The Sports Encyclopedia: BASEBALL

David S. Neft · Roland T. Johnson · Richard M. Cohen

GROSSET & DUNLAP
A Filmways Company
Publishers New York

PUBLISHED SIMULTANEOUSLY IN CANADA
LIBRARY OF CONGRESS CATALOG CARD NUMBER: 73-15137
ISBN: 0-448-12243-X (Paperback edition)
ISBN: 0-448-13354-7 (Library edition)

PRINTED IN THE UNITED STATES OF AMERICA

Contents

1946-1960 GOIN' FOR THE PUMP 275

1961-1975 UNLOCKING THE FLOODGATES 357

LEADERS AND FEATURES 467

Preface

The Sports Encyclopedia: Baseball is the first reference book in a continuing series of major sports encyclopedias. This book, in particular, marks the first major reference book to appear on baseball since 1969. The previous effort, *The Baseball Encyclopedia,* represented, to that time, the most complete compendium on the subject ever offered. As we were proud to play a major role in the development of that effort, so are we proud to be the authors of this book. Yet beyond simply presenting baseball statistics again, it is our belief that we have presented a different format which adds another dimension to the study of the records and performances of former seasons. Instead of primarily presenting an alphabetical list of all ballplayers, we have placed the emphasis on the season so that the reader will be able to perceive baseball as a team sport from year to year and follow the ballplayers and their achievements in more direct relationship to one another.

In using such a format, we have also taken a certain license to arrange the history of baseball into various time periods, complete with its own leaders' section and lifetime registers, to give a truer perspective to the game of baseball as it has changed throughout the years. More importantly though, and perhaps out of a greater consideration for the economics of book buying, we planned the book in a way which makes it possible to purchase the greatest amount of information for the lowest price of any similar book in the marketplace.

This book, of course, could not have been accomplished by four individuals alone. Baseball is simply too expansive a subject to allow such an undertaking. It is, therefore, appropriate that the organizations and individuals who assisted in the preparation of the manuscript not only receive the recognition they deserve, but also be given a rousing "thank you" for their fine and untiring efforts in our and all of baseball's behalf:

Consultants in the preparation of the manuscript–
N. Richard Anderson and John G. Hogrogian.
Baseball Hall of Fame–
Paul Kerr, President
Jack Redding, Librarian
Cliff Kachline, Historian, with special thanks for his continuing effort to collect demographic questionnaires for every man who ever played in the major leagues.
Office of the Commissioner of Baseball–
Joe Reichler, Director of Public Relations
National League–
Dave Grote, Director of Public Relations
American League–
Bob Holbrook, Executive Assistant
Tom Monahan, Director of Publicity
Society for American Baseball Research, a huge effort coordinated by Bill Haber, Staten Island, N. Y., included:

Arthur Ahrens, Chicago, Ill.
William Balza, Beaver Dam, Wis.
Bob Brauner, Brookline, Mass.
Frank Caruso, Olympia, Wash.
John Clark, Regina, Sas., Canada
Arthur Craig, Belmont, Mass.
Bob Davis, Washington, D.C.
Ted DiTullio, Bronx, N.Y.
Ron Liebman, Queens, N.Y.
John O'Malley, New York, N.Y.
Dan Dischley, Lake Ronkonkoma, N.Y.
John England, Fort Smith, Ark.
Paul Frisz, Terre Haute, Ind.
Larry Fritsch, Stevens Point, Wis.
Vic Frolund, Youngstown, Ohio
Dan Ginsburg, Pittsburgh, Pa.
Ray Gonzalez, Woodside, N.Y.
Bill Gustafson, San Jose, Calif.
Tom Hufford, Pulaski, Va.
Larry Kelley, Meridian, Idaho
Stanley Kuminski, Brooklyn, N.Y.
Irv Lerner, Philadelphia, Pa.
Bill Loughman, Elmhurst, Ill.
Jim MacAlister, Philadelphia, Pa.
Stan Makowsky, Brooklyn, N.Y.
Bob McConnell, Wilmington, Del.
Fred McKie, Penns Grove, N.J.
Jim McLean, Rockford, Ill.
Doug McWilliams, Berkeley, Calif.
Peter Molin, Arlington, Va.
Ray Nemec, Downers Grove, Ill.
Robert Oliver, Salem, Ore.
Pete Palmer, Lexington, Mass.
John Pardon, Croton-on-Hudson, N.Y.
Paul Quinn, Chicago, Ill.
Owen Ricker, Regina, Sask., Canada
Emil Rothe, Chicago, Ill.
Tom Shea, Hingham, Mass.
Joe Simenic, Cleveland, Ohio
Jack Smalling, Ames, Iowa
John Stirling, Indianapolis, Ind.
Neil Sussman, Ft. Lauderdale, Fla.
John Tattersall, Havertown, Pa.
Bob Thing, Skowhegan, Maine
Bill Weiss, San Mateo, Calif.
Ralph Winnie, Seattle, Wash.
Daniel Woods, Hyde Park, Maine
R. H. Ziegler, Manhattan, Kan.

Grosset and Dunlap–
Robert Markel, Editor-in-chief
Irving Ross, Production Director
Joe Sandler, Production
George Paturzo, Designer

The author's wives, (a special thanks for their faith and cooperation throughout the project): Naomi Neft, Judy Johnson, Nancy Cohen, and Thea Deutsch.

Since we are fallible human beings, we know that readers will find errors in this book. In order to keep future editions as accurate and complete as possible, we would appreciate corrections and additions being sent to us at:

SPORTS PRODUCTS INC.
632 North Mountain Road
Newington, Conn. 06111

Codes and Explanations

In each section of the book, codes, unfamiliar abbreviations, and bold facing may be shown. The following, by section, is an explanation of this matter:

Yearly Statistical Sections

Age—The age shown for each player is as of July 1 of that year.

Average Team Age—(Appears on the line which shows the team's totals.) For batters, the age shown is the average age based on those men who had at least 1 at bat per game scheduled. For pitchers, the age shown is the average age based on those men who appeared in at least 15 games.

Traded Players—Whenever a number or numbers appear before a player's name, such as 1, 2, 3, 4, 5, or 13, 14, 15, 24, 25, it indicates that he played for more than one team *that year*. For example, 2 would mean that the team he is shown with is his *second* team that year. On the other hand, 13 would mean that the player started the year with that team, was traded, and returned to that team again.

Bold Facing—Indicates league leaders.

Grouped Players—Certain players may be grouped together because of a lack of space on the page. When they do appear in such groupings, the information shown indicates the following:

Batters—Jones 24 L 3-7—Last Name, Age, Bats (Left, Right, or Both), Hits, At Bats.

Pitchers—Smith 21 R 0-1—Last Name, Age, Throws (Left or Right), Won and Lost Record.

Team Name Line—Shown alongside the name of each team is Position Finished, Won-Lost Record, Winning Percentage, Games Behind, and Manager. If a team had more than one manager, the won and lost record and the winning percentage for each manager is shown.

Partial Innings Pitched—Whenever a .1 is shown under the IP (Innings Pitched) Column, it indicates 1/3 of an inning pitched.

Career Interruptions—Whenever a symbol appears in parenthesis after a player's name, i.e., Jones (XX), it indicates a career interruption of 30 days or more duration, or a career ending injury or illness. The explanation to these symbols may be found under Career Interruption Codes on this page.

World Series Sections

Bold Facing—In the individual game line score totals, it indicates winning and losing pitchers and winning and losing team. In the composite box score totals, it indicates that the player led the Series in the indicated category.

Register Sections

Players have been assigned to the various register sections according to what time period they played the most. The only exception to this is that anybody who played mostly in the nineteenth century but overlapped his career into the twentieth century, would appear in the 1901-1919 Period Register Section.

Men who were primarily non-pitchers are included in the pitcher register only if they pitched in 5 or more games.

The information which appears in each Period Register Section, in addition to the player's lifetime statistics, is as follows:

Last name, Use name (name player was known as), Middle names, and nicknames, the last of which appear in parenthesis ( ):

Ruth, Babe—George Herman (The Sultan of Swat)

For Latin ballplayers, where the mother's maiden name became part of the player's name, the information is indicated by brackets [ ] which appear between the middle name and the nickname. Such as in the case of Luis Aparicio:

Aparicio, Luis—Luis Ernesto [Monteil] (Little Louie)

If a player used another name other than that he was "born as", his real name is indicated in parenthesis ( ) after the last name and use name. Such as in the case of Max Carey:

Carey (Carnarius), Max (Maximilian)—Max George (Scoops)

Manager—Whenever an M appears before a year or years it indicates that the player was a manager.

League Abbreviations—Each of the league affiliations is abbreviated and stands for the following: AA—American Association, AL—American League, FL—Federal League, NL—National League, PL—Players League, UA—Union Association.

Other Major League Sports—Certain players also played professional basketball or football. Such information is indicated with the league in abbreviations. These abbreviations stand for the following: NBL—National Basketball League, NBA—National Basketball Association, NFL—National Football League, AAFC—All-American Football Conference, BAA—Basketball Association of America, ABL—American Basketball League.

Career Interruptions—If an abbreviation other than a league follows the year played, it means a career end or full year missed because of certain prevailing reasons. The explanation of these abbreviations may be found under the Career Interruption Codes on this page.

Career Interruption Codes

AA – Injured in automobile accident
AJ – Arm injury
BA – Broken arm
BC – Broken or dislocated collarbone
BE – Broken bone in elbow
BF – Broken bone in foot
BG – Broken finger
BH – Broken bone in hand
BJ – Broken jaw
BK – Broken bone in knee
BL – Broken leg
BN – Broken ankle
BP – Broken hip bone
BR – Broken rib or ribs
BS – Broken bone in shoulder
BT – Broken toe
BW – Broken wrist
BX – Broken spine
BY – Broken cheek bone
BZ – Broken nose
CJ – Face injury
CN – Concussion
CP – Blood poisoning
DD – Died during the season or the following off-season
DE – Declared ineligible by commissioner or league president
DL – Declared ineligible for life by commissioner
DO – Declared ineligible for playing in outlaw league
DP – On team for entire year—but did not play
DU – Unofficially declared ineligible for life
EJ – Elbow injury
FA – Finger amputated
FJ – Foot or heel injury
FR – Badly burned
FS – Fractured skull
GJ – Groin injury
GW – Gunshot wounds
HJ – Hand injury
HO – Holdout
IJ – Eye injury
IL – Illness
JA – In jail for assault
JJ – Injury or on disabled list—type of injury unknown
JL – Returned to Japanese League
JT – Jumped team
KB – Killed by pitched ball
KJ – Knee injury
KP – Kept out of lineup as part of A.L.-N.L. peace agreement in 1903
LA – Leg amputated
LJ – Leg or thigh injury
ML – Special military leave to play baseball
MM – Merchant marine
MS – Military service
NJ – Ankle injury
PB – Head injury from pitched ball
PJ – Hip injury
QJ – Brain injury
RC – Retired to coach
RJ – Finger injury
RL – Reported late in order to finish school year
RP – Attended to personal business
RR – Refused to report
SA – Sore arm
SC – Barred by court injunction
SJ – Shoulder injury or shoulder separation
SL – Suspended by commissioner or league president
SM – Suspended for playing in the Mexican League
ST – Suspended by team
SU – Suspended for hitting or abusing umpire
TJ – Chest injury
UJ – Side injury
VJ – Rib injury
VR – Voluntarily retired
WJ – Wrist injury
WW – Voluntarily retired to work in plants producing war material.
XJ – Back injury
YJ – Head injury

The Great Mississippi

FOR LEE ALLEN,
who called one night
on his way back to Cooperstown
to say he had discovered the sun.

THE GREAT MISSISSIPPI

Up from the grasslands,
The plains, the cities,
Up from the vastness
  of the land itself;
Up
Up
Up
To The Great Mississippi.

Up to that First Field
  bathed in sun,
Basking in the glory
  of its birth,
Immersed in future time.

Further up slides the sun.

Up
To the Red Stockings from Cincinnati,
The Original Magnificent Machine,
The dynasty without a future.
Up
To the National Association,
Swaying in its greatness.

Further up slides the sun.

Through the mouth of history
  slide provocative names
Once breathed on the lips
  of dreamers.

In what fine grave
  do the
Elizabeth Resolutes,
Troy Haymakers,
And
Lord Baltimores
  now rest?

Upmovingup
To expanding cities
  pocketed
In gray concrete.

(Can you hear the shrill and melodic chant
  of the Train Conductor
  calling out his roll?)

:NewYawkHartferdBosstonPhilaDELphia
LouievilleCINCINnatiShecargo and
  SaintLouieeeeeee.

Up up up
Up
To the Great Mississippi.

THE GRAND CENTRAL HOTEL

No sun,
Now rubble,
The collected debris
  of memories
Echoes
An anguished ring
  through the corridors
Of Manhattan Canyons:

Where are we going?

From where
To where
Do we step?

December . . . a month . . . a day . . . a time
logged on the fresh pages of history . . .
the first and only real entry . . . a league
. . . a new league . . . a microscopic legion of
men bearing witness to the birth, unfurling
its colors on an industrial land to detract

from the former failure . . .

The National Association is dead,
Long live the National League!

From rubble to rubble,
From dust to dust,
New fortresses
Stretch their fledgling arms
And puncture the sky
With abbreviated zeal.

Like so many transients
Awaiting a derailed train,
The others come
And never go.

The American Association is dead
The Union Association is dead
The Players League is dead.
All gone,
All dead,

Long live the National League!

THE AMERICAN LEAGUE

After the rubble—
  the dust,
The coat of dust
  hovering over sidewalks,
Into the cracks of time.

Dust races in the sunlight.

Fresh footprints,
Permanent steps
  on the floor of history.

The steps of giants,
Of circus performers,
And
Golden-armed magicians
  traipsing
Through sun-filled cities
And sunless nights
In search of permanence.

Brave Mack,
Cornelius Alexander McGillicuddy
Mack
Mack the Master,
  the tall, lean visionary
  who led a white elephant
And
  of course
Notwithstandingnotwithout
  in center ring
The acrobat from Georgia
The acrobat who spelled
  his name
CAPITAL C
  little o
  little b
  little b
The frenzied acrobat
  who danced on the wall of greatness
With razor feet,
Who cut his image
  in swirls of blood.

O,
The sawdust stained with blood,
The dripping pattern
  of immortal footprints
Imprinted on the souls
  of ordinary men.

Dust races in the sunlight
But the sun cannot speak.

1919

Before the threat
And dismal cold gray
  of mourning
Came the sun.

And Charlie Comiskey
  should've turned in his sleep
  should've turned in his sleep
  should've turned . . .

Insane sun
Floating above the earth
Like some extravagant madman
Spending next year's allowance.

The same burning sun
In the same afternoons
In all the cities
East
  and somewhat
West
  of the
Great Mississippi.

  should've turned in his sleep

Too many
Suns
In too many
Cities

Too many
Faces
in the face of it
All.

How much grief?
Too
Much
Grief.
Too many faces
Too many suns
Far too many of too many things
Far too many of too many things.

  should've turned in his sleep

More like Dali,
  less Victoria,
The playing field becomes a landscape
Fixed and isolated and trapped
Between the borders of its own fabrication.

The stadium faces
Blur
  in the afternoon sun
The celebration
Ends
  in the afternoon sun
The victory becomes
Defeat
  in the afternoon sun.

Morality
Victoria Escaped
Insane sun.

How much of how many things?

The death of honor
The end of a fading
And final trust.

  should've turned in his sleep

And as
The unsettling dust
Settles in the throat of all men
There are not enough beers
In all the bars
In all the worlds
To flush out the stale bitterness
Of too many afternoons
In too many suns.

And Charlie Comiskey
  woke up
  and deposited the nightmare
  in the pillow of his dream.

THE BABE

Jovial Giant squashed between
Greatness and an empty childhood;
Juxtaposed in time and play.

Mirthmaker,
Charmer,
Crowd-pleaser,
Lover,
King.

A crown of gold
A golden crown
A golden statue
A statue of gold.

We
Toast you with gauntlets of gold
And crown you with our passion.
We
Celebrate your proud head
Tipped upward and framed by a golden sun.

We
Chill in your stretching shadow
Which blocks the sun.

Can you remember
All the autographs inked in hysteria?
Or
The pennants
Nailed
On flagpoles atop the stadium roof?
Nailed
By the bludgeoning power of your power.

The wind makes those flags
Dance in the sky,
And their sound is the sound
Of seagulls—
Returning home to dine.

A FISHERMAN'S TALE

Ernest
Hemingway
Immortalized
Joe
DiMaggio
And
Joe
DiMaggio
Immortalized
Himself
And
So
Did
Ted Williams,
  that wonderful slugger from Boston.

JACKIE

He waited
In the whiteness of the afternoon sun;
Black man on green ground.
He waited
In the shadows and touched
  the hand of history;
Black man on green ground.
He waited
In the silence of his tongue;
Black man on green ground.
He waited
In the path of words
  which broke his bones;
Black man on green ground.
He waited
As few men have ever
  waited
And endured
Before a multitude
  as no man before.

O,
To have conquered the white sun,
  blinding
To have sailed the sun and ridden
  its joy
  in tears
And
  in laughter.

To have ridden the white sun,
  blinding
And to be
  struck
  struck
  struck
    by the rising
Of
Your
Own
Black
Sun.

Your crown was white;
. . . and waited.

TWENTY-SIX YEARS NOW

After the war
After white on white on white
After Robinson.

Yes,
Twenty-six
  years now
Twenty-six years
Twenty-six years
  have come
And
Gone.

And the once empty rosters are no longer
Empty
  of our faces,
No longer
Empty
  as the face of my mother
That day
My father spoke.

I remember the gloom of my father's words
And what they did to my mother's face
And what they did to my heart
—Those words my daddy spoke.

Daddy told about
Josh Gibson
And how he was
Swatting white balls
In black parks
  while Ruth and fellows
  like Foxx
Were
Making hay.

Daddy told about
Satch, Ole Satch
Lean and hummin'
Told about
Ole Satch
And how when Satch was
Striking black leather
In places
Like
Chattanooga
And Birmingham
And Pittsburgh
And Bismarck
And Cleveland
And Wichita
And Kansas City
And Havana and
Told when
Satch was doing all those things
How
  Grove and Dean and Feller
Were
Making hay.

Yes,
Twenty-six years
  since my father's words
Twenty-six years
  since his death.

He had a belly laugh

My daddy did
And his laugh
  if ever such a sound could reach your ears
Would be filled with the
Loud
  and
Quiet joy
That men such as
  Mays and Robinson and Aaron
Could have given him.

Not their booming home runs and feats of magic

Just their faces
Just their faces
Just their faces
  now.

NO. 714

On the
21st day of July
Henry Aaron
  slapped Home Run No. 700
And smiled
  in the quiet way in which
He smiles.

On the
17th day of August
Henry Aaron
  slapped Home Run No. 703
And wondered
  if his wrists would not give way
And cheat him.

On the
3rd day of September
Henry Aaron
  slapped Home Run No. 707
  slapped Home Run No. 708
And thought
  of the stars.

On the
17th day of September
Henry Aaron
  slapped Home Run No. 711
And said
  it wasn't important
  anymore
There was
  time.

On the
22nd day of September
Henry Aaron
  slapped Home Run No. 712
And wondered
  if nature understood
  the struggle
Of men.

The sun is awesome and
  does not compromise.

On the
29th day of September
Henry Aaron
  slapped Home Run No. 713
And forgot
all the cruelty sent by mail.

A child walks
To the edge of the water
And efforts in the sand
  of the afternoon sun
  to save
Stale castles
Too illiterate
  to fall.

On the
30th day of September
Henry Aaron
  singled three times
And then went home
To wait
  the summer.

BEYOND THE GREAT MISSISSIPPI

After St. Louis
We crowded our caravans
And headed
West,
Uncautiously moving
Toward the sun.

Moved
Until
We reached
The waters of the Pacific,
Until
We seeded
Unknown soil.

And some of the seedlings took and some died.

Moved
Southward
And even
Northward
Beyond
Familiar borders.

And the land
Which once selfishly
  nestled its offspring
In limited embrace
Now
Extended its arms
To all
  who chanced the journey.

And the sun
No longer shone
In the same afternoons
In the same cities.

—*Jordan A. Deutsch*
OCTOBER, 1973

1876-1900
A Journey Through a Once and Distant Time

If H. G. Wells actually built his time machine and one could be transported back in time, the chances are that any similarity between the game of the twentieth century and the game as played through 1892, would simply be an illusion in the eye of the beholder. While struggling to see which men, let alone a league, could survive the rigors of implanting a new, national pastime, the playing rules, those necessary guidelines which were needed to bring continuity to the sport, were being changed continually. Beyond some of the rules, which are humorous in retrospect (such as before 1887, when the batter had the right to call for a high or low pitch), there are those rules which make it impossible to compare and judge the player performance pre-1893 with the standards of play as they are known today. The most relevant fact supporting this statement is the 1893 rule change which lengthened the pitching distance to 60 feet, 6 inches—a distance still used in all of professional baseball. Interestingly enough, in the search for an equitable separation of batter and pitcher, the distance started out at 45 feet. In 1881 five feet were tacked on and remained the same until the start of the 1893 season. Perhaps as important as the pitching distance was the pitcher's delivery which, until 1883, was underhanded. Getting to first base via a walk was a difficult chore for most of the seventies and eighties. It was not until 1889 that four balls got a batter to first. Before then it took anywhere from nine, in 1879, to five, in 1887. Yet while the batter couldn't get a "cheap ticket" to the first sack, neither could he easily be victimized by the fast ball. The three-strike rule was not adopted until 1888, refined in 1895 (a strike being charged on a foul tip), and made uniform in 1903 when a foul tip caught after two strikes resulted in an out. It was not until 1891 that baseball instituted the substitution rule, which previously had only been allowed in the case of injury or permission by the other team.

Scoring rules also added to the distortion in early statistical tabulation. These include the 1887 rule which credited a base on balls as a hit and the 1876 rule which charged the batter with a time at bat on a base on balls (both of these distortions are not used in this book). Stolen base statistics, which began in 1886, credited a runner for each base advanced on another player's hit. It was not until 1898 that this rule was changed to the one used today. In trying to determine how to classify base on balls, wild pitch, hit batter, and balks, the poor moundsman got it all lumped in the single category of "error". This was the ruling established in 1883, reversed in 1887, reestablished in 1888, and finally abolished in 1889—the same year the sacrifice bunt was first recognized, although charging the batter with a time at bat.

But baseball in its youth was more than the evolution of rule changes. There were the individuals, and the leagues, of which four fought for dominance in the last quarter century of the 1800's. In 1876, following the demise of the National Association, a league simply classified as "professional" and not major due to its erratic scheduling, came the National League. Organized on February 2, 1876, and mostly due to the efforts of William A. Hulbert, owner of the Chicago Cubs, a league constitution was drafted which called for a tight organization and a firm schedule of games. Hulbert took over the reins of league presidency in 1877 from Morgan G. Bulkeley, and although his iron fisted leadership was able to right scandal, end jumping franchises, and fatten the anemic coffers, it also led to the first rival league. Hulbert saw fit to throw Cincinnati out of the league after the 1880 season for permitting games on the sabbath and liquor in the stands. It was this move which led to the formation of the American Association in 1882. Headed by Justin Thorner, of Cincinnati, and H. D. "Denny" Knight, of Pittsburgh, the new league not only succeeded in raiding players, but allowed the scheduling of Sunday games while cutting ticket prices from 50 to 25 cents. Hulbert died in 1882 and A. G. Mills, the new National League President, saw the inevitable and sued for peace in time to save his league from ruin. Out of the "laying down of arms" came the National Agreement, a document which not only led to mutual protection over player contracts, but brought about the first post-season championships between the two leagues in 1884.

That same year the Union Association headed by Henry V. Lucus, a St. Louis millionaire, came into being. But unlike the player raiding which led to the success of the American Association, the Union Associations' tactics only resulted in their downfall. Both the other leagues raided enough of the new league's players so that at season's end only five of the original 12 franchises remained intact, and the Union Association was merely another page in baseball's history. In 1890, as the result of an organization begun in 1885, baseball's newest league came into existence. Called the Players' League, and made up mostly of available stars at the time, the new league was born out of the frustration of limited salaries, unjust fines, and the reserve clause. But a lack of administrative leadership and heavy gate competition ended their efforts after a year. It was their existence, as well as their demise, which consequently brought an end to the American Association after the 1891 season. Upset over the reassignment of Players' League personnel, the league withdrew from the National Agreement. This time, however, its 25 cent admission price could not support the finances which were needed for another war with the National League. Of the eight teams in the league, four went by the way of history and the other four joined the National League to bring their circuit to 12 clubs—an ill-devised structure which lasted through the 1899 season when four teams were dropped. It was a move which two years later led to the birth of the strongest rival the National League had ever known.

1876—1900 SINGLE SEASON LEADERS

BATTING

Batting Average

1	Tip O'Neill	1887	StL	N	.442a
2	Hugh Duffy	1894	Bos	N	.438
3	Willie Keeler	1897	Bal	N	.432
4	Ross Barnes	1876	Chi	N	.429b
5	Denny Lyons	1887	Phi	AA	.425a
6	Jesse Burkett	1895	Cle	N	.423
7	Pete Browning	1887	Lou	AA	.418a
8	Fred Dunlap	1884	StL	U	.415
9	Jesse Burkett	1896	Cle	N	.410
10	Ed Delahanty	1899	Phi	N	.408
11	Fred Clarke	1897	Lou	N	.406
12	Sam Thompson	1894	Phi	N	.404
13	Jesse Burkett	1899	StL	N	.402
14	Ed Delahanty	1894	Phi	N	.400

a-Bases on balls not counted as Hit
b-Bases on balls not counted as At Bat

Hits

1	Willie Keeler	1897	Bal	N	243
2	Jesse Burkett	1896	Cle	N	240
3	Denny Lyons	1887	Phi	AA	237
4	Hugh Duffy	1894	Bos	N	236
5	Jesse Burkett	1895	Cle	N	235
6	Ed Delahanty	1899	Phi	N	234
7	Jesse Burkett	1899	StL	N	228
8	Tip O'Neill	1887	StL	AA	227
9	Pete Browning	1887	Lou	AA	226
10	Billy Hamilton	1894	Phi	N	223

Slugging Average

1	Tip O'Neill	1887	StL	AA	.708a
2	Hugh Duffy	1894	Bos	N	.679
3	Sam Thompson	1894	Phi	N	.666
4	Sam Thompson	1895	Phi	N	.657
5	Bill Joyce	1894	Was	N	.633
6	Fred Dunlap	1884	StL	U	.625
7	Ed Delahanty	1896	Phi	N	.610
8	Ed Delahanty	1895	Phi	N	.599
9	Denny Lyons	1887	Phi	AA	.591a
10	Ed Delahanty	1893	Phi	N	.588

a-Bases on balls not counted as Hit

Home Runs

1	Ned Williamson	1884	Chi	N	27
2	Fred Pfeffer	1884	Chi	N	25
	Buck Freeman	1899	Was	N	25
4	Abner Dalrymple	1884	Chi	N	22
5	Cap Anson	1884	Chi	N	21
6	Sam Thompson	1889	Phi	N	20
7	Billy O'Brien	1887	Was	N	19
	Harry Stovey	1889	Phi	AA	19
	Bug Holliday	1889	Cin	AA	19
	Ed Delahanty	1893	Phi	N	19

Runs Batted In

1	Sam Thompson	1887	Det	N	166
2	Sam Thompson	1895	Phi	N	165
3	Cap Anson	1886	Chi	N	147
4	Ed Delahanty	1893	Phi	N	146
5	Hugh Duffy	1894	Bos	N	145
6	Hardy Richardson	1890	Bos	P	144
7	Sam Thompson	1894	Phi	N	141
8	Ed Delahanty	1899	Phi	N	137
9	Joe Kelley	1895	Bal	N	134
	Steve Brodie	1895	Bal	N	134

Triples

1	Perry Werden	1893	StL	N	33
	Dave Orr	1886	NY	AA	33
3	Heinie Reitz	1894	Bal	N	29
4	Harry Davis	1897	Pit	N	28
5	Jimmy Williams	1899	Pit	N	27
6	Sam Thompson	1894	Phi	N	26
	Roger Connor	1894	NY-StL	N	26
	George Treadway	1894	Bkn	N	26
	George Davis	1893	NY	N	26
	Buck Freeman	1899	Was	N	26

Runs

1	Billy Hamilton	1894	Phi	N	196
2	Tom Brown	1891	Bos	AA	177
3	Joe Kelley	1894	Bal	N	167
4	Tip O'Neill	1887	StL	AA	166
	Billy Hamilton	1895	Phi	N	166
6	Willie Keeler	1894	Bal	N	164
7	Arlie Latham	1887	StL	AA	163
8	Fred Dunlap	1884	StL	U	161
	Willie Keeler	1895	Bal	N	161
	Hugh Duffy	1890	Chi	P	161

Doubles

1	Ed Delahanty	1899	Phi	N	56
2	Ned Williamson	1883	Chi	N	50
	Hugh Duffy	1894	Bos	N	50
4	Joe Kelley	1894	Bal	N	48
5	Ed Delahanty	1895	Phi	N	47
	Honus Wagner	1899	Lou	N	47
7	Tip O'Neill	1887	StL	AA	46
8	Honus Wagner	1900	Pit	N	45
	Walt Wilmot	1894	Chi	N	45
10	Denny Lyons	1887	Phi	AA	43

Bases on Balls

1	John Crooks	1892	StL	N	136
2	Billy Hamilton	1894	Phi	N	126
3	John McGraw	1899	Bal	N	124
4	Bill Joyce	1890	Bkn	P	123
5	John Crooks	1893	StL	N	121
6	Cupid Childs	1893	Cle	N	120
7	Dummy Hoy	1891	StL	AA	119
8	Yank Robinson	1889	StL	AA	118
9	Cupid Childs	1892	Cle	N	117
10	Yank Robinson	1888	StL	AA	116
	Jim McTamany	1889	Col	AA	116
	Roger Connor	1892	Phi	N	116

PITCHING

Wins

1	Old Hoss Radbourn	1884	Prov	N	60
2	John Clarkson	1885	Chi	N	53
3	Guy Hecker	1884	Lou	AA	52
4	Old Hoss Radbourn	1883	Prov	N	49
	John Clarkson	1889	Bos	N	49
6	Al Spalding	1876	Chi	N	47
	Charlie Buffinton	1884	Bos	N	47
8	Pud Galvin	1883	Buf	N	46
	Pud Galvin	1884	Buf	N	46
	Matt Kilroy	1887	Bal	AA	46

Winning Percentage

1	Fred Goldsmith	1880	Chi	N	.880
2	Old Hoss Radbourn	1884	Prov	N	.833
3	Jay Hughes	1899	Bkn	N	.824
4	Bill Hoffer	1895	Bal	N	.811
5	Mickey Welch	1885	NY	N	.800
	Jocko Flynn	1886	Chi	N	.800
7	Bill Hoffer	1896	Bal	N	.788
8	Al Spalding	1876	Chi	N	.783
	Jovett Meekin	1894	NY	N	.783
10	Cy Young	1895	Cle	N	.778

Losses

1	John Coleman	1883	Phi	N	48
2	Will White	1880	Cin	N	43
3	Larry McKeon	1884	Ind	AA	41
4	Jim McCormick	1879	Cle	N	40
	George Bradley	1879	Troy	N	40
6	Pud Galvin	1880	Buf	N	37
	Henry Porter	1888	KC	AA	37
	George Cobb	1892	Bal	N	37
9	Stump Weidman	1886	KC	N	36
10	Jim Devlin	1876	Lou	N	35
	Adonis Terry	1884	Bkn	AA	35
	Florence Sullivan	1884	Pit	AA	35
	Hardie Henderson	1885	Bal	AA	35

Earned Run Average

1	George Bradley	1876	StL	N	1.23
2	George Bradley	1880	Prov	N	1.38
3	Old Hoss Radbourn	1884	Prov	N	1.45
4	Monte Ward	1878	Prov	N	1.51
5	Pud Galvin	1876	Lou	N	1.56
6	Tim Keefe	1885	NY	N	1.58
7	Silver King	1888	StL	AA	1.64
8	Mickey Welch	1885	NY	N	1.65
9	Candy Cummings	1876	Har	N	1.67
10	Tommy Bond	1876	Har	N	1.68

Innings Pitched

1	Will White	1879	Cin	N	680
2	Old Hoss Radbourn	1884	Prov	N	679
3	Guy Hecker	1884	Lou	AA	671
4	Jim McCormick	1880	Cle	N	658
5	Pud Galvin	1883	Buf	N	656
6	Pud Galvin	1884	Buf	N	636
7	Old Hoss Radbourn	1883	Prov	N	632
8	Bill Hutchison	1892	Chi	N	627
9	John Clarkson	1885	Chi	N	623
10	Jim Devlin	1876	Lou	N	622

Strikeouts

1	Matt Kilroy	1886	Bal	AA	513
2	Toad Ramsey	1886	Lou	AA	499
3	One Arm Daily	1884	C-P–Was	U	483
4	Old Hoss Radbourn	1884	Prov	N	441
5	Charlie Buffinton	1884	Bos	N	417
6	Guy Hecker	1884	Lou	AA	385
7	Bill Sweeney	1884	Bal	U	384
8	Pud Galvin	1884	Buf	N	369
9	Mark Baldwin	1889	Col	AA	368
10	Tim Keefe	1883	NY	AA	361

Games Pitched

1	Will White	1879	Cin	N	76
	Pud Galvin	1883	Buf	N	76
	Old Hoss Radbourn	1883	Prov	N	76
4	Old Hoss Radbourn	1884	Prov	N	75
	Guy Hecker	1884	Lou	AA	75
	Bill Hutchison	1892	Chi	N	75
7	Lee Richmond	1880	Wor	N	74
	Jim McCormick	1880	Cle	N	74
9	John Clarkson	1889	Bos	N	73
10	Pud Galvin	1884	Buf	N	72

Shutouts

1	George Bradley	1876	StL	N	16
2	Tommy Bond	1879	Bos	N	12
	Pud Galvin	1884	Buf	N	12
	Ed Morris	1886	Pit	AA	12
5	Old Hoss Radbourn	1884	Prov	N	11
	Dave Foutz	1886	StL	AA	11
7	Jim McCormick	1884	CleN-Cin	U	10
	John Clarkson	1885	Chi	N	10
9	Tommy Bond	1878	Bos	N	9
	George Derby	1881	Det	N	9
	Cy Young	1892	Cle	N	9

1876-1900 PERIOD LEADERS

BATTING

Batting Average
(Minimum 1000 Games or 4000 At Bats)

1	Willie Keeler	1892-00	.385
2	Jesse Burkett	1890-00	.363
3	Billy Hamilton	1888-00	.348
4	Pete Browning	1882-94	.347
5	Joe Kelley	*1891-00	.345
6	Ed Delahanty	1888-00	.343
7	Dan Brouthers	1879-96	.343
8	Cap Anson	*1876-97	.333
9	Sam Thompson	1885-98	.333
10	Hugh Duffy	1888-00	.331

Hits

1	Cap Anson	*1876-97	3022
2	Roger Connor	*1880-97	2460
3	Jim O'Rourke	1876-03	2299
4	Dan Brouthers	1879-96	2288
5	Biddy McPhee	*1882-99	2287
6	George Van Haltren	1887-00	2276
7	Jimmy Ryan	1885-00	2264
8	Hugh Duffy	1888-00	2200
9	Ed Delahanty	1888-00	2171
10	Monte Ward	*1878-94	2122

Slugging Average
(Minimum 1000 Games or 4000 At Bats)

1	Dan Brouthers	1879-96	.520
2	Sam Thompson	1885-98	.504
3	Joe Kelley	1891-00	.498
4	Ed Delahanty	1888-00	.495
5	Roger Connor	*1880-97	.486
6	Harry Stovey	*1880-93	.485
7	Willie Keeler	1892-00	.483
8	Jesse Burkett	1890-00	.476
9	Pete Browning	*1882-94	.474
10	Mike Tiernan	*1887-99	.464

Home Runs

1	Roger Connor	*1880-97	137
2	Sam Thompson	1885-98	128
3	Harry Stovey	*1880-93	121
4	Hugh Duffy	1888-00	106
	Dan Brouthers	1879-96	106
	Mike Tiernan	*1887-99	106
7	Jimmy Ryan	1885-00	105
8	Cap Anson	*1876-97	97
9	Fred Pfeffer	*1882-97	95
10	Herman Long	1889-00	87

Runs Batted In

1	Cap Anson	*1876-97	1879
2	Roger Connor	*1880-97	1323
3	Sam Thompson	1885-98	1296
4	Dan Brouthers	1879-96	1294
5	Hugh Duffy	1888-00	1248
6	Ed Delahanty	1888-00	1242
7	Jake Beckley	1888-00	1170
8	Ed McKean	*1887-99	1124
9	Biddy McPhee	*1882-99	1067
10	Fred Pfeffer	*1882-97	1019

Triples

1	Roger Connor	*1880-97	227
2	Dan Brouthers	1879-96	212
3	Jake Beckley	1888-00	191
4	Harry Stovey	*1880-93	185
5	Buck Ewing	*1880-97	179
6	Biddy McPhee	*1882-99	170
7	Mike Tiernan	*1887-99	159
8	Sam Thompson	1885-98	155
9	Ed McKean	*1887-99	153
10	Ed Delahanty	1888-00	150

Runs

1	Cap Anson	*1876-97	1728
2	Biddy McPhee	*1882-99	1674
3	Billy Hamilton	1888-00	1620
4	Roger Connor	*1880-97	1607
5	Tom Brown	*1882-98	1524
6	Don Brouthers	1879-96	1513
7	George Van Haltren	1887-00	1511
8	Jimmy Ryan	1885-00	1507
9	Hugh Duffy	1888-00	1497
10	Harry Stovey	*1880-93	1488

Doubles

1	Cap Anson	*1876-97	530
2	Dan Brouthers	1879-96	446
3	Roger Connor	*1880-97	429
4	Ed Delahanty	1888-00	418
5	Jim O'Rourke	1876-93	385
6	Jimmy Ryan	1885-00	381
7	Paul Hines	*1876-91	355
8	King Kelly	*1878-93	351
9	Harry Stovey	*1880-93	348
10	Sam Thompson	1885-98	326

Bases on Balls

1	Billy Hamilton	1888-00	1123
2	Roger Connor	*1880-97	1002
3	Biddy McPhee	*1882-99	981
4	Cupid Childs	1888-00	961
5	Cap Anson	*1876-97	952
6	Dummy Hoy	1888-99	877
7	Dan Brouthers	1879-96	840
8	Mike Griffin	*1887-98	809
9	Billy Nash	*1884-98	804
10	George Van Haltren	1887-00	772

PITCHING

Wins

1	Pud Galvin	*1879-92	361
2	Tim Keefe	*1880-93	343
3	John Clarkson	*1882-94	327
4	Mickey Welch	*1880-92	311
5	Kid Nichols	1890-00	310
6	Old Hoss Radbourn	*1881-91	308
7	Tony Mullane	*1881-94	286
8	Cy Young	1890-00	285
9	Gus Weyhing	1887-00	266
10	Jim McCormick	*1878-87	264

Winning Percentage
(Minimum 100 Wins)

1	Bob Caruthers	*1884-92	.682
2	Larry Corcoran	*1880-87	.658
3	Kid Nichols	1890-00	.655
4	John Clarkson	*1882-94	.650
5	Cy Young	1890-00	.631
6	Tommy Bond	*1876-84	.625
7	Clark Griffith	1891-00	.619
8	Old Hoss Radbourn	*1881-91	.617
9	Jack Stivetts	*1889-99	.616
10	Monte Ward	*1878-84	.608

Losses

1	Pud Galvin	*1879-92	309
2	Gus Weyhing	1887-00	228
3	Tim Keefe	*1880-93	224
4	Jim McCormick	*1878-87	214
5	Tony Mullane	*1881-94	213
6	Mickey Welch	*1880-92	207
7	Jim Whitney	*1881-90	204
8	Adonis Terry	*1884-97	197
9	Old Hoss Radbourn	*1881-91	191
10	John Clarkson	*1882-94	176

Earned Run Average

(not available)

Innings Pitched

1	Pud Galvin	*1879-92	5941
2	Tim Keefe	*1880-93	5070
3	Mickey Welch	*1880-92	4781
4	Tony Mullane	*1881-94	4545
5	John Clarkson	*1882-94	4537
6	Old Hoss Radbourn	*1881-91	4535
7	Gus Weyhing	1887-00	4304
8	Jim McCormick	*1878-87	4275
9	Kid Nichols	1890-00	4221
10	Cy Young	1890-00	4044

Strikeouts

1	Tim Keefe	*1880-93	2531
2	John Clarkson	*1882-94	1978
3	Amos Rusie	1889-98	1928
4	Mickey Welch	*1880-92	1846
5	Old Hoss Radbourn	*1881-91	1830
6	Tony Mullane	*1881-94	1812
7	Pud Galvin	*1879-92	1799
8	Jim McCormick	*1878-87	1704
9	Charlie Buffinton	*1882-92	1700
10	Gus Weyhing	1887-90	1662

Games Pitched

1	Pud Galvin	*1879-92	697
2	Tim Keefe	*1880-93	602
3	Mickey Welch	*1880-92	564
4	Tony Mullane	*1881-94	557
5	Gus Weyhing	1887-00	535
6	John Clarkson	*1882-94	531
7	Old Hoss Radbourn	*1881-91	528
8	Kid Nichols	1890-00	519
9	Cy Young	1890-00	505
10	Jim McCormick	*1878-87	492

Shutouts

1	Pud Galvin	*1879-92	56
2	Mickey Welch	*1880-92	41
3	Kid Nichols	1890-00	40
4	Tim Keefe	*1880-93	39
5	John Clarkson	*1882-94	37
6	Tommy Bond	*1876-84	36
	Will White	*1877-86	36
8	Old Hoss Radbourn	*1881-91	34
9	Jim McCormick	*1878-87	33
10	Cy Young	1890-00	32

*—Entire major league career

1876-1883 SUMMARY

FINAL STANDINGS

Team	W	L	Pct.	GB	Runs	Opp.R
1876 National League						
Chicago	**52**	**14**	**.788**	–	**624**	257
St. Louis	45	19	.703	6	386	**229**
Hartford	47	21	.691	6	429	261
Boston	39	31	.557	15	471	450
Louisville	30	36	.455	22	280	344
New York	21	35	.375	26	260	412
Philadelphia	14	45	.237	34.5	378	534
Cincinnati	9	56	.138	42.5	238	579
1877 National League						
Boston	**42**	**18**	**.700**	–	**419**	**263**
Louisville	35	25	.583	7	339	288
Brooklyn	31	27	.534	10	341	311
St. Louis	28	32	.467	14	284	318
Chicago	26	33	.441	15.5	[illegible]	[illegible]
Cincinnati	15	42	.263	25.5	291	485
1878 National League						
Boston	**41**	**19**	**.683**	–	298	**241**
Cincinnati	37	23	.617	4	333	281
Providence	33	27	.550	8	353	337
Chicago	30	30	.500	11	**371**	331
Indianapolis	24	36	.400	17	293	328
Milwaukee	15	45	.250	26	256	386
1879 National League						
Providence	**59**	**25**	**.702**	–	**612**	355
Boston	54	30	.643	5	562	**348**
Buffalo	46	32	.590	10	394	365
Chicago	46	33	.582	10.5	437	411
Cincinnati	43	37	.538	14	485	464
Cleveland	27	55	.329	31	322	461
Syracuse	22	48	.314	30	276	462
Troy	19	56	.253	35.5	321	543
1880 National League						
Chicago	**67**	**17**	**.798**	–	**538**	317
Providence	52	32	.619	15	419	**299**
Cleveland	47	37	.560	20	387	337
Troy	41	42	.494	25.5	392	438
Worcester	40	43	.482	26.5	412	370
Boston	40	44	.476	27	416	456
Buffalo	24	58	.293	42	331	502
Cincinnati	21	59	.263	44	296	472
1881 National League						
Chicago	**56**	**28**	**.667**	–	**550**	**379**
Providence	47	37	.560	9	447	426
Buffalo	45	38	.542	10.5	440	447
Detroit	41	43	.488	15	439	429
Troy	39	45	.464	17	399	429
Boston	38	45	.458	17.5	349	410
Cleveland	36	48	.429	20	392	414
Worcester	32	50	.390	23	410	492
1882 National League						
Chicago	**55**	**29**	**.655**	–	**604**	**353**
Providence	52	32	.619	3	463	356
Boston	45	39	.536	10	472	414
Buffalo	45	39	.536	10	500	461
Cleveland	42	40	.512	12	402	411
Detroit	42	41	.506	12.5	407	488
Troy	35	48	.422	19.5	430	522
Worcester	18	66	.214	37	379	652
1882 American Association						
Cincinnati	**55**	**25**	**.688**	–	**489**	**268**
Philadelphia	41	34	.547	11.5	406	389
Louisville	42	38	.525	13	443	352
Pittsburgh	39	39	.500	15	428	418
St. Louis	37	43	.463	18	399	496
Baltimore	19	54	.260	32.5	273	515
1883 National League						
Boston	**63**	**35**	**.643**	–	669	456
Chicago	59	39	.602	4	**679**	540
Providence	58	40	.592	5	636	**436**
Cleveland	55	42	.567	7.5	476	443
Buffalo	52	45	.536	10.5	614	576
New York	46	50	.479	16	530	577
Detroit	40	58	.408	23	524	650
Philadelphia	17	81	.173	46	437	887
1883 American Association						
Philadelphia	**66**	**32**	**.673**	–	**720**	547
St. Louis	65	33	.663	1	549	409
Cincinnati	61	37	.622	5	662	413
New York	54	42	.563	11	498	**405**
Louisville	52	45	.536	13.5	564	562
Columbus	32	65	.330	33.5	476	659
Pittsburgh	31	67	.316	35	525	728
Baltimore	28	68	.292	37	471	742

BATTING LEADERS

(Bases on balls not counted as At Bat)

Name	Pos.	Team	G	AB	R	H	2B	3B	HR	RBI	BB	BA	SA
Cap Anson	3B	Chi	66	309	63	110	13	6	2	59	12	.356	.456
Ross Barnes	2B	Chi	66	322	**126**	**138**	**23**	11	1	59	**20**	**.429**	**.578**
George Hall	OF	Phi	60	268	51	98	8	**12**	**5**	45	8	.366	.541
Paul Hines	OF	Chi	64	305	62	101	21	3	2	59	1	.331	.439
Cal McVey	1B-P	Chi	63	308	62	107	15	0	1	53	2	.347	.406
Levi Meyerle	3B	Phi	55	256	46	87	12	8	0	34	3	.340	.449
Jim O'Rourke	OF	Bos	70	312	61	102	15	1	2	43	15	.327	.401
Johnny Peters	SS	Chi	66	316	70	111	14	2	1	47	3	.351	.418
Lipman Pike	OF	StL	63	282	55	91	19	10	1	50	8	.323	.472
Deacon White	C	Chi	66	303	66	104	18	1	1	**60**	7	.343	.419
Cap Anson	3B-C	Chi	59	255	52	86	**20**	1	0	32	9	.337	.424
John Cassidy	OF	Bkn	60	251	43	95	10	5	0	27	3	.378	.458
George Hall	OF	Lou	61	270	53	87	15	8	0	26	12	.322	.437
Charley Jones	OF	Cin-Chi-Cin	57	240	53	75	12	10	2	38	15	.313	.471
Cal McVoy	C-3B-P	Chi	60	266	58	98	9	7	0	36	8	.368	.455
Jim O'Rourke	OF	Bos	61	265	**68**	96	16	4	0	23	**20**	.362	.457
Lipman Pike	OF-2B	Cin	58	263	45	78	12	4	**4**	23	9	.297	.420
Deacon White	1B-OF	Bos	59	266	51	**103**	14	**11**	2	**49**	8	**.387**	**.545**
Cap Anson	OF	Chi	59	256	54	86	12	2	0	40	13	.336	.398
Lew Brown	C-1B	Prov	57	238	44	75	**18**	7	1	43	7	.315	.462
Abner Dalrymple	OF	Mil	60	267	52	95	10	4	0	15	6	**.356**	.423
Bob Ferguson	SS	Chi	60	255	44	88	10	2	0	39	10	.345	.400
Dick Higham	OF	Prov	60	273	**60**	86	17	4	1	29	5	.315	.418
Paul Hines	OF	Prov	60	248	40	87	12	4	**4**	**50**	2	.351	.480
Orator Shaffer	OF	Ind	60	253	48	87	17	6	0	30	13	.344	.458
Joe Start	1B	Chi	60	**281**	58	**97**	12	5	1	27	2	.345	.434
Cap Anson	1B	Chi	49	221	41	72	22	1	0	34	2	.326	.434
Paul Hines	OF	Prov	84	**406**	81	**145**	23	8	2	52	8	**.357**	.468
Charley Jones	OF	Bos	83	355	**85**	112	24	9	**9**	**62**	**29**	.315	.510
King Kelly	3B-OF-C	Cin	76	342	78	118	22	**14**	2	47	8	.348	.509
Jim O'Rourke	OF-1B	Prov	80	359	69	126	17	12	1	46	13	.351	.474
John O'Rourke	OF	Bos	70	308	69	105	17	11	6	**62**	8	.341	**.526**
Joe Start	1B	Prov	65	311	70	99	11	5	2	37	7	.318	.405
Deacon White	C-OF	Cin	77	330	55	109	16	8	1	52	6	.330	.436
Ned Williamson	3B	Chi	77	314	65	94	20	13	1	36	24	.299	.455
Tom York	OF	Prov	80	339	69	104	25	5	1	50	19	.307	.419
Cap Anson	1B	Chi	84	346	52	117	22	1	1	**74**	14	.338	.416
Tom Burns	SS	Chi	82	323	46	100	17	3	0	43	12	.310	.381
Roger Connor	3B	Troy	83	340	53	113	17	10	3	47	13	.332	.459
Abner Dalrymple	OF	Chi	86	**374**	**91**	**124**	25	12	0	36	3	.332	.463
George Gore	OF	Chi	75	312	69	114	21	2	2	47	21	**.365**	**.465**
Paul Hines	OF	Prov	82	356	61	109	19	2	3	35	13	.306	.396
Charley Jones	OF	Bos	64	269	43	80	15	4	5	37	11	.297	.439
King Kelly	OF-C-3B	Chi	82	335	71	98	13	11	1	60	12	.293	.406
Jim O'Rourke	OF-INF-C	Bos	84	355	70	100	18	11	**6**	45	21	.282	.445
Harry Stovey	OF-1B	Wor	81	345	72	89	18	**14**	**6**	28	12	.258	.443
Cap Anson	1B	Chi	84	343	66	**137**	25	7	1	**82**	26	**.399**	**.522**
Charlie Bennett	C	Det	76	299	44	90	19	7	7	64	18	.301	.482
Dan Brouthers	OF-1B	Buf	65	270	60	86	15	7	**8**	44	18	.319	.515
Abner Dalrymple	OF	Chi	81	362	72	117	21	4	1	37	15	.323	.412
Buttercup Dickerson	OF	Wor	80	367	48	116	17	5	1	31	8	.316	.398
Fred Dunlap	2B	Cle	78	345	59	112	25	4	3	24	18	.325	.446
George Gore	OF	Chi	73	309	**86**	92	20	8	1	44	27	.298	.424
King Kelly	OF	Chi	80	353	84	114	**28**	3	2	55	16	.323	.436
Jack Rowe	C	Buf	61	246	36	82	11	**11**	1	43	1	.333	.480
Joe Start	1B	Prov	79	348	56	114	12	6	0	29	9	.328	.397
Cap Anson	1B	Chi	82	348	69	126	30	8	1	**83**	20	.362	.503
Charlie Bennett	C-3B	Det	80	328	40	100	15	10	5	48	20	.305	.457
Dan Brouthers	1B	Buf	84	351	71	**129**	25	11	6	63	21	**.368**	**.553**
Roger Connor	1B-OF-3B	Troy	79	339	63	111	22	**17**	4	42	13	.327	.528
George Gore	OF	Chi	84	367	**99**	117	14	7	3	51	**29**	.319	.420
Paul Hines	OF	Prov	84	379	73	117	28	10	4	34	10	.308	.467
King Kelly	SS-OF-C	Chi	84	377	81	115	**36**	5	1	55	10	.305	.435
Joe Start	1B	Prov	82	356	58	117	9	9	0	48	11	.329	.404
Jim Whitney	P-OF	Bos	60	246	48	80	18	8	5	48	24	.325	.524
George Wood	OF	Det	81	360	63	95	12	11	**7**	27	14	.264	.417
Pete Browning	2B-SS-3B	Lou	69	288	64	110	**19**	3	5		26	**.382**	**.521**
Hick Carpenter	3B	Cin	80	350	78	**128**	15	5	1	67	10	.354	.446
Mike Mansell	OF	Pit	79	347	59	96	18	**16**	2		7	.277	.438
Jack O'Brien	C-OF	Phi	62	240	44	73	13	3	3	37	13	.304	.421
Pop Snyder	C	Cin	72	308	49	89	12	2	1	50	9	.289	.351
Ed Swartwood	OF	Pit	76	325	**86**	107	18	11	5		21	.329	.498
Oscar Walker	OF	StL	76	318	48	74	15	7	**7**		10	.233	.390
Chicken Wolf	OF	Lou	78	320	46	94	11	8	0		9	.294	.378
Dan Brouthers	1B	Buf	97	420	83	**156**	39	**17**	3	**97**	16	**.371**	**.567**
Jack Burdock	2B	Bos	96	400	80	132	27	7	5	88	14	.330	.470
Roger Connor	1B	NY	96	401	80	145	28	14	1	50	25	.362	.509
Fred Dunlap	2B	Cle	90	383	79	126	34	2	4	37	22	.329	.460
Buck Ewing	C-OF-2B	NY	85	369	88	113	9	13	**10**	41	20	.306	.482
George Gore	OF	Chi	91	392	105	131	27	9	2	52	27	.334	.464
Joe Hornung	OF	Bos	98	446	**106**	124	25	13	8	66	8	.278	.446
John Morrill	1B	Bos	97	404	83	129	33	15	6	68	15	.319	.520
Jim O'Rourke	OF-C	Buf	93	430	99	141	30	7	1	38	16	.328	.437
Ezra Sutton	3B	Bos	94	414	101	134	28	15	3	73	17	.324	.486
Pete Browning	OF-SS-3B	Lou	84	360	95	121	14	11	4		23	.336	.469
Hick Carpenter	3B	Cin	94	432	99	133	18	4	3	40	18	.308	.389
Jim Clinton	OF	Bal	94	400	69	122	16	8	0		27	.305	.385
Charlie Comiskey	1B	StL	96	404	76	120	17	9	2	64	11	.297	.399
Charley Jones	OF	Cin	90	390	83	116	16	11	11	80	20	.297	.479
Mike Moynahan	SS	Phi	93	392	90	111	17	10	2	67	30	.283	.393
Jack Nelson	SS	NY	96	413	75	123	19	6	0		31	.291	.373
Long John Reilly	1B	Cin	97	436	103	126	21	14	9	79	9	.289	.463
Harry Stovey	1B	Phi	94	412	**110**	127	**32**	8	**14**	66	26	.308	**.527**
Ed Swartwood	1B-OF	Pit	95	417	86	**154**	24	8	3		24	**.369**	.487

PITCHING LEADERS

Name	Team	W	L	Pct.	G	IP	H	BB	SO	ShO	E.R.A.
Tommy Bond	Har	32	13	.711	45	408	355	13	88	6	1.68
Joe Borden	Bos	12	12	.500	29	218	257	**51**	34	2	2.89
Foghorn Bradley	Bos	11	9	.550	22	173	201	16	16	1	2.49
George Bradley	StL	45	19	.703	64	573	470	38	103	**16**	**1.23**
Candy Cummings	Har	16	8	.667	24	216	215	14	26	5	1.67
Jim Devlin	Lou	30	**35**	.462	**68**	**622**	566	37	**122**	5	1.56
Lon Knight	Phi	10	23	.303	34	282	383	34	12	0	2.62
Jack Manning	Bos	15	6	.714	34	197	213	32	24	0	2.14
Bobby Mathews	NY	21	34	.382	56	516	**693**	24	37	2	2.86
Al Spalding	Chi	**47**	13	**.783**	61	529	542	26	39	8	1.75
Joe Blong	StL	11	10	.524	25	187	203	38	51	0	2.74
Tommy Bond	Bos	**40**	17	**.702**	58	521	530	36	**170**	**6**	**2.11**
George Bradley	Chi	19	26	.422	50	394	452	39	59	2	3.31
Candy Cummings	Cin	5	14	.263	19	156	219	13	11	0	4.34
Jim Devlin	Lou	35	**25**	.583	**61**	**559**	**617**	41	141	4	2.25
Terry Larkin	Bkn	29	**25**	.537	56	501	510	**53**	96	4	2.14
Bobby Mathews	Cin	3	12	.200	15	120	200	17	9	0	4.04
Tricky Nichols	StL	18	23	.439	42	350	376	**53**	80	1	2.60
Tommy Bond	Bos	**40**	19	**.678**	**59**	**533**	**571**	33	**182**	**9**	2.06
Tom Healey	Prov-Ind	7	7	.500	14	113	125	20	20	0	2.39
Terry Larkin	Chi	29	26	.527	56	506	511	31	163	1	2.24
Jim McCormick	Ind	5	8	.385	14	117	128	15	36	1	1.69
Ed (The Only) Nolan	Ind	13	22	.371	38	347	359	**56**	125	1	2.57
Monte Ward	Prov	22	13	.629	37	334	308	34	116	6	**1.51**
Sam Weaver	Mil	12	**31**	.279	45	383	371	21	95	1	1.95
Will White	Cin	29	21	.580	52	468	477	45	169	5	1.79
Tommy Bond	Bos	42	19	.689	64	555	543	24	155	**12**	**1.96**
George Bradley	Troy	13	**40**	.245	54	487	590	26	133	3	2.85
Pud Galvin	Buf	37	27	.578	66	593	585	31	136	6	2.28
Frank Hankinson	Chi	15	10	.600	26	231	248	27	69	2	2.50
Terry Larkin	Chi	31	23	.574	58	513	514	30	142	3	2.44
Bobby Mathews	Prov	13	6	.684	27	189	194	26	90	0	2.29
Harry McCormick	Syr	18	33	.353	54	457	517	31	96	5	2.99
Jim McCormick	Cle	20	**40**	.333	62	546	582	**74**	197	3	2.42
Monte Ward	Prov	**44**	18	**.710**	70	587	571	36	**239**	2	2.15
Will White	Cin	43	31	.581	**76**	**680**	**676**	68	232	4	1.99
Tommy Bond	Bos	26	29	.473	63	493	559	45	118	3	2.67
George Bradley	Prov	12	9	.571	28	196	158	6	54	4	**1.38**
Larry Corcoran	Chi	43	14	.754	63	536	404	**99**	**268**	5	1.95
Pud Galvin	Buf	20	37	.351	58	459	528	32	128	5	2.71
Fred Goldsmith	Chi	22	3	**.880**	26	210	189	18	90	4	1.75
Jim McCormick	Cle	**45**	28	.616	**74**	**658**	**585**	75	260	7	1.85
Lee Richmond	Wor	34	33	.507	**74**	591	541	74	243	5	2.15
Monte Ward	Prov	40	23	.635	70	595	501	45	230	**8**	1.74
Mickey Welch	Troy	34	30	.531	65	574	575	80	123	4	2.54
Will White	Cin	18	**43**	.295	62	517	550	56	161	3	2.14
Larry Corcoran	Chi	**31**	14	.689	45	397	380	78	150	4	2.31
George Derby	Det	29	26	.527	56	495	505	86	**212**	**9**	2.20
Pud Galvin	Buf	29	24	.538	56	474	546	46	136	5	2.39
Fred Goldsmith	Chi	25	13	.658	39	330	328	44	76	5	2.59
Jim McCormick	Cle	26	30	.464	59	526	484	84	178	2	2.45
Old Hoss Radbourn	Prov	25	11	**.694**	41	325	309	64	117	3	
Lee Richmond	Wor	25	27	.481	53	462	547	68	156	3	
Monte Ward	Prov	18	18	.500	39	330	326	53	119	3	
Mickey Welch	Troy	20	18	.526	39	359	360	78	140	4	
Jim Whitney	Bos	**31**	**33**	.484	**66**	**552**	**548**	**90**	162	6	2.43
Larry Corcoran	Chi	27	12	**.692**	39	356	281	63	170	3	1.95
Pud Galvin	Buf	28	22	.560	52	445	476	40	162	3	
Fred Goldsmith	Chi	28	16	.636	45	405	377	38	107	4	2.42
Tim Keefe	Troy	17	26	.395	43	375	368	81	116	1	
Bobby Mathews	Bos	19	14	.576	34	285	278	22	153	0	3.03
Jim McCormick	Cle	**36**	29	.554	**68**	**596**	**550**	**103**	200	4	
Old Hoss Radbourn	Prov	31	19	.620	55	474	429	51	**201**	**5**	1.93
Monte Ward	Prov	19	13	.594	33	278	261	36	72	4	2.40
Stump Weidman	Det	26	20	.565	46	411	391	39	161	4	2.63
Jim Whitney	Bos	24	22	.522	49	420	404	41	180	3	2.66
Denny Driscoll	Pit	13	9	.591	23	201	162	12	59	0	
Doc Landis	Phi-Bal	12	**29**	.293	44	358	**425**	47	75	0	
Harry McCormick	Cin	13	12	.520	25	220	177	42	33	3	
Jumbo McGinnis	StL	25	20	.556	45	388	391	53	134	3	
Tony Mullane	Lou	30	24	.556	**55**	460	418	**78**	**170**	5	
Harry Salisbury	Pit	20	18	.526	38	335	315	37	135	1	
Sam Weaver	Phi	26	15	.634	42	371	374	35	104	2	
Will White	Cin	**40**	12	**.769**	54	**480**	411	71	122	**8**	
Charlie Buffinton	Bos	24	13	.649	43	333	346	51	188	4	3.11
Larry Corcoran	Chi	31	21	.596	56	474	483	82	216	3	
One Arm Daily	Cle	24	18	.571	45	380	360	**99**	171	4	
Pud Galvin	Buf	46	29	.613	**76**	**656**	676	50	279	**5**	
Fred Goldsmith	Chi	28	18	.609	46	383	456	39	82	2	
Jim McCormick	Cle	27	13	**.675**	43	341	316	65	145	1	1.82
Old Hoss Radbourn	Prov	**49**	25	.662	**76**	632	563	56	315	4	
Stump Weidman	Det	19	23	.452	52	402	435	72	183	3	
Mickey Welch	NY	27	21	.563	54	426	431	66	144	4	
Jim Whitney	Bos	38	22	.833	62	514	492	35	**345**	1	2.21
George Bradley	Phi	17	7	.708	27	217	221	23	58	0	
Denny Driscoll	Pit	18	21	.462	41	333	426	39	79	1	
Guy Hecker	Lou	26	23	.531	51	451	509	72	153	3	
Tim Keefe	NY	41	27	.603	**68**	**619**	486	98	**361**	5	
Bobby Mathews	Phi	30	14	.682	44	381	396	31	203	1	
Jumbo McGinnis	StL	29	15	.659	45	377	320	69	131	**6**	
Frank Mountain	Col	26	**33**	.441	59	503	**546**	**123**	159	4	
Tony Mullane	StL	36	15	**.706**	54	467	377	74	196	3	
Sam Weaver	Lou	26	22	.542	48	419	468	38	116	4	
Will White	Cin	**43**	22	.662	65	577	473	104	141	**6**	

1884-1887 SUMMARY

1884 National League

FINAL STANDINGS

Team	W	L	Pct.	GB	Runs	Opp.R
Providence	84	28	.750	–	.665	388
Boston	73	38	.658	10.5	684	468
Buffalo	64	47	.577	19.5	700	626
Chicago	62	50	.554	22	834	647
New York	62	50	.554	22	693	623
Philadelphia	39	73	.348	45	549	824
Cleveland	35	77	.313	49	458	716
Detroit	28	84	.250	56	445	736

BATTING LEADERS

Name	Pos.	Team	G	AB	R	H	2B	3B	HR	RBI	BB	BA	SA
Cap Anson	1B	Chi	111	471	108	159	32	3	21	102	29	.338	.552
Dan Brouthers	1B	Buf	90	381	80	124	22	16	14	79	33	.325	.577
Roger Connor	2B-OF-3B	NY	112	462	93	146	27	4	4	82	38	.316	.418
Abner Dalrymple	OF	Chi	110	516	110	160	17	9	22	69	14	.310	.506
King Kelly	OF-C-SS-3B	Chi	107	448	120	153	30	5	13	95	46	.341	.518
Jim O'Rourke	OF-1B-C	Buf	104	448	112	157	27	9	5	63	35	.350	.484
Fred Pfeffer	2B	Chi	111	463	104	134	11	10	25	101	25	.289	.518
Ezra Sutton	3B	Bos	106	447	97	156	26	6	3	61	29	.349	.454
Deacon White	3B	Buf	106	436	80	142	14	12	5	74	32	.325	.447
Ned Williamson	3B	Chi	106	413	82	115	18	7	27	84	42	.278	.552

PITCHING LEADERS

Name	Team	W	L	Pct.	G	IP	H	BB	SO	ShO	E.R.A.
Charlie Buffinton	Bos	47	16	.746	67	587	506	76	417	8	2.09
Larry Corcoran	Chi	35	23	.603	60	517	473	116	272	7	
Charlie Ferguson	Phi	21	24	.467	50	417	443	93	194	2	
Pud Galvin	Buf	46	22	.676	72	636	566	63	369	12	2.02
John Harkins	Cle	12	32	.273	46	391	399	108	192	3	
Jim McCormick*	Cle	19	22	.463	42	359	357	75	218	3	2.83
Old Hoss Radbourn	Prov	60	12	.833	75	679	528	98	441	11	1.45
Charlie Sweeney**	Prov	17	7	.708	27	221	153	29	143	3	
Mickey Welch	NY	39	21	.650	65	557	528	146	345	4	
Jim Whitney	Bos	22	14	.611	38	336	272	27	270	6	

1884 American Association

FINAL STANDINGS

Team	W	L	Pct.	GB	Runs	Opp.R
New York	75	32	.701	–	734	423
Columbus	69	39	.639	6.5	585	459
Louisville	68	40	.630	7.5	573	425
St. Louis	67	40	.626	8	658	539
Cincinnati	68	41	.624	8	754	512
Baltimore	63	43	.594	11.5	636	515
Philadelphia	61	46	.570	14	700	546
Toledo	46	58	.442	27.5	463	571
Brooklyn	40	64	.385	33.5	476	644
Richmond	12	30	.286	30.5	194	294
Pittsburgh	30	78	.278	45.5	406	725
Indianapolis	29	78	.271	46	462	755
Washington	12	51	.190	41	248	481

BATTING LEADERS

Name	Pos.	Team	G	AB	R	H	2B	3B	HR	RBI	BB	BA	SA
Sam Barkley	2B	Tol	104	433	71	130	39	9	1		22	.300	.439
Pete Browning	3B-OF-1B	Lou	105	454	101	155	34	8	4	47	13	.341	.478
Dude Esterbrook	3B	NY	112	477	110	150	29	11	1		12	.314	.428
Frank Fennelly	SS	Was-Cin	90	380	94	124	22	15	4		31	.326	.495
Sadie Houck	SS	Phi	110	473	93	143	19	14	0		7	.302	.402
Charley Jones	OF	Cin	113	475	113	153	22	19	7	71	37	.322	.493
Ted Larkin	OF	Phi	87	328	61	97	19	9	3	37	15	.296	.436
Fred Lewis	OF	StL	72	307	60	99	23	3	0		17	.322	.417
Biddy McPhee	2B	Cin	113	462	106	135	10	7	5	64	27	.292	.377
Dave Orr	1B	NY	110	460	83	162	32	13	9	112	5	.352	.537
Long John Reilly	1B	Cin	106	457	114	155	24	19	11	91	5	.339	.547
Chief Roseman	OF	NY	107	437	97	129	16	11	4		21	.295	.410
Harry Stovey	1B	Phi	106	443	126	146	25	25	10	83	26	.330	.567
Ed Swartwood	OF-1B	Pit	102	397	74	131	19	6	0		33	.330	.408
Chicken Wolf	OF	Lou	112	498	79	151	24	11	3	73	4	.303	.414

PITCHING LEADERS

Name	Team	W	L	Pct.	G	IP	H	BB	SO	ShO	E.R.A.
Bob Emslie	Bal	32	18	.640	50	455	419	88	264	4	
Dave Foutz	StL	17	7	.708	25	207	167	36	95	2	
Guy Hecker	Lou	52	20	.722	75	671	526	56	385	6	
Hardie Henderson	Bal	27	22	.551	52	439	382	116	346	4	
Tim Keefe	NY	37	17	.685	58	483	378	75	317	4	
Jack Lynch	NY	39	14	.736	54	487	410	42	286	5	
Bobby Mathews	Phi	30	18	.625	49	431	401	49	286	3	
Jumbo McGinnis	StL	24	16	.600	40	354	331	35	141	5	
Ed Morris	Col	35	13	.729	52	430	335	51	302	3	
Frank Mountain	Col	24	17	.585	42	361	289	78	156	5	
Billy Mountjoy	Cin	20	12	.625	33	289	274	43	96	3	
Tony Mullane	Tol	35	25	.583	68	576	485	90	329	8	
Billy Taylor***	Phi	18	12	.600	30	260	232	44	130	1	
Adonis Terry	Bkn	19	35	.352	57	485	487	75	233	3	
Will White	Cin	34	18	.654	52	456	479	74	118	7	

1884 Union Association

FINAL STANDINGS

Team	W	L	Pct.	GB	Runs	Opp.R
St. Louis	94	19	.832	–	887	429
Milwaukee	8	4	.667	35.5	53	34
Cincinnati	69	36	.657	21	703	466
Baltimore	58	47	.552	32	662	627
Boston	58	51	.532	34	636	558
Chicago-Pitt.	41	50	.451	42	438	482
Washington	47	65	.420	46.5	572	679
Philadelphia	21	46	.313	50	414	545
St. Paul	2	6	.250	39.5	24	57
Altoona	6	19	.240	44	90	216
Kansas City	16	63	.203	61	311	618
Wilmington	2	16	.111	44.5	35	114

BATTING LEADERS

Name	Pos.	Team	G	AB	R	H	2B	3B	HR	RBI	BB	BA	SA
Phil Baker	1B-OF-C	Was	86	371	75	107	12	5	1		11	.288	.356
Dick Burns	OF	Cin	79	350	84	107	17	12	4		5	.306	.457
Cannonball Crane	OF-C	Bos	101	428	83	122	23	6	13		14	.285	.458
Fred Dunlap	2B	StL	101	448	161	186	39	8	13		29	.415	.625
Jack Gleason	3B	StL	92	395	90	128	30	2	3		23	.324	.433
Bill Harbidge	OF	Cin	82	341	59	95	12	5	2		25	.279	.361
Bill Hawes	OF-1B	Cin	79	349	80	97	7	4	4		6	.278	.355
Buster Hoover	OF	Phi	63	275	76	100	20	8	0		15	.364	.495
Harry Moore	OF	Was	111	461	77	155	23	5	1		19	.336	.414
Joe Quinn	1B	StL	103	429	74	116	21	1	0		9	.270	.324
Dave Rowe	OF	StL	109	485	95	142	32	11	3		10	.293	.423
Emmett Seery	OF	Bal-KC	106	467	115	146	26	7	2		21	.313	.411
Orator Shaffer	OF	StL	106	467	130	168	40	10	2		30	.360	.501
Jumbo Shoeneck	1B	Bal-C+P	106	426	61	131	24	2	2		8	.308	.387

PITCHING LEADERS

Name	Team	W	L	Pct.	G	IP	H	BB	SO	ShO	E.R.A.
Jersey Bakely	Phi-Wil-KC	16	30	.348	46	395	443	81	226	1	
Tommy Bond	Bos	12	9	.571	23	189	185	14	128	0	
Henry Boyle	StL	15	3	.833	19	150	118	10	88	2	
George Bradley	Cin	25	15	.625	41	342	350	23	168	3	
Walter Burke	Bos	19	15	.559	38	322	326	31	255	0	
Dick Burns	Cin	23	15	.605	40	330	298	47	167	1	
One Arm Daily	C-P-Was	28	28	.500	58	501	446	72	483	4	
Charlie Gagus	Was	10	9	.526	23	170	143	38	156	0	
Jim McCormick*	Cin	21	3	.875	24	210	151	14	125	7	
Dupee Shaw	Bos	21	15	.583	39	316	227	50	309	5	
Bill Sweeney	Bal	40	21	.656	62	538	522	74	384	6	
Charlie Sweeney**	StL	24	7	.774	33	271	207	13	192	3	
Billy Taylor***	StL	25	4	.862	33	263	222	40	154	2	
Bill Wise	Was	23	18	.561	50	371	383	60	268	4	

1885 National League

FINAL STANDINGS

Team	W	L	Pct.	GB	Runs	Opp.R
Chicago	87	25	.777	–	834	470
New York	85	27	.759	2	691	370
Philadelphia	56	54	.509	30	513	511
Providence	53	57	.482	33	442	531
Boston	46	66	.411	41	528	589
Detroit	41	67	.380	44	514	582
Buffalo	38	74	.339	49	495	761
St. Louis	36	72	.333	49	390	593

BATTING LEADERS

Name	Pos.	Team	G	AB	R	H	2B	3B	HR	RBI	BB	BA	SA
Cap Anson	1B	Chi	112	464	100	144	35	7	7	108	34	.310	.461
Dan Brouthers	1B	Buf	98	407	87	146	27	13	7	59	34	.359	.541
Roger Connor	1B	NY	110	455	102	169	23	15	1	65	51	.371	.495
Abner Dalrymple	OF	Chi	113	492	109	135	27	12	11	61	46	.274	.445
Buck Ewing	C-OF	NY	81	342	81	104	14	11	6	63	13	.304	.462
George Gore	OF	Chi	109	441	115	138	19	12	5	57	68	.313	.444
King Kelly	OF-C	Chi	107	438	124	126	24	7	9	75	46	.288	.436
Jim O'Rourke	OF	NY	112	477	119	143	21	15	5	42	40	.300	.438
Hardy Richardson	2B-OF	Buf	96	426	90	136	17	9	6	44	20	.319	.444
Ezra Sutton	3B	Bos	108	449	78	140	23	8	4	47	17	.312	.425

PITCHING LEADERS

Name	Team	W	L	Pct.	G	IP	H	BB	SO	ShO	E.R.A.
Charlie Buffinton	Bos	22	27	.449	51	434	425	112	242	6	2.80
John Clarkson	Chi	53	16	.768	70	623	497	97	308	10	1.81
Ed Daily	Phi	26	23	.531	50	440	370	90	140	4	2.21
Charlie Ferguson	Phi	26	19	.578	48	405	345	81	197	5	2.13
Tim Keefe	NY	32	13	.711	46	398	297	103	230	7	1.58
Jim McCormick	Prov-Chi	21	7	.750	28	252	221	60	96	3	2.39
Old Hoss Radbourn	Prov	26	20	.565	58	509	521	111	218	3	2.26
Dupee Shaw	Prov	23	26	.469	49	400	343	99	194	6	2.63
Mickey Welch	NY	44	11	.800	56	492	372	131	258	7	1.65
Jim Whitney	Bos	18	32	.360	51	441	503	37	200	2	3.00

1885 American Association

FINAL STANDINGS

Team	W	L	Pct.	GB	Runs	Opp.R
St. Louis	79	33	.705	–	677	461
Cincinnati	63	49	.563	16	642	575
Pittsburgh	56	55	.505	22.5	548	539
Philadelphia	55	57	.491	24	764	691
Brooklyn	53	59	.473	26	624	650
Louisville	53	59	.473	26	562	598
New York	44	64	.407	33	527	688
Baltimore	41	68	.376	36.5	541	683

BATTING LEADERS

Name	Pos.	Team	G	AB	R	H	2B	3B	HR	RBI	BB	BA	SA
Steve Brady	OF	NY	108	433	60	128	14	5	3	58	25	.296	.372
Tom Brown	OF	Pit	108	437	81	133	16	12	4	68	35	.304	.423
Pete Browning	OF	Lou	113	479	98	176	32	10	9	73	25	.367	.532
John Coleman	OF	Phi	97	401	71	124	15	12	2	70	25	.309	.421
Frank Fennelly	SS	Cin	112	455	82	118	14	17	10	89	38	.259	.431
Charley Jones	OF	Cin	112	492	109	161	19	19	4	35	21	.327	.467
Ted Larkin	OF	Phi	108	455	114	154	40	13	8	88	26	.338	.536
Dave Orr	1B	NY	107	443	76	162	29	21	6	77	8	.366	.567
Long John Reilly	1B	Cin	106	461	92	142	18	11	5	60	11	.308	.427
Harry Stovey	1B-OF	Phi	112	480	130	164	27	11	13	75	39	.342	.525

PITCHING LEADERS

Name	Team	W	L	Pct.	G	IP	H	BB	SO	ShO	E.R.A.
Bob Caruthers	StL	40	13	.755	53	482	430	57	190	6	
Dave Foutz	StL	33	14	.702	47	408	351	92	147	2	
Guy Hecker	Lou	30	23	.566	53	480	454	54	209	2	
Hardie Henderson	Bal	26	35	.426	61	539	539	117	263	0	
Jack Lynch	NY	23	21	.523	44	379	410	42	177	1	
Bobby Mathews	Phi	30	17	.638	48	422	394	57	286	2	
Larry McKeon	Cin	20	13	.606	33	290	273	50	117	2	
Ed Morris	Pit	39	24	.619	63	581	459	101	298	7	
Henry Porter	Bkn	33	21	.611	54	482	427	110	197	2	
Will White	Cin	17	15	.531	34	293	295	64	80	2	

1886 National League

FINAL STANDINGS

Team	W	L	Pct.	GB	Runs	Opp.R
Chicago	90	34	.726	–	900	555
Detroit	87	36	.707	2.5	829	538
New York	75	44	.630	12.5	692	558
Philadelphia	71	43	.623	14	621	498
Boston	56	61	.479	30.5	657	661
St. Louis	43	79	.352	46	547	712
Kansas City	30	91	.248	58.5	494	872
Washington	28	92	.233	60	445	791

BATTING LEADERS

Name	Pos.	Team	G	AB	R	H	2B	3B	HR	RBI	BB	BA	SA
Cap Anson	1B	Chi	105	504	117	187	34	11	10	147	55	.371	.522
Dan Brouthers	1B	Det	121	489	139	181	41	16	11	72	66	.370	.587
Roger Connor	1B	NY	118	485	105	172	30	19	7	71	41	.355	.538
Jack Glasscock	SS	StL	121	486	96	158	28	8	3	40	38	.325	.434
George Gore	OF	Chi	118	444	150	135	19	13	6	62	102	.304	.446
Paul Hines	OF-3B-1B	Was	121	487	80	152	25	7	9	56	35	.312	.448
King Kelly	OF-C	Chi	118	451	155	175	31	11	4	80	83	.388	.532
Hardy Richardson	OF-2B	Det	125	538	125	189	27	11	11	61	46	.351	.504
Jack Rowe	SS	Det	111	468	97	142	21	8	6	88	26	.303	.421
Sam Thompson	OF	Det	122	503	100	156	19	14	8	89	35	.310	.451

PITCHING LEADERS

Name	Team	W	L	Pct.	G	IP	H	BB	SO	ShO	E.R.A.
Lady Baldwin	Det	42	13	.764	56	487	371	100	323	7	2.22
Dan Casey	Phi	25	19	.568	44	369	326	104	193	4	2.44
John Clarkson	Chi	35	17	.673	55	467	419	86	313	3	2.41
Charlie Ferguson	Phi	32	9	.780	48	396	317	69	212	4	1.91
Jocko Flynn	Chi	24	6	.800	32	257	207	63	146	2	2.24
Charlie Getzein	Det	31	11	.738	43	387	388	85	172	1	3.00
Tim Keefe	NY	42	20	.677	64	540	478	100	291	2	2.53
Jim McCormick	Chi	31	11	.738	42	348	341	100	172	2	2.84
Old Hoss Radbourn	Bos	27	30	.474	58	509	521	111	218	3	3.01
Mickey Welch	NY	33	22	.600	59	500	514	163	272	1	2.99

1886 American Association

FINAL STANDINGS

Team	W	L	Pct.	GB	Runs	Opp.R
St. Louis	93	46	.669	–	944	592
Pittsburgh	80	57	.584	12	810	647
Brooklyn	76	61	.555	16	832	832
Louisville	66	70	.485	25.5	833	805
Cincinnati	65	73	.471	27.5	883	865
Philadelphia	63	72	.467	28	772	942
New York	53	82	.393	38	628	766
Baltimore	48	83	.366	41	625	878

BATTING LEADERS

Name	Pos.	Team	G	AB	R	H	2B	3B	HR	RBI	BB	BA	SA
Pete Browning	OF	Lou	112	469	88	159	29	7	3		29	.339	.443
Bob Caruthers	P-OF	StL	86	313	91	107	22	12	3	61	64	.342	.518
Guy Hecker	P-1B-OF	Lou	84	345	76	118	13	5	4		32	.342	.443
Ted Larkin	OF	Phi	139	563	136	184	34	17	2	74	59	.327	.458
Arlie Latham	3B	StL	134	578	153	175	23	9	1	47	55	.303	.379
Fred Lewis	OF	Cin	77	324	72	103	14	6	2	32	20	.318	.417
Biddy McPhee	2B	Cin	140	562	139	153	24	11	7	70	59	.272	.391
Tip O'Neill	OF	StL	138	575	105	195	29	15	3	107	47	.339	.457
Dave Orr	1B	NY	136	566	90	196	27	33	7	91	17	.346	.548
Harry Stovey	OF-1B	Phi	123	486	115	154	26	13	7	59	64	.317	.467

PITCHING LEADERS

Name	Team	W	L	Pct.	G	IP	H	BB	SO	ShO	E.R.A.
Al Atkinson	Phi	25	17	.595	45	397	414	101	154	1	
Bob Caruthers	StL	30	14	.682	44	387	323	86	166	2	
Dave Foutz	StL	41	15	.732	59	504	418	144	283	11	
Pud Galvin	Pit	29	21	.580	50	435	457	75	72	2	
Guy Hecker	Lou	26	23	.531	49	420	390	118	133	2	
Matt Kilroy	Bal	29	34	.460	68	582	474	182	513	5	
Ed Morris	Pit	41	20	.672	64	555	455	118	326	12	
Tony Mullane	Cin	31	27	.534	63	529	500	166	250	1	
Henry Porter	Bkn	28	20	.583	48	424	439	114	163	1	
Toad Ramsey	Lou	38	27	.585	67	590	447	207	499	3	

1887 National League

FINAL STANDINGS

Team	W	L	Pct.	GB	Runs	Opp.R
Detroit	79	45	.637	–	969	714
Philadelphia	75	48	.610	3.5	901	702
Chicago	71	50	.587	6.5	813	716
New York	68	55	.553	10.5	816	723
Boston	61	60	.504	16.5	831	792
Pittsburgh	55	69	.444	24	621	750
Washington	46	76	.377	32	601	818
Indianapolis	37	89	.294	43	628	965

BATTING LEADERS

(Bases on balls not counted as Hit)

Name	Pos.	Team	G	AB	R	H	2B	3B	HR	RBI	BB	BA	SA
Cap Anson	1B	Chi	122	472	107	164	33	13	7	102	60	.347	.517
Dan Brouthers	1B	Det	122	499	153	168	35	20	12	101	71	.337	.559
Roger Connor	1B	NY	127	471	113	134	26	22	17	104	75	.285	.541
Jerry Denny	3B	Ind	122	510	86	165	34	12	11	97	13	.324	.502
King Kelly	OF-2B-C	Bos	114	470	119	152	34	11	8	63	55	.323	.494
Billy O'Brien	1B	Was	113	453	71	126	16	12	19	73	21	.278	.492
Hardy Richardson	2B-OF	Det	120	542	130	177	26	18	9	91	31	.327	.491
Jack Rowe	SS	Det	123	536	134	170	30	10	6	96	39	.317	.444
Sam Thompson	OF	Det	127	544	118	202	29	23	11	166	32	.371	.570
Sam Wise	SS-OF-2B	Bos	110	455	95	151	27	17	9	86	36	.332	.525

PITCHING LEADERS

Name	Team	W	L	Pct.	G	IP	H	BB	SO	ShO	E.R.A.
Charlie Buffinton	Phi	21	17	.553	40	332	352	92	160	1	3.66
Dan Casey	Phi	28	13	.683	45	390	377	115	119	4	2.86
John Clarkson	Chi	38	21	.644	60	523	513	92	237	2	3.08
Charlie Ferguson	Phi	21	10	.677	37	297	297	47	125	2	3.00
Pud Galvin	Pit	28	21	.571	49	441	490	67	76	2	3.29
Charlie Getzein	Det	29	13	.690	43	367	373	106	135	2	3.73
Tim Keefe	NY	35	19	.648	56	479	449	108	186	2	3.10
Kid Madden	Bos	22	14	.611	37	321	317	122	81	3	3.79
Mickey Welch	NY	23	15	.605	41	346	339	91	115	2	3.36
Jim Whitney	Was	24	21	.533	47	406	439	42	146	3	3.22

1887 American Association

FINAL STANDINGS

Team	W	L	Pct.	GB	Runs	Opp.R
St. Louis	95	40	.704	–	1131	761
Cincinnati	81	54	.600	14	892	745
Baltimore	77	58	.570	18	975	861
Louisville	76	60	.559	19.5	956	854
Philadelphia	64	69	.481	30	893	890
Brooklyn	60	74	.448	34.5	904	918
New York	44	89	.331	50	754	1093
Cleveland	39	92	.298	54	729	1112

BATTING LEADERS

(Bases on balls counted at Hit)

Name	Pos.	Team	G	AB	R	H	2B	3B	HR	RBI	BB	BA	SA
Pete Browning	OF	Lou	134	541	133	226	36	18	4		55	.418	.573
Oyster Burns	SS-3B	Bal	140	548	120	182	33	20	10	99	63	.332	.520
Bob Caruthers	OF-P	StL	98	359	94	129	23	9	7	73	66	.359	.532
Charlie Comiskey	1B	StL	125	536	136	180	22	6	4	103	27	.336	.422
Jumbo Davis	3B-SS	Bal	130	488	81	150	23	19	8	109	28	.307	.482
Dave Foutz	OF-P-1B	StL	103	425	79	152	26	13	4	108	23	.358	.508
Denny Lyons	3B	Phi	137	558	128	237	43	16	6	102	47	.425	.591
Tip O'Neill	OF	StL	123	513	166	227	46	24	14	123	50	.442	.708
Dave Orr	1B	NY	85	343	62	125	24	11	2	66	22	.364	.516
Harry Stovey	OF-1B	Phi	124	489	124	163	29	12	4	76	56	.333	.466

PITCHING LEADERS

Name	Team	W	L	Pct.	G	IP	H	BB	SO	ShO	E.R.A.
Bob Caruthers	StL	29	9	.763	39	341	337	61	74	2	3.35
Dave Foutz	StL	25	12	.676	40	339	369	90	94	1	3.74
Matt Kilroy	Bal	46	20	.697	69	589	585	157	217	6	2.87
Silver King	StL	34	11	.756	46	390	401	109	128	2	3.53
Tony Mullane	Cin	31	17	.646	48	416	414	121	97	6	3.50
Toad Ramsey	Lou	37	27	.578	65	561	542	167	355	0	
Ed Seward	Phi	25	25	.500	55	474	448	140	155	3	
Elmer Smith	Cin	33	18	.647	52	447	400	126	176	3	2.74
Phenomenal Smith	Bal	25	30	.455	58	490	526	176	206	1	3.58
Gus Weyhing	Phi	26	25	.510	55	466	465	167	193	2	

FINAL STANDINGS

Team	W	L	Pct.	GB	Runs	Opp.R
1888 National League						
New York	84	47	.641	–	659	479
Chicago	77	58	.570	9	734	659
Philadelphia	69	61	.531	14.5	535	509
Boston	70	64	.522	15.5	669	619
Detroit	68	63	.519	16	721	629
Pittsburgh	66	58	.493	19.5	534	580
Indianapolis	50	85	.370	36	603	731
Washington	48	86	.358	37.5	482	731
1888 American Association						
St. Louis	92	43	.681	–	789	501
Brooklyn	88	52	.629	6.5	758	584
Philadelphia	81	52	.609	10	827	594
Cincinnati	80	54	.597	11.5	745	628
Baltimore	57	80	.416	36	653	779
Cleveland	50	82	.379	40.5	651	839
Louisville	48	87	.356	44	689	870
Kansas City	43	89	.326	47.5	579	896
1889 National League						
New York	83	43	.659	–	935	708
Boston	83	45	.648	1	826	626
Chicago	67	65	.508	19	867	814
Philadelphia	63	64	.496	20.5	742	748
Pittsburgh	61	71	.462	25	726	801
Cleveland	61	72	.459	25.5	656	720
Indianapolis	59	75	.440	28	819	894
Washington	41	83	.331	41	632	892
1889 American Association						
Brooklyn	93	44	.679	–	995	706
St. Louis	90	45	.667	2	957	680
Philadelphia	75	58	.564	16	880	787
Cincinnati	76	63	.547	18	897	769
Baltimore	70	65	.519	22	791	795
Columbus	60	78	.435	33.5	779	924
Kansas City	55	82	.401	38	852	1031
Louisville	27	111	.196	66.5	632	1091
1890 National League						
Brooklyn	86	43	.667	–	884	620
Chicago	84	53	.613	6	847	692
Philadelphia	78	54	.591	9.5	823	707
Cincinnati	77	55	.583	10.5	753	633
Boston	76	57	.571	12	763	593
New York	63	68	.481	24	713	698
Cleveland	44	88	.333	43.5	630	832
Pittsburgh	23	113	.169	66.5	597	1235
1890 American Association						
Louisville	88	44	.667	–	819	588
Columbus	79	55	.590	10	831	617
St. Louis	78	58	.574	12	870	736
Toledo	68	64	.515	20	739	689
Rochester	63	63	.500	22	709	711
Syracuse	55	72	.433	30.5	698	831
Philadelphia	54	78	.409	34	702	945
Brooklyn-Balt.	41	92	.308	47.5	674	925
1890 Players League						
Boston	81	48	.628	–	992	767
Brooklyn	76	56	.576	6.5	964	893
New York	74	57	.565	8	1018	875
Chicago	75	62	.547	10	886	770
Philadelphia	68	63	.519	14	941	855
Pittsburgh	60	68	.469	20.5	835	892
Cleveland	55	75	.423	26.5	849	1027
Buffalo	36	96	.273	46.5	793	1199
1891 National League						
Boston	87	51	.630	–	847	658
Chicago	82	53	.607	3.5	832	730
New York	71	61	.538	13	754	711
Philadelphia	68	69	.496	18.5	756	773
Cleveland	65	74	.468	22.5	835	888
Brooklyn	61	76	.445	25.5	765	820
Cincinnati	56	81	.409	30.5	646	790
Pittsburgh	55	80	.407	30.5	679	744
1891 American Association						
Boston	93	42	.689	–	1028	675
St. Louis	86	52	.623	8.5	976	753
Baltimore	72	63	.533	21	850	798
Philadelphia	73	66	.525	22	817	794
Cinc.-Milw.	64	72	.471	29.5	776	799
Columbus	61	76	.445	33	702	777
Louisville	55	84	.396	40	713	890
Washington	43	92	.319	50	691	1067
1892 National League						
Boston	102	48	.680	–	862	649
Cleveland	93	56	.624	8.5	855	613
Brooklyn	95	59	.617	9	935	733
Philadelphia	87	66	.569	16.5	860	690
Cincinnati	82	68	.547	20	766	731
Pittsburgh	80	73	.523	35.5	802	796
Chicago	70	76	.479	30	635	735
New York	71	80	.470	31.5	811	826
Louisville	63	89	.414	40	649	804
Washington	58	93	.384	44.5	731	869
St. Louis	56	94	.373	46	703	922
Baltimore	46	101	.313	54.5	779	1020

BATTING LEADERS

Name	Pos.	Team	G	AB	R	H	2B	3B	HR	RBI	BB	BA	SA
Cap Anson	1B	Chi	134	515	101	177	17	12	12	84	47	.344	.493
Jake Beckley	1B	Pit	71	283	35	97	16	3	1	27	7	.343	.431
Dan Brouthers	1B	Det	129	522	118	160	35	13	9	66	68	.306	.475
Roger Connor	1B	NY	134	481	98	140	15	17	14	71	73	.291	.480
Buck Ewing	C-3B	NY	103	415	83	127	17	15	6	58	24	.306	.463
Dick Johnston	OF	Bos	135	585	102	173	33	17	12	68	15	.296	.472
King Kelly	C-OF	Bos	105	440	85	140	20	11	9	71	31	.318	.475
Jimmy Ryan	OF	Chi	130	549	115	182	37	7	16	64	35	.332	.512
Mike Tiernan	OF	NY	113	443	75	130	14	8	9	52	42	.293	.422
Deacon White	3B	Det	125	527	75	157	20	5	4	71	21	.298	.378
Pete Browning	OF	Lou	99	384	59	120	23	8	3	72	37	.313	.438
Oyster Burns	OF-SS	Bal-Bkn	129	528	95	158	27	13	6	67	38	.299	.434
Hub Collins	OF-2B-SS	Bkn	126	516	133	164	31	12	2	53	50	.318	.436
Ted Larkin	1B	Phi	135	544	97	154	27	10	7	101	33	.283	.408
Denny Lyons	3B	Phi	111	446	98	145	21	5	6	83	41	.325	.435
Ed McKean	SS-OF	Cle	130	542	92	161	23	13	6	68	28	.297	.421
Tip O'Neill	OF	StL	130	530	106	176	23	9	5	98	44	.332	.438
Dave Orr	1B	Bkn	95	393	57	119	20	5	1	59	7	.303	.387
Long John Reilly	1B	Cin	127	527	112	167	28	14	13	103	17	.324	.509
Harry Stovey	OF	Phi	130	538	128	171	25	21	9	65	62	.318	.493
Cap Anson	1B	Chi	134	518	99	177	30	6	7	117	86	.342	.463
Dan Brouthers	1B	Bos	126	485	105	181	25	8	7	118	66	.373	.501
Roger Connor	1B	NY	131	496	117	157	32	17	13	130	93	.317	.528
Jerry Denny	3B	Ind	133	578	96	163	24	0	18	112	27	.282	.417
Hugh Duffy	OF	Chi	136	584	144	182	21	7	12	89	46	.312	.433
Buck Ewing	C	NY	96	407	91	133	23	14	4	87	37	.327	.482
Jack Glasscock	SS	Ind	134	582	128	209	39	2	7	85	31	.359	.469
Jimmy Ryan	OF-SS	Chi	135	576	140	187	30	12	17	72	70	.325	.477
Sam Thompson	OF	Phi	128	533	103	158	35	4	20	111	36	.296	.490
Mike Tiernan	OF	NY	122	499	146	167	23	13	11	73	96	.335	.499
Lou Bierbauer	2B	Phi	130	549	80	172	27	7	7	105	29	.313	.426
Oyster Burns	OF	Bkn	132	499	104	157	19	11	5	100	68	.315	.427
Billy Hamilton	OF	KC	137	532	145	160	15	15	3	77	87	.301	.402
Bug Holliday	OF	Cin	135	562	107	193	28	7	19	104	43	.343	.520
Ted Larkin	1B	Phi	133	516	108	167	26	11	3	74	83	.324	.434
Denny Lyons	3B	Phi	131	507	131	171	34	4	9	82	79	.327	.473
Tip O'Neill	OF	StL	133	534	125	180	32	8	9	110	72	.337	.478
Dave Orr	1B	Col	134	560	70	182	31	11	4	87	9	.325	.441
Harry Stovey	OF	Phi	138	546	154	180	37	14	19	119	77	.330	.553
Tommy Tucker	1B	Bal	134	526	103	197	22	11	5	99	42	.375	.487
Cap Anson	1B	Chi	139	504	102	157	16	4	7	107	113	.312	.401
Oyster Burns	OF	Bkn	119	472	102	134	22	13	13	128	51	.284	.468
Jack Clements	C	Phi	97	381	64	120	23	8	7	74	45	.315	.472
Jack Glasscock	SS	NY	124	512	91	172	33	10	1	66	41	.336	.445
Billy Hamilton	OF	Phi	123	496	131	161	10	9	2	49	83	.325	.393
George Pinckney	3B	Bkn	126	485	115	150	20	9	7	83	80	.309	.431
Long John Reilly	1B	Cin	133	553	114	166	25	25	6	86	16	.300	.468
Sam Thompson	OF	Phi	132	549	114	172	38	9	4	102	42	.313	.437
Mike Tiernan	OF	NY	133	553	130	168	25	20	13	59	68	.304	.492
Walt Wilmot	OF	Chi	139	571	114	159	15	12	13	98	64	.278	.415
Count Campau	OF	StL	74	310	68	85	9	11	10	75	26	.274	.471
Cupid Childs	2B	Syr	136	494	109	170	32	14	2	89	72	.344	.478
Sandy Griffin	OF	Roc	107	407	85	124	28	4	5	53	50	.305	.430
Spud Johnson	OF	Col	137	545	106	193	23	18	1	113	48	.354	.468
Denny Lyons	3B	Phi	88	327	79	116	29	5	7	73	57	.351	.538
Tommy McCarthy	OF-3B	StL	132	539	134	189	26	9	6	69	66	.351	.466
Jack O'Connor	C	Col	118	446	89	152	14	10	2	66	38	.341	.430
Ed Swartwood	OF	Tol	126	463	106	143	23	11	3	64	80	.309	.425
Perry Werden	1B	Tol	129	502	113	142	22	20	6	72	78	.283	.442
Chicken Wolf	OF	Lou	134	538	100	197	29	11	4	98	43	.366	.483
Jake Beckley	1B	Pit	121	517	109	168	41	20	9	119	42	.325	.534
Pete Browning	OF	Cle	118	488	114	191	41	7	5	93	75	.391	.535
Roger Connor	1B	NY	123	484	134	180	25	15	14	104	88	.372	.572
Hugh Duffy	OF	Chi	137	591	161	194	33	14	7	82	59	.328	.467
Buck Ewing	C	NY	83	349	99	122	20	15	8	72	39	.350	.562
George Gore	OF	NY	93	400	131	134	25	8	10	55	77	.335	.513
Jim O'Rourke	OF	NY	111	469	112	172	31	7	9	115	33	.367	.520
Dave Orr	1B	Bkn	107	464	98	180	30	13	6	124	30	.388	.547
Hardy Richardson	OF	Bos	130	554	125	184	31	16	13	144	52	.332	.516
Monte Ward	SS	Bkn	128	558	135	207	14	10	4	60	51	.371	.453
Cap Anson	1B	Chi	136	537	82	158	25	9	8	120	75	.294	.419
Pete Browning	OF	Cin-Pit	101	398	62	129	22	5	3	61	51	.324	.427
Jack Clements	C	Phi	105	416	57	127	29	4	4	74	43	.305	.423
Roger Connor	1B	NY	129	477	110	140	27	12	6	94	83	.293	.438
Billy Hamilton	OF	Phi	133	529	142	179	21	6	2	60	102	.338	.412
Bug Holliday	OF	Cin	110	440	75	140	19	8	9	84	37	.318	.459
Herman Long	SS	Bos	139	577	130	166	21	12	10	77	80	.288	.418
Jim O'Rourke	OF	NY	136	554	94	167	27	8	5	95	26	.301	.406
Harry Stovey	OF	Bos	133	545	118	152	33	19	16	95	78	.279	.497
Mike Tiernan	OF	NY	133	540	111	164	30	12	16	72	69	.304	.493
Dan Brouthers	1B	Bos	130	486	117	170	26	20	5	108	87	.350	.516
Tom Brown	OF	Bos	137	589	177	189	29	21	6	72	70	.321	.472
Charlie Duffee	OF	Col	137	552	86	166	28	4	10	90	42	.301	.420
Hugh Duffy	OF	Bos	127	536	134	180	23	10	9	109	61	.336	.466
Duke Farrell	3B-C-OF	Bos	122	473	108	143	19	13	12	110	59	.302	.474
Denny Lyons	3B	StL	120	451	124	142	24	3	11	84	88	.315	.455
Tommy McCarthy	OF	StL	136	578	127	179	20	8	8	95	50	.310	.413
Jocko Milligan	C-1B	Phi	118	455	75	138	35	12	11	106	56	.303	.505
Tip O'Neill	OF	StL	129	521	112	167	29	3	10	95	62	.321	.445
George Van Haltren	OF	Bal	139	566	136	180	19	15	9	83	71	.318	.452
Dan Brouthers	1B	Bkn	152	588	121	197	33	20	5	124	84	.335	.485
Oyster Burns	OF	Bkn	139	545	94	168	25	18	4	96	65	.308	.442
Cupid Childs	2B	Cle	144	552	135	185	15	12	3	53	117	.335	.422
Roger Connor	1B	Phi	153	558	122	159	31	11	12	73	116	.285	.444
Ed Delahanty	OF	Phi	120	470	78	147	33	19	6	91	31	.313	.502
Hugh Duffy	OF	Bos	146	609	125	184	25	13	5	81	60	.302	.411
Buck Ewing	1B-C	NY	97	394	58	126	12	15	8	77	38	.320	.487
Billy Hamilton	OF	Phi	136	539	131	178	18	7	3	53	81	.330	.406
Bug Holliday	OF	Cin	149	600	114	172	23	15	13	91	57	.287	.440
Ted Larkin	1B	Was	116	450	73	127	16	5	8	96	39	.282	.393
Jimmy Ryan	OF	Chi	127	508	102	147	21	12	10	65	61	.289	.437
Sam Thompson	OF	Phi	151	602	109	183	31	8	9	104	59	.304	.427
Mike Tiernan	OF	NY	114	451	80	134	15	11	5	66	57	.297	.412
George Van Haltren	OF	Bal	148	604	116	179	23	13	7	62	76	.296	.412

PITCHING LEADERS

Name	Team	W	L	Pct.	G	IP	H	BB	SO	ShO	E.R.A.
Charlie Buffinton	Phi	28	17	.622	46	400	324	59	199	3	1.91
John Clarkson	Bos	33	20	.623	54	483	448	119	223	3	2.76
Pete Conway	Det	30	14	.682	45	391	315	57	176	4	2.26
Pud Galvin	Pit	23	25	.479	50	437	446	53	107	6	2.64
Tim Keefe	NY	35	11	.761	51	434	316	91	333	8	1.74
Gus Krock	Chi	25	14	.641	39	340	295	45	161	4	2.44
Ed Morris	Pit	29	24	.547	55	480	470	74	135	5	2.31
Ben Sanders	Phi	19	10	.655	31	275	240	33	121	4	1.90
Bill Sowders	Bos	19	15	.559	36	317	278	73	132	2	2.07
Mickey Welch	NY	26	19	.578	47	425	328	108	167	5	1.93
Jersey Bakley	Cle	25	33	.431	61	533	518	128	212	4	2.97
Bob Caruthers	Bkn	29	15	.659	44	392	337	53	140	4	2.39
Icebox Chamberlin	Lou-StL	25	11	.694	38	308	238	86	176	2	2.19
Nat Hudson	StL	26	10	.722	39	333	283	59	130	5	2.54
Mickey Hughes	Bkn	25	13	.658	40	363	281	98	159	2	2.13
Silver King	StL	45	21	.682	66	586	437	76	258	6	1.64
Tony Mullane	Cin	26	16	.619	44	380	341	75	186	4	2.84
Ed Seward	Phi	34	19	.642	57	519	388	127	272	6	2.01
Lee Viau	Cin	27	14	.659	42	388	331	110	164	1	2.64
Gus Weyhing	Phi	28	18	.609	47	404	314	111	204	3	2.25
Ed Beatin	Cle	20	16	.556	36	318	316	141	126	3	3.57
Henry Boyle	Ind	21	21	.500	46	379	422	95	97	2	3.92
Charlie Buffinton	Phi	26	17	.605	47	380	390	121	153	2	3.24
John Clarkson	Bos	49	19	.721	73	620	589	203	284	8	2.73
Pud Galvin	Pit	23	16	.590	41	341	392	78	77	4	4.17
Tim Keefe	NY	28	13	.683	47	364	310	151	209	3	3.31
Darby O'Brien	Cle	22	17	.564	41	347	345	167	122	1	4.15
Old Hoss Radbourn	Bos	20	11	.645	33	277	282	72	99	1	3.67
Harry Staley	Pit	21	26	.447	49	420	434	116	159	1	3.51
Mickey Welch	NY	27	12	.692	45	364	340	149	125	3	3.02
Mark Baldwin	Col	27	34	.443	63	514	458	274	368	6	3.61
Bob Caruthers	Bkn	40	12	.769	56	445	444	104	118	7	3.13
Icebox Chamberlin	StL	33	14	.702	53	422	376	165	202	2	2.96
Jesse Duryea	Cin	30	16	.652	53	401	372	127	183	2	2.56
Frank Foreman	Bal	25	21	.543	51	414	364	137	180	5	3.52
Matt Kilroy	Bal	29	25	.537	59	481	476	142	217	5	2.84
Silver King	StL	33	17	.660	56	458	462	125	188	3	3.14
Jack Stivetts	StL	12	7	.632	26	192	153	68	143	2	2.25
Adonis Terry	Bkn	21	16	.568	41	326	285	126	186	2	3.29
Gus Weyhing	Phi	30	20	.600	52	450	428	161	219	3	3.18
Bob Caruthers	Bkn	23	11	.676	37	300	292	87	64	1	3.09
John Clarkson	Bos	26	18	.591	44	383	370	140	138	2	3.27
Kid Gleason	Phi	39	17	.696	60	506	479	167	222	6	2.63
Bill Hutchison	Chi	42	25	.627	71	603	505	199	289	5	2.70
Tom Lovett	Bkn	31	11	.738	44	372	327	141	124	4	2.78
Pat Luby	Chi	20	9	.690	34	268	226	95	85	0	3.19
Kid Nichols	Bos	27	19	.587	48	427	374	112	222	7	2.21
Billy Rhines	Cin	28	17	.622	46	401	337	113	182	6	1.95
Amos Rusie	NY	29	34	.460	67	549	436	289	341	4	2.64
Adonis Terry	Bkn	25	16	.610	46	370	362	133	185	1	2.94
Bob Barr	Roc	28	25	.528	57	493	458	219	209	3	
Icebox Chamberlin	StL-Col	14	9	.609	30	210	176	96	128	6	
Red Ehret	Lou	25	14	.641	43	359	351	79	174	4	
Hank Gastright	Col	26	14	.650	48	401	312	135	199	4	
Egyptian Healy	Tol	22	23	.489	46	389	326	127	225	2	
Sadie McMahon	Phi-B-B	36	21	.632	60	509	498	166	291	1	
Toad Ramsey	StL	26	16	.619	44	349	325	102	257	1	
Fred Smith	Tol	19	14	.576	35	286	273	90	116	2	
Jack Stivetts	StL	29	20	.592	54	419	399	179	289	3	
Scott Stratton	Lou	34	15	.694	50	431	398	61	207	4	
Mark Baldwin	Chi	33	24	.579	59	501	498	249	211	1	3.31
Bill Daley	Bos	20	12	.625	34	235	246	167	110	2	3.60
Henry Gruber	Cle	21	20	.512	48	383	464	204	110	1	4.28
Ad Gumbert	Bos	24	11	.686	39	277	338	86	81	1	3.96
Silver King	Chi	32	22	.593	56	461	420	163	185	4	2.69
Phil Knell	Phi	21	11	.656	35	287	287	166	99	2	3.83
Hank O'Day	NY	22	13	.629	43	329	356	163	94	1	4.21
Old Hoss Radbourn	Bos	27	12	.692	41	343	352	100	80	1	3.31
Harry Staley	Pit	21	25	.457	46	388	392	74	145	3	3.22
Gus Weyhing	Bkn	30	16	.652	49	390	419	179	177	3	3.60
Mark Baldwin	Pit	22	28	.440	53	438	385	227	197	2	2.75
John Clarkson	Bos	34	18	.654	55	461	435	154	141	3	2.79
John Ewing	NY	21	8	.724	33	269	237	105	138	5	2.28
Kid Gleason	Phi	24	19	.558	53	418	431	165	100	1	3.51
Bill Hutchison	Chi	43	19	.694	66	561	508	178	261	4	2.81
Tom Lovett	Bkn	24	18	.571	44	366	361	129	129	3	3.69
Kid Nichols	Bos	30	17	.638	52	426	413	103	240	5	2.39
Amos Rusie	NY	33	20	.623	61	500	391	262	337	6	2.57
Harry Staley	Pit-Bos	23	14	.622	40	324	313	80	139	1	2.58
Cy Young	Cle	27	20	.574	55	424	431	140	147	0	2.84
Charlie Buffinton	Bos	28	9	.757	48	364	303	120	158	2	2.55
Icebox Chamberlin	Phi	22	23	.489	49	406	397	206	204	0	4.21
Cannonball Crane	C-M	14	17	.452	32	250	183	102	94	2	
George Haddock	Bos	34	11	.756	51	380	330	137	169	5	2.49
Phil Knell	Col	27	27	.500	58	462	363	226	228	5	2.92
Willie McGill	C-M-StL	21	13	.618	43	314	294	168	173	1	3.35
Sadie McMahon	Bal	34	25	.576	61	503	493	149	219	5	2.81
Darby O'Brien	Bos	19	13	.594	40	269	300	127	87	0	3.65
Jack Stivetts	StL	33	22	.600	64	440	357	232	259	3	2.86
Gus Weyhing	Phi	31	20	.608	52	450	428	161	219	3	3.18
John Clarkson	Bos-Cle	24	16	.600	45	389	350	132	139	5	2.48
Nig Cuppy	Cle	28	12	.700	47	376	333	121	103	1	2.51
George Haddock	Bkn	31	13	.705	46	381	340	163	153	3	3.14
Bill Hutchison	Chi	37	34	.521	75	627	572	187	316	5	2.74
Frank Killen	Was	30	23	.566	60	460	448	182	147	2	3.31
Tony Mullane	Cin	21	10	.677	37	295	222	127	109	3	2.59
Kid Nichols	Bos	35	16	.686	53	454	404	121	187	5	2.83
Amos Rusie	NY	31	30	.508	64	532	405	267	288	2	2.88
Harry Staley	Bos	24	11	.686	37	300	273	97	93	3	3.03
Ed Stein	Bkn	27	18	.600	48	377	310	150	190	6	2.84
Jack Stivetts	Bos	33	14	.702	53	415	346	171	180	3	3.04
Scott Stratton	Lou	21	20	.512	42	352	342	70	93	2	2.91
Gus Weyhing	Phi	30	21	.588	59	470	411	168	202	6	2.66
Cy Young	Cle	36	11	.766	53	453	363	118	168	9	1.93

1893—1900 SUMMARY

1893 National League

FINAL STANDINGS

Team	W	L	Pct.	GB	Runs	Opp.R
Boston	**86**	**43**	**.667**	–	1008	795
Pittsburgh	81	48	.628	5	970	**766**
Cleveland	73	55	.570	12.5	976	839
Philadelphia	72	57	.558	14	**1011**	841
New York	68	64	.515	19.5	941	845
Brooklyn	65	63	.508	20.5	775	845
Cincinnati	65	63	.508	20.5	759	814
Baltimore	60	70	.462	26.5	820	893
Chicago	56	71	.441	29	829	874
St. Louis	57	75	.432	30.5	745	829
Louisville	50	75	.400	34	759	942
Washington	40	89	.310	46	722	1032

BATTING LEADERS

Name	Pos.	Team	G	AB	R	H	2B	3B	HR	RBI	BB	BA	SA
Jesse Burkett	OF	Cle	124	480	144	179	23	15	6	82	98	.373	.521
George Davis	3B	NY	133	533	112	199	23	26	11	119	42	.373	.536
Ed Delahanty	OF	Phi	132	**588**	145	218	31	20	**19**	**146**	47	.371	**.588**
Hugh Duffy	OF	Bos	131	537	**149**	203	23	7	6	118	50	**.378**	.480
Buck Ewing	OF	Cle	114	477	116	177	27	17	6	122	41	.371	.537
Billy Hamilton	OF	Phi	82	349	111	138	21	7	5	44	63	.395	.539
Tommy McCarthy	OF	Bos	116	441	108	159	30	6	5	111	64	.361	.490
Ed McKean	SS	Cle	125	510	100	166	26	23	4	133	50	.325	.490
Jake Stenzel	OF	Pit	128	500	119	183	27	21	7	103	77	.366	.546
Patsy Tebeau	1B-3B	Cle	115	446	90	160	**35**	7	2	102	32	.359	.482
Sam Thompson	OF	Phi	130	583	130	**220**	33	14	11	126	50	.377	.539
Mike Tiernan	OF	NY	124	471	113	154	19	12	15	102	72	.327	.514
George Van Haltren	OF	Pit	124	502	129	176	14	11	3	79	75	.350	.440
Monte Ward	2B	NY	135	557	129	194	26	8	2	77	47	.348	.434

PITCHING LEADERS

Name	Team	W	L	Pct.	G	IP	H	BB	SO	ShO	E.R.A.
Theo Breitenstein	StL	19	20	.487	48	383	359	156	102	1	**3.17**
Kid Carsey	Phi	22	12	.647	39	318	375	124	50	1	4.81
Frank Dwyer	Cin	18	14	.563	37	287	332	93	53	1	4.14
Red Ehret	Pit	17	17	.500	39	314	322	115	70	**4**	3.44
Kid Gleason	StL	21	25	.457	48	380	436	187	86	1	4.62
Brickyard Kennedy	Bkn	26	19	.578	46	383	376	168	107	2	3.71
Frank Killen	Pit	**34**	10	**.773**	55	415	401	140	99	2	3.64
Sadie McMahon	Bal	24	16	.600	43	346	378	156	79	0	4.37
Kid Nichols	Bos	33	13	.717	52	425	426	118	94	1	3.52
Amos Rusie	NY	33	20	.623	**56**	**482**	**451**	**218**	**208**	**4**	3.23
Ed Stein	Bkn	19	14	.576	37	298	294	119	81	1	3.78
Jack Stivetts	Bos	19	13	.594	37	284	315	115	61	1	4.40
Gus Weyhing	Phi	24	16	.600	42	345	399	145	101	2	4.75
Cy Young	Cle	32	16	.667	53	423	442	103	102	1	3.36

1894 National League

Team	W	L	Pct.	GB	Runs	Opp.R
Baltimore	**89**	**39**	**.695**	–	1171	820
New York	88	44	.667	3	940	**789**
Boston	83	49	.629	8	**1222**	1002
Philadelphia	71	57	.555	18	1143	966
Brooklyn	70	61	.534	20.5	1021	1007
Cleveland	68	61	.527	21.5	932	896
Pittsburgh	65	65	.500	25	955	972
Chicago	57	75	.432	34	1041	1066
St. Louis	56	76	.424	35	771	954
Cincinnati	55	75	.423	35	910	1085
Washington	45	87	.341	46	882	1122
Louisville	36	94	.277	54	692	1001

Name	Pos.	Team	G	AB	R	H	2B	3B	HR	RBI	BB	BA	SA
Cap Anson	1B	Chi	83	347	87	137	26	6	5	99	40	.395	.548
Dan Brouthers	1B	Bal	123	528	137	182	33	25	9	128	67	.345	.553
Lave Cross	3B	Phi	120	543	128	211	32	12	7	125	29	.389	.530
Bill Dahlen	SS-3B	Chi	121	508	150	184	30	14	15	107	76	.362	.565
Ed Delahanty	OF	Phi	114	497	149	199	36	16	4	131	60	.400	.561
Hugh Duffy	OF	Bos	124	539	160	**236**	**50**	13	**18**	**145**	66	**.438**	**.679**
Billy Hamilton	OF	Phi	131	559	**196**	223	22	14	4	87	**126**	.399	.510
Bug Holliday	OF	Cin	122	519	125	199	24	8	13	119	40	.383	.536
Willie Keeler	OF	Bal	128	593	164	218	25	24	5	94	40	.368	.516
Joe Kelley	OF	Bal	129	509	167	199	48	17	6	111	107	.391	.587
Bobby Lowe	2B	Bos	133	**615**	158	210	35	12	17	115	50	.341	.520
Ed McKean	SS	Cle	130	561	115	199	29	16	8	128	49	.355	.506
Jake Stenzel	OF	Pit	131	523	148	184	40	20	13	121	75	.352	.579
Sam Thompson	OF	Phi	102	458	115	185	29	26	13	141	40	.404	.666

Name	Team	W	L	Pct.	G	IP	H	BB	SO	ShO	E.R.A.
Theo Breitenstein	StL	27	25	.519	**56**	**447**	**497**	191	140	1	4.79
Nig Cuppy	Cle	23	17	.575	43	316	381	128	65	**3**	4.56
Frank Dwyer	Cin	18	19	.486	45	348	471	106	49	1	5.07
Clark Griffith	Chi	21	11	.656	36	261	328	85	71	0	4.93
Brickyard Kennedy	Bkn	22	20	.524	48	361	445	149	107	0	4.91
Sadie McMahon	Bal	25	8	.758	35	276	317	111	60	0	4.21
Jouett Meekin	NY	**36**	10	**.783**	52	409	404	171	133	1	3.70
Win Mercer	Was	16	23	.410	49	333	431	125	69	0	3.76
Kid Nichols	Bos	32	13	.711	50	407	488	121	113	**3**	4.75
Amos Rusie	NY	**36**	13	.735	54	444	426	**200**	**195**	**3**	**2.78**
Ed Stein	Bkn	26	14	.650	45	359	396	171	84	2	4.54
Jack Stivetts	Bos	28	13	.683	45	338	429	127	76	0	4.90
Jack Taylor	Phi	24	10	.706	41	298	347	96	76	1	4.08
Cy Young	Cle	25	22	.532	52	409	488	106	108	2	3.94

1895 National League

Team	W	L	Pct.	GB	Runs	Opp.R
Baltimore	**87**	**43**	**.669**	–	1009	**646**
Cleveland	84	46	.646	3	917	720
Philadelphia	78	53	.595	9.5	**1068**	957
Chicago	72	58	.554	15	866	854
Brooklyn	71	60	.542	16.5	867	834
Boston	71	60	.542	16.5	907	826
Pittsburgh	71	61	.538	17	811	787
Cincinnati	66	64	.508	21	903	864
New York	66	65	.504	21.5	852	834
Washington	43	85	.336	43	837	1048
St. Louis	39	92	.298	48.5	747	1032
Louisville	35	96	.267	52.5	698	1090

Name	Pos.	Team	G	AB	R	H	2B	3B	HR	RBI	BB	BA	SA
Steve Brodie	OF	Bal	130	528	84	193	26	11	2	134	26	.365	.468
Jesse Burkett	OF	Cle	132	555	149	**235**	21	15	5	83	74	**.423**	.542
Ed Delahanty	OF	Phi	116	481	148	192	**47**	8	11	106	86	.399	.599
Hugh Duffy	OF	Bos	131	540	113	190	25	6	9	100	63	.352	.470
Billy Hamilton	OF	Phi	121	517	**166**	203	19	8	7	74	**96**	.393	.493
Hughie Jennings	SS	Bal	131	528	159	204	40	8	4	125	24	.386	.515
Willie Keeler	OF	Bal	131	560	161	221	23	15	4	78	37	.395	.511
Joe Kelley	OF	Bal	131	510	148	189	26	21	10	134	77	.371	.563
Bill Lange	OF	Chi	122	479	120	186	29	15	10	98	55	.388	.574
John McGraw	3B	Bal	93	385	109	144	15	7	2	48	60	.374	.465
Ed McKean	SS	Cle	132	**573**	131	197	26	17	8	119	45	.344	.490
Jake Stenzel	OF	Pit	131	520	115	200	38	13	7	97	57	.385	.548
Sam Thompson	OF	Phi	119	533	131	210	42	**22**	**18**	**165**	31	.394	**.657**
Mike Tiernan	OF	NY	120	474	128	168	23	19	7	70	66	.354	.527

Name	Team	W	L	Pct.	G	IP	H	BB	SO	ShO	E.R.A.
Theo Breitenstein	StL	18	**30**	.375	54	430	458	**178**	127	1	4.44
Kid Carsey	Phi	26	15	.634	44	342	**460**	118	64	0	4.92
Dad Clark	NY	18	14	.563	37	282	336	60	67	1	3.38
Nig Cuppy	Cle	25	15	.625	47	353	384	95	91	1	3.54
Clark Griffith	Chi	25	13	.658	42	353	434	91	79	0	3.93
Pink Hawley	Pit	32	21	.604	**56**	**444**	449	122	142	**4**	**3.18**
George Hemming	Bal	20	13	.606	34	262	288	96	43	1	4.05
Bill Hoffer	Bal	30	7	**.811**	41	314	206	124	00	**4**	3.21
Kid Nichols	Bos	30	14	.682	48	380	417	86	140	1	3.41
Billy Rhines	Cin	20	12	.625	38	268	322	76	72	0	4.80
Amos Rusie	NY	24	23	.511	49	393	384	159	**201**	**4**	3.73
Jack Taylor	Phi	26	13	.667	41	335	403	83	93	1	4.49
Adonis Terry	Chi	23	13	.639	38	311	346	131	88	0	4.80
Cy Young	Cle	**35**	10	.778	47	370	363	75	121	**4**	3.24

1896 National League

Team	W	L	Pct.	GB	Runs	Opp.R
Baltimore	**90**	**39**	**.698**	–	**995**	662
Cleveland	80	48	.625	9.5	840	650
Cincinnati	77	50	.606	12	783	**620**
Boston	74	57	.565	17	860	761
Chicago	71	57	.555	18.5	815	799
Pittsburgh	66	63	.512	24	787	741
New York	64	67	.489	27	829	821
Philadelphia	62	68	.477	28.5	890	891
Brooklyn	58	73	.443	33	692	764
Washington	58	73	.443	33	818	920
St. Louis	40	90	.308	50.5	593	929
Louisville	38	93	.290	53	653	997

Name	Pos.	Team	G	AB	R	H	2B	3B	HR	RBI	BB	BA	SA
Jesse Burkett	OF	Cle	133	**585**	**159**	**240**	26	16	6	72	49	**.410**	.540
Cupid Childs	2B	Cle	132	502	109	175	22	10	1	106	100	.348	.438
Bill Dahlen	SS	Chi	125	476	137	172	24	18	9	74	64	.361	.544
Ed Delahanty	OF-1B	Phi	123	505	131	199	**42**	14	**13**	**126**	62	.394	**.610**
Billy Hamilton	OF	Bos	131	523	153	190	26	8	3	52	**110**	.363	.461
Hughie Jennings	SS	Bal	129	523	125	208	24	9	0	121	19	.398	.478
Bill Joyce	3B-2B	Was-NY	129	477	125	154	26	12	**13**	93	101	.323	.509
Willie Keeler	OF	Bal	127	546	154	214	22	13	4	02	37	.392	.502
Joe Kelley	OF	Bal	130	516	147	191	27	17	8	100	91	.370	.535
Tom McCreery	OF	Lou	115	441	87	155	23	**21**	7	65	42	.351	.546
Elmer Smith	OF	Pit	120	475	118	170	22	14	6	94	74	.358	.501
Jake Stenzel	OF	Pit	112	467	104	171	26	13	2	82	32	.366	.490
Mike Tiernan	OF	NY	133	526	132	190	22	15	7	89	77	.361	.500
George Van Haltren	OF	NY	133	564	138	199	19	**21**	5	74	55	.353	.488

Name	Team	W	L	Pct.	G	IP	H	BB	SO	ShO	E.R.A.
Nig Cuppy	Cle	25	15	.625	46	358	388	75	86	1	3.12
Frank Dwyer	Cin	25	10	.714	36	289	321	60	57	3	3.15
Red Ehret	Cin	18	15	.545	34	277	298	74	60	2	3.41
Clark Griffith	Chi	22	13	.629	36	318	370	70	81	0	3.54
Pink Hawley	Pit	21	21	.500	49	378	382	157	137	2	3.60
Bill Hoffer	Bal	26	7	**.788**	35	309	317	95	93	3	3.38
Frank Killen	Pit	29	15	.659	**52**	**432**	476	119	134	**5**	3.52
Jouett Meekin	NY	26	13	.667	42	334	378	127	110	0	3.83
Win Mercer	Was	25	19	.568	46	366	456	117	94	2	4.13
Kid Nichols	Bos	**30**	15	.667	49	372	387	101	102	3	**2.83**
Arlie Pond	Bal	15	8	.652	28	214	232	57	80	2	3.49
Jack Stivetts	Bos	22	13	.629	42	329	353	99	71	2	4.10
Jack Taylor	Phi	21	20	.512	45	359	459	112	97	1	4.79
Cy Young	Cle	29	16	.644	51	414	**477**	62	**140**	**5**	3.24

1897 National League

Team	W	L	Pct.	GB	Runs	Opp.R
Boston	**93**	**39**	**.705**	–	**1025**	**665**
Baltimore	90	40	.692	2	964	674
New York	83	48	.634	9.5	895	695
Cincinnati	76	56	.576	17	763	705
Cleveland	69	62	.527	23.5	773	680
Brooklyn	61	71	.462	32	802	845
Washington	61	71	.462	32	781	793
Pittsburgh	60	71	.458	32.5	676	835
Chicago	59	73	.447	34	832	894
Philadelphia	55	77	.417	38	752	792
Louisville	52	78	.400	40	669	859
St. Louis	29	102	.221	63.5	588	1083

Name	Pos.	Team	G	AB	R	H	2B	3B	HR	RBI	BB	BA	SA
Jesse Burkett	OF	Cle	128	519	128	199	28	8	2	60	76	.383	.480
Fred Clarke	OF	Lou	129	525	122	213	28	15	5	66	45	.406	.545
Jimmy Collins	3B	Bos	133	529	102	183	25	11	6	**132**	41	.346	.469
George Davis	SS	NY	131	525	114	188	34	11	10	131	41	.358	.522
Ed Delahanty	OF	Phi	129	530	110	200	37	15	5	96	60	.377	.532
Hugh Duffy	OF	Bos	134	554	131	189	23	10	**11**	129	52	.341	.478
Billy Hamilton	OF	Bos	125	506	**153**	174	17	6	3	61	**105**	.344	.419
Hughie Jennings	SS	Bal	115	436	131	154	22	9	2	79	42	.353	.454
Willie Keeler	OF	Bal	128	562	147	**243**	25	18	1	74	35	**.432**	.546
Joe Kelley	OF	Bal	129	503	113	196	31	9	5	118	70	.390	.517
Nap Lajoie	1B	Phi	127	545	107	198	37	25	10	127	15	.363	**.578**
Bill Lange	OF	Chi	117	482	119	170	23	14	5	83	48	.353	.490
Chick Stahl	OF	Bos	112	468	111	168	26	12	4	97	38	.359	.491
Jake Stenzel	OF	Bal	131	536	112	188	**40**	8	5	116	36	.351	.483

Name	Team	W	L	Pct.	G	IP	H	BB	SO	ShO	E.R.A.
Theo Breitenstein	Cin	23	12	.657	40	320	345	91	98	2	3.63
Joe Corbett	Bal	24	8	.750	37	313	330	115	149	1	3.11
Clark Griffith	Chi	21	19	.525	41	343	410	86	102	1	3.72
Bill Hoffer	Bal	22	10	.688	38	303	350	104	62	1	4.31
Fred Klobedanz	Bos	25	8	**.758**	38	309	344	125	92	2	4.60
Ted Lewis	Bos	20	12	.625	38	290	316	125	65	2	3.85
Jouett Meekin	NY	20	11	.645	37	304	328	99	83	2	3.76
Win Mercer	Was	24	21	.533	45	332	395	102	88	**3**	3.25
Kid Nichols	Bos	**30**	11	.732	**46**	**368**	362	68	127	2	2.64
Jerry Nops	Bal	20	7	.741	30	221	235	52	69	1	2.81
Billy Rhines	Cin	20	15	.571	41	289	311	86	65	1	4.08
Amos Rusie	NY	29	18	.617	38	322	314	87	135	2	**2.54**
Cy Seymour	NY	20	14	.588	38	278	254	**164**	149	2	3.37
Cy Young	Cle	21	18	.538	**46**	335	391	49	88	2	3.79

1898 National League

Team	W	L	Pct.	GB	Runs	Opp.R
Boston	**102**	**47**	**.685**	–	872	**614**
Baltimore	96	53	.644	6	**933**	623
Cincinnati	92	60	.605	11.5	831	740
Chicago	85	65	.567	17.5	828	679
Cleveland	81	68	.544	21	730	683
Philadelphia	78	71	.523	24	823	784
New York	77	73	.513	25.5	837	800
Pittsburgh	72	76	.486	29.5	634	694
Louisville	70	81	.464	33	728	833
Brooklyn	54	91	.372	46	638	811
Washington	51	101	.336	52.5	704	939
St. Louis	39	111	.260	63.5	571	929

Name	Pos.	Team	G	AB	R	H	2B	3B	HR	RBI	BB	BA	SA
John Anderson	OF-1B	Bkn-Was	134	518	81	153	32	**22**	9	81	29	.295	**.494**
Jesse Burkett	OF	Cle	148	624	115	**215**	18	9	0	42	69	.345	.402
Jimmy Collins	3B	Bos	152	600	106	202	34	4	**15**	111	40	.337	.482
Ed Delahanty	OF	Phi	143	547	114	183	37	11	4	92	77	.335	.464
Hugh Duffy	OF	Bos	151	561	97	179	12	3	9	109	59	.319	.399
Billy Hamilton (KJ)	OF	Bos	110	417	111	153	16	4	3	50	87	.367	.446
Hughie Jennings	SS	Bal	143	533	136	173	24	9	1	87	78	.325	.409
Willie Keeler	OF	Bal	128	564	126	214	10	2	1	44	31	.379	.410
Joe Kelley	OF	Bal	124	467	71	153	17	15	3	110	56	.328	.448
Nap Lajoie	2B	Phi	147	610	113	200	**40**	10	5	**127**	21	.328	.451
Bill Lange	OF	Chi	111	439	79	147	19	11	5	68	35	.335	.462
John McGraw	3B	Bal	142	521	**142**	174	7	10	0	53	**112**	.334	.386
Jimmy Ryan	OF	Chi	143	569	121	185	31	13	4	79	73	.325	.446
Elmer Smith	OF	Cin	123	483	76	166	22	9	1	66	69	.344	.433

Name	Team	W	L	Pct.	G	IP	H	BB	SO	ShO	E.R.A.
Nixey Callahan	Chi	20	11	.645	31	274	267	71	73	2	2.46
Bert Cunningham	Lou	28	15	.651	44	362	387	65	34	0	3.16
Clark Griffith	Chi	26	10	.722	38	326	305	64	97	4	**1.88**
Pink Hawley	Cin	26	12	.684	43	331	357	91	69	3	3.37
Ted Lewis	Bos	25	8	**.758**	41	313	267	109	72	1	2.90
Al Maul	Bal	20	7	.741	28	240	207	49	31	1	2.10
Doc McJames	Bal	27	14	.659	45	374	327	113	178	2	2.36
Kid Nichols	Bos	29	12	.707	**50**	388	316	85	138	5	2.13
Wiley Piatt	Phi	24	14	.632	39	306	285	97	121	**6**	3.18
Jack Powell	Cle	24	15	.615	42	342	328	112	93	**6**	3.00
Cy Seymour	NY	25	17	.595	45	357	313	**213**	**239**	4	3.18
Jesse Tannehill	Pit	24	14	.632	43	327	338	63	93	5	2.94
Vic Willis	Bos	23	12	.657	41	311	264	148	160	1	2.84
Cy Young	Cle	25	14	.641	46	378	387	41	101	1	2.52

1899 National League

Team	W	L	Pct.	GB	Runs	Opp.R
Brooklyn	**101**	**47**	**.682**	–	892	658
Boston	95	57	.625	8	858	**645**
Philadelphia	94	58	.618	9	**916**	743
Baltimore	86	62	.581	15	827	691
St. Louis	84	67	.556	18.5	819	739
Cincinnati	83	67	.553	19	856	770
Pittsburgh	76	73	.510	25.5	834	765
Chicago	75	73	.507	26	812	763
Louisville	75	77	.493	28	827	775
New York	60	90	.400	42	734	863
Washington	54	98	.355	49	743	983
Cleveland	20	134	.130	84	529	1252

Name	Pos.	Team	G	AB	R	H	2B	3B	HR	RBI	BB	BA	SA
Jake Beckley	1B	Cin	135	519	87	173	23	18	3	99	40	.333	.464
Jesse Burkett	OF	StL	138	567	115	228	17	10	7	71	67	.402	.504
Fred Clarke	OF	Lou	148	601	124	209	21	11	5	70	49	.348	.444
George Davis	SS	NY	111	413	69	144	25	4	1	57	37	.349	.436
Ed Delahanty	OF	Phi	145	573	133	**234**	**56**	9	9	**137**	55	**.408**	**.585**
Elmer Flick	OF	Phi	125	486	101	167	21	14	2	98	42	.344	.457
Buck Freeman	OF	Was	155	587	107	187	20	26	**25**	122	23	.319	.569
Willie Keller	OF	Bkn	143	571	**141**	215	13	14	1	61	37	.377	.454
Nap Lajoie (KJ)	2B	Phi	76	308	70	117	17	11	6	70	12	.380	.565
John McGraw	3B	Bal	118	402	140	157	13	3	1	33	**124**	.390	.445
Chick Stahl	OF	Bos	148	578	123	201	22	17	8	53	72	.348	.486
Fred Tenney	1B	Bos	150	597	114	209	22	18	1	67	63	.350	.452
Honus Wagner	3B-OF	Lou	**145**	549	102	197	47	13	7	113	40	.359	.530
Jimmy Williams	3B	Pit	153	621	126	219	31	**27**	9	116	60	.353	.533

Name	Team	W	L	Pct.	G	IP	H	BB	SO	ShO	E.R.A.
Nixey Callahan	Chi	21	12	.636	35	294	327	76	77	3	3.06
Red Donahue	Phi	22	7	.759	35	279	292	63	51	4	3.39
Chick Fraser	Phi	21	13	.618	35	271	278	85	68	4	3.35
Clark Griffith	Chi	22	13	.629	38	320	329	65	73	0	2.78
Noodles Hahn	Cin	23	7	.767	38	309	280	68	**145**	4	2.68
Jay Hughes	Bkn	**28**	6	**.824**	35	292	250	119	99	3	2.68
Frank Kitson	Bal	20	16	.556	40	330	329	66	75	3	2.75
Sam Leever	Pit	20	23	.465	**51**	**379**	353	122	121	4	3.18
Joe McGinnity	Bal	**28**	17	.622	48	366	358	93	74	4	2.68
Kid Nichols	Bos	21	17	.553	42	343	326	82	108	4	2.99
Wiley Piatt	Phi	23	15	.605	39	305	323	86	89	2	3.45
Jesse Tannehill	Pit	23	14	.622	40	313	354	51	61	3	2.73
Vic Willis	Bos	27	10	.730	41	343	277	117	120	**5**	**2.49**
Cy Young	StL	26	15	.634	44	369	368	44	111	4	2.59

1900 National League

Team	W	L	Pct.	GB	Runs	Opp.R
Brooklyn	**82**	**54**	**.603**	–	**816**	722
Pittsburgh	79	60	.568	4.5	733	**612**
Philadelphia	75	63	.543	8	810	792
Boston	66	72	.478	17	778	739
Chicago	65	75	.464	19	635	751
St. Louis	65	75	.464	19	744	748
Cincinnati	62	77	.446	21.5	703	745
New York	60	78	.435	23	713	823

Name	Pos.	Team	G	AB	R	H	2B	3B	HR	RBI	BB	BA	SA
Jake Beckley	1B	Cin	139	559	99	192	26	9	2	94	40	.343	.433
Jesse Burkett	OF	StL	142	560	88	202	14	12	7	68	62	.361	.466
Ed Delahanty	1B	Phi	131	542	82	173	32	10	1	109	41	.319	.421
Elmer Flick	OF	Phi	138	547	106	207	33	16	11	**110**	56	.378	.558
Billy Hamilton	OF	Bos	136	524	103	174	19	5	1	47	107	.332	.393
Willie Keeler	OF	Bkn	137	568	106	**208**	11	14	4	68	30	.366	.456
Nap Lajoie	2B	Phi	102	451	95	156	32	12	7	92	10	.346	.517
Herman Long	SS	Bos	124	483	80	124	18	2	**12**	66	44	.256	.377
Roy Thomas	OF	Phi	140	529	**131**	167	25	3	0	33	**115**	.316	.374
Honus Wagner	OF	Pit	**135**	528	107	201	**45**	**22**	4	100	41	**.381**	**.572**

Name	Team	W	L	Pct.	G	IP	H	BB	SO	ShO	E.R.A.
Bill Carrick	NY	19	**21**	.471	**45**	342	**415**	92	63	1	3.53
Bill Dinneen	Bos	21	15	.583	40	321	304	105	107	1	3.11
Chick Fraser	Phi	16	10	.615	29	223	250	93	58	1	3.15
Noodles Hahn	Cin	16	21	.762	38	303	296	88	127	**4**	3.30
Brickyard Kennedy	Bkn	22	15	.595	42	292	316	111	75	2	3.91
Joe McGinnity	Bkn	**29**	9	**.763**	44	**343**	350	**113**	93	1	2.94
Deacon Phillippe	Pit	19	12	.613	38	279	274	42	75	1	2.84
Jesse Tannehill	Pit	20	7	.741	29	234	247	43	50	2	2.88
Rube Waddell	Pit	9	11	.450	29	209	176	55	**130**	2	**2.37**
Cy Young	StL	20	18	.526	41	.321	337	36	115	**4**	3.00

1876-1900 STARS

(Only those stars who did not appear in a single major league game after 1900, the 1876-1900 stars who played after 1900 are included in the1901-1919 list)

BATTERS

USE NAME-GIVEN NAMES (NICKNAMES)-MAIN POSITION(S)	TEAM BY YEAR	BIRTH DATE	BIRTH PLACE	DEATH DATE	B	T	HGT	WGT	G	AB	R	H	2B	3B	HR	RBI	BB	BA	SA
									LIFETIME BATTING TOTALS										
Anson, Cap-Adrian Constantine (Pop)-1B	76-97,M79-97ChiN M98NYN	4-17-52	Marshalltown, Iowa	4-14-22	R	R	6'1	227	2268	9067	1728	3022	530	126	97	1879	952	.333	.452
Brown, Tom-Thomas T.-OF	82BalAA 83-84ColAA 85-86PitAA 87PitN 87IndN 88-89BosN 90BosP 91BosAA 92-94LouN 95StLN 95-98,M97-98WasN	9-21-60	Liverpool, England	10-27-27	L	R	5'10	168	1783	7338	1524	1952	238	137	65		749	.266	.362
Browning, Pete-Louis Rogers (The Gladiator)-OF	82-89LouAA 90CleP 91PitN 91CinN 92LouN 92CinN 93LouN 94StLN 94BknN	7-17-58	Louisville, Ky.	9-10-05	R	R	6'	180	1180	4795	950	1164	292	89	46		465	.347	.474
Burns, Oyster-Thomas P.-OF	84WilU 84-88BalAA 88-89BknAA 90-95BknN 95NYN	9- 6-62	Philadelphia, Pa.	11-16-28	R	R	5'8	183	1178	4615	876	1388	228	131	65	834	464	.301	.449
Comiskey, Charlie-Charles Albert (Commy, The Old Roman)-1B	82-89,M83,85-89StLAA 90,M90ChiP 91,M91StLAA 92-94,M92-94CinN	8-15-59	Chicago, Ill.	10-26-31	R	R	6'	180	1385	5801	981	1543	199	69	29	883	197	.266	.339
Connor, Roger-Roger-1B	80-82TroyN 83-89,91,93-94NYN 90NYP 92PhiN 94-97,M96StLN	7- 1-57	Waterbury, Conn.	1- 4-31	L	L	6'3	220	1987	7732	1607	2460	429	227	137	1323	1002	.318	.486
Dalrymple, Abner-Abner Frank-OF	78MilN 79-86ChiN 87-88PitN 91C-MAA	9- 9-57	Warren, Ill.	1-25-39	L	R	5'10	175	941	4131	812	1195	216	81	43	407	204	.289	.412
Denny, Jerry-Jeremiah Dennis-3B	81-85ProvN 86StLN 87-89IndN 90-91NYN 91CleN 91PhiN 93-94LouN	3-16-59	New York, N.Y.	8-16-27	R	R	5'11	180	1234	4925	709	1284	238	74	74	667	173	.261	.384
Dunlap, Fred-Frederick C. (Sure Shot)-2B	80-83CleN 84StLU 85-86StLN 86-87DetN 88-90,M89PitN 90NYP 91WasAA	5-21-59	Philadelphia, Pa.	12- 1-02	R	R	5'8	165	955	3939	750	1176	224	53	41		283	.299	.414
Ewing, Buck-William-C,1B,OF	80-82TroyN 83-39NYN 90,M90NYP 91-92NYN 93-94CleN 95-97,M95-99CinN MOONYN	10-17-59	Hoaglands, Ohio	10-20-06	R	R	5'10	188	1281	5318	1118	1633	237	179	71	884	392	.307	.459
Glasscock, Jack-John Wesley (Pebbly Jack)-SS	79-84CleN 84CinU 85-86StLN 87-89,M89IndN 90-91NYN 92-93StLN 93-94PitN 95LouN 95WasN	7-22-59	Wheeling, W.Va.	2-24-47	R	R	5'8	160	1721	6955	1150	2038	309	95	27	847	439	.293	.376
Gore, George-George F.-OF	79-86ChiN 87-89NYN 90NYP 91-92NYN 92StLN	5- 3-52	Saccarappa, Me.	9-16-33	L	R	5'11	195	1301	5324	1324	1611	257	95	46	617	717	.303	.412
Griffin, Mike-Michael Joseph-OF	87-89BalAA 90PhiP 91-98BknN	3-20-65	Utica, N.Y.	4-10-08	L	R	5'7	160	1508	5908	1401	1775	316	106	41	719	809	.300	.411
Hines, Paul-Paul A.-OF	76-77ChiN 78-85ProvN 86-87WasN 88-89IndN 90PitN 90BosN 91WasAA	3- 1-62	Washington, D.C.	7-10-35	R	R	5'9	173	1471	6207	1073	1864	355	78	56	751	366	.300	.410
Holliday, Bug-James Wear-OF	89CinAA 90-98CinN	2- 8-67	St. Louis, Mo.	2-15-10	R	R	5'7	165	920	3604	733	1152	155	70	65	617	359	.320	.456
Jones (Rippay), Charley (Benjamin Wesley)-Charles Wesley-OF	76-77CinN 77ChiN 77-78CinN 79-80BosN 81-82SL 83-87CinAA 87NYAA 88KCAA	4-30-50	Alamance Co., N.C.	Deceased	R	R	5'11	202	880	3665	720	1103	171	101	55	582	237	.301	.448
Kelly, King-Michael Joseph-OF,C	78-79CinN 80-86ChiN 87-89BosN 90,M90BosP 91,M91C-MAA 91BosAA 91-92BosN 93NYN	12-31-57	Troy, N.Y.	11- 8-94	R	R	5'10	180	1443	5901	1367	1813	351	105	69	951	549	.307	.437
Lange, Bill-William Alexander (Little Eva)-OF	93-99ChiN	6- 6-71	San Francisco, Cal.	7-23-50	R	R	6'2	210	808	3194	692	1072	142	83	39	577	350	.336	.469
Larkin, Ted-Henry E.-1B,OF	84-89PhiAA 90,M90CleP 91PhiAA 92-93WasN	1-12-60	Reading, Pa.	1-31-42	R	R			1182	4691	933	1450	263	111	53	836	484	.309	.446
Lyons, Denny-Dennis Patrick Aloysius-3B	85ProvN 86-90PhiAA 91StLAA 92NYN 93-94PitN 95StLN 96-97PitN	3-12-66	Cincinnati, Ohio	1- 2-29	R	R	5'10	185	1129	4236	932	1368	237	73	62	755	621	.323	.457
McCarthy, Tommy-Thomas Francis Michael-OF	84BosU 85BosN 86-87PhiN 88-91StLAA 92-95BosN 96BknN	7-24-64	Boston, Mass.	8- 5-22	R	R	5'7	170	1269	5104	1062	1499	194	58	44	757	537	.294	.380
McKean, Ed-Edward John (Mac)-SS	87-88CleAA 89-98CleN 99StLN	6- 6-64	Grafton, Ohio	8-16-19	R	R	5'9	160	1655	6842	1213	2079	270	153	66	1124	635	.304	.417
McPhee, Biddy-John Alexander-2B	82-89CinAA 90-99,M01-02CinN	11- 1-59	Massena, N.Y.	1- 3-42	R	R	5'8	152	2127	8293	1674	2287	309	170	52	1067	981	.276	.373
Nash, Billy-William Mitchell-3B	84RicAA 85-89BosN 90BosP 91-95BosN 96-98,M96PhiN	6-24-65	Richmond, Va.	11-15-29	R	R	5'8	167	1543	5778	1077	1603	264	91	61	977	804	.277	.386
O'Neill, Tip-James Edward-OF	83NYN 84-89StLAA 90ChiP 91StLAA 92CinN	5-25-58	Woodstock, Canada	12-31-15	R	R	6'1	187	1048	4254	871	1389	212	98	52	757	421	.327	.459
Orr, Dave-David L.-1B	83NYN 83-87,M87NYAA 88BknAA 89ColAA 90BknP	9-29-59	New York, N.Y.	6- 3-15	R	R	5'6	160	788	3271	536	1141	197	110	37	627	98	.349	.510
Pfeffer, Fred-Nathaniel Frederick (Dandelion)-2B	82TroyN 83-89ChiN 90ChiP 91ChiN 92-95,M92LouN 96NYN 96-97ChiN	3-17-60	Louisville, Ky.	4-10-32	R	R	5'10	168	1667	6507	1090	1677	233	117	95	1019	527	.258	.373
Reilly, Long John-John Good-1B	80CinN 83-89CinAA 90-91CinN	10- 5-58	Cincinnati, Ohio	5-31-37	R	R	6'3	178	1135	4658	898	1341	215	138	69	740	156	.288	.438
Richardson, Hardy-Abram Harding (Old True Blue)-2B,OF,3B	79-85BufN 86-88DetN 89BosN 90BosP 91BosAA 92WasN 92NYN	4-21-55	Clarksboro, N.J.	1- 4-31	R	R	5'9	170	1316	5593	1112	1676	305	124	73	816	377	.300	.438
Rowe, Jack-John Charles-SS,C,OF	79-85BufN 86-88DetN 89PitN 90,M90BufP	12- 8-57	Harrisburg, Pa.	4-26-11	L	R	5'8	170	1034	4366	765	1249	201	89	28	645	224	.286	.392
Start, Joe-Joseph (Old Reliable)-1B	76NYN 77BknN 78ChiN 79-85ProvN 86WasN	10-14-42	New York, N.Y.	3-27-27	L	L	5'9	165	786	3402	590	1020	108	53	7	357	150	.300	.369
Stenzel (Stelzle), Jake-Jacob Charles-OF	90ChiN 92-96PitN 97-98BalN 98-99StLN 99CinN	6-24-67	Cincinnati, Ohio	1- 6-19	R	R	5'10	168	762	2992	662	1028	189	72	33	533	299	.344	.488
Stovey (Stow), Harry-Harry Duffield-OF,1B	80-82WorN 83-89PhiAA 90BosP 91-92BosN 92-93BalN 93BknN	12-20-56	Philadelphia, Pa.	9-20-37	R	R	5'11	180	1482	6072	1488	1866	348	185	121	907	661	.307	.485
Sutton, Ezra-Ezra Ballou-3B,SS	76PhiN 77-88BosN	9-17-50	Seneca Falls, N.Y.	6-20-07	R	R	5'8	153	1019	4226	734	1215	187	71	21	518	164	.288	.380
Tebeau, Patsy-Oliver Wendell-1B,3B	87ChiN 89CleN 90,M90CleP 91-98,M91-98CleN 99-00,M99-00StLN	12- 5-64	St. Louis, Mo.	5-15-18	R	R			1159	4555	667	1288	202	57	27	736	319	.283	.370
Tiernan, Mike-Michael Joseph (Silent Mike)-OF	87-99NYN	1-21-67	Trenton, N.J.	11- 9-18	L	L	5'11	165	1475	5878	1312	1843	248	159	106	849	747	.311	.464
Tucker, Tommy-Thomas Joseph-1B	87-89BalAA 90-97BosN 97WasN 98BknN 98StLN 99CleN	10-28-63	Holyoke, Mass.	10-22-35	B	R	5'11	165	1686	6461	1083	1888	238	86	42	932	479	.292	.375
Ward, Monte-John Montgomery-SS,2B,P,OF (See Pitchers below)	78-82ProvN 83-89,M84NYN 90,M90BknP 91-92,M91-92BknN 93-94,M93-94NYN	3- 3-60	Bellefonte, Pa.	3- 4-25	L (Bats Both 88)	R	5'9	165	1811	7568	1403	2122	232	96	25	867	420	.280	.346
White, Deacon, James Laurie-3B,C,1B,OF	76ChiN 77BosN 78-80,M79CinN 81-85BufN 86-88DetN 89PitN 90BufP	12- 7-47	Caton, N.Y.	7- 7-39	L	R	5'11	175	1289	5294	840	1607	205	73	18	756	292	.304	.380
Williamson, Ned-Edward Nagle-3B,SS	78IndN 79-89ChiN 90ChiP	10-24-55	Philadelphia, Pa.	3- 3-94	R	R	5'11	180	1192	4523	802	1153	230	83	63	667	506	.255	.384
Wolf, Chicken-William Van Winkle-OF	82-91,M89LouAA 92StLN	5-12-62	Louisville, Ky.	5-16-03	R	R			1201	4975	779	1451	214	109	17		229	.292	.389
Wright, George-George-SS	76-78BosN 79,M79ProvN 80-81BosN 82ProvN	1-28-47	Yonkers, N.Y.	8-21-37	R	R	5'9	150	329	1495	264	384	53	20	2	132	43	.257	.323

PITCHERS

All pitchers with at least 150 Wins

USE NAME-GIVEN NAMES (NICKNAMES)	TEAM BY YEAR	BIRTH DATE	BIRTH PLACE	DEATH DATE	B	T	HGT	WGT	W	L	PCT	G	GS	CG	IP	H	BB	SO	ShO	ERA	ERA-NA*
									LIFETIME PITCHING TOTALS												
Baldwin, Mark-Marcus Elmore	87-88ChiN 89ColAA 90ChiP 91-93PitN 93NYN	10-29-63	Pittsburgh, Pa.	11-10-29	R	R	6'	190	156	165	.486	347	328	296	2812	2699	1307	1354	14	3.36	none
Bond, Tommy-Thomas Henry	76HarN 77-81BosN 82,M82WorN 84BosU 84IndAA	4- 2-56	Granard, Ireland	1-24-41	R	R	5'7	160	192	115	.625	322	314	294	2779	2857	178	860	36	2.15	84
Buffinton, Charlie-Charles G.	82-86BosN 87-89PhiN 90,M90PhiP 91BosAA 92BalN 93HO	6-14-61	Fall River, Mass.	9-23-07	R	R	6'1	180	230	151	.604	414	396	351	3403	3344	856	1700	27	2.96	none
Caruthers, Bob-Robert Lee (Parisian Bob)	84-87StLAA 88-89BknAA 90-91BknN 92StLN 93ChiN-CinN (sore arm-OF-did not pitch)	1- 5-64	Memphis, Tenn.	8- 5-11	L	R	5'7	138	217	101	.682	341	310	298	2829	2678	597	900	24	3.16	84-86
Chamberlin, Icebox-Elton P.	86-88LouAA 88-90StLAA 90ColAA 91PhiAA 92-94CinN 96CleN	11- 5-67	Buffalo, N.Y.	9-22-29	R	R	5'9	168	157	123	.561	321	301	264	2522	2446	1065	1133	15	3.56	86-87,90
Clarkson, John-John Gibson	82WorN 84-87ChiN 88-92BosN 92-94CleN	7- 1-61	Cambridge, Mass.	2- 4-09	R	R	5'10	150	327	176	.650	531	518	485	4537	4295	1191	1978	37	2.84	84
Corcoran, Larry-Lawrence J.	80-85ChiN 85-86NYN 86WasN 87IndN	8-10-59	Brooklyn, N.Y.	10-14-91		R			173	90	.658	277	268	256	2393	2147	496	1103	23	2.27	83-84
Dwyer, Frank-John Francis	88-89ChiN 90ChiP 91C-MAA 92StLN 92-99CinN M02DetA	3-25-68	Lee, Mass.	2- 4-43	R	R	5'8	145	173	141	.551	365	318	270	2809	3301	764	563	12	3.85	none
Galvin, Pud-James Francis (Gentle Jeems, The Little Steam Engine)	79-85,M85BufN 85-86PitAA 87-89PitN 90PitP 91-92PitN 92StLN	12-25-55	St. Louis, Mo.	3- 7-02	R	R	5'8	190	361	309	.539	697	682	639	5941	6352	744	1799	56	2.94	81-83, 85AA-86
Hecker, Guy-Guy Jackson	82-89LouAA 90,M90PitN	4- 3-56	Youngville, Pa.	12- 4-38	R	R			174	147	.542	334	320	310	2905	2905	489	1099	15	4.46	82-87
Hutchison, Bill-William Forrest (Wild Bill)	89-95ChiN 97StLN	12-17-59	New Haven, Conn.	3-19-26	R	R	5'9	175	182	158	.535	373	345	319	3066	3110	1128	1231	21	3.59	none
Keefe, Tim-Timothy John (Sir Timothy)	80-82TroyN 83-84NYAA 85-89NYN 90NYP 91NYN 91-93PhiN	1- 1-57	Cambridge, Mass.	4-23-33	R	R	5'10	185	342	224	.604	600	594	552	5052	4442	1224	2521	39	2.65	81-84
Killen, Frank-Frank Bissell	91C-MAA 92WasN 93-98PitN 98-99WasN 99BosN 00ChiN	11-30-70	Pittsburgh, Pa.	12- 3-39	L	L	6'1	200	164	111	.596	321	300	253	2511	2730	822	725	13	3.79	none
King (Koenig), Silver-Charles Frederick	86KCN 87-89StLAA 90ChiP 91PitN 92-93NYN 93CinN 94-95VR 96-97WasN	1-11-68	St. Louis, Mo.	5-19-38	R	R	5'10	180	206	152	.575	398	371	329	3190	3105	970	1229	20	3.15	none
Mathews, Bobby-Robert T.	76NYN 77CinN 79,81ProvN 81-82BosN 83-87PhiAA	11-21-51	Baltimore, Md.	4-17-98	R	R	5'5	145	167	136	.551	323	315	289	2734	3008	336	1199	9	2.95	83-87
McCormick, Jim-James	78IndN 79-84,M79-80CleN 84CinU 85ProvN 85-86ChiN 87PitN	-56	Paterson, N.J.	3-10-18	R	R	5'10	226	264	214	.552	492	485	466	4275	4092	749	1704	33	2.49	82,84U
McMahon, Sadie-John Joseph	89-90PhiAA 90B-BAA 91BalAA 92-96BalN 97BknN	9-19-67	Wilmington, Del.	2-20-54	R	R	5'9	185	177	124	.588	321	305	279	2634	2726	945	967	14	3.56	90
Meekin, Jouett-Jouett	91LouAA 92LouN 92-93WasN 94-99NYN 99BosN 00PitN	2-21-67	New Albany, Ind.	12-14-44	R	R	6'1	180	156	138	.531	324	308	270	2603	2831	1058	900	9	4.07	none
Morris, Ed-Edward (Cannonball)	84ColAA 85-86PitAA 87-89PitN 90PitP	9-29-59	Brooklyn, N.Y.	4-12-37	R	L		156	172	125	.579	311	307	297	2678	2468	498	1217	29	3.49	84-86
Mullane, Tony-Anthony John (Count, The Apollo of the Box)	81DetN 82LouAA 83StLAA 84TolAA 85DE 06-89CinAA 90 93CinN 93-94BalN 94CleN	1-20-59	Cork, Ireland	4-25-44	B (Bats Left-82 (Occasionally pitched left-handed))	R	5'10	165	286	213	.573	557	505	469	4545	4203	1409	1812	31	3.46	82-84,86
Radbourn, Old Hoss-Charles Gardner	80BufN 81-85ProvN 86-89BosN 90BosP 91CinN	12-11-54	Rochester, N.Y.	2- 5-97	R	R	5'9	168	308	191	.617	528	503	489	4535	4335	875	1830	34	2.81	83-83
Stivetts, Jack-John Elmer (Happy Jack)	89-91StLAA 92-98BosN 99CleN	3-31-68	Ashland, Pa.	4-18-30	R	R	6'2	185	205	128	.616	386	332	278	2887	2905	1155	1223	14	3.77	90
Terry, Adonis-William J.	84-89BknAA 90-91BknN 92BalN 92-94PitN 94-97ChiN	8- 7-64	Westfield, Mass.	2-24-15	R	R			205	197	.510	441	407	368	3522	3519	1301	1555	18	3.76	84-87
Ward, Monte-John Montgomery (See Batters above)	78-82ProvN 83-84NYN	3- 3-60	Bellefonte, Pa.	3- 4-25	L	R	5'9	165	158	102	.608	291	261	244	2462	2317	253	920	24	2.03	81,84
Welch, Michey-Michael Francis (Smiling Mickey)	80-82TroyN 83-92NYN	7- 4-59	Brooklyn, N.Y.	7-30-41	R	R	5'8	160	311	207	.600	564	548	524	4781	4576	1297	1846	41	2.68	81-84
White, Will-William Henry (Whoop-La)	77BosN 78-80CinN 81DetN 82-86,M84CinAA	10-11-54	Caton, N.Y.	8-31-11	B	R	5'9	175	227	167	.576	403	401	394	3542	3440	496	1041	36	2.06	82-85
Whitney, Jim-James E. (Long Jim, Grasshopper Jim)	81-85BosN 86KCN 87-88WasN 89IndN 90PhiAA 91DD	-56	Binghamton, N.Y.	5-21-91	L	R			191	204	.484	413	396	377	3496	3607	411	1571	26	3.06	84

* Years for which E.R.A. is not available, not included in lifetime E.R.A.

1901-1919
When the Ball Was Dead and the Bases Alive with the Scurrying of Feet

In an era when leg power dominated and the same lifeless baseball was kept in play throughout the game, the celebrated home run was not the master weapon of the diamond. A study of the final 1901 statistics more than substantiates this fact as the St. Louis Cardinals, with a major league-leading 39 home runs, finished fourth, as compared with the Chicago White Sox, who took the American League crown behind the speed and cunning which accounted for 280 stolen bases, tops in both circuits.

Yet more than the runner, the game belonged to the pitcher. The parks were large and lacked the enclosures which could invite the long ball. The "spitter", which led to an entire array of trick pitches, was legal and a deadly weapon if one could master the art. There were a few, however, whose pitching mastery enabled them to accomplish their tasks on sheer talent alone, sans the spit ball or the trickery other men may have been forced to resort to using. Those who led the list of the seemingly immortals included Cy Young, Walter Johnson, Christy Mathewson, and Grover Cleveland "Pete" Alexander, a phenomenal golden-armed quartet which accounted for over 1600 victories in their careers.

In order to combat the mound opposition and survive the disadvantages of their trade, batters were forced to use an entirely different set of tactics than they might employ if playing in the latter part of the twentieth century. Instead of attacking *the pitch,* the hitter played it *defensively* and hit, when he could, *where the ball was pitched.* The players used heavy bats, choking-up and punching or hitting the ball down rather than going for the scalding line-drive shots so frequent in later eras. The result of this style of play made speed a vital factor, and bunting and stealing to squeeze out a run became the prevailing strategy of the times.

Mostly, it was hit and run and go for average, and the man who most typified such execution was Ty Cobb, Detroit's frantic base running demon, who stole 754 bases in the years 1905-1919 while hitting for a .373 average and leading the American League in batting 12 times. Cobb, who used aggressiveness and spikes to accomplish much of his record, was so brilliant a performer that his contemporaries were almost shadowed into obscurity. The point could not be made any stronger than as in the case of Shoeless Joe Jackson, who hit .408 in 1911 and .395 in 1912—only to find himself a frustrated bridesmaid to the fleet-footed Cobb. The National League's counterpart to Cobb was Honus Wagner who proved nearly as talented as a hitter and far more gracious as a human being. In his years with Pittsburgh, which ran from 1900-1917, Wagner nailed down eight batting titles and almost 700 stolen bases. Wagner also had the satisfaction when he met Cobb on the field for the first and only time during the 1909 World Series to outdo his rival in batting and stolen bases.

More than the individuals, the most important historical event of the age was the birth of the American League. While the older National League circuit had spilled into the twentieth century and had its roots as early as 1876, the American League did not strike up its colors until 1901. Mostly because of the leadership and imagination of its chief founder, Ban Johnson, the new league was able to find an equal place in the American limelight. Although peace between the two leagues did not come until 1903—after many battles had been fought and emotions worn thin—baseball found itself with the first true franchise stablization in history. Except for the American League's switching of Milwaukee to St. Louis in 1902 and Baltimore to New York in 1903, baseball had come upon a suitable geographical mix that would survive for fifty years, or at least as long as the limited scope of railroad travel would permit. Yet before the era could wind itself down, two other events were to take place—both disarming in their emergence. The first occurred in 1914 when the Federal League—a minor circuit—declared itself "major", mostly by using the same tactics of player raiding as Johnson had done in 1901. But whereas the public could withstand two leagues, it could not afford the luxury of all three. The third league lasted through the season of 1915 and left in its wake a string of new ballparks—the most notable being Wrigley Field. To get rid of the Federal League cost a reported $300,000, a figure which was cheap when compared to the holocaust which was to dawn in 1919.

It was in that year when key players on the Chicago White Sox threw away their good names and their careers by throwing the World Series to the underdog Cincinnati Reds. The events surrounding the scandal did not come to light until 1920, and was so staggering a revelation that it looked as though professional baseball would have to close its doors in shame. There was no doubt that it would take a miracle or two to save the game from premature extinction.

1901—1919 SINGLE SEASON LEADERS

BATTING

Batting Average

1	Nap Lajoie-Phi. (A)	1901	.422
2	Ty Cobb-Det. (A)	1911	.420
3	Ty Cobb-Det. (A)	1912	.410
4	Joe Jackson-Cle. (A)	1911	.408
5	Joe Jackson-Cle. (A)	1912	.395
6	Ty Cobb-Det. (A)	1913	.390
7	Tris Speaker-Cle. (A)	1916	.386
8	Ty Cobb-Det. (A)	1910	.385
9	Ty Cobb-Det. (A)	1919	.384
	Nap Lajoie-Cle. (A)	1910	.384

Hits

1	Ty Cobb-Det. (A)	1911	248
2	Joe Jackson-Cle. (A)	1911	233
3	Nap Lajoie-Phi. (A)	1901	229
4	Jesse Burkett-St.L. (N)	1901	228
5	Nap Lajoie-Cle. (A)	1910	227
	Ty Cobb-Det. (A)	1912	227
7	Joe Jackson-Cle. (A)	1912	226
8	Ty Cobb-Det. (A)	1917	225
9	Tris Speaker-Bos. (A)	1912	222
10	Cy Seymour-Cin. (N)	1905	219

Slugging Average

1	Babe Ruth-Bos. (A)	1919	.657
2	Nap Lajoie-Phi. (A)	1901	.635
3	Ty Cobb-Det. (A)	1911	.621
4	Ed Delahanty-Was. (A)	1902	.590
	Joe Jackson-Cle. (A)	1911	.590
6	Ty Cobb-Det. (A)	1912	.586
7	Joe Jackson-Cle. (A)	1912	.579
8	Heinie Zimmerman-Chi. (N)	1912	.571
	Ty Cobb-Det. (A)	1917	.571
10	Gavvy Cravath-Phi. (N)	1913	.568

Doubles

1	Tris Speaker-Bos. (A)	1912	53
2	Nap Lajoie-Cle. (A)	1910	51
3	Nap Lajoie-Cle. (A)	1904	50
4	Nap Lajoie-Cle. (A)	1906	49
5	Nap Lajoie-Cle. (A)	1901	48
6	Harry Davis-Phi. (A)	1905	47
	Ty Cobb-Det. (A)	1911	47
8	John Anderson-Mil. (A)	1901	46
	Tris Speaker-Bos (A)	1914	46
10	Bobby Veach-Det. (A)	1919	45

Runs Batted In

1	Frank Baker-Phi. (A)	1912	130
2	Gavvy Cravath-Phi. (N)	1913	128
3	Ty Cobb-Det. (A)	1911	127
4	Honus Wagner-Pit. (N)	1901	126
5	Nap Lajoie-Phi. (A)	1901	125
6	Sherry Magee-Phi. (N)	1910	123
7	Buck Freeman-Bos. (A)	1902	121
	Cy Seymour-Cin. (N)	1905	121
9	Sam Crawford-Det. (A)	1910	120
10	Ty Cobb-Det. (A)	1907	119

Triples

1	Owen Wilson-Pit. (N)	1912	36
2	Joe Jackson-Cle. (A)	1912	26
	Sam Crawford-Det. (A)	1914	26
4	Sam Crawford-Det. (A)	1903	25
	Larry Doyle-N.Y. (N)	1911	25
	Tommy Long-St.L. (N)	1915	25
7	Ty Cobb-Det. (A)	1911	24
8	Sam Crawford-Cin. (N)	1902	23
	Ty Cobb-Det. (A)	1912	23
	Sam Crawford-Det. (A)	1913	23
	Ty Cobb-Det. (A)	1917	23

Runs

1	Ty Cobb-Det. (A)	1911	147
2	Nap Lajoie-Phi. (A)	1901	145
3	Ty Cobb-Det. (A)	1915	144
4	Jesse Burkett-St.L. (N)	1901	139
5	Ginger Beaumont-Pit. (N)	1903	137
	Eddie Collins-Phi. (A)	1912	137
7	Tris Speaker-Bos. (A)	1912	136
8	Tommy Leach-Pit. (N)	1909	126
	Donie Bush-Det. (A)	1911	126
	Joe Jackson-Cle. (A)	1911	126

Home Runs

1	Babe Ruth-Bos. (A)	1919	29
2	Gavvy Cravath-Phi. (N)	1915	24
3	Wildfire Schulte-Chi. (N)	1911	21
4	Gavvy Cravath-Phi. (N)	1913	19
	Gavvy Cravath-Phi. (N)	1914	19
6	Fred Luderus-Phi. (N)	1913	18
	Vic Saier-Chi. (N)	1914	18
8	Hal Chase-Buf. (F)	1915	17
9	Sam Crawford-Cin. (N)	1901	16
	Socks Seybold-St.L. (A)	1902	16

Bases on Balls

1	Jimmy Sheckard-Chi. (N)	1911	147
2	Jimmy Sheckard-Chi. (N)	1912	122
3	Topsy Hartsel-Phi. (A)	1905	121
4	Eddie Collins-Chi. (A)	1915	119
5	Donie Bush-Det. (A)	1915	118
	Ty Cobb-Det. (A)	1915	118
	Burt Shotton-St.L. (A)	1915	118
8	Donie Bush-Det. (A)	1912	117
9	Miller Huggins-St.L. (N)	1910	116
10	Donie Bush-Det. (A)	1914	112

Stolen Bases

1	Ty Cobb-Det. (A)	1915	96
2	Clyde Milan-Was. (A)	1912	88
3	Ty Cobb-Det. (A)	1911	83
4	Eddie Collins-Phi. (A)	1910	81
5	Bob Bescher-Cin. (A)	1911	80
6	Ty Cobb-Det. (A)	1909	76
7	Benny Kauff-Ind. (F)	1914	75
8	Clyde Milan-Was. (A)	1913	74
	Fritz Maisel-N.Y. (A)	1914	74
10	Bob Bescher-Cin. (N)	1910	70

Strikeouts*

1	Gus Williams-St.L. (A)	1914	120
2	Danny Moeller-Was. (A)	1913	103
3	Ed McDonald-Bos. (N)	1912	91
4	Danny Moeller-Was. (A)	1914	89
	Gavvy Cravath-Phi. (N)	1916	89
6	Doug Baird-Pit. (N)	1915	88
7	Gus Williams-St.L. (A)	1913	87
8	Doc Lavan-St.L. (A)	1915	83
9	Ray Chapman-St.L. (A)	1915	82
	Wally Pipp-N.Y. (A)	1916	82

*Strikeouts not available for N.L. before 1910; for A.L. before 1913; and not available at all for Federal League.

At Bats

1	Patsy Dougherty-Bos. + N.Y. (A)	1904	647
2	Jimmy Collins-Bos. (A)	1904	633
3	George Stone-St.L. (A)	1905	632
4	Eddie Grant-Phi. (N)	1909	631
5	Tom Jones-St.L. (A)	1904	625
6	Jimmy Barrett-Det. (A)	1904	624
	Elmer Flick-Cle. (A)	1906	624
	Vin Campbell-Bos. (N)	1912	624
9	Jack Tobin-St.L. (F)	1915	623
	George Burns-N.Y. (A)	1916	623

PITCHING

Wins

1	Jack Chesbro-N.Y. (A)	1904	41
2	Ed Walsh-Chi. (A)	1908	40
3	Christy Mathewson-N.Y. (N)	1908	37
4	Walter Johnson-Was. (A)	1913	36
5	Joe McGinnity-N.Y. (N)	1904	35
6	Smokey Joe Wood-Bos. (A)	1912	34
7	Cy Young-Bos. (A)	1901	33
	Christy Mathewson-N.Y. (N)	1904	33
	Pete Alexander-Phi. (N)	1916	33
10	Cy Young-Bos. (A)	1902	32
	Christy Mathewson-N.Y. (N)	1905	32
	Walter Johnson-Was. (A)	1912	32

Winning Percentage

1	Smokey Joe Wood-Bos. (A)	1912	.872
2	Wild Bill Donovan-Det. (A)	1907	.862
3	Chief Bender-Phi. (A)	1914	.850
4	Tom Hughes-Bos. (N)	1916	.842
5	Walter Johnson-Was. (A)	1913	.837
6	King Cole-Chi. (N)	1910	.833
7	Ed Reulbach-Chi. (N)	1906	.826
8	Jack Chesbro-Pit. (N)	1902	.824
9	Chief Bender-Phi. (A)	1910	.821
10	Joe McGinnity-N.Y. (N)	1904	.814

Losses

1	Vic Willis-Bos. (N)	1905	29
2	Pete Dowling-Mil. + Cle. (A)	1901	27
	Dummy Taylor-N.Y. (N)	1901	27
	Jack Townsend-Was. (A)	1904	27
	George Bell-Bkn. (N)	1910	27
6	Gus Dorner-Cin. + Bos. (N)	1906	26
	Bob Groom-Was. (A)	1909	26
8	Patsy Flaherty-Chi. (A)	1903	25
	Oscar Jones-Bkn. (N)	1904	25
	Vic Willis-Bos. (N)	1904	25
	Harry McIntire-Bkn. (N)	1905	25
	Irv Young-Bos. (N)	1906	25
	Stony McGlynn-St. L. (N)	1907	25
	Bugs Raymond-St. L. (N)	1908	25
	Walter Johnson-Was. (A)	1909	25

Earned Run Average

1	Dutch Leonard-Bos. (A)	1914	1.01
2	Three Finger Brown-Chi. (N)	1906	1.04
3	Walter Johnson-Was. (A)	1913	1.09
4	Christy Mathewson-N.Y. (N)	1909	1.14
5	Jack Pfiester-Chi. (N)	1907	1.15
6	Addie Joss-Cle. (A)	1908	1.16
7	Carl Lundgren-Chi. (N)	1907	1.17
8	Pete Alexander-Phi. (N)	1915	1.22
9	Cy Young-Bos. (A)	1908	1.26
10	Christy Mathewson-N.Y. (N)	1905	1.27
	Ed Walsh-Chi. (A)	1910	1.27
	Walter Johnson-Was. (A)	1918	1.27

Saves

1	Three Finger Brown-Chi. (N)	1911	13
2	Chief Bender-Phi. (A)	1913	12
3	Harry Cheney-Chi. (N)	1913	11
	Dave Danforth-Chi. (A)	1917	11
5	Ed Walsh-Chi. (A)	1912	10
	Hugh Bedient-Buf. (F)	1915	10
7	Tom Hughes-Bos. (N)	1915	9
	Bob Shawkey-N.Y. (A)	1916	9
9	Frank Arrellanes-Bos. (A)	1909	8
	Red Ames-St.L. (N)	1916	8

Bases on Balls

1	Bob Harmon-St. L. (N)	1911	181
2	Elmer Myers-Phi. (A)	1916	168
3	Weldon Wyckoff-Phi. (A)	1915	165
4	Earl Moore-Phi. (N)	1911	164
5	Marty O'Toole-Pit. (N)	1912	159
6	Grover Lowdermilk-St.L. + Det.	1915	157
7	Wild Bill Donovan-Bkn. (N)	1901	152
8	Chick Fraser-Bos. (N)	1905	149
	Al Schulz-Buf. (F)	1915	149
10	Orvie Overall-Cin. (N)	1905	147

Games Pitched

1	Ed Walsh-Chi. (A)	1908	66
2	Ed Walsh-Chi. (A)	1912	62
3	Dave Davenport-St.L. (A)	1916	59
4	Ed Walsh-Chi. (A)	1907	56
	Christy Mathewson-N.Y. (N)	1908	56
	Ed Walsh-Chi. (A)	1911	56
	Reb Russell-Chi. (A)	1916	56
8	Joe McGinnity-N.Y. (N)	1903	55
	Jack Chesbro-N.Y. (A)	1904	55
	Dave Davenport-St.L. (F)	1915	55

Strikeouts

1	Rube Waddell-Phi. (A)	1904	349
2	Walter Johnson-Was. (A)	1910	313
3	Walter Johnson-Was (A)	1912	303
4	Rube Waddell-Phi. (A)	1903	302
5	Rube Waddell-Phi. (A)	1905	287
6	Ed Walsh-Chi. (A)	1908	269
7	Christy Mathewson-N.Y. (N)	1903	267
8	Christy Mathewson-N.Y. (N)	1908	259
9	Smokey Joe Wood-Bos. (A)	1912	258
10	Ed Walsh-Chi. (A)	1911	255

Games Started

1	Jack Chesbro-N.Y. (A)	1904	51
2	Ed Walsh-Chi. (A)	1908	49
3	Joe McGinnity-N.Y. (N)	1903	48
4	Vic Willis-Bos. (N)	1902	46
	Christy Mathewson-N.Y. (N)	1904	46
	Rube Wadell-Phi. (A)	1904	46
	Ed Walsh-Chi. (A)	1906	46
	Dave Davenport-St.L. (F)	1915	46
9	Jack Powell-N.Y. (A)	1904	45
	Pete Alexander-Phi. (N)	1916	45

Shutouts

1	Pete Alexander-Phi. (N)	1916	16
2	Jack Coombs-Phi. (A)	1910	13
3	Ed Walsh-Chi. (A)	1908	12
	Walter Johnson-Was. (A)	1913	12
	Pete Alexander-Phi. (N)	1915	12
6	Christy Mathewson-N.Y. (N)	1908	11
7	Cy Young-Bos. (A)	1904	10
	Ed Walsh-Chi. (A)	1906	10
	Smokey Joe Wood-Bos. (A)	1912	10
	Walter Johnson-Was. (A)	1914	10
	Dave Davenport-St.L. (F)	1915	10

Complete Games

1	Jack Chesbro-N.Y. (A)	1904	48
2	Vic Willis-Bos. (N)	1902	45
3	Joe McGinnity-N.Y. (N)	1903	44
4	George Mullin-Det. (A)	1904	42
	Ed Walsh-Chi. (A)	1908	42
6	Noodles Hahn-Cin. (N)	1901	41
	Cy Young-Bos. (A)	1902	41
	Irv Young-Bos. (N)	1905	41
9	Cy Young-Bos. (A)	1904	40
10	Joe McGinnity-Bal. (A)	1901	39
	Bill Dinneen-Bos. (A)	1902	39
	Jack Taylor-St.L. (N)	1904	39
	Rube Waddell-Phi. (A)	1904	39
	Vic Willis-Bos. (N)	1904	39

Innings Pitched

1	Ed Walsh-Chi. (A)	1908	464
2	Jack Chesbro-N.Y. (A)	1904	455
3	Joe McGinnity-N.Y. (N)	1903	434
4	Ed Walsh-Chi. (A)	1907	422
5	Vic Willis-Bos. (N)	1902	410
6	Joe McGinnity-N.Y. (N)	1904	408
7	Ed Walsh-Chi. (A)	1912	393
	Dave Davenport-St.L. (F)	1915	393
9	Christy Mathewson-N.Y. (N)	1908	391
10	Jack Powell-N.Y. (A)	1904	390

1901-1919 PERIOD LEADERS

BATTING

Batting Average
(Minimum 1000 Games or 4000 At Bats)

1	Ty Cobb	1905-19	.372
2	Joe Jackson	1908-19	.353
3	Tris Speaker	1907-19	.338
4	Nap Lajoie	1901-16	.332
5	Honus Wagner	1901-17	.325
6	Eddie Collins	1906-19	.325
7	Sam Crawford	1901-17	.311
8	Ginger Beaumont	1901-10	.310
9	Frank Baker	1908-19	.309
10	Stuffy McInnis	1909-19	.309

Hits

1	Sam Crawford	1901-17	2821
2	Honus Wagner	1901-17	2769
3	Ty Cobb	1905-19	2716
4	Nap Lajoie	1901-16	2523
5	Sherry Magee	*1904-19	2169
6	Hal Chase	*1905-19	2156
7	Tris Speaker	1907-19	2019
8	Tommy Leach	1901-18	1990
9	Eddie Collins	1906-19	1979
10	Ed Konetchy	1907-19	1854

Slugging Average
(Minimum 1000 Games or 4000 At Bats)

1	Ty Cobb	1905-19	.517
2	Joe Jackson	1908-19	.509
3	Gavvy Cravath	1908-19	.478
4	Tris Speaker	1907-19	.476
5	Honus Wagner	1901-17	.462
6	Sam Crawford	1901-17	.453
7	Nap Lajoie	1901-16	.445
8	Frank Baker	1908-19	.442
9	Elmer Flick	1901-10	.434
10	Sherry Magee	*1904-19	.427

Home Runs

1	Gavvy Cravath	1908-19	118
2	Wildfire Schulte	*1904-18	93
3	Sam Crawford	1901-17	90
4	Fred Luderus	1909-19	84
5	Sherry Magee	*1904-19	83
6	Frank Baker	1908-19	80
7	Honus Wagner	1901-17	78
8	Larry Doyle	1907-19	70
9	Ty Cobb	1905-19	68
	Harry Davis	1901-17	68

Runs Batted In

1	Sam Crawford	1901-17	1446
2	Honus Wagner	1901-17	1375
3	Ty Cobb	1905-19	1211
4	Sherry Magee	*1904-19	1177
5	Nap Lajoie	1901-16	1141
6	Hal Chase	*1905-19	941
7	Frank Baker	1908-19	880
8	Ed Konetchy	1907-19	847
9	Tris Speaker	1907-19	805
10	Heinie Zimmerman	*1907-19	796

Triples

1	Sam Crawford	1901-17	289
2	Ty Cobb	1905-19	212
3	Honus Wagner	1901-17	209
4	Sherry Magee	*1904-19	166
5	Tommy Leach	1901-18	162
6	Ed Konetchy	1907-19	160
7	Tris Speaker	1907-19	149
8	Joe Jackson	1908-19	148
9	Fred Clarke	1901-15	143
10	Eddie Collins	1906-19	131

Runs

1	Ty Cobb	1905-19	1415
2	Honus Wagner	1901-17	1413
3	Sam Crawford	1901-17	1300
4	Tommy Leach	1901-18	1258
5	Eddie Collins	1906-19	1135
6	Sherry Magee	*1904-19	1113
7	Donie Bush	1908-19	1085
8	Nap Lajoie	1901-16	1080
9	Jimmy Sheckard	1901-13	1053
10	Tris Speaker	1907-19	1051

Doubles

1	Nap Lajoie	1901-16	513
2	Honus Wagner	1901-17	511
3	Sam Crawford	1901-17	439
4	Ty Cobb	1905-19	431
5	Sherry Magee	*1904-19	425
6	Tris Speaker	1907-19	395
7	Hal Chase	*1905-19	324
8	Harry Davis	1901-17	311
9	Jimmy Sheckard	1901-13	299
	Ed Konetchy	1907-19	299

Bases on Balls

1	Donie Bush	1908-19	1007
2	Miller Huggins	*1904-16	1002
3	Jimmy Sheckard	1901-13	994
4	Eddie Collins	1906-19	907
5	Honus Wagner	1901-17	836
6	Roy Thomas	1901-11	812
7	Topsy Hartsel	1901-11	807
8	Johnny Evers	1902-17	777
9	Tommy Leach	1901-18	762
10	Tris Speaker	1907-19	745

Stolen Bases

1	Ty Cobb	1905-19	756
2	Honus Wagner	1901-17	601
3	Eddie Collins	1906-19	563
4	Clyde Milan	1907-19	480
5	Sherry Magee	*1904-19	441
6	Bob Bescher	1908-18	427
7	Max Carey	1910-19	392
8	Frank Chance	1901-14	378
9	Donie Bush	1908-19	377
10	Tris Speaker	1907-19	373

PITCHING

Wins

1	Christy Mathewson	1901-16	374
2	Eddie Plank	*1901-17	325
3	Walter Johnson	1907-19	296
4	Three Finger Brown	*1903-16	239
5	George Mullin	*1902-15	229
6	Cy Young	1901-11	226
7	Chief Bender	*1903-17	210
8	G.C. "Pete" Alexander	1911-19	208
9	Ed Walsh	*1904-17	194
10	Doc White	1901-10	190

Winning Percentage
(Minimum 100 Wins)

1	Sam Leever	1901-10	.707
2	G.C. "Pete" Alexander	1911-19	.675
3	Christy Mathewson	1901-16	.670
4	Joe Ward	1908-19	.669
5	Three Finger Brown	*1903-16	.653
6	Deacon Phillippe	1901-11	.652
7	Ed Reulbach	*1905-17	.632
8	Eddie Plank	*1901-17	.627
9	Addie Joss	*1902-10	.626
10	Jack Chesbro	1901-09	.622

Losses

1	Jack Powell	1901-12	193
	Eddie Plank	*1901-17	193
3	George Mullin	*1902-15	192
4	Walter Johnson	1907-19	191
5	Christy Mathewson	1901-16	184
6	Long Tom Hughes	1901-13	174
7	Red Ames	*1903-19	167
8	Vic Willis	1901-10	165
9	Doc White	1901-10	154
10	Earl Moore	*1901-14	153

Earned Run Average
(Minimum 1500 Innings Pitched or 100 Wins)

1	Walter Johnson	1907-19	1.65
2	Ed Walsh	*1904-17	1.82
3	Addie Joss	*1902-10	1.88
4	Joe Wood	1908-19	2.00
5	Three Finger Brown	*1903-16	2.06
6	G.C. "Pete" Alexander	1911-19	2.09
7	Rube Waddell	1901-10	2.11
8	Christy Mathewson	1901-16	2.11
9	Cy Young	1901-11	2.12
10	Dutch Leonard	1913-19	2.23

Saves

1	Three Finger Brown	*1903-16	49
2	Ed Walsh	*1904-17	40
3	Chief Bender	*1903-17	36
	Red Ames	*1903-19	36
5	Hooks Wiltse	*1904-15	34
6	Slim Sallee	1908-19	32
7	Christy Mathewson	1901-16	28
8	Eddie Plank	*1901-17	25
	Doc Crandall	*1908-18	25
10	Walter Johnson	1907-19	24
	Joe McGinnity	1901-08	24

Strikeouts

1	Walter Johnson	1907-19	2611
2	Christy Mathewson	1901-16	2487
3	Eddie Plank	*1901-17	2246
4	Rube Waddell	1901-10	2137
5	Ed Walsh	*1904-17	1736
6	Chief Bender	*1903-17	1711
7	Red Ames	*1903-19	1662
8	Cy Young	1901-11	1563
9	G.C. "Pete" Alexander	1911-19	1540
10	Wild Bill Donovan	1901-18	1492

Games Pitched

1	Christy Mathewson	1901-16	629
2	Eddie Plank	*1901-17	622
3	Walter Johnson	1907-19	543
4	Red Ames	*1903-19	533
5	George Mullin	*1902-15	488
6	Three Finger Brown	*1903-16	481
7	Eddie Cicotte	1905-19	465
8	Chief Bender	*1903-17	458
9	Ed Walsh	*1904-17	430
10	Doc White	1901-10	427

Shutouts

1	Walter Johnson	1907-19	88
2	Christy Mathewson	1901-16	77
3	G.C. "Pete" Alexander	1911-19	68
4	Eddie Plank	*1901-17	67
5	Ed Walsh	*1904-17	58
6	Three Finger Brown	*1903-16	56
7	Rube Waddell	1901-10	47
8	Doc White	*1901-13	46
9	Cy Young	1901-11	45
	Addie Joss	*1902-10	45

Games Started

1	Christy Mathewson	1901-16	550
2	Eddie Plank	*1901-17	527
3	Walter Johnson	1907-19	438
4	George Mullin	*1902-15	428
5	Cy Young	1901-11	370
	Jack Powell	1901-12	370
7	Red Ames	*1903-19	367
8	Vic Willis	1901-10	366
9	Doc White	*1901-13	363
10	Chief Bender	*1903-17	335

Innings Pitched

1	Christy Mathewson	1901-16	4748
2	Eddie Plank	*1901-17	4507
3	Walter Johnson	1907-19	4099
4	George Mullin	*1902-15	3687
5	Cy Young	1901-11	3313
6	Red Ames	*1903-19	3195
7	Three Finger Brown	*1903-16	3171
8	Jack Powell	1901-12	3159
9	Doc White	*1901-13	3050
10	Chief Bender	*1903-17	3016

Complete Games

1	Christy Mathewson	1901-16	433
2	Eddie Plank	*1901-17	410
3	Walter Johnson	1907-19	389
4	George Mullin	*1902-15	353
5	Cy Young	1901-11	332
6	Vic Willis	1901-10	302
7	Jack Powell	1901-12	296
8	Wild Bill Donovan	1901-18	279
9	Three Finger Brown	*1903-16	271
10	Doc White	*1901-13	262

*—Entire major league career

⊜ ⊜ 1901 A.L.—A Name by Any Other Was Not the Same ⊜ ⊜

The celebration did not equal the event. The bands and fanfare were noticeably absent, and only in the minds of those who fostered the dream was there any clamor at all. What had occurred, for the first time since the collapse of the American Association in 1891, was the unveiling of a second major league circuit. The bosses of the National League welcomed their rivals, the American League, with disdain and fear—elements necessary to give an underdog the impetus to survive.

The new league was first conceived and nurtured in the minds of League President Ban Johnson and White Sox owner Charlie Comiskey. Becoming head of the minor Western League in 1893, Johnson turned the league into the strongest of the minors within two years; this he accomplished by arranging for solid ownership of each of his franchises and by strongly backing his umpires in all disputes, thus assuring the fans that orderly games would be played. By 1896, the wheels were turning in Johnson's head; if the National League should decide to drop any of its 12 franchises, he would be ready to place a team in that territory. As fans continued to come to the firmly controlled games, each year in the late 1890's became a financial success for this regional Midwestern league.

Johnson upgraded his league even more in the century-turning year of 1900. The National League cut back that year to eight franchises, and Johnson moved a team into the abandoned Cleveland area. In addition, he won reluctant consent from the established Cubs; in return, Johnson agreed to abide by the National Agreement which defined his circuit as a minor league. Finally, Johnson conceptually broadened the geographical boundaries of the loop by changing the name from the Western League to the American League. Nevertheless, the league remained a minor circuit in 1900, with all its franchises located in the Midwest and with no pretext of hiring the best baseball talent in the United States.

In 1901, Johnson made his move; with full consent of the team owners, he withdrew from the National Agreement and announced plans to operate independently as a second major league. Expansion into the East erased the regional character of the league; Boston, Philadelphia, Baltimore, and Washington were chosen as sites, the first two being long-time citadels of National League strength. To obtain players, the American League raided the senior loop's rosters for stars as well as everyday players. Large salaries were offered by those financially sound owners Johnson had arranged for his loop. National League contracts were honored, but the new league did not recognize the reserve clause. An incipient players' association found that the new league strengthened its bargaining position; one of its major objectives was to prevent the trading of players to cities to which they did not wish to report—a right which became lost when both leagues came to peaceful terms in 1903.

When the American League's first season opened, each team found itself infused with talent from the older league. Perhaps the brightest star that first year was Nap Lajoie, second baseman for the Philadelphia Athletics, who copped the first American League batting title after jumping over from the rival Phillies. In addition to hitting a prodigious .422, Lajoie also drove in 125 runs and hit 14 home runs to capture the Triple Crown. Connie Mack was on hand to manage his first Athletics' squad and previewed one of his most prominent collegiate finds in 25-year-old Eddie Plank, a 17-game winner fresh from Gettysburg College. Jimmy Collins jumped the Boston National League team to manage and star for the new American League Boston entry and gloated on the arm of his leading pitcher, Cy Young, who came from St. Louis. Young, an 11-year National League veteran, turned in 33 victories to pace the junior circuit. John McGraw played third base while piloting the Baltimore Orioles, and his charges numbered veteran catcher Wilbert Robinson, young catcher Roger Bresnahan, and star hurler Joe McGinnity, a 28-game winner in the older loop in 1900. The new Chicago club got double duty out of Clark Griffith, who managed the club while leading the pitching staff with 24 victories. All of these men, with Johnson and Comiskey, were to eventually earn baseball's accolades by being enshrined in the Baseball Hall of Fame.

The White Sox took the first American League title by four games over a Boston club which suffered a late season pitching collapse. Prophetically, the Philadelphia A's played the best ball in the league during the final two months, giving evidence of better things to come. More important, the new clubs in Boston and Chicago outdrew the established National League teams. Despite litigation pending in the courts and a declared state of war with the old league, the American League was off and running. In fact, there was evidence that the National League would have to divide the spotlight for some time to come.

1901 AMERICAN LEAGUE

NAME	G by POS	B	AGE	G	AB	R	H	2B	3B	HR	RBI	BB	SO	SB	BA	SA
CHICAGO 1st 83-53 .610		**CLARK GRIFFITH**														
	TOTALS		30	137	4725	**819**	1303	173	89	32	656	**475**		**280**	.276	.370
Frank Isbell	1B137, 2B2, 3B1, SS1, P1	L	25	137	556	93	143	15	8	3	70	36		**52**	.257	.329
Sam Mertes	2B132, OF5	R	28	137	545	94	151	16	17	5	98	52		46	.277	.396
Frank Shugart	SS107	L	34	107	415	62	104	9	12	2	47	28		12	.251	.345
Fred Hartman	3B119		33	120	473	77	146	23	13	3	89	25		31	.309	.431
Fielder Jones	OF133	L	29	133	521	120	162	16	3	2	65	84		38	.311	.365
Dummy Hoy	OF132	L	39	131	536	113	157	23	11	2	60	**86**		30	.293	.400
Herm McFarland	OF132	L	31	132	473	83	130	21	9	4	59	75		33	.275	.383
Billy Sullivan	C97, 3B1	R	26	98	367	54	90	15	6	4	56	10		12	.245	.351
Joe Sugden	C42, 1B5	B	30	48	159	22	45	7	1	0	19	13		5	.283	.333
Nixey Callahan (BA)	P27, 3B6, 2B2	R	27	45	118	15	39	7	3	1	19	10		10	.331	.466
2 Jimmy Burke	SS31, 3B11	R	26	42	148	20	39	5	0	0	21	12		11	.264	.297
Clark Griffith	P35	R	31	35	89	21	27	3	1	2	14	23		0	.303	.427
2 Pop Foster	OF9		23	12	35	4	10	2	2	1	6	4		0	.286	.543
Dave Brain	2B5	R	24	5	20	2	7	1	0	0	5	1		0	.350	.400
BOSTON 2nd 79-57 .581 4		**JIMMY COLLINS**														
	TOTALS		28	138	4866	759	1353	183	104	**37**	632	331		157	.278	.381
Buck Freeman	1B128, 2B1, OF1	L	29	129	489	84	169	22	15	12	114	44		14	.346	.520
Hobe Ferris	2B138, SS1	R	23	138	523	68	131	16	15	2	63	23		13	.250	.350
Freddy Parent	SS138	R	25	138	517	87	158	23	9	4	59	41		16	.306	.408
Jimmy Collins	3B138	R	31	138	563	109	185	42	16	6	94	34		18	.329	**.492**
Charlie Hemphill	OF136	L	25	136	545	71	142	10	10	3	62	39		11	.261	.332
Chick Stahl	OF131	L	28	130	512	106	159	22	16	6	72	54		29	.311	.439
Tommy Dowd	OF137, 1B2, 3B1	R	32	138	594	104	159	18	7	3	52	38		33	.268	.337
Ossee Schreckengost	C72, 1B4	R	26	86	280	37	85	13	5	0	38	19		6	.304	.386
Lou Criger	C68, 1B8	R	29	76	268	26	62	6	3	0	24	11		7	.231	.276
Charlie Jones	OF10		25	10	41	6	6	2	0	0	6	1		2	.146	.195
Larry McLean	1B5	R	19	9	19	4	4	1	0	0	2	0		1	.211	.263
Harry Gleason	3B1	R	26	1	1	0	1	0	0	0	0	0		1	1.000	1.000
Jack Slattery	C1	R	24	1	3	1	1	0	0	0	1	1		0	.333	.333
DETROIT 3rd 74-61 .548 8.5		**GEORGE STALLINGS**														
	TOTALS		28	136	4676	742	1303	180	80	29	611	380		204	.279	.370
Pop Dillon	1B74	L	27	74	281	40	81	14	6	1	42	15		14	.288	.391
Kid Gleason	2B135	B	34	135	547	82	150	16	12	3	75	41		32	.274	.364
Kid Elberfeld	SS121	R	26	122	436	78	135	21	11	3	76	57		24	.310	.428
Doc Casey	3B127	L	30	128	540	105	153	16	9	2	46	32		34	.283	.357
Ducky Holmes	OF131	L	32	131	537	90	158	28	10	4	62	37		35	.294	.406
Jimmy Barrett	OF135	L	26	135	542	110	159	16	9	4	65	76		26	.293	.378
Doc Nance	OF132	R	24	132	461	72	129	24	5	3	66	51		9	.280	.373
Fritz Buelow	C69	R	25	70	231	28	52	5	5	2	29	11		2	.225	.316
S. McAllister	C35, 1B28, OF11, 3B10, SS3	B	26	90	306	45	92	9	4	3	57	15		17	.301	.386
Al Shaw	C42, 1B9, 3B2, SS1	R	26	55	171	20	46	7	0	1	23	10		2	.269	.327
Davey Crockett	1B27		25	28	102	10	29	2	2	0	14	6		1	.284	.343
1 Harry Lockhead	SS1			1	4	2	2	0	0	0	0	0		0	.500	.500

NAME	T	AGE	W	L	PCT	SV	G	GS	CG	IP	H	BB	SO	ShO	ERA
		27	**83**	53	**.610**	3	137	137	110	**1218**	1250	312	394	**11**	**2.98**
Clark Griffith	R	31	24	7	**.774**	1	35	30	26	267	275	50	67	**5**	2.66
Roy Patterson	R	24	20	16	.556	0	41	35	30	312	345	62	127	4	3.88
Nixey Callahan (BA)	R	27	15	7	.682	0	27	22	20	215	195	50	70	1	2.43
Jack Katoll	R	29	13	12	.520	0	27	25	19	208	231	53	59	0	2.81
John Skopec	L	21	6	3	.667	0	9	9	6	68	62	45	24	0	3.18
2 Wiley Piatt	L	26	2	2	.500	1	7	6	4	52	42	14	19	1	2.77
1 Zaza Harvey	L	22	3	6	.333	1	16	9	5	92	91	34	27	0	3.62
Frank Dupee	R	24	0	0	.000	0	1	1	0	0	0	3	0	0	∞
John McAleese	R	22	0	0	.000	0	1	0	0	3	7	1	1	0	9.00
Frank Isbell	R	25	0	0	.000	0	1	0	0	1	2	0	0	0	9.00
		27	79	57	.581	1	138	138	123	1217	1178	294	**396**	7	3.04
Cy Young	R	34	**33**	10	.767	0	43	41	38	371	324	37	**158**	**5**	**1.63**
George Winter	R	23	16	10	.615	0	28	28	26	241	234	66	63	1	2.80
Ted Lewis	R	28	16	16	.500	1	39	34	31	316	299	91	103	1	3.53
Fred Mitchell	R	23	6	9	.400	0	17	13	10	109	115	51	34	0	3.80
Nig Cuppy	R	31	4	6	.400	0	13	11	9	93	111	14	22	0	4.16
Win Kellum	L	25	2	3	.400	0	6	6	5	48	61	7	8	0	6.38
Garry Prentiss	R	25	1	0	1.000	0	2	1	1	10	7	6	0	0	1.80
Jake Volz	R	23	1	0	1.000	0	1	1	1	7	6	9	5	0	9.00
Deacon Morrissey			0	0	.000	0	1	0	0	4	5	2	1	0	2.25
1 Frank Foreman	R	38	0	1	.000	0	1	1	1	8	8	2	1	0	9.00
Charlie Beville			0	2	.000	0	2	2	1	9	8	9	1	0	4.00
		25	74*	61	.548	3	136	136	118	1189	1328	313	307	8	3.30
Roscoe Miller	R	24	23	13	.639	1	38	36	35	332	339	98	79	3	2.95
Ed Siever	L	23	18	11	.620	0	38	33	30	289	334	65	85	2	3.24
Joe Yeager	R	25	12	12	.500	1	26	25	22	200	209	46	38	2	2.61
Jack Cronin	R	27	12	16	.429	1	30	28	21	220	261	42	62	1	3.89
Emil Frisk	R	25	5	4	.556	0	11	7	6	75	94	26	22	0	4.32
Ed High	L		2	1	.667	0	4	1	1	18	21	6	4	0	3.50
Frank Owen	R	21	1	4	.200	0	8	5	3	56	70	30	17	0	4.34

*One win by Forfeit

PHILADELPHIA 4th 74-62 .544 9 — **CONNIE MACK**

NAME	G by POS	B	AGE	G	AB	R	H	2B	3B	HR	RBI	BB	SO	SB	BA	SA
TOTALS			27	137	**4882**	805	**1409**	**239**	87	35	**665**	301		173	.289	.395
Harry Davis	1B117	R	27	117	496	92	152	28	10	8	76	23		21	.306	.452
Nap Lajoie	2B119, SS12	R	25	131	543	**145**	**229**	**48**	13	**14**	**125**	24		27	**.422**	**.635**
2 Joe Dolan	SS61, 3B35, 2B1, OF1		28	98	338	50	73	21	2	1	38	26		3	.216	.299
Lave Cross	3B100	R	35	100	420	82	139	31	11	2	73	19		21	.332	.471
Socks Seybold	OF100, 1B14	R	30	114	457	74	152	25	12	8	90	40		14	.334	.492
Dave Fultz	OF106, 2B18, SS9	R	26	132	561	95	164	17	9	0	52	32		36	.292	.355
Matty McIntyre	OF82	L	21	82	308	38	85	12	4	0	46	30		11	.276	.341
Mike Powers	C111, 1B3	R	30	116	431	53	108	26	5	1	47	18		10	.251	.341
Jack Hayden	OF50		20	51	211	35	56	6	4	0	17	18		4	.265	.332
1 Phil Geier	OF50, SS2, 3B1	R	24	50	211	42	49	5	2	0	23	24		7	.232	.275
2 Bones Ely	SS45	R	28	45	171	11	37	6	2	0	16	3		6	.216	.275
2 Farmer Steelman	C14, OF12		26	27	88	5	23	2	0	0	7	10		4	.261	.284
Harry Smith (RJ)	C9, OF1	R	26	11	34	3	11	1	0	0	3	2		1	.324	.353
2 Harry Lockhead	SS9			9	34	3	3	0	0	0	2	3		0	.088	.088
Morgan Murphy	C8, 1B1	R	34	9	28	5	6	1	0	0	6	0		1	.214	.250
Fred Ketchum	OF5	L	25	5	22	5	5	0	0	0	2	0		0	.227	.227
2 Tom Leahy	OF2, SS1, C1	R	32	5	15	1	5	1	0	0	1	1		0	.333	.400
Bob Lindermann	OF3			3	9	0	1	0	0	0	0	0		0	.111	.111
Charlie Carr	1B2	R	24	2	8	0	1	0	0	0	0	0		0	.125	.125
Billy Lauder	3B2	R	27	2	8	1	1	0	0	0	0	0		0	.125	.125
Bob McKinney	2B1, 3B1		25	2	2	0	0	0	0	0	0	0		0	.000	.000

NAME	T	AGE	W	L	PCT	SV	G	GS	CG	IP	H	BB	SO	ShO	ERA
		28	74	62	.544	2	137	137	**124**	1201	1346	374	350	6	4.00
Chick Fraser	R	30	20	15	.571	1	40	37	35	331	344	**132**	110	2	3.81
Bill Bernhard	R	30	17	11	.607	0	31	27	26	257	328	50	58	1	4.52
Eddie Plank	L	25	17	13	.567	0	33	32	28	261	254	68	90	1	3.31
2 Snake Wiltse	L	29	14	5	.737	0	19	19	18	166	185	35	40	2	3.58
1 Wiley Piatt	L	26	6	12	.333	1	18	16	15	140	176	60	45	0	4.63
1 Dummy Leitner	R	30	0	0	.000	0	1	0	0	2	1	1	1	0	0.00
2 Bock Baker		22	0	1	.000	0	1	1	0	6	6	6	1	0	10.50
Peter Loos			0	1	.000	0	1	1	0	1	2	4	0	0	27.00
John McPherson		32	0	1	.000	0	1	1	0	4	7	4	0	0	11.25
Bill Milligan	L	24	0	3	.000	0	6	3	2	33	43	14	5	0	4.36

BALTIMORE 5th 68-65 .511 13.5 — **JOHN McGRAW**

NAME	G by POS	B	AGE	G	AB	R	H	2B	3B	HR	RBI	BB	SO	SB	BA	SA
TOTALS			27	134	4589	761	1348	179	**111**	24	633	369		207	**.294**	**.397**
Warren Hart	1B58			58	206	33	64	3	5	0	23	20		7	.311	.374
Jimmy Williams	2B130	R	24	130	501	113	159	26	**21**	7	96	56		21	.317	.495
Bill Keister	SS112	R	26	115	442	78	145	20	**21**	2	93	18		24	.328	.482
John McGraw (KJ)	3B69	L	28	73	230	73	81	13	9	0	28	61		25	.352	.487
Cy Seymour	OF133, 1B1	L	28	137	552	85	167	20	8	1	77	28		33	.303	.373
Jim Jackson	OF96	R	23	99	364	42	91	17	3	2	50	20		11	.250	.330
Mike Donlin	OF74, 1B47	L	23	122	481	108	164	22	14	5	67	53		32	.341	.476
Roger Bresnahan	C69, OF8, 3B4, 2B2, P2	R	22	86	293	40	77	9	9	1	32	23		10	.263	.365
2 Jack Dunn	3B67, SS19, P9, OF1, 2B1	R	28	96	362	41	90	9	4	0	36	21		10	.249	.296
Steve Brodie	OF83	L	32	84	309	41	96	5	6	2	41	25		10	.311	.385
Wilbert Robinson (RJ)	C67	R	38	71	241	34	72	13	3	0	26	10		9	.299	.378
Harry Howell	P37, OF9, SS6, 1B2, 2B1	R	24	53	188	26	41	10	5	2	26	5		7	.218	.356
Frank Foutz	1B20	R	24	20	72	13	17	4	1	2	14	8		0	.236	.403
George Rohe	1B8, 3B6	R	25	14	36	7	10	2	0	0	4	5		1	.278	.333
Walter Snodgrass	OF2			3	10	0	1	0	0	0	1	0		0	.100	.100
2 Tim Jordan	1B1	L	22	1	3	0	0	0	0	0	0	0		0	.000	.000
Tacks Latimer	C1		**23**	1	4	0	1	0	0	0	0	0		0	.250	.250

NAME	T	AGE	W	L	PCT	SV	G	GS	CG	IP	H	BB	SO	ShO	ERA
		30	68	65*	.511	5	134	134	115	1158	1313	344	271	4	3.73
Joe McGinnity	R	30	26	19	.573	**3**	**48**	**43**	**39**	**382**	**412**	96	75	1	3.56
Harry Howell	R	24	14	21	.400	0	37	34	32	295	333	79	93	1	3.66
2 Frank Foreman	R	38	13	7	.650	1	24	22	18	191	225	58	41	1	3.68
Jerry Nops	L	26	11	10	.524	1	27	23	17	177	192	59	43	1	4.07
2 Jack Dunn	R	28	3	3	.500	0	9	6	6	60	74	21	5	0	3.60
W. A. Kearns			1	0	1.000	0	3	1	1	17	30	9	5	0	6.35
Roger Bresnahan	R	22	0	1	.000	0	2	1	0	6	10	4	3	0	6.00
1 Stan Yerkes			0	1	.000	0	1	1	1	8	12	2	4	0	6.75
Crazy Schmidt	L	35	0	2	.000	0	4	3	1	23	25	16	2	0	1.96

***1 loss by forfeit**

WASHINGTON 6th 61-73 .455 21 — **JIMMY MANNING**

NAME	G by POS	B	AGE	G	AB	R	H	2B	3B	HR	RBI	BB	SO	SB	BA	SA
TOTALS			29	138	4772	683	1282	191	83	33	561	356		127	.269	.364
Mike Grady	1B59, C30, OF3	R	31	94	347	57	99	17	10	9	56	27		14	.285	.470
John Farrell	2B72, OF62, 3B1		24	135	555	100	151	32	11	3	63	52		25	.272	.386
Billy Clingman	SS137	B	31	137	480	66	116	10	7	2	56	42		10	.242	.304
Bill Coughlin	3B137	R	22	137	508	77	141	17	13	6	68	25		15	.278	.398
Sam Dungan	OF104, 1B35	R	35	138	559	70	179	26	12	1	72	40		9	.320	.415
2 Irv Waldron	OF78	R	25	79	**332#**	54	107	14	3	0	23	22		8	.322	.383
1 Pop Foster	OF102, SS2		23	103	392	65	109	16	9	6	54	41		10	.278	.411
Boileryard Clarke	C107, 1B3	R	32	110	422	58	118	15	5	3	54	23		7	.280	.360
Joe Quinn	2B66	R	36	66	266	33	67	10	2	2	34	11		7	.252	.331
Dale Gear	OF34, P24	R	29	58	199	17	47	9	2	0	20	4		2	.236	.302
Win Mercer	P24, OF16, 1B7, SS1, 3B1	R	27	51	140	26	42	7	2	0	16	23		10	.300	.379
Bill Everett	1B33		32	33	115	14	22	3	2	0	8	15		7	.191	.252
1 Jack O'Brien	OF11	L	28	11	45	5	8	0	0	0	5	3		2	.178	.178
Charlie Luskey	OF8, C3	R	25	11	41	8	8	3	1	0	3	2		0	.195	.317
1 Tim Jordan	1B6	L	22	6	20	2	4	1	0	0	2	3		0	.200	.250
Ben Harrison	OF1			1	2	0	0	0	0	0	0	1		0	.000	.000

NAME	T	AGE	W	L	PCT	SV	G	GS	CG	IP	H	BB	SO	ShO	ERA
		26	61	73*	.455	1	138	138	118	1183	**1396**	284	308	8	4.09
Casey Patten	L	25	17	10	.630	0	32	30	26	254	285	74	109	4	3.93
Watty Lee	L	21	16	16	.500	0	36	33	25	262	328	45	63	2	4.40
Bill Carrick	R	27	14	22	.389	0	42	37	34	324	367	93	70	0	3.75
Win Mercer	R	27	9	13	.409	1	24	22	19	180	217	50	31	1	4.55
Dale Gear	R	29	5	11	.313	0	24	16	14	163	199	22	35	1	4.03

#Waldron, also with Milwaukee, league leader in AB with 598

***1 loss by forfeit**

CLEVELAND 7th 55-82 .401 28.5 — **JIMMY McALEER**

NAME	G by POS	B	AGE	G	AB	R	H	2B	3B	HR	RBI	BB	SO	SB	BA	SA
TOTALS			29	138	4833	666	1311	197	68	12	523	243		125	.271	.348
Candy LaChance	1B133	B	31	133	548	81	166	22	9	1	75	7		11	.303	.381
Erve Beck	2B132	R	22	135	539	78	156	26	8	6	79	23		7	.289	.401
Frank Scheibeck	SS92	R	36	93	329	33	70	11	3	0	38	18		3	.213	.264
Bill Bradley	3B133, P1	R	23	133	516	95	153	28	13	1	55	26		18	.296	.407
2 Jack O'Brien	OF92, 3B1	L	28	92	375	54	106	14	5	0	39	22		13	.283	.347
Ollie Pickering	OF137	L	31	137	547	102	169	25	6	0	40	58		36	.309	.377
Jack McCarthy (KJ)	OF86	L	32	86	343	60	110	14	7	0	32	30		9	.321	.402
Bob Wood	C84, 3B4, OF3, 1B1, 2B1, SS1	R	35	98	346	45	101	23	3	1	49	12		6	.292	.384
2 Zaza Harvey	OF45		22	45	170	21	60	5	5	1	24	9		15	.353	.459
1 George Yeager	C25, 1B5, OF3, 2B2		28	39	139	13	31	5	0	0	14	4		2	.223	.259
2 Joe Connor	C32, OF4, SS1	R	26	37	121	13	17	3	1	0	6	7		2	.140	.182
Frank Genins	OF26		34	26	101	15	23	5	0	0	9	8		3	.228	.277
Danny Shay	SS19	R	24	19	75	4	17	2	2	0	10	2		0	.227	.307
Tom Donovan	OF18, P1	R	21	18	71	9	18	3	1	0	5	0		1	.254	.324
Jim McGuire	SS18		26	18	69	4	16	2	0	0	3	0		0	.232	.261
2 Truck Eagan	2B5, 3B1		24	5	18	2	3	0	1	0	2	1		0	.167	.278
1 Billy Hallman	SS5	R	34	5	19	2	4	0	0	0	3	2		0	.211	.211
Jimmy McAleer	OF2, 3B1, P1	R	36	3	7	0	1	0	0	0	0	0		0	.143	.143
D. F. Gallagher	OF2			2	4	0	0	0	0	0	0	0		0	.000	.000
Ed Cermak	OF1	R	19	1	4	0	0	0	0	0	0	0		0	.000	.000
Frank Cross	OF1		28	1	5	0	3	0	0	0	0	0		0	.600	.600
Russ Hall	SS1		29	1	4	2	2	0	0	0	0	0		0	.500	.500
Harry Hogan	OF1		25	1	4	0	0	0	0	0	0	0		0	.000	.000
Paddy Livingston	C1	R	21	1	2	0	0	0	0	0	0	0		0	.000	.000

NAME	T	AGE	W	L	PCT	SV	G	GS	CG	IP	H	BB	SO	ShO	ERA
		29	55†	82	.401	3	138	138	122	1182	1365	**464**	334	7	4.12
Earl Moore	R	21	16	14	.533	0	31	30	28	251	234	107	99	4	**2.90**
2 Pete Dowling	L		8	**22***	.267	0	33	30	28	256	269	104	99	2	3.87
Ed Scott	R	30	7	6	.538	0	17	16	11	125	149	38	23	0	4.39
Bill Hoffer	R	30	6	7	.462	**3**	16	10	10	99	113	35	19	0	4.55
Bill Hart		35	6	12	.333	0	20	19	16	158	180	57	48	0	3.76
Harry McNeal	R	23	5	6	.455	0	12	10	9	85	120	30	15	0	4.45
Jack Bracker	R	20	4	8	.333	0	12	12	12	100	137	31	18	0	6.21
Dick Braggins	R	21	1	2	.333	0	4	3	2	32	44	15	1	0	4.78
Bill Cristall	L	22	1	4	.200	0	6	6	5	48	54	30	12	1	4.87
1 Gus Weyhing	R	34	0	0	.000	0	2	1	0	11	20	5	0	0	8.18
1 Bock Baker		22	0	1	.000	0	1	1	1	8	23	6	0	0	5.63
Bill Bradley		23	0	0	.000	0	1	0	0	1	4	0	0	0	0.00
Tom Donovan		28	0	0	.000	0	1	0	0	7	16	3	0	0	5.14
Jimmy McAleer		36	0	0	.000	0	1	0	0	.1	2	3	0	0	0.00

***Dowling, also with Milwaukee, league leader in L with 27**

† win by forfeit

MILWAUKEE 8th 48-89 .350 35.5 — **HUGH DUFFY**

NAME	G by POS	B	AGE	G	AB	R	H	2B	3B	HR	RBI	BB	SO	SB	BA	SA
TOTALS			27	139	4795	641	1250	192	66	26	513	325		176	.261	.345
John Anderson	1B125, OF13	B	27	138	576	90	190	46	7	8	99	24		35	.330	.476
Billy Gilbert	2B127	R	25	127	492	77	133	14	7	0	43	31		19	.270	.327
Wid Conroy	SS118, 3B12	R	26	131	503	74	129	20	6	5	64	36		21	.256	.350
1 Jimmy Burke	3B64	R	26	64	233	24	48	8	0	0	26	17		6	.206	.240
Bill Hallman	OF139		25	139	549	70	135	27	6	2	47	41		12	.246	.328
Hugh Duffy	OF77	R	34	78	286	41	88	14	8	2	45	16		13	.308	.434
1 Irv Waldron	OF62	R	25	62	**266#**	48	79	8	6	0	29	16		12	.297	.372
Billy Maloney	C72, OF8	L	23	86	290	42	85	3	4	0	22	7		11	.293	.331
Bill Friel	3B61, OF28, 2B9, SS6	L	25	106	376	51	100	13	7	4	35	23		15	.266	.370
George Hogriever	OF54	R	32	54	221	25	52	10	2	0	16	30		7	.235	.299
1 Joe Connor	C30, 2B1, 3B1, OF1	R	26	38	102	10	28	3	1	1	9	6		4	.275	.353
2 Jiggs Donahue	C19, 1B13	L	21	37	108	10	33	4	4	0	16	10		4	.305	.417
1 Tom Leahy	C28, OF2, 2B1	R	32	33	99	18	24	6	2	0	10	11		3	.242	.343
Ed Bruyette	OF21, 2B3, SS1, 3B1			26	82	7	15	3	0	0	4	12		1	.183	.220
Davy Jones	OF14	L	21	14	52	12	9	0	0	3	5	11		4	.173	.346
George Bone	SS12		26	12	43	6	13	2	0	0	6	4		0	.302	.349
2 Phil Geier	OF8, 3B3	R	24	11	39	4	7	1	1	0	1	5		4	.179	.256
Lou Gertenrich	OF1	R	26	2	3	1	1	0	0	0	0	0		0	.333	.333
John Butler	C1			1	3	0	0	0	0	0	0	1		0	.000	.000
George McBride	SS3	R	20	1	4	0	0	0	0	0	0	1		0	.000	.000

NAME	T	AGE	W	L	PCT	SV	G	GS	CG	IP	H	BB	SO	ShO	ERA
		26	48	**89**	.350	6	139	139	107	1218	1383	395	376	3	4.06
Bill Reidy	R	27	15	18	.454	1	37	33	28	301	364	62	50	2	4.22
Bert Husting	R	23	9	15	.375	2	34	26	19	217	234	95	67	0	4.27
Ned Garvin	R	27	8	21	.275	2	37	27	22	257	258	90	122	1	3.47
Pink Hawley (IL)	R	28	7	13	.350	0	26	23	17	182	228	41	50	0	4.60
Tully Sparks	R	24	6	17	.260	0	29	26	18	210	228	93	62	0	3.51
1 Pete Dowling	L		3	**5***	.375	1	10	4	3	50	71	14	25	0	5.58

***Dowling, also with Cleveland, league leader in L with 27**

#Waldron, also with Washington, league leader in AB with 598

1901 N.L.—Breaking Up That Old Monopoly

While the upstart American League was playing its first major league schedule, the established National League had finished its 25th campaign and was established as the bastion of baseball in the United States. Since its founding in 1876, the league had weathered rule changes, shifting franchises, and competition from three rival leagues, establishing its durability and supremacy in the young field of professional baseball. The most vigorous competition had come from the American Association, an innovative organization which was launched in 1882 and which bit the dust financially after the 1891 season. For the greater part of the nineties, the National League reigned supreme over the game, but this domination brought its own troubles. The league expanded from eight to twelve teams in 1892, and some teams like Louisville and Washington spent an entire decade light-years from the first division. In an era dominated on the field by Baltimore and Boston, cooperation and collusion among the owners was the keynote off the field. Late in the era, ownership of two clubs by one group of individuals crept into the loop's structure; Baltimore and Brooklyn came under common management, as did Cleveland with St. Louis and Pittsburgh with Louisville. These abuses did not lead to fixing games, but all the better players in the interlocking ownership generally were concentrated on one team, leaving their counterpart much weaker. In response to such imbalances, the league in 1900 cut down to eight teams, dropping Baltimore, Louisville, Cleveland, and Washington, leaving a circuit of New York, Brooklyn, Boston, Philadelphia, Pittsburgh, Chicago, Cincinnati, and St. Louis—a structure which would stand undisturbed until 1953.

The entry of the American League onto the big league stage in 1901 created more than a second major league. It additionally opened a predicted escape value for the athletes. The National League had always assumed a high-handed stance with the players, and the athletes viewed with satisfaction the bidding war between the new rival and the old monolith. About thirty 1900 regulars jumped over to the junior loop, including stars Nap Lajoie, John McGraw, Jimmy Collins, Joe McGinnity, Clark Griffith, and Cy Young. The new league occupied three of the abandoned National League cities of the 1890's, and new teams were placed in direct competition with the clubs in Boston, Philadelphia, and Chicago.

On the field, the East Coast teams were more severely hurt by the raids than the Western teams. The Pittsburgh Pirates attained first place on June 16, and pulled away from runner-up Philadelphia in September to win the championship by 7½ games. Two of the shining lights of the squad were pirated from Louisville during the days of the interlocking ownership; Fred Clarke managed the team and hit .316 as the left fielder, and Honus Wagner alternated among three positions in the field while batting .353. Deacon Phillippe and Jack Chesbro gave the Bucs two 20-game winners on the mound. The second-place Phillies were hurt by the loss of Lajoie to the American League but still packed dynamite in the bats of Ed Delahanty and Elmer Flick. Champion Brooklyn fell to third place because of a slump in hitting and the defection of pitching ace "Iron Man" Joe McGinnity.

Four baseball immortals topped the batting lists. Jesse Burkett hit .382 to lead the league and bring St. Louis into the first division. Philadelphia's Ed Delahanty and Wee Willie Keeler of Brooklyn followed close on Burkett's heels, while Sam Crawford of Cincinnati hit 16 home runs to lead the circuit. As Brooklyn proudly displayed the league's biggest winner, Wild Bill Donovan, their local rivals, the New York Giants, unveiled the phenomenal arm of Christy Mathewson, a 20-game winner in his first full season.

After the 1901 season, the league owners split into two factions; four owners wanted Al Spalding to assume the league presidency to lead the war against the new league, and four owners supported the incumbent, Nick Young. This deadlock caused a halt in league business during the winter, and resulted in a three-man directorate of John T. Brush, A. H. Soden, and James A. Hart to assume direction of the shaken circuit.

1901 NATIONAL LEAGUE

NAME	G by POS	B	AGE	G	AB	R	H	2B	3B	HR	RBI	BB	SO	SB	BA	SA
PITTSBURGH 1st 90-49 .647		FRED CLARKE														
TOTALS			29	140	4913	776	1407	182	92	28	636	386		203	.286	.378
Kitty Bransfield	1B139	R	26	139	565	92	165	26	17	0	91	29		28	.292	.398
Claude Ritchey	2B139, SS1	B	27	140	540	66	160	20	4	1	74	47		15	.296	.354
1 Bones Ely	SS64, 3B1	R	38	65	240	18	50	6	3	0	28	6		5	.208	.258
Tommy Leach	3B92, SS4	R	23	95	375	62	112	13	13	1	44	20		16	.299	.411
2 Lefty Davis	OF86	L	26	87	335	87	105	8	11	2	33	56		22	.313	.421
Ginger Beaumont	OF133	L	24	132	555	118	182	14	6	8	72	44		32	.328	.418
Fred Clarke	OF127, SS1, 3B1	L	28	129	525	118	166	26	14	6	60	51		22	.316	.453
Chief Zimmer	C68	R	40	69	236	17	52	7	3	0	21	20		6	.220	.275
Honus Wagner	SS61, OF54, 3B24, 2B1	R	27	141	556	100	196	**39**	10	6	**126**	53		**48**	.353	.491
Jack O'Connor	C59	R	32	61	202	16	39	7	3	0	22	10		2	.193	.257
2 George Yeager	C20, 3B4, 1B1		28	26	91	9	24	2	1	0	10	4		1	.264	.308
Ed Poole	P12, OF12, 2B1, 3B1	R	26	26	78	6	16	4	0	1	4	4		1	.205	.295
3 Jimmy Burke	3B14	R	26	14	51	4	10	0	0	0	4	4		0	.196	.196
Lew Carr	SS9, 3B1	R	28	9	28	2	7	1	1	0	4	2		0	.250	.357
Jud Smith	3B6	R	32	6	21	1	3	1	0	0	0	3		0	.143	.190
1 Truck Eagan	SS3		24	4	12	0	1	0	0	0	2	0		1	.083	.083
1 Elmer Smith	OF1	L	33	4	4	0	0	0	0	0	0	2		0	.000	.000
1 Jiggs Donahue	C1, OF1	L	21	2	0	1	0	0	0	0	0	0		0	.000	.000
Terry Turner	3B2	R	20	2	7	0	3	0	0	0	1	0		0	.429	.429
PHILADELPHIA 2nd 83-57 .593 7.5		BILL SHETTSLINE														
TOTALS			29	140	4793	668	1275	194	58	24	553	**430**		199	.266	.346
Hughie Jennings	1B80, 2B1, SS1	R	32	81	302	38	83	22	2	1	39	25		13	.274	.371
2 Billy Hallman	2B90, 3B33	R	34	123	445	46	82	13	5	0	38	26		13	.184	.236
Monte Cross	SS139	R	31	139	483	49	95	14	1	1	44	52		24	.197	.236
Harry Wolverton	3B93		27	93	379	42	117	15	4	0	43	22		13	.309	.369
Elmer Flick	OF138	L	25	138	542	111	182	31	17	8	88	52		26	.336	.500
Roy Thomas	OF129	L	27	129	479	102	148	5	2	1	28	**100**		27	.309	.334
Ed Delahanty	OF84, 1B58	R	33	138	538	106	192	38	16	8	108	65		28	.357	.532
Ed McFarland	C74	R	26	74	295	33	84	14	2	1	32	18		11	.285	.356
2 Shad Barry	2B35, 3B16, OF13, SS1	R	24	67	252	35	62	10	0	1	22	15		13	.246	.298
1 Jimmy Slagle	OF48	L	27	48	183	20	37	6	2	1	20	16		5	.202	.273
Klondike Douglass	C41, 1B6, OF2	L	29	51	173	14	56	6	1	0	23	11		10	.324	.370
Al Orth	P35, OF4	R	28	41	128	14	36	6	0	1	15	3		3	.281	.352
Fred Jacklitsch (BG)	C30, 3B1	R	25	33	120	14	30	4	3	0	24	12		2	.250	.333
Doc White	P31, OF1	L	22	27	95	15	26	3	1	1	11	2		11	.274	.358
George Browne	OF8	L	25	8	26	2	5	1	0	0	4	1		2	.192	.231
Bert Conn	2B5		21	5	18	2	4	1	0	0	0	0		0	.222	.278
1 Joe Dolan	2B10		28	10	37	0	3	0	0	0	2	2		0	.081	.081
BROOKLYN 3rd 79-57 .581 9.5		NED HANLON														
TOTALS			30	137	4879	744	1399	**206**	93	32	633	312		178	**.287**	**.387**
Joe Kelley	1B115, 3B5	R	29	120	493	77	152	21	12	4	65	40		20	.308	.424
Tom Daly	2B133	R	35	133	520	88	164	38	10	3	90	42		31	.315	.444
Bill Dahlen	SS129, 2B2	R	31	130	513	69	134	17	10	4	82	30		23	.261	.357
2 Charlie Irwin	3B65	R	32	65	242	25	52	13	2	0	20	14		4	.215	.285
Willie Keeler	OF125, 3B10, 2B3	L	29	136	589	124	209	16	15	2	43	21		31	.355	.443
Tom McCreery	OF82, 1B4, SS2	R	26	91	335	47	97	11	14	3	53	32		13	.290	.433
Jimmy Sheckard	OF121, 3B12	L	22	133	558	116	197	31	**19**	11	104	47		42	.353	**.536**
Deacon McGuire	C81, 1B3	R	35	85	301	28	89	16	4	0	40	18		4	.296	.375
Duke Farrell	C59, 1B17	R	34	80	284	38	84	10	6	1	31	7		7	.296	.384
2 Cozy Dolan	OF64	L	28	66	253	33	66	11	1	0	29	17		7	.261	.312
Frank Gatins	3B46, SS5		30	50	197	21	45	7	2	1	21	5		6	.228	.299
1 Lefty Davis	OF24, 2B1	L	26	25	91	11	19	2	0	0	7	10		4	.209	.231
John Gochnaur	SS3	R	25	3	11	1	4	0	0	0	2	1		1	.364	.364
Hugh Hearne	C2	R	28	2	5	1	2	0	0	0	3	0		0	.400	.400
1 Farmer Steelman	C1		26	1	3	0	1	0	0	0	0	0		0	.333	.333

NAME	T	AGE	W	L	PCT	SV	G	GS	CG	IP	H	BB	SO	ShO	ERA
		28	**90**	49	**.647**	4	140	140	119	1245	1198	244	505	**15**	**2.58**
Deacon Phillippe	R	29	22	12	.647	2	37	32	30	296	274	38	103	1	2.22
Jack Chesbro	R	27	21	10	**.677**	1	36	28	26	288	261	52	129	**6**	2.37
Jesse Tannehill	L	26	18	10	.643	1	32	30	25	252	240	36	118	4	**2.18**
Sam Leever (SA)	R	29	14	5	.737	0	21	20	18	176	182	39	82	2	2.86
2 Ed Doheny	L	26	6	2	.750	0	11	10	6	77	68	22	28	1	1.99
Ed Poole	R	26	5	4	.556	0	12	10	8	80	78	30	26	1	3.60
George Merritt	R	21	3	0	1.000	0	3	3	3	24	28	5	5	0	4.88
1 Snake Wiltse	L	29	1	4	.200	0	7	5	3	44	57	13	10	0	4.30
1 Rube Waddell	L	24	0	2	.000	0	2	2	0	8	10	9	4	0	9.00
		26	83	57	.593	2	140	140	125	1247	1221	259	480	**15**	2.87
Al Orth	R	28	20	12	.625	1	35	33	30	282	250	32	92	**6**	2.27
Red Donahue	R	28	21	13	.618	1	35	34	34	304	307	60	89	1	2.61
Bill Duggleby	R	28	19	12	.613	0	34	28	25	276	294	40	94	5	2.87
Doc White	L	22	14	13	.518	0	31	27	22	237	241	56	132	0	3.19
Jack Townsend	R	22	9	6	.600	0	19	16	14	144	118	64	72	2	3.44
1 Jack Dunn	R	28	0	1	.000	0	2	2	0	5	11	7	1	0	19.80
		27	79	57	.581	**5**	137	137	111	1214	1244	**435**	583	7	3.14
Wild Bill Donovan	R	24	**25**	15	.625	**3**	**45**	38	36	351	324	**152**	226	2	2.77
Frank Kitson	R	29	19	11	.633	2	38	32	26	281	312	67	127	5	2.98
Jay Hughes	R	27	17	12	.586	0	31	29	24	251	265	102	96	0	3.26
2 Doc Newton	L	23	6	5	.545	0	13	12	9	105	110	30	45	0	2.83
Doc McJames (DD)	R	27	5	6	.455	0	13	12	6	91	104	40	42	0	4.75
Brickyard Kennedy (SA)	R	33	3	5	.375	0	14	8	6	85	80	24	28	0	3.07
Gene McCann	R	25	2	3	.400	0	6	5	3	34	34	16	9	0	3.44
Kid Carsey	R	30	1	0	1.000	0	2	0	0	7	9	3	4	0	10.29
Clarence Wright	R	22	1	0	1.000	0	1	1	1	9	6	1	6	0	1.00

ST. LOUIS 4th 76-64 .543 14.5 — PATSY DONOVAN

	NAME	G by POS	B	AGE	G	AB	R	H	2B	3B	HR	RBI	BB	SO	SB	BA	SA
	TOTALS			30	142	5039	792	1430	187	94	39	657	314		190	.284	.381
	Dan McGann	1B103	B	29	103	426	72	123	14	10	6	56	16		16	.289	.411
	Dick Padden	2B115, SS8	R	30	123	489	71	125	17	7	2	62	31		26	.256	.331
	Bobby Wallace	SS134	R	27	135	556	69	179	34	16	2	91	20		17	.322	.451
	Otto Krueger	3B142	R	24	142	520	77	143	16	12	2	79	50		19	.275	.363
	Patsy Donovan	OF129	R	36	129	524	91	154	23	6	1	73	27		24	.294	.366
	Snags Heidrick	OF118		24	118	502	94	170	24	12	6	67	21		32	.339	.470
	Jesse Burkett	OF142	L	32	142	597	139	228	21	17	10	75	59		27	.382	.524
	Jack Ryan	C65, 2B9, 1B5, OF3	R	32	83	300	27	59	6	5	0	31	7		5	.197	.250
	Art Nichols	C47, OF40	R	29	93	308	50	75	11	3	1	33	10		14	.244	.308
	Pop Schriver	C24, 1B19	R	35	53	166	17	45	7	3	1	23	12		2	.271	.367
1	Pete Childs	2B19, OF2, SS1		29	29	79	12	21	1	0	0	8	14		0	.200	.278
	Bill Richardson	1B15		23	15	52	7	11	2	0	2	7	6		1	.212	.365
	Mike Heydon	C13, OF1		26	16	43	2	9	1	1	1	6	5		2	.209	.349

	NAME	T	AGE	W	L	PCT	SV	G	GS	CG	IP	H	BB	SO	ShO	ERA
			25	76	64	.543	5	142	142	118	1270	1333	332	445	5	3.68
	Jack Harper	R	23	23	13	.639	0	39	37	28	309	294	99	128	1	3.61
	Jack Powell	R	26	19	19	.500	3	45	37	33	338	351	50	133	2	3.54
	Willie Sudhoff	R	26	17	11	.607	2	38	26	25	276	281	92	78	1	3.52
	Ed Murphy	R	24	10	9	.526	0	23	21	16	165	201	32	42	0	4.20
2	Stan Yerkes			3	1	.750	0	4	4	4	34	35	6	15	0	3.18
	Mike O'Neill	L	23	2	2	.500	0	5	4	4	41	29	10	16	1	1.32
	Cowboy Jones	L	26	2	6	.250	0	10	9	7	76	97	22	25	0	4.50
	Farmer Burns	R		0	0	.000	0	1	0	0	1	2	1	0	0	9.00
2	Chauncey Fisher	R	29	0	0	.000	0	1	0	0	3	7	1	0	0	15.00
	Bob Wicker	R	23	0	0	.000	0	1	0	0	3	4	1	2	0	0.00
1	Bill Magee	R	33	0	0	.000	0	1	1	0	8	8	4	3	0	4.50
	Ted Breitenstein	L	32	0	3	.000	0	3	3	1	15	24	14	3	0	6.60

BOSTON 5th 69-69 .500 20.5 — FRANK SELEE

	NAME	G by POS	B	AGE	G	AB	R	H	2B	3B	HR	RBI	BB	SO	SB	BA	SA
	TOTALS			29	140	4746	530	1180	135	36	28	449	303		158	.249	.310
	Fred Tenney	1B113, C2	L	29	113	457	63	127	13	2	1	22	37		15	.278	.322
	Gene DeMontreville	2B120, 3B20	R	27	140	570	83	174	14	5	5	72	17		23	.305	.374
	Herman Long	SS138	L	35	138	518	55	118	15	8	3	68	25		19	.238	.305
	Bobby Lowe	3B111, 2B18	R	32	129	491	47	125	11	1	3	47	17		22	.255	.299
2	Jimmy Slagle	OF66	L	27	66	255	35	69	7	0	0	7	34		14	.271	.298
	Billy Hamilton	OF99	L	35	102	349	70	102	11	2	3	38	64		19	.292	.361
	Dick Cooley	OF53, 1B10	L	28	63	240	27	62	13	3	0	27	14		5	.258	.338
	Mal Kittredge	C113	R	31	114	381	24	96	14	0	2	40	32		2	.252	.304
	Pat Moran	C28, 1B13, 3B4, SS3, OF3, 2B1	R	25	52	180	12	38	5	1	2	18	3		3	.211	.283
	Fred Crolius	OF49		24	49	200	22	48	4	1	1	13	9		6	.240	.285
	Kid Nichols	P38, OF7, 1B5	B	31	55	163	16	46	8	7	4	28	8		0	.282	.491
1	Frank Murphy	OF45		21	45	176	13	46	5	3	1	18	4		6	.261	.341
	Daff Gammons	OF23, 2B2, 3B1	R	25	28	93	10	18	0	1	0	10	3		5	.194	.215
2	Elmer Smith	OF15	L	33	16	57	5	10	2	1	0	3	6		2	.175	.246
	Pat Carney	OF13	L	24	13	55	6	16	2	1	0	6	3		0	.291	.364
	Joe Rickert	OF13	R	24	13	60	6	10	1	2	0	1	3		1	.167	.250
1	Shad Barry	OF11	R	24	11	40	3	7	2	0	0	6	2		1	.175	.225
	Fred Brown	OF5	R	22	7	14	1	2	0	0	0	2	0		0	.143	.143
	George Grosart	OF7		22	7	26	4	3	0	0	0	1	0		0	.115	.115
	Billy Lush	OF7	B	27	7	27	2	5	1	1	0	3	3		0	.185	.296
	John Hinton	3B4			4	13	0	1	0	0	0	0	2		0	.077	.077

	NAME	T	AGE	W	L	PCT	SV	G	GS	CG	IP	H	BB	SO	ShO	ERA
			28	69	69	.500	2	140	140	128	1263	1196	349	558	11	2.90
	Kid Nichols	R	31	20	15	.571	0	38	34	33	321	306	90	143	4	3.22
	Vic Willis	R	25	18	17	.514	2	38	35	33	305	262	78	133	6	2.36
	Bill Dinneen	R	25	16	19	.457	0	37	34	31	309	295	77	141	0	2.94
	Togie Pittinger	R	30	13	16	.448	0	34	33	27	281	288	76	129	1	3.01
	Bob Lawson	R	24	2	2	.500	0	6	4	4	46	45	28	12	0	3.33

CHICAGO 6th 53-86 .381 37 — TOM LOFTUS

	NAME	G by POS	B	AGE	G	AB	R	H	2B	3B	HR	RBI	BB	SO	SB	BA	SA
	TOTALS			27	140	4844	578	1250	153	61	18	481	314		204	.258	.326
	Jack Doyle	1B75	R	31	73	278	19	67	10	2	0	39	7		11	.241	.291
	Cupid Childs	2B63	L	33	63	237	23	61	9	0	0	21	30		3	.257	.295
	Barry McCormick	SS112, 3B3		26	115	427	45	100	15	6	1	32	31		12	.234	.304
	Fred Raymer	3B82, SS29, 1B5, 2B3	R	25	120	463	41	108	14	2	0	43	11		18	.233	.272
	Frank Chance (BW)	OF50, C13, 1B6	R	23	66	228	37	66	11	4	0	36	29		30	.289	.373
	Danny Green	OF133	L	24	133	537	82	168	16	12	6	61	40		31	.313	.421
	Topsy Hartsel	OF140	L	27	140	558	111	187	25	16	7	54	74		41	.335	.475
	Johnny Kling	C69, 1B1, OF1	R	26	74	253	25	67	5	3	0	21	9		7	.265	.308
	C. Dexter	1B54, 3B25, OF21, 2B13, C3		25	116	460	46	123	9	5	1	66	16		22	.267	.315
2	Mike Kahoe	C63, 1B6	R	27	67	237	21	53	12	2	1	21	8		5	.224	.304
2	Pete Childs	2B60		29	60	210	23	48	5	1	0	14	26		4	.229	.262
	Jocko Menefee	OF24, P21, 1B2, 2B1	R	33	48	152	19	39	5	3	0	13	8		4	.257	.329
1	Cozy Dolan	OF41	L	28	43	171	29	45	1	2	0	16	7		3	.263	.292
	Jim Delahanty	3B17, 2B1	R	22	17	63	4	12	2	0	0	4	3		5	.190	.222
	Bill Gannon	OF15			15	61	2	9	0	0	0	0	1		5	.148	.148
	Mike Hickey	3B10	R	29	10	37	4	6	0	0	0	3	2		1	.162	.162
	Larry Hoffman	3B5, 2B1		18	6	22	2	7	1	0	0	6	0		1	.318	.364
	Henry Croft	OF3			3	12	1	4	0	0	0	4	0		0	.333	.333
	Germany Schaefer	2B1, 3B1	R	24	2	5	0	3	1	0	0	0	2		0	.600	.800

	NAME	T	AGE	W	L	PCT	SV	G	GS	CG	IP	H	BB	SO	ShO	ERA
			26	53	86	.381	0	140	140	131	1242	1348	324	586	2	3.33
2	Rube Waddell	L	24	14	14	.500	0	29	28	26	244	239	66	168	0	2.80
	Jack Taylor	R	27	13	19	.406	0	33	31	30	276	341	44	68	0	3.36
	Long Tom Hughes	R	22	10	23	.303	0	37	35	32	308	309	115	225	1	3.24
	Jocko Menefee	R	33	8	12	.400	0	21	20	19	182	201	34	55	0	3.81
	Mal Eason	R	22	8	17	.320	0	27	25	23	221	246	60	68	1	3.58
	Charlie Ferguson		26	0	0	.000	0	1	0	0	2	1	2	0	0	0.00
	Bert Cunningham	R	35	0	1	.000	0	1	1	1	9	11	3	2	0	5.00

NEW YORK 7th 52-85 .380 37 — GEORGE DAVIS

	NAME	G by POS	B	AGE	G	AB	R	H	2B	3B	HR	RBI	BB	SO	SB	BA	SA
	TOTALS			29	141	4839	544	1225	167	46	19	458	303		133	.253	.318
	John Ganzel	1B138	R	26	138	526	42	113	13	3	2	66	20		6	.215	.262
	Ray Nelson	2B39	R	25	39	130	12	26	2	0	0	7	10		3	.200	.215
	George Davis	SS113, 3B17	B	30	130	495	69	153	21	6	7	65	40		26	.309	.418
	Sammy Strang	3B91, 2B37, OF5, SS4	B	24	135	493	55	139	14	6	1	34	59		40	.282	.341
2	Algie McBride	OF65	L	32	68	264	27	74	11	0	2	29	12		3	.280	.345
	George Van Haltren	OF135, P1	L	35	133	544	83	186	22	7	1	47	51		25	.342	.414
	Kip Selbach	OF125	R	29	125	502	89	145	29	6	1	56	45		8	.289	.376
	John Warner	C84	L	28	87	291	19	70	6	1	0	20	3		3	.241	.268
	C. Hickman	OF50, SS23, 3B15, P9, 2B7, 1B2	R	25	112	401	43	115	20	6	4	62	15		6	.287	.397
	Frank Bowerman	C46, 2B3, SS3, 3B3, 1B1	R	32	56	180	20	39	5	3	0	14	7		3	.217	.278
	Danny Murphy	2B28	R	24	28	102	6	19	3	0	0	6	4		1	.186	.216
	Broadway Aleck Smith	C25		30	26	78	5	11	0	0	0	6	0		2	.141	.141
	Jimmy Jones	OF20, P1	R	24	21	91	10	19	4	3	0	5	4		2	.209	.319
	Curt Bernard	OF15, 2B4, SS2, 3B1	L	23	23	76	11	17	0	2	0	6	7		2	.224	.276
	Charlie Buelow (KJ)	3B17, 2B2	R	24	22	72	3	8	4	0	0	4	2		0	.111	.167
	Jim Miller	2B18			18	58	3	8	0	0	0	3	6		1	.138	.138
2	Frank Murphy	OF12	R	21	12	48	4	6	0	0	0	2	3		1	.125	.125
	Heinie Smith	2B7, P2	R	29	9	29	5	6	2	1	1	4	1		1	.207	.448
	Joe Wall	C2, OF1	L	27	4	8	0	4	0	0	0	1	0		0	.500	.500

	NAME	T	AGE	W	L	PCT	SV	G	GS	CG	IP	H	BB	SO	ShO	ERA
			25	52	85	.380	1	141	141	118	1232	1389	377	542	11	3.87
	Christy Mathewson	R	22	20	17	.541	0	40	38	36	336	288	97	221	5	2.41
	Dummy Taylor	R	26	18	27	.400	0	45	43	37	353	377	112	136	4	3.19
	Bill Phyle (ST)	R	26	7	10	.412	1	24	19	16	169	208	54	62	0	4.26
	Charlie Hickman	R	25	3	5	.375	0	9	9	6	65	76	26	11	0	4.57
1	Ed Doheny	L	26	2	5	.286	0	10	6	6	74	88	17	36	0	4.50
	Roger Denzer	R	29	2	5	.286	0	11	9	3	62	69	5	22	1	3.34
	Harry Felix	R	24	0	0	.000	0	1	0	0	2	3	0	0	0	0.00
	Ike Van Zandt		24	0	0	.000	0	2	0	0	13	16	8	2	0	6.92
1	Chauncey Fisher	R	29	0	1	.000	0	1	1	0	4	11	2	1	0	15.75
	Larry Hesterfer	L	23	0	1	.000	0	1	1	1	6	15	3	2	0	7.50
	Jimmy Jones	R	24	0	1	.000	0	1	1	1	5	6	2	3	0	10.80
	Heinie Smith	R	29	0	1	.000	0	2	1	1	13	24	5	5	0	8.31
	George Van Haltren	L	35	0	1	.000	0	1	0	0	6	12	6	2	0	3.00
	Dummy Deegan			0	2	.000	0	2	1	1	17	27	6	8	0	6.35
2	Dummy Leitner	R	30	0	2	.000	0	2	2	2	18	27	4	3	0	4.50
	Albany Livingstone			0	2	.000	0	2	0	0	12	26	7	6	0	9.00
	Al Maul	R	35	0	2	.000	0	3	3	2	19	39	8	5	0	11.37
	Willie Mills	R	23	0	2	.000	0	2	2	2	16	21	4	3	0	8.44
2	Bill Magee	R	33	0	4	.000	0	6	5	4	42	56	11	14	0	6.00

CINCINNATI 8th 52-87 .374 38 — BID McPHEE

	NAME	G by POS	B	AGE	G	AB	R	H	2B	3B	HR	RBI	BB	SO	SB	BA	SA
	TOTALS			27	142	4914	561	1232	173	70	38	476	323		137	.251	.338
	Jake Beckley	1B140	L	33	140	590	70	177	39	13	3	79	28		6	.300	.425
	Harry Steinfeldt	3B55, 2B50	R	23	105	382	40	95	18	7	6	47	28		10	.249	.380
	Maggie Magoon	SS112, 2B15	R	26	127	460	47	116	16	7	1	53	52		15	.252	.324
1	Charlie Irwin	3B67	R	32	67	260	25	62	12	2	0	25	14		13	.238	.300
	Sam Crawford	OF126	L	21	131	523	89	175	22	16	16	104	37		12	.335	.530
	John Dobbs	OF100, 3B8	L	25	109	435	71	119	17	4	2	27	36		19	.274	.345
	Dick Harley	OF133	L	28	133	535	69	146	13	2	4	27	31		37	.273	.327
	Bill Bergen	C87	R	28	87	308	15	55	6	4	1	17	8		2	.179	.234
	Heinie Peitz	C49, 2B21, 3B6, 1B2	R	20	82	269	24	82	13	5	1	24	23		3	.305	.401
	Bill Fox	2B44	B	29	44	163	9	29	2	1	0	7	4		9	.178	.202
	Harry Bay	OF40	L	23	41	157	25	33	1	2	1	3	13		4	.210	.261
	Tommy Corcoran (IL)	SS30	R	32	31	114	13	21	4	2	0	15	11		7	.184	.254
1	Algie McBride	OF28	L	32	30	123	19	29	7	0	2	18	7		0	.236	.341
	Pete O'Brien	2B15	L	25	16	54	1	11	1	0	1	3	2		0	.204	.278
	Pat Hurley	C7			9	21	1	1	0	0	0	0	1		1	.048	.048
	Emil Haberer	3B3, 1B2	R	23	6	18	2	3	0	1	0	1	3		0	.167	.278
	Jack Heileman	3B4, 2B1	R	28	5	15	1	2	1	0	0	1	0		0	.133	.200
1	Mike Kahoe	C4	R	27	4	13	0	4	0	0	0	0	1		0	.308	.308

	NAME	T	AGE	W	L	PCT	SV	G	GS	CG	IP	H	BB	SO	ShO	ERA
			26	52	87	.374	0	142	142	126	1266	1469	365	542	4	4.17
	Noodles Hahn	L	22	22	19	.537	0	42	42	41	375	370	69	239	2	2.71
	Bill Phillips	R	32	14	18	.438	0	37	36	29	281	364	67	109	1	4.64
1	Doc Newton	L	23	4	13	.235	0	20	18	17	168	190	59	65	0	4.12
	Archie Stimmel	R	28	4	14	.222	0	20	18	14	153	170	44	55	1	4.12
	Barney McFadden	R	27	3	4	.429	0	8	5	4	46	54	40	11	0	6.07
	Len Swormstedt	R		2	1	.667	0	3	3	3	26	19	5	13	0	1.73
	Charlie Case	R	21	1	2	.333	0	3	3	3	27	34	6	5	0	4.67
	Whitey Guese	R	28	1	4	.200	0	6	5	4	44	62	14	11	0	6.14
	Jack Sutthoff	R	28	1	6	.143	0	10	4	4	70	82	39	12	0	5.53
	Crese Heismann	L	21	0	1	.000	0	3	2	1	14	18	6	6	0	5.79
	Doc Parker	R	27	0	1	.000	0	1	1	1	8	26	2	0	0	15.75
	Amos Rusie	R	30	0	1	.000	0	3	2	2	22	43	3	6	0	8.59
2	Gus Weyhing	R	34	0	1	.000	0	1	1	1	9	11	2	3	0	3.00
	Dick Scott	R	19	0	2	.000	0	3	2	2	21	26	9	7	0	5.14

⊜ ⊜ 1902 A. L.—Checkmate ⊜ ⊜

Midway through its second season, the American League found its Baltimore outpost in the hands of the enemy, making the completion of the loop schedule a muddy issue. Baltimore manager John McGraw was constantly running afoul of League President Ban Johnson. Several times during the 1901 and 1902 seasons he was suspended by Johnson for harassing the league umpires and when Little Napoleon continued his arbiter-baiting, Johnson dry-docked him indefinitely in July. McGraw decided not to take such treatment lying down and started negotiations which resulted in the Orioles being bought by John T. Brush, Chairman of the National League Executive Committee. With the enemy within its walls, the American League suffered a severe body blow; the new owner released McGraw, Joe McGinnity, Roger Bresnahan, Dan McGann, Cy Seymour, Joe Kelley, and Jack Cronin to sign with National League clubs, leaving Baltimore with a skeleton crew. When, on July 17, the Orioles could not field a team to meet St. Louis, Johnson used a league regulation to revoke the Baltimore franchise. He planned to operate the team for the rest of the season on league funds, arranged for each team to contribute players to stock the sabotaged team, and appointed local hero, Wilbert Robinson, to manage the reconstructed squad. The Orioles finished last, but that they finished the schedule at all represented a triumph of American League resiliency and solidarity.

Johnson, however, had more problems in 1902 than McGraw. The Pennsylvania Supreme Court presented the new loop with a courtroom setback by ordering Nap Lajoie, Bill Bernhard, and Chick Fraser to leave the Athletics and rejoin the Phillies, the club they had left the year before. Fraser returned to the National League club, but Johnson found his loophole in the Quaker state law and kept Lajoie and Bernhard by transferring their contracts to Cleveland; whenever the Ohio team visited Philadelphia, Lajoie and Bernhard spent a paid vacation in Atlantic City. Other states involved in the squabble ruled against the reserve clause, and Johnson's jumpers were allowed to remain with their new clubs.

St. Louis replaced Milwaukee in the 1902 circuit, and the new club raided the St. Louis Cardinals, of the old league, for several top players, luring Jesse Burkett, Bobby Wallace, Dick Padden, John Heidrick, Jack Harper, and Jack Powell into its fold. St. Louis represented the fourth city in which the two leagues both fielded teams and, in every instance, the new team outdrew the National League team. High salaries continued to induce stars to join American League teams. Besides the St. Louis jumpers, Ed Delahanty, Elmer Flick, and Red Donahue were the top names among those who left the National League for greener American League pastures.

Connie Mack won his first pennant by directing the Athletics to a good second half, which gave them the championship over the new St. Louis Browns. Even with the loss of Lajoie, Mack could field a hard-hitting lineup led by third baseman Lave Cross, and rightfielder Socks Seybold; six .300 hitters dotted the Athletic scorecard, making Lajoie's loss less noticeable. The pitching staff survived the loss of Bernard when Mack purchased lefty Rube Waddell in May from Los Angeles of the California League. Daffy to a fault and colorful to an extreme, the brash Waddell used a blazing fastball to post a 24-7 season mark with a league-leading 210 strikeouts. Steady Eddie Plank developed into a star in his second season by chalking up 20 victories. St. Louis, Boston, and Chicago pursued hotly but could not catch the stretch-running A's. Washington's Ed Delahanty led all batters with a .376 average, while Cy Young of Boston again paced the pitchers with 32 wins.

At the season's end, the Baltimore situation was settled by transferring the franchise to New York, where players for the new squad were pirated from the senior loop. This move, along with the other calamities during the season, convinced the National League that peace was cheaper than war and in January, 1903, the National League decided to sit down and talk to the American League. The senior circuit first proposed a merger, which Johnson wisely refused. After many words and abandoned strategies, the final treaty recognized both leagues as majors, agreed to respect the contracts and reserve clauses of all teams, and allowed the American League to keep practically all the players it had corralled from the National League. When the negotiations were over, the senior circuit was not certain what it had won, but only that it had neutralized the enemy.

And that was a victory.

1902 AMERICAN LEAGUE

NAME	G by POS	B	AGE	G	AB	R	H	2B	3B	HR	RBI	BB	SO	SB	BA	SA
PHILADELPHIA 1st 83-53 .610	**CONNIE MACK**															
TOTALS			29	137	4762	**775**	1369	235	67	38	**673**	343		201	.287	.389
Harry Davis	1B128, OF5	R	28	132	555	87	171	**43**	7	6	92	30		31	.308	.443
Danny Murphy	2B76	R	25	76	291	48	91	12	8	1	48	13		12	.313	.419
Monte Cross	SS137	R	32	137	497	72	115	22	2	3	59	32		17	.231	.302
Lave Cross	3B137	R	36	137	558	90	189	37	8	0	108	27		26	.339	.440
Socks Seybold	OF136	R	31	137	523	91	166	27	11	**16**	97	43		5	.317	.503
Dave Fultz	OF114, 2B16	R	27	129	506	**109**	153	20	5	1	49	62		44	.302	.368
Topsy Hartsel	OF137	L	28	137	545	**109**	154	20	12	5	58	**87**		**47**	.283	.391
2 Ossee Schreckengost	C71, 1B7, OF1	R	27	79	284	45	92	17	2	2	43	9		3	.324	.419
Mike Powers	C68, 1B3	R	31	71	246	35	65	7	1	2	39	14		3	.264	.325
Louis Castro	2B36, OF3, SS1	R	25	42	143	18	35	8	1	1	15	4		2	.245	.336
Eddie Plank	P36	L	26	36	120	15	35	6	1	0	16	3		4	.292	.358
Rube Waddell (JT)	P33	L	25	34	112	8	32	6	2	1	18	4		1	.286	.402
2 Frank Bonner	2B11		32	11	44	2	8	0	0	0	3	0		0	.182	.182
1 Elmer Flick	OF11	L	26	11	37	15	11	2	1	0	3	6		4	.297	.405
Farmer Steelman	C5, OF5		27	10	32	1	6	1	0	0	6	2		2	.188	.219
1 Nap Lajoie (HO)	2B1	R	26	1	4	0	1	0	0	0	1	0		1	.250	.250
ST. LOUIS 2nd 78-58 .574 5	**JIMMY McALEER**															
TOTALS			28	140	4736	619	1254	208	61	29	520	373		137	.265	.353
John Anderson	1B126, OF3	B	28	126	524	60	149	29	6	4	85	21		15	.284	.385
Dick Padden	2B117	R	31	117	413	54	109	26	3	1	40	30		11	.264	.349
Bobby Wallace	SS131, OF1, P1	R	28	133	495	71	142	33	9	1	63	45		19	.287	.396
Barry McCormick	3B132, SS7, OF1		27	139	504	55	124	14	4	3	51	37		10	.246	.308
2 Charlie Hemphill	OF101, 2B2	L	26	103	416	67	132	14	11	6	58	44		23	.317	.447
Snags Heidrick	OF109, SS1, 3B1, P1		25	110	447	75	129	19	10	3	56	34		17	.289	.396
Jesse Burkett	OF137, SS1, 3B1, P1	L	33	137	549	99	168	29	9	5	52	71		22	.306	.418
Joe Sugden	C61, 1B4, P1	B	31	69	208	24	48	7	2	0	15	20		2	.230	.284
Friel	OF33, 2B25, 1B10, 3B8, SS3, C1, P1	L	26	80	267	26	64	9	2	2	20	14		4	.240	.311
2 Mike Kahoe	C53	R	28	55	197	21	48	9	2	2	28	6		4	.244	.340
Jiggs Donahue	C23, 1B5	L	22	29	84	10	21	1	1	1	7	12		1	.250	.321
1 Billy Maloney	OF23, C7	L	24	30	112	8	23	3	0	0	11	6		0	.205	.232
1 Davy Jones	OF15	L	22	15	49	4	11	1	1	0	3	6		5	.224	.286
Jimmy McAleer	OF2	R	37	2	3	0	2	0	0	0	0	0		0	.667	.667
BOSTON 3rd 77-60 .562 6.5	**JIMMY COLLINS**															
TOTALS			28	138	**4875**	664	1356	195	95	42	572	275		132	.278	.383
Candy LaChance	1B138	B	32	138	541	60	151	13	4	6	56	18		8	.279	.351
Hobe Ferris	2B134	R	24	134	499	57	122	16	14	8	63	21		11	.244	.381
Freddy Parent	SS138	R	26	138	**567**	91	156	31	8	3	62	24		16	.275	.374
Jimmy Collins	3B107	R	32	105	425	71	138	21	10	6	61	24		11	.325	.459
Buck Freeman	OF138	L	30	138	569	76	177	37	20	11	**121**	32		15	.311	.504
Chick Stahl	OF125	L	29	127	507	92	161	25	10	2	58	37		18	.318	.418
Patsy Dougherty	OF102, 3B1	L	25	108	438	77	150	12	6	0	34	42		20	.342	.397
Lou Criger	C80, OF1	R	30	83	266	32	68	16	6	0	28	27		7	.256	.361
Harry Gleason	3B35, OF23, 2B4	R	27	71	240	30	54	5	5	2	25	10		6	.225	.313
John Warner	C64	L	29	65	222	19	52	5	7	0	12	13		0	.234	.320
1 Charley Hickman	OF27	R	26	28	108	13	**32***	5	2	3	16	3		1	.296	.463
Gary Wilson	2B2	R	25	2	8	0	1	0	0	0	1	0		0	.125	.125

NAME	T	AGE	W	L	PCT	SV	G	GS	CG	IP	H	BB	SO	ShO	ERA
		26	**83**	53	**.610**	3	137	137	114	1216	1292	368	**455**	5	3.29
Rube Waddell (JT)	L	25	24	7	**.774**	1	33	27	26	276	224	64	**210**	3	2.05
Eddie Plank	L	26	20	15	.571	0	36	32	31	300	319	61	107	1	3.30
2 Bert Husting	R	24	14	5	.737	0	32	27	17	204	240	91	44	1	3.79
1 Snake Wiltse	L	30	8	8	.500	1	19	17	13	138	182	41	28	0	5.15
Highball Wilson	R		7	4	.636	0	13	10	8	96	103	19	18	0	2.44
2 Fred Mitchell	R	24	5	8	.385	1	18	14	9	108	120	59	22	0	3.58
Andy Coakley	R	19	2	1	.667	0	3	3	3	27	25	9	9	0	2.67
1 Bill Bernhard (HO)	R	31	1	0	1.000	0	1	1	1	9	7	3	1	0	1.00
1 Bill Duggleby	R	29	1	1	.500	0	2	2	2	17	19	4	4	0	3.18
Ed Kenna	R	24	1	1	.500	0	2	1	1	17	19	11	5	0	5.29
Jim Porter			0	1	.000	0	1	1	1	8	12	5	2	0	3.38
Clarence Quinn			0	1	.000	0	1	1	1	8	12	1	3	0	4.50
Tom Walker	R	20	0	1	.000	0	1	1	1	8	10	0	2	0	5.63
		27	78	58	.574	**5**	140	140	120	**1244**	1273	343	348	7	3.34
Red Donahue	R	29	22	11	.667	0	35	34	33	316	322	65	63	2	2.76
Jack Powell	R	27	22	17	.564	**3**	42	39	36	328	320	93	137	3	3.21
Jack Harper	R	24	17	10	.630	0	29	26	20	222	224	81	74	2	4.14
Willie Sudhoff	R	27	11	13	.458	2	30	25	20	220	213	67	42	0	2.86
2 Charlie Shields	L	22	3	0	1.000	0	4	4	3	30	37	7	6	0	3.30
Bill Reidy	R	28	3	5	.375	0	12	9	7	95	111	13	16	0	4.45
Harry Kane	L	18	0	1	.000	0	4	1	1	23	34	16	7	0	5.48
Jesse Burkett	L	33	0	1	.000	0	1	0	0	1	4	1	2	0	9.00
Bill Friel	R	26	0	0	.000	0	1	0	0	4	4	0	0	0	4.50
John Heidrick		25	0	0	.000	0	1	0	0	1	0	0	0	0	0.00
Joe Sugden	R	31	0	0	.000	0	1	0	0	1	1	0	0	0	0.00
Bobby Wallace	R	28	0	0	.000	0	1	1	0	2	3	0	1	0	0.00
		28	77	60	.562	1	138	138	123	1238	1217	326	431	6	**3.02**
Cy Young	R	35	**32**	11	.744	0	**46**	**43**	**41**	**385**	350	53	160	3	2.15
Bill Dinneen	R	26	21	**21**	.500	0	42	42	39	371	348	99	136	2	2.94
George Winter (IL)	R	24	11	9	.550	0	20	20	18	168	149	53	51	0	3.00
2 Tully Sparks	R	25	7	8	.467	0	17	15	15	143	151	40	37	1	3.46
1 Garry Prentiss	R	26	2	2	.500	0	7	4	3	41	55	10	9	0	5.27
2 Long Tom Hughes (SA)	R	23	2	4	.333	0	9	8	4	49	51	24	15	0	3.31
Doc Adkins	R	29	1	1	.500	0	4	2	1	20	30	7	3	0	4.05
Nick Altrock	L	25	1	2	.333	1	3	2	1	18	19	7	5	0	2.00
1 Bert Husting	R	24	0	1	.000	0	1	1	1	8	15	8	4	0	9.00
1 Fred Mitchell	R	24	0	1	.000	0	1	0	0	4	8	5	2	0	11.25
Dave Williams	L		0	0	.000	0	3	0	0	19	22	11	7	0	5.21
Pep Deininger	L	24	0	0	.000	0	2	1	0	12	19	9	2	0	9.75

***Hickman, also with Cleveland, league leader in H with 194**

CHICAGO 4th 74-60 .552 8 — CLARK GRIFFITH

NAME	G by POS	B	AGE	G	AB	R	H	2B	3B	HR	RBI	BB	SO	SB	BA	SA
TOTALS			28	138	4654	675	1248	170	50	14	537	411		265	.268	.335
Frank Isbell	1B133, SS4, C1, P1	L	26	137	515	62	130	14	4	4	59	14		38	.252	.318
Tom Daly	2B137	B	36	137	489	57	110	22	3	1	54	55		19	.225	.288
George Davis	SS129, 1B3	B	31	132	480	77	143	27	7	3	93	65		33	.298	.402
1 Sammy Strang	3B137	B	25	137	536	108	158	18	5	3	46	76		38	.295	.364
Danny Green	OF129	L	25	129	481	77	150	16	11	0	62	53		35	.312	.391
Fielder Jones	OF135	L	30	135	532	98	171	16	5	0	54	57		33	.321	.370
S. Mertes	OF120, SS5, C2, 1B1, 2B1, 3B1, P1	R	29	129	497	60	140	23	7	1	79	37		46	.282	.362
Billy Sullivan	C70, 1B2, OF2	R	27	76	263	36	64	12	3	1	26	6		11	.243	.323
Ed McFarland	C69, 1B1	R	27	75	246	29	56	9	2	1	25	19		8	.228	.293
Nixey Callahan	P35, OF23, SS1	R	28	70	218	27	51	7	2	0	13	6		4	.234	.284
1 Herm McFarland	OF7	L	32	7	27	5	5	0	0	0	4	2		1	.185	.185
Ed Hughes	C1	R	22	1	4	0	1	0	0	0	0	0		0	.250	.250

NAME	T	AGE	W	L	PCT	SV	G	GS	CG	IP	H	BB	SO	ShO	ERA
		28	74	60	.552	1	138	138	116	1221	1269	331	346	11	3.41
Roy Patterson	R	25	20	12	.625	0	34	30	26	268	262	67	61	2	3.06
Nixey Callahan	R	28	16	14	.533	0	35	31	29	282	287	89	75	2	3.61
Clark Griffith	R	32	15	9	.625	0	28	24	20	213	247	47	51	3	4.18
Wiley Piatt	L	27	12	13	.480	0	32	30	22	246	263	66	96	2	3.51
1 Ned Garvin	R	28	9	10	.474	1	23	19	16	175	169	43	55	2	2.21
Sam Mertes	R	29	1	0	1.000	0	1	0	0	8	6	0	0	0	1.13
John Durham	R	20	1	1	.500	0	3	3	3	20	21	16	3	0	5.85
Frank Isbell	R	26	0	1	.000	0	1	1	0	1	3	1	1	0	9.00
1 Jack Katoll	R	30	0	0	.000	0	1	0	0	1	1	0	2	0	0.00
2 Dummy Leitner	R	31	0	0	.000	0	1	0	0	4	9	2	0	0	13.50
1 Sam McMackin			0	0	.000	0	1	0	0	3	1	0	2	0	0.00

CLEVELAND 5th 69-67 .507 14 — BILL ARMOUR

NAME	G by POS	B	AGE	G	AB	R	H	2B	3B	HR	RBI	BB	SO	SB	BA	SA
TOTALS			28	137	4840	686	**1401**	248	68	33	582	308		140	**.289**	.389
2 Charley Hickman	1B98, 2B3, P1	R	26	102	427	60	162*	31	10	8	94	12		9	.379	.555
2 Nap Lajoie	2B86	R	26	86	348	81	128	34	5	7	64	19		18	.368	.555
John Gochnaur	SS127	R	26	127	459	45	85	16	4	0	37	38		7	.185	.237
Bill Bradley	3B137	R	24	136	549	106	187	39	12	11	77	27		12	.341	.515
2 Elmer Flick	OF110	L	26	110	427	68	126	20	11	2	61	47		20	.295	.407
2 Harry Bay	OF107	L	24	108	455	71	132	10	5	0	23	36		22	.290	.334
Jack McCarthy	OF95	L	33	95	359	45	102	31	5	0	41	24		12	.284	.398
Harry Bemis	C87, OF2, 2B1	L	28	93	317	42	99	12	7	1	29	19		3	.312	.404
Bob Wood	C52, 1B16, OF2, 2B1, 3B1	R	36	81	258	23	76	18	2	0	40	27		1	.295	.380
Ollie Pickering	OF64, 1B2	L	32	69	293	46	75	5	2	3	26	19		22	.256	.317
1 Frank Bonner	2B34		32	34	132	14	37	6	0	0	14	5		1	.280	.326
1 Jack Thoney	2B14, SS11, OF2	R	22	28	105	14	30	7	1	0	11	9		4	.286	.371
1 Charlie Hemphill	OF19	L	26	25	94	14	25	2	0	0	11	5		4	.266	.287
1 Ossee Schreckengost	1B17	R	27	18	74	5	25	0	0	0	9	0		2	.338	.338
ZaZa Harvey	OF12		23	12	46	5	16	2	0	0	5	3		1	.348	.391
3 Hal O'Hagan	1B3		28	3	13	2	5	2	0	0	1	0		2	.385	.538
Peaches Graham	2B1	R	25	2	6	0	2	0	0	0	1	1		0	.333	.333
George Starnagle	C1	R	28	1	3	0	0	0	0	0	0	0		0	.000	.000

NAME	T	AGE	W	L	PCT	SV	G	GS	CG	IP	H	BB	SO	ShO	ERA
		25	69	67	.507	4	137	137	116	1204	1199	**411**	361	**16**	3.28
2 Bill Bernhard	R	31	17	6	.739	1	27	24	22	217	169	34	57	3	2.20
Earl Moore	R	22	17	17	.500	1	36	34	29	293	304	**101**	84	4	2.95
Addie Joss	R	22	16	13	.552	1	32	29	28	269	225	75	106	**5**	2.78
Clarence Wright	R	23	7	10	.412	1	21	18	15	148	150	75	52	1	3.95
Gus Dorner	R	25	3	1	.750	0	4	4	4	36	33	13	5	1	1.26
Charlie Smith	R	22	2	1	.667	0	3	3	2	20	23	5	5	1	4.05
Dike Varney	L	21	2	1	.667	0	3	3	0	15	14	12	7	0	6.00
Otto Hess	L	23	2	3	.400	0	7	4	4	44	67	23	13	0	5.93
Ginger Clark	R	23	1	0	1.000	0	1	0	0	6	10	3	1	0	6.00
Jack Lundbom	R	25	1	1	.500	0	8	3	1	34	48	16	7	0	6.62
1 Dummy Taylor	R	27	1	3	.250	0	4	4	4	34	37	8	8	1	1.59
2 Charley Hickman	R	26	0	1	.000	0	1	1	1	8	11	5	1	0	7.88
1 Dummy Leitner	R	31	0	1	.000	0	1	1	0	8	11	1	0	0	4.50
Lou Polchow		21	0	1	.000	0	1	1	1	8	9	4	2	0	5.63
Ed Walker	L	27	0	1	.000	0	1	1	1	8	11	3	1	0	3.38
Oscar Streit	L	28	0	7	.000	0	8	7	4	52	72	25	10	0	5.19
Cal Vasbinder	R	21	0	0	.000	0	2	0	0	5	5	8	2	0	9.00

*Hickman, also with Boston, league leader in H with 194

WASHINGTON 6th 61-75 .449 22 — TOM LOFTUS

NAME	G by POS	B	AGE	G	AB	R	H	2B	3B	HR	RBI	BB	SO	SB	BA	SA
TOTALS			30	138	4734	707	1338	**262**	66	**47**	606	329		121	.283	**.396**
Scoops Carey	1B120	R	31	120	452	46	142	35	11	0	60	20		3	.314	.440
2 Jack Doyle	2B68, 1B7, OF4, C1	R	32	78	315	50	75	15	2	1	20	29		7	.238	.308
Bones Ely	SS105	R	39	105	381	39	100	11	2	1	62	21		3	.262	.310
Bill Coughlin	3B66, SS31, 2B26	R	23	121	470	84	140	27	4	6	71	26		32	.298	.411
Watty Lee	OF95, P13	L	22	109	391	61	100	21	5	4	45	33		8	.256	.366
Jimmy Ryan	OF120	R	39	120	482	92	153	32	6	6	44	43		13	.317	.446
Ed Delahanty	OF111, 1B13	R	34	123	473	103	178	41	15	10	93	62		14	**.376**	**.590**
Boileryard Clarke	C87	R	33	87	291	31	78	16	0	6	40	23		1	.268	.385
Bill Keister	OF65, 2B40, 3B14, SS2	R	27	119	483	82	145	33	9	9	90	14		27	.300	.462
13 Lew Drill	C53, OF8, 2B5, 3B1	R	25	71	221	33	58	10	4	1	29	26		5	.262	.357
1 Harry Wolverton	3B59		28	59	249	35	62	8	3	1	23	13		8	.249	.317
Jake Atz	2B3	R	23	3	10	1	1	0	0	0	0	0		0	.100	.100
Tim Donahue (DD)	C3	L	32	3	8	0	2	0	0	0	1	0		0	.250	.250
Joe Stanley	OF3	B	21	3	12	2	4	0	0	0	1	0		0	.333	.333

NAME	T	AGE	W	L	PCT	SV	G	GS	CG	IP	H	BB	SO	ShO	ERA
		27	61	75	.449	2	138	138	**130**	1208	1403	312	300	2	4.36
Al Orth	R	29	19	18	.514	0	38	37	36	324	**367**	40	76	1	3.97
Casey Patten	L	26	17	17	.500	1	36	34	33	300	331	89	92	1	4.05
Bill Carrick	R	28	12	17	.414	0	31	30	28	258	344	72	36	0	4.85
Jack Townsend	R	23	9	16	.360	0	27	26	22	220	233	89	71	0	4.46
Watty Lee	L	22	4	6	.400	1	13	10	10	98	118	20	24	0	5.05
2 Cy Vorhees		27	0	1	.000	0	1	1	1	8	10	2	1	0	4.50

DETROIT 7th 52-83 .385 30.5 — FRANK DWYER

NAME	G by POS	B	AGE	G	AB	R	H	2B	3B	HR	RBI	BB	SO	SB	BA	SA
TOTALS			29	137	4644	566	1167	141	55	22	488	359		130	.251	.320
1 Pop Dillon	1B66	L	28	66	243	21	50	6	3	0	22	16		2	.206	.255
Kid Gleason	2B118	B	35	118	441	42	109	11	4	1	38	25		17	.247	.297
Kid Elberfeld	SS130	R	27	130	487	70	129	16	7	1	64	55		20	.265	.333
Doc Casey	3B132	L	31	132	520	69	142	18	7	3	55	44		22	.273	.352
Ducky Holmes	OF92	L	33	92	362	50	93	15	4	2	33	28		16	.257	.337
Jimmy Barrett	OF136	L	27	136	509	93	154	19	6	4	44	74		24	.303	.387
Dick Harley	OF125	L	29	125	491	59	138	9	8	2	44	36		20	.281	.344
Deacon McGuire	C70	R	36	73	229	27	52	14	1	2	23	24		0	.227	.323
Fritz Buelow	C63, 1B2	R	26	66	224	23	50	5	2	2	29	9		3	.223	.290
13 McA'ster	1B26, OF12, C9, SS6, 3B6, 2B3	B	27	66	229	19	48	5	2	1	32	5		1	.210	.262
Joe Yeager	P19, OF13, 2B12, SS3, 3B1		26	50	161	17	39	6	5	1	23	5		0	.242	.360
2 Erve Beck	1B36, OF5	R	23	41	162	23	48	4	0	2	22	4		3	.296	.358
George Mullin	P35, OF4	R	21	40	120	20	39	4	3	0	11	8		1	.325	.408
Pete Lepine	OF19, 1B8	L	25	30	96	8	20	3	2	1	19	8		1	.208	.313
1 Harry Arndt	OF10, 1B1		23	10	34	4	5	0	1	0	7	6		0	.147	.206
John O'Connell	2B6, 1B2		30	8	22	1	4	0	0	0	0	3		0	.182	.182
E. Poste	OF3			3	12	2	1	0	0	0	2	0		0	.083	.083
Lou Schiappacasse	OF2	R	21	2	5	0	0	0	0	0	1	1		0	.000	.000

NAME	T	AGE	W	L	PCT	SV	G	GS	CG	IP	H	BB	SO	ShO	ERA
		25	52	83	.385	4	137	137	116	1191	1267	370	245	9	3.56
Win Mercer	R	28	15	18	.455	1	35	33	28	282	282	80	40	4	3.03
George Mullin	R	21	14	15	.483	0	35	30	25	260	282	95	78	0	3.67
Ed Siever	L	24	8	13	.381	1	25	23	17	188	166	32	36	4	**1.91**
1 Roscoe Miller	R	25	6	11	.353	1	20	18	15	149	158	57	39	1	3.68
Joe Yeager	R	26	6	12	.333	0	19	15	14	140	171	41	28	0	4.82
Wish Egan	R	21	1	2	.333	0	3	3	2	22	23	6	0	0	2.86
Rube Kisinger	R	25	1	4	.200	0	5	5	5	43	48	14	7	0	3.14
Arch McCarthy			1	7	.125	1	10	8	8	72	90	31	10	0	6.13
John Terry			0	1	.000	0	1	1	1	5	8	1	0	0	3.60
1 Jack Cronin	R	28	0	0	.000	0	4	0	0	17	26	8	5	0	9.53
Tom Fisher	R	21	0	0	.000	0	1	0	0	4	4	1	0	0	0.00
2 Sam McMackin			0	0	.000	0	1	1	1	8	9	4	2	0	3.38

BALTIMORE 8th 50-88 .362 34 — JOHN McGRAW 28-34 .452 WILBERT ROBINSON 22-54 .289

NAME	G by POS	B	AGE	G	AB	R	H	2B	3B	HR	RBI	BB	SO	SB	BA	SA
TOTALS			28	141	4760	715	1318	202	**107**	33	598	**417**		189	.277	.385
1 Dan McGann	1B68	B	30	68	251	42	79	10	7	0	42	19		19	.315	.410
Jimmy Williams	2B104, 3B19, 1B1	R	25	125	498	83	156	27	**21**	8	83	36		14	.313	.500
Billy Gilbert	SS129	R	26	129	445	74	109	12	3	2	38	45		38	.245	.299
1 Roger Bresnahan	3B30, C22, OF15	R	23	65	234	31	64	9	6	4	34	21		11	.274	.415
1 Cy Seymour	OF72	L	29	72	270	38	75	8	8	3	41	18		13	.278	.400
2 Herm McFarland	OF61	L	32	61	242	54	78	19	6	3	36	36		10	.322	.488
Kip Selbach	OF127	R	30	128	503	86	161	27	9	3	60	58		22	.320	.427
Wilbert Robinson	C87	R	39	92	336	39	98	14	7	1	57	12		11	.292	.384
Harry Howell	2B26, 3B15, SS11	R	25	96	347	42	93	16	11	2	42	18		7	.268	.395
2 Harry Arndt	OF62, 2B4, 3B2, SS1		23	68	248	41	63	7	4	2	28	35		9	.254	.339
1 Joe Kelley	OF48, 3B8, 1B5	R	30	61	222	50	69	16	7	1	34	34		12	.311	.459
B. Aleck Smith	C27, 1B7, OF4, 2B3, 3B1		31	41	145	10	34	3	0	0	21	8		5	.234	.255
Tom Jones	1B37, 2B1	R	25	37	159	22	45	8	4	0	14	2		1	.283	.384
I. I. Mathison	3B28, SS1	R		29	91	12	24	2	1	0	7	9		2	.264	.308
Andy Oyler	3B20, OF3, SS2, 2B1	R	22	27	77	9	17	1	0	1	6	8		3	.221	.273
1 John McGraw	3B19	L	29	20	63	14	18	3	2	1	3	17		5	.286	.444
2 George Yeager	C11		29	11	38	3	7	1	0	0	1	2		0	.184	.211
Bill Mellor (NJ)	1B10	R	28	10	36	4	13	3	0	0	5	3		1	.361	.444
1 Jimmy Sheckard	OF4	L	23	4	16	3	4	1	0	0	0	1		2	.250	.313
2 Sport McAllister	2B2, 1B1	B	27	3	11	0	1	0	0	0	1	1		0	.091	.091
2 Jack Thoney (BG)	3B3	R	22	3	11	1	0	0	0	0	0	1		1	.000	.000
2 Pop Dillon	1B2	L	28	2	7	1	2	0	1	0	0	2		0	.286	.571
2 Lew Drill	C1, 1B1	R	25	2	8	2	2	0	0	0	0	0		0	.250	.250
Bill Burns				1	1	0	1	0	0	0	0	0		0	1.000	1.000
2 Ernie Courtney	3B1	L	23	1	4	3	2	0	1	0	1	1		0	.500	1.000
Tim Jordan	OF1	L	23	1	4	0	0	0	0	0	0	0		0	.000	.000

NAME	T	AGE	W	L	PCT	SV	G	GS	CG	IP	H	BB	SO	ShO	ERA
		28	50	**88**	.362	0	141	141	119	1210	**1531**	354	258	3	4.31
1 Joe McGinnity	R	31	13	10	.565	0	25	23	19	199	219	46	39	0	3.35
Harry Howell	R	25	9	14	.391	0	26	23	19	199	243	48	33	1	4.12
1 Long Tom Hughes	R	23	7	6	.538	0	13	13	12	108	120	32	45	1	3.92
2 Snake Wiltse	L	30	7	10	.412	0	19	18	18	164	215	51	37	0	5.10
1 Charlie Shields	L	22	5	11	.313	0	23	15	10	142	201	32	28	1	4.25
2 Jack Cronin	R	20	3	5	.375	0	10	8	8	76	66	24	20	0	2.61
2 Jack Katoll	R	30	3	10	.231	0	15	13	13	123	175	32	25	0	4.02
Ike Butler	R	28	2	11	.154	0	16	14	12	116	168	45	13	0	5.35
Ernie Ross	L	22	1	1	.500	0	2	2	2	17	20	12	2	0	7.41
2 Dad Hale	R	23	0	1	.000	0	3	2	1	14	21	6	6	0	4.50
Bob Lawson	R	25	0	2	.000	0	3	2	1	13	21	3	5	0	4.85
Frank Foreman	R	39	0	2	.000	0	2	2	2	16	28	6	2	0	6.19
2 Garry Prentiss (DD)	R	26	0	2	.000	0	2	2	0	7	14	5	1	0	10.29
2 Crese Heismann	L	22	0	3	.000	0	3	3	2	16	20	12	2	0	8.44

1902 N.L.—The Worst Laid Plans . . .

Another year of war with the American League brought an element of battle fatigue to the National League in 1902. A three-man Executive Committee, chaired by John T. Brush, directed the war effort during the season, chalking up its greatest triumph when it purchased the Baltimore American League team and sabotaged it by releasing its better players to sign National League contracts. That victory was short-lived, as the disemboweled Baltimore team was replanted in New York at the season's close by the new league, thus rivaling the Giants in Gotham. To add insult to injury, the new New York club stocked its roster by raiding the National League pantry for players.

A hollow victory was won when the Pennsylvania Supreme Court ruled that Nap Lajoie, Bill Bernhard, and Chick Fraser had to leave the Philadelphia Athletics to return to the rival Phillies, to whom they were bound by the reserve clause. Fraser returned, but Lajoie and Bernhard evaded the court order by joining the Cleveland American team and keeping out of Pennsylvania all season. In addition to not retaining these two, the Phillies lost Elmer Flick, Ed Delahanty, Red Donahue, and Al Orth to further American League raids. Outside of Pennsylvania, state courts generally ruled against the reserve clause and, thus, in favor of the new loop.

The Pittsburgh Pirates managed to avoid any losses to the American League's raiding tactics for the second consecutive year, and the strong Buc squad trounced all the weakened competition in waltzing to a repeat championship by a margin of 27½ games over distant runner-up Brooklyn. The Pirate total of 103 wins topped any team's record in the 27-year history of the league and, after May 4, no team could show its heels to the flying Bucs. League batting champ, Ginger Beaumont, manager Fred Clarke, and Honus Wagner all swung hot bats through the year, and Jack Chesbro, Jesse Tannehill, and Deacon Phillippe gave the Bucs three 20-win aces, with Chesbro's 28 wins topping the league's hurlers. In addition, third sacker Tommy Leach led the circuit in home runs with six clouts.

Brooklyn's second-place finish was due in good measure to Willie Keeler's .342 batting and good pitching by Frank Kitson and Wild Bill Donovan. After losing its entire offense and top pitchers to the new league in two years, Philadelphia dropped into seventh place. The New York Giants got off to a dismal start, and even the infusion of Baltimore talent could not stop a basement finish; nevertheless, new manager John McGraw, Joe McGinnity, Roger Bresnahan, and Dan McGann would all serve the Giants well in the years to come.

Peace talks were opened with the American League during the winter with the National League first seeking a merger between the two loops. The American League, united behind Ban Johnson, preferred to retain its own identity, and the peace treaty signed in January, 1903, allowed just that. Both leagues would recognize each other as equals, both would honor each other's reserve lists and contracts, and most of the players currently in the American League were permitted to remain there. The junior loop could follow its plan to invade New York in return for a pledge to leave Pittsburgh to the Pirates. The Giants objected to the treaty's allowance of the American League's moving to New York, and Brooklyn took issue with permanently losing the players who had jumped to the rival league, but a reluctant consensus was reached, putting an end to the two-year baseball war and getting down to the sport at hand.

Events followed each other rapidly after the conclusion of the playing season. New raids by the American League stripped Brooklyn of Wee Willie Keeler, Frank Kitson, and Wild Bill Donovan, relieved Pittsburgh of Jesse Tannehill and Jack Chesbro, and took Sam Crawford off Cincinnati's hands. The controlling ownership of the New York Giants was purchased by John T. Brush, and his position as head of the Executive Committee was rendered obsolete by the election of Harry Pulliam of Pittsburgh as President of the National League in December.

1902 NATIONAL LEAGUE

NAME	G by POS	B	AGE	G	AB	R	H	2B	3B	HR	RBI	BB	SO	SB	BA	SA
PITTSBURGH 1st 103-36 .741		FRED CLARKE														
TOTALS			28	142	4976	775	1410	189	94	19	660	372		228	.286	.374
Kitty Bransfield (KJ)	1B101	R	27	102	412	50	127	21	9	1	69	17		24	.308	.410
Claude Richey	2B114, OF1	B	28	115	405	54	112	13	1	2	55	53		10	.277	.328
Wid Conroy	SS95, OF3	R	25	99	365	55	89	10	6	1	47	24		10	.244	.312
Tommy Leach	3B134	R	24	135	514	97	144	21	20	6	85	45		29	.280	.434
Lefty Davis (BN)	OF59	L	27	59	232	52	65	7	3	0	20	35		19	.280	.336
Ginger Beaumont	OF130	L	25	131	544	101	194	21	6	0	67	39		33	.357	.417
Fred Clarke (FG)	OF113	L	29	114	461	104	148	27	14	2	53	51		34	.321	.453
Harry Smith	C50	R	27	50	185	14	35	4	1	0	12	4		4	.189	.222
Honus Wagner	OF61, SS44, 1B32, 2B1, P1	R	28	137	538	105	177	33	16	3	91	43		43	.329	.467
Jimmy Burke	2B27, OF18, 3B9, SS4	R	27	60	203	24	60	12	2	0	26	17		9	.296	.374
Jack O'Connor	C42, 1B6, OF1	R	33	49	170	13	50	1	2	1	28	3		2	.294	.341
Chief Zimmer	C41	R	41	42	142	13	38	4	2	0	17	11		4	.268	.324
Jesse Tannehill	P26, OF16	B	27	44	148	27	43	6	1	1	17	12		3	.291	.365
Jimmy Sebring	OF19	L	20	19	80	15	26	4	4	0	15	5		2	.325	.475
Eddie Phelps	C13, 1B5	R	23	18	61	5	13	1	0	0	6	4		2	.213	.230
Fred Crolius	OF9		25	9	38	4	10	2	1	0	7	0		0	.263	.368
George Merritt	OF2		22	2	9	2	3	1	0	0	2	0		0	.333	.444
Lee Fohl	C1	L	31	1	3	0	0	0	0	0	1	0		0	.000	.000
Mike Hopkins	C1	R	29	1	2	0	2	1	0	0	0	0		0	1.000	1.500
Bill Miller	OF1			1	5	0	1	0	0	0	2	0		0	.200	.200
BROOKLYN 2nd 75-63 .543 27.5		NED HANLON														
TOTALS			29	141	4845	564	1242	147	49	19	476	319		145	.256	.319
Tom McCreery	1B108, OF4	R	27	112	430	49	105	8	4	4	57	29		16	.244	.309
Tim Flood	2B132, OF1	R	25	132	476	43	104	11	4	3	51	23		8	.218	.277
Bill Dahlen	SS138	R	32	136	520	68	139	26	7	2	74	43		29	.267	.356
Charlie Irwin	3B130, SS1	R	33	131	458	59	125	14	0	2	43	39		13	.273	.317
Willie Keeler	OF133	L	30	132	556	84	188	18	7	0	38	21		23	.338	.396
Cozy Dolan	OF141	L	29	141	592	72	166	16	7	1	54	33		24	.280	.336
2 Jimmy Sheckard	OF123	L	23	122	480	84	131	20	10	4	37	57		25	.273	.381
Hugh Hearne	C65	R	29	66	231	22	65	10	0	0	28	16		3	.281	.325
Duke Farrell	C49, 1B24	R	35	74	264	14	64	5	2	0	24	12		6	.242	.277
Ed Wheeler	3B11, 2B10, SS5		23	30	96	4	12	0	0	0	5	3		1	.125	.125
Lew Ritter	C16	R	26	16	57	5	12	1	0	0	2	1		2	.211	.228
Rube Ward	OF11		23	13	31	4	9	1	0	0	2	2		0	.290	.323
George Hildebrand	OF11	R	23	11	41	3	9	1	0	0	5	3		0	.220	.244
Tacks Latimer	C8		24	8	24	0	1	0	0	0	0	0		0	.042	.042
2 Joe Wall	C5	L	28	5	18	0	3	0	0	0	0	3		0	.167	.167
Nig Fuller	C3	R		3	9	0	0	0	0	0	1	0		0	.000	.000
Pat Deisel	C1	R	26	1	3	0	2	0	0	0	1	1		0	.667	.667
BOSTON 3rd 73-64 .533 29		AL BUCKENBERGER														
TOTALS			28	142	4728	571	1178	142	39	14	453	398		189	.249	.305
Fred Tenney	1B134	L	30	134	491	88	154	16	3	2	30	73		21	.314	.371
Gene DeMontreville	2B112, SS10	R	28	125	483	50	130	18	5	0	53	12		27	.269	.327
Herman Long	SS107, 2B13	L	36	120	432	41	98	9	0	2	44	31		22	.227	.262
Ed Gremminger	3B140	R	28	140	522	55	134	20	12	1	65	39		7	.257	.347
Pat Carney	OF137, P2	L	25	137	522	75	141	17	4	2	65	42		27	.270	.330
Billy Lush	OF116, 3B1	B	28	120	413	68	92	8	1	2	19	76		30	.223	.262
Dick Cooley	OF127, 1B7	L	29	135	548	73	162	26	8	0	58	34		27	.296	.372
Mal Kittredge	C72	R	32	80	255	18	60	7	0	2	30	24		4	.235	.286
Pat Moran	C71, 1B3, OF1	R	26	80	251	22	60	5	5	1	24	17		6	.239	.311
1 Ernie Courtney	OF39, SS3	L	23	48	165	23	36	3	0	0	17	13		3	.218	.236
2 Charlie Dexter	SS22, 2B19, OF7, 3B1		26	48	183	33	47	3	0	1	18	16		16	.257	.290
Fred Brown	OF2	R	23	2	6	1	2	1	0	0	0	0		0	.333	.500
George Grosart (DD) 23																

NAME	T	AGE	W	L	PCT	SV	G	GS	CG	IP	H	BB	SO	ShO	ERA
		28	103	36	.741	3	142	142	131	1265	1142	250	564	21	2.30
Jack Chesbro	R	28	28	6	.824	1	35	33	31	286	242	62	136	8	2.17
Jesse Tannehill	L	27	20	6	.769	0	26	24	23	231	203	25	100	2	1.95
Deacon Phillippe	R	30	20	9	.690	0	31	30	29	272	265	26	122	5	2.05
Ed Doheny (IL)	L	27	16	4	.800	0	22	21	19	188	161	61	88	2	2.54
Sam Leever (SA)	R	30	16	7	.696	2	28	26	23	222	203	31	86	4	2.39
Warry McLaughlin		26	3	0	1.000	0	3	3	3	26	27	9	13	0	2.77
Harv Cushman		24	0	4	.000	0	4	4	3	26	30	31	12	0	7.27
1 Ed Poole	R	27	0	0	.000	0	1	0	0	8	7	3	2	0	1.13
Honus Wagner	R	28	0	0	.000	0	1	0	0	5	4	2	5	0	0.00
		27	75	63	.543	3	141	141	131	1256	1113	363	536	14	2.69
Frank Kitson	R	30	19	12	.613	0	31	30	28	260	251	48	107	3	2.84
Wild Bill Donovan	R	25	17	15	.531	1	35	33	30	298	250	111	170	4	2.78
Jay Hughes	R	28	15	11	.577	0	31	30	27	254	228	55	94	0	2.87
Doc Newton	L	24	15	14	.517	2	31	28	26	264	208	87	107	4	2.42
2 LeRoy Evans	R	28	5	6	.455	0	13	11	11	97	91	33	35	2	2.69
John McMackin	R	24	2	2	.500	0	4	4	4	32	34	11	6	0	3.09
2 Ned Garvin	R	28	1	1	.500	0	2	2	2	18	15	4	7	1	1.00
Gene McCann	R	26	1	2	.333	0	3	3	3	30	32	12	9	0	2.40
Lafe Winham	L	20	0	0	.000	0	1	0	0	3	4	2	1	0	0.00
		28	73	64	.533	4	142	142	124	1260	1233	372	523	14	2.61
Togie Pittinger	R	31	27	15	.643	0	46	40	36	389	360	128	174	7	2.52
Vic Willis	R	26	27	19	.587	3	51	46	45	410	372	101	225	4	2.20
John Malarkey (IL)		30	9	11	.450	1	21	19	17	170	158	58	39	1	2.59
2 Mal Eason	R	23	9	14	.391	0	27	26	20	206	237	59	50	2	2.75
Fred Klobedanz	L	31	1	0	1.000	0	1	1	1	8	9	2	4	0	1.13
Pat Carney	L	25	0	1	.000	0	2	1	0	5	6	3	3	0	9.00
Bob Dresser	L	23	0	1	.000	0	1	1	1	9	12	0	8	0	3.00
1 Dad Hale	R	23	0	3	.000	0	8	6	3	47	69	18	12	0	6.32
Sammy Curran		27	0	0	.000	0	1	0	0	7	6	0	3	0	1.29
Red Long	R	25	0	0	.000	0	1	1	1	8	4	3	5	0	1.13

CINCINNATI 4th 70-70 .500 33.5 — BID McPHEE 27-37 .422 FRANK BANCROFT 10-7 .588 JOE KELLEY 33-26 .559

NAME	G by POS	B	AGE	G	AB	R	H	2B	3B	HR	RBI	BB	SO	SB	BA	SA
TOTALS			29	141	4908	632	1383	188	77	18	531	297		131	.282	.362
Jake Beckley	1B129, P1	L	34	129	532	82	176	21	7	5	69	34		16	.331	.425
Heinie Peitz	2B45, C47, 3B6, 1B6	R	29	112	387	54	122	22	5	1	60	24		7	.315	.406
Tommy Corcoran	SS137, 2B1	R	33	137	537	54	135	20	4	0	54	11		23	.251	.304
Harry Steinfeldt	3B129, OF1	R	24	129	479	53	133	20	7	1	49	24		12	.278	.355
Sam Crawford	OF140	L	22	140	555	94	185	16	**23**	3	78	47		15	.333	.461
Dummy Hoy	OF72	L	40	72	279	48	82	16	2	2	20	41		12	.294	.387
1 John Dobbs	OF63	L	26	63	256	39	76	7	3	1	16	19		7	.297	.359
Bill Bergen	C89	R	29	89	322	19	58	8	3	0	36	14		2	.180	.224
2 Cy Seymour	OF61, 3B1, P1	L	29	60	235	28	82	8	2	2	37	12		10	.349	.426
1 Erve Beck	2B32, 1B6, OF6	R	23	48	187	19	57	10	3	1	20	3		2	.305	.406
Maggie Magoon	2B41, SS3	R	27	45	162	29	44	9	2	0	23	13		7	.272	.352
2 Joe Kelley	OF20, 2B10, 3B9, SS2	R	30	37	156	24	51	8	2	1	12	15		3	.327	.423
Mike Donlin (JA)	OF32, SS1, P1	L	24	34	143	30	42	4	5	0	9	9		9	.294	.392
Bill Phillips	P33	R	33	38	114	11	39	1	3	0	11	6		1	.342	.404
2 Billy Maloney	OF18, C7	L	24	27	89	13	22	4	0	1	7	2		8	.247	.326
Jack Morrissey	2B11, OF1	B	25	12	39	5	11	1	1	0	3	4		0	.282	.359
1 Harry Bay	OF3	L	24	6	16	3	6	0	0	0	1	2		0	.375	.375

NAME	T	AGE	W	L	PCT	SV	G	GS	CG	IP	H	BB	SO	ShO	ERA
		27	70	70	.500	1	141	141	130	1239	1228	352	430	9	2.67
Noodles Hahn	L	23	23	12	.657	0	36	36	35	321	282	58	142	6	1.77
Bill Phillips	R	33	16	16	.500	0	33	33	30	269	267	55	85	0	2.51
2 Ed Poole	R	27	12	4	.750	0	16	16	16	138	129	54	55	2	2.15
2 Henry Thielman	R	21	9	15	.375	1	25	23	22	211	201	78	49	0	3.24
Bob Ewing (KJ)	R	29	5	6	.455	0	15	12	10	118	126	47	44	0	2.97
1 Clarence Curry	R	23	3	4	.429	0	10	7	6	65	70	17	20	1	3.74
1 Crese Heismann	L	22	2	1	.667	0	5	3	2	33	33	10	15	0	2.45
Jake Beckley	L	34	0	1	.000	0	1	1	0	4	9	1	2	0	6.75
Martin Glendon		26	0	1	.000	0	1	1	0	3	5	4	0	0	12.00
Cy Hooker	R	22	0	1	.000	0	1	1	1	8	11	0	0	0	4.50
Len Swormstedt	R		0	2	.000	0	2	2	2	18	22	5	3	0	4.00
Rube Vickers	R	24	0	3	.000	0	3	3	3	21	31	8	6	0	6.00
Archie Stimmel	R	29	0	4	.000	0	4	3	3	26	37	12	7	0	3.46
Mike Donlin (JA)	L	24	0	0	.000	0	1	0	0	1	1	0	0	0	0.00
2 Cy Seymour	L	29	0	0	.000	0	1	0	0	3	4	3	2	0	9.00

CHICAGO 5th 68-69 .496 34 — FRANK SELEE

NAME	G by POS	B	AGE	G	AB	R	H	2B	3B	HR	RBI	BB	SO	SB	BA	SA
TOTALS			26	141	4802	530	1200	131	40	6	423	353		**222**	.250	.298
Frank Chance	1B38, C29, OF4	R	24	73	236	40	67	8	4	1	31	35		28	.284	.364
Bobby Lowe	2B117, 3B2	R	33	119	472	41	116	13	3	0	31	11		16	.246	.286
Joe Tinker	SS124, 3B8	R	21	133	501	54	137	17	5	2	54	26		28	.273	.339
Germany Schaefer	3B75, 1B3, OF2, SS1	R	25	81	291	32	57	2	3	0	14	19		12	.196	.223
2 Davy Jones (IL)	OF64	L	22	64	243	41	74	12	3	0	14	38		12	.305	.379
2 John Dobbs	OF59	L	26	59	235	31	71	8	2	0	35	18		3	.302	.353
Jimmy Slagle	OF113	L	28	115	454	64	143	11	4	0	28	53		40	.315	.357
Johnny Kling	C112, SS1	R	27	114	434	50	124	15	6	0	57	29		23	.286	.348
1 Charlie Dexter	3B39, 1B22, OF10		26	69	266	30	60	12	0	2	26	19		13	.226	.293
J. Menefee	P22, OF22, 1B19, 3B2, 2B1	R	34	65	216	24	50	4	1	0	15	15		4	.231	.259
Dakin Miller	OF51	L	24	51	187	17	46	4	1	0	13	7		10	.246	.278
Art Williams	OF24, 1B19		24	47	160	17	37	3	0	0	14	15		9	.231	.250
Bunk Congalton	OF45		27	45	179	14	40	3	0	1	24	7		3	.223	.257
1 Hal O'Hagen	1B31		28	31	108	10	21	1	3	0	10	11		8	.194	.259
Johnny Evers	2B18, SS8	L	20	25	89	7	20	0	0	0	2	3		1	.225	.225
Fred Clark	1B12	L	28	12	43	1	8	1	0	0	2	4		1	.186	.209
Jim Murray	OF12	R	24	12	47	3	8	0	0	0	1	2		0	.170	.170
Larry Schlafly	OF5, 2B4, 3B2	R	23	10	31	5	10	0	3	0	5	6		2	.323	.516
1 Mike Kahoe	C4, 3B2, SS1	R	28	7	18	0	4	1	0	0	2	0		0	.222	.278
Mike Lynch	OF7		25	7	28	4	4	0	0	0	0	2		0	.143	.143
Mike Jacobs	SS5			5	19	1	4	0	0	0	2	0		0	.211	.211
Ed Glenn	SS2	R	28	2	7	0	0	0	0	0	0	1		0	.000	.000
2 Jack Hendricks	OF2	L	27	2	7	0	4	0	1	0	0	0		0	.571	.857

2 Sammy Strang 25 B 4-11, Pete Lamer 28 2-9, Chick Pedroes 32 0-6, R. E. Hildebrand 0-4, Ed Hughes 0-3, Snapper Kennedy 24 R 0-5

NAME	T	AGE	W	L	PCT	SV	G	GS	CG	IP	H	BB	SO	ShO	ERA
		27	68	69	.496	2	141	141	**132**	**1275**	1235	279	437	17	**2.21**
Jack Taylor	R	28	23	11	.676	1	36	33	33	325	271	43	83	7	**1.33**
Jocko Menefee	R	34	12	10	.545	0	22	21	20	197	202	26	60	4	2.42
Pop Williams	R	28	11	16	.407	0	31	31	26	254	259	63	94	1	2.52
Carl Lundgren	R	22	9	9	.500	0	18	18	17	160	158	45	68	1	1.97
Jim St. Vrain		19	4	6	.400	0	12	11	10	95	88	25	51	1	2.08
Bob Rhoades	R	22	4	8	.333	1	16	12	12	118	131	42	43	1	3.20
Alex Hardy	L	25	2	2	.500	0	4	4	4	35	29	12	12	1	3.60
1 Mal Eason	R	23	1	1	.500	0	2	2	2	18	21	2	4	0	1.00
Jim Gardner	R	27	1	2	.333	0	3	3	2	25	23	10	6	0	2.88
Deacon Morrissey			1	3	.250	0	5	5	5	40	40	8	13	0	2.25
Fred Glade	R	26	0	1	.000	0	1	1	1	8	13	3	3	0	9.00

ST. LOUIS 6th 56-78 .418 44.5 — PATSY DONOVAN

NAME	G by POS	B	AGE	G	AB	R	H	2B	3B	HR	RBI	BB	SO	SB	BA	SA
TOTALS			29	140	4751	517	1226	116	37	10	402	273		158	.258	.304
Kitty Brashear	1B67, 2B21, OF16, SS3	R	24	110	388	36	107	8	2	1	40	32		9	.276	.314
John Farrell	2B118, SS21		25	138	565	68	141	13	5	0	25	43		9	.250	.290
Otto Krueger	SS107, 3B18	R	25	128	467	55	124	7	8	0	46	29		14	.266	.315
Fred Hartman	3B105, SS4, 1B3		34	114	416	30	90	10	3	0	52	14		14	.216	.255
Patsy Donovan	OF126	R	37	126	502	68	155	12	4	0	35	28		41	.309	.349
Homer Smoot	OF129	L	24	129	518	58	161	19	4	3	48	23		20	.311	.380
George Barclay	OF137		26	137	543	79	163	14	2	3	53	31		30	.300	.350
Jack Ryan	C66, 1B4, 3B4, 2B2, SS1	R	33	76	267	23	48	4	4	0	14	4		2	.180	.225
Art Nichols (JJ)	1B56, C11, OF4	R	30	73	251	36	67	12	0	1	31	21		18	.267	.327
Jack O'Neill	C59	R	29	63	192	13	27	1	1	0	12	13		2	.141	.156
Mike O'Neill	P36, OF3	L	24	51	135	21	43	5	3	2	15	2		0	.319	.444
Jack Calhoun	3B12, 1B5, OF1	R	22	20	64	3	10	2	1	0	8	8		1	.156	.219
Art Weaver	C11		23	11	33	2	6	2	0	0	3	1		0	.182	.242
Doc Hazelton	1B7		25	7	23	0	3	0	0	0	0	2		0	.130	.130
Rudy Kling	SS4	R	32	4	10	1	2	0	0	0	0	4		1	.200	.200
Otto Williams	SS2	R	24	2	5	0	2	0	0	0	2	1		1	.400	.400
Soldier Boy Murphy	3B1		23	1	3	1	2	1	0	0	1	1		0	.667	1.000

NAME	T	AGE	W	L	PCT	SV	G	GS	CG	IP	H	BB	SO	ShO	ERA
		24	56	78	.418	**4**	140	140	112	1228	**1399**	338	400	7	3.47
Mike O'Neill	L	24	16	15	.516	2	36	32	29	288	297	66	105	2	2.91
Stan Yerkes			12	**21**	.364	0	39	37	27	273	341	79	81	1	3.66
Ed Murphy	R	25	10	6	.625	1	23	17	12	164	187	31	37	1	3.02
2 Clarence Curry	R	23	7	5	.583	0	15	12	10	125	125	35	30	2	2.59
Bob Wicker	R	24	5	12	.294	0	22	16	14	152	159	45	78	1	3.20
Wiley Dunham			2	3	.400	1	7	5	3	38	47	13	15	0	5.68
Alex Pearson	R	25	2	6	.250	0	11	10	8	82	90	22	24	0	3.95
Bill Popp	R	25	2	6	.250	0	9	7	5	60	87	26	20	0	4.95
Chappie McFarland	R		0	1	.000	0	2	1	1	11	11	3	3	0	5.73
Jim Hackett	R	24	0	3	.000	0	4	3	3	30	46	16	7	0	6.30
Joe Adams	L	24	0	0	.000	0	1	0	0	4	9	2	0	0	9.00

PHILADELPHIA 7th 56-81 .409 46 — BILL SHETTSLINE

NAME	G by POS	B	AGE	G	AB	R	H	2B	3B	HR	RBI	BB	SO	SB	BA	SA
TOTALS			28	138	4615	484	1139	110	43	5	389	356		108	.247	.293
Hughie Jennings	1B69, SS5, 2B4	R	33	78	289	31	80	16	3	1	32	14		8	.277	.363
Pete Childs	2B123		30	123	403	25	78	5	0	0	25	34		6	.194	.206
Rudy Hulswitt	SS125, 3B3	R	25	128	497	59	135	11	7	0	38	30		12	.272	.322
Billy Hallman	3B72	R	35	73	254	14	63	8	4	0	35	14		9	.248	.311
Shad Barry	OF137, 1B1	R	25	138	543	65	156	20	6	3	58	44		14	.287	.363
Roy Thomas	OF138	L	28	138	500	89	143	4	7	0	24	**107**		17	.286	.322
1 George Browne	OF70	L	26	70	281	41	73	7	1	0	26	16		11	.260	.292
Red Dooin	C84, OF6	R	23	94	333	20	77	7	3	0	35	10		8	.231	.270
Klondike Douglass	1B69, C29, OF10	L	30	109	408	37	95	12	3	0	37	23		6	.233	.277
Henry Krug	OF28, 2B13, SS9, 3B6	R	25	53	198	20	45	3	3	0	14	7		2	.227	.273
Doc White	P36, OF19	L	23	61	179	17	47	3	1	1	15	11		5	.263	.307
Fred Jacklitsch	C29, OF1	R	26	38	114	8	23	4	0	0	8	9		2	.202	.237
2 Harry Wolverton	3B34		28	34	136	12	40	3	2	0	16	9		3	.294	.346
Patsy Greene	3B19		27	19	65	6	11	1	0	0	1	2		2	.169	.185
Bill Thomas	OF3, 1B1, 2B1	R	24	6	17	1	2	0	0	0	0	1		0	.118	.118
Tom Fleming	OF5		28	5	16	2	6	0	0	0	2	1		0	.375	.375
Bill Clay	OF3	R	27	3	8	1	2	0	0	0	1	0		0	.250	.250
Nap Shea	C3	R	28	3	8	1	1	0	0	0	0	1		0	.125	.125

Howard Berry 29 B 1-4, Frank Maher 0-0, Tom Maher 0-1, Ed Watkins 0-3

NAME	T	AGE	W	L	PCT	SV	G	GS	CG	IP	H	BB	SO	ShO	ERA
		27	56	81	.409	3	138	138	118	1211	1323	334	504	8	3.50
Doc White	L	23	16	20	.444	1	36	35	34	306	277	72	185	3	2.53
Chick Fraser	R	31	12	13	.480	0	27	26	24	224	238	74	97	3	3.42
2 Bill Duggleby	R	29	11	17	.393	1	33	28	25	259	282	57	60	0	3.37
Ham Iburg	R	24	11	18	.379	0	30	30	20	236	286	62	106	1	3.89
1 Cy Vorhees		27	3	3	.500	0	10	4	3	54	63	20	24	1	3.83
2 Bill Magee	R	34	2	4	.333	0	8	6	6	54	61	18	15	0	3.67
Harry Felix	R	25	1	3	.250	0	9	5	3	45	61	11	10	0	5.60
Barney McFadden	R	28	0	1	.000	0	1	1	1	9	14	7	3	0	8.00
Jesse Whiting			0	1	.000	0	1	1	1	9	13	6	0	0	5.00
Bill Wolfe			0	1	.000	0	1	1	1	9	11	4	3	0	4.00
Bill Salisbury		26	0	0	.000	0	2	1	0	6	15	2	0	0	13.50
Henry Fox			0	0	.000	1	1	0	0	1	2	1	1	0	18.00

NEW YORK 8th 48-88 .353 53.5 — HORACE FOGEL 18-23 .439 HEINIE SMITH 5-27 .156 JOHN McGRAW 25-38 .397

NAME	G by POS	B	AGE	G	AB	R	H	2B	3B	HR	RBI	BB	SO	SB	BA	SA
TOTALS			29	139	4571	401	1088	147	34	8	336	252		187	.238	.290
2 Dan McGann	1B61	B	30	61	226	26	68	6	7	0	21	12		12	.301	.389
Heinie Smith	2B138	R	30	138	511	46	129	19	2	0	33	17		32	.252	.297
Joe Bean	SS48	R	28	48	176	13	39	2	1	0	5	5		9	.222	.244
Billy Lauder	3B121, OF4	R	28	125	482	41	114	20	1	1	44	10		19	.237	.288
Jack Dunn	OF43, SS36, 3B18, P3, 2B2	R	29	100	342	26	72	11	1	0	14	20		13	.211	.249
Steve Brodie	OF109	L	33	109	417	35	117	8	2	3	42	22		11	.281	.332
Jimmy Jones	OF67	R	25	67	249	16	59	11	1	0	19	13		7	.237	.289
Frank Bowerman	C98, 1B3	R	33	105	372	37	94	13	6	0	26	13		13	.253	.320
2 George Browne	OF53	L	26	53	216	30	69	9	5	0	14	9		13	.319	.407
2 R. Bresnahan	OF27, C16, 1B4, SS4, 3B1	R	23	51	178	16	52	13	3	1	22	16		6	.292	.416
1 Jack Doyle	1B49	R	32	50	190	25	57	12	1	1	19	10		10	.300	.389
1 George Yeager	C27, 1B3, OF1		29	38	108	6	22	2	1	0	9	11		1	.204	.241
Jim Jackson	OF34	R	24	35	110	14	20	5	1	0	13	15		6	.182	.245
2 John McGraw	SS34	L	29	36	106	13	24	0	0	0	5	26		7	.226	.226
24 Hal O'Hagan	1B18, OF8		28	26	84	5	12	2	1	0	8	2		3	.143	.190
George VanHaltren (BN)	OF24	L	36	26	96	14	24	1	2	0	7	17		7	.250	.302
Roy Clark	OF20	L	28	21	76	4	11	1	0	0	3	1		5	.145	.158
Heinie Wagner	SS17	R	21	17	56	4	12	1	0	0	2	0		3	.214	.232
1 Jack Hendricks	OF7	L	27	8	26	1	6	2	0	0	0	2		2	.231	.308
Jim Delahanty	OF7	R	23	7	26	3	6	1	0	0	3	1		0	.231	.269
1 Joe Wall	OF3	L	28	6	14	2	5	2	0	0	0	2		0	.357	.500
Libe Washburn	OF3		28	6	9	1	4	0	0	0	0	2		1	.444	.444
John Robinson	C3	R		4	9	0	0	0	0	0	0	0		0	.000	.000

Jim McDonald 3-9, John O'Neill 0-8, Jim Callahan 0-4, Chick Hartley R 0-4

NAME	T	AGE	W	L	PCT	SV	G	GS	CG	IP	H	BB	SO	ShO	ERA
		27	48	**88**	.353	1	139	139	118	1226	1193	332	501	11	2.82
Christy Mathewson	R	23	14	17	.452	0	34	32	29	277	241	73	159	**8**	2.11
2 Joe McGinnity	R	31	8	8	.500	0	19	16	16	153	122	32	67	1	2.06
1 LeRoy Evans	R	28	8	12	.400	0	23	17	17	176	186	58	48	0	3.17
2 Dummy Taylor	R	27	7	15	.318	0	26	25	18	201	194	55	87	0	2.28
3 Jack Cronin	R	28	5	6	.455	0	13	12	11	114	105	18	52	0	2.45
1 Tully Sparks	R	25	4	11	.267	1	15	13	11	115	123	40	40	0	3.76
Brickyard Kennedy (IL)	R	34	1	4	.200	0	6	6	4	39	44	16	9	1	3.92
2 Roscoe Miller	R	25	1	8	.111	0	10	9	7	73	77	11	15	0	4.56
John Burke		25	0	1	.000	0	2	1	1	14	21	3	3	0	5.79
1 Henry Thielman	R	21	0	1	.000	0	2	2	0	6	8	6	5	0	1.50
Bob Blewett	L	25	0	2	.000	0	5	3	2	28	39	7	8	0	4.82
Jack Dunn	R	29	0	3	.000	0	3	2	2	27	28	12	6	0	3.67
1 Bill Magee	R	34	0	0	.000	0	2	1	0	5	5	1	2	0	3.60

1903 The First Embarrassment of a New Peace

The raiding stopped, the polemics ceased, and peace came to the baseball world under a new National Agreement between two equal leagues. The players and managers now concentrated on the ballfield, while the owners concentrated on the turnstiles which clicked at a record pace.

The Pittsburgh Pirates breezed to their third straight National League pennant in an easier race than the final margin of 6½ games would indicate. The heavy-hitting Pirates were never out of the top spot after June 19, staving off threats from New York and Chicago. Honus Wagner took down his second batting crown with a .355 average, while Fred Clarke and Ginger Beaumont, as usual, placed among the league leaders. On the mound, Sam Leever won 25 games and Deacon Phillippe 24 at the head of the pennant column. The Giants rose into second place in the first full year of John McGraw's leadership. Baltimore expatriate Roger Bresnahan swung the stick at a .350 pace, and fellow re-jumper Joe McGinnity teamed up with Christy Mathewson to give the Giants a pair of 30-win aces; the influx of Baltimore talent triggered a rise from sixth to runner-up and an increase in the gate despite fan competition from the new New York Highlanders in the American League.

The success of the new American League club in New York removed any doubts of the major league status of the circuit. Playing in the freshly-opened Highlander Park in upper Manhattan, the new club in town got away to a slow start but rallied to finish in the first division; the squad which boasted of Willie Keeler, Jack Chesbro, and Clark Griffith carved for itself a new following out of the Gotham fandom and planted a seed which would bloom into baseball's most successful franchise. At the top of the standings, Boston danced home first with 14½ games to spare, spurred on by Cy Young's 28 wins—tops in the league for the third time. Connie Mack's A's slumped into a distant runner-up spot due to a falloff in hitting.

The two pennant winners became teams of destiny when owners, Barney Dreyfus of Pittsburgh and Henry Killilea of Boston, agreed in August to pit their front-running clubs against each other in the fall in a nine-game series for the "world's" championship. The handshake arrangement between the two magnates set up the first World Series and the first inter-league championship series since the 1890 match of the National League and American Association champs.

A large crowd of 16,242 assembled in Boston on October 1, to witness the first World Series game, a match-up between the legendary Cy Young and Pirate ace Deacon Phillippe. Young's fastballs met a hostile reception as the Bucs belted him for four runs in the top of the first, while Phillippe struck out ten Boston batters on the way to a 7-3 victory. Pittsburgh's Jimmy Sebring spiced the victory with the first home run in the fall classic. After four games, the Bucs had three wins in hand, but Bill Dinneen and Young came back to win two games each as Boston swept the next four to take the first World Series title. Dinneen won three games for the winners, while Chick Stahl and Hobe Ferris led the Boston offense. Phillippe was the victor in all three Pirate victories, as his pitching partner, Sam Leever, was soundly hit in both his appearances.

Before the books on the 1903 season could be closed, two tragic footnotes to baseball would have to be added to the history of the game. The first occurred in January, as 28-year-old Detroit pitcher Win Mercer committed suicide by gas inhalation in San Francisco, thus ending a nine-year major league career. The second tragedy provided the basis for one of baseball's most clouded mysteries. It involved Washington's Ed Delahanty, a superstar who dominated the averages of his time, three times rising above the .400 barrier and once taking league batting honors with the Phillies in 1899 with a .410 mark. Delahanty, known to have bouts of drunkenness, reportedly left his team in Detroit to return East to recover from illness. While aboard the New York Central train heading to New York, the train crossed a bridge over Niagara Falls. What happened aboard the train—whether Delahanty lost his balance and fell while searching out the bar car, committed suicide, or got into a brawl and was thrown from the train—is still unknown. The only known fact is that the talented athlete was found below the falls two days later on July 4. His sensational death made newspaper headlines at the time, and his 16-year batting mark of .346 was enough to place him in the Hall of Fame, and fourth lifetime in the history of baseball behind Ty Cobb, Rogers Hornsby, and Shoeless Joe Jackson.

1903 AMERICAN LEAGUE

NAME	G by POS	B	AGE	G	AB	R	H	2B	3B	HR	RBI	BB	SO	SB	BA	SA
BOSTON 1st 91-47 .659			**JIMMY COLLINS**													
TOTALS			30	141	**4919**	**707**	**1336**	222	**113**	**48**	**609**	262		141	**.272**	**.392**
Candy LaChance	1B141	B	33	141	522	60	134	22	6	1	53	28		12	.257	.328
Hobe Ferris	2B139, SS2	R	25	141	525	69	132	19	7	9	66	25		11	.251	.366
Freddy Parent	SS139	R	27	139	560	83	170	31	17	4	80	13		24	.304	.441
Jimmy Collins	3B130	R	33	130	541	87	160	34	17	5	72	24		22	.296	.449
Buck Freeman	OF141	L	31	141	565	74	161	39	21	**13**	**104**	30		4	.285	.497
Chick Stahl (JJ)	OF74	L	30	78	298	60	83	11	6	2	44	28		14	.279	.376
Patsy Dougherty	OF139	L	26	139	**590**	**106**	**195**	19	12	4	59	33		35	.331	.424
Lou Criger	C96	R	31	96	317	41	61	7	10	3	31	26		5	.192	.306
Jack O'Brien	OF71, 3B11, 2B4, SS1	L	30	96	338	44	71	14	4	3	38	21		10	.210	.302
Cy Young	P40	R	36	41	137	21	44	6	3	1	14	4		2	.321	.431
Jake Stahl	C28, OF1	R	24	40	92	14	22	3	5	2	8	4		1	.239	.446
Long Tom Hughes	P33		24	33	93	14	26	4	2	1	13	3		1	.280	.398
Duke Farrell (BL)	C17	R	36	17	52	5	21	5	1	0	8	5		1	.404	.538
Broadway Aleck Smith	C10		32	11	33	4	10	1	0	0	4	0		0	.303	.333
George Stone		L	25	2	2	0	0	0	0	0	0	0		0	.000	.000
Harry Gleason	3B2	R	28	6	13	3	2	1	0	0	2	0		0	.154	.231
PHILADELPHIA 2nd 75-60 .556 14.5			**CONNIE MACK**													
TOTALS			30	137	4673	597	1236	228	68	31	502	268		157	.264	.362
Harry Davis	1B104, OF2	R	29	101	403	74	120	29	7	5	55	24		24	.298	.436
Danny Murphy	2B133	R	26	133	512	65	141	29	11	1	60	13		17	.275	.381
Monte Cross	SS137, 2B1	R	33	137	470	44	116	21	2	3	45	49		31	.247	.319
Lave Cross	3B136, 1B1	R	37	137	554	61	162	23	5	2	90	10		13	.292	.363
Socks Seybold	OF120, 1B18	R	32	137	531	78	159	**43**	8	8	84	38		5	.299	**.456**
Ollie Pickering	OF135	L	33	137	512	93	144	18	6	1	36	53		40	.281	.346
Topsy Hartsel	OF96	L	29	98	373	65	116	19	14	5	26	49		13	.311	.477
Ossee Schreckengost	C77, 1B10	R	28	92	306	26	78	13	4	3	30	11		0	.255	.353
Mike Powers	C66, 1B7	R	32	75	247	19	56	11	1	0	23	5		1	.227	.279
Danny Hoffman	OF62, P1	L	23	74	248	29	61	5	7	2	22	6		7	.246	.347
Bert Daly	2B4, 3B3, SS1	R	22	10	21	2	4	0	2	0	4	1		0	.190	.381
John Kalahan	C1	R	24	1	5	0	0	0	0	0	0	0		0	.000	.000
Ed Hilley	3B1	R	24	1	3	1	1	0	0	0	0	1		0	.333	.333
CLEVELAND 3rd 77-63 .550 15			**BILL ARMOUR**													
TOTALS			28	140	4773	639	1265	**231**	95	31	550	259		**175**	.265	.373
Charley Hickman	1B125, 2B7	R	27	130	518	67	171	31	11	12	97	17		15	.330	.502
Nap Lajoie	2B122, 1B1, 3B1	R	27	126	488	90	173	40	13	7	93	24		22	**.355**	**.533**
John Gochnaur	SS134	R	27	134	438	48	81	16	4	0	48	48		10	.185	.240
Bill Bradley	3B136	R	25	137	543	103	171	35	22	6	68	25		23	.315	.494
Elmer Flick	OF140	L	27	142	529	84	158	22	16	2	51	51		27	.299	.412
Harry Bay	OF140	L	25	140	579	94	169	15	12	1	35	29		**45**	.292	.364
1 Jack McCarthy	OF108	L	34	108	415	47	110	20	8	0	43	19		15	.265	.352
Harry Bemis	C74, 1B10, 2B1	L	29	92	314	31	82	20	3	1	41	8		5	.261	.354
Fred Abbott	C71, 1B3	R	28	77	255	25	60	11	3	1	25	7		8	.235	.314
Jack Thoney	OF24, 2B5, 3B2	R	23	32	122	10	25	3	0	1	9	2		7	.205	.254
Billy Clingman	2B11, SS7, 3B3	B	33	21	64	10	18	1	1	0	7	11		2	.281	.328
Jack Hardy	OF5	R	26	5	19	1	3	1	0	0	1	1		1	.158	.211
1 Jack Slattery	1B2	R	26	4	11	1	0	0	0	0	0	0		0	.000	.000
Happy Jack Iott	OF3	R	26	3	10	1	2	0	0	0	0	2		1	.200	.200
Hugh Hill			23	1	1	0	0	0	0	0	0	0		0	.000	.000

NAME	T	AGE	W	L	PCT	SV	G	GS	CG	IP	H	BB	SO	ShO	ERA
		28	**91**	47	**.659**	3	141	141	123	**1255**	1142	269	579	**20**	**2.56**
Cy Young	R	36	**28**	9	**.757**	2	40	35	**34**	**342**	294	37	176	**7**	2.08
Long Tom Hughes	R	24	20	7	.741	0	33	31	25	245	232	60	112	5	2.57
Bill Dinneen	R	27	21	11	.656	1	37	35	32	299	255	66	148	6	2.23
Norwood Gibson	R	26	13	11	.542	0	24	21	17	183	166	65	76	2	3.20
George Winter	R	25	9	8	.529	0	24	18	14	178	182	37	64	0	3.08
1 Nick Altrock (IL)	L	26	0	1	.000	0	1	1	1	8	13	4	3	0	9.00
		24	75	60	.556	1	137	137	112	1207	1124	315	**728**	10	2.98
Eddie Plank	L	27	23	16	.590	0	**43**	**40**	33	336	317	65	176	3	2.38
Rube Waddell	L	26	22	16	.579	0	39	38	**34**	324	274	85	**302**	4	2.44
Chief Bender	R	20	17	15	.531	0	36	33	29	270	239	65	127	2	3.07
Weldon Henley	R	22	12	9	.571	0	29	21	13	186	186	67	86	1	3.92
Conny McGeehan		19	1	0	1.000	0	3	0	0	10	9	1	4	0	4.50
Lee Fairbank	R	22	0	0	.000	0	4	1	1	24	33	12	10	0	4.88
Clarence Quinn			0	0	.000	0	2	0	0	9	11	5	1	0	5.00
Ed Pinnance	R	**23**	0	1	.000	1	2	1	0	7	5	2	2	0	2.57
Andy Coakley	R	20	0	3	.000	0	6	3	2	38	48	11	20	0	5.45
Danny Hoffman	L	23	0	0	.000	0	1	0	0	3	2	2	0	0	3.00
		25	77	63	.550	2	140	140	**125**	1244	1161	271	521	**20**	2.66
Earl Moore	R	23	20	8	.714	1	28	26	26	239	189	56	142	3	**1.77**
Addie Joss	R	23	18	13	.581	0	33	32	32	293	239	43	126	3	2.15
Bill Bernhard (BG)	R	32	14	6	.700	0	20	19	18	166	151	21	60	3	2.11
2 Red Donahue	R	30	7	9	.430	0	16	15	14	137	142	12	45	4	2.43
Jesse Stovall	R	27	5	1	.833	0	6	6	6	57	44	21	12	2	2.05
Gus Dorner	R	26	3	5	.375	1	12	8	4	74	83	24	28	2	3.28
Ed Killian	L	26	3	5	.375	0	9	8	7	62	61	13	18	3	2.47
2 Bob Rhoades	R	23	2	3	.400	0	5	5	5	41	55	3	21	0	5.27
1 Clarence Wright	R	24	3	9	.250	0	15	12	8	102	122	58	42	0	5.74
Martin Glendon		27	1	2	.333	0	3	3	3	28	20	7	9	0	0.96
Alex Pearson	R	26	1	2	.333	0	4	3	2	30	34	3	12	0	3.60
Bill Pounds			0	0	.000	0	1	0	0	5	8	0	2	0	10.80
Ed Walker	L	28	0	0	.000	0	3	3	0	12	13	10	4	0	5.25

NEW YORK 4th 72-62 .537 17 — CLARK GRIFFITH

NAME	G by POS	B	AGE	G	AB	R	H	2B	3B	HR	RBI	BB	SO	SB	BA	SA
TOTALS			29	136	4565	579	1136	193	62	18	474	332		160	.249	.330
John Ganzel	1B129	R	28	129	476	62	132	25	7	3	71	30		9	.277	.378
Jimmy Williams	2B132	R	26	132	502	60	134	30	12	3	82	39		9	.267	.392
2 Kid Elberfeld	SS90	R	28	90	349	49	100	18	5	0	45	22		16	.287	.367
Wid Conroy	3B123, SS4	R	26	126	503	74	137	23	12	1	45	32		33	.272	.372
Willie Keeler	OF128, 3B4	L	31	132	515	98	164	13	7	0	32	32		25	.318	.371
Herm McFarland	OF103	L	33	103	362	41	88	16	9	5	45	46		13	.243	.378
Lefty Davis	OF102, SS1	L	28	104	372	54	88	10	0	0	25	43		11	.237	.263
Monte Beville	C75, 1B3	L	28	82	258	23	50	14	1	0	29	16		4	.194	.256
Dave Fultz	OF77, 3B2	R	28	79	295	39	66	12	1	0	25	25		29	.224	.271
Jack O'Connor (ST)	C63, 1B1	R	34	64	212	13	43	4	1	0	12	8		4	.203	.231
1 Ernie Courtney	SS19, 2B4, 1B1	L	24	25	79	7	21	3	3	1	8	7		1	.266	.418
1 Herman Long	SS22	L	37	22	80	6	15	3	0	0	8	2		3	.188	.225
Pat McCauley	C6		33	6	19	0	1	0	0	0	1	0		0	.053	.053
Jack Zalusky	C6, 1B1	R	24	7	16	2	5	0	0	0	1	1		0	.313	.313
1 Patsy Greene	3B2, SS1		28	4	13	1	4	1	0	0	0	0		0	.308	.385
Tim Jordan	1B2	L	24	2	8	2	1	0	0	0	0	0		0	.125	.125
Fred Holmes	1B1	R		1	0	0	0	0	0	0	0	1		0	.000	.000

NAME	T	AGE	W	L	PCT	SV	G	GS	CG	IP	H	BB	SO	ShO	ERA
		29	72	62	.537	2	136	136	111	1201	1171	245	463	7	3.08
Jack Chesbro	R	29	21	15	.583	0	40	36	33	325	300	74	147	1	2.77
Jesse Tannehill	L	28	15	15	.500	0	32	31	22	240	258	34	106	2	3.26
Clark Griffith	R	33	14	10	.583	0	25	24	22	213	201	33	69	2	2.70
Harry Howell	R	26	10	7	.588	0	25	15	13	156	140	44	62	0	3.52
Bill Wolfe	R	27	6	9	.400	0	20	16	12	148	143	26	48	1	2.98
2 John Deering	R	25	3	1	.750	0	9	7	6	60	59	18	14	1	3.75
Ambrose Puttmann	L	22	2	0	1.000	0	3	2	1	19	16	4	0	0	0.95
Elmer Bliss	R	28	1	0	1.000	0	1	0	0	5	4	0	2	0	0.00
Doc Adkins	R	30	0	1	.000	1	2	1	0	7	10	5	0	0	7.71
Ed Quick	L		0	1	.000	0	1	1	0	4	5	1	1	0	4.50
Snake Wiltse	L	31	0	3	.000	1	4	3	2	25	35	6	6	0	5.40

DETROIT 5th 65-71 .478 25 — WIN MERCER (DD) 0-0 .000 ED BARROW 65-71 .478

NAME	G by POS	B	AGE	G	AB	R	H	2B	3B	HR	RBI	BB	SO	SB	BA	SA
TOTALS			29	137	4582	567	1229	162	91	12	451	292		128	.268	.351
Charlie Carr	1B135	R	26	135	548	59	154	23	11	2	79	10		10	.281	.374
Heinie Smith	2B93	R	31	93	336	36	75	11	3	1	22	19		12	.223	.283
S. McAllister	SS46, C18, OF5, 3B4, 1B1	B	28	78	265	31	69	8	2	0	22	10		5	.260	.306
Joe Yeager	3B107, SS1, P1		27	109	402	36	103	15	6	0	43	18		9	.256	.323
Sam Crawford	OF137	L	23	137	545	93	181	23	**25**	4	89	25		23	.332	.488
Jimmy Barrett	OF136	L	28	136	517	95	163	13	10	2	31	**74**		27	.315	.391
Billy Lush	OF101, 3B12, 2B3, SS1	B	29	119	423	71	116	18	14	1	33	70		14	.274	.390
Deacon McGuire	C69, 1B1	R	37	72	248	15	62	12	1	0	21	19		3	.250	.306
Fritz Buelow	C60, 1B2	R	27	63	192	24	41	3	6	1	13	6		4	.214	.307
2 Herman Long	SS38, 2B31	L	37	69	239	21	53	12	0	0	23	10		11	.222	.272
George Mullin	P41, OF1	R	22	46	126	11	35	9	1	1	12	2		1	.278	.389
1 Kid Elberfeld	SS34, 3B1	R	28	35	132	29	45	5	3	0	19	11		6	.341	.424
1 Doc Gessler	OF28	L	22	29	105	9	25	5	4	0	12	3		1	.238	.362
2 Ernie Courtney	3B13, SS9	L	24	23	74	7	17	0	0	0	6	5		1	.230	.230
John Burns	2B11	R	26	11	37	2	10	0	0	0	3	1		0	.270	.270
Soldier Boy Murphy	SS5		24	5	22	1	4	1	0	0	1	0		0	.182	.227
Simon Nicholls	SS2	L	20	2	8	0	3	0	0	0	0	0		0	.375	.375
2 Patsy Greene	3B1		28	1	3	0	0	0	0	0	0	0		0	.000	.000
Sam McMackin (DD)																
Win Mercer (DD) 28																

NAME	T	AGE	W	L	PCT	SV	G	GS	CG	IP	H	BB	SO	ShO	ERA
		26	65	71	.478	3	137	137	123	1196	1169	**336**	554	15	2.75
George Mullin	R	22	19	14	.576	**3**	41	36	31	321	284	**106**	170	6	2.24
Wild Bill Donovan	R	26	17	16	.515	0	35	34	**34**	307	247	95	187	4	2.29
Frank Kitson	R	31	15	15	.500	0	31	28	28	258	277	38	102	2	2.58
Rube Kisinger	R	26	7	9	.438	0	16	14	13	119	118	27	33	2	2.95
1 John Deering	R	25	3	6	.333	0	10	8	5	61	77	24	14	0	3.84
John Skopec	L	23	2	2	.500	0	6	5	3	39	46	13	14	0	3.46
Mal Eason	R	24	2	4	.333	0	7	6	6	56	60	19	21	1	3.38
Alex Jones	L	36	0	2	.000	0	2	2	0	9	19	6	2	0	12.00
Harry Kane	L	19	0	2	.000	0	3	3	2	18	26	8	10	0	8.50
Joe Yeager		27	0	1	.000	0	1	1	1	9	15	0	1	0	4.00

ST. LOUIS 6th 65-74 .468 26.5 — JIMMY McALEER

NAME	G by POS	B	AGE	G	AB	R	H	2B	3B	HR	RBI	BB	SO	SB	BA	SA
TOTALS			28	139	4639	500	1133	166	68	12	408	271		101	.244	.317
John Anderson	1B133, OF7	B	29	138	550	65	156	34	8	2	78	23		16	.284	.385
Bill Friel	2B63, 3B24, OF9	L	27	97	351	46	80	11	8	0	25	23		4	.228	.305
Bobby Wallace	SS135	R	29	136	519	63	127	20	17	1	54	28		11	.245	.355
Hunter Hill	3B86		24	86	317	30	77	11	3	0	25	8		2	.243	.297
Charlie Hemphill	OF104	L	27	105	383	36	94	6	3	3	29	23		16	.245	.300
Snags Heidrick	OF119, C1		26	120	461	55	129	20	15	1	42	19		19	.280	.395
Jesse Burkett	OF132	L	34	133	514	74	152	20	7	3	40	52		16	.296	.379
Mike Kahoe	C71, OF2	R	29	77	244	26	46	7	5	0	23	11		1	.189	.258
Joe Sugden	C66, 1B8	B	32	79	243	25	52	4	0	0	22	25		5	.214	.230
1 Barry McCormick	2B28, 3B28, SS4		28	61	207	13	45	6	1	1	16	18		5	.217	.271
2 Joe Martin	OF38, 2B6, 3B1	L	27	44	173	18	37	6	4	0	7	6		0	.214	.295
Dick Padden (RJ)	2B29	R	22	29	94	7	19	3	0	0	6	9		5	.202	.234
Ben Bowcock	2B14		23	14	50	7	16	3	1	1	10	3		1	.320	.480
Pinky Swander	OF14	L	22	14	51	9	14	2	2	0	6	10		0	.275	.392
Owen Shannon	C8, 1B1	R	17	9	28	1	6	2	0	0	3	1		0	.214	.286
Claude Gouzzie	2B1	R	32	1	1	0	0	0	0	0	0	0		0	.000	.000

NAME	T	AGE	W	L	PCT	SV	G	GS	CG	IP	H	BB	SO	ShO	ERA
		28	65	74	.468	**5**	139	139	124	1222	1220	237	511	12	2.77
Willie Sudhoff	R	28	21	16	.511	1	38	35	30	294	262	56	104	5	2.27
Jack Powell	R	28	15	19	.441	2	38	34	33	306	294	58	169	4	2.91
Ed Siever	L	25	14	15	.483	0	31	27	24	254	245	39	90	1	2.48
1 Red Donahue	R	30	7	6	.538	1	16	15	14	131	145	22	51	0	2.75
Barney Pelty	R	22	3	3	.500	1	7	6	5	49	49	15	20	0	2.39
2 Clarence Wright	R	24	2	4	.333	0	8	8	7	61	73	16	37	1	3.69
John Terry			1	0	1.000	0	3	1	1	18	21	4	2	0	2.50
2 LeRoy Evans	R	29	1	4	.200	0	7	7	4	54	66	14	24	0	4.17
1 Bill Reidy	R	29	1	5	.167	0	5	5	5	43	53	7	8	1	3.98
Cy Morgan	R	24	0	2	.000	0	2	1	1	13	12	6	6	0	4.15

CHICAGO 7th 60-77 .438 30.5 — NIXEY CALLAHAN

NAME	G by POS	B	AGE	G	AB	R	H	2B	3B	HR	RBI	BB	SO	SB	BA	SA
TOTALS			29	138	4670	516	1152	176	49	14	436	325		180	.247	.314
Frank Isbell	1B117, 3B19, 2B2, SS1, OF1	L	27	138	546	52	132	25	9	2	59	12		26	.242	.332
2 Maggie Magoon	2B94	R	28	94	334	32	76	11	3	0	25	30		4	.228	.278
Lee Tannehill	SS138	R	22	138	503	48	113	14	3	2	50	25		10	.225	.276
Nixey Callahan	3B102, OF8, P3	R	29	118	439	47	128	26	5	2	56	20		24	.292	.387
Danny Green	OF133	L	26	135	499	75	154	26	7	6	62	47		29	.309	.425
Fielder Jones	OF136	L	31	136	530	71	152	18	5	0	45	47		21	.287	.340
2 Ducky Holmes	OF82, 3B3	L	34	86	344	53	96	7	5	0	18	25		25	.279	.328
Ed McFarland	C56, 1B1	R	28	61	201	15	42	7	2	1	19	14		3	.209	.279
Bill Hallman	OF57		27	63	207	29	43	7	4	0	18	31		11	.208	.280
2 Jack Slattery	C56, 1B5	R	26	63	211	8	46	3	2	0	20	2		2	.218	.251
1 Tom Daly	2B43	B	37	43	150	20	31	11	0	0	19	20		6	.207	.280
Billy Sullivan (IL)	C31	R	28	32	111	10	21	4	0	1	7	5		3	.189	.252
1 Cozy Dolan	1B19, OF4	L	30	27	104	16	27	5	1	0	7	6		5	.260	.327
Pep Clark	3B15	R	20	15	65	7	20	4	2	0	9	2		5	.308	.431

NAME	T	AGE	W	L	PCT	SV	G	GS	CG	IP	H	BB	SO	ShO	ERA
		25	60	77	.438	**5**	138	138	114	1235	1233	287	391	9	3.02
Doc White	L	24	17	16	.515	0	37	36	29	300	258	69	114	3	2.13
Roy Patterson	R	26	14	15	.483	2	34	30	26	293	275	69	89	2	2.70
Patsy Flaherty	L	27	11	**25**	.306	0	40	34	29	294	**338**	50	65	2	3.73
Frank Owen	R	23	8	12	.400	1	26	20	15	167	167	44	66	1	3.50
1 Davey Dunkle	R	30	5	4	.556	1	12	7	6	82	96	31	26	0	4.06
2 Nick Altrock	L	26	4	3	.571	1	12	8	6	71	59	19	19	1	2.15
Nixey Callahan	R	29	1	2	.333	0	3	3	3	28	40	5	12	0	4.50

WASHINGTON 8th 43-94 .314 47.5 — TOM LOFTUS

NAME	G by POS	B	AGE	G	AB	R	H	2B	3B	HR	RBI	BB	SO	SB	BA	SA
TOTALS			30	140	4613	437	1066	172	72	17	372	257		131	.231	.311
Boileryard Clarke	1B88, C37	R	34	126	465	35	111	14	6	2	38	15		12	.239	.308
2 Barry McCormick	2B63		28	63	219	14	47	10	2	0	23	10		3	.215	.279
Charlie Moran (LJ)	SS96, 2B2		24	98	373	41	84	14	5	1	24	33		8	.225	.298
Bill Coughlin	3B119, SS4, 2B2	R	24	125	470	57	118	18	3	1	31	9		30	.251	.309
Watty Lee	OF47, P22	L	23	75	231	17	48	8	4	0	13	18		5	.208	.277
Jimmy Ryan	OF114	R	40	114	436	41	107	26	4	7	46	17		11	.245	.372
Kip Selbach	OF140, 3B1	R	31	140	533	68	134	23	12	3	49	41		20	.251	.356
2 Mal Kittredge	C60	R	33	60	192	8	41	4	1	0	16	10		1	.214	.245
R. Robinson	2B45, OF30, SS24, 3B5			103	373	41	79	10	8	1	20	33		16	.212	.290
Al Orth	P36, SS7, OF4, 1B2	R	30	55	162	19	49	9	7	0	11	4		3	.302	.444
Lew Drill	C47, 1B3	R	26	51	154	11	39	9	3	0	23	15		4	.253	.351
Scoops Carey (BZ)	1B47	R	32	48	183	8	37	3	2	0	23	4		0	.202	.240
Ed Delahanty (DD)	OF40, 1B1	R	35	43	156	22	52	11	1	1	21	12		3	.338	.436
1 Joe Martin	2B15, 3B13, OF7	R	27	35	119	11	27	4	5	0	7	5		2	.227	.345
Jack Hendricks	OF32	L	28	32	112	10	20	1	3	0	4	13		3	.179	.241
1 Ducky Holmes	OF14, 3B4, 2B2	L	34	21	71	13	16	3	1	1	8	5		10	.225	.338
Gene DeMontreville (BF)	2B11, SS1	R	29	11	40	0	12	2	0	0	3	0		0	.300	.350
Champ Osteen	SS10	L	26	10	40	4	8	0	2	0	4	2		0	.200	.300

NAME	T	AGE	W	L	PCT	SV	G	GS	CG	IP	H	BB	SO	ShO	ERA
		26	43	**94**	.314	3	140	140	122	1224	**1333**	306	452	6	3.82
Al Orth	R	30	10	21	.323	2	36	32	30	280	326	62	88	2	4.34
Casey Patten	L	27	10	23	.303	1	36	34	32	300	313	80	133	0	3.60
Watty Lee	L	23	8	13	.381	0	22	20	15	167	169	40	70	2	3.07
Highball Wilson	R		8	18	.308	0	30	28	25	242	269	43	56	1	3.31
2 Davey Dunkle	R	30	5	8	.385	0	14	13	10	108	111	33	51	0	4.25
Jack Townsend	R	24	2	11	.154	0	20	13	10	127	145	48	54	0	4.75

PITTSBURGH 1st 91-49 .650 — **FRED CLARKE**

NAME	G by POS	B	AGE	G	AB	R	H	2B	3B	HR	RBI	BB	SO	SB	BA	SA
TOTALS			27	141	4991	792	1430	208	110	34	650	364		172	.287	.393
Kitty Bransfield	1B127	R	28	127	505	69	134	23	7	2	57	33		13	.265	.350
Claude Ritchey	2B137	B	29	138	506	66	145	28	10	0	59	55		15	.287	.381
Honus Wagner	SS111, OF12, 1B6	R	29	129	512	97	182	30	19	5	101	44		46	.355	.518
Tommy Leach	3B127	R	25	127	507	97	151	16	17	7	87	40		22	.298	.438
Jimmy Sebring	OF124	L	21	124	506	71	140	16	13	4	64	32		20	.277	.383
Ginger Beaumont	OF141	L	26	141	613	137	209	30	6	7	68	44		23	.341	.444
Fred Clarke	OF101, SS2	L	30	104	427	88	150	32	15	5	70	41		21	.351	.532
Eddie Phelps	C76, 1B3	R	24	81	273	32	77	7	3	2	31	17		2	.282	.352
Otto Krueger	SS29, OF28, 3B13, 2B3	R	26	80	256	42	63	6	8	1	20	21		5	.246	.344
Harry Smith (RJ)	C60, OF1	R	28	61	212	15	37	3	2	0	19	12		2	.175	.208
Brickyard Kennedy (PJ)	P18	R	34	23	58	7	21	4	3	0	10	2		0	.362	.534
2 Art Weaver	C11, 1B5	R	24	16	48	8	11	0	1	0	3	2		0	.229	.271
Joe Marshall	OF3, SS3, 2B1			10	23	2	6	1	2	0	2	0		0	.261	.478
George Merritt	OF7, P1		23	9	27	4	4	0	1	0	3	2		1	.148	.222
Fred Carisch	C4	R	21	5	18	4	6	4	0	1	5	0		0	.333	.722
Eude Curtis	OF5		26	5	19	2	8	1	0	0	3	1		0	.421	.474
Hans Lobert	3B3, 2B1, SS1	R	21	5	13	1	1	1	0	0	0	1		1	.077	.154
Solly Hofman	OF2	R	20	3	2	1	0	0	0	0	0	0		0	.000	.000
Bill Gray	OF2	R	30	2	6	1	2	0	0	0	1	1		0	.333	.333
Ernie Diehl	OF1	R	25	1	3	0	1	0	0	0	0	0		0	.333	.333
Lou Gertenrich	OF1	R	28	1	3	0	0	0	0	0	0	0		0	.000	.000

NAME	T	AGE	W	L	PCT	SV	G	GS	CG	IP	H	BB	SO	ShO	ERA
		31	91	49	.650	5	141	141	117	1251	1215	384	454	15	2.91
Sam Leever	R	31	25	7	.781	1	36	34	30	284	255	60	90	7	2.06
Deacon Phillippe	R	31	24	9	.727	2	36	33	31	289	269	29	123	4	2.43
Ed Doheny (IL)	L	28	16	8	.667	2	27	25	22	223	209	89	75	2	3.19
Brickyard Kennedy (PJ)	R	35	9	6	.600	0	18	15	10	125	130	57	39	0	3.46
Bucky Veil	R	21	5	3	.625	0	12	6	4	71	70	36	20	0	3.80
Kaiser Wilhelm	R	29	5	3	.625	0	12	9	7	86	88	25	20	1	3.24
Lafe Winham	L	21	3	1	.750	0	5	4	3	36	33	21	22	1	2.25
Gus Thompson	R	26	2	2	.500	0	5	4	3	43	52	16	22	0	3.56
Cy Falkenberg	R	23	2	5	.286	0	10	6	3	56	65	32	24	0	3.86
George Merritt	R	23	0	0	.000	0	1	0	0	4	4	1	2	0	2.25
Lew Moren	R	19	0	1	.000	0	1	1	1	6	9	2	2	0	9.00
Doc Scanlan	R	22	0	1	.000	0	1	1	1	9	5	6	0	0	4.00
Jack Pfiester	L	25	0	3	.000	0	3	3	2	19	26	10	15	0	6.16

NEW YORK 2nd 84-55 .604 6.5 — **JOHN McGRAW**

NAME	G by POS	B	AGE	G	AB	R	H	2B	3B	HR	RBI	BB	SO	SB	BA	SA
TOTALS			30	142	4741	729	1290	181	49	20	570	379		264	.272	.344
Dan McGann	1B129	B	31	129	482	75	130	21	6	3	50	32		36	.270	.357
Billy Gilbert	2B128	R	27	128	413	62	104	9	0	1	40	41		37	.252	.281
Charlie Babb	SS113, 3B8	B	30	121	424	68	105	15	8	0	46	45		22	.248	.321
Billy Lauder	3B108	R	29	108	395	52	111	13	0	0	53	14		19	.281	.314
George Browne	OF141	L	27	141	591	105	185	20	3	3	45	43		27	.313	.372
Roger Bresnahan	OF84, 1B13, C11, 3B4	R	24	113	406	87	142	30	8	4	55	61		34	.350	.493
Sam Mertes	OF137, 1B1, C1	R	30	138	517	100	145	32	14	7	104	61		45	.280	.437
John Warner	C85	L	30	89	285	38	81	8	5	0	34	7		5	.284	.347
George Van Haltren	OF75	L	37	84	280	42	72	6	1	0	28	28		14	.257	.286
Jack Dunn	SS27, 3B25, 2B19, OF1	R	30	78	257	35	62	15	1	0	37	15		12	.241	.307
Frank Bowerman	C55, 1B4, OF1	R	34	64	210	22	58	6	2	1	31	6		5	.276	.338
Christy Mathewson	P45	R	24	45	124	13	28	3	0	1	20	8		1	.226	.274
John McGraw	OF2, 2B2, SS1, 3B1	L	30	12	11	2	3	0	0	0	1	1		1	.273	.273
George Davis (KP)	SS4	B	32	4	15	2	4	0	0	0	1	1		0	.267	.267

NAME	T	AGE	W	L	PCT	SV	G	GS	CG	IP	H	BB	SO	ShO	ERA
		28	84	55	.604	8	142	142	116	1262	1257	371	628	8	2.95
Joe McGinnity	R	32	31	20	.608	2	55	48	44	434	391	109	171	3	2.43
Christy Mathewson	R	24	30	13	.698	2	45	42	37	366	321	100	267	3	2.26
Dummy Taylor	R	28	13	13	.500	0	33	31	18	245	306	89	94	1	4.22
Jack Cronin	R	29	6	4	.600	1	20	11	8	116	130	37	50	0	3.80
Red Ames	R	20	2	0	1.000	0	2	2	2	14	5	8	14	1	1.29
Roscoe Miller	R	26	2	5	.286	3	15	8	6	85	101	24	30	0	4.13
Bill Bartley	R	18	0	0	.000	0	1	0	0	3	3	4	2	0	0.00

CHICAGO 3rd 82-56 .594 8 — **FRANK SELEE**

NAME	G by POS	B	AGE	G	AB	R	H	2B	3B	HR	RBI	BB	SO	SB	BA	SA
TOTALS			26	139	4733	695	1300	191	62	9	548	422		259	.275	.347
Frank Chance	1B121, C2	R	25	125	441	83	144	24	10	2	81	78		67	.327	.440
Johnny Evers	2B110, SS11, 3B2	L	21	124	464	70	136	27	7	0	52	19		25	.293	.381
Joe Tinker	SS107, 3B17	R	22	124	460	67	134	21	7	2	70	37		27	.291	.380
Doc Casey	3B112	L	32	112	435	56	126	8	3	1	40	19		11	.290	.329
Dick Harley	OF103	L	30	104	386	72	89	9	1	0	33	45		27	.231	.259
Davy Jones	OF130	L	23	130	497	64	140	18	3	1	62	53		15	.282	.336
Jimmy Slagle	OF139	L	29	139	543	104	162	20	6	0	44	81		33	.298	.357
Johnny Kling	C132	R	28	132	491	67	146	29	13	3	68	22		23	.297	.428
2 Otto Williams	SS26, 2B7, 1B3, 3B1	R	25	38	130	14	29	5	0	0	13	4		8	.223	.262
Bobby Lowe (BK)	2B22, 1B6, 3B1	R	34	32	105	14	28	5	3	0	15	4		5	.267	.371
Tommy Raub	C12, 1B6, OF5, 3B4	R	32	36	84	6	19	3	2	0	7	5		3	.226	.310
2 Jack McCarthy	OF24	L	34	24	101	11	28	5	0	0	14	4		8	.277	.327
1 John Dobbs	OF16	L	27	16	61	8	14	1	1	0	4	7		0	.230	.279
Jim Cook	OF5, 2B2, 1B1	R	23	8	26	3	4	1	0	0	2	2		1	.154	.192
Bill Hanlon	1B8			8	21	4	2	0	0	0	2	6		1	.095	.095
George Moriarty	3B1	R	18	1	5	1	0	0	0	0	0	0		0	.000	.000
Larry McLean	C1	R	21	1	4	0	0	0	0	0	1	1		0	.000	.000

NAME	T	AGE	W	L	PCT	SV	G	GS	CG	IP	H	BB	SO	ShO	ERA
		28	82	56	.594	6	139	139	117	1240	1182	354	451	6	2.77
Jack Taylor	R	29	21	14	.600	1	37	33	33	312	277	57	83	1	2.45
Jake Weimer	L	29	20	8	.714	0	35	33	27	282	241	104	128	3	2.30
2 Bob Wicker	R	25	20	9	.690	1	32	27	24	247	236	74	110	1	3.02
Carl Lundgren	R	23	11	9	.550	3	27	20	16	193	191	60	67	0	2.94
Jacko Menefee	R	35	8	10	.444	0	20	17	13	147	157	38	39	1	3.00
Alex Hardy	L	26	1	1	.500	0	3	3	1	13	21	7	4	0	6.23
2 Clarence Currie	R	24	1	2	.333	1	6	3	2	33	35	9	9	0	3.00
1 Jack Doscher	L	22	0	1	.000	0	1	1	0	3	6	2	5	0	12.00
Peaches Graham	R	26	0	1	.000	0	1	1	0	5	9	3	4	0	5.40
1 Pop Williams	R	29	0	1	.000	0	1	1	1	5	9	0	2	0	5.40

CINCINNATI 4th 74-65 .532 16.5 — **JOE KELLEY**

NAME	G by POS	B	AGE	G	AB	R	H	2B	3B	HR	RBI	BB	SO	SB	BA	SA
TOTALS			31	141	4857	764	1399	228	92	28	652	403		144	.288	.390
Jake Beckley	1B119	L	35	120	459	85	150	29	10	2	81	42		23	.327	.447
2 Tom Daly	2B79	B	37	80	307	42	90	14	9	1	38	16		5	.293	.407
Tommy Corcoran	SS115	R	34	115	459	61	113	18	7	2	73	12		12	.246	.329
Harry Steinfeldt	3B104, SS14	R	25	118	439	71	137	32	12	6	83	47		6	.312	.481
2 Cozy Dolan	OF93	L	30	93	385	64	111	20	3	0	58	28		11	.288	.356
Cy Seymour	OF135	L	30	135	558	85	191	25	15	7	72	33		25	.342	.478
Mike Donlin	OF118, 1B7	L	25	126	496	110	174	25	18	7	67	56		26	.351	.516
Heinie Peitz	C78, 1B11, 3B9, 2B4	R	30	105	358	45	93	15	3	0	42	37		7	.260	.318
Joe Kelley	OF67, SS12, 2B11, 3B8, 1B6	R	31	105	383	85	121	22	4	3	45	51		18	.316	.418
Bill Bergen	C58	R	30	58	207	21	47	4	2	0	19	7		2	.227	.266
1 Maggie Magoon	2B32, 3B9	R	28	42	139	6	30	6	0	0	9	19		2	.216	.259
Jack Morrissey	2B17, OF8, SS2	B	26	29	89	14	22	1	0	0	9	14		3	.247	.258
Charlie DeArmond	3B11	R	26	11	39	10	11	2	1	0	7	3		1	.282	.385
Pete Cregan	OF6	R	28	6	19	0	2	0	0	0	0	1		0	.105	.105
Emil Haberer	C4	R	25	5	13	1	1	0	0	0	0	2		0	.077	.077
Lee Fohl	C4	L	32	4	14	3	5	1	1	0	2	0		0	.357	.571
Pat Deisel	C1	R	27	2	0	0	0	0	0	0	0	1		0	.000	.000
Harry Wood	OF2	L		2	3	0	0	0	0	0	0	1		0	.000	.000
Dan Kerwin	OF2	L	23	2	6	1	4	1	0	0	1	2		0	.667	.833

NAME	T	AGE	W	L	PCT	SV	G	GS	CG	IP	H	BB	SO	ShO	ERA
		29	74	65	.532	1	141	141	126	1230	1277	378	480	11	3.07
Noodles Hahn	L	24	22	12	.647	0	34	34	34	296	297	47	127	5	2.52
Jack Sutthoff	R	30	16	10	.615	0	30	27	21	225	207	79	76	3	2.80
Bob Ewing	R	30	14	13	.519	1	29	28	27	247	254	64	104	1	2.77
Ed Poole	R	28	8	13	.381	0	25	21	18	184	188	77	73	1	3.28
Bill Phillips	R	34	7	6	.538	0	16	13	11	118	134	30	46	1	3.36
Jack Harper	R	25	7	8	.467	0	17	15	13	135	143	70	45	0	4.33
Cy Hooker	R	23	0	0	.000	0	1	0	0	2	2	2	0	0	0.00
Jimmy Wiggs	R	26	0	1	.000	0	2	1	0	5	12	2	2	0	5.40
Rip Reagan	R	21	0	2	.000	0	3	2	2	18	40	7	7	0	6.00

BROOKLYN 5th 70-66 .515 19 — **NED HANLON**

NAME	G by POS	B	AGE	G	AB	R	H	2B	3B	HR	RBI	BB	SO	SB	BA	SA
TOTALS			27	139	4534	666	1201	177	56	15	539	522		273	.265	.339
Jack Doyle	1B139	R	33	139	524	84	164	27	6	0	91	54		34	.313	.387
Tim Flood	2B84, SS2, OF1	R	26	89	309	27	77	15	2	0	32	15		14	.249	.311
Bill Dahlen	SS138	R	33	138	474	71	124	17	9	1	64	82		34	.262	.342
Sammy Strang	3B124, OF8, 2B3	B	26	135	508	101	138	21	5	0	38	75		46	.272	.333
Judge McCredie	OF56	L	26	56	213	40	69	5	0	0	20	24		10	.324	.347
2 John Dobbs	OF110	L	27	111	414	61	98	15	7	2	59	48		23	.237	.321
Jimmy Sheckard	OF139	L	24	139	515	99	171	29	9	9	75	75		67	.332	.476
Lew Ritter	C74, OF2	R	27	78	259	26	61	9	6	0	37	19		9	.236	.317
Dutch Jordan	2B54, 3B18, OF4, 1B1	R	23	78	267	27	63	11	1	0	21	19		9	.236	.285
Fred Jacklitsch	C53, 2B1, OF1	R	27	60	176	31	47	8	3	1	21	33		4	.267	.364
2 Doc Gessler	OF43	L	22	49	154	20	38	8	3	0	18	17		9	.247	.330
1 Tom McCreery	OF38	R	28	40	141	13	37	5	2	0	10	20		5	.262	.326
Hugh Hearne	C17, 1B2	R	30	26	57	8	16	3	2	0	4	3		2	.281	.404
Ed Householder	OF12		33	12	43	5	9	0	0	0	9	2		3	.209	.209
Henry Thielman	OF5, P4	R	22	9	23	3	5	1	0	1	2	5		0	.217	.391
Hughie Jennings	OF4	R	34	6	17	2	4	0	0	0	1	1		1	.235	.235
Matt Broderick	2B1	R	26	2	2	0	0	0	0	0	1	0		0	.000	.000
Frank McManus	C2		27	2	7	0	0	0	0	0	0	0		0	.000	.000
Ed Hug	C1	R	22	1	0	0	0	0	0	0	0	1		0	.000	.000

NAME	T	AGE	W	L	PCT	SV	G	GS	CG	IP	H	BB	SO	ShO	ERA
		28	70	66	.515	4	139	139	118	1221	1276	377	438	11	3.44
Henry Schmidt	R	30	22	13	.629	2	40	36	29	301	321	120	96	5	3.83
Oscar Jones	R	24	19	14	.576	0	38	36	31	324	320	77	95	4	2.94
Ned Garvin	R	29	15	18	.455	2	38	34	30	298	277	84	154	2	3.08
2 Bill Reidy	R	29	6	7	.462	0	15	13	11	104	130	14	21	0	3.46
1 LeRoy Evans	R	29	5	9	.357	0	15	12	9	110	121	41	42	0	3.27
Grant Thatcher	R	26	3	1	.750	0	4	4	4	28	33	7	9	0	2.89
2 Jack Doscher	L	22	0	0	.000	0	3	0	0	7	8	9	4	0	7.71
2 Bill Pounds			0	0	.000	0	1	0	0	6	8	2	2	0	6.00
Rube Vickers	R	25	0	1	.000	0	4	1	1	14	27	9	5	0	10.93
Henry Thielman	R	22	0	3	.000	0	4	3	3	29	31	14	10	0	4.66

NAME	G by POS	B	AGE	G	AB	R	H	2B	3B	HR	RBI	BB	SO	SB	BA	SA
BOSTON 6th 58-80 .420 32	AL BUCKENBERGER															
TOTALS			27	140	4682	575	1145	176	47	25	479	398		159	.245	.318
Fred Tenney	1B122	L	31	122	447	79	140	22	3	3	41	70		21	.313	.396
Ed Abbaticchio	2B116, SS17	R	26	136	489	61	111	18	5	1	46	52		23	.227	.290
Harry Aubrey	SS94, 2B1, OF1		22	96	325	26	69	8	2	0	27	18		7	.212	.249
Ed Gremminger	3B140	R	29	140	511	57	135	24	9	5	56	31		12	.264	.376
Pat Carney	OF92, P10, 1B1	L	26	110	392	37	94	12	4	1	49	28		10	.240	.298
Charlie Dexter	OF106, SS9, C6		27	123	457	82	102	15	1	3	34	61		32	.223	.280
Dick Cooley	OF126, 1B13	L	30	138	553	76	160	26	10	1	70	44		27	.289	.378
Pat Moran	C107, 1B1	R	27	109	389	40	102	25	5	7	54	29		8	.262	.406
Joe Stanley	OF77, SS1, P1	B	22	86	308	40	77	12	5	1	47	18		10	.250	.331
Frank Bonner	2B24, SS22		33	48	173	11	38	5	0	1	10	7		2	.220	.266
1 Mal Kittredge	C30	R	33	32	99	10	21	2	0	0	6	11		1	.212	.232
2 Tom McCreery	OF23	R	28	23	83	15	18	2	1	1	10	9		6	.217	.301

NAME	T	AGE	W	L	PCT	SV	G	GS	CG	IP	H	BB	SO	ShO	ERA
		30	58	80	.420	1	140	140	125	1229	1310	**460**	516	5	3.34
Togie Pittinger	R	32	18	**22**	.450	1	44	39	35	352	**396**	**143**	140	0	3.48
Vic Willis	R	27	12	17	.414	0	33	32	29	278	256	88	125	2	2.98
John Malarkey		31	11	16	.407	0	32	27	25	253	266	96	98	2	3.09
Wiley Piatt	L	28	9	15	.375	0	25	23	18	181	198	61	100	0	3.18
Pat Carney	L	26	4	5	.444	0	10	9	9	78	93	31	29	0	4.04
3 Pop Williams	R	29	4	5	.444	0	10	10	9	83	97	37	20	1	4.12
Joe Stanley	R	22	0	0	.000	0	1	0	0	4	4	4	4	0	9.00

NAME	G by POS	B	AGE	G	AB	R	H	2B	3B	HR	RBI	BB	SO	SB	BA	SA
PHILADELPHIA 7th 49-86 .363 39.5	CHIEF ZIMMER															
TOTALS			29	139	4781	618	1283	186	62	12	500	338		120	.268	.341
Klondike Douglass	1B97	L	31	105	377	43	96	5	4	1	36	28		6	.255	.297
Kid Gleason	2B102, OF4	B	36	106	412	65	117	19	6	1	49	23		12	.284	.367
Rudy Hulswitt	SS138	R	26	138	519	56	128	22	9	1	58	28		10	.247	.329
Harry Wolverton	3B123		29	123	494	72	152	13	12	0	53	18		10	.308	.383
Bill Keister	OF100	R	28	100	400	53	128	27	7	3	63	14		11	.320	.445
Roy Thomas	OF130	L	29	130	477	88	156	11	2	1	27	**107**		17	.327	.365
Shad Barry	OF107, 1B30, 3B1	R	26	138	550	75	152	24	5	1	60	30		26	.276	.344
Frank Roth	C60, 3B1	R	24	68	220	27	60	11	4	0	22	9		3	.273	.359
John Titus	OF72	L	27	72	280	38	80	15	6	2	34	19		5	.286	.404
B. Hallman	2B22, 3B19, 1B9, OF4, SS3	R	36	63	198	20	42	11	2	0	17	16		2	.212	.288
Red Dooin	C51, 1B1, OF1	R	24	62	188	18	41	5	1	0	14	8		9	.218	.255
Chief Zimmer	C35	R	42	37	118	9	26	3	1	1	19	9		3	.220	.288
Roy Brashear	2B18, 1B2	R	29	20	75	9	17	3	0	0	4	6		2	.227	.267
Dutch Rudolph		L	20	1	1	0	0	0	0	0	0	0		0	.000	.000
John Walsh	3B1			1	3	0	0	0	0	0	0	0		0	.000	.000

NAME	T	AGE	W	L	PCT	SV	G	GS	CG	IP	H	BB	SO	ShO	ERA
		28	49	86	.363	3	139	139	**126**	1212	1347	425	381	5	3.97
Bill Duggleby	R	30	13	18	.419	2	36	30	28	264	318	79	57	3	3.75
Chick Fraser	R	32	12	17	.414	1	31	29	26	250	260	97	104	1	4.50
Fred Mitchell	R	25	11	15	.423	0	28	28	24	227	250	102	69	1	4.48
Tully Sparks	R	26	11	15	.423	0	28	28	27	248	248	56	88	0	2.72
2 Pop Williams	R	29	1	1	.500	0	2	2	2	18	21	6	8	0	3.00
John McFetridge		33	1	11	.083	0	14	13	11	103	120	49	31	0	4.89
Warry McLaughlin		27	0	2	.000	0	3	2	2	23	38	11	3	0	7.04
Fred Burchall	L	23	0	3	.000	0	6	3	2	44	48	14	12	0	2.86
Libe Washburn		29	0	4	.000	0	4	4	4	35	44	11	9	0	4.37

NAME	G by POS	B	AGE	G	AB	R	H	2B	3B	HR	RBI	BB	SO	SB	BA	SA
ST. LOUIS 8th 43-94 .314 46.6	PATSY DONOVAN															
TOTALS			28	139	4689	505	1176	138	65	8	407	277		171	.251	.313
Jim Hackett	1B89, P7	R	25	99	351	24	80	13	8	0	36	19		2	.228	311
John Farrell	2B118, OF12		26	130	519	83	141	25	8	1	32	48		17	.272	.356
Dave Brain	SS72, 3B46	R	24	119	464	44	107	8	15	1	60	25		21	.231	.319
Jimmy Burke	3B93, 2B15, OF5	R	28	115	431	55	123	13	3	0	42	23		28	.285	.329
Patsy Donovan	OF105	R	38	105	410	63	134	15	3	0	40	25		25	.327	.378
Homer Smoot	OF129	L	25	129	500	67	148	22	8	4	49	32		17	.296	.396
George Barclay	OF107		27	108	419	37	104	10	8	0	42	15		12	.248	.310
Jack O'Neill	C74	R	30	75	246	23	58	9	1	0	27	13		11	.236	.280
Jack Ryan	C47, 1B18, SS2	R	34	67	227	18	54	5	1	1	10	10		2	.238	.282
1 Otto Williams	SS52, 2B1	R	25	53	187	10	38	4	2	0	9	9		6	.203	.246
John Dunleavy	OF38, P14		23	61	193	23	48	3	3	0	10	13		10	.249	.295
Art Nichols	1B25, OF7, C2	R	31	36	120	13	23	2	0	0	9	12		9	.192	.208
Mike O'Neill	P19, OF13	L	25	41	110	12	25	2	2	0	6	8		3	.227	.282
Lee DeMontreville	SS15, 2B4, OF1	R	23	26	70	8	17	3	1	0	7	8		3	.243	.314
1 Art Weaver	C16		24	16	49	4	12	0	0	0	5	4		1	.245	.245
Harry Berte	2B3, SS1		31	4	15	1	5	0	0	0	1	1		0	.333	.333
John Coveney	C4		23	4	14	0	2	0	0	0	0	0		0	.143	.143
Lou Ury	1B2			2	7	0	1	0	0	0	0	0		0	.143	.143

NAME	T	AGE	W	L	PCT	SV	G	GS	CG	IP	H	BB	SO	ShO	ERA
		25	43	**94**	.314	2	139	139	111	1182	**1353**	430	419	4	3.76
Three Finger Brown	R	26	9	13	.409	0	26	24	19	201	231	59	83	1	2.60
Chappie McFarland	R		9	18	.333	0	28	26	25	229	253	48	76	1	3.07
John Dunleavy		23	6	8	.429	0	14	13	9	102	101	57	51	0	4.06
1 Bob Rhoades	R	23	5	8	.385	0	17	13	12	129	154	47	52	1	4.60
Ed Murphy	R	26	4	8	.333	0	15	12	9	106	108	38	16	0	3.31
1 Clarence Currie	R	24	4	12	.250	1	22	16	13	148	155	60	52	1	4.01
Mike O'Neill	L	25	4	13	.235	0	19	17	12	115	184	43	39	0	4.77
Jim Hackett	R	25	1	4	.200	1	7	6	5	48	47	18	21	0	3.75
War Sanders	L	25	1	6	.143	0	8	6	3	40	48	21	9	0	6.08
John Lovett		26	0	0	.000	0	3	1	0	5	6	5	3	0	5.40
Larry Milton			0	0	.000	0	1	0	0	4	3	1	0	.0	2.25
Ed Taylor			0	0	.000	0	1	0	0	3	0	0	1	0	0.00
1 Bob Wicker	R	25	0	0	.000	0	1	0	0	5	4	3	3	0	0.00
Hal Betts	R		0	1	.000	0	1	1	1	9	11	5	2	0	10.00
Pat Hynes		19	0	1	.000	0	1	1	1	9	10	6	1	0	4.00
Charlie Moran	R	25	0	1	.000	0	3	2	2	24	30	19	7	0	5.25
Stan Yerkes			0	1	.000	0	1	1	0	5	8	0	3	0	1.80

WORLD SERIES – BOSTON (AL) 5 PITTSBURGH (NL) 3

LINE SCORES

TEAM	1	2	3	4	5	6	7	8	9	10	11	12	R	H	E
Game 1 October 1 at Boston															
PIT (NL)	4	0	1	1	0	0	1	0	0				7	12	2
BOS (AL)	0	0	0	0	0	0	2	0	1				3	6	4
Phillippe Young															
Game 2 October 2 at Boston															
PIT	0	0	0	0	0	0	0	0	0				0	3	2
BOS	2	0	0	0	0	1	0	0	X				3	9	0
Leever, Veil (2) **Dinneen**															
Game 3 October 3 at Boston															
PIT	0	1	2	0	0	0	0	1	0				4	7	0
BOS	0	0	0	1	0	0	0	1	0				2	4	2
Phillippe Hughes, Young (3)															
Game 4 October 6 at Pittsburgh															
BOS	0	0	0	0	1	0	0	0	3				4	9	1
PIT	1	0	0	0	1	0	3	0	X				5	12	1
Dinneen **Phillippe**															
Game 5 October 7 at Pittsburgh															
BOS	0	0	0	0	0	6	4	1	0				11	14	2
PIT	0	0	0	0	0	0	0	2	0				2	6	4
Young Kennedy, Thompson (8)															
Game 6 October 8 at Pittsburgh															
BOS	0	0	3	0	2	0	1	0	0				6	10	1
PIT	0	0	0	0	0	0	3	0	0				3	0	0
Dinneen Leever															
Game 7 October 10 at Pittsburgh															
BOS	2	0	0	2	0	2	0	1	0				7	11	4
PIT	0	0	0	1	0	1	0	0	1				3	10	3
Young Phillippe															
Game 8 October 13 at Boston															
PIT	0	0	0	0	0	0	0	0	0				0	4	3
BOS	0	0	0	2	0	1	0	0	X				3	8	0
Dinneen Phillippe															

COMPOSITE BATTING

NAME	POS	G	AB	R	H	2B	3B	HR	RBI	BA
Boston (AL)										
Totals		8	232	39	71	4	16	2	**34**	.252
Collins	3B	8	**36**	5	9	1	2	0	1	.250
Dougherty	OF	8	34	3	8	0	2	**2**	5	.235
Stahl	OF	8	33	6	10	1	3	0	3	.303
Freeman	OF	8	32	6	9	0	3	0	4	.281
Parent	SS	8	32	**8**	9	0	3	0	4	.281
Ferris	2B	8	31	3	9	0	1	0	**5**	.290
LaChance	1B	8	27	5	6	**2**	1	0	4	.222
Criger	C	8	26	1	6	0	0	0	4	.231
Young	P	4	15	1	2	0	1	0	3	.133
Dinneen	P	4	12	1	3	0	0	0	0	.250
Farrell	PH	2	2	0	0	0	0	0	1	.000
O'Brien	PH	2	2	0	0	0	0	0	0	.000
Hughes	P	1	0	0	0	0	0	0	0	.000
Pittsburgh (NL)										
Totals		8	270	24	64	7	9	1	21	.237
Beaumont	OF	8	34	6	9	0	1	0	1	.265
Clarke	OF	8	34	3	9	**2**	1	0	**2**	.265
Leach	3B	8	33	3	9	0	**4**	0	**7**	.273
Sebring	OF	8	30	3	**11**	0	1	1	**3**	**.367**
Bransfield	1B	8	29	3	6	0	2	0	1	.207
Wagner	SS	8	27	2	6	1	0	0	3	.222
Ritchey	2B	8	27	2	3	1	0	0	2	.111
Phelps	C	8	26	1	6	**2**	0	0	1	.231
Phillippe	P	5	18	1	4	0	0	0	1	.222
Leever	P	2	4	0	0	0	0	0	0	.000
Smith	C	1	3	0	0	0	0	0	0	.000
Kennedy	P	1	2	0	1	1	0	0	0	.500
Veil	P	1	2	0	0	0	0	0	0	.000
Thompson	P	1	1	0	0	0	0	0	0	.000

COMPOSITE PITCHING

NAME	G	IP	H	BB	SO	W	L	SV	ERA
Boston (AL)									
Totals	8	71	64	14	45	5	3	0	2.15
Dinneen	4	35	29	**8**	**28**	**3**	1	0	2.06
Young	4	34	31	4	17	2	1	0	1.85
Hughes	1	2	4	2	0	0	1	0	9.00
Pittsburgh (NL)									
Totals	8	70	71	14	29	3	5	0	3.73
Phillippe	5	**44**	**38**	3	22	**3**	**2**	0	2.86
Leever	2	10	13	3	2	0	**2**	0	5.40
Veil	1	7	6	**5**	1	0	0	0	1.29
Kennedy	1	7	11	3	3	0	1	0	5.14
Thompson	1	2	3	0	1	0	0	0	4.50

1904 A. L.—Chesbro and the One That Got Away

Despite his three 20-win seasons since 1901, no one expected Jack Chesbro to have the sort of year he did for the New York Highlanders, turning in a masterful pitching performance and keeping them in the pennant race practically single-handedly. The stocky 30-year-old right-hander won 41 games, a modern baseball record which stands today; he started 51 games and completed all but three of them, a feat of stamina necessitated by the aging of Clark Griffith and the illness of Al Orth.

With Chesbro winning and winning, the Highlanders stayed in the midst of a five-team dogfight for the American League crown. In the final week, it came down to New York and the Boston Pilgrims, and the schedule-maker had shown enough foresight to match these two contenders against each other on the final weekend. The Highlanders took a half-game lead with a victory on October 7, but Boston swept a doubleheader the next day to go back in front by a game-and-a-half. A doubleheader on the tenth would settle it, with New York needing a sweep to cop the title. Jack Chesbro was handed the ball by manager Clark Griffith while Bill Dineen was given the call for Boston. As the enthusiastic 28,000 New York fans positioned themselves for the dramatics which were to unfold on the last day of the regular season, hopes were high for the Highlanders to win their first American League pennant; after all, New York was starting out with a plus 40-game winner, while all Boston had on the mound was a 22-game winner in Dineen.

In the third inning Chesbro started the action with a triple to right field. But he was left stranded, and the game went into the fifth inning before New York scored two runs behind three hits and two walks to take a 2-0 lead. In the seventh, with the score still at 2-0, a throwing error to the plate by second baseman Jimmy Williams allowed Boston to tie the game. Then, in the ninth, Chesbro gave a single to Lou Criger who, after a sacrifice and a ground out, found himself on third base. Chesbro's 42nd victory, or at least the thought of it, went the same route as the Highlanders' pennant dreams, as Happy Jack uncorked a wild pitch to allow Criger home with what turned out to be the winning run. Surprisingly enough, New York held on to take the meaningless second game, 1-0, in ten innings.

Boston's tooth and nail struggle for the pennant gave the American League its first repeat champion. Manager Jimmy Collins fielded a lineup which included stars, Chick Stahl, Buck Freeman, Freddy Parent, and Collins himself. Boston's long suit, though, was pitching; 37-year-old Cy Young kept rolling along with 26 wins, including a perfect game, and Bill Dineen and Jesse Tannehill each chipped in with 20-win seasons. The New York club continued its hot work of late 1903 by staying in contention all the way; Chesbro was the main shoulder at the wheel, but Willie Keeler's batting and Jack Powell's pitching also merited star acclaim. Chicago, Cleveland, and Philadelphia all had a chance to reach the top as late as September.

Nap Lajoie of Cleveland socked the ball at a .381 clip, nailing down his third American League batting crown in four years; Willie Keeler was runner-up with a .343 mark. Of the six .300 hitters in the league, Cleveland fielded three of them—Lajoie, Elmer Flick, and Bill Bradley. The hitting generally fell off as the league adopted the foul-strike rule, making all fouls before two strikes count as a strike. The National League had held the rule for two years, and this attempt to speed up play represented one of the major changes in the rules of the game of baseball.

Chesbro's 41 victories far and away paced the league in that department; Cy Young, unseated as leading winner for the first time since the league was formed, placed second with 26 wins. While Chesbro was setting a season mark for victories, Philadelphia's Rube Waddell blazed his way to a new strikeout record with 349. Addie Joss of Cleveland exhibited enough control to deny the trio at least one major pitching honor with his 1.59 E.R.A.

The American and National Leagues coexisted without incident during the season, but the fall witnessed an unfortunate turn of events. Down the stretch, the Highlanders and Pilgrims both offered to meet the National League champion New York Giants at the conclusion of the season to determine a world's champion. President John T. Brush of the Giants refused the offers, stating that the National League was the premier baseball organization in America and that its prestige should not be jeopardized by contending for a crown with minor leagues. With this snub, Brush declined to play the Series into which the champion owners of 1903 had voluntarily entered. Despite heavy press criticism, Brush remained adamant; later, Giant manager John McGraw admitted the chief responsibility for the decision, owing to his personal coolness towards American League President Ban Johnson. The second World Series went unplayed, and Boston claimed the title for itself by default.

1904 AMERICAN LEAGUE

NAME	G by POS	B	AGE	G	AB	R	H	2B	3B	HR	RBI	BB	SO	SB	BA	SA
BOSTON 1st 95-59 .617		JIMMY COLLINS														
TOTALS			31	157	5231	608	1294	194	**105**	26	522	347		101	.247	.340
Candy LaChance	1B157	B	34	157	573	55	130	19	5	1	47	23		7	.227	.283
Hobe Ferris	2B156	R	26	156	563	50	120	23	10	3	63	23		7	.213	.306
Freddy Parent	SS155	R	28	155	591	85	172	22	9	6	77	28		20	.291	.389
Jimmy Collins	3B156	R	34	156	633	85	168	32	13	3	67	27		19	.265	.371
Buck Freeman	OF157	L	32	157	598	64	166	20	19	7	84	32		11	.278	.410
Chick Stahl	OF157	L	31	157	583	84	173	27	**22**	3	67	64		13	.297	.434
2 Kip Selbach	OF98	R	32	98	376	50	97	19	8	0	30	48		10	.258	.351
Lou Criger	C95	R	32	98	299	34	63	10	5	2	34	27		1	.211	.298
Duke Farrell	C56	R	37	68	198	11	42	9	2	0	15	15		1	.212	.278
1 Patsy Dougherty	OF49	L	27	49	**195***	**33***	53	5	4	0	4	25		10	.272	.338
1 Bill O'Neill	OF9, SS2	B	24	17	51	7	10	1	0	0	5	2		0	.196	.216
2 Bob Unglaub	2B3, 3B2, SS1	R	22	9	13	1	2	1	0	0	2	1		0	.154	.231
Tom Doran	C11	L	24	12	32	1	4	0	1	0	0	4		1	.125	.188
NEW YORK 2nd 92-59 .609 1.5		CLARK GRIFFITH														
TOTALS			28	155	5220	598	**1354**	195	91	27	499	312		163	.259	.347
John Ganzel	1B118, 2B9, SS1	R	29	130	465	50	121	16	10	6	48	24		13	.260	.376
Jimmy Williams	2B146	R	27	146	559	62	147	31	7	2	74	38		14	.263	.354
Kid Elberfeld (LJ)	SS122	R	29	122	445	54	114	12	5	2	46	37		16	.256	.319
Wid Conroy	3B110, SS27, OF3	R	27	140	489	58	119	18	12	1	52	43		30	.243	.335
Willie Keeler	OF142	L	32	143	539	76	185	13	10	2	40	35		22	.343	.416
John Anderson	OF11, 1B33	B	30	143	558	62	155	27	12	3	82	23		20	.278	.385
2 Patsy Dougherty	OF106	L	27	106	**452***	**80***	128	13	10	6	22	19		11	.283	.396
Deacon McGuire	C97, 1B1	R	28	101	322	17	67	12	2	0	20	27		2	.208	.258
Dave Fultz	OF90	R	29	97	339	39	93	17	4	2	32	24		17	.274	.366
Red Kleinow	C62, 3B2, OF1	R	24	68	209	12	43	8	4	0	16	15		4	.206	.282
2 Jack Thoney	3B26, OF10	R	24	36	128	17	24	4	2	0	12	8		9	.188	.250
Champ Osteen	3B17, SS8, 1B4	L	27	28	107	15	21	1	4	2	9	1		0	.196	.336
1 Monte Beville	1B4, C3	L	29	9	22	2	6	2	0	0	2	2		0	.273	.364
1 Bob Unglaub	3B4, SS1	R	22	6	19	2	4	0	0	0	2	0		0	.211	.211
Orth Collins	OF5	L	24	5	17	3	6	1	1	0	1	1		0	.353	.529
Frank McManns	C4		28	4	7	0	0	0	0	0	0	0		0	.000	.000
Elmer Bliss	OF1	R	29	1	1	0	0	0	0	0	0	0		0	.000	.000
CHICAGO 3rd 89-65 .578 6		NIXEY CALLAHAN 22-18 .550 FIELDER JONES 67-47 .588														
TOTALS			29	156	5027	600	1217	193	68	14	519	**373**		**216**	.242	.316
Jiggs Donahue	1B101	L	24	102	367	47	92	9	8	1	48	25		21	.251	.327
Gus Dundon	2B103, 3B3, SS2	R	29	108	373	40	85	9	3	0	36	30		19	.228	.268
George Davis	SS152	B	33	152	558	74	143	25	14	1	69	43		32	.256	.357
Lee Tannehill	3B153	R	23	153	547	50	125	31	5	0	61	20		14	.229	.303
Danny Green	OF146	L	27	147	536	83	142	16	10	2	62	63		28	.265	.343
Fielder Jones	OF149	L	32	149	547	72	133	14	5	3	42	53		25	.243	.303
Nixey Callahan	OF104, 2B28	R	30	132	482	66	126	23	2	0	54	39		29	.261	.317
Billy Sullivan	C107	R	29	108	371	29	85	18	4	1	44	12		11	.229	.307
Frank Isbell	1B57, 2B27, OF5, SS4	L	28	96	314	27	66	10	3	1	34	16		19	.210	.271
Ducky Holmes	OF63	L	35	68	251	42	78	11	9	1	19	14		13	.311	.438
Ed McFarland	C49	R	29	50	160	22	44	11	3	0	20	17		2	.275	.381
Charlie Jones	OF5		28	5	17	2	4	0	1	0	1	1		0	.235	.353
Mike Heydon	C4		29	4	10	0	1	1	0	0	1	1		0	.100	.200
13Frank Huelsman	OF1	R	30	4	7	0	1	1	0	0	0	0		0	.143	.286
Claude Berry	C3	R	24	3	1	1	0	0	0	0	0	1		0	.000	.000

NAME	T	AGE	W	L	PCT	SV	G	GS	CG	IP	H	BB	SO	ShO	ERA
		29	**95**	59	**.617**	1	157	157	**148**	1406	1208	233	612	21	**2.12**
Cy Young	R	37	26	16	.619	1	43	41	40	380	327	29	200	**10**	1.97
Bill Dinneen	R	28	23	14	.622	0	37	37	37	336	283	63	153	5	2.20
Jesse Tannehill	L	29	21	11	.656	0	33	31	30	282	256	33	116	4	2.04
Norwood Gibson	R	27	17	14	.548	0	33	32	29	273	216	81	112	1	2.21
George Winter	R	26	8	4	.667	0	20	16	12	136	126	27	31	1	2.32

***Dougherty, also with New York, league leader in AB with 647 and R with 113**

NAME	T	AGE	W	L	PCT	SV	G	GS	CG	IP	H	BB	SO	ShO	ERA
		30	92	59	.609	1	155	155	123	1381	1180	311	684	15	2.57
Jack Chesbro	R	30	**41**	12	**.774**	0	**55**	**51**	**48**	**455**	338	88	239	6	1.82
Jack Powell	R	29	23	19	.548	0	47	45	38	390	340	92	202	3	2.44
2 Al Orth	R	31	11	3	.786	0	20	18	11	138	122	19	47	2	2.67
1 Long Tom Hughes	R	25	7	12	.368	0	19	18	12	136	141	48	75	1	3.71
Clark Griffith	R	34	6	5	.545	1	16	11	8	100	91	16	36	1	2.88
Ambrose Puttmann	L	23	2	2	.500	0	9	3	2	49	40	17	26	1	2.76
Walter Clarkson	R	25	2	3	.400	0	13	4	2	66	63	25	43	0	5.05
2 Ned Garvin	R	30	0	2	.000	0	2	2	0	12	14	2	8	0	2.25
1 Bill Wolfe	R	28	0	1	.000	0	7	3	2	34	31	4	8	0	3.18

***Dougherty, also with Boston, league leader in AB with 647 and R with 113**

NAME	T	AGE	W	L	PCT	SV	G	GS	CG	IP	H	BB	SO	ShO	ERA
		25	89	65	.578	**3**	156	156	134	1380	1161	303	550	**26**	2.30
Nick Altrock	L	27	21	13	.618	0	38	36	31	307	274	48	87	6	2.96
Frank Owen	R	24	21	15	.583	1	37	36	34	315	243	61	103	4	1.94
Frank Smith	R	24	16	10	.615	0	26	23	22	202	157	58	107	4	2.09
Doc White	L	25	16	10	.615	0	30	30	23	228	201	68	115	7	1.78
Roy Patterson	R	27	9	9	.500	0	22	17	14	165	148	24	64	4	2.29
Ed Walsh	R	23	5	5	.500	1	18	8	6	111	90	32	57	1	2.59
1 Patsy Flaherty	L	28	1	2	.333	0	5	5	4	43	36	10	14	0	2.09
Tom Dougherty	R	23	0	0	.000	1	1	0	0	2	0	0	0	0	0.00
Elmer Stricklett	R	27	0	1	.000	0	1	1	0	7	12	2	3	0	10.29

CLEVELAND 4th 86-65 .570 7.5 — BILL ARMOUR

	NAME	G by POS	B	AGE	G	AB	R	H	2B	3B	HR	RBI	BB	SO	SB	BA	SA
	TOTALS			27	154	5152	647	1340	225	90	27	553	307		178	.260	.354
1	Charley Hickman	1B40, 2B45, OF1	R	28	86	337	34	97	22	10	4	45	13		9	.288	.448
	Nap Lajoie	2B95, SS44, 1B2	R	28	140	554	92	211	50	14	6	102	27		31	.381	.554
	Terry Turner (IL)	SS111	R	23	111	404	41	95	9	6	1	45	11		5	.235	.295
	Bill Bradley	3B154	R	26	154	607	95	182	31	8	5	83	26		27	.300	.402
	Elmer Flick	OF144, 2B6	L	28	149	575	95	174	31	17	6	56	51		42	.303	.447
	Harry Bay	OF132	L	26	132	506	69	122	12	9	3	36	43		38	.241	.318
	Billy Lush	OF138	B	30	138	477	76	123	13	8	1	50	72		12	.258	.325
	Harry Bemis	C79, 1B13, 2B1	L	30	97	336	35	76	11	6	0	25	8		6	.226	.295
	George Stovall	1B38, 2B9, OF3, 3B1	R	25	51	182	18	54	9	1	1	31	2		4	.297	.374
	Fred Abbott	C33, 1B7	R	29	41	130	14	22	4	2	0	12	6		2	.169	.231
2	Fritz Buelow	C42	R	28	42	119	11	21	4	1	0	5	11		2	.176	.227
2	Charlie Carr	1B32	R	27	32	120	9	27	5	1	0	7	4		0	.225	.283
	Bill Schwartz	1B22, 3B1	R	20	24	86	5	13	2	0	0	0	0		4	.151	.174
	Claude Rossman	OF17	L	23	18	62	5	13	5	0	0	6	0		0	.210	.290
	Rube Vinson	OF15		25	15	49	12	15	1	0	0	2	10		2	.306	.327
	Harry Ostdiek	C7	R	23	7	18	1	3	0	1	0	3	3		1	.167	.278
	Mike Donovan	SS1	R	22	2	2	0	0	0	0	0	0	0		0	.000	.000

	NAME	T	AGE	W	L	PCT	SV	G	GS	CG	IP	H	BB	SO	ShO	ERA
			27	86	65	.570	1	154	154	141	1357	1273	285	627	20	2.22
	Bill Bernhard	R	33	21	13	.618	1	38	37	35	321	323	55	137	4	2.13
	Red Donahue	R	31	19	14	.576	0	35	32	30	277	281	49	127	6	2.40
	Addie Joss (IL)	R	24	14	9	.609	0	25	24	20	192	160	30	83	5	1.59
	Earl Moore	R	24	13	11	.542	0	26	24	22	228	186	61	139	1	2.25
	Bob Rhoades	R	24	10	9	.526	0	22	19	18	175	175	48	72	0	2.88
	Otto Hess	L	25	9	7	.563	0	21	16	15	151	134	31	64	4	1.67
	John Hickey	R	22	0	2	.000	0	2	2	1	12	14	11	5	0	7.50

PHILADELPHIA 5th 81-70 .536 12.5 — CONNIE MACK

	NAME	G by POS	B	AGE	G	AB	R	H	2B	3B	HR	RBI	BB	SO	SB	BA	SA
	TOTALS			31	155	5088	557	1266	197	77	31	486	313		137	.249	.336
	Harry Davis	1B102	R	30	102	403	54	124	22	12	12	62	23		15	.308	.511
	Danny Murphy	2B150	R	27	149	550	80	158	29	18	7	77	22		22	.287	.444
	Monte Cross	SS153	R	34	153	503	33	95	23	4	1	38	46		19	.189	.256
	Lave Cross	3B155	R	38	155	607	80	177	29	10	1	71	13		13	.290	.377
	Socks Seybold	OF129, 1B13	R	33	143	511	55	144	25	11	3	64	42		12	.282	.391
	Ollie Pickering	OF121	L	34	124	455	56	103	10	3	0	30	45		17	.226	.262
	Topsy Hartsel	OF147	L	30	147	534	79	135	17	12	2	25	75		19	.253	.341
	Ossee Schreckengost	C84, 1B9	R	29	95	311	23	58	9	1	1	21	5		3	.186	.232
	Mike Powers	C56, OF1	R	33	57	184	11	35	3	0	0	11	6		3	.190	.207
	Danny Hoffman (IJ)	OF51	L	24	53	204	31	61	7	5	3	24	5		9	.299	.426
13	Jim Mullin	1B26, 2B5, SS2, OF1	R	20	41	110	9	24	1	0	1	9	5		4	.218	.255
	Pete Noonan	C22, 1B10	R	22	39	114	13	23	3	1	2	13	1		1	.202	.298
	Lou Bruce	OF25, P2, 2B1, 3B1	L	27	30	101	9	27	3	0	0	8	5		2	.267	.297

	NAME	T	AGE	W	L	PCT	SV	G	GS	CG	IP	H	BB	SO	ShO	ERA
			25	81	70	.536	0	155	155	137	1361	1149	366	887	26	2.35
	Eddie Plank	L	28	26	17	.605	0	43	43	37	357	309	86	201	7	2.14
	Rube Waddell	L	27	26	17	.605	0	46	46	39	383	307	91	349	8	1.62
	Weldon Henley	R	23	14	17	.452	0	36	34	31	296	245	76	130	5	2.52
	Andy Coakley	R	21	4	4	.500	0	8	8	8	62	50	23	33	2	2.03
	Chief Bender	R	21	10	11	.476	0	29	20	18	204	167	59	149	4	2.87
	Fred Applegate	R	25	1	2	.333	0	3	3	3	21	29	8	12	0	6.43
	Lou Bruce	R	27	0	0	.000	0	2	0	0	11	11	2	2	0	4.91
	John Barthold	R	22	0	1	.000	0	4	0	0	11	12	8	5	0	4.91
	Lee Fairbank	R	23	0	1	.000	0	3	1	1	17	19	13	6	0	6.35

ST. LOUIS 6th 65-87 .428 29 — JIMMY McALEER

	NAME	G by POS	B	AGE	G	AB	R	H	2B	3B	HR	RBI	BB	SO	SB	BA	SA
	TOTALS			29	156	5291	481	1266	153	53	10	406	332		150	.239	.294
	Tom Jones	1B134, 2B23, OF4	R	27	156	625	53	152	15	10	2	68	15		16	.243	.309
	Dick Padden	2B132	R	33	132	453	42	108	19	4	0	36	40		23	.238	.298
	Bobby Wallace	SS139	R	30	139	550	57	150	28	4	2	69	42		19	.273	.349
2	Charlie Moran	3B81, OF1		25	82	272	15	47	3	1	0	14	25		2	.173	.191
	Charlie Hemphill	OF108, 2B1	L	28	114	438	47	112	13	2	2	45	35		23	.256	.308
	Snags Heidrick	OF130		27	133	538	66	147	14	10	1	36	16		35	.273	.342
	Jesse Burkett	OF147	L	35	147	576	72	157	15	9	2	27	78		12	.273	.340
	Joe Sugden	C79, 1B28	B	33	104	347	25	91	6	3	0	30	28		6	.262	.297
	Mike Kahoe	C69	R	30	72	236	9	51	6	1	0	12	8		4	.216	.250
	Pat Hynes	OF63, P5		20	66	254	23	60	7	3	0	15	3		3	.236	.287
1	Hunter Hill	3B56, OF1		25	58	219	19	47	3	0	0	14	6		4	.215	.228
	Harry Gleason (PB)	SS20, 3B20, 2B5, OF1	R	29	46	155	10	33	7	1	0	6	4		1	.213	.271
4	Frank Huelsman	OF18	R	30	20	68	6	15	2	1	0	1	6		0	.221	.279
	Jack O'Connor	C14	R	35	14	47	4	10	1	0	0	2	2		0	.213	.234
	Gene DeMontreville	2B3	R	30	4	9	0	1	0	0	0	0	2		0	.111	.111
	Art Bader	OF1	R	17	2	3	0	0	0	0	0	0	1		0	.000	.000
	Pinky Swander		L	23	1	1	0	0	0	0	0	0	0		0	.000	.000
	Harry Vahrenhorst		R	19	1	1	0	0	0	0	0	0	0		0	.000	.000

	NAME	T	AGE	W	L	PCT	SV	G	GS	CG	IP	H	BB	SO	ShO	ERA
			27	65	87	.428	2	156	156	135	1410	1335	333	577	13	2.83
	Fred Glade	R	28	18	16	.529	1	35	34	30	289	248	58	156	6	2.27
	Barney Pelty	R	23	14	18	.438	1	39	35	31	301	270	77	126	2	2.84
	Harry Howell	R	27	13	21	.382	0	34	33	32	300	254	60	122	2	2.19
	Ed Siever	L	26	11	15	.423	0	29	24	19	217	235	65	77	2	2.65
	Willie Sudhoff	R	29	8	14	.364	0	27	24	20	222	232	54	63	1	3.77
	Pat Hynes		20	1	0	1.000	0	5	2	1	26	35	7	6	0	6.23
	Clarence Wright	R	25	0	1	.000	0	1	1	0	4	10	2	3	0	13.50
	Cy Morgan	R	25	0	2	.000	0	8	3	2	51	51	10	24	0	3.71

DETROIT 7th 62-90 .408 32 — ED BARROW 32-46 .410 BOBBY LOWE 30-44 .405

	NAME	G by POS	B	AGE	G	AB	R	H	2B	3B	HR	RBI	BB	SO	SB	BA	SA
	TOTALS			28	162	5321	505	1231	154	69	11	431	344		112	.231	.292
1	Charlie Carr	1B92	R	27	92	360	29	77	13	3	0	40	14		6	.214	.267
2	Bobby Lowe	2B140	R	35	140	506	47	105	14	6	0	40	17		15	.208	.259
	Charley O'Leary	SS135	R	22	135	456	39	97	10	3	1	16	21		9	.213	.254
	Ed Gremminger	3B83	R	30	83	309	18	66	13	3	1	28	14		3	.214	.285
	Sam Crawford	OF150	L	24	150	571	46	141	21	17	2	73	44		20	.247	.354
	Jimmy Barrett	OF162	L	29	162	624	83	167	10	5	0	31	79		15	.268	.300
	Matty McIntyre	OF152	L	24	152	578	74	146	11	10	2	46	44		11	.253	.317
	Bob Wood	C47	R	38	49	175	15	43	6	2	1	17	5		1	.246	.320
	R. Robinson	SS30, 3B26, OF20, 2B19			101	320	30	77	13	6	0	37	29		14	.241	.319
2	Bill Coughlin	3B56	R	25	56	206	22	47	6	0	0	17	5		1	.228	.257
2	Monte Beville	C30, 1B24	L	29	54	174	14	36	5	1	0	13	8		2	.207	.247
	George Mullin	OF2	R	23	52	151	14	46	11	2	0	8	10		1	.305	.404
2	Lew Drill	C49, 1B2	R	27	51	160	7	39	6	1	0	13	20		2	.244	.294
1	Fritz Buelow	C42	R	28	42	136	6	15	1	1	0	5	8		2	.110	.132
2	Charley Hickman	1B39	R	28	42	144	18	35	6	6	2	22	11		3	.243	.410
	John Burns	2B4	R	27	4	16	3	2	0	0	0	1	1		1	.125	.125
2	Frank Huelsman	OF4	R	30	4	18	1	6	1	0	0	4	1		1	.333	.389
1	Frank McManus	C1		28	1	0	0	0	0	0	0	0	0		0	.000	.000

	NAME	T	AGE	W	L	PCT	SV	G	GS	CG	IP	H	BB	SO	ShO	ERA
			27	62	90	.408	3	162	162	143	1430	1345	433	556	15	2.77
	Wild Bill Donovan	R	27	17	16	.515	0	34	34	30	293	251	94	137	3	2.46
	George Mullin	R	23	16	24	.400	1	45	44	42	382	345	131	161	7	2.40
	Ed Killian	L	27	15	20	.429	1	40	34	32	332	293	93	124	4	2.44
	Frank Kitson	R	32	10	12	.455	1	26	24	19	200	211	38	69	0	3.06
	Charlie Jaeger		29	2	3	.400	0	8	6	5	49	49	15	13	0	2.57
	Jesse Stovall	R	28	2	13	.133	0	22	17	13	147	170	45	41	1	4.41
	Cy Ferry	R	25	0	1	.000	0	3	1	1	13	12	11	4	0	6.23
	Bugs Raymond	R	22	0	1	.000	0	5	2	1	15	14	6	7	0	3.00

WASHINGTON 8th 38-113 .252 55.5 — MAL KITTREDGE 1-16 .059 PATSY DONOVAN 37-97 .257

	NAME	G by POS	B	AGE	G	AB	R	H	2B	3B	HR	RBI	BB	SO	SB	BA	SA
	TOTALS			29	157	5149	437	1170	171	57	10	348	283		150	.227	.288
	Jake Stahl	1B119, OF23	R	25	142	520	54	136	29	12	3	50	21		25	.262	.381
	Barry McCormick	2B113		29	113	404	36	88	11	1	0	39	27		9	.218	.250
	Joe Cassidy	SS99, OF32, 3B23	R	21	152	581	63	140	12	19	1	33	15		17	.241	.332
2	Hunter Hill	3B71, OF5		25	77	290	18	57	6	1	0	17	11		10	.197	.224
	Patsy Donovan	OF122	R	39	125	434	32	104	6	0	0	19	24		16	.240	.253
2	Bill O'Neill	OF93, 2B3	B	24	95	365	33	89	10	1	1	16	22		22	.244	.285
5	Frank Huelsman	OF84	R	30	84	303	21	75	19	4	2	30	24		6	.248	.356
	Mal Kittredge	C79	R	34	81	265	11	64	7	0	0	24	8		2	.242	.268
	Boileryard Clarke	C52, 1B29	R	35	85	275	23	58	8	1	0	17	17		5	.211	.247
1	Bill Coughlin	3B64	R	25	65	265	28	73	15	4	0	17	9		10	.275	.362
1	Charlie Moran	SS61, 3B1		25	62	243	27	54	10	0	0	7	23		7	.222	.263
1	Kip Selbach	OF48	R	32	48	178	15	49	8	4	0	14	24		9	.275	.365
1	Lew Drill	C29, OF14	R	27	46	142	17	38	7	2	1	11	21		3	.268	.366
1	Al Orth (IL)	OF18, P10	L	31	31	102	7	22	3	1	0	11	1		2	.216	.265
2	Jim Mullin	2B27	R	20	27	102	10	19	2	2	0	4	4		3	.186	.245
1	Jack Thoney	OF17	R	24	17	70	6	21	3	0	0	6	1		2	.300	.343
	Lefty Herring	1B10, OF5	L	24	15	46	3	8	1	0	0	2	7		0	.174	.196
	Rabbitt Nill	2B15	R	22	15	48	4	8	0	1	0	3	5		0	.167	.208
	Izzy Hoffman	OF9	L	29	10	30	1	3	1	0	0	1	2		0	.100	.133

	NAME	T	AGE	W	L	PCT	SV	G	GS	CG	IP	H	BB	SO	ShO	ERA
			26	38	113	.252	3	157	157	137	1360	1487	347	533	7	3.62
	Casey Patten	L	28	15	21	.417	2	45	39	37	358	367	79	150	2	3.07
2	Bill Wolfe	R	28	6	9	.400	0	17	16	13	127	131	22	44	2	3.26
	Beany Jacobson	L	23	5	23	.179	0	33	30	23	254	276	57	75	1	3.54
	Jack Townsend	R	25	5	27	.156	0	36	34	31	291	319	100	143	2	3.59
1	Al Orth (IL)	R	31	3	4	.429	0	10	7	7	74	88	15	23	0	4.74
	Davey Dunkle	R	31	2	9	.182	0	12	11	7	74	95	23	23	0	4.99
2	Long Tom Hughes	R	25	2	14	.125	1	16	14	14	124	133	34	48	0	3.48
	Del Mason	R	20	0	3	.000	0	5	3	2	33	45	13	16	0	6.00
	Highball Wilson	R		0	3	.000	0	3	3	3	25	33	4	11	0	4.68

⊜ ⊜ 1904 N. L.—One Iron Hand, Two Iron Arms, and Only a Pennant . . . ⊜ ⊜

Giant fans had been waiting for a pennant for 15 years, and all that was needed, it seemed, was a firm hand at the tiller. The Giants received such a hand, and none in the history of baseball was any firmer. John McGraw joined a last-place Giant squad in 1902, brought it in second the next year, and whipped it home first by a wide margin in 1904. The Little Napoleon had played on championship teams during his days at Baltimore, but the 1904 pennant was his maiden victory as a manager. McGraw built the Giants up by adding new talent; he brought several teammates with him from Baltimore in 1902, and several other key players were enrolled through trades and careful scouting of the minors. Primarily though, McGraw booted his club to the top by insulting, cajoling, and taunting each player to do his best. He was a tough disciplinarian; an icy glare from McGraw could chill any ballplayer and freeze his nerves. As compensation, he insisted that all his men be well paid, since a man good enough to play for him deserved a top salary. McGraw approached the style of the stern platoon sergeant—hated and feared by some, but respected by all.

On the way to their first title since 1889, the Giants started out of the gate fast and sprinted through the summer before pulling away from the pack. Three key additions bolstered the New York lineup, which amassed 106 victories, a new major league record at the time. Mike Donlin came over in mid-season from Cincinnati to add punch to the outfield, and the infield was greatly strengthened by the insertion of rookie Art Devlin at third and the purchase of veteran shortstop Bill Dahlen from Brooklyn. No one Giant performed spectacularly at bat, but solid stick work was consistently turned in by outfielder Sam Mertes, first sacker Dan McGann, and shortstop Dahlen. The good offense was matched by the best pitching in the league, with the Giants allowing their opponents the smallest sum of runs of any team. An earlier version of the M&M boys made news in the big town; Iron Man Joe McGinnity won 35 games during the year, barely surpassing teammate Christy Mathewson's total of 33. As if these two were not enough, Dummy Taylor developed into a good enough hurler to chalk up 21 victories.

The rest of the teams contented themselves with striving for the leftovers. Chicago caught fire in September and leapfrogged over Pittsburgh and Cincinnati into second place. The Cubs continued assembling parts for future pennant winners, adding Three Finger Brown to the pitching staff to go with their already assembled double-play combination of Joe Tinker, Johnny Evers, and Frank Chance. Chicago lived on pitching and defense in 1904, while Cincinnati lived by the bat. The champion Pirates limped home in fourth place, severely hampered by Deacon Phillippe's illness and Fred Clarke's bad leg. The Bucs made the first division in good measure on the strength of Honus Wagner's .349 batting, good for his second straight batting crown.

All the cheers for the Giants turned sour when president John T. Brush announced that his team would not compete against the American League champion at the season's end. Despite fierce press criticism, Brush stood on his decision, attributed overtly to the American League's being an inferior circuit not worthy of playing the National League for a championship. More realistically, however, the true cause of the refusal rested in Brush's ire at having American League competition in New York and in McGraw's personal antipathy towards junior circuit president Ban Johnson, which resulted from a 1902 dispute between the two men when McGraw was in the American League.

National League president Harry Pulliam supported Brush, stating that the 1903 Series had been a voluntary arrangement, and that no obligatory agreement had ever been reached. But during the off-season, Brush himself seized the opportunity for immortality by proposing that the autumn classic be made an annual and compulsory affair. The proposal was adopted, and the "Brush Rules" governing the Series in playing and financial matters up to the present were used to set the firm standards for the annual world's championship.

1904 NATIONAL LEAGUE

NAME	G by POS	B	AGE	G	AB	R	H	2B	3B	HR	RBI	BB	SO	SB	BA	SA
NEW YORK 1st 106-47 .693		JOHN McGRAW														
TOTALS			29	157	5150	744	1347	202	65	31	564	434		283	.262	.344
Dan McGann	1B141	B	32	141	517	81	148	22	6	6	71	36		42	.286	.387
Billy Gilbert	2B146	R	28	146	478	57	121	13	3	1	54	46		33	.253	.299
Bill Dahlen	SS145	R	34	145	523	70	140	26	2	2	**80**	44		47	.268	.337
Art Devlin	3B130	R	24	130	474	81	133	16	8	1	66	62		33	.281	.354
George Browne	OF149	L	28	150	596	**99**	169	16	5	4	39	39		24	.284	.347
R. Bresnahan	OF93, 1B10, SS4, 2B1, 3B1	R	25	109	402	81	114	22	7	5	33	58		13	.284	.410
Sam Mertes	OF147, SS1	R	31	148	532	83	147	28	11	4	78	54		47	.276	.393
John Warner	C86	L	31	86	287	29	57	5	1	1	15	14		7	.199	.233
Frank Bowerman	C79, 1B9, 2B2, P1	R	35	93	289	38	67	11	4	2	27	16		7	.232	.318
Jack Dunn	3B28, SS10, 2B9, OF7, P1	R	31	64	181	27	56	12	2	1	19	11		11	.309	.414
1 Moose McCormick	OF55	L	23	59	203	28	54	9	5	1	26	13		13	.266	.374
2 Mike Donlin	OF37	L	26	42	132	17	37	7	3	2	14	10		1	.280	.424
24 Doc Marshall	C3, OF2, 2B1	R	29	11	17	3	6	1	0	0	2	1		0	.353	.412
John McGraw	2B2, SS2	R	31	5	12	0	4	0	0	0	0	3		0	.333	.333
Dan Brouthers	1B1	L	46	2	5	0	0	0	0	0	0	0		0	.000	.000
Jim O'Rourke	C1	R	51	1	4	1	1	0	0	0	0	0		0	.250	.250
CHICAGO 2nd 93-60 .608 13		FRANK SELEE														
TOTALS			28	156	5210	597	1294	157	62	22	470	298		227	.248	.315
Frank Chance	1B123, C1	R	26	124	451	89	140	16	10	6	49	36		42	.310	.430
Johnny Evers	2B152	L	22	152	532	49	141	14	7	0	47	28		26	.265	.318
Joe Tinker	SS140, OF1	R	23	141	488	55	108	12	13	3	41	29		41	.221	.318
Doc Casey	3B134, C2	L	33	136	548	71	147	20	4	1	43	18		21	.268	.325
Davy Jones	OF97	L	24	98	336	44	82	11	5	3	39	41		14	.244	.333
Jack McCarthy	OF115	L	35	115	432	36	114	14	2	0	51	23		14	.264	.306
Jimmy Slagle	OF120	L	30	120	481	73	125	12	10	1	31	41		28	.260	.333
Johnny Kling	C104, OF10, 1B6	R	29	123	452	41	110	18	0	2	46	16		7	.243	.296
2 Shad Barry	OF30, 1B18, 3B16, SS8, 2B2	R	27	73	263	29	69	7	2	1	26	17		12	.262	.316
O. Williams	OF21, 1B11, SS10, 2B6, 3B6	R	26	57	185	21	37	4	1	0	8	13		9	.200	.232
Bob Wicker	P30, OF20	R	26	50	155	17	34	1	0	0	9	4		4	.219	.226
Jack O'Neill	C49	R	31	51	168	8	36	5	0	1	19	6		1	.214	.262
Harry McChesney	OF22	R	24	22	88	9	23	6	2	0	11	4		2	.261	.375
Wildfire Schulte	OF20	L	21	20	84	16	24	4	3	2	13	2		1	.286	.476
Broadway Aleck Smith	OF6, C1, 3B1		33	10	29	2	6	1	0	0	1	3		1	.207	.241
Solly Hofman	OF6, SS1	R	21	7	26	7	7	0	0	1	4	1		2	.269	.385
George Moriarty	3B2, OF2	R	19	4	13	0	0	0	0	0	0	1		0	.000	.000
Ike Van Zandt	OF3		27	3	11	0	0	0	0	0	0	0		0	.000	.000
Bill Carney	OF2		26	2	7	0	0	0	0	0	0	1		0	.000	.000
Dutch Rudolph	OF2	L	21	2	3	0	1	0	0	0	0	0		0	.333	.333
Fred Holmes	C1	R		1	3	1	1	1	0	0	0	0		0	.333	.667
Harry Stanton	C1			1	3	0	0	0	0	0	0	0		0	.000	.000
CINCINNATI 3rd 88-65 .575 18		JOE KELLEY														
TOTALS			29	157	**5231**	692	1332	189	92	21	561	399		179	.255	.338
Joe Kelley	1B117, OF6, 2B1	R	32	123	449	75	126	21	13	0	63	49		15	.281	.385
Miller Huggins	2B140	B	25	140	491	96	129	12	7	2	30	88		13	.263	.328
Tommy Corcoran	SS150	R	35	150	578	55	133	17	9	2	74	19		19	.230	.301
Harry Steinfeldt (LJ)	3B98	R	26	99	349	35	85	11	6	1	52	29		16	.244	.318
Cozy Dolan	OF102, 1B24	L	31	129	465	88	132	8	10	6	51	39		19	.284	.383
Cy Seymour	OF130	L	31	131	531	71	166	26	13	5	58	29		11	.313	.439
Fred Odwell	OF126, 2B1	R	31	129	468	75	133	22	10	1	58	26		30	.284	.380
Admiral Schlei	C88	R	26	97	291	25	69	8	3	0	32	17		7	.237	.285
Orville Woodruff	3B61, 2B17, SS8, OF1	R	27	87	306	20	58	14	3	0	20	19		9	.190	.255
Heinie Peitz	C64, 1B18, 3B1	R	31	84	272	32	66	13	2	1	30	14		1	.243	.316
1 Mike Donlin (ST)	OF53, 1B6	L	26	60	236	42	84	11	7	1	38	18		21	.356	.475
2 Jimmy Sebring	OF56	L	22	56	222	22	50	9	2	0	24	14		8	.225	.284
Gabby Street	C11	R	21	11	33	1	4	1	0	0	0	1		2	.121	.152
Peaches O'Neill	C5, 1B1	R	24	8	15	0	4	0	0	0	1	1		0	.267	.267

NAME	T	AGE	W	L	PCT	SV	G	GS	CG	IP	H	BB	SO	ShO	ERA
		26	**106**	47	**.693**	**15**	157	157	127	**1397**	1151	349	**707**	**21**	**2.17**
Joe McGinnity	R	33	**35**	8	**.814**	**6**	**51**	44	38	**408**	307	86	144	**9**	**1.61**
Christy Mathewson	R	24	33	12	.733	1	48	**46**	33	368	306	78	**212**	4	2.03
Dummy Taylor	R	29	21	15	.583	0	37	36	29	296	231	75	138	5	2.34
Hooks Wiltse	L	23	13	3	.813	3	24	16	14	165	150	61	105	2	2.84
Red Ames	R	21	4	6	.400	3	16	13	11	115	94	38	93	1	2.27
Jack Dunn	R	31	0	0	.000	1	1	0	0	4	3	3	1	0	4.50
Bill Milligan	L	27	0	1	.000	2	5	1	1	25	36	4	6	0	5.40
2 Claude Elliot	R	24	0	2	.000	0	3	1	1	15	21	3	8	0	3.00
Frank Bowerman	R	35	0	0	.000	0	1	0	0	1	3	1	0	0	9.00
		27	93	60	.608	6	156	156	139	1384	1150	402	618	18	2.30
Jake Weimer	L	30	20	14	.588	0	37	37	31	307	229	97	177	5	1.91
Buttons Briggs	R	28	19	11	.633	3	34	30	28	277	252	77	112	3	2.05
Carl Lundgren	R	24	17	10	.630	1	31	27	25	242	203	77	106	2	2.60
Bob Wicker	R	26	17	8	.680	0	30	27	23	229	201	58	99	4	2.67
Three Finger Brown	R	27	15	10	.600	1	26	23	21	212	155	50	81	4	1.87
1 Frank Corridon	R	23	5	5	.500	0	12	10	9	100	88	37	34	0	3.06
Dango Groth	R	19	0	2	.000	1	3	2	2	16	22	6	9	0	5.63
		27	88	65	**.575**	2	157	157	142	1384	1256	343	502	12	2.35
Jack Harper	R	27	23	8	.742	0	35	35	31	285	262	85	125	6	2.37
Win Kellum	L	28	14	9	.609	2	31	24	22	225	206	46	70	1	2.60
Tom Walker	R	22	15	10	.600	0	24	24	22	217	196	53	64	2	2.24
Noodles Hahn	L	25	16	18	.471	0	35	34	33	298	258	35	98	2	2.05
Bob Ewing	R	31	11	13	.458	0	26	24	22	212	198	58	99	0	2.46
1 Claude Elliott	R	24	3	1	.750	0	9	6	4	58	53	23	19	1	2.95
1 Jack Sutthoff	R	31	6	6	.500	0	12	10	8	90	83	43	27	0	2.30

PITTSBURGH 4th 87-66 .569 19 — FRED CLARKE

NAME	G by POS	B	AGE	G	AB	R	H	2B	3B	HR	RBI	BB	SO	SB	BA	SA
TOTALS			27	156	5160	675	1333	164	**102**	15	522	391		178	.258	.338
Kitty Bransfield	1B139	R	29	139	520	47	116	17	9	0	60	22		11	.223	.290
Claude Ritchey	2B156, SS2	B	30	156	544	79	143	22	12	0	51	59		12	.263	.347
Honus Wagner	SS121, OF8, 1B3, 2B2	R	30	132	490	97	171	**44**	14	4	75	59		**53**	**.349**	**.520**
Tommy Leach	3B146	R	26	146	579	92	149	15	12	2	56	45		23	.257	.335
1 Jimmy Sebring	OF80	L	22	80	305	28	82	11	7	0	32	17		8	.269	.351
Ginger Beaumont	OF153	L	27	153	**615**	97	**185**	12	12	3	54	34		28	.301	.374
Fred Clarke (LJ)	OF70	L	31	72	278	51	85	7	11	0	25	22		11	.306	.410
Eddie Phelps	C91, 1B1	R	25	94	302	29	73	5	3	0	28	15		2	.242	.278
Otto Krueger	OF33, SS32, 3B10	R	27	86	268	34	52	6	2	1	26	29		8	.194	.243
2 Moose McCormick	OF66	L	23	66	238	25	69	10	6	2	23	13		6	.290	.408
Harry Smith	C44, OF3	R	29	47	141	17	35	3	1	0	18	16		5	.248	.284
Fred Carisch	C22, 1B14	R	22	37	125	9	31	3	1	0	8	9		3	.248	.288
Jack Gilbert	OF25		28	25	87	13	21	0	0	0	3	12		3	.241	.241
Bull Smith	OF13			13	42	2	6	0	1	0	0	1		0	.143	.190
Ernie Diehl	OF7, SS4	R	26	12	37	6	6	0	0	0	4	6		3	.162	.162
Harry Cassady	OF12		23	12	44	8	9	0	0	0	3	2		2	.205	.205
Jimmy Archer	C7, OF1	R	21	7	20	1	3	0	0	0	1	0		0	.150	.150
Tom Stankard	SS1, 3B1	R	22	2	2	0	0	0	0	0	0	0		0	.000	.000
1 Bobby Lowe		R	35	1	1	0	0	0	0	0	0	0		0	.000	.000
Jack Rafter	C1	R	29	1	3	0	0	0	0	0	0	0		0	.000	.000

NAME	T	AGE	W	L	PCT	SV	G	GS	CG	IP	H	BB	SO	ShO	ERA
		28	87	66	.569	1	156	156	133	1348	1273	379	455	14	2.89
2 Patsy Flaherty	L	28	19	9	.679	0	29	28	28	242	210	59	54	5	2.05
Sam Leever	R	32	18	11	.621	0	34	32	26	253	224	54	63	0	2.17
Mike Lynch	L	29	15	11	.577	0	27	24	24	223	200	91	95	1	2.70
Charlie Case	R	24	10	5	.667	0	18	17	14	141	129	31	49	3	2.94
Deacon Phillippe (IL)	R	32	10	10	.500	1	21	19	17	167	183	26	82	3	3.23
Roscoe Miller	R	27	7	8	.467	0	19	17	11	134	133	39	35	2	3.36
Chick Robitaille	R	25	4	3	.571	0	9	8	8	66	52	13	34	0	1.91
Jack Pfiester	L	26	1	1	.500	0	3	2	1	20	28	9	6	0	7.20
Howie Camnitz	R	22	1	3	.250	0	10	2	2	49	48	20	21	0	4.22
Watty Lee	L	24	1	2	.333	0	5	3	1	23	34	9	5	0	8.61
1 Doc Scanlan	R	23	1	3	.250	0	4	3	1	22	21	20	10	0	4.91
Lew Moren	R	20	0	0	.000	0	1	0	0	4	7	4	0	0	9.00
Bucky Veil	R	22	0	0	.000	0	1	1	0	5	4	4	1	0	5.40

ST. LOUIS 5th 75-79 .487 31.5 — KID NICHOLS

NAME	G by POS	B	AGE	G	AB	R	H	2B	3B	HR	RBI	BB	SO	SB	BA	SA
TOTALS			28	155	5104	602	1292	175	66	24	456	343		199	.253	.327
Jake Beckley	1B142	L	36	142	551	72	179	22	9	1	67	35		17	.325	.403
John Farrell	2B130		27	131	509	72	130	23	3	0	20	46		16	.255	.312
Danny Shay	SS97, 2B2	R	27	99	340	45	87	11	1	1	18	39		36	.256	.303
Jimmy Burke	3B118	R	29	118	406	37	92	10	3	0	37	15		17	.227	.266
Spike Shannon	OF133	B	26	134	500	84	140	10	3	1	26	50		34	.280	.318
Homer Smoot	OF137	L	26	137	520	58	146	23	6	3	66	37		23	.281	.365
1 George Barclay	OF103		28	103	375	41	75	7	4	1	28	12		14	.200	.248
Mike Grady	C77, 1B11, 2B3, 3B1	R	34	101	323	44	101	15	11	5	43	31		6	.313	.474
Dave Brain	SS59, 3B30, OF19, 2B13, 1B4	R	24	127	488	57	130	24	12	7	72	17		18	.266	.408
John Dunleavy	OF44, P7		24	51	172	23	40	7	3	1	14	16		8	.233	.326
Dave Zearfoss	C25	R	36	27	80	7	17	2	0	0	9	10		0	.213	.238
Larry McLean	C24	R	22	27	84	5	14	2	1	0	4	4		1	.167	.214
Hugh Hill	OF23	R	24	23	93	13	21	2	1	3	4	2		3	.226	.366
Bill Byers	C16, 1B1	R		19	60	3	13	0	0	0	4	1		0	.217	.217
Simmy Murch	2B6, 3B6, SS1	R	23	13	51	3	7	1	0	0	1	1		0	.137	.157
John Butler	C12	R	24	12	37	0	6	1	0	0	1	4		0	.162	.189
1 She Donahue	2B3, SS1	R	27	4	15	1	4	0	0	0	2	0		3	.267	.267
Charlie Swindells	C3	R	25	3	8	0	1	0	0	0	0	0		0	.125	.125

NAME	T	AGE	W	L	PCT	SV	G	GS	CG	IP	H	BB	SO	ShO	ERA
		30	75	79	.487	2	155	155	**146**	1368	1286	319	529	7	2.64
Jack Taylor	R	30	21	19	.565	1	41	39	**39**	352	297	82	103	2	2.22
Kid Nichols	R	34	21	13	.618	1	36	35	35	317	268	50	134	3	2.02
Chappie McFarland	R		14	17	.452	0	32	31	28	270	266	56	111	1	3.20
Mike O'Neill	L	26	10	14	.417	0	25	24	23	220	229	50	68	1	2.09
Joe Corbett (IL)	R	28	5	9	.357	0	14	14	12	109	110	51	68	0	4.38
Jim McGinley	R	25	2	1	.667	0	3	3	3	27	28	6	6	0	2.00
War Sanders	L	26	1	2	.333	0	4	3	1	19	25	1	11	0	4.74
John Dunleavy		24	1	4	.200	0	7	5	5	55	63	23	28	0	4.42

BROOKLYN 6th 56-97 .366 50 — NED HANLON

NAME	G by POS	B	AGE	G	AB	R	H	2B	3B	HR	RBI	BB	SO	SB	BA	SA
TOTALS			26	154	4916	497	1142	159	53	15	390	411		205	.232	.295
Pop Dillon	1B134	L	30	135	511	60	132	18	6	0	31	40		13	.258	.317
Dutch Jordan	2B70, 3B11, 1B4	R	24	87	252	21	45	10	2	0	19	13		7	.179	.234
Charlie Babb	SS151	B	31	151	521	49	138	18	3	0	53	53		34	.265	.311
Dude McCormick (BA)	3B104, 2B1	R	21	105	347	28	64	5	4	0	27	43		22	.184	.222
Harry Lumley	OF150	L	23	150	577	79	161	23	**18**	**9**	78	41		30	.279	.428
John Dobbs	OF92, 2B2, SS2	L	28	101	363	36	90	16	2	0	30	28		11	.248	.303
Jimmy Sheckard	OF141, 2B2	L	25	143	507	70	121	23	6	1	46	56		21	.239	.314
Bill Bergen	C93, 1B1	R	31	96	329	17	60	4	2	0	12	9		3	.182	.207
Doc Gessler	OF88, 1B1, 2B1	L	23	104	341	41	99	18	4	2	28	30		13	.290	.384
Sammy Strang (IL)	2B63, 3B12, SS1	B	27	77	271	28	52	11	0	1	9	45		16	.192	.244
Lew Ritter	C57, 2B5, 3B1	R	28	72	214	23	53	4	1	0	19	20		17	.248	.276
Heinie Batch	3B28	R	24	28	94	9	24	1	2	2	7	1		6	.255	.372
Fred Jacklitsch	1B11, 2B8, C5	R	28	26	77	8	18	3	1	0	8	7		7	.234	.299
1 Jack Doyle	1B8	R	34	8	22	2	5	1	0	0	2	6		1	.227	.273
Charlie Loudenslager	2B1		23	1	2	0	0	0	0	0	0	0		0	.000	.000
1 Deacon Van Buren		L	33	1	1	0	1	0	0	0	0	0		0	1.000	1.000

NAME	T	AGE	W	L	PCT	SV	G	GS	CG	IP	H	BB	SO	ShO	ERA
		29	56	97	.366	2	154	154	135	1337	1281	414	453	12	2.70
Oscar Jones	R	25	17	**25**	.405	0	46	41	38	377	**387**	92	96	0	2.75
Jack Cronin	R	30	12	23	.343	0	40	34	33	307	284	79	110	4	2.70
2 Doc Scanlan	R	23	7	6	.538	0	13	12	11	104	94	40	40	3	2.16
Ed Poole	R	29	7	14	.333	1	25	23	19	178	178	74	67	1	3.39
1 Ned Garvin	R	30	6	14	.300	0	23	22	16	182	141	78	86	2	1.68
Doc Reisling	R	29	3	4	.429	0	7	7	6	51	45	10	19	1	2.12
2 Fred Mitchell	R	26	2	5	.286	0	8	8	8	66	73	23	16	1	3.82
Bull Durham	R	23	1	0	1.000	0	2	2	1	11	10	5	1	0	3.27
Grant Thatcher	R	27	1	0	1.000	0	1	0	0	9	9	2	4	0	4.00
Jack Doscher	L	23	0	1	.000	0	2	0	0	6	1	1	2	0	0.00
Joe Koukalik	R	24	0	1	.000	0	1	1	1	8	10	4	1	0	1.13
Bill Reidy	R	30	0	4	.000	1	6	4	2	38	49	6	11	0	4.50

BOSTON 7th 55-98 .359 51 — AL BUCKENBERGER

NAME	G by POS	B	AGE	G	AB	R	H	2B	3B	HR	RBI	BB	SO	SB	BA	SA
TOTALS			27	155	5135	491	1217	153	50	24	394	316		143	.237	.300
Fred Tenney	1B144, OF4	L	32	147	533	76	144	17	9	1	37	57		17	.270	.341
Fred Raymer	2B114	R	28	114	419	28	88	12	3	1	27	13		17	.210	.260
Ed Abbaticchio	SS154	R	27	154	579	76	148	18	10	3	54	40		24	.256	.337
Jim Delahanty	3B113, 2B18, OF9, P1	R	25	142	499	56	142	27	8	3	60	27		16	.285	.389
Rip Cannell	OF93	L	24	100	346	32	81	5	1	0	18	23		10	.234	.254
Phil Geier	OF137, 3B7, 2B5, SS1	R	27	149	580	70	141	17	2	1	27	56		18	.243	.284
Dick Cooley	OF116, 1B6	L	31	122	467	41	127	18	7	5	70	24		14	.272	.373
Tom Needham	C77, OF1	R	25	84	269	18	70	12	3	4	19	11		3	.260	.372
Pat Moran	C72, 3B39, 1B12	R	28	113	398	26	90	11	3	4	34	18		10	.226	.299
Pat Carney	OF71, P4, 1B1	L	27	78	279	24	57	5	2	0	11	12		6	.204	.237
2 George Barclay	OF24		28	24	93	5	21	3	1	0	10	2		3	.226	.280
Bill Lauterborn	2B20	R	25	20	69	7	19	2	0	0	2	1		1	.275	.304
3 Doc Marshall	C10, OF1	R	29	13	43	3	9	0	1	0	2	2		2	.209	.256
Kid O'Hara	OF8	B	28	8	29	3	6	0	0	0	0	4		1	.207	.207
Joe Stanley	OF3	B	23	3	8	0	0	0	0	0	0	0		0	.000	.000
Gene McAuliffe	C1	R	32	1	2	0	1	0	0	0	0	0		0	.500	.500
Andy Sullivan	SS1		19	1	1	0	0	0	0	0	0	1		0	.000	.000
John White	OF1	R	26	1	5	1	0	0	0	0	0	0		0	.000	.000

NAME	T	AGE	W	L	PCT	SV	G	GS	CG	IP	H	BB	SO	ShO	ERA
		26	55	98	.359	0	155	155	136	1348	1405	**500**	544	13	3.43
Vic Willis	R	28	18	**25**	.419	0	43	43	**39**	350	357	109	196	2	2.85
Kaiser Wilhelm	R	30	15	21	.417	0	39	36	30	288	316	74	73	3	3.69
Togie Pittinger	R	23	14	21	.400	0	38	38	35	335	298	**144**	146	5	2.66
Tom Fisher	R	23	6	15	.286	0	31	21	19	214	257	82	84	2	4.25
Ed McNichol			2	13	.133	0	17	15	12	122	120	74	39	1	4.28
Joe Stewart	R	25	0	0	.000	0	2	0	0	9	12	4	1	0	9.64
Pat Carney	L	27	0	3	.000	0	4	2	1	26	40	12	5	0	5.88
Jim Delahanty	R	25	0	0	.000	0	1	0	0	3	5	1	0	0	0.00

PHILADELPHIA 8th 52-100 .342 53.5 — HUGH DUFFY

NAME	G by POS	B	AGE	G	AB	R	H	2B	3B	HR	RBI	BB	SO	SB	BA	SA
TOTALS			27	155	5103	571	1268	170	54	23	469	377		159	.248	.316
2 Jack Doyle	1B65, 2B1	R	34	66	236	20	52	10	3	1	22	19		4	.220	.301
Kid Gleason	2B152, 3B1	B	37	153	587	61	161	23	6	0	42	37		17	.274	.334
Rudy Hulswitt	SS113	R	27	113	406	36	99	11	4	1	36	16		8	.244	.298
Harry Wolverton (RJ)	3B102		30	102	398	43	106	15	5	0	49	26		18	.266	.329
Sherry Magee	OF94, 1B1	R	19	95	364	51	101	15	12	3	57	14		11	.277	.409
Roy Thomas	OF139	L	30	139	496	92	144	6	6	3	29	**102**		28	.290	.345
John Titus	OF140	L	28	146	504	60	148	25	5	4	55	46		15	.294	.387
Red Dooin	C96, 1B4, OF3, 3B1	R	25	108	355	41	86	11	4	6	36	8		15	.242	.346
Johnny Lush (DO)	1B62, OF33, P7	L	18	106	369	39	102	22	3	2	42	27		12	.276	.369
Frank Roth	C67, 1B1, 2B1	R	25	81	229	28	59	8	1	1	20	12		0	.258	.314
2 She Donahue	SS29, 3B24, 1B3, 2B2	R	27	58	200	21	43	4	0	0	14	3		7	.215	.235
Bob Hall	3B20, SS15, 1B11	R	25	46	163	11	26	4	0	0	17	14		5	.160	.184
1 Shad Barry	OF32, 3B1	R	27	35	122	15	25	2	0	0	3	11		2	.205	.221
Hugh Duffy	OF14	R	37	18	46	10	13	1	1	0	5	13		3	.283	.348
2 Deacon Van Buren	OF12	L	33	12	43	2	10	2	0	0	3	3		2	.233	.279
1 Doc Marshall	C7	R	29	8	20	1	2	0	0	0	1	0		0	.100	.100
Jesse Purnell	3B7	L	23	7	19	2	2	0	0	0	1	4		1	.105	.105
Klondike Douglass	1B3	L	32	3	10	1	3	0	0	0	1	0		0	.300	.300
Tom Fleming	OF1	R	30	3	6	0	0	0	0	0	0	0		0	.000	.000
Herman Long	2B1	L	38	1	4	0	1	0	0	0	0	0		0	.250	.250
Butch Rementer	C1			1	2	0	0	0	0	0	0	0		0	.000	.000

NAME	T	AGE	W	L	PCT	SV	G	GS	CG	IP	H	BB	SO	ShO	ERA
		30	52	**100**	.342	2	155	155	131	1339	**1418**	425	469	9	3.39
Chick Fraser	R	24	14	24	.368	1	42	36	32	302	287	100	127	2	3.25
Bill Duggleby	R	31	12	14	.462	1	32	27	22	224	265	53	55	2	3.78
Tully Sparks	R	27	7	16	.304	0	26	25	19	201	208	43	67	3	2.64
2 Frank Corridon	R	23	6	5	.545	0	12	11	11	94	88	28	44	1	2.20
1 Fred Mitchell	R	26	4	7	.364	0	13	13	11	109	133	25	29	0	3.39
2 Jack Sutthoff	R	31	6	13	.316	0	19	18	17	164	172	71	46	0	3.68
Ralph Caldwell	L	20	2	3	.400	0	6	5	5	41	40	15	30	0	4.17
John McPherson		36	1	10	.091	0	15	12	11	128	130	46	32	1	3.66
Tom Barry		25	0	1	.000	0	1	1	0	1	6	1	1	0	27.00
John Brackinridge	R	23	0	1	.000	0	7	1	0	34	37	16	11	0	5.56
Johnny Lush (DO)	L	18	0	6	.000	0	7	6	3	43	52	27	27	0	3.56

1905 Whitewashing the Elephants

In a pitcher's year which saw only two regular .300 hitters in the American League, the Philadelphia team batting average of .255 was good enough to score a league-leading 617 runs and bring Connie Mack his second championship in four years. The White Elephants' return to the top after two years, and their jump from a 1904 fifth-place finish, came about via Harry Davis' team-leading .284 batting average and the arms of southpaws, Rube Waddell and Eddie Plank, who again turned in excellent years but were complemented by the development of Chief Bender and Andy Coakley into reliable starters. The foursome, although mostly accounting for a team E.R.A. of 2.19 and capturing almost every statistical pitching category, had to take a back seat in team earned run honors to the Chicago White Sox, who walked off with the crown on a brilliant 1.99 performance.

Although Chicago's pitching was rich enough to make the race a photo-finish between themselves and the Athletics, the first three months of the campaign saw the struggle for first place between Chicago and the heavy-hitting Cleveland team. The two swapped the top spot through July, while the Athletics paced themselves in a close, third-place berth. Cleveland dropped off after playing-manager, Nap Lajoie, the league's best hitter in 1904, was sidelined in July with blood poisoning, and, on August 2, the Mackmen double-timed ahead of Chicago into first place. With Cleveland fading away, and Chicago's weak hitting catching up with them, the Athletics widened the gap in August and seemingly iced away the crown.

But the White Sox hung tight and started melting away the Athletics' lead until, on September 28, it stood at three percentage points with Chicago coming into Philadelphia for a three-game set. The tired Athletics rallied their forces to take two of the three games to all but finish Chicago—a job which was done by the lowly St. Louis Browns, who beat the hitless wonders twice in the final week to allow the Athletics to walk in with a two-game margin championship.

Chicago consolation came in Ed Walsh, the spit-balling wonder, who opened his major league career by winning eight of eleven decisions while posting a 2.17 E.R.A. The Detroit Tigers moved from seventh to third on the arms of George Mullin, Ed Killian, and Wild Bill Donovan. But a more important event was the arrival of young Ty Cobb, who hit .240 as a part-time outfielder. While the Tigers were moving toward the light of day, the 1904 championship Boston Red Sox pulled a reversal and were never in the race, as they wound up fourth. Despite the addition of hard-hitting Jesse Burkett from St. Louis, only Jess Tannehill provided consistency on the mound for the Beantowners. Bill Dineen flattened out at 14-14 after a 23-victory season, and 38-year-old Cy Young posted his worst record since breaking into baseball in 1890. Cleveland's Lajoie, the holder of a partial season's .329 average, surrendered the batting title to teammate Elmer Flick, who was joined in the magic .300 circle only by New York's Willie Keeler. The American League's final individual highlight, or at least one worthy of mention, was Jack Chesbro, who went from his record 41-victory 1904 season to a substantial but more realistic 20 wins.

In the National League, John McGraw kept his Giants on top from April 23, on to repeat as champions. Pittsburgh kept within striking distance for most of the summer and made a move to close the gap in August but fell back in the fall, when they were unable to maintain the momentum picked up during the dog-days of late summer. The Giants again possessed the most powerful attack in the league, featuring Mike Donlin's .356 clouting. Roger Bresnahan hit .302 and handled a mound staff which included 32-game winner, Christy Mathewson, 20-game aces, Red Ames and Joe McGinnity, and solid starters, Hooks Wiltse, and Dummy Taylor. Pittsburgh received .363 batting from Honus Wagner and good pitching from Sam Leever and returning Deacon Phillippe, but was simply unable to put all the pieces together. Wagner himself was unhorsed after two years as batting champion by Cincinnati's Cy Seymour.

After a one-year interruption, the World Series resumed with a dazzling exhibition of pitching dominance. The rested Giants downed the tired Athletics in five games, with each game incredibly being a shutout. Mathewson established himself as an early Series hero by tossing three whitewashings at the Athletics while teammate McGinnity accounted for New York's other shutout. In the phenomenal pitcher's battle, Philadelphia's only three runs of the Series came in Bender's second-game win. The victory, in addition to avenging the senior circuit's loss in 1903, was a great personal satisfaction to McGraw, who got the one-upmanship in his long-standing feud with American League President Ban Johnson.

1905 AMERICAN LEAGUE

NAME	G by POS	B	AGE	G	AB	R	H	2B	3B	HR	RBI	BB	SO	SB	BA	SA
PHILADELPHIA 1st 92-56 .622		**CONNIE MACK**														
	TOTALS		29	152	5107	**617**	**1300**	**256**	51	24	**511**	376		189	**.255**	**.339**
Harry Davis	1B149	R	31	149	602	**92**	171	**47**	6	**8**	**83**	43		36	.284	.422
Danny Murphy	2B150	R	28	150	533	71	148	36	4	6	71	42		23	.278	.394
Jack Knight	SS81, 3B2	R	19	88	325	28	66	12	1	3	29	9		4	.203	.274
Lave Cross	3B147	R	39	147	583	68	155	26	5	0	77	26		8	.266	.328
Socks Seybold	OF132	R	34	132	488	64	132	36	5	6	59	42		5	.270	.402
Danny Hoffman	OF119	L	25	119	454	64	119	10	10	1	35	33		**46**	.262	.335
Topsy Hartsel	OF147	L	31	148	533	87	147	22	8	0	28	**121**		36	.276	.347
Ossee Schreckengost	C112, 1B2	R	30	121	416	30	113	19	6	0	45	3		9	.272	.346
Monte Cross	SS76, 2B2	R	35	78	248	28	67	17	2	0	24	19		8	.270	.355
Bris Lord	OF60, 3B1	R	21	66	238	38	57	14	0	0	13	14		3	.239	.298
13Mike Powers	C40	R	34	40	121	8	18	0	0	0	10	3		4	.149	.149
Harry Barton	C13, 1B2, 3B2, OF1	B	30	29	60	5	10	2	1	0	3	3		2	.167	.233
CHICAGO 2nd 92-60 .605 2		**FIELDER JONES**														
	TOTALS		30	157	5109	613	1212	200	55	11	487	439		194	.237	.304
Jiggs Donahue	1B149	L	25	149	533	71	153	24	2	1	76	44		32	.287	.345
Gus Dundon (CJ)	2B104, SS2	R	30	106	364	30	70	7	3	0	22	23		14	.192	.228
George Davis	SS157	B	34	157	550	74	153	28	3	1	55	60		31	.278	.345
Lee Tannehill	3B142	R	24	142	480	38	96	17	2	0	39	45		8	.200	.244
Danny Green	OF107	L	28	112	379	56	92	13	6	0	44	53		11	.243	.309
Fielder Jones	OF153	L	33	153	568	91	139	17	12	2	38	73		20	.245	.327
Ducky Holmes	OF89	L	36	92	328	42	66	15	2	0	22	19		11	.201	.259
Billy Sullivan	C93, 1B2, 3B1	R	30	99	323	25	65	10	3	2	26	13		14	.201	.269
Nixey Callahan	OF93	R	31	96	345	50	94	18	6	1	43	29		26	.272	.368
Frank Isbell	2B42, OF40, 1B9, SS2	L	29	94	341	55	101	21	11	2	45	15		15	.296	.440
Ed McFarland	C70	R	30	80	250	24	70	13	4	0	31	23		5	.280	.364
George Rohe	3B17, 2B16	R	29	34	113	14	24	1	0	1	12	12		2	.212	.248
Hub Hart	C6	L	27	10	17	2	2	0	0	0	4	3		0	.118	.118
DETROIT 3rd 79-74 .516 15.5		**BILL ARMOUR**														
	TOTALS		28	153	4968	511	1208	190	54	13	421	375		129	.243	.311
Pinky Lindsay	1B88		26	88	329	38	88	14	1	0	31	18		10	.267	.316
Germany Schaefer	2B151, SS3	R	28	153	554	64	135	17	9	2	47	45		19	.244	.318
Charley O'Leary	SS148	R	23	148	512	47	109	13	1	0	33	29		13	.213	.242
Bill Coughlin	3B137	R	26	138	489	48	123	20	6	0	44	34		16	.252	.317
Sam Crawford	OF103, 1B51	L	25	153	575	73	171	40	10	6	75	50		22	.297	.433
Dick Cooley	OF97	L	32	99	377	25	93	11	9	1	32	26		7	.247	.332
Matty McIntyre	OF131	L	25	131	495	59	130	21	5	0	30	48		9	.263	.325
Lew Drill	C70	R	28	71	211	17	55	9	0	0	24	32		7	.261	.303
1 Charley Hickman	OF47, 1B12	R	29	59	213	21	47	12	3	2	20	12		3	.221	.333
Bobby Lowe	OF25, 3B22, 2B6, SS4, 1B1	R	36	60	181	17	35	7	2	0	9	13		3	.193	.254
Ty Cobb	OF41	L	18	41	150	19	36	6	0	1	15	10		2	.240	.300
2 John Warner	C36	L	32	36	119	12	24	2	3	0	7	8		2	.202	.269
2 Tom Doran	C32	L	25	34	94	8	15	3	0	0	4	8		2	.160	.191
Jimmy Barrett	OF18	L	30	20	67	2	17	1	0	0	3	6		0	.254	.269
John Sullivan	C12		32	12	31	4	5	0	0	0	4	4		0	.161	.161
Bob Wood	C7	R	39	8	24	1	2	1	0	0	0	1		0	.083	.125
2 Nig Clarke	C2	L	22	3	7	1	3	0	0	1	1	0		0	.429	.857

NAME	T	AGE	W	L	PCT	SV	G	GS	CG	IP	H	BB	SO	ShO	ERA
		25	**92**	56	**.622**	7	152	152	117	1383	1137	409	**895**	**20**	2.19
Rube Waddell	L	28	**26**	11	.703	**4**	**46**	34	27	329	231	90	**287**	7	**1.48**
Eddie Plank	L	29	25	12	.676	0	41	**41**	**35**	347	287	75	210	4	2.26
Andy Coakley	R	22	20	7	**.741**	0	35	31	21	255	227	73	145	3	1.84
Chief Bender	R	22	16	11	.593	3	35	23	18	229	193	90	142	4	2.83
Weldon Henley	R	24	4	12	.250	0	25	19	13	184	155	67	82	2	2.59
Jimmy Dygert	R	20	1	3	.250	0	6	3	2	35	41	11	24	0	4.37
Joe Myers	R	23	0	0	.000	0	1	1	1	5	3	3	5	0	3.60
		26	92	60	.605	3	157	157	131	**1427**	1163	329	613	17	**1.99**
Frank Owen	R	25	22	14	.611	0	42	38	32	334	276	56	125	3	2.10
Nick Altrock	L	28	21	11	.656	2	38	34	31	316	274	63	97	3	1.88
Frank Smith	R	25	19	13	.594	0	39	31	27	292	215	107	171	4	2.13
Dock White	L	26	18	14	.563	0	36	32	25	260	204	58	120	4	1.77
Ed Walsh	R	24	8	3	.727	1	22	13	9	137	121	29	71	1	2.17
Roy Patterson	R	28	4	5	.444	0	13	9	7	89	73	16	29	1	1.82
		28	79	74	.516	2	153	153	124	1348	1226	**474**	578	16	2.83
Ed Killian	L	28	22	15	.595	1	39	37	33	313	263	102	110	**8**	2.27
George Mullin	R	24	22	18	.550	0	44	**41**	**35**	**348**	**303**	**138**	168	0	2.51
Will Bill Donovan	R	28	18	14	.563	0	34	32	27	281	236	101	135	5	2.59
Frank Kitson	R	33	11	15	.423	1	33	26	21	226	230	57	78	3	3.46
Eddie Cicotte	R	21	1	1	.500	0	3	1	1	18	25	5	6	0	3.50
Jimmy Wiggs (HO)	R	28	3	3	.500	0	7	7	4	41	30	29	37	0	3.29
John Eubank	R	32	2	0	1.000	0	3	2	0	17	13	3	1	0	2.18
Andy Bruckmiller	R	23	0	0	.000	0	1	0	0	1	4	1	1	0	27.00
Walt Justis	R	21	0	0	.000	0	2	0	0	3	4	6	0	0	9.00
George Disch		26	0	2	.000	0	8	3	1	48	43	8	14	0	2.62
Gene Ford	R	24	0	2	.000	0	7	1	1	35	51	14	20	0	5.66
Charlie Jackson	R	23	0	2	.000	0	2	2	1	11	14	7	3	0	5.73
Frosty Thomas	R	24	0	2	.000	0	2	1	0	6	10	3	5	0	7.50

BOSTON 4th 78-74 .513 16

JIMMY COLLINS

NAME	G by POS	B	AGE	G	AB	R	H	2B	3B	HR	RBI	BB	SO	SB	BA	SA
TOTALS			32	153	5031	583	1177	165	69	**29**	488	**486**		131	.234	.311
Moose Grimshaw	1B74	B	29	85	285	39	68	8	2	4	35	21		4	.239	.323
Hobe Ferris	2B140, OF1	R	27	141	523	51	115	24	16	6	59	23		11	.220	.361
Freddy Parent	SS153	R	29	153	602	55	141	16	5	0	33	47		25	.234	.277
Jimmy Collins	3B131	R	35	131	508	66	140	25	5	4	65	37		18	.276	.368
Kip Selbach	OF116	R	33	124	418	54	103	16	6	4	47	67		12	.246	.342
Chick Stahl	OF134	L	32	134	500	61	129	18	4	0	47	50		18	.258	.310
Jesse Burkett	OF149	L	36	149	573	78	147	13	13	4	47	67		13	.257	.346
Lou Criger	C109	R	33	109	313	33	62	6	7	1	36	54		5	.198	.272
Buck Freeman	1B72, OF51, 3B2	L	33	130	455	59	109	20	8	3	49	46		8	.240	.338
Bob Unglaub	3B21, 2B8, 1B2	R	23	43	121	18	27	5	1	0	11	6		2	.223	.281
Charlie Armbruster (RJ)	C35	R	23	35	91	13	18	4	0	0	6	18		3	.198	.242
John Godwin	OF6, 2B5		28	13	37	4	13	1	0	0	10	3		3	.351	.378
Art McGovern	C15	R	23	15	44	1	5	1	0	0	1	4		0	.114	.136
Candy LaChance	1B12	B	35	12	41	1	6	1	0	0	5	6		0	.146	.171
Pop Rising	3B4			8	18	2	2	1	1	0	2	2		0	.111	.278
Duke Farrell (LJ)	C7	R	38	7	21	2	6	1	0	0	2	1		0	.286	.333
1 Tom Doran	C1	L	25	2	2	0	0	0	0	0	0	0		0	.000	.000
Frank Owens	C1	R	19	1	2	0	0	0	0	0	0	0		0	.000	.000

NAME	T	AGE	W	L	PCT	SV	G	GS	CG	IP	H	BB	SO	ShO	ERA
		30	78	74	.513	5	153	153	125	1356	1198	292	652	15	2.84
Jesse Tannehill	L	30	22	10	.688	1	36	31	27	272	238	59	113	6	2.48
Cy Young	R	38	18	19	.486	0	38	34	32	321	248	30	210	5	1.82
Bill Dinneen	R	29	14	14	.500	1	31	29	23	244	235	50	97	2	3.73
George Winter	R	27	14	16	.467	3	35	27	24	264	249	54	119	2	2.97
Norwood Gibson	R	28	4	7	.364	0	23	17	9	134	118	55	67	0	3.69
Ed Hughes	R	25	3	1	.750	0	6	4	2	33	38	9	8	0	4.64
Ed Barry	L		1	2	.333	0	7	5	2	41	38	15	18	0	2.85
Joe Harris	R	23	1	2	.333	0	3	3	3	23	16	8	14	0	2.35
Hank Olmsted	R	26	1	2	.333	0	3	3	3	25	18	12	6	0	3.24

CLEVELAND 5th 76-78 .494 19

NAP LAJOIE

NAME	G by POS	B	AGE	G	AB	R	H	2B	3B	HR	RBI	BB	SO	SB	BA	SA
TOTALS			28	154	5130	559	**1309**	211	**72**	18	482	286		188	**.255**	.335
Charlie Carr	1B87	R	28	89	306	29	72	12	4	1	31	13		12	.235	.310
Nap Lajoie (JJ)	2B59, 1B5	R	29	65	249	29	82	13	2	2	41	17		11	.329	.422
Terry Turner	SS154	R	24	154	582	48	153	16	14	4	72	14		17	.263	.359
Bill Bradley	3B145	R	27	145	537	63	144	34	6	0	51	27		22	.268	.354
Elmer Flick	OF130, 2B1	L	29	131	496	71	152	29	**19**	4	64	53		35	**.306**	**.466**
Harry Bay	OF143	L	27	143	550	90	164	18	10	0	22	36		36	.298	.367
Jim Jackson	OF105, 3B3	R	27	108	421	58	108	12	4	2	31	34		15	.257	.318
Fritz Buelow	C59,OF8, 1B3, 3B2	R	29	74	236	11	41	4	1	1	18	6		7	.174	.212
George Stovall	1B59, 2B46, OF4	R	26	111	419	41	114	31	3	1	47	13		13	.272	.368
Harry Bemis	C58, 2B4, 3B2, 1B1	L	31	69	226	27	66	13	3	0	28	13		3	.292	.376
Otto Hess	OF27, P26	L	26	54	175	15	44	8	1	2	13	7		2	.251	.343
13 Nig Clarke	C41	L	22	42	123	11	24	6	1	0	9	11		0	.195	.260
Nick Kahl (IL)	2B31, SS1, OF1	R	26	39	131	16	29	4	1	0	21	4		1	.221	.267
Rube Vinson	OF36		26	38	133	12	26	3	1	0	9	7		4	.195	.233
Jap Barbeau	2B11	R	23	11	37	1	10	1	1	0	2	1		1	.270	.351
Bunk Congalton	OF12			12	47	4	17	0	0	0	5	2		3	.362	.362
Howard Wakefield	C8	R	21	9	25	3	4	0	0	0	1	0		0	.160	.160
Eddie Grant	2B2	L	22	2	8	1	3	0	0	0	0	0		0	.375	.375
Emil Leber	3B2	R	24	2	6	1	0	0	0	0	0	1		0	.000	.000

NAME	T	AGE	W	L	PCT	SV	G	GS	CG	IP	H	BB	SO	ShO	ERA
		28	76	78	.494	1	154	154	**139**	1363	**1251**	334	555	16	2.85
Addie Joss	R	25	20	11	.645	0	33	32	31	286	246	46	132	3	2.01
Bob Rhoades	R	25	17	11	.607	0	28	26	24	235	219	55	61	4	2.83
Earl Moore	R	25	15	15	.500	0	31	30	28	269	232	92	131	3	2.64
Otto Hess	L	26	10	14	.417	0	26	25	22	214	179	72	109	4	3.15
Red Donahue	R	32	6	11	.353	0	20	17	13	138	132	25	45	1	3.39
Bill Bernhard	R	34	6	14	.300	1	22	19	17	174	185	34	56	0	3.36
Hi West	R	20	2	2	.500	0	6	4	4	33	43	10	15	1	4.09
Cy Ferry	R	26	0	0	.000	0	1	1	0	2	3	0	2	0	13.50
Jack Halla	L	21	0	0	.000	0	3	0	0	13	12	0	4	0	2.77

NEW YORK 6th 71-78 .477 21.5

CLARK GRIFFITH

NAME	G by POS	B	AGE	G	AB	R	H	2B	3B	HR	RBI	BB	SO	SB	BA	SA
TOTALS			29	152	4957	587	1228	163	61	23	480	360		**200**	.248	.319
Hal Chase	1B122, 2B1, SS1	R	22	126	465	60	116	16	6	3	49	15		22	.249	.329
Jimmy Williams	2B129	R	28	129	470	54	107	20	8	6	62	50		14	.228	.343
Kid Elberfeld	SS108	R	30	111	390	48	102	18	2	0	53	23		18	.262	.318
Joe Yeager	3B90, SS21		29	115	401	53	107	16	7	0	42	25		8	.267	.342
Willie Keeler	OF139, 2B12, 3B3	L	33	149	560	81	169	14	4	4	38	43		19	.302	.363
Dave Fultz	OF122	R	30	130	422	49	98	13	3	0	42	39		44	.232	.277
Patsy Dougherty	OF108, 3B1	L	28	116	418	56	110	9	6	3	29	28		17	.263	.335
Red Kleinow (RJ)	C83, 1B3	R	25	88	253	23	56	6	3	1	24	20		7	.221	.281
Wid Conroy	3B48 OF21, SS18, 1B9, 2B3	R	28	102	385	55	105	19	11	2	25	32		25	.273	.395
Deacon McGuire	C71	R	39	72	228	9	50	7	2	0	33	18		3	.219	.268
Eddie Hahn	OF43	L	29	43	160	32	51	5	0	0	11	25		1	.319	.350
1 John Anderson	OF22, 1B3	B	31	32	99	12	23	3	1	0	14	8		9	.232	.283
Jim Cockman	3B13	R	32	13	38	5	4	0	0	0	2	4		2	.105	.105
Frank LaPorte	2B11	R	25	11	40	4	16	1	0	1	12	1		1	.400	.500
2 Mike Powers	1B7, C4	R	34	11	33	3	6	1	0	0	2	1		0	.182	.212
Frank Delahanty	1B5, OF3	R	22	9	27	0	6	1	0	0	2	1		0	.222	.259
Joe Connor	C6, 1B2	R	30	8	22	4	5	1	0	0	2	3		1	.227	.273
Rube Oldring	SS8	R	21	8	30	2	9	0	1	1	6	2		4	.300	.467
Fred Curtis	1B2			2	9	0	2	1	0	0	2	1		1	.222	.333
Phil Cooney	3B1	R	18	1	3	0	0	0	0	0	0	0		0	.000	.000
Jack Doyle	1B1	R	35	1	3	0	0	0	0	0	0	0		0	.000	.000
Fred Jacklitsch	C1	R	29	1	3	1	0	0	0	0	1	1		0	.000	.000
Joe McCarthy	C1	R	23	1	2	0	0	0	0	0	0	0		0	.000	.000
John Ganzel (HO) 30																

NAME	T	AGE	W	L	PCT	SV	G	GS	CG	IP	H	BB	SO	ShO	ERA
		30	71	78	.477	**9**	152	152	88	1354	1235	396	642	10	2.92
Jack Chesbro	R	31	20	15	.571	0	41	38	24	303	262	71	156	1	2.20
Al Orth	R	32	18	18	.500	1	40	37	26	305	273	61	121	4	2.86
1 Jack Powell	R	30	9	13	.409	1	36	23	13	202	214	57	84	1	3.52
Bill Hogg		25	9	12	.429	1	39	22	9	205	178	101	125	2	3.20
Clark Griffith	R	35	8	6	.571	3	25	7	4	103	82	15	46	2	1.66
Ambrose Puttmann	L	24	2	7	.222	1	17	9	5	86	79	37	39	0	4.29
Louis LeRoy	R	26	1	1	.500	0	3	3	2	24	26	1	8	0	3.75
Walter Clarkson	R	26	2	2	.500	1	9	4	3	46	40	13	35	0	3.91
Doc Newton	L	27	2	2	.500	1	11	7	2	60	61	24	15	0	2.10
Art Goodwin		29	0	0	.000	0	1	0	0	.1	2	2	0	0	81.00
Wilbur Good	L	19	0	2	.000	0	5	2	0	19	18	14	13	0	4.74

WASHINGTON 7th 64-87 .424 29.5

JAKE STAHL

NAME	G by POS	B	AGE	G	AB	R	H	2B	3B	HR	RBI	BB	SO	SB	BA	SA
TOTALS			27	156	5009	560	1117	193	68	22	483	298		169	.223	.302
Jake Stahl	1B140	R	26	141	501	66	122	22	12	5	66	28		41	.244	.365
2 Charley Hickman	2B85, 1B3	R	29	88	360	48	112	26	9	2	46	9		3	.311	.450
Joe Cassidy	SS151	R	22	151	576	67	124	16	4	1	43	25		23	.215	.262
Hunter Hill (IL)	3B103		26	104	374	37	78	12	1	1	24	32		10	.209	.254
2 John Anderson	OF89, 1B4	B	31	93	400	50	116	21	6	1	38	22		22	.290	.380
Charlie Jones	OF142		29	142	544	68	113	18	4	2	41	31		24	.208	.267
Frank Huelsman	OF123	R	31	126	421	48	114	28	8	3	62	31		11	.271	.397
Mike Heydon	C77		30	77	245	20	47	7	4	1	26	21		5	.192	.265
Rabbitt Nill	3B54, 2B33, SS6	R	23	103	319	46	58	7	3	3	31	33		12	.182	.251
Punch Knoll	OF70, C5, 1B2	R	23	85	244	24	52	10	5	0	29	9		3	.213	.295
Mal Kittredge	C75	R	35	76	238	16	39	8	0	0	14	15		1	.164	.197
Jim Mullin	2B39, 1B7	R	21	50	163	18	31	7	6	0	13	5		5	.190	.307
Joe Stanley	OF27	B	24	28	92	13	24	2	1	1	17	7		4	.261	.337
Harry Cassady	OF9		24	9	30	1	4	0	0	0	1	0		0	.133	.133
Claude Rothgeb	OF3	B	25	6	13	2	2	0	0	0	0	0		1	.154	.154
Hughie Tate	OF3	R	25	4	10	1	3	0	1	0	2	0		1	.300	.500
Denny Sullivan	OF3	L	22	3	11	0	0	0	0	0	0	1		0	.000	.000
Shag Shaughnessy	OF1	R	22	1	3	0	0	0	0	0	0	0		0	.000	.000

NAME	T	AGE	W	L	PCT	SV	G	GS	CG	IP	H	BB	SO	ShO	ERA
		27	64	87	.424	5	156	156	118	1362	1250	385	539	11	2.87
Long Tom Hughes	R	26	16	16	.500	1	39	35	26	291	239	79	149	5	2.35
Casey Patten	L	29	16	20	.444	0	42	37	29	310	300	86	113	2	3.14
Bill Wolfe	R	29	9	14	.391	2	28	24	17	182	162	37	52	1	2.57
Beany Jacobson (IL)	L	24	8	9	.471	1	22	17	12	144	139	35	50	0	3.31
Jack Townsend	R	26	7	16	.304	0	34	24	22	263	247	84	102	0	2.63
Cy Falkenberg	R	25	4	4	.500	1	12	10	6	75	71	31	35	2	3.84
Harry Hardy		29	2	1	.667	0	3	2	2	24	20	6	10	0	1.88
Rick Adams	L	26	2	6	.250	0	11	6	3	63	63	24	25	1	3.57
Moxie Manuel	R	23	0	1	.000	0	3	1	1	10	9	3	3	0	5.40

ST. LOUIS 8th 54-99 .353 40.5

JIMMY McALEER

NAME	G by POS	B	AGE	G	AB	R	H	2B	3B	HR	RBI	BB	SO	SB	BA	SA
TOTALS			29	156	**5204**	509	1205	153	49	16	415	362		130	.232	.289
Tom Jones	1B135	R	28	135	504	44	122	16	2	0	48	30		5	.242	.282
Ike Rockenfield	2B95	R	28	95	322	40	70	12	0	0	16	46		11	.217	.255
Bobby Wallace	SS156	R	31	156	587	67	159	29	9	1	59	45		13	.271	.356
Harry Gleason	3B144, 2B6	R	30	150	535	45	116	11	5	1	57	34		23	.217	.262
Emil Frisk	OF116	L	29	127	429	58	112	11	6	3	36	42		7	.261	.336
Ben Koehler	OF127, 1B12, 2B6	R	28	142	536	55	127	14	6	2	47	32		22	.237	.297
George Stone	OF154	L	27	154	**632**	76	**187**	26	13	7	52	44		26	.296	.411
Joe Sugden	C71, 1B9	B	34	85	266	21	46	4	0	0	23	23		3	.173	.188
Ike Van Zandt	OF74, 1B1, P1		28	94	322	31	75	15	1	1	20	7		7	.233	.295
Frank Roth	C29	R	26	35	107	9	25	3	0	0	7	6		1	.234	.262
Tubby Spencer	C34	R	21	35	115	6	27	1	2	0	11	7		2	.235	.278
Charlie Moran	2B21, 3B7		26	28	82	6	16	1	0	0	5	10		3	.195	.207
Art Weaver	C28		26	28	92	5	11	2	1	0	3	1		0	.120	.163
Charlie Starr	2B16, 3B6		26	24	97	9	20	0	0	0	6	7		0	.206	.206
Dick Padden (IL)	2B16	R	34	16	58	5	10	1	1	0	4	3		3	.172	.224
Charlie Gibson	C1	R	28	1	3	0	0	0	0	0	0	0		0	.000	.000
Branch Rickey	C1	L	23	1	3	0	0	0	0	0	0	0		0	.000	.000
John Heidrick (VR) 28																

NAME	T	AGE	W	L	PCT	SV	G	GS	CG	IP	H	BB	SO	ShO	ERA
		28	54	**99**	.353	3	156	156	133	1385	1245	389	633	10	2.74
Harry Howell	R	28	14	21	.400	0	38	37	**35**	323	252	101	198	4	1.98
Barney Pelty	R	24	13	14	.481	1	31	28	26	259	222	68	114	1	2.75
Willie Sudhoff	R	30	10	20	.333	0	32	30	23	244	222	78	70	1	2.99
Jim Buchanan	R	27	6	10	.375	2	22	15	12	141	149	27	54	1	3.51
Fred Glade	R	29	7	**24**	.226	0	32	32	28	275	257	58	127	2	2.81
2 Jack Powell	R	30	2	1	.667	0	3	3	3	28	22	5	12	0	1.61
Cy Morgan	R	26	2	6	.250	0	13	8	5	77	82	37	44	1	3.62
Harry Ables	L	20	0	3	.000	0	6	3	1	31	37	13	11	0	3.77
Ike Van Zandt		28	0	0	.000	0	1	0	0	7	2	2	3	0	0.00
Jack O'Connor (IL) 38															

NEW YORK 1st 105-48 .686 — JOHN McGRAW

NAME	G by POS	B	AGE	G	AB	R	H	2B	3B	HR	RBI	BB	SO	SB	BA	SA
TOTALS			30	155	5094	780	1392	191	88	39	642	517		291	.273	.368
Dan McGann	1B136	B	33	136	491	88	147	23	14	5	75	55		22	.299	.434
Billy Gilbert	2B115	R	29	115	376	45	93	11	3	0	24	41		11	.247	.293
Bill Dahlen	SS147, OF1	R	35	148	520	67	126	20	4	7	81	62		37	.242	.337
Art Devlin	3B153	R	25	153	525	74	129	14	7	2	61	66		59	.246	.310
George Browne	OF127	L	29	127	536	95	157	16	14	4	43	20		26	.293	.397
Mike Donlin	OF150	L	27	150	606	124	216	31	16	7	80	56		33	.356	.495
Sam Mertes	OF150	R	32	150	551	81	154	27	17	5	108	56		52	.279	.417
Roger Bresnahan	C87, OF8	R	26	104	331	58	100	18	3	0	46	50		11	.302	.375
Sammy Strang	2B47, OF38, SS9, 1B1, 3B1	B	28	111	294	51	76	9	4	3	29	58		23	.259	.347
Frank Bowerman	C72, 1B17, 2B1	R	36	98	297	37	80	8	1	3	41	12		6	.269	.333
Boileryard Clarke	1B17, C12	R	36	31	50	2	9	0	0	1	4	4		1	.180	.240
Offa Neal	3B3, 2B1	L	29	4	13	0	0	0	0	0	0	0		0	.000	.000
John McGraw	OF1	L	32	3	0	0	0	0	0	0	0	0		1	.000	.000
Moonlight Graham	OF1	L	28	1	0	0	0	0	0	0	0	0		0	.000	.000
1 Bob Hall	OF1	R	26	1	3	1	1	0	0	0	0	0		0	.333	.333

NAME	T	AGE	W	L	PCT	SV	G	GS	CG	IP	H	BB	SO	ShO	ERA
		27	105	48	.686	15	155	155	117	1370	1160	364	760	17	2.39
Christy Mathewson	R	26	32	8	.800	2	43	37	32	339	252	64	206	8	1.27
Joe McGinnity	R	34	22	16	.579	3	46	38	26	320	289	71	125	2	2.87
Red Ames	R	22	22	8	.733	0	34	31	21	263	220	105	198	2	2.74
Dummy Taylor	R	30	15	9	.625	0	32	28	18	213	200	51	91	4	2.66
Hooks Wiltse	L	24	14	6	.700	4	32	19	18	197	158	61	120	1	2.47
Claude Elliott	R	25	0	1	.000	6	10	2	2	38	41	12	20	0	4.03

PITTSBURGH 2nd 96-57 .627 9 — FRED CLARKE

NAME	G by POS	B	AGE	G	AB	R	H	2B	3B	HR	RBI	BB	SO	SB	BA	SA
TOTALS			29	155	5213	692	1385	190	91	22	564	382		202	.266	.350
Del Howard	1B90, OF28, P1	L	27	123	435	56	127	18	5	2	63	27		19	.292	.370
Claude Ritchey	2B153, SS2	B	31	153	533	54	136	29	6	0	52	51		12	.255	.332
Honus Wagner	SS145, OF2	R	31	147	548	114	199	32	14	6	101	54		57	.363	.505
2 Dave Brain	3B78, SS4	R	26	85	307	31	79	17	6	3	46	15		8	.257	.381
Otis Clymer	OF89, 1B1	L	28	96	365	74	108	11	5	0	23	19		23	.296	.353
Ginger Beaumont	OF97	L	28	103	384	60	126	12	8	3	40	22		21	.328	.424
Fred Clarke	OF137	L	32	141	525	95	157	18	15	2	51	55		24	.299	.402
Heinie Deitz	C87, 2B1	R	32	88	278	18	62	10	0	0	27	24		2	.223	.259
Tommy Leach	OF71, 3B58, 2B2, SS2	R	27	131	499	71	128	10	14	2	53	37		17	.257	.345
Bill Clancey	1B52, OF4		27	56	227	23	52	11	3	2	34	4		3	.229	.330
George Gibson	C44	R	24	46	135	14	24	2	2	2	14	15		2	.178	.267
Doc Hillebrand	1B16, P10, OF7, C3	R	25	39	110	9	26	3	2	0	7	6		1	.236	.300
Bob Ganley	OF32	L	30	32	127	12	40	1	2	0	7	8		3	.315	.354
Fred Carisch	C30	R	23	32	107	7	22	0	3	0	8	2		1	.206	.262
1 George McBride	3B17, SS8	R	24	27	87	9	19	4	0	0	7	6		2	.218	.264
Steamer Flanagan	OF5	L	24	7	25	7	7	1	1	0	3	1		3	.280	.400
Jim Wallace	OF7	L	23	7	29	3	6	1	0	0	3	3		2	.207	.241
Otto Knabe	3B3	R	21	3	10	0	3	1	0	0	2	3		0	.300	.400
Harry Smith (AJ)	C1	R	30	1	3	0	0	0	0	0	1	0		1	.000	.000

NAME	T	AGE	W	L	PCT	SV	G	GS	CG	IP	H	BB	SO	ShO	ERA
		29	96	57	.627	6	155	155	113	1383	1270	389	512	12	2.86
Deacon Phillippe	R	33	22	13	.629	0	38	33	25	279	235	48	133	5	2.19
Sam Leever	R	33	19	6	.760	1	33	29	20	230	199	54	81	3	2.70
Mike Lynch	L	30	17	8	.680	2	33	22	13	206	191	107	106	0	3.80
Charlie Case	R	25	12	10	.545	1	31	24	18	217	202	66	57	3	2.57
Patsy Flaherty	L	29	9	10	.474	1	27	20	15	188	197	49	44	0	3.49
Chick Robitaille	R	26	8	5	.615	0	17	12	10	120	126	28	32	0	2.93
Lefty Leifield	L	21	5	2	.714	0	8	7	6	56	52	14	10	1	2.89
Doc Hillebrand	L	25	4	2	.667	1	10	6	4	61	43	19	37	0	2.80
George Moore	R	32	0	0	.000	0	1	0	0	3	2	0	1	0	0.00
Ed Kinsella	R	23	0	1	.000	0	3	2	2	17	19	3	11	0	2.65
Del Howard	R	27	0	0	.000	0	1	0	0	6	4	1	0	0	0.00

CHICAGO 3rd 92-61 .601 13 — FRANK SELEE 52-38 .578 FRANK CHANCE 40-23 .635

NAME	G by POS	B	AGE	G	AB	R	H	2B	3B	HR	RBI	BB	SO	SB	BA	SA
TOTALS			28	155	5108	667	1249	157	82	12	522	448		267	.245	.314
Frank Chance	1B115	R	27	118	392	92	124	16	12	2	70	78		38	.316	.434
Johnny Evers (HJ)	2B99	L	23	99	340	44	94	11	2	1	37	27		19	.276	.329
Toe Tinker	SS149	R	24	149	547	70	135	18	8	2	66	34		31	.247	.320
Doc Casey	3B142, SS1	L	34	144	526	66	122	21	10	1	56	41		22	.232	.316
Billy Maloney	OF145	L	27	145	558	78	145	17	14	2	56	43		59	.260	.351
Jimmy Slagle	OF155	L	31	155	568	96	153	19	4	0	37	97		27	.269	.317
Wildfire Schulte	OF123	L	22	123	493	67	135	15	14	1	47	32		16	.274	.367
Johnny Kling	C106, OF4, 1B1	R	30	111	380	26	83	8	6	1	52	28		13	.218	.279
Solly Hofman	2B59, 1B9, SS9, 3B3, OF3	R	22	86	287	43	68	14	4	1	38	20		15	.237	.324
Jack McCarthy	OF37, 1B6	L	36	59	170	16	47	4	3	0	14	10		8	.276	.335
Jack O'Neill	C50	R	32	53	172	16	34	4	2	0	12	8		6	.198	.244
1 Shad Barry	1B26	R	28	27	104	10	22	2	0	0	10	5		5	.212	.231
Hans Lobert	3B13, OF1	R	23	14	46	7	9	2	0	0	1	3		4	.196	.239

NAME	T	AGE	W	L	PCT	SV	G	GS	CG	IP	H	BB	SO	ShO	ERA
		26	92	61	.601	2	155	155	133	1407	1135	385	627	23	2.04
Jake Weimer	L	31	18	12	.600	1	33	30	26	250	212	80	107	2	2.27
Three Finger Brown (JJ)	R	28	18	10	.643	0	30	24	24	249	219	44	89	4	2.17
Ed Reulbach	R	22	18	14	.562	1	34	29	28	292	208	73	152	5	1.42
Carl Lundgren	R	25	13	5	.722	0	23	19	16	169	132	53	69	3	2.24
Bob Wicker	R	27	13	7	.650	0	22	22	17	178	139	47	86	4	2.02
Buttons Briggs	R	29	8	8	.500	0	20	20	13	168	141	52	68	5	2.14
Big Jeff Pfeffer	R	23	4	5	.444	0	15	11	9	101	84	36	56	0	2.50

PHILADELPHIA 4th 83-69 .546 21.5 — HUGH DUFFY

NAME	G by POS	B	AGE	G	AB	R	H	2B	3B	HR	RBI	BB	SO	SB	BA	SA
TOTALS			28	155	5243	708	1362	187	82	16	567	406		180	.260	.336
Kitty Bransfield	1B151	R	30	151	580	55	150	23	9	3	76	27		27	.259	.345
Kid Gleason	2B155	B	38	155	608	95	150	17	7	1	50	45		16	.247	.303
Mickey Doolan	SS135	R	25	136	492	53	125	27	11	1	48	24		17	.254	.360
Ernie Courtney	3B155	L	26	155	601	77	165	14	7	2	77	47		17	.275	.331
John Titus	OF147	L	29	147	548	99	169	36	14	2	89	69		11	.308	.436
Roy Thomas	OF147	L	31	147	562	118	178	11	6	0	31	93		23	.317	.358
Sherry Magee	OF155	R	20	155	603	100	180	24	17	5	98	44		48	.299	.420
Red Dooin	C107, 3B1	R	26	113	380	45	95	13	5	0	36	10		12	.250	.311
Fred Abbott	C34,1B5	R	30	42	128	9	25	6	1	0	12	6		4	.195	.258
Otto Krueger	SS23, OF6, 3B1	R	28	46	114	10	21	1	1	0	12	13		1	.184	.211
Hugh Duffy	OF8	R	38	15	40	7	12	2	1	0	3	1		0	.300	.400
Mike Kahoe	C15	R	31	16	51	2	13	2	0	0	4	1		1	.255	.294
Red Munson	C8		21	9	26	1	3	1	0	0	2	0		0	.115	.154

NAME	T	AGE	W	L	PCT	SV	G	GS	CG	IP	H	BB	SO	ShO	ERA
		31	83	69	.546	5	155	155	119	1399	1303	411	516	12	2.81
Togie Pittinger	R	34	23	15	.605	2	46	37	29	337	311	104	136	4	3.10
Bill Duggleby	R	32	18	17	.514	0	38	36	27	289	270	83	75	1	2.46
Tully Sparks	R	28	14	11	.560	1	34	29	20	260	217	73	98	3	2.18
Frank Corridon	R	24	10	13	.435	1	35	26	18	212	203	57	79	1	3.48
2 Kid Nichols	R	35	10	6	.625	0	17	16	15	139	129	28	50	1	2.27
Jack Sutthoff	R	32	3	4	.429	0	13	6	4	78	82	36	26	1	3.81
Johnny Lush	L	19	2	0	1.000	0	2	2	1	17	12	8	8	0	1.59
King Brady	R	24	1	1	.500	0	2	2	2	13	19	2	3	0	3.46
Ralph Caldwell	L	21	1	1	.500	1	7	2	1	34	44	7	29	0	4.24
Harry Kane	L	21	1	1	.500	0	2	2	2	17	12	8	12	1	1.59
Buck Washer	R	22	0	0	.000	0	1	0	0	3	4	5	0	0	6.00

CINCINNATI 5th 79-74 .516 26 — JOE KELLEY

NAME	G by POS	B	AGE	G	AB	R	H	2B	3B	HR	RBI	BB	SO	SB	BA	SA
TOTALS			27	155	5205	736	1401	160	101	27	611	434		181	.269	.354
2 Shad Barry	1B123, OF2	R	28	125	494	90	160	11	12	1	56	33		16	.324	.401
Miller Huggins	2B149	B	26	149	564	117	154	11	8	1	38	103		27	.273	.326
Tommy Corcoran	SS151	R	36	151	605	70	150	21	11	2	85	23		28	.248	.329
Harry Steinfeldt	3B103, 1B1, 2B1, OF1	R	27	114	384	49	104	16	9	1	39	30		15	.271	.367
Fred Odwell	OF126	R	32	130	468	79	113	10	9	9	65	26		21	.241	.359
Cy Seymour	OF149	L	32	149	581	95	219	40	21	8	121	51		21	.377	.559
Joe Kelley	OF85, 1B2	R	33	90	321	43	89	7	6	1	37	27		8	.277	.346
Admiral Schlei	C89, 1B6	R	27	99	314	32	71	8	3	1	36	22		9	.226	.280
Al Bridwell	3B43, OF18, 2B7, SS5, 1B1	L	21	82	254	17	64	3	1	0	17	19		8	.252	.272
Jimmy Sebring	OF56	L	23	58	217	31	62	10	5	2	28	14		11	.286	.406
Eddie Phelps	C44	R	26	44	156	18	36	5	3	0	18	12		4	.231	.301
13 Gabby Street	C27	R	22	31	93	8	23	5	1	0	8	6		1	.247	.323
1 Cozy Dolan	1B13, OF9	L	32	22	77	7	18	2	1	0	4	7		2	.234	.286
Bill Hinchman	OF12, 3B4, 1B1	R	32	17	51	10	13	4	1	0	10	13		4	.255	.373
Johnny Siegle	OF16	R	30	17	56	9	17	1	2	1	8	7		0	.304	.446
Cliff Blankenship	1B15	R	25	19	56	8	11	1	1	0	7	4		1	.196	.250
Mike Mowrey	3B7	R	21	7	30	4	8	1	0	0	6	1		0	.267	.300

NAME	T	AGE	W	L	PCT	SV	G	GS	CG	IP	H	BB	SO	ShO	ERA
		27	79	74	.516	2	155	155	119	1366	1409	439	547	10	3.01
Bob Ewing	R	32	20	11	.645	0	40	34	30	312	284	79	164	4	2.51
Orvie Overall	R	24	17	23	.425	0	42	39	32	318	290	147	173	2	2.86
Charlie Chech	R	27	14	14	.500	0	39	25	20	268	300	77	79	1	2.89
Tom Walker	R	23	10	6	.625	0	23	19	12	145	171	44	28	1	3.23
Jack Harper	R	27	9	14	.391	1	26	23	15	179	189	69	70	1	3.87
Noodles Hahn (SA)	L	26	5	3	.625	0	13	8	5	77	85	9	17	1	2.81
Rip Vowinkel	R	20	3	3	.500	0	6	6	4	45	52	10	7	0	4.20
Ollie Johns	L	25	1	0	1.000	1	4	1	1	18	31	4	8	0	3.50
Ernie Baker	R	29	0	0	.000	0	1	0	0	4	7	0	1	0	4.50

ST. LOUIS 6th 58-96 .377 47.5

KID NICHOLS 19-29 .396 JIMMY BURKE 17-32 .347 STANLEY ROBISON 22-35 .386

NAME	G by POS	B	AGE	G	AB	R	H	2B	3B	HR	RBI	BB	SO	SB	BA	SA
TOTALS			28	154	5066	534	1254	140	85	20	446	391		162	.248	.321
Jake Beckley	1B134	L	37	134	514	48	147	20	10	1	57	30		12	.286	.370
Harry Arndt	2B90, OF9, 3B7, SS5		26	113	415	40	101	11	6	2	36	24		13	.243	.313
2 George McBride	SS80, 1B1	R	24	81	281	22	61	1	2	2	34	14		10	.217	.256
Jimmy Burke	3B122	R	30	122	431	34	97	9	5	1	30	21		15	.225	.276
John Dunleavy (LJ)	OF118, 2B1		25	119	435	52	105	8	8	1	25	55		15	.241	.303
Homer Smoot	OF138	L	27	139	534	73	166	21	16	4	58	33		21	.311	.433
Spike Shannon	OF140	B	27	140	544	73	146	16	3	0	41	47		27	.268	.309
Mike Grady	C71, 1B20	R	35	100	311	41	89	20	7	4	41	33		15	.286	.434
Danny Shay (FA)	2B39, SS39	R	28	78	281	30	67	12	1	0	28	35		11	.238	.288
Josh Clarke	OF26, 2B16, SS4	L	26	50	167	31	43	3	2	3	18	27		8	.257	.353
1 Dave Brain	SS29, 3B6, OF6	R	26	44	158	11	36	4	5	1	17	8		4	.228	.335
1 John Warner	C41	L	32	41	137	9	35	2	2	1	12	6		2	.255	.321
Tom Leahy	C29	R	36	35	97	3	22	1	3	0	7	8		0	.227	.299
Art Hoelskoetter	3B20, 2B3, P1	R	22	24	83	7	20	2	1	0	5	3		1	.241	.289
Dave Zearfuss	C19	R	37	20	51	2	8	0	1	0	2	4		0	.157	.196
Rube DeGroff	OF15		25	15	56	3	14	2	1	0	5	5		1	.250	.321
John Himes	OF11			12	41	3	6	0	0	0	0	1		0	.146	.146
John Farrell	2B7		28	7	24	6	4	0	1	0	1	4		1	.167	.250
Simmy Murch	2B2, SS1		24	3	9	0	1	0	0	0	0	0		0	.111	.111
Gerry Shea	C2		23	2	6	0	2	0	0	0	0	0		0	.333	.333

NAME	T	AGE	W	L	PCT	SV	G	GS	CG	IP	H	BB	SO	ShO	ERA
		26	58	96	.377	2	154	154	135	1348	1431	367	411	10	3.59
Jake Thielman	R	26	15	16	.484	0	32	29	26	242	265	62	87	0	3.50
Jack Taylor	R	31	15	21	.417	1	37	34	34	309	302	85	102	3	3.44
Chappie McFarland	R		9	18	.333	1	31	28	22	250	281	65	85	3	3.82
Buster Brown	R	23	8	11	.421	0	23	21	17	179	172	62	57	3	2.97
Wish Egan	R	24	5	15	.250	0	23	19	18	171	189	39	29	0	3.58
Win Kellum	L	29	3	3	.500	0	11	7	5	74	70	10	19	1	2.92
Bill Campbell	L	31	1	1	.500	0	2	2	2	17	27	7	2	0	7.41
Sandy McDougal		27	1	4	.200	0	5	5	5	45	50	12	10	0	3.40
1 Kid Nichols	R	35	1	5	.167	0	7	7	5	52	64	18	16	0	5.37
Art Hoelskoetter	R	22	0	1	.000	0	1	1	1	6	6	5	4	0	1.50
Jim McGinley	R	26	0	1	.000	0	1	1	0	3	5	2	0	0	15.00

BOSTON 7th 51-103 .331 54.5

FRED TENNEY

NAME	G by POS	B	AGE	G	AB	R	H	2B	3B	HR	RBI	BB	SO	SB	BA	SA
TOTALS			28	156	5190	467	1217	148	52	17	387	302		132	.234	.293
Fred Tenney	1B148, P1	L	33	149	549	84	158	18	3	0	28	67		17	.288	.332
Fred Raymer	2B134, 1B1, OF1	R	29	137	498	26	105	14	2	0	31	8		15	.211	.247
Ed Abbaticchio	SS152, OF1	R	28	153	**610**	70	170	25	12	3	41	35		30	.279	.374
Harry Wolverton	3B122		31	122	463	38	104	15	7	2	55	23		10	.225	.300
2 Cozy Dolan	OF111, 1B2, P2	L	32	112	433	44	119	11	7	3	48	27		21	.275	.353
Rip Cannell	OF154	L	25	154	567	52	140	14	4	0	36	51		17	.247	.286
Jim Delahanty	OF124, P1	R	26	125	461	50	119	11	8	5	55	28		12	.258	.349
Pat Moran	C78	R	29	85	267	22	64	11	5	2	22	8		3	.240	.341
Tom Needham	C77, OF3, 1B2	R	26	83	271	21	59	6	1	2	17	24		3	.218	.269
Bill Lauterborn	3B29, 2B23, SS3, OF2	R	26	67	200	11	37	1	1	0	9	12		1	.185	.200
Bud Sharpe	OF42, C3, 1B1	L	23	46	170	8	31	3	2	0	11	7		0	.182	.224
George Barclay (IL)	OF28		29	29	108	5	19	1	0	0	7	2		2	.176	.185
Allie Strobel	3B4, OF1	R	21	5	19	1	2	0	0	0	2	0		0	.105	.105
Dave Murphy	SS2, 3B1			3	11	0	2	0	0	0	1	0		0	.182	.182
2 Gabby Street	C3	R	22	3	12	0	2	0	0	0	0	0		1	.167	.167
Bill McCarthy	C1			1	3	0	0	0	0	0	0	0		0	.000	.000

NAME	T	AGE	W	L	PCT	SV	G	GS	CG	IP	H	BB	SO	ShO	ERA
		30	51	103	.331	0	156	156	139	1383	1390	433	533	13	3.52
Irv Young	L	27	20	21	.488	0	43	42	41	378	337	71	156	6	2.90
Chick Fraser	R	34	14	21	.400	0	39	38	35	334	320	149	130	2	3.29
Vic Willis	R	29	11	29	.275	0	41	41	36	342	340	107	149	4	3.21
Kaiser Wilhelm	R	31	4	23	.148	0	34	27	23	242	287	75	76	0	4.54
Dick Harley	R	30	2	5	.286	0	9	4	4	66	72	19	19	1	4.64
Frank Hershey		27	0	1	.000	0	1	1	0	4	5	2	1	0	6.75
Jake Volz	R	27	0	2	.000	0	3	2	0	9	12	8	1	0	10.00
Jim Delahanty	R	26	0	0	.000	0	1	1	0	2	5	0	0	0	4.50
2 Cozy Dolan	L	32	0	1	.000	0	2	0	0	4	7	1	1	0	9.00
Fred Tenney	L	33	0	0	.000	0	1	0	0	2	5	1	0	0	4.50

BROOKLYN 8th 48-104 .316 56.5

NED HANLON

NAME	G by POS	B	AGE	G	AB	R	H	2B	3B	HR	RBI	BB	SO	SB	BA	SA
TOTALS			27	155	5100	506	1255	154	60	29	430	327		186	.246	.317
Doc Gessler	1B107, OF12	L	24	126	431	44	125	17	4	3	46	38		26	.290	.369
Charlie Malay	2B75, OF25, SS1	B	26	102	349	33	88	7	2	1	31	22		13	.252	.292
Phil Lewis	SS118	R	21	118	433	32	110	9	2	3	33	16		16	.254	.305
Heinie Batch	3B145	R	25	145	568	64	143	20	11	5	49	26		21	.252	.352
Harry Lumley	OF129	L	24	130	505	50	148	19	10	7	47	36		22	.293	.412
John Dobbs	OF123	L	29	123	460	59	117	21	4	2	36	31		15	.254	.330
Jimmy Sheckard	OF129	L	26	130	480	58	140	20	11	3	41	61		23	.292	.398
Lew Ritter	C84, OF4, 3B2	R	29	92	311	32	68	10	5	1	28	15		16	.219	.293
Bill Bergen	C76	R	32	79	247	12	47	3	2	0	22	7		4	.190	.219
Charlie Babb	SS36, 1B31, 3B5, 2B2	B	32	75	235	27	44	8	2	0	17	27		10	.187	.238
2 Bob Hall	OF42, 2B7, 1B3	R	26	56	203	21	48	4	1	2	15	11		8	.236	.296
Red Owens	2B43	R	30	43	168	14	36	6	2	1	20	6		1	.214	.292
John Hummel	2B30	R	22	30	109	19	29	3	4	0	7	9		6	.266	.367
Fred Mitchell	P12, 1B7, 3B4, SS1, OF1	R	27	27	79	4	15	0	0	0	8	4		0	.190	.190
Ed McGamwell	1B4		27	4	16	0	4	0	0	0	0	1		0	.250	.250
Ad Yale	1B4		35	4	13	1	1	0	0	0	1	1		0	.077	.077

NAME	T	AGE	W	L	PCT	SV	G	GS	CG	IP	H	BB	SO	ShO	ERA
		26	48	**104**	.316	3	155	155	125	1347	1416	**476**	556	7	3.76
Doc Scanlan	R	24	15	11	.577	0	33	28	22	250	220	104	135	2	2.92
Harry McIntire	R	27	8	25	.242	1	40	35	29	309	**340**	101	135	1	3.70
Elmer Stricklett	R	28	8	19	.296	1	33	28	25	237	259	71	77	1	3.34
Oscar Jones	R	26	8	15	.348	1	29	20	14	174	197	56	66	0	4.66
Mal Eason	R	26	5	21	.192	0	27	27	20	207	230	72	64	3	4.30
Fred Mitchell	R	27	3	7	.300	0	12	10	9	96	107	38	44	0	4.78
Jack Doscher	L	24	1	5	.167	0	12	7	6	71	60	30	33	0	3.17
Doc Reisling	R	30	0	1	.000	0	2	0	0	3	3	4	2	0	3.00

WORLD SERIES – NEW YORK (NL) 4 PHILADELPHIA (AL) 1

LINE SCORES

TEAM	1	2	3	4	5	6	7	8	9	10	11	12	R	H	E
Game 1 October 9 at Philadelphia															
NY (NL)	0	0	0	0	2	0	0	0	1				3	10	1
PHI (AL)	0	0	0	0	0	0	0	0	0				0	4	0
Mathewson				Plank											
Game 2 October 10 at New York															
PHI	0	0	1	0	0	0	0	2	0				3	6	2
NY	0	0	0	0	0	0	0	0	0				0	4	2
Bender				McGinnity, Ames (9)											
Game 3 October 12 at Philadelphia															
NY	2	0	0	0	5	0	0	0	2				9	8	1
PHI	0	0	0	0	0	0	0	0	0				0	4	5
Mathewson				Coakley											
Game 4 October 13 at New York															
PHI	0	0	0	0	0	0	0	0	0				0	5	2
NY	0	0	0	1	0	0	0	0	X				1	4	1
Plank				McGinnity											
Game 5 October 14 at New York															
PHI	0	0	0	0	0	0	0	0	0				0	6	0
NY	0	0	0	0	1	0	0	1	X				2	5	1
Bender				Mathewson											

COMPOSITE BATTING

NAME	POS	G	AB	R	H	2B	3B	HR	RBI	BA
New York (NL)										
Totals		5	153	15	31	7	0	0	13	.203
Browne	OF	5	**22**	2	4	0	0	0	1	.182
Donlin	OF	5	19	**4**	**5**	1	0	0	1	.263
McGann	1B	5	17	1	4	**2**	0	0	**4**	.235
Gilbert	2B	5	17	1	4	0	0	0	2	.235
Mertes	OF	5	17	2	3	1	0	0	2	.176
Bresnahan	C	5	16	3	**5**	**2**	0	0	1	**.313**
Devlin	3B	5	16	0	4	1	0	0	1	.250
Dahlen	SS	5	15	1	0	0	0	0	1	.000
Mathewson	P	3	8	1	2	0	0	0	0	.250
McGinnity	P	2	5	0	0	0	0	0	0	.000
Strang	PH	1	1	0	0	0	0	0	0	.000
Ames	P	1	0	0	0	0	0	0	0	.000
Philadelphia (AL)										
Totals		5	155	3	25	5	0	0	2	.161
Davis	1B	5	20	0	4	1	0	0	0	.200
Lord	OF	5	20	0	2	0	0	0	2	.100
L. Cross	3B	5	19	0	2	0	0	0	0	.105
Hartsel	OF	5	17	1	**5**	1	0	0	0	.294
M. Cross	SS	5	17	0	3	0	0	0	0	.176
Murphy	2B	5	16	0	3	1	0	0	0	.188
Seybold	OF	5	16	0	2	0	0	0	0	.125
Schreckengost	C	3	9	2	2	1	0	0	0	.222
Powers	C	3	7	0	1	1	0	0	0	.143
Plank	P	2	6	0	1	0	0	0	0	.167
Bender	P	2	5	0	0	0	0	0	0	.000
Coakley	P	1	2	0	0	0	0	0	0	.000
Hoffman	PH	1	1	0	0	0	0	0	0	.000

COMPOSITE PITCHING

NAME	G	IP	H	BB	SO	W	L	SV	ERA
New York (NL)									
Totals	5	45	25	5	25	4	1	0	0.00
Mathewson	3	**27**	**14**	1	**18**	**3**	0	0	**0.00**
McGinnity	2	17	10	3	6	1	1	0	**0.00**
Ames	1	1	1	1	1	0	0	0	0.00
Philadelphia (AL)									
Totals	5	43	31	15	26	1	4	0	1.47
Bender	2	17	9	**6**	13	1	1	0	1.06
Plank	2	17	**14**	4	11	0	**2**	0	1.59
Coakley	1	9	**8**	5	2	0	1	0	**2.00**

1906 West Side, South Side, It's Still Chicago

After 19 years of pennant drought in the National League stronghold of Chicago, the rains of victory were finally in sight. Followers of the American League's Chicago team, the White Sox, had tasted success in the first year of the junior league's formation in 1901, and were not as hungry for the pennant. But rooters of the Chicago Cubs, the National League's entry in that city since 1876, had not been able to have a happy winter since the summer of '86.

When the victory rain did come, it came in buckets, and not only on the Cubs, but the White Sox and the entire city of Chicago as well. Indeed, 1906 was a happy and delirious time for the Chicago baseball fan. He could sit back in October with a sporting appetite as satiated as a physical hunger is by a Thanksgiving dinner. After all, the wonderful town had been treated to a full fare of exciting and varied baseball all summer. With both the Cubs and White Sox fighting for first place, fans turned out in droves for each team, making the Chicago entries tops in attendance in both leagues. As a result, the fans were treated to a double helping of pennant topped by a calorie-rich dessert of World Series.

The New York Giants stayed with the Cubs until June, but fell back when the Bruins shifted into top speed and stayed there all summer. Never running into a slump, the Cubs chalked up an unprecedented 116 victories, wiping out the Giants' 1904 record of 106 wins. A mediocre attack became the bane of opposing pitchers with the pre-season addition of third sacker Harry Steinfeldt, a .327 swinger who gave extra bite to the middle of the batting order. Playing-manager Frank Chance hit over .310 for the fourth straight year, and catcher Johnny Kling shot from .218 the previous year to a robust .312 batting mark. Joe Tinker, Johnny Evers, and Chance made the infield airtight and helped the pitchers allow the lowest total of runs of any team since the turn of the century. Three Finger Brown, in winning 26 games, proved the big reason why the Cubs stayed away from any slumps. Rookie southpaw Jack Pfiester contributed 20 victories, big Ed Reulbach 19, Carl Lundgren 17, and Orvie Overall came over from Cincinnati in mid-season to add 12 victories to the Cubs' record win column.

While fans could go to the west side to see the Cubs rolling up victories at an astonishing clip, they could also travel down to the south side to see their "Hitless Wonders", the weak-hitting White Sox, in a dogfight for the American League flag. In early August, the White Sox found themselves in fourth place behind the front-running Atheletics, New York, and Cleveland. Then, in a masterful stroke of strategic genius, manager Fielder Jones led his charges on a 19-game winning streak, which toppled the A's and installed the Chisox in first place. With the Athletics fading fast, the Sox and New York battled through September for the first-place plum which the Sox finally grasped in the season's final week.

In their three-game victory margin, the Chisox depended on pitching and defense to carry an attack where only two men hit over .260 as the team itself finished with the lowest batting average in the league. Frank Owen and funnyman Nick Altrock gave the Sox a pair of 20-win aces, as spitballer Ed Walsh and practicing dentist Doc White proved the strongest in the earned run department, with White taking league honors with a 1.52 mark. New York and Cleveland flexed the biggest offensive muscles in the league but had to take a back seat to the Midway weaklings, who made an art out of defense.

When it came to the World Series, the White Sox upset their crosstown rivals by outpitching them for a six-game victory. Bad fielding by the Cubs gave Altrock a 2-1 triumph over Brown in the curtain raiser, and Walsh and White accounted for three more notches in the White Sox ledger to down the Cubs for a major surprise. Adding insult to injury, the anemic White Sox attack came alive in games five and six and slashed out with 12-and 14-hit barrages to send starters, Reulbach and Brown, to early showers before sending the fans to the street, where they could make their way home in the comfort that would enable them to enter the coming chill of winter in the warmth of victory.

1906 AMERICAN LEAGUE

NAME	G by POS	B	AGE	G	AB	R	H	2B	3B	HR	RBI	BB	SO	SB	BA	SA
CHICAGO 1st 93-58 .616	FIELDER JONES															
	TOTALS		30	154	4921	570	1132	152	52	6	444	**453**		214	.230	.286
Jiggs Donahue	1B154	L	26	154	556	70	143	17	6	1	57	48		36	.257	.315
Frank Isbell	2B132, OF14, C1, P1	L	30	143	549	71	153	18	11	0	57	30		37	.279	.352
George Davis	SS129, 2B1	B	35	133	484	63	134	25	6	0	80	41		27	.277	.353
Lee Tannehill	3B99, SS17	R	25	116	378	26	69	8	3	0	33	31		7	.183	.220
Bill O'Neill	OF93	B	26	94	330	37	82	4	1	1	21	22		19	.248	.276
Fielder Jones	OF144	L	34	144	496	77	114	22	4	2	34	83		26	.230	.302
2 Eddie Hahn	OF130	L	30	130	484	80	110	7	5	0	27	69		19	.227	.262
Billy Sullivan	C118	R	31	118	387	37	83	18	4	1	33	22		10	.214	.289
2 Patsy Dougherty	OF74	L	29	75	253	30	59	9	4	1	27	19		11	.233	.312
George Rohe	3B57, 2B5, OF1	R	30	75	225	14	58	5	1	0	25	16		8	.258	.289
Gus Dundon	2B18, SS14	R	31	33	96	7	13	1	0	0	4	11		4	.135	.146
Hub Hart	C15	L	28	17	37	1	6	0	0	0	0	2		0	.162	.162
Frank Roth	C15	R	27	16	51	4	10	1	1	0	7	3		1	.196	.255
Frank Hemphill	OF13	R	28	13	40	0	3	0	0	0	2	9		1	.075	.075
Babe Towne	C12	L	26	13	36	3	10	0	0	0	6	7		0	.278	.278
Ed McFarland	C3	R	31	7	22	0	3	1	0	0	3	3		0	.136	.182
Rube Vinson	OF4		27	7	24	2	6	0	0	0	3	2		1	.250	.250
Lee Quillen	SS3	R	24	4	9	1	3	0	0	0	0	0		1	.333	.333
NEW YORK 2nd 90-61 .596 3	CLARK GRIFFITH															
	TOTALS		27	155	5095	641	1345	166	**77**	17	528	331		192	.266	.339
Hal Chase	1B150, 2B1	R	23	151	597	84	193	23	10	0	76	13		28	.323	.395
Jimmy Williams	2B139	R	29	139	501	62	139	25	7	3	77	44		8	.277	.373
Kid Elberfeld (JJ)	SS98	R	31	99	346	59	106	12	4	2	31	30		19	.306	.382
Frank LaPorte	3B114, 2B5, OF1	R	26	123	454	60	120	23	9	2	54	22		10	.264	.368
Willie Keeler	OF152	L	34	152	592	96	180	9	3	2	33	40		23	.304	.340
2 Danny Hoffman (KJ)	OF98	L	26	100	320	34	82	10	6	0	23	27		32	.256	.325
Frank Delahanty	OF92	R	23	92	307	37	73	11	8	2	41	16		11	.238	.345
Red Kleinow	C95, 1B1	R	26	96	268	30	59	9	3	0	31	24		8	.220	.276
Wid Conroy	OF97, SS49, 3B2	R	29	148	567	67	139	17	10	4	54	47		32	.245	.332
George Moriarty	3B39, OF15, 1B5, 2B1	R	21	65	197	22	46	7	7	0	23	17		8	.234	.340
Joe Yeager	SS22, 2B13, 3B3		30	57	123	20	37	6	1	0	12	13		3	.301	.366
Deacon McGuire	C49, 1B1	R	40	51	144	11	43	5	0	0	14	12		3	.299	.333
Ira Thomas	C42	R	25	44	115	12	23	1	2	0	15	8		2	.200	.243
1 Patsy Dougherty	OF12	L	29	12	52	3	10	2	0	0	4	0		0	.192	.231
1 Eddie Hahn	OF7	L	30	11	22	2	2	1	0	0	1	3		2	.091	.136
John Ganzel (HO) 31																
CLEVELAND 3rd 89-64 .582 5	NAP LAJOIE															
	TOTALS		28	157	**5414**	**663**	**1511**	**240**	73	11	**548**	330		203	**.279**	**.356**
Claude Rossman	1B105, OF1	L	25	118	396	49	122	13	2	1	53	17		11	.308	.359
Nap Lajoie	2B130, 3B15, SS7	R	30	152	602	88	**214**	**49**	7	0	91	30		20	.355	.460
Terry Turner	SS147	R	25	147	584	85	170	27	7	2	62	35		27	.291	.372
Bill Bradley (BA)	3B82	R	28	82	302	32	83	15	2	2	25	18		13	.275	.358
Bunk Congalton	OF114		31	117	419	51	134	13	5	2	50	24		12	.320	.389
Elmer Flick	OF150, 2B8	L	30	157	**624**	**98**	194	33	**22**	1	62	54		**39**	.311	.439
Jim Jackson	OF105	R	28	105	374	44	80	13	2	0	38	38		25	.214	.259
Harry Bemis	C81	L	32	93	297	28	82	13	5	2	30	12		8	.276	.374
George Stovall	1B55, 3B30, 2B19	R	27	116	443	54	121	19	5	0	37	8		15	.273	.339
Harry Bay (NJ)	OF68	L	28	68	280	47	77	8	3	0	14	26		17	.275	.325
Nig Clarke	C54	L	23	57	179	22	64	12	4	1	21	13		3	.358	.486
Jap Barbeau	3B32, SS6	R	24	42	129	8	25	5	3	0	12	9		5	.194	.279
Fritz Buelow	C33, 1B1	R	30	34	86	7	14	2	0	0	7	9		0	.163	.186
Ben Caffyn	OF29		26	30	103	16	20	4	0	0	3	12		2	.194	.233
Joe Birmingham	OF9	R	21	9	37	4	11	2	1	0	6	1		2	.297	.405
2 Mal Kittredge	C1	R	26	1	3	0	0	0	0	0	0	0		0	.000	.000
Bill Shipke	2B2	R	23	2	6	0	0	0	0	0	0	0		0	.000	.000

NAME	T	AGE	W	L	PCT	SV	G	GS	CG	IP	H	BB	SO	ShO	ERA
		27	93	58	.616	9	154	154	117	1375	1212	255	543	**32**	2.13
Frank Owen	R	26	22	13	.629	2	42	36	27	293	289	54	66	7	2.33
Nick Altrock	L	29	20	13	.606	1	38	30	25	288	269	42	99	4	2.06
Doc White	L	27	18	6	.750	0	28	24	20	219	160	38	95	7	**1.52**
Ed Walsh	R	25	17	13	.567	**3**	41	31	24	278	215	58	171	**10**	1.88
Roy Patterson	R	29	10	7	.588	1	21	18	12	142	119	17	45	3	2.09
Frank Smith	R	26	5	5	.500	2	20	13	8	122	124	37	53	1	3.39
Lou Fiene	R	21	1	1	.500	0	6	2	1	31	35	9	12	0	2.90
Frank Isbell	R	30	0	0	.000	0	1	0	0	2	1	0	2	0	0.00
		29	90*	61	.596	5	155	155	99	1358	1236	351	605	18	2.78
Al Orth	R	33	**27**	17	.614	0	45	39	**36**	**339**	**317**	66	133	3	2.34
Jack Chesbro	R	32	24	16	.600	1	**49**	**42**	24	325	314	75	152	4	2.96
Bill Hogg		26	14	13	.519	0	28	25	15	206	171	72	107	3	2.93
Walter Clarkson	R	27	9	4	.692	1	32	16	9	151	135	55	64	3	2.32
Doc Newton	L	28	6	5	.545	0	21	15	6	125	118	33	52	2	3.17
Noodles Hahn	L	27	3	2	.600	0	6	6	3	42	38	6	17	1	3.86
Louis LeRoy	R	27	2	0	1.000	1	11	2	1	45	33	12	28	0	2.20
Slow Joe Doyle	R	24	2	2	.500	0	9	6	3	45	34	13	28	2	2.40
Clark Griffith	R	26	2	2	.500	2	17	2	1	60	58	15	16	0	3.00
Cy Barger	R	21	0	0	.000	0	2	1	0	5	7	3	3	0	10.80
Tom Hughes	R	22	1	0	1.000	0	3	1	1	15	11	1	5	0	4.20
*One win by forfeit															
		28	89	64	.582	5	157	157	**133**	**1413**	1197	365	530	27	**2.09**
Bob Rhoades	R	26	22	10	.688	1	38	34	31	315	259	92	89	7	1.80
Addie Joss	R	26	21	9	.700	1	34	31	28	282	220	43	106	9	1.72
Otto Hess	L	27	20	17	.541	**3**	43	36	33	334	274	85	167	7	1.83
Bill Bernhard	R	35	16	15	.516	0	31	30	23	255	235	47	85	2	2.54
Harry Eells	R	25	4	5	.444	0	14	8	6	86	77	48	35	1	2.62
Jack Townsend	R	27	3	7	.300	0	17	12	8	93	92	31	31	1	2.90
Glenn Liebhardt	R	23	2	0	1.000	0	2	2	2	18	13	1	9	0	1.50
Earl Moore (HO)	R	26	1	1	.500	0	5	4	2	30	27	18	8	0	3.90

PHILADELPHIA 4th 78-67 .538 12 — CONNIE MACK

NAME	G by POS	B	AGE	G	AB	R	H	2B	3B	HR	RBI	BB	SO	SB	BA	SA
TOTALS			29	149	4883	555	1206	213	49	**31**	489	385		166	.247	.330
Harry Davis	1B145	R	32	145	551	94	161	40	8	**12**	**96**	49		23	.292	.459
Danny Murphy	2B119	R	29	119	448	48	135	24	7	2	60	21		17	.301	.400
Monte Cross	SS134	R	36	134	445	32	89	23	3	0	40	50		22	.200	.265
Jack Knight	3B67, 2B7	R	20	74	253	29	49	7	2	3	20	19		6	.194	.273
Socks Seybold	OF114	R	35	116	411	41	130	21	3	5	59	30		9	.316	.418
Bris Lord	OF115	R	22	118	434	50	101	13	7	1	44	27		12	.233	.302
Topsy Hartsel	OF144	L	32	144	533	96	136	21	9	1	30	**88**		31	.255	.334
Ossee Schreckengost	C89, 1B4	R	31	98	338	29	96	20	1	1	41	10		5	.284	.358
Harry Armbruster	OF74	L	24	91	265	40	63	6	3	2	24	43		13	.238	.306
Rube Oldring (BN)	3B49, SS3, 2B2, 1B1	R	22	59	174	15	42	10	1	0	19	2		7	.241	.310
Mike Powers	C57, 1B1	R	35	58	185	5	29	1	0	0	7	1		2	.157	.162
Art Brouthers	3B33		23	36	144	18	30	5	1	0	14	5		4	.208	.257
Dave Shean	2B22	R	28	22	75	7	16	3	2	0	3	5		6	.213	.307
Simon Nicholls	SS12	L	23	12	44	1	8	1	0	0	1	3		0	.182	.205
Claude Berry	C10	R	26	10	30	2	7	0	0	0	2	2		1	.233	.233
Jim Byrnes	C8	R	26	9	23	2	4	0	1	0	0	0		0	.174	.261
1 Danny Hoffman	OF7	L	26	7	22	4	5	0	0	0	0	3		1	.227	.227
Ed Lennox	3B6	R	20	6	17	1	1	1	0	0	0	1		0	.059	.118
Eddie Collins	SS3, 3B1	L	19	6	17	1	4	0	0	0	0	0		0	.235	.235
Willy Fetzer		L	22	1	1	0	0	0	0	0	0	0		0	.000	.000
1 Jack Hannifan			23	1	1	0	1	0	0	0	0	0		0	1.000	1.000

NAME	T	AGE	W	L	PCT	SV	G	GS	CG	IP	H	BB	SO	ShO	ERA
		25	78	67*	.538	7	149	149	107	1322	1135	425	**749**	18	2.60
Eddie Plank	L	30	19	5	**.792**	0	26	25	21	212	173	51	108	5	2.25
Rube Waddell	L	29	16	16	.500	1	43	34	22	273	221	92	**196**	8	2.21
Chief Bender	R	23	15	10	.600	**3**	36	27	24	238	208	48	159	0	2.53
Jimmy Dygert	R	21	10	13	.435	1	35	25	15	214	175	91	106	4	2.69
Jack Coombs	R	23	10	11	.476	1	23	18	13	173	144	68	90	1	2.50
Andy Coakley (IL)	R	23	7	8	.467	0	22	16	10	149	144	44	59	0	3.14
Bill Bartley	R	21	0	0	.000	1	3	0	0	9	10	6	6	0	9.00
Mike Cunningham	R		1	0	1.000	0	5	1	1	28	29	9	15	0	3.21
Jim Holmes		23	0	1	.000	0	3	1	0	9	10	8	1	0	4.00
Hack Schumann	R	21	0	2	.000	0	4	2	1	18	21	8	9	0	4.00

*1 loss by forfeit

ST. LOUIS 5th 76-73 .510 16 — JIMMY McALEER

NAME	G by POS	B	AGE	G	AB	R	H	2B	3B	HR	RBI	BB	SO	SB	BA	SA
TOTALS			28	154	5053	559	1250	145	60	20	456	366		222	.247	.312
Tom Jones	1B143	R	29	144	539	51	136	22	6	0	30	24		27	.252	.315
Pete O'Brien	2B120, 3B20, SS11	L	30	151	524	44	122	9	4	2	57	42		25	.233	.277
Bobby Wallace	SS138	R	32	139	476	64	123	24	7	2	67	58		24	.258	.351
Roy Hartzell	3B103, SS6, 2B2	L	24	113	404	43	86	7	0	0	24	19		21	.213	.230
Harry Niles	OF108, 3B34	R	25	142	541	71	124	14	4	2	31	46		30	.229	.281
Charlie Hemphill	OF154	L	30	154	585	90	169	19	12	4	62	43		33	.289	.383
George Stone	OF154	L	28	154	581	91	208	24	19	6	71	52		35	**.358**	**.496**
Jack O'Connor	C57	R	37	61	186	8	37	0	0	0	11	2		5	.199	.199
Ben Koehler	OF52, 2B7, SS1, 3B1	R	29	66	186	27	41	1	1	0	15	24		9	.220	.237
Branch Rickey	C54, OF1	L	24	64	201	22	57	8	3	3	24	16		4	.284	.398
Tubby Spencer	C54	R	21	58	188	15	33	6	1	0	17	7		4	.176	.218
Ike Rockenfield	2B26	R	29	27	89	3	21	4	0	0	8	1		0	.236	.281
Lou Nordyke	1B12	R	29	25	53	4	13	1	0	0	7	10		3	.245	.264
John Heidrick (VR) 29																

NAME	T	AGE	W	L	PCT	SV	G	GS	CG	IP	H	BB	SO	ShO	ERA
		28	76	73	.510	5	154	154	**133**	1358	1132	314	568	17	2.23
Barney Pelty	R	25	17	12	.586	2	34	30	25	261	189	59	92	4	1.59
Harry Howell	R	29	15	13	.536	1	35	33	30	277	233	61	140	6	2.11
Fred Glade	R	30	15	15	.500	0	35	32	28	267	215	59	96	4	2.36
Jack Powell (ST)	R	31	13	14	.481	1	28	26	25	244	196	55	132	3	1.77
Beany Jacobson	L	25	9	9	.500	0	24	15	12	155	146	27	53	0	2.50
Ed Smith	R	27	7	10	.412	1	19	18	13	155	153	53	45	0	3.72

DETROIT 6th 71-78 .477 21 — BILL ARMOUR

NAME	G by POS	B	AGE	G	AB	R	H	2B	3B	HR	RBI	BB	SO	SB	BA	SA
TOTALS			26	151	4927	516	1194	154	64	10	409	333		205	.242	.306
Pinky Lindsay	1B122, 2B17, 3B1		27	141	499	59	112	16	2	0	33	45		18	.224	.265
Germany Schaefer	2B114, SS7	R	29	124	446	48	106	14	3	2	42	32		31	.238	.296
Charley O'Leary	SS127	R	24	128	443	34	97	13	2	2	34	17		8	.219	.271
Bill Coughlin	3B147	R	27	147	498	54	117	15	5	2	60	36		31	.235	.297
Sam Crawford	OF116, 1B32	L	26	145	563	65	166	23	16	2	72	38		24	.295	.403
Ty Cobb (IL)	OF96	L	19	98	358	45	113	13	7	1	34	19		23	.316	.399
Matty McIntyre	OF133	L	26	133	493	63	128	19	11	0	39	56		29	.260	.343
Boss Schmidt	C67	B	25	68	216	13	47	4	3	0	10	6		1	.218	.264
Davy Jones	OF84	L	26	84	323	41	84	12	2	0	24	41		21	.260	.310
Freddie Payne	C47, OF17	R	25	72	222	23	60	5	5	0	20	13		4	.270	.338
1 John Warner	C49	L	33	50	153	15	37	4	2	0	10	12		4	.242	.294
Bobby Lowe (IL)	SS19, 2B17, 3B5	R	37	41	145	11	30	3	0	1	12	4		3	.207	.248
Sam Thompson	OF8	L	46	8	31	4	7	0	1	0	3	1		0	.226	.290
Frank Scheibeck	2B3	R	41	3	10	1	1	0	0	0	0	2		0	.100	.100
Gus Hetling	3B2	R	20	2	7	0	1	0	0	0	0	0		0	.143	.143

NAME	T	AGE	W	L	PCT	SV	G	GS	CG	IP	H	BB	SO	ShO	ERA
		30	71	78	.477	5	151	151	128	1334	**1398**	389	469	7	3.06
George Mullin	R	25	21	18	.538	0	40	40	35	330	315	**108**	123	2	2.78
Ed Siever	L	28	14	10	.583	1	30	25	20	223	240	45	71	1	2.70
Red Donahue	R	33	13	14	.481	0	28	28	26	241	260	54	82	3	2.73
Ed Killian (IL)	L	29	9	6	.600	2	21	16	14	150	165	54	47	0	3.42
Will Bill Donovan	R	29	9	15	.375	0	25	25	22	212	221	72	85	0	3.14
John Eubank	R	33	4	10	.286	2	24	12	7	135	147	35	38	1	3.53
Jimmy Wiggs	R	29	1	1	.500	0	4	1	0	10	11	7	7	0	5.40
Jack Rowan	R	19	0	1	.000	0	1	1	1	9	15	6	0	0	11.00
Ed Willett	R	22	0	3	.000	0	3	3	3	25	24	8	16	0	3.96

WASHINGTON 7th 55-95 .367 37.5 — JAKE STAHL

NAME	G by POS	B	AGE	G	AB	R	H	2B	3B	HR	RBI	BB	SO	SB	BA	SA
TOTALS			29	151	4966	518	1181	144	65	26	433	306		**233**	.238	.309
Jake Stahl	1B136	R	27	137	482	38	107	9	8	0	51	21		30	.222	.274
Larry Schlafly	2B123	R	27	123	426	60	105	13	8	2	30	50		29	.246	.329
Dave Altizer	SS113, OF2	L	29	115	433	56	111	9	5	1	27	35		37	.256	.307
Lave Cross	3B130	R	40	130	494	55	130	14	6	1	46	28		19	.263	.322
C. Hickman (IL)	OF95, 1B18, 3B5, 2B1	R	30	120	451	53	128	26	4	9	57	14		9	.284	.419
Charlie Jones	OF128, 2B1		30	131	497	56	120	11	11	3	42	24		34	.241	.326
John Anderson	OF151	B	32	151	583	62	158	25	4	3	70	19		**39**	.271	.343
Howard Wakefield	C60	R	22	77	211	17	59	9	2	1	21	7		6	.280	.355
Rabbitt Nill	SS31, 2B25, 3B15, OF15	R	24	89	315	37	74	8	2	0	15	47		16	.235	.273
Joe Stanley	OF64, P1	B	25	73	221	18	36	0	4	0	9	20		6	.163	.199
Mike Heydon (BG)	C49		31	49	145	14	23	7	1	0	10	14		2	.159	.221
2 John Warner	C32	L	33	32	103	5	21	4	1	1	9	2		3	.204	.291
1 Mal Kittredge	C27	R	36	27	78	5	14	0	0	0	3	1		0	.179	.179
Otto Williams	SS8, 2B6, 1B2, 3B1	R	28	20	51	3	7	0	0	0	2	2		0	.137	.137
Pat Duff			31	1	1	0	0	0	0	0	0	0		0	.000	.000
Warren Shanabrook	3B1	R	25	1	2	0	0	0	0	0	0	0		0	.000	.000
Joe Cassidy (DD) 23																

NAME	T	AGE	W	L	PCT	SV	G	GS	CG	IP	H	BB	SO	ShO	ERA
		29	55	95	.367	1	151	151	115	1323	1331	**451**	558	12	3.25
Casey Patten	L	30	19	15	.559	0	38	32	28	283	253	79	96	6	2.16
Cy Falkenberg	R	26	14	19	.424	1	40	36	30	299	277	**108**	178	2	2.86
Charlie Smith	R	26	9	16	.360	0	33	22	17	235	250	75	105	2	2.91
Long Tom Hughes	R	27	7	17	.292	0	30	24	18	204	230	81	90	1	3.62
Frank Kitson	R	34	6	16	.272	0	30	21	15	197	196	57	59	1	3.65
Con Starkel	R	25	0	0	.000	0	1	0	0	3	7	2	1	0	18.00
Sam Edmonston	L	22	0	1	.000	0	2	1	1	10	10	2	0	0	4.50
Chink Wilson			0	1	.000	0	1	1	1	7	3	2	1	0	2.57
Willie Sudhoff	R	31	0	2	.000	0	9	5	0	20	30	9	7	0	9.00
Clyde Goodwin	R	19	0	2	.000	0	4	3	1	22	20	13	9	0	4.50
Harry Hardy		30	0	3	.000	0	5	3	2	20	35	12	4	0	9.00
Bill Wolfe	R	30	0	3	.000	0	4	3	2	20	17	10	8	0	4.05
Joe Stanley	R	25	0	0	.000	0	1	0	0	3	3	1	0	0	12.00

BOSTON 8th 49-105 .318 45.5 — JIMMY COLLINS 44-92 .324 CHICK STAHL 5-13 .278

NAME	G by POS	B	AGE	G	AB	R	H	2B	3B	HR	RBI	BB	SO	SB	BA	SA
TOTALS			28	155	5168	462	1223	160	75	13	408	298		99	.237	.304
Moose Grimshaw (JJ)	1B110	B	30	110	428	46	124	16	12	0	48	23		5	.290	.383
Hobe Ferris	2B126, 3B4	R	28	130	495	47	121	25	13	2	44	10		8	.244	.360
Freddy Parent	SS143, 2B6	R	30	149	600	67	141	14	10	1	49	31		16	.235	.297
Red Morgan	3B88		22	88	307	20	66	6	3	1	21	16		7	.215	.264
Jack Hayden (SL)	OF85	R	25	85	322	22	80	6	4	1	14	17		6	.248	.301
Chick Stahl	OF155	R	33	155	595	62	170	24	6	4	51	47		13	.286	.366
John Hoey	OF94		24	94	361	27	88	8	4	0	24	14		10	.244	.288
Charlie Armbruster	C66, 1B1	R	24	72	201	9	29	6	1	0	6	25		2	.144	.184
Buck Freeman	OF65, 1B43, 3B4	L	34	121	392	42	98	20	8	1	30	28		5	.250	.349
J. Godwin (LJ)	3B27, SS14, OF10, 2B3, 1B1		29	66	193	11	36	2	1	0	15	6		6	.187	.207
Kip Selbach	OF58	R	34	60	228	15	48	9	2	0	23	18		7	.211	.268
Bob Peterson	C30, 2B3, 1B2, OF1			39	118	10	24	1	1	1	9	11		1	.203	.254
Bill Carrigan	C35	R	22	37	109	5	23	0	0	0	10	5		3	.211	.211
Jimmy Collins (KJ)	3B32	R	36	37	142	17	39	9	4	1	16	4		1	.275	.415
Jesse Tannehill	P27	L	31	31	79	12	22	2	2	0	4	6		1	.278	.354
Charlie Graham (SA)	C27	R	28	30	90	10	21	1	0	1	12	10		1	.233	.278
Chet Chadbourne	2B11, SS1	L	21	11	43	7	13	1	0	0	3	3		1	.302	.326
Heinie Wagner	2B9	R	25	9	32	1	9	0	0	0	4	1		2	.281	.281
Lou Criger (IL)	C6	R	34	7	17	0	3	1	0	0	1	1		1	.176	.235
Tom Doran	C2	L	26	2	3	1	0	0	0	0	0	0		0	.000	.000

NAME	T	AGE	W	L	PCT	SV	G	GS	CG	IP	H	BB	SO	ShO	ERA
		30	49	**105**	.318	6	155	155	124	1382	1360	285	549	6	3.41
Jesse Tannehill	L	31	13	11	.542	0	27	26	18	196	207	39	82	2	3.17
Cy Young	R	39	13	**21**	.382	2	39	34	28	288	288	25	140	0	3.19
Bill Dinneen	R	30	8	19	.296	0	28	27	22	219	209	52	60	1	2.92
George Winter (IL)	R	28	6	18	.250	2	29	22	18	208	215	38	72	1	4.11
Ralph Glaze	R	25	4	6	.400	0	19	10	7	123	110	32	56	0	3.59
Joe Harris	R	24	2	**21**	.087	2	30	24	20	235	211	67	99	1	3.52
Rube Kroh	L	19	1	0	1.000	0	1	1	1	9	2	4	5	1	0.00
Len Swormstedt	R		1	1	.500	0	3	2	2	21	17	0	6	0	1.29
Frank Oberlin	R	30	1	3	.250	0	4	4	4	34	38	13	13	0	3.18
Ed Hughes	R	26	0	0	.000	0	2	0	0	10	15	3	3	0	5.40
Norwood Gibson	R	29	0	2	.000	0	5	2	1	19	25	7	3	0	5.21
Ed Barry	L		0	3	.000	0	3	3	3	21	23	5	10	0	6.00

CHICAGO 1st 116-36 .763 — FRANK CHANCE

NAME	G by POS	B	AGE	G	AB	R	H	2B	3B	HR	RBI	BB	SO	SB	BA	SA
TOTALS			27	154	5018	704	1316	181	71	20	539	448		283	.262	.339
Frank Chance	1B136	R	28	136	474	103	151	24	10	3	71	70		57	.319	.430
Johnny Evers	2B153, 3B1	L	24	154	533	65	136	17	6	1	51	36		49	.255	.315
Joe Tinker	SS147, 3B1	R	25	148	523	75	122	18	4	1	64	43		30	.233	.289
Harry Steinfeldt	3B150, 2B1	R	28	151	539	81	176	27	10	3	83	47		29	.327	.430
Wildfire Schulte	OF146	L	23	146	563	77	158	18	13	7	60	31		25	.281	.396
Jimmy Slagle	OF127	L	32	127	498	71	119	8	6	0	33	63		25	.239	.279
Jimmy Sheckard	OF149	L	27	149	549	90	144	27	10	1	45	67		30	.262	.353
Johnny Kling	C96, OF3	R	31	107	343	45	107	15	8	2	46	23		14	.312	.420
Pat Moran	C61	R	30	70	226	22	57	13	1	0	35	7		6	.252	.319
Solly Hofman	OF23, 1B21, SS9, 2B4, 3B4	R	23	64	195	30	50	2	3	2	20	20		13	.256	.328
2 Doc Gessler	OF21, 1B1	L	25	34	83	8	21	3	0	0	10	12		4	.253	.289
Tom Walsh	C2	R	21	2	1	0	0	0	0	0	0	0		0	.000	.000
1 Pete Noonan	1B1	R	24	5	3	0	1	0	0	0	0	0		0	.333	.333
Bull Smith				1	1	0	0	0	0	0	0	0		0	.000	.000

NAME	T	AGE	W	L	PCT	SV	G	GS	CG	IP	H	BB	SO	ShO	ERA
		27	116	36	.763	10	154	154	125	1379	1018	446	702	28	1.76
Three Finger Brown	R	29	26	6	.813	3	36	32	27	277	198	61	144	9	1.04
Jack Pfiester	L	28	20	8	.714	0	31	29	20	242	173	63	153	4	1.56
Ed Reulbach	R	23	19	4	.826	3	33	24	20	218	129	92	94	6	1.65
Carl Lundgren	R	26	17	6	.739	2	27	24	21	208	160	89	103	5	2.21
2 Orvie Overall	R	25	12	3	.800	1	18	14	13	144	116	51	94	2	1.88
2 Jack Taylor	R	32	12	3	.800	0	17	16	15	147	116	39	34	2	1.84
1 Fred Beebe	R	25	7	1	.875	1	14	6	4	70	56	32	55*	0	2.70
1 Bob Wicker	R	28	3	5	.375	0	10	8	5	72	70	19	25	0	3.00
2 Jack Harper	R	28	0	0	.000	0	1	1	0	1	0	0	0	0	0.00

*Beebe, also with St. Louis, league leader in SO with 171

NEW YORK 2nd 96-56 .632 20 — JOHN McGRAW

NAME	G by POS	B	AGE	G	AB	R	H	2B	3B	HR	RBI	BB	SO	SB	BA	SA
TOTALS			31	152	4768	625	1217	162	53	15	513	563		288	.255	.321
Dan McGann	1B122	R	34	134	451	62	107	14	8	0	37	60		30	.237	.304
Billy Gilbert	2B98	R	30	104	307	44	71	6	1	1	27	12		22	.231	.267
Bill Dahlen	SS143	R	36	143	471	63	113	18	3	1	49	76		16	.240	.297
Art Devlin	3B148	R	26	148	498	76	149	23	8	2	65	74		54	.299	.390
George Browne (IL)	OF121	L	30	122	477	61	126	10	4	0	38	27		32	.264	.302
2 Cy Seymour	OF72	L	33	72	269	35	86	12	3	4	42	18		20	.320	.431
2 Spike Shannon	OF76	B	28	76	287	42	73	5	1	0	25	34		18	.254	.279
Roger Bresnahan	C82, OF40	R	27	124	405	69	114	22	4	0	43	81		25	.281	.356
Sammy Strang	2B57, OF39, SS4, 3B3, 1B1	B	29	113	313	50	100	16	4	4	49	54		21	.319	.435
Frank Bowerman	C67, 1B20	R	37	103	285	23	65	7	3	1	42	15		5	.228	.284
1 Sam Mertes	OF71	R	33	71	253	37	60	9	6	1	33	29		21	.237	.332
Mike Donlin (BL)	OF29, 1B1	L	28	37	121	15	38	5	1	1	14	11		9	.314	.397
1 Doc Marshall	OF16, C13, 1B2	R	31	38	102	8	17	3	2	0	7	7		7	.167	.235
Broadway Aleck Smith	C8, 1B3, OF1		35	16	28	0	5	0	0	0	2	1		1	.179	.179
2 Jack Hannifan	SS6, 3B3, 2B1	R	23	10	30	4	6	0	1	0	3	2		1	.200	.267
Frank Burke	OF4		26	8	9	2	3	1	1	0	1	1		1	.333	.667
Matty Fitzgerald	C3	R	25	4	6	2	4	0	0	0	2	0		1	.667	.667
John McGraw	3B1	L	33	4	2	0	0	0	0	0	0	1		0	.000	.000

NAME	T	AGE	W	L	PCT	SV	G	GS	CG	IP	H	BB	SO	ShO	ERA
		27	96	56	.632	18	152	152	105	1334	1207	394	639	16	2.49
Joe McGinnity	R	35	27	12	.692	2	45	37	32	340	316	71	105	3	2.25
Christy Mathewson	R	27	22	12	.647	1	38	35	22	267	262	77	128	5	2.97
Dummy Taylor	R	31	17	9	.654	0	31	27	13	213	186	57	91	2	2.20
Hooks Wiltse	L	25	16	11	.593	6	38	26	21	249	227	58	125	1	2.27
Red Ames (KJ)	R	23	12	10	.545	1	31	25	15	203	166	93	156	1	2.66
Cecil Ferguson	R	19	2	1	.667	7	22	1	1	52	43	24	32	1	2.60
Henry Mathewson	R	21	0	1	.000	1	2	1	1	10	7	14	2	0	5.40

PITTSBURGH 3rd 93-60 .608 23.5 — FRED CLARKE

NAME	G by POS	B	AGE	G	AB	R	H	2B	3B	HR	RBI	BB	SO	SB	BA	SA
TOTALS			29	154	5030	622	1313	164	67	12	497	424		162	.261	.327
Jim Nealon	1B154		21	154	556	82	142	21	12	3	83	53		15	.255	.353
Claude Ritchey	2B151	B	32	152	484	46	130	21	5	1	62	68		6	.269	.339
Honus Wagner	SS137, OF2, 3B1	R	32	142	516	103	175	38	9	2	71	58		53	.339	.459
Tommy Sheehan	3B90	R	28	95	315	28	76	6	3	1	34	18		13	.241	.289
Bob Ganley	OF134	L	31	137	511	63	132	7	6	0	31	41		19	.258	.295
Ginger Beaumont (LJ)	OF78	L	29	80	310	48	82	9	3	2	32	19		1	.265	.332
Fred Clarke	OF110	L	33	118	417	69	129	14	13	1	39	40		18	.309	.412
George Gibson	C81	R	25	81	259	8	46	6	1	0	20	16		1	.178	.208
Tommy Leach	3B65, OF60, SS1	R	28	133	476	66	136	10	7	1	39	33		21	.286	.342
Dutch Meier	OF52, SS17	R	27	82	273	32	70	11	4	0	16	13		4	.256	.326
2 Eddie Phelps	C40	R	27	43	118	9	28	3	1	0	12	9		1	.237	.280
Heinie Peitz	C38	R	23	40	125	13	30	8	0	0	20	13		1	.240	.304
Bill Hallman	OF23		30	23	89	12	24	3	1	1	6	15		3	.270	.360
Otis Clymer (BN)	OF11	L	29	11	45	7	11	0	1	0	1	3		1	.244	.289
Otis Abstein	2B3, OF2	R	23	8	20	2	4	0	0	0	3	0		2	.200	.200
Alan Storke	3B2, SS1	R	21	5	12	1	3	1	0	0	1	1		1	.250	.333
Fred Carisch	C4	R	24	4	12	0	1	0	0	0	0	1		1	.083	.083
Harry Smith (IL)	C1	R	31	1	1	0	0	0	0	0	0	1		0	.000	.000

NAME	T	AGE	W	L	PCT	SV	G	GS	CG	IP	H	BB	SO	ShO	ERA
		30	93	60	.608	2	154	154	116	1358	1234	309	532	26	2.21
Vic Willis	R	30	22	13	.629	1	41	36	32	322	295	76	124	6	1.73
Sam Leever	R	34	22	7	.759	0	36	31	25	260	232	48	76	6	2.32
Lefty Leifield	L	22	18	13	.581	1	37	31	24	256	214	68	111	8	1.86
Deacon Phillippe	R	34	15	10	.600	0	33	24	19	219	216	26	90	3	2.47
Mike Lynch	R	31	6	5	.545	0	18	12	7	119	101	31	48	0	2.42
Doc Hillebrand	L	26	3	2	.600	0	7	5	4	53	42	21	32	1	2.21
1 Ed Karger	L	23	2	3	.400	0	6	2	0	28	21	9	8	0	1.93
Howie Camnitz	R	24	1	0	1.000	0	2	1	1	9	6	5	5	1	2.00
King Brady	R	25	1	1	.500	0	3	2	1	23	30	4	14	0	2.35
Charlie Case	R	26	1	1	.500	0	2	2	1	11	8	5	3	0	5.73
2 Chappie McFarland	R		1	3	.250	0	6	5	2	35	39	7	11	1	2.57
Lou Manske	L	21	1	0	1.000	0	2	1	0	8	12	5	6	0	5.63
Bert Maxwell	R	19	0	1	.000	0	1	1	0	8	8	2	1	0	5.63
Irish McIlveen	L	25	0	1	.000	0	2	1	0	7	10	2	3	0	7.71

PHILADELPHIA 4th 71-82 .464 45.5 — HUGH DUFFY

NAME	G by POS	B	AGE	G	AB	R	H	2B	3B	HR	RBI	BB	SO	SB	BA	SA
TOTALS			27	154	4911	530	1183	197	47	12	444	432		180	.241	.307
Kitty Bransfield	1B139	R	31	140	524	47	144	28	5	1	60	16		12	.275	.353
Kid Gleason	2B135	B	39	135	494	47	112	17	2	0	34	36		17	.227	.269
Mickey Doolan	SS154	R	26	154	535	41	123	19	7	1	55	27		16	.230	.297
Ernie Courtney	3B96, 1B13, OF3, SS1	R	27	116	398	53	94	12	2	0	42	45		6	.236	.276
John Titus	OF142	L	30	145	484	67	129	22	5	1	57	78		12	.267	.339
Roy Thomas	OF142	L	32	142	493	81	125	10	7	0	16	107		22	.254	.302
Sherry Magee	OF154	R	21	154	563	77	159	36	8	6	67	52		55	.282	.407
Red Dooin	C107	R	27	113	351	25	86	19	1	0	32	13		15	.245	.305
Johnny Lush	P37, OF22, 1B2	L	20	76	212	28	56	7	1	0	15	14		6	.264	.307
Paul Sentell	3B33, 2B19, OF2, SS1	R	26	63	192	19	44	5	1	1	14	14		15	.229	.281
Jerry Donovan	C52, OF1, SS1	R	29	61	166	11	33	4	0	0	15	6		2	.199	.223
Joe Ward	3B27, 2B3, SS1	R	21	35	129	12	38	8	6	0	11	5		2	.295	.450
Ches Crist	C6	R	24	6	11	1	0	0	0	0	0	0		0	.000	.000
Harry Houston	C2	R	22	2	4	0	0	0	0	0	0	1		0	.000	.000
Hugh Duffy		R	39	1	1	0	0	0	0	0	0	0		0	.000	.000

NAME	T	AGE	W	L	PCT	SV	G	GS	CG	IP	H	BB	SO	ShO	ERA
		28	71	82	.464	5	154	154	108	1354	1201	436	500	20	2.58
Tully Sparks	R	29	19	16	.543	3	42	37	29	317	244	62	114	6	2.16
Johnny Lush	L	20	18	15	.545	0	37	35	24	281	254	119	151	4	2.37
Bill Duggleby	R	33	13	19	.406	2	42	30	22	280	241	66	83	5	2.25
Lew Richie	R	22	9	11	.450	0	33	22	14	206	170	79	65	3	2.40
Togie Pittinger	R	35	8	10	.444	0	20	16	9	130	128	50	43	2	3.39
Jim McClosky		23	3	2	.600	0	9	4	3	41	46	9	6	0	2.85
Harry Kane	L	22	1	3	.250	0	6	3	2	28	28	18	14	0	3.86
Charlie Roy	R	22	0	1	.000	0	7	1	0	18	24	5	6	0	5.00
Kid Nichols	R	26	0	1	.000	0	4	2	1	11	17	13	1	0	9.82
Walter Moser	R	25	0	4	.000	0	6	4	4	43	49	15	17	0	3.56

BROOKLYN 5th 66-86 .434 50 — PATSY DONOVAN

NAME	G by POS	B	AGE	G	AB	R	H	2B	3B	HR	RBI	BB	SO	SB	BA	SA
TOTALS			28	153	4897	495	1156	141	68	25	407	388		175	.236	.308
Tim Jordan	1B126	L	27	129	450	67	118	20	8	12	78	59		16	.262	.422
Whitey Alperman	2B104, SS24, 3B1	R	26	128	441	38	111	15	7	3	46	6		13	.252	.338
Phil Lewis	SS135	R	22	136	452	40	110	8	4	0	37	43		14	.243	.279
Doc Casey	3B149	L	33	149	571	71	133	17	8	0	34	52		22	.233	.291
Harry Lumley	OF131	L	25	133	484	72	157	23	12	9	61	48		35	.324	.477
Billy Maloney	OF151	L	28	151	566	71	125	15	7	0	32	49		38	.221	.272
Jack McCarthy	OF86	L	37	91	322	23	98	13	1	0	35	20		9	.304	.351
Bill Bergen	C103	R	33	103	353	9	56	3	3	0	19	7		2	.159	.184
John Hummel	2B50, OF21, 1B15	R	23	97	286	20	57	6	4	1	21	36		10	.199	.259
Lew Ritter	C53, OF9, 1B3, 3B2	R	30	73	226	22	47	1	3	0	15	16		6	.208	.239
Heinie Batch (IL)	OF50, 3B2	R	26	59	203	23	52	7	6	0	11	15		3	.256	.350
1 Doc Gessler	1B9	L	25	9	33	3	8	1	2	0	4	3		3	.242	.394
Patsy Donovan	OF6	R	41	7	21	1	5	0	0	0	0	0		0	.238	.238
Phil Reardon	OF4	R	22	5	14	0	1	0	0	0	0	0		0	.071	.071
John Butler	C1	R	26	1	0	0	0	0	0	0	0	0		0	.000	.000

NAME	T	AGE	W	L	PCT	SV	G	GS	CG	IP	H	BB	SO	ShO	ERA
		27	66	86	.434	11	153	153	119	1349	1255	453	476	22	3.13
Doc Scanlan	R	25	18	13	.581	2	38	33	28	288	230	127	120	6	3.19
Elmer Stricklett	R	29	14	18	.438	5	41	35	28	292	273	77	88	5	2.71
Harry McIntire	R	28	13	21	.382	3	39	31	25	276	254	89	121	4	2.97
Jim Pastorius	L	24	10	14	.417	0	29	24	16	212	225	69	58	3	3.61
Mal Eason	R	27	10	17	.370	1	34	26	18	227	212	74	64	3	3.25
Jesse Whiting			1	1	.500	0	3	2	2	25	26	6	7	1	2.88
Hub Knolls	R	22	0	0	.000	0	2	0	0	7	13	2	3	0	3.86
Jack Doscher (JT)	L	25	0	1	.000	0	2	1	1	14	12	4	10	0	1.29
3 Chappie McFarland	R		0	1	.000	0	1	1	1	9	10	5	5	0	8.00

NAME	G by POS	B	AGE	G	AB	R	H	2B	3B	HR	RBI	BB	SO	SB	BA	SA
CINCINNATI 6th 64-87 .424 51.5		**NED HANLON**														
TOTALS			29	155	5025	530	1198	140	71	16	454	395		170	.238	.304
Snake Deal	1B65	R	27	65	231	13	48	4	3	0	21	6		15	.208	.251
Miller Huggins	2B146	B	27	146	545	81	159	11	7	0	26	71		41	.292	.338
Tommy Corcoran	SS117	R	37	117	430	29	89	13	1	1	33	19		8	.207	.249
Jim Delahanty	3B105, SS5, OF2	R	27	115	379	63	106	21	4	1	39	45		21	.280	.364
Frank Jude	OF80	R	21	80	308	31	64	6	4	1	31	16		7	.208	.263
1 Cy Semour	OF79	L	33	79	307	35	79	7	2	4	38	24		9	.257	.332
Joe Kelley	OF122, 1B3, SS1, 3B1	R	34	129	465	43	106	19	11	1	53	44		9	.228	.323
Admiral Schlei	C91, 1B21	R	20	116	388	44	95	13	8	4	54	29		7	.245	.351
Hans Lobert	3B35, SS31, 2B10, OF1	R	24	79	268	39	83	5	5	0	19	19		20	.310	.366
1 Shad Barry	1B43, OF30	R	29	73	279	38	80	10	5	1	33	26		11	.287	.369
2 Homer Smoof	OF59	L	28	60	220	11	57	8	1	1	17	13		0	.259	.318
Fred Odwell	OF57	R	33	58	202	20	45	5	4	0	21	15		11	.223	.287
Paddy Livingston	C47	R	26	50	139	8	22	1	4	0	8	12		0	.158	.223
Charlie Carr	1B22	R	29	22	94	9	18	2	3	0	10	2		0	.191	.277
Johnny Siegle (LJ)	OF21	R	31	22	68	4	8	2	2	0	7	3		0	.118	.206
Mike Mowrey	3B15, SS1, 2B1	R	22	21	53	3	17	3	0	0	6	5		2	.321	.377
Bill Hinchman	OF16	R	23	18	54	7	11	1	1	0	1	8		2	.204	.259
Larry McLean	C12	R	24	12	35	3	7	2	0	0	2	4		0	.200	.257
1 Eddie Phelps	C12	R	27	12	40	3	11	0	2	1	5	3		2	.275	.450

Jimmy Barrett (KJ) 31 L 0-12, Oscar Stanage 23 R 0-1, Eddie Tiemeyer 21 R 2-11

NAME	T	AGE	W	L	PCT	SV	G	GS	CG	IP	H	BB	SO	ShO	ERA
		32	64	87	.424	5	155	155	126	1370	1248	470	567	11	2.69
Jake Weimer	L	32	20	14	.588	1	41	39	31	305	263	99	141	6	2.21
Bob Ewing	R	33	13	14	.481	0	33	32	26	288	248	60	145	2	2.37
Chick Fraser (HO)	R	35	10	20	.333	0	31	28	25	236	221	80	58	2	2.67
2 Bob Wicker	R	28	6	14	.300	0	20	17	14	150	150	46	69	0	2.70
1 Orvie Overall	R	25	3	5	.375	0	13	10	6	82	77	46	33	0	4.28
Charley Hall	R	20	4	6	.400	1	14	9	9	95	86	50	49	1	3.32
Bill Essick	R	24	2	1	.667	0	6	4	3	39	39	16	16	0	3.00
1 Carl Druhot	L	23	2	2	.500	0	4	3	1	25	27	7	14	0	4.32
Charlie Chech	R	28	1	4	.200	3	11	5	5	66	59	24	17	0	2.32
1 Jack Harper (RJ)	R	28	1	4	.200	0	5	5	3	37	38	20	10	0	4.14
1 Gus Dorner	R	29	1	1*	.500	0	2	1	1	15	16	4	5	0	1.20
Leo Hafford		22	1	1	.500	0	3	1	1	19	13	11	5	0	0.95
Eddie Tiemeyer	R	21	0	0	.000	0	1	0	0	1	1	1	1	0	0.00
Del Mason	R	22	0	1	.000	0	2	1	1	12	10	6	4	0	4.50

*Dorner, also with Boston, league leader in L with 26

NAME	G by POS	B	AGE	G	AB	R	H	2B	3B	HR	RBI	BB	SO	SB	BA	SA
ST. LOUIS 7th 52-98 .347 63		**JOHN McCLOSKEY**														
TOTALS			29	154	**5075**	475	1195	137	69	10	362	361		110	.235	.296
Jake Beckley	1B85	L	38	87	320	29	79	16	6	0	44	13		3	.247	.334
Pug Bennett	2B153	R	32	153	**595**	66	156	16	7	1	34	56		20	.262	.318
George McBride	SS90	R	25	90	313	24	53	8	2	0	13	17		5	.169	.208
Harry Arndt	3B65, 1B1, OF1		27	69	256	30	69	7	9	2	26	19		5	.270	.391
Al Burch	OF91	L	22	91	335	40	89	5	1	0	11	37		15	.266	.287
2 Homer Smoot	OF86	L	28	86	343	41	85	9	10	0	31	11		3	.248	.332
1 Spike Shannon	OF80	B	28	80	302	36	78	4	0	0	25	36		15	.258	.272
Mike Grady	C60, 1B38	R	36	97	280	33	70	11	3	3	27	48		5	.250	.343
Hoelskoeltter	3B53, SS16, P12, OF12, 2B1	R	23	94	317	21	71	6	3	0	14	4		2	.224	.262
2 Shad Barry	OF35, 1B21, 3B6	R	29	62	237	26	59	9	1	0	12	15		6	.249	.295
2 Sam Mertes	OF53	R	33	53	191	20	47	7	4	0	19	16		10	.246	.325
Forrest Crawford	SS39, 3B6		25	45	145	8	30	3	1	0	11	7		1	.207	.241
Red Murray	OF34, C7	R	22	46	144	10	37	9	7	1	16	9		5	.257	.438
John Himes	OF40			40	155	10	42	6	2	0	14	7		4	.271	.329
2 Pete Noonan	C23, 1B16	R	24	44	125	8	21	1	3	1	9	11		1	.168	.248
2 Doc Marshall	C38	R	31	39	123	6	34	4	1	0	10	6		1	.276	.326
Joe Marshall	OF23, 1B4			33	95	2	15	1	2	0	7	6		0	.158	.211
Tommy Raub	C22	R	35	24	78	9	22	2	4	0	2	4		2	.282	.410
Bill Phyle	3B21		31	22	73	6	13	3	1	0	4	5		2	.178	.247
Joe McCarthy	C15	R	24	15	37	3	9	2	0	0	2	2		0	.243	.297
Tom O'Hara	OF14		20	14	53	8	16	1	0	0	0	3		3	.302	.321
Ed Holly	SS10	R	26	10	34	1	2	0	0	0	7	5		0	.059	.059

Ducky Holmes 22 5-27, Eddie Zimmerman 23 R 3-14, Jack Slattery 29 R 2-7, Rube DeGroff 26 0-4

NAME	T	AGE	W	L	PCT	SV	G	GS	CG	IP	H	BB	SO	ShO	ERA
		26	52	98	.347	2	154	154	118	1354	1246	**479**	559	4	3.04
2 Fred Beebe	R	25	9	9	.500	0	20	19	16	161	115	68	**116**	1	3.02
1 Jack Taylor	R	32	8	9	.471	0	17	17	17	155	133	47	27	1	2.15
Buster Brown	R	24	8	16	.333	0	32	27	21	238	208	112	109	0	2.65
2 Carl Druhot	L	23	6	7	.462	0	15	13	12	130	117	46	45	1	2.63
2 Ed Karger	L	23	5	16	.238	1	25	20	17	192	193	43	73	0	2.72
Stony McGlynn	R	34	2	2	.500	0	6	6	6	48	43	15	25	0	2.44
Charlie Rhodes	R	21	3	4	.429	0	9	6	3	45	37	20	32	0	3.40
1 Chappie McFarland	R		2	1	.667	1	6	4	2	37	33	8	16	0	1.95
Ambrose Puttmann	L	25	1	2	.333	0	4	4	0	19	23	9	12	0	5.21
Wish Egan	R	25	2	9	.182	0	16	12	7	86	97	27	23	0	4.60
Gus Thompson	R	29	2	11	.154	0	17	12	8	103	111	25	36	0	4.28
Art Hoelskoetter	R	23	2	4	.333	0	12	3	2	58	53	34	20	0	4.66
Art Fromme	R	23	1	2	.333	0	3	3	3	25	19	10	11	1	1.44
Irv Higginbotham	R	24	1	4	.200	0	7	6	4	47	50	11	14	0	3.26
Babe Adams	R	24	0	1	.000	0	1	1	0	4	9	2	0	0	13.50
Jake Thielman	R	27	0	1	.000	0	1	1	0	5	5	2	0	0	3.60

*Beebe, also with Chicago, league leader in SO with 171

NAME	G by POS	B	AGE	G	AB	R	H	2B	3B	HR	RBI	BB	SO	SB	BA	SA
BOSTON 8th 49-102 .325 66.5		**FRED TENNEY**														
TOTALS			27	152	4925	408	1115	136	43	16	330	356		93	.226	.281
Fred Tenney	1B143	L	34	143	544	61	154	12	8	1	28	58		17	.283	.340
Allie Strobel	2B93, SS6, OF1	R	22	100	317	28	64	10	3	1	24	29		2	.202	.262
Al Bridwell	SS119, OF1	L	22	120	459	41	104	9	1	0	22	44		6	.227	.251
Dave Brain	3B139	R	27	139	525	43	131	19	5	5	45	29		11	.250	.333
Cozy Dolan	OF144, 2B7, P2, 1B1	L	33	152	549	54	136	20	4	0	39	55		17	.248	.299
Johnny Bates	OF140	L	24	140	504	52	127	21	5	6	54	36		9	.252	.349
Del Howard	OF87, 2B45, SS14, 1B2	L	28	147	545	46	142	19	8	1	54	26		17	.261	.330
Tom Needham	C76, 2B5, 1B2, 3B1, OF1	R	27	83	285	11	54	8	2	1	12	13		3	.189	.242
Sam Brown	C35, OF13, 3B12, 1B3, 2B2	R	28	71	231	12	48	6	1	0	20	13		4	.208	.242
Big Jeff Pfeffer	P35, OF14	R	24	60	158	10	31	3	3	1	11	5		4	.196	.272
Jack O'Neill	C48, 1B2, OF1	R	33	61	167	14	30	5	1	0	4	12		0	.180	.222
Gene Good (AJ)	OF34	L	23	34	119	4	18	0	0	0	0	13		2	.151	.151
Happy Jack Cameron	OF16, P2		21	18	61	3	11	0	0	0	4	2		0	.180	.180
Frank Connaughton	SS11, 2B1	R	37	12	44	3	9	0	0	0	1	3		1	.205	.205
Ches Spencer	OF8	L	23	8	27	1	4	1	0	0	0	0		0	.148	.185
Bunny Madden	OF4	L	22	4	15	1	4	0	0	0	0	1		0	.267	.267
Ernie Diehl	OF2, SS1	R	27	3	11	1	5	0	1	0	0	0		0	.455	.636

Jack Schulte 24 R 0-7, Ed Abbaticchio (HO) 29

NAME	T	AGE	W	L	PCT	SV	G	GS	CG	IP	H	BB	SO	ShO	ERA
		27	49	**102**	.325	0	152	152	**137**	1318	**1291**	436	562	10	3.18
Irv Young	L	28	16	25	.390	0	43	**41**	**37**	**358**	**349**	83	151	4	2.92
Big Jeff Pfeffer	R	24	13	22	.371	0	35	35	33	302	270	114	158	4	2.95
Vive Lindaman	R	28	12	23	.343	0	39	37	32	307	303	90	115	2	2.43
2 Gus Dorner	R	29	8	**25***	.242	0	34	32	29	257	264	103	104	0	3.89
Happy Jack Cameron		21	0	0	.000	0	2	1	0	6	4	6	2	0	0.00
Bill McCarthy		24	0	0	.000	0	1	0	0	2	2	3	0	0	9.00
Jim Maroney	L	22	0	3	.000	0	3	3	3	27	28	12	11	0	5.33
Roy Witherup	R	19	0	3	.000	0	8	3	3	46	59	19	14	0	6.26
Cozy Dolan		33	0	1	.000	0	2	0	0	12	12	6	7	0	4.50

*Dorner, also with Cincinnati, league leader in L with 26

WORLD SERIES – CHICAGO (AL) 4 CHICAGO (NL) 2

LINE SCORES

TEAM	1	2	3	4	5	6	7	8	9	10	11	12	R	H	E
Game 1 October 9 at West Side Park															
CHI (AL)	0	0	0	0	1	1	0	0	0				2	4	1
CHI (NL)	0	0	0	0	0	1	0	0	0				1	4	2
Altrock		**Brown**													
Game 2 October 10 at Comiskey Park															
CHI (NL)	0	3	1	0	0	1	0	2	0				7	10	2
CHI (AL)	0	0	0	0	1	0	0	0	0				1	1	2
Reulbach		**White**, Owen (4)													
Game 3 October 11 at West Side Park															
CHI (AL)	0	0	0	0	0	3	0	0	0				3	4	1
CHI (NL)	0	0	0	0	0	0	0	0	0				0	2	2
Walsh		**Pfiester**													
Game 4 October 12 at Comiskey Park															
CHI (NL)	0	0	0	0	0	0	1	0	0				1	7	1
CHI (AL)	0	0	0	0	0	0	0	0	0				0	2	1
Brown		**Altrock**													
Game 5 October 13 at West Side Park															
CHI (AL)	1	0	2	4	0	1	0	0	0				8	12	6
CHI (NL)	3	0	0	1	0	2	0	0	0				6	6	0
Walsh, White (7)				Reulbach, **Pfiester** (3), Overall (4)											
Game 6 October 14 at Comiskey Park															
CHI (NL)	1	0	0	0	1	0	0	0	1				3	7	0
CHI (AL)	3	4	0	0	0	0	0	1	X				8	14	3
Brown, Overall (2)				**White**											

COMPOSITE BATTING

NAME	POS	G	AB	R	H	2B	3B	HR	RBI	BA
Chicago (AL)										
Totals		6	187	22	37	10	3	0	19	.198
Isbell	2B	6	**26**	**4**	**8**	**4**	0	0	4	.308
Hahn	OF	6	22	**4**	6	0	0	0	0	.273
Rohe	3B	6	21	2	7	1	**2**	0	4	**.333**
Jones	OF	6	21	**4**	2	0	0	0	0	.095
Sullivan	C	6	21	0	0	0	0	0	0	.000
Dougherty	OF	6	20	1	2	0	0	0	1	**.100**
Donahue	1B	6	18	0	6	2	1	0	4	**.333**
Davis	SS	3	13	**4**	4	3	0	0	**6**	.308
Tannehill	SS	3	9	1	1	0	0	0	0	.111
Altrock	P	2	4	0	1	0	0	0	0	.250
Walsh	P	2	4	1	0	0	0	0	0	.000
White	P	3	3	0	0	0	0	0	0	.000
Owen	P	1	2	0	0	0	0	0	0	.000
McFarland	PH	1	1	0	0	0	0	0	0	.000
O'Neill	OF	1	1	1	0	0	0	0	0	.000
Towne	PH	1	1	0	0	0	0	0	0	.000
Chicago (NL)										
Totals		6	184	18	36	9	0	0	11	.196
Schulte	OF	6	**26**	1	7	3	0	0	3	.269
Hofman	OF	6	23	3	7	1	0	0	2	.304
Chance	1B	6	21	3	5	1	0	0	0	.238
Sheckard	OF	6	21	0	0	0	0	0	1	.000
Steinfeldt	3B	6	20	2	5	1	0	0	2	.250
Evers	2B	6	20	2	3	1	0	0	1	.150
Tinker	SS	6	18	**4**	3	0	0	0	1	.167
Kling	C	6	17	2	3	1	0	0	0	.176
Brown	P	3	6	0	2	0	0	0	0	.333
Overall	P	2	4	1	1	1	0	0	0	.250
Reulbach	P	2	3	0	0	0	0	0	1	.000
Moran	PH	2	2	0	0	0	0	0	0	.000
Pfeister	P	2	2	0	0	0	0	0	0	.000
Gessler	PH	2	1	0	0	0	0	0	0	.000

COMPOSITE PITCHING

NAME	G	IP	H	BB	SO	W	L	SV	ERA
Chicago (AL)									
Totals	6	54	36	18	28	4	2	1	1.50
Altrock	2	18	11	2	5	1	1	0	**1.00**
Walsh	2	15	7	6	**17**	**2**	0	0	1.20
White	**3**	15	12	7	4	1	1	1	1.80
Owen	1	6	6	3	2	0	0	0	3.00
Chicago (NL)									
Totals	6	53	37	18	35	2	4	0	3.40
Brown	**3**	**19.2**	**14**	4	12	1	**2**	0	3.20
Overall	2	12	10	3	8	0	0	0	2.25
Reulbach	2	11	6	**8**	4	1	0	0	2.45
Pfiester	2	10.1	7	3	11	0	**2**	0	6.10

1907 A Peach in the Summer and a Goat in the Fall

The city of Detroit got its start in professional baseball in 1881 as tenants of the National League. The franchise lasted until 1888, a year after the club captured its only pennant. It was not until 1901 that Detroit got another team—this time, as members of the newly established American League. The best the Tigers could do in those six years were two third-place berths. Previously, the championship had been confined to the cities of Chicago, Philadelphia, and Boston. Yet, before the season would be officially closed, the territorial pennant map would see expansion into the future motor city of the world.

One of the key figures in Detroit's new destiny was long-time National Leaguer Hughie Jennings, who took over the reins of the Tigers in the spring and guided them into the hallowed turf of the championship in his first try as manager. Under Jennings' hand, the league watched in surprise as the 1906 sixth-place Tigers rose to the top like cream—a major reason being the maturing of young outfielder Ty Cobb into a star of commanding presence on the field. The 20-year-old Georgia Peach, in his third year with the Tigers, blossomed into a batting terror by socking the ball at a .350 clip to win his first batting championship. The pugnacious right fielder rang fear into the hearts of infielders just as much as pitchers with his league-leading 49 stolen bases, achieved mostly via a style of sliding in high with razor-honed spikes.

With Cobb batting cleanup, Sam Crawford saw enough good pitches in the third slot to bat a rousing .323—enough to place him second in the league behind Cobb. The duo helped make the Tigers' attack the best in the league, even though the entire team belted only 11 home runs—a credible amount considering it was the era of the dead ball. Veteran Wild Bill Donovan and lefty Ed Killian each won 25 games for the Tigers, while George Mullin chalked up 20 wins but only broke even, as he lost 20 games in a workhorse season of 357 innings.

In reaching for the first American League pennant, Detroit did not have an easy time of it. As of late September, the Tigers were fighting for the flag with Philadelphia, Chicago, and Cleveland, with the issue finally coming down to a crucial series with Philadelphia. With the two teams tied for the top, the Tigers came into Philadelphia on September 27, and knocked off the A's to take over the lead. In the second game of the set, the two nines battled to a 17-inning draw, enabling Detroit to leave with a slim edge which they never relinquished. The late season slump of Rube Waddell, and Chief Bender's sore arm, severely hurt the chances of Philadelphia in the final decisive weeks. Chicago held the best hand of hurlers, aced by 27-game winner Doc White and 24-game winner Ed Walsh but, this time, could not overcome the lack of batting punch in the lineup, while Cleveland could not quite make up for Nap Lajoie's .299 batting average—the worst in his 12-year career.

The National League witnessed the "collapse" of the Cubs to 107 wins, nine less than the previous year but still enough for a 17-game margin over the runner-up Pirates. While four teams threatened in the junior loop, all hands conceded the senior circuit crown to Chicago early in the summer. The heart of the Cubs could be found in the infield in playing-manager Frank Chance, Johnny Evers, Joe Tinker, and forgotten-man Harry Steinfeldt, who covered the diamond with an airtight blanket which smothered many an opponents' rally. In addition to their defensive play, Chance and Steinfeldt also supplied the team's offensive power.

The Cubs' pitching department was headed by Orvie Overall, who proved the winningest of five solid starters in a complement which included Three Finger Brown, Carl Lundgren, Jack Pfiester, and Ed Reulbach.

For the second year in a row, the Cubs were favored to win the Series. This time they did not fail, taking four straight from Detroit after an opening game tie called because of darkness. Pfiester, Reulbach, Overall, and Brown all turned in complete game victories in holding the Tigers to only six runs in the five-game set—a pitching success summed up in Crawford's .238 batting average and Cobb's weak .200 mark.

Coupled with the pitching corps spectacular 0.75 E.R.A., was Chicago's superb running game. Led by Jimmy Slagle's six thefts, the Cubs racked up a Series record 18 steals. Slagle, who only managed 28 steals during the regular season, also knocked in four runs—the most RBI's in the Series—and provided the go-ahead run in the Cubs' first victory. Steinfeldt's .471 and Evers' .350 hitting, which led the Cubs' offense, also aided in bringing Chicago its first world's title.

A tragic footnote to the season occurred in spring training when Chick Stahl, the playing-manager of the American League Boston club, violently ended his life on March 28, by drinking carbolic acid. Although it was known that Stahl, only 34, was despondent, the reason for his suicide was never learned.

1907 AMERICAN LEAGUE

NAME	G by POS	B	AGE	G	AB	R	H	2B	3B	HR	RBI	BB	SO	SB	BA	SA
DETROIT 1st 92-58 .613		**HUGHIE JENNINGS**														
TOTALS			26	153	5201	**696**	**1382**	179	**75**	11	**551**	315		192	**.266**	**.335**
Claude Rossman	1B153	L	26	153	571	60	158	21	8	0	69	33		20	.277	.342
Red Downs	2B80, OF20, SS1, 3B1	R	23	105	374	28	82	13	5	1	42	13		3	.219	.289
Charley O'Leary	SS138	R	25	139	465	61	112	19	1	0	34	32		11	.241	.286
Bill Coughlin	3B133	R	28	134	519	80	126	10	2	0	46	35		15	.243	.270
Ty Cobb	OF150	L	20	150	605	97	**212**	29	15	5	**119**	24		**49**	**.350**	**.473**
Sam Crawford	OF144, 1B2	L	27	144	582	**102**	188	34	17	4	81	37		18	.323	.460
Davy Jones	OF126	L	27	126	491	101	134	10	6	0	27	60		30	.273	.318
Boss Schmidt	C103	B	26	104	349	32	85	6	6	0	23	5		8	.244	.295
G. Schaefer	2B74, SS18, 3B14, OF1	R	30	109	372	45	96	12	3	1	32	30		21	.258	.315
George Mullin	P46	R	26	70	157	16	34	5	3	0	13	12		2	.217	.287
Freddie Payne	C46, OF5	R	26	53	169	17	28	2	2	0	14	7		4	.166	.201
Ed Killian	P41, OF2, 1B1	L	30	46	122	16	39	5	3	0	11	4		3	.320	.410
Matty McIntyre	OF20	L	27	20	81	6	23	1	1	0	9	7		3	.284	.321
Jimmy Archer	C17, 2B1	R	24	18	42	6	5	0	0	0	0	4		0	.119	.119
Bobby Lowe	3B10, OF4, SS2	R	38	17	37	2	9	2	0	0	5	4		0	.243	.297
Tex Erwin	C4	L	21	4	5	0	1	0	0	0	1	1		0	.200	.200
Hughie Jennings	2B1, SS1	R	38	1	4	0	1	1	0	0	0	0		0	.250	.500
Red Killefer	OF1	R	23	1	4	0	0	0	0	0	0	0		0	.000	.000
PHILADELPHIA 2nd 88-57 .607 1.5		**CONNIE MACK**														
TOTALS			31	150	5002	582	1277	**220**	45	**22**	485	384		138	.255	.330
Harry Davis	1B149	R	33	149	582	84	155	**37**	8	**8**	87	42		20	.266	.399
Danny Murphy	2B122	R	30	124	469	51	127	23	3	2	57	30		11	.271	.345
Simon Nicholls	SS82, 2B28, 3B13	L	24	126	460	75	139	12	2	0	23	24		13	.302	.337
2 Jimmy Collins	3B100	R	37	102	372	39	102	22	1	0	35	24		4	.274	.339
Socks Seybold	OF147	R	36	147	564	58	153	29	4	5	92	40		10	.271	.363
Rube Oldring	OF117	R	23	117	441	48	126	27	8	1	40	7		29	.286	.390
Topsy Hartsel	OF143	L	33	143	507	93	142	23	6	3	29	**106**		20	.280	.367
Ossee Schreckengost	C99, 1B2	R	32	101	356	30	97	16	3	0	38	17		4	.272	.334
Monte Cross	SS74	R	37	77	248	37	51	9	5	0	18	39		17	.206	.282
Mike Powers	C59	R	36	59	159	9	29	3	0	0	9	7		1	.182	.201
Bris Lord	OF53, P1	R	23	57	170	12	31	3	0	1	11	14		2	.182	.218
1 Jack Knight	3B38	R	21	38	130	9	29	7	1	0	12	10		1	.223	.292
Eddie Collins	SS6	L	20	14	20	0	5	0	0	0	2	0		0	.250	.250
Claude Berry	C8	R	27	8	19	2	4	2	0	0	1	2		0	.211	.316
CHICAGO 3rd 87-64 .576 5.5		**FIELDER JONES**														
TOTALS			32	157	5079	584	1205	147	34	5	474	**421**		175	.237	.283
Jiggs Donahue	1B157	L	27	157	**609**	75	158	16	5	0	68	28		27	.259	.302
Frank Isbell	2B119, OF5, SS1, P1	L	31	125	486	60	118	19	7	0	41	22		22	.243	.311
George Davis	SS131	B	36	132	466	59	111	18	2	1	52	47		15	.238	.292
George Rohe	3B76, 2B39, SS30	R	31	144	494	46	105	11	2	2	51	39		16	.213	.255
Eddie Hahn	OF156	L	31	156	592	87	151	9	7	0	45	84		17	.255	.294
Fielder Jones	OF154	L	35	154	559	72	146	18	1	0	47	67		17	.261	.297
Patsy Dougherty	OF148	L	30	148	533	69	144	17	2	1	59	36		33	.270	.315
Billy Sullivan	C108, 2B1	R	32	112	339	30	59	8	4	0	36	21		6	.174	.221
Ed McFarland	C43	R	32	52	138	11	39	9	1	0	8	12		3	.283	.362
Lee Quillin	3B48	R	25	49	151	17	29	5	0	0	14	10		8	.192	.225
Lee Tannehill (NJ)	3B31, SS2	R	26	33	108	9	26	2	0	0	11	8		3	.241	.259
Hub Hart	C25	L	29	29	70	6	19	1	0	0	7	5		1	.271	.286
Mike Welday	OF15	L	27	24	35	2	8	1	1	0	0	6		0	.229	.314
2 Charley Hickman	OF3	R	31	21	23	1	6	2	0	0	1	4		0	.261	.348
Jake Atz	3B2	R	28	3	7	0	1	0	0	0	0	0		0	.143	.143
2 Charlie Armbruster	C1	R	25	1	3	0	0	0	0	0	0	1		0	.000	.000

NAME	T	AGE	W	L	PCT	SV	G	GS	CG	IP	H	BB	SO	ShO	ERA
		30	**92**	58	**.613**	6	153	153	120	1371	1281	380	512	15	2.33
Wild Bill Donovan	R	30	25	4	**.862**	1	32	28	27	271	222	82	123	3	2.19
Ed Killian	L	30	25	13	.658	0	41	34	29	314	286	91	96	3	1.78
George Mullin	R	26	20	20	.500	3	46	42	35	357	**346**	106	146	5	2.60
Ed Siever	L	29	19	10	.655	1	39	33	22	275	256	52	88	3	2.16
John Eubank	R	34	2	3	.400	0	15	8	4	81	88	20	17	1	2.67
Ed Willett	R	23	1	5	.167	0	10	6	1	49	47	20	27	0	3.67
Herm Malloy		22	0	1	.000	0	1	1	1	8	13	5	6	0	5.63
Elijah Jones	R	25	0	2	.000	1	4	1	1	16	23	4	9	0	5.06
		26	88	57	.607	7	150	150	106	1354	106	378	**789**	**27**	2.35
Eddie Plank	L	31	24	16	.600	0	43	40	33	344	282	85	183	**8**	2.20
Jimmy Dygert	R	22	20	9	.690	2	42	28	18	262	200	85	151	5	2.34
Rube Waddell	L	30	19	13	.594	0	44	33	20	285	234	73	**232**	7	2.15
Chief Bender	R	24	16	8	.667	3	33	24	20	219	185	34	112	4	2.05
Jack Coombs (AJ)	R	24	6	9	.400	2	23	17	10	133	109	64	73	2	3.11
Rube Vickers	R	29	2	2	.500	0	10	4	3	50	44	12	21	1	3.42
Charlie Fritz	L	25	1	0	1.000	0	1	1	0	3	0	3	1	0	3.00
Bill Bartley	R	22	0	2	.000	0	15	3	2	56	44	19	16	0	2.25
George Craig	L	19	0	0	.000	0	2	0	0	2	2	3	0	0	9.00
Sam Hope		28	0	0	.000	0	1	0	0	.1	3	0	0	0	0.00
Bris Lord	R	23	0	0	.000	0	1	0	0	1	3	0	0	0	9.00
		28	87	64	.576	7	157	157	112	1406	1279	305	604	17	**2.22**
Doc White	L	28	**27**	13	.675	2	46	35	24	291	270	38	141	7	2.26
Ed Walsh	R	26	24	18	.571	2	**56**	**46**	**37**	**422**	341	87	206	5	**1.60**
Frank Smith	R	27	22	11	.667	0	41	37	29	310	280	**111**	139	3	2.47
Nick Altrock	L	30	8	12	.400	1	30	21	15	214	210	31	61	1	2.57
Roy Patterson	R	30	4	6	.400	0	19	13	4	96	105	18	27	1	2.63
Frank Owen	R	27	2	3	.400	0	11	4	2	47	43	13	15	0	2.49
Frank Isbell	R	31	0	0	.000	1	1	0	0	.1	0	0	0	0	0.00
Lou Fiene	R	22	0	1	.000	1	6	1	1	26	30	7	15	0	4.15

CLEVELAND 4th 85-67 .559 8 — NAP LAJOIE

NAME	G by POS	B	AGE	G	AB	R	H	2B	3B	HR	RBI	BB	SO	SB	BA	SA
TOTALS			28	158	5068	528	1221	182	68	11	433	335		193	.241	.310
George Stovall	1B122, 3B2	R	28	124	466	38	110	18	7	1	36	18		13	.236	.311
Nap Lajoie	2B128, 1B9	R	31	137	509	53	152	32	6	2	63	30		24	.299	.397
Terry Turner	SS145	R	26	148	524	57	127	20	7	0	46	19		27	.242	.307
Bill Bradley	3B139	R	29	139	498	48	111	20	1	0	34	35		20	.223	.267
Elmer Flick	OF147	L	31	147	549	78	166	17	18	3	58	64		41	.302	.415
Joe Birmingham	OF134, SS3	R	22	138	476	55	112	10	10	1	33	16		23	.235	.305
Bill Hinchman	OF150, 1B4, 2B1	R	24	152	514	62	117	19	9	1	50	47		15	.228	.305
Nig Clarke	C115	L	24	120	390	44	105	19	6	3	33	35		3	.269	.372
Harry Bemis	C51, 1B2	L	33	65	172	12	43	7	0	0	19	7		5	.250	.291
1 Pete O'Brien	2B17, 3B14, SS9	L	31	43	145	9	33	5	2	0	6	7		1	.228	.290
Harry Bay (KJ)	OF31	L	29	34	95	14	17	1	1	0	7	10		7	.179	.211
Howard Wakefield	C11	R	23	26	37	4	5	2	0	0	3	3		0	.135	.189
Pete Lister	1B22	R	25	22	65	5	18	2	0	0	4	3		2	.277	.308
Frank Delahanty	OF15	R	24	15	52	3	9	0	1	0	4	4		2	.173	.212
Harry Hinchman	2B15	B	28	15	51	3	11	3	1	0	9	5		2	.216	.314
2 Rabbit Nill	3B9, SS2	R	25	12	43	5	12	1	0	0	2	3		2	.279	.302
1 Bunk Congalton	OF6		32	9	22	2	4	0	0	0	2	4		0	.182	.182

NAME	T	AGE	W	L	PCT	SV	G	GS	CG	IP	H	BB	SO	ShO	ERA
		27	85	67	.559	5	158	158	127	1393	1253	362	513	20	2.26
Addie Joss	R	27	27	11	.711	2	42	38	34	339	279	54	127	6	1.83
Glenn Liebhardt	R	24	18	14	.563	1	38	34	27	280	254	85	110	4	2.06
Bob Rhoades	R	27	15	14	.517	1	35	31	23	275	258	84	76	5	2.29
Jake Thielman	R	28	11	8	.579	0	20	18	18	166	151	34	56	3	2.33
Otto Hess (LJ)	L	28	6	6	.500	1	17	14	7	93	84	37	36	0	2.90
2 Walter Clarkson (JJ)	R	28	4	6	.400	0	17	10	9	91	77	29	32	1	1.98
Heinie Berger	R	25	3	3	.500	0	14	7	5	87	74	20	50	1	3.00
Bill Bernhard	R	36	0	4	.000	0	8	4	3	42	58	11	19	0	3.21
1 Earl Moore	R	27	1	1	.500	0	3	2	1	19	18	8	7	0	4.74

NEW YORK 5th 70-78 .473 21 — CLARK GRIFFITH

NAME	G by POS	B	AGE	G	AB	R	H	2B	3B	HR	RBI	BB	SO	SB	BA	SA
TOTALS			28	152	5042	604	1257	150	67	14	497	304		206	.250	.314
Hal Chase	1B121, OF4	R	24	125	498	72	143	23	3	2	68	19		32	.287	.357
Jimmy Williams	2B139	R	30	139	504	53	136	17	11	2	63	35		14	.270	.359
Kid Elberfeld	SS118	R	32	120	447	61	121	16	7	0	51	36		22	.271	.336
G. Moriarty	3B91, 1B22, OF9, 2B8, SS1	R	22	126	437	51	121	16	5	0	43	25		28	.277	.338
Willie Keeler	OF107	L	35	107	423	50	99	6	5	0	17	15		7	.234	.272
Danny Hoffman	OF135	L	27	136	517	81	131	10	3	4	46	42		30	.253	.308
Wid Conroy	OF100, SS38	R	30	140	530	58	124	12	11	3	51	30		41	.234	.315
Red Kleinow	C86, 1B1	R	27	90	269	30	71	6	4	0	26	24		5	.264	.316
Frank LaPorte	3B64, OF63, 1B1	R	27	130	470	56	127	20	11	0	48	27		10	.270	.360
Ira Thomas	C66, 1B2	R	26	80	208	20	40	5	4	1	24	10		5	.192	.269
Branch Rickey	OF22, C11, 1B9	L	25	52	137	16	25	1	3	0	15	11		4	.182	.234
Al Orth	P36, OF1	R	34	44	105	11	34	6	0	1	13	4		1	.324	.410
Jack Bell	OF17	R	26	17	52	4	11	2	1	0	3	3		4	.212	.288
Neal Ball	SS11, 2B5	R	26	15	44	5	9	1	1	0	4	1		1	.205	.273
Walter Blair	C7	R	23	7	22	1	4	0	0	0	1	2		0	.182	.182
Baldy Louden	3B3	R	23	4	9	4	1	0	0	0	0	2		1	.111	.111
1 Deacon McGuire	C1	R	41	1	1	0	0	0	0	0	0	0		0	.000	.000

NAME	T	AGE	W	L	PCT	SV	G	GS	CG	IP	H	BB	SO	ShO	ERA
		29	70	78	.473	7	152	152	93	1334	1327	428	511	9	3.03
Al Orth	R	34	14	21	.400	1	36	33	21	249	244	53	78	1	2.60
Bill Hogg		27	11	8	.579	0	25	21	13	167	173	83	64	0	3.07
Slow Joe Doyle	R	25	11	11	.500	1	29	23	15	194	169	67	94	1	2.64
Jack Chesbro (NJ)	R	33	9	10	.474	0	30	25	17	206	192	46	78	1	2.53
Doc Newton	L	29	7	10	.412	0	19	15	10	133	132	31	70	0	3.18
Tacks Neuer		27	4	2	.667	0	7	6	6	54	40	19	22	3	2.17
Bob Keefe	R	25	4	2	.667	2	19	3	0	58	60	20	20	0	2.48
2 Frank Kitson	R	35	3	1	.750	1	12	4	3	61	75	17	14	0	3.10
2 Earl Moore	R	28	2	6	.250	1	12	9	3	64	72	30	28	0	3.94
Tom Hughes	R	21	2	1	.667	0	4	3	2	27	16	11	10	0	2.67
Roy Castleton	L	21	1	1	.500	0	3	2	1	16	11	3	3	0	2.81
Lew Brockett	R	26	1	3	.250	0	8	4	1	46	58	26	13	0	6.26
Cy Barger	R	22	0	0	.000	0	1	0	0	6	10	1	0	0	3.00
1 Walter Clarkson	R	28	1	1	.500	1	5	2	0	17	19	8	3	0	6.35
Clark Griffith	R	37	0	0	.000	0	4	0	0	8	15	6	5	0	9.00
Ray Tift	R	23	0	0	.000	0	4	1	0	19	33	4	6	0	4.74
Rube Manning	R	24	0	1	.000	0	1	1	1	9	8	3	3	0	3.00

ST. LOUIS 6th 69-83 .454 24 — JIMMY McALEER

NAME	G by POS	B	AGE	G	AB	R	H	2B	3B	HR	RBI	BB	SO	SB	BA	SA
TOTALS			29	155	5224	538	1324	154	64	9	433	370		144	.253	.313
Tom Jones	1B155	R	30	155	549	53	137	17	3	0	34	34		24	.250	.291
Harry Niles	2B116, OF1	R	26	120	492	65	142	9	5	2	35	28		19	.289	.339
Bobby Wallace	SS147	R	33	147	538	56	138	19	7	0	70	54		16	.257	.318
Joe Yeager	3B92, 2B17, SS10		31	123	436	32	104	21	7	1	44	31		11	.239	.326
Ollie Pickering	OF150	L	37	151	576	63	159	15	10	0	60	35		15	.276	.337
Charlie Hemphill	OF153	L	31	153	603	66	156	20	9	0	38	51		14	.259	.322
George Stone	OF155	L	29	155	596	77	191	14	13	4	59	59		23	.320	.408
Tubby Spencer	C63	R	22	71	230	27	61	11	1	1	25	7		1	.265	.335
Roy Hartzell	3B38, 2B15, SS2, OF2	L	25	60	220	20	52	3	5	0	13	11		7	.236	.295
Jim Stephens	C56	R	23	58	173	15	35	6	3	0	11	15		3	.202	.272
Jim Delahanty	3B21, OF4, 2B2	R	28	33	95	8	21	3	0	0	6	5		6	.221	.253
Fritz Buelow	C25	R	31	26	75	9	11	1	0	0	1	7		0	.147	.160
Jack O'Connor	C25	R	38	25	89	2	14	2	0	0	4	0		0	.157	.180
Kid Butler	2B11, 3B5, SS1	R	19	20	59	4	13	2	0	0	6	2		1	.220	.254
Emil Frisk		L	31	4	4	0	1	0	0	0	0	1		0	.250	.250
Jimmy McAleer		R	42	2	0	0	0	0	0	0	0	0		0	.000	.000
John Heidrick (VR) 30																

NAME	T	AGE	W	L	PCT	SV	G	GS	CG	IP	H	BB	SO	ShO	ERA
		30	69	83	.454	8	155	155	129	1381	1254	352	463	15	2.61
Harry Howell	R	30	16	15	.516	3	42	35	26	316	258	88	118	2	1.94
Fred Glade	R	31	13	9	.591	0	24	22	18	202	187	45	71	2	2.67
Jack Powell	R	32	14	16	.467	0	32	31	27	256	229	62	96	4	2.67
Barney Pelty	R	26	12	21	.364	1	36	31	29	273	234	64	85	5	2.57
Bill Dinneen	R	31	7	11	.389	4	24	16	15	155	153	33	38	2	2.44
Bill Bailey	L	18	4	1	.800	0	6	5	3	48	39	15	17	0	2.44
Cy Morgan	R	28	1	5	.167	0	10	6	4	55	77	17	14	0	6.05
Billy McGill	R	27	1	0	1.000	0	2	2	1	18	22	2	8	0	3.50
Beany Jacobson	L	26	1	5	.167	0	7	7	6	57	55	26	16	0	3.00

BOSTON 7th 59-90 .396 32.5 — CY YOUNG 3-4 .429 GEORGE HUFF 3-5 .375 BOB UNGLAUB 8-20 .286 DEACON McGUIRE 45-61 .425

NAME	G by POS	B	AGE	G	AB	R	H	2B	3B	HR	RBI	BB	SO	SB	BA	SA
TOTALS			30	155	5238	466	1223	155	48	18	405	305		124	.234	.292
Bob Unglaub	1B139	R	25	139	544	49	138	17	13	1	62	23		14	.254	.338
Hobe Ferris	2B150	R	29	150	561	41	135	25	2	4	60	10		11	.241	.314
Heinie Wagner (JJ)	SS109, 2B1, 3B1	R	26	111	385	29	82	10	4	2	21	31		20	.213	.275
2 Jack Knight	3B96, SS4	R	21	100	369	28	78	9	3	2	29	19		8	.211	.268
2 Bunk Congalton	OF126		32	127	496	44	142	11	8	2	47	20		13	.286	.353
Denny Sullivan	OF143	L	24	144	551	73	135	18	0	1	26	44		16	.245	.283
Jimmy Barrett (KJ)	OF99	L	32	106	390	52	95	11	6	1	28	38		3	.244	.310
Lou Criger	C75	R	35	75	226	12	41	4	0	0	14	19		2	.181	.199
Freddy Parent	OF47, SS43, 3B7, 2B5	R	31	114	409	51	113	19	5	1	26	22		12	.276	.355
Al Shaw	C73, 1B1	R	32	76	198	10	38	1	3	0	7	18		4	.192	.227
Moose Grimshaw	OF23, 1B15, SS2	B	31	64	181	19	37	7	2	0	33	16		6	.204	.265
1 Jimmy Collins	3B39	R	37	39	151	12	44	7	0	0	10	10		4	.291	.338
John Hoey	OF21		25	39	96	7	21	2	1	0	8	1		2	.219	.260
1 Charlie Armbruster	C21	R	25	23	60	2	6	1	0	0	0	8		1	.100	.117
Chet Chadbourne	OF10	L	22	10	38	0	11	0	0	0	1	7		1	.289	.289
Harry Lord	3B10	L	25	10	38	4	6	1	0	0	3	1		1	.158	.184
Tris Speaker	OF4	L	19	7	19	0	3	0	0	0	1	1		0	.158	.158
2 Deacon McGuire		R	41	6	4	1	3	0	0	1	1	0		0	.750	1.500
Buck Freeman	OF3	L	35	4	12	1	2	0	0	1	2	3		0	.167	.417
Bob Peterson	C4			4	13	1	1	0	0	0	0	0		0	.077	.077
George Whiteman	OF2	R	24	3	11	0	2	0	0	0	1	0		0	.182	.182
Chick Stahl (DD) 34																

NAME	T	AGE	W	L	PCT	SV	G	GS	CG	IP	H	BB	SO	ShO	ERA
		30	59	90	.396	8	155	155	100	1414	1222	337	517	17	2.45
Cy Young	R	40	22	15	.595	3	43	37	33	343	286	51	147	6	1.99
George Winter	R	29	11	16	.407	1	35	27	21	257	198	61	88	4	2.07
Ralph Glaze	R	26	9	13	.409	0	32	21	11	182	150	48	68	1	2.32
2 Cy Morgan	R	28	7	6	.538	0	16	13	9	114	77	34	50	2	1.97
Jesse Tannehill	L	32	6	7	.462	1	18	16	10	131	131	20	29	2	2.47
Tex Pruiett		24	3	11	.214	3	35	17	6	174	166	59	54	2	3.10
1 Frank Oberlin	R	31	1	4	.200	0	12	4	2	46	48	24	18	0	4.30
2 Beany Jacobson	L	26	0	1	.000	0	2	1	0	2	2	3	1	0	9.00
Ed Barry			0	1	.000	0	2	2	1	17	13	5	6	0	2.12
Fred Burchell	L	27	0	1	.000	0	2	1	0	10	8	2	6	0	2.70
Elmer Steele	R	23	0	1	.000	0	4	1	0	11	11	1	10	0	1.64
1 Bill Dinneen	R	31	0	4	.000	0	5	5	3	33	42	8	8	0	5.18
Rube Kroh	L	20	0	4	.000	0	7	5	1	34	33	8	8	0	2.65
Joe Harris	R	25	0	7	.000	0	12	5	3	59	57	13	24	0	3.05

WASHINGTON 8th 49-102 .325 43.5 — JOE CANTILLON

NAME	G by POS	B	AGE	G	AB	R	H	2B	3B	HR	RBI	BB	SO	SB	BA	SA
TOTALS			30	154	5105	506	1243	137	57	12	414	390		223	.243	.300
John Anderson	1B61, OF26	B	33	87	333	33	96	12	4	0	44	34		19	.288	.348
2 Jim Delahanty	2B68, 3B27, OF9, 1B4	R	28	109	404	44	118	18	7	2	54	36		18	.292	.386
Dave Altizer	SS71, 1B50, OF26	L	30	147	540	60	145	15	5	2	42	34		38	.269	.326
Bill Shipke	3B63	R	24	64	189	17	37	3	2	1	9	15		6	.196	.249
Bob Ganley	OF154	L	32	154	605	73	167	10	5	1	35	54		40	.276	.314
Charlie Jones	OF111, 2B5, 1B4, SS2		31	121	437	48	116	14	10	0	37	22		26	.265	.343
2 Otis Clymer (NJ)	OF51, 1B1	L	30	57	206	30	65	5	5	1	16	18		18	.316	.403
John Warner (RJ)	C64	L	34	72	207	11	53	5	0	0	17	12		3	.256	.280
1 Rabbit Nill	2B32, OF25, 3B1	R	25	66	215	21	47	7	3	0	25	15		6	.219	.279
Mike Heydon	C57		32	62	164	14	30	3	0	0	9	25		3	.183	.201
1 Charley Hickman	1B30, OF18, 2B3, P1	R	31	60	198	20	55	9	4	1	23	14		4	.278	.379
Tony Smith	SS51	R	23	51	139	12	26	1	1	0	8	18		3	.187	.209
Clyde Milan	OF47	L	21	48	183	22	51	3	3	0	9	8		8	.279	.328
Nig Perrine	2B24, SS18, 3B2	R	22	44	146	13	25	4	0	0	15	13		10	.171	.212
Lave Cross	3B41	R	41	41	161	13	32	8	0	0	10	10		3	.199	.248
2 Pete O'Brien	3B26, SS13, 2B1	L	31	39	134	6	25	3	1	0	12	12		4	.187	.224
Cliff Blankenship (BG)	C22, 1B9	R	27	37	102	4	23	2	0	0	6	3		3	.225	.245
Bill Kay	OF12	L	29	25	60	8	20	1	1	0	7	0		0	.333	.383
Bruno Block	C21	R	22	24	57	3	8	2	1	0	2	2		0	.140	.211
Larry Schlafly	2B24	R	28	24	74	10	10	0	0	1	4	22		7	.135	.176
2 Mike Kahoe	C15	R	32	17	47	3	9	1	0	0	1	0		0	.191	.213
Owen Shannon	C4	R	21	4	7	0	1	0	0	0	0	0		0	.143	.143

NAME	T	AGE	W	L	PCT	SV	G	GS	CG	IP	H	BB	SO	ShO	ERA
		28	49	102	.325	4	154	154	106	1352	1381	341	567	11	3.11
Casey Patten	L	31	12	17	.414	0	36	29	20	237	272	63	58	1	3.57
Charlie Smith	R	27	9	20	.310	0	36	31	21	259	254	51	119	3	2.61
Long Tom Hughes	R	28	8	13	.381	3	34	23	18	211	206	47	102	2	3.11
Walter Johnson	R	19	5	9	.357	0	14	12	11	111	98	17	68	2	1.86
Cy Falkenberg	R	27	6	18	.250	1	32	24	17	234	195	77	108	1	2.35
Oscar Graham	L	30	4	10	.286	0	20	14	6	104	116	29	44	0	3.98
Henry Gehring		26	3	7	.300	0	15	9	8	87	92	14	31	2	3.31
2 Frank Oberlin	R	31	2	7	.222	0	11	8	3	49	57	12	18	0	4.59
Bull Durham	R	26	0	0	.000	0	2	0	0	5	10	4	1	0	12.60
Sam Edmonston	L	23	0	0	.000	0	1	0	0	3	8	1	0	0	9.00
1 Charley Hickman	R	31	0	0	.000	0	1	0	0	5	4	5	2	0	3.60
Sam Lanford	R	21	0	0	.000	0	2	1	0	7	10	5	2	0	5.14
John McDonald	R		0	0	.000	0	1	0	0	6	12	2	3	0	9.00
Doc Tonkin	L	25	0	0	.000	0	1	0	0	3	6	5	0	0	6.00
1 Frank Kitson	R	35	0	1	.000	0	5	3	2	32	41	9	11	0	3.94

CHICAGO 1st 107-45 .704 — FRANK CHANCE

NAME	G by POS	B	AGE	G	AB	R	H	2B	3B	HR	RBI	BB	SO	SB	BA	SA
TOTALS			28	156	4892	571	1224	162	48	13	450	435		235	.250	.311
Frank Chance	1B109	R	29	111	382	58	112	19	2	1	50	51		35	.293	.361
Johnny Evers	2B151	L	25	151	508	66	127	18	4	2	51	39		46	.250	.313
Joe Tinker	SS113	R	26	117	402	36	89	11	3	1	36	25		20	.221	.271
Harry Steinfeldt	3B151	R	29	152	542	52	144	25	5	1	70	37		19	.266	.336
Wildfire Schulte (GJ)	OF92	L	24	97	342	44	98	14	7	2	32	22		7	.287	.386
Jimmy Slagle	OF136	L	33	136	489	71	126	6	6	0	32	76		28	.258	.294
Jimmy Sheckard	OF142	L	28	143	484	76	129	23	1	1	36	76		31	.267	.324
Johnny Kling	C98, 1B2	R	32	104	334	44	95	15	8	1	43	27		9	.284	.386
S. Hofman	OF69, SS42, 1B18, 3B4, 2B3	R	24	134	470	67	126	11	3	1	36	41		29	.268	.311
Pat Moran	C59	R	31	65	198	8	45	5	1	1	19	10		5	.227	.278
2 Del Howard	1B33, OF8	L	29	51	148	10	34	2	2	0	13	6		3	.230	.270
1 Newt Randall	OF21		26	22	78	6	16	4	2	0	4	8		2	.205	.308
Kid Durbin	P5, OF5	L	20	11	18	2	6	0	0	0	0	1		0	.333	.333
1 Mike Kahoe	C3, 1B1	R	32	5	10	0	4	0	0	0	1	0		0	.400	.400
1 Bill Sweeney	SS3	R	21	3	10	1	1	0	0	0	1	1		1	.100	.100
Heinie Zimmerman	2B4, SS1, OF1	R	20	5	9	0	2	1	0	0	1	0		0	.222	.333
Jack Hardy	C1	R	30	1	4	0	1	0	0	0	0	0		0	.250	.250
Jack Harper (HO) 29																

NAME	T	AGE	W	L	PCT	SV	G	GS	CG	IP	H	BB	SO	ShO	ERA
TOTALS		29	107	45	.704	7	156	156	114	1373	1054	402	586	30	1.73
Orvie Overall	R	26	23	8	.742	3	36	31	26	268	201	69	141	8	1.68
Three Finger Brown	R	30	20	6	.769	3	34	27	20	233	180	40	107	6	1.39
Carl Lundgren	R	27	18	7	.720	0	28	25	21	207	130	92	84	7	1.17
Ed Reulbach	R	24	17	4	.810	0	27	22	16	192	147	64	96	4	1.69
Jack Pfiester	L	29	15	9	.625	0	30	22	13	195	143	48	90	3	1.15
Chick Fraser	R	36	8	5	.615	1	22	15	9	138	112	46	41	2	2.28
Jack Taylor	R	33	6	5	.545	0	18	13	8	123	127	33	22	0	3.29
Kid Durbin	L	20	0	1	.000	1	5	1	1	17	14	10	5	0	5.29

PITTSBURGH 2nd 91-63 .591 17 — FRED CLARKE

NAME	G by POS	B	AGE	G	AB	R	H	2B	3B	HR	RBI	BB	SO	SB	BA	SA
TOTALS			28	157	4957	634	1261	133	78	19	465	403		[illegible]	.254	.324
Jim Nealon	1B104	R	22	105	381	29	98	10	8	0	47	23		11	.257	.325
Ed Abbaticchio	2B147	R	30	147	496	63	130	14	7	2	82	65		35	.262	.331
Honus Wagner	SS138, 1B4	R	33	142	515	98	180	38	14	6	82	46		61	.350	.513
Alan Storke	3B67, 1B23, 2B7, SS5	R	22	112	357	24	92	6	6	1	39	16		6	.258	.317
Goat Anderson	OF117, 2B5		27	127	413	73	85	3	1	1	12	80		27	.206	.225
Tommy Leach	OF111, 3B33, SS6, 2B1	R	29	149	547	102	166	19	12	4	43	40		43	.303	.404
Fred Clarke	OF144	L	34	148	501	97	145	18	13	2	59	68		37	.289	.389
George Gibson	C109, 1B1	R	26	113	382	28	84	8	7	3	35	18		2	.220	.301
Bill Hallman	OF84	R	31	94	302	39	67	6	2	0	15	33		21	.222	.255
Tommy Sheehan (HJ)	3B57, SS10	R	29	75	226	23	62	2	3	0	25	23		10	.274	.310
Eddie Phelps	C35, 1B1	R	28	43	113	11	24	1	0	0	12	9		1	.212	.221
Harry Swacina	1B26	R	25	26	95	9	19	1	1	0	10	4		1	.200	.232
Harry Smith	C18	R	32	18	38	4	10	1	0	0	1	4		0	.263	.289
1 Otis Clymer	OF15, 1B1	L	30	22	66	8	15	2	0	0	4	5		4	.227	.258
Danny Moeller	OF11	B	22	11	42	4	12	1	1	0	3	4		2	.286	.357
Harl Maggart	OF2	L	24	3	6	1	0	0	0	0	0	2		1	.000	.000
Bill McKechnie	3B2, 2B1	B	20	3	8	0	1	0	0	0	0	0		0	.125	.125
Marc Campbell	SS2	L	22	2	4	0	1	0	0	0	1	1		0	.250	.250
George Kelsey	C2			2	5	1	2	0	0	0	0	0		0	.400	.400

NAME	T	AGE	W	L	PCT	SV	G	GS	CG	IP	H	BB	SO	ShO	ERA
TOTALS		30	91	63	.591	5	157	157	111	1363	1207	368	497	24	2.30
Vic Willis	R	31	22	11	.667	1	39	37	27	293	234	69	107	6	2.33
Lefty Leifield	L	23	20	16	.556	1	40	33	24	286	270	100	112	6	2.33
Sam Leever	R	35	14	9	.609	0	31	24	17	217	182	46	65	5	1.66
Deacon Phillippe	R	35	13	11	.542	2	35	26	17	214	214	36	61	1	2.61
Howie Camnitz	R	25	13	8	.619	1	31	19	15	180	135	59	85	4	2.15
Nick Maddox	R	20	5	1	.833	0	6	6	6	54	32	13	38	1	0.83
2 Bill Dubbleby	R	34	2	2	.500	0	9	3	1	40	34	12	4	1	2.70
1 Mike Lynch (IL)	L	32	2	2	.500	0	7	4	2	36	37	22	9	0	2.25
King Brady	R	26	0	0	.000	0	1	0	0	2	2	1	0	0	0.00
Connie Walsh		25	0	0	.000	0	1	0	0	1	1	1	0	0	9.00
2 Harry Wolter	L	22	0	0	.000	0	1	0	0	2	3	2	0	0	4.50
Babe Adams	R	25	0	2	.000	0	4	3	1	22	40	3	11	0	6.95
Bill Otey	L	20	0	1	.000	0	3	2	1	16	23	4	5	0	4.50

PHILADELPHIA 3rd 83-64 .565 21.5 — BILLY MURRAY

NAME	G by POS	B	AGE	G	AB	R	H	2B	3B	HR	RBI	BB	SO	SB	BA	SA
TOTALS			27	149	4725	514	1113	162	65	12	424	424		154	.236	.305
Kitty Bransfield	1B92	R	32	94	348	25	81	15	2	0	38	14		8	.233	.287
Otto Knabe	2B121, OF5	R	23	129	444	67	113	16	9	1	34	52		18	.255	.338
Mickey Doolan	SS145	R	27	145	509	33	104	19	7	1	47	25		18	.204	.275
E. Courtney	3B75, 1B48, OF4, 2B2, SS2	L	28	130	440	42	107	17	4	2	43	55		6	.243	.314
John Titus	OF142	L	31	145	523	72	144	23	12	3	63	47		9	.275	.382
Roy Thomas	OF121	L	33	121	419	70	102	15	3	1	23	83		11	.243	.301
Sherry Magee	OF139	R	22	140	503	75	165	28	12	4	85	53		46	.328	.455
Red Dooin	C94, 2B1, OF1	R	28	101	313	18	66	8	4	0	14	15		10	.211	.262
Eddie Grant	3B74	L	24	74	268	26	65	4	3	0	19	10		10	.243	.280
Fred Jacklitsch	C58, 1B6, OF1	R	31	73	202	19	43	7	0	0	17	27		7	.213	.248
Ossie Osborn	OF36, 1B1	L	23	56	163	22	45	2	3	0	9	3		4	.276	.325
Kid Gleason	2B26, 1B4, SS4, OF1	B	40	36	126	11	18	3	0	0	6	7		3	.143	.167
Johnny Lush	P8, OF4	L	21	17	40	5	8	1	1	0	5	1		1	.200	.275
Paul Sentell	SS2, OF1	R	27	3	3	0	0	0	0	0	0	1		0	.000	.000

NAME	T	AGE	W	L	PCT	SV	G	GS	CG	IP	H	BB	SO	ShO	ERA
TOTALS		27	83	64	.565	4	149	149	110	1299	1095	422	499	21	2.43
Tully Sparks	R	30	22	8	.733	1	33	31	24	265	221	51	90	3	2.00
Frank Corridon	R	26	18	14	.563	2	37	32	23	274	228	89	131	3	2.46
Lew Moren	R	23	11	18	.379	1	37	31	21	255	202	101	98	3	2.54
Togie Pittinger	R	36	9	5	.643	0	16	12	8	102	101	35	37	1	3.00
2 Buster Brown	R	25	9	6	.600	0	21	16	13	130	118	56	38	4	2.42
Lew Richie	R	23	6	6	.500	0	25	12	9	117	88	38	40	2	1.77
George McQuillan	R	22	4	0	1.000	0	6	5	5	41	21	11	28	3	0.66
1 Johnny Lush	L	21	3	5	.375	0	8	8	5	57	48	21	20	2	3.00
Harry Coveleski	L	21	1	0	1.000	0	4	0	0	20	10	3	6	0	0.00
1 Bill Duggleby	R	34	0	2	.000	0	5	2	2	29	43	11	8	0	7.45
Jim McClosky		24	0	0	.000	0	3	0	0	9	15	6	3	0	7.00

NEW YORK 4th 82-71 .536 25.5 — JOHN McGRAW

NAME	G by POS	B	AGE	G	AB	R	H	2B	3B	HR	RBI	BB	SO	SB	BA	SA
TOTALS			32	155	4874	573	1222	160	48	23	475	516		205	.251	.317
Dan McGann (BA)	1B81	B	35	81	262	29	78	9	1	2	36	29		9	.298	.363
Larry Doyle	2B69	L	20	69	227	16	59	3	0	0	16	20		3	.260	.273
Bill Dahlen	SS143	R	37	143	464	40	96	20	1	0	34	51		11	.207	.254
Art Devlin	3B140, SS3	R	27	143	491	61	136	16	2	1	54	63		38	.277	.324
George Browne	OF121	L	31	127	458	54	119	11	10	5	37	31		15	.260	.360
Cy Seymour	OF126	L	34	131	473	46	139	25	8	3	75	36		21	.294	.400
Spike Shannon	OF155	B	29	155	585	104	155	12	5	1	33	82		33	.265	.308
Roger Bresnahan	C95, 1B6, OF2, 3B1	R	28	110	328	57	83	9	7	4	38	61		15	.253	.360
Sammy Strang	OF70, 2B13, 3B7, 1B5, SS1	B	30	123	306	56	77	20	4	4	30	60		21	.252	.382
Frank Bowerman	C62, 1B29	R	38	96	311	31	81	8	2	0	32	17		11	.260	.299
Tommy Corcoran	2B62	R	38	62	226	21	60	9	2	0	24	7		9	.265	.323
Jack Hannifan	1B29, 3B10, SS9, OF2	R	24	56	149	16	34	7	3	1	15	15		6	.228	.336
Danny Shay	2B13, SS9, OF2	R	30	35	79	10	15	1	1	1	6	12		5	.190	.266
Fred Merkle	1B15	R	18	15	47	0	12	1	0	0	5	1		0	.255	.277
Harry Curtis	C6		24	6	9	2	2	0	0	0	1	2		2	.222	.222
Matty Fitzgerald	C6	R	26	7	15	1	2	1	0	0	1	0		0	.133	.200
Monte Pfyl	1B1	R	23	1	0	0	0	0	0	0	0	0		0	.000	.000
Ham Wade	OF1	R	26	1	0	0	0	0	0	0	0	0		0	.000	.000
Mike Donlin (HO) 29																

NAME	T	AGE	W	L	PCT	SV	G	GS	CG	IP	H	BB	SO	ShO	ERA
TOTALS		28	82	71	.536	13	155	155	109	1371	1219	369	655	19	2.45
Christy Mathewson	R	28	24	13	.649	2	41	36	31	315	250	53	178	8	2.00
Joe McGinnity	R	36	18	18	.500	4	47	34	23	310	320	58	120	3	3.16
Hooks Wiltse	L	26	13	12	.520	2	33	21	14	190	171	48	79	3	2.18
Dummy Taylor	R	32	11	7	.611	1	28	21	11	171	145	46	56	3	2.42
Red Ames	R	24	10	12	.455	1	39	26	17	233	184	108	146	2	2.16
Cecil Ferguson	R	20	3	1	.750	1	15	5	4	64	63	20	37	0	2.11
2 Mike Lynch	L	32	3	6	.333	1	12	10	7	72	68	30	34	0	3.38
Henry Mathewson	R	22	0	0	.000	1	1	0	0	1	1	0	0	0	0.00
Roy Beecher	R	23	0	2	.000	0	2	2	2	14	17	6	5	0	2.57

BROOKLYN 5th 65-83 .439 40 — PATSY DONOVAN

NAME	G by POS	B	AGE	G	AB	R	H	2B	3B	HR	RBI	BB	SO	SB	BA	SA
TOTALS			28	153	4895	446	1135	142	63	18	380	336		121	.232	.298
Tim Jordan	1B143	L	28	147	485	43	133	15	8	4	53	74		10	.274	.363
Whitey Alperman	2B115, 3B14, SS12	R	27	141	558	44	130	23	16	2	39	13		5	.233	.342
Phil Lewis	SS136	R	23	136	475	52	118	11	1	0	30	23		16	.248	.276
Doc Casey	3B138	L	36	141	527	55	122	19	3	0	19	34		16	.231	.279
Harry Lumley	OF118	L	26	127	454	47	121	23	11	9	66	31		18	.267	.425
Billy Maloney	OF144	L	29	144	502	51	115	7	10	0	32	31		25	.229	.283
Heinie Batch	OF102, 3B2, 2B1, SS1	R	27	116	388	38	96	10	3	0	31	23		7	.247	.289
Lew Ritter	C89	R	31	93	271	15	55	6	1	0	17	18		5	.203	.232
John Hummel	2B44, OF33, 1B12, SS8	R	24	107	342	41	80	12	3	3	31	26		8	.234	.313
Bill Bergen	C51	R	34	51	138	2	22	3	0	0	14	1		1	.159	.181
2 Al Burch	OF36, 2B1	L	23	40	120	12	35	2	2	0	12	11		5	.292	.342
John Butler	C28, OF1	R	27	30	79	6	10	1	0	0	2	9		0	.127	.139
Jack McCarthy	OF25	L	38	25	91	4	20	2	0	0	8	2		4	.220	.242
Patsy Donovan	OF1	R	42	1	1	0	0	0	0	0	0	0		0	.000	.000
Pat Hurley	C1	R		1	2	0	0	0	0	0	0	1		0	.000	.000
Ed McLane	OF1		25	1	2	0	0	0	0	0	0	0		0	.000	.000

NAME	T	AGE	W	L	PCT	SV	G	GS	CG	IP	H	BB	SO	ShO	ERA
TOTALS		27	65	83	.439	1	153	153	125	1356	1218	463	479	20	2.38
Jim Pastorius	L	25	16	12	.571	0	28	26	20	222	218	77	70	4	2.35
Nap Rucker	L	22	15	13	.536	0	37	30	26	275	242	80	131	4	2.06
Elmer Stricklett	R	30	12	14	.462	0	29	26	25	230	211	65	69	4	2.27
George Bell	R	32	8	16	.333	1	35	27	20	264	222	77	88	3	2.25
Harry McIntire	R	29	7	15	.318	0	28	22	19	200	178	79	49	3	2.38
Doc Scanlan	R	26	6	8	.429	0	17	15	10	107	90	61	59	2	3.20
Weldon Henley	R	26	1	5	.167	0	7	7	5	56	54	21	11	0	3.05
Jesse Whiting			0	0	.000	0	1	0	0	3	3	3	2	0	12.00

CINCINNATI 6th 66-87 .431 41.5 — **NED HANLON**

NAME	G by POS	B	AGE	G	AB	R	H	2B	3B	HR	RBI	BB	SO	SB	BA	SA
TOTALS			28	156	4966	524	1226	126	**90**	15	443	372		158	.247	.318
John Ganzel	1B143	R	32	145	531	61	135	20	**16**	2	64	29		9	.254	.363
Miller Huggins	2B156	B	28	156	561	64	139	12	4	1	31	**83**		28	.248	.289
Hans Lobert	SS142, 3B5	R	25	148	537	61	132	9	12	1	41	37		30	.246	.313
Mike Mowrey	3B127, SS11	R	23	138	448	43	113	16	6	1	44	35		10	.252	.321
Mike Mitchell	OF146, 1B2	R	27	148	558	64	163	17	12	3	47	37		17	.292	.382
Art Kruger	OF96	R	26	100	317	25	74	10	9	0	28	18		10	.233	.322
Fred Odwell	OF84, 2B1	R	34	94	274	24	74	5	7	0	24	22		10	.270	.339
Larry McLean	C89, 1B13	R	25	113	374	35	108	9	9	0	54	13		4	.289	.361
John Kane (JJ)	OF42, 3B25, SS6, 2B2	R	23	79	262	40	65	9	4	3	19	22		20	.248	.347
Admiral Schlei (RJ)	C67, 1B3, OF2	R	29	84	246	28	67	3	2	0	27	28		5	.272	.301
Lefty Davis	OF70	L	32	73	266	28	61	5	5	1	25	23		9	.229	.297
Dode Paskert	OF16	R	25	16	50	10	14	4	0	1	8	2		2	.280	.420
Mike O'Neill	OF9	L	29	9	29	5	2	0	2	0	2	2		1	.069	.207
Chick Autry	OF7	L	22	7	25	3	5	0	0	0	0	1		0	.200	.200
1 Harry Wolter	OF4	L	22	4	15	1	2	0	0	0	1	0		0	.133	.133
Bill McCarthy	C3			3	8	1	1	0	0	0	0	0		0	.125	.125
Eddie Tiemeyer		R	22	1	0	1	0	0	0	0	0	1		0	.000	.000
Pete Lamer	C1		33	1	2	0	0	0	0	0	0	0		0	.000	.000

NAME	T	AGE	W	L	PCT	SV	G	GS	CG	IP	H	BB	SO	ShO	ERA
		27	66	87	.431	2	156	156	118	1351	1223	444	481	10	2.41
Andy Coakley	R	24	17	16	.515	1	37	30	21	265	269	79	89	1	2.34
Bob Ewing	R	34	17	19	.472	0	41	37	32	333	279	85	147	2	1.73
Jake Weimer	L	33	11	14	.440	0	29	26	19	209	165	63	67	3	2.41
Roy Hitt	L	20	6	10	.375	0	21	18	14	153	143	56	63	2	3.41
Del Mason	R	23	5	12	.294	0	25	17	13	146	144	55	45	1	3.14
Charley Hall	R	21	4	2	.667	0	11	8	5	68	51	43	25	0	2.51
Bill Campbell	L	33	3	0	1.000	0	3	3	3	21	19	3	4	0	2.14
Fred Smith	R	28	2	7	.222	1	18	9	6	85	90	24	19	0	2.86
Bob Spade	R	30	1	2	.333	0	3	3	3	27	21	9	7	1	1.00
Frank Leary (DD)		26	0	1	.000	0	2	1	0	8	7	6	4	0	1.13
Bill Essick	R	25	0	2	.000	0	3	2	2	22	23	8	7	0	2.86
Cotton Minahan	R	24	0	2	.000	0	2	2	1	14	12	13	4	0	1.29

BOSTON 7th 58-90 .392 47 — **FRED TENNEY**

NAME	G by POS	B	AGE	G	AB	R	H	2B	3B	HR	RBI	BB	SO	SB	BA	SA
TOTALS			28	152	**5020**	503	1222	142	61	22	395	413		120	.243	.309
Fred Tenney	1B149	L	35	150	554	83	151	18	8	0	26	82		15	.273	.334
Claude Ritchey	2B144	B	33	144	499	45	127	17	4	2	51	50		8	.255	.317
Al Bridwell	SS140	L	23	140	509	49	111	8	2	0	26	61		17	.218	.242
Dave Brain	3B130	R	28	133	509	60	142	24	9	**10**	56	29		10	.279	.420
Johnny Bates	OF120	L	25	126	447	52	116	18	12	2	49	39		11	.260	.367
Ginger Beaumont	OF149	L	30	150	580	67	**187**	19	14	4	62	37		25	.322	.424
2 Newt Randall	OF73		26	75	258	16	55	6	3	0	15	19		4	.213	.260
Tom Needham	C78, 1B1	R	28	86	260	19	51	6	2	1	19	18		4	.196	.246
Sam Brown	C63, 1B2	R	29	70	208	17	40	6	0	0	14	12		0	.192	.221
2 B. Sweeney	3B23, SS15, OF11, 2B5, 1B1	R	21	58	191	24	50	2	0	0	18	15		8	.262	.272
1 Del Howard	OF45, 2B3	L	29	50	187	20	51	4	2	1	13	11		11	.273	.332
Frank Burke	OF36	R	27	43	129	6	23	0	1	0	8	11		3	.178	.194
Izzy Hoffman	OF19	L	32	19	86	17	24	3	1	0	3	6		2	.279	.337
Jim Ball	C10		22	10	36	3	6	2	0	0	3	2		0	.167	.222
Jess Orndorff	C5	B	26	5	17	0	2	0	0	0	0	0		0	.118	.118
Joe Knotts	C3			3	8	0	0	0	0	0	0	1		0	.000	.000
Oscar Westerberg	SS2			2	6	0	2	0	0	0	1	1		0	.333	.333
Tom Asmussen	C2		30	2	5	0	0	0	0	0	0	0		0	.000	.000
Bob Brush	1B1		32	2	2	0	0	0	0	0	0	0		0	.000	.000
Cozy Dolan (DD) 34																

NAME	T	AGE	W	L	PCT	SV	G	GS	CG	IP	H	BB	SO	ShO	ERA
		28	58	90	.392	2	152	152	121	1339	**1324**	458	426	9	3.33
Patsy Flaherty	L	31	12	15	.444	0	27	25	23	217	197	59	34	0	2.70
Gus Dorner	R	30	12	16	.429	0	36	31	24	271	253	92	85	2	3.12
Vive Lindaman	R	29	11	15	.423	1	34	28	24	260	252	108	90	2	3.63
Irv Young	L	29	10	23	.303	1	40	32	22	245	287	58	86	3	3.97
Big Jeff Pfeffer (AJ)	R	25	6	8	.429	0	19	16	12	144	129	61	65	1	3.00
Jake Boultes	R	22	5	9	.529	0	24	12	11	140	140	50	49	0	2.70
Frank Barberich	R	25	1	1	.500	0	2	2	1	12	19	5	1	0	6.00
Sammy Frock	R	23	1	2	.333	0	5	3	3	33	28	11	12	1	3.00
Ernie Lindeman	R	24	0	0	.000	0	1	1	0	6	6	4	3	0	6.00
Rube Dessau	R	24	0	1	.000	0	2	2	1	9	13	10	1	0	11.00

ST. LOUIS 8th 52-101 .340 55.5 — **JOHN McCLOSKEY**

NAME	G by POS	B	AGE	G	AB	R	H	2B	3B	HR	RBI	BB	SO	SB	BA	SA
TOTALS			27	156	5008	419	1163	121	51	19	331	312		125	.232	.288
Ed Konetchy	1B91	R	21	91	331	34	83	11	8	3	30	26		13	.251	.360
Pug Bennett	2B83, 3B3	R	33	87	324	20	72	8	2	0	21	21		7	.222	.259
Ed Holly	SS147, 2B3	R	27	150	545	55	125	18	3	1	40	36		16	.229	.279
Bobby Byrne	3B148, SS1	R	22	149	559	55	143	11	5	0	29	35		21	.256	.293
Shad Barry (KJ)	OF81	R	30	81	294	30	73	5	2	0	19	28		4	.248	.279
John Burnett	OF59			59	206	18	49	8	4	0	12	15		5	.238	.316
Red Murray	OF131	R	33	132	485	46	127	10	10	7	46	24		23	.262	.367
Doc Marshall	C83	R	32	84	268	19	54	8	2	2	18	12		2	.201	.269
Hoelskoetter	2B72, 1B27, OF8, C8, 3B2, P2	R	24	119	397	21	98	6	3	2	28	27		5	.247	.292
Pete Noonan	C70	R	25	74	237	19	53	7	3	1	16	9		3	.224	.291
John Kelly	OF52		28	53	197	12	37	5	0	0	6	13		7	.188	.213
1 Al Burch	OF48	L	23	48	154	18	35	3	1	0	5	17		7	.227	.260
Tom O'Hara	OF47		21	48	173	11	41	2	1	0	5	12		1	.237	.260
Jake Beckley	1B32	L	39	32	115	6	24	3	0	0	7	1		0	.209	.235
Buck Hopkins	OF15	R	24	15	44	7	6	3	0	0	3	10		2	.136	.205
3 Harry Wolter	OF9, P3	L	22	16	47	4	16	0	0	0	6	3		1	.340	.340
Harry Arndt	1B4, 3B3		28	11	32	3	6	1	0	0	2	1		0	.188	.219
Al Shaw	OF9	L	26	9	25	2	7	0	0	0	1	3		1	.280	.280
Forrest Crawford (DD)	SS7		26	7	22	0	5	0	0	0	3	2		0	.227	.227
Joe Delahanty	OF7	L	31	7	22	3	7	0	0	1	2	0		3	.318	.455
John Baxter	1B6			6	21	1	4	0	0	0	0	0		0	.190	.190

NAME	T	AGE	W	L	PCT	SV	G	GS	CG	IP	H	BB	SO	ShO	ERA
		26	52	**101**	.340	2	156	156	**127**	1366	1212	**500**	594	20	2.69
Ed Karger	L	24	15	19	.441	1	39	33	29	314	257	65	137	6	2.04
Stony McGlynn	R	35	14	**25**	.359	1	45	**39**	**33**	**352**	**329**	**112**	109	3	2.91
Fred Beebe	R	26	7	19	.269	0	31	29	24	238	192	109	141	4	2.72
2 Johnny Lush	L	21	7	10	.412	0	20	19	15	144	132	42	71	4	2.50
Art Fromme	R	23	5	13	.278	0	23	16	13	146	138	67	67	2	2.90
Bugs Raymond	R	25	2	4	.333	0	8	6	6	65	56	21	34	1	1.66
1 Buster Brown	R	25	1	6	.143	0	9	8	6	64	57	45	17	0	3.38
3 Harry Wolter	L	22	1	2	.333	0	3	3	1	23	27	18	8	0	4.30
Carl Druhot	L	24	0	1	.000	0	1	1	0	2	3	4	1	0	18.00
Charlie Shields	L	27	0	2	.000	0	3	2	0	7	12	7	1	0	9.00
Art Hoelskoetter	R	24	0	0	.000	0	2	0	0	11	9	10	8	0	5.73

WORLD SERIES – CHICAGO (NL) 4 DETROIT (AL) 0 One Tie Game

LINE SCORES

TEAM	1	2	3	4	5	6	7	8	9	10	11	12	R	H	E
Game 1 October 8 at Chicago															
DET (AL)	0	0	0	0	0	0	0	3	0	0	0	0	3	9	3
CHI (NL)	0	0	0	1	0	0	0	0	2	0	0	0	3	10	5
Donovan — Overall, Reulbach (10)															
Game 2 October 9 at Chicago															
DET	0	1	0	0	0	0	0	0	0				1	9	1
CHI	0	1	0	2	0	0	0	0	X				3	9	1
Mullin — **Pfiester**															
Game 3 October 10 at Chicago															
DET	0	0	0	0	0	1	0	0	0				1	6	1
CHI	0	1	0	3	1	0	0	0	X				5	10	1
Siever, Killian (5) — **Reulbach**															
Game 4 October 11 at Detroit															
CHI	0	0	0	0	2	0	3	0	1				6	7	2
DET	0	0	0	1	0	0	0	0	0				1	5	2
Overall — Donovan															
Game 5 October 12 at Detroit															
CHI	1	1	0	0	0	0	0	0	0				2	7	1
DET	0	0	0	0	0	0	0	0	0				0	7	2
Brown — **Mullin**															

COMPOSITE BATTING

NAME	POS	G	AB	R	H	2B	3B	HR	RBI	BA
Chicago (NL)										
Totals		5	167	19	43	6	1	0	16	.257
Slagle	OF	5	**22**	3	6	0	0	0	**4**	.273
Sheckard	OF	5	21	0	5	**2**	0	0	2	.238
Evers	2B-SS	5	20	2	7	**2**	0	0	1	.350
Schulte	OF	5	20	3	5	0	0	0	2	.250
Kling	C	5	19	2	4	0	0	0	1	.211
Steinfeldt	3B	5	17	2	**8**	1	1	0	2	**.471**
Chance	1B	4	14	3	3	1	0	0	0	.214
Tinker	SS	5	13	**4**	2	0	0	0	1	.154
Overall	P	2	5	0	1	0	0	0	2	.200
Reulbach	P	2	5	0	1	0	0	0	1	.200
Howard	1B	2	5	0	1	0	0	0	0	.200
Brown	P	1	3	0	0	0	0	0	0	.000
Pfiester	P	1	2	0	0	0	0	0	0	.000
Zimmerman	2B	1	1	0	0	0	0	0	0	.000
Moran	PH	1	0	0	0	0	0	0	0	.000
Detroit (AL)										
Totals		5	172	6	36	1	2	0	6	.209
Crawford	OF	5	21	1	5	1	0	0	3	.238
Schaefer	2B	5	21	1	3	0	0	0	0	.143
Rossman	1B	5	20	1	8	0	1	0	2	.400
Coughlin	3B	5	20	0	5	0	0	0	0	.250
Cobb	OF	5	20	1	4	0	1	0	0	.200
Jones	OF	5	17	1	6	0	0	0	0	.353
O'Leary	SS	5	17	0	1	0	0	0	0	.059
Schmidt	C	4	12	0	2	0	0	0	0	.167
Donovan	P	2	8	0	0	0	0	0	0	.000
Mullin	P	2	6	0	0	0	0	0	0	.000
Payne	C	2	4	0	1	0	0	0	1	.250
Archer	C	1	3	0	0	0	0	0	0	.000
Killian	P	1	2	1	1	0	0	0	0	.500
Siever	P	1	1	0	0	0	0	0	0	.000

COMPOSITE PITCHING

NAME	G	IP	H	BB	SO	W	L	SV	ERA
Chicago (NL)									
Totals	5	48	36	9	22	4	0	0	0.75
Overall	**2**	18	14	4	11	1	0	0	1.00
Reulbach	**2**	12	6	3	4	1	0	0	0.75
Brown	1	9	7	1	4	1	0	0	**0.00**
Pfiester	1	9	9	1	3	1	0	0	1.00
Detroit (AL)									
Totals	5	46	43	12	26	0	4	0	2.15
Donovan	**2**	**21**	17	6	**16**	0	1	0	1.71
Mullin	**2**	17	16	**6**	8	0	**2**	0	2.12
Killian	1	4	3	1	1	0	0	0	2.25
Siever	1	4	7	0	1	0	1	0	4.50

1908 Forty-Five Feet Toward Immortality

Fred Tenney woke up on September 23rd in the throes of a lumbago attack, and 19-year-old substitute Fred Merkle was sent in to take his place at first base. As events turned out, fate would treat Merkle unkindly that day. With 25,000 fans assembled in the Polo Grounds, the second-place Chicago Cubs were playing the leading Giants with only percentage points separating the clubs. A 1-1 tie held fast until the Giants came to bat in the bottom of the ninth. There were two outs: Moose McCormick was on third and young Merkle perched on first after singling to right. (What follows is one account of the many which were offered of what is still known as the greatest goof of all time.) Al Bridwell lashed a Jack Pfiester serve into center field for a clean single, scoring McCormick and apparently ending the game. However, as the crowd started surging onto the field, Merkle, halfway to second, immediately sprinted for the clubhouse without bothering to touch second base, the common practice at the time. With the jubilant New York fans already piling onto the playing field, Cub second baseman Johnny Evers realized that Merkle would be forced out at second for the third out, thereby nullifying the run. Evers called frantically for center fielder Solly Hofman to throw him the ball, but Hofman—unable to clearly see Evers in the crowd—overshot his mark with a heave towards first base. Giant first base coach Joe McGinnity realized what was happening, outwrestled Cub shortstop Joe Tinker for the ball, and with Tinker on his back heaved it toward shortstop. Floyd Kroh, a second-line Cub pitcher who was not even in the game, saw a spectator pick up the ball, demanded it, and slugged the customer when he would not cough it up. Kroh retrieved the ball from the now-prone fan, worked his way through the still-unaware crowd, and handed the ball to Evers on second. Umpire Hank O'Day was supposedly watching the whole affair; he called Merkle out and disallowed the run, using darkness as an excuse to call the game a tie. The Giants screamed bloody murder when notified in the clubhouse that their victory was rescinded, but league president Harry Pulliam upheld O'Day's decision. The matter finally went before the Board of Directors who, on October 5, sustained Pulliam's decision. The game grew in proportion when the Cubs and Giants finished the regular season with identical 98-55 records. The tie was rescheduled for October 8, and a record 35,000 spectators crammed into the Polo Grounds and watched Three-Finger Brown, in relief, best Christy Mathewson in a 4-2 come-from-behind Chicago victory, which gave the Cubs their third consecutive National League crown.

The Cubs fielded a solid, balanced squad, good in all departments and expected to repeat as champions. The Giants relied on a strong offense led by Mike Donlin and a thin pitching staff aced by Mathewson and Hooks Wiltse to challenge all the way, and the Pirates—eliminated only on the last day of the season—also fielded a balanced squad led by superstar Honus Wagner, the National League batting leader for the sixth time.

The National League held no monopoly on tight races as the Detroit Tigers repeated as champions only by defeating the White Sox on the final day of the season in one of the tightest races ever staged in the American League. Detroit, Cleveland, and Chicago all battled for the top into the final two days of the season, with the Tigers finishing half a game and .004 percentage points ahead of Chicago. Detroit's victory was blemished somewhat by a rain-out game they did not have to make up. The White Sox did not figure to win the pennant, but got as far as they did because of the iron-man work of spitballer Ed Walsh. Starting regularly with two days rest, relieving between starts, and winning an incredible 40 games over the course of 464 innings, Walsh turned in one of the finest pitching efforts in history. He also took part in the greatest pitching duel ever staged under pressure conditions when, on October 2, against Cleveland, he gave up four hits and struck out 15, only to be victimized 1-0 by the perfect game performance of Addie Joss.

The World Series proved anticlimactic as the favored Cubs disappointed no one in disposing of the Tigers in five games despite Ty Cobb's .368 swinging. Frank Chance, Johnny Evers, and Joe Tinker starred for the Cubs at bat and afield, while Orvie Overall and Three-Finger Brown accounted for all the victories on the mound to end a circus-like season which, oddly enough, would be remembered only for the "bonehead" play of an inexperienced youngster.

1908 AMERICAN LEAGUE

NAME	G by POS	B	AGE	G	AB	R	H	2B	3B	HR	RBI	BB	SO	SB	BA	SA
DETROIT 1st 90-63 .588	**HUGHIE JENNINGS**															
TOTALS			27	153	5109	**645**	**1347**	**199**	86	19	**520**	320		165	**.264**	**.347**
Claude Rossman	1B138	L	27	138	524	45	154	33	13	2	71	27		8	.294	.418
Red Downs	2B82, 3B1	R	24	84	289	29	64	10	3	1	35	5		2	.221	.287
Germany Schaefer	SS68, 2B58, 3B29	R	31	153	584	96	151	20	10	3	52	37		40	.259	.342
Bill Coughlin	3B119	R	29	119	405	32	87	5	1	0	23	23		10	.215	.232
Ty Cobb	OF150	L	21	150	581	88	**188**	**36**	**20**	4	**108**	34		39	**.324**	**.475**
Sam Crawford	OF134, 1B17	L	28	152	**591**	102	184	33	16	**7**	80	37		15	.311	.457
Matty McIntyre	OF151	L	28	151	569	**105**	168	24	13	0	28	83		20	.295	.383
Boss Schmidt	C121	B	27	122	419	45	111	14	3	1	38	16		5	.265	.320
Charley O'Leary (IL)	SS64, 2B1	R	26	65	211	21	53	9	3	0	17	9		4	.251	.322
Davy Jones	OF32	L	28	56	121	17	25	2	1	0	10	13		11	.207	.240
Ira Thomas	C29	R	27	40	101	6	31	1	0	0	8	5		0	.307	.317
Red Killefer	2B16, SS7, 3B4	R	24	28	75	9	16	1	0	0	11	3		4	.213	.227
Donie Bush	SS20	B	20	20	68	13	20	1	1	0	4	7		2	.294	.338
Freddie Payne (BG)	C16, OF2	R	27	20	45	3	3	0	0	0	2	3		1	.067	.067
Clay Perry	3B5	R	26	5	11	0	2	0	0	0	0	0		0	.182	.182
CLEVELAND 2nd 90-64 .584 .5	**NAP LAJOIE**															
TOTALS			28	157	5108	570	1221	188	58	18	458	364		169	.239	.309
George Stovall	1B132, OF5, SS1	R	29	138	534	71	156	29	6	2	45	17		14	.292	.380
Nap Lajoie	2B156, 1B1	R	32	157	581	77	168	32	6	2	74	47		15	.289	.375
George Perring	SS48, 3B41	R	23	89	310	23	67	8	5	0	19	16		0	.216	.274
Bill Bradley	3B116, SS21	R	30	148	548	70	133	24	7	1	46	29		18	.243	.318
Bill Hinchman	OF75, SS51, 1B4	R	25	137	464	55	107	23	8	6	59	38		9	.231	.353
Joe Birmingham(AJ)	OF121, SS1	R	23	122	413	32	88	10	1	2	38	19		15	.213	.257
Josh Clarke	OF131	L	29	131	492	70	119	8	4	1	21	76		37	.242	.280
Nig Clarke	C90	L	25	97	290	34	70	8	6	1	27	30		6	.241	.321
Harry Bemis	C76, 1B2	L	34	91	277	23	62	9	1	0	33	7		14	.224	.264
Charley Hickman	OF28, 1B20, 2B1	R	32	65	197	16	46	6	1	2	16	9		2	.234	.305
Terry Turner	OF36, SS17	R	27	60	201	21	48	11	1	0	19	15		18	.239	.303
Wilbur Good	OF42	L	22	46	154	23	43	1	3	1	14	13		7	.279	.344
2 Dave Altizer	OF24, SS3	L	31	29	89	11	19	1	2	0	5	7		7	.213	.270
Rabbit Nill	SS6, OF2, 2B1	R	26	10	23	3	5	0	0	0	1	0		0	.217	.217
Homer Davidson	C5, OF1	R	23	9	4	2	0	0	0	0	0	0		1	.000	.000
Elmer Flick(IL)	OF9	L	32	9	35	4	8	1	1	0	2	3		0	.229	.314
Otto Hess	P4, OF4	L	29	8	14	0	0	0	0	0	0	1		0	.000	.000
Grover Land	C8	R	23	8	16	1	3	0	0	0	2	0		0	.188	.188
2 Denny Sullivan	OF2	L	25	3	6	0	0	0	0	0	0	0		0	.000	.000
Harry Bay		L	30	2	0	0	0	0	0	0	0	0		0	.000	.000
2 Deacon McGuire	1B1	R	42	1	4	0	1	1	0	0	2	0		0	.250	.500
CHICAGO 3rd 88-64 .579 1.5	**FIELDER JONES**															
TOTALS			32	156	5027	535	1127	145	41	3	430	**463**		209	.224	.271
Jiggs Donahue	1B83	L	28	93	304	22	62	8	2	0	22	25		14	.204	.243
George Davis	2B95, SS23, 1B4	B	37	128	419	41	91	14	1	0	26	41		22	.217	.255
Freddy Parent(KJ)	SS118	R	32	119	391	28	81	7	5	0	35	50		9	.207	.251
Lee Tannehill	3B136, SS5	R	27	141	482	44	104	15	3	0	35	25		6	.216	.259
Eddie Hahn	OF118	L	32	122	447	58	112	12	8	0	21	39		11	.251	.313
Fielder Jones	OF149	L	36	149	529	92	134	11	7	1	50	86		26	.253	.306
Patsy Dougherty	OF138	L	31	138	482	68	134	11	6	0	45	58		**47**	.278	.326
Billy Sullivan	C137	R	33	137	430	40	82	8	4	0	29	22		15	.191	.228
John Anderson	OF90, 1B9	B	34	123	355	36	93	17	1	0	47	30		21	.262	.315
Frank Isbell	1B65, 2B18	L	32	84	320	31	79	15	3	1	49	19		18	.247	.322
Jake Atz	2B46, SS18, 3B1	R	29	83	206	24	40	3	0	0	27	31		9	.194	.209
Al Shaw	C29	R	33	32	49	0	4	1	0	0	2	2		0	.082	.102
Billy Purtell	3B25	R	22	26	69	3	9	2	0	0	3	2		2	.130	.159
Art Weaver	C15		29	15	35	1	7	1	0	0	1	1		0	.200	.229
2 Ossee Schreckengost	C6	R	33	6	16	1	3	0	0	0	0	1		0	.188	.188

NAME	T	AGE	W	L	PCT	SV	G	GS	CG	IP	H	BB	SO	ShO	ERA
		27	**90**	63	**.588**	6	153	153	**120**	1374	**1313**	318	553	14	2.40
Ed Summers	R	23	24	12	.667	1	40	32	24	301	271	55	103	4	1.64
Wild Bill Donovan	R	31	18	7	.720	0	29	28	25	243	210	53	141	6	2.07
George Mullin	R	27	17	12	.586	1	39	30	26	291	301	71	121	1	3.09
Ed Willett (NJ)	R	24	15	9	.625	1	30	22	18	197	186	60	77	2	2.28
Ed Killian	L	31	11	10	.524	1	27	23	15	181	170	53	47	0	2.98
2 George Winter	R	30	2	5	.286	1	7	6	5	56	49	7	25	0	1.61
Ed Siever	L	30	2	6	.250	0	11	9	4	62	74	13	23	1	3.48
George Suggs	R	25	1	0	1.000	1	6	1	1	27	32	2	8	0	1.67
Herm Malloy		23	0	2	.000	0	3	2	2	17	20	4	8	0	3.71
		27	**90**	64	.584	5	157	157	108	**1422**	1172	328	548	18	**2.02**
Addie Joss	R	28	24	11	.686	2	42	35	29	325	232	30	130	9	**1.16**
Bob Rhoades	R	28	18	12	.600	0	37	30	20	270	229	73	62	1	1.77
Glenn Liebhardt	R	25	15	16	.484	0	39	26	19	262	222	81	146	3	2.20
Heinie Berger	R	26	13	8	.619	0	29	24	16	199	152	66	101	0	2.13
Charlie Chech	R	30	11	7	.611	0	27	20	14	166	136	34	51	4	1.73
1 Jake Thielman	R	29	4	3	.571	0	11	8	5	62	59	9	15	0	3.63
2 Cy Falkenberg	R	28	2	5	.286	0	8	7	2	44	52	10	17	0	4.09
Ed Foster			1	0	1.000	2	6	1	1	21	16	12	11	0	2.14
Jack Ryan	R	23	1	0	1.000	1	8	1	1	36	27	2	7	0	2.25
Bill Lattimore	L	24	1	2	.333	0	4	4	1	24	24	7	5	1	4.50
Otto Hess	L	29	0	0	.000	0	4	0	0	7	11	1	2	0	5.14
Walter Clarkson	R	29	0	0	.000	0	2	1	0	3	6	2	1	0	12.00
Jack Graney	L	22	0	0	.000	0	2	0	0	3	6	1	0	0	6.00
		28	88	64	.579	**13**	156	156	107	1414	1170	284	623	22	2.22
Ed Walsh	R	27	**40**	15	**.727**	**7**	**66**	**49**	**42**	**464**	**343**	56	**269**	**12**	1.42
Doc White	L	29	18	13	.581	0	41	37	24	296	267	69	126	5	2.55
Frank Smith(JT)	R	28	17	16	.515	1	41	35	24	298	213	73	129	3	2.02
Frank Owen	R	28	6	8	.429	0	25	14	5	140	142	37	48	1	3.41
Nick Altrock	L	31	3	7	.300	4	23	13	8	136	127	18	21	1	2.71
Moxie Manuel	R	26	3	4	.429	1	18	6	3	60	52	25	25	0	3.30
Andy Nelson			1	0	1.000	0	2	1	0	9	11	4	1	0	2.00
Lou Fiene	R	23	0	1	.000	0	1	1	1	9	9	1	3	0	4.00
Fred Olmsted	R	26	0	0	.000	0	1	0	0	2	6	1	1	0	13.50

ST. LOUIS 4th 83-69 .546 6.5 — JIMMY McALEER

NAME	G by POS	B	AGE	G	AB	R	H	2B	3B	HR	RBI	BB	SO	SB	BA	SA
TOTALS			29	155	5152	543	1261	173	56	20	447	343		126	.245	.312
Tom Jones	1B155	R	31	155	549	43	135	14	2	1	50	30		18	.246	.284
Jimmy Williams	2B148	R	31	148	539	63	127	20	7	4	53	55		7	.236	.321
Bobby Wallace	SS137	R	34	137	487	59	123	24	4	1	60	52		5	.253	.324
Hobe Ferris	3B148	R	30	148	555	54	150	26	7	2	74	14		6	.270	.353
Roy Hartzell	OF82, SS18, 3B7, 2B4	L	26	115	422	41	112	5	6	2	32	19		24	.265	.320
Danny Hoffman	OF99	L	28	99	363	41	91	9	7	1	25	23		17	.251	.322
George Stone	OF148	L	30	148	588	89	165	21	8	5	31	55		20	.281	.369
Tubby Spencer	C89	R	23	91	286	19	60	6	1	0	28	17		1	.210	.238
Charlie Jones	OF72		32	74	263	37	61	11	2	0	17	14		14	.232	.289
Dode Criss	P9, OF7, 1B1	L	23	64	82	15	28	6	0	0	14	9		1	.341	.415
Al Schweitzer	OF55	R	25	64	182	22	53	4	2	1	14	20		6	.291	.352
Jim Stephens	C45	R	24	47	150	14	30	4	1	0	6	9		0	.200	.240
2 Syd Smith	C25	R	24	27	76	6	14	4	4	0	5	4		2	.184	.342
Snags Heidrick	OF25		31	26	93	8	20	2	2	1	6	1		3	.215	.312
1 Bert Blue	C8	R	31	11	25	2	9	1	2	1	1	3		0	.360	.560
Joe Yeager (IL)	2B4, SS1		32	10	15	3	5	1	0	0	1	1		2	.333	.400

NAME	T	AGE	W	L	PCT	SV	G	GS	CG	IP	H	BB	SO	ShO	ERA
		29	83	69	.546	3	155	155	107	1397	1151	387	607	16	2.15
Rube Waddell	L	31	19	14	.576	3	43	36	25	286	223	90	232	5	1.89
Harry Howell	R	31	18	8	.692	0	41	32	27	324	279	70	117	2	1.89
Jack Powell	R	33	16	13	.552	0	33	32	23	256	208	47	85	6	2.11
Bill Dinneen	R	32	14	7	.667	0	27	16	11	167	133	53	39	1	2.10
Barney Pelty	R	27	7	4	.636	0	20	13	7	122	104	32	36	2	1.99
Bill Graham	L		6	7	.462	0	21	13	7	117	104	32	47	0	2.31
Bill Bailey	L	19	3	5	.375	0	22	12	7	107	85	50	42	0	3.03
Dode Criss	R	23	0	1	.000	0	9	1	0	18	15	13	9	0	6.50

BOSTON 5th 75-79 .487 15.5 — DEACON McGUIRE 53-62 .461 — FRED LAKE 22-17 .564

NAME	G by POS	B	AGE	G	AB	R	H	2B	3B	HR	RBI	BB	SO	SB	BA	SA
TOTALS			28	155	5047	565	1243	116	**88**	14	444	289		168	.246	.312
2 Jake Stahl	1B79	R	28	79	258	29	64	9	11	0	23	20		14	.248	.368
Amby McConnell	2B126, SS3	L	25	140	502	77	140	10	6	2	43	38		31	.279	.335
Heinie Wagner	SS153	R	27	153	526	62	130	11	5	1	46	27		20	.247	.293
Harry Lord	3B143	L	26	145	558	61	145	15	6	2	37	22		23	.260	.319
Doc Gessler	OF126	L	27	128	435	55	134	13	14	3	63	51		19	.308	.423
1 Denny Sullivan	OF99	L	25	101	353	33	85	7	7	0	25	14		15	.241	.300
Jack Thoney	OF101	R	28	109	416	58	106	5	9	2	30	13		16	.255	.325
Lou Criger	C84	R	36	84	237	12	45	4	2	0	25	13		1	.190	.224
Gavvy Cravath	OF77, 1B5	R	27	94	277	43	71	10	11	1	34	38		6	.256	.383
1 Bob Unglaub	1B72	R	26	72	266	23	70	11	3	1	25	7		6	.263	.338
2 Frank LaPorte	2B27, 3B12, OF5	R	28	62	156	14	37	1	3	0	15	12		3	.237	.282
Bill Carrigan (IL)	C47, 1B3	R	24	57	149	13	35	5	2	0	14	3		1	.235	.295
Pat Donahue	C32, 1B3	R	23	35	86	8	17	2	0	1	6	9		0	.198	.256
Tris Speaker	OF31	L	20	31	118	12	26	2	3	0	9	4		2	.220	.288
Jim McHale	OF19	R	32	21	67	9	15	2	2	0	7	4		4	.224	.313
Ed McFarland	C13	R	33	19	48	5	10	2	1	0	4	1		0	.208	.292
2 Harry Niles	2B8, SS2	R	27	17	33	4	9	0	0	1	3	6		3	.273	.364
John Hoey	OF11		26	13	43	5	7	0	0	0	3	0		1	.163	.163
Walter Carlisle	OF3	L	24	3	10	0	1	0	0	0	0	1		1	.100	.100
Jimmy Barrett	OF2	L	33	2	8	0	1	0	0	0	1	1		0	.125	.125
Larry Gardner	3B2	L	22	2	6	0	3	0	0	0	1	0		0	.500	.500
1 Deacon McGuire		R	42	1	1	0	0	0	0	0	0	0		0	.000	.000
Harry Ostdiek	C1	R	27	1	3	0	0	0	0	0	0	0		0	.000	.000

NAME	T	AGE	W	L	PCT	SV	G	GS	CG	IP	H	BB	SO	ShO	ERA
		29	75	79	.487	7	155	155	102	1381	1200	364	624	12	2.27
Cy Young	R	41	21	11	.656	2	36	33	30	299	230	37	150	3	1.26
Cy Morgan	R	29	13	13	.500	2	30	26	17	205	166	90	99	2	2.46
Eddie Cicotte	R	24	11	12	.478	2	39	24	17	207	198	59	95	2	2.43
Fred Burchell	L	28	10	8	.556	0	31	19	9	180	161	65	94	0	2.95
Elmer Steele	R	24	5	7	.417	0	16	13	9	118	85	13	37	1	1.83
Frank Arellanes	R	26	4	3	.571	0	11	8	6	79	60	18	33	1	1.82
1 George Winter	R	30	4	14	.222	0	22	17	8	148	150	34	55	0	3.04
Ralph Glaze	R	27	2	2	.500	0	10	3	2	35	43	5	13	0	3.34
Tex Pruiett		25	2	7	.222	1	13	6	1	59	55	21	28	1	1.98
Doc McMahon	R	21	1	0	1.000	0	1	1	1	9	14	0	3	0	3.00
King Brady	R	27	1	0	1.000	0	1	1	1	9	8	0	3	1	0.00
Smokey Joe Wood	R	18	1	1	.500	0	6	2	1	23	14	16	11	1	2.35
2 Casey Patten	L	32	0	1	.000	0	1	1	0	3	8	1	0	0	15.00
Charlie Hartman		19	0	0	.000	0	1	0	0	2	1	2	1	0	4.50
1 Jesse Tannehill	L	33	0	0	.000	0	1	1	0	5	4	3	2	0	3.60
2 Jake Thielman	R	29	0	0	.000	0	1	0	0	1	3	0	0	0	27.00

PHILADELPHIA 6th 68-85 .444 22 — CONNIE MACK

NAME	G by POS	B	AGE	G	AB	R	H	2B	3B	HR	RBI	BB	SO	SB	BA	SA
TOTALS			30	157	5064	487	1131	183	49	**21**	392	368		116	.223	.291
Harry Davis	1B147	R	34	147	513	65	127	23	9	5	62	61		20	.248	.357
Danny Murphy	OF84, 2B56, 1B2	R	31	142	525	51	139	28	6	4	66	32		16	.265	.364
Simon Nicholls	SS120, 2B23, 3B7	L	25	150	550	58	119	17	3	4	31	35		14	.216	.280
Jimmy Collins	3B115	R	38	115	433	34	94	14	3	0	30	20		5	.217	.263
Jack Coombs	OF47, P26	B	25	78	220	24	56	9	5	1	23	9		6	.255	.355
Rube Oldring (IL)	OF116	R	24	116	434	38	96	14	2	1	39	18		13	.221	.270
Topsy Hartsel	OF129	L	34	129	460	73	112	16	6	4	29	**93**		15	.243	.330
1 Ossee Schreckengost	C66, 1B1	R	33	71	207	16	46	7	1	0	16	6		1	.222	.266
Eddie Collins	2B47, SS28, OF10	L	21	102	330	39	90	18	7	1	40	16		8	.273	.379
Mike Powers	C60, 1B2	R	37	62	172	8	31	6	1	0	7	5		1	.180	.227
Socks Seybold (JJ)	OF34	R	37	48	130	5	28	2	0	0	3	12		2	.215	.231
1 Syd Smith	C36, 1B6, OF2	R	24	46	128	8	26	8	0	1	10	4		0	.203	.289
Jack Barry	2B20, SS14, 3B3	R	21	40	135	13	30	4	3	0	8	10		5	.222	.296
Frank Manush	3B20, 2B2	R	24	23	77	6	12	2	1	0	0	2		2	.156	.208
Scotty Barr	2B11, 3B4, 1B2, OF2	R	21	19	56	4	8	2	0	0	1	3		0	.143	.179
1 Herbie Moran	OF19	L	24	19	59	4	9	0	0	0	4	6		1	.153	.153
Jack Lapp	C13	L	23	13	35	4	5	0	1	0	1	5		0	.143	.200
Amos Strunk	OF11	L	19	12	34	4	8	1	0	0	0	4		0	.235	.265
Frank Baker	3B9	L	22	9	31	5	9	3	0	0	2	0		0	.290	.387
Jack Fox	OF8	R	23	9	30	2	6	0	0	0	0	0		2	.200	.200
Shag Shaughnessy	OF8	R	25	8	29	2	9	0	0	0	1	2		3	.310	.310
2 Bert Blue	C6	R	31	6	19	2	3	0	0	0	1	0		0	.158	.158
Joe Jackson	OF5	L	18	5	23	0	3	0	0	0	3	0		0	.130	.130
Ben Egan	C2	R	24	2	6	1	1	1	0	0	0	1		0	.167	.333

NAME	T	AGE	W	L	PCT	SV	G	GS	CG	IP	H	BB	SO	ShO	ERA
		26	68	85	.444	8	157	157	102	1377	1186	409	**740**	**23**	2.57
Rube Vickers	R	30	18	19	.486	2	53	33	21	300	264	71	156	6	2.34
Eddie Plank	L	32	14	16	.467	2	34	28	21	245	202	46	135	4	2.17
Jimmy Dygert	R	23	11	15	.423	1	41	27	15	239	184	**97**	164	5	2.86
Chief Bender	R	25	8	9	.471	1	18	17	14	139	121	21	85	2	1.75
Jack Coombs	R	25	7	5	.583	1	26	18	10	153	130	64	80	4	2.00
Biff Schlitzer	R	23	6	8	.429	0	24	18	11	131	110	45	57	2	3.16
Nick Carter	R	29	2	5	.286	1	14	6	2	61	58	17	17	0	2.95
Harry Krause	L	20	1	1	.500	0	4	2	2	21	20	4	10	0	2.57
Jack Flater	R	27	1	3	.250	0	5	3	3	39	35	12	8	0	2.08
Doc Martin	R	20	0	1	.000	0	1	1	0	2	2	3	2	0	13.50
Gus Salve	L	22	0	1	.000	0	1	1	1	9	9	8	5	0	2.00
Al Kellog	L		0	2	.000	0	3	3	2	17	20	9	8	0	5.82
Bert Maxwell	R	21	0	0	.000	0	4	0	0	13	23	9	7	0	11.08
Eddie Files	R	25	0	0	.000	0	2	0	0	9	8	3	6	0	6.00

WASHINGTON 7th 67-85 .441 22.5 — JOE CANTILLON

NAME	G by POS	B	AGE	G	AB	R	H	2B	3B	HR	RBI	BB	SO	SB	BA	SA
TOTALS			28	155	5040	479	1185	131	74	8	378	368		170	.235	.295
Jerry Freeman	1B154	L	26	154	531	45	134	15	5	1	45	36		6	.252	.305
Jim Delahanty	2B79	R	29	83	287	33	91	11	4	1	30	24		16	.317	.394
George McBride	SS155	R	27	155	518	47	120	10	6	0	34	41		12	.232	.274
Bill Shipke	3B110, 2B1	R	25	111	341	40	71	7	8	0	20	38		15	.208	.276
Ollie Pickering	OF98	L	38	113	373	45	84	7	4	2	30	28		13	.225	.282
Clyde Milan	OF122	L	22	130	485	55	116	10	12	1	32	38		29	.239	.315
Bob Ganley	OF150	L	33	150	549	61	131	19	9	1	36	45		30	.239	.311
Gabby Street	C128	R	25	131	394	31	81	12	7	1	32	40		5	.206	.279
Otis Clymer	OF82, 2B13, 3B2	L	31	110	368	32	93	11	4	1	35	20		19	.253	.313
2 Bob Unglaub	3B39, 2B27, 1B4	R	26	72	276	23	85	10	5	0	29	8		8	.308	.380
1 Dave Altizer	2B38, 3B16, 1B4, SS1	L	31	67	205	19	46	1	1	0	18	13		8	.224	.239
John Warner (KJ)	C41, 1B1	L	35	51	116	8	28	2	1	0	8	8		7	.241	.276
Eli Cates	P19, 2B3	R	31	40	59	5	11	1	1	0	3	6		0	.186	.237
Bob Edmundson	OF24	R	29	26	80	5	15	4	1	0	2	7		0	.188	.263
Jesse Tannehill (AJ)	P10	B	33	26	43	1	11	1	0	0	3	2		0	.256	.279
Mike Kahoe	C11	R	33	17	27	1	5	1	0	0	0	0		0	.185	.222

NAME	T	AGE	W	L	PCT	SV	G	GS	CG	IP	H	BB	SO	ShO	ERA
		27	67	85	.441	8	155	155	105	1395	1238	347	649	13	2.34
Long Tom Hughes	R	29	18	15	.545	4	43	31	24	276	224	77	165	3	2.22
Walter Johnson (IL)	R	20	14	14	.500	1	36	29	23	257	196	52	160	6	1.65
Charlie Smith	R	28	8	13	.381	1	26	22	13	184	166	60	83	0	2.40
1 Cy Falkenberg	R	28	6	2	.750	1	17	8	5	85	70	21	34	1	1.91
Bill Burns (BR)	L	28	6	11	.353	0	23	19	11	165	135	18	55	2	1.69
Burt Keeley	R	28	6	11	.353	1	28	17	12	170	173	48	68	1	2.96
Eli Cates	R	31	4	8	.333	0	19	10	7	115	112	32	33	0	2.50
2 Jesse Tannehill (AJ)	L	33	2	4	.333	0	10	9	5	72	77	23	14	0	3.75
Roy Witherup	R	21	2	4	.333	0	6	6	4	48	51	8	31	0	3.00
1 Casey Patten	L	32	1	2	.333	0	4	3	1	18	25	6	6	0	3.50
Henry Gehring		27	0	1	.000	0	3	1	0	5	9	2	0	0	14.40

NEW YORK 8th 51-103 .331 39.5 — CLARK GRIFFITH 24-32 .429 — KID ELBERFELD 27-71 .276

NAME	G by POS	B	AGE	G	AB	R	H	2B	3B	HR	RBI	BB	SO	SB	BA	SA
TOTALS			28	155	5036	456	1187	142	51	12	372	288		**230**	.236	.291
Hal Chase (JT)	1B98, 2B3, OF3, 3B1	R	25	106	405	50	104	11	3	1	36	15		27	.257	.306
1 Harry Niles	2B85, OF7	R	27	96	361	43	90	14	6	4	24	25		18	.249	.355
Neal Ball	SS130, 2B1	R	27	132	446	34	110	16	2	0	38	21		32	.247	.291
Wid Conroy	3B119, 2B12, OF10	R	31	141	531	44	126	22	3	1	39	14		23	.237	.296
Willie Keeler	OF88	L	36	91	323	38	85	3	1	1	14	31		14	.263	.288
Charlie Hemphill	OF142	L	32	142	505	62	150	12	9	0	44	59		42	.297	.356
1 Jake Stahl	OF67, 1B6	R	28	74	274	34	70	18	5	2	42	11		16	.255	.380
Red Kleinow (BG)	C89, 2B2	R	28	96	279	16	47	3	2	1	13	22		5	.168	.204
George Moriarty	1B52, 3B28, OF10, 2B4	R	23	101	348	25	82	12	1	0	27	11		22	.236	.276
Walter Blair	C60, OF9, 1B3	R	24	76	211	9	40	5	1	1	13	11		4	.190	.237
Irish McIlveen	OF44	L	27	44	169	17	36	3	3	0	8	14		6	.213	.266
1 Frank LaPorte	2B26, OF11	R	28	39	145	7	38	3	5	0	15	8		3	.262	.352
Frank Delahanty	OF36	R	25	37	125	12	32	1	2	0	10	10		9	.256	.296
Queenie O'Roarke	OF14, SS11, 2B4, 3B3	R	24	34	108	5	25	1	0	0	3	4		4	.231	.241
Ed Sweeney	C25, 1B1, OF1	R	19	32	82	4	12	2	0	0	2	5		0	.146	.171
Birdie Cree	OF21	R	25	21	78	5	21	0	2	0	4	7		1	.269	.321
Earl Gardner	2B20	R	23	20	75	7	16	2	0	0	4	1		0	.213	.240
Kid Elberfeld (LJ)	SS17	R	33	19	56	11	11	3	0	0	5	6		1	.196	.250
Mike Donovan	3B5	R	26	5	19	2	5	1	0	0	2	0		0	.263	.316

NAME	T	AGE	W	L	PCT	SV	G	GS	CG	IP	H	BB	SO	ShO	ERA
		30	51	**103**	.331	6	155	155	91	1363	1286	**457**	584	11	3.16
Jack Chesbro	R	34	14	20	.412	3	45	31	21	289	271	67	124	3	2.93
Rube Manning	R	25	13	16	.448	2	41	26	19	245	228	86	113	2	2.94
Joe Lake	R	26	9	**22**	.290	0	38	27	19	269	252	77	118	2	3.18
Doc Newton	L	30	4	6	.400	1	23	13	6	88	78	41	49	1	2.97
Bill Hogg		28	4	15	.211	0	24	21	6	152	155	63	72	0	3.02
Pete Wilson	L	22	3	3	.500	0	6	6	4	39	27	33	28	1	3.46
Al Orth	R	35	2	13	.133	0	21	17	8	139	134	30	22	1	3.43
Slow Joe Doyle	R	26	1	1	.500	0	12	4	2	48	42	14	20	1	2.63
Jack Warhop	R	23	1	2	.333	0	5	4	3	36	40	8	11	0	4.50
Andy O'Connor	R	23	0	1	.000	0	1	1	1	8	15	7	5	0	10.13
Fred Glade (SA)	R	32	0	4	.000	0	5	5	2	32	30	14	11	0	4.22
Harry Billiard	R	22	0	0	.000	0	5	0	0	14	13	13	9	0	2.57
Hippo Vaughn (HJ)	L	20	0	0	.000	0	2	0	0	2	1	4	2	0	4.50

CHICAGO 1st 99-55 .643 — **FRANK CHANCE**

	NAME	G by POS	B	AGE	G	AB	R	H	2B	3B	HR	RBI	BB	SO	SB	BA	SA
	TOTALS			29	158	5085	625	1267	197	56	19	492	418		212	.249	.321
	Frank Chance	1B126	R	30	129	452	65	123	27	4	2	55	37		27	.272	.363
	Johnny Evers	2B123	L	26	126	416	83	125	19	6	0	37	66		36	.300	.375
	Joe Tinker	SS157	R	27	157	548	67	146	23	14	6	68	32		30	.266	.392
	Harry Steinfeldt	3B150	R	30	150	539	63	130	20	6	1	62	36		12	.241	.306
	Wildfire Schulte	OF102	R	25	102	386	42	91	20	2	1	43	29		15	.236	.306
	Jimmy Slagle	OF101	L	34	104	352	38	78	4	1	0	26	43		17	.222	.239
	Jimmy Sheckard	OF115	L	29	115	403	54	93	18	3	2	22	62		18	.231	.305
	Johnny Kling	C117, OF6, 1B2	R	33	126	424	51	117	23	5	4	59	21		16	.276	.382
	Solly Hofman	OF50, 1B37, 2B22, 3B9	R	25	120	411	55	100	15	5	2	42	33		15	.243	.319
	Del Howard	OF81, 1B5	L	30	96	315	42	88	7	3	1	26	23		11	.279	.330
	Pat Moran	C45	R	32	50	150	12	39	5	1	0	12	13		6	.260	.307
	Heinie Zimmerman	2B20, OF8, 3B1, SS1	R	21	46	113	17	33	4	1	0	9	1		2	.292	.345
	Kid Durbin	OF11	L	21	14	28	3	7	1	0	0	0	2		0	.250	.286
2	Doc Marshall	C4, OF3	R	33	12	20	4	6	0	1	0	3	0		0	.300	.400
	Jack Hayden	OF11	R	27	11	45	3	9	2	0	0	2	1		1	.200	.244
	Vin Campbell		L	20	1	1	0	0	0	0	0	0	0		0	.000	.000

	NAME	T	AGE	W	L	PCT	SV	G	GS	CG	IP	H	BB	SO	ShO	ERA
			30	99	55	.643	12	158	158	108	1434	1137	437	668	27	2.14
	Three Finger Brown	R	31	29	9	.763	5	44	31	27	312	214	49	123	9	1.47
	Ed Reulbach	R	25	24	7	.774	1	46	35	25	298	227	106	133	7	2.02
	Orvie Overall (HJ)	R	27	15	11	.577	4	37	27	16	225	165	78	167	4	1.92
	Jack Pfiester	L	30	12	10	.545	0	33	29	18	252	204	70	117	3	2.00
	Chick Fraser	R	37	11	9	.550	2	26	17	11	163	141	61	66	2	2.26
	Carl Lundgren	R	28	6	9	.400	0	23	15	9	139	149	56	38	1	4.21
2	Andy Coakley	R	25	2	0	1.000	0	4	3	2	20	14	6	7	1	0.90
	Rube Kroh	L	21	0	0	.000	0	2	1	0	12	9	4	11	0	1.50
	Bill Mack	L	23	0	0	.000	0	2	0	0	6	5	1	2	0	3.00
	Carl Spongberg	R	24	0	0	.000	0	1	0	0	7	9	6	4	0	9.00

NEW YORK 2nd (Tie) 98-56 .636 1 — **JOHN McGRAW**

	NAME	G by POS	B	AGE	G	AB	R	H	2B	3B	HR	RBI	BB	SO	SB	BA	SA
	TOTALS			29	157	5006	652	1339	182	43	20	562	494		181	.267	.333
	Fred Tenney	1B156	L	36	156	583	101	149	20	1	2	49	72		17	.256	.304
	Larry Doyle	2B102	L	21	104	377	65	116	16	9	0	33	22		17	.308	.398
	Al Bridwell	SS147	L	24	147	467	53	133	14	1	0	40	52		20	.285	.319
	Art Devlin	3B157	R	28	157	534	59	135	18	4	2	45	62		19	.253	.313
	Mike Donlin	OF155	L	30	155	593	71	198	26	13	6	106	23		30	.334	.452
	Cy Seymour	OF155	L	35	156	587	60	157	23	2	5	92	30		18	.267	.339
1	Spike Shannon	OF74	B	30	77	268	34	60	2	1	1	21	28		13	.224	.250
	Roger Bresnahan	C139	R	29	140	449	70	127	25	3	1	54	83		14	.283	.359
2	Moose McCormick	OF65	L	27	73	252	31	76	16	3	0	32	4		6	.302	.389
	Buck Herzog (WJ)	2B42, SS11, 3B3, OF1	L	29	64	160	38	48	6	2	0	11	36		16	.300	.363
	Tom Needham	C47	R	29	54	91	8	19	3	0	0	11	12		0	.209	.242
	Fred Merkle	1B11, OF5, 2B1, 3B1	R	19	38	41	6	11	2	1	1	7	4		0	.268	.439
2	Shad Barry	OF31	R	31	37	67	5	10	1	1	0	5	9		1	.149	.194
	Sammy Strang	2B14, OF5, SS3	B	31	28	53	8	5	0	0	0	2	23		5	.094	.094
2	Dave Brain	2B3, OF3, 3B2, SS1	R	29	11	17	2	3	0	0	0	1	2		1	.176	.176
	Fred Snodgrass	C3	R	20	6	4	2	1	0	0	0	1	0		1	.250	.250
	Josh Devore	OF2	L	20	5	6	1	1	0	0	0	2	1		1	.167	.167
	Steve Evans	OF1	L	23	2	2	0	1	0	0	0	0	0		0	.500	.500
1	Jack Hannifan	OF1	R	25	1	2	0	0	0	0	0	0	0		0	.000	.000
	Art Wilson		R	22	1	0	0	0	0	0	0	0	0		0	.000	.000

	NAME	T	AGE	W	L	PCT	SV	G	GS	CG	IP	H	BB	SO	ShO	ERA
			29	98	56	.636	18	157	157	95	1411	1214	288	656	24	2.14
	Christy Mathewson	R	29	37	11	.771	5	56	44	34	391	285	42	259	11	1.43
	Hooks Wiltse	L	27	23	14	.622	2	44	38	30	330	266	73	118	7	2.24
	Doc Crandall	R	20	12	12	.500	0	32	24	13	215	198	59	77	0	2.93
	Joe McGinnity	R	37	11	7	.611	3	37	20	7	186	192	37	55	5	2.27
	Dummy Taylor	R	33	8	5	.615	2	27	15	6	128	127	34	50	1	2.32
	Red Ames (IL)	R	25	7	4	.636	1	18	15	5	114	96	27	81	0	1.82
	Rube Marquard	L	18	0	1	.000	0	1	1	0	5	6	2	2	0	3.60
	Bill Malarkey	L	29	0	2	.000	2	15	0	0	35	31	10	12	0	2.57
	Roy Beecher	R	24	0	0	.000	1	2	0	0	6	11	3	0	0	7.50
	Bull Durham	R	27	0	0	.000	0	1	0	0	2	2	1	2	0	9.00

PITTSBURGH 2nd (Tie) 98-56 .636 1 — **FRED CLARKE**

	NAME	G by POS	B	AGE	G	AB	R	H	2B	3B	HR	RBI	BB	SO	SB	BA	SA
	TOTALS			29	155	5109	585	1263	162	98	25	496	420		186	.247	.332
	Harry Swacina	1B50	R	26	53	176	7	38	6	1	0	13	5		4	.216	.261
	Ed Abbaticchio	2B144	R	31	146	500	43	125	16	7	1	61	58		22	.250	.316
	Honus Wagner	SS151	R	34	151	568	100	201	39	19	10	109	54		53	.354	.542
	Tommy Leach	3B150, OF2	R	30	152	583	93	151	24	16	5	41	54		24	.259	.381
	Owen Wilson	OF144	L	24	144	529	47	120	8	7	3	43	22		12	.227	.285
2	Roy Thomas	OF101	L	34	102	386	52	99	11	10	1	24	49		11	.256	.345
	Fred Clarke	OF151	L	35	151	551	83	146	18	15	2	53	65		24	.265	.363
	George Gibson	C140	R	27	143	486	37	111	19	4	2	45	19		4	.228	.296
	Alan Storke (RL)	1B49, 3B6, 2B1	R	23	64	202	20	51	5	3	1	12	9		4	.252	.322
	Jim Kane	1B40	L	25	55	145	16	35	3	3	0	22	12		5	.241	.303
	Danny Moeller	OF27	B	23	36	109	14	21	3	1	0	9	9		4	.193	.239
	Eddie Phelps	C20	R	29	34	64	3	15	2	2	0	11	2		0	.234	.328
2	Spike Shannon	OF32	B	30	32	127	10	25	0	2	0	12	9		5	.197	.228
	Doc Gill	1B25	R	29	27	76	10	17	0	1	0	14	11		3	.224	.250
1	Beals Becker	OF17	L	21	20	65	4	10	0	1	0	0	2		2	.154	.185
	Charlie Starr	2B12, SS5, 3B2		29	20	59	8	11	2	0	0	8	13		6	.186	.220
	Paddy O'Connor	C4	R	28	12	16	1	3	0	0	0	2	0		0	.188	.188
	Hunky Shaw		B	23	1	1	0	0	0	0	0	0	0		0	.000	.000
	John Sullivan	C1		35	1	1	0	0	0	0	0	0	0		0	.000	.000
	Cy Neighbors	OF1		28	1	0	0	0	0	0	0	0	0		0	.000	.000

	NAME	T	AGE	W	L	PCT	SV	G	GS	CG	IP	H	BB	SO	ShO	ERA
			28	98	56	.636	9	155	155	100	1402	1142	406	468	24	2.12
	Nick Maddox	R	21	23	8	.742	1	36	32	22	261	209	90	70	4	2.28
	Vic Willis	R	32	23	11	.676	0	41	38	25	305	239	69	97	7	2.07
	Howie Camnitz	R	26	16	9	.640	2	38	26	17	237	182	69	118	3	1.56
	Sam Leever	R	36	15	7	.682	2	38	20	14	193	179	41	28	4	2.10
	Lefty Leifield	L	24	15	14	.517	2	34	26	18	219	168	86	87	5	2.10
2	Irv Young	L	30	4	3	.571	1	16	7	3	90	73	21	31	1	2.00
	Chick Brandom	R	21	1	0	1.000	1	3	1	1	17	13	4	8	0	0.53
	Bob Vail	R	26	1	2	.333	0	4	1	0	15	15	7	9	0	6.00
1	Harley Young	L		0	2	.000	0	8	3	0	48	40	10	17	0	2.25
	Deacon Phillippe	R	36	0	0	.000	0	5	0	0	12	20	3	1	0	11.25
2	Tom McCarthy	R	24	0	0	.000	0	2	1	0	6	3	6	1	0	0.00
	Doc Hillebrand	L	28	0	0	.000	0	1	0	0	1	1	0	1	0	0.00

PHILADELPHIA 4th 83-71 .539 16 — **BILLY MURRAY**

	NAME	G by POS	B	AGE	G	AB	R	H	2B	3B	HR	RBI	BB	SO	SB	BA	SA
	TOTALS			27	155	5012	503	1223	194	68	11	400	334		200	.244	.316
	Kitty Bransfield	1B143	R	33	144	527	53	160	25	7	3	71	23		30	.304	.395
	Otto Knabe	2B151	R	24	151	555	63	121	26	8	0	27	49		27	.218	.294
	Mickey Doolan	SS129	R	28	129	445	29	104	25	4	2	49	17		5	.234	.321
	Eddie Grant	3B134, SS13	L	25	147	598	69	146	13	8	0	32	35		27	.244	.293
	John Titus	OF149	L	32	149	539	75	154	24	5	2	48	53		27	.286	.360
	Ossie Osborn	OF152	L	24	152	555	62	148	19	12	2	44	30		16	.267	.355
	Sherry Magee	OF142	R	23	143	508	79	144	30	16	2	57	49		40	.283	.417
	Red Dooin	C132	R	29	133	435	28	108	17	4	0	41	17		20	.248	.306
	Ernie Courtney	3B22, 1B13, 2B5, SS2	L	29	60	160	14	29	3	0	0	6	15		1	.181	.200
	Fred Jacklitsch	C30	R	32	37	86	6	19	3	0	0	7	14		3	.221	.256
	Wally Clement	OF8	L	26	16	36	0	8	3	0	0	1	0		2	.222	.306
	Dave Shean	SS14	R	30	14	48	4	7	2	0	0	2	1		1	.146	.188
1	Moose McCormick	OF5	L	27	11	22	0	2	0	0	0	2	2		0	.091	.091
	Charlie Johnson	OF4	L	23	6	16	2	4	0	1	0	2	1		0	.250	.375
1	Roy Thomas	OF6	L	34	6	24	2	4	0	0	0	0	2		0	.167	.167
	Kid Gleason	2B1, OF1	B	41	2	1	0	0	0	0	0	0	0		0	.000	.000
	Pep Deininger	OF1	L	30	1	0	0	0	0	0	0	0	0		0	.000	.000

	NAME	T	AGE	W	L	PCT	SV	G	GS	CG	IP	H	BB	SO	ShO	ERA
			26	83	71	.539	6	155	155	116	1393	1167	379	476	22	2.10
	George McQuillan	R	23	23	17	.575	2	48	42	32	360	263	91	114	7	1.52
	Tully Sparks	R	31	16	15	.516	2	33	31	24	263	251	51	85	2	2.60
	Frank Corridon	R	27	14	10	.583	1	27	24	18	208	178	48	50	2	2.51
	Lew Moren	R	24	8	9	.471	0	28	16	9	154	146	49	72	4	2.92
	Bill Foxen	L	24	7	7	.500	0	22	16	10	147	126	53	52	2	1.96
	Lew Richie	R	24	7	10	.412	1	25	15	13	158	125	49	58	2	1.82
	Harry Coveleski	L	22	4	1	.800	0	6	5	5	44	29	12	22	2	1.23
	Harry Hoch	R	21	2	1	.667	0	3	3	2	26	20	13	4	0	2.77
	Earl Moore	R	28	2	1	.667	0	3	3	3	26	20	8	16	1	0.00
	Buster Brown	R	26	0	0	.000	0	3	0	0	7	9	5	3	0	2.57

CINCINNATI 5th 73-81 .474 26 — **JOHN GANZEL**

	NAME	G by POS	B	AGE	G	AB	R	H	2B	3B	HR	RBI	BB	SO	SB	BA	SA
	TOTALS			28	155	4879	488	1108	129	77	14	398	372		196	.227	.294
	John Ganzel	1B108	R	33	112	388	32	97	16	10	1	53	19		6	.250	.351
	Miller Huggins	2B135	B	29	135	498	65	119	14	5	0	23	58		30	.239	.287
	Rudy Hulswitt	SS118, 2B1	R	31	119	386	27	88	5	7	1	28	30		7	.228	.285
	Hans Lobert	3B99, SS35, OF21	R	26	155	570	71	167	17	18	4	63	46		47	.293	.407
	Mike Mitchell	OF118, 1B1	R	28	119	406	41	90	9	6	1	37	46		18	.222	.281
	John Kane	OF127, 2B1	R	24	130	455	61	97	11	7	3	23	43		30	.213	.288
	Dode Paskert	OF116	R	26	118	395	40	96	14	4	1	36	27		25	.243	.306
	Admiral Schlei	C88	R	30	92	300	31	66	6	4	1	22	22		2	.220	.277
	Larry McLean	C69, 1B19	R	26	99	309	24	67	9	4	1	28	15		2	.217	.282
	Mike Mowrey (KJ)	3B56, SS3, OF3	R	24	77	227	17	50	9	1	0	23	12		5	.220	.269
	Bob Bescher	OF32	B	24	32	114	16	31	5	5	0	17	9		10	.272	.404
	Dick Hoblitzell	1B29	L	19	29	114	8	29	3	2	0	8	7		2	.254	.316
	Dick Bayless	OF19	L	26	19	71	7	16	1	0	1	3	6		0	.225	.282
	Dick Egan	2B18	R	24	18	68	8	14	3	1	0	5	2		7	.206	.279
1	Dave Brain (IL)	OF16	R	29	16	55	4	6	0	0	0	1	8		0	.109	.109
	Tom Daley	OF13	L	23	14	46	5	5	0	0	0	1	3		1	.109	.109
	Bob Coulson	OF6	R	21	8	18	3	6	1	1	0	1	3		0	.333	.500
	Bill McGilvray		L	25	2	2	0	0	0	0	0	0	0		0	.000	.000
	Bunny Pearce (NJ)	C2	R	23	2	2	0	0	0	0	0	0	0		0	.000	.000

	NAME	T	AGE	W	L	PCT	SV	G	GS	CG	IP	H	BB	SO	ShO	ERA
			30	73	81	.474	8	155	155	110	1384	1218	415	433	17	2.37
	Bob Spade	R	31	17	12	.586	1	35	28	22	249	230	85	74	3	2.75
	Bob Ewing	R	35	17	15	.531	3	37	32	23	294	247	57	95	4	2.20
	Bill Campbell	L	34	12	13	.480	2	35	24	19	221	203	44	73	2	2.61
	Jake Weimer	L	34	8	7	.533	0	15	15	9	117	110	50	36	2	2.38
1	Andy Coakley	R	25	8	18	.308	2	32	28	20	242	219	64	61	4	1.86
	Jean Dubuc	R	19	5	6	.455	0	15	9	7	85	62	41	32	1	2.75
	Jack Rowan	R	21	3	3	.500	0	8	7	4	49	46	16	24	1	1.84
	Marty O'Toole	R	20	1	0	1.000	0	3	2	1	15	15	7	5	0	2.40
	Jake Volz	R	30	1	2	.333	0	7	4	1	23	16	12	6	0	3.52
	Jack Doscher (BL)	L	27	1	3	.250	0	7	4	3	44	31	22	7	0	1.84
	Ralph Savidge	R	29	0	1	.000	0	4	1	1	21	18	8	7	0	2.57
1	Tom McCarthy	R	24	0	1	.000	0	1	1	0	4	6	3	3	0	9.00
	Bill Tozer	R	25	0	0	.000	0	4	0	0	11	11	4	5	0	1.64
1	Charlie Rhodes	R	23	0	0	.000	0	1	0	0	4	1	2	4	0	0.00
	Bert Sincock	L	20	0	0	.000	0	1	0	0	5	3	0	1	0	3.60

BOSTON 6th 63-91 .409 36 — **JOE KELLEY**

NAME	G by POS	B	AGE	G	AB	R	H	2B	3B	HR	RBI	BB	SO	SB	BA	SA
TOTALS			31	156	5131	537	1228	137	43	17	426	414		134	.239	.293
Dan McGann	1B121, 2B9	B	36	135	475	52	114	8	5	2	55	38		9	.240	.291
Claude Ritchey	2B120	B	34	121	421	44	115	10	3	2	36	50		7	.273	.325
Bill Dahlen	SS144	R	38	144	524	50	125	23	2	3	48	35		10	.239	.307
Bill Sweeney	3B123, SS2, 2B1	R	22	127	418	44	102	15	3	0	40	45		17	.244	.294
George Browne	OF138	L	32	138	536	61	122	10	6	1	34	36		17	.228	.274
Ginger Beaumont	OF121	L	31	125	476	66	127	20	6	2	52	42		13	.267	.347
Johnny Bates	OF117	L	26	127	445	48	115	14	6	1	29	35		25	.258	.324
Frank Bowerman (HJ)	C63, 1B11	R	38	86	254	16	58	8	1	1	25	13		4	.228	.280
Peaches Graham	C62, 2B5	R	31	75	215	22	59	5	0	0	22	23		4	.274	.298
2 Jack Hannifan	3B35, 2B22, SS15, OF7	R	25	74	257	30	53	6	2	2	22	28		7	.206	.268
Joe Kelley	OF38, 1B10	R	36	62	228	25	59	8	2	2	17	27		5	.259	.338
2 Beals Becker	OF43	L	21	43	171	13	47	3	1	0	7	7		7	.275	.304
Harry Smith	C38	R	33	41	130	13	32	2	2	1	16	7		2	.246	.315
Fred Stem	1B18	L	22	19	72	9	20	0	1	0	3	2		1	.278	.306
2 Herbie Moran	OF8	L	24	8	29	3	8	0	0	0	2	2		1	.276	.276
Jim Ball	C6		23	6	15	1	1	0	0	0	0	1		0	.067	.067
Walt Thomas	SS5			5	13	2	2	0	0	0	1	3		2	.154	.154

NAME	T	AGE	W	L	PCT	SV	G	GS	CG	IP	H	BB	SO	ShO	ERA
		28	63	91	.409	1	156	156	92	1405	1262	423	416	14	2.79
Cecil Ferguson (AJ)	R	21	12	11	.522	0	37	20	13	208	168	84	98	3	2.47
Vive Lindaman	R	30	12	16	.429	1	43	30	21	271	246	70	68	2	2.36
Patsy Flaherty	L	32	12	18	.400	0	31	31	21	244	221	81	50	0	3.25
Gus Dorner	R	31	8	19	.296	0	38	28	14	216	176	77	41	3	3.54
3 Tom McCarthy (BH)	R	24	6	3	.667	0	14	11	7	94	77	28	27	2	1.63
1 Irv Young	L	30	4	8	.333	0	16	11	7	85	94	19	32	1	2.86
Tom Tuckey	L		3	3	.500	0	8	8	3	72	60	20	26	1	2.50
Jake Boultes	R	23	3	5	.375	0	17	5	1	75	80	8	28	0	3.00
Bill Chappelle	R	24	2	4	.333	0	13	7	3	70	60	17	23	1	1.80
Al Mattern	R	25	1	3	.250	0	5	3	1	30	30	6	8	1	2.10
2 Harley Young	L		0	1	.000	0	6	2	1	27	29	4	12	0	3.33
Big Jeff Pfeffer (AJ)	R	26	0	0	.000	0	4	0	0	10	18	8	3	0	12.60
Chick Maloney	R	22	0	0	.000	0	1	0	0	2	3	1	0	0	4.50

BROOKLYN 7th 53-101 .344 46 — **PATSY DONOVAN**

NAME	G by POS	B	AGE	G	AB	R	H	2B	3B	HR	RBI	BB	SO	SB	BA	SA
TOTALS			28	154	4897	375	1044	110	60	28	306	323		113	.213	.277
Tim Jordan	1B146	L	29	148	515	58	127	18	5	12	60	59		9	.247	.371
Harry Pattee	2B74	L	26	80	264	19	57	5	2	0	9	25		24	.216	.250
Phil Lewis	SS116	R	24	118	415	22	91	5	6	1	30	13		9	.219	.267
Tommy Sheehan	3B145	R	30	146	468	45	100	18	2	0	29	53		9	.214	.261
Harry Lumley	OF116	L	27	127	440	36	95	13	12	4	39	29		4	.216	.327
Billy Maloney	OF103, C4	L	30	113	359	31	70	5	7	3	17	24		14	.195	.273
Al Burch	OF116	L	24	123	456	45	111	8	4	2	18	33		15	.243	.292
Bill Bergen	C99	R	35	99	302	8	53	8	2	0	15	5		1	.175	.215
John Hummel	OF95, 2B43, SS9, 1B8	R	25	154	594	51	143	11	12	4	41	34		20	.241	.320
W. Alperman (BN)	2B42, 3B9, OF5, SS2	R	28	70	213	17	42	3	1	0	15	9		2	.197	.235
Tommy McMillian	SS29, OF14	R	20	43	147	9	35	3	0	0	3	9		5	.238	.259
Lew Ritter	C37	R	32	38	99	6	19	2	1	0	2	7		0	.192	.232
Joe Dunn	C20	R	23	20	64	3	11	3	0	0	5	0		0	.172	.219
Tom Catterson	OF18	L	23	19	68	5	13	1	1	1	2	5		0	.191	.279
Alex Farmer	C11	R	28	12	30	1	5	1	0	0	2	1		0	.167	.200
Simmy Murch	1B2	R	27	6	11	1	2	1	0	0	0	1		0	.182	.273

NAME	T	AGE	W	L	PCT	SV	G	GS	CG	IP	H	BB	SO	ShO	ERA
		29	53	101	.344	4	154	154	118	1369	1165	444	535	20	2.47
Nap Rucker	L	23	17	19	.472	1	42	35	30	333	265	125	199	6	2.08
Kaiser Wilhelm	R	34	16	22	.571	0	42	36	33	332	266	83	99	6	1.87
Harry McIntire	R	30	11	20	.355	2	40	35	26	288	259	90	108	4	2.69
George Bell	R	33	4	15	.211	1	29	21	12	155	162	45	63	2	3.60
Jim Pastorius	L	26	4	20	.167	0	28	25	16	214	171	74	54	2	2.44
Jim Holmes		25	1	4	.200	0	13	1	1	40	37	20	10	0	3.38
Abe Kruger	R	23	0	1	.000	0	2	1	0	6	5	3	2	0	4.50
Pembroke Finlayson	R	19	0	0	.000	0	1	0	0	.1	0	4	0	0	135.00

ST. LOUIS 8th 49-105 .318 50 — **JOHN McCLOSKEY**

NAME	G by POS	B	AGE	G	AB	R	H	2B	3B	HR	RBI	BB	SO	SB	BA	SA
TOTALS			27	154	4959	372	1105	134	57	17	301	282		150	.223	.283
Ed Konetchy	1B154	R	22	154	545	46	135	19	12	5	50	38		16	.248	.354
Billy Gilbert	2B89	R	32	89	276	12	59	7	0	0	10	20		6	.214	.239
Patsy O'Rourke	SS53	R	27	53	164	8	32	4	2	0	16	14		2	.195	.244
Bobby Byrne	3B122, SS4	R	23	127	439	27	84	7	1	0	14	23		16	.191	.212
Red Murray	OF154	R	24	154	593	64	167	19	15	7	62	37		48	.282	.400
Al Shaw	OF91, SS4, 3B1	L	27	107	367	40	97	13	4	1	19	25		9	.264	.330
Joe Delahanty	OF138	L	32	140	499	37	127	14	11	1	44	32		11	.255	.333
Bill Ludwig	C62	R	26	66	187	15	34	2	2	0	8	16		3	.182	.214
Chappie Charles	2B65, SS31, 3B23	R	27	121	454	39	93	14	3	1	17	19		15	.205	.256
1 Shad Barry	OF69, SS2	R	31	74	268	24	61	8	1	0	11	19		9	.228	.265
Art Hoelskoetter	C41, 3B2, 1B1, 2B1	R	25	62	155	10	36	7	1	0	6	6		1	.232	.290
Jack Bliss	C43	R	26	44	136	9	29	4	0	1	5	8		3	.213	.265
Champ Osteen	SS17, 3B12	L	31	29	112	2	22	4	0	0	11	0		0	.196	.232
Tom Reilly	SS29	R	23	29	81	5	14	1	0	1	3	2		4	.173	.222
Wilbur Murdock	OF16			27	62	5	16	3	0	0	5	3		4	.258	.306
Walter Morris	SS23	R	28	23	73	1	13	1	1	0	2	0		1	.178	.219
Charlie Moran	C16	R	30	21	63	2	11	1	2	0	2	0		0	.175	.254
Ralph McLaurin	OF6		23	8	22	2	5	0	0	0	0	0		0	.227	.227
1 Doc Marshall	C6	R	33	6	14	0	1	0	0	0	1	0		0	.071	.071

NAME	T	AGE	W	L	PCT	SV	G	GS	CG	IP	H	BB	SO	ShO	ERA
		26	49	105	.318	4	154	154	97	1368	1217	430	528	13	2.64
Bugs Raymond	R	26	15	25	.375	2	48	37	23	324	236	95	145	5	2.03
Johnny Lush	L	22	11	18	.379	1	38	32	23	251	221	57	93	3	2.12
Fred Beebe	R	27	5	13	.278	0	29	19	12	174	134	66	72	0	2.64
Art Fromme	R	24	5	13	.278	0	20	14	9	116	102	50	62	2	2.72
Ed Karger	L	25	4	9	.308	0	22	15	9	141	148	50	34	1	3.06
Slim Sallee	L	23	3	8	.273	0	25	12	7	129	144	36	39	1	3.14
Irv Higginbotham	R	26	3	8	.273	0	19	11	7	107	113	33	38	1	3.20
2 Charlie Rhodes	R	23	1	2	.333	0	4	4	3	33	23	12	15	0	3.00
Ollie Baldwin			1	3	.250	0	4	4	0	15	16	11	5	0	6.00
Stony McGlynn	R	36	1	6	.143	1	16	6	4	76	76	17	23	0	3.43
Fred Gaiser		23	0	0	.000	0	1	0	0	2	4	3	2	0	9.00

WORLD SERIES – CHICAGO (NL) 4 DETROIT (AL) 1

LINE SCORES

TEAM	1	2	3	4	5	6	7	8	9	10	11	12	R	H	E
Game 1 October 10 at Detroit															
CHI (NL)	0	0	4	0	0	0	1	0	5				10	14	2
DET (AL)	1	0	0	0	0	0	3	2	0				6	10	4
Reulbach, Overall (7), **Brown (8)** — Killian, **Summers (3)**															
Game 2 October 11 at Chicago															
DET	0	0	0	0	0	0	0	0	1				1	4	1
CHI	0	0	0	0	0	0	0	6	X				6	7	1
Donovan — **Overall**															
Game 3 October 12 at Chicago															
DET	1	0	0	0	0	5	0	2	0				8	11	4
CHI	0	0	0	3	0	0	0	0	0				3	7	2
Mullin — **Pfiester**, Reulbach (9)															
Game 4 October 13 at Detroit															
CHI	0	0	2	0	0	0	0	0	1				3	10	0
DET	0	0	0	0	0	0	0	0	0				0	4	1
Brown — **Summers**, Winter (9)															
Game 5 October 14 at Detroit															
CHI	1	0	0	0	1	0	0	0	0				2	10	0
DET	0	0	0	0	0	0	0	0	0				0	3	0
Overall — **Donovan**															

COMPOSITE BATTING

NAME	POS	G	AB	R	H	2B	3B	HR	RBI	BA
Chicago (NL)										
Totals		5	164	24	48	4	2	1	20	.293
Sheckard	OF	5	21	2	5	2	0	0	1	.238
Evers	2B	5	20	5	7	1	0	0	2	.350
Chance	1B	5	19	4	8	0	0	0	2	.421
Hofman	OF	5	19	2	6	0	1	0	4	.316
Tinker	SS	5	19	2	5	0	0	1	4	.263
Schulte	OF	5	18	4	7	0	1	0	2	.389
Steinfeldt	3B	5	16	3	4	0	0	0	3	.250
Kling	C	5	16	2	4	1	0	0	2	.250
Overall	P	3	6	0	2	0	0	0	0	.333
Brown	P	2	4	0	0	0	0	0	0	.000
Reulbach	P	2	3	0	0	0	0	0	0	.000
Pfiester	P	1	2	0	0	0	0	0	0	.000
Howard	PH	1	1	0	0	0	0	0	0	.000
Detroit (AL)										
Totals		5	158	15	32	5	0	0	14	.203
Crawford	OF	5	21	2	5	1	0	0	1	.238
Cobb	OF	5	19	3	7	1	0	0	4	.368
Rossman	1B	5	19	3	4	0	0	0	3	.211
O'Leary	SS	5	19	2	3	0	0	0	0	.158
McIntyre	OF	5	18	2	4	1	0	0	0	.222
Schaefer	3B-2B	5	16	0	2	0	0	0	0	.125
Schmidt	C	4	14	0	1	0	0	0	1	.071
Coughlin	3B	3	8	0	1	0	0	0	1	.125
Downs	2B	2	6	1	1	1	0	0	1	.167
Summers	P	2	5	0	1	0	0	0	1	.200
Thomas	C	2	4	0	2	1	0	0	1	.500
Donovan	P	2	4	0	0	0	0	0	0	.000
Mullin	P	1	3	1	1	0	0	0	1	.333
Jones	PH	3	2	1	0	0	0	0	0	.000
Killian	P	1	0	0	0	0	0	0	0	.000
Winter	P	2	0	0	0	0	0	0	0	.000

COMPOSITE PITCHING

NAME	G	IP	H	BB	SO	W	L	SV	ERA
Chicago (NL)									
Totals	5	45	32	12	26	4	1	0	2.60
Overall	3	18.1	7	7	15	2	0	0	0.98
Brown	2	11	6	1	5	2	0	0	0.00
Pfiester	1	8	10	3	1	0	1	0	7.88
Reulbach	2	7.2	9	1	5	0	0	0	4.70
Detroit (AL)									
Totals	5	44	48	13	26	1	4	0	3.68
Donovan	2	17	17	4	10	0	2	0	4.24
Summers	2	14.2	18	4	7	0	2	0	4.30
Mullin	1	9	7	1	8	1	0	0	0.00
Killian	1	2.1	5	3	1	0	0	0	11.57
Winter	1	1	1	1	0	0	0	0	0.00

1909 Cobb—Everything but the Last Laugh

After winning three straight National League pennants, and coming up on the long end of the 1908 Merkle incident, the Chicago Cubs entered the season confident of an unprecedented fourth consecutive senior circuit title. The Cubs got off to a slow start out of the gate, due largely to the holdout of catcher Johnny Kling and the nervous breakdown of second baseman Johnny Evers, but from May until the season's end, the team played championship ball. Three Finger Brown, Orvie Overall, and Ed Reulbach all pitched effectively, forming the heart of a hill staff that was the heart of the Cubs. The Cubs wound up with 104 victories, five more than the 1908 champions, but had to settle for a disappointing second-place finish. While Chicago played good ball for five months, the Pittsburgh Pirates were consistent winners all year, starting fast and never leaving first place after May 5. Honus Wagner proved the difference as he led the Pirates to the crown afield as well as at bat, winning his fourth consecutive batting crown with a .339 average and knocking in 100 runs to take honors also in that category. Manager Fred Clarke and rookie second baseman Dots Miller also produced well with the bat, contributing to the best offense in the league. Vic Willis and Howie Camnitz chalked up 20-win seasons on the mound for the 110-victory winning Pirates. The rest of the teams trailed badly, with only the Cubs and the New York Giants closer than 30 games to the top.

As a three-pennant streak ended in the National League, the same streak was achieved in the American League. The Detroit Tigers overcame a mid-season slump to chalk up their third straight crown. The Mackmen of Philadelphia were expected to be second-division residents, but the rebuilt Athletics held the lead for most of August before the champion Tigers came on with a rush to reclaim the throne. The Tigers flashed strong teeth with Ty Cobb and Sam Crawford filling the center of the lineup. Good claws were evident in a pitching staff aced by 29-victory winner George Mullin and 22-game winner Ed Willett. Outside of Mullin and Willett, the only American League pitcher to win 20 games was Frank Smith of the White Sox.

Compared to the Tiger veteran lineup, the Athletics were babes in arms, sporting a new trio of infielders in Eddie Collins, Frank Baker, and Jack Barry. The Athletic pitching staff of Ed Plank, Chief Bender, Cy Morgan, and Harry Krause was the league's best, but the Tiger attack prevailed in the flag chase. Cobb dominated the offensive statistics, pacing the loop in batting average with .377, home runs with 9, and runs batted in with 107. In addition to becoming the second man in modern baseball to capture the Triple Crown, Cobb also took stolen base honors with 76 swipes.

The Series was anticipated as a match between stars, Ty Cobb and Honus Wagner, but a Pirate second-line pitcher named Babe Adams stole the spotlight with three complete game victories in leading the Pirates to the championship over the Tigers in seven games. Adams posted a 12-3 mark during the regular season as a rookie spot starter and reliever, and manager Clarke fingered him a surprise opening game pitcher. A victory in game one was repeated in games five and seven to etch Adams' name into the record books. As far as the Wagner-Cobb duel was concerned, the Flying Dutchman bested the Georgia Peach .333-.231 in batting and 6-2 in stolen bases.

Institutions came and passed for the national pastime in 1909. Harry C. Pulliam's six-year reign as National League President came to an end with his nervous breakdown and his suicide by pistol in New York on July 29. On a less morbid note, Forbes Field in Pittsburgh and Shibe Park in Philadelphia opened their gates for the first time, gates which would not be boarded up until 60 years had passed and countless memorable moments in baseball had occurred on their playing fields. Of all the events that were to occur, the one that never came about in the expanse of Forbes Field was a no-hitter, leaving that park the only one in all of baseball history to close its doors without the incident of such notoriety.

1909 AMERICAN LEAGUE

NAME	G by POS	B	AGE	G	AB	R	H	2B	3B	HR	RBI	BB	SO	SB	BA	SA
DETROIT 1st 98-54 .645		HUGHIE JENNINGS														
TOTALS			27	158	5095	666	1360	209	58	19	521	397		280	.267	.342
1 Claude Rossman	1B75	L	28	82	287	16	75	8	3	0	39	13		10	.261	.310
1 Germany Schaefer	2B86, OF1	R	32	87	280	26	70	12	0	0	22	14		12	.250	.293
Donie Bush	SS157	B	21	157	532	114	145	18	2	0	33	**88**		53	.273	.314
George Moriarty	3B106, 1B24	R	24	133	473	43	129	20	4	1	39	24		34	.273	.338
Ty Cobb	OF156	L	22	156	573	**116**	**216**	33	10	**9**	**107**	48		**76**	**.377**	**.517**
Sam Crawford	OF139, 1B17	L	29	156	589	83	185	**35**	14	6	97	47		30	.314	.452
Matty McIntyre	OF122	L	29	125	476	65	116	18	9	1	34	54		13	.244	.326
Boss Schmidt	C81, OF1	B	28	84	253	21	53	8	2	1	28	7		7	.209	.269
Oscar Stanage	C77	R	26	77	252	17	66	8	6	0	21	11		2	.262	.341
Charles O'Leary	3B54, 2B15, SS4, OF2	R	27	76	261	29	53	10	0	0	13	6		9	.203	.241
Davy Jones	OF57	L	29	69	204	44	57	2	2	0	10	28		12	.279	.309
2 Jim Delahanty	2B46	R	30	46	150	29	38	10	1	0	20	17		9	.253	.333
2 Tom Jones	1B44	R	32	44	153	13	43	9	0	0	18	5		9	.281	.340
1 Red Killefer	2B17, OF1	R	25	23	61	6	17	2	2	1	4	3		2	.279	.426
Heinie Beckendorf	C15	R	25	15	27	1	7	1	0	0	1	2		0	.259	.296
Joe Casey	C3	R	21	3	5	1	0	0	0	0	0	1		0	.000	.000
Del Gainer	1B2	R	22	2	5	0	1	0	0	0	0	0		0	.200	.200
Hughie Jennings	1B2	R	40	2	4	1	2	0	0	0	2	0		0	.500	.500
PHILADELPHIA 2nd 95-58 .621 3.5		CONNIE MACK														
TOTALS			28	153	4905	600	1259	186	**87**	**22**	498	403		205	.257	**343**
Harry Davis	1B149	R	35	149	530	73	142	22	11	4	75	51		20	.268	.374
Eddie Collins	2B152, SS1	L	22	153	572	104	198	30	10	3	56	62		67	.346	.449
Jack Barry	SS124	R	22	124	409	56	88	11	2	1	23	44		17	.215	.259
Frank Baker	3B146	L	23	148	541	73	165	27	**19**	4	85	26		20	.305	.447
Danny Murphy	OF149	R	32	149	541	61	152	28	14	5	69	35		19	.281	.412
Rube Oldring	OF89, 1B1	R	25	90	326	39	75	13	7	2	28	20		17	.230	.331
2 Bob Ganley	OF77	L	34	80	274	32	54	4	2	0	9	28		16	.197	.226
Ira Thomas	C84	R	28	84	256	22	57	9	3	0	31	18		4	.223	.281
Topsy Hartsel	OF74	L	35	83	267	30	72	4	4	1	18	48		3	.270	.326
Heinie Heitmuller	OF60	L	26	64	210	36	60	9	8	0	15	18		7	.286	.405
Paddy Livingston	C64	R	29	64	175	15	41	6	4	0	15	15		4	.234	.314
Scotty Barr	OF15, 1B7	R	22	22	51	5	4	1	0	0	1	11		2	.078	.098
Jack Lapp	C19	L	24	21	56	8	19	3	1	0	10	3		1	.339	.429
Simon Nicholls	SS14, 3B5, 1B1	L	26	21	71	10	15	2	1	0	3	3		0	.211	.268
Stuffy McInnis	SS14	R	18	19	46	4	11	0	0	1	4	2		0	.239	.304
Amos Strunk	OF9	L	20	11	35	1	4	0	0	0	2	1		2	.114	.114
Morrie Rath	SS4, 3B2	L	22	7	26	4	7	1	0	0	3	2		1	.269	.308
Joe Jackson	OF4	L	19	5	17	3	5	0	0	0	3	1		0	.294	.294
Ed Larkin	C2	R	24	2	6	0	1	0	0	0	1	1		0	.167	.167
Harry Curry	2B1	R	16	1	4	1	1	0	0	0	0	0		0	.250	.250
Mike Powers(DD)	C1	R	38	1	4	1	1	0	0	0	0	0		0	.250	.250
BOSTON 3rd 88-63 .583 9.5		FRED LAKE														
TOTALS			26	152	4964	590	1306	151	69	20	474	348		215	.263	.333
Jake Stahl	1B126	R	29	127	435	62	128	19	12	6	60	43		16	.294	.434
Amby McConnell	2B121	L	26	121	453	59	108	7	8	0	36	34		26	.238	.289
Heinie Wagner	SS123, 2B1	R	28	124	430	51	110	16	7	1	49	35		18	.256	.333
Harry Lord	3B134	L	27	136	534	85	166	12	7	0	31	20		36	.311	.360
1 Doc Gessler	OF111, 1B1	L	28	111	386	56	115	24	1	0	46	31		16	.298	.365
Tris Speaker	OF142	L	21	143	544	73	168	26	13	7	77	38		35	.309	.443
Harry Niles	OF117, 3B13, SS9, 2B5	R	28	145	546	64	134	12	5	1	38	39		27	.245	.291
Bill Carrigan	C77, 1B8	R	25	94	280	27	83	13	2	1	36	17		2	.296	.368
Harry Hooper	OF74	L	21	81	255	29	72	3	4	0	12	16		15	.282	.325
Pat Donahue	C58	R	24	64	176	14	42	4	1	2	25	17		2	.239	.307
Harry Wolter	1B17, P10, OF9	L	24	54	119	14	29	2	4	2	10	9		2	.244	.378
Charlie French	2B28, SS23	L	25	51	167	13	42	3	1	0	13	15		8	.251	.281
Tubby Spencer	C26	R	25	28	74	6	12	1	0	0	9	6		2	.162	.176
Larry Gardner	3B8, SS5	L	23	19	37	8	11	1	2	0	5	4		1	.297	.432
Jack Thoney(NJ)	OF10	R	29	13	40	1	5	1	0	0	3	2		2	.125	.150
Tom Madden	C7	R	26	10	17	0	4	0	0	0	1	0		0	.235	.235
Babe Danzig	1B3	R	22	6	13	0	2	0	0	0	0	2		0	.154	.154
Paul Howard	OF6	R	25	6	15	2	3	1	0	0	2	3		0	.200	.267
Steve Yerkes		R	21	2	2	0	1	0	0	0	0	0		0	.500	.500

NAME	T	AGE	W	L	PCT	SV	G	GS	CG	IP	H	BB	SO	ShO	ERA
		27	**98**	54	**.645**	14	158	158	**117**	1420	1254	359	528	16	2.26
George Mullin	R	28	**29**	9	**.763**	1	40	35	29	304	258	78	124	3	2.22
Ed Willett	R	25	22	9	.710	1	41	34	25	293	239	76	89	3	2.33
Ed Summers	R	24	19	9	.679	1	35	32	24	282	243	52	107	3	2.23
Ed Killian	L	32	11	9	.550	1	25	19	14	173	150	49	54	3	1.72
Wild Bill Donovan	R	32	8	7	.533	2	21	17	13	140	121	60	76	4	2.31
Ralph Works	R	21	3	1	.750	3	16	4	4	64	62	17	31	0	1.97
Kid Speer	L	23	3	3	.500	2	12	8	4	76	88	13	12	0	2.84
George Suggs	R	26	2	3	.400	1	9	4	2	44	34	10	18	0	2.05
Elijah Jones	R	27	1	1	.500	0	2	2	0	10	10	0	2	0	2.70
Bill Lelivelt	R	24	0	2	.000	1	4	2	1	20	27	2	4	0	4.50
Ed Lafitte	R	23	0	1	.000	1	3	1	1	14	22	2	11	0	3.86
		27	95	58	.621	5	153	153	111	1388	1069	386	**728**	**27**	**1.92**
Eddie Plank	L	33	19	10	.655	0	34	33	24	275	215	62	132	3	1.70
Chief Bender	R	26	18	8	.692	1	34	29	24	250	196	45	161	5	1.66
Harry Krause	L	21	18	8	.692	1	32	21	16	213	151	49	139	7	**1.39**
2 Cy Morgan	R	30	16	11	.593	0	28	26	21	229	152	71	81	5	1.65
Jack Coombs	R	26	12	11	.522	1	31	25	19	206	156	73	97	6	2.32
Jimmy Dygert	R	24	8	5	.615	1	32	12	6	137	117	50	79	1	2.43
Rube Vickers	R	31	3	2	.600	1	18	3	1	56	60	19	25	0	3.38
John Kull	L	27	1	0	1.000	0	1	0	0	3	3	5	4	0	3.00
1 Biff Schlitzer	R	24	0	3	.000	0	4	3	0	13	13	7	6	0	5.54
Tommy Atkins	L	21	0	0	.000	0	1	1	0	6	6	5	4	0	4.50
		25	88	63	.583	**19**	152	152	75	1358	1214	384	555	10	2.60
Frank Arellanes	R	27	16	12	.571	**8**	45	30	17	231	192	43	82	1	2.18
Eddie Cicotte	R	25	13	5	.722	1	27	15	10	160	117	56	82	1	1.97
Smokey Joe Wood(KJ)	R	19	11	7	.611	2	24	19	13	159	121	43	88	4	2.21
Charlie Chech	R	31	7	5	.583	0	17	13	6	107	107	27	40	1	2.94
Charlie Hall	R	23	6	4	.600	0	11	7	3	60	59	17	27	0	2.55
2 Ed Karger	L	26	5	3	.625	0	12	6	3	68	71	22	17	0	3.18
Jack Ryan	R	24	4	3	.571	0	13	8	2	61	65	20	24	0	3.23
2 Biff Schlitzer	R	24	4	5	.444	1	13	8	5	76	81	19	24	0	3.20
Ray Collins	L	22	4	3	.571	0	12	8	4	74	70	18	31	2	2.80
Elmer Steele	R	25	4	2	.667	3	16	8	2	76	75	15	32	0	2.84
2 Charlie Smith	R	29	3	0	1.000	0	3	3	2	25	23	2	11	0	2.16
Fred Burchell	L	29	3	4	.429	0	10	5	1	52	51	11	12	0	2.94
Harry Wolter	L	24	3	3	.500	1	10	6	0	53	53	28	20	0	3.91
Larry Pape	R	26	2	0	1.000	2	11	3	2	58	46	12	18	1	2.01
1 Cy Morgan	R	30	2	6	.250	1	12	10	5	65	52	31	30	0	2.35
Bill Mathews	R	31	1	0	1.000	0	5	1	0	17	16	10	6	0	3.18
2 Jack Chesbro	R	35	0	1	.000	0	1	1	0	6	7	4	3	0	4.50
Chet Nourse	R	21	0	0	.000	0	3	0	0	5	5	5	3	0	7.20
Fred Anderson	R	23	0	0	.000	0	1	1	0	8	3	1	5	0	1.13

CHICAGO 4th 78-74 .513 20 — BILLY SULLIVAN

NAME	G by POS	B	AGE	G	AB	R	H	2B	3B	HR	RBI	BB	SO	SB	BA	SA
TOTALS			30	159	5017	494	1110	145	56	4	393	441		211	.221	.275
Frank Isbell	1B101, OF9, 2B5	L	33	120	433	33	97	17	6	0	33	23		23	.224	.291
Jake Atz	2B118, OF3, SS1	R	30	119	381	39	90	18	3	0	22	38		14	.236	.299
Freddy Parent	SS98, OF37, 2B1	R	33	136	472	61	123	10	5	0	30	46		32	.261	.303
Lee Tannehill	3B91, SS64	R	28	155	531	39	118	21	5	0	47	31		12	.222	.281
Eddie Hahn (BC)	OF76	L	33	76	287	30	52	6	0	1	16	31		9	.181	.213
Dave Altizer	OF62, 1B45	L	32	116	382	47	89	6	7	1	20	39		27	.233	.293
Patsy Dougherty	OF138	L	32	139	491	71	140	23	13	1	55	51		36	.285	.391
Billy Sullivan	C97	R	34	97	265	11	43	3	0	0	16	17		9	.162	.174
Billy Purtell	3B71, 2B32	R	23	103	361	34	93	9	3	0	40	19		14	.258	.299
Doc White	OF40, P24	L	30	72	192	24	45	1	5	0	7	33		7	.234	.292
Frank Owens	C57	R	23	64	174	12	35	4	1	0	17	8		3	.201	.236
Frank Smith	P51	R	29	53	127	11	22	6	3	0	20	10		0	.173	.268
Willis Cole	OF46	R	27	46	165	17	39	7	3	0	16	16		3	.236	.315
Freddie Payne (NJ)	C27, OF3	R	28	32	82	8	20	2	0	0	12	5		0	.244	.268
Bob Messenger	OF31	B	25	31	112	18	19	1	1	0	0	13		7	.170	.196
Mike Welday	OF20	L	29	29	74	3	14	0	0	0	5	4		2	.189	.189
George Davis	1B17, 2B2	B	38	28	68	5	9	1	0	0	2	10		4	.132	.147
1 Gavvy Cravath	OF18	R	28	19	50	7	9	0	0	1	8	19		3	.180	.240
Barney Reilly	2B11, OF1	R	25	12	25	3	5	0	0	0	3	3		2	.200	.200
Cuke Barrows	OF5	R	25	5	20	1	3	0	0	0	2	0		0	.150	.150

1 Jiggs Donahue 29 L 0-4, 2 Ham Patterson 31 R 0-3

NAME	T	AGE	W	L	PCT	SV	G	GS	CG	IP	H	BB	SO	ShO	ERA
		26	78	74	.513	6	159	159	112	1437	1190	341	671	26	2.04
Frank Smith	R	29	25	17	.595	1	51	41	37	365	278	70	177	7	1.80
Ed Walsh	R	28	15	11	.577	2	31	28	20	230	166	50	127	8	1.41
Jim Scott	R	20	12	12	.500	1	36	29	19	250	194	93	135	4	2.30
Doc White	L	30	11	9	.550	1	24	21	14	178	149	31	77	3	1.72
2 Bill Burns	L	29	7	13	.350	0	22	19	8	174	169	35	52	3	1.97
Fred Olmsted	R	27	3	2	.600	0	8	6	5	55	52	12	21	0	1.80
Rube Suter	L	21	2	3	.400	1	18	6	3	87	72	28	53	1	2.48
Lou Fiene	R	24	2	5	.286	0	13	6	4	72	75	18	24	0	4.13
Frank Owen	R	29	1	1	.500	0	3	2	1	16	19	3	3	0	4.50
1 Nick Altrock	L	32	0	1	.000	0	1	1	1	9	16	1	2	0	5.00

NEW YORK 5th 74-77 .490 23.5 — GEORGE STALLINGS

NAME	G by POS	B	AGE	G	AB	R	H	2B	3B	HR	RBI	BB	SO	SB	BA	SA
TOTALS			28	153	4981	591	1234	143	61	16	473	407		187	.248	.311
Hal Chase (IL)	1B118, SS1	R	26	118	474	60	134	17	3	4	63	20		25	.283	.357
Frank LaPorte	2B83	R	29	89	309	35	92	19	3	0	31	18		5	.298	.379
Jack Knight	SS78, 1B19, 2B18	R	23	116	360	46	85	8	5	0	40	37		15	.236	.286
Jimmy Austin	3B111, SS23, 2B1	B	29	136	437	37	101	11	5	1	39	32		30	.231	.286
Willie Keeler	OF95	L	37	99	360	44	95	7	5	1	32	24		10	.264	.319
Ray Demmitt	OF109	L	25	123	427	68	105	12	12	4	30	55		16	.246	.358
Clyde Engle	OF134	R	25	135	492	66	137	20	5	3	71	47		18	.278	.358
Red Kleinow	C77	R	29	78	206	24	47	11	4	0	15	25		7	.228	.320
Kid Elberfeld	SS61, 3B43	R	34	106	379	47	90	9	5	0	26	28		23	.237	.288
Birdie Cree	OF77, SS6, 2B4, 3B1	R	26	104	343	48	90	6	3	2	27	30		10	.262	.315
Charlie Hemphill	OF45	L	33	73	181	23	44	5	1	0	10	32		10	.243	.282
Ed Sweeney	C62, 1B3	R	20	67	176	19	47	3	0	0	21	16		3	.267	.284
Walter Blair	C42	R	25	42	110	5	23	2	2	0	11	7		2	.209	.264
Earl Gardner	2B22	R	24	22	85	12	28	4	0	0	15	3		4	.329	.376
George McConnell	1B11, P2	R	31	13	43	4	9	0	1	0	5	1		1	.209	.256
1 Joe Ward	2B7, 1B1	R	24	9	28	3	5	0	0	0	0	1		2	.179	.179
1 Neal Ball	2B8	R	28	8	29	5	6	1	1	0	3	3		2	.207	.310

Bobby Vaughn 24 R 2-14, Irish McIlveen 28 L 0-3, Eddie Tiemeyer 24 R 3-8, Johnny Wanner 23 1-8

NAME	T	AGE	W	L	PCT	SV	G	GS	CG	IP	H	BB	SO	ShO	ERA
		26	74	77	.490	14	153	153	94	1332	1223	422	597	16	2.68
Joe Lake	R	27	14	11	.560	2	31	26	17	215	180	59	117	3	1.88
Jack Warhop	R	24	13	15	.464	4	36	23	21	243	197	81	95	2	2.41
Lew Brockett	R	28	10	8	.556	1	26	18	10	152	148	59	70	3	2.37
Jack Quinn (IL)	R	25	9	5	.643	2	23	11	8	119	110	24	36	0	1.97
Slow Joe Doyle	R	27	8	6	.571	0	17	15	8	126	103	37	57	3	2.57
Tom Hughes	R	25	7	8	.467	3	24	16	9	119	109	37	69	2	2.65
Rube Manning	R	26	7	11	.389	2	26	21	11	173	167	48	71	2	3.17
Pete Wilson	L	23	5	6	.455	0	14	12	7	94	82	43	44	1	3.16
Al Orth	R	36	1	0	1.000	0	1	1	0	3	6	1	1	0	12.00
George McConnell	R	31	0	1	.000	0	2	1	0	4	3	3	4	0	2.25
1 Jack Chesbro	R	35	0	3	.000	0	9	4	2	50	70	13	17	0	6.30
Doc Newton	L	31	0	3	.000	0	4	4	1	22	27	11	11	0	2.86
Dick Carroll		24	0	0	.000	0	2	1	0	5	7	1	1	0	3.60
Russ Ford	R	26	0	0	.000	0	1	0	0	3	4	4	2	0	9.00
Butch Schmidt	L	22	0	0	.000	0	1	0	0	5	10	1	2	0	7.20

CLEVELAND 6th 71-82 .464 27.5 — NAP LAJOIE 57-57 .500, DEACON McGUIRE 14-25 .359

NAME	G by POS	B	AGE	G	AB	R	H	2B	3B	HR	RBI	BB	SO	SB	BA	SA
TOTALS			27	155	5044	519	1214	173	81	10	407	283		173	.241	.313
George Stovall	1B145	R	30	145	565	60	139	17	10	2	49	6		25	.246	.322
Nap Lajoie (WJ)	2B120, 1B8	R	33	128	469	56	152	33	7	1	47	35		13	.324	.431
2 Neal Ball	SS95	R	28	96	324	29	83	13	2	1	25	17		17	.256	.318
Bill Bradley	3B87, 2B3, 1B3	R	31	95	334	30	62	6	3	0	22	19		8	.186	.222
Wilbur Good	OF80	L	23	94	318	33	68	6	5	0	17	28		13	.214	.264
Joe Birmingham (EJ)	OF98	R	24	100	343	29	99	10	5	1	38	19		12	.289	.356
Bill Hinchman	OF131, SS6	R	26	139	457	57	118	20	13	2	53	41		22	.258	.372
Ted Easterly	C76	L	24	98	287	32	75	14	10	1	27	13		8	.261	.390
George Perring	3B66, SS11, 2B8	R	24	88	283	26	63	10	9	0	20	19		6	.223	.322
Bris Lord	OF69	R	25	69	249	26	67	7	3	1	25	8		10	.269	.333
Elmer Flick	OF61	L	33	66	235	28	60	10	2	0	15	22		9	.255	.315
Nig Clarke	C44	L	26	55	164	15	45	4	2	0	14	9		1	.274	.323
Terry Turner (JJ)	2B26, SS26	R	28	53	208	25	52	7	4	0	16	14		14	.250	.322
Harry Bemis	C36	L	35	42	123	4	23	2	3	0	13	0		2	.187	.252
Duke Reilley	OF18	R	24	20	62	10	13	0	0	0	0	4		5	.210	.210
Dolly Stark	SS19	R	24	19	60	4	12	0	0	0	1	6		4	.200	.200
Miles Netzel	3B6, OF2		23	10	37	2	7	1	0	0	3	3		1	.189	.216
Bob Higgins	C8	R	22	8	23	0	2	0	0	0	0	0		0	.087	.087

Tom Raftery 27 R 7-32, Josh Clarke 30 L 0-12, Walt Doan 22 L 1-9, Denny Sullivan (IL) 26 L 1-2

NAME	T	AGE	W	L	PCT	SV	G	GS	CG	IP	H	BB	SO	ShO	ERA
		31	71	82	.464	2	155	155	110	1366	1211	349	569	15	2.39
Cy Young	R	42	19	15	.559	0	35	34	30	295	267	59	109	3	2.26
Addie Joss	R	29	14	13	.519	0	33	28	24	243	198	31	67	4	1.70
Heinie Berger	R	27	13	14	.481	1	34	29	19	257	221	58	162	4	2.63
Cy Falkenberg	R	29	10	9	.526	0	24	18	13	165	135	50	82	2	2.40
Bob Rhoades	R	29	5	9	.357	0	20	15	9	133	124	50	46	2	2.91
Jerry Upp	L	25	2	1	.667	0	7	4	2	27	26	12	13	0	1.67
Cail Sitton	R	26	2	2	.500	0	14	5	3	50	50	16	16	0	2.88
Harry Otis	L	22	2	2	.500	0	5	3	0	26	26	18	6	0	1.38
Glenn Liebhardt	R	26	2	4	.333	0	12	4	1	52	54	16	15	0	2.94
Harry Ables	L	24	1	1	.500	0	5	3	3	30	26	10	24	0	2.10
Willie Mitchell	L	19	1	2	.333	0	3	3	3	23	18	10	8	0	1.57
Red Booles	L	28	0	1	.000	0	4	1	0	23	20	8	6	0	1.96
Walt Doane	R	22	0	1	.000	0	1	1	0	5	10	1	2	0	5.40
Fred Winchell		27	0	3	.000	1	4	3	0	14	16	2	7	0	6.43
Lucky Wright	R	29	0	5	.000	0	5	4	3	23	20	8	6	0	3.91

ST. LOUIS 7th 61-89 .407 36 — JIMMY McALEER

NAME	G by POS	B	AGE	G	AB	R	H	2B	3B	HR	RBI	BB	SO	SB	BA	SA
TOTALS			30	154	4964	443	1152	116	45	11	352	331		136	.232	.280
1 Tom Jones	1B95, 3B2	R	32	97	337	30	84	9	3	0	29	18		13	.249	.294
Jimmy Williams	2B109	R	32	110	374	32	73	3	6	0	22	29		6	.195	.235
Bobby Wallace	SS87, 3B29	R	35	116	403	36	96	12	2	1	35	38		7	.238	.285
Hobe Ferris	3B114, 2B34	R	31	148	556	36	120	18	5	3	58	12		11	.216	.282
Roy Hartzell	OF85, SS65, 2B1	L	27	152	595	64	161	12	5	0	32	29		14	.271	.308
Danny Hoffman	OF109	L	29	110	387	44	104	6	7	2	26	41		24	.269	.336
George Stone (NJ)	OF81	L	31	83	310	33	89	5	4	1	15	24		8	.287	.339
Lou Criger	C73	R	37	74	212	15	36	1	1	0	9	25		2	.170	.184
Art Griggs	1B49, OF40, 2B8, SS1	R	25	108	364	38	102	17	5	0	43	24		11	.280	.354
John McAleese	OF79, 3B2		30	85	267	33	57	7	0	0	12	32		18	.213	.240
Jim Stephens	C72	R	25	79	223	18	49	5	0	3	18	13		5	.220	.283
Bill Bailey	P32, OF3	L	20	38	77	1	22	1	1	0	7	3		1	.286	.325
Dode Criss	P11	L	24	35	48	2	14	6	1	0	7	0		0	.292	.458
Al Schweitzer	OF22	R	26	27	76	7	17	2	0	0	2	5		3	.224	.250
Walt Devoy	OF16, 1B3		24	19	69	7	17	3	1	0	8	3		4	.246	.319
Ned Crompton	OF17	L	20	17	63	7	10	2	1	0	2	7		1	.159	.222
1 Ham Patterson	1B6, OF6	R	31	17	49	2	10	1	0	0	5	0		1	.204	.224
Burt Shotton	OF17	L	24	17	61	5	16	0	1	0	0	5		3	.262	.295
Wib Smith	C13, 1B1	L	22	17	42	3	8	0	0	0	2	0		0	.190	.190
Bill Killefer	C11	R	21	11	29	0	4	0	0	0	1	0		2	.138	.138
2 Claude Rossman	OF2	L	28	2	8	0	1	0	0	0	0	0		0	.125	.125

NAME	T	AGE	W	L	PCT	SV	G	GS	CG	IP	H	BB	SO	ShO	ERA
		29	61	89	.407	5	154	154	105	1355	1287	383	620	21	2.88
Jack Powell	R	34	12	16	.429	3	34	27	18	239	221	42	82	4	2.11
Barney Pelty	R	28	11	10	.524	0	27	23	17	199	158	53	88	5	2.31
Rube Waddell	L	32	11	13	.458	1	31	28	16	220	204	57	141	5	2.37
Bill Bailey	L	20	9	12	.429	0	32	20	17	199	174	75	114	1	2.44
Bill Graham (BG)	L		8	14	.364	1	34	21	13	187	171	60	82	3	3.13
Bill Dinneen	R	33	6	7	.462	0	17	13	8	112	112	29	26	3	3.46
Harry Howell	R	32	1	1	.500	0	10	3	0	37	42	8	16	0	3.16
Jack Gilligan	R	23	1	2	.333	0	3	3	3	23	28	9	4	0	5.48
Chuck Rose	L	23	1	2	.333	0	3	3	3	25	32	7	6	0	5.40
Dode Criss	R	24	1	5	.167	0	11	6	3	55	53	32	43	0	3.44
Bill McCorry	R	21	0	2	.000	0	2	2	2	15	29	6	10	0	9.00
Phil Stremmel	R	29	0	2	.000	0	2	2	2	18	20	4	6	0	4.50
Ed Kusel		23	0	3	.000	0	3	3	3	24	43	1	2	0	7.13

WASHINGTON 8th 42-110 .276 56 — JOE CANTILLON

NAME	G by POS	B	AGE	G	AB	R	H	2B	3B	HR	RBI	BB	SO	SB	BA	SA
TOTALS			28	156	4982	382	1112	148	41	9	306	321		136	.223	.275
2 Jiggs Donahue	1B81	L	29	84	283	13	67	12	1	0	28	22		9	.237	.286
1 Jim Delahanty	2B85	R	30	90	302	18	67	13	5	1	21	23		4	.222	.308
George McBride	SS155	R	28	155	504	38	118	16	0	0	34	36		17	.234	.266
Wid Conroy	3B120, 2B13, OF5, SS1	R	32	139	488	44	119	13	4	1	20	37		24	.244	.293
Jack Lelivelt	OF91	L	23	91	318	25	93	8	6	0	24	19		8	.292	.355
Clyde Milan	OF120	L	23	130	400	36	80	12	4	1	15	31		10	.200	.258
2 George Browne	OF101	L	33	103	393	40	107	15	5	1	16	17		13	.272	.344
Gabby Street	C137	R	26	137	407	25	86	12	1	0	29	26		2	.211	.246
Bob Unglaub	1B57, OF43, 2B25, 3B4	R	27	130	480	43	127	14	9	3	41	22		15	.265	.350
Otis Clymer (LJ)	OF41	L	32	45	138	11	27	5	2	0	6	17		7	.196	.261
2 Red Killefer	OF24, 3B6, C3, 2B3, SS1	R	25	40	121	11	21	1	0	0	5	13		4	.174	.182
Cliff Blankenship	C17, OF4	R	29	39	60	4	15	0	0	0	9	0		2	.250	.250
2 Germany Schaefer	2B32, 3B1	R	32	37	128	13	31	5	1	1	4	6		2	.242	.320
Jack Slattery	1B11, C5	R	32	32	56	4	12	2	0	0	6	2		1	.214	.250
Warren Miller	OF15			26	51	5	11	0	0	0	1	4		0	.216	.216
Bill Yohe	3B19		29	21	72	6	15	2	0	0	4	3		2	.208	.236
Jerry Freeman	1B14, OF1	L	27	19	48	2	8	0	1	0	3	4		3	.167	.208
1 Bob Ganley	OF17	L	34	19	63	5	16	3	0	0	5	1		4	.254	.302
2 Doc Gessler	OF16, 1B1	L	28	17	54	10	13	2	1	0	8	12		4	.241	.315
Bob Kelly	3B10, 2B3, OF1	R	24	17	42	3	6	2	1	0	1	3		1	.143	.238
Jesse Tannehill	OF9, P3	B	34	16	36	2	6	1	0	0	1	5		0	.167	.194

Jack Hardy 32 R 4-24, Bill Shipke 26 R 2-16, Orth Collins 29 L 0-7, Mike Kahoe 34 R 1-8, 2 Gavvy Cravath 28 R 0-5, Tom Crooke 2-7, Frank Hemphill 31 R 0-3, 2 Jimmy Sebring 27 L 0-0

NAME	T	AGE	W	L	PCT	SV	G	GS	CG	IP	H	BB	SO	ShO	ERA
		27	42	110	.276	3	156	156	99	1375	1288	424	653	10	3.04
Walter Johnson	R	21	13	25	.342	1	40	36	27	297	247	84	164	4	2.21
Bob Groom	R	24	6	26	.188	1	44	31	17	261	218	105	131	1	2.86
Dolly Gray	L	30	5	19	.208	0	36	26	19	218	210	77	87	0	3.59
Long Tom Hughes	R	30	4	8	.333	1	22	13	7	120	113	33	77	2	2.70
Dixie Walker	R	22	3	1	.750	0	4	4	4	36	31	6	25	0	2.50
1 Charlie Smith	R	29	3	12	.200	0	23	15	7	146	140	37	72	1	3.27
Doc Reisling (DE)	R	34	2	4	.333	0	10	6	6	67	70	17	22	1	2.42
Roy Witherup	R	22	2	6	.250	0	12	8	5	68	79	20	26	0	4.24
1 Bill Burns	L	29	1	0	1.000	0	6	4	1	29	25	7	13	0	1.24
Jesse Tannehill	L	34	1	1	.500	0	3	2	2	21	19	5	8	1	3.43
Nick Altrock	L	32	1	3	.250	0	9	5	2	38	55	5	9	0	5.45
Frank Oberlin	R	33	1	3	.250	0	9	4	1	41	41	16	13	0	3.73
Bill Foreman			0	2	.000	0	2	2	1	11	8	7	2	0	4.91
Joe Ohl	L	21	0	0	.000	0	4	0	0	9	7	1	2	0	2.00
Joe Hovlik	R	24	0	0	.000	0	3	0	0	6	13	3	1	0	4.50
Burt Keeley	R	29	0	0	.000	0	2	0	0	7	12	1	0	0	11.57
Orth Collins	R	29	0	0	.000	0	1	0	0	1	0	0	1	0	0.00

PITTSBURGH 1st 110-42 .724 — FRED CLARKE

NAME	G by POS	B	AGE	G	AB	R	H	2B	3B	HR	RBI	BB	SO	SB	BA	SA
TOTALS			28	154	5129	701	1332	218	92	25	585	479		185	.260	.353
Bill Abstein	1B135	R	26	137	512	51	133	20	10	1	70	27		16	.260	.344
Dots Miller	2B150	R	22	151	560	71	156	31	13	3	87	39		14	.279	.396
Honus Wagner	SS136, OF1	R	35	137	495	92	168	39	10	5	100	66		35	.339	.489
1 Jap Barbeau	3B85	R	27	91	350	60	77	16	3	0	25	37		19	.220	.283
Owen Wilson	OF154	L	25	154	569	64	155	22	12	4	59	19		17	.272	.374
Tommy Leach	OF138, 3B13	R	31	151	587	126	153	29	8	6	43	66		27	.261	.368
Fred Clarke	OF152	L	36	152	550	97	158	16	11	3	68	80		31	.287	.373
George Gibson	C150	R	28	150	510	42	135	25	9	2	52	44		9	.265	.361
Ham Hyatt	OF6, 1B2	L	24	48	67	9	20	3	4	0	7	3		1	.299	.463
2 Bobby Byrne	3B46	R	24	46	168	31	43	6	2	0	7	32		8	.256	.315
1 Alan Storke	1B18, 3B14	R	24	37	118	12	30	5	2	0	12	7		1	.254	.331
Ed Abbaticchio	SS18, 2B4, OF1	R	32	36	87	13	20	0	0	1	16	19		2	.230	.264
1 Ward Miller	OF14	L	24	15	56	2	8	0	1	0	4	4		2	.143	.179
Mike Simon	C9	R	26	11	18	2	3	0	0	0	2	1		0	.167	.167
Paddy O'Connor	C3, 3B1	R	29	9	16	1	5	1	0	0	3	0		0	.313	.375
2 Kid Durbin		L	22	1	0	0	0	0	0	0	0	0		0	.000	.000

NAME	T	AGE	W	L	PCT	SV	G	GS	CG	IP	H	BB	SO	ShO	ERA
		30	110	42	.724	11	154	154	93	1402	1174	320	490	20	2.07
Howie Camnitz	R	27	25	6	.806	3	41	30	20	283	207	68	133	5	1.62
Vic Willis	R	33	22	11	.667	1	39	35	24	290	243	83	95	4	2.23
Lefty Leifield	L	25	19	8	.704	0	32	27	13	202	172	54	43	3	2.36
Nick Maddox	R	22	13	8	.619	0	31	27	17	203	173	39	56	4	2.22
Babe Adams	R	27	12	3	.800	2	25	12	7	130	88	23	65	3	1.11
Sam Leever	R	37	8	1	.889	2	19	4	2	70	74	14	23	0	2.83
Deacon Phillippe	R	37	8	3	.727	0	22	12	7	132	121	14	38	1	2.32
Sammy Frock	R	25	2	1	.667	1	8	4	3	36	44	4	11	0	2.50
Chick Brandom	R	22	1	0	1.000	2	13	2	0	41	33	10	21	0	1.10
Bill Powell	R	24	0	1	.000	0	3	1	0	7	7	6	2	0	3.86
Harry Camnitz	R	24	0	0	.000	0	1	0	0	4	6	1	1	0	4.50
Gene Moore	L	23	0	0	.000	0	1	0	0	2	4	3	2	0	18.00
Charlie Wacker	R		0	0	.000	0	1	0	0	2	2	1	0	0	0.00

CHICAGO 2nd 104-49 .680 6.5 — FRANK CHANCE

NAME	G by POS	B	AGE	G	AB	R	H	2B	3B	HR	RBI	BB	SO	SB	BA	SA
TOTALS			28	155	4999	632	1227	203	60	20	496	420		187	.245	.322
Frank Chance (BS)	1B92	R	31	93	324	53	88	16	4	0	46	30		29	.272	.346
Johnny Evers	2B126	L	27	127	463	88	122	19	6	1	24	73		28	.263	.337
Joe Tinker	SS143	R	28	143	516	56	132	26	11	4	57	17		23	.256	.372
Harry Steinfeldt	3B151	R	31	151	528	73	133	27	6	2	59	57		22	.252	.337
Wildfire Schulte	OF140	L	26	140	500	57	142	16	11	4	60	24		23	.264	.357
Solly Hofman	OF153	R	26	153	527	60	150	21	4	2	58	53		20	.285	.351
Jimmy Sheckard	OF148	L	30	148	525	81	134	29	5	1	43	72		15	.255	.335
Jimmy Archer	C80	R	26	80	261	31	60	9	2	1	30	12		5	.230	.291
Pat Moran	C74	R	33	77	246	18	54	11	1	1	23	16		2	.220	.285
Del Howard	1B57	L	31	69	203	25	40	4	2	1	24	18		6	.197	.251
Heinie Zimmerman	SS12	R	22	65	183	23	50	9	2	0	21	3		7	.273	.344
Joe Stanley	OF16	B	28	22	52	4	7	1	0	0	2	6		0	.135	.154
John Kane	OF8, SS3, 3B3, 2B2	R	25	20	45	6	4	1	0	0	5	2		1	.089	.111
Tom Needham	C7	R	30	13	28	3	4	0	0	0	0	0		0	.143	.143
1 George Browne	OF12	L	33	12	39	7	8	0	1	0	1	5		3	.205	.256
Fred Luderus	1B11	L	23	11	37	8	11	1	1	1	9	3		0	.297	.459
Bill Davison	OF2	R	22	2	7	2	1	0	0	0	0	1		1	.143	.143
Johnny Kling (HO) 34																

NAME	T	AGE	W	L	PCT	SV	G	GS	CG	IP	H	BB	SO	ShO	ERA
		28	104	49	.680	11	155	155	111	1399	1094	364	680	31	1.75
Three Finger Brown	R	32	27	9	.750	7	50	34	32	343	246	53	172	8	1.31
Orvie Overall	R	28	20	11	.645	3	38	32	23	285	204	80	205	9	1.42
Ed Reulbach	R	26	19	10	.655	0	35	32	23	263	194	82	105	6	1.78
Jack Pfiester	L	31	17	6	.739	0	29	25	13	197	179	49	73	5	2.42
Rube Kroh	L	22	9	4	.692	0	17	13	10	120	97	30	51	1	1.65
2 Irv Higginbotham	R	27	5	2	.714	1	19	6	4	78	64	20	32	0	2.19
Rip Hagerman (PJ)	R	21	4	4	.500	0	13	7	4	70	64	28	32	1	1.82
Ray Brown		20	1	0	1.000	0	1	1	1	9	5	4	2	0	2.00
King Cole	R	23	1	0	1.000	0	1	1	1	9	6	3	1	1	0.00
Rudy Schwenk		25	1	1	.500	0	3	2	0	4	16	3	3	0	13.50
Carl Lundgren	R	29	0	1	.000	0	2	1	0	4	6	4	0	0	4.50
Andy Coakley	R	26	0	1	.000	0	1	1	0	2	7	3	1	0	18.00
2 Pat Ragan	R	20	0	0	.000	0	2	0	0	4	4	1	2	0	2.25
Chick Fraser	R	38	0	0	.000	0	1	0	0	3	2	4	1	0	0.00

NEW YORK 3rd 92-61 .601 18.5 — JOHN McGRAW

NAME	G by POS	B	AGE	G	AB	R	H	2B	3B	HR	RBI	BB	SO	SB	BA	SA
TOTALS			28	157	5218	622	1327	173	68	26	510	530		234	.254	.328
Fred Tenney	1B98	L	37	101	375	43	88	8	2	3	30	52		8	.235	.291
Larry Doyle	2B144	L	22	147	570	86	172	27	11	6	49	45		31	.302	.419
Al Bridwell	SS145	L	25	145	476	59	140	11	5	0	55	67		32	.294	.338
Art Devlin	3B143	R	29	143	491	61	130	19	8	0	56	65		26	.265	.336
Red Murray	OF149	R	25	149	570	74	150	15	12	7	91	45		48	.263	.368
Bill O'Hara	OF115	L	25	115	360	48	85	9	3	1	30	41		31	.236	.286
Moose McCormick	OF110	L	28	110	413	68	120	21	8	3	27	49		4	.291	.402
Admiral Schlei	C89	R	31	92	279	25	68	12	0	0	30	40		4	.244	.287
Chief Meyers	C64	R	28	90	220	15	61	10	5	1	30	22		3	.277	.382
Cy Seymour (JJ)	OF74	L	36	80	280	37	87	12	5	1	30	25		14	.311	.400
Fred Merkle	1B70, 2B1	R	20	79	236	15	45	9	1	0	20	16		8	.191	.237
Buck Herzog	OF29, 2B4, 3B4, SS1	R	23	42	130	16	24	2	0	0	8	13		2	.185	.200
Tillie Shafer	3B16, 2B13, OF2	B	20	38	84	11	15	2	1	0	7	14		6	.179	.226
Art Fletcher	SS19, 2B5, 3B5	R	24	29	98	7	21	0	1	0	6	1		0	.214	.235
Fred Snodgrass	OF20, C2, 1B1	R	21	28	70	10	21	5	0	1	6	7		10	.300	.414
Josh Devore (IL)	OF12	L	21	22	28	6	4	1	0	0	1	2		3	.143	.179
Art Wilson	C19	R	23	19	42	4	10	2	1	0	5	4		0	.238	.333
Arlie Latham	2B2	R	49	4	2	1	0	0	0	0	0	0		1	.000	.000
Mike Donlin (VR) 31																

NAME	T	AGE	W	L	PCT	SV	G	GS	CG	IP	H	BB	SO	ShO	ERA
		25	92	61	.601	15	157	157	105	1441	1248	397	695	16	2.27
Christy Mathewson	R	30	25	6	.806	2	37	33	26	275	192	36	149	8	1.14
Hooks Wiltse	L	28	20	11	.645	3	37	30	22	269	228	51	119	4	2.01
Bugs Raymond	R	27	18	12	.600	0	39	31	18	270	239	87	121	2	2.47
Red Ames	R	26	15	10	.600	1	34	26	20	244	217	81	116	2	2.69
Doc Crandall	R	21	6	4	.600	6	30	7	4	122	117	33	55	0	2.88
Rube Marquard	L	19	5	13	.278	1	29	21	8	173	155	73	109	0	2.60
Louis Drucke	R	20	2	1	.667	0	3	3	2	24	20	13	8	0	2.25
Dutch Klawitter	R	21	1	1	.500	1	6	3	2	27	24	13	6	0	2.00
George Daly	R	21	0	3	.000	0	3	3	3	21	31	8	8	0	6.00
Bull Durham	R	28	0	0	.000	1	4	0	0	11	15	2	2	0	3.27
Red Waller		26	0	0	.000	0	1	0	0	1	3	0	1	0	0.00
Jake Weimer	L	35	0	0	.000	0	1	0	0	3	7	0	1	0	9.00

CINCINNATI 4th 77-76 .503 33.5 — CLARK GRIFFITH

NAME	G by POS	B	AGE	G	AB	R	H	2B	3B	HR	RBI	BB	SO	SB	BA	SA
TOTALS			26	157	5088	603	1273	159	72	22	507	478		280	.250	.323
Dick Hoblitzell	1B142	L	20	142	517	59	159	23	11	4	67	44		17	.308	.418
Dick Egan	2B116, SS10	R	25	127	480	59	132	14	3	2	53	37		39	.275	.329
Tom Downey	SS119, C1	R	25	119	416	39	96	9	6	1	32	32		16	.231	.288
Hans Lobert	3B122	R	27	122	425	50	90	13	5	4	52	48		30	.212	.294
Mike Mitchell	OF144, 1B1	R	29	145	523	83	162	17	17	4	86	57		37	.310	.430
Rebel Oakes	OF113	L	22	120	415	55	112	10	5	3	31	40		23	.270	.340
Bob Bescher	OF117	B	25	124	446	73	107	17	6	1	34	56		54	.240	.312
Larry McLean (BK)	C95	R	27	95	324	26	83	12	2	2	36	21		1	.256	.324
Dode Paskert	OF82, 1B6	R	28	104	322	49	81	7	4	0	33	34		23	.252	.298
Miller Huggins	2B31, 3B15	B	30	57	159	18	34	3	1	0	6	28		11	.214	.245
Frank Roth	C54	R	30	56	147	12	35	7	2	0	16	6		5	.238	.313
2 Ward Miller	OF26	L	24	43	113	17	35	3	1	0	4	6		9	.310	.354
1 Mike Mowrey	3B22, SS13	R	25	38	115	10	22	5	0	0	5	20		2	.191	.235
Tommy Clarke	C17	R	21	18	52	5	13	3	2	0	10	6		3	.250	.385
2 Chappie Charles	2B10, SS3	R	28	13	43	3	11	2	0	0	5	4		2	.256	.302
Roy Ellam	SS9	R	23	10	21	4	4	0	1	1	4	7		1	.190	.429
1 Chick Autry	1B9	L	24	9	33	3	6	2	0	0	4	2		1	.182	.242
1 Kid Durbin		L	22	6	5	1	1	0	0	0	0	1		0	.200	.200
Bill Moriarty	SS6	R	26	6	20	1	4	1	0	0	1	0		2	.200	.250
Emil Haberer	C4	R	31	5	16	1	3	1	0	0	2	0		0	.188	.250
Claire Patterson	OF2	L	21	4	8	0	1	0	0	0	1	0		0	.125	.125
Si Pauxtis	C4	R	23	4	8	2	1	0	0	0	0	0		0	.125	.125
Cozy Dolan	3B3	R	26	3	6	2	1	0	0	0	0	2		0	.167	.167
Doc Johnston	1B3	L	21	3	10	1	0	0	0	0	1	0		0	.000	.000
Swat McCabe	OF3	L	27	3	11	2	6	1	0	0	0	1		1	.545	.636
Mike Konnick	C2	R	20	2	5	0	2	1	0	0	1	0		0	.400	.600
Bunny Pearce	C2	R	24	2	2	0	0	0	0	0	0	0		0	.000	.000
Del Young	OF2	L	23	2	7	0	2	0	0	0	1	1		0	.286	.286
Ezra Midkiff	3B1	L	26	1	2	0	0	0	0	0	0	0		0	.000	.000

NAME	T	AGE	W	L	PCT	SV	G	GS	CG	IP	H	BB	SO	ShO	ERA
		27	77	76	.503	8	157	157	91	1407	1233	510	477	10	2.52
Art Fromme	R	25	19	13	.594	2	37	34	22	279	195	101	126	4	1.90
Harry Gaspar	R	26	18	11	.621	2	44	29	19	260	228	57	65	4	2.01
Jack Rowan	R	22	11	12	.478	0	38	23	14	226	185	104	81	0	2.79
Bob Ewing	R	36	11	12	.478	0	31	29	14	218	195	63	86	2	2.44
Bill Campbell	L	35	7	11	.389	2	30	15	7	148	162	39	37	0	2.68
Bob Spade (HO)	R	32	5	5	.500	0	14	13	8	98	91	39	31	0	2.85
Jean Dubuc	R	20	3	5	.375	1	19	5	2	71	72	46	19	0	3.68
Tom Cantwell	R	20	1	0	1.000	0	6	1	1	22	16	7	7	0	1.64
Roy Castleton	L	23	1	1	.500	0	4	1	1	14	14	6	5	0	1.93
1 Ed Karger	L	26	1	3	.250	0	9	5	1	34	26	30	8	0	4.50
1 Pat Ragan	R	20	0	1	.000	0	2	0	0	8	7	4	2	0	3.38
Jack Bushelman	R	23	0	1	.000	0	1	1	1	7	7	4	3	0	2.57
Clark Griffith	R	39	0	1	.000	0	1	1	1	6	11	2	3	0	6.00
Chet Carmichael	R	21	0	0	.000	0	2	0	0	7	9	3	2	0	0.00
2 Bill Chappelle	R	25	0	0	.000	1	1	0	0	4	5	2	0	0	2.25
Ralph Savidge	R	30	0	0	.000	0	1	0	0	4	10	3	2	0	22.50

PHILADELPHIA 5th 74-79 .484 36.5 — BILLY MURRAY

NAME	G by POS	B	AGE	G	AB	R	H	2B	3B	HR	RBI	BB	SO	SB	BA	SA
TOTALS			28	154	5036	515	1228	185	53	12	417	370		185	.244	.309
Kitty Bransfield	1B138	R	34	140	527	47	154	27	6	1	59	18		17	.292	.372
Otto Knabe	2B110, OF1	R	25	114	402	40	94	13	3	0	34	35		9	.234	.281
Mickey Doolan	SS147	R	29	147	493	39	108	12	10	1	35	37		10	.219	.290
Eddie Grant	3B154	L	26	154	631	75	170	18	4	1	37	35		28	.269	.315
John Titus	OF149	L	33	151	540	69	146	22	6	3	46	66		23	.270	.350
2 Johnny Bates	OF73	L	27	77	266	43	78	11	1	1	15	28		22	.293	.353
Sherry Magee	OF143	R	24	143	522	60	141	33	14	2	66	44		38	.270	.398
Red Dooin	C140	R	30	141	468	42	105	14	1	2	38	21		14	.224	.271
2 Joe Ward	2B48, SS8, 1B5, OF2	R	24	74	184	21	49	8	2	0	23	9		7	.266	.332
Ossie Osborn	OF54	L	25	58	189	14	35	4	1	0	19	12		6	.185	.217
Pep Deininger	OF45, 2B1	L	31	55	169	22	44	9	0	0	16	11		5	.260	.314
1 Dave Shean	2B14, 1B11, OF3, SS1	R	31	36	112	14	26	2	2	0	4	14		3	.232	.286
Marty Martel	C12	R	26	24	41	1	11	3	1	0	7	4		0	.268	.390
Fred Jacklitsch	C11, 2B1	R	33	20	32	6	10	1	1	0	1	10		1	.313	.406
1 Wally Clement		L	27	3	3	0	0	0	0	0	0	0		0	.000	.000
2 Charlie Starr			30	3	3	0	0	0	0	0	0	0		0	.000	.000
Ben Froelich	C1	R	21	1	1	0	0	0	0	0	0	0		0	.000	.000
Ed McDonough	C1		22	1	1	0	0	0	0	0	0	0		0	.000	.000

NAME	T	AGE	W	L	PCT	SV	G	GS	CG	IP	H	BB	SO	ShO	ERA
		27	74	79	.484	6	154	154	89	1391	1190	472	612	17	2.44
Earl Moore	R	29	18	12	.600	0	38	34	24	300	238	108	173	4	2.10
Lew Moren	R	25	16	15	.516	1	40	31	19	258	226	93	110	2	2.65
George McQuillan (IL)	R	24	13	16	.448	2	41	28	16	248	202	54	96	4	2.14
Frank Corridon	R	28	11	7	.611	0	27	19	11	171	147	61	69	3	2.11
Harry Coveleski	L	23	6	10	.375	1	24	17	8	122	109	49	56	2	2.73
Tully Sparks	R	32	6	11	.353	0	24	16	6	122	126	32	40	1	2.95
Bill Foxen	L	25	3	7	.300	0	18	7	5	83	65	32	37	1	3.36
1 Lew Richie	R	25	1	1	.500	1	11	1	0	45	40	18	11	0	2.00
1 Buster Brown	R	27	0	0	.000	0	7	1	0	25	22	16	10	0	3.24
Frank Scanlan	L	19	0	0	.000	1	6	0	0	11	8	5	5	0	1.64
Ben Van Dyke	L	21	0	0	.000	0	2	0	0	7	7	4	5	0	3.68

BROOKLYN 6th 55-98 .359 55.5 — **HARRY LUMLEY**

NAME	G by POS	B	AGE	G	AB	R	H	2B	3B	HR	RBI	BB	SO	SB	BA	SA
TOTALS			27	155	5056	442	1157	176	59	16	370	330		141	.229	.296
Tim Jordan	1B95	L	30	103	330	47	90	20	3	3	36	59		13	.273	.379
Whitey Alperman	2B108	R	29	111	420	35	104	19	12	1	41	2		7	.248	.357
Tommy McMillian	SS105, 2B2, 3B1	R	21	108	373	18	79	15	1	0	24	20		11	.212	.257
Ed Lennox	3B121	R	23	126	435	33	114	18	9	2	44	47		11	.262	.359
Harry Lumley (SJ)	OF52	L	28	55	172	13	43	8	3	0	14	16		1	.250	.331
Al Burch	OF151, 1B1	L	25	152	601	80	163	20	6	1	30	51		38	.271	.329
2 Wally Clement	OF88	L	27	92	340	35	87	8	4	0	17	18		11	.256	.303
Bill Bergen	C112	R	36	112	346	16	48	1	1	1	15	10		4	.139	.156
John Hummel	1B54, 2B38, SS36, OF5	R	26	146	542	54	152	15	9	4	52	22		16	.280	.363
P. McElveen	3B37, OF13, SS10, 1B5, 2B5	R	25	81	258	22	51	8	1	3	25	14		6	.198	.271
Joe Kustus	OF50	R		53	173	12	25	5	0	1	11	11		9	.145	.191
Doc Marshall	C49, OF1	R	34	50	149	7	30	7	1	0	10	6		3	.201	.262
George Hunter	OF23, P16	B	22	44	123	8	28	7	0	0	8	9		1	.228	.285
Zack Wheat	OF26	L	23	26	102	15	31	7	3	0	4	6		1	.304	.431
1 Jimmy Sebring	OF25	L	27	25	81	11	8	1	1	0	5	11		3	.099	.136
Red Downey	OF19	L	20	19	78	7	20	1	0	0	8	2		4	.256	.269
Joe Dunn	C7	R	24	10	25	1	4	1	0	0	2	0		0	.160	.200
Tom Catterson	OF6	L	24	9	18	0	4	0	0	0	1	3		0	.222	.222
Lee Meyer	SS7			7	23	1	3	0	0	0	0	2		0	.130	.130
Hy Myers	OF6	R	20	6	22	1	5	1	0	0	6	2		1	.227	.273
Harry Redmond	2B5		21	6	19	3	0	0	0	0	1	0		0	.000	.000

NAME	T	AGE	W	L	PCT	SV	G	GS	CG	IP	H	BB	SO	ShO	ERA
		29	55	98	.359	3	155	155	126	1384	1277	528	594	17	3.10
George Bell	R	34	16	15	.516	1	33	30	29	256	236	73	95	6	2.71
Nap Rucker	L	24	13	19	.406	1	38	33	28	309	245	101	201	6	2.24
Doc Scanlan	R	28	8	7	.533	0	19	17	12	141	125	65	72	2	2.94
Harry McIntire	R	31	7	17	.292	1	32	26	20	228	200	91	84	2	3.63
George Hunter	L	22	4	10	.286	0	16	13	10	113	104	38	43	0	2.47
Kaiser Wilhelm	R	35	3	13	.188	0	22	17	14	163	176	59	45	1	3.26
Eddie Dent	R	21	2	4	.333	0	6	5	4	42	47	15	17	0	4.29
Elmer Knetzer	R	23	1	3	.250	0	5	4	3	36	33	22	7	0	3.00
Jim Pastorius	L	27	1	9	.100	0	12	9	5	80	91	58	23	0	5.74
Sam Fletcher	R		0	1	.000	0	1	1	1	9	13	2	5	0	8.00
Pembroke Finlayson	R	20	0	0	.000	0	1	0	0	7	7	4	2	0	5.14

ST. LOUIS 7th 54-98 .355 56 — **ROGER BRESNAHAN**

NAME	G by POS	B	AGE	G	AB	R	H	2B	3B	HR	RBI	BB	SO	SB	BA	SA
TOTALS			27	154	5108	583	1242	148	56	15	479	568		161	.243	.303
Ed Konetchy	1B152	R	23	152	576	88	165	23	14	4	80	65		25	.286	.396
1 Chappie Charles	2B71, SS28, 3B2	R	28	99	339	33	80	7	3	0	29	31		7	.236	.274
Rudy Hulswitt	SS65, 2B12	R	32	82	289	21	81	8	3	0	29	19		7	.280	.329
1 Bobby Byrne	3B105	R	24	105	421	61	90	13	6	1	33	46		21	.214	.280
Steve Evans	OF141, 1B2	L	24	143	498	67	129	17	6	2	56	66		14	.259	.329
Al Shaw	OF92	L	28	114	331	45	82	12	7	2	34	55		15	.248	.344
Rube Ellis	OF145	L	23	149	575	76	154	10	9	3	46	54		16	.268	.332
Eddie Phelps	C82	R	30	100	306	43	76	13	1	0	22	39		7	.248	.297
Joe Delahanty	OF63, 2B48	L	33	123	411	28	88	16	4	2	54	42		10	.214	.287
Roger Bresnahan	C59, 2B9, 3B1	R	30	72	234	27	57	4	1	0	23	46		11	.244	.269
2 Alan Storke	SS44, 2B4, 1B1	R	24	48	174	11	49	5	0	0	10	12		5	.282	.310
2 Jap Barbeau	3B46	R	27	47	175	23	44	3	0	0	5	28		14	.251	.269
Jack Bliss	C32	R	27	35	113	12	25	2	1	1	8	12		2	.221	.283
Howard Murphy	OF19	L	27	25	60	3	12	0	0	0	3	4		1	.200	.200
Champ Osteen	SS16	L	32	16	45	6	9	1	0	0	7	7		1	.200	.222
Billy Gilbert	2B12	R	33	12	29	4	5	0	0	0	1	4		1	.172	.172
2 Mike Mowrey	2B7, 3B2	R	25	12	29	3	7	1	0	0	4	4		1	.241	.276

Bob James 22 L 6-21, Tom Reilly 24 R 2-7, Charlie Enwright 21 L 1-7, Coonie Blank 0-2

NAME	T	AGE	W	L	PCT	SV	G	GS	CG	IP	H	BB	SO	ShO	ERA
		22	54	98	.355	4	154	154	84	1380	1368	483	435	4	3.41
Fred Beebe	R	28	15	21	.417	1	44	34	18	288	256	104	105	1	2.81
Johnny Lush	L	23	11	18	.379	0	34	28	21	221	215	69	66	2	3.14
Slim Sallee	L	24	10	11	.476	0	32	27	12	219	223	59	55	1	2.42
Bob Harmon	R	21	6	11	.353	0	21	17	10	159	155	65	48	0	3.68
Festus Higgins	R	16	3	3	.500	0	16	5	5	66	68	17	15	0	4.50
Charlie Rhodes	R	24	3	5	.375	0	12	10	4	61	55	33	25	0	3.98
Les Backman	R	21	3	11	.214	0	21	14	8	128	146	39	35	0	4.15
1 Irv Higginbotham	R	27	1	0	1.000	0	3	1	1	11	5	2	2	0	1.64
1 Forrest More	R	25	1	5	.167	0	15	3	1	50	48	20	17	0	5.04
John Raleigh	L	19	1	10	.091	0	15	10	3	81	85	21	26	0	3.78
Steve Melter	R		0	1	.000	3	23	1	0	64	79	20	24	0	3.52
Grover Lowdermilk	R	24	0	2	.000	0	7	3	1	29	28	30	14	0	6.21
Harry Sullivan	L	21	0	0	.000	0	2	1	0	1	4	2	1	0	36.00
Joe Bernard			0	0	.000	0	1	0	0	1	1	2	2	0	0.00

BOSTON 8th 45-108 .294 65.5 — **FRANK BOWERMAN 23-55 .295 HARRY SMITH 22-53 .293**

NAME	G by POS	B	AGE	G	AB	R	H	2B	3B	HR	RBI	BB	SO	SB	BA	SA
TOTALS			28	155	5017	427	1121	124	43	15	338	400		135	.223	.274
Fred Stem	1B68	L	23	73	245	13	51	2	3	0	11	12		5	.208	.241
2 Dave Shean	2B72	R	31	75	267	32	66	11	4	1	29	17		14	.247	.330
Jack Coffey	SS73	R	22	73	257	21	48	4	4	0	20	11		2	.187	.233
Bill Sweeney	3B112, SS26	R	23	138	493	44	120	19	3	1	36	37		25	.243	.300
Beals Becker	OF152	L	22	152	562	60	138	15	6	6	24	47		21	.246	.326
Ginger Beaumont	OF111	L	32	123	407	35	107	11	4	0	60	35		12	.263	.310
Roy Thomas	OF71	L	35	83	281	36	74	9	1	0	11	47		5	.263	.302
Peaches Graham	C76, OF6, SS1, 3B1	R	32	92	267	27	64	6	3	0	17	24		7	.240	.285
Fred Beck	OF57, 1B33	L	22	96	334	20	66	4	6	3	27	17		5	.198	.272
Bill Dahlen	SS49, 2B6, 3B2	R	39	69	197	22	46	6	1	2	16	29		4	.234	.305
2 Chick Autry	1B61, OF4	L	24	65	199	16	39	4	0	0	13	21		5	.196	.216
1 Johnny Bates	OF60	L	27	63	236	27	68	15	3	1	23	20		15	.288	.390
1 Charlie Starr	2B54, SS6, 3B3		30	61	216	16	48	2	3	0	6	31		7	.222	.259
Harry Smith	C31	R	34	43	113	9	19	4	1	0	4	5		3	.168	.221
Gus Getz	3B36, 2B2, SS2	R	19	40	148	6	33	2	0	0	9	1		2	.223	.236
Frank Bowerman	C27	R	39	33	99	6	21	2	0	0	4	2		0	.212	.232
Claude Ritchey	2B25	B	35	30	87	4	15	1	0	0	3	8		1	.172	.184
Al Shaw	C13	R	34	17	41	1	4	0	0	0	0	5		0	.098	.098
Bill Rariden	C13	R	21	13	42	1	6	1	0	0	1	4		1	.143	.167
Hosea Siner	3B5, 2B1, SS1	R	24	10	23	1	3	0	0	0	1	2		0	.130	.130

Herbie Moran 25 L 7-31, Bill Dam 24 1-2, Ernie Diehl 30 R 2-4

NAME	T	AGE	W	L	PCT	SV	G	GS	CG	IP	H	BB	SO	ShO	ERA
		26	45	108	.294	6	155	155	98	1371	1329	543	414	12	3.20
Al Mattern	R	26	16	20	.444	3	47	32	24	316	322	108	98	2	2.85
2 Lew Richie	R	25	7	7	.500	2	22	13	9	132	118	44	42	2	2.32
Kirby White	R	25	6	13	.316	0	23	19	11	148	134	80	53	0	3.22
Cecil Ferguson	R	22	5	23	.179	0	36	30	19	227	235	83	87	3	3.72
Cliff Curtis	R	26	4	5	.444	0	10	9	8	83	53	30	22	2	1.41
2 Buster Brown	R	27	4	10	.286	0	18	17	8	123	108	56	32	2	3.15
1 Bill Chappelle	R	25	1	1	.500	0	5	3	2	29	31	11	8	0	1.86
Gus Dorner	R	32	1	2	.333	1	5	2	0	25	17	17	7	0	2.52
Vive Lindaman	R	31	1	6	.143	0	15	6	6	66	75	28	13	1	4.64
Chick Evans	R	19	0	3	.000	0	4	3	1	22	25	14	11	0	4.50
2 Forrest More	R	25	0	4	.000	0	10	4	3	49	47	20	10	0	4.41
Tom McCarthy	R	25	0	5	.000	0	8	7	3	46	47	28	11	0	3.52
Tom Tuckey	L		0	9	.000	0	17	10	4	91	104	22	16	0	4.25
Cush Cooney	R	22	0	0	.000	0	3	0	0	6	4	2	3	0	1.50
Jake Boultes	R	24	0	0	.000	0	1	0	0	8	9	0	1	0	6.75

WORLD SERIES – PITTSBURGH (NL) 4 DETROIT (AL) 3

LINE SCORES

TEAM	1	2	3	4	5	6	7	8	9	10	11	12	R	H	E
Game 1 October 8 at Pittsburgh															
DET (AL)	1	0	0	0	0	0	0	0	0				1	6	4
PIT (NL)	0	0	0	1	2	1	0	0	X				4	5	0
Mullin — Adams															
Game 2 October 9 at Pittsburgh															
DET	0	2	3	0	2	0	0	0	0				7	9	3
PIT	2	0	0	0	0	0	0	0	0				2	5	1
Donovan — Camnitz, Willis (3)															
Game 3 October 11 at Detroit															
PIT	5	1	0	0	0	0	0	0	2				8	10	3
DET	0	0	0	0	0	0	4	0	2				6	10	5
Maddox — Summers, Willett (1), Works (8)															
Game 4 October 12 at Detroit															
PIT	0	0	0	0	0	0	0	0	0				0	5	6
DET	0	2	0	3	0	0	0	0	X				5	8	0
Leifield, Phillippe (5) — Mullin															
Game 5 October 13 at Pittsburgh															
DET	1	0	0	0	0	2	0	1	0				4	6	1
PIT	1	1	1	0	0	0	4	1	X				8	10	2
Summers, Willett (8) — Adams															
Game 6 October 14 at Detroit															
PIT	3	0	0	0	0	0	0	0	1				4	7	3
DET	1	0	0	2	1	1	0	0	X				5	10	3
Willis, Camnitz (6), Phillippe (7) — Mullin															
Game 7 October 16 at Detroit															
PIT	0	2	0	2	0	3	0	1	0				8	7	0
DET	0	0	0	0	0	0	0	0	0				0	6	3
Adams — Donovan, Mullin (4)															

COMPOSITE BATTING

NAME	POS	G	AB	R	H	2B	3B	HR	RBI	BA
Pittsburgh (NL) Totals		7	223	34	50	13	1	2	25	.224
Miller	2B	7	28	2	7	1	0	0	4	.250
Abstein	1B	7	26	3	6	2	0	0	2	.231
Wilson	OF	7	26	2	4	1	0	0	1	.154
Leach	OF-3B	7	25	8	9	4	0	0	2	.360
Gibson	C	7	25	2	6	2	0	0	2	.240
Wagner	SS	7	24	4	8	2	1	0	6	.333
Byrne	3B	7	24	5	6	1	0	0	0	.250
Clarke	OF	7	19	7	4	0	0	2	7	.211
Adams	P	3	9	0	0	0	0	0	0	.000
Willis	P	2	4	0	0	0	0	0	0	.000
Hyatt	OF	2	4	1	0	0	0	0	1	.000
Maddox	P	1	4	0	0	0	0	0	0	.000
O'Connor	PH	1	1	0	0	0	0	0	0	.000
Abbaticchio	PH	1	1	0	0	0	0	0	0	.000
Camnitz	P	2	1	0	0	0	0	0	0	.000
Leifield	P	1	1	0	0	0	0	0	0	.000
Phillippe	P	2	1	0	0	0	0	0	0	.000
Detroit (AL) Totals		7	233	28	55	16	0	2	26	.236
D. Jones	OF	7	30	6	7	0	0	1	1	.233
Crawford	OF-1B	7	28	4	7	3	0	1	4	.250
Delahanty	2B	7	26	2	9	4	0	0	4	.346
Cobb	OF	7	26	3	6	3	0	0	5	.231
T. Jones	1B	7	24	3	6	1	0	0	2	.250
Bush	SS	7	23	5	6	1	0	0	3	.261
Moriarty	3B	7	22	4	6	1	0	0	1	.273
Schmidt	C	6	18	0	4	2	0	0	4	.222
Mullin	P	6	16	1	3	1	0	0	0	.188
Stanage	C	2	5	0	1	0	0	0	2	.200
Donovan	P	2	4	0	0	0	0	0	0	.000
McIntyre	OF	4	3	0	0	0	0	0	0	.000
Summers	P	2	3	0	0	0	0	0	0	.000
O'Leary	3B	1	3	0	0	0	0	0	0	.000
Willett	P	2	2	0	0	0	0	0	0	.000
Works	P	1	0	0	0	0	0	0	0	.000

COMPOSITE PITCHING

NAME	G	IP	H	BB	SO	W	L	SV	ERA
Pittsburgh (NL) Totals	7	61	55	20	22	4	3	0	2.80
Adams	3	27	18	6	11	3	0	0	1.33
Willis	2	11.1	10	8	3	0	1	0	3.97
Maddox	1	9	10	2	4	1	0	0	1.00
Phillippe	2	6	2	1	2	0	0	0	0.00
Leifield	1	4	7	1	0	0	1	0	11.25
Camnitz	2	3.2	8	2	2	0	1	0	9.82
Detroit (AL) Totals	7	61	50	20	34	3	4	0	3.10
Mullin	4	32	23	8	20	2	1	0	2.25
Donovan	2	12	7	8	7	1	1	0	3.00
Summers	2	7.1	13	4	4	0	2	0	8.60
Willett	2	7.2	3	0	1	0	0	0	0.00
Works	1	2	4	0	2	0	0	0	9.00

1910 The Day It All Became "Official"

U.S. President William H. Taft opened the 1910 baseball season by throwing out the first ball. His actions served to mark baseball as the "official" national pastime and advanced the state of the political art into the twentieth century. Those in attendance at the game, including Vice President James Sherman, hailed the unprecedented event. Washington's pitcher, Walter Johnson, responded to the turnout of the robust chief executive by turning in a one-hit performance and blanking the Philadelphia Athletics, 1-0. Taft's presence, although getting the season off on a respected high note, was not an omen of prosperity, either for the Senators who finished last, or for a season whose attendance would be cut by poor early season weather and pennant races which were virtually over by July 1.

The Philadelphia Athletics recovered from that opening day whitewash by playing winning ball all year. Three-time champion Detroit stayed in the running for a fourth crown until the Athletics pulled away from the field in June and July. Philadelphia's attack boasted of three .300 hitters in Eddie Collins, Danny Murphy, and Rube Oldring but, as usual, the pitching staff was the spearhead of the team. Jack Coombs won 31 games in developing into a star hurler and pitched 46 consecutive scoreless innings at one stage in the season. Chief Bender notched 23 victories, and Eddie Plank and Cy Morgan were also consistent winners for the American League's first 100-victory team. Detroit's offense remained strong, but the Tiger's pitching fell apart, prompting a fall into third place behind the surprising New York Yankees.

Ty Cobb took his fourth straight batting crown with a .385 mark, edging Nap Lajoie by .001. Lajoie paced the league in hits with 227, and Boston's Jake Stahl led all batters with 10 homers.

Pittsburgh's 1909 National League pennant victory turned out only to be an interlude in the reign of the Chicago Cubs as kingpins in the senior loop. Finishing 13 games ahead of the field, the Cubs easily won their fourth pennant in five years, never leaving first after May. As usual, the Cubs' infield was airtight with Tinker, Evers, and Chance on duty, and outfielders, Solly Hofman and Wildfire Schulte, supplying much of the drive in the attack. Three Finger Brown lodged his usual 25 victories, but the key mound development turned out to be King Cole, who became an unexpected 20-game winner in his first full season. The Giants came in second, running into hot and cold streaks all year; Christy Mathewson provided a rare element of consistency in winning 27 games. Pittsburgh's collapse could be traced to their pitching. Although Babe Adams registered 18 victories, Howie Camnitz fell off from 24 to 12 victories. Vic Willis, who won 23 games in 1909 for the Bucs, spent the season with St. Louis where he compiled a dismal 9-12 mark.

Connie Mack led his Athletics into the World Series against the Cubs with great confidence in his pitching staff, a confidence which was amply rewarded by five complete games in five contests. Jack Coombs hurled three complete game victories, while Chief Bender won one and lost one while pitching two complete games. Using only two pitchers, the Athletics used a full lineup to rack up a .316 team batting mark, with Eddie Collins and Frank Baker logging .400 averages. The Chicago batters were held to a collective .222, winning only a ten-inning fourth-game from Connie Mack's White Elephants.

During the season, both leagues introduced a new "jack-rabbit" ball. Although modestly boosting run and home run production, it was inevitable that the "livelier" ball would drastically alter baseball's playing style before the century was much older.

1910 AMERICAN LEAGUE

NAME	G by POS	B	AGE	G	AB	R	H	2B	3B	HR	RBI	BB	SO	SB	BA	SA
PHILADELPHIA 1st 102-48 .680		CONNIE MACK														
TOTALS			28	155	5167	672	**1376**	**194**	**106**	19	541	409		207	**.266**	**.356**
Harry Davis	1B139	R	36	139	492	61	122	19	4	1	41	53		17	.248	.309
Eddie Collins	2B153	L	23	153	583	81	188	16	15	3	81	49		**81**	.322	.417
Jack Barry	SS145	R	23	145	487	64	126	19	5	3	60	52		14	.259	.337
Frank Baker	3B146	L	24	146	561	83	159	25	15	2	74	34		21	.283	.392
Danny Murphy	OF151	R	33	151	560	70	168	28	18	4	64	31		18	.300	.436
Rube Oldring	OF134	R	26	134	546	79	168	27	14	4	57	23		17	.308	.430
Topsy Hartsel	OF83	L	36	90	285	45	63	10	3	0	22	58		11	.221	.277
Jack Lapp	C63	L	25	71	192	18	45	4	3	0	17	20		0	.234	.286
2 Bris Lord	OF71	R	26	72	288	55	80	16	12	1	20	23		6	.278	.427
Ira Thomas	C60	R	29	60	180	14	50	8	2	1	19	6		2	.278	.361
Eddie Plank	P38	L	34	38	86	6	11	2	0	0	8	2		0	.128	.151
Stuffy McInnis	SS17, 2B5, 3B4, OF1	R	19	38	73	10	22	2	4	0	12	7		3	.301	.438
Paddy Livingston	C37	R	30	37	120	11	25	4	3	0	9	6		2	.208	.292
Ben Houser(SJ)	1B26	L	26	34	69	9	13	3	2	0	7	7		0	.188	.290
Heinie Heitmuller	OF28	L	27	31	111	11	27	2	2	0	7	7		6	.243	.297
1 Morrie Rath	3B11, 2B3	L	23	18	26	3	4	0	0	0	1	5		0	.154	.154
Amos Strunk	OF14	L	21	16	48	9	16	0	1	0	2	3		4	.333	.375
24Pat Donahue	C14	R	26	15	37	2	6	0	0	0	4	3		1	.162	.162
Claude Derrick	SS1	R	24	1	1	0	0	0	0	0	0	0		0	.000	.000
Earle Mack	C1	L	20	1	4	0	2	0	1	0	0	0		0	.500	1.000
NEW YORK 2nd 88-63 .583 14.5		GEORGE STALLINGS 76-61 .555						HAL CHASE 9-2 .818								
TOTALS			27	156	5050	629	1252	163	75	20	492	**464**		**288**	.248	.322
Hal Chase	1B130	R	27	130	524	67	152	20	5	3	73	16		40	.290	.365
Frank LaPorte	2B79, OF24, 3B15	R	30	124	432	43	114	14	6	2	67	33		16	.264	.338
Jack Knight	SS79, 1B23, 2B7, 3B4, OF1	R	24	117	414	58	129	25	4	3	45	34		23	.312	.413
Jimmy Austin	3B133	B	30	133	432	46	94	11	4	2	36	47		22	.218	.275
Harry Wolter	OF130	L	25	135	479	42	128	15	9	4	42	66		39	.267	.361
Charlie Hamphill	OF94	L	34	102	351	45	84	9	4	0	21	55		19	.239	.288
Birdie Cree	OF134	R	27	134	467	58	134	19	16	4	73	40		28	.287	.422
Ed Sweeney	C78	R	21	78	215	25	43	4	4	0	13	17		12	.200	.256
Bert Daniels	OF85, 3B6, 1B4	R	27	95	356	68	90	13	8	1	17	41		41	.253	.343
Earl Gardner	2B70	R	25	86	271	36	66	4	2	1	24	21		9	.244	.284
Roxy Roach	SS58, OF9	R	25	70	220	27	47	9	2	0	20	29		15	.214	.273
Fred Mitchell	C68	R	32	68	196	16	45	7	2	0	18	9		6	.230	.286
Eddie Foster	SS22	R	23	30	83	5	11	2	0	0	1	8		2	.133	.157
Lou Criger(IL)	C27	R	38	27	69	3	13	2	0	0	4	10		0	.188	.217
Walter Blair	C6	R	26	6	22	2	5	0	1	0	2	0		0	.227	.318
Les Channell(BL)	OF6	L	24	6	19	3	6	0	0	0	3	2		2	.316	.316
1 Red Kleinow (SA)	C5	R	30	6	12	2	5	0	0	0	2	1		2	.417	.417
1 Clyde Engle	OF3	R	26	5	13	0	3	0	0	0	0	2		1	.231	.231
Joe Walsh	C1		22	1	3	0	0	0	0	0	2	0		0	.000	.000
Bunny Madden		L	26	1	1	0	0	0	0	0	0	0		0	.000	.000
Larry McClure	OF1	R	24	1	1	0	0	0	0	0	0	0		0	.000	.000
Lew Brockett (HO) 29																
Bill Hogg(DD)29																
DETROIT 3rd 86-68 .558 18		HUGHIE JENNINGS														
TOTALS			28	155	5048	**679**	1319	192	73	26	**548**	459		249	.261	.344
Tom Jones	1B135	R	33	135	432	32	110	13	4	0	45	35		22	.255	.303
Jim Delahanty	2B106	R	31	106	378	67	111	16	3	2	45	43		15	.294	.368
Donie Bush	SS141, 3B1	B	22	142	496	90	130	13	4	3	34	**78**		49	.262	.323
George Moriarty	3B134	R	25	136	490	53	123	24	3	2	60	33		33	.251	.324
Sam Crawford	OF153, 1B1	L	30	154	588	83	170	26	**19**	5	**120**	37		20	.289	.423
Ty Cobb	OF137	L	23	140	509	**106**	196	36	13	8	91	64		65	**.385**	**.554**
Davy Jones	OF101	L	30	113	377	77	100	6	6	0	24	51		25	.265	.313
Oscar Stanage	C84	R	27	88	275	24	57	7	4	2	25	20		1	.207	.284
Matty McIntyre	OF77	L	30	83	305	40	72	15	5	0	25	39		4	.236	.318
Boss Schmidt	C66	B	29	71	197	22	51	7	7	1	23	2		2	.259	.381
Charley O'Leary	2B38, SS16, 3B6	R	28	65	211	23	51	7	1	0	9	9		7	.242	.284
Hack Simmons	1B22, 3B7, OF2	R	25	42	110	12	25	3	1	0	9	10		1	.227	.273
Chick Lathers	3B13, 2B7, SS4	L	21	41	82	4	19	2	0	0	3	8		0	.232	.256
Joe Casey	C22	R	22	23	62	3	12	3	0	0	2	2		1	.194	.242
Jay Kirke	2B7, OF1	L	22	8	25	3	5	1	0	0	3	1		1	.200	.240
1 Heinie Beckendorf	C2	R	26	3	13	0	3	0	0	0	2	1		0	.231	.231

NAME	T	AGE	W	L	PCT	SV	G	GS	CG	IP	H	BB	SO	ShO	ERA
		27	**102**	48	**.680**	8	155	155	**123**	1422	1103	450	**789**	**24**	**1.78**
Jack Coombs	R	27	**31**	9	.775	2	**45**	38	35	353	248	115	224	**13**	1.30
Chief Bender	R	27	23	5	**.821**	1	30	28	25	250	182	47	155	3	1.58
Cy Morgan	R	31	18	12	.600	0	36	34	23	291	214	**117**	134	3	1.55
Eddie Plank	L	34	16	10	.615	2	38	32	22	250	218	55	123	1	2.02
Harry Krause	L	22	6	6	.500	0	16	11	9	112	99	42	60	2	2.89
Jimmy Dygert	R	25	4	4	.500	1	19	8	6	99	81	49	59	1	2.55
Tommy Atkins	L	22	3	2	.600	2	15	3	2	57	53	23	29	0	2.68
Lefty Russell	L	19	1	0	1.000	0	1	1	1	9	8	2	5	1	0.00
		25	88	63	.583	10	156	156	110	1411	1238	364	654	14	2.59
Russ Ford	R	27	26	6	.813	1	36	33	29	300	194	70	209	8	1.65
Jack Quinn	R	26	18	12	.600	0	35	31	20	237	214	58	82	0	2.43
Jack Warhop	R	25	14	14	.500	2	37	27	20	254	219	79	75	0	2.87
Hippo Vaughn	L	22	13	11	.542	2	30	25	18	222	190	58	107	5	1.83
Tom Hughes	R	26	7	9	.438	1	23	15	11	152	153	37	64	0	3.49
Ray Fisher	R	22	5	3	.625	1	17	7	3	92	95	18	42	0	2.93
Rube Manning	R	27	2	4	.333	0	16	9	4	75	80	25	25	0	3.72
John Frill	L	31	2	2	.500	1	10	5	3	48	55	5	27	1	4.50
Ray Caldwell	R	22	1	0	1.000	2	6	2	1	19	19	9	17	0	3.79
1 Slow Joe Doyle	R	28	0	2	.000	0	3	2	1	12	19	5	6	0	8.25
		27	86	68	.558	5	155	155	108	1375	1257	460	532	17	2.84
George Mullin	R	29	21	12	.636	0	38	32	27	289	260	102	98	5	2.87
Wild Bill Donovan	R	33	18	7	.720	0	26	23	20	209	184	61	107	3	2.41
Ed Willett	R	26	16	11	.593	0	37	25	18	224	175	74	65	4	2.37
Ed Summers	R	25	12	12	.500	1	30	25	18	220	211	60	82	1	2.53
Sailor Stroud	R	25	5	9	.357	1	28	15	7	130	123	41	63	3	3.26
Ed Killian	L	33	4	3	.571	0	11	9	5	74	75	27	20	1	3.04
Hub Pernoll	L	22	4	3	.571	0	11	5	4	55	54	14	25	0	2.94
Ralph Works	R	22	3	6	.333	1	18	10	5	86	73	39	36	0	3.56
Frank Browning	R	27	2	2	.500	2	11	6	2	42	51	10	16	0	3.00
Art Loudell	R	25	1	1	.500	0	5	2	1	21	23	14	12	0	3.43
Marv Peasley	L	20	0	1	.000	0	2	1	0	10	13	11	4	0	8.10
Bill Lelivelt	R	25	0	1	.000	0	1	1	1	9	6	3	2	0	1.00
Dave Skeels	R	17	0	0	.000	0	1	1	0	6	9	4	2	0	12.00

BOSTON 4th 81-72 .529 22.5 — PATSY DONOVAN

NAME	G by POS	B	AGE	G	AB	R	H	2B	3B	HR	RBI	BB	SO	SB	BA	SA
TOTALS			25	158	5205	637	1350	175	87	43	527	430		194	.259	.351
Jake Stahl	1B142	R	30	144	531	68	144	19	16	10	77	42		22	.271	.424
Larry Gardner	2B113	L	24	113	413	55	117	12	10	2	36	41		8	.283	.375
Heinie Wagner	SS140	R	29	142	491	61	134	26	7	1	52	44		26	.273	.360
Harry Lord	3B70, SS1	L	28	77	288	25	72	5	5	1	32	14		17	.250	.313
Harry Hooper	OF155	L	22	155	584	81	156	9	10	2	27	62		40	.267	.327
Tris Speaker	OF140	L	22	141	538	92	183	20	14	7	65	52		35	.340	.468
Duffy Lewis	OF149	R	21	151	541	64	153	29	7	8	68	32		10	.283	.407
Bill Carrigan	C110	R	26	114	342	36	85	11	1	3	53	23		10	.249	.313
2 Clyde Engle	3B51, 2B27, OF15, SS7	R	26	106	363	59	96	18	7	2	38	31		12	.264	.369
2 Red Kleinow (SA)	C49	R	30	50	147	9	22	1	0	1	8	20		3	.150	.177
2 Billy Purtell	3B41, SS8	R	24	49	168	15	35	1	2	1	15	18		2	.208	.256
Hugh Bradley	1B21, C3, OF1	R	25	32	83	8	14	6	2	0	7	5		2	.169	.289
1 Harry Niles	OF15	R	29	18	57	6	12	3	0	1	3	4		1	.211	.316
Tom Madden	C12	R	27	14	35	4	13	3	0	0	4	3		0	.371	.457
1 Amby McConnell	2B10	L	27	12	36	6	6	0	0	0	1	5		4	.167	.167
1 Charlie French	2B8	L	26	9	40	4	8	1	0	0	3	1		0	.200	.225

Dutch Lerchen 21 R 0-15, Hap Myers (IL) 22 R 2-6, Pat Donahue 26 R 0-4, Ed Hearn R 21 0-2, Ralph Pond 22 1-4, Doc Moskiman 30 R 1-9, Jack Thoney (JJ) 29

NAME	T	AGE	W	L	PCT	SV	G	GS	CG	IP	H	BB	SO	ShO	ERA
TOTALS		25	81	72	.529	9	158	158	100	1429	1236	414	670	11	2.46
Eddie Cicotte	R	26	15	11	.577	0	36	30	20	250	213	86	104	3	2.74
Ray Collins	L	23	13	11	.542	2	35	26	18	245	205	41	109	4	1.62
Charley Hall	R	24	11	9	.550	5	35	16	13	189	142	73	95	0	1.91
Charlie Smith	R	30	12	6	.667	0	24	18	11	156	141	35	53	0	2.30
Smokey Joe Wood	R	20	12	13	.480	0	35	17	14	199	155	56	145	3	1.68
Ed Karger	L	27	11	7	.611	1	27	25	16	183	162	53	81	1	3.20
Frank Arellanes	R	28	4	6	.400	0	28	13	2	100	106	24	33	0	2.88
Ben Hunt	L	22	2	4	.333	0	7	7	3	47	45	20	19	0	4.02
2 Frank Smith	R	30	1	2	.333	0	4	3	2	28	22	11	8	0	4.82
Frank Barberich	R	28	0	0	.000	0	2	0	0	5	7	2	0	0	7.20
Louis LeRoy	R	31	0	0	.000	0	1	0	0	4	7	2	3	0	11.25
Chris Mahoney	R	25	0	1	.000	1	2	1	0	11	16	5	6	0	3.27
Marty McHale (SA)	R	21	0	2	.000	0	2	2	1	14	15	6	14	0	4.50

CLEVELAND 5th 71-81 .467 32 — DEACON McGUIRE

NAME	G by POS	B	AGE	G	AB	R	H	2B	3B	HR	RBI	BB	SO	SB	BA	SA
TOTALS			29	161	5359	539	1310	185	63	9	460	366		189	.244	.308
George Stovall	1B132, 2B2	R	31	142	521	47	136	19	4	0	52	14		16	.261	.313
Nap Lajoie	2B149, 1B10, SS4	R	34	159	**591**	92	**227**	**51**	7	4	76	60		26	.384	.514
Terry Turner (JJ)	SS94, 3B46, 2B9	R	29	150	574	71	132	14	6	0	33	53		31	.230	.275
Bill Bradley	3B61	R	32	61	214	12	42	3	0	0	12	10		6	.196	.210
Jack Graney	OF114	L	24	116	454	62	107	13	9	1	31	37		18	.236	.311
Joe Birmingham	OF103, 3B1	R	25	104	364	41	84	11	2	0	35	23		18	.231	.272
13Art Kruger	OF62	R	29	62	223	19	38	6	3	0	14	20		12	.170	.224
Ted Easterly	C66, OF30	L	25	110	363	34	111	16	6	0	55	21		10	.306	.383
2 Harry Niles	OF56, SS7, 3B5	R	29	70	240	25	51	6	4	1	18	15		9	.213	.283
Harry Bemis (BG)	C46	L	36	61	167	11	36	5	1	1	16	5		3	.216	.275
1 Bris Lord	OF55	R	26	56	201	21	44	5	6	0	17	12		4	.219	.303
Neal Ball	SS27, 2B6, OF6, 3B3	R	29	53	119	12	25	3	1	0	12	9		4	.210	.252
George Perring	3B33, 1B4	R	25	39	122	14	27	6	3	0	8	3		3	.221	.320
Grover Land	C33	R	25	34	111	4	23	0	0	0	7	2		1	.207	.207
2 Morrie Rath	3B22, SS1	L	23	24	67	5	13	3	0	0	0	10		2	.194	.239
Elmer Flick	OF18	L	34	24	68	5	18	2	1	1	7	10		1	.265	.368
Nig Clarke (IL)	C17	L	27	21	58	4	9	2	0	0	2	8		0	.155	.190
Joe Jackson	OF20	L	20	20	75	15	29	2	5	1	11	8		4	.387	.587

Cotton Knaupp 20 R 14-59, Ed Hohnhorst 25 L 20-62, Art Thomason 21 L 9-57, Roger Peckinpaugh 19 R 9-45, Dave Callahan 21 L 8-44, Syd Smith 26 R 9-27
Jack Adams 19 B 3-13, Herman Bronkie 25 R 2-9, Simon Nicholls 27 L 0-0, 3 Pat Donahue 26 R 0-4, Deacon McGuire 44 R 1-3, Jim Rutherford 23 L 1-2

NAME	T	AGE	W	L	PCT	SV	G	GS	CG	IP	H	BB	SO	ShO	ERA
TOTALS		27	71	81	.467	**14**	161	161	92	**1462**	**1386**	487	614	13	2.89
Cy Falkenberg	R	30	14	13	.519	4	37	29	18	257	246	75	107	3	2.94
Willie Mitchell	L	20	12	8	.600	1	35	18	11	184	155	55	102	1	2.59
Specs Harkness	R	22	9	7	.563	3	26	16	6	136	132	55	60	1	3.04
Cy Young	R	43	7	10	.412	0	21	20	14	163	149	27	58	1	2.54
George Kahler	R	20	6	4	.600	0	12	12	8	95	80	46	38	2	1.61
Elmer Koestner	R	24	5	10	.333	4	27	13	8	145	145	63	44	1	3.04
1 Fred Linke	L		5	6	.455	1	22	13	6	123	115	49	52	1	3.29
Addie Joss (SA)	R	30	5	5	.500	0	13	12	9	107	96	18	49	1	2.27
Heinie Berger	R	28	4	4	.500	0	13	8	2	65	57	32	24	0	3.05
Harry Fanwell	R	23	2	9	.182	1	17	11	5	92	87	38	30	1	3.62
Fred Blanding	R	22	2	2	.500	0	6	5	4	45	43	12	25	1	2.80
Walt Doan	R	23	0	0	.000	0	6	0	0	18	31	8	7	0	5.50
Casey Kirsch	R	22	0	0	.000	0	2	0	0	3	5	1	5	0	6.00
Ben DeMott	R	21	0	3	.000	0	6	4	1	28	45	8	13	0	5.46

CHICAGO 6th 68-85 .444 35.5 — HUGH DUFFY

NAME	G by POS	B	AGE	G	AB	R	H	2B	3B	HR	RBI	BB	SO	SB	BA	SA
TOTALS			27	156	5028	456	1062	115	58	7	351	403		183	.211	.261
Chick Gandil	1B74, OF2	R	22	77	275	21	53	7	3	2	21	24		12	.193	.262
Rollie Zeider	2B87, SS45, 3B4	R	26	136	498	57	108	9	2	0	31	62		49	.217	.243
Lena Blackburne	SS74	R	23	75	242	16	42	3	1	0	10	19		4	.174	.194
1 Billy Purtell	3B102	R	24	102	368	21	86	5	3	1	36	21		5	.234	.272
Shano Collins	OF65, 1B27	R	24	97	315	29	62	10	8	1	24	25		10	.197	.289
Paul Meloan	OF65	L	21	65	222	23	54	6	6	0	23	17		4	.243	.324
Patsy Dougherty	OF121	L	33	127	443	45	110	8	6	1	43	41		22	.248	.300
Freddie Payne	C78, OF2	R	29	91	257	17	56	5	4	0	19	11		6	.218	.268
Freddy Parent (BG)	OF62, 2B11, SS4, 3B1	R	34	81	258	23	46	6	1	1	16	29		14	.178	.221
Lee Tannehill (JJ)	SS38, 1B23, 3B6	R	29	67	230	17	51	10	0	1	21	11		3	.222	.278
Doc White	P33, OF14	L	31	56	126	14	25	1	2	0	8	14		2	.198	.238
Bruno Block	C47	R	25	55	152	12	32	1	1	0	9	13		3	.211	.230
2 Charlie French	2B28, OF16	L	26	45	170	17	28	1	1	0	4	10		5	.165	.182
Billy Sullivan (JJ)	C45	R	35	45	142	10	26	4	1	0	6	7		0	.183	.225
2 Harry Lord	3B44	L	28	44	165	26	49	6	3	0	10	14		17	.297	.370
Charlie Mullen	1B37, OF2	R	21	41	123	15	24	2	1	0	13	4		4	.195	.228
2 Amby McConnell (IL)	2B32	L	27	32	119	13	33	2	3	0	5	7		4	.277	.345
2 George Browne	OF29	L	34	30	112	17	27	4	1	0	4	12		6	.241	.295
Dutch Zwilling	OF27	L	21	27	87	7	16	5	0	0	5	11		1	.184	.241
Felix Chouinard	OF23, 2B1	R	22	24	82	6	16	3	2	0	9	8		4	.195	.280
Willis Cole	OF22	R	28	22	80	6	14	2	1	0	2	4		0	.175	.225
Eddie Hahn	OF15	L	34	15	53	2	6	2	0	0	1	7		0	.113	.151
Red Kelly	OF14	R	25	14	45	6	7	0	1	0	1	7		0	.156	.200
Bob Messenger	OF9	B	26	9	26	7	6	0	1	0	4	4		3	.231	.308
Cuke Barrows	OF6	R	26	6	20	0	4	0	0	0	1	3		0	.200	.200
Red Bowser	OF1		24	1	2	0	0	0	0	0	0	0		0	.000	.000

NAME	T	AGE	W	L	PCT	SV	G	GS	CG	IP	H	BB	SO	ShO	ERA
TOTALS		28	68	85	.444	10	156	156	103	1430	1130	381	785	23	2.01
Ed Walsh	R	29	18	**20**	.474	**6**	**45**	36	33	370	242	61	258	7	**1.27**
Doc White	L	31	15	13	.536	1	33	29	20	246	219	50	111	2	2.57
Fred Olmsted	R	28	10	12	.455	1	32	20	14	184	174	50	68	4	1.95
Franke Lange	R	26	9	4	.692	0	23	15	6	131	93	54	98	1	1.66
Jim Scott	R	21	8	18	.308	2	41	23	14	230	182	86	135	2	2.43
1 Frank Smith	R	30	4	9	.308	0	19	15	9	129	91	40	50	3	2.03
Irv Young	L	32	4	8	.333	0	27	17	7	136	122	39	64	4	2.71
1 Bill Burns	L	30	0	0	.000	0	1	0	0	.1	0	1	0	0	0.00
Chief Chovneau	R	20	0	1	.000	0	1	1	0	5	7	0	1	0	3.60

WASHINGTON 7th 66-85 .437 36.5 — JIMMY McALEER

NAME	G by POS	B	AGE	G	AB	R	H	2B	3B	HR	RBI	BB	SO	SB	BA	SA
TOTALS			29	157	4983	498	1175	145	46	9	393	449		192	.236	.289
Bob Unglaub	1B124	R	28	124	431	29	101	9	4	0	44	21		21	.234	.274
Red Killefer	2B88, OF12	R	26	106	345	35	79	17	1	0	24	29		17	.229	.284
George McBride	SS154	R	29	154	514	54	118	19	4	1	55	61		11	.230	.288
Kid Elberfeld	3B113, 2B10, SS3	R	35	127	455	53	114	9	2	2	42	35		19	.251	.292
Doc Gessler	OF144	L	29	145	487	58	126	17	11	2	50	62		18	.259	.351
Clyde Milan	OF142	L	24	142	531	89	148	17	6	0	16	71		44	.279	.333
Jack Lelivelt	OF89, 1B7	L	24	110	347	40	92	10	3	0	33	40		20	.265	.311
Gabby Street	C86	R	27	89	257	13	52	6	0	1	16	23		1	.202	.237
Wid Conroy	3B48, OF46, 2B5	R	33	105	351	36	89	11	3	1	27	30		11	.254	.311
Germany Schaefer	2B35, OF26, 3B2	R	33	74	229	27	63	6	5	0	14	25		17	.275	.345
2 Heinie Beckendorf	C36	R	20	37	97	8	15	1	0	0	10	5		0	.155	.165
Eddie Ainsmith	C30	R	18	33	104	4	20	1	2	0	9	6		0	.192	.240
John Henry	C18, 1B10	R	20	28	87	2	13	1	1	0	5	2		2	.149	.184
Bill Cunningham	2B22	R	22	22	74	3	22	5	1	0	14	12		4	.297	.392
Doc Ralston	OF22	R	24	22	73	4	15	1	0	0	3	3		2	.205	.219
Jock Somerlott	1B16	R	27	16	63	6	14	0	0	0	2	3		2	.222	.222
Tom Crooke	1B5			8	21	1	4	1	0	0	1	1		0	.190	.238
1 George Browne	OF5	L	34	7	22	1	4	0	0	0	0	1		0	.182	.182
Jack Hardy	C4, OF1	R	33	7	8	1	2	0	0	0	0	0		0	.250	.250

NAME	T	AGE	W	L	PCT	SV	G	GS	CG	IP	H	BB	SO	ShO	ERA
TOTALS		27	66	85	.437	5	157	157	119	1376	1223	374	675	19	2.45
Walter Johnson	R	22	25	17	.595	2	**45**	**42**	**38**	**374**	**269**	76	**313**	8	1.35
Bob Groom	R	25	12	17	.414	0	34	30	22	258	255	77	98	3	2.75
Dixie Walker	R	23	11	11	.500	0	29	26	16	199	167	68	85	3	3.30
Doc Reisling (IL)	R	35	9	10	.474	2	30	20	13	191	185	44	57	2	2.54
Dolly Gray	L	31	8	19	.338	0	34	29	21	229	216	64	84	3	2.63
Frank Oberlin	R	34	1	6	.143	0	8	6	6	57	52	23	18	0	3.00
Bill Foreman			0	0	.000	0	1	0	0	1	1	0	0	0	9.00
Joe Hovlik	R	25	0	0	.000	0	1	0	0	2	6	0	0	0	13.50
Dutch Hinrichs	R	21	0	1	.000	1	3	0	0	7	10	3	5	0	2.57
Bill Otey	L	23	0	1	.000	0	9	1	1	35	40	6	12	0	3.35
Charlie Moyer		24	0	3	.000	0	6	3	2	25	22	13	3	0	3.24
Jimmy Sebring (DD) 27															

ST. LOUIS 8th 47-107 .305 57 — JACK O'CONNOR

NAME	G by POS	B	AGE	G	AB	R	H	2B	3B	HR	RBI	BB	SO	SB	BA	SA
TOTALS			28	157	5077	454	1115	131	60	12	347	415		169	.220	.276
Pat Newman	1B103	R	29	103	384	45	83	3	8	2	26	29		16	.216	.281
Frank Truesdale	2B123	B	24	123	415	39	91	7	2	1	25	48		29	.219	.253
Bobby Wallace	SS98, 3B40	R	36	138	508	47	131	19	7	0	37	49		12	.258	.323
Roy Hartzell	3B89, SS38, OF23	L	28	151	542	52	118	13	5	2	30	49		18	.218	.271
Al Schweitzer	OF109	R	27	113	379	37	87	11	2	2	37	36		26	.230	.285
Danny Hoffman	OF106	L	30	106	380	20	90	11	5	0	27	34		16	.237	.292
George Stone	OF147	L	32	152	562	60	144	17	12	0	40	48		20	.256	.329
Jim Stephens	C96	R	26	99	299	24	72	3	7	0	23	16		2	.241	.298
Art Griggs	OF49, 2B41, 1B17, SS3, 3B3	R	26	123	416	28	98	22	5	2	30	25		11	.236	.327
Bill Killefer	C73	R	22	74	193	14	24	2	2	0	7	12		0	.124	.155
Dode Criss	1B12, P6	L	25	70	91	11	21	4	2	1	11	11		2	.231	.352
Red Corriden	SS14, 3B12	R	22	26	84	19	13	3	0	1	4	13		5	.155	.226
Hub Northen	OF26	L	24	26	96	6	19	1	0	1	16	5		2	.198	.208
Bill Abstein	1B23	R	27	25	87	1	13	2	0	0	3	2		3	.149	.172
Red Fisher	OF19	L	23	23	72	5	9	2	1	0	3	8		5	.125	.181
Sled Allen	C12, 1B1	R	23	14	23	3	3	1	0	0	1	1		0	.130	.174
Ray Demmitt	OF8	L	26	10	23	4	4	1	0	0	2	3		0	.174	.217
Mal McDonald	3B10			10	32	4	5	0	0	0	1	1		0	.156	.156

Bert Graham 24 B 3-26, Tommy Mee 20 R 3-19, Joe Crisp 20 R 0-1, Roy Janson 20 R 4-5, Jack O'Connor 41 R 0-0

NAME	T	AGE	W	L	PCT	SV	G	GS	CG	IP	H	BB	SO	ShO	ERA
TOTALS		27	47	**107**	.305	4	157	157	100	1391	1356	**532**	557	9	3.09
Joe Lake	R	28	11	18	.379	2	35	29	24	261	243	77	141	1	2.21
Jack Powell	R	35	7	11	.389	0	21	18	16	129	121	28	52	3	2.30
Red Nelson	R	24	5	1	.833	0	7	6	6	60	57	14	30	1	2.55
Barney Pelty	R	29	5	10	.333	0	27	18	12	165	157	70	48	3	3.49
Roy Mitchell	R	25	4	2	.667	0	6	6	6	52	43	12	23	0	2.60
Farmer Ray	R	23	4	10	.286	0	21	16	11	141	146	49	35	0	3.57
Bill Bailey	L	21	3	18	.143	1	34	20	13	192	186	97	90	0	3.29
Rube Waddell	L	33	3	1	.750	1	10	2	0	33	31	11	16	0	3.55
Dode Criss	R	25	2	1	.667	0	6	0	0	19	12	9	9	0	1.42
Mark Hall	R	22	1	7	.125	0	8	7	5	46	50	31	25	0	4.30
Ed Kinsella	R	28	1	3	.250	0	10	5	2	50	62	16	10	0	3.78
2 Bob Spade	R	33	1	3	.250	0	7	5	2	35	34	17	8	1	4.37
Ray Boyd	R	23	0	2	.000	0	3	2	1	14	16	5	6	0	4.50
Bill Crouch	L	23	0	0	.000	0	1	1	1	8	6	7	2	0	3.38
Jack Gilligan	R	24	0	3	.000	0	9	5	2	39	37	28	10	0	3.69
Bill Graham	L		0	8	.000	0	9	6	1	43	46	13	12	0	3.56
Harry Howell	R	33	0	0	.000	0	1	0	0	3	7	2	1	0	12.00
2 Fred Linke	L		0	1	.000	0	3	3	0	17	24	13	5	0	4.24
Alex Malloy	R	23	0	6	.000	0	7	6	4	53	47	17	27	0	2.55
Phil Stremmel	R	30	0	2	.000	0	5	2	2	29	31	16	7	0	3.72

CHICAGO 1st 104-50 .675 — **FRANK CHANCE**

NAME	G by POS	B	AGE	G	AB	R	H	2B	3B	HR	RBI	BB	SO	SB	BA	SA
TOTALS			29	154	4977	711	1333	219	**84**	**34**	586	542	501	173	.268	.366
Frank Chance	1B87	R	32	88	295	54	88	12	8	0	36	37	15	16	.298	.393
Johnny Evers	2B125	L	28	125	433	87	114	11	7	0	28	108	18	28	.263	.321
Joe Tinker	SS131	R	29	133	473	48	136	25	9	3	69	24	35	20	.288	.397
Harry Steinfeldt	3B128	R	32	129	448	70	113	21	1	2	58	36	29	10	.252	.317
Wildfire Schulte	OF150	L	27	151	559	93	168	29	15	**10**	68	39	57	22	.301	.460
Solly Hofman	OF110, 1B24, 3B1	R	27	136	477	83	155	24	16	3	86	65	34	29	.325	.461
Jimmy Sheckard	OF143	L	31	144	507	82	130	27	6	5	51	83	53	22	.256	.363
Johnny Kling	C86	R	35	91	297	31	80	17	2	2	32	37	27	3	.269	.360
H. Zimmerman	2B33, SS26, 3B22, OF4, 1B1	R	23	99	335	35	95	16	6	3	38	20	36	7	.284	.394
Jimmy Archer	C49, 1B40	R	27	98	313	36	81	17	6	2	41	14	49	6	.259	.371
Ginger Beaumont	OF56	L	33	76	172	30	46	5	1	2	22	28	14	4	.267	.343
John Kane	OF18, 2B6, 3B4, SS2	R	26	32	62	11	15	0	0	1	12	9	10	2	.242	.290
Tom Needham	C27, 1B1	R	31	31	76	9	14	3	1	0	10	10	10	1	.184	.250
1 Fred Luderus	1B17	L	24	24	54	5	11	1	1	0	3	4	3	0	.204	.259
1 Doc Miller		L	27	1	1	0	0	0	0	0	0	0	0	0	.000	.000

NAME	T	AGE	W	L	PCT	SV	G	GS	CG	IP	H	BB	SO	ShO	ERA
		29	**104**	50	**675**	13	154	154	99	1379	1171	474	609	**25**	**2.51**
Three Finger Brown	R	33	25	13	.658	**7**	46	31	**27**	295	256	64	143	**7**	1.86
King Cole	R	24	20	4	**.833**	1	33	29	21	240	174	130	114	4	1.80
Harry McIntire	R	32	13	9	.591	0	28	19	10	176	152	50	65	2	3.07
Orvie Overall (SA)	R	29	12	6	.667	1	23	21	11	145	106	54	92	4	2.66
Ed Reulbach (IL)	R	27	12	8	.600	0	24	23	13	173	161	49	55	1	3.12
2 Lew Richie	R	26	11	4	.733	4	30	11	8	130	117	51	53	3	2.70
Jack Pfiester	L	32	6	3	.667	0	14	13	5	100	82	26	34	2	1.80
Rube Kroh (ST)	L	23	3	1	.750	0	6	4	1	34	33	15	16	0	4.50
Big Jeff Pfeffer	R	28	1	0	1.000	0	13	1	1	41	43	16	11	0	3.29
Orlie Weaver	R	22	1	2	.333	0	7	2	2	32	34	15	22	0	3.66
Alex Carson	R	29	0	0	.000	0	2	0	0	7	6	1	2	0	3.86
2 Bill Foxen	L	26	0	0	.000	0	2	0	0	5	7	3	2	0	9.00

NEW YORK 2nd 91-63 .591 13 — **JOHN McGRAW**

NAME	G by POS	B	AGE	G	AB	R	H	2B	3B	HR	RBI	BB	SO	SB	BA	SA
TOTALS			26	155	5061	**715**	**1391**	204	83	31	**621**	562	489	282	**.275**	**.366**
Fred Merkle	1B144	R	21	144	506	75	148	35	14	4	70	44	59	23	.292	.441
Larry Doyle	2B151	L	23	151	575	97	164	21	14	8	69	71	26	39	.285	.412
Al Bridwell	SS141	L	26	142	492	74	136	15	7	0	48	73	23	14	.276	.335
Art Devlin	3B147	R	30	147	493	71	128	17	5	2	67	62	32	28	.260	.327
Red Murray	OF148	R	26	149	553	78	153	27	8	4	87	52	51	57	.277	.376
Fred Snodgrass	OF101, 1B9, 3B1, C1	R	22	120	396	69	127	22	8	2	44	71	52	33	.321	.432
Josh Devore	OF130	L	22	133	490	92	149	11	10	2	27	46	67	43	.304	.300
Chief Meyers	C117	R	29	127	365	25	104	18	0	1	62	40	18	5	.285	.342
Beals Becker	OF45, 1B1	L	23	80	126	18	36	2	4	3	24	14	25	11	.286	.437
Cy Seymour	OF76	L	37	79	287	32	76	9	4	1	40	23	18	10	.265	.334
Admiral Schlei	C49	R	32	55	99	10	19	2	1	0	8	14	10	4	.192	.232
Art Fletcher	SS22, 2B11, 3B11	R	25	51	125	12	28	2	1	0	13	4	9	9	.224	.256
Doc Crandall	P42, SS1	R	22	45	73	10	25	2	4	1	13	5	7	0	.342	.521
Tillie Shafer	3B8, 2B2, SS2	R	21	29	21	5	4	1	0	0	1	0	6	0	.190	.238
Art Wilson	C25, 1B1	R	24	26	52	10	14	4	1	0	5	9	6	2	.269	.385
Willie Keeler	OF2	L	38	19	10	5	3	0	0	0	0	3	1	1	.300	.300
Hank Gowdy	1B5	R	20	7	14	1	3	1	0	0	2	2	3	1	.214	.286
1 Elmer Zacher	OF1	R	26	1	0	0	0	0	0	0	0	0	0	0	.000	.000
Mike Donlin (VR) 32																
Fred Tenney (CJ) 38																

NAME	T	AGE	W	L	PCT	SV	G	GS	CG	IP	H	BB	SO	ShO	ERA
		26	91	63	.591	10	155	155	96	1392	1290	397	**717**	9	2.68
Christy Mathewson	R	31	**27**	9	.750	0	38	35	**27**	318	292	60	184	1	1.90
Doc Crandall	R	22	17	4	.810	5	42	18	13	208	194	43	73	2	2.55
Hooks Wiltse	L	29	14	12	.538	2	36	30	18	235	232	52	88	2	2.72
Red Ames	R	27	12	11	.522	0	33	23	13	190	161	63	94	3	2.22
Louis Drucke	R	21	12	10	.545	0	34	27	15	215	174	82	151	0	2.47
Rube Marquard	L	20	4	4	.500	0	13	8	2	71	65	40	52	0	4.44
Bugs Raymond	R	28	4	11	.267	0	19	11	6	99	106	40	55	0	3.82
Walt Dickson	R	27	1	0	1.000	0	12	1	0	20	31	9	9	0	5.40
Dutch Klawitter	R	22	0	0	.000	0	1	0	0	1	2	2	0	0	9.00
Ed Hendricks	L	24	0	1	.000	1	4	1	1	12	12	4	2	0	3.75
Dick Rudolph	R	22	0	1	.000	2	3	1	1	12	21	2	9	0	7.50

PITTSBURGH 3rd 86-67 .562 17.5 — **FRED CLARKE**

NAME	G by POS	B	AGE	G	AB	R	H	2B	3B	HR	RBI	BB	SO	SB	BA	SA
TOTALS			28	154	5125	655	1364	214	83	33	543	437	524	148	.266	.360
Jack Flynn (KJ)	1B93	R	26	96	332	32	91	10	2	6	52	30	47	6	.274	.370
Dots Miller	2B117, SS2	R	23	120	444	45	101	13	10	1	48	33	41	11	.227	.309
Honus Wagner	SS138, 1B11, 2B2	R	36	150	556	90	**178**	34	8	4	81	59	47	24	.320	.432
Bobby Byrne	3B148	R	25	148	602	101	**178**	**43**	12	2	52	66	27	36	.296	.417
Owen Wilson	OF146	L	26	146	536	59	148	14	13	4	50	21	68	8	.276	.373
Tommy Leach	OF131, SS2, 2B1	R	32	135	529	83	143	24	5	4	52	38	62	18	.270	.357
Fred Clarke	OF118	L	37	123	429	57	113	23	9	2	63	53	23	12	.263	.373
George Gibson	C143	R	29	143	482	53	125	22	6	3	44	47	31	7	.259	.349
Vin Campbell	OF74	L	22	97	282	42	92	9	5	4	21	26	23	17	.326	.436
Ham Hyatt	1B38, OF4	L	25	74	175	19	46	5	6	1	30	8	14	3	.263	.377
Bill McKechnie	2B36, SS14, 3B8, 1B4	B	23	71	212	23	46	1	2	0	12	11	23	4	.217	.241
Mike Simon	C14	R	27	22	50	3	10	0	1	0	5	1	2	1	.200	.240
Jack Kading	1B8	R	25	8	23	5	7	2	1	0	4	4	5	0	.304	.478
Paddy O'Connor	C1	R	30	6	4	0	1	0	0	0	0	1	1	0	.250	.250
2 Bud Sharpe	1B4	L	28	4	16	2	3	0	1	0	1	0	2	0	.188	.313
Alex McCarthy	SS3	R	22	3	12	1	1	0	1	0	0	0	2	0	.083	.250
1 Ed Abbaticchio	SS1	R	33	3	3	0	0	0	0	0	0	0	0	0	.000	.000
Max Carey	OF2	B	20	2	6	2	3	0	1	0	2	2	1	0	.500	.833

NAME	T	AGE	W	L	PCT	SV	G	GS	CG	IP	H	BB	SO	ShO	ERA
		30	86	67	.562	12	154	154	73	1376	1254	392	479	13	2.83
Babe Adams	R	28	18	9	.667	0	34	30	16	245	217	60	101	3	2.24
Lefty Leifield	L	26	15	12	.556	2	40	30	13	218	197	67	64	3	2.65
Deacon Phillippe	R	38	14	2	.875	4	31	8	5	122	111	9	30	1	2.29
Howie Camnitz	R	28	12	13	.480	2	38	31	16	260	246	61	120	1	3.22
2 Kirby White	R	26	10	9	.526	2	30	21	7	153	142	75	42	3	3.47
Sam Leever	R	38	6	5	.545	2	26	8	4	111	104	25	33	0	2.76
Bill Powell	R	25	4	6	.400	0	12	9	4	75	65	34	23	2	2.40
Lefty Webb	L	25	2	1	.667	0	7	3	2	27	29	9	6	0	5.67
Gene Moore	L	24	2	1	.667	0	4	1	0	17	19	7	9	0	3.18
Nick Maddox	R	23	2	3	.400	0	20	7	2	87	73	28	29	0	3.41
Jack Ferry	R	23	1	2	.333	0	6	3	2	31	26	8	12	0	2.32
1 Sammy Frock	R	26	0	1	.000	0	1	0	0	1	2	2	1	0	4.50
Elmer Steele	R	26	0	3	.000	0	3	3	2	24	19	3	7	0	2.25
Skip Dowd	R	21	0	0	.000	0	1	0	0	2	4	2	1	0	0.00
Jack Mercer	L	20	0	0	.000	0	1	0	0	1	0	2	1	0	0.00

PHILADELPHIA 4th 78-75 .510 25.5 — **RED DOOIN**

NAME	G by POS	B	AGE	G	AB	R	H	2B	3B	HR	RBI	BB	SO	SB	BA	SA
TOTALS			29	157	**5171**	674	1319	**223**	71	22	565	506	559	199	.255	.338
Kitty Bransfield	1B110	R	35	123	427	39	102	17	4	3	52	20	34	10	.239	.319
Otto Knabe	2B136	R	26	137	510	73	133	18	6	1	44	47	42	15	.261	.325
Mickey Doolan	SS148	R	30	148	536	58	141	31	6	2	57	35	56	16	.263	.354
Eddie Grant	3B152	R	27	152	579	70	155	15	5	1	67	39	54	25	.268	.316
John Titus	OF142	L	34	143	535	91	129	26	5	3	35	93	44	20	.241	.325
Johnny Bates	OF131	L	28	135	498	91	152	26	11	3	61	61	49	31	.305	.420
Sherry Magee	OF154	R	25	154	519	**110**	172	39	17	6	**123**	94	36	49	**.331**	**.507**
Red Dooin (BN)	C91, OF3	R	31	103	331	30	80	13	4	0	30	22	17	10	.242	.305
Jimmy Walsh	OF27, 2B26, SS9, 3B5	R	24	88	242	28	60	8	3	3	31	25	38	5	.248	.343
Pat Moran	C56	R	34	68	199	13	47	7	1	0	11	17	16	6	.236	.281
Joe Ward	1B32, SS1, 3B1	R	25	48	124	11	18	2	1	0	13	3	11	1	.145	.177
Fred Jacklitsch	C13, 1B2, 2B1, 3B1	R	34	25	51	7	10	3	0	0	2	5	9	0	.196	.255
Roy Thomas	OF20	L	36	23	71	7	13	0	2	0	4	7	5	4	.183	.239
2 Fred Luderus	1B19	L	24	21	68	10	20	5	2	0	14	9	5	2	.294	.426
Ed McDonough	C4		23	5	9	1	1	0	0	0	0	0	1	0	.111	.111
John Castle	OF2		27	3	4	1	1	0	0	0	0	0	0	1	.250	.250
Harry Cheek	C2			2	4	1	2	1	0	0	0	0	0	0	.500	.750

NAME	T	AGE	W	L	PCT	SV	G	GS	CG	IP	H	BB	SO	ShO	ERA
		27	78	75	.510	9	157	157	84	1411	1297	547	657	16	3.05
Earl Moore	R	30	22	15	.595	0	46	35	19	283	228	121	**185**	6	2.58
Bob Ewing	R	37	16	14	.533	0	34	32	20	255	235	86	102	4	3.00
Lew Moren	R	26	13	14	.481	1	34	26	12	205	207	82	74	1	3.56
George McQuillan	R	25	9	6	.600	1	24	17	13	152	109	50	71	3	**1.60**
Eddie Stack	R	22	6	7	.462	0	20	16	7	117	115	34	48	1	4.00
1 Bill Foxen	L	26	5	5	.500	0	16	9	5	78	73	40	33	0	2.54
Ad Brennan	L	28	3	0	1.000	0	19	5	2	73	72	28	28	0	2.34
Lou Schettler	R	24	2	6	.250	1	27	7	3	107	96	51	62	0	3.20
George Chalmers	R	22	1	1	.500	0	4	3	2	22	21	11	12	0	5.32
Jim Maroney	L	26	1	2	.333	1	12	2	1	42	43	11	13	0	2.14
Bill Culp	R	23	0	0	.000	1	4	0	0	7	8	4	4	0	7.71
Patsy Flaherty	L	34	0	0	.000	0	1	0	0	.1	1	1	0	0	0.00
Bert Humphries	R	29	0	0	.000	2	5	0	0	10	13	3	3	0	4.50
Barney Slaughter	R	25	0	1	.000	1	8	1	0	18	21	11	7	0	5.50
Charlie Girard		24	0	2	.000	1	7	1	0	27	33	12	11	0	6.34
Tully Sparks	R	33	0	2	.000	0	3	3	0	15	22	2	4	0	6.00

CINCINNATI 5th 75-79 .487 29 — **CLARK GRIFFITH**

NAME	G by POS	B	AGE	G	AB	R	H	2B	3B	HR	RBI	BB	SO	SB	BA	SA
TOTALS			26	156	5121	620	1326	150	79	23	526	529	515	**310**	.259	.333
Dick Hoblitzell	1B148, 2B7	L	21	155	**611**	85	170	24	13	4	70	47	32	28	.278	.380
Dick Egan	2B131, SS3	R	26	135	474	70	116	11	5	0	46	53	38	41	.245	.289
2 Tommy McMillian	SS82	R	22	82	248	20	46	0	3	0	13	31	23	7	.185	.210
Hans Lobert (XJ)	3B90	R	28	93	314	43	97	6	6	3	40	30	9	41	.309	.395
Mike Mitchell	OF149, 1B7	R	30	156	583	79	167	16	**18**	5	88	59	56	35	.286	.401
Dode Paskert	OF139, 1B2	R	29	144	506	63	152	21	5	2	46	70	60	51	.300	.374
Bob Bescher	OF150	B	26	150	589	95	147	20	10	4	48	81	75	**70**	.250	.338
Larry McLean	C119	R	28	127	423	27	126	14	7	2	71	26	23	4	.298	.378
Tom Downey	SS68, 3B41	R	26	111	378	43	102	9	3	2	32	34	28	12	.270	.325
Ward Miller	OF26	L	25	81	126	21	30	6	0	0	10	22	13	10	.238	.286
Tommy Clarke	C56	R	22	64	151	19	42	6	5	1	20	19	17	1	.278	.404
Frank Roth	C4, OF1	R	31	26	29	3	7	2	0	0	3	0	2	1	.241	.310
Art Phelan	3B8, 2B5, OF3, SS1	R	22	23	42	7	9	0	0	0	4	7	6	5	.214	.214
Orville Woodruff	3B17, 2B4	R	33	21	61	6	9	1	0	0	2	7	8	2	.148	.164
Mickey Corcoran	2B14	R	27	14	46	3	10	3	0	0	7	5	9	0	.217	.283
Swat McCabe	OF9	L	28	13	35	3	9	1	0	0	5	1	2	0	.257	.286
Jim Doyle	3B3, OF1	R	28	7	13	1	2	2	0	0	1	0	2	0	.154	.308
Chappie Charles	SS4	R	29	4	15	1	2	0	1	0	0	0	1	0	.133	.267
Dave Altizer	SS3	L	33	3	10	3	6	0	0	0	0	3	0	0	.600	.600
George Wheeler		R	28	3	3	0	0	0	0	0	0	0	2	0	.000	.000
Bob Meinke	SS2	R	23	2	1	0	0	0	0	0	0	0	0	0	.000	.000
Rabbit Robinson	3B2			2	7	0	0	0	0	0	1	1	0	0	.000	.000
Joe Burns (IL)		L	21	1	1	0	1	0	0	0	0	0	0	1	1.000	1.000
Ned Crompton	OF1	L	21	1	2	0	0	0	0	0	0	0	2	0	.000	.000
Clark Griffith		R	40	1	0	0	0	0	0	0	0	0	0	0	.000	.000
Mike Konnick	SS1	R	21	1	3	0	0	0	0	0	0	1	0	0	.000	.000

NAME	T	AGE	W	L	PCT	SV	G	GS	CG	IP	H	BB	SO	ShO	ERA
		27	75	79	.487	11	156	156	86	1387	1334	528	497	15	3.08
George Suggs	R	28	19	11	.633	3	35	30	23	266	248	48	91	2	2.40
Harry Gaspar	R	27	15	17	.469	**7**	48	31	16	275	257	75	74	4	2.59
Jack Rowan	R	23	14	13	.519	1	42	30	18	261	242	105	108	4	2.93
Fred Beebe	R	29	12	15	.444	0	35	26	11	214	193	94	93	2	3.07
2 Bill Burns	L	30	8	13	.381	0	31	21	13	179	183	49	57	2	3.48
Art Fromme (IL)	R	26	3	4	.429	0	11	5	1	49	44	39	10	0	2.94
Rube Benton	L	23	1	1	.500	0	12	2	0	38	44	23	15	0	4.74
Harry Coveleski	L	24	1	1	.500	0	7	4	2	39	35	42	27	0	5.31
Roy Castleton	L	24	1	2	.333	0	4	2	1	14	15	6	5	0	3.21
1 Bob Spade	R	33	1	2	.333	0	3	3	1	17	35	9	1	0	6.89
Wingo Anderson	L	23	0	0	.000	0	7	2	0	17	16	17	11	0	4.76
2 Slow Joe Doyle	R	28	0	0	.000	0	5	0	0	11	16	11	4	0	6.54
Tom Cantwell	R	21	0	0	.000	0	2	0	0	1	2	3	0	0	18.00
Walt Slagle	R	31	0	0	.000	0	1	0	0	1	0	3	0	0	9.00
Mysterious Walker	R	26	0	0	.000	0	1	0	0	3	4	4	1	0	3.00

BROOKLYN 6th 64-90 .416 40 — **BILL DAHLEN**

	NAME	G by POS	B	AGE	G	AB	R	H	2B	3B	HR	RBI	BB	SO	SB	BA	SA
	TOTALS			26	156	5125	497	1174	166	73	25	408	434	**706**	151	.229	.305
	Jake Daubert	1B144	L	26	144	552	67	146	15	15	8	50	47	53	23	.264	.389
	John Hummel	2B153	R	27	153	578	67	141	21	13	5	74	57	**81**	21	.244	.351
	Tony Smith	SS101, 3B6	R	26	106	321	31	58	10	1	1	16	69	53	9	.181	.227
	Ed Lennox	3B100	R	24	110	367	19	95	19	4	3	32	36	39	7	.259	.357
	Jack Dalton	OF72	R	25	77	273	33	62	9	4	1	21	26	30	5	.227	.300
	Bill Davidson	OF131	R	23	136	509	48	121	13	7	0	34	24	54	27	.238	.291
	Zack Wheat	OF156	L	24	156	606	78	172	36	15	2	55	47	80	16	.284	.403
	Bill Bergen	C89	R	37	89	249	11	40	2	1	0	14	6	39	0	.161	.177
	Al Burch	OF70, 1B13	L	26	103	352	41	83	8	3	1	20	22	30	13	.236	.284
	Tex Erwin	C68	L	24	81	202	15	38	3	1	1	10	24	12	3	.188	.228
	Pryor McElveen	3B54, SS6, 2B3, C1	R	26	74	213	19	48	8	3	1	26	22	47	6	.225	.305
	Hap Smith	OF16	L	26	35	76	6	18	2	0	0	5	4	14	4	.237	.263
	Otto Miller	C28	R	21	31	66	5	11	3	0	0	2	2	19	1	.167	.212
	Dolly Stark	SS30	R	25	30	103	7	17	3	0	0	8	7	19	2	.165	.194
	Bob Coulson	OF25	R	23	25	89	14	22	3	4	1	13	6	14	9	.247	.404
1	Tommy McMillian	SS23	R	22	23	74	2	13	1	0	0	2	6	10	4	.176	.189
	Harry Lumley	OF4	L	29	8	21	3	3	0	0	0	0	3	6	0	.143	.143
	Tim Jordan (KJ)		L	31	5	5	1	1	0	0	1	3	0	2	0	.200	.800
	Bill Dahlen		R	40	3	2	0	0	0	0	0	0	0	0	0	.000	.000
	George Hunter	OF1	B	23	1	0	0	0	0	0	0	0	0	0	0	.000	.000

NAME	T	AGE	W	L	PCT	SV	G	GS	CG	IP	H	BB	SO	ShO	ERA
		29	64	90	.416	5	156	156	**103**	**1420**	1331	545	555	15	3.07
Nap Rucker	L	25	17	18	.486	0	41	**39**	**27**	**320**	**293**	84	147	6	2.59
Cy Barger	R	25	15	15	.500	1	35	30	25	272	267	107	87	2	2.88
George Bell	R	35	10	**27**	.270	1	44	36	25	310	267	82	102	4	2.64
Doc Scanlan	R	29	9	11	.450	2	34	25	14	217	175	116	103	0	2.61
Elmer Knetzer	R	24	7	5	.583	0	20	15	10	133	122	60	56	3	3.18
Kaiser Wilhelm	R	36	3	7	.300	0	15	5	0	68	88	18	17	0	4.76
Rube Dessau	R	27	2	3	.400	1	19	0	0	51	67	29	24	0	5.82
Fred Miller	L	24	1	1	.500	0	6	2	0	21	25	13	2	0	4.71
George Crable	L	24	0	0	.000	0	2	1	1	7	5	5	3	0	5.14
Frank Schneiberg		28	0	0	.000	0	1	0	0	1	5	4	0	0	63.00
Sandy Burk	R	23	0	3	.000	0	4	3	1	19	17	27	14	0	6.16

ST. LOUIS 7th 63-90 .412 40.5 — **ROGER BRESNAHAN**

	NAME	G by POS	B	AGE	G	AB	R	H	2B	3B	HR	RBI	BB	SO	SB	BA	SA
	TOTALS			26	153	4912	637	1217	167	70	15	527	**655**	581	179	.248	.319
	Ed Konetchy	1B144, P1	R	24	144	520	87	157	23	16	3	78	78	59	18	.302	.425
	Miller Huggins	2B151	B	31	151	547	101	145	15	6	1	36	**116**	46	34	.265	.320
	Arnold Hauser	SS117, 3B1	R	21	119	375	37	77	7	2	2	36	49	39	15	.205	.251
	Mike Mowrey	3B141	R	26	143	489	69	138	24	6	2	70	67	38	21	.282	.368
	Steve Evans	OF141, 1B10	L	25	151	506	73	122	21	8	2	73	78	63	10	.241	.326
	Rebel Oakes	OF127	L	23	131	468	50	118	14	6	0	43	38	38	18	.252	.308
	Rube Ellis	OF141	L	24	142	550	87	142	18	8	4	54	62	70	25	.258	.342
	Ed Phelps	C80	R	31	93	270	25	71	4	2	0	37	36	29	9	.263	.293
	Roger Bresnahan	C77, OF2, P1	R	31	88	234	35	65	15	3	0	27	55	17	13	.278	.368
	Rudy Hulswitt	SS30, 2B2	R	33	63	133	9	33	7	2	0	14	13	10	5	.248	.331
2	Elmer Zacher	OF36, 2B1	R	26	47	132	7	28	5	1	0	10	10	19	3	.212	.265
	Frank Betcher	SS12, 3B7, 2B6, OF2	B	22	35	89	7	18	2	0	0	6	7	14	1	.202	.225
	Ody Abbott	OF21	R	23	22	70	2	13	2	1	0	6	6	20	3	.186	.243
	Jack Bliss	C13	R	28	16	33	2	2	0	0	0	3	4	8	0	.061	.061
	Bill O'Hara	OF4, 1B1, P1	L	26	9	20	1	3	0	0	0	2	1	3	0	.150	.150
	Jap Barbeau	3B6, 2B1	R	28	7	21	4	4	0	1	0	2	3	3	0	.190	.286
	Billy Kelly	C1	R	24	2	2	1	0	0	0	0	0	1	0	0	.000	.000
	Ernie Lush	OF1		25	1	4	0	0	0	0	0	0	1	1	0	.000	.000
	Alan Storke (DD) 25																

NAME	T	AGE	W	L	PCT	SV	G	GS	CG	IP	H	BB	SO	ShO	ERA
		26	63	90	.412	**14**	153	153	83	1337	**1396**	541	466	3	3.78
Johnny Lush	L	24	14	13	.519	1	36	24	13	225	235	70	54	1	3.20
Bob Harmon	R	22	13	15	.464	2	43	33	15	236	227	**133**	87	0	4.46
Vic Willis	R	34	9	12	.429	3	33	23	12	212	224	61	67	1	3.35
Slim Sallee (ST)	L	25	7	8	.467	2	18	13	9	115	112	24	46	1	2.97
Les Backman	R	22	6	7	.462	2	26	11	6	116	117	53	41	0	3,03
Frank Corridon	R	29	6	14	.300	3	30	18	9	156	168	55	51	0	3.81
Bill Steele	R	24	4	4	.500	1	9	8	8	72	71	24	25	0	3.25
Roy Golden	R	21	2	3	.400	0	7	6	3	43	44	33	31	0	4.39
Cy Alberts	R	28	1	2	.333	0	4	3	2	28	35	20	10	0	6.11
Bunny Hearn	L	19	1	3	.250	0	5	5	4	39	49	16	14	0	5.08
Rube Geyer	R	25	0	1	.000	0	4	0	0	4	5	3	5	0	4.50
Festus Higgins	R	17	0	1	.000	0	2	0	0	10	15	7	1	0	4.50
Elmer Rieger	R	21	0	2	.000	0	13	2	0	21	26	7	9	0	6.25
Ed Zmich	L	25	0	5	.000	0	9	6	2	36	38	29	19	0	6.25
Roger Bresnahan	R	31	0	0	.000	0	1	0	0	3	6	1	0	0	0.00
Bill Chambers	R	20	0	0	.000	0	1	0	0	1	1	0	0	0	0.00
Ed Konetchy	R	24	0	0	.000	0	1	0	0	4	4	1	0	0	4.50
Bill O'Hara	L	26	0	0	.000	0	1	0	0	1	0	0	0	0	0.00
Harry Patton			0	0	.000	0	1	0	0	4	4	2	2	0	2.25
Charlie Pickett			0	0	.000	0	2	0	0	6	7	2	2	0	1.50
John Raleigh	L	20	0	0	.000	0	3	1	0	5	8	0	2	0	9.00

BOSTON 8th 53-100 .346 50.5 — **FRED LAKE**

	NAME	G by POS	B	AGE	G	AB	R	H	2B	3B	HR	RBI	BB	SO	SB	BA	SA
	TOTALS			28	157	5123	495	1260	173	49	31	421	359	540	152	.246	.317
1	Bud Sharpe	1B113	L	28	115	439	30	105	14	3	0	29	14	31	4	.239	.285
	Dave Shean	2B148	R	32	150	543	52	130	12	7	3	36	42	45	16	.239	.304
	Bill Sweeney	SS110, 3B21, 1B17	R	24	150	499	43	133	22	4	5	46	61	28	25	.267	.357
	Buck Herzog	3B105	R	24	106	380	51	95	20	3	3	32	30	34	13	.250	.342
2	Doc Miller	OF130	L	27	130	482	48	138	27	4	3	55	33	52	17	.286	.378
	Fred Beck	OF134, 1B19	L	23	154	571	52	157	32	9	**10**	64	19	55	8	.275	.415
	Cush Collins	OF151	B	28	151	584	67	141	6	7	3	40	43	48	36	.241	.291
	Peaches Graham	C87, 3B2, 1B1, OF1	R	33	110	291	31	82	13	2	0	21	33	15	5	.282	.340
	Harry Smith	C38	R	35	70	147	8	35	4	0	1	15	5	14	5	.238	.286
	Gus Getz	3B22, 2B13, OF8, SS4	R	20	54	144	14	28	0	1	0	7	6	10	2	.194	.208
2	Ed Abbaticchio	SS46, 2B1	R	33	52	178	20	44	4	2	0	10	12	16	2	.247	.292
	Bill Rariden	C49	R	22	49	137	15	31	5	1	1	14	12	22	1	.226	.299
	Wilbur Good	OF23	L	24	23	86	15	29	5	4	0	11	6	13	5	.337	.488
	Herbie Moran	OF20	L	26	20	67	11	8	0	0	0	3	13	14	6	.119	.119
	Pete Burg	3B12, SS1	R	28	13	46	7	15	0	1	0	10	7	12	5	.326	.370
	Rube Sellers	OF9	R	29	12	32	3	5	0	0	0	2	6	5	1	.156	.156
	Marty Martel	1B10	R	27	10	31	0	4	0	0	0	1	2	3	0	.129	.129
	Bill Cooney	OF2		23	8	12	2	3	0	0	0	1	2	0	0	.250	.250
	Fred Liese			24	5	4	0	0	0	0	0	0	1	2	0	.000	.000
	Fred Lake		R	43	3	1	0	0	0	0	0	0	1	0	0	.000	.000
	Rowdy Elliott	C1	R	19	3	2	0	0	0	0	0	0	0	0	0	.000	.000
2	Art Kruger		R	29	1	1	0	0	0	0	0	0	0	0	0	.000	.000
	Jimmy Riley		R	29	1	1	0	0	0	0	0	0	1	1	0	.000	.000

	NAME	T	AGE	W	L	PCT	SV	G	GS	CG	IP	H	BB	SO	ShO	ERA
			25	53	**100**	.346	9	157	157	74	1390	1328	**599**	531	12	3.22
	Al Mattern	R	27	16	19	.457	1	**51**	37	17	305	288	121	94	6	2.98
2	Sammy Frock	R	26	11	19	.367	2	45	29	15	255	245	91	170	2	3.21
	Buster Brown	R	28	9	23	.281	2	46	29	16	263	251	94	88	1	2.67
	Cecil Ferguson	R	23	8	7	.533	0	26	14	10	123	110	58	40	1	3.80
	Cliff Curtis	R	27	6	24	.200	2	43	37	12	251	251	124	75	2	3.55
	Billy Burke	L	20	1	0	1.000	0	19	1	1	64	68	29	22	0	4.08
	Chick Evans	R	20	1	1	.500	1	13	1	0	31	28	27	12	0	5.23
1	Kirby White	R	26	1	2	.333	0	3	3	3	26	15	12	6	0	1.38
	Ralph Good	R	24	0	0	.000	0	2	0	0	9	6	2	4	0	2.00
	Lefty Tyler	L	20	0	0	.000	0	2	0	0	11	11	6	6	0	2.46
	Jiggs Parson	R	24	0	2	.000	0	10	4	0	35	35	26	7	0	3.86
1	Lew Richie	R	26	0	3	.000	0	4	2	0	16	20	9	7	0	2.81

WORLD SERIES – PHILADELPHIA (AL) 4 CHICAGO (NL) 1

LINE SCORES

TEAM	1	2	3	4	5	6	7	8	9	10	11	12	R	H	E
Game 1 October 17 at Philadelphia															
CHI (NL)	0	0	0	0	0	0	0	0	1				1	3	1
PHI (AL)	0	2	1	0	0	0	0	1	X				4	7	2
Overall, McIntire (4)			**Bender**												
Game 2 October 18 at Philadelphia															
CHI	1	0	0	0	0	0	1	0	1				3	8	3
PHI	0	0	2	0	1	0	6	0	X				9	14	4
Brown, Richie (8)			**Coombs**												
Game 3 October 20 at Chicago															
PHI	1	2	5	0	0	0	4	0	0				12	15	1
CHI	1	2	0	0	0	0	0	2	0				5	6	5
Coombs			Reulbach, **McIntire** (3), Pfiester (3)												
Game 4 October 22 at Chicago															
PHI	0	0	1	2	0	0	0	0	0	0			3	11	3
CHI	1	0	0	1	0	0	0	0	1	1			4	9	1
Bender			Cole, **Brown** (9)												
Game 5 October 23 at Chicago															
PHI	1	0	0	0	1	0	0	5	0				7	9	1
CHI	0	1	0	0	0	0	0	1	0				2	9	2
Coombs			**Brown**												

COMPOSITE BATTING

NAME	POS	G	AB	R	H	2B	3B	HR	RBI	BA
Philadelphia (AL) Totals		5	177	35	56	19	1	1	**30**	.316
Baker	3B	5	**22**	6	**9**	3	0	0	4	.409
Lord	OF	5	**22**	3	4	2	0	0	1	.182
Collins	2B	5	21	5	**9**	**4**	0	0	3	**.429**
Murphy	OF	5	20	**6**	7	3	0	1	**9**	.350
Strunk	OF	4	18	2	5	1	1	0	2	.278
Davis	1B	5	17	5	6	3	0	0	2	.353
Barry	SS	5	17	3	4	2	0	0	3	.235
Coombs	P	3	13	0	5	1	0	0	3	.385
Thomas	C	4	12	2	3	0	0	0	1	.250
Bender	P	2	6	1	2	0	0	0	1	.333
Hartsel	OF	1	5	2	1	0	0	0	0	.200
Lapp	C	1	4	0	1	0	0	0	1	.250
Chicago (NL) Totals		5	158	15	35	11	1	0	13	.222
Steinfeldt	3B	5	20	0	2	1	0	0	1	.100
Tinker	SS	5	18	2	6	2	0	0	0	.333
Chance	1B	5	17	1	6	1	1	0	4	.353
Schulte	OF	5	17	3	6	3	0	0	2	.353
Zimmerman	2B	5	17	0	4	1	0	0	2	.235
Hofman	OF	5	15	2	4	0	0	0	2	.267
Sheckard	OF	5	14	5	4	2	0	0	1	.286
Kling	C	5	13	0	1	0	0	0	0	.077
Archer	1B-C	3	11	1	2	1	0	0	0	.182
Brown	P	3	7	0	0	0	0	0	0	.000
Beaumont	PH	3	2	1	0	0	0	0	0	.000
Cole	P	1	2	0	0	0	0	0	0	.000
Pfiester	P	1	2	0	0	0	0	0	0	.000
McIntire	P	2	1	0	0	0	0	0	0	.000
Needham	PH	1	1	0	0	0	0	0	0	.000
Overall	P	1	1	0	0	0	0	0	0	.000
Kane	PR	1	0	0	0	0	0	0	0	.000
Reulbach	P	1	0	0	0	0	0	0	0	.000
Richie	P	1	0	0	0	0	0	0	0	.000

COMPOSITE PITCHING

NAME	G	IP	H	BB	SO	W	L	SV	ERA
Philadelphia (AL) Totals	5	45.2	35	18	31	4	1	0	2.76
Coombs	**3**	**27**	23	**14**	**17**	**3**	0	0	3.33
Bender	2	18.2	12	4	14	1	1	0	**1.93**
Chicago (NL) Totals	5	44	56	17	24	1	4	0	4.70
Brown	**3**	18	**23**	7	14	1	**2**	0	5.50
Cole	1	8	10	3	5	0	0	0	3.38
Pfiester	1	6.2	9	1	1	0	0	0	0.00
McIntire	2	5.1	4	3	3	0	1	0	6.75
Overall	1	3	6	1	1	0	1	0	9.00
Reulbach	1	2	3	2	0	0	0	0	9.00
Richie	1	1	1	0	0	0	0	0	0.00

1911 The Fire Fighters of Philadelphia

It seemed that Fate would frown on the New York Giants in 1911 when the Polo Grounds caught fire on April 14, and was extensively damaged. The orphaned Giants were taken into Highlander Park by the Yankees, but this was hardly an auspicious manner in which to begin a season. Despite the spring mishap, John McGraw's men stayed close to the pace-setting Chicago Cubs during the summer before taking off in August and leaving the pack behind. The Giants' hot streak dated from the time utility man Art Fletcher was given the shortstop job, and Buck Herzog was reacquired from Boston to fill the third base slot. Staying free of injuries, the Giants passed the Cubs on August 24, and wrapped up the pennant with 20 victories in their final 24 games. The injury-plagued Cubs could not match the Giant pace and had to settle for a second-place finish, 7½ games back. Perhaps aiding the Giants most of all down the stretch was moving back into the rebuilt Polo Grounds in September.

The Giants' victory could be found in Rube Marquard who, after two years of mediocrity, fulfilled the promise that had prompted McGraw to shell out $11,000 to purchase his contract in 1908. The left-handed hurler developed into the league's top southpaw, winning 24 games and leading the league in strikeouts. He formed a counterpoint to righty Christy Mathewson, giving McGraw the top pitching duo in baseball. Larry Doyle, Art Fletcher, and Chief Meyers posted .300 averages for the Giants, and Fred Merkle provided power and run production for the offense.

Honus Wagner took his eighth and last batting crown with a .334 mark, and Wildfire Schulte of Chicago won the home run title with a tremendous total of 21 circuit blasts, the best power mark since 1899. Eight pitchers chalked up 20 victories, with rookie Grover "Pete" Alexander of the Phillies leading the way with 28.

The American League race was a two-team affair as the Philadelphia Athletics and Detroit Tigers ran away from the rest of the field. Philadelphia started slowly, while Detroit began the year as a hot team. The Athletics righted themselves and played winning ball from May on to stay hot on Detroit's tail throughout the summer. Both teams possessed high octane offenses, but Connie Mack's pitching staff gave the Athletics the edge. Behind ace pitchers, Jack Coombs and Eddie Plank, Philadelphia passed the Tigers on August 4, and did not stop until they had the pennant won by 13½ games. The Athletic infield of Stuffy McInnis, Eddie Collins, Jack Barry, and Frank Baker became known as the $100,000 infield, and a team batting mark of .296 enabled the strong pitching staff to win 101 games.

Ty Cobb and Sam Crawford formed the most feared batting tandem in the league, but mediocre pitching negated their efforts and failed to give Detroit the balance to overhaul the Athletics. Cobb won his fifth consecutive batting title with a career-high .420 mark, although rookie outfielder Joe Jackson of the Cleveland Indians threatened him all the way with a .408 average—the highest runner-up average ever recorded in baseball. Philadelphia's Frank Baker led all batters with 11 homers, and teammate Jack Coombs led in wins with 28.

The Athletics' pitchers continued to handcuff batters in the World Series as they held the Giants to a .175 batting average and 13 runs in a six-game Series won by the Mackmen. Bender, Coombs, and Plank all pitched complete game victories, but the star of the Series was Athletic third baseman Frank Baker. Besides hitting .375, his home run in the second game beat Rube Marquard, and another homer in the ninth inning of the third game off Christy Mathewson tied the score. The third baseman's power performance was substantial enough to have the press immediately dub him as Home Run Baker—one of the early heroes of Series play.

1911 AMERICAN LEAGUE

NAME	G by POS	B	AGE	G	AB	R	H	2B	3B	HR	RBI	BB	SO	SB	BA	SA
PHILADELPHIA 1st 101-50 .669		CONNIE MACK														
TOTALS			27	152	5199	**861**	1540	233	93	35	**692**	424		226	**.296**	**.397**
Stuffy McInnis	1B97, SS24	R	20	126	468	76	150	20	10	3	77	25		23	.321	.425
Eddie Collins	2B132	L	24	132	493	92	180	22	13	3	73	62		38	.365	.481
Jack Barry	SS127	R	24	127	442	73	117	18	7	1	63	38		30	.265	.344
Frank Baker	3B148	L	25	148	592	96	198	38	4	**11**	115	40		38	.334	.468
Danny Murphy	OF136, 2B4	R	34	141	508	104	167	27	11	6	66	50		22	.329	.461
Rube Oldring	OF119	R	27	121	495	84	147	11	14	3	59	21		21	.297	.394
Bris Lord	OF132	R	27	134	574	92	178	36	11	3	55	35		15	.310	.427
Ira Thomas	C103	R	30	103	297	33	81	14	3	0	39	23		4	.273	.340
Amos Strunk	OF62, 1B2	L	22	74	215	42	55	7	2	1	21	35		13	.256	.321
Jack Lapp	C57, 1B4	L	26	68	167	35	59	10	3	1	26	24		4	.353	.467
Harry Davis	1B53	R	37	57	183	27	36	9	1	1	22	24		2	.197	.273
Jack Coombs	P47	R	28	52	141	31	45	6	1	2	23	8		5	.319	.418
Claude Derrick	2B20, SS6, 1B3, 3B2	R	25	36	100	14	23	1	2	0	5	7		7	.230	.280
Paddy Livingston(NJ)	C26	R	31	27	71	9	17	4	0	0	8	7		1	.239	.296
Topsy Hartsel	OF10	R	37	25	38	8	9	2	0	0	1	8		0	.237	.289
Chester Emerson	OF7	L	21	7	18	2	4	0	0	0	0	6		1	.222	.222
1 Willie Hogan	OF6	R	26	7	19	1	2	1	0	0	2	0		0	.105	.158
Earle Mack	3B2	L	21	2	4	0	0	0	0	0	0	0		0	.000	.000

NAME	T	AGE	W	L	PCT	SV	G	GS	CG	IP	H	BB	SO	ShO	ERA
		29	**101**	50	**669**	15	152	152	97	1376	1343	487	739	13	3.01
Jack Combs	R	28	**28**	12	.700	3	47	**40**	26	337	**360**	119	185	1	3.53
Eddie Plank	L	35	22	8	.733	5	40	30	24	257	237	77	149	**6**	2.10
Chief Bender	R	28	17	5	.773	4	31	24	16	216	198	58	114	3	2.17
Cy Morgan	R	32	15	7	.682	1	38	30	15	250	217	113	136	2	2.70
Harry Krause	L	23	11	8	.579	2	27	19	12	169	155	47	85	1	3.04
Dave Danforth	L	21	5	2	.714	0	14	2	1	34	29	17	21	0	3.71
Elmer Leonard	R	22	2	2	.500	0	5	1	1	19	26	10	10	0	2.84
Doc Martin	R	23	1	2	.333	0	11	3	1	38	40	17	21	0	4.50
Boardwalk Brown	R	24	0	1	.000	0	2	1	1	12	12	2	6	0	4.50
Howard Armstrong	R	21	0	1	.000	0	1	0	0	3	3	1	0	0	0.00
Lefty Russell	L	20	0	2	.000	0	7	2	0	32	45	18	7	0	7.60
Lep Long	R	22	0	0	.000	0	4	0	0	8	15	5	4	0	4.50
Allan Collamore	R	24	0	0	.000	0	2	0	0	2	6	3	1	0	36.00

NAME	G by POS	B	AGE	G	AB	R	H	2B	3B	HR	RBI	BB	SO	SB	BA	SA
DETROIT 2nd 89-65 .578 13.5		HUGHIE JENNINGS														
TOTALS			27	154	5294	831	**1544**	230	**96**	30	657	471		**276**	.292	.388
Jim Delahanty	1B72, 2B59, 3B12	R	32	144	542	83	184	30	14	3	94	56		15	.339	.463
Charley O'Leary	2B67, 3B6	R	29	74	256	29	68	8	2	0	25	21		10	.266	.313
Donie Bush	SS150	B	23	150	561	126	130	18	5	1	36	**98**		42	.232	.287
George Moriarty	3B129, 1B1	R	26	130	478	51	116	20	4	1	60	27		28	.243	.308
Sam Crawford	OF146	L	31	146	574	109	217	36	14	7	115	61		37	.378	.526
Ty Cobb	OF146	L	24	146	591	**147**	**248**	**47**	**24**	8	**127**	44		**83**	**.420**	**.621**
Davy Jones	OF92	L	31	98	341	78	93	10	0	0	19	41		25	.273	.302
Oscar Stanage	C141	R	28	141	503	45	133	13	7	3	51	20		3	.264	.336
Delos Drake	OF83, 1B2	R	24	95	315	37	88	9	9	1	36	17		20	.279	.375
Del Gainer (BW)	1B69	R	24	70	248	32	75	11	4	2	25	20		10	.302	.403
George Mullin(IL)	P30	R	30	40	98	4	28	7	2	0	5	10		1	.286	.398
Biff Schaller	OF16, 1B1	L	21	40	60	8	8	0	1	1	7	4		1	.133	.217
Chick Lathers	2B9, 3B8, SS4, 1B3	L	22	29	45	5	10	1	0	0	4	5		0	.222	.244
Boss Schmidt (AJ)	C9, OF1	B	30	28	46	4	13	2	1	0	2	0		0	.283	.370
Paddy Baumann	2B23, OF3	R	25	26	94	8	24	2	4	0	11	6		1	.255	.362
Joe Casey	C12, OF3	R	23	15	33	2	5	0	0	0	3	3		0	.152	.152
Guy Tutweiler	2B6, OF3	L	21	13	32	3	6	2	0	0	3	2		0	.188	.250
Jack Ness	1B12	R	25	12	39	6	6	0	0	0	2	2		0	.154	.154
Squanto Wilson	C5	B	22	5	16	2	3	0	0	0	0	2		0	.188	.188

NAME	T	AGE	W	L	PCT	SV	G	GS	CG	IP	H	BB	SO	ShO	ERA
		27	89	65	.578	8	154	154	**108**	**1388**	**1514**	460	538	8	3.73
George Mullin(IL)	R	30	18	10	.643	0	30	29	25	234	245	61	87	2	3.08
Ed Willett	R	27	13	14	.481	2	38	27	15	231	261	80	86	2	3.66
Ralph Works	R	23	11	5	.688	1	30	15	9	167	173	67	68	3	3.88
Ed Lafitte	R	25	11	8	.579	1	29	20	15	172	205	52	63	0	3.92
Edgar Summers	R	26	11	11	.500	2	30	20	13	179	189	51	65	0	3.67
Wild Bill Donovan	R	34	10	9	.526	1	20	19	15	168	160	64	81	1	3.32
Bill Covington	R	24	7	1	.875	1	17	6	5	84	94	33	29	0	4.07
Jack Lively	R	26	7	5	.583	0	18	14	10	114	143	34	45	0	4.58
Clarence Mitchell	L	20	1	0	1.000	0	5	1	0	14	20	7	4	0	8.36
Wiley Taylor	R	23	0	2	.000	0	3	2	1	19	18	10	9	0	3.79
Pug Cavet	L	21	0	0	.000	0	1	1	0	4	6	1	1	0	4.50

NAME	G by POS	B	AGE	G	AB	R	H	2B	3B	HR	RBI	BB	SO	SB	BA	SA
CLEVELAND 3rd 80-73 .523 22		DEACON McGUIRE 6-11 3.53						GEORGE STOVALL 74-62 .544								
TOTALS			28	156	**5314**	691	1500	238	81	20	579	354		209	.282	.369
George Stovall	1B118, 2B2	R	32	126	458	48	124	17	7	0	79	21		11	.271	.338
Neal Ball	2B95, 3B17, SS1	R	30	116	412	45	122	14	9	3	47	27		21	.296	.396
Ivy Olson	SS139, 3B1	R	25	140	545	89	142	20	8	1	50	34		20	.261	.332
Terry Turner	3B94, 2B14, SS10	R	30	117	417	59	105	16	9	0	28	34		29	.252	.333
Joe Jackson	OF147	L	21	147	571	126	233	45	19	7	83	56		41	.408	.590
Joe Birmingham	OF101, 3B16	R	26	125	447	55	136	18	5	2	51	15		16	.304	.380
Jack Graney	OF142	L	25	146	527	84	142	25	5	1	45	66		21	.269	.342
Gus Fisher	C58, 1B1	L	25	70	203	20	53	6	3	0	12	7		6	.261	.320
Ted Easterly	OF54, C23	L	26	99	287	34	93	19	5	1	37	8		6	.324	.436
Nap Lajoie	1B41, 2B37	R	35	90	315	36	115	20	1	2	60	26		13	.365	.454
Syd Smith	C48, 1B1, 3B1	R	27	58	154	8	46	8	1	1	21	11		0	.299	.383
Hank Butcher	OF34	R	24	38	133	21	32	7	3	1	11	11		9	.241	.361
Grover Land	C34, 1B1	R	26	35	107	5	15	1	2	0	10	3		2	.140	.187
Art Griggs (JJ)	2B11, OF4, 3B3, 1B1	R	27	27	68	7	17	3	2	1	7	5		1	.250	.397
Bill Lindsay	3B15, 2B1	L	30	19	66	6	16	2	0	0	5	1		2	.242	.273
Cotton Knaupp	SS13	R	21	13	39	2	4	1	0	0	0	0		0	.103	.128
Jack Mills	3B7	L	21	13	17	5	5	0	0	0	1	1		1	.294	.294
Steve O'Neill	C9	R	19	9	27	1	4	1	0	0	1	4		2	.148	.185
Dave Callahan	OF3	L	22	5	12	1	4	0	1	0	0	1		0	.333	.500
Tim Hendryx	3B2	R	20	2	4	0	1	0	0	0	0	0		0	.250	.250
Jack Adams	C2	B	20	2	5	0	1	0	0	0	0	1		0	.200	.200
Herman Bronkie	3B2	R	26	2	6	0	1	0	0	0	0	0		0	.167	.167
Addie Joss(DD)31																
Simon Nichols(DD)28																

NAME	T	AGE	W	L	PCT	SV	G	GS	CG	IP	H	BB	SO	ShO	ERA
		24	80	73	.523	10	156	156	93	1382	1376	**550**	673	6	3.37
Vean Gregg	L	26	23	7	**.767**	0	34	26	22	244	172	86	125	5	**1.81**
Gene Krapp	R	24	12	8	.600	3	34	26	14	215	182	**136**	130	1	3.43
George Kahler	R	21	9	8	.529	2	30	17	10	154	153	66	97	0	3.28
Cy Falkenberg	R	31	8	5	.615	1	15	13	7	107	117	24	46	0	3.28
Fred Blanding	R	23	7	11	.389	2	29	16	11	176	190	60	80	0	3.68
Willie Mitchell	L	21	7	14	.333	1	30	22	9	177	190	60	78	0	3.76
Bill James	R	24	3	4	.429	0	8	6	4	52	58	32	21	0	4.84
1 Cy Young	R	44	3	4	.429	0	7	7	4	46	54	13	20	0	3.92
Earl Yingling	L	22	2	1	.667	0	4	3	1	22	30	9	6	0	4.50
Specs Harkness	R	23	2	2	.500	0	12	6	3	52	62	21	25	0	4.33
Hi West	R	26	2	4	.333	1	13	8	3	65	84	18	17	0	3.74
Pat Paige	R	26	1	0	1.000	0	2	1	1	16	21	7	6	0	4.50
Jim Baskette	R	23	1	2	.333	0	4	2	2	21	21	9	8	0	3.43
Josh Swindell	R	27	0	1	.000	0	4	1	1	17	19	4	6	0	2.12
Bugs Reisigl	R	23	0	1	.000	0	2	1	1	13	13	3	6	0	6.23
Ben DeMott	R	22	0	1	.000	0	1	1	0	4	10	2	2	0	11.25

CHICAGO 4th 77-74 .510 24 — HUGH DUFFY

NAME	G by POS	B	AGE	G	AB	R	H	2B	3B	HR	RBI	BB	SO	SB	BA	SA
TOTALS			30	154	5210	717	1399	179	92	20	593	385		201	.269	.350
Shano Collins	1B97, 2B3, OF3	R	25	106	370	48	97	16	12	4	48	20		14	.262	.403
Amby McConnell (LJ)	2B103	L	28	104	396	45	111	11	5	1	34	23		7	.280	.341
Lee Tannehill	SS102, 2B27, 3B8, 1B5	R	30	141	516	60	131	17	6	0	49	32		0	.254	.310
Harry Lord	3B138	L	29	141	561	103	180	18	18	3	61	32		43	.321	.433
Matty McIntyre	OF146	L	31	146	569	102	184	19	11	1	52	64		17	.323	.401
Ping Bodie	OF128, 2B16	R	23	145	551	75	159	27	13	4	97	49		14	.289	.407
Nixey Callahan	OF114	R	37	120	466	64	131	13	5	3	60	15		45	.281	.350
Billy Sullivan	C89	R	36	89	256	26	55	9	3	0	31	16		1	.215	.273
Patsy Dougherty	OF56	L	34	76	211	39	61	10	9	0	32	26		19	.289	.422
Rollie Zeider	1B29, SS17, 3B10, 2B9	R	27	73	217	39	55	3	0	2	21	29		28	.253	.295
Freddie Payne	C56	R	30	66	133	14	27	2	1	1	19	8		6	.203	.256
Frank Lange	P29	R	27	54	76	7	22	6	2	0	16	7		0	.289	.421
Ray Corhan (JJ)	SS43	R	23	43	131	14	28	6	2	0	8	15		2	.214	.290
Bruno Block	C38	R	26	39	115	11	35	6	1	1	18	6		0	.304	.400
Charlie Mullen	1B20	R	22	20	59	7	12	2	1	0	5	5		1	.203	.271
Felix Chouinard	2B4, OF4	R	23	14	17	3	3	0	0	0	0	0		0	.176	.176
Cuke Barrows	OF13	R	27	13	46	5	9	2	0	0	4	7		2	.196	.239
Bob Messenger	OF4	B	27	13	17	4	2	0	1	0	0	3		0	.118	.235
Tex Jones	1B9	R	25	9	31	4	6	1	0	0	4	3		1	.194	.226
Ralph Kreitz	C7	R	25	7	17	0	4	1	0	0	0	2		0	.235	.294

Freddy Parent 35 R 4-9, Marty Berghammer 25 L 0-5, Jimmy Johnston 21 R 0-2, Wally Mayer 21 R 0-3, 1 Paul Meloan 22 L 1-3, Lena Blackburne (KJ) 24

NAME	T	AGE	W	L	PCT	SV	G	GS	CG	IP	H	BB	SO	ShO	ERA
		28	77	74	.510	**19**	154	154	86	1366	1349	384	**752**	**14**	3.02
Ed Walsh	R	30	27	18	.600	**7**	**56**	37	33	**369**	327	72	**255**	5	2.22
Jim Scott	R	22	14	11	.560	2	39	26	14	202	195	81	128	3	2.63
Doc White	L	32	10	14	.417	3	34	29	16	214	219	35	72	4	2.99
Frank Lange	R	27	8	8	.500	0	29	22	8	162	151	77	104	1	3.22
Fred Olmsted	R	29	6	6	.500	3	25	11	7	118	146	30	45	1	4.19
Irv Young	L	33	5	6	.455	2	24	11	2	93	99	25	40	0	4.36
Joe Benz	R	27	3	2	.600	0	12	6	2	56	52	13	28	0	2.25
Joe Hovlik	R	26	2	0	1.000	1	12	3	1	47	47	20	24	0	3.06
Jesse Baker	L	23	2	7	.222	1	22	8	3	94	101	30	51	0	3.93
George Mogridge	L	22	0	2	.000	0	4	1	0	13	12	1	5	0	5.38

BOSTON 5th 78-75 .510 24 — PATSY DONOVAN

NAME	G by POS	B	AGE	G	AB	R	H	2B	3B	HR	RBI	BB	SO	SB	BA	SA
TOTALS			25	153	5024	680	1379	203	66	**35**	559	**506**		190	.274	.362
Clyde Engle	1B65, 3B51, 2B13, OF10	R	27	146	514	58	139	13	3	2	48	51		24	.270	.319
Heinie Wagner	2B40, SS32	R	30	80	261	34	67	13	8	1	38	29		15	.257	.379
Steve Yerkes	SS116, 2B14, 3B11	R	23	142	502	70	140	24	3	1	57	52		14	.279	.345
Larry Gardner	3B72, 2B62	L	25	138	492	80	140	17	8	4	44	64		27	.285	.376
Harry Hooper	OF130	L	23	130	524	93	163	20	6	4	45	73		38	.311	.395
Tris Speaker	OF138	L	23	141	510	88	167	34	13	8	70	59		25	.327	.492
Duffy Lewis	OF125	R	22	130	469	64	144	32	4	7	86	25		11	.307	.437
Bill Carrigan (BH)	C62, 1B6	R	27	72	232	29	67	6	1	1	30	26		5	.289	.336
Rip Williams (BL)	1B57, C38	R	29	95	284	36	68	8	5	0	31	24		9	.239	.303
Les Nunamaker	C59	R	22	62	183	18	47	4	3	0	19	12		1	.257	.311
Joe Riggert	OF38	R	24	50	146	19	31	4	4	2	13	12		5	.212	.336
Olaf Hendriksen	OF25	L	23	27	93	17	34	2	1	0	8	14		4	.366	.409
Billy Purtell	3B16, 2B3, SS3, OF1	R	25	27	82	5	23	5	3	0	7	1		1	.280	.415
Jack Thoney		R	30	26	20	5	5	0	0	0	2	0		1	.250	.250
John Lewis	2B18	R	23	18	59	7	16	0	0	0	6	7		2	.271	.271
2 Hap Myers	1B12	R	23	13	38	3	14	2	0	0	0	4		4	.368	.421
Hugh Bradley (BL)	1B12	R	26	12	41	9	13	2	0	1	4	2		1	.317	.439
Hal Janvrin	3B5, 1B4	R	18	9	27	2	4	1	0	0	1	3		0	.148	.185

Walt Lonergan 25 R 7-26, 1 Red Kleinow 31 R 3-14, Hy Gunning 22 L 1-9, 1 Tom Madden 28 R 3-15, Les Wilson 25 L 0-7,
Swede Carlstrom 24 R 1-6, Tony Tonneman 29 R 1-5, Tracey Baker 19 R 0-0, Joe Giannini 22 L 1-2

NAME	T	AGE	W	L	PCT	SV	G	GS	CG	IP	H	BB	SO	ShO	ERA
		26	78	75	.510	16	153	153	87	1364	1314	475	713	10	**2.73**
Smokey Joe Wood	R	21	23	17	.575	5	44	33	25	277	226	76	231	5	2.02
Larry Pape	R	28	11	8	.579	2	27	19	10	176	167	63	49	2	2.46
Ray Collins	L	24	11	12	.478	2	31	24	14	204	189	46	88	0	2.39
Eddie Cicotte	R	27	11	15	.423	0	35	25	16	221	236	73	106	1	2.81
Charley Hall	R	25	8	7	.533	5	32	10	6	147	149	72	83	0	3.74
Buck O'Brien	R	29	5	1	.833	0	6	5	5	48	30	21	31	2	0.38
Ed Karger	L	28	5	8	.385	1	25	18	6	131	134	42	57	0	3.37
Jack Killilay	R	24	3	2	.600	1	14	7	1	61	65	36	28	0	3.54
2 Judge Nagel	R	31	1	1	.500	0	5	1	0	27	27	6	12	0	3.33
1 Walter Moser	R	30	0	1	.000	0	6	3	1	25	37	11	11	0	3.96
Jack Bushelman	R	25	0	1	.000	0	3	1	1	12	8	10	5	0	3.00
Casey Hageman	R	24	0	2	.000	0	2	2	2	17	16	5	8	0	2.12
Marty McHale	R	22	0	0	.000	0	4	1	0	9	19	3	3	0	10.00
Blaine Thomas	R	23	0	0	.000	0	2	2	0	5	3	7	0	0	0.00
1 Charlie Smith	R	31	0	0	.000	0	1	1	0	2	2	1	0	0	9.00
1 Frank Smith	R	31	0	0	.000	0	1	1	0	2	6	3	1	0	18.00

NEW YORK 6th 76-76 .500 25.5 — HAL CHASE

NAME	G by POS	B	AGE	G	AB	R	H	2B	3B	HR	RBI	BB	SO	SB	BA	SA
TOTALS			27	153	5056	686	1375	190	**96**	25	577	493		270	.272	.362
Hal Chase	1B124, OF7, 2B2, SS1	R	28	133	527	82	166	32	7	3	62	21		36	.315	.419
Earl Gardner	2B101	R	26	102	357	36	94	13	2	0	39	20		14	.263	.311
Jack Knight	SS82, 1B27, 2B21, 3B1	R	25	132	470	69	126	16	7	3	62	42		18	.268	.351
Roy Hartzell	3B124, SS12, OF8	L	29	144	527	67	156	17	11	3	91	63		22	.296	.387
Harry Wolter	OF113, 1B2	L	26	122	434	78	132	17	15	4	36	62		28	.304	.440
Bert Daniels	OF120	R	28	131	462	74	132	16	9	2	31	48		40	.286	.372
Birdie Cree	OF137, SS4, 2B1	R	28	137	520	90	181	30	22	4	88	56		48	.348	.513
Walter Blair	C84, 1B1	R	27	85	222	18	43	9	2	0	26	16		2	.194	.252
Ed Sweeney	C83	R	22	83	229	17	53	6	5	0	18	14		8	.231	.301
Otie Johnson (AJ)	SS47, 2B15, 3B4	B	27	71	209	21	49	9	6	3	36	39		12	.234	.378
Charlie Hemphill (IL)	OF56	L	35	69	201	32	57	4	2	1	15	37		9	.284	.338
Bob Williams	C20	R	17	20	47	3	9	2	0	0	8	5		1	.191	.234
Cozy Dolan	3B19	R	28	19	69	19	21	1	2	0	6	8		12	.304	.377
Justin Fitzgerald	OF9	L	21	16	37	6	10	1	0	0	6	4		4	.270	.297
Stubby Magner	SS6, 2B5	R	23	13	33	3	7	0	0	0	4	4		1	.212	.212
Roxey Roach	SS8, 2B5	R	26	13	40	4	10	2	1	0	2	6		0	.250	.350
Ed Wilkinson	OF3, 2B1	R	21	10	13	2	3	0	0	0	1	0		0	.231	.231
Guy Zinn	OF8	L	24	9	27	5	4	0	2	0	1	4		0	.148	.296
Johnnie Priest	2B5, 3B2	R	20	7	21	2	3	0	0	0	2	2		3	.143	.143

Bill Bailey 29 L 1-9, Gene Elliott 23 L 1-13, Mike Handiboe 23 L 1-15, Harry Curry 18 R 2-11, Joe Walsh 23 2-9

NAME	T	AGE	W	L	PCT	SV	G	GS	CG	IP	H	BB	SO	ShO	ERA
		26	76	76	.500	9	153	153	91	1361	1404	406	667	5	3.54
Russ Ford	R	28	22	11	.667	1	37	33	26	281	251	76	158	0	2.28
Ray Caldwell	R	23	14	14	.500	3	41	27	19	255	240	79	145	1	3.35
Jack Warhop	R	26	12	13	.480	1	31	25	17	210	239	44	71	1	4.16
Ray Fisher	R	23	10	11	.476	1	29	22	8	172	178	55	99	3	3.24
Jack Quinn	R	27	7	10	.412	3	40	16	7	175	203	41	71	0	3.75
Hippo Vaughn (IL)	L	23	8	10	.444	0	26	18	11	146	158	54	74	0	4.37
Lew Brockett	R	30	3	4	.429	0	16	8	2	75	73	39	25	0	4.68
Harry Ables	L	26	0	1	.000	0	3	2	0	11	16	7	6	0	9.82
Andy Coakley	R	28	0	1	.000	0	2	1	1	12	20	2	4	0	5.25
Red Hoff	L	20	0	1	.000	0	5	1	0	21	21	7	10	0	2.14
Ed Klepfer	R	23	0	0	.000	0	2	0	0	4	5	2	4	0	6.75

WASHINGTON 7th 64-90 .416 38.5 — JIMMY McALEER

NAME	G by POS	B	AGE	G	AB	R	H	2B	3B	HR	RBI	BB	SO	SB	BA	SA
TOTALS			28	154	5062	624	1307	159	53	16	493	466		215	.258	.320
Germany Schaefer	1B108, OF7	R	34	125	440	74	147	14	7	0	45	57		22	.334	.398
Bill Cunningham	2B93	R	23	94	331	34	63	10	5	3	37	19		10	.190	.278
George McBride	SS154	R	30	154	557	58	131	11	4	0	59	52		15	.235	.269
Wid Conroy	3B85, OF15, 2B1	R	34	106	349	40	81	11	4	2	28	20		12	.232	.304
Doc Gessler	OF126, 1B1	L	30	128	450	65	127	19	5	4	78	74		29	.282	.373
Clyde Milan	OF154	L	25	154	**616**	109	194	24	8	3	35	74		58	.315	.394
Tilly Walker	OF94	R	23	98	356	44	99	6	4	2	39	15		12	.278	.334
Gabby Street	C71	R	28	72	216	16	48	7	1	0	14	14		4	.222	.264
Kid Elberfeld	2B66, 3B54	R	36	127	404	58	110	19	4	0	47	65		24	.272	.339
John Henry	C51, 1B30	R	21	85	261	24	53	5	0	0	21	25		8	.203	.222
Jack Lelivelt	OF49, 1B7	L	25	72	225	29	72	12	4	0	22	22		7	.320	.409
Eddie Ainsmith	C49	R	19	61	149	12	33	2	3	0	14	10		5	.221	.275
Dixie Walker	P32	R	24	34	66	6	20	2	0	0	5	3		0	.303	.333
Ray Morgan	3B25	R	22	25	89	11	19	2	0	0	5	4		2	.213	.236
Warren Miller	OF9			21	34	3	5	0	0	0	0	0		0	.147	.147
Tommy Long	OF13	R	21	14	48	1	11	3	0	0	5	1		4	.229	.292
Jock Somerlott	1B12	R	28	13	40	2	7	0	0	0	2	0		2	.175	.175
Bull Smith				1	0	0	0	0	0	0	0	0		0	.000	.000

NAME	T	AGE	W	L	PCT	SV	G	GS	CG	IP	H	BB	SO	ShO	ERA
		27	64	90	.416	6	154	154	106	1354	1471	410	628	13	3.52
Walter Johnson	R	23	25	13	.658	1	40	37	**36**	323	292	70	207	**6**	1.89
Bob Groom	R	26	13	17	.433	2	37	32	20	255	280	67	135	2	3.82
Long Tom Hughes	R	32	10	17	.370	2	34	27	17	223	251	77	86	2	3.47
Dixie Walker	R	24	8	14	.364	1	32	24	15	186	205	50	65	2	3.38
Charlie Becker	L	23	3	5	.375	0	11	5	5	71	80	23	31	1	4.06
Carl Cashion	R	20	2	3	.400	0	11	9	5	71	67	47	26	0	4.19
Dolly Gray	L	32	2	13	.133	0	28	15	6	121	160	40	42	0	5.06
Bill Otey	L	24	1	4	.200	0	12	2	0	50	68	15	16	0	6.30
Fred Sherry	R	22	0	4	.000	0	10	3	2	52	63	19	20	0	4.33

ST. LOUIS 8th 45-107 .296 56.5 — BOBBY WALLACE

NAME	G by POS	B	AGE	G	AB	R	H	2B	3B	HR	RBI	BB	SO	SB	BA	SA
TOTALS			27	152	5005	567	1192	187	63	17	473	460		125	.238	.311
John Black	1B54	R	21	54	186	13	28	4	0	0	7	10		4	.151	.172
Frank LaPorte	2B133, 3B3	R	31	136	507	71	159	37	12	2	82	34		4	.314	.446
Bobby Wallace	SS124, 2B1	R	37	125	410	35	95	12	2	0	31	46		8	.232	.271
Jimmy Austin	3B148	B	31	148	541	84	141	25	11	2	45	69		26	.261	.359
Al Schweitzer	OF68	R	28	76	237	31	51	11	4	0	34	43		12	.215	.295
Burt Shotton	OF139	L	26	139	572	85	146	11	8	0	36	51		26	.255	.302
2 Willie Hogan	OF117, 1B5	R	26	123	443	53	115	17	8	2	62	43		18	.260	.348
Nig Clarke	C73, 1B4	L	28	82	256	22	55	10	1	0	18	26		2	.215	.262
Jim Stephens	C66	R	27	70	212	11	49	5	5	0	17	17		1	.231	.302
2 Paul Meloan	OF54	L	22	64	206	30	54	11	2	3	14	15		7	.262	.379
Dode Criss	1B14, P4	L	26	58	83	10	21	3	1	2	15	11		0	.253	.386
Ed Hallinan	SS34, 2B15, 3B3	R	22	52	169	13	35	3	1	0	14	14		4	.207	.237
Jim Murray	OF25	R	33	31	102	8	19	5	0	3	11	5		0	.186	.324
Pete Compton	OF28	L	21	28	107	9	29	4	0	0	5	8		2	.271	.308
Paul Krichell	C25	R	28	28	82	6	19	3	0	0	8	4		2	.232	.268
Joe Kutina	1B26	R	26	26	101	12	26	6	2	3	15	2		2	.257	.446
Danny Hoffman	OF23	L	31	24	81	11	17	3	2	0	7	12		3	.210	.296
Pat Newman	1B20	R	30	20	62	11	12	4	0	0	5	12		4	.194	.258
Dave Rowan	1B18	L	28	18	65	7	25	1	1	0	11	4		0	.385	.431
1 Hap Myers	1B11	R	23	11	37	4	11	1	0	0	1	1		0	.297	.324
Gus Williams	OF7	L	23	9	26	1	7	3	0	0	0	0		0	.269	.385

Allie Moulton 25 R 1-15, Clyde Southwick 24 L 3-12, Al Clancy 22 R 0-5, Red Gust 23 R 0-12, Joe Crisp 21 R 1-1, Elmer Duggan 27 L 0-4, Frank Truesdale 25 B 0-0

NAME	T	AGE	W	L	PCT	SV	G	GS	CG	IP	H	BB	SO	ShO	ERA
		27	45	**107**	.296	3	152	152	92	1342	1465	463	383	7	3.83
Joe Lake	R	29	10	15	.400	0	30	25	14	215	245	40	69	2	3.30
Jack Powell	R	36	8	**19**	.296	1	31	27	18	208	224	44	52	1	3.29
Barney Pelty	R	30	7	15	.318	0	28	22	18	207	197	69	59	1	2.83
Earl Hamilton	L	19	5	12	.294	1	32	17	10	177	191	69	55	0	3.97
Roy Mitchell	R	26	4	8	.333	0	28	12	8	134	134	45	40	1	3.83
Red Nelson	R	25	3	9	.250	1	16	13	6	81	103	44	24	0	5.22
Lefty George	L	24	3	10	.231	0	27	13	6	116	136	51	23	1	4.19
Elmer Brown	R	28	2	1	.667	0	5	3	1	16	16	14	5	1	6.75
Mack Allison	R	24	2	1	.667	0	3	3	3	26	24	5	2	0	2.08
Ed Hawk	R	21	1	4	.200	0	5	4	4	38	38	8	14	0	3.31
Howie Gregory	R	24	0	1	.000	0	3	1	0	7	11	4	1	0	5.14
2 Walter Moser	R	30	0	2	.000	0	2	2	0	3	11	4	2	0	24.00
Dode Criss	R	26	0	2	.000	0	4	2	0	18	24	10	9	0	8.50
Curly Brown	L	22	0	2	.000	0	3	2	2	23	22	5	8	0	2.74
George Curry	R	22	0	3	.000	0	3	3	0	16	19	24	2	0	7.32
Bill Bailey	L	22	0	3	.000	0	7	2	2	32	42	16	8	0	4.50
Bill Harper	R	22	0	0	.000	0	2	0	0	8	9	4	6	0	6.75
Jeff Pfeffer	R	23	0	0	.000	0	2	0	0	10	11	4	4	0	7.20
1 Joe Willis	L	21	0	0	.000	0	1	1	0	7	8	3	0	0	5.14

NEW YORK 1st 99-54 .647 — JOHN McGRAW

NAME	G by POS	B	AGE	G	AB	R	H	2B	3B	HR	RBI	BB	SO	SB	BA	SA
TOTALS			26	154	5006	756	1399	225	103	41	651	530	506	347	.279	.390
Fred Merkle	1B148	R	22	149	541	80	153	24	10	12	84	43	60	49	.283	.431
Larry Doyle	2B141	L	24	143	526	102	163	25	25	13	77	71	39	38	.310	.527
1 Al Bridwell	SS76	L	27	76	263	28	71	10	1	0	31	33	10	8	.270	.316
Art Devlin	3B79, 1B6, 2B6, SS6	R	31	95	260	42	71	16	2	0	25	42	19	9	.273	.350
Red Murray	OF131	R	27	140	488	70	142	27	15	3	78	43	37	48	.291	.426
Fred Snodgrass	OF149, 1B1, 2B1	R	23	151	534	83	157	27	10	1	77	72	59	51	.294	.388
Josh Devore	OF149	L	23	149	565	96	158	19	10	3	50	81	69	61	.280	.365
Chief Meyers	C128	R	30	133	391	48	130	18	9	1	61	25	33	7	.332	.432
Art Fletcher	SS74, 3B21, 2B13	R	26	112	326	73	104	17	8	1	37	30	27	20	.319	.429
Beals Becker	OF55	L	24	88	172	28	45	11	1	1	20	26	22	19	.262	.355
2 Buck Herzog	3B65, 2B3, SS1	R	25	69	247	37	66	14	4	1	26	14	19	22	.267	.368
Art Wilson	C64	R	25	66	109	17	33	9	1	1	17	19	12	6	.303	.431
Doc Crandall	P41, SS6, 2B3	R	23	61	113	12	27	1	4	2	21	8	16	2	.239	.372
1 Mike Donlin	OF3	L	33	12	12	3	4	0	0	1	1	0	1	2	.333	.583
Grover Hartley	C10	R	22	11	18	1	4	2	0	0	1	1	1	1	.222	.333
Gene Paulette	1B7, SS1, 3B1	R	19	10	12	1	2	0	0	0	1	0	1	0	.167	.167
George Burns	OF6	R	21	6	17	2	1	0	0	0	0	1	0	0	.059	.059
1 Hank Gowdy	1B2	R	21	4	4	1	1	1	0	0	0	2	0	0	.250	.500
Admiral Schlei		R	33	1	1	0	0	0	0	0	0	0	1	0	.000	.000

NAME	T	AGE	W	L	PCT	SV	G	GS	CG	IP	H	BB	SO	ShO	ERA
		26	99	54	.647	13	154	154	95	1368	1267	369	771	18	2.69
Christy Mathewson	R	32	26	13	.667	3	45	37	29	307	303	38	141	5	1.99
Rube Marquard	L	21	24	7	.774	3	45	33	22	278	221	106	237	5	2.49
Doc Crandall	R	23	15	5	.750	5	41	15	9	199	199	51	94	2	2.63
Hooks Wiltse	L	30	12	9	.571	0	30	24	11	187	177	39	92	4	3.28
Red Ames	R	28	11	10	.524	2	34	23	13	205	170	54	118	1	2.68
Bugs Raymond	R	29	6	4	.600	0	17	9	4	82	73	33	39	1	3.30
Louis Drucke	R	22	4	4	.500	0	15	10	4	76	83	41	42	0	4.02
Bert Maxwell	R	24	1	2	.333	0	4	3	3	31	37	7	8	0	2.90
Charlie Faust		30	0	0	.000	0	2	0	0	2	2	0	0	0	4.50
Dick Rudolph	R	23	0	0	.000	0	1	0	0	2	2	0	0	0	9.00

CHICAGO 2nd 92-62 .597 7.5 — FRANK CHANCE

NAME	G by POS	B	AGE	G	AB	R	H	2B	3B	HR	RBI	BB	SO	SB	BA	SA
TOTALS			27	157	5130	757	1335	218	101	54	626	585	617	214	.260	.374
Vic Saier	1B73	L	20	86	259	42	67	15	1	1	37	25	37	11	.259	.336
Heinie Zimmerman	2B108, 3B20, 1B11	R	24	143	535	80	164	22	17	9	85	25	50	23	.307	.462
Joe Tinker	SS143	R	30	144	536	61	149	24	12	4	69	39	31	30	.278	.390
Jim Doyle	3B127	R	29	130	472	69	133	23	12	5	62	40	54	19	.282	.413
Wildfire Schulte	OF154	L	28	154	577	105	173	30	21	21	107	76	68	23	.300	.534
Solly Hofman	OF107, 1B36	R	28	143	512	66	129	17	2	2	70	66	40	30	.252	.305
Jimmy Sheckard	OF156	L	32	156	539	121	149	26	11	4	50	147	58	32	.276	.388
Jimmy Archer	C102, 1B10, 2B1	R	28	116	387	41	98	18	5	4	41	18	43	5	.253	.357
2 Wilbur Good	OF40	L	25	58	145	27	39	5	4	2	21	11	17	10	.269	.400
Dave Shean	2B23, SS19, 3B1	R	33	54	145	17	28	4	0	0	15	8	15	4	.193	.221
Johnny Evers (IL)	2B33, 3B11	L	29	46	155	29	35	4	3	0	7	34	10	6	.226	.290
2 Peaches Graham	C28	R	34	36	71	6	17	3	0	0	8	11	8	2	.239	.282
Frank Chance (NJ)	1B29	R	33	31	87	23	21	6	3	1	17	25	13	9	.241	.414
1 Al Kaiser	OF23	R	24	27	84	16	21	0	5	0	7	7	12	6	.250	.369
1 Johnny Kling	C25	R	36	27	80	8	14	3	2	1	5	8	14	1	.175	.300
Tom Needham	C23	R	32	27	62	4	12	2	0	0	5	9	14	2	.194	.226
2 Bill Collins	OF4	B	29	7	5	2	1	1	0	0	0	1	3	0	.200	.400
2 Kitty Bransfield	1B3	R	36	3	10	0	4	2	0	0	0	2	2	0	.400	.600
Orvie Overall (VR) 30																

NAME	T	AGE	W	L	PCT	SV	G	GS	CG	IP	H	BB	SO	ShO	ERA
		28	92	62	.597	16	157	157	85	1411	1270	525	582	11	2.90
Three Finger Brown	R	34	21	11	.656	13	53	27	21	270	267	55	129	0	2.80
King Cole	R	25	18	7	.720	0	32	27	13	221	188	99	101	2	3.13
Ed Reulbach	R	28	16	9	.640	0	33	29	15	222	191	103	79	2	2.96
Lew Richie	R	27	15	11	.577	1	36	28	18	253	213	103	78	4	2.31
Harry McIntire	R	33	11	7	.611	0	25	17	9	149	147	33	56	1	4.11
2 Charlie Smith	R	31	3	2	.600	0	7	5	3	38	31	7	11	1	1.42
1 Orlie Weaver	R	23	3	2	.600	0	6	4	1	44	29	17	20	1	2.04
Larry Cheney	R	25	1	0	1.000	0	3	1	0	10	8	3	11	0	0.00
Fred Toney	R	23	1	1	.500	0	18	4	1	67	55	35	27	0	2.42
Bill Foxen	L	27	1	1	.500	0	3	1	0	13	12	12	6	0	2.08
Reggie Richter	R	24	1	3	.250	2	22	5	0	55	62	20	34	0	3.11
2 Cliff Curtis	R	28	1	2	.333	0	4	1	0	7	7	5	4	0	3.86
Cy Slapnicka	R	25	0	2	.000	0	3	2	1	24	21	7	10	0	3.38
Jack Pfiester	L	33	0	4	.000	0	6	5	3	34	34	18	15	0	3.97
1 Hank Griffin	R	25	0	0	.000	0	1	1	0	1	1	3	1	0	18.00
Ernie Ovitz	R	25	0	0	.000	0	1	0	0	2	3	3	0	0	4.50
2 Jack Rowan	R	24	0	0	.000	0	1	0	0	2	1	2	0	0	4.50

PITTSBURGH 3rd 85-69 .552 14.5 — FRED CLARKE

NAME	G by POS	B	AGE	G	AB	R	H	2B	3B	HR	RBI	BB	SO	SB	BA	SA
TOTALS			29	155	5137	744	1345	206	106	48	633	525	583	160	.262	.371
Newt Hunter	1B61	R	31	65	209	35	53	10	6	2	24	25	43	9	.254	.388
Dots Miller	2B129	R	24	137	470	82	126	17	8	6	78	51	48	17	.268	.377
Honus Wagner	SS101, 1B28, OF1	R	37	130	473	87	158	23	16	9	89	67	34	20	.334	.507
Bobby Byrne	3B152	R	26	153	598	96	155	24	17	2	52	67	41	23	.259	.366
Owen Wilson	OF146	L	27	148	544	72	163	34	12	12	107	41	55	10	.300	.472
Max Carey	OF122	B	21	129	427	77	110	15	10	5	43	44	75	27	.258	.375
Fred Clarke	OF101	L	38	110	392	73	127	25	13	5	49	53	27	10	.324	.492
George Gibson	C98	R	30	100	311	32	65	12	2	0	19	29	16	3	.209	.260
Tommy Leach	OF89, SS13, 3B1	R	33	108	386	60	92	12	6	3	43	46	50	19	.238	.324
Bill McKechnie	1B57, 2B17, SS12, 3B6	B	24	104	321	40	73	8	7	2	37	28	18	9	.227	.315
Mike Simon	C68	R	28	71	215	19	49	4	3	0	22	10	14	1	.228	.274
Alex McCarthy	SS33, 2B11, 3B1, OF1	R	23	50	150	18	36	5	1	2	31	14	24	4	.240	.327
Vin Campbell	OF21	L	23	42	93	12	29	3	1	0	10	8	7	6	.312	.366
Jack Flynn	1B13, OF1	R	27	33	59	5	12	0	1	0	3	9	8	0	.203	.237
Brown Keene	1B1	R	20	6	7	0	0	0	0	0	0	1	4	0	.000	.000
Billy Kelly	C1	R	25	6	8	0	1	0	0	0	0	0	2	0	.125	.125
Jerry Dorsey	OF1		26	2	6	0	0	0	0	0	0	0	1	0	.000	.000
Mickey Keliher	1B2	L	21	2	7	0	0	0	0	0	0	0	5	0	.000	.000
John Shovlin		R	20	2	1	1	0	0	0	0	0	0	1	0	.000	.000

NAME	T	AGE	W	L	PCT	SV	G	GS	CG	IP	H	BB	SO	ShO	ERA
		26	85	69	.552	11	155	155	91	1380	1249	375	605	13	2.84
Babe Adams	R	29	22	12	.647	0	40	37	24	293	253	42	133	6	2.34
Howie Camnitz	R	29	20	15	.571	1	40	33	18	268	245	84	139	1	3.14
Lefty Leifield	L	27	16	16	.500	1	42	37	26	318	301	82	111	2	2.63
1 Elmer Steele	R	27	9	9	.500	2	31	16	7	166	153	31	52	2	2.60
Jack Ferry	R	24	6	4	.600	3	26	8	4	86	83	27	32	1	3.11
1 Judge Nagle	R	31	4	2	.667	1	8	3	1	27	33	6	11	0	3.66
Claude Hendrix	R	22	4	6	.400	1	22	12	6	119	85	53	57	1	2.73
Marty O'Toole (SA)	R	23	3	2	.600	0	5	5	3	38	28	20	34	0	2.37
Harry Gardner	R	22	1	1	.500	2	13	3	2	42	39	20	24	0	4.50
Hank Robinson	L	21	0	1	.000	0	5	0	0	13	13	5	8	0	2.77
Kirby White	R	27	0	1	.000	0	2	1	0	3	3	1	1	0	9.00
Deacon Phillippe	R	39	0	0	.000	0	3	0	0	6	5	2	3	0	7.50
Dick Cottrell	L	22	0	0	.000	0	1	0	0	1	4	1	0	0	9.00
Sherry Smith	L	20	0	0	.000	0	1	0	0	1	4	1	0	0	36.00

PHILADELPHIA 4th 79-73 .520 19.5 — RED DOOIN

NAME	G by POS	B	AGE	G	AB	R	H	2B	3B	HR	RBI	BB	SO	SB	BA	SA
TOTALS			28	153	5044	658	1307	214	56	60	564	490	588	153	.259	.359
Fred Luderus	1B146	L	25	146	551	69	166	24	11	16	99	40	76	6	.301	.472
Otto Knabe	2B142	R	27	142	528	99	125	15	6	1	42	94	35	23	.237	.294
Mickey Doolan	SS145	R	31	146	512	51	122	23	6	1	49	44	65	14	.238	.313
Hans Lobert	3B147	R	29	147	541	94	154	20	9	9	72	66	31	40	.285	.405
John Titus (BL)	OF60	L	35	76	236	35	67	14	1	8	26	32	16	3	.284	.453
Dode Paskert	OF153	R	29	153	560	96	153	18	5	4	47	70	70	28	.273	.345
Sherry Magee (SJ)	OF120	R	26	121	445	79	128	32	5	15	94	49	33	22	.288	.483
Red Dooin (BL)	C74	R	32	74	247	18	81	15	1	1	16	14	12	6	.328	.409
J. Walsh	OF48, 2B14, SS9, 3B7, C4, 1B1	R	25	94	289	29	78	20	3	1	31	21	30	5	.270	.370
2 Fred Beck	OF61	L	24	66	210	26	59	8	3	3	25	17	21	3	.281	.390
Pat Moran	C32	R	35	34	103	2	19	3	0	0	8	3	13	0	.184	.214
2 Tom Madden (RJ)	C22	R	28	28	76	4	21	1	1	0	4	0	13	0	.276	.316
Harry Welchonce	OF17	L	27	26	66	9	14	4	0	0	6	7	8	0	.212	.273
1 Kitty Bransfield	1B8	R	36	23	43	4	11	1	1	0	3	0	5	1	.256	.326
Clarence Lehr	OF5, 2B4, SS4	R	25	23	27	2	4	0	0	0	2	0	7	0	.148	.148
Roy Thomas	OF11	L	37	21	30	5	5	2	0	0	2	8	6	0	.167	.233
Dick Cotter	C17	R	20	20	46	2	13	0	0	0	5	5	7	1	.283	.283
Tubby Spencer	C11	R	27	11	32	2	5	1	0	1	3	3	7	0	.156	.281
Bill Killefer	C6	R	23	6	16	3	3	0	0	0	2	0	2	0	.188	.188
Paddy Mayes	OF2	L	26	5	5	1	0	0	0	0	0	1	2	0	.000	.000
2 Red Kleinow	C4	R	31	4	8	0	1	0	0	0	0	0	1	0	.250	.250
Hughie Miller		R	23	1	0	0	0	0	0	0	0	0	0	0	.000	.000
John Quinn	C1	R	25	1	2	0	0	0	0	0	0	0	0	0	.000	.000

NAME	T	AGE	W	L	PCT	SV	G	GS	CG	IP	H	BB	SO	ShO	ERA
		27	79	73	.520	10	153	153	90	1373	1285	598	697	20	3.30
Pete Alexander	R	24	28	13	.683	3	48	37	31	367	285	129	227	7	2.57
Earl Moore	R	31	15	19	.441	1	42	36	21	308	265	164	174	5	2.63
George Chalmers	R	23	13	10	.565	4	38	22	11	209	196	101	101	3	3.10
Eddie Stack	R	23	5	5	.500	0	13	10	5	78	67	41	36	1	3.57
2 Bill Burns	L	31	4	7	.364	1	21	14	8	121	132	26	47	3	3.42
Ad Brennan	L	29	3	1	.750	0	5	3	1	23	22	12	12	0	3.52
1 Bert Humphries	R	30	3	1	.750	1	11	5	2	41	56	10	13	0	4.17
Fred Beebe	R	30	3	4	.429	0	9	8	3	48	52	24	20	0	4.50
1 Jack Rowan	R	24	3	4	.429	0	12	6	2	45	59	20	17	0	4.70
3 Cliff Curtis	R	28	2	1	.667	0	8	5	3	45	45	15	13	1	2.60
Bert Hall	R	22	0	1	.000	0	7	1	0	18	19	13	8	0	4.00
Buck Stanley	L	21	0	1	.000	0	4	0	0	11	14	9	5	0	6.54
Bob Ewing	R	38	0	2	.000	0	4	3	1	24	29	14	12	0	7.88
Toots Shultz	R	22	0	3	.000	0	5	3	2	25	30	15	9	0	9.36
Jake Smith			0	0	.000	0	2	0	0	5	3	2	1	0	0.00
Troy Puckett	R	21	0	0	.000	0	1	0	0	2	4	2	1	0	13.50
Jimmy Walsh	R	25	0	1	.000	0	1	0	0	3	7	1	1	0	12.00

ST. LOUIS 5th 75-74 .503 22 — ROGER BRESNAHAN

NAME	G by POS	B	AGE	G	AB	R	H	2B	3B	HR	RBI	BB	SO	SB	BA	SA
TOTALS			26	158	5132	671	1295	199	85	27	567	592	650	175	.252	.340
Ed Konetchy	1B158	R	25	158	571	90	165	38	13	6	88	81	63	27	.289	.433
Miller Huggins	2B136	B	32	138	509	106	133	19	2	1	24	96	52	37	.261	.312
Arnold Hauser	SS134, 3B2	R	22	136	515	61	124	11	8	3	46	26	67	24	.241	.311
Mike Mowrey	3B134, SS1	R	27	137	471	59	126	29	7	0	61	59	46	15	.268	.359
Steve Evans	OF150	L	26	154	547	74	161	24	13	5	71	46	52	13	.294	.413
Rebel Oakes	OF151	L	24	154	551	69	145	13	6	2	59	41	35	25	.263	.319
Rube Ellis	OF148	L	25	155	555	69	139	20	10	3	66	66	64	9	.250	.339
Jack Bliss	C84, SS1	R	29	97	258	36	59	6	4	1	27	42	25	5	.229	.295
Roger Bresnahan	C77, 2B2	R	32	81	227	22	63	17	8	3	41	45	19	4	.278	.463
Wally Smith	3B26, SS25, 2B8, OF1	R	22	81	194	23	42	6	5	2	19	21	33	5	.216	.330
Otto McIver	OF17	B	26	30	62	11	14	2	1	1	9	9	14	0	.226	.339
Denny Wilie	OF15	L	20	28	51	10	12	3	1	0	3	8	11	3	.235	.333
Lee Magee	2B18, SS3	B	22	26	69	9	18	1	1	0	8	8	8	4	.261	.304
Ivy Wingo	C18	L	20	25	57	4	12	2	0	0	3	3	7	0	.211	.246
Jim Clark	OF8	R	23	14	18	2	3	0	1	0	3	3	4	2	.167	.278
Hap Morse	SS2, OF1	R	24	8	4	0	0	0	0	0	0	1	2	0	.000	.000
Dan McGeehan	2B3	R	26	3	9	0	2	0	0	0	1	0	1	0	.222	.222
Ed Conwell	3B1	R	21	1	1	0	0	0	0	0	0	0	1	0	.000	.000
Frank Gilhooley	OF1	L	19	1	0	0	0	0	0	0	0	0	0	0	.000	.000
Milt Reed		L	20	1	1	0	0	0	0	0	0	0	0	0	.000	.000

NAME	T	AGE	W	L	PCT	SV	G	GS	CG	IP	H	BB	SO	ShO	ERA
		24	75	74	.503	10	158	158	88	1402	1296	701	561	6	3.68
Bob Harmon	R	23	23	16	.590	4	51	41	28	348	290	181	144	2	3.13
Bill Steele	R	25	18	19	.486	3	43	34	23	287	287	113	115	1	3.74
Slim Sallee	L	26	15	9	.625	3	36	30	18	245	234	64	74	1	2.76
Rube Geyer	R	26	9	6	.600	0	29	11	7	149	141	56	46	1	3.26
Roy Golden	R	22	4	9	.308	0	30	25	6	149	127	129	81	0	5.01
Lou Lowdermilk	L	24	3	4	.429	0	16	3	3	65	72	29	20	0	3.46
Ed Zmich	L	26	1	0	1.000	0	4	0	0	13	8	8	4	0	2.08
Harry Camnitz	R	26	1	0	1.000	0	2	0	0	2	0	1	2	0	0.00
Gene Woodburn	R	24	1	5	.167	0	11	6	1	38	22	40	23	0	5.45
Grover Lowdermilk	R	26	0	1	.000	0	11	2	1	33	37	33	15	1	7.36
2 Joe Willis	L	21	0	1	.000	0	2	2	1	15	13	4	5	0	4.20
George Zachert	L	26	0	2	.000	0	4	1	0	7	17	6	6	0	11.57
Gene Dale	R	22	0	2	.000	0	5	2	0	15	13	16	13	0	6.60
Jack McAdams	R	24	0	0	.000	0	6	0	0	10	7	5	4	0	3.60
Jack Reis	R	21	0	0	.000	0	3	0	0	9	5	8	4	0	1.00
Bunny Hearn	L	20	0	0	.000	0	2	0	0	3	7	0	1	0	12.00
Roy Radebough	R	27	0	0	.000	0	2	1	0	10	6	4	1	0	2.70
Pete Standridge	R	20	0	0	.000	0	2	0	0	5	10	4	3	0	9.00

CINCINNATI 6th 70-83 .458 29 — CLARK GRIFFITH

NAME	G by POS	B	AGE	G	AB	R	H	2B	3B	HR	RBI	BB	SO	SB	BA	SA
TOTALS			26	159	5291	682	1379	180	105	21	595	578	594	289	.261	.346
Dick Hoblitzell	1B158	L	22	158	**622**	81	180	19	13	11	91	42	44	32	.289	.415
Dick Egan	2B152	R	27	153	558	80	139	11	5	1	56	59	50	37	.249	.292
Tom Downey	SS93, 2B6, 3B5, 1B2, OF1	R	27	111	360	50	94	16	7	0	36	44	38	10	.261	.344
Eddie Grant	3B122, SS11	L	28	136	458	49	102	12	7	1	53	51	47	28	.223	.286
Mike Mitchell	OF140	R	31	142	529	74	154	22	22	2	84	44	34	35	.291	.427
Johnny Bates	OF147	R	29	148	518	89	151	24	13	1	61	103	59	33	.292	.394
Bob Bescher	OF153	B	27	153	599	106	165	32	10	1	45	102	**78**	**80**	.275	.367
Larry McLean	C98	R	29	107	328	24	94	7	2	0	34	20	18	1	.287	.320
Tommy Clarke (XJ)	C81, 1B1	R	23	86	203	20	49	6	7	1	25	25	22	4	.241	.355
Jimmy Esmond	SS44, 3B14, 2B2	R	21	73	198	27	54	4	6	1	11	17	30	7	.273	.369
Armando Marsans	OF34, 1B1, 3B1	R	24	58	138	17	36	2	2	0	11	15	11	11	.261	.304
1 Fred Beck	OF16, 1B6	L	24	41	87	7	16	1	2	2	20	1	13	2	.184	.310
Dave Altizer	SS23, 1B1, 2B1, OF1	L	34	37	75	8	17	4	1	0	4	9	5	2	.227	.307
Hank Severeid	C22	R	20	37	56	5	17	6	1	0	10	3	6	0	.304	.446
Rafael Almeida	3B27, 2B1, SS1	R	23	36	96	9	30	5	1	0	15	9	16	3	.313	.385
Mike Balenti	SS2, OF1	R	24	8	8	2	2	0	0	0	0	0	1	3	.250	.250
Danny Mahoney		R	22	1	0	0	0	0	0	0	0	0	0	0	.000	.000
1 Hub Northen		L	25	1	0	0	0	0	0	0	0	0	0	0	.000	.000

NAME	T	AGE	W	L	PCT	SV	G	GS	CG	IP	H	BB	SO	ShO	ERA
		28	70	83	.458	12	159	159	77	**1425**	1410	476	557	4	3.26
George Suggs	R	29	15	13	.536	0	36	29	17	261	258	79	91	1	3.00
Bob Keefe	R	29	12	13	.480	3	39	26	15	234	196	76	105	0	2.69
Art Fromme	R	27	10	11	.476	0	38	26	11	208	190	79	107	1	3.46
2 Frank Smith	R	31	10	14	.417	1	34	18	10	176	198	55	67	0	3.99
Harry Gaspar	R	**28**	10	17	.370	4	44	32	11	254	272	69	76	2	3.29
2 Bert Humphries	R	30	4	3	.571	0	14	7	3	65	62	18	16	0	2.35
Ray Boyd	R	24	3	2	.600	1	7	4	3	44	34	19	20	0	2.66
Rube Benton	L	24	3	3	.500	0	6	6	5	46	44	23	28	0	2.00
George McQuillan	R	26	2	6	.250	0	19	5	2	77	92	31	28	0	4.68
1 Bill Burns	L	31	1	0	1.000	1	6	3	0	18	17	3	5	0	3.00
Jack Compton	R	29	0	1	.000	1	8	3	0	25	19	15	6	0	3.96
Barney Schreiber	L	29	0	0	.000	1	3	0	0	10	19	2	5	0	5.40
Herb Juul	L	25	0	0	.000	0	1	0	0	4	3	4	2	0	4.50
Jesse Tannehill	L	36	0	0	.000	0	1	0	0	4	6	3	1	0	6.75

BROOKLYN 7th 64-86 .427 33.5 — BILL DAHLEN

NAME	G by POS	B	AGE	G	AB	R	H	2B	3B	HR	RBI	BB	SO	SB	BA	SA
TOTALS			27	154	5059	539	1198	151	71	28	465	425	**683**	184	.237	.311
Jake Daubert	1B149	L	27	149	573	89	176	17	8	5	45	51	56	32	.307	.391
John Hummel	2B127, 1B4, SS2	R	28	137	477	54	129	21	11	5	58	67	66	16	.270	.392
Bert Tooley	SS114	R	24	119	433	55	89	11	3	1	29	53	63	18	.206	.252
Eddie Zimmerman	3B122	R	28	122	417	31	77	10	7	3	36	34	37	9	.185	.264
Bob Coulson	OF145	R	24	146	521	52	122	23	7	0	50	42	**78**	32	.234	.305
Bill Davidson	OF74	R	24	87	292	33	68	3	4	1	26	16	21	18	.233	.281
Zack Wheat	OF136	L	25	140	534	55	153	26	13	5	76	29	58	21	.287	.412
Bill Bergen	C84	R	38	84	227	8	30	3	1	0	10	14	42	2	.132	.154
Tex Erwin	C74	L	25	91	218	30	59	13	2	7	34	31	23	5	.271	.445
Dolly Stark	SS34, 2B18, 3B3	R	26	70	193	25	57	4	1	0	19	20	24	6	.295	.326
Cy Barger	P30, OF11, 1B1	R	26	57	145	16	33	1	1	0	9	5	20	2	.228	.248
Al Burch	OF43, 2B3	L	27	54	167	18	38	2	3	0	7	15	22	3	.228	.275
Red Smith	3B28	R	21	28	111	10	29	6	1	0	19	5	13	5	.261	.333
Otto Miller	C22	R	22	25	62	7	13	2	2	0	8	0	4	2	.210	.306
Jud Daley	OF16	L	27	19	65	8	15	2	1	0	7	2	8	2	.231	.292
2 Hub Northen	OF19	L	25	19	76	16	24	2	2	0	1	14	9	4	.316	.395
Pryor McElveen	2B5, SS1	R	27	16	31	1	6	0	0	0	5	0	3	0	.194	.194
Hy Myers	OF13	R	22	13	43	2	7	1	0	0	0	2	3	1	.163	.186
Tony Smith	SS10, 2B3	R	27	13	40	3	6	1	0	0	2	8	7	1	.150	.175

George Browne 35 L 4-12, Al Humphrey 25 L 5-27, Larry LeJeune 25 R 3-19, Bob Higgins 24 R 3-10, Bill Dahlen 41 R 0-3

NAME	T	AGE	W	L	PCT	SV	G	GS	CG	IP	H	BB	SO	ShO	ERA
		27	64	86	.427	10	154	154	81	1372	1310	566	533	14	3.39
Nap Rucker	L	26	22	18	.550	4	48	33	23	316	255	110	190	5	2.72
Elmer Knetzer	R	25	11	12	.430	0	35	20	11	204	202	93	66	3	3.49
Cy Barger	R	26	11	15	.423	0	30	30	21	217	224	71	60	1	3.53
George Bell	R	36	5	6	.455	0	19	12	6	101	123	28	28	2	4.28
Bill Schardt	R	25	5	15	.250	4	39	22	10	195	190	91	77	1	3.60
Pat Ragan	R	22	4	3	.571	1	22	7	5	94	81	31	39	2	2.11
Doc Scanlan	R	30	3	10	.231	1	22	15	3	114	101	69	45	0	3.64
Eddie Dent	R	23	2	1	.667	0	5	3	1	32	30	10	3	0	3.65
Sandy Burk	R	24	1	3	.250	0	13	7	1	58	54	47	15	0	5.12
Walt Miller	R	26	0	1	.000	0	3	2	0	11	16	6	0	0	6.55
Jack Ryan	R	26	0	1	.000	0	3	1	0	6	9	4	1	0	3.00
Raleigh Aitchison	L	23	0	1	.000	0	1	0	0	1	1	1	0	0	0.00
2 Elmer Steele	R	27	0	0	.000	0	5	2	0	23	24	5	9	0	3.13

BOSTON 8th 44-107 .291 54 — FRED TENNEY

NAME	G by POS	B	AGE	G	AB	R	H	2B	3B	HR	RBI	BB	SO	SB	BA	SA
TOTALS			28	156	**5308**	699	**1417**	**249**	54	37	594	554	577	169	.267	.355
Fred Tenney	1B93, OF2	L	39	102	369	52	97	13	4	1	36	50	17	5	.263	.328
Bill Sweeney	2B136	R	25	137	523	92	164	33	6	3	63	77	26	33	.314	.417
1 Buck Herzog	SS74, 3B4	R	25	79	294	53	91	19	5	5	41	33	21	26	.310	.459
S. Ingerton	3B58, OF43, 1B17, 2B11, SS4	R	25	136	521	63	130	24	4	5	61	39	68	6	.250	.340
Doc Miller	OF146	L	28	146	577	69	**192**	36	3	7	91	43	43	32	.333	.442
2 Mike Donlin	OF56	L	33	56	222	33	70	16	1	2	34	22	17	7	.315	.423
2 Al Kaiser	OF58	R	24	65	197	20	40	5	2	2	15	10	26	4	.203	.279
2 Johnny Kling	C71, 3B1	R	36	75	241	32	54	8	1	2	24	30	29	0	.224	.290
Bill Rariden	C65, 3B3, 2B1	R	23	70	246	22	56	9	0	0	21	21	18	3	.228	.264
Jack Spratt	SS26, 2B5, 3B4, OF4	L	22	62	154	22	37	4	4	2	13	13	25	1	.240	.357
Ed McDonald	3B53, SS1	R	24	54	175	28	36	7	3	1	21	40	39	11	.206	.297
2 Al Bridwell	SS51	L	27	51	182	29	53	5	0	0	10	33	8	2	.291	.319
1 Wilbur Good	OF43	L	25	43	165	21	44	9	3	0	15	12	22	3	.267	.358
George Jackson	OF39	R	29	39	147	28	51	11	2	0	25	12	21	12	.347	.449
Patsy Flaherty	OF19, P4	L	35	38	94	9	27	3	2	2	20	8	11	2	.287	.426
1 Peaches Graham	C26	R	34	33	88	7	24	6	1	0	12	14	5	2	.273	.364
Josh Clarke	OF30	L	32	32	120	16	28	7	3	1	4	29	22	6	.233	.367
2 Hank Gowdy	1B26, C1	R	21	29	97	9	28	4	2	0	16	4	19	2	.289	.371
Art Butler	3B14, 2B4, SS1	R	23	27	68	11	12	2	0	0	2	6	6	0	.176	.206
Bill Jones	OF18	L	24	24	51	6	11	2	1	0	3	15	7	1	.216	.294
Ben Houser	1B20	L	27	20	71	11	18	1	0	1	9	8	6	2	.254	.310
Jay Kirke	OF14, 1B3, 2B1, SS1, 3B1	L	23	20	89	9	32	5	5	0	12	2	6	3	.360	.528

Harry Steinfeldt (BG) 33 R 16-63, 1 Bill Collins 29 B 6-44, Herman Young 25 R 6-25, Bert Weeden 28 L 0-1

NAME	T	AGE	W	L	PCT	SV	G	GS	CG	IP	H	BB	SO	ShO	ERA
		26	44	**107**	.291	7	156	156	73	1374	**1570**	672	486	5	5.08
Buster Brown	R	29	8	18	.309	2	42	25	13	241	258	116	76	0	4.29
Big Jeff Pfeffer	R	29	7	5	.583	2	26	6	4	97	116	57	24	1	4.73
Lefty Tyler	L	21	7	10	.412	0	28	20	10	165	150	109	90	1	5.08
Hub Perdue (AJ)	R	29	6	10	.375	1	24	19	9	137	180	41	40	0	5.00
2 Cy Young	R	44	4	5	.444	0	11	11	8	80	83	15	35	2	3.71
Al Mattern	R	28	4	15	.211	0	33	21	11	186	228	63	51	0	4.99
Ed Donnelly	R	30	3	2	.600	0	5	4	4	37	33	9	16	1	2.43
2 Orlie Weaver	R	23	3	12	.200	0	27	17	4	121	140	84	50	0	6.47
Cecil Ferguson	R	24	1	3	.250	0	6	3	0	24	40	12	4	0	9.75
1 Cliff Curtis	R	28	1	8	.111	1	12	9	5	77	79	34	23	0	4.44
Jiggs Parson	R	25	0	1	.000	0	7	0	0	25	36	15	7	0	6.48
Sammy Frock	R	27	0	1	.000	0	4	1	1	16	29	5	8	0	5.63
Billy Burke	L	21	0	1	.000	0	2	1	0	3	6	5	1	0	21.00
Patsy Flaherty	L	35	0	2	.000	0	4	2	1	14	21	8	0	0	7.07
Brad Hogg	R	23	0	3	.000	1	8	3	2	26	33	14	8	0	6.58
Bill McTigue	L	20	0	5	.000	0	14	8	0	37	37	49	23	0	7.05
2 Hank Griffin	R	25	0	6	.000	0	15	6	1	83	96	34	30	0	5.20
Fuller Thompson	R	22	0	0	.000	0	3	0	0	5	5	2	0	0	3.60

WORLD SERIES – PHILADELPHIA (AL) 4 NEW YORK (NL) 2

LINE SCORES

TEAM	1	2	3	4	5	6	7	8	9	10	11	12	R	H	E
Game 1 October 14 at New York															
PHI (AL)	0	1	0	0	0	0	0	0	0				1	6	2
NY (NL)	0	0	0	1	0	0	1	0	X				2	5	0
Bender / **Mathewson**															
Game 2 October 16 at Philadelphia															
NY	0	1	0	0	0	0	0	0	0				1	5	3
PHI	1	0	0	0	0	2	0	0	X				3	4	0
Marquard, Crandall (8) / **Plank**															
Game 3 October 17 at New York															
PHI	0	0	0	0	0	0	0	0	1	0	2		3	9	2
NY	0	0	1	0	0	0	0	0	0	0	1		2	3	5
Coombs / Mathewson															
Game 4 October 24 at Philadelphia															
NY	2	0	0	0	0	0	0	0	0				2	7	3
PHI	0	0	0	3	1	0	0	0	X				4	11	1
Mathewson, Wiltse (8) / **Bender**															
Game 5 October 25 at New York															
PHI	0	0	3	0	0	0	0	0	0	0			3	7	1
NY	0	0	0	0	0	0	1	0	2	1			4	9	2
Coombs, **Plank** (10) / Marquard, Ames (4), **Crandall** (8)															
Game 6 October 26 at Philadelphia															
NY	1	0	0	0	0	0	0	0	1				2	4	3
PHI	0	0	1	4	0	1	7	0	X				13	13	5
Ames, Wiltse (5), Marquard (7) / **Bender**															

COMPOSITE BATTING

NAME	POS	G	AB	R	H	2B	3B	HR	RBI	BA
Philadelphia (AL) Totals		6	205	27	50	15	0	3	21	.244
Lord	OF	6	**27**	2	5	2	0	0	1	.185
Oldring	OF	6	25	2	5	2	0	1	3	.200
Baker	3B	6	24	**7**	**9**	2	0	**2**	**5**	**.375**
Davis	1B	6	24	3	5	1	0	0	**5**	.208
Murphy	OF	6	23	4	7	3	0	0	3	.304
Collins	2B	6	21	4	6	1	0	0	1	.286
Barry	SS	6	19	2	7	**4**	0	0	2	.368
Thomas	C	4	12	1	1	0	0	0	1	.083
Bender	P	3	11	0	1	0	0	0	0	.091
Coombs	P	2	8	1	2	0	0	0	0	.250
Lapp	C	2	8	1	2	0	0	0	0	.250
Plank	P	2	3	0	0	0	0	0	0	.000
McInnis	1B	1	0	0	0	0	0	0	0	.000
Strunk	PH	1	0	0	0	0	0	0	0	.000
New York (NL) Totals		6	189	13	33	11	1	0	10	.175
Devore	OF	6	24	1	4	1	0	0	3	.167
Doyle	2B	6	23	3	7	3	1	0	1	.304
Fletcher	SS	6	23	1	3	1	0	0	1	.130
Herzog	3B	6	21	3	4	2	0	0	0	.190
Murray	OF	6	21	0	0	0	0	0	0	.000
Meyers	C	6	20	2	6	2	0	0	2	.300
Merkle	1B	6	20	1	3	1	0	0	1	.150
Snodgrass	OF	6	19	1	2	0	0	0	1	.105
Mathewson	P	3	7	0	2	0	0	0	0	.286
Becker	PH	3	3	0	0	0	0	0	0	.000
Crandall	P	3	2	1	1	1	0	0	1	.500
Ames	P	2	2	0	1	0	0	0	0	.500
Marquard	P	3	2	0	0	0	0	0	0	.000
Wiltse	P	2	1	0	0	0	0	0	0	.000
Wilson	C	1	1	0	0	0	0	0	0	.000

COMPOSITE PITCHING

NAME	G	IP	H	BB	SO	W	L	SV	ERA
Philadelphia (AL) Totals	6	55.2	33	14	44	4	2	0	1.29
Bender	**3**	26	16	**8**	**20**	**2**	1	0	**1.04**
Coombs	2	20	11	6	16	1	0	0	1.35
Plank	2	9.2	6	0	8	1	1	0	1.86
New York (NL) Totals	6	54	50	4	31	2	4	0	2.83
Mathewson	**3**	**27**	**25**	2	13	1	**2**	0	2.00
Marquard	**3**	11.2	9	1	8	0	1	0	1.54
Ames	2	8	6	1	6	0	1	0	2.25
Crandall	2	4	2	0	2	1	0	0	0.00
Wiltse	2	3.1	8	0	2	0	0	0	18.90

1912 All for One and All to Sixth

Ty Cobb, who had been the heart of a Tiger team that finished near the top for five years, all too often displayed an extreme battling attitude on the field. Finally, on May 15, Cobb's anger and aggressiveness caught up with him. During a game in New York, Cobb went into the grandstands after a heckler and handed him a sound thrashing before park police could break it up. American League President Ban Johnson suspended Cobb indefinitely, and the entire roster of the Detroit club supported Cobb by refusing to take the field unless the suspension was lifted. Johnson was adamant and so were the Tigers. The strike was on. On May 18, Detroit manager Hughie Jennings was forced to field a pickup team of collegians, sandlotters, and aging coaches against the Philadelphia Athletics; the A's laughed themselves to a 23-2 victory over the one-day major leaguers. Another such game was to be played on May 20, but Connie Mack graciously allowed it to be postponed. The Tiger players finally rescinded and took the field on May 21. Cobb was reinstated on May 26, but poor morale and weak pitching tumbled the Tigers into a sixth-place finish.

While tempers were flaring in Detroit, clear heads and a new field boss were prevailing in Boston, where the fifth-place 1911 Red Sox moved to a new American League record for victories—105—and their third junior circuit pennant. Under new manager Jake Stahl, the Sox played steady ball all year and avoided any prolonged slumps in finishing 14 games ahead of the pack. An excellent attack centered around outfielders, Tris Speaker and Duffy Lewis, and the arm of Smokey Joe Wood, who proved to be the team star. Wood, a ripe 22-year-old veteran of four years, used a smoking fastball to win 34 games against 5 losses and finish second in strikeouts only to the whiff master himself, Walter Johnson. The Red Sox victory was even more pleasant in light of the fact that Fenway Park opened its gates in April for the first time, and by October it had an American League pennant flying high over its freshly painted enclosures.

Another 1911 second division club, the Washington Senators, also surprised experts by rushing into second place. Streaks of 17 and 10 wins punctuated the season, and Walter Johnson's 32 victories and Clyde Milan's 88 stolen bases were high points of manager Clark Griffith's first year at the helm of the Nats. The Philadelphia Athletics got off to their usual slow start but could not come back any farther than third place; injuries and weakened pitching relegated the White Elephants to an also-ran role.

Whereas the Giants had won the National League crown with a late-season rush in 1911, they repeated in 1912 by rushing out to an early lead and never giving it up. A slump in July and August took some wind out of the sails of what appeared to be a record-breaking season but could not even threaten New York's perch on top. Rube Marquard won a record 19 consecutive games on the way to 26 victories, while Christy Mathewson brought home his 23 wins on schedule. A burly rookie spitballer, Jeff Tesreau, joined these two as a mound ace for John McGraw by winning 17 games and leading the league in E.R.A. Fred Merkle and Larry Doyle sparked the best offense in the league.

Good pitching enabled the Pirates to finish second, but the aging and ailing Cubs limped home in third. Frank Chance no longer played, Three Finger Brown was on the downhill side of his career, and Solly Hofman was traded off, signifying the breakup of the champion Cubs at the turn of the decade.

The Series lasted eight games, due to a tie game before Boston defeated the Giants for the championship. In a pitcher's series, Joe Wood played the star's role, winning three games and losing one.

One face during the season was noticeably absent. Cy Young, after 22 years of pitching and 511 victories, announced his retirement in the spring, thus ending one of baseball's legendary careers and certainly taking with him a winning statistic that would never again be equaled.

1912 AMERICAN LEAGUE

NAME	G by POS	B	AGE	G	AB	R	H	2B	3B	HR	RBI	BB	SO	SB	BA	SA
BOSTON 1st 105-47 .691	JAKE STAHL															
TOTALS			27	154	5071	**800**	1404	**269**	84	**29**	**654**	**565**		185	.277	**.380**
Jake Stahl	1B92	R	32	95	326	40	98	21	6	3	60	31		13	.301	.429
Steve Yerkes	2B131	R	24	131	523	73	132	22	6	0	42	41		4	.252	.317
Heinie Wagner	SS144	R	31	144	504	75	138	25	6	2	68	62		21	.274	.359
Larry Gardner	3B143	L	26	143	517	88	163	24	18	3	86	56		25	.315	.449
Harry Hooper	OF147	L	24	147	590	98	143	20	12	2	53	66		29	.242	.327
Tris Speaker	OF153	L	24	153	580	136	222	**53**	12	10	90	82		52	.383	.567
Duffy Lewis	OF154	R	23	154	581	85	165	36	9	6	109	52		9	.284	.408
Bill Carrigan	C87	R	28	87	266	24	70	7	1	0	24	38		7	.263	.297
Clyde Engle	1B25, 2B15, 3B11, SS2, OF1	R	28	57	171	32	40	5	3	0	18	28		12	.234	.298
Hick Cady(NJ)	C43, 1B4	R	26	47	135	19	35	13	2	0	9	10		0	.259	.385
Smokey Joe Wood	P43	R	22	43	124	17	36	13	1	1	13	11		0	.290	.435
Hugh Bradley	1B40	R	27	40	137	16	26	11	1	1	19	15		3	.190	.307
Olaf Henriksen	OF10	L	24	37	56	20	18	3	1	0	8	14		0	.321	.411
Les Nunamaker	C35	R	23	35	103	15	26	5	2	0	6	6		2	.252	.340
2 Neal Ball	2B17	R	32	18	45	10	9	2	0	0	6	3		5	.200	.244
Marty Krug	SS9, 2B4	R	23	16	39	6	12	2	1	0	7	5		2	.308	.410
Pinch Thomas	C12	L	24	12	30	0	6	0	0	0	5	2		1	.200	.200
WASHINGTON 2nd 91-61 .599 14	CLARKE GRIFFITH															
TOTALS			26	154	5074	698	1298	202	86	20	575	472		**274**	.256	.341
Chick Gandil	1B117	R	24	117	443	59	135	20	15	2	81	27		21	.305	.431
Ray Morgan	2B75, SS4, 3B1	R	23	80	273	40	65	10	7	1	30	29		11	.238	.337
George McBride	SS152	R	31	152	521	56	118	13	7	1	52	38		17	.226	.284
Eddie Foster	3B154	R	25	154	**618**	98	176	34	9	2	70	53		27	.285	.379
Danny Moeller	OF132	B	27	132	519	90	143	26	10	6	46	52		30	.276	.399
Clyde Milan	OF154	L	26	154	601	105	184	19	11	1	79	63		**88**	.306	.379
Howard Shanks	OF113	R	21	115	399	52	92	14	7	1	48	40		21	.231	.308
John Henry (KJ)	C63	R	22	63	191	23	37	4	1	0	9	31		10	.194	.225
Eddie Ainsmith	C58	R	20	60	186	22	42	7	2	0	22	14		4	.226	.285
Germany Schaefer	OF19, 1B15, 2B15, P1	R	35	60	166	21	41	7	3	0	19	23		11	.247	.325
Rip Williams	C45	R	30	57	157	14	50	11	4	0	22	7		2	.318	.439
Walter Johnson	P50	R	24	55	144	16	38	6	4	2	20	7		2	.264	.403
2 Frank LaPorte	2B37	R	32	39	136	13	42	9	1	0	17	12		3	.309	.390
Tilly Walker	OF31, 2B1	R	24	36	110	22	30	2	1	0	9	8		11	.273	.309
Jack Knight	2B27, 1B5	R	26	32	93	10	15	2	1	0	9	16		4	.161	.204
Jack Flynn	1B20	R	28	20	71	9	12	4	1	0	5	7		2	.169	.254
Duke Kenworthy	OF10	B	25	12	38	6	9	1	0	0	2	2		3	.237	.263
Bill Cunningham	2B7	R	24	7	27	5	5	1	0	1	8	3		2	.185	.333
Roy Moran	OF5	R	27	5	13	1	2	0	0	0	0	8		3	.154	.154
Roxey Roach	SS2	R	27	2	2	1	1	0	0	1	1	0		0	.500	2.000
Joe Agler		L	25	1	1	0	0	0	0	0	0	0		0	.000	.000
Dave Howard		R	23	1	0	0	0	0	0	0	0	0		0	.000	.000
Tommy Long		R	22	1	1	0	0	0	0	0	0	0		0	.000	.000
Jack Ryan	3B1	R	43	1	1	0	0	0	0	0	0	0		0	.000	.000
PHILADELPHIA 3rd 90-62 .592 15	CONNIE MACK															
TOTALS			26	153	5111	780	**1442**	204	**108**	22	620	485		258	**.282**	.377
Stuffy McInnis	1B153	R	21	153	568	83	186	25	13	3	101	49		27	.327	.433
Eddie Collins	2B153	L	25	153	543	**137**	189	25	11	0	64	101		63	.348	.435
Jack Barry	SS139	R	25	139	483	76	126	19	9	0	55	47		22	.261	.337
Frank Baker	3B149	L	26	149	577	116	200	40	21	**10**	**130**	50		40	.347	.541
Bris Lord	OF96	R	28	96	378	63	90	12	9	0	25	34		15	.238	.317
Rube Oldring	OF97	R	28	98	395	61	119	14	5	1	24	10		17	.301	.370
Amos Strunk	OF118	L	23	120	412	58	119	13	12	3	63	47		29	.289	.400
Jack Lapp	C82	L	27	90	281	26	82	15	6	1	35	19		3	.292	.399
Harl Maggert	OF61	L	29	72	242	39	62	8	6	1	13	36		10	.256	.351
Ben Egan	C46	R	28	48	138	9	24	3	4	0	13	6		3	.174	.254
Ira Thomas	C46	R	31	46	139	14	30	4	2	1	13	8		3	.216	.295
Danny Murphy	OF36	R	35	36	130	27	42	6	2	2	20	16		8	.323	.446
Eddie Murphy	OF33	L	20	33	142	24	45	4	1	0	6	11		7	.317	.359
Jimmy Walsh	OF30	L	26	31	107	11	27	8	2	0	15	12		7	.252	.364
Claude Derrick	SS18	R	26	21	58	7	14	0	1	0	7	5		1	.241	.276
Howard Fahey	3B2, 2B1, SS1	R	20	5	8	0	0	0	0	0	0	0		0	.000	.000
Joe Mathes	3B4	B	20	4	14	0	2	0	0	0	0	0		0	.143	.143
Chester Emerson		L	22	1	1	0	0	0	0	0	0	0		0	.000	.000

NAME	T	AGE	W	L	PCT	SV	G	GS	CG	IP	H	BB	SO	ShO	ERA
		25	**105**	47	**.691**	8	154	154	**110**	1362	1243	385	712	**18**	2.76
Smokey Joe Wood	R	22	**34**	5	**.872**	1	43	38	**35**	344	267	82	258	**10**	1.91
Hugh Bedient	R	22	20	9	.690	3	41	28	19	231	206	55	122	0	2.92
Buck O'Brien	R	30	19	13	.594	1	37	34	26	276	237	90	115	2	2.57
Charley Hall	R	26	15	8	.652	2	34	21	10	191	178	70	83	2	3.02
Ray Collins(KJ)	L	25	14	8	.636	0	27	23	17	199	192	42	82	4	2.54
Jack Bushelman	R	26	1	0	1.000	0	3	0	0	8	9	5	5	0	4.50
Larry Pape	R	29	1	1	.500	1	13	2	1	49	74	16	17	0	4.96
1 Eddie Cicotte	R	28	1	3	.250	0	9	6	2	46	58	15	20	0	5.67
Ben Van Dyke	L	24	0	0	.000	0	3	1	0	14	13	7	8	0	3.21
Casey Hageman	R	25	0	0	.000	0	2	1	0	1	5	3	1	0	36.00
Doug Smith	L	19	0	0	.000	0	1	0	0	3	4	0	1	0	3.00
		25	91	61	.599	9	154	154	99	1376	1219	525	**828**	12	**2.69**
Walter Johnson	R	24	32	12	.727	3	50	37	34	368	259	76	**303**	7	**1.39**
Bob Groom	R	27	24	13	.649	1	43	40	29	316	287	94	179	2	2.62
Long Tom Hughes	R	33	13	10	.565	1	31	26	11	196	201	78	108	1	2.94
Carl Cashion	R	21	11	6	.647	1	26	17	13	170	150	103	84	1	3.18
2 Hippo Vaughn	L	24	4	3	.571	0	12	8	4	81	75	43	49	0	2.89
Dixie Walker	R	25	3	4	.429	0	9	8	5	60	72	18	29	0	5.25
Joe Engel	R	19	2	5	.286	1	17	10	2	75	70	50	29	0	3.96
2 Barney Pelty	R	31	1	6	.143	0	11	4	1	44	40	10	15	0	3.28
Paul Musser	R	23	1	0	1.000	1	7	2	0	21	16	16	10	0	2.57
Jerry Akers	R	24	0	0	.000	1	5	1	0	20	24	15	11	0	4.95
Charlie Becker	L	24	0	0	.000	0	4	0	0	9	8	6	5	0	3.00
Joe Boehling	L	21	0	0	.000	0	3	0	0	5	4	6	2	0	7.20
Bert Gallia	R	20	0	0	.000	0	2	0	0	2	0	3	0	0	0.00
Lefty Schegg	L	22	0	0	.000	0	2	1	0	5	7	4	3	0	3.60
Nick Altrock	L	35	0	1	.000	0	1	0	0	1	1	2	0	0	18.00
Clark Griffith	R	42	0	1	.000	0	1	0	0	0	1	0	0	0	∞
Herb Herring	R	20	0	0	.000	0	1	0	0	1	1	1	0	0	0.00
1 Steve White	R	27	0	0	.000	0	1	0	0	1	2	0	1	0	0.00
Germany Schaefer	R	34	0	0	.000	0	1	0	0	1	1	0	0	0	0.00
		27	90	62	.592	13	153	153	100	1357	1273	518	601	9	3.32
Eddie Plank	L	36	26	6	.813	2	37	30	24	260	234	83	110	3	2.21
Jack Coombs	R	29	21	10	.677	3	40	32	23	262	227	94	120	1	3.29
Chief Bender	R	29	13	8	.619	2	27	19	12	171	169	33	90	1	2.74
Boardwalk Brown	R	25	13	11	.542	1	34	24	16	199	204	87	64	3	3.66
Duke Houck	R	20	8	8	.500	1	30	17	12	181	148	74	75	0	2.93
Cy Morgan	R	33	3	8	.273	1	16	14	5	94	75	51	47	0	3.74
Stan Coveleski	R	23	2	1	.667	0	5	2	2	21	18	4	9	1	3.43
2 Roy Crabb	R	21	2	4	.333	0	7	7	3	43	48	17	12	0	3.77
Roger Salmon	L	21	1	0	1.000	0	2	1	0	5	7	4	5	0	9.00
Herb Pennock	L	18	1	2	.333	2	17	2	1	50	48	30	38	0	4.50
1 Harry Krause	L	24	0	2	.000	1	4	2	0	5	10	2	3	0	14.40
Lefty Russell	L	21	0	2	.000	0	5	2	2	17	18	14	9	0	7.42
Hardin Barry	R	21	0	0	.000	0	3	0	0	13	18	4	3	0	7.62
Dave Danforth	L	22	0	0	.000	0	3	0	0	20	26	12	8	0	4.05
Doc Martin	R	24	0	0	.000	0	2	0	0	4	5	5	4	0	11.25
Bullet Joe Bush	R	19	0	0	.000	0	1	1	0	8	14	4	3	0	7.88
Slim Harrell	R	21	0	0	.000	0	1	0	0	3	4	0	1	0	0.00

CHICAGO 4th 78-76 .506 28 — NIXEY CALLAHAN

NAME	G by POS	B	AGE	G	AB	R	H	2B	3B	HR	RBI	BB	SO	SB	BA	SA
TOTALS			27	158	5181	640	1321	174	80	17	537	423		205	.255	.329
Rollie Zeider	1B66, 3B56, SS1	R	28	129	420	57	103	12	10	1	42	50		47	.245	.329
Morrie Rath	2B157	L	25	157	591	104	161	10	2	1	19	95		30	.272	.301
Buck Weaver	SS147	B	21	147	523	55	117	21	8	1	43	9		12	.224	.300
Harry Lord	3B106, OF45	L	30	151	570	81	152	19	12	5	54	52		28	.267	.368
Shano Collins	OF105, 1B46	R	26	153	575	75	168	34	10	2	81	29		26	.292	.397
Ping Bodie	OF130	R	24	137	472	58	139	24	7	5	72	43		12	.294	.407
Nixey Callahan	OF107	R	38	111	408	45	111	9	7	1	52	12		19	.272	.336
Walt Kuhn	C75	R	28	75	178	16	36	7	0	0	10	20		5	.202	.242
Chick Mattick	OF78	R	25	88	285	45	74	7	9	1	35	27		15	.260	.358
Bruno Block	C48	R	27	46	136	8	35	5	6	0	26	7		1	.257	.382
Matty McIntyre	OF45	L	32	45	84	10	14	0	0	0	10	14		3	.167	.167
Billy Sullivan (SJ)	C39	R	37	39	91	9	19	2	1	0	15	9		0	.209	.253
Jac Fournier	1B17	L	19	35	73	5	14	5	2	0	2	4		1	.192	.315
Babe Borton	1B30	L	23	31	105	15	39	3	1	0	17	8		1	.371	.419
2 Ted Easterly	C10, OF1	L	27	30	55	5	20	2	0	0	14	2		1	.364	.400
Ray Schalk	C23	R	19	23	63	7	18	2	0	0	8	3		2	.286	.317
Ernie Johnson	SS16	L	24	18	42	7	11	0	1	0	5	1		0	.262	.310
Cuke Barrows	OF3	R	28	8	13	0	3	0	0	0	2	2		1	.231	.231
Wally Mayer	C6	R	22	7	9	1	0	0	0	0	0	1		0	.000	.000

Lena Blackburne (ST) 25 R 0-1, Mutz Ens 27 L 0-6, Lee Tannehill (BA) 31 R 0-3, Joe Berrens 1-4, Polly McLarry 21 L 0-2, Kid Gleason 45 B 1-2,1 Del Paddock 25 L 0-1, Polly Wolfe 23 L 0-1

NAME	T	AGE	W	L	PCT	SV	G	GS	CG	IP	H	BB	SO	ShO	ERA
		28	78	76	.506	15	158	158	84	1412	1397	426	697	14	3.06
Ed Walsh	R	31	27	17	.614	10	62	41	32	393	392	94	254	6	2.15
Joe Benz	R	26	12	18	.400	0	41	31	11	238	230	70	96	3	2.92
Frank Lange	R	28	10	10	.500	3	31	21	11	165	165	68	96	2	3.28
2 Eddie Cicotte	R	28	9	7	.563	0	20	18	13	152	159	37	70	1	2.84
Doc White	L	33	8	9	.471	0	32	19	9	172	172	47	57	1	3.24
Rube Peters	R	26	5	6	.455	0	28	11	4	109	134	33	39	0	4.11
George Mogridge	L	23	3	4	.429	2	17	7	2	65	69	16	31	0	3.99
Jim Scott (IL)	R	23	2	2	.500	0	6	4	2	38	36	15	23	1	2.13
Harry Smith	R	22	1	0	1.000	0	1	1	0	5	6	0	1	0	1.80
Wiley Taylor	R	24	1	1	.500	0	3	3	0	20	21	14	4	0	4.95
Phil Douglas	R	22	0	1	.000	0	3	1	0	12	21	6	7	0	7.50
Walt Johnson	R	19	0	0	.000	0	4	0	0	14	11	10	8	0	3.21
Rip Jordan (BL)	R	22	0	0	.000	0	3	0	0	10	13	0	0	0	6.30
Ralph Bell	L	21	0	0	.000	0	3	0	0	6	8	8	5	0	9.00
1 Roy Crabb	R	21	0	1	.000	0	2	1	0	9	6	4	3	0	1.00
Flame Delhi	R	19	0	0	.000	0	1	0	0	3	7	3	2	0	9.00
Fred Lamline	R	24	0	0	.000	0	1	0	0	2	7	2	1	0	31.50

CLEVELAND 5th 75-78 .490 30.5 — HARRY DAVIS 54-71 .432 JOE BIRMINGHAM 21-7 .750

NAME	G by POS	B	AGE	G	AB	R	H	2B	3B	HR	RBI	BB	SO	SB	BA	SA
TOTALS			26	155	5134	680	1403	218	77	10	561	407		194	.273	.352
Art Griggs	1B71	R	28	89	273	29	83	16	7	0	39	33		10	.304	.414
Nap Lajoie (XJ)	2B97, 1B20	R	36	117	448	66	165	34	4	0	90	28		18	.368	.462
Roger Peckinpaugh	SS67	R	21	69	236	18	50	4	1	1	22	16		11	.212	.250
Terry Turner	3B103	R	31	103	370	54	114	14	4	0	33	31		19	.308	.368
Joe Jackson	OF150	L	22	152	572	121	226	44	26	3	90	54		35	.395	.579
Joe Birmingham	OF96, 1B9	R	27	107	369	49	94	19	3	0	45	26		15	.255	.322
Buddy Ryan	OF90	L	26	93	328	53	89	12	9	1	31	30		12	.271	.372
Steve O'Neill (BG)	C67	R	20	68	215	17	49	4	0	0	14	12		2	.228	.247
Ivy Olson	SS56, 3B35, 2B21, OF3	R	26	123	467	68	118	13	1	0	33	21		16	.253	.285
Jack Graney (JJ)	OF75	L	26	78	264	44	64	13	2	0	20	50		9	.242	.307
1 Ted Easterly	C51	L	27	63	186	17	55	4	0	1	21	7		3	.296	.333
Doc Johnston	1B41	L	24	43	164	22	46	7	4	1	11	11		8	.280	.390
1 Neal Ball (BG)	2B37	R	31	37	132	12	30	4	1	0	14	9		7	.227	.273
Ray Chapman	SS31	R	21	31	109	29	34	6	3	0	19	10		10	.312	.422
Hank Butcher	OF20	R	25	24	82	9	16	4	1	1	10	6		1	.195	.305
Fred Carisch	C23	R	30	25	70	4	19	3	1	0	5	1		3	.271	.343
Tim Hendryx	OF22	R	21	23	70	9	17	2	4	1	14	8		3	.243	.429
Bill Hunter	OF16	L	28	21	55	6	9	2	0	0	2	10		0	.164	.200
Jack Adams	C20	B	21	20	54	5	11	2	1	0	6	4		0	.204	.278

Paddy Livingston 32 R 11-47, Art Hauger 18 L 1-18, Ed Hohnhorst 27 L 11-54, Howard Baker 24 R 5-30, Ken Nash 23 B 4-23, Herman Bronkie 27 R 0-16, Jack Kibble 20 B 0-8, Moxie Meixel 24 L 1-2, Lou Nagelsen 25 R 0-3, Harry Davis 38 R 0-5, Hack Eibel 18 L 0-3, Harvey Grubb 21 R 0-0

NAME	T	AGE	W	L	PCT	SV	G	GS	CG	IP	H	BB	SO	ShO	ERA
		24	75	78	.490	8	155	155	96	1353	1367	523	622	7	3.30
Vean Gregg	L	27	20	13	.606	2	37	34	26	271	242	90	184	1	2.59
Fred Blanding	R	24	18	14	.563	2	39	31	24	262	259	79	75	1	2.92
George Kahler	R	22	12	19	.387	1	41	32	17	246	263	121	104	3	3.70
Bill Steen	R	24	9	8	.529	0	26	16	6	143	163	45	61	1	3.78
Jim Baskette	R	24	8	4	.667	0	29	11	7	116	109	46	51	1	3.18
Willie Mitchell	L	22	5	8	.385	2	29	15	9	164	149	56	94	0	2.80
Gene Krapp	R	25	2	5	.286	0	9	7	4	59	57	42	22	0	4.57
Bert Brenner	R	24	1	0	1.000	0	2	1	1	13	14	4	3	0	2.77
Lefty James	L	23	0	1	.000	1	3	1	0	6	8	4	2	0	7.50
2 Harry Krause	L	24	0	1	.000	0	2	2	0	5	11	2	1	0	10.80
Lefty George	L	25	0	5	.000	0	11	5	2	44	69	18	18	0	4.91
Bill James	R	24	0	0	.000	0	3	0	0	14	15	9	5	0	4.50
Roy Walker	R	19	0	0	.000	0	2	0	0	3	0	3	1	0	0.00
Jim Neher	R	23	0	0	.000	0	1	0	0	1	0	0	0	0	0.00
Ernie Wolf	R	23	0	0	.000	0	1	0	0	6	8	4	1	0	6.00

DETROIT 6th 69-84 .451 36.5 — HUGHIE JENNINGS

NAME	G by POS	B	AGE	G	AB	R	H	2B	3B	HR	RBI	BB	SO	SB	BA	SA
TOTALS			28	154	5141	720	1375	189	86	19	569	530		270	.267	.349
George Moriarty	1B71, 3B33	R	27	105	375	38	93	23	1	0	54	26		27	.248	.315
Baldy Louden	2B86, 3B26, SS5	R	28	121	403	57	97	12	4	1	36	58		28	.241	.298
Donie Bush	SS144	B	24	144	511	107	118	14	8	2	38	117		35	.231	.301
Charlie Deal	3B41	R	20	41	142	13	32	4	2	0	11	9		4	.225	.282
Sam Crawford	OF149	L	32	149	581	81	189	30	21	4	109	42		41	.325	.470
Ty Cobb	OF140	L	25	140	553	119	227	30	23	7	83	43		61	.410	.586
Davy Jones	OF81	L	32	97	316	54	93	5	2	0	24	38		16	.294	.323
Oscar Stanage	C119	R	29	119	394	35	103	9	4	0	41	34		3	.261	.305
Jim Delahanty	2B44, OF33	R	33	78	266	34	76	14	1	0	41	42		9	.286	.346
Ossie Vitt	OF27, 3B24, 2B15	R	22	73	273	39	67	4	4	0	19	18		17	.245	.289
Del Gainer	1B50	R	25	51	179	28	43	5	6	0	20	18		14	.240	.335
Red Corriden	3B25, 2B7, SS3	R	24	38	138	22	28	6	0	0	5	15		4	.203	.246
George Mullin	P30	R	31	38	90	13	25	5	1	0	12	17		0	.278	.356
Eddie Onslow	1B35	L	19	35	128	11	29	1	2	1	13	3		3	.227	.289
Jack Onslow	C31	R	23	31	69	7	11	1	0	0	4	10		1	.159	.174
Brad Kocher	C23	R	24	24	63	5	13	3	1	0	9	2		0	.206	.286
Bobby Veach	OF22	L	24	23	79	8	27	5	1	0	15	5		2	.342	.430
Paddy Baumann	3B6, 2B5, OF1	R	26	13	42	3	11	1	0	0	7	6		4	.262	.286
Hank Perry	OF7	L	25	13	36	3	6	1	0	0	0	3		0	.167	.194

Al Bashang 23 B 1-12, Red McDermott 22 R 4-15, Charley O'Leary 30 R 2-10, Jack Smith 18 0-0, Ed Irvin 30 2-3, Hughie Jennings 43 R 0-1, Bill Leinhauser 18 R 0-4, Billy Maharg 25 0-1, Jim McGarr 23 0-4, Dan McGarvey 0-3, Deacon McGuire 46 B 1-2, Pat Meany 20 0-2, Ollie O'Mara 21 R 0-4, Joe Sugden 41 B 1-4, Hap Ward 0-2

NAME	T	AGE	W	L	PCT	SV	G	GS	CG	IP	H	BB	SO	ShO	ERA
		27	69	84	.451	6	154	154	104	1358	1424	517	506	7	3.78
Jean Dubuc	R	23	17	10	.630	3	37	26	23	250	217	109	97	2	2.77
Ed Willett	R	28	17	15	.531	0	37	31	24	284	281	84	89	1	3.29
George Mullin	R	31	12	17	.414	0	30	29	22	226	214	92	88	2	3.54
2 Joe Lake	R	30	9	12	.429	2	26	14	12	163	190	39	86	0	3.10
1 Ralph Works	R	24	5	10	.333	1	27	17	9	157	185	66	64	1	4.24
Bill Covington	R	25	3	4	.429	0	14	9	2	63	58	30	19	1	4.14
Ed Summers	R	27	2	1	.667	0	3	3	1	17	16	3	5	0	4.72
Wild Bill Donovan	R	35	1	0	1.000	0	3	1	0	10	5	2	6	0	0.90
George Boehler	R	20	1	2	.333	0	4	4	2	31	49	14	13	0	6.68
Bill Jensen	R	23	1	1	.500	0	4	3	1	25	30	14	4	0	5.40
Bill Burns	L	32	1	4	.200	0	6	5	2	39	52	9	6	0	5.31
Hooks Dauss	R	22	0	1	.000	0	2	2	2	17	11	9	7	0	3.18
Pat McGehee	R	23	0	0	.000	0	1	1	0	0	1	1	0	0	0.00
Allan Traverse	R	20	0	1	.000	0	1	1	1	8	26	7	1	0	15.75
Bun Troy	R	23	0	1	.000	0	1	1	0	7	9	3	1	0	5.14
Harry Moran	L	23	0	1	.000	0	5	2	1	15	19	12	3	0	4.80
Charlie Wheatley	R	19	0	4	.000	0	5	5	2	35	45	17	14	0	6.17
Hub Pernoll	L	24	0	0	.000	0	3	0	0	9	9	4	3	0	6.00
Ed Lafitte (ST)	R	26	0	0	.000	0	1	0	0	2	2	2	0	0	13.50
Alex Remneas	R	26	0	0	.000	0	1	0	0	2	5	0	0	0	22.50

ST. LOUIS 7th 53-101 .344 53 — BOBBY WALLACE 12-27 .308 GEORGE STOVALL 41-74 .357

NAME	G by POS	B	AGE	G	AB	R	H	2B	3B	HR	RBI	BB	SO	SB	BA	SA
TOTALS			29	157	5081	556	1263	166	71	19	468	449		176	.249	.320
George Stovall	1B94	R	33	115	398	35	101	17	5	0	45	14		11	.254	.322
Del Pratt	2B121, SS21, OF8, 3B1	R	24	151	570	76	172	26	15	5	69	36		24	.302	.426
Bobby Wallace	SS86, 3B10, 2B2	R	38	99	323	39	78	14	5	0	31	43		3	.241	.316
Jimmy Austin	3B149	B	32	149	536	57	135	14	8	2	44	38		28	.252	.319
Pete Compton	OF72	L	22	100	268	26	75	6	4	2	30	21		11	.280	.354
Burt Shotton	OF154	L	27	154	580	87	168	15	8	2	40	86		35	.290	.353
Willie Hogan	OF99	R	27	107	360	32	77	10	2	1	36	34		17	.214	.261
Jim Stephens	C66	R	28	74	205	13	51	7	5	0	22	7		3	.249	.332
1 Frank LaPorte	2B39, OF32	R	32	80	266	32	83	11	4	1	38	20		7	.312	.395
Joe Kutina	1B51, OF1	R	27	67	205	18	42	9	3	1	18	13		0	.205	.293
Gus Williams	OF62	L	24	64	216	32	63	13	7	2	32	27		18	.292	.444
Paul Krichell	C57	R	29	57	167	19	35	6	0	0	8	19		2	.217	.255
Walt Alexander	C37	R	21	37	97	5	17	4	0	0	5	8		1	.175	.216
Heinie Jantzen	OF31	R	22	31	119	10	22	0	1	1	8	4		3	.185	.227
Ed Hallinan	SS26	R	23	28	86	11	19	2	0	0	1	5		3	.221	.244
John Daley	SS17	R	23	17	52	7	9	0	0	1	3	9		4	.173	.231

Bunny Brief 19 R 13-42, Eddie Miller 23 R 9-46, Bill Brown 18 L 4-20, George Alton 21 R 4-17, Frank Crossin 21 R 5-22, Charlie Snell 19 R 4-19, Harry Smoyer 22 3-14, Doc Shanley 22 R 0-8, Phil Ketter 2-6, Tom Tennant 29 L 0-2, Lou Criger 40 R 0-2, C.Miller 0-2, Lou Proctor 0-0, Fred Walden 22 R 0-0

NAME	T	AGE	W	L	PCT	SV	G	GS	CG	IP	H	BB	SO	ShO	ERA
		26	53	101	.344	7	157	157	89	1370	1433	442	547	8	3.71
George Baumgardner	R	20	11	14	.440	0	30	26	19	218	222	79	102	2	3.38
Earl Hamilton	L	20	11	14	.440	2	41	26	17	250	228	86	139	1	3.24
Jack Powell	R	37	9	16	.360	0	32	28	21	235	248	52	67	0	3.11
Mack Allison	R	25	6	17	.261	1	31	20	11	169	171	49	43	1	3.62
Elmer Brown	R	29	5	8	.385	1	23	11	2	120	122	42	45	1	3.00
Roy Mitchell	R	27	3	4	.429	0	13	8	5	62	81	17	22	0	4.65
1 Joe Lake	R	30	2	7	.222	0	11	6	4	57	70	16	28	0	4.42
Willie Adams	R	21	2	3	.400	0	13	5	0	46	50	19	16	0	3.92
Carl Weilman	L	22	2	4	.333	1	9	6	5	48	42	3	24	2	2.81
Curly Brown	L	23	1	3	.250	0	16	5	2	65	69	35	28	1	4.84
1 Barney Pelty	R	31	1	5	.167	0	6	6	2	39	43	15	10	0	5.56
Buddy Napier	R	22	0	2	.000	1	7	2	0	25	33	5	10	0	5.04
1 Red Nelson	R	26	0	3	.000	1	8	3	0	18	21	13	9	0	7.00
Bill Bailey	L	23	0	1	.000	0	3	2	1	11	15	10	2	0	9.00
1 John Frill	L	33	0	0	.000	0	3	3	0	4	16	1	2	0	22.50
Frank Spencer	R	26	0	0	.000	0	1	0	0	2	2	0	0	0	0.00

NEW YORK 8th 50-102 .329 55 — HARRY WOLVERTON

NAME	G by POS	B	AGE	G	AB	R	H	2B	3B	HR	RBI	BB	SO	SB	BA	SA
TOTALS			26	153	5095	632	1320	168	79	18	502	463		247	.259	.334
Hal Chase	1B121, 2B8	R	29	131	522	61	143	21	9	4	58	17		33	.274	.372
Hack Simmons	2B88, 1B13, SS4	R	27	110	401	45	96	17	2	0	41	33		19	.239	.292
Jack Martin	SS64, 3B4, 2B1	R	25	69	231	30	52	6	1	0	17	37		14	.225	.260
2 Del Paddock	3B41, 2B2, OF1	L	25	45	156	26	45	5	3	1	14	23		9	.288	.378
Guy Zinn	OF106	L	25	106	401	56	105	15	10	6	55	50		17	.262	.394
Roy Hartzell	OF55, 3B56, SS10, 2B2	L	30	123	416	50	113	10	11	1	38	64		20	.272	.356
Bert Daniels	OF131	R	29	133	496	72	136	25	11	2	41	51		37	.274	.381
Ed Sweeney	C108	R	23	110	351	37	94	12	1	0	30	27		6	.268	.308
Dutch Sterrett	OF37, 1B17, C10, 2B1	R	22	66	230	30	61	4	7	1	32	11		8	.265	.357
Birdie Cree (BW)	OF50	R	29	50	190	25	63	11	6	0	22	20		12	.332	.453
Earl Gardner	2B43	R	27	43	160	14	45	3	1	0	26	5		11	.281	.313
George McConnell	P23, 1B2	R	34	42	91	11	27	4	2	0	8	4		0	.297	.385
Tommy McMillan	SS41	R	24	41	149	24	34	2	0	0	12	15		18	.228	.242
Russ Ford	P36, 2B2, OF2	R	29	40	112	15	32	8	0	1	8	6		2	.286	.384
Bill Strumpf	SS26, 2B8, 3B4, 1B1, OF1	R	20	40	129	8	31	0	0	0	10	6		5	.240	.240
Jack Lelivelt	OF36	L	26	36	149	12	54	6	7	2	23	4		7	.362	.537
Harry Wolverton	3B7		38	33	50	6	15	1	0	0	4	2		1	.300	.360
Gabby Street	C28	R	29	28	88	4	16	1	1	0	6	7		1	.182	.216
Pat Maloney	OF20	R	24	22	79	9	17	1	0	0	4	6		3	.215	.228

Ezra Midkiff 29 L 21-86, Bob Williams 18 R 6-44, 1 Cozy Dolan 29 R 12-60, Curt Coleman 25 L 9-37, Harry Wolter (RJ) 27 L 11-32, John Dowd 21 R 6-31, Klondike Smith 25 L 5-27, Benny Kauff 22 L 3-11, Gus Fisher 26 L 1-10, Bill Otis 22 L 1-20, Jack Little 21 R 3-12, Johnnie Priest 21 R 1-2, George Batten 20 R 0-3, Homer Thompson 20 R 0-0

NAME	T	AGE	W	L	PCT	SV	G	GS	CG	IP	H	BB	SO	ShO	ERA
		27	50	102	.329	3	153	153	109	1335	1448	436	637	3	4.13
Russ Ford	R	29	13	21	.382	0	36	35	32	292	317	79	112	0	3.55
Jack Warhop	R	27	10	19	.345	3	39	22	16	258	256	59	110	0	2.86
George McConnell	R	34	8	12	.400	0	23	20	19	177	172	52	91	0	2.75
Ray Caldwell	R	24	8	16	.333	0	30	26	14	183	196	67	95	3	4.47
Jack Quinn	R	28	5	7	.417	0	18	11	7	103	139	23	47	0	5.77
Ray Fisher	R	24	2	8	.200	0	17	13	5	90	107	32	47	0	5.90
1 Hippo Vaughn	L	24	2	8	.200	0	15	10	5	63	66	37	46	0	5.14
Al Schulz	L	23	1	1	.500	0	3	1	1	16	11	11	8	0	2.25
George Davis	R	22	1	4	.200	0	10	7	5	54	61	28	22	0	6.50
Red Hoff	L	21	0	1	.000	0	5	1	0	16	20	6	14	0	6.75
Carl Thompson	R	22	0	2	.000	0	7	2	1	33	43	13	15	0	6.00
Ray Keating	R	20	0	3	.000	0	6	5	3	36	36	18	21	0	5.75
George Shears	L	22	0	0	.000	0	4	0	0	15	24	11	9	0	5.40

1912 NATIONAL LEAGUE

NEW YORK 1st 103-48 .682 — **JOHN McGRAW**

NAME	G by POS	B	AGE	G	AB	R	H	2B	3B	HR	RBI	BB	SO	SB	BA	SA
TOTALS			26	154	5067	**823**	1451	231	89	**47**	**702**	522	497	**319**	**.286**	.393
Fred Merkle	1B129	R	23	129	479	82	148	22	6	11	84	42	70	37	.309	.449
Larry Doyle	2B143	L	25	143	558	98	184	33	8	10	90	56	20	36	.330	.471
Art Fletcher	SS126, 2B2, 3B1	R	27	129	419	64	118	17	9	1	57	16	29	16	.282	.372
Buck Herzog	3B140	R	26	140	482	72	127	20	9	2	47	57	34	37	.263	.355
Red Murray	OF143	R	28	143	549	83	152	26	20	3	92	27	45	38	.277	.413
Beals Becker	OF117	L	25	125	402	66	106	18	8	6	58	54	35	30	.264	.393
Fred Snodgrass	OF116, 1B28, 2B1	R	24	146	535	91	144	24	9	3	69	70	65	43	.269	.364
Chief Meyers	C122	R	31	126	371	60	133	16	5	6	54	47	20	8	.358	.477
Josh Devore	OF96	L	24	106	327	66	90	14	6	2	37	51	43	27	.275	.373
Tillie Shafer	SS31, 2B20, 3B7	B	23	78	163	48	47	4	1	0	23	30	19	22	.288	.325
Art Wilson	C61	R	26	65	121	17	35	6	0	3	19	13	14	2	.289	.413
Doc Crandall	P37, 2B2, 1B1	R	24	50	80	9	25	6	2	0	19	6	7	0	.313	.438
Moose McCormick	OF6, 1B1	L	31	42	39	4	13	4	1	0	8	6	9	1	.333	.487
George Burns	OF23	R	22	29	51	11	15	4	0	0	3	8	8	7	.294	.373
Heinie Groh (JJ)	2B12, SS7, 3B6	R	22	27	48	8	13	2	1	0	3	8	7	6	.271	.354
Grover Hartley	C25	R	23	25	34	3	8	2	1	0	7	8	4	2	.235	.353
Dave Robertson	1B1	L	22	3	2	0	1	0	0	0	1	0	1	1	.500	.500

NAME	T	AGE	W	L	PCT	SV	G	GS	CG	IP	H	BB	SO	ShO	ERA
		27	103	48	.682	**15**	154	154	93	1370	1352	338	652	8	**2.58**
Rube Marquard	L	22	**26**	11	.703	1	43	38	22	295	286	80	175	1	2.57
Christy Mathewson	R	33	23	12	.657	4	43	34	27	**310**	311	34	134	0	2.12
Jeff Tesreau	R	23	17	7	.708	1	36	28	19	243	177	106	119	3	**1.96**
Doc Crandall	R	24	13	7	.650	2	37	10	7	162	181	35	60	1	3.61
Red Ames	R	29	11	5	.688	2	33	22	9	179	194	35	83	2	2.46
Hooks Wiltse	L	31	9	6	.600	3	28	17	5	134	140	28	58	0	3.16
Lore Bader	R	24	2	0	1.000	0	2	1	1	10	9	6	3	0	0.90
LaRue Kirby	R	22	1	0	1.000	0	3	1	1	11	13	6	2	0	5.73
Al Demaree	R	25	1	0	1.000	0	2	2	1	16	17	2	11	1	1.69
Louis Drucke	R	23	0	0	.000	1	1	0	0	2	5	1	0	0	13.50
Ted Goulait	R	22	0	0	.000	0	1	1	1	7	11	4	6	0	6.43
Ernie Shore	R	21	0	0	.000	1	1	0	0	1	8	1	1	0	27.00

PITTSBURGH 2nd 93-58 .616 10 — **FRED CLARKE**

NAME	G by POS	B	AGE	G	AB	R	H	2B	3B	HR	RBI	BB	SO	SB	BA	SA
TOTALS			28	152	5252	751	**1493**	222	**129**	39	657	420	514	177	.284	**398**
Dots Miller	1B147	R	25	148	567	74	156	33	12	4	87	37	45	18	.275	.397
Alex McCarthy	2B105, 3B4	R	24	111	401	53	111	12	4	1	41	30	36	8	.277	.334
Honus Wagner	SS143	R	38	145	558	91	181	35	20	7	**102**	59	38	26	.324	.496
Bobby Byrne	3B130	R	27	100	630	99	152	31	11	3	35	54	40	20	.288	.405
Mike Donlin	OF62	L	34	77	244	27	77	9	8	2	35	20	16	8	.316	.443
Owen Wilson	OF152	L	28	152	583	80	175	19	**36**	11	95	35	67	16	.300	.513
Max Carey	OF150	B	22	150	587	114	177	23	8	5	66	61	79	45	.302	.394
George Gibson	C94	R	31	95	300	23	72	14	3	2	35	20	16	0	.240	.327
Billy Kelly	C39	R	26	48	132	20	42	3	2	1	11	2	16	8	.318	.394
Claude Hendrix	P39	R	23	46	121	25	39	10	6	1	15	3	18	1	.322	.529
Ham Hyatt	OF15, 1B3	L	27	46	97	13	28	3	1	0	22	6	8	2	.289	.340
Art Butler	2B43	R	24	43	154	19	42	4	2	1	17	15	11	2	.273	.344
Mike Simon	C40	L	21	42	113	10	34	2	1	0	11	5	9	1	.301	.336
Eddie Mensor	OF32	B	22	39	99	19	26	3	2	0	1	23	12	10	.263	.333
Jim Viox	3B10, SS8, OF3, 2B1	R	21	33	70	8	13	2	3	1	7	3	5	2	.186	.343
1 Tommy Leach	OF24	R	34	28	97	24	29	4	2	0	19	12	9	6	.299	.381
Bill McKechnie	3B15, SS4, 2B3, 1B2	B	25	24	73	8	18	0	1	0	4	2	1	2	.247	.274
2 Solly Hofman	OF15	R	29	17	53	7	15	4	1	0	2	5	6	0	.283	.396
Stump Edington	OF14	L	20	15	53	4	16	0	2	0	12	3	1	0	.302	.377
Wally Rehg	OF2	R	23	8	9	1	0	0	0	0	0	2	1	0	.000	.000
Stan Gray	1B4	R	23	6	20	4	5	0	1	0	2	0	3	0	.250	.350

Ovid Nicholson 23 L 5-11, Ona Dodd 25 R 0-9, Mickey Keliher 22 L 0-0, Rivington Bisland 22 R 0-1, 1 Earl Blackburn 19 R 0-0, Ralph Capron 19 L 0-0

NAME	T	AGE	W	L	PCT	SV	G	GS	CG	IP	H	BB	SO	ShO	ERA
		26	93	58	.616	7	152	152	**94**	1385	1268	497	**664**	**18**	2.85
Claude Hendrix	R	23	24	9	**.727**	1	39	32	25	289	256	105	176	4	2.58
Howie Camnitz	R	30	22	12	.647	2	41	32	22	277	256	82	121	2	2.83
Marty O'Toole	R	24	15	17	.469	0	37	36	17	275	237	**159**	150	5	2.72
Hank Robinson	L	22	12	7	.626	2	33	16	11	175	146	30	79	0	2.26
Babe Adams	R	30	11	8	.579	0	28	21	11	170	169	35	63	2	2.92
Wilbur Cooper	L	20	3	0	1.000	0	6	4	0	38	32	15	30	2	1.66
Jack Ferry	R	25	2	0	1.000	1	11	3	1	39	33	23	10	1	3.00
2 King Cole	R	26	2	2	.500	0	12	4	2	49	61	18	11	0	6.43
Ed Warner	L	23	1	1	.500	0	11	3	1	45	40	18	13	1	3.60
1 Lefty Leifield	L	28	1	2	.333	0	6	1	1	24	29	10	8	1	4.12
Sherry Smith	L	21	0	0	.000	1	3	0	0	4	6	1	3	0	6.75
Harry Gardner	R	23	0	0	.000	0	1	0	0	.1	3	1	0	0	0.00

CHICAGO 3rd 91-59 .607 11.5 — **FRANK CHANCE**

NAME	G by POS	B	AGE	G	AB	R	H	2B	3B	HR	RBI	BB	SO	SB	BA	SA
TOTALS			29	152	5048	756	1398	**245**	91	43	639	**560**	615	164	.277	.387
Vic Saier	1B120	L	21	122	451	74	130	25	14	2	61	34	65	11	.288	.419
Johnny Evers	2B143	L	30	143	478	73	163	23	11	1	63	74	18	16	.341	.441
Joe Tinker	SS142	R	31	142	550	80	155	24	7	0	75	38	21	25	.282	.351
Heinie Zimmerman	3B121, 1B22	R	25	145	557	95	**207**	**41**	14	**14**	99	38	60	23	**.372**	**.571**
Wildfire Schulte	OF139	L	29	139	553	90	146	27	11	13	64	53	70	17	.264	.423
2 Tommy Leach	OF73, 3B4	R	34	82	265	50	64	10	3	2	32	55	20	14	.242	.325
Jimmy Sheckard	OF146	L	33	146	523	85	128	22	10	3	47	**122**	81	15	.245	.342
Jimmy Archer	C118	R	29	120	385	35	109	20	2	5	58	22	36	7	.283	.384
Ward Miller	OF64	L	27	86	241	45	74	11	4	0	22	26	18	11	.307	.386
2 Red Downs	2B16, SS9, 3B5	R	28	43	95	9	25	4	3	1	14	9	17	5	.263	.400
Wilbur Good	OF10	L	26	39	35	7	5	0	0	0	1	3	7	3	.143	.143
1 Solly Hofman (IL)	OF27, 1B9	R	29	36	125	28	34	11	0	0	18	22	13	5	.272	.360
Tom Needham	C32	R	33	33	90	12	16	5	0	0	10	7	13	3	.178	.233
Cy Williams	OF22	L	24	28	62	3	15	1	1	0	1	6	14	2	.242	.290
Ed Lennox	3B24	R	26	27	81	13	19	4	1	1	16	12	10	1	.235	.346
Dick Cotter	C24	R	21	26	54	6	15	0	2	0	10	6	13	1	.278	.352
2 Tom Downey	SS5, 3B3, 2B1	R	28	13	22	4	4	0	2	0	4	1	5	0	.182	.364

Charlie Moore 27 R 2-9, Frank Chance 34 R 1-5, Mike Hechinger 22 R 0-3, Harry Chapman 24 R 1-4, George Yantz 25 R 1-1

NAME	T	AGE	W	L	PCT	SV	G	GS	CG	IP	H	BB	SO	ShO	ERA
		30	91	59	.607	9	152	152	80	1359	1307	493	554	14	3.42
Larry Cheney	R	26	**26**	10	.722	0	42	37	**28**	303	262	111	140	4	2.85
Lew Richie	R	28	16	8	.667	0	39	27	15	238	222	74	69	4	2.95
Jimmy Lavender	R	28	16	13	.552	3	42	31	15	252	240	89	109	3	3.03
Ed Reulbach	R	29	10	6	.625	4	39	19	8	169	161	60	75	0	3.78
2 Lefty Leifield	L	28	7	2	.778	0	13	9	4	71	68	21	23	1	2.41
Charlie Smith	R	32	7	4	.636	1	20	5	1	94	92	31	47	0	4.21
Three Finger Brown	R	35	5	6	.455	0	15	8	5	89	92	20	34	2	2.63
Jim Maroney	L	28	1	1	.500	1	10	3	1	24	25	17	5	0	4.50
Fred Toney	R	24	1	2	.333	0	9	2	0	24	21	11	9	0	5.25
1 King Cole	R	26	1	2	.333	0	8	3	0	19	36	8	9	0	10.89
Harry McIntire	R	34	1	2	.333	0	4	3	2	24	22	6	8	0	3.75
Len Madden	L	21	0	1	.000	0	6	2	0	12	16	9	5	0	3.00
Grover Lowdermilk	R	27	0	1	.000	0	2	1	1	13	17	14	8	0	9.69
Rudy Sommers	R	23	0	1	.000	0	1	0	0	3	4	2	2	0	3.00
George Pearce	L	24	0	0	.000	0	3	2	0	15	15	12	9	0	5.40
Dick Cottrell	L	23	0	0	.000	0	1	0	0	4	8	1	1	0	9.00
Bill Powell	R	27	0	0	.000	0	1	0	0	2	2	1	0	0	9.00
Joe Vernon	R	22	0	0	.000	0	1	0	0	4	4	6	1	0	11.25
Orvie Overall (VR) 31															

CINCINNATI 4th 75-78 .490 29 — **HANK O'DAY**

NAME	G by POS	B	AGE	G	AB	R	H	2B	3B	HR	RBI	BB	SO	SB	BA	SA
TOTALS			27	155	5115	656	1310	183	89	21	565	479	492	248	.256	.339
Dick Hoblitzell	1B147	L	23	148	558	73	164	32	12	2	85	48	28	23	.294	.405
Dick Egan	2B149	R	28	149	507	69	125	14	5	0	52	56	26	24	.247	.294
Jimmy Esmond	SS74	R	22	82	231	24	45	5	3	1	40	20	31	11	.195	.255
Art Phelan	3B127, 2B3	R	24	130	461	56	112	9	11	3	54	46	37	25	.243	.330
Mike Mitchell	OF144	R	32	147	552	60	156	14	13	4	78	41	43	23	.283	.377
Armando Marsans	OF98, 1B6	R	25	110	416	59	132	19	7	1	38	20	17	35	.317	.404
Bob Bescher	OF143	B	28	145	548	**120**	154	29	11	4	38	83	61	**67**	.281	.396
Larry McLean	C98	R	30	102	333	17	81	15	1	1	27	18	15	1	.243	.303
Eddie Grant	SS56, 3B15	L	29	96	255	37	61	6	1	2	20	18	27	11	.239	.294
Johnny Bates	OF65	L	30	81	239	45	69	12	7	1	29	47	16	10	.289	.410
Tommy Clarke	C63	R	24	72	146	19	41	7	2	0	22	28	14	9	.281	.356
Tex McDonald	SS42	L	23	61	140	16	36	3	4	1	15	13	24	5	.257	.357
Hank Severeid	C20, 1B7, OF6	R	21	50	114	10	27	0	3	0	13	8	11	0	.237	.289
Pete Knisely	OF13, 2B3, SS1	R	28	21	67	10	22	7	3	0	7	4	5	3	.328	.522
Rafael Almeida	3B16	R	24	16	59	9	13	4	3	0	10	5	8	0	.220	.390
Andy Kyle	OF7	L	22	9	21	3	7	1	0	0	4	4	2	0	.333	.381
2 Earl Blackburn	C1	R	19	1	0	0	0	0	0	0	0	1	0	0	.000	.000

NAME	T	AGE	W	L	PCT	SV	G	GS	CG	IP	H	BB	SO	ShO	ERA
		29	75	78	.490	10	155	155	86	1378	1455	452	561	12	3.42
George Suggs	R	30	19	16	.543	3	42	36	25	303	**320**	56	104	5	2.94
Rube Benton	L	25	18	21	.462	2	**50**	**39**	22	302	316	118	162	2	3.10
Art Fromme	R	28	16	18	.471	0	43	37	23	296	285	88	120	3	2.74
Bert Humphries	R	31	9	11	.450	2	30	15	9	159	162	36	58	2	3.22
Jim Bagby	R	22	2	0	1.000	0	5	1	0	17	17	9	10	0	3.18
Frank Gregory	R	23	2	0	1.000	0	4	2	1	16	19	7	4	0	4.50
2 John Frill	L	33	1	0	1.000	0	3	2	0	15	19	1	4	0	6.00
Howard McGraner	L	22	1	0	1.000	0	4	0	0	19	22	7	5	0	7.11
Ed Donalds	R	27	1	0	1.000	0	1	0	0	4	7	0	1	0	4.50
Gene Packard	L	24	1	0	1.000	0	1	1	1	9	7	4	2	0	3.00
Frank Smith	R	32	1	1	.500	0	7	3	1	23	34	15	5	0	6.26
2 Ralph Works	R	24	1	1	.500	0	3	1	1	10	4	5	5	0	2.70
Frank Harter	R	25	1	2	.333	0	o	3	1	29	25	11	12	0	3.11
Bob Keefe	R	30	1	3	.250	2	17	6	0	69	78	33	29	0	5.22
Harry Gaspar	R	**29**	1	3	.250	0	7	6	2	37	38	16	13	0	4.14
Dixie Davis	R	21	0	1	.000	0	7	0	0	27	25	16	12	0	2.66
Gene Moore	L	26	0	1	.000	1	5	2	0	15	17	11	6	0	4.80
Sam Fletcher			0	0	.000	0	2	0	0	10	15	11	3	0	11.70
Ben Taylor			0	0	.000	0	2	0	0	6	9	3	2	0	3.00
Bill Cramer	R	21	0	0	.000	0	1	0	0	2	6	0	2	0	0.00
Bill Doak	R	21	0	0	.000	0	1	1	0	2	4	1	0	0	4.50
Hanson Horsey	R	22	0	0	.000	0	1	0	0	4	14	3	0	0	22.50
Bill Prough	R	**24**	0	0	.000	0	1	0	0	3	7	1	0	1	6.00
Chuck Thompkins	R	22	0	0	.000	0	1	0	0	3	5	0	1	0	0.00

PHILADELPHIA 5th 73-79 .480 30.5 — **RED DOOIN**

NAME	G by POS	B	AGE	G	AB	R	H	2B	3B	HR	RBI	BB	SO	SB	BA	SA
TOTALS			30	152	5077	670	1354	244	68	43	570	464	615	159	.267	.368
Fred Luderus	1B146	L	26	148	572	77	147	31	5	10	69	44	65	8	.257	.381
Otto Knabe	2B123	R	28	126	426	56	120	11	4	0	46	55	20	16	.282	.326
Mickey Doolan	SS146	R	32	146	532	47	137	26	6	1	62	34	59	6	.258	.335
Hans Lobert	3B64	R	30	65	257	37	84	12	5	2	33	19	13	13	.327	.436
Gavvy Cravath	OF113	R	31	130	436	63	124	30	9	11	70	47	77	15	.284	.470
Dode Paskert	OF141, 2B2, 3B1	R	30	145	540	102	170	37	5	2	43	91	67	36	.315	.413
Sherry Magee	OF124, 1B6	R	27	132	464	79	142	25	9	6	66	55	54	30	.306	.438
Bill Killefer	C85	R	24	85	268	18	60	6	3	1	21	4	14	6	.224	.280
Red Dooin	C58	R	33	69	184	20	43	9	0	0	22	5	12	8	.234	.283
2 Doc Miller	OF40	L	29	67	177	24	51	12	5	0	21	9	13	3	.288	.412
1 Tom Downey	3B46, SS3	R	28	54	171	27	50	6	3	1	23	21	20	3	.292	.380
Jimmy Walsh	2B31, 3B12, C5	R	26	51	150	16	40	6	3	2	19	8	20	3	.267	.387
1 John Titus	OF42	L	36	45	157	43	43	9	5	3	22	33	14	6	.274	.452
John Dodge	3B23, 2B5, SS1	R	23	30	92	3	11	1	0	0	3	4	11	2	.120	.130
Peaches Graham	C19	R	35	24	59	6	17	1	0	1	4	8	5	1	.288	.356
Jack Boyle	3B6, SS2	L	22	15	25	4	7	1	0	0	2	1	5	0	.280	.320
Pat Moran	C13	R	36	13	26	3	1	1	0	0	1	1	7	0	.115	.154
2 Cozy Dolan	3B11	R	29	11	50	8	14	2	2	0	7	1	10	3	.280	.400
George Mangus	OF5	L	22	10	25	2	5	3	0	0	3	1	6	0	.200	.320
Bill Brinker	3B2, OF2	B	28	9	18	1	4	1	0	0	2	2	3	0	.222	.278
George Browne	3B1	L	36	6	5	0	1	0	0	0	0	1	0	0	.200	.200

Gene Steinbrenner 19 R 2-9, Hal Savage L 0-3, Mike Loan 17 R 1-2

NAME	T	AGE	W	L	PCT	SV	G	GS	CG	IP	H	BB	SO	ShO	ERA
		26	73	79	.480	9	152	152	82	1355	1381	515	616	10	3.25
Pete Alexander	R	25	19	17	.528	3	46	34	26	**310**	289	105	**195**	3	2.82
Tom Seaton	R	**24**	16	12	.571	2	44	27	16	255	246	106	118	2	3.28
Ad Brennan	L	30	11	9	.550	2	27	19	13	174	185	49	78	1	3.57
Eppa Rixey	L	21	10	10	.500	0	23	20	10	162	147	54	59	3	2.50
Earl Moore	R	32	9	14	.391	0	31	24	10	182	186	77	79	1	3.31
George Chalmers	R	24	3	4	.429	0	12	8	3	58	64	37	22	0	3.26
2 Red Nelson	R	26	2	0	1.000	0	4	2	1	19	25	6	2	0	3.79
1 Cliff Curtis	R	29	2	5	.286	0	10	8	2	50	55	17	20	0	3.24
Toots Schultz	R	23	1	4	.200	1	22	4	1	59	75	35	20	0	4.58
Erskine Mayer	R	23	0	1	.000	0	7	1	0	21	27	7	5	0	6.43
Rube Marshall	R	21	0	1	.000	0	2	1	0	3	12	1	2	0	21.00
Happy Finneran	R	20	0	2	.000	1	14	4	0	46	50	10	10	0	2.55
Huck Wallace	L	29	0	0	.000	0	4	0	0	5	7	4	4	0	0.00
Hank Ritter	R	18	0	0	.000	0	3	0	0	6	5	5	1	0	4.50
Frank Nicholson	R	22	0	0	.000	0	2	0	0	4	8	2	1	0	6.75

ST. LOUIS 6th 63-90 .412 36 — ROGER BRESNAHAN

NAME	G by POS	B	AGE	G	AB	R	H	2B	3B	HR	RBI	BB	SO	SB	BA	SA
TOTALS			26	153	5092	659	1366	190	77	27	561	508	620	193	.268	.352
Ed Konetchy	1B142, OF1	R	26	143	538	81	169	26	13	8	82	62	66	25	.314	.455
Miller Huggins	2B114	B	33	120	431	82	131	15	4	0	29	87	31	35	.304	.357
Arnold Hauser	SS132	R	23	133	479	73	124	14	7	1	42	39	69	26	.259	.324
Mike Mowrey	3B108	R	28	114	408	59	104	13	8	2	50	46	29	19	.255	.341
Steve Evans	OF134	L	27	135	491	59	139	23	9	6	72	36	51	11	.283	.403
Rebel Oakes	OF136	L	25	136	495	57	139	19	5	3	58	31	24	26	.281	.358
Lee Magee	OF85, 2B23, 1B6, SS1	B	23	128	458	60	133	13	8	0	40	39	29	16	.290	.354
Ivy Wingo	C92	L	21	100	310	38	82	18	0	2	44	23	45	8	.265	.394
Rube Ellis	OF76	L	26	109	305	47	82	18	2	4	33	34	36	6	.269	.380
Wally Smith	3B32, SS22, 1B6	R	23	75	219	22	56	5	5	0	26	29	27	4	.256	.324
Jack Bliss	C41	R	30	49	114	11	28	3	1	0	18	19	14	3	.246	.289
Roger Bresnahan	C28	R	33	48	108	8	36	7	2	1	15	14	9	4	.333	.463
Denny Wilie	OF16	L	21	30	48	2	11	0	1	0	6	7	9	0	.229	.271
Bad News Galloway	2B16, SS1	B	24	21	54	4	10	2	0	0	4	5	8	2	.185	.222
Frank Gilhooley	OF11	L	20	13	49	5	11	0	0	0	2	3	8	0	.224	.224
Elmer Miller	OF11	R	21	12	37	5	7	1	0	0	3	4	9	1	.189	.216
Possum Whitted	3B12	R	22	12	46	7	12	3	0	0	7	3	5	1	.261	.326
Frank Snyder	C11	R	19	11	18	2	2	0	0	0	0	2	7	1	.111	.111

John Kelleher 18 R 4-12, Ted Cather 23 R 8-19, Roy Rolling 25 R 3-15, Jim Clark 24 R 0-1, Ed Burns 23 R 0-1, Jack Mercer 22 L 0-1, Mike Murphy 23 R 0-1

NAME	T	AGE	W	L	PCT	SV	G	GS	CG	IP	H	BB	SO	ShO	ERA
		25	63	90	.412	12	153	153	62	1353	1466	**560**	487	6	3.85
Bob Harmon	R	24	18	18	.500	0	43	34	15	268	284	116	73	3	3.93
Slim Sallee	L	27	16	17	.485	**6**	48	32	20	294	289	72	108	3	2.60
Bill Steele	R	26	9	13	.409	2	40	25	7	194	245	66	67	0	4.69
Rube Geyer	R	27	7	14	.333	0	41	18	6	181	191	84	61	0	3.28
Joe Willis	L	22	4	9	.308	2	31	17	4	130	143	62	55	0	4.43
Dan Griner	R	24	3	4	.429	0	12	7	2	54	59	15	20	0	3.17
Phil Redding	R	22	2	1	.667	0	3	3	2	25	31	11	9	0	5.04
Pol Perritt	R	19	1	1	.500	0	6	3	1	31	25	10	13	0	3.19
Lou Lowdermilk	L	25	1	1	.500	1	4	1	1	15	14	9	2	0	3.00
2 Sandy Burk	R	25	1	3	.250	1	12	4	2	45	37	12	17	0	2.40
Gene Woodburn	R	25	1	4	.200	0	20	5	1	48	60	42	25	0	5.63
Gene Dale	R	23	0	5	.000	0	19	3	1	62	76	51	37	0	6.53
Wheezer Dell	R	25	0	0	.000	0	3	0	0	2	3	3	0	0	13.50
Roland Howell	R	20	0	0	.000	0	3	0	0	2	5	5	0	0	22.50
Bob Ewing	R	39	0	0	.000	0	1	1	0	1	2	1	0	0	0.00
George Zackert	L	27	0	0	.000	0	1	0	0	1	2	1	0	0	18.00

BROOKLYN 7th 58-95 .379 46 — BILL DAHLEN

NAME	G by POS	B	AGE	G	AB	R	H	2B	3B	HR	RBI	BB	SO	SB	BA	SA
TOTALS			26	153	5141	651	1377	220	73	32	561	490	584	179	.268	.358
Jake Daubert	1B143	L	28	145	559	81	172	19	16	3	66	48	45	29	.308	.415
George Cutshaw	2B91, 3B5, SS1	R	24	102	357	41	100	14	4	0	28	31	16	16	.280	.342
Bert Tooley	SS76	R	25	77	265	34	62	6	5	2	37	19	21	12	.234	.317
Red Smith	3B125	R	22	128	486	75	139	28	6	4	57	54	51	22	.286	.393
Hub Northen	OF102	L	26	118	412	54	116	26	6	3	46	41	46	8	.282	.396
Herbie Moran	OF129	L	28	130	508	77	140	18	10	1	40	69	38	28	.276	.356
Zack Wheat	OF122	L	26	123	453	70	138	28	7	8	65	39	40	16	.305	.450
Otto Miller	C94	R	23	98	316	35	88	18	1	1	31	18	50	11	.278	.351
John Hummel	2B58, OF44, 1B11	R	29	122	411	55	116	21	7	5	54	49	55	7	.282	.404
Bobby Fisher	SS74, 2B1, 3B1	R	25	82	257	27	60	10	3	0	26	14	32	7	.233	.296
Jud Daley	OF55	L	28	61	199	22	51	9	1	1	13	24	17	2	.256	.327
Tex Erwin	C41	L	26	59	133	14	28	3	0	2	14	18	16	1	.211	.278
Eddie Phelps	C32	R	33	52	111	8	32	4	3	0	23	16	15	1	.288	.378
Enos Kirkpatrick	3B29, SS3	R	26	32	94	13	18	1	1	0	0	9	15	5	.191	.223
Casey Stengel	OF17	L	21	17	57	9	18	1	0	1	13	15	9	5	.316	.386
1 Red Downs	2B9	R	28	9	32	2	8	3	0	0	3	1	5	3	.250	.344
Dolly Stark	SS7	R	27	8	22	2	4	0	0	0	2	1	3	2	.182	.182
Bob Higgins	C1	R	25	1	2	0	0	0	0	0	0	0	1	0	.000	.000

NAME	T	AGE	W	L	PCT	SV	G	GS	CG	IP	H	BB	SO	ShO	ERA
		25	58	95	.379	8	153	153	71	1357	1399	510	553	10	3.64
Nap Rucker	L	27	18	21	.462	4	45	34	23	298	272	72	151	**6**	2.21
Eddie Stack	R	24	7	5	.583	1	28	17	4	142	139	55	45	0	3.36
Elmer Knetzer	R	26	7	9	.438	0	33	16	4	140	135	70	61	1	4.56
Pat Ragan	R	23	7	18	.280	1	36	26	12	208	211	65	101	1	3.63
Earl Yingling	L	23	6	11	.353	0	25	16	12	163	186	56	51	0	3.59
Maury Kent	R	26	5	5	.500	0	20	9	2	93	107	46	24	1	4.84
2 Cliff Curtis	R	29	4	7	.364	1	19	9	3	80	72	37	22	0	3.94
Frank Allen	L	22	3	9	.250	0	20	15	5	109	119	57	58	1	3.63
Cy Barger	R	27	1	9	.100	0	16	11	6	94	120	42	30	0	5.46
Bill Schardt	R	26	0	1	.000	1	7	0	0	21	25	6	7	0	4.28
1 Sandy Burk	R	25	0	0	.000	0	2	0	0	8	9	3	2	0	3.38
Eddie Dent	R	24	0	0	.000	0	1	0	0	1	4	1	1	0	36.00

BOSTON 8th 52-101 .340 52 — JOHNNY KLING

NAME	G by POS	B	AGE	G	AB	R	H	2B	3B	HR	RBI	BB	SO	SB	BA	SA
TOTALS			28	153	**5361**	693	1465	227	68	35	605	454	**691**	137	.273	.361
Ben Houser	1B83	L	28	108	332	38	95	17	3	8	52	22	29	1	.286	.428
Bill Sweeney	2B153	R	26	153	593	84	204	31	13	1	100	68	34	27	.344	.445
Frank O'Rourke	SS59	R	17	61	196	11	24	3	1	0	16	11	50	1	.122	.148
Ed McDonald	3B118	R	25	121	459	70	119	23	6	2	34	70	**91**	22	.259	.349
2 John Titus	OF96	L	36	96	345	56	112	23	6	2	48	49	20	5	.325	.443
Vin Campbell	OF144	L	24	145	**624**	102	185	32	9	3	48	32	44	19	.296	.391
George Jackson	OF107	R	30	110	397	55	104	13	5	4	48	38	72	22	.262	.350
Johnny Kling	C74	R	37	81	252	26	80	10	3	2	30	15	30	3	.317	.405
Art Devlin	1B69, SS26, 3B26, OF1	R	32	124	436	59	126	18	8	0	54	51	37	11	.289	.367
Jay Kirke	OF71, 3B32, 1B1	L	24	103	359	53	115	11	4	4	62	9	46	7	.320	.407
Bill Rariden	C73	R	24	79	247	27	55	3	1	1	14	18	35	3	.223	.255
1 Doc Miller	OF50	L	27	51	201	26	47	8	1	2	24	14	17	6	.234	.313
Hank Gowdy	C22, 1B7	R	22	44	96	16	26	6	1	3	10	16	13	3	.271	.448
Al Bridwell (FJ)	SS31	L	20	31	106	6	25	5	1	0	14	7	6	2	.236	.302
Jack Spratt	SS23	L	23	27	89	6	23	3	2	3	15	7	11	2	.258	.438
Rabbit Maranville	SS26	R	20	26	86	8	18	2	0	0	8	9	14	1	.209	.233
Al Kaiser	OF4	R	25	4	13	0	0	0	0	0	0	0	3	0	.000	.000
Joe Schultz	2B4	R	18	4	12	1	3	1	0	0	4	0	2	0	.250	.333
Dave Shean	SS4	R	34	4	10	1	3	0	0	0	0	1	2	0	.300	.300
Bill Jones		L	25	3	2	0	1	0	0	0	2	0	1	0	.500	.500
Gil Whitehouse	C2	B	18	2	6	0	0	0	0	0	0	0	3	0	.000	.000
Mike Gonzalez	C1	R	21	1	2	0	0	0	0	0	0	1	1	0	.000	.000
Art Schwind	3B1	B	20	1	2	0	1	0	0	0	0	0	0	0	.500	.500

NAME	T	AGE	W	L	PCT	SV	G	GS	CG	IP	H	BB	SO	ShO	ERA
		29	52	**101**	.340	5	153	153	92	**1391**	**1544**	521	542	4	4.17
Hub Perdue	R	30	13	16	.448	3	37	30	20	249	295	54	101	1	3.80
Otto Hess	L	33	12	17	.414	0	33	31	21	254	270	90	80	1	3.76
Lefty Tyler	L	22	12	**22**	.353	0	42	29	18	256	262	126	144	0	4.19
Ed Donnelly	R	31	5	10	.333	0	37	18	10	184	225	72	67	0	4.36
Buster Brown	R	30	4	15	.211	0	31	21	13	168	146	66	68	1	4.00
Walt Dickson	R	29	3	19	.136	1	36	20	9	189	233	61	47	1	3.86
Bill McTigue	L	21	2	0	1.000	0	10	1	1	35	39	18	17	0	5.40
Brad Hogg	R	24	1	1	.500	1	10	1	0	31	37	16	12	0	6.97
Al Mattern	R	29	0	1	.000	0	2	1	0	6	10	1	3	0	7.50
Hank Griffin	R	26	0	0	.000	0	3	0	0	2	3	3	0	0	22.50
Rube Kroh	L	25	0	0	.000	0	3	1	0	6	8	6	1	0	6.00
2 Steve White	R	27	0	0	.000	0	3	0	0	6	9	5	2	0	6.00
King Brady	R	31	0	0	.000	0	2	0	0	3	5	3	0	0	18.00
Bill Brady	R	24	0	0	.000	0	1	0	0	1	2	0	0	0	0.00

WORLD SERIES – BOSTON (AL) 4 NEW YORK (NL) 3 (One Tie)

LINE SCORES

TEAM	1	2	3	4	5	6	7	8	9	10	11	12	R	H	E
Game 1 October 8 at New York															
BOS (AL)	0	0	0	0	0	1	3	0	0				4	6	1
NY (NL)	0	0	2	0	0	0	0	0	1				3	8	1
Wood	**Tesreau**, Crandall (8)														
Game 2 October 9 at Boston															
NY	0	1	0	1	0	0	0	3	0	1	0		6	11	5
BOS	3	0	0	0	1	0	0	1	0	1	0		6	10	1
Mathewson	Collins, Hall (8), Bedient (11)						Game called by darkness								
Game 3 October 10 at Boston															
NY	0	1	0	0	1	0	0	0	0				2	7	1
BOS	0	0	0	0	0	0	0	0	1				1	7	0
Marquard	**O'Brien**, Bedient (9)														
Game 4 October 11 at New York															
BOS	0	1	0	1	0	0	0	0	1				3	8	1
NY	0	0	0	0	0	0	1	0	0				1	9	1
Wood	**Tesreau**, Ames (8)														
Game 5 October 12 at Boston															
NY	0	0	0	0	0	0	1	0	0				1	3	1
BOS	0	0	2	0	0	0	0	0	X				2	5	1
Mathewson	**Bedient**														
Game 6 October 14 at New York															
BOS	0	2	0	0	0	0	0	0	0				2	7	2
NY	5	0	0	0	0	0	0	0	X				5	11	2
O'Brien, Collins (2)	**Marquard**														
Game 7 October 15 at Boston															
NY	6	1	0	0	0	2	1	0	1				11	16	4
BOS	0	1	0	0	0	0	2	1	0				4	9	3
Tesreau	**Wood**, Hall (2)														
Game 8 October 16 at Boston															
NY	0	0	1	0	0	0	0	0	0	1			2	9	2
BOS	0	0	0	0	0	0	1	0	0	2			3	8	5
Mathewson	Bedient, **Wood** (8)														

COMPOSITE BATTING

NAME	POS	G	AB	R	H	2B	3B	HR	RBI	BA
Boston (AL)										
Totals		8	273	25	60	14	6	1	21	.220
Stahl	1B	8	32	3	**8**	2	0	0	2	**.250**
Yerkes	2B	8	32	3	**8**	0	**2**	0	4	**.250**
Lewis	OF	8	32	4	**6**	3	0	0	2	**.188**
Hooper	OF	8	31	3	9	2	1	0	2	.290
Speaker	OF	8	30	4	9	1	**2**	0	2	.300
Wagner	SS	8	30	1	5	1	0	0	0	.167
Gardner	3B	8	28	4	5	2	1	1	4	.179
Cady	C	7	22	1	3	0	0	0	1	.136
Wood	P	4	7	1	2	0	0	0	1	.286
Carrigan	C	2	7	0	0	0	0	0	0	.000
Bedient	P	4	6	0	0	0	0	0	0	.000
Collins	P	2	5	0	0	0	0	0	0	.000
Hall	P	2	4	0	3	1	0	0	0	.750
Engle	PH	3	3	1	1	1	0	0	2	.333
O'Brien	P	2	2	0	0	0	0	0	0	.000
Hendriksen	PH-PR	2	1	0	1	1	0	0	1	1.000
Ball	PH	1	1	0	0	0	0	0	0	.000
New York (NL)										
Totals		8	274	31	74	14	4	1	25	.270
Merkle	1B	8	**33**	5	9	2	1	0	3	**.273**
Doyle	2B	8	**33**	5	8	1	0	1	2	.242
Snodgrass	OF	8	**33**	2	7	2	0	0	2	.212
Murray	OF	8	31	5	10	**4**	1	0	**5**	.323
Herzog	3B	8	30	**6**	**12**	**4**	1	0	4	**.400**
Meyers	C	8	28	2	10	0	1	0	3	.357
Fletcher	SS	8	28	1	5	1	0	0	3	.179
Devore	OF	7	24	4	6	0	0	0	0	.250
Mathewson	P	3	12	0	2	0	0	0	0	.167
Tesreau	P	3	8	0	3	0	0	0	2	**.375**
McCormick	PH	5	4	0	1	0	0	0	1	.250
Becker	OF	2	4	1	0	0	0	0	0	.000
Marquard	P	2	4	0	0	0	0	0	0	.000
Wilson	C	2	1	0	1	0	0	0	0	1.000
Crandall	P	1	1	0	0	0	0	0	0	.000
Shafer	SS	3	0	0	0	0	0	0	0	.000
Ames	P	1	0	0	0	0	0	0	0	.000

COMPOSITE PITCHING

NAME	G	IP	H	BB	SO	W	L	SV	ERA
Boston (AL)									
Totals	8	74	74	22	39	4	3	0	2.80
Wood	**4**	22	**27**	3	**21**	**3**	1	0	3.68
Bedient	**4**	18	10	7	7	1	0	0	1.00
Collins	2	14.1	14	0	6	0	0	0	1.88
Hall	2	10.2	11	9	1	0	0	0	3.38
O'Brien	2	9	12	3	4	0	**2**	0	5.00
New York (NL)									
Totals	8	73.2	60	19	36	3	4	0	1.71
Mathewson	3	**28.2**	23	5	10	0	**2**	0	1.26
Tesreau	3	23	19	**11**	15	1	**2**	0	3.13
Marquard	2	18	14	2	9	2	0	0	**0.50**
Crandall	1	2	1	0	2	0	0	0	0.00
Ames	1	2	3	1	0	0	0	0	4.50

1913 Offenses and Defenses Along the Eastern Front

A pennant race was nary in sight as the Athletics and Giants ran away and hid from their competitors. Connie Mack's Athletics quickly squelched any suspense in the American League chase by moving out into first place in late April and never relinquishing the position. The Athletic pitching suffered from the loss of Jack Coombs to illness, but Mack covered himself by using veterans, Eddie Plank and Chief Bender, in double duty as starters and as relievers for young starters, Broadwalk Brown, Joe Bush, and Duke Houck. For a change, the Athletic offense carried the main responsibility for victory. Stuffy McInnis, Eddie Collins, and Frank Baker all hit .320 or better, and Baker won his third consecutive homer title with a total of 12. These three, along with shortstop Jack Barry, had earned the respect of fans as the class infield of their era.

Washington again captured second place, due to good pitching, and the batting duo of Nap Lajoie and Joe Jackson propelled Cleveland into third place. Boston fell from first in 1912 to a distant fourth place, costing Manager Jake Stahl his job in mid-season, less than a year after winning the World Series. More than the Red Sox hitters' inability to match their 1912 run production, the big blow to Boston was Joe Wood's broken hand, which limited him to nine victories. Detroit went through the season without the confrontation which troubled them in 1912, but were again relegated to a dismal sixth-place finish because of poor pitching.

The National League race also revealed no surprises as the New York Giants recovered from a slow start to coast to a third consecutive pennant. A pitching staff led by three 20-game winners, screwballer Christy Mathewson, fastballer Rube Marquard, and spitballer Jeff Tesreau, allowed the lowest total of runs in the league. Infielders, Larry Doyle and Art Fletcher, acted as sparkplugs for a Giant attack, which was third in the loop in run production.

The Philadelphia Phillies surpised all by finishing in second place, 12½ games out. Young pitchers, Tom Seaton and Grover "Pete" Alexander, excelled in 20-game winning seasons, and Gavvy Cravath led the attack with a .341 mark and a league-pacing 19 home runs.

The Cubs finished third in a year of rebuilding under the new managership of second baseman Johnny Evers. Former manager Frank Chance was released before the season began, pitcher Ed Reulbach was traded to Brooklyn, and shortstop Joe Tinker and pitching ace Three Finger Brown were dispatched to Cincinnati. All things considered, Evers' feat of bringing the Cubs home third was an admirable achievement. His two former cohorts, Chance and Tinker, did not fare as well in their new managerial roles. Chance managed the New York Yankees and Tinker the Reds, with both clubs finishing a poor seventh. Brooklyn finished sixth with batting champ Jack Daubert, a rookie outfielder named Casey Stengel, and a new home in Ebbets Field.

John McGraw again had no luck in the World Series as Mack's Athletics defeated McGraw's Giants in five games. The Giant pitchers shaped up better on paper, but Bender, Plank, and Bush all pitched complete game victories for the Mackmen. Frank Baker and Eddie Collins were Series stars with .400 batting marks.

The end of the season was marked by the announcement that the Federal League, an independent minor circuit, planned to expand to major league status by raiding the rosters of the National and American League teams. The Federals showed their serious intentions by signing Joe Tinker and Three Finger Brown to contracts soon after the season's end. It seemed that baseball would have to contend with its own war, much as would Europe, also preparing to protect itself against a more ominous intruder.

1913 AMERICAN LEAGUE

PHILADELPHIA 1st 96-57 .627 — CONNIE MACK

NAME	G by POS	B	AGE	G	AB	R	H	2B	3B	HR	RBI	BB	SO	SB	BA	SA
TOTALS			25	153	5044	**794**	**1412**	**223**	80	**33**	**660**	**534**	547	221	**.280**	**.375**
Stuffy McInnis	1B148	R	22	148	543	79	177	30	4	4	90	45	31	16	.326	.418
Eddie Collins	2B148	L	26	148	534	**125**	184	23	13	3	73	85	37	54	.345	.453
Jack Barry	SS134	R	26	134	455	62	125	20	6	3	85	44	32	15	.275	.365
Frank Baker	3B149	L	27	149	565	116	190	34	9	**12**	**117**	63	31	34	.336	.492
Eddie Murphy	OF135	L	21	136	508	105	150	14	7	1	30	70	44	21	.295	.356
Jimmy Walsh	OF88	L	27	94	303	56	77	16	5	0	27	38	40	15	.254	.340
Rube Oldring	OF136, SS5	R	29	136	538	101	152	27	9	5	71	34	37	40	.283	.394
Jack Lapp	C77, 1B1	L	28	81	238	23	54	4	4	1	20	37	26	1	.227	.290
Amos Strunk	OF80	L	24	93	292	30	89	11	12	0	46	29	23	14	.305	.425
Wally Schang	C71	B	23	76	207	32	55	16	3	3	30	34	44	4	.266	.415
Tom Daley	OF38	L	28	59	141	13	36	2	1	0	11	13	28	4	.255	.284
Danny Murphy	OF9	R	36	40	59	3	19	5	1	0	6	4	8	0	.322	.441
Bill Orr	SS16, 1B3, 2B2, 3B2	R	22	27	67	6	13	1	1	0	7	4	10	1	.194	.239
Ira Thomas	C21	R	32	21	53	3	15	4	1	0	6	4	8	0	.283	.396
Harry Davis	1B6	R	39	7	17	2	6	2	0	0	4	1	4	0	.353	.471
George Brickley	OF4	R	18	5	12	0	2	0	1	0	0	0	4	0	.167	.333
Harry Fritz	3B5	R	22	5	13	1	0	0	0	0	0	2	4	0	.000	.000
2 Doc Lavan	SS5	R	22	5	14	1	1	0	1	0	1	0	0	0	.071	.214

Wickey McAvoy 18 R 1-9, Press Cruthers 22 R 3-12, Joe Giebel 21 R 1-3, Monte Peffer 22 R 0-3

NAME	T	AGE	W	L	PCT	SV	G	GS	CG	IP	H	BB	SO	ShO	ERA
		25	**96**	57	**.627**	21	153	153	69	1351	1200	**532**	630	15	3.20
Chief Bender	R	30	21	10	.677	**12**	48	22	16	237	208	59	135	2	2.21
Boardwalk Brown	R	26	17	11	.607	1	43	35	11	235	200	87	70	3	2.95
Eddie Plank	L	37	18	10	.643	4	41	29	18	243	211	57	151	7	2.59
Duke Houck	R	21	14	6	.700	0	41	19	4	176	147	122	71	1	4.14
Bullet Joe Bush	R	20	14	6	.700	3	39	15	5	200	199	66	81	1	3.83
Bob Shawkey	R	22	8	5	.615	0	18	15	8	111	92	50	52	1	2.35
Herb Pennock	L	19	2	1	.667	0	14	4	1	33	30	22	17	0	5.18
Weldon Wyckoff	R	21	2	4	.333	0	17	7	3	62	56	46	31	0	4.36
John Taff	R	23	0	1	.000	1	7	1	0	18	22	5	9	0	6.50
Pat Bohen	R	22	0	1	.000	0	1	1	1	8	3	2	5	0	1.13
Charlie Boardman	L	20	0	2	.000	0	2	2	1	9	10	6	4	0	2.00
Dave Morey	R	24	0	0	.000	0	2	0	0	4	2	2	1	0	4.50
Jack Coombs (IL)	R	30	0	0	.000	0	2	2	0	5	5	6	0	0	10.80
Dick Cottrell	L	24	0	0	.000	0	2	1	1	10	15	2	3	0	5.40

WASHINGTON 2nd 90-64 .584 6.5 — CLARK GRIFFITH

NAME	G by POS	B	AGE	G	AB	R	H	2B	3B	HR	RBI	BB	SO	SB	BA	SA
TOTALS			26	155	**5074**	596	1281	156	80	20	484	440	595	**287**	.252	.327
Chick Gandil	1B145	R	25	148	550	61	175	25	8	1	72	36	33	22	.318	.398
Ray Morgan	2B133, SS4	R	24	137	481	58	131	19	8	0	57	68	63	19	.272	.345
George McBride	SS150	R	32	150	499	52	107	18	7	1	52	43	46	12	.214	.285
Eddie Foster(IL)	3B105	R	26	106	409	56	101	11	5	1	41	36	31	22	.247	.306
Danny Moeller	OF153	B	28	153	589	88	139	15	10	5	42	72	**103**	62	.236	.321
Clyde Milan	OF154	L	27	154	579	92	173	18	9	3	54	58	25	**74**	.299	.377
Howard Shanks	OF109	R	22	109	390	38	99	11	5	1	37	15	40	24	.254	.315
John Henry	C96	R	23	96	273	26	61	8	4	1	26	30	43	5	.223	.293
Eddie Ainsmith	C79, P1	R	21	79	229	26	49	4	4	2	20	12	41	17	.214	.293
Frank LaPorte	3B46, 2B13, OF12	R	33	79	242	25	61	5	4	0	18	17	16	10	.252	.306
Rip Williams	C18, 1B8, OF5	R	31	65	106	9	30	6	2	1	12	9	16	3	.283	.406
G. Schaefer	2B17, 1B5, 3B2, OF1, P1	R	36	52	100	17	32	1	1	0	7	15	12	6	.320	.350
Joe Gedeon	OF14, 3B8, 2B2, SS1, P1	R	19	27	71	3	13	1	2	1	6	1	6	3	.183	.296
Jack Calvo	OF12	L	29	16	33	5	8	0	0	1	2	1	4	0	.242	.333
Merito Acosta	OF7	L	17	9	20	3	6	0	1	0	1	4	2	2	.300	.400
Ben Spencer	OF8	L	23	8	21	2	6	1	1	0	2	2	4	0	.286	.429
Bill Morley	2B1	R	23	2	3	0	0	0	0	0	0	0	0	0	.000	.000
Jack Ryan	C1	R	44	1	1	0	0	0	0	0	0	0	0	0	.000	.000
Carl Cashion(AJ)	P4, OF3	L	22	7	12	1	3	0	0	0	2	1	1	0	.250	.250

NAME	T	AGE	W	L	PCT	SV	G	GS	CG	IP	H	BB	SO	ShO	ERA
		25	90	64	.584	**22**	155	155	80	**1396**	1175	465	**757**	**22**	2.72
Walter Johnson	R	25	**36**	7	**.837**	3	47	36	**30**	**346**	230	38	**243**	**12**	**1.09**
Joe Boehling	L	22	17	7	.708	4	38	25	18	235	197	82	110	3	2.14
Bob Groom	R	28	16	16	.500	0	37	36	18	264	258	81	156	4	3.24
Joe Engel	R	20	8	9	.471	1	36	23	6	165	124	85	70	2	3.05
Long Tom Hughes	R	32	4	12	.250	7	36	13	4	130	129	61	59	0	4.29
Slim Love	L	22	1	0	1.000	1	5	1	0	17	14	6	5	0	1.59
Doc Ayres	R	23	2	1	.333	1	4	2	1	18	12	4	17	1	1.50
2 George Mullin	R	32	3	5	.375	0	12	9	3	57	69	25	14	0	5.05
Harry Harper	L	18	0	0	.000	0	4	0	0	13	10	5	9	0	3.47
Mutt Williams	R	21	0	0	.000	0	1	1	0	4	4	2	1	0	4.50
Carl Cashion(AJ)	R	22	1	1	.500	0	4	3	0	9	7	14	3	0	6.00
Bert Gallia	R	21	1	5	.167	3	31	4	0	96	85	46	46	0	4.13
Nick Altrock	L	36	0	0	.000	0	4	0	0	9	7	4	2	0	5.00
Jack Bentley	L	18	1	0	1.000	1	3	1	0	11	5	2	5	0	0.00
John Wilson	L	23	0	0	.000	0	3	0	0	4	4	3	1	0	4.50
Tom Drohan	R	25	0	0	.000	0	2	0	0	2	5	0	2	0	9.00
Jim Shaw	R	19	0	1	.000	0	2	1	0	13	8	7	14	0	2.08
Eddie Ainsmith	R	21	0	0	.000	0	1	0	0	.1	2	0	0	0	54.00
Rex Dawson	R	24	0	0	.000	0	1	0	0	1	1	0	0	0	0.00
Joe Gedeon	R	20	0	0	.000	0	1	0	0	0	0	0	0	0	0.00
Clark Griffith	R	43	0	0	.000	0	1	0	0	1	1	0	0	0	0.00
Doc Hedgpeth	L	24	0	0	.000	1	1	0	0	1	1	0	0	0	0.00
Germany Schaefer	R	36	0	0	.000	0	1	0	0	.1	2	0	0	0	54.00

CLEVELAND 3rd 86-66 .566 9.5 — JOE BIRMINGHAM

NAME	G by POS	B	AGE	G	AB	R	H	2B	3B	HR	RBI	BB	SO	SB	BA	SA
TOTALS			25	155	5030	631	1348	205	74	16	527	420	557	191	.268	.348
Doc Johnston	1B133	L	25	133	530	74	135	19	12	2	39	35	65	19	.255	.347
Nap Lajoie	2B126	R	37	137	465	66	156	25	2	1	68	33	17	17	.335	.404
Ray Chapman	SS138	R	22	140	508	78	131	19	7	3	39	46	51	29	.258	.341
Ivy Olson	3B73, 1B22, 2B1	R	27	104	370	47	92	13	3	0	32	22	28	7	.249	.300
Joe Jackson	OF148	L	23	148	528	109	**197**	**39**	17	7	71	80	26	26	.373	**.551**
Nemo Leibold	OF72	L	21	84	286	37	74	11	6	0	12	21	43	16	.259	.339
Jack Graney	OF148	L	27	148	517	56	138	18	12	3	68	48	55	27	.267	.366
Fred Carisch	C79	R	31	81	222	11	48	4	2	0	26	21	19	6	.216	.252
Terry Turner	3B71, 2B25, SS21	R	32	120	388	60	96	13	4	0	44	55	35	13	.247	.302
Steve O'Neill	C78	R	21	78	234	19	69	13	3	0	29	10	24	5	.295	.376
Buddy Ryan	OF67, 1B1	L	27	73	243	26	72	6	1	0	32	11	13	9	.296	.329
Joe Birmingham(BF)	OF37	R	28	47	131	16	37	9	1	0	15	8	22	7	.282	.366
2 Jack Lelivelt		L	27	23	23	0	9	2	0	0	7	0	3	1	.391	.478
Ray Bates	3B12, OF2	R	23	20	30	4	5	0	2	0	4	3	9	3	.167	.300
Grover Land(JJ)	C17	R	28	17	47	3	11	1	0	0	9	4	1	1	.234	.255
George Dunlop	SS4, 3B3	R	24	7	17	3	4	1	0	0	0	0	5	0	.235	.294
1 Johnny Beall		L	31	6	6	0	1	0	0	0	1	0	2	0	.167	.167
Larry Kopf	2B3, 3B1	B	22	5	9	1	2	0	0	0	1	0	0	0	.222	.222
Ernie Krueger	C4	R	22	5	6	0	0	0	0	0	0	0	2	0	.000	.000
Eddie Edmonson	1B1, OF1	L	23	2	5	0	0	0	0	0	0	0	0	0	.000	.000

George Young 23 L 0-2, Johnny Bassler 18 L 0-2, Josh Billings 21 R 0-3, 1 Roger Peckinpaugh 22 R 0-0, Billy Southworth 20 L 0-0, Josh Swindell 29 R 0-0

NAME	T	AGE	W	L	PCT	SV	G	GS	CG	IP	H	BB	SO	ShO	ERA
		26	86	66	.566	4	155	155	95	1387	1278	502	689	18	2.52
Cy Falkenberg	R	33	23	10	.700	0	39	36	23	276	238	88	166	6	2.22
Vean Gregg	L	28	20	13	.606	3	44	34	23	286	258	**124**	166	3	2.23
Fred Blanding	R	25	15	10	.600	0	41	22	14	215	234	72	63	3	2.55
Willie Mitchell	L	23	14	8	.636	0	34	22	14	217	153	88	141	4	1.74
George Kahler	R	23	5	11	.313	0	24	15	5	118	118	32	43	0	3.15
Bill Steen (BW)	R	25	4	5	.444	1	22	13	8	128	113	49	57	2	2.46
Nick Cullop	L	25	3	7	.300	0	23	8	4	98	105	35	30	0	4.41
Lefty James	L	24	2	2	.500	0	11	4	4	39	42	9	18	0	3.00
Jim Baskette	R	25	0	0	.000	0	2	1	0	5	8	2	0	0	5.40
Lynn Brenton	R	22	0	0	.000	0	1	0	0	2	4	0	2	0	9.00
Lee Dashner	L	26	0	0	.000	0	1	0	0	2	0	0	2	0	4.50
Luke Glavenich	R	20	0	0	.000	0	1	0	0	1	3	3	1	0	9.00
Dave Gregg	R	22	0	0	.000	0	1	0	0	1	2	0	0	0	18.00

BOSTON 4th 79-71 .527 — JACK STAHL 39-41 .488 — BILL CARRIGAN 40-30 .571

	NAME	G by POS	B	AGE	G	AB	R	H	2B	3B	HR	RBI	BB	SO	SB	BA	SA
	TOTALS			26	151	4965	630	1334	220	101	17	531	466	534	189	.269	.364
	Clyde Engle	1B133, OF2	R	29	143	498	75	144	17	12	2	50	53	41	28	.289	.384
	Steve Yerkes	2B129	R	25	136	483	67	129	29	6	1	48	50	32	11	.267	.358
	Heinie Wagner (SA)	SS105, 2B4	R	32	110	365	43	83	14	8	2	34	40	29	9	.227	.326
	Larry Gardner	3B130	L	27	131	473	64	133	17	10	0	63	47	34	18	.281	.359
	Harry Hooper	OF147	L	25	148	586	100	169	29	12	4	40	60	51	26	.288	.399
	Tris Speaker	OF139	L	25	141	520	94	190	35	22	3	71	65	22	46	.365	.535
	Duffy Lewis	OF142	R	24	149	551	54	164	31	12	0	90	30	55	12	.298	.397
	Bill Carrigan	C81	R	29	85	256	17	62	15	5	0	28	27	26	6	.242	.340
	Hal Janvrin	SS48, 3B19, 2B8, 1B6	R	20	86	276	18	57	5	1	3	25	23	27	17	.207	.264
	Hick Cady	C38	R	27	39	96	10	24	5	2	0	6	5	14	1	.250	.344
	Pinch Thomas	C30	L	25	37	91	6	26	1	2	1	15	2	11	1	.286	.374
	Olaf Henriksen (IL)	OF7	L	25	30	40	8	15	1	0	0	2	7	5	3	.375	.400
	Wally Rehg	OF27	R	24	30	101	13	28	3	2	0	9	2	7	4	.277	.347
	Les Nunamaker	C27	R	24	29	65	9	14	5	2	0	9	8	8	2	.215	.354
	Neal Ball	2B10, SS8, 3B1	R	33	21	58	9	10	2	0	0	4	9	13	3	.172	.207
	Bill Mundy	1B14	L	24	15	47	4	12	0	0	0	4	4	12	0	.255	.255
	Wally Snell	C1	R	24	5	8	1	3	0	0	0	0	0	0	1	.375	.375
	Jake Stahl		R	33	2	2	0	0	0	0	0	0	0	1	0	.000	.000

	NAME	T	AGE	W	L	PCT	SV	G	GS	CG	IP	H	BB	SO	ShO	ERA
	TOTALS		26	79	71	.527	15	151	151	87	1355	1318	441	709	11	2.93
	Ray Collins	L	26	19	8	.704	0	30	30	19	247	242	37	88	3	2.63
	Hugh Bedient	R	23	15	14	.517	5	43	29	19	259	255	67	122	1	2.78
	Dutch Leonard	L	21	14	16	.467	1	42	27	14	259	245	94	144	2	2.39
	Smokey Joe Wood (BH)	R	23	11	5	.688	3	23	18	12	146	120	61	123	1	2.29
	Earl Moseley	R	28	9	5	.643	0	24	15	7	121	105	49	62	3	3.12
	Charley Hall	R	27	4	4	.500	5	35	4	2	105	97	46	48	0	3.43
1	Buck O'Brien	R	31	4	9	.308	0	15	12	6	90	103	35	54	0	3.70
	Rube Foster	R	25	3	4	.429	1	19	8	4	68	64	28	36	1	3.18
	Fred Anderson	R	27	0	6	.000	0	10	8	4	57	84	21	32	0	6.00
	Paul Maloy	R	21	0	0	.000	0	2	0	0	2	2	1	0	0	9.00
	Esty Chaney	R	22	0	0	.000	0	1	0	0	1	1	2	0	0	9.00

CHICAGO 5th 78-74 .513 17.5 — NIXEY CALLAHAN

	NAME	G by POS	B	AGE	G	AB	R	H	2B	3B	HR	RBI	BB	SO	SB	BA	SA
	TOTALS			25	153	4822	486	1139	157	66	23	410	398	550	156	.236	.310
2	Hal Chase	1B102	R	30	102	384	49	110	11	10	2	39	16	41	9	.286	.383
	Morrie Rath	2B86	L	26	90	295	37	59	2	0	0	12	46	22	22	.200	.207
	Buck Weaver	SS151	B	22	151	533	51	145	17	8	4	52	15	60	20	.272	.356
	Harry Lord	3B150	L	31	150	547	62	144	18	12	1	42	45	39	24	.263	.346
	Shano Collins	OF147	R	27	148	535	53	128	26	9	1	47	32	60	22	.239	.327
	Ping Bodie	OF119	R	25	127	406	39	107	14	8	8	48	35	57	5	.264	.397
	Chick Mattick	OF63	R	26	68	207	15	39	8	1	0	11	18	16	3	.188	.237
	Ray Schalk	C125	R	20	128	401	38	98	15	5	1	38	27	36	14	.244	.314
	Joe Berger	2B69, SS4, 3B1	R	26	77	223	27	48	6	2	2	20	36	28	5	.215	.287
	Jack Fournier	1B29, OF23	L	20	68	171	20	40	8	5	1	23	21	23	9	.234	.357
	Larry Chappell	OF59	L	23	60	208	20	48	8	1	0	15	18	22	7	.231	.279
	Ted Easterly	C19	L	28	60	97	3	23	1	0	0	8	4	9	2	.237	.247
	Biff Schaller	OF32	L	23	34	96	12	21	3	0	0	4	20	16	5	.219	.250
1	Babe Borton	1B26	L	24	28	80	9	22	5	0	0	13	23	5	1	.275	.338
	Walt Kuhn	C24	R	29	26	50	5	8	1	0	0	5	13	8	1	.160	.180
2	Johnny Beall	OF17	L	31	17	60	10	16	0	1	2	3	0	0	1	.267	.400
1	Rollie Zeider	3B6, 1B3, 2B1	R	29	13	20	4	7	0	0	0	2	4	1	3	.350	.350

Jim Breton 21 R 5-30, Davy Jones 33 L 6-21, Edd Roush 20 L 1-10, Nixey Callahan 39 R 2-9, Don Rader 19 L 1-3, Tom Daly 21 R 0-3, Billy Meyer 21 R 1-1

	NAME	T	AGE	W	L	PCT	SV	G	GS	CG	IP	H	BB	SO	ShO	ERA
	TOTALS		27	78	74	.513	9	153	153	86	1360	1189	438	602	16	2.33
	Red Russell	L	24	22	16	.579	4	51	36	25	316	249	79	122	7	1.91
	Jim Scott	R	24	20	20	.500	1	48	38	27	312	252	86	158	4	1.91
	Eddie Cicotte	R	29	18	12	.600	1	41	30	18	268	224	73	121	3	1.58
	Ed Walsh (SA)	R	32	8	3	.727	1	16	14	7	98	91	39	34	1	2.57
	Joe Benz	R	27	7	10	.412	2	33	17	7	151	146	59	79	1	2.74
	Doc White	L	34	2	4	.333	0	19	8	2	103	106	39	39	0	3.50
	Frank Lange	R	29	1	3	.250	0	12	3	0	41	46	20	20	0	4.83
	Pop Boy Smith	R	21	0	2	.000	0	15	2	0	32	31	11	13	0	3.38
	Frank Miller	R	27	0	1	.000	0	1	1	0	2	4	3	2	0	22.50
2	Buck O'Brien	R	31	0	3	.000	0	6	3	0	18	21	13	4	0	4.00
	Bill Lathrop	R	21	0	0	.000	0	6	0	0	17	16	12	9	0	4.24
	Jim Scoggins	L	21	0	0	.000	0	1	1	0	0	0	1	0	0	0.00
	Bob Smith	R	21	0	0	.000	0	1	0	0	2	3	3	1	0	13.50

Lena Blackburne (ST) 26

DETROIT 6th 66-87 .431 30 — HUGHIE JENNINGS

	NAME	G by POS	B	AGE	G	AB	R	H	2B	3B	HR	RBI	BB	SO	SB	BA	SA
	TOTALS			27	153	5064	624	1344	180	101	24	519	496	501	218	.265	.355
	Del Gainer	1B102	R	26	104	363	47	97	16	8	2	25	30	45	10	.267	.372
	Ossie Vitt	2B78, 3B17, OF2	R	23	99	359	45	86	11	3	2	33	31	18	5	.240	.304
	Donie Bush	SS152	B	25	152	593	98	149	19	10	1	40	80	32	44	.251	.322
	George Moriarty	3B93, OF7	R	28	102	347	29	83	5	2	0	30	24	25	33	.239	.265
	Sam Crawford	OF140, 1B13	L	33	153	610	78	193	32	23	9	83	52	28	13	.316	.489
	Ty Cobb	OF118	L	26	122	428	70	167	18	16	4	67	58	31	52	.390	.535
	Bobby Veach	OF136	L	25	137	494	54	133	22	10	0	64	53	31	22	.269	.354
	Oscar Stanage	C77	R	30	80	241	19	54	13	2	0	21	21	35	5	.224	.295
	Hugh High	OF50	L	25	80	183	18	42	6	1	0	16	28	24	6	.230	.273
	Baldy Louden	2B32, 3B26, SS6, OF5	R	29	72	191	28	46	4	5	0	23	24	22	6	.241	.314
	Jean Dubuc	P36, OF3	R	24	68	135	17	36	5	3	2	11	2	17	1	.267	.393
	Red McKee	C61	L	22	67	187	18	53	3	4	1	20	21	21	7	.283	.358
	Paddy Baumann	2B48	R	27	49	191	31	57	7	4	1	22	16	18	4	.298	.393
	Henri Rondeau	C14, 1B6	R	26	35	70	5	13	2	0	0	5	14	16	1	.186	.214
	Ed Willett	P34	R	29	35	92	8	26	4	1	1	13	3	23	0	.283	.380
	Frank Gibson	C19, OF1	L	22	20	57	8	8	1	0	0	2	3	9	2	.140	.158
	Eddie Onslow	1B17	L	20	17	55	7	14	1	0	0	8	5	9	1	.255	.273
1	Charlie Deal	3B15	R	21	16	50	3	11	0	2	0	3	1	7	2	.220	.300
	Guy Tutweiler	3B14	L	23	14	47	4	10	0	1	0	7	4	12	2	.213	.255
	Les Hennessey	2B9	R	19	12	22	2	3	0	0	0	0	3	6	2	.136	.136
	Wally Pipp	1B10	L	20	12	31	3	5	0	3	0	5	2	6	0	.161	.355

Al Platte 23 L 2-18, Joe Burns 24 L 5-13, Pepper Peploski 21 R 2-4, Ray Powell 24 L 0-0, Steve Partenheimer 21 R 0-2

	NAME	T	AGE	W	L	PCT	SV	G	GS	CG	IP	H	BB	SO	ShO	ERA
	TOTALS		25	66	87	.431	5	153	153	90	1360	1359	504	468	3	3.41
	Jean Dubuc	R	24	16	14	.533	0	36	28	22	243	228	91	73	1	2.89
	Hooks Dauss	R	23	13	12	.520	1	33	29	22	225	188	82	107	1	2.68
	Ed Willett	R	29	13	14	.481	0	34	30	19	242	237	89	59	0	3.09
	Mark Hall (NJ)	R	25	9	12	.429	0	30	21	8	165	154	79	69	1	3.27
	Joe Lake	R	31	8	7	.533	1	28	12	6	137	149	24	35	0	3.28
	Ralph Comstock	R	22	2	5	.286	1	10	7	1	60	90	16	37	0	5.40
1	George Mullin	R	32	1	6	.143	0	7	7	4	52	53	18	16	0	2.77
	Will House	R	22	1	2	.333	0	19	2	0	54	64	17	16	0	5.17
	Dutch Klawitter	R	25	1	2	.333	0	8	3	1	32	39	15	10	0	5.91
	Carl Zamloch	R	23	1	6	.143	1	17	5	3	70	66	23	28	0	2.71
	Lefty Williams	L	20	1	3	.250	1	5	4	3	29	34	4	9	0	4.97
	George Boehler	R	21	0	1	.000	0	1	1	1	8	11	6	2	0	6.75
	Lou North	R	22	0	1	.000	0	1	1	0	6	10	9	3	0	15.00
	Erwin Renfer	R	17	0	1	.000	0	1	1	0	6	5	3	1	0	6.00
	Al Clauss	L	22	0	1	.000	0	5	1	0	13	11	12	1	0	4.84
	Heinie Elder	L	22	0	0	.000	0	1	0	0	3	4	5	0	0	9.00
	Burt Grover (BH)	R	23	0	0	.000	0	2	1	0	11	9	7	2	0	3.28
	Charlie Harding	R	22	0	0	.000	0	1	0	0	2	3	1	0	0	4.50
	Lefty Lorenzen	L	20	0	0	.000	0	1	0	0	2	4	3	0	0	18.00

Ed Lafitte (ST) 27

NEW YORK 7th 57-94 .377 38 — FRANK CHANCE

	NAME	G by POS	B	AGE	G	AB	R	H	2B	3B	HR	RBI	BB	SO	SB	BA	SA
	TOTALS			27	153	4880	529	1157	154	45	9	430	534	617	203	.237	.293
	Jack Knight	1B50, 2B21	R	27	70	250	24	59	10	0	0	24	25	27	7	.236	.276
	Roy Hartzel	2B81, OF30, 3B21, SS4	L	31	141	490	60	127	18	1	0	38	67	40	26	.259	.300
2	Roger Peckinpaugh	SS93	R	22	95	340	35	91	10	7	1	32	24	47	19	.268	.347
	Ezra Midkiff	3B76, SS4, 2B2	L	30	83	284	22	56	9	1	0	14	12	33	9	.197	.236
	Bert Daniels	OF87	R	30	93	320	52	69	13	5	0	22	44	36	27	.216	.288
	Harry Wolter	OF121	L	28	126	425	53	108	18	6	2	43	80	50	13	.254	.339
	Birdie Cree	OF144	R	30	145	534	51	145	25	6	1	63	50	51	22	.272	.346
	Ed Sweeney	C112, 1B1	R	24	117	351	35	93	10	2	2	40	37	41	11	.265	.322
	Ray Caldwell	P27, OF3	L	25	55	97	10	28	3	2	0	11	3	15	3	.289	.361
	Fritz Maisel	3B51	R	23	51	187	33	48	4	3	0	12	34	20	25	.257	.310
2	Rollie Zeider (CJ)	SS23, 2B19, 1B4, 3B2	R	29	49	159	15	37	2	0	0	12	25	9	3	.233	.245
2	Bill McKechnie	2B27, SS7, 3B2	B	26	44	112	7	15	0	0	0	8	8	17	2	.134	.134
	Ray Fisher	P43	R	25	43	79	5	22	2	0	0	3	1	15	1	.278	.304
1	Hal Chase	1B29, 2B5, OF5	R	30	39	146	15	31	2	4	0	9	11	13	5	.212	.281
	Dick Gossett	C38	R	21	39	105	9	17	2	0	0	9	10	22	1	.162	.181
2	Babe Borton	1B33	L	24	33	108	8	14	1	0	1	11	18	19	1	.130	.167
	Harry Williams	1B27	R	23	27	82	18	21	3	1	1	12	15	10	6	.256	.354
	Frank Gilhooley	OF24	L	21	24	85	10	29	2	1	0	14	4	9	6	.341	.388
	Claud Derrick	SS14, 3B4, 2B1	R	27	22	65	7	19	1	0	1	7	5	8	2	.292	.354
	Dutch Sterrett	1B6, C1, OF1	R	23	21	35	0	6	0	0	0	3	1	5	1	.171	.171
	Doc Cook	OF20	L	22	20	72	9	19	2	1	0	1	10	4	1	.264	.319

Bill Holden 23 R 16-53, 1 Jack Lelivelt 27 L 6-28, Joe Smith 19 R 5-32, Bill Stumpf 21 R 6-29, Frank Chance 35 R 5-24, George Whiteman 30 R 11-32, Ralph Young 23 B 1-15, Bob Williams 19 R 3-19, Luke Boone 23 R 4-12, Bill Reynolds 28 R 0-5, Dan Costello 21 L 1-2, Joe Hanson 0-2

	NAME	T	AGE	W	L	PCT	SV	G	GS	CG	IP	H	BB	SO	ShO	ERA
	TOTALS		27	57	94	.377	6	153	153	78	1344	1318	455	530	7	3.27
	Ray Fisher	R	25	11	17	.393	0	43	31	15	246	244	71	92	1	3.19
	Russ Ford	R	30	11	18	.379	3	33	28	16	237	244	58	72	1	2.66
	Ray Caldwell	R	25	9	8	.529	1	27	16	15	164	131	60	87	2	2.43
	Al Schulz	L	24	8	14	.364	0	38	22	9	193	197	69	77	0	3.73
	Ray Keating	R	21	6	12	.333	0	28	21	9	151	147	51	83	2	3.22
	George McConnell	R	35	5	15	.250	2	35	20	9	180	162	60	72	0	3.20
	Jack Warhop (SA)	R	28	4	4	.500	0	15	7	1	62	69	33	11	0	3.77
	Marty McHale	R	24	2	4	.333	0	7	6	4	49	49	10	11	1	2.94
	Cy Pieh	R	26	1	0	1.000	0	4	0	0	10	10	7	6	0	4.50
	George Clark	L	22	0	1	.000	0	11	1	0	19	22	19	5	0	9.00
	Ed Klepfer	R	25	0	1	.000	0	8	1	0	25	38	12	10	0	7.56
	Red Hoff	L	22	0	0	.000	0	2	0	0	3	0	1	2	0	0.00
	Jim Hanley			0	0	.000	0	1	0	0	4	5	4	2	0	6.75

ST. LOUIS 8th 57-96 .373 39 — GEORGE STOVALL 50-84 .373 — JIMMY AUSTIN 2-6 .250 — BRANCH RICKEY 5-6 .454

	NAME	G by POS	B	AGE	G	AB	R	H	2B	3B	HR	RBI	BB	SO	SB	BA	SA
	TOTALS			27	155	5031	528	1193	179	73	18	422	449	769	209	.237	.312
	George Stovall	1B76	R	34	89	303	34	87	14	3	1	24	7	23	7	.287	.363
	Del Pratt	2B146, 1B9	R	25	155	592	60	175	31	13	2	87	40	57	37	.296	.402
	Mike Balenti	SS56, OF8	R	26	70	211	17	38	2	4	0	11	6	32	3	.180	.227
	Jimmy Austin	3B142	B	33	142	489	56	130	18	6	2	42	45	51	37	.266	.339
	Gus Williams	OF143	L	25	147	538	72	147	21	16	5	53	57	87	31	.273	.400
	Burt Shotton	OF146	L	28	147	549	105	163	23	8	1	28	99	63	43	.297	.373
	Johnny Johnston	OF106	L	23	109	380	37	85	14	4	2	27	42	51	11	.224	.297
	Sam Agnew	C103	R	26	104	307	27	64	9	5	2	24	20	49	11	.208	.290
	Dunny Brief	1B62, OF8	R	20	84	258	24	56	11	6	1	26	21	46	3	.217	.318
	Pete Compton	OF21	L	23	61	100	14	18	5	2	2	17	13	13	2	.180	.330
	Bobby Wallace (BH)	SS38, 3B7	R	39	53	147	11	31	5	0	0	21	14	16	1	.211	.245
	Bill McAllester	C37	R	23	47	85	3	13	4	0	0	6	11	12	2	.153	.200
1	Doc Lavan	SS46	R	22	46	149	8	21	2	1	0	4	10	46	3	.141	.168
	Walt Alexander	C43	R	22	43	110	5	15	2	1	0	7	4	36	1	.136	.173
	Tilly Walker	OF23	R	25	23	85	7	25	4	1	0	11	2	9	5	.294	.365
	Dee Walsh	SS22, 3B1	B	23	23	53	8	9	0	1	0	5	6	11	3	.170	.208
	Sam Covington	1B16	L	20	20	60	3	9	0	1	0	4	4	6	3	.150	.183
	Rivington Bisland	SS12	R	23	12	44	3	6	0	0	0	3	2	5	0	.136	.136

George Maisel 21 R 3-18, Buzzy Wares 27 R 10-35, Tod Sloan 22 L 7-26, Ernie Walker 22 L 3-14, Frank Crossin 22 R 1-4, Charlie Flanagan 21 R 0-3,
Fred Graff 24 R 2-5, Walt Meinert 22 L 3-8, Luther Bonin 25 L 0-1, George Tomer 17 L 0-1

	NAME	T	AGE	W	L	PCT	SV	G	GS	CG	IP	H	BB	SO	ShO	ERA
	TOTALS		24	57	96	.373	4	155	155	101	1382	1369	454	476	13	3.06
	Earl Hamilton	L	21	13	12	.520	1	31	24	19	217	197	83	101	3	2.57
	Roy Mitchell	R	28	13	16	.448	1	33	27	21	245	265	47	59	4	3.02
	George Baumgardner	R	21	10	19	.345	1	38	31	22	253	267	84	78	2	3.13
	Carl Weilman	L	23	10	20	.333	0	39	28	17	252	262	60	79	1	3.39
	Walt Leverenz	L	24	6	17	.261	1	30	27	14	203	159	89	87	2	2.57
	Dwight Stone	R	26	2	6	.250	0	18	7	3	91	94	46	37	1	3.56
	Hal Schwenk	L	22	1	0	1.000	0	1	1	1	11	12	4	3	0	3.27
	Curly Brown	L	24	1	1	.500	0	2	2	1	14	12	4	3	0	2.57
	Mack Allison	R	26	1	3	.250	0	11	4	2	51	52	13	12	0	2.30
	Willie Adams	R	22	0	0	.000	0	4	0	0	9	12	4	5	0	10.00
	Wiley Taylor	R	25	0	2	.000	0	5	4	1	32	33	16	12	0	4.78
	Sam Powell			0	0	.000	0	2	0	0	2	1	2	0	0	0.00
	Pete Schmidt	L		0	0	.000	1	1	0	0	2	3	2	0	0	4.50

NEW YORK 1st 101-51 .664 — JOHN McGRAW

NAME	G by POS	B	AGE	G	AB	R	H	2B	3B	HR	RBI	BB	SO	SB	BA	SA
TOTALS			26	156	5218	684	1427	226	70	31	580	444	501	**296**	**.273**	.361
Fred Merkle	1B153	R	24	153	563	78	147	30	12	3	69	41	60	35	.261	.373
Larry Doyle	2B130	L	26	132	482	67	135	25	6	5	73	59	29	38	.280	.388
Art Fletcher	SS136	R	28	136	538	76	160	20	9	4	71	24	35	32	.297	.390
Buck Herzog	3B84, 2B2	R	27	96	290	46	83	15	3	3	31	22	12	23	.286	.390
Red Murray	OF147	R	29	147	520	70	139	21	3	2	59	34	28	35	.267	.331
Fred Snodgrass	OF133, 1B3, 2B1	R	25	141	457	65	133	21	6	3	49	53	44	27	.291	.383
George Burns	OF150	R	23	150	605	81	173	37	4	2	54	58	**74**	40	.286	.370
Chief Meyers	C116	R	32	120	378	37	118	18	5	3	47	37	22	7	.312	.410
Tillie Shafer	3B79, 2B25, SS17, OF15	B	24	138	508	74	146	17	12	5	52	61	55	32	.287	.398
Moose McCormick	OF15	L	32	57	80	9	22	2	3	0	15	5	13	0	.275	.375
Art Wilson	C49, 1B2	R	27	54	79	5	15	0	1	0	8	11	11	1	.190	.215
13Doc Crandall	P35, 2B2	R	25	46	47	7	15	4	1	0	4	3	8	0	.319	.447
2 Larry McLean	C28	R	31	30	75	3	24	4	0	0	9	4	4	1	.320	.373
Claude Cooper	OF15	L	20	27	30	11	9	4	0	0	4	4	6	3	.300	.433
2 Eddie Grant	3B5, 2B3, SS1	L	30	27	20	8	4	1	0	0	1	2	2	1	.200	.250
Grover Hartley	C21, 1B1	R	24	23	19	4	6	0	0	0	0	1	2	4	.316	.316
Jim Thorpe	OF9	R	25	19	35	6	5	0	0	1	2	1	9	2	.143	.229
1 Josh Devore	OF8	L	25	16	21	4	4	0	1	0	1	3	4	6	.190	.286
Milt Stock	SS1	R	19	7	17	2	3	1	0	0	1	2	1	2	.176	.235
1 Heinie Groh	3B2, SS1	R	23	4	2	0	0	0	0	0	0	0	1	0	.000	.000
Joe Evers		L	21	1	0	0	0	0	0	0	0	0	0	0	.000	.000
Howard Merritt	OF1	R	18	1	0	0	0	0	0	0	0	0	0	0	.000	.000

NAME	T	AGE	W	L	PCT	SV	G	GS	CG	IP	H	BB	SO	ShO	ERA
		28	**101**	51	**.664**	**17**	156	156	82	1420	1276	315	651	11	**2.43**
Christy Mathewson	R	34	25	11	.694	2	40	35	25	306	**291**	21	93	4	**2.06**
Rube Marquard	L	23	23	10	.697	3	42	33	20	288	248	49	151	4	2.50
Jeff Tesreau	R	24	22	13	.629	0	41	**38**	17	282	222	119	167	1	2.17
Al Demaree	R	26	13	4	.765	2	31	24	11	200	176	38	76	2	2.21
2 Art Fromme	R	29	11	6	.644	0	26	12	3	112	112	29	50	0	4.01
13Doc Crandall	R	25	4	4	.500	6	35	3	2	98	102	24	42	0	2.84
1 Red Ames	R	30	2	1	.667	1	8	5	2	42	35	8	30	0	2.57
Bunny Hearn	L	22	1	1	.500	0	2	2	1	13	13	7	8	0	2.77
Rube Schauer	R	22	0	1	.000	0	3	1	1	12	14	9	7	0	7.50
Hooks Wiltse	L	32	0	0	.000	3	17	2	0	58	53	8	25	0	1.55
Ferdie Schupp	L	22	0	0	.000	0	5	1	0	12	10	3	2	0	0.75

PHILADELPHIA 2nd 88-63 .583 12.5 — RED DOOIN

NAME	G by POS	B	AGE	G	AB	R	H	2B	3B	HR	RBI	BB	SO	SB	BA	SA
TOTALS			29	159	**5400**	693	**1433**	**257**	78	**73**	597	383	578	156	.265	**.382**
Fred Luderus	1B155	L	27	155	588	67	154	32	7	18	86	34	51	5	.262	.432
Otto Knabe	2B148	R	29	148	571	70	150	25	7	2	53	45	26	14	.263	.342
Mickey Doolan	SS148, 2B3	R	33	151	518	32	113	12	6	1	43	24	68	17	.218	.270
Hans Lobert	3B145, SS3, 2B1	R	31	150	573	98	172	28	11	7	55	42	34	41	.300	.424
Gavvy Cravath	OF141	R	32	147	525	78	**179**	34	14	**19**	**128**	55	63	10	.341	**.568**
Dode Paskert	OF120	R	31	124	454	83	119	21	9	4	29	65	69	12	.262	.374
Sherry Magee	OF123, 1B4	R	28	138	470	92	144	36	6	11	70	38	36	23	.306	.479
Bill Killefer	C118, 1B1	R	25	120	360	25	88	14	3	0	24	4	17	2	.244	.300
2 Beals Becker	OF77, 1B1	L	26	88	306	53	99	19	10	9	44	22	30	11	.324	.539
Doc Miller	OF12	L	30	69	87	9	30	6	0	0	11	6	6	2	.345	.414
1 Cozy Dolan	OF12, SS10, 2B9, 3B4, 1B1	R	30	55	126	15	33	4	0	0	8	1	21	9	.262	.294
Red Dooin	C50	R	34	55	129	6	33	4	1	0	13	3	9	1	.256	.302
Dan Howley	C22	R	27	26	32	5	4	2	0	0	2	4	4	3	.125	.188
Jimmy Walsh	2B6, SS3, 3B1, OF1	R	27	26	30	3	10	4	0	0	5	1	5	1	.333	.467
3 Josh Devore	OF14	L	25	23	39	9	11	1	0	0	5	4	7	0	.282	.308
2 Bobby Byrne	3B15	R	28	19	58	9	13	1	0	1	4	5	3	2	.224	.293

Ed Burns 24 R 6-30, Milt Reed 22 L 6-24, Vern Duncan 23 L 5-12, 1 John Dodge 24 R 1-3, Ralph Capron 20 L 0-1, Pat Moran 37 R 0-1

NAME	T	AGE	W	L	PCT	SV	G	GS	CG	IP	H	BB	SO	ShO	ERA
		26	88	63	.583	11	159	159	77	**1455**	1407	**512**	**667**	**10**	3.15
Tom Seaton	R	**25**	**27**	12	.692	1	52	35	21	**322**	262	**136**	**168**	6	2.60
Pete Alexander	R	26	22	8	.733	2	47	35	23	306	288	75	159	**7**	2.79
Ad Brennan	L	31	14	12	.538	1	40	25	12	207	204	46	94	1	2.39
Eppa Rixey	L	22	9	5	.643	2	35	19	9	156	148	56	75	2	3.11
Erskine Mayer	R	24	9	9	.500	1	39	20	7	171	172	46	51	2	3.11
2 Howie Camnitz	R	31	3	3	.500	1	9	5	1	49	49	23	21	0	3.67
George Chalmers	R	25	3	10	.231	1	26	13	4	116	133	51	46	0	4.81
1 Earl Moore	R	33	1	3	.250	1	12	4	0	52	50	40	24	0	5.02
Rube Marshall	R	22	0	1	.000	1	14	3	0	45	54	22	18	0	4.60
Doc Imlay	R	24	0	0	.000	0	9	0	0	14	19	7	7	0	7.07
Happy Finnernan	R	21	0	0	.000	0	3	0	0	5	12	2	0	0	7.20
1 Red Nelson	R	27	0	0	.000	0	2	0	0	8	9	4	3	0	2.25
Jim Haislip	R	21	0	0	.000	0	1	0	0	3	4	3	0	0	6.00
Ray Hartranft			0	0	.000	0	1	0	0	1	3	1	1	0	9.00

CHICAGO 3rd 88-65 .575 13.5 — JOHNNY EVERS

NAME	G by POS	B	AGE	G	AB	R	H	2B	3B	HR	RBI	BB	SO	SB	BA	SA
TOTALS			29	154	5010	**720**	1286	194	**96**	59	**617**	**553**	634	181	.257	.369
Vic Saier	1B148	L	22	148	518	93	149	14	**21**	14	92	62	62	26	.288	.477
Johnny Evers	2B135	L	31	135	444	81	126	20	5	3	49	50	14	11	.284	.372
Al Bridwell	SS135	L	29	135	405	35	97	6	6	1	37	74	28	12	.240	.291
Heinie Zimmerman	3B125	R	26	127	447	69	140	28	12	9	95	41	40	18	.313	.490
Wildfire Schulte	OF129	L	30	131	495	85	138	28	6	9	68	39	68	21	.279	.414
Tommy Leach	OF119, 3B2	R	35	130	454	**99**	131	23	10	6	32	77	44	21	.289	.423
1 Mike Mitchell	OF81	R	33	81	278	37	72	11	6	4	35	32	33	15	.259	.385
Jimmy Archer	C103, 1B8	R	30	110	367	38	98	14	7	2	44	19	27	4	.267	.360
Art Phelan	2B46, 3B38, SS1	R	25	90	259	41	65	11	6	2	35	29	25	8	.251	.363
Ward Miller	OF63	L	28	80	203	23	48	5	7	1	16	34	33	13	.236	.345
Roger Bresnahan	C58	R	34	68	161	20	37	5	2	1	21	21	11	7	.230	.304
Wilbur Good	OF26	L	27	49	91	11	23	3	2	1	12	11	16	5	.253	.363
Cy Williams	OF44	L	25	49	156	17	35	3	3	4	32	5	26	5	.224	.359
Red Corriden	SS36, 2B2, 3B1	R	25	45	97	13	17	3	0	2	9	9	14	4	.175	.268
1 Otis Clymer	OF26	L	36	30	105	16	24	5	1	0	7	14	18	9	.229	.295
Tom Needham	C14, 1B1	R	34	20	42	5	10	4	1	0	11	4	8	0	.238	.381
Tuffy Stewart	OF1	L	29	9	8	1	1	1	0	0	2	2	5	1	.125	.250

Bubbles Hargrave 20 R 1-3, Milo Allison 22 L 2-6, 1 Mike Hechinger 23 R 0-2, Chick Keating 21 R 1-5, Pete Knisely 29 R 0-2, Fritz Mollwitz 23 R 3-7, Ed McDonald 26 R 0-0

NAME	T	AGE	W	L	PCT	SV	G	GS	CG	IP	H	BB	SO	ShO	ERA
		29	88	65	.575	15	154	154	89	1372	1330	478	556	12	3.13
Larry Cheney	R	27	21	14	.667	**11**	**54**	36	25	305	271	98	136	2	2.57
Bert Humphries	R	32	16	4	**.800**	1	28	20	13	181	169	24	61	2	2.69
George Pearce	L	25	13	5	.722	0	25	21	14	163	137	59	73	3	2.32
Jimmy Lavender	R	29	10	14	.417	2	40	20	10	204	206	98	91	0	3.66
Charlie Smith	R	33	7	9	.438	0	20	17	8	138	138	34	47	1	2.55
Hippo Vaughn	L	25	5	1	.833	0	7	6	5	56	37	27	36	2	1.45
2 Eddie Stack	R	25	4	2	.667	1	11	7	3	51	56	15	28	1	4.24
Orvie Overall	R	32	4	5	.444	0	11	9	6	68	73	26	30	1	3.31
Fred Toney	R	25	2	2	.500	0	7	5	2	39	52	22	12	0	6.00
Lew Richie	R	29	2	4	.333	0	16	6	1	65	77	30	15	0	5.82
Doc Watson	L	28	1	0	1.000	0	1	1	1	9	8	6	1	0	1.00
Zip Zabel	R	22	1	0	1.000	0	1	1	0	5	3	1	0	0	0.00
2 Earl Moore	R	33	1	1	.500	0	7	2	0	28	34	12	12	0	4.50
1 Ed Reulbach	R	30	1	3	.250	0	10	2	1	39	41	21	10	0	4.38
Lefty Leifield	L	29	0	1	.000	0	6	1	0	21	28	5	4	0	5.57

PITTSBURGH 4th 78-71 .523 21.5 — FRED CLARKE

NAME	G by POS	B	AGE	G	AB	R	H	2B	3B	HR	RBI	BB	SO	SB	BA	SA
TOTALS			28	155	5252	673	1383	210	86	35	570	391	545	181	.263	.356
Dots Miller	1B150, SS3	R	26	154	580	75	158	24	20	7	90	37	52	20	.272	.419
Jim Viox	2B124, SS10	R	22	137	492	86	156	32	8	2	65	64	28	14	.317	.427
Honus Wagner	SS105	R	39	114	413	51	124	18	4	3	56	26	40	21	.300	.385
1 Bobby Byrne	3B110	R	28	113	448	54	121	22	0	1	47	29	28	10	.270	.326
Owen Wilson	OF155	L	29	155	580	71	154	12	14	10	73	32	62	9	.266	.386
2 Mike Mitchell	OF54	R	33	54	199	25	54	8	2	1	16	14	15	7	.271	.347
Max Carey	OF154	B	23	154	**620**	**99**	172	23	10	5	49	55	67	**61**	.277	.371
Mike Simon	C92	R	30	92	255	23	63	6	2	1	17	10	15	3	.247	.298
Art Butler	2B27, SS24, 3B2, OF2	R	25	82	214	40	60	9	3	0	20	32	14	9	.280	.350
Ham Hyatt	1B5, OF5	L	28	63	81	8	27	6	2	4	16	3	8	0	.333	.605
George Gibson (BN)	C48	R	32	48	118	6	33	4	2	0	12	10	8	2	.280	.347
Billy Kelly	C40	R	27	48	82	11	22	2	2	0	9	2	12	1	.268	.341
Eddie Mensor	OF18, 2B1, SS1	B	23	44	56	9	10	1	0	0	1	8	13	2	.179	.196
Babe Adams	P43	R	31	43	114	13	33	6	2	0	13	1	16	0	.289	.377
Fred Kommers	OF40	L	27	40	155	14	36	5	4	0	22	10	29	1	.232	.316
2 Cozy Dolan	3B35	R	30	35	133	22	27	5	2	0	9	15	14	14	.203	.271
Alex McCarthy	SS12, 3B12, 2B6	R	25	31	74	7	15	5	0	0	10	7	7	1	.203	.270
Everett Booe	OF22	L	23	29	80	9	16	0	2	0	2	6	9	2	.200	.250
Solly Hofman	OF24	R	30	28	83	11	19	5	2	0	7	8	6	3	.229	.337
Bob Coleman	C24	R	22	24	50	5	9	2	0	0	9	7	8	0	.180	.220
Roy Wood	OF8, 1B1	R	20	14	35	4	10	4	0	0	2	1	8	0	.286	.400
Fred Clarke	OF2	L	40	9	13	0	1	1	0	0	0	0	0	0	.077	.154

Gil Britton 21 R 0-12, Jake Kafora 24 R 0-1

NAME	T	AGE	W	L	PCT	SV	G	GS	CG	IP	H	BB	SO	ShO	ERA
		26	78	71	.523	7	155	155	74	1400	1344	434	590	9	2.90
Babe Adams	R	31	21	10	.677	0	43	37	24	314	271	49	144	4	2.15
Hank Robinson	L	23	14	9	.609	0	43	23	8	196	184	41	50	1	2.39
Claude Hendrix	R	24	14	15	.483	3	42	25	17	241	216	89	138	2	3.84
George McQuillan	R	28	8	6	.571	1	25	16	7	142	144	35	59	0	3.42
Marty O'Toole (IL)	R	25	6	8	.429	1	26	15	7	145	148	55	58	0	3.29
1 Howie Camnitz	R	31	6	17	.261	2	36	22	5	192	203	84	64	1	3.75
Wilbur Cooper	L	21	5	3	.625	0	30	9	3	93	98	45	39	1	3.29
Bill Luhrsen	R	29	3	1	.750	0	5	3	2	29	25	16	11	0	2.48
Jack Ferry	R	26	1	0	1.000	0	4	0	0	5	4	2	2	0	5.40
Joe Conzelman	R	23	0	1	.000	0	3	2	1	15	13	5	9	0	1.20
Jack Scheneberg	R	25	0	1	.000	0	1	1	0	6	10	2	1	0	6.00
Eddie Eayrs	L	22	0	0	.000	0	2	0	0	8	8	6	5	0	2.25
Bernie Duffy	R	19	0	0	.000	0	3	2	0	11	18	3	8	0	5.72
Al Mamaux	R	19	0	0	.000	0	1	0	0	3	2	2	2	0	3.00

Mike Donlin (VR) 35

BOSTON 5th 69-82 .457 31.5 — GEORGE STALLINGS

NAME	G by POS	B	AGE	G	AB	R	H	2B	3B	HR	RBI	BB	SO	SB	BA	SA
TOTALS			26	154	5145	641	1318	191	60	32	533	488	**641**	177	.256	.335
Hap Myers	1B135	R	25	140	524	74	143	20	1	2	50	38	48	57	.273	.326
Bill Sweeney	2B137	R	27	139	502	65	129	17	6	0	47	66	50	18	.257	.315
Rabbit Maranville	SS143	R	21	143	571	68	141	13	8	2	48	68	62	25	.247	.308
Art Devlin	3B69	R	33	73	210	19	48	7	5	0	12	29	17	8	.229	.310
John Titus	OF75	L	37	87	269	33	80	14	2	5	38	35	22	4	.297	.420
Les Mann	OF120	R	19	120	407	54	103	24	7	3	51	18	73	7	.253	.369
Joe Connolly	OF124	L	25	126	427	79	120	18	11	5	57	66	47	18	.281	.410
Bill Rariden	C87	R	25	95	246	31	58	9	2	3	30	30	21	5	.236	.325
Fred Smith	3B59, 2B14, SS11, OF4	R	21	92	285	35	65	9	3	0	27	29	55	7	.228	.281
Bert Whaling	C77	R	25	79	211	22	51	8	2	0	25	10	32	3	.242	.299
Bris Lord	OF62	R	29	73	235	22	59	12	1	6	26	8	22	7	.251	.387
2 Tex McDonald	3B31, 2B6, OF1	L	24	62	145	24	52	4	4	0	18	15	17	4	.359	.441
Cy Seymour	OF18	L	40	39	73	2	13	2	0	0	10	7	7	2	.178	.205
Tommy Griffith	OF35	L	23	37	127	16	32	4	1	1	12	9	8	1	.252	.323
Guy Zinn	OF35	L	26	36	138	15	41	8	2	1	15	4	23	3	.297	.406
Otto Hess	P29	L	34	35	83	9	26	0	1	2	11	7	15	0	.313	.410
Butch Schmidt	1B22	L	26	22	78	6	24	2	2	1	14	2	5	1	.308	.423
Jay Kirke	OF13	L	25	18	38	3	9	2	0	0	3	1	6	0	.237	.289
Wilson Collins	OF9	R	24	16	3	3	1	0	0	0	0	0	0	0	.333	.333

Drummond Brown 28 R 11-34, 2 Otis Clymer 36 L 12-37, 2 Charlie Deal 21 R 11-36, Joe Schultz 19 R 4-18, Bill Calhoun 23 L 1-13, Oscar Dugey 25 R 2-8, Fred Mitchell 35 R 1-3,
Rex DeVogt 25 R 0-6, Hank Gowdy 23 R 3-5, George Jackson 31 R 3-10, Art Bues 25 R 0-1, Jeff McCleskey 21 L 0-3, Walt Tragesser 26 R 0-0, 1 Bill McKechnie 26 B 0-4, Bill McTigue 22 R 0-0

NAME	T	AGE	W	L	PCT	SV	G	GS	CG	IP	H	BB	SO	ShO	ERA
		27	69	82	.457	3	154	154	**105**	1373	1343	419	597	12	3.19
Hud Perdue	R	31	16	13	.552	1	38	32	16	212	201	39	91	3	3.27
Lefty Tyler	L	23	16	17	.485	2	39	34	**28**	290	245	108	143	4	2.79
Dick Rudolph	R	25	14	13	.519	0	33	22	17	249	258	59	109	1	2.93
Otto Hess	L	34	7	17	.292	0	29	27	19	218	231	70	80	2	3.84
Walt Dickson	R	30	6	7	.462	0	19	15	8	128	118	45	47	0	3.23
Bill James	R	21	6	10	.375	0	24	14	10	136	134	57	73	1	2.78
Jack Quinn	R	29	4	3	.571	0	8	7	6	56	55	7	33	1	2.43
Lefty Gervais	L	22	0	1	.000	0	5	2	1	16	18	4	1	0	5.63
Gene Cocreham	R	28	0	1	.000	0	1	1	0	8	13	4	3	0	7.88
Win Noyes	R	24	0	0	.000	0	11	0	0	21	22	6	5	0	4.72
Paul Strand	L	19	0	0	.000	0	7	0	0	17	22	12	6	0	2.12
Buster Brown	R	31	0	0	.000	0	2	0	0	13	19	3	3	0	4.84
George Davis	R	23	0	0	.000	0	2	0	0	8	7	5	3	0	4.50

Ben Houser (KJ) 29

BROOKLYN 6th 65-84 .436 34.5 — BILL DAHLEN

NAME	G by POS	B	AGE	G	AB	R	H	2B	3B	HR	RBI	BB	SO	SB	BA	SA
TOTALS			26	152	5165	595	1394	193	86	39	502	361	555	188	.270	.363
Jake Daubert	1B138	L	29	139	508	76	178	17	7	2	52	44	40	25	**.350**	.423
George Cutshaw	2B147	R	25	147	592	72	158	23	13	7	80	39	22	39	.267	.385
Bobby Fisher	SS131	R	26	132	474	42	124	11	10	4	54	10	43	16	.262	.352
Red Smith	3B151	R	23	151	540	70	160	**40**	10	6	76	45	67	22	.296	.441
Herbie Moran	OF129	L	29	132	515	71	137	15	5	0	26	45	29	21	.266	.315
Casey Stengel	OF119	L	22	124	438	60	119	16	8	7	43	56	58	19	.272	.393
Zack Wheat	OF135	L	27	138	535	64	161	28	10	7	58	25	45	19	.301	.430
Otto Miller	C103, 1B1	R	24	104	320	26	87	11	7	0	26	10	31	7	.272	.350
John Hummel	OF28, SS17, 1B6, 2B3	R	30	67	198	20	48	7	7	2	24	13	23	4	.242	.379
Bill Fischer	C51	L	22	62	165	16	44	9	4	1	12	10	5	0	.267	.388
Enos Kirkpatrick	SS10, 1B8, 2B6, 3B4	R	27	48	89	13	22	4	1	1	5	3	18	5	.247	.348
Earl Yingling	P26	L	24	40	60	11	23	1	0	0	5	9	8	0	.383	.400
Benny Meyer	OF27, C1	R	25	38	87	12	17	0	1	1	10	10	14	8	.195	.253
Leo Callahan	OF8	L	22	33	41	6	7	3	1	0	3	4	5	0	.171	.293
Bill Collins	OF27	B	31	32	95	8	18	1	0	0	4	8	11	2	.189	.200
Tex Erwin (BA)	C13	L	27	20	31	6	8	1	0	0	3	4	5	0	.258	.290
Eddie Phelps	C4	R	34	15	18	0	4	0	0	0	0	1	2	0	.222	.222
2 Mike Hechinger	C4	R	23	9	11	1	2	1	0	0	0	0	2	0	.182	.273
Lew McCarty	C9	R	24	9	26	1	6	0	0	0	2	2	0	0	.231	.231
Al Scheer	OF6	L	24	6	22	3	5	0	0	0	0	2	4	1	.227	.227
Ray Mowe	SS2	L	23	5	9	0	1	0	0	0	0	0	1	0	.111	.111

NAME	T	AGE	W	L	PCT	SV	G	GS	CG	IP	H	BB	SO	ShO	ERA
		26	65	84	.436	7	152	152	70	1373	1287	439	548	9	3.13
Pat Ragan	R	24	15	18	.455	0	44	32	14	265	284	64	109	0	3.77
Nap Rucker	L	28	14	15	.483	3	41	33	16	260	236	67	111	4	2.87
Earl Yingling	L	24	8	8	.500	0	26	13	8	147	158	10	40	2	2.57
Cliff Curtis	R	30	8	9	.471	2	30	16	5	152	145	55	57	0	3.26
2 Ed Reulbach	R	30	7	6	.538	0	15	12	8	110	77	34	46	2	2.05
Bull Wagner	R	25	4	2	.667	0	18	1	0	71	77	30	11	0	5.45
1 Eddie Stack	R	25	4	4	.500	0	23	9	4	87	79	32	34	1	2.38
Frank Allen	L	23	4	18	.182	2	34	25	11	175	144	81	82	0	2.83
Mysterious Walker	R	29	1	3	.250	0	11	8	3	58	44	35	35	0	3.57
Jeff Pfeffer	R	25	0	1	.000	0	5	2	1	24	28	13	13	0	3.38
Maury Kent	R	27	0	0	.000	0	3	0	0	7	5	3	1	0	2.57
Elmer Brown	R	30	0	0	.000	0	3	1	0	13	6	10	6	0	2.08
Bill Hall	R	21	0	0	.000	0	3	0	0	5	4	5	3	0	5.40

Elmer Knetzer (HO) 27

CINCINNATI 7th 64-89 .418 37.5 — JOE TINKER

NAME	G by POS	B	AGE	G	AB	R	H	2B	3B	HR	RBI	BB	SO	SB	BA	SA
TOTALS			28	156	5132	607	1339	170	**96**	27	541	458	579	226	.261	.347
Dick Hoblitzell	1B134	L	24	137	502	59	143	23	7	3	62	35	26	18	.285	.376
2 Heinie Groh	2B113, SS4	R	23	117	397	51	112	19	5	3	48	38	36	24	.282	.378
Joe Tinker	SS101, 3B9	R	32	110	382	47	121	20	13	1	57	20	26	10	.317	.445
2 John Dodge	3B91	R	24	94	323	35	78	8	8	4	45	10	34	11	.241	.353
Johnny Bates	OF111	L	31	131	407	63	113	13	7	6	51	67	30	21	.278	.388
Armando Marsans	OF94, 1B22, 3B2, SS1	R	26	118	435	49	129	7	6	0	38	17	25	37	.297	.340
Bob Bescher	OF138	B	29	141	511	86	132	22	11	1	37	**94**	68	38	.258	.350
Tommy Clarke	C100	R	25	114	330	29	87	11	8	1	38	39	40	2	.264	.355
Johnny Kling	C63	R	38	80	209	20	57	7	6	0	23	14	14	2	.273	.364
Marty Berghammer	SS53, 2B13	L	25	74	188	25	41	4	1	1	13	10	29	16	.218	.266
2 Josh Devore	OF57	L	25	66	217	30	58	6	4	3	14	12	21	17	.267	.373
Dick Egan	2B30, SS17, 3B2	R	29	60	195	15	55	7	3	0	22	15	13	6	.282	.349
Rafael Almeida	3B37, OF3, SS2, 2B1	R	25	50	130	14	34	4	2	3	21	11	16	4	.262	.392
2 Jimmy Sheckard	OF38	L	34	47	116	16	22	1	3	0	7	27	16	6	.190	.250
1 Beals Becker	OF28	L	26	30	108	11	32	5	3	0	14	6	12	0	.296	.398
1 Eddie Grant	3B26	L	30	27	94	12	20	1	0	0	9	11	10	7	.213	.223
Al Wickland	OF24	L	25	26	79	7	17	5	5	0	8	6	19	3	.215	.405
Earl Blackburn	C12	R	20	17	27	1	7	0	0	0	3	2	5	2	.259	.259
1 Tex McDonald	SS1	L	24	11	10	1	3	0	0	0	2	0	1	0	.300	.300

Hank Severeid 22 R 0-6, Bill Hobbs 20 R 0-4, Karl Meister 22 R 2-7, Harry Chapman 25 R 1-2, Bert Niehoff 29 R 0-8, Mark Stewart 23 L 0-1

NAME	T	AGE	W	L	PCT	SV	G	GS	CG	IP	H	BB	SO	ShO	ERA
		29	64	89	.418	10	156	156	71	1380	1398	456	522	10	3.46
Chief Johnson	R	27	14	16	.467	0	44	31	13	269	251	86	107	3	3.01
Rube Benton (JJ)	L	26	11	7	.611	0	23	22	9	144	140	60	68	1	3.50
Three Finger Brown	R	36	11	12	.478	6	39	16	11	173	174	44	41	1	2.92
2 Red Ames	R	30	11	13	.458	2	31	24	12	187	185	70	80	1	2.89
George Suggs	R	31	8	15	.348	2	36	22	9	199	220	35	73	2	4.03
Gene Packard	L	25	7	11	.389	0	39	21	9	191	208	64	73	2	2.97
Frank Harter	R	26	1	1	.500	0	17	2	0	47	47	19	10	0	3.83
1 Art Fromme	R	29	1	4	.200	0	9	7	2	56	55	21	24	0	4.18
Chick Smith	L	20	0	1	.000	0	5	1	0	18	15	11	11	0	3.50
Ralph Works	R	25	0	1	.000	0	5	2	0	15	15	8	4	0	7.80
Dick Robertson	R	22	0	1	.000	0	2	1	1	10	13	9	1	0	7.20
Bill Powell	R	28	0	1	.000	0	1	1	0	.1	2	2	0	0	54.00
Harry McIntire	R	35	0	1	.000	0	1	0	0	1	3	0	0	0	27.00
Joe McManus	R	25	0	0	.000	0	1	0	0	2	3	4	1	0	18.00
Jack Rowan	R	26	0	4	.000	0	5	5	5	39	37	9	21	0	3.00
Ernie Herbert	R	26	0	0	.000	0	6	0	0	17	12	5	5	0	2.12
2 Red Nelson	R	27	0	0	.000	0	2	0	0	2	6	4	0	0	31.50
Fred Betts			0	0	.000	0	1	0	0	3	1	3	0	0	3.00
Francis Harrington	R	24	0	0	.000	0	1	0	0	4	6	1	1	0	9.00
Cy Morgan	R	34	0	1	.000	0	1	1	0	2	5	1	2	0	18.00

ST. LOUIS 8th 51-99 .340 49 — MILLER HUGGINS

NAME	G by POS	B	AGE	G	AB	R	H	2B	3B	HR	RBI	BB	SO	SB	BA	SA
TOTALS			27	152	4952	523	1221	152	72	14	427	450	573	171	.247	.315
Ed Konetchy	1B139, P1	R	27	139	502	74	137	18	17	7	68	53	41	27	.273	.418
Miller Huggins	2B112	B	34	120	381	73	109	12	0	0	27	91	49	23	.286	.318
Charley O'Leary	SS102, 2B15	R	31	120	404	32	88	15	5	0	31	20	34	3	.218	.280
Mike Mowrey	3B130	R	29	131	449	61	116	18	4	0	33	53	40	21	.258	.316
Steve Evans	OF74, 1B1	L	28	97	245	18	61	15	6	1	31	20	28	5	.249	.371
Rebel Oakes	OF144	L	26	146	537	59	156	14	5	0	49	43	32	22	.291	.335
Lee Magee	OF107, 2B21, 1B6, SS2	B	24	136	529	53	140	13	7	2	31	34	30	23	.265	.327
Ivy Wingo	C97, 1B5, OF1	L	22	111	305	25	78	5	8	2	35	17	41	18	.256	.344
P. Whitted	OF40, SS37, 3B21, 2B7, 1B2	R	23	122	402	44	89	10	5	0	38	31	44	9	.221	.271
Ted Cather	OF57, 1B1, P1	R	24	67	183	16	39	8	4	0	12	9	24	7	.213	.301
1 Jimmy Sheckard	OF46	L	34	52	136	18	27	2	1	0	17	41	25	5	.199	.228
1 Larry McLean	C42	R	31	48	152	7	41	9	0	0	12	6	9	0	.270	.329
Pete Hildebrand	C22, OF1	R	28	26	55	3	9	2	0	0	1	1	10	1	.164	.200
Skipper Roberts	C16	L	25	26	41	4	6	2	0	0	3	3	13	1	.146	.195
Arnold Hauser (IL)	SS8, 2B4	R	24	22	45	3	13	0	3	0	9	2	2	1	.289	.422
Finners Quinlan	OF12	L	25	13	50	1	8	0	0	0	1	1	9	0	.160	.160
Zinn Beck	SS5, 3B5	R	27	10	30	4	5	1	0	0	2	4	10	1	.167	.200
Wes Callahan	SS6	R	24	7	14	0	4	0	0	0	1	2	2	1	.286	.286
Frank Snyder	C7	R	20	7	21	1	4	0	1	0	2	0	4	0	.190	.286

Chuck Miller 23 L 2-12, Heinie Peitz 40 R 1-4, 2 Doc Crandall 25 R 0-2, Al Cabrera 30 0-2, John Vann 20 R 0-1, Jim Whelan 23 R 0-1

NAME	T	AGE	W	L	PCT	SV	G	GS	CG	IP	H	BB	SO	ShO	ERA
		25	51	**99**	.340	11	152	152	73	1349	**1423**	476	464	6	4.24
Slim Sallee	L	28	18	15	.545	5	49	31	17	273	254	59	105	3	2.70
Dan Griner	R	25	10	**22**	.313	0	34	34	18	225	279	66	79	1	5.08
Bob Harmon	R	25	8	21	.276	2	42	27	16	273	291	99	66	1	3.92
Pol Perritt	R	20	6	14	.300	0	36	21	8	175	205	64	64	0	5.25
Bill Steele	R	27	4	4	.500	0	12	9	2	54	58	18	10	0	5.00
Bill Doak	R	22	2	8	.200	1	15	12	5	93	79	39	51	1	3.10
Ed Konetchy	R	27	1	0	1.000	0	1	0	0	5	1	4	3	0	0.00
Rube Geyer	R	28	1	5	.167	1	30	4	2	79	83	38	21	0	5.27
Harry Trekell	R	20	0	1	.000	0	7	1	1	30	25	8	15	0	4.50
Walt Marbet	R	22	0	1	.000	0	3	1	0	3	9	4	1	0	18.00
Ben Hunt	L	25	0	1	.000	0	2	1	0	8	6	9	6	0	3.38
Sandy Burk	R	26	1	2	.333	1	19	5	0	70	81	33	29	0	5.14
Dick Niehaus	L	20	0	2	.000	0	3	3	2	24	20	13	4	0	4.13
Bill Hopper	R	22	0	3	.000	0	3	3	2	24	20	8	3	0	3.75
Joe Willis	L	23	0	0	.000	1	7	0	0	10	9	11	6	0	7.20
Ted Cather	R	24	0	0	.000	0	1	0	0	.1	1	2	0	0	54.00
Phil Redding	R	23	0	0	.000	0	1	0	0	3	2	1	1	0	6.00

WORLD SERIES – PHILADELPHIA (AL) 4 NEW YORK (NL) 1

LINE SCORES

TEAM	1	2	3	4	5	6	7	8	9	10	11	12	R	H	E
Game 1 October 7 at New York															
PHI (AL)	0	0	0	3	2	0	0	1	0				6	11	1
NY (NL)	0	0	1	0	3	0	0	0	0				4	11	0
Bender	**Marquard**, Crandall (6), Tesreau (8)														
Game 2 October 8 at Philadelphia															
NY	0	0	0	0	0	0	0	0	0	3			3	7	2
PHI	0	0	0	0	0	0	0	0	0	0			0	8	2
Mathewson	**Plank**														
Game 3 October 9 at New York															
PHI	3	2	0	0	0	0	2	1	0				8	12	1
NY	0	0	0	0	1	0	1	0	0				2	5	1
Bush	**Tesreau**, Crandall (7)														
Game 4 October 10 at Philadelphia															
NY	0	0	0	0	0	0	3	2	0				5	8	2
PHI	0	1	0	3	2	0	0	0	X				6	9	0
Bender	**Demaree**, Marquard (5)														
Game 5 October 11 at New York															
PHI	1	0	2	0	0	0	0	0	0				3	6	1
NY	0	0	0	0	1	0	0	0	X				1	2	2
Plank	**Mathewson**														

COMPOSITE BATTING

NAME	POS	G	AB	R	H	2B	3B	HR	RBI	BA
Philadelphia (AL)										
Totals		5	174	23	46	4	4	2	21	.204
Oldring	OF	5	**22**	**5**	6	0	1	0	0	.273
E. Murphy	OF	5	**22**	2	5	0	0	0	0	.227
Baker	3B	5	20	2	**9**	0	0	1	**7**	.450
Barry	SS	5	20	3	6	**3**	0	0	2	.300
Collins	2B	5	19	**5**	8	0	**2**	0	3	.421
McInnis	1B	5	17	1	2	1	0	0	2	.118
Strunk	OF	5	17	3	2	0	0	0	0	.118
Schang	C	4	14	2	5	0	1	1	6	.357
Bender	P	2	8	0	0	0	0	0	**0**	.000
Plank	P	2	7	0	1	0	0	0	**1**	.143
Bush	P	1	4	0	1	0	0	0	0	.250
Lapp	C	1	4	0	1	0	0	0	0	.250
New York (NL)										
Totals		5	164	15	33	3	1	1	15	.201
Doyle	2B	5	20	1	3	0	0	0	2	.150
Burns	OF	5	19	2	3	2	0	0	1	.158
Shafer	OF-3B	5	19	2	3	1	1	0	1	.158
Herzog	3B	5	19	1	1	0	0	0	0	.053
Fletcher	SS	5	18	1	5	0	0	0	4	.278
Murray	OF	5	16	2	4	0	0	0	1	.250
Merkle	1B	4	13	3	3	0	0	1	3	.231
McLean	C	5	12	0	6	0	0	0	2	**.500**
Mathewson	P	2	5	1	3	0	0	0	1	.600
Crandall	P	4	4	0	0	0	0	0	0	.000
Meyers	C	1	4	0	0	0	0	0	0	.000
Snodgrass	1B-OF	2	3	0	1	0	0	0	0	.333
Wilson	C	3	3	0	0	0	0	0	0	.000
McCormick	PH	2	2	1	1	0	0	0	0	.500
Wiltse	1B	2	2	0	0	0	0	0	0	.000
Tesreau	P	2	2	0	0	0	0	0	0	.000
Marquard	P	2	1	0	0	0	0	0	0	.000
Grant	PH-PR	2	1	1	0	0	0	0	0	.000
Demaree	P	1	1	0	0	0	0	0	0	.000
Cooper	PR	2	0	0	0	0	0	0	0	.000

COMPOSITE PITCHING

NAME	G	IP	H	BB	SO	W	L	SV	ERA
Philadelphia (AL)									
Totals	5	46	33	8	19	4	1	0	2.15
Plank	2	**19**	9	3	7	1	1	0	**0.95**
Bender	2	18	**19**	1	**9**	**2**	0	0	4.00
Bush	1	9	5	**4**	3	1	0	0	1.00
New York (NL)									
Totals	5	45	46	7	16	1	4	0	3.80
Mathewson	2	**19**	14	2	7	1	1	0	**0.95**
Marquard	2	9	10	3	3	0	1	0	7.00
Tesreau	2	8.1	11	1	4	0	1	0	6.48
Crandall	2	4.2	4	0	2	0	0	0	3.86
Demaree	1	4	7	1	0	0	1	0	4.50

1914 The Miracle in Boston

Europe had broken out into war in the spring, and the world of baseball followed suit with its first war between leagues since the American League was formed in 1901. The Federal League set up shop as a third major league and proceeded to raid both established leagues for players. The National League lost more players to the Feds than the American, but the National was compensated by one of the most exciting pennant races in its history.

John McGraw led his Giants out to a substantial lead in June, apparently on the way to a fourth straight pennant. Though Rube Marquard was losing more than he was winning, Christy Mathewson and Jeff Tesreau were piling up enough victories to keep the Giants on top, despite slumps by Red Murray and Larry Doyle.

The Boston Braves, mired in last place as late as July 18, were a club made up of castoffs who had finished fifth the previous year. Then, suddenly, around mid-July the Braves caught fire and started moving up. Behind the direction of dapper manager George Stallings, the Braves moved into fourth place on July 21, and kept going until reaching second place August 12. Bill James, Dick Rudolph, and Lefty Tyler assumed practically all the Brave pitching chores during the drive, and all three were consistent winners. Joe Connolly represented the only .300 hitter on the club, but ex-Cub Johnny Evers and shortstop Rabbit Maranville provided solid infielding around second base in addition to clutch stick work. The Braves poked their heads into the clouds of first place on September 2, and passed the slumping Giants for keeps on September 8, capping a drive of 34 wins in 44 tries. The Braves, so recently doormats, kept winning until the season's end, finishing 10½ games over the faded Giants and writing the greatest comeback story in baseball's annals.

The American League race exhibited none of the drama of the pennant chase—the Philadelphia Athletics were expected to win, and they did so quite handily. Connie Mack's machine ground out 749 runs, tops in the league, as Stuffy McInnis, Eddie Collins, and Frank Baker provided teeth for the Philadelphia attack. With Jack Coombs again out with illness, Chief Bender and Eddie Plank provided the mound savvy and were helped by young hurlers, Bob Shawkey and Joe Bush.

The Red Sox came in second, relying on good pitching to keep the team in contention. Manager Bill Carrigan had "The Grey Eagle," Tris Speaker, as the heart of his lineup, and Ray Collins and Dutch Leonard developed into top starters. Joe Wood could not return to his form of 1912, as he again won only nine games. A more historical note out of Boston occurred in September, when the Red Sox purchased from Providence, of the International League, a promising young pitcher named Babe Ruth.

The World Series promised to be an easy Athletic win, but the momentum which swept the Braves on to their pennant crested and broke over the back of Philadelphia. Boston won the first game behind Dick Rudolph, 7-1, and the upset materialized as the Braves swept the next 3 games to shut the Mackmen out of the win column. The Boston staff of Rudolph, James, and Tyler held the Athletics to a .172 batting average, while Boston's hot hitters included Johnny Evers at .438 and catcher Hank Gowdy at .545.

The Series marked the end of the line for the 1914 edition of Connie Mack's Athletics. Mack could not meet the salary demands of star players who were being wooed by the Federal League, so he began selling most of his top players to other teams in the circuit to keep the American League intact. Breaking up the perennially tough Athletics spelled disaster to Mack's dynasty, and the Tall Tactician would have to rebuild his team over the course of a dozen years before they could return to the status of contenders.

1914 AMERICAN LEAGUE

NAME	G by POS	B	AGE	G	AB	R	H	2B	3B	HR	RBI	BB	SO	SB	BA	SA
PHILADELPHIA 1st 99-53 .651		**CONNIE MACK**														
TOTALS			26	157	5126	749	1392	165	80	29	627	545	517	231	.272	.352
Stuffy McInnis	1B149	R	23	149	576	74	181	12	8	1	95	19	27	25	.314	.368
Eddie Collins	2B152	L	27	152	526	122	181	23	14	2	85	97	31	58	.344	.452
Jack Barry	SS140	R	27	140	467	57	113	12	0	0	42	53	34	22	.242	.268
Frank Baker	3B149	L	28	150	570	84	182	23	10	9	89	53	37	19	.319	.442
Eddie Murphy	OF148	L	22	148	573	101	156	12	9	3	43	87	46	36	.272	.340
Amos Strunk	OF120	L	25	122	404	58	111	15	3	2	45	57	38	25	.275	.342
Rube Oldring	OF117	R	30	119	466	68	129	21	7	3	49	18	35	14	.277	.371
Wally Schang	C100	B	24	107	307	44	88	11	8	3	45	32	33	7	.287	.404
Jack Lapp	C67	L	29	69	199	22	46	7	2	0	19	31	14	1	.231	.286
2 Jimmy Walsh	OF56, 1B3, 3B3, SS1	L	28	67	216	35	51	11	6	3	36	30	27	6	.236	.384
Larry Kopf	SS13, 3B8, 2B5	B	23	35	69	8	13	2	2	0	12	8	14	6	.188	.275
1 Tom Daley	OF24	L	29	29	86	17	22	1	3	0	7	12	14	4	.256	.337
Chick Davies	OF10, P1	L	22	19	46	6	11	3	1	0	5	5	13	1	.239	.348
Shag Thompson	OF8	L	21	16	29	3	5	0	1	0	2	7	8	1	.172	.241
Bill Orr	SS6, 3B1	R	23	10	24	3	4	1	1	0	1	2	5	1	.167	.292
Wickey McAvoy	C8	R	19	18	16	1	2	0	1	0	0	0	4	0	.125	.250
Harry Davis	1B1	R	40	5	7	0	3	0	0	0	2	1	0	0	.429	.429
Press Cruthers	2B4	R	23	4	15	1	3	0	1	0	0	0	4	0	.200	.333
Dean Sturgis	C1	R	21	4	4	1	1	0	0	0	0	1	2	0	.250	.250
Sam Crane	SS2	R	19	2	6	0	0	0	0	0	0	2	3	0	.000	.000
Earle Mack	1B2	L	24	2	8	0	0	0	0	0	1	0	0	1	.000	.000
Ferdie Moore	1B2		18	2	4	1	2	0	0	0	1	0	2	0	.500	.500

John Coyle 0-2, Ben Rochefort 17 L 1-2, Charlie Sweeney 0-1, Ira Thomas 33 R 0-3

NAME	T	AGE	W	L	PCT	SV	G	GS	CG	IP	H	BB	SO	ShO	ERA
		25	99	53	.651	13	157	157	88	1404	1264	521	720	22	2.78
Chief Bender	R	31	17	3	850	0	28	23	14	179	159	55	107	7	2.26
Bullet Joe Bush	R	21	17	12	.586	2	38	22	14	206	184	81	109	2	3.06
Bob Shawkey	R	23	16	8	.667	2	38	31	18	237	223	75	89	5	2.73
Eddie Plank	L	38	15	7	.683	2	34	22	11	185	178	42	110	4	2.87
Herb Pennock	L	20	11	4	.733	3	28	14	8	152	136	65	90	3	2.78
Weldon Wyckoff	R	22	11	8	.579	2	32	20	11	185	153	103	86	0	3.02
Rube Bressler	L	19	10	3	.769	2	29	10	8	148	112	56	96	1	1.76
Chick Davies	L	22	1	0	1.000	0	1	1	1	9	8	3	4	0	1.00
1 Boardwalk Brown	R	27	1	6	.143	0	15	8	2	66	64	26	20	0	4.09
Jack Coombs	R	31	0	1	.000	0	2	2	0	8	8	3	1	0	4.50
Bill Jensen	R	25	0	1	.000	0	1	1	1	9	7	2	1	0	2.00
1 Duke Houck	R	22	0	0	.000	0	3	3	0	11	14	6	4	0	3.27
Charlie Boardman	L	21	0	0	.000	0	2	0	0	7	10	4	2	0	5.14
Fred Worden			0	0	.000	0	1	0	0	2	8	0	1	0	18.00

NAME	G by POS	B	AGE	G	AB	R	H	2B	3B	HR	RBI	BB	SO	SB	BA	SA
BOSTON 2nd 91-62 .595 8.5		**BILL CARRIGAN**														
TOTALS			25	160	5117	588	1278	226	85	18	513	490	549	177	.250	.338
2 Dick Hoblitzell	1B68	L	25	68	229	31	73	10	3	0	33	19	21	12	.319	.389
1 Steve Yerkes	2B91	R	26	92	293	23	64	17	2	1	23	14	23	5	.218	.300
Everett Scott	SS143	R	21	144	539	66	129	15	6	2	37	32	43	9	.239	.301
Larry Gardner	3B153	L	28	155	553	50	143	23	19	3	68	35	39	16	.259	.385
Harry Hooper	OF140	L	26	141	530	85	137	23	15	1	41	58	47	19	.258	.364
Tris Speaker	OF156, 1B1, P1	L	26	158	571	100	193	46	18	4	90	77	25	42	.338	.503
Duffy Lewis	OF142	R	25	146	510	53	142	37	9	2	79	57	41	22	.278	.398
Bill Carrigan	C78	R	30	81	178	18	45	5	1	1	22	40	18	1	.253	.309
Hal Janvrin	2B57, 1B56, SS20, 3B6	R	21	143	492	65	117	18	6	1	51	38	50	29	.238	.305
Wally Rehg	OF42	R	25	84	151	14	33	4	2	0	11	18	11	5	.219	.272
Pinch Thomas	C61, 1B1	L	26	63	130	9	25	1	0	0	5	18	17	1	.192	.200
Hick Cady	C58	R	28	61	159	14	41	6	1	0	8	12	22	2	.258	.308
Olaf Henriksen	OF27	L	26	61	95	16	25	2	1	1	5	22	12	5	.263	.337
1 Clyde Engle	1B29, 2B5, 3B2	R	30	55	134	14	26	2	0	0	9	14	11	4	.194	.209
2 Del Gainer (JJ)	1B18, 2B11	R	27	38	84	11	20	9	2	2	13	8	14	2	.238	.464
Bill Swanson	2B6, 3B3, SS1	B	25	11	20	0	4	2	0	0	0	3	4	0	.200	.300
Larry Pratt	C5	R	26	5	4	0	0	0	0	0	0	0	4	0	.000	.000
1 Les Nunamaker	C2, 1B1	R	25	4	5	0	1	0	0	0	0	1	0	0	.200	.200
Squanto Wilson	1B1	B	25	1	0	0	0	0	0	0	0	0	0	0	.000	.000

NAME	T	AGE	W	L	PCT	SV	G	GS	CG	IP	H	BB	SO	ShO	ERA
		25	91	62	.595	11	160	160	87	1434	1212	397	605	26	2.35
Ray Collins	L	27	20	13	.606	0	39	30	16	272	252	56	72	7	2.51
Dutch Leonard	L	22	19	5	.792	4	36	25	17	223	141	60	174	7	1.01
Rube Foster(KJ)	R	26	14	8	.636	0	32	27	17	213	162	52	92	6	1.65
Smokey Joe Wood	R	24	9	3	.750	1	18	14	11	113	94	34	67	1	2.63
Ernie Shore	R	23	9	4	.692	2	20	16	9	140	103	34	51	1	1.99
Hugh Bedient	R	24	8	12	.400	3	42	16	7	177	185	45	70	0	3.61
2 Vean Gregg	L	29	4	4	.500	0	13	10	4	76	78	41	26	0	3.56
1 Rankin Johnson	R	26	4	9	.308	0	16	13	4	99	92	34	24	2	3.10
Babe Ruth	L	19	2	1	.667	0	4	3	1	23	21	7	3	0	3.91
2 Guy Cooper	R	21	1	1	.500	0	9	1	0	22	23	9	5	0	5.32
1 Fritz Coumbe	L	24	1	2	.333	1	17	5	1	62	49	16	17	0	1.45
Ed Kelly	R	24	0	0	.000	0	3	0	0	2	1	1	4	0	0.00
Matt Zeiser	R	25	0	0	.000	0	2	0	0	10	9	8	0	0	1.80
Tris Speaker	L	26	0	0	.000	0	1	0	0	1	2	0	0	0	9.00

Heinie Wagner (IL) 32

NAME	G by POS	B	AGE	G	AB	R	H	2B	3B	HR	RBI	BB	SO	SB	BA	SA
WASHINGTON 3rd 81-73 .526 19		**CLARK GRIFFITH**														
TOTALS			28	157	5108	572	1245	176	81	18	470	470	640	220	.244	.320
Chick Gandil	1B145	R	26	145	526	48	136	24	10	3	75	44	44	30	.259	.359
Ray Morgan	2B146	R	25	147	491	50	126	22	8	1	49	62	34	24	.257	.340
George McBride	SS156	R	33	156	503	49	102	12	4	0	24	43	70	12	.203	.243
Eddie Foster	3B156	R	27	156	616	82	174	16	10	2	50	60	47	31	.282	.351
Danny Moeller	OF150	B	29	151	571	83	143	19	10	1	45	71	89	26	.250	.324
Clyde Milan(JJ)	OF113	L	28	115	437	63	129	19	11	1	39	32	26	38	.295	.396
Howard Shanks	OF139	R	23	143	500	44	112	22	10	4	64	29	51	18	.224	.332
John Henry	C91	R	24	91	261	22	44	7	4	0	20	37	47	7	.169	.226
Rip Williams	C44, 1B8, OF1	R	32	81	169	17	47	6	4	1	22	13	19	2	.278	.379
Eddie Ainsmith(BW)	C51	R	22	58	151	11	34	7	0	0	13	9	28	8	.225	.272
2 Mike Mitchell	OF53	R	34	55	193	20	55	5	3	1	20	22	19	9	.285	.358
Wally Smith	2B12, 1B7, SS7, 3B5, OF1	R	25	45	97	11	19	4	1	0	8	3	12	3	.196	.258
Merito Acosta	OF24	L	18	38	74	10	19	2	2	0	4	11	18	3	.257	.338
Germany Schaefer	2B3, OF3	R	37	25	29	6	7	1	0	0	2	3	5	4	.241	.276
Charlie Pick	OF7	L	26	10	23	0	9	0	0	0	1	4	4	1	.391	.391
Joe Gedeon	OF3	R	20	3	2	0	0	0	0	0	1	0	1	0	.000	.000
Doug Neff	SS3	R	22	3	2	0	0	0	0	0	0	0	0	0	.000	.000
Irish Meusel	OF1	R	21	1	2	0	0	0	0	0	0	0	0	0	.000	.000
Tom Wilson	C1	R	25	1	1	0	0	0	0	0	0	0	0	0	.000	.000

NAME	T	AGE	W	L	PCT	SV	G	GS	CG	IP	H	BB	SO	ShO	ERA
		22	81	73	.526	16	157	157	75	1421	1170	520	784	24	2.54
Walter Johnson	R	26	28	18	.635	1	51	40	33	372	287	74	225	10	1.71
Jim Shaw	R	20	15	17	.469	4	48	31	15	257	198	137	164	5	2.70
Joe Boehling	L	23	12	8	.600	1	27	24	14	196	180	76	91	2	3.03
Doc Ayres	R	24	12	16	.429	2	49	31	8	265	221	54	148	3	2.55
Joe Engel	R	21	7	5	.583	2	35	15	1	124	108	75	41	0	2.98
Jack Bentley	L	19	5	7	.417	4	30	12	3	125	110	53	55	2	2.38
Harry Harper	L	19	2	1	.667	0	23	3	1	57	45	35	50	0	3.47
Carl Cashion	R	23	0	1	.000	0	2	1	0	5	4	6	1	0	10.80
Mutt Williams	R	22	0	0	.000	1	5	0	0	7	5	4	3	0	5.14
Bert Gallia	R	22	0	0	.000	0	2	0	0	6	3	4	4	0	4.50
Jim Stevens	R	24	0	0	.000	0	2	0	0	3	4	2	0	0	9.00
Nick Altrock	L	37	0	0	.000	0	1	0	0	1	3	0	0	0	0.00
Frank Barron	L	23	0	0	.000	0	1	0	0	1	1	0	1	0	0.00
Clark Griffith	R	44	0	0	.000	1	1	0	0	1	1	0	1	0	0.00

Heinie Wagner (IL) 32

DETROIT 4th 80-73 .523 19.5 — HUGHIE JENNINGS

NAME	G by POS	B	AGE	G	AB	R	H	2B	3B	HR	RBI	BB	SO	SB	BA	SA
TOTALS			26	157	5102	615	1318	195	84	25	513	557	537	211	.258	.344
George Burns	1B137	R	21	137	478	55	139	22	5	5	57	32	56	23	.291	.389
Martv Kavanagh	2B115, 1B4	R	23	127	439	60	109	21	6	4	35	41	42	16	.248	.351
Donie Bush	SS157	B	26	157	596	97	150	18	4	0	32	**112**	54	35	.252	.295
George Moriarty (BG)	3B126, 1B3	R	29	130	465	56	118	19	5	1	40	39	27	34	.254	.323
Sam Crawford	OF157	L	34	157	582	74	183	22	**26**	8	**104**	69	31	25	.314	.483
Ty Cobb(BR)	OF96	L	27	97	345	69	127	22	11	2	57	57	22	35	**.368**	**.513**
Bobby Veach	OF145	L	26	149	531	56	146	19	14	1	72	50	29	20	.275	.369
Oscar Stanage	C122	R	31	122	400	16	77	8	4	0	25	24	58	2	.193	.233
Hugh High	OF53	L	26	80	184	25	49	5	3	0	17	26	21	7	.266	.326
Jean Dubuc	P36	R	25	70	124	9	28	8	1	1	11	7	11	1	.226	.331
Harry Heilmann	OF29, 1B16, 2B6	R	19	67	182	25	41	8	1	2	18	22	29	1	.225	.313
Ossie Vitt (BW)	2B36, 3B16, OF2, SS1	R	24	66	195	35	49	7	0	0	8	31	8	10	.251	.287
Del Baker	C38	R	22	43	70	4	15	2	1	0	1	6	9	0	.214	.271
Red McKee	C27	L	23	32	64	7	12	1	1	0	8	14	16	1	.188	.234
Billy Purtell	3B16, 2B1, SS1	R	28	26	76	4	13	4	0	0	3	2	7	0	.171	.224

Paddy Baumann 28 R 0-11, 1 Ray Demmitt 30 L 0-0, 1 Del Gainer 27 R 0-0, Fred McMullin 22 R 0-1

NAME	T	AGE	W	L	PCT	SV	G	GS	CG	IP	H	BB	SO	ShO	ERA
		25	80	73	.523	13	157	157	81	1412	1285	498	567	14	2.86
Harry Covelski	L	28	22	12	.647	2	44	36	23	303	251	100	124	5	2.49
Hooks Dauss	R	24	18	15	.545	**4**	45	35	22	302	286	87	150	3	2.86
Jean Dubuc	R	25	13	14	.481	1	36	27	15	224	216	76	70	2	3.46
Pug Cavet	L	24	7	7	.500	2	31	14	6	151	129	44	51	1	2.45
Alex Main	R	30	6	6	.500	3	32	12	5	138	131	59	55	1	2.67
Ross Reynolds	R	24	5	3	.625	1	26	7	3	78	62	39	31	1	2.08
Mark Hall	R	26	4	6	.400	0	25	8	1	90	80	27	10	0	2.70
George Boehler	R	22	2	3	.400	0	18	6	2	63	54	48	37	0	3.57
Red Oldham	L	20	2	4	.333	0	9	7	3	45	42	8	23	0	3.40
Ed McCreery	R	23	1	0	1.000	0	3	1	0	4	6	3	4	0	11.25
Johnny Williams (IL)	R	24	0	3	.000	0	4	3	1	11	17	5	4	0	6.54
Lefty Williams	L	21	0	0	.000	0	1	1	0	1	3	2	0	0	0.00

ST. LOUIS 5th 71-82 .464 28.5 — BRANCH RICKEY

NAME	G by POS	B	AGE	G	AB	R	H	2B	3B	HR	RBI	BB	SO	SB	BA	SA
TOTALS			27	159	5101	523	1241	185	75	17	430	423	**863**	233	.243	.319
John Leary	1B130, C15	R	23	144	533	35	141	28	7	0	45	10	71	9	.265	.343
Del Pratt	2B152, OF5, SS1	R	26	158	584	85	165	34	13	5	65	50	45	37	.283	.411
Doc Lavan	SS73	R	23	74	239	21	63	7	4	1	21	17	39	6	.264	.339
Jimmy Austin	3B127	B	34	130	466	55	111	16	4	0	30	40	59	20	.238	.290
Gus Williams	OF141	L	26	143	499	51	126	19	6	4	47	36	**120**	35	.253	.339
Burt Shotton	OF152	L	29	154	579	82	156	19	9	0	38	64	66	40	.269	.333
Tilly Walker	OF145	R	26	151	517	67	154	24	16	6	78	51	72	29	.298	.441
Sam Agnew	C113	R	27	113	311	22	66	5	4	0	16	24	63	10	.212	.254
Ivon Howard	3B33, 1B28, OF2, SS1	B	31	81	209	21	51	6	2	0	20	28	42	14	.244	.292
Buzzy Wares	SS68, 2B8	R	28	81	215	20	45	10	1	0	23	28	35	10	.209	.265
Ernie Walker	OF36	L	23	71	131	19	39	5	3	1	14	13	26	6	.298	.405
Frank Crossin	C41	R	23	43	90	5	11	1	1	0	5	10	10	3	.122	.156
Eddie Miller	1B8, 2B5, OF5, 3B2	R	25	34	58	8	8	0	1	0	4	4	13	1	.138	.172
Bill Rumler	C9, OF6	R	23	33	46	2	8	1	0	0	6	3	12	2	.174	.196
Bobby Wallace (FR)	SS19, 3B2	R	40	26	73	3	16	2	1	0	5	5	13	1	.219	.274
Joe Jenkins	C9	R	23	19	32	0	4	1	1	0	0	1	11	2	.125	.219
Tim Bowden	OF4	L	22	7	9	0	2	0	0	0	0	1	6	0	.222	.222
Bob Clemens	OF5	R	27	7	13	1	3	0	1	0	3	2	1	0	.231	.385
Dick Kauffman	1B6	R	26	7	15	1	4	1	0	0	2	0	3	0	.267	.333
Dee Walsh	SS7	B	24	7	23	1	2	0	0	0	1	2	4	1	.087	.087

George Hale 19 R 2-11, 1 Jack Enzenroth 28 R 1-6, Ed Hemingway 21 B 0-6, Dutch Bold 19 R 0-1, Branch Rickey 32 L 0-2, Bob Messenger 30 B 0-2, Dutch Schirick 24 R 0-0

NAME	T	AGE	W	L	PCT	SV	G	GS	CG	IP	H	BB	SO	ShO	ERA
		25	71	82	.464	9	159	159	80	1411	1309	540	553	14	2.84
Carl Weilman	L	24	18	13	.581	0	44	36	20	299	260	84	119	3	2.08
Earl Hamilton	L	22	17	18	.486	2	44	35	20	302	265	100	111	5	2.50
Bill James	R	27	15	14	.517	0	44	35	19	284	269	109	109	3	2.85
George Baumgardner	R	22	14	13	.519	3	45	18	9	184	152	84	93	2	2.79
Roy Mitchell	R	29	4	5	.444	**4**	28	9	4	103	134	38	38	0	4.37
Wiley Taylor	R	26	2	5	.286	0	16	8	2	50	41	25	20	1	3.42
Walt Leverenz	L	25	1	12	.077	0	27	16	5	111	107	63	41	0	3.81
Harry Hoch	R	27	0	2	.000	0	15	2	1	54	55	27	13	0	3.00
Grover Baichley	R	24	0	0	.000	0	4	0	0	7	9	3	3	0	5.14
Ernie Manning	R	23	0	0	.000	0	4	0	0	10	11	3	3	0	3.60
Allan Sothoron	R	21	0	0	.000	0	1	0	0	6	6	4	3	0	6.00

CHICAGO 6th (Tie) 70-84 .455 30 — NIXEY CALLAHAN

NAME	G by POS	B	AGE	G	AB	R	H	2B	3B	HR	RBI	BB	SO	SB	BA	SA
TOTALS			26	157	5040	487	1205	161	71	19	390	408	609	167	.239	.311
Jack Fournier	1B97, OF6	L	29	109	379	44	118	14	9	6	44	31	44	10	.311	.443
Lena Blackburne	2B143	R	27	144	474	52	105	10	5	1	35	66	58	25	.222	.270
Buck Weaver	SS134	B	23	136	541	64	133	20	9	2	28	20	40	14	.246	.327
Jim Breton	3B79	R	22	81	231	21	49	7	2	0	24	24	42	9	.212	.260
Shano Collins	OF154	R	28	154	598	61	164	34	9	3	65	27	49	30	.274	.376
Ping Bodie	OF95	R	26	107	327	21	75	9	5	3	29	21	35	12	.229	.315
2 Ray Demmit	OF142	L	30	146	515	63	133	13	12	2	46	61	48	12	.258	.342
Ray Schalk	C124	R	21	135	392	30	106	13	2	0	36	38	24	24	.270	.314
Tom Daly	OF23, 3B5, C4, 1B2	R	22	61	133	13	31	2	0	0	8	7	13	3	.233	.248
1 Hal Chase	1B58	R	31	58	206	27	55	10	5	0	20	23	19	9	.267	.364
Scotty Alcock	3B48, 2B1	R	28	54	156	12	27	4	2	0	7	7	14	4	.173	.224
Joe Berger	SS27, 2B12, 3B7	R	27	47	148	11	23	3	1	0	3	13	9	2	.155	.189
Wally Mayer	C33, 3B1	R	24	39	85	7	14	3	1	0	5	14	23	1	.165	.224
Braggo Roth	OF34	R	21	34	126	14	37	4	6	1	10	8	25	3	.294	.444
Larry Chappell	OF9	L	24	21	39	3	9	0	0	0	1	4	11	0	.231	.231
Harry Lord (JT)	3B19, OF1	L	32	21	69	8	13	1	1	1	3	5	3	2	.188	.275
Walt Kuhn	C16	R	30	17	40	4	11	1	0	0	0	8	11	2	.275	.300
Howard Baker	3B15	R	26	15	47	4	13	1	1	0	5	3	8	2	.277	.340
Carl Manda	2B7	R	27	9	15	2	4	0	0	0	1	3	3	1	.267	.267
Polly Wolfe	OF8	L	25	9	28	0	6	0	0	0	0	3	6	1	.214	.214

Cecil Coombs 26 R 4-23, Charlie Kavanagh 21 R 1-5, Delos Brown 21 R 0-1, Irv Porter 26 B 1-4, Hank Schreiber 22 R 0-2, Billy Sullivan 39 R 0-0

NAME	T	AGE	W	L	PCT	SV	G	GS	CG	IP	H	BB	SO	ShO	ERA
		27	70	84	.455	15	157	157	74	1399	1207	401	660	17	2.48
Jim Scott	R	25	14	18	.438	2	43	33	12	253	228	75	138	2	2.84
Joe Benz	R	28	14	**19**	.424	3	48	35	16	283	245	66	142	4	2.26
Eddie Cicotte	R	30	11	16	.407	3	45	29	15	269	220	72	122	4	2.04
Red Faber	R	25	10	9	.526	**4**	40	20	11	181	154	64	88	2	2.68
Mellie Wolfgang	R	24	9	5	.643	2	24	11	9	119	96	32	50	2	1.89
Reb Russell	L	25	8	12	.400	1	38	23	8	167	168	33	79	1	2.91
Ed Walsh	R	33	2	3	.400	0	8	5	3	45	33	20	15	1	2.80
Hi Jasper	R	33	1	0	1.000	0	16	0	0	32	22	20	19	0	3.38
Bill Lathrop	R	22	1	2	.333	0	19	1	0	48	41	19	7	0	2.63

NEW YORK 6th (Tie) 70-84 .455 30 — FRANK CHANCE 61-76 .445 — ROGER PECKINPAUGH 9-8 .529

NAME	G by POS	B	AGE	G	AB	R	H	2B	3B	HR	RBI	BB	SO	SB	BA	SA
TOTALS			26	157	4992	536	1144	149	52	12	416	**577**	711	**251**	.229	.287
Charlie Mullen	1B93	R	25	93	323	33	84	8	0	0	44	33	55	11	.260	.285
Luke Boone	2B90, 3B9	R	24	106	370	34	82	8	2	0	21	31	41	10	.222	.254
Roger Peckinpaugh	SS157	R	23	157	570	55	127	14	6	3	51	51	73	38	.223	.284
Fritz Maisel	3B148	R	24	149	548	78	131	23	9	2	47	76	69	**74**	.239	.325
Doc Cook	OF126	L	28	131	470	59	133	11	3	1	40	44	60	26	.283	.326
Birdie Cree	OF76	R	31	77	275	45	85	18	5	0	40	30	24	4	.309	.311
Roy Hartzell	OF128, 2B5	L	32	137	481	55	112	15	9	1	32	68	38	22	.233	.308
Ed Sweeney	C78	R	25	87	258	25	55	8	1	1	22	35	30	19	.213	.264
2 Les Nunamaker	C70, 1B5	R	25	87	257	19	68	10	3	2	29	22	34	11	.265	.350
Frank Truesdale	2B67, 3B4	B	28	77	217	23	46	4	0	0	13	39	35	11	.212	.230
2 Tom Daley	OF57	L	29	67	191	36	48	6	4	0	9	38	13	8	.251	.325
Ray Caldwell	P31, 1B6	L	26	59	113	9	22	4	0	0	10	7	24	2	.195	.230
Harry Williams	1B48	R	24	59	178	9	29	5	2	1	17	26	26	3	.163	.230
1 Bill Holden	OF45	R	24	50	165	12	30	3	2	0	12	16	26	2	.182	.224
1 Jimmy Walsh	OF41	L	28	43	136	13	26	1	3	1	11	29	21	6	.191	.265
Dick Gossett	C9	R	22	9	21	3	3	0	0	0	1	5	5	0	.143	.143
Angel Aragon	OF1	R	20	6	7	1	1	0	0	0	0	1	2	0	.143	.143
Jay Rogers	C4	R	25	5	8	0	0	0	0	0	0	0	4	0	.000	.000
Harry Kingman	1B1	L	22	4	3	0	0	0	0	0	0	1	2	0	.000	.000
Charlie Meara	OF3	L	23	4	7	2	2	0	0	0	1	2	2	0	.286	.286
Bill Reynolds	C1	R	29	4	5	0	2	0	0	0	0	0	3	0	.400	.400

Joe Harris 23 R 0-1, Pi Schwert 21 R 0-5, Alex Burr 20 R 0-0, Frank Chance 36 R 0-0, Frank Gilhooley 22 L 2-3, Les Channell 28 L 1-1, Bill Schwarz 23 0-1

NAME	T	AGE	W	L	PCT	SV	G	GS	CG	IP	H	BB	SO	ShO	ERA
		26	70	84	.455	7	157	157	**97**	1397	1277	390	563	5	2.82
Ray Caldwell	R	26	17	9	.654	2	31	23	22	213	153	51	92	1	1.94
Ray Fisher	R	26	10	12	.455	1	29	26	17	209	177	61	86	2	2.28
King Cole	R	28	11	9	.550	0	33	15	8	142	151	51	43	2	3 29
Jack Warhop	R	29	8	15	.348	0	37	23	15	217	182	44	56	0	2.37
Ray Keating	R	22	7	11	.389	1	34	25	13	210	198	67	109	0	2.96
Marty McHale	R	25	7	16	.304	2	31	23	12	191	195	33	75	0	2.97
2 Boardwalk Brown	R	27	5	5	.500	1	20	14	8	122	123	42	57	0	3.25
Cy Pieh	R	27	4	4	.500	0	18	4	1	62	68	29	24	0	5.08
1 Al Schulz	L	25	1	3	.250	0	6	4	1	28	27	10	18	0	4.82
1 Guy Cooper	R	21	0	0	.000	0	1	0	0	3	3	2	3	0	9.00

CLEVELAND 8th 51-102 .333 48.5 — JOE BIRMINGHAM

NAME	G by POS	B	AGE	G	AB	R	H	2B	3B	HR	RBI	BB	SO	SB	BA	SA
TOTALS			26	157	**5157**	538	1262	178	70	10	438	450	685	167	.245	.312
Doc Johnston	1B89, OF2	L	26	103	340	43	83	15	1	0	23	28	46	14	.244	.294
Nap Lajoie	2B80, 1B31	R	38	121	419	37	108	14	3	0	50	32	15	14	.268	.305
Ray Chapman (NJ)	SS72, 2B33	R	23	106	375	59	103	16	10	2	42	48	48	24	.275	.387
Terry Turner	3B103, 2B17	R	33	120	428	43	105	14	9	1	33	44	36	17	.245	.327
Joe Jackson	OF119	L	24	122	453	61	153	22	13	3	53	41	34	22	.338	.464
Nemo Leibold	OF107	L	22	114	402	46	106	13	3	0	32	54	56	12	.264	.311
Jack Graney	OF127	L	28	130	460	63	122	17	10	1	39	67	46	20	.265	.352
Steve O'Neill	C81, 1B1	R	22	86	269	28	68	12	2	0	20	15	35	1	.253	.312
Ivy Olson	SS31, 2B23, 3B19, OF6, 1B3	R	28	89	310	22	75	6	2	1	20	13	24	15	.242	.284
Roy Wood	OF41, 1B20	R	21	72	220	24	52	6	3	1	15	13	26	6	.236	.305
Jay Kirke	OF42, 1B18	L	26	67	242	18	66	10	2	1	25	7	30	5	.273	.343
Johnny Bassler	C25, 3B1, OF1	L	19	43	77	5	14	1	1	0	6	15	8	3	.182	.221
Bill Wambsganss	SS36, 2B4	R	20	43	143	12	31	6	2	0	12	8	24	2	.217	.287
Fred Carisch	C38	R	32	40	102	8	22	3	2	0	5	12	18	2	.216	.284
Jack Lelivelt	OF12, 1B1	L	28	32	64	6	21	5	1	0	13	2	10	2	.328	.438
Ben Egan	C27	R	30	29	88	7	20	2	1	0	11	3	20	0	.227	.273
Larry Pezold	3B20, OF1	R	21	23	71	4	16	0	1	0	5	9	6	2	.225	.254
Joe Birmingham	OF14	R	29	19	47	2	6	0	0	0	4	2	5	0	.128	.128
Rivington Bisland	SS15, 3B1	R	24	18	57	9	6	1	0	0	2	6	2	2	.105	.123
Walter Barbare (JJ)	3B14, SS1	R	22	15	52	6	16	2	2	0	5	2	5	1	.308	.423

Elmer Smith 21 L 17-53, Josh Billings (JJ) 22 R 2-8, Bruce Hartford 22 R 4-22, Frank Mills 19 L 1-8, Tinsley Ginn 22 L 0-1, Al Cypert 24 R 0-1, George Dunlop 25 R 0-3, Tom Reilly 29 R 0-1

NAME	T	AGE	W	L	PCT	SV	G	GS	CG	IP	H	BB	SO	ShO	ERA
		25	51	**102**	.333	2	157	157	69	1392	**1365**	**666**	688	10	3.20
Willie Mitchell	L	24	13	17	.433	0	39	32	16	257	228	124	179	3	3.19
Bill Steen (DW)	R	26	9	14	.391	0	30	22	13	201	201	68	97	1	2.60
Rip Hagerman	R	26	9	15	.375	0	37	26	12	198	189	118	112	3	3.09
1 Vean Gregg	L	29	8	3	.727	0	17	12	6	97	88	48	56	1	3.06
Allan Collamore	R	27	3	7	.300	0	28	8	3	105	100	49	32	0	3.26
Fred Blanding	R	26	3	9	.250	1	29	12	5	116	133	54	35	0	3.96
Abe Bowman	R	21	2	7	.222	0	22	10	2	73	74	45	27	1	4.44
Al Tedrow	L	22	1	2	.333	0	4	3	1	22	19	14	4	0	1.22
Paul Carter	R	20	1	3	.250	0	5	4	1	25	35	5	9	0	2.88
2 Fritz Coumbe	L	24	1	5	.167	0	14	5	2	55	59	16	22	0	3.28
Guy Morton	R	21	1	13	.070	1	25	13	5	128	116	55	80	1	3.02
Harley Dillinger	L	19	0	1	.000	0	11	2	1	34	41	25	11	0	4.50
Lloyd Bishop	R	24	0	1	.000	0	3	1	0	8	14	3	1	0	5.63
George Kahler	R	24	0	1	.000	0	2	1	1	14	17	7	3	0	3.86
1 Nick Cullop	L	26	0	1	.000	0	1	0	0	3	4	1	3	0	3.00
Lefty James	L	25	0	3	.000	0	17	6	1	51	44	32	16	0	3.18
George Beck	R	25	0	0	.000	0	1	0	0	1	1	0	0	0	0.00
Omer Benn	R	24	0	0	.000	0	1	0	0	1	0	0	1	0	0.00
Sad Sam Jones	R	21	0	0	.000	0	1	0	0	3	2	2	0	0	3.00

BOSTON 1st 94-59 .614 — GEORGE STALLINGS

NAME	G by POS	B	AGE	G	AB	R	H	2B	3B	HR	RBI	BB	SO	SB	BA	SA
TOTALS			25	158	5206	657	1307	213	60	35	572	502	617	139	.251	.335
Butch Schmidt	1B147	L	27	147	537	67	153	17	9	1	71	43	55	14	.285	.356
Johnny Evers	2B139	L	32	139	491	81	137	20	3	1	40	87	26	12	.279	.338
Rabbit Maranville	SS156	R	22	156	586	74	144	23	6	4	78	45	56	28	.246	.326
Charlie Deal	3B74, SS1	R	22	79	257	17	54	13	2	0	23	20	23	4	.210	.276
Larry Gilbert	OF60	L	22	72	224	32	60	6	1	5	25	26	34	3	.268	.371
Les Mann	OF123	R	20	126	389	44	96	16	11	4	40	24	50	9	.247	.375
Joe Connolly	OF118	L	26	120	399	64	122	28	10	9	65	49	36	12	.306	.494
Hank Gowdy	C115, 1B9	R	24	128	366	42	89	17	6	3	46	48	40	14	.243	.347
2 P. Whitted	OF38, 2B15, 3B5, 1B4, SS3	R	24	66	218	36	57	11	4	2	31	18	18	10	.261	.376
2 Red Smith	3B60	R	24	60	207	30	65	17	1	3	37	28	24	4	.314	.449
Bert Whaling	C59	R	26	60	172	18	36	7	0	0	12	21	28	2	.209	.250
Oscar Dugey	OF17, 2B16, 3B1	R	26	58	109	17	21	2	0	1	10	10	15	10	.193	.239
2 Josh Devore	OF42	L	26	51	128	22	29	4	0	1	5	18	14	2	.227	.281
2 Ted Cather	OF48	R	25	50	145	19	43	11	2	0	27	7	28	7	.297	.400
2 Herbie Moran	OF41	L	30	41	154	24	41	3	1	0	4	17	11	4	.266	.299
Jim Murray	OF32	R	36	39	112	10	26	4	2	0	12	6	24	2	.232	.304
1 Jack Martin	3B27, 1B1, 2B1	R	27	33	85	10	18	2	0	0	5	6	7	0	.212	.235
Otto Hess	P14, 1B5	L	35	31	47	5	11	1	0	1	6	1	11	0	.234	.319
Wilson Collins	OF19	R	25	27	35	5	9	0	0	0	1	2	8	0	.257	.257
Tommy Griffith	OF14	L	24	16	48	3	5	0	0	0	1	2	6	0	.104	.104
Clancy Tyler	C6	R	22	6	19	2	2	0	0	0	2	1	5	0	.105	.105
Clarence Kraft	1B1	R	27	3	3	0	1	0	0	0	0	0	1	0	.333	.333
Billy Martin	SS1	R	20	1	3	0	0	0	0	0	0	0	0	0	.000	.000

NAME	T	AGE	W	L	PCT	SV	G	GS	CG	IP	H	BB	SO	ShO	ERA
		24	94	59	.614	5	158	158	104	1421	1272	477	606	18	2.74
Dick Rudolph	R	26	27	10	.730	0	42	36	31	336	288	61	138	6	2.36
Bill James	R	22	26	7	.788	2	46	37	30	332	261	118	156	4	1.90
Lefty Tyler	L	24	16	14	.533	2	38	34	21	271	247	101	140	5	2.69
Paul Strand (SA)	L	20	6	2	.750	0	16	3	1	55	47	23	33	0	2.45
Dick Crutcher	R	24	5	6	.455	0	33	15	5	159	169	66	48	1	3.46
Otto Hess	L	35	5	6	.455	1	14	11	7	89	89	33	24	1	3.03
George Davis	R	24	3	3	.500	0	9	6	4	56	42	26	26	1	3.38
Gene Cocreham	R	29	3	4	.429	0	15	3	1	45	48	27	15	0	4.80
1 Hub Perdue	R	32	2	5	.286	0	9	9	2	51	60	11	13	0	5.82
Tom Hughes	R	30	1	0	1.000	0	2	2	1	17	14	4	11	0	2.65
Dolf Luque	R	23	0	1	.000	0	2	1	1	9	5	4	1	0	4.00
Dick Cottrell	L	25	0	1	.000	0	1	1	0	1	2	3	1	0	9.00
Buster Brown (DD) 32															

NEW YORK 2nd 84-70 .545 10.5 — JOHN McGRAW

NAME	G by POS	B	AGE	G	AB	R	H	2B	3B	HR	RBI	BB	SO	SB	BA	SA
TOTALS			27	156	5146	672	1363	222	59	30	566	447	479	239	.265	.348
Fred Merkle	1B146	R	25	146	512	71	132	25	7	7	63	52	80	23	.258	.375
Larry Doyle	2B145	L	27	145	539	87	140	19	8	5	63	58	25	17	.260	.353
Art Fletcher	SS135	R	29	135	514	62	147	26	8	2	79	22	37	15	.286	.379
Milt Stock	3B113, SS1	R	20	115	365	52	96	17	1	3	41	34	21	11	.263	.340
Fred Snodgrass	OF96, 1B14, 2B1, 3B1	R	26	113	392	54	103	20	4	0	44	37	43	25	.263	.334
Bob Bescher	OF126	B	30	135	512	82	138	23	4	6	35	45	48	36	.270	.365
George Burns	OF154	R	24	154	561	100	170	35	10	3	60	89	53	62	.303	.417
Chief Meyers	C126	R	33	134	381	33	109	13	5	1	55	34	25	4	.286	.354
Eddie Grant	3B52, SS21, 2B16	L	31	88	282	34	78	7	1	0	29	23	21	11	.277	.309
Red Murray	OF49	R	30	86	139	19	31	6	3	0	23	9	7	11	.223	.309
Dave Robertson	OF71	L	24	82	256	25	68	12	3	2	32	10	26	9	.266	.359
Larry McLean	C74	R	32	79	154	8	40	6	0	0	14	4	9	4	.260	.299
Mike Donlin		L	36	35	31	1	5	1	1	1	3	3	5	0	.161	.355
Sandy Piez	OF4	R	25	35	8	9	3	0	1	0	3	0	1	4	.375	.625
Jim Thorpe	OF4	R	26	30	31	5	6	1	0	0	2	0	4	1	.194	.226
Elmer Johnson	C11	R	30	11	12	0	2	1	0	0	0	1	3	0	.167	.250
Ben Dyer	SS6, 2B1	R	21	7	4	1	1	0	0	0	0	0	1	1	.250	.250
Harry Smith	C4	R	24	5	7	0	3	0	0	0	2	3	1	1	.429	.429
Des Beatty	SS1, 3B1	R	21	2	3	0	0	0	0	0	1	0	0	0	.000	.000
Fred Brainerd	2B2	R	22	2	5	1	1	0	0	0	0	1	0	0	.200	.200
Walter Holke	1B2	B	21	2	6	0	2	0	0	0	0	0	0	0	.333	.333

NAME	T	AGE	W	L	PCT	SV	G	GS	CG	IP	H	BB	SO	ShO	ERA
		29	84	70	.545	9	156	156	88	1391	1298	367	563	20	2.94
Jeff Tesreau	R	25	26	10	.722	1	42	40	26	322	238	128	189	8	2.38
Christy Mathewson	R	35	24	13	.649	2	41	35	29	312	314	23	80	5	3.00
Rube Marquard	L	24	12	22	.353	2	39	33	15	268	261	47	92	4	3.06
Al Demaree	R	27	10	17	.370	0	38	30	13	224	219	77	89	2	3.09
Art Fromme	R	30	9	5	.643	2	38	12	3	138	142	44	57	1	3.20
Hank Ritter	R	20	1	0	1.000	0	1	0	0	8	4	4	4	0	1.13
Hooks Wiltse	L	33	1	1	.500	1	20	0	0	38	41	12	19	0	2.84
2 Marty O'Toole	R	26	1	1	.500	0	10	5	2	34	34	12	13	0	4.24
Eric Erickson	R	22	0	1	.000	0	1	1	0	5	8	3	3	0	0.00
Ferdie Schupp	L	23	0	0	.000	1	8	0	0	17	19	9	9	0	5.82
Rube Schauer	R	23	0	0	.000	0	6	0	0	22	16	8	6	0	3.28
Al Huenke	R	23	0	0	.000	0	1	0	0	2	2	0	2	0	4.50

ST. LOUIS 3rd 81-72 .529 13 — MILLER HUGGINS

NAME	G by POS	B	AGE	G	AB	R	H	2B	3B	HR	RBI	BB	SO	SB	BA	SA
TOTALS			27	157	5046	558	1249	203	65	33	461	445	618	204	.248	.333
Dots Miller	1B98, SS53, 2B5	R	27	155	573	67	166	27	10	4	88	34	52	16	.290	.393
Miller Huggins	2B147	B	35	148	509	85	134	17	4	1	24	105	63	32	.263	.318
Art Butler	SS84, OF1	R	26	86	274	29	55	12	3	1	24	39	23	14	.201	.277
Zinn Beck	3B122, SS16	R	28	137	457	42	106	15	11	3	45	28	32	14	.232	.333
Owen Wilson	OF154	L	30	154	580	64	150	27	12	9	73	32	66	14	.259	.393
Lee Magee	OF102, 1B40, 2B6	B	25	142	529	59	150	23	4	2	40	42	24	36	.284	.353
Cozy Dolan	OF97, 3B29	R	31	126	421	76	101	16	3	4	32	55	74	42	.240	.321
Frank Snyder	C98	R	21	100	326	19	75	15	4	1	25	13	28	1	.230	.310
Walton Cruise	OF81	L	24	95	256	20	58	9	3	4	28	25	42	3	.227	.332
Ivy Wingo	C70	L	23	80	237	24	71	8	5	4	26	18	17	15	.300	.426
Lee Dressen	1B38	L	24	46	103	16	24	2	1	0	7	11	20	2	.233	.272
1 Ted Cather	OF28	R	25	39	99	11	27	7	0	0	13	3	15	4	.273	.343
Chuck Miller	OF19	L	24	36	36	4	7	1	0	0	2	3	9	2	.194	.222
2 Joe Riggert	OF30	R	27	34	89	9	19	5	2	0	8	5	14	4	.213	.315
Ken Nash	SS10, 2B6, SS3	B	25	24	51	4	14	3	1	0	6	6	10	0	.275	.373
1 Possum Whitted	3B11, OF3, 2B1	R	24	20	31	3	4	1	0	0	1	0	3	1	.129	.161
Jack Roche	C9	R	23	12	9	1	6	2	1	0	3	0	1	1	.667	1.111
Paddy O'Connor	C7	R	34	10	9	0	0	0	0	0	0	2	2	0	.000	.000
Bruno Betzel	2B4, 3B1	R	19	7	9	2	0	0	0	0	0	1	1	0	.000	.000
Rolla Daringer	SS1	L	24	2	4	1	2	1	0	0	0	1	2	0	.500	.750

NAME	T	AGE	W	L	PCT	SV	G	GS	CG	IP	H	BB	SO	ShO	ERA
		26	81	72	.529	12	157	157	83	1425	1279	422	531	16	2.38
Bill Doak	R	23	19	6	.760	1	36	33	16	256	193	87	118	7	1.72
Slim Sallee	L	29	18	17	.514	6	46	30	18	282	252	72	105	3	2.11
Pol Perritt	R	21	16	13	.552	2	41	32	18	286	248	93	115	3	2.36
Dan Griner	R	26	9	13	.409	2	37	16	11	179	163	57	74	2	2.51
2 Hub Perdue	R	32	8	8	.500	1	22	19	12	153	160	35	43	0	2.83
Hank Robinson	L	24	7	8	.467	0	26	16	6	126	128	32	30	1	3.00
1 Bill Steele	R	28	2	2	.500	0	17	2	0	53	55	7	16	0	2.72
Dick Niehaus	L	21	1	0	1.000	0	8	1	1	17	18	8	6	0	3.18
1 Casey Hageman	R	27	1	4	.200	0	12	7	1	55	43	20	21	0	2.46
Steamboat Williams	R	22	0	1	.000	0	5	1	0	11	13	6	2	0	6.55
Bill Hopper	R	23	0	0	.000	0	3	0	0	5	6	5	1	0	3.60
Arnold Hauser (IL) 25															

CHICAGO 4th 78-76 .506 16.5 — HENRY F. O'DAY

NAME	G by POS	B	AGE	G	AB	R	H	2B	3B	HR	RBI	BB	SO	SB	BA	SA
TOTALS			29	156	5050	605	1229	199	74	42	502	501	577	164	.243	.337
Vic Saier	1B153	L	23	153	537	87	129	24	8	18	72	94	61	19	.240	.415
Bill Sweeney	2B134	R	28	134	463	45	101	14	5	1	38	53	15	18	.218	.276
Red Corriden	SS96, 3B8, 2B3	R	26	107	318	42	73	9	5	3	29	35	33	13	.230	.318
Heinie Zimmerman	3B119, SS15, 2B12	R	27	146	564	75	167	36	12	4	87	20	46	17	.296	.424
Wilbur Good	OF154	L	28	154	580	70	158	24	7	2	43	53	74	31	.272	.348
Tommy Leach	OF137, 3B16	R	36	153	577	80	152	24	9	7	46	79	50	16	.263	.373
Wildfire Schulte	OF134	L	31	137	465	54	112	22	7	5	61	39	55	16	.241	.351
Roger Bresnahan	C85, 2B14, OF1	R	35	101	248	42	69	10	4	0	24	49	20	14	.278	.351
Jimmy Archer (EJ)	C76	R	31	79	248	17	64	9	2	0	19	9	9	1	.258	.310
Cy Williams	OF27	L	26	55	94	12	19	2	2	0	5	13	13	2	.202	.266
Jimmy Johnston	OF28, 2B4	R	24	50	101	9	23	3	2	1	8	4	9	3	.228	.327
Pete Knisely	OF16	R	30	37	69	5	9	0	1	0	5	5	6	0	.130	.159
2 Claud Derrick	SS28	R	28	28	96	5	21	3	1	0	13	5	13	2	.219	.271
Art Phelan	3B7, 2B3, SS2	R	26	25	46	5	13	2	1	0	3	4	3	0	.283	.370
Bubbles Hargrave	C16	R	21	23	36	3	8	2	0	0	2	0	4	2	.222	.278
Chick Keating	SS16	R	22	20	30	3	3	0	1	0	0	6	9	0	.100	.167
Bobby Fisher	SS15	R	27	15	50	5	15	2	2	0	5	3	4	2	.300	.420
Art Bues	3B12	R	26	14	45	3	10	1	1	0	4	5	6	1	.222	.289
1 Fritz Mollwitz	1B4, OF1	R	24	13	20	0	3	0	0	0	1	0	3	1	.150	.150

2 Johnny Bates 32 L 1-8, Tom Needham 35 R 2-17, Tuffy Stewart 30 L 0-1, Milo Allison 23 L 1-1, Herman Bronkie 29 R 1-1, Earl Tyree 24 R 0-4

NAME	T	AGE	W	L	PCT	SV	G	GS	CG	IP	H	BB	SO	ShO	ERA
		28	78	76	.506	11	156	156	70	1389	1169	528	651	14	2.71
Hippo Vaughn	L	26	21	13	.618	1	42	35	23	294	236	109	165	4	2.05
Larry Cheney	R	28	20	18	.526	5	50	40	21	311	239	140	157	6	2.55
Jimmy Lavender	R	30	11	11	.500	0	37	28	11	214	191	87	87	2	3.07
Bert Humphries	R	33	10	11	.476	0	34	22	8	171	162	37	62	2	2.68
George Pearce	L	26	8	12	.333	1	30	16	4	141	122	65	78	0	3.51
Zip Zabel	R	23	4	4	.500	3	29	7	2	128	104	45	50	0	2.18
Charlie Smith	R	34	2	4	.333	0	16	5	1	54	49	15	17	0	3.83
2 Casey Hageman	R	27	2	1	.667	1	16	1	0	47	44	12	17	0	3.45
1 Elmer Koestner	R	28	0	0	.000	0	4	0	0	6	6	4	6	0	3.00
George McConnell	R	36	0	1	.000	0	1	1	0	7	3	3	3	0	1.29
Eddie Stack	R	26	0	1	.000	0	7	1	0	16	13	11	9	0	5.06

BROOKLYN 5th 75-79 .487 19.5 — WILBERT ROBINSON

NAME	G by POS	B	AGE	G	AB	R	H	2B	3B	HR	RBI	BB	SO	SB	BA	SA
TOTALS			26	154	5152	622	1386	172	90	31	529	376	559	173	.269	.355
Jake Daubert	1B126	L	30	126	474	89	156	17	7	6	45	30	34	25	.329	.432
George Cutshaw	2B153	R	26	153	583	69	150	22	12	2	78	30	32	34	.257	.346
Dick Egan	SS83, 3B10, OF3, 2B2, 1B1	R	30	106	337	30	76	10	3	1	21	22	25	8	.226	.282
1 Red Smith	3B90	R	24	90	330	39	81	10	8	4	48	30	26	11	.245	.361
Casey Stengel	OF121	L	23	126	412	55	130	13	10	4	60	56	55	19	.316	.425
Jack Dalton	OF116	R	29	128	442	65	141	13	8	1	45	53	39	19	.319	.391
Zack Wheat	OF144	L	28	145	533	66	170	26	9	9	89	47	50	20	.319	.452
Lew McCarty	C84	R	25	90	284	20	72	14	2	1	30	14	22	1	.254	.327
John Hummel	1B36, OF19, 2B1, SS1	R	31	73	208	25	55	8	9	0	20	16	25	5	.264	.389
Hy Myers	OF60	R	25	70	227	35	65	3	9	0	17	7	24	2	.286	.379
Ollie O'Mara (BL)	SS63	R	23	67	247	41	65	10	2	1	7	16	26	14	.263	.332
Gus Getz	3B55	R	24	55	210	13	52	8	1	0	20	2	15	9	.248	.295
Otto Miller	C50	R	25	54	169	17	39	6	1	0	9	7	20	0	.231	.278
Bill Fischer	C30	L	23	43	105	12	27	1	2	0	8	8	12	1	.257	.305
Kid Elberfeld	SS18, 2B1	R	39	30	62	7	14	1	0	0	1	2	4	0	.226	.242
1 Joe Riggert	OF20	R	27	27	83	6	16	1	3	2	6	4	20	2	.193	.349
1 Tex Erwin	C4	L	28	9	11	0	5	0	0	0	1	2	1	1	.455	.455

NAME	T	AGE	W	L	PCT	SV	G	GS	CG	IP	H	BB	SO	ShO	ERA
		26	75	79	.487	11	154	154	80	1368	1282	466	605	11	2.82
Jeff Pfeffer	R	26	23	12	.657	4	43	34	27	315	264	91	135	3	1.97
Raleigh Aitchison	L	26	12	7	.632	0	26	17	8	172	156	60	87	3	2.67
Pat Ragan	R	25	10	15	.400	3	38	26	14	208	214	85	106	1	2.99
Ed Reulbach	R	31	11	18	.379	3	44	29	14	256	228	83	119	3	2.64
1 Frank Allen	L	24	8	14	.364	0	36	21	10	171	165	57	68	1	3.11
Nap Rucker	L	29	7	6	.538	0	16	16	5	104	113	27	35	0	3.38
Elmer Brown	R	31	2	2	.500	0	11	4	1	37	33	23	22	0	3.89
Johnny Enzmann	R	24	1	0	1.000	0	7	1	0	19	21	8	5	0	4.74
Charlie Schmutz	R	24	1	3	.250	0	18	5	1	57	57	13	21	0	3.33
2 Bill Steele	R	28	0	1	.000	1	8	1	0	16	17	7	3	0	5.63
Bull Wagner	R	26	0	1	.000	0	6	0	0	12	14	12	4	0	6.75

PHILADELPHIA 6th 74-80 .481 20.5 — RED DOOIN

NAME	G by POS	B	AGE	G	AB	R	H	2B	3B	HR	RBI	BB	SO	SB	BA	SA
TOTALS			29	154	5110	651	1345	211	52	**62**	564	472	570	145	.263	**.362**
Fred Luderus	1B121	L	28	121	443	55	110	16	5	12	55	33	31	2	.248	.388
Bobby Bryne	2B101, 3B22	R	29	126	467	61	127	12	1	0	26	45	44	9	.272	.302
2 Jack Martin	SS83	R	27	83	292	26	74	5	3	0	21	27	29	6	.253	.291
Hans Lobert	3B133, SS2	R	32	135	505	83	139	24	5	1	52	49	32	31	.275	.349
Gavvy Cravath	OF143	R	33	149	499	76	149	27	8	**19**	100	83	72	14	.299	.499
Dode Paskert	OF128, SS4	R	32	132	451	59	119	25	6	3	44	56	68	23	.264	.366
Beals Becker	OF126	L	27	138	514	76	167	25	5	9	66	37	59	16	.325	.446
Bill Killefer	C90	R	26	98	299	27	70	10	1	0	27	8	17	3	.234	.274
Sherry Magee	OF67, SS39, 1B32, 2B8	R	29	146	544	96	**171**	**39**	11	15	**103**	55	42	25	.314	**.509**
Ed Burns	C55	R	25	70	139	8	36	3	4	0	16	20	12	5	.259	.338
Hal Irelan	2B44, SS3, 1B2, 3B2	B	23	67	165	16	39	8	0	1	16	21	22	3	.236	.303
Red Dooin	C40	R	35	53	118	10	21	2	0	1	8	4	14	4	.178	.220
Milt Reed	SS22, 2B11, 3B1	L	23	44	107	10	22	2	1	0	2	10	13	4	.206	.243
1 Josh Devore	OF9	L	26	30	53	5	16	2	0	0	7	4	5	0	.302	.340
Dummy Murphy	SS9	R	24	9	26	1	4	1	0	0	3	0	4	0	.154	.192
Pat Hilly	OF4	R	27	8	10	2	3	0	0	0	1	1	5	0	.300	.300
Fred Mollenkamp	1B3		24	3	8	0	1	0	0	0	0	2	0	0	.125	.125
Frank Fletcher		R	23	1	1	0	0	0	0	0	0	0	1	0	.000	.000
Pat Moran	C1	R	38	1	0	0	0	0	0	0	1	0	0	0	.000	.000
George McAvoy				1	1	0	0	0	0	0	0	0	0	0	.000	.000

NAME	T	AGE	W	L	PCT	SV	G	GS	CG	IP	H	BB	SO	ShO	ERA
		24	74	80	.481	7	154	154	85	1379	**1403**	452	650	14	3.06
Pete Alexander	R	27	**27**	15	.643	1	46	39	**32**	**355**	**327**	76	**214**	6	2.38
Erskine Mayer	R	25	21	19	.525	2	48	39	24	321	308	91	116	4	2.58
Ben Tincup	R	23	7	10	.412	2	28	17	9	155	165	62	108	3	2.61
Rube Marshall	R	23	6	7	.462	1	27	19	7	134	144	50	49	0	3.76
Joe Oeschger	R	23	4	8	.333	1	32	10	5	124	129	54	47	0	3.77
Stan Baumgartner	L	21	3	2	.600	0	15	3	2	60	60	16	24	1	3.30
Eddie Matteson	R	29	3	2	.600	0	15	3	2	58	58	23	28	0	3.10
Eppa Rixey	L	23	2	11	.154	0	24	15	2	103	124	45	41	0	4.37
Elmer Jacobs	R	21	1	3	.250	0	14	7	1	51	65	20	17	0	4.76
George Chalmers	R	26	0	3	.000	0	3	2	1	18	23	15	6	0	5.50

PITTSBURGH 7th 69-85 .448 25.5 — FRED CLARKE

NAME	G by POS	B	AGE	G	AB	R	H	2B	3B	HR	RBI	BB	SO	SB	BA	SA
TOTALS			28	158	5145	503	1197	148	79	18	437	416	608	147	.233	.303
Ed Konetchy	1B154	R	28	154	563	56	140	23	9	4	51	32	48	20	.249	.343
Jim Viox	2B138, SS2, OF2	R	23	143	506	52	134	18	5	1	57	63	33	9	.265	.326
Honus Wagner	SS132, 3B17, 1B1	R	40	150	552	60	139	15	9	1	50	51	51	23	.252	.317
Mike Mowrey	3B78	R	30	79	284	24	72	7	5	1	25	22	20	8	.254	.324
1 Mike Mitchell	OF76	R	34	76	273	31	64	11	5	2	23	16	16	5	.234	.333
Joe Kelly	OF138	R	24	141	508	47	113	19	9	1	48	39	59	21	.222	.301
Max Carey	OF154	B	24	156	**593**	76	144	25	**17**	1	31	59	56	38	.243	.347
George Gibson	C101	R	33	102	274	19	78	9	5	0	30	27	27	4	.285	.354
Ham Hyatt	1B7, C1	L	29	74	79	2	17	3	1	1	15	7	14	1	.215	.316
Bob Coleman	C72	R	23	73	150	11	40	4	1	1	14	15	32	3	.267	.327
Alex McCarthy	3B36, 2B10, SS6	R	26	57	173	14	26	0	1	1	14	6	17	2	.150	.179
Joe Leonard	3B38, SS1	L	19	53	126	17	25	2	2	0	4	12	21	4	.198	.246
Zip Collins	OF49	L	22	49	182	14	44	2	0	0	15	8	10	3	.242	.253
Eddie Mensor	OF25	B	24	44	89	15	18	2	1	1	6	22	13	2	.202	.281
Jimmy Kelly	OF7	L	24	32	44	4	10	2	1	0	3	2	3	0	.227	.318
Dan Costello	OF20	L	22	21	64	7	19	1	0	0	5	8	16	2	.297	.313
Jake Kafora	C17	R	25	21	23	2	3	0	0	0	0	0	6	0	.130	.130
Wally Gerber	SS17	R	22	17	54	5	13	1	1	0	5	2	8	0	.241	.296
Ike McAuley	SS5, 3B3, 2B2,	R	20	15	24	3	3	0	0	0	0	0	8	0	.125	.125

Paddy Siglin 22 R 6-39, Bobby Schang 27 R 8-35, Fritz Scheeren 23 R 9-31, Clarence Berger 19 L 1-13, Syd Smith 30 R 3-11, Pete Falsey 23 L 0-1, Bill Wagner 20 R 0-1, Fred Clarke 41 L 0-2, Sam Brenegan 23 L 0-0, Pat Killhullen 23 R 0-1, Ralph Shafer 20 0-0

NAME	T	AGE	W	L	PCT	SV	G	GS	CG	IP	H	BB	SO	ShO	ERA
		26	69	85	.448	11	158	158	86	1405	1272	392	488	10	2.70
Wilbur Cooper	L	22	16	15	.516	0	40	34	19	267	246	79	102	0	2.12
Babe Adams	R	32	13	16	.448	1	40	35	19	283	253	39	91	3	2.45
George McQuillan	R	29	13	17	.433	4	45	28	15	259	248	60	96	0	2.99
Bob Harmon	R	26	13	17	.433	3	37	30	19	245	226	55	61	2	2.53
Al Mamaux	R	20	5	2	.714	0	13	6	4	63	41	24	30	2	1.71
Joe Conzelman	R	24	5	6	.455	2	33	9	4	101	88	40	39	1	2.94
Erv Kantlehner	L	21	3	2	.600	0	21	5	3	67	51	39	26	2	3.09
1 Marty O'Toole	R	26	1	8	.111	1	19	9	1	92	92	47	36	0	4.70
Herb Kelly	L	22	0	2	.000	0	5	2	2	26	24	7	6	0	2.43
Pat Bohen	R	23	0	0	.000	0	1	0	0	1	2	2	0	0	18.00
Dixie McArthur	R	22	0	0	.000	0	1	0	0	1	1	0	1	0	0.00

CINCINNATI 8th 60-94 .390 34.5 — BUCK HERZOG

NAME	G by POS	B	AGE	G	AB	R	H	2B	3B	HR	RBI	BB	SO	SB	BA	SA
TOTALS			27	157	4991	530	1178	142	64	16	432	441	**627**	224	.236	.300
1 Dick Hoblitzell	1B75	L	25	78	248	31	52	8	7	0	26	26	26	7	.210	.298
Heinie Groh	2B134, SS2	R	24	139	455	59	131	18	4	2	32	64	28	24	.288	.358
Buck Herzog	SS137, 1B2	R	28	138	498	54	140	14	8	1	40	42	27	46	.281	.347
Bert Niehoff	3B134, 2B3	R	30	142	484	46	117	16	9	4	49	38	77	20	.242	.337
1 Herbie Moran	OF107	L	30	107	395	43	93	10	5	1	35	41	29	26	.235	.294
Bert Daniels	OF71	R	31	71	269	29	59	9	7	0	19	19	40	14	.219	.305
George Twombly	OF68	R	22	68	240	22	56	0	5	0	19	14	27	12	.233	.275
Tommy Clarke	C108	R	26	113	313	30	82	13	7	2	25	31	30	6	.262	.367
Mike Gonzalez	C83	R	23	95	176	19	41	6	0	0	10	13	16	2	.233	.267
Doc Miller	OF47	L	31	93	192	8	49	7	2	0	33	16	18	4	.255	.313
Marty Berghammer	SS33, 2B13	L	26	77	112	6	25	2	0	0	6	10	18	4	.223	.241
Bill Kellogg	1B38, 2B11, OF2, 3B1	R	30	71	126	14	22	0	1	0	7	14	28	7	.175	.190
1 Johnny Bates	OF57	L	32	67	163	36	40	7	5	2	15	29	18	4	.245	.387
Earl Yingling	P34, OF13	L	25	61	120	9	23	2	0	1	11	9	15	3	.192	.233
Maury Uhler	OF36	R	27	46	56	12	12	2	0	0	3	5	11	4	.214	.250
Red Killefer	OF35, 2B5, 3B1	R	30	42	141	16	39	6	1	0	12	20	18	11	.277	.333
Fritz Vonkolnitz	3B20, OF11, C2, 1B1	R	21	41	104	8	23	2	0	0	6	6	16	4	.221	.240
1 Armando Marsans	OF36	R	27	36	124	16	37	3	0	0	22	14	6	13	.298	.323

1 Johnny Rawlings 21 R 13-60, 2 Fritz Mollwitz 24 R 18-111, Tiny Graham 21 R 14-61, Harry LaRoss 23 R 11-48, Howard Lohr 22 R 10-47, 2 Tex Erwin 28 L 11-35,
2 Bill Holden 24 R 6-28, Norm Glockson 20 R 0-12, Kid McLaughlin 26 L 0-2, 1 Claud Derrick 28 R 2-6, Ed Kippert 34 R 0-2

NAME	T	AGE	W	L	PCT	SV	G	GS	CG	IP	H	BB	SO	ShO	ERA
		25	60	**94**	.390	**15**	157	157	74	1387	1259	489	607	14	2.94
Rube Benton	L	27	17	18	.437	2	41	31	16	271	223	95	121	5	2.96
Red Ames	R	31	15	**23**	.395	**6**	47	36	18	297	274	94	128	3	2.64
Phil Douglas	R	24	11	18	.379	1	45	25	13	239	186	92	121	0	2.56
Earl Yingling	L	25	8	13	.381	0	34	27	8	198	207	54	80	3	3.45
Pete Schneider	R	21	5	13	.278	1	29	20	11	144	143	56	62	1	2.81
1 Dave Davenport	R	24	2	2	.500	2	10	6	3	54	38	30	22	1	2.50
King Lear	R	23	1	2	.333	1	17	4	3	56	55	19	20	1	3.05
Jack Rowan	R	27	1	3	.250	2	12	2	0	39	38	10	16	0	3.46
Paul Fittery	L	26	0	2	.000	0	8	4	2	44	41	12	21	0	3.07
Pete Fahrer	R	24	0	0	.000	0	5	0	0	8	8	4	2	0	1.13
2 Elmer Koestner	R	28	0	0	.000	0	5	1	0	18	18	9	6	0	4.50
Karl Adams	R	22	0	0	.000	0	4	0	0	8	14	5	5	0	9.00
Bob Ingersoll	R	31	0	0	.000	0	4	0	0	6	5	5	2	0	3.00
Pat Griffin	R	21	0	0	.000	0	1	0	0	1	3	2	0	0	9.00
1 Chief Johnson	R	28	0	0	.000	0	1	1	0	4	6	2	1	0	6.75

WORLD SERIES – BOSTON (NL) 4 PHILADELPHIA (AL) 0

LINE SCORES

TEAM	1	2	3	4	5	6	7	8	9	10	11	12	R	H	E
Game 1 October 9 at Philadelphia															
BOS (NL)	0	2	0	0	1	3	0	1	0				7	11	2
PHI (AL)	0	1	0	0	0	0	0	0	0				1	5	0
Rudolph — Bender, Wyckoff (6)															
Game 2 October 10 at Philadelphia															
BOS	0	0	0	0	0	0	0	0	1				1	7	1
PHI	0	0	0	0	0	0	0	0	0				0	2	1
James — Plank															
Game 3 October 12 at Boston															
PHI	1	0	0	1	0	0	0	0	0	2	0	0	4	8	2
BOS	0	1	0	1	0	0	0	0	0	2	0	1	5	9	1
Bush — Tyler, **James (10)**															
Game 4 October 13 at Boston															
PHI	0	0	0	0	1	0	0	0	0				1	7	0
BOS	0	0	0	1	2	0	0	0	X				3	6	0
Shawkey, Pennock (6) — **Rudolph**															

COMPOSITE BATTING

NAME	POS	G	AB	R	H	2B	3B	HR	RBI	BA
Boston (NL)										
Totals		4	135	16	33	6	2	1	14	.244
Schmidt	1B	4	**17**	2	5	0	0	0	2	.294
Evers	2B	4	16	2	7	0	0	0	2	.438
Deal	3B	4	16	1	2	2	0	0	0	.125
Whitted	OF	4	14	2	3	0	1	0	2	.214
Maranville	SS	4	13	1	4	0	0	0	**3**	.308
Moran	OF	3	13	2	1	1	0	0	0	.077
Gowdy	C	4	11	**3**	**6**	**3**	**1**	**1**	**3**	**.545**
Connolly	OF	3	9	1	1	0	0	0	1	.111
Mann	OF	3	7	1	2	0	0	0	1	.286
Rudolph	P	2	6	1	2	0	0	0	0	.333
Cather	OF	1	5	0	0	0	0	0	0	.000
James	P	2	4	0	0	0	0	0	0	.000
Tyler	P	1	3	0	0	0	0	0	0	.000
Devore	PH	1	1	0	0	0	0	0	0	.000
Gilbert	PH	1	0	0	0	0	0	0	0	.000
Philadelphia (AL)										
Totals		4	128	6	22	9	0	0	5	.172
Baker	3B	4	16	0	4	2	0	0	2	.250
Murphy	OF	4	16	2	3	2	0	0	0	.188
Oldring	OF	4	15	0	1	0	0	0	0	.067
Collins	2B	4	14	0	3	0	0	0	1	.214
McInnis	1B	4	14	2	2	1	0	0	0	.143
Barry	SS	4	14	1	1	0	0	0	0	.071
Schang	C	4	12	1	2	1	0	0	0	.167
Strunk	OF	2	7	0	2	0	0	0	0	.286
Walsh	OF	3	6	0	2	1	0	0	1	.333
Bush	P	1	5	0	0	0	0	0	0	.000
Shawkey	P	1	2	0	1	1	0	0	1	.500
Bender	P	1	2	0	0	0	0	0	0	.000
Plank	P	1	2	0	0	0	0	0	0	.000
Wyckoff	P	1	1	0	1	1	0	0	0	1.000
Lapp	C	1	1	0	0	0	0	0	0	.000
Pennock	P	1	1	0	0	0	0	0	0	.000

COMPOSITE PITCHING

NAME	G	IP	H	BB	SO	W	L	SV	ERA
Boston (NL)									
Totals	4	39	22	13	28	4	0	0	1.15
Rudolph	**2**	**18**	**12**	4	**15**	**2**	0	0	0.50
James	**2**	11	2	**6**	9	**2**	0	0	**0.00**
Tyler	1	10	8	3	4	0	0	0	3.60
Philadelphia (AL)									
Totals	4	37	33	15	18	0	4	0	3.41
Bush	4	11	9	4	4	0	1	0	3.27
Plank	1	9	7	4	6	0	1	0	1.00
Bender	6	5.1	8	2	3	0	1	0	10.13
Shawkey	2	5	4	2	0	0	1	0	3.60
Wyckoff	1	3.2	3	1	2	0	0	0	2.45
Pennock	1	3	2	2	3	0	0	0	0.00

1914 F. L.—Gilmore's Green Glory

Like the new leagues of the present era, the Federal League was born with high hopes and plenty of money. When Chicago businessman, James A. Gilmore, became president of the minor Federal League in 1913, he planned to turn the sectional midwest loop into a national major league. Using broad strokes and rosy colors, Gilmore painted a picture of baseball as a profitable financial venture and lined up backing for most of the eight franchises in his loop. Leading industrialists, such as Phil Ball, Charles Weeghman, and Robert Ward, backed franchises with visions of sizeable profits and free advertising from their nationally-known clubs.

With a bankroll intact, confidence soaring, and the reality of risk neatly tucked away in the unknown and optimistic future, Gilmore proclaimed the Federal League as a third major league in 1914 and stated that his loop would not honor the "monopolistic" reserve clause set up by the baseball establishment. Big money was freely waved around, and the first major catch for the Feds was star shortstop Joe Tinker, signed to manage and play for the Chicago Whales. Other established players followed Tinker on the golden brick road into the new league. Some older players past their prime cashed in one last big paycheck by signing with the Feds; Three Finger Brown and Solly Hofman of the old Cub champions, George Mullin of the Tiger triple pennant winners, Danny Murphy of Connie Mack's Athletics, and veteran National Leaguers, Howie Camnitz and Al Bridwell, brought along their names but little of their former skills. Some younger veterans joined the loop, among them star-hurler Tom Seaton, the Phillies' double-play tandem of Otto Knabe and Mickey Doolan, outfielder Rebel Oakes, and pitchers, Doc Crandall, Russ Ford, Bob Groom, Cy Falkenburg, and Claude Hendrix. Star first-sacker Hal Chase, always amenable to a well-greased palm, jumped the White Sox in mid-season to join the Feds. Minor leaguers, major league rejects, and youngsters filled the remainder of the berths. Overtures were made to superstars, Ty Cobb, Tris Speaker, and Walter Johnson, but they stayed put when their salaries were boosted by sweating American League moguls.

The 1914 season opened with franchises bucking the established competition in Brooklyn, Chicago, St. Louis, and Pittsburgh, and with teams in the minor AAA cities of Baltimore, Buffalo, Kansas City, and Indianapolis. New parks were constructed in all eight cities and were ready for the openers. Chicago's entry played in what was eventually called Wrigley Field.

As the season progressed, attendance was not far behind the established loops, but all three circuits suffered from having the paying public spread thinly among three markets. The Feds' gate was boosted by a spirited pennant race in which almost every team, at one time or another, contended. Indianapolis and Chicago raced neck and neck into the final week, with Chicago losing a slight lead over the Hoosiers by dropping a doubleheader to the Kansas City Packers on October 6, which allowed the Indianians to finally grab the brass ring.

A 24-year-old bon vivant on the order of Joe Namath paced the Hoosiers and became the league's top star. Outfielder Benny Kauff led the loop in batting and stolen bases and lived in a style befitting a champ, which included, among other indulgences, diamond rings and silk underwear. Frank Laporte provided solid batting behind Kauff, and Cy Falkenberg paced the Indianapolis hurlers with 25 victories. Bill McKechnie and Edd Roush were other youngsters on the flag-winners who would make names for themselves in future campaigns. The runner-up Chicago Whales fielded Joe Tinker, Dutch Zwilling (a star slugger who would later flop in the National League), and Max Flack (a .247 hitter who would later play 10 years in the senior circuit). Other league stars included established hurlers, Hendrix and Seaton, the ever-ready Hal Chase, ex-Cardinal Steve Evans, and Senator reject Duke Kenworthy.

As the year closed, the Feds continued to wave hefty contracts under star noses. Although it was a tactic that would eventually harm all the owners, the money was welcomed by the players themselves who, long frustrated by a closed market, found it profitable.

1914 FEDERAL LEAGUE

NAME	G by POS	B	AGE	G	AB	R	H	2B	3B	HR	RBI	BB	SO	SB	BA	SA
INDIANAPOLIS 1st 88-65 .575		BILL PHILLIPS														
TOTALS			27	157	5176	762	1474	230	90	33	629	470		273	.285	.383
Charlie Carr	1B115	R	37	115	441	44	129	11	10	3	69	26		19	.293	.383
Frank LaPorte	2B132	R	34	133	505	86	157	27	12	4	107	36		15	.311	.436
Jimmy Esmond	SS151	R	24	151	542	74	160	23	15	2	49	40		25	.295	.404
Bill McKechnie	3B149	B	27	149	571	107	174	22	6	2	38	53		47	.305	.375
Benny Kauff	OF154	L	24	154	571	120	211	44	13	8	95	72		75	.370	.534
Vin Campbell	OF132	L	26	134	544	92	173	23	11	7	44	37		26	.318	.439
Al Scheer	OF102, 2B4, SS1	L	25	120	363	63	111	23	6	3	45	49		9	.306	.427
Bill Rariden	C130	R	26	131	396	44	93	15	5	0	47	61		12	.235	.298
Edd Roush	OF43, 1B2	L	21	74	165	26	55	6	5	1	30	6		12	.333	.448
Al Kaiser(IL)	OF50, 1B1	R	27	59	187	22	43	10	0	1	16	17		6	.230	.299
George Mullin	P36	R	33	43	77	11	24	5	3	0	21	11		0	.312	.455
Carl Vandagrift	2B28, 3B12, SS5	R	31	43	136	25	34	4	0	0	9	9		7	.250	.279
Biddy Dolan	1B31			32	103	13	23	4	2	1	15	12		5	.223	.330
Bill Warren	C23	L	27	26	50	5	12	2	0	0	5	5		2	.240	.280
George Textor	C21	B	25	22	57	2	10	0	0	0	4	2		0	.175	.175
1 Everett Booe	OF5, SS3	L	24	20	31	5	7	1	0	0	6	7		4	.226	.258
Frank Rooney	1B9			12	35	1	7	0	1	1	8	1		2	.200	.343
CHICAGO 2nd 87-67 .565 1.5		JOE TINKER														
TOTALS			26	157	5098	621	1314	227	50	51	544	520		171	.258	.352
Fred Beck	1B157	L	27	157	555	51	155	23	4	11	77	44		9	.279	.395
Jack Farrell	2B155, SS3	B	22	156	524	58	123	23	4	0	35	52		12	.235	.294
Joe Tinker(BR)	SS125	R	33	127	440	53	114	22	7	2	46	38		24	.259	.355
Rollie Zeider	3B117, SS1	R	30	120	456	59	120	15	2	1	36	44		35	.263	.311
Al Wickland	OF157	L	26	157	536	74	148	31	10	6	68	81		17	.276	.405
Dutch Zwilling	OF154	L	25	154	592	91	185	38	8	15	95	46		21	.313	.480
Max Flack	OF133	L	24	134	502	66	124	15	3	2	39	51		37	.247	.301
Art Wilson	C132	R	28	137	440	78	128	31	8	10	64	70		13	.291	.466
Harry Fritz	3B46, SS9, 2B1	R	23	65	174	16	37	5	1	0	13	18		2	.213	.253
Austin Walsh	OF30	L	22	57	121	14	29	6	1	1	10	4		0	.240	.331
Jim Stanley	SS40, 3B3, 2B1, OF1	B	25	54	98	13	19	3	0	0	4	19		2	.194	.224
Bruno Block	C33	R	29	43	100	8	19	4	1	0	13	11		1	.190	.250
Bill Jackson	OF6, 1B4	L	33	26	25	2	1	0	0	0	1	3		0	.040	.040
Count Clemens	C8	R	27	13	27	4	4	0	0	0	2	3		0	.148	.148
Leo Kavanagh	SS5	R	19	5	11	0	3	0	0	0	1	1		0	.273	.273
2 Skipper Roberts		L	26	4	3	0	1	0	0	0	1	1		0	.333	.333
Jack Kading		R	29	3	3	0	0	0	0	0	0	0		0	.000	.000
Jimmy Smith	SS3	R	19	3	6	1	3	1	0	0	1	0		0	.500	.667
BALTIMORE 3rd 84-70 .545 4.5		OTTO KNABE														
TOTALS			30	160	5120	645	1374	222	67	32	551	487		152	.268	.357
Harry Swacina	1B158	R	32	158	617	70	173	26	8	0	90	14		15	.280	.348
Otto Knabe	2B144	R	30	146	470	45	107	25	3	2	42	53		10	.228	.306
Mickey Doolan	SS145	R	34	144	486	58	119	25	6	1	53	40		34	.245	.327
Jimmy Walsh	3B113, 2B1, SS1, OF1	R	28	120	428	54	132	25	4	10	65	22		18	.308	.456
Benny Meyer	OF132, SS4	R	26	143	500	76	152	18	10	5	40	71		23	.304	.410
Vern Duncan	OF148, OF8, 2B1	L	24	157	557	99	160	20	8	2	53	67		13	.287	.363
Hack Simmons	OF73, 2B26, 1B4, SS2, 3B1	R	29	114	352	50	95	16	5	1	38	32		7	.270	.352
Fred Jacklitsch	C118	R	38	122	337	40	93	21	4	2	48	52		7	.276	.380
Harvey Russell	C47, SS1, OF1	L	27	81	168	18	39	3	2	0	13	18		2	.232	.274
Guy Zinn(BL)	OF57	L	27	61	225	30	63	10	6	3	25	16		6	.280	.418
3 Johnny Bates	OF59	L	32	59	190	24	58	6	3	1	29	38		6	.305	.384
E. Kirkpatrick (BL)	3B36, SS11, OF3, 1B1	R	28	55	174	22	44	7	2	2	16	18		10	.253	.351
1 Medric Boucher	C7, 1B1, OF1	R	25	16	16	2	5	1	1	0	2	1		0	.313	.500
2 Fred Kommers	OF12	L	28	16	42	5	9	1	0	1	1	7		0	.214	.310
2 Doc Kerr	C13, 1B1	B		14	34	4	9	1	1	0	1	1		1	.265	.353
Frank Lobert	3B7, 2B1	R	30	11	30	3	6	0	1	0	2	0		0	.200	.267
John McCandless	OF8	L	19	11	31	5	8	0	1	0	1	3		0	.258	.323
3 Felix Chouinard	OF2	R	27	5	9	3	4	0	0	0	1	0		0	.444	.444

NAME	T	AGE	W	L	PCT	SV	G	GS	CG	IP	H	BB	SO	ShO	ERA
		29	88	65	.575	9	157	157	104	1398	1352	476	664	15	3.06
Cy Falkenberg	R	34	25	16	.610	3	49	43	33	377	332	89	236	9	2.22
Earl Moseley	R	29	19	18	.514	1	43	38	29	317	303	123	205	4	3.47
George Kaiserling	R	21	17	10	.630	0	37	33	20	275	288	72	75	1	3.11
George Mullin	R	33	14	10	.583	2	36	20	11	203	202	91	74	1	2.70
Harry Billiard	R	28	8	7	.533	2	32	16	5	126	117	63	45	0	3.71
Charlie Whitehouse	L	20	2	0	1.000	0	8	2	2	26	34	5	10	0	4.85
2 Ed Henderson	L	24	1	0	1.000	0	2	1	1	10	8	4	1	0	4.50
Katsey Keifer	R	22	1	0	1.000	0	1	1	1	9	6	2	2	0	2.00
Frank Harter	R	27	1	2	.333	0	6	1	1	25	33	7	8	0	3.96
Ralph McConnaughey	R	25	0	2	.000	0	7	2	1	26	23	16	7	0	4.85
Clarence Woods	R	23	0	0	.000	1	2	0	0	2	1	2	1	0	4.50
Fred Ostendorf	L	23	0	0	.000	0	1	0	0	2	5	2	0	0	22.50
		26	87	67	.565	8	157	157	93	1420	1204	393	650	17	2.44
Claude Hendrix	R	25	29	10	.744	5	49	37	34	362	262	77	189	6	1.69
Erv Lange	R	26	12	11	.522	2	36	22	10	190	162	55	87	2	2.23
Max Fiske	R	25	12	12	.500	0	38	22	7	198	161	59	87	0	3.14
2 Rankin Johnson	R	26	9	5	.643	0	16	14	12	120	88	29	60	2	1.58
1 Doc Watson	L	29	9	8	.529	1	26	18	10	172	145	49	69	3	2.04
Ad Brennan	L	32	5	5	.500	0	16	11	5	86	84	21	31	1	3.56
Tom McGuire	R	22	5	6	.455	0	24	12	7	131	143	57	37	0	3.71
Mike Prendergast	L	25	5	9	.357	0	30	19	7	136	131	40	71	1	2.38
Dave Black	L	22	1	0	1.000	0	8	1	1	25	28	4	19	0	6.12
Babe Sherman	R	22	0	1	.000	0	1	1	0	.1	0	2	0	0	0.00
		30	84	70	.545	13	160	160	88	1392	1389	392	732	15	3.13
Jack Quinn	R	30	26	14	.650	1	46	42	27	343	335	65	164	4	2.60
George Suggs	R	31	24	14	.632	4	46	38	26	319	322	57	132	6	2.91
Kaiser Wilhelm	R	40	12	17	.414	5	47	27	11	244	263	81	113	1	4.02
Frank Smith	R	34	10	8	.556	2	39	22	9	175	180	47	83	1	2.98
Bill Bailey	L	25	7	9	.438	0	19	18	10	129	106	68	131	1	3.07
Snipe Conley	R	20	4	6	.400	1	35	11	4	125	112	47	86	2	2.52
Ducky Yount	R	28	1	1	.500	0	13	1	1	41	44	19	19	0	4.18
John Ridgeway	R	23	0	1	.000	0	4	1	0	9	20	3	2	0	11.00
Vern Hughes	L	21	0	0	.000	0	3	0	0	6	5	3	0	0	3.00
John Allen	R	23	0	0	.000	0	1	0	0	2	2	2	2	0	18.00

BUFFALO 4th 80-71 .530 7 — **LARRY SCHLAFLY**

NAME	G by POS	B	AGE	G	AB	R	H	2B	3B	HR	RBI	BB	SO	SB	BA	SA
TOTALS			28	155	5064	620	1264	177	74	38	508	430		228	.250	.336
Joe Agler	1B76, OF54	L	27	135	463	82	126	17	6	0	20	77		21	.272	.335
Tom Downey	2B129, SS16, 3B5	R	30	151	541	69	118	20	3	2	42	40		35	.218	.277
Baldy Louden	SS115	R	30	126	431	73	135	11	4	6	63	52		35	.313	.399
• Fred Smith	3B127, SS19, 1B1	R	22	145	473	48	104	12	10	2	45	49		24	.220	.300
2 Tex McDonald	OF61, 2B10	L	25	69	250	32	74	13	6	3	32	20		11	.296	.432
Charlie Hanford	OF155	R	33	155	597	83	174	28	13	13	90	32		37	.291	.447
1 Frank Delahanty	OF78	R	31	79	274	29	55	4	7	2	27	23		21	.201	.288
Walter Blair	C128	R	30	128	378	22	92	11	2	0	33	32		6	.243	.283
Del Young	OF41	L	28	80	174	17	48	5	5	4	22	3		0	.276	.431
2 Hal Chase	1B73	R	31	75	291	43	103	19	9	3	48	6		10	.354	.512
2 Everett Booe	OF58, SS8, 3B2, 2B1	L	24	76	241	29	54	9	2	0	14	21		8	.224	.278
Art LaVigne	C34, 1B3	R	29	51	90	10	14	2	0	0	4	7		0	.156	.178
Larry Schlafly	2B23, 1B7, 3B1, OF1, C1	R	35	51	127	16	33	7	1	2	19	12		3	.260	.378
Nick Allen	C26	R	25	32	63	3	15	1	0	0	4	3		4	.238	.254
2 Clyde Engle	3B23, OF9	R	30	32	110	12	28	4	1	0	12	11		5	.255	.309
Luther Bonin	OF20	L	26	20	76	6	14	4	1	0	4	7		3	.184	.263
Bill Collins	OF15	B	32	21	47	6	7	2	2	0	2	1		0	.149	.277
Del Wertz	SS1	R	23	3	0	1	0	0	0	0	0	0		0	.000	.000
Ned Pettigrew		R	32	2	2	0	0	0	0	0	0	0		0	.000	.000
Jack Snyder	C1	R	22	1	0	0	0	0	0	0	0	1		0	.000	.000

NAME	T	AGE	W	L	PCT	SV	G	GS	CG	IP	H	BB	SO	ShO	ERA
		28	80	71	.530	16	155	155	89	1387	1249	505	662	15	3.16
Russ Ford	R	31	21	6	.778	6	35	26	19	247	190	41	123	5	1.82
Gene Krapp	R	27	16	14	.533	0	36	29	18	253	198	115	106	1	2.49
Fred Anderson	R	28	13	15	.464	0	37	28	21	260	243	64	144	2	3.08
Earl Moore	R	34	11	15	.423	2	36	27	14	195	184	99	96	2	4.29
Harry Moran	L	25	10	7	.588	2	34	16	7	154	159	53	73	2	4.27
2 Al Schulz	L	25	9	12	.429	2	27	23	10	171	160	77	87	0	3.37
Joe Houser	L	22	0	1	.000	0	7	2	0	23	21	20	6	0	5.48
Eddie Porray	R	25	0	1	.000	0	3	3	0	10	18	7	0	0	4.50
Bob Brown	R	23	0	0	.000	3	15	1	0	37	39	16	13	0	3.40
Dan Woodman	R	20	0	0	.000	1	13	0	0	34	30	11	13	0	2.39
Biff Schlitzer	R	29	0	0	.000	0	3	0	0	3	7	2	1	0	18.00

BROOKLYN 5th 77-77 .500 11.5 — **BILL BRADLEY**

NAME	G by POS	B	AGE	G	AB	R	H	2B	3B	HR	RBI	BB	SO	SB	BA	SA
TOTALS			28	157	**5221**	662	1402	225	85	42	573	404		220	.269	.368
Hap Myers	1B88	R	26	92	305	61	67	10	5	1	29	44		43	.220	.295
Solly Hofman	2B108, 1B22, OF21, SS1	R	31	147	515	65	148	25	12	5	83	54		34	.287	.412
Eddie Gagnier	SS88, 3B6	R	31	94	337	22	63	12	2	0	25	13		8	.187	.234
Tex Westerzil	3B149	R	23	149	534	54	137	18	10	0	66	34		17	.257	.328
Steve Evans	OF112, 1B27	L	29	145	514	93	179	41	**15**	12	96	50		18	.348	**.556**
Al Shaw	OF102	L	33	112	376	81	122	27	7	5	49	44		24	.324	.473
Claude Cooper	OF101	L	21	113	399	56	96	14	11	2	25	26		25	.241	.346
Grover Land	C97	R	29	102	335	24	92	6	2	0	29	12		7	.275	.304
George Anderson	OF92	L	24	98	364	58	115	13	3	3	24	31		16	.316	.393
Al Halt	SS71, 2B3, OF1	L	23	80	261	26	61	6	2	3	25	13		11	.234	.307
Jim Delahanty	2B55, 1B5	R	35	74	214	28	62	13	5	0	15	25		4	.290	.397
Frank Owens	C58	R	28	58	184	15	51	7	3	2	20	9		2	.277	.380
Danny Murphy	OF46	R	37	50	161	16	50	9	0	4	32	17		4	.311	.441
Art Griggs	1B27, OF1	R	30	40	112	10	32	6	1	1	15	5		1	.286	.384
2 Felix Chouinard	OF21	R	27	32	79	7	20	1	2	0	8	4		3	.253	.316
Art Watson	C18	R	28	22	46	7	13	4	1	1	3	1		0	.283	.478
Bill Bradley		R	36	7	6	1	3	1	0	0	3	0		0	.500	.667
Rinaldo Williams	3B4	L	20	4	15	1	4	2	0	0	0	0		0	.267	.400

NAME	T	AGE	W	L	PCT	SV	G	GS	CG	IP	H	BB	SO	ShO	ERA
		25	77	77	.500	9	157	157	91	1386	1375	**559**	636	11	3.33
Tom Seaton	R	26	25	14	.641	2	44	38	26	303	299	102	172	7	3.03
Ed Lafitte	R	28	18	15	.545	2	42	33	23	291	260	**127**	137	0	2.63
Happy Finnernan	R	22	12	11	.522	1	27	23	13	175	153	60	54	2	3.19
Bill Chappelle (JJ)	R	30	4	2	.667	0	16	6	4	74	71	29	31	0	3.16
Jim Bluejacket	R	26	4	5	.444	1	17	7	3	67	77	19	29	1	3.76
Don Marion	R	23	3	2	.600	0	17	9	4	89	97	38	41	0	3.94
Bert Maxwell	R	27	3	4	.429	1	12	8	6	71	76	24	19	1	3.29
Rube Peters	R	28	2	2	.500	0	11	3	1	38	52	16	13	0	3.79
2 Three Finger Brown	R	37	2	5	.286	0	9	8	5	58	63	18	32	0	4.19
2 Duke Houck	R	22	2	6	.250	0	17	9	3	92	95	43	45	0	3.13
Rudy Sommers	L	25	2	7	.222	2	23	8	2	82	88	34	40	0	4.06
Fin Wilson	L	24	0	1	.000	0	2	1	1	7	7	11	4	0	7.71
Herold Juul	R	21	0	3	.000	0	9	3	0	29	26	31	16	0	6.21
Esty Chaney	R	23	0	0	.000	0	1	0	0	4	7	2	1	0	6.75
Lee McGraw	R	24	0	0	.000	0	1	0	0	2	0	0	2	0	0.00
Joe Vernon	R	24	0	0	.000	0	1	1	0	3	4	5	0	0	12.00

KANSAS CITY 6th 67-84 .444 20 — **GEORGE STOVALL**

NAME	G by POS	B	AGE	G	AB	R	H	2B	3B	HR	RBI	BB	SO	SB	BA	SA
TOTALS			28	154	5127	644	1369	226	77	39	557	399		171	.267	.364
George Stovall	1B116, 3B1	R	35	122	448	50	121	20	5	7	75	23		8	.270	.384
Duke Kenworthy	2B145	B	27	146	545	93	173	40	14	**15**	91	36		37	.317	.525
Pep Goodwin	SS67, 3B40, 1B1	L	22	112	374	38	88	15	6	1	32	27		4	.235	.316
George Perring	3B101, 1B41, SS1, P1	R	29	144	496	68	138	28	10	2	69	59		7	.278	.387
Grover Gilmore	OF132	L	25	139	530	91	152	25	5	1	32	37		23	.287	.358
Art Kruger	OF120	R	33	122	441	45	114	24	7	4	47	23		11	.259	.372
Chet Chadbourne	OF146	L	29	147	581	92	161	22	8	1	37	69		42	.277	.348
Ted Easterly	C128	L	29	134	436	58	146	20	12	1	67	31		10	.335	.443
Cad Coles	OF39, 1B3	L	25	78	194	17	49	7	3	1	25	5		6	.253	.335
Cliff Daringer	SS24, 3B19, 2B14	L	29	64	160	12	42	2	1	0	16	11		9	.263	.288
2 Johnny Rawlings	SS61	R	21	61	196	18	41	3	0	0	15	22		6	.209	.224
Fred Potts	OF31	L	27	41	102	14	27	4	0	1	9	25		7	.265	.333
Drummond Brown	C23, 1B2	R	29	31	58	4	11	3	0	0	5	7		1	.190	.241
2 Jack Enzenroth	C24	R	28	26	67	7	12	4	1	0	5	5		0	.179	.269
W. Van Tappen	SS8, 3B6, 2B1	R	23	18	39	1	8	1	0	1	3	1		1	.205	.308

NAME	T	AGE	W	L	PCT	SV	G	GS	CG	IP	H	BB	SO	ShO	ERA
		26	67	84	.444	12	154	154	82	1361	1387	445	600	10	3.41
Gene Packard	L	26	20	14	.588	5	42	34	24	302	282	88	154	4	2.89
2 Nick Cullop	L	26	14	19	.424	1	44	36	22	296	256	87	149	4	2.34
2 Chief Johnson	R	28	9	10	.474	0	20	19	12	134	157	33	78	2	3.16
Dwight Stone	R	27	8	14	.364	0	39	22	6	187	205	77	88	0	4.33
Ben Harris	R	25	7	7	.500	1	31	14	5	154	179	41	40	0	4.09
Pete Henning	R	26	5	10	.333	2	28	14	7	138	153	58	45	0	4.83
Dan Adams	R	25	4	9	.308	3	36	14	6	136	141	52	38	0	3.51
George Hogan		28	0	1	.000	0	4	1	0	13	12	7	7	0	4.15
George Perring	R	29	0	0	.000	0	1	0	0	1	2	1	0	0	9.00
Ducky Swann	R	22	0	0	.000	0	1	0	0	1	0	1	1	0	0.00

PITTSBURGH 7th 64-86 .427 22.5 — **DOC GESSLER 6-12 .333 REBEL OAKES 58-74 .439**

NAME	G by POS	B	AGE	G	AB	R	H	2B	3B	HR	RBI	BB	SO	SB	BA	SA
TOTALS			29	154	5114	605	1339	180	**90**	34	520	410		153	.262	.352
Hugh Bradley	1B118	R	29	118	427	41	131	20	6	0	61	27		7	.307	.382
John Lewis	2B115, SS1	R	26	117	394	32	92	14	5	1	48	17		9	.234	.302
Ed Holly	SS94, 2B1, OF2	R	34	100	350	28	86	9	4	0	26	17		14	.246	.294
Ed Lennox	3B123	R	28	124	430	71	134	25	10	11	84	71		19	.312	.493
Hal Savage	OF93, 3B29, SS11, 2B3	L		132	479	81	136	9	9	1	26	67		17	.284	.347
Rebel Oakes	OF145	L	27	145	571	82	178	18	10	7	75	35		28	.312	.415
Davy Jones	OF93	L	34	97	352	58	96	9	8	2	24	42		15	.273	.361
Claude Berry	C122	R	34	124	411	35	98	18	9	2	36	26		6	.238	.341
Cy Rheam	1B43, 3B13, 2B11, OF1	R	20	73	214	15	45	5	3	0	20	9		6	.210	.262
Mike Menoskey	OF41	L	19	68	140	26	37	4	1	2	9	16		5	.264	.350
1 Tex McDonald	OF29, 2B27, SS5	L	25	67	223	27	71	16	7	3	29	13		9	.318	.493
13 Skipper Roberts	C23, OF1	L	26	62	94	12	22	4	2	1	8	2		3	.234	.351
1 Doc Kerr	C18	B		42	71	3	17	4	2	1	7	10		0	.239	.394
2 Frank Delahanty	OF36, 2B4	R	31	41	159	25	38	4	4	1	7	11		7	.239	.333
2 Steve Yerkes	SS39	R	26	39	142	18	48	9	5	1	25	11		2	.338	.493
Ralph Mattis	OF24	R	23	36	85	14	21	4	1	0	8	9		2	.247	.318
Bob Coulson	OF18	R	27	18	64	7	13	1	0	0	3	7		2	.203	.219
1 Felix Chouinard	2B4, OF3, SS1	R	27	9	30	2	9	1	0	1	3	0		1	.300	.433
Jim Scott	SS8	R	27	8	24	2	6	1	0	0	1	5		1	.250	.292
Madden	C1			2	2	0	1	0	0	0	1	0		0	.500	.500
2 Medric Boucher		R	25	1	1	0	0	0	0	0	0	0		0	.000	.000

NAME	T	AGE	W	L	PCT	SV	G	GS	CG	IP	H	BB	SO	ShO	ERA
		29	64	86	.427	6	154	154	97	1370	1416	444	510	9	3.56
Elmer Knetzer	R	28	20	12	.625	1	37	30	20	272	257	88	146	3	2.88
Howie Camnitz	R	32	14	19	.424	1	36	34	20	262	256	90	82	1	3.23
Cy Barger	R	29	10	16	.385	1	33	26	18	228	252	63	70	1	4.34
Walt Dickson	R	31	9	19	.321	1	40	32	19	257	262	74	63	3	3.15
George LaClaire	R	27	5	2	.714	0	22	7	5	103	99	25	49	1	4.02
Mysterious Walker	R	30	4	16	.200	0	35	21	12	169	197	74	79	0	4.32
2 Frank Allen	L	24	1	0	1.000	0	1	1	1	7	9	0	3	0	5.14
Willie Adams	R	23	1	1	.500	2	15	2	1	55	70	22	14	0	3.76
1 Ed Henderson	L	24	0	1	.000	0	6	1	1	16	14	8	4	0	3.94

ST. LOUIS 8th 62-89 .411 25 — **THREE FINGER BROWN 50-63 .442 FIELDER JONES 12-26 .316**

NAME	G by POS	B	AGE	G	AB	R	H	2B	3B	HR	RBI	BB	SO	SB	BA	SA
TOTALS			27	154	5078	565	1254	193	65	26	480	503		113	.247	.326
Hughie Miller	1B130	R	26	132	490	51	109	20	5	0	46	27		4	.222	.284
Doc Crandall	2B63, P27, SS1, OF1	R	26	118	278	40	86	16	5	2	41	58		3	.309	.424
Al Bridwell	SS103, 2B11	L	30	117	381	46	90	6	5	1	33	71		9	.236	.286
Al Boucher	3B147	R	32	147	516	62	119	26	4	2	49	52		13	.231	.308
Jack Tobin	OF132	L	22	137	530	80	143	24	11	7	35	51		20	.270	.396
Ward Miller	OF111	L	29	121	402	49	118	17	7	4	50	59		18	.294	.400
Delos Drake	OF116, 1B18	R	27	138	514	51	129	18	8	3	42	31		17	.251	.335
Mike Simon	C78	R	31	93	276	21	57	11	2	0	21	18		2	.207	.261
John Misse	2B50, SS48, 3B2	R	**29**	99	306	28	60	8	1	0	22	36		3	.196	.229
G. Hartley	C32, 2B13, 1B9, 3B3, OF2	R	25	86	213	24	61	15	2	1	25	12		4	.286	.390
1 Fred Kommers	OF67	L	28	76	244	33	75	9	8	3	41	24		7	.307	.447
Harry Chapman	C51, 1B1, 2B1, OF1	R	26	64	181	16	38	2	1	0	14	13		2	.210	.232
LaRue Kirby	OF50	B	24	52	195	21	48	6	3	2	18	14		5	.246	.338
Joe Mathes (JJ)	2B23	B	22	26	85	10	25	3	0	0	6	9		1	.294	.329
Manuel Cueto	3B10, SS5, 2B2	R	22	19	43	2	4	0	0	0	2	5		0	.093	.093
2 Armando Marsans (SC)	2B7, SS2	R	27	9	40	5	14	0	2	0	2	3		4	.350	.450
Fielder Jones		L	42	5	3	0	1	0	0	0	0	1		0	.333	.333

NAME	T	AGE	W	L	PCT	SV	G	GS	CG	IP	H	BB	SO	ShO	ERA
		29	62	**89**	.411	6	154	154	97	1367	**1418**	409	661	9	3.59
Doc Crandall	R	26	13	9	.591	0	27	21	18	196	194	52	84	1	3.54
Bob Groom	R	29	13	**20**	.394	1	42	34	23	281	281	75	167	1	3.24
1 Three Finger Brown	R	37	12	6	.667	0	26	18	13	175	172	43	81	2	3.29
2 Dave Davenport	R	**24**	8	13	.381	4	33	26	13	216	204	80	142	2	3.46
Hank Keupper	L	27	8	20	.286	0	42	25	12	213	256	49	70	1	4.27
Ed Willett	R	30	4	16	.200	0	27	21	14	175	208	56	73	0	4.22
2 Doc Watson	L	29	3	4	.429	0	9	7	4	56	41	24	18	2	1.93
Ernie Herbert	R	27	1	1	.500	1	18	2	0	50	56	27	24	0	3.78
Ted Welch	R	21	0	0	.000	0	3	0	0	6	6	3	2	0	6.00

1915 F. L.—A Short Life

The Federal League began its second year in the courts and ended it as a mere footnote in the history of the national pastime. An antitrust suit against organized baseball was filed in January in the United States District Court in Chicago. The presiding judge in the suit was Kenesaw M. Landis, later to become baseball's first commissioner. Litigation continued through the spring and summer, as the baseball wars resumed both on the field and on the dotted line.

Two plums were plucked for the Feds when star hurlers, Eddie Plank and Chief Bender, were induced to leave Connie Mack's Athletics. Two veteran National League pitchers who had seen better years—Ed Reulbach and Hooks Wiltse—also joined the new loop, as did young hitters, Ed Konetchy and Lee Magee. Several lesser lights came along with the "names" to strengthen the Federal playing ranks this second time around.

As the curtain rose on the playing season, 1914 champion Indianapolis no longer graced the circuit. The Hoosier franchise had been transferred to Newark, New Jersey, for economic reasons. Another close race evolved, with Chicago, St. Louis, and Pittsburgh racing head-and-head down the stretch. The Chicago Whales, managed by Joe Tinker, received offensive firepower from Dutch Zwilling and Max Flack, and uncovered a pair of surprise pitching aces in 37-year-old George McConnell and 38-year-old Three Finger Brown. St. Louis was paced by star hurlers, Eddie Plank, Doc Crandall, and Dave Davenport, and Pittsburgh's shining light was first-sacker Ed Konetchy.

Going into the final day of the season, one game separated the three contenders. After a doubleheader split between Chicago and Pittsburgh and a St. Louis victory, the smoke cleared on a .001 pennant-winning margin for Chicago over St. Louis. Pittsburgh, incredibly enough, finished third, one-half game and .004 percentage points behind. Chicago had played two fewer games than St. Louis, due to rainouts. Under today's practices, the race would not have ended there. Nevertheless, the exciting finish marked the second straight attractive race for the Feds.

Individual heroics spiced the play throughout. Bennie Kauff, sold to Brooklyn by the defunct Indianapolis club, again paced the league's batters with a .342 mark and led in stolen bases. In the pitching ranks, 6'3" George McConnell won 25 games for Chicago to lead the circuit.

As the season went on, Judge Landis urged the parties before the bench to discuss an amicable settlement. Finally, due to mounting losses and the possible U.S. entry into The Great War, the Feds were forced to sue for peace. The treaty was signed on December 21, with several key arrangements. Charles Weeghman, owner of the Chicago club, was permitted to purchase the Chicago Cubs, and St. Louis' Phil Ball was able to buy the Browns. All Federal players, except the Chicago and St. Louis squads, were to be sold to the highest bidder, and all remaining contracts continued as the responsibility of the Federal League owners. Several Federal owners were to be reimbursed for their losses and long-term leases on ball parks.

Out of the debris came the beginning—as well as the end—of certain careers. Several players who made their debut in the Federal League went on to successful careers in the established circuits. They included Bennie Kauff (for whom the New York Giants paid a record $35,000), Edd Roush, Jack Tobin, Howard Ehmke, and Max Flack. Among those who saw the last of full-time playing activity in what had been described as "the outlaw league" were Joe Tinker, Three Finger Brown, George Mullin, Al Bridwell, Howie Camnitz, and Hooks Wiltse.

The peace settlement made no provision for the Baltimore owners, who were simply left out in the cold. The jilted owners responded with an antitrust suit, which resulted in Justice Oliver Wendell Holmes' edict in 1922 "that baseball is exempt from antitrust regulations due to its peculiar nature." And, as history would bear witness, the effects of the edict and the Federal League were not at all short-range.

1915 FEDERAL LEAGUE

NAME	G by POS	B	AGE	G	AB	R	H	2B	3B	HR	RBI	BB	SO	SB	BA	SA
CHICAGO 1st 86-66 .566		**JOE TINKER**														
TOTALS			26	155	5133	641	1320	185	77	**50**	558	444		161	.257	.352
Fred Beck	1B117	L	28	121	373	35	83	9	3	5	38	24		4	.223	.303
Rollie Zeider	2B83, 3B30, SS21	R	31	130	493	65	115	24	2	0	34	43		16	.233	.290
Harry Fritz	3B70, 2B6, SS1	R	24	79	236	27	59	8	4	3	26	13		4	.250	.356
1 Jimmy Smith	SS92, 2B1	B	20	95	318	32	69	11	4	4	30	14		4	.217	.314
Max Flack	OF138	L	25	141	523	88	164	20	14	3	45	40		37	.314	.423
Dutch Zwilling	OF148, 1B3	L	26	150	548	65	157	32	7	13	**94**	67		24	.286	.442
Les Mann	OF130, SS1	R	21	135	468	75	143	14	**19**	4	58	36		18	.306	.442
Art Wilson	C87	R	29	96	269	44	82	11	2	7	31	65		8	.305	.439
Bill Fischer	C80	L	24	105	292	30	96	15	4	4	50	24		5	.329	.449
Charlie Hanford	OF43	R	34	77	179	27	43	4	5	0	22	12		10	.240	.318
Jack Farrell	2B70, SS1	B	23	70	222	27	48	10	1	0	14	25		8	.216	.270
Bill Jackson	1B36, OF1	L	34	50	98	15	16	1	0	1	12	14		3	.163	.204
24Tex Westerzil	3B48	R	24	49	164	15	40	4	1	0	14	8		2	.244	.280
Three Finger Brown	P35, OF1	R	38	36	82	10	24	2	1	0	6	3		0	.293	.341
Joe Tinker	SS16, 2B5, 3B4	R	34	30	69	7	19	2	1	0	9	13		3	.275	.333
1 Al Wickland	OF24	L	27	30	86	11	21	2	2	1	5	13		3	.244	.349
Joe Weiss	1B29	R	21	29	85	6	19	1	2	0	11	3		0	.224	.282
2 Mickey Doolan	SS24	R	35	24	86	9	23	1	1	0	9	2		5	.267	.302
Arnold Hauser(IL)	SS16, 3B6	R	26	23	54	6	11	1	0	0	4	5		2	.204	.222
Charlie Pechous	3B18	R	18	18	51	4	9	3	0	0	4	4		1	.176	.235
Count Clemens	C9, 2B2	R	28	11	22	3	3	1	0	0	3	1		0	.136	.182
ST. LOUIS 2nd 87-67 .565 0		**FIELDER JONES**														
TOTALS			27	159	**5145**	634	1344	199	**81**	23	547	**576**		195	.261	.345
Babe Borton	1B159	L	26	159	549	**97**	157	20	14	3	83	**92**		17	.286	.390
Bobby Vaughn	2B127, SS12, 3B8	R	30	144	521	69	146	19	9	0	32	58		24	.280	.351
Ernie Johnson	SS152	L	27	152	512	58	123	18	10	7	67	46		32	.240	.355
Charlie Deal	3B65	R	23	65	223	21	72	12	4	1	27	12		10	.323	.426
Jack Tobin	OF158	L	23	158	**623**	91	**186**	29	14	6	51	68		31	.299	.403
Delos Drake	OF97, 1B1	R	28	102	343	32	91	23	4	1	41	23		6	.265	.364
Ward Miller	OF154	L	30	154	536	80	164	19	9	1	63	79		33	.306	.381
Grover Hartley	C113, 1B1	R	26	117	395	47	107	20	6	1	50	42		10	.271	.359
Doc Crandall	P51	R	27	84	141	18	40	2	2	1	19	27		4	.284	.348
Al Bridwell	2B42, 3B15, 1B1	L	31	65	175	20	40	3	2	0	9	25		6	.229	.269
Harry Chapman	C53	R	27	62	186	19	37	6	3	1	29	22		4	.199	.280
LaRue Kirby	OF52, P1	R	25	61	178	15	38	7	2	0	16	17		3	.213	.275
Art Kores	3B60	R	28	60	201	18	47	9	2	1	22	21		6	.234	.313
Armando Marsans	OF35	R	28	36	124	16	22	3	0	0	6	14		5	.177	.202
2 Jimmy Walsh	3B9	R	29	17	31	5	6	1	0	0	1	3		1	.194	.226
3 Tex Westerzil	3B8	R	24	8	24	1	5	1	0	0	4	2		2	.208	.250
Fielder Jones	OF3	L	43	7	6	1	0	0	0	0	0	0		0	.000	.000
Hughie Miller	1B6	R	27	7	6	0	3	1	0	0	3	0		0	.500	.667
1 Pete Compton	OF2	L	25	2	8	0	2	0	0	0	3	0		0	.250	.250
PITTSBURGH 3rd 86-67 .562 .5		**REBEL OAKES**														
TOTALS			29	156	5040	592	1318	180	80	20	507	448		224	.262	.341
Ed Konetchy	1B152	R	29	152	578	79	179	31	18	10	93	41		27	.310	.478
Steve Yerkes	2B114, SS8	R	27	121	434	44	125	17	8	1	49	30		17	.288	.371
Marty Berghammer	SS132	L	27	132	469	96	114	10	6	0	33	83		26	.243	.290
Mike Mowrey	3B151	R	31	151	521	56	147	27	5	1	49	66		40	.282	.359
Jimmy Kelly	OF148	L	25	148	524	68	154	12	17	4	50	35		38	.294	.405
Rebel Oakes	OF153	L	28	153	580	55	161	24	5	0	82	37		21	.278	.336
2 Al Wickland	OF109	L	27	110	389	63	117	12	8	1	30	52		23	.301	.380
Claude Berry	C99	R	35	100	292	32	56	11	1	1	26	29		7	.192	.247
John Lewis	2B45, SS11, OF6, 1B5, 3B1	R	27	82	231	24	61	6	5	0	26	8		7	.264	.333
Paddy O'Connor	C66	R	35	70	219	15	50	10	1	0	16	14		4	.228	.283
Ed Lennox	3B3	R	29	55	53	1	16	3	1	1	9	7		0	.302	.453
Cy Rheam	OF22, 1B1	R	21	34	69	10	12	0	0	1	5	1		4	.174	.217
1 Hugh Bradley	OF15	R	30	26	66	3	18	4	1	0	6	4		2	.273	.364
Ed Holly	SS11, 3B3	R	35	16	42	8	11	2	0	0	5	5		3	.262	.310
Mike Menosky	OF9	L	20	17	21	3	2	0	0	0	1	2		2	.095	.095
Frank Delahanty	OF11	R	32	14	42	3	10	1	0	0	3	1		0	.238	.262
Davy Jones	OF13	L	35	14	49	6	16	0	1	0	4	6		1	.327	.367
Hal Savage	OF3, 3B1	L		14	21	0	3	0	0	0	0	1		0	.143	.143
Orie Kerlin	C3	L	24	3	1	0	0	0	0	0	0	0		0	.000	.000

NAME	T	AGE	W	L	PCT	SV	G	GS	CG	IP	H	BB	SO	ShO	ERA
		31	86	66	**.566**	10	155	155	97	1398	1232	402	576	21	2.64
George McConnell	R	37	**25**	**10**	**.714**	1	44	35	23	303	262	89	151	4	2.20
Three Finger Brown	R	38	17	8	.680	4	35	25	17	236	189	64	95	3	2.10
Claude Hendrix	R	26	16	15	.516	4	40	31	26	285	256	84	107	5	3.00
Mike Prendergast	L	26	14	12	.538	0	42	30	16	254	220	67	95	3	2.48
1 Dave Black	L	23	6	7	.462	0	25	10	2	121	104	33	43	0	2.45
2 Bill Bailey	L	26	3	1	.750	0	5	5	3	33	23	10	24	3	2.18
Ad Brennan	L	33	3	9	.250	0	19	13	7	106	117	30	40	2	3.74
1 Rankin Johnson	R	27	2	4	.333	1	11	6	3	57	58	23	19	0	4.42
Henry Rasmussen		22	0	0	.000	0	2	0	0	2	3	2	2	0	13.50
		30	**87**	67	.565	9	159	159	94	**1426**	1267	396	**698**	**24**	2.73
Dave Davenport	R	**25**	22	18	.550	1	**55**	**46**	**30**	**393**	300	96	**229**	**10**	2.20
Eddie Plank	L	39	21	11	.656	3	42	31	23	268	212	54	147	6	2.08
Doc Crandall	R	27	21	15	.583	1	51	33	22	313	**307**	77	117	4	2.59
Bob Groom	R	30	11	11	.500	2	37	26	11	209	200	73	111	4	3.27
Doc Watson	L	30	9	9	.500	0	33	20	6	136	132	58	45	0	3.97
Ed Willett	R	31	2	3	.400	2	17	2	1	53	61	18	19	0	4.58
Ernie Herbert	R	28	1	0	1.000	0	11	1	1	48	48	18	23	0	3.38
LaRue Kirby		25	0	0	.000	0	1	0	0	7	7	2	7	0	5.14
		28	86	67	.562	12	156	156	88	1382	1273	441	517	16	2.79
Frank Allen	L	25	23	13	.639	0	41	37	24	283	230	100	127	6	2.51
Elmer Knetzer	R	29	18	14	.563	3	41	33	22	279	256	89	120	3	2.58
Clint Rogge	R	25	17	11	.607	0	37	31	17	254	240	93	93	5	2.55
Cy Barger	R	30	9	8	.529	6	34	13	8	153	130	47	47	1	2.29
Walt Dickson	R	32	7	5	.583	0	27	11	4	97	115	33	36	0	4.18
Bunny Hearn	L	24	6	11	.353	0	29	17	8	176	187	37	49	1	3.38
2 Ralph Comstock	R	24	3	3	.500	2	12	7	3	53	44	7	18	0	3.23
Sandy Burk (DE)	R	28	2	0	1.000	0	2	2	1	18	8	11	9	0	1.00
1 George LaClaire	R	28	1	2	.333	1	14	3	1	46	43	13	10	0	3.33
Howie Camnitz	R	33	0	0	.000	0	4	2	0	20	19	11	6	0	4.50
Al Braithwood	L	23	0	0	.000	0	2	0	0	3	0	0	2	0	0.00
Johnny Miljus	R	20	0	0	.000	0	1	0	0	1	1	0	0	0	0.00

KANSAS CITY 4th 81-71 .529 5.5

GEORGE STOVALL

NAME	G by POS	B	AGE	G	AB	R	H	2B	3B	HR	RBI	BB	SO	SB	BA	SA
TOTALS			30	153	4937	547	1206	200	66	28	483	368		144	.244	.329
George Stovall	1B129	R	36	130	481	48	112	21	3	0	43	29		8	.233	.289
Duke Kenworthy	2B108, OF7	B	28	122	396	59	118	30	7	3	52	28		20	.298	.432
Johnny Rawlings	SS120	R	22	120	398	40	85	9	2	2	24	27		17	.214	.261
George Perring	3B102, 1B31, 2B31, SS1	R	30	153	553	67	143	23	7	7	68	57		10	.259	.364
Grover Gilmore	OF119	L	26	119	411	53	117	22	15	1	47	26		19	.285	.418
Chet Chadbourne	OF152	L	30	152	587	75	133	16	9	1	35	62		29	.227	.290
Al Shaw	OF124	L	34	132	448	67	126	22	10	6	67	46		15	.281	.415
Ted Easterly	C88	L	30	110	309	32	84	12	5	3	32	21		2	.272	.372
Pop Goodwin	SS42, 2B23	L	23	81	229	22	54	5	1	0	16	15		6	.236	.266
Art Kruger	OF66	R	34	80	240	24	57	9	2	2	26	12		5	.238	.317
Drummond Brown	C65, 1B1	R	30	77	227	13	55	10	1	1	26	12		3	.242	.308
Bill Bradley	3B61	R	37	66	203	16	39	10	1	0	9	9		6	.192	.251
Jack Enzenroth	C8	R	29	14	19	3	3	0	0	0	3	6		0	.158	.158

NAME	T	AGE	W	L	PCT	SV	G	GS	CG	IP	H	BB	SO	ShO	ERA
TOTALS		28	81	72	.529	11	153	153	95	1359	1210	390	526	16	2.82
Nick Cullop	L	27	22	11	.667	2	44	36	22	302	278	67	111	3	2.44
Gene Packard	L	27	20	12	.625	2	42	31	21	282	250	74	108	5	2.68
Chief Johnson	R	29	17	17	.500	2	46	34	19	281	253	71	118	4	2.75
Alex Main	R	31	13	14	.481	3	35	28	18	230	181	75	91	2	2.54
Pete Henning	R	27	9	15	.375	2	40	20	15	207	181	76	73	1	3.17
Babe Blackburn	R	20	0	1	.000	0	7	2	0	16	19	13	7	0	8.44
Dan Adams	R	26	0	2	.000	0	11	2	0	35	41	13	16	0	4.63
Joe Gingras	R	22	0	0	.000	0	2	0	0	4	6	1	2	0	6.75
Ben Harris	R	29	0	0	.000	0	1	0	0	2	1	0	0	0	0.00

NEWARK 5th 80-72 .526 6

BILL PHILLIPS 26-27 .491 BILL McKECHNIE 54-45 .546

NAME	G by POS	B	AGE	G	AB	R	H	2B	3B	HR	RBI	BB	SO	SB	BA	SA
TOTALS			28	155	5097	585	283	**210**	80	17	487	438		184	.252	.334
Emil Huhn	1B101, C16	R	23	124	415	34	94	18	1	1	41	28		13	.227	.282
Frank LaPorte	2B146	R	35	148	550	55	139	28	10	2	56	48		14	.253	.351
Jimmy Esmond	SS155	R	27	155	569	79	147	20	10	5	62	59		18	.258	.355
Bill McKechnie	3B117, OF1	B	28	126	448	49	115	22	5	1	43	41		28	.257	.335
Vin Campbell	OF126	L	27	127	525	78	163	18	10	1	44	29		24	.310	.389
Edd Roush	OF144	L	22	145	550	73	164	22	10	3	60	38		28	.298	.391
Al Scheer	OF155	L	26	155	546	75	146	25	14	2	60	65		31	.267	.375
Bill Rariden	C142	R	27	142	444	49	120	30	7	0	40	60		8	.270	.369
Germany Schaefer	OF17, 1B13, 3B9, 2B2	R	38	59	154	26	33	5	3	0	8	25		3	.214	.286
Rupert Mills	1B37	R	22	41	134	12	27	5	1	0	16	6		6	.201	.254
Johnny Strands	3B12, 2B9, OF2	R	29	35	75	7	14	3	1	1	11	6		1	.187	.293
Gil Whitehouse	OF28, C1, P1	B	21	35	120	16	27	6	2	0	9	6		3	.225	.308
Ted Reed	3B20	R	24	20	77	5	20	1	2	0	4	2		1	.260	.325
3 Hugh Bradley	1B8	R	30	12	33	0	5	0	0	0	2	2		2	.152	.152
2 Larry Pratt	C3	R	27	5	4	2	2	2	0	0	0	3		2	.500	1.000
Bill Warren	1B1, C1	L	28	5	3	0	1	0	0	0	0	0		0	.333	.333
George Textor	C3	B	26	3	6	1	2	0	0	0	0	0		0	.333	.333

NAME	T	AGE	W	L	PCT	SV	G	GS	CG	IP	H	BB	SO	ShO	ERA
TOTALS		29	80	72	.526	7	155	155	**100**	1407	1308	453	581	16	**2.60**
Ed Reulbach	R	32	21	10	.677	1	33	30	23	270	233	69	117	4	2.23
George Kaiserling	R	22	15	15	.500	2	41	29	16	261	246	73	75	5	2.24
Herb Moseley	R	30	15	15	.500	1	38	32	22	268	222	99	142	5	**1.91**
Harry Moran	L	26	13	9	.591	0	34	23	13	206	193	66	87	2	2.53
1 Cy Falkenberg	R	35	9	11	.450	1	25	21	14	172	175	47	76	0	3.24
Charlie Whitehouse	L	21	2	2	.500	0	11	3	1	40	46	17	18	0	4.28
George Mullin	R	34	2	2	.500	0	5	4	3	32	41	16	14	0	5.91
2 Tom Seaton	R	27	2	6	.250	1	12	10	7	75	61	21	28	0	2.28
Chick Brandom	R	28	1	1	.500	0	16	1	1	50	55	15	15	0	3.42
Harry Billiard	R	29	0	1	.000	1	14	2	0	28	32	28	7	0	5.79
Fred Trautman	R	33	0	0	.000	0	1	0	0	3	4	1	2	0	6.00
Gil Whitehouse		21	0	0	.000	0	1	0	0	1	0	1	0	0	0.00

BUFFALO 6th 74-78 .487 12

LARRY SCHLAFLY 14-29 .326 WALTER BLAIR 1-1 .500 HARRY LORD 59-48 .551

NAME	G by POS	B	AGE	G	AB	R	H	2B	3B	HR	RBI	BB	SO	SB	BA	SA
TOTALS			30	153	5065	574	1261	193	68	40	500	420		184	.249	.338
Hal Chase	1B143, OF1	R	32	145	566	85	161	33	10	**17**	89	20		23	.284	.468
Baldy Louden	2B88, SS27, 3B19	R	31	141	469	67	132	18	5	4	48	64		30	.281	.367
Roxey Roach	SS92	R	30	92	346	35	93	20	3	2	31	17		11	.269	.361
Harry Lord	3B92, OF1	L	33	97	359	50	97	12	6	1	21	21		15	.270	.345
Jack Dalton	OF119	R	30	132	437	68	128	17	3	2	46	50		28	.293	.359
Clyde Engle	OF100, 2B21, 3B17, 1B1	R	31	141	501	56	131	22	8	3	71	34		24	.261	.355
2 Benny Meyer	OF88	R	27	93	333	37	77	8	6	1	29	40		9	.231	.300
Walter Blair	C97	R	31	98	290	23	65	15	3	2	20	18		4	.224	.317
Solly Hofman	OF82, 1B11, 3B4, 2B2, SS1	R	32	109	346	29	81	10	6	0	27	30		12	.234	.298
Tom Downey	2B48, 3B35, SS2, 1B1	R	31	92	282	24	56	9	1	1	19	26		11	.199	.248
Tex McDonald	OF65	L	26	87	251	31	68	9	6	6	39	27		5	.271	.426
Nick Allen	C80	R	26	84	215	14	44	7	1	0	17	18		4	.205	.247
1 Fred Smith	SS32, 3B1	R	23	35	114	8	27	2	4	0	11	13		2	.237	.325
1 Joe Agler	OF20, 1B1	L	28	25	73	11	13	1	2	0	2	20		2	.178	.247
2 Art Watson	C6, OF1	R	29	22	30	6	14	1	0	1	13	0		0	.467	.600
Del Young	OF3	L	29	12	15	0	2	0	0	0	0	1		1	.133	.133
2 Eddie Gagnier	2B1	R	32	1	2	0	0	0	0	0	0	0		0	.000	.000

NAME	T	AGE	W	L	PCT	SV	G	GS	CG	IP	H	BB	SO	ShO	ERA
TOTALS		26	74	78	.487	11	153	153	79	1360	1271	**553**	594	14	3.38
Al Schulz	L	26	21	14	.600	0	42	38	25	310	264	**149**	160	5	3.08
Fred Anderson	R	29	19	13	.594	0	36	28	14	240	192	72	142	5	2.51
Hugh Bedient	R	25	16	18	.471	**10**	53	30	16	269	284	69	106	2	3.18
Gene Krapp	R	28	9	19	.321	0	38	30	14	231	188	123	93	1	3.51
Russ Ford	R	32	5	9	.357	0	21	15	7	127	140	48	34	0	4.54
Rube Marshall	R	24	2	1	.667	0	21	4	2	59	62	33	21	0	3.97
2 Ed Lafitte	R	29	2	2	.500	1	14	5	1	50	53	22	17	0	3.42
Howard Ehmke	R	21	0	2	.000	0	18	2	0	54	69	25	18	0	5.50
Dan Woodman	R	21	0	0	.000	0	5	1	0	15	14	9	1	0	4.20
2 George La Claire	R	28	0	0	.000	0	1	0	0	3	4	1	2	0	6.00
Bob Smith	R	23	0	0	.000	0	1	0	0	1	1	2	0	0	18.00

BROOKLYN 7th 70-82 .461 16

LEE MAGEE 53-64 .453 JOHN GANZEL 17-18 .486

NAME	G by POS	B	AGE	G	AB	R	H	2B	3B	HR	RBI	BB	SO	SB	BA	SA
TOTALS			26	153	5035	**647**	**1348**	205	75	36	**561**	473		**249**	**.268**	**.360**
Hap Myers	1B107	R	27	118	341	61	98	9	1	1	36	32		28	.287	.328
Lee Magee	2B115, 1B2	B	26	121	452	87	146	19	10	4	49	22		34	.323	.436
2 Fred Smith	SS94, 3B15	R	23	110	385	41	95	16	6	5	58	25		21	.247	.358
Al Halt	3B111, SS40	L	24	151	524	41	131	22	7	3	64	39		20	.250	.336
George Anderson	OF134	L	25	136	511	70	135	23	9	2	39	52		20	.264	.356
Benny Kauff	OF136	L	25	136	483	92	165	23	11	12	83	85		**55**	**.342**	**.509**
Claude Cooper	OF121, 1B32	L	22	153	527	75	155	26	12	2	63	77		31	.294	.400
Grover Land	C81	R	30	96	290	25	75	13	2	0	22	6		3	.259	.317
1 Steve Evans	OF61, 1B1	L	30	63	216	44	64	**14***	4	3	30	35		7	.296	.440
Mike Simon	C45	R	32	47	142	7	25	5	1	0	12	9		1	.176	.225
Ty Helfrich	2B34, OF1	R	24	43	104	12	25	6	0	0	5	15		2	.240	.298
2 Hugh Bradley	1B26, OF7, C1	R	30	37	126	7	31	3	2	0	18	4		6	.246	.302
1 Tex Westerzil	3B31	R	24	36	106	13	33	3	3	0	21	21		8	.311	.396
2 Harry Smith	C19, OF1	R	25	28	65	5	13	0	0	1	4	7		2	.200	.246
Art Griggs	1B5, OF1	R	31	27	38	4	11	1	0	1	2	3		0	.289	.395
Dave Howard	2B12, OF2, SS1, 3B1	R	26	24	36	5	8	1	0	0	1	1		0	.222	.250
1 Eddie Gagnier	SS13, 2B6	R	32	20	50	8	13	1	0	0	4	10		2	.260	.280
1 Larry Pratt	C17	R	27	20	49	5	9	1	0	1	2	2		2	.184	.265
Jim Delahanty	2B4	R	36	17	25	0	6	1	0	0	2	3		1	.240	.280
Milt Reed	SS10	L	24	10	31	2	9	1	1	0	8	2		2	.290	.387
1 Art Watson	C7	R	29	9	19	4	5	0	3	0	1	3		0	.263	.579
Tiny Tesch	2B3	B	**25**	8	7	2	2	1	0	0	2	0		0	.286	.429
Danny Murphy	2B1, OF1	R	38	5	12	0	2	0	0	0	0	0		0	.167	.167
Felix Chouinard	OF2	R	28	4	4	1	2	0	0	0	2	0		0	.500	.500
Dick Wright	C3	R	25	4	5	0	0	0	0	0	0	0		0	.000	.000
Frank Kane	OF2	L	20	3	10	2	2	0	1	0	2	0		0	.200	.400

NAME	T	AGE	W	L	PCT	SV	G	GS	CG	IP	H	BB	SO	ShO	ERA
TOTALS		28	70	82	.461	**16**	153	153	78	1356	1299	536	467	10	3.37
Don Marion	R	24	12	9	.571	0	35	25	15	208	193	64	46	2	3.20
1 Tom Seaton	R	**27**	12	11	.522	3	32	23	13	189	199	99	86	0	4.57
Jim Bluejacket (LJ)	R	27	10	11	.476	0	24	21	10	163	155	75	48	2	3.15
Happy Finneran	R	23	10	12	.455	2	37	24	12	215	197	87	68	1	2.80
Bill Upham	R	27	6	8	.429	5	33	11	4	121	129	40	46	2	3.05
1 Ed Lafitte	R	29	6	9	.400	0	17	16	7	118	126	57	34	0	3.97
2 Frank Smith	R	35	5	2	.714	0	15	5	4	63	69	18	24	1	3.14
2 Cy Falkenberg	R	35	3	3	.500	0	7	7	5	48	31	12	20	1	1.50
Hooks Wiltse	L	34	3	5	.375	5	18	3	1	59	49	7	17	0	2.29
Mysterious Walker	R	31	2	4	.333	1	13	7	2	66	61	22	28	0	3.68
Fin Wilson	L	**25**	1	8	.111	0	18	11	5	102	85	53	47	0	3.79
Bill Herring	R	21	0	0	.000	0	3	0	0	3	5	2	3	0	15.00

*Evans, also with Baltimore, league leader in 2B with 34

BALTIMORE 8th 47-107 .305 40

OTTO KNABE

NAME	G by POS	B	AGE	G	AB	R	H	2B	3B	HR	RBI	BB	SO	SB	BA	SA
TOTALS			29	154	5060	550	1235	196	53	36	465	470		128	.244	.325
Harry Swacina	1B75, 2B1	R	33	85	301	24	74	13	1	1	38	9		9	.246	.306
Otto Knabe	2B94, OF1	R	31	100	319	38	80	16	2	1	25	37		7	.251	.323
1 Mickey Doolan	SS119	R	35	119	404	41	75	13	7	2	21	24		10	.186	.267
1 Jimmy Walsh	3B106	R	29	106	401	43	121	20	1	9	60	21		12	.302	.424
2 Steve Evans	OF88, 1B4	L	30	88	340	50	107	**20***	6	1	37	28		8	.315	.418
Vern Duncan	OF124, 3B21, 2B1	L	25	146	531	68	142	18	4	2	43	54		19	.267	.328
John McCandless	OF105	L	20	117	406	47	87	6	7	5	34	41		9	.214	.300
Frank Owens	C99	R	29	99	334	32	84	14	7	3	28	17		4	.251	.362
Guy Zinn	OF88	L	28	102	312	30	84	18	3	5	43	35		2	.269	.394
2 Joe Agler	1B58, OF4, 2B3	L	28	72	214	28	46	4	2	0	14	34		15	.215	.252
Enos Kirkpatrick	3B28, 2B21, 1B5, SS5	R	29	68	171	22	41	8	2	0	19	24		12	.240	.310
Harvey Russell	C21	L	28	53	73	5	19	1	2	0	11	14		1	.260	.329
Fred Jacklitsch	C45, SS1	R	39	49	135	20	32	9	0	2	13	31		2	.237	.348
John Gallagher	2B37, SS5, 3B1	R	21	40	126	11	25	4	0	0	4	5		1	.198	.230
Hack Simmons	2B13, OF13	R	30	39	88	8	18	7	1	1	14	10		1	.205	.341
1 Benny Meyer	OF34	R	27	35	120	20	29	2	0	0	5	37		6	.242	.258
2 Jimmy Smith	SS33	R	20	33	100	9	19	1	1	1	11	11		3	.176	.231
Ken Crawford	1B14, OF4			23	82	4	20	2	1	0	7	1		0	.244	.293
Dave Hickman	OF20	R	21	20	81	7	17	4	1	1	7	4		5	.210	.321
Karl Kolseth	1B6	L	23	6	23	1	6	1	1	0	1	1		0	.261	.391
Doc Kerr	C2, 1B1	B		3	6	1	2	0	0	0	0	1		0	.333	.333
Wally Reinicker	3B3			3	8	0	1	0	0	0	0	0		0	.125	.125
Charlie Eakle	2B2		27	2	7	0	2	1	0	0	0	0		1	.286	.429
Clarence Forsythe	3B1			1	3	0	0	0	0	0	0	1		0	.000	.000
Charlie Maisel	C1	R	21	1	4	0	0	0	0	0	0	0		0	.000	.000
Charlie Miller				1	1	0	0	0	0	0	0	0		0	.000	.000

NAME	T	AGE	W	L	PCT	SV	G	GS	CG	IP	H	BB	SO	ShO	ERA
TOTALS		29	47	**107**	.305	7	154	154	85	1360	**1455**	466	570	5	3.96
George Suggs	R	32	11	17	.393	3	35	25	12	233	288	68	71	0	4.13
Jack Quinn	R	31	9	**22**	.290	1	44	31	21	274	289	63	118	0	3.45
2 Rankin Johnson	R	27	7	11	.389	1	23	19	12	151	143	58	62	2	3.34
1 Bill Bailey	L	26	6	19	.240	0	36	23	11	190	179	115	98	2	4.64
1 Frank Smith	R	35	4	4	.500	0	17	9	2	89	108	31	37	0	4.65
Chief Bender	R	32	4	16	.200	1	26	23	15	178	198	37	89	0	3.99
Charlie Young	R	21	2	3	.400	0	9	5	1	35	39	21	13	0	5.91
Larry Douglas	R	25	1	0	1.000	0	2	0	0	3	3	2	1	0	3.00
2 Dave Black	L	23	1	3	.250	0	8	4	1	34	32	15	10	0	3.71
Snipe Conley	R	21	1	4	.200	0	25	6	4	86	97	32	40	0	4.29
3 George La Claire	R	28	1	8	.111	1	18	9	6	84	76	22	30	1	2.46
Tom Vereker			0	0	.000	0	2	0	0	3	3	2	1	0	15.00
Kaiser Wilhelm	R	41	0	0	.000	0	1	0	0	1	0	0	0	0	0.00

*Evans, also with Brooklyn, league leader in 2B with 34

1915 The White Elephant Crumbles

It was much like yesterday's victor reentering the arena without the armor or weapons that brought glory a time before.

The Athletics entered the season with the American League championship but without the players that won it. Financial pressures had caused manager Connie Mack to sell most of his high-salaried veteran players for whom the rival Federal League had created a bull market. Ace pitchers, Eddie Plank and Chief Bender, had signed with the Federal League and Eddie Collins and Ed Murphy went to the Chicago White Sox during the winter. Jack Coombs was released by Mack and picked up by Brooklyn. In addition to these divestments, Frank Baker decided to pack baseball in to devote full time to his farm. Mack, nevertheless, felt he could defend the championship with the good young talent he had held in reserve behind his veterans. The kids, however, fell on their faces at bat and on the mound, and the A's fell deep into the second division from the very start. On the way to 109 losses, the worst record in the Athletics' 15-year history, Mack continued unloading during the season, sending Bob Shawkey to the Yankees and Jack Barry and Herb Pennock to the Red Sox.

Barry played in his third World Series in so many years as the Boston Red Sox edged the fast-closing Detroit Tigers for first place. The Tigers held the top spot for most of the first half, but a slump enabled the Bosox to take over the lead which they never relinquished. Tris Speaker and Duffy Lewis starred with the bat for Boston, and deep pitching gave the Red Sox an edge over the rest of the circuit. Five starters won 14 or more games: righties, Rube Foster, Ernie Shore, and Joe Wood, and lefties, Dutch Leonard and Babe Ruth. In addition, rookie submarine pitcher Carl Mays provided the best relief work in the league. Ruth won 18 games in his first full season, while unveiling a glimpse of things to come as he led the champions in home runs with four blasts in 92 times at bat. Detroit finished 2½ games out with Ty Cobb, Sam Crawford, and rookie Tommy Veach leading the attack. Cobb won his ninth consecutive batting title with a .369 mark, while setting a modern stolen base record with 96 thefts.

While the Athletics were plummeting into the depths of the American League basement, the crosstown rival Philadelphia Phillies shot from a fifth-place finish the previous year into the National League pennant. Rookie manager Pat Moran led his team to eight wins in a row to start the year, and a first-half challenge from the Cubs faded after June to leave the Phillies alone at the top. The two team stars were 31-game winner Grover "Pete" Alexander and league homer-champ Gavvy Cravath, but a strong supporting cast included 21-game winner Erskine Mayer, first baseman Fred Luderus, and slick-fielding rookie shortstop Dave "Beauty" Bancroft. Boston again made a late season rush, but injuries to Bill James and Johnny Evers limited their rise to second place this time around. New manager Wilbert Robinson led a Brooklyn team without stars into a surprising third-place finish. The New York Giants fell with a thud into last place; Larry Doyle and Jeff Tesreau continued to star but Christy Mathewson, Rube Marquard, and Fred Snodgrass—among others—had bad years to cut the heart out of the Giants.

By the time the World Series was over, Boston again claimed the championship. This time, however, it belonged to the Red Sox, who won it in a slightly less impressive way than the Braves. Alexander held Boston to one run in winning the first game of the Series for the Phillies, but the Red Sox pitchers took over to win the next four games by holding Philadelphia to a Series .182 batting average.

The Federal League ended its existence at the end of the season, putting an end to the three league setup and the two years of financial hardship on practically all teams, thus again allowing baseball to relax. The settlement with the Federal League cost $300,000. It was indeed an expensive page in baseball's history.

1915 AMERICAN LEAGUE

NAME	G by POS	B	AGE	G	AB	R	H	2B	3B	HR	RBI	BB	SO	SB	BA	SA
BOSTON 1st 101-50 .669	**BILL CARRIGAN**															
	TOTALS		27	155	5024	668	1308	202	76	14	575	527	476	118	.260	.339
Dick Hoblitzell	1B117	L	26	124	399	54	113	15	12	2	61	38	26	9	.283	.396
Heinie Wagner	2B79, 3B1, OF1	R	34	84	267	38	64	11	2	0	29	37	34	8	.240	.296
Everett Scott	SS100	R	22	100	359	25	72	11	0	0	28	17	21	4	.201	.231
Larry Gardner(JJ)	3B127	L	29	127	430	51	111	14	6	1	55	39	24	11	.258	.326
Harry Hooper	OF147	L	27	149	566	90	133	20	13	2	51	89	36	22	.235	.327
Tris Speaker	OF150	L	27	150	547	108	176	25	12	0	69	81	14	29	.322	.411
Duffy Lewis	OF152	R	26	152	557	69	162	31	7	2	76	45	63	14	.291	.382
Pinch Thomas	C82	L	27	86	203	21	48	4	4	0	21	13	20	3	.236	.296
Hal Janvrin	SS64, 3B20, 2B8	R	22	99	316	41	85	9	1	0	37	14	27	8	.269	.304
Del Gainer	1B56, OF6	R	28	82	200	30	59	5	8	1	29	21	31	7	.295	.415
2 Jack Barry	2B78	R	28	78	248	30	65	13	2	0	26	24	11	0	.262	.331
Hick Cady	C77	R	29	78	205	25	57	10	2	0	17	19	25	0	.278	.346
Olaf Henriksen	OF25	L	27	73	92	9	18	2	2	0	13	18	7	1	.196	.261
Bill Carrigan	C44	R	31	46	95	10	19	3	0	0	7	16	12	0	.200	.232
Babe Ruth	P32	L	20	42	92	16	29	10	1	4	21	9	23	0	.315	.576
Rube Foster	P37	R	27	40	83	10	23	7	0	1	9	6	18	0	.277	.398
Mike McNally	3B18, 2B5	R	21	23	53	7	8	0	1	0	0	3	7	0	.151	.189
2 Bill Rodgers	2B6	L	27	11	6	2	0	0	0	0	0	3	2	0	.000	.000
Chick Shorten	OF5	L	23	6	14	1	3	1	0	0	0	0	2	0	.214	.286
Pat Haley	C4	R	24	5	7	2	1	1	0	0	0	1	0	0	.143	.286
Wally Rehg	OF1	R	26	5	5	2	1	0	0	0	0	0	1	1	.200	.200
DETROIT 2nd 100-54 .649 2.5	**HUGHIE JENNINGS**															
	TOTALS		27	156	**5128**	**778**	**1372**	**207**	94	23	**647**	**681**	527	**241**	**.268**	**.358**
George Burns	1B104	R	22	105	392	49	99	18	3	5	50	22	51	9	.253	.352
Ralph Young	2B119	B	25	123	378	44	92	6	5	0	31	53	31	12	.243	.286
Donie Bush	SS155	B	27	155	561	99	128	12	8	1	44	118	44	35	.228	.283
Ossie Vitt	3B151, 2B2	R	25	152	560	116	140	18	13	1	48	80	22	26	.250	.334
Sam Crawford	OF156	L	35	156	612	81	183	31	**19**	5	**112**	66	29	24	.299	.436
Ty Cobb	OF156	L	28	156	563	**144**	**208**	31	13	3	99	118	43	**96**	**.369**	.487
Bobby Veach	OF152	L	27	152	569	81	178	**40**	10	3	**112**	68	43	16	.313	.434
Oscar Stanage	C100	R	32	100	300	27	67	9	2	1	31	20	41	5	.223	.277
Marty Kavanagh	1B44, 2B42, SS2, OF2	R	24	113	332	55	98	14	13	3	49	42	44	8	.295	.443
Del Baker	C61	R	23	68	134	16	33	3	3	0	15	15	15	3	.246	.313
Jean Dubuc	P39	R	26	60	112	7	23	2	1	0	14	8	15	0	.205	.241
Red McKee	C35	L	24	55	106	10	29	5	0	1	17	13	16	1	.274	.349
1 Baby Doll Jacobson	1B10, OF7	R	24	37	65	5	14	6	2	0	4	5	14	0	.215	.369
George Moriarty	3B12, 1B1, 2B1, OF1	R	30	31	38	2	8	1	0	0	0	5	7	1	.211	.237
Frank Fuller	2B9, SS1	B	22	14	32	6	5	0	0	0	2	9	7	2	.156	.156
John Peters	C1	R	21	1	3	0	0	0	0	0	0	0	1	0	.000	.000
Marc Hall(DD)27																
CHICAGO 3rd 93-61 .604 9.5	**PANTS ROWLAND**															
	TOTALS		24	155	4918	717	1269	163	**102**	25	598	583	575	233	.258	.348
Jack Fournier	1B65, OF57	L	22	126	422	86	136	20	18	5	77	64	37	21	.322	**.491**
Eddie Collins	2B155	L	28	155	521	118	173	22	10	4	77	**119**	27	46	.332	.436
Buck Weaver	SS148	B	24	148	563	83	151	18	11	3	49	32	58	24	.268	.355
Lena Blackburne	3B83, SS9	R	28	96	283	33	61	5	1	0	25	35	34	13	.216	.240
2 Eddie Murphy	OF70	L	23	70	273	51	86	11	5	0	26	39	12	20	.315	.392
Happy Felsch	OF118	R	23	121	427	65	106	18	11	3	53	51	59	16	.248	.363
Shano Collins	OF104, 1B47	R	29	153	576	73	148	24	17	2	85	28	50	38	.257	.368
Ray Schalk	C134	R	22	135	413	46	110	14	4	1	54	62	21	15	.266	.327
1 Braggo Roth	3B35, OF30	R	22	70	240	44	60	6	10	**3***	35	29	50	12	.250	.396
Bunny Brief	1B46	R	22	48	154	13	33	6	2	2	17	16	28	8	.214	.318
2 Joe Jackson	OF46	L	25	46	162	21	43	4	5	2	36	24	12	6	.265	.389
Finners Quinlan	OF32	L	27	42	114	11	22	3	0	0	7	4	11	3	.193	.219
2 Nemo Leibold	OF22	L	23	36	74	10	17	1	0	0	11	15	11	1	.230	.243
Tom Daly	C19, 1B1	R	23	29	47	5	9	1	0	0	3	5	9	0	.191	.213
Pete Johns	3B28	R	22	28	100	7	21	2	1	0	11	8	11	2	.210	.250
Wally Mayer	C20	R	25	22	54	3	12	3	1	0	5	5	8	0	.222	.315
Jim Breton	3B14, 2B1, SS1	R	23	16	36	3	5	1	0	0	1	5	9	2	.139	.167
Ray Demmitt	OF3	L	31	9	6	0	0	0	0	0	0	1	2	0	.000	.000
1 Howard Baker		R	27	2	2	0	0	0	0	0	0	0	2	0	.000	.000
Larry Chappell		R	25	1	1	0	0	0	0	0	0	0	0	0	.000	.000
Charlie Jackson		L	21	1	1	0	0	0	0	0	0	0	1	0	.000	.000

NAME	T	AGE	W	L	PCT	SV	G	GS	CG	IP	H	BB	SO	ShO	ERA
		25	**101**	50	**.669**	16	155	155	82	1397	1164	446	634	16	2.39
Rube Foster	R	27	20	8	.714	1	37	33	22	255	217	86	82	5	2.12
Ernie Shore	R	24	19	8	.704	0	38	32	17	247	207	66	102	4	1.64
Babe Ruth	L	20	18	6	**.750**	0	32	28	16	218	166	85	112	1	2.44
Smokey Joe Wood	R	25	14	5	.737	4	25	16	10	157	120	44	63	3	**1.49**
Dutch Leonard	L	23	14	7	.667	1	32	21	10	183	130	67	116	2	2.36
Vean Gregg(SA)	L	30	5	3	.625	3	18	9	3	75	71	32	43	1	3.36
Ray Collins	L	28	5	7	.416	1	25	9	2	105	101	31	43	0	4.28
Carl Mays	R	23	4	6	.400	**6**	38	6	2	132	119	21	65	0	2.59
1 Ralph Comstock	R	24	2	0	1.000	0	3	0	0	9	10	2	1	0	2.00
2 Herb Pennock	L	21	0	0	.000	0	5	1	0	14	23	10	7	0	9.64
Guy Cooper	R	22	0	0	.000	0	1	0	0	2	0	2	0	0	0.00
		25	100	54	.649	**20**	156	156	86	**1413**	1259	489	550	9	2.86
Harry Coveleski	L	29	23	13	.639	4	**50**	38	20	313	**271**	87	150	1	2.44
Hooks Dauss	R	25	23	13	.639	3	46	35	27	310	261	112	132	1	2.50
Jean Dubuc	R	26	17	12	.586	2	39	33	22	258	231	88	74	5	3.21
Bernie Boland	R	23	13	6	.684	2	45	18	8	203	167	75	72	1	3.10
2 Bill James	R	28	7	3	.700	0	11	9	3	67	57	33	24	1	2.42
2 Bill Steen	R	27	5	1	.888	4	20	7	3	79	83	22	28	0	2.73
2 Grover Lowdermilk	R	30	4	0	1.000	0	7	5	0	28	17	24	18	0	4.18
Pug Cavet	L	25	4	3	.571	1	17	7	2	71	83	22	26	0	4.06
Red Oldham	L	21	3	0	1.000	4	17	2	1	58	52	17	17	0	2.79
George Boehler	R	23	1	2	.333	0	8	0	0	15	19	4	7	0	1.80
Ross Reynolds	R	25	0	1	.000	0	4	2	0	11	17	5	2	0	6.54
Razor Ledbetter	R	20	0	0	.000	0	1	0	0	1	1	0	0	0	0.00
		27	93	61	.604	9	155	155	92	1401	1242	350	635	17	2.43
Jim Scott	R	26	24	11	.686	2	48	35	23	296	256	78	120	**7**	2.04
Red Faber	R	26	24	13	.649	2	**50**	32	22	300	264	99	182	3	2.55
Joe Benz	R	29	15	11	.577	0	39	28	17	238	209	43	81	2	2.12
Eddie Cicotte	R	31	13	12	.520	3	39	26	15	223	216	48	106	1	3.03
Reb Russell	L	26	11	11	.500	2	41	25	10	229	215	47	90	3	2.59
Ed Walsh	R	34	3	0	1.000	0	3	3	3	27	19	7	12	1	1.33
Mellie Wolfgang	R	25	2	2	.500	0	17	2	0	54	39	12	21	0	1.83
1 Ed Klepfer	R	27	1	0	1.000	0	3	2	1	13	11	5	3	0	2.77
Hi Jasper	R	34	0	1	.000	0	3	2	1	16	8	9	15	0	4.50
Dixie Davis	R	24	0	0	.000	0	2	0	0	3	2	2	2	0	0.00
Walt Johnson	R	22	0	0	.000	0	1	0	0	2	3	0	3	0	9.00

***Roth, also with Cleveland, League Leader in HR with 7**

WASHINGTON 4th 85-68 .556 17 — CLARK GRIFFITH

NAME	G by POS	B	AGE	G	AB	R	H	2B	3B	HR	RBI	BB	SO	SB	BA	SA
TOTALS			27	155	5029	571	1225	152	79	12	465	458	541	186	.244	.312
Chick Gandil	1B134	R	27	136	485	53	141	20	15	2	64	29	33	20	.291	.406
Ray Morgan (ST)	2B57, SS2, 3B2	R	26	62	193	21	45	5	4	0	21	30	15	6	.233	.301
George McBride	SS146	R	34	146	476	54	97	8	6	1	30	29	60	10	.204	.252
Eddie Foster	3B79, 2B75	R	28	154	618	75	170	25	10	0	52	48	30	20	.275	.348
Danny Moeller	OF116	B	30	118	438	65	99	11	10	2	23	59	63	32	.226	.311
Clyde Milan	OF151	L	29	153	573	83	165	13	7	2	66	53	32	40	.288	.346
Howard Shanks	OF80, 3B49, 2B10	R	24	141	492	52	123	19	8	0	47	30	42	12	.250	.321
John Henry	C94	R	25	95	277	20	61	9	2	1	22	36	28	10	.220	.278
Rip Williams	C40, 1B15, 3B1	R	33	91	197	14	48	8	4	0	31	18	20	4	.244	.325
Merito Acosta	OF53	L	19	72	163	20	34	4	1	0	18	28	15	8	.209	.245
Tom Connolly	3B24, OF19, SS4	L	22	50	141	14	26	3	2	0	7	14	19	5	.184	.234
Eddie Ainsmith (KJ)	C42	R	23	47	120	13	24	4	2	0	6	10	18	7	.200	.267
Doug Neff	3B12, 2B10, SS7	R	23	30	60	1	10	1	0	0	4	4	6	1	.167	.183
Jim Shaw	P25	R	21	25	43	2	10	2	0	0	3	3	20	0	.233	.279
Turner Barber	OF19	L	21	20	53	9	16	1	1	0	6	6	7	0	.302	.358
Charlie Jamieson	OF17	L	22	17	68	9	19	3	2	0	7	6	9	0	.279	.382
Manny Kopp	OF9	B	23	16	32	2	8	0	0	0	0	5	7	1	.250	.250
Henri Rondeau	OF11	R	28	14	40	3	7	0	0	0	4	4	3	1	.175	.175
Joe Judge	1B10, OF2	L	21	12	41	7	17	2	0	0	9	4	6	2	.415	.463
Sam Mayer	OF9, 1B1, P1	R	22	11	29	5	7	0	0	1	4	4	2	1	.241	.345
Horace Milan	OF10	R	21	11	27	6	11	1	1	0	7	8	7	2	.407	.519
Carl Sawyer	2B6, SS4	R	24	10	32	8	8	1	0	0	3	4	5	2	.250	.281
Charlie Pick		L	27	3	2	0	0	0	0	0	0	0	0	0	.000	.000

NAME	T	AGE	W	L	PCT	SV	G	GS	CG	IP	H	BB	SO	ShO	ERA
		23	85	68	.556	14	155	155	87	1394	116	455	715	19	2.30
Walter Johnson	R	27	27	13	.675	5	47	39	35	337	258	56	203	7	1.55
Bert Gallia	R	23	16	10	.615	1	43	29	14	260	220	64	130	3	2.28
Doc Ayres	R	25	16	9	.625	3	40	16	8	211	178	38	96	2	2.22
Joe Boehling	L	24	12	13	.500	0	40	32	14	229	217	119	108	2	3.22
Harry Harper	L	20	5	4	.555	1	19	10	5	86	66	40	54	2	1.78
Jim Shaw	R	21	5	12	.294	2	25	18	7	133	102	76	78	1	2.50
George Dumont	R	19	2	1	.667	0	6	4	3	40	23	12	18	2	2.03
Sam Rice	R	25	1	0	1.000	0	4	2	1	18	13	9	9	0	2.00
Joe Engel	R	22	1	3	.250	0	11	3	0	34	30	19	9	0	3.18
Bill Hopper	R	24	0	1	.000	1	13	0	0	31	39	16	8	0	4.64
Jack Bentley	L	20	0	2	.000	0	4	2	0	11	8	3	0	0	0.82
Nick Altrock	L	38	0	0	.000	1	1	0	0	3	7	1	2	0	9.00
Sam Mayer	R	22	0	0	.000	0	1	0	0	0	0	2	0	0	0.00

NEW YORK 5th 69-83 .454 32.5 — WILD BILL DONOVAN

NAME	G by POS	B	AGE	G	AB	R	H	2B	3B	HR	RBI	BB	SO	SB	BA	SA
TOTALS			27	154	4982	583	1162	167	50	31	459	570	668	198	.233	.305
Wally Pipp	1B134	L	22	136	479	59	118	20	13	4	60	66	81	18	.246	.367
Luke Boone	2B115, SS12, 3B3	R	25	130	431	44	88	12	2	5	43	41	53	14	.204	.276
Roger Peckinpaugh	SS142	R	24	142	540	67	119	18	7	5	44	49	72	19	.220	.307
Fritz Maisel	3B134	R	25	135	530	77	149	16	6	4	46	48	35	51	.281	.357
Doc Cook	OF131	L	29	132	476	70	129	16	5	2	33	62	43	29	.271	.338
Hugh High	OF117	L	27	119	427	51	110	19	7	1	43	62	47	22	.258	.342
Roy Hartzell	OF107, 2B5, 3B2	L	33	119	387	39	97	11	2	3	60	57	37	7	.251	.313
Les Nunamaker	C77, 1B2	R	26	87	249	24	56	6	3	0	17	23	24	3	.225	.273
Paddy Baumann	2B43, 3B19	R	29	76	219	30	64	13	1	2	28	28	32	9	.292	.388
Birdie Cree	OF53	R	32	74	196	23	42	8	2	0	15	36	22	7	.216	.276
Ray Caldwell	P36	R	27	72	144	27	35	4	1	4	20	9	32	4	.243	.368
Ed Sweeney	C53	R	26	53	137	12	26	2	0	0	5	25	12	3	.190	.204
Charlie Mullen	1B27	R	26	40	90	11	24	1	0	0	7	10	12	5	.267	.278
Elmer Miller	OF26	R	24	26	83	4	12	1	0	0	3	4	14	0	.145	.157
2 Walt Alexander	C24	R	24	25	68	7	17	4	0	1	5	13	16	2	.250	.353
Tim Hendryx	OF12	R	24	13	40	4	8	2	0	0	1	4	2	0	.200	.250
1 Ed Barney	OF10	L	25	11	36	1	7	0	0	0	8	3	6	2	.194	.194
Tom Daley	OF2	L	30	10	8	2	2	0	0	0	1	2	2	1	.250	.250
Ernie Krueger	C8	R	24	10	29	3	5	1	0	0	0	0	5	0	.172	.207
Skeeter Shelton	OF10	R	27	10	40	1	1	0	0	0	0	2	10	0	.025	.025

Pi Schwert 22 R 5-18, Gene Layden 21 L 2-7, Roxy Walters 22 R 1-3, Frank Gilhooley 23 L 0-4

NAME	T	AGE	W	L	PCT	SV	G	GS	CG	IP	H	BB	SO	ShO	ERA
		27	69	83	.454	2	154	154	100	1383	1272	517	559	11	3.09
Ray Caldwell	L	27	19	16	.543	0	36	35	31	305	266	107	130	3	2.89
Ray Fisher	R	27	18	11	.621	0	30	28	19	248	219	62	97	4	2.10
Jack Warhop	R	30	7	9	.438	0	21	19	12	143	164	52	34	0	3.96
Cy Pieh	R	28	4	5	.444	1	21	8	3	94	78	39	46	2	2.87
2 Bob Shawkey	R	24	4	7	.364	0	16	9	5	86	78	35	31	0	3.24
Boardwalk Brown	R	28	3	6	.333	0	19	10	5	97	95	47	34	0	4.08
Ray Keating	R	23	3	6	.333	0	11	10	8	79	66	45	37	1	3.65
Marty McHale	R	26	3	7	.300	0	13	11	6	78	86	19	25	0	4.27
Cliff Markle	R	21	2	0	1.000	0	3	2	2	23	15	6	12	0	0.39
King Cole	R	29	2	3	.400	1	10	6	2	51	41	22	19	0	3.18
George Mogridge	L	26	2	3	.400	0	6	6	3	41	33	11	11	1	1.76
Dan Tipple	R	25	1	1	.500	0	3	2	2	19	14	11	14	0	2.84
Allen Russell	R	21	1	2	.333	0	5	3	1	27	21	21	21	0	2.67
Dick Cottrell	L	26	0	1	.000	0	7	0	0	21	29	7	7	0	3.43
Will Bill Donovan	R	38	0	3	.000	0	9	1	0	34	35	10	17	0	4.76
2 Dazzy Vance	R	24	0	3	.000	0	8	3	1	28	23	16	18	0	3.54
Neal Brady	R	18	0	0	.000	0	2	1	0	9	9	7	6	0	3.00

ST. LOUIS 6th 63-91 .409 39.5 — BRANCH RICKEY

NAME	G by POS	B	AGE	G	AB	R	H	2B	3B	HR	RBI	BB	SO	SB	BA	SA
TOTALS			27	159	5112	521	1255	166	65	19	439	472	765	202	.246	.315
John Leary	1B53, C11	R	24	75	227	19	55	10	0	0	15	5	36	2	.242	.286
Del Pratt	2B158	R	27	159	602	61	175	31	11	3	78	26	43	32	.291	.394
Doc Lavan	SS157	R	24	157	514	44	112	17	7	1	48	42	83	13	.218	.284
Jimmy Austin	3B141	B	35	141	477	61	127	6	6	1	30	64	60	18	.266	.310
Dee Walsh	OF45, 3B2, 2B1, SS1, P1	B	23	59	150	13	33	5	0	0	6	14	25	6	.220	.253
Tilly Walker	OF139	R	27	144	510	53	137	20	7	5	49	36	77	20	.269	.365
Burt Shotton	OF154	L	30	156	559	93	158	18	11	1	30	118	62	43	.283	.360
Sam Agnew	C102	R	28	104	295	18	60	4	2	0	19	12	36	5	.203	.231
Ivon Howard	1B48, 3B23, OF17, SS2, 2B1	B	32	113	324	43	90	10	7	2	43	43	48	29	.278	.370
George Sisler	1B37, OF29, P15	L	22	81	274	28	78	10	2	3	29	7	27	10	.285	.369
Hank Severeid	C64	R	24	80	203	12	45	6	1	1	22	16	25	2	.222	.276
Ernie Walker	OF33	L	24	50	109	15	23	4	2	0	9	23	32	5	.211	.284
Gus Williams	OF35	L	27	45	119	15	24	2	2	1	11	6	16	11	.202	.277
Dick Kauffman (AJ)	1B32, OF1	R	27	37	124	9	32	8	2	0	14	5	27	0	.258	.355
2 Baby Doll Jacobson	OF32	R	24	34	115	13	24	8	1	1	9	10	26	3	.209	.304
Bill Lee	OF15, 3B1	R	20	18	59	2	11	1	0	0	4	6	5	1	.186	.203
Muddy Ruel	C6	R	19	10	14	0	0	0	0	0	1	5	5	0	.000	.000

Bobby Wallace 41 R 3-13, George O'Brien 25 R 2-9, Pat Parker 22 R 1-6, Mike Dalrymple 0-2,
Ray Schmandt 19 R 0-4, 1 Walt Alexander 24 R 0-1, Chris Burkam 22 0-1, Shorty Dee 25 R 0-3

NAME	T	AGE	W	L	PCT	SV	G	GS	CG	IP	H	BB	SO	ShO	ERA
		25	63	91	.409	5	159	159	76	1403	1256	612	566	6	3.07
Carl Weilman	L	25	18	18	.500	4	47	31	19	296	240	83	125	3	2.34
Earl Hamilton	L	23	9	17	.346	0	35	27	13	204	203	69	63	1	2.87
1 Grover Loudermilk	R	30	9	19	.321	0	38	29	14	222	183	133	130	1	3.12
1 Bill James	R	28	6	10	.375	1	34	23	8	170	155	92	58	0	3.60
Ernie Koob	L	22	5	6	.455	0	28	13	6	134	119	50	37	0	2.35
George Sisler	L	22	4	4	.500	0	15	8	6	70	62	38	41	0	2.83
Tim McCabe	R	20	3	1	.750	0	7	4	4	42	25	9	17	1	2.36
Jim Park	R	22	2	0	1.000	0	3	3	1	23	18	9	5	0	1.17
Parson Perryman	R	26	2	3	.400	0	24	3	0	50	52	16	19	0	3.96
Red Hoff	L	24	2	2	.500	0	11	3	2	44	26	24	23	0	1.23
Pete Sims	R	24	1	0	1.000	0	3	2	0	8	6	6	4	0	4.50
Walt Leverenz	L	26	1	2	.333	0	5	1	0	9	11	8	3	0	8.00
Tom Phillips	R	26	1	3	.250	0	5	4	1	27	28	12	5	0	3.00
Allan Sothoron	R	22	0	1	.000	0	3	1	0	4	8	5	2	0	6.75
Harry Hoch	R	28	0	3	.000	0	12	3	1	40	52	26	9	0	7.20
George Baumgardner	R	23	0	2	.000	0	7	1	1	22	29	11	6	0	4.50
Rollin Cook	R	24	0	0	.000	0	5	0	0	14	16	9	7	0	7.07
Alex Remneas	R	29	0	0	.000	0	2	0	0	6	3	3	5	0	1.50
Johnny Tillman	R	21	0	0	.000	0	2	1	0	10	6	4	6	0	0.90

Carl East 20 R 0-0, Reeves McKay L 0-0, Scott Perry 24 R 0-0, Dee Walsh 25 0-0

CLEVELAND 7th 57-95 .375 44.5 — JOE BIRMINGHAM 12-16 .429 — LEE FOHL 45-79 .363

NAME	G by POS	B	AGE	G	AB	R	H	2B	3B	HR	RBI	BB	SO	SB	BA	SA
TOTALS			25	154	5030	539	1210	169	79	20	456	490	681	138	.241	.317
Jay Kirke	1B87	L	27	87	339	35	105	19	2	2	40	14	21	5	.310	.395
Bill Wambsganss	2B78, 3B35	R	21	121	375	30	73	4	4	0	21	36	50	8	.195	.227
Ray Chapman	SS154	R	24	154	570	101	154	14	17	3	67	70	82	36	.270	.370
Walter Barbare	3B68, 1B1	R	23	77	246	15	47	3	1	0	11	10	27	6	.191	.211
Elmer Smith	OF123	L	22	144	476	37	118	23	12	3	67	36	75	10	.248	.366
1 Nemo Leibold	OF53	L	23	57	207	28	53	5	4	0	4	24	16	5	.256	.319
Jack Graney	OF115	L	29	116	404	42	105	20	7	1	56	59	29	12	.260	.351
Steve O'Neill	C115	R	23	121	386	32	91	14	2	2	34	26	41	2	.236	.298
1 Joe Jackson	OF49, 1B27	L	25	82	299	42	99	16	9	3	45	28	11	10	.331	.475
Terry Turner	2B51, 3B20	R	34	75	262	35	66	14	1	0	14	29	13	12	.252	.313
Billy Southworth	OF44	L	22	60	177	25	39	2	5	0	8	36	12	2	.220	.288
Denny Wilie	OF35	L	24	45	131	14	33	4	1	2	10	26	18	2	.252	.344
Ben Egan	C40	R	31	42	120	4	13	3	0	0	6	8	14	0	.108	.133
Joe Evans	3B30, 2B2	R	20	42	109	17	28	4	2	0	11	22	18	6	.257	.330
2 Braggo Roth	OF39	R	22	39	144	23	43	4	7	4*	20	22	22	14	.299	.507
Jack Hammond	2B19	R	24	35	84	9	18	2	1	0	4	1	19	0	.214	.262
Roy Wood	1B21, OF2	R	22	33	78	5	15	2	1	0	3	2	13	1	.192	.244
Pete Shields	1B23	R	23	23	72	4	15	6	0	0	6	4	14	3	.208	.292

1 Bill Rodgers 27 L 14-45, Jim Eschen 23 R 10-42, Tex Hoffman 21 L 2-13, Ben Paschal 1-9, Josh Billings 23 R 4-21, Homer Haworth 19 L 1-7, Lee Gooch 25 R 1-2

NAME	T	AGE	W	L	PCT	SV	G	GS	CG	IP	H	BB	SO	ShO	ERA
		24	57	95	.375	12	154	154	62	1372	1287	518	610	11	3.13
Guy Morton	R	22	16	15	.516	1	34	27	15	240	189	60	134	6	2.14
Willie Mitchell	L	25	11	14	.440	1	36	30	12	236	210	84	149	1	2.82
Rip Hagerman	R	27	6	13	.316	0	29	22	7	151	156	77	69	0	3.52
Roy Walker	R	22	5	9	.357	1	25	15	4	131	122	65	57	0	3.98
Fritz Coumbe	L	25	4	7	.364	2	30	12	4	114	123	37	37	1	3.47
Oscar Harstad	R	23	3	6	.333	1	32	7	4	82	81	35	35	0	3.40
Sad Sam Jones	R	22	3	8	.273	5	48	9	2	146	131	63	42	0	3.64
Clarence Garrett	R	24	2	2	.500	0	4	4	2	23	19	6	5	0	2.35
Lynn Brenton	R	24	2	3	.400	0	11	5	1	51	60	20	18	1	3.35
Allan Collamore	R	28	2	5	.286	0	11	6	5	64	52	22	15	2	2.39
Paul Carter	R	21	1	2	.333	1	11	2	2	42	44	18	14	0	3.21
1 Bill Steen	R	27	1	4	.200	0	10	7	2	45	51	15	22	0	5.00
2 Ed Klepfer	R	27	1	6	.143	0	8	7	2	43	47	11	13	0	2.09
Abe Bowman	R	22	0	1	.000	0	2	1	0	1	1	3	0	0	27.00
Herb Hill	R	22	0	0	.000	0	1	0	0	2	1	2	0	0	0.00

*Roth, also with Chicago, league leader in HR with 7

PHILADELPHIA 8th 43-109 .283 58.5 — CONNIE MACK

NAME	G by POS	B	AGE	G	AB	R	H	2B	3B	HR	RBI	BB	SO	SB	BA	SA
TOTALS			26	154	5081	545	1204	183	72	16	440	436	634	127	.237	.311
Stuffy McInnis	1B119	R	24	119	456	44	143	14	4	0	49	14	17	8	.314	.362
Nap Lajoie	2B110, SS10, 1B5, 3B2	R	39	129	490	40	137	24	5	1	61	11	16	10	.280	.355
Larry Kopf	SS74, 3B42, 2B2	B	24	118	386	39	87	10	2	1	33	41	45	5	.225	.269
Wally Schang	3B43, OF41, C26	B	25	116	359	64	89	9	11	1	44	66	47	18	.248	.343
Jimmy Walsh	OF109, 3B2, 1B1	L	29	117	417	48	86	15	6	1	20	57	64	22	.206	.278
Amos Strunk	OF111, 1B19	L	26	132	485	76	144	28	16	1	45	56	45	17	.297	.427
Rube Oldring	OF96, 3B6	R	31	107	408	49	101	23	3	6	42	22	21	11	.248	.363
Jack Lapp	C89, 1B12	L	30	112	312	26	85	16	5	2	31	30	29	5	.272	.375
Lew Malone	2B43, 3B12, OF4, SS2	R	18	76	201	17	41	4	4	1	17	21	40	7	.204	.279
Wickey McAvoy	C64	R	20	68	184	12	35	7	2	0	6	11	32	0	.190	.250
1 Eddie Murphy	OF58, 3B6	L	23	68	260	37	60	3	4	0	17	29	15	13	.231	.273
Chick Davies	OF32, P4	L	23	56	132	13	24	5	3	0	11	14	31	2	.182	.265
1 Jack Barry	SS54	R	28	54	194	16	43	6	2	0	15	15	9	6	.222	.273
Tom Healy	3B17, SS1	R	19	23	77	11	17	1	0	0	5	6	4	0	.221	.234
Shag Thompson	OF7	L	22	17	33	5	11	2	0	0	2	4	6	0	.333	.394
Harry Damrau	3B16	R	23	16	56	4	11	1	0	0	3	5	17	1	.196	.214

Bill Bankston 22 L 5-36, Socks Seibold 19 R 3-26, Sam Crane 20 R 2-23, Cy Perkins 19 R 4-20, Sam McConnell 20 L 2-11,
Harry Davis 41 R 1-3, Owen Conway 24 1-15, Buck Danner 24 R 3-12, Bill Haeffner 20 R 1-4, Henry Bostock 20 R 0-7,
Al Edwards 19 0-5, Fred Lear 21 R 0-2, Bunny Corcoran 20 0-4, Ira Thomas 34 R 0-0, Frank Baker 29 (HO)

NAME	T	AGE	W	L	PCT	SV	G	GS	CG	IP	H	BB	SO	ShO	ERA
		22	43	109	.283	2	154	154	78	1348	1358	827	588	6	4.33
Weldon Wyckoff	R	23	10	22	.313	1	43	34	20	276	238	165	157	1	3.52
1 Bob Shawkey	R	24	6	6	.500	0	17	13	7	100	103	38	56	1	4.05
Bullet Joe Bush	R	22	5	15	.250	0	25	18	8	146	137	89	89	0	4.13
Tom Knowlson	R	20	4	7	.364	0	18	9	8	101	99	60	24	0	3.47
Tom Sheehan	R	21	4	8	.333	0	15	13	8	102	131	38	22	1	4.15
Rube Bressler	L	20	4	17	.190	0	32	20	7	178	183	118	69	1	5.21
1 Herb Pennock	L	21	3	5	.375	1	11	8	3	44	46	29	24	1	5.32
Bill Morrisette	R	22	2	0	1.000	0	4	1	1	20	15	5	11	0	1.35
Cap Crowell	R	22	2	6	.250	0	10	8	4	54	56	47	15	0	5.50
Joe Sherman	R	24	1	0	1.000	0	2	1	1	15	15	1	5	0	2.40
Elmer Myers	R	21	1	0	1.000	0	1	1	1	9	2	5	12	1	0.00
Chick Davies	L	23	1	2	.333	0	4	2	0	15	20	12	2	0	9.00
Bill Meehan	R	23	0	1	.000	0	1	1	0	4	7	3	4	0	11.25
Tink Turner	R	25	0	1	.000	0	1	1	0	2	5	3	0	0	22.50
Carl Ray	L	26	0	1	.000	0	2	1	0	7	11	6	6	0	5.14
Jack Harper	R	21	0	1	.000	0	3	0	0	9	5	1	3	0	3.00
Jack Richardson	R	22	0	1	.000	0	3	3	2	24	21	14	11	0	2.63

Harry Eccles 21 L 0-1, Bud Davis 25 R 0-2, Bruno Haas 24 L 0-2, Harry Weaver 20 R 0-2,
Dana Fillingim 21 R 0-4, Jack Nabors 27 R 0-5, Walter Ancker 21 R 0-0, Squiz Pillon 21 L 0-0,
H. B. Cone 0-0, Bob Pepper 20 R 0-0

PHILADELPHIA 1st 90-62 .592 — PAT MORAN

NAME	G by POS	B	AGE	G	AB	R	H	2B	3B	HR	RBI	BB	SO	SB	BA	SA
TOTALS			28	153	4916	589	1216	202	39	**58**	486	460	600	121	.247	.340
Fred Luderus	1B141	L	29	141	499	55	157	36	7	7	62	42	36	9	.315	.457
Bert Niehoff	2B148	R	31	148	529	61	126	27	2	2	49	30	63	21	.238	.308
Dave Bancroft	SS153	B	24	153	563	85	143	18	2	7	30	77	62	15	.254	.330
Bobby Byrne	3B105	R	30	105	387	50	81	6	4	0	21	39	28	4	.209	.245
Gavvy Cravath	OF150	R	34	150	522	**89**	149	31	7	**24**	**115**	**86**	77	11	.285	**.510**
Dode Paskert	OF92, 1B5	R	33	109	328	51	80	17	4	3	39	35	38	9	.244	.348
Possum Whitted	OF119, 1B7	R	25	128	448	46	126	17	3	1	43	29	47	24	.281	.339
Bill Killefer	C105	R	27	105	320	26	76	9	2	0	24	18	14	5	.238	.278
Beals Becker	OF98	L	28	112	338	38	83	16	4	11	35	26	48	12	.246	.414
Milt Stock	3B55, SS4	R	21	69	227	37	59	7	3	1	15	22	26	6	.260	.330
Ed Burns	C67	R	26	67	174	11	42	5	0	0	16	20	12	1	.241	.270
Oscar Dugey	2B14	R	27	42	39	4	6	1	0	0	0	7	5	2	.154	.179
Bud Weiser	OF20	R	24	37	64	6	9	2	0	0	8	7	12	2	.141	.172
Jack Adams	C23, 1B1	B	24	24	27	1	3	0	0	0	2	2	3	0	.111	.111

NAME	T	AGE	W	L	PCT	SV	G	GS	CG	IP	H	BB	SO	ShO	ERA
TOTALS		27	**90**	62	**.592**	8	153	153	**98**	1374	1161	342	652	**20**	**2.17**
Pete Alexander	R	28	**31**	10	**.756**	3	49	42	**36**	**376**	253	64	**241**	**12**	**1.22**
Erskine Mayer	R	26	21	15	.583	2	43	33	20	275	240	59	114	2	2.36
Al Demaree	R	28	14	11	.560	1	32	26	13	210	201	58	69	3	3.04
Eppa Rixey	L	24	11	12	.478	1	29	22	10	177	163	64	88	2	2.39
George Chalmers	R	27	8	9	.471	1	26	20	13	170	159	45	82	1	2.49
2 George McQuillan	R	30	4	3	.571	0	9	8	5	64	60	11	13	0	2.11
Joe Oeschger	R	24	1	0	1.000	0	6	1	1	24	21	9	8	0	3.38
Stan Baumgartner	L	22	0	2	.000	0	16	1	0	48	38	23	27	0	2.44
Ben Tincup	R	24	0	0	.000	0	10	0	0	31	26	9	10	0	2.03

BOSTON 2nd 83-69 .546 7 — GEORGE STALLINGS

NAME	G by POS	B	AGE	G	AB	R	H	2B	3B	HR	RBI	BB	SO	SB	BA	SA
TOTALS			28	157	5070	582	1219	**231**	57	17	496	**549**	620	121	.240	.319
Butch Schmidt	1B127	L	28	127	458	46	115	26	7	2	60	36	59	3	.251	.352
Johnny Evers	2B83	L	33	83	278	38	73	4	1	1	22	50	16	7	.263	.295
Rabbit Maranville	SS149	R	23	149	509	51	124	23	6	2	43	45	65	18	.244	.324
Red Smith	3B157	R	25	157	549	66	145	34	4	2	65	67	49	10	.264	.352
Herbie Moran	OF123	L	31	130	419	59	84	13	5	0	21	66	41	16	.200	.255
Sherry Magee	OF134, 1B22	R	30	156	571	72	160	34	12	2	87	54	39	15	.280	.392
Joe Connolly	OF93	L	27	104	305	48	91	14	8	0	23	39	35	13	.298	.397
Hank Gowdy	C118	R	25	118	316	27	78	15	3	2	30	41	34	10	.247	.332
Ed Fitzpatrick	2B71, OF29	R	25	105	303	54	67	19	3	0	24	43	36	13	.221	.304
2 Dick Egan	OF24, 2B22, SS10, 1B9, 3B4	R	31	83	220	20	57	9	1	0	21	28	18	3	.259	.309
Bert Whaling	C72	R	27	72	190	10	42	6	2	0	13	8	38	0	.221	.274
Larry Gilbert	OF27	L	23	45	106	11	16	4	0	0	4	11	13	4	.151	.189
Ted Cather	OF40	R	26	40	102	10	21	3	1	2	18	15	19	2	.206	.314
2 Pete Compton	OF35	L	25	35	116	10	28	7	1	1	12	8	11	4	.241	.345
Paul Strand	P6, OF5	R	21	24	22	3	2	0	0	0	2	0	4	0	.091	.091
2 Fred Snodgrass	OF18, 1B5	R	27	23	79	10	22	2	0	0	9	7	9	0	.278	.304
Walt Tragesser	C7	R	28	7	7	1	0	0	0	0	0	0	2	0	.000	.000
2 Zip Collins	OF5	L	23	5	14	3	4	1	1	0	0	2	1	1	.286	.500
Joe Shannon	OF4, 2B1	R	18	5	10	3	2	0	0	0	1	0	3	0	.200	.200
Earl Blackburn	C3	R	22	3	6	0	1	0	0	0	0	2	1	0	.167	.167
Fletcher Low	3B1	R	22	1	4	1	1	0	1	0	1	0	0	0	.250	.750
Red Shannon	2B1	B	18	1	3	0	0	0	0	0	0	0	0	0	.000	.000

NAME	T	AGE	W	L	PCT	SV	G	GS	CG	IP	H	BB	SO	ShO	ERA
TOTALS		27	83	69	.546	13	157	157	95	1406	1257	366	630	15	2.57
Dick Rudolph	R	27	22	19	.537	1	44	**43**	30	341	**304**	64	147	3	2.38
Tom Hughes	R	31	16	14	.533	**9**	**50**	25	17	280	208	58	171	4	2.12
2 Pat Ragan	R	26	15	12	.556	0	33	26	13	227	208	59	81	3	2.46
Lefty Tyler	L	25	10	9	.526	0	32	24	15	205	182	84	89	1	2.85
Bill James (SJ)	R	23	5	4	.556	0	13	10	4	68	68	22	23	0	3.04
Art Nehf	L	22	5	4	.556	0	12	10	6	78	60	21	[illegible]	1	[illegible]
Jesse Barnes	R	22	4	0	1.000	0	9	3	2	45	41	10	16	0	1.40
George Davis	R	25	3	3	.500	0	15	9	4	73	85	19	26	0	3.82
Dick Crutcher	R	25	2	2	.500	2	14	4	1	44	50	16	17	0	4.29
Paul Strand	L	21	1	1	.500	1	6	2	2	23	26	3	13	0	2.35
Otto Hess	L	36	0	1	.000	0	4	1	1	14	16	6	5	0	3.86
Dolf Luque	R	24	0	0	.000	0	2	1	0	5	6	4	3	0	3.60
Gene Cocreham	R	30	0	0	.000	0	1	0	0	2	3	0	0	0	4.50

BROOKLYN 3rd 80-72 .526 10 — WILBERT ROBINSON

NAME	G by POS	B	AGE	G	AB	R	H	2B	3B	HR	RBI	BB	SO	SB	BA	SA
TOTALS			26	154	5120	536	1268	165	75	14	449	313	496	131	.248	.317
Jake Daubert	1B150	L	31	150	544	62	164	21	8	2	47	57	48	11	.301	.381
George Cutshaw	2B154	R	27	154	566	68	139	18	9	0	62	34	35	28	.246	.309
Ollie O'Mara	SS149	R	24	149	577	77	141	26	3	0	31	51	40	11	.244	.300
Gus Getz	3B128, SS2	R	25	130	477	39	123	10	5	2	46	8	14	19	.258	.312
Casey Stengel	OF129	L	24	132	459	52	109	20	12	3	50	34	46	5	.237	.353
Hy Myers	OF153	R	26	153	605	69	150	21	7	2	46	17	51	19	.248	.316
Zack Wheat	OF144	L	29	146	528	64	136	15	12	5	66	52	42	21	.258	.360
Otto Miller	C84	R	26	84	254	20	57	4	6	0	25	6	28	3	.224	.287
Lew McCarty	C84	R	26	84	276	19	66	9	4	0	19	7	23	7	.239	.301
1 Joe Schultz	3B55, SS1	R	21	56	120	13	35	3	2	0	4	10	18	3	.292	.350
John Hummel	OF20, 1B11, SS1	R	32	53	100	6	23	2	3	0	8	6	11	1	.230	.310
Jack Coombs	P29	R	32	29	75	8	21	1	1	0	5	2	17	0	.280	.320
Bill Zimmerman	OF18	R	26	22	57	3	16	2	0	0	7	4	8	1	.281	.316
Red Smyth	OF9	L	22	19	22	3	3	1	0	0	3	4	2	1	.136	.182
2 Ivy Olson	2B10, SS7, 3B1, OF1	R	29	18	26	2	2	0	1	0	3	1	0	0	.077	.154
Al Nixon	OF14	R	29	14	26	3	6	1	0	0	2	2	4	1	.231	.269
Mack Wheat	C8	R	22	8	14	0	1	0	0	0	0	0	5	0	.071	.071
1 Dick Egan		R	31	3	3	0	0	0	0	0	0	0	0	0	.000	.000
John Karst (BN)	3B1	L	21	1	0	0	0	0	0	0	0	0	0	0	.000	.000

NAME	T	AGE	W	L	PCT	SV	G	GS	CG	IP	H	BB	SO	ShO	ERA
TOTALS		27	80	72	.526	8	154	154	87	1390	1252	473	499	16	2.65
Jeff Pfeffer	R	27	19	14	.576	3	40	34	26	292	243	76	84	6	2.10
Jack Coombs	R	32	15	10	.600	0	29	24	17	196	166	91	56	2	2.57
Sherry Smith	L	24	14	8	.636	2	29	20	11	174	169	42	52	2	2.59
Wheezer Dell	R	28	11	10	.524	1	40	24	12	215	166	100	94	4	2.34
Nap Rucker	L	30	9	4	.692	1	19	15	7	123	134	28	38	1	2.41
2 Phil Douglas	R	25	5	5	.500	0	20	13	5	117	104	17	63	1	2.61
Ed Appleton	R	23	4	10	.286	0	34	10	5	138	133	66	50	0	3.33
2 Rube Marquard	L	25	2	2	.500	1	6	3	0	25	29	5	13	0	6.12
1 Pat Ragan	R	26	1	0	1.000	0	5	0	0	20	11	8	7	0	0.90
Duster Mails	L	19	0	1	.000	0	2	0	0	5	6	5	3	0	3.60
Leon Cadore	R	24	0	2	.000	0	7	2	1	21	28	8	12	0	5.57
2 Larry Cheney	R	29	0	2	.000	0	5	4	1	27	16	17	11	0	1.67
Raleigh Aitchison	L	27	0	4	.000	0	7	5	2	33	36	6	14	0	4.91
Elmer Brown	R	32	0	0	.000	0	1	0	0	2	4	3	1	0	9.00
Charlie Schmutz	R	25	0	0	.000	0	1	0	0	4	7	1	1	0	6.75

CHICAGO 4th 73-80 .477 17.5 — ROGER BRESNAHAN

NAME	G by POS	B	AGE	G	AB	R	H	2B	3B	HR	RBI	BB	SO	SB	BA	SA
TOTALS			29	156	5114	570	1246	212	66	53	485	393	639	166	.244	**.342**
Vic Saier	1B139	L	24	144	497	74	131	35	11	11	64	64	62	29	.264	.445
Heinie Zimmerman	2B100, 3B36, SS4	R	28	139	520	65	138	28	11	3	62	21	33	19	.265	.379
Bobby Fisher	SS147	R	28	147	568	70	163	22	5	5	53	30	51	9	.287	.370
Art Phelan	3B110, 2B24	R	27	133	448	41	98	16	7	3	35	55	42	12	.219	.306
Wilbur Good	OF125	L	29	128	498	66	126	18	9	2	27	34	65	19	.253	.337
Cy Williams	OF149	L	27	151	518	59	133	22	6	13	64	26	49	15	.257	.398
Wildfire Schulte	OF147	L	32	151	550	66	137	20	6	12	62	49	68	19	.249	.373
Jimmy Archer	C88	R	32	97	309	21	75	11	5	1	27	11	38	5	.243	.320
Roger Bresnahan	C68	R	36	77	221	19	45	8	1	1	19	29	23	19	.204	.262
Polly McLarry	1B25, 2B20	L	24	68	127	16	25	3	0	1	12	14	20	2	.197	.244
Pete Knisely	OF34, 2B9	R	31	64	134	12	33	9	0	0	17	15	18	1	.246	.313
2 Red Murray	OF39, 2B1	R	31	51	144	20	43	6	1	0	11	8	8	6	.299	.354
2 Alex McCarthy	2B12, 3B12, SS1	R	27	23	72	4	19	3	0	1	6	5	7	2	.264	.347
Bubbles Hargrave	C9	R	22	15	19	2	3	0	1	0	2	1	5	0	.158	.263
Eddie Mulligan	SS10, 3B1	R	20	11	22	5	8	1	0	0	2	5	1	2	.364	.409
2 Joe Schultz	2B2	R	21	7	8	1	2	0	0	0	3	0	2	0	.250	.250
Red Corriden	3B1, OF1	R	27	6	3	1	0	0	0	0	0	2	1	0	.000	.000
John Fluhrer	OF2	R	21	6	6	0	2	0	0	0	0	1	0	1	.333	.333
Chick Keating	SS2	R	23	4	8	1	0	0	0	0	0	0	3	1	.000	.000
Bob O'Farrell	C2	R	18	2	3	0	1	0	0	0	0	0	0	0	.333	.333
Jack Wallace	C2	R	24	2	7	1	2	0	0	0	1	0	2	0	.286	.286

NAME	T	AGE	W	L	PCT	SV	G	GS	CG	IP	H	BB	SO	ShO	ERA
TOTALS		27	73	80	.477	8	156	156	71	1399	1272	480	**657**	18	3.11
Hippo Vaughn	L	27	20	12	.625	1	41	34	18	270	240	77	148	4	2.87
George Pearce	L	27	13	9	.591	0	36	20	8	176	158	77	96	2	3.32
Jimmy Lavender	R	31	10	16	.385	4	41	24	13	220	178	67	117	1	2.58
1 Larry Cheney	R	29	8	9	.471	0	25	18	6	131	120	55	68	2	3.57
Bert Humphries	R	34	8	13	.381	3	31	22	10	172	183	23	45	4	2.30
Zip Zabel	R	24	7	10	.412	0	36	17	8	163	124	84	60	3	3.20
Pete Standridge	R	24	4	1	.800	0	29	3	2	112	120	36	42	0	3.62
Brad Hogg	R	27	1	0	1.000	0	2	2	1	13	12	6	0	1	2.08
3 Phil Douglas	R	25	1	1	.500	0	4	4	2	25	17	7	18	1	2.16
Karl Adams	R	23	1	9	.100	0	26	12	3	107	105	43	57	0	4.71
Ed Schorr	R	24	0	0	.000	0	2	0	0	6	9	5	3	0	7.50
Bob Wright	R	23	0	0	.000	0	2	0	0	4	6	0	3	0	2.25

PITTSBURGH 5th 73-81 .474 18 — FRED CLARKE

NAME	G by POS	B	AGE	G	AB	R	H	2B	3B	HR	RBI	BB	SO	SB	BA	SA
TOTALS			29	156	5113	557	1259	197	91	24	464	419	656	**182**	.246	.334
Doc Johnston	1B147	L	27	147	543	71	144	19	12	5	64	38	40	26	.265	.372
Jim Viox	2B135, 3B13, OF2	R	24	150	503	56	129	17	8	2	45	75	31	12	.256	.334
Honus Wagner	SS131, 2B12, 1B10	R	41	156	566	68	155	32	17	6	78	39	64	22	.274	.422
Doug Baird	3B120, OF20, 2B3	R	23	145	512	49	112	26	12	1	53	37	**88**	29	.219	.322
Bill Hinchman	OF156	R	32	156	577	72	177	33	14	5	77	48	75	17	.307	.438
1 Zip Collins	OF101	L	23	106	354	51	104	8	5	1	23	24	38	6	.294	.353
Max Carey	OF139	B	25	140	564	76	143	26	5	3	27	57	58	**36**	.254	.333
George Gipson	C120	R	34	120	351	28	88	15	6	1	30	31	25	5	.251	.336
Dan Costello	OF17	L	22	71	125	16	27	4	1	0	11	7	23	7	.216	.264
Wally Gerber	SS23, 3B23, 2B2	R	23	56	144	8	28	2	2	0	7	9	16	6	.194	.208
1 Bobby Schang	C44	R	28	56	125	13	23	6	3	0	4	14	32	2	.184	.280
2 Ed Barney	OF26	L	25	32	99	16	27	1	2	0	5	11	12	7	.273	.323
Leo Murphy	C34	R	26	34	41	4	4	0	0	0	4	4	12	0	.098	.098
1 Alex McCarthy	2B9, SS5, 3B4, 1B1	R	27	21	49	3	10	0	1	0	3	5	10	1	.204	.245
Larry Lejeune	OF18	R	29	18	65	4	11	0	1	0	2	2	7	4	.169	.200
Paddy Siglin	2B1	R	23	6	7	1	2	0	0	0	0	1	2	1	.286	.286
Ike McAuley	SS5	R	21	5	15	0	2	1	0	0	0	0	6	0	.133	.200
Bill Wagner	C3	R	21	5	5	0	0	0	0	0	0	1	2	0	.000	.000
Fritz Scheeren	OF1	R	24	4	3	0	0	0	0	0	0	0	0	0	.000	.000
Pat Ducan	OF1	R	21	3	5	0	1	0	0	0	0	0	1	0	.200	.200
Fred Clarke	OF1	L	42	1	2	0	1	0	0	0	0	0	0	0	.500	.500
Harry Daubert		R	20	1	1	0	0	0	0	0	0	0	1	0	.000	.000
Syd Smith		R	31	1	1	0	0	0	0	0	0	0	0	0	.000	.000

NAME	T	AGE	W	L	PCT	SV	G	GS	CG	IP	H	BB	SO	ShO	ERA
TOTALS		26	73	81	.474	11	156	156	91	1380	1229	384	544	18	2.60
Al Mamaux	R	21	21	8	.724	0	38	31	17	252	182	96	152	8	2.03
Bob Harmon	R	27	16	17	.485	1	37	32	25	270	242	62	86	5	2.50
Babe Adams	R	33	14	14	.500	2	40	30	17	245	229	34	62	2	2.87
1 George McQuillan (SA)	R	30	8	10	.444	1	30	20	9	149	160	39	56	0	2.84
Erv Kantlehner	L	22	5	12	.294	3	29	18	10	163	135	58	64	1	2.26
Wilbur Cooper	L	23	5	16	.238	4	38	21	11	186	180	52	71	1	3.29
Carmen Hill	R	19	2	1	.667	0	8	3	2	47	42	13	24	1	1.15
Joe Conzelman	R	25	1	1	.500	0	18	1	0	47	41	20	22	0	3.45
Herb Kelly	L	23	1	1	.500	0	5	1	0	11	10	4	6	0	4.09
Phil Slattery	L	22	0	0	.000	0	3	0	0	8	5	1	1	0	0.00
1 Dazzy Vance	R	24	0	1	.000	0	1	1	0	3	3	5	0	0	9.00

NAME	G by POS	B	AGE	G	AB	R	H	2B	3B	HR	RBI	BB	SO	SB	BA	SA
ST. LOUIS 6th 72-81 .471 18.5	**MILLER HUGGINS**															
TOTALS			28	157	5106	**590**	1297	159	**92**	20	483	457	**658**	162	**.254**	.333
Dots Miller	1B83, 2B55, 3B9, SS3	R	28	150	553	73	146	17	10	2	72	43	48	27	.264	.342
Miller Huggins	2B107	B	36	107	353	57	85	5	2	2	24	74	68	13	.241	.283
Art Butler	SS130	R	27	130	469	73	119	12	5	1	31	47	34	26	.254	.307
Bruno Betzel	3B105, 2B3, SS2	R	20	117	367	42	92	12	4	0	27	18	48	10	.251	.305
Tommy Long	OF140	R	25	140	507	61	149	21	**25**	2	61	31	50	19	.294	.446
Owen Wilson	OF107	L	31	107	348	33	96	13	6	3	39	19	43	8	.276	.374
Bob Bescher	OF130	B	31	130	486	71	128	15	7	4	34	52	53	27	.263	.348
Frank Snyder	C144	R	22	144	473	41	141	22	7	2	55	39	49	3	.298	.387
Cozy Dolan	OF98	R	32	111	322	53	90	14	9	2	38	34	37	17	.280	.398
Ham Hyatt	1B81, OF25	L	30	106	295	23	79	8	9	2	46	28	24	3	.268	.376
Zinn Beck	3B62, SS4, 2B2	R	29	70	223	21	52	9	4	0	15	12	31	3	.233	.309
Mike Gonzalez	C31, 1B8	R	24	51	97	12	22	2	2	0	10	8	9	4	.227	.289
Jack Roche	C4	R	24	46	39	2	8	0	1	0	6	4	8	1	.205	.256
Rogers Hornsby	SS18	R	19	18	57	5	14	2	0	0	4	2	6	0	.246	.281
Rolla Daringer	SS10	L	25	10	23	3	2	0	0	0	0	9	5	0	.087	.087
Harry Glenn	C5	L	25	6	16	1	5	0	0	0	1	3	0	0	.313	.313
Jack Smith	OF4	L	20	4	16	2	3	0	1	0	0	1	5	0	.188	.313
Don Brown	OF1	R	18	1	2	0	1	0	0	0	0	2	1	0	.500	.500
CINCINNATI 7th 71-83 .461 20	**BUCK HERZOG**															
TOTALS			28	160	**5231**	516	**1323**	194	84	15	425	360	512	156	.253	.331
Fritz Mollwitz	1B153	R	25	153	525	36	136	21	3	1	51	15	49	19	.259	.316
3 Bill Rodgers	2B56, SS6, 3B1, OF1	L	27	72	213	20	51	13	4	0	12	11	29	8	.239	.338
Buck Herzog	SS153, 1B2	R	29	155	579	61	153	14	10	1	42	34	21	35	.264	.328
Heinie Groh	3B131, 2B29	R	25	160	587	72	170	32	9	3	50	50	33	12	.290	.390
Tommy Griffith	OF160	L	25	160	583	59	179	31	16	4	85	41	34	6	.307	.436
Red Killefer	OF153, 1B2	R	31	155	555	75	151	25	11	1	41	38	33	12	.272	.362
Tommy Leach	OF96	R	37	107	335	42	75	7	5	0	17	56	38	20	.224	.275
Ivy Wingo	C97, OF1	L	24	119	339	26	75	11	6	3	29	13	33	10	.221	.316
Tommy Clarke	C72	R	27	96	226	23	65	7	2	0	21	33	22	7	.288	.336
Joe Wagner	2B46, SS12, 3B2	R	26	75	197	17	35	5	2	0	13	8	35	4	.178	.223
Ken Williams	OF62	L	25	71	219	22	53	10	4	0	16	15	20	4	.242	.324
1 Ivy Olson	2B37, 3B15, 1B7	R	29	63	207	18	48	5	4	0	14	12	13	10	.232	.295
F. VonKolnitz	3B18, SS6, 1B3, C2, OF1	R	22	50	78	6	15	4	1	0	6	7	11	1	.192	.269
George Twombly	OF46	R	23	46	66	5	13	0	1	0	5	8	8	5	.197	.227
Johnny Beall	OF10	L	33	10	34	3	8	1	0	0	3	5	10	0	.235	.265
1 Red Dooin	C10	R	36	10	31	2	10	0	0	0	0	2	5	1	.323	.323
NEW YORK 8th 69-83 .454 21	**JOHN McGRAW**															
TOTALS			28	155	5218	582	1312	195	68	24	**501**	315	547	155	.251	.329
Fred Merkle	1B111, OF29	R	26	140	505	52	151	25	3	4	62	36	39	20	.299	.384
Larry Doyle	2B147	L	28	150	591	86	**189**	**40**	10	4	70	32	28	22	**.320**	.442
Art Fletcher	SS149	R	30	149	562	59	143	17	7	3	74	6	36	12	.254	.326
Hans Lobert	3B106	R	33	106	386	46	97	18	4	0	38	25	24	14	.251	.319
Dave Robertson	OF138	L	25	141	544	72	160	17	10	3	58	22	52	22	.294	.379
1 Fred Snodgrass	OF75	R	27	80	252	36	49	9	0	0	20	35	33	11	.194	.230
George Burns	OF155	R	25	155	**622**	83	169	27	14	3	51	56	57	27	.272	.375
Chief Meyers	C110	R	34	110	289	24	67	10	5	1	26	26	18	4	.232	.311
Fred Brainerd	1B45, 3B16, SS9, 2B1, OF1	R	23	91	249	31	50	7	2	1	21	21	44	6	.201	.257
Eddie Grant	3B55, 2B9, 1B1, SS1	L	32	87	192	18	40	2	1	0	10	9	20	5	.208	.229
2 Red Dooin	C46	R	36	46	124	9	27	2	2	0	9	3	15	0	.218	.266
1 Red Murray	OF34	R	31	45	127	12	28	1	2	3	11	7	15	2	.220	.331
Charlie Babington	OF12, 1B1	R	20	28	33	5	8	3	1	0	2	0	4	1	.242	.394
1 Harry Smith	C18	R	25	21	32	1	4	0	1	0	3	6	12	0	.125	.188
Lew Wendell	C18	R	23	20	36	0	8	1	1	0	5	2	7	0	.222	.306
Marty Becker	OF16	B	21	17	52	5	13	2	0	0	3	2	9	3	.250	.288
George Kelly	1B9, OF4	R	19	17	38	2	6	0	0	1	4	1	9	0	.158	.237
Jim Thorpe	OF15	R	27	17	52	8	12	3	1	0	1	2	16	4	.231	.327
Larry McLean (ST)	C12	R	33	13	33	0	5	0	0	0	4	0	1	0	.152	.152
2 Bobby Schang	C6	R	28	12	21	1	3	0	0	0	1	4	5	1	.143	.143
Merwin Jacobson	OF5	L	21	8	24	0	2	0	0	0	0	1	5	0	.083	.083
Ben Dyer	3B6, SS1	R	22	7	19	4	4	0	1	0	0	4	3	0	.211	.316
Brad Kocher	C3	R	27	4	11	3	5	0	1	0	2	0	1	0	.455	.636
2 Howard Baker	3B1	R	27	1	3	0	0	0	0	0	0	0	0	0	.000	.000

NAME	T	AGE	W	L	PCT	SV	G	GS	CG	IP	H	BB	SO	ShO	ERA
		27	72	81	.471	9	157	157	79	1401	1320	402	538	12	2.88
Bill Doak	R	24	16	18	.471	1	38	36	19	276	263	85	124	3	2.64
Lee Meadows	R	20	13	11	.542	0	39	26	14	244	232	88	104	1	2.99
Slim Sallee	L	30	13	17	.433	3	46	33	17	275	245	57	91	2	2.85
2 Red Ames	R	32	9	3	.750	1	15	14	8	113	93	32	48	2	2.47
Hank Robinson	L	25	7	8	.467	0	32	15	6	143	128	35	57	1	2.45
Hub Perdue	R	33	6	12	.333	1	31	13	5	115	141	19	29	1	4.23
Dan Griner	R	27	5	11	.313	3	37	18	9	150	137	46	46	2	2.82
Dick Niehaus	I	22	2	1	.667	0	15	2	0	45	48	22	21	0	4.00
Charlie Boardman	L	22	1	0	1.000	0	3	1	1	19	12	15	7	0	1.42
Fred Lamline	R	23	0	0	.000	0	4	0	0	19	21	3	11	0	2.84
		26	71	**83**	.461	**12**	160	160	80	**1432**	1304	**497**	572	19	2.84
Gene Dale	R	26	18	17	.514	3	49	35	20	297	256	**107**	104	4	2.45
Fred Toney	R	27	15	6	.714	2	36	23	18	223	160	73	108	6	1.57
Pete Schneider	R	22	13	**19**	.406	2	48	35	16	276	254	104	108	5	2.48
1 Rube Benton	L	28	9	13	.409	4	35	21	6	176	165	67	83	2	3.32
King Lear	R	24	6	10	.375	0	40	15	9	168	169	45	46	0	3.00
Limb McKenry	R	26	5	5	.500	0	21	11	5	110	94	39	37	0	2.94
Lefty George	L	28	2	2	.500	0	5	3	2	28	24	8	11	1	3.86
1 Red Ames	R	32	2	4	.333	1	17	7	4	68	82	24	26	1	4.50
1 Phil Douglas	R	25	1	5	.167	0	8	7	0	47	53	23	29	0	5.36
Curly Brown	L	26	0	2	.000	0	7	3	0	27	26	6	13	0	4.67
Ray Callahan	L	23	0	0	.000	0	3	0	0	6	12	1	4	0	9.00
Harry McCluskey	L	23	0	0	.000	0	3	0	0	5	4	0	2	0	5.40
Al Cochran	R	24	0	0	.000	0	1	0	0	2	5	0	1	0	9.00
		26	69	**83**	.454	9	155	155	78	1385	**1350**	325	637	15	3.11
Jeff Tesreau	R	26	19	16	.543	3	43	38	24	306	235	75	176	8	2.29
Pol Perritt	R	22	12	18	.400	0	35	30	16	220	226	59	91	4	2.66
Sailor Stroud	R	30	11	9	.550	1	32	22	8	184	194	35	62	0	2.79
1 Rube Marquard	L	25	9	8	.529	2	27	20	10	169	178	33	79	2	3.73
Chirsty Mathewson	R	36	8	14	.364	0	27	24	11	186	199	20	57	1	3.58
2 Rube Benton	L	28	4	5	.444	1	10	7	3	61	57	9	26	0	2.80
Hank Ritter	R	21	2	1	.667	2	22	2	0	58	66	15	35	0	4.65
Rube Schauer	R	24	2	8	.200	0	32	7	4	105	101	35	65	0	3.51
Ferdie Schupp	L	24	1	0	1.000	0	23	1	0	55	57	29	28	0	5.07
Fred Herbert	R	28	1	1	.500	0	2	2	1	17	12	4	6	0	1.06
Art Fromme	R	31	0	1	.000	0	4	1	0	12	15	2	4	0	6.00
Emilio Palmero	L	20	0	2	.000	0	3	2	1	12	10	9	8	0	3.00

WORLD SERIES – BOSTON (AL) 4 PHILADELPHIA (NL) 1

LINE SCORES

TEAM	1	2	3	4	5	6	7	8	9	10	11	12	R	H	E
Game 1 October 8 at Philadelphia															
BOS (AL)	0	0	0	0	0	0	0	1	0				1	8	1
PHI (NL)	0	0	0	1	0	0	0	2	X				3	5	1
Shore **Alexander**															
Game 2 October 9 at Philadelphia															
BOS	1	0	0	0	0	0	0	0	1				2	10	0
PHI	0	0	0	0	1	0	0	0	0				1	3	1
Foster **Mayer**															
Game 3 October 11 at Boston															
PHI	0	0	1	0	0	0	0	0	0				1	3	0
BOS	0	0	0	1	0	0	0	0	1				2	6	1
Alexander **Leonard**															
Game 4 October 12 at Boston															
PHI	0	0	0	0	0	0	0	1	0				1	7	0
BOS	0	0	1	0	0	1	0	0	X				2	8	1
Chalmers **Shore**															
Game 5 October 13 at Philadelphia															
BOS	0	1	1	0	0	0	0	2	1				5	10	1
PHI	2	0	0	2	0	0	0	0	0				4	9	1
Foster **Mayer, Rixey (3)**															

COMPOSITE BATTING

NAME	POS	G	AB	R	H	2B	3B	HR	RBI	BA
Boston (AL)										
Totals		5	159	12	42	2	2	3	11	.264
Hooper	OF	5	**20**	**4**	7	0	0	**2**	3	.350
Lewis	OF	5	18	1	**8**	1	0	1	5	**.444**
Scott	SS	5	18	0	1	0	0	0	0	.056
Speaker	OF	5	17	2	5	0	1	0	0	.294
Gardner	3B	5	17	2	4	0	1	0	0	.235
Barry	2B	5	17	1	3	0	0	0	1	.176
Hoblitzell	1B	5	16	1	5	0	0	0	1	.313
Foster	P	2	8	0	4	1	0	0	1	.500
Cady	C	4	6	0	2	0	0	0	0	.333
Shore	P	2	5	0	1	0	0	0	0	.200
Thomas	C	2	5	0	1	0	0	0	0	.200
Gainor	1B	1	3	1	1	0	0	0	0	.333
Leonard	P	1	3	0	0	0	0	0	0	.000
Henriksen	PH	2	2	0	0	0	0	0	0	.000
Carrigan	C	1	2	0	0	0	0	0	0	.000
Janvrin	SS	1	1	0	0	0	0	0	0	.000
Ruth	PH	1	1	0	0	0	0	0	0	.000
Philadelphia (NL)										
Totals		5	148	10	27	4	1	1	9	.182
Paskert	OF	5	19	2	3	0	0	0	0	.158
Bancroft	SS	5	17	2	5	0	0	0	1	.294
Stock	3B	5	17	1	2	1	0	0	0	.118
Luderus	1B	5	16	1	7	**2**	0	1	**6**	.438
Burns	C	5	16	1	3	0	0	0	0	.188
Cravath	OF	5	16	2	2	1	1	0	1	.125
Niehoff	2B	5	16	1	1	0	0	0	0	.063
Whitted	OF-1B	5	15	0	1	0	0	0	1	.067
Alexander	P	2	5	0	1	0	0	0	0	.200
Mayer	P	2	4	0	0	0	0	0	0	.000
Chalmers	P	1	3	0	1	0	0	0	0	.333
Rixey	P	1	2	0	1	0	0	0	0	.500
Byrne	PH	1	1	0	0	0	0	0	0	.000
Killefer	PH	1	1	0	0	0	0	0	0	.000
Becker	OF	2	0	0	0	0	0	0	0	.000
Dugey	PR	2	0	0	0	0	0	0	0	.000

COMPOSITE PITCHING

NAME	G	IP	H	BB	SO	W	L	SV	ERA
Boston (AL)									
Totals	5	44	27	10	25	4	1	0	1.84
Foster	2	**18**	12	2	**13**	**2**	0	0	2.00
Shore	2	17	12	**8**	6	1	1	0	2.12
Leonard	1	9	3	0	6	1	0	0	**1.00**
Philadelphia (NL)									
Totals	5	43.2	42	11	25	1	4	0	2.30
Alexander	2	17.2	14	4	10	1	1	0	1.53
Mayer	2	11.1	**16**	2	7	0	1	0	2.38
Chalmers	1	8	8	3	6	0	1	0	2.25
Rixey	1	6.2	4	2	2	0	1	0	4.05

⊖ ⊖ 1916 Streaking to Nowhere ⊖ ⊖

Of the 86 games won by the Giants, half were won in an unusual manner. In fact, the entire season included the sublime and ridiculous for Giant rooters. After losing eight straight games at home and unable to get going, the Giants took to the road and won 17 straight. But their brief fling at glory quickly waned, prompting manager John McGraw to quickly rebuild the team. He got rid of Bill McKechnie, Fred Merkle, and Larry Doyle. His one-time ace, Christy Mathewson, went to Cincinnati to manage, while Buck Herzog, the Reds' manager, came to New York as a utility infielder. McGraw also acquired Heinie Zimmerman from the Cubs to bolster the infield.

New blood seemed to be the answer as the Giants entered September and made a frantic dash down the stretch, winning a record 26 in a row at home and almost pulling off the impossible, before falling to Boston on the 30th and winding up seven games out in fourth place. Other streaks, which mostly added up to zero, included Washington's 16 in a row on the road, the Browns' 14 in a row, and the Athletics' 20 in a row—the last of which came on the downside and accounted for an experiment of young players by Connie Mack which did not work and cost him 117 losses, the most ever in the American League to that time. Individual streaks were made by Zack Wheat of the Dodgers and Sherry Magee of the Braves. Wheat hit in 29 straight games, and Magee handled 170 chances in left field before making a miscue.

Close races in both leagues helped offset bad weather and the costly financial burden of the Federal League settlement. In the National League, Brooklyn survived a tough race to win their first pennant by a scant margin. Philadelphia and Boston were alive going into the last week, but were forced to play in a pair of double headers and took turns eliminating each other. The Phillies, although dethroned, again produced the most prolific hurler of the year in Grover "Pete" Alexander, who registered 16 shutouts, 33 victories, and a low 1.55 E.R.A. Third-place Boston was unable to overcome injuries which took their toll on Sherry Magee, Tom Hughes and Johnny Evers, the first two suffering broken bones and Evers an attack of neuritis in his throwing arm. Before the season started, Frank Chance had his choice of 50 players with which to form a club. As a result of the Federal League settlement, he had the roster of the disbanded Chicago Federal League team in addition to his own Cubs and still could do no better than fifth place. One bright spot came from the last-place Cardinals: Rogers Hornsby played his first full year and hit .313.

In the American League, the Red Sox proved the most adept at musical chairs and won their second pennant in a row. Before the season started, they sold Tris Speaker to Cleveland, after Speaker and the Red Sox owners could not agree on Speaker's 1916 contract. Speaker's roommate and friend, pitcher Smokey Joe Wood, then held out for the entire year until he was also dealt to Cleveland. Luckily, Tilly Walker handled Speaker's post adequately, and a young lefthander, Babe Ruth, blossomed to win 23 games and post the lowest E.R.A. in the league with 1.75.

Detroit's Ty Cobb, although managing to lead the league with 68 stolen bases, lost the batting title for the first time in ten years, losing it to Speaker, who hit .386 to the Georgia Peach's .371.

The World Series was a case of Red Sox pitching and defense against Brooklyn's superiority with the bat. The former proved more meaningful, and Boston decisively beat Brooklyn four games to one.

1916 AMERICAN LEAGUE

NAME	G by POS	B	AGE	G	AB	R	H	2B	3B	HR	RBI	BB	SO	SB	BA	SA
BOSTON 1st 91-63 .591		**BILL CARRIGAN**														
TOTALS			27	156	5017	548	1245	196	56	14	454	464	482	129	.248	.318
Dick Hoblitzell	1B126	L	27	130	417	57	108	17	1	0	39	47	28	10	.259	.305
Jack Barry	2B94	R	29	94	330	28	67	6	1	0	20	17	24	8	.203	.227
Everett Scott	SS121, 2B1, 3B1	R	23	123	366	37	85	19	2	0	27	23	24	8	.232	.295
Larry Gardner	3B147	L	30	148	493	47	152	19	7	2	62	48	27	12	.308	.387
Harry Hooper	OF151	L	28	151	575	75	156	20	11	1	37	80	35	27	.271	.350
Tilly Walker	OF128	R	28	128	467	68	124	29	11	3	46	23	45	14	.266	.394
Duffy Lewis	OF151	R	27	152	563	56	151	29	5	1	56	33	56	16	.268	.343
Pinch Thomas	C90	L	28	99	216	21	57	10	1	1	21	33	13	4	.264	.333
Hal Janvrin	SS59, 2B39, 1B4, 3B3	R	23	117	310	26	69	11	4	0	26	32	32	6	.223	.284
Mike McNally	2B35, 3B14, SS7, OF1	R	22	87	135	28	23	0	0	0	9	10	19	9	.170	.170
Hick Cady	C63, 1B3	R	30	78	162	5	31	6	3	0	13	15	16	0	.191	.265
Olaf Henriksen	OF31	L	28	68	99	13	20	2	2	0	11	19	15	2	.202	.263
Babe Ruth	P44	L	21	67	136	18	37	5	3	3	15	10	23	0	.272	.419
Del Gainer	1B48, 2B2	R	29	56	142	14	36	6	0	3	18	10	24	5	.254	.359
Chick Shorten	OF33	L	24	53	112	14	33	2	1	0	11	10	8	1	.295	.330
Sam Agnew	C38	R	29	40	67	4	14	2	1	0	7	6	4	0	.209	.269
Bill Carrigan	C27	R	32	33	63	7	17	2	1	0	11	11	3	2	.270	.333
2 Jimmy Walsh	OF6, 3B2	L	30	13	16	5	2	0	0	0	2	4	2	3	.125	.125
Heinie Wagner	3B4, 2B1, SS1	R	35	6	8	2	4	1	0	0	0	3	0	2	.500	.625
1 Pat Haley		R	25	1	1	0	0	0	0	0	0	0	1	0	.000	.000
CHICAGO 2nd 89-65 .578 2		**PANTS ROWLAND**														
TOTALS			26	155	5081	601	1277	194	**100**	17	484	447	591	197	.251	.339
Jack Fournier	1B85, OF1	L	23	105	313	36	75	13	9	3	44	36	40	19	.240	.367
Eddie Collins	2B155	L	29	155	545	87	168	14	17	0	52	86	36	40	.308	.396
Zeb Terry	SS93	R	25	94	269	20	51	8	4	0	17	33	36	4	.190	.249
Buck Weaver	3B85, SS66	B	25	151	582	78	132	27	6	3	38	30	48	22	.227	.309
Shano Collins	OF136, 1B4	R	30	143	527	74	128	28	12	0	42	59	51	16	.243	.342
Happy Felsch	OF141	R	24	146	546	73	164	24	12	7	70	31	67	13	.300	.427
Joe Jackson	OF155	L	26	155	592	91	202	40	**21**	3	78	46	25	24	.341	.495
Ray Schalk	C124	R	23	129	410	36	95	12	9	0	41	41	31	30	.232	.305
Jack Ness	1B69	R	30	75	258	32	69	7	5	1	34	9	32	4	.267	.345
Fred McMullin (JJ)	3B63, SS2, 2B1	R	24	68	187	8	48	3	0	0	10	19	30	9	.257	.273
Eddie Murphy	OF24, 3B1	L	24	51	105	14	22	5	1	0	4	9	5	3	.210	.276
Nemo Leibold	OF24	L	24	45	82	5	20	1	2	0	13	7	7	7	.244	.305
Jack Lapp	C34	L	31	40	101	6	21	0	1	0	7	8	10	1	.208	.228
Byrd Lynn	C13	R	27	31	40	4	9	1	0	0	3	4	7	2	.225	.250
Fritz VonKolnitz	3B13	R	23	24	44	1	10	3	0	0	7	2	6	0	.227	.295
Ziggy Hasbrouck	1B7	R	22	9	8	1	1	0	0	0	0	1	2	0	.125	.125
Ceylon Wright	SS8	L		8	18	0	0	0	0	0	0	1	7	0	.000	.000
George Moriarty	1B1, 3B1	R	31	7	5	1	1	0	0	0	0	2	0	0	.200	.200
Ted Jourdan		L	20	3	2	0	0	0	0	0	0	1	1	2	.000	.000
Ray Shook		R	25	1	0	0	0	0	0	0	0	0	0	0	.000	.000
Joe Fautsch		R	27	1	1	0	0	0	0	0	0	0	0	0	.000	.000
DETROIT 3rd 87-67 .565 4		**HUGHIE JENNINGS**														
TOTALS			28	155	5193	**673**	**1371**	202	96	17	**560**	545	529	190	**.264**	**.350**
George Burns	1B124	R	23	135	479	60	137	22	6	4	73	22	30	12	.286	.382
Ralph Young	2B146, SS6, 3B1	B	26	153	528	60	139	16	6	1	45	62	43	20	.263	.322
Donie Bush	SS144	B	28	145	550	73	124	5	9	0	34	75	42	19	.225	.267
Ossie Vitt	3B151, SS2	R	26	153	597	88	135	17	12	0	42	75	28	18	.226	.295
Harry Heilmann	OF77, 1B30, 2B9	R	21	136	451	57	127	30	11	2	73	42	40	9	.282	.410
Ty Cobb	OF143, 1B1	L	29	145	542	**113**	201	31	10	5	68	78	39	**68**	.371	.493
Bobby Veach	OF150	L	28	150	566	92	173	33	15	3	91	52	41	24	.306	.433
Oscar Stanage	C94	R	33	94	291	16	69	17	3	0	30	17	48	3	.237	.316
Sam Crawford	OF79, 1B2	L	36	100	322	41	92	11	13	0	42	37	10	10	.286	.401
Del Baker	C59	R	24	61	98	7	15	4	0	0	6	11	8	2	.153	.194
1 Marty Kavanagh	OF11, 2B2, 3B2	R	25	58	78	6	11	4	0	0	5	9	15	0	.141	.192
George Harper (BL)	OF14	L	24	44	56	4	9	1	0	0	3	5	8	0	.161	.179
Red McKee	C26	L	25	32	76	3	16	1	2	0	4	6	11	0	.211	.276
Frank Fuller	2B8, SS1	B	23	20	10	2	1	0	0	0	1	1	4	3	.100	.100
Tubby Spencer	C19	R	32	19	54	7	20	1	1	1	10	6	6	2	.370	.481
Jack Dalton	OF4	R	31	8	11	1	2	0	0	0	0	0	5	0	.182	.182
George Maisel	3B3	R	24	7	5	2	0	0	0	0	0	0	2	0	.000	.000
Ben Dyer	SS4	R	23	4	14	4	4	1	0	0	1	1	1	0	.286	.357
Bert Ellison	3B2	R	20	2	7	0	1	0	0	0	1	0	1	0	.143	.143
Billy Sullivan	C1	R	41	1	0	0	0	0	0	0	0	0	0	0	.000	.000

NAME	T	AGE	W	L	PCT	SV	G	GS	CG	IP	H	BB	SO	ShO	ERA
		26	**91**	63	**.591**	16	156	156	76	1411	1221	463	584	**23**	2.47
Babe Ruth	L	21	23	12	.657	1	44	**40**	23	324	230	118	170	**9**	**1.75**
Dutch Leonard	L	24	18	11	.621	5	48	34	17	274	244	66	144	6	2.36
Carl Mays	R	24	18	13	.581	3	44	25	14	245	208	74	76	2	2.39
Ernie Shore	R	25	17	10	.630	1	38	27	10	226	221	49	62	3	2.63
Rube Foster	R	28	13	8	.619	3	33	20	9	182	173	86	53	3	3.07
Vean Gregg	L	31	2	5	.286	0	21	7	3	78	71	30	41	0	3.00
Sad Sam Jones	R	23	0	1	.000	1	12	0	0	27	25	10	7	0	3.67
1 Marty McHale	R	27	0	1	.000	0	2	1	0	6	7	4	1	0	3.00
Herb Pennock	L	22	0	2	.000	1	9	2	0	27	23	8	12	0	3.00
2 Weldon Wyckoff (SA)	R	24	0	0	.000	1	8	0	0	23	19	18	18	0	4.70
Smokey Joe Wood (HO) 26															
		29	89	65	.578	16	155	155	73	1412	1189	405	644	18	**2.36**
Reb Russell	L	27	17	11	.607	4	56	26	16	264	207	42	112	5	2.42
Eddie Cicotte	R	32	16	7	**.696**	4	44	20	11	187	138	70	91	2	1.78
Red Faber	R	27	16	9	.640	2	35	25	15	205	167	61	87	3	2.02
Lefty Williams	L	23	13	7	.650	1	43	25	10	224	220	65	138	2	2.89
Joe Benz	R	30	9	5	.643	0	28	16	6	142	108	32	57	4	2.03
Jim Scott	R	27	9	14	.391	2	32	20	8	165	155	53	71	1	2.73
Dave Danforth	L	26	5	5	.500	2	28	8	1	94	87	37	49	0	3.26
Mellie Wolfgang	R	26	4	6	.400	1	27	14	6	127	103	42	36	1	1.98
Ed Walsh	R	35	0	1	.000	0	2	1	0	3	4	3	3	0	3.00
		26	87	67	.565	12	155	155	81	1410	1254	578	531	9	2.97
Harry Coveleski	L	30	21	11	.656	2	44	39	22	324	278	63	108	3	1.97
Hooks Dauss	R	26	19	12	.613	4	39	29	18	239	220	90	95	1	3.20
Bernie Boland	R	24	10	3	.769	1	46	9	5	130	111	73	99	1	3.95
Jean Dubuc	R	27	10	10	.500	1	36	16	8	170	134	84	40	1	2.96
2 Willie Mitchell	L	26	7	5	.583	0	23	17	7	128	119	48	60	2	3.30
George Cunningham	R	21	7	10	.412	2	35	14	5	150	146	74	68	0	2.76
Bill James	R	29	7	12	.368	2	30	20	8	152	141	79	61	0	3.67
Howard Ehmke	R	22	3	1	.750	0	5	4	4	37	34	15	15	0	3.16
2 Earl Hamilton	L	24	2	2	.500	0	5	5	3	37	34	22	7	1	2.68
George Boehler	R	24	1	1	.500	0	5	2	1	13	12	9	8	0	4.85
Bill McTigue	L	25	0	1	.000	0	3	0	0	5	5	5	1	0	5.40
Eric Erickson	R	24	0	0	.000	0	8	0	0	16	13	8	7	0	2.81
Deacon Jones	R	22	0	0	.000	0	1	0	0	7	7	5	2	0	2.57
1 Grover Lowdermilk	R	31	1	1	.000	0	1	0	0	.1	0	3	0	0	0.00

NEW YORK 4th 80-74 .519 11 — WILL BILL DONOVAN

NAME	G by POS	B	AGE	G	AB	R	H	2B	3B	HR	RBI	BB	SO	SB	BA	SA
TOTALS			26	156	**5200**	575	1277	194	59	**35**	492	516	**632**	179	.246	.326
Wally Pipp	1B148	L	23	151	545	70	143	20	14	**12**	93	54	**82**	16	.262	.417
Joe Gedeon	2B122	R	22	122	435	50	92	14	4	0	27	40	61	14	.211	.262
Roger Peckinpaugh	SS146	R	25	146	552	65	141	22	8	4	58	62	50	18	.255	.346
Frank Baker	3B96	L	30	100	360	46	97	23	2	10	52	36	30	15	.269	.428
Frank Gilhooley	OF57	L	24	58	223	40	62	5	3	1	10	37	17	6	.278	.341
Lee Magee	OF128, 2B2	B	27	131	510	57	131	18	4	3	45	50	31	29	.257	.325
Hugh High	OF109	L	28	115	377	44	99	13	4	1	28	47	44	13	.263	.326
Les Nunamaker	C79	R	27	91	260	25	77	14	7	0	28	34	21	4	.296	.404
Paddy Baumann	OF28, 3B26, 2B9	R	30	79	237	35	68	5	3	1	25	19	16	10	.287	.346
Roxy Walters	C65	R	23	66	203	13	54	9	3	0	23	14	42	2	.266	.340
Charlie Mullen	2B20, 1B17, OF6	R	27	59	146	11	39	9	1	0	18	9	13	7	.267	.342
Fritz Maisel	OF26, 3B11, 2B4	R	26	53	158	18	36	5	0	0	7	20	18	4	.228	.259
Luke Boone	3B25, SS12, 2B7	R	26	46	124	14	23	4	0	1	8	8	10	7	.185	.242
Ray Caldwell	P21, OF3	L	28	45	93	6	19	2	0	0	4	2	17	1	.204	.226
Elmer Miller	OF42	R	25	43	152	12	34	3	2	1	18	11	18	8	.224	.289
Rube Oldring	OF43	R	32	43	158	17	37	8	0	1	12	12	13	6	.234	.304
Walt Alexander	C27	R	25	36	78	8	20	6	1	0	3	13	20	0	.256	.359
Roy Hartzell	OF28	L	34	33	64	12	12	1	0	0	7	9	3	1	.188	.203
Tim Hendryx	OF15	R	25	15	62	10	18	7	1	0	5	8	6	4	.290	.435

Angel Aragon 22 R 5-27, 1 Solly Hofman 33 R 8-27, Doc Cook 30 L 1-10, Germany Schaefer 39 R 0-0

NAME	T	AGE	W	L	PCT	SV	G	GS	CG	IP	H	BB	SO	ShO	ERA
		26	80	74	.519	**18**	156	156	83	1428	1249	476	616	10	2.77
Bob Shawkey	R	25	24	14	.632	**9**	53	27	21	277	204	81	122	4	2.21
Nick Cullop	L	28	13	6	.684	1	28	22	9	167	151	32	77	0	2.05
Ray Fisher	R	28	10	8	.556	3	31	21	9	179	191	51	56	1	3.17
Allen Russell	R	22	6	10	.375	5	34	18	8	171	138	75	104	1	3.21
George Mogridge	L	27	6	12	.333	0	31	21	9	195	174	45	66	1	2.31
Urban Shocker	R	25	5	3	.625	0	12	9	4	82	67	32	43	1	2.63
Ray Keating	R	24	5	6	.455	0	14	12	6	91	91	37	35	0	3.07
Ray Caldwell	R	28	5	12	.294	0	21	18	14	166	142	65	76	1	2.98
Cliff Markle	R	22	4	3	.471	0	11	7	3	46	41	31	14	1	4.50
Slim Love	L	25	2	0	1.000	0	20	1	0	48	46	23	21	0	4.88
Jesse Buckles	L	26	0	0	.000	0	2	0	0	4	3	1	0	0	2.25
Mike Cantwell	L	20	0	0	.000	0	1	0	0	2	0	2	0	0	0.00
Wild Bill Donovan	R	39	0	0	.000	0	1	0	0	1	1	1	0	0	0.00
King Cole (DD) 29															

ST. LOUIS 5th 79-75 .513 12 — FIELDER JONES

NAME	G by POS	B	AGE	G	AB	R	H	2B	3B	HR	RBI	BB	SO	SB	BA	SA
TOTALS			28	158	5159	591	1262	181	50	14	499	**627**	610	**234**	.245	.308
George Sisler	1B139, OF3, P3	L	23	151	580	83	177	21	11	4	76	40	37	34	.305	.400
Del Pratt	2B158	R	28	158	596	64	159	35	12	5	**103**	54	56	26	.267	.391
Doc Lavan	SS106	R	25	110	343	32	81	13	1	0	19	32	38	7	.236	.280
Jimmy Austin	3B124	B	36	129	411	55	85	15	6	1	28	74	59	19	.207	.280
Ward Miller	OF135, 2B1	L	31	146	485	72	129	17	5	1	50	72	76	25	.266	.328
Armando Marsans	OF150	R	29	151	528	51	134	12	1	1	60	57	41	46	.254	.286
Burt Shotton	OF157	L	31	157	**618**	97	174	23	6	1	36	**111**	67	41	.282	.343
Hank Severeid	C89, 1B1, 3B1	R	25	100	293	23	80	8	2	0	34	26	17	3	.273	.314
Grover Hartley	C75	R	27	89	222	19	50	8	0	0	12	30	24	4	.225	.261
Jack Tobin	OF41	L	24	77	150	16	32	4	1	0	10	12	13	7	.213	.253
Ernie Johnson	SS60, 3B12	L	28	74	236	29	54	9	3	0	19	30	23	13	.229	.292
Babe Burton	1B22	L	27	66	98	10	22	1	2	1	12	19	13	1	.224	.306
Bill Rumler	C9	R	25	27	37	6	12	3	0	0	10	3	7	0	.324	.405
1 Charlie Deal	3B22, 2B1	R	24	23	74	7	10	1	0	0	10	6	8	4	.135	149
Harry Chapman	C14	R	28	18	31	2	3	0	0	0	0	2	5	0	.097	.097
Bobby Wallace	3B9, SS5	R	42	14	18	0	5	0	0	0	1	2	1	0	.278	.278

Bill Lee 21 R 2-11, Gene Paulette 24 R 2-4, George Hale 21 R 0-1, Vern Clemons 24 R 1-7, Ray Kennedy 21 R 0-1

NAME	T	AGE	W	L	PCT	SV	G	GS	CG	IP	H	BB	SO	ShO	ERA
		28	79	75	.513	12	158	158	71	**1444**	1292	478	505	9	2.58
Carl Weilman	L	26	17	18	.486	2	46	31	19	276	237	76	91	1	2.15
Eddie Plank	L	40	15	15	.500	4	37	26	17	236	203	67	88	3	2.33
Bob Groom	R	31	14	9	.609	3	41	26	6	217	174	98	92	1	2.57
Dave Davenport	R	26	12	11	.522	1	**59**	31	13	291	267	100	129	1	2.85
Ernie Koob (IL)	L	23	11	8	.579	2	33	20	10	167	153	56	26	2	2.53
13 Earl Hamilton	R	24	5	7	.417	0	23	13	2	95	101	30	25	0	3.32
Tim McCabe	R	21	2	0	1.000	0	13	0	0	26	29	7	7	0	3.12
George Baumgardner	R	24	1	0	1.000	0	4	2	0	8	12	5	4	0	7.88
George Sisler	L	23	1	2	.333	0	3	3	3	27	18	6	12	1	1.00
Jim Park	R	23	1	4	.200	0	26	6	1	79	69	25	26	0	2.62
Bill Fincher	R	22	0	1	.000	0	12	0	0	21	22	7	5	0	2.14
Doc Crandall	R	28	0	0	.000	0	2	0	0	1	7	1	0	0	36.00

CLEVELAND 6th 77-77 .500 14 — LEE FOHL

NAME	G by POS	B	AGE	G	AB	R	H	2B	3B	HR	RBI	BB	SO	SB	BA	SA
TOTALS			27	157	5064	630	1264	**233**	66	16	533	522	605	160	.250	.331
Chick Gandil	1B145	R	28	146	533	51	138	26	9	0	72	36	48	13	.259	.341
Ivon Howard	2B65, 1B7	B	33	81	246	20	46	11	5	0	23	30	34	9	.187	.272
Bill Wambsganss	SS106, 2B24, 3B5	R	22	136	475	57	117	14	4	0	45	41	40	13	.246	.293
Terry Turner	3B77, 2B42	R	35	124	428	52	112	15	3	0	38	40	29	15	.262	.311
Braggo Roth	OF112	R	23	125	409	50	117	19	7	4	72	38	48	29	.286	.396
Tris Speaker	OF151	L	28	151	546	102	**211**	**41**	8	2	79	82	20	35	**.386**	**.502**
Jack Graney	OF154	L	30	155	589	106	142	**41**	14	5	54	102	72	10	.241	.384
Steve O'Neill	C128	R	24	130	378	30	89	23	0	0	29	24	33	2	.235	.296
Ray Chapman (KJ)	SS52, 3B36, 2B16	R	25	109	346	50	80	10	5	0	27	50	46	21	.231	.289
1 Elmer Smith	OF57	L	23	79	213	25	59	15	3	3	40	18	35	3	.277	.418
Joe Evans	3B28	R	21	33	82	4	12	1	0	0	1	7	12	4	.146	.159
Tom Daly	C25, OF1	R	24	31	73	3	16	1	1	0	8	1	2	0	.219	.260
2 Danny Moeller	OF8, 2B1	B	31	25	30	5	2	0	0	0	1	5	6	2	.067	.067
Josh Billings	C12	R	24	22	31	2	5	0	0	0	1	2	11	0	.161	.161
Bob Coleman	C12	R	25	19	28	3	6	2	0	0	4	7	6	0	.214	.286
2 Marty Kavanagh	2B9, 1B1, 3B1	R	25	19	44	4	11	2	1	1	10	2	5	0	.250	.409
Hank DeBerry	C14	R	21	15	33	7	9	4	0	0	4	6	9	0	.273	.394
Milo Allison	OF5	L	25	14	18	10	5	0	0	0	0	6	1	0	.278	.278
Walter Barbare	3B12	R	24	13	48	3	11	1	0	0	3	4	9	0	.229	.250
Clyde Engle	3B7, 1B2, OF1	R	32	11	26	1	4	0	0	0	1	0	6	0	.154	.154

Al Bergman 25 R 3-14, Lou Guisto 22 R 3-19, 1 Larry Chappell 26 L 0-2, 1 Joe Leonard 22 L 0-2, Howard Lohr 24 R 1-7, Jack Bradley 22 R 0-3, Ollie Welf 27R 0-0

NAME	T	AGE	W	L	PCT	SV	G	GS	CG	IP	H	BB	SO	ShO	ERA
		27	77	77	.500	16	157	157	65	1416	**1383**	467	537	9	2.99
Stan Coveleski	R	27	16	14	.533	3	45	27	11	232	247	58	76	1	3.41
Jim Bagby	R	26	16	16	.500	5	48	27	14	279	253	67	88	3	2.55
Guy Morton (LJ)	R	23	12	6	.667	0	27	18	9	150	139	42	88	0	2.88
Fritz Coumbe	L	26	7	5	.583	0	29	13	7	120	121	27	39	2	2.03
Fred Beebe	R	35	6	3	.667	2	20	12	5	101	92	37	32	1	2.41
Ed Klepfer	R	28	6	7	.462	2	31	13	4	143	136	46	62	1	2.52
Al Gould	R	23	6	7	.417	1	30	9	6	107	101	40	41	1	2.52
Otis Lambeth	R	26	3	3	.500	1	15	9	3	74	69	38	28	0	2.92
2 Joe Boehling	L	25	3	4	.429	0	12	9	3	61	63	23	18	0	2.66
Pop Boy Smith	R	24	1	2	.333	0	5	3	0	26	25	11	4	0	3.81
1 Willie Mitchell	L	26	1	5	.167	2	12	6	1	44	55	19	24	0	5.11
2 Grover Lowdermilk	R	31	1	5	.167	0	10	9	2	51	52	45	28	0	5.82
2 Marty McHale	R	27	0	0	.000	0	5	0	0	11	10	6	2	0	5.73
Ken Penner	R	20	0	0	.000	0	4	2	0	13	14	4	5	0	4.15
Rip Hagerman	R	28	0	0	.000	0	2	0	0	4	5	2	1	0	11.25
Shorty DesJardien	R	22	0	0	.000	0	1	0	0	1	1	1	0	0	18.00
Red Gunkel	R	22	0	0	.000	0	1	0	0	1	0	1	1	0	0.00

WASHINGTON 7th 76-77 .497 14.5 — CLARK GRIFFITH

NAME	G by POS	B	AGE	G	AB	R	H	2B	3B	HR	RBI	BB	SO	SB	BA	SA
TOTALS			28	159	5113	534	1239	170	60	12	468	535	597	185	.242	.306
Joe Judge (IL)	1B103	L	22	103	336	42	74	10	8	0	28	54	44	18	.220	.298
Ray Morgan	2B82, SS9, 1B3, 3B1	R	27	99	315	41	84	12	4	1	29	59	29	14	.267	.340
George McBride	SS139	R	35	139	466	36	106	15	4	1	36	23	58	8	.227	.283
Eddie Foster	3B84, 2B72	R	29	158	606	75	153	18	9	1	44	68	26	23	.252	.317
1 Danny Moeller	OF65	B	31	78	240	30	59	8	1	1	23	30	35	13	.246	.300
Clyde Milan	OF149	L	30	150	565	58	154	14	3	1	45	56	31	34	.273	.313
Howard Shanks	OF88, 3B31, SS8, 1B7	R	25	140	471	51	119	15	7	1	48	41	34	23	.253	.321
John Henry	C116	R	26	117	305	28	76	12	3	0	46	49	40	12	.249	.308
Rip Williams	1B34, C23, 3B1	R	34	76	202	16	54	10	2	0	20	15	19	5	.267	.337
Charlie Jamieson	OF41, 1B4, P1	L	23	64	145	16	36	4	0	0	13	18	18	5	.248	.276
Sam Rice	OF46, P5	L	26	58	197	26	59	8	3	1	17	15	13	4	.299	.386
Eddie Ainsmith	C46	R	24	51	100	11	17	4	0	0	8	8	14	3	.170	.210
Henri Rondeau	OF48	R	29	50	162	20	36	5	3	1	28	18	18	7	.222	.309
2 Elmer Smith	OF45	L	23	45	168	12	36	10	3	2	27	18	28	4	.214	.345
2 Joe Leonard	3B42	L	21	42	168	20	46	7	0	0	14	22	23	4	.274	.315
Patsy Gharrity	C18, 1B15	R	24	39	92	8	21	5	1	0	9	8	18	2	.228	.304
Carl Sawyer	2B6, SS5, 3B1	R	25	16	31	3	6	1	0	0	2	4	4	3	.194	.226
Turner Barber	OF9	L	22	15	33	3	7	0	1	1	5	2	3	0	.212	.364

Mike Menosky 21 L 6-37, Merito Acosta 20 L 1-7

NAME	T	AGE	W	L	PCT	SV	G	GS	CG	IP	H	BB	SO	ShO	ERA
		24	76	77	.497	9	159	159	84	1432	1271	540	**706**	11	2.66
Walter Johnson	R	28	**25**	20	.556	1	48	38	**36**	**371**	**290**	132	**228**	3	1.89
Bert Gallia	R	24	17	13	.567	3	49	31	13	284	278	99	120	1	2.76
Harry Harper	L	21	15	10	.600	0	36	34	12	250	209	101	149	2	2.45
1 Joe Boehling	L	25	8	10	.444	1	27	19	7	140	134	54	52	2	3.09
Doc Ayres	R	26	5	9	.357	2	43	17	7	157	173	52	69	0	3.78
Jim Shaw	R	22	3	8	.273	1	26	9	5	106	86	50	44	2	2.63
George Dumont	R	20	2	3	.400	1	17	5	2	53	37	17	21	0	3.06
Claude Thomas	L	26	1	2	.333	0	7	4	1	28	27	12	7	1	4.18
Sam Rice	R	26	0	1	.000	0	5	1	0	21	18	10	3	0	3.00
Molly Craft	R	20	0	1	.000	0	2	1	1	11	12	6	9	0	3.27
Marv Goodwin	R	25	0	0	.000	0	3	0	0	6	5	3	1	0	3.00
Jack Bentley	L	21	0	0	.000	0	2	0	0	1	0	1	1	0	0.00
Charlie Jamieson	L	23	0	0	.000	0	1	0	0	2	2	3	2	0	4.50

PHILADELPHIA 8th 36-117 .235 54.5 — CONNIE MACK

NAME	G by POS	B	AGE	G	AB	R	H	2B	3B	HR	RBI	BB	SO	SB	BA	SA
TOTALS			27	154	5010	447	1212	169	65	19	380	406	631	151	.242	.313
Stuffy McInnis	1B140	R	25	140	512	42	151	25	3	1	60	25	19	7	.295	.361
Nap Lajoie	2B105, 1B5, OF2	R	40	113	426	33	105	14	4	2	35	14	26	15	.246	.312
Whitey Witt	SS142	L	20	143	563	64	138	16	15	2	36	55	71	19	.245	.337
Charlie Pick	3B108, OF8	L	28	121	398	29	96	10	3	0	20	40	24	25	.241	.281
1 Jimmy Walsh	OF113, 1B1	L	30	114	390	42	91	13	6	1	27	54	36	27	.233	.305
Amos Strunk	OF143, 1B7	L	27	150	544	71	172	30	9	3	49	66	59	21	.316	.421
Wally Schang	OF61, C36	B	26	110	338	41	90	15	8	7	38	38	44	14	.266	.420
Billy Meyer	C48	R	24	50	138	12	32	2	2	1	12	8	11	3	.232	.297
Lee McElwee	3B30, SS1	R	22	54	155	9	41	3	0	0	10	8	17	0	.265	.284
Lee King	OF22, SS11, 3B5, 2B2	R	22	42	144	13	27	1	2	0	8	7	15	4	.188	.222
Otis Lawrey	2B29, OF5	L	22	41	123	10	25	0	0	0	4	9	21	4	.203	.203
1 Rube Oldring	OF40	R	32	40	146	10	36	8	3	0	14	9	9	1	.247	.342
Val Picinich	C37	R	19	40	118	8	23	3	1	0	5	6	33	1	.195	.237
2 Pat Haley	C33	R	25	34	108	8	25	5	0	0	4	6	19	0	.231	.278
Bill Stellbauer	OF14	R	22	25	48	2	13	2	1	0	5	6	7	2	.271	.354
Roy Grover	2B20	R	24	20	77	8	21	1	2	0	7	6	10	5	.273	.338
Les Lanning	OF9, P6	L	21	19	33	5	6	2	0	0	1	10	9	0	.182	.242
Harland Rowe	3B7, OF1	L	20	17	36	2	5	1	0	0	3	2	8	0	.139	.167
Shag Thompson	OF7	L	23	15	17	4	0	0	0	0	0	7	6	1	.000	.000
Don Brown	OF12	R	19	14	42	6	10	2	1	1	5	4	9	0	.238	.405
Mike Murphy	C12	R	27	14	27	0	3	0	0	0	1	1	3	0	.111	.111
Ralph Mitterling	OF12	R	26	13	39	1	6	0	0	0	2	3	6	0	.154	.154
Charlie Grimm	OF7	L	17	12	22	0	2	0	0	0	0	2	4	0	.091	.091

Doc Carroll 24 R 2-22, Buck Thrasher 26 L 9-29, Tom Healy 20 R 6-23, Lew Malone 19 R 0-4, Harry Davis 42 R 1-6, Bill Johnson 23 L 4-15, Sam Crane 21 R 1-4

NAME	T	AGE	W	L	PCT	SV	G	GS	CG	IP	H	BB	SO	ShO	ERA
		24	36	**117**	.235	3	154	154	**94**	1344	1311	**715**	575	11	3.84
Bullet Joe Bush	R	23	15	**24**	.385	0	40	33	25	287	222	130	157	8	2.57
Elmer Myers	R	22	14	23	.378	1	44	35	31	315	280	**168**	182	2	3.66
Rube Parnham	R	22	2	1	.667	0	4	3	2	25	27	13	8	0	0.36
Jing Johnson	R	21	2	9	.182	0	12	12	8	84	90	39	25	0	3.75
Socks Seibold	R	20	1	2	.333	0	3	2	1	22	22	9	5	1	4.09
Tom Sheehan	R	22	1	16	.063	0	38	17	8	188	197	94	54	0	3.69
Jack Nabors	R	28	1	18	.048	1	40	29	11	213	206	95	74	0	3.46
1 Weldon Wyckoff	R	24	0	1	.000	0	7	2	1	21	20	20	4	0	5.57
Carl Ray	L	27	0	1	.000	0	3	2	0	9	9	14	5	0	5.00
Mike Driscoll	R	23	0	1	.000	0	1	0	0	5	6	2	0	0	5.40
Rube Bressler	L	21	0	2	.000	0	4	2	0	15	16	14	8	0	6.60
Les Lanning	L	21	0	3	.000	0	6	3	1	24	38	17	9	0	8.25
George Hesselbacher	R	21	0	4	.000	0	6	4	2	26	37	22	6	0	7.27
Cap Crowell	R	23	0	6	.000	0	9	6	1	40	43	34	15	0	4.73
Marsh Williams	R	23	0	6	.000	0	10	4	3	51	71	31	17	0	7.94
Harry Weaver	R	21	0	0	.000	0	3	0	0	8	14	5	2	0	10.13
Axel Lindstrom	R	20	0	0	.000	1	1	0	0	4	2	0	1	0	4.50
Bill Morrisette	R	23	0	0	.000	0	1	0	0	4	6	5	2	0	6.75
Jack Richardson	R	23	0	0	.000	0	1	0	0	1	2	1	1	0	27.00
Doc Whittaker	R	22	0	0	.000	0	1	0	0	2	3	2	0	0	4.50

BROOKLYN 1st 94-60 .610 — WILBERT ROBINSON

NAME	G by POS	B	AGE	G	AB	R	H	2B	3B	HR	RBI	BB	SO	SB	BA	SA
TOTALS			29	156	5234	585	**1366**	195	80	28	493	355	550	187	**.261**	**.345**
Jake Daubert	1B126	L	32	127	478	75	151	16	7	3	33	38	39	21	.316	.397
George Cutshaw	2B154	R	28	154	581	58	151	21	4	2	63	25	32	27	.260	.320
Ivy Olson	SS103, 2B3, 1B1	R	30	108	351	29	89	13	4	1	38	21	27	14	.254	.322
Mike Mowrey	3B144	R	32	144	495	57	121	22	6	0	60	50	60	16	.244	.313
Jimmy Johnston	OF106	R	26	118	425	58	107	13	8	1	26	35	38	22	.252	.327
Hy Myers	OF106	R	27	113	412	54	108	12	14	3	36	21	35	17	.262	.381
Zack Wheat	OF149	L	30	149	568	76	177	32	13	9	73	43	49	19	.312	**.461**
Chief Meyers	C74	R	35	80	239	21	59	10	3	0	21	26	15	2	.247	.314
Casey Stengel	OF121	L	25	127	462	66	129	27	8	8	53	33	51	11	.279	.424
Otto Miller	C69	R	27	73	216	16	55	9	2	1	17	7	29	6	.255	.329
Ollie O'Mara	SS51	R	25	72	193	18	39	5	2	0	15	12	20	10	.202	.249
1 Lew McCarty	C27, 1B17	R	27	55	150	17	47	6	1	0	13	14	16	4	.313	.367
Jeff Pfeffer	P41, OF4	R	28	43	122	5	34	2	2	0	12	4	32	2	.279	.328
Gus Getz	3B20, SS7, 1B3	R	26	40	96	9	21	1	2	0	8	0	5	9	.219	.271
2 Fred Merkle	1B15, OF4	R	27	23	69	6	16	1	0	0	2	7	4	2	.232	.246
Dave Hickman	OF3	R	22	9	5	3	1	0	0	0	0	2	0	1	.200	.200
Hack Miller	OF3	R	22	3	3	0	1	0	1	0	1	1	1	0	.333	1.000
Bunny Fabrique	SS2	B	28	2	2	0	0	0	0	0	0	0	1	0	.000	.000

John Kelleher 22 R 0-3, Red Smyth 23 L 0-5, Mack Wheat 23 R 0-2, Artie Dede 20 R 0-1, Al Nixon 30 R 2-2

NAME	T	AGE	W	L	PCT	SV	G	GS	CG	IP	H	BB	SO	ShO	ERA
		29	**94**	60	**.610**	9	156	156	96	**1427**	1201	372	634	22	**2.12**
Jeff Pfeffer	R	28	25	11	.694	1	41	37	30	329	274	63	128	6	1.91
Larry Cheney	R	30	18	12	.600	0	41	32	15	253	178	105	166	5	1.92
Sherry Smith	L	25	14	10	.583	1	36	23	15	219	193	45	67	4	2.34
Rube Marquard	L	26	13	6	.684	5	36	20	15	205	169	38	107	2	1.58
Jack Coombs	R	33	13	8	.619	0	27	21	10	159	136	44	47	3	2.66
Wheezer Dell	R	29	8	9	.471	1	32	16	9	155	143	43	76	2	2.26
Nap Rucker	L	31	2	1	.667	0	9	4	1	37	34	7	14	0	1.70
Ed Appleton	R	24	1	2	.333	1	14	3	1	47	49	18	14	0	3.06
Duster Mails	L	20	0	1	.000	0	11	0	0	17	15	9	13	0	3.71
Leon Cadore	R	25	0	0	.000	0	1	0	0	6	10	0	2	0	4.50

PHILADELPHIA 2nd 91-62 .595 2.5 — PAT MORAN

NAME	G by POS	B	AGE	G	AB	R	H	2B	3B	HR	RBI	BB	SO	SB	BA	SA
TOTALS			29	154	4985	581	1244	**223**	53	42	486	399	571	149	.250	.341
Fred Luderus	1B146	L	30	146	508	52	143	26	3	5	53	41	32	8	.281	.374
Bert Niehoff	2B146, 3B1	R	32	146	548	65	133	42	4	4	61	37	57	20	.243	.356
Dave Bancroft	SS142	B	25	142	477	53	101	10	0	3	33	74	57	15	.212	.252
Milt Stock	3B117, SS15	R	22	132	509	61	143	25	6	1	43	27	33	21	.281	.360
Gavvy Cravath	OF130	R	35	137	448	70	127	21	8	11	70	64	**89**	9	.283	.440
Dode Paskert	OF146, SS1	R	34	149	555	82	155	30	7	8	46	54	76	22	.279	.402
Possum Whitted	OF136, 1B16	R	26	147	526	68	148	20	12	6	68	19	46	29	.281	.399
Bill Killefer	C91	R	28	97	286	22	62	5	4	3	27	8	14	2	.217	.294
Ed Burns	C75, SS1, OF1	R	27	78	219	14	51	8	1	0	14	16	18	3	.233	.279
Wilbur Good	OF46	L	30	75	136	25	34	4	3	1	15	8	13	7	.250	.346
Claude Cooper	OF29, 1B1	L	23	56	104	9	20	2	0	0	11	7	15	1	.192	.212
Bobby Byrne	3B40	R	31	48	141	22	33	10	1	0	9	14	7	6	.234	.319
Oscar Dugey	2B12	R	28	41	50	9	11	3	0	0	1	9	8	3	.220	.280
Jack Adams (HJ)	C11	B	25	11	13	2	3	0	0	0	1	0	3	0	.231	.231
Bud Weiser	OF4	R	25	4	10	1	3	1	0	0	1	0	3	0	.300	.400
Bob Gandy	OF1	L	22	1	2	0	0	0	0	0	0	0	1	0	.000	.000
Billy Maharg	OF1		29	1	1	0	0	0	0	0	0	0	0	0	.000	.000
Ben Tincup				1	1	0	0	0	0	0	0	0	0	0	.000	.000

NAME	T	AGE	W	L	PCT	SV	G	GS	CG	IP	H	BB	SO	ShO	ERA
		29	91	62	.595	9	154	154	**97**	1382	1238	295	601	**24**	2.36
Pete Alexander	R	29	**33**	12	.733	3	48	**45**	**38**	**389**	**323**	50	**167**	**16**	**1.55**
Eppa Rixey	L	25	22	10	.688	0	38	33	20	287	239	74	134	3	1.85
Al Demaree	R	29	19	14	.576	1	39	35	25	285	252	48	130	2	2.62
Erskine Mayer	R	27	7	7	.500	0	28	16	7	140	148	33	62	2	3.15
Chief Bender	R	33	7	7	.500	3	27	13	4	123	137	34	43	0	3.73
Joe Oeschger	R	25	1	0	1.000	0	14	0	0	30	18	14	17	0	2.40
George Chalmers	R	28	1	4	.200	0	12	8	2	54	49	19	21	0	3.17
George McQuillan	R	31	1	7	.125	2	21	3	1	62	58	15	22	0	2.76
Gary Fortune	R	21	0	1	.000	0	1	1	0	5	2	4	3	0	3.60
2 Erv Kantlehner	L	23	0	0	.000	0	3	0	0	4	7	3	2	0	9.00
Stan Baumgartner	L	23	0	0	.000	0	1	0	0	4	5	1	0	0	2.25

BOSTON 3rd 89-63 .586 4 — GEORGE STALLINGS

NAME	G by POS	B	AGE	G	AB	R	H	2B	3B	HR	RBI	BB	SO	SB	BA	SA
TOTALS			28	158	5075	542	1181	166	73	22	472	**437**	646	141	.233	.307
Ed Konetchy	1B158	R	30	158	566	76	147	29	13	3	70	43	46	13	.260	.373
Johnny Evers (AJ)	2B71	L	34	71	241	33	52	4	1	0	15	40	19	5	.216	.241
Rabbit Maranville	SS155	R	24	155	604	79	142	16	13	4	38	50	69	32	.235	.325
Red Smith	3B150	R	26	150	509	48	132	16	10	3	60	53	55	13	.259	.348
Joe Wilhoit	OF108	L	24	116	383	44	88	13	4	2	38	27	45	18	.230	.300
Fred Snodgrass	OF110	R	28	112	382	33	95	13	5	1	32	34	54	14	.249	.317
Sherry Magee	OF120, 1B2, SS1	R	31	120	419	44	101	17	5	3	54	44	52	10	.241	.327
Hank Gowdy	C116	R	26	118	349	32	88	12	1	1	34	24	33	8	.252	.301
Zip Collins	OF78	L	24	93	268	39	56	1	6	1	18	18	42	4	.209	.269
Dick Egan	2B53, SS12, 3B8	R	32	83	238	23	53	8	3	0	16	19	21	2	.223	.282
Ed Fitzpatrick	2B46, OF28	R	26	83	216	17	46	8	0	1	18	15	26	5	.213	.264
Joe Connolly	OF31	L	28	62	110	11	25	5	2	0	12	14	13	5	.227	.309
Earl Blackburn	C44	R	23	47	110	12	30	4	4	0	7	9	21	2	.273	.382
Walt Tragesser	C29	R	29	41	54	3	11	1	0	0	4	5	10	0	.204	.222
Lefty Tyler	P34	L	26	39	93	10	19	3	1	3	20	9	15	0	.204	.355
1 Pete Compton	OF30	L	26	34	98	13	20	2	0	0	8	7	7	5	.204	.224
2 Larry Chappell	OF14	L	26	20	53	4	12	1	1	0	9	2	8	1	.226	.283
Fred Bailey	OF2	L	20	6	10	0	1	0	0	0	1	0	3	0	.100	.100
Art Rico	C4	R	19	4	4	0	0	0	0	0	0	0	0	0	.000	.000
Joe Mathes	2B2	B	24	2	0	0	0	0	0	0	0	0	0	0	.000	.000

NAME	T	AGE	W	L	PCT	SV	G	GS	CG	IP	H	BB	SO	ShO	ERA
		27	89	63	.586	11	158	158	**97**	1416	1206	325	**644**	21	2.19
Dick Rudolph	R	28	19	12	.613	3	41	38	27	312	266	38	133	5	2.16
Lefty Tyler	L	26	17	10	.630	1	34	28	21	249	200	58	117	6	2.02
Tom Hughes	R	32	16	3	**.842**	5	40	14	7	161	121	51	97	1	2.35
Pat Ragan	R	27	9	9	.500	0	28	23	14	182	143	47	94	3	2.08
Frank Allen	L	26	8	2	.800	1	19	14	7	113	102	31	63	2	2.07
Art Nehf	L	23	7	5	.583	0	22	12	6	121	110	20	36	1	2.01
Ed Reulbach	R	33	7	6	.538	0	21	11	6	109	99	41	47	0	2.48
Jesse Barnes	R	23	6	14	.300	1	33	18	9	163	154	37	55	3	2.37
1 Elmer Knetzer	R	30	0	2	.000	0	2	0	0	5	11	2	2	0	7.20

Bill James (SJ) 24

NEW YORK 4th 86-66 .566 7 — JOHN McGRAW

NAME	G by POS	B	AGE	G	AB	R	H	2B	3B	HR	RBI	BB	SO	SB	BA	SA
TOTALS			28	155	5152	**597**	1305	188	74	42	**500**	356	558	**206**	.253	.343
1 Fred Merkle	1B112	R	27	112	401	45	95	19	3	7	44	33	46	17	.237	.352
1 Larry Doyle	2B113	L	29	113	441	55	118	24	10	2	47	27	23	17	.268	.381
Art Fletcher	SS133	R	31	133	500	53	143	23	8	3	66	13	36	15	.286	.382
1 Bill McKechnie	3B71	B	29	71	260	22	64	9	1	0	17	7	20	7	.246	.288
Dave Robertson	OF144	L	26	150	587	88	180	18	8	**12**	69	14	56	21	.307	.426
Benny Kauff	OF154	L	26	154	552	71	146	22	15	9	74	68	65	40	.264	.408
George Burns	OF155	R	26	155	**623**	**105**	174	24	8	5	41	63	47	37	.279	.368
Bill Rariden	C119	R	28	120	351	23	78	9	3	1	29	55	32	4	.222	.274
2 Buck Herzog	2B44, 3B27, SS9	R	30	77	280	40	73	10	4	0	25	22	24	19	.261	.325
George Kelly	1B13, OF12, 3B1	R	20	49	76	4	12	2	1	0	3	6	24	1	.158	.211
Hans Lobert	3B20	R	34	48	76	6	17	3	2	0	11	5	8	2	.224	.316
2 Heinie Zimmerman	3B40	R	29	40	151	22	41	4	0	0	**19***	7	10	9	.272	.298
1 Edd Roush	OF15	L	23	39	69	4	13	0	1	0	5	1	4	4	.188	.217
Walter Holke	1B34	B	23	34	111	16	39	4	2	0	13	6	16	10	.351	.423
Brad Kocher	C30	R	28	34	65	1	7	2	0	0	1	2	10	0	.108	.138
2 Lew McCarty	C24	R	27	25	68	6	27	3	4	0	9	7	9	0	.397	.559
1 Herb Hunter	3B6, 1B2	L	20	21	28	3	7	0	0	1	4	0	5	0	.250	.357
2 Mickey Doolan	SS16, 2B2	R	36	18	51	4	12	3	1	1	3	2	4	1	.235	.392
Red Dooin	C15	R	37	15	17	1	2	0	0	0	0	0	3	0	.118	.118

Fred Brainerd 24 R 0-7, 2 Red Killefer 32 R 1-1, Lew Wendell 24 R 0-2, Duke Kelleher 22 0-0, Joe Rodriquez 21 R 0-0, Heinie Stafford 24 R 0-1

NAME	T	AGE	W	L	PCT	SV	G	GS	CG	IP	H	BB	SO	ShO	ERA
		27	86	66	.566	12	155	155	88	1397	1267	310	638	22	2.60
Pol Perritt	R	23	18	11	.621	2	40	28	17	251	243	56	115	5	2.62
Rube Benton	L	29	16	8	.667	2	38	30	15	239	210	58	115	3	2.86
Jeff Tesreau	R	27	14	14	.500	2	40	33	23	268	249	65	113	5	2.92
Ferdie Schupp	L	25	9	3	.750	1	30	11	8	140	79	37	86	4	0.90
2 Slim Sallee	L	31	9	4	.692	0	15	11	7	112	96	10	35	2	1.37
Fred Anderson	R	30	9	13	.409	2	38	27	13	188	206	38	98	2	3.40
George Smith	R	24	3	0	1.000	0	9	1	0	21	14	6	9	0	2.57
Sailor Stroud	R	31	3	2	.600	1	10	4	0	47	47	9	16	0	2.68
1 Christy Mathewson	R	37	3	4	.429	2	12	6	4	66	59	7	16	1	2.32
Hank Ritter	R	22	1	0	1.000	0	3	0	0	5	3	0	3	0	0.00
Rube Schauer	R	25	1	4	.200	0	19	3	1	46	44	16	24	0	2.93
Emilio Palmero	L	21	0	3	.000	0	4	1	0	16	17	8	8	0	7.88

*Zimmerman, also with Chicago, league leader in RB1 with 83

CHICAGO 5th 67-86 .438 26.5 — JOE TINKER

NAME	G by POS	B	AGE	G	AB	R	H	2B	3B	HR	RBI	BB	SO	SB	BA	SA
TOTALS			27	156	5179	520	1237	194	56	**46**	456	399	**662**	133	.239	.325
Vic Saier	1B147	L	25	147	498	60	126	25	3	7	50	79	68	20	.253	.357
2 Otto Knabe	2B42, SS1, 3B1, OF1	R	32	51	145	17	40	8	0	0	7	9	18	3	.276	.331
Chuck Wortman	SS69	R	24	69	234	17	47	4	2	2	16	18	22	4	.201	.261
1 Heinie Zimmerman	3B75, 2B14, SS4	R	29	107	398	54	116	25	5	6	**64***	16	33	15	.291	.425
Max Flack	OF136	L	26	141	465	65	120	14	3	3	20	42	43	24	.258	.320
Cy Williams	OF116	L	28	118	405	55	113	19	9	**12**	66	51	64	6	.279	.459
Les Mann	OF115	R	22	127	415	46	113	13	9	2	29	19	31	11	.272	.361
Jimmy Archer	C65, 3B1	R	33	77	205	11	45	6	2	1	30	12	24	3	.220	.283
R. Zeider	3B55, 2B33, OF7, SS5, 1B2	R	32	98	345	29	81	11	2	1	22	26	26	9	.235	.287
1 Wildfire Schulte	OF65	L	33	72	230	31	68	11	1	5	27	20	35	9	.296	.417
1 Bill Fischer	C56	L	25	65	179	15	35	9	2	1	14	11	8	2	.196	.285
Eddie Mulligan	SS58	R	21	58	189	13	29	3	4	0	9	8	30	1	.153	.212
Joe Kelly	OF46	R	26	54	169	18	43	7	1	2	15	9	16	10	.254	.343
Steve Yerkes	2B41	R	28	44	137	12	36	6	2	1	10	9	7	1	.263	.358
1 Alex McCarthy	2B34, SS3	R	28	37	107	10	26	2	3	0	6	11	7	1	.243	.318
2 Art Wilson	C34	R	30	36	114	5	22	3	1	0	5	6	14	1	.193	.237
Dutch Zwilling	OF10	L	27	35	53	4	6	1	0	1	8	4	6	0	.113	.189
2 Fritz Mollwitz	1B19, OF6	R	26	33	71	1	19	2	0	0	11	7	6	4	.268	.296
1 Mickey Doolan	SS24	R	36	28	70	4	15	2	1	0	5	8	7	0	.214	.271
Rowdy Elliott	C18	R	25	23	55	5	14	3	0	0	3	3	5	1	.255	.309
Charlie Pechous	3B22	R	19	22	69	5	10	1	1	0	4	3	21	1	.145	.188
Earl Smith	OF7	B	25	14	27	2	7	1	1	0	4	2	5	1	.259	.370

2 Larry Doyle 29 L 15-38, Joe Tinker 35 R 1-10, Nick Allen 27 R 1-16, 2 Solly Hofman 33 R 5-16, Merwin Jacobson 22 L 3-13, 2 Charlie Deal 24 R 2-8,
2 Herb Hunter 20 L 0-4, Marty Shay 18 R 2-7, John O'Connor 0-0, Bob O'Farrell 19 R 0-0, Eddie Sicking 19 R 0-1, Count Clemens 29 R 0-15

NAME	T	AGE	W	L	PCT	SV	G	GS	CG	IP	H	BB	SO	ShO	ERA
		30	67	86	.438	13	156	156	72	1417	1265	365	616	17	2.65
Hippo Vaughn	L	28	17	15	.531	1	44	35	21	294	269	67	144	4	2.20
Gene Packard	L	28	10	6	.625	5	37	15	5	155	154	38	36	2	2.79
Jimmy Lavender	R	32	10	14	.417	2	36	25	9	188	163	62	91	4	2.82
Claude Hendrix	R	27	8	16	.333	2	36	24	15	218	193	67	117	3	2.68
Tom Seaton	R	28	6	6	.500	1	31	14	4	121	108	43	45	0	3.27
Mike Prendergast	L	27	6	11	.353	2	35	10	4	152	127	23	56	2	2.31
George McConnell	R	38	4	12	.250	0	28	20	8	171	137	35	82	1	2.58
Scott Perry	R	25	2	1	.667	0	4	3	2	28	30	3	10	1	2.57
Paul Carter	R	22	2	2	.500	0	8	5	2	36	26	17	14	0	2.75
Three Finger Brown	R	39	2	3	.400	0	12	4	2	48	52	9	21	0	3.94
George Pearce	L	28	0	0	.000	0	4	1	0	4	6	1	0	0	2.25

*Zimmerman, also with New York, league leader in RBI with 83

PITTSBURGH 6th 65-89 .422 29

NAME	G by POS	B	AGE	G	AB	R	H	2B	3B	HR	RBI	BB	SO	SB	BA	SA
TOTALS			27	157	5181	484	1246	147	91	20	406	372	618	173	.240	.316
Doc Johnston	1B110	L	28	114	404	33	86	10	10	0	39	20	42	17	.213	.287
Jack Farmer	2B31, OF15, SS4, 3B1	R	23	55	166	10	45	6	4	0	14	7	24	1	.271	.355
Honus Wagner	SS92, 1B24, 2B4	R	42	123	432	45	124	15	9	1	39	34	36	11	.287	.370
Doug Baird	3B80, 2B29, OF16	R	24	128	430	41	93	10	7	1	28	24	49	20	.216	.279
Bill Hinchman	OF124, 1B31	R	33	152	555	64	175	18	16	4	76	54	61	10	.315	.427
Max Carey	OF154	B	26	154	599	90	158	23	11	7	42	59	58	63	.264	.374
2 Wildfire Schulte	OF48	L	33	55	177	12	45	5	3	0	14	17	19	5	.254	.316
Walter Schmidt	C57	R	29	64	184	16	35	1	2	2	15	10	13	3	.190	.250
Joe Schultz	2B24, 3B24, OF6, SS1	R	22	77	204	18	53	8	2	0	22	7	14	6	.260	.319
Dan Costello	OF41	L	24	60	159	11	38	1	3	0	8	6	23	3	.239	.283
1 Art Wilson	C39	R	30	53	128	11	33	5	2	1	12	13	27	4	.258	.352
2 Alex McCarthy	SS39, 2B7, 3B5	R	28	50	146	11	29	3	0	0	3	15	10	3	.199	.219
Ed Barney	OF40	L	26	45	137	16	27	4	0	0	9	23	15	8	.197	.226
Hooks Warner	3B42, 2B1	L	22	44	168	12	40	1	1	2	14	6	19	6	.238	.292
Carson Bigbee	2B23, OF19, 3B1	L	21	43	164	17	41	3	6	0	3	7	14	8	.250	.341
Jim Viox	2B25, 3B11	R	25	43	132	12	33	7	0	1	17	17	11	2	.250	.326
2 Bill Fischer	C35	R	25	42	113	11	29	7	1	1	6	10	3	1	.257	.363
Jimmy Smith	SS27, 3B6	B	21	36	96	4	18	1	1	0	5	6	22	0	.188	.219
George Gibson	C29	R	35	33	84	4	17	2	2	0	4	3	7	0	.202	.274
1 Otto Knabe	2B28	R	32	28	89	4	17	3	1	0	9	6	6	1	.191	.247
Bill Wagner	C15	R	22	19	38	2	9	0	2	0	2	5	8	0	.237	.342
Ray O'Brien	OF14	L	23	16	57	5	12	3	2	0	3	1	14	0	.211	.333

Jesse Altenburg 23 L 6-14, Lee King 23 R 2-18, Frank Symkal 26 R 3-10, 2 Pete Compton 26 L 1-16, Ike McAuley 22 R 2-8, Paddy Siglin 24 R 1-4, Bill Batsch 24 R 0-0, Wilbur Fisher 21 L 0-1, Billy Gleason 21 R 0-2, Newt Halliday 19 R 0-1, Gene Madden 26 L 0-1

NAME	T	AGE	W	L	PCT	SV	G	GS	CG	IP	H	BB	SO	ShO	ERA
		26	65	89	.422	7	157	157	88	1420	1277	443	596	10	2.76
Al Mamaux	R	22	21	15	.583	2	45	38	26	310	264	136	163	1	2.53
Wilbur Cooper	L	24	12	11	.522	2	42	23	16	246	189	74	111	2	1.87
Bob Harmon	R	28	8	11	.421	0	31	17	10	173	175	39	62	2	2.81
Frank Miller	R	30	7	10	.412	1	30	20	10	173	135	49	88	2	2.29
Elmer Jacobs	R	23	6	10	.375	0	34	17	8	153	151	38	46	0	2.94
1 Erv Kantlehner	L	23	5	15	.250	2	34	21	7	165	151	57	49	2	3.16
Burleigh Grimes	R	22	2	3	.400	0	6	5	4	46	40	10	20	0	2.35
Bill Evans	R	23	2	5	.286	0	13	6	3	63	57	16	21	0	3.00
Babe Adams	R	34	2	9	.182	0	16	10	4	72	91	12	22	1	5.75
Paul Carpenter	R	21	0	0	.000	0	5	0	0	8	8	4	5	0	1.13
Carmen Hill	R	20	0	0	.000	0	2	0	0	6	11	5	5	0	9.00
Jack Scott	R	24	0	0	.000	0	1	0	0	5	5	3	4	0	10.80

CINCINNATI 7th (Tie) 60-93 .392 33.5 BUCK HERZOG 34-49 .410 IVY WINGO 1-1 .500 CHRISTY MATHEWSON 25-43 .368

NAME	G by POS	B	AGE	G	AB	R	H	2B	3B	HR	RBI	BB	SO	SB	BA	SA
TOTALS			28	155	5254	505	1336	187	88	14	422	362	573	157	.254	.331
Hal Chase	1B98, OF25, 2B16	R	33	142	542	66	184	29	12	4	82	19	48	22	.339	.459
Baldy Louden	2B108, SS23	R	32	134	439	38	96	16	4	1	32	54	54	12	.219	.280
1 Buck Herzog	SS65, 3B12, OF1	R	30	79	281	30	75	14	2	1	24	21	12	15	.267	.342
Heinie Groh	3B110, 2B33, SS5	R	26	149	553	85	149	24	14	2	28	84	34	13	.269	.374
Tommy Griffith	OF155	L	26	155	595	50	158	28	7	2	61	36	37	16	.266	.346
2 Edd Roush	OF69	L	23	69	272	34	78	7	14	0	15	13	19	15	.287	.415
Greasy Neale	OF133	L	24	138	530	53	139	13	5	0	20	19	79	17	.262	.306
Ivy Wingo	C107	L	25	119	347	30	85	8	11	2	40	25	27	4	.245	.349
Tommy Clarke	C51	R	28	78	177	10	42	10	1	0	17	24	20	8	.237	.305
1 Red Killefer	OF68	R	32	70	234	29	57	9	1	1	18	21	8	7	.244	.303
1 Fritz Mollwitz	1B54	R	26	65	183	12	41	4	4	0	16	5	12	6	.224	.290
Bobby Fisher	SS29, 2B6, OF1	R	29	61	136	9	37	4	3	0	11	8	14	7	.272	.346
Clarence Mitchell	P29, 1B9, OF3	L	25	56	117	11	28	2	1	0	11	4	6	1	.239	.274
Frank Emmer	SS29, OF2, 2B1, 3B1	R	20	42	89	8	13	3	1	0	2	7	27	1	.146	.202
Emil Huhn	C18, 1B14, OF1	R	24	37	94	4	24	3	2	0	3	2	11	0	.255	.330
2 Bill McKechnie	3B35	B	29	37	130	4	36	3	0	0	10	3	12	4	.277	.300
Larry Kopf	SS11	B	25	11	40	2	11	2	0	0	5	1	8	1	.275	.325
Paul Smith	OF10	L	28	10	44	5	10	0	1	0	1	1	8	3	.227	.273

Ken Williams (JJ) 26 L 3-27, Johnny Beall 34 L 7-21, Bill Hobbs 23 R 2-11, Bill Rodgers 28 L 0-4, George Twombly 24 R 0-5

NAME	T	AGE	W	L	PCT	SV	G	GS	CG	IP	H	BB	SO	ShO	ERA
		27	60	93	.392	6	155	155	86	1408	1356	458	569	7	3.10
Fred Toney	R	28	14	17	.452	1	41	38	21	300	247	78	146	3	2.28
Clarence Mitchell	L	25	11	10	.524	0	29	24	17	195	211	45	52	1	3.14
Pete Schneider	R	23	10	19	.345	1	44	31	16	274	259	82	117	3	2.69
Al Schulz	L	27	8	19	.296	2	44	22	10	215	208	93	95	0	3.14
Earl Moseley	R	31	7	10	.412	1	31	15	7	150	145	69	60	0	3.90
2 Elmer Knetzer	R	30	5	12	.294	1	36	16	12	171	161	45	70	0	2.89
Gene Dale (ST)	R	27	3	4	.429	0	17	5	2	70	80	33	23	0	5.14
2 Christy Mathewson	R	37	1	0	1.000	0	1	1	1	9	15	1	3	0	8.00
Limb McKenry	R	27	1	1	.500	0	6	1	0	15	14	8	2	0	4.20
Jim Bluejacket	R	28	0	1	.000	0	3	2	0	7	12	3	1	0	7.71
Twink Twining	R	22	0	0	.000	0	1	0	0	2	4	1	0	0	13.50

ST. LOUIS 7th (Tie) 60-93 .392 33.5 MILLER HUGGINS

NAME	G by POS	B	AGE	G	AB	R	H	2B	3B	HR	RBI	BB	SO	SB	BA	SA
TOTALS			26	153	5030	476	1223	155	74	25	413	335	651	182	.243	.318
Dots Miller	1B93, 2B38, SS21, 3B1	R	29	143	505	47	120	22	7	1	46	40	49	18	.238	.315
Bruno Betzel	2B113, 3B33, OF7	R	21	142	510	49	119	15	11	1	37	39	77	22	.233	.312
Roy Corhan	SS84	R	28	92	295	30	62	6	3	0	18	20	31	15	.210	.251
Rogers Hornsby	3B83, SS45, 1B15, 2B1	R	20	139	495	63	155	17	15	6	65	40	63	17	.313	.444
Tommy Long	OF106	R	26	119	403	37	118	11	10	1	33	10	43	21	.293	.377
Jack Smith	OF120	L	21	130	357	43	87	6	5	6	34	20	50	24	.244	.339
Bob Bescher	OF151	B	32	151	561	78	132	24	8	6	43	60	50	39	.235	.339
Mike Gonzalez	C93, 1B13	R	25	118	331	33	79	15	4	0	29	28	18	5	.239	.308
Frank Snyder	C72, 1B46, SS1	R	23	132	406	23	105	12	4	0	39	18	31	7	.259	.308
Owen Wilson	OF113	L	32	120	355	30	85	8	2	3	32	20	46	4	.239	.299
Art Butler	OF15, 2B8, SS1, 3B1	R	28	86	110	9	23	5	0	0	7	7	12	3	.209	.255
Zinn Beck (KJ)	3B52, 1B1, 2B1	R	30	62	184	8	41	7	1	0	10	14	21	3	.223	.272
Tony Brottem	C15, OF2	R	24	26	33	3	6	1	0	0	4	3	10	1	.182	.212
Miller Huggins	2B7	B	37	18	9	2	3	0	0	0	0	2	3	0	.333	.333
Sammy Bohne	SS14	R	19	14	38	3	9	0	0	0	0	4	6	3	.237	.237
Stuffy Stewart	2B8	R	22	9	17	0	3	0	0	0	1	0	3	0	.176	.176
Walton Cruise	OF2	L	26	3	3	0	2	0	0	0	0	1	0	0	.667	.667

Jack Roche (ST) 25

NAME	T	AGE	W	L	PCT	SV	G	GS	CG	IP	H	BB	SO	ShO	ERA
		27	60	93	.392	15	153	153	58	1355	1331	445	529	11	3.14
Bill Doak	R	25	12	8	.600	0	29	26	11	192	177	55	82	3	2.63
Lee Meadows	R	21	12	23	.343	2	51	36	11	289	261	119	120	1	2.58
Red Ames	R	33	11	16	.407	8	45	22	10	228	225	57	98	2	2.64
Steamboat Williams	R	24	6	7	.462	1	36	8	5	105	121	27	25	0	4.20
1 Slim Sallee	L	31	5	5	.500	1	16	17	4	70	75	23	28	2	3.47
Hi Jasper	R	35	5	6	.455	1	21	11	2	107	97	42	37	0	3.28
Bob Steele	L	22	5	15	.250	0	29	22	7	148	156	42	67	1	3.41
Milt Watson	R	23	4	6	.400	0	18	13	5	103	109	33	27	2	3.06
Joe Lotz	R	25	0	3	.000	0	12	3	1	40	31	17	18	0	4.28
Charley Hall	R	30	0	4	.000	1	10	5	2	43	45	14	15	0	5.44
Murphy Currie	R	22	0	0	.000	0	6	0	0	14	7	9	8	0	1.93
Dan Griner	R	28	0	0	.000	1	4	0	0	11	15	3	3	0	4.09
Cy Warmoth	L	23	0	0	.000	0	3	0	0	5	12	4	1	0	14.40

WORLD SERIES – BOSTON (AL) 4 BROOKLYN (NL) 1

LINE SCORES

TEAM	1	2	3	4	5	6	7	8	9	10 11 12	R	H	E
Game 1 October 7 at Boston													
BKN (NL)	0	0	0	1	0	0	0	0	4		5	10	4
BOS (AL)	0	0	1	0	1	0	3	1	X		6	8	1
Marquard, Pfeffer (8) **Shore**, Mays (9)													
Game 2 October 9 at Boston (14 Innings)													
BKN	1	0	0	0	0	0	0	0	0	0 0 0 0 0	1	6	2
BOS	0	0	1	0	0	0	0	0	0	0 0 0 0 1	2	7	1
Smith **Ruth**													
Game 3 October 10 at Brooklyn													
BOS	0	0	0	0	0	2	1	0	0		3	7	1
BKN	0	0	1	1	2	0	0	0	X		4	10	0
Mays, Foster (6) **Coombs**, Pfeffer (7)													
Game 4 October 11 at Brooklyn													
BOS	0	3	0	1	1	0	1	0	0		6	10	1
BKN	2	0	0	0	0	0	0	0	0		2	5	4
Leonard **Marquard**, Cheney (5), Rucker (8)													
Game 5 October 12 at Boston													
BKN	0	1	0	0	0	0	0	0	0		1	3	3
BOS	0	1	2	0	1	0	0	0	X		4	7	2
Pfeffer, Dell (8) **Shore**													

COMPOSITE BATTING

NAME	POS	G	AB	R	H	2B	3B	HR	RBI	BA
Boston (AL)										
Totals		5	164	21	39	7	6	2	18	.238
Janvrin	2B	5	23	2	5	3	0	0	1	.217
Hooper	OF	5	21	6	7	1	1	0	1	.333
Lewis	OF	5	17	3	6	2	1	0	1	.353
Hoblitzell	1B	5	17	3	4	1	1	0	2	.235
Gardner	3B	5	17	2	3	0	0	2	6	.176
Scott	SS	5	16	1	2	0	1	0	1	.125
Walker	OF	3	11	1	3	0	1	0	1	.273
Shorten	OF	2	7	0	4	0	0	0	2	.571
Thomas	C	3	7	0	1	0	1	0	0	.143
Shore	P	2	7	0	0	0	0	0	0	.000
Ruth	P	1	5	0	0	0	0	0	1	.000
Cady	C	2	4	1	1	0	0	0	0	.250
Carrigan	C	1	3	0	2	0	0	0	1	.667
Walsh	OF	1	3	0	0	0	0	0	0	.000
Leonard	P	1	3	0	0	0	0	0	0	.000
Gainor	PH	1	1	0	1	0	0	0	1	1.000
Mays	P	2	1	0	0	0	0	0	0	.000
Foster	P	1	1	0	0	0	0	0	0	.000
Henriksen	PH	1	0	1	0	0	0	0	0	.000
McNally	PR	1	0	1	0	0	0	0	0	.000
Brooklyn (NL)										
Totals		5	170	13	34	2	5	1	11	.200
Myers	OF	5	22	2	4	0	0	1	3	.182
Wheat	OF	5	19	2	4	0	1	0	1	.211
Cutshaw	2B	5	19	2	2	1	0	0	2	.105
Mowrey	3B	5	17	2	3	0	0	0	1	.176
Daubert	1B	4	17	1	3	0	1	0	0	.176
Olson	SS	5	16	1	4	0	1	0	2	.250
Stengel	OF	4	11	2	4	0	0	0	0	.364
Johnston	OF	3	10	1	3	0	1	0	0	.300
Meyers	C	3	10	0	2	0	1	0	0	.200
Miller	C	2	8	0	1	0	0	0	0	.125
Smith	P	1	5	0	1	1	0	0	0	.200
Pfeffer	P	4	4	0	1	0	0	0	0	.250
Merkle	1B	3	4	0	1	0	0	0	1	.250
Coombs	P	1	3	0	1	0	0	0	1	.333
Marquard	P	2	3	0	0	0	0	0	0	.000
Getz	PH	1	1	0	0	0	0	0	0	.000
O'Mara	PH	1	1	0	0	0	0	0	0	.000
Cheney	P	1	0	0	0	0	0	0	0	.000
Dell	P	1	0	0	0	0	0	0	0	.000
Rucker	P	1	0	0	0	0	0	0	0	.000

COMPOSITE PITCHING

NAME	G	IP	H	BB	SO	W	L	SV	ERA
Boston (AL)									
Totals	5	49	34	14	19	4	1	1	1.47
Shore	2	17.2	12	4	9	2	0	0	1.53
Ruth	1	14	6	3	4	1	0	0	0.64
Leonard	1	9	5	4	3	1	0	0	1.00
Mays	2	5.1	8	3	2	0	1	1	5.06
Foster	1	3	3	0	1	0	0	0	0.00
Brooklyn (NL)									
Totals	5	47.1	39	18	25	1	4	1	3.04
Smith	1	13.1	7	6	2	0	1	0	1.35
Marquard	2	11	12	6	9	0	2	0	6.55
Pfeffer	3	10.2	7	4	5	0	1	1	1.69
Coombs	1	6.1	7	1	1	1	0	0	4.26
Cheney	1	3	4	1	5	0	0	0	3.00
Rucker	1	2	1	0	3	0	0	0	0.00
Dell	1	1	1	0	0	0	0	0	0.00

1917 Little Napoleon Returns to the Front

The genius of John McGraw, who was aptly dubbed "Little Napoleon", lay in his ability to motivate his players. But his rebuilding of the Giants into pennant winners in 1917 underscored his administrative ability. Two years before, the Giants had fallen into the basement, and 1916 had proved to be a year of streaks and slumps. This year, the Gotham club reached the top of the heap to stay, on June 27, and won easily over the second-place Phillies by ten games. McGraw completely revised his infield, using young Walter Holke at first, three-time Giant Buck Herzog at second, and heavy-hitting ex-Cub Heinie Zimmerman at third—to go along with holdover shortstop Art Fletcher. Federal League standout Benny Kauff starred in center field, and right fielder Dave Robertson hit 12 home runs to form, with Zimmerman, the power punch of the team. McGraw needed new starting pitchers and found able arms in lefties, Ferdie Schupp, Slim Sallee, and Rube Benton and righty Pol Perritt.

The Phillies were done in by a mid-season batting slump which affected the entire lineup. Grover "Pete" Alexander had 30 victories for the third time in as many years, and Gavvy Cravath again led the batting attack for the Phils. Johnny Evers was purchased from Boston to fill the keystone slot, but age had taken its toll on the old Cub star and he could manage to hit only .224. Third-place St. Louis had the league's worst pitching, but its second-best hitter in young Rogers Hornsby. Cincinnati also held a batting ace in Edd Roush, another Federal League discovery, who won the batting crown with a .341 mark. In the second division, Brooklyn fell from the pennant the year before into a dismal seventh place finish. The failure of the pitching staff, Jake Daubert's average, and Zack Wheat's inability to contribute the extra base hits he did in 1916 were chiefly responsible for Brooklyn's sudden turnaround. Boston also was expected to contend but was fortunate to barely beat out Brooklyn for sixth place.

The Chicago White Sox capped a three-year rise under manager Pants Rowland by winning the American League title over the Red Sox by nine games. Boston and Chicago kept trading the first and second slots until the White Sox staked a permanent claim on the lead on August 18. Good pitching and hitting made the Chisox the class of the league. Outfielders, Happy Felsch and Joe Jackson, were .300 hitters, and pitcher Eddie Cicotte led the way in wins with 28 and E.R.A. with 1.53. Rookie Swede Risberg came through at shortstop with a good glove that tied together the inner defense, permitting Buck Weaver to play regularly at third base.

The Red Sox entered their title defense under a new manager, Jack Barry, but a record almost identical to their 1916 winning season could only net them a runner-up position. The hitting fell off from recent years, but young pitchers, Babe Ruth and Carl Mays, both logged 20-win seasons.

Ty Cobb returned to the batting throne for the tenth time in 11 seasons after a one-year sabbatical, and his .383 mark easily led young runner-up George Sisler and third-placer Tris Speaker, both of whom hit over .350.

When the World Series dawned on October 6, McGraw found himself in the fall classic for the fifth time. His fortunes had not improved since his first visit to the Series in 1906, when he came out a winner. Ed Cicotte took a close 2-1 opening game win en route to a six-game White Sox Series victory. Red Faber won the other three games for the White Sox by hurling complete victories and winning once in relief. Veteran Eddie Collins led the White Sox in batting, but New York's Dave Robertson paced all hitters with a .500 average for the Series.

Four future Hall of Famers hung up their spikes in 1917. Sam Crawford was reduced to a pinch hitter for Detroit, and he ended a career as one of the early American League's top sluggers. Eddie Plank wound up his 17-year career with 325 victories, all but 21 of which were earned in the American League—the crafty southpaw providing ace pitching on Connie Mack's early pennant winners. Johnny Evers hit a paltry .214 for the Braves and Phillies and that prompted the 35-year-old second baseman to pack it in. Finally, Honus Wagner ended his 21-year career, at age 43, as a part-time first sacker for Pittsburgh—the all-time great shortstop retiring with eight National League batting crowns to his credit.

1917 AMERICAN LEAGUE

NAME	G by POS	B	AGE	G	AB	R	H	2B	3B	HR	RBI	BB	SO	SB	BA	SA
CHICAGO 1st 100-54 .649		PANTS ROWLAND														
TOTALS			26	156	5057	**657**	1281	152	**81**	18	**535**	522	479	**219**	.253	.326
Chick Gandil	1B149	R	29	149	553	53	151	9	7	0	57	30	36	16	.273	.315
Eddie Collins	2B156	L	30	156	564	91	163	18	12	0	67	89	16	53	.289	.363
Swede Risberg	SS146	R	22	149	474	59	96	20	8	1	45	59	65	16	.203	.285
Buck Weaver	3B107, SS10	B	26	118	447	64	127	16	5	3	32	27	29	19	.284	.362
Nemo Leibold	OF122	L	25	125	428	59	101	12	6	0	29	74	34	27	.236	.292
Happy Felsch	OF152	R	25	152	575	75	177	17	10	6	102	33	52	26	.308	.403
Joe Jackson	OF145	L	27	146	538	91	162	20	17	5	75	57	25	13	.301	.429
Ray Schalk	C139	R	24	140	424	48	96	12	5	2	51	59	27	19	.226	.292
Shano Collins	OF73	R	31	82	252	38	59	13	3	1	14	10	27	14	.234	.321
Fred McMullin	3B52, SS2	R	25	59	194	35	46	2	1	0	12	27	17	9	.237	.258
Eddie Murphy	OF9	L	25	53	51	9	16	2	1	0	16	5	1	4	.314	.392
Byrd Lynn	C29	R	28	35	72	7	16	2	0	0	5	7	11	1	.222	.250
Ted Jourdan	1B14	L	21	17	34	2	5	0	1	0	2	1	3	0	.147	.206
Joe Jenkins		R	26	10	9	0	1	0	0	0	2	0	5	0	.111	.111
Ziggy Hasbrouck	2B1	R	23	2	1	1	0	0	0	0	0	0	0	0	.000	.000
Zeb Terry	SS1	R	26	2	1	0	0	0	0	0	0	2	0	0	.000	.000
2 Bobby Byrne	2B1	R	32	1	1	0	0	0	0	0	0	0	0	0	.000	.000
Jack Fournier		L	24	1	1	0	0	0	0	0	0	0	1	0	.000	.000
BOSTON 2nd 90-62 .592 9		JACK BARRY														
TOTALS			29	157	5048	556	1243	198	64	14	476	466	473	105	.246	.319
Dick Hoblitzell	1B118	L	28	120	420	49	108	19	7	1	47	46	22	12	.257	.343
Jack Barry	2B116	R	30	116	388	45	83	9	0	2	30	47	27	12	.214	.253
Everett Scott	SS157	R	24	157	528	40	127	24	7	0	50	20	46	12	.241	.313
Larry Gardner	3B146	L	31	146	501	53	133	23	7	1	61	54	37	16	.265	.345
Harry Hooper	OF151	L	29	151	559	89	143	21	11	3	45	80	40	21	.256	.349
Tilly Walker	OF96	R	28	106	337	41	83	18	7	2	37	25	38	6	.246	.359
Duffy Lewis	OF150	R	28	150	553	55	167	29	9	1	65	29	54	8	.302	.392
Sam Agnew	C85	R	30	85	260	17	54	6	2	0	16	19	30	2	.208	.246
Pinch Thomas	C77	L	29	83	202	24	48	7	0	0	24	27	9	2	.238	.272
Chick Shorten	OF43	L	25	69	168	12	30	4	2	0	16	10	10	2	.179	.226
Jimmy Walsh	OF47	L	31	57	185	25	49	6	3	0	12	25	14	6	.265	.330
Hal Janvrin	2B38, SS10, 1B1	R	24	55	127	21	25	3	0	0	8	11	13	2	.197	.220
Del Gainer	1B50	R	30	52	172	28	53	10	2	2	19	15	21	1	.308	.424
Babe Ruth	P41	L	22	52	123	14	40	6	3	2	12	12	18	0	.325	.472
Mike McNally	3B14, SS9, 2B6	R	23	42	50	9	15	1	0	0	2	6	3	3	.300	.320
Hick Cady	C14	R	31	17	46	4	7	1	1	0	2	1	6	0	.152	.217
Olap Henriksen		L	29	15	12	1	1	0	0	0	1	3	4	0	.083	.083
Jimmy Cooney	2B10, SS1	R	22	11	36	4	8	1	0	0	3	6	2	0	.222	.250
Wally Mayer	C4	R	27	4	12	2	2	0	0	0	0	5	2	0	.167	.167
CLEVELAND 3rd 88-66 .571 12		LEE FOHL														
TOTALS			25	156	4994	584	1224	**218**	64	13	475	**549**	**596**	210	.245	.322
Joe Harris	1B95, OF5, 3B1	R	26	112	369	40	112	22	4	0	65	55	32	11	.304	.385
Bill Wambsganss	2B138, 1B2	R	23	141	499	52	127	17	6	0	43	37	42	16	.255	.313
Ray Chapman	SS156	R	26	156	563	98	170	28	13	2	36	61	65	52	.302	.409
Joe Evans	3B127	R	22	132	385	36	73	4	5	2	33	42	44	12	.190	.242
Braggo Roth	OF135	R	24	145	495	69	141	30	9	1	72	52	**73**	51	.285	.388
Tris Speaker	OF142	L	29	142	523	90	184	42	11	2	60	67	14	30	.352	.486
Jack Graney	OF145	L	31	146	535	87	122	29	7	3	35	**94**	49	16	.228	.325
Steve O'Neill	C127	R	25	129	370	21	68	10	2	0	29	41	55	2	.184	.222
Lou Guisto	1B59	R	23	73	200	9	37	4	2	0	29	25	18	3	.185	.225
Terry Turner	3B40, 2B23, SS1	R	26	69	180	16	37	7	0	0	15	14	19	4	.206	.244
Josh Billings	C48	R	25	66	129	8	23	3	2	0	9	8	21	2	.178	.233
2 Elmer Smith	OF40	L	24	64	161	21	42	5	1	3	22	13	18	6	.261	.360
Milo Allison	OF11	R	26	32	35	4	5	0	0	0	0	9	7	3	.143	.143
Ivon Howard	3B6, 2B4, OF4	B	34	27	39	7	4	0	0	0	0	3	5	1	.103	.103
Hank DeBerry	C9	R	22	25	33	3	9	2	0	0	1	2	7	0	.273	.333
1 Ray Miller	1B4	L	29	19	21	1	4	1	0	0	2	8	3	0	.190	.238
Marty Kavanagh	OF2	R	26	14	14	1	0	0	0	0	0	3	2	0	.000	.000
Ferd Eunick	3B1	R	25	1	2	0	0	0	0	0	0	0	0	0	.000	.000

NAME	T	AGE	W	L	PCT	SV	G	GS	CG	IP	H	BB	SO	ShO	ERA
		28	**100**	54	**.649**	**23**	156	156	79	**1424**	1236	413	517	**21**	**2.16**
Eddie Cicotte	R	33	**28**	12	.700	4	49	35	29	**347**	246	70	150	7	**1.53**
Lefty Williams	L	24	17	8	.680	1	45	29	8	230	221	81	85	1	2.97
Red Faber	R	28	16	13	.552	3	41	29	17	248	224	85	84	3	1.92
Reb Russell	L	28	15	5	**.750**	4	35	24	11	189	170	32	54	5	1.95
Dave Danforth	L	27	11	6	.647	**11**	**50**	9	1	173	155	74	79	1	2.65
Joe Benz	R	31	7	3	.700	0	19	13	7	95	76	23	25	2	2.46
Jim Scott (MS)	R	28	6	7	.462	0	24	17	6	125	126	42	37	2	1.87
Mellie Wolfgang (JJ)	R	27	0	0	.000	0	5	0	0	18	18	6	3	0	5.00
		26	90	62	.592	6	157	157	**115**	1421	1197	413	509	15	2.20
Babe Ruth	L	22	24	13	.649	2	41	38	**35**	326	244	108	128	6	2.02
Carl Mays	R	25	22	9	.710	0	35	33	27	289	230	74	91	2	1.74
Dutch Leonard	L	25	16	17	.485	1	37	36	26	294	257	72	144	4	2.17
Ernie Shore	R	26	13	10	.565	1	29	27	14	227	201	55	57	1	2.22
Rube Foster (AJ)	R	29	8	7	.533	0	17	16	9	125	108	53	34	1	2.52
Herb Pennock	L	23	5	5	.500	1	24	5	4	101	90	23	35	1	3.30
Lore Bader (BJ)	R	29	2	0	1.000	0	15	1	0	38	48	18	14	0	2.37
Sad Sam Jones	R	24	0	1	.000	1	9	1	0	16	15	6	5	0	4.50
Weldon Wyckoff	R	25	0	0	.000	0	1	0	0	5	4	4	1	0	1.80
		27	88	66	.571	20	156	156	74	1413	1270	438	451	19	2.52
Jim Bagby	R	27	23	13	.639	6	49	37	26	321	**277**	73	83	7	1.96
Stan Coveleski	R	28	19	14	.576	4	45	36	25	298	202	94	133	**9**	1.81
Ed Klepfer	R	29	14	4	.778	1	41	27	9	213	208	55	66	1	2.37
Guy Morton	R	24	10	10	.500	2	35	18	6	161	158	59	62	1	2.74
Fritz Coumbe	L	27	8	6	.571	4	34	10	4	134	119	35	30	1	2.15
Otis Lambeth	R	27	7	6	.538	2	26	10	2	97	97	30	27	0	3.15
Al Gould	R	24	4	4	.500	0	27	7	1	94	95	52	24	0	3.64
Red Torkelson	R	23	2	1	.667	0	4	3	0	22	33	13	10	0	7.77
Joe Boehling	L	26	1	6	.143	0	12	7	1	46	50	16	11	0	4.70
Pop Boy Smith	R	25	0	1	.000	0	6	0	0	9	14	4	3	0	8.00
Smokey Joe Wood (SA)	R	27	0	1	.000	1	5	1	0	16	17	7	2	0	3.38
George Dickerson	R	24	0	0	.000	0	1	0	0	1	0	0	0	0	0.00

DETROIT 4th 78-75 .510 21.5 — **HUGHIE JENNINGS**

NAME	G by POS	B	AGE	G	AB	R	H	2B	3B	HR	RBI	BB	SO	SB	BA	SA
TOTALS			28	154	5093	639	**1317**	204	76	26	**535**	483	476	163	**.259**	**.344**
George Burns	1B104	R	24	119	407	42	92	14	10	1	40	15	33	3	.226	.317
Ralph Young	2B141	B	27	141	503	64	116	18	2	1	35	61	35	8	.231	.280
Donie Bush	SS147	B	29	147	581	**112**	163	18	3	0	24	80	40	34	.281	.322
Ossie Vitt	3B140	R	27	140	512	65	130	13	6	0	47	56	15	18	.254	.303
Harry Heilmann	OF123, 1B27	R	22	150	556	57	156	22	11	5	86	41	54	11	.281	.387
Ty Cobb	OF152	L	30	152	**588**	107	**225**	**44**	**23**	7	102	61	34	**55**	**.383**	**.571**
Bobby Veach	OF154	L	29	154	571	79	182	31	12	8	**103**	61	44	21	.319	.457
Oscar Stanage	C95	R	34	99	297	19	61	14	1	0	30	20	35	3	.205	.259
Tubby Spencer	C62	R	33	70	192	13	46	8	3	0	22	15	15	0	.240	.313
Sam Crawford	1B15, OF3	L	37	61	104	6	18	4	0	2	12	4	6	0	.173	.269
George Harper	OF31	L	25	47	117	6	24	3	0	0	12	11	15	2	.205	.231
Bob Jones	2B18, 3B8	L	27	46	77	16	12	1	2	0	2	4	8	3	.156	.221
Ben Dyer	SS14, 3B8	R	24	30	67	6	14	5	0	0	0	2	17	3	.209	.284
Archie Yelle	C24	R	25	25	51	4	7	1	0	0	0	5	4	2	.137	.157
Fred Nicholson	OF3	R	22	13	14	4	4	1	0	0	1	1	2	0	.286	.357
Bert Ellison	1B9	R	21	9	29	2	5	1	2	1	4	6	3	0	.172	.448
Ira Flagstead	OF2	R	23	4	4	0	0	0	0	0	0	0	1	0	.000	.000
2 Tony DeFate	2B1	R	22	3	2	1	0	0	0	0	0	0	1	0	.173	.269
Frank Walker		R	22	2	2	0	0	0	0	0	0	0	1	0	.000	.000

NAME	T	AGE	W	L	PCT	SV	G	GS	CG	IP	H	BB	SO	ShO	ERA
		26	78	75	.510	15	154	154	78	1396	1209	504	516	20	2.56
Hooks Dauss	R	27	17	14	.548	2	37	31	22	271	243	87	102	6	2.42
Bernie Boland	R	25	16	11	.593	6	43	28	13	238	192	95	89	3	2.68
Bill James	R	30	13	10	.565	1	34	23	10	198	163	96	62	2	2.09
Willie Mitchell	L	27	12	8	.600	0	30	22	12	185	172	46	80	5	2.19
Howard Ehmke	R	23	10	15	.400	2	35	25	13	206	174	88	90	4	2.97
Deacon Jones	R	23	4	4	.500	0	24	6	2	77	69	26	28	0	2.92
Harry Coveleski	L	31	4	6	.400	0	16	11	2	69	70	14	15	0	2.61
George Cunningham	R	22	2	7	.222	4	44	8	4	139	113	51	49	0	2.91
Johnny Couch	R	26	0	0	.000	0	3	0	0	13	13	1	1	0	2.77

WASHINGTON 5th 74-79 .484 25.5 — **CLARK GRIFFITH**

NAME	G by POS	B	AGE	G	AB	R	H	2B	3B	HR	RBI	BB	SO	SB	BA	SA
TOTALS			26	157	**5142**	543	1238	173	70	4	462	500	574	166	.241	.304
Joe Judge	1B100	L	23	102	393	62	112	15	15	2	30	50	40	17	.285	.415
Ray Morgan	2B95, 3B3	R	28	101	338	32	90	9	1	1	33	40	29	7	.266	.308
Howard Shanks	SS90, OF26, 1B2	R	26	126	430	45	87	15	5	0	28	33	37	15	.202	.260
Eddie Foster	3B86, 2B57	R	30	143	554	66	130	16	8	0	43	46	23	11	.235	.292
Sam Rice	OF155	L	27	155	586	77	177	25	7	0	69	50	41	35	.302	.369
Clyde Milan	OF153	L	31	155	579	60	170	15	4	0	48	58	26	20	.294	.333
Mike Menosky	OF94	L	22	114	322	46	83	12	10	1	34	45	55	22	.258	.366
Eddie Ainsmith	C119	R	25	125	350	38	67	17	4	0	42	40	48	16	.191	.263
Joe Leonard	3B67, 1B20, SS1, OF1	L	22	99	297	30	57	6	7	0	23	45	40	6	.192	.259
Patsy Gharrity	1B46, C5, OF1	R	25	76	176	15	50	5	0	0	18	14	18	7	.284	.313
John Henry	C59	R	27	65	163	10	31	6	0	0	18	24	16	1	.190	.227
George McBride	SS41, 3B6, 2B2	R	36	50	141	6	27	3	0	0	9	10	17	1	.191	.213
1 Elmer Smith	OF29	L	24	35	117	8	26	4	3	0	17	5	14	1	.222	.308
Sam Crane	SS32	R	22	32	95	6	17	2	0	0	4	4	14	0	.179	.200
Horace Milan	OF23	R	23	31	73	8	21	3	1	0	9	4	9	4	.288	.356
Charlie Jamieson	OF9, P1	L	24	20	35	4	6	2	0	0	2	6	5	0	.171	.229
Bill Murray	2B6, SS1	R	23	8	21	2	3	0	1	0	4	2	2	1	.143	.238

NAME	T	AGE	W	L	PCT	SV	G	GS	CG	IP	H	BB	SO	ShO	ERA
		25	74	79	.484	7	157	157	84	1415	1228	536	**637**	20	2.77
Walter Johnson	R	29	23	16	.590	1	47	34	30	328	259	67	**188**	8	2.30
Jim Shaw	R	23	15	14	.517	1	47	31	15	266	233	**123**	118	2	3.21
Doc Ayres	R	27	11	10	.524	1	40	15	12	208	192	59	78	3	2.16
Harry Harper	L	22	11	12	.478	0	31	31	10	179	145	106	99	4	3.02
Bert Gallia	R	25	9	13	.409	1	42	23	9	208	191	93	84	1	2.99
George Dumont	R	21	5	14	.263	1	37	23	8	205	171	76	65	2	2.55
Molly Craft	R	21	0	0	.000	1	8	0	0	14	17	8	2	0	3.86
Doc Waldbauer	R	25	0	0	.000	1	2	0	0	5	10	2	2	0	7.20
1 Charlie Jamieson	L	24	0	0	.000	0	1	0	0	2	10	2	1	0	45.00

NEW YORK 6th 71-82 .464 28.5 — **WILD BILL DONOVAN**

NAME	G by POS	B	AGE	G	AB	R	H	2B	3B	HR	RBI	BB	SO	SB	BA	SA
TOTALS			25	155	5136	524	1226	172	52	**27**	445	496	535	136	.239	.308
Wally Pipp	1B155	L	24	155	587	82	143	29	12	**9**	70	60	66	11	.244	.380
Fritz Maisel	2B100, 3B7	R	27	113	404	46	80	4	4	0	20	36	18	29	.198	.228
Roger Peckinpaugh	SS148	R	26	148	543	63	141	24	7	0	41	64	46	17	.260	.330
Frank Baker	3B146	L	31	146	553	57	156	24	2	6	71	48	27	18	.282	.365
Elmer Miller	OF112	R	26	114	379	43	95	11	3	3	35	40	44	11	.251	.319
Tim Hendryx	OF107	R	26	125	393	43	98	14	7	5	44	62	45	6	.249	.359
Hugh High	OF100	L	29	103	365	37	86	11	6	1	19	48	31	8	.236	.307
Les Nunamaker	C91	R	28	104	310	22	81	9	2	0	33	21	25	5	.261	.303
Ray Caldwell	P32, OF8	L	29	63	124	12	32	6	1	2	12	16	16	2	.258	.371
Roxy Walters	C57	R	24	61	171	16	45	2	0	0	14	9	22	2	.263	.275
Frank Gilhooley (AJ-BC)	OF46	L	25	54	165	14	40	6	1	0	8	30	13	6	.242	.291
1 Lee Magee	OF50	B	28	51	173	17	38	4	1	0	8	13	18	3	.220	.254
Paddy Baumann	2B18, OF7, 3B1	R	31	49	110	10	24	2	1	0	8	4	9	2	.218	.255
Joe Gedeon	2B31	R	23	33	117	15	28	7	0	0	8	7	13	4	.239	.299
2 Armando Marsans(BL)	OF25	R	30	25	88	10	20	4	0	0	15	8	3	6	.227	.273
Walt Alexander (RJ)	C20	R	26	20	51	1	7	2	1	0	4	4	11	1	.137	.216
Angel Aragon	OF6, 3B4, SS2	R	23	14	45	2	3	1	0	0	2	2	2	0	.067	.089
Chick Fewster	2B11	R	21	11	36	2	8	0	0	0	1	5	5	1	.222	.222
Bill Lamar	OF11	L	20	11	41	2	10	0	0	0	3	0	2	1	.244	.244
Sammy Vick	OF10	R	22	10	36	4	10	3	0	0	2	1	6	2	.278	.361
Aaron Ward	SS7	R	20	8	26	0	3	0	0	0	1	1	5	0	.115	.115

Muddy Ruel 21 R 2-17, Howie Camp 24 L 6-21, Rube Oldring (VR) 33

NAME	T	AGE	W	L	PCT	SV	G	GS	CG	IP	H	BB	SO	ShO	ERA
		27	71	82	.464	7	155	155	87	1411	1280	427	571	9	2.66
Bob Shawkey	R	26	13	15	.464	1	32	26	16	236	207	72	97	1	2.44
Ray Caldwell	R	29	13	16	.448	1	32	29	21	236	199	76	102	1	2.86
George Mogridge	L	28	9	11	.450	0	29	25	15	196	185	39	46	1	2.98
Urban Shocker	R	26	8	5	.615	1	26	13	7	145	124	46	68	0	2.61
Ray Fisher	R	29	8	9	.471	0	23	18	12	144	126	43	64	3	2.19
Allen Russell	R	23	7	8	.467	2	25	10	6	104	89	39	55	0	2.25
Slim Love	L	26	6	5	.545	1	33	9	2	130	115	57	82	0	2.35
Nick Cullop	L	29	5	9	.357	0	30	18	5	146	161	31	27	2	3.33
Ed Monroe	R	24	1	0	1.000	1	9	1	1	29	35	6	12	0	3.41
Neal Brady	R	20	1	0	1.000	0	2	1	0	9	6	5	4	0	2.00
Bob McGraw	R	22	0	1	.000	0	2	2	1	11	9	3	3	0	0.82
John Enright	R	21	0	1	.000	0	1	1	0	5	5	3	1	0	5.40
Bill Piercy	R	21	0	1	.000	0	1	1	1	9	9	2	4	0	3.00
Hank Thormahlen	L	20	0	1	.000	0	1	1	0	8	9	4	5	0	2.25
Walt Smallwood	R	24	0	0	.000	0	2	0	0	2	1	1	1	0	0.00

ST. LOUIS 7th 57-97 .370 43 — **FIELDER JONES**

NAME	G by POS	B	AGE	G	AB	R	H	2B	3B	HR	RBI	BB	SO	SB	BA	SA
TOTALS			28	155	5090	511	1249	183	63	15	425	405	540	157	.245	.315
George Sisler	1B133, 2B2	L	24	135	539	60	190	30	9	2	52	30	19	37	.353	.453
Del Pratt	1B119, 1B4	R	29	123	450	40	111	22	8	1	53	33	36	18	.247	.338
Doc Lavan (AJ)	SS110, 2B7	R	26	118	355	19	85	8	5	0	30	19	34	5	.239	.290
Jimmy Austin	3B121, SS6	B	37	125	455	61	109	18	8	0	19	50	46	13	.240	.314
Tod Sloan	OF77	L	26	109	313	32	72	6	2	2	25	28	34	8	.230	.281
Baby Doll Jacobson	OF131, 1B11	R	26	148	529	53	131	23	7	4	55	31	67	10	.248	.340
Burt Shotton	OF107	L	32	118	398	47	89	9	1	1	20	62	47	16	.224	.259
Hank Severeid	C139, 1B1	R	26	143	501	45	133	23	4	1	57	28	20	6	.265	.333
Ernie Johnson	SS39, 2B18, 3B14	L	29	80	199	28	49	6	2	2	20	12	16	13	.246	.327
Bill Rumler	OF9	R	26	78	88	7	23	3	4	1	16	8	9	2	.261	.420
1 Armando Marsans	OF67, 3B5, 2B1	R	30	75	257	31	59	12	0	0	20	20	6	11	.230	.276
Earl Smith	OF51	B	26	52	199	31	56	7	7	0	10	15	21	5	.281	.387
Ward Miller	OF25	L	32	43	82	13	17	1	1	1	2	16	15	7	.207	.280
George Hale	C28	R	22	38	61	4	12	2	1	0	8	10	12	0	.197	.262
2 Lee Magee	3B20, 2B6, 1B5, OF1	B	28	36	112	11	19	1	0	0	4	6	6	3	.170	.179
Grover Hartley (JT)	C4, SS1, 3B1	R	28	19	13	2	3	0	0	0	0	2	1	0	.231	.231
Ray Demmitt	OF14	L	33	14	53	6	15	1	2	0	7	0	8	1	.283	.377
Wally Gerber	SS12, 2B2	R	25	14	39	2	12	1	1	0	2	3	2	1	.308	.385
1 Gene Paulette	1B5, 2B3, 3B1	R	25	12	22	3	4	0	0	0	0	3	3	0	.182	.182
Duke Kenworthy	2B4	B	30	5	10	1	1	0	0	0	1	1	1	1	.100	.100

Scrappy More 24 R 1-8, Ed Murray 22 R 0-1, Ott Neu 22 R 0-0, Tom Richardson 23 R 0-1

NAME	T	AGE	W	L	PCT	SV	G	GS	CG	IP	H	BB	SO	ShO	ERA
		27	57	97	.370	12	155	155	65	1385	**1320**	537	429	12	3.20
Dave Davenport	R	27	17	17	.500	2	47	**39**	19	281	273	105	100	2	3.07
Allan Sothoron	R	24	14	**19**	.424	4	48	33	17	277	259	96	85	3	2.83
Bob Groom	R	32	8	**19**	.296	3	38	28	11	233	193	95	82	4	2.94
Ernie Koob	L	24	6	14	.300	1	39	18	3	134	139	57	47	1	3.90
Eddie Plank	L	41	5	6	.455	1	20	13	8	131	105	38	26	1	1.79
Tom Rogers	R	25	3	6	.333	0	24	8	3	109	112	44	27	0	3.88
Grover Lowdermilk	R	32	2	1	.667	0	3	2	2	19	16	4	9	1	1.42
Jim Park	R	24	1	1	.500	0	13	0	0	20	27	12	9	0	6.75
Carl Weilman (IL)	L	27	1	2	.333	0	5	3	0	19	19	6	9	0	1.89
Speed Martin	R	23	0	3	.000	0	9	2	0	16	20	5	5	0	5.63
Earl Hamilton	L	25	0	9	.000	1	27	8	2	83	86	41	19	0	3.14
Rasty Wright	R	21	0	0	.000	0	16	1	0	40	48	10	5	0	5.40
Vince Molyneaux (JT)	R	28	0	0	.000	0	7	0	0	22	18	20	4	0	4.91
Tim McCabe (IL)	R	22	0	0	.000	0	1	0	0	2	4	4	2	0	27.00
Kewpie Pennington	R	20	0	0	.000	0	1	0	0	1	1	0	0	0	0.00

PHILADELPHIA 8th 55-98 .359 44.5 — **CONNIE MACK**

NAME	G by POS	B	AGE	G	AB	R	H	2B	3B	HR	RBI	BB	SO	SB	BA	SA
TOTALS			26	154	5111	527	1296	177	62	17	457	435	519	112	.254	.322
Stuffy McInnis	1B150	R	26	150	567	50	172	19	4	0	44	33	19	18	.303	.351
Roy Grover	2B139	R	25	141	482	45	108	15	7	0	34	43	53	12	.224	.284
Whitey Witt	SS111, OF7, 3B6	L	21	128	452	62	114	13	4	0	28	65	45	12	.252	.299
Ray Bates	3B124	R	27	127	485	47	115	20	7	2	66	21	39	12	.237	.320
2 Charlie Jamieson	OF83	L	24	85	345	41	92	6	2	0	27	37	36	8	.267	.296
Amos Strunk	OF146	L	28	148	540	83	152	26	7	1	45	68	37	16	.281	.361
Ping Bodie	OF145, 1B1	R	29	148	557	50	162	28	11	7	74	53	40	13	.291	.418
Wally Schang	C79, 3B12, OF7	B	27	118	316	41	90	14	9	3	36	29	24	6	.285	.415
Billy Meyer	C55	R	25	62	162	9	38	5	1	0	9	7	14	0	.235	.278
Bill Johnson	OF30	L	24	48	109	7	19	2	2	1	8	8	14	4	.174	.257
Joe Dugan	SS39, 2B2	R	20	43	134	9	26	8	0	0	16	3	16	0	.194	.254
Pat Haley	C34	R	26	41	98	7	27	2	1	0	11	4	12	2	.276	.316
Otis Lawry	2B17, OF1	L	23	30	55	7	9	1	0	0	1	2	9	1	.164	.182
Buck Thrasher	OF22	L	27	23	77	5	18	2	1	0	2	3	12	0	.234	.286
Pug Griffin	1B3	R	21	18	25	4	5	1	0	1	3	1	9	1	.200	.360
Lee Gooch	OF16	R	27	17	59	4	17	2	0	1	8	4	10	0	.288	.373
Eddie Palmer	3B13, SS1	R	24	16	52	7	11	1	0	0	5	7	7	1	.212	.231
Ralph Sharman	OF10	R	22	13	37	2	11	2	1	0	2	3	2	1	.297	.405
Red Shannon	SS10	B	20	11	35	8	10	0	0	0	7	6	9	2	.286	.286
Wickey McAvoy	C8	R	22	10	24	1	6	1	0	1	4	0	3	0	.250	.417
Cy Perkins	C6	R	21	6	18	1	3	0	0	0	2	2	1	0	.167	.167

Gene Bailey 23 R 1-12, Pat French 23 R 0-2, Windy Bradshaw 21 L 0-4, Val Picinich 20 R 2-6, Harry Davis 43 R 0-1

NAME	T	AGE	W	L	PCT	SV	G	GS	CG	IP	H	BB	SO	ShO	ERA
		26	55	**98**	.359	6	154	154	80	1366	1310	**562**	516	8	3.27
Bullet Joe Bush	R	24	11	17	.393	1	37	31	17	233	207	111	121	4	2.47
Win Noyes	R	28	10	10	.500	1	27	22	11	171	156	77	64	1	2.95
Jing Johnson	R	22	9	12	.429	0	34	23	13	191	184	56	55	0	2.78
Elmer Myers	R	23	9	16	.360	3	38	23	13	202	221	79	88	2	4.41
Rube Schauer	R	26	7	16	.304	0	33	21	10	215	209	69	62	0	3.14
Socks Seibold	R	21	4	16	.200	1	33	15	9	160	141	85	55	1	3.94
Rollie Naylor	R	25	2	2	.500	0	5	5	3	33	30	11	11	0	1.64
Cy Falkenberg	R	37	2	6	.250	0	15	8	4	81	86	26	35	0	3.33
Dave Keefe	R	20	1	0	1.000	0	3	0	0	5	5	4	1	0	1.80
Rube Parnham	R	23	0	1	.000	0	2	2	0	11	12	9	4	0	4.09
Walt Johnson	R	24	0	2	.000	0	4	2	0	14	15	5	8	0	7.07
Walter Anderson	L	19	0	0	.000	0	14	2	0	39	32	21	10	0	3.00
Jack Nabors	R	29	0	0	.000	0	2	0	0	3	2	1	2	0	3.00
Eddie Bacon		22	0	0	.000	0	1	0	0	6	5	7	0	0	6.00
Red Hill	L	23	0	0	.000	0	1	0	0	3	5	1	0	0	6.00

NEW YORK 1st 98-56 .636 — JOHN McGRAW

NAME	G by POS	B	AGE	G	AB	R	H	2B	3B	HR	RBI	BB	SO	SB	BA	SA
TOTALS			28	158	5211	635	1360	170	71	39	537	373	533	162	.261	.343
Walter Holke	1B153	B	24	153	527	55	146	12	7	2	55	34	54	13	.277	.338
Buck Herzog	2B113	R	31	114	417	69	98	10	8	2	31	31	36	12	.235	.312
Art Fletcher	SS151	R	32	151	557	70	145	24	5	4	56	23	28	12	.260	.343
Heinie Zimmerman	3B149, 2B5	R	30	150	585	61	174	22	9	5	102	16	43	13	.297	.391
Dave Robertson	OF140	L	27	142	532	64	138	16	9	12	54	10	47	17	.259	.391
Benny Kauff	OF153	L	27	153	559	89	172	22	4	5	68	59	54	30	.308	.388
George Burns	OF152	R	27	152	597	103	180	25	13	5	45	75	55	40	.302	.412
Bill Rariden	C100	R	29	101	266	20	72	10	1	0	25	42	17	3	.271	.316
Lew McCarty	C54	R	28	56	162	15	40	3	2	2	19	14	6	1	.247	.327
Hans Lobert	3B21	R	35	50	52	4	10	1	0	1	5	5	5	2	.192	.269
Jimmy Smith	2B29, SS7	B	22	36	96	12	22	5	1	0	2	9	18	6	.229	.302
George Gibson	C35	R	36	35	82	1	14	3	0	0	5	7	2	1	.171	.207
Joe Wilhoit	OF11	L	25	34	50	9	17	2	2	0	8	8	5	0	.340	.460
1 Pete Kilduff	2B21, SS5, 3B1	R	24	31	78	12	16	3	0	1	12	4	11	2	.205	.282
2 Jim Thorpe	OF18	R	29	26	57	12	11	3	2	0	4	8	10	1	.193	.316
Red Murray	OF11, C1	R	33	22	22	1	1	1	0	0	3	4	3	0	.045	.091
Al Baird	2B7, SS3	R	22	10	24	1	7	0	0	0	4	2	2	2	.292	.292
Jack Onslow	C9	R	28	9	8	1	2	1	0	0	0	0	1	0	.250	.375
1 Ernie Krueger	C6	R	26	8	10	0	0	0	0	0	0	0	4	0	.000	.000
Ed Hemingway	3B7	B	24	7	25	3	8	1	1	0	1	2	1	2	.320	.440
Joe Rodriguez	1B7	R	22	7	20	2	4	0	1	0	2	2	1	2	.200	.300
Ross Youngs	OF7	B	20	7	26	5	9	2	3	0	1	1	5	1	.346	.654

NAME	T	AGE	W	L	PCT	SV	G	GS	CG	IP	H	BB	SO	ShO	ERA
		29	98	56	.631	14	158	158	92	1427	1221	327	551	17	2.27
Ferdie Schupp	L	26	21	7	.750	0	36	32	25	272	202	70	147	6	1.95
Slim Sallee	L	32	18	7	.720	4	34	24	18	216	199	34	54	1	2.17
Pol Perritt	R	24	17	7	.708	1	35	26	14	215	186	45	72	5	1.88
Rube Benton	L	30	15	9	.625	3	35	25	14	215	190	41	70	3	2.72
Jeff Tesreau	R	28	13	8	.619	2	33	20	11	184	168	58	85	1	3.08
Fred Anderson	R	31	8	8	.500	3	38	18	8	162	122	34	69	1	1.44
2 Al Demaree	R	30	4	5	.444	0	15	11	1	78	70	17	23	0	2.65
1 George Kelly	R	21	1	0	1.000	0	1	0	0	5	4	1	2	0	0.00
Jim Middleton	R	28	1	1	.500	1	13	0	0	36	35	8	9	0	2.75
Ad Swigler	R	21	0	1	.000	0	1	1	0	6	7	8	4	0	6.00
George Smith	R	25	0	3	.000	0	14	1	1	38	38	11	16	0	2.84

PHILADELPHIA 2nd 87-65 .572 10 — PAT MORAN

NAME	G by POS	B	AGE	G	AB	R	H	2B	3B	HR	RBI	BB	SO	SB	BA	SA
TOTALS			31	154	5084	578	1262	225	60	38	526	435	533	109	.248	.339
Fred Luderus	1B154	L	31	154	522	57	136	24	4	5	72	65	35	5	.261	.351
Bert Niehoff	2B96, 1B7, 3B6	R	33	114	361	30	92	17	4	2	42	23	29	8	.255	.341
Dave Bancroft	SS120, 2B3, OF2	B	26	127	478	56	116	22	5	4	43	44	42	14	.243	.335
Milt Stock	3B133, SS19	R	23	150	564	76	149	27	6	3	53	51	34	25	.264	.349
Gavvy Cravath	OF139	R	36	140	503	70	141	29	16	12	83	70	57	6	.280	.473
Dode Paskert	OF138	R	35	141	546	78	137	27	11	4	43	62	63	19	.251	.363
Possum Whitted	OF141, 1B10, 2B1	R	27	149	553	69	155	24	9	3	70	30	56	10	.280	.373
Bill Killefer	C120	R	29	125	409	28	112	12	0	0	31	15	21	4	.274	.303
2 Wildfire Schulte	OF42	L	34	64	149	21	32	10	0	1	15	16	22	4	.215	.302
2 Johnny Evers (AJ)	2B49, 3B7	L	35	56	183	20	41	5	1	1	12	30	13	8	.224	.279
Oscar Dugey	2B15, OF4	R	29	44	72	12	14	4	1	0	9	4	9	2	.194	.278
Jack Adams	C38, 1B1	B	26	43	107	4	22	4	1	1	7	0	20	0	.206	.290
Claude Cooper	OF12	L	24	24	29	5	3	1	0	0	1	5	4	0	.103	.138
Ed Burns	C15	R	28	20	49	2	10	1	0	0	6	1	5	2	.204	.224
Patsy McGaffigan	SS17, OF1	R	28	19	60	5	10	1	0	0	6	0	7	1	.167	.183
1 Bobby Byrne	3B4	R	32	13	14	1	5	0	0	0	0	1	2	0	.357	.357
Harry Pearce	SS4	R	27	7	16	2	4	3	0	0	2	0	4	0	.250	.438

NAME	T	AGE	W	L	PCT	SV	G	GS	CG	IP	H	BB	SO	ShO	ERA
		29	87	65	.572	5	154	154	103	1389	1258	327	617	22	2.46
Pete Alexander	R	30	30	13	.698	0	45	44	35	388	336	58	201	8	1.86
Eppa Rixey	L	26	16	21	.432	1	39	36	23	281	249	67	121	4	2.27
Joe Oeschger	R	26	15	14	.517	1	42	30	18	262	241	72	123	5	2.75
Erskine Mayer	R	28	11	6	.647	0	28	18	11	160	160	33	64	1	2.76
Chief Bender	R	34	8	2	.800	2	20	10	8	113	84	26	43	4	1.67
Jimmy Lavender	R	33	6	8	.429	1	28	14	7	129	119	44	52	0	3.56
Paul Fittery	L	29	1	1	.500	0	17	2	1	56	69	27	13	0	4.50

Stan Baumgartner (VR) 24

ST. LOUIS 3rd 82-70 .539 15 — MILLER HUGGINS

NAME	G by POS	B	AGE	G	AB	R	H	2B	3B	HR	RBI	BB	SO	SB	BA	SA
TOTALS			25	154	5083	531	1271	159	93	26	436	359	652	159	.250	.333
2 Gene Paulette	1B93	R	25	95	332	32	88	21	7	0	34	16	16	9	.265	.370
Dots Miller	2B92, 1B46, SS11	R	30	148	544	61	135	15	9	2	45	33	52	14	.248	.320
Rogers Hornsby	SS144	R	21	145	523	86	171	24	17	8	66	45	34	17	.327	.484
2 Doug Baird	3B103, OF2	R	25	104	364	38	92	19	12	0	24	23	52	18	.253	.371
Tommy Long	OF137	R	27	144	530	49	123	12	14	3	41	37	44	21	.232	.325
Jack Smith	OF128	L	22	137	462	64	137	16	11	3	34	38	65	25	.297	.398
Walton Cruise	OF152	L	27	153	529	70	156	20	10	5	59	38	73	16	.295	.399
Frank Snyder	C94	R	24	115	313	18	74	9	2	1	33	27	43	4	.236	.288
Bruno Betzel	2B75, OF23, 3B4	R	22	106	328	24	71	4	3	1	17	20	47	9	.216	.256
Mike Gonzalez	C68, 1B18, OF1	R	26	106	290	28	76	8	1	1	28	22	24	12	.262	.307
Fred Smith	3B51, 2B2, SS1	R	25	56	165	11	30	0	2	1	17	17	22	4	.182	.224
Bob Bescher	OF32	B	33	42	110	10	17	1	1	1	8	20	13	3	.155	.209
2 Red Smyth	OF23	L	24	38	72	5	15	0	2	0	4	4	9	3	.208	.264
1 Tony DeFate	3B5, 2B1	R	22	14	14	0	2	0	0	0	1	4	5	0	.143	.143
Stuffy Stewart	OF7, 2B2	R	23	13	9	4	0	0	0	0	0	0	4	0	.000	.000
Bobby Wallace	3B5, SS2	R	43	8	10	0	1	0	0	0	2	0	1	0	.100	.100
John Brock	C4	R	19	7	15	4	6	1	0	0	2	0	2	2	.400	.467
Paddy Livingston	C6	R	37	7	20	0	4	0	0	0	2	0	1	2	.200	.200
Ike McAuley	SS3	R	23	3	7	0	2	0	0	0	1	0	1	0	.286	.286
Jack Roche	C1	R	26	1	1	0	0	0	0	0	0	0	0	0	.000	.000

NAME	T	AGE	W	L	PCT	SV	G	GS	CG	IP	H	BB	SO	ShO	ERA
		26	82	70	.539	10	154	154	66	1392	1257	421	502	16	3.03
Bill Doak	R	26	16	20	.444	2	44	37	16	281	257	85	111	3	3.11
Lee Meadows	R	22	15	9	.625	2	43	37	18	265	253	90	100	4	3.09
Red Ames	R	34	15	10	.600	3	43	19	10	209	189	57	62	2	2.71
Milt Watson	R	24	10	13	.435	0	41	20	5	161	149	51	45	3	3.52
Oscar Horstman	R	26	9	4	.692	1	35	11	4	138	111	54	50	1	3.46
2 Gene Packard	L	29	9	6	.600	2	34	11	6	153	138	25	44	0	2.47
Marv Goodwin	R	26	6	4	.600	0	14	12	6	85	70	19	38	3	2.22
George Pearce	L	29	1	1	.500	0	5	0	0	10	7	3	4	0	3.60
1 Bob Steele	L	23	1	3	.250	0	12	6	1	42	33	19	23	0	3.21
Jakie May	L	21	0	0	.000	0	15	1	0	29	29	11	18	0	3.41
Lou North	R	26	0	0	.000	0	5	0	0	11	14	4	4	0	4.09
Bruce Hitt	R	19	0	0	.000	0	2	0	0	4	7	1	1	0	9.00
Tim Murchison	L	20	0	0	.000	0	1	0	0	1	0	2	2	0	0.00

CINCINNATI 4th 78-76 .506 20 — CHRISTY MATHEWSON

NAME	G by POS	B	AGE	G	AB	R	H	2B	3B	HR	RBI	BB	SO	SB	BA	SA
TOTALS			29	157	5251	601	1385	196	100	26	513	312	477	153	.264	.354
Hal Chase	1B151	R	34	154	602	71	167	28	15	4	86	15	49	21	.277	.394
Dave Shean	2B131	R	39	131	442	36	93	9	5	2	35	22	39	10	.210	.267
Larry Kopf	SS145	B	26	148	573	81	146	19	8	2	26	28	48	17	.255	.326
Heinie Groh	3B154, 2B2	R	27	156	599	91	182	39	11	1	53	71	30	15	.304	.411
Tommy Griffith	OF100	L	27	115	363	45	98	18	7	1	45	19	23	5	.270	.366
Edd Roush	OF134	L	24	136	522	82	178	19	14	4	67	27	24	21	.341	.454
Greasy Neale	OF119	L	25	121	385	40	113	14	9	3	33	24	36	25	.294	.400
Ivy Wingo	C120	L	26	121	399	37	106	16	11	2	39	25	13	9	.266	.376
1 Jim Thorpe	OF69	R	29	77	251	29	62	2	8	4	36	6	35	11	.247	.367
Tommy Clarke	C29	R	29	58	110	11	32	3	3	1	13	11	12	2	.291	.400
Manuel Cueto	OF38, 2B6, C5	R	25	56	140	10	28	3	0	1	11	16	17	4	.200	.243
Bill McKechnie (BH)	2B26, SS13, 3B4	B	30	48	134	11	34	3	1	0	15	7	7	5	.254	.291
Clarence Mitchell	P32, 1B6, OF5	L	26	47	90	13	25	3	0	0	5	5	5	0	.278	.311
2 Sherry Magee	OF41, 1B2	R	32	45	137	17	44	8	4	0	23	16	7	4	.321	.438
Emil Huhn	C15	R	25	23	51	2	10	1	2	0	3	2	5	1	.196	.294
Dutch Ruether	P7	L	23	19	24	1	5	2	0	0	1	3	6	1	.208	.292
Harry Smith	C7	R	27	8	17	0	2	0	0	0	1	2	7	0	.118	.118
Gus Getz	2B4, 3B3	R	27	7	14	2	4	0	0	0	3	3	0	0	.286	.286

NAME	T	AGE	W	L	PCT	SV	G	GS	CG	IP	H	BB	SO	ShO	ERA
		25	78	76	.506	6	157	157	94	1405	1363	404	492	11	2.66
Fred Toney	R	29	24	16	.600	1	43	42	31	340	300	77	123	7	2.20
Pete Schneider	R	24	20	19	.513	0	46	42	25	342	316	119	142	0	1.97
Mike Regan	R	29	11	10	.524	0	32	26	16	216	228	41	50	1	2.71
Hod Eller	R	22	10	5	.667	1	37	11	7	152	131	37	77	1	2.37
Clarence Mitchell	L	26	9	15	.375	1	32	20	10	159	166	34	37	2	3.23
Jimmy Ring	R	22	3	7	.300	2	24	7	3	88	90	35	33	0	4.40
Dutch Reuther	L	23	1	2	.333	0	7	4	0	36	43	14	12	0	3.50
Roy Sanders	R	24	0	1	.000	0	2	2	1	14	12	16	3	0	4.50
Joe Engel	R	24	0	1	.000	0	1	1	1	8	12	6	2	0	5.63
Elmer Knetzer	R	31	0	0	.000	1	11	0	0	27	29	12	7	0	3.00
2 Scott Perry	R	26	0	0	.000	0	4	1	0	13	17	8	4	0	6.92
Rube Bressler	L	22	0	0	.000	0	2	1	0	9	15	5	2	0	6.00
Herman Pillette	R	21	0	0	.000	0	1	0	0	1	4	0	0	0	18.00

CHICAGO 5th 74-80 .481 24 — FRED MITCHELL

NAME	G by POS	B	AGE	G	AB	R	H	2B	3B	HR	RBI	BB	SO	SB	BA	SA
TOTALS			28	157	5135	552	1229	194	67	17	458	415	599	127	.239	.313
2 Fred Merkle	1B140, OF6	R	28	146	549	65	146	30	9	3	57	42	60	13	.266	.370
Larry Doyle	2B128	L	30	135	476	48	121	19	5	6	61	48	28	5	.254	.353
Chuck Wortman	SS65, 2B1, 3B1	R	25	75	190	24	33	4	1	0	9	18	23	6	.174	.205
Charlie Deal	3B130	R	25	135	449	46	114	11	3	0	47	19	18	10	.254	.292
Max Flack	OF117	L	27	131	447	65	111	18	7	0	21	51	34	17	.248	.320
Cy Williams	OF136	L	29	138	468	53	113	22	4	5	42	38	78	8	.241	.338
Les Mann	OF116	R	23	117	444	63	121	19	10	1	44	27	46	14	.273	.367
Art Wilson	C75	R	31	81	211	17	45	9	2	2	25	32	36	6	.213	.303
Harry Wolter	OF97, 1B1	L	32	117	353	44	88	15	7	0	28	38	40	7	.249	.331
Rollie Zeider	SS48, 3B26, 2B24, 1B1, OF1	R	33	108	354	36	86	14	2	0	27	28	30	17	.243	.294
Rowdy Elliott	C73	R	26	85	223	18	56	8	5	0	28	11	11	4	.251	.332
2 Pete Kilduff	SS51, 2B5	R	24	56	202	23	56	9	5	0	15	12	19	11	.277	.371
Pickles Dillhoefer	C37	R	22	42	95	3	12	1	1	0	8	2	9	1	.126	.158
1 Dutch Ruether	P10, 1B5	L	23	31	44	3	12	1	3	0	11	8	11	0	.273	.432
Morrie Schick	OF12	R	25	14	34	3	5	0	0	0	3	3	10	0	.147	.147
Paddy Driscoll	2B8, 3B2, SS1	R	22	13	28	2	3	1	0	0	3	2	6	2	.107	.143
Charlie Pechous	3B7, SS5	R	20	13	41	2	10	0	0	0	1	2	9	1	.244	.244
1 Harry Wolfe	OF2, SS1	R	23	9	5	1	2	0	0	0	1	1	1	0	.400	.400
Turner Barber	OF7	L	23	7	28	2	6	1	0	0	2	2	8	1	.214	.250
Roy Leslie	1B6	R	22	7	19	1	4	0	0	0	1	1	5	1	.211	.211
Vic Saier (BL)	1B6	L	26	6	21	5	5	1	0	0	2	2	1	0	.238	.286
Herb Hunter	2B1, 3B1	L	21	3	3	0	0	0	0	0	0	0	0	0	.000	.000
Bill Marriott	OF1	L	24	2	6	0	0	0	0	0	0	0	1	0	.000	.000

Bob O'Farrell 20 R 3-8, Jimmy Archer (VR) 34 R 0-2, Earl Blackburn 24 R 0-2

NAME	T	AGE	W	L	PCT	SV	G	GS	CG	IP	H	BB	SO	ShO	ERA
		27	74	80	.481	9	157	157	79	1404	1303	374	654	14	2.62
Hippo Vaughn	L	29	23	13	.639	0	41	39	27	296	255	91	195	5	2.01
Phil Douglas	R	25	14	20	.412	1	51	37	20	293	269	50	151	5	2.55
Claude Hendrix	R	28	10	12	.455	1	40	21	13	215	202	72	81	1	2.60
Vic Aldridge	R	23	6	6	.500	2	30	5	1	107	100	37	44	1	3.11
Tom Seaton	R	29	5	4	.556	1	16	9	3	75	60	23	27	1	2.52
Paul Carter	R	23	5	8	.385	2	23	13	6	113	115	19	34	0	3.27
1 Al Demaree	R	30	5	9	.357	1	24	18	6	141	125	37	43	1	2.55
Mike Prendergast	L	28	3	6	.333	1	35	8	1	99	112	21	43	0	3.36
1 Dutch Ruether	L	23	2	0	1.000	0	10	4	1	36	37	12	23	0	2.50
Harry Weaver	R	22	1	1	.500	0	4	2	1	20	17	7	8	0	2.70
Roy Walker	R	24	0	1	.000	0	2	1	0	7	8	5	4	0	3.86
1 Gene Packard	L	29	0	0	.000	0	2	0	0	2	3	0	1	0	9.00

BOSTON 6th 72-81 .471 25.5 — GEORGE STALLINGS

NAME	G by POS	B	AGE	G	AB	R	H	2B	3B	HR	RBI	BB	SO	SB	BA	SA
TOTALS			28	157	5201	536	1280	169	75	22	452	427	587	155	.246	.320
Ed Konetchy	1B129	R	31	130	474	56	129	19	13	2	54	36	40	16	.272	.380
Johnny Rawlings	2B96, SS17, 3B1, OF1	R	24	122	371	37	95	9	4	2	31	38	32	12	.256	.318
Rabbit Maranville	SS142	R	25	142	561	69	146	19	13	3	43	40	47	27	.260	.357
Red Smith	3B147	R	27	147	505	60	149	31	6	2	62	53	61	16	.295	.392
Wally Rehg	OF86	R	28	86	341	48	92	12	6	1	31	24	32	13	.270	.349
Ray Powell	OF88	L	28	88	357	42	97	10	4	4	30	24	54	12	.272	.356
Joe Kelly	OF116	R	27	116	445	41	99	9	8	3	36	26	45	21	.222	.299
Walt Tragesser	C98	R	30	98	297	23	66	10	2	0	25	15	36	5	.222	.269
1 Sherry Magee	OF65, 1B2	R	32	72	246	24	63	8	4	1	29	13	23	7	.256	.333
Ed Fitzpatrick	2B22, OF19, 3B15	R	27	63	178	20	45	8	4	0	17	12	22	4	.253	.343
Lefty Tyler	P32, 1B11	L	27	61	134	8	31	4	0	0	11	17	19	0	.231	.261
1 Joe Wilhoit	OF52	L	25	54	186	20	51	5	0	1	10	17	15	5	.274	.317
Fred Bailey	OF27	L	21	50	110	9	21	2	1	1	5	9	25	3	.191	.255
Hank Gowdy (MS)	C49	R	27	49	154	12	33	7	0	0	14	15	13	2	.214	.260
George Twombly	OF29, 1B1	R	25	32	102	8	19	1	1	0	9	18	5	4	.186	.216
Mike Massey	2B25	B	23	31	91	12	18	0	0	0	2	15	15	2	.198	.198
2 Chief Meyers	C24	R	36	25	68	5	17	4	4	0	4	4	4	0	.250	.426
1 Johnny Evers	2B24	L	35	24	83	5	16	0	0	0	0	13	8	1	.193	.193
Sam Covington	1B17	L	24	17	66	8	13	2	0	1	10	5	5	1	.197	.273

Art Rico 20 R 4-14, Zip Collins 25 L 4-27, Larry Chappell 27 L 0-2, Hank Schreiber 25 R 2-7, Fred Jacklitsch 41 R 0-0

NAME	T	AGE	W	L	PCT	SV	G	GS	CG	IP	H	BB	SO	ShO	ERA
		27	72	81	.471	3	157	157	105	1425	1309	371	593	19	2.77
Art Nehf	L	24	17	8	.680	0	38	23	17	233	197	39	101	5	2.16
Lefty Tyler	L	27	14	12	.538	1	32	28	22	239	203	86	98	4	2.52
Dick Rudolph	R	29	13	13	.500	0	32	30	22	243	252	54	96	5	3.41
Jesse Barnes	R	24	13	**21**	.382	1	50	33	27	295	261	50	107	2	2.68
Pat Ragan	R	28	6	9	.400	1	30	13	5	148	138	35	61	1	2.92
Tom Hughes (XJ)	R	33	5	3	.625	0	11	8	6	74	54	30	40	2	1.95
Frank Allen	L	27	3	11	.214	0	29	14	2	112	124	47	56	0	3.94
Jack Scott	R	25	1	2	.333	0	7	3	3	40	36	5	21	0	1.80
Ed Reulbach	R	34	0	1	.000	0	5	2	0	22	21	15	9	0	2.86
Ed Walsh	R	36	0	1	.000	0	4	3	1	18	22	9	4	0	3.50
Cal Crum	R	25	0	0	.000	0	1	0	0	1	1	1	0	0	0.00

Bill James (SJ) 25
1 Scott Perry (JT) 26

BROOKLYN 7th 70-81 .464 26.5 — WILBERT ROBINSON

NAME	G by POS	B	AGE	G	AB	R	H	2B	3B	HR	RBI	BB	SO	SB	BA	SA
TOTALS			25	156	**5251**	511	1299	159	78	25	429	334	527	130	.247	.322
Jake Daubert	1B125	L	33	125	468	59	122	4	4	2	30	51	30	11	.261	.299
George Cutshaw	2B134	R	29	135	487	42	126	17	7	4	49	21	26	22	.259	.347
Ivy Olson	SS133, 3B6	R	31	139	580	64	156	18	5	2	38	14	34	6	.269	.328
Mike Mowrey	3B80, 2B2	R	33	83	271	20	58	9	5	0	25	29	25	7	.214	.284
Casey Stengel	OF150	L	26	150	549	69	141	23	12	6	73	60	62	18	.257	.375
Dave Hickman	OF101	R	23	114	370	46	81	15	4	6	36	17	66	14	.219	.330
Zack Wheat	OF98	L	31	109	362	38	113	15	11	1	41	20	18	5	.312	.423
Otto Miller	C91	R	28	92	274	19	63	5	4	1	17	14	29	5	.230	.288
Hy Myers (SJ)	OF66, 1B22, 2B19, 3B15	R	28	120	471	37	126	15	10	1	41	18	25	5	.268	.348
J. Johnston	OF92, 1B14, SS4, 2B3, 3B3	R	27	103	330	33	89	10	4	0	25	23	28	16	.270	.324
Frank O'Rourke	3B58	R	22	64	198	18	47	7	1	0	15	14	25	11	.237	.283
1 Chief Meyers	C44	R	36	47	132	8	28	3	0	0	3	13	7	4	.212	.235
2 Ernie Krueger	C23	R	26	31	81	10	22	2	2	1	6	5	7	1	.272	.383
1 Red Smyth	3B4, OF2	L	24	29	24	5	3	0	0	0	1	4	6	0	.125	.125
Mack Wheat	C18, OF9	R	24	29	60	2	8	1	0	0	0	1	12	1	.133	.150
Bunny Fabrique	SS21	B	29	25	88	8	18	3	0	1	3	8	9	0	.205	.273

Jack Snyder 25 R 3-11, Bill Leard 31 R 0-3, 1 Fred Merkle 28 R 1-8, Lew Malone 20 R 0-0

NAME	T	AGE	W	L	PCT	SV	G	GS	CG	IP	H	BB	SO	ShO	ERA
		29	70	81	.464	9	156	156	99	1421	1288	405	582	7	2.78
Rube Marquard	L	27	19	12	.613	0	37	29	14	233	200	60	117	2	2.55
Leon Cadore	R	26	13	13	.500	3	37	30	21	264	231	63	115	1	2.45
Sherry Smith	L	26	12	12	.500	3	38	23	15	211	210	51	58	0	3.33
Jeff Pfeffer	R	29	11	15	.423	0	30	30	24	266	225	66	115	3	2.23
Larry Cheney	R	31	8	12	.400	2	35	24	14	210	185	73	102	1	2.36
Jack Coombs	R	34	7	11	.389	0	31	14	9	141	147	49	34	0	3.96
Jack Russell	L	21	0	1	.000	0	5	1	1	16	12	6	1	0	4.50
Johnny Miljus	R	22	0	1	.000	0	4	1	1	15	14	8	9	0	0.60
Wheezer Dell	R	30	0	4	.000	1	17	4	0	58	55	25	28	0	3.72
Paul Wachtel	R	29	0	0	.000	0	2	0	0	6	9	4	3	0	10.50
Dick Durning	L	24	0	0	.000	0	1	0	0	1	0	0	0	0	0.00

Duster Mails (MS) 21

PITTSBURGH 8th 51-103 .331 47 — NIXEY CALLAHAN 20-40 .333 HONUS WAGNER 1-4 .200 HUGO BEZDEK 30-59 .337

NAME	G by POS	B	AGE	G	AB	R	H	2B	3B	HR	RBI	BB	SO	SB	BA	SA
TOTALS			28	157	5169	464	1230	160	61	9	396	399	580	150	.238	.298
Honus Wagner (HO)	1B47, 3B18, 2B2, SS1	R	43	74	230	15	61	7	1	0	24	24	17	5	.265	.304
Jake Pitler	2B106, OF3	R	23	109	382	39	89	8	5	0	23	30	24	6	.233	.280
Chuck Ward	SS112, 2B8, 3B5	R	22	125	423	25	100	12	3	0	43	32	43	5	.236	.279
Tony Boeckel	3B62	R	24	64	219	16	58	11	1	0	23	8	31	6	.265	.324
Lee King	OF102	R	24	111	381	32	95	14	5	1	35	15	58	8	.249	.320
Max Carey	OF153	B	27	155	588	82	174	21	12	1	51	58	38	**46**	.296	.378
Carson Bigbee	OF107, 2B16, SS2	L	22	133	469	46	112	11	6	0	21	37	16	19	.239	.288
Bill Fischer	C69, 1B2	L	26	95	245	25	70	9	2	3	25	27	19	11	.286	.376
Walter Schmidt	C61	R	30	72	183	9	45	7	0	0	17	11	11	4	.246	.284
Bill Hinchman (BL)	OF48, 1B20	R	34	69	244	27	46	5	5	2	29	33	27	5	.189	.275
Bill Wagner	C37, 1B12	R	23	53	151	15	31	7	2	0	9	11	22	1	.205	.278
Alex McCarthy	3B26, 2B13, SS9	R	29	49	151	15	33	4	0	0	8	11	13	1	.219	.245
1 Doug Baird	3B41, 2B2	R	25	43	135	17	35	6	1	0	18	20	19	8	.259	.319
Charlie Jackson	OF36	L	23	41	121	7	29	3	2	0	1	10	22	4	.240	.298
Adam Debus	SS21, 3B18	R	24	38	131	9	30	5	4	0	7	7	14	2	.229	.328
Fritz Mollwitz	1B36, 2B1	R	27	36	140	15	36	4	1	0	12	8	8	4	.257	.300
Bunny Brief	1B34	R	24	36	115	15	25	5	1	2	11	15	21	4	.217	.330
1 Wildfire Schulte	OF28	L	34	30	103	11	22	5	1	0	7	10	14	5	.214	.282
Buster Caton	SS14	R	20	14	57	6	12	1	2	0	4	6	7	0	.211	.298
Don Flinn	OF12	R	24	14	37	1	11	1	1	0	1	1	6	1	.297	.378
Billy Gleason	2B13	R	22	13	42	3	7	1	0	0	0	5	5	1	.167	.190

Jesse Altenburg 24 L 3-17, Red Smith 25 R 3-21, 2 Joe Wilhoit 25 L 2-10, 2 George Kelly 21 R 2-23, 2 Ray Miller 29 L 4-27, Billy Webb 22 R 3-15, Fred Blackwell 21 L 2-10, Hooks Warner 23 L 1-5, Ben Shaw 24 R 0-2, 2 Harry Wolfe 23 R 0-5, Arch Reilly 25 R 0-0

NAME	T	AGE	W	L	PCT	SV	G	GS	CG	IP	H	BB	SO	ShO	ERA
		25	51	**103**	.331	6	157	157	84	1418	1318	**432**	509	17	3.01
Wilbur Cooper	L	25	17	11	.607	1	40	34	23	298	276	54	99	7	2.36
Frank Miller	R	31	10	19	.345	1	38	28	14	224	216	60	92	5	3.16
Hal Carlson	R	23	7	11	.389	1	34	17	9	161	140	49	68	1	2.91
Elmer Jacobs	R	24	6	19	.240	2	38	25	10	227	214	76	58	1	2.81
2 Bob Steele	L	23	5	11	.313	1	27	19	13	180	158	53	82	1	2.75
Burleigh Grimes	R	23	3	16	.158	0	37	17	8	194	186	70	72	1	3.53
Al Mamaux (ST)	R	23	2	11	.154	0	16	13	5	86	92	50	22	0	5.23
Elmer Ponder	R	24	1	1	.500	0	3	2	1	21	12	6	11	1	1.71
Bill Evans (IL)	R	24	0	4	.000	0	8	2	1	27	24	14	5	0	3.33

WORLD SERIES – CHICAGO (AL) 4 NEW YORK (NL) 2

LINE SCORES

TEAM	1	2	3	4	5	6	7	8	9	10	11	12	R	H	E
Game 1 October 6 at Chicago															
NY (NL)	0	0	0	0	1	0	0	0	0				1	7	1
CHI (AL)	0	0	1	1	0	0	0	0	X				2	7	1
Sallee	**Cicotte**														
Game 2 October 7 at Chicago															
NY	0	2	0	0	0	0	0	0	0				2	8	1
CHI	0	2	0	5	0	0	0	0	X				7	14	1
Schupp, **Anderson** (2), Perritt (4), Tesreau (8)	**Faber**														
Game 3 October 10 at New York															
CHI	0	0	0	0	0	0	0	0	0				0	5	3
NY	0	0	0	2	0	0	0	0	X				2	8	2
Cicotte	**Benton**														
Game 4 October 11 at New York															
CHI	0	0	0	0	0	0	0	0	0				0	7	0
NY	0	0	0	1	1	0	1	2	X				5	10	1
Faber, Danforth (8)	**Schupp**														
Game 5 October 13 at Chicago															
NY	2	0	0	2	0	0	1	0	0				5	12	3
CHI	0	0	1	0	0	1	3	3	X				8	14	6
Sallee, Perritt (8)	Russell, Cicotte (1), Williams (7), **Faber** (8)														
Game 6 October 15 at New York															
CHI	0	0	0	3	0	0	0	0	1				4	7	1
NY	0	0	0	0	2	0	0	0	0				2	6	3
Faber	**Benton**, Perritt (6)														

COMPOSITE BATTING

NAME	POS	G	AB	R	H	2B	3B	HR	RBI	BA
Chicago (AL) Totals		6	197	21	54	6	0	1	18	.274
McMullin	3B	6	24	1	3	1	0	0	2	.125
Jackson	OF	6	23	**4**	7	0	0	0	2	.304
Gandil	1B	6	23	1	6	1	0	0	**5**	.261
E. Collins	2B	6	22	**4**	9	1	0	0	2	.409
Felsch	OF	6	22	**4**	6	1	0	1	3	.273
Weaver	SS	6	21	3	7	1	0	0	1	.333
J. Collins	OF	6	21	2	6	1	0	0	0	.286
Schalk	C	6	19	1	5	0	0	0	0	.263
Faber	P	4	7	0	1	0	0	0	0	.143
Cicotte	P	3	7	0	1	0	0	0	0	.143
Leibold	OF	2	5	1	2	0	0	0	2	.400
Risberg	PH	2	2	0	1	0	0	0	1	.500
Lynn	PH	1	1	0	0	0	0	0	0	.000
Danforth	P	1	0	0	0	0	0	0	0	.000
Russell	P	1	0	0	0	0	0	0	0	.000
Williams	P	1	0	0	0	0	0	0	0	.000
New York (NL) Totals		6	199	17	51	5	4	2	16	.256
Fletcher	SS	6	**25**	2	5	1	0	0	0	.200
Kauff	OF	6	**25**	2	4	1	0	**2**	**5**	.160
Zimmerman	3B	6	**25**	1	3	0	1	0	0	.120
Herzog	2B	6	24	1	6	0	1	0	2	.250
Robertson	OF	6	22	3	**11**	1	1	0	1	**.500**
Burns	OF	6	22	3	5	0	0	0	2	.227
Holke	1B	6	21	2	6	**2**	0	0	1	.286
Rariden	C	5	13	2	5	0	0	0	2	.385
Sallee	P	2	6	0	1	0	0	0	1	.167
McCarty	C	3	5	1	2	0	1	0	1	.400
Schupp	P	2	4	0	1	0	0	0	1	.250
Benton	P	2	4	0	0	0	0	0	0	.000
Perritt	P	3	2	0	2	0	0	0	0	1.000
Wilhoit	PH	2	1	0	0	0	0	0	0	.000
Thorpe	OF	1	0	0	0	0	0	0	0	.000
Anderson	P	1	0	0	0	0	0	0	0	.000
Tesreau	P	1	0	0	0	0	0	0	0	.000

COMPOSITE PITCHING

NAME	G	IP	H	BB	SO	W	L	SV	ERA
Chicago (AL) Totals	6	52	51	6	27	4	2	0	2.77
Faber	**4**	**27**	21	3	9	**3**	1	0	2.33
Cicotte	3	23	**23**	2	**13**	1	1	0	1.95
Williams	1	1	2	0	3	0	0	0	9.00
Danforth	1	1	3	0	2	0	0	0	18.00
Russell	1	0	2	1	0	0	0	0	∞
New York (NL) Totals	6	51	54	11	28	2	4	0	3.00
Sallee	2	15.1	20	**4**	4	0	**2**	0	5.28
Benton	2	14	9	1	8	1	1	0	**0.00**
Schupp	2	10.1	11	2	9	1	0	0	1.74
Perritt	3	8.1	9	3	3	0	0	0	2.16
Anderson	1	2	5	0	3	0	1	0	18.00
Tesreau	1	1	0	1	1	0	0	0	0.00

1918 The "Non-Essential" Season

With America entering full force into World War I, baseball could not continue unscathed. Many players were taken by the draft, some enlisted in the armed forces, and others went to work in war industries. In June, Provost Marshall General Crowder issued a "work-or-fight" order, forcing all draft-age men into either the military or essential industries. Baseball was ruled "non-essential", and a schedule curtailed to September 2, could be completed only in a period of grace granted by Secretary of War Baker. Labor Day marked the end of the war-shortened race—any further play could only be carried on by teams of the old and very young. Even before September, many players and managers were drafted or left their teams, making it a season of scrambling for players and make-shift teams.

The Boston Red Sox won the American League pennant by 2½ games over Cleveland. Despite losing playing-manager Jack Barry and left fielder Duffy Lewis to the military, Boston's good fortunes lay in having Babe Ruth. The baby-faced strong man filled in for Lewis and responded by hitting 11 home runs and batting .300, while still finding time to win 13 games on the mound. Carl Mays gathered 21 wins to his credit, and Boston manager Ed Barrow was able to obtain Stuffy McInnis, Amos Strunk, Wally Schang, and Joe Bush from the Athletics to plug up other holes. The Indians were hurt by the suspension of star Tris Speaker for the balance of the season for his assaulting umpire Tom Connelly in a home play dispute in a game at Philadelphia on August 28. Speaker and pitcher-turned-outfielder Joe Wood proved to be the big bats for the Indians. The White Sox were hard hit by the war and fell to sixth; Red Faber and Swede Risberg were drafted, and Joe Jackson, Happy Felsch, and Lefty Williams all left to do war work.

Ty Cobb collected his eleventh batting title, while Ruth's power performance was enough to help him garner his first home run crown by tying Tilly Walker of Philadelphia. Ruth also came through in the clutch by batting in 66 runs, good enough for a third-place tie with Joe Wood of Cleveland. Walter Johnson continued to dominate the pitching statistics by leading in wins, E.R.A., strikeouts, and tying in shutouts with Carl Mays of Boston.

Despite the fall of the White Sox, the Chicago Cubs upheld the Windy City's honor by waltzing into the National League pennant by 10½ games. The Cubs had purchased star pitcher Grover "Pete" Alexander from the Phillies during the winter, but he was drafted after only three games. Nevertheless, the Cubs were mostly a blend of veterans who played solid ball all year. Rookie Charlie Hollocher hit .316 and played good shortstop, and ex-Giant Fred Merkle also provided heavy stick work. Pitchers, Hippo Vaughn, Lefty Tyler, and Claude Hendrix, all won consistently, enabling the Cubs to coast in first.

The runner-up Giants felt the pinch of the war more than the Cubs. Benny Kauff hit .315 in 67 games and was then drafted. Pitcher Rube Benton enlisted, and Jeff Tesreau and Walter Holke left for the war industries. In addition, Ferdie Schupp and Heinie Zimmerman had off-years, leaving rookie outfielder Ross Youngs the only true bright spot by season's end.

Secretary of War Baker permitted the World Series to go on, and the Red Sox beat the Cubs four games to two. Babe Ruth pitched a shutout in game one and extended his record scoreless innings' streak in Series play to 29 2/3 innings before the Cubs scored against him in the fourth game. This record would stand until broken by Whitey Ford of the Yankees in 1961. In addition to Ruth, Mays also took two games in what was marked as a pitcher's Series, as both teams collected a grand total of 19 runs—the lowest Series run total since the classic pitcher's confrontation of 1905, which produced five shutouts in five games and only 18 runs.

1918 AMERICAN LEAGUE

BOSTON 1st 75-51 .595 — ED BARROW

NAME	G by POS	B	AGE	G	AB	R	H	2B	3B	HR	RBI	BB	SO	SB	BA	SA
TOTALS			29	126	3982	473	990	159	54	15	390	406	324	110	.249	.327
Stuffy McInnis (MS)	1B94, 3B23	R	27	117	423	40	115	11	5	0	56	19	10	10	.272	.322
Dave Shean	2B115	R	40	115	425	58	112	16	3	0	34	40	25	11	.264	.315
Everett Scott	SS126	R	25	126	443	40	98	11	5	0	43	12	16	11	.221	.269
Fred Thomas (MS)	3B41, SS1	R	25	44	144	19	37	2	1	1	11	15	20	4	.257	.306
Harry Hooper	OF126	L	30	126	474	81	137	26	13	1	44	75	25	24	.289	.405
Amos Strunk	OF113	L	29	114	413	50	106	18	9	0	35	36	13	20	.257	.344
Babe Ruth	OF59, P20, 1B13	L	23	95	317	50	95	26	11	**11**	66	57	**58**	6	.300	**.555**
Sam Agnew	C72	R	31	72	199	11	33	8	0	0	6	11	26	0	.166	.206
Wally Schang	C57, OF16, 3B5, SS1	B	28	88	225	36	55	7	1	0	20	46	35	4	.244	.284
George Whiteman	OF69	R	35	71	214	24	57	14	0	1	28	20	9	9	.266	.346
Carl Mays	P35	R	26	38	104	10	30	3	3	0	5	9	15	1	.288	.375
Bullet Joe Bush	P36	R	25	36	98	8	27	3	2	0	14	6	11	0	.276	.347
Wally Mayer (MS)	C23	R	28	26	49	7	11	4	0	0	5	7	7	0	.224	.306
George Cochran	3B23, SS1		29	25	63	8	8	0	0	0	3	11	7	3	.127	.127
Dick Hoblitzell (MS)	1B19	L	29	25	69	4	11	1	0	0	4	8	3	3	.159	.174
Jack Stansbury	3B18, OF2	R	32	20	47	3	6	1	0	0	2	6	3	0	.128	.149
2 Jack Coffey	3B14, 2B1	R	31	15	44	5	7	1	0	1	2	3	2	2	.159	.250
Frank Truesdale	2B10	B	32	15	36	6	10	1	0	0	2	4	5	1	.278	.306
Walter Barbare	3B11, SS1	R	26	13	29	2	5	3	0	0	2	0	1	1	.172	.276
Hack Miller	OF10	R	24	12	29	2	8	2	0	0	4	0	4	0	.276	.345

Heinie Wagner 36 R 1-8, Eusebio Gonzalez 25 R 1-2, Red Bluhm 24 R 0-1, Jack Barry (MS) 31, Jimmy Cooney (MS) 23, Paul Musser (MS) 29, Del Gainor (MS) 31, Hal Janvrin (MS) 25, Duffy Lewis (MS) 30, Mike McNally (MS) 24, Chick Shorten (MS) 26, Jimmy Walsh (MS) 22

NAME	T	AGE	W	L	PCT	SV	G	GS	CG	IP	H	BB	SO	ShO	ERA
		25	75	51	.595	2	126	126	105	1120	931	380	392	25	2.31
Carl Mays	R	26	21	13	.618	0	35	33	**30**	293	230	81	114	**8**	2.21
Sad Sam Jones	R	25	16	5	**.762**	0	24	21	16	184	151	70	44	5	2.25
Bullet Joe Bush	R	25	15	15	.500	2	36	31	26	273	241	91	125	7	2.11
Babe Ruth	L	23	13	7	.650	0	20	19	18	166	125	49	40	1	2.22
Dutch Leonard (MS)	L	26	8	6	.571	0	16	16	12	126	119	53	47	3	2.71
Vince Molyneaux	R	29	1	0	1.000	0	6	0	0	11	3	8	1	0	3.27
Lore Bader	R	30	1	3	.250	0	5	4	2	27	26	12	10	1	3.33
Dick McCabe	R	22	0	1	.000	0	3	1	0	10	13	2	3	0	2.70
Jean Dubuc	R	29	0	1	.000	0	2	1	1	11	11	5	1	0	4.09
Walt Kinney	L	24	0	0	.000	0	5	0	0	15	5	8	4	0	1.80
Bill Pertica	R	21	0	0	.000	0	1	0	0	3	3	0	1	0	3.00
Weldon Wyckoff	R	26	0	0	.000	0	1	0	0	2	4	1	2	0	0.00

Herb Pennock (MS) 24

CLEVELAND 2nd 73-54 .575 2.5 — LEE FOHL

NAME	G by POS	B	AGE	G	AB	R	H	2B	3B	HR	RBI	BB	SO	SB	BA	SA
TOTALS			28	129	4166	**510**	1084	**176**	**67**	9	**423**	**492**	386	**165**	**.260**	**.341**
Doc Johnston	1B73	L	30	74	273	30	62	12	2	0	25	26	19	12	.227	.286
Bill Wambsganss (MS)	2B87	R	24	87	315	34	93	15	2	0	40	21	21	16	.295	.356
Ray Chapman	SS128, OF1	R	27	128	446	**84**	119	19	8	1	32	**84**	46	30	.267	.352
Joe Evans (MS)	3B74	R	23	79	243	38	64	6	7	1	22	30	29	7	.263	.358
Braggo Roth	OF106	R	25	106	375	53	106	21	12	1	59	53	41	35	.283	.411
Tris Speaker	OF127	L	30	127	471	73	150	**33**	11	0	61	64	9	27	.318	.435
Smokey Joe Wood	OF95, 2B19, 1B4	R	28	119	422	41	125	22	4	5	66	36	38	8	.296	.403
Steve O'Neill	C113	R	26	114	359	34	87	8	7	1	35	48	22	5	.242	.312
Terry Turner	3B46, 2B26, SS1	R	37	74	233	24	58	7	2	0	23	22	15	6	.249	.296
Jack Graney	OF45	L	32	70	177	27	42	7	4	0	9	28	13	3	.237	.322
Eddie Miller	1B22, OF4	R	29	32	96	9	22	4	3	0	3	12	10	2	.229	.333
Pinch Thomas	C24	L	30	32	73	2	18	0	1	0	5	6	6	0	.247	.274
Rip Williams	1B21, C1	R	36	28	71	5	17	2	2	0	7	9	6	2	.239	.324
Al Halt	3B14, 2B4, SS4, 1B2	L	27	26	69	9	12	2	0	0	1	9	12	4	.174	.203
Bob Bescher	OF17	B	34	25	60	12	20	2	1	0	6	17	5	3	.333	.400
1 Marty Kavanagh	1B12	R	27	13	38	4	8	2	0	0	6	7	7	1	.211	.263
Jack Farmer	3B5	R	25	7	9	1	2	0	0	0	1	0	3	2	.222	.222
1 Gus Getz	OF3	R	28	6	15	2	2	1	0	0	0	4	1	0	.133	.200
Josh Billings (MS)	C1	R	26	2	3	0	1	0	0	0	0	0	0	0	.333	.333

Eddie Onslow 25 L 1-6, Hick Cady (JJ) 32 R 0-0, John Peters 24 R 0-1, Germany Schaefer 41 R 0-5, Hank DeBerry (MS) 23, Lou Guisto (MS) 24, Joe Harris (MS) 27, Elmer Smith (MS) 25

NAME	T	AGE	W	L	PCT	SV	G	GS	CG	IP	H	BB	SO	ShO	ERA
		28	73	54	.575	**13**	129	129	80	1161	1126	343	364	6	2.64
Stan Coveleski	R	29	22	13	.629	1	38	33	25	311	261	76	87	2	1.82
Jim Bagby	R	28	17	16	.515	**6**	**45**	31	23	271	274	78	57	2	2.69
Guy Morton	R	25	14	8	.636	0	30	28	13	215	189	77	123	1	2.64
Fritz Coumbe	L	28	13	7	.650	3	30	17	11	150	164	52	41	1	3.06
Johnny Enzmann	R	28	5	7	.417	2	30	14	8	137	130	29	38	0	2.36
Bob Groom	R	33	2	2	.500	0	14	5	0	43	70	18	8	0	7.12
George McQuillan	R	33	0	1	.000	1	5	1	0	23	25	4	7	0	2.35
Otis Lambeth (MS)	R	28	0	0	.000	0	2	0	0	7	10	6	3	0	6.43
2 Ad Brennan	L	36	0	0	.000	0	1	0	0	3	3	3	0	0	3.00
Roy Wilkinson	R	24	0	0	.000	0	1	0	0	1	0	0	0	0	0.00

Ed Klepfer (MS) 30
Red Torkelson (MS) 24

WASHINGTON 3rd 72-56 .563 4 — CLARK GRIFFITH

NAME	G by POS	B	AGE	G	AB	R	H	2B	3B	HR	RBI	BB	SO	SB	BA	SA
TOTALS			29	130	**4472**	461	**1144**	156	48	5	404	376	361	137	.256	.316
Joe Judge	1B130	L	24	130	502	56	131	23	7	1	46	49	32	20	.261	.341
Ray Morgan	2B80, OF2	R	29	88	300	25	70	11	1	0	30	28	14	4	.233	.277
Doc Lavan	SS117, OF1	R	27	117	464	44	129	17	2	0	45	14	21	12	.278	.323
Eddie Foster	3B127, 2B2	R	31	129	**519**	70	147	13	3	0	29	41	20	12	.283	.320
Wildfire Schulte	OF75	L	35	93	267	35	77	14	3	0	44	47	36	5	.288	.363
Clyde Milan	OF124	L	32	128	503	56	146	18	5	0	56	36	14	26	.290	.346
Burt Shotton	OF122	L	33	126	505	68	132	16	7	0	21	67	28	25	.261	.321
Eddie Ainsmith (MS)	C89	R	26	96	292	22	62	10	9	0	20	29	44	6	.212	.308
Howard Shanks	OF64, 2B48, 3B3	R	27	120	436	42	112	19	4	1	56	31	21	23	.257	.326
Walter Johnson	P39, OF4	R	30	65	150	10	40	4	4	1	18	9	18	2	.267	.367
Val Picinich (MS)	C46	R	21	47	148	13	34	3	2	1	12	9	25	0	.230	.297
George McBride	SS14, 2B2	R	37	18	53	2	7	0	0	0	1	0	11	1	.132	.132
Joe Casey	C8	R	30	9	17	3	4	0	0	0	2	2	2	0	.235	.235
Sam Rice (MS)	OF6	L	28	7	23	3	8	1	0	0	3	2	0	1	.348	.391
Patsy Gharrity (VR)		R	26	4	4	0	1	1	0	0	2	0	1	0	.250	.500
1 Merito Acosta		L	22	3	2	0	0	0	0	0	0	0	1	0	.000	.000

Bob Berman 19 R 0-0, Joe Leonard (MS) 23, Mike Menosky (MS) 23, Horace Milan (MS) 24

NAME	T	AGE	W	L	PCT	SV	G	GS	CG	IP	H	BB	SO	ShO	ERA
		26	72	56	.563	8	130	130	75	**1227**	1021	395	505	20	**2.14**
Walter Johnson	R	30	**23**	13	.639	3	39	29	29	325	241	70	**162**	**8**	**1.27**
Jim Shaw	R	24	16	12	.571	1	41	30	14	241	201	90	129	4	2.43
Harry Harper	L	23	11	10	.524	1	35	32	14	244	182	104	78	3	2.18
Doc Ayres	R	28	11	12	.478	3	40	24	11	220	215	63	67	4	2.82
Eddie Matteson	R	33	5	3	.625	0	14	6	2	68	57	15	17	0	1.72
Ed Hovlik	R	26	2	1	.667	0	8	2	1	28	25	10	10	0	1.29
Ing Hansen	R	20	1	0	1.000	0	5	0	0	9	10	3	2	0	3.00
Nellie Reese	L	19	1	0	1.000	0	2	0	0	2	3	4	1	0	0.00
George Dumont	R	22	1	1	.500	0	4	1	1	14	18	6	12	0	5.14
Earl Yingling (MS)	L	29	1	2	.333	0	5	2	2	38	30	12	15	0	2.13
Nick Altrock	L	41	0	2	.000	0	5	3	1	24	24	6	5	0	3.00
Molly Craft (MS)	R	22	0	0	.000	0	3	0	0	7	5	1	5	0	1.29
1 Ad Brennan	L	36	0	0	.000	0	2	1	0	5	7	5	0	0	5.40
Garland Buckeye	L	20	0	0	.000	0	1	0	0	2	3	6	2	0	18.00

NEW YORK 4th 60-63 .488 13.5 — MILLER HUGGINS

NAME	G by POS	B	AGE	G	AB	R	H	2B	3B	HR	RBI	BB	SO	SB	BA	SA
TOTALS			28	126	4224	491	1085	160	45	20	406	367	370	88	.257	.330
Wally Pipp (MS)	1B91	L	25	91	349	48	106	15	9	2	44	22	34	11	.304	.415
Del Pratt	2B126	R	30	126	477	65	131	19	7	2	55	35	26	12	.275	.356
Roger Peckinpaugh	SS122	R	27	122	446	59	103	15	3	0	43	43	41	12	.231	.278
Frank Baker	3B126	L	32	126	504	65	154	24	5	6	62	38	13	8	.306	.409
Frank Gilhooley	OF111	L	26	112	427	58	118	13	5	1	23	53	24	7	.276	.337
Elmer Miller	OF62	R	27	67	202	18	49	9	2	1	22	19	17	2	.243	.322
Ping Bodie	OF90	R	30	91	324	36	83	12	6	3	46	27	24	6	.256	.358
Truck Hannah	C88	R	27	90	250	24	55	6	0	2	21	51	25	5	.220	.268
Ray Caldwell	P24, OF19	L	30	65	151	13	44	10	0	1	18	13	23	2	.291	.377
Hoxy Walters	C50, OF9	R	25	64	191	18	38	5	1	0	12	9	18	3	.199	.236
Ham Hyatt	OF25, 1B5	L	33	53	131	11	30	8	0	2	10	8	8	1	.299	.336
Armando Marsans	OF36	R	31	37	123	13	29	5	1	0	9	5	3	3	.236	.293
Bill Lamar (MS)	OF27	L	21	28	110	12	25	3	0	0	2	6	2	2	.227	.255
Jack Fournier	1B27	L	25	27	100	9	35	6	1	0	12	7	7	7	.350	.430
John Hummel	OF15, 1B3, 2B1	R	35	22	61	9	18	1	2	0	4	11	8	3	.295	.377
Aaron Ward (MS)	SS11, 2B4, OF4	R	21	20	32	2	4	1	0	0	1	2	7	1	.125	.156
Zinn Beck	1B5	R	32	11	8	0	0	0	0	0	1	0	1	0	.000	.000
Hugh High	OF4	L	30	7	10	1	0	0	0	0	0	1	1	0	.000	.000
Chick Fewster	2B2	R	22	5	2	1	1	0	0	0	0	0	0	0	.500	.500
Muddy Ruel (MS)	C2	R	22	3	6	0	2	0	0	0	0	2	1	1	.333	.333
Sammy Vick (MS)	OF1	R	23	2	3	1	2	0	0	0	1	0	0	0	.667	.667
Paddy O'Connor	C1	R	38	1	3	0	1	0	0	0	0	0	1	0	.333	.333

Howie Camp (MS) 25

NAME	T	AGE	W	L	PCT	SV	G	GS	CG	IP	H	BB	SO	ShO	ERA
TOTALS		26	60	63	.488	11	126	126	59	1148	1103	463	369	9	3.03
George Mogridge	L	29	16	13	.552	6	45	19	13	230	232	43	62	1	2.27
Slim Love	L	27	13	12	.520	1	38	29	13	229	207	116	95	1	3.07
Ray Caldwell	R	30	9	8	.529	1	24	21	14	177	173	62	59	1	3.05
Allen Russell	R	24	8	11	.421	3	27	18	7	141	139	73	54	2	3.26
Hank Thormahlen	L	21	7	3	.700	0	16	12	5	113	85	52	22	3	2.47
Ray Keating	R	26	2	2	.500	0	15	6	1	48	39	30	16	0	3.94
Hank Robinson	L	28	2	4	.333	0	11	3	1	48	47	16	14	0	3.00
2 Happy Finneran	R	26	2	6	.250	0	23	13	4	114	134	35	34	0	3.79
Bob Shawkey (MS)	R	27	1	1	.500	0	3	2	1	16	7	10	3	1	1.13
Bob McGraw (MS)	R	23	0	1	.000	0	1	1	0	0	0	4	0	0	∞
Roy Sanders	R	24	0	2	.000	0	6	2	0	26	28	16	8	0	4.15
Dazzy Vance	R	27	0	0	.000	0	2	0	0	2	9	2	0	0	18.00
Walter Bernhardt	R	25	0	0	.000	0	1	0	0	1	0	0	0	0	0.00
Alex Ferguson (MS)	R	21	0	0	.000	0	1	0	0	2	2	2	1	0	0.00
Ed Monroe (MS)	R	25	0	0	.000	0	1	0	0	2	1	2	1	0	4.50

Neal Brady (MS) 21
Ray Fisher (MS) 30
Ernie Shore (MS) 27
Walt Smallwood (MS) 25

ST. LOUIS 5th 58-64 .475 15 — FIELDER JONES 23-24 .489 JIMMY AUSTIN 6-8 .429 JIMMY BURKE 29-32 .475

NAME	G by POS	B	AGE	G	AB	R	H	2B	3B	HR	RBI	BB	SO	SB	BA	SA
TOTALS			28	124	4019	426	1040	152	40	5	360	397	340	138	.259	.320
George Sisler	1B114, P2	L	25	114	452	69	154	21	9	2	41	40	17	45	.341	.440
Joe Gedeon	2B123	R	24	123	441	39	94	14	3	1	41	27	29	7	.213	.265
Jimmy Austin	SS57, 3B48	B	38	110	367	42	97	14	4	0	20	53	32	18	.264	.324
Fritz Maisel	3B79, OF1	R	28	90	284	43	66	4	2	0	16	46	17	11	.232	.261
Ray Demmitt	OF114	L	34	116	405	45	114	23	5	1	61	38	35	10	.281	.370
Jack Tobin	OF122	L	26	122	480	59	133	19	5	0	36	48	26	13	.277	.338
Earl Smith	OF81	B	27	89	286	28	77	10	5	0	32	13	16	13	.269	.339
Les Nunamaker	C81, 1B1, OF1	R	29	85	274	22	71	9	2	0	22	28	16	6	.259	.307
Tim Hendryx	OF65	R	27	88	219	22	61	14	3	0	33	37	35	5	.279	.370
Wally Gerber (MS)	SS56	R	26	56	171	10	41	4	0	0	10	19	11	2	.240	.263
Hank Severeid (MS)	C42	R	27	51	133	8	34	4	0	0	11	18	4	4	.256	.286
Pete Johns	1B10, SS4, 3B4, OF4, 2B2	R	29	46	89	5	16	1	1	0	11	4	6	0	.180	.213
Ernie Johnson	SS11, 3B1	L	30	29	34	7	9	1	0	0	0	0	2	4	.265	.294
George Hale	C11	R	23	12	30	0	4	1	0	0	1	1	5	0	.133	.167
Ken Williams (MS)		L	28	2	1	0	0	0	0	0	1	1	0	0	.000	.000

Baby Doll Jacobson (MS) 27, Bill Rumler (MS) 27, Ted Sloan (MS) 27

NAME	T	AGE	W	L	PCT	SV	G	GS	CG	IP	H	BB	SO	ShO	ERA
TOTALS		26	58	64	.475	7	124	124	67	1111	993	402	346	7	2.75
Allan Sothoron	R	25	13	12	.520	0	29	24	14	209	152	67	71	2	1.94
Dave Davenport	R	28	10	11	.476	1	31	22	12	180	182	69	60	2	3.25
Rasty Wright	R	22	8	2	.800	0	18	13	6	111	99	18	25	1	2.51
Tom Rogers	R	23	8	10	.444	2	29	16	11	154	148	49	29	0	3.27
Bert Gallia	R	26	7	6	.538	0	19	17	10	124	126	61	48	1	3.48
Urban Shocker (MS)	R	27	6	5	.545	2	14	9	7	95	69	40	33	0	1.80
Duke Houck	R	26	2	4	.333	2	27	2	0	72	58	29	29	0	2.38
Lefty Leifield	L	34	2	6	.250	0	15	6	3	67	61	19	22	1	2.55
Grover Lowdermilk	R	33	2	6	.250	0	13	11	4	80	74	38	25	0	3.15
Bugs Bennett	R	26	0	2	.000	0	4	2	0	10	12	7	0	0	3.60
George Sisler	L	25	0	0	.000	0	2	1	0	8	10	4	4	0	4.50
Tim McCabe	R	23	0	0	.000	0	1	0	0	1	2	1	0	0	18.00

Ernie Koob (MS) 25

CHICAGO 6th 57-67 .460 17 — PANTS ROWLAND

NAME	G by POS	B	AGE	G	AB	R	H	2B	3B	HR	RBI	BB	SO	SB	BA	SA
TOTALS			28	124	4132	457	1057	136	54	9	375	375	358	116	.256	.321
Chick Gandil	1B114	R	30	114	439	49	119	18	4	0	55	27	19	9	.271	.330
Eddie Collins (MS)	2B96	L	31	97	330	51	91	8	2	2	30	73	13	22	.276	.330
Buck Weaver	SS98, 3B11, 2B1	B	27	112	420	37	126	12	5	0	29	11	24	20	.300	.352
Fred McMullin	3B69, 2B1	R	26	70	235	32	65	7	0	1	16	25	26	7	.277	.319
Eddie Murphy	OF63, 2B8	L	26	91	286	36	85	9	3	0	23	22	18	6	.297	.350
Shano Collins	OF92, 1B5, 2B1	R	32	103	365	30	100	18	11	1	56	17	19	7	.274	.392
Nemo Leibold	OF114	L	26	116	440	57	110	14	6	1	31	63	32	13	.250	.316
Ray Schalk	C106	R	25	108	333	35	73	6	3	0	22	36	22	12	.219	.255
Risberg (MS)	SS30, 3B24, 2B12, 1B7, OF3	R	23	82	273	36	70	12	3	1	27	23	32	5	.256	.333
Happy Felsch (WW)	OF53	R	26	53	206	16	52	2	5	1	20	15	13	6	.252	.325
Wilbur Good	OF35	L	32	35	148	24	37	9	4	0	11	11	16	1	.250	.365
Otto Jacobs	C21	R	29	29	73	4	15	3	1	0	3	5	8	0	.205	.274
Babe Pinelli	3B24	R	22	24	78	7	18	1	1	1	7	7	8	3	.231	.308
Joe Jackson (HO-WW)	OF17	L	28	17	65	9	23	2	2	1	20	8	1	3	.354	.492
Johnny Mostil	2B9	R	22	10	33	4	9	2	2	0	4	1	6	1	.273	.455
Al DeVormer	C6, OF1	R	26	8	19	2	5	2	0	0	0	0	4	1	.263	.368
Ted Jourdan (MS)	1B2	L	22	7	10	1	1	0	0	0	1	0	0	0	.100	.100
Byrd Lynn	C4	R	29	5	8	0	2	0	0	0	0	2	1	0	.250	.250
Kid Willson		L	22	4	1	2	0	0	0	0	0	1	1	0	.000	.000
Pat Hargrove (MS)		R	22	2	2	0	0	0	0	0	0	0	0	0	.000	.000

Joe Jenkins (MS) 27
Tom McGuire (MS) 26

NAME	T	AGE	W	L	PCT	SV	G	GS	CG	IP	H	BB	SO	ShO	ERA
TOTALS		28	57	67	.460	6	124	124	76	1126	1092	300	349	10	2.69
Eddie Cicotte	R	34	12	19	.387	2	38	30	24	266	275	40	104	1	2.64
Frank Shellenback	R	19	10	12	.455	1	28	20	10	183	180	74	47	3	2.66
Joe Benz	R	32	7	8	.467	0	29	17	10	154	156	28	30	1	2.51
Lefty Williams (WW)	L	25	6	4	.600	1	15	14	7	106	76	47	30	2	2.72
Reb Russell	L	29	6	5	.545	0	19	14	10	125	117	33	38	2	2.59
Dave Danforth	L	28	6	15	.286	2	39	13	5	139	148	40	48	0	3.43
Red Faber (MS)	R	29	5	1	.833	0	11	9	5	81	70	23	26	1	1.22
Jack Quinn	R	34	5	1	.833	0	6	5	5	51	38	7	22	0	2.29
Mellie Wolfgang	R	28	0	1	.000	0	4	0	0	8	12	3	1	0	5.63
1 Roy Mitchell	R	33	0	1	.000	0	2	2	0	12	18	4	3	0	7.50
Ed Corey (BN)	R	18	0	0	.000	0	1	0	0	2	2	1	0	0	4.50

Jim Scott (MS) 30

DETROIT 7th 55-71 .437 20 — HUGHIE JENNINGS

NAME	G by POS	B	AGE	G	AB	R	H	2B	3B	HR	RBI	BB	SO	SB	BA	SA
TOTALS			29	128	4262	473	1063	141	56	13	393	452	380	123	.249	.318
Harry Heilmann (MS)	OF40, 1B37, 2B2	R	23	79	286	34	79	10	6	5	39	35	10	13	.276	.406
Ralph Young	2B91	B	28	91	298	31	56	7	1	0	21	54	17	15	.188	.218
Donie Bush	SS128	B	30	128	500	74	117	10	3	0	22	79	31	9	.234	.266
Ossie Vitt	3B66, 2B9, OF3	R	28	81	267	29	64	5	2	0	17	32	6	5	.240	.273
George Harper	OF64	L	26	69	227	19	55	5	2	0	16	18	14	3	.242	.282
Ty Cobb	OF93, 1B13, 3B2, P2	L	31	111	421	83	161	19	14	3	64	41	21	34	.382	.515
Bobby Veach	OF127, P1	L	30	127	499	59	139	21	13	3	78	35	23	21	.279	.391
Archie Yelle	C52	R	26	56	144	7	25	3	0	0	7	9	15	0	.174	.194
Bob Jones	3B63, 1B6	L	28	74	287	43	79	14	4	0	21	17	16	7	.275	.352
Tubby Spencer	C48, 1B1	R	34	66	155	11	34	8	1	0	8	19	18	1	.219	.284
Frank Walker	OF45	R	23	55	167	10	33	10	3	1	20	7	29	3	.198	.311
Oscar Stanage (BG)	C47, 1B5	R	35	54	186	9	47	4	0	1	14	11	18	2	.253	.290
Lee Dressen	1B30	L	28	31	107	10	19	1	2	0	3	21	10	2	.178	.224
Art Griggs	1B25	R	34	28	99	11	36	8	0	0	16	10	5	2	.364	.444
1 Jack Coffey	2B22	R	31	22	67	7	14	0	2	0	4	8	5	2	.209	.269
Ben Dyer (MS)	1B2, OF2, P2, 2B1	R	25	13	18	1	5	0	0	0	2	0	6	0	.278	.278
3 Marty Kavanagh	1B12	R	27	13	44	2	12	3	0	0	9	11	6	0	.273	.341
Bert Ellison (MS)	OF4, 2B3	R	22	7	23	1	6	1	0	0	2	3	1	1	.261	.304
Harry Curry	2B5	R	29	5	20	1	5	1	0	0	0	0	1	0	.250	.300
Joe Cobb (MS)		R	23	1	0	0	0	0	0	0	0	1	0	0	.000	.000
Hughie Jennings	1B1	R	49	1	0	0	0	0	0	0	0	0	0	0	.000	.000

Ira Flagstead (MS) 24
Fred Nicholson (MS) 23

NAME	T	AGE	W	L	PCT	SV	G	GS	CG	IP	H	BB	SO	ShO	ERA
TOTALS		26	55	71	.437	8	128	128	74	1161	1130	437	371	8	3.40
Bernie Boland	R	26	14	10	.583	0	29	25	14	204	176	67	63	4	2.65
Hooks Dauss	R	28	13	16	.448	3	33	26	21	250	243	58	73	1	2.99
Rudy Kallio	R	25	8	13	.381	0	30	22	10	181	178	76	70	2	3.63
George Cunningham	R	23	6	7	.462	1	27	14	10	140	131	38	39	0	3.15
Bill James (MS)	R	31	6	11	.353	0	19	18	8	122	127	68	42	1	3.76
Eric Erickson (MS)	R	26	4	5	.444	1	12	9	8	94	81	29	48	0	2.49
Deacon Jones	R	24	2	2	.500	2	21	4	1	67	60	38	12	0	3.09
Wild Bill Donovan	R	41	1	0	1.000	0	2	1	0	6	5	1	1	0	1.50
1 Happy Finneran	R	26	1	2	.333	1	5	2	0	14	22	8	2	0	9.64
Charley Hall	R	32	0	1	.000	0	6	1	0	13	14	6	2	0	6.92
Harry Coveleski	L	32	0	1	.000	0	3	1	1	14	17	6	3	0	3.86
Willie Mitchell (MS)	L	28	0	1	.000	0	1	1	0	4	3	5	2	0	9.00
Bill Bailey	L	29	0	2	.000	0	8	4	1	38	53	26	13	0	5.92
Herb Hall	R	24	0	0	.000	0	3	0	0	6	12	7	1	0	15.00
Ty Cobb	R	31	0	0	.000	0	2	0	0	4	6	2	0	0	4.50
Ben Dyer (MS)	R	25	0	0	.000	0	2	0	0	2	0	0	0	0	0.00
Bobby Veach	R	30	0	0	.000	0	1	0	0	2	2	2	0	0	4.50

Johnny Couch (MS) 27
Howard Ehmke (MS) 24

PHILADELPHIA 8th 52-76 .406 24 — CONNIE MACK

NAME	G by POS	B	AGE	G	AB	R	H	2B	3B	HR	RBI	BB	SO	SB	BA	SA
TOTALS			25	130	4278	412	1039	124	44	22	356	343	485	83	.243	.308
George Burns	1B128, OF2	R	25	130	505	61	178	22	9	6	70	23	25	8	.352	.467
Jimmy Dykes (MS)	2B56, 3B1	R	21	59	186	13	35	3	3	0	13	19	32	3	.188	.237
Joe Dugan	SS85, 2B35	R	21	120	406	25	79	11	3	3	34	16	55	4	.195	.259
Larry Gardner	3B127	L	32	127	463	50	132	22	6	1	52	43	22	9	.285	.365
Charlie Jamieson	OF102, P5	L	25	110	416	50	84	11	2	0	11	54	30	11	.202	.238
Tilly Walker	OF109	R	30	114	414	56	122	20	0	11	48	41	44	8	.295	.423
Manny Kopp (MS)	OF96	B	26	96	363	60	85	7	7	0	18	42	55	22	.234	.292
Wickey McAvoy	C74, 1B1, OF1, P1	R	23	83	271	14	66	5	3	0	32	13	23	5	.244	.284
Red Shannon	SS45, 2B26	B	21	72	225	23	54	6	5	0	16	42	52	5	.240	.311
Cy Perkins	C60	R	22	68	218	9	41	4	1	1	14	8	15	1	.188	.229
2 Merito Acosta	OF45	L	22	49	169	3	8	1	0	0	2	2	16	0	.140	.158
Rube Oldring	OF30, 2B2, 3B2	R	34	49	133	5	31	2	1	0	11	8	10	0	.233	.263
Claude Davidson	2B15, OF8, 3B1	L	21	31	81	4	15	1	0	0	4	5	9	0	.185	.198
Jake Munch	1B2, OF2	L	27	22	30	3	8	0	1	0	0	0	5	0	.267	.333
Frank Fahey	OF5, P3	R	22	10	17	2	3	1	0	0	1	0	3	0	.176	.235

Gene Bailey (MS) 24, Ray Bates (MS) 25, Pat Haley (MS) 27, Otis Lawry (MS) 24, Whitey Witt (MS) 22

NAME	T	AGE	W	L	PCT	SV	G	GS	CG	IP	H	BB	SO	ShO	ERA
TOTALS		27	52	76	.406	7	130	130	80	1156	1105	479	279	12	3.22
Scott Perry	R	27	21	19	.525	1	44	36	30	332	295	111	81	3	1.98
Vean Gregg	L	33	8	14	.364	2	30	25	17	199	180	67	63	3	3.12
Mule Watson	R	21	6	10	.375	0	21	19	11	142	139	44	30	3	3.36
Willie Adams	R	27	6	12	.333	0	32	14	7	169	164	97	39	0	4.42
Elmer Myers (MS)	R	24	4	8	.333	1	18	15	5	95	101	42	17	1	4.64
Bob Geary (MS)	R	27	3	5	.375	3	16	7	6	87	94	31	22	2	2.69
Charlie Jamieson	L	25	2	1	.667	0	5	2	1	23	24	13	2	0	4.30
Tom Zachary (MS)	L	22	1	0	1.000	0	2	2	0	8	9	7	1	0	5.63
Roy Johnson	R	22	1	5	.167	0	10	8	3	50	47	27	14	0	3.42
Bill Pierson	L	19	0	1	.000	0	8	1	0	22	20	20	6	0	3.27
Vic Keen	R	19	0	1	.000	0	1	1	0	8	9	1	1	0	3.38
Frank Fahey	R	22	0	0	.000	0	3	0	0	9	5	14	1	0	6.00
Red Shea	R	19	0	0	.000	0	3	0	0	9	14	2	2	0	4.00
Ed Holmes	R		0	0	.000	0	2	0	0	2	4	1	0	0	13.50
Lou Bauer	R	19	0	0	.000	0	1	0	0	0	0	2	0	0	∞
Wickey McAvoy	R	23	0	0	.000	0	1	0	0	1	0	0	0	0	0.00

Walter Anderson (MS) 20, Jing Johnson (MS) 23, Dave Keefe (MS) 21, Rollie Naylor (MS) 26, Win Noyes (MS) 29, Socks Seibold (MS) 22

CHICAGO 1st 84-45 .651 — FRED MITCHELL

NAME	G by POS	B	AGE	G	AB	R	H	2B	3B	HR	RBI	BB	SO	SB	BA	SA
TOTALS			29	131	4325	538	1147	164	53	21	438	358	343	159	.265	.342
Fred Merkle	1B129	R	29	129	482	55	143	25	5	3	65	35	36	21	.297	.388
Rollie Zeider	2B79, 1B1, 3B1	R	34	82	251	31	56	3	2	0	26	23	20	16	.223	.251
Charlie Hollocher	SS131	L	22	131	509	72	161	23	6	2	38	47	30	26	.316	.397
Charlie Deal	3B118	R	26	119	414	43	99	9	3	2	34	21	13	11	.239	.290
Max Flack	OF121	L	28	123	478	74	123	17	10	4	41	56	19	17	.257	.360
Dode Paskert	OF121, 3B6	R	36	127	461	69	132	24	3	3	59	53	49	20	.286	.371
Les Mann	OF129	R	24	129	489	69	141	27	7	2	55	38	45	21	.288	.384
Bill Killefer	C104	R	30	104	331	30	77	10	3	0	22	17	10	5	.233	.281
Turner Barber	OF27, 1B4	L	24	55	123	11	29	3	2	0	10	9	16	3	.236	.293
Bob O'Farrell	C45	R	21	52	113	9	32	7	3	1	14	10	15	0	.283	.425
Pete Kilduff (MS)	2B30	R	25	30	93	7	19	2	2	0	13	7	7	1	.204	.269
Charlie Pick	2B20, 3B8	L	30	29	89	13	29	4	1	0	12	14	4	7	.326	.393
Bill McCabe	2B13, OF4	B	23	29	45	9	8	0	1	0	5	4	7	2	.178	.222
Chuck Wortman	2B8, SS4	R	26	17	17	4	2	0	0	1	3	1	2	3	.118	.294
Rowdy Elliott (MS)	C5	R	27	5	10	0	0	0	0	0	0	2	1	0	.000	.000
Fred Lear		R	24	2	1	0	0	0	0	0	0	1	0	0	.000	.000
Tommy Clarke	C1	R	30	1	0	0	0	0	0	0	0	0	0	0	.000	.000
Tom Daly	C1	R	26	1	1	0	0	0	0	0	0	0	0	0	.000	.000

Paddy Driscoll (MS) 23, Bill Marriott (MS) 25, Morrie Schick (MS) 26

NAME	T	AGE	W	L	PCT	SV	G	GS	CG	IP	H	BB	SO	ShO	ERA
		28	84	45	.651	8	131	131	92	1197	1050	296	472	23	2.18
Hippo Vaughn	L	30	22	10	.688	0	35	33	27	290	216	76	148	8	1.74
Claude Hendrix	R	29	20	7	.741	0	32	27	21	233	229	54	86	3	2.78
Lefty Tyler	L	28	19	8	.704	1	33	30	22	269	218	67	102	8	2.01
Phil Douglas	R	28	10	9	.526	2	25	19	11	157	145	31	51	2	2.12
Speed Martin	R	24	5	2	.714	1	9	5	4	54	47	14	16	1	1.83
Paul Carter	R	24	3	2	.600	2	21	4	1	73	78	19	13	0	2.71
Pete Alexander (MS)	R	31	2	1	.667	0	3	3	3	26	19	3	15	0	1.73
Harry Weaver (MS)	R	23	2	2	.500	1	8	3	1	33	27	7	9	1	2.18
Roy Walker	R	25	1	3	.250	1	13	7	2	43	50	15	20	0	2.72
Vic Aldridge (MS)	R	24	0	1	.000	0	3	0	0	12	11	6	10	0	1.50
Buddy Napier	R	28	0	0	.000	0	1	0	0	7	10	4	2	0	5.14

NEW YORK 2nd 71-53 .573 10.5 — JOHN McGRAW

NAME	G by POS	B	AGE	G	AB	R	H	2B	3B	HR	RBI	BB	SO	SB	BA	SA
TOTALS			28	124	4164	480	1081	150	53	13	400	271	365	130	.260	.330
Walter Holke (WW)	1B88	B	25	88	326	38	82	17	4	1	27	10	26	10	.252	.337
Larry Doyle (IL)	2B73	L	31	75	257	38	67	7	4	3	36	37	10	10	.261	.354
Art Fletcher	SS124	R	33	124	468	51	123	20	2	0	47	18	20	12	.263	.314
Heinie Zimmerman	3B100, 1B19	R	31	121	463	43	126	19	10	1	56	13	23	14	.272	.363
Ross Youngs	OF120	L	21	124	474	70	143	16	8	1	25	44	49	10	.302	.376
Benny Kauff (MS)	OF67	L	28	67	270	41	85	19	4	2	39	16	30	9	.315	.437
George Burns	OF119	R	28	119	465	80	135	22	6	4	51	43	37	40	.290	.389
Lew McCarty	C75	R	29	86	257	16	69	7	3	0	24	17	13	3	.268	.319
Bill Rariden	C63	R	30	69	183	15	41	5	1	0	17	15	15	1	.224	.262
Joe Wilhoit	OF55	L	26	64	135	13	37	3	3	0	15	17	14	4	.274	.341
Jim Thorpe	OF44	R	30	58	113	15	28	4	4	1	11	4	18	3	.248	.381
Joe Rodriguez	2B40, 1B8, 3B2	R	23	50	125	15	20	0	2	0	15	12	3	6	.160	.192
Eddie Sicking (MS)	3B24, 2B18, SS2	R	21	46	132	9	33	4	0	0	12	6	11	2	.250	.280
Pete Compton	OF19	L	28	21	60	5	13	0	1	0	5	5	4	2	.217	.250
Jay Kirke	1B16	L	30	17	56	1	14	1	0	0	3	1	3	0	.250	.268
2 Bert Niehoff (BL)	2B7	R	34	7	23	3	6	0	0	0	1	0	4	0	.261	.261
George Gibson	C4	R	37	4	2	0	1	1	0	0	0	0	0	0	.500	1.000

Al Baird (MS) 23
George Kelly (MS) 22
Dave Robertson (MS) 28

NAME	T	AGE	W	L	PCT	SV	G	GS	CG	IP	H	BB	SO	ShO	ERA
		29	71	53	.573	11	124	124	74	1112	1002	228	330	18	2.64
Pol Perritt	R	25	18	13	.581	0	35	31	19	233	212	38	60	6	2.74
Red Causey	R	24	11	6	.647	2	29	18	10	158	143	42	48	2	2.79
Al Demaree	R	31	8	6	.571	1	26	14	8	142	143	25	39	2	2.47
Slim Sallee	L	33	8	8	.500	2	18	16	12	132	122	12	33	1	2.25
Jesse Barnes (MS)	R	25	6	1	.857	0	9	9	4	55	53	10	12	2	1.80
2 Fred Toney	R	30	6	2	.750	1*	11	9	7	85	55	7	19	1	1.69
Fred Anderson (MS)	R	32	4	2	.667	3	18	4	2	71	62	17	24	1	2.66
Jeff Tesreau (WW)	R	29	4	4	.500	0	12	9	3	74	61	21	31	1	2.31
2 Bob Steele	L	24	3	5	.375	1	12	7	5	66	56	11	24	1	2.59
2 George Smith	R	26	2	3	.400	0	5	2	1	27	26	6	4	0	4.00
Rube Benton (MS)	L	31	1	2	.333	0	3	3	2	24	17	3	9	0	1.88
Ferdie Schupp (AJ)	L	27	0	1	.000	0	10	2	1	33	42	27	22	0	7.64
Jack Ogden	R	20	0	0	.000	0	5	0	0	9	8	3	1	0	3.00
Waite Hoyt	R	18	0	0	.000	0	1	0	0	1	0	0	2	0	0.00
George Ross	L	26	0	0	.000	1	1	0	0	2	2	3	2	0	0.00

*Toney, also with Cincinnati, tied for league lead in SV with 3

CINCINNATI 3rd 68-60 .531 15.5 — CHRISTY MATHEWSON 61-57 .517 HEINIE GROH 7-3 .700

NAME	G by POS	B	AGE	G	AB	R	H	2B	3B	HR	RBI	BB	SO	SB	BA	SA
TOTALS			29	129	4265	538	1185	165	84	15	447	304	303	128	.278	.366
Hal Chase (ST)	1B67, OF2	R	35	74	259	30	78	12	6	2	38	13	15	5	.301	.417
Lee Magee	2B114, 3B3	B	29	119	459	62	133	22	13	0	28	28	19	19	.290	.394
Lena Blackburne	SS125	R	31	125	435	35	99	8	10	1	45	25	30	6	.228	.299
Heinie Groh	3B126	R	28	126	493	88	158	28	3	1	37	54	24	11	.320	.396
Tommy Griffith	OF118	L	28	118	427	47	113	10	4	2	48	39	30	10	.265	.321
Edd Roush	OF113	L	25	113	435	61	145	18	10	5	62	22	10	24	.333	.455
Greasy Neale	OF102	L	26	107	371	59	100	11	11	1	32	24	38	23	.270	.367
Ivy Wingo	C93, OF5	L	27	100	323	36	82	15	6	0	31	19	18	6	.254	.337
Sherry Magee	1B66, OF38, 2B6	R	33	115	400	46	119	15	13	2	76	37	18	14	.298	.415
Manuel Cueto	OF19, 2B10, SS9, C6	R	26	48	108	14	32	5	1	0	14	19	5	4	.296	.361
Nick Allen (MS)	C31	R	29	37	96	6	25	2	2	0	5	4	7	0	.260	.323
Pete Schneider	P33	R	25	36	83	11	24	3	2	1	7	0	12	0	.289	.410
Harry Smith	C6, OF1	R	28	13	27	4	5	1	2	0	4	3	6	1	.185	.370
3 Jimmy Archer	C7, 1B1	R	35	9	26	3	7	1	0	0	2	1	3	0	.269	.308

Pat Duncan (MS) 24
Larry Kopf (MS) 27
Morrie Rath (MS) 31

NAME	T	AGE	W	L	PCT	SV	G	GS	CG	IP	H	BB	SO	ShO	ERA
		26	68	60	.531	6	129	129	84	1143	1136	381	321	14	3.00
Hod Eller	R	23	16	12	.571	1	37	22	14	218	205	59	84	0	2.35
Pete Schneider	R	25	10	15	.400	0	33	30	17	218	213	117	51	2	3.51
Jimmy Ring	R	23	9	5	.643	0	21	18	13	142	130	48	26	4	2.85
Rube Bressler (MS)	L	23	8	15	.615	0	17	13	10	128	124	39	37	0	2.46
Dolf Luque	R	27	6	3	.667	0	12	10	9	83	84	32	26	1	3.80
1 Fred Toney	R	30	6	10	.375	2*	21	19	9	137	148	31	32	1	2.89
Mike Regan	R	30	5	5	.500	2	22	6	4	80	77	29	15	3	3.26
2 Roy Mitchell	R	33	4	0	1.000	0	5	3	3	36	27	5	9	2	0.75
Snipe Conley	R	24	2	0	1.000	1	5	0	0	14	17	5	2	0	5.14
1 George Smith	R	26	2	3	.400	0	10	6	4	55	71	11	19	1	4.09
Larry Jacobus	R	24	0	1	.000	0	5	0	0	17	25	1	8	0	5.82
Dutch Ruether (MS)	L	24	0	1	.000	0	2	2	1	10	10	3	10	0	2.70
Jesse Haines	R	24	0	0	.000	0	1	0	0	5	5	1	2	0	1.80

*Toney, also with New York, tied for league lead in SV with 3

PITTSBURGH 4th 65-60 .520 17 — HUGO BEZDEK

NAME	G by POS	B	AGE	G	AB	R	H	2B	3B	HR	RBI	BB	SO	SB	BA	SA
TOTALS			27	126	4091	466	1016	107	72	15	391	371	285	200	.248	.321
Fritz Mollwitz	1B119	R	28	119	432	43	116	12	7	0	45	23	24	23	.269	.329
George Cutshaw	2B126	R	30	126	463	56	132	16	10	5	68	27	18	25	.285	.395
Buster Caton (MS)	SS79	R	21	80	303	37	71	5	7	0	17	32	16	12	.234	.297
Bill McKechnie	3B126	B	31	126	435	34	111	13	9	2	43	24	22	12	.255	.340
Billy Southworth	OF64	L	25	64	246	37	84	5	7	2	43	26	9	19	.341	.443
Max Carey	OF126	B	28	126	468	70	128	14	6	3	48	62	25	58	.274	.348
Carson Bigbee	OF92	L	23	92	310	47	79	11	3	1	19	42	10	19	.255	.319
Walter Schmidt	C104	R	31	105	323	31	77	6	3	0	27	17	19	7	.238	.276
Bill Hinchman	OF40, 1B3	R	35	50	111	10	26	5	2	0	13	15	8	1	.234	.315
Casey Stengel (MS)	OF27	L	27	39	122	18	30	4	1	1	12	16	14	11	.246	.320
Lee King (MS)	OF36	R	25	36	112	9	26	3	2	1	11	11	15	3	.232	.321
Tommy Leach	OF23, SS3	R	40	30	72	14	14	2	3	0	5	19	5	2	.194	.306
Luke Boone	SS26, 2B1	R	28	27	91	7	18	3	0	0	3	8	6	1	.198	.231
Roy Ellam	SS26	R	32	26	77	9	10	1	1	0	2	17	17	2	.130	.169
1 Jimmy Archer	C21, 1B1	R	35	24	58	4	9	1	2	0	3	1	6	0	.155	.241
Ben Shaw (MS)	1B9, C5	R	25	21	36	5	7	1	0	0	2	2	2	0	.194	.222
Red Smith	C10	R	26	15	24	1	4	1	0	0	3	3	0	0	.167	.208
Fred Blackwell (MS)	C8	L	22	8	13	1	2	0	0	0	4	3	4	0	.154	.154
2 Gus Getz	3B2	R	28	7	10	0	2	0	0	0	0	0	1	0	.200	.200
Jake Pitler	2B1	R	24	2	1	1	0	0	0	0	0	1	0	2	.000	.000

Tony Boeckel (MS) 25
Adam Debus (MS) 25
Charlie Jackson (MS) 24
Ray Miller (MS) 30, Hooks Warner (MS) 24, Billy Webb (MS) 22

NAME	T	AGE	W	L	PCT	SV	G	GS	CG	IP	H	BB	SO	ShO	ERA
		28	65	60	.520	7	126	126	85	1140	1005	299	367	10	2.48
Wilbur Cooper	L	26	19	14	.576	3	38	29	26	273	219	65	117	3	2.11
Frank Miller	R	32	11	8	.579	0	23	23	14	170	152	37	47	2	2.38
2 Erskine Mayer	R	29	9	3	.750	0	15	14	11	123	122	27	25	1	2.27
Roy Sanders	R	25	7	9	.438	1	28	14	6	156	135	52	55	1	2.60
Earl Hamilton (MS)	L	26	6	0	1.000	0	6	6	6	54	47	13	20	1	0.83
Ralph Comstock	R	27	5	6	.455	1	15	8	6	81	78	14	44	0	3.00
1 Bob Steele	L	24	2	3	.400	1	10	4	2	49	44	17	21	1	3.31
Carmen Hill	R	22	2	3	.400	0	6	4	3	44	24	17	15	0	1.23
Bob Harmon	R	30	2	7	.222	0	16	9	5	82	76	12	7	0	2.63
Babe Adams	R	36	1	1	.500	0	3	3	2	23	15	4	6	0	1.17
Cy Slapnicka	R	32	1	4	.200	1	7	6	4	49	50	22	3	0	4.78
1 Elmer Jacobs	R	25	0	1	.000	0	8	4	0	23	31	14	2	0	5.87
Hal Carlson (MS)	R	24	0	1	.000	0	3	2	0	12	12	5	5	0	3.75

Bill Evans (MS) 25
Elmer Ponder (MS) 25

BROOKLYN 5th 57-69 .452 25.5 — WILBERT ROBINSON

NAME	G by POS	B	AGE	G	AB	R	H	2B	3B	HR	RBI	BB	SO	SB	BA	SA
TOTALS			30	126	4212	360	1052	121	62	10	303	212	326	113	.250	.315
Jake Daubert	1B105	L	34	108	396	50	122	12	15	2	47	27	18	10	.308	.429
Mickey Doolan	2B91	R	38	92	308	14	55	8	2	0	18	22	24	8	.179	.218
Ivy Olson	SS126	R	32	126	506	63	121	16	4	1	17	27	18	21	.239	.292
Ollie O'Mara	3B121	R	27	121	450	29	96	8	1	1	24	7	18	11	.213	.242
Jimmy Johnston	OF96, 1B21, 3B4, 2B1	R	28	123	484	54	136	16	8	0	27	33	31	22	.281	.347
Hy Myers	OF107	R	29	107	407	36	104	9	8	4	40	20	26	17	.256	.346
Zack Wheat	OF105	L	32	105	409	39	137	15	3	0	51	16	17	9	.335	.386
Otto Miller	C62, 1B1	R	29	75	228	8	44	6	1	0	8	9	20	1	.193	.228
Mack Wheat	C38, OF7	R	25	57	157	11	34	7	1	1	3	8	24	2	.217	.293
Dave Hickman (MS)	OF46	R	24	53	167	14	39	4	7	1	16	8	31	5	.234	.359
Jack Coombs	P27, OF13	B	35	46	113	6	19	3	2	0	3	7	5	1	.168	.230
Ray Schmandt	2B34	R	22	34	114	11	35	5	4	0	18	7	7	1	.307	.421
Ernie Krueger (MS)	C23	R	27	30	87	4	25	4	2	0	7	4	9	2	.287	.379
2 Jimmy Archer	C7	R	35	9	22	3	6	0	1	0	0	1	5	0	.273	.364
Al Nixon	OF4	R	32	6	11	1	5	0	0	0	0	0	0	0	.455	.455
Frank O'Rourke	2B2, OF1	R	23	4	12	0	2	0	0	0	2	1	3	0	.167	.167
Al Bashang	OF1	B	29	2	5	0	1	0	0	0	0	0	0	0	.200	.200
Red Sheridan (MS)	2B2	R	21	2	4	0	1	0	0	0	0	1	0	1	.250	.250
Chuck Ward (MS)	3B2	R	23	2	6	0	2	0	0	0	3	0	0	0	.333	.333

Lew Malone (MS) 21

NAME	T	AGE	W	L	PCT	SV	G	GS	CG	IP	H	BB	SO	ShO	ERA
		29	57	69	.452	2	126	126	85	1131	1024	320	395	17	2.81
Burleigh Grimes	R	24	19	9	.679	1	40	28	19	270	210	76	113	7	2.13
Larry Cheney	R	32	11	13	.458	1	32	21	15	201	177	74	83	0	3.00
Rube Marquard	L	28	9	18	.333	0	34	29	19	239	231	59	89	4	2.64
Jack Coombs	R	35	8	14	.364	0	27	22	16	189	191	49	44	2	3.81
3 George Smith	R	26	4	1	.800	0	8	5	4	50	43	5	18	0	2.34
Dick Robertson	R	27	3	6	.333	0	13	9	7	87	87	28	18	1	2.59
Leon Cadore (MS)	R	27	1	0	1.000	0	2	2	1	17	6	2	5	1	0.53
Jeff Pfeffer (MS)	R	30	1	0	1.000	0	1	1	1	9	2	3	1	1	0.00
Dan Griner	R	30	1	5	.167	0	11	6	3	54	47	15	22	1	2.17
Al Mamaux	R	24	0	1	.000	0	2	1	0	8	14	2	2	0	6.75
Harry Heitmann (MS)	R	21	0	1	.000	0	1	1	0	.1	4	0	0	0	8.00
Clarence Mitchell (MS)	L	27	0	1	.000	0	1	1	0	.1	4	0	0	0	8.00
Dick Durning	L	25	0	0	.000	0	1	0	0	2	3	4	0	0	13.50
Jake Hehl	R	18	0	0	.000	0	1	0	0	1	0	0	0	0	0.00
Lefty Herrmann	L	25	0	0	.000	0	1	0	0	1	0	1	0	0	0.00
Norman Plitt	R	25	0	0	.000	0	1	0	0	2	3	1	0	0	4.50
Jack Russell (MS)	L	22	0	0	.000	0	1	0	0	1	2	1	0	0	18.00

Johnny Miljus (MS) 23
Sherry Smith (MS) 27
Duster Mails (MS) 22

PHILADELPHIA 6th 55-68 .447 26 — PAT MORAN

NAME	G by POS	B	AGE	G	AB	R	H	2B	3B	HR	RBI	BB	SO	SB	BA	SA
TOTALS			29	125	4192	429	1022	158	28	25	376	346	400	97	.244	.313
Fred Luderus	1B125	L	32	125	468	54	135	23	2	5	67	42	33	4	.288	.378
Patsy McGaffigan (MS)	2B53, SS1	R	29	54	192	17	39	3	2	1	8	16	23	3	.203	.255
Dave Bancroft	SS125	B	27	125	499	69	132	19	4	0	26	54	36	11	.265	.319
Milt Stock	3B123	R	24	123	481	62	132	14	1	1	42	35	22	20	.274	.314
Gavvy Cravath	OF118	R	37	121	426	43	99	27	5	8	54	54	46	7	.232	.376
Cy Williams	OF91	L	30	94	351	49	97	14	1	6	39	27	30	10	.276	.373
Irish Meusel	OF120, 2B4	R	25	124	473	47	132	25	6	4	62	30	21	18	.279	.383
Jack Adams	C76	B	27	84	227	10	40	4	0	0	12	10	26	5	.176	.194
Ed Burns	C68	R	29	68	184	10	38	1	1	0	9	20	9	1	.207	.223
Justin Fitzgerald	OF57	L	28	66	133	21	39	8	0	0	6	13	6	3	.293	.353
Harry Pearce	2B46, SS2, 1B1, 3B1	R	28	60	164	16	40	3	2	0	18	9	31	5	.244	.287
Ed Hemingway	2B25, 3B3, 1B1	B	25	33	108	7	23	4	1	0	12	7	9	4	.213	.269
Possum Whitted	OF22, 1B1	R	28	24	86	7	21	4	0	0	3	4	10	4	.244	.291
Pickles Dillhoefer (MS)	C6	R	23	8	11	0	1	0	0	0	0	1	1	2	.091	.091

Mickey Devine 26 R 1-8, Ty Pickup 20 R 1-1, Claude Cooper (MS) 25

NAME	T	AGE	W	L	PCT	SV	G	GS	CG	IP	H	BB	SO	ShO	ERA
		27	55	68	.447	6	125	125	78	1140	1086	369	312	10	3.15
Brad Hogg	R	30	13	13	.500	1	29	25	17	228	201	61	81	3	2.53
Mike Prendergast	L	29	13	14	.481	1	33	30	20	252	257	46	41	0	2.89
2 Elmer Jacobs	R	25	9	5	.643	1	18	14	12	123	91	42	33	3	2.41
1 Erskine Mayer	R	29	7	4	.636	0	13	13	7	104	108	26	16	0	3.12
Joe Oeschger	R	27	6	18	.250	3	30	23	13	184	159	83	60	2	3.03
Milt Watson	R	25	5	7	.417	0	23	11	6	113	126	36	29	0	3.42
Alex Main	R	34	2	2	.500	0	8	4	1	35	30	16	14	1	4.63
Ben Tincup (MS)	R	27	0	1	.000	0	8	1	0	17	24	6	6	0	7.41
Dixie Davis (MS)	R	27	0	2	.000	0	17	2	1	47	43	30	18	0	3.06
Gary Fortune	R	23	0	2	.000	0	5	2	1	31	41	19	10	0	8.13
Frank Woodward (MS)	R	24	0	0	.000	0	2	0	0	6	6	4	4	0	6.00

Stan Baumgartner (VR) 25
Eppa Rixey (MS) 27

BOSTON 7th 53-71 .427 28.5 — GEORGE STALLINGS

NAME	G by POS	B	AGE	G	AB	R	H	2B	3B	HR	RBI	BB	SO	SB	BA	SA
TOTALS			29	124	4162	424	1014	107	59	13	353	350	438	83	.244	.307
Ed Konetchy	1B112, OF6, P1	R	32	119	437	33	103	15	5	2	56	32	35	5	.236	.307
Buck Herzog	2B99, 1B12, SS7	R	32	118	473	57	108	12	6	0	26	29	28	10	.228	.279
Johnny Rawlings	SS71, 2B20, OF18	R	25	111	410	32	85	7	3	0	21	30	31	10	.207	.239
Red Smith	3B119	R	28	119	429	55	128	20	3	2	65	45	47	8	.298	.373
Al Wickland	OF95	L	30	95	332	55	87	7	13	4	32	53	39	12	.262	.398
Ray Powell (MS)	OF53	L	29	53	188	31	40	7	5	0	20	29	30	2	.213	.303
Roy Massey	OF45, 1B4, SS1, 3B1	L	27	66	203	20	59	6	2	0	18	23	20	1	.291	.340
Art Wilson	C85	R	32	89	280	15	69	8	2	0	19	24	31	5	.246	.289
Joe Kelly (MS)	OF45	R	28	47	155	20	36	2	4	0	15	6	12	12	.232	.297
John Henry	C38	R	28	43	102	6	21	2	0	0	4	10	15	0	.206	.225
Wally Rehg (MS)	OF38	R	29	40	133	6	32	5	1	1	12	5	14	3	.241	.316
Jimmy Kelly	OF35	L	28	35	146	19	48	1	4	0	4	9	9	4	.329	.390
Jimmy Smith	SS9, 2B7, OF6, 3B5	B	23	34	102	8	23	3	4	1	14	3	13	1	.225	.363
Zeb Terry (MS)	SS27	R	27	28	105	17	32	2	2	0	8	8	14	1	.305	.362
Chet Chadbourne	OF27	L	33	27	104	9	27	2	1	0	6	5	5	5	.260	.298
Rip Conway (MS)	2B5, 3B1	L	22	14	24	4	4	0	0	0	2	2	4	1	.167	.167
Doc Crandall	P5, OF3	R	30	14	28	1	8	0	0	0	2	4	3	0	.286	.286
Bill Wagner	C13	R	24	13	47	2	10	0	0	1	7	4	5	0	.213	.277
Rabbit Maranville (MS)	SS11	R	26	11	38	3	12	0	1	0	3	4	0	0	.316	.368
Buzz Murphy	OF9	L	23	9	32	6	12	2	3	1	9	3	5	0	.375	.719
Walt Tragresser (MS)	C7	R	31	7	1	0	0	0	0	0	0	0	0	0	.000	.000
Fred Bailey (MS)		L	22	4	4	1	1	0	0	0	0	0	1	0	.250	.250

Sam Covington (MS) 25 L 1-3, Tom Miller 20 L 0-2, Doc Bass 1-1, Paul Johnson 21 R 0-0, Hank Gowdy (MS) 28, Art Rico (MS) 21, Hank Schreiber (MS) 26

NAME	T	AGE	W	L	PCT	SV	G	GS	CG	IP	H	BB	SO	ShO	ERA
		28	53	71	.427	0	124	124	96	1117	1111	277	340	13	2.90
Art Nehf	L	25	15	15	.500	0	32	31	28	284	274	76	96	2	2.69
Dick Rudolph	R	30	9	10	.474	0	21	20	15	154	144	30	48	3	2.57
Pat Ragan	R	29	8	17	.320	0	30	25	15	206	212	54	68	2	3.23
Dana Fillingim (MS)	R	24	7	6	.538	0	14	13	10	113	99	28	29	4	2.23
Bunny Hearn	L	27	5	6	.455	0	17	12	9	126	119	29	30	1	2.50
Jake Northrop	R	30	5	1	.833	0	7	4	4	40	26	3	4	1	1.35
Hugh McQuillan	R	20	1	0	1.000	0	1	1	1	9	7	5	1	0	3.00
Bill Upham	R	30	1	1	.500	0	3	2	2	21	28	1	8	0	5.14
Doc Crandall	R	30	1	2	.333	0	5	3	3	34	39	4	4	0	2.38
Lefty George	L	31	1	5	.167	0	9	5	4	54	56	21	22	0	2.33
Cal Crum	R	26	0	1	.000	0	1	1	0	2	6	3	0	0	18.00
Ed Konetchy	R	32	0	1	.000	0	1	1	1	8	14	2	3	0	6.75
Tom Hughes	R	34	0	2	.000	0	3	3	1	18	17	6	9	0	3.50
Hugh Canavan (MS)	L	21	0	4	.000	0	11	3	3	47	70	15	18	0	6.32

Bill James (MS) 26

ST. LOUIS 8th 51-78 .395 33 — JACK HENDRICKS

NAME	G by POS	B	AGE	G	AB	R	H	2B	3B	HR	RBI	BB	SO	SB	BA	SA
TOTALS			25	131	**4369**	454	1066	147	64	**27**	388	329	**461**	119	.244	.325
G. Paulette	1B97, SS12, 2B7, OF6, 3B2, C1, P1	R	26	125	461	33	126	15	3	0	52	27	16	11	.273	.319
Bobby Fisher	2B63	R	31	63	246	36	78	11	3	2	20	15	11	7	.317	.411
Rogers Hornsby	SS109, OF2	R	22	115	416	51	117	19	11	5	60	40	43	8	.281	.416
Doug Baird (MS)	3B81, SS1, OF1	R	26	82	316	41	78	12	8	2	25	25	42	25	.247	.354
Walton Cruise (MS)	OF65	L	28	70	240	34	65	5	4	6	39	30	26	2	.271	.400
Cliff Heathcote	OF88	L	20	88	348	37	90	12	3	4	32	20	40	12	.259	.345
Austin McHenry	OF80	R	22	80	272	32	71	12	6	1	29	21	24	8	.261	.360
Mike Gonzalez	C100, OF5, 1B2	R	27	117	349	33	88	13	4	3	20	39	30	14	.252	.338
Bruno Betzel	3B34, OF21, 2B10	R	23	76	230	18	51	6	7	0	13	12	16	8	.222	.309
Charlie Grimm	1B42, OF2, 3B1	L	19	50	141	11	31	7	0	0	12	6	15	2	.220	.270
Jack Smith (MS)	OF42	L	23	42	166	24	35	2	1	0	4	7	21	5	.211	.235
Red Smyth	OF25, 2B11	L	25	40	113	19	24	1	2	0	4	16	11	3	.212	.257
Frank Snyder (MS)	C27, 1B3	R	25	39	112	5	28	7	1	0	10	6	13	4	.250	.330
George Anderson	OF35	L	28	35	132	20	39	4	5	0	6	15	7	0	.295	.402
Bobby Wallace	2B17, SS12, 3B1	R	44	32	98	3	15	1	0	0	4	6	9	1	.153	.163
John Brock	C18, OF1	R	20	27	52	9	11	2	0	0	4	3	10	5	.212	.250
1 Bert Niehoff	2B22	R	34	22	84	5	15	2	0	0	5	3	10	2	.179	.202
Johnny Beall	OF18	L	36	19	49	2	11	1	0	0	6	3	6	0	.224	.245
Herman Bronkie	3B18	R	33	18	68	7	15	3	0	1	7	2	4	0	.221	.309
2 Marty Kavanagh	OF8, 2B4	R	27	12	44	6	8	1	0	1	8	3	1	1	.182	.273
Dutch Distel	2B5, SS2, OF1	R	22	8	17	3	3	1	1	0	1	2	3	0	.176	.353

Chick Mattick 31 R 2-14, Dick Wheeler 20 R 0-6, Bob Larmore 21 R 2-7, Tony Brottem (MS) 26 R 0-4, Ted Menze 20 R 0-3, Dots Miller (MS) 31

NAME	T	AGE	W	L	PCT	SV	G	GS	CG	IP	H	BB	SO	ShO	ERA
		26	51	**78**	.395	5	131	131	72	1193	**1148**	352	361	3	2.96
Gene Packard	L	30	12	12	.500	2	30	23	10	182	184	33	46	1	3.51
Red Ames	R	35	9	14	.391	1	27	25	17	207	192	52	68	0	2.30
Bill Doak	R	27	9	15	.375	1	31	23	16	211	191	60	74	1	2.43
Lee Meadows	R	23	8	14	.364	1	30	21	12	165	176	56	49	0	3.60
Bill Sherdel	L	21	6	12	.333	0	35	17	9	182	174	49	40	1	2.72
Jakie May (MS)	L	22	5	6	.455	0	29	16	6	153	149	69	61	0	3.82
Rankin Johnson	R	30	1	1	.500	0	6	1	0	23	20	7	4	0	2.74
Oscar Tuero	R	25	1	2	.333	0	11	3	2	44	32	10	13	0	1.02
Oscar Horstmann (MS)	R	27	0	2	.000	0	9	2	0	23	29	14	6	0	5.48
Earl Howard	R	22	0	0	.000	0	1	0	0	2	0	2	0	0	0.00
Gene Paulette	R	26	0	0	.000	0	1	0	0	.1	1	0	0	0	0.00

Marv Goodwin (MS) 27
Lou North (MS) 27
Bruce Hitt (MS) 20

WORLD SERIES – BOSTON (AL) 4 CHICAGO (NL) 2

LINE SCORES

TEAM	1	2	3	4	5	6	7	8	9	10	11	12	R	H	E
Game 1 September 5 at Chicago															
BOS (AL)	0	0	0	1	0	0	0	0	0				1	5	0
CHI (NL)	0	0	0	0	0	0	0	0	0				0	6	0
Ruth Vaughn															
Game 2 September 6 at Chicago															
BOS	0	0	0	0	0	0	0	0	1				1	6	1
CHI	0	3	0	0	0	0	0	0	X				3	7	1
Bush **Tyler**															
Game 3 September 7 at Chicago															
BOS	0	0	0	2	0	0	0	0	0				2	7	0
CHI	0	0	0	0	1	0	0	0	0				1	7	1
Mays Vaughn															
Game 4 September 9 at Boston															
CHI	0	0	0	0	0	0	0	2	0				2	7	1
BOS	0	0	0	2	0	0	0	1	X				3	4	0
Tyler, Douglas (8) **Ruth**, Bush (9)															
Game 5 September 10 at Boston															
CHI	0	0	1	0	0	0	0	2	0				3	7	0
BOS	0	0	0	0	0	0	0	0	0				0	5	0
Vaughn Jones															
Game 6 September 11 at Boston															
CHI	0	0	0	1	0	0	0	0	0				1	3	2
BOS	0	0	2	0	0	0	0	0	X				2	5	0
Tyler, Hendrix (8) **Mays**															

COMPOSITE BATTING

NAME	POS	G	AB	R	H	2B	3B	HR	RBI	BA
Boston (AL)										
Totals		6	172	9	32	2	3	0	6	.186
Strunk	OF	6	**23**	1	4	1	1	0	0	.174
Scott	SS	6	21	0	2	0	0	0	1	.095
McInnis	1B	6	20	2	5	0	0	0	1	.250
Whiteman	OF	6	20	2	5	0	1	0	1	.250
Hooper	OF	6	20	0	4	0	0	0	0	.200
Shean	2B	6	19	2	4	1	0	0	0	.211
Thomas	3B	6	16	0	2	0	0	0	0	.125
Schang	C	5	9	1	4	0	0	0	1	.444
Agnew	C	4	9	0	0	0	0	0	0	.000
Ruth	P-OF	3	5	0	1	0	1	0	2	.200
Mays	P	2	5	1	1	0	0	0	0	.200
Bush	P	2	2	0	0	0	0	0	0	.000
Dubuc	PH	1	1	0	0	0	0	0	0	.000
Miller	PH	1	1	0	0	0	0	0	0	.000
Jones	P	1	1	0	0	0	0	0	0	.000
Chicago (NL)										
Totals		6	176	10	37	5	1	0	10	.210
Mann	OF	6	22	0	5	**2**	0	0	**2**	.227
Hollocher	SS	6	21	2	4	0	1	0	1	.190
Paskert	OF	6	21	0	4	1	0	0	2	.190
Flack	OF	6	19	2	5	0	0	0	0	.263
Pick	2B	6	18	2	**7**	1	0	0	0	**.389**
Merkle	1B	6	18	1	5	0	0	0	1	.278
Deal	3B	6	17	0	3	0	0	0	0	.176
Killefer	C	6	17	2	2	1	0	0	2	.118
Vaughn	P	3	10	0	0	0	0	0	0	.000
Tyler	P	3	5	0	1	0	0	0	2	.200
O'Farrell	C	3	3	0	0	0	0	0	0	.000
Barber	PH	3	2	0	0	0	0	0	0	.000
Hendrix	P	2	1	0	1	0	0	0	0	1.000
Wortman	2B	1	1	0	0	0	0	0	0	.000
McCabe	PR-PH	3	1	1	0	0	0	0	0	.000
Zeider	3B	2	0	0	0	0	0	0	0	.000
Douglas	P	1	0	0	0	0	0	0	0	.000

COMPOSITE PITCHING

NAME	G	IP	H	BB	SO	W	L	SV	ERA
Boston (AL)									
Totals	6	53	37	18	14	4	2	0	1.70
Mays	2	18	10	3	5	**2**	0	0	**1.00**
Ruth	2	17	13	7	4	**2**	0	0	1.06
Bush	2	9	7	3	0	0	1	**1**	3.00
Jones	1	9	7	5	5	0	1	0	3.00
Chicago (NL)									
Totals	6	52	32	16	21	2	4	0	1.04
Vaughn	**3**	**27**	17	5	**17**	1	2	0	**1.00**
Tyler	**3**	23	14	**11**	4	1	1	0	1.17
Douglas	1	1	1	0	0	0	1	0	0.00
Hendrix	1	1	0	0	0	0	0	0	0.00

1919 Prelude to Disaster

After war had shortened the 1918 baseball season, peace and the national pastime each staged comebacks in this year of the armistice. A nation of baseball fans turned out at the ball parks in swarms in individual pursuit of a "return to normalcy", and interest in the game surpassed any level since the Federal League conflict. The highest number of fans since 1912 attended the World Series between the favored Chicago White Sox and the lightly-held Cincinnati Reds, and this nightcap to the season, experimentally lengthened to nine games, showed the Reds easily downing the Sox five games to three. The educated opinion on the Series outcome postulated that Chicago had been tired out by a rigorous pennant race, while Cincinnati had saved its strength by clinching its pennant early.

The shiny Series cup concealed the corruption within. The public did not yet know that seven White Sox players had agreed to throw the Series in return for $100,000 from gambling interests. The average fan could not realize that Joe Jackson's .375 batting average only camouflaged his intentional failings in clutch situations, and the man in the bleachers did not suspect that star Sox pitchers, Eddie Cicotte and Lefty Williams, were being shelled from the mound because of lack of effort to fire the ball. Had the public known of the sordid deal, they would have better appreciated the gutty performance of pitcher Dicky Kerr, who won two games despite the treason of half the team behind him in the field. But the public did not know and would not until September of the following year. There were only some unsupported rumors about White Sox' dishonesty, thus making the 1919 World Series a simple upset victory and a fitting end to a good season.

Fate would have been kinder if it had not allowed the White Sox to edge out the Cleveland Indians for the American League flag. But Joe Jackson and Happy Felsch, both Series throwers, and Eddie Collins, not involved in the fix, provided too much talent to keep Chicago away from the pennant. The trio sparked the league's best offense, while Eddie Cicotte and Lefty Williams proved a pair of aces on the hill. Freshman manager Kid Gleason led his charges into first place on July 10, and strong challenges by the Indians and the New York Yankees could not budge the Sox from that top spot the rest of the way. Regardless of the World Series fix, the Sox had to honestly fight down to the wire to win by a 3½ game final bulge over the Indians for the pennant.

The Cincinnati Reds became a part of baseball's notoriety by winning the National League pennant over the New York Giants, whom they caught in August and then turned away in two crucial series late in the season. The Reds, in winning their first senior circuit title, piled up a final nine-game margin, sparked by the batting of Edd Roush and Heinie Groh and the pitching of Slim Sallee, Hod Eller, and Dutch Reuther. Although the stirring Series win seemingly capped a glorious Cincinnati season, in retrospect one overlooks that the Reds won—remembering only that the White Sox threw it all away.

For the runner-up Giants, their season was brightened by Jesse Barnes, who returned from the military to lead the circuit with his 25 wins. Another war-time returnee, Grover "Pete" Alexander, posted a 16-11 mark with a league-leading 1.72 E.R.A.—a fine performance, especially when coupled with teammate Hippo Vaughn's 21 wins and 1.79 E.R.A., but not enough to help Chicago repeat as league champions.

The year, in addition to bringing later disaster, also ushered in a legend which would eventually restore the faith of the game. A free-swinging young slugger by the name of Babe Ruth became the sensation of baseball by developing into the greatest power-hitter in history. The pitcher-turned-outfielder set a new season's home run record by clouting 29 circuit-blasts, eclipsing Ned Williamson's mark of 27 set in 1884 for Chicago. The lusty Ruth also found time to pitch 17 games for the Red Sox. It was a herculean feat, yet not enough to prevent the Beantowners from falling from the top in 1918 to a sixth-place finish. Boston's fall from glory was attributed in large measure to star pitcher Carl Mays' jumping of the team and subsequent sale to the Yankees—a deal which triggered a severe internal squabble within the American League. Boston owner Harry Frazee's troubles due to a deserting star and second-division finish did not end there. He found himself pinched for funds and restocked his empty coffers by selling the fabulous Ruth to the Yankees during the winter for $125,000, thus enabling New York to begin the greatest dynasty in the history of baseball.

1919 AMERICAN LEAGUE

NAME	G by POS	B	AGE	G	AB	R	H	2B	3B	HR	RBI	BB	SO	SB	BA	SA
CHICAGO 1st 88-52 .629	KID GLEASON															
TOTALS			28	140	4675	**668**	**1343**	218	70	25	**571**	427	358	**150**	**.287**	.380
Chick Gandil	1B115	R	31	115	441	54	128	24	7	1	60	20	20	10	.290	.383
Eddie Collins	2B140	L	32	140	518	87	165	19	7	4	80	68	27	**33**	.319	.405
Swede Risberg	SS97, 1B22	R	24	119	414	48	106	19	6	2	38	35	38	19	.256	.345
Buck Weaver	3B97, SS43	B	28	140	**571**	89	169	33	9	3	75	11	21	22	.296	.401
Nemo Leibold	OF122	L	27	122	434	81	131	18	2	0	26	72	30	17	.302	.353
Happy Felsch	OF135	R	27	135	502	68	138	34	11	7	86	40	35	19	.275	.428
Joe Jackson	OF139	L	29	139	516	79	181	31	14	7	96	60	10	9	.351	.506
Ray Schalk	C129	R	26	131	394	57	111	9	3	0	34	51	25	11	.282	.320
Shano Collins	OF46, 1B8	R	33	63	179	21	50	6	3	1	16	7	11	3	.279	.363
Fred McMullin	3B46, 2B5	R	27	60	170	31	50	8	4	0	19	11	18	4	.294	.388
Eddie Murphy	OF6	L	27	30	35	8	17	4	0	0	5	7	0	0	.486	.600
Byrd Lynn	C28	R	30	29	66	4	15	4	0	0	4	4	9	0	.227	.288
Joe Jenkins	C4	R	28	11	19	0	3	1	0	0	1	1	1	1	.158	.211
Hervey McClellan	3B3, SS2	R	24	7	12	2	4	0	0	0	1	1	1	0	.333	.333
CLEVELAND 2nd 84-55 .604 3.5	LEE FOHL 45-34 .570 TRIS SPEAKER 39-21 .650															
TOTALS			29	139	4565	634	1268	**254**	71	25	547	**498**	367	113	.278	**381**
Doc Johnston	1B98	L	31	102	331	42	101	17	3	1	33	25	18	21	.305	.384
Bill Wambsganss	2B139	R	25	139	526	60	146	17	6	2	60	32	24	18	.278	.344
Ray Chapman	SS115	R	28	115	433	75	130	23	10	3	53	31	38	18	.300	.420
Larry Gardner	3B139	L	33	139	524	67	157	29	7	2	79	39	29	7	.300	.393
Elmer Smith	OF111	L	26	114	395	60	110	24	6	9	54	41	30	15	.278	.438
Tris Speaker	OF134	L	31	134	494	83	146	38	12	2	63	73	12	15	.296	.433
Jack Graney	OF125	L	33	128	461	79	108	22	8	1	30	**105**	39	7	.234	.323
Steve O'Neill	C123	R	27	125	398	46	115	35	7	2	47	48	21	4	.289	.427
Smokey Joe Wood	OF64, P1	R	29	72	192	30	49	10	5	1	27	32	21	3	.255	.375
Joe Harris	1B46, SS4	R	28	62	184	30	69	16	1	1	46	33	21	2	.375	.489
Pinch Thomas	C21	L	31	34	46	2	5	0	0	0	2	4	3	0	.109	.109
Harry Lunte	SS24	R	26	26	77	2	15	2	0	0	2	1	7	0	.195	.221
Les Nunamaker	C16	R	30	26	56	6	14	1	1	0	7	2	6	0	.250	.304
Charlie Jamieson	P4, OF3	L	26	26	17	3	6	2	1	0	2	0	2	2	.353	.588
Joe Evans	SS6	R	24	21	14	9	1	0	0	0	0	2	1	1	.071	.071
NEW YORK 3rd 80-59 .576 7.5	MILLER HUGGINS															
TOTALS			28	141	**4775**	582	1275	193	49	**45**	499	386	479	101	.267	.356
Wally Pipp	1B138	L	26	138	523	74	144	23	10	7	50	39	42	9	.275	.398
Del Pratt	2B140	R	31	140	527	69	154	27	7	4	56	36	24	22	.292	.393
Roger Peckinpaugh	SS121	R	28	122	453	89	138	20	2	7	33	59	37	10	.305	.404
Frank Baker	3B141	L	33	141	567	70	166	22	1	10	83	44	18	13	.293	.388
Sammy Vick	OF100	R	24	106	407	59	101	15	9	2	27	35	55	9	.248	.344
Ping Bodie	OF134	R	31	134	475	45	132	27	8	6	59	36	46	15	.278	.406
Duffy Lewis	OF141	R	30	141	559	67	152	23	4	7	89	17	42	8	.272	.365
Muddy Ruel	C81	R	23	81	233	18	56	6	0	0	31	34	26	4	.240	.266
Chick Fewster	OF41, SS23, 2B4, 3B2	R	23	81	244	38	69	9	3	1	15	34	36	8	.283	.357
Truck Hannah	C73, 1B1	R	28	75	227	14	54	8	3	1	20	22	19	0	.238	.313
Aaron Ward	1B5, 3B3, SS2, 2B1	R	22	27	34	5	7	2	0	0	2	5	6	0	.206	.265
Al Wickland	OF15	L	31	26	46	2	7	1	0	0	1	2	10	0	.152	.174
Lefty O'Doul	P3, OF1	L	22	19	16	2	4	0	0	0	1	1	2	1	.250	.250
George Halas	OF6	B	25	12	22	0	2	0	0	0	0	0	8	0	.091	.091
1 Bill Lamar	OF3, 1B1	L	22	11	16	1	3	1	0	0	0	2	1	1	.188	.250
Frank Gleich	OF4	L	25	5	4	0	1	0	0	0	1	1	0	0	.250	.250
Fred Hofmann	C1	R	25	1	1	0	0	0	0	0	0	0	0	0	.000	.000
Frank Kane		L	24	1	1	0	0	0	0	0	0	0	0	0	.000	.000
Curt Walker		L	22	1	1	0	0	0	0	0	0	0	0	0	.000	.000

NAME	T	AGE	W	L	PCT	SV	G	GS	CG	IP	H	BB	SO	ShO	ERA
		30	**88**	52	**.629**	2	140	140	**87**	1266	1245	342	468	14	3.04
Eddie Cicotte	R	35	**29**	7	**.806**	1	40	35	**29**	**307**	256	49	110	5	1.82
Lefty Williams	L	26	23	11	.676	0	41	**40**	27	297	265	58	125	5	2.64
Dickie Kerr	L	25	13	8	.619	0	39	17	10	212	208	64	79	1	2.89
Red Faber	R	30	11	9	.550	0	25	20	9	162	185	45	45	0	3.83
2 Grover Lowdermilk	R	34	5	5	.500	0	20	11	5	97	95	43	43	0	2.78
3 Bill James	R	32	3	1	.750	0	5	5	3	39	39	14	11	2	2.54
Roy Wilkinson	R	25	1	1	.500	0	4	1	1	22	21	10	5	1	2.05
Dave Danforth	L	29	1	2	.333	1	15	1	0	42	58	20	17	0	7.71
Frank Shellenback	R	20	1	3	.250	0	8	4	2	35	40	16	10	0	5.14
2 Erskine Mayer	R	30	1	3	.250	0	6	2	0	24	30	11	9	0	8.25
John Sullivan	L	25	0	1	.000	0	4	2	1	15	24	8	9	0	4.20
Charlie Robertson	R	23	0	1	.000	0	1	1	0	2	5	0	1	0	9.00
Joe Benz	R	33	0	0	.000	0	1	0	0	2	2	0	0	0	0.00
Tom McGuire	R	27	0	0	.000	0	1	0	0	3	5	3	0	0	9.00
2 Win Noyes	R	30	0	0	.000	0	1	1	0	6	10	0	4	0	7.50
3 Pat Ragan	R	30	0	0	.000	0	1	0	0	1	1	0	0	0	0.00
Reb Russell (SA)	L	30	0	0	.000	0	1	0	0	0	1	1	0	0	0.00
		27	84	55	.604	**9**	139	139	80	1255	1242	362	432	10	2.92
Stan Coveleski	R	30	24	12	.667	3	43	34	24	296	**286**	60	118	4	2.52
Jim Bagby	R	29	17	11	.607	3	35	32	21	241	258	44	61	0	2.80
George Uhle	R	20	10	5	.667	0	26	12	7	127	129	43	50	1	2.91
Guy Morton	R	26	10	9	.526	0	26	20	9	147	128	47	64	3	2.82
Elmer Myers	R	25	8	7	.533	0	23	15	6	135	134	43	38	1	3.73
2 Ray Caldwell	R	31	5	1	.833	0	6	6	4	53	33	19	24	1	1.70
Hi Jasper	R	38	4	5	.444	0	12	10	5	83	83	28	25	0	3.58
Tom Phillips	R	30	3	2	.600	0	22	3	2	55	55	34	18	0	2.95
Johnny Enzmann	R	29	2	2	.500	1	14	4	2	55	67	8	13	0	2.29
Fritz Coumbe	L	29	1	1	.500	1	8	2	0	24	32	9	7	0	5.25
Tony Faeth	R	25	0	0	.000	0	6	0	0	18	13	10	7	0	0.50
Ed Klepfer	R	31	0	0	.000	0	5	0	0	7	12	6	7	0	7.71
Charlie Jamieson	L	26	0	0	.000	0	4	1	0	13	12	8	0	0	5.54
Joe Engel	R	26	0	0	.000	0	1	0	0	0	0	3	0	0	∞
Smokey Joe Wood	R	29	0	0	.000	1	1	0	0	1	0	0	0	0	0.00
		28	80	59	.576	7	141	141	85	1303	1143	433	500	14	**2.78**
Bob Shawkey	R	28	20	11	.645	4	41	27	22	261	218	92	122	3	2.72
Jack Quinn	R	35	15	15	.500	0	38	31	18	264	242	65	97	4	2.63
Hank Thormahlen	L	22	13	9	.591	1	30	25	13	189	155	61	62	2	2.62
George Mogridge	L	30	10	7	.588	0	35	18	13	187	159	46	58	3	2.50
1 Allen Russell	R	25	4	5	.444	**2***	23	9	4	91	89	32	50	1	3.46
2 Carl Mays	R	27	9	3	.750	0	13	13	12	120	96	37	54	1	1.65
Ernie Shore	R	28	5	8	.385	0	20	13	3	95	105	44	24	0	4.17
Luke Nelson	R	25	3	0	1.000	0	9	1	0	24	22	11	11	0	3.00
Pete Schneider	R	26	0	1	.000	0	7	4	0	29	19	22	11	0	3.41
1 Bob McGraw (MS)	R	24	1	0	1.000	0	6	C	0	16	11	10	3	0	3.38
Lefty O'Doul	L	22	0	0	.000	0	3	0	0	5	7	4	2	0	3.60
Walt Smallwood (MS)	R	26	0	0	.000	0	6	0	0	22	20	9	6	0	4.91

*Russell, also with Boston, league leader in SV with 6

DETROIT 4th 80-60 .571 8 — HUGHIE JENNINGS

NAME	G by POS	B	AGE	G	AB	R	H	2B	3B	HR	RBI	BB	SO	SB	BA	SA
TOTALS			28	140	4665	620	1319	222	84	23	544	429	427	121	.283	.381
Harry Heilmann	1B140	R	24	140	537	74	172	30	15	8	93	37	41	7	.320	.477
Ralph Young	2B121, SS4	B	29	125	456	63	96	13	5	1	25	53	32	8	.211	.268
Donie Bush	SS129	B	31	129	509	82	124	11	6	0	26	75	36	22	.244	.289
Bob Jones	3B127	L	29	127	439	37	114	18	6	1	57	34	39	11	.260	.335
Ira Flagstead	OF83	R	25	97	287	43	95	22	3	5	41	35	39	6	.331	.481
Ty Cobb	OF123	L	32	124	497	92	191	36	13	1	70	38	22	28	.384	.515
Bobby Veach	OF138	L	31	139	538	87	191	45	17	3	101	33	33	19	.355	.519
Eddie Ainsmith	C106	R	27	114	364	42	99	17	12	3	32	45	30	9	.272	.409
Chick Shorten	OF75	L	27	95	270	37	85	9	3	0	22	22	13	5	.315	.370
Bert Ellison	2B25, OF10, SS1	R	23	56	134	18	29	4	0	0	11	13	24	4	.216	.246
Ben Dyer	3B23, SS11, OF1	R	26	44	85	11	21	4	0	0	15	8	19	0	.247	.294
Oscar Stanage	C36, 1B1	R	36	38	120	9	29	4	1	1	15	7	12	1	.242	.317
Archie Yelle	C5	R	27	5	4	1	0	0	0	0	0	1	0	0	.000	.000
1 Snooks Dowd		R	21	1	0	0	0	0	0	0	0	0	0	0	.000	.000

NAME	T	AGE	W	L	PCT	SV	G	GS	CG	IP	H	BB	SO	ShO	ERA
		27	80	60	.571	5	140	140	85	1256	1254	431	428	10	3.30
Hooks Dauss	R	29	21	9	.700	0	34	32	22	256	262	63	73	2	3.55
Howard Ehmke	R	25	17	10	.630	0	33	31	20	249	255	107	79	2	3.18
Dutch Leonard	L	27	14	13	.519	0	29	28	18	217	212	65	102	4	2.78
Bernie Boland	R	27	14	16	.467	1	35	30	18	243	222	80	71	1	3.04
Slim Love	L	28	5	4	.556	2	22	8	4	90	92	40	46	0	3.00
2 Doc Ayres	R	29	5	3	.625	0	24	5	3	94	88	28	32	1	2.68
1 Bill James	R	32	2	0	1.000	0	2	1	0	9	12	5	3	0	6.00
George Cunningham	R	24	1	1	.500	1	17	0	0	48	54	15	11	0	4.88
Willie Mitchell	L	29	1	2	.333	0	3	2	0	14	12	10	4	0	5.14
1 Eric Erickson	R	27	0	2	.000	0	3	2	0	15	17	10	4	0	6.60
Rudy Kallio	R	26	0	0	.000	1	12	1	0	22	28	8	3	0	5.73

ST. LOUIS 5th (Tie) 67-72 .482 20.5 — JIMMY BURKE

NAME	G by POS	B	AGE	G	AB	R	H	2B	3B	HR	RBI	BB	SO	SB	BA	SA
TOTALS			30	140	4671	535	1234	187	73	31	460	391	443	74	.264	.355
George Sisler	1B131	L	26	132	511	96	180	31	15	10	83	27	20	28	.352	.530
Joe Gedeon	2B118	R	25	120	437	57	111	13	4	0	27	50	35	4	.254	.302
Wally Gerber	SS140	R	27	140	462	43	105	14	6	1	37	49	36	1	.227	.290
Jimmy Austin	3B98	B	39	106	396	54	94	9	9	1	21	42	31	8	.237	.313
Earl Smith (JJ)	OF68	B	28	88	252	21	63	12	5	1	36	18	27	1	.250	.349
Baby Doll Jacobson	OF105, 1B8	R	28	120	455	70	147	31	8	4	51	24	47	9	.323	.453
Jack Tobin	OF123	L	27	127	486	54	159	22	7	6	57	36	24	8	.327	.438
Hank Severeid	C103	R	28	112	351	16	87	12	2	0	36	21	13	2	.248	.293
Ray Demmitt	OF49	L	35	79	202	19	48	11	2	1	19	14	27	3	.238	.327
Herman Bronkie	3B34, 2B16, 1B2	R	34	67	196	23	50	6	4	0	14	23	23	2	.255	.327
Ken Williams (JJ)	OF63	L	29	65	227	32	68	10	5	6	35	26	25	7	.300	.467
Josh Billings	C27, 1B1	R	27	38	76	9	15	1	1	0	3	1	12	0	.197	.237
Wally Mayer	C25	R	29	30	62	2	14	4	1	0	5	8	11	0	.226	.323
Tod Sloan	OF20	L	28	27	63	9	15	1	3	0	6	12	3	0	.238	.349
Joe Schepner	3B13	R	23	14	48	2	10	4	0	0	6	1	5	0	.208	.292
Pat Collins	C5	R	22	10	20	2	3	1	0	0	1	4	2	0	.150	.200
John Shovlin	2B9	R	28	9	35	4	7	0	0	0	1	5	2	0	.200	.200
Gene Robertson	SS2	L	19	5	7	1	1	0	0	0	0	1	2	0	.143	.143

NAME	T	AGE	W	L	PCT	SV	G	GS	CG	IP	H	BB	SO	ShO	ERA
		28	67	72	.482	6	140	140	77	1256	1255	421	415	14	3.13
Allan Sothoron	R	26	20	13	.606	3	40	30	21	270	256	87	106	3	2.20
Urban Shocker	R	28	13	11	.542	0	30	25	13	211	193	55	86	5	2.69
Bert Gallia	R	27	12	14	.462	2	34	25	14	222	220	92	83	1	3.61
Carl Weilman (XJ)	L	29	10	6	.625	0	20	20	12	148	133	45	44	3	2.07
Lefty Leifield	L	35	6	4	.600	0	19	9	6	92	96	25	18	2	2.93
Ernie Koob	L	26	2	3	.400	0	25	4	0	66	77	23	11	0	4.64
Dave Davenport	R	29	2	11	.154	1	24	16	5	123	135	41	37	0	3.95
Elam Vangilder	R	23	1	0	1.000	0	3	1	1	13	15	3	6	0	2.08
Bill Bayne	L	20	1	1	.500	0	2	2	1	12	16	6	0	0	5.25
1 Tom Rogers	R	24	0	1	.000	0	2	0	0	1	7	0	1	0	27.00
Rolla Mapel	L	29	0	3	.000	0	4	3	2	20	17	17	2	0	4.50
Rasty Wright	R	23	0	5	.000	0	24	5	2	63	79	20	14	0	5.57
1 Grover Loudermilk	R	34	0	0	.000	0	7	0	0	12	6	4	6	0	0.75
Hal Haid	R	21	0	0	.000	0	1	0	0	2	5	3	1	0	18.00

BOSTON 5th (Tie) 66-71 .482 20.5 — ED BARROW

NAME	G by POS	B	AGE	G	AB	R	H	2B	3B	HR	RBI	BB	SO	SB	BA	SA
TOTALS			26	138	4548	565	1188	181	49	33	494	471	411	108	.261	.344
Stuffy McInnis	1B118	R	28	120	440	32	134	12	5	1	58	23	11	8	.305	.361
2 Red Shannon	2B79	B	22	80	290	36	75	11	7	0	17	17	42+	7	.259	.345
Everett Scott	SS138	R	26	138	507	41	141	19	0	0	38	19	26	8	.278	.316
Ossie Vitt	3B133	R	29	133	469	64	114	10	3	0	40	44	11	9	.243	.277
Harry Hooper	OF128	L	31	128	491	76	131	25	6	3	49	79	28	23	.267	.360
2 Braggo Roth	OF55	R	26	63	227	32	58	9	4	0	23	24	32	9	.256	.330
Babe Ruth	OF111, P17, 1B4	L	24	130	432	103	139	34	12	29	114	101	58	7	.322	.657
Wally Schang	C103	B	24	113	330	43	101	16	3	0	55	71	42	15	.306	.373
1 Amos Strunk	OF48	L	30	48	184	27	50	11	3	0	17	13	13	3	.272	.364
2 Bill Lamar	OF36	L	22	48	148	18	43	5	1	0	14	5	9	3	.291	.338
Roxy Walters	C47	R	26	48	135	7	26	2	0	0	9	7	15	1	.193	.207
Frank Gilhooley	OF33	L	27	48	112	14	27	4	0	0	1	12	8	2	.241	.277
Del Gainer	1B21, OF18	R	31	47	118	9	28	6	2	0	13	13	15	5	.237	.322
Mike McNally	SS11, 3B11, 2B3	R	25	33	42	10	11	4	0	0	6	1	2	4	.262	.357
Jack Barry	2B31	R	32	31	108	13	26	5	1	0	2	5	5	2	.241	.306
Dave Shean	2B29	R	41	29	100	4	14	0	0	0	8	5	7	1	.140	.140
Joe Wilhoit	OF5	L	27	6	18	7	6	0	0	0	2	5	2	1	.333	.333
Norm McNeil	C5	R	26	5	9	0	3	0	0	0	1	1	0	0	.333	.333

Dick Hoblitzell (MS) 30

NAME	T	AGE	W	L	PCT	SV	G	GS	CG	IP	H	BB	SO	ShO	ERA
		26	66	71	.482	7	138	138	85	1222	1251	420	380	15	3.30
Herb Pennock	L	25	16	8	.667	0	32	26	16	219	223	48	70	5	2.71
Sad Sam Jones	R	26	12	20	.375	0	35	31	21	245	258	95	67	5	3.75
2 Allen Russell	R	25	9	4	.692	4*	21	11	9	120	105	39	63	1	2.55
Babe Ruth	L	24	8	5	.615	2	17	15	12	133	148	58	30	0	2.98
1 Carl Mays	R	27	7	11	.389	1	21	16	11	145	131	40	53	2	2.48
1 Ray Caldwell	R	31	7	4	.636	0	18	12	5	86	88	30	22	1	3.77
Waite Hoyt	R	19	4	6	.400	0	13	11	6	105	99	22	28	1	3.26
2 Bill James	R	32	3	5	.375	0	13	7	4	73	78	39	12	0	4.07
2 Bob McGraw	R	24	0	2	.000	0	10	1	0	27	33	17	6	0	6.67
Paul Musser (MS)	R	30	0	2	.000	0	5	4	1	20	26	8	14	0	4.05
George Dumont	R	23	0	4	.000	0	13	2	0	35	45	19	12	0	4.37
Bullet Joe Bush (SA)	R	26	0	0	.000	0	3	2	0	9	11	4	3	0	5.00
George Winn	L	21	0	0	.000	0	3	0	0	5	6	1	0	0	7.20

*Russell, also with New York, league leader in SV with 6
+Shannon, also with Philadelphia, league leader in SO with 70

WASHINGTON 7th 56-84 .400 32 — CLARK GRIFFITH

NAME	G by POS	B	AGE	G	AB	R	H	2B	3B	HR	RBI	BB	SO	SB	BA	SA
TOTALS			27	142	4757	533	1238	177	63	24	459	416	511	142	.260	.339
Joe Judge	1B133	L	25	135	521	83	150	33	12	2	31	81	35	23	.288	.409
1 Hal Janvrin	2B56, SS2	R	26	61	208	17	37	4	1	1	13	19	17	8	.178	.221
Howard Shanks	SS94, 2B34, OF6	R	28	135	491	33	122	8	7	1	54	25	48	13	.248	.299
Eddie Foster	3B115	R	32	120	478	57	126	12	5	0	26	33	21	20	.264	.310
Sam Rice	OF141	L	29	141	557	80	179	23	9	3	71	42	26	26	.321	.411
Clyde Milan (IL)	OF86	L	33	88	321	43	92	12	6	0	37	40	16	11	.287	.361
Mike Menosky	OF103	L	24	116	342	62	98	15	3	6	39	44	46	13	.287	.401
Val Picinich	C69	R	22	80	212	18	58	12	3	3	22	17	43	6	.274	.401
Patsy Gharrity	C60, OF33, 1B7	R	27	111	347	35	94	19	4	2	43	25	39	4	.271	.366
Buzz Murphy	OF73	L	24	79	252	19	66	7	4	0	28	19	32	5	.262	.321
Joe Leonard	2B28, 3B25, 1B4, OF1	L	24	71	198	26	51	8	3	2	20	20	28	3	.258	.359
Sam Agnew	C36	R	32	42	98	6	23	7	0	0	10	10	8	1	.235	.306
Frank Ellerbe	SS28	R	23	28	105	13	29	4	1	0	16	2	15	5	.276	.333
2 Roy Grover	2B24	R	27	24	75	6	14	0	0	0	7	6	10	2	.187	.187
George McBride	SS15	R	38	15	40	3	8	1	1	0	4	3	6	0	.200	.275
Bucky Harris	2B8	R	22	8	28	0	6	2	0	0	4	1	3	0	.214	.286
Ike Davis	SS4	R	24	8	14	0	0	0	0	0	0	0	6	0	.000	.000
Claude Davidson	3B2	L	22	2	7	1	3	0	0	0	0	1	1	0	.429	.429
Jesse Baker	SS1	R	23	1	0	0	0	0	0	0	0	0	0	0	.000	.000
Frank Kelliher		L	20	1	1	0	0	0	0	0	0	0	0	0	.000	.000
Danny Silva	3B1	R	22	1	4	0	1	0	0	0	0	0	0	0	.250	.250
George Twombly	OF1	R	27	1	4	0	0	0	0	0	0	0	0	0	.000	.000

NAME	T	AGE	W	L	PCT	SV	G	GS	CG	IP	H	BB	SO	ShO	ERA
		25	56	84	.400	8	142	142	69	1274	1237	451	536	12	3.01
Walter Johnson	R	31	20	14	.588	2	39	29	27	290	235	51	147	7	1.49
Jim Shaw	R	25	16	17	.485	4	45	38	23	307	274	101	128	3	2.73
Harry Harper	L	24	6	21	.222	0	35	30	8	208	220	97	87	0	3.72
2 Eric Erickson	R	27	6	10	.375	0	20	15	7	132	130	63	86	1	3.95
Harry Courtney	L	20	3	0	1.000	0	4	3	3	26	25	19	6	1	2.77
Al Schacht	R	26	2	0	1.000	0	2	2	1	15	14	4	4	0	2.40
1 Doc Ayres	R	29	1	6	.143	0	11	5	0	44	52	17	12	0	2.86
Ed Gill	R	22	1	1	.500	0	16	2	0	37	38	21	7	0	4.86
Tom Zachary (MS)	L	23	1	5	.167	0	17	7	0	62	68	20	9	0	2.90
Charlie Whitehouse	L	25	0	1	.000	0	6	1	0	12	13	6	5	0	4.50
Bill Snyder	R	21	0	1	.000	0	2	1	0	8	6	3	5	0	1.13
Dick Robertson	R	28	0	2	.000	0	7	4	0	28	25	9	7	0	2.25
1 Harry Thompson	L	26	0	3	.000	1	12	2	0	43	48	8	10	0	3.56
Molly Craft	R	23	0	3	.000	0	16	2	0	49	59	18	17	0	3.86
Ed Hovlik	R	27	0	0	.000	1	3	0	0	6	12	9	3	0	12.00
Clarence Fisher	R	20	0	0	.000	0	2	0	0	4	8	3	1	0	13.50
Nick Altrock	L	42	0	0	.000	0	1	0	0	0	4	0	0	0	∞
Rip Jordan	R	29	0	0	.000	0	1	1	0	4	6	2	2	0	11.25

PHILADELPHIA 8th 36-104 .257 52 — CONNIE MACK

NAME	G by POS	B	AGE	G	AB	R	H	2B	3B	HR	RBI	BB	SO	SB	BA	SA
TOTALS			25	140	4730	459	1156	175	71	35	396	349	565	103	.244	.334
George Burns	1B86, OF34	R	26	126	470	63	139	29	9	8	57	19	18	15	.296	.447
1 Red Shannon	2B37	B	22	39	155	14	42	7	2	0	14	12	28*	9	.271	.342
Joe Dugan	SS98, 2B4, 3B2	R	22	104	387	25	105	17	2	1	30	11	30	9	.271	.333
Fred Thomas	3B124	R	26	124	453	42	96	11	10	2	23	43	52	12	.212	.294
Manny Kopp	OF65	B	27	75	235	34	53	2	4	1	12	42	43	16	.226	.281
Tilly Walker	OF115	R	31	125	456	47	133	30	6	10	64	26	41	8	.292	.450
Whitey Witt	OF59, 2B56, 3B2	L	23	122	460	56	123	15	6	0	33	46	26	11	.267	.326
Cy Perkins	C87, SS8	R	23	101	305	22	77	12	7	2	29	27	22	2	.252	.357
Dick Burrus	1B38, OF10	L	21	70	194	17	50	3	4	0	8	9	25	2	.258	.314
Wickey McAvoy	C57	R	24	62	170	10	24	5	2	0	11	14	21	1	.141	.194
2 Amos Strunk	OF52	L	30	60	194	15	41	6	4	0	13	23	15	3	.211	.284
Walt Kinney	P43, OF1	L	25	57	88	11	25	6	0	1	11	10	15	0	.284	.386
1 Braggo Roth	OF48	R	26	48	195	33	63	13	8	5	29	15	21	11	.323	.549
Terry Turner	SS19, 2B17, 3B1	R	38	38	127	7	24	3	0	0	6	5	9	2	.189	.213
1 Roy Grover	2B12, 3B3	R	27	22	56	8	13	1	0	0	2	5	6	0	.232	.250
Jimmy Dykes	2B16	R	22	17	49	4	9	1	0	0	1	7	11	0	.184	.204
Chick Galloway	SS17	R	22	17	63	2	9	0	0	0	4	1	8	0	.143	.143
Ivy Griffin	1B17	L	23	17	68	5	20	2	2	0	6	3	10	0	.294	.382
Frank Welch	OF15	R	21	15	54	5	9	1	1	2	7	7	10	0	.167	.333
Al Wingo	OF15	L	21	15	59	9	18	1	3	0	2	4	12	0	.305	.424
2 Snooks Dowd	2B3, SS2, 3B1, OF1	R	21	13	18	4	3	0	0	0	6	0	5	2	.167	.167
Charlie High	OF9	L	20	11	29	2	2	0	0	0	1	3	4	2	.069	.069
Bob Allen	OF6	R	23	9	22	3	3	1	0	0	0	3	7	0	.136	.182
Art Ewoldt	3B9	R	25	9	32	2	7	1	0	0	2	1	5	0	.219	.250
Lena Styles	C8	R	19	8	22	0	6	1	0	0	5	1	6	0	.273	.318
Lew Groh	3B1	R	35	2	4	0	0	0	0	0	0	0	2	0	.000	.000
Johnny Walker	C3	R	22	3	9	0	0	0	0	0	0	0	2	0	.000	.000

Ray Haley (MS) 28, Otis Lawrey (MS) 25

NAME	T	AGE	W	L	PCT	SV	G	GS	CG	IP	H	BB	SO	ShO	ERA
		26	36	104	.257	2	140	140	72	1239	1371	503	417	1	4.26
Jing Johnson	R	24	9	15	.375	0	34	25	12	202	222	62	67	0	3.61
Walt Kinney	L	25	9	15	.375	1	43	21	13	203	199	91	97	0	3.64
Rollie Naylor	R	27	5	18	.217	0	31	23	17	205	210	64	68	0	3.34
2 Tom Rogers	R	24	4	12	.250	0	23	18	7	140	152	60	37	1	4.31
Scott Perry	R	28	4	17	.190	1	25	21	12	184	193	72	38	0	3.57
Socks Seibold	R	23	2	3	.400	0	14	4	1	46	58	26	19	0	5.28
Walter Anderson	L	21	1	0	1.000	0	3	0	0	14	13	8	10	0	3.86
Jimmy Zinn	R	24	1	3	.250	0	5	3	2	26	38	10	9	0	6.23
1 Win Noyes	R	30	1	5	.167	0	10	6	3	49	66	15	20	0	5.69
2 Harry Thompson	L	26	0	1	.000	0	3	0	0	12	16	3	1	0	6.75
Mule Watson	R	22	0	1	.000	0	4	2	0	14	17	7	6	0	7.07
Danny Boone	R	24	0	1	.000	0	3	2	0	15	24	10	1	0	6.60
Charlie Eckert	R	20	0	1	.000	0	2	1	1	16	17	3	6	0	3.94
Dave Keefe	R	22	0	1	.000	0	1	1	1	9	8	3	5	0	4.00
Ray Roberts	R	23	0	2	.000	0	3	2	0	14	21	3	2	0	7.71
Bob Hasty	R	23	0	2	.000	0	2	2	1	12	15	4	5	0	5.25
Pat Martin	L	25	0	2	.000	0	2	2	1	11	11	8	6	0	4.09
Lefty York	L	23	0	2	.000	0	2	2	0	4	13	5	2	0	27.00
Bob Geary	R	28	0	3	.000	0	9	2	1	32	32	18	9	0	4.78
Bill Grevell	R	21	0	0	.000	0	5	2	0	12	15	18	3	0	14.25
Mike Kircher	R	21	0	0	.000	0	2	0	0	8	15	3	2	0	7.88
Bill Pierson	L	20	0	0	.000	0	2	1	0	8	9	8	4	0	3.38
Willie Adams	R	28	0	0	.000	1	1	0	0	5	7	2	0	0	3.60

*Shannon, also with Boston, league leader in SO with 70

CINCINNATI 1st 96-44 .686 — PAT MORAN

	NAME	G by POS	B	AGE	G	AB	R	H	2B	3B	HR	RBI	BB	SO	SB	BA	SA
	TOTALS			29	140	4577	578	1204	135	**83**	20	489	**405**	368	143	.263	.342
	Jake Daubert	1B140	L	35	140	537	79	148	10	12	2	44	35	23	11	.276	.350
	Morrie Rath	2B138	L	32	138	537	77	142	13	1	1	29	64	24	17	.264	.298
	Larry Kopf	SS135	B	28	135	503	51	136	18	5	0	58	28	27	18	.270	.326
	Heinie Groh	3B121	R	29	122	448	79	139	17	11	5	63	56	26	21	.310	.431
	Greasy Neale	OF138	L	27	139	500	57	121	10	12	1	54	47	51	28	.242	.316
	Edd Roush	OF133	L	26	133	504	73	162	19	12	4	71	42	19	20	**.321**	.431
	Rube Bressler	OF48, P13	R	24	61	165	22	34	3	4	2	17	23	15	2	.206	.309
	Ivy Wingo	C75	L	28	76	245	30	67	12	6	0	27	23	19	4	.273	.371
	Bill Rariden	C70	R	31	74	218	16	47	6	3	1	24	17	19	4	.216	.284
	Sherry Magee	OF47, 2B1, 3B1	R	34	56	163	11	35	6	1	0	21	26	19	4	.215	.264
	Hod Eller	P38	R	24	38	93	10	26	3	3	1	13	0	16	2	.280	.409
	Pat Duncan (MS)	OF27	R	25	31	90	9	22	3	3	2	17	8	7	2	.244	.411
	Manuel Cueto	OF25, 3B1	R	27	29	88	10	22	2	0	0	4	10	4	5	.250	.273
	Jimmy Smith	3B6, SS5, 2B4, OF4	B	24	28	40	9	11	1	3	1	10	4	8	1	.275	.525
	Hank Schreiber	3B17, SS2	R	27	19	58	5	13	4	0	0	4	0	12	0	.224	.293
	Nick Allen	C12	R	30	15	25	7	8	0	1	0	5	2	6	0	.320	.400
	Charlie See	OF4	L	22	8	14	1	4	0	0	0	1	1	0	0	.286	.286
	Wally Rehg	OF5	R	30	5	12	1	2	0	0	0	3	1	0	0	.167	.167
2	Billy Zitzmann	OF1	R	21	2	1	0	0	0	0	0	0	0	0	0	.000	.000

	NAME	T	AGE	W	L	PCT	SV	G	GS	CG	IP	H	BB	SO	ShO	ERA
			28	**96**	44	**.686**	9	140	140	89	1274	1104	298	407	**23**	2.23
	Slim Sallee	L	34	21	7	.750	0	29	28	22	228	221	20	24	4	2.05
	Hod Eller	R	24	20	9	.690	2	38	30	16	248	216	50	137	7	2.40
	Dutch Ruether	L	25	19	6	**.760**	0	33	29	20	243	195	**83**	78	3	1.81
	Ray Fisher	R	31	14	5	.737	1	26	20	12	174	141	38	41	5	2.17
	Jimmy Ring	R	24	10	9	.526	3	32	18	12	183	150	51	61	2	2.26
	Dolf Luque	R	28	9	3	.750	3	30	9	6	106	89	36	40	2	2.63
	Rube Bressler	L	24	2	4	.333	0	13	4	1	42	37	8	13	0	3.43
	Ed Gerner	L	21	1	0	1.000	0	5	1	0	17	22	3	2	0	3.18
	Roy Mitchell	R	34	0	1	.000	0	7	1	0	31	32	9	10	0	2.32
	Mike Regan	R	31	0	0	.000	0	1	0	0	2	1	0	1	0	0.00

NEW YORK 2nd 87-53 .621 9 — JOHN McGRAW

	NAME	G by POS	B	AGE	G	AB	R	H	2B	3B	HR	RBI	BB	SO	SB	BA	SA
	TOTALS			29	140	4664	**605**	1254	204	64	40	**505**	328	407	157	**.269**	**.366**
	Hal Chase (DU)	1B107	R	36	110	408	58	116	17	7	5	45	17	40	16	.284	.397
	Larry Doyle	2B100	L	32	113	381	61	110	14	10	7	52	31	17	12	.289	.433
	Art Fletcher	SS127	R	34	127	488	54	135	20	5	3	54	9	28	6	.277	.357
	Heinie Zimmerman (DU)	3B123	R	32	123	444	56	113	20	6	4	58	21	30	8	.255	.354
	Ross Youngs	OF130	L	22	130	489	73	152	**31**	7	2	43	51	47	24	.311	.415
	Benny Kauff	OF134	L	29	135	491	73	136	27	7	10	67	39	45	21	.277	.422
	George Burns	OF139	R	29	139	534	**86**	162	30	9	2	46	**82**	37	**40**	.303	.404
	Lew McCarty	C59	R	30	85	210	17	59	5	4	2	21	18	15	2	.281	.371
	Mike Gonzalez	C52, 1B4	R	28	58	158	18	30	6	0	0	8	20	9	3	.190	.228
	Frankie Frisch	2B29, 3B28, SS1	B	20	53	190	21	43	3	2	2	24	4	14	15	.226	.295
	Al Baird	2B24, SS9, 3B5	R	24	38	83	8	20	1	0	0	5	5	9	3	.241	.253
	George Kelly	1B32	R	23	32	107	12	31	6	2	1	14	3	15	1	.290	.411
2	Frank Snyder	C31	R	26	32	92	7	21	6	0	0	11	8	9	1	.228	.293
	Jigger Statz	OF18, 2B5	R	21	21	60	7	18	2	1	0	6	3	8	2	.300	.367
	Earl Smith	C14, 2B1	L	22	21	36	5	9	2	1	0	8	3	3	1	.250	.361
	Lee King	OF7	R	26	21	20	5	2	1	0	0	1	1	6	0	.100	.150
1	Eddie Sicking	SS6	R	22	6	15	2	5	0	0	0	3	1	0	0	.333	.333
	Jimmy Cooney	SS4, 2B1	R	24	5	14	3	3	0	0	0	1	0	0	0	.214	.214
	Chick Bowen	OF2	R	21	3	5	0	1	0	0	0	1	1	2	0	.200	.200
	Bob Kinsella	OF3	L	20	3	9	1	2	0	0	0	0	0	3	1	.222	.222
1	Jim Thorpe	OF2	R	31	2	3	0	1	0	0	0	1	0	0	0	.333	.333
1	Dave Robertson		L	29	1	0	0	0	0	0	0	0	0	0	0	.000	.000

	NAME	T	AGE	W	L	PCT	SV	G	GS	CG	IP	H	BB	SO	ShO	ERA
			28	87	53	.621	**13**	140	140	72	1256	1153	305	340	11	2.70
	Jesse Barnes	R	26	**25**	9	.735	1	38	34	23	296	263	35	92	4	2.40
	Rube Benton	L	32	17	11	.607	2	35	28	11	209	181	52	53	1	2.63
	Fred Toney	R	31	13	6	.684	1	24	20	14	181	157	35	40	4	1.84
2	Art Nehf	L	26	9	2	.818	0	13	12	9	102	70	19	24	2	1.50
1	Red Causey	R	25	9	3	.750	0	19	16	6	105	99	38	25	0	[illegible]
	Jean Dubuc	R	30	6	4	.600	3	36	5	1	132	119	37	32	0	2.66
2	Phil Douglas	R	29	2	4	.333	0	8	6	4	51	53	6	21	0	2.12
2	Pat Ragan	R	30	1	0	1.000	0	7	1	1	23	19	14	7	0	1.57
	Pol Perritt	R	26	1	1	.500	1	11	3	0	19	27	12	2	0	7.11
	Bill Hubbell	R	22	1	1	.500	0	2	2	2	18	19	2	3	0	2.00
	Jesse Winters	R	25	1	2	.333	3	16	2	0	28	39	13	6	0	5.46
	Rosy Ryan	R	21	1	2	.333	0	4	3	1	20	20	9	7	0	3.15
1	Ferdie Schupp (AJ)	L	28	1	3	.250	1	9	4	0	32	32	18	17	0	5.63
2	Joe Oeschger	R	28	0	1	.000	0	5	1	0	8	12	2	3	0	4.50
	Colonel Snover	L	24	0	1	.000	0	2	1	0	9	7	3	4	0	1.00
	Bob Steele	L	25	0	1	.000	0	1	0	0	3	3	2	0	0	6.00
1	George Smith	R	27	0	2	.000	0	3	2	0	11	18	4	0	0	5.73
	Johnny Jones	R	26	0	0	.000	1	2	0	0	7	9	3	3	0	5.14
	Virgil Barnes	R	22	0	0	.000	0	1	0	0	2	6	1	1	0	18.00

CHICAGO 3rd 75-65 .536 21 — FRED MITCHELL

	NAME	G by POS	B	AGE	G	AB	R	H	2B	3B	HR	RBI	BB	SO	SB	BA	SA
	TOTALS			29	140	4581	454	1174	166	58	21	387	298	359	150	.256	.332
	Fred Merkle	1B132	R	30	133	498	52	133	20	6	3	62	33	35	20	.267	.349
1	Charlie Pick	2B71, 3B3	L	31	75	269	27	65	8	6	0	18	14	12	17	.242	.316
	Charlie Hollocher	SS115	L	23	115	430	51	116	14	5	3	26	44	19	16	.270	.347
	Charlie Deal	3B116	R	27	116	405	37	117	23	5	2	52	12	12	11	.289	.385
	Max Flack	OF116	L	29	116	469	71	138	20	4	6	35	34	13	18	.294	.392
	Dode Paskert	OF80	R	37	88	270	21	53	11	3	2	29	28	33	7	.196	.281
1	Les Mann	OF78	R	25	80	299	31	68	8	8	1	22	11	29	12	.227	.318
	Bill Killefer	C100	R	31	103	315	17	90	10	2	0	22	15	8	5	.286	.330
2	Lee Magee	OF44, SS13, 3B10, 2B7	B	30	79	267	36	78	12	4	1	17	18	16	14	.292	.378
	Turner Barber	OF68	L	25	76	230	26	72	9	4	0	21	14	17	7	.313	.387
2	Buck Herzog	2B52	R	33	52	193	15	53	4	4	0	17	10	7	12	.275	.337
	Bob O'Farrell	C38	R	22	49	125	11	27	4	2	0	9	7	10	2	.216	.280
	Fred Lear	1B9, 2B9, SS3	R	25	40	76	8	17	3	1	1	11	8	11	2	.224	.329
	Bill McCabe	OF19, SS4, 3B1	B	24	33	84	8	13	3	1	0	5	9	15	3	.155	.214
1	Pete Kilduff	3B14, 2B8, SS7	R	26	31	88	5	24	4	2	0	8	10	5	1	.273	.364
2	Dave Robertson	OF25	L	29	27	96	8	20	2	0	1	10	1	10	3	.208	.260
	Tom Daly	C18	R	27	25	50	4	11	0	1	0	1	2	5	0	.220	.260
	Barney Friberg	OF7	R	19	8	20	0	4	1	0	0	1	0	2	0	.200	.250
	Hal Reilly	OF1			1	3	0	0	0	0	0	0	0	1	0	.000	.000

	NAME	T	AGE	W	L	PCT	SV	G	GS	CG	IP	H	BB	SO	ShO	ERA
			28	75	65	.536	5	140	140	80	1265	1127	294	**495**	21	**2.21**
	Hippo Vaughn	L	31	21	14	.714	1	38	**37**	25	**307**	264	62	**141**	4	1.79
	Pete Alexander	R	32	16	11	.593	1	30	27	20	235	180	38	121	**9**	**1.72**
1	Phil Douglas	R	29	10	6	.625	0	25	19	8	162	133	34	63	4	2.00
	Claude Hendrix	R	30	10	14	.206	0	33	25	15	206	208	42	69	2	2.62
	Speed Martin	R	25	8	8	.500	2	35	14	7	164	158	52	54	2	2.47
	Paul Carter	R	25	5	4	.556	1	28	7	2	85	81	28	17	0	2.65
	Sweetbreads Bailey	R	24	3	5	.375	0	21	5	0	71	75	20	19	0	3.17
	Lefty Tyler	L	29	2	2	.500	0	6	5	3	30	20	13	9	0	2.10
	Harry Weaver	R	24	0	1	.000	0	2	1	0	3	6	2	1	0	12.00
	Joel Newkirk	R	23	0	0	.000	0	1	0	0	2	2	3	1	0	13.50

PITTSBURGH 4th 71-68 .511 24.5 — HUGO BEZDEK

	NAME	G by POS	B	AGE	G	AB	R	H	2B	3B	HR	RBI	BB	SO	SB	BA	SA
	TOTALS			28	139	4538	472	1132	130	82	17	394	344	381	**196**	.249	.325
	Vic Saier	1B51	L	28	58	166	19	37	3	3	2	17	18	13	5	.223	.313
	George Cutshaw	2B139	R	31	139	512	49	124	15	8	3	51	30	22	36	.242	.320
	Zeb Terry	SS127	R	28	129	472	46	107	12	6	0	27	31	26	12	.227	.278
	Walter Barbare	3B80, 2B1	R	27	85	293	34	80	11	5	1	34	18	18	11	.273	.355
1	Casey Stengel	OF87	L	28	89	321	38	94	10	10	4	43	35	35	12	.293	.424
	Carson Bigbee	OF124	L	24	125	478	61	132	11	4	2	27	37	26	31	.276	.328
	Billy Southworth	OF121	L	26	121	453	56	127	14	**14**	4	61	32	22	23	.280	.400
	Walter Schmidt	C85	R	32	85	267	23	67	9	2	0	29	23	9	5	.251	.300
	Max Carey (IL)	OF63	B	29	66	244	41	75	10	2	0	9	25	24	18	.307	.365
1	Fritz Mollwitz	1B52, OF2	R	29	56	168	11	29	2	4	0	12	15	18	9	.173	.232
1	Tony Boeckel	3B45	R	26	45	152	18	38	9	2	0	16	18	20	11	.250	.336
	Cliff Lee	C28, OF6	R	22	42	112	5	22	2	4	0	2	6	8	2	.196	.286
	Buster Caton	SS17, 3B11, OF1	R	22	39	102	13	18	1	2	0	5	12	10	2	.176	.225
2	Possum Whitted	1B33, 3B2, OF1	R	29	35	131	15	51	7	7	0	21	6	4	7	.389	.550
	Wilbur Cooper	P35	R	27	35	101	9	29	2	2	0	7	4	9	5	.287	.347
	Fred Nicholson	OF17, 1B1	R	24	30	66	8	18	2	2	1	6	6	11	2	.273	.409
	Fred Blackwell	C22	L	23	24	65	3	14	3	0	0	4	3	9	0	.215	.262
	Ed Sweeney	C15	R	30	17	42	0	4	1	0	0	0	5	6	1	.095	.119
	Charlie Grimm	1B11	L	20	12	44	6	14	1	3	0	6	2	4	1	.318	.477
1	Billy Zitzmann	OF8	R	21	11	26	5	5	1	0	0	2	0	6	2	.192	.231
	Hooks Warner	3B3	L	25	6	8	0	1	0	0	0	2	3	1	0	.125	.125

Adam Debus (MS) 26, Bill McKechnie (VR) 32

	NAME	T	AGE	W	L	PCT	SV	G	GS	CG	IP	H	BB	SO	ShO	ERA
			30	71	68	.511	4	139	139	92	1249	1113	263	391	16	2.88
	Wilbur Cooper	L	27	19	13	.594	1	35	32	**27**	287	229	74	106	4	2.67
	Babe Adams	R	37	17	10	.630	1	34	29	23	263	213	23	92	6	1.98
	Frank Miller	R	33	13	12	.520	0	32	26	16	202	170	34	59	3	3.03
	Hal Carlson	R	25	8	10	.444	0	22	14	7	141	114	39	49	1	2.23
	Earl Hamilton	L	27	8	11	.421	1	28	19	10	160	167	49	39	1	3.32
1	Erskine Mayer	R	30	5	3	.625	1	18	10	6	88	100	12	20	0	4.50
	John Wisner	R	19	1	0	1.000	0	4	1	1	19	12	7	4	0	0.95
	Bill Evans	R	26	0	4	.000	0	7	3	2	37	41	18	15	0	5.59
	Elmer Ponder (MS)	R	26	0	5	.000	0	9	5	0	47	55	6	6	0	4.02
	Carmen Hill	R	23	0	0	.000	0	4	0	0	5	12	1	1	0	9.00

BROOKLYN 5th 69-71 .493 27 — WILBERT ROBINSON

	NAME	G by POS	B	AGE	G	AB	R	H	2B	3B	HR	RBI	BB	SO	SB	BA	SA
	TOTALS			29	141	**4844**	525	**1272**	167	66	25	452	258	405	112	.263	.340
	Ed Konetchy	1B132	R	33	132	486	46	145	24	9	1	47	29	39	14	.298	.391
	Jimmy Johnston	2B87, OF14, 1B2, SS1	R	29	117	405	56	114	11	4	1	23	29	26	11	.281	.336
	Ivy Olson	SS140	R	33	140	**590**	73	**164**	14	9	1	38	30	12	26	.278	.337
	Lew Malone	3B47, 2B2, SS2	R	22	51	162	9	33	7	3	0	11	6	18	1	.204	.284
	Tommy Griffith	OF125	L	29	125	484	65	136	18	4	6	57	23	32	8	.281	.372
	Hy Myers	OF131	R	30	133	512	62	157	23	**14**	5	**73**	23	34	13	.307	**.436**
	Zack Wheat	OF137	L	33	137	536	70	159	23	11	5	62	33	27	15	.297	.409
	Ernie Krueger	C66	R	28	80	226	24	56	7	4	5	36	19	25	4	.248	.381
	Dave Hickman	OF29	R	25	57	104	14	20	3	1	0	11	6	17	2	.192	.240
	Otto Miller	C51	R	30	51	164	18	37	5	0	0	5	7	14	2	.226	.256
	Ray Schmandt	2B18, 1B12, 3B6	R	23	47	127	8	21	4	0	0	10	4	13	0	.165	.197
1	Lee Magee	2B36, 3B9	B	30	45	181	16	43	7	2	0	7	5	8	5	.238	.298
	Chuck Ward	3B45	R	24	45	150	7	35	1	2	0	8	7	11	0	.233	.267
	Mack Wheat	C38	R	26	41	112	5	23	3	0	0	8	2	22	1	.205	.232
2	Pete Kilduff	3B26, 2B1	R	26	32	73	9	22	3	1	0	8	12	11	5	.301	.370
3	Doug Baird	3B17	R	27	20	60	6	11	0	1	0	8	1	10	3	.183	.217
	Horace Allen	OF2	L	20	4	7	0	0	0	0	0	0	0	2	0	.000	.000
	Tom Fitzsimmons	3B4	R	29	4	4	1	0	0	0	0	0	1	2	0	.000	.000
	Ollie O'Mara	3B2	R	28	2	7	1	0	0	0	0	0	0	0	0	.000	.000

	NAME	T	AGE	W	L	PCT	SV	G	GS	CG	IP	H	BB	SO	ShO	ERA
			27	69	71	.493	1	141	141	**98**	**1281**	1256	292	476	12	2.73
	Jeff Pfeffer	R	31	17	13	.567	0	30	30	26	267	270	49	92	4	2.66
	Leon Cadore	R	28	14	12	.538	0	35	27	16	251	228	39	94	3	2.37
	Burleigh Grimes (JJ)	R	25	10	11	.476	0	25	21	13	181	179	60	82	1	3.48
	Al Mamaux	R	25	10	12	.455	0	30	22	16	199	174	66	80	2	2.67
	Clarence Mitchell	L	28	7	5	.583	0	23	11	9	109	123	23	43	0	3.06
	Sherry Smith	L	28	7	12	.368	1	30	19	13	173	181	29	40	2	2.24
	Rube Marquard (BL)	L	29	3	3	.500	0	8	7	3	59	54	10	29	0	2.29
1	Larry Cheney	R	33	1	3	.250	0	9	4	2	39	45	14	14	0	4.15
	Lafayette Henion	R	20	0	0	.000	0	1	0	0	3	2	2	2	0	6.00

BOSTON 6th 57-82 .410 38.5 — GEORGE STALLINGS

NAME	G by POS	B	AGE	G	AB	R	H	2B	3B	HR	RBI	BB	SO	SB	BA	SA
TOTALS			29	140	4746	465	1201	142	62	24	399	355	**481**	145	.253	.324
Walter Holke	1B136	B	26	137	518	48	151	14	6	0	48	21	25	19	.292	.342
1 Buck Herzog	2B70, 1B1	R	33	73	275	27	77	8	5	1	25	13	11	16	.280	.356
Rabbit Maranville	SS131	R	27	131	480	44	128	18	10	5	43	36	23	12	.267	.377
2 Tony Boeckel	3B93	R	26	95	365	42	91	11	5	1	26	35	13	10	.249	.315
Ray Powell	OF122	L	30	123	470	51	111	12	12	2	33	41	**79**	16	.236	.326
Joe Riggert	OF61	R	32	63	240	34	68	8	5	4	17	25	30	9	.283	.408
2 Walton Cruise	OF66	L	29	73	241	23	52	7	0	1	21	17	29	8	.216	.257
Hank Gowdy	C74, 1B1	R	29	78	219	18	61	8	1	1	22	19	16	5	.279	.338
Red Smith	OF48, 3B23	R	29	87	241	24	59	6	0	1	25	40	22	6	.245	.282
Johnny Rawlings	2B58, OF12, SS5	R	26	77	275	30	70	8	2	1	16	16	20	10	.255	.309
Art Wilson	C64, 1B1	R	33	71	191	14	49	8	1	0	16	25	19	2	.257	.309
2 Jim Thorpe	OF38, 1B2	R	31	60	156	16	51	7	3	1	25	6	30	7	.327	.429
2 Les Mann	OF40	R	25	40	145	15	41	6	4	3	20	9	14	7	.283	.441
2 Charlie Pick	2B21, 3B5, OF3, 1B2	L	31	34	114	12	29	1	1	1	7	7	5	4	.254	.307
1 Lena Blackburne	3B24, 1B1, 2B1, SS1	R	32	31	80	5	21	3	1	0	4	6	7	3	.263	.325
1 Walt Tragresser	C14	R	32	20	40	3	7	2	0	0	3	2	10	1	.175	.225
Joe Kelly	OF16	R	29	18	64	5	9	1	0	0	3	0	11	2	.141	.156
Dizzy Nutter	OF12	L	25	18	52	4	11	0	0	0	3	4	5	1	.212	.212
Dixie Carroll	OF13	L	28	15	49	10	13	3	1	0	7	7	1	5	.265	.367
Mickey O'Niel	C11	R	21	11	28	3	6	0	0	0	1	1	7	0	.214	.214
Hod Ford	SS8, 3B2	R	21	10	28	4	6	0	1	0	3	2	6	0	.214	.286
Lloyd Christenbury	OF7	L	25	7	31	5	9	1	0	0	4	2	2	0	.290	.323

Tom Miller 21 L 2-6, Gene Bailey 25 R 2-6, Lee King 25 R 0-1, Sam White 24 R 0-1, Art Rico (DD) 22

NAME	T	AGE	W	L	PCT	SV	G	GS	CG	IP	H	BB	SO	ShO	ERA
		27	57	82	.410	9	140	140	79	1271	1313	337	374	5	3.17
Dick Rudolph	R	31	13	**18**	.419	2	37	32	24	274	**282**	54	76	2	2.17
1 Art Nehf	L	26	8	9	.471	0	22	19	13	169	151	40	53	1	3.09
Ray Keating	R	27	7	11	.389	0	22	13	9	136	129	45	48	1	2.98
Al Demaree	R	32	6	6	.500	3	25	13	6	128	147	35	34	0	3.80
Jack Scott	R	27	6	6	.500	1	19	12	7	104	109	39	44	0	3.12
Dana Fillingim	R	25	6	13	.316	2	32	19	9	186	185	39	50	0	3.39
3 Joe Oeschger	R	28	4	2	.667	0	7	7	4	57	83	21	16	1	2.53
2 Red Causey	R	25	4	5	.444	0	10	10	3	69	81	20	14	0	4.57
Hugh McQuillan	R	21	2	3	.400	1	16	7	2	60	66	14	13	0	3.45
Jake Northrop	R	31	1	5	.167	0	11	3	2	37	43	10	9	0	4.62
2 Larry Cheney	R	33	0	2	.000	0	8	2	0	33	35	15	13	0	3.55
1 Pat Ragan	R	30	0	2	.000	0	4	3	0	13	16	3	3	0	6.92
Bill James	R	27	0	0	.000	0	1	0	0	5	6	2	1	0	3.60

ST. LOUIS 7th 54-83 .394 40.5 — BRANCH RICKEY

NAME	G by POS	B	AGE	G	AB	R	H	2B	3B	HR	RBI	BB	SO	SB	BA	SA
TOTALS			26	138	4588	463	1175	163	52	18	398	304	418	148	.256	.326
Dots Miller	1B68, 2B28	R	32	101	346	38	80	10	4	1	24	13	23	6	.231	.292
Milt Stock	2B77, 3B58	R	25	135	492	56	151	16	4	0	52	49	21	17	.307	.356
Doc Lavan	SS99	R	28	100	356	25	86	12	2	1	25	11	30	4	.242	.295
Rogers Hornsby	3B72, SS37, 2B25, 1B5	R	23	138	512	68	163	15	9	8	71	48	41	17	.318	.430
Jack Smith	OF111	L	24	119	408	47	91	16	3	0	15	26	29	30	.223	.277
Cliff Heathcote	OF101, 1B2	L	21	114	401	53	112	13	4	1	29	20	41	26	.279	.339
Austin McHenry	OF103	R	23	110	371	41	106	19	11	1	47	19	57	7	.286	.404
Vern Clemons	C75	R	27	88	239	14	63	13	2	2	22	26	13	4	.264	.360
Joe Schultz	OF49, 2B5	R	25	88	229	24	58	9	1	2	21	11	7	4	.253	.328
Burt Shotton	OF67	L	34	85	270	35	77	13	5	1	20	22	25	17	.285	.381
1 Frank Snyder	C48, 1B1	R	26	50	154	7	28	4	2	0	14	5	13	2	.182	.234
Pickles Dillhoefer	C39	R	24	45	108	11	23	3	2	0	12	8	6	5	.213	.278
1 Gene Paulette	1B35, SS3	R	27	43	144	11	31	6	0	0	11	9	6	4	.215	.257
2 Fritz Mollwitz	1B25	R	29	25	83	7	19	3	0	0	5	7	3	2	.229	.265
2 Doug Baird	3B8, 2B1, OF1	R	27	16	33	4	7	0	1	0	4	2	3	2	.212	.273
Roy Leslie	1B9	R	24	12	24	2	5	1	0	0	4	4	3	0	.208	.250
1 Walton Cruise	OF5, 1B2	L	29	9	21	0	2	1	0	0	0	1	6	0	.095	.143
Sam Fishburne	1B1, 2B1	R	26	9	6	0	2	1	0	0	2	0	0	0	.333	.500
2 Hal Janvrin	2B2, SS1, 3B1	R	26	7	14	1	3	1	0	0	1	2	2	0	.214	.286

Bobby Fisher 32 R 3-11, Wally Kimmick 22 R 0-1, 2 Mike Pasquariello 20 R 0-1

NAME	T	AGE	W	L	PCT	SV	G	GS	CG	IP	H	BB	SO	ShO	ERA
		26	54	83	.394	8	138	138	55	1217	1146	**415**	414	6	3.23
Bill Doak	R	28	13	14	.481	0	31	29	13	203	182	55	69	3	3.10
Marv Goodwin	R	28	11	9	.550	0	33	17	7	179	163	33	48	0	2.51
Oscar Tuero	R	26	5	7	.417	**4**	**45**	17	4	155	137	42	45	0	3.19
Bill Sherdel	L	22	5	9	.357	1	36	10	7	137	137	42	52	0	3.48
2 Ferdie Schupp	L	28	4	4	.500	0	10	9	6	70	55	30	37	0	3.73
1 Lee Meadows	R	24	4	10	.286	0	22	12	3	92	100	30	28	1	3.03
1 Red Ames	R	36	3	5	.375	1	23	7	1	70	88	25	19	0	4.89
2 Frank Woodward	R	25	3	5	.375	1	17	7	2	72	65	28	18	0	2.63
2 Elmer Jacobs	R	26	3	6	.333	1	17	8	4	85	81	25	31	1	2.54
Jakie May	L	23	3	12	.200	0	28	19	8	126	99	87	58	1	3.21
Oscar Horstmann	R	28	0	1	.000	0	6	2	0	15	14	12	5	0	3.00
Bill Bolden	R	26	0	1	.000	0	3	1	0	12	17	4	4	0	5.25
Roy Parker	R	22	0	0	.000	0	2	0	0	2	6	1	0	0	31.50
Willis Koenigsmark	R	23	0	0	.000	0	1	0	0	0	2	1	0	0	∞
Art Reinhart	L	20	0	0	.000	0	1	0	0	0	0	0	0	0	0.00

PHILADELPHIA 8th 47-90 .343 47.5 — JACK COOMBS 18-44 .290 GAVVY CRAVATH 29-46 .387

NAME	G by POS	B	AGE	G	AB	R	H	2B	3B	HR	RBI	BB	SO	SB	BA	SA
TOTALS			29	138	4746	510	1191	**208**	50	**42**	436	323	469	114	.251	.342
Fred Luderus	1B138	L	33	138	509	60	149	30	6	5	49	54	48	6	.293	.405
2 Gene Paulette	2B53, OF10, 1B1	R	27	67	243	20	63	8	3	1	31	19	10	10	.259	.329
Dave Bancroft(JJ)	SS88	B	28	92	335	45	91	13	7	0	25	31	30	8	.272	.352
2 Lena Blackburne	3B72, 1B1, 2B1, SS1	R	32	72	291	32	58	10	5	2	19	10	22	2	.199	.289
Leo Callahan	OF58	L	28	81	235	26	54	14	4	1	9	29	19	5	.230	.336
Cy Williams	OF108	L	31	109	435	54	121	21	1	9	39	30	43	9	.278	.393
Irish Meusel	OF128	R	26	135	521	65	159	26	7	5	59	15	13	24	.305	.411
Jack Adams	C73	B	28	78	232	14	54	7	2	1	17	6	27	4	.233	.293
Gavvy Cravath	OF56	R	38	83	214	34	73	18	5	**12**	45	35	21	8	.341	.640
1 Possum Whitted	OF47, 2B20, 1B2	R	29	78	289	32	72	14	1	3	32	14	20	5	.249	.336
Harry Pearce	2B43, SS23, 3B2	R	29	68	244	24	44	3	3	0	9	8	27	6	.180	.217
1 Doug Baird	3B66	R	27	66	242	33	61	13	3	2	30	22	28	13	.252	.355
2 Eddie Sicking	SS35, 2B21	R	22	61	185	16	40	2	1	0	15	8	17	4	.216	.238
2 Walt Tragresser	C34	R	32	35	114	7	27	7	0	0	8	9	31	4	.237	.298
Hick Cady	C29	R	33	34	98	6	21	6	0	1	19	4	8	1	.214	.306
Nig Clarke	C22	L	36	26	62	4	15	3	0	0	2	4	5	1	.242	.290

Bevo LeBourveau 24 L 17-63, Bert Yeabsley 25 R 0-0, Doc Wallace 25 R 1-4, Pat Cavanaugh 19 R 0-1, 1 Mike Pasquariello 20 R 1-1, Lou Raymond 24 R 1-2, 2 Casey Stengel (ST) 28, Stan Baumgartner (VR) 26

NAME	T	AGE	W	L	PCT	SV	G	GS	CG	IP	H	BB	SO	ShO	ERA
		27	47	**90**	.343	2	138	138	93	1243	**1391**	408	397	6	4.17
2 Lee Meadows	R	24	8	10	.444	0	18	17	15	149	128	49	88	3	2.48
Gene Packard	L	31	6	8	.429	1	21	16	10	134	167	30	24	1	4.16
1 Frank Woodward	R	25	6	9	.400	0	17	12	6	101	109	35	27	0	4.72
1 Elmer Jacobs	R	26	6	10	.375	0	17	15	13	129	150	44	37	0	3.84
Eppa Rixey (MS)	L	28	6	12	.333	0	23	18	11	154	160	50	63	1	3.97
2 George Smith	R	27	5	11	.313	0	31	20	11	185	194	46	42	1	3.21
Brad Hogg	R	31	5	12	.294	0	22	19	13	150	163	55	48	0	4.44
Milt Watson	R	26	2	4	.333	0	8	4	3	47	51	19	12	0	5.17
3 Larry Cheney	R	33	2	5	.286	0	9	6	5	57	69	28	25	0	4.58
Mike Cantwell	L	23	1	3	.250	0	5	3	2	27	36	9	6	0	5.67
1 Joe Oeschger	R	28	0	1	.000	0	5	4	2	38	52	16	5	0	5.92
Mike Prendergast	L	30	0	1	.000	0	5	0	0	15	20	10	5	0	8.40
Pat Murray	L	21	0	2	.000	0	8	2	1	34	50	12	11	0	6.35
2 Red Ames	R	36	0	2	.000	1	3	2	1	16	26	3	4	0	6.19
Rags Faircloth	R	26	0	0	.000	0	2	0	0	2	5	0	0	0	9.00
Lefty Weinert	L	17	0	0	.000	0	1	0	0	4	11	2	0	0	18.00

WORLD SERIES – CINCINNATI (NL) 5 CHICAGO (AL) 3

LINE SCORES

TEAM	1	2	3	4	5	6	7	8	9	10	11	12	R	H	E
Game 1 October 1 at Cincinnati															
CHI (AL)	0	1	0	0	0	0	0	0	0				1	6	1
CIN (NL)	1	0	0	5	0	0	2	1	X				9	14	1
Cicotte, Wilkinson (4), Lowdermilk (8) — **Ruether**															
Game 2 October 2 at Cincinnati															
CHI	0	0	0	0	0	0	2	0	0				2	10	1
CIN	0	0	0	3	0	1	0	0	X				4	4	2
Williams — **Sallee**															
Game 3 October 3 at Chicago															
CIN	0	0	0	0	0	0	0	0	0				0	3	1
CHI	0	2	0	1	0	0	0	0	X				3	7	0
Fisher, Luque (8) — **Kerr**															
Game 4 October 4 at Chicago															
CIN	0	0	0	0	2	0	0	0	0				2	5	2
CHI	0	0	0	0	0	0	0	0	0				0	3	2
Ring — **Cicotte**															
Game 5 October 6 at Chicago															
CIN	0	0	0	0	0	4	0	0	1				5	4	0
CHI	0	0	0	0	0	0	0	0	0				0	3	3
Eller — **Williams**, Mayer (9)															
Game 6 October 7 at Cincinnati															
CHI	0	0	0	0	1	3	0	0	0	1			5	10	3
CIN	0	0	2	2	0	0	0	0	0	0			4	11	0
Kerr — Ruether, **Ring** (6)															
Game 7 October 8 at Cincinnati															
CHI	1	0	1	0	2	0	0	0	0				4	10	1
CIN	0	0	0	0	0	1	0	0	0				1	7	4
Cicotte — **Sallee**, Fisher (5), Luque (6)															
Game 8 October 9 at Chicago															
CIN	4	1	0	0	1	3	0	1	0				10	16	2
CHI	0	0	1	0	0	0	0	4	0				5	10	1
Eller — **Williams**, James (1), Wilkinson (6)															

COMPOSITE BATTING

NAME	POS	G	AB	R	H	2B	3B	HR	RBI	BA
Cincinnati (NL)										
Totals		8	251	35	64	10	7	0	34	.255
Rath	2B	8	31	5	7	1	0	0	2	.226
Daubert	1B	8	29	4	7	0	1	0	1	.241
Groh	3B	8	29	**6**	5	2	0	0	2	.172
Neale	OF	8	28	3	10	1	1	0	4	.357
Roush	OF	8	28	**6**	6	2	1	0	7	.214
Kopf	SS	8	27	3	6	0	**2**	0	3	.222
Duncan	OF	8	26	3	7	2	0	0	**8**	.269
Rariden	C	5	19	0	4	0	0	0	2	.211
Wingo	C	3	7	1	4	0	0	0	1	.571
Eller	P	2	7	2	2	1	0	0	0	.286
Ruether	P	3	6	2	4	1	**2**	0	4	.667
Ring	P	2	5	0	0	0	0	0	0	.000
Sallee	P	2	4	0	0	0	0	0	0	.000
Magee	PH	2	2	0	1	0	0	0	0	.500
Fisher	P	2	2	0	1	0	0	0	0	.500
Luque	P	2	1	0	0	0	0	0	0	.000
Smith	PR	1	0	0	0	0	0	0	0	.000
Chicago (AL)										
Totals		8	263	20	59	10	3	1	17	.224
Weaver	3B	8	**34**	4	11	**4**	1	0	0	.324
Jackson	OF	8	32	5	**12**	3	0	**1**	6	**.375**
E. Collins	2B	8	31	2	7	1	0	0	1	.226
Gandil	1B	8	30	1	7	0	1	0	5	.233
Felsch	OF	8	26	2	5	1	0	0	3	.192
Risberg	SS	8	25	3	2	0	1	0	0	.080
Schalk	C	8	23	1	7	0	0	0	2	.304
Leibold	OF	5	18	0	1	0	0	0	0	.056
S. Collins	OF	4	16	2	4	1	0	0	0	.250
Cicotte	P	3	8	0	0	0	0	0	0	.000
Kerr	P	2	6	0	1	0	0	0	0	.167
Williams	P	3	5	0	1	0	0	0	0	.200
McMullin	PH	2	2	0	1	0	0	0	0	.500
Murphy	PH	3	2	0	0	0	0	0	0	.000
Wilkinson	P	2	2	0	0	0	0	0	0	.000
James	P	1	2	0	0	0	0	0	0	.000
Lynn	C	1	1	0	0	0	0	0	0	.000
Lowdermilk	P	1	0	0	0	0	0	0	0	.000
Mayer	P	1	0	0	0	0	0	0	0	.000

COMPOSITE PITCHING

NAME	G	IP	H	BB	SO	W	L	SV	ERA
Cincinnati (NL)									
Totals	8	72	59	15	30	5	3	0	1.62
Eller	2	18	13	2	**15**	**2**	0	0	2.00
Ring	2	14	7	6	4	1	1	0	**0.64**
Ruether	2	14	12	4	1	1	0	0	2.57
Sallee	2	13.1	**19**	1	2	1	1	0	1.35
Fisher	2	7.2	7	2	2	0	1	0	2.35
Luque	2	5	1	0	6	0	0	0	0.00
Chicago (AL)									
Totals	8	71	64	25	22	3	5	0	3.42
Cicotte	**3**	**21.2**	**19**	5	7	1	2	0	2.91
Kerr	2	19	14	3	6	**2**	0	0	1.42
Williams	**3**	16.1	12	**8**	4	0	**3**	0	6.61
Wilkinson	2	7.1	9	4	3	0	0	0	1.23
James	1	4.2	8	3	2	0	0	0	5.79
Mayer	1	1	0	1	0	0	0	0	0.00
Lowdermilk	1	1	2	1	0	0	0	0	9.00

USE NAME – GIVEN NAMES (NICKNAMES)	TEAM BY YEAR	BIRTH DATE	BIRTH PLACE	DEATH DATE	B	T	HGT	WGT	G	AB	R	H	2B	3B	HR	RBI	BB	SO	SB	BA	SA
									LIFETIME BATTING TOTALS												
Abbaticchio, Ed-Edward James	97-98PhiN 03-05BosN 06HO 07-10PitN 10BosN	4-15-77	Latrobe, Pa.	1- 6-57	R	R	5'11	170	850	3032	356	772	99	44	11	324	289		142	.255	.327
Abbott (Winbigler), Fred-Harry Frederick	03-04CleA 05PhiN	10-22-74	Versailles, Ohio	6-11-35	R	R			160	513	48	107	21	6	1	49	19		14	.209	.279
Abbott, Ody-Ody Cleon (Toby)	10StLN	9- 5-86	New Eagle, Pa.	4-13-33	R	R	6'2	180	22	70	2	13	2	1	0	6	6	20	3	.186	.243
Abstein, Bill-William Henry (Big Bill)	06,09PitN 10StLA	2- 2-83	St. Louis, Mo.	4- 8-40	R	R	6'2	185	170	619	54	150	22	10	1	76	29		21	.242	.315
Acosta, Merito-Balmadero Pedro	13-16,18WasA 18PhiA	6- 2-96	Havana, Cuba	11-16-63	L	L	5'7	140	175	435	56	111	9	7	0	37	63	46	17	.255	.308
Adams, Jack-John Bertram	10-12CleA 15-19PhiN	6-21-91	Wharton, Tex.	6-24-40	B	R	6'1	185	267	678	37	137	17	4	2	45	23		9	.202	.248
Agler, Joe-Joseph Abram	12WasA 14-15BufF 15BalF	6-12-87	Coshocton, Ohio	4-26-71	L	L	5'11	165	233	751	121	185	22	10	0	36	131		38	.246	.302
Agnew, Sam-Samuel Lester	13-15StLA 16-18BosA 19WasA	4-12-87	Farmington, Mo.	7-19-51	R	R	5'11	185	560	1537	105	314	41	14	2	98	102	216	29	.204	.253
Ainsmith, Eddie-Edward Wilbur	10-18WasA 19-21DetA 21-23StLN 23BknN 24NYN	2- 4-92	Cambridge, Mass.		R	R	5'11	180	1068	3048	299	707	108	54	22	317	263		86	.232	.324
Aiton, George-George Wilson (Bill)	12StLA	12-29-90	Kingman, Kans.		B	R	5'11	175	8	17	1	4	0	0	0	1	4		0	.235	.235
Alcock, Scotty-John Forbes	14ChiA	11-29-85	Wooster, Ohio	1-30-73	R	R	5'9	160	54	156	12	27	4	2	0	7	7	14	4	.173	.224
Alexander, Walt-Walter Ernest	12-13,15StLA 15-17NYA	3- 5-91	Marietta, Ga.		R	R	5'10	165	162	405	26	76	18	3	1	24	42	83	5	.188	.254
Allen, Bob-Robert	19PhiA	-96			R	R	5'10	180	9	22	3	3	1	0	0	0	3	7	0	.136	.182
Allen, Horace-Horace Tanner (Pug)	19BknN	6-11-99	DeLand, Fla.		L	R	6'	187	4	7	0	0	0	0	0	0	0	2	0	.000	.000
Allen, Nick-Artemus Ward	14-15BufF 16ChiN 18-20CinN	9-14-88	Norton, Kans.	10-16-39	R	R	6'2	200	216	500	41	116	13	5	0	36	33		8	.232	.278
Allen, Sled-Fletcher Manson	10StLA	8-23-86	West Plains, Mo.	10-16-59	R	R	6'1	180	14	23	3	3	1	0	0	1	1		0	.130	.174
Allison, Milo-Milo Henry (Pete)	13-14ChiN 16-17CleA	10-16-90	Elk Rapids, Mich.	6-18-57	L	R	6'	163	49	60	15	13	0	0	0	0	15	9	4	.217	.217
Almeida, Rafael-Rafael D.	11-13CinN	7-30-87	Havana, Cuba	3- -68	R	R	5'9	164	102	285	32	77	13	6	3	46	25	40	7	.270	.389
Alperman, Whitey-Charles Augustus	06-09BknN	11-11-79	Etna, Pa.	12-25-42	R	R	5'10	180	450	1632	134	387	60	36	7	141	30		27	.237	.331
Altenburg, Jesse-Jesse Howard (Chip)	16-17PitN	1- 2-93	Ashley, Mich.	3-12-73	L	R	5'8	158	19	31	3	9	1	1	0	3	1	5	0	.290	.387
Altizer, Dave-David Tildon (Filipino)	06-08WasA 08CleA 09ChiA 10-11CinN	11- 6-76	Pearl, Ill.	5-14-64	L	R	5'10	160	514	1734	204	433	36	21	4	116	140		119	.250	.302
Anderson (Jendrus), George-George Andrew Jendrus	14-15BknF 18StLN	9-26-89	Cleveland, Ohio	3-20-62	L	R	5'8	160	269	1007	149	289	40	17	5	69	98		36	.287	.375
Anderson, Goat-Edward John	07PitN	1-13-80	Cleveland, Ohio	3-15-23		R			127	413	73	85	3	1	1	12	80		27	.206	.225
Anderson, John-John Joseph (Honest John)	94-98BknN 98WasN 99BknN 01MilA 02-03StLA 04-05NYA 05-07WasA 08ChiA	12-14-73	Sarpsborg, Norway	7-23-49	B	R	6'2	180	1620	6343	866	1852	326	126	48	976	310		347	.292	.406
Aragon, Angel-Angel Valdez Sr. (Bing, Pete)	14,16-17NYA	8- 2-93	Havana, Cuba	1-24-52	R	R	5'5	150	33	79	4	9	1	0	0	5	5	6	2	.114	.127
Archer, Jimmy-James Patrick	04PitN 07DetA 09-17ChiN 18PitN 18BknN 18CinN	5-13-83	Dublin, Ireland	3-29-58	R	R	5'10	176	846	2645	247	660	106	34	16	296	124		36	.250	.333
Armbruster, Charlie-Charles A.	05-07BosA 07ChiA	-82	Cincinnati, Ohio		R	R	5'9	180	131	355	24	53	11	1	0	12	52		6	.149	.186
Armbruster, Harry-Harry (Buster, Army)	06PhiA	3-20-82	Cincinnati, Ohio	12-10-53	L	L	5'10	190	91	265	40	63	6	3	2	24	43		13	.238	.306
Arndt, Harry-Harry J.	02DetA 02BalA 05-07StLN	2-12-79	South Bend, Ind.	3-25-21					271	985	118	244	26	20	6	99	85		27	.248	.333
Asmussen, Tom-Thomas William	07BosN	9-26-76	Chicago, Ill.	8-21-63		R			2	5	0	0	0	0	0	0	0		0	.000	.000
Atz, Jake-Jacob Henry	02WasA 07-09ChiA	7- 1-79	Washington, D.C.	5-22-45	R	R	5'9	160	208	604	64	132	21	3	0	49	69		23	.219	.263
Aubrey, Harry-Harvey Herbert	03BosN	7- 5-80	St. Joseph, Mo.			R			96	325	26	69	8	2	0	27	18		7	.212	.249
Austin, Jimmy-James Philip (Pepper)	09-10NYA 11-23,25-26,29,M13,18,23StLA	12- 8-79	Swansea, Wales	3- 6-65	B	R	5'7	155	1580	5388	661	1328	174	76	13	390	592		244	.246	.314
Autry, Chick-William Askew	07,09CinN 09BosN	1- 2-85	Humboldt, Tenn.		L	L	5'11	168	81	257	22	50	6	0	0	17	24		6	.195	.218
Babb, Charlie-Charles Amos	03NYN 04-05BknN	2-20-73	Milwaukie, Ore.	3-20-54	B	R	5'10	165	347	1180	144	287	41	13	0	116	125		66	.243	.300
Babington, Charlie-Charles Percy	15NYN	5- 4-95	Cranston, R.I.	3-22-57	R	R	6'	170	28	33	5	8	3	1	0	2	0	4	1	.242	.394
Bader, Art-Arthur Herman	04StLA	9-21-86	St. Louis, Mo.	4- 5-57	R	R	5'10	170	2	3	0	0	0	0	0	0	1		0	.000	.000
Bailey, Bill-Harry Lewis	11NYA	11-19-81	Shawnee, Ohio	10-27-67	L	R	5'10	170	5	9	1	1	0	0	0	0	0		0	.111	.111
Bailey, Fred-Frederick Middleton (Penny)	16-18BosN	8-16-95	Mt. Hope, W.Va.	8-16-72	L	L	5'11	150	60	124	10	23	2	1	1	6	9	29	5	.185	.242
Baird, Al-Albert Wells	17NYN 18MS 19NYN	6- 2-95	Cleburne, Tex.		R	R	5'9	160	48	107	9	27	1	0	0	9	7	11	3	.252	.262
Baird, Doug-Howard Douglas	15-17PitN 17-18StLN 19PhiN 19StLN 19-20BknN 20NYN	9-27-91	St. Charles, Mo.	6-13-67	R	R	5'9	148	617	2106	230	492	86	45	6	191	157	295	118	.234	.326
Baker, Del-Delmer David	14-16,M33,38-42DetA	5- 3-92	Sherwood, Ore.		R	R	5'11	176	172	302	27	63	9	4	0	22	32	32	5	.209	.265
Baker, Frank-John Franklin (Home Run)	08-14PhiA 15HO 16-19,20VR 21-22NYA	3-13-86	Trappe, Md.	6-28-63	L	R	5'11	173	1575	5983	887	1838	311	103	96	987	473		235	.307	.442
Baker, Howard-Howard Francis	12CleA 14-15ChiA 15NYN	3- 1-88	Bridgeport, Conn.	1-16-64	R	R	5'11	175	29	82	5	18	1	1	0	7	8	10	2	.220	.256
Baker (Silverman), Jesse (Michael)-Jesse	19WasA	-96			R	R	5'4	140	1	0	0	0	0	0	0	1	0	0	0	–	–
Baker, Tracy-Tracy Lee	11BosA	11- 7-91	Pendleton, Ore.	3-14-75	R	R	6'1	180	1	0	0	0	0	0	0	0	0	0	0	–	–
Balenti, Mike-Michael Richard	11CinN 13StLA	7- 3-86	Calumet, Okla.	8- 4-55	R	R	6'1	175	78	219	19	40	2	4	0	11	6	33	6	.183	.228
Ball, Jim-James Chandler	07-08BosN	-85	Harford Co., Md.			R			16	51	4	7	2	0	0	3	3		0	.137	.176
Ball, Neal-Cornelius	07-09NYA 09-12CleA 12-13BosA	4-22-81	Grand Haven, Mich.	10-15-57	R	R	5'7	145	496	1609	161	404	56	17	4	151	99		92	.251	.314
Bankston, Bill-Wilborn Everett	15PhiA	5-25-93	Barnesville, Ga.	2-26-70	L	R	5'11	180	11	36	6	5	1	1	1	2	2	5	1	.139	.306
Barbeau, Jap-William Joseph	05-06CleA 09PitN 09-10StLN	6-10-82	New York, N.Y.	9-10-69	R	R	5'5	140	198	712	96	160	25	8	0	46	78		39	.225	.282
Barclay, George-George Oliver (Deerfoot)	02-04StLN 04-05BosN	5-16-76	Millville, Pa.	4- 2-09		R	5'10	162	401	1538	167	382	35	15	4	140	62		61	.248	.298
Barney, Ed-Edmund J.	15NYA 15-16PitN	1-23-90	Amery, Wis.	10- 4-67	L	R	5'10	178	88	272	33	61	5	2	0	22	37	33	17	.224	.257
Barr, Scotty-Hyder Edward	09-09PhiA	10- 6-86	Bristol, Tenn.	12- 2-34	R	R	6'	175	41	107	9	12	3	0	0	2	14		2	.112	.140
Barrett, Jimmy-James Erigena	99-00CinN 01-05DetA 06CinN 07-08BosA	3-28-75	Athol, Mass.	10-24-21	L	L	5'9	170	866	3304	581	962	82	48	16	255	440		145	.291	.360
Barrows, Cuke-Roland	09-12ChiA	10-20-83	Gray, Me.	2-10-55	R	L	5'8	158	32	99	6	19	2	0	0	9	12		3	.192	.212
Barry, Jack-John Joseph	08-15PhiA 15-17,M17BosA 18MS 19BosA	4-26-87	Meriden, Conn.	4-23-61	R	R	5'9	158	1222	4146	533	1009	142	38	10	429	396		153	.243	.303
Barry, Shad-John C.	99WasN 00-01BosN 01-04PhiN 04-05ChiN 05-06CinN 06-08StLN 08NYN	9-28-76	Newburgh, N.Y.	11-27-36	R	R			1100	4007	515	1075	130	48	10	391	279		143	.268	.332
Barton, Harry-Harry Lamb	05PhiA	1-20-75	Chester, Pa.	1-25-55	B	R	5'6	155	29	60	5	10	2	1	0	3	3		2	.167	.233
Bashang, Al-Albert C.	12DetA 18BknN	8-22-88	Cincinnati, Ohio	6-23-67	B	R	5'8	150	7	17	3	2	0	0	0	0	3		0	.118	.118
Bass, Doc-William C.	18BosN		Cincinnati, Ohio						1	1	1	1	0	0	0	0	0	0	0	1.000	1.000
Batch, Heinie-Emil (Ace)	04-07BknN	1-21-80	Brooklyn, N.Y.	8-23-26	R	R	5'7	170	348	1253	134	315	38	22	7	98	65		37	.251	.334
Bates, Johnny-John William	06-09BosN 09-10PhiN 11-14CinN 14ChiN 14BalF	1-10-82	Steubenville, Ohio	2-10-49	L	L	5'7	168	1163	3921	572	1088	167	73	25	417	504		187	.277	.376
Bates, Ray-Raymond	13CleA 17PhiA 18MS	2- 8-90	Paterson, N.J.	8-15-70	R	R	6'	168	147	515	51	120	20	9	2	70	24	48	15	.233	.318
Batsch, Bill-William McKinley	16PitN	5-18-92	Mingo Junction, Ohio	12-31-63	R	R	5'10	168	1	0	0	0	0	0	0	0	1	0	0	–	–
Batten, George-George Burnett	12NYA	10- 7-91	Haddonfield, N.J.	8- 4-72	R	R	5'11	165	1	3	0	0	0	0	0	0	0		0	.000	.000
Baumann, Paddy-Charles John	11-14DetA 15-17NYA	12-20-85	Indianapolis, Ind.	11-20-69	R	R	5'9	160	295	904	118	248	30	13	4	101	81		30	.274	.350
Baxter, John-John	07StLN		Spokane, Wash.						6	21	1	4	0	0	0	0	0		0	.190	.190
Bay, Harry-Harry Elbert (Deerfoot)	01-02CinN 02-08CleA	1-17-78	Pontiac, Ill.	3-20-52	L	L	5'8	138	673	2638	413	720	65	42	5	141	195		169	.273	.335
Bayless, Dick-Harry Owen	08CinN	-82	Joplin, Mo.	12-16-20	L	R	5'9	178	19	71	7	16	1	0	1	3	6		0	.225	.282
Beall, Johnny-John Woolf	13CleA 13ChiA 15-16CinN 18StLN	3-12-82	Beltsville, Md.		L	R	6'	180	58	170	18	43	4	1	3	17	11	25	2	.253	.341
Bean, Joe-Joseph William	02NYN	3-18-74	Boston, Mass.	2-15-61	R	R	5'8	138	48	176	13	39	2	1	0	5	5		9	.222	.244
Beatty, Des-Aloysius Desmond (Desperate)	14NYN	4- 7-93	Baltimore, Md.	10- 6-69	R	R	5'8	158	2	3	0	0	0	0	0	1	0	0	0	.000	.000
Beaumont, Ginger-Clarence Howeth	99-06PitN 07-09BosN 10ChiN	7-23-76	Rochester, Wis.	4-10-56	L	R	5'8	190	1463	5647	953	1754	182	82	39	617	425		243	.311	.393
Beck, Erve-Erwin Thomas (Dutch)	99BknN 01CleA 02CinN 02DetA	7-19-78	Toledo, Ohio	12-22-16	R	R	5'10	168	232	912	122	265	42	11	9	123	30		12	.291	.390
Beck, Fred-Frederick Thomas	09-10BosN 11CinN 11PhiN 14-15ChiF	11-17-86	Havana, Ill.	3-12-62	L	L	6'1	180	635	2130	191	536	77	27	34	251	122		31	.252	.361
Beck, Zinn-Zinn Bertram	13-16StLN 18NYA	9-30-85	Steubenville, Ohio		R	R	5'10	160	290	902	75	204	32	16	3	73	58	95	21	.226	.307
Beckendorf, Heinie-Henry Ward	09-10DetA 10WasA	6-15-84	New York, N.Y.	9-15-49	R	R	5'9	174	55	137	9	25	2	0	0	13	8		0	.182	.197
Becker, Beals-David Beals	08PitN 08-09BosN 10-12NYN 13CinN 13-15PhiN	7- 5-86	El Dorado, Kans.	8-16-43	L	L	5'11	176	876	2764	367	763	114	43	45	292	241		129	.276	.397
Becker, Marty-Martin Henry	15NYN	12-25-93	Tiffin, Ohio	9-25-57	B	R	5'7	168	17	52	5	13	2	0	0	3	2	9	3	.250	.288
Beckley, Jake-Jacob Peter (Eagle Eye)	88-89PitN 90PitP 91-96PitN 96-97NYN 97-03CinN 04-07StLN	8- 4-67	Hannibal, Mo.	6-25-18	L	L	5'10	200	2383	9476	1601	2930	455	246	87	1574	616		335	.309	.437
Bell (Baerwald), Jack (Rudolph Fred)-John	07NYA	1- 1-81	Wausau, Wis.	7-28-55	R	R	5'8	158	17	52	4	11	2	1	0	3	3		4	.212	.288
Bemis, Harry-Harry Parker	02-10CleA	2- 1-74	Farmington, N.H.	5-23-47	L	R	5'6	155	703	2229	213	569	92	29	5	234	79		49	.255	.329
Bennett, Pug-Justin Titus	06-07StLN	2-20-74	Ponca, Neb.	9-12-35	R	R	5'11	165	240	919	86	228	24	9	1	55	77		27	.248	.297
Bergen, Bill-William Aloysius	01-03CinN 04-11BknN	6-13-73	N. Brookfield, Mass.	12-19-43	R	R	6'	184	947	3028	138	516	45	21	2	193	88		23	.170	.201
Berger, Clarence-Clarence Edward	14PitN	11- 1-94	East Cleveland, Ohio	6-30-59	L	R	6'	185	6	13	2	1	0	0	0	0	1	4	0	.077	.077
Berger, Joe-Joseph August (Fats)	13-14ChiA	12-20-86	St. Louis, Mo.	3- 6-56	R	R	5'10	170	124	371	38	71	9	3	2	23	49	37	7	.191	.248
Berghammer, Marty-Martin Andrew (Pepper)	11ChiA 13-14CinN 15PitF	6-18-88	Elliott, Pa.	12-21-57	L	R	5'11	165	285	774	136	180	16	7	1	52	103		46	.233	.275
Bergman, Al-Alfred Henry (Dutch)	16CleA	9-27-90	Peru, Ind.	6-20-61	R	R	5'7	155	8	14	2	3	0	1	0	0	2	4	0	.214	.357
Berman, Bob-Robert Leon	18WasA	1-24-99	New York, N.Y.		R	R	5'7	155	2	0	0	0	0	0	0	0	0	0	0	–	–
Bernard, Curt-Curtis Henry	00-01NYN	2-18-78	Parkersburg, W.Va.	4-10-55	L	R	5'10	150	42	146	20	34	2	2	0	14	13		5	.233	.274
Berrens, Joe-Joseph	12ChiA		St. John's, Canada						2	4	1	1	0	0	0	0	0		0	.250	.250
Berry, Claude-Claude Elzy (Admiral)	04ChiA 06-07PhiA 14-15PitF	2- 4-80	Losantville, Ind.	2- 1-74	R	R	5'7	165	245	753	72	165	31	10	3	65	60		14	.219	.299
Berry, Howard-Joseph Howard Sr. (Hodge)	02PhiN	9-10-72	Wheeling, W.Va.	3-13-61	B	R	5'9	172	1	4	0	1	0	0	0	1	1		1	.250	.250
Berte, Harry-Harry	03StLN	5-10-72	Covington, Ky.			R			4	15	1	5	0	0	0	1	1		0	.333	.333

USE NAME – GIVEN NAMES (NICKNAMES)	TEAM BY YEAR	BIRTH DATE	BIRTH PLACE	DEATH DATE	B	T	HGT	WGT	G	AB	R	H	2B	3B	HR	RBI	BB	SO	SB	BA	SA
									LIFETIME BATTING TOTALS												
Bescher, Bob-Robert Henry	08-13CinN 14NYN 15-17StLN 18CleA	2-25-84	London, Ohio	11-29-42	B	L	6'1	200	1228	4536	749	1171	190	74	28	345	619		427	.258	.351
Betcher (Bettger), Frank-Franklin Lyle	10StLN	2-15-88	Philadelphia, Pa.		B	R	5'11	173	35	89	7	18	2	0	0	6	7	14	1	.202	.225
Betzel, Bruno-Christian Frederick Albert John Henry David	14-18StLN	12- 6-94	Chattanooga, Ohio	2- 7-65	R	R	5'9	158	448	1444	135	333	37	25	2	94	90	189	49	.231	.295
Beville, Monte-Henry Monte	03-04NYA 04DetA	2-24-75	Dublin, Ind.	1-24-55	L	R	5'11	180	145	454	39	92	21	2	0	44	26		6	.203	.258
Billings, Josh-John Augustus	13-18CleA 19-23StLA	11-30-91	Grantville, Kans.		R	R	5'11	165	240	488	44	106	12	5	0	29	23	73	5	.217	.262
Birmingham, Joe-Joseph Lee (Dode)	06-14,M12-15CleA	8- 6-84	Elmira, N.Y.	4-24-46	R	R	5'10	185	771	2627	283	667	89	28	6	265	129		108	.254	.316
Bisland, Rivington-Rivington Martin	12PitN 13StLA 14CleA	2-17-90	New York, N.Y.	1-11-73	R	R	5'9	155	31	102	12	12	1	0	0	5	8	7	2	.118	.127
Black (Haddow), John-John Falcnor	11StLA	2-23-90	Covington, Ky.		R	R	6'1	185	54	186	13	28	4	0	0	7	10		4	.151	.172
Blackburn, Earl-Earl Stuart	12PitN 12-13CinN 15-16BosN 17ChiN	11- 1-92	Leesville, Ohio	8- 3-66	R	R	5'11	180	71	145	13	38	4	4	0	10	14	27	4	.262	.345
Blackburne, Lena-Russell Aubrey (Slats) (See P20-45)	10ChiA 11KJ 12ChiA 18ChiN 19BosN 19PhiN 27,29,M28-29ChiA	10-23-86	Clifton Heights, Pa.	2-29-68	R	R	5'11	160	548	1807	174	387	39	23	4	139	162		54	.214	.268
Blackwell, Fred-Fredrick William (Blacky)	17-19PitN	9- 7-95	Bowling Green, Ky.		L	R	5'10	160	35	88	5	18	3	0	0	10	6	16	0	.205	.239
Blair, Walter-Walter Allen (Heavy)	07-11NYA 14-15,M15BufF	10-13-83	Landrus, Pa.	8-20-48	R	R	6'	185	442	1255	80	272	42	11	3	106	86		18	.217	.275
Blank, Coonie	09StLN								1	2	0	0	0	0	0	0	0		0	.000	.000
Blankenship, Cliff-Clifford Douglas	05CinN 07,09WasA	4-10-80	Columbus, Ga.	4-26-56	R	R	5'10	165	95	218	16	49	3	1	0	22	7		6	.225	.248
Bliss, Elmer-Elmer Ward (See P01-19)	03-04NYA	3- 9-75	Penfield, Pa.	3-18-62	L	R	6'	180	2	4	0	0	0	0	0	0	0		0	.000	.000
Bliss, Jack-John Joseph Albert	08-12StLN	1- 9-82	Vancouver, Wash.	10-23-68	R	R	5'10	185	241	654	70	143	15	6	3	61	85		13	.219	.274
Block (Blochowitz), Bruno-James John	07WasA 10-12ChiA 14ChiF	3-13-85	Wiscon. Rapids, Wis.	8- 6-37	R	R	5'8	185	207	560	42	129	18	10	1	68	39		5	.230	.304
Blue, Bert-Bird Wayne	08StLA 08PhiA	12-14-76	Bettsville, Ohio	12-14-28	R	R	6'3	200	17	44	4	12	1	2	1	2	3		0	.273	.455
Bluhm, Red-Harvey Fred	18BosA	6-27-94	Cleveland, Ohio	5- 7-52	R	R	5'11	165	1	1	0	0	0	0	0	0	0	0	0	.000	.000
Bodie (Pezzolo), Ping (Francesco Stephano)-Frank Stephan	11-14ChiA 17PhiA 18-21NYA	10- 8-87	San Francisco, Cal.	12- 7-61	R	R	5'8	195	1049	3670	392	1011	169	72	43	516	312		83	.275	.396
Bold, Dutch-Charles Dickens	14StLA	10-27-94	Karlskrona, Sweden		R	R	6'2	185	2	1	0	0	0	0	0	0	0	1	0	.000	.000
Bone, George-George Drummond	01MilA	8-27-74	New Haven, Conn.	5-28-18		R			12	43	6	13	2	0	0	6	4		0	.302	.349
Bonin, Luther-Ernest Luther	13StLA 14BufF	1-13-88	Green Hill, Ind.	1- 3-66	L	R	5'9	178	21	77	6	14	4	1	0	4	7		3	.182	.260
Bonner, Frank-Frank J. (The Human Flea)	94-95BalN 95StLN 96BknN 99WasN 02CleA 02PhiA 03BosN	8-20-69	Lowell, Mass.	12-31-05		R			240	941	114	239	44	7	4	115	55		32	.254	.328
Booe, Everett-Everett Little	13PitN 14IndF 14BufF	9-28-90	Mocksville, N.C.	5-21-69	L	R	5'8	165	125	352	43	77	10	4	0	22	34		14	.219	.270
Boone, Luke-Luke Joseph (Danny)	13-16NYA 18PitN	5- 6-90	Pittsburgh, Pa.		R	R	5'9	160	314	1028	102	215	27	4	6	76	91	111	32	.209	.261
Borton, Babe-William Baker	12-13ChiA 13NYA 15StLF 16StLA	8-14-88	Marion, Ill.	7-29-54	L	L	6'	178	317	940	139	254	30	17	5	136	160		21	.270	.354
Bostick (Lifsit), Henry Henry Landers	15PhiA	1-12-95	Boston, Mass.		R	R			2	7	1	0	0	0	0	0	0	1	0	.000	.000
Boucher, Al-Alexander Francis (Bo)	14StLF	11-13-81	Franklin, Mass.	6-23-74	R	R	5'8	156	147	516	62	119	26	4	2	49	52		13	.231	.308
Boucher, Medric-Medric T.	14BalF 14PitF	-89			R	R	5'10	165	17	17	2	5	1	1	0	2	1		0	.294	.471
Bowcock, Ben-Benjamin F.	03StLA	10-28-79	Fall River, Mass.						14	50	7	16	3	1	1	10	3		1	.320	.480
Bowden, Tim-David Timon	14StLA	8-15-91	McDonough, Ga.	10-25-49	L	R	5'10	175	7	9	0	2	0	0	0	0	1	6	0	.222	.222
Bowen, Chick-Emmons Joseph	19NYN	7-26-97	New Haven, Conn.	8- 9-48	R	R	5'7	165	2	3	1	1	0	0	0	1	1	2	0	.333	.333
Bowerman, Frank-Frank Eugene (Mike)	95-98BalN 98-99PitN 00-07NYN 08-09,M09BosN	12- 5-68	Romeo, Mich.	11-30-48	R	R	6'1	195	1040	3383	345	861	100	38	13	392	129		86	.255	.318
Bowser, Red-James H.	10ChiA	-86	Greensburg, Pa.						1	2	0	0	0	0	0	0	0		0	.000	.000
Boyle, Jack-John Bellew	12PhiN	7- 9-89	Morris, Ill.	4- 3-71	L	R	5'11	165	15	25	4	7	1	0	0	2	1	5	0	.280	.320
Bradley, Bill-William Joseph	99-00ChiN 01-10CleA 14,M14BknF 15KCF	2-13-78	Cleveland, Ohio	3-11-54	R	R	6'	185	1460	5452	761	1484	273	84	34	552	290		193	.272	.372
Bradley, Hugh-Hugh Frederick	10-12BosA 14-15PitF 15BknF 15NwkF	5-23-85	Grafton, Mass.	1-26-49	R	R			277	913	84	238	46	12	2	117	59		23	.261	.344
Bradley, Jack-John Thomas	16CleA	9-20-93	Denver, Colo.	3-18-69	R	R	5'11	175	2	3	0	0	0	0	0	0	0	1	0	.000	.000
Bradshaw, Windy-Dallas Carl (Rabbit)	17PhiA	11-23-95	Wolf Creek, Ill.	12-11-39	L	R	5'7	145	2	4	0	0	0	0	0	0	0	1	0	.000	.000
Brady, Fred (See Larry Kopf)																					
Brain, Dave-David Leonard	01ChiA 03-05StLN 05PitN 06-07BosN 08CinN 08NYN	1-24-79	Hereford, England	5-25-59	R	R	5'10	170	679	2543	254	641	97	52	27	303	134		73	.252	.363
Brainerd, Fred-Frederick	14-16NYN	2-17-92	Champaign, Ill.	4-17-59	R	R	6'	176	95	261	32	51	7	2	1	21	22	44	6	.195	.249
Bransfield, Kitty-William Edward	98BosN 01-04PitN 05-11PhiN 11ChiN	1- 7-75	Worcester, Mass.	5- 1-47	R	R	5'11	207	1330	4997	530	1350	225	77	14	637	221		175	.270	.354
Brashear, Kitty-Norman C.	02StLN	8-27-77	Mansfield, Ohio	12-23-34	R	R	5'11	205	110	388	36	107	8	2	1	40	32		9	.276	.314
Brashear, Roy-Roy Parks	99LouN 03PhiN	1- 3-74	Ashtabula, Ohio	4-20-51					23	77	9	18	3	0	0	4	6		2	.234	.273
Brenegan, Sam-Olaf Selmer	14PitN	9- 1-90	Galesville, Wis.	4-20-56	L	R	6'2	185	1	0	0	0	0	0	0	0	0	0	0	–	–
Bresnahan, Roger-Roger Philip (The Duke of Tralee)	97WasN 00ChiN 01-02BalA 02-08NYN 09-12,M09-12StLN 13-15,M15ChiN	6-11-79	Toledo, Ohio	12- 4-44	R	R	5'9	200	1445	4479	683	1251	223	71	26	530	714		211	.279	.378
Breton, Jim-John Frederick	13-15ChiA	7-15-91	Chicago, Ill.	5-30-73	R	R	5'10	178	107	297	25	59	9	3	0	27	30	56	11	.199	.249
Brickley, George-George Vincent	13PhiA	7-19-94	Everett, Mass.	2-23-47	R	R	5'9	180	5	12	0	2	0	1	0	0	0	4	0	.167	.333
Bridwell, Al-Albert Henry	05CinN 06-07BosN 08-11NYN 11-12BosN 13ChiN 14-15StLF	1- 4-84	Friendship, Ohio	1-23-69	L	R	5'9	150	1251	4169	457	1064	95	32	2	348	559		136	.255	.295
Brief (Bordetzki), Bunny (Antonio)-Anthony Vincent	12-13StLA 15ChiA 17PitN	7- 3-92	Remus, Mich.	2-10-63	R	R	6'1	185	183	569	61	127	25	9	5	59	58		17	.223	.325
Brinker, Bill-William Hutchinson (Dode)	12PhiN	8-30-83	Warrensburg, Mo.	2-18-65	B	R	6'1	190	9	18	1	4	1	0	0	2	2	3	0	.222	.278
Britton, Gil-Stephen Gilbert	13PitN	9-21-91	Parsons, Kans.		R	R	5'10	160	3	12	0	0	0	0	0	0	0	2	0	.000	.000
Brock, John-John Roy	17-18StLN	10-16-97	Hamilton, Ill.	10-27-51	R	R	5'7	165	34	67	13	17	3	0	0	6	3	12	7	.254	.299
Broderick, Matt-Matthew T.	03BknN	12- 2-76	Lattimer Mines, Pa.	2-22-41	R	R	5'6	135	2	2	0	0	0	0	0	0	0		0	.000	.000
Brodie, Steve-Walter Scott	90-91BosN 92-93StLN 93-96BalN 97-98PitN 98-99BalN 01BalA 02NYN	9-11-68	Warrenton, Va.	10-30-35	L	R	5'9	176	1439	5686	873	1740	193	89	25	901	420		310	.308	.386
Bronkie, Herman-Herman Charles (Dutch)	10-12CleA 14ChiN 18StLN 19,22StLA	3-30-85	S. Manchester, Conn.	5-27-68	R	R	5'9	165	121	360	40	87	14	5	1	24	33		3	.242	.317
Brouthers, Art-Arthur H.	06PhiA	11-25-82	Montgomery, Ala.	9-28-59		R			36	144	18	30	5	1	0	14	5		4	.208	.257
Brouthers, Dan-Dennis Joseph (Big Dan)	79-80TroyN 81-85BufN 86-88DetN 89BosN 90BosP 91BosAA 92-93BknN 94-95BalN 95LouN 96PhiN 04NYN	5- 8-58	Sylvan Lake, N.Y.	8- 2-32	L	L	6'2	207	1665	6682	1513	2288	446	212	106	1294	840	239	261	.342	.520
Brown, Bill-William Verna	12StLA	7- 8-93	Coleman, Tex.	5-13-65	L	L	5'8	185	9	20	0	4	0	0	0	1	0		0	.200	.200
Brown, Delos-Delos Hight	14ChiA	10- 4-92	Anna, Ill.	12-21-64	R	R	5'9	160	1	1	0	0	0	0	0	0	0	1	0	.000	.000
Brown, Don-James Donaldson (Moose)	15StLN 16PhiA	3-31-97	Laurel, Ind.		R	R			15	44	6	11	2	1	1	5	6	10	0	.250	.409
Brown, Drummond-Drummond Nichols	13BosN 14-15KCF	1-31-85	Taft, Cal.	1-24-27	R	R	6'	180	123	319	20	77	14	1	2	33	21		4	.241	.310
Brown, Fred-Fred Herbert	01-02BosN	4-12-79	Ossipee, N.H.	2- 3-55	R	R	5'10	180	9	20	2	4	1	0	0	2	0		0	.200	.250
Brown, Sam-Samuel Wakefield	06-07BosN	5-21-78	Webster, Pa.	11- 8-31	R	R			141	439	29	88	12	1	0	34	25		4	.200	.232
Browne, George-George Edward	01-02PhiN 02-07NYN 08BosN 09ChiN 09-10WasA 10ChiA 11BknN 12PhiN	1-12-76	Richmond, Va.	12- 9-20	L	R	5'10	160	1102	4300	614	1176	119	55	18	303	259		190	.273	.339
Bruce, Lou-Louis R.	04PhiA	1-16-77	St. Regis, N.Y.	2- 9-68	L	R	5'5	145	30	101	9	27	3	0	0	8	5		2	.267	.297
Brush, Bob-Robert	07BosN	3- 8-75	Osage, Iowa	4- 2-44					2	2	0	0	0	0	0	0	0		0	.000	.000
Bruyette, Ed-Edward T.	01MilA		Aurora, Ill.			R			26	82	7	15	3	0	0	4	12		1	.183	.220
Buelow, Charlie-Charles John	01NYN	1-12-77	Dubuque, Iowa	3- 4-51	R	R			22	72	3	8	4	0	0	4	2		0	.111	.167
Buelow, Fritz-Frederick William	99-00StLN 01-04DetA 04-06CleA 07StLA	2-13-76	Berlin, Germany	12-27-33	R	R			430	1331	125	256	25	18	6	112	69		20	.192	.252
Bues, Art-Arthur Frederick	13BosN 14ChiN	3- 3-88	Milwaukee, Wis.	11- 7-54	R	R	5'11	184	16	46	3	10	1	1	0	4	5	7	1	.217	.283
Burch, Al-Albert William	06-07StLN 07-11BknN	10- 7-83	Albany, N.Y.	10- 5-26	L	R	5'8	160	611	2185	254	554	48	20	4	103	186		96	.254	.299
Burg, Pete-Joseph Peter	10BosN	6- 4-82	Chicago, Ill.	4-28-69	R	R	5'10	165	13	46	7	15	0	1	0	10	7	12	5	.326	.370
Burkam, Chris-Chauncey DePew	15StLA	10-13-92	Benton Harbor, Mich.	5- 9-64	L	R	5'11	175	1	1	0	0	0	0	0	0	0	1	0	.000	.000
Burke, Frank-Frank Aloysius	06NYN 07BosN	2-16-80	Carbon Co., Pa.	9-17-46		R			51	138	8	26	1	2	0	9	12		4	.188	.225
Burke, Jimmy-James Timothy (Sunset Jimmy)	98CleN 99StLN 01MilA 01ChiA 01-02PitN 03-05,M05StLN M18-20StLA	10-12-74	St. Louis, Mo.	3-26-42	R	R			550	1947	200	475	58	13	1	187	112		87	.244	.289
Burkett, Jesse-Jesse Cail (The Crab) (See P01-19)	90NYN 91-98CleN 99-01StLN 02-04StLA 05BosA	12- 4-68	Wheeling, W.Va.	5-27-53	L	L	5'8	155	2063	8389	1708	2872	314	185	75	952	1029		392	.342	.451
Burnett, John-John P.	07StLN								59	206	18	49	8	4	0	12	15		5	.238	.316
Burns, Bill-William	02BalA		Hagerstown, Md.						1	1	0	1	0	0	0	0	0		0	1.000	1.000
Burns, Ed-Edward James	12StLN 13-18PhiN	10-31-88	San Francisco, Cal.	6- 1-42	R	R	5'9	175	321	796	48	183	21	6	0	65	83	59	14	.230	.271
Burns, George-George Joseph	11-21NYN 22-24CinN 25PhiN	11-24-89	Utica, N.Y.	8-15-66	R	R	5'7	160	1853	7241	1188	2077	362	108	41	611	872	565	383	.287	.384
Burns, Joe-Joseph Francis	10CinN 13DetA	3-26-89	Ipswich, Mass.		L	L	5'11	170	5	14	0	6	0	0	0	1	2	4	1	.429	.429
Burns, John-John Joseph	03-04DetA	5-13-77	Moosic, Pa.	6-24-57	R	R	5'10	160	15	53	5	12	0	0	0	4	2		1	.226	.226
Burr, Alex-Alexander Thomson	14NYA	11- 1-93	Chicago, Ill.	11- 1-18	R	R	6'3	190	1	0	0	0	0	0	0	0	0	0	0	–	–
Bush, Donie-Owen Joseph (Ownie)	08-21DetA 21-23,M23WasA M27-29PitN M30-31ChiA M33CinN	10- 8-87	Indianapolis, Ind.	3-28-72	B	R	5'6	140	1945	7206	1280	1803	186	74	9	436	1158		405	.250	.300
Butcher, Hank-Henry Joseph	11-12CleA	7-12-86	Chicago, Ill.		R	R	5'10	180	62	215	30	48	11	4	2	21	17		10	.223	.340
Butler (Bouthillier), Art-Arthur Edward	11BosN 12-13PitN 14-16StLN	12-19-87	Fall River, Mass.		R	R	5'9	160	454	1289	181	311	44	13	3	101	146	100	54	.241	.303
Butler, John-John Albert (01 played as Fred King)	01MilA 04StLN 06-07BknN	7-26-79	Boston, Mass.		R	R	5'7	170	44	119	6	16	2	0	0	3	13		0	.134	.152
Butler, Kid-Willis Everett	07StLA	8- 9-87	Franklin, Pa.	2-22-64	R	R	5'11	155	20	59	4	13	2	0	0	6	2		1	.220	.254
Byers, Bill-John William (Big Bill)	04StLN		Baltimore, Md.		R	R			19	60	3	13	0	0	0	4	1		0	.217	.217

USE NAME – GIVEN NAMES (NICKNAMES)	TEAM BY YEAR	BIRTH DATE	BIRTH PLACE	DEATH DATE	B	T	HGT	WGT	LIFETIME BATTING TOTALS G	AB	R	H	2B	3B	HR	RBI	BB	SO	SB	BA	SA
Byrne, Bobby-Robert Matthew	07-09StLN 09-13PitN 13-17PhiN 17ChiA	12-31-84	St. Louis, Mo.		R	R	5'7	145	1283	4831	667	1225	186	60	10	329	456		176	.254	.323
Byrnes, Jim-James Joseph	06PhiA	1- 5-80	San Francisco, Cal.	7-31-41	R	R	5'9	150	9	23	2	4	0	1	0	0	0		0	.174	.261
Cabrera, Al-Alfredo A.	13StLN	-83	Canary Islands		R				1	2	0	0	0	0	0	0	0	0	0	.000	.000
Cady, Hick-Forrest LeRoy	12-17BosA 18CleA 19PhiN	1-26-86	Bishop Hill, Ill.	3- 3-46	R	R	6'2	179	355	901	83	216	47	11	1	74	67	91	4	.240	.320
Caffyn, Ben-Benjamin Thomas	06CleA	2-10-80	Peoria, Ill.	11-22-42					30	103	16	20	4	0	0	3	12		2	.194	.233
Caldwell, Ray-Raymond Benjamin (Slim) (See P01-19)	10-18NYA 19BosA 19-21CleA	4-26-88	Corydon, Pa.	8-17-67	L	R	6'2	190	582	1164	137	289	46	8	8	114	78	158	23	.248	.322
Calhoun, Bill-William Davitte (Mary)	13BosN	6-23-90	Rockmart, Ga.	2-11-55	L	L	6'	180	6	13	0	1	0	0	0	0	0	3	0	.077	.077
Calhoun, Jack-John Charles (Red)	02StLN	12-14-79	Pittsburgh, Pa.	2-27-47	R	R	6'	185	20	64	3	10	2	1	0	8	8		1	.156	.219
Callahan, Dave-David Joseph	10-11CleA	7-20-88	Seneca, Ill.	10-28-69	L	R	5'10	165	18	56	7	12	1	1	0	2	5		5	.214	.268
Callahan, Jim-James J.	02NYN		Philadelphia, Pa.						1	4	0	0	0	0	0	0	1		0	.000	.000
Callahan, Leo-Leo David	13BknN 19PhiN	8- 9-90	Boston, Mass.		L	L	5'6	142	114	276	32	61	17	5	1	12	33	24	5	.221	.330
Callahan, Nixey-James Joseph (See P01-19)	94PhiN 97-00ChiN 01-05,11-13,M03-04,12-14ChiA M16-17PitN	3-18-74	Fitchburg, Mass.	10- 4-34	R	R	5'10	180	922	3296	440	906	137	46	11	394	159		185	.275	.354
Callahan, Wes-Wesley LeRoy	13StLN	7- 3-88	Lyons, Ind.	9-13-53	R	R	5'7	155	7	14	0	4	0	0	0	1	2	2	1	.286	.286
Calvo (Del Calvo), Jack-Jacinto [Gonzalez]	13,20WasA	6-11-94	Havana, Cuba	6-15-65	L	L	5'11	185	33	56	10	9	0	1	1	4	3	6	0	.161	.250
Cameron, Happy Jack-John William	06BosN	-85	Boston, Mass.						18	61	3	11	0	0	0	4	2		0	.180	.180
Camp, Howie-Howard Lee (Red)	17NYA 18MS	7- 1-93	Munford, Ala.	5- 8-60	L	R	5'9	169	5	21	3	6	1	0	0	0	1	2	0	.286	.333
Campbell, Marc-Marc Thaddeus (Hutch)	07PitN	11-29-84	Punxsutawney, Pa.	2-13-46	L	R	5'10	155	2	4	0	1	0	0	0	1	1		0	.250	.250
Campbell, Vin-Arthur Vincent	08CinN 10-11PitN 12BosN 14IndF 15NwkF	1-30-88	St. Louis, Mo.	11-16-69	L	R	6'	185	546	2069	326	642	85	36	15	167	132		92	.310	.408
Cannell, Rip-Virgin Wirt	04-05BosN	1-23-80	South Bridgton, Me.	8-26-48	L	R	5'10	180	254	913	84	221	19	5	0	54	74		27	.242	.274
Capron, Ralph-Ralph Earl	12PitN 13PhiN	3-11-93	Minneapolis, Minn.	Deceased	L	R	5'11	165	3	1	1	0	0	0	0	0	0	0	0	.000	.000
Carey, Scoops-George C.	95BalN 98LouN 02-03WasA	12- 4-70	East Liverpool, Ohio	12-17-16	R	R			299	1150	114	316	60	20	1	159	52		6	.275	.364
Carisch, Fred-Frederick Behlmer	03-06PitN 12-14CleA 23DetA	11-14-81	Fountain City, Wis.		R	R	5'10	174	226	656	43	149	17	9	1	57	46		16	.227	.285
Carlisle, Walter-Walter G. (Rosy)	08BosA	7- 6-83	Yeadon, England	3-27-45	L	L			3	10	0	1	0	0	0	0	1		1	.100	.100
Carlstrom, Swede-Albin Oscar	11BosA	10-26-86	Elizabeth, N.J.	4-28-35	R	R	5'11	175	2	6	0	1	0	0	0	0	0		0	.167	.167
Carney, Bill-William J.	04ChiN	-78	St. Paul, Minn.						2	7	0	0	0	0	0	0	1		0	.000	.000
Carney, Pat-Patrick Joseph (Doc) (See P01-19)	01-04BosN	8- 7-76	Holyoke, Mass.	1- 9-53	L	L			338	1248	142	308	36	11	3	131	85		43	.247	.300
Carr, Charlie-Charles Carbitt	98WasN 01PhiA 03-04DetA 04-05CleA 06CinN 14IndF	12-27-76	Coatesville, Pa.	11-25-32	R	R	6'2	195	507	1948	185	492	68	32	6	240	71		48	.253	.330
Carr, Lew-Lewis Smith	01PitN	8-15-72	Union Springs, N.Y.	6-15-54	R	R	6'2	200	9	28	2	7	1	1	0	4	2		0	.250	.357
Carrigan, Bill-William Francis (Rough)	06,08-16,M13-16,27-29BosA	10-22-83	Lewiston, Me.	7- 8-69	R	R	5'11	175	706	1970	196	506	67	14	6	235	206		37	.257	.314
Carroll, Dixie-Dorsey Lee	19BosN	5-19-91	Paducah, Ky.		L	R	5'11	165	15	49	10	13	3	1	0	7	7	1	5	.265	.367
Carroll, Doc-Ralph Arthur (Red)	16PhiA	12-28-91	Worcester, Mass.		R	R	6'	170	10	22	1	2	0	0	0	0	1	8	0	.091	.091
Casey, Doc-James Patrick	98-99WasN 99-00,06-07BknN 01-02DetA 03-05ChiN	3-15-71	Lawrence, Mass.	12-31-36	L	R	5'6		1116	4340	585	1120	136	52	9	354	270		194	.258	.320
Casey, Joe-Joseph Felix	09-11DetA 18WasA	8-15-87	Boston, Mass.	6- 2-66	R	R	5'9	180	50	117	9	21	3	0	0	7	8		1	.179	.205
Cassady, Harry-Harry D.	04PitN 05WasA	7-20-80	Bellflower, Ill.						21	74	9	13	0	0	0	4	2		2	.176	.176
Cassidy, Joe-Joseph Phillip	04-05WasA	2- 8-83	Chester, Pa.	3-25-06	R	R			303	1157	130	264	28	23	2	76	40		40	.228	.297
Castle, John-John Francis	10PhiN	6- 1-83	Honeybrook, Pa.	4-15-29					3	4	1	1	0	0	0	0	0	0	1	.250	.250
Castro, Louis-Louis M. (Jud)	02PhiA	-77	Colombia		R	R			42	143	18	35	8	1	1	15	4		2	.245	.336
Caton, Buster-James Howard (Howdy)	17-20PitN	7-16-96	Zanesville, Ohio	1- 8-48	R	R	5'6	165	231	814	85	184	18	16	0	53	83	52	18	.226	.287
Catterson, Tom-Thomas Henry	08-09BknN	8-25-84	Warwick, R.I.	2- 5-20	L	L	5'10	170	28	86	5	17	1	1	1	3	8		0	.198	.267
Cavanaugh, Pat-Patrick John	19PhiN	-00	Reading, Pa.						1	1	0	0	0	0	0	0	0	1	0	.000	.000
Cermak, Ed-Edward	01CleA	3-10-82	Cleveland, Ohio	11-22-11	R	R	5'11	170	1	4	0	0	0	0	0	0	0		0	.000	.000
Chadbourne, Chet-Chester James (Pop)	06-07BosA 14-15KCF 18BosN	10-26-84	Parkman, Me.	6-23-43	L	R	5'9	170	347	1353	183	345	41	18	2	82	146		78	.255	.316
Chance, Frank-Frank Leroy (Husk, The Peerless Leader)	98-12,M05-12ChiN 13-14,M13-14NYA M23BosA	9- 9-77	Fresno, Cal.	9-15-24	R	R	6'	190	1281	4278	795	1273	195	80	20	597	554		405	.298	.395
Channell, Les-Lester Clark (Goat, Gint)	10,14NYA	3- 3-86	Crestline, Ohio	5- 8-54	L	L	6'	180	7	20	3	7	1	0	0	3	2		2	.350	.400
Chapman, Harry-Harry E.	12ChiN 13CinN 14-15StLF 16StLA	10-26-87	Severance, Kans.	10-21-18	R	R	5'11	160	147	404	38	80	8	5	1	44	37		7	.198	.250
Chapman, Ray-Raymond Johnson	12-20CleA	1-15-91	Beaver Dam, Ky.	8-17-20	R	R	5'10	170	1050	3785	671	1053	162	81	17	364	452		233	.278	.377
Chappell, Larry-LaVerne Ashford	13-15ChiA 16CleA 16-17BosN	2-19-90	McClusky, Ill.	11- 8-18	L	L	6'2	186	109	305	27	69	9	2	0	26	25	42	9	.226	.269
Charles (Achenbach), Chappie (Charles Shuh)-Raymond	08-09StLN 09-10CinN	3-25-81	Phillipsburg, N.J.	8- 4-59	R	R	5'11	175	237	851	76	186	23	7	1	51	54		24	.219	.266
Chase, Hal-Harold Homer (Prince Hal)	05-13,M10-11NYA 13-14ChiA 14-15BufF 16-18CinN 19NYN 19DU	2-13-83	Los Gatos, Cal.	5-18-47	R	L	6'	175	1917	7416	980	2156	324	124	57	941	276		363	.291	.391
Cheek, Harry-Harry G.	10PhiN		Kansas City, Mo.			R			2	4	1	2	1	0	0	0	0	0	0	.500	.750
Childs, Cupid-Clarence L.	88PhiN 90SyrAA 91-98CleN 99StLN 00-01ChiN	8- 8-67	Calvert Co., Md.	11- 8-12	L	R			1463	5624	1218	1757	200	102	20	743	991		285	.312	.395
Childs, Pete-George Peter	01StLN 01ChiN 02PhiN	11-15-71	Philadelphia, Pa.	2-15-22		R			212	692	60	147	11	1	0	47	74		10	.212	.231
Chouinard, Felix-Felix George	10-11ChiA 14PitF 14BknF 14BalF 15BknF	-88	Chicago, Ill.	Deceased	R	R	5'7	150	88	221	22	54	5	4	1	23	12		8	.244	.317
Clancey, Bill-William Edward	05PitN	4-12-78	Redfield, N.Y.	2-10-48		R			56	227	23	52	11	3	2	34	4		3	.229	.330
Clancy, Al-Albert Harrison	11StLA	8-14-88	Las Cruces, N.M.	10-17-51	R	R	5'10	175	3	5	0	0	0	0	0	0	0		0	.000	.000
Clark, Fred-Alfred Robert (Dad)	02ChiN	7-16-73	San Francisco, Cal.	7-26-56	L	R	5'11	170	12	43	1	8	1	0	0	2	4		1	.186	.209
Clark, Jim-James F.	11-12StLN	12-26-87	Brooklyn, N.Y.		R	R	5'11	175	16	19	2	3	0	1	0	3	3	5	2	.158	.263
Clark, Pep-Harry	03ChiA	3-18-83	Union City, Ohio	6- 8-65	R	R	5'7	175	15	65	7	20	4	2	0	9	2		5	.308	.431
Clark, Roy-Roy Elliott (Pepper)	02NYN	5-11-74	New Haven, Conn.	11- 1-25	L	R	5'8	170	21	76	4	11	1	0	0	3	1		5	.145	.158
Clarke, Boileryard-William Jones	93-98BalN 99-00BosN 01-04WasA 05NYN	10-18-68	New York, N.Y.	7-29-59	R	R			941	3314	395	860	112	33	20	429	176		50	.260	.331
Clarke, Fred-Fred Clifford (Cap)	94-99,M97-99LouN 00-15,M00-15PitN	10- 3-72	Winterset, Iowa	8-14-40	L	R	5'10	165	2243	8584	1620	2703	358	219	66	1014	874		527	.315	.431
Clarke, Josh-Joshua Baldwin (Pepper)	98LouN 05StLN 08-09CleA 11BosN	3- 8-79	Winfield, Kans.	7- 2-62	L	R	5'10	180	223	809	118	193	18	9	5	43	135		51	.239	.302
Clarke, Nig-Jay Justin	05CleA 05DetA 05-10CleA 11StLA 19PhiN 20PitN	12-15-82	Amherstburg, Canada	6-15-49	L	R	5'8	165	506	1536	157	390	64	20	6	127	138		16	.254	.333
Clarke, Tommy-Thomas Aloysius	09-17CinN 18ChiN	5- 9-88	New York, N.Y.	8-14-45	R	R	5'11	175	700	1708	166	453	66	37	6	191	216		42	.265	.358
Clay, Bill-Frederick C.	02PhiN	11-23-74	Baltimore, Md.	10-12-17		R			3	8	1	2	0	0	0	1	0		0	.250	.250
Clemens, Bob-Robert Baxter	14StLA	8- 9-86	Mt. Hebron, Mo.	4- 5-64	R	R	5'9	163	7	13	1	3	0	1	0	3	2	1	0	.231	.285
Clemens (Ulatowski), Count-Clement Lambert	14-15ChiF 16ChiN	11-21-86	Chicago, Ill.	11- 2-67	R	R	5'11	176	34	64	7	7	1	0	0	5	5		0	.109	.125
Clement, Wally-Wallace Oakes	08-09PhiN 09BknN	7-21-81	Auburn, Me.	11- 1-53	L	R	5'11	175	111	379	35	95	11	4	0	18	18		13	.251	.301
Clingman, Billy-William Frederick	90CinN 91CinAA 95PitN 96-99LouN 00ChiN 01WasA 03CleA	11-21-69	Cincinnati, Ohio	5-14-58	B	R	5'11	150	817	2870	406	709	87	33	8	300	303		96	.247	.309
Clymer, Otis-Otis Edgar	05-07PitN 07-09WasA 13ChiN 13BosN	2-27-77	Pine Grove, Pa.	2-27-26	L	R	5'11	180	385	1330	182	355	42	19	2	98	99		83	.267	.332
Cobb (Serafin), Joe-Joseph Stanley	18DetA	1-24-95	Hudson, Pa.	12-24-47	R	R	5'9	170	1	0	0	0	0	0	0	0	1	0	0	–	–
Cobb, Ty-Tyrus Raymond (The Georgia Peach)	05-26,M21-26DetA 27-28PhiA	12-18-86	Narrows, Ga.	7-17-61	L	R	6'1	175	3034	11437	2245	4192	724	297	118	1933	1249		892	.367	.513
Cochran, George-George Leslie	18BosA	2-12-89	Rusk, Tex.			R			25	63	8	8	0	0	0	3	11	7	3	.127	.127
Cockman, Jim-James	05NYA	4-26-73	Guelph, Canada	9-28-47	R	R	5'6	145	13	38	5	4	0	0	0	2	4		2	.105	.105
Coffey, Jack-John Francis	09BosN 18DetA 18BosA	1-28-87	New York, N.Y.	2-14-66	R	R	5'11	178	110	368	33	69	5	6	1	26	22		6	.188	.242
Cole, Willis-Willis Russell	09-10ChiA	1- 6-82	Milton Junction, Wis.	10-11-65	R	R	5'8	170	68	245	23	53	9	4	0	18	20		3	.216	.286
Coleman, Bob-Robert Hunter	13-14PitN 16CleA M44-45BosN	9-26-90	Huntingburg, Ind.	7-16-59	R	R	6'2	190	116	228	19	55	8	1	1	27	29	46	3	.241	.298
Coleman, Curt-Curtis Hancock	12NYA	2-18-87	Salem, Ore.		L	R	5'11	180	12	37	8	9	4	0	0	4	7		0	.243	.351
Coles, Cad-Cadwallader R.	14KCF	1-17-89	Rock Hill, S.C.	6-30-42	L	R	6'	174	78	194	17	49	7	3	1	25	5		6	.253	.335
Collins, Bill-William Shirley	10-11BosN 11ChiN 13BknN 14BufF	3-27-82	Chestertown, Ind.	6-26-61	B	R	6'	170	228	775	91	173	11	10	3	54	54		42	.223	.275
Collins, Eddie-Edward Trowbridge Sr. (Cocky) (Played as Eddie Sullivan 06)	06-14PhiA 15-26,M25-26ChiA 27-30PhiA	5- 2-87	Millerton, N.Y.	3-25-51	L	R	5'9	175	2826	9949	1818	3311	437	186	47	1299	1503		743	.333	.428
Collins, Jimmy-James Joseph	95BosN 95LouN 96-00BosN 01-07,M01-06BosA 07-08PhiA	1-16-70	Buffalo, N.Y.	3- 6-43	R	R	5'7	160	1718	6792	1057	1999	333	117	65	983	426		188	.294	.407
Collins, Orth-Orth Stein (Buck)	04NYA 09WasA	4-27-80	Lafayette, Ind.	12-13-49	L	R	6'	150	13	24	3	6	1	1	0	1	1		0	.250	.375
Collins, Shano-John Francis	10-20ChiA 21-25,M31-32BosA	12- 4-85	Charlestown, Mass.	9-10-55	R	R	6'	185	1799	6386	747	1687	309	133	22	705	331		225	.264	.365
Collins, Wilson-Cyril Wilson	13-14BosN	5- 7-89	Pulaski, Tenn.	2-28-41	R	R	5'9	165	43	38	8	10	0	0	0	1	2	9	0	.263	.263
Collins, Zip-John Edgar	14-15PitN 15-17BosN 21PhiA	5- 2-92	Brooklyn, N.Y.		L	L	5'11	158	286	916	124	232	17	14	2	63	58	100	15	.253	.309
Compton, Pete-Anna Sebastian (Bash)	11-13StLA 15StLF 15-16BosN 16PitN 18NYN	9-28-89	San Marcos, Tex.		L	L	5'11	170	286	773	78	186	24	8	5	80	64		26	.241	.312
Congalton, Bunk-William Millar	02ChiN 05-07CleA 07BosA	1-24-75	Guelph, Canada	8-19-37					310	1163	115	337	27	13	5	128	57		31	.290	.348
Conn, Bert-Albert Thomas (See P01-19)	98,00-01PhiN	9-22-79	Philadelphia, Pa.	11- 2-44		R			12	30	7	8	2	1	0	2	0		0	.267	.400
Connaughton, Frank-Frank H.	94BosN 96NYN 06BosN	1- 1-69	Clinton, Mass.	12- 2-42	R	R			144	525	89	146	13	4	4	77	44		21	.278	.341
Connolly, Joe-Joseph Aloysius	13-16BosN	2-12-88	N. Smithfield, R.I.	9- 1-43	L	R	5'7	165	412	1241	202	358	65	31	14	157	168	131	48	.288	.425
Connolly, Tom-Thomas Francis (Blackie)	15WasA	12-30-92	Boston, Mass.		L	R	5'11	175	50	141	14	26	3	2	0	7	14	19	5	.184	.234

USE NAME – GIVEN NAMES (NICKNAMES)	TEAM BY YEAR	BIRTH DATE	BIRTH PLACE	DEATH DATE	B	T	HGT	WGT	G	AB	R	H	2B	3B	HR	RBI	BB	SO	SB	BA	SA
					LIFETIME BATTING TOTALS																
Connor, Joe-Joseph Francis	95StLN 00BosN 01MilA 01CleA 05NYA	12- 8-74	Waterbury, Conn.	11- 8-57	R	R	6'2	185	92	271	29	54	7	2	1	22	18		8	.199	.251
Conroy, Wid-William Edward	01MilA 02PitN 03-08NYA 09-11WasA	4- 5-77	Camden, N.J.	12- 6-59	R	R	5'9	158	1377	5061	605	1257	176	82	22	452	345		262	.248	.329
Conway, Owen-Owen Sylvester	15PhiA	10-23-90	New York, N.Y.	3-13-42		R			4	15	2	1	0	0	0	0	0	3	0	.067	.067
Conway, Rip-Richard Daniel	18BosN	4-18-96	White Bear, Minn.	12- 3-71	L	R	5'6	160	14	24	4	4	0	0	0	2	2	4	1	.167	.167
Conwell, Ed-Edward James (Irish)	11StLN	1-29-90	Chicago, Ill.		R	R	5'11	155	1	1	0	0	0	0	0	0	0	1	0	.000	.000
Cook, Doc-Luther Almus	13-16NYA	6-24-86	Witt, Tex.	6-30-73	L	R	6'	170	286	1028	138	282	29	9	3	75	116	109	56	.274	.329
Cook, Jim-James Fitchie	03ChiN	11-10-79	Dundee, Ill.	6-17-49	R	R	5'9	163	8	26	3	4	1	0	0	2	2		1	.154	.192
Cooley, Dick-Duff C. (Sir Richard)	93-96StLN 96-99PhiN 00PitN 01-04BosN 05DetA	3-29-73	Leavenworth, Kans.	8- 9-37	L	R			1311	5361	846	1582	179	106	26	558	365		233	.295	.383
Coombs, Cecil-Cecil Lysander	14ChiA	3-18-88	Moweaqua, Ill.		R	R	5'9	160	7	23	1	4	1	0	0	1	1	7	0	.174	.217
Cooney, Cush-William A	09-10BosN	4- 4-87	Boston, Mass.	11- 6-28		R			13	22	2	6	0	0	0	1	2		0	.273	.273
Cooney (Cohen), Phil-Phillip	05NYA	9-14-86	Paterson, N.J.		R	R	5'8	155	1	3	0	0	0	0	0	0	0		0	.000	.000
Cooper, Claude-Claude William	13NYN 14-15BknF 16-17PhiN 18MS	4- 1-93	Troupe, Tex.	1-21-74	L	L	5'9	158	373	1089	156	283	47	23	4	104	119		60	.260	.356
Corcoran, Bunny-Arthur Andrew	15PhiA	11-23-94	Roxbury, Mass.	7-27-58		R			1	4	0	0	0	0	0	0	0	2	0	.000	.000
Corcoran, Mickey-Michael Joseph	10CinN	8-26-82	Buffalo, N.Y.	12- 9-50	R	R	5'8	165	14	46	3	10	3	0	0	7	5	9	0	.217	.283
Corcoran, Tommy-Thomas William (Tommy the Cork)	90PhiP 91PhiAA 92-96BknN 97-06CinN 07NYN	1- 4-69	New Haven, Conn.	6-25-60	R	R	5'10	164	2199	8776	1179	2248	288	151	34	1135	382		415	.256	.335
Corhan, Roy-Roy George (Irish)	11ChiA 16StLN	10-21-87	Indianapolis, Ind.	11-24-58	R	R	5'9	165	135	426	44	90	12	5	0	26	35		17	.211	.263
Corriden, Red-John Michael Sr.	10StLA 12DetA 13-15ChiN M50ChiA	9- 4-87	Logansport, Ind.	9-28-59	R	R	5'9	165	222	640	97	131	21	5	6	47	74		26	.205	.281
Costello, Dan-Daniel Francis (Dashing Dan)	13NYA 14-16PitN	9- 9-91	Jessup, Pa.	3-26-36	L	R	5'11	175	154	350	35	85	6	4	0	24	21	62	12	.243	.283
Cotter, Dick-Richard Raphael	11PhiN 12ChiN	10-23-90	Manchester, N.H.		R	R	5'11	172	46	100	8	28	0	2	0	15	11	20	2	.280	.320
Coughlin, Bill-William Paul (Scranton Bill)	99WasN 01-04WasA 04-08DetA	7-12-78	Scranton, Pa.	5- 7-43	R	R	5'9	180	1047	3855	484	972	133	39	15	380	203		162	.252	.319
Coulson, Bob-Robert Jackson	08CinN 10-11BknN 14PitF	6-17-87	Donora, Pa.	9-11-53	R	R	5'10	175	197	692	76	163	28	12	1	67	58		43	.236	.315
Courtney, Ernie-Ernest E.	02BosN 02BalA 03NYA 03DetA 05-08PhiN	-79	Des Moines, Iowa		L	R			558	1921	226	471	52	17	5	200	188		35	.245	.298
Coveney, John-John Patrick	03StLN	-80	South Natick, Mass.			R			4	14	0	2	0	0	0	0	0		0	.143	.143
Covington, Sam-Clarence Otto	13StLA 17-18BosN	12-17-92	Henryville, Tenn.	1- 4-63	L	R	6'1	190	40	129	11	23	2	1	1	14	9	11	4	.178	.233
Coyle, John-John	14PhiA					R			1	2	0	0	0	0	0	0	0	2	0	.000	.000
Crandall, Doc-James Otis (See P01-19)	08-13NYN 13StLN 13NYN 14-15StLF 16StLA 18BosN	10- 8-87	Wadena, Ind.	8-17-51	R	R	5'10	180	500	887	109	253	35	19	9	126	118		9	.285	.398
Crane, Sam-Samuel Byren (Red)	14-16PhiA 17WasA 20-21CinN 22BknN	9-13-94	Harrisburg, Pa.	11-12-55	R	R	5'11	154	174	495	51	103	19	2	0	30	29	46	7	.208	.255
Cravath, Gavvy-Clifford Carlton (Cactus)	08BosA 09ChiA 09WasA 12-20,M19-20PhiN	3-23-81	Escondido, Cal.	5-23-63	R	R	5'10	186	1219	3950	575	1134	232	83	119	719	561		89	.287	.478
Crawford, Forrest-Forrest	06-07StLN	5-10-81	Rockdale, Tex.	3-27-08	L	R			52	167	8	35	3	1	0	14	9		1	.210	.240
Crawford, Ken-Kenneth	15BalF		Pittsburgh, Pa.		L				23	82	4	20	2	1	0	7	1		0	.244	.293
Crawford, Sam-Samuel Earl (Wahoo Sam)	99-02CinN 03-17DetA	4-18-80	Wahoo, Neb.	6-15-68	L	L	6'	190	2517	9579	1392	2964	455	312	97	1524	760		367	.309	.452
Cree, Birdie-William Franklin	08-15NYA	10-22-82	Khedive, Pa.	11- 8-42	R	R	5'6	150	742	2603	345	761	117	62	11	332	269		132	.292	.398
Cregan, Pete-Peter James (Peekskill Pete)	99NYN 03CinN	4-13-75	Kingston, N.Y.	5-18-45	R	R	5'7	150	7	21	0	2	0	0	0	0	1		0	.095	.095
Criger, Lou-Louis	96-98CleN 99-00StLN 01-08BosA 09StLA 10NYA 12StLA	2- 3-72	Elkhart, Ind.	5-14-34	R	R	6'	150	1012	3199	337	706	87	49	11	342	309		58	.221	.289
Crisp, Joe-Joseph Shelby	10-11StLA	7- 8-89	Higginsville, Mo.	2- 5-39	R	R	6'3	200	2	2	0	1	0	0	0	0	0		0	.500	.500
Criss, Dode-Dode (See P01-19)	08-11StLA	3-12-85	Sherman, Miss.	9- 8-55	L	R	6'2	200	227	304	38	84	19	4	3	47	31		3	.276	.395
Crist, Ches-Chester Arthur (Squack)	06PhiN	2-10-82	Cozadale, Ohio	1- 7-57	R	R	5'11	165	6	11	1	0	0	0	0	0	0		0	.000	.000
Crockett, Davey-Daniel Solomon	01DetA	10- 5-75	Lammoor, Va.	2-23-61					28	102	10	29	2	2	0	14	6		1	.284	.343
Croft, Henry-Henry T.	99LouN 99PhiN 01ChiN		Chicago, Ill.	Deceased					7	21	1	5	0	0	0	4	1		0	.238	.238
Crolius, Fred-Fred Joseph	01BosN 02PitN	12-16-76	Jersey City, N.J.	8-25-60					58	238	26	58	6	2	1	20	9		6	.244	.298
Crompton, Ned-Edward	09StLA 10CinN	2-12-89	Liverpool, England	9-28-50	L	R	5'10	175	18	65	7	10	2	1	0	2	7		1	.154	.215
Crooke, Tom-Thomas A.	09-10WasA		Washington, D.C.	4- 5-29		R			11	28	3	6	2	0	0	3	3		1	.214	.286
Cross, Frank-Frank Atwell (Mickey)	01CleA	1-20-73	Cleveland, Ohio	11- 2-32		R			1	5	0	3	0	0	0	0	0		0	.600	.600
Cross, Lave-Lafayette Napoleon	87-88LouAA 89PhiAA 90PhiP 91PhiAA 92-97PhiN 98StLN 99,M99CleN 99-00StLN 00BknN 01-05PhiA 06-07WasA	5-12-66	Milwaukee, Wis.	9- 6-27	R	R	5'8	155	2265	9065	1349	2645	402	134	47	1368	464		307	.292	.381
Cross, Monte-Montford Montgomery	92BalN 94-95PitN 96-97StLN 98-01PhiN 02-07PhiA	8-31-69	Philadelphia, Pa.	6-21-34	R	R			1679	5813	718	1376	234	68	30	621	616		316	.237	.316
Crossin, Frank-Frank Patrick	12-14StLA	6-15-91	Avondale, Pa.	12- 6-65	R	R	5'10	160	55	116	8	17	1	1	0	7	12	11	4	.147	.172
Cruise, Walton-Walton Edwin	14,16-19StLN 19-24BosN	5- 6-90	Childersburg, Ala.	1- 9-75	L	R	6'	175	736	2321	293	644	83	39	30	272	238	250	49	.277	.386
Cruthers, Press-Charles Preston	13-14PhiA	9- 8-90	Marshallton, Del.		R	R	5'9	152	7	27	1	6	1	1	0	0	0	4	0	.222	.333
Cueto, Manuel-Manuel (Potato)	14StLF 17-19CinN	2- 8-92	Guanajay, Cuba	6-29-42	R	R	5'8	160	150	379	36	86	10	1	1	31	50		13	.227	.266
Cunningham, Bill-William James	10-12WasA	6- 9-88	Schenectady, N.Y.	2-21-46	R	R	5'9	170	123	432	42	90	16	6	4	59	34		16	.208	.301
Cunningham, George-George Harold (See P01-19)	16-19,21DetA	7-13-94	Sturgeon Lake, Minn.	3-10-72	R	R	5'11	185	162	210	27	47	6	3	1	13	36	67	2	.224	.295
Curry, Harry-James L.	09PhiA 11NYA 18DetA	3-10-93	Camden, N.J.	8- 2-38	R	R	5'11	160	10	35	5	8	1	0	0	0	1		0	.229	.257
Curtis, Fred-Frederick	05NYA		Sau. Ste. Marie, Mich.						2	9	0	2	1	0	0	2	1		1	.222	.333
Curtis, Eude-Eugene	03PitN	5- 7-77	Bethany, W.Va.	1- 2-18					5	19	2	8	1	0	0	3	1		0	.421	.474
Curtis, Harry-Harry Albert	07NYN	2-19-83	Portland, Me.	8- 1-51		R			6	9	2	2	0	0	0	1	2		2	.222	.222
Cutshaw, George-George William (Clancy)	12-17BknN 18-21PitN 22-23DetA	7-29-87	Wilmington, Ill.	8-22-73	R	R	5'9	160	1516	5621	629	1487	195	89	25	653	300	242	271	.265	.344
Cypert, Al-Alfred Boyd (Cy)	14CleA	8- 7-89	Little Rock, Ark.	1- 9-73	R	R	5'10	150	1	1	0	0	0	0	0	0	0	1	0	.000	.000
Dahlen, Bill-William Frederick (Bad Bill)	91-98ChiN 99-03BknN 04-07NYN 08-09BosN 10-11,M10-13BknN	1- 5-70	Nelliston, N.Y.	12- 5-50	R	R	5'9	180	2442	9019	1594	2478	403	166	84	1233	1064		587	.275	.384
Daley, John-John Francis	12StLA	5-25-89	Pittsburgh, Pa.		R	R	5'7	155	17	52	7	9	0	0	1	3	9		4	.173	.231
Daley, Jud-Judson Lawrence	11-12BknN	3-14-84	S. Coventry, Conn.	1-26-67	L	R	5'8	172	80	264	30	66	11	2	1	20	26	25	4	.250	.318
Daley, Tom-Thomas Francis (Pete)	08CinN 13-14PhiA 14-15NYA	11-13-84	DuBois, Pa.	12- 2-34	L	R	5'5	168	179	472	73	113	9	8	0	29	68		18	.239	.292
Dalrymple, Mike-Michael	15StLA		St. Louis, Mo.			R			2	2	0	0	0	0	0	0	0	0	0	.000	.000
Dalton, Jack-Talbot Percy	10,14BknN 15BufF 16DetA	7- 3-84	Henderson, Tenn.		R	R	5'10	187	345	1163	167	333	39	15	4	112	129		52	.286	.356
Daly, Bert-Albert Joseph	03PhiA	4- 8-81	Bayonne, N.J.	9- 3-52	R	R	5'9	170	10	21	2	4	0	2	0	4	1		0	.190	.381
Daly, Tom-Thomas Daniel (Kid)	13-15ChiA 16CleA 18-21ChiN	12-12-91	St. John, Canada	11- 7-46	R	R	5'11	170	243	540	49	129	17	3	0	55	25	43	5	.239	.281
Daly, Tom-Thomas Peter (Tido)	87-88ChiN 89WasN 90-96,90-01BknN 02-03ChiA 03CinN	2- 7-66	Philadelphia, Pa.	10-29-39	B	R	5'7	170	1560	5671	1030	1588	261	103	49	811	687		403	.280	.388
Dam, Bill-Elbridge Rust	09BosN	4- 4-85	Cambridge, Mass.	6-22-30					1	2	1	1	1	0	0	0	1		0	.500	1.000
Damrau, Harry-Harry Robert	15PhiA	-92	New York, N.Y.	2- -21	R	R	5'10	178	16	56	4	11	1	0	0	3	5	17	1	.196	.214
Daniels, Bert-Bernard Elmer	10-13NYA 14CinN	10-31-82	Danville, Ill.	6- 6-58	R	R	5'9	180	523	1903	295	486	76	40	5	130	203		159	.255	.345
Danner, Buck-Henry Frederick	15PhiA	6- 8-91	Dedham, Mass.	9-19-49	R	R	5'6	135	3	12	1	3	0	0	0	0	0	1	1	.250	.250
Danzig, Babe-Harold P.	09BosA	4-30-87	Binghamton, N.Y.	7-14-31	R	R	6'2	205	6	13	0	2	0	0	0	0	2		0	.154	.154
Daringer, Cliff-Clifford Clarence (Shanty)	14KCF	4-10-85	Hayden, Ind.	12-26-71	L	R	5'7	155	64	160	12	42	2	1	0	16	11		9	.263	.288
Daringer, Rolla-Rolla Harrison	14-15StLN	11-15-89	North Vernon, Ind.	5-23-74	L	R	5'10	155	12	27	4	4	1	0	0	0	10	7	0	.148	.185
Daubert, Harry-Harry J. (Jake)	15PitN	8- 7-94	Columbus, Ohio	1- -44	R	R	6'	160	1	1	0	0	0	0	0	0	0	1	0	.000	.000
Daubert, Jake-Jacob Ellsworth	10-18BknN 19-24CinN	4-17-84	Shamokin, Pa.	10- 9-24	L	L	5'10	160	2014	7673	1117	2326	250	165	56	722	623	489	251	.303	.401
Davidson, Bill-William J.	09ChiN 10-11BknN	5-10-87	Lafayette, Ind.	3-12-15	R	R	5'10	170	225	808	83	190	16	11	1	60	41	76	46	.235	.286
Davidson, Claude-Claude Boucher (Davey)	18PhiA 19WasA	10-13-96	Roxbury, Mass.	4-18-56	L	R	5'11	155	33	88	5	18	1	0	0	4	6	10	0	.205	.216
Davidson, Homer-Homer Hurd (Divvy)	08CleA	10-14-84	Cleveland, Ohio	7-26-48	R	R	5'10	155	9	4	2	0	0	0	0	0	0		1	.000	.000
Davies, Chick-Lloyd Garrison (See P20-45)	14-15PhiA 25-26NYN	3- 6-92	Peabody, Mass.	9- 5-73	L	L	5'8	145	117	202	24	39	8	4	0	17	22	50	3	.193	.272
Davis, George-George Stacey	90-92CleN 93-01,03,M95,00-01NYN 02,04-09ChiA	8-23-70	Cohoes, N.Y.	10-17-40	B	R	5'9	180	2378	9027	1546	2683	442	167	73	1432	870		632	.297	.407
Davis, Harry-Harry H (Jasper)	95-96NYN 96-98PitN 98LouN 98-99WasN 01-11PhiA 12,M12CleA 13-17PhiA	7-10-73	Philadelphia, Pa.	8-11-47	R	R	5'10	180	1748	6625	986	1836	364	143	74	952	525		312	.277	.408
Davis, Lefty-Alfonzo DeFord	01BknN 01-02PitN 03NYA 07CinN	2- 4-75	Nashville, Tenn.	2- 7-19	L	L			348	1296	232	338	32	19	3	110	167		65	.261	.322
Deal, Charlie-Charles Albert	12-13DetA 13-14BosN 15StLF 16 StLA 16-21ChiN	10-30-91	Wilkinsburg, Pa.		R	R	5'11	160	850	2930	295	732	104	34	11	318	135		65	.257	.327
Deal, Snake-John Wesley	06CinN	1-21-79	Conshohocken, Pa.	5- 9-44	R	R	6'	164	65	231	13	48	4	3	0	21	6		15	.208	.251
DeArmond, Charlie-Charles Hommer (Hummer)	03CinN	2-13-77	Okeana, Ohio	12-17-33	R	R	5'10	165	11	39	10	11	2	1	0	7	3		1	.282	.385
Debus, Adam-Adam Joseph	17PitN 18-19MS	10- 7-92	Chicago, Ill.		R	R	5'10	150	38	131	9	30	5	4	0	7	7	14	2	.229	.328
Dede, Artie-Arthur Richard	16BknN	7-12-95	Brooklyn, N.Y.	9- 6-71	R	R	5'9	155	1	1	0	0	0	0	0	0	0	0	0	.000	.000
Dee, Shorty-Maurice Leo	15StLA	10- 4-89	Halifax, Canada	8-12-71	R	R	5'6	155	1	3	1	0	0	0	0	0	1	0	0	.000	.000
DeFate, Tony-Clyde Herbert	17StLN 17DetA	2-22-95	Kansas City, Mo.	9- 3-63	R	R	5'8	158	17	16	1	2	0	0	0	1	4	6	0	.125	.125
DeGroff, Rube-Edward Arthur	05-06StLN	9- 2-79	Hyde Park, N.Y.	12-17-55					16	60	4	14	2	1	0	5	5		1	.233	.300
Deininger, Pep-Otto Charles (See P01-19)	02BosA 08-09PhiN	10-10-77	Wasseralfingen, Germ.	9-25-50	L	L	5'8	180	58	175	22	46	10	1	0	16	11		5	.263	.331
Deisel, Pat-Edward	02BknN 03CinN	4-29-76	Ripley, Ohio	4-17-48	R	R	5'10	180	3	3	0	2	0	0	0	1	2		0	.667	.667

USE NAME – GIVEN NAMES (NICKNAMES)	TEAM BY YEAR	BIRTH DATE	BIRTH PLACE	DEATH DATE	B	T	HGT	WGT	G	AB	R	H	2B	3B	HR	RBI	BB	SO	SB	BA	SA
									LIFETIME BATTING TOTALS												
Delahanty, Ed-Edward James (Big Ed)	88-89PhiN 90CleP 91-01PhiN 02-03WasA	10-30-67	Cleveland, Ohio	7- 2-03	R	R	6'1	170	1828	7493	1596	2593	508	182	100	1464	741		478	.346	.502
Delahanty, Frank-Frank George (Pudgie)	05-06,08NYA 07CleA 14BufF 14-15PitF	1-29-83	Cleveland, Ohio	7-22-66	R	R	5'9	160	287	986	109	223	22	22	5	94	66		50	.226	.308
Delahanty, Jim-James Christopher	01ChiN 02NYN 04-05BosN 06CinN 07StLA	6-20-79	Cleveland, Ohio	10-17-53	R	R	5'10	170	1186	4091	520	1159	191	60	18	489	378		151	.283	.373
	07-09WasA 09-12DetA 14-15BknF																				
Delahanty, Joe-Joseph Nicholas	07-09StLN	10-18-75	Cleveland, Ohio	1- 9-36	L	R	5'9	168	270	932	68	222	30	15	4	100	74		24	.238	.315
Demmitt, Ray-Charles Raymond	09NYA 10StLA 14DetA 14-15ChiA 17-19StLA	2- 2-84	Illiopolis, Ill.	2-19-56	L	R			498	1631	205	419	61	33	8	165	172		42	.257	.349
DeMontreville, Gene-Eugene	94PitN 95-97WasN 98-99BalN 99ChiN 00BknN	3-26-74	St. Paul, Minn.	2-18-35	R	R	5'8	165	913	3589	535	1106	129	32	17	497	174		235	.308	.376
	01-02BosN 03WasA 04StLA																				
DeMontreville, Lee-Leon	03StLN	9-23-79	St. Paul, Minn.	3-22-62	R	R	5'7	140	26	70	8	17	3	1	0	7	8		3	.243	.314
Derrick, Claude-Claude Lester (Deek)	10-12PhiA 13NYA 14CinN 14ChiN	6-11-86	Burton, Ga.	7-15-74	R	R	6'	175	110	326	35	79	6	4	1	33	22		13	.242	.294
Devlin, Art-Arthur McArthur	04-11NYN 12-13BosN	10-16-79	Washington, D.C.	9-18-48	R	R	6'	175	1313	4412	603	1185	164	57	10	505	576		285	.269	.338
DeVogt, Rex-Rex Eugene	13BosN	1- 4-88	Clare, Mich.	11- 9-35	R	R	5'10	170	3	6	0	0	0	0	0	0	0	3	0	.000	.000
Devore, Josh-Joshua D.	08-13NYN 13CinN 13-14PhiN 14BosN	11-13-87	Murray City, Ohio	10- 6-54	L	L	5'8	175	601	1874	331	520	58	31	11	149	222		160	.277	.359
Devoy, Walt-Walter Joseph	09StLA	3-14-85	St. Louis, Mo.	12-17-53					19	69	7	17	3	1	0	8	3		4	.246	.319
Dexter, Charlie-Charles	96-99LouN 00-02ChiN 02-03BosN	6-15-76	Evansville, Ind.	6- 9-34					763	2867	429	756	91	23	16	346	198		182	.264	.328
Diehl, Ernie-Ernest Guy	03-04PitN 06,09BosN	10- 2-77	Cincinnati, Ohio	11- 6-58	R	R	6'1	190	17	55	8	14	1	1	0	4	6		3	.255	.309
Dillon, Pop-Frank Edward	99-00PitN 01-02DetA 02BalA 04BknN	10-17-73	Normal, Ill.	9-12-31	L	R			312	1180	146	298	44	16	1	116	78		31	.253	.319
Distel, Dutch-George Adam	18StLN	4-15-96	Madison, Ind.	2-12-67	R	R	5'9	165	8	17	3	3	1	1	0	1	2	3	0	.176	.353
Dobbs, Johnny-John Gordon	01-02CinN 02-03ChiN 03-05BknN	6- 3-76	Chattanooga, Tenn.	9- 9-34	L	R	5'9	170	582	2224	305	585	85	23	7	207	187		78	.263	.331
Dodd, Ona-Ona Melvin	12PitN	10-14-86	Springtown, Tex.	3-31-29	R	R	5'8	150	5	9	0	0	0	0	0	1	1	3	0	.000	.000
Dodge, John-John Lewis	12-13PhiN 13CinN	4-27-89	Bolivar, Tenn.	6-19-16	R	R	5'11	165	127	418	38	90	9	8	4	48	16	45	13	.215	.304
Dolan, Biddy-E.L.	14IndF				R	R			32	103	13	23	4	2	1	15	12		5	.223	.330
Dolan (Alberts), Cozy (James) Alvin James	09CinN 11-12NYA 12-13PhiN 13PitN	12- 6-82	Oshkosh, Wis.	12-10-58	R	R	5'10	180	378	1187	210	299	43	21	6	111	121		102	.252	.339
	14-15StLN 22NYN																				
Dolan, Cozy-Patrick Henry (See P01-19)	95-96BosN 00-01ChiN 01-02BknN	12- 3-72	Cambridge, Mass.	3-29-07	L	L	5'10	160	830	3173	428	856	99	37	10	015	227		114	.270	.334
	03ChiA 03-05CinN 05-06BosN																				
Dolan, Joe-Joseph	96-97LouN 99-01PhiN 01PhiA	2-24-73	Baltimore, Md.	3-24-38		R			319	1148	140	247	37	10	6	122	72		30	.215	.280
Donahue, Jiggs-John Augustus	00-01PitN 01MilA 02StLA 04-09ChiA 09WasA	7-13-79	Springfield, Ohio	7-19-13	L	L	6'1	178	812	2858	320	731	91	30	4	327	215		145	.256	.313
Donahue, Pat-Patrick William	08-10BosA 10PhiA 10CleA 10PhiA	11- 3-84	Springfield, Ohio	1-31-66	R	R	6'	175	118	307	24	65	6	1	3	35	29		3	.212	.267
Donahue, She-Charles Michael	04StLN 04PhiN	6-29-77	Oswego, N.Y.	8-28-47	R	R			62	215	22	47	4	0	0	16	3		10	.219	.237
Donahue, Tim-Timothy Cornelius	91BosAA 95-00ChiN 02WasA	6- 8-70	Raynham, Mass.	6-12-02	L	R			454	1493	197	360	56	11	2	163	142		55	.241	.297
Donlin, Mike-Michael (Turkey Mike)	99-00StLN 01BalA 02-04CinN 04-06NYN	5-30-78	Erie, Pa.	9-24-33	L	L	5'9	170	1050	3859	670	1287	174	98	51	543	312		210	.334	.469
	07HO 08NYN 09-10VR 11NYN 11BosN 12PitN 13VR 14NYN																				
Donovan, Jerry-Jeremiah Francis	06PhiN	9- 3-76	Lock Haven, Pa.	6-27-38	R	R			61	166	11	33	4	0	0	15	6		2	.199	.223
Donovan, Mike-Michael Berchman	04CleA 08NYA	10-18-81	Brooklyn, N.Y.	2- 3-38	R	R	5'8	155	7	21	2	5	1	0	0	2	0		0	.238	.286
Donovan, Patsy-Patrick Joseph	90BosN 90BknN 91LouAA 91WasAA 92WasN	3-16-65	Queenstown, Ireland	12-25-53	R	L	5'11	175	1817	7450	1324	2266	213	72	16	737	453		528	.304	.359
	92-99,M97,99PitN 00-03,M01-03StLN 04,M04WasA 06-07,M06-08BknN M10-11BosA																				
Donovan, Tom-Thomas J.	01CleA	7- 7-79	Lock Haven, Pa.	2-20-55	R	R	6'2	168	18	71	9	18	3	1	0	5	0		1	.254	.324
Dooin, Red-Charles Sebastian	02-14,M10-14PhiN 15CinN 15-16NYN	6-12-79	Cincinnati, Ohio	5-14-52	R	R	5'9	165	1290	4004	333	961	139	31	10	344	155		133	.240	.298
Doolan (Doolittle), Mickey-Michael Joseph	05-13PhiN 14-15BalF 15ChiF	5- 7-80	Ashland, Pa.	11- 1-51	R	R	5'10	170	1727	5968	513	1377	246	81	15	554	370		178	.231	.307
	16ChiN 16NYN 18BknN																				
Doran, Tom-Thomas J.	04-05BosA 05DetA 06BosA	2- 2-80	Westchester Co., N.Y.	6-22-10	L	L			50	131	10	19	3	1	0	4	12		3	.145	.183
Dorsey, Jerry-Jeremiah	11PitN	-85	Oakland, Cal.						2	6	0	0	0	0	0	0	0	1	0	.000	.000
Dougherty, Patsy-Patrick Henry	02-04BosA 04-06NYA 06-11ChiA	10-27-76	Andover, N.Y.	4-30-40	L	R	6'2	190	1233	4558	677	1294	138	78	17	413	378		261	.284	.360
Douglass, Klondike-William Bigham	96-97StLN 98-04PhiN	5-10-72	Boston, Pa.	12-13-53	L	R	6'	200	746	2797	371	775	83	30	10	275	227		93	.277	.339
Dowd, John-John Leo	12NYA	1- 3-91	S. Weymouth, Mass.		R	R	5'8	170	10	31	1	6	1	0	0	0	6		0	.194	.226
Dowd, Snooks-Raymond Bernard	19DetA 19PhiA 26BknN	12-20-97	Springfield, Mass.	4- 4-62	R	R	5'8	163	16	26	4	3	0	0	0	6	0	5	2	.115	.115
Dowd, Tommy-Thomas Jefferson (Buttermilk Tommy)	91BosAA 91WasAA 92WasN	4-20-69	Holyoke, Mass.	7- 2-33	R	R			1313	5478	904	1491	160	87	23	501	369		384	.272	.346
	93-97,M96-97StLN 97PhiN 98StLN 99CleN 01BosA																				
Downey, Red-Alexander Cummings	09BknN	2- 6-89	Aurora, Ind.	7-10-49	L	L	5'11	174	19	78	7	20	1	0	0	8	2		4	.256	.269
Downey, Tom-Thomas Edward	09-11ChiN 12PhiN 12ChiN 14-15BufF	1- 1-84	Lawrence, Mass.	8- 3-61	R	R	5'10	178	651	2170	256	520	69	25	7	188	198		87	.240	.304
Downs, Red-Jerome Willis	07-08DetA 12BknN 12ChiN	8-23-83	Neola, Iowa	10-12-39	R	R	5'11	175	241	790	68	179	30	11	3	94	28		13	.227	.304
Doyle, Jack-John Joseph (Dirty Jack)	89-90ColAA 91-92CleN 92-95,M95NYN	10-25-69	Killorgin, Ireland	12-31-58	R	R	5'9	155	1542	6013	997	1814	305	66	25	968	437		558	.302	.387
	96-97BalN 98,M98WasN 98-00NYN 01ChiN 02NYN 02WasA 03-04BknN 04PhiN 05NYA																				
Doyle, Jim-James Francis	10CinN 11ChiN	12-25-81	Syracuse, N.Y.	2- 1-12	R	R	5'10	168	137	485	70	135	25	12	5	63	40	56	19	.278	.410
Doyle, Larry-Lawrence Joseph (Laughing Larry)	07-16NYN 16-17ChiN 18-20NYN	7-31-86	Caseyville, Ill.	3- 1-74	L	R	5'10	165	1766	6509	960	1887	299	123	74	793	625		298	.290	.408
Drake, Delos-Delos Daniel	11DetA 14-15StLF	12- 3-86	Girard, Ohio	10- 3-65	R	L	5'11	170	335	1172	120	308	50	21	5	119	71		43	.263	.354
Dressen, Lee-Leo August	14StLN 18DetA	7-23-89	Ellinwood, Kans.	6-30-31	L	L	6'	165	77	210	26	43	3	3	0	10	32	30	4	.205	.248
Drill, Lew-Lewis L	02WasA 02BalA 02-04WasA 04-05DetA	5- 9-77	Browerville, Minn.	7- 4-69	R	R	5'6	186	292	896	87	231	41	10	2	100	114		21	.258	.333
Driscoll, Paddy-John Leo 20-29 played in N.F.L.	17ChiN 18MS	1-11-95	Evanston, Ill.	6-29-68	R	R	5'8	155	13	28	2	3	1	0	0	3	2	6	2	.107	.143
21-22,56-57 Head Coach in N.F.L.																					
Duff, Pat-Patrick Henry	06WasA	5- 6-75	Providence, R.I.	9-11-25		R			1	1	0	0	0	0	0	0	0		0	.000	.000
Duffy, Hugh-Hugh	88-89ChiN 90ChiP 91BosAA 92-00BosN 01,M01MilA	11-26-66	Cranston, R.I.	10-19-54	R	R	5'7	168	1733	7024	1555	2313	310	117	108	1301	662		599	.329	.453
	04-06,M04-06PhiN M10-11ChiA M21-22BosA																				
Dugey, Oscar-Oscar Joseph	13-14BosN 15-17PhiN 20BosN	10-25-87	Palestine, Tex.	1- 1-66	R	R	5'8	160	195	278	45	54	10	1	1	20	31	38	17	.194	.248
Duggan, Elmer-James Elmer (Mer)	11StLA	6- 3-84	Whiteland, Ind.	12- 5-51	L	L	5'10	165	1	4	1	0	0	0	0	1	1		0	.000	.000
Duncan, Vern-Vernon Van Duke	13PhiN 14-15BalF	1- 6-90	Clayton, N.C.	6- 1-54	L	R	5'9	155	311	1100	170	307	39	12	4	97	121		32	.279	.347
Dundon, Gus-Agustus	04-06ChiA	7-10-74	Columbus, Ohio	9- 1-40	R	R	5'10	165	247	833	77	168	17	6	0	62	64		37	.202	.236
Dungan, Sam-Samuel Morrison	92-94ChiN 94LouN 00ChiN 01WasA	1-29-66	Ferndale, Cal.	3-16-39	R				382	1521	213	467	74	26	3	196	116		40	.307	.396
Dunleavy, John-John Francis (See P01-19)	03-05StLN	9-14-79	Harrison, N.J.	4-12-44					231	800	98	193	18	14	2	49	84		33	.241	.306
Dunlop, George-George Henry	13-14CleA	7-19-88	Meriden, Conn.	Deceased	R	R	5'10	170	8	20	3	4	1	0	0	0	1	6	0	.200	.250
Dunn, Jack-John Joseph (See P01-19)	97-00BknN 00-01PhiN 01BalA 02-04NYN	10- 6-72	Meadville, Pa.	10-22-28	R	R			488	1612	196	398	55	10	1	164	83		57	.247	.301
Dunn, Joe-Joseph Edward	08-09BknN	3-11-85	Springfield, Ohio	3-19-44	R	R	5'9	160	30	89	4	15	4	0	0	7	0		0	.169	.213
Durbin, Kid-Blaine Alphonsus	07-08ChiN 09CinN 09PitN	9-10-86	Kans.	9-11-43	L	L	5'8	155	32	51	6	14	1	0	0	0	4		0	.275	.294
Dyer, Ben-Benjamin Franklin	14-15NYN 16-19DetA	2-13-93	Chicago, Ill.	8- 7-59	R	R	5'10	170	105	207	27	49	10	1	0	18	15	47	4	.237	.295
Eagan, Truck-Charles Eugene	01PitN 01CleA	8-10-76	San Francisco, Cal.	3-19-49	R	R	5'11	190	9	30	2	4	0	1	0	4	1		1	.133	.200
Eakle, Charlie-Charles Emory	15BalF	9-27-87	Md.	6-15-59					2	7	0	2	1	0	0	0	0		1	.286	.429
Easterly, Ted-Theodore Harrison	09-12CleA 12-13ChiA 14-15KCF	4-20-85	Lincoln, Neb.	7- 6-51	L	R	5'8	165	704	2020	215	607	88	38	7	261	107		42	.300	.392
Edington, Stump-Jacob Frank	12PitN	7- 4-91	Koleen, Ind.	11-29-69	L	L	5'8	170	15	53	4	16	0	2	0	12	3	1	0	.302	.377
Edmondson, Bob-Robert E.	08WasA	4-30-79	Paris, Ky.	8-14-31	R	R	5'11	185	26	80	5	15	4	1	0	2	7		0	.188	.263
Edmonson, Eddie-Earl Edward (Axel)	13CleA	11-20-89	Hopewell, Pa.	5-10-71	L	R	6'	175	2	5	0	0	0	0	0	0	0	0	0	.000	.000
Edwards, Al-Albert	15PhiA	-96	Freeport, N.Y.			R			2	5	0	0	0	0	0	0	0	3	0	.000	.000
Egan, Ben-Arthur Augustus	08,12PhiA 14-15CleA	11-20-83	Augusta, N.Y.	2-18-68	R	R	6'	195	121	352	21	58	9	5	0	30	18		3	.165	.219
Egan, Dick-Richard Joseph	08-13CinN 14-15BknN 15-16BosN	6-23-84	Portland, Ore.	6-30-47	R	R	5'11	165	917	3080	374	767	87	29	4	292	291		167	.249	.300
Elberfeld, Kid-Norman Arthur (The Tabasco Kid)	98PhiN 99CinN 01-03DetA	4-13-75	Pomeroy, Ohio	1-13-44	R	R	5'7	158	1293	4561	647	1234	166	58	10	535	427		209	.271	.339
	03-09,M08NYA 10-11WasA 14BknN																				
Ellam, Roy-Roy (Slippery, Whitey)	09CinN 18PitN	2- 8-86	Conshohocken, Pa.	10-28-48	R	R	5'10	203	36	98	13	14	1	2	1	6	24		3	.143	.224
Elliott, Gene-Eugene Birminghouse	11NYA	2- 8-88	Fayette City, Pa.		L	R	5'7	150	5	13	1	1	1	0	0	1	2		0	.077	.154
Elliott, Rowdy-Harold H.	10BosN 16-18ChiN 20BknN	7- 8-90	Bloomington, Ill.	2-12-34	R	R			157	402	36	97	15	5	1	44	19	23	5	.241	.311
Ellis, Rube-George William	09-12StLN	11-17-85	Downey, Cal.	3-13-38	L	L	6'	170	555	1985	279	517	66	29	14	199	216		56	.260	.344
Ellison, Bert-Herbert Spencer	16-20DetA	11-15-95	Rutland, Ark.	8-11-55	R	R	5'11	170	135	348	32	75	13	4	1	39	30	55	9	.216	.284
Ely, Bones-Frederick William	84BufN 86LouAA 90SyrAA 91BknN 92BalN	6- 7-63	Girard, Pa.	1-10-52	R	R	6'1	155	1340	5127	649	1330	146	70	24	652	256		164	.259	.329
	93-95StLN 96-01PitN 01PhiA 02WasA																				
Emerson, Chester-Chester Arthur (Chuck)	11-12PhiA	10-27-89	Stow, Me.	7- 2-71	L	R	5'8	165	8	19	2	4	0	0	0	0	6		1	.211	.211
Engle, Clyde-Arthur Clyde (Hack)	09-10NYA 10-14BosA 14-15BufF 16CleA	3-19-84	Dayton, Ohio	12-26-39	R	R	5'8	190	831	2822	373	748	101	39	12	318	271		128	.265	.341
Ens, Mutz-Anton	12ChiA	11- 8-84	St. Louis, Mo.	6-28-50	L	L	6'1	185	3	6	0	0	0	0	0	0	0		0	.000	.000
Enwright, Charlie-Charles Michael	09StLN	10- 6-87	Sacramento, Cal.	1-19-17	L	R			3	7	1	1	0	0	0	1	2		0	.143	.143
Enzenroth, Jack-Clarence Herman	14StLA 14-15KCF	11- 4-85	Mineral Point, Wis.	2-21-44	R	R	5'10	164	43	92	10	16	4	1	0	8	13		0	.174	.239
Erwin, Tex-Ross Emil	07DetA 10-14BknN 14CinN	12-22-85	Forney, Tex.	4- 5-53	L	R	6'	185	276	635	70	150	23	3	11	70	82	61	10	.236	.334
Eschen, Jim-James Godrich	15CleA	8-21-91	Brooklyn, N.Y.	9-27-60	R	R	5'10	160	15	42	11	10	1	0	0	2	5	9	0	.238	.262
Esmond, Jimmy-James J.	11-12CinN 14IndF 15NwkF	10- 8-89	Albany, N.Y.	6-26-48	R	R	5'10	167	461	1540	204	406	52	34	9	162	136		61	.264	.359
Eunick, Ferd-Fernandas Bowen (Dutch)	17CleA	4-22-92	Baltimore, Md.	12- 9-59	R	R	5'6	160	1	2	0	0	0	0	0	0	0	0	0	.000	.000
Evans, Steve-Louis Richard	08NYN 09-13StLN 14-15BknF 15BalF	2-17-85	Cleveland, Ohio	12-28-43	L	L			978	3359	478	963	175	67	32	466	359		86	.287	.407
Everett, Bill-William L.	95-00ChiN 01WasA	12-13-68	Fort Wayne, Ind.	1-19-38		R			697	2839	535	909	82	39	11	341	212		199	.320	.388

USE NAME – GIVEN NAMES (NICKNAMES)	TEAM BY YEAR	BIRTH DATE	BIRTH PLACE	DEATH DATE	LIFETIME BATTING TOTALS																
					B	T	HGT	WGT	G	AB	R	H	2B	3B	HR	RBI	BB	SO	SB	BA	SA
Evers, Joe-Joseph Francis	13NYN	9-10-91	Troy, N.Y.	1- 4-49	L	R	5'9	135	1	0	0	0	0	0	0	0	0	0	0	–	–
Evers, Johnny-John Joseph (Crab, The Trogan)	02-13,M13 ChiN 14-17BosN 17PhiN M21ChiN 22,M24ChiA 29BosN	7-21-81	Troy, N.Y.	3-28-47	L	R	5'9	125	1782	6134	919	1658	216	70	12	538	779		324	.270	.334
Ewoldt, Art-Arthur Lee (Sheriff)	19PhiA	1- 8-94	Paullina, Iowa		R	R	5'10	165	9	32	2	7	1	0	0	2	1	5	0	.219	.250
Fabrique, Bunny-Albert LaVerne	16-17BknN	12-23-87	Clinton, Mich.	1-10-60	B	R	5'8	150	27	90	8	18	3	0	1	3	8	10	0	.200	.267
Fahey, Frank-Francis Raymond	18PhiA	1-22-96	Milford, Mass.	3-19-54	B	R	6'1	190	10	17	2	3	1	0	0	1	0	3	0	.176	.235
Fahey, Howard-Howard Simpson (Cap, Kid)	12PhiA	6-24-92	Medford, Mass.	10-24-71	R	R	5'7	145	5	8	0	0	0	0	0	0	0		0	.000	.000
Falsey, Pete-Peter James	14PitN	4-24-91	New Haven, Conn.		L	L	5'6	132	3	1	0	0	0	0	0	0	0	1	0	.000	.000
Farmer, Alex-Alexander Johnson	08BknN	5- 9-80	New York, N.Y.	3- 5-20	R	R	6'	175	12	30	1	5	1	0	0	2	1		0	.167	.200
Farmer, Jack-Floyd Haskell	16PitN 18CleA	7-14-92	Granville, Tenn.	5-21-70	R	R	6'	180	62	175	11	47	6	4	0	15	7	27	3	.269	.349
Farrell, Duke-Charles Andrew	88-89ChiN 90ChiP 92BosAA 92PitN 93WasN 94-96NYN 96-99WasN 99-02BknN 03-05BosA	8-31-66	Oakdale, Mass.	2-15-25	B	R	6'2	180	1566	5623	826	1575	211	123	51	912	477		150	.280	.389
Farrell, Jack-John J	14-15ChiF	6-16-92	Chicago, Ill.	3-24-18	B	R	5'8	145	226	746	85	171	33	5	0	49	77		20	.229	.287
Farrell, John-John Stephen	01WasA 02-05StLN	12- 4-76	Covington, Ky.	5-14-21		R			541	2172	329	567	93	28	4	141	193		68	.261	.335
Fautsch, Joe-Joseph Roamon	16ChiA	2-28-87	Minneapolis, Minn.	3-16-71	R	R	5'10	162	1	1	0	0	0	0	0	0	0	0	0	.000	.000
Felsch, Happy-Oscar Emil	15-20ChiA 20DL	8-22-91	Milwaukee, Wis.	8-17-64	R	L	5'10	170	749	2812	385	825	135	64	38	446	207	251	88	.293	.427
Ferris, Hobe-Albert Sayles	01-07BosA 08-09StLA	12- 7-77	Providence, R.I.	3-18-38	R	R	5'10	170	1286	4800	473	1146	192	89	39	550	161		89	.239	.340
Fetzer, Willy-William McKinnon	06PhiA	6-24-84	Concord, N.C.	5- 3-59	L	R	5'10	180	1	1	0	0	0	0	0	0	0		0	.000	.000
Fischer, Bill-William Charles	13-14BknN 15ChiF 16ChiN 16-17PitN	3- 2-91	New York, N.Y.	9- 4-45	L	R	6'	174	412	1099	109	301	50	15	10	115	90		20	.274	.374
Fishburn, Sam-Samuel E.	19StLN	5-15-93	Haverhill, Mass.	4-11-65	R	R	5'9	157	9	6	0	2	1	0	0	2	0	0	0	.333	.500
Fisher, Bobby-Robert Taylor	12-13BknN 14-15ChiN 16CinN 18-19StLN	11- 3-86	Nashville, Tenn.	8- 4-63	R	R	5'11	170	503	1742	189	480	61	26	11	170	80	157	48	.276	.359
Fisher, Gus-Augustus Harris	11CleA 12NYA	10-21-85	Pottsborough, Tex.	4- 8-72	L	R	5'10	175	74	213	21	54	6	3	0	12	7		6	.254	.310
Fisher, Red-John Gus	10StLA	6-22-87	Pittsburgh, Pa.	2- 1-40	L	R			23	72	5	9	2	1	0	3	8		5	.125	.181
Fisher, Wilbur-Wilbur McCullough	16PitN	7-18-94	Chesapeake, Ohio	10-24-60	L	R	6'	174	1	1	0	0	0	0	0	0	0	0	0	.000	.000
Fitzgerald, Justin-Justin Howard	11NYA 18PhiN	6-22-90	San Mateo, Cal.	1-17-45	L	R	5'8	160	82	170	27	49	9	0	0	12	17		7	.288	.341
Fitzgerald, Matty-Matthew William	06-07NYN	8-31-80	Albany, N.Y.	9-22-49	R	R	6'	185	11	21	3	6	1	0	0	3	0		1	.286	.333
Fitzpatrick, Ed-Edward Henry	15-17BosN	12- 9-89	Phillipsburg, Pa.	10-23-65	R	R	5'8	165	251	697	91	158	35	7	1	59	70	84	22	.227	.301
Fitzsimmons, Tom-Thomas William	19BknN	4- 6-90	Oakland, Cal.	12-20-71	R	R	6'1	190	4	4	1	0	0	0	0	0	1	2	0	.000	.000
Flack, Max-Max John	14-15ChiF 16-22ChiN 22-25StLN	2- 5-90	Belleville, Ill.	7-31-75	L	L	5'7	148	1411	5252	783	1461	212	72	35	391	474		200	.278	.366
Flanagan, Charlie-Charles James	13StLA	12-13-91	Oakland, Cal.	1- 8-30	R	R	6'	175	4	3	0	0	0	0	0	0	1	0	0	.000	.000
Flanagan, Steamer-James Paul	05PitN	4-20-81	Kingston, Pa.	4-21-47	L	L	6'1	185	7	25	7	7	1	1	0	3	1		3	.280	.400
Fleming, Tom-Thomas Vincent (Sleuth)	99NYN 02,04PhiN	11-20-73	Philadelphia, Pa.	12-26-57			5'11	155	28	92	11	24	1	0	0	6	2		1	.261	.272
Fletcher, Art-Arthur	09-20NYN 20PhiN 21VR 22,M23-26PhiN M29NYA	1- 5-85	Collinsville, Ill.	2- 6-50	R	R	5'10	170	1529	5541	684	1534	238	77	32	675	203		159	.277	.365
Fletcher, Frank-O. Frank	14PhiN	3 6 91	Hildreth, Ill.	10- 7-74	R	R	5'9	161	1	1	0	0	0	0	0	0	0	1	0	.000	.000
Flick, Elmer-Elmer Harrison	98-01PhiN 02PhiA 02-10CleA	1-11-76	Bedford, Ohio	1- 9-71	L	R	5'9	168	1483	5597	948	1765	268	169	48	756	597		341	.315	449
Flinn, Don-Don Raphael	17PitN	11-17-92	Bluffdale, Tex.	3- 9-59	R	R	6'1	185	14	37	1	11	1	1	0	1	1	6	1	.297	.378
Flood, Tim-Timothy A.	99StLN 02-03BknN	3-13-77	Montgomery City, Mo.	6-15-29	R	R			231	816	70	190	26	6	3	86	42		23	.233	.293
Fluhrer, John-John L.	15ChiN	1- 3-94	Adrian, Mich.	7-17-46	R	R	5'9	165	6	6	0	2	0	0	0	0	1	0	1	.333	.333
Flynn, Jack-John Anthony	10-11PitN 12WasA	9- 7-83	Providence, R.I.	3-23-35	R	R	6'	175	149	462	46	115	14	4	6	60	46		8	.249	.335
Fohl, Lee-Leo Alexander	02PitN 03CinN M15-19CleA M21-23StLA M24-26BosA	11-28-70	Pittsburgh, Pa.	10-30-65	L	R	5'10	175	5	17	3	5	1	1	0	3	0		0	.294	.471
Foley, Pat (See Willie Greene)																					
Forsythe, Clarence-Clarence	15BalF		St. Louis, Mo.			R			1	3	0	0	0	0	0	0	1		0	.000	.000
Foster, Eddie-Edward Cunningham (Kid)	10NYA 12-19WasA 20-22BosA 22-23StLA	2-13-87	Chicago, Ill.	1-15-37	R	R	5'6	145	1499	5652	732	1490	191	71	6	446	528		195	.264	.326
Foster, Pop-Clarence Francis	98-00NYN 01WasA 01ChiA	4- 8-78	New Haven, Conn.	4-16-44		R			261	922	146	263	37	19	10	137	76		17	.285	.399
Foutz, Frank-Frank Hayes	01BalA	4- 8-77	Baltimore, Md.	12-25-61	R	R			20	72	13	17	4	1	2	14	8		0	.236	.403
Fox, Bill-William Henry	97WasN 01CinN	1-15-72	Fiskdale, Mass.	5- 7-46	B	R	5'11	160	48	177	13	33	2	1	0	7	5		9	.186	.209
Fox, Jack-John Paul	08PhiA	5-21-85	Reading, Pa.	6-28-63	R	R	5'10	185	9	30	2	6	0	0	0	0	0		2	.200	.200
Freeman, Buck-John Frank	91WasAA 98-99WasN 00BosN 01-07BosA	10-30-71	Catasauqua, Pa.	6-25-49	L	L	5'9	150	1126	4211	583	1238	202	130	82	713	272		93	.294	.462
Freeman, Jerry-James Jeremiah	08-09WasA	-82	Oakland, Cal.		L				173	579	47	142	15	6	1	48	40		9	.245	.297
French, Charlie-Charles Calvin	09-10BosA 10ChiA	10-12-83	Indianapolis, Ind.	3-30-62	L	R	5'6	140	105	377	34	78	5	2	0	20	26		13	.207	.231
French, Pat-Frank Alexander	17PhiA	9-22-93	Dover, N.H.	7-13-69	R	R	6'1	180	3	2	0	0	0	0	0	0	0	0	0	.000	.000
Friel, Bill-William Edward	01MilA 02-03StLA	4- 1-76	Renovo, Pa.	12-24-59	L	R			283	994	123	244	33	17	6	80	60		23	.245	.331
Frisk, Emil-John Emil (See P01-19)	99CinN 01DetA 05,07StLA	10-15-75	Kalkaska, Mich.	1-27-22	L	R	6'1	190	160	506	73	135	15	6	4	45	48		7	.267	.344
Fritz, Harry-Harry Koch (Dutchman)	13PhiA 14-15ChiF	9-30-90	Philadelphia, Pa.	11- 4-74	R	R	5'8	170	149	423	44	96	13	5	3	39	33		6	.227	.303
Froelich, Ben-William Palmer	09PhiN	11-12-87	Pittsburgh, Pa.	9- 1-16	R	R			1	1	0	0	0	0	0	0	0		0	.000	.000
Fuller, Frank-Frank Edward (Rabbit)	15-16DetA 23BosA	1- 1-93	Detroit, Mich.	10-29-65	B	R	5'7	150	40	63	11	11	0	0	0	3	11	12	6	.175	.175
Fuller, Nig-Charles F.	02BknN				R	R			3	9	0	0	0	0	0	1	0		0	.000	.000
Fultz, Dave-David Lewis	98-99PhiN 99BalN 01-02PhiA 03-05NYA	5-29-75	Staunton, Va.	10-29-59	R	R	5'11	170	644	2393	369	651	86	26	3	223	201		190	.272	.333
Gagnier, Eddie-Edward James	14-15BknF 15BufF	4-16-83	Paris, France	9-13-46	R	R	5'9	170	115	389	30	76	13	2	0	29	23		10	.195	.239
Gainer, Del-Dellos Clinton (Sheriff)	09,11-14DetA 14-17,19BosA 18MS 22StLN	11-10-86	Montrose, W.Va.	1-29-47	R	R	6'	180	546	1608	218	438	75	36	14	185	149		54	.272	.390
Gallagher, D.F.-D.F.	01CleA								2	4	0	0	0	0	0	0	0		0	.000	.000
Gallagher, John-John C.	15BalF	-94	Pittsburgh, Pa.		R	R	5'10	156	40	126	11	25	4	0	0	4	5		1	.198	.230
Galloway, Bad News-James Cato	12StLN	9-16-87	Iredell, Tex.	5- 3-50	B	R	6'3	187	21	54	4	10	2	0	0	4	5	8	2	.185	.222
Gammons, Daff-John Ashley	01BosN	3-17-76	New Bedford, Mass.	9-24-63	R	R	5'11	170	28	93	10	18	0	1	0	10	3		5	.194	.215
Gandil, Chick-Charles Arnold	10ChiA 12-15WasA 16CleA 17-19ChiA 20HO-DL	1-19-88	St. Paul, Minn.	12-13-70	R	R	6'1	190	1147	4245	449	1176	173	78	11	557	273		153	.277	.362
Gandy, Bob-Robert Brinkley (String)	16PhiN	8-25-93	Jacksonville, Fla.	6-19-45	L	R	6'3	180	1	2	0	0	0	0	0	0	0	1	0	.000	.000
Ganley, Bob-Robert Stephen	05-06PitN 07-09WasA 09PhiA	4-23-75	Lowell, Mass.	10-10-45	L	L			572	2129	246	540	44	24	2	123	177		112	.254	.300
Gannon, Bill-William G.	98StLN 01ChiN		New Haven, Conn.	4-26-27					16	64	2	9	0	0	0	0	1		5	.141	.141
Ganzel, John-John Henry	98PitN 00ChiN 01NYN 03-04NYA 05-06HO 07-08,M08CinN M15BknF	4- 7-75	Racine, Wis.	1-14-59	R	R	6'	195	747	2718	281	682	104	50	18	336	136		46	.251	.346
Gardner, Earl-Earl M.	08-12NYA	1-24-85	Sparta, Ill.	3- 2-43	R	R	5'11	160	273	948	105	249	26	5	1	108	50		38	.263	.304
Gardner, Larry-William Lawrence	08-17BosA 18PhiA 19-24CleA	5-13-86	Enosburg Falls, Vt.		L	R	5'8	165	1922	6684	867	1931	300	129	27	929	654		165	.289	.385
Gatins, Frank-Frank Anthony	98WasN 01BknN	3- 6-71	Johnstown, Pa.	11- 8-11					66	253	26	59	9	2	1	26	8		6	.233	.296
Gear, Dale-Dale Dudley (See P01-19)	96-97CleN 01WasA	2- 2-72	Lone Elm, Kans.	9-23-51	R	R	5'11	165	69	238	25	57	11	3	0	25	8		4	.239	.311
Gedeon, Joe-Elmer Joseph	13-14WasA 16-17NYA 18-20StLA 20DL	12- 5-93	Sacramento, Cal.	5-19-41	R	R	6'	167	581	2109	259	515	82	19	2	171	180	181	33	.244	.304
Geier, Phil-Louis Phillip (Little Phil)	96-97PhiN 00CinN 01PhiA 01MilA 04BosN	11- 3-76	Washington, D.C.	9-25-67	R	R	5'7	145	349	1312	199	330	30	12	2	102	154		54	.252	.297
Genins, Frank-C. Frank (Frenchy)	92CinN 92StLN 95PitN 01CleA	11- 2-66	St. Louis, Mo.	9-30-22		R			147	511	74	116	19	0	2	44	43		27	.227	.276
Gertenrich, Lou-Louis Wilhelm	01MilA 03PitN	5- 4-75	Chicago, Ill.	10-23-33	R	R	5'8	175	3	6	1	1	0	0	0	0	0		0	.167	.167
Gessler, Doc-Harry Homer	03DetA 03-06BknN 06ChiN 08-09BosA 09-11WasA M14PitF	12-23-80	Indiana, Pa.	12-26-24	L	R			880	2959	369	831	127	49	14	363	333		142	.281	.371
Getz, Gus-Gustave (Gee-Gee)	09-10BosN 14-16BknN 17CinN 18CleA 18PitN	8- 3-89	Pittsburgh, Pa.	5-28-69	R	R	5'11	165	339	1114	85	265	22	9	2	93	24	46	41	.238	.279
Giannini, Joe-Joseph Francis	11BosA	9- 8-88	San Francisco, Cal.	9-26-42	L	R	5'8	155	1	2	0	1	1	0	0	0	0		0	.500	1.000
Gibson, Charlie-Charles E.	05StLA	-77	Philadelphia, Pa.		R	R	5'8	160	12	15	1	2	0	0	0	1	2	0	0	.133	.133
Gibson, George-George C. (Moon)	05-16PitN 17-18NYN M20-22PitN M25ChiN M32-34PitN	7-22-80	London, Canada	1-25-67	R	R	5'11	190	1213	3776	295	893	142	49	15	345	286		40	.236	.312
Giebel, Joe-Joseph Henry	13PhiA	11-30-91	Washington, D.C.		R	R	5'10	175	1	3	0	1	0	0	0	0	0	1	0	.333	.333
Gilbert, Billy-William Oliver	01MilA 02BalA 03-06NYN 08-09StLN	6-21-76	Tullytown, Pa.	8- 8-27	R	R	5'4	153	850	2816	375	695	72	17	5	237	270		167	.247	.290
Gilbert, Jack-John Robert (Jackrabbit)	98WasN 98NYN 04PitN	9-14-75	Rhinebeck, N.Y.	7- 7-41					28	96	13	23	0	0	0	4	13		5	.240	.240
Gilbert, Larry-Lawrence William	14-15BosN	12- 2-91	New Orleans, La.	2-17-65	L	L	5'9	158	117	330	43	76	10	1	5	29	37	47	7	.230	.312
Gilhooley, Frank-Frank Patrick (Flash)	11-12StLN 13-18NYA 19BosA	6-10-92	Toledo, Ohio	7-11-59	L	R	5'8	155	312	1068	141	289	30	10	2	58	140	80	37	.271	.323
Gill, Doc-Warren Darst	08PitN	12-21-78	Ladoga, Ind.	11-26-52	R	R	6'1	175	27	76	10	17	0	1	0	14	11		3	.224	.250
Gilmore, Grover-Ernest Grover	14-15KCF	11- 1-88	Chicago, Ill.	11-25-19	L	L	5'9	170	258	941	144	269	47	20	2	79	63		42	.286	.385
Ginn, Tinsley-Tinsley Rucker	14CleA	9-26-91	Royston, Ga.	8-30-31	L	R	5'9	180	2	1	0	0	0	0	0	0	0	0	0	.000	.000
Gleason, Harry-Harry Gilbert	01-03BosA 04-05StLA	3-28-75	Camden, N.J.	10-21-61	R	R	5'6	150	274	944	88	206	24	11	3	90	48		31	.218	.276
Gleason, Kid-William J. (See P01-19)	88-91PhiN 92-94StLN 94-95BalN 96-00NYN 01-02DetA 03-08PhiN 12,M19-23ChiA	10-26-66	Camden, N.J.	1- 2-33	B	R	5'7	158	1969	7445	1017	1951	216	85	15	823	500		332	.262	.320
Glenn, Ed-Edward D.	98WasN 98NYN 02ChiN	-74	Ludlow, Ky.	12- 6-11	R	R			5	15	1	1	0	0	0	0	4		1	.067	.067
Glenn, Harry-Harry Melville (Husky)	15StLN	6- 9-90	Shelburn, Ind.	10-12-18	L	R	6'	185	6	16	1	5	0	0	0	1	3	0	0	.313	.313
Glockson, Norm-Norman Stanley	14CinN	6-15-94	Blue Island, Ill.	8- 5-55	R	R	6'2	200	7	12	0	0	0	0	0	0	1	6	0	.000	.000

USE NAME – GIVEN NAMES (NICKNAMES)	TEAM BY YEAR	BIRTH DATE	BIRTH PLACE	DEATH DATE	B	T	HGT	WGT	G	AB	R	H	2B	3B	HR	RBI	BB	SO	SB	BA	SA
									LIFETIME BATTING TOTALS												
Gochnaur, John-John Peter	01BknN 02-03CleA	9-12-75	Altoona, Pa.	9-27-29	R	R	5'9	160	264	908	94	170	32	8	0	87	87		18	.187	.240
Godwin, John-John Henry (Bunny)	05-06BosA	3-10-77	East Liverpool, Ohio	5- 5-56	R	R	6'	190	79	230	15	49	3	1	0	25	9		9	.213	.235
Gonzalez, Eusebio-Eusebio Miguel [Lopez] (Papo)	18BosA	7-13-92	Havana, Cuba		R	R	5'10	165	2	2	1	1	0	1	0	0	0	0	0	.500	1.500
Gooch, Lee-Lee Currin	15CleA 17PhiA	2-23-90	Oxford, N.C.	5-18-66	R	R	6'	190	19	61	4	18	2	0	1	8	4	10	0	.295	.377
Good, Gene-Eugene J.	06BosN	12-13-82	Roxbury, Mass.	8- 6-47	L	L	5'6	130	2	3	0	0	0	0	0	0	0	2	0	.000	.000
Good, Wilbur-Wilbur David (Lefty) (See P01-19)	05NYA 08-09CleA 10-11BosN	9-28-85	Punxsutawney, Pa.	12-30-63	L	L	5'6	165	750	2634	324	609	84	44	9	187	190		104	.258	.342
	11-15ChiN 16PhiN 18ChiA																				
Goodwin, Pep-Claire Vernon	14-15KCF	12-19-91	Pocatello, Idaho	2-15-72	L	R	5'10	160	193	603	60	142	20	7	1	48	42		10	.235	.297
Gossett, Dick-John Star	13-14NYA	8-21-91	Dennison, Ohio	10- 6-62	R	R	5'11	185	48	126	12	20	2	0	0	10	15	27	1	.159	.175
Gouzzie, Claude-Claude	03StLA	-71	Pa.	9-21-07	R	R	5'9	170	1	1	0	0	0	0	0	0	0		0	.000	.000
Gowdy, Hank-Henry Morgan (Harry)	10-11NYN 11-17BosN 18MS 19-23BosN	8-24-89	Columbus, Ohio	8- 1-66	R	R	6'2	182	1050	2735	270	738	122	27	21	322	311	247	59	.270	.327
	23-25NYN 29-30BosN																				
Grady, Mike-Michael William	94-97PhiN 97StLN 98-00NYN 01WasA 04-06StLN	12-23-69	Kennett Square, Pa.	12- 3-43	R	R	5'11	190	914	2991	487	885	155	68	35	459	311		111	.296	.428
Graff, Fred-Frederick Gottlieb	13StLA	8-25-89	Canton, Ohio		R	R	5'10	164	4	5	1	2	1	0	0	2	3	3	0	.400	.600
Graham, Bert-Bert	10StLA	4- 3-86	Tilton, Ill.	6-19-71	B	R	6'1	187	8	26	1	3	2	1	0	5	1		0	.115	.269
Graham, Charlie-Charles Henry	06BosA	4-25-78	Santa Clara, Cal.	8-29-48	R	R	5'11	180	30	90	10	21	1	0	1	12	10		1	.233	.278
Graham, Moonlight-Archibald Wright	05NYN	11- 9-76	Fayetteville, N.C.	8-25-65	L	R	5'10	170	1	0	0	0	0	0	0	0	0	0	0	–	–
Graham, Peaches-George Frederick (See P01-19)	02CleA 03ChiN 08-11BosN	3-23-77	Aledo, Ill.	7-25-39	R	R	5'9	180	373	999	99	265	34	6	1	85	114		21	.265	.314
	11ChiN 12PhiN																				
Graham, Tiny-Dawson Francis	14CinN	12- 9-92	Nashville, Tenn.	12-29-62	R	R	6'2	185	25	61	5	14	1	0	0	3	3	10	1	.230	.246
Graney, Jack-John Gladstone (See P01-19)	08,10-22CleA	6-10-86	St. Thomas, Canada		L	L	5'9	180	1402	4705	706	1178	219	79	18	420	712		148	.250	.342
Grant, Eddie-Edward Leslie (Harvard Eddie)	05CleA 07-10PhiN 11-13CinN 13-15NYN	5-21-83	Franklin, Mass.	10- 5-18	L	R	5'11	170	990	3385	399	844	79	30	5	277	233		153	.249	.295
Gray, Bill-William	00PitN	11- 1-73	Saw Mill Run, Pa.	9- 7-33	R	R	5'10	145	2	6	1	2	0	0	0	1	1		0	.333	.333
Gray, Stan-Stanley Oscar (Dolly)	12PitN	12-10-88	Ladonia, Tex.	10-11-64	R	R	6'1	184	6	20	4	5	0	1	0	2	0	3	0	.250	.350
Green, Danny-Edward	98-01ChiN 02-05ChiA	11- 6-76	Burlington, N.J.	11- 9-14	L				923	3481	551	1024	123	65	29	422	315		192	.294	.392
Greene, Patsy-Patrick Joseph (Played as Pat Foley 02)	02PhiN 03NYA 03DetA	3-20-75	Providence, R.I.	10-20-34	R	R			24	81	7	15	2	0	0	1	2		2	.185	.210
Gremminger, Ed-Lorenzo Edward (Battleship)	95CleN 02-03BosN 04DetA	3-30-74	Canton, Ohio	5-26-42	R	R	6'1	200	382	1422	140	357	58	24	7	164	89		23	.251	.340
Griffin, Pug-Francis Arthur	17PhiA 20NYN	4-24-96	Lincoln, Neb.	10-12-51	R	R	5'11	187	23	29	4	6	1	0	1	3	2	11	1	.207	.345
Griffith, Tommy-Thomas Herman	13-14BosN 15-18CinN 19-25BknN 25ChiN	10-26-89	Prospect, Ohio	4-13-67	L	R	5'10	175	1401	4947	589	1383	208	72	52	619	351	262	70	.280	.382
Griggs, Art-Art Carle	09-10StLA 11-12CleA 14-15BknF 18DetA	10-10-83	Topeka, Kans.	12-19-38	R	R	5'11	185	442	1370	127	379	73	20	5	152	105		36	.277	.370
Grimshaw, Moose-Myron Frederick	05-07BosA	11-30-75	St. Johnsville, N.Y.	12-11-36	B	R	6'1	173	259	894	104	229	31	16	4	116	60		15	.256	.340
Groh, Heinie-Henry Knight	12-13NYN 13-21,M18CinN 22-26NYN 27PitN	9-18-89	Rochester, N.Y.	8-22-68	R	R	5'8	158	1676	6074	920	1774	308	87	26	566	696	345	180	.292	.384
Groh, Lew-Lewis Carl (Silver)	19PhiA	10-16-83	Rochester, N.Y.	10-20-60	R	R			2	4	0	0	0	0	0	0	0	2	0	.000	.000
Grosart, George-George Albert	01BosN	-79	Meadville, Pa.	4-18-02					7	26	4	3	0	0	0	1	0		0	.115	.115
Grover, Roy-Roy Arthur	16-17,19PhiA 19WasA	1-17-92	Snohomish, Wash.		R	R	5'8	150	207	690	67	156	17	9	0	50	60	79	19	.226	.277
Grubb, Harvey-Harvey Harrison	12CleA	9-18-90	Lexington, N.C.	1-25-70	R	R	6'	189	1	0	0	0	0	0	0	0	0	0	0	–	–
Gunning, Hy-Hyland	11BosA	8- 6-88	Maplewood, N.J.	3-28-75	L	R	6'1	189	4	9	0	1	0	0	0	2	2		0	.111	.111
Gust, Red-Ernest Herman Frank	11StLA	1-24-88	Bay City, Mich.	10-26-45	R	R	6'	170	3	12	0	0	0	0	0	0	0		0	.000	.000
Haberer, Emil-Emil Karl	01,03,09CinN	2- 2-78	Cincinnati, Ohio	10-19-51	R	R	6'1	204	16	47	4	7	1	1	0	3	5		0	.149	.213
Hackett, Jim-James Joseph (Sunny Jim) (See P01-19)	02-03StLN	10- 1-77	Jacksonville, Ill.	3-28-61	R	R	6'2	185	105	372	26	86	14	8	0	40	21		3	.231	.312
Hahn, Eddie-William Edgar	05-06NYA 06-10ChiA	8-27-75	Nevada, Ohio	11-29-41	L	R		160	553	2045	291	484	42	20	1	122	258		59	.237	.278
Halas, George-George Stanley 20-29 played in N.F.L.	19NYA	2- 2-94	Chicago, Ill.		B	R	6'	164	12	22	0	2	0	0	0	0	0	8	0	.091	.091
20-29,33-42,46-55,58-68 head coach in N.F.L.																					
Hale, George-George Wagner (Ducky)	14,16-18StLA	8- 3-94	Dexter, Kans.	11- 1-45	R	R	5'10	160	60	103	5	18	3	1	0	9	11	21	0	.175	.223
Haley, Pat-Raymond Timothy	15-16BosA 16-17PhiA 18-19MS	1-23-91	Danbury, Iowa		R	R	5'11	180	81	214	17	53	8	1	0	15	11	32	2	.248	.294
Hall, Bob-Robert Prill	04PhiN 05NYN 05BknN	12-20-78	Baltimore, Md.	12- 1-50	R	R	5'10	158	103	369	33	75	8	1	2	32	25		13	.203	.247
Hall, Russ-Robert Russell	98StLN 01CleA	9-29-71	Shelbyville, Ky.	7- 1-37		R			40	147	15	38	1	1	0	10	7		1	.259	.279
Halliday, Newt-Newton	16PitN	-97	Chicago, Ill.		R	R	6'1	175	1	1	0	0	0	0	0	0	0	1	0	.000	.000
Hallinan, Ed-Edward S.	11-12StLA	8-23-88	San Francisco, Cal.	8-24-40	R	R	5'9	168	80	255	24	54	5	1	0	15	19		7	.212	.239
Hallman, Bill-William Harry	01MilA 03ChiA 06-07PitN	3-15-76	Philadelphia, Pa.	4-23-50					319	1147	150	269	43	13	3	86	120		47	.235	.303
Hallman, Billy-William Wilson	88-89PhiN 90PhiP 91PhiAA 92-97PhiN	3-31-67	Pittsburgh, Pa.	9-11-20	R	R			1501	5999	943	1664	243	86	20	769	425		205	.277	.357
	97,M97StLN 98BknN 01CleA 01-03PhiN																				
Halt, Al-Alva William	14-15BknF 18CleA	11-23-90	Sandusky, Ohio	1-22-73	L	R	6'	180	257	854	76	204	30	9	6	90	61		35	.239	.316
Hamilton, Billy-William Robert (Sliding Billy)	88-89KCAA 90-95PhiN 96-01BosN	2-16-66	Newark, N.J.	12-15-40	L	L	5'6	165	1582	6262	1690	2157	225	94	40	736	1187		937	.344	.430
Hammond, Jack-Walter Charles (Wobby)	15,22CleA 22PitN	2-26-91	Amsterdam, N.Y.	3- 4-42	R	R	5'11	170	45	99	13	22	2	1	0	4	2	19	0	.222	.263
Handiboe, Mike-Aloysius James (Coalyard Mike)	11NYA	7-21-87	Washington, D.C.	1-31-53	L	L	5'10	155	5	15	0	1	0	0	0	0	2		0	.067	.067
Hanford, Charlie-Charles Joseph	14BuffF 15ChiF	6- 3-81	Tunstall, England	7-19-63	R	R	5'6	145	232	776	110	217	32	18	13	112	44		47	.280	.418
Hanlon, Bill-William (Big Bill)	03ChiN		Cal.						8	21	4	2	0	0	0	2	6		1	.095	.095
Hannah, Truck-James Harrison	18-20NYA	6- 5-91	Larimore, N.D.		R	R	6'1	190	244	736	62	173	25	4	5	66	97	79	7	.235	.300
Hannifan, Jack-John Joseph	06PhiA 06-08NYN 08BosN	2-25-83	Holyoke, Mass.	10-27-45	R	R	5'11	167	142	439	50	94	13	6	3	40	45		14	.214	.292
Hanson, Joe-Joseph	13NYA		St. Louis, Mo.			R			1	2	0	0	0	0	0	0	0	0	0	.000	.000
Hardy, Jack-John Doolittle	03CleA 07ChiN 09-10WasA	6-23-77	Cleveland, Ohio	10-20-21	R	R	6'	185	23	55	5	10	1	0	0	5	2		1	.182	.200
Hargrove, Pat-William Patrick	18ChiA	5-10-96	Palmyra Ct. H., Kans.		R	R	5'10	158	2	2	0	0	0	0	0	0	0	0	0	.000	.000
Harley, Dick-Richard Joseph	97-98StLN 99CleN 00-01CinN 02DetA 03ChiN	9-25-72	Philadelphia, Pa.	4- 3-52	L	R	5'10	165	743	2881	388	756	59	28	10	236	223		135	.262	.313
Harrison, Ben-Leo J.	01WasA								1	2	0	0	0	0	0	0	1		0	.000	.000
Hart, Hub-James Henry	05-07ChiA	2- 2-78	Everett, Mass.	10-10-60	L	R	5'11	170	56	124	9	27	1	0	0	11	10		1	.218	.226
Hart, Warren-Warren F.	01BalA								58	206	33	64	3	5	0	23	20		7	.311	.374
Hartford, Bruce-Bruce	14CleA	5-14-92	Chicago, Ill.	Deceased	R	R	6'	190	8	22	5	4	1	0	0	0	4	9	0	.182	.227
Hartley, Chick-Walter Scott	02NYN	8-22-80	Philadelphia, Pa.	7-18-48	R	R	5'8	180	1	4	0	0	0	0	0	0	0		0	.000	.000
Hartley, Grover-Grover Allen (Slick)	11-13NYN 14-15StLF 16-17StLA 24-26NYN	7- 2-88	Osgood, Ind.	10-19-64	R	R	5'11	175	566	1321	135	352	61	11	3	144	135		29	.266	.336
	27BosA 28DP 29-30CleA 34StLA																				
Hartman, Fred-Frederick Orrin (Dutch)	94PitN 97StLN 98-99NYN 01ChiA 02StLN	4-25-68	Pittsburgh, Pa.	11-11-38		R			583	2246	298	620	75	46	10	332	118		87	.276	.364
Hartsel, Topsy-Tully Frederick	98-99LouN 00CinN 01ChiN 02-11PhiA	6-26-74	Polk, Ohio	10-14-44	L	L	5'5	155	1351	4834	824	1334	183	92	31	341	837		247	.276	.371
Hartzell, Roy-Roy Allen	06-10StLA 11-16NYA	7- 6-81	Golden, Colo.	11- 6-61	L	R	5'8	155	1288	4548	503	1146	112	55	12	397	455		182	.252	.309
Harvey, Zaza-Ervin King (Silent) (See P01-19)	00ChiN 01ChiA 01-02CleA	1- 5-79	Saratoga, Cal.	6- 3-54		L			76	259	37	86	10	6	1	32	14		17	.332	.429
Hasbrook, Ziggy-Robert Lyndon	16-17ChiA	11-21-93	Grundy Center, Iowa		R	R	6'1	180	11	9	2	1	0	0	0	0	1	2	0	.111	.111
Hauger, Art-John Arthur	12CleA	11-18-93	Delhi, Ohio	8- 2-44	L	R	5'11	168	15	18	0	1	0	0	0	0	1		0	.056	.056
Hauser, Arnold-Arnold George (Pee-Wee)	10-13StLN 14IL 15ChiF	9-25-88	Chicago, Ill.	5-22-66	R	R	5'6	145	433	1468	180	349	33	20	6	137	121		68	.238	.300
Haworth, Homer-Howard Homer	15CleA	8-27-95	Newburg, Ore.		L	R	5'10	165	7	7	0	1	0	0	0	1	2	2	0	.143	.143
Hayden, Jack-John Francis	01PhiA 06BosA 08ChiN	10-21-80	Bryn Mawr, Pa.	8- 3-42					147	578	60	145	14	8	1	33	36		11	.251	.308
Hazleton, Doc-Willard Carpenter	02StLN	8-28-76	Strafford, Vt.	3-17-41					7	23	0	3	0	0	0	0	2		0	.130	.130
Healy, Tom-Thomas Fitzgerald	15-16PhiA	10-30-95	Altoona, Pa.		R	R	6'	172	29	100	15	23	2	1	0	7	7	6	1	.230	.270
Hearn, Ed-Edmund	10BosA	9-17-88	Ventura, Cal.	9- 8-52	R	R	5'9	160	2	2	0	0	0	0	0	0	0		0	.000	.000
Hearne, Hugh-Hugh Joseph (Hughie)	01-03BknN	4-18-73	Troy, N.Y.	9-22-32	R	R	5'8	182	94	293	31	83	13	2	0	35	19		5	.283	.341
Hechinger, Mike-Michael Vincent	12-13ChiN 13BknN	2-14-90	Chicago, Ill.	8-13-67	R	R	6'	175	13	16	1	2	1	0	0	0	2	2	0	.125	.188
Heidrick, Snags-R. Emmett	98CleN 99-01StLN 02-04,08StLA 05-07VR	7-29-76	Queenstown, Pa.	1-20-16					758	3049	470	915	109	74	16	342	146		181	.300	.400
Heileman, Jack-John George	01CinN	8-10-72	Cincinnati, Ohio	7-19-40	R	R	5'10	155	5	15	1	2	1	0	0	1	0		0	.133	.200
Heitmuller, Heinie-William Frederick	09-10PhiA	-83	San Francisco, Cal.	10- 8-12	L	R	6'2	215	95	321	47	87	11	10	0	22	25		13	.271	.368
Helfrick, Ty-Emory Wilbur	15BknF	10- 9-90	Pleasantville, N.J.	3-18-55	R	R	5'10	178	43	104	12	25	6	0	0	5	15		2	.240	.298
Hemingway, Ed-Edson Marshall	14StLA 17NYN 18PhiN	5- 8-93	Sheridan, Mich.	7- 5-69	B	R	5'11	165	43	138	10	31	5	2	0	13	10	11	7	.225	.290
Hemphill, Charlie-Charles Judson (Eagle Eye)	99StLN 99CleN 01BosA 02CleA	4-20-76	Greenville, Mich.	6-22-53	L	L	5'9	160	1240	4539	581	1230	118	69	22	421	435		209	.271	.342
	02-04,06-07StLA 08-11NYA																				
Hemphill, Frank-Frank Vernon	06ChiA 09WasA	5-13-78	Greenville, Mich.	11-16-50	R	R	5'11	165	14	43	0	3	0	0	0	2	9		1	.070	.070
Hendricks, Jack-John Charles	02NYN 02ChiN 03WasA M18StLN M24-29CinN	4- 9-75	Joliet, Ill.	5-13-43	L	L	5'11	160	42	145	11	30	3	4	0	4	15		5	.207	.283
Hendryx, Tim-Timothy Green	11-12CleA 15-17NYA 18StLA 20-21BosA	1-31-91	LeRoy, Ill.		R	R	5'9	170	414	1288	152	355	68	22	6	191	185		26	.276	.377
Hennessy, Les-Lester Baker	13DetA	12-12-93	Lynn, Mass.		R	R	6'	190	12	22	2	3	0	0	0	0	3	6	2	.136	.136
Henriksen,, Olaf-Olaf (Swede)	11-17BosA	4-26-88	Kirkerup, Denmark	10-17-62	L	L	5'7	158	311	487	84	131	12	7	1	48	97		15	.269	.329
Henry, John-John T.	10-17WasA 18BosN	12-26-89	Amherst, Mass.	11-24-41	R	R	6'	180	683	1920	161	397	54	15	2	171	244		55	.207	.254
Herring, Lefty-Silas Clarke	99WasN 04WasA	3- 4-80	Philadelphia, Pa.		L	L	5'11	160	17	47	4	9	1	0	0	2	8		0	.191	.213

USE NAME – GIVEN NAMES (NICKNAMES)	TEAM BY YEAR	BIRTH DATE	BIRTH PLACE	DEATH DATE	B	T	HGT	WGT	LIFETIME BATTING TOTALS												
									G	AB	R	H	2B	3B	HR	RBI	BB	SO	SB	BA	SA
Herzog, Buck-Charles Lincoln	08-09NYN 10-11BosN 11-13NYN 14-16,M14-16CinN 16-17NYN 18-19BosN 19-20ChiN	7- 9-85	Baltimore, Md.	9- 4-53	R	R	5'11	160	1493	5284	705	1370	191	75	20	445	427		312	.259	.335
Hetling, Gus-August Julius	06DetA	11-21-85	St. Louis, Mo.	10-13-62	R	R	5'10	165	2	7	0	1	0	0	0	0	0		0	.143	.143
Heydon, Mike-Michael Edward (Ed)	98BalN 99WasN 01StLN 04ChiA 05-07WasA	7-15-74	Mo.	10-13-13		R			214	619	52	111	19	6	2	53	70		12	.179	.239
Hickey, Mike-Michael Edward	99BosN 01ChiN	12-25-71	Chicopee, Mass.	6-11-18	R	R			11	40	4	7	0	0	0	3	2		1	.175	.175
Hickman, Charley-Charles Taylor (Piano Legs) (See P01-19)	97-99BosN 00-01NYN 02BosA 02-04CleA 04-05DetA 05-07WasA 07ChiA 08CleA	3- 4-76	Taylortown, Pa.	4-19-34	R	R	5'9	185	1074	3968	480	1199	212	87	58	614	153		76	.302	.443
Hickman, Dave-David James	15BalF 16-19BknN	5-19-94	Union City, Tenn.		R	R	5'7	170	253	727	84	158	26	13	8	70	37	114	27	.217	.322
Higgins, Bob-Robert Stone	09CleA 11-12BknN	9-23-86	Fayetteville, Tenn.	5-25-41	R	R	5'8	176	13	35	1	6	0	0	0	2	1	1	1	.143	.143
High, Hugh-Hugh Jenken (Bunny, Lefty)	13-14DetA 15-18NYA	10-24-87	Pottstown, Pa.	11-16-62	L	L	5'7	155	504	1546	176	386	54	21	3	123	212	168	56	.250	.318
Hildebrand, George-George Albert	02BknN	9- 6-78	San Francisco, Cal.	5-30-60	R	R	5'8	170	11	41	3	9	1	0	0	5	3		0	.220	.244
Hildebrand, Pete-Palmer Marion	13StLN	12-23-84	Schauck, Ohio	1-25-60	R	R	5'11	180	26	55	3	9	2	0	0	1	1	10	1	.164	.200
Hildebrand, R.E.-R.E.	02ChiN								1	4	1	0	0	0	0	0	1		0	.000	.000
Hill, Hugh-Hugh Ellis	03CleA 04StLN	7-21-79	Ringgold, Ga.	9- 6-58					24	94	13	21	2	1	3	4	2		3	.223	.362
Hill, Hunter-Hunter Benjamin	03-04StLA 04-05WasA	6-21-79	Austin, Tex.	2-22-59		R			325	1200	104	259	32	5	1	80	57		26	.216	.253
Hillebrand, Doc-Homer Hiller Henry (See P01-19)	05-06,08PitN	10-10-79	Freeport, Ill.	1-23-74	R	L	5'8	165	47	131	10	31	4	2	0	10	7		1	.237	.298
Hilley, Ed-Edward Garfield (Whitey)	03PhiA	6-17-79	Cleveland, Ohio	11-14-56	R	R	5'10	170	1	3	1	1	0	0	0	0	1		0	.333	.333
Hilly (Hilgerink), Pat-William Edward	14PhiN	2-24-87	Fostoria, Ohio	7-25-53	R	R	5'11	180	8	10	2	3	0	0	0	1	1	5	0	.300	.300
Himes, John-John H.	05-06StLN								52	196	13	48	5	2	0	14	8		4	.245	.291
Hinchman, Bill-William White	05-06CinN 07-09CleA 15-18,20PitN	4- 4-83	Philadelphia, Pa.	2-21-63	R	R	5'11	190	908	3043	364	793	128	69	20	369	298		85	.261	.368
Hinchman, Harry-Harry Sibley	07CleA	8- 4-78	Philadelphia, Pa.	1-19-33	B	R	5'11	165	15	51	3	11	3	1	0	9	5		2	.216	.314
Hinton, John-John R.	01BosN		Altoona, Pa.			R			4	13	0	1	0	0	0	0	2		0	.077	.077
Hobbs, Bill-William Lee	13,16CinN	5- 7-93	Grant's Lick, Ky.	1- 5-45	R	R	5'9	155	10	15	1	2	1	0	0	1	2	3	1	.133	.200
Hoblitzell, Dick-Richard Carleton	08-14CinN 14-18BosA 19-20MS	10-26-88	Waverly, W.Va.	11-14-62	L	L	6'	172	1314	4706	591	1310	194	88	27	593	407		173	.278	.374
Hoelskoetter, Art-Arthur H. (Holley, Hoss) (See P01-19) (Played as Art Hostetter 07-08)	05-08StLN	9-30-82	St. Louis, Mo.	8- 3-54	R	R	6'2		300	952	59	225	21	8	2	53	40		9	.236	.282
Hoey, John-John B.	06-08BosA	11-10-81	Watertown, Mass.	11-11-47					146	500	39	116	10	5	0	35	15		13	.232	.272
Hoffman, Danny-Daniel John	03-06PhiA 06-07NYA 08-11StLA	3-10-80	Canton, Conn.	3-14-22	L	L	5'9	175	828	2976	359	761	71	52	13	235	226		185	.256	.328
Hoffman, Izzy-Harry C.	04WasA 07BosN	1- 5-75	Bridgeport, N.J.	11-13-42	L	L			29	116	18	27	4	1	0	4	8		2	.233	.284
Hoffman, Larry-Lawrence Charles	01ChiN	7-18-82	Chicago, Ill.	12-29-48		R			6	22	2	7	1	0	0	6	0		1	.318	.364
Hoffman, Tex-Edward Adolph	15CleA	11-30-93	San Antonio, Tex.	5-19-47	B	R	5'9	195	9	13	1	2	0	0	0	2	1	5	0	.154	.154
Hofman, Solly-Arthur Frederick (Circus Solly)	03PitN 04-12ChiN 12-13PitN 14BknN 15BufF 16NYA 16ChiN	10-29-82	St. Louis, Mo.	3-10-56	R	R	6'	160	1194	4072	554	1095	162	60	19	495	421		208	.269	.352
Hogan, Harry-Harry S.	01CleA	11- 1-75	Syracuse, N.Y.	1-25-34					1	4	0	0	0	0	0	0	0		0	.000	.000
Hogan, Willie-William Henry (Happy)	11PhiA 11-12StLA	9-14-84	North San Juan, Cal.	9-28-74	R	R	5'10	175	237	822	86	194	28	10	3	100	77		35	.236	.305
Hogriever, George-George C.	95CinN 01MilA	3-17-69	Cincinnati, Ohio	1-26-61	R	R	5'8	160	121	458	86	118	18	9	2	50	66		47	.258	.349
Hohnhurst, Ed-Edward Henry	10,12CleA	1-31-85	Cincinnati, Ohio	3-28-16	L	L	6'1	175	31	116	13	31	4	1	0	8	6		8	.267	.319
Holden, Bill-William Paul	13-14NYA 14CinN	9- 7-89	Birmingham, Ala.	9-14-71	R	R	6'	170	79	246	20	52	6	3	0	21	27	36	2	.211	.260
Holly, Ed-Edward William	06-07StLN 14-15PitF	7- 6-79	Chicago, Ill.	11-27-73	R	R	5'10	165	276	971	92	224	29	7	1	78	63		33	.231	.278
Holmes, Ducky-Howard Elbert	06StLN	7- 8-83	Dayton, Ohio	9-18-45		R			9	27	2	5	0	0	0	2	2		0	.185	.185
Holmes, Ducky-James William	95-97LouN 97NYN 98StLN 98-99BalN 01-02DetA 03WasA 03-05ChiA	1-28-69	Des Moines, Iowa	8- 6-32	L	R	5'6	170	931	3586	545	1017	143	59	17	374	236		244	.284	.371
Holmes, Fred-Frederick	03NYA 04ChiN		Chicago, Ill.		R	R			2	3	1	1	1	0	0	0	1		0	.333	.667
Hooper, Harry-Harry Bartholomew	09-20BosA 21-25ChiA	8-24-87	Bell Station, Cal.	12-17-74	L	R	5'10	168	2308	8784	1429	2466	389	160	75	817	1136		375	.281	.387
Hopkins, Mike-Michael Joseph (Skinner)	02PitN	11- 1-72	Glasgow, Scotland	2- 5-72	R	R	5'8	160	1	2	0	2	1	0	0	0	0	0	0	1.000	1.500
Hopkins, Buck-John Winton (Sis)	07StLN	1- 3-83	Grafton, Va.	10- 2-29	R	R	5'10	165	15	44	7	6	3	0	0	3	10		2	.136	.205
Householder, Ed-Edward H.	03BknN	10-12-69	Pittsburgh, Pa.	7- 3-24					12	43	5	9	0	0	0	9	2		3	.209	.209
Houser, Ben-Benjamin Franklin	10PhiA 11-12BosN 13KJ	11-30-83	Shenandoah, Pa.	1-15-52	L	L	6'1	185	162	472	58	126	21	5	9	68	37		3	.267	.390
Howard, Dave-David Austin (Del)	12WasA 15BknF	5- 1-89	Washington, D.C.	1-26-56	R	R	5'11	165	25	36	6	8	1	0	0	1	1		0	.222	.250
Howard, Del-George Elmer	05PitN 06-07BosN 07-09ChiN	12-24-77	Kenney, Ill.	12-24-56	L	R	6'	180	536	1833	199	482	54	22	6	193	111		67	.263	.326
Howard, Ivon-Ivon Chester	14-15StLA 16-17CleA	10-12-82	Kenney, Ill.	3-30-67	B	R	5'10	170	302	818	91	191	27	14	2	86	104	129	53	.233	.304
Howard, Paul-Paul Joseph (Del)	09BosA	5-20-84	Boston, Mass.	8-29-68	R	R	5'8	170	6	15	2	3	1	0	0	2	3		0	.200	.267
Howell, Henry-Harry (Handsome Harry) (See P01-19)	98BknN 99BalN 00BknN 01-02BalA 03NYA 04-10StLA	11-14-76	Brooklyn, N.Y.	5-22-56	R	R			457	1395	143	301	59	26	10	130	64		20	.216	.317
Howley, Dan-Daniel Philip (Dapper Dan)	13PhiN M27-29StLA M30-32CinN	10-16-85	East Weymouth, Mass.	3-10-44	R	R	6'	167	26	32	5	4	2	0	0	2	4	4	3	.125	.188
Hoy, Dummy-William Ellsworth	88-89WasN 90BufP 91StLAA 92-93WasN 94-97CinN 98-99LouN 01ChiA 02CinN	5-23-62	Houckstown, Ohio	12-15-61	L	R	5'4	148	1795	7098	1424	2067	237	118	40	726	1004		607	.291	.375
Huelsman, Frank-Frank Elmer	97StLN 04ChiA 04DetA 04ChiA 04StLA 04-05WasA	6- 5-74	St. Louis, Mo.	6- 9-59	R	R	6'2	210	240	824	76	213	52	13	5	97	62		18	.258	.371
Hug, Ed-Edward Ambrose	03BknN	7-14-80	Fayetteville, Ohio	5-11-53	R	R			1	0	0	0	0	0	0	0	1	0	0	–	–
Huggins, Miller-Miller James (Hug, The Mighty Mite)	04-09CinN 10-16,M13-17StLN M18-29NYA	3-27-79	Cincinnati, Ohio	9-25-29	B	R	5'6	140	1585	5557	947	1474	146	50	9	318	1002		324	.265	.314
Hughes, Ed-Edward	02ChiN								1	3	0	0	0	0	0	0	0		0	.000	.000
Hughes, Ed-Edward H. (See P01-19)	02ChiA 05-06BosA	-80	Chicago, Ill.		R	R	6'1	180	9	21	2	4	0	0	0	2	0		0	.190	.190
Huhn, Emil-Emil Hugo (Hap)	15NwkF 16-17CinN	3-10-92	North Vernon, Ind.	9- 5-25	R	R	6'	180	184	560	40	128	22	5	1	47	32		14	.229	.291
Hulswitt, Rudy-Rudolph Edward	99LouN 02-04PhiN 08CinN 09-10StLN	2-23-77	Newport, Ky.	1-16-50	R	R	5'8	165	644	2230	208	564	64	32	3	203	136		49	.253	.314
Hummel, John-John Edwin (Silent John)	05-15BknN 18NYA	4- 4-83	Bloomsburg, Pa.	5-18-59	R	R	5'11	160	1161	3906	421	991	128	84	29	394	346		117	.254	.352
Humphrey, Al-Albert	11BknN	2-28-86	Ashtabula, Ohio	5-13-61	L	R	5'11	180	8	27	4	5	0	0	0	0	3	7	0	.185	.185
Hunter, Bill-William Ellsworth	12CleA	7- 8-86	Buffalo, N.Y.	4-10-34	L	L	5'7	155	21	55	6	9	2	0	0	2	10		0	.164	.200
Hunter, George-George Henry (See P01-19)	09-10BknN	7- 8-86	Buffalo, N.Y.	1-11-68	B	L	5'8	165	45	123	8	28	7	0	0	8	9		1	.228	.285
Hunter, Herb-Herbert Harrison	16NYN 16-17ChiN 20BosA 21StLN	12-25-95	Boston, Mass.	7-25-70	L	R	6'	165	39	49	8	8	0	0	1	4	2	6	0	.163	.224
Hunter, Newt-Frederick Creighton	11PitN	1- 5-80	Chillicothe, Ohio	10-26-63	R	R	6'	180	65	209	35	53	10	6	2	24	25	43	9	.254	.388
Hurley, Pat-Patrick	01CinN 07BknN				R	R			10	23	1	1	0	0	0	0	2		1	.043	.043
Huston, Harry-Harry Emanuel Kress	06PhiN	10-14-83	Bellefontaine, Ohio	10-13-69	R	R	5'9	168	2	4	0	0	0	0	0	0	1		0	.000	.000
Hyatt, Ham-Robert Hamilton	09-10,12-14PitN 15StLN 18NYA	11- 1-84	Buncombe Co., N.C.	9-11-63	L	R	6'1	185	464	925	85	247	36	23	10	146	63		11	.267	.388
Hynes, Pat-Patrick J. (See P01-19)	03StLN 04StLA	3-12-84	St. Louis, Mo.	3- 2-07					67	257	23	60	7	3	0	15	3		3	.233	.284
Ingerton, Scotty-William John	11BosN	1- 8-89	Rapid City, S.D.	6-15-56	R	R	6'1	172	136	521	63	130	24	4	5	61	39	68	6	.250	.340
Iott (Hoyot) Happy Jack-Frederick John (Biddo)	03CleA	1- 7-76	Houlton, Me.	2-17-41	R	R	5'10	175	3	10	1	2	0	0	0	0	2		1	.200	.200
Irelan, Hal-Harold (Grump)	14PhiN	8- 5-90	Burnettsville, Ind.	7-16-44	B	R	5'7	165	67	165	16	39	8	0	1	16	21	22	3	.236	.303
Irvin, Ed-William Edward	12DetA	-82	Philadelphia, Pa.	2-18-16		R			1	3	0	2	0	2	0	0	0		0	.667	2.000
Irwin, Charlie-Charles E.	93-95ChiN 96-01CinN 01-02BknN	2-15-69	Sheffield, Ill.	9-21-25	R	R	5'10	160	990	3683	554	991	144	47	16	488	286		191	.269	.347
Isbell, Frank-William Frank (Bald Eagle) (See P01-19)	98ChiN 01-09ChiA	8-21-75	Delevan, N.Y.	7-15-41	L	R	5'11	190	1119	4217	500	1056	158	62	13	455	190		253	.250	.327
Jacklitsch, Fred-Frederick Lawrence	00-02PhiN 03-04BknN 05NYA 07-10PhiN 14-15BalF 17BosN	5-24-76	Brooklyn, N.Y.	7-18-37	R	R	5'9	180	490	1344	160	327	64	12	5	153	201		35	.243	.320
Jackson, Bill-William Riley	14-15ChiF	4- 4-81	Pittsburgh, Pa.	9-26-58	L	L	6'	150	76	123	17	17	1	0	1	13	17		3	.138	.171
Jackson, Charlie-Charles Herbert (Lefty)	15ChiA 17PitN 18MS	2- 7-94	Granite City, Ill.	5-27-68	L	L	5'9	150	42	122	7	29	3	2	0	1	10	23	4	.238	.295
Jackson, George-George Christopher (Hickory)	11-13BosN	1- 2-82	Springfield, Mo.	11-25-72	R	R	6'	180	152	554	85	158	24	7	4	73	50	95	34	.285	.375
Jackson, Jim-James Benner	01BalA 02NYN 05-06CleA	11-28-77	Philadelphia, Pa.	10- 9-55	R	R			347	1269	158	299	47	10	4	132	107		57	.236	.298
Jackson, Joe-Joseph W. (Shoeless Joe)	08-09PhiA 10-15CleA 15-20ChiA 20DL	7-16-89	Brandon Mills, S.C.	12- 5-51	L	R	6'	180	1330	4981	873	1774	307	168	54	785	519		202	.356	.518
Jacobs, Mike-Morris Elmore	02ChiN								5	19	1	4	0	0	0	2	0		0	.211	.211
Jacobs, Otto-Otto Albert	18ChiA	4-19-89	Chicago, Ill.	11-19-55	R	R	5'9	180	29	73	4	15	3	1	0	3	5	8	0	.205	.274
James, Bob-Berton Hulon	09StLN	7- 7-86	Adamsville, Ky.		L	R	5'11	175	6	21	1	6	0	0	0	0	4		1	.286	.286
Jansen, Roy-Raymond W.	10StLA	-90	St. Louis, Mo.		R	R	5'11	165	1	5	0	4	0	0	0	0	0		0	.800	.800
Jantzen, Heinie-Walter C.	12StLA	-90	Chicago, Ill.		R	R	5'11	170	31	119	10	22	0	1	1	8	4		3	.185	.227
Janvrin, Hal-Harold Chandler (Childe Harold)	11,13-17BosA 18MS 19WasA 19-21StLN 21-22BknN	8-27-92	Haverhill, Mass.	3- 2-62	R	R	5'11	168	756	2221	250	515	68	18	6	210	171		79	.232	.287
Jenkins, Joe-Joseph Daniel	14StLA 17ChiA 18MS 19ChiA	10-12-90	Shelbyville, Tenn.	6-21-74	R	R	5'11	170	40	60	0	8	2	1	0	3	2	17	3	.133	.200
Jennings, Hughie-Hugh Ambrose (Ee-Yah)	91LouAA 92-93LouN 93-99BalN 99-00BknN 01-02PhiN 03BknN 07,09,12,18,M07-20DetA	4- 2-69	Pittston, Pa.	2- 1-28	R	R	5'8	165	1274	4884	996	1530	227	88	18	840	347		372	.313	.407
Johns, Pete-William R.	15ChiA 18StLA	1-17-89	Cleveland, Ohio	8- 9-64	R	R	5'10	165	74	189	12	37	3	2	0	22	12	17	2	.196	.233
Johnson, Bill-William Lawrence	16-17PhiA	10-18-92	Chicago, Ill.	11- 5-50	L	R	5'11	170	52	124	8	23	3	2	1	9	8	18	4	.185	.266
Johnson, Charlie-Charles Cleveland (Home Run)	08PhiN	3-12-85	Slatington, Pa.	8-28-40	L	L	5'9	150	6	16	2	4	0	1	0	2	1		0	.250	.375

USE NAME – GIVEN NAMES (NICKNAMES)	TEAM BY YEAR	BIRTH DATE	BIRTH PLACE	DEATH DATE	B	T	HGT	WGT	G	AB	R	H	2B	3B	HR	RBI	BB	SO	SB	BA	SA
					LIFETIME BATTING TOTALS																
Johnson, Elmer-Elmer Ellsworth (Hickory)	14NYN	6-12-84	Beard, Ind.	10-31-66	R	R	5'9	185	11	12	0	2	1	0	0	0	1	3	0	.167	.250
Johnson, Ote-Otis L. (Home Run)	11NYA	11- 5-83	Muncie, Ind.	11- 9-15	B	R	5'9	185	71	209	21	49	9	6	3	36	39		12	.234	.378
Johnson, Walter-Walter Perry (The Big Train, Barney) (See P01-19)		11- 6-87	Humboldt, Kans.	12-10-46	R	R	6'1	200	937	2329	242	549	94	41	24	256	113		13	.236	.342
	07-27,M29-32WasA M33-35CleA																				
Johnston, Doc-Wheeler Roger	09CinN 12-14CleA 15-16PitN 18-21CleA 22PhiA	9- 9-87	Chattanooga, Tenn.	2-17-61	L	L	6'	170	1055	3774	478	992	154	68	14	379	264		139	.263	.351
Johnston, Johnny-John Thomas	13StLA	3-28-90	Longview, Tex.	3- 7-40	L	R	5'11	172	109	380	37	85	14	4	2	27	42	51	11	.224	.297
Jones, Bill-William Dennis (Midget)	11-12BosN	4- 8-87	Hartland, Canada	10-10-46	L	R	5'6	157	27	53	6	12	2	1	0	5	15	8	1	.226	.302
Jones, Charlie-Charles C. (Casey)	01BosA 04ChiA 05-07WasA 08StLA	6- 2-76	Butler, Pa.	4- 2-47		R			483	1799	217	420	56	28	5	144	93		100	.233	.304
Jones, Davy-David Jefferson (Kangaroo)	01MilA 02StLA 02-04ChiN 06-12DetA	6-30-80	Cambria, Wis.	3-31-72	L	R	5'10	165	1085	3772	643	1020	98	40	9	289	478		207	.270	.325
	13ChiA 14-15PitF																				
Jones, Fielder-Fielder Allison	96-00BknN 01-08,M04-08ChiA 14-15,M14-15StLF	8-13-71	Shinglehouse, Pa.	3-13-34	L	R	5'11	180	1787	6761	1181	1929	200	76	22	633	817		359	.285	.348
	M16-18StLA																				
Jones, Jimmy-James Tilford (Sheriff)	97LouN 01-02NYN	12-25-76	London, Ky.	5- 6-53	R	R	5'10	150	90	344	28	79	16	4	0	24	18		9	.230	.299
Jones, Tex-William Roderick	11ChiA	8- 4-85	Marion, Kans.	2-26-38	R	R	6'1	190	9	31	4	6	1	0	0	4	3		1	.194	.226
Jones, Tom-Thomas	02BalA 04-09StLA 09-10DetA	1-22-77	Honesdale, Pa.	6-21-23	R	R	6'1	195	1058	3847	341	964	123	34	3	336	193		135	.251	.303
Jordan, Dutch-Adolf Otto	03-04BknN	1- 5-80	Pittsburgh, Pa.	12-23-72	R	R	5'10	185	165	519	48	108	21	3	0	40	32		16	.208	.260
Jordan, Tim-Timothy Joseph	01WasA 01-02BalA 03NYA 06-10BknN	2-14-79	New York, N.Y.	9-13-49	L	L	6'1	170	542	1820	220	474	74	24	22	232	254		48	.260	.380
Joyce, Mike (See Mike O'Neill-see P01-19)																					
Jude, Frank-Frank	06CinN	-85	Mahnomen Co., Minn.	5- 4-61	R	R	5'7	150	80	308	31	64	6	4	1	31	16		7	.208	.263
Kading, Jack-John Frederick	10PitN 14ChiF	11-27-84	Waukesha, Wis.	6- 2-64	R	R	6'3	190	11	26	5	7	2	1	0	4	4		0	.269	.423
Kafora, Jake-Frank Jacob (Tomatoes)	13-14PitN	10-16-88	Detroit, Mich.	3-23-28	R	R	6'	180	22	24	3	3	0	0	0	0	0	7	0	.125	.125
Kahl, Nick-Nicholas Alexander	05CleA	4-10-79	Coulterville, Ill.	7-13-59	R	R	5'9	185	39	131	16	29	4	1	0	21	4		1	.221	.267
Kahoe, Mike-Michael Joseph	95,99-01CinN 01-02ChiN 02-04StLA 05PhiN 07ChiN	9- 3-73	Yellow Springs, Ohio	5-14-49	R	R	6'	190	410	1311	103	278	44	14	4	105	39		21	.212	.276
	07-09WasA																				
Kaiser, Al-Alfred Edward (Deerfoot)	11ChiN 11-12BosN 14IndF	8- 3-86	Cincinnati, Ohio	4-11-69	R	R	5'10	180	155	481	58	104	15	7	3	38	34		10	.216	.295
Kalahan, John-John Joseph	03PhiA	9-30-78	Philadelphia, Pa.	6-20-52	R	R	6'	165	1	5	0	0	0	0	0	0	0		0	.000	.000
Kane (Kiley), Frank-Francis Thomas (Sugar)	15BknF 19NYA	3- 9-95	Whitman, Mass.	12- 2-62	L	R	5'11	175	4	11	2	2	0	1	0	2	0		0	.182	.364
Kane, Jim-James J.	08PitN	11-27-82	Scranton, Pa.	10- 2-47	L	L			55	145	16	35	3	3	0	22	12		5	.241	.303
Kane, John-John Francis	07-08CinN 09-10ChiN	10-24-83	Pittsburg, Kans.	1-28-34	R	R	5'6	138	261	824	118	181	21	11	7	59	76		53	.220	.297
Karst, John-John Gottlieb (King)	15BknN	10-15-93	Philadelphia, Pa.		L	R	5'11	175	1	0	0	0	0	0	0	0	0	0	0	–	–
Kauff, Benny-Benjamin Michael (The Ty Cobb of the Feds)	13NYA 14IndF	1- 5-90	Pomeroy, Ohio	11-17-61	L	L	5'8	157	859	3094	521	961	169	57	49	454	367		234	.311	.450
	15BknF 16-20NYN 21DL																				
Kauffman, Dick-Howard Richard	14-15StLA	6-22-88	East Lewisburg, Pa.	4-16-48	R	R	6'3	190	44	139	10	36	9	2	0	16	5	30	0	.259	.353
Kavanagh, Charlie-Charles Hugh (Silk)	14ChiA	6- 9-93	Chicago, Ill.		R	R	5'9	165	5	5	0	1	0	0	0	0	0	2	0	.200	.200
Kavanagh, Leo-Leo Daniel	14ChiF	8- 9-94	Chicago, Ill.	8-10-50	R	R	5'9	180	5	11	0	3	0	0	0	1	1		0	.273	.273
Kavanagh, Marty-Martin Joseph	14-16DetA 16-18CleA 18StLN 18DetA	6-13-91	Harrison, N.J.	7-28-60	R	R	6'	187	369	1033	138	257	47	20	9	122	118	122	26	.249	.359
Kay, Bill-Walter Brocton (King Bill)	07WasA	2- 5-78	New Castle, Va.	12- 3-45	L	R	6'2	180	25	60	8	20	1	1	0	7	0		0	.333	.383
Keating, Chick-Walter Francis	13-15ChiN 26PhiN	8- 8-91	Philadelphia, Pa.	7-13-59	R	R	5'9	155	30	45	5	4	1	1	0	0	6	13	1	.089	.156
Keeler, Willie-William Henry (Wee Willie)	92-93NYN 93BknN 94-98BalN	3- 3-72	Brooklyn, N.Y.	1- 1-23	L	L	5'4	140	2125	8570	1720	2955	234	155	34	810	524		519	.345	.420
	99-02BknN 03-09NYA 10NYN																				
Keene, Brown-William Brown (Rebel)	11PitN	-91	Atlanta, Ga.		R	R	6'	181	6	7	0	0	0	0	0	0	1	4	0	.000	.000
Keister, Bill-William Hoffman (Wagon Tongue)	96BalN 98BosN 99BalN 00StLN	8-17-74	Baltimore, Md.	8-19-24	R	R			621	2435	401	759	133	63	17	399	90		134	.312	.439
	01BalA 02WasA 03PhiN																				
Keliher, Mickey-Maurice Michael	11-12PitN	1-11-90	Washington, D.C.	9- 7-30	L	L	6'	175	4	7	1	0	0	0	0	0	0	5	0	.000	.000
Kelleher, Duke-Albert Aloysius	16NYN	9-30-93	New York, N.Y.	9-28-47		R			1	0	0	0	0	0	0	0	0	0	0	–	–
Kelley, Joe-Joseph James	91BosN 92PitN 92-98BalN 99-01BknN 02BalA	12- 9-71	Cambridge, Mass.	8-14-43	R	R	5'11	190	1836	6989	1425	2245	353	189	66	1194	911		458	.321	.454
	02-06,M02-05CinN 08,M08BosN																				
Kelliher, Frank-Frank Mortimer (Yucca)	19WasA	5-23-99	Somerville, Mass.	3- 4-56	L	L	5'9	175	1	1	0	0	0	0	0	0	0	0	0	.000	.000
Kellogg, Bill-William Dearstyne	14CinN	5-25-84	Albany, N.Y.	12-12-71	R	R	5'10	153	71	126	14	22	0	1	0	7	14	28	7	.175	.190
Kelly, Billy-William Joseph	10StLN 11-13PitN	5- 1-86	Baltimore, Md.	6- 3-40	R	R	6'	183	104	224	32	65	5	4	1	20	5	30	9	.290	.362
Kelly, Bob-Robert Brown (Speed)	09WasA	8-19-84	Bryan, Ohio	5- 6-49	R	R			17	42	3	6	2	1	0	1	3		1	.143	.238
Kelly (Taggart), Jimmy-James Robert	14PitN 15PitF 18BosN	2- 1-90	Bloomfield, N.J.		L	R	5'10	180	215	714	91	212	15	22	4	57	46		42	.297	.396
Kelly, Joe-Joseph Herbert	14PitN 16ChiN 17-19BosN	9-23-89	Weir City, Kans.		R	R	5'10	175	376	1341	131	300	38	22	6	117	80	143	66	.224	.298
Kelly, John-John B.	07StLN	3-13-79	Clifton Heights, Pa.	3-19-44			5'9	165	53	197	12	37	5	0	0	6	13		7	.188	.213
Kelly, Red-Albert Michael	10ChiA	11-15-84	Union, Ill.	2- 4-61	R	R	5'11	165	14	45	6	7	0	1	0	1	7		0	.156	.200
Kelsey, George-George W.	07PitN		Ohio			R			2	5	1	2	0	0	0	0	0		0	.400	.400
Kennedy, Ray-Raymond Lincoln	16StLA	5-19-95	Pittsburgh, Pa.	1-18-69	R	R	5'9	165	1	1	0	0	0	0	0	0	0	0	0	.000	.000
Kennedy, Snapper-Sherman Montgomery	02ChiN	11- 1-77	Conneaut, Ohio	-44					1	5	0	0	0	0	0	0	0		0	.000	.000
Kenworthy, Duke-William Jennings	12WasA 14-15KCF 17StLA	7- 4-86	Cambridge, Ohio	9-21-50	B	R	5'7	165	285	989	159	301	71	21	18	146	67		61	.304	.473
Kerlin, Orie-Orie Milton (Cy)	15PitF	1-23-91	Summerfield, La.		L	R	5'7	150	3	1	0	0	0	0	0	0	0		0	.000	.000
Kerr, Doc-John Jonas	14PitF 14-15BalF		Baltimore, Md.	6- 9-37	B	R	5'10	190	59	111	8	28	5	3	1	8	12		1	.252	.378
Kerwin, Dan-Daniel P.	03CinN	7- 9-79	Philadelphia, Pa.		L	L	5'9	164	2	6	1	4	1	0	0	1	2		0	.667	.833
Ketchum, Fred-Frederick L.	99LouN 01PhiA	7-27-75	Elmira, N.Y.	3-12-08	L	R			20	83	18	24	1	0	0	7	0		4	.289	.301
Ketter, Phil-Philip	12StLA		Hutchinson, Kans.			R			2	6	1	2	0	0	0	0	0		0	.333	.333
Kibble, Jack-John Wesley (Happy)	12CleA	1- 2-92	Seatonville, Ill.		B	R	5'9	154	5	8	1	0	0	0	0	0	0		0	.000	.000
Kilhullen, Pat-Joseph Isadore	14PitN	8-10-90	Carbondale, Pa.	11- 2-22	R	R	5'9	175	1	1	0	0	0	0	0	0	0	0	0	.000	.000
Killefer, Bill-William Lavier (Reindeer Bill)	09-10StLA 11-17PhiN	10-10-87	Bloomingdale, Mich.	7- 2-60	R	R	5'10	200	1035	3150	237	751	86	21	4	240	113		39	.238	.283
	18-21,M21-25ChiN M30-33StLA																				
Killefer, Red-Wade (Lollypop)	07-09DetA 09-10WasA 14-16CinN 16NYN	4-13-84	Bloomingdale, Mich.	9- 4-58	R	R	5'9		467	1537	181	381	61	16	3	116	128		57	.248	.314
King, Fred (See John Butler)																					
King, Lee-Lee	16PhiA 19BosN	3-28-94	Waltham, Mass.	9- 7-38	R	R	5'10	150	44	145	13	27	1	2	0	8	7	15	4	.186	.221
Kingman, Harry-Henry Lees	14NYA	4- 3-92	Tientsin, China		L	L	6'1	165	4	3	0	0	0	0	0	0	1	2	0	.000	.000
Kinsella, Bob-Robert Francis	19-20NYN	1- 5-99	Springfield, Ill.	12-30-51	L	R	5'9	165	4	12	1	3	0	0	0	1	0	5	1	.250	.250
Kippert, Ed-Edward August	14CinN	1- 3-80	Detroit, Mich.	6- 3-60	R	R	5'10	180	2	2	0	0	0	0	0	0	0	0	0	.000	.000
Kirby, LaRue-LaRue (See P01-19)	12NYN 14-15StLF	12-30-89	Eureka, Mich.	6-10-61	B	R	6'	185	116	378	37	87	14	5	2	34	31		8	.230	.310
Kirke, Jay-Judson Fabian	10DetA 11-13BosN 14-15CleA 18NYN	6-16-88	Fleischmanns, N.Y.	8-31-68	L	R	6'1	195	320	1148	122	346	49	13	7	148	35		21	.301	.385
Kirkpatrick, Enos-Enos Claire	12-13BknN 14-15BalF	12- 9-85	Pittsburgh, Pa.	4-14-64	R	R	5'11	185	203	528	70	125	20	6	3	46	54		32	.237	.314
Kittredge (Kitteridge), Mal-Malachi J.	90-97ChiN 98-99LouN 99WasN	10-12-69	Clinton, Mass.	9-12-27	R	R	5'7	170	1212	4005	376	882	110	31	17	390	314		65	.220	.276
	01-03BosN 03-06,M04WasA 06CleA																				
Kleinow, Red-John Peter (Doc)	04-10NYA 10-11BosA 11PhiN	7-20-79	Milwaukee, Wis.	10- 9-29	R	R	5'10	165	584	1665	146	354	45	20	3	135	153		42	.213	.269
Kling, Johnny-John Gradwohl (Noisy)	00-08ChiN 09HO 10-11ChiN 11-12,M12BosN	2-25-75	Kansas City, Mo.	1-31-47	R	R	5'9	160	1260	4241	474	1149	176	64	20	513	281		121	.271	.357
	13CinN																				
Kling, Rudy-Rudolph A.	02StLN	3-23-70	St. Louis, Mo.	3-14-37	R	R			4	10	1	2	0	0	0	0	4		1	.200	.200
Knabe, Otto-Franz Otto (Frank, Dutch)	05PitN 07-13PhiN 14-15,M14-15BalF	6-12-84	Carrick, Pa.	5-17-61	R	R	5'8	175	1275	4469	572	1103	177	50	8	365	485		143	.247	.314
	16PitN 16ChiN																				
Knaupp, Cotton-Henry Antone	10-11CleA	8-13-89	San Antonio, Tex.	7- 6-67	R	R	5'9	165	31	98	5	18	4	1	0	11	8		4	.184	.245
Knight, Jack-John Wesley (Schoolboy)	05-07PhiA 07BosA 09-11NYA 12WasA 13NYA	10- 6-85	Philadelphia, Pa.	12-19-65	R	R	6'2	180	767	2664	301	636	96	24	14	270	211		86	.239	.309
Knisely, Pete-Peter Cole	12CinN 13-15ChiN	8-11-83	Waynesburg, Pa.	7- 1-48	R	R	5'9	185	124	272	27	64	16	4	0	29	24	30	4	.235	.324
Knoll, Punch-Charles Elmer	05WasA	10- 7-81	Evansville, Ind.	2- 7-60	R	R	5'7	170	85	244	24	52	10	5	0	29	9		3	.213	.295
Knotts, Joe-Joseph	07BosN		York, Pa.			R			3	8	0	0	0	0	0	0	1		0	.000	.000
Kocher, Brad-Bradley Wilson	12DetA 15-16NYN	1-16-88	White Haven, Pa.	2-13-65	R	R	5'11	188	62	139	9	25	5	2	0	12	4		0	.180	.245
Koehler, Ben-Bernard James	05-06StLA	1-26-77	Schoerndorn, Germany	5-21-61	R	R	5'10	175	208	722	82	168	15	7	2	62	56		31	.233	.281
Kolseth, Karl-Karl Dickey (Koley)	15BalF	12-25-92	Cambridge, Mass.	5- 3-56	L	R	6'	182	6	23	1	6	1	1	0	1	1		0	.261	.391
Kommers, Fred-Fred Raymond (Bugs)	13PitN 14StLF 14BalF	3-31-86	Chicago, Ill.	6-14-43	L	R	6'	175	132	441	52	120	15	12	4	64	41		8	.272	.388
Konetchy, Ed-Edward Joseph (Big Ed)	07-13StLN 14PitN 15PitF 16-18BosN	9- 3-85	LaCrosse, Wis.	5-27-47	R	R	6'2	195	2084	7649	971	2146	344	181	74	992	689		255	.281	.402
	19-21BknN 21PhiN																				
Konnick, Mike-Michael Aloysius	09-10CinN	1-13-89	Glen Lyon, Pa.	7- 9-71	R	R	5'9	180	3	8	0	2	1	0	0	1	1	0	0	.250	.375
Kopf, Larry-William Lorenz	13CleA 14-15PhiA 16-17CinN 18MS 19-21CinN	11- 3-90	Bristol, Conn.		B	R	5'9	160	850	3009	348	749	83	30	5	266	242	214	72	.249	.301
(Played as Fred Brady 13)	22-23BosN																				
Kopp, Manny-Merlin Henry	15WasA 18-19PhiA	1- 2-92	Toledo, Ohio	5- 6-60	B	R	5'6	158	187	630	96	146	9	11	1	30	89	105	39	.232	.286
Kores, Art-Arthur Emil (Dutch)	15StLF	7-22-86	Milwaukee, Wis.	11- -74	R	R	5'9	167	60	201	18	47	9	2	1	22	21		6	.234	.313
Kraft, Clarence-Clarence Otto (Big Boy)	14BosN	6- 9-87	Evansville, Ind.	3-26-58	R	R	6'	190	3	3	0	1	0	0	0	0	0	1	0	.333	.333
Kreitz, Ralph-Ralph Wesley (Red)	11ChiA	11-13-85	Plum Creek, Neb.	7-20-41	R	R	5'9	175	7	17	0	4	1	0	0	0	2		0	.235	.294
Krichell, Paul-Paul Bernard	11-12StLA	12-19-82	New York, N.Y.	6- 4-57	R	R	5'7	150	85	243	25	54	9	0	0	16	23		4	.222	.259
Krueger, Ernie-Ernest George	13CleA 15NYA 17NYN 17-21BknN 25CinN	12-27-90	Chicago, Ill.		R	R	5'10	185	318	836	87	220	33	14	11	93	64	85	12	.263	.376

USE NAME – GIVEN NAMES (NICKNAMES)	TEAM BY YEAR	BIRTH DATE	BIRTH PLACE	DEATH DATE	B	T	HGT	WGT	G	AB	R	H	2B	3B	HR	RBI	BB	SO	SB	BA	SA
					LIFETIME BATTING TOTALS																
Krueger, Otto-Arthur William ('Oom Paul)	99CleN 00-02StLN 03-04PitN 05PhiN	9-17-76	Chicago, Ill.	2-20-61	R	R	5'7	165	507	1704	230	427	40	33	5	196	160		48	.251	.322
Krug, Henry-Henry Charles	02PhiN	12- 4-76	San Francisco, Cal.	1-14-08	R	R			53	198	20	45	3	3	0	14	7		2	.227	.273
Kruger, Art-Arthur T.	07CinN 10CleA 10BosN 10CleA 14-15KCF	3-16-81	San Antonio, Tex.	11-28-49	R	R	6'	185	365	1222	113	283	49	21	6	115	73		38	.232	.321
Kuhn, Walt-Walter Charles (Red)	12-14ChiA	2- 2-84	Frenso, Cal.	6-14-35	R	R	5'7	162	118	268	25	55	9	0	0	15	41		8	.205	.239
Kustus, Joe-Julius	09BknN		Detroit, Mich.		R	R			53	173	12	25	5	0	1	11	11		9	.145	.191
Kutina, Joe-Joseph Peter	11-12StLA	1-16-85	Chicago, Ill.	4-13-45	R	R	6'2	205	93	306	30	68	15	5	4	33	15		2	.222	.343
Kyle, Andy-Andrew Ewing	12CinN	10-29-89	Toronto, Canada	9- 6-71	L	L	5'8	160	9	21	3	7	1	0	0	4	4	2	0	.333	.381
LaChance, Candy-George Joseph	93-98BknN 99BalN 01CleA 02-05BosA	2-15-70	Waterbury, Conn.	8-18-32	B	R			1261	4934	681	1382	199	89	39	690	219		210	.280	.380
Lajoie, Nap-Napoleon (Larry)	96-00PhiN 01-02PhiA 02-14,M05-09CleA 15-16PhiA	9- 5-75	Woonsocket, R.I.	2 7-59	R	R	6'1	195	2480	9589	1502	3251	650	163	82	1599	516		395	.339	.466
Lake, Fred-Frederick Lovett	91BosN 94LouN 97BosN 98PitN M08-09BosA	10-16-66	Nova Scotia, Canada	11-24-31	R	R			48	123	12	29	7	0	1	16	17		4	.236	.317
	10,M10BosN																				
Lamer, Pete-Pierre	02ChiN 07CinN	-74	Hoboken, N.J.	10-24-31		R			3	11	2	2	0	0	0	0	0		0	.182	.182
Land, Grover-Grover Cleveland	08,10-11,13CleA 14-15BknF	9-22-84	Frankfort, Ky.	7-22-58	R	R			292	906	62	219	26	5	2	79	27		14	.242	.288
Lanning, Les-Lester Alfred (Red)	16PhiA	5-13-95	Harvard, Ill.	6-13-62	L	L	5'9	165	19	33	5	6	2	0	0	1	10	9	0	.182	.242
LaPorte, Frank-Frank Breyfogle (Pot)	05-08NYA 08BosA 09-10NYA 11-12StLA	2- 6-80	Uhrichsville, Ohio	9-25-39	R	R	5'8	175	1193	4212	501	1185	198	80	14	560	288		101	.281	.376
	12-13WasA 14IndF 15NwkF																				
Lapp, Jack-John Walker	08-15PhiA 16ChiA	9-10-84	Frazer, Pa.	2- 6-20	L	R	5'8	185	565	1581	168	416	59	26	5	166	177		16	.263	.343
Larkin, Ed-Edward Francis	09PhiA	7- 1-85	Wyalusing, Pa.	3-28-34	R	R			2	6	0	1	0	0	0	1	1		0	.167	.167
Larmore, Bob-Robert McCahan (Red)	18StLN	12- 6-96	Anderson, Ind.	1-15-64	R	R	5'10	185	4	7	0	2	0	0	0	1	0	2	0	.286	.286
LaRoss, Harry-Harry Raymond (Spike)	14CinN	1- 2-91	Easton, Pa.	-54	R	R	5'11	170	22	48	7	11	1	0	0	5	2	10	4	.229	.250
Latham, Arlie-Walter Arlington (The Freshest Man on Earth)	80BufN 83-89StLAA 90ChiP	3-15-60	West Lebanon, N.H.	11-29-52	R	R	5'8	150	1621	6815	1470	1851	249	86	27	641	589		791	.272	.345
	90-95CinN 96,M96StLN 99WasN 09NYN												For Latham, Stolen Bases include the years, 86-09								
Lathers, Chick-Charles Ten Eyck	10-11DetA	10-22-88	Detroit, Mich.	7-26-71	L	R	6'	180	70	127	9	29	3	0	0	7	13		0	.228	.252
Latimer, Tacks-Clifford Wesley	98NYN 99LouN 00PitN 01BalA 02BknN	11-30-77	Loveland, Ohio	4-24-36		R			27	86	5	19	3	0	0	7	2		1	.221	.256
Lauder, Billy-William	98-99PhiN 01PhiA 02-03NYN	2-23-74	New York, N.Y.	5-20-33	R	R	5'10	160	481	1823	207	476	64	14	6	254	77		60	.261	.321
Lauterborn, Bill-William Bernard	04-05BosN	6- 9-79	Hornell, N.Y.	4-19-65	R	R	5'6	140	87	269	18	56	3	1	0	11	13		2	.208	.227
Lavan, Doc-John Leonard	13StLA 13PhiA 14-17StLA 18WasA 19-24StLN	10-28-90	Grand Rapids, Mich.	5-30-52	R	R	5'8	151	1162	3891	338	954	134	45	7	377	209	376	71	.245	.308
LaVigne, Art-Arthur David	14BufF	1-26-85	Worcester, Mass.	7-18-50	R	R	5'10	162	51	90	10	14	2	0	0	4	7		0	.156	.178
Lawry, Otis-Otis Carroll (Rabbit)	16-17PhiA 18-19MS	11- 1-93	Fairfield, Me.	10-23-65	L	R	5'8	133	71	178	17	34	1	0	0	5	11	30	5	.191	.197
Layden, Gene-Eugene Francis	15NYA	3-14-94	Pittsburgh, Pa.		L	L	5'10	160	3	7	2	2	0	0	0	0	0	1	0	.286	.286
Leach, Tommy-Thomas William (Tommy the Wee)	98-99LouN 00-12PitN 12-14ChiN	11- 4-77	French Creek, N.Y.	9-29-69	R	R	5'6	150	2147	7954	1352	2144	277	170	62	810	820		364	.270	.371
	15CinN 18PitN																				
Leahy, Tom-Thomas Joseph	97PitN 97-98WasN 09MilA 01PhiA 05StLN	6- 2-69	New Haven, Conn.	6-12-51		R			131	411	55	106	15	10	0	42	44		17	.258	.343
Lear, Fred-Frederick Francis (King)	15PhiA 18-19ChiN 20NYN	4- 7-94	New York, N.Y.	10-13-55	R	R			75	166	20	39	3	2	2	18	17	28	2	.235	.313
Leard, Bill-William Wallace (Wild Bill)	17BknN	10-14-85	Oneida, N.Y.	1-15-70	R	R	5'10	155	3	3	0	0	0	0	0	0	0	1	0	.000	.000
Leary, John-John Louis (Jack)	14-15StLA	5- 2-91	Waltham, Mass.	8-18-61	R	R	5'11	180	219	760	54	196	38	7	0	60	15	107	11	.258	.326
Leber, Emil-Emil Bohmiel	05CleA	5-15-81	Cleveland, Ohio	11- 6-24	R	R	5'11	170	2	6	1	0	0	0	0	0	1		0	.000	.000
Lee, Bill-William Joseph	15-16StLA	1- 9-95	Bayonne, N.J.		R	R	5'9	165	25	70	3	13	1	0	0	4	7	6	1	.186	.200
Lee, Watty-Wyatt Arnold (See P01-19)	01-03WasA 04PitN	8-12-79	Lynch's Station, Va.	3- 6-36	L	L	5'10	170	235	763	94	185	35	13	4	70	58		13	.242	.338
Lehr, Clarence-Clarence Emanuel (King)	11PhiN	5-16-86	Escanaba, Mich.	1-31-48	R	R	5'11	165	23	27	2	4	0	0	0	2	0	7	0	.148	.148
Leibold, Nemo-Harry Loran	13-15CleA 15-20ChiA 21-23BosA 23-25WasA	2-17-92	Butler, Ind.		L	R	5'6	157	1258	4167	638	1109	145	48	4	283	571	335	133	.266	.327
Leinhauser, Bill-William Charles	12DetA	11- 4-93	Philadelphia, Pa.		R	R	5'10	150	1	4	0	0	0	0	0	0	0		0	.000	.000
LeJeune, Larry-Sheldon Aldenbert	11BknN 15PitN	7-22-85	Chicago, Ill.	4-21-52	R	R	6'	185	24	84	6	14	0	1	0	4	4	15	6	.167	.190
Lelivelt, Jack-John Frank	09-11WasA 12-13NYA 13-14CleA	11-14-85	Chicago, Ill.	1-20-41	L	L	5'11	175	381	1154	114	347	43	22	2	126	89		46	.301	.381
Lennox, Ed-James Edgar (Eggie)	06PhiA 09-10BknN 12ChiN 14-15PitF	11- 3-85	Camden, N.J.	10-26-39	R	R	5'10	174	448	1383	138	379	70	25	18	185	174		38	.274	.400
Leonard, Joe-Joseph Howard	14PitN 16CleA 16-17WasA 18MS 19-20WasA	11-15-94	West Chicago, Ill.	5- 1-20	L	R	5'7	156	269	791	94	179	23	12	2	61	99	113	17	.226	.293
Lepine, Pete-Louis Joseph	02DetA	9- 5-76	Montreal, Canada	12- 3-49	L	L			30	96	8	20	3	2	1	19	8		1	.208	.313
Lerchen, Dutch-Bertram Roe	10BosA	4- 4-89	Detroit, Mich.	1- 7-62	R	R	5'9	165	6	15	1	0	0	0	0	0	1		0	.000	.000
Lewis, Duffy-George Edward	10-17BosA 18MS 19-20NYA 21WasA	4-18-88	San Francisco, Cal.		R	R	5'10	165	1459	5351	612	1518	289	68	38	793	352		113	.284	.384
Lewis, John-John D.	11BosA 14-15PitF	-88	Pittsburgh, Pa.		R	R	5'8	158	217	684	63	169	20	10	1	80	32		18	.247	.310
Lewis, Phil-Philip	05-08BknN	10- 7-83	Pittsburgh, Pa.	8- 8-59	R	R	6'	195	508	1775	146	429	33	13	4	130	95		55	.242	.282
Liese, Fred-Frederick Richard	10BosN	10- 7-85	Wis.	6-30-67					5	4	0	0	0	0	0	0	1	2	0	.000	.000
Lindermann, Bob-Robert J.	01PhiA		Chester, Pa.		R	R			3	9	0	1	0	0	0	0	0		0	.111	.111
Lindsay, Bill-William Gibbons	11CleA	2-24-81	Madison, N.C.	7-14-63	L	R	5'10	165	19	66	6	16	2	0	0	5	1		2	.242	.273
Lindsay, Pinky-Christian H.	05-06DetA	7-21-78	Monaca, Pa.	1-25-41					229	828	97	200	30	3	0	64	63		28	.242	.285
Lister, Pete-Morris Elmer	07CleA	7-21-81	Savanna, Ill.	5-12-48					22	65	5	18	2	0	0	4	3		2	.277	.308
Little, Jack-William Arthur	12NYA	3-12-91	Mart, Tex.	7-27-61	R	R	5'11	175	3	12	2	3	0	0	0	0	1		2	.250	.250
Livingston, Paddy-Patrick Joseph	01CleA 06CinN 09-11PhiA 12CleA 17StLN	1-14-80	Cleveland, Ohio		R	R	5'8	197	205	574	48	120	17	12	0	45	41		9	.209	.280
Loan, Mike-William Joseph	12PhiN	9-27-94	Philadelphia, Pa.	11-21-66	R	R	5'11	185	1	2	1	1	0	0	0	0	0	0	0	.500	.500
Lobert, Frank-Frank John	14BalF	11-26-83	Williamsport, Pa.	5-29-32	R	R	6'	180	11	30	3	6	0	1	0	2	0		0	.200	.267
Lobert, Hans-John Bernard	03PitN 05ChiN 06-10ChiN 11-14PhiN 15-17NYN M38,42PhiN	10-18-81	Wilmington, Del.	9-14-68	R	R	5'9	170	1317	4563	640	1252	159	82	32	482	395		316	.274	.366
Lockhead, Harry-Harry P.	99CleN 01DetA 01PhiA		Cal.	Deceased		R			156	585	56	127	8	1	1	45	24		21	.217	.239
Lohr, Howard-Howard Sylvester	14CinN 16CleA	6- 3-92	Philadelphia, Pa.		R	R	6'	165	21	54	6	11	1	1	0	8	0	9	3	.204	.259
Lonergan, Walt-Walter E.	11BosA	9-22-85	Boston, Mass.	1-23-58	R	R	5'7	156	10	26	2	7	0	0	0	1	1		1	.269	.269
Long, Herman-Herman C. (Germany)	89KCAA 90-02BosN 03NYA 03DetA 04PhiN	4-13-66	Chicago, Ill.	9-17-09	L	R	5'8	160	1870	7657	1458	2142	317	98	92	1056	612		554	.280	.383
Long, Tommy-Thomas Augustus	11-12WasA 15-17StLN	6- 1-90	Mitchum, Ala.	6-15-72	R	R	5'10	165	418	1489	148	401	47	49	6	140	79		65	.269	.379
Lord, Bris-Bristol Robotham	05-07PhiA 09-10CleA 10-12PhiA 13BosN	9-21-83	Upland, Pa.	11-13-64	R	R	5'9	185	741	2767	379	707	119	49	13	236	175		74	.256	.348
Lord, Harry-Harry Donald	07-10BosA 10-14ChiA 15,M15BufF	3- 8-82	Porter, Me.	8- 9-48	L	R	5'10	165	972	3689	505	1024	107	70	14	294	226		206	.278	.356
Louden, Baldy-William	07NYA 12-13DetA 14-15BufF 16CinN	8-27-83	Pittsburgh, Pa.	12- 8-35	R	R	5'11	175	598	1942	267	507	61	22	12	202	254		112	.261	.334
Loudenslager, Charlie-Charles Edward	04BknN	5-21-81	Baltimore, Md.	10-31-33		R	5'9	186	1	2	0	0	0	0	0	0	0		0	.000	.000
Low, Fletcher-Fletcher	15BosN	4- 7-93	Essex, Mass.	6- 6-73	R	R	5'10	175	1	4	1	1	0	1	0	1	0	0	0	.250	.750
Lowe, Bobby-Robert Lincoln (Link)	90-01BosN 02-03ChiN 04PitN 04-07,M04DetA	7-10-68	Pittsburgh, Pa.	12- 8-51	R	R	5'10	150	1814	7020	1129	1925	230	85	71	982	473		310	.274	.362
Luderus, Fred-Frederick William	09-10ChiN 10-20PhiN	9-12-85	Milwaukee, Wis.	1- 4-61	L	R	5'11	185	1346	4851	570	1344	251	54	84	642	414		55	.277	.403
Ludwig, Bill-William Lawrence	08StLN	5-27-82	Louisville, Ky.	9- 5-47	R	R			66	187	15	34	2	2	0	8	16		3	.182	.214
Lumley, Harry-Harry G. (Judge)	04-10,M09BknN	9-29-80	Forest City, Pa.	5-22-38	L	R	5'10	183	730	2653	300	728	109	66	38	305	204		110	.274	.408
Lunte, Harry-Harry August	19-20CleA	9-15-92	St. Louis, Mo.	7-27-65	R	R	5'11	165	49	148	8	29	2	0	0	9	6	13	0	.196	.209
Lush, Billy-William Lucas	95-97WasN 01-02BosN 03DetA 04CleA	11-10-73	Bridgeport, Conn.	8-28-51	B	R	5'8	165	497	1717	291	427	49	35	8	152	291		79	.249	.332
Lush, Ernie-Ernest Benjamin	10StLN	10-31-84	Bridgeport, Conn.	2-26-37		L			1	4	0	0	0	0	0	0	1	1	0	.000	.000
Lush, Johnny-John Charles (See P01-19)	04-07PhiN 07-10StLN	10- 8-85	Williamsport, Pa.	11-18-46	L	L	5'9	165	369	993	107	252	40	11	2	94	69		28	.254	.322
Luskey, Charlie-Charles Melton	01WasA	4- 6-76	Washington, D.C.	12-20-62	R	R	5'7	165	11	41	8	8	3	1	0	3	2		0	.195	.317
Lynch, Mike-Michael Joseph	02ChiN	9-10-76	St. Paul, Minn.	4- 2-47					7	28	4	4	0	0	0	0	2		0	.143	.143
Lynn, Byrd,-Byrd	16-20ChiA	3-13-89	Unionville, Ill.	2- 5-40	R	R	5'11	165	116	211	15	50	9	1	0	15	18	31	3	.237	.289
Mack (McGillicuddy), Earle-Earle Thaddeus	10-11,14PhiA	2- 1-90	Philadelphia, Pa.	2- 5-67	L	R	5'8	140	5	16	0	2	0	1	0	1	0		1	.125	.250
Madden	14PitF		Pittsburgh, Pa.						2	2	0	1	0	0	0	0	1		0	.500	.500
Madden, Bunny-Thomas J.	06BosN 10NYA	-84			L	L			5	16	1	4	0	0	0	0	1		0	.250	.250
Madden, Gene-Eugene	16PitN	6- 5-90	Elm Grove, W.Va.	4- 6-49	L	R	5'10	155	1	1	0	0	0	0	0	0	0	0	0	.000	.000
Madden, Tom-Thomas Francis	09-11BosA 11PhiN	9-14-82	Boston, Mass.	1-20-54	R	R	5'10	190	56	143	10	41	4	1	0	11	13		0	.287	.327
Magee (Hoernschemeyer), Lee-Leopold Christopher	11-14StLN 15,M15BknF	6- 4-89	Cincinnati, Ohio	3-14-66	B	R	5'11	165	1014	3739	467	1029	133	54	12	277	265		186	.275	.349
	16-17NYA 17StLA 18CinN 19BknN 19ChiN 20DL																				
Magee, Sherry-Sherwood Robert	04-14PhiN 15-17BosN 17-19CinN	8- 6-84	Clarendon, Pa.	3-13-29	R	R	5'11	180	2085	7441	1113	2169	425	166	83	1177	737		441	.291	.427
Maggert, Harl-Harl Vess	07PitN 12PhiA	2-13-83	Cromwell, Ind.	1- 7-63	L	R	5'8	155	75	248	40	62	8	6	1	13	38		11	.250	.343
Magner, Stubby-Edmund Burke	11NYA	2-20-88	Kalamazoo, Mich.	9- 6-56	R	R	5'3	135	13	33	3	7	0	0	0	4	4		1	.212	.212
Magoon, Maggie-George Henry (Topsy)	98BknN 99BalN 99ChiN 01-03CinN 03ChiA	3-27-75	St. Albans, Me.	12- 6-43	R	R	5'9	165	521	1836	197	441	60	16	2	201	194		49	.240	.294
Maharg, Bill-William	12DetA 16PhiN	3-19-87	Philadelphia, Pa.			R			2	2	0	0	0	0	0	0	0		0	.000	.000
Maher, Frank-Frank	02PhiN		Philadelphia, Pa.			R			1	0	0	0	0	0	0	0	0	0	0	–	–
Maher, Tom-Thomas	02PhiN		Philadelphia, Pa.						2	1	0	0	0	0	0	0	0		0	.000	.000
Mahoney, Danny-Daniel Joseph	11CinN	9- 6-88	Haverhill, Mass.	9-28-60	R	R	5'6	145	1	0	0	0	0	0	0	0	0	0	0	–	–
Maisel, Charlie-Charles Louis	15BalF	4-21-94	Catonsville, Md.	8-25-53	R	R	6'		1	4	0	0	0	0	0	0	0		0	.000	.000
Maisel, Fritz-Frederick Charles (Flash)	13-17NYA 18StLA	12-23-89	Catonsville, Md.	4-22-67	R	R	5'7	170	591	2111	295	510	56	24	6	148	260	177	194	.242	.299
Malay, Charlie-Charles Francis	05BknN	6-13-79	Brooklyn, N.Y.	9-18-49	B	R	5'11	175	102	349	33	88	7	2	1	31	22		13	.252	.292

USE NAME – GIVEN NAMES (NICKNAMES)	TEAM BY YEAR	BIRTH DATE	BIRTH PLACE	DEATH DATE	B	T	HGT	WGT	G	AB	R	H	2B	3B	HR	RBI	BB	SO	SB	BA	SA
					LIFETIME BATTING TOTALS																
Malone, Lew-Lewis Aloysius	15-16PhiA 17BknN 18MS 19BknN	3-13-97	Baltimore, Md.	2-17-72	R	R	5'11	175	133	367	28	74	11	7	1	28	28	60	8	.202	.278
Maloney, Bill-William Alphonse	01MilA 02StLA 02CinN 05ChiN 06-08BknN	6- 5-78	Lewiston, Me.	9- 2-60	L	R	5'10	177	696	2476	294	585	54	42	6	177	162		155	.236	.299
Maloney, Pat-Patrick William	12NYA	1-19-88	Grosvenordale, Conn.		R	R	6'	150	22	79	9	17	1	0	0	4	6		3	.215	.228
Manda, Carl-Carl Alan	14ChiA	11-16-86	Little River, Kans.		R	R	5'10	170	9	15	2	4	0	0	0	1	3	3	1	.267	.267
Mangus, George-George Graham	12PhiN	5-22-90	Red Creek, N.Y.	8-10-33	L	R	5'11	165	10	25	2	5	3	0	0	3	1	6	0	.200	.320
Mann, Les-Leslie	13-14BosN 15ChiF 16-19ChiN 19-20BosN 21-23StLN 23CinN	11-18-93	Lincoln, Neb.	1-14-62	R	R	5'9	172	1498	4714	678	1331	205	106	44	503	324		192	.282	.399
	24-27BosN 27-28NYN																				
Manush, Frank-Frank Benjamin	08PhiA	9-18-83	Tuscumbia, Ala.	1- 5-65	R	R	5'10	175	23	77	6	12	2	1	0	0	2		2	.156	.208
Marsans, Armando-Armando	11-14CinN 14-15StLF 16-17StLA 17-18NYA	10- 3-86	Matanzas, Cuba	9- 3-60	R	R	5'10	157	655	2273	267	612	67	19	2	221	173		171	.269	.318
Marshall, Doc-William Riddle	04PhiN 04NYN 04BosN 04,06NYN 06-08StLN	9-22-75	Butler, Pa.	12-11-59	R	R	6'1	185	261	756	51	159	23	8	2	54	34		15	.210	.270
	08ChiN 09BknN																				
Marshall, Joe-Joseph H.	03PitN 06StLN		Troy, N.Y.	-32					43	118	4	21	2	4	0	9	6		0	.178	.263
Martel, Marty-Leon Alphonse (Doc)	09PhiN 10BosN	1-29-83	Weymouth, Mass.	10-11-47	R	R	6'	185	34	72	1	15	3	1	0	8	6		0	.208	.278
Martin, Billy-William Lloyd	14BosN	2-13-94	Washington, D.C.	9-14-49	R	R	5'8	170	1	3	0	0	0	0	0	0	0	0	0	.000	.000
Martin, Jack-John Christopher	12NYA 14BosN 14PhiN	4-19-87	Plainfield, N.J.		R	R	5'7	150	185	608	66	144	13	4	0	43	70		20	.237	.271
Martin, Joe-Joseph Samuel (Silent Joe)	03WasA 03StLA	1- 1-76	Hollidaysburg, Pa.	5-25-64	L	R	5'9	155	79	292	29	64	10	9	0	14	11		2	.219	.315
Massey, Mike-William Herbert	17BosN	9-28-93	Galveston, Tex.	10-17-71	B	R	5'11	168	31	91	12	18	0	0	0	2	15	15	2	.198	.198
Massey, Roy-Roy Hardee (Red)	18BosN	10- 9-90	Sevierville, Tenn.	6-23-54	L	R	5'11	170	66	203	20	59	6	2	0	18	23	20	1	.291	.340
Mathes, Joe-Joseph John	12PhiA 14StLF 16BosN	7-28-91	Milwaukee, Wis.		B	R	6'	180	32	99	10	27	3	0	0	6	9		1	.273	.303
Mathison, I.I.-I.I.	02BalA		Baltimore, Md.			R			29	91	12	24	2	1	0	7	9		2	.264	.308
Mattick, Chick-Walter Joseph	12-13ChiA 18StLN	3-12-87	St. Louis, Mo.	11- 5-68	R	R	5'10	180	164	506	60	115	15	10	1	47	47		18	.227	.302
Mattis, Ralph-Ralph (Matty)	14PitF	8-24-90	Roxborough, Pa.	9-13-60	R	R	5'11	172	36	85	14	21	4	1	0	8	9		2	.247	.318
Maul, Al-Albert Joseph (Smiling Al) (See P01-19)	84PhiU 07PhiN 88 89PitN	10- 9-65	Philadelphia, Pa.	5- 3-58	R	R	6'	175	401	1350	191	328	44	30	7	179	182		46	.243	.336
	90PitP 91PitN 93-97WasN 97-98BalN 99BknN 00PhiN 01NYN																				
Mayer (Erskine), Sam-Samuel Frankel (Craven)	15WasA	2-28-93	Atlanta, Ga.	7- 1-62	R	L	5'8	155	11	29	3	7	0	0	1	4	4	2	1	.241	.345
Mayer, Wally-Walter A. (Kid)	11-12,14-15ChiA 17-18BosA 19StLA	8- 3-89	Cincinnati, Ohio	11-18-51	R	R	5'11	168	129	274	22	53	14	3	0	20	42		1	.100	[illegible]
Mayes, Paddy-Adair Bushyhead	11PhiN	3-17-85	Locust Grove, Okla.	5-28-62	L	R	5'11	160	5	5	1	0	0	0	0	0	1	2	0	.000	.000
McAleer, Jimmy-James Robert	89CleN 90CleP 91-98CleN 01,M01CleA	7-10-64	Youngstown, Ohio	4-29-31	R	R	6'	175	1017	3972	614	1031	114	38	13	469	365		262	.260	.317
	02,07,M02-09StLA M10-11WasA																				
McAleese, John-John James (See P01-19)	01ChiA 09StLA	8-22-78	Sharon, Pa.	11-14-50		R			86	268	33	57	7	0	0	12	32		18	.213	.239
McAllester, Bill-William Lusk	13StLA	12-29-89	Chattanooga, Tenn.	3- 3-70	R	R	5'11	170	47	85	3	13	4	0	0	6	11	12	2	.153	.200
McAllister, Sport-Lewis William (See P01-19)	96-99CleN 01-02DetA 02BalA	7-23-74	Austin, Miss.	7-17-62	B	R	5'11	180	416	1441	154	357	35	18	5	164	67		33	.248	.307
	02-03DetA																				
McAuley, Ike-James Earl	14-16PitN 17StLN 25ChiN	8-19-93	Wichita, Kans.	4- 6-28	R	R	5'9	150	64	179	14	44	8	2	0	13	11	28	1	.246	.313
McAuliffe, Gene-Eugene Leo	04BosN	2-28-72	Randolph, Mass.	4-29-53	R	R	6'1	180	1	2	0	1	0	0	0	0	0		0	.500	.500
McAvoy, George-George H.	14PhiN								1	1	0	0	0	0	0	0	0	0	0	.000	.000
McAvoy, Wickey-James Eugene	13-15,17-19PhiA	10-20-94	Rochester, N.Y.	-73	R	R	5'11	172	235	674	38	134	18	8	1	53	38	87	6	.199	.254
McBride, Algie-Algernon Briggs	96ChiN 98-01CinN 01NYN	5-23-69	Martinsville, Ind.	1-10-56	L	L	5'9	152	401	1581	256	463	58	26	12	179	132		37	.293	.385
McBride, George-George Florian	01MilA 05PitN 05-06StLN 08-20,M21WasA	11-20-80	Milwaukee, Wis.	7- 2-73	R	R	5'11	170	1656	5518	516	1201	140	47	7	447	419		133	.218	.264
McCabe, Bill-William Francis	18-20ChiN 20BknN	10-28-94	Chicago, Ill.		B	R	5'9	180	106	199	28	32	3	2	0	13	15	28	6	.161	.196
McCabe, Swat-James Arthur	09-10CinN	11-20-81	Towanda, Pa.	12- 9-44	L		5'10		16	46	5	15	2	0	0	5	1		1	.326	.370
McCandless, John-John C.	14-15BalF	-95	Pittsburgh, Pa.		L	R	6'	170	128	437	52	95	6	8	5	35	44		9	.217	.302
McCarthy, Alex-Alexander George	10-15PitN 15-16ChiN 16-17PitN	5-12-88	Chicago, Ill.		R	R	5'9	150	432	1335	136	306	34	11	5	122	104	133	23	.229	.282
McCarthy, Bill-William John	05BosN 07CinN		Boston, Mass.			R			4	11	1	1	0	0	0	0	0		0	.091	.091
McCarthy, Jack-John A.	93-94CinN 98-99PitN 00ChiN 01-03CleA 03-05ChiN 06-07BknN	3-26-69	Gilbertville, Mass.	9-11-31	L	L	5'9	155	1091	4196	549	1206	169	68	8	475	268		152	.287	.366
McCarthy, Joe-Joseph N.	05NYA 06StLN	12-25-81	Syracuse, N.Y.	1-12-37	R	R			16	39	3	9	2	0	0	2	2		0	.231	.282
McCarty, Lew-George Lewis	13-16BknN 16-20NYN 20-21StLN	11-17-88	Milton, Pa.	6- 9-30	R	R	5'11	192	532	1479	113	393	47	20	5	137	102	107	20	.266	.335
McCauley, Pat-Patrick M.	93StLN 96WasN 03NYA	6-10-70	Ware, Mass.	1-23-17		R			37	119	14	23	3	0	2	12	7		3	.193	.269
McChesney, Harry-Harry Vincent (Pud)	04ChiN	6- 1-80	Pittsburgh, Pa.	8-11-60	R	R	5'9	165	22	88	9	23	6	2	0	11	4		2	.261	.375
McCleskey, Jeff-Jefferson Lamar	13BosN	-92	Americus, Ga.	-71	L	R	5'11	160	2	3	0	0	0	0	0	0	1	0	0	.000	.000
McClure, Hal-Harold Murray (Mac)	10NYA	10- 3-85	Wayne, W.Va.	8-31-49	R	R	5'6	130	1	1	0	0	0	0	0	0	0		0	.000	.000
McConnell, Amby-Ambrose Moses	08-10BosA 10-11ChiA	4-29-83	North Pownal, Vt.	5-20-42	L	R	5'7	150	409	1506	200	398	30	22	3	119	107		72	.264	.319
McConnell, Sam-Samuel Faulkner	15PhiA	6- 8-95	Philadelphia, Pa.		L	R	5'6	150	6	11	1	2	1	0	0	0	1	3	0	.182	.273
McCormick, Barry-William J.	95LouN 96-01ChiN 02-03StLA 03-04WasA	12-25-74	Cincinnati, Ohio	1-28-56		R			987	3637	432	865	112	43	15	417	280		136	.238	.305
McCormick, Dude-Michael J.	04BknN	-83	Jersey City, N.J.	11-19-53	R	R			105	347	28	64	5	4	0	27	43		22	.184	.222
McCormick, Moose-Harry Elwood	04NYN 04PitN 08PhiN 08-09,12-13NYN	2-28-81	Philadelphia, Pa.	7- 9-62	L	L	5'11	180	418	1247	165	356	62	26	6	133	92		30	.285	.391
McCredie, Judge-Walter Henry	03BknN	11-29-76	Manchester, Iowa	7-29-34	L	R	6'2	195	56	213	40	69	5	0	0	20	24		10	.324	.347
McCreery, Tom-Thomas Livingston	97-97LouN 97-98NYN 98-00PitN 01-03BknN 03BosN	10-19-74	Beaver, Pa.	7- 3-41	B	R	5'11	180	796	2965	468	859	100	77	26	387	308		118	.290	.402
McDermott, Red-Frank A. (Irish)	12DetA	11-12-89	Philadelphia, Pa.	9-11-64	R	R	5'6	150	5	15	2	4	1	0	0	0	0		1	.267	.333
McDonald, Ed-Edward C.	11-12BosN 13ChiN	10-28-86	Albany, N.Y.	3-11-46	R	R	6'	180	176	634	98	155	30	9	3	55	110	130	33	.244	.334
McDonald, Jim-James	02NYN		Philadelphia, Pa.						2	9	0	3	0	0	0	1	0		0	.333	.333
McDonald, Mal-Joseph Malcolm	10StLA				R	R	5'11	175	10	32	4	5	0	0	0	1	1		0	.156	.156
McDonald (Crabtree), Tex-Charles C.	12-13CinN 13BosN 14PitF 14-15BufF	1-31-89	Farmersville, Tex.	3-31-43	L	R	5'10	160	357	1019	131	304	45	27	13	135	88		34	.298	.434
McDonough, Ed-Edward	09-10 PhiN	9-13-86	Elgin, Ill.	9- 2-26		R			6	10	1	1	0	0	0	0	0	1	0	.100	.100
McElveen, Pryor-Pryor Mynatt (Humpy)	09-11BknN	11- 5-83	Atlanta, Ga.	10-27-51	R	R	5'10	168	171	502	42	105	16	4	4	56	36		12	.209	.281
McElwee, Lee-Leland Stanford	16PhiA	5-23-94	La Mesa, Cal.	2- 8-57	R	R	5'10	160	54	155	9	41	3	0	0	10	8	17	0	.265	.284
McFarland, Ed-Edward William	93CleN 96-97StLN 97-01PhiN 02-07ChiA 08BosA	8- 3-74	Cleveland, Ohio	11-28-59	R	R	5'10	180	886	3001	396	819	147	50	13	384	254		72	.273	.368
McFarland, Herm-Hermas Walter	96LouN 98CinN 01-02ChiA 02BalA 03NYA	3-11-70	Des Moines, Iowa	9-21-35	L	R			348	1266	202	338	61	28	13	167	175		66	.267	.390
McGaffigan, Patsy-Mark Andrew	17-18PhiN	9-12-88	Carlyle, Ill.	12-22-40	R	R	5'8	140	73	252	22	49	4	2	1	14	16	30	4	.194	.238
McGamwell, Ed-Edward M.	05BknN	1-10-78	Buffalo, N.Y.	11- 1-50					4	16	0	4	0	0	0	0	1		0	.250	.250
McGann, Dan-Dennis Lawrence	95LouN 96BosN 98BalN 99BknN 99WasN 00-01StLN	7-15-71	Shelbyville, Ky.	12-13-10	B	R	5'9	190	1456	5300	853	1512	188	102	42	736	437		288	.285	.383
	02BalA 02-07NYN 08BosN																				
McGarr, Jim-James Vincent (Reds)	12DetA	11- 9-88	Philadelphia, Pa.				5'9	170	1	4	0	0	0	0	0	0	0		0	.000	.000
McGarvey, Dan-Daniel	12DetA								1	3	0	0	0	0	0	0	1		0	.000	.000
McGeehan, Dan-Daniel DeSales	11StLN	6- 7-85	Jeddo, Pa.	7-12-55	R	R	5'6	135	3	9	0	2	0	0	0	1	0	1	0	.222	.222
McGilvray, Bill-William Alexander (Big Bill)	08CinN	4-29-83	Portland, Ore.	5-23-52	L	L	6'	160	2	2	0	0	0	0	0	0	0		0	.000	.000
McGovern, Art-Arthur John	05BosA	2-27-82	St. John, Canada	11-14-15	R	R		160	15	44	1	5	1	0	0	1	4		0	.114	.136
McGraw, John-John Joseph (Muggsy, Little Napoleon)	91BalAA 92-99,M99BalN	4- 7-73	Truxton, N.Y.	2-25-34	L	R	5'7	155	1093	3928	1021	1312	124	72	13	462	836		441	.334	.412
	00StLN 01-02,M01-02BalA 02-06,M02-32NYN																				
McGuire, Deacon-James Thomas	84TolAA 85DetN 86-88PhiN 88DetN 88CleAA	11- 2-65	Youngstown, Ohio	10-31-36	B	R	6'1	185	1777	6239	770	1737	298	75	45	850	515		137	.278	.372
	90RocAA 91WasAA 92-99,M98WasN 99-01BknN 02-03DetA 04-07NYA																				
	07-08,M07-08BosA 08,10,M09-11CleA 12DetA																				
McGuire, Jim-James A.	01CleA	2- 4-75	Dunkirk, N.Y.	1-26-17		R			18	69	4	16	2	0	0	3	0		0	.232	.261
McHale, Jim-James Bernard	08BosA	12-17-75	Miners Mills, Pa.	6-18-59																	
McIlveen, Irish-Henry Cooke (See P01-19)	06PitN 08-09NYA	7-27-80	Belfast, Ireland	10-18-60	L	L	5'11	180	53	177	18	38	3	3	0	8	15		6	.215	.266
McInnis, Stuffy-John Phalen (Jack)	09-17PhiA 18-21BosA 22CleA 23-24BosN	9-19-90	Gloucester, Mass.	2-16-60	R	R	5'9	162	2128	7822	872	2406	312	101	20	1060	380		172	.308	.381
	25-26PitN 27,M27PhiN																				
McIntyre, Matty-Matthew W.	01PhiA 04-10DetA 11-12ChiA	6-12-80	Stonington, Conn.	4- 2-20	L	L	5'11	175	1068	3958	562	1066	140	69	4	319	439		120	.269	.343
McIver, Otto-Edward Otto	11StLN	7-26-84	Greenville, Tex.	5- 4-54	B	L	5'11	175	30	62	11	14	2	1	1	9	9	14	0	.226	.339
McKechnie, Bill-William Boyd (Deacon)	07,10-12PitN 13BosN 13NYA 14IndF	8- 7-86	Wilkinsburg, Pa.	10-29-65	B	R	5'10	160	844	2841	319	716	84	33	8	240	188		127	.252	.313
	15,M15NwkF 16NYN 16-17CinN 18PitN 19VR 20,M22-26PitN M28-29StLN																				
	M30-37BosN M38-46CinN																				
McKee, Red-Ray	13-16DetA	7-20-90	Shawnee, Ohio	8- 5-72	L	R	5'11	180	186	433	38	110	10	7	2	49	54	64	9	.254	.323
McKinney, Bob-Robert Francis	01PhiA	10- 4-75	McSherrystown, Pa.	8-19-46					2	2	0	0	0	0	0	0	0		0	.000	.000
McLane, Ed-Edward Cameron	07BknN	8-20-81	Weston, Mass.						1	2	0	0	0	0	0	0	0		0	.000	.000
McLarry, Polly-Howard Zell	12ChiA 15ChiN	3-25-91	Leonard, Tex.	11- 4-71	L	R	6'	185	70	129	16	25	3	0	1	12	14		2	.194	.240
McLaughlin, Kid-James Anson (Sunshine)	14CinN	4-12-88	Randolph, N.Y.	11-17-34	L	R	5'9	158	3	2	1	0	0	0	0	0	0	0	0	.000	.000
McLaurin, Ralph-Ralph Edgar	08StLN	5-23-85	Kissimmee, Fla.	2-11-43					8	22	2	5	0	0	0	0	0		0	.227	.227
McLean, Larry-John Bannerman	01BosA 03ChiN 04StLN 06-12CinN 13StLN 13-15NYN	7-18-81	Cambridge, Mass.	3-14-21	R	R	6'5	228	862	2647	183	694	90	26	6	298	136		20	.262	.323
McManus, Frank-Francis E.	99WasN 03BknN 04DetA 04NYA	9-21-75	Lawrence, Mass.	9- 1-23		R			14	35	3	8	1	0	0	2	2		3	.229	.257
McMillian, Tommy-Thomas Law (Rebel)	08-10BknN 10CinN 12NYA	4-17-88	Pittston, Pa.	7-15-66	R	R	5'5	130	297	991	73	207	21	4	0	54	81		45	.209	.238

For D. McGuire, Stolen Bases include the years, 86-12

USE NAME – GIVEN NAMES (NICKNAMES)	TEAM BY YEAR	BIRTH DATE	BIRTH PLACE	DEATH DATE	B	T	HGT	WGT	G	AB	R	H	2B	3B	HR	RBI	BB	SO	SB	BA	SA
					LIFETIME BATTING TOTALS																
McMullin, Fred-Frederick William	14DetA 16-20ChiA 20DL	10-13-91	Scammon, Kans.	11-21-52	R	R	5'11	170	304	914	120	234	21	9	1	70	91	105	30	.256	.302
McNeil, Norm-Norman Francis	19BosA	10-22-92	Chicago, Ill.	4-11-42	R	R	5'11	180	5	9	0	3	0	0	0	1	1	0	0	.333	.333
Meany, Pat-Patrick	12DetA	-92	Philadelphia, Pa.	10-20-22		R			1	2	0	0	0	0	0	0	1		0	.000	.000
Meara, Charlie-Charles Edward (Goggy)	14NYA	4-13-91	New York, N.Y.	2- 8-62	L	R	5'10	160	4	7	2	2	0	0	0	1	2	2	0	.286	.286
Mee, Tommy-Thomas William (Judge)	10StLA	3-18-90	Chicago, Ill.		R	R	5'8	165	8	19	1	3	2	0	0	1	0		0	.158	.263
Meier, Dutch-Arthur Ernst	06PitN	3-30-79	St. Louis, Mo.	3-23-48	R	R	5'10	175	82	273	32	70	11	4	0	16	13		4	.256	.326
Meinert, Walt-Walter Henry	13StLA	12-11-90	New York, N.Y.	11- 9-58	L	L	5'7	150	4	8	1	3	0	0	0	0	1	3	0	.375	.375
Meinke, Bob-Robert Bernard	10CinN	6 25 87	Chicago, Ill.	12-29-52	R	R	5'10	135	2	1	0	0	0	0	0	0	1	0	0	.000	.000
Meister, Karl-Karl Daniel (Dutch)	13CinN	5-15-91	Marietta, Ohio	8-15-67	R	R	6'	178	4	7	1	2	1	0	0	2	0	4	0	.286	.429
Meixell, Moxie-Merten Merrill	12CleA	10- 8-87	Lake Crystal, Minn.		L	R	5'10	168	2	2	0	1	0	0	0	0	0		0	.500	.500
Mellor, Bill-William Harpin	02BalA	6- 6-74	Camden, N.J.	11- 4-40	R	R	6'		10	36	4	13	3	0	0	5	3		1	.361	.444
Meloan, Paul-Paul B. (Molly)	10-11ChiA 11StLA	8-23-88	Paynesville, Mo.	2-11-50	L	R	5'10	175	130	431	53	109	17	8	3	38	32		11	.253	.350
Menefee, Jocko-John (See P01-19)	92PitN 93-94LouN 94-95PitN 98NYN 00-03ChiN	1-15-68	W. Va.	3-11-53	R	R	6'		219	676	74	151	15	7	0	57	52		14	.223	.266
Mensor, Eddie-Edward E. (Midget)	12-14PitN	11-22-89	Woodville, Ore.		B	R	5'6	145	127	244	43	54	6	3	1	8	53	38	14	.221	.283
Menze, Ted-Theodore Charles	18StLN	11- 4-97	St. Louis, Mo.	12-23-69	R	R	5'9	172	1	3	0	0	0	0	0	0	0	2	0	.000	.000
Mercer, Jack-John Locke (See P01-19)	10PitN 12StLN	6-22-90	Taylortown, La.		L	L	5'10	155	2	1	0	0	0	0	0	0	0	0	0	.000	.000
Mercer, Win-George Barclay (See P01-19)	94-99WasN 00NYN 01WasA 02DetA	6-20-74	Chester, W.Va.	1-12-03	R	R	5'7	140	561	1739	276	509	35	23	7	197	141		88	.293	.351
Merkle, Fred-Frederick Charles	07-16NYN 16-17BknN 17-20ChiN 25-26NYA	12-20-88	Watertown, Wis.	3- 2-56	R	R	6'1	190	1638	5782	720	1580	290	81	60	733	454		272	.273	.383
Merritt, George-George Washington (See P01-19)	01-03PitN	4-14-80	Paterson, N.J.	2-21-38		R			15	47	8	10	1	2	0	5	2		1	.213	.319
Merritt, Howard-John Howard (Lefty)	13NYN	10- 6-94	Plantersville, Miss.	11- 3-55	R	L	5'11	170	1	0	0	0	0	0	0	0	0	0	0	–	–
Mertes, Sam-Samuel Blair (Sandow)	96PhiN 98-00ChiN 01-02ChiA 03-06NYN 06StLN	8- 6-72	San Francisco, Cal.	3-11-45	R	R	5'10	185	1183	4393	696	1230	191	109	40	721	422		395	.280	.400
Messenger, Bob-Charles Walter	09-11ChiA 14StLA	3-19-84	Bangor, Me.	7-10-51	B	R	5'9	165	54	157	29	27	1	3	0	4	20		10	.172	.217
Meyer, Benny-Benjamin (Earache)	13BknN 14-15BalF 15BufF 25PhiN	1- 1-88	Hematite, Mo.	2- 6-74	R	R	5'9	170	310	1041	146	276	29	17	7	84	158		46	.265	.346
Meyer, Billy-William Adam	13ChiA 16-17PhiA M48-52PitN	1-14-92	Knoxville, Tenn.	3-31-57	R	R	5'9	170	113	301	15	71	7	3	1	21	15	25	3	.236	.289
Meyer, Lee-Lee	09BknN					R			7	23	1	3	0	0	0	0	2		0	.130	.130
Meyers, Chief-John Tortes	09-15NYN 16-17BknN 17BosN	7-29-80	Riverside, Cal.	7-25-71	R	R	5'11	194	992	2834	276	826	120	41	14	363	274		44	.291	.378
Midkiff, Ezra-Ezra Millington (Salt Rock)	09CinN 12-13NYA	11-13-82	Salt Rock, W.Va.	3-21-57	L	R	5'10	180	105	372	31	77	10	1	0	23	19		13	.207	.239
Milan, Clyde-Jesse Clyde (Deerfoot)	07-22,M22WasA	3-16-86	Linden, Tenn.	3- 3-53	L	R	5'9	168	1981	7359	1004	2099	240	105	17	617	685		494	.285	.353
Milan, Horace-Horace Robert	15,17WasA 18MS	4- 7-94	Linden, Tenn.	7- -55	R	R	5'9	175	42	100	14	32	4	2	0	16	12	16	6	.320	.400
Miller, Bill-William	02PitN		Cleveland, Ohio						1	5	0	1	0	0	0	2	0		0	.200	.200
Miller, C.-C.	12StLA					R			1	2	0	0	0	0	0	0	0		0	.000	.000
Miller, Charlie-Charles Hess	15BalF	12-30-77	Conestoga Center, Pa.	1-13-51					1	1	0	0	0	0	0	0	0		0	.000	.000
Miller, Chuck-Charles Marion	13-14StLN	9-18-89	Woodville, Ohio	6-16-61	L	L	5'7	150	40	48	4	9	1	0	0	3	3	11	2	.188	.208
Miller, Dakin-Dakin Evans	02ChiN	9- 2-77	Malvern, Iowa	4-20-50	L	R	5'10	175	51	187	17	46	4	1	0	13	7		10	.246	.278
Miller, Doc-Roy Oscar	10ChiN 10-12BosN 12-13PhiN 14CinN	-83	San Francisco, Cal.	7-30-38	L	L	5'10	170	557	1717	184	507	96	15	12	235	121	149	64	.295	.390
Miller, Dots-John Barney	09-13PitN 14-17StLN 18MS 19StLN 20-21PhiN	8- 9-86	Kearny, N.J.	9- 5-23	R	R	5'11	170	1589	5805	711	1526	232	108	32	715	391		177	.263	.357
Miller, Eddie-Edwin J.	12,14StLA 18CleA	11-24-88	Annville, Pa.		R	R	6'	180	79	200	21	39	5	4	0	12	18		4	.195	.260
Miller, Elmer-Elmer	12StLN 15-18,21-22NYA 22BosA	7-28-90	Sandusky, Ohio	11-28-44	R	R	6'	175	413	1414	170	343	43	20	16	151	113	140	29	.243	.335
Miller, Hughie-Hugh Stanley (Cotton)	11PhiN 14-15StLF	12-28-87	St. Louis, Mo.	12-24-45	R	R	6'1	175	140	496	51	112	21	5	0	49	27		4	.226	.288
Miller, Jim-James (Rabbit)	01NYN		Pittsburgh, Pa.	2- 8-37					18	58	3	8	0	0	0	3	6		1	.138	.138
Miller, Otto-Lowell Otto (Moonie)	10-22BknN	6- 1-89	Minden, Neb.	3-29-62	R	R	6'	196	927	2836	229	695	97	33	5	231	104	301	40	.245	.308
Miller, Ray-Raymond P.	17CleA 17PitN 18MS	2-12-88	Pittsburgh, Pa.	4- 7-27	L	L	5'10	168	25	48	2	8	2	0	0	2	10	6	0	.167	.208
Miller, Tom-Thomas Royall	18-19BosN	7- 5-97	Powhatan Ct. House, Va.		L	R	5'11	180	9	8	2	2	0	0	0	0	0	1	1	.250	.250
Miller, Ward-Ward Taylor (Windy)	09PitN 09-10CinN 12-13ChiN 14-15StLF 16-17StLA	7- 5-84	Mt. Carroll, Ill.	9- 4-58	L	R	5'11	177	769	2244	322	623	79	35	8	221	318		128	.278	.355
Miller, Warren-Warren W.	09,11WasA								47	85	8	16	0	0	0	1	4		0	.188	.188
Mills, Frank-Frank LeMoyne	14CleA	5-13-95	Knoxville, Ohio		L	R	6'	180	4	8	0	1	0	0	0	0	1	2	0	.125	.125
Mills, Jack-Abbott Paige	11CleA	10-23-89	S. Williamstown, Mass.	6- 3-73	L	R	6'	165	13	17	5	5	0	0	0	1	1		1	.294	.294
Mills, Rupert-Rupert Frank	15NwkF	10-12-92	Newark, N.J.	7-20-29	R	R	6'2	185	41	134	12	27	5	1	0	16	6		6	.201	.254
Misse, John-John Beverly	14StLF	5-30-85	Highland, Kans.	3-18-70	R	R	5'9	150	99	306	28	60	8	1	0	22	36		3	.196	.229
Mitchell (Yapp), Fred-Frederick Francis (See P01-19)	01-02BosA 02PhiA 03-04PhiN 04-05BknN 10NYA 13BosN M17-20ChiN M21-23BosN	6- 5-78	Cambridge, Mass.	10-13-70	R	R	5'9	185	202	572	55	120	16	7	0	52	22		8	.210	.262
Mitchell, Mike-Michael Francis	07-12CinN 13ChiN 13-14PitN 14WasA	12-12-79	Springfield, Ohio	7-16-61	R	R	6'1	185	1123	4094	514	1137	130	104	27	514	368		202	.278	.380
Mitterling, Ralph-Ralph (Sarge)	16PhiA	4-19-90	Freeburg, Pa.	1-22-56	R	R	5'10	165	13	39	1	6	0	0	0	2	3	6	0	.154	.154
Moeller, Danny-Daniel Edward	07-08PitN 12-16WasA 16CleA	3-23-85	DeWitt, Iowa	4-14-51	B	R	5'11	165	704	2538	379	618	83	43	15	192	302		171	.243	.328
Mollenkamp, Fred-Frederick Henry	14PhiN	3-15-90	Cincinnati, Ohio	11- 1-48					3	8	0	1	0	0	0	0	2	0	0	.125	.125
Mollwitz, Fritz-Frederick August (Zip)	13-14ChiN 14-16CinN 16ChiN 17-19PitN 19StLN	6-16-90	Coburg, Germany	10- 3-67	R	R	6'2	170	534	1740	138	420	50	19	1	158	83	132	70	.241	.294
Moore, Charley-Charles Welsey	12ChiN	12- 1-04	Jackson Co., Ind.	7-29-70	R	R	5'10	160	5	9	2	2	0	1	0	2	0	1	0	.222	.444
Moore, Ferdie-Ferdinand Depage	14PhiA	2-21-96	Camden, N.J.	5- 6-47					2	4	1	2	0	0	0	1	0	2	0	.500	.500
Moore, Scrappy-William Allen	17StLA	12-16-92	St. Louis, Mo.	10-13-64	R	R	5'8	153	4	8	1	1	0	0	0	0	1	0	0	.125	.125
Moran, Charley-Charles Barthell (Uncle Charley) (See P01-19)	03,08StLN	2-22-78	Nashville, Tenn.	6-14-49	R	R	5'5	180	25	77	4	17	1	2	0	3	0		1	.221	.286
Moran, Charlie-Charles Vincent	03-04WasA 04-05StLA	3-26-79	Washington, D.C.	4-11-34		R			270	970	89	201	28	6	1	50	91		20	.207	.252
Moran, Herbie-John Herbert	08PhiA 08-10BosN 12-13BknN 14CinN 14-15BosN	2-16-84	Costello, Pa.	9-21-54	L	R	5'6	150	595	2177	300	527	60	26	2	135	264		103	.242	.296
Moran, Pat-Patrick Joseph	01-05BosN 06-09ChiN 10-14,M15-18PhiN M19-23CinN	2- 7-76	Fitchburg, Mass.	3- 7-24	R	R	5'10	180	818	2634	198	618	102	24	18	262	142		55	.235	.312
Moran, Roy-Roy Ellis (Deedle)	12WasA	9-17-84	Vincennes, Ind.	7-18-66	R	R	5'8	155	5	13	1	2	0	0	0	0	8		3	.154	.154
Morgan, Ray-Raymond Caryll	11-18WasA	6-14-89	Baltimore, Md.	2-15-40	R	R	5'8	155	739	2480	278	630	90	33	4	254	320		87	.254	.322
Morgan, Red-James Edward	06BosA	10- 6-83	Council Bluffs, Iowa	Deceased		R			88	307	20	66	6	3	1	21	16		7	.215	.264
Moriarty, Bill-William Joseph	09CinN	-83	Chicago, Ill.	12-25-16	R	R	6'2	180	6	20	1	4	1	0	0	1	0		2	.200	.250
Moriarty, George-George Joseph	03-04ChiN 06-08NYA 09-15DetA 16ChiA M27-28DetA	7- 7-84	Chicago, Ill.	4- 8-64	R	R	6'	185	1071	3671	372	920	147	32	5	376	234		248	.251	.312
Morley, Bill-William M.	13WasA	-90	Staten Island, N.Y.		R	R	5'11	170	2	3	0	0	0	0	0	0	0	0	0	.000	.000
Morris, Walter-John Walter	08StLN	1-31-80	Rockwall, Tex.	8- 2-61	R	R	5'11		23	73	1	13	1	1	0	2	0		1	.178	.219
Morrissey, Jack-John Albert (King)	02-03CinN	5- 2-76	Lansing, Mich.	10-30-36	B	R	5'10	160	41	128	19	33	2	1	0	12	18		3	.258	.289
Morse, Hap-Peter Raymond	11StLN	12- 6-86	St. Paul, Minn.	6-19-74	R	R	5'8	160	4	8	0	0	0	0	0	0	1	2	0	.000	.000
Moskiman, Doc-William Bankhead	10BosA	12-20-79	Oakland, Cal.	1-11-53	R	R	6'	170	5	9	1	1	0	0	0	1	2		0	.111	.111
Moulton, Allie-Albert Theodore	11StLA	1-16-86	Medway, Mass.		R	R	5'6	155	4	15	4	1	0	0	0	1	4		0	.067	.067
Mowe, Ray-Raymond Benjamin	13BknN	7-12-89	Rochester, Ind.	8-14-68	L	R	5'7	160	5	9	0	1	0	0	0	0	0	1	0	.111	.111
Mowrey, Mike-Harry Harlan	05-09CinN 09-13StLN 14PitN 16-17BknN	4-20-84	Brown's Mill, Pa.	3-20-47	R	R	5'8	160	1275	4290	485	1099	184	53	7	461	469		167	.256	.329
Mullen, Charlie-Charles George	14-16NYA	3-15-89	Seattle, Wash.	6- 6-63	R	R	5'10	155	253	741	77	183	22	3	0	87	61		28	.247	.285
Mullin, George-George Joseph (Wabash George) (See P01-19)	02-13DetA 13WasA 14IndF 15NwkF	7- 4-80	Toledo, Ohio	1- 7-44	R	R	5'11	188	615	1531	163	401	70	23	3	137	122		10	.262	.344
Mullin, Jim-James Henry	04PhiA 04WasA 04PhiA 05WasA	10-16-83	New York, N.Y.	1-24-25	R	R	5'10	173	118	375	37	74	10	8	1	26	14		12	.197	.275
Munch, Jake-Jacob Ferdinand	18PhiA	11-16-90	Morton, Pa.	6- 8-66	L	L	6'2	170	22	30	3	8	0	1	0	0	0	5	0	.267	.333
Mundy, Bill-William Edward	13BosA	6-28-89	Salineville, Ohio	9-23-58	L	L	5'10	154	15	47	4	12	0	0	0	4	4	12	0	.255	.255
Munson, Red-Clarence Hanford	05PhiN	7-31-83	Cincinnati, Ohio	Deceased		R			9	26	1	3	1	0	0	2	0		0.	.115	.154
Murch, Simmy-Simeon T.	04-05StLN 08BknN	11-21-80	Castine, Me.	6- 6-39	R	R	6'2	230	22	71	4	10	2	0	0	1	2		0	.141	.169
Murdock, Wilbur-Wilbur E.	08StLN								27	62	5	16	3	0	0	5	3		4	.258	.306
Murphy, Buzz-Robert R.	18BosN 19WasA	4-26-95	Denver, Colo.	5-11-38	L	L			88	284	25	78	9	7	1	37	22	37	5	.275	.366
Murphy, Danny-Daniel Francis	00-01NYN 02-13PhiA 14-15BknF	8-11-76	Philadelphia, Pa.	11-22-55	R	R	5'9	175	1514	5461	713	1574	288	103	44	708	338		194	.288	.403
Murphy, Dave-David Francis (Dirty)	05BosN	5- 4-76	Adams, Mass.	4- 8-40		R			3	11	0	2	0	0	0	1	0		0	.182	.182
Murphy, Dummy-Herbert Courtland	14PhiN	-90	Indianapolis, Ind.	8-10-62	R	R	5'10	165	9	26	1	4	1	0	0	3	0	4	0	.154	.192
Murphy, Eddie-John Edward (Honest Eddie)	12-15PhiA 15-21ChiA 26PitN	10- 2-91	Hancock, N.Y.	2-21-69	L	R	5'10	155	760	2373	411	680	66	32	4	195	294		111	.207	.340
Murphy, Frank-Frank Morton	01BosN 01NYN	-80	Hackensack, N.J.	11- 2-12					57	224	17	52	5	3	1	20	7		7	.232	.295
Murphy, Howard-Howard	09StLN	-82	Milton, Okla.	9- 5-26					25	60	3	12	0	0	0	3	4		1	.200	.200
Murphy, Leo-Leo Joseph (Red)	15PitN	1- 7-89	Terre Haute, Ind.	8-12-60	R	R	6'1	180	34	41	4	4	0	0	0	4	4	12	0	.098	.098
Murphy, Mike-Michael Jerome	12StLN 16PhiA	8-19-88	Forestville, Pa.	10-27-52	R	R	5'9	170	15	28	0	3	0	0	0	2	1	3	0	.107	.107

									LIFETIME BATTING TOTALS												
USE NAME – GIVEN NAMES (NICKNAMES)	TEAM BY YEAR	BIRTH DATE	BIRTH PLACE	DEATH DATE	B	T	HGT	WGT	G	AB	R	H	2B	3B	HR	RBI	BB	SO	SB	BA	SA
Murphy, Morg-Morgan Edward	90BosP 91BosAA 92-95CinN 96-97StLN 98PitN	2-14-67	E. Providence, R.I.	10- 3-38	R	R	5'8	160	562	1973	251	446	59	13	10	227	157		55	.226	.284
	98,00PhiN 01PhiA																				
Murphy, Soldier Boy-John P.	02StLN 03DetA	-79	New Haven, Conn.	6- 1-14					6	25	2	6	2	0	0	2	1		0	.240	.320
Murray, Bill-William Allenwood	17WasA	9- 6-93	Vinalhaven, Me.	9-14-43	R	R	5'11	165	8	21	2	3	0	1	0	4	2	2	1	.143	.238
Murray, Ed-Edward Francis	17StLA	5- 8-95	Mystic, Conn.	11- 8-70	R	R	5'6	145	1	1	0	0	0	0	0	0	0	1	0	.000	.000
Murray, Jim-James Oscar	02ChiN 11StLA 14BosN	1-16-78	Galveston, Tex.	4-25-45	R	L	5'10	180	82	261	21	53	9	2	3	24	13		2	.203	.287
Murray, Red-John Joseph	06-08StLN 09-15NYN 15ChiN 17NYN	3- 4-84	Arnot, Pa.	12- 4-58	R	R	5'10	190	1264	4334	555	1170	168	96	37	579	299		321	.270	.379
Myers, Hap-Ralph Edward	10BosA 11StLA 11BosA 13BosN 14-15BknF	4- 8-88	San Francisco, Cal.	6-30-67	R	R	6'3	175	377	1251	203	335	42	7	4	116	119		132	.268	.322
Myers, Hy-Henry Harrison	09,11,14-22BknN 23-25StLN 25CinN 25StLN	4-27-89	East Liverpool, Ohio	5- 1-65	R	R	5'9	175	1310	4910	555	1380	179	100	32	559	195	360	107	.281	.378
Nagelsen (Nageleisen), Lou-Louis Marcellus	12CleA	6-29-87	Piqua, Ohio	10-22-65	R	R	6'2	180	2	3	0	0	0	0	0	0	0		0	.000	.000
Nance (Cooper), Doc-William G. (Kid)	97-98LouN 01DetA	8- 2-76	Fort Worth, Tex.	5-28-58	R	R			188	657	110	183	34	7	7	99	83		14	.279	.384
Nash, Ken-Kenneth Leland	12CleA 14StLN	7-14-88	S. Weymouth, Mass.		B	R	5'8	140	35	74	6	18	3	1	0	6	9		0	.243	.311
Neal, Offa-Theophilus Fountain	05NYN	6- 5-76	Logan, Ill.	4-11-50	L	R	6'	185	4	13	0	0	0	0	0	0	0		0	.000	.000
Neale, Greasy-Alfred Earle	16-20CinN 21PhiN 21-22CinN 23VR 24CinN	11- 5-91	Parkersburg, W.Va.	11- 2-73	L	R	6'	170	768	2661	321	688	71	50	8	200	201	281	139	.259	.332
41-50 head coach in N.F.L.																					
Nealon, Jim-James Joseph	06-07PitN	12-15-84	Sacramento, Cal.	4- 2-10					259	937	111	240	31	20	3	130	76		26	.256	.342
Needham, Tom-Thomas J. (Deerfoot)	04-07BosN 08NYN 09-14ChiN	4- 7-79	Ireland	12-13-26	R	R	5'10	180	523	1491	113	311	50	10	8	117	109		20	.209	.272
Neff, Doug-Douglas Williams	14-15WasA	10- 8-91	Harrisonburg, Va.	5-23-32	R	R	5'9	140	33	62	1	10	1	0	0	4	4	6	1	.161	.177
Neighbors, Cy-Cecil F.	08PitN	9-23-80	Mo.	5-20-64					1	0	0	0	0	0	0	0	0	0	0	–	–
Nelson (Kellogg), Ray (Raymond Nelson)-Raymond (Kell)	01NYN	8- 4-75	Holyoke, Mass.	1- 8-61	R	R	5'9	150	39	130	12	26	2	0	0	7	10		3	.200	.215
Ness, Jack-John Charles	11DetA 16ChiA	11-11-85	Chicago, Ill.	12- 3-57	R	R	6'2	165	87	297	38	75	7	5	1	36	11		4	.253	.320
Netzel, Milo-Miles A.	09CleA	5-12-86	Eldred, Pa.	3-18-38		R			10	37	2	7	1	0	0	3	3		1	.189	.216
Neu, Otto-Otto Adam	17StLA	9-24-94	Springfield, Ohio	9-19-32	R	R	5'11	170	1	0	0	0	0	0	0	0	0	0	0	–	–
Newnam, Pat-Patrick Henry	10-11StLA	12-10-80	Hemstead, Tex.	6-20-38	R	R	6'	180	123	446	50	95	7	0	3	31	41		20	.213	.278
Nicholls, Simon-Simon Burdette	03DetA 06-09PhiA 10CleA	7-18-82	Germantown, Md.	3-12-11	L	R			314	1133	144	284	32	6	4	58	65		27	.251	.300
Nichols (Meikle), Art-Arthur Francis	98-00ChiN 01-03StLN	7-14-71	Manchester, N.H.	8- 9-45	R	R	5'10	175	241	793	112	194	28	3	2	89	50		51	.245	.295
Nicholson, Ovid-Ovid Edward	12PitN	12-30-88	Salem, Ind.	3-24-68	L	R	5'9	155	6	11	2	5	0	0	0	3	1	2	0	.455	.455
Niehoff, Bert-John Albert	13-14CinN 15-17PhiN 18StLN 18NYN	5-13-84	Louisville, Colo.	12- 8-74	R	R	5'10	170	581	2037	210	489	104	19	12	207	131	242	71	.240	.327
Niles, Harry-Herbert Clyde	06-07StLA 08NYA 08-10BosA 10CleA	9-10-80	Buchanan, Mich.	4-18-53	R	R	5'8	175	608	2270	278	562	58	24	12	152	163		107	.248	.310
Nill, Rabbit-George Charles	04-07WasA 07-08CleA	7-14-81	Fort Wayne, Ind.	5-24-62	R	R	5'7	160	295	963	116	204	23	9	3	77	103		36	.212	.264
Noonan, Pete-Peter John	04PhiA 06ChiN 06-07StLN	11-24-81	W. Stockbridge, Mass.	1-11-65	R	R	6'	180	163	479	40	98	11	7	4	38	21		5	.205	.282
Nordyke, Lou-Louis Ellis	06StLA	8- 7-76	Brighton, Iowa	9-27-45	R	R	6'	185	25	53	4	13	1	0	0	7	10		3	.245	.264
Northen, Hub-Hubbard Elwin	10StLA 11CinN 11-12BknN	8-16-85	Atlanta, Tex.	10- 1-47	L	L	5'8	175	164	584	76	159	29	8	3	63	60		14	.272	.365
Nunamaker, Les-Leslie Grant	11-14BosA 14-17NYA 18StLA 19-22CleA	1-25-89	Malcolm, Neb.	11-14-38	R	R	6'2	190	715	1990	194	533	75	30	2	215	176		36	.268	.339
Nutter, Dizzy-Everett Clarence	19BosN	8-27-93	Roseville, Ohio	7-25-58	L	R	5'10	160	18	52	4	11	0	0	0	3	4	5	1	.212	.212
Oakes, Rebel-Ennis Telfair	09CinN 10-13StLN 14-15,M14-15PitF	12-17-86	Homer, La.	2-29-48	L	R	5'9	170	985	3617	427	1009	112	42	15	397	265		163	.279	.346
O'Brien, George-George Joseph	15StLA	11- 4-89	Cleveland, Ohio	3-24-66	R	R	6'	185	3	9	1	2	0	0	0	0	1	2	0	.222	.222
O'Brien, Jack-John Joseph	99WasN 01WasA 01CleA 03BosA	2- 5-73	Watervliet, N.Y.	6-10-33	L	R	6'1	165	321	1217	166	313	38	14	9	133	77		44	.257	.334
O'Brien, Pete-Peter J.	01CinN 06StLA 07CleA 07WasA	-76	Binghamton, N.Y.	1-31-17	L	R	5'7	170	249	857	60	191	18	7	3	78	63		30	.223	.271
O'Brien, Ray-Raymond Joseph	16PitN	10-31-92	St. Louis, Mo.	3-31-42	L	L	5'9	175	16	57	5	12	3	2	0	3	1	14	0	.211	.333
O'Connell, John-John Joseph	91BalAA 02DetA	5-16-72	Lawrence, Mass.	Deceased					16	51	3	9	1	0	0	7	6		2	.176	.196
O'Connor, Jack-John Joseph (Peach Pie)	87-88CinAA 89-91ColAA 92-98CleN	6- 2-69	St. Louis, Mo.	11-14-37	R	R	5'10	170	1434	5346	693	1430	201	66	18	738	301		215	.267	.340
	99-00StLN 00-02PitN 03NYA 04,06-07,10,M10StLA																				
O'Connor, John-John J.	16ChiN					R			1	0	0	0	0	0	0	0	0	0	0	–	–
O'Connor, Paddy-Patrick Francis	08-10PitN 14StLN 15PitF 18NYA	8- 4-79	Windsor Locks, Conn.	8-17-50	R	R	5'8	168	108	267	17	60	11	1	0	21	17		4	.225	.273
Odwell, Fred-Frederick William (Fritz)	04-07CinN	9-25-72	Downsville, N.Y.	8-19-48	R	R	5'9	160	411	1412	198	365	42	30	10	168	89		72	.258	.352
O'Hagan, Hal-Harold P.	92WasN 02ChiN 02NYN 02CleA 02NYN	9-30-73	Washington, D.C.	1-14-13			6'	173	61	209	18	39	5	4	0	19	13		13	.187	.249
O'Hara, Bill-William Alexander	09NYN 10StLN	8-14-83	Toronto, Canada	1-15-31	L	R	5'10		124	380	49	88	9	3	1	32	42		31	.232	.279
O'Hara, Kid-James Francis	04BosN	12-19-75	Wilkes-Barre, Pa.	12- 1-54	B	R	5'7	152	8	29	3	6	0	0	0	0	4		1	.207	.207
O'Hara, Tom-Thomas F.	06-07StLN	7-13-85	Waverly, N.Y.	6- 8-54					62	226	19	57	3	1	0	5	15		4	.252	.274
Oldring, Rube-Reuben Henry	05NYA 06-16PhiA 16NYA 17VR 18PhiA	5-30-84	New York, N.Y.	9- 9-61	R	R	5'10	186	1237	4690	616	1268	205	75	28	471	206		197	.270	.364
O'Leary, Charley-Charles Timothy	04-12DetA 13StLN 34StLA	10-15-81	Chicago, Ill.	1- 6-41	R	R	5'7	165	954	3230	317	731	104	18	3	213	164		74	.226	.272
Olson, Ivy-Ivan Massie	11-15CleA 15-24BknN	10-14-85	Kansas City, Mo.	9- 1-65	R	R	5'11	175	1572	6111	730	1575	191	69	13	446	285		156	.258	.318
O'Mara, Ollie-Oliver Edward	12DetA 14-16,18-19BknN	3- 8-91	St. Louis, Mo.		R	R	5'8	140	412	1478	166	341	49	8	2	77	86	105	46	.231	.279
O'Neill, Bill-William John	04BosA 04WasA 06ChiA	1-22-80	St. John, Canada	7-27-20	B	R			206	746	77	181	15	2	2	42	46		41	.243	.276
O'Neill, Jack-John Joseph	02-03StLN 04-05ChiN 06BosN	1-10-73	Maam, Ireland	6-29-35	R	R	5'10	165	303	945	74	185	24	5	1	74	52		20	.196	.235
O'Neill, John-John J.	99,02NYN		New York, N.Y.			R			4	15	0	0	0	0	0	0	0		0	.000	.000
O'Neill, Mike-Michael Joyce (See P01-19)	01-14StLN 07CinN	9- 7-77	Galway, Ireland	8-12-59	L	L	5'11	185	137	380	50	97	14	9	2	41	20		4	.255	.355
(Played as Mike Joyce 01)																					
O'Neill, Peaches-Philip Bernard	04CinN	8-30-79	Anderson, Ind.	8- 2-55	R	R	5'11	165	8	15	0	4	0	0	0	1	1		0	.267	.267
O'Neill, Steve-Stephen Francis	11-23CleA 24BosA 25NYA 27-28StLA	7- 6-91	Minooka, Pa.	1-26-62	R	R	5'10	175	1586	4795	448	1259	248	34	13	537	592		30	.263	.337
	M35-37CleA M43-48DetA M50-51BosA M52-54PhiN																				
Onslow, Eddie-Edward Joseph	12-13DetA 18CleA 27WasA	2-17-93	Meadville, Pa.		L	L	6'	170	63	207	23	48	3	2	1	22	9		4	.232	.280
Onslow, Jack-John James	12DetA 17NYN M49-50ChiA	10-13-88	Scottdale, Pa.	12-22-60	R	R	5'11	180	40	77	8	13	2	0	0	4	10		1	.169	.195
Orndorff, Jess-Jesse Walworth Thayer	07BosN	1-15-81	Chicago, Ill.	9-28-60	B	R	6'	168	5	17	0	2	0	0	0	0	0		0	.118	.118
O'Rourke, Jim-James Henry (Orator Jim)	76-78BosN 79ProvN 80BosN	8-24-52	Bridgeport, Conn.	1- 8-19	R	R	5'8	185	1762	7368	1439	2300	385	139	51	1010	481	349	211	.312	.423
	81-84,M81-84BufN 85-89NYN 90NYP 91-92NYN 93,M93WasN 04NYN								For Jim O'Rourke, Stolen Bases includes the years, 86-04												
O'Rourke, Patsy-Joseph Leo Sr.	08StLN	4-13-81	Philadelphia, Pa.	4-18-56	R	R	5'7	160	53	164	8	32	4	2	0	16	14		2	.195	.244
O'Rourke, Queenie-James Stephen	08NYA	12-26-83	Bridgeport, Conn.	12-22-55	R	R	5'7	150	34	108	5	25	1	0	0	3	4		4	.231	.241
Orr, Billy-William John	13-14PhiA	4-22-91	San Francisco, Cal.	3-10-67	R	R	5'11	168	37	91	9	17	2	2	0	8	6	15	2	.186	.221
Orth, Al-Albert Lewis (The Curveless Wonder) (See P01-19)	95-01PhiN	9- 5-72	Tipton, Ind.	10- 8-48	L	R	6'	200	603	1683	184	461	60	30	12	184	51		39	.274	.367
	02-04WasA 04-09NYA																				
Osborn, Ossie-Wilfred Pearl (Green, Fred)	07-09PhiN	11-28-83	Nevada, Ohio	9- 2-54	L	R	5'9	178	266	907	98	228	25	16	2	72	45		26	.251	.321
Ostdiek, Harry-Harry Girard	04CleA 08BosA	4-12-81	Ottumwa, Iowa	5- 6-56	R	R	5'11	185	8	21	1	3	0	1	0	3	3		1	.143	.238
Osteen, Champ-James Champlin	03WasA 04NYA 08-09StLN	2-24-77	Hendersonville, N.C.	12-14-62	L	R	5'8	150	83	304	27	60	6	6	2	31	10		1	.197	.276
Otis, Bill-Paul Franklin	12NYA	12-24-89	Scituate, Mass.		L	R	5'10	150	4	20	1	1	0	0	0	2	3		0	.050	.050
Owens, Frank-Frank Walter (Yip)	05BosA 09ChiA 14BknF 15BalF	1-26-86	Toronto, Canada	7- 2-58	R	R	6'	170	222	694	59	170	25	11	5	65	34		9	.245	.334
Owens, Red-Thomas Llewellyn	99PhiN 05BknN	11- 1-74	Pottsville, Pa.	8-21-52	R	R			51	189	14	37	6	2	1	21	8		1	.196	.265
Oyler, Andy-Andrew Paul (Pepper)	02BalA	5- 5-80	Newville, Pa.	10-24-70	R	R	5'8	138	27	77	9	17	1	0	1	6	8		3	.221	.273
Padden, Dick-Richard Joseph (Brains)	96-98PitN 99WasN 01StLN 02-05StLA	9-17-70	Martins Ferry, Ohio	10-31-22	R	R	5'10	165	873	3160	421	811	116	46	11	334	224		131	.257	.333
Paddock, Del-Delmar Harold	12ChiA 12NYA	6- 6-87	Volga, S.D.	2- 6-52	L	R	5'9	165	46	157	26	45	5	3	1	14	23		9	.287	.376
Palmer, Eddie-Edwin Henry (Baldy)	17PhiA	6- 1-93	Petty, Tex.		R	R	5'9	175	16	52	7	11	1	0	0	5	7	7	1	.212	.231
Parent, Freddy-Frederick Alfred	99StLN 01-07BosA 08-11ChiA	11-25-75	Biddeford, Me.	11- 2-72	R	R	5'5	148	1327	4984	633	1306	180	74	20	471	333		184	.262	.340
Parker, Pat-Clarence Perkins	15StLA	5-22-93	Somerville, Mass.	3-21-67	R	R	5'7	160	3	6	0	1	0	0	0	1	0	3	0	.167	.167
Partenheimer, Steve-Harold Philip	13DetA	8-30-91	Greenfield, Mass.	6-16-71	R	R	5'8	145	1	2	0	0	0	0	0	0	0	0	0	.000	.000
Paskert, Dode-George Henry	07-10CinN 11-17PhiN 18-20ChiN 21CinN	8-28-81	Cleveland, Ohio	2-12-59	R	R	5'11	165	1716	6017	868	1613	279	77	42	577	715		293	.268	.361
Pasquariello-Mike-Michael John	19PhiN 19StLN	11- 7-98	Philadelphia, Pa.	4- 5-65	R	R	5'11	167	2	2	1	1	0	0	0	0	0	1	0	.500	.500
Pattee, Harry-Harry Ernest	08BknN	1-17-82	Charlestown, Mass.	7-17-71	L	R	5'8	150	80	264	19	57	5	2	0	9	25		24	.216	.250
Patterson, Claire-Lorenzo Claire	09CinN	10- 5-87	Arkansas City, Kans.	3-28-13	L	R	6'	180	4	8	0	1	0	0	0	1	0		0	.125	.125
Patterson, Ham-Hamilton	09StLA 09ChiA	10-13-77	Belleville, Ill.	11-25-45	R	R	6'2	185	18	52	4	10	1	0	0	5	1		1	.192	.212
Paulette, Gene-Eugene Edward	11NYN 16-17StLA 17-19StLN 19-20PhiN 21DL	5-26-92	Centralia, Ill.	2- 8-66	R	R	6'	150	500	1780	160	478	66	19	2	165	108	69	43	.269	.330
Pauxtis, Si-Simon Francis	09CinN	7-20-85	Pittston, Pa.	3-13-61	R	R	6'	175	4	8	2	1	0	0	0	0	0		0	.125	.125
Payne, Freddie-Frederick Thomas (Doc)	06-08DetA 09-11ChiA	9- 2-80	Camden, N.Y.	1-16-54	R	R	5'10	162	334	908	82	194	16	12	1	86	47		21	.214	.261
Pearce, Bunny-William C.	08-09CinN	3-17-85	Corning, Ohio	5-22-33	R	R	6'1	185	4	4	0	0	0	0	0	0	0		0	.000	.000
Pearce, Harry-Harry James	17-19PhiN	7-12-89	Philadelphia, Pa.	1- 8-42	R	R	5'9	158	135	424	42	88	9	5	0	29	17	62	11	.208	.252
Pechous, Charlie-Charles Edward	15ChiF 16-17ChiN	10- 5-96	Chicago, Ill.		R	R	6'	170	53	161	11	29	4	1	0	9	9		3	.180	.217
Peckinpaugh, Roger-Roger Thorpe	10,12-13CleA 13-21,M14NYA 22-26WasA	2- 5-91	Wooster, Ohio		R	R	5'10	165	2012	7233	1006	1876	256	75	48	739	814		207	.259	.335
	27ChiA M28-33,41CleA																				
Pedroes, Chick-Charles P.	02ChiN	10-27-69	Chicago, Ill.	8- 6-27					2	6	0	0	0	0	0	0	0		0	.000	.000
Peffer, Monte-Monte	13PhiA	-91	New York, N.Y.		R	R	5'4	147	1	3	0	0	0	0	0	0	0	1	0	.000	.000
Peitz, Heinie-Henry Clement	92-95StLN 96-04CinN 05-06PitN 13StLN	11-28-72	St. Louis, Mo.	10-23-43	R	R	5'11	165	1230	4114	542	1128	192	65	16	560	409		94	.274	.364

USE NAME – GIVEN NAMES (NICKNAMES)	TEAM BY YEAR	BIRTH DATE	BIRTH PLACE	DEATH DATE	B	T	HGT	WGT	G	AB	R	H	2B	3B	HR	RBI	BB	SO	SB	BA	SA
Peploski, Pepper-Joseph Aloysius	13DetA	9-12-91	Brooklyn, N.Y.	-47	R	R	5'8	155	2	4	1	2	0	0	0	0	0	0	0	.500	.500
Perrine, Nig-John Grover	07WasA	1-14-85	Clinton, Wis.	8-13-48	R	R	5'9	160	44	146	13	25	4	1	0	15	13		10	.171	.212
Perring, George-George Wilson	08-10CleA 14-15KCF	8-13-84	Sharon, Wis.	8-20-60	R	R	6'	190	513	1764	198	438	75	34	9	183	154		26	.248	.345
Perry, Clay-Clayton Shields	08DetA	12-18-81	Rice Lake, Wis.	1-16-54	R	R	5'10	175	5	11	0	2	0	0	0	0	0		0	.182	.182
Perry, Hank-William Henry (Socks)	12DetA	7-28-86	Howell, Mich.	7-18-56	L	R	5'11	195	13	36	3	6	1	0	0	0	3		0	.167	.194
Peterson, Bob-Robert A.	06-07BosA		Philadelphia, Pa.			R			43	131	11	25	1	1	1	9	11		1	.191	.237
Pettigrew, Ned-Jim Ned	14BufF	8-25-81	Honey Grove, Tex.	8-20-52	R	R	5'10	175	2	2	0	0	0	0	0	0	0		0	.000	.000
Pezold, Larry-Lorenz Johannes	14CleA	6-22-93	New Orleans, La.	10-22-57	R	R	5'9	175	23	71	4	16	0	1	0	5	9	6	2	.225	.254
Pfyl, Monte-Meinhard Charles	07NYN 09-13DO	5-11-84	St. Louis, Mo.	10-18-45	L	L	6'3	190	1	0	0	0	0	0	0	0	0	0	0	–	–
Phelan, Art-Arthur Thomas (Dugan)	10,12CinN 13-15ChiN	8-14-87	Niantic, Ill.	12-27-64	R	R	5'8	160	401	1256	150	297	38	25	8	131	141	113	50	.236	.326
Phelps, Eddie-Edward Jaykill (Yaller)	02-04,06-08PitN 05-06CinN 09-10StLN 12-13BknN	3- 3-79	Albany, N.Y.	1-31-42	R	R	5'10	185	629	1832	186	460	45	20	3	205	163		31	.251	.302
Phyle, Bill-William Joseph (See P01-19)	98-99ChiN 01NYN 06StLN	6-25-75	Duluth, Minn.	8- 7-53		R			61	182	17	32	5	1	0	8	9		2	.176	.214
Pick, Charlie-Charles Thomas	14-15WasA 16PhiA 18-19ChiN 19-20BosN	4-10-88	Brookneal, Va.	6-26-54	L	R	5'10	160	367	1278	115	333	39	17	3	86	102	60	64	.261	.325
Pickering, Ollie-Oliver Daniel	96-97LouN 97CleN 01-02CleA 03-04PhiA 07StLA 08WasA	4- 9-70	Olney, Ill.	1-20-52	L	R	5'11	170	885	3347	500	910	97	39	9	287	286		198	.272	.332
Pickup, Ty-Clarence William	18PhiN	10-29-97	Philadelphia, Pa.	8- 2-74	R	R	6'	180	1	1	0	1	0	0	0	0	0	0	0	1.000	1.000
Piez, Sandy-Charles William	14NYN	10-13-88	New York, N.Y.	12-29-30	R	R	5'10	170	35	8	9	3	0	1	0	3	0	1	4	.375	.625
Pitler, Jake-Jacob Albert	17-18PitN	4-22-94	New York, N.Y.	2- 3-68	R	R	5'8	150	111	383	40	89	8	5	0	23	31	24	8	.232	.279
Platte, Al-Alfred Frederick Joseph	13DetA	4-13-90	Grand Rapids, Mich.		L	L	5'7	160	7	18	1	2	1	0	0	0	1	1	0	.111	.167
Pond, Ralph-Ralph Benjamin	10BosA	5- 4-88	Eau Claire, Wis.	9- 8-47					1	4	0	1	0	0	0	0	0		1	.250	.250
Porter, Irv-Irving Marble	14ChiA	5-17-88	Lynn, Mass.	2-20-71	B	R	5'9	155	1	4	1	1	0	0	0	0	0	1	0	.250	.250
Poste, E.-E.	02DetA								3	12	2	1	0	0	0	2	0		0	.083	.083
Potts, Fred-John Frederick	14KCF	2- 6-87	Tipp City, Ohio	9- 5-62	L	R	5'7	165	41	102	14	27	4	0	1	9	25		7	.265	.333
Powers, Mike-Michael Riley	98-99LouN 99WasN 01-05PhiA 05NYA 05-09PhiA	9-22-70	Pittsfield, Mass.	4-26-09	R	R			643	2079	184	453	72	13	4	199	72		27	.218	.271
Pratt, Del-Derrill Burnham	12-17StLA 18-20NYA 21-22BosA 23-24DetA	1-10-88	Walhalla, S.C.		R	R	5'11	175	1835	6826	856	1996	392	117	43	966	513		246	.292	.403
Pratt, Larry-Lester John	14BosA 15BknF 15NwkF	10- 8-87	Gibson City, Ill.	1- 8-69	R	R	6'	183	30	57	7	11	3	0	1	2	5		4	.193	.298
Priest, Johnnie-John Gooding	11-12NYA	6-23-91	St. Joseph, Mo.		R	R	5'11	170	9	23	3	4	0	0	0	3	2		3	.174	.174
Proctor, Lou	12StLA								1	0	0	0	0	0	0	0	1	0	0	–	–
Purnell, Jesse-Jesse Rhoades (Scrappy)	04PhiN	5-11-81	Glenside, Pa.	7- 4-66	L	R	5'5	140	7	19	2	2	0	0	0	1	4		1	.105	.105
Purtell, Billy-William Patrick	08-10ChiA 10-11BosA 14DetA	1- 6-86	Columbus, Ohio	3-17-62	R	R	5'9	165	333	1124	82	259	26	11	2	104	63		24	.230	.278
Quillin, Lee-Leon Abner	06-07ChiA	5- 5-82	North Branch, Minn.	5-14-65	R	R	5'10	165	53	160	18	32	5	0	0	14	10		9	.200	.231
Quinlan, Finners-Thomas Finners	13StLN 15ChiA	10-21-87	Scranton, Pa.	2-17-66	L	L	5'8	154	55	164	12	30	3	0	0	8	5	20	3	.183	.201
Quinn, Joe-Joseph J.	84StLU 85-86StLN 88-89BosN 90BosP 91-92BosN	12-25-64	Sydney, Australia	11-12-40	R	R	5'7	158	1759	6841	887	1799	226	69	29	794	364		278	.263	.329
	93-96,M95StLN 96-98BalN 98StLN 99,M99CleN 00StLN 00CinN 01WasA												For Joe Quinn, Stolen Bases includes the years, 86-01								
Quinn, John John Edward (Pit)	11PhiN	9-12-85	Framingham, Mass.	4- 9-56	R	R	6'2	185	1	2	0	0	0	0	0	0	0	0	0	.000	.000
Rafter, Jack-John Cornelius	04PitN	2-20-75	Troy, N.Y.	1- 5-43	R	R	5'8	165	1	3	0	0	0	0	0	0	0		0	.000	.000
Raftery (Rafferty), Tom-Thomas Francis	09CleA	10- 5-81	Boston, Mass.	12-31-54	R	R			8	32	6	7	2	1	0	0	4		1	.219	.344
Ralston, Doc-Samuel Beryl	10WasA	8- 3-85	Pierpont, Ohio	8-29-50	R	R	6'	185	22	73	4	15	1	0	0	3	3		2	.205	.219
Randall, Newt-Newton J.	07ChiN 07BosN	2- 3-81	New Lowell, Canada	5- 3-55			5'10		97	336	22	71	10	5	0	19	27		6	.211	.271
Rariden, Bill-William Angel (Bedford Bill)	09-13BosN 14IndF 15NwkF 16-18NYN	2- 4-88	Bedford, Ind.	8-28-42	R	R	5'10	168	982	2877	272	682	105	24	7	272	340		47	.237	.298
	19-20CinN																				
Rath, Morrie-Morris Charles	09-10PhiA 10CleA 12-13ChiA 18MS 19-20CinN	12-25-86	Mobeetie, Tex.	11-18-45	L	R	5'8	160	563	2048	291	521	36	7	4	92	258		82	.254	.285
Raub, Tommy-Thomas Jefferson	03ChiN 06StLN	12- 1-70	Raubsville, Pa.	2-16-49	R	R	5'10	155	60	162	15	41	5	6	0	9	9		5	.253	.358
Raymer, Fred-Frederick Charles	01ChiN 04-05BosN	11-12-75	Leavenworth, Kans.	6-12-57	R	R	5'11	185	371	1380	95	301	40	7	1	101	32		50	.218	.259
Raymond, Lou-Louis Anthony	19PhiN	12-11-94	Buffalo, N.Y.		R	R	5'10	187	1	2	0	1	0	0	0	0	0	0	0	.500	.500
Reardon, Phil-Philip Michael	06BknN	10- 3-83	Brooklyn, N.Y.	9-28-20	R	R			5	14	0	1	0	0	0	0	0		0	.071	.071
Redmond, Harry-Harry John	09BknN	9-13-87	Cleveland, Ohio	7-10-60		R			6	19	3	0	0	0	0	1	0		0	.000	.000
Reed, Milt-Milton D.	11StLN 13-14PhiN 15BknF	7- 4-90	Atlanta, Ga.		L	R	5'9	150	68	163	16	37	4	2	0	10	13		7	.227	.276
Reed, Ted-Ralph Edwin	15NwkF	10-18-90	Beaver, Pa.	2-16-59	R	R	5'11	190	20	77	5	20	1	2	0	4	2		1	.260	.325
Rehg, Wally-Walter Phillip	12PitN 13-15BosA 17-18BosN 19CinN	8-31-88	Summerfield, Ill.	4- 5-46	R	R	5'8	160	258	752	85	188	24	11	2	66	52	66	26	.250	.319
Reilley, Duke-Alexander Aloysius (Midget)	09CleA	8-25-84	Chicago, Ill.	3- 4-68	R	R	5'4	148	20	62	10	13	0	0	0	0	4		5	.210	.210
Reilly, Arch-Archer Edwin	17PitN	8-17-91	Alton, Ill.	11-29-63	R	R	5'10	163	1	0	0	0	0	0	0	0	0	0	0	–	–
Reilly, Barney-Bernard Eugene	09ChiA	2- 7-84	Brockton, Mass.	11-15-34	R	R	6'	175	12	25	3	5	0	0	0	3	3		2	.200	.200
Reilly, Hal-Harold J.	19ChiN								1	3	0	0	0	0	0	0	0	1	0	.000	.000
Reilly, Tom-Thomas Henry	08-09StLN 14CleA	8- 3-84	St. Louis, Mo.	10-19-18	R	R			35	89	5	16	1	1	1	5	2		4	.180	.247
Reinicker (Smith), Wally-Walter	15BalF								3	8	0	1	0	0	0	0	0		0	.125	.125
Rementer, Butch-Willis J.	04PhiN		Philadelphia, Pa.			R			1	2	0	0	0	0	0	0	0		0	.000	.000
Reynolds, Bill-William Dee	13-14NYA	8-14-84	Eastland, Tex.	6- 5-24	R	R	6'	190	9	10	0	2	0	0	0	0	0	4	0	.200	.200
Rheam, Cy-Kenneth Johnston	14-15PitF	9-28-93	Pittsburgh, Pa.	10-23-47	R	R	6'	175	107	283	25	57	5	3	1	25	10		10	.201	.251
Richardson, Bill-William Hezekiah	01StLN	10- 8-77	Decatur Co., Ind.	4-11-54					15	52	7	11	2	0	2	7	6		1	.212	.365
Richardson, Tom-Thomas Mitchell	17StLA	8- 7-83	Louisville, Ill.	11-15-39	R	R	6'	190	1	1	0	0	0	0	0	0	0	0	0	.000	.000
Rickert, Joe-Joseph Francis (Diamond Joe)	98PitN 01BosN	12-12-76	London, Ohio	10-15-43	R	R	5'10	165	15	66	6	11	1	2	0	1	3		1	.167	.242
Rickey, Branch-Wesley Branch (The Mahatma)	05-06StLA 07NYA 14,M13-15StLA	12-20-81	Stockdale, Ohio	12- 9-65	L	R	5'9	175	119	343	38	82	9	6	3	39	27		8	.239	.327
	M19-25StLN																				
Rico, Art-Arthur Raymond	16-17BosN 18MS	7-23-96	Roxbury, Mass.	1- 3-19	R	R	5'9	185	17	18	1	4	1	0	0	2	0	2	0	.222	.278
Riggert, Joe-Joseph Aloysius	11BosA 14BknN 14StLN 19BosN	12-11-86	Janesville, Wis.	12-10-73	R	R	5'9	170	174	558	68	134	18	14	8	44	46		20	.240	.366
Riley, Jimmy-James Joseph	10BosN	11-10-86	Buffalo, N.Y.	3-25-49	R	R	6'	165	6	14	1	0	0	0	0	0	3	3	0	.000	.000
Risberg, Swede-Charles August	17-20ChiA 20DL	10-13-94	San Francisco, Cal.	10-13-75	R	R	6'	175	476	1619	196	394	72	27	6	175	148	180	52	.243	.332
Rising, Pop-Perry Sumner	05BosA		Industry, Pa.						8	18	2	2	1	1	0	2	2		0	.111	.278
Ritchey, Claude-Claude Cassius (Little All Right)	97CinN 98-99LouN	10- 5-73	Emlenton, Pa.	11- 8-51	B	R	5'6	167	1671	5929	711	1636	217	67	18	673	607		149	.276	.344
	00-06PitN 07-09BosN																				
Ritter, Lew-Lewis Elmer (Old Dog)	02-08BknN	9- 7-75	Liverpool, Pa.	5-27-52	R	R	5'9	150	462	1437	129	315	33	17	1	120	96		55	.219	.268
Roach, Roxey-Wilbur Charles	10-11NYA 12WasA 15BufF	11-28-82	Anita, Pa.	12-26-47	R	R	5'11	160	177	608	67	151	31	6	3	54	52		26	.248	.334
Roberts, Skipper-Clarence Ashley	13StLN 14PitF 14ChiF 14PitF	1-11-88	Wardner, Idaho	12-24-63	L	R	5'10	175	82	138	16	29	6	2	1	12	6		4	.210	.304
Robertson, Dave-Davis Aydelotte	12,14-17NYN 18MS 19NYN 19-21ChiN 21PitN 22NYN	9-25-89	Portsmouth, Va.	11- 5-70	L	L	6'	186	804	2830	366	812	117	44	47	364	113	262	94	.287	.409
Robinson, John-John (Bridgeport)	02NYN		E. Greenwich, Conn.			R			4	9	0	0	0	0	0	0	0		0	.000	.000
Robinson, Rabbit-Clyde	03WasA 04DetA 10CinN		Ashtabula, Ohio	4-16-15		R			200	700	71	156	23	14	1	58	63		30	.223	.300
Robinson, Wilbert-Wilbert (Uncle Robbie)	86-90PhiAA 90-91BalAA 92-99BalN	6- 2-63	Bolton, Mass.	8- 8-34	R	R	5'8	215	1361	5046	637	1399	211	54	18	740	286		227	.277	.351
	00StLN 01-02,M02BalA M14-31BknN																				
Roche, Jack-John Joseph (Red)	14-15StLN 16ST 17StLN	11-22-90	Los Angeles, Cal.		R	R	6'1	178	59	49	3	14	2	2	0	9	4	9	2	.286	.408
Rochefort (Gilbert), Ben (Bennett Harold Rochefort)-Bennett Harold	14PhiA	8-15-96	Camden, N.J.		L	R	6'2	185	1	2	0	1	0	0	0	0	0	1	0	.500	.500
Rockenfield, Ike-Issac Broc	05-06StLA	11- 3-76	Omaha, Neb.	2-21-27	R	R	5'7	150	122	411	43	91	16	0	0	24	47		11	.221	.260
Rodgers, Bill-Wilbur Kincaid (Raw Meat Bill)	15CleA 15BosA 15-16CinN	4-18-87	Pleasant Ridge, Ohio		L	R	5'8	160	102	268	30	65	15	4	0	19	22	40	11	.243	.328
Rodriguez, Joe-Jose (El Hombre Goma)	16-18NYN	2-23-94	Havana, Cuba	3-23-48	R	R	6'	170	58	145	17	24	0	3	0	17	14	4	8	.166	.207
Rogers, Jay-Jay Lewis	14NYA	8- 3-88	Sandusky, N.Y.	7- 1-64	R	R	5'11	178	5	8	0	0	0	0	0	0	0	4	0	.000	.000
Rohe, George-George Anthony (Whitey)	01BalA 05-07ChiA	9-15-75	Cincinnati, Ohio	6-10-57	R	R	5'9	165	267	868	81	197	19	3	3	92	72		27	.227	.266
Rolling, Ray-Raymond Copeland	12StLN	9- 8-86	Martinsburg, Mo.	8-25-66	R	R	5'10	160	5	15	0	3	0	0	0	0	0	5	0	.200	.200
Rondeau, Henri-Henri Joseph	13DetA 15-16WasA	5- 5-87	Danielson, Conn.	5-28-43	R	R	5'10	175	99	272	28	56	7	3	1	37	36	37	9	.206	.265
Rooney, Frank-Frank L.	14IndF								12	35	1	7	0	1	1	8	1		2	.200	.343
Rossman, Claude-Claude R.	04,06CleA 07-09DetA 09StLA	6-17-81	Philmont, N.Y.	1-16-28	L	L			511	1848	175	523	80	26	3	238	90		49	.283	.359
Roth, Braggo-Robert Frank	14-15ChiA 15-18CleA 19PhiA 19BosA 20WasA 21NYA	8-28-92	Burlington, Wis.	9-11-36	R	R	5'7	170	811	2831	427	804	138	73	30	422	335	389	189	.284	.416
Roth, Frank-Francis Charles	03-04PhiN 05StLA 06ChiA 09-10CinN	10-11-78	Chicago, Ill.	3-27-55	R	R	5'10	160	282	783	83	196	32	8	1	75	36		19	.250	.315
Rothgeb, Claude-Claude James	05WasA	1- 1-80	Milford, Ill.	7- 6-44	B	R	6'	190	6	13	2	2	0	0	0	0	0		1	.154	.154
Rowan (Drohan), Dave-David	11StLA	12- 6-82	Elona, Canada	7-30-55	L	L	5'11	175	18	65	7	25	1	1	0	11	4		0	.385	.431
Rowe, Harland-Harland Stimson (Hypie)	16PhiA	4-20-96	Springvale, Me.	5-26-69	L	R	6'1	170	17	36	2	5	1	0	0	3	2	8	0	.139	.167
Rudolph, Dutch-John Herman	03PhiN 04ChiN	7-10-82	Natrona, Pa.	4-17-67	L	L	5'10	160	3	4	0	1	0	0	0	0	0		0	.250	.250
Rumler, Bill-William George	14,16-17StLA 18MS	3-27-91	Milford, Neb.	5-26-66	R	R	6'1	190	138	171	15	43	7	4	1	32	14	28	4	.251	.357
Russell, Harvey-Harvey Holmes	14-15BalF	1-10-87	Marshall, Va.		L	R	5'9	163	134	241	23	58	4	4	0	24	32		3	.241	.290
Rutherford, Jim-James Hollis	10CleA	9-26-86	Stillwater, Minn.	9-18-56	L	R	6'1	180	1	2	0	1	0	0	0	0	0		0	.500	.500

USE NAME – GIVEN NAMES (NICKNAMES)	TEAM BY YEAR	BIRTH DATE	BIRTH PLACE	DEATH DATE	B	T	HGT	WGT	G	AB	R	H	2B	3B	HR	RBI	BB	SO	SB	BA	SA
					LIFETIME BATTING TOTALS																
Ryan, Buddy-John Budd	12-13CleA	10- 6-85	Kans.	7- 9-56	L	R	5'9	172	166	571	79	161	18	10	1	63	41		13	.282	.354
Ryan, Jack-John Bennett	89-91LouAA 94-96BosN 98BknN 99BalN 01-03StLN	11-12-68	Haverhill, Mass.	Deceased	R	R	5'10	165	616	2199	245	479	71	30	4	193	85		26	.218	.283
	12-13WasA																				
Ryan, Jimmy-James E.	85-89ChiN 90ChiP 91-00ChiN 02-03WasA	2-11-63	Clinton, Mass.	10-26-23	R	L	5'9	162	2008	8165	1640	2524	439	153	118	1093	803		434	.309	.444
										For Jimmy Ryan, Stolen Bases includes the years, 86-03											
Saier, Vic-Victor Sylvester	11-17ChiN 19PitN	5- 4-91	Lansing, Mich.	5-14-67	L	R	5'11	185	864	2947	454	774	142	61	55	395	378	369	121	.263	.408
Savage, Hal-Harold James	12PhiN 14-15PitF		Bridgeport, Conn.	Deceased	L	R			148	503	82	139	9	9	1	26	69		17	.276	.336
Sawyer, Carl-Carl Everett (Huck)	15-16WasA	10-19-90	Seattle, Wash.	1-18-57	R	R			26	63	11	14	2	0	0	5	8	9	5	.222	.254
Schaefer, Germany-Herman A.	01-02ChiN 05-09DetA 09-14WasA 15NwkF 16NYA 18CleA	2- 4-77	Chicago, Ill.	5-16-19	R	R	5'9	175	1143	3783	497	972	117	48	9	308	333		201	.257	.320
Schalk, Ray-Raymond William (Cracker)	12-28,M27-28ChiA 29NYN	8-12-92	Harvey, Ill.	5-19-70	R	R	5'9	165	1760	5306	579	1345	199	49	11	594	638		176	.253	.316
Schaller, Biff-Walter	11DetA 13ChiA	9-23-89	Chicago, Ill.	10- 9-39	L	R	5'11	168	74	156	20	29	3	1	1	11	24		6	.186	.237
Schang, Bobby-Robert Martin	14-15PitN 15NYN 27StLN	12- 7-86	Wales Center, N.Y.	8-29-66	R	R	5'7	165	82	186	14	35	7	4	0	6	18	47	3	.188	.269
Scheer, Al-Allan G.	13BknN 14IndF 15NwkF	10-21-88	Dayton, Ohio	5- 6-59	L	R	5'9	165	281	931	141	262	48	20	5	105	116		41	.281	.392
Scheeren, Fritz-Frederick (Dutch)	14-15PitN	7- 1-91	Kokomo, Ind.	6-17-73	R	R	6'	180	15	34	4	9	0	1	1	2	1	6	1	.265	.412
Scheibeck, Frank-Frank	87CleAA 88DetN 90TolAA 94PitN 94-95,99WasN 01CleA	6-28-65	Detroit, Mich.	10-22-56	R	R			389	1401	214	327	37	18	2	146	182		93	.233	.290
	06DetA																				
Schepner, Joe-Joseph Maurice (Gentleman Joe)	19StLA	8-10-95	Aliquippa, Pa.	7-25-59	R	R	5'10	170	14	48	2	10	4	0	0	6	1	5	0	.208	.292
Schiappacasse, Lou-Louis Joseph	02DetA	3-29-81	Ann Arbor, Mich.	9-19-10	R				2	5	0	0	0	0	0	1	1		0	.000	.000
Schick, Morrie-Maurice Francis	17ChiN 18MS	4-17-92	Chicago, Ill.		R	R	5'11	170	14	34	3	5	0	0	0	3	3	10	0	.147	.147
Schirick, Dutch-Harry Ernest	14StLA	6-15-90	Ruby, N.Y.	11-12-68	R	R	5'8	160	1	0	0	0	0	0	0	0	1	0	2	–	–
Schlafly, Larry-Harry Linton	02ChiN 06-07WasA 14,M14-15BufF	9-20-78	Port Washington, Ohio	6-29-19	R	R	5'11	182	208	658	91	158	20	12	5	58	90		41	.240	.330
Schlei, Admiral-George Henry	04-08CinN 09-11NYN	1-12-78	Cincinnati, Ohio	1-24-58	R	R	5'10	185	636	1918	195	455	52	21	6	209	172		38	.237	.296
Schmidt, Boss-Charles	06-11DetA	9-12-80	Coal Hill, Ark.	11-14-32	B	R	5'11	200	477	1480	137	360	41	22	3	124	36		23	.243	.307
Schmidt, Butch-Charles John (See P01-19)	09NYA 13-15BosN	7-19-86	Baltimore, Md.	9- 4-52	L	L	6'	175	297	1075	119	292	45	19	4	145	81		18	.272	.358
Schreckengost, Ossee-Ossee Freeman	97LouN 98CleN 99StLN 99CleN 99StLN	4-11-75	New Bethlehem, Pa.	7- 9-14	R	R			892	3048	304	830	130	34	9	338	102		45	.272	.346
	01BosA 02CleA 02-08PhiA 08ChiA																				
Schreiber, Hank-Henry Walter	14ChiA 17BosN 18MS 19CinN 21NYN 26ChiN	7-12-91	Cleveland, Ohio	2-21-68	R	R	5'11	165	36	91	10	18	5	0	0	6	1	16	0	.198	.253
Schriver, Pop-William Frederick	86BknAA 88-90PhiN 91-94ChiN 95NYN 97CinN	7-11-65	Brooklyn, N.Y.	12-27-32	R	R	5'11	175	796	2705	362	715	112	40	16	375	223		54	.264	.353
	98-00PitN 01StLN																				
Schulte, Jack-John Herman Frank	06BosN	11-15-81	Cincinnati, Ohio	8-17-75	R	R	5'9	180	2	7	0	0	0	0	0	0	0		0	.000	.000
Schulte, Wildfire-Frank M.	04-16ChiN 16-17PitN 17PhiN 18WasA	9-17-82	Cohocton, N.Y.	10- 2-49	L	R	5'10	170	1805	6531	906	1766	288	124	93	792	545		233	.270	.395
Schwartz, Bill-William Charles (Blab)	04CleA	4-22-84	Cleveland, Ohio	8-29-61	R	R	6'2	185	24	86	5	13	2	0	0	0	0		4	.151	.174
Schwarz, Bill-William DeWitt	14NYA	1-30-91	Birmingham, Ala.	6-24-49		R			1	1	0	0	0	0	0	0	0	1	0	.000	.000
Schweitzer, Al-Albert Casper (Cheese)	08-11StLA	12-23-82	Cincinnati, Ohio	1-27-69	R	R	5'6	170	280	874	97	208	28	8	3	87	104		47	.238	.299
Schwert, Pi-Pius Louis	14-15NYA	11-22-92	Angola, N.Y.	3-11-41	R	R	5'11	160	11	23	6	5	3	0	0	6	3	8	0	.217	.348
Schwind, Art-Arthur E.	12BosN	-92	Ottawa, Canada		B	R	5'8	150	1	2	0	1	0	0	0	0	0	0	0	.500	.500
Scott, Jim-James Walter	14PitF	-87		5-12-72	R	R	5'9	165	8	24	2	6	1	0	0	1	5		1	.250	.292
Sebring, Jimmy-James Dennison	02-04PitN 04-05CinN 09BknN 09WasA	3-25-82	Liberty, Pa.	12-22-09	L	L	6'	180	363	1411	178	368	51	32	6	168	93		52	.261	.355
Selbach, Kip-Albert Karl	94-98WasN 99CinN 00-01NYN 02BalA 03-04WasA 04-06BosA	3-24-72	Columbus, Ohio	2-17-56	R	R	5'7	190	1608	6140	1067	1816	291	154	44	779	783		335	.296	.415
Sellers, Rube-Oliver	10BosN	3- 7-81	Duquesne, Pa.	1-14-52	R	R	5'10	180	12	32	3	5	0	0	0	2	6	5	1	.156	.156
Sentell, Paul-Leopold Theodore	06-07PhiN	8-27-79	New Orleans, La.	4-27-23	R	R	5'9	176	66	195	19	44	5	1	1	14	15		15	.226	.277
Seybold, Socks-Ralph Orlando	99CinN 01-08PhiA	11-23-70	Washingtonville, O.	12-22-21	R	R	5'11	175	996	3701	479	1083	213	55	51	556	293		64	.293	.421
Seymour, Cy-James Bentley (See P01-19)	96-00NYN 01-02BalA 02-06CinN	12- 9-72	Albany, N.Y.	9-20-19	L	L	6'	200	1524	5657	738	1720	232	97	52	799	354		218	.304	.407
	06-10NYN 13BosN																				
Shafer, Ralph-Ralph Newton	14PitN	3-17-94	Cincinnati, Ohio	2- 5-50			5'11		1	0	0	0	0	0	0	0	0	0	0	–	–
Shafer, Tillie-Arthur Joseph	09-10,12-13NYN	3-22-89	Los Angeles, Cal.	1-10-62	B	R	5'10	165	283	776	138	212	24	14	5	83	105		60	.273	.360
Shanabrook, Warren-Warren H.	06WasA	11-30-80	Massillon, Ohio	3-10-64	R	R	6'	170	1	2	0	0	0	0	0	0	0		0	.000	.000
Shanks, Howard-Howard Samuel (Hank)	12-22WasA 23-24BosA 25NYA	7-21-90	Chicago, Ill.	7-30-41	R	R	5'11	170	1664	5699	604	1440	212	97	25	620	415		185	.253	.337
Shanley, Doc-Harry Root	12StLA	1-30-90	Granbury, Tex.	12-13-34	R	R	5'11	174	5	8	1	0	0	0	0	1	2		0	.000	.000
Shannon, Joe-Joseph Aloysius	15BosN	2-11-97	Jersey City, N.J.	7-28-55	R	R	5'11	170	5	10	3	2	0	0	0	1	0	3	0	.200	.200
Shannon, Owen-Owen Dennis Ignatius	03StLA 07WasA	12-22-85	Omaha, Neb.	4-10-18	R	R			13	35	1	7	2	0	0	3	1		0	.200	.257
Shannon, Red-Maurice Joseph	15BosN 17-19PhiA 19BosA 20WasA 20-21PhiA 26ChiN	2-11-97	Jersey City, N.J.	4-12-70	B	R	5'11	170	310	1070	124	277	38	22	0	91	109	178	21	.259	.336
Shannon, Spike-William Porter	04-06StLN 06-08NYN 08PitN	2- 7-78	Pittsburgh, Pa.	5-16-40	B	R	5'11	180	694	2613	383	677	49	15	3	183	286		145	.259	.293
Sharman, Ralph-Ralph Edward	17PhiA	4-11-95	Cleveland, Ohio	5-24-18	R	R	5'11	176	13	37	2	11	2	1	0	2	3	2	1	.297	.405
Sharpe, Bud-Bayard Heston	05,10BosN 10PitN	8- 6-81	West Chester, Pa.	5-31-16	L	R			165	625	40	139	17	6	0	41	21		4	.222	.269
Shaughnessy, Shag-Francis Joseph	05WasA 08PhiA	4- 8-83	Amboy, Ill.	5-15-69	R	R	6'1	185	9	32	2	9	0	0	0	1	2		3	.281	.281
Shaw, Al-Albert Simpson	07-09StLN 14BknF 15KCF	3- 1-81	Toledo, Ohio	12-30-74	L	R	5'8	165	474	1547	235	434	74	28	14	170	173		64	.281	.392
Shaw, Al-Alfred (Shoddy)	01DetA 07BosA 08ChiA 09BosN	10- 3-74	Burslem, England	3-25-58	R	R	5'8	160	180	459	31	92	9	3	1	32	35		6	.200	.240
Shaw, Ben-Benjamin Nathaniel	17-18PitN	6-18-93	La Center, Ky.	3-16-59	R	R	5'11	190	23	38	5	7	1	0	0	2	2	2	0	.184	.211
Shaw, Hunky-Royal N.	08PitN	9-29-84	Yakima, Wash.	7- 3-69	B	R	5'8	165	1	1	0	0	0	0	0	0	0		0	.000	.000
Shay, Danny-Daniel C.	04-05StLN 07NYN	11- 8-76	Springfield, Ohio	12- 1-27		R			231	775	89	186	26	5	2	62	88		52	.240	.294
Shea, Gerry-Gerald J.	05StLN	7-26-81	St. Louis, Mo.	5- 4-64		R	5'7	160	2	6	0	2	0	0	0	0	0		0	.333	.333
Shea, Nap-John Edward	02PhiN	5-23-74	Ware, Mass.	7- 8-68	R	R	5'5	155	3	8	1	1	0	0	0	0	1		0	.125	.125
Shean, Dave-David William	06PhiA 08-09PhiN 09-10BosN 11ChiN 12BosN 17ChiN	5-23-78	Ware, Mass.	5-22-63	R	R	5'11	175	630	2167	225	495	59	23	6	166	155		66	.228	.285
	18-19BosA																				
Sheckard, Jimmy-Samuel James Tilden	97-98BknN 99BalN 00-01BknN 02BalA	11-23-78	Upper Chanceford, Pa.	1-15-47	L	R	5'9	175	2121	7603	1296	2097	356	138	56	813	1135		475	.276	.381
	02-05BknN 06-12ChiN 13StLN 13CinN																				
Sheehan, Tommy-Thomas H.	06-07PitN 08BknN	11- 6-77	Sacramento, Cal.	5-22-59	R	R	5'8	160	316	1009	96	238	26	8	1	88	94		32	.236	.280
Shelton, Skeeter-Andrew Kemper	15NYA	6-29-88	Huntington, W.Va.	1- 9-54	R	R			10	40	1	1	0	0	0	0	2	10	0	.025	.025
Sheridan, Red-Eugene Anthony (Gene)	18,20BknN	11-14-96	Brooklyn, N.Y.		R	R	5'10	160	5	6	0	1	0	0	0	0	1	1	1	.167	.167
Shields, Pete-Frank LeRoy	15CleA	9-21-91	Swiftwater, Miss.	2-11-61	R	R	6'	175	23	72	4	15	6	0	0	6	4	14	3	.208	.292
Shipke (Shipkrethaver), Bill-William Martin (Skipper Bill)	06CleA 07-09WasA	11-18-82	St. Louis, Mo.	9-10-40	R	R	5'7	145	186	552	59	110	11	10	1	29	55		21	.199	.261
Shook, Ray-Raymond Curtis	16ChiA	11-18-90	Perry, Ohio	9-16-70	R	R	5'7	155	1	0	0	0	0	0	0	0	0	0	0	–	–
Shotton, Burt-Burton Edwin (Barney)	09,11-17StLA 18WasA 19-23StLN	10-18-84	Brownhelm, Ohio	7-29-62	L	R	5'11	175	1388	4949	747	1338	154	65	9	290	714		294	.270	.333
	M28-33PhiN M34CinN M47,48-50BknN																				
Shovlin, John-John Joseph	11PitN 19-20StLA	1-14-91	Drifton, Pa.		R	R	5'7	163	18	43	7	9	0	0	0	3	5	3	0	.209	.209
Shugart, Frank-William Frank	90ChiP 91-93PitN 93-94StLN 95LouN 97PhiN 01ChiA	-67	Chicago, Ill.	Deceased	L	R			742	2987	483	802	111	80	21	384	218		132	.268	.380
Sicking, Eddie-Edward Joseph	16ChiN 18-19NYN 19PhiN 20NYN 20CinN 27PitN	3-30-97	St. Bernard, Ohio		R	R	5'9	165	203	597	51	135	13	2	0	59	39	43	14	.226	.255
Siegle, Johnny-John Herbert	05-06CinN	7- 8-74	Urbana, Ohio		R	R	5'10	165	39	124	13	25	3	4	1	15	10		0	.202	.315
Siglin, Paddy-Wesley Peter	14-16PitN	9-24-91	Aurelia, Iowa	8- 5-56	R	R	5'10	160	23	50	5	9	0	0	0	2	5	10	2	.180	.180
Silva, Danny-Daniel James	19WasA	10- 5-96	Everett, Mass.	4- 4-74	R	R	6'	170	1	4	0	1	0	0	0	0	0	0	0	.250	.250
Simmons, Hack-George Washington	10DetA 12NYA 14-15BalF	1-29-85	Brooklyn, N.Y.	4-26-42	R	R	5'8	180	305	951	115	234	43	9	2	102	85		28	.246	.317
Simon, Mike-Michael Edward	09-13PitN 14StLF 15BknF	4-13-83	Hayden, Ind.	6-10-63	R	R	5'11	188	378	1069	85	241	28	10	1	90	54		9	.225	.273
Siner, Hosea-Hosea John	09BosN	3-20-85	Shelburn, Ind.	6-11-48	R	R	5'10	185	10	23	1	3	0	0	0	1	2		0	.130	.130
Slagle, Jimmy-James Franklin (Rabbit, Shorty)	99WasN 00-01PhiN 01BosN	7-11-73	Worthville, Pa.	5-10-56	L	R			1298	4998	779	1348	128	55	2	344	619		273	.270	.319
	02-08ChiN																				
Slattery, Jack-John Terrence	01BosA 03CleA 03ChiA 06StLN 09WasA M28BosN	1- 6-77	Boston, Mass.	7-17-49	R	R	6'2	190	103	288	14	61	5	2	0	27	6		3	.212	.243
Sloan, Tod-Yale Yeastman	13,17StLA 18MS 19StLA	12-24-90	Madisonville, Tenn.	9-12-56	L	R	6'	175	143	402	43	94	8	5	2	33	41	46	9	.234	.294
Smith, Broadway Aleck-Alexander Benjamin	97-99BknN 99BalN 00BknN 01NYN	-71	New York, N.Y.	7- 9-19		R			283	948	108	251	32	11	1	130	26		38	.265	.325
	02BalA 03BosA 04ChiN 06NYN																				
Smith, Bull-Louis	04PitN 06ChiN 11WasA					R			15	43	2	6	0	1	0	0	1		0	.140	.186
Smith, Elmer-Elmer Ellsworth (Mike) (See P01-19)	86-89CinAA 92-97PitN	3-23-68	Pittsburgh, Pa.	11- 3-45	L	L	5'11	178	1233	4675	931	1462	202	131	37	661	636		243	.313	.436
	98-00CinN 00NYN 01PitN 01BosN																				
Smith, Fred-Frederick Vincent	13BosN 14-15BufF 15BknF 17StLN	7-29-91	Cleveland, Ohio	5-28-61	R	R	5'11	185	438	1422	143	321	39	25	8	158	133		58	.226	.305
Smith, Hap-Henry Joseph	10BknN	7-14-83	Coquille, Ore.	2-26-61	L	R	6'	185	35	76	6	18	2	0	0	5	4	14	4	.237	.263
Smith, Harry-Harry Thomas	01PhiA 02-07PitN 08-10, M09BosN	10-31-74	Yorkshire, England	2-17-33	R	R			343	1004	83	214	22	7	2	89	55		23	.213	.255
Smith, Harry-James Harry	14-15NYN 15BknF 17-18CinN	5-15-90	Baltimore, Md.	4- 1-22	R	R	5'10	180	75	148	10	27	1	3	1	14	21	26	4	.182	.250
Smith, Heinie-George Henry	97-98LouN 99PitN 01-02,M02NYN 03DetA	10-24-71	Pittsburgh, Pa.	6-25-39	R	R	5'9	160	309	1120	117	269	43	7	3	91	51		54	.240	.299
Smith (Coffey), Jack-John Joseph	12DetA	8- 8-93	Oswaya, Pa.			R			1	0	0	0	0	0	0	0	0	0	0	–	–
Smith, Jimmy-James Lawrence	14-15ChiF 15BalF 16PitN 17NYN 18BosN 19CinN	5-15-95	Pittsburgh, Pa.	1- 1-74	B	R	5'10	152	370	1127	119	247	32	15	12	101	63		18	.219	.306
	21-22PhiN				Bats Right 14																

USE NAME – GIVEN NAMES (NICKNAMES)	TEAM BY YEAR	BIRTH DATE	BIRTH PLACE	DEATH DATE	B	T	HGT	WGT	G	AB	R	H	2B	3B	HR	RBI	BB	SO	SB	BA	SA
					LIFETIME BATTING TOTALS																
Smith (Persico), Joe-Salvatore Giuseppe	13NYA	12-29-93	New York, N.Y.		R	R	5'7	170	13	32	1	5	0	0	0	2	1	14	1	.156	.156
Smith, Jud-Judson Grant	93CinN 93StLN 96PitN 98WasN 01PitN	1-13-69	Green Oak, Mich.	12- 7-47	R	R			102	344	49	96	11	5	4	37	37		14	.279	.375
Smith, Klondike-Armstrong Frederick	12NYA	1- 4-87	London, England	11-15-59	L	L	5'9	165	7	27	0	5	1	0	0	0	0		1	.185	.222
Smith, Paul-Paul Stoner	16CinN	5- 7-88	Mt. Zion, Ill.	7- 3-58	L	R	6'1	190	10	44	5	10	0	1	0	1	1	8	3	.227	.273
Smith, Red-James Carlisle	11-14BknN 14-19BosN	4- 6-90	Greenville, S.C.	10-10-66	R	R	5'11	165	1117	3907	477	1087	208	49	27	514	420	415	117	.278	.377
Smith, Red-Willard Jehu	17-18PitN	4-11-92	Logansport, Ind.	7-17-72	R	R	5'8	165	26	45	2	7	2	0	0	5	6	4	1	.156	.200
Smith, Syd-Sydney E.	08PhiA 08StLA 10-11CleA 14-15PitN	8-31-83	Smithville, S.C.	6 5-61	R	R	5'10	190	146	397	24	98	21	5	2	40	22		2	.247	.340
Smith, Tony-Anthony (Irish)	07WasA 10-11BknN	5-14-84	Chicago, Ill.	2-27-64	R	R	5'9	150	170	500	46	90	12	2	1	26	95		13	.180	.218
Smith, Wally-Wallace H.	11-12StLN 14WasA	3-13-89	Philadelphia, Pa.		R	R	5'11	180	201	510	56	117	15	11	2	53	53	72	12	.229	.314
Smith, Wib-Wilbur Floyd	09StLA	8-30-86	Evart, Mich.	11-18-59	L	R	5'10	165	17	42	3	8	0	0	0	2	0		0	.190	.190
Smoot, Homer-Homer	02-06StLN 06CinN	3-23-78	Galestown, Md.	3-25-28	L	R	5'10	180	680	2635	308	763	102	45	15	269	149		84	.290	.380
Smoyer (Smowrey), Harry-Henry Neitz	12StLA	4-25-90	Fredericksburg, Pa.	2-28-58		R			6	14	1	3	0	0	0	0	2		0	.214	.214
Smykal (Smejkal), Frank-Frank John	16PitN	10-13-89	Chicago, Ill.	8-11-50	R	R	5'7	150	6	10	1	3	0	0	0	2	3	1	1	.300	.300
Smyth, Red-James Daniel	15-17BknN 17-18StLN	1-30-93	Holly Springs, Miss.	4-14-58	L	R	5'9	152	128	236	32	45	2	4	0	12	28	31	7	.191	.233
Snell, Charlie-Charles A.	12StLA	11-29-92	Reading, Pa.		R	R	5'11	160	8	19	0	4	1	0	0	0	3		0	.211	.263
Snell, Wally-Walter Henry (Doc)	13BosA	5-19-89	Bridgewater, Mass.		R	R	5'8	167	5	8	1	3	0	0	0	0	0	0	1	.375	.375
Snodgrass, Fred-Fred Carlisle (Snow)	08-15NYN 15-16BosN	10-19-87	Ventura, Cal.	4- 5-74	R	R	5'11	175	923	3101	453	852	143	42	11	351	386		215	.275	.359
Snodgrass, Walter-Walter Amzi	01BalA		Springfield, Ohio				5'10	165	3	10	0	1	0	0	0	1	0		0	.100	.100
Snyder, Jack-John William	14BufF 17BknN	-92	Allegheny Co., Pa.		R	R	5'9	170	8	11	1	3	0	0	0	1	1		0	.273	.273
Somerlott, Jock-John Wesley	10-11WasA	10-26-82	Flint, Ind.	4-21-65	R	R	6'	160	29	103	8	21	0	0	0	4	3		4	.204	.204
Southwick, Clyde-Clyde Aubra	11StLA	11- 3-86	Maxwell, Iowa	10-14-61	L	R	6'	180	4	12	3	3	0	0	0	0	1		0	.250	.250
Speaker, Tris-Tristram E (The Grey Eagle)	07-15BosA 16-26,M19-26CleA 27WasA	4- 4-88	Hubbard, Tex.	12- 8-58	L	L	5'11	193	2789	10208	1881	3515	793	223	117	1527	1381		433	.344	.500
	28PhiA																				
Spencer, Ben-Lloyd Bennet	13WasA	5-15-90	Patapsco, Md.	9- 1-70	L	L	5'8	160	8	21	2	6	1	1	0	2	2	4	0	.286	.429
Spencer, Ches-Chester Arthur	06BosN	3- 4-83	South Webster, Ohio	11-10-38	L	R	6'	180	8	27	1	4	1	0	0	0	0		0	.148	.185
Spencer, Tubby-Edward Russell	05-08StLA 09BosA 11PhiN 16-18DetA	1-26-84	Oil City, Pa.	2- 1-45	R	R	5'10	215	449	1326	106	298	43	10	3	133	87		13	.225	.279
Spratt, Jack-Henry Lee	11-12BosN	7-10-88	Broadford, Va.	7- 3-69	L	R	5'8	175	89	243	28	60	7	6	5	28	20	36	3	.247	.387
Stafford, Heinie-Henry Alexander	16NYN	11- 1-91	Orleans, Vt.	1-29-72	R	R	5'7	160	1	1	0	0	0	0	0	0	0	0	0	.000	.000
Stahl, Chick-Charles Sylvester	97-00BosN 01-06,M06BosA	1-10-73	Fort Wayne, Ind.	3-28-07	L	L			1302	5062	856	1552	218	116	37	622	470		173	.307	.417
Stahl, Jake-Garland	03BosA 04-06,M05-06WasA 08NYA 08-10BosA 11VR	4-13-79	Elkhart, Ind.	9-18-22	R	R	6'2	195	981	3421	405	891	149	87	31	437	221		178	.260	.382
	12-13,M12-13BosA																				
Stanage, Oscar-Oscar Harland	06CinN 09-20,25DetA	3-17-83	Tulare, Cal.	11-11-64	R	R	5'11	190	1094	3503	248	819	123	34	8	321	219		30	.234	.295
Stankard, Tom-Thomas Francis	04PitN	3-20-82	Waltham, Mass.	6-13-58	R	R	6'1	190	2	2	0	0	0	0	0	0	0		0	.000	.000
Stanley, Jim-James F.	14ChiF	-89			B	R	5'6	148	54	98	13	19	3	0	0	4	19		2	.194	.224
Stanley, Joe-Joseph Bernard	97WasN 02WasA 03 04BosN 05 06WasA 09ChiN	4- 2-81	Washington, D.C.	9-13-67	B	R	5'9	150	216	694	77	148	15	10	2	76	51		20	.213	.272
Stansbury, Jack-John James	18BosA	12- 6-85	Phillipsburg, N.J.	12-26-70	R	R	5'9	165	20	47	3	6	1	0	0	2	6	3	0	.128	.149
Stanton, Harry-Harry Andrew	00StLN 04ChiN		St. Louis, Mo.			R			2	3	0	0	0	0	0	0	0		0	.000	.000
Stark, Dolly-Monroe Randolph	09CleA 10-12BknN	1-19-85	Ripley, Miss.	12- 1-24	R	R	5'9	160	127	378	38	90	7	1	0	30	34		14	.238	.262
Starnagle (Steuernagel), George-George Henry	02CleA	10- 6-73	Belleville, Ill.	2-15-46	R	R	5'11	175	1	3	0	0	0	0	0	0	0		0	.000	.000
Starr, Charlie-Charles Watkin	05StLA 08PitN 09BosN 09PhiN	8-30-78	Pike Co., Ohio	10-18-37		R			108	375	33	79	4	3	0	20	51		13	.211	.237
Steelman, Farmer-Morris James	99LouN 00-01BknN 01-02PhiA	6-29-75	Millville, N.J.	9-16-44		R			43	142	8	31	3	1	0	15	14		6	.218	.254
Steinbrenner, Gene-Eugene Gass	12PhiN	11-17-92	Pittsburgh, Pa.	4-25-70	R	R	5'9	155	3	9	0	2	1	0	0	1	0	3	0	.222	.333
Steinfeldt, Harry-Harry M.	98-05CinN 06-10ChiN 11BosN	9-29-77	St. Louis, Mo.	8-17-14	R	R	5'10	180	1645	5898	762	1575	282	91	27	762	471		189	.267	.359
Stellbauer, Bill-William Jennings	16PhiA	3-20-94	Bremond, Tex.	2-16-74	R	R	5'10	175	25	48	2	13	2	1	0	5	6	7	2	.271	.354
Stem, Fred-Frederick Boothe	08-09BosN	9-22-85	Oxford, N.C.	9- 5-64	L	R	6'2	160	92	317	22	71	2	4	0	14	14		6	.224	.256
Stengel, Casey-Charles Dillon (The Old Professor)	12-17BknN 18-19PitN	7-30-90	Kansas City, Mo.	9-29-75	L	L	5'11	175	1277	4288	575	1219	182	89	60	535	437	453	131	.284	.410
	20-21PhiN 21-23NYN 24-25BosN M34-36BknN M38-43BosN M49-60NYA M62-65NYN																				
Stephens, Jim-James Walter (Little Nemo)	07-12StLA	12-10-83	Salineville, Ohio	1- 2-65	R	R	5'6	157	427	1262	95	286	30	21	3	97	77		14	.227	.291
Sterrett, Dutch-Charles Hurlbut	12-13NYA	10- 1-89	Milroy, Pa.	12- 9-65	R	R	5'11	165	87	265	30	67	4	7	1	35	12		9	.253	.332
Stewart, Mark-Mark (Big Slick)	13CinN	10-11-89	Whitlock, Tenn.	1-17-32	L	R	6'1	180	1	1	0	0	0	0	0	0	0	0	0	.000	.000
Stewart, Tuffy-Charles Eugene	13-14ChiN	7-31-83	Chicago, Ill.	11-18-34	L	L	5'10	167	11	9	1	1	1	0	0	2	2	5	1	.111	.222
Stone, George-George Robert	03BosA 05-10StLA	9- 3-77	Lost Nation, Iowa	1- 3-45	L	L	5'7	175	848	3271	426	984	107	69	23	268	282		132	.301	.397
Storke, Alan-Alan Marshall	06-09PitN 09StLN	9-27-84	Auburn, N.Y.	3-18-10	R	R			266	863	68	225	22	11	2	74	45		17	.261	.319
Stovall, George-George Thomas (Firebrand)	04-11,M11CleA 12-13,M12-13StLA	11-23-78	Independence, Mo.	11- 5-51	R	R	6'2	180	1409	5218	544	1375	231	59	15	563	172		145	.264	.339
	14-15,M14-15KCF																				
Strands, Johnny-John Lawrence	15NwkF	12- 5-85	Chicago, Ill.	1-19-57	R	R	5'10	165	35	75	7	14	3	1	1	11	6		1	.187	.293
Strang (Nicklin), Sammy (Samuel Strang)-Samuel Nicklin (The Dixie Thrush)	96LouN	12-16-76	Chattanooga, Tenn.	3-13-32	B	R			901	2925	479	787	112	28	16	253	464		219	.269	.343
	00ChiN 01NYN 02ChiA 02ChiN 03-04BknN 05-08NYN																				
Street, Gabby-Charles Evard (Old Sarge)	04-05CinN 05BosN 05CinN 08-11WasA	9-30-82	Huntsville, Ala.	2- 6-51	R	R	5'11	180	503	1501	98	312	44	11	2	105	119		17	.208	.256
	12NYA 31,M29-33StLN M38StLA																				
Strobel, Allie-Albert Irving	05-06BosN	6-11-84	Boston, Mass.	2-10-55	R	R	6'	160	105	336	29	66	10	3	1	26	29		2	.196	.253
Strunk, Amos-Amos Aaron	08-17PhiA 18-19BosA 19-20PhiA 20-24ChiA 24PhiA	1-22-89	Philadelphia, Pa.		L	L	5'11	175	1507	4994	695	1415	212	96	15	528	573		185	.283	.373
Stumpf, Bill-William Frederick	12-13NYA	3-21-92	Baltimore, Md.	2-14-66	R	R	6'	175	52	158	13	37	1	0	0	11	9		5	.234	.241
Sturgis, Dean-Dean Donnell	14PhiA	12- 1-92	Beloit, Kans.	6- 4-50	R	R	6'1	180	4	4	1	1	0	0	0	0	1	2	0	.250	.250
Sugden, Joe-Joseph	93-97PitN 98StLN 99CleN 01ChiA 02-05StLA 12DetA	7-31-70	Philadelphia, Pa.	6-28-59	B	R	5'10	180	822	2703	295	695	72	24	3	283	220		49	.257	.305
Sullivan, Andy-Andrew R.	04BosN	8-30-84	Southborough, Mass.	2-14-20		R			1	1	0	0	0	0	0	0	1		0	.000	.000
Sullivan, Billy-William Joseph Sr.	99-00BosN 01-12,14,M09ChiA 16DetA	2- 1-75	Oakland, Wis.	1-28-65	R	R	5'9	155	1143	3651	363	775	118	33	20	378	170		99	.212	.279
Sullivan, Denny-Dennis William	05WasA 07-08BosA 08-09CleA	9-28-82	Hillsboro, Wis.	6- 2-56	L	R			254	923	106	221	25	7	1	51	59		31	.239	.285
Sullivan, Eddie (See Eddie Collins)																					
Sullivan, John-John Eugene	05DetA 08PitN	2-16-73	Ill.	6- 5-24		R			13	32	4	5	0	0	0	4	4		0	.156	.156
Swacina, Harry-Harry Joseph (Swats)	07-08PitN 14-15BalF	8-22-81	St. Louis, Mo.	6-21-44	R	R	6'2	190	322	1189	110	304	46	11	1	151	32		29	.256	.315
Swander, Pinky-Edward O.	03-04StLA	7- 4-80	Portsmouth, Ohio	10-24-44	L	R	5'9	180	15	52	9	14	2	2	0	6	10		0	.269	.385
Swanson, Bill-William Andrew	14BosA	10-12-88	New York, N.Y.	10-14-54	B	R	5'7	140	11	20	0	4	2	0	0	0	3	4	0	.200	.300
Sweeney, Bill-William John	07ChiN 07-13BosN 14ChiN	3- 6-86	Covington, Ky.	5-26-48	R	R	5'10	175	1039	3692	442	1004	153	40	11	389	423		172	.272	.344
Sweeney, Charlie-Charles A.	14PhiA								1	1	0	0	0	0	0	0	0	1	0	.000	.000
Sweeney, Ed-Edward Francis	08-15NYA 19PitN	7-19-88	Chicago, Ill.	7- 4-47	R	R	6'1	200	644	1841	174	427	48	13	3	151	181		63	.232	.277
Swindells, Charlie-Charles Jay	04StLN	10-26-78	Rockford, Ill.	7-22-40	R	R	5'11	180	3	8	0	1	0	0	0	0	0		0	.125	.125
Tannehill, Jesse-Jesse Niles (See P01-19)	94CinN 97-02PitN 03NYA	7-14-74	Dayton, Ky.	9-22-56	B	L	5'8	150	505	1409	191	361	59	23	6	143	105		19	.256	.344
	04-08BosA 08-09WasA 11CinN				Bats Left 03																
Tannehill, Lee-Lee Ford	03-12ChiA	10-26-80	Dayton, Ky.	2-16-38	R	R	5'11	170	1089	3778	331	833	135	27	3	346	229		63	.220	.273
Tate, Hughie-Hugh Henry	05WasA	5-19-80	Everett, Pa.	8- 7-56	R	R	5'11	190	4	10	1	3	0	1	0	2	0		1	.300	.500
Tennant, Tom-Thomas Francis	12StLA	7- 3-82	Monroe, Wis.	2-15-55	L	L	5'11	165	2	2	1	0	0	0	0	0	0		0	.000	.000
Tenney, Fred-Frederick	94-07,M05-07BosN 08-09NYN 11,M11BosN	11-26-71	Georgetown, Mass.	7- 3-52	L	L	5'9	155	1980	7587	1271	2239	264	80	22	688	874		285	.295	.360
Tesch, Tiny-Albert John	15BknF	1-27-90	Jersey City, N.J.	8- 3-47	B	R	5'10	155	8	7	2	2	1	0	0	2	0		0	.286	.429
Textor, George-George Bernhardt (Tex)	14IndF 15NwkF	12-27-88	Newport, Ky.	3-11-54	B	R	5'10	174	25	63	3	12	0	0	0	4	2		0	.190	.190
Thomas, Bill-William Miskey	02PhiN	12- 8-77	Norristown, Pa.	1-14-50	R	R	5'10	190	6	17	1	2	0	0	0	0	1		0	.118	.118
Thomas, Fred-Frederick Harvey	18BosA 19-20PhiA 20WasA	12-19-92	Milwaukee, Wis.		R	R	5'10	160	247	859	88	193	19	14	4	45	84	90	24	.225	.293
Thomas, Ira-Ira Felix	06-07NYA 08DetA 09-15PhiA	1-22-81	Ballston Spa, N.Y.	10-11-58	R	R	6'	190	481	1352	124	327	46	17	3	155	82		20	.242	.308
Thomas, Pinch-Chester David (Goat)	12-17BosA 18-21CleA	1-24-88	Camp Point, Ill.	12-24-53	L	R	5'9	173	476	1035	88	245	27	8	2	102	118		12	.237	.284
Thomas, Roy-Roy Allen	99-08PhiN 08PitN 09BosN 10-11PhiN	3-24-74	Norristown, Pa.	11-20-59	L	L	5'11	150	1472	5292	1008	1539	99	54	7	299	1042		251	.291	.334
Thomas, Walt-Walter W.	08BosN					R			5	13	2	2	0	0	0	1	3		2	.154	.154
Thomason, Art-Arthur Wilson (Sillie)	10CleA	2-12-89	Liberty, Mo.	5- 2-44	L	L	5'8	150	17	57	3	9	0	1	0	2	5		3	.158	.193
Thompson, Homer-Thomas Homer	12NYA	6- 1-92	Spring City, Tenn.	9-12-57	R	R	5'9	160	1	0	0	0	0	0	0	0	0	0	0	–	–
Thompson, Sam-Samuel Luther (Big Sam)	85-88DetN 89-98PhiN 06DetA	3- 5-60	Danville, Ind.	11- 7-22	L	L	6'3	207	1406	5972	1259	1984	326	156	128	1299	450		235	.332	.503
										For Sam Thompson, Stolen Bases includes the years 86-06											
Thompson, Shag-James Alfred	14-16PhiA	4-29-93	Haw River, N.C.		L	R	5'8	165	48	79	12	16	2	1	0	4	18	20	2	.203	.253
Thoney (Thoeny), Jack-John (Bullet Jack)	02CleA 02BalA 03CleA 04WasA 04NYA	12- 8-79	Fort Thomas, Ky.	10-24-48	R	R	5'10	175	264	912	112	216	23	12	3	73	36		42	.237	.298
	08-09,11BosA																				
Thorpe, Jim-James Francis	13-15NYN 17CinN 17-19NYN 19BosN	5-28-88	Prague, Okla.	3-28-53	R	R	6'1	200	289	698	91	176	20	18	7	82	27	122	29	.252	.362
20-26 played in N.F.L.																					

USE NAME – GIVEN NAMES (NICKNAMES)	TEAM BY YEAR	BIRTH DATE	BIRTH PLACE	DEATH DATE	B	T	HGT	WGT	G	AB	R	H	2B	3B	HR	RBI	BB	SO	SB	BA	SA
									LIFETIME BATTING TOTALS												
Thrasher, Buck-Frank Edward	16-17PhiA	8- 6-89	Watkinsville, Ga.	6-12-38	L	R	6'	182	30	106	9	27	4	2	0	6	5	13	0	.255	.330
Tiemeyer, Eddie-Edward Carl	06-07CinN 09NYA	5- 9-85	Cincinnati, Ohio	9-27-46	R	R	5'11	185	9	19	5	5	1	0	0	0	3		0	.263	.316
Tinker, Joe-Joseph Bert	02-12ChiN 13,M13CinN 14-15,M14-15ChiF 16,M16ChiN	7-27-80	Muscotah, Kans.	7-27-48	R	R	5'9	175	1805	6445	776	1698	263	114	31	782	416		342	.263	.354
Titus, John-John Franklin (Silent John)	03-12PhiN 12-13BosN	2-21-76	St. Clair, Pa.	1- 8-43	L	L	5'9	166	1402	4960	738	1401	253	72	38	561	620		140	.282	.385
Tomer, George-George	13StLA	11-26-95	Perry, Iowa		L	R	6'	180	1	1	0	0	0	0	0	0	0	1	0	.000	.000
Tonneman, Tony-Charles Richard	11BosA	9-10-81	Chicago, Ill.	8- 7-51	R	R	5'10	175	2	5	0	1	1	0	0	3	1		0	.200	.400
Tooley, Bert-Albert	11-12BknN	8-30-86	Howell, Mich.		R	R	5'10	155	196	698	89	151	17	8	3	66	72	84	30	.216	.277
Towne, Babe-Jay King	06ChiA	3-12-80	Coon Rapids, Iowa	10-29-38	L	R		190	13	36	3	10	0	0	0	6	7		0	.278	.278
Tragesser, Walt-Walter Joseph	13,15-19BosN 19-20PhiN	6-14-87	Lafayette, Ind.	12-14-70	R	R	6'	175	272	689	54	148	31	3	6	66	35	125	14	.215	.295
Truesdale, Frank-Frank D.	10-11StLA 14NYA 18BosA	12-12-85	Kirkwood, Mo.		B	R	5'8	145	216	668	69	147	12	2	1	40	91		41	.220	.249
Turner, Terry-Terrence Lamont (Cotton Top)	01PitN 04-18CleA 19PhiA	2-28-81	Sandy Lake, Pa.	7-18-60	R	R	5'8	150	1665	5917	698	1497	207	77	8	528	435		256	.253	.318
Tutwiler, Guy-Guy Isbell (King Tut)	11,13DetA	7-17-89	Coalburg, Ala.	8-15-30	L	R	6'	175	27	79	7	16	2	1	0	10	6		2	.203	.253
Twombly, George-George Frederick (Silent George)	14-16CinN 17BosN 19WasA	6- 4-92	Boston, Mass.	2-17-75	R	R	5'9	165	150	417	35	88	1	7	0	33	41	41	21	.211	.247
Tyler, Clancy-Frederick Franklin	14BosN	12-16-91	Derry, N.H.	10-14-45	R	R	5'10	180	6	19	2	2	0	0	0	2	1	5	0	.105	.105
Tyree, Earl-Earl Carlton	14ChiN	3- 4-90	Huntsville, Ill.	5-17-54	R	R	5'8	160	1	4	1	0	0	0	0	0	0	0	0	.000	.000
Uhler, Maury-Maurice W.	14CinN	12-14-86	Pikesville, Md.	5- 4-18	R	R	5'11	165	46	56	12	12	2	0	0	3	5	11	4	.214	.250
Unglaub, Bob-Robert Alexander	04NYA 04-05,07-08,M07BosA 08-10WasA	7-31-81	Baltimore, Md.	11-29-16	R	R	5'11	178	595	2150	188	554	67	35	5	215	88		66	.258	.328
Ury, Lou-Louis	03StLN		Fort Smith, Ark.			R			2	7	0	1	0	0	0	0	0		0	.143	.143
Vahrenhorst, Harry-Harry Henry (Dutch)	04StLA	2-13-85	St. Louis, Mo.	10-10-43	R	R	6'1	175	1	1	0	0	0	0	0	0	0		0	.000	.000
Van Buren, Deacon-Edward Eugene	04BknN 04PhiN	12-14-70	La Salle Co., Ill.	6-29-57	L	R	5'10	175	13	44	2	11	2	0	0	3	3		2	.250	.295
Vandagrift, Carl-Carl William	14IndF	4-22-83	Cantrall, Ill.	10- 9-20	R	R	5'8	155	43	136	25	34	4	0	0	9	9		7	.250	.279
Van Haltren, George-George Edward Martin (See P01-19)	87-89ChiN 90BknP	3-30-66	St. Louis, Mo.	9-29-45	L	L	5'11	170	1979	8007	1650	2558	293	159	69	1014	868		564	.319	.422
	91,M91BalAA 92,M92BalN 92-93PitN 94-03NYN																				
Vann, John-John Silas	13StLN	6- 7-93	Fairland, Okla.	6-10-58	R	R			1	1	0	0	0	0	0	0	0	1	0	.000	.000
Van Tappen, W.-W.	14KCF	-91			R	R	5'8	158	18	39	1	8	1	0	1	3	1		1	.205	.308
Van Zandt, Ike-Charles Isaac	01NYN 04ChiN 05StLA	-77	Brooklyn, N.Y.	9-14-08					100	339	32	76	15	1	1	20	7		7	.224	.283
Vaughn, Bobby-Robert	09NYA 15StLF	6- 4-85	Stamford, N.Y.	4-11-65	R	R	5'9	150	149	535	70	148	19	9	0	32	59		25	.277	.346
Veach, Bobby-Robert Hayes	12-23DetA 24-25BosA 25NYA 25WasA	6-29-88	Island, Ky.	8- 7-45	L	R	5'11	160	1821	6659	953	2064	393	147	64	1166	571		195	.310	.442
Vick, Sammy-Samuel Bruce	17-20NYA 21BosA	4-12-95	Batesville, Miss.		R	R	5'10	163	213	641	90	159	28	11	2	50	51	91	12	.248	.335
Vinson, Rube-Ernest Augustus	04-05CleA 06ChiA	3-20-79	Dover, Del.	10-12-51			5'9	168	60	206	26	47	4	1	0	14	19		7	.228	.257
Viox, Jim-James Henry	12-16PitN	12-30-90	Lockland, Ohio	1- 6-69	R	R	5'7	150	506	1703	214	465	76	24	7	191	222	108	39	.273	.358
Vitt, Ossie-Oscar Joseph	12-18DetA 19-21BosA M38-40CleA	1- 4-90	San Francisco, Cal.	1-31-63	R	R	5'10	150	1062	3760	560	894	106	48	4	294	455		114	.238	.295
Von Kolnitz, Fritz-Alfred Holmes	14-15CinN 16ChiA	5-20-93	Charleston, S.C.	3-18-48	R	R	5'10	175	115	226	15	48	9	1	0	19	15	33	5	.212	.261
Wade, Ham-Abraham Lincoln	07NYN	12-20-80	Spring City, Pa.	7-21-68	R	R	5'8	155	1	0	0	0	0	0	0	0	0	0	0	–	–
Wagner, Bill-William Joseph	14-17PitN 18BosN	1- 2-94	Jessup, Iowa	1-11-51	R	R	6'	187	93	242	19	50	7	4	1	18	21	37	1	.207	.281
Wagner, Heinie-Charles F.	02NYN 06-13BosA 14IL 15-16,18,M30BosA	9-23-80	New York, N.Y.	3-20-43	R	R	5'9	183	983	3333	400	834	128	47	10	343	310		144	.250	.326
Wagner, Honus-John Peter (The Flying Dutchman)	97-99LouN 00-17,M17-PitN	2-24-74	Carnegie, Pa.	12- 6-55	R	R	5'11	200	2792	10427	1740	3430	651	252	101	1732	963		720	.329	.469
Wagner, Joe-Joseph Bernard	15CinN	4-24-89	New York, N.Y.	11-15-48	R	R	5'11	165	75	197	17	35	5	2	0	13	8	35	4	.178	.223
Wakefield, Howard-Howard John	05CleA 06WasA 07CleA	4- 2-84	Bucyrus, Ohio	4-16-41	R	R			112	273	24	68	11	2	1	25	10		6	.249	.315
Walden, Fred-Thomas Fred	12StLA	6-25-90	Fayette, Mo.	9-27-55	R	R			1	0	0	0	0	0	0	0	0	0	0	–	–
Waldron, Irv-Irving	01MilA 01WasA	1-21-76	Queens, N.Y.	7-22-44	R	R			141	598	102	186	22	9	0	52	38		20	.311	.378
Walker, Ernie-Ernest Robert	13-15StLA	9-17-90	Blossburg, Ala.	4- 1-65	L	R	6'	165	128	254	34	65	9	5	1	25	36	63	11	.256	.343
Walker, Tilly-Clarence William	11-12WasA 13-15StLA 16-17BosA 18-23PhiA	9- 4-87	Denver, Colo.	9-20-59	R	R	5'11	175	1421	5067	696	1423	244	71	118	679	415		130	.281	.427
Wall, Joe-Joseph Francis (Gummy)	01-02NYN 02BknN	7-24-73	Brooklyn, N.Y.	7-17-36	L	L			15	40	2	12	2	0	0	1	5		0	.300	.350
Wallace, Bobby-Rhoderick John (Rhody) (See P01-19)	94-98CleN 99-01StLN	11- 4-73	Pittsburgh, Pa.	11- 3-60	R	R	5'8	170	2385	8629	1056	2308	395	149	35	1121	774		209	.267	.360
	02-16,M11-12StLA 17-18StLN M37CinN																				
Wallace, Doc-Frederick Renshaw	19PhiN	9-20-93	Church Hill, Md.	12-31-64	R	R	5'6	135	2	4	0	1	0	0	0	0	0	1	0	.250	.250
Wallace, Jack-Clarence Eugene	15ChiN	8- 6-90	Winnfield, La.	10-15-60	R	R	5'11	175	2	7	1	2	0	0	0	1	0	2	0	.286	.286
Wallace, Jim-James L.	05PitN	11-14-81	Boston, Mass.	5-16-53	L	L			7	29	3	6	1	0	0	3	3		2	.207	.241
Walsh, Austin-Austin	14ChiF	-92			L	L	5'11	175	57	121	14	29	6	1	1	10	4		0	.240	.331
Walsh, Dee-Leo Thomas	13-15StLA	3-28-90	St. Louis, Mo.	7-14-71	B	R	5'9	165	89	226	22	44	5	1	0	12	22	40	10	.195	.226
Walsh, Jimmy-James Charles	12-13PhiA 14NYA 14-16PhiA 16-17BosA 18MS	9-22-85	Kallila, Ireland	7- 3-62	L	R	5'10	170	536	1770	235	409	70	31	6	150	249		92	.231	.316
Walsh, Jimmy-Michael Timothy (Runt)	10-13PhiN 14-15BalF 15StLF	3-25-86	Lima, Ohio	1-21-47	R	R	5'9	174	502	1571	178	447	84	14	25	212	101		45	.285	.404
Walsh, Joe-Joseph Francis	10-11NYA	10-14-87	Waterbury, Conn.	1- 6-67		R			5	12	2	2	1	0	0	2	0		0	.167	.250
Walsh, John-John	03PhiN		Wilkes-Barre, Pa.			R			1	3	0	0	0	0	0	0	0		0	.000	.000
Walsh, Tom-Thomas Joseph	06ChiN	2-28-85	Davenport, Iowa	3-16-63	R	R	5'11	170	2	1	0	0	0	0	0	0	0		0	.000	.000
Wanner, Johnny-Clarence Curtis	09NYA	11-29-85	Geneseo, Ill.	5-28-19					3	8	0	1	0	0	0	0	2		1	.125	.125
Ward, Chuck-Charles William	17PitN 18-22BknN	7-30-94	St. Louis, Mo.	4- 4-69	R	R	6'2	180	236	769	52	175	20	6	0	72	51	67	7	.228	.269
Ward, Hap	12DetA								1	2	0	0	0	0	0	0	0		0	.000	.000
Ward, Joe-Joseph	06PhiN 09NYA 09-10PhiN	9- 2-84	Philadelphia, Pa.	8-11-34	R	R			166	465	47	110	18	9	0	47	18		12	.237	.314
Ward, Rube-John Andrew	02BknN	2- 6-79	New Lexington, Ohio	1-17-45					13	31	4	9	1	0	0	2	2		0	.290	.323
Wares, Buzzy-Clyde Ellsworth	13-14StLA	3-23-86	Vandalia, Mich.	5-26-64	R	R	5'10	150	91	250	25	55	12	1	0	24	29	38	12	.220	.276
Warner, Hooks-Hoke Hayden	16-17PitN 18MS 19PitN 21ChiN	5-22-94	Del Rio, Tex.	2-19-47	L	R	5'10	170	67	219	16	50	2	1	2	19	11	22	7	.228	.274
Warner, John-John Joseph	95BosN 95-96LouN 96-01NYN 02BosA 03-04NYN 05StLN	8-15-72	New York, N.Y.	12-21-43	L	R			1066	3474	340	866	80	35	6	304	181		86	.249	.298
	05-06DetA 06-08WasA																				
Warren, Bill-William H.	14IndF 15NwkF	2-11-87	Cairo, Ill.		L	R	5'8	165	31	53	5	13	2	0	0	6	5		2	.245	.283
Washburn, Libe-Libe	02NYN 03PhiN	6-16-74	Lynn, N.H.	3-22-40					14	27	2	7	0	0	0	1	3		1	.259	.259
Watkins, Ed-Edward	02PhiN								1	3	0	0	0	0	0	0	1		0	.000	.000
Watson, Art-Arthur S.	14-15BknF 15BufF	-86	Chicago, Ill.		R	R	5'10	175	53	95	17	32	5	4	2	17	4		0	.337	.537
Weaver, Art-Arthur Coggshall	02-03STLN 03PitN 05StLA 08ChiA	4- 7-79	Wichita, Kans.	3-23-17		R			86	257	20	47	5	2	0	15	9		1	.183	.218
Weaver, Buck-George Davis	12-20ChiA 20DL	8-18-90	Stowe, Pa.	1-31-56	B	R	5'11	170	1254	4810	625	1310	199	69	21	421	183		172	.272	.356
Webb, Billy-William Joseph	17PitN 18MS	6-25-95	Chicago, Ill.	1-12-43	R	R	5'10	160	5	15	1	3	0	0	0	0	2	3	0	.200	.200
Weeden, Bert-Charles Albert	11BosN	12-21-82	Northwood, N.H.	1- 7-39	L	L	6'	200	1	1	0	0	0	0	0	0	0	0	0	.000	.000
Weiser, Bud-Harry Budson	15-16PhiN	1- 8-91	Shamokin, Pa.	7-31-61	R	R	5'11	165	41	74	7	12	3	0	0	9	7	15	2	.162	.203
Weiss, Joe-Joseph Harold	15ChiF	1-27-94	Chicago, Ill.		R	R	6'	165	29	85	6	19	1	2	0	11	3		0	.224	.282
Welchonce, Harry-Harry Monroe	11PhiN	11-20-83	North Point, Pa.		L	R	5'11	170	26	66	9	14	4	0	0	6	7	8	0	.212	.273
Welday, Mike-Lyndon Earl	07,09ChiA	12-19-79	Conway, Iowa	5-28-42	L	L			53	109	5	22	1	1	0	5	10		2	.202	.229
Welf, Ollie-Oliver Henry	16CleA	1-17-89	Cleveland, Ohio	6-15-67	R	L	5'9	160	1	0	0	0	0	0	0	0	0	0	0	–	–
Wertz, Del-Dwight Lewis	14BufF	-91			R	R	5'6	155	3	0	1	0	0	0	0	0	0	0	0	–	–
Westerberg, Oscar-Oscar	07BosN			4-17-09		R			2	6	0	2	0	0	0	1	1		0	.333	.333
Wisterzil, Tex-George J.	14-15BknF 15ChiF 15StLF 15ChiF	3- 7-91	Detroit, Mich.	6-27-64	R	R	5'9	150	242	828	83	215	26	14	0	105	65		29	.260	.325
Whaling, Bert-Albert James	13-15BosN	6-22-88	Los Angeles, Cal.	1-21-65	R	R	6'	185	211	573	50	129	21	4	0	50	39	98	5	.225	.276
Wheat, Mack-McKinley Davis	15-19BknN 20-21PhiN	6- 9-93	Polo, Mo.		R	R	5'11	167	225	602	34	123	23	5	4	35	19	102	7	.204	.279
Wheat, Zack-Zachariah Davis (Buck)	09-26BknN 27PhiA	5-23-86	Hamilton, Mo.	3-11-72	L	R	5'10	170	2410	9106	1289	2884	476	172	132	1248	650		205	.317	.450
Wheeler (Maynard), Dick (Richard Wheeler)-Richard	18StLN	1-14-98	Keene, N.H.	2-12-62	R	R	5'11	185	3	6	0	0	0	0	0	0	0	3	0	.000	.000
Wheeler, Ed-Edward W.	02BknN	6-15-79	Sherman, Mich.	8-15-60	R	R			30	96	4	12	0	0	0	5	3		1	.125	.125
Wheeler, George-George Harrison (Heavy)	10CinN	11-10-81	Shelburn, Ind.	6-14-18	R	R	5'9	180	3	3	0	0	0	0	0	0	0	2	0	.000	.000
Whelan, Jim-James Frank	13StLN	-90			R	R	5'8	165	1	1	0	0	0	0	0	0	0	0	0	.000	.000
White, Doc-Guy Harris (See P01-19)	01-02PhiN 03-13ChiA	4- 9-79	Washington, D.C.	2-19-69	L	L	6'1	165	547	1279	147	277	22	13	2	76	147		32	.217	.259
White, John-John Wallace (Doc)	04BosN	1-19-78	Indianapolis, Ind.	9-30-63	R	R	5'6		1	5	1	0	0	0	0	0	0		0	.000	.000
White, Sam-Samuel	19BosN	-95			R	R	6'	180	1	1	0	0	0	0	0	0	0	0	0	.000	.000
Whitehouse, Gil-Gilbert Arthur	12BosN 15NwkF	10-15-93	Somerville, Mass.	2-14-26	B	R	5'10	170	37	126	16	27	6	2	0	9	6		3	.214	.294
Whiteman, George-George	07BosA 17NYA 18BosA	12-23-82	Peoria, Ill.	2-10-47	R	R	5'7	160	85	257	32	70	17	1	1	31	27		11	.272	.358
Whitted, Possum-George Bostic	12-14StLN 14BosN 15-19PhiN 19-21PitN 22BknN	2- 4-90	Durham, N.C.	10-16-62	R	R	5'8	168	1024	3628	440	978	145	60	23	451	215	310	116	.270	.362
Wickland, Al-Albert	13CinN 14-15ChiF 15PitF 18BosN 19NYA	1-27-88	Chicago, Ill.		L	L	5'7	155	444	1468	212	397	58	38	12	144	207		58	.270	.386
Wilhoit, Joe-Joseph William	16-17BosN 17PitN 17-18NYN 19BosA	12-20-91	Hiawatha, Kans.	9-25-30	L	R	6'2	175	283	782	93	201	23	9	3	73	75	82	28	.257	.321
Wilie, Denny-Denney Earnest	11-12StLN 15CleA	9-22-90	Mt. Calm, Tex.	6-20-66	L	L	5'8	155	103	230	26	56	7	3	2	19	41	38	5	.243	.326

USE NAME – GIVEN NAMES (NICKNAMES)	TEAM BY YEAR	BIRTH DATE	BIRTH PLACE	DEATH DATE	LIFETIME BATTING TOTALS																
					B	T	HGT	WGT	G	AB	R	H	2B	3B	HR	RBI	BB	SO	SB	BA	SA
Wilkinson, Ed-Edward E.	11NYA	-90	San Francisco, Cal.		R	R	5'10	154	10	13	2	3	0	0	0	1	0		0	.231	.231
Williams, Art-Arthur Frank	02ChiN	8-26-77	Somerville, Mass.	-35		R			47	160	17	37	3	0	0	14	15		9	.231	.250
Williams, Bob-Robert Elias	11-13NYA	4-27-94	Monday, Ohio	8- 6-62	R	R	6'	190	46	110	10	18	3	0	0	11	15		1	.164	.191
Williams, Gus-August Joseph (Gloomy Gus)	11-15StLA	5- 7-88	Omaha, Neb.	4-16-64	L	L	6'	185	403	1398	171	367	58	31	12	143	126		95	.263	.374
Williams, Harry-Harry Peters	13-14NYA	6-23-90	Omaha, Neb.	12-21-63	R	R	6'2	200	86	260	27	50	8	3	2	29	41	36	9	.192	.269
Williams, Jimmy-James Thomas (Buttons)	99-00PitN 01-02BalA 03-07NYA 08-09StLA	12-20-76	St. Louis, Mo.	1-16-65	R	R	5'9	175	1457	5483	775	1507	243	137	49	796	474		159	.275	.396
Williams, Otto-Otto George	02-03StLN 03-04ChiN 06WasA	11- 2-77	Newark, N.J.	3-19-37	R	R			170	568	48	113	13	3	0	34	29		24	.203	.237
Williams, Rinaldo-Rinaldo Lewis	14BknF	12-18-93	Santa Cruz, Cal.	4-24-66	L	R			4	15	1	4	2	0	0	0	0		0	.267	.400
Williams, Rip-Alva Mitchel	11BosA 12-16WasA 18CleA	1-31-82	Carthage, Ill.	7-23-33	R	R	5'11	172	493	1186	111	314	51	23	2	145	95		27	.265	.352
Wilson, Art-Arthur Earl (Dutch)	08-13NYN 14-15ChiF 16PitN 16-17ChiN 18-20BosN 21CleA	12-11-85	Macon, Ill.	6-12-60	R	R	5'8	170	812	2056	237	536	96	22	24	226	292		50	.261	.364
Wilson, Gary-James Gary	02BosA	1-12-77	Baltimore, Md.	5- 1-69	R	R	5'7	168	2	8	0	1	0	0	0	1	0		0	.125	.125
Wilson, Les-Lester Wilbur (Tug)	11BosA	7-17-85	St. Louis, Mich.	4- 4-69	L	R	5'11	170	5	7	0	0	0	0	0	0	2		0	.000	.000
Wilson, Owen-John Owen (Chief)	08-13PitN 14-16StLN	8-21-83	Austin, Tex.	2-22-54	L	R	6'2	185	1280	4624	520	1246	157	114	59	571	241		98	.269	.391
Wilson, Squanto-George Frank	11DetA 14BosA	3-29-89	Old Town, Me.	3-26-67	B	R	5'9	170	6	16	2	3	0	0	0	0	2		0	.188	.188
Wilson, Tom-Thomas C.	14WasA	-89			R	R	6'1	170	1	1	0	0	0	0	0	0	0	0	0	.000	.000
Wingo, Ivy-Ivey Brown	11-14StLN 15-26,29,M16CinN	7- 8-90	Gainesville, Ga.	3- 1-41	L	R	5'10	160	1326	4001	363	1039	147	81	25	455	264	285	87	.260	.356
Wolfe, Harry-Harry	17ChiN 17PitN	7- 7-93	Cleveland, Ohio		R	R	5'8	160	12	10	1	2	0	0	0	1	2	5	0	.200	.200
Wolfe, Polly-Roy Chamberlain	12,14ChiA	9- 1-88	Knoxville, Ill.	11-21-38	L	R	5'10	170	10	29	0	6	0	0	0	0	3		1	.207	.207
Wolter, Harry-Harry Meigs (See P01-19)	07CinN 07PitN 07StLN 09BosA 10-13NYA 17ChiN	7-11-84	Monterey, Cal.	7- 7-70	L	L	5'10	175	587	1905	286	514	69	42	12	167	268		95	.270	.369
Wolverton, Harry-Harry Sterling	98-00ChiN 00-01PhiN 02WasA 02-04PhiN 05BosN 12,M12NYA	12- 6-73	Mt. Vernon, Ohio	2- 4-37		R	5'11	205	779	2993	345	834	94	52	7	352	166		81	.279	.352
Wood, Bob-Robert Lynn	98-00CinN 01-02CleA 04-05DetA	7-28-65	Thorn Hill, Ohio	5-22-43	R	R			379	1232	146	347	70	15	2	168	89		14	.282	.368
Wood, Harry-Harry	03CinN		Baltimore, Md.		L	R	5'10	155	2	3	0	0	0	0	0	0	1		0	.000	.000
Wood, Joe-Joseph (Smokey Joe) (See P01-19)	08-15BosA 16HO 17-22CleA	10-25-89	Kansas City, Mo.		R	R	5'11	180	695	1952	267	553	118	30	24	325	208		23	.283	.411
Wood, Roy-Roy Winton (Woody)	13PitN 14-15CleA	8-29-92	Monticello, Ark.	4- 6-74	R	R	6'	175	119	333	33	77	12	4	1	20	16	47	7	.231	.300
Woodruff, Orville-Orville Francis (Sam)	04,10CinN	12-27-76	Chilo, Ohio	7-22-37	R	R	5'9	160	108	367	26	67	15	3	0	22	26		11	.183	.240
Wortman, Chuck-William Lewis	16-18ChiN	1- 5-92	Baltimore, Md.		R	R	5'7	150	161	441	45	82	8	3	3	28	37	47	13	.186	.238
Wright, Ceylon-Edward Yatman	16ChiA		Chicago, Ill.		L	R	5'9	150	8	18	0	0	0	0	0	0	1	7	0	.000	.000
Wright, Dick-William James	15BknF	5- 5-90	Worcester, N.Y.	1-24-52	R	R	5'10	170	4	5	0	0	0	0	0	0	0		0	.000	.000
Yale, Ad-William M.	05BknN	4-17-70	Bristol, Conn.	4-27-48					4	13	1	1	0	0	0	1	1		0	.077	.077
Yantz, George-George Webb	12ChiN	7-27-86	Louisville, Ky.	2-26-67	R	R	5'6	168	1	1	0	1	0	0	0	0	0	0	0	1.000	1.000
Yeabsley, Bert-Robert Watkins	19PhiN	12-17-93	Philadelphia, Pa.	2- 8-61	R	R	5'9	175	3	0	0	0	0	0	0	0	1	0	0	–	–
Yeager, George-George E.	96-99BosN 01CleA 01PitN 02NYN 02BalA	6- 4-73	Cincinnati, Ohio	Deceased		R			211	694	89	164	25	6	5	73	45		9	.236	.311
Yeager, Joe-Joseph F. (Little Joe) (See P01-19)	98-00BknN 01-03DetA 05-06NYA 07-08StLA	8-28-75	Philadelphia, Pa.	7- 2-37		R			572	1844	203	467	77	29	4	201	110		37	.253	.333
Yelle, Archie-Archie Joseph	17-19DetA	6-11-92	Saginaw, Mich.		R	R	5'10	170	86	199	12	32	4	0	0	7	15	19	2	.161	.181
Yerkes, Steve-Stephen Douglas	09,11-14BosA 14-15PitF 16ChiN	5-15-88	Hatboro, Pa.	1-31-71	R	R	5'9	165	707	2516	307	675	124	32	6	254	207		54	.268	.350
Yohe, Bill-William F.	09WasA	9- 2-79	Mattoon, Ill.			R	5'8	180	21	72	6	15	2	0	0	4	3		2	.208	.236
Young, Del-Delmer John	09CinN 14-15BufF	10-24-85	Macon City, Mo.	12-17-59	L	R	5'11	195	94	196	17	52	5	5	4	23	5		1	.265	.403
Young, George-George Joseph	13CleA	4- 1-90	Brooklyn, N.Y.	3-13-50	L	R	5'10	180	2	2	0	0	0	0	0	0	0	0	0	.000	.000
Young, Herman-Herman John	11BosN	4-14-86	Roxbury, Mass.	12-13-66	R	R	5'8	155	9	25	2	6	0	0	0	0	0	3	0	.240	.240
Young, Ralph-Ralph Stuart (Pep)	13NYA 15-21DetA 22PhiA	9-19-89	Philadelphia, Pa.	1-24-65	B	R	5'9	165	1022	3643	480	898	108	30	4	254	495	235	92	.247	.296
Zacher, Elmer-Elmer Henry (Silver)	10NYN 10StLN	9-17-83	Buffalo, N.Y.	12-20-44	R	R	5'9	190	48	132	7	28	5	1	0	10	10	19	3	.212	.265
Zalusky, Jack-John Francis	03NYA	6-22-79	Minneapolis, Minn.	8-11-35	R	R	5'11	172	7	16	2	5	0	0	0	1	1		0	.313	.313
Zearfoss, Dave-David William Tilden	96-98NYN 04-05StLN	1- 1-68	Schenectady, N.Y.	9-12-45		R			72	201	15	42	3	3	0	17	19		1	.209	.254
Zeider, Rollie-Rollie Hubert (Bunions)	10-13ChiA 13NYA 14-15ChiF 16-18ChiN	11-16-83	Auburn, Ind.	9-12-67	R	R	5'10	162	938	3213	392	768	93	22	5	253	334		223	.239	.286
Zimmer, Chief-Charles Louis	84DetN 86NYAA 87-88CleAA 89-99CleN 99LouN 00-02PitN 03,M03PhiN	11-23-60	Marietta, Ohio	8-22-49	R	R	6'	190	1277	4528	622	1227	221	80	26	625	390		158	.271	.372
													For Zimmer, Stolen Bases includes the years, 86-03								
Zimmerman, Bill-William H.	15BknN	1-20-89	Kengen, Germany	10- 4-52	R	R	5'8	172	22	57	3	16	2	0	0	7	4	8	1	.281	.316
Zimmerman, Eddie-Edward Desmond	06StLN 11BknN	1- 4-83	Oceanic, N.J.	5- 6-45	R	R	5'9	160	127	431	31	80	10	7	3	37	34		9	.186	.262
Zimmerman, Heinie-Henry	07-16ChiN 16-19NYN 19DU	2- 9-87	New York, N.Y.	3-14-69	R	R	5'11	176	1456	5304	695	1566	275	105	58	796	242		175	.295	.419
Zinn, Guy-Guy	11-12NYA 13BosN 14-15BalF	2-13-87	Hallbrook, W.Va.	10- 6-49	L	R	5'10	170	314	1103	136	297	51	23	15	139	109		28	.269	.398
Zwilling, Dutch-Edward Harrison	10ChiA 14-15ChiF 16ChiN	11- 2-88	St. Louis, Mo.		L	L	5'6	160	366	1280	167	364	76	15	29	202	128		46	.284	.435

USE NAME – GIVEN NAMES (NICKNAMES)	TEAM BY YEAR	BIRTH DATE	BIRTH PLACE	DEATH DATE	B	T	HGT	WGT	W	L	PCT	SV	G	GS	CG	IP	H	BB	SO	ShO	ERA	AB	H	HR	BA
									LIFETIME PITCHING TOTALS													BATTING TOTALS			
Ables, Harry-Harry Terrell (Hal, Hans)	05StLA 09CleA 11NYA	10- 4-84	Terrell, Tex.	2- 8-51	R	L	6'2	200	1	5	.167	0	14	8	4	72	79	30	41	0	4.00	26	0	0	.000
Adams, Babe-Charles Benjamin	06StLN 07,09-16,18-26PitN*	5-18-82	Tipton, Ind.	7-27-68	L	R	5'11	185	194	140	.581	15	482	355	206	2995	2841	430	1036	44	2.76	1019	216	3	.212
Adams, Dan-Daniel Leslie	14-15KCF	6-19-89	St. Louis, Mo.	10- 6-64	R	R	5'11	165	4	11	.267	3	47	16	6	171	182	65	54	0	3.74	55	8	1	.145
Adams, Joe-Joseph Edward (Wagon Tongue)	02StLN	10-28-77	Cowden, Ill.	10- 8-52	R	L	6'	190	0	0	–	0	1	0	0	4	9	2	0	0	9.00	2	0	0	.000
Adams, Karl-Karl Tutwiler (Rebel)	14CinN 15ChiN	8-11-91	Colombus, Ga.	9-17-67	R	R	6'2	170	1	9	.100	0	30	12	3	115	119	48	62	0	5.01	32	1	0	.031
Adams, Rick-Reuben Alexander	05WasA	12-24-78	Paris, Tex.	3-10-55	L	L	6'	165	2	6	.250	0	11	6	3	63	63	24	25	1	3.57	23	4	0	.174
Adams, Willie-James Irwin	12-13StLA 14PitF 18-19PhiA	9-27-90	Clearfield, Pa.	6-18-37	R	R	6'4	180	9	16	.360	2	65	21	8	284	303	144	74	0	4.37	88	9	0	.102
Adkins, Doc-Merle Theron (Babe)	02BosA 03NYA	8- 5-72	Troy, Wis.	9-12-55	R	R	5'11	220	1	2	.333	1	6	3	1	27	40	12	3	0	5.00	12	2	0	.167
Aitchison, Raleigh-Raleigh Leonidas (Redskin)	11,14-15BknN	12- 5-87	Tyndall, S.D.	9-26-58	R	L	5'11	175	12	12	.500	0	34	22	10	206	193	67	101	3	3.01	59	10	0	.169
Akers, Jerry-Albert Earl	12WasA	11- 1-87	Shelbyville, Ind.		R	R	5'11	175	0	0	–	1	5	1	0	20	24	15	11	0	4.95	6	2	0	.333
Alberts, Cy-Frederick Joseph	10StLN	1-14-82	Grand Rapids, Mich.	8-27-17	R	R	6'	230	1	2	.333	0	4	3	2	28	35	20	10	0	6.11	7	0	0	.000
Alexander, Pete-Grover Cleveland	11-17PhiN 18-26ChiN 26-29StLN	2-26-87	Elba, Neb.	11- 4-50	R	R	6'1	185	373	208	.642	32	696	598	439	5189	4868	953	2199	88	2.56	1810	378	11	.209
	30PhiN																								
Allen, Frank-Frank Leon	12-14BknN 14-15PitF 16-17BosN	8-26-89	Newbern, Ala.	7-30-33	R	L	5'8	175	50	67	.427	3	180	127	60	970	893	373	457	10	2.93	288	39	2	.135
Allen, John-John Marshall	14BalF	10-27-90	Berkeley Spr., W. Va.	9-24-67	R	R	6'1	170	0	0	–	0	1	0	0	2	2	2	2	0	18.00	0	0	0	–
Allison, Mack-Mack Pendleton	11-13StLA	1-23-87	Owensboro, Ky.	3-13-64	R	R	6'1	185	9	21	.300	1	45	27	16	246	247	67	57	1	3.18	76	9	0	.118
Altrock, Nick-Nicholas	98LouN 02-03BosA 03-09ChiA	9-15-76	Cincinnati, Ohio	1-20-65	B	L	5'10	197	82	72	.532	11	218	161	128	1515	1455	272	425	16	2.67	552	97	2	.176
	09,12-15,18-19,24,29,31,33WasA																								
Ames, Red-Leon Kessling	03-13NYN 13-15CinN 15-19StLN 19PhiN	8- 2-82	Warren, Ohio	10- 8-36	B	R	5'10	185	183	167	.523	36	533	367	209	3195	2896	1034	1662	26	2.63	1014	143	3	.141
Ancker, Walter-Walter (Liver, Gee)	15PhiA	4-10-94	New York, N.Y.	2-13-54	R	R	6'1	190	0	0	–	0	4	1	0	18	19	17	4	0	3.50	6	0	0	.000
Anderson, Fred-John Fred (Spitball)	09,13BosA 14-15BufF 16-18NYN	12-11-85	Calahan, N.C.	11- 8-57	R	R	6'2	180	53	57	.482	8	178	114	62	986	912	247	514	11	2.86	312	41	0	.131
Anderson, Walter-Walter Carl (Lefty)	17PhiA 18MS 19PhiA	9-25-97	Grand Rapids, Mich.		L	L	6'2	160	1	0	1.000	0	17	2	0	53	45	29	20	0	3.23	11	3	0	.273
Anderson, Wingo-Wingo Charlie	10CinN	8-13-86	Alvarado, Tex.	12-19-50	R	L	5'10	150	0	0	–	0	7	2	0	17	16	17	11	0	4.76	5	1	0	.200
Applegate, Fred-Frederick Romaine (Snitz)	04PhiA	5- 9-79	Bradford, Pa.	4-21-00	R	R	6'2	180	1	2	.333	0	3	3	3	21	29	8	12	0	6.43	7	2	0	.286
Appleton, Ed-Edward Samuel (Whitey, Roastie)	15-16BknN	2-29-92	Arlington, Tex.	1-27-32	R	R	6'2	185	5	12	.294	1	48	13	0	100	112	84	64	0	3.26	56	9	0	.161
Arellanes, Frank-Frank Julian	08-10BosA	1-28-82	Santa Cruz, Cal.	12-13-18	R	R	5'11	175	24	21	.533	8	74	51	25	410	358	85	148	2	2.28	142	24	1	.169
Armstrong, Howard-Howard Elmer	11PhiA	12- 2-89	East Claridon, O.	3- 8-26	R	R	5'9	165	0	1	.000	0	1	0	0	3	3	1	0	0	0.00	1	0	0	.000
Atkins, Tommy-Francis Montgomery	09-10PhiA	12- 9-87	Ponca, Neb.	5- 7-56	L	L	5'10	165	3	2	.600	2	16	4	2	63	59	28	33	0	2.86	19	2	0	.105
Ayers, Doc-Yancy Wyatt	13-19WasA 19-21DetA	5-20-90	Fancy Gap, Va.	5-26-68	R	R	6'1	185	70	80	.467	13	299	138	59	1429	1357	379	622	16	2.84	420	72	0	.171
Backman, Les-Lester John	09-10StLN	3-20-88	Cleves, Ohio		R	R	6'	195	9	18	.333	2	47	25	14	244	263	92	76	0	3.61	74	8	0	.108
Bacon, Eddie-Edgar Suter	17PhiA	4- 8-95	Franklin Co., Ky.	10- 2-63					0	0	–	0	1	0	0	6	5	7	0	0	6.00	6	3	0	.500
Bader, Lore-Lore Verne (King)	12NYN 17-18BosA	4-27-88	Bader, Ill.	6- 2-73	L	R	6'	175	5	3	.625	0	22	6	3	75	83	36	27	1	2.52	22	4	0	.182
Bagby, Jim-James Charles Jacob Sr. (Sarge)	12CinN 16-22CleA 23PitN	10- 5-89	Barnett, Ga.	7-28-54	B	R	6'1	180	127	87	.593	28	316	209	132	1828	1884	458	450	15	3.10	660	144	2	.218
Baichley, Grover-Grover Cleveland	14StLA	1- 7-90	Toledo, Ill.	6-30-56	R	R	5'9	165	0	0	–	0	4	0	0	7	9	3	3	0	5.14	1	0	0	.000
Bailey, Bill-William F.	07-12StLA 14-15BalF 15ChiF 18DetA 21-22StLN	4-12-89	Fort Smith, Ark.	11- 2-26	L	L	5'11	165	37	78	.322	1	203	117	71	1086	1035	527	570	8	3.56	366	71	0	.194
Baker, Bock-Charles	01CleA 01PhiA	7-17-78	Troy, N.Y.						0	2	.000	0	2	2	1	14	29	12	1	0	7.71	7	1	0	.143
Baker, Ernie-Ernest Gould	05CinN	8- 8-75	Concord, Mich.	10-25-45	R	R	5'10	160	0	0	–	0	1	0	0	4	7	0	1	0	4.50	2	0	0	.000
Baker, Jesse-Jesse Ormand	11ChiA	6- 3-88	Anderson I., Wash.	9-26-72	L	L	5'11	188	2	7	.222	1	22	8	3	94	101	30	51	0	3.93	29	3	0	.103
Baldwin, Ollie-Oliver F.	08StLN		Youngstown, Ohio						1	3	.250	0	4	4	0	15	16	11	5	0	6.00	6	0	0	.000
Barberich, Frank-Frank Frederick	07BosN 10BosA	2- 3-82	Queens, N.Y.	5- 1-65	B	R	5'10	175	1	1	.500	0	4	2	1	17	26	7	1	0	6.35	5	0	0	.000
Barger, Cy-Enos Bolivar	06-07NYA 10-12BknN 14-15PitF	5-18-85	Jamestown, Ky.	9-23-64	L	R	6'	160	46	63	.422	8	151	111	78	975	1010	334	297	5	3.56	428	97	0	.227
Barron, Frank-Frank John	14WasA	8- 6-90	St. Mary's, W. Va.	9-18-64	L	L	6'1	175	0	0	–	0	1	0	0	1	1	0	1	0	0.00	0	0	0	–
Barry, Ed-Edward (Jumbo)	05-07BosA		Freeport, Ind.			L			1	6	.143	0	12	10	6	79	74	25	34	0	3.53	23	2	0	.087
Barry, Hardin-Hardin (Finn)	12PhiA	3-26-91	Susanville, Cal.	11- 5-69	R	R	6'	195	0	0	–	0	3	0	0	13	18	4	3	0	7.62	4	0	0	.000
Barry, Tom-Thomas Arthur	04PhiN	4-10-79	St. Louis, Mo.	6- 4-46					0	1	.000	0	1	1	0	1	6	1	1	0	27.00	0	0	0	–
Barthold, John-John Francis (Hans)	04PhiA	4-14-82	Philadelphia, Pa.	11- 4-46	B	R	5'11	180	0	1	.000	0	4	0	0	11	12	8	5	0	4.91	3	1	0	.333
Bartley, Bill-William Jackson	03NYN 06-07PhiA	1- 8-85	Cincinnati, Ohio	5-17-65	R	R	5'11	190	0	0	–	1	19	3	2	68	57	29	24	0	3.04	25	3	0	.120
Baskette, Jim-James Blain (Big Jim)	11-13CleA	12-10-87	Athens, Tenn.	7-30-42	R	R	6'2	185	9	6	.600	0	35	14	9	142	138	57	59	1	3.30	47	8	0	.170
Bauer, Lou-Louis Walter (Kid)	18PhiA	11-30-98	Egg Harbor C., N.J.		R	R	6'	175	0	0	–	0	1	0	0	0	0	2	0	0	∞	0	0	0	–
Baumgardner, George-George Washington	12-16StLA	7-22-91	Barboursville, W. Va.	12-13-70	L	R	5'11	178	36	48	.429	4	124	78	51	685	682	263	283	6	3.22	215	31	0	.144
Beck,George-George F.	14CleA	-89	Moline, Ill.		R	R	5'11	162	0	0	–	0	1	0	0	1	1	0	0	0	0.00	0	0	0	–
Becker, Charlie-Charles S. (Buck)	11-12WasA	10-14-88	Washington, D.C.	7-30-28	L	L	6'2	180	3	5	.375	0	15	5	5	80	88	29	36	1	3.94	24	6	0	.250
Bedient, Hugh-Hugh Carpenter	12-14BosA 15BufF	10-23-89	Gerry, N.Y.	7-21-65	R	R	6'	185	59	53	.527	21	179	103	61	936	930	236	420	3	3.09	286	38	0	.133
Beebe, Fred-Frederick Leonard	06ChiN 06-09StLN 10CinN 11PhiN 16CleA	12-31-80	Lincoln, Neb.	10-30-57	R	R	6'1	190	63	85	.426	4	202	153	93	1294	1090	534	634	9	2.86	457	72	0	.158
Beecher, Roy-LeRoy (Colonel)	07-08NYN	5-10-84	Swanton, Ohio	10-11-52	L	R	6'2	180	0	2	.000	1	4	2	2	20	28	9	5	0	4.05	8	1	0	.125
Bell, George-George Glenn (Farmer)	07-11BknN	11- 2-74	Greenwood, N.Y.	12-25-41	R	R	6'	195	43	79	.352	4	160	126	92	1086	1010	305	376	17	2.85	351	48	0	.137
Bell, Ralph-Ralph Albert	12ChiA	11-16-90	Kohoka, Mo.	10-18-59	L	L	5'11	170	0	0	–	0	3	0	0	6	8	8	5	0	9.00	2	0	0	.000
Bender, Chief-Charles Albert	03-14PhiA 15BalF 16-17PhiN 25ChiA	5- 5-83	Brainerd, Minn.	5-22-54	R	R	6'2	185	210	128	.621	36	459	335	257	3017	2645	712	1711	41	2.46	1147	243	6	.212
Benn, Omer-Henry Omer	14CleA	1-25-90	Viola, Wis.	6- 4-67	R	R	6'	190	0	0	–	0	1	0	0	1	0	0	1	0	0.00	0	0	0	–
Benton, Rube-John Clebon	10-15CinN * 15-21NYN 22DE 23-25CinN	6-27-87	Clinton, N.C.	12-12-37	R	L	6'1	190	156	145	.518	21	437	305	145	2518	2472	712	950	24	3.09	825	142	1	.172
*-pitched in 1 game for Pit N–game protested and all records ordered thrown out by N.L. president																									
Benz, Joe-Joseph Louis (Blitzen, Butcher Boy)	11-19ChiA	1-21-86	New Alsace, Ind.	4-22-57	R	R	6'2	190	74	76	.493	5	250	163	76	1359	1224	334	538	17	2.42	441	61	0	.138
Berger, Heinie-Charles	07-10CleA	1- 7-82	LaSalle, Ill.	2-10-54		R			32	29	.532	1	90	68	42	608	504	176	337	5	2.56	206	27	0	.131
Bernard, Joe-Joseph	09StLN								0	0	–	0	1	0	0	1	1	2	2	0	0.00	0	0	0	–
Bernhard, Bill-William Henry (Strawberry Bill)	99-00PhiN	3-16-71	Clarence, N.Y.	3-30-49	R	R	6'4	225	112	82	.577	5	231	200	175	1792	1860	365	545	14	3.04	721	130	0	.180
	01-02PhiA 02-07CleA																								
Bernhardt, Walter-WalterJacob	18NYA	5-20-93	Pleasant Valley, Pa.	7-26-58	R	R	6'2	195		0	–	0	1	0	0	1	0	0	0	0	0.00	0	0	0	–
Betts, Fred-Fred W.	13CinN		Cincinnati, Ohio						0	0	–	0	1	0	0	3	1	3	0	0	3.00	1	0	0	.000
Betts, Hal-Harold M. (Chubby)	03StLN		Alton, Ill.		R	R	5'10	200	0	1	.000	0	1	1	1	9	11	5	2	0	10.00	3	0	0	.000
Beville, Charlie-Charles E. (Candy)	01BosA								0	2	.000	0	2	2	1	9	8	9	1	0	4.00	7	2	0	.286
Billiard, Harry-Harry P.	08NYA 14IndF 15NwkF	11-21-85	Wooster, Ohio	6- 3-23	R	R			8	8	.500	3	51	18	5	168	162	104	61	0	3.96	49	10	0	.204
Bishop, Lloyd-Lloyd Clifton	14CleA	4-25-90	Conway Sprs., Kans.	6-18-68	R	R	6'	175	0	1	.000	0	3	1	0	8	14	3	1	0	5.63	2	0	0	.000
Black, Dave-David	14-15ChiF 15BalF 23BosA	4-19-92	Chicago, Ill.	10-27-36	L	L	6'2	175	8	10	.444	0	43	15	4	181	166	52	72	0	3.18	61	11	0	.180
Blackburn, Babe-Foster Edwin	15KCF 21ChiA	1- 6-95	Chicago, Ill.		R	R	6'	200	0	1	.000	0	8	2	0	17	19	14	7	0	7.94	4	0	0	.000
Blanding, Fred-Frederick James (Fritz)	10-14CleA	2- 8-88	Redlands, Calif.	7-16-50	R	R	6'	185	45	46	.495	5	144	86	58	814	859	277	278	5	3.13	301	65	1	.216
Blewett, Bob-Robert Lawrence	02NYN	6-28-77	Fond du Lac, Wis.	3-17-58	L	L	5'11	170	0	2	.000	0	5	3	2	28	39	7	8	0	4.82	10	0	0	.000
Bliss, Elmer-Elmer Ward	03NYA	3- 9-75	Penfield, Pa.	3-18-62	L	R	6'	180	1	0	1.000	0	1	0	0	5	4	0	2	0	0.00	(See B01-19)			
Bluejacket (Smith), Jim-James	14-15BknF 16CinN	7- 8-87	Adair, Okla.	3-26-47	R	R	6'2	200	14	17	.452	1	44	30	13	237	244	97	78	3	3.46	85	11	0	.129
Boardman, Charlie-Charles Louis	13-14PhiA 15StLN	3-27-93	Seneca Falls, N.Y.	8-10-68	L	L	6'2	194	1	2	.333	0	7	3	2	35	32	25	13	0	2.31	12	2	0	.167
Boehler, George-George Henry	12-16DetA 20-21StLA 23PitN 26BknN	1- 2-92	Lawrenceburg, Ind.	6-23-58	R	R	6'2	180	7	13	.350	0	60	18	7	201	231	134	91	0	4.75	60	14	0	.233
Boehling, Joe-John Joseph	12-16WasA 16-17,20CleA	3-20-91	Richmond, Va.	9- 8-41	L	L	5'11	168	53	49	.520	6	162	118	57	924	861	386	396	9	2.97	311	66	1	.212
Bohen, Pat-Leo Ignatius	13PhiA 14PitN	9-30-90	Oakland, Iowa	4- 9-42	R	R	5'8	160	0	1	.000	0	2	1	1	9	5	4	5	0	3.00	4	0	0	.000
Boland, Bernie-Bernard Anthony	15-20DetA 21StLA	1-21-92	Rochester, N.Y.		R	R	5'8	168	68	52	.567	10	210	119	59	1063	925	432	364	10	3.24	327	45	0	.138
Bolden, Bill-William Horace (Big Bill)	19StLN	5- 9-93	Dandridge, Tenn.	12- 8-66	R	R	6'4	200	0	1	.000	0	3	1	0	12	17	4	4	0	5.25	3	1	0	.333
Booles, Red-Seabron Jesse	09CleA	7-14-80	Bernice, La.	3-16-55	L	L	5'10	150	0	1	.000	0	4	1	0	23	20	8	6	0	1.96	6	1	0	.167
Boultes, Jake-Jake John	07-09BosN	8- 6-84	St. Louis, Mo.	12-24-55		R			8	14	.364	0	42	17	12	223	229	58	78	0	2.95	92	13	0	.141
Bowman, Abe-Alvah Edson	14-15CleA	1-25-93	Greenup, Ill.		R	R	6'1	190	2	8	.200	0	24	11	2	74	75	48	27	1	4.74	21	1	0	.048
Boyd, Ray-Raymond C.	10StLA 11CinN	2-11-87	Hortonville, Ind.	2-11-20	R	R	5'10	160	3	4	.429	1	10	6	4	58	50	24	26	0	3.10	17	2	0	.118
Bracken, Jack-John James	01CleA	4-14-81	Cleveland, Ohio	7-16-54	R	R	5'11	175	4	8	.333	0	12	12	12	100	137	31	18	0	6.21	44	10	0	.227
Brackenridge, John-John Givler	04PhiN	12-24-80	Harrisburg, Pa.	3-20-53	R	R	6'		0	1	.000	0	7	1	0	34	37	16	11	0	5.56	13	2	0	.154
Brady, Bill-William A.	12BosN	-88		4-12-17		R			0	0	–	0	1	0	0	1	2	0	0	0	0.00	0	0	0	–
Brady, King-James Ward	05PhiN 06-07PitN 08BosA 12BosN	5-28-81	Elmer, N.J.	8-21-47	R	R	6'	190	3	2	.600	0	9	5	4	50	64	10	20	1	3.10	18	2	0	.111
Braggins, Dick-Richard Realf	01CleA	12-25-79	Mercer, Pa.	8-16-63	R	R	5'11	170	1	2	.333	0	4	3	2	32	44	15	1	0	4.78	13	2	0	.154
Braithwood, Al-Alfred	15PitF	2-15-92	Braceville, Ill.	11-24-60	R	L	6'1	145	0	0	–	0	2	0	0	3	0	0	2	0	0.00	0	0	0	–
Brandom, Chick-Chester Milton	08-09PitN 15NwkF	3-31-87	Coldwater, Kans.	10- 7-58	R	R	5'10	170	3	1	.750	3	32	4	2	108	101	29	44	0	2.08	27	4	0	.148
Breitenstein, Theo-Theodore P.	91StLAA 92-96StLN 97-00CinN 01StLN	6- 1-69	St. Louis, Mo.	5- 3-35	L	L	5'9	150	165	170	.496	3	379	341	300	2965	3091	1203	889	12	4.04	1320	289	4	.219

USE NAME – GIVEN NAMES (NICKNAMES)	TEAM BY YEAR	BIRTH DATE	BIRTH PLACE	DEATH DATE	B	T	HGT	WGT	W	L	PCT	SV	G	GS	CG	IP	H	BB	SO	ShO	ERA	AB	H	HR	BA
					LIFETIME PITCHING TOTALS																	BATTING TOTALS			
Brennan, Ad-Addison Foster	10-13PhiN 14-15ChiF 18WasA 18CleA	7-18-81	LaHarpe, Kans.	1- 7-62	L	L	5'11	170	39	36	.520	3	129	77	40	677	694	194	283	5	3.11	220	48	1	.218
Brenner, Bert-Delbert Henry (Dutch)	12CleA	7-18-87	Minneapolis, Minn.	4-11-71	R	R	6'	175	1	0	1.000	0	2	1	1	13	14	4	3	0	2.77	5	0	0	.000
Bressler, Rube-Raymond Bloom	14-16PhiA 17-20CinN	10-23-94	Coder, Pa.	11- 7-66	R	L	6'	187	26	31	.456	2	107	52	27	540	511	242	229	3	3.40	(See B20-45)			
Briggs, Buttons-Herbert Theodore	96-98,04-05ChiN	7- 8-75	Poughkeepsie, N.Y.	2- 8-11	R	R	6'1	180	45	47	.489	4	106	97	84	856	879	332	338	8	3.41	319	50	1	.157
Brockett, Lew-Lewis Albert (King)	07,09NYA 10HO 11NYA	7-23-80	Brownsville, Ill.	9-19-60	R	R	5'10	168	14	15	.483	1	50	30	13	273	279	124	108	3	3.66	121	33	0	.273
Brown, Boardwalk-Carroll William	11-14PhiA 14-15NYA	2-20-87	Woodbury, N.J.		R	R	6'1	178	39	40	.494	3	133	92	43	731	698	291	251	6	3.47	258	38	1	.147
Brown, Bob-Robert M.	14BufF	91			R	R	6'6	165	16	21	.432	1	79	49	13	363	360	193	159	2	4.49	9	2	0	.222
Brown, Buster-Charles Edward	05-07StLN 07-09PhiN 09-13BosN	8-31-81	Boone, Iowa	2- 9-14	R	R			51	105	.327	4	234	165	107	1451	1368	631	501	11	3.21	522	95	3	.182
Brown, Curly-Charles Roy (Lefty)	11-13StLA 15CinN	12- 9-88	Spring Hill, Kans.	6-10-68	L	L	5'10	165	2	8	.200	0	28	12	5	129	129	50	52	1	4.19	49	11	0	.224
Brown, Elmer-Elmer Young (Shook)	11-12StLA 13-15BknN	3-25-83	Southport, Ind.	1-23-55	L	R	5'11	172	9	11	.450	1	43	19	4	188	181	92	79	2	3.49	59	8	0	.136
Brown, Ray-Paul Percival	09ChiN	1-31-89	Chicago, Ill.	5-29-55					1	0	1.000	0	1	1	1	9	5	4	2	0	2.00	5	0	0	.000
Brown, Three Finger-Mordecai Peter Centennial (Miner)	03StLN	10-19-76	Nyesville, Ind.	2-14-48	B	R	5'10	175	239	127	.653	49	481	332	271	3171	2708	673	1374	56	2.06	1143	235	2	.206
	04-12ChiN 13CinN 14,M14StLF 14BknF 15ChiF 16ChiN																								
Browning, Frank-Frank	10DetA	10-29-82	Falmouth, Ky.	5-20-48	R	R	5'5	145	2	2	.500	2	11	6	2	42	51	10	16	0	3.00	14	0	0	.000
Bruckmiller, Andy-Andrew	05DetA	1- 1-82	McKeesport, Pa.	1-12-70	R	R	5'11	175	0	0	–	0	1	0	0	0	3	1	0	0	∞	1	0	0	.000
Buchanan, Jim-James Forrest	05StLA	7- 7-77	Chatham Hill, Va.	6-15-49	R	R	5'10	165	6	10	.375	2	22	15	12	141	149	27	54	1	3.51	46	7	0	.152
Buckles, Jess-Jesse Robert (Jim)	16NYA	5-20-90	LaVerne, Cal.		L	L	6'2	205	0	0	–	0	2	0	0	4	3	1	2	0	2.25	1	0	0	.000
Burchell, Fred-Frederick Duff	03PhiN 07-09BosA	7-14-79	Perth Amboy, N.J.	11-20-51	R	L	5'11		13	16	.448	0	49	28	12	286	268	92	124	0	2.93	109	24	0	.220
Burk, Sandy-Charles Sanford	10-12BknN 12-13StLN 15PitF	4-22-87	Columbus, Ohio	10-11-34	R	R	5'8	155	5	11	.313	2	52	21	5	218	206	133	86	0	4.25	67	6	0	.090
Burke, Billy-William Ignatius	10-11BosN	7-11-89	Clinton, Mass.	2- 9-67	L	L	5'10	165	1	1	.500	0	21	2	1	67	74	34	23	0	4.84	22	5	0	.227
Burke, John-John Patrick	02NYN	1-27-77	Hazelton, Pa.	8- 4-50					0	1	.000	0	2	1	1	14	21	3	3	0	5.79	13	2	0	.154
Burkett, Jesse-Jesse Cail (The Crab)	90NYN 94CleN 02StLA	12- 4-68	Wheeling, W.Va.	5-27-53	L	L	5'8	155	1	12	.077	0	23	12	6	123	144	94	84	0	5.56	(See B01-19)			
Burns, Bill-William Thomas (Sleepy Bill)	08-09WasA 09-10ChiA	1-29-80	San Saba, Tex.	6- 6-53	B	L	6'2	195	28	48	.368	2	116	85	43	726	713	148	235	10	2.69	244	48	0	.197
	10-11CinN 11 PhiN 12DetA																								
Burns, Farmer-James	01StLN		Ashtabula, Ohio			R			0	0	–	0	1	0	0	1	2	1	0	0	9.00	0	0	0	–
Bushelman, Jack-John Francis	09CinN 11-12BosA	8-29-85	Cincinnati, Ohio	10-26-55	R	R	6'2	175	1	2	.333	0	7	2	2	27	24	19	13	0	3.33	7	0	0	.000
Butler, Ike-Isaac Burr	02BalA	8-22-73	Langston, Mich.	3-17-48		R			2	11	.154	0	16	14	12	116	168	45	13	0	5.35	53	6	0	.113
Caldwell, Ralph-Ralph Grant (Lefty)	04-05PhiN	1-18-84	Philadelphia, Pa.	8- 5-69	L	L	5'9	155	3	4	.429	1	13	7	6	75	84	22	59	0	4.20	33	8	0	.242
Caldwell, Ray-Raymond Benjamin (Slim)	10-18NYA 19BosA 19-21CleA	4-26-88	Corydon, Pa.	8-17-67	L	R	6'2	190	133	120	.526	14	343	261	185	2242	2085	737	1005	16	3.21	(See B01-19)			
Callahan, Nixey-James Joseph	94PhiN 97-00ChiN	3-18-74	Fitchburg, Mass.	10- 4-34	R	R	5'10	180	100	75	.571	2	195	177	169	1602	1748	437	445	11	3.39	(See B01-19)			
	01-03,M03-04,12-14ChiA M16-17PitN																								
Callahan, Ray-Raymond James (Pat)	15CinN	8-29-91	Ashland, Wis.	1-23-73	L	L	5'10	170	0	0	–	0	3	0	0	6	12	1	4	0	9.00	3	1	0	.333
Camnitz, Harry-Henry Richardson	09PitN 11StLN	10-26-84	McKinney, Ky.	1- 6-51	R	R	6'1	168	1	0	1.000	0	3	0	0	6	6	2	3	0	3.00	2	0	0	.000
Camnitz, Howie-Samuel Howard (Red)	04,06-12PitN 13PhiN 14-15PitF	8-22-81	Covington, Ky.	3- 2-60	L	R	5'9	169	133	105	.559	15	326	237	137	2086	1052	656	915	19	2.75	677	92	1	.136
Campbell, Bill-William James	05StLN 07-09CinN	11- 5-73	Pittsburgh, Pa.	10- 6-57	L	L	5'10	165	23	25	.479	4	70	44	31	407	411	93	116	2	2.81	130	15	0	.115
Canavan, Hugh-Hugh Edward (Hugo)	18BosN	5-13-97	Worcester, Mass.	9- 4-67	L	L	5'8	160	0	4	.000	0	11	3	3	47	70	15	18	0	6.32	21	2	0	.095
Cantwell, Mike-Michael Joseph	16NYA 19-20PhiN	1-15-96	Washington, D.C.	1- 5-53	R	R	6'1	168	1	6	.143	0	11	4	2	52	61	26	14	0	4.67	16	3	0	.188
Cantwell, Tom-Thomas Aloysius	09-10CinN	12-23-88	Washington, D.C.	4- 1-68	L	L	5'10	155	1	0	1.000	0	8	1	1	23	18	10	7	0	2.35	5	3	0	.600
Carmichael, Chet-Chester Keller	09CinN	1- 9-88	Eaton, Ind.	8-23-60	R	R	5'11	200	0	0	–	0	2	0	0	7	9	3	2	0	0.00	2	0	0	.000
Carney, Pat-Patrick Joseph (Doc)	02-04BosN	8- 7-76	Holyoke, Mass.	1- 9-53	L	L			4	9	.308	0	16	12	10	109	139	46	37	0	4.71	(See B01-19)			
Carpenter, Paul-Paul Calvin	16PitN	8-12-94	Granville, Ohio	3-14-68	R	R	5'11	165	0	0	–	0	5	0	0	8	8	4	5	0	1.13	2	0	0	.000
Carrick, Bill-William Martin (Doughnut Bill)	98-00NYN 01-02WasA	9- 5-73	Erie, Pa.	3- 7-32		R			64	86	.427	0	167	155	138	1326	1650	400	239	4	4.13	502	81	0	.161
Carroll, Dick-Richard T.	09NYA	7-21-84	Cleveland, Ohio	11-22-45					0	0	–	0	2	1	0	5	7	1	1	0	3.60	2	1	0	.500
Carsey, Kid-Wilfred	91WasAA 92-97PhiN 97-98StLN 99CleN 99WasN	10-22-70	New York, N.Y.	Deceased	R	R	5'7	168	117	134	.466	3	294	256	218	2222	2780	796	484	4	4.95	1012	216	2	.213
	99NYN 01BknN																								
Carson, Alex-Alexander James (Soldier)	10ChiN	5- 1-81	N.J.	8-18-54		R			0	0	–	0	2	0	0	7	6	1	2	0	3.86	1	0	0	.000
Carter, Nick-Conrad Powell	08PhiA	5-19-79	Oatlands, Va.	11-23-61	L	R	5'8	126	2	5	.286	1	14	6	2	61	58	17	17	0	2.95	20	2	0	.100
Carter, Paul-Paul Warren (Nick)	14-15CleA 16-20ChiN	5- 1-94	Lake Park, Ga.		L	R	6'3	175	20	27	.426	8	127	43	16	480	510	142	115	0	3.32	152	30	0	.197
Case, Charlie-Charles Emmett	01CinN 04-06PitN	9- 7-79	Rural, Ohio	4-16-64	R	R	6'	170	24	18	.571	1	54	46	36	396	373	108	114	6	2.93	133	18	0	.135
Cashion, Carl-Jay Carl	11-14WasA	6- 6-91	Mecklenburg, N.C.	11-17-35	L	R	6'2	200	14	11	.560	1	43	30	18	255	228	170	114	1	3.71	153	37	2	.242
Castleton, Roy-Roy J.	07NYA 09-10CinN	-86	Salt Lake City, U.		L	L	5'11	167	3	4	.429	0	11	5	3	44	40	15	13	0	2.66	13	2	0	.154
Cates, Eli-Eli Eldo	08WasA	1-26-77	Greensfork, Ind.	5-29-64	R	R	5'9	175	4	8	.333	0	19	10	7	115	112	32	33	0	2.50	59	11	0	.186
Cavet, Pug-Tiller H.	11,14-15DetA	12-26-89	McGregor, Tex.	8- 4-66	L	L	6'3	176	11	10	.524	3	49	22	8	226	218	67	78	1	2.99	72	11	0	.153
Chalmers, George-George W. (Dut)	10-16PhiN	6- 7-88	Edinburgh, Scot.	8- 5-60	R	R	6'1	189	29	41	.414	6	121	76	36	647	645	279	290	4	3.41	209	34	0	.163
Chambers, Bill-William Christopher	10StLN	9-13-89	Cameron, W.Va.	3-27-62	R	R	5'9	185	0	0	–	0	1	0	0	1	1	0	0	0	0.00	0	0	0	–
Chaney, Estey,Estey Clyon	13BosA 14BknF	1-29-91	Hadley, Pa.	2- 5-52	R	R	5'11	170	0	0	–	0	2	0	0	5	8	4	1	0	7.20	1	0	0	.000
Chappelle, Bill-William Hogan (Big Bill)	08-09BosN 09CinN 14BknF	3-22-84	Waterloo, N.Y.	12-31-44	R	R	6'2	206	7	7	.500	1	35	16	9	177	167	59	62	1	2.39	56	5	1	.089
Chech, Charlie-Charles William	05-06CinN 08-CleA 09BosA	4-27-78	Madison, Wis.	1-31-38	R	R	5'11	190	33	31	.516	3	94	63	45	607	602	162	187	6	2.52	198	30	0	.152
Cheney, Larry-Laurance Russell	11-15ChiN 15-19BknN 19BosN 19PhiN	5- 2-86	Belleville, Kans.	1- 6-69	R	R	6'1	185	116	100	.537	19	313	225	132	1880	1605	733	926	20	2.70	617	115	1	.186
Chesbro, Jack-John Dwight (Happy Jack)	99-02PitN 03-09NYA 09BosA	6- 5-74	N. Adams, Mass.	11- 6-31	R	R	5'9	180	198	130	.604	7	392	332	261	2898	2642	690	1265	33	2.68	1098	215	5	.196
Chouneau (Cadreau), Chief-William	10ChiA	9- 2-89	Cloquet, Minn.	9-17-48	R	R	5'9	150	0	1	.000	0	1	1	0	5	7	0	1	0	3.60	1	0	0	.000
Cicotte, Eddie-Edward Victor	05DetA 08-12BosA 12-20ChiA 20DL	6-19-84	Detroit, Mich.	5- 5-69	B	R	5'9	175	209	149	.584	23	502	359	248	3224	2897	827	1374	35	2.37	1063	197	0	.185
Clark, Geroge-George Myron	13NYA	5-19-91	Smithland, Iowa	11-14-40	R	L	6'	190	0	1	.000	0	11	1	0	19	22	19	5	0	9.00	4	2	0	.500
Clark, Ginger-Harvey Daniel	02CleA	3- 7-79	Wooster, Ohio	5-10-43	R	R	5'11	165	1	0	1.000	0	1	0	0	6	10	3	1	0	6.00	4	2	0	.500
Clarkson, Walter-Walter Hamilton	04-07NYA 07-08CleA	11- 3-78	Cambridge, Mass.	10-10-46	R	R	5'10	150	18	16	.529	3	78	37	23	374	340	132	178	4	3.18	132	20	0	.152
Clauss, Al-Albert Stanley (Lefty)	13DetA	6-24-91	New Haven, Conn.	9-13-52	L	L	5'10	178	0	2	.000	0	5	1	0	13	11	12	1	0	4.85	4	0	0	.000
Coakley, Andy-Andrew James	02-06PhiA 07-08CinN 08-09ChiN 11NYA	11-20-82	Providence, R.I.	9-27-63	L	R	6'	165	60	59	504	3	150	124	88	1073	1023	314	428	11	2.36	355	42	0	.118
(Played as Jack McAllister 02)																									
Cochran, Al-Alvah Jackson (Goat)	15CinN	1-31-91	Concord, Ga.	5-23-47	R	R	5'9	175	0	0	–	0	1	0	0	2	5	0	1	0	9.00	0	0	0	–
Cocreham, Gene-Eugene	13-15BosN	11-14-84	Luling, Tex.	12-27-45	R	R	6'3	192	3	5	.375	0	17	4	1	55	64	31	18	0	5.24	14	1	0	.071
Cole, King-Leonard Leslie	09-12ChiN 12PitN 14-15NYA	4-15-86	Toledo, Iowa	1- 6-16	R	R	6'1	170	55	27	.671	2	129	85	47	731	657	331	298	9	3.12	249	43	0	.173
Collamore, Allan-Allan Edward	11PhiA 14-15CleA	6- 5-87	Worcester, Mass.		R	R	6'	170	5	12	.294	0	40	14	8	171	158	74	48	2	3.32	55	7	0	.127
Collins, Ray-Raymond Williston	09-15BosA	2-11-87	Colchester, Vt.	1- 9-70	L	L	6'1	185	86	62	.581	5	199	150	90	1346	1251	271	513	20	2.51	419	69	1	.165
Compton, Jack-Harry Leroy	11CinN	3- 9-82	Lancaster, Ohio		R	R	5'9	157	0	1	.000	1	8	3	0	25	19	15	6	0	3.96	6	2	0	.333
Comstock, Ralph-Ralph Remick (Commy)	13DetA 15BosA 15PitF 18PitN	11-24-90	Sylvania, Ohio	9-13-66	R	R	5'10	168	11	14	.440	6	40	22	10	203	222	39	100	0	3.72	66	10	0	.152
Cone, H.B.-H.B.	15PhiA		Tex.						0	0	–	0	1	1	0	1	5	0	0	0	27.00	0	0	0	–
Conley, Snipe-James Patrick	14-15BalF 18CinN	4-25-94	Cressona, Pa.		R	R	5'11	179	7	10	.412	2	65	17	8	225	226	84	128	2	3.36	63	11	0	.175
Conn, Bert-Albert Thomas	98,00PhiN	9-22-79	Philadelphia, Pa.	11- 2-44		R			0	3	.000	0	5	2	1	24	42	18	5	0	7.88	(See B01-19)			
Conzelman, Joe-Joseph Harrison	13-15PitN	7-14-89	Bristol, Conn.		R	R	6'	170	6	8	.429	2	54	12	5	163	142	65	70	1	2.93	42	4	0	.095
Cook Rollin-Rollin Edward	15StLA	10- 5-90	Toledo, Ohio	8-11-75	R	R	5'9	152	0	0	–	0	5	0	0	14	16	9	7	0	7.07	4	1	0	.250
Coombs, Jack-John Wesley (Colby Jack)	06-14PhiA 15-18BknN	11-18-82	LeGrand, Iowa	4-15-57	B	R	6'	185	158	111	.587	13	355	273	188	2320	2034	841	1052	35	2.78	1110	261	4	.235
	M19PhiN 20DetA																								
Cooper, Guy-Guy Evans (Rebel)	14NYA 14-15BosA	1- 8-93	Rome, Ga.	8 2-51	B	R	6'1	185	1	1	.500	0	11	1	0	27	26	13	8	0	5.33	8	0	0	.000
Cooper, Wilbur-Arley Wilbur	12-24PitN 25-26ChiN 26DetA	2-24-92	Bearsville, W.Va.	8- 7-73	R	L	5'11	175	216	178	.548	14	517	406	279	3482	3415	853	1252	36	2.89	1227	293	6	.239
Corbett, Joe-Joseph A.	95WasN 96-97BalN 04StLN	12- 4-75	San Francisco, Cal.	5- 2-45	R	R			32	21	.604	1	62	57	52	482	497	192	248	1	3.42	220	53	0	.241
Corey, Ed-Edward N.	18ChiA	4-10-00	Chicago, Ill.		R	R			0	0	–	0	1	0	0	2	2	1	0	0	4.50	1	0	0	.000
Corridon, Frank-Frank J. (Fiddler)	04ChiN 04-05,07-09PhiN 10StLN	11-25-80	Newport, R.I.	2-21-41	R	R	6'	170	70	68	.507	7	180	140	99	1216	1100	375	458	10	2.81	445	80	1	.180
Cottrell, Dick-Ensign Stover	11PitN 12ChiN 13PhiA 14BosN 15NYA	8-29-88	Hoosick Falls, N.Y.	2-27-47	L	L	5'9	173	0	2	.000	0	12	2	1	37	58	14	12	0	4.86	12	1	0	.083
Coumbe, Fritz-Frederick Nicholas	14BosA 14-19CleA 20-21CinN	12-13-89	Antrim, Pa.		L	L	5'10	152	38	38	.500	12	193	70	32	762	773	217	212	5	2.80	252	52	1	.206
Coveleski (Kowalewski), Harry-Harry Frank (The Giant Killer)		4-23-86	Shamokin, Pa.	8- 4-50	B	L	6'	180	82	55	.599	9	198	151	83	1248	1070	376	511	13	2.39	418	79	0	.189
	07-09PhiN 10CinN 14-18DetA																								
Covington, Bill-William Wilkes (Tex)	11-12DetA	3-19-87	Henryville, Tenn.	12-10-31	L	R	6'1	175	10	5	.667	1	31	15	7	147	152	63	48	1	4.10	47	8	0	.170
Crabb, Roy-James Roy	12ChiA 12PhiA	8-23-90	Monticello, Iowa	3- 3-40	R	R	5'11	160	2	5	.286	0	9	8	3	52	54	21	15	0	3.29	19	0	0	.000
Crable, George-George E.	10BknN	-86	Brooklyn, N.Y.		L	L	6'1	190	0	0	–	0	2	1	1	7	5	5	3	0	5.14	2	0	0	.000
Craft, Molly-Maurice Montague	16-19WasA	11-28-95	Portsmouth, Va.		R	R	6'2	165	0	4	.000	1	29	3	1	81	93	33	33	0	3.56	26	3	0	.115
Craig, George-George McCarthy (Lefty)	07PhiA	11-15-87	Philadelphia, Pa.	4-23-11		L			0	0	–	0	2	0	0	2	2	3	0	0	9.00	1	0	0	.000
Cramer, Bill-William Wendell	12CinN	5-21-91	Bedford, Ind.	9-11-66	R	R	6'	175	0	0	–	0	1	0	0	2	6	0	2	0	0.00	6	0	0	.000
Crandall, Doc-James Otis	08-13NYN 13StLN 13NYN 14-15StLF	10- 8-87	Wadena, Ind.	8-17-51	R	R	5'10	180	102	62	.622	25	302	134	91	1548	1538	379	606	10	2.92	(See B01-19)			
	16StLA 18BosN																								
Criss, Dode-Dode	08-11StLA	3-12-85	Sherman, Miss.	9- 8-55	L	R	6'2	200	3	9	.250	0	30	9	3	110	104	64	70	0	4.42	(See B01-19)			

									LIFETIME PITCHING TOTALS													BATTING TOTALS			
USE NAME – GIVEN NAMES (NICKNAMES)	TEAM BY YEAR	BIRTH DATE	BIRTH PLACE	DEATH DATE	B	T	HGT	WGT	W	L	PCT	SV	G	GS	CG	IP	H	BB	SO	ShO	ERA	AB	H	HR	BA
Cristall, Bill-William Arthur (Lefty)	01CleA	9-12-78	Odessa, Russia	1-28-39	L	L	5'7	145	1	4	.200	0	6	6	5	48	54	30	12	1	4.88	20	7	0	.350
Cronin, Jack-John J.	95BknN 98PitN 99CinN 01-02DetA 02BalA	5-26-74	Staten Island, N.Y.	7-13-29	R	R	6'	200	42	58	.420	4	128	102	88	924	973	235	318	6	3.40	367	66	0	.180
	02-03NYN 04BknN																								
Crouch, Bill-William Henry (Skip)	10StLA	12- 3-86	Marshallton, Del.	12-22-45	L	L	6'1	210	0	0	–	0	1	1	1	8	6	7	2	0	3.38	3	0	0	.000
Crowell, Cap-Minot Joy	15-16PhiA	9- 5-92	Roxbury, Mass.	9-30-62	R	R	6'1	178	2	11	.154	0	19	14	5	94	99	81	30	0	5.17	34	5	0	.147
Crum, Cal-Calvin Carl	17-18BosN	-92	Mattoon, Ill.		R	R	6'1	175	0	1	.000	0	2	1	0	3	7	4	0	0	12.00	1	0	0	.000
Crutcher, Dick-Richard Louis	14-15BosN	11-25-89	Frankfort, Ky.	6-19-52	R	R	5'9	148	7	8	.467	2	47	19	6	203	219	82	65	1	3.64	67	11	0	.164
Cullop, Nick-Norman Andrew	13-14CleA 14-15KCF 16-17NYA 21StLA	9-17-87	Chilhowie, Va.	4-15-61	R	L	5'11	172	57	55	.509	4	174	121	62	1024	973	259	400	9	2.73	329	49	0	.149
Culp, Bill-William Edward	10PhiN	6-11-87	Bellaire, Ohio	9- 3-69	B	R	6'1	165	0	0	–	1	4	0	0	7	8	4	4	0	7.71	2	0	0	.000
Cunningham, Bert-Ellsworth Elmer	87BknAA 88-89BalAA 90PhiP	11-25-65	Wilmington, Del.	5-14-52	R	R			145	168	.463	2	341	310	286	2727	3063	1064	718	4	4.22	1175	252	9	.214
	90BufP 91BalAA 95-99LouN 00-01ChiN																								
Cunningham, George-George Harold	16-19DetA	7-13-94	Sturgeon Lake, Minn.	3-10-72	R	R	5'11	185	16	25	.390	8	123	36	19	477	444	178	167	0	3.13	(See B01-19)			
Cunningham, Mike-Rudolph	06PhiA		Kershaw, S.C.			R			0	0	–	0	5	1	1	28	29	9	15	0	3.21	12	4	0	.333
Cuppy (Koppe), Nig-George Joseph	92-98CleN 99StLN 00BosN 01BosA	7- 3-69	Logansport, Ind.	7-27-22	R	R	5'7	160	161	100	.617	5	302	262	224	2284	2520	609	504	9	3.49	945	222	1	.235
Curran, Sammy-Simon Francis	02BosN	10-30-74	Dorchester, Mass.	5-19-36					0	0	–	0	1	0	0	7	6	0	3	0	1.29	2	0	0	.000
Currie, Clarence-Clarence F.	02CinN 02-03StLN 03ChiN	12-30-78	Glencoe, Canada	7-15-41	R	R			15	23	.395	2	53	38	31	371	385	121	111	3	3.39	129	20	0	.155
Currie, Murphy-Murphy Archibald	16StLN	8-31-93	Fayetteville, N.C.	6-22-39	R	R	5'11	165	0	0	–	0	6	0	0	14	7	9	8	0	1.93	3	0	0	.000
Curry, George-George James (Soldier Boy)	11StLA	12-21-88	Bridgeport, Conn.	10- 5-63	R	R	6'	185	0	3	.000	0	3	3	0	16	19	24	2	0	7.31	5	0	0	.000
Curtis, Cliff-Clifton Garfield	09-11BosN 11ChiN 11-12PhiN 12-13BknN	7- 3-82	Delaware, Ohio	4-23-43	R	R	6'2	180	28	61	.315	6	136	94	38	745	707	317	236	5	3.31	246	39	0	.159
Cushman, Harv-Harvey Barnes	02PitN	7- 5-77	Rockland, Me.	12-27-20					0	4	.000	0	4	4	3	26	30	31	12	0	7.27	10	2	0	.200
Dale, Gene-Emmett Eugene	11-12StLN 15-16CinN	6-16-89	St. Louis, Mo.	3-20-58	R	R	6'3	190	21	28	.429	3	90	45	23	444	425	207	177	4	3.59	139	31	0	.223
Daley, George-George Joseph (Pecks)	09NYN	7-28-87	Buffalo, N.Y.	12-12-57	R	R	5'10	175	0	3	.000	0	3	3	3	21	31	8	8	0	6.00	9	1	0	.111
Dashner, Lee-Lee Claire (Lefty)	13CleA	4-25-87	Renault, Ill.	12-16-59	B	L	5'11	192	0	0	–	0	1	0	0	2	0	0	2	0	4.50	0	0	0	–
Dauss, Hooks-George August	12-26DetA	9-22-89	Indianapolis, Ind.	7-27-63	R	R	5'10	168	221	182	.548	41	538	388	245	3391	3407	1064	1201	21	3.32	1124	212	6	.189
Davenport, Dave-David W. (Big Dave)	14CinN 14-15StLF	2-20-90	DeRidder, La.	10-16-54	R	R	6'6	220	75	85	.469	12	259	186	95	1538	1399	521	719	18	2.93	472	49	1	.104
	16-19StLA																								
Davis, Bud-John Wilbur (Country)	15PhiA	12- 7-89	Merry Point, Va.	5-26-67	L	R	6'	207	0	2	.000	0	18	2	2	67	65	59	18	0	4.03	26	8	0	.308
Davis, George-George Allen (Iron)	12NYA 13-15BosN	3- 9-90	Lancaster, N.Y.	6- 4-61	B	R	5'10	175	7	10	.412	0	36	22	13	191	195	78	77	1	4.48	61	11	0	.180
Dawson, Rex-Rexford Paul	13WasA	2-10-89	Skagit Co., Wash.	10-20-58	L	R	6'	185	0	0	–	0	1	0	0	1	1	0	0	0	0.00	0	0	0	–
Deegan, Dummy-W. John	01NYN		New York, N.Y.						0	2	.000	0	2	1	1	17	27	6	8	0	6.35	5	0	0	.000
Deering, John-John Thomas	03DetA 03NYA	6-25-78	Lynn, Mass.	2-15-43		R			6	7	.462	0	19	15	11	121	136	42	28	1	3.79	47	9	0	.191
Deininger, Pep-Otto Charles	02BosA	10-10-77	Wasseralfingen, Ger.	9-25-50	L	L	5'8	180	0	0	–	0	2	1	0	12	19	9	2	0	9.75	(See B01-19)			
Delhi, Flame-Lee William	12ChiA	11- 5-92	Harqua Hala, Ariz.	5- 9-66	R	R	6'2	198	0	0	–	0	1	0	0	3	7	3	2	0	9.00	0	0	0	–
Dell, Wheezer-William George	12StLN 15-17BknN	6-11-87	Tuscarora, Nev.	8-24-66	R	R	6'4	210	19	23	.452	3	92	44	21	430	367	171	198	6	2.55	126	15	0	.119
Demaree, Al-Albert Wentworth	12-14NYN 15-16PhiN 17ChiN	9- 8-86	Quincy, Ill.	4-30-62	L	R	6'	170	80	72	.526	9	232	173	84	1425	1350	337	514	14	2.77	456	54	0	.118
	17-18NYN 19BosN																								
DeMott, Ben-Benyew Harrison	10-11CleA	4- 2-89	Green Village, N.J.	7- 5-63	R	R	6'	192	0	4	.000	0	7	5	1	32	55	10	15	0	6.19	18	3	0	.167
Dent, Eddie-Elliott Estill	09,11-12BknN	12- 8-87	Baltimore, Md.	11-23-74	R	R	6'1	190	4	5	.444	0	12	8	5	75	81	26	21	0	4.44	26	2	0	.077
Denzer, Roger-Roger (Peaceful Valley)	97ChiN 01NYN	10- 5-71	LeSever, Minn.	9-18-49	L	R	6'	180	5	11	.313	0	23	19	11	157	194	39	39	1	4.41	61	8	0	.131
DesJardien, Shorty-Paul Raymond 20-21 played in N.F.L.	16CleA	8-24-93	Coffeyville, Kans.	3- 7-56	R	R	6'4	205	0	0	–	0	1	0	0	1	1	1	0	0	18.00	0	0	0	–
Dessau, Rube-Frank Rolland	07BosN 10BknN	3-29-83	New Galilee, Pa.	5- 6-52	B	R	5'11	175	2	4	.333	1	21	2	1	60	80	39	25	0	6.60	19	1	0	.053
Dickerson, George-George Clark	17CleA	12- 1-92	Renner, Tex.	7- 9-38	R	R	6'1	170	0	0	–	0	1	0	0	1	0	0	0	0	0.00	0	0	0	–
Dickson, Walt-Walter R. (Hickory)	10NYN 12-13BosN 14-15PitF	-83	Greenville, Tex.	12-10-18	R	R	5'11	175	26	50	.342	2	134	79	40	701	759	222	202	4	3.59	223	30	0	.135
Dillinger, Harley-Harley Hugh (Hoke, Lefty)	14CleA	10-30-94	Pomeroy, Ohio	1- 8-59	R	L	5'11	175	0	1	.000	0	11	2	1	34	41	25	11	0	4.50	10	0	0	.000
Dinneen, Bill-William Henry (Big Bill)	98-99WasN 00-01BosN	4- 5-76	Syracuse, N.Y.	1-13-55	R	R	6'1	190	174	178	.494	6	391	353	306	3075	2957	829	1127	23	3.01	1132	218	1	.193
	02-07BosA 07-09StLA																								
Disch, George-George Charles	05DetA	3-15-79	Lincoln, Mo.	8-25-50					0	2	.000	0	8	3	1	48	43	8	14	0	2.63	19	2	0	.105
Doak, Bill-William Leopold (Spittin' Bill)	12CinN 13-24StLN	1-28-91	Pittsburgh, Pa.	11-26-54	R	R	6'	165	169	157	.518	16	453	368	162	2782	2676	851	1014	36	2.98	905	115	1	.127
	24BknN 25-26VR 27-28BknN 29StLN																								
Doane, Walt-Walter Rudolph	09-10CleA	3-12-87	Bellevue, Idaho	10-19-35	L	R	6'	165	0	1	.000	0	7	1	0	23	41	9	9	0	5.48	16	3	0	.188
Doheny, Ed-Edward R.	95-01NYN 01-03PitN	11-24-74	Northfield, Vt.	12-29-16	L	L	5'10	165	79	82	.491	2	183	168	140	1393	1412	665	567	6	3.75	563	112	3	.199
Dolan, Cozy-Patrick Henry	95-96,05-06BosN	12- 3-72	Cambridge, Mass.	3-29-07	L	L	5'10	160	12	13	.480	1	35	26	21	255	289	101	69	3	4.45	(See B01-19)			
Donahue, Red-Francis Rostell	93NYN 95-97StLN 98-01PhiN	1-23-73	Waterbury, Conn.	8-25-13	R	R			168	169	.499	4	368	340	312	2975	3384	690	788	25	3.61	1147	174	1	.152
	02-03StLA 03-05,CleA 06DetA																								
Donalds, Ed-Edward Alexander (Skipper)	12CinN	6-22-85	Gallipolis, Ohio	7- 3-50	R	R	5'11	180	1	0	1.000	0	1	0	0	4	7	0	1	0	4.50	1	0	0	.000
Donnelly, Ed-Edward	11-12BosN	7-29-80	Hampton, N.Y.	11-28-57	R	R	6'1	205	8	12	.400	0	42	22	14	221	258	81	83	1	4.03	83	20	0	.241
Donovan, Wild Bill-William Edward	98WasN 99-02BknN 03-12DetA	10-13-76	Lawrence, Mass.	12- 9-23	R	R	5'11	190	187	138	.575	9	378	327	289	2968	2631	1059	1552	35	2.69	1300	252	6	.194
	15-16,M15-17NYA 18DetA M21PhiN																								
Dorner, Gus-Augustus	02-03CleA 06CinN 06-09BosN	8-18-76	Chambersburg, Pa.	5- 4-56	R	R	5'10	176	36	69	.343	2	131	106	76	894	842	330	275	8	3.33	308	46	0	.149
Doscher, Jack-John Henry Jr.	03ChiN 03-06BknN 08CinN	7-27-80	Troy, N.Y.	5-27-71	L	L	6'1	170	2	11	.154	0	27	13	10	145	118	68	61	0	2.86	50	5	0	.100
Dougherty, Tom-Thomas James (Sugar Boy)	04ChiA	5-30-81	Chicago, Ill.	11- 6-53	L	R			0	0	–	0	1	0	0	2	0	0	0	0	0.00	1	0	0	.000
Douglas, Larry-Howard Lawrence	15BalF	6- 5-90	Jellico, Tenn.	11- 4-49	R	R	6'3	175	1	0	1.000	0	2	0	0	3	3	2	1	0	3.00	0	0	0	–
Douglas, Phil-Philip Brooks (Shufflin' Phil)	12ChiA 14-15CinN	6-17-90	Cedartown, Ga.	8- 1-52	R	R	6'4	190	94	93	.503	8	299	200	95	1708	1626	411	683	20	2.80	561	90	2	.160
	15BknN 15-19ChiN 19-22NYN 22DL																								
Dowd, Skip-James Joseph	10PitN	2-16-89	Holyoke, Mass.	12-20-60	R	R	5'10	160	0	0	–	0	1	0	0	2	4	2	1	0	0.00	0	0	0	–
Dowling, Pete-Henry Peter	97-99LouN 01MilA 01CleA		Ky.	6-30-05		L			38	65	.369	1	117	102	92	908	984	339	299	2	3.87	357	71	1	.199
Doyle, Slow Joe-Judd Bruce	06-10NYA 10CinN	9-15-81	Clay Center, Kans.	11-21-47	L	R	5'8	150	22	22	.500	1	75	50	29	437	383	147	209	7	2.84	135	22	0	.163
Dresser, Bob-Robert U.	02BosN	10- 4-78	Newton, Mass.	7-27-24		L			0	1	.000	0	1	1	1	9	12	0	8	0	3.00	4	1	0	.250
Driscoll, Mike-Michael Columbus	16PhiA	10-19-92	Rockland, Mass.	3-21-53	R	R	6'1	160	0	1	.000	0	1	0	0	5	6	2	0	0	5.40	2	0	0	.000
Drohan, Tom-Thomas F.	13WasA	8-26-87	Fall River, Mass.	9-17-26	R	R	5'10	175	0	0	–	0	2	0	0	2	5	0	2	0	9.00	0	0	0	–
Drucke, Louis-Louis Frank	09-12NYN	12- 3-88	Waco, Tex.	9-22-55	R	R	6'1	188	18	15	.545	1	53	40	21	317	282	137	201	0	2.90	101	18	1	.178
Druhot, Carl-Carl A.	06CinN 06-07StLN	9- 1-82	Ohio	2-11-18	L	L	5'7	150	8	10	.444	0	20	17	13	157	147	57	60	1	3.10	65	15	0	.231
Dubuc, Jean-Jean Joseph Octave (Chauncey)	08-09CinN 12-16DetA 18BosA	9-15-88	St. Johnsbury, Vt.	8-28-58	R	R	5'10	185	87	76	.540	12	256	150	101	1444	1290	577	438	12	3.04	652	150	4	.230
	19NYN 20DL																								
Duffy, Bernie-Bernard Allen	13PitN	8-18-93	Vinson, Okla.	2- 9-62	R	R	5'11	180	0	0	–	0	3	2	0	11	18	3	8	0	5.73	4	1	0	.250
Duggleby, Bill-William James (Frosty Bill)	98,01PhiN 02PhiA	3-17-74	Utica, N.Y.	8-30-44		R			92	105	.467	6	240	191	158	1732	1836	423	452	17	3.19	645	107	6	.166
	02-07PhiN 07PitN																								
Dumont, George-George Henry (Pea Soup)	15-18WasA 19BosA	11-13-95	Minneapolis, Minn.	10-13-56	R	R	5'10	160	10	23	.303	2	77	35	14	347	294	130	128	4	2.85	94	6	0	.064
Dunham, Wiley-Wiley H.	02StLN		Piketon, Ohio						2	3	.400	1	7	5	3	38	47	13	15	0	5.68	12	1	0	.083
Dunkle, Davey-Edward Perks	97-98PhiN 99WasN 03ChiA 03-04WasA	8-19-72	Philipsburg, Pa.	11-19-41	B	R	6'2	220	18	30	.375	1	61	47	36	420	503	162	139	0	5.04	164	31	0	.189
Dunleavy, John-John Francis	03-04StLN	9-14-79	Harrison, N.J.	4-12-44					7	12	.368	0	21	18	14	157	164	80	79	0	4.18	(See B01-19)			
Dunn, Jack-John Joseph	97-00BknN 00-01PhiN 01BalA 02,04NYN	10- 6-72	Meadville, Pa.	10-22-28	R	R			63	59	.516	3	142	118	103	1077	1217	334	171	3	4.11	(See B01-19)			
Dupee, Frank-Frank Oliver	01ChiA	4-29-77	Monkton, Vt.	8-14-56		R	6'1	200	0	0	–	0	1	1	0	0	0	3	0	0	∞	0	0	0	–
Durham, Bull-Louis G.	04BknN 07WasA 08-09NYN	-81	Bolivar, N.Y.			R			1	0	1.000	1	9	2	1	29	37	12	6	0	5.28	7	1	0	.143
Durham, John-John Garfield	02ChiA	10- 7-81	Douglass, Kans.	5- 7-49	R	R	6'	175	1	1	.500	0	3	3	3	20	21	16	3	0	5.85	15	1	0	.067
Durning Dick-Richard Knott	17-18BknN	10-10-92	Louisville, Ky.	9-23-48	L	L	6'2	178	0	0	–	0	2	0	0	3	3	4	0	0	9.00	0	0	0	–
Dygert, Jimmy-James Henry (Sunny Jim)	05-10PhiA	7- 5-84	Utica, N.Y.	2- 8-36	R	R	5'10	185	54	49	.524	6	175	103	62	986	798	383	583	16	2.65	336	47	1	.140
Eason, Mal-Malcolm Wayne (Kid)	00-02ChiN 02BosN 03DetA 05-06BknN	3-13-79	Brookville, Pa.	4-16-70		R			36	74	.327	1	125	113	90	944	1015	289	273	10	3.39	356	43	0	.121
East, Carl-Carlton William	15StLA	8-27-94	Rome, Ga.	1-15-53	L	R	6'2	178	0	0	–	0	1	1	0	3	6	2	1	0	18.00	(See B20-45)			
Eccles, Harry-Harry Josiah (Bugs)	15PhiA	7- 9-93	Kennedy, N.Y.	6- 2-55	L	L	6'2	170	0	1	.000	0	5	1	0	21	18	6	13	0	6.86	6	1	0	.167
Edmonston, Sam-Samuel Sherwood	06-07WasA	8-30-83	Washington, D.C.		L	L	5'11	185	0	1	.000	0	3	1	1	13	18	3	0	0	5.54	5	1	0	.200
Eells, Harry-Harry Archibald	06CleA	2-14-81	Ida Grove, Iowa	10-15-40	R	R	6'3	190	4	5	.444	0	14	8	6	86	77	48	35	1	2.62	32	6	0	.188
Egan, Wish-Aloysius Jerome	02DetA 05-06StLN	6-16-81	Evart, Mich.	4-13-51	R	R	6'3	185	8	26	.235	0	42	34	27	279	309	72	52	0	3.84	96	10	0	.104
Elder, Heinie-Henry Knox	13DetA	8-23-90	Seattle, Wash.		L	L			0	0	–	0	1	0	0	3	4	5	0	0	9.00	1	0	0	.000
Eller, Hod-Horace Owen	17-21CinN	7- 5-94	Muncie, Ind.	7-18-61	R	R	5'11	185	61	40	.604	5	160	88	52	862	806	213	381	10	2.62	308	68	1	.221
Elliott, Claude-Claude Judson	04CinN 04-05NYN	11-17-79	Pardeeville, Wis.	6-21-23	R	R	6'	190	3	4	.429	6	22	9	7	111	115	38	47	1	3.32	45	9	1	.200
Engel, Joe-Joseph William	12-15WasA 17CinN 19CleA 20WasA	3-12-93	Washington, D.C.	6-12-69	R	R	6'1	183	18	23	.439	4	102	52	10	408	344	242	151	2	3.38	104	7	0	.067
Enright, John-John Percy	17NYA	-96	Fort Worth, Tex.		R	R	5'11	177	0	1	.000	0	1	1	0	5	5	3	1	0	5.40	1	0	0	.000
Enzmann, Johnny-John	14BknN 18-19CleA 20PhiN	3- 4-90	Brooklyn, N.Y.		R	R	5'10	165	10	12	.455	2	67	20	11	270	297	61	91	0	2.83	92	13	0	.141
Essick, Bill-William Earl (Vinegar Bill)	06-07CinN	12-18-81	Grand Ridge, Ill.	10-11-51		R			2	3	.400	0	9	6	5	61	62	24	23	0	2.95	21	1	0	.048
Eubank, John-John Franklin (Honest John)	05-07DetA	9- 9-72	Servia, Ind.	11- 3-58	L	R	6'2	215	8	13	.381	2	42	22	11	233	248	58	56	2	3.13	102	20	0	.196
Evans, Bill-William James	16-17PitN 18MS 19PitN	2-10-93	Reidsville, N.C.	12-21-46	R	R	6'	175	2	13	.133	0	28	11	6	127	122	48	41	0	3.83	40	4	0	.100

USE NAME – GIVEN NAMES (NICKNAMES)	TEAM BY YEAR	BIRTH DATE	BIRTH PLACE	DEATH DATE	B	T	HGT	WGT	W	L	PCT	SV	G	GS	CG	IP	H	BB	SO	ShO	ERA	AB	H	HR	BA
									LIFETIME PITCHING TOTALS													BATTING TOTALS			
Evans, Chick-Charles Franklin	09-10BosN	10-15-89	Franklin, Vt.	9- 2-16	R	R			1	4	.200	2	17	4	1	53	53	41	23	0	4.92	19	1	0	.053
Evans, LeRoy-LeRoy	97StLN 97LouN 98-99WasN 02NYN 02-03BknN 03StLA	3-19-74	Knoxville, Tenn.	Deceased	R	R	6'	180	30	42	.417	0	84	68	57	614	673	233	211	2	3.66	201	32	0	.159
Ewing, Bob-George Lemuel (Long Bob)	02-09CinN 10-11PhiN 12StLN	4-24-73	New Hampshire, O.	6-20-47	R	R	6'5	175	124	119	.510	4	291	264	205	2302	2097	614	998	19	2.49	872	170	3	.195
Fahrer, Pete-Clarence Willie	14CinN	3-10-90	Holgate, Ohio	6-10-67	L	R	6'	190	0	0	–	0	5	0	0	8	8	4	2	0	1.13	1	0	0	.000
Fairbank, Lee-James Lee (Smoky)	03-04PhiA	3-17-81	Deansboro, N.Y.	12-27-55	R	R	5'10	185	0	1	.000	0	7	2	2	41	52	25	16	0	5.49	16	1	0	.063
Faircloth, Rags-James Lamar	19PhiN	8-19-92	Kenton, Tenn.		R	R	5'11	160	0	0	–	0	2	0	0	2	5	0	0	0	9.00	0	0	0	–
Falkenberg, Cy-Frederick Peter	03PitN 05-08WasA 08-11, 13CleA 14IndF 15NwkF 15BknF 17PhiA	12-17-79	Chicago, Ill.	4-14-61	R	R	6'5	180	128	126	.504	13	330	268	180	2276	2090	690	1164	27	2.68	771	117	1	.152
Fanwell, Harry-Harry Clayton	10CleA	10-16-86	Patapsco, Md.	7-15-65	B	R	6'	175	2	9	.182	1	17	11	5	92	87	38	30	1	3.62	30	1	0	.033
Faust, Charlie-Charles Victor (Victory)	11NYN	10- 9-80	Marion, Kans.	6-18-15					0	0	–	0	2	0	0	2	2	0	0	0	4.50	0	0	0	–
Felix, Harry-Harry	01NYN 02PhiN	-77	Brooklyn, N.Y.	10-18-61	R	R	5'7	160	1	3	.250	0	10	5	3	47	64	11	10	0	5.36	38	5	0	.132
Ferguson, Cecil-George Cecil	06-07NYN 08-11BosN	8-19-86	Ellsworth, Kans.	9- 5-43	R	R	5'10	165	29	46	.387	8	142	73	47	698	659	281	298	8	3.34	218	41	1	.188
Ferguson, Charlie-Charles Augustus	01ChiN	5-10-75	Okemos, Mich.	5-17-31					0	0	–	0	1	0	0	2	1	2	0	0	0.00	1	0	0	.000
Ferry, Cy-Alfred Joseph	04DetA 05CleA	9-27-78	Hudson, N.Y.	9-27-38	R	R	6'1	170	0	1	.000	0	4	2	1	15	15	11	6	0	7.20	7	2	0	.286
Ferry, Jack-John Francis	10-13PitN	4- 7-87	Pittsfield, Mass.	8-29-54	R	R	5'11	175	10	6	.625	4	47	14	7	161	146	60	56	2	3.02	51	13	0	.255
Fiene, Lou-Louis Henry (Big Finn)	06-09ChiA	12-29-84	Fort Dodge, Iowa	12-22-64	R	R	6'	175	3	8	.273	1	26	10	7	138	149	35	54	0	3.85	53	6	0	.113
Files, Eddie-Charles Edward	08PhiA	5-19-83	Portland, Me.	5-10-54	R	R			0	0	–	0	2	0	0	9	8	3	6	0	6.00	3	0	0	.000
Fincher, Bill-William Allen	16StLA	5-26-94	Atlanta, Ga.	5- 8-46	R	R	6'1	180	0	1	.000	0	12	0	0	21	22	7	5	0	2.14	4	1	0	.250
Finlayson, Pembroke-Pembroke	08-09BknN	7-31-88	Cheraw, S.C.	3- 6-12	R	R			0	0	–	0	2	0	0	7	7	8	2	0	11.57	3	0	0	.000
Finneran, Happy-Joseph Ignatius (Smokey Joe)	12-13PhiN 14-15BknF 18DetA 18NYA	10-29-91	East Orange, N.J.	2- 3-42	R	R	5'10	169	25	33	.431	5	109	66	29	569	568	202	168	3	3.31	184	31	0	.168
Fisher, Chauncey-Chauncey Burr (Peach)	93-94CleN 94,96CinN 97BknN 01NYN 01StLN	1- 8-72	Anderson, Ind.	4-27-39	R	R	5'11	175	19	29	.396	3	65	44	36	436	583	140	80	3	5.37	176	38	1	.216
Fisher, Ray-Raymond Lyle	10-17NYA 18MS 19-20CinN 21DL	10- 4-87	Middlebury, Vt.		R	R	5'11	180	98	95	.508	8	279	208	110	1755	1667	481	680	20	2.82	587	105	2	.179
Fisher, Tom-Thomas Chalmers (Red)	02DetA 04BosN	11- 1-80	Anderson, Ind.	9- 3-72	R	R	5'11	175	6	15	.286	0	32	21	19	218	261	83	84	2	4.17	101	21	2	.208
Fiske, Max-Maximilian Patrick (Ski)	14ChiF	10-12-88	Chicago, Ill.	5-15-28	R	R	6'	210	12	12	.500	0	38	22	7	198	161	59	87	0	3.14	68	16	0	.235
Fittery, Paul-Paul Clarence	14CinN 17PhiN	10-10-87	Lebanon, Pa.	1-28-74	B	L	5'8	168	1	3	.250	0	25	6	3	100	110	39	34	0	3.87	39	3	0	.077
Flaherty, Patsy-Patrick Joseph	99LouN 00PitN 03-04ChiA 04-05PitN 07-08BosN 10PhiN 11BosN	1-23-76	Carnegie, Pa.	1-23-68	L	L	5'8	165	66	85	.437	1	173	150	125	1303	1292	331	271	7	3.10	624	123	6	.197
Flater, Jack-John William	08PhiA	9-22-80	Sandymount, Md.	3-20-70	R	R	5'10	175	1	3	.250	0	5	3	3	39	35	12	8	0	2.08	15	2	0	.133
Fletcher, Sam-Samuel S.	09BknN 12CinN		Altoona, Pa.			R	6'2	210	0	1	.000	0	3	1	1	19	28	13	8	0	9.95	7	2	0	.286
Ford, Gene-Eugene Wyman	05DetA	4-16-81	Milton, Canada	8-23-73	R	R	6'	170	0	0	–	0	6	1	0	16	23	15	2	0	10.69	10	0	0	.000
Ford, Russ-Russell William	09-13NYA 14-15BufF	4-25-83	Brandon, Canada	1-24-60	R	R	5'11	175	98	71	.580	11	199	170	129	1487	1340	376	710	14	2.59	506	106	1	.209
Foreman, Bill-William	09-10WasA		Pa.						0	2	.000	0	3	2	1	12	9	7	2	0	5.25	3	1	0	.333
Foreman, Frank-Francis Isaiah	84ChiU 84KCU 85,89BalAA 90-91CinN 91WasAA 92WasN 92BalN 93NYN 95-96CinN 01BosA 01-02BalA	5- 1-63	Baltimore, Md.	11-19-57	R	R	6'	160	100	93	.518	4	230	206	170	1728	1863	661	591	8	3.95	742	167	9	.225
Foster, Ed-Edward Lee	08CleA			3- 2-29					1	0	1.000	2	6	1	1	21	16	12	11	0	2.14	6	0	0	.000
Foster, Rube-George	13-17BosA	1- 5-88	Lehigh, Okla.		R	R	5'8	160	58	35	.624	5	138	104	61	843	724	305	297	16	2.35	270	58	1	.215
Fox, Henry-Henry H.	02PhiN								0	0	–	1	1	0	0	1	2	1	1	0	18.00	0	0	0	–
Foxen, Bill-William Aloysius	08-10PhiN 10-11ChiN	5-31-84	Tenafly, N.J.	4-17-37	L	L	5'11	165	16	20	.444	0	61	33	20	326	283	140	130	3	2.57	106	15	1	.142
Fraser, Chick-Charles Carrolton	96-98LouN 98CleN 99-00PhiN 01PhiA 02-04PhiN 05BosN 06CinN 07 09ChiN		Chicago, Ill.	5- 8-40	R	R	5'10	188	176	208	.458	7	433	389	342	3355	3460	1332	1098	22	3.68	1319	236	3	.179
Frill, John-John Edmond	10NYA 12StLA 12CinN	4- 3-79	Reading, Pa.	9-29-18	R	L	5'10	170	3	2	.600	1	16	10	3	67	90	7	33	1	5.91	24	4	0	.167
Frisk, Emil-John Emil	99CinN 01DetA	10-15-75	Kalkaska, Mich.	1-27-22	L	R	6'1	190	8	10	.444	0	20	16	15	143	175	43	39	0	4.15	(See B01-19)			
Fritz, Charlie-Charles Cornelius	07PhiA	6-18-82	Mobile, Ala.	7-31-44		L			1	0	1.000	0	1	1	0	3	0	3	1	0	3.00	1	0	0	.000
Frock, Sammy-Samuel W.	07BosN 09-10PitN 10-11BosN	12-23-83	Baltimore, Md.	11- 3-25	R	R	6'	168	14	24	.368	3	63	38	22	342	348	113	202	3	3.24	117	20	0	.171
Fromme, Art-Arthur Henry	06-08StLN 09-13CinN 13-15NYN	9- 3-83	Quincy, Ill.	8-24-56	R	R	6'	178	80	90	.471	4	252	167	90	1437	1297	530	638	14	2.91	476	77	0	.162
Gaiser, Fred-Fred Jacob	08StLN	4- 8-85	Stuttgart, Germany	11-14-18					0	0	–	0	1	0	0	2	4	3	2	0	9.00	1	0	0	.000
Gallia, Bert-Melvin Allys	12-17WasA 18-20StLA 20PhiN	10-14-91	Beeville, Tex.		R	R	6'	165	64	68	.485	12	242	135	61	1278	1210	494	550	7	3.13	412	69	1	.167
Gardner, Harry-Harry	11-12PitN	9-20-88	Portland, Ore.	8- 2-61	R	R	6'2	180	1	1	.500	2	14	3	2	42	42	21	24	0	4.50	14	3	0	.214
Gardner, Jim-James Anderson	95,97-99PitN 02ChiN	10- 4-74	Pittsburg, Pa.	4-24-05		R			25	23	.521	0	59	49	37	422	468	130	115	1	3.86	226	41	1	.181
Garrett, Clarence-Clarence Raymond (Laz)	15CleA	3- 6-91	Reader, W. Va.		R	R	6'5	185	2	2	.500	0	4	4	2	23	19	6	5	0	2.35	8	0	0	.000
Garvin, Ned-Virgil Lee	96PhiN 99-00ChiN 01MilA 02ChiA 02-04BknN 04NYA	1- 1-74	Navasota, Tex.	6-16-08	R	R	6'3	160	59	97	.378	5	181	158	134	1400	1320	413	612	13	2.72	496	60	0	.121
Gaspar, Harry-Harry Lambert	09-12CinN	4-28-83	Kingsley, Iowa	5-14-40	R	R	6'	180	44	48	.478	13	143	98	48	826	795	217	228	10	2.69	266	36	0	.135
Gear, Dale-Dale Dudley	96CleN 01WasA	2- 2-72	Lone Elm, Kans.	9-23-51	R	R	5'11	165	5	13	.278	0	27	18	16	186	234	28	41	1	4.21	(See B01-19)			
Geary, Bob-Robert Norton (Speed)	18-19PhiA 21CinN	5-10-91	Cincinnati, Ohio		R	R	5'11	168	4	9	.308	3	35	10	7	148	164	51	41	2	3.47	45	11	0	.244
Gehring, Henry-Henry	07-08WasA	1-24-81	St. Paul, Minn.	4-18-12					3	8	.273	0	18	10	8	92	101	16	31	2	3.91	48	11	1	.229
George, Lefty-Thomas Edward	11StLA 12CleA 15CinN 18BosN	8-13-86	Pittsburgh, Pa.	5-13-55	L	L	6'	155	6	22	.214	0	52	26	14	242	285	98	74	2	3.87	92	14	0	.152
Gerner, Ed-Edwin Frederick (Lefty)	19CinN	7-22-97	Philadelphia, Pa.	5-15-70	L	L	5'8	175	1	0	1.000	0	5	1	0	17	22	3	2	0	3.18	6	1	0	.167
Gervais, Lefty-Lucien Edward	13BosN	7- 6-90	Grover, Wis.	10-19-50	L	L	5'10	165	0	1	.000	0	5	2	1	16	18	4	1	0	5.63	5	0	0	.000
Geyer, Rube-Jacob Bowman	10-13StLN	3-22-85	Pittsburgh, Pa.			R			17	26	.395	1	104	33	15	413	420	181	133	1	3.66	133	26	0	.195
Gibson, Norwood-Norwood Ringold	03-06BosA	3-11-77	Peoria, Ill.	7- 7-59	R	R	5'10	165	32	32	.500	0	85	72	56	609	525	208	258	3	2.93	206	28	0	.136
Gill, Ed-Edward James	19WasA	8- 7-96	Somerville, Mass.		L	R	5'11	180	1	1	.500	0	16	2	0	37	38	21	7	0	4.86	7	0	0	.000
Gilligan, Jack-John Patrick	09-10StLA	10-18-85	Chicago, Ill.		B	R	6'	190	1	5	.167	0	12	8	5	62	65	37	14	0	4.35	24	4	0	.167
Gingras, Joe-Joseph John	15KCF	1-10-93	New York, N.Y.	9- 6-47	R	R	6'2	188	0	0	–	0	2	0	0	4	6	1	2	0	6.75	1	0	0	.000
Girard, Charlie-Charles A.	10PhiN	-86	Brooklyn, N.Y.						0	2	.000	1	7	1	0	27	33	12	11	0	6.33	8	1	0	.125
Glade, Fred-Frederick Monroe	02ChiN 04-07StLA 08NYA	1-25-76	Dubuque, Iowa	11-21-34	R	R	6'1	200	53	69	.434	1	132	126	107	1073	950	237	464	14	2.62	381	57	0	.150
Glavenich, Luke-Luke Frank	13CleA	1-17-93	Jackson, Cal.	5-22-35	R	R	5'9	189	0	0	–	0	1	0	0	1	3	3	1	0	9.00	0	0	0	–
Glaze, Ralph-Daniel Ralph	06-08BosA	3-13-81	Denver, Colo.	10-31-68	R	R	5'9	165	15	21	.417	0	61	34	20	340	303	85	137	1	2.89	129	22	1	.171
Gleason, Kid-William J.	88-91PhiN 92-94StLN 94-95BalN M19-23ChiA	10-26-66	Camden, N.J.	1- 2-33	B	R	5'7	158	136	129	.513	6	299	266	240	2389	2552	906	744	11	3.79	(See B01-19)			
Glendon, Martin-Martin H.	02CinN 03CleA	-76	Chicago, Ill.				5'11	180	1	3	.250	0	4	4	3	31	25	11	9	0	2.03	9	0	0	.000
Golden, Roy-Roy Kramer	10-11StLN	7-12-88	Madisonville, Ill.	10- 4-61	R	R	6'1	195	6	12	.333	0	37	31	9	192	171	162	112	0	4.88	59	9	0	.153
Good, Ralph-Ralph Nelson	10BosN	4-25-86	Monticello, Me.	11-24-65	R	R	6'	165	0	0	–	0	2	0	0	9	6	2	4	0	2.00	3	0	0	.000
Good-Wilbur-Wilbur David (Lefty)	05NYA	9-28-85	Punxsutawney, Pa.	12-30-63	L	L	5'6	165	0	2	.000	0	5	2	0	19	18	14	13	0	4.74	(See B01-19)			
Goodwin, Art-Arthur Ingram	05NYA	2-27-76	Whitley Twnsp., Pa.	6-19-43					0	0	–	0	1	0	0	.1	2	2	0	0	81.00	0	0	0	–
Goodwin, Clyde-Clyde Samuel	06WasA	11-12-86	Shade, Ohio	10-12-63	R	R	5'11	145	0	2	.000	0	4	3	1	22	20	13	9	0	4.50	5	1	0	.200
Goodwin, Marv-Marvin Mardo	16WasA 17StLN 18MS 19-22StLN 25CinN	1-16-91	Gordonsville, Va.	10-21-25	R	R	6'	175	21	25	.457	2	102	48	19	447	467	100	121	3	3.30	129	24	0	.186
Goulait, Ted-Theodore Lee (Snooze)	12NYN	8-11-89	St. Clair, Mich.	7-15-36	R	R	5'9	172	0	0	–	0	1	1	1	7	11	4	6	0	6.43	2	1	0	.500
Gould, Al-Albert Frank (Pudgy)	16-17CleA	1-20-93	Muscatine, Iowa		R	R	5'6	160	9	11	.450	1	57	16	7	201	196	92	65	1	3.04	53	8	0	.151
Graham, Bill-William	08-10StLA					L			14	29	.326	1	64	40	21	347	321	105	141	3	2.90	118	17	0	.144
Graham, Oscar-Oscar M.	07WasA	-77	Manilla, Iowa	9-16-31		L			4	10	.286	0	20	14	6	104	116	29	44	0	3.98	48	11	1	.229
Graham, Peaches-George Frederick	03ChiN	3-23-77	Aledo, Ill.	7-25-39	R	R	5'9	180	0	1	.000	0	1	1	0	5	9	3	4	0	5.40	(See B01-19)			
Graney, Jack-John Gladstone	08CleA	6-10-86	St. Thomas, Canada		L	L	5'9	180	0	0	–	0	2	0	0	3	6	1	0	0	6.00	(See B01-19)			
Gray, Dolly-William Denton	09-11WasA	12- 4-78	Ishpeming, Mich.	4- 4-56	L	L	6'2	160	15	51	.227	0	98	70	46	568	586	181	213	3	3.52	218	44	0	.202
Gregg, Dave-David Charles (Highpockets)	13CleA	3-14-91	Chehalis, Wash.	11-12-65	R	R	6'3	185	0	0	–	0	1	0	0	1	2	0	0	0	18.00	0	0	0	–
Gregg, Vean-Sylveanus Augustus	11-14CleA 14-16BosA 18PhiA 25WasA	4-13-85	Chehalis, Wash.	7-29-64	L	L	6'1	185	92	64	.590	12	240	162	105	1400	1248	556	722	14	2.69	457	78	0	.171
Gregory, Frank-Frank Ernst	12CinN	7-25-90	Spring Valley, Wis.	11- 5-55	R	R	5'11	185	2	0	1.000	0	4	2	1	16	19	7	4	0	4.50	5	1	0	.200
Gregory, Howie-Howard Watterson	11StLA	11-18-86	Hannibal, Mo.	5-30-70	L	R	6'	175	0	1	.000	0	3	1	0	7	11	4	1	0	5.14	2	0	0	.000
Grevell, Bill-William	19PhiA	3- 5-98	Williamstown, N.J.	6-20-23	R	R	5'11	170	0	0	–	0	5	2	0	12	15	18	3	0	14.25	5	0	0	.000
Griffin, Hank-John Linton	11ChiN 11-12BosN	-86			R	R			0	6	.000	0	19	7	1	86	100	40	31	0	5.76	30	7	0	.233
Griffin, Pat-Patrick Richard	14CinN	5- 6-93	Niles, Ohio	6- 7-27	R	R	6'2	180	0	0	–	0	1	0	0	1	3	2	0	0	9.00	0	0	0	–
Griffith, Clark-Clark Calvin (The Old Fox)	91StLAA 91BosAA 93-00ChiN 01-02,M01-02ChiA 03-07,M03-08NYA 09-10,M09-11CinN 12-14,M12-20WasA	11-20-69	Stringtown, Mo.	10-27-55	R	R	5'6	156	235	143	.622	9	453	372	337	3388	3670	774	955	22	3.31	1380	322	8	.233
Griner, Dan-Donald Dexter (Rusty)	12-16StLN 18BknN	3- 7-88	Centerville, Tenn.	6- 3-50	L	R	6'1	200	28	55	.337	6	135	81	43	673	700	202	244	6	3.49	219	52	0	.237
Groom, Bob-Robert	09-13WasA 14-15StLF 16-17StLA 18CleA	9-12-84	Belleville, Ill.	2-19-48	R	R	6'2	175	119	150	.442	13	367	288	157	2337	2216	783	1159	22	3.10	764	98	0	.128
Groth, Dango-Ernest John	04ChiN	12-24-84	Cedarburg, Wis.	5-23-50	R	R	5'11	175	0	2	.000	1	3	2	2	16	22	6	9	0	5.63	6	0	0	.000
Grover, Burt-Charles Burt (Bugs)	13DetA	6-20-90	Vanceton, Ohio	5-24-71	L	R	6'1	185	0	0	–	0	2	1	0	11	9	7	2	0	3.27	3	0	0	.000
Guese, Whitey-Theodore	01CinN	1-23-73	New Bremen, Ohio	4- 8-51	R	R	6'	200	1	4	.200	0	6	5	4	44	62	14	11	0	6.14	15	3	0	.200
Gunkel, Red-Woodward William	16CleA	4-15-94	Sheffield, Ill.	4-19-54	B	R	5'8	158	0	0	–	0	1	0	0	1	0	1	1	0	0.00	0	0	0	–

									LIFETIME PITCHING TOTALS													BATTING TOTALS			
USE NAME – GIVEN NAMES (NICKNAMES)	TEAM BY YEAR	BIRTH DATE	BIRTH PLACE	DEATH DATE	B	T	HGT	WGT	W	L	PCT	SV	G	GS	CG	IP	H	BB	SO	ShO	ERA	AB	H	HR	BA
Haas, Bruno-Bruno Philip (Boon) 21 played in N.F.L.	15PhiA	5- 5-91	Worcester, Mass.	6- 5-52	B	L	5'10	180	0	2	.000	0	6	2	1	14	23	28	7	0	12.21	18	1	0	.056
Hackett, Jim-James Joseph (Sunny Jim)	02-03StLN	10- 1-77	Jacksonville, Ill.	3-28-61	R	R	6'2	185	1	7	.125	1	11	9	8	78	93	34	28	0	4.73	(See B01-19)			
Hafford, Leo-Leo Edgar	06CinN	9-17-83	Somerville, Mass.	10- 2-11			6'	170	1	1	.500	0	3	1	1	19	13	11	5	0	0.95	9	2	0	.222
Hageman, Casey-Kurt Moritz	11-12BosA 14StLN 14ChiN	5-12-87	Mt. Oliver, Pa.	4- 1-64	R	R	5'10	186	3	7	.300	1	32	11	3	120	108	40	47	0	3.08	35	9	0	.257
Hagerman, Rip-Zeriah Zequiel	09ChiN 14-16 CleA	6-20-88	Lyndon, Kans.	1-29-30	R	R	6'2	200	19	32	.385	0	81	55	23	432	414	225	214	4	3.08	123	8	0	.065
Hahn, Noodles-Frank George	99-05CinN 06NYA	4-29-79	Nashville, Tenn.	2- 6-60	L	L	5'9	160	130	94	.580	0	242	230	211	2021	1906	380	912	25	2.55	733	129	2	.176
Haislip, Jim-James Clifton (Slim)	13PhiN	8- 4-91	Farmersville, Tex.	1-22-70	R	R	6'3	186	0	0	–	0	1	0	0	3	4	3	0	0	6.00	1	0	0	.000
Hale, Dad-Ray Luther	02BosN 02BalA	2-18-79	Allegan, Mich.	2- 1-46	R	R	5'10	180	0	4	.000	0	11	8	4	61	90	24	18	0	5.90	20	0	0	.000
Hall, Bert-Herbert Ernest	11PhiN	10-15-88	Portland, Ore.	7-18-48	R	R	5'10	185	0	1	.000	0	7	1	0	18	19	13	8	0	4.00	3	1	0	.333
Hall, Bill-William Bernard	13BknN	2-22-92	Charleston, W. Va.		R	R	6'	180	0	0	–	0	3	0	0	5	4	5	3	0	5.40	1	0	0	.000
Hall (Ciolo), Charley (Carlos)-Charles Louis (Sea Lion)	06-07CinN 09-13BosA 16StLN 18DetA	7-27-85	Ventura, Cal.	12- 6-43	L	R	6'1	187	53	45	.541	20	188	81	50	911	821	391	427	3	3.08	371	73	2	.197
Hall, Herb-Herbert Silas (Iron Duke)	18DetA	6- 5-94	Steelville, Ill.	7- 3-70	B	R	6'4	220	0	0	–	0	3	0	0	6	12	7	1	0	15.00	1	0	0	.000
Hall, Mark-Marcus	10StLA 13-14DetA	8-12-87	Joplin, Mo.	2-24-15	R	R			14	25	.359	0	63	36	14	301	292	137	112	1	3.26	83	6	0	.072
Halla, Jack-John Arthur	05CleA	5-13-84	St. Louis, Mo.	9-30-47	L	L	5'11	175	0	0	–	0	3	0	0	13	12	0	4	0	2.77	4	1	0	.250
Hamilton, Earl-Earl Andrew	11-16StLA 16DetA 16-17StLA 18-23PitN 24PhiN	7-19-91	Gibson City, Ill.	11-17-68	L	L	5'8	160	117	147	.443	13	410	262	140	2342	2319	773	790	16	3.16	733	112	0	.153
Hanley, Jim-James Patrick	13NYA		Providence, R.I.	Deceased					0	0	–	0	1	0	0	4	5	4	2	0	6.75	1	0	0	.000
Hansen, Ing-Roy Inglof	18WasA	3- 6-98	Beloit, Wis.		R	R	6'	165	1	0	1.000	0	5	0	0	9	10	3	2	0	3.00	0	0	0	–
Harding, Charlie-Charlies H. (Slim)	13DetA	1- 3-91	Nashville, Tenn.		R	R	6'2	172	0	0	–	0	1	0	0	2	3	1	0	0	4.50	0	0	0	–
Hardy, Alex-David Alexander	02-03ChiN	-77	Toronto, Canada	4-22-40		L			3	3	.500	0	7	7	5	48	50	19	16	1	4.31	20	4	0	.200
Hardy, Harry-Harry	05-06WasA	11- 5-75	Steubenville, Ohio	9- 4-43					2	4	.333	0	8	5	4	44	55	18	14	0	5.11	15	1	0	.067
Harkness, Specs-Frederick Harvey	10-11CleA	12-13-87	Los Angeles, Cal.	5-16-52	R	R	5'11	180	11	9	.550	3	38	22	9	188	194	76	85	1	3.40	69	13	0	.188
Harley, Dick-Henry Risk	05BosN	8-18-74	Springfield, Ohio	5-16-61	R	R			2	5	.286	0	9	4	4	66	72	19	19	1	4.64	22	1	0	.045
Harmon, Bob-Robert Greene (Hickory Bob)	09-13StLN 14-16,18PitN	10-15-87	Liberal, Mo.	11-27-61	B	R	6'	187	107	133	.446	12	321	240	143	2054	1966	702	634	15	3.33	692	127	1	.184
Harper, Bill-William Homer (Blue Sleeve)	11StLA	6-14-89	Bertrand, Mo.	6-17-51	B	R	6'1	180	0	0	–	0	2	0	0	8	9	4	6	0	6.75	3	0	0	.000
Harper, Harry-Harry Clayton	13-19 WasA 20BosA 21NYA 23BknN	4-24-95	Hackensack, N.J.	4-23-63	L	L	6'2	165	59	76	.437	2	219	170	65	1257	1100	582	623	12	2.86	402	59	0	.147
Harper, Jack-Charles William	99CleN 00-01StLN 02StLA 03-06CinN 06ChiN 07HO	4- 2-78	Franklin, Pa.	9-30-50	R	R	6'	178	81	62	.566	1	158	148	115	1208	1198	438	466	10	3.58	451	84	1	.186
Harper, Jack-John Wesley	15PhiA	8- 5-93	Hendricks, W. Va.	6-18-27	R	R	5'11	180	0	1	.000	0	3	0	0	9	5	1	3	0	3.00	2	0	0	.000
Harrell, Slim-Oscar Martin	12PhiA	7-31-90	Grandview, Tex.	4-30-71	R	R	6'3	180	0	0	–	0	1	0	0	3	4	0	1	0	0.00	1	0	0	.000
Harrington, Francis-Andrew Francis	13CinN	11-13-88	Wakefield, Mass.	11-12-38	R	R	6'	193	0	0	–	0	1	0	0	4	6	1	1	0	9.00	2	1	0	.500
Harris, Ben-Benjamin F.	14-15KCF	-89	Nashville, Tenn.		R	R	6'	195	7	7	.500	1	32	14	5	156	180	41	40	0	4.04	45	9	0	.200
Harris, Joe-Joseph White	05-07BosA	2- 1-82	Melrose, Mass.	4-12-66	R	R	6'1	198	3	30	.091	2	45	32	26	317	284	88	137	1	3.35	111	18	0	.162
Harstad, Oscar-Oscar Theander	15CleA	5-24-92	Parkland, Wash.		R	R	6'	174	3	6	.333	1	32	7	4	82	81	35	35	0	3.40	16	2	0	.125
Hart, Bill-William Franklin	86-87PhiAA 92BknN 95PitN 96-97StLN 98PitN 01CleA	7-19-65	Louisville, Ky.	9-19-36					65	110	.371	3	206	190	162	1583	1819	704	431	5	4.60	748	154	4	.206
Harter, Frank-Franklin Pierce (Chief)	12-13CinN 14IndF	9-19-86	Keyesport, Ill.	4-14-59	R	R	5'11	165	3	5	.375	0	29	6	2	101	105	37	30	0	3.65	33	3	0	.091
Hartman, Charlie-Charlies Otto	08BosA	8-10-88	Los Angeles, Cal.	10-22-60					0	0	–	0	1	0	0	2	1	2	1	0	4.50	0	0	0	–
Hartranft, Ray-Raymond Charles	13PhiN								0	0	–	0	1	0	0	1	3	1	1	0	9.00	0	0	0	–
Harvey, Zaza-Ervin King (Silent)	00ChiN 01ChiA	1- 5-79	Saratoga, Cal.	6- 3-54		L			3	6	.333	1	17	9	5	96	94	35	27	0	3.47	(See B01-19)			
Hawk, Ed-Edward	11StLA	5-11-90	Neosho, Mo.	3-26-36	L	R	5'11	175	1	4	.200	0	5	4	4	38	38	8	14	0	3.32	13	2	0	.154
Hawley, Pink-Emerson P.	92-94StLN 95-97PitN 98-99CinN 00NYN 01MilA	12- 5-72	Beaver Dam, Wis.	9-19-38	L	R	5'10	185	165	177	.482	3	393	344	297	3011	3334	973	869	11	3.97	1195	297	11	.249
Hearn, Bunny-Bunn	10-11StLN 13NYN 15PitF 18,20BosN	5-21-91	Chapel Hill, N.C.	10-19-59	L	L	5'11	190	13	24	.351	0	66	40	24	400	429	100	111	2	3.56	133	24	1	.180
Hedgpeth, Doc-Harry Malcolm	13WasA	9- 4-88	Fayetteville, N.C.	7-30-66	L	L	6'1	194	0	0	–	0	1	0	0	1	1	0	0	0	0.00	0	0	0	–
Hehl, Jake-Herman Charles	18BknN	12- 8-99	Brooklyn, N.Y.	7- 4-61	R	R	5'11	180	0	0	–	0	1	0	0	1	0	0	0	0	0.00	0	0	0	–
Heismann, Crese-Christian Ernest	01-02CinN 02BalA	4-16-80	Cincinnati, Ohio	11-19-51	R	L	6'2	175	2	5	.286	0	11	8	5	63	71	28	23	0	4.71	26	6	0	.231
Heitmann, Harry-Harry Anton	18BknN	10- 6-96	Albany, N.Y.	12-15-58	R	R	6'1	205	0	1	.000	0	1	1	0	.1	4	0	0	0	108.00	0	0	0	–
Henderson, Ed-Edward J.	14PitF 14IndF	-90	New York, N.Y.		L	L	5'9	168	1	1	.500	0	8	2	2	26	22	12	5	0	4.15	7	0	0	.000
Hendricks, Ed-Edward (Big Ed)	10NYN	6-20-86	Zeeland, Mich.	11-28-30	L	L	6'3	200	0	1	.000	1	4	1	1	12	12	4	2	0	3.75	4	0	0	.000
Hendrix, Claude-Claude Raymond	11-13PitN 14-15ChiF 16-20ChiN 21DU	4-13-89	Olathe, Kans.	3-22-44	R	R	6'	195	144	116	.554	17	360	257	184	2372	2123	697	1092	27	2.65	922	222	13	.241
Henion, Lafayette-Lafayette M.	19BknN	-99	San Diego, Cal.	7-22-55	R	R	5'11	154	0	0	–	0	1	0	0	3	2	2	2	0	6.00	1	0	0	.000
Henley, Weldon-Weldon	03-05PhiA 07BknN	10-20-80	Jasper, Ga.	11-16-60	R	R	6'	175	31	42	.425	0	97	81	62	722	640	231	309	8	2.94	261	48	0	.184
Henning, Pete-Ernest Herman	14-15KCF	12-28-87	Crown Ppoint, Ind.	11- 4-39	R	R	6'1	185	14	25	.359	4	68	34	22	345	334	134	118	1	3.83	112	22	0	.196
Herbert, Ernie-Ernie Albert (Tex)	13CinN 14-15StLF	1-30-87	Hale, Mo.	1-13-68	R	R	5'10	165	2	1	.667	1	35	3	1	115	116	50	52	0	3.37	35	13	0	.371
Herbert (Kemman), Fred (Herbert Frederick)-Frederick	15NYN	3- 4-87	LaGrange, Ill.	5-29-63	R	R	6'	185	1	1	.500	0	2	2	1	17	12	4	6	0	1.06	6	1	0	.167
Herrmann, Lefty-Martin John	18BknN	1-10-93	Oldenburg, Ind.	9-11-56	L	L	5'10	150	0	0	–	0	1	0	0	1	0	1	0	0	0.00	0	0	0	–
Herrell, Walt-Walter W.	11WasA		Washington, D.C.						0	0	–	0	1	0	0	2	5	2	0	0	18.00	1	0	0	.000
Herring, Bill-William Francis (Smoke)	15BknF	10-31-93	New York, N.Y.	9-10-62	R	R	6'3	185	0	0	–	0	3	0	0	3	5	2	3	0	15.00	0	0	0	–
Herring, Herb-Herbert Lee	12WasA	7-22-91	Danville, Ark.	4-22-64	R	R	5'11	178	0	0	–	0	1	0	0	1	1	1	0	0	0.00	0	0	0	–
Hershey, Frank-Frank	05BosN	12-13-77	Gorham, N.Y.	12-15-49					0	1	.000	0	1	1	0	4	5	2	1	0	6.75	1	0	0	.000
Hess, Otto-Otto C.	02,04-08CleA 12-15BosN	10-10-78	Berne, Switzerland	2-25-26	L	L	6'1	170	71	88	.447	5	198	165	129	1418	1355	448	580	19	2.98	716	154	5	.215
Hesselbacher, George-George Edward	16PhiA	1-18-95	Philadelphia, Pa.		R	R	6'2	175	0	4	.000	0	6	4	2	26	37	22	6	0	7.27	8	1	0	.125
Hesterfer, Larry-Lawrence	01NYN	6- 9-78	Newark, N.J.	9-22-43	R	L	5'8	150	0	1	.000	0	1	1	1	6	15	3	2	0	7.50	2	0	0	.000
Hickey, John-John W.	04CleA	11- 3-81	Minneapolis, Minn.	12-28-41		R			0	2	.000	0	2	2	1	12	14	11	5	0	7.50	5	0	0	.000
Hickman, Charley, Charles Taylor (Piano Legs)	97-99BosN 01NYN 02CleA 07WasA	3- 4-76	Taylortown, Pa.	4-19-34	R	R	5'9	185	12	8	.600	4	30	22	15	185	175	94	37	3	4.28	(See B01-19)			
Higginbotham, Irv-Irving Clinton	06,08-09StLN 09ChiN	4-26-82	Homer, Neb.	6-12-59	R	R	6'1	196	10	14	.417	1	48	24	16	243	232	66	86	1	2.81	85	15	0	.176
Higgins, Festus-Festus Edward	09-10StLN	-93	Cincinnati, Ohio	10- 4-24	R	R			3	4	.429	0	18	5	5	76	83	24	16	0	4.50	26	6	0	.231
High, Ed-Edward (Lefty)	05DetA		Baltimore, Md.			L			2	1	.667	0	4	1	1	18	21	6	4	0	3.50	7	0	0	.000
Hill, Herb-Herbert	15CleA	8-19-92	Dallas, Tex.		R	R	5'11	175	0	0	–	0	1	0	0	2	1	2	0	0	0.00	0	0	0	–
Hill, Red-Clifford J.	17PhiA	1-25-94	Marshall, Tex.	8-13-38	B	L			0	0	–	0	1	0	0	3	5	1	0	0	6.00	0	0	0	–
Hillebrand, Doc-Homer Hiller Henry	05-06,08PitN	10-10-79	Freeport, Ill.	1-23-74	R	L	5'8	165	7	4	.636	1	18	11	8	115	86	40	70	1	2.50	(See B01-19)			
Hinrichs, Dutch-William Louis	10WasA	4-27-89	Orange, Cal.	8-18-72	R	R	6'3	195	0	1	.000	1	3	0	0	7	10	3	5	0	2.57	4	0	0	.000
Hitt, Bruce-Bruce Smith	17StLN 18MS	3-14-98	Comanche, Tex.	11-10-73	R	R	6'1	190	0	0	–	0	2	0	0	4	7	1	1	0	9.00	1	0	0	.000
Hitt, Roy-Roy Wesley (Rhino)	07CinN	6-22-87	Carleton, Neb.	2- 8-56	L	L	5'10	200	6	10	.375	0	21	18	14	153	143	56	63	2	3.41	56	10	0	.179
Hock, Harry-Harry Keller	08PhiN 14-15StLA	1- 9-87	Woodside, Del.		R	R	5'10	165	2	6	.250	0	30	8	4	120	127	66	26	0	4.35	33	4	0	.121
Hoelskoetter, Art-Arthur H. (Holley, Hoss) (Played as Art Hostetter 07)	05-07StLN	9-30-82	St. Louis, Mo.	8- 3-54	R	R	6'2		2	5	.286	0	15	4	3	75	68	49	32	0	4.56	(See B01-19)			
Hoff, Red-Chester Cornelius	11-13NYA 15StLA	5- 8-91	Ossining, N.Y.		L	L	5'9	162	2	4	.333	0	23	5	2	84	67	38	49	0	2.46	34	7	0	.206
Hoffer, Bill-William Leopold (Wizard)	95-98 BalN 98-99 PitN 01CleA	11- 8-70	Cedar Rapids, Ia.	7-21-59	R	R	5'9	155	95	45	.679	3	161	142	125	1254	1333	453	314	10	3.75	563	129	1	.229
Hogan, George-George Emmet	14KCF	9-25-85	Marion, Ohio	2-28-22					0	1	.000	0	4	1	0	13	12	7	7	0	4.15	4	0	0	.000
Hogg, Bill-William (Buffalo Bill)	05-08NYA	-80	Port Huron, Mich.	12- 8-09					38	49	.437	1	116	89	43	730	677	319	368	5	3.06	246	28	1	.114
Hogg, Brad-Carter Bradley	11-12BosN 15ChiN 18-19PhiN	3-26-88	Buena Vista, Ga.	4- 2-35	L	R	6'	185	20	29	.408	3	71	50	33	448	446	152	149	4	3.70	162	40	0	.247
Holmes, Ed-Edward M.	18PhiA					R			0	0	–	0	2	0	0	2	4	1	0	0	13.50	0	0	0	–
Holmes, Jim-James Scott	06PhiA 08BknN	8- 2-82	Lawrenceburg, Ky.	3-10-60					1	5	.167	0	16	2	1	49	47	28	11	0	3.49	18	4	0	.222
Hooker (Hock), Cy (Cyrus)-William E.	02-03CinN	-80	Richmond, Va.	8-21-11		R			0	1	.000	0	2	1	1	10	13	2	0	0	3.60	4	0	0	.000
Hope, Sam-Samuel	07PhiA	12- 4-78	Brooklyn, N.Y.	6-30-46					0	0	–	0	1	0	0	.1	3	0	0	0	0.00	0	0	0	–
Hooper, Bill-William Booth (Bird Dog)	13-14StLN 15WasA	8-26-90	Jackson, Tenn.	1-14-65	R	R	6'	175	0	4	.000	1	19	3	2	60	65	29	12	0	4.20	13	4	0	.308
Horsey, Hanson-Hanson Galena	12CinN	11-26-89	Galena, Md.	12- 1-49	R	R	5'11	165	0	0	–	0	1	0	0	4	14	3	0	0	22.50	2	0	0	.000
Horstmann, Oscar-Oscar Theodore	17-19StLN	6- 2-91	Alma, Mo.		R	R	5'11	165	9	7	.563	1	50	15	4	176	154	80	61	1	3.68	52	10	0	.192
Houck, Duke-Byron Simon	12-14PhiA 14BknF 18StLA	8-28-91	Prosper, Minn.	6-17-69	R	R	6'	175	26	24	.520	3	118	50	19	532	462	274	224	1	3.30	175	20	1	.114
House, Will-Willard Edwin	13DetA	10- 3-90	Cabool, Mo.	11-16-23	R	R	6'3	190	1	2	.333	0	19	2	0	54	64	17	16	0	5.17	10	0	0	.000
Houser, Joe-Joseph William	14BufF	7- 3-91	Steubenville, Ohio	1- 3-53	L	L	5'9	160	0	1	.000	0	7	2	0	23	21	20	6	0	5.48	7	1	0	.143
Hovlik, Ed-Edward Charles (Hick)	18-19WasA	8-20-91	Cleveland, Ohio	3-19-55	R	R	6'	180	2	1	.667	1	11	2	1	34	37	19	13	0	3.18	10	1	0	.100
Hovlik, Joe-Joseph (Brick)	09-10WasA 11ChiA	8-16-84	Czechoslovakia	11- 3-51	R	R	5'10	185	2	0	1.000	1	16	3	1	55	66	23	25	0	3.60	15	1	0	.067
Howard, Earl-Earl N.	18StLN	6-25-96	Everett, Pa.	4- -37	R	R	6'1	160	0	0	–	0	1	0	0	2	0	2	0	0	0.00	0	0	0	–

									LIFETIME PITCHING TOTALS													BATTING TOTALS			
USE NAME – GIVEN NAMES (NICKNAMES)	TEAM BY YEAR	BIRTH DATE	BIRTH PLACE	DEATH DATE	B	T	HGT	WGT	W	L	PCT	SV	G	GS	CG	IP	H	BB	SO	ShO	ERA	AB	H	HR	BA
Howell, Henry-Harry (Handsome Harry)	98BknN 99BalN 00BknN 09-02BalA 03NYA 04-10StLA	11-14-76	Brooklyn, N.Y.	5-22-56	R	R			132	141	.484	5	340	282	244	2567	2435	677	986	20	2.74	(See B01-19)			
Howell, Roland-Roland Boatner (Billiken)	12StLN	1- 3-92	Napolenville, La		R	R	6'4	210	0	0	–	0	3	0	0	2	5	5	0	0	22.50	0	0	0	–
Huenke, Al-Albert John	14NYN	6-26-91	New Bremen, Ohio		R	R	6'	175	0	0	–	0	1	0	0	2	2	0	2	0	4.50	1	0	0	.000
Hughes, Ed-Edward H.	05-06BosA	-80	Chicago, Ill.		R	R	6'1	180	3	1	.750	0	8	4	2	43	53	12	11	0	4.81	(See B01-19)			
Hughes, Jay-James Jay	98BalN 99,01-02BknN	1-22-74	Sacramento, Cal.	6- 2-24	R	R	6'	190	81	40	.669	0	135	129	112	1098	1011	376	370	8	3.00	453	102	3	.225
Hughes, Long Tom-Thomas J.	00-01ChiN 02BalA 02-03BosA 04NYA 05-09,11-13WasA	11-26-78	Chicago, Ill.	2- 8-56	R	R	5'11	165	129	175	.424	20	399	314	227	2644	2610	853	1368	24	3.09	958	190	6	.198
Hughes, Tom-Thomas L.	06-07,09-10NYA 14-18BosN	1-28-84	Coal Creek, Colo.	11- 1-61	R	R	6'2	175	55	40	.579	18	160	87	55	863	703	235	476	9	2.56	285	37	3	.130
Hughes, Vern-Vernon Alexander (Lefty)	14BalF	4-15-93	Etna, Pa.	9-26-61	L	L	5'10	155	0	0	–	0	3	0	0	6	5	3	0	0	3.00	1	0	0	.000
Humphries, Bert-Albert	10-11PhiN 11-12CinN 13-15ChiN	9-26-80	California, Pa.	9-21-45	R	R	5'11	182	50	43	.538	9	153	91	45	797	807	151	258	10	2.78	247	46	0	.186
Hunt, Ben-Benjamin Franklin (Highpockets)	10BosA 13StLN	-88	Eufaula, Okla.		L	L	6'1	190	2	5	.286	0	9	8	3	55	51	29	25	0	3.93	20	1	0	.050
Hunter, George-George Henry	09BknN	7- 8-86	Buffalo, N.Y.	1-11-68	B	L	5'8	165	4	10	.286	0	16	13	10	113	104	38	43	0	2.47	(See B01-19)			
Husting, Bert-Berthold Juneau (Pete)	00PitN 01MilA 02BosA 02PhiA	3- 6-78	Fond du Lac, Wis.	9- 3-48	R	R			23	21	.523	2	69	54	37	437	499	199	122	1	4.16	183	33	1	.180
Hynes, Pat-Patrick J.	03StLN 04StLA	3-12-84	St. Louis, Mo.	3-12-07					1	1	.500	0	6	3	2	35	45	13	7	0	5.66	(See B01-19)			
Iburg, Ham-Herman Edward	02PhiN	10-29-77	San Francisco, Cal.	2-11-45	R	R	5'11	165	11	18	.379	0	30	30	20	236	286	62	106	1	3.89	87	12	0	.138
Imlay, Doc-Harry Miller	13PhiN	1-12-89	Allentown, N.J.	10- 7-48	R	R	6'	168	0	0	–	0	9	0	0	14	19	7	7	0	7.07	3	0	0	.000
Ingersoll, Bob-Robert Randolph	14CinN	1- 8-83	Rapid City, S.D.	1-13-27	R	R	5'11	175	0	0	–	0	4	0	0	6	5	5	2	0	3.00	1	1	0	1.000
Isbell, Frank-William Frank (Bald Eagle)	98ChiN 01-02,06-07ChiA	8-21-75	Delevan, N.Y.	7-15-41	L	R	5'11	190	4	7	.364	1	17	10	7	85	92	43	19	0	3.60	(See B01-19)			
Jackson, Charlie-Charles W.	05DetA	-82	Iowa			R			0	2	.000	0	2	2	1	11	14	7	3	0	5.73	4	1	0	.250
Jacobs, Elmer-William Elmer	14PhiN 16-68PitN 18-19PhiN 19-20StLN 24-25ChiN 27ChiA	8-10-92	Salem, Mo.	2-10-58	R	R	6'	165	50	81	.382	7	250	133	65	1189	1223	423	336	8	3.55	347	56	0	.161
Jacobson, Beany-Albert L.	04-05WasA 06-07StLA 07BosA	6- 5-81	Pt. Washington, Wis.	1-31-33		L			23	46	.333	1	88	70	53	612	618	148	195	1	3.19	208	24	0	.115
Jacobus, Larry-Stuart Louis	18CinN	12-18-93	Cincinnati, Ohio	8-19-65	B	R	6'2	186	0	1	.000	0	5	0	0	17	25	1	8	0	5.82	5	0	0	.000
Jaeger, Charlie-Charles Thomas	04DetA	4-17-75	Ottawa, Ill.	9-27-42					2	3	.400	0	8	6	5	49	49	15	13	0	2.57	17	1	0	.059
James, Bill-William Henry (Big Bill)	11-12CleA 14-15StLA 15-19DetA 19BosA 19ChiA	1-20-87	Detroit, Mich.	5-24-42	B	R	6'4	195	65	70	.481	4	203	147	67	1180	1112	576	408	9	3.21	358	51	0	.142
James, Bill-William Lawrence (Seattle Bill)	13-15BosN 16-17SJ 18MS 19BosN	3-12-92	Iowa Hill, Cal.	3-10-71	L	R	6'3	196	37	21	.638	2	84	61	44	541	469	199	253	5	2.28	199	46	0	.231
James, Lefty-William A.	12-14CleA	7- 1-89	Glenroy, Ohio	5- 3-33	R	L	5'11	175	2	6	.250	1	31	11	5	96	94	45	36	0	3.38	28	3	0	.107
Jamieson, Charlie-Charles Devine	16WasA 17-18PhiA 19,22CleA	2- 7-93	Paterson, N.J.	10-27-69	L	L	5'9	165	2	1	.667	0	13	3	1	48	55	30	7	0	6.19	(See B20-45)			
Jasper, Hi-Harry W.	14-15ChiA 16StLN 19CleA	11-15-80	St. Louis, Mo.	5-22-37	R	R	5'11	180	10	12	.455	1	52	23	8	238	210	99	96	0	3.48	74	12	1	.162
Jensen, Bill-William	12DetA 14PhiA	11-23-88	New Haven, Conn.		L	R	5'11	170	1	2	.333	0	5	4	2	34	37	16	5	0	4.50	13	0	0	.000
Johns, Ollie-Oliver Tracy	05CinN	8-21-79	Trenton, Ohio	6-17-61	L	L			1	0	1.000	1	4	1	1	18	31	4	8	0	3.50	5	1	0	.200
Johnson, Chief-George Howard (Murphy, Big Murph)	13-14CinN 14-15KCF	3-30-86	Winnebago, Neb.	6-11-22	R	R	5'11	190	40	43	.482	2	111	85	44	688	667	192	304	9	2.86	224	27	3	.121
Johnson, Jing-Russell Conwell	16-17PhiA 18MS 19,27-28PhiA	10- 9-94	Parker Ford, Pa.	12- 6-50	R	R	5'9	172	24	38	.387	0	101	64	36	548	559	179	171	0	3.33	174	32	2	.184
Johnson, Rankin-Adam Rankin Sr. (Tex)	14BosA 14-15ChiF 15BalF 18StLN	2- 4-88	Burnet, Tex.	7- 2-72	R	R	6'1	185	23	30	.434	2	72	53	31	450	401	151	169	6	2.92	144	18	0	.125
Johnson, Roy-Roy (Hardrock)	18PhiA M44ChiN	10- 1-95	Madill, Okla.		R	R	6'	185	1	5	.167	0	10	8	3	50	47	27	14	0	3.42	15	1	0	.067
Johnson, Walt-Ellis Walter	12,15ChiA 17PhiA	12- 8-92	Minneapolis, Minn.	1-14-65	R	R	6'1	185	0	2	.000	0	9	2	0	30	29	15	19	0	5.40	4	0	0	.000
Johnson, Walter-Walter Perry (Barney, The Big Train)	07-27WasA M29-32WasA M33-35CleA	11- 6-87	Humboldt, Kans.	12-10-46	R	R	6'1	200	416	279	.599	36	802	666	532	5926	4927	1404	3506	112	2.17	(See B01-19)			
Jones, Alex-Alexander H.	89PitN 92LouN 92WasN 94PhiN 03DetA	-67	Bradford, Pa.	Deceased		L			9	16	.360	0	26	24	18	201	199	77	65	1	3.72	79	13	0	.165
Jones, Cowboy-Albert Edward (Bronco)	98CleN 99-01StLN	8-23-74	Golden, Colo.	2- 8-58	L	L	5'11	160	25	35	.417	0	70	66	52	526	618	155	147	3	3.61	202	32	0	.158
Jones, Deacon-Carroll Elmer	16-18DetA	12-20-93	Arcadia, Kans.	12-28-52	R	R	6'1	174	6	6	.500	2	46	10	3	151	136	69	45	0	2.98	44	5	0	.114
Jones, Elijah-Elijah Albert	07,09DetA	1-27-82	Oxford, Mich.	4-28-43	R	R			1	3	.250	1	6	3	1	26	33	4	11	0	4.15	8	1	0	.125
Jones, Oscar-Oscar Winfield (Flip Flap)	03-05BknN	1-21-79	London Grove, Pa.	10- 8-46	R	R	5'7	163	44	54	.449	1	113	97	83	875	904	225	257	4	3.20	327	69	0	.211
Jordan, Rip-Raymond Willis (Lanky)	12ChiA 19WasA	9-28-89	Portland, Me.	6- 5-60	L	R	6'	172	0	0	–	0	4	1	0	14	19	2	2	0	7.71	5	0	0	.000
Joss, Addie-Adrian	02-10CleA 10IL	4-12-80	Juneau, Wis.	4-14-11	R	R	6'3	185	159	95	.626	6	287	261	235	2336	1895	370	926	45	1.88	817	118	1	.144
Joyce, Mike (See Mike O'Neill)																									
Justis, Walt-Walter Newton (Smoke)	05DetA	8-17-83	Moores Hill, Ind.	10- 4-41	R	R	5'8	195	0	0	–	0	2	0	0	3	4	6	0	0	9.00	1	0	0	.000
Juul, Herold-Earl Herold	14BknF	5-21-93	Chicago, Ill.	1- 4-42	R	R	5'9	150	0	3	.000	0	9	3	0	29	26	31	16	0	6.21	9	2	0	.222
Juul. Herb Herbert Victor	11CinN	2- 2-86	Chicago, Ill.	11-14-28	L	L	5'11	150	0	0	–	0	1	0	0	4	3	4	2	0	4.50	2	0	0	.000
Kahler, George-George Runnells (Krum)	10-14CleA	9- 6-89	Athens, Ohio	2- 7-24	R	R	6'	183	32	43	.427	3	109	77	41	627	631	272	285	5	3.17	207	25	0	.121
Kaiserling, George-George (Shiny)	14IndF 15NwkF	5-12-93	Steubenville, Ohio	3- 2-18	R	R	6'	180	32	25	.561	2	78	62	36	536	534	145	150	6	2.69	177	23	0	.130
Kallio, Rudy-Rudolph	18-19DetA 25BosA	12-14-92	Portland, Ore.		R	R	5'10	160	9	17	.346	1	49	27	10	222	234	93	75	2	4.18	66	11	0	.167
Kane (Cohen), Harry-Harry (Klondike)	02StLA 03DetA 05-06PhiN	7-27-83	Hamburg, Ark.	9-15-32	L	L			2	7	.222	0	15	9	7	86	100	50	43	1	4.81	30	3	0	.100
Kantlehner, Erv-Erving Leslie	14-16PitN 16PhiN	7-31-92	San Jose, Cal.		L	L	6'	190	13	29	.310	5	87	44	20	399	344	157	141	5	2.84	113	24	0	.212
Karger, Ed-Edwin	06PitN 06-08StLN 09CinN 09-11BosA	5- 6-83	San Angelo, Cal.	9- 9-57	R	L	5'11	175	48	68	.414	3	165	123	81	1091	1012	314	415	8	2.79	400	88	6	.220
Katoll, Jack-John (Big Jack)	98-99ChiN 01-02ChiA 02BalA	6-24-72	Germany	6-18-55	R	R	6'4	200	17	24	.415	0	47	41	35	361	432	90	90	0	3.32	149	20	1	.134
Kearns, W.A.-W.A.	01BalA		Chicago, Ill.						1	0	1.000	0	3	1	1	17	30	9	5	0	6.35	7	1	0	.143
Keating, Ray-Raymond Herbert	12-16,18NYA 19BosN	7-21-91	Bridgeport, Conn.	12-29-63	R	R	5'11	185	30	51	.370	1	130	92	49	751	706	293	349	4	3.30	247	42	1	.170
Keefe, Bob-Robert Francis	07NYA 11-12CinN	6-16-82	Folsom, Cal.	12- 7-64	R	R	5'11	155	17	18	.486	7	75	35	15	361	334	129	154	0	3.14	107	10	0	.093
Keeley, Burt-Burton Elwood (Speed)	08-09WasA	11- 2-79	Wilmington, Ill.	5- 3-52	R	R	5'9	170	6	11	.353	1	30	17	12	177	185	49	68	1	3.31	51	6	0	.118
Keifer, Katsey-Sherman C.	14IndF	-92			B	R			1	0	1.000	0	1	1	1	9	6	2	2	0	2.00	3	1	0	.333
Kellogg, Al-Albert C. (Lefty)	08PhiA					L			0	2	.000	0	3	3	2	17	20	9	8	0	5.82	8	1	0	.125
Kellum, Win-Winford Ansley	01BosA 04CinN 05StLN	4-11-76	Waterford, Canada	8-10-51	B	L	5'8	160	19	15	.559	2	48	37	32	347	337	63	97	2	3.19	125	21	0	.168
Kelly, Ed-Edward L.	14BosA	-90	Spokane, Wash.		R	R	5'11	173	0	0	–	0	3	0	0	2	1	1	4	0	0.00	1	0	0	.000
Kelly, Herb-Herbert Barrett (Moke)	14-15PitN	6- 4-92	Mobile, Ala.	5-18-73	L	L	5'9	160	1	3	.250	0	10	3	2	37	34	11	12	0	2.92	11	3	0	.273
Kenna, Ed-Edward Benninghaus (The Pitching Poet)	02PhiA	10-17-77	Charleston, W.Va.	3-22-12		R	6'	180	1	1	.500	0	2	1	1	17	19	11	5	0	5.29	8	1	0	.125
Kennedy, Brickyard-William P.	92-01BknN 02NYN 03PitN	10- 7-67	Bellaire, Ohio	9-23-15	R	R	5'11	160	182	163	.528	9	405	353	293	3021	3276	1201	797	12	3.96	1274	341	1	.268
Kent, Maury-Maurice Allen	12-13BknN	9-17-85	Marshalltown, Iowa	4-19-66	R	R	6'	168	5	5	.500	0	23	9	2	100	112	49	25	1	4.68	38	8	0	.211
Keupper, Hank-Henry J.	14StLF	6-24-87	Staunton, Ill.	8-14-60	L	L	6'1	180	8	20	.286	0	42	25	12	213	256	49	70	1	4.27	68	17	0	.250
Killian, Ed-Edwin Henry (Twilight Ed)	03CleA 04-10DetA	11-12-76	Racine, Wis.	7-18-28	L	L	5'11	170	100	81	.552	6	213	180	149	1599	1463	482	516	22	2.38	609	127	0	.209
Killilay, Jack-John William	11BosA	5-24-87	Leavenworth, Kans.	10-21-68	R	R	5'11	165	4	3	.571	1	14	7	1	61	65	36	28	0	3.54	24	1	0	.042
Kinney, Walt-Walter William	18BosA 19-20,23PhiA	9- 9-93	Denison, Tex.	7- 1-71	L	L	6'2	186	11	20	.355	1	63	30	18	291	274	136	129	1	3.59	125	35	2	.280
Kinsella, Ed-Edward William (Rube)	05PitN 10StLA	1-15-82	Lexington, Ill.		R	R	6'1	175	1	4	.200	0	13	7	4	67	81	19	21	0	3.49	15	3	0	.200
Kirby, LaRue-LaRue	12NYN 15StLF	12-30-89	Eureka, Mich.	6-10-61	B	R	6'	185	1	0	1.000	0	4	1	1	18	20	8	9	0	5.50	(See B01-19)			
Kirsch, Casey-Harry Louis	10CleA	10-17-87	Pittsburgh, Pa.	12-25-25	R	R	5'11	170	0	0	–	0	2	0	0	3	5	1	5	0	6.00	0	0	0	–
Kisinger, Rube-Charles Samuel	02-03DetA	12-13-76	Adrian, Mich.	7-14-41	R	R	6'	190	8	13	.381	0	21	19	18	162	166	41	40	2	3.00	66	9	0	.136
Kitson, Frank-Frank L.	98-99BalN 00-02BknN 03-05DetA 06-07WasA 07NYA	4-11-72	Hopkins, Mich.	4-14-30	L	R	5'10	150	126	117	.519	8	303	248	211	2217	2328	488	729	20	3.17	972	234	4	.241
Klawitter, Dutch-Albert C.	09-10NYN 13DetA	4-12-88	Wilkes-Barre, Pa.	2- 2-50	R	R	5'11	187	2	3	.400	1	15	6	3	60	65	30	16	0	4.20	20	3	0	.150
Klepfer, Ed-Edward Lloyd (Big Ed)	11-13NYA 15ChiA 15-17CleA 18MS 19CleA	3-17-88	Summerville, Pa.	8- 9-50	R	R	6'	185	22	18	.550	3	98	50	16	448	457	137	165	2	2.81	125	6	0	.048
Klobedanz, Fred Frederick Augustus	96-99,02BosN	6-13-71	Waterbury, Conn.	4-12-40	L	L	5'11	190	52	26	.667	0	89	85	69	702	742	266	181	2	4.12	317	86	7	.271
Knetzer, Elmer-Elmer Ellsworth (Baron)	09-12BknN 13HO 14-15PitF 16BosN 16-17CinN	7-22-85	Carrick, Pa.		R	R	5'10	180	69	69	.500	6	220	134	82	1267	1206	481	535	13	3.15	386	42	0	.109
Knolls, Hub-Oscar Edward	06BknN	12-18-83	Medaryville, Ind.	7- 1-46		R			0	0	–	0	2	0	0	7	13	2	3	0	3.86	1	1	0	1.000
Knowlson, Tom-Thomas H.	15PhiA	-95	Ridgway, Pa.		B	R	5'11	178	4	7	.364	0	18	9	8	101	99	60	24	0	3.48	36	3	0	.083
Koenigsmark, Willis-Willis Thomas	19StLN	2-27-90	Waterloo, Ill.	7- 1-72	R	R	6'4	180	0	0	–	0	1	0	0	0	2	1	0	0	∞	0	0	0	–
Koestner, Elmer-Elmer Joseph (Bob)	10CleA 14ChiN 14CinN	11-30-85	Piper City, Ill.	10-27-59	R	R	6'1	175	5	10	.333	4	36	14	8	170	169	76	56	1	3.18	54	17	0	.315
Koob, Ernie-Ernest Gerald	15-17StLA 18MS 19StLA	9-11-92	Keeler, Mich.	11-12-41	L	L	5'10	160	24	31	.436	3	125	55	19	501	488	186	121	3	3.13	128	9	0	.070
Koukalik, Joe-Joseph	04BknN	3- 3-80	Chicago, Ill.	12-27-45	R	R	5'8	160	0	1	.000	0	1	1	1	8	10	4	1	0	1.13	3	0	0	.000
Krapp, Gene-Eugene H. (Rubber Arm)	11-12CleA 14-15BufF	5-12-87	Rochester, N.Y.	4-13-23	R	R	5'7	168	39	46	.459	3	117	92	50	758	625	416	351	3	3.23	243	44	0	.181
Krause, Harry-Harry William (Hal)	08-12PhiA 12CleA	7-12-87	San Francisco, Cal.	10-23-40	B	L	5'10	165	36	26	.581	4	85	57	39	525	446	146	298	10	2.50	185	36	0	.195
Kroh, Rube-Floyd Myron	06-07BosA 08-10ChiN 12BosN	8-25-86	Friendship, N.Y.	3-17-44	L	L	6'2	186	13	9	.591	0	36	25	13	215	182	67	92	2	2.30	72	13	0	.181
Kruger, Abe-Abraham	08BknN	2-14-85	Morris Run, Pa.	7- 4-62	R	R	6'2	190	0	1	.000	0	2	1	0	6	5	3	2	0	4.50	2	0	0	.000
Kull, John-John A.	09PhiA	6-24-82	Shenandoah, Pa.	3-30-36	L	L	6'2	190	1	0	1.000	0	1	0	0	3	3	5	4	0	3.00	1	1	0	1.000
Kusel, Ed-Edward	09StLA	2-15-86	Cleveland, Ohio	10-20-48					0	3	.000	0	3	3	3	24	43	1	2	0	7.13	4	0	0	.000
LaClaire, George-George Lewis (Frenchy)	14-15PitF 15BufF 15BalF	10-18-86	Milton, Vt.	10-10-18	R	R	5'9	170	7	12	.368	2	55	19	12	236	222	61	91	2	3.36	71	9	0	.127
Lafitte, Ed-Edward Francis	09,11-12DetA 13ST 14-15BknF 15BufF	4- 7-86	New Orleans, La.	4-12-71	R	R	6'2	188	37	35	.514	5	106	75	47	647	668	262	262	0	3.34	245	54	2	.220

USE NAME – GIVEN NAMES (NICKNAMES)	TEAM BY YEAR	BIRTH DATE	BIRTH PLACE	DEATH DATE	B	T	HGT	WGT	W	L	PCT	SV	G	GS	CG	IP	H	BB	SO	ShO	ERA	AB	H	HR	BA
									LIFETIME PITCHING TOTALS													BATTING TOTALS			
Lake, Joe-Joseph Henry	08-09NYA 10-12StLA 12-13DetA	12- 6-81	Brooklyn, N.Y.	6-30-50	R	R	6'	185	63	92	.406	7	199	139	96	1317	1329	332	594	8	2.85	480	101	3	.210
Lambeth, Otis-Otis Samuel	16-18CleA	5-13-90	Berlin, Kans.		R	R	6'	175	10	9	.526	3	43	19	5	178	176	74	58	0	3.19	60	10	0	.167
Lamline, Fred-Frederick Arthur (Dutch, Punk)	12ChiA 15StLN	8-14-87	Port Huron, Mich.	9-20-70	R	R	5'11	171	0	0	–	0	5	0	0	21	28	5	12	0	5.57	8	1	0	.125
Lanford, Sam-Lewis Grover	07WasA	1- 8-86	Woodruff, S.C.	9-14-70	L	R	5'9	155	0	0	–	0	2	1	0	7	10	5	2	0	5.14	3	1	0	.333
Lange, Erv-Erwin Henry	14ChiF	8-12-87	Forest Park, Ill.	4-24-71	R	R	5'10	145	12	11	.522	2	36	22	10	190	162	55	87	2	2.23	51	9	0	.176
Lange, Frank-Frank Herman (Seagan)	10-13ChiA	10-28-83	Columbus, Wis.	12-26-45	R	R	5'11	160	28	25	.528	3	95	61	25	499	455	219	318	4	2.96	210	52	0	.248
Lathrop, Bill-William George	13-14ChiA	8-12-91	Hanover, Wis.	11-20-58	R	R	6'2	184	1	2	.333	0	25	1	0	65	57	31	16	0	3.05	16	0	0	.000
Lattimore, Bill-William Hershel (Slothful Bill, Tex)	08CleA	5-25-84	Roxton, Tex.	10-30-19	L	L	5'9	165	1	2	.333	0	4	4	1	24	24	7	5	1	4.50	9	4	0	.444
Lavender, Jimmy-James Sanford	12-16ChiN 17PhiN	3-25-84	Barnesville, Ga.	1-12-60	R	R	5'11	165	63	76	.453	12	224	142	65	1207	1097	447	547	10	3.09	374	54	0	.144
Lawson, Bob-Robert Baker	01BosN 02BalA	8-23-76	Brookneal, Va.	10-28-52	R	R	5'10	170	2	4	.333	0	9	6	5	59	66	31	17	0	3.66	33	5	1	.152
Lear, King-Charles Bernard	14-15CinN	1-23-91	Greencastle, Pa.			R	6'	175	7	12	.368	1	57	19	12	224	224	64	66	1	3.01	63	11	0	.175
Leary, Frank-Francis Patrick	07CinN	2-26-81	Wayland, Mass.	10- 4-07					0	1	.000	0	2	1	0	8	7	6	4	0	1.13	2	0	0	.000
Ledbetter, Razor-Ralph Overton	15DetA	12- 8-94	Rutherford C., N.C.	2- 1-69	R	R	6'3	190	0	0	–	0	1	0	0	1	1	0	0	0	0.00	0	0	0	–
Lee, Watty-Wyatt Arnold	01-03WasA 04PitN	8-12-79	Lynch's Sta., Va.	3- 6-36	L	L	5'10	171	29	37	.439	1	76	66	51	550	649	114	162	4	4.29	(See B01-19)			
Leever, Sam-Samuel (The Goshen Schoolmaster)	98-10PitN	12-23-71	Goshen, Ohio	5-19-53	R	R	5'10	175	193	101	.656	13	388	299	241	2661	2449	587	847	38	2.47	991	185	2	.187
Leifield, Lefty-Albert Peter	05-12PitN 12-13ChiN 18-20StLA	9- 5-83	Trenton, Ill.	10-10-70	L	L	6'1	165	124	96	.564	7	296	217	138	1838	1673	554	616	33	2.47	611	107	0	.175
Leitner, Dummy-George Michael	01PhiA 01NYN 02CleA 02ChiA	6-19-71	Parkton, Md.	2-20-60	L	R	5'7	120	0	3	.000	0	5	3	2	32	48	8	4	0	5.34	15	2	0	.133
Lelivelt, Bill-William John	09-10DetA	10-21-84	Chicago, Ill.	2-14-68	R	R	6'	195	0	3	.000	1	5	3	2	29	33	5	6	0	3.41	8	3	0	.375
Leonard, Dutch-Hubert Benjamin	13-18BosA 19-21DetA 22VR 23ST	4-16-92	Birmingham, Ohio	7-11-52	L	L	5'10	185	138	111	.554	14	330	271	152	2187	2021	662	1157	32	2.77	716	124	0	.173
	24-25DetA																								
Leonard, Elmer-Elmer Ellsworth (Tiny)	11PhiA	11-12-88	Napa, Cal.		R	R	6'3	210	2	2	.500	0	5	1	1	19	26	10	10	0	2.84	7	2	0	.286
LaRoy, Louis-Louis Paul (Chief)	05-06NYA 10BosA	2-18-79	Omro, Wis.	10-10-44	R	R	5'10	180	3	1	.750	1	15	5	3	73	66	15	39	0	3.21	23	3	0	.130
Leverenz, Walt-Walter Fred (Tiny, Lefty)	13-15StLA	7-21-88	Chicago, Ill.	[illegible]	L	L	5'10	175	8	31	.205	1	62	44	19	323	277	160	131	2	3.15	102	18	0	.176
Lewis, Ted-Edward Morgan (Parson)	96-00BosN 01BosA	12-25-72	Machynlleth, Wales	5-24-36	R	R	5'10	158	92	63	.594	4	183	153	136	1405	1379	511	[illegible]	7	[illegible]	[illegible]	120	0	.220
Liebhardt, Glenn-Glenn John	06-09CleA	3-10-83	Milton, Ind.	7-13-56	R	R	5'10	175	37	34	.521	1	91	66	49	612	543	183	280	7	2.18	190	28	0	.147
Lindaman, Vive-Vivan Alexander	06-09BosN	10-28-77	Charles City, Iowa	2-13-27	R	R	6'1	200	36	60	.375	2	131	101	82	904	876	296	286	7	2.92	303	46	0	.152
Lindeman, Ernie-Ernest	07BosN	6-10-83	New York, N.Y.	12-27-51	R	R			0	0	–	0	1	1	0	6	6	4	3	0	6.00	2	1	0	.500
Lindstrom, Axel-Axel Olaf	16PhiA	8-26-95	Gustavsburg, Sweden	6-24-40	R	R	5'10	180	0	0	–	1	1	0	0	4	2	0	1	0	4.50	2	1	0	.500
Linke, Fred-Frederick L. (Laddie)	10CleA 10StLA				L	L	6'	170	5	7	.417	1	25	16	6	140	139	62	57	1	3.41	49	8	0	.163
Lively, Jack-Henry Everett	11DetA	5-29-85	Joppa, Ala.	12- 5-67	L	R	5'9	185	7	5	.583	0	18	14	10	114	143	34	45	0	4.58	43	11	0	.256
Livingston, Albany-Albany	01NYN		New York, N.Y.	1-21-14					0	0	–	0	2	0	0	12	26	7	6	0	9.00	6	1	0	.167
Long, Les-Lester	11PhiA	7-12-88	Summit, N.J.	10-21-58	R	R	5'10	153	0	0	–	0	4	0	0	8	15	5	4	0	4.50	3	0	0	.000
Long, Red-Nelson	02BosN	9-28-76	Burlington, Canada	8-11-29	R	R	6'1	190	0	0	–	0	1	1	1	8	4	3	5	0	1.13	3	0	0	.000
Loos, Peter-Peter	01PhiA		Philadelphia, Pa.						0	1	.000	0	1	1	0	1	2	4	0	0	27.00	0	0	0	–
Lorenzen, Lefty-Adolph Andreas	13DetA	1-12-93	Davenport, Iowa	3- 5-63	L	L	5'10	164	0	0	–	0	1	0	0	2	4	3	0	0	18.00	2	1	0	.500
Lotz, Joe-Joseph Peter (Smokey)	16StLN	1- 2-91	Remsen, Iowa	1- 1-71	R	R	5'9	175	0	3	.000	0	12	3	1	40	31	17	18	0	4.28	12	4	0	.333
Loudell, Art-Arthur	10DetA	-85				R			1	1	.500	0	5	2	1	21	23	14	12	0	3.43	7	1	0	.143
Love, Slim-Edward Haughton	13WasA 16-18NYA 19-20DetA	8- 1-90	Love, Miss.	11-30-42	L	L	6'7	195	27	21	.563	5	119	48	19	518	480	246	251	1	3.04	156	30	0	.192
Lovett, John-John	03StLN	5- 6-77	Monday, Ohio	12- 5-37					0	0	–	0	3	1	0	5	6	5	3	0	5.40	3	1	0	.333
Lowdermilk, Grover-Grover Cleveland (Slim)	09,11StLN 12ChiN	1-15-85	Sandborn, Ind.	3-31-68	R	R	6'4	190	23	40	.365	0	122	73	30	590	534	376	296	3	3.81	191	25	0	.131
	15StLA 15-16DetA 16CleA 17-19StLA 19-20ChiA																								
Lowdermilk, Lou-Louis Bailey	11-12StLN	2-23-87	Sandborn, Ind.		R	L	6'1	180	4	5	.444	1	20	4	4	80	86	38	22	0	3.38	22	3	0	.136
Luhrsen, Bill-William Ferdinand (Wild Bill)	13PitN	4-14-84	Buckley, Ill.	**8-15-73**	R	R	5'9	165	3	1	.750	0	5	3	2	29	25	16	11	0	2.48	10	0	0	.000
Lundbom, Jack-John Frederick	02CleA	3-10-77	Manistee, Mich.	10-31-49	R	R	6'2	187	1	1	.500	0	8	3	1	34	48	16	7	0	6.62	15	4	0	.267
Lundgren, Carl-Carl Leonard	02-09ChiN	2-16-80	Marengo, Ill.	8-21-34	**R**	**R**	**5'11**	**175**	91	56	.619	6	179	149	125	1322	1129	476	535	19	2.42	460	72	0	.157
Lush, Johnny-John Charles	04-07PhiN 07-10StLN	10- 8-85	Williamsport, Pa.	11-18-46	L	L	5'9	165	66	85	.437	2	182	154	105	1239	1169	413	490	16	2.68	(See B01-19)			
Lynch, Mike-Michael Joseph	04-07PitN 07NYN	**6-28-75**	Holyoke, Mass.	4- 2-27	**R**	**L**	**5'10**	**155**	43	32	.573	3	97	72	53	656	597	281	292	1	3.05	246	50	0	.203
Mack, Bill-William Francis	08ChiN	2-12-85	Elmira, N.Y.	9-30-71	L	L	6'1	155	0	0	–	0	2	0	0	6	5	1	2	0	3.00	3	2	0	.667
Madden, Len-Leonard Joseph (Lefty)	12ChiN	7- 2-90	Toledo, Ohio	9- 9-49	L	L	6'2	165	0	1	.000	0	6	2	0	12	16	9	5	0	3.00	4	1	0	.250
Maddox, Nick-Nicholas	07-10PitN	11- 9-86	Gavanstown, Md.	11-27-54	L	R	6'	175	43	20	.683	1	93	72	47	605	487	170	193	9	2.29	209	51	0	.244
Magee, Bill-William M.	97-99LouN 99PhiN 99WasN 01StLN 01-02NYN	1-11-68	Boston, Mass.	Deceased	R	R	5'10	154	30	50	.375	0	106	88	69	742	837	350	161	5	4.94	283	50	0	.177
	02PhiN																								
Mahoney, Chris-Christopher John (Steve)	10BosA	6-11-85	Milton, Mass.	7-15-54	R	R	5'9	165	0	1	.000	1	2	1	0	11	16	5	6	0	3.27	7	1	0	.143
Main, Alex-Miles Grant	14DetA 15KCF 18PhiN	5-13-84	Montrose, Mich.	12-29-65	L	R	6'5	195	21	22	.488	6	75	44	24	403	342	150	160	4	2.77	127	20	0	.157
Malarkey, Bill-William John	08NYN	11-26-78	Port Byron, Ill.	12-12-56	R	L	5'10	185	0	2	.000	2	15	0	0	35	31	10	12	0	2.57	6	0	0	.000
Malarkey, John-John S.	94-96WasN 99ChiN 02-03BosN	5-10-72	Springfield, Ohio	10-29-49			5'11	155	22	38	.367	3	80	59	51	566	629	227	179	3	3.64	207	35	1	.169
Malloy, Alex-Archibald Alexander (Lick)	10StLA	10-31-86	Laurinburg, N.C.	3- 1-61	R	R	6'2	180	0	6	.000	0	7	6	4	53	47	17	27	0	2.55	16	1	0	.063
Malloy, Herm-Herman (Tug)	07-08DetA	6- 1-85	Massillon, Ohio	5- 9-42	R	R	6'		0	3	.000	0	4	3	3	25	33	9	14	0	4.32	13	4	0	.308
Maloney, Chic-Charles Michael	08BosN	5-22-86	Cambridge, Mass.	1-17-67	R	R	5'8	155	0	0	–	0	1	0	0	2	3	1	0	0	4.50	0	0	0	–
Maloy, Paul-Paul Augustus (Biff)	13BosA	6- 4-92	Bascom, Ohio		R	R	6'	185	0	0	–	0	2	0	0	2	2	1	0	0	9.00	0	0	0	–
Mamaux, Al-Albert Leon	13-17PitN 18-23BknN 24NYA	5-30-94	Pittsburgh, Pa.	1- 2-63	R	R	6'	168	76	67	.531	10	254	140	78	1294	1138	511	625	15	2.89	422	77	1	.182
Manning, Ernie-Ernest Devon (Ed)	14StLA	10- 9-90	Florala, Ala.	**4-28-73**	L	R	6'	175	0	0	–	0	4	0	0	10	11	3	3	0	3.60	4	0	0	.000
Manning, Rube-Walter S. (Speedy)	07-10NYA	4-29-83	Chambersburg, Pa.	4-23-30	R	R	6'	180	22	32	.407	4	84	57	35	502	483	162	212	4	3.14	180	33	0	.183
Manske, Lou-Louis Hugo	06PitN	7- 4-84	Milwaukee, Wis.	4-27-63	L	L	6'		1	0	1.000	0	2	1	0	8	12	5	6	0	5.63	4	0	0	.000
Manuel, Moxie-Mark Garfield	05WasA 08ChiA	10-16-81	Metropolis, Ill.	4-26-24	R	R	5'11	170	3	**5**	.375	1	21	7	4	70	61	28	28	0	3.60	20	2	0	.100
Mapel, Rolla-Rolla Hamilton (Lefty)	19StLA	3- 9-90	Lee's Summit, Mo.	4- 6-66	L	L	5'11	165	0	3	.000	0	4	3	2	20	17	17	2	0	4.50	6	1	0	.167
Marbet, Walt-Walter William	13StLN	9-13-90	Plymouth Co., Iowa	9-24-56	R	R	6'1	175	0	1	.000	0	3	1	0	3	9	4	1	0	18.00	0	0	0	–
Marion, Don-Donald George	14-15BknF	7-31-90	Cleveland, Ohio	1-19-33	R	R	6'1	187	15	11	.577	0	52	34	19	297	290	102	87	2	3.42	110	20	0	.182
Maroney, Jim-James Francis	06BosN 10PhiN 12ChiN	12- 4-83	Boston, Mass.	2- -29	L	L			2	6	.250	2	25	8	5	93	96	40	29	0	3.68	26	4	0	.154
Marquard, Rube-Richard William	08-15NYN 15-20BknN 21CinN	10- 9-89	Cleveland, Ohio		B	L	6'3	180	201	177	.532	19	536	403	197	3309	3233	858	1593	30	3.07	1107	198	1	.179
	22-25BosN																								
Marshall, Rube-Roy DeVerne	12-14PhiN 15BufF	7-19-90	Salineville, Ohio		R	R	5'11	170	8	10	.444	2	64	27	9	241	272	106	90	0	4.18	71	12	0	.169
Martin, Doc-Harold Winthrop	08,11-12PhiA	9-23-87	Roxbury, Mass.	4-15-35	R	R	5'11	165	1	3	.250	0	14	4	1	44	47	25	27	0	5.52	18	3	0	.167
Mason, Del-Adelbert William	04WasA 06-07CinN	10-29-83	Newfane, N.Y.	12-31-62	R	R	6'	160	5	16	.238	0	32	21	16	191	199	74	65	1	3.72	64	8	0	.125
Mathewson, Christy-Christopher (Big Six)	00-16NYN 16,M16-18CinN	8-12-78	Factoryville, Pa.	10- 7-25	R	R	6'2	195	374	187	.667	28	634	551	434	4778	4216	838	2502	77	2.13	1684	362	7	.215
Mathewson, Henry-Henry	06-07NYN	12-24-86	Factoryville, Pa.	7- 1-17	R	R	6'3	175	0	1	.000	2	3	1	1	11	8	14	2	0	4.91	2	0	0	.000
Mattern, Al-Alonzo Albert	08-12BosN	6-16-83	West Rush, N.Y.	11- 6-58	L	R	5'10	165	36	59	.379	4	138	94	53	843	878	299	254	9	3.37	272	45	0	.165
Matteson, Eddie-Henry Edson	14PhiN 18WasA	9- 7-84	**Guys Mills, Pa.**	**9- 1-43**	R	R	5'10	160	8	5	.615	0	29	9	4	126	115	38	45	0	2.36	41	6	0	.146
Matthews, Bill-William Calvin	09BosA	1-12-78	Mahanoy City, Pa.	1-23-46		R			1	0	1.000	0	5	1	0	17	16	10	6	0	3.18	8	0	0	.000
Maul, Al-Albert Joseph (Smiling Al)	84PhiU 87PhiN 88-89PitN	10- 9-65	Philadelphia, Pa.	5- 3-58	R	R	6'	175	85	78	.521	1	187	167	143	1433	1659	518	346	4	4.42	(See B01-19)			
	90PitP 91PitN 93-97WasN 97-98BalN 99BknN 00PhiN 01NYN																								
Maxwell, Bert-James Albert	06PitN 08PhiA 11NYN 14BknF	10-17-86	Texarkana, Ark.	12-10-61	B	R	6'	180	4	7	.364	1	21	12	9	123	144	42	35	1	4.17	40	3	0	.075
Mayer (Erskine), Erskine (James)-Erskine John (Erk)	12-18PhiN	1-16-89	Atlanta, Ga.	3-10-57	R	R	6'	168	91	70	.565	6	245	166	93	1427	1415	345	482	12	2.96	453	84	2	.185
	18-19PitN 19ChiA																								
McAdams, Jack-George D.	11StLN	12-17-86	Benton, Ark.	5-21-37	R	R	6'1	170	0	0	–	0	6	0	0	10	7	5	4	0	3.60	1	0	0	.000
McAleese, John-John James	01ChiA	**8-22-78**	Sharon, Pa.	**11-14-50**		R			0	0	–	0	1	0	0	3	7	1	1	0	9.00	(See B01-19)			
McAllister, Jack (See Andy Coakley)																									
McAllister, Sport-Lewis William	96-99CleN	7-23-74	Austin, Miss.	7-17-62	B	R	5'11	180	4	7	.364	0	17	11	10	113	140	44	21	0	5.34	(See B01-19)			
McArthur, Dixie-Oland Alexander	14PitN	2- 1-92	Vernon, Ala.		R	R	6'1	185	0	0	–	0	1	0	0	1	1	0	1	0	0.00	0	0	0	–
McCabe, Dick-Richard James	18BosA 22ChiA	2-21-96	Mamaroneck, N.Y.	4-11-50	R	R	5'10	159	1	1	.500	0	6	1	0	13	17	2	4	0	3.46	2	0	0	.000
McCabe, Tim-Timothy	15-18StLA	10-19-94	Ironton, Mo.		R	R	6'	190	5	1	.833	0	22	4	4	71	60	21	26	1	3.55	19	1	0	.053
McCann, Gene-Henry Eugene	01-02BknN	6-13-76	Baltimore, Md.	4-26-43		R			3	5	.375	0	9	8	6	64	66	28	18	0	2.95	22	1	0	.045
McCarthy, Arch-Archibald J.	02DetA		Ypsilanti, Mich						1	7	.125	1	10	8	8	72	90	31	10	0	6.13	28	2	0	.071
McCarthy, Bill-William Thomas	06BosN	4-11-82	Ashland, Mass.	**5-22-39**					0	0	–	0	1	0	0	2	2	3	0	0	9.00	1	0	0	.000
McCarthy, Tom-Thomas Patrick	08CinN 08PitN 08-09BosN	5-22-84	Fort Wayne, Ind.	3-28-33		R			6	9	.400	0	25	20	10	150	133	65	42	2	2.34	57	8	0	.140
McClosky, Jim-James John	06-07PhiN	8-20-82	Wyoming, Pa.	6- 5-19					3	2	.600	0	12	4	3	50	61	15	9	0	3.60	19	3	0	.158
McCluskey, Harry-Harry Robert (Lefty)	15CinN	3-29-92	Clay Center, Ohio	6- 7-62	L	L	5'11	173	0	0	–	0	3	0	0	5	4	0	2	0	5.40	2	0	0	.000
McConnaughey, Ralph-Ralph J.	14IndF	-89			R	R	5'8	166	0	2	.000	0	7	2	1	26	23	16	7	0	4.85	8	1	0	.125
McConnell, George-George Neely	09,12-13NYA 14ChiN 15ChiF 16ChiN	9-16-77	Shelbyville, Tenn.	5-10-64	R	R	6'3	190	42	51	.452	3	133	97	59	842	739	242	403	5	2.60	385	88	1	.229
McCorry, Bill-William Charles	09StLA	7- 9-87	Saranac Lake, N.Y.	3-22-73	L	R	5'9	157	0	2	.000	0	2	2	2	15	29	6	10	0	9.00	5	0	0	.000

					LIFETIME PITCHING TOTALS																	BATTING TOTALS			
USE NAME – GIVEN NAMES (NICKNAMES)	TEAM BY YEAR	BIRTH DATE	BIRTH PLACE	DEATH DATE	B	T	HGT	WGT	W	L	PCT	SV	G	GS	CG	IP	H	BB	SO	ShO	ERA	AB	H	HR	BA
McCreery, Ed-Edward P.	14DetA	-91	Filer, Idaho	Deceased					1	0	1.000	0	3	1	0	4	6	3	4	0	11.25	1	0	0	.000
McDonald, John-John J.	07WasA					R			0	0	–	0	1	0	0	6	12	2	3	0	9.00	3	1	0	.333
McDougal, Sandy-James A.	05StLN	2-18-78	Buffalo, N.Y.	10- 4-10					1	4	.200	0	5	5	5	45	50	12	10	0	3.40	15	2	0	.133
McFadden, Barney-Bernard Joseph	01CinN 02PhiN	2-22-74	Eckley, Pa.	4-28-24	R	R	6'1	195	3	5	.375	0	9	6	5	55	68	47	14	0	6.38	23	3	0	.130
McFarland, Chappie-Charles A.	02-06StLN 06PitN 06BknN		St. Louis, Mo.	12-15-24		R			35	59	.372	2	106	96	81	841	893	192	307	6	3.35	293	42	0	.143
McFetridge, John-John R.	90,03PhiN	8-25-69	Philadelphia, Pa.	1-10-17					2	11	.154	0	15	14	12	112	125	51	35	0	4.58	38	9	0	.237
McGeehan, Conny-Cornelius Bernard	03PhiA	10 6-83	Drifton, Pa.	7- 4-07					1	0	1.000	0	3	0	0	10	9	1	4	0	4.50	6	0	0	.000
McGehee, Pat-Patrick Henry	12DetA	7- 2-88	Meadville, Miss.	12-30-46	L	R	6'2	180	0	0	–	0	1	1	0	0	1	1	0	0	0.00	0	0	0	–
McGill, Billy-William John (Parson)	07StLA	6-29-80	Galva, Kans.	8- 7-59	R	R			1	0	1.000	0	2	2	1	18	22	2	8	0	3.50	9	0	0	.000
McGinley, Jim-James William	04-05StLN	10- 2-78	Groveland, Mass.	9-20-61	R	R	5'9	165	2	2	.500	0	4	4	3	30	33	8	6	0	3.30	12	2	0	.167
McGinnity, Joe-Joseph Jerome (Iron Man)	99BalN 00BknN 01-02BalA 02-08NYN	3-19-71	Rock Island, Ill.	11-14-29	R	R	5'11	206	248	144	.633	26	465	381	314	3441	3276	812	1068	32	2.65	1298	250	0	.193
McGlynn, Stony-Ulysses Simpson Grant	06-08StLN	5-26-72	Lancaster, Pa.	8-26-41	R	R	5'11	185	17	33	.340	2	67	51	43	476	448	144	157	3	2.95	168	28	0	.167
McGraner, Howard-Howard (Muck)	12CinN	9-11-89	Hamley Run, Ohio	10-22-52	L	L	5'7	155	1	0	1.000	0	4	0	0	19	22	7	5	0	7.11	8	2	0	.250
McGraw, Lee-James Leo	14BknF	-90		11-14-18	R	R	6'	160	0	0	–	0	1	0	0	2	0	0	2	0	0.00	0	0	0	–
McGuire, Tom-Thomas Patrick (Elmer)	14ChiF 18MS 19ChiA	2- 1-92	Chicago, Ill.	12- 7-59	R	R	6'	175	5	6	.455	0	25	12	7	134	148	60	37	0	3.83	71	19	1	.268
McHale, Marty-Martin Joseph	10-11BosA 13-15NYA 16BosA 16CleA	10-30-88	Stoneham, Mass.		R	R	5'11	174	12	30	.286	2	64	44	23	358	381	81	131	1	3.57	107	15	0	.140
McIlveen, Irish-Henry Cooke	06PitN	7-27-80	Belfast, N. Ireland	10-18-60	L	L	5'11	180	0	1	.000	0	2	1	0	7	10	2	3	0	7.71	(See B01-19)			
McIntire, Harry-John Reed (Rocks)	05-09BknN 10-12ChiN 13CinN	1-11-78	Detroit, Mich.	1- 9-49	R	R	5'11	180	71	117	.378	7	237	188	140	1651	1555	539	626	17	3.22	615	134	2	.218
McJames (James), Doc-James McCutchen	95-97WasN 98-BalN 99,01BknN	8-27-73	Williamsburg, S.C.	9-23-01		R			76	77	.497	4	178	162	137	1361	1414	563	593	6	3.43	537	84	0	.156
McKay, Reeves-Reeves H.	15StLA					L			0	0	–	0	1	0	0	1	1	0	0	0	9.00	0	0	0	–
McKenry, Limb-Frank Gordon (Big Pete)	15-16CinN	8-13-88	Piney Flats, Tenn.	11- 1-56	R	R	6'4	205	6	6	.500	0	27	12	5	125	108	47	39	0	3.10	38	7	0	.184
McLaughlin, Warry-Warren A.	00PhiN 02PitN 03PhiN	1-22-76	N. Plainfield, N.J.	10-22-23					3	2	.600	0	7	5	5	55	69	26	17	0	4.75	23	7	0	.304
McMackin, John-John Weaver (Spartanburg John)	02BknN	3- 6-78	Spartanburg, S.C.	9-25-56	R	R	5'11	165	2	2	.500	0	4	4	4	32	34	11	6	0	3.09	11	2	0	.182
McMackin, Sam-Samuel	02ChiA 02DetA		Cleveland, Ohio	2-11-03					0	0	–	0	2	1	1	11	10	4	4	0	2.45	5	2	0	.400
McMahon, Doc-Henry John	08BosA	12-19-86	Woburn, Mass.	12-11-29					1	0	1.000	0	1	1	1	9	14	0	3	0	3.00	5	2	0	.400
McManus, Joe-Joab Logan	13CinN	9- 7-87	Palmyra, Ill.	12-23-55	R	R	6'1	185	0	0	–	0	1	0	0	2	3	4	1	0	18.00	0	0	0	–
McNeal, Harry-John Harley	01CleA	8-11-77	Iberia, Ohio	1-11-45	R	R	6'3	175	5	6	.455	0	12	10	9	85	120	30	15	0	4.45	37	6	0	.162
McNichol, Ed-Edward	04BosN		Wheeling, W.Va						2	13	.133	0	17	15	12	122	120	74	39	1	4.28	43	4	0	.093
McPherson, John-John Jacob	01PhiA 04PhiN	3- 9-69	Easton, Pa.	9-30-41					1	11	.083	0	16	13	11	132	137	50	32	1	3.89	48	3	0	.063
McQuillan, George-George Watt	07-10PhiN 11CinN 13-15PitN 15-16PhiN 18CleA	5- 1-85	Brooklyn, N.Y.	3-30-40	R	R	5'11	175	85	89	.489	14	273	173	105	1577	1382	401	590	17	2.38	469	55	0	.117
McTigue, Bill-William Patrick (Pud, Lefty)	11-13BosN 16DetA	6- 3-91	Nashville, Tenn	5- 8-20	L	L	6'1	170	2	6	.250	0	27	9	1	77	81	72	41	0	6.19	26	2	0	.077
Meehan, Bill-William Thomas	15PhiA	9- 3-91	Osceola, Pa.						0	1	.000	0	1	1	0	4	7	3	4	0	11.25	1	1	0	1.000
Melter, Steve-Stephen B.	09StLN					R			0	1	.000	3	23	1	0	64	79	20	24	0	3.52	15	2	0	.133
Menefee, Jocko-John	92PitN 93-94LouN 94-95PitN 98NYN 00-03ChiN	1-15-68	W.Va.	3-11-53	R	R	6'		56	69	.448	0	139	125	111	1110	1290	273	293	7	3.82	(See B01-19)			
Mercer, Jack-John Locke	10PitN	6-22-90	Taylortown, La.		L	L	5'10	155	0	0	–	0	1	0	0	1	0	2	1	0	0.00	(See B01-19)			
Mercer, Win-George Barclay	94-99WasN 00NYN 01WasA 02DetA	6-20-74	Chester, W.Va.	1-12-03	R	R	5'7	140	135	164	.452	9	330	298	252	2466	3057	752	525	11	3.98	(See B01-19)			
Merritt, George-George Washington	01,03PitN	4-14-80	Paterson, N.J.	2-21-38		R			3	0	1.000	0	4	3	3	28	32	6	7	0	4.50	(See B01-19)			
Miller, Frank-Frank Lee (Bullet)	13ChiA 16-19PitN 22-23BosN	3-13-86	Salem, Mich.	2-19-74	R	R	6'	188	52	66	.441	4	163	127	68	1010	944	254	359	14	3.01	325	38	0	.117
Miller, Fred-Frederick Holman (Speedy)	10BknN	6-28-86	Fairfield, Ind.	5- 2-53	L	L	6'2	190	1	1	.500	0	6	2	0	21	25	13	2	0	4.71	8	2	0	.250
Miller, Roscoe-Roscoe Clyde (Roxy, Rubberlegs)	01-02DetA 02-03NYN 04PitN 04PitN	12- 2-76	Croydon, Ind.	4-18-13	R	R	6'2	190	39	45	.464	5	102	88	74	772	808	229	198	6	3.45	288	46	0	.160
Miller, Walt-Walter W.	11BknN	10-19-84	Gas City, Ind.	3- 1-56	R	R	5'11	180	0	1	.000	0	3	2	0	11	16	6	0	0	6.55	4	0	0	.000
Milligan, Bill-William J.	01PhiA 04NYN	-77	Buffalo, N.Y.	9- 3-28	R	L			0	4	.000	2	11	4	3	58	79	18	11	0	4.81	24	6	1	.250
Mills, Willie-William Grant (Wee Willie)	01NYN	8-15-77	Schenevus, N.Y.	7- 5-14	R	R	5'7	150	0	2	.000	0	2	2	2	16	21	4	3	0	8.44	6	1	0	.167
Milton, Larry-S. Lawrence	03StLN		Pittsburg, Kans.						0	0	–	0	1	0	0	4	3	1	0	0	2.25	2	1	0	.500
Minahan, Cotton-Edmund Joseph	07CinN	12-10-82	Springfield, Ohio	5-20-58	R	R	6'	190	0	2	.000	0	2	2	1	14	12	13	4	0	1.29	5	0	0	.000
Mitchell (Yapp), Fred-Frederick Francis	01-02BosA 02PhiA 03-04PhiN 04-05BknN M17-20ChiN M21-23BosN	6- 5-78	Cambridge, Mass.	10-13-70	R	R	5'9	185	31	52	.373	1	97	86	71	719	806	303	216	2	4.09	(See B01-19)			
Mitchell, Roy-Albert Roy	10-14StLA 18ChiA 18-19CinN	4-19-85	Belton, Tex.	9- 8-59	R	R	5'9	170	32	37	.464	5	122	68	47	675	734	177	204	7	3.43	235	44	0	.187
Mitchell, Willie-William	09-16CleA 16-19DetA	12- 1-89	Pleasant Grove, Miss.	11-23-73	R	L	6'	176	84	92	.477	7	275	190	94	1632	1464	605	921	16	2.86	530	69	0	.130
Molyneaux, Vince-Vincent Leo	17StLA 18BosA	8-17-88	Lewiston, N.Y.	5- 4-50	R	R	6'	180	1	0	1.000	0	13	0	0	33	21	28	5	0	4.36	6	0	0	.000
Monroe, Ed-Edward Oliver (Peck)	17-18NYA	2-22-93	Louisville, Ky.	4-29-69	R	R	6'5	187	1	0	1.000	1	10	1	1	31	36	8	13	0	3.48	12	2	0	.167
Moore, Earl-Earl Alonzo (Crossfire, Big Ebbie)	01-07CleA 07NYA 08-13PhiN 13ChiN 14BufF	7-29-79	Pickerington, Ohio	11-28-61	R	R	6'	190	164	153	.517	7	387	324	230	2767	2467	1102	1397	34	2.78	944	134	0	.142
Moore, Gene-Eugene Sr. (Blue Goose)	09-10PitN 12CinN	11- 9-85	Lancaster, Tex.	8-31-38	L	L	6'2	185	2	2	.500	1	10	3	0	34	40	21	17	0	4.76	11	0	0	.000
Moore, George-George Raymond	05PitN	11-25-72	Cambridge, Mass.	11-17-48	B	R	5'10	165	0	0	–	0	1	0	0	3	2	0	1	0	0.00	1	0	0	.000
Moran, Charley-Charles Barthell (Uncle Charley)	03StLN	2-22-78	Nashville, Tenn.	6-14-49	R	R	5'5	180	0	1	.000	0	3	2	2	24	30	19	7	0	5.25	(See B01-19)			
Moran, Harry-Harry Edwin	12DetA 15BufF 15NwkF	4- 2-89	Slater, W.Va.	11-28-62	L	L	6'1	165	23	17	.575	1	73	41	21	375	371	131	163	4	3.34	117	22	0	.188
More, Forrest-Forrest	09StLN 09BosN	9-30-83	Hayden, Ind.	8-17-68	R	R	6'	180	2	10	.167	0	25	7	4	99	95	40	27	0	4.73	28	3	0	.107
Moren, Lew-Lewis Howard (Hicks)	03-04PitN 07-10PhiN	8- 4-83	Pittsburgh, Pa.	11- 2-66	R	R	5'11	150	48	57	.457	3	141	105	62	882	797	331	356	10	2.95	291	39	0	.134
Morey, Dave-David Beale	13PhiA	2-25-89	Malden, Mass.		L	R	6'	185	0	0	–	0	2	0	0	4	2	2	1	0	4.50	1	0	0	.000
Morgan, Cy-Harry Richard	03-05,07StLA 07-09BosA 09-12PhiA 13CinN	11-10-78	Pomeroy, Ohio	6-28-62	R	R	6'	175	77	79	.494	5	210	172	107	1445	1180	578	667	15	2.51	489	61	0	.125
Morrissey, Deacon-Frank Frederick	01BosA 02ChiN		Baltimore, Md.						1	3	.250	0	6	5	5	44	45	10	14	0	2.25	25	2	0	.080
Morton, Guy-Guy Sr. (The Alabama Blossom)	14-24CleA	6- 1-93	Vernon, Ala.	10-18-34	R	R	6'2	175	97	86	.535	6	316	184	80	1629	1520	583	830	20	3.13	548	86	0	.157
Moseley, Earl-Earl Victor	13BosA 14IndF 15NwkF 16CinN	9- 7-84	Middleburg, Ohio	7- 1-63	R	R	5'9	168	50	48	.510	3	136	100	65	856	775	340	469	12	3.01	280	32	0	.114
Moser, Walter-Walter Frederick	06PhiN 11BosA 11StLA	2-27-81	Concord, N.C.	12-10-46	R	R	5'9	170	0	7	.000	0	14	9	5	71	97	30	30	0	4.56	22	1	0	.045
Moyer, Charlie-Charles Edward	10WasA	8-15-85	Andover, Ohio						0	3	.000	0	6	3	2	25	22	13	3	0	3.24	8	1	0	.125
Mullin, George-George Joseph (Wabash George)	02-13DetA 13WasA 14IndF 15NwkF	7- 4-80	Toledo, Ohio	1- 7-44	R	R	5'11	188	229	192	.544	11	488	428	353	3687	3518	1238	1482	34	2.82	(See B01-19)			
Murphy, Ed-Edward J.	98PhiN 01-03StLN	1-22-77	Auburn, N.Y.	1-29-35		R			25	26	.490	1	68	53	39	465	537	111	103	1	3.64	203	50	1	.246
Murray, Pat-Patrick Joseph	19PhiN	7-18-97	Scottsville, N.Y.		R	L	6'	175	0	2	.000	0	8	2	1	34	50	12	11	0	6.35	12	0	0	.000
Musser, Paul-Paul	12WasA 18MS 19BosA	6-24-89	Millheim, Pa.	7- 7-73	R	R	6'	175	1	2	.333	1	12	6	1	41	42	24	24	0	3.29	15	0	0	.000
Myers, Elmer-Elmer Glenn	15-18PhiA 19-20CleA 20-22BosA	3- 2-94	York Springs, Pa.		R	R	6'2	185	55	72	.433	6	185	127	78	1102	1148	440	428	8	4.06	412	93	0	.226
Myers, Joe-Joseph William	05PhiA	3-18-82	Wilmington, Del.	2-11-56	R	R			0	0	–	0	1	1	1	5	3	3	5	0	3.60	2	0	0	.000
Nabors, Jack-Herman John	15-17PhiA	11-19-87	Montevallo, Ala.	11-20-23	R	R	6'3	185	1	25	.038	1	52	36	13	270	266	131	94	0	3.87	85	9	0	.106
Nagle, Judge-Walter Harold (Lucky)	11PitN 11BosA	3-10-80	Santa Rosa, Cal.	5-27-71	R	R	6'	176	5	3	.625	1	13	4	1	54	60	12	23	0	3.50	17	2	0	.118
Neher, Jim-James Gilmore	12CleA	2- 5-89	Rochester, N.Y.	11-11-51	R	R	5'11	185	0	0	–	0	1	0	0	1	0	0	0	0	0.00	0	0	0	–
Nelson, Andy-Andrew (Peaches)	08ChiA								1	0	1.000	0	2	1	0	9	11	4	1	0	2.00	2	0	0	.000
Nelson, Luke-Luther Martin	19NYA	12- 4-93	Cable, Ill.		R	R	6'	180	3	0	1.000	0	9	1	0	24	22	11	11	0	3.00	7	1	0	.143
Nelson (Horazdovsky), Red-Albert Francis	10-12StLA 12-13PhiN 13CinN	5-19-86	Cleveland, Ohio	10-26-56	R	R	5'11	190	10	13	.435	2	39	24	13	188	221	85	68	1	4.55	66	12	1	.182
Neuer, Tacks-John S.	07NYA	-80	Hazleton, Pa.						4	2	.667	0	7	6	6	54	40	19	22	3	2.17	21	2	0	.095
Newton, Doc-Eustace James	00-01CinN 01-02BknN 05-09NYA	10-26-77	Mt. Carmel, Ind.	5-14-31	L	L	6'	185	53	72	.424	3	177	139	99	1200	1179	416	502	8	3.23	436	75	0	.172
Nichols, Kid-Charles Augustus	90-01BosN 04-05,M04-05StLN 05-06PhiN	9-14-69	Madison, Wis.	4-11-53	B	R	5'10	175	362	203	.641	16	621	562	533	5061	4912	1268	1868	48	2.95	2055	467	16	.227
Nicholson, Frank-Frank Collins	12PhiN	8-29-89	Berlin, Pa.	11-10-72	R	R	6'2	175	0	0	–	0	2	0	0	4	8	2	1	0	6.75	0	0	0	–
Niehaus, Dick-Richard J.	13-15StLN 20CleA	10-24-92	Covington, Ky.	3-12-57	L	L	5'11	165	4	5	.444	2	45	9	3	126	128	59	43	0	3.79	34	8	0	.235
Nops, Jerry-Jeremiah H.	96PhiN 96-99BalN 00BknN 01BalA	6-23-75	Toledo, Ohio	3-26-37		L			72	44	.621	1	136	122	99	989	1083	281	294	7	3.69	383	87	0	.227
Northrop, Jake-George Howard	18-19BosN	3- 5-88	Monroeton, Pa.	11- 6-45	L	R	5'11	170	6	6	.500	0	18	7	6	77	69	13	13	1	2.92	21	6	0	.286
Nourse, Chet-Chester Linwood	09BosA	8- 7-87	Ipswich, Mass.	4-20-58	R	R	6'3	185	0	0	–	0	3	0	0	5	5	5	3	0	7.20	2	0	0	.000
Noyes, Win-Winfield Charles	13BosN 17PhiA 18MS 19PhiA 19ChiA	6-16-89	Pleasanton, Neb.	4- 8-69	R	R	6'	180	11	15	.423	1	49	29	14	247	254	98	93	1	3.75	74	10	0	.135
Oberlin, Frank-Frank Rufus (Flossie)	06-07BosA 07,09-10WasA	3-29-76	Elsie, Mich.	1- 6-52	R	R	6'1	165	6	23	.207	0	44	26	16	227	236	88	80	0	3.77	77	8	0	.104
O'Brien, Buck-Thomas Joseph	11-13BosA 13ChiA	5-10-82	Brockton, Mass.	7-25-59	R	R	5'10	180	28	26	.519	1	64	54	37	433	391	159	204	4	2.62	143	20	0	.140
O'Connor, Andy-Andrew James	08NYA	9-14-84	Roxbury, Mass.		R	R	6'	160	0	1	.000	0	1	1	1	8	16	7	5	0	10.13	3	0	0	.000
Ohl, Joe-Joseph Earl	09WasA	1-10-88	Jobstown, N.J.	12-18-51	L	L			0	0	–	0	4	0	0	9	7	1	2	0	2.00	2	0	0	.000
Olmsted, Fred-Fredrick D. (Omy)	08-11ChiA	11-21-81		6-16-72	R	R	5'11	170	19	20	.487	4	66	37	26	359	378	93	135	5	2.73	124	19	0	.153
Olmsted, Hank-Henry Theodore	05BosA	1-12-79	Saginaw Bay, Mich.	1- 6-69	R	R	5'8	147	1	2	.333	0	3	3	3	25	18	12	6	0	3.24	8	1	0	.125
O'Neill, Mike-Michael Joyce (Played as Mike Joyce 01)	01-04StLN	9- 7-77	Galway, Ireland	8-12-59	L	L	5'11	185	32	44	.421	2	85	77	68	664	739	169	228	4	2.86	(See B01-19)			

USE NAME – GIVEN NAMES (NICKNAMES)	TEAM BY YEAR	BIRTH DATE	BIRTH PLACE	DEATH DATE	B	T	HGT	WGT	W	L	PCT	SV	G	GS	CG	IP	H	BB	SO	ShO	ERA	AB	H	HR	BA
									LIFETIME PITCHING TOTALS													BATTING TOTALS			
Orth, Al-Albert Lewis (The Curveless Wonder)	95-01PhiN 02-04WasA	9- 5-72	Tipton, Ind.	10- 8-48	L	R	6'	200	203	183	.526	8	440	394	324	3355	3564	661	948	28	3.37	(See B01-19)			
	04-09NYA																								
Ostendorf, Fred-Frederick K.	14IndF	8- 5-90	Baltimore, Md.	3- 2-65	L	L	6'	169	0	0	–	0	1	0	0	2	5	2	0	0	22.50	1	0	0	.000
Otey, Bill-William Tilford (Steamboat Bill)	07PitN 10-11WasA	12-16-86	Dayton, Ohio	4-23-31	L	L	6'2	181	1	6	.143	0	24	5	2	101	131	25	33	0	4.99	34	7	0	.206
Otis, Harry-Harry George (Cannonball)	09CleA	10- 5-86	W. New York, N.J.		R	L	6'	180	2	2	.500	0	5	3	0	26	26	18	6	0	1.38	9	1	0	.111
O'Toole, Marty-Martin James	08CinN 11-14PitN 14NYN	11-27-87	Framingham, Mass.	2-18-49	R	R	5'11	175	27	36	.429	2	100	72	31	599	554	300	296	5	3.29	211	43	0	.204
Overall, Orvie-Orval	05-06CinN 06-10ChiN 11-12VR 13ChiN	2- 2-81	Visalia, Cal.	7-14-47	B	R	6'2	214	106	72	.596	12	218	182	133	1535	1232	551	935	30	2.23	526	94	2	.179
Ovitz, Ernie-Ernest Gayheart	11ChiN	10- 7-85	Mineral Point, Wis.		R	R	5'8	156	0	0	–	0	1	0	0	2	3	3	0	0	4.50	0	0	0	–
Owen, Frank-Frank Malcolm (Yip)	01DetA 03-09ChiA	12-23-79	Ypsilanti, Mich.	11-27-42		R			83	69	.546	4	194	155	119	1368	1249	298	443	16	2.55	483	77	2	.159
Packard, Gene-Eugene Milo	12-13CinN 14-15KCF 16-17ChiN	7-13-87	Colorado Spr., Colo.	5-19-59	L	L	5'10	155	85	69	.552	17	248	152	86	1410	1393	356	488	15	3.01	502	103	2	.205
	17-18StLN 19PhiN																								
Paige, Pat-George L.	11CleA	-85	Paw Paw, Mich.		R	R	5'10	175	1	0	1.000	0	2	1	1	16	21	7	6	0	4.50	7	1	0	.143
Pape, Larry-Lawrence Albert	09,11-12BosA	-83	Norwood, Ohio	7-21-18	R	R	5'11	175	14	9	.609	5	51	24	13	283	287	91	84	3	2.80	102	20	0	.196
Park, Jim-James	15-17StLA	11-10-92	Richmond, Ky.	12-17-70	R	R	6'2	175	4	5	.444	0	42	9	2	122	114	46	40	0	3.02	32	6	0	.188
Parker, Doc-Harley Park	93,95-96ChiN 01CinN	6-14-74	Theresa, N.Y.	3- 3-41	R	R	6'2	200	5	9	.357	1	18	14	13	134	196	39	24	1	5.91	62	17	0	.274
Parker, Roy-Roy W.	19StLN	-97			R	R	6'2	185	0	0	–	0	2	0	0	2	6	1	0	0	31.50	0	0	0	–
Parnham, Rube-James Arthur	16-17PhiA	2- 1-94	Heidelberg, Pa.	11-25-63	R	R	6'3	185	2	2	.500	0	6	5	2	36	39	22	12	0	1.50	14	3	0	.214
Parson, Jiggs-William Edwin	10-11BosN	12-28-85	Parker, S.D.	5-19-67	R	R	6'2	180	0	3	.000	0	17	4	0	60	71	41	14	0	4.95	22	3	0	.136
Pastorious, Jim-James W.	06-09BknN	7-12-81	Pittsburgh, Pa.	5-10-41	L	L	5'9	165	31	55	.360	0	97	84	57	728	705	278	205	9	3.11	231	35	0	.152
Patten, Casey-Case Lyman	01-08WasA 08BosA	5- 7-76	Westport, N.Y.	5-31-35	B	L	6'	175	107	126	.459	4	270	239	206	2063	2154	557	757	16	3.36	746	94	2	.126
Patterson, Roy-Roy Lewis (The Boy Wonder)	01-07ChiA	12-17-76	Stoddard, Wis.	4-14-53	R	R	6'	185	81	70	.536	3	184	152	119	1365	1327	273	442	17	2.75	495	77	1	.156
Patton, Harry-Harry O.	10StLN		Davenport, Iowa						0	0	–	0	1	0	0	4	4	2	2	0	2.25	0	0	0	–
Pearce, George-George Thomas	12-16ChiN 17StLN	1-10-88	Aurora, Ill.	10-11-35	L	L	5'10	175	36	27	[illegible]	1	105	66	28	600	515	317	260	5	3.11	166	20	0	.120
Pearson, Alex-Alexander Franklin	02StLN 03CleA	3- 9-77	Greensboro, Pa.	10-30-66	R	R	5'10	160	3	8	.273	0	15	13	10	112	124	25	36	0	3.86	46	10	0	.217
Peasley, Marv-Marvin Warren	10DetA	7-16-89	Jonesport, Me.	12-27-48	L	L	6'1	175	0	1	.000	0	2	1	0	10	13	11	4	0	8.10	3	0	0	.000
Pelty, Barney-Barney (The Yiddish Curver)	03-12StLA 12WasA	9-10-80	Farmington, Mo.	5-24-39	R	R	5'9	175	91	118	.435	6	266	216	173	1918	1663	532	693	23	2.62	701	101	0	.144
Pennington-Kewpie-George Louis	17StLA	9-24-96	New York, N.Y.	5- 3-53	R	R	5'8	170	0	0	–	0	1	0	0	1	1	0	0	0	0.00	0	0	0	–
Pepper, Bob-Robert Ernest	15PhiA	5- 3-95	Rooston, Pa.	4- 8-68	R	R	6'2	178	0	0	–	0	1	0	0	5	6	4	0	0	1.80	2	0	0	.000
Perdue, Hub-Herbert Rodney (The Gallatin Squash)	11-14BosN 14-15StLN	6- 7-82	Bethpage, Tenn.	10-31-68	R	R	5'10	192	51	64	.443	7	161	122	64	917	1037	199	317	5	3.86	300	42	0	.140
Pernoll, Hub-Henry Hubbard	10,12DetA	3-14-88	Grant's Pass, Ore.	2-18-44	R	L	5'8	175	4	3	.571	0	14	5	4	64	63	18	28	0	3.38	19	1	0	.053
Perritt, Pol-William Dayton	12-14StLN 15-21NYN 21DetA	8-30-92	Arcadia, La.	10-15-47	R	R	6'2	172	92	78	.541	8	256	177	93	1470	1416	390	543	23	2.89	477	72	0	.151
Perry, Scott-Herbert Scott	15StLA 16ChiN 17BosN 17CinN 18-21PhiA	4-17-91	**Dennison, Tex.**	10-27-59	L	R	6'1	190	41	68	.376	4	132	104	69	893	927	284	231	5	3.07	296	40	1	.135
Perryman, Parson-Emmett Key	15StLA	10-24-88	Everette Sprs., Ga.	9-12-66	R	R	6'4	193	2	3	.400	0	24	3	0	50	52	16	19	0	3.96	6	0	0	.000
Peters, Rube-Oscar C.	12ChiA 14BknF	3-15-86	Grand Fork, Ill.		R	R	6'	185	7	8	.467	0	39	14	5	147	186	49	52	0	4.04	42	7	0	.167
Pfeffer, Big Jeff-Francis Xavier	05ChiN 06-08BosN 10ChiN 11BosN	3-31-82	Champaign, Ill.	12-19-54	R	R	6'1	185	31	40	.437	2	112	69	59	695	660	292	317	6	3.30	323	66	2	.204
Pfeffer, Jeff-Edward Joseph	11StLA 13-21BknN 21-24StLN 24PitN	3- 4-88	Seymour, Ill.	8-15-72	R	R	6'3	210	158	112	.585	10	347	280	194	2407	2320	592	836	28	2.77	874	180	0	.206
Pfiester (Hagenbush), Jack-John Albert (Jack the Giant Killer)	03-04PitN 01-11ChiN	5-24-78	Cincinnati, Ohio	9- 3-53	R	L	6'	170	72	44	.621	0	149	128	75	1059	869	293	503	17	2.04	349	36	0	.103
Phillippe Deacon-Charles Louis	99LouN 00-13PitN	5-23-72	Rural Retreat, Va.	3-30-52	L	R	6'1	180	187	108	.634	12	372	288	242	2608	2518	363	929	27	2.58	976	186	3	.191
Phillips, Bill-William Corcoran (Whoa Bill, Silver Bill)	90PitN	11- 9-68	Allenport, Pa.	10-25-41	R	R	5'11	180	69	74	.483	3	176	152	120	1295	1477	363	374	6	4.09	541	122	0	.226
	95,99-03CinN 14IndFM15NwkF																								
Phyle, Bill-William Joseph	98-99ChiN 01NYN	6-25-75	Duluth, Minn.	8- 7-53		R			11	19	.367	2	37	31	28	276	324	89	76	2	3.95	(See B01-19)			
Piatt, Wiley-Wiley Harlan (Iron Man)	98-00PhiN 01PhiA 01-02ChiA 03BosN	7-13-74	Blue Creek, Ohio		L	L	5'10	175	85	80	.515	2	182	170	139	1391	1481	455	517	12	3.60	535	130	0	.243
Pickett, Charlie-Charles A.	10StLN		Columbus, Ohio						0	0	–	0	2	0	0	6	7	2	2	0	1.50	0	0	0	–
Pieh, Cy-Edwin John	13-15NYA	9-29-86	Wannikee, Wis.	9-12-45	R	R	6'2	190	9	9	.500	1	43	12	4	166	156	75	76	2	3.80	51	5	0	.098
Pierson, Bill-William Morris (Wild Bill)	18-19,24PhiA	6-14-99	Atlantic City, N.J.	2-20-59	L	L	6'2	180	0	1	.000	0	11	2	0	33	32	31	10	0	3.27	7	2	0	.286
Pillion, Squiz-Cecil Randolph	15PhiA	4-13-94	Hartford, Conn.	9-30-62	L	L	6'	178	0	0	–	0	2	0	0	5	10	2	0	0	7.20	1	0	0	.000
Pinnance, Ed-Edward D. (Peanuts)	03PhiA	**10-22-79**	Walpole I., Canada	12-12-44		R			0	1	.000	0	2	1	0	7	5	2	2	0	2.57	3	0	0	.000
Pittinger, Togie-Charles Reno (Horse Race)	00-04BosN 05-07PhiN	-71	Greencastle, Pa.	1-14-09		R			114	113	.502	3	262	228	187	2040	2017	734	832	20	3.10	744	92	1	.124
Plank, Eddie-Edward Stewart (Gettysburg Eddie)	01-14PhiA 15StLF	8-31-75	Gettysburg, Pa.	2-24-26	L	L	5'11	175	325	193	.627	25	622	527	410	4507	3956	1072	2246	67	2.34	1607	331	3	.206
	16-17StLA																								
Polchow, Lou-Louis William	02CleA	3-14-81	Mankato, Minn.	8-15-12					0	1	.000	0	1	1	1	8	9	4	2	0	5.63	4	0	0	.000
Poole, Ed-Edward I. (Pee Wee)	00-02PitN 02-03CinN 04BknN	9- 7-74	Canton, Ohio	3-11-19	R	R	6'	175	33	35	.485	1	80	70	61	595	584	238	226	5	3.04	279	51	2	.183
Popp, Bill-William Peter	02StLN	6- 7-77	St. Louis, Mo.	9- 7-09		R			2	6	.250	0	9	7	5	60	87	26	20	0	4.95	21	1	0	.048
Porray, Eddie-Edmund Joseph	14BufF	12- 5-88	on ship-Atlantic O.	7-13-54	R	R	5'11	170	0	1	.000	0	3	3	0	10	18	7	0	0	4.50	4	0	0	.000
Porter, Jim-James	02PhiA		Bloomington, Ill.						0	1	.000	0	1	1	1	8	12	5	2	0	3.38	3	0	0	.000
Pounds, Bill-William Charles	03CleA 03BknN		Paterson, N.J.						0	0	–	0	2	0	0	11	16	2	4	0	8.18	5	3	0	.600
Powell, Bill-William Burris	09-10PitN 12ChiN 13CinN	5- 8-85	Grafton, W.Va.	9-28-67	R	R	6'2	182	4	8	.333	0	17	11	4	84	76	43	25	2	2.89	26	7	0	.269
Powell, Jack-John Joseph (Red)	97-98CleN 99-01StLN 02-03StLA	7- 9-74	Bloomington, Ill.	10-17-44	R	R	5'11	195	248	255	.493	14	577	517	424	4387	4319	1021	1621	47	2.97	1618	309	7	.191
	04-05NYA 05-12StLA																								
Powell, Sam-Samuel	13StLA								0	0	–	0	2	0	0	2	1	2	0	0	0.00	0	0	0	–
Prendergast, Mike-Michael Thomas	14-15ChiF 16-17ChiN 18-19PhiN	12-15-88	Arlington, Ill.	11-18-67	R	L	5'10	165	41	53	.436	4	180	97	48	908	867	207	311	6	2.74	279	32	0	.115
Prentiss (Wilson), Garry-George Pepper (Kitten) (Played as George Wilson 01)	01-02BosA 02BalA	6-10-76	Wilmington, Del.	9- 8-02	B	R	5'11	175	3	4	.429	0	11	7	4	58	76	21	10	0	5.28	23	6	0	.261
Prough, Bill-Herschel Clinton	12CinN	**11-28-87**	**Markle, Ind.**	**12-29-36**	R	R	6'3	185	0	0	–	0	1	0	0	3	7	1	1	0	6.00	1	0	0	.000
Pruiett, Tex-Charles LeRoy	07-08BosA	4-10-83	Osgood, Ind.	3- 6-53					5	18	.217	4	48	23	7	233	221	80	82	3	2.82	67	9	0	.134
Puckett, Troy-Troy Levi	11PhiN	12-10-89	Winchester, Ind.	4-13-71	L	R	6'2	186	0	0	–	0	1	0	0	2	4	2	1	0	13.50	0	0	0	–
Puttmann, Ambrose-Ambrose Nicholas	03-05NYA 06StLN	9- 9-80	Cincinnati, Ohio	6-21-36		L	**6'4**	**185**	7	11	.389	1	33	18	8	173	158	67	85	1	3.59	63	18	0	.286
Quick, Ed-Edwin S.	03NYA		Baltimore, Md.			L			0	1	.000	0	1	1	0	4	5	1	1	0	4.50	1	0	0	.000
Quinn, Clarence-Clarence C.	02-03PhiA								0	1	.000	0	3	1	1	17	23	6	4	0	4.76	6	2	0	.333
Radebaugh, Roy-Roy	11StLN	2-22-84	Champaign, Ill.	1-17-45	R	R	5'7	160	0	0	–	0	2	1	0	10	6	4	1	0	2.70	3	0	0	.000
Ragan, Pat-Don Carlos Patrick	09CinN 09ChiN 11-15BknN 15-19BosN	11-15-88	Blanchard, Iowa	9- 4-56	R	R	5'10	185	76	104	.422	6	283	182	93	1610	1555	470	680	13	2.99	544	84	1	.154
	19NYN 19ChiA 23PhiN																								
Raleigh, John-John Austin	09-10StLN	4-21-90	Elkhorn, Wis.	8-24-55	R	L			1	10	.091	0	18	11	3	86	93	21	28	0	4.08	24	2	0	.083
Rasmussen, Henry-Henry	15ChiF	-93	Chicago, Ill.						0	0	–	0	2	0	0	2	3	2	2	0	13.50	1	0	0	.000
Ray, Carl-Carl Grady	15-16PhiA	1-31-89	Danbury, N.C.	4- 3-70	L	L	5'11	170	0	2	.000	0	5	3	0	16	20	20	11	0	5.06	5	0	0	.000
Ray, Farmer-Robert Henry	10StLA	9-17-86	Fort Lyon, Colo.	3-11-63	L	R	5'11	160	4	10	.286	0	21	16	11	141	146	49	35	0	3.57	40	7	0	.175
Raymond, Bugs-Arthur Lawrence	04DetA 07-08StLN 09-11NYN	2-24-82	Chicago, Ill.	9- 7-12	**R**	**R**	**5'10**	**180**	45	57	.441	2	136	96	58	855	724	282	401	9	2.48	263	42	0	.160
Reagan, Rip-Arthur	03CinN	-82	Fort Scott, Kans.		R	R	5'11	170	0	2	.000	0	3	2	2	18	40	7	7	0	6.00	8	2	0	.250
Redding, Phil-Philip Hayden	12-13StLN	1-25-90	Crystal Sprs., Miss.	3-31-28	L	R	5'11	190	2	1	.667	0	4	3	2	28	33	12	10	0	5.14	9	0	0	.000
Rees, Nellie-Stanley Milton	18WasA	2-25-99	Cynthiana, Ky.	8-30-37	L	L	6'3	190	1	0	1.000	0	2	0	0	2	3	4	1	0	0.00	0	0	0	–
Regan, Mike-Michael John	17-19CinN	11-19-87	Phoenix, N.Y.	5-22-61	R	R	5'11	165	16	15	.516	2	55	32	20	298	306	70	66	4	2.84	103	23	0	.223
Reidy, Bill-William Joseph	96NYN 99BknN 01MilA 02-03StLA	10- 9-73	Cleveland, Ohio	10-14-15	R	R	5'10	175	25	39	.391	3	79	66	55	601	740	106	109	3	4.18	245	39	0	.159
	03-04BknN																								
Reis, Jack-Harrie Crane	11StLN	6-14-90	Cincinnati, Ohio	7-20-39	R	R	5'10	160	0	0	–	0	3	0	0	9	5	8	4	0	1.00	2	0	0	.000
Reisigl, Bugs-Jacob	11CleA	12-12-87	Brooklyn, N.Y.	2-24-57	R	R	5'10	175	0	1	.000	0	2	1	1	13	13	3	6	0	6.23	5	0	0	.000
Reisling, Doc-Frank Carl	04-05BknN 06-08DE 09-10WasA	7-25-74	Martins Ferry, O.	3- 4-55	R	R	5'10	180	14	19	.424	2	49	33	25	312	303	75	100	4	2.45	98	18	0	.184
Remneas, Alex-Alexander Norman	12DetA 15StLA	**2-21-86**	Minneapolis, Minn.		R	R	6'1	180	0	0	–	0	3	0	0	8	8	3	5	0	6.75	1	0	0	.000
Renfer, Erwin-Erwin Arthur	13DetA	12-11-95	Elgin, Ill.	10-26-58	R	R	6'	180	0	1	.000	0	1	1	0	6	5	3	1	0	6.00	2	0	0	.000
Reulbach, Ed-Edward Marvin (Big Ed)	05-13ChiN 13-14BknN 15NwkF	12- 1-82	Detroit, Mich.	7-17-61	R	R	6'1	190	182	106	.632	13	399	299	200	2633	2117	892	1137	40	2.28	862	127	1	.147
	15-17BosN																								
Reynolds, Ross-E. Ross	14-15DetA	8-20-89	Edwards Co., Tex.		R	R	6'2	185	5	4	.556	1	30	9	3	89	79	44	33	1	2.63	24	1	0	.042
Rhoads, Bob-Robert Barton (Dusty)	02ChiN 03StLN 03-09CleA	10- 4-79	Wooster, Ohio	2-12-67	R	R	6'1	215	98	84	.538	3	218	185	154	1691	1604	494	522	21	2.61	642	121	2	.188
Rhodes, Charlie-Charles Anderson	06StLN 08CinN 08-09StLN	4- 7-85	Caney, Kans.	10-26-18	R	R	5'7	160	7	11	.389	0	26	20	10	143	116	67	76	0	3.46	48	10	0	.208
Rice, Sam-Edgar Charles	15-16WasA	2-20-90	Morocco, Ind.	**10-13-74**	L	R	5'9	150	1	1	.500	0	9	3	1	39	31	19	12	0	2.54	(See B20-45)			
Richardson, Jack-John William	15-16PhiA	10- 3-92	Central City, Ill.	1-18-70	B	R	6'3	197	0	1	.000	0	4	3	2	25	23	15	12	0	3.60	8	0	0	.000
Richie, Lew-Lewis A.	06-09PhiN 09-10BosN 10-13ChiN	8-23-83	Ambler, Pa.	8-15-36	R	R	5'8	165	74	65	.532	9	241	137	87	1360	1190	495	438	20	2.54	443	65	0	.147
Richter, Reggie-Emil Henry	11ChiN	9-14-88	Dusseldorf, Germany	8- 3-34	R	R	6'2	180	1	3	.250	2	22	5	0	55	62	20	34	0	3.11	10	1	0	.100
Ridgeway, John-John A.	14BalF	-91	Philadelphia, Pa.		L	R	5'11	174	0	1	.000	0	4	1	0	9	20	3	2	0	11.00	1	0	0	.000
Rieger, Elmer-Elmer Jay	10StLN	2-25-89	Perris, Cal.	10-21-59	B	R	6'	175	0	2	.000	0	13	2	0	21	26	7	9	0	5.57	3	0	0	.000
Ritter, Hank-William Herbert	12PhiN 14-16NYN	10-12-93	McCoysville, Pa.	9- 3-64	R	R	6'	180	4	1	.800	2	29	2	0	77	78	24	43	0	3.97	20	2	0	.100

USE NAME – GIVEN NAMES (NICKNAMES)	TEAM BY YEAR	BIRTH DATE	BIRTH PLACE	DEATH DATE	LIFETIME PITCHING TOTALS																	BATTING TOTALS			
					B	T	HGT	WGT	W	L	PCT	SV	G	GS	CG	IP	H	BB	SO	ShO	ERA	AB	H	HR	BA
Roberts, Ray-Raymond	19PhiA	8-24-95	Cruger, Miss.	1-30-62	L	R	5'11	180	0	2	.000	0	3	2	0	14	21	3	2	0	7.71	4	1	0	.250
Robertson, Dick-Richard J.	13CinN 18BknN 19WasA	-91	Washington, D.C.		R	R	5'9	160	3	9	.250	0	22	14	8	125	125	46	26	1	2.88	40	9	0	.225
Robinson (Roberson), Hank-John Henry (Rube)	11-13PitN 14-15StLN 18NYA	8-16-89	Floyd, Ark.	7- 3-65	R	L	6'1	175	42	37	.532	2	150	73	32	701	646	159	238	3	2.53	218	37	0	.170
Robitaille, Chick- Joseph Anthony	04-05PitN	3- 2-79	Whitehall, N.Y.	7-30-47	R	R	5'8	150	12	8	.600	0	26	20	18	186	178	41	66	0	2.56	66	8	0	.121
Rogers, Tom-Thomas Andrew (Shotgun)	17-19StLA 19PhiA 21NYA	2-12-92	Scottville, Ky.	3- 7-36	R	R	6'1	195	15	30	.333	3	83	42	21	415	431	162	94	1	3.95	134	30	1	.224
Rogge, Clint-Francis Clinton	15PitF 21CinN	7-19-89	Memphis, Mich.	1- 6-69	L	R	5'10	185	18	13	.581	0	43	34	17	289	283	102	105	5	2.74	91	15	0	.165
Rose, Chuck-Charles Alfred	09StLA	9- 1-85	Macon, Mo.	8- 4-61	L	L	5'8	158	1	2	.333	0	3	3	3	25	32	7	6	0	5.40	7	1	0	.143
Ross, Ernie-Ernest Bertram (Curly)	02BalA	3 31-80	Toronto, Canada	3-28-50	L	L	5'8	160	1	1	.500	0	2	2	2	17	20	12	2	0	7.41	8	0	0	.000
Ross, George-George Sidney	18NYN	6-27-92	Kentfield, Cal.	4-22-35	L	L	5'10	175	0	0	–	1	1	0	0	2	2	3	2	0	0.00	1	0	0	.000
Rowan, Jack-John Albert	06DetA 08-10, 13-14CinN 11PhiN 11ChiN	6-16-87	New Castle, Pa.	9-29-66	R	R	6'1	210	32	40	.444	3	119	74	44	671	623	272	267	5	3.07	199	30	0	.151
Roy, Charlie-Charles Robert	06PhiN	6-22-84	Beaulieu, Minn.	2-10-50	R	R	5'10	190	0	1	.000	0	7	1	0	18	24	5	6	0	5.00	7	0	0	.000
Rucker, Nap-George Napoleon	07-16BknN	9-30-84	Crabapple, Ga.	12-19-70	R	L	5'11	200	134	134	.500	14	336	272	186	2375	2089	701	1217	38	2.42	805	157	1	.195
Rudolph, Dick-Richard (Baldy)	10-11NYN 13-20BosN 21DP 22-23,27BosN	8-25-87	New York, N.Y.	10-20-49	B	R	5'9	160	122	108	.530	8	279	241	172	2048	1971	402	786	26	2.66	698	131	2	.188
					Bats Right 10-18																				
Rusie, Amos-Amos Wilson (The Hoosier Thunderbolt)	89IndN 90-95NYN 96HO 97-98NYN 99-00HO 01CinN	5-30-71	Mooresville, Ind.	12- 6-42	R	R	6'1	200	248	170	.593	5	462	427	392	3769	3384	1704	1934	30	3.08	1721	430	8	.250
Russell, Lefty-Clarence Dixon	10-12PhiA	7- 8-90	Baltimore, Md.	1-22-62	L	L	6'1	165	1	4	.200	0	13	5	3	58	71	34	21	1	6.36	20	5	0	.250
Russell, Reb-Ewell Albert	13-19ChiA	4-12-89	Jackson, Miss.	9-30-73	L	L	5'11	185	79	60	.568	15	241	148	80	1290	1127	267	495	23	2.34	(See B20-45)			
Ruth, Babe-George Herman (The Sultan of Swat)	14-19BosA 20-21,30,33NYA	2- 6-95	Baltimore, Md.	8-16-48	L	L	6'2	215	93	44	.679	5	163	147	107	1221	974	441	488	17	2.28	(See B20-45)			
Ryan, Jack-Jack (Gulfport)	08CleA 09BosA 11BknN	9-19-84	Lawrenceville, Ill.	10-16-49	R	R	5'10	165	5	4	.556	1	24	10	3	103	101	26	32	0	2.88	31	5	0	.161
St. Vrain, Jim-James H.	02ChiN	6- 6-83	Monroe Co., Mo.	6-12-37			5'9	175	4	6	.400	0	12	11	10	95	88	25	51	1	2.08	31	3	0	.097
Salisbury, Bill-William A.	02PhiN	-76	Iowa						0	0	–	0	2	1	0	6	15	2	0	0	13.50	1	0	0	.000
Sallee, Slim-Harry Franklin (Scatter)	08-16StLN 16-18NYN 19-20CinN 20-21NYN	2- 3-85	Higginsport, Ohio	3-23-50	L	L	6'3	170	173	143	.547	36	475	307	188	2819	2726	572	835	25	2.57	923	157	2	.170
Salmon, Roger-Roger Elliott	12PhiA	5-11-91	Newark, N.J.	6-17-74	L	L	6'2	170	1	0	1.000	0	2	1	0	5	7	4	5	0	9.00	1	0	0	.000
Salve, Gus-Augustus William	08PhiA	12-29-85	Boston, Mass.	5-29-71	L	L	6'	190	0	1	.000	0	1	1	1	9	9	8	5	0	2.00	4	0	0	.000
Sanders, Roy-Roy Garvin (Butch, Pep)	17CinN 18PitN	8- 1-92	Stafford, Kans.	1-17-50	R	R	6'	195	7	10	.412	1	30	16	7	170	147	68	58	1	2.75	59	8	0	.136
Sanders, Roy-Roy L. (Simon)	18NYA 20StLA	-94			R	R	6'	185	1	3	.250	0	14	3	0	43	48	33	10	0	4.60	11	0	0	.000
Sanders, War-Warren Williams	03-04StLN	8- 2-77	Maynardville, Tenn.	8- 3-62	R	L	5'10	160	2	8	.200	0	12	9	4	59	73	22	20	0	5.64	21	1	0	.048
Savidge, Ralph-Ralph Austin (The Human Whipcord)	08-09CinN	2- 3-79	Jerseytown, Pa.	7-22-59	R	R	6'2	210	0	1	.000	0	5	1	1	25	28	11	9	0	5.76	8	0	0	.000
Scanlan, Doc-William Dennis	03-04PitN 04-07BknN 08IL 09-11BknN	3- 7-81	Syracuse, N.Y.	5-29-49	L	R	5'8	165	67	70	.489	5	181	149	102	1252	1061	608	584	15	3.00	416	78	0	.188
Scanlan, Frank-Frank Aloysius (Dreamy)	09PhiN	4-28-90	Syracuse, N.Y.	4- 9-69	R	L	6'1	175	0	0	–	1	6	0	0	11	8	5	5	0	1.64	4	0	0	.000
Schardt, Bill-Wilburt (Big Bill)	11-12BknN	1-20-86	Cleveland, Ohio	7-26-64	R	R	6'4	210	5	16	.238	5	46	22	10	216	215	97	84	1	3.67	65	10	0	.154
Schauer (Dimitrihoff), Rube (Dimitri Ivanovich)-Alexander John	13-16NYN 17PhiA	3-19-91	Odessa, Russia	4-15-57	R	R	6'2	192	10	29	.266	0	93	32	16	400	384	137	164	0	3.35	121	16	0	.132
Schegg (Price), Lefty-Gilbert Eugene	12WasA	8-28-89	Leesville, Ohio			L			0	0	–	0	2	1	0	5	7	4	3	0	3.60	2	0	0	.000
Scheneberg, Jack-John Bluford	13PitN 20StLA	11-20-87	Guyandotte, W.Va.	9-26-50	B	R	6'	180	0	1	.000	0	2	1	0	8	17	3	1	0	11.25	2	1	0	.500
Schettler, Lou-Louis Martin	10PhiN	6-12-86	Pittsburgh, Pa.	5- 1-60	R	R	5'11	160	2	6	.250	1	27	7	3	107	96	51	62	0	3.20	41	7	0	.171
Schlitzer, Biff-Victor Joseph	08-09PhiA 09BosA 14Buff	12- 4-84	Rochester, N.Y.	1- 4-48	R	R	5'11	175	10	16	.385	1	44	29	16	223	211	73	88	2	3.51	80	16	0	.200
Schmidt, Butch-Charles John	09NYA	7-19-86	Baltimore, Md.	9- 4-52	L	L	6'	175	0	0	–	0	1	0	0	5	10	1	2	0	7.20	(See B01-19)			
Schmidt, Henry-Henry M.	03BknN	6-26-73	Brownsville, Tex.	4-23-26	R	R	5'8	150	22	13	.629	2	40	36	29	301	321	120	96	5	3.83	107	21	1	.196
Schmidt, Pete-Herman	13StLA		St. Louis, Mo.			L			0	0	–	1	1	0	0	2	3	2	0	0	4.50	0	0	0	–
Schmit, Crazy-Frederic M. (Germany)	90PitN 92-93BalN 93NYN 99CleN 01BalA	12-13-66	Chicago, Ill.	10- 5-40	L	L	5'10	165	7	36	.163	0	54	48	37	361	464	185	93	1	5.46	157	24	0	.153
Schmutz, Charlie-Charlies Otto (King)	14-15BknN	1- 1-90	San Diego, Cal.	6-27-62	R	R	6'3	195	1	3	.250	0	19	5	1	61	64	14	22	0	3.54	17	3	0	.176
Schneiberg, Frank-Frank Frederick	10BknN	3-12-82	Milwaukee, Wis.	5-18-48					0	0	–	0	1	0	0	1	5	4	0	0	63.00	0	0	0	–
Schneider, Pete-Peter Joseph	14-18CinN 19NYA	8-20-92	Los Angeles, Cal.	6- 1-57	R	R	6'1	194	58	86	.403	4	207	162	85	1283	1204	500	491	11	2.62	434	96	5	.221
Schorr, Ed-Edward Walter	15ChiN	2-14-91	Bremen, Ohio	9-12-69	R	R	6'1	180	0	0	–	0	2	0	0	6	9	5	3	0	7.50	2	1	0	.500
Schreiber, Barney-David Henry	11CinN	5- 8-82	Waverly, Ohio	10- 6-64	L	L	6'	185	0	0	–	1	3	0	0	10	19	2	5	0	5.40	3	0	0	.000
Schulz, Al-Albert Christopher (Heinie, Lefty)	12-14NYA 14-15BufF 16CinN	5-12-89	Toledo, Ohio	12-13-31	R	L	6'1	182	48	63	.432	4	160	110	56	933	867	409	445	5	3.32	304	47	1	.155
Schumann, Hack-Carl J.	06PhiA	8-13-84	Buffalo, N.Y.	3-25-46		R			0	2	.000	0	4	2	1	18	21	8	9	0	4.00	6	0	0	.000
Schupp, Ferdie-Ferdinand Maurice	13-19NYN 19-21StLN 21BknN 22ChiA	1-16-91	Louisville, Ky.	12-16-71	R	L	5'10	150	61	39	.610	6	216	120	62	1054	938	464	553	11	3.32	321	58	1	.181
Schwenck, Rudy-Rudolph Christian	09ChiN	4- 6-84	Louisville, Ky.	11-27-41					1	1	.500	0	3	2	0	4	16	3	3	0	13.50	4	1	0	.250
Schwenk, Hal-Harold Edward	13StLA	8-23-90	Schuylkill Hvn., Pa.	9- 4-55	L	L	6'	174	1	0	1.000	0	1	1	1	11	12	4	3	0	3.27	3	1	0	.333
Scoggins, Jim-Lynn J. (Lefty)	13ChiA	7-19-91	Kileen, Tex.	8-16-23	L	L	5'11	165	0	0	–	0	1	1	0	0	0	1	0	0	0.00	0	0	0	–
Scott, Dick-Amos Richard	01CinN	2- 5-82	Bethel, Ohio	4-11-11	R	R	6'	180	0	2	.000	0	3	2	2	21	26	9	7	0	5.14	9	0	0	.000
Scott, Ed-Edward	00CinN 01CleA	8-12-70	Walbridge, Ohio	11- 1-33	R	R			24	26	.480	1	60	52	43	448	529	104	115	0	3.98	171	29	2	.170
Scott, Jim-James (Death Valley Jim)	09-17ChiA 18MS	4-23-88	Deadwood, S.D.	4- 7-57	R	R	6'1	215	109	113	.491	12	317	225	125	1871	1624	609	945	26	2.32	614	79	1	.129
Seaton, Tom-Thomas Gordon	12-13PhiN 14-15BknF 15NwkF 16-17ChiN	8-30-87	Blair, Neb.	4-10-40	B	R	6'	175	93	65	.589	11	231	156	90	1340	1235	530	644	16	3.14	451	84	4	.186
Seymour, Cy-James Bentley	96-00NYN 02CinN	12- 9-72	Albany, N.Y.	9-20-19	L	L	6'	200	63	54	.538	1	140	123	105	1033	953	661	584	6	3.76	(See B01-19)			
Shaw, Jim-James Aloysius (Grunting Jim)	13-21WasA	8-13-93	Pittsburgh, Pa.	1-27-62	R	R	6'	180	82	99	.453	17	287	194	96	1599	1446	688	767	17	3.07	528	86	4	.163
Shears, George-George Penfield	12NYA	4-13-90	Marshall, Mo.		R	L	6'3	180	0	0	–	0	4	0	0	15	24	11	9	0	5.40	6	1	0	.167
Shellenback, Frank-Frank Victor	18-19ChiA	12-16-98	Joplin, Mo.	8-17-69	R	R	6'2	192	11	15	.423	1	36	24	12	218	220	90	57	3	3.05	65	8	0	.123
Sherman, Babe-Daniel L.	14ChiF	-92	Conn.		R	R	5'6	145	0	1	.000	0	1	1	0	.1	0	2	0	0	0.00	0	0	0	–
Sherman, Joe-Joel Powers	15PhiA	11- 4-90	Yarmouth, Mass.		R	R	6'	165	1	0	1.000	0	2	1	1	15	15	1	5	0	2.40	6	2	0	.333
Sherry (Schuerholz), Fred-Fred Peter	11WasA	6-13-89	Honesdale, Pa.	7-27-75	R	R	6'	170	0	4	.000	0	10	3	2	52	63	19	20	0	4.33	19	3	0	.158
Shields, Charlie-Charles S.	02BalA 02StLA 07StLN	12-10-79	Jackson, Tenn.	8-27-53	L	L			8	14	.364	0	30	21	13	179	250	46	35	1	4.27	63	14	0	.222
Shore, Ernie-Ernest Grady	12NYN 14-17RosA 18MS 19-20NYA	3-24-91	East Bend, N.C.		R	R	6'4	220	65	42	.607	6	160	120	55	980	906	270	309	9	2.47	321	39	0	.121
Shultz, Toots-Wallace Luther	11-12PhiN	10-10-88	Homestead, Pa.	1-30-59	R	R	5'10	175	1	7	.125	1	27	7	3	84	105	50	29	0	6.00	29	7	0	.241
Siever, Ed-Edward T.	01-02DetA 03-04StLA 06-08DetA	4- 2-78	Lewistown, Ill.	2- 5-20	L	L			86	80	.518	3	203	174	136	1508	1550	311	470	14	2.60	523	81	0	.155
Sims, Pete-Clarence	15StLA	5-24-91	Crown City, Ohio	12- 2-68	R	R	5'11	165	1	0	1.000	0	3	2	0	8	6	6	4	0	4.50	1	1	0	1.000
Sincock, Bert-Herbert Sylvester	08CinN	9- 8-87	Barkerville, Can.	8- 1-46	L	L	5'10	165	0	0	–	0	1	0	0	5	3	0	1	0	3.60	2	0	0	.000
Sisler, George-George Harold (Gorgeous George)	15-16,18,20,25-26,M24-26StLA 28BosN	3-24-93	Manchester, Ohio	3-26-73	L	L	5'11	170	5	6	.455	2	24	12	9	111	91	52	63	1	2.35	(See B20-45)			
Sitton, Carl-Carl Vetter	09CleA	9-22-82	Pendleton, S.C.	9-11-31	R	R	5'10	170	2	2	.500	0	14	5	3	50	50	16	16	0	2.88	13	2	0	.154
Skeels, Dave-David	10DetA	12-29-92	Wash.	12- 2-26	L	R	6'1	187	0	0	–	0	1	1	0	6	9	4	2	0	12.00	3	0	0	.000
Skopec, John-John S. (Buckshot)	01ChiA 03DetA	5- 8-80	Chicago, Ill.	10-12-12	L	L	5'10	190	8	5	.615	0	15	14	9	107	108	58	38	0	3.28	43	12	1	.279
Slagle, Walt-Walter Jennings	10CinN	12-15-78	Kenton, Ohio	6-17-74	B	R	6'	165	0	0	–	0	1	0	0	1	0	3	0	0	9.00	0	0	0	–
Slapnicka, Cy-Cyril Charles	11ChiN 18PitN	3-23-86	Cedar Rapids, Iowa		B	R	5'10	165	1	6	.143	1	10	8	5	73	71	29	13	0	4.32	23	3	0	.130
Slattery, Phil-Philip Ryan	15PitN	2-25-93	Harper, Iowa	3-12-68	R	L	5'11	160	0	0	–	0	3	0	0	8	5	1	1	0	0.00	1	0	0	.000
Slaughter, Barney-Byron Atkins	10PhiN	10- 6-84	Smyrna, Del.	5-17-61	R	R	5'11	165	0	1	.000	1	8	1	0	18	21	11	7	0	5.50	5	1	0	.200
Smallwood, Walt-Walter Clayton	17NYA 18MS 19NYA	4-24-93	Dayton, Md.		R	R	6'2	190	0	0	–	0	8	0	0	24	21	10	7	0	4.50	5	0	0	.000
Smith, Bob-Robert Ashley	13ChiA 15BufF	7-19-91	Hardwick, Vt.	4-29-67	R	R	5'11	160	0	0	–	0	2	0	0	3	4	5	1	0	15.00	0	0	0	–
Smith, Charlie-Charles E.	02CleA 06-09WasA 09-11BosA 11-14ChiN	4-20-80	Cleveland, Ohio		R	R	6'1	185	65	87	.428	2	212	147	86	1351	1309	353	570	9	2.81	447	67	1	.150
Smith, Chick-John William	13CinN	12- 2-92	Dayton, Ky.	10-11-35	L	L	5'8	165	0	1	.000	0	5	1	0	18	15	11	11	0	3.50	4	0	0	.000
Smith, Doug-Douglass Weldon	12BosA	5-25-93	Miller's Fls., Mass.		L	L	5'10	168	0	0	–	0	1	0	0	3	4	0	1	0	3.00	0	0	0	–
Smith, Ed-Rhesa Edward	06StLA	2-21-70	Mentone, Ind.	3-20-55	R	R	5'11	170	7	10	.412	1	19	18	13	155	153	53	45	0	3.72	54	11	0	.204
Smith, Elmer-Elmer Ellsworth (Mike)	86-89CinAA 92,94PitN 98CinN	3-23-68	Pittsburgh, Pa.	11- 3-45	L	L	5'11	178	76	58	.567	0	150	137	123	1219	1175	438	526	9	3.24	(See B01-19)			
Smith (Schmidt), Frank-Frank Elmer (Nig)	04-10ChiA 10-11BosA 11-12CinN 14-15BalF 15BknF	10-28-79	Pittsburgh, Pa.	11- 3-52	R	R	5'10	194	138	113	.550	7	354	256	184	2275	1975	676	1051	27	2.59	766	156	2	.204
Smith, Fred-Frederick C.	07CinN	11-24-78	New Diggins, Wis.	2- 4-64	R	R	5'10	186	2	7	.222	1	18	9	5	85	90	24	19	0	2.86	28	3	0	.107
Smith, Harry-Harrison Morton	12ChiA	8-20-89	Union, Neb.	7-26-64	R	R	5'9	160	1	0	1.000	0	1	1	0	5	6	0	1	0	1.80	1	0	0	.000
Smith, Jake-Jacob G.	11PhiN		DuBois, Pa.						0	0	–	0	2	0	0	5	3	2	1	0	0.00	3	0	0	.000
Smith, Pop Boy-Clarence Ossie	13ChiA 16-17CleA	5-23-92	Newport, Tenn.	2-16-24	R	R	6'1	176	1	5	.167	0	26	5	0	67	70	26	20	0	4.16	13	2	0	.154
Snover, Colonel-Colonel Lester (Bosco)	19NYN	5-16-95	Hallstead, Pa.	4-30-60	L	L	6'	200	0	1	.000	0	2	1	0	9	7	3	4	0	1.00	2	0	0	.000
Sommers, Rudy-Rudolph	12ChiN 14BknF 26-27BosA	10-30-88	Cincinnati, Ohio	3-18-49	B	L	5'11	170	2	8	.200	2	33	8	2	101	113	53	44	0	4.81	26	7	0	.269
Spade, Bob-Robert	07-10CinN 10StLA	1- 4-77	Akron, Ohio	9- 7-24	R	R	5'10	190	25	24	.510	1	62	52	36	426	411	159	121	5	2.96	144	32	0	.222
Sparks, Tully-Tully Frank	97PhiN 99PitN 01MilA 02NYN 02BosA 03-10PhiN	4-18-77	Monroe, La.	7-15-37	R	R			120	138	.465	8	315	269	202	2337	2231	629	778	19	2.79	796	91	0	.114

		BIRTH		DEATH	LIFETIME PITCHING TOTALS																	BATTING TOTALS			
USE NAME – GIVEN NAMES (NICKNAMES)	TEAM BY YEAR	DATE	BIRTH PLACE	DATE	B	T	HGT	WGT	W	L	PCT	SV	G	GS	CG	IP	H	BB	SO	ShO	ERA	AB	H	HR	BA
Speer, Kid-George Nathan	09DetA	6-16-86	Corning, Mo.	1-13-46	L	L			3	3	.500	2	12	8	4	76	88	13	12	0	2.84	25	3	0	.120
Spencer, Frank-Frank G.	12StLA	-86	Minneapolis, Minn.		R	R	5'10	172	0	0	–	0	1	0	0	2	2	0	0	0	0.00	0	0	0	–
Spongberg, Carl-Carl Gustav	08ChiN	5-21-84	Idaho Falls, Idaho	7-21-38	R	R	6'2	208	0	0	–	0	1	0	0	7	9	6	4	0	9.00	3	2	0	.667
Stack, Eddie-William Edward	10-11PhiN 12-13BknN 13-14ChiN	10-24-87	Chicago, Ill.	8-28-58	R	R	6'	175	26	24	.520	2	102	60	23	491	469	188	200	4	3.52	157	17	0	.108
Standridge, Pete-Alfred Peter	11StLN 15ChiN	4-25-91	Black Diamond, Wash.	8- 2-63	R	R	6'	180	4	1	.800	0	31	3	2	117	130	40	45	0	3.85	41	9	0	.220
Stanley, Buck-John Leonard	11PhiN	11-13-89	Washington, D.C.	8-13-40	L	L	5'10	160	0	1	.000	0	4	0	0	11	14	9	5	0	6.55	4	0	0	.000
Starkel, Con-Conrad	06WasA	11-16-80	Germany	1-19-33	R	R	6'	200	0	0	–	0	1	0	0	3	7	2	1	0	18.00	0	0	0	–
Steele, Bill-William Mitchell (Big Bill)	10-14StLN 14BknN	10- 5-85	Milford, Pa.	10-19-49	R	R			37	43	.463	7	129	79	40	677	733	235	236	1	4.02	231	47	0	.203
Steele, Bob-Robert Wesley	16-17StLN 17-18PitN 18-19NYN	3-29-94	Cassburn, Canada	1-27-62	B	L	5'10	175	16	38	.296	3	91	58	28	488	450	144	217	4	3.04	178	40	0	.225
Steele, Elmer-Elmer Rae	07-09BosA 10-11PitN 11BknN	5-17-84	Muitzeskill, N.Y.	3- 9-66	B	R	5'11	200	18	22	.450	5	75	43	20	418	367	68	147	3	2.41	144	19	0	.132
Steen, Bill-William John	12-15CleA 15DetA	11-11-87	Pittsburgh, Pa.		R	R	6'	172	28	34	.452	5	108	65	32	597	611	199	265	4	3.05	204	42	0	.206
Stevens, Jim-James Arthur (Steve)	14WasA	8-25-89	Williamsburg, Md.	9-25-66	R	R	5'11	180	0	0	–	0	2	0	0	3	4	2	0	0	9.00	1	0	0	.000
Stewart, Joe-Joseph Lawrence (Ace)	04BosN	3-11-79	Monroe, N.C.	2- 9-13		R	5'11	175	0	0	–	0	2	0	0	9	12	4	1	0	10.00	5	1	0	.200
Stimmel, Archie-Archibald May (Lumbago)	00-02CinN	5-30-73	Woodsboro, Md.	8-18-58	R	R	6'	175	5	19	.208	0	26	22	18	192	225	60	64	1	4.22	77	8	0	.104
Stone, Dwight-Dwight Ely	13StLA 14KCF	8- 2-86	Holt Co., Neb.		R	R	6'1	170	10	20	.333	0	57	29	9	278	299	123	125	1	4.08	91	16	1	.176
Stovall, Jesse-Jesse Cramer (Scout)	03CleA 04DetA	7-24-75	Independence, Mo.	7-12-55	L	R	6'	175	7	14	.333	0	28	23	19	204	214	66	53	3	3.75	78	12	0	.154
Strand, Paul-Paul Edward	13-15BosN	12-19-93	Carbonado, Wash.	7- 2-74	R	L	6'	190	7	3	.700	1	29	5	3	95	95	38	52	0	2.37	(See B20-45)			
Streit, Oscar-Oscar William	99BosN 02CleA	7- 7-73	Florence, Ala.	10-10-35	L	L	6'5	190	1	7	.125	0	10	8	5	67	87	40	10	0	5.51	26	4	0	.154
Stremmel, Phil-Philip	09-10StLA	4-16-80	Zanesville, Ohio	12-26-47	R	R	6'	175	0	4	.000	0	7	4	4	47	51	20	13	0	4.02	14	1	0	.071
Stricklett, Elmer-Elmer Griffin	04ChiA 05-07BknN	8-29-76	Glasco, Kans.	6- 7-64	R	R	5'6	140	34	52	.395	6	104	90	78	766	755	215	237	10	2.84	269	45	0	.167
Stroud, Sailor-Ralph Vivian	10DetA 15-16NYN	5-15-85	Ironia, N.J.	4-11-70	R	R	6'	160	19	20	.487	3	70	40	15	361	364	85	141	3	2.94	109	11	0	.101
Sudhoff, Willie-John William (Wee Willie)	97-98StLN 99CleN	9-17-74	St. Louis, Mo.	5-25-17	R	R	5'7	165	100	136	.424	6	279	240	200	2082	2171	607	518	10	3.60	822	149	1	.181
	99-01StLN 02-05StLA 06WasA																								
Suggs, George-George Franklin	08-09DetA 10-13CinN 14-15BalF	7- 7-82	Kinston, N.C.	4- 4-49	R	R	5'7	168	99	89	.527	17	245	185	115	1652	1722	355	588	18	3.11	549	112	1	.204
Sullivan, Harry-Harry Andrew	09StLN	4-12-88	Rockford, Ill.	9-22-19	L	L			0	0	–	0	2	1	0	1	4	2	1	0	36.00	1	0	0	.000
Sullivan, John-John Jeremiah (Lefty)	19ChiA	5-31-94	Chicago, Ill.	7- 7-58	L	L	5'11	165	0	1	.000	0	4	2	1	15	24	8	9	0	4.20	3	0	0	.000
Summers, Ed-Oron Edgar (Kickapoo)	08-12DetA	12- 5-84	Ladoga, Ind.	5-12-53	B	R	6'2	180	68	45	.602	5	138	112	80	999	930	221	362	8	2.42	352	57	2	.162
Suter, Rube-Harry Richard	09ChiA	9-15-87	Independence, Mo.	7-24-71	L	L	5'10	190	2	3	.400	1	18	6	3	87	72	28	53	1	2.48	32	3	0	.094
Sutthoff, Jack-John Gerhard (Sunny Jack)	98WasN 99StLN	6-29-73	Cincinnati, Ohio	8- 3-42	R	R	5'9	175	33	42	.440	0	88	68	56	653	664	287	196	4	3.56	242	35	0	.145
	01,03-04CinN 04-05PhiN																								
Swann, Ducky-Henry	14KCF	-92			R	R	6'1	165	0	0	–	0	1	0	0	1	0	1	1	0	0.00	0	0	0	–
Swigler, Ad-Adam William (Doc)	17NYN	9-21-95	Philadelphia, Pa.	2- 5-75	R	R	5'10	180	0	1	.000	0	1	1	0	6	7	8	4	0	6.00	2	0	0	.000
Swindell, Josh-Joshua Ernest	11,13CleA	7- 5-83	Rose Hill, Kans.	3-19-69	R	R	6'	180	0	1	.000	0	4	1	1	17	19	4	6	0	2.12	4	1	0	.250
Swormstedt, Len-Leonard B.	01-02CinN 06BosA		Cincinnati, Ohio	4-30-15	R	R	5'11	165	3	4	.429	0	8	7	7	65	58	10	22	0	2.22	23	1	0	.043
Taff, John-John G.	13PhiA	-90	Austin, Tex.	5-15-61	R	R	6'	170	0	1	.000	1	7	1	0	18	22	5	9	0	6.50	5	1	0	.200
Tannehill, Jesse-Jesse Niles	94CinN 97-02PitN 03NYA 04-08BosA	7-14-74	Dayton, Ky.	9-22-56	B	L	5'8	150	194	119	.620	8	357	318	263	2751	2787	477	940	34	2.78	(See B01-19)			
	08-09WasA 11CinN				Bats Left-03																				
Taylor, Ben-Benjamin	12CinN					R	5'11	163	0	0	.000	0	2	0	0	6	9	3	2	0	3.00	2	0	0	.000
Taylor, Dummy-Luther Haden	00-01NYN 02CleA 02-08NYN	2-21-75	Oskaloosa, Kans.	8-22-58	R	R	6'1	160	115	106	.520	3	274	237	160	1916	1877	551	767	21	2.75	645	93	0	.144
Taylor, Ed-Edward	03StLN								0	0	–	0	1	0	0	3	0	0	1	0	0.00	1	0	0	.000
Taylor, Jack-John W.	98-03ChiN 04-06StLN 06-07ChiN	1-14-74	Straightville, O.	3- 4-38	R	R	5'10	170	151	140	.519	5	310	286	278	2617	2502	582	657	19	2.67	1059	235	2	.222
Taylor, Wiley-Philip Wiley	11DetA 12ChiA 13-14StLA	3-18-88	Wamego, Kans.	7- 8-54	R	R	6'1	175	3	10	.231	0	27	17	4	121	113	65	45	1	4.09	33	2	0	.061
Tedrow, Al-Allen Seymour	14CleA	12-14-91	Westerville, Ohio	1-23-58	R	L	6'	180	1	2	.333	0	4	3	1	22	19	14	4	0	1.23	6	1	0	.167
Terry, John-John	02DetA 03StLA		St. Louis, Mo.						1	1	.500	0	4	2	2	23	29	5	2	0	2.74	11	0	0	.000
Tesreau, Jeff-Charles Monroe	12-18NYN	3- 5-89	Silver Mine, Mo.	9-24-46	R	R	6'2	218	115	72	.615	9	247	206	123	1679	1350	572	880	27	2.43	574	124	2	.216
Thatcher, Grant-Ulysses Grant	03-04BknN	2-23-77	Maytown, Pa.	3-17-36		R	5'10	180	4	1	.800	0	5	4	4	37	42	9	13	0	3.16	15	3	0	.200
Thielman, Henry-Henry Joseph	02NYN 02CinN 03BknN	10- 3-80	St. Cloud, Minn.	9- 2-42	R	R	5'11	175	9	19	.321	1	31	28	25	246	240	98	64	0	3.37	123	18	1	.146
Thielman, Jake-John Peter	05-06StLN 07-08CleA 08BosA	5-20-79	St. Cloud, Minn.	1-28-28	R	R	6'	175	31	28	.525	0	65	56	49	475	483	107	158	3	3.16	175	42	0	.240
Thomas, Blaine-Blaine M.	11BosA	-88	Payson, Ariz.	8-21-15	R	R	5'11	175	0	0	–	0	2	2	0	5	3	7	0	0	0.00	2	1	0	.500
Thomas, Claude-Claude Alfred (Lefty)	16WasA	5-15-90	Stanberry, Mo.	3- 6-46	L	L	6'1	180	1	2	.333	0	7	4	1	28	27	12	7	1	4.18	10	1	0	.100
Thomas, Frosty-Forrest	05DetA	5-23-81	Faucett, Mo.	3-18-70	R	R	6'	185	0	2	.000	0	2	1	0	6	10	3	5	0	7.50	2	0	0	.000
Thompson, Carl-Thomas Carl	12NYA	11- 7-89	Spring City, Tenn.	1-16-63	R	R			0	2	.000	0	7	2	1	33	43	13	15	0	6.00	10	3	0	.300
Thompson, Fuller-Fuller Weidner	11BosN	5- 1-89	Los Angeles, Cal.	2-19-72	R	R	5'11	164	0	0	–	0	3	0	0	5	5	2	0	0	3.60	0	0	0	–
Thompson, Gus-John Gustav	03PitN 06StLN	6-22-77	Humboldt, Iowa	3-28-58	R	R	6'2	185	4	13	.235	0	22	16	11	146	163	41	58	0	4.07	50	10	0	.200
Thompson, Harry-Harold	19WasA 19PhiA	3-25-93	Nanticoke, Pa.	2-14-51	L	L	5'8	150	0	4	.000	1	15	2	0	55	64	11	11	0	4.25	38	8	0	.211
Thormahlen, Hank-Herbert Ehler (Lefty)	17-20NYA 21BosA 25BknN	7- 5-96	Jersey City, N.J.	2- 6-55	L	L	6'	180	30	29	.508	2	104	63	26	565	550	203	148	5	3.33	173	29	0	.168
Tift, Ray-Raymond Frank	07NYA	6-21-84	Fitchburg, Mass.	3-29-45		R			0	0	–	0	4	1	0	19	33	4	6	0	4.74	5	0	0	.000
Tillman, Johnny-John Lawrence	15StLA	10- 6-93	Bridgeport, Conn.	4- 7-64	B	R	5'11	170	0	0	–	0	2	1	0	10	6	4	6	0	0.90	3	0	0	.000
Tincup, Ben-Austin Ben	14-16,18PhiN 28ChiN	12-14-90	Adair, Okla.		L	R	6'1	180	7	11	.389	2	48	18	9	212	229	78	127	3	3.10	74	10	0	.135
Tipple, Dan-Daniel E. (Big Dan, Rusty)	15NYA	2-13-90	Rockford, Ill.	3-26-60	R	R	6'	176	1	1	.500	0	3	2	2	19	14	11	14	0	2.84	6	0	0	.000
Tompkins, Chuck-Charles Herbert	12CinN	9- 1-89	Prescott, Ark.		R	R	6'	185	0	0	–	0	1	0	0	3	5	0	1	0	0.00	1	1	0	1.000
Toney, Fred-Frederick Arthur	11-13ChiN 15-18CinN 18-22NYN 23StLN	12-11-87	Nashville, Tenn.	3-11-53	R	R	6'2	195	137	102	.573	12	336	271	158	2206	2037	583	718	28	2.69	744	118	3	.159
Tonkin, Doc-Harry Glenville	07WasA	8-11-81	Concord, N.H.	5-30-59	L	L			0	0	–	0	1	0	0	3	6	5	0	0	6.00	2	2	0	1.000
Torkelson, Red-Chester LeRoy	17CleA 18MS	3-19-94	Chicago, Ill.	9-22-64	R	R	6'	175	2	1	.667	0	4	3	0	22	33	13	10	0	7.77	9	2	0	.222
Townsend, Jack-John (Happy)	01PhiN 02-05WasA 06CleA	4- 9-79	Townsend, Del.	12-21-63	R	R	6'	190	34	84	.288	0	153	125	107	1138	1154	416	473	5	2.88	427	71	1	.166
Tozer, Bill-William Louis	08CinN	7- 3-82	St. Louis, Mo.	2-23-55	R	R	6'	200	0	0	–	0	4	0	0	11	11	4	5	0	1.64	2	0	0	.000
Trautman, Fred-Frederick Orlando	15NwkF	3-24-92	Bucyrus, Ohio	2-15-64	R	R	6'1	175	0	0	–	0	1	0	0	3	4	1	2	0	6.00	1	0	0	.000
Travers, Allan-Aloysius Joseph	12DetA	5- 7-92	Philadelphia, Pa.	4-19-68	R	R	6'1	180	0	1	.000	0	1	1	1	8	26	7	1	0	15.75	3	0	0	.000
Trekell, Harry-Harry Roy	13StLN	11-18-92	Breda, Ill.	11- 4-65	R	R	6'1	170	0	1	.000	0	7	1	1	30	25	8	15	0	4.50	9	1	0	.111
Troy, Bun-Robert	12DetA	8-22-88	Germany	10- 7-18	R	R	6'4	195	0	1	.000	0	1	1	0	7	9	3	1	0	5.14	2	0	0	.000
Tuckey, Tom-Thomas H.	08-09BosN		Birmingham, Eng.			L			3	12	.200	0	25	18	7	163	164	42	42	1	3.48	49	5	0	.102
Tuero, Oscar-Oscar [Monzon]	18-20StLN	12-17-92	Havana, Cuba		R	R	5'8	158	6	9	.400	4	58	20	6	200	174	53	58	0	2.88	51	11	0	.216
Turner, Tink-Thomas Lovatt	15PhiA	2-20-90	Swarthmore, Pa.	2-25-62	R	R	6'1	190	0	1	.000	0	1	1	0	2	5	3	0	0	22.50	0	0	0	–
Twining, Twink-Howard Earle (Doc)	16CinN	5-30-94	Horsham, Pa.	6-14-73	R	R	6'	168	0	0	–	0	1	0	0	2	4	1	0	0	13.50	0	0	0	–
Tyler, Lefty-George Albert	10-17BosN 18-21ChiN	12-14-89	Derry, N.H.	9-29-53	L	L	5'10	175	127	118	.518	7	323	265	182	2228	1990	829	1003	31	2.95	870	189	4	.217
Upham, Bill-William Lawrence	15BknF 18BosN	4- 4-88	Akron, Ohio	9-14-59	B	R	6'	178	7	9	.438	5	36	13	6	142	157	41	54	2	3.36	45	6	0	.133
Upp, Jerry-George Henry	09CleA	12-10-83	Sandusky, Ohio	6-30-37		L			2	1	.667	0	7	4	2	27	26	12	13	0	1.67	9	2	0	.222
Vail, Bob-Robert Garfield (Doc)	08PitN	9-24-81	Linneus, Me.	-53	R	R	5'10	165	1	2	.333	0	4	1	0	15	15	7	9	0	6.00	3	1	0	.333
Van Dyke, Ben-Benjamin Harrison	09PhiN 12BosA	8-15-88	Clintonville, Pa.	10-22-73	R	L	6'1	150	0	0	–	0	5	1	0	21	20	11	13	0	3.43	7	1	0	.143
Van Haltren, George-George Edward Martin	87-88ChiN 90BknP	3-30-66	St. Louis, Mo.	9-29-45	L	L	5'11	170	41	29	.586	4	93	68	65	690	810	244	281	5	4.05	(See B01-19)			
	91,M91BalAA 92,M92BalN 95-96,00-01NYN																								
Varney, Dike-Lawrence Delano	02CleA	8- 9-80	Dover, N.H.	4-23-50	L	L	6'	165	2	1	.667	0	3	3	0	15	14	12	7	0	6.00	6	1	0	.167
Vasbinder, Cal-Moses Calhoun	02CleA	7-19-80	Scio, Ohio	12-22-50	R	R			0	0	–	0	2	0	0	5	5	8	2	0	9.00	2	1	0	.500
Vaughn, Hippo-James Leslie	08,10-11NYA 12WasA 13-21ChiN	4- 9-88	Weatherford, Tex.	5-29-66	B	L	6'4	215	178	137	.565	6	390	332	216	2731	2461	817	1416	40	2.49	921	159	3	.173
Veil, Bucky-Frederick William	03-04PitN	8- 2-81	Tyrone, Pa.	4-16-31	R	R	5'10	165	5	3	.625	0	13	7	4	76	74	40	21	0	3.91	30	7	0	.233
Vereker, Tom-Thomas	15BalF								0	0	–	0	2	0	0	3	3	2	1	0	15.00	0	0	0	–
Vernon, Joe-Joseph Henry	12ChiN 14BknF	11-25-89	Mansfield, Mass.	3-13-55	R	R			0	0	–	0	2	1	0	7	8	11	1	0	11.57	3	0	0	.000
Vickers, Rube-Harry Porter	02CinN 03BknN 07-09PhiA	5-17-78	Pittsford, Mich.	12- 9-58	R	R	6'2	225	23	27	.460	3	88	44	29	441	426	119	213	7	3.04	163	26	0	.160
Volz, Jake-Jacob Phillip (Silent Jake)	01BosA 05BosN 08CinN	4- 4-78	San Antonio, Tex.	8-11-62	R	R	5'10	175	2	4	.333	0	11	7	2	39	34	29	12	0	6.00	10	1	0	.100
Vorhees, Cy-Henry Bert	02PhiN 02WasA	9-30-74	Lodi, Ohio	2- 8-10					3	4	.429	0	11	5	4	62	73	22	25	1	3.92	23	9	0	.391
Vowinkel, Rip-John Henry	05CinN	11-18-84	Oswego, N.Y.	7-13-66	R	R	5'10	195	3	3	.500	0	6	6	4	45	52	10	7	0	4.20	14	1	0	.071
Wachtel, Paul-Paul Horine	17BknN	4-30-88	Myersville, Md.	12-15-64	R	R	5'11	175	0	0	–	0	2	0	0	6	9	4	3	0	10.50	3	1	0	.333
Wacker, Charlie-Charles	09PitN		New Albany, Ind.		R	R			0	0	–	0	1	0	0	2	2	1	0	0	0.00	0	0	0	–
Waddell, Rube-George Edward	97,99LouN 00-01PitN 01ChiN	10-13-76	Bradford, Pa.	4- 1-14	R	L	6'1	196	196	138	.587	12	407	340	261	2962	2460	803	2316	50	2.16	1062	171	4	.161
	02-07PhiA 08-10StLA																								
Wagner, Bull-William George	13-14BknN	1- 1-88	Lilley, Mich.	10- 2-67	R	R	6'	225	4	3	.571	0	24	1	0	83	91	42	15	0	5.64	27	6	0	.222
Waldbauer, Doc-Albert Charles	17WasA	2-22-92	Richmond, Va.	7-16-69	R	R	6'2	190	0	0	–	1	2	0	0	5	10	2	2	0	7.20	1	0	0	.000
Walker, Dixie-Ewart Gladstone	09-12WasA	6- 1-87	Brownsville, Pa.	11-14-65	L	R	6'1	192	25	30	.455	1	74	62	40	481	475	142	204	5	3.52	164	33	0	.201

USE NAME – GIVEN NAMES (NICKNAMES)	TEAM BY YEAR	BIRTH DATE	BIRTH PLACE	DEATH DATE	LIFETIME PITCHING TOTALS																	BATTING TOTALS			
					B	T	HGT	WGT	W	L	PCT	SV	G	GS	CG	IP	H	BB	SO	ShO	ERA	AB	H	HR	BA
Walker, Ed-Edward Harrison	02-03CleA	8-11-74	Cambois, England	9-29-47	L	L	6'5	242	0	1	.000	0	4	4	1	20	24	13	5	0	4.50	6	1	0	.167
Walker, Mysterious-Frederick Mitchell	10CinN 13BknN 14PitF 15BknF	3-21-84	Utica, Neb.	2- 1-58	R	R			7	23	.233	1	60	36	17	296	306	135	143	0	4.01	99	15	0	.152
Walker, Tom-Thomas William	02PhiA 04-05CinN	8- 1-81	Philadelphia, Pa.	7-10-44	R	R	5'11	170	25	17	.595	0	48	44	35	370	377	97	94	3	2.70	132	17	0	.129
Wallace, Bobby-Rhoderick John (Rhody)	94-96CleN 02,M11-12StLA M37CinN	11- 4-73	Pittsburgh, Pa.	11- 3-60	R	R	5'8	170	24	21	.533	1	57	48	38	402	469	158	120	3	3.89	(See B01-19)			
Wallace, Huck-Harry Clinton (Lefty)	12PhiN	7-27-82	Richmond, Ind.	7- 6-51	L	L	5'6	160	0	0	–	0	4	0	0	5	7	4	4	0	0.00	0	0	0	–
Waller, Red-John Francis	09NYN	-83	Washington, D.C.	2- 9-15					0	0	–	0	1	0	0	1	3	0	1	0	0.00	0	0	0	–
Walsh, Connie-Cornelius	07PitN	4-23-82	St. Louis, Mo.	4- 5-53					0	0	–	0	1	0	0	1	1	1	0	0	9.00	0	0	0	–
Walsh, Ed-Edward Augustine (Big Ed)	04-16ChiA 17BosN	5-14-81	Plains, Pa.	5-26-59	R	R	6'1	193	194	128	.602	40	430	315	250	2965	2346	617	1736	58	1.82	1085	208	3	.192
Warhop (Wauhop), Jack-John Milton (Chief, Crab)	08-15NYA	7- 4-84	Hinton, W. Va.	10- 4-60	R	R	5'9	168	69	91	.431	10	221	150	105	1423	1366	400	463	3	3.09	495	77	0	.156
Warner, Ed-Edward Emory	12PitN	6-20-89	Fitchburg, Mass.	2- 5-54	R	L	5'10	165	1	1	.500	0	11	3	11	45	40	18	13	1	3.60	15	2	0	.133
Washer, Buck-William	05PhiN	10-11-82	Akron, Ohio	12- 8-55	R	R	5'10	175	0	0	–	0	1	0	0	3	4	5	0	0	6.00	1	0	0	.000
Watson, Doc-Charles John	13ChiN 14ChiF 14-15StLF	1-30-85	Ohio	12-30-49	R	L	5'10	170	22	21	.512	1	69	46	21	373	326	137	133	5	2.70	112	12	0	.107
Watson, Milt-Milton W.	16-17StLN 18-19PhiN	-93	Paris, Tex.		R	R	6'	185	21	30	.412	0	90	48	19	424	435	139	113	5	3.57	139	16	0	.115
Weaver, Harry-Harry A.	15-16PhiA 17-19ChiN	2-26-95	Clarendon, Pa.		R	R	5'11	160	3	6	.333	1	19	8	4	82	82	31	21	1	3.62	22	5	0	.227
Weaver, Orlie-Orville Forest (Buck)	10-11ChiN 11BosN	6- 4-88	Newport, Tenn.	12-28-70	R	R	6'3	180	7	15	.318	0	40	23	7	197	203	116	92	1	5.03	71	8	0	.113
Webb, Lefty-Cleon Earl	10PitN	3- 1-85	Mt. Gilead, Ohio	1-12-58	B	L	5'11	165	2	1	.667	0	7	3	2	27	29	9	6	0	5.67	10	2	0	.200
Weilman (Weilenmann), Carl-Carl Woolworth (Zeke)	12-17StLA 18IL 19-20StLA	11-29-89	Hamilton, Ohio	5-25-24	L	L	6'5	187	85	94	.475	9	240	179	105	1521	1394	418	536	14	2.67	505	86	0	.170
Weimer, Jake-Jacob (Tornado Jake)	03-05ChiN 06-08CinN 09NYN	11-29-73	Ottumwa, Iowa	6-17-28	L	L	5'11	175	97	69	.584	2	191	180	143	1473	1227	493	657	21	2.23	540	115	1	.213
Welch, Ted-Theodore	14StLF	-93			L	R	5'9	160	0	0	–	0	3	0	0	6	6	3	2	0	6.00	1	0	0	.000
West, Hi-James Hiram	05,11CleA	8- 8-84	Roseville, Ill.	5-25-63	R	R	6'	185	4	6	.400	1	19	12	7	98	127	28	32	1	3.86	36	4	0	.111
Weyhing, Gus-August	87-89PhiAA 90BknP 91PhiAA 92-95PhiN 95-PitN 95-96LouN 97VR 98-99WasN 00StLN 00BknN 01CleA 01CinN	9-29-66	Louisville, Ky.	9- 4-55	R	R	5'10	145	266	229	.537	4	538	503	448	4324	4562	1566	1665	28	3.89	1835	308	3	.168
Wheatley, Charlie-Charles	12DetA	6-27-93	Rosedale, Kans.		R	R	5'11	174	0	4	.000	0	5	5	2	35	45	17	14	0	6.17	12	0	0	.000
White, Doc-Guy Harris	01-02PhiN 03-13ChiA	4- 9-79	Washington, D.C.	2-19-69	L	L	6'1	165	190	154	.552	8	427	362	262	3050	2743	670	1384	46	2.38	(See B01-19)			
White, Kirby-Oliver Kirby (Redbuck)	09-10BosN 10-11PitN	1- 3-84	Hillsboro, Ohio	4-22-43	L	R	6'	190	17	25	.405	2	58	44	21	330	294	168	102	3	3.25	103	22	0	.214
White, Steve-Stephen Vincent	12WasA 12BosN	12-21-84	Dorchester, Mass.	1-29-75	R	R	5'10	160	0	0	–	0	4	0	0	7	11	5	3	0	5.14	3	0	0	.000
Whitehouse, Charlie-Charles Evis (Lefty)	14IndF 15NwkF 19WasA	1-25-94	Charleston, Ill.	7-19-60	B	L	6'	152	4	3	.571	0	25	6	3	78	93	28	33	0	4.50	19	0	0	.000
Whiting, Jesse-Jesse W.	02PhiN 06-07BknN								1	2	.333	0	5	3	3	37	42	15	9	1	4.14	15	4	0	.267
Whittaker, Doc-Walter Elton	16PhiA	6-11-94	Chelsea, Mass.	8- 7-65	L	R	5'9	165	0	0	–	0	1	0	0	2	3	2	0	0	4.50	0	0	0	–
Wicker, Bob-Robert Kitridge	01-03StLN 03-06ChiN 06CinN	5-25-78	Lawrence Co., Ind.	1-22-55	R	R	5'11	180	64	55	.538	1	138	117	97	1036	963	293	472	10	2.73	477	98	0	.205
Wiggs, Jimmy-James Alvin (Big Jim)	03CinN 05-06DetA	9- 1-76	Trondheim, Norway	1-20-63	B	R	6'4	200	4	5	.444	0	13	9	4	56	53	38	46	0	3.86	19	3	0	.158
Wilhelm, Kaiser-Irvin Key	03PitN 04-05BosN 08-10BknN 14-15BalF 21,M21-22PhiN	1-26-74	Wooster, Ohio	5-21-36	R	R	6'	162	58	106	.354	5	216	157	118	1432	1495	418	444	12	3.44	507	78	0	.154
Willett, Ed-Robert Edgar	06-13DetA 14-15StLF	3- 7-84	Norfolk, Va.	5-10-34	R	R	6'	183	103	99	.510	6	274	201	138	1773	1719	565	600	12	3.08	652	130	5	.199
Williams, Dave-David Owen	02BosA		Scranton, Pa.		R	L			0	0	–	0	3	0	0	19	22	11	7	0	5.21	9	3	0	.333
Williams, Johnny-John Brodie (Honolulu Johnny)	14DetA	7-16-89	Honolulu, Hawaii	9- 8-63	R	R	6'	180	0	3	.000	0	4	3	1	11	17	5	4	0	6.55	3	0	0	.000
Williams, Lefty-Claud Preston	13-14DetA 16-20ChiA 20DL	3- 9-93	Aurora, Mo.	11- 4-59	R	L	5'9	160	81	47	.633	4	189	151	81	1186	1121	347	515	10	3.13	384	61	0	.159
Williams, Marsh-Marshall McDiarmid (Cap)	16PhiA	2-21-93	Faison, N.C.	2-22-35	R	R	6'2	175	0	6	.000	0	10	4	3	51	71	31	17	0	7.94	19	2	0	.105
Williams, Mutt-David Carter	13-14WasA	7-31-91	Ozark, Ark.	3-30-62	R	R	6'2	185	0	0	–	1	6	1	0	11	9	6	4	0	4.91	2	1	0	.500
Williams, Pop-Walter Merrill	98WasN 02-03ChiN 03PhiN 03BosN	5-19-74	Bowdoinham, Me.	8- 4-59	R	R			16	25	.390	0	46	46	40	377	418	113	127	2	3.20	175	38	0	.217
Williams, Steamboat-Rees Gephardt	14,16StLN	1-31-92	Cascade, Mont.		L	R			6	8	.429	1	41	9	5	116	134	33	27	0	4.42	25	5	0	.200
Willis, Joe-Joseph Denk	11StLA 11-13StLN	4- 9-90	Coal Grove, Ohio	12- 4-66	R	L	6'1	185	4	10	.286	3	41	20	5	161	173	80	66	0	4.61	48	6	0	.125
Willis, Vic-Victor Gazaway	98-05BosN 06-09PitN 10StLN	4-12-76	Iron Hill, Md.	8- 3-47	R	R	6'3	205	243	203	.545	13	513	471	388	3997	3621	1212	1652	50	2.63	1492	248	1	.166
Wilson, Chink-Howard William	06WasA								0	1	.000	0	1	1	1	7	3	2	1	0	2.57	2	0	0	.000
Wilson, Fin-Finis Elbert	14-15BknF	12- 9-89	East Fork, Ky.	3- 9-59	L	L	6'1	185	1	9	.100	0	20	12	6	109	92	64	51	0	4.05	37	12	0	.324
Wilson, George (See George Prentiss)																									
Wilson, Highball-Howard P.	99CleN 02PhiA 03-04WasA		Philadelphia, Pa.	Deceased		R			15	26	.366	0	47	42	37	371	417	71	86	1	3.30	132	26	0	.197
Wilson, John-John Nicodemus (Lefty)	13WasA	6-15-90	Boonsboro, Md.	9-23-54	R	L	6'1	185	0	0	–	0	3	0	0	4	4	3	1	0	4.50	0	0	0	–
Wilson, Pete-Peter Alec	08-09NYA	10- 9-85	Springfield, Mass.	6- 5-57		L			8	9	.471	0	20	18	11	133	109	76	72	2	3.25	47	5	0	.106
Wiltse, Hooks-George LeRoy	04-14NYN 15BknF	9- 7-80	Hamilton, N.Y.	1-21-59	R	L	6'	185	138	90	.605	34	357	226	154	2111	1892	498	965	27	2.48	743	156	2	.210
Wiltse, Snake-Lewis DeWitt	01PitN 01-02PhiA 02BalA 03NYA	12- 5-71	Bouckville, N.Y.	8-25-28	R	L			30	29	.508	2	68	62	54	537	674	146	121	2	4.59	284	79	2	.278
Winchell (Cook), Fred-Frederick Russell	09CleA	1-23-82	Arlington, Mass.	8- 8-58					0	3	.000	1	4	3	0	14	16	2	7	0	6.43	5	1	0	.200
Winham, Lafe-Lafayette Sharkey	02BknN 03PitN	10-23-81	Brooklyn, N.Y.	9-12-51	L	L	5'11	200	3	1	.750	0	6	4	3	39	37	23	23	1	2.08	16	1	0	.063
Winter, George-George Lovington (Sassafras)	01-08BosA 08DetA	4-27-78	New Providence, Pa.	5-26-51		R			81	100	.448	7	220	181	146	1656	1552	377	568	9	2.87	589	114	1	.194
Witherup, Roy-Foster LeRoy	06BosN 08-09WasA	7-26-86	N. Washington, Pa.	12-23-41	R	R	6'	185	4	13	.235	0	26	17	12	162	189	47	71	0	4.44	52	6	0	.115
Wolf, Ernie-Ernest A.	12CleA	2- 2-89	Newark, N.J.	5-23-64	R	R	5'11	174	0	0	–	0	1	0	0	6	8	4	1	0	6.00	2	0	0	.000
Wolfe, Bill-William	02PhiN		Jersey City, N.J.						0	1	.000	0	1	1	1	9	11	4	3	0	4.00	3	1	0	.333
Wolfe, Bill-William O.	03-04NYA 04-06WasA	1- 7-76	Independence, Pa.	2-27-53	R	R			21	36	.368	2	76	62	46	510	484	99	160	4	2.96	172	19	1	.110
Wolfgang, Mellie-Meldon John	14-18ChiA	3-20-90	Albany, N.Y.	6-30-47	R	R	5'9	160	15	14	.517	3	77	27	15	326	268	95	111	3	2.18	103	19	0	.184
Wolter, Harry-Harry Meigs	07PitN 07StLN 09BosA	7-11-84	Monterey, Cal.	7- 7-70	L	L	5'10	175	4	5	.444	1	14	9	1	78	83	48	28	0	4.04	(See B01-19)			
Woods, Clarence-Clarence	14IndF	6-11-92	Ohio Co., Ind.	7- 2-69	R	R	6'5	230	0	0	–	1	2	0	0	2	1	2	1	0	4.50	0	0	0	–
Wood, Joe-Joseph (Smokey Joe)	08-15BosA 16HO 17,19-20CleA	10-25-89	Kansas City, Mo.		R	R	5'11	180	115	57	.669	18	225	158	121	1436	1138	421	989	28	2.03	(See B01-19)			
Woodburn, Gene-Eugene Stewart	11-12StLN	8-20-86	Bellaire, Ohio	1-18-61	R	R	6'	175	2	9	.182	0	31	11	2	86	82	82	48	0	5.55	19	1	0	.053
Woodman, Dan-Daniel Courtenay (Cocoa)	14-15BufF	7- 8-93	Danvers, Mass.	12-14-62	R	R	5'8	160	0	0	–	1	18	1	0	49	44	20	14	0	2.94	11	2	0	.182
Woodward, Frank-Frank Russell	18-19PhiN 19StLN 21-22WasA 23ChiA	5-17-94	New Haven, Conn.	6-11-61	R	R	5'10	175	9	15	.375	1	42	21	8	194	199	74	55	0	4.22	57	9	0	.158
Worden, Fred	14PhiA								0	0	–	0	1	0	0	2	8	0	1	0	18.00	1	0	0	.000
Works, Ralph-Ralph Talmadge (Judge, Big Fellow)	09-12DetA 12-13CinN	3-16-88	Payson, Ill.	8-10-41	R	R	6'2	185	23	24	.489	6	99	49	28	499	512	202	208	4	3.79	175	28	0	.160
Wright, Bob-Robert Cassius	15ChiN	12-13-91	Greensburg, Ind.		R	R	6'1	175	0	0	–	0	2	0	0	4	6	0	3	0	2.25	0	0	0	–
Wright, Clarence-Clarence Eugene	01BknN 02-03CleA 03-04StLA	12-11-78	Cleveland, Ohio	10-29-30	R	R			13	22	.371	1	46	40	31	324	361	152	140	2	4.50	138	23	1	.167
Wright, Lucky-William Simmons (William the Red, Deacon)	09CleA	2-21-80	Tontogany, Ohio	7- 8-41	R	R	6'	178	0	5	.000	0	5	4	3	23	20	8	6	0	3.91	7	0	0	.000
Wyckoff, Weldon-John Weldon	13-16PhiA 16-18BosA	2-19-92	Williamsport, Pa.	5- 8-61	R	R	6'1	175	23	35	.397	4	109	63	35	574	494	357	299	1	3.55	208	31	1	.149
Yeager, Joe-Joseph F. (Little Joe)	98-00BknN 01-03DetA	8-28-75	Philadelphia, Pa.	7- 2-37		R			35	48	.422	2	94	80	73	705	805	188	145	3	3.74	(See B01-19)			
Yerkes, Stan-Stanley (Yank)	01BalA 01-03StLN		Boston, Mass.	7-28-40					15	24	.385	0	45	43	32	320	396	87	103	1	3.66	108	14	0	.130
Yingling, Earl-Earl Hershey (Chink)	11CleA 12-13BknN 14CinN 18WasA	10-29-88	Chillicolthe, Ohio	10- 2-62	L	L	5'11	180	25	35	.417	0	94	61	31	568	611	141	192	5	3.22	270	72	1	.267
Young, Charlie-Charles V.	15BalF	-94	Trenton, N.J.		B	R	5'10	155	2	3	.400	0	9	5	1	35	39	21	13	0	5.91	9	2	0	.222
Young, Cy-Denton True	90-98CleN 99-00StLN 01-08,M07BosA 09-11CleA 11BosN	3-29-67	Gilmore, Ohio	11- 4-55	R	R	6'2	210	511	313	.620	18	906	816	750	7357	7092	1217	2803	77	2.63	2955	629	18	.213
Young, Harley-Harley E. (Cy the Third)	08PitN 08BosN		Kans.			L			0	3	.000	0	14	5	1	76	69	14	29	0	2.61	22	3	0	.136
Young, Irv-Irving Melrose (Young Cy, Cy the Second)	05-08BosN 08PitN 10-11ChiA	7-21-77	Columbia Falls, Me.	1-14-35	L	L	5'10	180	63	94	.401	4	209	161	119	1385	1361	316	560	19	3.11	475	60	0	.126
Yount, Ducky-Herbert Macon	14BalF	12- 7-85	Newton, N.C.	5- 7-70	R	R	6'2	178	1	1	.500	0	13	1	1	41	44	19	19	0	4.17	12	1	0	.083
Zabel, Zip George Washington	13-15ChiN	2-18-91	Wetmore, Kans.	5-31-70	R	R	6'1	185	12	14	.462	3	66	25	10	296	231	130	110	3	2.71	94	11	0	.117
Zackert, George-George Carl	11-12StLN	12-24-84	St. Joseph, Mo.		L	L	6'	177	0	2	.000	0	5	1	0	8	19	7	6	0	12.38	2	0	0	.000
Zamloch, Carl-Carl Eugene	13DetA	10- 6-89	Oakland, Cal.	8-19-63	R	R	6'1	176	1	6	.143	1	17	5	3	70	66	23	28	0	2.44	22	4	0	.182
Zeiser, Matt-Matthew J.	14BosA	9-25-88	Chicago, Ill.		R	R	5'10	170	0	0	–	0	2	0	0	10	9	8	0	0	1.80	3	0	0	.000
Zmich, Ed-Edward Albert (Ike)	10-11StLN	10- 1-84	Cleveland, Ohio	8-20-50	L	L	6'	180	1	5	.167	0	13	6	2	49	46	37	23	0	5.14	17	1	0	.059

1920-1945
Then There Was Ruth, the Yankees, and the Things You Could Count On

The era of baseball marked by the greatest stability the game has ever known, was ushered in by the ouster of eight Chicago White Sox players. Their exile from the diamonds of professional baseball came as a result of their throwing the 1919 World Series to the Cincinnati Reds. The man responsible for the punishment was Judge Kennesaw Mountain Landis, baseball's first commissioner.

Landis was appointed in 1920, the year the scandal broke. Although his stern actions helped restore the public's confidence, it served only half a measure in preserving the good name of the sport. What the public needed most was a hero of fantasy proportions—a knight who could enter the hallowed grounds of major league baseball and destroy the evil with one stab of his mighty lance, someone to cleanse the tarnished name while setting the turnstiles into a frenzied motion. But a knight did not come. Instead, it was a king. They dubbed him the Sultan of Swat and he honored the sobriquet by belting home runs at an unprecidented clip.

The Sultan, the Bambino, the Babe, was George Herman Ruth, who came from the Boston Red Sox to the New York Yankees in 1920 for the tidy sum of $125,000. Ruth's life style and power not only renewed the public's enthusiasm, but set an entirely new strategy in motion. Aided by a livelier ball, Ruth hit 54 home runs during his first season in New York, an unthinkable amount when compared to the 29 he poled the year before, which had then set the all-time single season's mark.

Along with Ruth came the New York Yankees, who had lingered in the depths of the second division for most of their existence in the American League. It wasn't until 1921 that they collected their first pennant in the beginning of what was to be the most successful dynasty in baseball history. Yet beyond the Yankees and Ruth himself, was the influence of the home run ball. Its affects produced a profound change in the style of the game. The emphasis, especially in the American League where power hitters abounded, moved away from bunting and stealing, mostly because of such men as Lou Gehrig, Joe DiMaggio, Hank Greenberg, Jimmie Foxx, Al Simmons, and Ted Williams, a marvelous collection of super heroes who accounted for over 2500 home runs.

The advent of power hitting did more than alter the face of the game. With its coming was the imbalance that is inevitable with such a drastic change. Those who paid the heaviest price were baseball's minority breed, the pitcher. Once a feared and revered figure, he became the object of many a cannon blast. At the same time as baseball had cleansed its ranks of those who soiled the good name of the game, it also saw fit to sanitize the batter-pitcher relationship. The spitball, the most famous of all trick pitches, was abolished in 1920, although a few pitchers were still allowed to use it. To further complicate the pitcher's life, new balls were introduced into play sooner to give the batter an advantage he had never enjoyed. Following these demoralizing blows to the mound corps came the new stadiums, built between 1909 and 1923 in such places as Detroit, St. Louis, Brooklyn, and New York. All of these stadiums were enclosed with distances to tempt the most mediocre of power hitters.

The combination of the livelier ball and easier home run barriers gave the pitcher an entirely different set of stragegies. Instead of finding all batters choking up and waiting to punch the ball where they could, the pitcher was faced with some players starting to swing up and go for the long ball, as well as trying to pull nearly everything that was offered across the plate. To say the least, it was not a happy time for those trying to eke out a living atop a mound of dirt. To add insult to injury, men such as Dale Alexander and Zeke Bonura, who would have been denied entrance to the major leagues during earlier days, suddenly found themselves in major league uniforms because of their ability to merely hit a baseball.

With the pitcher reduced to a more subdued role and with the sudden infusion of power, baseball emerged into the more rampant pace of the twentieth century. More accurately, it joined the exaggerated motion of the Roaring Twenties. As baseball began churning out its greatest stars, attendance swelled and salaries began to spiral to add to the growing aura of the sport, while at the same time lifting the average ballplayer to first class citizenry. Of course, no one equalled the money which Ruth earned. In his heyday he made $80,000 a season—a staggering amount considering low taxes and the depression. But while Ruth's salary symbolized the emergence of the Yankees as a structure of power and money, it by no means typified the economics of the times. The chemistry of Ruth and the Yankees was simply that perfect mixture which nature seems to produce once in every century.

Although not as dramatic and as sudden in coming as Ruth, was another occurrence that was to have a more lasting effect on the game of baseball. In the 1920's, Branch Rickey, general manager of the St. Louis Cardinals, established a string of farm clubs where young and inexpensively signed St. Louis talent could be nurtured. Rickey, in effect, had created St. Louis' own minor league system, and it was successful enough to not only produce Stan Musial, one of the greatest players the National League was to ever have, but also to give the Cardinals a dynasty that was nearly as successful as the Yankees. Rickey later made the same contribution to the Brooklyn Dodgers—an influence that soon changed the way all ball clubs acquired most of their new players.

1920—1945 SINGLE SEASON LEADERS

BATTING

Batting Average

1	Rogers Hornsby-St.L. (N)	1924	.424
2	George Sisler-St.L. (A)	1922	.420
3	George Sisler-St.L. (A)	1920	.407
4	Ted Williams-Bos. (A)	1941	.406
5	Rogers Hornsby-St.L. (N)	1925	.403
	Harry Heilmann-Det. (A)	1923	.403
7	Rogers Hornsby-St.L. (N)	1922	.401
	Bill Terry-N.Y. (N)	1930	.401
	Ty Cobb-Det. (A)	1922	.401
10	Lefty O'Doul-Phi. (N)	1929	.398
	Harry Heilman-Det. (A)	1927	.398

Hits

1	George Sisler-St.L. (A)	1920	257
2	Lefty O'Doul-Phi. (N)	1929	254
	Bill Terry-N.Y. (N)	1930	254
4	Al Simmons-Phi. (A)	1925	253
5	Rogers Hornsby-St.L. (N)	1922	250
	Chuck Klein-Phi. (N)	1930	250
7	George Sisler-St.L. (A)	1922	246
8	Heinie Manush-St.L. (A)	1928	241
	Babe Herman-Bkn. (N)	1930	241
10	Harry Heilmann-Det. (A)	1921	237
	Paul Waner-Pit. (N)	1927	237
	Joe Medwick-St.L. (N)	1937	237

Slugging Average

1	Babe Ruth-N.Y. (A)	1920	.847
2	Babe Ruth-N.Y. (A)	1921	.846
3	Babe Ruth-N.Y. (A)	1927	.772
4	Lou Gehrig-N.Y. (A)	1927	.765
5	Babe Ruth-N.Y. (A)	1923	.764
6	Rogers Hornsby-St.L. (N)	1925	.756
7	Jimmie Foxx-Phi. (A)	1932	.749
8	Babe Ruth-N.Y. (A)	1924	.739
9	Babe Ruth-N.Y. (A)	1926	.737
10	Ted Williams-Bos. (A)	1941	.735

Doubles

1	Earl Webb-Bos. (A)	1931	67
2	George Burns-Cle. (A)	1926	64
	Joe Medwick-St.L. (N)	1936	64
4	Hank Greenberg-Det. (A)	1934	63
5	Paul Waner-Pit. (N)	1932	62
6	Charlie Gehringer-Det. (A)	1936	60
7	Tris Speaker-Cle. (A)	1923	59
	Chuck Klein-Phi. (N)	1930	59
9	Billy Herman-Chi. (N)	1935	57
	Billy Herman-Chi. (N)	1936	57

Runs Batted In

1	Hack Wilson-Chi. (N)	1930	190
2	Lou Gehrig-N.Y. (A)	1931	184
3	Hank Greenberg-Det. (A)	1937	183
4	Lou Gehrig-N.Y. (A)	1927	175
	Jimmie Foxx-Bos. (A)	1938	175
6	Lou Gehrig-N.Y. (A)	1930	174
7	Babe Ruth-N.Y. (A)	1921	171
8	Chuck Klein-Phi. (N)	1930	170
	Hank Greenberg-Det. (A)	1935	170
10	Jimmie Foxx-Phi. (A)	1932	169

Triples

1	Kiki Cuyler-Pit. (N)	1925	26
2	Earl Combs-N.Y. (A)	1927	23
	Adam Comorosky-Pit. (N)	1930	23
4	Hy Myers-Bkn. (N)	1920	22
	Jake Daubert-Cin. (N)	1922	22
	Paul Waner-Pit. (N)	1926	22
	Earle Combs-N.Y. (A)	1930	22
	Snuffy Stirnweiss-N.Y. (A)	1945	22
9	Edd Roush-Cin. (N)	1924	21
	Earle Combs-N.Y. (A)	1928	21

Runs

1	Babe Ruth-N.Y. (A)	1921	177
2	Lou Gehrig-N.Y. (A)	1936	167
3	Babe Ruth-N.Y. (A)	1928	163
	Lou Gehrig-N.Y. (A)	1931	163
5	Babe Ruth-N.Y. (A)	1920	158
	Babe Ruth-N.Y. (A)	1927	158
	Chuck Klein-Phi. (N)	1930	158
8	Rogers Hornsby-Chi. (N)	1929	156
9	Kiki Cuyler-Chi. (N)	1930	155
10	Lefty O'Doul-Phi. (N)	1929	152
	Woody English-Chi. (N)	1930	152
	Al Simmons-Phi. (A)	1930	152
	Chuck Klein-Phi. (N)	1932	152

Home Runs

1	Babe Ruth-N.Y. (A)	1927	60
2	Babe Ruth-N.Y. (A)	1921	59
3	Jimmie Foxx-Phi. (A)	1932	58
	Hank Greenberg-Det. (A)	1938	58
5	Hack Wilson-Chi. (N)	1930	56
6	Babe Ruth-N.Y. (A)	1920	54
	Babe Ruth-N.Y. (A)	1928	54
8	Jimmie Foxx-Bos. (A)	1938	50
9	Babe Ruth-N.Y. (A)	1930	49
	Lou Gehrig-N.Y. (A)	1934	49
	Lou Gehrig-N.Y. (A)	1936	49

Bases on Balls

1	Babe Ruth-N.Y. (A)	1923	170
2	Babe Ruth-N.Y. (A)	1920	148
	Eddie Stanky-St.L. (N)	1945	148
4	Ted Williams-Bos. (A)	1941	145
	Ted Williams-Bos. (A)	1942	145
6	Babe Ruth-N.Y. (A)	1921	144
	Babe Ruth-N.Y. (A)	1926	144
8	Babe Ruth-N.Y. (A)	1924	142
9	Babe Ruth-N.Y. (A)	1927	138
10	Babe Ruth-N.Y. (A)	1930	136

Stolen Bases

1	Sam Rice-Was. (A)	1920	63
2	Ben Chapman-N.Y. (A)	1931	61
	George Case-Was. (A)	1943	61
4	Wally Moses-Chi. (A)	1943	56
5	Snuffy Stirnweiss-N.Y. (A)	1944	55
6	Max Carey-Pit. (N)	1920	52
7	Max Carey-Pit. (N)	1922	51
	George Sisler-St.L. (A)	1922	51
	Max Carey-Pit. (N)	1923	51
	George Case-Was. (A)	1939	51

Strikeouts

1	Vince DiMaggio-Bos. (N)	1938	134
2	Chet Ross-Bos. (N)	1940	127
3	Vince DiMaggio-Pit. (N)	1943	126
4	Jimmie Foxx-Bos. (A)	1936	119
5	Dolph Camilli-Bkn. (N)	1941	115
6	Dolph Camilli-Phi. (N)	1935	113
7	Vince DiMaggio-Bos. (N)	1937	111
8	Dolph Camilli-Bkn. (N)	1939	107
9	Frankie Crosetti-N.Y. (A)	1937	105
	Chet Laabs-St.L. (A)	1943	105

At Bats

1	Woody Jensen-Pit. (N)	1936	696
2	Lloyd Waner-Pit. (N)	1931	681
	Jo-Jo Moore-N.Y. (N)	1935	681
4	Rabbit Maranville-Pit. (N)	1922	672
5	Jack Tobin-St.L. (A)	1921	671
6	Al Simmons-Phi. (A)	1932	670
7	Buddy Lewis-Was. (A)	1937	668
8	Billy Herman-Chi. (N)	1935	666
9	Taylor Douthit-St.L. (N)	1930	664
10	Lloyd Waner-Pit. (N)	1929	662

PITCHING

Wins

1	Jim Bagby-Cle. (A)	1920	31
	Lefty Grove-Phi. (A)	1931	31
3	Dizzy Dean-St.L. (N)	1934	30
4	Hal Newhouser-Det. (A)	1944	29
5	Dazzy Vance-Bkn. (N)	1924	28
	Lefty Grove-Phi. (A)	1930	28
	Dizzy Dean-St.L. (N)	1935	28
8	Pete Alexander-Chi. (N)	1920	27
	Carl Mays-N.Y. (A)	1921	27
	Urban Schocker-St.L. (A)	1921	27
	Eddie Rommel-Phi. (A)	1922	27
	Dolf Luque-Cin. (N)	1923	27
	George Uhle-Cle. (A)	1926	27
	Bucky Walters-Cin. (N)	1939	27
	Bob Feller-Cle. (A)	1940	27
	Dizzy Trout-Det. (A)	1944	27

Winning Percentage

1	Johnny Allen-Cle. (A)	1937	.938
2	Freddie Fitzsimmons-Bkn. (N)	1940	.889
3	Lefty Grove-Phi. (A)	1931	.886
4	Lefty Grove-Phi. (A)	1930	.848
5	Emil Yde-Pit. (N)	1924	.842
	Schoolboy Rowe-Det. (A)	1940	.842
7	Lefty Gomez-N.Y. (A)	1934	.839
8	Spud Chandler-N.Y. (A)	1943	.833
9	Elmer Riddle-Cin. (N)	1941	.826
10	Dazzy Vance-Bkn. (N)	1924	.824

Losses

1	Paul Derringer-St.L. + Cin. (N)	1933	23
2	Scott Perry-Phi. (A)	1920	25
	Red Ruffing-Bos. (A)	1928	25
	Ben Cantwell-Bos. (N)	1935	25
5	Pat Caraway-Chi. (A)	1931	24
	Sam Gray-St.L. (A)	1931	24
7	Rollie Naylor-Phi. (A)	1920	22
	Eddie Rommel-Phi. (A)	1921	23
	Dolf Luque-Cin. (N)	1922	23
10	Eppa Rixey-Phi. (N)	1920	22
	Red Ruffing-Bos. (A)	1929	22
	Si Johnson-Cin. (N)	1934	22
	Hugh Mulcahy-Phi. (N)	1940	22

E.R.A.

1	Spud Chandler-N.Y. (A)	1943	1.64
2	Carl Hubbell-N.Y. (N)	1933	1.66
3	Howie Pollet-St.L. (N)	1943	1.75
4	Mort Cooper-St.L. (N)	1942	1.77
5	Hal Newhouser-Det. (A)	1945	1.81
6	Larry French-Bkn. (N)	1942	1.82
7	Max Lanier-St.L. (N)	1943	1.90
8	Pete Alexander-Chi. (N)	1920	1.91
9	Dolf Luque-Cin. (N)	1923	1.93
10	Lon Warneke-Chi. (N)	1933	2.01

Saves

1	Firpo Marberry-Was. (A)	1926	22
2	Johnny Murphy-N.Y. (A)	1939	19
3	Clint Brown-Chi. (A)	1937	18
	Clint Brown-Chi. (A)	1939	18
5	Al Benton-Det. (A)	1940	17
6	Firpo Marberry-Was. (A)	1924	15
	Firpo Marberry-Was. (A)	1925	15
	Jack Quinn-Bkn. (N)	1931	15
	Johnny Murphy-N.Y. (A)	1941	15
	Ace Adams-N.Y. (N)	1945	15
	Andy Karl-Phi. (N)	1945	15

Bases on Balls

1	Bob Feller-Cle. (A)	1938	208
2	Bob Feller-Cle. (A)	1941	194
3	Bobo Newsom-St.L (A)	1938	192
4	Bump Hadley-Chi. + St.L. (A)	1932	171
5	Bobo Newsom-Was. + Bos. (A)	1937	167
6	Johnny Vander Meer-Cin. (N)	1943	162
7	Dixie Davis-St.L. (A)	1920	149
	Bobo Newsom-St.L. (A)	1934	149
9	Vern Kennedy-Chi. (A)	1936	147
10	Bob Feller-Cle. (A)	1939	143

Games Pitched

1	Ace Adams-N.Y. (N)	1943	70
2	Andy Karl-Phi. (N)	1945	67
3	Ace Adams-N.Y. (N)	1944	65
	Ace Adams-N.Y. (N)	1945	65
5	Firpo Marberry-Was. (A)	1926	64
6	Joe Heving-Cle. (A)	1944	63
7	Clint Brown-Chi. (A)	1939	61
	Ace Adams-N.Y. (N)	1942	61
9	Garland Braxton-Was. (A)	1927	59
10	Russ Van Atta-N.Y. + St.L. (A)	1935	58

Strikeouts

1	Dazzy Vance-Bkn. (N)	1924	262
2	Bob Feller-Cle. (A)	1940	261
3	Bob Feller-Cle. (A)	1941	260
4	Bob Feller-Cle. (A)	1939	246
5	Bob Feller-Cle. (A)	1938	240
6	Van Lingle Mungo-Bkn. (N)	1936	238
7	Bobo Newsom-St.L. (A)	1938	226
8	Dazzy Vance-Bkn. (N)	1925	221
9	Hal Newhouser-Det. (A)	1945	212
10	Lefty Grove-Phi. (A)	1930	209

Games Started

1	George Uhle-Cle. (A)	1923	44
2	Bill Voiselle-N.Y. (N)	1944	41
3	Pete Alexander-Chi. (N)	1920	40
	Stan Coveleski-Cle. (A)	1921	40
	George Uhle-Cle. (A)	1922	40
	George Casper-Phi. (A)	1938	40
	Bobo Newsom-St.L. (A)	1938	40
	Bob Feller-Cle. (A)	1941	40
	Dizzy Trout-Det. (A)	1944	40
10	39 starts=9 times by 8 men		

Shutouts

1	Carl Hubbell-N.Y. (N)	1933	10
	Mort Cooper.St.L. (N)	1942	10
3	Bill Lee-Chi. (N)	1938	9
4	Babe Adams-Pit. (N)	1920	8
	Hal Newhouser-Det. (A)	1945	8
6	Pete Alexander-Chi. (N)	1920	7
	Hal Schumacher-N.Y. (N)	1933	7
	Dizzy Dean-St.L. (N)	1934	7
	Whit Wyatt-Bkn. (N)	1941	7
	Hi Bithorn-Chi. (N)	1943	7
	Mort Cooper-St.L. (N)	1944	7
	Dizzy Trout-Det. (A)	1944	7

Complete Games

1	Pete Alexander-Chi. (N)	1920	33
	Burleigh Grimes-Bkn. (N)	1923	33
	Dizzy Trout-Det. (A)	1944	33
4	Red Faber-Chi. (A)	1921	32
	George Uhle-Cle. (A)	1926	32
6	Urban Shocker-St.L. (A)	1921	31
	Red Faber-Chi. (A)	1922	31
	Wes Ferrell-Bos. (A)	1935	31
	Bobo Newsom-St.L. (A)	1938	31
	Bucky Walters-Cin. (N)	1939	31
	Bob Feller-Cle. (A)	1940	31

Innings Pitched

1	Pete Alexander-Chi. (N)	1920	363
2	George Uhle-Cle. (A)	1923	358
3	Red Faber-Chi. (A)	1922	353
4	Dizzy Trout-Det. (A)	1944	352
5	Urban Shocker-St.L. (A)	1922	348
6	Bob Feller-Cle. (A)	1941	343
7	Jim Bagby-Cle. (A)	1920	340
8	Carl Mays-N.Y. (A)	1921	337
9	Red Faber-Chi. (A)	1921	331
	Burleigh Grimes-Pit. (N)	1928	331

1920-1945 PERIOD LEADERS

BATTING

Batting Average
(Minimum 1000 Games or 4000 At Bats)

1	Rogers Hornsby	1920-37	.374
2	Harry Heilmann	1920-32	.361
3	Ty Cobb	1920-28	.357
4	Al Simmons	*1924-44	.355
5	Tris Speaker	1920-28	.354
6	Babe Ruth	1920-35	.347
7	Eddie Collins	1920-30	.346
8	George Sisler	1920-30	.344
9	Bill Terry	*1923-36	.341
10	Lou Gehrig	*1923-39	.340

Hits

1	Paul Waner	*1926-45	3152
2	Al Simmons	*1924-44	2927
3	Mel Ott	1926-45	2871
4	Charlie Gehringer	*1924-42	2839
5	Frankie Frisch	1920-37	2837
6	Goose Goslin	*1921-38	2735
7	Lou Gehrig	*1923-39	2721
8	Jimmie Foxx	*1925-45	2646
9	Doc Cramer	1929-45	2603
10	Sam Rice	1920-34	2561

Slugging Average
(Minimum 1000 Games or 4000 At Bats)

1	Babe Ruth	1920-35	.708
2	Lou Gehrig	*1923-39	.632
3	Rogers Hornsby	1920-37	.621
4	Jimmie Foxx	*1925-45	.609
5	Hank Greenberg	1930-45	.602
6	Harry Heilmann	1920-32	.558
7	Ken Williams	1920-29	.547
8	Hack Wilson	*1923-34	.545
9	Chuck Klein	*1928-44	.543
10	Mel Ott	1926-45	.536

Home Runs

1	Babe Ruth	1920-35	665
2	Jimmie Foxx	*1925-45	534
3	Mel Ott	1926-45	510
4	Lou Gehrig	*1923-39	493
5	Al Simmons	*1924-44	307
6	Chuck Klein	*1928-44	300
7	Bob Johnson	*1933-45	288
8	Rogers Hornsby	1920-37	274
9	Hank Greenberg	1930-45	262
10	Goose Goslin	*1921-38	248

Runs Batted In

1	Lou Gehrig	*1923-39	1991
2	Babe Ruth	1920-35	1982
3	Jimmie Foxx	*1925-45	1921
4	Mel Ott	1926-45	1856
5	Al Simmons	*1924-44	1827
6	Goose Goslin	*1921-38	1609
7	Charlie Gehringer	*1924-42	1427
8	Joe Cronin	*1926-45	1423
9	Jim Bottomley	*1922-37	1422
10	Joe Medwick	1932-45	1335

Triples

1	Paul Waner	*1926-45	190
2	Goose Goslin	*1921-38	173
3	Sam Rice	1920-34	165
4	Pie Traynor	*1920-37	164
5	Lou Gehrig	*1923-39	162
6	Heinie Manush	*1923-39	160
7	Kiki Cuyler	*1921-38	157
8	Earle Combs	*1924-35	154
9	Jim Bottomley	*1922-37	151
10	Al Simmons	*1924-44	149

Runs

1	Babe Ruth	1920-35	1972
2	Lou Gehrig	*1923-39	1888
3	Mel Ott	1926-45	1857
4	Charlie Gehringer	*1924-42	1774
5	Jimmie Foxx	*1925-45	1751
6	Paul Waner	*1926-45	1626
7	Frankie Frisch	1920-37	1511
8	Al Simmons	*1924-44	1507
9	Goose Goslin	*1921-38	1483
10	Sam Rice	1920-34	1328

Doubles

1	Paul Waner	*1926-45	603
2	Charlie Gehringer	*1924-42	574
3	Al Simmons	*1924-44	539
4	Lou Gehrig	*1923-39	535
5	Joe Medwick	1932-45	524
6	Joe Cronin	*1926-45	514
7	Goose Goslin	*1921-38	500
8	Heinie Manush	*1923-39	491
9	Mel Ott	1926-45	487
10	Jim Bottomley	*1922-37	465

Bases on Balls

1	Babe Ruth	1920-35	1867
2	Mel Ott	1926-45	1700
3	Lou Gehrig	*1923-39	1510
4	Jimmie Foxx	*1925-45	1452
5	Charlie Gehringer	*1924-42	1185
6	Max Bishop	*1924-35	1153
7	Lu Blue	*1921-33	1092
8	Paul Waner	*1926-45	1091
9	Bob Johnson	*1933-45	1073
10	Harlond Clift	*1934-45	1070

Stolen Bases

1	Frankie Frisch	1920-37	404
2	Max Carey	1920-29	346
3	Kike Cuyler	*1921-38	328
4	George Case	1937-45	316
5	Ben Chapman	1930-45	287
6	Sam Rice	1920-34	285
7	Gee Walker	*1931-45	223
8	George Sisler	1920-30	221
9	Charlie Gehringer	*1924-42	181
10	Eddie Collins	1920-30	180

Strikeouts

1	Jimmie Foxx	*1925-45	1311
2	Babe Ruth	1920-35	1146
3	Dolf Camilli	*1933-45	961
4	Mel Ott	1926-45	881
5	Tony Lazzeri	*1926-39	864
6	Bob Johnson	*1933-45	851
7	Vince DiMaggio	1937-45	825
8	Jimmy Dykes	1920-39	806
9	Frankie Crosetti	1932-45	789
10	Lou Gehrig	*1923-39	788

*—Entire major league career

PITCHING

Wins

1	Lefty Grove	*1925-41	300
2	Red Ruffing	1924-45	265
3	Ted Lyons	1923-42	259
4	Carl Hubbell	*1920-43	253
5	Burleigh Grimes	1920-34	236
6	Waite Hoyt	1920-38	233
7	Paul Derringer	*1931-45	223
8	Earl Whitehill	*1923-39	218
9	Freddie Fitzsimmons	*1925-43	217
10	Mel Harder	1928-45	212

Winning Percentage
(Minimum 100 Wins)

1	Lefty Grove	*1925-41	.680
2	Mort Cooper	1938-45	.675
3	Bob Feller	1936-45	.663
4	Johnny Allen	*1932-44	.654
5	Lefty Gomez	*1930-43	.649
6	Dizzy Dean	1930-41	.644
7	Carl Mays	1920-29	.636
8	Ray Kremer	*1924-33	.627
9	Urban Shocker	1920-28	.627
10	Firpo Marberry	*1923-36	.623

Losses

1	Ted Lyons	1923-42	226
2	Red Ruffing	1924-45	219
3	Paul Derringer	*1931-45	212
4	Bobo Newsom	1929-45	189
5	Tom Zachary	1920-36	186
6	Earl Whitehill	*1923-39	185
7	Sad Sam Jones	1920-35	181
8	Mel Harder	1928-45	178
9	Waite Hoyt	1920-38	176
10	Burleigh Grimes	1920-34	173

Earned Run Average
(Minimum 1500 Innings Pitched or 100 Wins)

1	Mort Cooper	1938-45	2.80
2	Carl Hubbell	*1928-43	2.98
3	Dizzy Dean	1930-41	3.05
4	Lefty Grove	*1925-41	3.06
5	G.C. "Pete" Alexander	1920-30	3.09
6	Bob Feller	1936-45	3.15
7	Lon Warneke	*1930-45	3.18
8	Bucky Walters	1934-45	3.21
9	Dazzy Vance	1922-35	3.22
10	Dolf Luque	1920-35	3.24

Saves

1	Firpo Marberry	*1923-36	101
2	John Murphy	1932-43	97
3	Clint Brown	*1928-42	64
4	Joe Heving	*1930-45	63
5	Lefty Grove	*1925-41	55
6	Jack Quinn	1920-33	52
	Waite Hoyt	1920-38	52
8	Ace Adams	1941-45	49
	Wilcy Moore	*1927-33	49
10	Mace Brown	1935-43	47

Strikeouts

1	Lefty Grove	*1925-41	2266
2	Dazzy Vance	1922-35	2027
3	Red Ruffing	1924-45	1957
4	Bobo Newsom	1929-45	1834
5	Carl Hubbell	*1928-43	1677
6	Tommy Bridges	1930-45	1657
7	Paul Derringer	*1931-45	1507
8	Lefty Gomez	*1930-43	1468
9	Charlie Root	*1923-41	1459
10	Earl Whitehill	*1923-39	1350

Games Pitched

1	Waite Hoyt	1920-38	661
2	Charlie Root	*1923-41	632
3	Lefty Grove	*1925-41	616
4	Red Ruffing	1924-45	607
5	Ted Lyons	1923-42	589
6	Paul Derringer	*1931-45	579
7	Larry French	*1929-42	570
8	Mel Harder	1928-45	554
	Jesse Haines	1920-37	554
10	Firpo Marberry	*1923-36	551

Shutouts

1	Red Ruffing	1924-45	43
2	Larry French	*1929-42	40
3	Bucky Walters	1934-45	38
4	Carl Hubbell	*1928-43	36
5	Lefty Grove	*1925-41	32
	Paul Derringer	*1931-45	32
	Tommy Bridges	1930-45	32
8	Lon Warneke	*1930-45	31
9	Dazzy Vance	1922-35	30
	Freddie Fitzsimmons	1925-43	30

Games Started

1	Red Ruffing	1924-45	519
2	Ted Lyons	1923-42	479
3	Earl Whitehill	*1923-39	473
4	Lefty Grove	*1925-41	457
5	Paul Derringer	*1931-45	445
6	Carl Hubbell	*1928-43	431
7	Freddie Fitzsimmons	*1925-43	426
8	Sad Sam Jones	1920-35	425
9	Burleigh Grimes	1920-34	424
10	Bobo Newsom	1929-45	413

Innings Pitched

1	Red Ruffing	1924-45	4228
2	Ted Lyons	1923-42	4119
3	Lefty Grove	*1925-41	3940
4	Waite Hoyt	1920-38	3656
5	Paul Derringer	*1931-45	3646
6	Carl Hubbell	*1928-43	3591
7	Earl Whitehill	*1923-39	3563
8	Burleigh Grimes	1920-34	3486
9	Sad Sam Jones	1920-35	3263
10	Mel Harder	1928-45	3254

Complete Games

1	Ted Lyons	1923-42	351
2	Red Ruffing	1924-45	330
3	Lefty Grove	*1925-41	300
4	Burleigh Grimes	1920-34	270
5	Carl Hubbell	*1928-43	260
6	Paul Derringer	*1931-45	251
7	Wes Ferrell	*1927-41	227
	Earl Whitehill	*1923-39	227
9	Bobo Newsom	1929-45	220
	Waite Hoyt	1920-38	220

Complete Game Percentage
(Complete Games as a percentage of Games Started – minimum 175 Games Started)

1	Ted Lyons	1923-42	73.3
2	Wes Ferrell	*1927-41	70.3
3	Jim Tobin	*1937-45	68.7
4	Wilbur Cooper	1920-26	68.0
5	Red Lucas	*1923-38	67.8
6	Bob Feller	1936-45	67.4
7	Dizzy Dean	1930-41	67.2
8	G.C. "Pete" Alexander	1920-30	66.8
9	Carl Mays	1920-29	66.0
10	Lefty Grove	*1925-41	65.6

1920 Here Come De Judge

The cheers and heroics of the 1920 season were overshadowed by the sordid and the tragic, and off-the-field developments elicited more interest from the public than did the actual playing; indeed, courtroom revelations made it debatable whether baseball contests deserved any serious following at all. Rumors had drifted about since the past autumn that some members of the Chicago White Sox had been bought by gamblers to throw the 1919 World Series and in September a Chicago grand jury hung baseball's dirty laundry out for an airing. Confessions from Ed Cicotte and Joe Jackson confirmed that Cicotte, Jackson, Lefty Williams, Chick Gandil, Swede Risberg, Fred McMullin, and Happy Felsch had, indeed, agreed to dump the Series in return for $100,000 from New York gambling interests, of which only $20,000 was delivered and that Buck Weaver had, at least, concealed his knowledge of the fix. The shock wave hit the National Pastime with many repercussions. The most immediate result was the suspension of the soiled Sox by Chicago owner Charles Comiskey, thus ruining his club's pennant chances for 1920 in a close title race with the Cleveland Indians. Another revelation stemming from the grand jury was that three National League players, Hal Chase, Heinie Zimmerman, and Lee Magee, had been barred after the 1919 season, without publicity, for throwing games; indeed, Chase was exposed as a major go-between in the Series fix.

A less immediate result of the scandal was the reorganization of baseball's government. The office of Commissioner was created and Judge Kenesaw M. Landis of Chicago was appointed to fill it at a salary of $42,500 yearly. To take the position, Landis demanded and received strong discretionary powers. He proved uncompromising and despotic, but provided a stern paternal image for the game.

Tragedy descended onto the ball field August 16, at the Polo Grounds in New York. Yankee pitcher Carl Mays had a reputation for brushing batters back, but a fast ball that eluded him skulled Cleveland's Ray Chapman, leaving him a limp figure in the dust and lime around home plate. Without regaining consciousness, Chapman died the next day—the first and only fatality of major league baseball.

Cleveland's morale sunk to zero after shortstop Chapman's death, but Manager Tris Speaker proved magnificent at rallying his men together. A close fight with the White Sox and Yankees was won in September by the Indians when shortstop Joe Sewell and pitcher Walter Mails were recalled and chipped in with key performances. The Sox stayed close all year, despite dissension between "honest" and "crooked" players, and might have won it again, to the embarrassment of all baseball, had not stars, Jackson, Weaver, Felsch, Cicotte, and Williams been exposed by the grand jury and thrown off the team with only two weeks remaining in the season.

The disgrace of the Black Sox scandal was softened by the unprecedented power of Babe Ruth's bat, aided my a much livelier ball. In 1919, the New York Yankees shelled out $177,500 to the money-poor Red Sox for Ruth and Carl Mays—obtaining Mays during that season and Ruth in the winter. Mays, despite the Chapman tragedy, led New York pitchers in 1920 with 26 wins, while Ruth, now a full-time outfielder, found the Polo Grounds cozy enough to clout 54 round-trippers, an outrageous total that surpassed any one team's total output—setting a homer record which few expected ever to be equalled. But the new infusion of talent could not better the Yankees' third-place 1919 finish. Their one consolation was a closer pennant loss and the optimism that they would dominate the future.

Bothered by a bad knee, Ty Cobb gave up his batting title to young George Sisler of St. Louis. Prophetically though, Cobb's remaining nine years, which would be good enough to be desired by any ball player, would never again produce a batting title.

Brooklyn won the National League pennant behind good pitching aced by spitballer Burleigh Grimes. Wilbert Robinson's Dodgers beat out the Giants by seven games for the top spot, but dropped the Series to the Indians in another five-of-nine classic. Cleveland needed only seven games to claim the crown.

Led by Stan Coveleski's three route-going victory pitching performances, Bill Wambsganss' unassisted triple play—the only one in Series history, and Elmer Smith's grand slam—the first in Series history, the door on baseball's greatest season of extremes was finally closed.

1920 AMERICAN LEAGUE

NAME	G by POS	B	AGE	G	AB	R	H	2B	3B	HR	RBI	BB	SO	SB	BA	SA
CLEVELAND 1st 98-56 .636		**TRIS SPEAKER**														
TOTALS			29	154	5196	**857**	1574	**300**	**95**	35	**758**	**576**	379	73	.303	.417
Doc Johnston	1B147	L	32	147	535	68	156	24	10	2	71	28	32	13	.292	.385
Bill Wambsganss	2B153	R	26	153	565	83	138	16	11	1	55	54	26	9	.244	.317
Ray Chapman (KB)	SS111	R	29	111	435	97	132	27	8	3	49	52	38	13	.303	.423
Larry Gardner	3B154	L	34	154	597	72	185	31	11	3	118	53	25	3	.310	.414
Elmer Smith	OF129	L	27	129	456	82	144	37	10	12	103	53	35	5	.316	.520
Tris Speaker	OF149	L	32	150	552	137	214	**50**	11	8	107	97	13	10	.388	.562
Charlie Jamieson	OF98, 1B4	L	27	108	370	69	118	17	7	1	40	41	26	2	.319	.411
Steve O'Neill	C148	R	28	149	489	63	157	39	5	3	55	69	39	3	.321	.440
Jack Graney	OF47	L	34	62	152	31	45	11	1	0	13	27	21	4	.296	.382
Smokey Joe Wood	OF54, P1	R	30	61	137	25	37	11	2	1	30	25	16	1	.270	.401
Joe Evans	OF43, SS6	R	25	56	172	32	60	9	9	0	23	15	3	6	.349	.506
2 George Burns	1B12	R	27	44	56	7	15	4	1	0	13	4	3	1	.268	.375
Les Nunamaker	C17, 1B6	R	31	34	54	10	18	3	3	0	14	4	5	1	.333	.500
Harry Lunte	SS21, 2B3	R	27	23	71	6	14	0	0	0	7	5	6	0	.197	.197
Joe Sewell	SS22	L	21	22	70	14	23	4	1	0	12	9	4	1	.329	.414
Pinch Thomas	C7	L	32	9	9	2	3	1	0	0	0	3	1	0	.333	.444
Joe Harris (DO) 29																
CHICAGO 2nd 96-58 .623 2		**KID GLEASON**														
TOTALS			29	154	5330	794	1569	267	94	37	702	473	355	111	.294	.401
Shano Collins	1B117, OF12	R	34	133	495	70	150	21	10	1	63	23	24	12	.303	.392
Eddie Collins	2B153	L	33	153	601	115	222	37	13	3	75	69	19	19	.369	.489
Swede Risberg (DL)	SS124	R	25	126	458	53	122	21	10	2	65	31	45	12	.266	.369
Buck Weaver (DL)	3B126, SS25	B	29	151	630	104	210	35	8	2	75	28	23	19	.333	.424
Nemo Leibold (BH)	OF108	L	28	108	413	61	91	16	3	1	28	55	30	7	.220	.281
Happy Felsch (DL)	OF142	R	28	142	556	88	188	40	15	14	115	37	25	8	.338	.540
Joe Jackson (DL)	OF145	L	30	146	570	105	218	42	**20**	12	121	56	14	9	.382	.589
Ray Schalk	C151	R	27	151	485	64	131	25	5	1	61	68	19	10	.270	.348
Eddie Murphy	OF19, 3B3	L	28	58	118	22	40	2	1	0	19	12	4	1	.339	.373
2 Amos Strunk	OF49	L	31	51	183	32	42	7	1	1	14	28	15	1	.230	.295
Ted Jourdan	1B40	L	24	48	150	16	36	6	1	0	8	17	17	3	.240	.293
Fred McMullin (DL)	3B29, 2B3, SS1	R	28	46	127	14	25	1	4	0	13	9	13	1	.197	.268
Byrd Lynn	C14	R	31	16	25	0	8	2	1	0	3	1	3	0	.320	.480
Hervey McClellan	SS4, 3B2	R	25	10	18	4	6	1	1	0	5	4	1	2	.333	.500
Bibb Falk	OF4	L	21	7	17	1	5	1	1	0	2	0	5	0	.294	.471
Bubber Jonnard	C1	R	22	2	5	0	0	0	0	0	0	0	1	0	.000	.000
Chick Gandil (HO-DL) 32																
NEW YORK 3rd 95-59 .617 3		**MILLER HUGGINS**														
TOTALS			28	154	5176	838	1448	268	71	**115**	747	539	**626**	64	.280	**.426**
Wally Pipp	1B153	L	27	153	610	109	171	30	14	11	76	48	54	4	.280	.430
Del Pratt	2B154	R	32	154	574	84	180	37	8	4	97	50	24	12	.314	.427
Roger Peckinpaugh	SS137	R	29	139	534	109	144	26	6	8	54	72	47	8	.270	.386
Aaron Ward	3B114, SS12	R	23	127	496	62	127	18	7	11	54	33	**84**	7	.256	.387
Babe Ruth	OF139, 1B2, P1	L	25	142	458	**158**	172	36	9	**54**	**137**	**148**	80	14	.376	**.847**
Ping Bodie	OF129	R	32	129	471	63	139	26	12	7	79	40	30	6	.295	.446
Duffy Lewis (KJ)	OF99	R	31	107	365	34	99	8	1	4	61	24	32	2	.271	.332
Muddy Ruel	C80	R	24	82	261	30	70	14	1	1	15	15	18	4	.268	.341
Bob Meusel	OF64, 3B45, 1B2	R	23	119	460	75	151	40	7	11	83	20	72	4	.328	.517
Truck Hannah	C78	R	29	79	259	24	64	11	1	2	25	24	35	2	.247	.320
Sammy Vick	OF33	R	25	51	118	21	26	7	1	0	11	14	20	1	.220	.297
Frank Gleich	OF15	L	26	24	41	6	5	0	0	0	3	6	10	0	.122	.122
Chick Fewster	SS5, 2B2	R	24	21	21	8	6	1	0	0	1	7	2	0	.286	.333
Fred Hofmann	C14	R	26	15	24	3	7	0	0	0	1	1	2	0	.292	.292
Joe Lucey	2B1, SS1	R	25	3	3	0	0	0	0	0	0	0	0	0	.000	.000
Ray French	SS1	R	25	2	2	2	0	0	0	0	1	0	1	0	.000	.000
Tom Connelly		L	21	1	1	0	0	0	0	0	0	0	0	0	.000	.000
Frank Baker (VR) 34																

NAME	T	AGE	W	L	PCT	SV	G	GS	CG	IP	H	BB	SO	ShO	ERA
		28	**98**	56	**.636**	7	154	154	93	1376	1448	401	466	10	3.41
Jim Bagby	R	30	**31**	12	**.721**	0	**48**	**39**	**30**	**340**	**338**	79	73	3	2.89
Stan Coveleski	R	31	24	14	.632	2	41	37	26	315	284	65	**133**	3	2.48
Ray Caldwell	R	32	20	10	.667	0	34	33	20	238	286	63	80	0	3.86
Guy Morton	R	27	8	6	.571	1	29	17	5	137	140	57	72	1	4.47
Duster Mails	L	24	7	0	1.000	0	9	8	6	63	54	18	25	2	1.85
George Uhle	R	21	4	5	.444	1	27	6	2	85	98	29	27	0	5.18
1 Elmer Myers	R	26	2	4	.333	1	16	7	2	71	93	23	16	0	4.82
Dick Niehaus	L	27	1	2	.333	2	19	3	0	40	42	16	12	0	3.60
Bob Clark	R	22	1	2	.333	0	11	2	2	42	59	13	8	1	3.43
Joe Boehling	L	29	0	1	.000	0	3	2	0	13	16	10	4	0	4.85
Tony Faeth	R	26	0	0	.000	0	13	0	0	25	31	20	14	0	4.32
Tim Murchison	L	23	0	0	.000	0	2	0	0	5	3	4	0	0	0.00
George Ellison	R	23	0	0	.000	0	1	0	0	1	0	2	1	0	0.00
Smokey Joe Wood	R	30	0	0	.000	0	1	0	0	2	4	2	1	0	22.50
		29	96	58	.623	10	154	154	**112**	1386	1467	405	438	8	3.59
Red Faber	R	31	23	13	.639	1	40	**39**	28	319	332	88	108	1	2.99
Lefty Williams (DL)	L	27	22	14	.611	0	39	38	26	299	302	90	128	0	3.91
Dickie Kerr	L	26	21	9	.700	5	45	28	20	254	266	72	72	3	3.37
Eddie Cicotte (DL)	R	36	21	10	.677	2	37	35	28	303	316	74	87	4	3.27
Roy Wilkinson	R	26	7	9	.437	2	34	11	9	145	162	48	30	0	4.03
George Payne	R	26	1	1	.500	0	12	0	0	30	39	9	7	0	5.40
Shovel Hodge	R	26	1	1	.500	0	4	2	1	20	15	12	5	0	.225
Joe Kiefer	R	20	0	1	.000	0	2	1	0	5	7	5	1	0	14.40
Spencer Heath	R	25	0	0	.000	0	4	0	0	7	19	2	0	0	15.43
Grover Lowdermilk	R	35	0	0	.000	0	3	0	0	5	9	5	0	0	7.20
		28	95	59	.617	11	154	154	88	1368	1414	420	480	**16**	**3.31**
Carl Mays	R	28	26	11	.703	2	45	37	26	312	310	84	92	**6**	3.06
Bob Shawkey	R	29	20	13	.606	2	38	31	20	268	246	85	126	5	**2.45**
Jack Quinn	R	36	18	10	.643	3	41	31	16	253	271	48	101	2	3.20
Rip Collins	R	24	14	8	.636	1	36	20	12	187	171	79	66	3	3.18
Hank Thormahlen	L	23	9	6	.600	1	29	14	5	143	178	43	35	0	4.16
George Mogridge	L	31	5	9	.357	1	26	15	7	125	146	36	35	0	4.32
Ernie Shore	R	29	2	2	.500	1	14	5	2	44	61	21	12	0	4.90
Babe Ruth	L	25	1	0	1.000	0	1	1	0	4	3	2	0	0	4.50
Bob McGraw	R	25	0	0	.000	0	15	0	0	27	24	20	11	0	4.67
Lefty O'Doul	L	23	0	0	.000	0	2	0	0	4	4	2	2	0	4.50

ST. LOUIS 4th 76-77 .497 21.5 — JIMMY BURKE

NAME	G by POS	B	AGE	G	AB	R	H	2B	3B	HR	RBI	BB	SO	SB	BA	SA
TOTALS			29	154	5358	797	1651	279	83	50	708	427	339	120	.308	.419
George Sisler	1B154, P1	L	27	154	631	137	257	49	18	19	122	46	19	42	.407	.632
Joe Gedeon	2B153	R	26	153	606	95	177	33	6	0	61	55	36	1	.292	.366
Wally Gerber	SS154	R	28	154	584	70	163	26	2	2	60	58	32	4	.279	.341
Jimmy Austin	3B75	B	40	83	280	38	76	11	3	1	32	31	15	2	.271	.343
Jack Tobin	OF147	L	28	147	593	94	202	34	10	4	62	39	23	21	.341	.452
Baby Doll Jacobson	OF154, 1B1	R	29	154	609	97	216	34	14	9	122	46	37	11	.355	.501
Ken Williams	OF138	L	30	141	521	90	160	34	13	10	72	41	26	18	.307	.480
Hank Severeid	C117	R	29	123	422	46	117	14	5	2	49	33	11	5	.277	.348
Earl Smith	3B70, OF15	L	29	103	353	45	108	21	0	3	55	13	18	11	.306	.436
Josh Billings	C40	R	28	66	155	19	43	5	2	0	11	11	10	1	.277	.335
Pat Collins	C7	R	23	23	28	5	6	1	0	0	6	3	5	0	.214	.250
Frank Thompson	3B14, 2B2	R	26	22	53	7	9	0	0	0	5	13	10	1	.170	.170
Lyman Lamb	OF7	R	25	9	24	4	9	2	0	0	4	0	7	2	.375	.458
John Shovlin	SS5	R	29	7	7	2	2	0	0	0	2	0	0	0	.286	.286
Dutch Wetzel	OF5	R	26	6	19	5	9	1	1	0	5	4	1	0	.474	.632
Billy Mullen		R	24	1	1	0	0	0	0	0	0	0	0	0	.000	.000
Dud Lee	SS1	L	20	1	2	2	2	0	0	0	1	0	0	1	1.000	1.000

Johnnie Heving 24 R 0-1, Marty McManus 20 R 1-3, Earl Pruess 25 R 0-0, Paul Speraw 26 R 0-2

NAME	T	AGE	W	L	PCT	SV	G	GS	CG	IP	H	BB	SO	ShO	ERA
		26	76	77	.497	14	154	154	84	1379	1481	578	444	9	4.03
Urban Shocker	R	29	20	10	.667	5	38	28	22	246	224	70	107	5	2.71
Dixie Davis	R	29	18	12	.600	0	38	31	22	269	250	149	85	0	3.18
Carl Weilman	L	30	9	13	.409	2	30	24	13	183	201	61	45	1	4.47
Allan Sothoron	R	27	8	15	.348	2	36	26	12	218	263	89	81	1	4.71
Bill Burwell	R	25	6	4	.600	4	33	2	0	113	133	42	30	0	3.66
Bill Bayne	L	21	5	6	.455	0	18	13	6	100	102	41	38	1	3.69
Elam Vangilder	R	24	3	8	.273	0	24	13	4	105	131	40	25	0	5.49
Adrian Lynch	R	23	2	0	1.000	0	5	3	1	22	23	17	8	0	5.32
Ray Richmond	R	24	2	0	1.000	0	2	2	1	17	18	9	4	0	6.35
Joe DeBerry	R	23	2	4	.333	0	10	7	3	55	65	20	12	1	4.90
Roy Sanders	R	26	1	1	.500	0	8	1	0	17	20	17	2	0	5.29
George Boehler	R	28	0	1	.000	0	3	1	0	7	10	4	2	0	7.71
1 Bert Gallia	R	28	0	1	.000	0	2	1	0	4	8	3	0	0	6.75
Hod Leverette	R	31	0	2	.000	0	3	2	0	10	9	12	0	0	5.40
Lefty Leifield	L	36	0	0	.000	0	4	0	0	9	17	3	3	0	7.00
Jack Scheneberg	R	32	0	0	.000	0	1	0	0	2	7	1	0	0	27.00
George Sisler	L	27	0	0	.000	1	1	0	0	1	0	0	2	0	0.00

BOSTON 5th 72-81 .471 25.5 — ED BARROW

NAME	G by POS	B	AGE	G	AB	R	H	2B	3B	HR	RBI	BB	SO	SB	BA	SA
TOTALS			28	154	5199	650	1397	216	71	22	575	533	429	98	.269	.350
Stuffy McInnis	1B148	R	29	148	559	50	166	21	3	2	71	18	19	6	.297	.356
Mike McNally	2B76, SS8, 1B6	R	26	93	312	42	80	5	1	0	23	31	24	13	.256	.279
Everett Scott	SS154	R	27	154	569	41	153	21	12	4	61	21	15	4	.269	.369
Eddie Foster	3B88, 2B21	R	33	117	386	48	100	17	6	0	41	42	17	10	.259	.334
Mike Menosky	OF141	L	25	141	532	80	158	24	9	3	64	65	52	23	.297	.393
Jim Hendryx	OF98	R	29	99	363	54	119	21	5	0	73	42	27	7	.328	.413
Harry Hooper	OF139	L	32	139	536	91	167	30	17	7	53	88	27	16	.312	.470
Roxy Walters	C85, 1B2	R	27	88	258	25	51	11	1	0	28	30	21	2	.198	.248
Wally Schang	C73, OF40	B	30	122	387	58	118	30	7	4	51	64	37	7	.305	.450
Ossie Vitt	3B64, 2B21	R	30	87	296	50	65	10	4	1	28	43	10	5	.220	.291
Benn Karr	P26	L	26	57	75	8	21	5	0	1	15	6	18	0	.280	.387
Cliff Brady	2B53	R	23	53	180	16	41	5	1	0	12	13	12	0	.228	.267
2 Gene Bailey	OF40	R	26	46	135	14	31	2	0	0	5	9	15	2	.230	.244
Hack Eibel	OF5, P3, 1B1	L	26	29	43	4	8	2	0	0	6	3	6	1	.186	.233
Hob Hiller	3B6, SS5, 2B2, OF1	R	27	17	29	4	5	1	1	0	2	2	5	0	.172	.276
Ben Paschal	OF7	R	24	9	28	5	10	0	0	0	5	5	2	1	.357	.357
Mickey Devine	C5	R	28	8	12	1	2	0	0	0	0	1	2	1	.167	.167
Bert Chaplin	C2	L	26	4	5	2	1	1	0	0	1	4	1	0	.200	.400
Herb Hunter	OF4	L	24	4	12	2	1	0	0	0	0	1	1	0	.083	.083
George Orme	OF3	R	28	4	6	4	2	0	0	0	1	3	0	0	.333	.333

Paddy Smith 26 L 0-2, 2 Jigger Statz 22 R 0-3, Ray Grimes 26 R 1-4, Dick Hoblitzell (MS) 31

NAME	T	AGE	W	L	PCT	SV	G	GS	CG	IP	H	BB	SO	ShO	ERA
		25	72	81	.471	6	154	154	91	1395	1481	461	481	11	3.83
Herb Pennock	L	26	16	13	.552	2	37	31	19	242	244	61	68	4	3.68
Bullet Joe Bush	R	27	15	15	.500	1	35	32	18	244	287	94	88	0	4.24
Sad Sam Jones	R	27	13	16	.448	0	37	33	20	274	302	79	86	3	3.94
2 Elmer Myers	R	26	9	1	.900	0	12	10	9	97	90	24	34	1	2.13
Waite Hoyt	R	20	6	6	.500	1	22	11	6	121	123	47	45	2	4.39
Allen Russell	R	26	5	6	.455	1	16	10	7	108	100	38	53	0	3.00
Harry Harper	L	25	5	14	.263	0	27	22	11	163	163	66	71	1	3.03
Benn Karr	R	26	3	8	.273	1	26	2	0	92	109	24	21	0	4.80
Gary Fortune	R	25	0	2	.000	0	14	3	1	42	46	23	10	0	5.79
Hack Eibel	L	26	0	0	.000	0	3	0	0	10	10	3	5	0	3.60
Hal Deviney	R	27	0	0	.000	0	1	0	0	3	7	2	0	0	15.00

WASHINGTON 6th 68-84 .447 29 — CLARK GRIFFITH

NAME	G by POS	B	AGE	G	AB	R	H	2B	3B	HR	RBI	BB	SO	SB	BA	SA
TOTALS			27	153	5251	723	1526	233	81	36	620	433	543	161	.291	.386
Joe Judge	1B124	L	26	126	493	103	164	19	15	5	51	65	34	12	.333	.462
Bucky Harris	2B135	R	23	137	506	76	152	26	6	1	68	41	36	16	.300	.381
Jim O'Neill	SS80, 2B2	R	27	86	294	27	85	17	7	1	40	13	30	7	.289	.405
Frank Ellerbe	3B75, SS19, OF1	R	24	101	336	38	98	14	2	0	36	19	23	5	.292	.345
Braggo Roth	OF128	R	27	138	468	80	136	23	8	9	92	75	57	24	.291	.432
Sam Rice	OF153	L	30	153	624	83	211	29	9	3	80	39	23	63	.338	.428
Clyde Milan	OF123	L	34	126	506	70	163	22	5	3	41	28	12	10	.322	.403
Patsy Gharrity	C120, 1B7, OF1	R	28	131	428	51	105	18	3	3	44	37	52	6	.245	.322
H. Shanks	3B63, OF35, 1B14, 2B5, SS1	R	29	128	444	56	119	16	7	4	37	29	43	11	.268	.363
1 Red Shannon	SS31, 2B16, 3B15	B	23	62	222	30	64	8	7	0	30	22	32	2	.288	.387
Val Picinich	C45	R	23	48	133	14	27	6	2	3	14	9	33	0	.203	.346
Frank Brower	OF20, 1B9, 3B1	L	27	36	119	21	37	7	2	1	13	9	11	1	.311	.429
Jack Calvo	OF10	L	36	17	23	5	1	0	1	0	2	2	2	0	.043	.130
Ricardo Torres	1B7, C5	R	26	16	30	8	10	1	0	0	3	1	4	0	.333	.367
Frank O'Rourke	SS13, 3B1	R	25	14	54	8	16	1	0	0	5	2	5	2	.296	.315
George McBride	SS13	R	39	13	41	6	9	1	0	0	3	2	3	0	.220	.244
Doc Prothro	SS2, 3B2	R	26	6	13	2	5	0	0	0	2	0	4	0	.385	.385
Bobby LaMotte	SS1, 3B1	R	22	4	3	0	0	0	0	0	0	1	1	0	.000	.000
Bill Hollahan	3B3	R	23	3	4	0	1	0	0	0	1	1	2	1	.250	.250
2 Fred Thomas	3B2	R	27	3	7	0	1	0	0	0	0	0	1	0	.143	.143
Ed Johnson	OF2	L	21	2	8	0	2	0	0	0	1	0	0	0	.250	.250

Elmer Bowman 23 R 0-1, Allie Watt 20 R 1-1, Joe Leonard (DD) 25 L 0-0

NAME	T	AGE	W	L	PCT	SV	G	GS	CG	IP	H	BB	SO	ShO	ERA
		26	68	84	.447	10	153	153	80	1367	1521	520	418	10	4.17
Tom Zachary	L	24	15	16	.484	2	44	30	18	263	289	78	53	3	3.76
Eric Erickson	R	28	12	16	.429	1	39	28	12	239	231	128	87	0	3.84
Jim Shaw	R	26	11	18	.378	1	38	32	17	236	285	87	88	0	4.28
Walter Johnson (LJ-SA)	R	32	8	10	.444	3	21	15	12	144	135	27	78	4	3.13
Harry Courtney	L	21	8	11	.421	0	37	24	10	188	223	77	48	1	4.74
Al Schact	R	27	6	4	.600	1	22	11	5	99	130	30	19	1	4.45
Jose Acosta	R	29	5	4	.556	1	17	5	4	83	92	26	9	1	4.01
Bill Snyder	R	22	2	1	.667	1	16	4	1	54	59	28	17	0	4.17
Harry Biemiller	R	22	1	0	1.000	0	5	2	1	17	21	13	10	0	4.76
Clarence Fisher	R	21	0	1	.000	0	2	0	0	4	5	5	0	0	9.00
Duke Shirey	R	22	0	1	.000	0	2	1	0	4	5	2	0	0	6.75
Gus Bono	R	25	0	2	.000	0	4	1	0	12	17	6	4	0	9.00
Leon Carlson	R	25	0	0	.000	0	3	0	0	12	14	2	3	0	3.75
Joe Gleason	R	24	0	0	.000	0	3	0	0	8	14	6	2	0	13.50
Jerry Conway	L	19	0	0	.000	0	1	0	0	2	1	1	0	0	0.00
Joe Engel	R	27	0	0	.000	0	1	0	0	2	0	4	0	0	18.00

DETROIT 7th 61-93 .396 37 — HUGHIE JENNINGS

NAME	G by POS	B	AGE	G	AB	R	H	2B	3B	HR	RBI	BB	SO	SB	BA	SA
TOTALS			29	155	5215	651	1408	228	72	30	560	479	391	76	.270	.359
Harry Heilmann	1B122, OF21	R	25	145	543	66	168	28	5	9	89	39	32	3	.309	.429
Ralph Young	2B150	B	30	150	594	84	173	21	6	0	33	85	30	8	.291	.347
Donie Bush	SS140	B	32	141	506	85	133	18	5	1	33	73	32	15	.263	.324
Babe Pinelli	3B74, SS18, 2B1	R	24	102	284	33	65	9	3	0	21	25	16	6	.229	.282
Chick Shorten	OF99	L	28	116	364	35	105	9	6	1	40	28	14	2	.288	.354
Ty Cobb (LJ)	OF112	L	33	112	428	86	143	28	8	2	63	58	28	14	.334	.451
Bobby Veach	OF154	L	32	154	612	92	188	39	15	11	113	36	22	11	.307	.474
Oscar Stanage	C77	R	37	78	238	12	55	17	0	0	17	14	21	0	.231	.303
Ira Flagstead	OF82	R	26	110	311	40	73	13	5	3	35	37	27	3	.235	.338
Bob Jones	3B67, 2B5, SS1	L	30	81	265	35	66	6	3	1	18	22	13	3	.249	.306
Sammy Hale	3B16, OF4, 2B1	R	23	76	116	13	34	3	3	1	14	5	15	2	.293	.397
Eddie Ainsmith	C61	R	28	69	186	19	43	5	3	1	19	14	19	4	.231	.306
Bert Ellison	1B38, OF4, 3B1	R	24	61	155	11	34	7	2	0	21	8	26	4	.219	.290
Clyde Manion	C30	R	23	32	80	4	22	4	1	0	8	4	7	0	.275	.350
Larry Woodall	C15	R	25	18	49	4	12	1	0	0	5	2	6	0	.245	.265
Clarence Huber	3B11	R	23	11	42	4	9	2	1	0	5	0	5	0	.214	.310
Dave Claire	SS3	R	22	3	7	1	1	0	0	0	0	0	0	0	.143	.143

NAME	T	AGE	W	L	PCT	SV	G	GS	CG	IP	H	BB	SO	ShO	ERA
		27	61	93	.396	7	155	155	76	1385	1487	561	483	7	4.04
Howard Ehmke	R	26	15	18	.455	3	38	33	23	268	250	124	98	1	3.29
Hooks Dauss	R	30	13	21	.382	0	38	32	18	270	308	84	82	0	3.56
Dutch Leonard	L	28	10	17	.370	0	28	27	10	191	192	63	76	3	4.34
Red Oldham	L	26	8	13	.381	1	39	23	11	215	248	91	62	1	3.85
Doc Ayres	R	30	7	14	.333	1	46	22	9	209	217	62	103	2	3.88
Allen Conkwright	R	23	2	1	.667	1	5	2	0	19	29	16	4	0	7.10
John Bogart	R	19	2	1	.667	0	4	3	0	24	16	18	5	0	3.00
Roy Crumpler	L	23	1	0	1.000	0	2	2	1	13	17	11	2	0	5.54
Bill Morrisette	R	27	1	1	.500	0	8	3	1	27	25	19	15	0	4.33
Mutt Wilson	R	23	1	1	.500	0	3	2	1	13	12	5	4	0	3.46
Frank Okrie	L	23	1	2	.333	0	21	1	1	41	44	18	9	0	5.27
Ernie Alten	L	25	0	1	.000	0	14	1	0	23	40	9	4	0	9.00
Harry Baumgartner	R	27	0	1	.000	0	9	0	0	18	18	6	7	0	4.00
Bernie Boland	R	28	0	2	.000	0	4	3	1	17	23	14	4	0	7.94
John Glaiser	R	25	0	0	.000	1	9	1	0	17	23	8	3	0	6.35
Red Cox	R	25	0	0	.000	0	3	0	0	5	9	3	1	0	5.40
Jack Coombs	R	37	0	0	.000	0	2	0	0	6	7	2	1	0	3.00

Cy Fried 22 L 0-0, Slim Love 29 L 0-0, Lou Vedder 23 R 0-0

PHILADELPHIA 8th 48-106 .312 50 — CONNIE MACK

NAME	G by POS	B	AGE	G	AB	R	H	2B	3B	HR	RBI	BB	SO	SB	BA	SA
TOTALS			25	156	5258	557	1326	219	49	44	470	356	594	51	.252	.338
Ivy Griffin	1B126, 2B2	L	24	129	467	46	111	15	1	0	20	15	49	3	.238	.274
Jimmy Dykes	2B108, 3B36	R	23	142	546	81	140	25	4	8	35	52	73	6	.256	.361
Chick Galloway	SS84, 2B4, 3B3	R	23	98	298	28	60	9	3	0	18	22	22	2	.201	.252
1 Fred Thomas	3B61, SS12	R	27	76	255	27	59	6	3	1	11	26	17	8	.231	.290
1 Amos Strunk	OF54	L	31	58	202	23	60	9	3	0	20	21	9	0	.297	.371
Frank Welch	OF97	R	22	100	360	43	93	17	5	4	40	26	41	2	.258	.367
Tilly Walker	OF149	R	32	149	585	79	157	23	7	17	82	40	59	9	.268	.419
Cy Perkins	C146, 2B1	R	24	148	492	40	128	24	6	5	52	28	35	5	.260	.364
Joe Dugan	3B59, 2B32, SS32	R	23	123	491	65	158	40	5	3	60	19	51	5	.322	.442
Dick Burrus	1B31, OF2	L	22	71	135	11	25	8	0	0	10	5	7	0	.185	.244
Glen Myatt	OF37, C21	L	22	70	196	14	49	8	3	0	18	12	22	1	.250	.321
Whitey Witt	OF50, 2B11, SS2	L	24	65	218	29	70	11	3	1	25	27	16	2	.321	.413
Lyle Bigbee	OF12, P12	L	26	37	70	4	13	1	0	1	8	8	10	1	.186	.243
2 Red Shannon	SS24	B	23	25	88	4	15	1	1	0	3	4	12	1	.170	.205
Lena Styles	C9, 1B7	R	20	24	50	5	13	3	1	0	5	6	7	1	.260	.360
Frank Walker	OF24	R	25	24	91	10	21	2	2	0	10	5	14	0	.231	.297
1 George Burns	OF13	R	27	22	60	1	14	3	0	1	7	6	7	4	.233	.333
Paul Johnson	OF18	R	23	18	72	6	15	0	0	0	5	4	8	1	.208	.208
Charlie High	OF17	L	21	17	65	7	20	2	1	1	6	3	6	0	.308	.415
Emmett McCann	SS11	R	18	13	34	4	9	1	1	0	3	3	1	0	.265	.353
Bill Kelly	1B2	R	20	9	13	0	3	1	0	0	0	0	2	0	.231	.308
Johnny Walker	C6	R	23	9	22	0	5	1	0	0	5	0	1	0	.227	.273

Dan Kerns 0-1, Ed Wingo 24 R 1-4

NAME	T	AGE	W	L	PCT	SV	G	GS	CG	IP	H	BB	SO	ShO	ERA
		24	48	106	.312	2	156	156	81	1380	1612	461	423	5	3.92
Scott Perry	R	29	11	25	.306	1	42	34	20	264	310	65	79	1	3.62
Rollie Naylor	R	28	10	23	.303	0	42	36	20	251	306	86	90	0	3.47
Slim Harriss	R	23	9	14	.391	0	31	25	11	192	226	57	60	0	4.08
Eddie Rommel	R	22	7	7	.500	1	33	12	8	174	165	43	43	2	2.84
Dave Keefe	R	23	6	7	.462	0	31	13	7	130	129	30	41	1	2.97
Walt Kinney	L	26	2	4	.333	0	10	8	5	61	59	28	19	1	3.10
Bob Hasty	R	24	1	3	.250	0	19	4	1	72	91	28	12	0	5.00
Pat Martin	L	26	1	4	.200	0	8	5	2	32	48	25	14	0	6.19
Roy Moore	L	21	1	13	.071	0	24	16	7	133	161	64	45	0	4.67
John Slappey	L	21	0	1	.000	0	3	1	0	6	15	4	1	0	7.50
Bill Knowlton	R	27	0	1	.000	0	1	1	0	6	9	3	5	0	4.50
Fred Heimach	L	19	0	1	.000	0	1	1	0	5	13	1	0	0	14.40
Lyle Bigbee	R	26	0	3	.000	0	12	0	0	45	66	25	12	0	8.00
Charlie Eckert	R	21	0	0	.000	0	2	0	0	6	8	1	1	0	4.50
W. W. Shanner	R		0	0	.000	0	1	0	0	4	6	1	1	0	6.75

BROOKLYN 1st 93-61 .604 — WILBERT ROBINSON

NAME	G by POS	B	AGE	G	AB	R	H	2B	3B	HR	RBI	BB	SO	SB	BA	SA
TOTALS			31	155	5399	660	1493	205	**99**	28	566	359	391	70	.277	.367
Ed Konetchy	1B130	R	34	131	497	62	153	22	12	5	63	33	18	3	.308	.431
Pete Kilduff	2B134, 3B5	R	27	141	478	62	130	26	8	0	58	58	43	2	.272	.360
Ivy Olson	SS125, 2B21	R	34	143	637	71	162	13	11	1	46	20	19	4	.254	.314
Jimmy Johnston	3B146, OF7, SS3	R	30	155	635	87	185	17	12	1	52	43	23	19	.291	.361
Tommy Griffith	OF92	L	30	93	334	41	87	9	4	2	30	15	18	3	.260	.329
Hy Myers	OF152, 3B2	R	31	154	582	83	177	36	**22**	4	80	35	54	9	.304	.462
Zack Wheat	OF148	L	34	148	583	89	191	26	13	9	73	48	21	8	.328	.463
Otto Miller	C89	R	31	90	301	16	87	9	2	0	33	9	18	0	.289	.332
Bernie Neis	OF83	R	24	95	249	38	63	11	2	2	22	26	35	9	.253	.337
Clarence Mitchell	P19, 1B11, OF4	L	29	55	107	9	25	2	2	0	11	8	9	1	.234	.290
Ernie Krueger	C46	R	29	52	146	21	42	4	2	1	17	16	13	2	.288	.363
Burleigh Grimes	P40	R	26	43	111	9	34	8	3	0	16	8	21	2	.306	.432
Rowdy Elliott	C39	R	29	41	112	13	27	4	0	1	13	3	6	0	.241	.304
2 Bill McCabe	SS13, OF6, 2B4, 3B3	B	25	41	68	10	10	0	0	0	3	2	6	1	.147	.147
Ray Schmandt	1B20	R	24	28	63	7	15	2	1	0	7	3	4	1	.238	.302
Bill Lamar	OF12	L	23	24	44	5	12	4	0	0	4	0	1	0	.273	.364
Chuck Ward (IL)	SS19	R	25	19	71	7	11	1	0	0	4	3	3	1	.155	.169
2 Wally Hood	OF5	R	25	7	14	4	2	1	0	0	1	4	4	2	.143	.214
1 Doug Baird	3B2	R	28	6	6	1	2	0	0	0	1	2	1	0	.333	.333
Zack Taylor	C9	R	21	9	13	3	5	2	0	0	5	0	2	0	.385	.538
Jack Sheehan	SS2, 3B1	B	27	3	5	0	2	1	0	0	0	1	0	0	.400	.600
Red Sheridan	SS3	R	23	3	2	0	0	0	0	0	0	0	1	0	.000	.000

NAME	T	AGE	W	L	PCT	SV	G	GS	CG	IP	H	BB	SO	ShO	ERA
		29	**93**	61	**.604**	10	155	155	89	**1427**	1381	327	**553**	17	**2.62**
Burleigh Grimes	R	26	23	11	**.676**	2	40	33	25	304	271	67	131	5	2.22
Jeff Pfeffer	R	32	16	9	.640	0	30	28	20	215	225	45	80	2	3.01
Leon Cadore	R	29	15	14	.517	0	35	30	16	254	256	56	79	4	2.62
Al Mamaux	R	26	12	8	.600	4	41	18	9	191	172	63	101	2	2.68
Sherry Smith	L	29	11	9	.550	3	33	12	6	136	134	27	33	2	1.85
Rube Marquard	L	30	10	7	.588	0	28	26	10	190	181	35	89	1	3.22
Clarence Mitchell	L	29	5	2	.714	1	19	7	3	79	85	23	18	1	3.08
Johnny Miljus	R	25	1	0	1.000	0	9	0	0	23	24	4	9	0	3.13
George Mohart	R	28	0	1	.000	0	13	1	0	36	33	7	13	0	1.75

NEW YORK 2nd 86-68 .558 7 — JOHN McGRAW

NAME	G by POS	B	AGE	G	AB	R	H	2B	3B	HR	RBI	BB	SO	SB	BA	SA
TOTALS			27	155	5309	**682**	1427	210	76	46	560	**432**	**545**	131	.269	.363
George Kelly	1B155	R	24	155	590	69	157	22	11	11	**94**	41	**92**	6	.266	.397
Larry Doyle	2B133	L	33	137	471	48	134	21	2	4	50	47	28	11	.285	.363
2 Dave Bancroft	SS108	B	29	108	442	79	132	29	7	0	31	33	32	7	.299	.396
Frankie Frisch	3B109, SS2	B	21	110	440	57	123	10	10	4	77	20	18	34	.280	.375
Ross Youngs	OF153	L	23	153	581	92	204	27	14	6	78	75	55	18	.351	.477
Lee King	OF84	R	27	93	261	32	72	11	4	7	42	21	38	3	.276	.429
George Burns	OF154	R	30	154	631	**115**	181	35	9	6	46	**76**	48	22	.287	.399
Frank Snyder	C84	R	27	87	264	26	66	13	4	3	27	17	18	2	.250	.364
Earl Smith	C82	L	23	91	262	20	77	7	1	1	30	18	16	5	.294	.340
Benny Kauff	OF51	L	30	55	157	31	43	12	3	3	26	25	14	3	.274	.446
1 Eddie Sicking	3B28, 2B15, SS3	R	23	46	134	11	23	3	1	0	9	10	10	6	.172	.209
Vern Spencer	OF40	L	24	45	140	15	28	2	3	0	19	11	17	4	.200	.257
1 Art Fletcher	SS41	R	35	41	171	21	44	7	2	0	24	1	15	3	.257	.322
1 Lew McCarty	C5	R	31	36	38	2	5	0	0	0	0	4	2	2	.132	.132
Fred Lear	3B24, 2B1	R	26	31	87	12	22	0	1	1	7	8	15	0	.253	.310
Bummer Grimes	2B21	R	26	26	57	5	9	1	0	0	3	3	8	1	.158	.175
Al LeFevre	3B9, 2B6, 3B1	L	21	17	27	5	4	0	1	0	0	0	13	0	.148	.222
1 Jigger Statz	OF12	R	22	16	30	0	4	0	1	0	5	2	9	0	.133	.200
Mike Gonzalez	C8	R	29	11	13	1	3	0	0	0	0	3	1	1	.231	.231
Curt Walker	OF4	L	23	8	14	0	1	0	0	0	0	1	3	0	.071	.071
2 Doug Baird	3B4	R	28	7	8	0	1	0	0	0	0	1	3	0	.125	.125
Pug Griffin	OF2	R	24	5	4	0	1	0	0	0	0	1	2	0	.250	.250
Alex Gaston	C3	R	27	4	10	2	1	0	0	0	1	1	2	0	.100	.100
Eddie Brown	OF2	R	28	3	8	1	1	1	0	0	0	0	3	0	.125	.250
Bob Kinsella	OF1	L	21	1	3	0	1	0	0	0	1	0	2	0	.333	.333

NAME	T	AGE	W	L	PCT	SV	G	GS	CG	IP	H	BB	SO	ShO	ERA
		29	86	68	.558	9	155	155	86	1409	1379	297	380	**18**	2.80
Fred Toney	R	32	21	11	.656	1	42	37	17	278	266	57	81	4	2.65
Art Nehf	L	27	21	12	.636	0	40	33	22	281	273	45	79	5	3.08
Jesse Barnes	R	27	20	15	.571	0	43	35	23	293	271	56	63	2	2.65
Phil Douglas	R	30	14	10	.583	2	46	21	10	226	225	55	71	3	2.71
Rube Benton	L	33	9	16	.360	2	33	25	12	193	222	31	52	4	3.03
2 Slim Sallee	L	35	1	0	1.000	0	5	1	1	17	16	0	2	0	1.59
1 Bill Hubbell	R	23	0	1	.000	2	14	0	0	30	26	15	8	0	2.10
Rosy Ryan	R	22	0	1	.000	0	3	1	1	15	14	4	5	0	1.80
Virgil Barnes	R	23	0	1	.000	0	1	1	0	7	9	1	2	0	3.86
Tom Grubbs	R	26	0	1	.000	0	1	1	0	5	9	0	0	0	7.20
Jesse Winters	R	26	0	0	.000	0	21	0	0	46	37	28	14	0	3.52
Pol Perritt	R	27	0	0	.000	2	8	0	0	15	9	4	3	0	1.80
Claude Davenport	R	22	0	0	.000	0	1	0	0	2	2	1	0	0	4.50
Jean Dubuc (DL) 31															

CINCINNATI 3rd 82-71 .536 10.5 — PAT MORAN

NAME	G by POS	B	AGE	G	AB	R	H	2B	3B	HR	RBI	BB	SO	SB	BA	SA
TOTALS			30	154	5176	639	1432	169	76	18	546	382	367	158	.277	.349
Jake Daubert	1B140	L	36	142	553	97	168	28	13	4	48	47	29	11	.304	.423
Morrie Rath	2B126, 3B1, OF1	L	33	129	506	61	135	7	4	2	28	36	24	10	.267	.308
Larry Kopf	SS123, 2B2, 3B2, OF1	B	29	126	458	56	112	15	6	0	59	35	24	14	.245	.303
Heinie Groh	3B144, SS1	R	30	145	550	86	164	28	12	0	49	60	29	16	.298	.393
Greasy Neale	OF150	L	28	150	530	55	135	10	7	3	46	45	48	29	.255	.317
Edd Roush	OF139, 1B11, 2B1	L	27	149	579	81	196	22	16	4	90	42	22	36	.339	.453
Pat Duncan	OF154	R	26	154	576	75	170	16	11	2	83	42	42	18	.295	.372
Ivy Wingo	C107, 2B2	L	29	108	364	32	96	11	5	2	38	19	13	6	.264	.338
Sam Crane	SS25, 3B10, 2B4, OF3	R	25	54	144	20	31	4	0	0	9	7	9	5	.215	.243
Charlie See	OF17, P1	L	23	47	82	9	25	4	0	0	15	1	7	2	.305	.354
Nick Allen	C36	R	31	43	85	10	23	3	1	0	4	6	11	0	.271	.329
Bill Rariden	C37	R	32	39	101	9	25	3	0	0	10	5	0	2	.248	.277
2 Eddie Sicking	2B25, SS9, 3B2	R	23	37	123	12	33	3	0	0	17	13	5	2	.268	.293
Rube Bressler	P10, OF3, 1B2	R	25	21	30	4	8	1	0	0	3	1	4	1	.267	.300

NAME	T	AGE	W	L	PCT	SV	G	GS	CG	IP	H	BB	SO	ShO	ERA
		29	82	71	.536	9	154	154	90	1418	1327	393	435	12	2.84
Jimmy Ring	R	25	17	16	.515	1	42	33	18	293	268	92	73	1	3.22
Dutch Ruether	L	26	16	12	.571	3	37	33	23	266	235	96	99	5	2.47
Dolf Luque	R	29	13	9	.591	1	37	23	10	208	168	60	72	1	2.51
Hod Eller	R	25	13	12	.520	0	35	22	15	210	208	52	76	2	2.96
Ray Fisher	R	32	10	11	.476	1	33	22	10	201	189	50	56	1	2.73
1 Slim Sallee	L	35	5	6	.455	2	21	12	6	116	129	16	13	0	3.34
Buddy Napier	R	30	4	2	.667	0	9	5	5	49	47	7	17	1	1.29
Rube Bressler	L	25	2	0	1.000	0	10	2	1	20	24	2	4	1	1.80
Lynn Brenton	R	29	2	1	.667	1	5	1	1	18	17	4	13	0	5.00
Fritz Coumbe	L	30	0	1	.000	0	3	0	0	15	17	4	7	0	4.80
Dazzy Swartz	R	23	0	1	.000	0	1	1	1	12	17	2	2	0	4.50
George Lowe	R	25	0	0	.000	0	1	0	0	2	1	1	0	0	0.00
Charlie See	L	23	0	0	.000	0	1	0	0	6	6	4	3	0	6.00
Jack Theis	R	28	0	0	.000	0	1	0	0	2	1	3	0	0	0.00

PITTSBURGH 4th 79-75 .513 14 — GEORGE GIBSON

NAME	G by POS	B	AGE	G	AB	R	H	2B	3B	HR	RBI	BB	SO	SB	BA	SA
TOTALS			27	155	5219	530	1342	162	90	16	449	374	405	**181**	.257	.332
Charlie Grimm	1B148	L	21	148	533	38	121	13	7	2	54	30	40	7	.227	.289
George Cutshaw	2B129	R	32	131	488	56	123	16	8	0	47	23	10	17	.252	.318
Buster Caton	SS98	R	23	98	352	29	83	11	5	0	27	33	19	4	.236	.295
Possum Whitted	3B125, 1B10, OF1	R	30	134	494	53	129	11	12	1	74	35	36	11	.261	.338
Billy Southworth	OF142	L	27	146	546	64	155	17	13	2	53	52	20	23	.284	.374
Max Carey	OF129	B	30	130	485	74	140	18	4	1	35	59	31	**52**	.289	.348
Carson Bigbee	OF133	L	25	137	550	78	154	19	15	4	32	45	28	31	.280	.391
Walter Schmidt	C92	R	33	94	310	22	86	8	4	0	20	24	15	9	.277	.329
Fred Nicholson	OF58	R	25	99	247	33	89	16	7	4	30	18	31	9	.360	.530
Walter Barbare (BJ)	SS34, 2B12, 3B5	R	28	57	186	9	51	5	2	0	12	9	11	5	.274	.323
Bill Haeffner	C52	R	25	54	175	8	34	4	1	0	14	8	14	1	.194	.229
Bill McKechnie	3B20, SS10, 2B6, 1B1	B	33	40	133	13	29	3	1	1	13	4	7	7	.218	.278
Cliff Lee	C19, OF2	R	23	37	76	9	18	2	2	0	8	4	14	0	.237	.316
Bill Hinchman		R	37	18	16	0	3	0	0	0	1	1	3	0	.188	.188
Pie Traynor	SS17	R	20	17	52	6	11	3	1	0	2	3	6	1	.212	.308
Clyde Barnhart	3B12	R	24	12	46	5	15	4	2	0	5	1	2	1	.326	.500
Cotton Tierney	2B10, SS2	R	26	12	46	4	11	5	0	0	8	3	4	1	.239	.348
Homer Summa	OF6	L	21	10	22	1	7	1	1	0	1	3	1	1	.318	.455
Nig Clarke	C3	L	37	3	7	0	0	0	0	0	0	2	4	0	.000	.000
1 Wally Hood		R	25	2	1	1	0	0	0	0	0	1	0	1	.000	.000

NAME	T	AGE	W	L	PCT	SV	G	GS	CG	IP	H	BB	SO	ShO	ERA
		28	79	75	.513	10	155	155	92	1416	1389	280	444	17	2.89
Wilbur Cooper	L	28	24	15	.615	2	44	37	28	327	307	52	114	3	2.39
Babe Adams	R	38	17	13	.567	2	35	33	19	263	240	18	84	**8**	2.16
Hal Carlson	R	26	14	13	.519	3	39	31	16	247	262	63	62	3	3.35
Elmer Ponder	R	27	11	15	.423	0	33	23	13	196	182	40	62	2	2.62
Earl Hamilton	L	28	10	13	.435	3	39	23	12	230	223	69	74	0	3.25
Johnny Morrison	R	24	1	0	1.000	0	2	1	1	7	4	1	3	1	0.00
Jimmy Zinn	R	25	1	1	.500	0	6	3	2	31	32	5	18	0	3.48
John Wisner	R	20	1	3	.250	0	17	2	1	45	46	10	13	0	3.40
Johnny Meador	R	27	0	2	.000	0	12	2	0	36	48	7	5	0	4.25
Sherrif Blake	R	20	0	0	.000	0	6	0	0	13	21	6	7	0	8.31
13 Mule Watson	R	23	0	0	.000	0	5	0	0	11	15	7	1	0	9.00
Whitey Glazner	R	27	0	0	.000	0	2	0	0	9	9	2	1	0	3.00

CHICAGO 5th (Tie) 75-79 .487 18 — FRED MITCHELL

NAME	G by POS	B	AGE	G	AB	R	H	2B	3B	HR	RBI	BB	SO	SB	BA	SA
TOTALS			29	154	5117	619	1350	223	67	34	535	428	421	115	.264	.354
Fred Merkle	1B85, OF1	R	31	92	330	33	94	20	4	3	38	24	32	3	.285	.397
Zeb Terry	SS70, 2B63	R	29	133	496	56	139	26	9	0	52	44	22	12	.280	.369
Charlie Hollocher (IL)	SS80	L	24	80	301	53	96	17	2	0	22	41	15	20	.319	.389
Charlie Deal	3B128	R	28	129	450	48	108	10	5	3	39	20	14	5	.240	.304
Max Flack	OF132	L	30	135	520	85	157	30	6	4	49	52	15	13	.302	.406
Dode Paskert	OF137	R	38	139	487	57	136	22	10	5	71	64	58	16	.279	.396
Dave Robertson	OF134	L	30	134	500	68	150	29	11	10	75	40	44	17	.300	.462
Bob O'Farrell	C86	R	23	94	270	29	67	11	4	3	19	34	23	1	.248	.352
Turner Barber	1B69, OF17, 2B2	L	26	94	340	27	90	10	5	0	50	9	26	5	.265	.324
Buck Herzog	2B59, 3B28, 1B1	R	34	91	305	39	59	9	2	0	19	20	21	8	.193	.236
Babe Twombly	OF45, 2B2	L	24	78	183	25	43	1	1	2	14	17	20	5	.235	.284
Bill Killefer (BG)	C61	R	32	62	191	16	42	7	1	0	16	8	5	2	.220	.267
Barney Friberg	2B24, OF24	R	20	50	114	11	24	5	1	0	7	6	20	2	.211	.272
Tom Daly	C29	R	28	44	90	12	28	6	0	0	13	2	6	1	.311	.378
Bill Marriott	2B14	L	27	14	43	7	12	4	2	0	5	6	5	1	.279	.465
Hal Leathers	SS6, 2B3	L	21	9	23	3	7	1	0	1	1	1	1	1	.304	.478
1 Bill McCabe		B	25	3	2	1	0	0	0	0	0	0	0	0	.000	.000
Sumpter Clarke	3B1	R	22	1	3	0	1	0	0	0	0	0	1	0	.333	.333
Lee Magee (DL) 31																

NAME	T	AGE	W	L	PCT	SV	G	GS	CG	IP	H	BB	SO	ShO	ERA
		29	75	79	.487	9	154	154	**95**	1389	1459	382	508	13	3.27
Pete Alexander	R	33	**27**	14	.659	5	46	**40**	**33**	**363**	**335**	69	**173**	7	**1.91**
Hippo Vaughn	L	32	19	16	.543	0	40	38	24	301	301	81	131	4	2.54
Lefty Tyler	L	30	11	12	.478	0	27	27	18	193	193	57	57	2	3.31
Claude Hendrix	R	31	9	12	.429	0	27	23	12	204	216	54	72	0	3.57
Speed Martin	R	26	4	15	.211	2	35	13	6	136	165	50	44	0	4.83
Paul Carter	R	26	3	6	.333	2	31	8	2	106	131	36	14	0	4.67
Chippy Gaw	R	28	1	1	.500	0	6	1	0	13	16	3	4	0	4.85
Sweetbreads Bailey	R	25	1	2	.333	0	21	1	0	37	55	11	8	0	7.06
Joel Newkirk	R	24	0	1	.000	0	2	1	0	7	8	6	2	0	5.14
Virgil Cheeves	R	19	0	0	.000	0	5	2	0	18	16	7	3	0	3.50
Percy Jones	L	20	0	0	.000	0	4	0	0	7	15	3	0	0	11.57
Joe Jaeger	R	25	0	0	.000	0	2	0	0	3	6	4	0	0	12.00
Ted Turner	R	28	0	0	.000	0	1	0	0	1	2	1	0	0	18.00

ST. LOUIS 5th (Tie) 75-79 .487 18 — **BRANCH RICKEY**

NAME	G by POS	B	AGE	G	AB	R	H	2B	3B	HR	RBI	BB	SO	SB	BA	SA
TOTALS			27	155	**5495**	675	**1589**	**238**	96	32	**600**	373	484	126	**.289**	**.385**
Jack Fournier	1B138	L	27	141	530	77	162	33	14	3	61	42	42	26	.306	.438
Rogers Hornsby	2B149	R	24	149	589	96	**218**	**44**	20	9	**94**	60	50	12	**.370**	**.559**
Doc Lavan	SS138	R	29	142	516	52	149	21	10	1	63	19	38	11	.289	.374
Milt Stock	3B155	R	26	155	**639**	85	204	28	6	0	76	40	27	15	.319	.382
Joe Schultz	OF80	R	26	99	320	38	84	5	5	0	32	21	11	5	.263	.309
Cliff Heathcote	OF129	L	22	133	489	55	139	18	8	3	56	25	31	21	.284	.372
Austin McHenry	OF133	R	24	137	504	66	142	19	11	10	65	25	73	8	.282	.423
Vern Clemons	C103	R	28	112	338	17	95	10	6	1	36	30	12	1	.281	.355
Jack Smith	OF83	L	25	91	313	53	104	22	5	1	28	25	23	14	.332	.444
Hal Janvrin	SS27, 1B25, OF20, 2B6	R	27	87	270	33	74	8	4	1	28	17	19	5	.274	.344
Pickles Dillhoefer	C74	R	25	76	224	26	59	8	3	0	13	13	7	2	.263	.326
Burt Shotton	OF51	L	35	62	180	28	41	5	0	1	12	18	14	5	.228	.272
Mike Knode	OF9, 2B4, SS2, 3B2	L	24	42	65	11	15	1	1	0	12	5	6	0	.231	.277
Tim Griesenbeck	C3	R	22	5	3	1	1	0	0	0	0	0	0	0	.333	.333
2 Lew McCarty	C3	R	31	5	7	0	2	0	0	0	0	5	0	0	.286	.286
Heinie Mueller	OF4	L	20	4	22	0	7	1	0	0	1	2	4	1	.318	.364
George Gilham	C1	R	20	1	3	0	0	0	0	0	0	0	1	0	.000	.000
Ed Hock	OF1	L	21	1	0	0	0	0	0	0	0	0	0	0	.000	.000
Bill Schindler	C1	R	23	1	2	0	0	0	0	0	0	0	1	0	.000	.000

NAME	T	AGE	W	L	PCT	SV	G	GS	CG	IP	H	BB	SO	ShO	ERA
		27	75	79	.487	**12**	155	155	72	**1427**	**1488**	**479**	529	9	3.43
Bill Doak	R	29	20	12	.625	1	39	37	20	270	256	80	90	5	2.53
Ferdie Schupp	L	29	16	13	.552	0	38	37	17	251	246	**127**	119	0	3.51
Jesse Haines	R	26	13	20	.394	2	**47**	37	19	302	303	80	120	4	2.98
Bill Sherdel	L	23	11	10	.524	**6**	43	7	4	170	183	40	74	0	3.28
Elmer Jacobs	R	27	4	8	.333	1	23	9	1	78	91	33	21	0	5.19
Lou North	R	29	3	2	.600	1	24	6	3	88	90	32	37	0	3.27
Marv Goodwin	R	29	3	8	.273	1	32	12	3	116	153	28	23	0	4.97
Mike Kitcher	R	22	2	1	.667	0	9	3	1	37	50	5	5	0	5.35
George Lyons	R	29	2	1	.667	0	7	2	1	23	21	9	5	0	3.13
Jakie May	L	24	1	4	.200	0	16	5	3	71	65	37	33	0	3.04
Hal Kime	L	21	0	0	.000	0	4	0	0	7	9	2	1	0	2.57
Bob Glenn		26	0	0	.000	0	2	0	0	2	2	0	0	0	0.00
Walt Schulz	R	20	0	0	.000	0	2	0	0	6	10	2	0	0	6.00
George Scott	R	23	0	0	.000	0	2	0	0	6	4	3	1	0	4.50
Oscar Tuero	R	27	0	0	.000	0	2	0	0	1	5	1	0	0	36.00

BOSTON 7th 62-90 .408 30 — **GEORGE STALLINGS**

NAME	G by POS	B	AGE	G	AB	R	H	2B	3B	HR	RBI	BB	SO	SB	BA	SA
TOTALS			28	153	5218	523	1358	168	86	23	456	385	488	88	.260	.339
Walter Holke	1B143	B	27	144	551	53	162	15	11	3	64	28	31	4	.294	.377
Charlie Pick	2B94	L	32	95	383	34	105	16	6	2	28	23	11	10	.274	.363
Rabbit Maranville	SS133	R	28	134	493	48	131	19	15	1	43	28	24	14	.266	.371
Tony Boeckel	3B149, SS3, 2B1	R	27	153	582	70	156	28	5	3	62	38	50	18	.268	.349
Walton Cruise	OF82	L	30	91	288	40	80	7	5	1	21	31	26	5	.278	.347
Ray Powell	OF147	L	31	147	609	69	137	12	12	6	29	44	83	10	.225	.314
Les Mann	OF110	R	26	115	424	48	117	7	8	3	32	38	42	7	.276	.351
Mickey O'Neil	C105, 2B1	R	22	112	304	19	86	5	4	0	28	21	20	4	.283	.326
Hod Ford	2B59, SS18, 1B4	R	22	88	257	16	62	12	5	1	30	18	25	3	.241	.339
Eddie Eayrs	OF63, P7	L	29	87	244	31	80	5	2	1	24	30	18	4	.328	.377
John Sullivan	OF66, 1B6	R	30	81	250	36	74	14	4	1	28	29	29	3	.296	.396
Hank Gowdy	C74	R	30	80	214	14	52	11	2	0	18	20	15	6	.243	.313
L. Christenbury	OF14, SS7, 2B6, 3B2	L	26	65	106	17	22	2	2	0	14	13	12	0	.208	.264
Art Wilson	3B6, C2	R	34	16	19	0	1	0	0	0	0	1	1	0	.053	.053
1 Gene Bailey	OF8	R	26	13	24	2	2	0	0	0	0	3	3	0	.083	.083
Oscar Dugey		R	32	5	0	2	0	0	0	0	0	0	0	0	.000	.000
1 Johnny Rawlings	2B1	R	27	5	3	0	0	0	0	0	2	0	1	0	.000	.000
Red Torphy	1B3	R	28	3	15	1	3	2	0	0	2	0	1	0	.200	.333
Tom Whelan	1B1	R	26	1	1	0	0	0	0	0	0	1	1	0	.000	.000

NAME	T	AGE	W	L	PCT	SV	G	GS	CG	IP	H	BB	SO	ShO	ERA
		27	62	90	.408	6	153	153	93	1386	1464	415	368	13	3.54
Joe Oeschger	R	29	15	13	.536	0	38	30	20	299	294	99	80	5	3.46
Dana Fillingim	R	26	12	21	.364	0	37	30	22	272	292	79	66	2	3.11
Hugh McQuillan	R	22	11	15	.423	5	38	27	17	226	230	70	53	1	3.55
Jack Scott	R	28	10	21	.323	1	44	32	22	291	308	85	94	3	3.53
2 Mule Watson	R	23	5	4	.556	0	13	10	4	75	79	17	16	2	3.60
Dick Rudolph	R	32	4	8	.333	0	18	12	3	89	104	24	24	0	4.04
Leo Townsend	L	29	2	2	.500	0	7	1	1	24	18	2	0	0	1.50
Johnny Jones	R	27	1	0	1.000	0	3	1	0	10	16	5	6	0	6.30
Al Pierotti	R	24	1	1	.500	0	6	2	2	25	23	9	12	0	2.88
Eddie Eayrs	L	29	1	2	.333	0	7	3	0	26	36	12	7	0	5.54
Bunny Hearn	L	29	0	3	.000	0	11	4	2	43	54	11	9	0	5.65
Ira Townsend	R	26	0	0	.000	0	4	1	0	7	10	2	1	0	1.29

PHILADELPHIA 8th 62-91 .405 30.5 — **GAVVY CRAVATH**

NAME	G by POS	B	AGE	G	AB	R	H	2B	3B	HR	RBI	BB	SO	SB	BA	SA
TOTALS			29	153	5264	565	1385	229	54	**64**	483	283	531	100	.263	.364
Gene Paulette	1B139, SS2	R	28	143	562	59	162	16	6	1	36	33	16	9	.288	.343
2 Johnny Rawlings	2B97	R	27	98	384	39	90	19	2	3	30	22	25	9	.234	.318
2 Art Fletcher	SS101	R	35	102	379	36	112	25	7	4	38	15	28	4	.296	.430
Ralph Miller	3B91, 1B3, SS2, OF1	R	24	97	338	28	74	14	1	0	28	11	32	3	.219	.266
Casey Stengel	OF118	L	29	129	445	53	130	25	6	9	50	38	35	7	.292	.436
Cy Williams	OF147	L	32	148	590	88	192	36	10	**15**	72	32	45	18	.325	.497
Irish Meusel	OF129, 1B3	R	27	138	518	75	160	27	8	14	69	32	27	17	.309	.473
Mack Wheat	C74	R	27	78	230	15	52	10	3	3	20	8	35	3	.226	.335
Dots Miller	2B59, 3B17, SS12, 1B9, OF1	R	33	98	343	41	87	12	2	1	27	16	17	13	.254	.309
Bevo LeBourveau	OF72	L	25	84	261	29	67	7	2	3	13	11	36	9	.257	.333
Russ Wrightstone	3B56, SS2, 2B1	L	27	76	206	23	54	6	1	3	17	10	25	3	.262	.345
Walt Tragresser	C52	R	33	62	176	17	37	11	1	6	26	4	36	4	.210	.386
Frank Withrow	C48	R	29	48	132	8	24	4	1	0	12	8	26	0	.182	.227
Gavvy Cravath	OF5	R	39	46	45	2	13	5	0	1	11	9	12	0	.289	.467
1 Dave Bancroft	SS42	B	29	42	171	23	51	7	2	0	5	9	12	1	.298	.363
Fred Luderus	1B7	L	34	16	32	1	5	2	0	0	4	3	6	0	.156	.219
Walt Walsh		R	23	2	0	0	0	0	0	0	0	0	0	0	.000	.000

NAME	T	AGE	W	L	PCT	SV	G	GS	CG	IP	H	BB	SO	ShO	ERA
		27	62	**91**	.405	11	153	153	77	1381	1480	444	419	8	3.63
Lee Meadows	R	25	16	14	.533	0	35	33	19	247	249	90	95	3	2.84
George Smith	R	28	13	18	.419	2	43	28	10	251	265	51	51	2	3.44
Eppa Rixey	L	29	11	**22**	.333	2	41	33	25	284	288	69	109	1	3.48
2 Bill Hubbell	R	23	9	9	.500	2	24	20	9	150	176	42	26	1	3.84
Red Causey	R	26	7	14	.333	3	35	26	11	181	203	79	30	1	4.33
Johnny Enzmann	R	30	2	3	.400	0	16	1	1	59	79	16	35	0	3.82
2 Bert Gallia	R	28	2	6	.250	2	18	5	1	72	79	29	35	0	4.50
Huck Betts	R	23	1	1	.500	0	27	4	1	88	86	33	18	0	3.58
Lefty Weinert	L	18	1	1	.500	0	10	2	0	22	27	19	10	0	6.14
Mike Cantwell	L	24	0	3	.000	0	5	1	0	23	25	15	8	0	3.91
Jimmie Keenan	L	31	0	0	.000	0	1	0	0	3	3	1	2	0	3.00

Stan Baumgartner (VR) 27

WORLD SERIES – CLEVELAND (AL) 5 BROOKLYN (NL) 2

LINE SCORES

TEAM	1	2	3	4	5	6	7	8	9	10	11	12	R	H	E
Game 1 October 5 at Brooklyn															
CLE (AL)	0	2	0	1	0	0	0	0	0				3	5	0
BKN (NL)	0	0	0	0	0	0	1	0	0				1	5	1
Coveleski / **Marquard**, Mamaux (7), Cadore (9)															
Game 2 October 6 at Brooklyn															
CLE	0	0	0	0	0	0	0	0	0				0	7	1
BKN	1	0	1	0	1	0	0	0	X				3	7	0
Bagby, Uhle (7) / **Grimes**															
Game 3 October 7 at Brooklyn															
CLE	0	0	0	1	0	0	0	0	0				1	3	1
BKN	2	0	0	0	0	0	0	0	X				2	6	1
Caldwell, Mails (1), Uhle (8) / **S. Smith**															
Game 4 October 9 at Cleveland															
BKN	0	0	0	1	0	0	0	0	0				1	5	1
CLE	2	0	2	0	0	1	0	0	X				5	12	2
Cadore, Mamaux (2), Marquard (3), Pfeffer (6) / **Coveleski**															
Game 5 October 10 at Cleveland															
BKN	0	0	0	0	0	0	0	0	1				1	13	1
CLE	4	0	0	3	1	0	0	0	X				8	12	2
Grimes, Mitchell (4) / **Bagby**															
Game 6 October 11 at Cleveland															
BKN	0	0	0	0	0	0	0	0	0				0	3	0
CLE	0	0	0	0	0	1	0	0	X				1	7	3
S. Smith / **Mails**															
Game 7 October 12 at Cleveland															
BKN	0	0	0	0	0	0	0	0	0				0	5	2
CLE	0	0	0	1	1	0	1	0	X				3	7	3
Grimes, Mamaux (8) / **Coveleski**															

COMPOSITE BATTING

NAME	POS	G	AB	R	H	2B	3B	HR	RBI	BA
Cleveland (AL) Totals		7	217	21	53	9	2	2	17	.244
Wambsganss	2B	7	26	3	4	0	0	0	1	.154
Speaker	OF	7	25	**6**	8	2	1	0	1	.320
Gardner	3B	7	24	1	5	1	0	0	2	.208
Sewell	SS	7	23	0	4	0	0	0	0	.174
O'Neill	C	7	21	1	7	3	0	0	2	**.333**
Jamieson	OF	6	15	2	5	1	0	0	1	**.333**
E. Smith	OF	5	13	1	4	0	1	1	**5**	.308
Evans	OF	4	13	0	4	0	0	0	0	.308
D. Johnston	1B	5	11	1	3	0	0	0	0	.273
Burns	1B	5	10	1	3	1	0	0	2	.300
Wood	OF	4	10	2	2	1	0	0	0	.200
Coveleski	P	3	10	2	1	0	0	0	0	.100
Bagby	P	2	6	1	2	0	0	1	3	.333
Mails	P	2	5	0	0	0	0	0	0	.000
Graney	OF	3	3	0	0	0	0	0	0	.000
Nunamaker	C	2	2	0	1	0	0	0	0	.500
Uhle	P	2	0	0	0	0	0	0	0	.000
Caldwell	P	1	0	0	0	0	0	0	0	.000
Lunte	2B	1	0	0	0	0	0	0	0	.000
Thomas	C	1	0	0	0	0	0	0	0	.000
Brooklyn (NL) Totals		7	215	8	44	5	1	0	8	.205
Wheat	OF	7	**27**	2	**9**	2	0	0	2	**.333**
Myers	OF	7	26	0	6	0	0	0	1	.231
Olson	SS	7	25	2	8	1	0	0	0	.320
Konetchy	1B	7	23	0	4	0	1	0	2	.174
Griffith	OF	7	21	1	4	2	0	0	3	.190
Kilduff	2B	7	21	0	2	0	0	0	0	.095
J. Johnston	3B	4	14	2	3	0	0	0	0	.214
Miller	C	6	14	0	2	0	0	0	0	.143
Sheehan	3B	3	11	0	2	0	0	0	0	.182
Grimes	P	3	6	1	2	0	0	0	0	.333
Krueger	C	4	6	0	1	0	0	0	0	.167
S. Smith	P	2	6	0	0	0	0	0	0	.000
Neis	OF	4	5	0	0	0	0	0	0	.000
Mitchell	P	2	3	0	1	0	0	0	0	.333
Lamar	PH	3	3	0	0	0	0	0	0	.000
Mamaux	P	3	1	0	0	0	0	0	0	.000
Marquard	P	2	1	0	0	0	0	0	0	.000
Pfeffer	P	1	1	0	0	0	0	0	0	.000
Schmandt	PH	1	1	0	0	0	0	0	0	.000

McCabe PR 0-0, Cadore P 0-0

COMPOSITE PITCHING

NAME	G	IP	H	BB	SO	W	L	SV	ERA
Cleveland (AL) Totals	7	61	44	10	20	5	2	0	0.88
Coveleski	**3**	**27**	15	2	**8**	**3**	0	0	0.67
Mails	2	15.2	6	6	6	1	0	0	**0.00**
Bagby	2	15	20	1	3	1	1	0	1.80
Uhle	2	3	1	0	3	0	0	0	0.00
Caldwell	1	.1	2	1	0	0	1	0	27.00
Brooklyn (NL) Totals	7	59	53	21	21	2	5	0	2.44
Grimes	**3**	19.1	**23**	**9**	4	1	**2**	0	4.19
S. Smith	2	17	10	3	3	1	1	0	0.53
Marquard	2	9	7	3	6	0	1	0	1.00
Mitchell	1	4.2	3	3	1	0	0	0	0.00
Mamaux	**3**	4	2	0	5	0	0	0	4.50
Pfeffer	1	3	4	2	1	0	0	0	3.00
Cadore	2	2	4	1	1	0	1	0	9.00

⊖ ⊖ 1921 The Year They Took the Series Underground ⊖ ⊖

In 1906, the city of Chicago had enjoyed the privilege of monopolizing the World Series. This happened when the Cubs and White Sox both managed to win their respective flags at the same time. In 1921, the city of New York duplicated the achievement and even added an oddity to the feat. New York made full use of its underground railroad system to provide baseball with the first subway World Series.

New York had the Giants and Dodgers. But, since both were in the National League, it meant that only the Yankees had to be included if such an historic occasion was to occur. The Yankees had never before won a pennant, but thanks to the bat of Babe Ruth, a Cleveland team hurt by injuries to Tris Speaker and Steve O'Neill, and running out of gas down the backstretch, the American League occupants in New York racked up their first pennant in late September.

It was an exciting enough race to attract fan interest, but those who came out to the ball park did so more to see Ruth than the Yankees. The Sultan of Swat became the talk of the baseball world by popping home runs at an unprecedented rate, chalking up 59 clouts in his ledger by the time the season ended. Ruth grew into the biggest drawing card in sports' history, bringing fans out in droves at home and on the road and, in good measure, overcoming the effect of the 1919 World Series scandal on the game's public image. In addition to his 59 homers, Ruth also amassed 170 runs batted in, tops in the majors, while swinging the wood to a .378 tune, a performance that perhaps is regarded as the most outstanding set of statistics ever aggregated in a single season. But all in all, Ruth was denied the Triple Crown, as he finished third in hitting. And for all of his future greatness, it was destined that this achievement of batting would never be his.

Ruth's supporting cast on the attack included Bob Meusel, A.L. runner-up in homers and third in runs batted in, and clutch-hitting first baseman Wally Pipp. The unheralded Yankee pitching staff turned in the best performance in the league—Carl Mays racked up 27 victories, and newly-acquired, Waite Hoyt, and Bob Shawkey won 19 and 18 games apiece. Despite these assets, the Yankees could not shake the pre-season favorite Indians until September, and the final margin of victory was only 4½ games.

Joining the Yankees in the Subway Series were the Giants as John McGraw led his team to the top of the National League for the seventh time during his 19-year tenure in New York. The Pittsburgh Pirates used good pitching to remain ahead of the pack going into August, but a five-game series sweep in late August by McGraw's boys turned the tide against the Bucs. Good baseball down the stretch enabled the heavy-hitting Giants to overtake slumping Pittsburgh in September and win the crown by four games. George Kelly led the league with 23 home runs and drove in 122 runs for the Giants, and Frankie Frisch and Ross Youngs spiced high batting averages with 100 RBI's each. Dave Bancroft hit .318 while playing standout ball at shortstop, and Emil "Irish" Meusel hit .329 after joining the team in mid-season from Philadelphia.

The anticipated best of nine Subway Series got off to a surprising start when Carl Mays and Waite Hoyt threw shutouts to give the Yankees a two-game lead. But the Yankees could only win one of the next three games before a bad arm prevented Ruth from making any further appearances. The Giants then proceeded to take the next three games and the world championship. Ruth managed only one homer, but he alone of the Yankees' batters was able to hit .300, a mark attained by five Giants.

After the Series, Ruth and Bob Meusel took part in a barnstorming tour, which Judge Landis had ruled unallowed. Landis backed up his tough stance with fines, which covered the players' Series shares, and suspensions of the two until May 20, of the following season. And all in one motion, baseball knew it had an uncompromising boss and a travelling hero.

1921 AMERICAN LEAGUE

NAME	G by POS	B	AGE	G	AB	R	H	2B	3B	HR	RBI	BB	SO	SB	BA	SA
NEW YORK 1st 98-55 .641		MILLER HUGGINS														
TOTALS			28	153	5249	**948**	1576	285	87	**134**	**861**	588	**567**	89	.300	**.464**
Wally Pipp	1B153	L	28	153	588	96	174	35	9	8	97	45	28	17	.296	.427
Aaron Ward	2B123, 3B33	R	24	153	556	77	170	30	10	5	75	42	68	6	.306	.423
Roger Peckinpaugh	SS149	R	30	149	577	128	166	25	7	8	71	84	44	2	.288	.397
Frank Baker	3B83	L	35	94	330	46	97	16	2	9	71	26	12	8	.294	.436
Bob Meusel	OF147	R	24	149	598	104	190	40	16	24	135	34	**88**	17	.318	.559
Elmer Miller	OF56	R	30	56	242	41	72	9	8	4	36	19	16	2	.298	.450
Babe Ruth	OF152, 1B2, P2	L	26	152	540	**177**	204	44	16	**59**	**171**	**144**	81	17	.378	**.846**
Wally Schang	C132	B	31	134	424	77	134	30	5	6	55	78	35	7	.316	.453
Mike McNally	3B48, 2B16	R	27	71	215	36	56	4	2	1	24	14	15	5	.260	.312
Chick Fewster	OF43, 2B15	R	25	66	207	44	58	19	0	1	19	28	43	4	.280	.386
Carl Mays	P49	R	29	51	143	18	49	5	1	2	22	4	7	0	.343	.434
Braggo Roth	OF37	R	28	43	152	29	43	9	2	2	10	19	20	1	.283	.408
Chicken Hawks	OF15	L	25	41	73	16	21	2	3	2	15	5	12	0	.288	.479
Bob Shawkey (LJ)	P38	R	30	38	90	13	27	2	1	1	11	2	13	0	.300	.378
Ping Bodie	OF25	R	33	31	87	5	15	2	2	0	12	8	8	0	.172	.241
Fred Hofmann	C18, 1B1	R	27	23	62	7	11	1	1	1	5	5	13	0	.177	.274
Al DeVormer	C17	R	29	22	49	6	17	4	0	0	7	2	4	2	.347	.429
Johnny Mitchell	SS7, 2B5	B	26	13	42	4	11	1	0	0	2	4	4	1	.262	.286
Tom Connelly	OF3	L	22	4	5	0	1	0	0	0	0	1	0	0	.200	.200
Frank Gleich (IL) 27																
CLEVELAND 2nd 94-60 .610 4.5		TRIS SPEAKER														
TOTALS			29	154	5383	925	1656	**355**	90	42	845	**614**	376	58	.308	.430
Doc Johnston	1B116	L	33	118	384	53	114	20	7	2	44	29	15	2	.297	.401
Bill Wambsganss	2B103, 3B2	R	27	107	410	80	117	28	5	2	46	44	27	13	.285	.393
Joe Sewell	SS154	L	22	154	572	101	182	36	12	4	91	80	17	7	.318	.444
Larry Gardner	3B152	L	35	153	586	101	187	32	14	3	115	65	16	3	.319	.437
Elmer Smith	OF127	L	28	129	431	98	125	28	9	16	84	56	46	0	.290	.508
Tris Speaker	OF128	L	33	132	506	107	183	**52**	14	3	74	68	12	2	.362	.538
Charlie Jamieson	OF137	L	28	140	536	94	166	33	10	1	45	67	27	8	.310	.414
Steve O'Neill	C105	R	29	106	335	39	108	22	1	1	50	57	22	0	.322	.403
George Burns	1B73	R	28	84	244	52	88	21	4	0	48	13	19	2	.361	.480
Jack Graney	OF32	L	35	68	107	19	32	3	0	2	18	20	9	1	.299	.383
Smokey Joe Wood	OF64	R	31	66	194	32	71	16	5	4	60	25	17	2	.366	.562
Riggs Stephenson	2B54, 3B2	R	23	65	206	45	68	17	2	2	34	23	15	4	.330	.461
Joe Evans	OF47	R	26	57	153	36	51	11	0	0	21	19	5	4	.333	.405
Les Nunamaker	C46	R	32	46	131	16	47	7	2	0	24	11	8	1	.359	.443
Ginger Shinault	C20	R	28	22	29	5	11	1	0	0	3	6	5	1	.379	.414
Pinch Thomas	C19	L	33	21	35	1	9	3	0	0	4	10	2	0	.257	.343
Tex Jeanes	OF4	R	20	4	2	2	1	0	0	0	2	1	0	0	.500	.500
Luke Sewell	C3	R	20	3	6	0	0	0	0	0	1	0	3	0	.000	.000
Lou Guisto	1B1	R	27	2	2	0	1	0	0	0	1	0	1	0	.500	.500
Art Wilson	C2	R	35	2	1	0	0	0	0	0	0	0	0	0	.000	.000
ST. LOUIS 3rd 81-73 .526 17.5		LEE FOHL														
TOTALS			27	154	5442	835	1655	246	**106**	67	720	413	407	92	.304	.425
George Sisler	1B138	L	28	138	582	125	216	38	18	12	104	34	27	**35**	.371	.560
Marty McManus	2B96, 3B13, 1B10, SS2	R	21	121	412	49	107	19	8	3	64	27	30	5	.260	.367
Wally Gerber (BH)	SS113	R	29	114	436	55	121	12	9	2	48	34	19	3	.278	.360
2 Frank Ellerbe	3B105	R	25	105	430	65	124	20	12	2	48	22	42	1	.288	.405
Jack Tobin	OF150	L	29	150	**671**	132	236	31	18	8	59	35	22	7	.352	.487
Baby Doll Jacobson	OF141, 1B11	R	30	151	599	90	211	38	14	5	90	42	30	8	.352	.487
Ken Williams	OF145	L	31	146	547	115	190	31	7	24	117	74	42	20	.347	.561
Hank Severeid	C126	R	30	143	472	66	153	23	7	2	78	42	9	7	.324	.415
Dud Lee	SS31, 2B30, 3B3	L	21	72	180	18	30	4	2	0	11	14	34	1	.167	.211
Dutch Wetzel	OF27	R	27	61	119	16	25	2	0	2	10	9	20	0	.210	.277
Pat Collins	C31	R	24	58	111	9	27	3	0	1	10	16	17	1	.243	.297
Lyman Lamb	3B23, 2B7, OF6	R	26	45	134	18	34	9	2	1	17	4	12	0	.254	.373
Jimmy Austin (BA)	SS14, 2B6, 3B2	B	41	27	66	8	18	2	1	0	2	4	7	2	.273	.333
Billy Gleason	2B25	R	26	26	74	6	19	0	1	0	8	6	6	0	.257	.284
1 Earl Smith	3B13, OF4	B	30	25	78	7	26	4	2	2	14	3	4	0	.333	.513
Josh Billings	C12	R	29	20	46	2	10	0	0	0	4	0	7	0	.217	.217
Billy Mullen	3B2	R	25	4	4	0	0	0	0	0	0	2	1	0	.000	.000
Jim Riley	2B4	L	26	4	11	0	0	0	0	0	0	1	3	0	.000	.000
Luke Stuart	2B3	R	29	3	3	2	1	0	0	1	2	0	1	0	.333	1.333

NAME	T	AGE	W	L	PCT	SV	G	GS	CG	IP	H	BB	SO	ShO	ERA
		28	**98**	55	**.641**	15	153	153	**92**	1374	1461	470	**481**	7	**3.79**
Carl Mays	R	29	**27**	9	**.750**	**7**	**49**	38	30	**337**	332	76	70	1	3.04
Waite Hoyt	R	21	19	13	.594	3	44	32	21	282	301	81	102	1	3.10
Bob Shawkey (LJ)	R	30	18	12	.600	2	38	31	18	245	245	86	126	3	4.08
Rip Collins	R	25	11	5	.688	0	28	16	7	137	158	78	64	1	5.45
Jack Quinn	R	37	8	7	.533	0	33	13	6	129	158	32	44	0	3.49
Bill Piercy	R	25	5	4	.556	0	14	10	5	82	82	28	35	1	2.86
Harry Harper (BG)	L	26	4	3	.571	0	8	7	4	53	52	25	22	0	3.74
Alex Ferguson	R	24	3	1	.750	1	17	4	1	56	64	27	9	0	5.95
Babe Ruth	L	26	2	0	1.000	0	2	1	0	9	14	9	2	0	9.00
Tom Sheehan	R	27	1	0	1.000	1	12	1	0	33	43	19	7	0	5.45
Tom Rogers	R	29	0	1	.000	1	5	0	0	11	12	9	0	0	7.36
		28	94	60	.610	14	154	154	81	1378	1534	431	475	**11**	3.90
Stan Coveleski	R	32	23	13	.639	2	43	**40**	29	316	341	84	99	2	3.36
George Uhle	R	22	16	13	.552	2	41	28	13	238	288	63	63	2	4.01
Duster Mails	L	25	14	8	.636	2	34	24	10	194	210	89	87	2	3.94
Jim Bagby	R	31	14	12	.538	4	40	26	12	192	238	44	37	0	4.69
3 Allan Sothoron	R	28	12	4	.750	0	22	16	10	145	146	58	61	2	3.23
Guy Morton	R	28	8	3	.727	0	30	6	2	108	98	32	45	2	2.75
Ray Caldwell	R	33	6	6	.500	4	37	13	5	147	159	49	76	1	4.90
Ted Odenwald	L	19	1	0	1.000	0	10	0	0	17	16	6	4	0	1.59
Bernie Henderson	R	22	0	1	.000	0	2	1	0	3	5	0	1	0	9.00
Bob Clark	R	23	0	0	.000	0	5	0	0	9	23	6	2	0	15.00
Jesse Petty	L	26	0	0	.000	0	4	0	0	9	10	0	0	0	2.00
Joe Harris (DO) 30															
		26	81	73	.526	9	154	154	79	1381	1543	**557**	478	9	4.61
Urban Shocker	R	30	**27**	12	.692	4	47	39	31	327	345	86	132	4	3.55
Dixie Davis	R	30	16	16	.500	0	40	36	20	265	279	**123**	100	2	4.45
Bill Bayne	L	22	11	5	.688	3	47	14	7	164	167	80	82	1	4.72
Elam Vangilder	R	25	11	12	.478	0	31	21	10	180	196	67	48	1	3.95
Ray Kolp	R	26	8	7	.533	0	37	18	5	167	208	51	43	1	4.96
Emilio Palmero	L	26	4	7	.364	0	24	9	4	90	109	49	26	0	5.00
Bill Burwell	R	26	2	4	.333	2	33	3	1	84	102	29	17	0	5.14
1 Allan Sothoron	R	28	1	2	.333	0	5	4	1	28	33	8	9	0	5.14
Bernie Boland	R	29	1	4	.200	0	8	6	0	28	34	28	6	0	9.00
Joe DeBerry	R	24	0	1	.000	0	10	1	0	12	15	10	1	0	6.75
Ray Richmond	R	25	0	1	.000	0	7	1	0	15	23	14	7	0	11.40
Nick Cullop	L	33	0	2	.000	0	4	1	0	12	18	6	3	0	8.25
George Boehler	R	29	0	0	.000	0	1	0	0	1	1	0	0	0	0.00
Dutch Henry	L	19	0	0	.000	0	1	0	0	2	2	0	1	0	4.50
2 Bugs Bennett	R	29	0	0	.000	0	3	1	0	6	11	6	3	0	13.50

WASHINGTON 4th 80-73 .523 18 — GEORGE McBRIDE

NAME	G by POS	B	AGE	G	AB	R	H	2B	3B	HR	RBI	BB	SO	SB	BA	SA
TOTALS			29	154	5294	704	1468	240	96	42	609	462	470	111	.277	.383
Joe Judge	1B152	L	27	153	622	87	187	26	11	7	72	68	35	21	.301	.412
Bucky Harris	2B154	R	24	154	584	82	169	22	8	0	54	54	39	29	.289	.354
Frank O'Rourke	SS122	R	26	123	444	51	104	17	8	3	54	26	56	6	.234	.329
Howard Shanks	3B154	R	30	154	562	81	170	25	19	7	69	57	38	11	.302	.452
Clyde Milan	OF98	L	35	112	406	55	117	19	11	1	40	37	13	4	.288	.397
Sam Rice	OF141	L	31	143	561	83	185	39	13	4	79	38	10	25	.330	.467
Bing Miller	OF109	R	26	114	420	57	121	28	8	9	71	25	50	3	.288	.457
Patsy Gharrity	C115	R	29	121	387	62	120	19	8	7	55	45	44	4	.310	.455
Frank Brower	OF47, 1B4	L	28	83	203	31	53	12	3	1	35	18	7	1	.261	.365
2 Earl Smith	OF43, 3B1	L	30	59	180	20	39	5	2	2	12	10	19	1	.217	.300
Val Picinich	C45	R	24	45	141	10	39	9	0	0	12	16	21	0	.277	.340
Duffy Lewis	OF27	R	32	27	102	11	19	4	1	0	14	8	10	1	.186	.245
2 Donie Bush	SS21	B	33	23	84	15	18	1	0	0	2	12	4	2	.214	.226
Bobby LaMotte	SS12	R	23	16	41	5	8	0	0	0	2	5	0	0	.195	.195
Goose Goslin	OF14	L	20	14	50	8	13	1	1	1	6	5	5	0	.260	.380
1 Frank Ellerbe	3B1	R	25	10	10	1	2	0	1	0	2	0	2	0	.200	.400
1 Tony Brottem	C4	R	29	4	7	1	1	0	0	0	0	2	1	0	.143	.143
George Foss	3B2	R	24	4	7	0	0	0	0	0	0	0	1	0	.000	.000
Ricardo Torres	C2	R	27	2	3	1	1	0	0	0	0	1	1	0	.333	.333

NAME	T	AGE	W	L	PCT	SV	G	GS	CG	IP	H	BB	SO	ShO	ERA
		28	80	73	.523	10	154	154	80	1384	1568	442	452	8	3.97
George Mogridge	L	32	18	14	.563	0	38	36	21	288	301	66	101	4	3.00
Tom Zachary	L	25	18	16	.529	1	39	31	17	250	314	59	53	1	3.96
Walter Johnson	R	33	17	14	.548	1	35	32	25	264	265	92	143	1	3.51
Eric Erickson	R	29	8	10	.444	0	32	22	9	179	181	65	71	2	3.62
Al Schacht	R	28	6	6	.500	1	29	5	2	83	110	27	15	0	4.88
Harry Courtney	L	22	6	9	.400	1	30	15	3	133	159	71	26	0	5.62
Jose Acosta	R	30	5	4	.556	3	33	7	2	116	148	36	30	0	4.35
Jim Shaw	R	27	1	0	1.000	3	15	4	0	40	59	17	4	0	7.43
Tom Phillips	R	32	1	0	1.000	0	1	1	1	9	9	3	2	0	2.00
Nemo Gaines (ML)	L	23	0	0	.000	0	4	0	0	5	5	2	1	0	0.00
Frank Woodward	R	27	0	0	.000	0	3	1	0	11	11	3	4	0	5.73
Red Bird	L	31	0	0	.000	0	1	0	0	5	5	1	2	0	5.40
Ralph Miller	L	22	0	0	.000	0	1	0	0	1	0	0	0	0	0.00
Vance McIlree	R	23	0	0	.000	0	1	0	0	1	1	0	0	0	9.00

BOSTON 5th 75-79 .487 23.5 — HUGH DUFFY

NAME	G by POS	B	AGE	G	AB	R	H	2B	3B	HR	RBI	BB	SO	SB	BA	SA
TOTALS			30	154	5206	668	1440	248	69	17	584	428	329	83	.277	.361
Stuffy McInnis	OF152	R	30	152	584	72	179	31	10	0	74	21	9	2	.307	.394
Del Pratt	2B134	R	33	135	521	80	169	36	10	5	100	44	10	8	.324	.461
Everett Scott	SS154	R	28	154	576	65	151	21	9	1	60	27	21	5	.262	.335
Eddie Foster	3B94, 2B22	R	34	120	412	51	117	18	6	0	30	57	15	13	.284	.357
Shano Collins	OF138, 1B3	R	35	141	542	63	155	29	12	4	65	18	38	15	.286	.406
Nemo Leibold	OF117	L	29	123	467	88	143	26	6	0	30	41	27	13	.306	.388
Mike Menosky	OF133	L	26	133	477	77	143	18	5	3	43	60	45	12	.300	.377
Muddy Ruel	C109	R	25	113	358	41	99	21	1	1	43	41	15	2	.277	.349
Ossie Vitt	3B71, OF3, 1B2	R	31	78	232	29	44	11	1	0	12	45	13	1	.190	.246
Roxy Walters	C54	R	28	54	169	17	34	4	1	0	13	10	11	3	.201	.237
Bullet Joe Bush	P37, OF4	R	28	51	120	19	39	5	4	0	14	3	14	2	.325	.433
Tim Hendryx (BG)	OF41	R	30	49	137	10	33	8	2	0	21	24	13	1	.241	.328
Sammy Vick	OF14, C1	R	26	44	77	5	20	3	1	0	9	1	10	0	.260	.325
Pinky Pittinger	OF27, 3B3, SS2, 2B1	R	22	40	91	6	18	1	0	0	5	4	13	3	.198	.209
Ernie Neitzke	OF8, P2	R	26	11	25	3	6	0	0	0	1	4	4	0	.240	.240
Jack Perrin	OF4	L	23	4	13	3	3	0	0	0	1	0	3	0	.231	.231
Bert Chaplin	C1	L	27	3	2	0	0	0	0	0	0	0	1	0	.000	.000
Hob Hiller		R	28	1	1	0	0	0	0	0	0	0	0	0	.000	.000

NAME	T	AGE	W	L	PCT	SV	G	GS	CG	IP	H	BB	SO	ShO	ERA
		27	75	79	.487	5	154	154	88	1364	1521	452	446	9	3.99
Sad Sam Jones	R	28	23	16	.590	1	40	38	25	299	318	78	98	5	3.22
Bullet Joe Bush	R	28	16	9	.640	1	37	31	20	254	244	93	96	3	3.51
Herb Pennock	L	27	12	14	.462	0	32	32	15	223	268	59	91	1	4.03
Benn Karr	R	27	8	7	.533	0	26	7	5	118	123	38	37	0	3.66
Elmer Myers	R	27	8	12	.400	0	30	20	11	172	217	53	40	0	4.87
Allen Russell	R	27	7	11	.389	3	39	14	8	173	204	77	60	0	4.11
Hank Thormahlen	L	24	1	7	.125	0	23	9	3	96	101	34	17	0	4.50
Curt Fullerton	R	22	0	1	.000	0	4	1	1	15	22	10	4	0	9.00
2 Allan Sothoron	R	28	0	2	.000	0	2	2	0	6	15	5	2	0	13.50
Ernie Neitzke	R	26	0	0	.000	0	2	0	0	7	8	4	1	0	6.43
Sam Dodge	R	31	0	0	.000	0	1	0	0	1	1	1	0	0	9.00

DETROIT 6th 71-82 .464 27 — TY COBB

NAME	G by POS	B	AGE	G	AB	R	H	2B	3B	HR	RBI	BB	SO	SB	BA	SA
TOTALS			29	154	5461	883	**1724**	268	100	58	800	582	376	95	**.316**	.433
Lu Blue	1B152	B	24	153	585	103	180	33	11	5	75	103	47	13	.308	.427
Ralph Young	2B106	B	31	107	401	70	120	8	3	0	29	69	23	11	.299	.334
1 Donie Bush	SS81, 2B23	B	33	104	402	72	113	6	5	0	27	45	23	8	.281	.321
Bob Jones	3B141	L	31	141	554	82	168	23	9	1	72	37	24	8	.303	.383
Harry Heilmann	OF145, 1B4	R	26	149	602	114	**237**	43	14	19	139	53	37	2	**.394**	.606
Ty Cobb	OF121	L	34	128	507	124	197	37	16	12	101	56	19	22	.389	.596
Bobby Veach	OF149	L	33	150	612	110	207	43	13	16	128	48	31	14	.338	.529
Johnny Bassler	C115	L	26	119	388	37	119	18	5	0	56	58	16	2	.307	.379
Chick Shorten	OF52, C1	L	29	92	217	33	59	11	3	0	23	20	11	2	.272	.350
Ira Flagstead	SS55, OF12, 2B8, 3B1	R	27	85	259	40	79	15	1	0	31	21	21	7	.305	.371
Joe Sargent	2B24, 3B23, SS19	R	27	66	178	21	45	8	5	2	22	24	26	2	.253	.388
Larry Woodall	C24	R	26	46	80	10	29	4	1	0	14	6	7	1	.363	.438
1 Eddie Ainsmith	C34	R	29	35	98	6	27	5	2	0	12	13	7	1	.276	.367
Howard Ehmke	P30	R	27	30	74	9	21	3	1	0	9	1	7	0	.284	.351
Herm Merritt	SS17	R	20	20	46	3	17	1	2	0	6	1	5	1	.370	.478
Clyde Manion	C4	R	24	12	10	0	2	0	0	0	2	2	2	0	.200	.200
Sammy Hale		R	24	9	2	2	0	0	0	0	0	0	1	0	.000	.000
Sam Barnes	2B2	L	21	7	11	2	2	1	0	0	0	2	1	0	.182	.273
Jackie Tavener	SS2	L	23	2	4	0	0	0	0	0	0	0	1	0	.000	.000
George Cunningham	OF1	R	26	1	0	0	0	0	0	0	0	0	0	0	.000	.000
Clarence Huber	3B1	R	24	1	0	0	0	0	0	0	0	0	0	0	.000	.000

NAME	T	AGE	W	L	PCT	SV	G	GS	CG	IP	H	BB	SO	ShO	ERA
		28	71	82	.464	**17**	154	154	73	1386	1634	495	452	4	4.40
Howard Ehmke	R	27	13	14	.481	0	30	22	13	196	220	81	68	1	4.55
Dutch Leonard	L	29	11	13	.458	1	36	32	16	245	273	63	120	1	3.75
Red Oldham	L	27	11	14	.440	1	40	28	12	229	258	81	67	1	4.25
Hooks Dauss	R	31	10	15	.400	1	32	28	16	233	275	81	68	0	4.33
Bert Cole	L	23	7	4	.636	1	20	11	7	110	134	36	22	1	4.25
Suds Sutherland	R	27	6	2	.750	0	13	8	3	58	80	18	18	0	4.97
Jim Middleton	R	32	6	11	.353	7	38	10	2	122	149	44	31	0	5.01
Slicker Parks	R	25	3	2	.600	0	10	1	0	25	33	16	10	0	5.76
Carl Holling	R	24	3	7	.300	4	35	11	4	136	162	58	38	0	4.30
2 Pol Perritt	R	28	1	0	1.000	0	4	2	0	13	18	7	3	0	4.85
Lefty Stewart	L	20	0	0	.000	1	5	0	0	9	20	5	4	0	12.00
Jim Walsh	L	26	0	0	.000	0	3	0	0	4	2	1	3	0	2.25
Doc Ayres	R	31	0	0	.000	0	2	1	0	4	9	2	0	0	9.00
Danny Boone	R	26	0	0	.000	1	1	0	0	2	1	2	0	0	0.00

CHICAGO 7th 62-92 .403 36.5 — KID GLEASON

NAME	G by POS	B	AGE	G	AB	R	H	2B	3B	HR	RBI	BB	SO	SB	BA	SA
TOTALS			29	154	5329	683	1509	242	82	35	608	445	474	97	.283	.379
Earl Sheely	1B154	R	28	154	563	68	171	25	6	11	95	57	34	4	.304	.428
Eddie Collins	2B136	L	34	139	526	79	177	20	10	2	58	66	11	12	.337	.424
Ernie Johnson	SS141	L	33	142	613	93	181	28	7	1	51	29	24	22	.295	.369
Eddie Mulligan	3B152, SS1	R	26	152	609	82	153	21	12	1	45	32	53	13	.251	.330
Harry Hooper (BH)	OF108	L	33	108	419	74	137	26	5	8	58	55	21	13	.327	.470
Amos Strunk	OF111	L	32	121	401	68	133	19	10	3	69	38	27	7	.332	.451
Bibb Falk	OF149	L	22	152	585	62	167	31	11	5	82	37	69	4	.285	.402
Ray Schalk	C126	R	28	128	416	32	105	24	4	0	47	40	36	3	.252	.329
Johnny Mostil	OF91, 2B1	R	25	100	326	43	98	21	7	3	42	28	35	10	.301	.436
Hervey McClellan	2B20, SS15, OF15, 3B5	R	26	63	196	20	35	4	1	1	14	14	18	2	.179	.224
Yam Yaryan	C34	R	28	45	102	11	31	8	2	0	15	9	16	0	.304	.422
George Lees	C16	R	26	20	42	3	9	2	0	0	4	0	3	0	.214	.262
Fred Bratchi	OF5	R	29	16	28	0	8	1	0	0	3	0	2	0	.286	.321
Red Ostergard		L	23	12	11	2	4	0	0	0	0	0	2	0	.364	.364
Elmer Leifer	3B1, OF1	L	28	9	10	0	3	0	0	0	1	0	4	0	.300	.300
Eddie Murphy		L	29	6	5	1	1	0	0	0	0	0	0	0	.200	.200
Frank Pratt		L	23	1	1	0	0	0	0	0	0	0	0	0	.000	.000

NAME	T	AGE	W	L	PCT	SV	G	GS	CG	IP	H	BB	SO	ShO	ERA
		27	62	92	.403	9	154	154	86	1365	1603	549	392	7	4.94
Red Faber	R	32	25	15	.625	1	43	39	**32**	331	293	87	124	4	**2.48**
Dickie Kerr	L	27	19	17	.528	1	44	37	25	309	**357**	96	80	3	4.72
Shovel Hodge	R	27	6	8	.429	2	36	11	6	143	191	54	25	0	6.54
Roy Wilkinson	R	27	4	20	.174	3	36	22	11	198	259	78	50	0	5.14
Doug McWeeney	R	24	3	6	.333	2	27	9	4	98	127	45	46	0	6.06
Jack Russell	L	25	2	5	.286	0	11	8	4	66	82	35	15	0	5.32
Dominick Mulrennan	R	27	2	8	.200	0	12	10	3	56	84	36	10	0	7.24
Cy Twombly	R	24	1	2	.333	0	7	4	0	28	26	25	7	0	5.79
Jack Wieneke	L	27	0	1	.000	0	10	3	0	25	39	17	10	0	8.28
Sarge Connally	R	22	0	1	.000	0	5	2	0	22	29	10	6	0	6.54
Lum Davenport	L	21	0	3	.000	0	13	2	0	35	41	32	9	0	6.94
Lee Thompson	L	23	0	3	.000	0	4	4	0	21	32	6	4	0	8.14
1 Bugs Bennett	R	29	0	3	.000	0	3	2	1	18	19	16	2	0	6.00
Russ Pence	R	21	0	0	.000	0	4	0	0	5	6	7	2	0	9.00
Hod Fenner	R	23	0	0	.000	0	2	1	0	7	14	3	1	0	7.71
John Michaelson	R	27	0	0	.000	0	2	0	0	3	4	1	1	0	9.00
Babe Blackburn	R	26	0	0	.000	0	1	0	0	1	0	1	1	0	0.00

PHILADELPHIA 8th 53-100 .346 45 — CONNIE MACK

NAME	G by POS	B	AGE	G	AB	R	H	2B	3B	HR	RBI	BB	SO	SB	BA	SA
TOTALS			24	155	**5465**	657	1497	256	64	82	601	424	561	68	.274	.389
Johnny Walker	1B99, C7	R	24	113	423	41	109	14	5	2	45	9	29	5	.258	.329
Jimmy Dykes	2B155	R	24	155	613	88	168	32	13	16	77	60	75	6	.274	.447
Chick Galloway	SS110, 3B20, 2B1	R	24	131	465	42	123	28	5	3	47	29	43	12	.265	.366
Joe Dugan	3B119	R	24	119	461	54	136	22	6	10	58	28	45	5	.295	.434
Whitey Witt	OF154	L	25	154	629	100	198	31	11	4	45	77	52	16	.315	.418
Frank Welch	OF104	R	23	115	403	48	115	18	6	7	45	34	43	6	.285	.412
Tilly Walker	OF142	R	33	142	556	89	169	32	5	23	101	73	41	3	.304	.504
Cy Perkins	C141	R	25	141	538	58	155	31	4	12	73	32	32	5	.288	.428
Frank Brazill	1B36, 3B9	L	21	66	177	17	48	3	1	0	19	23	21	2	.271	.299
Emmett McCann	SS32, 3B9, 2B2, 1B1, C1	R	19	52	157	15	35	5	0	0	15	4	6	2	.223	.255
Paul Johnson	OF32	R	24	48	127	17	40	6	2	1	10	9	17	0	.315	.417
Glenn Myatt	C27	L	23	44	69	6	14	2	0	0	5	6	7	0	.203	.232
Ivy Griffin	1B28	L	25	39	103	14	33	4	2	0	13	5	6	1	.320	.398
Zip Collins	OF21	L	29	24	71	14	20	5	1	0	5	6	5	1	.282	.380
Frank Walker	OF19	R	26	19	66	6	15	3	0	1	6	8	11	1	.227	.318
Bill Barrett	SS7, P4, 3B2, 1B1	R	21	14	30	3	7	2	1	0	3	0	5	0	.233	.367
Frank Callaway	SS14	R	23	14	50	7	12	1	1	0	2	2	11	1	.240	.300
Ben Mallonee	OF6	L	27	7	24	2	6	1	0	0	0	1	1	1	.250	.292
Lena Styles	C2	R	21	4	5	0	1	0	0	0	0	0	2	0	.200	.200
Elmer Yoter		R	21	3	3	0	0	0	0	0	0	0	1	0	.000	.000
Dot Fulghum	SS1	R	20	2	2	0	0	0	0	0	0	1	1	0	.000	.000
Red Shannon		B	24	1	1	0	0	0	0	0	0	0	0	0	.000	.000

NAME	T	AGE	W	L	PCT	SV	G	GS	CG	IP	H	BB	SO	ShO	ERA
		24	53	**100**	.346	7	155	155	75	**1403**	**1645**	548	431	1	4.61
Eddie Rommel	R	23	16	**23**	.410	3	46	32	20	285	312	87	71	0	3.95
Slim Harriss	R	24	11	16	.407	2	39	28	14	228	258	73	92	0	4.27
Roy Moore	L	22	10	10	.500	0	29	26	12	192	206	122	64	0	4.50
Bob Hasty	R	25	5	16	.238	0	35	22	9	179	238	40	46	0	4.88
Scott Perry	R	30	3	6	.333	1	12	8	5	70	77	24	19	0	4.11
Rollie Naylor	R	29	3	13	.188	0	32	19	6	169	214	55	39	0	4.84
Dave Keefe	R	24	2	9	.182	1	44	12	4	173	214	64	68	0	4.68
Bill Barrett	R	21	1	0	1.000	0	4	0	0	5	2	9	2	0	7.20
Fred Heimach	L	20	1	0	1.000	0	1	1	1	9	7	1	1	1	0.00
Harvey Freeman	R	23	1	4	.200	0	18	4	2	51	65	35	5	0	7.24
Arliss Taylor			0	1	.000	0	1	1	0	2	7	2	0	0	22.50
Jim Sullivan	R	27	0	2	.000	0	2	2	2	17	20	7	8	0	3.18
Lefty Wolf	L	21	0	0	.000	0	8	0	0	15	15	16	12	0	7.20
Bill Bishop	L	20	0	0	.000	0	2	0	0	7	8	10	4	0	9.00
Ray Miner	L	24	0	0	.000	0	1	0	0	1	2	3	0	0	36.00

NEW YORK 1st 94-59 .614 — JOHN McGRAW

NAME	G by POS	B	AGE	G	AB	R	H	2B	3B	HR	RBI	BB	SO	SB	BA	SA
TOTALS			27	153	5278	840	1575	237	93	75	748	469	390	137	.298	.421
George Kelly	1B149	R	25	149	587	95	181	42	9	23	122	40	73	4	.308	.528
2 Johnny Rawlings	2B86, SS1	R	28	86	307	40	82	8	1	1	30	18	19	4	.267	.309
Dave Bancroft	SS153	B	30	153	606	121	193	26	15	6	67	66	23	17	.318	.441
Frankie Frisch	3B93, 2B61	B	22	153	618	121	211	31	17	8	100	42	28	49	.341	.485
Ross Youngs	OF137	L	24	141	504	90	165	24	16	3	102	71	47	21	.327	.456
George Burns	OF149, 3B1	R	31	149	605	111	181	28	9	4	61	80	24	19	.299	.395
2 Irish Meusel	OF62	R	28	62	243	37	80	12	6	2	36	15	12	5	.329	.453
Frank Snyder	C101	R	28	108	309	36	99	13	2	8	45	27	24	3	.320	.453
Earl Smith	C78	L	24	89	229	35	77	8	4	10	51	27	8	4	.336	.537
Eddie Brown	OF30	R	29	70	128	16	36	6	2	0	12	4	11	1	.281	.359
1 Curt Walker	OF58	L	24	64	192	30	55	13	5	3	35	15	8	4	.286	.453
1 Goldie Rapp	3B56	B	29	58	181	21	39	9	1	0	15	15	13	3	.215	.276
Bill Cunningham	OF20	R	25	40	76	10	21	2	1	1	12	3	3	0	.276	.368
1 Lee King	OF35, 1B1	R	28	39	94	17	21	4	2	0	7	13	6	0	.223	.309
Bill Patterson	3B14, SS7	R	24	23	35	5	14	0	0	1	5	2	5	0	.400	.486
Alex Gaston	C11	R	28	20	22	1	5	1	1	0	3	1	9	0	.227	.364
1 John Monroe	2B8, SS1	L	22	19	21	4	3	0	0	1	3	3	6	0	.143	.286
2 Casey Stengel	OF18	L	30	18	22	4	5	1	0	0	2	1	5	0	.227	.273
Mike Gonzalez	1B6, C2	R	30	13	24	3	9	1	0	0	0	1	0	0	.375	.417
Howard Berry	2B7	B	26	9	6	0	2	0	1	0	2	1	1	0	.333	.667
Hank Schreiber	2B2, SS2, 3B1	R	29	4	6	2	2	0	0	0	2	1	1	0	.333	.333
Joe Connolly	OF1	R	25	2	4	0	0	0	0	0	0	1	1	0	.000	.000
Wally Kopf	3B2	B	21	2	3	0	1	0	0	0	0	1	1	0	.333	.333
Bud Heine	2B1	L	20	1	2	0	0	0	0	0	0	0	0	0	.000	.000
1 Butch Henline		R	26	1	1	0	0	0	0	0	0	0	1	0	.000	.000
Jim Mahady	2B1	R	20	1	0	0	0	0	0	0	0	0	0	0	.000	.000

Benny Kauff (DL) 31

NAME	T	AGE	W	L	PCT	SV	G	GS	CG	IP	H	BB	SO	ShO	ERA
		30	94	59	.614	18	153	153	71	1372	1497	295	357	9	3.56
Art Nehf	L	28	20	10	.667	1	41	34	18	261	266	55	67	2	3.62
Fred Toney	R	33	18	11	.621	3	42	32	16	249	274	65	63	1	3.61
Jesse Barnes	R	28	15	9	.625	6	42	31	15	259	298	44	56	1	3.10
Phil Douglas	R	31	15	10	.600	2	40	27	13	222	266	55	55	3	4.21
Rosy Ryan	R	23	7	10	.412	3	36	16	5	147	140	32	58	0	3.74
Slim Sallee	L	36	6	4	.600	2	37	0	0	96	115	14	23	0	3.65
Rube Benton (DE)	L	34	5	2	.714	0	18	9	3	72	72	17	11	1	2.87
Red Shea	R	22	5	2	.714	0	9	2	1	32	28	2	10	0	3.09
1 Pol Perritt	R	28	2	0	1.000	0	5	1	0	12	17	2	5	0	3.75
2 Red Causey	R	27	1	1	.500	0	7	1	0	15	13	6	1	0	2.40
Walt Zink	R	21	0	0	.000	0	2	0	0	4	4	3	1	0	2.25
Claude Jonnard	R	24	0	0	.000	1	1	0	0	4	4	0	7	0	0.00

PITTSBURGH 2nd 90-63 .588 4 — GEORGE GIBSON

NAME	G by POS	B	AGE	G	AB	R	H	2B	3B	HR	RBI	BB	SO	SB	BA	SA
TOTALS			29	154	5379	692	1533	231	104	37	623	341	371	134	.285	.387
Charlie Grimm	1B150	L	22	151	562	62	154	21	17	7	71	31	38	6	.274	.409
George Cutshaw	2B84	R	33	98	350	46	119	18	4	0	53	11	11	14	.340	.414
Rabbit Maranville	SS153	R	29	153	612	90	180	25	12	1	70	47	38	25	.294	.379
Clyde Barnhart	3B118	R	25	124	449	66	116	15	13	3	62	32	36	3	.258	.370
Possum Whitted	OF102, 1B7	R	31	108	403	60	114	23	7	7	63	26	21	5	.283	.427
Max Carey	OF139	B	31	140	521	85	161	34	4	7	56	70	30	37	.309	.430
Carson Bigbee	OF146	L	26	147	632	100	204	23	17	3	42	41	19	21	.323	.427
Walter Schmidt	C111	R	34	114	393	30	111	9	3	0	38	12	13	10	.282	.321
Cotton Tierney	2B72, 3B32, OF4, SS3	R	27	117	442	49	132	22	8	3	52	24	31	4	.299	.405
2 Dave Robertson	OF58	L	31	60	230	29	74	18	3	6	48	12	16	4	.322	.504
2 Tony Brottem	C29	R	29	30	91	6	22	2	0	0	9	3	11	0	.242	.264
Ray Rohmwer	OF10	L	26	30	40	6	10	3	2	0	6	4	8	0	.250	.425
Johnny Mokan	OF15	R	25	19	52	7	14	3	2	0	9	5	3	0	.269	.404
Bill Skiff	C13	R	25	16	45	7	13	2	0	0	11	0	4	1	.289	.333
Johnny Gooch	C13	B	23	13	38	2	9	0	0	0	3	3	3	1	.237	.237
Pie Traynor	3B3, SS1	R	21	7	19	0	5	0	0	0	2	1	2	0	.263	.263
Mike Wilson	C5	R	24	5	4	0	0	0	0	0	0	0	0	0	.000	.000
Kiki Cuyler	OF1	R	21	1	3	0	0	0	0	0	0	0	1	0	.000	.000
Bill Warwick	C1	R	23	1	1	0	0	0	0	0	0	0	0	0	.000	.000

NAME	T	AGE	W	L	PCT	SV	G	GS	CG	IP	H	BB	SO	ShO	ERA
		29	90	63	.588	10	154	154	88	1416	1448	322	500	10	3.16
Wilbur Cooper	L	29	22	14	.611	0	38	38	29	327	341	80	134	2	3.25
Whitey Glazner	R	28	14	5	.737	1	36	25	15	234	214	58	88	0	2.77
Babe Adams	R	39	14	5	.737	0	25	20	11	160	155	18	55	2	2.65
Earl Hamilton	L	29	13	15	.464	0	35	30	12	225	237	58	59	2	3.36
Johnny Morrison	R	25	9	7	.563	0	21	17	11	144	131	33	52	3	2.88
Jimmy Zinn	R	26	7	6	.538	4	32	9	5	127	159	30	49	1	3.68
Chief Yellowhorse (GJ)	R	23	5	3	.625	1	10	4	1	48	45	13	19	0	3.00
Hal Carlson	R	27	4	8	.333	4	31	10	3	110	121	23	37	0	4.26
1 Elmer Ponder	R	28	2	0	1.000	0	8	1	1	25	29	3	3	0	2.16
Lyle Bigbee	R	27	0	0	.000	0	5	0	0	8	4	4	1	0	1.13
Bill Hughes	R	24	0	0	.000	0	1	0	0	2	3	1	2	0	4.50
Phill Morrison	R	26	0	0	.000	0	1	0	0	1	1	0	1	0	0.00
Drew Rader	L	20	0	0	.000	0	1	0	0	2	2	0	0	0	0.00
Rip Wheeler	R	23	0	0	.000	0	1	0	0	3	6	1	0	0	9.00

ST. LOUIS 3rd 87-66 .569 7 — BRANCH RICKEY

NAME	G by POS	B	AGE	G	AB	R	H	2B	3B	HR	RBI	BB	SO	SB	BA	SA
TOTALS			26	154	5309	809	1635	260	88	83	733	382	452	94	.308	.437
Jack Fournier	1B149	L	28	149	574	103	197	27	9	16	86	56	48	20	.343	.505
Rogers Hornsby	2B142, OF6, SS3, 3B3, 1B1	R	25	154	592	131	235	44	18	21	126	60	48	13	.397	.639
Doc Lavan	SS150	R	30	150	560	58	145	23	11	2	82	23	30	7	.259	.350
Milt Stock	3B149	R	27	149	587	96	180	27	6	3	84	48	26	11	.307	.388
Jack Smith	OF103	L	26	116	411	86	135	22	9	7	33	21	24	11	.328	.477
Les Mann	OF 79	R	27	97	256	57	84	12	7	7	30	23	28	5	.328	.512
Austin McHenry	OF152	R	25	152	574	92	201	37	8	17	102	38	49	10	.350	.531
Vern Clemons	C109	R	29	117	341	29	109	16	2	2	48	33	17	0	.320	.396
Joe Schultz	OF67, 3B3, 1B2	R	27	92	275	37	85	20	3	6	45	15	11	4	.309	.469
Pickles Dillhoefer	C69	R	26	76	162	19	39	4	4	0	15	11	7	2	.241	.315
Cliff Heathcote (BP)	OF51	L	23	62	156	18	38	6	2	0	9	10	9	7	.244	.308
Heinie Mueller	OF54	L	21	55	176	25	62	10	6	1	34	11	22	2	.352	.494
Burt Shotton	OF11	L	36	38	48	9	12	1	1	1	7	7	4	0	.250	.375
2 Eddie Ainsmith	C23, 1B1	R	29	27	62	5	18	0	1	0	5	3	4	0	.290	.323
Specs Toporcer	2B12, SS2	L	22	22	53	4	14	1	0	0	2	3	4	1	.264	.283
1 Hal Janvrin	1B9, 2B1	R	28	18	32	5	9	1	0	0	5	1	0	1	.281	.313
Herb Hunter	1B1	L	25	9	2	3	0	0	0	0	0	1	0	0	.000	.000
Charlie Niebergall	C3	R	22	5	6	1	1	0	0	0	0	0	0	0	.167	.167
Walt Irwin		R	23	4	1	1	0	0	0	0	0	0	1	0	.000	.000
Reuben Ewing	SS1	R	21	3	1	0	0	0	0	0	0	0	1	0	.000	.000
Howie Jones	OF1	L	24	3	2	0	0	0	0	0	0	0	1	0	.000	.000
George Gilham		R	21	1	1	0	0	0	0	0	0	0	0	0	.000	.000
Lew McCarty		R	32	1	1	0	0	0	0	0	0	0	1	0	.000	.000

NAME	T	AGE	W	L	PCT	SV	G	GS	CG	IP	H	BB	SO	ShO	ERA
		28	87	66	.569	16	154	154	70	1372	1486	399	464	10	3.62
Jesse Haines	R	27	18	12	.600	0	37	29	13	244	261	56	84	2	3.50
Bill Doak	R	30	15	6	.714	1	32	28	13	209	224	37	83	1	2.58
Bill Pertica	R	24	14	10	.583	2	38	31	15	208	212	70	67	2	3.38
Roy Walker	R	28	11	12	.478	3	38	24	11	171	194	53	52	0	4.21
2 Jeff Pfeffer	R	33	9	3	.750	0	18	13	7	99	115	28	22	1	4.27
Bill Sherdel	L	24	9	8	.529	1	38	8	5	144	137	38	57	1	3.19
Lou North	R	30	4	4	.500	7	40	0	0	86	81	32	28	0	3.56
1 Ferdie Schupp	L	30	2	0	1.000	1	9	4	1	37	42	21	22	0	4.13
Bill Bailey	L	32	2	5	.286	0	19	6	3	74	95	22	20	1	4.26
Tink Riviere	R	21	1	0	1.000	0	18	2	0	38	45	20	15	0	6.16
Marv Goodwin	R	29	1	2	.333	1	14	4	1	36	47	9	7	0	3.75
Jakie May	L	25	1	3	.250	0	5	5	1	21	29	12	5	0	4.71
Mike Kircher	R	23	0	1	.000	0	3	0	0	3	4	1	2	0	9.00

BOSTON 4th 79-74 .516 15 — FRED MITCHELL

NAME	G by POS	B	AGE	G	AB	R	H	2B	3B	HR	RBI	BB	SO	SB	BA	SA
TOTALS			28	153	5385	721	1561	209	100	61	630	377	470	94	.290	.400
Walter Holke	1B150	R	28	150	579	60	151	15	10	3	63	17	41	8	.261	.337
Hod Ford	2B119, SS33	R	23	152	555	50	155	29	5	2	61	36	49	2	.279	.360
Walter Barbare	SS121, 2B8, 3B2	R	29	134	550	66	166	22	7	0	49	24	28	11	.302	.367
Tony Boeckel	3B153	R	28	153	592	93	185	20	13	10	84	52	41	20	.313	.441
Billy Southworth	OF141	L	28	141	569	86	175	25	15	7	79	36	13	22	.308	.441
Ray Powell	OF149	L	32	149	624	114	191	25	18	12	74	58	85	6	.306	.462
Walton Cruise	OF102, 1B2	L	31	108	344	47	119	16	7	8	55	48	24	10	.346	.503
Mickey O'Neil	C95	R	23	98	277	26	69	9	4	2	29	23	21	2	.249	.332
Fred Nicholson	OF59, 1B4, 2B2	R	26	83	245	36	80	11	7	5	41	17	29	5	.327	.490
Hank Gowdy	C53	R	31	64	164	17	49	7	2	2	17	16	11	2	.299	.402
Frank Gibson	C41	L	30	63	125	14	33	5	4	2	13	3	17	0	.264	.416
Lloyd Christenbury	2B32, SS2, 3B2	L	27	62	125	34	44	6	2	3	16	21	7	3	.352	.504
Al Nixon	OF45	R	35	55	138	25	33	6	3	1	9	7	11	3	.239	.348
Jack Scott	P47	L	29	51	88	14	30	5	1	1	12	5	7	0	.341	.455
1 John Sullivan		R	31	5	5	0	0	0	0	0	0	0	0	0	.000	.000

NAME	T	AGE	W	L	PCT	SV	G	GS	CG	IP	H	BB	SO	ShO	ERA
		25	79	74	.516	12	153	153	74	1385	1488	420	382	11	3.90
Joe Oeschger	R	30	20	14	.588	0	46	36	19	299	303	97	68	3	3.52
Dana Fillingim	R	27	15	10	.600	1	44	22	11	240	249	56	54	3	3.45
Jack Scott	R	29	15	13	.536	3	47	29	16	234	258	57	83	2	3.69
Mule Watson	R	24	14	13	.519	2	44	31	15	259	269	57	48	1	3.86
Hugh McQuillan	R	23	13	17	.433	5	45	31	13	250	284	90	94	2	4.00
Cy Morgan	R	24	1	1	.500	1	17	0	0	30	37	17	8	0	6.60
Garland Braxton	L	21	1	3	.250	0	17	2	0	37	44	17	16	0	4.87
Johnny Cooney	L	20	0	1	.000	0	8	1	0	21	19	10	9	0	3.86
Al Pierotti	R	25	0	1	.000	0	2	0	0	2	3	3	1	0	18.00
Leo Townsend	L	30	0	1	.000	0	1	1	0	1	2	3	0	0	36.00
Ira Townsend	R	27	0	0	.000	0	4	0	0	7	11	4	0	0	6.43
1 Eddie Eayrs	L	30	0	0	.000	0	2	0	0	5	9	9	1	0	16.20

Dick Rudolph (DP) 33

BROOKLYN 5th 77-75 .507 16.5 — WILBERT ROBINSON

NAME	G by POS	B	AGE	G	AB	R	H	2B	3B	HR	RBI	BB	SO	SB	BA	SA
TOTALS			31	152	5263	667	1476	209	85	59	584	325	400	91	.280	.386
Ray Schmandt	1B92	R	25	95	350	42	107	8	5	1	43	11	22	3	.306	.366
Pete Kilduff	2B105, 3B1	R	28	107	372	45	107	15	10	3	45	31	36	6	.288	.406
Ivy Olson	SS133, 2B20	R	35	151	652	88	174	22	10	3	35	28	26	4	.267	.345
Jimmy Johnston	3B150, SS3	R	31	152	624	104	203	41	14	5	56	45	26	28	.325	.460
Tommy Griffith	OF124	L	31	129	455	66	142	21	6	12	71	36	13	3	.312	.464
Hy Myers	OF124, 2B21, 3B1	R	32	144	549	51	158	14	4	4	68	22	51	8	.288	.350
Zack Wheat	OF148	L	35	148	568	91	182	31	10	14	85	44	19	11	.320	.484
Otto Miller	C91	R	32	91	286	22	67	8	6	1	27	9	26	2	.234	.315
Bernie Neis	OF77, 2B1	R	25	102	230	34	59	5	4	4	34	25	41	9	.257	.365
Ernie Krueger	C52	R	30	65	163	18	43	11	4	3	20	14	12	2	.264	.436
Wally Hood	OF20	R	26	56	65	16	17	1	2	1	4	9	14	2	.262	.385
1 Ed Konetchy	1B54	R	35	55	197	25	53	6	5	3	23	19	21	3	.269	.396
Dutch Ruether	P36	L	27	49	97	12	34	5	2	2	13	4	9	1	.351	.505
2 Hal Janvrin	SS17, 2B10, 1B8, 3B5, OF1	R	28	44	92	8	18	4	0	0	14	7	6	3	.196	.239
Zack Taylor	C30	R	22	30	102	6	20	0	2	0	8	1	8	2	.196	.235
Chuch Ward (XJ)	SS12	R	26	12	28	1	2	1	0	0	0	4	2	0	.071	.107
2 Eddie Eayrs	OF1	L	30	8	6	1	1	0	0	0	1	2	0	0	.167	.167

Jack Sheehan 28 B 0-12, Bill Lamar 24 L 1-3

NAME	T	AGE	W	L	PCT	SV	G	GS	CG	IP	H	BB	SO	ShO	ERA
		28	77	75	.507	12	152	152	82	1363	1556	361	471	8	3.70
Burleigh Grimes	R	27	22	13	.629	0	37	35	30	302	313	76	136	2	2.84
Leon Cadore	R	30	13	14	.481	0	35	30	12	212	243	46	79	1	4.16
Clarence Mitchell	L	30	11	9	.550	2	37	18	13	190	206	46	39	3	2.89
Dutch Ruether	L	27	10	13	.435	2	36	27	12	211	247	67	78	1	4.27
Sherry Smith	L	30	7	11	.389	4	35	17	9	175	232	34	36	0	3.91
Johnny Miljus	R	26	6	3	.667	1	28	9	3	94	115	27	37	0	4.21
Al Mamaux	R	27	3	3	.500	1	12	1	0	43	36	13	21	0	3.14
2 Ferdie Schupp	L	30	3	4	.429	2	20	7	1	61	75	27	26	0	4.57
Ray Gordinier	R	29	1	0	1.000	0	3	3	0	12	10	8	4	0	5.25
1 Jeff Pfeffer	R	33	1	5	.167	0	6	5	2	32	36	9	8	0	4.50
2 Sweetbreads Bailey	R	26	0	0	.000	0	7	0	0	24	35	7	6	0	5.25
George Mohart	R	29	0	0	.000	0	2	0	0	7	8	1	1	0	3.86

CINCINNATI 6th 70-83 .458 24 — PAT MORAN

NAME	G by POS	B	AGE	G	AB	R	H	2B	3B	HR	RBI	BB	SO	SB	BA	SA
TOTALS			28	153	5112	618	1421	221	94	20	560	375	308	117	.278	.370
Jake Daubert	1B136	L	37	136	516	69	158	18	12	2	64	24	16	12	.306	.399
Sammy Bohne	2B102, 3B53	R	24	153	613	98	175	28	16	3	44	54	38	26	.285	.398
Larry Kopf	SS93, 2B4, 3B3, OF1	B	30	107	367	36	80	8	3	1	25	43	20	3	.218	.264
Heinie Groh (HO)	3B97	R	31	97	357	54	118	19	6	0	48	36	17	22	.331	.417
Rube Bressler	OF85, 1B6	R	26	109	323	41	99	18	6	1	54	39	20	5	.307	.409
Edd Roush	OF108	L	28	112	418	68	147	27	12	4	71	31	8	19	.352	.502
Pat Duncan	OF145	R	27	145	532	57	164	27	10	2	60	44	33	7	.308	.408
Ivy Wingo	C92, OF1	L	30	97	295	20	79	7	6	3	38	21	14	3	.268	.363
Bubbles Hargrave	C73	R	28	93	263	28	76	17	8	1	38	12	15	4	.289	.426
Lew Fonseca	2B50, 1B16, OF16	R	22	82	297	38	82	10	3	1	41	8	13	2	.276	.340
Sam Crane	SS63, 3B2, OF1	R	26	73	215	20	50	10	2	0	16	14	14	2	.233	.298
2 Greasy Neale	OF60	L	29	63	241	39	58	10	5	0	12	22	16	9	.241	.324
Charlie See	OF30	L	24	37	106	11	26	5	1	1	7	7	5	3	.245	.340
Dode Paskert	OF24	R	39	27	92	8	16	1	1	0	4	4	8	0	.174	.207
Denny Williams	OF1	L	21	10	7	0	0	0	0	0	0	0	2	0	.000	.000

Astyanax Douglass 23 L 1-7, Wally Kimmick R 24 1-6, Kenny Hogan 18 L 0-2

NAME	T	AGE	W	L	PCT	SV	G	GS	CG	IP	H	BB	SO	ShO	ERA
		29	70	83	.458	9	153	153	83	1363	1500	305	408	7	3.46
Eppa Rixey	L	30	19	18	.514	1	40	36	21	301	324	66	76	2	2.78
Rube Marquard	L	31	17	14	.548	0	39	35	18	266	291	50	88	2	3.38
Dolf Luque	R	30	17	19	.472	3	41	36	25	304	318	64	102	3	3.38
Pete Donohue	R	20	7	6	.538	1	21	11	7	118	117	26	44	0	3.36
Fritz Coumbe	L	31	3	4	.429	1	28	6	3	87	89	21	12	0	3.20
Hod Eller	R	26	2	2	.500	1	13	3	0	34	46	15	7	0	5.03
Cliff Markle	R	27	2	6	.250	0	10	6	5	67	75	20	23	0	3.76
Bob Geary	R	30	1	1	.500	0	10	1	0	29	38	2	10	0	4.35
Clint Rogge	R	31	1	2	.333	0	6	3	0	35	43	9	12	0	4.11
Lynn Brenton	R	30	1	8	.111	1	17	9	2	60	80	17	19	0	4.05
Alan Clarke	L	25	0	1	.000	0	1	1	1	5	7	2	1	0	5.40
Buddy Napier	R	31	0	2	.000	1	22	6	1	57	72	13	14	0	5.53

Ray Fisher (DL) 33

CHICAGO 7th 64-89 .418 30 — JOHNNY EVERS 42-56 .429 BILL KILLEFER 22-33 .400

NAME	G by POS	B	AGE	G	AB	R	H	2B	3B	HR	RBI	BB	SO	SB	BA	SA
TOTALS			28	153	5321	668	1553	234	56	37	609	343	374	70	.292	.378
Ray Grimes	1B147	R	27	147	530	91	170	38	6	6	79	70	55	5	.321	.449
Zeb Terry	2B122	R	30	123	488	59	134	18	1	2	45	27	19	1	.275	.328
Charlie Hollocher	SS137	L	25	140	558	71	161	28	8	3	37	43	13	5	.289	.384
Charlie Deal	3B113	R	29	115	422	52	122	19	8	3	66	13	9	3	.289	.393
Max Flack	OF130	L	31	133	572	80	172	31	4	6	37	32	15	17	.301	.400
George Maisel	OF108	R	29	111	393	54	122	7	2	0	43	11	13	17	.310	.338
Turner Barber	OF123	L	27	127	452	73	142	14	4	1	54	41	24	5	.314	.369
Bob O'Farrell	C90	R	24	96	260	32	65	12	7	4	32	18	14	2	.250	.396
J. Kelleher	3B37, 2B27, 1B11, SS11, OF1	R	27	95	301	31	93	11	7	4	47	16	16	2	.309	.432
Babe Twombly	OF45	L	25	87	175	22	66	8	1	1	18	11	10	4	.377	.451
2 John Sullivan	OF65	R	31	76	240	28	79	14	4	4	41	19	26	3	.329	.471
Tom Daly	C47	R	29	51	143	12	34	7	1	0	22	8	8	1	.238	.301
Bill Killefer	C42	R	33	45	133	11	43	1	0	0	16	4	4	3	.323	.331
Pete Alexander	P31	R	34	31	95	8	29	3	1	1	14	2	13	0	.305	.389
Bill Marriott	2B6, SS1, 3B1, OF1	L	28	30	38	3	12	1	1	0	7	4	1	0	.316	.395
1 Dave Robertson	OF7	L	31	22	36	7	8	3	0	0	14	1	3	0	.222	.306
Hooks Warner	3B10	L	27	14	38	4	8	1	0	0	3	2	1	1	.211	.237
Carter Elliott	SS10	L	27	12	28	5	7	2	0	0	0	5	3	0	.250	.321
Red Thomas	OF8	R	23	8	30	5	8	3	0	1	5	4	5	0	.267	.267

Kettle Wirts 23 R 2-11, Joe Klugmann 26 R 6-21

NAME	T	AGE	W	L	PCT	SV	G	GS	CG	IP	H	BB	SO	ShO	ERA
		27	64	89	.418	7	153	153	73	1363	1605	409	441	7	4.39
Pete Alexander	R	34	15	13	.536	1	31	29	21	252	286	33	77	3	3.39
Virgil Cheeves	R	20	11	12	.478	0	37	22	9	163	192	47	39	1	4.64
Speed Martin	R	27	11	15	.423	1	37	28	13	217	245	68	86	1	4.36
Buck Freeman	R	24	9	10	.474	3	38	20	6	177	189	70	42	0	4.12
Lefty York	L	25	5	9	.357	1	40	10	4	139	170	63	57	1	4.73
Lefty Tyler	L	31	3	2	.600	0	10	6	4	50	59	14	8	0	3.24
Percy Jones	L	21	3	5	.375	0	32	5	1	99	116	39	46	0	4.55
2 Elmer Ponder	R	28	3	6	.333	0	16	11	5	89	117	17	31	0	4.75
Hippo Vaughn	L	33	3	11	.214	0	17	14	7	109	153	31	30	0	6.03
Tony Kaufmann	R	20	1	0	1.000	1	2	1	1	13	12	3	6	0	4.15
George Stueland	R	22	0	1	.000	0	2	1	0	11	11	7	4	0	5.73
Ollie Hanson	R	25	0	2	.000	0	2	2	1	9	9	6	2	0	7.00
Vic Keen	R	22	0	3	.000	0	5	4	1	25	29	9	9	0	4.68
1 Sweetbreads Bailey	R	26	0	0	.000	0	3	0	0	5	6	2	2	0	3.60
Oscar Fuhr	L	27	0	0	.000	0	1	0	0	4	11	0	2	0	9.00

Claude Hendrix (DU) 32

PHILADELPHIA 8th 51-103 .331 43.5 — WILD BILL DONOVAN 31-71 .304 KAISER WILHELM 20-32 .385

NAME	G by POS	B	AGE	G	AB	R	H	2B	3B	HR	RBI	BB	SO	SB	BA	SA
TOTALS			28	154	5329	617	1512	238	50	**88**	573	294	**615**	66	.284	.397
2 Ed Konetchy	1B71	R	35	72	268	38	86	17	4	8	59	21	17	3	.321	.504
Jimmy Smith	2B66	R	26	67	247	31	57	8	1	4	22	11	28	2	.231	.320
Frank Parkinson	SS105, 3B1	R	26	108	391	36	99	20	2	5	32	13	81	3	.253	.353
Russ Wrightstone	3B54, OF37, 2B4	L	28	109	372	59	110	13	4	9	51	18	20	4	.296	.425
Bevo LeBourveau	OF76	L	26	93	281	42	83	12	5	6	35	29	51	4	.295	.438
Cy Williams	OF146	L	33	146	562	67	180	28	6	18	75	30	32	5	.320	.488
1 Irish Meusel	OF85	R	28	84	343	59	121	21	7	12	51	18	17	8	.353	.560
Frank Bruggy	C86, 1B2	R	30	96	277	28	86	11	2	5	28	23	37	6	.310	.419
Cliff Lee	1B48, OF27, C2	R	24	88	286	31	88	14	4	4	29	13	34	5	.308	.427
Dots Miller	3B41, 1B38, 2B6	R	34	84	320	37	95	11	3	0	23	15	27	3	.297	.350
2 Lee King	OF57	R	28	64	216	25	58	19	4	4	32	8	37	1	.269	.449
1 Johnny Rawlings	2B60	R	28	60	254	20	74	14	2	1	16	8	12	4	.291	.374
Ralph Miller	SS46, 3B10	R	25	57	204	19	62	10	0	3	26	6	10	3	.304	.397
John Peters	C44	R	27	55	155	7	45	4	0	3	23	6	13	1	.290	.374
2 Goldie Rapp	3B50, 2B1	B	29	52	202	28	56	7	1	1	10	14	8	6	.377	.337
2 John Monroe	2B28, 3B9	L	22	41	133	13	38	4	2	1	8	11	9	2	.286	.368
2 Butch Henline	C32	R	26	33	111	8	34	2	0	0	8	2	6	1	.306	.324
1 Casey Stengel	OF24	L	30	24	59	7	18	3	1	0	4	6	7	1	.305	.390
1 Greasy Neale	OF22	L	29	22	57	7	12	1	0	0	1	14	9	3	.211	.228
2 Curt Walker	OF21	L	24	21	77	11	26	2	1	0	8	5	5	0	.338	.390
Lance Richbourg	2B4	L	23	10	5	2	1	1	0	0	0	0	3	1	.200	.400
Mack Wheat	C9	R	28	10	27	1	5	2	1	0	4	0	3	0	.185	.333
Don Rader	SS9	L	27	9	32	4	9	2	0	0	3	3	5	0	.281	.344

Art Fletcher (VR) 36, Gene Paulette (DL) 29

NAME	T	AGE	W	L	PCT	SV	G	GS	CG	IP	H	BB	SO	ShO	ERA
		26	51	**103**	.331	8	154	154	82	1349	**1665**	371	333	5	4.48
Lee Meadows	R	26	11	16	.407	0	28	27	15	194	226	62	52	2	4.31
Jimmy Ring	R	26	10	19	.345	1	34	30	21	246	258	88	88	0	4.25
Bill Hubbell	R	24	9	16	.360	2	36	30	15	220	269	38	43	1	4.34
Jesse Winters	R	27	5	10	.333	0	18	14	10	114	142	28	22	0	3.64
George Smith	R	29	4	**20**	.167	1	39	28	12	221	303	52	45	1	4.76
1 Red Causey	R	27	3	3	.500	0	7	7	4	51	58	11	8	0	2.82
Stan Baumgartner	L	28	3	6	.333	0	22	7	2	67	103	22	13	0	6.98
Huck Betts	R	24	3	7	.300	4	32	2	1	101	141	14	28	0	4.46
Lefty Weinert	L	19	1	0	1.000	0	8	0	0	12	8	5	2	0	1.50
Jimmie Keenan	L	32	1	2	.333	0	15	2	0	32	48	15	7	0	6.75
Duke Sedgwick	R	22	1	3	.250	0	16	5	1	71	81	32	21	0	4.94
Petie Behan	R	33	0	1	.000	0	2	2	1	11	17	1	3	0	5.73
Kaiser Wilhelm	R	47	0	0	.000	0	4	0	0	8	11	3	1	0	3.38

WORLD SERIES – NEW YORK (NL) 5 NEW YORK (AL) 3

LINE SCORES

TEAM	1	2	3	4	5	6	7	8	9	10	11	12	R	H	E
Game 1 October 5 at Polo Grounds															
NY (AL)	1	0	0	0	1	1	0	0	0				3	7	0
NY (NL)	0	0	0	0	0	0	0	0	0				0	5	0
Mays **Douglas**, Barnes (1)															
Game 2 October 6 at Polo Grounds															
NY (NL)	0	0	0	0	0	0	0	0	0				0	2	3
NY (AL)	0	0	0	1	0	0	0	2	X				3	3	0
Nehf **Hoyt**															
Game 3 October 7 at Polo Grounds															
NY (AL)	0	0	4	0	0	0	0	1	0				5	8	0
NY (NL)	0	0	4	0	0	0	8	1	X				13	20	0
Shawkey, **Quinn** (3), Collins (7), Rogers (7) Toney, **Barnes** (3)															
Game 4 October 9 at Polo Grounds															
NY (NL)	0	0	0	0	0	0	0	3	1				4	9	1
NY (AL)	0	0	0	0	1	0	0	0	1				2	7	1
Douglas **Mays**															
Game 5 October 10 at Polo Grounds															
NY (AL)	0	0	1	2	0	0	0	0	0				3	6	1
NY (NL)	1	0	0	0	0	0	0	0	0				1	10	1
Hoyt **Nehf**															
Game 6 October 11 at Polo Grounds															
NY (NL)	0	3	0	4	0	1	0	0	0				8	13	0
NY (AL)	3	2	0	0	0	0	0	0	0				5	7	2
Toney, **Barnes** (1) Harper, **Shawkey** (2), Piercy (9)															
Game 7 October 12 at Polo Grounds															
NY (AL)	0	1	0	0	0	0	0	0	0				1	8	1
NY (NL)	0	0	0	1	0	0	1	0	X				2	6	0
Mays **Douglas**															
Game 8 October 13 at Polo Grounds															
NY (NL)	1	0	0	0	0	0	0	0	0				1	6	0
NY (AL)	0	0	0	0	0	0	0	0	0				0	4	1
Nehf **Hoyt**															

COMPOSITE BATTING

NAME	POS	G	AB	R	H	2B	3B	HR	RBI	BA
New York (NL)										
Totals		8	264	29	71	13	4	2	28	.269
Burns	OF	8	**33**	2	**11**	**4**	1	0	2	.333
Bancroft	SS	8	**33**	3	5	1	0	0	3	.152
Rawlings	2B	8	30	2	10	3	0	0	4	.333
Frisch	3B	8	30	**5**	9	0	1	0	1	.300
Kelly	1B	8	30	3	7	1	0	0	4	.233
I. Meusel	OF	8	29	4	10	2	1	1	**7**	.345
Youngs	OF	8	25	3	7	1	1	0	4	.280
Snyder	C	7	22	4	8	1	0	1	3	**.364**
Barnes	P	3	9	3	4	0	0	0	0	.444
Nehf	P	3	9	0	0	0	0	0	0	.000
Douglas	P	3	7	0	0	0	0	0	0	.000
Smith	C	3	7	0	0	0	0	0	0	.000
Toney	P	2	0	0	0	0	0	0	0	.000
New York (AL)										
Totals		8	241	22	50	7	1	2	20	.207
Miller	OF	8	31	3	5	1	0	0	2	.161
B. Meusel	OF	8	30	3	6	2	0	0	3	.200
Peckinpaugh	SS	8	28	2	5	1	0	0	0	.179
Ward	2B	8	26	1	6	0	0	0	4	.231
Pipp	1B	8	26	1	4	1	0	0	2	.154
Schang	C	8	21	1	6	1	1	0	1	.286
McNally	3B	7	20	3	4	1	0	0	1	.200
Ruth	OF	6	16	3	5	0	0	1	4	.313
Fewster	OF	4	10	3	2	0	0	1	2	.200
Hoyt	P	3	9	0	2	0	0	0	1	.222
Mays	P	3	9	0	1	0	0	0	0	.111
Baker	3B	4	8	0	2	0	0	0	0	.250
Shawkey	P	2	4	2	2	0	0	0	0	.500
Quinn	P	1	2	0	0	0	0	0	0	.000
DeVormer	C	2	1	0	0	0	0	0	0	.000
Collins	P	1	0	0	0	0	0	0	0	.000
Harper	P	1	0	0	0	0	0	0	0	.000
Piercy	P	1	0	0	0	0	0	0	0	.000
Rogers	P	1	0	0	0	0	0	0	0	.000

COMPOSITE PITCHING

NAME	G	IP	H	BB	SO	W	L	SV	ERA
New York (NL)									
Totals	8	71	50	27	44	5	3	0	2.53
Nehf	3	26	13	**13**	8	1	**2**	0	1.38
Douglas	3	26	**20**	5	17	**2**	1	0	2.07
Barnes	3	16.1	10	6	**18**	**2**	0	0	1.65
Toney	2	2.2	7	3	1	0	0	0	23.63
New York (AL)									
Totals	8	70	71	22	38	3	5	0	3.09
Hoyt	3	**27**	18	11	**18**	**2**	1	0	**0.00**
Mays	3	26	**20**	0	9	1	**2**	0	1.73
Shawkey	2	9	13	6	5	0	1	0	7.00
Quinn	1	3.2	8	2	2	0	1	0	9.82
Harper	1	1.1	3	2	1	0	0	0	20.25
Rogers	1	1.1	3	0	1	0	0	0	6.75
Piercy	1	1	2	0	2	0	0	0	0.00
Collins	1	0.2	4	1	0	0	0	0	54.00

1922 It's a Bird, It's a plane, It's . . .

The fact that both pennant winners would repeat their 1921 championships paled into insignificance in face of the continuing trend to more home runs—a trend that would surely change the complexion of the national game. As the Roaring Twenties were reaching full stride, baseball too, hypoed its activity by spicing the 1922 season with 1,055 homers, a remarkable feat in comparison to five years before when both leagues combined for only 339 circuit clouts. Although the new slightly more lively ball introduced in 1909 started a slow rise in the home run totals, it was the outlawing of the spitball and other trick pitches in 1920 combined with the introduction of a really lively ball in 1920 (American League) and 1921 (National League) which was responsible for launching a skyrocketing acceleration in home run production in both leagues. Babe Ruth drew national attention to the majestic circuit clout. After watching Ruth's following and salary grow, an instantaneous chain reaction was set in motion, with the result that hitters concentrated more on hitting the long ball than on going for averages. If anything, the ball player found that the home run was the way to instant success and the knowledge that someone, somewhere, would have remembered him for being a colossus of strength, if only for a fleeting moment. Such was the effect of the new weapon that by the time the cheering subsided and the season closed, both leagues found their total earned run average had climbed to over four runs a game, a statistical embarrassment symptomatic of pitching's subservience to hitting in the lively post-war era.

Ironically, the man who altered baseball for all time was not in uniform for the start of the fireworks. Commissioner Landis had suspended Ruth and teammate Bob Meusel for barnstorming after the 1921 World Series, and not until May 20, were the two Yankee sluggers permitted to suit up. Although New York managed to stay on top of the American League, even before the return of the two outfielders, the charging St. Louis Browns edged past the Yankees to take a slight lead in July. The Brownies were winning consistently with good pitching and the best attack in the league by holding a hand of four eventual 100-RBI men in Marty McManus, Baby Doll Jacobson, Ken Williams, and George Sisler, who also won his second batting crown with a torrid .420 average. Yet, while the Browns were winning, so were the Yankees. And when both teams got together in St. Louis in mid-August, the Yankees were able to make the better of it to retake the top spot. Both teams stayed hot during the Indian summer, but the Yankees never relinquished their slight lead and finished in front with a paper-thin margin of one game. Nevertheless, the Browns' 93 wins made their 1922 edition the best club in the history of the franchise—a franchise which would end in 1953.

The National League race was dominated by the New York Giants, who led all year and held a seven-game margin at the finish. Irish Meusel, George Kelly, and Ross Youngs led a team attack which finished with a .304 batting average, and veteran Casey Stengel hit .368 after being installed in center field in mid-season. Ace pitcher Phil Douglas was 11-4 when he was barred in mid-season after writing a foolish letter implying that he would welcome a bribe to throw games, but his slack was taken up by Art Nehf, Rosie Ryan, Jesse Barnes, and free-agent signee Jack Scott, who recovered from a sore arm to win eight games after Douglas' ouster. Cincinnati threatened with its pitching, and the Cards and Pirates boasted of strong offenses, but none of them could overtake the Giants after New York's early-season getaway. Rogers Hornsby of St. Louis, singlehandedly kept the Cardinals in the first division by hitting .401, belting 42 home runs, and driving 152 runs across the plate, a performance which earned him the National League's first Triple Crown since Hugh Duffy turned the trick for Boston in 1894.

The Yankees came into the World Series with high hopes but flopped miserably, dropping four games while managing only a second-game tie. The Giant pitchers shut off the Yankee attack by holding Babe Ruth to a pitiful .118 mark. In comparison, Heinie Groh and Frankie Frisch of the Giants both posted .470 plus averages. The Series return to the best four-of-seven format also marked the first appearance of radio microphones at the fall classic.

1922 AMERICAN LEAGUE

NAME	G by POS	B	AGE	G	AB	R	H	2B	3B	HR	RBI	BB	SO	SB	BA	SA
NEW YORK 1st 94-60 .610		MILLER HUGGINS														
TOTALS			29	154	5245	758	1504	220	75	95	674	497	532	62	.287	.412
Wally Pipp	1B152	L	29	152	577	96	190	32	10	9	90	56	32	7	.329	.466
Aaron Ward	2B152, 3B2	R	25	154	558	69	149	19	5	7	68	45	64	7	.267	.357
Everett Scott	SS154	R	29	154	557	64	150	23	5	3	45	23	22	2	.269	.345
2 Joe Dugan	3B60	R	25	60	252	44	72	9	1	3	25	13	21	1	.286	.365
Bob Meusel (SL)	OF121	R	25	121	473	61	151	26	11	16	84	40	58	13	.319	.522
Whitey Witt	OF138	L	26	140	528	98	157	11	6	4	40	**89**	29	5	.297	.364
Babe Ruth (SL)	OF110, 1B1	L	27	110	406	94	128	24	8	35	99	84	80	2	.315	**.672**
Wally Schang	C119	B	32	124	408	46	130	21	7	1	53	53	36	12	.319	.412
Frank Baker (JJ)	3B60	L	36	69	234	30	65	12	3	7	36	15	14	1	.278	.444
Mike McNally	3B34, 2B9, SS4, 1B1	R	28	52	143	20	36	2	2	0	18	16	14	2	.252	.294
1 Elmer Miller	OF51	R	31	51	172	31	46	7	2	3	18	11	12	2	.267	.384
1 Chick Fewster	OF38, 2B2	R	26	44	132	20	32	4	1	1	9	16	23	2	.242	.311
Bullet Joe Bush (RJ)	P39	R	29	39	95	15	31	6	2	0	12	3	11	0	.326	.432
Fred Hofmann	C28	R	28	37	91	13	27	5	3	2	10	9	12	0	.297	.484
Norm McMillan	OF23, 3B5	R	26	33	78	7	20	1	2	0	11	6	10	4	.256	.321
Camp Skinner	OF4	L	25	27	33	1	6	0	0	0	2	0	4	1	.182	.182
Al DeVormer	C17, 1B1	R	30	24	59	8	12	4	1	0	11	1	6	0	.203	.305
2 Elmer Smith	OF10	L	29	21	27	1	5	0	0	1	5	3	5	0	.185	.296
1 Johnny Mitchell	SS4	B	27	4	4	1	0	0	0	0	0	0	1	0	.000	.000
ST. LOUIS 2nd 93-61 .604 1		LEE FOHL														
TOTALS			29	154	**5416**	**867**	**1693**	291	**94**	98	**785**	473	381	**135**	**.313**	.455
George Sisler	1B141	L	29	142	586	**134**	**246**	42	**18**	8	105	49	14	**51**	**.420**	.594
Marty McManus	2B153, 1B1	R	22	154	606	88	189	34	11	11	109	38	41	9	.312	.459
Wally Gerber	SS152	R	30	153	604	81	161	22	8	1	51	52	34	6	.267	.334
Frank Ellerbe (BK)	3B91	R	26	91	342	42	84	16	3	1	33	25	37	1	.246	.319
Jack Tobin	OF145	L	30	146	625	122	207	34	8	13	66	56	22	7	.331	.474
Baby Doll Jacobson	OF137, 1B7	R	31	145	555	88	176	22	16	9	102	46	36	19	.317	.463
Ken Williams	OF153	L	32	153	585	128	194	34	11	**39**	**155**	74	31	37	.332	.627
Hank Severeid	C134	R	31	137	517	49	166	32	7	3	78	28	12	1	.321	.427
Pat Collins	C27, 1B5	R	25	63	127	14	39	6	0	8	23	21	21	0	.307	.543
Chick Shorten	OF31	L	30	55	131	22	36	12	5	2	16	16	8	0	.275	.489
Elam Vangilder	P43	R	26	45	93	16	32	10	2	2	11	5	11	0	.344	.559
2 Eddie Foster	3B37	R	35	37	144	29	44	4	0	0	12	20	8	3	.306	.333
Herman Bronkie	3B18	R	37	23	64	7	18	4	1	0	2	6	7	0	.281	.375
Gene Robertson	3B7, SS6, 2B1	L	22	18	27	2	8	2	1	0	1	1	1	1	.296	.444
Jimmy Austin	3B11, 2B2	B	42	15	31	6	9	3	1	0	1	3	2	0	.290	.452
Cedric Durst	OF6	L	25	15	12	5	4	1	0	0	0	0	1	0	.333	.417
Josh Billings	C3	R	30	5	7	0	3	1	0	0	1	0	0	0	.429	.571
DETROIT 3rd 79-75 .513 15		TY COBB														
TOTALS			29	155	5377	828	1641	250	87	54	735	530	378	78	.305	.414
Lu Blue	1B144	B	25	145	584	131	175	31	9	6	45	82	48	8	.300	.414
George Cutshaw	2B132	R	34	132	499	57	133	14	8	2	61	20	13	11	.267	.339
Topper Rigney	SS155	R	25	155	536	68	161	17	7	2	63	68	44	17	.300	.369
Bob Jones	3B119	L	32	124	455	65	117	10	6	3	44	36	18	8	.257	.325
Harry Heilmann (BC)	OF115, 1B5	R	27	118	455	92	162	27	10	21	92	58	28	8	.356	.598
Ty Cobb	OF134	L	35	137	526	99	211	42	16	4	99	55	24	9	.401	.565
Bobby Veach	OF154	L	34	155	618	96	202	34	13	9	126	42	27	9	.327	.468
Johnny Bassler	C117	L	27	121	372	41	120	14	0	0	41	62	12	2	.323	.360
Dan Clark	2B38, OF5, 3B1	L	28	83	185	31	54	11	3	3	26	15	11	1	.292	.432
Fred Haney	3B44, 1B11, SS2	R	24	81	213	41	75	7	4	0	25	32	14	3	.352	.423
Larry Woodall	C39	R	27	50	125	19	43	2	2	0	18	8	11	0	.344	.392
Ira Flagstead	OF31	R	28	44	91	21	28	5	3	3	8	14	16	0	.308	.527
Bob Fothergill	OF39	R	24	42	152	20	49	12	4	0	29	8	9	1	.322	.454
Clyde Manion	C21, 1B1	R	25	42	69	9	19	4	1	0	12	4	6	0	.275	.362
Chick Gagnon	SS1, 3B1	R	24	9	4	2	1	0	0	0	0	0	2	0	.250	.250
John Mohardt	OF3	R	24	5	1	2	1	0	0	0	0	1	0	0	1.000	1.000
Dutch Leonard (VR) 30																

NAME	T	AGE	W	L	PCT	SV	G	GS	CG	IP	H	BB	SO	ShO	ERA
NEW YORK		27	**94**	60	**.610**	14	154	154	**98**	1394	1402	423	458	7	3.39
Bullet Joe Bush (RJ)	R	29	26	7	**.788**	3	39	30	20	255	240	85	92	0	3.32
Bob Shawkey	R	31	20	12	.625	1	39	33	19	300	286	98	130	3	2.91
Waite Hoyt	R	22	19	12	.613	0	37	31	17	265	271	76	95	3	3.43
Sad Sam Jones	R	29	13	13	.500	**8**	45	28	21	260	270	76	81	0	3.67
Carl Mays	R	30	12	14	.462	2	34	29	21	240	257	50	41	1	3.60
George Murray	R	23	4	2	.667	0	22	3	0	57	53	26	14	0	3.95
Clem Llewellyn	R	26	0	0	.000	0	1	0	0	1	1	0	0	0	0.00
Lefty O'Doul	L	25	0	0	.000	0	6	0	0	16	24	12	5	0	3.38
ST. LOUIS		27	93	61	.604	**22**	154	154	79	1392	1412	**419**	**534**	8	**3.38**
Urban Shocker	R	31	24	17	.585	3	48	38	29	348	**365**	57	**149**	2	2.97
Elam Vangilder	R	26	19	13	.594	4	43	30	19	245	248	48	63	3	3.42
Ray Kolp	R	27	14	4	.778	0	32	18	9	170	199	36	54	1	3.92
Dixie Davis	R	31	11	6	.647	0	25	25	7	174	162	87	65	2	4.09
Rusty Wright	R	26	9	7	.563	5	31	16	5	154	148	50	44	0	2.92
Hub Pruett	R	21	7	7	.500	7	39	8	4	120	99	59	70	0	2.32
Dave Danforth	L	32	5	2	.714	1	20	10	3	80	93	38	48	0	3.27
Bill Bayne	L	23	4	5	.444	2	26	9	3	93	86	27	38	0	4.55
Dutch Henry	L	20	0	0	.000	0	4	0	0	5	7	5	3	0	5.40
Heinie Meine	R	26	0	0	.000	0	1	0	0	4	5	2	0	0	4.50
DETROIT		26	79	75	.513	15	155	155	67	1391	1554	473	461	7	4.27
Herman Pillette	R	26	19	12	.613	1	40	37	18	275	270	95	71	4	2.84
Howard Ehmke	R	28	17	17	.500	1	45	30	16	280	299	101	108	1	4.21
Hooks Dauss	R	32	13	13	.500	4	39	25	12	219	251	59	78	1	4.19
Red Oldham	L	28	10	13	.435	3	43	27	9	212	256	59	72	0	4.67
Ole Olsen	R	27	7	6	.538	3	37	15	5	137	147	40	52	0	4.54
Syl Johnson	R	21	7	3	.700	1	29	8	3	97	99	30	29	0	3.71
Lil Stoner	R	23	4	4	.500	0	17	7	2	63	76	35	18	0	7.00
Bert Cole	L	24	1	6	.143	0	23	5	2	79	105	39	21	1	4.90
Carl Holling	R	25	1	1	.500	0	5	1	0	9	21	5	2	0	16.00
2 Roy Moore	L	23	0	0	.000	2	9	0	0	20	29	10	9	0	5.85
Ken Holloway	R	24	0	0	.000	0	1	0	0	1	1	0	1	0	0.00

CLEVELAND 4th 78-76 .506 16 — **TRIS SPEAKER**

NAME	G by POS	B	AGE	G	AB	R	H	2B	3B	HR	RBI	BB	SO	SB	BA	SA
TOTALS			30	155	5293	768	1544	320	73	32	698	554	331	89	.292	398
Stuffy McGinnis	1B140, C1	R	31	142	537	58	164	28	7	1	78	15	5	1	.305	.389
Bill Wambsganss	2B124, SS16, C1	R	28	143	538	89	141	22	6	0	47	60	26	17	.262	.325
Joe Sewell	SS139, 2B12	L	23	153	558	80	167	28	7	2	83	73	20	10	.299	.385
Larry Gardner	3B128	L	36	137	470	74	134	31	3	2	68	49	21	9	.285	.377
Smokey Joe Wood	OF140, 1B1	R	32	142	505	74	150	33	8	8	92	50	63	5	.297	.442
Tris Speaker	OF110	L	34	131	426	85	161	48	8	11	71	77	11	8	.378	.606
Charlie Jamieson	OF144, P2	L	29	145	567	87	183	29	11	3	57	54	22	15	.323	.429
Steve O'Neill	C130	R	30	133	392	33	122	27	4	2	65	73	25	2	.311	.416
Riggs Stephenson	3B33, 2B24, OF3	R	24	86	233	47	79	24	5	2	32	27	18	3	.339	.511
Joe Evans	OF49	R	27	75	145	35	39	6	2	0	22	8	4	11	.269	.338
Luke Sewell	C38	R	21	41	87	14	23	5	0	0	10	5	8	1	.264	.322
Jack Graney	OF13	L	36	37	58	6	9	0	0	0	2	9	12	0	.155	.155
Lou Guisto	1B24	R	28	35	84	7	21	10	1	0	9	2	7	0	.250	.393
Les Nunamaker	C15	R	33	25	43	8	13	2	0	0	7	4	3	0	.302	.349
Pat McNulty	OF22	L	23	22	59	10	16	2	1	0	5	9	5	4	.271	.339
Ginger Shinault	C11	R	29	13	15	1	2	1	0	0	0	0	2	0	.133	.200
Homer Summa	OF12	L	23	12	46	9	16	3	3	1	6	1	1	1	.348	.609
Joe Connolly	OF12	R	26	12	45	6	11	2	1	0	6	5	8	1	.244	.333
Ike Kahdot	3B2	R	20	4	2	0	0	0	0	0	0	0	1	0	.000	.000
Bill Doran	3B2	L	22	3	2	0	1	0	0	0	0	1	0	0	.500	.500
Joe Rabbitt	OF1	L	22	2	3	1	1	0	0	0	0	0	0	0	.333	.333
Chick Sorrells	SS1	R	25	2	1	0	0	0	0	0	0	0	0	0	.000	.000
1 Jack Hammond	2B1	R	31	1	4	1	1	0	0	0	0	0	0	0	.250	.250
Uke Clanton	1B1	L	24	1	1	0	0	0	0	0	0	0	1	0	.000	.000

NAME	T	AGE	W	L	PCT	SV	G	GS	CG	IP	H	BB	SO	ShO	ERA
		27	78	76	.506	7	155	155	76	1379	1605	464	489	14	4.60
George Uhle	R	23	22	16	.579	3	50	40	23	287	328	89	82	5	4.08
Stan Coveleski	R	33	17	14	.548	2	35	33	21	277	292	64	98	3	3.31
Guy Morton	R	29	14	9	.609	0	38	23	13	203	218	85	102	3	3.99
Duster Mails	L	26	4	7	.364	0	26	13	4	104	122	40	54	1	5.28
Jim Bagby	R	32	4	5	.444	1	25	10	4	98	134	39	25	0	6.34
Jim Lindsey	R	24	4	5	.444	1	29	5	0	84	105	24	29	0	6.00
Danny Boone	R	27	4	6	.400	0	11	10	4	75	07	19	9	2	4.08
Jim Joe Edwards	L	27	3	8	.273	0	25	7	0	88	113	40	44	0	4.70
Dewey Metivier	R	24	2	0	1.000	0	2	2	2	18	18	3	1	0	4.50
George Winn	L	24	1	2	.333	0	8	3	1	34	44	5	7	0	4.50
Allan Sothoron	R	29	1	3	.250	0	6	4	2	25	26	14	8	0	6.48
Phil Bedgood	R	24	1	0	1.000	0	1	1	1	9	7	4	5	0	4.00
2 Sherry Smith	L	31	1	0	1.000	0	2	2	1	16	18	3	4	0	3.38
Dave Keefe	R	25	0	0	.000	0	18	1	0	36	47	12	11	0	6.25
John Middleton	L	22	0	1	.000	0	2	1	0	7	8	6	2	0	7.71
Charlie Jamieson	L	29	0	0	.000	0	2	0	0	6	7	4	2	0	3.00
Joe Shaute	L	22	0	0	.000	0	2	0	0	4	7	3	3	0	18.00
Logan Drake	R	21	0	0	.000	0	1	0	0	3	4	2	1	0	3.00
George Edmondson	R	26	0	0	.000	0	2	0	0	2	4	0	0	0	9.00
Nellie Pott	L	22	0	0	.000	0	2	0	0	2	7	2	0	0	31.50
Ted Odenwald	L	20	0	0	.000	0	1	0	0	1	6	2	2	0	54.00
Doc Hamann	R	21	0	0	.000	0	1	0	0	0	3	3	0	0	∞
Tex Jeanes	R	21	0	0	.000	0	1	0	0	0	0	1	0	0	0.00

CHICAGO 5th 77-77 .500 17 — **KID GLEASON**

NAME	G by POS	B	AGE	G	AB	R	H	2B	3B	HR	RBI	BB	SO	SB	BA	SA
TOTALS			30	155	5267	691	1463	243	62	45	635	482	463	106	.278	.373
Earl Sheely	1B149	R	29	149	526	72	167	37	4	6	80	60	27	4	.317	.437
Eddie Collins	1B154	L	35	154	598	92	194	20	12	1	69	73	16	20	.324	.403
Ernie Johnson	SS141	L	34	145	603	85	153	17	3	0	56	40	30	21	.254	.292
Eddie Mulligan	3B86, SS7	R	27	103	372	39	87	14	8	0	31	22	32	7	.234	.315
Harry Hooper	OF149	L	34	152	602	111	183	35	8	11	80	68	33	16	.304	.444
John Mostil	OF123	R	26	132	458	74	139	28	14	7	70	38	39	14	.303	.472
Bibb Falk	OF129	L	23	131	483	58	144	27	1	12	79	27	55	2	.298	.433
Ray Schalk	C142	R	29	142	442	57	124	22	3	4	60	67	36	12	.281	.371
Amos Strunk	OF75, 1B9	L	33	92	311	36	90	11	4	0	33	33	28	9	.289	.350
Hervey McClellan	3B71, SS8, 3B2, OF1	R	27	91	301	28	68	17	3	2	28	16	32	3	.226	.322
Yam Yaryan	C25	R	29	36	71	9	14	2	0	2	9	6	10	1	.197	.310
Roy Graham	C3	R	27	5	3	0	0	0	0	0	0	0	0	0	.000	.000
John Jenkins	2B1, SS1	R	25	5	3	0	0	0	0	0	1	0	2	0	.000	.000
Hal Bubser		R	26	3	3	0	0	0	0	0	0	0	2	0	.000	.000
Jimmie Long	C2	R	24	3	3	0	0	0	0	0	0	1	0	0	.000	.000
Johnny Evers	2B1	L	40	1	3	0	0	0	0	0	1	2	0	0	.000	.000
Elmer Pence	OF1	R	21	1	0	0	0	0	0	0	0	0	0	0	.000	.000
Augie Swentor	C1	R	22	1	1	0	0	0	0	0	0	0	1	0	.000	.000
Dickie Kerr (HO) 28																

NAME	T	AGE	W	L	PCT	SV	G	GS	CG	IP	H	BB	SO	ShO	ERA
		27	77	77	.500	8	155	155	86	1407	1472	529	484	13	3.93
Red Faber	R	33	21	17	.553	2	43	38	31	353	334	83	148	4	2.80
Charlie Robertson	R	26	14	15	.483	0	37	34	21	272	294	89	83	3	3.64
Dixie Leverett	R	28	13	10	.565	2	33	27	16	225	224	79	60	4	3.32
Ted Blankenship	R	21	8	10	.444	1	24	15	7	128	124	47	42	0	3.80
Shovel Hodge	R	28	7	6	.538	1	35	8	2	139	154	65	37	0	4.14
2 Harry Courtney	L	23	5	6	.455	0	18	11	5	88	100	37	28	0	4.91
Ferdie Schupp	L	31	4	4	.500	0	18	12	3	74	79	66	38	1	6.08
Frank Mack	R	22	2	2	.500	0	8	4	1	34	36	16	11	1	3.71
Lum Davenport	L	22	1	1	.500	0	9	1	0	17	14	13	9	0	10.59
Larry Duff	R	24	1	1	.500	0	3	1	0	13	16	3	7	0	4.85
Dick McCabe	R	26	1	0	1.000	0	3	0	0	3	4	0	1	0	6.00
Jose Acosta	R	31	0	2	.000	0	5	1	0	15	25	6	6	0	8.40
Roy Wilkinson	R	28	0	1	.000	1	4	1	0	14	24	6	3	0	9.00
Homer Blankenship	R	19	0	0	.000	0	4	0	0	13	21	5	3	0	4.85
Doug McWeeney (ST)	R	25	0	1	.000	0	4	1	0	11	13	7	5	0	5.73
Jack Russell	L	26	0	1	.000	1	4	1	0	7	7	4	3	0	6.67
Emmett Bowles	R	23	0	0	.000	0	1	0	0	1	2	1	0	0	27.00
Ernie Cox	R	28	0	0	.000	0	1	0	0	1	1	2	0	0	18.00

WASHINGTON 6th 69-85 .448 25 — **CLYDE MILAN**

NAME	G by POS	B	AGE	G	AB	R	H	2B	3B	HR	RBI	BB	SO	SB	BA	SA
TOTALS			28	154	5201	650	1395	229	76	45	575	458	442	97	.268	.367
Joe Judge	1B148	L	28	148	591	84	174	32	15	10	81	50	20	5	.294	.450
Bucky Harris	1B154	R	25	154	602	95	162	24	8	2	40	52	38	25	.269	.346
Roger Peckinpaugh	SS147	R	31	147	520	62	132	14	4	2	48	55	36	11	.254	.308
Bobby LaMotte	3B62, SS6	R	24	68	214	22	54	10	2	1	23	15	21	6	.252	.332
Frank Brower	OF121, 1B7	L	29	139	471	61	138	20	6	9	71	52	25	8	.293	.418
Sam Rice	OF154	L	32	154	633	91	187	37	13	6	69	48	13	20	.295	.423
Goose Goslin (BW)	OF92	R	21	101	358	44	116	19	7	3	53	25	26	4	.324	.441
Patsy Gharrity (JJ)	C87	R	30	96	273	40	70	16	6	5	45	36	30	3	.256	.414
Howard Shanks	3B54, OF27	R	31	84	272	35	77	10	9	1	32	25	25	6	.283	.397
Val Picinich	C76	R	25	76	210	16	48	12	2	0	19	23	33	1	.229	.305
Earl Smith	OF49, 3B1	B	31	65	205	22	53	12	2	1	23	8	17	4	.259	.351
Clyde Milan	OF11	L	36	42	74	8	17	5	0	0	5	2	2	0	.230	.297
Donie Bush (IJ)	2B37, 2B1	B	34	41	134	17	32	4	1	0	7	21	7	1	.239	.284
Ed Goebel	OF15	R	22	37	59	13	16	1	0	1	3	8	16	1	.271	.339
Tom Zachary	P32	L	26	32	71	4	21	2	1	1	14	3	20	0	.296	.394
Ossie Bluege	3B17, SS2	R	21	19	61	5	12	1	0	0	2	7	7	1	.197	.213
Pete Lapan	C11	R	31	11	34	7	11	1	0	1	6	3	4	1	.324	.441
Ricardo Torres	C3	R	28	4	4	0	0	0	0	0	0	0	1	0	.000	.000
George McNamara	OF3	L	19	3	11	3	3	0	0	0	1	1	2	0	.273	.273

NAME	T	AGE	W	L	PCT	SV	G	GS	CG	IP	H	BB	SO	ShO	ERA
		29	69	85	.448	10	154	154	84	1362	1485	500	422	11	3.81
George Mogridge	L	33	18	13	.581	0	34	32	18	252	300	72	61	3	3.57
Walter Johnson	R	34	15	16	.484	4	41	31	23	280	283	99	105	4	2.99
Tom Zachary	L	26	15	10	.600	1	32	25	13	185	190	43	37	1	3.11
Ray Francis	L	29	7	18	.280	2	39	26	15	225	265	66	64	2	4.28
Eric Erickson	R	30	4	12	.250	2	30	17	6	142	144	73	61	0	4.94
Jim Brillheart	L	18	4	6	.400	1	31	10	3	120	120	72	47	0	3.60
Tom Phillips	R	33	3	7	.300	0	17	7	2	70	72	22	19	1	4.89
Joe Gleason	R	26	2	2	.500	0	8	5	3	41	53	18	12	0	4.61
Cy Warmoth	L	29	1	0	1.000	0	5	1	1	19	15	9	8	0	1.42
1 Harry Courtney	L	23	0	1	.000	0	5	0	0	10	11	9	4	0	3.60
Lucas Turk	R	24	0	0	.000	0	5	0	0	12	16	5	1	0	6.75
Chief Youngblood	R	22	0	0	.000	0	2	0	0	4	9	7	0	0	15.75
Slim McGrew	R	22	0	0	.000	0	1	0	0	2	4	2	1	0	9.00
Frank Woodward	R	28	0	0	.000	0	1	0	0	2	3	3	2	0	13.50

PHILADELPHIA 7th 65-89 .422 29 — **CONNIE MACK**

NAME	G by POS	B	AGE	G	AB	R	H	2B	3B	HR	RBI	BB	SO	SB	BA	SA
TOTALS			27	155	5241	705	1409	229	63	111	631	437	591	60	.269	.400
Joe Hauser	1B94	L	23	111	368	61	119	21	5	9	43	30	37	1	.323	.481
Ralph Young	2B120	B	32	125	470	62	105	19	2	1	35	55	21	8	.223	.279
Chick Galloway	SS155	R	25	155	571	83	185	26	9	6	69	39	38	10	.324	.433
Jimmy Dykes	3B140, 2B5	R	25	145	501	66	138	23	7	12	68	55	98	6	.275	.421
Frank Welch	OF104	R	24	114	375	43	97	17	3	11	49	40	40	3	.259	.408
Bing Miller	OF139	R	27	143	535	90	180	29	12	21	90	24	42	10	.336	.553
Tilly Walker	OF148	R	34	153	565	111	160	31	4	37	99	61	64	4	.283	.549
Cy Perkins	C141	R	26	148	505	58	135	20	6	6	69	40	30	1	.267	.366
Beauty McGowan	OF82	L	20	99	300	36	69	10	5	1	20	40	46	6	.230	.307
Doc Johnston	1B65	L	34	71	260	41	65	11	7	1	29	24	15	7	.250	.358
Frank Bruggy (JJ)	C31	R	31	53	111	10	31	7	0	0	9	6	11	1	.279	.342
Heinie Scheer	2B29, 3B10	R	22	51	135	10	23	3	0	4	12	3	25	1	.170	.281
Frank Callaway (KJ)	2B11, 3B5, SS4	R	24	29	48	5	13	0	2	0	4	0	13	0	.271	.354
Ollie Fuhrman	C4	B	25	6	6	1	2	1	0	0	1	0	0	0	.333	.500
Frank Brazill	3B2	L	22	6	13	0	1	0	0	0	1	0	1	0	.077	.077
Frank McCue	3B2	B	23	2	5	0	0	0	0	0	0	0	0	0	.000	.000
Johnny Berger	C2	R	20	2	1	0	1	0	0	0	0	0	0	1	1.000	1.000

NAME	T	AGE	W	L	PCT	SV	G	GS	CG	IP	H	BB	SO	ShO	ERA
		25	65	89	.422	6	155	155	73	1363	1573	469	373	4	4.59
Eddie Rommel	R	24	27	13	.675	2	51	33	22	294	294	63	54	3	3.28
Rollie Naylor	R	30	10	15	.400	0	35	26	11	171	212	51	37	0	4.74
Bob Hasty	R	26	9	14	.391	0	28	26	14	192	225	41	33	1	4.27
Slim Harriss	R	25	9	20	.310	3	47	32	13	230	262	94	102	0	5.01
Fred Heimach	L	21	7	11	.389	1	37	19	7	172	220	63	47	0	5.02
Curly Ogden	R	21	1	4	.200	0	15	6	4	72	59	33	20	0	3.12
Rube Yarrison	R	26	1	2	.333	0	18	1	0	34	50	12	10	0	8.21
Otto Rettig	R	28	1	2	.333	0	4	4	1	18	18	12	3	0	5.00
Jim Sullivan	R	28	0	2	.000	0	20	2	1	51	76	25	15	0	5.47
Charlie Eckert	R	23	0	2	.000	0	21	0	0	50	61	23	15	0	4.68
1 Roy Moore	L	23	0	3	.000	0	15	6	0	51	65	32	29	0	7.59
Gus Ketchum	R	25	0	1	.000	0	6	0	0	16	19	8	4	0	5.63
Red Schillings	R	22	0	0	.000	0	4	0	0	8	10	11	4	0	6.75
Harry O'Neill	R	25	0	0	.000	0	1	0	0	3	2	1	0	0	3.00

BOSTON 8th 61-93 .396 33 — **HUGH DUFFY**

NAME	G by POS	B	AGE	G	AB	R	H	2B	3B	HR	RBI	BB	SO	SB	BA	SA
TOTALS			27	154	6288	598	1392	250	55	45	510	366	455	60	.263	.357
George Burns	1B140	R	29	147	558	71	171	32	5	12	73	20	28	8	.306	.446
Del Pratt	2B154	R	34	154	607	73	183	44	7	6	86	53	20	7	.301	.427
2 Johnny Mitchell	SS58	B	27	59	203	20	51	4	1	1	8	16	17	1	.251	.296
1 Joe Dugan	3B63, SS20	R	25	84	341	45	98	22	3	3	38	9	28	2	.287	.396
Shano Collins	OF117, 1B1	R	36	135	472	33	128	24	7	1	52	7	16	7	.271	.358
Joe Harris	OF83, 1B21	R	31	119	408	53	129	30	9	6	54	30	15	2	.316	.478
Mike Menosky	OF103	L	27	126	406	61	115	16	5	3	32	40	33	9	.283	.369
Muddy Ruel	C112	R	26	116	361	34	92	15	1	0	28	41	26	4	.255	.302
Nemo Leibold	OF71	L	30	81	271	42	70	8	1	1	18	41	14	1	.258	.306
1 Elmer Smith	OF59	L	29	73	231	43	66	13	6	6	32	25	21	0	.286	.472
Frank O'Rourke	SS48, 3B19	R	27	67	216	28	57	14	3	1	17	20	28	6	.264	.370
Pinky Pittinger	3B31, SS29	R	23	66	186	16	48	3	0	0	7	9	10	2	.258	.274
Benn Karr	P41	L	20	66	98	7	21	2	0	0	4	4	7	1	.214	.235
1 Eddie Foster	3B28, SS2, C2	R	35	48	109	11	23	3	0	0	3	9	10	1	.211	.239
2 Elmer Miller	OF35	R	31	44	147	16	28	2	3	4	16	5	10	3	.190	.327
Roxy Walters	C36	R	29	38	98	4	19	2	0	0	6	6	8	0	.194	.214
Bert Chaplin	C21	L	28	28	69	8	13	1	1	0	6	9	9	2	.188	.232
2 Chick Fewster	3B23	R	26	23	83	8	24	4	1	0	9	6	10	8	.289	.361
Chick Maynard	SS12	L	25	12	24	1	3	0	0	0	0	3	2	0	.125	.125
Dick Reichle	OF6	L	25	6	24	3	6	1	0	0	0	0	2	0	.250	.292
Walt Lynch	C3	R	25	3	2	1	1	0	0	0	0	0	0	0	.500	.500

NAME	T	AGE	W	L	PCT	SV	G	GS	CG	IP	H	BB	SO	ShO	ERA
		28	61	93	.396	6	154	154	71	1373	1508	503	359	10	4.30
Rip Collins	R	26	14	11	.560	0	32	29	15	211	219	103	69	3	3.75
Jack Quinn	R	38	13	16	.464	0	40	32	16	256	263	59	67	4	3.48
Herb Pennock	L	28	10	17	.370	1	32	26	15	202	230	74	59	1	4.32
Alex Ferguson	R	25	9	16	.360	2	39	27	10	198	201	62	44	1	4.32
Allen Russell	R	28	6	7	.462	2	34	11	1	126	152	57	34	0	5.00
Benn Karr	R	28	5	12	.294	1	41	13	7	183	212	45	41	0	4.47
Bill Piercy (SL)	R	26	3	9	.250	0	29	12	7	121	140	62	24	1	4.69
Curt Fullerton	R	23	1	4	.200	0	31	3	0	64	70	35	17	0	5.48
Sam Dodge	R	32	0	0	.000	0	3	0	0	6	11	3	3	0	4.50
Elmer Myers	R	28	0	1	.000	0	3	1	0	6	10	3	1	0	16.50

NEW YORK 1st 93-61 .604 — **JOHN McGRAW**

NAME	G by POS	B	AGE	G	AB	R	H	2B	3B	HR	RBI	BB	SO	SB	BA	SA
TOTALS			28	156	5455	852	1661	253	90	80	756	448	421	116	.304	.428
George Kelly	1B151	R	26	151	592	96	194	33	8	17	107	30	65	12	.328	.497
Frankie Frisch	2B85, 3B53, SS1	B	23	132	514	101	168	16	13	5	51	47	13	31	.327	.438
Dave Bancroft	SS156	B	31	156	651	117	209	41	5	4	60	79	27	16	.321	.418
Heinie Groh	3B110	R	32	115	426	63	113	21	3	3	51	53	21	5	.265	.350
Ross Youngs	OF147	L	25	149	559	105	185	34	10	7	86	55	50	17	.331	.465
Casey Stengel	OF77	L	31	84	250	48	92	8	10	7	48	21	17	4	.368	.564
Irish Meusel	OF154	R	29	154	617	100	204	28	17	16	132	35	33	12	.331	.509
Frank Snyder	C97	R	29	104	318	34	109	21	5	5	51	23	25	1	.343	.487
Earl Smith	C75	L	25	90	234	29	65	11	4	9	39	37	12	1	.278	.474
Johnny Rawlings	2B77, 3B5	R	29	88	308	46	87	13	8	1	30	23	15	7	.282	.386
Bill Cunningham	OF71, 3B1	R	26	85	229	37	75	15	2	2	33	7	9	4	.328	.437
Ralph Shinners (PB)	OF37	R	26	56	135	16	34	4	2	0	15	5	22	3	.252	.311
Dave Robertson	OF8	L	32	42	47	5	13	2	0	1	3	3	7	0	.277	.383
2 Lee King	1B5, OF5	R	29	20	34	6	6	3	0	0	2	5	2	1	.176	.265
Alex Gaston	C13	R	29	16	26	1	5	0	0	0	1	0	3	1	.192	.192
Howard Berry		B	27	6	0	0	0	0	0	0	0	0	0	0	.000	.000
Freddie Maguire	2B3	R	23	5	12	4	4	0	0	0	1	0	1	1	.333	.333
Mahlon Higbee	OF3	R	20	3	10	2	4	0	0	1	5	0	2	0	.400	.700
Travis Jackson	SS3	R	18	3	8	1	0	0	0	0	0	0	2	0	.000	.000
Waddy MacPhee	3B2	R	22	2	7	2	2	0	1	0	0	1	0	0	.286	.571
Ike Boone		L	25	2	2	0	1	0	0	0	0	0	1	0	.500	.500
Cozy Dolan		R	39	1	0	0	0	0	0	0	0	0	0	0	.000	.000

NAME	T	AGE	W	L	PCT	SV	G	GS	CG	IP	H	BB	SO	ShO	ERA
		27	93	61	.604	15	156	156	76	1396	1454	393	388	7	3.45
Art Nehf	L	29	19	13	.594	1	37	35	20	268	286	64	60	3	3.29
Rosy Ryan	R	24	17	12	.586	3	46	20	12	192	194	74	75	1	3.00
Jesse Barnes	R	29	13	8	.619	0	37	30	14	213	236	38	52	2	3.51
Phil Douglas (DL)	R	32	11	4	.733	0	24	21	9	158	154	35	33	1	2.62
2 Jack Scott	R	30	8	2	.800	2	17	10	5	80	83	23	37	0	4.39
Claude Jonnard	R	25	6	1	.857	5	33	0	0	96	96	28	44	0	3.84
2 Hugh McQuillan	R	24	6	5	.545	1	15	13	5	94	111	34	24	0	3.83
Fred Toney (HO)	R	34	5	6	.455	0	13	12	6	86	91	31	10	0	4.19
Red Causey	R	28	4	3	.571	1	24	2	1	71	69	34	13	0	3.17
Carmen Hill	R	26	2	1	.667	0	8	4	0	28	33	5	6	0	4.82
Virgil Barnes	R	25	1	0	1.000	2	22	3	1	52	46	11	16	0	3.46
Clint Blume	R	23	1	0	1.000	0	1	1	1	9	7	1	2	0	1.00
Mike Cvengros	L	20	0	1	.000	0	1	1	1	9	6	3	3	0	4.00
Fred Johnson	R	28	0	2	.000	0	2	2	1	18	20	1	8	0	4.00
Red Shea	R	23	0	3	.000	0	11	2	0	23	22	11	5	0	4.70

Rube Benton (DE) 35

CINCINNATI 2nd 86-68 .558 7 — **PAT MORAN**

NAME	G by POS	B	AGE	G	AB	R	H	2B	3B	HR	RBI	BB	SO	SB	BA	SA
TOTALS			29	156	5282	766	1562	226	99	45	[illegible]	[illegible]	[illegible]	130	[illegible]	[illegible]
Jake Daubert	1B156	L	38	156	610	114	205	15	22	12	66	56	21	14	.336	.492
Sammy Bohne	2B85, SS22	R	25	112	383	53	105	14	5	3	51	39	18	13	.274	.360
Ike Caveney	SS118	R	27	118	394	41	94	12	9	3	54	29	33	6	.239	.338
Babe Pinelli	3B156	R	26	156	547	77	167	19	7	1	72	48	37	17	.305	.371
George Harper	OF109	L	30	128	430	67	146	22	8	2	68	35	22	11	.340	.442
George Burns	OF156	R	32	156	631	104	180	20	10	1	53	78	38	30	.285	.353
Pat Duncan	OF151	R	28	151	607	94	199	44	12	8	94	40	31	12	.328	.479
Bubbles Hargrave	C87	R	29	98	320	49	101	22	10	7	57	26	18	7	.316	.513
Lew Fonseca	2B71	R	23	81	291	55	105	20	3	4	45	14	18	7	.361	.491
Ivy Wingo	C78	L	31	80	260	24	74	13	3	3	45	23	11	1	.285	.392
Rube Bressler	1B3, OF2	R	27	52	53	7	15	0	2	0	8	4	4	1	.283	.358
Edd Roush (HO)	OF43	L	29	49	165	29	58	7	4	1	24	19	5	5	.352	.461
Wally Kimmick	SS30, 2B3, 3B1	R	25	39	89	11	22	2	1	0	12	3	12	0	.247	.292
Greasy Neale	OF16	L	30	25	43	11	10	2	1	0	2	6	3	5	.233	.326
Red Lutz	C1	R	23	1	1	0	1	1	0	0	0	0	0	0	1.000	2.000

NAME	T	AGE	W	L	PCT	SV	G	GS	CG	IP	H	BB	SO	ShO	ERA
		27	86	68	.558	3	156	156	88	1386	1481	326	357	8	3.53
Eppa Rixey	L	31	25	13	.658	0	40	38	20	[illegible]	[illegible]	45	80	2	3.54
Pete Donohue (AJ)	R	21	18	9	.667	1	33	30	18	242	257	43	66	2	3.12
Johnny Couch	R	31	16	9	.640	1	43	34	18	264	301	56	45	2	3.89
Dolf Luque	R	31	13	23	.361	0	39	32	18	261	266	72	79	0	3.31
Cactus Keck	R	23	7	6	.538	1	27	15	5	131	138	29	27	1	3.37
Cliff Markle	R	28	4	5	.444	0	25	3	2	76	75	33	34	1	3.79
John Gillespie	R	22	3	3	.500	0	31	4	1	78	84	29	21	0	4.50
Karl Schnell	R	22	0	0	.000	0	10	0	0	20	21	18	5	0	2.70
1 Jack Scott (AJ)	R	30	0	0	.000	0	1	0	0	1	2	1	0	0	9.00

PITTSBURGH (Tie) 3rd 85-69 .552 8 — **GEORGE GIBSON 32-33 .492 BILL McKECHNIE 53-36 .596**

NAME	G by POS	B	AGE	G	AB	R	H	2B	3B	HR	RBI	BB	SO	SB	BA	SA
TOTALS			27	155	5521	865	1698	239	110	52	777	423	326	145	.308	.419
Charlie Grimm	1B154	L	23	154	593	64	173	28	13	0	76	43	15	6	.292	.383
Cotton Tierney	2B105, OF2, SS1, 3B1	R	28	122	441	58	152	26	14	7	86	22	40	7	.345	.515
Rabbit Maranville	SS138, 2B18	R	30	155	672	115	198	26	15	0	63	61	43	24	.295	.378
Pie Traynor	3B124, SS18	R	22	142	571	89	161	17	12	4	81	27	28	17	.282	.375
Reb Russell	OF60	L	33	60	220	51	81	14	8	12	75	14	18	4	.368	.668
Max Carey	OF155	B	32	155	629	140	207	28	12	10	70	80	26	51	.329	.459
Carson Bigbee	OF150	L	27	150	614	113	215	29	15	5	99	56	13	24	.350	.471
Johnny Gooch	C103	B	24	105	353	45	116	15	3	1	42	39	15	1	.329	.397
Clyde Barnhart	OF26, 3B30	R	26	75	209	30	69	7	5	1	38	25	7	3	.330	.426
Ray Rohwer	OF30	L	27	53	129	19	38	6	3	3	22	10	17	1	.295	.457
Jewel Ens	2B29, 3B3, 1B2, SS1	R	32	47	142	18	42	7	3	0	17	7	9	3	.296	.387
Walter Schmidt (HO)	C40	R	35	40	152	21	50	11	1	0	22	1	5	2	.329	.414
Walter Mueller	OF31	R	27	32	122	21	33	5	1	2	18	5	7	1	.270	.377
1 Johnny Mokan	OF23	R	26	31	89	9	23	3	1	0	8	9	3	0	.258	.315
Jim Mattox	C21	L	25	29	51	11	15	1	1	0	3	1	3	0	.294	.353
Bubber Jonnard	C10	R	22	10	21	4	5	0	1	0	2	2	4	0	.238	.333
2 Jack Hammond	2B4	R	31	9	11	3	3	0	0	0	0	1	0	0	.273	.273
Stuffy Stewart	2B3	R	28	3	13	3	2	0	0	0	0	0	1	0	.154	.154
Jake Miller	OF3	R	25	3	11	0	1	0	0	0	0	2	0	1	.091	.091

Kiki Cuyler 22 R 0-0, Grover Lovelace 23 R 0-1, Art Merewether 19 R 0-1, Tom McNamara 26 R 0-1

NAME	T	AGE	W	L	PCT	SV	G	GS	CG	IP	H	BB	SO	ShO	ERA
		30	85	69	.552	7	155	155	88	1387	1613	358	490	15	3.98
Wilbur Cooper	L	30	23	14	.622	0	41	37	27	295	330	61	129	4	3.18
Johnny Morrison	R	26	17	11	.607	1	45	33	20	286	315	87	104	5	3.43
Earl Hamilton	L	30	11	7	.611	2	33	14	9	160	183	40	34	1	3.99
Whitey Glazner	R	29	11	12	.478	1	34	26	10	193	238	52	77	1	4.38
Hal Carlson	R	28	9	12	.429	2	39	18	6	145	193	58	64	0	5.71
Babe Adams	R	40	8	11	.421	0	27	19	12	171	191	15	39	4	3.58
Myrl Brown	R	27	3	1	.750	0	7	5	2	35	42	13	9	0	5.91
Chief Yellowhorse	R	24	3	1	.750	0	28	5	2	78	92	20	24	0	4.50
Bonnie Hollingsworth	R	26	0	0	.000	0	9	0	0	14	17	8	7	0	7.71
Rip Wheeler	R	24	0	0	.000	0	1	0	0	1	1	2	0	0	0.00
Jimmy Zinn	R	27	0	0	.000	1	5	0	0	10	11	2	3	0	1.80

ST. LOUIS (Tie) 3rd 85-69 .552 8 — **BRANCH RICKEY**

NAME	G by POS	B	AGE	G	AB	R	H	2B	3B	HR	RBI	BB	SO	SB	BA	SA
TOTALS			28	154	5425	863	1634	280	88	107	787	447	425	73	.301	.444
Jack Fournier	1B109, P1	L	29	128	404	64	119	23	9	10	61	40	21	6	.295	.470
Rogers Hornsby	2B154	R	26	154	623	141	250	46	14	42	152	65	50	17	.401	.722
Specs Toporcer	SS91, 3B6, 2B1, OF1	L	23	116	352	56	114	25	6	3	36	24	18	2	.324	.455
Milt Stock	3B149, SS1	R	28	151	581	85	177	33	9	5	79	42	29	7	.305	.418
2 Max Flack	OF66	L	32	66	267	46	78	12	1	2	21	31	11	3	.292	.367
Jack Smith	OF136	L	27	143	510	117	158	23	12	8	46	50	30	18	.310	.449
Joe Schultz	OF89	R	28	112	344	50	108	13	4	2	64	19	10	3	.314	.392
Eddie Ainsmith	C116	R	30	119	379	46	111	14	4	13	59	28	43	2	.293	.454
Doc Lavan	SS82, 3B5	R	31	89	264	24	60	8	1	0	27	13	10	3	.227	.265
Les Mann	OF57	R	28	84	147	42	51	14	1	2	20	16	12	0	.347	.497
Vern Clemons	C63	R	30	71	160	9	41	4	0	0	15	18	5	1	.256	.281
Austin McHenry (IL)	OF61	R	26	64	238	31	72	18	3	5	43	14	27	2	.303	.466
Heinie Mueller	OF44	L	22	61	159	20	43	7	2	3	26	14	18	2	.270	.396
Del Gainer	1B26, OF10	R	34	43	97	19	26	7	4	2	23	14	6	0	.268	.485
Jim Bottomley	1B34	L	22	37	151	29	49	8	5	5	35	6	13	3	.325	.543
Ray Blades	OF29, SS4, 3B1	R	25	37	130	27	39	2	4	3	21	25	21	3	.300	.446
1 Cliff Heathcote	OF32	L	24	34	98	11	24	5	2	0	14	9	4	0	.245	.337
Burt Shotton	OF3	L	37	34	30	5	6	1	0	0	2	4	6	0	.200	.233
Harry McCurdy	C9, 1B2	L	22	13	27	3	8	2	2	0	5	1	1	0	.296	.519
Ernie Vick	C3	R	21	3	6	1	2	2	0	0	0	0	0	0	.333	.667
Howard Freigau	SS2, 3B1	R	19	3	1	0	0	0	0	0	0	0	0	0	.000	.000

Pickles Dillhoefer (DD) 27

NAME	T	AGE	W	L	PCT	SV	G	GS	CG	IP	H	BB	SO	ShO	ERA
		29	85	69	.552	12	154	154	60	1302	1609	447	465	8	4.44
Jeff Pfeffer	R	34	19	12	.617	2	44	32	19	261	286	58	83	1	3.58
Bill Sherdel	L	25	17	13	.567	2	47	31	15	242	298	62	79	3	3.87
Jesse Haines	R	28	11	9	.550	0	29	26	11	183	207	45	62	2	3.84
Bill Doak	R	31	11	13	.458	2	37	29	8	180	222	69	73	2	5.55
Lou North	R	31	10	3	.769	4	53	11	4	150	164	64	84	0	4.44
Bill Pertica	R	25	8	8	.500	0	34	14	2	117	153	65	30	0	5.92
Epp Sell	R	25	4	2	.667	0	7	5	0	33	47	6	5	0	6.82
Clyde Barfoot	R	30	4	5	.444	2	42	2	1	118	139	30	19	0	4.19
Roy Walker	R	29	1	2	.333	0	12	2	0	32	34	15	14	0	4.78
Bill Bailey	L	33	0	2	.000	0	12	0	0	32	38	23	11	0	5.35
Sid Benton	R	26	0	0	.000	0	1	0	0	0	0	2	0	0	0.00
Eddie Dyer	L	21	0	0	.000	0	2	0	0	4	7	0	3	0	2.25
Jack Fournier	L	29	0	0	.000	0	1	0	0	1	0	0	0	0	0.00
Marv Goodwin	R	31	0	0	.000	0	2	0	0	4	3	3	0	0	2.25
Jack Knight	R	27	0	0	.000	0	1	1	0	4	9	3	1	0	9.00
Johnny Stuart	R	21	0	0	.000	0	2	1	0	2	2	2	1	0	9.00

CHICAGO 5th 80-74 .519 13 — **BILL KILLEFER**

NAME	G by POS	B	AGE	G	AB	R	H	2B	3B	HR	RBI	BB	SO	SB	BA	SA
TOTALS			26	156	5335	771	1564	248	71	42	667	525	447	97	.293	.390
Ray Grimes	1B138	R	28	138	509	99	180	45	12	14	99	75	33	7	.354	.572
Zeb Terry	2B125, SS4, 3B3	R	31	131	496	56	142	24	2	0	67	34	16	2	.286	.343
Charlie Hollocher	SS152	L	26	152	592	90	201	37	8	3	69	58	5	19	.340	.444
Marty Krug	3B104, 2B23, SS1	R	33	127	450	67	124	23	4	4	60	43	43	7	.276	.371
Barney Friberg	OF74, 1B6, 3B5, 2B3	R	22	97	296	51	92	8	2	0	23	37	37	8	.311	.351
Jigger Statz (BH)	OF110	B	24	110	462	77	137	19	5	1	34	41	31	16	.297	.366
Hack Miller	OF116	R	28	122	466	61	164	28	5	12	78	26	39	3	.352	.511
Bob O'Farrell	C125	R	25	128	392	68	127	18	8	4	60	79	34	5	.324	.441
Turner Barber	OF47, 1B16	L	28	84	226	35	70	7	4	0	29	30	9	7	.310	.376
2 Cliff Heathcote	OF60	L	22	76	243	37	68	8	7	1	34	18	15	5	.280	.383
Marty Callaghan	OF53	L	22	74	175	31	45	7	4	0	20	17	17	2	.257	.343
John Kelleher	3B46, SS7, 1B4	R	28	63	193	23	50	7	1	0	20	15	14	5	.259	.306
George Maisel	OF26	R	30	38	84	9	16	1	1	0	6	8	2	1	.190	.226
Gabby Hartnett	C27	R	21	31	72	4	14	1	1	0	4	6	8	1	.194	.236
Kettle Wirts	C27	R	24	31	58	7	10	2	0	1	6	12	15	0	.172	.259
1 Max Flack	OF17	L	32	17	54	7	12	1	0	0	6	2	4	2	.222	.241
Sparky Adams	2B11	R	27	11	44	5	11	0	1	0	3	4	3	1	.250	.295
Howie Fitzgerald	OF6	L	20	10	24	3	8	1	0	0	4	3	2	1	.333	.375
George Grantham	3B5	L	22	7	23	3	4	1	1	0	3	1	3	2	.174	.304
Butch Weis		L	19	2	2	2	1	0	0	0	0	0	0	0	.500	.500
Walt Golvin	1B2	L	28	2	2	0	0	0	0	0	1	0	0	0	.000	.000

Joe Klugman 27 R 0-2, Harvey Cotter 22 L 1-1

NAME	T	AGE	W	L	PCT	SV	G	GS	CG	IP	H	BB	SO	ShO	ERA
		25	80	74	.519	12	156	156	74	1398	1579	475	402	8	4.34
Pete Alexander	R	35	16	13	.552	1	33	31	20	246	283	34	48	1	3.62
Vic Aldridge	R	22	16	15	.516	0	36	34	20	258	287	56	66	2	3.52
Virgil Cheeves	R	21	12	11	.522	2	39	23	9	183	195	76	40	1	4.09
George Stueland	R	23	9	4	.692	0	35	12	4	113	129	49	44	0	5.81
Tiny Osborne	R	29	9	5	.643	3	41	14	7	184	183	95	81	1	4.50
Percy Jones	L	22	8	9	.471	1	44	26	7	162	197	68	45	2	4.78
Tony Kaufmann	R	21	7	13	.350	3	37	9	4	153	161	57	45	1	4.06
Speed Martin	R	28	1	0	1.000	0	1	1	0	6	10	2	2	0	7.50
Fred Fussel	L	26	1	1	.500	0	3	2	1	19	24	8	4	0	4.74
Vic Keen	R	23	1	2	.333	1	7	3	2	35	36	10	11	0	3.86
Uel Eubanks	R	20	0	0	.000	0	2	0	0	2	5	4	1	0	22.50
Ed Morris	R	22	0	0	.000	0	5	0	0	12	22	6	5	0	8.25
Buck Freeman	R	25	0	1	.000	1	11	1	0	26	47	10	10	0	8.66

NAME	G by POS	B	AGE	G	AB	R	H	2B	3B	HR	RBI	BB	SO	SB	BA	SA
BROOKLYN 6th 76-78 .494 17	WILBERT ROBINSON															
TOTALS			31	155	5413	743	1569	235	76	56	674	339	318	79	.290	.392
Ray Schmandt	1B110	R	26	110	396	54	106	17	3	2	44	21	28	6	.268	.341
Ivy Olson	2B85, SS51	R	36	136	551	63	150	26	6	1	47	25	10	8	.272	.347
Jimmy Johnston	2B62, SS50, 3B26	R	32	138	567	110	181	20	7	4	49	38	17	18	.319	.400
Andy High	3B130, SS22, 2B1	L	24	153	579	82	164	27	10	6	65	59	26	3	.283	.396
Tommy Griffith	OF82	L	32	99	329	44	104	17	8	4	49	23	10	7	.316	.453
Hy Myers	OF152, 2B1	R	33	153	618	82	196	20	9	6	89	13	26	9	.317	.408
Zack Wheat	OF152	L	36	152	600	92	201	29	12	16	112	45	22	9	.335	.503
Hank DeBerry	C81	R	27	85	259	29	78	10	1	3	35	20	9	4	.301	.382
Bert Griffith	OF77, 1B6	R	26	106	325	45	100	22	8	2	35	5	11	5	.308	.443
Dutch Ruether	P35	L	28	67	125	12	26	6	1	2	20	12	11	0	.208	.320
Bernie Neis	OF27	B	26	61	70	15	16	4	1	1	9	13	8	3	.229	.357
Otto Miller	C57	R	33	59	180	20	47	11	1	1	23	6	13	0	.261	.350
Clarence Mitchell (NJ)	1B42, P5	L	31	56	155	21	45	6	3	3	28	19	6	0	.290	.426
Bernie Hungling	C36	R	26	39	102	9	23	1	2	1	13	6	20	2	.225	.304
Chuck Ward (IL)	SS31, 3B2	R	27	33	91	12	25	5	1	0	14	5	8	1	.275	.352
Hal Janvrin	2B15, SS4, 3B2, 1B1, OF1	R	29	30	57	7	17	3	1	0	1	4	4	0	.298	.386
Sam Post	1B8	L	25	9	25	3	7	0	0	0	4	1	4	1	.280	.280
Zack Taylor	C6	R	23	7	14	0	3	0	0	0	2	1	1	0	.214	.214
Sam Crane	SS3	R	27	3	8	1	2	1	0	0	0	0	1	0	.250	.375
Wally Hood		R	27	2	0	2	0	0	0	0	0	0	0	0	.000	.000
Possum Whitted		R	32	1	1	0	0	0	0	0	0	0	0	0	.000	.000
PHILADELPHIA 7th 57-96 .373 35.5	KAISER WILHELM															
TOTALS			29	154	5459	738	1537	268	55	**116**	685	450	**611**	48	.282	.415
Roy Leslie	1B139	R	27	141	513	44	139	23	2	6	50	37	49	3	.271	.359
Frank Parkinson	2B139	R	27	141	545	86	150	18	6	15	70	55	**93**	3	.275	.413
Art Fletcher	SS106	R	37	110	396	46	111	20	5	7	53	21	14	3	.280	.409
Goldie Rapp	3B117, SS2	B	30	119	502	58	127	26	3	0	38	32	29	6	.253	.317
Curt Walker	OF147	L	25	148	581	102	196	36	11	12	89	56	46	11	.337	.499
Cy Williams	OF150	L	34	151	584	98	180	30	6	26	92	74	49	11	.308	.514
Cliff Lee	OF89, 1B18, 3B1	R	25	122	422	65	136	29	6	17	77	32	43	2	.322	.540
Butch Henline	C119	R	27	125	430	57	136	20	4	14	64	36	33	2	.316	.479
Russ Wrightstone	3B40, SS35, 1B2	L	29	99	331	56	101	18	6	5	33	28	17	4	.305	.441
Bevo LeBourveau	OF42	L	27	74	167	24	45	8	3	2	20	24	29	0	.269	.389
John Peters	C39	R	28	55	143	15	35	9	1	4	24	9	18	0	.245	.406
2 Johnny Mokan	OF37, 3B2	R	26	47	151	20	38	7	1	3	27	16	25	1	.252	.371
Jimmy Smith	SS23, 2B13, 3B1	B	27	38	114	13	25	1	0	1	6	5	9	1	.219	.254
Lee Meadows	P33	R	27	33	86	8	27	4	0	0	5	1	25	0	.314	.360
1 Lee King	OF15	R	29	19	53	8	12	5	1	2	13	8	6	0	.226	.472
Frank Withrow	C8	R	31	10	21	3	7	2	0	0	3	3	5	0	.333	.429
Stan Benton	2B5	L	20	6	19	1	4	1	0	0	3	2	1	0	.211	.263
BOSTON 8th 53-100 .346 39.5	FRED MITCHELL															
TOTALS			30	154	5161	596	1355	162	73	32	509	387	451	67	.263	.341
Walter Holke (LJ)	1B105	B	29	105	395	35	115	9	4	0	46	14	23	6	.291	.334
Larry Kopf	2B78, SS33, 3B13	B	31	126	466	59	124	6	3	1	37	45	22	8	.266	.298
Hod Ford	SS115, 2B28	R	24	143	515	58	140	23	9	2	60	30	36	2	.272	.363
Tony Boeckel	3B106	R	29	119	402	61	116	19	6	6	47	35	32	14	.289	.410
Walton Cruise	OF100, 1B2	L	32	104	352	51	98	15	10	4	46	44	20	4	.278	.412
Ray Powell	OF136	L	33	142	550	82	163	22	11	6	37	59	66	3	.296	.409
Al Nixon	OF79	R	36	86	318	35	84	14	4	2	22	9	19	6	.264	.352
Mickey O'Neil	C79	R	24	83	251	18	56	5	2	0	26	14	11	1	.223	.259
Walter Barbare	2B45, 3B38, 1B14	R	30	106	373	38	86	5	4	0	40	21	22	2	.231	.265
Hank Gowdy	C72, 1B1	R	32	92	221	23	70	11	1	1	27	24	13	2	.317	.389
Fred Nicholson	OF63	R	27	78	222	31	56	4	5	2	29	23	24	5	.252	.342
Lloyd Christenbury	OF32, 2B5, 3B2	L	28	71	152	22	38	5	2	1	13	18	11	2	.250	.329
Frank Gibson	C29, 1B20	L	31	66	164	15	49	7	2	3	20	10	27	4	.299	.421
Billy Southworth (LJ)	OF41	L	29	43	158	27	51	4	4	4	18	18	1	4	.323	.475
Bunny Roser	OF32	L	20	32	113	13	27	3	4	0	16	10	19	2	.239	.336
Snake Henry	1B18	L	26	18	66	5	13	4	1	0	5	2	8	2	.197	.288
Gil Gallagher	SS6	B	25	7	22	1	1	1	0	0	2	1	7	0	.045	.091

NAME	T	AGE	W	L	PCT	SV	G	GS	CG	IP	H	BB	SO	ShO	ERA
(Brooklyn)		29	76	78	.494	8	155	155	82	1383	1568	**490**	**499**	12	4.04
Dutch Ruether	L	28	21	12	.636	0	35	35	26	267	290	92	89	2	3.54
Dazzy Vance	R	31	18	12	.600	0	36	30	16	246	259	94	**134**	5	3.70
Burleigh Grimes	R	28	17	14	.548	1	35	34	18	256	318	84	99	1	4.75
Leon Cadore	R	31	8	15	.348	0	29	21	13	190	224	57	49	0	4.36
1 Sherry Smith	L	31	4	8	.333	2	28	9	3	109	128	35	15	1	4.55
Harry Shriver	R	25	4	6	.400	0	25	14	4	108	114	48	38	2	3.00
Art Decatur	R	28	3	4	.429	1	29	2	1	88	87	29	31	0	2.76
Al Mamaux	R	28	1	4	.200	3	37	7	1	88	97	33	35	0	3.68
Clarence Mitchell (NJ)	L	31	0	3	.000	0	5	3	0	13	28	7	1	0	13.85
Ray Gordinier	R	30	0	0	.000	0	5	0	0	11	13	8	5	0	9.00
Jim Murray	L	21	0	0	.000	1	4	0	0	6	8	3	3	0	4.50
Paul Schreiber	R	19	0	0	.000	0	1	0	0	1	2	0	0	0	0.00
(Philadelphia)		26	57	96	.373	5	154	154	73	1372	**1692**	460	394	6	4.64
Jimmy Ring	R	27	12	18	.400	1	40	33	17	249	292	**103**	116	0	4.59
Lee Meadows	R	27	12	18	.400	0	33	33	19	237	264	71	62	2	4.02
Lefty Weinert	L	20	8	11	.421	1	34	22	10	167	189	70	58	0	3.39
Bill Hubbell	R	25	7	15	.318	1	35	24	11	189	257	41	33	1	5.00
Jesse Winters	R	28	6	6	.500	2	34	9	4	138	176	56	29	0	5.35
George Smith	R	30	5	14	.263	0	42	18	6	194	250	35	44	1	4.78
Petie Behan	R	34	4	2	.667	0	7	5	3	47	49	14	13	1	2.49
John Singleton	R	25	1	10	.091	0	22	9	3	93	127	38	27	1	5.90
Huck Betts	R	25	1	0	1.000	0	7	0	0	15	23	8	4	0	9.60
Stan Baumgartner	L	29	1	1	.500	0	6	1	0	10	18	5	2	0	6.30
Letron Pinto	L	24	0	1	.000	0	9	0	0	25	31	14	4	0	5.04
Tom Sullivan	L	26	0	0	.000	0	3	0	0	8	16	5	2	0	11.25
(Boston)		27	53	**100**	.346	6	154	154	63	1348	1565	489	360	7	4.37
Frank Miller	R	36	11	13	.458	1	31	23	14	200	213	60	65	2	3.51
Rube Marquard	L	32	11	15	.423	1	39	24	7	198	255	66	57	0	5.09
Mule Watson	R	25	8	14	.364	1	41	29	8	201	262	59	53	1	4.70
Joe Oeschger	R	31	6	21	.222	1	46	23	10	196	234	81	51	1	5.05
1 Hugh McQuillan	R	24	5	10	.333	0	28	17	7	136	154	56	33	0	4.24
Dana Fillingim	R	28	5	9	.357	2	25	12	5	117	143	37	25	1	4.54
Tim McNamara	R	23	3	4	.429	0	24	5	4	71	55	26	16	2	2.41
Harry Hulihan	L	23	2	3	.400	0	7	6	2	40	40	26	16	0	3.15
Garland Braxton (IL)	L	22	1	2	.333	0	25	4	2	67	75	24	15	0	3.36
Johnny Cooney	L	21	1	2	.333	0	4	3	1	25	19	6	7	0	2.16
Joe Genewich	R	25	0	2	.000	0	6	2	1	23	29	11	4	0	7.04
Gene Lansing	R	24	0	1	.000	0	15	1	0	41	46	22	14	0	5.93
Jim Mathews	L	22	0	1	.000	0	3	1	0	10	5	6	0	0	3.60
Cy Morgan	R	25	0	0	.000	0	2	0	0	1	8	2	0	0	36.00
Dick Rudolph	R	34	0	2	.000	0	3	3	1	16	22	5	3	0	5.06
Al Yeargin	R	20	0	1	.000	0	1	1	1	7	5	2	1	0	1.29

WORLD SERIES – NEW YORK (NL) 4 NEW YORK (AL) 0 (one tie game)

LINE SCORES

TEAM	1	2	3	4	5	6	7	8	9	10	11	12	R	H	E
Game 1 October 4 at Polo Grounds															
NY (AL)	0	0	0	0	0	1	1	0	0				2	7	0
NY (NL)	0	0	0	0	0	0	0	3	X				3	11	3
Bush, Hoyt (8)	Nehf, **Ryan** (8)														
Game 2 October 5 at Polo Grounds															
NY (NL)	3	0	0	0	0	0	0	0	0	0			3	8	1
NY (AL)	1	0	0	1	0	0	0	1	0	0			3	8	0
J. Barnes	Shawkey	Stopped by darkness													
Game 3 October 6 at Polo Grounds															
NY (AL)	0	0	0	0	0	0	0	0	0				0	4	1
NY (NL)	0	0	2	0	0	0	1	0	X				3	12	1
Hoyt, Jones (8)	**Scott**														
Game 4 October 7 at Polo Grounds															
NY (NL)	0	0	0	0	4	0	0	0	0				4	9	1
NY (AL)	2	0	0	0	0	0	1	0	0				3	8	0
McQuillan	**Mays**, Jones (9)														
Games 5 October 8 at Polo Grounds															
NY (AL)	1	0	0	0	1	0	1	0	0				3	5	0
NY (NL)	0	2	0	0	0	0	0	3	X				5	10	0
Bush	**Nehf**														

COMPOSITE BATTING

NAME	POS	G	AB	R	H	2B	3B	HR	RBI	BA
New York (NL)										
Totals		5	162	18	50	2	1	1	18	.309
I. Meusel	OF	5	20	3	5	0	0	1	**7**	.250
Groh	3B	5	19	**4**	**9**	0	1	0	0	**.474**
Bancroft	SS	5	19	**4**	4	0	0	0	2	.211
Kelly	1B	5	18	0	5	0	0	0	2	.278
Frisch	2B	5	17	3	8	1	0	0	2	.471
Youngs	OF	5	16	2	6	0	0	0	2	.375
Snyder	C	4	15	1	5	0	0	0	0	.333
Cunningham	OF	4	10	0	2	0	0	0	2	.200
E. Smith	C	4	7	0	1	0	0	0	0	.143
Stengel	OF	2	5	0	2	0	0	0	0	.400
J. Scott	P	1	4	0	1	0	0	0	0	.250
McQuillan	P	1	4	1	1	1	0	0	0	.250
J. Barnes	P	1	4	0	0	0	0	0	0	.000
Nehf	P	2	3	0	0	0	0	0	0	.000
King	OF	2	1	0	1	0	0	0	1	1.000
Ryan	P	1	0	0	0	0	0	0	0	.000
New York (AL)										
Totals		5	158	11	32	6	1	2	11	.203
Pipp	1B	5	**21**	0	6	1	0	0	3	.286
B. Meusel	OF	5	20	2	6	1	0	0	2	.300
Dugan	3B	5	20	**4**	5	1	0	0	0	.250
Witt	OF	5	18	1	4	1	1	0	0	.222
Ruth	OF	5	17	1	2	1	0	0	1	.118
Schang	C	5	16	0	3	1	0	0	0	.188
E. Scott	SS	5	14	0	2	0	0	0	1	.143
Ward	2B	5	13	3	2	0	0	**2**	3	.154
Bush	P	2	6	0	1	0	0	0	1	.167
Shawkey	P	1	4	0	0	0	0	0	0	.000
Hoyt	P	2	2	0	1	0	0	0	0	.500
Elmer Smith	PH	2	2	0	0	0	0	0	0	.000
Mays	P	1	2	0	0	0	0	0	0	.000
McMillan	OF	1	2	0	0	0	0	0	0	.000
Baker	PH	1	1	0	0	0	0	0	0	.000
McNally	2B	1	0	0	0	0	0	0	0	.000
Jones	P	2	0	0	0	0	0	0	0	.000

COMPOSITE PITCHING

NAME	G	IP	H	BB	SO	W	L	SV	ERA
New York (NL)									
Totals	5	46	32	8	20	4	0	0	1.76
Nehf	**2**	**16**	11	3	**6**	1	0	0	2.25
J. Barnes	1	10	8	2	**6**	0	0	0	1.80
J. Scott	1	9	4	1	2	1	0	0	**0.00**
McQuillan	1	9	8	2	4	1	0	0	3.00
Ryan	1	2	1	0	2	1	0	0	0.00
New York (AL)									
Totals	5	43	50	12	15	0	4	0	3.35
Bush	**2**	15	**21**	5	**6**	0	**2**	0	4.80
Shawkey	1	10	8	2	4	0	0	0	2.70
Hoyt	**2**	8	11	2	4	0	1	0	1.13
Mays	1	8	9	2	1	0	1	0	4.50
Jones	**2**	2	1	1	0	0	0	0	0.00

1923 The Haunting Eviction

New York owned the baseball world. If there was any doubt to the claim, the final standings of 1921 and 1922 could easily back it up. During both previous seasons, the Giants and Yankees had won their league flags, and 1923 seemed to pose no problem for either of the clubs. But when problems from without are not present, the strife seems to manifest from within. Such was the case when an overabundance of success or jealousy of others good fortunes caused the Giants to inform Yankee owner Colonel Jacob Ruppert that his American Leaguers were no longer welcomed tenants in the Polo Grounds.

This decision sent the Colonel out to build Yankee Stadium—a 62,000-seat palace within ¼ mile of the National League park. With the most attractive stadium in the country, an exciting club, and a super drawing card in slugger Babe Ruth, the Yankees enjoyed a banner year at the gate and won a third consecutive American League pennant on the field. Although the Bambino swatted 41 homers into the friendly seats of the stadium, drove home 130 teammates, and batted a robust .393, the Yankee long suits were pitching and defense. A trade with Boston brought lefty Herb Pennock into the starting rotation with Joe Bush, Sam Jones, Bob Shawkey, and Waite Hoyt to form the class hill staff of the loop. A solid infield cut off many opponent's runs, and the attack led by Ruth, Bob Meusel, and Wally Pipp provided enough Yankee runs for a final 16-game pennant margin.

Detroit and Cleveland, both possessors of .300 team batting averages, were the distant runner-ups to the New Yorkers. The Tigers fielded a Hall of Fame outfield in batting leader Harry Heilmann, manager Ty Cobb, and rookie Heinie Manush, while Tris Speaker managed both the Indians and provided the sock with his .380 batting average and 130 runs batted in. Both clubs, though, lacked the pitching to finish closer to the top. The fall of 1922's contending St. Louis Browns into the second division was insured by the eye ailment which sidelined star first-sacker George Sisler for the entire campaign.

With their hometown rivals unfurling a championship and a new stadium, the Giants felt obligated to match the upstarts. To begin the promotional campaign, the Polo Grounds were embellished and enlarged to a capacity of 54,000 seats. To further woo spectators into their den, the Giants won their third straight championship in a close race with the Cincinnati Reds. While no slugger on the order of Ruth graced the Jints' lineup, Frankie Frisch starred in his own manner with a .348 batting mark and blazing speed afield and on the bases. While Ross Youngs belted only three homers, he hit .336 and covered right field more gracefully than the Babe. Highpockets Kelly provided solid batting, and Giant Irish Meusel enjoyed a better year than brother Yankee Bob. Dave Bancroft, as usual, played an air-tight shortstop, but his late-season bout with pneumonia gave rookie Travis Jackson an extended trial in his slot. The pitching staff flashed no aces, but enough numbers to get by, as Jack Scott and reliever Rosie Ryan led the staff with 16 victories apiece.

Cincinnati boasted of the loop's top pitching with 20-game winners, Dolf Luque, Eppa Rixey, and Pete Donohue, but lacked enough hitters like Edd Roush to overtake New York. Second-division clubs held the league batting stars, as Rogers Hornsby of the Cardinals won his fourth straight batting title, and Cy Williams the home run title to give his last-place Philadelphia Phillies' teammates something to cheer about.

For the third straight October, the World Series was played in New York, but this time in two parks. Casey Stengel won the opener in Yankee Stadium for the Giants with a ninth-inning inside-the-park home run and gave Art Nehf a 1-0 victory in game three with another circuit blast. But the Nationals won no other games, as the Yankees' attack found the Giants' pitchers easy marks. A six-game Series victory, spiced with three Ruth homers, marked the Yankees emergence from the underdog role in New York—a part which they had reluctantly held years since their birth in 1903.

1923 AMERICAN LEAGUE

NAME	G by POS	B	AGE	G	AB	R	H	2B	3B	HR	RBI	BB	SO	SB	BA	SA
NEW YORK 1st 98-54 .645		MILLER HUGGINS														
TOTALS			29	152	**5347**	823	1554	231	79	**105**	770	521	516	69	.291	**.422**
Wally Pipp	1B144	L	30	144	569	79	173	19	8	6	108	36	28	6	.304	.397
Aaron Ward	2B152	R	26	152	567	79	161	26	11	10	82	56	65	8	.284	.422
Everett Scott	SS152	R	30	152	533	48	131	16	4	6	60	13	19	1	.246	.325
Joe Dugan	3B146	R	26	146	**644**	111	182	30	7	7	67	25	41	4	.283	.384
Babe Ruth	OF148, 1B4	L	28	152	522	**151**	205	45	13	**41**	**131**	**170**	**93**	17	.393	**.764**
Whitey Witt	OF144	L	27	146	596	113	187	18	10	6	56	67	42	2	.314	.408
Bob Meusel	OF121	R	26	132	460	59	144	29	10	9	91	31	52	13	.313	.478
Wally Schang (GJ)	C81	B	33	84	272	39	75	8	2	2	29	27	17	3	.276	.342
Fred Hofmann	C70	R	29	72	238	24	69	10	4	3	26	18	27	2	.290	.403
Elmer Smith	OF47	L	30	70	183	30	56	6	2	7	35	21	21	3	.306	.475
Harvey Hendrick	OF12	L	25	37	66	9	18	3	1	3	12	2	8	3	.273	.485
Mike McNally	SS13, 3B7, 2B5	R	29	30	38	5	8	0	0	0	1	3	4	2	.211	.211
Hinkey Haines	OF14	R	24	28	25	9	4	2	0	0	3	4	5	3	.160	.240
Benny Bengough	C19	R	24	19	53	1	7	2	0	0	3	4	2	0	.132	.170
2 Ernie Johnson	SS15, 3B1	L	35	19	38	6	17	1	1	1	8	1	1	0	.447	.605
Lou Gehrig	1B9	L	20	13	26	6	11	4	1	1	9	2	5	0	.423	.769
Mike Gazella	SS4, 2B2, 3B2	R	26	8	13	2	1	0	0	0	1	2	3	0	.077	.077
DETROIT 2nd 83-71 .539 16		TY COBB														
TOTALS			29	155	5266	831	1579	270	69	41	739	596	385	87	.300	.401
Lu Blue	1B129	B	26	129	504	100	143	27	7	1	46	96	40	9	.284	.371
Fred Haney	2B69, 3B55, SS16	R	25	142	503	85	142	13	4	4	67	45	23	12	.282	.348
Topper Rigney	SS129	R	26	129	470	63	148	24	11	1	74	55	35	7	.315	.419
Bob Jones	3B97	L	33	100	372	51	93	15	4	1	40	29	13	7	.250	.320
Harry Heilmann	OF130, 1B12	R	28	144	524	121	211	44	11	18	115	74	40	8	**.403**	.632
Ty Cobb	OF141	L	36	145	556	103	189	40	7	6	88	66	14	9	.340	.469
Heinie Manush	OF79	L	21	109	308	59	103	20	5	4	54	20	21	3	.334	.471
Johnny Bassler	C128	L	28	135	383	45	114	12	3	0	49	76	13	2	.298	.345
Bobby Veach	OF85, C1	L	35	114	293	45	94	13	3	2	39	29	21	10	.321	.406
Bob Fothergill	OF68	R	25	101	241	34	76	18	2	1	49	12	19	4	.315	.419
Del Pratt	2B60, 1B17, 3B12	R	35	101	297	43	92	18	3	0	40	25	9	5	.310	.391
Larry Woodall	C60	R	28	71	148	20	41	12	2	1	19	22	9	2	.277	.405
George Cutshaw (IL)	2B43, 3B2	R	35	45	143	15	32	1	2	0	13	9	5	2	.224	.259
Clyde Manion	C3, 1B1	R	26	23	22	0	3	0	0	0	2	2	2	0	.136	.136
John Kerr	SS15	B	24	19	42	4	9	1	0	0	1	4	5	0	.214	.238
Les Burke	3B2, 2B1, C1	L	20	7	10	2	1	0	0	0	2	0	1	0	.100	.100
Fred Carisch	C2	R	41	2	0	0	0	0	0	0	0	0	0	0	.000	.000
1 Ira Flagstead		R	29	1	1	0	0	0	0	0	0	0	0	0	.000	.000
CLEVELAND 3rd 82-71 .536 16.5		TRIS SPEAKER														
TOTALS			28	153	5290	**888**	**1594**	**301**	75	59	**807**	**633**	384	86	**.301**	.420
Frank Brower	1B112, OF2	L	30	126	397	77	113	25	8	16	66	62	32	6	.285	.509
Bill Wambsganss	2B88, 3B4, SS2	R	29	101	345	59	100	20	4	1	59	43	15	12	.290	.380
Joe Sewell	SS151	L	24	153	533	98	195	41	10	3	109	98	12	9	.353	.479
Rube Lutzke	3B143	R	25	143	511	71	131	20	6	3	65	59	57	10	.256	.337
Homer Summa	OF136	L	24	137	525	92	172	27	6	3	69	33	20	9	.328	.419
Tris Speaker	OF150	L	35	150	574	133	218	**59**	11	17	130	93	15	10	.380	.610
Charlie Jamieson	OF152	L	30	152	**644**	130	**222**	36	12	2	51	80	37	19	.345	.447
Steve O'Neill	C111	R	31	113	330	31	82	12	0	0	50	64	34	0	.248	.285
Glen Myatt	C69	L	25	92	220	36	63	7	6	3	40	16	18	0	.286	.414
Riggs Stephenson	2B66, OF3, 3B1	R	25	91	301	48	96	20	6	5	65	15	25	6	.319	.475
George Uhle	P54	R	24	58	144	23	52	10	3	0	22	7	10	2	.361	.472
Joe Connolly	OF39	R	27	52	109	25	33	10	1	3	25	13	7	1	.303	.495
Larry Gardner	3B19	L	37	52	79	4	20	5	1	0	12	12	7	0	.253	.342
Lou Guisto	1B40	R	29	40	144	17	26	5	0	0	18	15	15	1	.181	.215
Ray Knode	1B21	L	22	22	38	7	11	0	0	2	4	2	4	1	.289	.447
Luke Sewell	C7	R	22	10	10	2	2	0	1	0	1	1	0	0	.200	.400
Wally Shaner	OF2, 3B1	R	23	3	4	1	1	0	0	0	0	1	1	0	.250	.250
Tom Gulley	OF1	L	23	2	3	1	1	1	0	0	0	0	0	0	.333	.667
Jackie Gallagher	OF1	L	21	1	1	0	1	0	0	0	1	0	0	0	1.000	1.000
Sumpter Clarke	OF1	R	25	1	3	0	0	0	0	0	0	0	0	0	.000	.000
Kenny Hogan		L	20	1	0	0	0	0	0	0	0	0	0	0	.000	.000

NAME	T	AGE	W	L	PCT	SV	G	GS	CG	IP	H	BB	SO	ShO	ERA
		29	**98**	54	**.645**	10	152	152	**102**	1367	1365	491	**506**	9	**3.66**
Sad Sam Jones	R	30	21	8	.724	4	39	27	18	243	239	69	68	3	3.63
Herb Pennock	L	29	19	6	**.760**	3	35	27	21	224	235	68	93	1	3.34
Bullet Joe Bush	R	30	19	15	.559	0	37	30	23	276	263	117	125	3	3.42
Waite Hoyt	R	23	17	9	.654	1	37	28	19	239	227	66	60	1	3.01
Bob Shawkey	R	32	16	11	.593	1	36	31	17	259	232	102	125	1	3.51
Carl Mays	R	31	5	2	.714	0	23	7	2	81	119	32	16	0	6.22
George Pipgras	R	23	1	3	.250	0	8	2	2	33	34	25	12	0	6.00
Oscar Roettger	R	23	0	0	.000	1	5	0	0	12	16	12	7	0	8.25
		27	83	71	.539	12	155	155	61	1374	1502	449	447	9	4.09
Hooks Daus	R	33	21	13	.615	3	50	39	22	316	331	78	105	4	3.62
Herman Pillette	R	27	14	**19**	.424	1	47	37	14	250	280	83	64	0	3.85
Bert Cole	L	25	13	5	.722	5	52	13	5	163	183	61	32	1	4.14
Syl Johnson	R	22	12	7	.632	0	37	18	7	176	181	47	93	1	3.99
Ken Hollaway	R	25	11	10	.524	1	42	24	7	194	232	75	55	1	4.45
Ray Francis	L	30	5	8	.385	1	33	6	0	79	95	28	27	0	4.45
Rip Collins	R	27	3	7	.300	0	17	13	3	92	104	22	25	1	4.88
Earl Whitehill	L	23	2	0	1.000	0	8	3	2	33	22	15	19	1	2.73
Ed Wells	L	23	0	0	.000	0	7	0	0	10	11	6	6	0	5.40
Ole Olsen	R	28	1	1	.500	0	17	2	1	41	42	17	12	0	6.37
Rufe Clarke	R	23	1	1	.500	0	5	0	0	6	6	6	2	0	4.50
Roy Moore	L	24	0	0	.000	1	3	0	0	12	15	11	7	0	3.00
Dutch Leonard (ST) 31															
		28	82	71	.536	11	153	153	77	1375	1517	466	407	**10**	3.91
George Uhle	R	24	**26**	16	.619	5	54	**44**	**29**	**358**	**378**	102	109	1	3.77
Stan Coveleski (IL)	R	34	13	14	.481	2	33	31	17	228	251	42	54	**5**	**2.76**
Joe Shaute	L	23	10	8	.556	0	33	16	7	172	176	53	61	0	3.52
Jim Joe Edwards	L	28	10	10	.500	1	38	21	8	179	200	75	68	1	3.73
Sherry Smith	L	32	9	6	.600	1	30	16	10	124	129	37	23	1	3.27
Guy Morton	R	30	6	6	.500	1	32	14	3	128	133	56	54	2	4.29
Dewey Metivier	R	25	4	2	.667	1	26	5	1	73	111	38	9	0	6.53
Danny Boone (SA)	R	28	4	6	.400	0	27	4	2	70	93	31	15	0	6.04
Phil Bedgood	R	25	0	2	.000	0	9	2	0	19	16	14	7	0	5.21
Logan Drake	R	22	0	0	.000	0	4	0	0	4	2	5	2	0	4.50
Emil Levsen	R	25	0	0	.000	0	3	0	0	4	4	0	1	0	0.00
Jim Sullivan	R	29	0	1	.000	0	3	0	0	5	10	5	4	0	14.40
George Edmondson	R	27	0	0	.000	0	1	0	0	4	8	3	0	0	11.25
Johnson Fry	R	21	0	0	.000	0	1	0	0	4	6	4	0	0	11.25
George Winn	L	25	0	0	.000	0	1	0	0	2	0	1	0	0	0.00

WASHINGTON 4th 75-78 .490 23.5 — DONIE BUSH

NAME	G by POS	B	AGE	G	AB	R	H	2B	3B	HR	RBI	BB	SO	SB	BA	SA
TOTALS			28	155	5244	720	1436	224	93	26	628	532	448	102	.274	.367
Joe Judge (KJ)	1B112	L	29	113	405	56	127	24	6	2	63	58	20	11	.314	.417
Bucky Harris	2B144, SS1	R	26	145	532	60	150	21	13	2	70	50	29	23	.282	.382
Roger Peckinpaugh	SS154	R	32	154	568	73	150	18	4	2	62	64	30	10	.264	.320
Ossie Bluege (KJ)	3B107, 2B2	R	22	109	379	48	93	15	7	2	42	48	53	5	.245	.338
Sam Rice	OF147	L	33	148	595	117	188	35	18	3	75	57	12	20	.316	.450
2 Nemo Leibold	OF84	L	31	95	315	68	96	13	4	1	22	53	16	7	.305	.381
Goose Goslin	OF149	L	22	150	600	86	180	29	18	9	99	40	53	7	.300	.463
Muddy Ruel	C133	R	27	136	449	63	142	24	3	0	54	55	21	4	.316	.383
Joe Evans	OF72, 3B21, 1B5	R	28	106	372	42	98	15	3	0	38	27	18	6	.263	.320
Patsy Gharrity	C35, 1B33	R	31	93	251	26	52	9	4	3	33	22	27	6	.207	.311
Pinky Hargrave	3B8, C5, OF1	R	27	33	59	4	17	2	0	0	8	2	6	0	.288	.322
Rip Wade	OF19	L	25	33	69	8	16	2	2	2	14	5	10	0	.232	.406
Jim O'Neill	2B8, 3B6, OF1	R	30	23	33	6	9	1	0	0	3	1	3	0	.273	.303
Pep Conroy (IL)	3B10, 1B6, OF1	R	24	18	60	6	8	2	2	0	2	4	9	0	.133	.233
Showboat Fisher	OF5	L	24	13	23	4	6	2	0	0	2	4	3	0	.261	.348
Donie Bush	3B6, 2B1	B	35	10	22	6	9	0	0	0	0	0	1	0	.409	.409
Bobby Murray	3B10	L	24	10	39	2	7	1	0	0	2	1	4	1	.179	.205
Doc Prothro	3B6	R	29	6	8	2	2	0	1	0	3	1	3	0	.250	.500
Carr Smith	OF4	R	22	5	9	0	1	1	0	0	1	0	0	0	.111	.222
Pete Lapan		R	32	2	2	0	0	0	0	0	0	0	0	0	.000	.000

Jim Riley 28 L 0-3, Jake Propst 28 L 0-1

NAME	T	AGE	W	L	PCT	SV	G	GS	CG	IP	H	BB	SO	ShO	ERA
TOTALS		30	75	78	.490	16	155	155	72	1375	1531	559	474	8	3.99
Walter Johnson	R	35	17	12	.586	4	43	35	18	262	267	69	130	3	3.54
George Mogridge	L	34	13	13	.500	1	33	28	18	211	228	56	62	3	3.11
Allen Russell	R	29	10	7	.588	9	52	6	4	181	177	77	67	0	3.03
Tom Zachary	L	27	10	16	.385	0	35	29	10	204	270	63	40	0	4.50
Paul Zahniser	R	26	9	10	.474	0	33	21	10	177	201	76	52	1	3.86
Cy Warmoth	L	30	7	5	.583	0	21	13	4	105	103	76	45	0	4.28
Firpo Marberry	R	24	4	0	1.000	0	11	4	2	45	42	17	18	0	2.80
Bonnie Hollingsworth	R	27	3	7	.300	0	17	8	1	73	72	50	26	0	4.07
Monroe Mitchell	R	21	2	4	.333	2	10	6	3	42	57	22	8	1	6.43
Jim Brillheart	L	19	0	1	.000	0	12	0	0	18	27	12	8	0	7.00
Skipper Friday	R	25	0	1	.000	0	7	2	1	30	35	22	9	0	6.90
Duke Sedgwick	R	24	0	1	.000	0	5	2	1	16	27	6	4	0	7.88
Slim McGrew	R	23	0	0	.000	0	3	0	0	5	11	3	1	0	12.60
Fred Schemanske	R	20	0	0	.000	0	1	0	0	1	3	0	0	0	27.00
Clay Roe	L	19	0	1	.000	0	1	1	0	2	0	6	2	0	0.00
Bob Potter	R	21	0	0	.000	0	1	0	0	3	11	4	1	0	21.00
Ted Wingfield	R	23	0	0	.000	0	1	0	0	1	0	0	1	0	0.00

ST. LOUIS 5th 74-78 .487 24 — LEE FOHL 51-49 .510 JIMMY AUSTIN 23-29 .442

NAME	G by POS	B	AGE	G	AB	R	H	2B	3B	HR	RBI	BB	SO	SB	BA	SA
TOTALS			29	154	5298	688	1489	248	62	82	613	442	423	64	.281	.398
2 Dutch Schleibner	1B127	R	32	127	444	50	122	19	6	4	52	39	60	3	.275	.372
Marty McManus	2B133, 1B20	R	23	154	582	86	180	35	10	15	94	49	50	14	.309	.481
Wally Gerber	SS154	R	31	154	605	85	170	26	3	1	62	54	50	4	.281	.331
Homer Ezzell	3B73, 2B8	R	27	88	275	31	68	6	0	0	14	15	20	4	.247	.269
Jack Tobin	OF151	L	31	151	637	91	202	32	15	13	73	42	13	8	.317	.476
Baby Doll Jacobson	OF146	R	32	147	592	76	183	29	6	8	81	29	27	6	.309	.419
Ken Williams	OF145	L	33	147	555	106	198	37	12	29	91	79	32	18	.357	.623
Hank Severeid	C116	R	32	122	432	50	133	27	6	3	51	31	11	3	.308	.419
Pat Collins	C47	R	26	85	181	9	32	8	0	3	30	15	45	0	.177	.271
Gene Robertson (VR)	3B74, 2B1	L	23	78	251	36	62	10	1	0	17	21	7	4	.247	.295
Cedric Durst	OF10, 1B8	L	26	45	85	12	18	2	0	5	11	8	14	0	.212	.412
Eddie Foster	2B20, 3B7	R	36	27	100	9	18	2	0	0	4	7	7	0	.180	.200
Bill Whaley	OF13	R	24	23	50	5	12	2	1	0	1	4	2	0	.240	.320
Frank Ellerbe	3B14	R	27	18	49	6	9	0	0	0	1	1	5	0	.184	.184
Johnny Schulte	1B1, C1	L	26	7	3	1	0	0	0	0	1	4	0	0	.000	.000
Herschel Bennett	OF1	L	26	5	4	0	0	0	0	0	0	1	1	0	.000	.000
Josh Billings	C4	R	31	4	9	0	0	0	0	0	0	0	2	0	.000	.000
Harry Rice		L	22	4	3	0	0	0	0	0	0	0	0	0	.000	.000
Jimmy Austin	C1	B	43	1	0	0	0	0	0	0	0	0	0	0	.000	.000
Bill Mizeur		L	23	1	1	0	0	0	0	0	0	0	0	0	.000	.000

Syl Simon 25 R 0-1, Chick Shorten (VR) 31, George Sisler (IJ) 30

NAME	T	AGE	W	L	PCT	SV	G	GS	CG	IP	H	BB	SO	ShO	ERA
TOTALS		28	74	78	.487	10	154	154	84	1373	1430	528	488	10	3.93
Urban Shocker	R	32	20	12	.625	5	43	35	25	277	292	49	109	3	3.41
Dave Danforth	L	33	16	14	.533	1	38	29	16	226	221	87	96	1	3.94
Elam Vangilder	R	27	16	17	.485	1	41	35	20	282	276	120	74	4	3.06
Rasty Wright	R	27	7	4	.636	0	20	8	4	83	107	34	26	0	6.40
Ray Kolp	R	28	5	12	.294	1	34	17	11	171	178	54	44	1	3.90
Dixie Davis	R	32	4	6	.400	0	19	17	5	109	106	63	36	1	3.64
Hub Pruett (BA)	L	22	4	7	.364	2	32	8	3	104	109	64	59	0	4.33
Bill Bayne	L	24	2	2	.500	0	19	2	0	46	49	31	15	0	4.50
Charlie Root	R	24	0	4	.000	0	27	2	0	60	68	18	27	0	5.70
George Grant	R	20	0	0	.000	0	4	0	0	9	15	3	2	0	5.00
1 Sloppy Thurston	R	24	0	0	.000	0	2	1	0	4	8	2	0	0	6.75
Jumbo Jim Elliott	L	22	0	0	.000	0	1	0	0	1	1	3	0	0	27.00

PHILADELPHIA 6th 69-83 .454 29 — CONNIE MACK

NAME	G by POS	B	AGE	G	AB	R	H	2B	3B	HR	RBI	BB	SO	SB	BA	SA
TOTALS			25	153	5196	661	1407	229	65	52	577	445	517	72	.273	.370
Joe Hauser	1B146	L	24	146	537	93	165	21	10	16	94	69	52	6	.307	.473
Jimmy Dykes	2B102, SS20, 3B2	R	26	124	416	50	105	28	1	4	43	35	40	6	.252	.353
Chick Galloway	SS134	R	26	134	504	64	140	18	9	2	62	37	30	12	.278	.361
Sammy Hale	3B107	R	26	115	434	68	125	22	8	3	51	17	31	8	.288	.396
Frank Welch	OF117	R	25	125	421	56	125	19	9	4	55	48	40	1	.297	.413
Wid Matthews	OF127	L	26	129	485	52	133	11	6	1	25	50	27	16	.274	.328
Bing Miller	OF119	R	28	123	458	68	137	25	4	12	64	27	34	9	.299	.450
Cy Perkins	C137	R	27	143	500	53	135	34	5	2	65	65	30	1	.270	.370
Beauty McGowan	OF79	L	21	95	287	41	73	9	1	1	19	36	25	4	.254	.303
Heinie Scheer	2B61	R	23	69	210	26	50	8	1	2	21	17	41	3	.238	.314
Fred Heimach	P40, 1B6	L	22	63	118	14	30	4	1	1	11	4	18	0	.254	.331
Harry Riconda	3B47, SS2	R	26	55	175	23	46	11	4	0	12	12	18	4	.263	.371
Frank Bruggy	C34, 1B5	R	32	54	105	4	22	3	0	1	6	4	9	1	.210	.267
Tilly Walker	OF26	R	35	52	109	12	30	5	2	2	16	14	11	1	.275	.413
Walt French	OF10	L	23	16	39	7	9	3	0	0	2	5	7	0	.231	.308
Chuck Rowland	C4	R	23	5	6	0	0	0	0	0	0	0	2	0	.000	.000
Doc Wood	SS3	R	23	3	3	0	1	0	0	0	0	0	0	0	.333	.333
John Jones	OF1	L	22	1	4	0	1	0	0	0	1	0	1	0	.250	.250

NAME	T	AGE	W	L	PCT	SV	G	GS	CG	IP	H	BB	SO	ShO	ERA
TOTALS		25	69	83	.454	12	153	153	65	1365	1465	550	400	6	4.08
Eddie Rommel	R	25	18	19	.486	5	56	31	19	298	306	108	76	3	3.27
Bob Hasty	R	27	13	15	.464	1	44	36	10	243	274	72	56	1	4.45
Rollie Naylor (LJ)	R	31	12	7	.632	0	26	20	9	143	149	59	27	2	3.46
Slim Harriss	R	26	10	16	.385	6	46	28	9	209	221	95	89	0	4.00
Fred Heimach	L	22	6	12	.333	0	40	19	10	208	238	69	63	0	4.33
2 Rube Walberg	L	23	4	8	.333	0	26	10	4	115	122	60	38	0	5.32
Roy Meeker	L	22	3	0	1.000	0	5	2	2	25	24	13	12	0	3.60
Denny Burns	R	25	2	1	.667	0	4	3	2	27	21	7	8	0	2.00
Curly Ogden	R	22	1	2	.333	0	18	2	0	46	63	32	14	0	5.67
Al Kellett	R	21	0	1	.000	0	5	0	0	10	11	8	1	0	6.30
Walt Kinney	L	29	0	1	.000	0	5	1	0	12	11	9	9	0	7.50
Hank Hulvey	R	25	0	1	.000	0	1	1	0	7	10	2	2	0	7.71
Harry O'Neill	R	26	0	0	.000	0	3	0	0	2	1	3	2	0	0.00
Chuck Wolfe	R	26	0	0	.000	0	3	0	0	10	6	8	1	0	3.60
Ren Kelly	R	23	0	0	.000	0	1	0	0	7	7	4	1	0	2.57
Doc Ozmer	R	22	0	0	.000	0	1	0	0	2	1	1	1	0	4.50

CHICAGO 7th 69-85 .448 30 — KID GLEASON

NAME	G by POS	B	AGE	G	AB	R	H	2B	3B	HR	RBI	BB	SO	SB	BA	SA
TOTALS			28	156	5246	692	1463	254	57	42	604	532	458	191	.279	.373
Earl Sheely	1B156	R	30	156	570	74	169	25	3	4	88	79	30	5	.296	.372
Eddie Collins	2B142	L	36	145	505	89	182	22	5	5	67	84	8	49	.360	.453
Hervey McClellan	SS139, 2B2	R	28	141	550	67	129	29	3	1	41	27	44	14	.235	.304
Willie Kamm	3B149	R	23	149	544	57	159	39	9	6	87	62	82	17	.292	.430
Harry Hooper	OF143	L	35	145	576	87	166	32	4	10	65	68	22	18	.288	.410
Johnny Mostil	OF143, 3B6, SS1	R	27	153	546	91	159	37	15	3	64	62	51	41	.291	.430
Bibb Falk	OF80	L	24	87	274	44	84	18	6	5	38	25	12	4	.307	.471
Ray Schalk	C121	R	30	123	382	42	87	12	2	1	44	39	28	6	.228	.277
Roy Elsh	OF57	R	27	81	209	28	52	7	2	0	24	16	23	15	.249	.301
Amos Strunk	OF4, 1B3	L	34	54	54	7	17	0	0	0	8	8	5	1	.315	.315
2 Sloppy Thurston	P44	R	24	45	79	10	25	5	1	0	4	2	6	0	.316	.405
Bill Barrett	OF40, 3B1	R	23	44	162	17	44	7	2	2	23	9	24	12	.272	.377
Roy Graham	C33	R	28	36	82	3	16	2	0	0	6	9	6	0	.195	.220
John Happenny	2B20, SS8	R	22	32	86	7	19	5	0	0	10	3	13	0	.221	.279
Buck Crouse	C22	L	26	23	70	6	18	2	1	1	7	3	4	0	.257	.357
Maurice Archdeacon	OF20	L	24	22	87	23	35	5	1	0	4	6	8	2	.402	.483
1 Ernie Johnson	SS12	L	35	12	53	5	10	2	0	0	1	3	5	2	.189	.226
Lou Rosenberg	2B2	R	20	3	4	0	1	0	0	0	0	0	1	0	.250	.250
Leo Taylor		R	22	2	0	0	0	0	0	0	0	0	0	0	.000	.000
Red Dorman	C1	R	25	1	2	0	1	0	0	0	0	0	0	0	.500	.500
Shine Cortazzo		R	18	1	1	0	0	0	0	0	0	0	0	0	.000	.000
Roxy Snipes		L	26	1	1	0	0	0	0	0	0	0	0	0	.000	.000

NAME	T	AGE	W	L	PCT	SV	G	GS	CG	IP	H	BB	SO	ShO	ERA
TOTALS		26	69	85	.448	11	156	156	74	1402	1512	534	467	5	4.03
Red Faber	R	34	14	11	.560	0	32	31	15	232	233	62	91	2	3.41
Charlie Robertson	R	27	13	18	.419	0	38	34	18	255	262	104	91	1	3.81
Mike Cvengros	L	21	12	13	.480	3	41	26	14	214	216	107	86	0	4.42
Dixie Leverett	R	29	10	13	.435	3	38	24	9	193	212	64	64	0	4.06
Ted Blankenship	R	22	9	14	.391	0	44	23	9	209	219	100	57	1	4.27
2 Sloppy Thurston	R	24	7	8	.467	4	44	12	8	192	223	36	55	0	3.05
Ted Lyons	R	22	2	1	.667	0	9	1	0	23	30	15	6	0	6.26
Homer Blankenship	R	20	1	1	.500	1	4	0	0	5	9	1	1	0	3.60
Claral Gillenwater	R	23	1	3	.250	0	5	3	1	21	28	6	2	1	5.57
Frank Mack	R	23	0	1	.000	0	11	0	0	23	23	11	6	0	4.30
Frank Woodward	R	29	0	1	.000	0	2	1	0	2	5	1	0	0	13.50
2 Leon Cadore	R	32	0	1	.000	0	1	1	0	2	6	2	3	0	27.00
Paul Castner	L	26	0	0	.000	0	6	0	0	10	14	5	0	0	6.30
Sarge Connally	R	24	0	0	.000	0	3	0	0	9	7	12	3	0	6.00
Lum Davenport	L	23	0	0	.000	0	2	0	0	4	7	4	1	0	6.75
Red Proctor	R	22	0	0	.000	0	2	0	0	4	11	2	0	0	13.50
Slim Embry	R	21	0	0	.000	0	1	0	0	3	7	2	1	0	9.00

Dickie Kerr (SL) 29
Doug McWenney (ST) 26

BOSTON 8th 61-91 .401 37 — FRANK CHANCE

NAME	G by POS	B	AGE	G	AB	R	H	2B	3B	HR	RBI	BB	SO	SB	BA	SA
TOTALS			29	154	5181	584	1354	253	54	34	525	391	480	80	.261	.351
George Burns	1B146	R	30	146	551	91	181	47	5	7	82	45	33	9	.328	.470
Chick Fewster	2B48, SS36	R	27	90	284	32	67	10	1	0	15	39	35	7	.236	.278
Johnny Mitchell	SS87, 2B5	B	28	92	347	40	78	15	4	0	19	34	18	7	.225	.291
Howard Shanks	3B83, 2B37, OF6, SS2	R	32	131	464	38	118	19	5	3	57	19	37	6	.254	.336
2 Ira Flagstead	OF102	R	29	109	382	55	119	23	4	8	53	37	26	8	.312	.455
Dick Reichle	OF93	L	26	122	361	40	93	17	3	1	39	22	34	3	.258	.330
Joe Harris	OF132, 1B9	R	32	142	483	82	162	28	11	13	76	52	27	7	.335	.520
Val Picinich	C81	R	26	87	268	33	74	21	1	2	31	46	32	3	.276	.384
Norm McMillan	3B67, 2B34, SS28	R	27	131	459	37	116	24	5	0	42	28	44	13	.253	.327
Shano Collins	OF89	R	37	97	342	41	79	10	5	0	18	11	29	7	.231	.289
Mike Menosky	OF49	L	28	84	188	22	43	8	4	0	25	22	19	3	.229	.314
Al DeVormer	C55, 1B2	R	31	74	209	20	54	7	3	0	18	6	21	3	.258	.321
Pinky Pittinger	2B42, SS10, 3B3	R	24	60	177	15	38	5	0	0	15	5	10	3	.215	.243
Roxy Walters	C36, 2B1	R	30	40	104	9	26	4	0	0	5	2	6	0	.250	.288
1 Nemo Leibold	OF10	L	31	12	18	1	2	0	0	0	0	1	2	0	.111	.111
John Donahue	OF9	B	29	10	36	5	10	4	0	0	1	4	5	0	.278	.389
Camp Skinner	OF2	L	26	7	13	1	3	2	0	0	1	0	0	0	.231	.385
Frank Fuller	2B6	B	30	6	21	3	5	0	0	0	0	1	1	1	.238	.238
Ike Boone	OF4	L	26	5	15	1	4	0	1	0	2	1	0	0	.267	.400

NAME	T	AGE	W	L	PCT	SV	G	GS	CG	IP	H	BB	SO	ShO	ERA
TOTALS		28	61	91	.401	11	154	154	78	1372	1534	520	412	3	4.20
Howard Ehmke	R	29	20	17	.541	3	43	39	28	317	318	119	121	2	3.78
Jack Quinn	R	39	13	17	.433	7	42	28	16	243	302	53	71	1	3.89
Alex Ferguson	R	26	9	13	.409	0	34	27	11	198	229	67	72	0	4.05
Bill Piercy	R	27	8	17	.320	0	30	24	11	187	193	73	51	0	3.42
George Murray	R	24	7	11	.389	0	39	18	5	178	190	87	40	0	4.90
Curt Fullerton	R	24	2	15	.118	1	36	16	7	142	167	71	37	0	5.13
Les Howe	R	27	1	0	1.000	0	12	2	0	30	23	7	7	0	2.40
Lefty O'Doul	L	26	1	1	.500	0	23	0	0	53	69	31	10	0	5.43
Dave Black	L	31	0	0	.000	0	2	0	0	1	2	0	0	0	0.00
Carl Stimson	R	28	0	0	.000	0	2	0	0	4	12	5	1	0	22.50
Clarence Blethen	R	29	0	0	.000	0	5	0	0	18	29	7	2	0	7.00

NEW YORK 1st 95-58 .621 — JOHN McGRAW

NAME	G by POS	B	AGE	G	AB	R	H	2B	3B	HR	RBI	BB	SO	SB	BA	SA
TOTALS			27	153	5452	**854**	**1610**	248	76	85	**790**	**487**	406	106	**.295**	**.415**
George Kelly	1B145	R	27	145	560	82	172	23	5	16	103	47	64	14	.307	.452
Frankie Frisch	2B135, 3B17	B	24	151	641	116	**223**	32	10	12	111	46	12	29	.348	.485
Dave Bancroft (IL)	SS96, 2B11	B	32	107	444	80	135	33	3	1	31	62	23	8	.304	.399
Heinie Groh	3B118	R	33	123	465	91	135	22	5	4	48	60	22	3	.290	.385
Ross Youngs	OF152	L	26	152	596	**121**	200	33	12	3	87	73	36	13	.336	.446
Jimmy O'Connell	OF64, 1B8	L	22	87	252	42	63	9	2	6	39	34	32	7	.250	.373
Irish Meusel	OF145	R	30	146	595	102	177	22	14	19	**125**	38	16	8	.297	.477
Frank Snyder	C112	R	30	120	402	37	103	13	6	5	63	24	29	5	.256	.356
Travis Jackson	SS60, 3B31, 2B1	R	19	96	327	45	90	12	7	4	37	22	40	3	.275	.391
Bill Cunningham	OF68, 2B4	R	27	79	203	22	55	7	1	5	27	10	9	5	.271	.389
Casey Stengel	OF57	L	32	75	218	39	74	11	5	5	43	20	18	6	.339	.505
2 Hank Gowdy	C43	R	33	53	122	13	40	6	3	1	18	21	9	2	.328	.451
Jack Bentley	P31	L	28	52	89	9	38	6	2	1	14	3	4	0	.427	.573
Freddie Maguire	2B16, 3B1	R	24	41	30	11	6	1	0	0	2	2	4	1	.200	.233
Jack Scott (LJ)	P40	L	31	40	79	12	25	4	0	1	10	3	5	1	.316	.405
Ralph Shinners	OF6	R	27	33	13	5	2	1	0	0	0	2	1	0	.154	.231
1 Earl Smith	C12	L	26	24	34	2	7	1	1	1	4	4	1	0	.206	.382
Alex Gaston	C21	R	30	22	39	3	8	2	0	1	5	0	6	0	.205	.333
Bill Terry	1B2	L	24	3	7	1	1	0	0	0	0	2	2	0	.143	.143
Hack Wilson	OF3	R	23	3	10	0	2	0	0	0	0	0	1	0	.200	.200
Moe Solomon	OF2	L	22	2	8	0	3	1	0	0	1	0	1	0	.375	.500

NAME	T	AGE	W	L	PCT	SV	G	GS	CG	IP	H	BB	SO	ShO	ERA
		27	**95**	58	**.621**	**18**	153	153	62	1377	1440	424	453	10	3.90
Rosy Ryan	R	25	16	5	.762	4	**45**	15	7	173	169	46	58	0	3.49
Jack Scott (LJ)	R	31	16	7	.696	1	40	25	9	220	223	65	79	3	3.89
Hugh McQuillan	R	25	15	14	.517	0	38	32	15	230	224	66	75	5	3.40
Jack Bentley	L	28	13	8	.619	3	31	26	12	183	198	67	80	1	4.48
Art Nehf	L	30	13	10	.565	2	34	27	7	196	219	49	50	1	4.50
2 Mule Watson	R	26	8	5	.615	0	17	15	8	108	117	21	26	0	3.42
Claude Jonnard	R	26	4	3	.571	**5**	**45**	1	1	96	105	35	45	0	3.28
1 Jesse Barnes	R	30	3	1	.750	1	12	4	1	36	48	13	12	0	6.25
Clint Blume	R	24	2	0	1.000	0	12	1	0	24	22	20	2	0	3.75
Fred Johnson	R	29	2	0	1.000	0	3	2	1	17	11	7	5	0	4.24
Virgil Barnes	R	26	2	3	.400	1	22	2	0	53	59	19	6	0	3.91
Dinty Gearin	L	25	1	1	.500	0	6	2	1	24	23	10	9	0	3.38
Walter Huntzinger	R	24	0	1	.000	0	2	1	0	8	9	1	2	0	7.88
Red Lucas	R	21	0	0	.000	1	3	0	0	5	9	4	3	0	0.00
1 Rube Walberg	L	23	0	0	.000	0	2	0	0	5	4	1	1	0	1.80

CINCINNATI 2nd 91-63 .591 4.5 — PAT MORAN

NAME	G by POS	B	AGE	G	AB	R	H	2B	3B	HR	RBI	BB	SO	SB	BA	SA
TOTALS			30	154	5278	708	1506	237	95	45	645	439	367	96	.285	.392
Jake Daubert	1B121	L	39	125	500	63	146	27	10	2	54	40	20	11	.292	.398
Sammy Bohne	2B96, 3B35, SS9, 1B1	R	26	139	539	77	136	18	10	3	47	48	37	16	.252	.340
Ike Caveney	SS138	R	28	138	488	58	135	21	9	4	63	26	41	5	.277	.381
Babe Pinelli (JJ)	3B116	R	27	117	423	44	117	14	5	0	51	27	29	10	.277	.333
George Burns	OF154	R	33	154	614	99	168	27	13	3	45	**101**	46	12	.274	.375
Edd Roush	OF137	L	30	138	527	88	185	**41**	18	6	88	46	16	10	.351	.531
Pat Duncan	OF146	R	29	147	566	92	185	26	8	7	83	30	27	15	.327	.438
Bubbles Hargrave	C109	R	30	118	378	54	126	23	9	10	78	44	22	4	.333	.521
Lew Fonseca	2B45, 1B14	R	24	65	237	33	66	11	4	3	28	9	16	4	.278	.397
George Harper	OF29	L	31	61	125	14	32	4	2	3	16	11	9	0	.256	.392
Ivy Wingo	C57	L	32	61	171	10	45	9	2	1	24	9	11	1	.263	.357
Rube Bressler	1B22, OF6	R	28	54	119	25	33	3	1	0	18	20	4	3	.277	.319
Rube Benton	P33	L	36	33	80	5	23	3	0	0	4	1	12	0	.288	.325
Wally Kimmick	2B17, 3B4, SS1	R	26	29	80	11	18	2	1	0	6	5	15	3	.225	.275
Boob Fowler	SS10	L	22	11	33	9	11	0	1	1	6	1	3	1	.333	.485
Eddie Pick	OF4	B	24	9	8	2	3	0	0	0	2	3	3	0	.375	.375
2 Les Mann		R	29	8	1	1	0	0	0	0	0	0	0	0	.000	.000
Gus Sanberg	C5	R	27	7	17	1	3	1	0	0	1	1	1	0	.176	.235
Ed Hock		L	24	2	0	0	0	0	0	0	0	0	0	0	.000	.000

Greasy Neale (VR) 31

NAME	T	AGE	W	L	PCT	SV	G	GS	CG	IP	H	BB	SO	ShO	ERA
		29	91	63	.591	9	154	154	88	1391	1465	359	450	11	**3.21**
Dolf Luque	R	32	**27**	8	**.771**	2	41	37	28	322	279	88	151	**6**	**1.93**
Eppa Rixey	L	32	20	15	.571	1	42	37	23	309	334	65	97	3	2.80
Pete Donahue	R	22	21	15	.583	3	42	36	19	274	304	68	84	2	3.38
Rube Benton	L	36	14	10	.583	1	33	26	15	219	243	57	59	0	3.66
Bill Harris	R	23	3	2	.600	0	22	3	1	70	79	18	18	0	5.14
Cactus Keck	R	24	3	6	.333	2	35	6	1	87	84	32	16	0	3.72
1 Johnny Couch	R	32	2	7	.222	0	19	8	1	69	98	15	14	0	6.00
Herb McQuaid	R	24	1	0	1.000	0	12	1	0	34	31	10	9	0	2.38
George Abrams	R	25	0	0	.000	0	3	0	0	5	10	3	1	0	9.00
Haddie Gill	L	24	0	0	.000	0	1	0	0	1	1	1	1	0	0.00
Karl Schnell	R	23	0	0	.000	0	1	0	0	1	2	2	0	0	36.00

PITTSBURGH 3rd 87-67 .565 8.5 — BILL McKECHNIE

NAME	G by POS	B	AGE	G	AB	R	H	2B	3B	HR	RBI	BB	SO	SB	BA	SA
TOTALS			29	154	5405	786	1592	224	**111**	49	701	407	362	154	.295	.404
Charlie Grimm	1B152	L	24	152	563	78	194	29	13	7	99	41	43	6	.345	.480
Johnny Rawlings	2B119	R	30	119	461	53	131	18	4	1	45	25	29	9	.284	.347
Rabbit Maranville	SS141	R	31	141	581	78	161	19	9	1	41	42	34	14	.277	.346
Pie Traynor	3B153	R	23	153	616	108	208	19	**19**	12	101	34	19	28	.338	.489
Clyde Barnhart	OF92	R	27	114	327	60	106	25	13	9	72	47	21	5	.324	.563
Max Carey	OF153	B	33	153	610	120	188	32	**19**	6	63	73	28	**51**	.308	.452
Carson Bigbee	OF122	L	28	123	499	79	149	18	7	0	54	43	15	10	.299	.363
Walter Schmidt	C96	R	36	97	335	39	83	72	2	0	37	22	12	10	.248	.281
Reb Russell	OF76	L	34	94	291	49	84	18	7	9	58	20	21	3	.289	.491
Johnny Gooch	C66	B	25	66	202	16	56	10	2	1	20	17	13	2	.277	.361
Walter Mueller	OF26	R	28	40	111	11	34	4	4	0	20	4	6	2	.306	.414
1 Cotton Tierney	2B29	R	29	29	120	22	35	5	2	2	23	2	10	2	.292	.417
Spencer Adams	2B11, SS6	L	25	25	56	11	14	0	1	0	4	6	6	2	.250	.286
Jim Mattox	C8	L	26	22	32	4	6	1	1	0	1	0	5	0	.188	.281
Jewel Ens	1B4, 3B3, SS1	R	33	12	29	3	8	1	1	0	5	0	3	2	.276	.376
Kiki Cuyler	OF11	R	23	11	40	4	10	1	1	0	2	5	3	2	.250	.325
Frank Luce	OF5	L	26	9	12	2	6	0	0	0	3	2	2	2	.500	.500
Eddie Moore	SS6	R	24	6	26	6	7	1	0	0	1	2	3	1	.269	.308
Eppie Barnes	1B1	L	22	2	2	0	1	0	0	0	0	0	1	0	.500	.500

NAME	T	AGE	W	L	PCT	SV	G	GS	CG	IP	H	BB	SO	ShO	ERA
		30	87	67	.565	9	154	154	92	1376	1313	402	414	5	3.87
Johnny Morrison	R	27	25	13	.658	2	42	37	27	302	287	110	114	2	3.49
Wilbur Cooper	L	31	17	**19**	.472	0	39	**38**	26	295	331	71	77	1	3.57
2 Lee Meadows	R	28	16	10	.615	0	31	25	17	227	250	44	66	1	3.01
Babe Adams	R	41	13	7	.650	1	26	22	11	159	196	25	38	0	4.42
Earl Hamilton	L	31	7	9	.438	1	28	15	5	141	148	42	42	0	3.77
Jim Bagby	R	33	3	2	.600	3	21	6	2	69	95	25	16	0	5.22
Ray Steineder	R	27	2	0	1.000	0	15	2	1	55	58	18	23	0	4.75
1 Whitey Glazner	R	30	2	1	.667	1	7	4	1	30	29	11	8	1	3.30
Earl Kunz	R	23	1	2	.333	1	21	2	1	46	48	24	12	0	5.48
George Boehler	R	31	1	3	.250	0	10	3	1	28	33	26	12	0	6.11
Arnie Stone	L	30	0	1	.000	0	9	0	0	12	19	4	2	0	8.25
Hal Carlson	R	29	0	0	.000	0	4	0	0	13	19	2	4	0	4.85

CHICAGO 4th 83-71 .539 12.5 — BILL KILLEFER

NAME	G by POS	B	AGE	G	AB	R	H	2B	3B	HR	RBI	BB	SO	SB	BA	SA
TOTALS			26	154	5259	756	1516	243	52	90	675	455	485	**181**	.288	.406
Ray Grimes (XJ)	1B62	R	29	64	216	32	71	7	2	2	36	24	17	5	.329	.407
George Grantham	2B150	L	23	152	570	81	160	36	8	8	70	71	**92**	43	.281	.414
Sparky Adams	SS79, OF1	R	28	95	311	40	90	12	0	4	35	26	10	20	.289	.367
Barney Friberg	3B146	R	23	146	547	91	174	27	11	12	88	45	49	13	.318	.473
Cliff Heathcote	OF112	L	25	117	393	48	98	14	3	1	27	25	22	32	.249	.308
Jigger Statz	OF154	R	25	154	**655**	110	209	33	8	10	70	56	42	29	.319	.440
Hack Miller	OF129	R	29	135	485	74	146	24	2	20	88	27	39	6	.301	.482
Bob O'Farrell	C124	R	26	131	452	73	144	25	4	12	84	67	38	10	.319	.471
Gabby Hartnett	C39, 1B31	R	22	85	231	28	62	12	2	8	39	25	22	4	.268	.442
Charlie Hollocher (IL)	SS65	L	27	66	260	46	89	14	2	1	28	26	5	9	.342	.423
John Kelleher	1B22, SS14, 3B11, 2B6	R	29	66	193	27	59	10	0	6	21	14	9	2	.306	.451
Marty Callaghan	OF38	L	23	61	129	18	29	1	3	0	14	8	18	2	.225	.279
Allen Elliott	1B52	L	25	53	168	21	42	8	2	2	29	2	12	3	.250	.357
Otto Vogel	OF24, 3B1	R	23	41	81	10	17	0	1	1	6	7	11	2	.210	.272
Denver Grigsby	OF22	L	22	24	72	8	21	5	2	0	5	7	5	1	.292	.417
Butch Weis	OF6	L	20	22	26	2	6	1	0	0	2	5	8	0	.231	.269
Kettle Wirts	C3	R	25	5	5	2	1	0	0	0	1	2	0	0	.200	.200

Bob Barrett 24 R 1-3, Pete Turgeon 26 R 1-6, Tony Murray 19 R 1-4

NAME	T	AGE	W	L	PCT	SV	G	GS	CG	IP	H	BB	SO	ShO	ERA
		26	83	71	.539	11	154	154	80	1367	1419	435	408	8	3.82
Pete Alexander	R	36	22	12	.647	2	39	36	26	305	308	30	72	3	3.19
Vic Aldridge	R	29	16	9	.640	0	30	30	15	217	209	67	64	2	3.48
Tony Kaufmann	R	22	14	10	.583	3	33	24	18	206	209	67	72	2	3.10
Vic Keen	R	24	12	8	.600	1	35	17	10	177	169	57	46	0	3.00
Tiny Osborne	R	30	8	15	.348	1	37	25	8	180	174	89	69	1	4.55
Virgil Cheeves	R	22	3	4	.429	0	19	8	0	71	89	37	13	0	6.21
Nick Dumovich	L	21	3	5	.375	1	28	8	1	94	118	45	23	0	4.60
Fred Fussell	L	27	3	5	.375	3	28	2	1	76	90	31	38	0	5.57
Phil Collins	R	21	1	0	1.000	0	1	1	0	5	8	1	2	0	3.60
Rip Wheeler	R	25	1	2	.333	0	3	3	1	24	28	5	5	0	4.88
George Stueland	R	24	0	1	.000	0	6	0	0	8	11	5	2	0	5.63
Guy Bush	R	21	0	0	.000	0	1	0	0	1	1	0	2	0	0.00
Ed Stauffer	R	25	0	0	.000	0	1	0	0	2	5	1	0	0	13.50

ST. LOUIS 5th 79-74 .516 16 — BRANCH RICKEY

NAME	G by POS	B	AGE	G	AB	R	H	2B	3B	HR	RBI	BB	SO	SB	BA	SA
TOTALS			27	154	**5526**	746	1582	**274**	76	63	676	438	446	89	.286	.398
Jim Bottomley	1B130	L	23	134	523	79	194	34	14	8	94	45	44	4	.371	.535
Rogers Hornsby (IL)	2B96, 1B10	R	27	107	424	89	163	32	10	17	83	55	29	3	**.384**	**.627**
H. Freigau	SS87, 2B16, 1B9, 3B1, OF1	R	20	113	358	30	94	18	1	1	35	25	36	5	.263	.327
Milt Stock	3B150, 2B1	R	29	151	603	63	174	33	3	2	96	40	21	9	.289	.363
Max Flack	OF121	L	33	128	505	82	147	16	9	3	28	41	16	7	.291	.376
Hy Myers	OF87	R	34	96	330	29	99	18	2	2	48	12	19	5	.300	.385
Jack Smith	OF109	L	28	124	407	98	126	16	6	5	41	27	20	32	.310	.415
1 Eddie Ainsmith	C80	R	31	82	263	22	56	11	6	3	34	22	19	4	.213	.335
Ray Blades	OF83, 3B4	R	26	98	317	48	78	21	5	5	44	37	46	4	.246	.391
Specs Toporcer	2B52, SS33, 1B1, 3B1	L	24	97	303	45	77	11	3	3	35	41	14	4	.254	.340
Heinie Mueller	OF74	L	23	78	265	39	91	16	9	5	41	18	16	4	.343	.528
Harry McCurdy	C58	L	23	67	185	17	49	11	2	0	15	11	11	3	.265	.346
Vern Clemons	C41	R	31	57	130	6	37	9	1	0	13	10	11	0	.285	.369
Doc Lavan	SS40, 3B4, 1B3, 2B1	R	32	50	111	10	22	6	0	1	12	9	7	0	.198	.279
Bill Sherdel	P39	L	26	45	83	13	28	2	0	1	9	7	8	0	.337	.398
1 Les Mann	OF26	R	29	38	89	20	33	5	2	5	11	9	5	0	.371	.640
Eddie Dyer	OF8, P4	L	22	35	45	17	12	3	0	2	5	3	5	1	.267	.467
Les Bell	SS15	R	21	15	51	5	19	2	1	0	9	9	7	1	.373	.451
Jake Flowers	SS7, 2B2, 3B2	R	21	13	32	0	3	1	0	0	2	2	7	1	.094	.125
Charlie Niebergall	C7	R	24	9	28	2	3	1	0	0	1	2	3	0	.107	.143
Taylor Douthit	OF7	R	22	9	27	3	5	0	2	0	0	0	4	1	.185	.333
Jimmy Hudgens	1B3, 2B1	L	20	6	12	2	3	1	0	0	0	3	3	0	.250	.333
Tige Stone	OF4, P1	R	21	5	1	0	1	0	0	0	0	0	0	0	1.000	1.000

George Kopshaw 27 R 1-5, Joe Schultz 29 R 2-7, Speed Walker 25 R 2-7, Burt Shotton 38 L 0-0, Austin McHenry (DD) 27

NAME	T	AGE	W	L	PCT	SV	G	GS	CG	IP	H	BB	SO	ShO	ERA
		30	79	74	.516	7	154	154	77	1398	1539	456	398	9	3.87
Jesse Haines	R	29	20	13	.606	0	37	36	23	266	283	75	73	1	3.11
Bill Sherdel	L	26	15	13	.536	2	39	26	14	225	270	59	78	0	4.32
Fred Toney	R	35	11	12	.478	0	29	28	16	197	211	61	48	1	3.84
Johnny Stuart	R	22	9	5	.643	3	37	10	7	150	139	70	55	1	4.26
Jeff Pfeffer	R	35	8	9	.471	0	26	18	7	152	171	40	32	1	4.03
Bill Doak	R	32	8	13	.381	0	30	26	7	185	199	69	53	3	3.26
Clyde Barfoot	R	31	3	3	.500	1	33	2	1	101	112	27	23	1	3.74
Lou North	R	32	3	4	.429	1	34	3	0	72	90	31	24	0	5.13
Eddie Dyer	L	22	2	1	.667	0	4	3	2	22	30	5	7	1	4.09
Epp Sell	R	26	0	1	.000	0	5	1	0	15	16	8	2	0	6.00
Tige Stone	R	21	0	0	.000	0	1	0	0	3	5	3	1	0	12.00
Fred Wiginton	R	25	0	0	.000	0	4	0	0	8	11	5	2	0	3.38
Bill Pertica	R	26	0	0	.000	0	1	1	0	2	2	3	0	0	4.50

BROOKLYN 6th 76-78 .494 19.5 — **WILBERT ROBINSON**

NAME	G by POS	B	AGE	G	AB	R	H	2B	3B	HR	RBI	BB	SO	SB	BA	SA
TOTALS			29	155	5476	753	1559	214	81	62	674	425	382	71	.285	.387
Jack Fournier	1B133	L	30	133	515	91	181	30	13	22	102	43	28	11	.351	.588
Jimmy Johnston	2B84, SS52, 3B14	R	33	151	625	111	203	29	11	4	60	53	15	16	.325	.426
Moe Berg	SS47, 2B1	R	21	49	129	9	24	3	2	0	6	2	5	1	.186	.240
Andy High	3B80, SS45, 2B5	L	25	123	426	51	115	23	9	3	37	47	13	4	.270	.387
Tommy Griffith	OF127	L	33	131	481	70	141	21	9	8	66	50	19	8	.293	.424
Bernie Neis	OF111	B	27	126	445	78	122	17	4	5	37	36	38	8	.274	.364
Gene Bailey	OF100, 1B5	R	29	127	411	71	109	11	7	1	42	43	34	9	.265	.333
Zack Taylor	C84	R	24	96	337	29	97	11	6	0	46	9	13	2	.288	.356
Zack Wheat (IL)	OF87	L	37	98	349	63	131	13	5	8	65	23	12	3	.375	.510
Ivy Olson	2B72, 3B4, SS2, 1B2	R	37	82	292	33	76	11	1	1	35	14	10	5	.260	.315
Bert Griffith	OF62	R	27	79	248	23	73	8	4	2	37	13	16	1	.294	.383
Hank DeBerry	C60	R	28	78	235	21	67	11	6	1	48	20	12	2	.285	.396
Bill McCarren	3B66, OF1	R	27	69	216	28	53	10	1	3	27	22	39	0	.245	.343
Ray French	SS30	R	28	43	73	14	16	2	1	0	7	4	7	0	.219	.274
Charlie Hargreaves	C15	R	26	20	57	5	16	0	0	0	4	1	2	0	.281	.281
1 Dutch Schliebner	1B19	R	32	19	76	11	19	4	0	0	4	5	7	1	.250	.303
Turner Barber	OF12	L	29	13	46	3	10	2	0	0	8	2	2	0	.217	.261
Billy Mullen	3B4	R	28	4	11	1	3	0	0	0	0	0	0	0	.273	.273

Stuffy Stewart 29 R 4-11, 2 Eddie Ainsmith 31 R 2-10, Bernie Hungling 27 R 0-4

NAME	T	AGE	W	L	PCT	SV	G	GS	CG	IP	H	BB	SO	ShO	ERA
		28	76	78	.494	5	155	155	94	1410	1522	477	549	8	3.73
Burleigh Grimes	R	29	21	18	.538	0	39	38	33	327	356	100	119	2	3.58
Dazzy Vance	R	32	18	15	.545	0	37	35	21	280	263	100	197	3	3.50
Dutch Ruether	L	29	15	14	.517	0	34	34	20	275	308	86	87	0	4.22
Leo Dickerman	R	26	8	12	.400	0	34	20	7	166	185	71	57	1	3.58
1 Leon Cadore	R	32	4	1	.800	0	8	4	3	36	39	13	5	0	3.25
Dutch Henry	L	21	4	6	.400	0	17	9	5	94	105	28	28	2	3.93
Art Decatur	R	29	3	3	.500	3	36	5	2	105	115	34	27	0	2.66
George Smith	R	31	3	6	.333	1	25	7	3	91	99	28	15	0	3.66
Harry Harper	L	28	0	1	.000	0	1	1	0	4	8	3	4	0	13.50
Al Mamaux	R	29	0	2	.000	0	5	1	0	13	20	6	5	0	8.31
Paul Schreiber	R	20	0	0	.000	1	9	0	0	15	16	8	4	0	4.20
Harry Shriver	R	26	0	0	.000	0	1	1	0	4	8	0	1	0	6.75

BOSTON 7th 54-100 .351 41.5 — **FRED MITCHELL**

NAME	G by POS	B	AGE	G	AB	R	H	2B	3B	HR	RBI	BB	SO	SB	BA	SA
TOTALS			29	155	5329	636	1455	213	58	32	569	429	404	57	.273	.353
Stuffy McInnis	1B154	R	32	154	607	70	191	23	9	2	95	26	12	7	.315	.392
Hod Ford	2B95, SS19	R	25	111	380	27	103	16	7	2	50	31	30	1	.271	.366
Bob Smith	SS101, 2B8	R	25	115	375	30	94	16	3	0	40	17	35	4	.251	.309
Tony Boeckel	3B147, SS1	R	30	148	568	72	169	32	4	7	79	51	31	11	.298	.405
Billy Southworth	OF151, 2B2	L	30	153	611	95	195	29	16	6	78	61	23	14	.319	.448
Ray Powell	OF84	L	34	97	338	57	102	20	4	4	38	45	36	1	.302	.420
Gus Felix	OF123, 2B5, 3B4	R	28	139	506	64	138	17	2	6	44	51	65	8	.273	.350
Mickey O'Neil	C95	R	25	96	306	29	65	7	4	0	20	17	14	3	.212	.261
Al Nixon	OF80	R	37	88	321	53	88	12	4	0	19	24	14	2	.274	.336
2 Earl Smith	C54	L	26	72	191	22	55	15	1	3	19	22	10	0	.288	.424
Art Conlon	2B36, SS6, 3B4	R	25	59	147	23	32	3	0	0	17	11	11	0	.218	.238
Bill Bagwell	OF22	L	27	56	93	8	27	4	2	2	10	6	12	0	.290	.441
Johnny Cooney	P23, OF11, 1B1	R	22	42	66	7	25	1	0	0	3	4	2	0	.379	.394
Frank Gibson	C20	B	32	41	50	13	15	1	0	0	5	7	7	0	.300	.320
Larry Kopf	SS37, 2B4	B	32	39	138	15	38	3	1	0	10	13	6	0	.275	.312
Al Hermann	2B15, 3B5, 1B4	R	22	31	93	2	22	4	0	0	11	0	7	3	.237	.280
1 Hank Gowdy	C15	R	33	23	48	5	6	1	1	0	5	15	5	1	.125	.188
Walton Cruise	OF9	L	33	21	38	4	8	2	0	0	0	3	2	1	.211	.263
Bob Emmerich	OF8	R	25	13	24	3	2	0	0	0	0	2	3	1	.083	.083
Snake Henry		L	27	11	9	1	1	0	0	0	2	1	1	0	.111	.111

Ernie Padgett 24 R 2-11, Dee Cousineau 24 R 2-2

NAME	T	AGE	W	L	PCT	SV	G	GS	CG	IP	H	BB	SO	ShO	ERA
		28	54	100	.351	7	155	155	54	1392	1662	394	351	13	4.22
Joe Genewich	R	26	13	14	.481	1	43	24	12	227	272	46	54	1	3.73
Rube Marquard	L	33	11	14	.440	0	38	29	11	239	265	65	78	3	3.73
2 Jesse Barnes	R	30	10	14	.417	2	31	23	12	195	204	43	41	5	2.77
Larry Benton	R	25	5	9	.357	0	35	9	1	128	141	57	42	0	4.99
Joe Oeschger	R	32	5	15	.250	2	44	19	6	166	227	54	33	1	5.69
Johnny Cooney	L	22	3	5	.375	0	23	8	5	98	92	22	23	2	3.31
Tim McNamara	R	24	3	13	.188	0	32	16	3	139	185	29	32	0	4.92
Joe Batchelder	L	24	1	0	1.000	0	4	1	1	9	12	1	2	0	7.00
1 Mule Watson	R	26	1	2	.333	1	11	4	1	31	42	20	10	0	5.23
Dick Rudolph	R	35	1	2	.333	0	4	4	1	19	27	10	3	1	3.80
Dana Fillingim	R	29	1	9	.100	0	35	12	1	100	141	36	27	0	5.22
Frank Miller	R	37	0	3	.000	1	8	6	0	39	54	11	6	0	4.62

PHILADELPHIA 8th 50-104 .325 45.5 — **ART FLETCHER**

NAME	G by POS	B	AGE	G	AB	R	H	2B	3B	HR	RBI	BB	SO	SB	BA	SA
TOTALS			28	155	5491	748	1528	259	39	112	677	414	556	70	.278	.401
Walter Holke	1B146, P1	B	30	147	562	64	175	31	4	7	70	16	37	7	.311	.418
2 Cotton Tierney	2B114, OF5, 3B2	R	29	121	480	68	152	31	1	11	65	24	42	3	.317	.454
Heinie Sand	SS120, 3B11	R	25	132	470	85	107	16	5	4	32	82	56	7	.228	.309
Russ Wrightstone	3B72, SS21, 2B9	L	30	119	392	59	107	21	7	7	57	21	19	5	.273	.416
Curt Walker	OF137, 1B1	L	26	140	527	66	148	26	5	5	66	45	31	12	.281	.378
Cy Williams	OF135	L	35	136	535	98	157	22	3	41	114	59	57	11	.293	.576
Johnny Mokan	OF105, 3B1	R	27	113	400	76	125	23	3	10	48	53	31	6	.313	.460
Butch Henline	C96, OF1	R	28	111	330	45	107	14	3	7	46	37	33	7	.324	.448
Cliff Lee	OF83, 1B16	R	26	107	355	54	114	20	4	11	47	20	39	3	.321	.493
Jimmie Wilson	C69, OF2	R	22	85	252	27	66	9	0	1	25	4	17	4	.262	.310
Frank Parkinson	2B37, SS15, 3B11	R	28	67	219	21	53	12	0	3	28	13	31	0	.242	.338
Clarence Mitchell	P29	L	32	53	78	10	21	3	2	1	9	4	11	0	.269	.397
Freddy Leach	OF26	L	25	52	104	5	27	4	0	1	16	3	14	1	.260	.327
Goldie Rapp	3B45	B	31	47	179	27	47	5	0	1	10	14	14	1	.263	.307
Carl Lord	3B14	R	23	17	47	3	11	2	0	0	2	2	3	0	.234	.277
Mickey O'Brien	C9	R	28	15	21	3	7	2	0	0	0	2	1	0	.333	.429
Andy Woehr	3B13	R	27	13	41	3	14	2	0	0	3	1	1	0	.341	.390
Lenny Metz	2B6, SS6	R	23	12	37	4	8	0	0	0	3	4	3	0	.216	.216
Tod Dennehy	OF9	L	24	9	24	4	7	2	0	0	2	1	3	0	.292	.375

Dixie Parker 28 L 1-5, Joe Bennett 22 R 0-0

NAME	T	AGE	W	L	PCT	SV	G	GS	CG	IP	H	BB	SO	ShO	ERA
		28	50	104	.325	8	155	155	68	1385	1801	549	384	3	5.30
Jimmy Ring	R	28	18	16	.529	0	39	36	23	313	336	115	112	0	3.77
Clarence Mitchell	L	32	9	10	.474	0	29	19	8	139	170	46	41	1	4.73
2 Whitey Glazner	R	30	7	14	.333	1	28	23	12	161	195	63	51	2	4.70
Lefty Weinert	L	21	4	17	.190	1	38	20	8	156	207	81	46	0	5.42
Petie Behan	R	35	3	12	.200	2	31	17	5	131	182	57	27	0	5.50
Huck Betts	R	26	2	4	.333	1	19	4	3	84	100	14	18	0	3.11
2 Johnny Couch	R	32	2	4	.333	0	11	7	2	65	91	21	18	0	5.26
Ralph Head	R	29	2	9	.182	0	35	13	5	132	185	57	24	0	6.68
1 Lee Meadows	R	28	1	3	.250	1	8	5	0	20	40	15	10	0	13.05
Bill Hubbell	R	26	1	6	.143	0	22	5	1	55	102	17	8	0	8.35
Jesse Winters	R	29	1	6	.143	1	21	6	1	78	116	39	23	0	7.38
Jim Bishop	R	25	0	3	.000	1	15	0	0	33	48	11	5	0	6.27
Broadway Jones	R	24	0	0	.000	0	3	0	0	8	5	7	1	0	9.00
Jim Grant	L	28	0	0	.000	0	2	0	0	4	10	4	0	0	13.50
Art Gardiner	R	23	0	0	.000	0	1	0	0	0	1	1	0	0	0.00
Walter Holke	B	30	0	0	.000	0	1	0	0	.1	1	0	0	0	0.00
Red Miller	R	26	0	0	.000	0	1	0	0	2	6	1	0	0	27.00
Pat Ragan	R	34	0	0	.000	0	1	0	0	3	6	0	0	0	6.00

WORLD SERIES – NEW YORK (AL) 4 NEW YORK (NL) 2

LINE SCORES

TEAM	1	2	3	4	5	6	7	8	9	10	11	12	R	H	E
Game 1 October 10 at Yankee Stadium															
NY (NL)	0	0	4	0	0	0	0	0	1				5	8	0
NY (AL)	1	2	0	0	0	0	1	0	0				4	12	1
Watson, **Ryan** (3) / Hoyt, **Bush** (3)															
Game 2 October 11 at Polo Grounds															
NY (AL)	0	1	0	2	1	0	0	0	0				4	10	0
NY (NL)	0	1	0	0	0	1	0	0	0				2	9	2
Pennock / **McQuillan**, Bentley (4)															
Game 3 October 12 at Yankee Stadium															
NY (NL)	0	0	0	0	0	0	1	0	0				1	4	1
NY (AL)	0	0	0	0	0	0	0	0	0				0	6	1
Nehf / **Jones**, Bush (9)															
Game 4 October 13 at Polo Grounds															
NY (AL)	0	6	1	1	0	0	0	0	0				8	13	1
NY (NL)	0	0	0	0	0	0	0	3	1				4	13	1
Shawkey, Pennock (8) / **J. Scott**, Ryan (2), McQuillan (2), Jonnard (8), Barnes (9)															
Game 5 October 14 at Yankee Stadium															
NY (NL)	0	1	0	0	0	0	0	0	0				1	3	2
NY (AL)	3	4	0	1	0	0	0	0	X				8	14	0
Bentley, J. Scott (2), Barnes (4), Jonnard (8) / **Bush**															
Game 6 October 15 at Polo Grounds															
NY (AL)	1	0	0	0	0	0	0	5	0				6	5	0
NY (NL)	1	0	0	1	1	1	0	0	0				4	10	1
Pennock, Jones (8) / **Nehf**, Ryan (8)															

COMPOSITE BATTING

NAME	POS	G	AB	R	H	2B	3B	HR	RBI	BA
New York (AL) Totals		6	205	30	60	8	4	5	29	.293
B. Meusel	OF	6	26	1	7	1	2	0	8	.269
Dugan	3B	6	25	5	7	2	1	1	5	.280
Witt	OF	6	25	1	6	2	0	0	4	.240
Ward	2B	6	24	4	10	0	0	1	2	.417
Scott	SS	6	22	2	7	0	0	0	3	.318
Schang	C	6	22	3	7	1	0	0	0	.318
Pipp	1B	6	20	2	5	0	0	0	2	.250
Ruth	OF-1B	6	19	8	7	1	1	3	3	.368
Bush	P	4	7	2	3	1	0	0	1	.429
Pennock	P	3	6	0	0	0	0	0	0	.000
Shawkey	P	1	3	0	1	0	0	0	1	.333
Jones	P	2	2	0	0	0	0	0	0	.000
Haines	OF	2	1	1	0	0	0	0	0	.000
Hendrick	PH	1	1	0	0	0	0	0	0	.000
Hofmann	PH	2	1	0	0	0	0	0	0	.000
Hoyt	P	1	1	0	0	0	0	0	0	.000
Johnson	SS	2	0	1	0	0	0	0	0	.000
New York (NL) Totals		6	201	17	47	2	3	5	17	.234
Frisch	2B	6	25	2	10	0	1	0	1	.400
I. Meusel	OF	6	25	3	7	1	1	1	2	.280
Bancroft	SS	6	24	1	2	0	0	0	1	.083
Youngs	OF	6	23	2	8	0	0	1	3	.348
Groh	3B	6	22	3	4	0	1	0	2	.182
Kelly	1B	6	22	1	4	0	0	0	1	.182
Snyder	C	5	17	1	2	0	0	1	2	.118
Stengel	OF	6	12	3	5	0	0	2	4	.417
Cunningham	OF	4	7	0	1	0	0	0	1	.143
Nehf	P	2	6	0	1	0	0	0	0	.167
Bentley	P	5	5	0	3	1	0	0	0	.600
Gowdy	C	3	4	0	0	0	0	0	0	.000
McQuillan	P	2	3	0	0	0	0	0	0	.000
Ryan	P	3	2	0	0	0	0	0	0	.000
Barnes	P	2	1	0	0	0	0	0	0	.000
Jackson	PH	1	1	0	0	0	0	0	0	.000
O'Connell	PH	2	1	0	0	0	0	0	0	.000
J. Scott	P	2	1	0	0	0	0	0	0	.000
Gearin	PR	1	0	0	0	0	0	0	0	.000
Jonnard	P	2	0	0	0	0	0	0	0	.000
Maquire	PR	2	0	1	0	0	0	0	0	.000
Watson	P	1	0	0	0	0	0	0	0	.000

COMPOSITE PITCHING

NAME	G	IP	H	BB	SO	W	L	SV	ERA
New York (AL) Totals	6	54	47	12	18	4	2	2	2.83
Pennock	3	17.1	19	1	8	2	0	1	3.63
Bush	3	16.2	7	4	5	1	1	0	1.08
Jones	2	10	5	2	3	0	1	1	0.90
Shawkey	1	7.2	12	4	2	1	0	0	3.52
Hoyt	1	2.1	4	1	0	0	0	0	15.43
New York (NL) Totals	6	53	60	20	22	2	4	0	4.25
Nehf	2	16.1	10	6	7	1	1	0	2.76
Ryan	3	9.1	11	3	3	1	0	0	0.96
McQuillan	2	9	11	4	3	0	1	0	5.00
Bentley	2	6.2	10	4	1	0	1	0	9.45
Barnes	2	4.2	4	0	4	0	0	0	0.00
J. Scott	2	3	9	1	2	0	1	0	12.00
Jonnard	2	2	1	1	1	0	0	0	0.00
Watson	1	2	4	1	1	0	0	0	13.50

1924 New York—Seven Flags in Four Years

When the season opened, the odds were greatly in favor of New York City taking another pennant, if not the Series. The odds' makers were well aware that no city, let alone a team, had ever been able to put four straight flags together. But no city ever had the advantage of New York. The Yankees and Giants were coming off the 1923 season with three consecutive pennants. Each had the talent to repeat and each virtually had the same team. If the Giants failed, there was always the Yankees and Babe Ruth.

In fact, the Yankees looked a cinch to repeat. Yet they, as the Giants, were in for a surprise—only one of which was to survive the unexpected. Manager John McGraw sized up his National League competition among Cincinnati, Chicago, and Pittsburgh. Little thought was given to the Brooklyn club, which had finished sixth in 1923.

Cincinnati had injury problems and never threatened. Chicago did threaten until their ace hurler, Grover "Pete" Alexander, broke his wrist in mid-August. But it was Pittsburgh, expected, and the Dodgers, unexpected, which proved to be a hindrance in the end. The Dodgers were greatly strengthened by manager Wilbert Robinson's shifting men at key positions and moving them from the bench to the starting lineup, as well as the remarkable pitching of Burleigh Grimes and Dazzy Vance, who fashioned 50 victories. Vance took league honors with 28 wins and a 2.16 E.R.A.

While the Dodgers, Giants, and Pirates were fighting to decide the pennant, baseball's most prolific hitter since Ty Cobb was trying to put some self-respect into the St. Louis lineup. Although the final results would be more remembered for the individual rather than the team, Rogers Hornsby was on his way to a fifth straight batting title with an average of .424, the highest ever recorded in the twentieth century.

By the time the dust of the last week settled, McGraw had won his fourth and unprecedented pennant by 1½ games over the Dodgers and three over Pittsburgh. The Yankees were not as fortunate. Their loss of the pennant by two games could be traced to the decline of the pitching staff which, except for Herb Pennock, fell off badly from their previous form. It could also be traced to Carl Mays, a temperamental on-again, off-again pitcher. The Yankees released Mays and Cincinnati picked him up. Mays, who had the misfortune to kill Ray Chapman with a pitched ball in 1920, went on to win 20 games.

Most of all, though, the Yankees' relegation to second place was a direct result of the Washington Senators who, for the first time in their history, found themselves winners. They became winners by surviving the Yankees with Ruth and his league-leading 46 homers and .378 batting average, as well as third place Detroit with five regulars over .300. The fact that Washington had survived to win the pennant could be credited to their masterful veteran Walter Johnson. He proved the mainstay of a corps of young moundsmen with his league-leading 23 wins and 2.72 E.R.A. Johnson's performance (adding up to 373 lifetime wins at the year's end) was not much different than the artistry he had provided Washington for 10 years. The difference this time was that he was not alone in his contribution: Goose Goslin hit .344, Sam Rice .334, and Joe Judge, .324. And George Mogridge and Tom Zachary combined for 31 wins.

The World Series, Johnson's first and McGraw's last, saw Johnson lose his first two starts. Then, in the eighth inning of the seventh and final game, Johnson entered as a reliever and held off the Giants until the 12th frame, when Earl McNeely made him a winner with a grounder that took a freak hop over Fred Lindstrom's head.

1924 AMERICAN LEAGUE

NAME	G by POS	B	AGE	G	AB	R	H	2B	3B	HR	RBI	BB	SO	SB	BA	SA
WASHINGTON 1st 92-62 .597	BUCKY HARRIS															
TOTALS			28	156	5304	755	1558	255	**88**	22	688	513	392	117	.294	.387
Joe Judge	1B140	L	30	140	516	71	167	38	9	3	79	53	21	13	.324	.450
Bucky Harris	2B143	R	27	143	544	88	146	28	9	1	58	56	41	19	.268	.358
Roger Peckinpaugh	SS155	R	33	155	523	72	142	20	5	2	73	72	45	11	.272	.340
Ossie Bluege	3B102, 2B10, SS4	R	23	117	402	59	113	15	4	2	49	39	36	7	.281	.353
Sam Rice	OF154	L	34	154	**646**	106	**216**	38	14	1	76	46	24	24	.334	.441
Nemo Liebold	OF70	L	32	84	246	41	72	6	4	0	20	42	10	6	.293	.350
Goose Goslin	OF154	L	23	154	579	100	199	30	17	12	**129**	68	29	16	.344	.516
Muddy Ruel	C147	R	28	149	501	50	142	20	2	0	57	62	20	7	.283	.331
Wid Matthews	OF44	L	27	53	169	25	51	10	4	0	13	11	4	3	.302	.408
Doc Prothro	3B45	R	30	46	159	17	53	11	5	0	24	15	11	4	.333	.465
Earl McNeely	OF42	R	26	43	179	31	59	5	6	0	15	5	21	3	.330	.425
Walter Johnson	P38	R	36	39	113	18	32	9	0	1	14	3	11	0	.283	.389
Tom Zachary	P33	L	28	33	72	7	22	1	0	0	8	5	8	0	.306	.319
Mule Shirley	1B25, C1	L	23	30	77	12	18	2	2	0	16	3	7	0	.234	.312
Tommy Taylor	3B16, 2B2, OF1	R	31	26	73	11	19	3	1	0	10	2	8	2	.260	.329
Pinky Hargrave	C8	R	28	24	33	3	5	1	1	0	5	1	4	0	.152	.242
Bennie Tate	C14	L	22	21	43	2	13	2	0	0	7	1	2	0	.302	.349
Showboat Fisher	OF11	L	25	15	41	7	9	1	0	0	6	6	6	2	.220	.244
Lance Richbourg	OF7	L	26	15	32	3	9	2	1	0	1	2	6	0	.281	.406
Ralph Miller	2B3	R	28	9	15	1	2	0	0	0	0	1	1	0	.133	.133
Bert Griffith	OF2	R	28	6	8	1	1	0	0	0	0	0	1	0	.125	.125
Carr Smith	OF4	R	23	5	10	1	2	0	0	0	0	0	3	0	.200	.200
2 Wade Lefler	OF1	L	28	5	8	0	5	3	0	0	4	0	0	0	.625	1.000
Chick Gagnon 26 R 1-5, Carl East 30 L 2-6, Patsy Gharrity (DE) 32																
NEW YORK 2nd 89-63 .586 2	MILLER HUGGINS															
TOTALS			29	153	5240	798	1516	218	86	**98**	734	478	420	69	.289	**.426**
Wally Pipp	1B153	L	31	153	589	88	174	30	**19**	9	113	51	36	12	.295	.457
Aaron Ward (LJ)	2B120, SS1	R	27	120	400	42	101	13	10	8	66	40	45	1	.253	.395
Everett Scott	SS153	R	31	153	548	56	137	12	6	4	64	21	15	3	.250	.316
Joe Dugan	3B148, 2B2	R	27	148	610	105	184	31	7	3	56	31	32	1	.302	.390
Babe Ruth	OF152	L	29	153	529	**143**	200	39	7	**46**	121	**142**	**81**	9	**.378**	**.739**
Whitey Witt	OF143	L	28	147	600	88	178	26	5	1	36	45	20	9	.297	.362
Bob Meusel	OF143, 3B2	R	27	143	579	93	188	40	11	12	120	32	43	26	.325	.494
Wally Schang	C106	B	34	114	356	46	104	19	7	5	52	48	43	2	.292	.427
Ernie Johnson	2B27, SS9, 3B2	L	36	64	119	24	42	4	8	3	12	11	7	1	.353	.597
Fred Hofmann	C54	R	30	62	166	17	29	6	1	1	11	12	15	2	.175	.241
Bullet Joe Bush	P39	R	31	60	124	13	42	9	3	1	14	7	6	0	.339	.484
Mike McNally	2B25, 3B13, SS6	R	30	49	69	11	17	0	0	0	2	7	5	1	.246	.246
Harvey Hendrick	OF17	L	26	40	76	7	20	0	0	1	11	2	7	1	.263	.303
Bob Shawkey	P38	R	33	38	69	12	22	4	1	1	15	7	5	0	.319	.449
Earle Combs (BN)	OF11	L	25	24	35	10	14	5	0	0	2	4	2	0	.400	.543
Shags Horan	OF13	R	28	22	31	4	9	1	0	0	7	1	5	0	.290	.323
Benny Bengough	C11	R	25	11	16	4	5	1	1	0	3	2	0	0	.313	.500
Lou Gehrig	1B2, OF1	L	21	10	12	2	6	1	0	0	6	3	2	0	.500	.583
Ben Paschal	OF4	R	28	4	12	2	3	1	0	0	3	1	0	0	.250	.333
Martin Autry 21 R 0-0, Mack Hillis 22 R 0-1																
DETROIT 3rd 86-68 .558 6	TY COBB															
TOTALS			29	156	**5389**	**849**	**1604**	**315**	76	35	**758**	**607**	400	100	**.298**	.404
Lu Blue	1B108	B	27	108	395	81	123	26	7	2	50	64	26	9	.311	.428
Del Pratt	2B63, 1B51, 3B4	R	36	121	429	56	130	32	3	1	77	31	10	6	.303	.399
Topper Rigney	SS146	R	27	147	499	81	144	29	9	4	93	102	39	11	.289	.407
Bob Jones	3B106	L	34	110	393	52	107	27	4	0	47	20	20	1	.272	.361
Harry Heilmann	OF147, 1B4	R	29	153	570	107	197	**45**	16	10	113	78	41	13	.346	.533
Ty Cobb	OF155	L	37	155	625	115	211	38	10	4	74	85	18	23	.338	.450
Heinie Manush	OF106, 1B1	L	22	120	422	83	122	24	8	9	68	27	30	14	.289	.448
Johnny Bassler	C121	L	29	124	379	43	131	20	3	1	68	62	11	2	.346	.422
Fred Haney	3B59, SS4, 2B3	R	26	86	256	54	79	11	1	1	30	39	13	7	.309	.371
Al Wingo	OF43	L	26	78	150	21	43	12	2	1	26	21	13	2	.287	.413
Les Burke	2B58, SS6	L	21	72	241	30	61	10	4	0	17	22	20	2	.253	.328
Larry Woodall	C62	R	29	67	165	23	51	9	2	0	24	21	5	0	.309	.388
Bob Fothergill	OF45	R	26	54	166	28	50	8	3	0	15	5	13	2	.301	.386
Frank O'Rourke	2B40, SS7	R	29	47	181	28	50	11	2	0	19	12	19	7	.276	.359
John Kerr	3B3, OF2	B	25	17	11	3	3	0	0	0	1	0	0	0	.273	.273
Clyde Manion	C3, 1B1	R	27	14	13	1	3	0	0	0	2	1	1	0	.231	.231
Charlie Gehringer	2B5	L	21	5	13	2	6	0	0	0	1	0	2	1	.462	.462

NAME	T	AGE	W	L	PCT	SV	G	GS	CG	IP	H	BB	SO	ShO	ERA
		29	**92**	62	**.597**	**25**	156	156	74	1383	1329	505	469	**13**	**3.34**
Walter Johnson	R	36	**23**	7	**.767**	0	38	**38**	20	278	233	77	**158**	**6**	**2.72**
George Mogridge	L	35	16	11	.593	0	30	30	13	213	217	61	48	2	3.76
Tom Zachary	L	28	15	9	.625	2	33	27	13	203	198	53	45	1	2.75
Firpo Marberry	R	25	11	12	.478	**15**	**50**	15	6	195	190	70	68	0	3.09
2 Curly Ogden	R	23	9	5	.643	0	16	16	9	108	83	51	23	3	2.58
Joe Martina	R	34	6	8	.429	0	24	13	8	125	129	56	57	0	4.68
Allen Russell	R	30	5	1	.833	8	37	0	0	82	83	45	17	0	4.39
Paul Zahniser	R	27	5	7	.417	0	24	14	5	92	98	49	28	1	4.40
By Speece	R	27	2	1	.667	0	21	1	0	54	60	27	15	0	2.67
Slim McGrew	R	24	0	1	.000	0	6	2	0	23	25	12	8	0	5.09
1 Ted Wingfield	R	24	0	0	.000	0	4	0	0	7	9	4	2	0	2.57
Nick Altrock	L	47	0	0	.000	0	1	0	0	2	4	0	0	0	0.00
		30	89	63	.586	13	153	153	76	1359	1483	522	**487**	**13**	3.86
Herb Pennock	L	30	21	9	.700	3	40	34	25	286	302	64	101	4	2.83
Waite Hoyt	R	24	18	13	.581	4	46	32	14	247	295	76	71	2	3.79
Bullet Joe Bush	R	31	17	16	.515	1	39	31	19	252	262	**109**	80	3	3.57
Bob Shawkey	R	33	16	11	.593	0	38	25	10	208	226	74	114	1	4.11
Sad Sam Jones	R	31	9	6	.600	3	36	21	8	179	187	76	53	3	3.62
Milt Gaston	R	28	5	3	.625	1	29	2	0	86	92	44	24	0	4.50
Walter Beall	R	24	2	0	1.000	0	4	2	0	23	19	17	18	0	3.52
Al Mamaux	R	30	1	1	.500	0	14	2	0	38	44	20	12	0	5.68
George Pipgras	R	24	0	1	.000	1	9	1	0	15	20	18	4	0	10.20
Cliff Markle	R	30	0	3	.000	0	7	3	0	23	29	20	7	0	9.00
Ben Shields	L	21	0	0	.000	0	2	0	0	2	6	2	3	0	27.00
Oscar Roettger	R	24	0	0	.000	0	1	0	0	0	1	2	0	0	0.00
		26	86	68	.558	20	156	156	60	**1391**	1582	465	439	5	4.20
Earl Whitehill	L	24	17	9	.654	0	35	32	16	233	260	79	65	2	3.86
Ken Hollaway	R	26	14	6	.700	3	49	14	5	181	209	61	46	0	4.08
Rip Collins	R	28	14	7	.667	0	34	30	11	216	199	63	75	1	3.21
Hooks Dauss	R	34	12	11	.522	6	40	10	5	131	155	40	44	0	4.60
Lil Stoner	R	25	11	11	.500	0	36	25	10	216	271	65	65	1	4.71
Ed Wells	L	24	6	8	.429	4	29	15	5	102	117	42	33	0	4.06
Syl Johnson	R	23	5	4	.556	3	29	9	2	104	117	42	55	0	4.93
Dutch Leonard	L	32	3	2	.600	1	8	7	3	49	65	16	25	0	4.78
Bert Cole	L	26	3	9	.250	2	27	11	2	108	134	35	16	1	4.75
Herman Pillette	R	28	1	1	.500	1	19	3	1	38	46	14	13	0	4.74
Willie Ludolph	R	24	0	0	.000	0	3	0	0	6	5	2	1	0	4.50
Rufe Clarke	R	24	0	0	.000	0	2	0	0	5	3	5	1	0	3.60
Ken Jones	R	20	0	0	.000	0	1	0	0	2	1	1	0	0	0.00

NAME	G by POS	B	AGE	G	AB	R	H	2B	3B	HR	RBI	BB	SO	SB	BA	SA
ST. LOUIS 4th 74-78 .487 17		GEORGE SISLER														
TOTALS			30	153	5236	769	1543	265	62	67	679	465	349	85	.295	.407
George Sisler	1B151	L	31	151	636	94	194	27	10	9	74	31	29	19	.305	.421
Marty McManus	2B119	R	24	123	442	71	147	23	5	5	80	55	40	13	.333	.441
Wally Gerber	SS147	R	32	148	496	61	135	20	4	0	55	43	34	4	.272	.329
Gene Robertson	3B110	L	24	121	439	70	140	26	4	4	52	36	14	3	.319	.424
Jack Tobin	OF131	L	32	136	569	87	170	30	8	2	48	50	12	6	.299	.390
Baby Doll Jacobson	OF152	R	33	152	579	103	184	41	12	19	97	35	45	6	.318	.528
Ken Williams	OF108	L	34	114	398	78	129	21	4	18	84	69	17	20	.324	.533
Hank Severeid	C130	R	33	137	432	37	133	23	2	4	48	36	15	1	.308	.398
Joe Evans	OF49	R	29	77	209	30	53	3	3	0	19	24	12	1	.254	.297
Norm McMillan	2B37, 3B17, SS7, 1B2	R	28	76	201	25	56	12	2	0	27	12	17	6	.279	.358
Harry Rice	3B15, 2B4, 1B2, SS2, OF2	L	23	44	93	19	26	7	0	0	15	7	5	1	.280	.355
Herschel Bennett (BA)	OF21	L	27	41	94	16	31	4	3	1	11	3	6	1	.330	.468
Pat Collins	C20	R	27	32	54	9	17	2	0	1	11	11	14	0	.315	.407
Tony Rego	C23	R	26	24	59	5	13	1	0	0	5	1	3	0	.220	.237
Syl Simon	3B6, SS5	R	26	23	32	5	8	1	1	0	6	3	5	0	.250	.344
1 Frank Ellerbe	3B21	R	28	21	61	7	12	3	0	0	2	2	3	0	.197	.246
Ellie Ellmore	OF3	L	24	7	17	2	3	3	0	0	0	1	3	0	.176	.353
Pat Burke	3B1	R	23	1	3	0	0	0	0	0	1	0	0	0	.000	.000
Bill Mizeur		L	24	1	1	0	0	0	0	0	0	0	0	0	.000	.000

NAME	T	AGE	W	L	PCT	SV	G	GS	CG	IP	H	BB	SO	ShO	ERA
		28	74	78	.487	7	153	153	66	1353	1511	517	386	11	4.58
Urban Shocker	R	33	16	13	.552	1	40	33	17	246	270	52	88	4	4.21
Dave Danforth	L	34	15	12	.556	4	41	27	12	220	246	69	65	1	4.50
Ernie Wingard	L	23	13	12	.520	1	36	26	14	218	215	85	23	0	3.51
Dixie Davis	R	33	11	13	.458	0	29	24	11	160	159	72	45	5	4.10
Ray Kolp	R	29	5	7	.417	0	25	12	5	97	131	25	29	1	5.66
Elam Vangilder	R	28	5	10	.333	1	43	18	5	145	183	55	49	0	5.77
George Lyons	R	33	3	2	.600	0	26	6	2	78	97	45	25	0	5.19
Hub Pruett	L	23	3	4	.429	0	33	1	0	65	64	42	27	0	4.57
Ollie Voight	R	24	1	0	1.000	0	8	1	0	16	21	13	4	0	5.63
George Grant	R	21	1	2	.333	0	22	2	0	51	69	25	11	0	6.35
Bill Bayne	L	25	1	3	.250	0	22	3	0	51	47	29	20	0	4.41
Bill Lasley	R	21	0	0	.000	0	2	0	0	4	7	2	0	0	6.75
Ed Barnhart	R	19	0	0	.000	0	1	0	0	1	0	2	0	0	0.00
Boom-Boom Beck	R	19	0	0	.000	0	1	0	0	1	2	1	0	0	0.00

NAME	G by POS	B	AGE	G	AB	R	H	2B	3B	HR	RBI	BB	SO	SB	BA	SA
PHILADELPHIA 5th 71-81 .467 20		CONNIE MACK														
TOTALS			27	152	5184	685	1459	251	59	63	608	374	**482**	79	.281	.389
Joe Hauser	1B146	L	25	149	562	97	162	31	8	27	115	56	52	7	.288	.516
Max Bishop	2B80	L	24	91	294	52	75	13	2	2	21	54	30	4	.255	.333
Chick Galloway	SS129	R	27	129	464	41	128	16	4	2	48	23	23	11	.276	.341
Harry Riconda	3B73, SS2, C1	R	27	83	281	34	71	16	3	1	21	27	43	3	.253	.342
Bing Miller	OF94, 1B7	R	29	113	398	62	136	22	4	6	62	12	24	11	.342	.462
Al Simmons	OF152	R	22	152	594	69	183	31	9	8	102	30	60	16	.308	.431
Bill Lamar	OF87	L	27	87	367	68	121	22	5	7	48	18	21	8	.330	.474
Cy Perkins	C128	R	28	128	392	31	95	19	4	0	32	31	20	3	.242	.311
Jimmy Dykes	2B77, 3B27, SS4	R	27	110	410	68	128	26	6	3	50	38	59	1	.312	.427
Frank Welch	OF74	R	26	94	293	47	85	13	2	5	31	35	27	2	.290	.399
Sammy Hale	3B55, OF5, SS1, C1	R	27	80	261	41	83	14	2	2	17	17	19	3	.318	.410
Fred Heimach	P40	L	23	58	90	14	29	3	2	0	12	3	8	1	.322	.400
Frank Bruggy	C44	R	33	50	113	9	30	6	0	0	8	8	15	4	.265	.319
Paul Strand	OF44	R	30	47	167	15	38	9	4	0	13	4	9	3	.228	.329
2 Amos Strunk	OF8	L	35	30	42	5	6	0	0	0	1	7	4	0	.143	.143
John Chapman	SS19	R	23	19	71	7	20	4	1	0	6	3	3	0	.282	.366
Charlie Gibson	C12	R	24	12	15	1	2	0	0	0	1	0	0	0	.133	.133
Ed Sherling		R	26	4	2	2	1	1	0	0	0	0	0	0	.500	1.000
Joe Greene		R	26	1	1	0	0	0	0	0	0	0	0	0	.000	.000

NAME	T	AGE	W	L	PCT	SV	G	GS	CG	IP	H	BB	SO	ShO	ERA
		26	71	81	.467	10	152	152	68	1345	1527	**597**	371	7	4.39
Eddie Rommel	R	26	18	15	.545	1	43	34	21	278	302	94	72	3	3.95
Fred Heimach	L	23	14	12	.538	0	40	26	10	198	243	60	60	0	4.73
Stan Baumgartner	L	31	13	6	.674	4	36	16	12	181	181	73	45	1	2.88
Sam Gray	R	26	8	7	.533	2	34	19	8	152	169	89	54	1	3.97
Denny Burns	R	26	6	8	.429	1	37	17	7	154	191	68	26	0	5.08
Slim Harriss	R	27	6	10	.375	2	36	12	4	123	138	62	45	1	4.68
Roy Meeker	L	23	5	12	.294	0	30	14	5	146	166	81	37	1	4.68
Bob Hasty	R	28	1	3	.250	0	18	4	0	53	57	30	15	0	5.60
Rollie Naylor	R	32	0	5	.000	0	10	7	1	38	53	20	10	0	6.39
Rube Walberg	L	24	0	0	.000	0	6	2	0	7	10	10	3	0	12.86
1 Curly Ogden	R	23	0	3	.000	0	5	1	0	13	14	7	4	0	4.85
Bill Pierson	L	25	0	0	.000	0	1	0	0	3	3	3	0	0	3.00

NAME	G by POS	B	AGE	G	AB	R	H	2B	3B	HR	RBI	BB	SO	SB	BA	SA
CLEVELAND 6th 67-86 .438 24.5		TRIS SPEAKER														
TOTALS			27	153	5332	755	1580	306	59	41	676	492	371	84	.296	.399
George Burns	1B127	R	31	129	462	64	143	37	5	4	66	29	27	14	.310	.437
Chick Fewster	2B94, 3B5	R	28	101	322	36	86	12	2	0	36	24	36	12	.267	.317
Joe Sewell	SS153	L	25	153	594	99	188	**45**	5	4	104	67	13	3	.316	.429
Rube Lutzke	3B103, 2B3	R	26	106	341	37	83	18	3	0	42	38	46	4	.243	.314
Homer Summa	OF95	L	25	111	390	55	113	21	6	2	38	11	16	4	.290	.390
Tris Speaker	OF128	L	36	135	486	94	167	36	9	9	65	72	13	5	.344	.510
Charlie Jamieson	OF143	L	31	143	594	98	213	34	8	3	53	47	15	21	.359	.458
Glenn Myatt	C95	L	26	105	342	55	117	22	7	8	73	33	12	6	.342	.518
Pat McNulty	OF75	L	25	101	291	46	78	13	5	0	26	33	22	10	.268	.347
Riggs Stephenson (LJ)	2B58, OF7	R	26	71	240	33	89	20	0	4	44	27	10	1	.371	.504
Frank Brower	1B26, P4, OF3	L	31	66	107	16	30	10	1	3	20	27	9	1	.280	.477
Luke Sewell	C57	R	23	63	165	27	48	9	1	0	17	22	13	1	.291	.358
George Uhle	P28	R	25	59	107	10	33	6	1	1	19	4	8	0	.308	.411
2 Frank Ellerbe	3B39, 2B2	R	28	46	120	7	31	1	3	1	14	1	9	0	.258	.342
Sumpter Clarke	OF33	R	26	45	104	17	24	6	1	0	11	6	12	0	.231	.308
Larry Gardner	3B8, 2B6	L	38	38	50	3	10	0	0	0	4	5	1	0	.200	.200
Roxy Walters	C25, 2B7	R	31	32	74	10	19	2	0	0	5	10	6	0	.257	.284
Elmer Yoter	3B19	R	24	19	66	3	18	1	1	0	7	5	8	0	.273	.318
Ray Knode	1B10	L	23	11	37	6	9	1	0	0	4	3	0	2	.243	.270
Tom Gulley	OF5	L	24	8	20	4	3	0	1	0	1	3	2	0	.150	.250
Joe Wyatt	OF4	R	23	4	11	1	2	0	0	0	1	2	1	0	.182	.182
Freddie Spurgeon	2B3	R	22	3	8	0	1	1	0	0	0	0	0	0	.125	.250
Kenny Hogan		L	21	2	1	0	0	0	0	0	0	0	0	0	.000	.000

NAME	T	AGE	W	L	PCT	SV	G	GS	CG	IP	H	BB	SO	ShO	ERA
		27	67	86	.438	7	153	153	**87**	1349	1603	503	312	7	4.40
Joe Shaute	L	24	20	**17**	.543	2	46	34	21	283	317	83	68	2	3.75
Stan Coveleski	R	35	15	16	.484	0	37	33	18	240	286	73	58	2	4.05
Sherry Smith	L	33	12	14	.462	1	39	27	20	248	267	42	31	2	3.01
George Uhle	R	25	9	15	.375	1	28	25	15	196	238	75	57	0	4.78
Jim Joe Edwards (KJ)	L	29	4	3	.571	0	10	7	5	57	64	34	15	1	2.84
Bud Messenger	R	26	2	0	1.000	0	5	2	1	25	28	14	4	0	4.32
Emil Levsen	R	26	1	1	.500	0	4	1	1	16	22	4	3	0	**4.50**
Carl Yowell	L	21	1	1	.500	0	4	2	2	27	37	13	8	0	6.67
Joe Dawson	R	26	1	2	.333	0	4	4	0	20	24	21	7	0	6.75
Watty Clark	L	22	1	3	.250	0	12	1	0	26	38	14	6	0	6.92
Dewey Metivier	R	26	1	5	.167	3	26	6	1	76	110	34	14	0	5.33
Luther Roy	R	21	0	5	.000	0	16	5	2	49	62	31	14	0	7.71
Guy Morton	R	31	0	1	.000	0	10	0	0	12	12	13	6	0	6.75
Virgil Cheeves	R	23	0	0	.000	0	8	1	0	17	26	17	2	0	7.94
Logan Drake	R	23	0	1	.000	0	5	1	0	11	18	10	8	0	10.64
George Edmondson	R	28	0	0	.000	0	5	1	0	8	10	5	3	0	9.00
Frank Brower	R	31	0	0	.000	0	4	0	0	10	7	4	0	0	0.90
Jim Lindsay	R	26	0	0	.000	0	3	0	0	3	8	3	0	0	21.00
Jake Miller	L	26	0	1	.000	0	2	2	1	12	13	5	4	0	3.00
Frank Wayenberg	R	25	0	0	.000	0	2	1	0	7	7	5	3	0	5.14
Bob Fitzke	R	23	0	0	.000	0	1	0	0	4	5	3	1	0	4.50
Bob Kuhn	R	24	0	1	.000	0	1	0	0	1	4	0	0	0	27.00

NAME	G by POS	B	AGE	G	AB	R	H	2B	3B	HR	RBI	BB	SO	SB	BA	SA
BOSTON 7th 67-87 .435 25		LEE FOHL														
TOTALS			31	157	5344	737	1481	302	63	30	666	604	418	79	.277	.374
Joe Harris	1B128, OF3	R	33	133	491	82	148	36	9	3	77	81	25	6	.301	.430
Bill Wambsganss	2B156	R	30	156	636	93	174	41	5	0	49	54	33	14	.274	.354
Dud Lee	SS90	L	24	94	288	36	73	9	4	0	29	40	**17**	8	.253	.313
Danny Clark	3B94	L	30	104	325	36	90	23	3	2	54	51	19	4	.277	.385
Ike Boone	OF124	L	27	128	486	71	162	30	4	13	96	55	32	2	.333	.492
Ira Flagstead	OF144	R	30	149	560	106	171	35	7	5	43	77	41	10	.305	.420
Bobby Veach	OF130	L	36	142	519	77	153	35	9	5	99	47	18	5	.295	.426
Steve O'Neill	C92	R	32	106	307	29	73	15	1	0	38	63	23	0	.238	.293
Homer Ezzell	3B63, SS21, C1	R	28	89	273	33	75	8	4	0	32	13	20	12	.275	.333
Shano Collins	OF56, 1B12	R	38	89	240	37	70	16	5	0	28	18	17	4	.292	.400
H. Shanks	SS38, 3B22, OF4, 1B2, 2B2	R	33	72	193	22	50	16	3	0	25	21	12	1	.259	.373
Val Picinich	C52	R	27	69	161	25	44	6	3	1	24	29	19	5	.273	.366
Phil Todt	1B18, OF4	L	22	52	103	17	27	8	2	1	14	6	9	0	.262	.408
Johnnie Heving	C29	R	28	45	109	15	31	5	1	0	11	10	7	0	.284	.349
Chappie Geygan	SS32	R	21	33	82	7	21	5	2	0	4	4	16	0	.256	.366
Denny Williams	OF19	L	24	25	85	17	31	3	0	0	4	10	5	3	.365	.400
Joe Connolly	OF3	R	28	14	10	1	1	0	0	0	1	2	2	0	.100	.100

NAME	T	AGE	W	L	PCT	SV	G	GS	CG	IP	H	BB	SO	ShO	ERA
		28	67	**87**	.435	16	157	157	73	1391	1563	523	414	8	4.35
Howard Ehmke	R	30	19	**17**	.528	4	45	36	26	**315**	324	81	119	4	3.46
Alex Ferguson	R	27	14	**17**	.452	2	41	32	15	238	259	108	78	0	3.78
Jack Quinn	R	40	12	13	.480	7	44	25	13	229	241	52	64	2	3.26
Curt Fullerton	R	25	7	12	.368	2	33	20	9	152	166	73	33	0	4.32
Bill Piercy	R	28	5	7	.417	0	23	18	3	121	156	66	20	0	5.95
Buster Ross	L	21	4	3	.571	1	30	2	1	93	109	30	16	1	3.48
Oscar Fuhr	L	30	3	6	.333	0	23	10	4	80	100	39	30	1	5.96
George Murray	R	25	2	9	.182	0	28	7	0	80	97	32	27	0	6.75
Les Howe	R	28	1	0	1.000	0	4	0	0	7	11	2	3	0	7.71
Hoge Workman	R	24	0	0	.000	0	11	0	0	18	25	11	7	0	8.50
Red Ruffing	R	20	0	0	.000	0	8	2	0	23	29	9	10	0	6.65
1 Ted Wingfield	R	24	0	2	.000	0	4	3	2	26	23	8	4	0	2.42
Clarence Winters		25	0	1	.000	0	4	2	0	7	22	4	3	0	20.57
Charley Jamerson	L	24	0	0	.000	0	1	0	0	1	1	3	0	0	18.00
Al Kellett	R	22	0	0	.000	0	1	0	0	0	0	2	0	0	∞
John Woods	R	26	0	0	.000	0	1	0	0	1	0	3	0	0	0.00

NAME	G by POS	B	AGE	G	AB	R	H	2B	3B	HR	RBI	BB	SO	SB	BA	SA
CHICAGO 8th 66-87 .431 25.5		JOHNNY EVERS														
TOTALS			29	154	5255	793	1512	254	58	41	710	604	418	**138**	.288	.382
Earl Sheely	1B146	R	31	146	535	84	171	34	3	3	103	95	28	7	.320	.411
Eddie Collins	2B150	L	37	152	556	108	194	27	7	6	86	89	16	**42**	.349	.455
Bill Barrett	SS77, OF27, 3B8	R	24	119	406	52	110	18	5	2	56	30	38	15	.271	.355
Willie Kamm	3B145	R	24	147	528	58	134	28	6	6	93	64	59	9	.254	.364
Harry Hooper	OF123	L	36	130	476	107	156	27	8	10	62	65	26	16	.328	.481
Johnny Mostil	OF105	R	28	118	385	75	125	22	5	4	49	45	41	7	.325	.439
Bibb Falk	OF134	L	25	138	526	77	185	37	8	6	99	47	21	6	.352	.487
Buck Crouse	C90	L	27	94	305	30	79	10	1	1	44	23	12	3	.259	.308
Maurice Archdeacon	OF77	L	25	95	288	59	92	9	3	0	25	40	30	11	.319	.372
Roy Elsh	OF38, 1B2	R	28	60	147	21	45	9	1	0	11	10	14	6	.306	.381
Ray Schalk	C56	R	31	57	153	15	30	4	2	1	11	21	10	1	.196	.268
Ray French	SS28, 2B3	R	29	37	112	13	20	4	0	0	11	10	13	3	.179	.214
H. McClellan (IL)	SS21, 2B7, 3B1, OF1	R	29	32	85	9	15	3	0	0	9	6	7	2	.176	.212
Ray Morehart	SS27, 2B2	L	24	31	100	10	20	4	2	0	8	17	7	3	.200	.280
Johnny Grabowski	C19	R	24	20	56	10	14	3	0	0	3	2	4	0	.250	.304
Bud Clancy	1B8	L	23	13	35	5	9	1	0	0	6	3	2	3	.257	.286
Ike Davis	SS10	R	29	10	33	5	8	1	1	0	4	2	5	0	.242	.333
Joe Burns	C6	R	24	8	19	1	2	0	0	0	0	0	2	0	.105	.105
Bill Black	2B1	L	24	6	5	0	1	0	0	0	0	0	0	0	.200	.200
Kettle Wirts	C5	R	26	6	12	0	1	0	0	0	0	2	2	1	.083	.083
Wally Dashiell	SS1	R	22	1	2	0	0	0	0	0	0	0	0	0	.000	.000
Frank Naleway	SS1	R	22	1	2	0	0	0	0	0	0	1	0	0	.000	.000

Bernie deViveirios 23 R 0-1, 1 Amos Strunk 35 L 0-1, Dickie Kerr (SL) 30

NAME	T	AGE	W	L	PCT	SV	G	GS	CG	IP	H	BB	SO	ShO	ERA
		26	66	**87**	.431	11	154	154	76	1367	**1635**	512	360	1	4.75
Sloppy Thurston	R	25	20	14	.588	1	38	36	**28**	291	**330**	60	37	1	3.80
Ted Lyons	R	23	12	11	.522	3	41	22	12	216	279	72	52	0	4.88
Red Faber (AJ)	R	35	9	11	.450	0	21	20	9	161	173	58	47	0	3.86
Ted Blankenship (ST)	R	23	7	6	.538	1	25	11	7	125	167	38	36	0	5.18
Sarge Connally	R	25	7	13	.350	6	44	13	6	160	177	68	55	0	4.05
Charlie Robertson (SA)	R	28	4	10	.286	0	17	14	5	97	108	54	29	0	5.01
Mike Cvengros	L	22	3	12	.200	0	26	15	2	106	119	67	36	0	5.86
Dixie Leverett	R	30	2	3	.400	0	21	11	4	99	123	41	29	0	5.82
Doug McWeeney	R	27	1	3	.250	0	13	5	2	43	47	17	18	0	4.60
Leo Mangum	R	28	1	4	.200	0	13	7	1	47	69	25	12	0	7.09
Happy Foreman	L	26	0	0	.000	0	3	0	0	4	7	4	1	0	2.25
Milt Steengrafe	R	24	0	0	.000	0	3	0	0	6	15	4	3	0	12.00
Bob Barnes	L	22	0	0	.000	0	2	0	0	5	14	0	1	0	18.00
Lum Davenport	L	24	0	0	.000	0	1	0	0	2	1	2	1	0	0.00
John Dobb	L	22	0	0	.000	0	2	0	0	2	4	1	2	0	9.00
Bob Lawrence	R	24	0	0	.000	0	1	0	0	1	1	1	1	0	9.00
Webb Schultz	R	26	0	0	.000	0	1	0	0	1	1	0	0	0	9.00

NEW YORK 1st 93-60 .608 — JOHN McGRAW

NAME	G by POS	B	AGE	G	AB	R	H	2B	3B	HR	RBI	BB	SO	SB	BA	SA
TOTALS			28	154	5445	857	1634	269	81	95	781	467	479	82	.300	.432
George Kelly	1B125, OF14, 2B5, 3B1	R	28	144	571	91	185	37	9	21	136	38	52	7	.324	.531
Frankie Frisch	2B143, SS10, 3B2	B	25	145	603	121	198	33	15	7	69	56	24	22	.328	.468
Travis Jackson	SS151	R	20	151	596	81	180	26	8	11	76	21	56	6	.302	.428
Heinie Groh	3B145	R	34	145	559	82	157	32	3	2	46	52	29	8	.281	.360
Ross Youngs	OF132, 2B2	L	27	133	526	112	187	33	12	10	74	77	31	11	.355	.521
Hack Wilson	OF103	R	24	107	383	62	113	19	12	10	57	44	46	4	.295	.486
Irish Meusel	OF138	R	31	139	549	75	170	26	9	6	102	33	18	11	.310	.423
Frank Snyder	C110	R	31	118	354	37	107	18	3	5	53	30	43	3	.302	.412
Billy Southworth	OF75	L	31	94	281	40	72	13	0	3	36	32	16	1	.256	.335
Hank Gowdy	C78	R	34	87	191	25	62	9	1	4	37	26	11	1	.325	.445
Bill Terry	1B42	L	25	77	163	26	39	7	2	5	24	17	18	1	.239	.399
Fred Lindstrom	2B23, 3B11	R	18	52	79	19	20	3	1	0	4	6	10	3	.253	.316
Jimmy O'Connell (DL)	OF29, 2B1	L	23	52	104	24	33	4	2	2	18	11	16	2	.317	.452
Art Nehf	P30, OF1	L	31	33	57	11	13	1	0	5	13	6	4	1	.228	.509
Eddie Ainsmith	C9	R	32	10	5	0	3	0	0	0	0	0	0	0	.600	.600
Grover Hartley	C3	R	35	4	7	1	2	1	0	0	1	1	0	1	.286	.429
Buddy Crump	OF1	L	22	1	4	0	0	0	0	0	1	0	1	0	.000	.000

NAME	T	AGE	W	L	PCT	SV	G	GS	CG	IP	H	BB	SO	ShO	ERA
TOTALS		26	93	60	.608	21	154	154	71	1379	1464	392	406	4	3.62
Jack Bentley	L	29	16	5	.762	1	28	24	13	188	196	56	60	1	3.78
Virgil Barnes	R	27	16	10	.615	3	35	29	15	229	239	57	59	1	3.07
Art Nehf	L	31	14	4	.778	2	30	20	11	172	167	42	72	0	3.67
Hugh McQuillan	R	26	14	8	.636	3	27	23	14	184	179	43	49	1	2.69
Rosy Ryan	R	26	8	6	.571	5	37	9	2	125	137	37	36	0	4.25
Mule Watson	R	27	7	4	.636	0	22	16	6	100	122	24	18	1	3.78
Wayland Dean	R	22	6	12	.333	0	26	20	6	126	139	45	39	0	5.00
Claude Jonnard	R	27	4	5	.444	5	34	3	1	90	80	24	40	0	2.40
Harry Baldwin	R	24	3	1	.750	0	10	2	1	34	42	11	5	0	4.23
1 Joe Oeschger	R	33	2	0	1.000	0	10	2	0	29	35	14	10	0	3.10
Walter Huntzinger	R	25	1	1	.500	1	12	2	0	32	41	9	6	0	4.50
Ernie Maun	R	23	1	1	.500	1	22	0	0	35	46	10	5	0	5.91
1 Dinty Gearin	L	26	1	2	.333	0	6	3	2	29	30	16	4	0	2.48
Leon Cadore	R	33	0	0	.000	0	2	0	0	4	2	3	2	0	0.00
Kent Greenfield	R	22	0	1	.000	0	1	1	0	3	9	1	1	0	15.00
Jack Scott (LJ) 32															

BROOKLYN 2nd 92-62 .597 1.5 — WILBERT ROBINSON

NAME	G by POS	B	AGE	G	AB	R	H	2B	3B	HR	RBI	BB	SO	SB	BA	SA
TOTALS			31	154	5339	717	1534	227	54	72	662	447	357	34	.287	.391
Jack Fournier	1B153	L	31	154	563	93	188	25	4	27	116	83	46	7	.334	.536
Andy High	2B133, SS17, 3B1	L	26	144	582	98	191	26	13	6	61	57	16	3	.328	.448
Johnny Mitchell	SS64	R	29	64	243	42	64	10	0	1	16	37	22	3	.263	.317
Milt Stock	3B142	R	30	142	561	66	136	14	4	2	52	26	32	3	.242	.292
Tommy Griffith	OF139	L	34	140	482	43	121	19	5	3	67	34	19	0	.251	.330
Eddie Brown	OF114	R	32	114	455	56	140	30	4	5	78	26	15	3	.308	.424
Zack Wheat	OF139	L	38	141	566	92	212	41	8	14	97	49	18	3	.375	.549
Zack Taylor	C93	R	25	99	345	36	100	9	4	1	39	14	14	0	.290	.348
Jimmy Johnston	SS63, 3B10, 1B4, OF1	R	34	86	315	51	94	11	2	2	29	27	10	5	.298	.365
Bernie Neis	OF62	B	28	80	211	43	64	8	3	4	26	27	17	4	.303	.427
Hank DeBerry	C63	R	29	77	218	20	53	10	3	3	26	20	21	0	.243	.358
Dick Loftus	OF29, 1B1	L	23	46	81	18	22	6	0	0	8	7	2	1	.272	.346
Burleigh Grimes	P38	R	30	40	124	11	37	3	0	0	7	5	13	1	.298	.323
Joe Klugman	2B28, SS1	R	29	31	79	7	13	2	1	0	3	2	9	0	.165	.215
Gene Bailey	OF17	R	30	18	46	7	11	3	0	1	4	7	6	1	.239	.370
Charlie Hargreaves	C9	R	27	15	27	4	11	2	0	0	5	1	1	0	.407	.481
Binky Jones	SS10	R	24	10	37	0	4	1	0	0	2	0	3	0	.108	.135
Ivy Olson	SS8, 2B2	R	38	10	27	0	6	1	0	0	0	3	1	0	.222	.259
Fred Johnston	2B1, 3B1	R	24	4	4	1	1	0	0	0	0	0	1	0	.250	.250

NAME	T	AGE	W	L	PCT	SV	G	GS	CG	IP	H	BB	SO	ShO	ERA
TOTALS		30	92	62	.597	5	154	154	97	1376	1432	403	638	10	3.64
Dazzy Vance	R	33	28	6	.824	0	35	34	30	309	238	77	262	3	2.16
Burleigh Grimes	R	30	22	13	.629	1	38	36	30	311	351	91	135	1	3.82
2 Bill Doak	R	33	11	5	.688	0	21	16	8	149	130	35	32	2	3.26
Art Decatur	R	30	10	9	.526	1	31	10	3	128	158	28	39	0	4.08
Dutch Ruether	L	30	8	13	.381	3	30	21	13	167	[illegible]	[illegible]	[illegible]	3	[illegible]
2 Tiny Osborne	R	31	6	5	.545	0	21	13	6	104	123	54	52	0	5.11
Rube Ehrhardt	R	29	5	3	.625	0	15	9	6	84	71	17	13	2	2.25
Bonnie Hollingsworth	R	28	1	0	1.000	0	3	1	1	8	7	9	6	0	6.75
Dutch Henry	L	22	1	2	.333	0	16	4	0	46	69	15	11	0	5.67
Jim Roberts	R	28	0	3	.000	0	11	5	0	25	41	8	10	0	7.56
1 Leo Dickerman	R	27	0	0	.000	0	7	2	0	20	20	16	9	0	5.40
Nelson Greene	L	23	0	1	.000	0	4	1	0	9	14	2	3	0	4.00
Rube Yarrison	R	28	0	2	.000	0	3	2	0	11	12	3	2	0	6.55
Tex Wilson	L	22	0	0	.000	0	2	0	0	4	7	1	1	0	13.50
Tom Long	L	26	0	0	.000	0	1	0	0	2	2	2	0	0	9.00

PITTSBURGH 3rd 90-63 .588 3 — BILL McKECHNIE

NAME	G by POS	B	AGE	G	AB	R	H	2B	3B	HR	RBI	BB	SO	SB	BA	SA
TOTALS			28	153	5288	724	1517	222	122	43	658	366	396	181	.287	.399
Charlie Grimm	1B151	L	25	151	542	53	156	25	12	2	63	37	22	3	.288	.389
Rabbit Maranville	2B152	R	32	152	594	62	158	33	20	2	71	35	53	18	.266	.399
Glenn Wright	SS153	R	23	153	616	80	177	28	18	7	111	27	52	14	.287	.425
Pie Traynor	3B141	R	24	142	545	86	160	26	13	5	82	37	26	24	.294	.417
Clyde Barnhart	OF88	R	28	102	344	49	95	6	11	3	51	30	17	8	.276	.384
Max Carey	OF149	B	34	149	599	113	178	30	9	7	55	58	17	49	.297	.412
Kiki Cuyler	OF114	R	24	117	466	94	165	27	16	9	85	30	62	32	.354	.539
Johnny Gooch	C69	B	26	70	224	26	65	6	5	0	25	16	12	1	.290	.362
Carson Bigbee	OF75	L	29	89	282	42	74	4	1	0	15	26	12	15	.262	.284
Eddie Moore	OF35, 3B13, 2B4	R	25	72	209	47	75	8	4	2	13	27	12	6	.359	.464
Walter Schmidt (RJ)	C57	R	37	58	177	16	43	3	2	1	20	13	5	6	.243	.299
2 Earl Smith	C35	L	27	39	111	12	41	10	1	4	21	13	4	2	.369	.586
Wilbur Cooper	P38	L	32	38	104	11	36	5	2	0	15	5	8	2	.346	.433
Walter Mueller	OF15	R	29	30	50	6	13	1	1	0	8	4	4	1	.260	.320
Cliff Knox	C6	B	22	6	18	1	4	0	0	0	2	2	0	0	.222	.222
Jewel Ens	1B5	R	34	5	10	2	3	0	0	0	0	0	3	0	.300	.300
Johnny Rawlings		R	31	3	3	0	1	0	0	0	2	0	0	0	.333	.333
Eppie Barnes	1B1	L	23	2	5	0	0	0	0	0	0	0	1	0	.000	.000

NAME	T	AGE	W	L	PCT	SV	G	GS	CG	IP	H	BB	SO	ShO	ERA
TOTALS		30	90	63	.588	5	153	153	85	1382	1387	323	364	15	3.27
Wilbur Cooper	L	32	20	14	.588	1	38	35	25	269	296	40	62	4	3.28
Ray Kremer	R	31	18	10	.643	1	41	30	17	259	262	51	64	4	3.20
Emil Yde	L	24	16	3	.842	0	33	22	14	194	171	62	53	4	2.83
Lee Meadows	R	29	13	12	.520	0	36	30	15	229	240	51	61	3	3.26
Johnny Morrison	R	28	11	16	.407	2	41	25	10	238	213	73	85	0	3.74
2 Jeff Pfeffer	R	36	5	3	.625	0	15	4	1	59	68	17	19	0	3.05
Arnie Stone	L	31	4	2	.667	0	26	2	1	64	57	15	7	0	2.95
Babe Adams (SA)	R	42	3	1	.750	0	9	3	2	40	31	3	5	0	1.13
Del Lundgren	R	23	0	1	.000	0	8	1	0	17	25	3	4	0	6.35
1 Ray Steineder	R	28	0	1	.000	0	5	0	0	3	6	5	0	0	12.00
Don Songer	L	25	0	0	.000	0	4	1	0	9	14	3	3	0	7.00
Buckshot May	R	24	0	0	.000	0	1	0	0	1	2	0	1	0	0.00
Fred Sale	R	22	0	0	.000	0	1	0	0	1	2	0	0	0	0.00

CINCINNATI 4th 83-70 .542 10 — PAT MORAN (DD) 48 0-0 .000 JACK HENDRICKS 83-70 .542

NAME	G by POS	B	AGE	G	AB	R	H	2B	3B	HR	RBI	BB	SO	SB	BA	SA
TOTALS			30	153	5301	649	1539	236	111	36	586	349	334	103	.290	.397
Jake Daubert	1B102	L	40	102	405	47	114	14	9	1	31	28	17	5	.281	.368
Hughie Critz	2B96, SS1	R	23	102	413	67	133	15	14	3	35	19	18	19	.322	.450
Ike Caveney (BT)	SS90, 2B5	R	29	95	337	36	92	19	1	4	32	14	21	2	.273	.371
Babe Pinelli	3B143	R	28	144	510	61	156	16	7	0	70	32	32	23	.306	.365
2 Curt Walker	OF109	L	27	109	397	55	119	21	10	4	46	44	15	7	.300	.433
Edd Roush	OF119	L	31	121	483	67	168	23	21	3	72	22	11	17	.348	.501
George Burns	OF90	R	34	93	336	43	86	19	2	2	33	29	21	3	.256	.342
Bubbles Hargrave	C91	R	31	98	312	42	94	19	10	3	33	30	20	2	.301	.455
Rube Bressler	1B50, OF49	R	29	115	383	41	133	14	13	4	49	22	20	9	.347	.483
Sammy Bohne	2B48, SS40, 3B12	R	27	100	349	42	89	15	9	4	46	18	24	9	.255	.384
Pat Duncan	OF83	R	30	96	319	34	86	21	6	2	37	20	23	1	.270	.392
Ivy Wingo	C65, 1B1	L	33	66	192	21	55	5	4	1	23	14	8	1	.286	.370
Boob Fowler	SS32, 2B4, 3B2	L	23	59	129	20	43	6	1	0	9	5	15	2	.333	.395
Chick Shorten	OF15	L	32	41	69	7	19	3	0	0	6	4	2	0	.275	.319
Carl Mays	P37	R	32	38	83	9	24	6	2	1	12	4	12	0	.289	.446
1 George Harper	OF22	L	32	28	74	7	20	3	0	0	3	13	5	1	.270	.311
Gus Sandberg	C24	R	28	24	52	1	9	0	0	0	3	2	7	0	.173	.173
Lew Fonseca	2B10, 1B6	R	25	20	57	5	13	2	1	0	9	4	4	1	.228	.298
Ed Hock	OF2	L	25	16	10	7	1	0	0	0	0	0	2	0	.100	.100
2 Cliff Lee	OF1	R	27	6	6	1	2	1	0	0	2	0	2	0	.333	.500
Greasy Neale	OF2	L	32	3	4	0	0	0	0	0	0	0	1	0	.000	.000
Eddie Pick	OF1	B	25	3	2	0	0	0	0	0	0	0	1	0	.000	.000
Jim Begley	2B2	R	21	2	5	1	1	0	0	0	0	2	0	0	.200	.200
Jack Blott	C1	R	21	2	1	0	0	0	0	0	0	0	0	0	.000	.000
Pat Moran (DD) 48																

NAME	T	AGE	W	L	PCT	SV	G	GS	CG	IP	H	BB	SO	ShO	ERA
TOTALS		31	83	70	.542	9	153	153	77	1378	1408	293	451	14	3.12
Carl Mays	R	32	20	9	.690	0	37	27	15	226	238	36	63	2	3.15
Pete Donohue	R	23	16	9	.640	0	35	32	16	222	248	36	72	3	3.61
Eppa Rixey	L	33	15	14	.517	1	35	29	15	238	219	47	57	4	2.76
Dolf Luque	R	33	10	15	.400	0	31	28	13	219	229	53	86	2	3.16
Tom Sheehan	R	30	9	11	.450	1	39	16	8	167	170	54	52	2	3.23
Rube Benton	L	37	7	9	.438	1	32	15	6	163	166	24	42	1	2.76
Pedro Dibut	R	31	3	0	1.000	0	7	2	2	37	24	12	15	0	2.19
Jakie May	L	28	3	3	.500	6	38	4	2	99	104	29	59	0	3.00
Bill Harris	R	24	0	0	.000	0	3	0	0	7	10	2	5	0	9.00

CHICAGO 5th 81-72 .529 12 — BILL KILLEFER

NAME	G by POS	B	AGE	G	AB	R	H	2B	3B	HR	RBI	BB	SO	SB	BA	SA
TOTALS			26	154	5134	698	1419	207	59	66	634	469	521	137	.276	.378
Harvey Cotter	1B90	L	24	98	310	39	81	16	4	4	33	36	31	3	.261	.377
George Grantham	2B118, 3B6	L	24	127	469	85	148	19	6	12	60	55	63	21	.316	.458
Sparky Adams	SS88, 2B19	R	29	117	418	66	117	11	5	1	27	40	20	15	.280	.337
Barney Friberg	3B142	R	24	142	495	67	138	19	3	5	82	66	53	19	.279	.360
Cliff Heathcote	OF111	L	26	113	392	66	121	19	7	0	30	28	28	26	.309	.393
Jigger Statz	OF131, 2B1	R	26	135	549	69	152	22	5	3	49	37	50	13	.277	.352
Denver Grigsby	OF121	L	23	124	411	58	123	18	2	3	48	31	47	10	.299	.375
Gabby Hartnett	C105	R	23	111	354	56	106	17	7	16	67	39	37	10	.299	.523
Charlie Hollocher (HO)	SS71	L	28	76	286	28	70	12	4	2	21	18	7	4	.245	.336
Bob O'Farrell	C57	R	27	71	183	25	44	6	2	3	28	30	13	2	.240	.344
Otto Vogel	OF53, 3B2	R	24	70	172	28	46	11	2	1	24	10	26	4	.267	.372
Bob Barrett	2B25, 1B10, 3B8	R	25	54	133	12	32	2	3	5	21	7	29	1	.241	.414
Hack Miller	OF32	R	30	53	131	17	44	8	1	4	25	8	11	1	.336	.504
Ray Grimes	1B50	R	30	51	177	33	53	6	5	5	34	28	15	4	.299	.475
Butch Weis	OF36	L	21	37	133	19	37	8	1	0	23	15	14	4	.278	.353
Tony Kaufmann	P34	R	23	35	76	6	24	5	0	1	14	3	10	0	.316	.421
Allen Elliott	1B10	L	26	10	14	0	2	0	0	0	0	0	1	0	.143	.143
Ralph Michaels	SS4	R	22	8	11	0	4	0	0	0	2	0	1	0	.364	.364
Howie Fitzgerald	OF5	L	22	7	19	1	3	0	0	0	2	0	2	0	.158	.158
John Churry	C3	R	23	6	7	0	1	1	0	0	0	2	0	0	.143	.286
Ted Kearns	1B4	R	24	4	16	0	4	0	1	0	1	1	1	0	.250	.375

NAME	T	AGE	W	L	PCT	SV	G	GS	CG	IP	H	BB	SO	ShO	ERA
TOTALS		27	81	72	.529	6	154	154	85	1381	1459	438	416	4	3.83
Tony Kaufmann	R	23	16	11	.593	0	34	26	16	208	218	66	79	3	4.02
Vic Aldridge	R	30	15	12	.556	0	32	32	20	244	261	80	74	0	3.50
Vic Keen	R	25	15	14	.517	3	40	28	15	235	242	80	75	0	3.79
Pete Alexander (BW)	R	37	12	5	.706	0	21	20	12	169	183	25	33	0	3.04
Elmer Jacobs	R	31	11	12	.478	1	38	22	13	190	181	72	50	1	3.74
Sheriff Blake	R	24	6	6	.500	1	29	11	4	106	123	44	42	0	4.59
Rip Wheeler	R	26	3	6	.333	0	29	4	0	101	103	21	16	0	3.92
Guy Bush	R	22	2	5	.286	0	16	8	4	81	91	24	36	0	4.00
George Milstead	L	21	1	1	.500	0	13	2	1	30	41	13	6	0	6.00
Ray Pierce	L	27	0	0	.000	0	6	0	0	7	7	4	2	0	7.71
1 Tiny Osborne	R	31	0	0	.000	1	2	0	0	3	3	2	2	0	3.00
Herb Brett	R	24	0	0	.000	0	1	1	0	5	6	7	1	0	5.40

ST. LOUIS 6th 65-89 .422 28.5 — BRANCH RICKEY

NAME	G by POS	B	AGE	G	AB	R	H	2B	3B	HR	RBI	BB	SO	SB	BA	SA
TOTALS			27	154	5349	740	1552	270	87	67	672	382	418	86	.290	.411
Jim Bottomley	1B133, 2B1	L	24	137	528	87	167	31	12	14	111	35	35	5	.316	.500
Rogers Hornsby	2B143	R	28	143	536	**121**	**227**	**43**	14	25	94	**89**	32	5	**.424**	**.696**
Jimmy Cooney	SS99, 3B7, 2B1	R	29	110	383	44	113	20	8	1	57	20	20	12	.295	.397
Howard Freigau	3B98, SS2	R	21	98	376	35	101	17	6	2	39	19	24	10	.269	.362
Jack Smith	OF114	L	29	124	459	91	130	18	6	2	33	33	27	24	.283	.362
Wattie Holm	OF64, C9, 3B4	R	22	81	293	40	86	10	4	0	23	8	16	1	.294	.355
Ray Blades	OF109, 2B7, 3B7	R	27	131	456	86	142	21	13	11	68	35	38	7	.311	.487
Mike Gonzalez	C119	R	33	120	402	34	119	27	1	3	53	24	22	1	.296	.391
Heinie Mueller	OF53, 1B27	L	24	92	296	39	78	12	6	2	37	19	16	8	.264	.365
Specs Toporcer	3B33, SS25, 2B3	L	25	70	198	30	62	10	3	1	24	11	14	2	.313	.409
Max Flack	OF52	L	34	67	209	31	55	11	3	2	21	21	5	3	.263	.373
Taylor Douthit	OF50	R	23	53	173	24	48	13	1	0	13	16	19	4	.277	.364
Eddie Dyer	P29, OF1	L	23	50	76	8	18	2	3	0	8	3	8	1	.237	.342
Hy Myers	OF22, 3B12, 2B3	R	35	43	124	12	26	5	1	1	15	3	10	1	.210	.290
Charlie Niebergall	C34	R	25	40	58	6	17	6	0	0	7	3	9	0	.293	.397
Vern Clemons	C17	R	32	25	56	3	18	3	0	0	6	2	3	0	.321	.375
Chick Hafey	OF24	R	21	24	91	10	23	5	2	2	22	4	8	1	.253	.418
Tommy Thevenow	SS23	R	20	23	89	4	18	4	1	0	7	1	6	1	.202	.270
Les Bell	SS17	R	22	17	57	5	14	3	2	1	5	3	7	0	.246	.421
Ernie Vick	C16	R	23	16	23	2	8	1	0	0	0	3	3	0	.348	.391
1 Joe Schultz	OF2	R	30	12	12	0	2	0	0	0	2	3	0	0	.167	.167

Ed Clough 17 L 1-14, Joe Bratcher 25 L 0-1, Doc Lavan 33 R 0-6, Ray Shepardson 27 R 0-6

NAME	T	AGE	W	L	PCT	SV	G	GS	CG	IP	H	BB	SO	ShO	ERA
		28	65	89	.422	6	154	154	79	1365	1528	**486**	393	7	4.15
Allan Sothoren	R	31	10	16	.385	0	29	28	16	197	209	84	62	**4**	3.56
Johnny Stuart	R	23	9	11	.450	0	28	22	13	159	167	60	54	0	4.75
Bill Sherdel	L	27	8	9	.471	1	35	10	6	169	188	38	57	0	3.41
Eddie Dyer	L	23	8	11	.421	0	29	15	7	137	174	51	23	1	4.60
Jesse Haines	R	30	8	19	.296	0	35	31	16	223	275	66	69	1	4.40
2 Leo Dickerman	R	27	7	4	.636	0	18	13	8	120	108	51	28	1	2.40
1 Jeff Pfeffer	R	36	4	5	.444	0	16	12	3	78	102	30	20	0	5.31
Hi Bell	R	26	3	8	.273	1	28	11	5	113	124	29	29	0	4.94
1 Bill Doak	R	33	2	1	.667	3	11	1	0	22	25	14	7	0	3.27
Flint Rhem	R	23	2	2	.500	1	6	3	3	32	31	17	20	0	4.50
Art Delaney	R	29	1	0	1.000	0	8	1	1	20	19	6	2	0	1.80
Jesse Fowler	L	25	1	1	.500	0	13	3	0	33	28	18	5	0	4.36
Pea Ridge Day	R	25	1	1	.500	0	3	3	1	18	22	6	3	0	4.50
Vince Shields	R	23	1	1	.500	0	2	1	0	12	10	3	4	0	3.00
1 Lou North	R	33	0	0	.000	0	6	0	0	15	15	9	8	0	6.60
Jack Berly	R	21	0	0	.000	0	4	0	0	8	8	4	2	0	5.63
Bob Vines	R	27	0	0	.000	0	2	0	0	11	23	0	0	0	9.00

PHILADELPHIA 7th 55-96 .364 37 — ART FLETCHER

NAME	G by POS	B	AGE	G	AB	R	H	2B	3B	HR	RBI	BB	SO	SB	BA	SA
TOTALS			29	152	5306	676	1459	256	56	94	615	382	452	57	.275	.397
Walter Holke	1B148	B	31	148	563	60	169	23	6	6	64	25	33	3	.300	.394
Hod Ford	2B145	R	26	145	530	58	144	27	5	3	53	27	40	1	.272	.358
Heinie Sand	SS137	R	26	137	539	79	132	21	6	6	40	52	57	5	.245	.340
Russ Wrightstone	3B97, 2B9, SS5, OF1	L	31	118	388	55	119	24	4	7	58	27	15	5	.307	.443
2 George Harper	OF109	L	32	109	411	68	121	26	6	16	55	38	23	10	.294	.504
Cy Williams	OF145	L	36	148	558	101	183	31	11	24	93	67	49	7	.328	.552
Johnny Mokan	OF94	R	28	96	366	50	95	15	1	7	44	30	27	7	.260	.363
Butch Henline	C83, OF2	R	29	115	289	41	82	18	4	5	35	27	15	1	.284	.426
Jimmie Wilson	C82, 1B2, OF1	R	23	95	280	32	78	16	3	6	39	17	12	5	.279	.421
2 Joe Schultz	OF76	R	30	88	284	35	80	15	1	5	29	20	18	6	.282	.394
Clarence Mitchell	P30	L	33	69	102	7	26	3	0	0	13	2	7	1	.255	.284
Frank Parkinson	3B28, SS21, 2B10	R	29	62	156	14	33	7	0	1	19	14	28	3	.212	.276
Andy Woehr	3B44, 2B1	R	28	50	152	11	33	4	5	0	17	5	8	2	.217	.309
Hal Carlson	P38	R	30	39	76	6	21	1	0	2	8	2	8	0	.276	.368
Fritz Henrich	OF32	L	25	36	90	4	19	4	0	0	4	2	12	0	.211	.256
1 Curt Walker	OF20	L	27	24	71	11	21	6	1	1	8	7	4	0	.296	.451
1 Cliff Lee	OF13, 1B4	R	27	21	56	4	14	3	2	1	7	2	5	0	.250	.429
Lew Wendell	C17	R	32	21	32	3	8	1	0	0	2	3	5	0	.250	.281

Freddy Leach 26 L 13-28, Lenny Metz 24 R 2-7, Spoke Emery 25 R 2-3

NAME	T	AGE	W	L	PCT	SV	G	GS	CG	IP	H	BB	SO	ShO	ERA
		30	55	96	.364	10	152	152	59	1355	**1689**	469	349	7	4.87
Bill Hubbell	R	27	10	9	.526	2	36	22	9	179	233	45	30	2	4.83
Jimmy Ring	R	29	10	12	.455	0	32	31	16	215	236	**108**	72	1	3.98
Hal Carlson	R	30	8	17	.320	2	38	24	12	204	267	55	66	1	4.85
Huck Betts	R	27	7	10	.412	2	37	9	2	144	160	42	46	0	4.31
Whitey Glazner	R	31	7	16	.304	0	35	24	8	157	210	63	41	2	5.85
Clarence Mitchell	L	33	6	13	.316	1	30	26	9	165	223	58	36	1	5.62
Johnny Couch	R	33	4	8	.333	3	37	6	3	137	170	39	23	0	4.73
2 Joe Oeschger	R	33	2	7	.222	0	19	8	0	65	88	16	8	0	4.43
2 Ray Steineder	R	28	1	1	.500	0	9	0	0	29	29	16	11	0	4.34
Bert Lewis	R	28	0	0	.000	0	12	0	0	18	23	7	3	0	6.00
Lefty Weinert	L	22	0	1	.000	0	8	1	0	15	10	11	7	0	2.40
Jim Bishop	R	26	0	1	.000	0	7	1	0	17	24	7	3	0	8.35
Earl Hamilton	L	32	0	1	.000	0	3	0	0	6	9	2	2	0	10.60
Lerton Pinto	L	26	0	0	.000	0	3	0	0	4	7	0	1	0	9.00

BOSTON 8th 53-100 .346 40 — DAVE BANCROFT

NAME	G by POS	B	AGE	G	AB	R	H	2B	3B	HR	RBI	BB	SO	SB	BA	SA
TOTALS			29	154	5283	520	1355	194	52	25	459	354	451	74	.256	.327
Stuffy McInnis	1B146	R	33	146	581	57	169	23	7	1	59	15	6	9	.291	.360
Cotton Tierney	2B115, 3B22	R	30	136	505	38	131	16	1	6	58	22	37	11	.259	.331
Bob Smith	SS80, 3B23	R	26	106	347	32	79	12	3	2	38	15	26	5	.228	.297
Ernie Padgett	3B113, 2B29	R	25	138	502	42	128	25	9	1	46	37	56	4	.255	.347
Casey Stengel	OF126	L	33	131	461	57	129	20	6	5	39	45	39	13	.280	.382
Frank Wilson	OF55	L	22	61	216	20	51	7	0	1	15	23	22	3	.237	.284
Bill Cunningham	OF109	R	28	114	437	44	119	15	8	1	40	32	27	8	.272	.350
Mickey O'Neil	C106	R	26	106	362	32	89	4	1	0	22	14	27	4	.246	.262
Frank Gibson	C46, 1B10, 3B2	L	33	90	229	25	71	15	6	1	30	10	23	1	.310	.441
Dave Bancroft (IL)	SS79	B	33	79	319	49	89	11	1	2	21	37	24	4	.279	.339
Ray Powell	OF46	L	35	74	188	21	49	9	1	1	15	21	28	1	.261	.335
Gus Felix	OF51	R	29	50	204	25	43	7	1	1	10	18	16	0	.211	.270
Johnny Cooney	P34, OF16, 1B1	R	23	55	130	10	33	2	1	0	4	9	5	0	.254	.285
1 Earl Smith	C13	L	27	33	59	1	16	3	0	0	8	6	3	0	.271	.322
Les Mann	OF28	R	30	32	102	13	28	7	4	0	10	8	10	1	.275	.422
Herb Thomas	OF32	R	22	32	127	12	28	4	1	1	8	9	8	5	.220	.291
Ed Sperber	OF17	L	29	24	59	8	17	2	0	1	12	10	9	3	.288	.373
Marty Shay	2B19, SS1	R	20	19	68	4	16	3	1	0	2	5	5	2	.235	.309

Walton Cruise 34 L 4-9, Hunter Lane 23 R 1-15, Eddie Phillips 23 R 0-3, Dee Cousineau 25 R 0-2, Al Hermann 23 R 0-1, John Kelleher 30 R 0-1, 1 Wade Lefler 28 L 0-1, Tony Boeckel (DD) 31

NAME	T	AGE	W	L	PCT	SV	G	GS	CG	IP	H	BB	SO	ShO	ERA
		26	53	**100**	.346	4	154	154	66	1379	1607	402	364	10	4.46
Jesse Barnes	R	31	15	**20**	.429	0	37	32	21	268	292	53	49	**4**	3.22
Joe Genewich	R	27	10	19	.345	1	34	27	11	200	258	65	43	2	5.22
Johnny Cooney	L	23	8	9	.471	2	34	19	12	181	176	50	67	2	3.18
Tim McNamara	R	25	8	12	.400	0	35	21	6	179	242	31	35	2	5.18
Larry Benton	R	26	5	7	.417	1	30	13	4	128	129	64	41	0	4.15
Dutch Stryker	R	28	3	8	.273	0	20	10	2	73	90	22	22	0	6.04
Rube Marquard (IL)	L	34	1	2	.333	0	6	6	1	36	33	13	10	0	3.00
2 Lou North	R	33	1	2	.333	0	9	4	1	35	45	19	11	0	5.40
Red Lucas	R	22	1	4	.200	0	27	4	1	84	112	18	30	0	5.14
Al Yeargin	R	22	1	11	.083	0	32	12	6	141	162	42	34	0	5.11
Kyle Graham	R	24	0	4	.000	0	5	4	1	33	33	11	15	0	3.82
Joe Muich	R	20	0	0	.000	0	3	0	0	9	19	5	1	0	11.00
Joe Batchelder (IL)	L	25	0	0	.000	0	3	0	0	5	4	2	2	0	3.60
Ike Kamp	L	23	0	1	.000	0	1	1	0	7	9	5	4	0	5.14
2 Dinty Gearin	L	26	0	1	.000	0	1	1	0	0	3	2	0	0	∞

WORLD SERIES – WASHINGTON (AL) 4 NEW YORK (NL) 3

LINE SCORES

TEAM	1	2	3	4	5	6	7	8	9	10	11	12	R	H	E
Game 1 October 4 at Washington															
NY (NL)	0	1	0	1	0	0	0	0	0	0	0	2	4	14	1
WAS	0	0	0	0	0	1	0	0	1	0	0	1	3	10	1
Nehf — Johnson															
Game 2 October 5 at Washington															
NY	0	0	0	0	0	0	1	0	2				3	6	0
WAS	2	0	0	0	1	0	0	0	1				4	6	1
Bentley — **Zachary**, Marberry (9)															
Game 3 October 6 at New York															
WAS	0	0	0	2	0	0	0	1	1				4	9	2
NY	0	2	1	1	0	1	0	1	X				6	12	0
Marberry, Russell (4), Martina (7), Speece (8) — **McQuillan**, Ryan (4), Jonnard (9), Watson (9)															
Game 4 October 7 at New York															
WAS	0	0	3	0	2	0	0	2	0				7	13	3
NY	1	0	0	0	0	1	0	1	1				4	6	1
Mogridge, Marberry (8) — **Barnes**, Baldwin (6), Dean (8)															
Game 5 October 8 at New York															
WAS	0	0	0	1	0	0	0	1	0				2	9	1
NY	0	0	1	0	2	0	0	3	X				6	13	0
Johnson — **Bentley**, McQuillan (8)															
Game 6 October 9 at Washington															
NY	1	0	0	0	0	0	0	0	0				1	7	1
WAS	0	0	0	0	2	0	0	0	X				2	4	0
Nehf, Ryan (8) — **Zachary**															
Game 7 October 10 at Washington															
NY	0	0	0	0	0	3	0	0	0	0	0	0	3	8	3
WAS	0	0	0	1	0	0	0	2	0	0	0	1	4	10	4
Barnes, Nehf (8), McQuillan (9), **Bentley** (11) — Ogden, Modgridge (1), Marberry (6), **Johnson** (9)															

COMPOSITE BATTING

NAME	POS	G	AB	R	H	2B	3B	HR	RBI	BA
Washington (AL)										
Totals		7	248	26	61	9	0	5	24	.246
Harris	2B	7	**33**	5	**11**	0	0	2	7	.333
Goslin	OF	7	32	4	**11**	1	0	**3**	**7**	.344
Rice	OF	7	29	2	6	0	0	0	1	.207
McNeely	OF	7	27	4	6	3	0	0	1	.222
Judge	1B	7	26	4	10	1	0	0	0	.385
Bluege	3B-SS	7	26	2	5	0	0	0	2	.192
Ruel	C	7	21	2	2	1	0	0	0	.095
Peckinpaugh	SS	4	12	1	5	2	0	0	2	.417
Miller	3B	4	11	0	2	0	0	0	2	.182
Johnson	P	3	9	0	1	0	0	0	0	.111
Leibold	OF	3	6	1	1	1	0	0	0	.167
Mogridge	P	2	5	0	0	0	0	0	0	.000
Zachary	P	2	5	0	0	0	0	0	0	.000
Shirley	PH	3	2	1	1	0	0	0	1	.500
Marberry	P	4	2	0	0	0	0	0	0	.000
Taylor	3B	3	2	0	0	0	0	0	0	.000
Tate	PH	3	0	0	0	0	0	0	1	.000
Martina	P	1	0	0	0	0	0	0	0	.000
Ogden	P	1	0	0	0	0	0	0	0	.000
Russell	P	1	0	0	0	0	0	0	0	.000
Speece	P	1	0	0	0	0	0	0	0	.000
New York (NL)										
Totals		7	253	27	66	9	2	4	22	.261
Kelly	OF-2B-1B	7	31	**7**	9	1	0	1	4	.290
Lindstrom	3B	7	30	1	10	2	0	0	4	.333
Frisch	2B-3B	7	30	1	10	**4**	1	0	0	.333
Wilson	OF	7	30	1	7	1	0	0	3	.233
Gowdy	C	7	27	4	7	0	0	0	2	.259
Youngs	OF	7	27	3	5	1	0	0	2	.185
Jackson	SS	7	27	3	2	0	0	0	1	.074
Terry	1B	5	14	3	6	0	1	1	1	**.429**
Meusel	OF	4	13	0	2	0	0	0	1	.154
Nehf	P	3	7	1	3	0	0	0	0	.429
Bentley	P	5	7	1	2	0	0	1	2	.286
Barnes	P	2	4	0	0	0	0	0	0	.000
Ryan	P	2	2	1	1	0	0	1	1	.500
McQuillan	P	3	1	0	1	0	0	0	1	1.000
Groh	PH	1	1	0	1	0	0	0	0	1.000
Southworth	OF	5	1	1	0	0	0	0	0	.000
Snyder	PH	1	1	0	0	0	0	0	0	.000
Baldwin	P	1	0	0	0	0	0	0	0	.000

Dean P 0-0, Jonnard P 0-0, Watson P 0-0

COMPOSITE PITCHING

NAME	G	IP	H	BB	SO	W	L	SV	ERA
Washington (AL)									
Totals	7	67	66	25	40	4	3	2	2.15
Johnson	3	**24**	**30**	**11**	**20**	1	**2**	0	2.25
Zachary	2	17.2	13	3	3	**2**	0	0	2.04
Mogridge	2	12	7	6	5	1	0	0	2.25
Marberry	**4**	8	9	4	10	0	1	**2**	**1.13**
Russell	1	3	4	0	0	0	0	0	3.00
Martina	1	1	0	0	1	0	0	0	0.00
Speece	1	1	3	0	0	0	0	0	9.00
Ogden	1	.1	0	1	1	0	0	0	0.00
New York (NL)									
Totals	7	66.2	61	29	34	3	4	2	3.24
Nehf	3	19.2	15	9	7	1	1	0	1.83
Bentley	3	17	18	8	10	1	2	0	3.71
Barnes	2	12.2	15	1	9	0	1	0	5.68
McQuillan	3	7	2	6	2	1	0	1	2.57
Ryan	2	5.2	7	4	3	0	0	0	3.18
Baldwin	1	2	1	0	1	0	0	0	0.00
Dean	1	2	3	0	2	0	0	0	4.50
Watson	1	.2	0	0	0	0	0	1	0.00
Jonnard	1	0	0	1	0	0	0	0	0.00

1925 The Abdominal Disaster That Ached a Dynasty

The world, or at least that part of it which included baseball in its territorial domain, was in for the greatest disillusionment since the 1919 World Series scandal. Oddly enough, the man most responsible for restoring the faith of the nation in the national game, also became the catalyst for destroying that faith again. This time, though, it was not the shock of immorality, but that baseball's super plus superstar was human after all.

Babe Ruth's popular image rested not only on his home run hitting, but also upon his prodigious appetites: for soda pop, for hot dogs, for alcohol, for steak, for women, for the night life, for the good life, for life itself. The Babe touched all bases, even off the diamond, and a winter of burning the candle at both ends inevitably caught up with him when he keeled over on April 8, as the Yankees were in the final stages of spring training. The press bellowed over Ruth's "bellyache" as the Bambino returned to New York for surgery to remove an intestinal abscess—an operation which would lay the slugger up until June. The Yankees had just missed out on a fourth straight pennant in 1924 and expected to return to the top once again. The absence of Ruth and the onslaughts of age, however, sapped the Bronx Bombers of their strength and desire, and the Yanks limped home a weak seventh. Even after his return, Ruth performed at less-than-peak efficiency, and a miserable season came to an early end for the Babe when manager Miller Huggins suspended him in September and slapped him with a record $5,000 fine for insubordination and constant breaking of club training rules. Out of the rubble, though, rose a new Yankee powerhouse. Lou Gehrig took over first base from Wally Pipp, Earle Combs established himself in center field, and shortstop Mark Koenig joined the team late in the year.

With the Yankees out of competition, the Senators and Athletics battled it out for the pennant, and the veteran Washington team pulled away from Connie Mack's young squad when the A's went into a 12-game tailspin in August. The Senators boasted of the league's best pitching in what was a hitter's year, as they posted a league-low 3.67 E.R.A. Thirty-seven-year-old Walter Johnson squeezed enough fastballs out of his right arm to win 20 games, while 35-year-old Stan Coveleski came over from Cleveland to notch 20 victories and 33-year-old Dutch Reuther chalked up 18 victories after being picked up on waivers from the National League. And when the aged starting staff ran into trouble, it fell back for help onto big Firpo Marberry, one of the first of baseball's great relief specialists, who posted a league-leading 15 saves. Twenty-eight-year-old Bucky Harris was the boy manager of the squad, and he and Roger Peckinpaugh held the defense together with their play at second base and shortstop.

The New York Giants dropped out of the first place slot after four straight National League pennants, giving way to a young Pittsburgh Pirate team. The Bucs defeated the Giants with a hard-hitting lineup, led by Max Carey and Kiki Cuyler, and a deep pitching staff which held no stars, but five solid starters. Rogers Hornsby proved to be the story of the year, winning the Triple Crown by hitting .403, swatting 39 homers, and driving 143 runs across the plate. In addition, the Cardinal second baseman succeeded Branch Rickey as manager after a slow start and brought the team up to a fourth place finish.

In the World Series, the Pirates became the first team in history to come back from a 3-1 deficit in games to win the championship. Although the Senators got stellar performances from Walter Johnson, Goose Goslin, Joe Harris, and Sam Rice, star shortstop Roger Peckinpaugh committed eight errors during the Series to keep the Bucs in the fray. The decisive seventh game was played in a steady downpour and was decided on Cuyler's double in the eighth inning, which scored the winning runs to defeat Walter Johnson and the Senators, 9 to 7.

1925 AMERICAN LEAGUE

NAME	G by POS	B	AGE	G	AB	R	H	2B	3B	HR	RBI	BB	SO	SB	BA	SA
WASHINGTON 1st 96-55 .636		BUCKY HARRIS														
TOTALS			30	152	5206	829	1577	251	72	56	747	533	427	**140**	.303	.411
Joe Judge	1B109	L	31	112	376	65	118	31	5	8	66	55	21	7	.314	.487
Bucky Harris	2B144	R	28	144	551	91	158	30	3	1	66	64	21	14	.287	.358
Roger Peckinpaugh	SS124, 1B1	R	34	126	422	67	124	16	4	4	64	49	23	13	.294	.379
Ossie Bluege	3B144, SS4	R	24	145	522	77	150	27	4	4	79	59	56	16	.287	.377
Sam Rice	OF152	L	35	152	649	111	227	31	13	1	87	37	10	26	.350	.442
Earl McNeely	OF112, 1B1	R	27	122	385	76	110	14	2	3	37	48	54	14	.286	.356
Goose Goslin	OF150	L	24	150	601	116	201	34	**20**	18	113	53	50	26	.334	.547
Muddy Ruel	C126, 1B1	R	29	127	393	55	122	9	2	0	54	63	16	4	.310	.346
2 Joe Harris	1B57, OF41	R	34	100	300	60	97	21	9	12	59	51	28	5	.323	.573
Nemo Leibold	OF26, 3B1	L	33	56	84	14	23	1	1	0	7	8	7	1	.274	.310
Dutch Ruether	P30, 1B1	L	31	55	108	18	36	3	2	1	15	10	8	0	.333	.426
2 Hank Severeid	C35	R	34	50	110	11	39	8	1	0	14	11	6	0	.355	.445
Spencer Adams	2B15, SS8, 3B3	L	27	39	55	11	15	4	1	0	4	5	4	1	.273	.382
Walter Johnson	P30	R	37	36	97	12	42	6	1	2	20	3	6	0	.433	.577
2 Everett Scott	SS30, 3B2	R	32	33	103	10	28	6	1	0	18	4	4	1	.272	.350
3 Bobby Veach	OF11	L	37	18	37	4	9	3	0	0	8	3	3	0	.243	.324
Bennie Tate	C14	L	23	16	27	0	13	3	0	0	7	2	2	0	.481	.593
Tex Jeanes	OF13	R	24	15	19	2	5	1	0	1	4	3	2	1	.263	.474
Mule Shirley	1B9	L	24	14	23	2	3	1	0	0	2	1	7	0	.130	.174
Mike McNally	3B7, SS2, 2B1	R	31	12	21	1	3	0	0	0	0	1	4	0	.143	.143

Wid Matthews 28 L 4-9, Stuffy Stewart 31 R 6-17, 1 Pinky Hargrave 23 R 3-6, Buddy Myer 21 L 2-8, Tubby McGee 26 R 0-3, 1 Roy Carlyle 26 L 0-1, Patsy Gharrity (DE) 23

NAME	T	AGE	W	L	PCT	SV	G	GS	CG	IP	H	BB	SO	ShO	ERA
		32	**96**	55	**.636**	**21**	152	152	69	1358	1426	543	464	9	**3.67**
Stan Coveleski	R	36	20	5	**.800**	0	32	32	15	241	230	73	58	3	**2.84**
Walter Johnson	R	37	20	7	.741	0	30	29	16	229	211	78	108	3	3.07
Dutch Ruether	L	31	18	7	.720	0	30	29	16	223	241	105	68	1	3.87
Tom Zachary	L	29	12	15	.444	2	38	33	11	218	247	74	58	1	3.84
Firpo Marberry	R	26	8	6	.571	**15**	**55**	0	0	93	84	45	53	0	3.48
3 Alex Ferguson	R	28	5	1	.833	0	7	6	3	55	52	23	24	0	3.27
1 George Mogridge	L	36	4	3	.571	0	10	8	3	53	56	18	13	0	3.40
Curly Ogden	R	24	3	1	.750	0	17	4	2	42	45	18	6	1	4.50
Vean Gregg	L	40	2	2	.500	2	26	5	1	74	87	38	18	0	4.14
Allen Russell	R	31	2	4	.333	2	32	2	0	69	85	37	25	0	5.74
Win Ballou	R	27	1	1	.500	0	10	1	1	28	38	13	13	0	4.50
Harry Kelley	R	19	1	1	.500	0	6	1	0	16	30	12	7	0	9.00
Jim Lyle	R	22	0	0	.000	0	1	0	0	3	5	1	3	0	6.00
Spence Pumpelly	R	32	0	0	.000	0	1	0	0	1	1	1	0	0	9.00
Lefty Thomas	L	21	0	2	.000	0	2	2	1	13	14	7	10	0	2.08

NAME	G by POS	B	AGE	G	AB	R	H	2B	3B	HR	RBI	BB	SO	SB	BA	SA
PHILADELPHIA 2nd 88-64 .579 8.5		CONNIE MACK														
TOTALS			27	153	5399	830	**1659**	298	79	76	767	453	432	67	**.307**	.434
Jim Poole	1B123	L	30	133	480	65	143	29	8	5	67	27	37	5	.298	.423
Max Bishop	2B104	L	25	105	368	66	103	18	4	4	27	87	37	5	.280	.383
Chuck Galloway	SS148	R	28	149	481	52	116	11	4	3	71	59	28	16	.241	.299
Sammy Hale	3B96, 2B1	R	28	110	391	62	135	30	11	8	63	17	27	7	.345	.540
Bing Miller	OF115, 1B12	R	30	124	474	78	151	29	10	10	81	19	14	11	.319	.485
Al Simmons	OF153	R	23	153	**658**	122	**253**	43	12	24	129	35	41	7	.384	.596
Bill Lamar	OF131	L	28	138	568	85	202	39	8	3	77	21	17	2	.356	.468
Mickey Cochrane	C133	L	22	134	420	69	139	21	5	6	55	44	19	7	.331	.448
Jimmy Dykes	3B64, 2B58, SS2	R	28	122	465	93	150	32	11	5	55	46	49	3	.323	.471
Frank Welch	OF57	R	27	85	202	40	56	5	4	4	41	29	14	2	.277	.401
Walt French	OF19	L	25	67	100	20	37	9	0	0	14	1	9	1	.370	.460
Cy Perkins	C58, 3B1	R	29	65	140	21	43	10	0	1	18	26	6	0	.307	.400
Bill Bagwell	OF4	L	29	36	50	4	15	2	1	0	10	2	2	0	.300	.380
Red Holt	1B25	L	30	27	88	13	24	7	0	1	8	12	9	0	.273	.386
Red Smith	SS16, 3B2	L	24	20	14	1	4	0	0	0	1	2	5	0	.286	.286
Charlie Berry	C4	R	22	10	14	1	3	1	0	0	3	0	2	0	.214	.286
Jimmie Foxx	C1	R	17	10	9	2	6	1	0	0	0	0	1	0	.667	.778
Carl Husta	SS6	R	23	6	22	2	3	0	0	0	2	2	3	0	.136	.136
Jim Keesey	1B2	R	22	5	5	1	2	0	0	0	1	0	2	0	.400	.400
1 Doc Gautreau	2B4	R	23	4	7	0	0	0	0	0	0	0	3	0	.000	.000
Charlie Engle	SS1	R	21	1	0	0	0	0	0	0	0	0	0	0	.000	.000

Joe Hauser (BK) 26

NAME	T	AGE	W	L	PCT	SV	G	GS	CG	IP	H	BB	SO	ShO	ERA
		29	88	64	.579	18	153	153	61	1373	1468	544	**495**	8	3.89
Eddie Rommel	R	27	**21**	10	.677	3	52	28	14	261	285	95	67	1	3.69
Slim Harriss	R	28	19	12	.613	1	46	**33**	15	252	263	95	95	2	3.50
Sam Gray (BG)	R	27	16	8	.667	3	32	28	14	196	199	63	80	4	3.39
Lefty Grove	L	25	10	12	.455	1	45	18	5	197	207	**131**	**116**	0	4.75
Rube Walberg	L	25	8	14	.364	7	53	20	7	192	197	77	82	0	3.98
Stan Baumgartner	L	32	6	3	.667	3	37	11	2	113	120	35	18	1	3.58
2 Jack Quinn	R	41	6	3	.667	0	18	14	4	100	119	16	19	0	3.87
Tom Glass	R	27	1	0	1.000	0	2	0	0	5	9	0	2	0	5.40
Art Stokes	R	28	1	1	.500	0	12	0	0	24	24	10	7	0	4.12
Elbert Andrews	R	23	0	0	.000	0	6	0	0	8	12	11	0	0	10.13
Fred Heimach (SJ)	L	24	0	1	.000	0	10	0	0	20	24	9	6	0	4.05
Lefty Willis	L	19	0	0	.000	0	1	1	0	5	9	2	3	0	10.80

NAME	G by POS	B	AGE	G	AB	R	H	2B	3B	HR	RBI	BB	SO	SB	BA	SA
ST. LOUIS 3rd 82-71 .536 15		GEORGE SISLER														
TOTALS			29	154	**5440**	897	1620	**304**	68	**110**	798	498	375	85	.298	**.439**
George Sisler	1B150, P1	L	32	150	649	100	224	21	15	12	105	27	24	11	.345	.479
Marty McManus	2B154, OF1	R	25	154	587	108	169	**44**	8	13	90	73	**69**	5	.288	.457
Bobby LaMotte	SS93, 3B3	R	27	97	356	61	97	20	4	2	51	34	22	5	.272	.368
Gene Robertson	3B154, SS1	L	25	154	582	97	158	26	5	14	76	81	30	10	.271	.405
Harry Rice	OF85, 1B3, 2B1, 3B1, C1	L	24	103	354	87	127	25	8	11	47	54	15	8	.359	.568
Baby Doll Jacobson	OF139	R	34	142	540	103	184	30	9	15	76	45	26	8	.341	.513
Ken Williams (PB)	OF102	L	35	102	411	83	136	31	5	25	105	37	14	10	.331	**.613**
Leo Dixon	C75	R	28	76	205	27	46	11	1	1	19	24	42	3	.224	.302
Herschel Bennett	OF73	L	28	93	298	46	83	11	6	2	37	18	16	4	.279	.376
Jack Tobin	OF39, 1B3	L	33	77	193	25	58	11	0	2	27	9	5	8	.301	.389
Wally Gerber (BL)	SS71	R	33	72	246	29	67	13	1	0	19	26	15	1	.272	.333
2 Pinky Hargrave	C62	R	29	67	225	34	64	15	2	8	43	13	13	2	.284	.476
Bullet Joe Bush	P33, OF1	R	32	57	102	10	26	12	0	2	18	6	8	2	.255	.431
Joe Evans	OF47	R	30	55	159	27	50	12	0	0	20	16	6	6	.314	.390
1 Hank Severeid	C31	R	34	34	109	15	40	9	0	1	21	11	2	0	.367	.477
Tony Rego	C19	R	27	20	32	5	13	2	1	0	3	3	2	0	.406	.531
Johnny Austin	3B1	B	45	1	1	0	0	0	0	0	0	0	0	0	.000	.000

NAME	T	AGE	W	L	PCT	SV	G	GS	CG	IP	H	BB	SO	ShO	ERA
		30	82	71	.536	10	154	154	67	**1393**	1598	**675**	419	7	4.85
Milt Gaston	R	29	15	14	.517	1	42	30	16	239	284	101	84	0	4.41
Bullet Joe Bush	R	32	14	14	.500	0	33	28	15	214	239	91	63	2	4.96
Elam Vangilder	R	29	14	8	.636	6	52	16	4	193	225	92	61	1	4.71
Dixie Davis	R	34	12	7	.632	1	35	23	9	180	192	106	58	0	4.60
Joe Giard	L	26	10	5	.667	0	30	21	9	161	179	87	43	4	5.03
Ernie Wingard	L	24	9	10	.474	0	32	18	8	153	184	77	20	0	5.06
Dave Danforth	L	35	7	9	.438	2	38	15	5	159	172	61	53	0	4.36
2 George Mogridge (AJ)	L	36	1	1	.500	0	2	2	1	15	17	5	8	0	6.00
George Blaeholder	R	21	0	0	.000	0	2	0	0	2	6	1	1	0	31.50
Chet Falk	L	20	0	0	.000	0	13	0	0	25	38	17	7	0	8.28
George Grant	R	22	0	2	.000	0	12	0	0	16	26	8	7	0	6.19
George Sisler	L	32	0	0	.000	0	1	0	0	2	1	1	1	0	0.00
Brad Springer	L	21	0	0	.000	0	2	0	0	3	1	7	0	0	3.00
Ed Stauffer	R	27	0	1	.000	0	20	1	0	30	34	21	13	0	5.41

DETROIT 4th 81-73 .526 16.5 — TY COBB

NAME	G by POS	B	AGE	G	AB	R	H	2B	3B	HR	RBI	BB	SO	SB	BA	SA
TOTALS			28	156	5371	903	1621	277	84	50	797	640	386	97	.302	.412
Lu Blue	1B148	B	28	150	532	91	163	18	9	3	94	83	29	19	.306	.391
Frank O'Rourke	2B118	R	30	124	482	88	141	40	7	5	57	32	37	5	.293	.436
Jackie Tavener	SS134	L	27	134	453	45	111	11	11	0	47	39	60	5	.245	.318
Fred Haney	3B107	R	27	114	398	84	111	15	3	0	40	66	29	11	.279	.332
Harry Heilmann	OF148	R	30	150	573	97	225	40	11	13	133	67	27	6	.393	.569
Ty Cobb	OF105, P1	L	38	121	415	97	157	31	12	12	102	65	12	13	.378	.598
Al Wingo	OF122	L	27	130	440	104	163	34	10	5	68	69	31	14	.370	.527
John Bassler	C118	L	30	121	344	40	96	19	3	0	52	74	6	1	.279	.352
Heinie Manush	OF73	L	23	99	277	46	84	14	3	5	47	24	21	8	.303	.430
Les Burke	2B52	L	22	77	180	32	52	6	3	0	24	17	8	4	.289	.356
Larry Woodall	C75	R	30	75	171	20	35	4	1	0	13	24	8	1	.205	.240
Bob Fothergill	OF59	R	27	71	204	38	72	14	0	2	28	6	3	2	.353	.451
Topper Rigney	SS51, 3B4	R	28	62	146	21	36	5	2	2	18	21	15	2	.247	.349
Johnny Neun	1B13	B	24	60	75	15	20	3	3	0	4	9	12	2	.267	.387
Bob Jones	3B46	L	35	50	148	18	35	6	0	0	15	9	5	1	.236	.277
Jack Warner	3B10	R	21	10	39	7	13	0	0	0	2	3	6	0	.333	.333
Charlie Gehringer	2B6	L	22	8	18	3	3	0	0	0	0	2	0	0	.167	.167
Oscar Stanage	C3	R	42	3	5	0	1	0	0	0	0	0	0	0	.200	.200
Andy Harrington		R	22	1	1	0	0	0	0	0	0	0	0	0	.000	.000

NAME	T	AGE	W	L	PCT	SV	G	GS	CG	IP	H	BB	SO	ShO	ERA
		28	81	73	.526	18	156	156	66	1384	1582	556	419	2	4.61
Hooks Dauss	R	35	16	11	.593	1	35	30	16	228	238	85	58	1	3.16
Ken Hollaway	R	27	13	4	.765	2	38	14	6	158	170	67	29	0	4.61
Earl Whitehill	L	25	11	11	.500	2	35	33	15	239	267	88	83	1	4.67
Dutch Leonard (SA)	L	33	11	4	.733	0	18	18	9	126	143	43	65	0	4.50
Lil Stoner	R	26	10	9	.526	1	34	18	8	152	166	53	51	0	4.26
Rip Collins	R	29	6	11	.353	0	26	20	5	140	149	52	33	0	4.56
Ed Wells	L	25	6	9	.400	2	35	14	5	134	190	62	45	0	6.19
Jess Doyle	R	27	4	7	.364	8	45	3	0	118	158	50	31	0	5.84
Ownie Carroll	R	22	2	2	.750	0	10	4	1	41	46	28	12	0	3.73
1 Bert Cole	L	27	2	3	.400	1	14	2	1	34	44	15	7	0	5.82
Ty Cobb	L	38	0	0	.000	1	1	0	0	1	0	0	0	0	0.00
Syl Johnson (BY)	R	24	0	2	.000	0	6	0	0	13	11	10	5	0	3.46
Bill Moore	R	22	0	0	.000	0	1	0	0	0	0	3	0	0	∞

CHICAGO 5th 79-75 .513 18.5 — EDDIE COLLINS

NAME	G by POS	B	AGE	G	AB	R	H	2B	3B	HR	RBI	BB	SO	SB	BA	SA
TOTALS			30	154	5224	811	1482	299	59	38	738	662	405	131	.284	.385
Earl Sheely	1B153	R	32	153	600	93	189	43	3	9	111	68	23	3	.315	.442
Eddie Collins (LJ)	2B116	L	38	118	425	80	147	26	3	3	80	87	8	19	.346	.442
Ike Davis	SS144	R	30	146	562	105	135	31	9	0	61	71	58	19	.240	.327
Willie Kamm	3B152	R	25	152	509	82	142	32	4	6	83	90	36	11	.279	.393
Harry Hooper	OF124	L	37	127	442	62	117	23	5	6	55	54	21	12	.265	.380
Johnny Mostil	OF153	R	29	153	605	135	181	36	16	2	50	90	52	43	.299	.421
Bibb Falk	OF154	L	26	154	602	80	181	35	9	4	99	51	25	4	.301	.409
Ray Schalk	C125	R	32	125	343	44	94	18	1	0	52	57	27	11	.274	.332
Bill Barrett	2B41, OF27, SS4, 3B4	R	25	81	245	44	89	23	3	3	40	24	27	5	.363	.518
Spence Harris	OF27	L	24	56	92	12	26	2	0	1	13	14	13	1	.283	.337
Buck Crouse	C48	L	28	54	131	18	46	7	0	2	25	12	4	1	.351	.450
Sloppy Thurston	P36	R	26	44	84	2	24	7	2	0	13	5	13	0	.286	.417
Roy Elsh	OF16, 1B3	R	29	32	48	6	9	1	0	0	4	5	7	2	.188	.208
Johnny Grabowski	C21	R	25	21	46	5	14	4	1	0	10	2	4	0	.304	.435
John Kane	SS8, 2B6	B	25	14	56	6	10	1	0	0	3	0	3	0	.179	.196
Maurice Archdeacon	OF1	L	28	10	9	2	1	0	0	0	0	2	1	0	.111	.111
1 George Bischoff	C4	R	30	7	11	1	1	0	0	0	0	1	5	0	.091	.091
Bud Clancy		L	24	4	3	0	0	0	0	0	0	1	0	0	.000	.000
Jule Mallonee	OF1	L	25	2	3	1	0	0	0	0	0	1	0	0	.000	.000
Leo Tankersley	C1	R	24	1	3	0	0	0	0	0	0	0	0	0	.000	.000

NAME	T	AGE	W	L	PCT	SV	G	GS	CG	IP	H	BB	SO	ShO	ERA
		27	79	75	.513	13	154	154	71	1369	1583	493	375	12	4.34
Ted Lyons	R	24	21	11	.656	3	43	32	19	263	274	83	45	5	3.25
Ted Blankenship	R	24	17	8	.680	1	40	23	16	222	218	69	81	3	3.16
Red Faber	R	36	12	11	.522	0	34	32	16	238	266	59	71	1	3.78
Sloppy Thurston	R	26	10	14	.417	1	36	25	9	175	250	47	35	0	6.17
Charlie Robertson	R	29	8	12	.400	0	24	23	6	137	181	47	27	2	5.26
Sarge Connally	R	26	6	7	.462	8	40	2	0	108	126	62	46	0	4.75
Mike Cvengros	L	23	3	9	.250	0	22	11	4	105	109	55	32	0	4.28
2 Jim Joe Edwards	L	30	1	2	.333	0	9	4	1	45	46	23	20	1	4.00
Leo Mangum	R	28	1	0	1.000	0	7	0	0	15	25	6	6	0	7.80
Ken Ash	R	23	0	0	.000	0	2	0	0	4	7	0	0	0	9.00
Chief Bender	R	42	0	0	.000	0	1	0	0	1	1	1	0	0	18.00
Jake Freeze	R	25	0	0	.000	0	2	0	0	4	5	3	1	0	2.25
Dickie Kerr	L	31	0	1	.000	0	12	2	0	37	45	18	4	0	5.11
Frank Mack	R	25	0	0	.000	0	8	0	0	13	24	13	6	0	9.69
Tink Riviere	R	25	0	0	.000	0	2	0	0	2	6	7	1	0	31.50

CLEVELAND 6th 70-84 .455 27.5 — TRIS SPEAKER

NAME	G by POS	B	AGE	G	AB	R	H	2B	3B	HR	RBI	BB	SO	SB	BA	SA
TOTALS			28	155	5436	782	1613	285	58	52	697	520	379	90	.297	.399
George Burns	1B126	R	32	127	488	69	164	41	4	6	79	24	24	16	.336	.473
Chick Fewster	2B86, 3B10, OF1	R	29	93	294	39	73	16	1	1	38	36	25	6	.248	.320
Joe Sewell	SS153, 2B3	L	26	155	608	78	204	37	7	1	98	64	4	7	.336	.424
Rube Lutzke	3B69, 2B10	R	27	81	238	31	52	9	0	1	16	26	29	2	.218	.269
Pat McNulty	OF111	L	26	118	373	70	117	18	2	6	43	47	23	7	.314	.421
Tris Speaker	OF109	L	37	117	429	79	167	35	5	12	87	70	12	5	.389	.578
Charlie Jamieson	OF135	L	32	138	557	109	165	24	5	4	42	72	26	14	.296	.379
Glenn Myatt	C98, OF1	L	27	106	358	51	97	15	9	11	54	29	24	2	.271	.455
Freddie Spurgeon	3B56, 2B46, SS3	R	23	107	376	50	108	9	3	0	32	15	21	8	.287	.327
Cliff Lee	OF70	R	28	77	230	43	74	15	6	4	42	21	33	2	.322	.491
Homer Summa	OF54, 3B2	L	26	75	224	28	74	10	1	0	25	13	6	3	.330	.384
Luke Sewell	C66, OF2	R	24	74	220	30	51	10	2	0	18	33	18	6	.232	.295
George Uhle	P29	R	26	55	101	10	29	3	3	0	13	7	7	0	.287	.376
Ray Knode (BZ)	1B34	L	24	45	108	13	27	5	0	0	11	10	4	3	.250	.296
Joe Klugmann	2B29, 1B4, 3B2	R	30	38	85	12	28	9	2	0	12	8	4	3	.329	.482
Johnny Hodapp	3B37	R	19	37	130	12	31	5	1	0	14	11	7	2	.238	.292
Sherry Smith	P31	L	34	31	92	9	28	3	1	1	15	6	13	1	.304	.391
Harvey Hendrick	1B3	L	27	25	28	2	8	1	2	0	9	3	6	0	.286	.464
Riggs Stephenson	OF16	R	27	19	54	8	16	3	1	1	9	7	3	1	.296	.444
Fred Eichrodt	OF13	R	22	15	52	4	12	3	1	0	4	2	7	0	.231	.327

Roxy Walters 32 R 4-20, Chuck Tolson 23 R 3-12, Jim Bedford 21 R 0-3, Frank McCrea 28 R 1-5, Dutch Ussat 21 R 0-1

NAME	T	AGE	W	L	PCT	SV	G	GS	CG	IP	H	BB	SO	ShO	ERA
		28	70	84	.455	9	155	155	93	1372	1604	493	345	6	4.49
Garland Buckeye	L	27	13	8	.619	0	30	18	11	153	161	58	49	1	3.65
George Uhle	R	26	13	11	.542	0	29	26	17	211	218	78	68	1	4.10
Benn Karr	R	31	11	12	.478	0	32	24	12	198	248	80	41	1	4.77
Sherry Smith	L	34	11	14	.440	1	31	30	22	237	296	48	30	1	4.86
Jake Miller	L	27	10	13	.435	2	32	22	13	190	207	62	51	0	3.31
Joe Shaute	L	25	4	12	.250	4	26	17	10	131	160	44	34	1	5.43
By Speece	R	28	3	5	.375	1	28	3	3	90	106	28	26	0	4.30
Carl Yowell	L	22	2	3	.400	1	12	4	1	36	40	17	12	0	4.50
Ray Benge	R	23	1	0	1.000	0	2	2	1	12	9	3	3	1	1.50
2 Bert Cole	L	27	1	1	.500	1	13	2	0	44	55	25	9	0	6.14
Emil Levsen	R	27	1	2	.333	0	4	3	2	24	30	16	9	0	5.62
1 Jim Joe Edwards	L	30	0	3	.000	0	13	3	1	36	60	23	12	0	8.25
Luther Roy	R	22	0	0	.000	0	6	1	0	10	14	11	1	0	3.60

NEW YORK 7th 69-85 .448 28.5 — MILLER HUGGINS

NAME	G by POS	B	AGE	G	AB	R	H	2B	3B	HR	RBI	BB	SO	SB	BA	SA
TOTALS			29	156	5353	706	1471	247	74	110	638	470	482	67	.275	.410
Lou Gehrig	1B114, OF6	L	22	126	437	73	129	23	10	20	68	46	49	6	.295	.531
Aaron Ward	2B113, 3B10	R	28	125	439	41	108	22	3	4	38	49	49	1	.246	.337
Pee Wee Wanninger	SS111, 3B3, 2B1	L	22	117	403	35	95	13	6	1	22	11	34	3	.236	.305
Joe Dugan	3B96	R	28	102	404	50	118	19	4	0	31	19	20	2	.292	.359
Babe Ruth (IL)	OF98	L	30	98	359	61	104	12	2	25	66	59	68	2	.290	.543
Earle Combs	OF150	L	26	150	593	117	203	36	13	3	61	65	43	12	.342	.462
Bob Meusel	OF131, 3B27	R	28	156	624	101	181	34	12	33	138	54	55	10	.290	.542
Benny Bengough	C94	R	26	95	283	17	73	14	2	0	23	19	9	0	.258	.322
Ben Paschal	OF66	R	29	89	247	49	89	16	5	12	56	22	29	14	.360	.611
Ernie Johnson	2B34, SS28, 3B2	L	37	76	170	30	48	5	1	5	17	8	10	6	.282	.412
Wally Schang	C58	B	35	73	167	17	40	8	1	2	24	17	9	3	.240	.335
Howard Shanks	3B26, 2B1, OF4	R	34	66	155	15	40	3	1	1	18	20	15	1	.258	.310
Wally Pipp (PB)	1B47	L	32	62	178	19	41	6	3	3	24	13	12	3	.230	.348
2 Bobby Veach	OF33	L	37	56	116	13	41	10	2	0	15	8	0	1	.353	.474
Waite Hoyt	P46	R	25	46	79	5	24	2	3	0	8	2	1	0	.304	.405
Steve O'Neill	C31	R	33	35	91	7	26	5	0	1	13	10	3	0	.286	.374
Whitey Witt	OF10	L	29	31	40	9	8	2	1	0	0	6	2	1	.200	.300
Frank Koenig	SS28	B	22	28	110	14	23	6	1	0	4	5	4	0	.209	.282
1 Everett Scott	SS18	R	32	22	60	3	13	0	0	0	4	2	2	0	.217	.217

Roy Luebbe 24 B 0-15, Fred Merkle 36 R 5-13, Fred Hofmann 31 R 0-2, Leo Durocher 19 R 0-1, Heinie Odom 24 B 1-1

NAME	T	AGE	W	L	PCT	SV	G	GS	CG	IP	H	BB	SO	ShO	ERA
		29	69	85	.448	13	156	156	80	1388	1560	505	492	8	4.33
Herb Pennock	L	31	16	17	.485	2	47	31	21	277	267	71	88	2	2.96
Sad Sam Jones	R	32	15	21	.417	2	43	31	14	247	267	104	92	1	4.62
Urban Shocker	R	34	12	12	.500	2	41	30	15	244	278	58	74	2	3.65
Waite Hoyt	R	25	11	14	.440	6	46	30	17	243	283	78	86	1	4.00
Bob Shawkey	R	34	6	14	.300	0	33	20	9	186	209	67	81	1	4.11
2 Alex Ferguson	R	28	4	2	.667	1	21	5	0	54	83	42	20	0	7.83
Ben Shields	L	22	3	0	1.000	0	4	2	2	24	24	12	5	0	4.88
Garland Braxton	L	25	1	1	.500	0	3	2	0	19	26	5	11	0	6.63
Hank Johnson	R	19	1	3	.250	0	24	4	2	67	88	37	25	1	6.85
Walter Beall	R	25	0	1	.000	0	8	1	0	11	11	19	8	0	13.09
Charlie Caldwell			0	0	.000	0	3	0	0	3	7	3	1	0	15.00
1 Ray Francis	L	32	0	0	.000	0	4	0	0	5	5	3	1	0	7.20
Jim Marquis	R	24	0	0	.000	0	2	0	0	7	12	6	0	0	10.29

BOSTON 8th 47-105 .309 49.5 — LEE FOHL

NAME	G by POS	B	AGE	G	AB	R	H	2B	3B	HR	RBI	BB	SO	SB	BA	SA
TOTALS			27	152	5166	639	1375	257	64	41	591	513	422	42	.266	.364
Phil Todt	1B140	L	23	141	544	62	151	29	13	11	75	44	29	3	.278	.439
Bill Wambsganss	2B103, 1B6	R	31	111	360	50	83	12	4	1	41	52	21	3	.231	.294
Dud Lee	SS84	L	25	84	266	22	57	7	3	0	19	34	19	2	.224	.275
Doc Prothro	3B108, SS3	R	31	119	415	44	130	23	3	0	51	52	21	9	.313	.383
Ike Boone	OF118	L	28	133	476	79	157	34	5	9	68	60	19	1	.330	.479
Ira Flagstead	OF144	R	31	148	572	84	160	38	2	6	61	63	30	5	.280	.385
2 Roy Carlyle	OF67	L	24	93	276	36	90	20	3	7	49	16	29	1	.326	.496
Val Picinich	C74, 1B2	R	28	90	251	31	64	21	0	1	25	33	21	2	.255	.351
Tex Vache	OF53	R	29	110	252	41	79	15	7	3	48	21	33	2	.313	.464
Denny Williams	OF52	L	25	68	218	28	50	1	3	0	13	17	11	2	.229	.261
Homer Ezzell	3B47, 2B9	R	29	58	186	40	53	6	4	0	15	19	18	9	.285	.360
Billy Rogell	2B49, SS6	B	20	58	169	12	33	5	1	0	17	11	17	0	.195	.237
Johnnie Heving	C34	R	29	45	119	14	20	7	0	0	6	12	7	0	.168	.227
Bud Connolly	SS34, 3B2	R	24	43	107	12	28	7	1	0	21	23	9	0	.262	.346
2 George Bischoff	C40	R	30	41	133	13	37	9	1	1	16	6	11	1	.278	.383
Jack Rothrock	SS22	B	20	22	55	6	19	3	3	0	7	3	7	0	.345	.509
Si Rosenthal	OF17	L	21	19	72	6	19	5	2	0	8	7	3	1	.264	.389
Al Stokes	C17	R	25	17	52	7	11	0	1	0	1	4	8	0	.212	.250
Tom Jenkins	OF15	L	27	15	64	9	19	2	1	0	5	3	4	0	.297	.359
Herb Welch	SS13	L	24	13	38	2	11	0	1	0	2	0	6	0	.289	.342

Mike Herrara 27 R 15-39, Turkey Gross 29 R 3-32, 1 Joe Harris 34 R 3-19, Chappie Geygan 22 R 2-11, Shano Collins 39 R 1-3, 1 Bobby Veach 37 L 1-5

NAME	T	AGE	W	L	PCT	SV	G	GS	CG	IP	H	BB	SO	ShO	ERA
		28	47	105	.309	6	152	152	68	1327	1615	510	310	6	4.96
Ted Wingfield	R	25	12	19	.387	2	41	26	18	254	267	92	30	2	3.96
Howard Ehmke	R	31	9	20	.310	1	34	31	22	261	285	85	95	0	3.70
Red Ruffing	R	21	9	18	.333	1	37	27	13	217	253	75	64	3	5.01
1 Jack Quinn	R	41	7	8	.467	0	19	15	8	105	140	26	24	0	4.37
Paul Zahniser	R	28	5	12	.294	1	37	21	7	177	232	89	30	1	5.15
Buster Ross	L	22	3	8	.273	0	33	8	0	94	119	40	15	0	6.21
Rudy Kallio	R	32	1	4	.200	0	7	4	0	19	28	9	2	0	7.58
Hal Neubauer	R	23	1	0	1.000	0	7	0	0	10	17	11	4	0	12.60
Bob Adams	R	23	0	0	.000	0	2	0	0	6	10	3	1	0	7.50
1 Alex Ferguson	R	28	0	2	.000	1	5	4	0	16	22	5	5	0	10.69
2 Ray Francis	L	32	0	2	.000	0	6	4	0	28	44	13	4	0	7.71
Oscar Fuhr	L	31	0	6	.000	0	39	6	0	91	138	30	27	0	6.63
Curt Fullerton	R	26	0	3	.000	0	4	2	0	23	22	9	3	0	3.13
Joe Kiefer	R	25	0	2	.000	0	2	2	0	15	20	9	4	0	6.00
Joe Lucey	R	28	0	1	.000	0	7	2	0	11	18	14	2	0	9.00

PITTSBURGH 1st 95-58 .621 — BILL McKECHNIE

NAME	G by POS	B	AGE	G	AB	R	H	2B	3B	HR	RBI	BB	SO	SB	BA	SA
TOTALS			28	153	5372	912	1651	316	105	78	820	499	363	159	.307	.449
George Grantham	1B102	L	25	114	359	74	117	24	6	8	52	50	29	14	.326	.493
Eddie Moore	2B122, OF15, 3B3	R	26	142	547	106	163	29	8	6	77	73	26	19	.298	.413
Glenn Wright	SS153, 3B1	R	24	153	614	97	189	32	10	18	121	31	32	3	.308	.480
Pie Traynor	3B150, SS1	R	25	150	591	114	189	39	14	6	106	52	19	15	.320	.464
Kiki Cuyler	OF153	R	25	153	617	**144**	**220**	43	**26**	18	102	58	56	41	.357	.598
Max Carey	OF130	B	35	133	542	109	186	39	13	5	44	66	19	**46**	.343	.491
Clyde Barnhart	OF138	R	29	142	539	85	175	32	11	4	114	59	25	9	.325	.447
Earl Smith	C96	L	28	109	329	34	103	22	3	8	64	31	13	4	.313	.471
Johnny Gooch	C76	B	27	79	215	24	64	8	4	0	30	20	16	1	.298	.372
Carson Bigbee	OF42	L	30	66	126	31	30	7	0	0	8	7	8	2	.238	.294
Stuffy McInnis	1B46	R	34	59	155	19	57	10	4	0	24	17	1	1	.368	.484
Johnny Rawlings	2B29	R	32	36	110	17	31	7	0	2	13	8	8	0	.282	.400
1 Al Niehaus	1B15	R	26	17	64	7	14	8	0	0	7	1	5	0	.219	.344
Roy Spencer	C11	R	25	14	28	1	6	1	0	0	2	1	3	1	.214	.250
Fresco Thompson	2B12	R	23	14	37	4	9	2	1	0	8	4	1	2	.243	.351
Mule Haas	OF2	L	21	4	3	1	0	0	0	0	0	0	1	0	.000	.000
Jewel Ens	1B3	R	35	3	5	2	1	0	0	1	2	0	1	0	.200	.800

NAME	T	AGE	W	L	PCT	SV	G	GS	CG	IP	H	BB	SO	ShO	ERA
		32	95	58	.621	13	153	153	77	1355	1526	387	386	2	3.87
Lee Meadows	R	30	19	10	.655	1	35	31	20	255	272	67	87	1	3.67
Ray Kremer	R	32	17	8	.680	2	40	27	14	215	232	47	62	0	3.68
Johnny Morrison	R	29	17	14	.548	**4**	**44**	26	10	211	245	60	60	0	3.88
Emil Yde	L	25	17	9	.654	0	33	28	13	207	254	75	41	0	4.13
Vic Aldridge	R	31	15	7	.682	0	30	26	14	213	218	74	88	1	3.63
Babe Adams	R	43	6	5	.545	3	33	10	3	101	129	17	18	0	5.44
Red Oldham	L	31	3	2	.600	1	11	4	3	53	66	18	10	0	3.91
2 Tom Sheehan	R	31	1	1	.500	2	23	0	0	57	63	13	13	0	2.68
Bud Culloton	R	29	0	1	.000	0	9	1	0	21	19	1	3	0	2.57
Lou Koupal	R	26	0	0	.000	0	6	0	0	9	14	7	0	0	9.00
Don Songer	L	26	0	1	.000	0	8	0	0	12	14	8	4	0	2.25

NEW YORK 2nd 86-66 .566 8.5 — JOHN McGRAW

NAME	G by POS	B	AGE	G	AB	R	H	2B	3B	HR	RBI	BB	SO	SB	BA	SA
TOTALS			27	152	5327	736	1507	239	61	**114**	682	411	494	79	.283	.415
Bill Terry	1B126	L	26	133	489	75	156	31	6	11	70	42	52	4	.319	.474
George Kelly	2B108, 1B25, OF17	R	29	147	586	87	181	29	3	20	99	35	54	5	.309	.471
Travis Jackson	SS110	R	21	112	411	51	117	15	2	9	59	24	43	8	.285	.397
Fred Lindstrom (BG)	3B96, 2B1, SS1	R	19	104	356	43	102	15	12	4	33	22	20	5	.287	.430
Ross Youngs	OF127, 2B3	L	28	130	500	82	132	24	6	6	53	66	51	17	.264	.372
Billy Southworth	OF119	L	32	123	473	79	138	19	5	6	44	51	11	6	.292	.391
Irish Meusel	OF126	R	32	135	516	82	169	35	8	21	111	26	19	5	.328	.548
Frank Snyder	C96	R	32	107	325	21	78	9	1	11	51	20	49	0	.240	.375
Frankie Frisch (NJ)	3B46, 2B42, SS39	B	26	120	502	89	166	26	6	11	48	32	14	21	.331	.472
Jack Bentley	P28, OF3, 1B1	L	30	64	99	10	30	5	2	3	18	9	11	0	.303	.485
Hack Wilson	OF50	R	25	62	180	28	43	7	4	6	30	21	33	5	.239	.422
Hank Gowdy	C41	R	35	47	114	14	37	4	3	3	19	12	7	0	.325	.491
Grover Hartley	C37, 1B8	R	36	46	95	9	30	1	1	0	8	8	3	2	.316	.347
Frank Walker	OF21	R	30	39	81	12	18	1	0	1	5	9	11	1	.222	.272
Doc Farrell	SS13, 3B7, 2B1	R	23	27	56	6	12	1	0	0	4	6	6	0	.214	.232
Heinie Groh (KJ)	3B16, 2B2	R	35	25	65	7	15	4	0	0	4	6	3	0	.231	.292
Mickey Devine	C11, 3B1	R	33	21	33	6	9	3	0	0	4	2	3	0	.273	.364
Pip Koehler	OF3	R	23	12	2	1	0	0	0	0	0	0	1	0	.000	.000
Hugh McMullen	C5	B	23	5	15	1	2	1	0	0	0	0	3	0	.133	.200
Earl Webb		L	26	4	3	0	0	0	0	0	0	1	1	0	.000	.000
Al Moore	OF2	R	22	2	8	0	1	0	0	0	0	1	2	0	.125	.125
Blackie Carter	OF1	R	22	1	4	0	0	0	0	0	0	0	1	0	.000	.000

NAME	T	AGE	W	L	PCT	SV	G	GS	CG	IP	H	BB	SO	ShO	ERA
		28	86	66	.566	8	152	152	80	1354	1532	408	446	6	3.94
Virgil Barnes	R	28	15	11	.577	2	32	27	17	222	242	53	53	1	3.53
Jack Scott	R	33	14	15	.483	3	36	28	18	240	251	55	87	2	3.15
Kent Greenfield	R	23	12	8	.600	0	29	21	12	172	195	64	66	0	3.87
Jack Bentley	L	30	11	9	.550	0	28	22	11	157	200	59	47	0	5.04
Art Nehf	L	32	11	9	.550	1	29	20	8	155	193	50	60	1	3.77
Wayland Dean	R	23	10	7	.588	1	33	14	6	151	169	50	53	1	4.65
Freddie Fitzsimmons	R	23	6	3	.667	0	10	8	6	75	70	18	17	1	2.64
Walter Huntzinger	R	26	5	1	.833	0	26	1	0	64	68	17	19	0	3.52
Hugh McQuillan	R	27	2	3	.400	1	14	11	2	70	95	23	23	0	6.04
Harry Baldwin	R	25	0	0	.000	0	1	0	0	1	3	1	0	0	9.00
Chick Davies	L	33	0	0	.000	0	2	1	0	7	13	4	5	0	6.43
John Wisner	R	25	0	0	.000	0	25	0	0	40	33	14	13	0	3.83

CINCINNATI 3rd 80-73 .523 15 — JACK HENDRICKS

NAME	G by POS	B	AGE	G	AB	R	H	2B	3B	HR	RBI	BB	SO	SB	BA	SA
TOTALS			29	153	5233	690	1490	221	90	44	624	409	327	108	.285	.387
2 Walter Holke	1B65	B	32	65	232	24	65	8	4	1	20	17	12	1	.280	.362
Hughie Critz	2B144	R	24	144	541	74	150	14	8	2	51	34	17	13	.277	.344
Ike Caveney	SS111	R	30	115	358	38	89	9	5	2	47	28	31	2	.249	.318
Babe Pinelli	3B109, SS17	R	29	130	492	68	139	33	6	2	49	22	28	8	.283	.386
Curt Walker	OF141	L	28	145	509	86	162	22	16	6	71	57	31	14	.318	.460
Edd Roush	OF134	L	32	134	540	91	183	28	16	8	83	35	14	22	.339	.494
Billy Zitzmann	OF89, SS1	R	27	104	301	53	76	13	3	0	21	35	22	11	.252	.316
Bubbles Hargrave	C84	R	32	87	273	28	82	13	6	2	33	25	23	4	.300	.414
Rube Bressler (NJ)	1B52, OF38	R	30	97	319	43	111	17	6	4	61	40	16	9	.348	.476
Elmer Smith	OF80	L	32	96	284	47	77	13	7	8	46	28	20	6	.271	.451
Chuck Dressen	3B47, 2B5, OF4	R	26	76	215	35	59	8	2	3	19	12	4	5	.274	.372
Sammy Bohne	SS49, 2B10, OF4, 1B2, 3B2	R	28	73	214	24	55	9	1	2	24	14	14	6	.257	.336
Ivy Wingo	C55	L	34	55	146	6	30	7	0	0	12	11	8	1	.205	.253
2 Al Niehaus	1B45	R	26	51	147	16	44	10	2	0	14	13	10	1	.299	.395
Pete Donohue	P42	R	24	43	109	13	32	3	1	1	12	4	9	0	.294	.367
Ernie Krueger	C30	R	34	37	88	7	27	4	0	1	7	6	8	1	.307	.386
2 Joe Schultz	OF15, 2B1	R	31	33	62	6	20	3	1	0	13	3	1	3	.323	.403
Astyanax Douglass	C7	L	27	7	17	1	3	0	0	0	1	1	3	0	.176	.176

Frank Bruggy 34 R 3-14, Boob Fowler 24 L 2-5, Jimmy Hudgens 22 L 3-7, Ollie Klee 25 L 0-1, 2 Hy Myers 36 R 1-6, Tom Sullivan 18 R 0-1, Jake Daubert (DD) 40

NAME	T	AGE	W	L	PCT	SV	G	GS	CG	IP	H	BB	SO	ShO	ERA
		31	80	73	.523	12	153	153	**92**	**1375**	1447	324	437	**11**	**3.38**
Eppa Rixey	L	34	21	11	.656	1	39	36	22	287	302	47	69	2	2.89
Pete Donohue	R	24	21	14	.600	2	42	**38**	**27**	**301**	310	49	78	3	3.08
Dolf Luque	R	34	16	18	.471	0	36	36	22	291	263	78	140	**4**	**2.63**
Rube Benton	L	38	9	10	.474	1	33	16	6	147	182	34	36	1	4.04
Jakie May	L	29	8	9	.471	2	36	12	7	137	146	45	74	1	3.88
Carl Mays (SA)	R	33	3	5	.375	2	12	5	3	52	60	13	10	0	3.29
Neal Brady	R	28	1	3	.250	1	20	3	2	64	73	20	12	0	4.64
1 Tom Sheehan	R	31	1	0	1.000	1	10	3	1	29	37	12	5	0	8.07
Harry Biemiller	R	27	0	1	.000	2	23	1	0	47	45	21	9	0	4.02
Pedro Dibut	R	32	0	0	.000	0	1	0	0	0	3	0	0	0	∞
Marv Goodwin	R	34	0	2	.000	0	4	3	2	21	26	5	4	0	4.71

ST. LOUIS 4th 77-76 .503 18 — BRANCH RICKEY 13-25 .342 — ROGERS HORNSBY 64-51 .557

NAME	G by POS	B	AGE	G	AB	R	H	2B	3B	HR	RBI	BB	SO	SB	BA	SA
TOTALS			27	153	5329	828	1592	292	80	109	752	446	414	70	.299	.445
Jim Bottomley	1B153	L	25	153	619	92	**227**	**44**	12	21	128	47	36	3	.367	.578
Rogers Hornsby	2B136	R	29	138	504	133	203	41	10	**39**	**143**	83	39	5	**.403**	**.756**
Specs Toporcer	SS66, 2B7	L	26	83	268	38	76	13	4	2	26	36	15	7	.284	.384
Les Bell	3B153, SS1	R	23	153	586	80	167	29	9	11	88	43	47	4	.285	.422
Chick Hafey	OF88	R	22	93	358	36	108	25	2	5	57	10	29	3	.302	.425
Heinie Mueller (BF)	OF72	L	25	78	243	33	76	16	4	1	26	17	11	0	.313	.424
Ray Blades	OF114, 3B1	R	28	122	462	112	158	37	8	12	57	59	47	6	.342	.535
2 Bob O'Farrell	C92	R	28	94	317	37	88	13	2	3	32	46	26	0	.278	.360
Jack Smith	OF64	L	30	80	243	53	61	11	4	4	31	19	13	20	.251	.379
Max Flack	OF59	L	35	79	241	23	60	7	8	0	28	21	9	5	.249	.344
Ralph Shinners	OF66	R	29	74	251	39	74	9	2	7	36	12	19	8	.295	.430
Jimmy Cooney	SS37, 2B15, OF1	R	30	54	187	27	51	11	2	0	18	4	5	1	.273	.353
Tommy Thevenow	SS50	R	21	50	175	17	47	7	2	0	17	7	12	3	.269	.331
Walter Schmidt	C31	R	38	37	87	9	22	2	1	0	9	4	3	1	.253	.299
Taylor Douthit	OF21	R	24	30	73	13	20	3	1	1	8	2	6	0	.274	.384
Art Reinhart	P20	L	26	28	67	9	22	2	1	0	7	2	10	0	.328	.388
1 Mike Gonzalez	C22	R	34	22	71	9	22	3	0	0	4	6	2	1	.310	.352
Ernie Vick	C9	R	24	14	32	3	6	2	1	0	3	3	1	0	.188	.313
Wattie Holm	OF13	R	23	13	58	10	12	1	1	0	2	3	1	1	.207	.259
Bill Warwick	C13	R	27	13	41	8	12	1	2	1	6	5	5	0	.293	.488
1 Howard Freigau	SS7, 2B1	R	22	9	26	2	4	0	0	0	0	2	1	0	.154	.154
13Hy Myers		R	36	2	2	1	1	0	0	0	0	0	0	0	1.000	1.000

NAME	T	AGE	W	L	PCT	SV	G	GS	CG	IP	H	BB	SO	ShO	ERA
		27	77	76	.503	7	153	153	82	1336	1480	470	428	8	4.36
Bill Sherdel	L	28	15	6	**.714**	1	32	21	17	200	216	42	53	2	3.11
Jesse Haines	R	31	13	14	.481	0	29	25	15	207	234	52	63	0	4.57
Art Reinhart	L	26	11	5	.688	0	20	16	15	145	149	47	26	1	3.04
Allan Sothoron	R	32	10	10	.500	0	28	23	8	156	173	63	67	2	4.04
Flint Rhem	R	24	8	13	.381	1	30	23	8	170	204	58	66	1	4.92
Duster Mails (SJ)	L	29	7	7	.500	0	21	14	9	131	145	58	49	0	4.60
Leo Dickerman	R	28	4	11	.267	1	29	20	7	131	135	79	40	2	5.56
Eddie Dyer (SA)	L	24	4	3	.571	3	27	5	1	82	93	24	25	0	4.17
Pea Ridge Day	R	26	2	4	.333	1	17	4	1	40	53	7	13	0	6.30
Johnny Stuart	R	24	2	2	.500	0	15	1	1	47	52	24	14	0	6.13
Wild Bill Hallahan	L	22	1	0	1.000	0	6	0	0	15	14	11	8	0	3.60
Ed Clough	L	18	0	1	.000	0	3	1	0	10	11	5	3	0	8.10
Gil Paulsen	R	22	0	0	.000	0	1	0	0	2	1	0	1	0	0.00

BOSTON 5th 70-83 .458 25 — DAVE BANCROFT

NAME	G by POS	B	AGE	G	AB	R	H	2B	3B	HR	RBI	BB	SO	SB	BA	SA
TOTALS			28	153	5365	708	1567	260	70	41	643	405	380	77	.292	.390
Dick Burrus	1B151	L	27	152	588	82	200	41	4	5	87	51	29	8	.340	.426
2 Doc Gautreau	2B68	R	23	68	279	45	73	13	3	0	23	35	13	11	.262	.330
Dave Bancroft	SS125	B	34	128	479	75	153	29	8	2	49	64	22	7	.319	.426
Bill Marriott	3B89, OF1	L	32	103	370	37	99	9	1	1	40	28	26	3	.268	.305
Jim Welsh	OF116, 2B3	L	22	122	484	69	151	25	8	7	63	20	24	7	.312	.440
Gus Felix	OF114	R	30	121	459	60	141	25	7	2	66	30	34	5	.307	.405
Bernie Neis	OF87	B	29	106	355	47	101	20	2	5	45	38	19	8	.285	.394
Frank Gibson	C86, 1B2	B	34	104	316	36	88	23	5	2	50	15	28	3	.278	.402
Dave Harris	OF90	R	25	92	340	49	90	8	7	5	36	27	44	6	.265	.374
Ernie Padgett	2B47, SS18, 3B7	R	26	86	256	31	78	9	7	0	29	14	14	3	.305	.395
Mickey O'Neil	C69	R	27	70	222	29	57	6	5	2	30	21	16	1	.257	.356
2 Andy High	3B60, 2B1	L	27	60	219	31	63	11	1	4	28	24	2	3	.288	.402
Les Mann	OF57	R	31	60	184	27	63	11	4	2	20	5	11	6	.342	.478
Bob Smith	SS21, 2B15, P13, OF1	R	27	58	174	17	49	9	4	0	23	5	6	2	.282	.379
Johnny Cooney	P31, 1B3, OF1	R	24	54	103	17	33	7	0	0	13	3	6	1	.320	.388
Oscar Siemer	C16	R	23	16	46	5	14	0	1	1	6	1	0	0	.304	.413
Casey Stengel	OF1	L	34	12	13	0	1	0	0	0	2	1	2	0	.077	.077
Frank Wilson	OF10	L	23	12	31	3	13	1	1	0	0	4	1	2	.419	.516
Hod Kibbie	2B8, SS3	R	21	11	41	5	11	2	0	0	2	5	6	0	.268	.317

Shanty Hogan 19 R 6-21, Red Lucas 23 L 3-20, Abe Hood 22 L 6-21, Herb Thomas 23 R 4-17, Ed Sperber 30 L 0-2, Dee Cousineau 26 R 0-0

NAME	T	AGE	W	L	PCT	SV	G	GS	CG	IP	H	BB	SO	ShO	ERA
		28	70	83	.458	4	153	153	77	1367	1567	458	351	5	4.39
Larry Benton	R	27	14	7	.667	1	31	21	16	183	170	70	49	2	3.10
Johnny Cooney	L	24	14	14	.500	0	31	29	20	246	267	50	65	2	3.48
Joe Genewich	R	28	12	10	.545	0	34	21	10	169	185	41	34	0	3.99
Jesse Barnes	R	32	11	16	.407	0	32	28	17	216	255	63	55	0	4.54
Kyle Graham	R	25	7	12	.368	1	34	23	5	157	177	62	32	0	4.41
Bob Smith	R	27	5	3	.625	0	13	10	6	93	110	36	19	0	4.45
Ike Kamp	L	24	2	4	.333	0	24	4	1	58	68	35	20	0	5.12
Rube Marquard	L	35	2	8	.200	0	26	8	0	72	105	27	19	0	5.75
Rosy Ryan	R	27	2	8	.200	2	37	7	1	123	152	52	48	0	6.29
Bill Vargus	L	25	1	1	.500	0	11	2	1	36	45	13	5	0	4.00
Bill Anderson	L	29	0	0	.000	0	2	0	0	3	5	2	1	0	9.00
Joe Batchelder	L	26	0	0	.000	0	4	0	0	7	10	1	2	0	5.14
Foster Edwards	R	21	0	0	.000	0	1	0	0	2	6	1	1	0	9.00
Tim McNamara	R	26	0	0	.000	0	1	0	0	.2	6	2	1	0	81.00
Joe Ogrodowski	R	18	0	0	.000	0	1	0	0	1	6	3	0	0	54.00

BROOKLYN 6th (Tie) 68-85 .444 27 — WILBERT ROBINSON

NAME	G by POS	B	AGE	G	AB	R	H	2B	3B	HR	RBI	BB	SO	SB	BA	SA
TOTALS			31	153	**5468**	786	1617	250	80	64	722	437	383	37	.296	.406
Jack Fournier	1B145	L	32	145	545	99	191	21	16	22	130	**86**	39	4	.350	.569
Milt Stock	2B141, 3B5	R	31	146	615	98	202	28	9	1	62	38	28	8	.328	.408
Johnny Mitchell	SS90	B	30	97	336	45	84	8	3	0	18	28	19	2	.250	.292
Jimmy Johnston	3B81, OF20, 1B8, SS2	R	35	123	431	63	128	13	3	2	43	45	15	7	.297	.355
Dick Cox	OF111	R	27	122	434	68	143	23	10	7	64	37	29	4	.329	.477
Eddie Brown	OF153	R	33	153	618	88	189	39	11	5	99	22	18	3	.306	.429
Zack Wheat	OF149	L	39	150	616	125	221	42	14	14	103	45	22	3	.359	.541
Zack Taylor	C96	R	26	109	352	33	109	16	4	3	44	17	19	0	.310	.403
Cotton Tierney	3B61, 1B1, 2B1	R	31	93	265	27	68	14	4	2	39	12	23	0	.257	.362
Hank DeBerry	C55	R	30	67	193	26	50	8	1	2	24	16	8	2	.259	.342
Hod Ford (HO)	SS66	R	27	66	216	32	59	11	0	1	15	26	15	0	.273	.338
Dick Loftus	OF38	L	24	51	131	16	31	6	0	0	13	5	5	2	.237	.282
Charlie Hargreaves	C18, 1B2	R	28	45	83	9	23	3	1	0	13	6	1	1	.277	.337
1 Andy High	2B11, 3B11, SS3	L	27	44	115	11	23	4	1	0	6	14	5	0	.200	.252
Chuck Corgan	SS14	B	22	14	47	4	8	1	1	0	0	3	9	0	.170	.234
1 Tommy Griffith	OF2	L	35	7	4	2	0	0	0	0	0	3	2	1	.000	.000
Roy Hutson	OF4	L	23	7	8	1	4	0	0	0	1	1	1	0	.500	.500
2 Bob Barrett		R	26	1	1	0	0	0	0	0	1	0	0	0	.000	.000
Jerry Standaert		R	23	1	1	0	0	0	0	0	0	0	1	0	.000	.000

NAME	T	AGE	W	L	PCT	SV	G	GS	CG	IP	H	BB	SO	ShO	ERA
		30	68	85	.444	4	153	153	82	1351	1608	477	**518**	4	4.77
Dazzy Vance	R	24	**22**	9	.710	0	31	31	26	265	247	66	**221**	**4**	3.53
Burleigh Grimes	R	31	12	**19**	.387	0	33	31	19	247	305	102	73	0	5.03
Rube Ehrhardt	R	30	10	14	.417	1	36	24	12	208	239	62	47	0	5.02
Jesse Petty	L	30	9	9	.500	0	28	22	7	153	188	47	39	0	4.88
Tiny Osborne	R	32	8	15	.348	1	41	22	10	175	210	75	59	0	4.94
2 Bill Hubbell	R	28	3	6	.667	1	33	5	3	87	120	24	16	0	5.28
Nelson Greene	L	24	2	0	1.000	1	11	0	0	22	45	7	4	0	10.64
Guy Cantrell	R	21	1	0	1.000	0	14	3	1	36	42	14	13	0	3.00
Joe Oeschger	R	34	1	2	.333	0	21	3	1	37	60	19	6	0	6.08
Lloyd Brown	L	20	0	3	.000	0	17	5	1	63	79	25	23	0	4.14
1 Art Decatur	R	31	0	0	.000	0	1	0	0	1	3	0	0	0	18.00
Jumbo Jim Elliott	L	24	0	2	.000	0	3	1	0	11	17	9	3	0	8.18
Bob McGraw	R	30	0	2	.000	0	2	2	2	20	14	13	3	0	3.15
Jim Roberts	R	29	0	0	.000	0	1	0	0	1	1	0	0	0	∞
Andy Rush	R	25	0	1	.000	0	4	2	0	10	16	5	4	0	9.00
Hank Thormahlen	L	28	0	3	.000	0	5	2	0	16	22	9	7	0	3.94
Bill Doak (VR) 34															

PHILADELPHIA 6th (Tie) 68-85 .444 27 — ART FLETCHER

NAME	G by POS	B	AGE	G	AB	R	H	2B	3B	HR	RBI	BB	SO	SB	BA	SA
TOTALS			29	153	5412	812	1598	288	58	100	731	456	**542**	48	.295	.425
Chicken Hawks	1B90	L	29	105	320	52	103	15	5	5	45	32	33	3	.322	.447
2 Barney Friberg	2B77, 3B14, C1, P1	R	25	91	304	41	82	12	1	5	22	39	35	1	.270	.365
Heinie Sand	SS143	R	27	148	496	69	138	30	7	3	55	64	65	1	.278	.385
Clarence Huber	3B120	R	28	124	436	46	124	28	5	5	54	17	33	3	.284	.406
Cy Williams	OF96	L	37	107	314	78	104	11	5	13	60	53	34	4	.331	.522
George Harper	OF126	L	33	132	495	86	173	35	7	18	97	28	32	10	.349	.558
George Burns	OF88	R	35	88	349	65	102	29	1	1	22	33	20	4	.292	.390
Jimmie Wilson	C89, OF1	R	24	108	335	42	110	19	3	3	54	32	25	5	.328	.430
Lew Fonseca	2B69, 1B55	R	26	126	467	78	149	30	5	7	60	21	42	6	.319	.450
Butch Henline	C68, OF1	R	30	93	263	43	80	12	5	8	48	24	16	3	.304	.479
R. Wrightstone	OF45, SS12, 3B11, 2B10, 1B6	L	32	92	286	48	99	18	5	14	61	19	18	0	.346	.591
Johnny Mokan	OF68	R	29	75	209	30	69	11	2	6	42	27	9	3	.330	.488
Wally Kimmick	SS28, 3B21, 2B13	R	28	70	141	16	43	3	2	1	10	22	26	0	.305	.376
Freddy Leach	OF65	L	27	65	292	47	91	15	4	5	28	5	21	1	.312	.442
Clarence Mitchell	P32, 1B2	L	34	52	92	7	18	2	0	0	13	5	9	2	.196	.217
1 Walter Holke	1B23	B	32	39	86	11	21	5	0	1	17	3	6	0	.244	.337
1 Joe Schultz	OF20	R	31	24	64	10	22	6	0	0	8	4	1	1	.344	.438
Lew Wendell	C9	R	33	18	26	0	2	0	0	0	3	1	3	0	.077	.077
Lenny Metz	SS9, 2B2	R	25	11	14	1	0	0	0	0	0	0	2	0	.000	.000
George Durning	OF4	R	23	5	14	3	5	0	0	0	1	2	1	0	.357	.357
Benny Meyer	2B1	R	37	1	1	1	1	1	0	0	0	0	0	0	1.000	2.000

NAME	T	AGE	W	L	PCT	SV	G	GS	CG	IP	H	BB	SO	ShO	ERA
		30	68	85	.444	9	153	153	69	1351	**1753**	444	371	8	5.02
Jimmy Ring	R	30	14	16	.467	0	38	37	21	270	**325**	**119**	93	1	4.37
Hal Carlson	R	31	13	14	.481	0	35	32	18	234	281	52	80	**4**	4.23
Clarence Mitchell	L	34	10	17	.370	1	32	26	12	199	245	51	46	1	5.29
Jack Knight	R	30	7	6	.538	3	33	11	4	105	161	36	19	0	6.86
Johnny Couch	R	34	5	6	.455	2	34	7	2	94	112	39	11	1	5.46
Ray Pierce	L	28	5	4	.556	0	23	8	4	90	134	24	18	0	5.50
Huck Betts	R	28	4	5	.444	1	35	7	1	97	146	38	28	0	5.57
2 Art Decatur	R	31	4	13	.235	2	25	15	4	128	170	35	31	0	5.27
Dutch Ulrich	R	25	3	3	.500	0	21	4	2	65	73	12	29	1	3.05
Claude Willoughby	R	26	2	1	.667	0	3	3	1	23	26	11	6	0	1.96
Dana Fillingim	R	31	1	0	1.000	0	5	1	0	9	19	6	2	0	10.00
Roy Crumpler	L	28	0	0	.000	0	3	1	0	5	8	2	1	0	7.20
2 Barney Friberg	R	25	0	0	.000	0	1	0	0	4	4	3	1	0	4.50
1 Bill Hubbell	R	28	0	0	.000	0	2	0	0	3	5	1	0	0	0.00
Skinny O'Neal	R	26	0	0	.000	0	11	1	0	20	35	12	6	0	9.45
Bob Vines	R	28	0	0	.000	0	3	0	0	4	9	3	0	0	11.25

CHICAGO 8th 68-86 .442 27.5 — BILL KILLEFER 33-42 .440 RABBIT MARANVILLE 23-30 .434 GEORGE GIBSON 12-14 .462

NAME	G by POS	B	AGE	G	AB	R	H	2B	3B	HR	RBI	BB	SO	SB	BA	SA
TOTALS			28	154	5353	723	1473	254	70	86	660	397	470	94	.275	.397
Charlie Grimm	1B139	L	26	141	519	73	159	29	5	10	76	38	25	4	.306	.439
Sparky Adams	2B144, SS5	R	30	149	**627**	95	180	29	8	2	48	44	15	26	.287	.368
Rabbit Maranville (BL)	SS74	R	33	75	266	37	62	10	3	0	23	29	20	6	.233	.293
2 Howard Freigau	3B96, SS17, 1B7	R	22	117	476	77	146	22	10	8	71	30	31	10	.307	.445
Cliff Heathcote	OF99	L	27	109	380	57	100	14	5	5	39	39	26	15	.263	.366
Mandy Brooks	OF89	R	26	90	349	55	98	25	7	14	72	19	28	10	.281	.513
Art Jahn	OF58	R	29	58	226	30	68	10	8	0	37	11	20	2	.301	.416
Gabby Hartnett	C110	R	24	117	398	61	115	28	3	24	67	36	**77**	1	.289	.555
2 Tommy Griffith	OF60	L	35	76	235	38	67	12	1	7	27	21	11	2	.285	.434
2 Mike Gonzalez	C50, 1B9	R	34	70	197	26	52	13	1	3	18	13	15	2	.264	.386
Butch Weis (IL)	OF47	L	22	67	180	16	48	5	3	2	25	23	22	2	.267	.361
Pinky Pittinger	SS24, 3B24	R	26	59	173	21	54	7	2	0	15	12	7	5	.312	.376
Denver Grigsby (BC)	OF39	L	24	51	137	20	35	5	0	0	20	19	12	1	.255	.292
1 Barney Friberg	3B26, OF12, 1B6, SS2	R	25	44	152	12	39	5	3	1	16	14	22	0	.257	.349
Jigger Statz	OF37	R	27	38	148	21	38	6	3	2	14	11	16	4	.257	.378
Ike McAuley	SS37	R	31	37	125	10	35	7	2	0	11	11	12	1	.280	.368
Hack Miller	OF21	R	31	24	86	10	24	3	2	2	9	2	9	0	.279	.430
Ralph Michaels	3B15, 1B1, 2B1, SS1	R	23	22	50	10	14	1	0	0	6	6	9	1	.280	.300
1 Bob O'Farrell	C3	R	28	17	22	2	4	0	1	0	3	2	5	0	.182	.273

NAME	T	AGE	W	L	PCT	SV	G	GS	CG	IP	H	BB	SO	ShO	ERA
		28	68	**86**	.442	10	154	154	75	1370	1575	**485**	435	5	4.41
Pete Alexander	R	38	15	11	.577	0	32	30	20	236	270	29	63	1	3.39
Tony Kaufmann	R	24	13	13	.500	2	31	23	14	196	221	77	49	2	4.50
Wilbur Cooper	L	33	12	14	.462	0	32	26	13	212	249	61	41	0	4.29
Sheriff Blake	R	25	10	18	.357	2	36	31	14	231	260	114	93	0	4.87
Guy Bush	R	23	6	13	.316	**4**	42	15	5	182	213	52	76	0	4.30
Percy Jones	L	25	6	6	.500	0	28	13	6	124	123	71	60	1	4.65
Elmer Jacobs	R	32	2	3	.400	1	18	4	1	56	63	22	19	1	5.14
Vic Keen	R	26	2	6	.250	1	30	8	1	83	125	41	19	0	6.29
Herb Brett	R	25	1	1	.500	0	10	1	0	17	12	3	6	0	3.71
George Milstead	L	22	1	1	.500	0	5	3	1	21	26	8	7	0	3.00
Jumbo Brown	R	18	0	0	.000	0	2	0	0	6	5	4	0	0	3.00
Bob Osborn	R	22	0	0	.000	0	1	0	0	2	6	0	0	0	0.00
George Stueland	R	26	0	0	.000	0	2	0	0	3	2	3	2	0	3.00

1 Bob Barrett 26 R 10-32, Alex Metzler 22 L 7-38. Joe Munson 25 L 13-35, Chink Taylor 27 R 0-6, Gale Staley 26 R 11-26, John Churry 24 R 3-6, Ted Kearns 25 R 1-2, Mel Kerr 22 L 0-0

WORLD SERIES – PITTSBURGH (NL) 4 WASHINGTON (AL) 3

LINE SCORES

TEAM	1	2	3	4	5	6	7	8	9	10	11	12	R	H	E
Game 1 October 7 at Pittsburgh															
WAS (AL)	0	1	0	0	2	0	0	0	1				4	8	1
PIT (NL)	0	0	0	0	1	0	0	0	0				1	5	0
Johnson — **Meadows**, Morrison (9)															
Game 2 October 8 at Pittsburgh															
WAS	0	1	0	0	0	0	0	0	1				2	8	2
PIT	0	0	0	1	0	0	0	2	X				3	7	0
Coveleski — **Aldridge**															
Game 3 October 10 at Washington															
PIT	0	1	0	1	0	1	0	0	0				3	8	3
WAS	0	0	1	0	0	1	2	0	X				4	10	1
Kremer — **Ferguson**, Marberry (8)															
Game 4 October 11 at Washington															
PIT	0	0	0	0	0	0	0	0	0				0	6	1
WAS	0	0	4	0	0	0	0	0	X				4	12	0
Yde, Morrison (3), Adams (8) — **Johnson**															
Game 5 October 12 at Washington															
PIT	0	0	2	0	0	0	2	1	1				6	13	0
WAS	1	0	0	1	0	0	1	0	0				3	8	1
Aldridge — **Coveleski**, Ballou (7), Zachary (8), Marberry (9)															
Game 6 October 13 at Pittsburgh															
WAS	1	1	0	0	0	0	0	0	0				2	6	2
PIT	0	0	2	0	1	0	0	0	X				3	7	1
Ferguson, Ballou (8) — **Kremer**															
Game 7 October 15 at Pittsburgh															
WAS	4	0	0	2	0	0	0	1	0				7	7	2
PIT	0	0	3	0	1	0	2	3	X				9	15	2
Johnson — Aldridge, Morrison (1), **Kremer** (5), Oldham (9)															

COMPOSITE BATTING

NAME	POS	G	AB	R	H	2B	3B	HR	RBI	BA
Pittsburgh (NL) Totals		7	230	25	61	12	2	4	25	.265
Barnhart	OF	7	28	1	7	1	0	0	5	.250
Wright	SS	7	27	3	5	1	0	1	3	.185
Traynor	3B	7	26	2	9	0	**2**	1	4	.346
Cuyler	OF	7	26	3	7	3	0	1	**6**	.269
Moore	2B	7	26	**7**	6	1	0	1	2	.231
Carey	OF	7	24	6	11	**4**	0	0	2	**.458**
Smith	C	6	20	0	7	1	0	0	0	.350
Grantham	1B	5	15	0	2	0	0	0	0	.133
McInnis	1B	4	14	0	4	0	0	0	1	.286
Kremer	P	3	7	0	1	0	0	0	1	.143
Aldridge	P	3	7	0	0	0	0	0	0	.000
Bigbee	PH	4	3	1	1	1	0	0	1	.333
Gooch	C	3	3	0	0	0	0	0	0	.000
Morrison	P	3	2	1	1	0	0	0	0	.500
Yde	P	2	1	1	0	0	0	0	0	.000
Meadows	P	1	1	0	0	0	0	0	0	.000
Adams	P	1	0	0	0	0	0	0	0	.000
Oldham	P	1	0	0	0	0	0	0	0	.000
Washington (AL) Totals		7	225	26	59	8	0	8	25	.262
Rice	OF	7	**33**	5	**12**	0	0	0	3	.364
Goslin	OF	7	26	6	8	1	0	**3**	**6**	.308
J. Harris	OF	7	25	5	11	2	0	**3**	**6**	.440
Peckinpaugh	SS	7	24	1	6	1	0	1	3	.250
Judge	1B	7	23	2	4	1	0	1	3	.174
B. Harris	2B	7	23	2	2	0	0	0	0	.087
Ruel	C	7	19	0	6	1	0	0	1	.316
Bluege	3B	5	18	2	5	1	0	0	2	.278
Johnson	P	3	11	0	1	0	0	0	0	.091
Myer	3B	3	8	0	2	0	0	0	0	.250
Ferguson	P	2	4	0	0	0	0	0	0	.000
Severeid	C	1	3	0	1	0	0	0	0	.333
Leibold	PH	3	2	1	1	1	0	0	0	.500
Adams	2B	2	1	0	0	0	0	0	0	.000
Coveleski	P	2	3	0	0	0	0	0	0	.000
Ruether	PH	1	1	0	0	0	0	0	0	.000
Veach	PH	2	1	0	0	0	0	0	1	.000
Ballou	P	2	0	0	0	0	0	0	0	.000
Marberry	P	2	0	0	0	0	0	0	0	.000
McNeely	OF	4	0	2	0	0	0	0	0	.000
Zachary	P	1	0	0	0	0	0	0	0	.000

COMPOSITE PITCHING

NAME	G	IP	H	BB	SO	W	L	SV	ERA
Pittsburgh (NL) Totals	7	61	59	17	32	4	3	1	3.69
Kremer	3	21	17	4	9	**2**	1	0	3.00
Aldridge	3	18.1	18	**9**	9	**2**	0	0	4.42
Morrison	3	9.1	11	1	7	0	0	0	2.89
Meadows	1	8	6	0	4	0	1	0	3.38
Yde	1	2.1	5	3	1	0	1	0	11.57
Adams	1	1	2	0	0	0	0	0	0.00
Oldham	1	1	0	0	2	0	0	1	0.00
Washington (AL) Totals	7	60	61	17	32	3	4	1	2.85
Johnson	3	**26**	**26**	4	**15**	**2**	1	0	**2.08**
Coveleski	2	14.1	16	5	3	0	2	0	3.77
Ferguson	2	14	13	6	11	1	1	0	3.21
Marberry	2	2.1	3	0	2	0	0	1	0.00
Ballou	2	1.2	0	1	1	0	0	0	0.00
Zachary	1	1.2	3	1	0	0	0	0	10.80

1926 The Spoils of Temperament

To say that the Cardinals were overdue would be an understatement. St. Louis had never seen a National League pennant flying over the city, and the last championship St. Louis team was the Browns in the American Association in 1888. Rogers Hornsby ended the drought by squeezing his Cards home two games ahead of the Cincinnati Reds. The Rajah took over the reins of the club from Branch Rickey in 1925 with the Cards in the basement and brought them up to a fourth-place finish.

Hornsby's managerial Midas touch continued to glint as his team edged into first place in early September to beat the Reds in head-on competition and lock up the 1926 crown. Hornsby, the batter, fell off from his spectacular 1925 Triple Crown performance but still managed to hit .317 and drive 93 Cards across the plate. Additional offensive fire power was generated by Sunny Jim Bottomley and Les Bell, who along with Hornsby, accounted for 313 runs batted in. Catcher Bob O'Farrell and shortstop Tommy Thevenow glued together the St. Louis defense, which often bailed out starters, Flint Rhem, Bill Sherdel, and Jesse Haines. The Reds came close with a good attack which featured the first catcher ever to win a major league batting crown in Bubbles Hargrave, while the Pirates fell off to a close third, despite a .336 season from rookie outfielder Paul Waner.

The Yankees seemed to have the American League pennant ready to hoist but had to fight off three late-season challengers before claiming the flag. With a ten-game lead in mid-August, the Yankees were expected to waltz home, but Cleveland, Philadelphia, and Washington made New York work for their return to the top. The Indians, led by Tris Speaker, came to within four games shortly after Labor Day before the Yankees stiffened.

The Athletics relied on a deep and talented pitching staff, led by Lefty Grove, to finish a strong third, and the Senators had to recover from a poor start to reach fourth place. Washington continued to torment opposing pitchers, but the Senators' trio of Walter Johnson, Stan Coveleski, and Dutch Reuther all fell off in their hurling, as age seemingly caught up with all three simultaneously, to end the team's brief dominance of glory. The Yankees blended established stars like Babe Ruth, Bob Meusel, and Joe Dugan, along with a brigade of younger talent in Lou Gehrig, Earle Combs, Mark Koenig, and rookie Tony Lazzeri to field a lineup which was the scourge of the league. No new names appeared in the pitching ledger, but Herb Pennock, Urban Shocker, and Waite Hoyt all had enough left to win consistently.

Although Ruth swatted four homers for the Yankees in the World Series, the 1926 fall classic is best remembered for the dramatic seventh and final game won by the Cardinals. St. Louis' Jesse Haines had been staked to a 3-1 lead in the fourth inning. In the seventh frame the score stood at 3-2 with three Yankees on base, young slugger Tony Lazzeri at bat, and two out. Hornsby, sensing disaster, stopped the action and waved 39-year-old Grover "Pete" Alexander into the fray.

In the twilight of a brilliant career, "Old Pete" had pitched his second complete game victory of the Series only the day before, and legend has it that he was sleeping off the affects of a celebration bender in the bullpen when Hornsby called him. Nonetheless, the veteran hiked up his trousers, strode to the mound, and dramatically fanned Lazzeri to end the threat. No Yankee reached base against Alexander until Ruth walked with two down in the ninth. With slugger Meusel at bat and Gehrig on deck, Ruth astonished everyone in the park—except the Cardinals—by lighting out for second. Bob O'Farrell had plenty of time to gun the ball down to Hornsby, who slapped the tag on the Babe to bring the first world's championship to St. louis.

The final postscript to the season proved that talent and a championship were not enough to gain lasting security. Hornsby, superb as a ball player, was equally difficult as a human being—so much so that his confrontations with Cardinal owner, Sam Breadon, found him traded to the Giants for Frankie Frisch when the 1927 season rolled around.

1926 AMERICAN LEAGUE

NAME	G by POS	B	AGE	G	AB	R	H	2B	3B	HR	RBI	BB	SO	SB	BA	SA
NEW YORK 1st 91-63 .591		**MILLER HUGGINS**														
TOTALS			27	155	5221	**847**	1508	262	75	**121**	**794**	**642**	**580**	79	.289	**437**
Lou Gehrig	1B155	L	23	155	572	135	179	47	**20**	16	107	105	72	6	.313	.549
Tony Lazzeri	2B149, SS5, 3B1	R	22	155	589	79	162	28	14	18	114	54	**96**	16	.275	.462
Mark Koenig	SS141	B	23	147	617	93	167	26	8	5	62	43	37	4	.271	.363
Joe Dugan	3B122	R	29	123	434	39	125	19	5	1	64	25	16	2	.288	.362
Babe Ruth	OF149, 1B2	L	31	152	495	**139**	184	30	5	**47**	**145**	**144**	76	11	.372	**.737**
Earle Combs	OF145	L	27	145	606	113	181	31	12	8	56	47	23	8	.299	.429
Bob Meusel(BF)	OF107	R	29	108	413	73	130	22	3	12	81	37	32	16	.315	.470
Pat Collins	C100	R	29	102	290	41	83	11	3	7	35	73	55	3	.286	.417
Ben Paschal	OF76	R	30	96	258	46	74	12	3	7	33	26	35	7	.287	.438
Mike Gazella	3B45, SS11	R	29	66	168	21	39	6	0	0	21	25	24	2	.232	.268
2 Hank Severeid	C40	R	35	41	127	13	34	8	1	0	13	13	4	1	.268	.346
Benny Bengough(SJ)	C35	R	27	36	84	9	32	6	0	0	14	7	4	1	.381	.452
2 Roy Carlyle	OF16	L	25	35	53	3	20	5	1	0	11	4	9	0	.377	.509
Spencer Adams	2B4, 3B1	L	28	28	25	7	3	1	0	0	1	3	7	1	.120	.160
Aaron Ward	2B4, 3B1	R	29	22	31	5	10	2	0	0	3	2	6	0	.323	.387
2 Dutch Ruether	P5	L	32	13	21	2	2	0	0	0	0	0	1	0	.095	.095
Bill Skiff	C6	R	30	6	11	0	1	0	0	0	0	0	1	0	.091	.091
Nick Cullop		R	25	2	2	0	1	0	0	0	0	0	1	0	.500	.500
Honey Barnes	C1	L	26	1	0	0	0	0	0	0	0	1	0	0	.000	.000
Kiddo Davis	OF1	R	24	1	0	0	0	0	0	0	0	0	0	0	.000	.000
Fred Merkle	1B1	R	37	1	2	0	0	0	0	0	0	0	0	0	.000	.000
CLEVELAND 2nd 86-66 .571 3		**TRIS SPEAKER**														
TOTALS			29	154	5293	738	1529	**333**	49	27	643	455	331	88	.289	.386
George Burns	1B151	R	33	151	603	97	**216**	**64**	3	4	114	28	33	13	.358	.494
Freddie Spurgeon	2B149	R	24	149	614	101	181	31	3	0	49	27	36	7	.295	.355
Joe Sewell	SS154	L	27	154	578	91	187	41	5	4	85	65	6	17	.324	.433
Rube Lutzke	3B142	R	28	142	475	42	124	28	6	0	59	34	35	6	.261	.345
Homer Summa	OF154	L	27	154	581	74	179	31	6	4	76	47	9	15	.308	.403
Tris Speaker	OF149	L	38	150	540	96	164	52	8	7	86	94	15	6	.304	.469
Charlie Jamieson	OF143	L	33	143	555	89	166	33	7	2	45	53	22	9	.299	.395
Luke Sewell	C125	R	25	126	433	41	103	16	4	0	46	36	27	9	.238	.293
Glenn Myatt	C35	L	28	56	117	14	29	5	2	0	13	13	13	1	.248	.325
Pat McNulty	OF9	L	27	48	56	3	14	2	1	0	6	5	9	0	.250	.321
Fred Eichrodt	OF27	R	23	37	80	14	25	7	1	0	7	2	11	1	.313	.425
Ernie Padgett	3B29, SS2	R	27	36	62	7	13	0	1	0	6	8	3	1	.210	.242
Ray Knode	1B11	L	25	31	24	6	8	1	1	0	2	2	3	0	.333	.458
Cliff Lee	OF9, C3	R	29	21	40	4	7	1	0	1	2	6	8	0	.175	.275
Guy Lacy	2B11, 3B2	L	29	13	24	2	4	0	0	1	2	2	2	0	.167	.292
Martin Autry(IL)	C3	R	23	3	7	1	1	0	0	0	0	1	0	0	.143	.143
Johnny Hodapp(BL)	3B3	R	20	3	5	0	1	0	0	0	0	0	1	0	.200	.200
PHILADELPHIA 3rd 83-67 .553 6		**CONNIE MACK**														
TOTALS			27	150	5046	677	1359	259	65	61	619	523	449	56	.269	.383
Jim Poole	1B101, OF1	L	31	112	361	49	106	23	5	8	63	23	25	4	.294	.452
Max Bishop	2B119	L	26	122	400	77	106	20	2	0	33	116	41	4	.265	.325
Chick Galloway	SS133	R	29	133	408	37	98	13	6	0	49	31	20	8	.240	.301
Sammy Hale	3B77, OF1	R	29	111	327	49	92	22	9	4	43	13	36	1	.281	.440
Walt French	OF98	L	26	112	397	51	121	18	7	1	36	18	24	2	.305	.393
Al Simmons	OF147	R	24	147	581	90	199	53	10	19	109	48	49	10	.343	.566
Bill Lamar	OF107	L	29	116	419	62	119	17	6	5	50	18	15	4	.284	.389
Mickey Cochrane	C115	L	23	120	370	50	101	8	9	8	47	56	15	5	.273	.408
Jimmy Dykes	3B77, 2B44, SS1	R	29	124	429	54	123	32	5	1	44	49	34	6	.287	.392
Joe Hauser	1B65	L	27	91	229	31	44	10	0	8	36	39	34	1	.192	.341
Frank Welch	OF49	R	28	75	174	26	49	8	1	4	23	26	9	2	.282	.408
Cy Perkins	C55	R	30	63	148	14	43	6	0	0	19	18	7	0	.291	.331
Bill Wambsganss	SS15, 2B8	R	32	54	54	11	19	3	0	0	1	8	8	1	.352	.407
1 Bing Miller	OF34, 1B1	R	31	38	110	13	32	6	2	2	13	11	6	4	.291	.436
Jimmie Foxx	C12, OF3	R	18	26	32	8	10	2	1	0	5	1	6	1	.313	.438
Alex Metzler	OF17	L	23	20	67	8	16	3	0	0	12	7	5	1	.239	.284
Dave Barbee	OF10	R	21	19	47	7	8	1	1	1	5	2	4	0	.170	.298
Charlie Engle	SS16	R	22	19	19	7	2	0	0	0	0	10	6	0	.105	.105
Frank Sigafoos	SS12	R	22	13	43	4	11	0	0	0	2	0	3	0	.256	.256
2 Tom Jenkins	OF6	L	28	6	23	3	4	2	0	0	0	0	2	0	.174	.261

NAME	T	AGE	W	L	PCT	SV	G	GS	CG	IP	H	BB	SO	ShO	ERA
		30	**91**	63	**.591**	20	155	155	64	1372	1442	478	486	4	3.86
Herb Pennock	L	32	23	11	.676	2	40	33	19	266	294	43	78	1	3.62
Urban Shocker	R	35	19	11	.633	2	41	33	19	258	272	71	59	0	3.38
Waite Hoyt	R	26	16	12	.571	4	40	27	12	218	224	62	79	1	3.84
Sad Sam Jones	R	33	9	8	.529	5	39	23	6	161	186	80	69	1	4.98
Bob Shawkey(BF)	R	35	8	7	.522	3	29	10	3	104	102	37	63	1	3.63
Myles Thomas	R	28	6	6	.500	0	33	13	3	140	140	65	38	0	4.24
Garland Braxton	L	26	5	1	.833	2	37	1	0	67	71	19	30	0	2.69
Walter Beall	R	26	2	4	.333	1	20	9	1	82	71	68	56	0	3.51
2 Dutch Ruether	L	32	2	3	.400	0	5	5	1	36	32	18	8	0	3.50
Herb McQuaid	R	27	1	0	1.000	0	17	1	0	38	48	13	6	0	6.16
Hank Johnson	R	20	0	0	.000	1	1	0	0	1	2	2	0	0	18.00
		29	88	66	.571	4	154	154	**96**	1374	1412	450	381	**11**	3.40
George Uhle	R	27	**27**	11	.711	1	39	**36**	**32**	**318**	**300**	**118**	159	3	2.83
Emil Levsen	R	28	16	13	.552	0	33	31	18	237	235	85	53	2	3.42
Joe Shaute	L	26	14	10	.583	1	34	25	15	207	215	65	47	1	3.52
Sherry Smith	L	35	11	10	.524	0	27	24	16	188	214	31	25	1	3.73
Jake Miller(SA)	L	28	7	4	.636	1	18	11	5	83	99	18	24	3	3.26
Garland Buckeye	L	28	6	9	.400	0	32	18	5	166	160	69	36	1	3.09
Benn Karr	R	32	5	6	.455	1	30	7	4	113	137	41	23	0	5.01
Ray Benge	R	24	1	0	1.000	0	8	0	0	12	15	4	3	0	3.75
Willis Hudlin	R	20	1	3	.250	0	8	2	1	32	25	13	6	0	2.81
Norm Lehr	R	25	0	0	.000	0	4	0	0	15	11	4	4	0	3.00
By Speece	R	29	0	0	.000	0	2	0	0	3	1	2	1	0	0.00
		31	83	67	.553	16	150	150	62	1346	1362	451	**571**	10	**3.00**
Lefty Grove	L	26	13	13	.500	6	45	33	20	258	227	101	**194**	1	**2.51**
2 Howard Ehmke	R	32	12	4	.750	0	20	18	10	147	125	50	55	1	2.82
Rube Walberg	L	26	12	10	.545	2	40	19	5	151	168	60	72	2	2.80
Sam Gray	R	28	11	12	.478	0	38	18	5	151	164	50	82	0	3.64
Eddie Rommel	R	28	11	11	.500	0	37	26	12	219	225	54	52	3	3.08
Jack Quinn	R	42	10	11	.476	1	31	21	8	164	191	36	58	3	3.40
Joe Pate	L	34	9	0	1.000	6	47	2	0	113	109	51	24	0	2.71
1 Slim Harriss	R	29	3	5	.375	0	12	10	2	57	66	22	13	0	4.10
Stan Baumgartner	L	33	1	1	.500	0	10	1	0	22	28	10	0	0	4.10
1 Fred Heimach	L	25	1	0	1.000	0	13	1	0	32	28	5	8	0	2.81
Lefty Willis	L	20	0	0	.000	1	13	1	0	32	31	12	13	0	1.41

WASHINGTON 4th 81-69 .540 8 — **BUCKY HARRIS**

NAME	G by POS	B	AGE	G	AB	R	H	2B	3B	HR	RBI	BB	SO	SB	BA	SA
TOTALS			29	152	5223	802	1525	244	97	43	721	555	369	122	.292	.401
Joe Judge	1B128	L	32	134	453	70	132	25	11	7	92	53	25	7	.291	.442
Bucky Harris	2B141	R	29	141	537	94	152	39	9	1	63	58	41	16	.283	.395
Buddy Myer	SS117, 3B8	L	22	132	434	66	132	18	6	1	62	45	19	10	.304	.380
Ossie Bluege	3B134, SS8	R	25	139	487	69	132	19	8	3	65	70	46	12	.271	.361
Sam Rice	OF152	L	36	152	641	98	216	32	14	3	76	42	20	25	.337	.445
Earl McNeely	OF120	R	28	124	442	84	134	20	12	0	48	44	28	18	.303	.403
Goose Goslin	OF147	L	25	147	567	105	201	26	15	17	108	63	38	8	.354	.543
Muddy Ruel	C117	R	30	117	368	42	110	22	4	1	53	61	14	7	.299	.389
Joe Harris	1B36, OF35	R	35	92	257	43	79	13	9	5	55	37	9	2	.307	.486
Stuffy Stewart	2B25, 3B1	R	32	62	63	27	17	6	1	0	9	6	6	8	.270	.397
Bennie Tate	C45	L	24	59	142	17	38	5	2	1	13	15	1	0	.268	.352
Roger Peckinpaugh	SS46, 1B1	R	35	57	147	19	35	4	1	1	14	28	12	3	.238	.299
1 Dutch Ruether	P23	L	32	47	92	6	23	2	0	1	11	6	10	0	.250	.304
1 Jack Tobin	OF7	L	34	27	33	5	7	0	1	0	3	0	0	0	.212	.273
1 Hank Severeid	C16	R	35	22	34	2	7	1	0	0	4	3	2	0	.206	.235
Tex Jeanes	OF14	R	25	21	30	6	7	2	0	0	3	0	3	0	.233	.300
Danny Taylor	OF12	R	25	21	50	10	15	0	1	1	5	5	7	1	.300	.400
Bobby Reeves	3B16, 2B1, SS1	R	22	20	49	4	11	0	1	0	7	6	9	1	.224	.265
Russ Ennis	C1	R	29	1	0	0	0	0	0	0	0	0	0	0	.000	.000
Patsy Gharrity (DE) 34																

NAME	T	AGE	W	L	PCT	SV	G	GS	CG	IP	H	BB	SO	ShO	ERA
TOTALS		30	81	69	.540	26	152	152	65	1349	1489	566	418	5	4.34
Walter Johnson	R	38	15	16	.484	0	33	33	22	262	259	73	125	2	3.61
Stan Coveleski	R	37	14	11	.560	1	36	34	11	245	272	81	50	3	3.12
1 Dutch Ruether	L	32	12	6	.667	0	23	23	9	169	214	66	48	0	4.85
Firpo Marberry	R	27	12	7	.611	22	64	5	3	138	120	66	43	0	3.00
General Crowder	R	27	7	4	.636	1	19	12	6	100	97	60	26	0	3.96
George Murray	R	27	6	3	.667	0	12	12	5	81	89	37	28	0	5.67
Curly Ogden	R	25	4	4	.500	0	22	9	4	96	114	45	21	0	4.31
Alex Ferguson	R	29	3	4	.429	1	19	4	0	40	69	18	16	0	7.69
Bill Morrell	R	26	3	3	.500	1	26	2	1	70	83	29	16	0	5.27
Dick Jones	R	24	2	1	.667	0	4	3	1	21	20	11	3	0	4.29
Emilio Palmero	L	31	2	2	.500	0	7	3	0	17	22	15	6	0	4.77
1 Bullet Joe Bush	R	33	1	8	.111	0	12	11	3	71	83	35	27	0	6.72
Bump Hadley	R	21	0	0	.000	0	1	0	0	3	6	2	0	0	12.00
Harry Kelley	R	20	0	0	.000	0	7	1	0	10	17	8	6	0	8.10
Frank Loftus	R	28	0	0	.000	0	1	0	0	1	3	2	0	0	9.00
Lefty Thomas	L	22	0	0	.000	0	6	0	0	9	8	10	3	0	5.00
Jimmie Uchrinscko	R	25	0	0	.000	0	3	0	0	8	13	8	0	0	10.12

CHICAGO 5th 81-72 .529 9.5 — **EDDIE COLLINS**

NAME	G by POS	B	AGE	G	AB	R	H	2B	3B	HR	RBI	BB	SO	SB	BA	SA
TOTALS			29	155	5220	730	1508	314	60	32	666	556	381	124	.289	.390
Earl Sheely	1B144	R	33	145	525	77	157	40	2	6	89	75	13	3	.299	.417
Eddie Collins	2B101	L	39	106	375	66	129	32	4	1	62	62	8	13	.344	.459
Bill Hunnefield	SS98, 3B17, 2B15	B	27	131	470	81	129	26	4	3	48	37	28	24	.274	.366
Willie Kamm	3B142	R	26	143	480	63	141	24	10	0	62	77	24	14	.294	.398
Bill Barrett	OF102, 1B2	R	26	111	368	46	113	31	4	6	61	25	26	9	.307	.462
Johnny Mostil	OF147	R	30	148	600	120	197	41	15	4	42	79	55	35	.328	.467
Bibb Falk	OF155	L	27	155	566	86	195	43	4	8	108	66	22	9	.345	.477
Ray Schalk	C80	R	33	82	226	26	60	9	1	0	32	27	11	5	.265	.314
Spence Harris	OF63	L	25	80	222	36	56	11	3	2	27	20	15	8	.252	.356
Ray Morehart	2B48	L	26	73	192	27	61	10	3	0	21	11	15	3	.318	.401
Buck Crouse	C45	L	29	49	135	10	32	4	1	0	17	14	7	0	.237	.281
Johnny Grabowski	C38, 1B1	R	26	48	122	6	32	1	1	1	11	4	15	0	.262	.311
Harry McCurdy	C25, 1B8	L	26	44	86	16	28	7	2	1	11	6	10	0	.326	.488
Moe Berg	SS31, 2B2, 3B1	R	24	41	113	4	25	6	0	0	7	6	9	0	.221	.274
1 Everett Scott	SS39	R	33	40	143	15	36	10	1	0	13	9	8	1	.252	.336
Tom Gulley	OF12	L	26	16	35	5	8	3	1	0	8	5	2	0	.229	.371
Bud Clancy	1B10	L	25	12	38	3	13	2	2	0	7	1	1	0	.342	.500
Pid Purdy	OF9	L	22	11	33	5	6	2	1	0	6	2	1	0	.182	.303
Pat Veltman	SS1	R	20	5	4	1	1	0	0	0	0	1	1	0	.250	.250

NAME	T	AGE	W	L	PCT	SV	G	GS	CG	IP	H	BB	SO	ShO	ERA
TOTALS		28	81	72	.529	12	155	155	85	1380	1426	506	458	11	3.74
Ted Lyons	R	25	18	16	.529	2	39	31	24	284	268	106	51	3	3.02
Red Faber	R	37	15	9	.625	0	27	25	13	185	203	57	65	1	3.55
Tommy Thomas	R	26	15	12	.556	2	44	32	13	249	225	110	127	2	3.80
Ted Blankenship (BG)	R	25	13	10	.565	1	29	26	15	209	217	65	66	1	3.62
Sarge Connally	R	27	6	5	.545	3	31	8	5	108	128	35	47	0	3.17
Jim Joe Edwards	L	31	6	9	.400	1	32	16	8	142	140	63	41	3	4.18
Sloppy Thurston	R	27	6	8	.429	3	31	13	6	134	164	36	35	1	5.04
Dixie Leverett	R	32	1	1	.500	0	6	3	1	24	31	7	12	0	6.00
Milt Steengrafe	R	26	1	1	.500	0	13	1	0	38	43	19	10	0	4.03
Les Cox	R	20	0	1	.000	0	2	0	0	5	6	5	3	0	5.40
Pryor McBee	L	25	0	0	.000	0	1	0	0	1	1	3	1	0	9.00

DETROIT 6th 79-75 .513 12 — **TY COBB**

NAME	G by POS	B	AGE	G	AB	R	H	2B	3B	HR	RBI	BB	SO	SB	BA	SA
TOTALS			28	157	5315	793	1547	281	90	36	717	599	423	88	.291	.398
Lu Blue	1B109, OF1	B	29	128	429	92	123	24	14	1	52	90	18	13	.287	.415
Charlie Gehringer	2B112, 3B6	L	23	123	459	62	127	19	17	1	48	30	42	9	.277	.399
Jackie Tavener	SS156	L	28	156	532	65	141	22	14	1	58	52	53	8	.265	.365
Jack Warner	3B95, SS3	R	22	100	311	41	78	8	6	0	34	38	24	8	.251	.315
Harry Heilmann	OF134	R	31	141	502	90	184	41	8	9	103	67	19	6	.367	.534
Heinie Manush	OF120	L	24	136	498	95	188	35	8	14	86	31	28	11	.378	.564
Bob Fothergill	OF103	R	28	110	387	63	142	31	7	3	73	33	23	4	.367	.506
Clyde Manion	C74	R	29	75	176	15	35	4	0	0	14	24	16	1	.199	.222
Frank O'Rourke	3B60, 2B41, SS10	R	31	111	363	43	88	16	1	1	41	35	33	8	.242	.300
Al Wingo	OF74, 3B2	L	28	108	298	45	84	19	0	1	45	52	32	4	.282	.356
Johnny Neun	1B49	B	25	97	242	47	72	14	4	0	15	27	26	4	.298	.388
Ty Cobb	OF55	L	39	79	233	48	79	18	5	4	62	26	2	9	.339	.511
Larry Woodall	C59	R	31	67	146	18	34	5	0	0	15	15	2	0	.233	.267
Johnny Bassler (BN)	C63	L	31	66	174	20	53	8	1	0	22	45	6	0	.305	.362
Les Burke	2B15, 3B7, SS1	L	23	38	75	9	17	1	0	0	4	7	3	1	.227	.240
Ray Hayworth	C8	R	22	12	11	1	3	0	0	0	5	1	1	0	.273	.273
Billy Mullen	3B9	R	31	11	13	2	1	0	0	0	0	5	1	1	.077	.077

NAME	T	AGE	W	L	PCT	SV	G	GS	CG	IP	H	BB	SO	ShO	ERA
TOTALS		28	79	75	.513	18	157	157	57	1395	1570	555	469	10	4.41
Earl Whitehill	L	26	16	13	.552	0	36	34	13	252	271	79	109	0	4.00
Hooks Dauss	R	36	12	6	.667	9	34	5	0	124	135	49	27	0	4.21
Sam Gibson	R	26	12	9	.571	2	35	24	16	196	199	75	61	2	3.49
Ed Wells	L	26	12	10	.545	0	36	26	9	178	201	76	58	4	4.15
Rip Collins	R	30	8	8	.500	1	30	13	5	122	128	44	44	3	2.73
Lil Stoner	R	27	7	10	.412	0	32	22	7	160	179	63	57	0	5.46
Augie Johns	L	26	6	4	.600	1	35	14	3	113	117	69	40	1	5.34
Ken Hollaway	R	28	4	6	.400	2	36	12	3	139	192	42	43	0	5.12
Clyde Barfoot	R	34	1	2	.333	2	11	1	0	31	42	9	7	0	4.94
George Smith	R	24	1	2	.333	0	23	1	0	44	55	33	15	0	6.95
2 Wilbur Cooper	L	34	0	4	.000	0	8	3	0	14	27	9	2	0	10.93
Jess Doyle	R	28	0	0	.000	1	2	0	0	4	6	1	2	0	4.25
Rudy Kneisch	L	27	0	1	.000	0	2	2	1	17	18	6	4	0	2.65

ST. LOUIS 7th 62-92 .403 29 — **GEORGE SISLER**

NAME	G by POS	B	AGE	G	AB	R	H	2B	3B	HR	RBI	BB	SO	SB	BA	SA
TOTALS			30	155	5259	682	1449	253	78	72	608	437	465	63	.276	.394
George Sisler	1B149, P1	L	33	150	613	78	178	21	12	7	71	30	30	12	.289	.398
Oscar Melillo (AJ)	2B88, 3B11	R	26	99	385	54	98	18	5	1	30	32	31	6	.255	.335
Wally Gerber	SS129	R	34	131	411	37	111	8	0	0	42	40	29	0	.270	.290
Marty McManus	3B84, 2B61, 1B4	R	26	149	549	102	156	30	10	9	68	55	62	5	.284	.424
2 Bing Miller	OF94	R	31	94	353	60	117	27	5	4	50	22	12	7	.331	.470
Harry Rice	OF133, 3B7, 2B4, SS2	L	25	148	578	86	181	27	10	9	59	63	40	10	.313	.441
Ken Williams	OF92, 2B1	L	36	108	347	55	97	15	7	17	74	39	23	5	.280	.510
Wally Shang	C82, OF3	B	36	103	285	36	94	19	5	8	50	32	20	5	.330	.516
Pinky Hargrave	C58	R	30	92	235	20	66	16	3	7	37	10	38	3	.281	.464
Herschel Bennett	OF50	L	29	80	225	33	60	14	2	1	26	22	21	2	.267	.360
Cedric Durst	OF57, 1B4	L	29	80	219	32	52	7	5	3	16	22	19	0	.237	.356
Gene Robertson	3B55, SS10, 2B3	L	26	78	247	23	62	12	6	1	19	17	10	5	.251	.360
1 Baby Doll Jacobson	OF50	R	35	50	182	18	52	15	1	2	21	9	14	1	.286	.412
Bobby LaMotte	SS30, 3B1	R	28	36	79	11	16	4	3	0	9	11	6	0	.202	.329
Leo Dixon (BW)	C33	R	29	33	89	7	17	3	1	0	8	11	14	1	.191	.247
Jimmy Austin	3B1	B	46	1	2	1	1	1	0	0	1	0	0	1	.500	1.000

NAME	T	AGE	W	L	PCT	SV	G	GS	CG	IP	H	BB	SO	ShO	ERA
TOTALS		28	62	92	.403	9	155	155	64	1368	1549	654	337	5	4.66
Tom Zachary	L	30	14	15	.483	0	34	31	18	247	264	97	53	3	3.61
Win Ballou	R	28	11	10	.500	2	43	13	5	154	186	71	59	0	4.79
Milt Gaston	R	30	10	18	.357	0	32	28	14	214	227	101	39	1	4.33
Elam Vangilder	R	30	9	11	.450	1	42	19	8	181	196	98	40	1	5.17
Ernie Wingard	L	25	5	8	.385	3	39	16	7	169	188	76	30	0	3.57
Chet Falk	L	21	4	4	.500	0	18	8	3	74	95	27	7	0	5.35
Dixie Davis	R	35	3	8	.273	1	27	7	2	83	93	40	39	0	4.66
Joe Giard	L	27	3	10	.231	0	22	16	2	90	113	67	18	0	7.00
Ernie Nevers	R	23	2	4	.333	0	11	7	4	75	82	24	16	0	4.44
Charlie Robertson	R	30	1	2	.333	0	8	7	1	28	38	21	13	0	8.36
Stew Bolen	L	23	0	0	.000	0	5	0	0	15	21	6	7	0	5.98
Claude Jonnard	R	29	0	2	.000	1	12	3	0	36	46	24	13	0	6.00
George Sisler	L	33	0	0	.000	1	1	0	0	2	0	2	3	0	0.00

BOSTON 8th 46-107 .301 44.5 — **LEE FOHL**

NAME	G by POS	B	AGE	G	AB	R	H	2B	3B	HR	RBI	BB	SO	SB	BA	SA
TOTALS			29	154	5185	562	1325	249	54	32	521	465	450	52	.256	.343
Phil Todt	1B154	L	24	154	599	56	153	19	12	7	69	40	38	3	.255	.362
Bill Regan	2B106	R	27	108	403	40	106	21	3	4	34	23	37	6	.263	.360
Topper Rigney	SS146	R	29	148	525	71	142	32	6	4	53	108	31	6	.270	.377
Fred Haney	3B137	R	28	138	462	47	102	15	7	0	52	74	28	13	.221	.284
2 Baby Doll Jacobson	OF98	R	35	98	394	44	120	36	1	6	69	22	22	4	.305	.447
Ira Flagstead (ST)	OF98	R	32	98	415	65	124	31	7	3	31	36	22	4	.299	.429
Si Rosenthal	OF67	L	22	104	285	34	76	12	3	4	34	19	18	4	.267	.372
Alex Gaston	C98	R	33	98	301	37	67	5	3	0	21	21	28	3	.223	.259
Mike Herrara	2B48, 3B16, SS4	R	28	74	237	20	61	14	1	0	19	15	13	0	.257	.325
Fred Bratchi	OF37	R	34	72	167	12	46	10	1	0	19	14	15	0	.275	.347
Wally Shaner	OF48	R	26	69	191	20	54	12	2	0	21	17	13	1	.283	.366
George Bischoff	C46	R	31	59	127	6	33	11	2	0	19	15	16	1	.260	.378
2 Jack Tobin	OF51	L	34	51	209	26	57	9	0	1	14	16	3	6	.273	.330
1 Roy Carlyle	OF37	L	25	45	164	22	47	6	2	2	16	4	18	0	.287	.384
Howie Fitzgerald	OF23	L	24	31	97	11	25	2	0	0	8	5	7	1	.258	.278
Al Stokes	C29	R	26	30	86	7	14	3	3	0	6	8	28	0	.163	.267
1 Tom Jenkins	OF13	L	28	21	50	3	9	1	1	0	6	3	7	0	.180	.240
Jack Rothrock	SS2	B	21	15	17	3	5	1	0	0	2	3	1	0	.294	.353
Emmett McCann	SS1, 3B1	R	24	6	3	0	0	0	0	0	0	1	1	0	.000	.000
Bill Moore	C5	L	24	5	18	2	3	0	0	0	0	0	4	0	.167	.167
Chappie Geygan	3B3	R	23	4	10	0	3	0	0	0	0	1	1	0	.300	.300
Boob Fowler	3B2	L	25	2	8	1	1	0	0	0	1	0	0	0	.125	.125
Dud Lee	SS2	L	26	2	7	2	1	0	0	0	0	0	0	0	.143	.143
Sam Langford		L	26	1	1	1	0	0	0	0	0	0	0	0	.000	.000

NAME	T	AGE	W	L	PCT	SV	G	GS	CG	IP	H	BB	SO	ShO	ERA
TOTALS		25	46	107	.301	5	154	154	53	1362	1520	546	336	6	4.72
Ted Wingfield	R	26	11	16	.407	3	43	20	9	191	220	50	30	1	4.43
Hal Wiltse	L	22	8	15	.348	0	37	29	9	196	201	99	59	1	4.22
2 Slim Harriss	R	29	6	10	.375	0	21	18	6	113	135	33	34	1	4.46
Red Ruffing	R	22	6	15	.286	2	37	22	6	166	169	68	58	0	4.39
Paul Zahniser	R	29	6	18	.250	0	30	24	7	172	213	69	35	1	4.97
Tony Welzer	R	27	4	3	.571	0	40	6	1	141	167	57	30	1	4.79
1 Howard Ehmke	R	32	3	10	.231	0	14	14	7	97	115	45	38	1	5.47
2 Fred Heimach	L	25	2	9	.182	0	20	13	6	102	119	42	17	0	5.65
Bill Clowers	L	28	0	0	.000	0	2	0	0	2	2	0	0	0	0.00
Happy Foreman	L	28	0	0	.000	0	3	0	0	7	3	5	3	0	3.86
Joe Kiefer	R	26	0	2	.000	0	11	1	0	30	29	16	4	0	4.80
Del Lundgren	R	25	0	2	.000	0	17	1	0	29	35	24	10	0	8.07
Danny MacFayden	R	21	0	1	.000	0	3	1	1	13	10	7	1	0	4.85
Buster Ross	L	23	0	1	.000	0	1	0	0	3	5	4	0	0	15.00
Jack Russell	R	20	0	5	.000	0	36	5	1	98	94	24	17	0	3.58
Rudy Sommers	L	37	0	0	.000	0	2	0	0	2	3	3	0	0	13.50

ST. LOUIS 1st 89-65 .578 — **ROGERS HORNSBY**

NAME	G by POS	B	AGE	G	AB	R	H	2B	3B	HR	RBI	BB	SO	SB	BA	SA
TOTALS			27	156	5381	817	1541	259	82	**90**	**756**	**478**	**518**	83	.286	**.415**
Jim Bottomley	1B154	L	26	154	603	98	180	**40**	14	19	**120**	58	52	4	.299	.506
Rogers Hornsby	2B134	R	30	134	527	96	167	34	5	11	93	61	39	3	.317	.463
Tommy Thevenow	SS156	R	22	156	563	64	144	15	5	2	63	27	26	8	.256	.311
Les Bell	3B155	R	24	155	581	85	189	33	14	17	100	54	62	9	.325	.518
2 Billy Southworth	OF99	L	33	99	391	76	124	22	6	11	69	26	9	13	.317	.488
Taylor Douthit	OF138	R	25	139	530	96	163	20	4	3	52	55	46	23	.308	.377
Ray Blades (JJ)	OF105	R	29	107	416	81	127	17	12	8	43	62	57	6	.305	.462
Bob O'Farrell	C146	R	29	147	492	63	144	30	9	7	68	61	44	1	.293	.433
Chick Hafey	OF54	R	23	78	225	30	61	19	2	4	38	11	36	2	.271	.427
Specs Toporcer	2B27, SS5, 3B1	L	27	64	88	13	22	3	2	0	9	8	9	1	.250	.330
Wattie Holm	OF39	R	24	55	144	18	41	5	1	0	21	18	14	3	.285	.333
1 Heinie Mueller	OF51	L	26	52	191	36	51	7	5	3	28	11	6	8	.267	.403
Jake Flowers	2B11, 1B3, SS1	R	24	40	74	13	20	1	0	3	9	5	9	1	.270	.405
Art Reinhart	P27	L	27	40	63	7	20	2	2	0	11	1	3	1	.317	.413
Ernie Vick	C23	R	25	24	51	6	10	2	0	0	4	3	4	0	.196	.235
Bill Warwick	C9	R	28	9	14	0	5	0	0	0	2	0	2	0	.357	.357
1 Jack Smith		L	31	1	1	0	0	0	0	0	0	0	1	0	.000	.000

NAME	T	AGE	W	L	PCT	SV	G	GS	CG	IP	H	BB	SO	ShO	ERA
TOTALS		29	**89**	65	**.578**	6	156	156	**90**	1399	1423	397	365	10	3.67
Flint Rhem	R	25	**20**	7	.741	0	34	34	20	258	241	75	72	1	3.21
Bill Sherdel	L	29	16	12	.571	0	34	29	17	235	255	49	59	3	3.49
Jesse Haines	R	32	13	4	.765	1	33	21	14	183	186	48	46	3	3.25
Vic Keen	R	27	10	9	.526	0	26	21	12	152	179	42	29	1	4.56
Art Reinhart	L	27	10	5	.667	0	27	11	9	143	159	47	26	0	4.22
2 Pete Alexander (SA-ST)	R	39	9	7	.563	2	23	16	11	148	136	24	35	2	2.92
Hi Bell	R	28	6	6	.500	2	27	7	3	85	82	17	27	0	3.18
Allan Sothoron	R	33	3	3	.500	0	15	4	1	43	37	16	19	0	4.19
Eddie Dyer	L	25	1	0	1.000	0	6	0	0	9	7	14	4	0	12.00
Wild Bill Hallahan	L	23	1	4	.200	0	19	3	0	57	45	32	28	0	3.63
Ed Clough	L	19	0	0	.000	0	1	0	0	2	5	3	0	0	22.50
1 Walter Huntzinger	R	27	0	4	.000	0	9	4	2	34	35	14	9	0	4.24
Syl Johnson	R	25	0	3	.000	1	19	6	1	49	54	15	10	0	4.22
Duster Mails	L	30	0	1	.000	0	1	0	0	1	2	1	1	0	0.00

CINCINNATI 2nd 87-67 .565 2 — **JACK HENDRICKS**

NAME	G by POS	B	AGE	G	AB	R	H	2B	3B	HR	RBI	BB	SO	SB	BA	SA
TOTALS			30	157	5320	747	**1541**	242	**120**	35	692	454	333	51	**.290**	.400
Wally Pipp	1B155	L	33	155	574	72	167	22	15	6	99	49	26	8	.291	.413
Hughie Critz	2B155	R	25	155	607	96	164	24	14	3	79	39	25	7	.270	.371
Frank Emmer	SS79	R	30	80	224	22	44	7	6	0	18	13	30	1	.196	.281
Chuck Dressen	3B123, SS1, OF1	R	27	127	474	70	120	27	11	4	48	49	31	0	.266	.395
Curt Walker	OF152	L	29	155	571	83	175	24	20	6	78	60	31	3	.306	.450
Edd Roush	OF143, 1B1	L	33	144	563	95	182	37	10	7	79	38	17	8	.323	.462
Cuckoo Christenson	OF93	L	26	114	329	41	115	15	7	0	41	40	18	8	.350	.438
Bubbles Hargrave	C93	R	33	105	326	42	115	22	8	6	62	25	17	2	**.353**	.525
Val Picinich	C86	R	29	89	240	33	63	16	1	2	31	29	22	4	.263	.363
Rube Bressler (IL)	OF80, 1B4	R	31	86	297	58	106	15	9	1	51	37	20	3	.357	.478
Babe Pinelli	3B40, SS27, 2B3	R	30	71	207	26	46	7	4	0	24	15	5	2	.222	.295
Red Lucas	P39, 2B1	L	24	66	76	15	23	4	4	0	14	10	13	0	.303	.461
Hod Ford	SS57	R	28	57	197	14	55	6	1	0	18	14	12	1	.279	.320
Billy Zitzmann	OF31	R	28	53	94	21	23	2	1	0	3	6	7	3	.245	.287
Pete Donohue	P47	R	25	47	106	8	33	5	2	0	14	5	8	0	.311	.396
Dolf Luque	P34	R	35	34	78	8	27	5	0	0	8	5	4	0	.346	.410
1 Sammy Bohne	SS20	R	29	25	54	8	11	0	2	0	5	4	8	1	.204	.278
Ethan Allen	OF9	R	22	18	13	3	4	1	0	0	0	0	3	0	.308	.385
Jimmy Hudgens	1B6	L	23	17	20	2	5	1	0	0	1	1	0	0	.250	.300
Ivy Wingo	C7	L	35	7	10	0	2	0	0	0	1	1	0	0	.200	.200
Howard Carter	2B3, SS1	R	21	5	1	0	0	0	0	0	0	0	0	0	.000	.000

2 Everett Scott (LJ) 33 R 4-6, Doc Prothro 32 R 1-5, Clyde Sukeforth 24 L 0-1

NAME	T	AGE	W	L	PCT	SV	G	GS	CG	IP	H	BB	SO	ShO	ERA
TOTALS		31	87	67	.565	8	157	157	88	**1409**	1449	324	424	**14**	3.42
Pete Donohue	R	25	**20**	14	.588	2	47	**38**	17	**286**	**298**	39	73	**5**	3.37
Carl Mays	R	34	19	12	.613	1	39	33	**24**	281	286	53	58	3	3.14
Eppa Rixey	L	35	14	8	.636	0	37	29	14	233	231	58	61	3	3.40
Dolf Luque	R	35	13	16	.448	0	34	30	16	234	231	77	83	1	3.42
Jakie May	L	30	10	9	.601	2	45	15	9	168	175	44	103	1	3.21
Red Lucas	R	24	8	5	.615	2	39	11	7	154	161	30	34	1	3.68
Pea Ridge Day	R	27	0	0	.000	0	4	0	0	7	13	2	2	0	7.71
Mul Holland	R	23	0	0	.000	0	3	0	0	7	3	5	0	0	1.29
Rufe Meadows	L	18	0	0	.000	0	1	0	0	.1	0	0	0	0	0.00
Roy Meeker	L	25	0	2	.000	0	7	1	1	21	24	9	5	0	6.43
2 Art Nehf	L	33	0	1	.000	0	7	0	0	17	25	5	4	0	3.71
Brad Springer	L	22	0	0	.000	0	1	0	0	1	2	2	1	0	9.00

Marv Goodwin (DD) 35

PITTSBURGH 3rd 84-69 .549 4.5 — **BILL McKECHNIE**

NAME	G by POS	B	AGE	G	AB	R	H	2B	3B	HR	RBI	BB	SO	SB	BA	SA
TOTALS			28	157	5312	769	1514	243	106	44	707	434	350	91	.285	.396
George Grantham	1B132	L	26	141	449	66	143	27	13	8	70	60	42	6	.318	.490
Hal Rhyne	2B66, SS44, 3B1	R	27	109	366	46	92	14	3	2	39	35	21	1	.251	.322
Glenn Wright	SS116	R	25	119	458	73	141	15	15	8	77	19	26	6	.308	.459
Pie Traynor	3B148, SS3	R	26	152	574	83	182	25	17	3	92	38	14	8	.317	.436
Paul Waner	OF139	L	23	144	536	101	180	35	**22**	8	79	66	19	11	.336	.528
1 Max Carey	OF82	B	36	86	324	46	72	14	5	0	28	30	14	10	.222	.296
Kiki Cuyler	OF157	R	26	157	614	**113**	197	31	15	8	92	50	66	**35**	.321	.459
Earl Smith	C98	L	29	105	292	29	101	17	2	2	46	28	7	1	.346	.438
Johnny Gooch	C80	B	28	86	218	19	59	15	1	1	42	20	14	1	.271	.362
Clyde Barnhart	OF61	R	30	76	203	26	39	3	0	0	10	23	13	1	.192	.207
Johnny Rawlings	2B59	R	33	61	181	27	42	6	0	0	20	14	10	3	.232	.265
Stuffy McInnis	1B40	R	35	47	127	12	38	6	1	0	13	7	3	1	.299	.362
1 Eddie Moore	2B24, 3B9, SS1	R	27	43	132	19	30	8	1	0	19	12	6	3	.227	.303
Carson Bigbee	OF21	L	31	42	68	15	15	3	1	2	4	3	0	2	.221	.382
Joe Cronin	2B27, SS7	R	19	38	83	9	22	2	2	0	11	6	15	0	.265	.337
Roy Spencer	C12	R	26	28	43	5	17	3	0	0	4	1	0	0	.395	.465
Fred Brickell	OF14	L	19	24	55	11	19	3	1	0	4	3	6	0	.345	.436
Walter Mueller	OF15	R	31	19	62	8	15	0	1	0	3	0	2	0	.242	.274
Eddie Murphy	OF3	L	34	16	17	3	2	0	0	0	6	3	0	0	.118	.118
Adam Comorosky	OF6	R	21	8	15	2	4	1	1	0	0	1	2	1	.267	.467

NAME	T	AGE	W	L	PCT	SV	G	GS	CG	IP	H	BB	SO	ShO	ERA
TOTALS		32	84	69	.549	**18**	157	157	83	1379	1422	455	387	12	3.67
Ray Kremer	R	33	**20**	6	**.769**	5	37	26	18	231	221	51	74	3	**2.61**
Lee Meadows	R	31	**20**	9	.690	0	36	31	15	227	254	52	54	1	3.96
Vic Aldridge	R	32	10	13	.435	1	30	26	12	190	204	73	61	1	4.07
Emil Yde	L	26	8	7	.533	0	37	22	12	187	181	81	34	1	3.66
Don Songer	L	27	7	8	.467	2	35	14	5	126	118	52	27	1	3.14
2 Bullet Joe Bush	R	33	6	6	.500	3	19	11	9	111	97	35	38	2	3.00
Johnny Morrison (ST)	R	30	6	8	.429	2	26	13	6	122	119	44	39	2	3.39
Carmen Hill	R	30	3	3	.500	0	6	6	4	40	42	9	8	1	3.38
Babe Adams	R	44	2	3	.400	3	19	0	0	37	51	8	7	0	6.08
Red Oldham	L	32	2	2	.500	2	17	2	0	42	56	18	16	0	5.57
Bud Culloton	R	30	0	0	.000	0	4	0	0	4	3	6	1	0	6.75
Lou Koupal	R	27	0	2	.000	0	6	2	1	20	22	8	7	0	3.15
Roy Mahaffey	R	23	0	0	.000	0	4	0	0	5	5	1	3	0	0.00
Chet Nichols	R	28	0	0	.000	0	3	0	0	8	13	5	2	0	7.88
Tom Sheehan	R	32	0	2	.000	0	9	4	1	31	36	12	16	0	6.68

CHICAGO 4th 82-72 .532 7 — **JOE McCARTHY**

NAME	G by POS	B	AGE	G	AB	R	H	2B	3B	HR	RBI	BB	SO	SB	BA	SA
TOTALS			28	155	5229	682	1453	**291**	49	66	630	445	447	85	.278	.390
Charlie Grimm	1B147	L	27	147	524	58	145	30	6	8	82	49	25	3	.277	.403
Sparky Adams	2B136, 3B19, SS2	R	31	154	**624**	95	193	35	3	0	39	52	27	27	.309	.375
Jimmy Cooney	SS141	R	31	141	513	52	129	18	5	1	47	23	10	11	.251	.312
Howard Freigau	3B135, SS2, OF1	R	23	140	508	51	137	27	7	3	51	43	42	6	.270	.368
Cliff Heathcote	OF133	L	28	139	510	98	141	33	3	10	53	58	30	18	.276	.412
Hack Wilson	OF140	R	26	142	529	97	170	36	8	**21**	109	**69**	61	10	.321	.539
Riggs Stephenson	OF74	R	28	82	281	40	95	18	3	3	44	31	16	2	.338	.456
Gabby Hartnett	C88	R	25	93	284	35	78	25	3	8	41	32	37	0	.275	.468
Mike Gonzalez	C78	R	35	80	253	24	63	13	3	1	23	13	17	3	.249	.336
Pete Scott	OF59, 3B1	R	27	77	189	34	54	13	1	3	34	22	31	3	.286	.413
Joe Kelly	OF39	L	26	65	176	16	59	15	3	0	32	7	11	0	.335	.455
Chuck Tolson	1B13	R	24	57	80	4	25	6	1	1	8	5	8	0	.313	.450
Joe Munson	OF28	L	26	33	101	17	26	2	2	3	15	8	4	0	.257	.406
Clyde Beck	2B30	R	24	30	81	10	16	0	0	1	4	7	15	0	.198	.235
Mandy Brooks	OF18	R	27	26	48	7	9	1	0	1	6	5	5	0	.188	.271
Red Shannon	SS13	B	29	19	51	9	17	5	0	0	4	6	3	0	.333	.431
Hank Schreiber	SS3, 3B3, 2B1	R	34	10	18	2	1	1	0	0	0	0	1	0	.056	.111

John Churry 25 R 0-4, Joe Graves L 20 0-5, Ralph Michaels 24 R 0-0

NAME	T	AGE	W	L	PCT	SV	G	GS	CG	IP	H	BB	SO	ShO	ERA
TOTALS		26	82	72	.532	14	155	155	77	1378	1407	**486**	508	13	**3.26**
Charlie Root	R	27	18	**17**	.514	2	42	32	21	271	267	62	127	2	2.82
Guy Bush	R	24	13	9	.591	2	35	16	7	157	149	42	32	2	2.87
Percy Jones	L	26	12	7	.632	2	30	20	10	160	151	90	80	2	3.09
Sherriff Blake	R	26	11	12	.478	1	39	27	11	198	204	**92**	95	4	3.59
Tony Kaufmann	R	25	9	7	.563	2	26	21	14	170	169	44	52	1	3.02
Bob Osborn	R	23	6	5	.545	1	31	15	6	136	157	58	43	0	3.64
Bill Piercy	R	30	6	5	.545	0	19	5	1	90	96	37	31	0	4.50
1 Pete Alexander	R	39	3	3	.500	0	7	7	4	52	55	7	12	0	3.46
Wilbur Cooper	L	34	2	1	.667	0	8	8	3	55	65	21	18	2	4.42
2 Walter Huntzinger	R	27	1	1	.500	2	11	0	0	29	26	8	4	0	0.93
George Milstead	L	23	1	5	.167	2	18	4	0	55	63	24	14	0	3.60
Johnny Welch	R	19	0	0	.000	0	3	0	0	4	5	1	0	0	2.25

NEW YORK 5th 74-77 .490 13.5 — **JOHN McGRAW**

NAME	G by POS	B	AGE	G	AB	R	H	2B	3B	HR	RBI	BB	SO	SB	BA	SA
TOTALS			27	151	5167	663	1435	214	58	73	617	339	420	**94**	.278	.384
George Kelly	1B114, 2B18	R	30	136	499	70	151	24	4	13	80	36	52	4	.303	.445
Frankie Frisch	2B127, 3B7	B	27	135	545	75	171	29	4	5	44	33	16	23	.314	.409
Travis Jackson	SS108, OF1	R	22	111	385	64	126	24	8	8	51	20	26	2	.327	.494
Fred Lindstrom	3B138, OF1	R	20	140	543	90	164	19	9	9	76	39	21	11	.302	.420
Ross Youngs (IL)	OF94	R	29	95	372	62	114	12	5	4	43	37	19	21	.306	.398
Ty Tyson	OF92	R	34	97	335	40	98	16	1	3	35	15	28	6	.293	.373
Irish Meusel	OF112	R	33	129	449	51	131	25	10	6	65	16	18	5	.292	.432
Paul Florence	C76	L	26	76	188	19	43	4	3	2	14	23	12	2	.229	.314
Bill Terry	1B38, OF14	L	27	98	225	26	65	12	5	5	43	22	17	3	.289	.453
2 Heinie Mueller	OF82	L	26	85	305	36	76	6	2	4	29	21	17	7	.249	.321
Doc Farrell	SS53, 2B3	R	24	67	171	19	49	10	1	2	23	12	17	4	.287	.392
Hugh McMullen	C56	B	24	57	91	5	17	2	0	0	6	2	18	1	.187	.209
Frank Snyder (BH)	C55	R	33	55	148	10	32	3	2	5	16	13	13	0	.216	.365
Jack Scott	P50	L	34	51	83	8	28	4	2	1	13	3	6	0	.337	.470
2 Jimmy Johnston	OF14	R	36	37	69	11	16	0	0	0	5	6	5	0	.232	.232
1 Billy Southworth	OF29	L	33	36	116	23	38	6	1	5	30	7	1	1	.328	.526
Mel Ott	OF10	L	17	35	60	7	23	2	0	0	4	1	9	1	.383	.417
Andy Cohen	2B10, SS10, 3B2	R	21	32	35	4	9	0	1	0	8	1	2	0	.257	.314
Al Moore	OF20	R	23	28	81	12	18	4	0	0	10	5	7	2	.222	.272
Grover Hartley	C13	R	37	13	21	0	1	0	0	0	0	5	0	0	.048	.048
Heinie Groh	3B7	R	36	12	35	2	8	2	0	0	3	2	3	0	.229	.286
Jack Cummings	C6	R	22	7	16	3	5	3	0	0	4	4	2	0	.313	.500
Blackie Carter	OF4	R	23	5	17	4	4	1	0	1	1	1	0	0	.235	.471

Mike Smith 21 L 1-7, Joe Connell 24 L 0-1, Pete Cote 23 R 0-1, Scottie Slayback 24 R 0-8, Fresco Thompson 24 R 5-8, Jim Boyle 22 R 0-0, Sam Hamby R 28 0-3

NAME	T	AGE	W	L	PCT	SV	G	GS	CG	IP	H	BB	SO	ShO	ERA
TOTALS		29	74	77	.490	15	151	151	61	1342	1370	427	419	4	3.77
Freddie Fitzsimmons	R	24	14	10	.583	0	37	26	12	219	224	58	48	0	2.88
Kent Greenfield	R	24	13	12	.520	1	39	28	8	223	206	82	74	1	3.96
Jack Scott	R	34	13	15	.464	5	**50**	22	13	226	242	53	82	0	4.34
Hugh McQuillan	R	28	11	10	.524	0	33	22	12	167	171	42	47	1	3.72
Jimmy Ring	R	31	11	10	.524	2	39	23	5	183	207	74	76	0	4.57
Virgil Barnes (JJ)	R	29	8	13	.381	1	31	25	9	185	183	56	54	2	2.87
Chick Davies	L	34	2	4	.333	**6**	38	1	0	89	96	35	27	0	3.94
John Wisner	R	26	2	2	.500	0	5	3	2	28	21	10	5	0	3.54
2 Jack Bentley	L	31	0	0	.000	0	1	0	0	2	0	2	1	0	0.00
Tim McNamera	R	27	0	0	.000	0	6	0	0	6	7	4	4	0	9.00
1 Art Nehf	L	33	0	0	.000	0	2	0	0	2	2	1	0	0	9.00
Joe Poetz	R	26	0	1	.000	0	2	1	0	8	5	8	0	0	3.38
Ned Porter	R	21	0	0	.000	0	2	0	0	2	2	0	1	0	4.50
Al Smith	R	22	0	0	.000	0	1	0	0	2	4	2	0	0	9.00

BROOKLYN 6th 71-82 .464 17.5 — WILBERT ROBINSON

NAME	G by POS	B	AGE	G	AB	R	H	2B	3B	HR	RBI	BB	SO	SB	BA	SA
TOTALS			31	155	5130	623	1348	246	62	40	568	475	464	76	.263	.358
Babe Herman	1B101, OF35	L	23	137	496	64	158	35	11	11	81	44	53	8	.319	.500
Chick Fewster	2B103	R	30	105	337	53	82	16	3	2	24	45	49	9	.243	.326
Johnny Butler	SS102, 3B42, 2B8	R	33	147	501	54	135	27	5	1	68	54	44	6	.269	.349
Bill Marriott	3B104	L	33	109	360	39	96	13	9	3	42	17	20	12	.267	.378
Dick Cox	OF117	R	28	124	398	53	118	17	4	1	45	46	20	6	.296	.367
Gus Felix	OF125	R	31	134	432	64	121	21	7	3	53	51	32	9	.280	.382
Zack Wheat	OF102	L	40	111	411	68	119	31	2	5	35	21	14	4	.290	.411
Mickey O'Neil	C74	R	28	75	201	19	42	5	3	0	20	23	8	3	.209	.264
Merwin Jacobson	OF86	L	32	110	288	41	71	9	2	0	23	36	24	5	.247	.292
Jack Fournier	1B64	R	33	87	243	39	69	9	2	11	48	30	16	0	.284	.473
Charlie Hargreaves	C70	R	29	85	208	14	52	13	2	2	23	19	10	1	.250	.361
Rabbit Maranville	SS60, 2B18	R	34	78	234	32	55	8	5	0	24	26	24	7	.235	.312
Jerry Standaert	2B21, 3B14, SS6	R	24	66	113	13	39	8	2	0	14	5	7	0	.345	.451
Whitey Witt	OF22	L	30	63	85	13	22	1	1	0	3	12	6	1	.259	.294
Hank DeBerry	C37	R	31	48	115	6	33	11	0	0	13	8	5	0	.287	.383
2 Sammy Bohne	2B31, 3B15	R	29	47	125	4	25	3	2	1	11	12	9	1	.200	.280
2 Max Carey	OF27	B	36	27	100	18	26	3	1	0	7	8	5	0	.260	.310
Moose Clabaugh	OF2	L	24	11	14	2	1	1	0	0	1	0	1	0	.071	.143

Milt Stock 32 R 0-8, Snooks Dowd 28 R 0-8

NAME	T	AGE	W	L	PCT	SV	G	GS	CG	IP	H	BB	SO	ShO	ERA
		32	71	82	.464	9	155	155	83	1362	1440	472	517	5	3.82
Jesse Petty	L	31	17	17	.500	1	38	33	23	276	246	79	101	1	2.84
Burleigh Grimes	R	32	12	13	.480	0	30	29	18	225	238	88	64	1	3.72
Doug McWeeney	R	29	11	13	.458	1	42	24	10	216	213	84	96	1	3.04
Jesse Barnes	R	33	10	11	.476	1	31	24	10	158	204	35	29	1	5.24
Bob McGraw	R	31	9	13	.409	1	33	21	10	174	197	67	49	0	4.60
Dazzy Vance	R	35	9	10	.474	1	24	22	12	169	172	58	140	1	3.89
Rube Ehrhardt	R	31	2	5	.286	4	44	1	0	97	101	35	25	0	3.90
George Boehler	R	34	1	0	1.000	0	10	1	0	35	42	23	10	0	4.37
Ray Moss	R	24	0	0	.000	0	1	0	0	1	3	0	0	0	9.00
Dutch Stryker	R	30	0	0	.000	0	2	0	0	2	8	1	0	0	27.00
Leon Williams	L	20	0	0	.000	0	8	0	0	8	16	2	3	0	5.63

Bill Doak (VR) 35

BOSTON 7th 66-86 .434 22 — DAVE BANCROFT

NAME	G by POS	B	AGE	G	AB	R	H	2B	3B	HR	RBI	BB	SO	SB	BA	SA
TOTALS			28	153	5216	624	1444	209	62	16	560	426	348	81	.277	.350
Dick Burrus	1B128	L	28	131	486	59	131	21	1	3	61	37	16	4	.270	.335
Doc Gautreau	2B74	R	24	79	266	36	71	9	4	0	8	35	24	17	.267	.331
Dave Bancroft	SS123, 3B2	B	35	127	453	70	141	18	6	1	44	64	29	3	.311	.384
Andy High	3B81, 2B49	L	28	130	476	55	141	17	10	2	66	39	9	4	.296	.387
Jim Welsh	OF129	L	23	134	490	69	136	18	11	3	57	33	28	6	.278	.378
2 Jack Smith	OF83	L	31	96	322	46	100	15	2	2	25	28	12	11	.311	.388
Eddie Brown	OF153	R	34	153	612	71	201	31	8	2	84	23	20	5	.328	.415
Zack Taylor	C123	R	27	125	432	36	110	22	3	0	42	28	27	1	.255	.319
Eddie Taylor	3B62, SS33	R	24	92	272	37	73	8	2	0	33	38	26	4	.268	.313
Frank Wilson	OF56	L	24	87	236	22	56	11	3	0	23	20	21	3	.237	.309
Johnny Cooney	1B31, P19, OF1	R	25	64	126	17	38	3	2	0	18	13	7	6	.302	.357
2 Eddie Moore	2B39, SS14, 3B1	R	27	54	184	17	49	3	2	0	15	16	12	6	.266	.304
Les Mann	OF46	R	32	50	129	23	39	8	2	1	20	9	9	5	.302	.419
Bob Smith	P33	R	28	40	84	10	25	6	2	0	13	2	4	0	.298	.417
Oscar Siemer	C30	R	24	31	73	3	15	1	0	0	6	3	7	0	.205	.219
Bernie Neis	OF20	B	30	30	93	16	20	5	2	0	8	8	10	4	.215	.312
Frank Gibson	C13	B	35	24	47	3	16	4	0	0	7	4	6	0	.340	.426
1 Jimmy Johnston	3B14, 2B2, OF1	R	36	23	57	7	14	1	0	1	5	10	3	2	.246	.316

Shanty Hogan 20 R 4-14, Harry Riconda 29 R 2-12, Sid Womack 29 R 0-3

NAME	T	AGE	W	L	PCT	SV	G	GS	CG	IP	H	BB	SO	ShO	ERA
		28	66	86	.434	9	153	153	60	1357	1536	455	408	9	4.03
Larry Benton	R	28	14	14	.500	1	43	27	12	232	244	81	103	1	3.84
Johnny Wertz	R	28	11	9	.550	0	32	23	7	189	212	47	65	1	3.29
Bob Smith	R	28	10	13	.435	1	33	23	14	193	199	75	44	4	3.92
Joe Genewich	R	29	8	16	.333	2	37	26	12	216	239	63	59	2	3.88
George Mogridge	L	37	6	10	.375	3	39	10	2	142	173	36	46	0	4.50
Hal Goldsmith	R	27	5	7	.417	0	19	15	5	101	135	28	16	0	4.37
Bunny Hearn	L	22	4	9	.308	2	34	12	3	117	121	56	40	0	4.23
Johnny Cooney	L	25	3	3	.500	0	19	8	3	83	106	29	23	1	4.01
Kyle Graham	R	26	3	3	.500	0	15	4	1	36	54	19	7	0	8.00
Foster Edwards	R	22	2	0	1.000	0	3	3	1	25	20	13	4	0	0.72
Rosy Ryan	R	28	0	2	.000	0	7	2	0	19	29	7	1	0	7.58
Bill Vargus	L	26	0	0	.000	0	4	0	0	3	4	1	0	0	3.00

PHILADELPHIA 8th 58-93 .384 29.5 — ART FLETCHER

NAME	G by POS	B	AGE	G	AB	R	H	2B	3B	HR	RBI	BB	SO	SB	BA	SA
TOTALS			31	152	5254	687	1479	244	50	75	632	422	479	47	.281	.390
1 Jack Bentley	1B56, P7	L	31	75	240	19	62	12	3	2	27	5	4	0	.258	.358
Barney Friberg	2B144	R	26	144	478	38	128	21	3	1	51	57	77	2	.268	.331
Heinie Sand	SS149	R	28	149	567	99	154	30	5	4	37	66	56	2	.272	.363
Clarence Huber	3B115	R	29	118	376	45	92	17	7	1	34	42	29	9	.245	.335
Cy Williams	OF93	L	38	107	336	63	116	13	4	18	53	38	35	2	.345	.568
Freddy Leach	OF123	L	28	129	492	73	162	29	7	11	71	16	33	6	.329	.484
Johnny Mokan	OF123	R	30	127	456	68	138	23	5	6	62	41	31	4	.303	.414
Jimmie Wilson	C79	R	25	90	279	40	85	10	2	4	32	25	20	3	.305	.398
R. Wrightstone	1B53, 3B37, 2B13, OF5	L	33	112	368	55	113	23	1	7	57	27	11	5	.307	.432
Butch Henline	C77, 1B4, OF2	R	31	99	283	32	80	14	1	2	30	21	18	1	.283	.360
Al Nixon	OF88	R	40	93	311	38	91	18	2	4	41	13	20	5	.293	.402
Wayland Dean	P33	L	24	63	102	11	27	4	0	3	19	5	26	0	.265	.392
George Harper	OF55	L	34	56	194	32	61	6	5	7	38	16	7	6	.314	.505
Ray Grimes	1B28	R	32	32	101	13	30	5	0	0	15	6	13	0	.297	.347
Wally Kimmick	1B5, SS4, 3B4, 2B1	R	29	20	28	0	6	2	1	0	2	3	7	0	.214	.357
Bubber Jonnard	C15	R	26	19	34	3	4	1	0	0	2	3	4	0	.118	.147
Bob Rice	3B15, 2B2, SS2	R	27	19	54	3	8	0	1	0	10	3	4	0	.148	.185
Dick Attreau	1B17	L	29	17	61	9	14	1	1	0	5	6	5	0	.230	.279
Ed Cotter	3B8, SS5	R	21	17	26	3	8	0	1	0	1	1	4	1	.308	.385
Denny Sothern	OF13	R	22	14	53	5	13	1	0	3	10	4	10	0	.245	.434
George Stutz	SS5	R	33	6	9	0	0	0	0	0	0	0	2	0	.000	.000

Joe Buskey 23 R 0-8, Lee Dunham 24 L 1-4, Chick Keating 34 R 0-2, Lew Wendell 34 R 0-4

NAME	T	AGE	W	L	PCT	SV	G	GS	CG	IP	H	BB	SO	ShO	ERA
		28	58	93	.384	5	152	152	68	1294	1699	454	331	5	5.19
Hal Carlson	R	32	17	12	.586	0	35	34	20	267	293	47	55	3	3.24
Clarence Mitchell	L	35	9	14	.391	1	28	25	12	179	232	55	52	0	4.58
Wayland Dean	R	24	8	16	.333	0	33	26	15	164	245	89	52	1	6.09
Dutch Ulrich	R	26	8	13	.381	1	45	17	8	148	178	37	52	1	4.07
Claude Willoughby	R	27	8	12	.400	1	47	18	6	168	218	71	37	0	5.95
Jack Knight	R	31	3	12	.200	2	35	15	5	143	206	48	29	0	6.61
Ed Baecht	R	19	2	0	1.000	0	28	1	1	56	73	28	14	0	6.11
Ray Pierce	L	29	2	7	.222	0	37	7	1	85	128	35	18	0	5.61
Ernie Maun	R	25	1	4	.200	0	14	5	0	38	57	18	9	0	6.39
1 Jack Bentley	L	31	0	2	.000	0	7	3	0	25	37	10	7	0	8.28
Art Decatur	R	32	0	0	.000	0	2	1	0	3	6	2	0	0	6.00
Mike Kelly	R	23	0	0	.000	0	4	0	0	7	9	4	2	0	9.00
Pete Rambo	R	19	0	0	.000	0	1	0	0	4	6	4	4	0	13.50
Lefty Taber	L	26	0	0	.000	0	6	0	0	8	8	5	0	0	7.88
Rusty Yarnell	R	23	0	1	.000	0	1	0	0	1	3	1	0	0	18.00

WORLD SERIES – ST. LOUIS (NL) 4 NEW YORK (AL) 3

LINE SCORES

TEAM	1	2	3	4	5	6	7	8	9	10	11	12	R	H	E
Game 1 October 2 at New York															
STL (NL)	1	0	0	0	0	0	0	0	0				1	3	1
NY (AL)	1	0	0	0	0	1	0	0	X				2	6	0
Sherdel, Haines (8) — Pennock															
Game 2 October 3 at New York															
STL	0	0	2	0	0	0	3	0	1				6	12	1
NY	0	2	0	0	0	0	0	0	0				2	4	0
Alexander — Shocker, Shawkey (8), Jones (9)															
Game 3 October 5 at St. Louis															
NY	0	0	0	0	0	0	0	0	0				0	5	1
STL	0	0	0	3	1	0	0	0	X				4	8	0
Reuther, Shawkey (5), Thomas (8) — Haines															
Game 4 October 6 at St. Louis															
NY	1	0	1	1	4	2	1	0	0				10	14	1
STL	1	0	0	3	0	0	0	0	1				5	14	0
Hoyt — Rhem, Reinhart (5), H. Bell (5), Hallahan (7), Keen (9)															
Game 5 October 7 at St. Louis															
NY	0	0	0	0	0	1	0	0	1	1			3	9	1
STL	0	0	0	1	0	0	1	0	0	0			2	7	1
Pennock — Sherdel															
Game 6 October 9 at New York															
STL	3	0	0	0	1	0	5	0	1				10	13	2
NY	0	0	0	1	0	0	1	0	0				2	8	1
Alexander — Shawkey, Shocker (7), Thomas (8)															
Game 7 October 10 at New York															
STL	0	0	0	3	0	0	0	0	0				3	8	0
NY	0	0	1	0	0	1	0	0	0				2	8	3
Haines, Alexander (7) — Hoyt, Pennock (7)															

COMPOSITE BATTING

NAME	POS	G	AB	R	H	2B	3B	HR	RBI	BA
St. Louis (NL)										
Totals		7	239	31	65	12	1	4	30	.272
Bottomley	1B	7	29	4	10	3	0	0	5	.345
Southworth	OF	7	29	6	10	1	1	1	4	.345
Hornsby	2B	7	28	2	7	1	0	0	4	.250
L. Bell	3B	7	27	4	7	1	0	1	6	.259
Hafey	OF	7	27	2	5	2	0	0	0	.185
Thevenow	SS	7	24	5	10	1	0	1	4	.417
O'Farrell	C	7	23	2	7	1	0	0	2	.304
Holm	OF	5	16	1	2	0	0	0	1	.125
Douthit	OF	4	15	3	4	2	0	0	1	.267
Alexander	P	3	7	1	0	0	0	0	0	.000
Haines	P	3	5	1	3	0	0	1	2	.600
Sherdel	P	2	5	0	0	0	0	0	0	.000
Flowers	PH	3	3	0	0	0	0	0	0	.000
Rhem	P	1	1	0	0	0	0	0	0	.000
H. Bell	P	1	0	0	0	0	0	0	0	.000
Hallahan	P	1	0	0	0	0	0	0	0	.000
Keen	P	1	0	0	0	0	0	0	0	.000
Reinhart	P	1	0	0	0	0	0	0	0	.000
Toporcer	PH	1	0	0	0	0	0	0	1	.000
New York (AL)										
Totals		7	223	21	54	10	1	4	20	.242
Koenig	SS	7	32	2	4	1	0	0	2	.125
Combs	OF	7	28	3	10	2	0	0	2	.357
Lazzeri	2B	7	26	2	5	1	0	0	3	.192
Dugan	3B	7	24	2	8	1	0	0	2	.333
Gehrig	1B	7	23	1	8	2	0	0	4	.348
Severeid	C	7	22	1	6	1	0	0	1	.273
Meusel	OF	7	21	3	5	1	1	0	0	.238
Ruth	OF	7	20	6	6	0	0	4	5	.300
Pennock	P	3	7	1	1	1	0	0	0	.143
Hoyt	P	2	6	0	0	0	0	0	0	.000
Paschal	PH	5	4	0	1	0	0	0	1	.250
Reuther	P	3	4	0	0	0	0	0	0	.000
Collins	C	3	2	0	0	0	0	0	0	.000
Shawkey	P	3	2	0	0	0	0	0	0	.000
Shocker	P	2	2	0	0	0	0	0	0	.000
Adams	PR	2	0	0	0	0	0	0	0	.000
Gazella	3B	1	0	0	0	0	0	0	0	.000
Jones	P	1	0	0	0	0	0	0	0	.000
Thomas	P	2	0	0	0	0	0	0	0	.000

COMPOSITE PITCHING

NAME	G	IP	H	BB	SO	W	L	SV	ERA
St. Louis (NL)									
Totals	7	63	54	31	31	4	3	1	2.71
Alexander	3	20.1	12	4	17	2	0	1	1.33
Sherdel	2	17	15	8	3	0	2	0	2.12
Haines	3	16.2	13	9	5	2	0	0	1.08
Rhem	1	4	7	2	4	0	0	0	6.75
H. Bell	1	2	4	1	1	0	0	0	9.00
Hallahan	1	2	2	3	1	0	0	0	4.50
Keen	1	1	0	0	0	0	0	0	0.00
Reinhart	1	0	1	4	0	0	1	0	∞
New York (AL)									
Totals	7	63	65	11	30	3	4	0	2.86
Pennock	3	22	13	4	8	2	0	0	1.23
Hoyt	2	15	19	1	10	1	1	0	1.20
Shawkey	3	10	8	2	7	0	1	0	5.40
Shocker	2	7.2	13	0	3	0	1	0	5.87
Ruether	1	4.1	7	2	1	0	1	0	4.16
Thomas	2	3	3	0	0	0	0	0	3.00
Jones	1	1	2	2	1	0	0	0	9.00

1927 The Finest Crop

By the time 1927 drew to a close, the Yankees owned every offensive statistic the American League could offer, with the exception of doubles and stolen bases. In fact, New York's attack was so devastating that by season's end it was unanimous that the junior circuit had experienced the strongest team ever to take the field. The results of the barrage was such that the pennant race became a pennant chase with the Yankees easily repeating as league champions.

Such was the attack that the Bronx Bombers did not leave first place for even one day as they finished with a 19-game lead over Philadelphia, the biggest winning margin in loop history. The Yankees chalked up 110 victories and a .714 percentage, both new American League records, and manager Miller Huggins had the best offense and best pitching in the League at his fingertips. Although Babe Ruth set a new single season's record for home runs by belting 60 circuit clouts, surprisingly little commotion was raised over this now-revered feat, simply because it was expected that the Bambino would knock even more homers next year. Young Lou Gehrig hit 47 round-trippers, joining the 32-year-old Ruth to form the most feared batting twosome in history. Tony Lazzeri and Bob Meusel joined this duo as 100-RBI men, and Earle Combs hit .356 in the leadoff slot. Thirty-year-old Wilcy Moore surfaced from the minors for the first time and won 19 games, posted the lowest E.R.A. in the league, and became the first sensational relief pitcher in a long chain of Yankee firemen. Connie Mack's Philadelphia Athletics climbed into second place as Al Simmons, Mickey Cochrane, Jimmie Foxx, and Lefty Grove showed the efficiency of Mack's rebuilding program. Ty Cobb also aided the team after his dismissal as Detroit manager and hit .357, enough to give him fifth-place league batting honors.

In contrast to the Yankee runaway, the Pittsburgh Pirates clinched the National League pennant on the final day of the season. The Bucs were the early season leaders, but the Chicago Cubs took the lead throughout August behind Hack Wilson's hitting and Charlie Root's pitching. The Cubs, however, faded as summer waned, and the Bucs seized first place on September 1, by beating Chicago 4 to 3 at Forbes Field. The Pirates stayed ahead the rest of the way, pursued hotly by the rallying Cardinals and the Giants. Paul Waner spearheaded the Pirates by brandishing a .380 cutlass and driving in 131 runs. Lloyd Waner, Pie Traynor, and Glenn Wright also starred with the stick for Pittsburgh, and when Kiki Cuyler was benched after a midseason run-in with Manager Donnie Bush, Clyde Barnhart stepped in with a .319 stick. Carmen Hill led the Pirate pitchers with 22 wins, while Lee Meadows and Ray Kremer each chipped in with 19 victories.

The World Series itself did nothing to dispel the Yankee might of the regular season. In fact, as more and more time separates that final season's stanza from the rest of history, the events of the Series are more attributed to the chilling display of power which took place before the cry of "play ball" was heard. Legend has it that the Pirates watched the Yankees destroy the baseball in batting practice the day before the World Series opener and were beaten before they began. But oddly enough, even though the Yankees swept the Series in four games, the Pirates outhit them in the first game, and only Ruth—in the last two games—hit the kind of blows the Bucs supposedly expected the entire lineup to deliver.

The season's end brought three departures from the major league stage of long-time leading characters. Ban Johnson resigned as American League President after heading that organization since before its inception as a major league in 1901. August Herrmann, who had been Chairman of the National Commission which governed baseball prior to the appointment of Judge Landis in 1920, resigned as Cincinnati President, and Washington's Walter Johnson left the game with 416 wins, 3,506 strikeouts, and a 2.17 E.R.A., all remarkable achievements in light of the fact that the Senators finished in the second division for ten of Johnson's 21 years.

1927 AMERICAN LEAGUE

NAME	G by POS	B	AGE	G	AB	R	H	2B	3B	HR	RBI	BB	SO	SB	BA	SA
NEW YORK 1st 110-44 .714	MILLER HUGGINS															
TOTALS			28	155	5347	975	1644	291	103	158	908	635	605	90	.307	.489
Lou Gehrig	1B155	L	24	155	584	149	218	52	18	47	175	109	84	10	.373	.765
Tony Lazzeri	2B113, SS38, 3B9	R	23	153	570	92	176	29	8	18	102	69	82	22	.309	.482
Mark Koenig	SS122	B	24	123	526	99	150	20	11	3	62	25	21	3	.285	.382
Joe Dugan	3B111	R	30	112	387	44	104	24	3	2	43	27	37	1	.269	.362
Babe Ruth	OF151	L	32	151	540	158	192	29	8	60	164	138	89	7	.356	.772
Earle Combs	OF152	L	28	152	648	137	231	36	23	6	64	62	31	15	.356	.511
Bob Meusal	OF131	R	30	135	516	75	174	47	9	8	103	45	58	24	.337	.510
Pat Collins	C89	R	30	92	251	38	69	9	3	7	36	54	24	0	.275	.418
Ray Morehart	2B53	L	27	73	195	45	50	7	2	1	20	29	18	4	.256	.328
Johnny Grabowski	C68	R	27	70	195	29	54	2	4	0	25	20	15	0	.277	.328
Cedric Durst	OF36, 1B2	L	30	65	129	18	32	4	3	0	25	6	7	0	.248	.326
Mike Gazella	3B44, SS6	R	30	54	115	17	32	8	4	0	9	23	16	4	.278	.417
Ben Paschal	OF27	R	31	50	82	16	26	9	2	2	16	4	10	0	.317	.549
Julie Wera	3B19	R	25	38	42	7	10	3	0	1	8	1	5	0	.239	.381
Benny Bengough	C30	R	28	31	85	6	21	3	3	0	10	4	4	0	.247	.353
PHILADELPHIA 2nd 91-63 .591 19	CONNIE MACK															
TOTALS			31	155	5296	841	1606	281	70	56	767	551	326	98	.303	.414
Jimmy Dykes	1B82, 3B25, 2B5, SS5, OF5, P2	R	30	121	417	61	135	33	6	3	60	44	23	2	.324	.453
Max Bishop	2B106	L	27	117	372	80	103	15	1	0	22	105	28	8	.277	.323
Joe Boley	SS114	R	30	118	370	49	115	18	8	1	52	26	14	8	.311	.411
Sammy Hale	3B128	R	30	131	501	77	157	24	8	5	81	32	32	11	.313	.423
Ty Cobb	OF126	L	40	134	490	104	175	32	7	5	93	67	12	22	.357	.482
Al Simmons(GJ)	OF105	R	25	106	406	86	159	36	11	15	108	31	30	10	.392	.645
Walt French	OF94	L	27	109	326	48	99	10	5	0	41	16	14	9	.304	.365
Mickey Cochrane	C123	L	24	126	432	80	146	20	6	12	80	50	7	9	.338	.495
Eddie Collins	2B56, SS1	L	40	95	225	50	76	12	1	1	15	60	9	6	.338	.413
Zack Wheat	OF62	L	41	88	247	34	80	12	1	1	38	18	5	2	.324	.393
Bill Lamar(ST)	OF79	B	30	84	324	48	97	23	3	4	47	16	10	4	.299	.426
Chick Galloway	SS61, 3B7	R	30	77	181	15	48	10	4	0	22	18	9	1	.265	.365
Jimmie Foxx	1B32, C5	R	19	61	130	23	42	6	5	3	20	14	11	2	.323	.515
Cy Perkins	C54, 1B1	R	31	59	137	11	35	7	2	1	15	12	8	0	.255	.358
Jim Poole	1B31	L	32	38	99	4	22	2	0	0	10	9	6	0	.222	.242
Dud Branom	1B26	L	29	30	94	8	22	1	0	0	13	2	5	2	.234	.245
3 Baby Doll Jacobson	OF14	R	36	17	35	3	8	3	0	1	5	0	3	0	.229	.400
Charlie Bates	OF9	R	21	9	38	5	9	2	2	0	3	5	3	0	.237	.395
Rusty Saunders	OF4	R	21	5	15	2	2	1	0	0	2	3	2	0	.133	.200
Joe Mellana	3B2	R	22	4	7	1	2	0	0	0	2	0	1	0	.286	.286
Joe Hauser(JJ)28																
WASHINGTON 3rd 85-69 .552 25	BUCKY HARRIS															
TOTALS			30	157	5389	782	1549	268	87	29	696	498	359	133	.287	.386
Joe Judge	1B136	L	33	137	522	68	161	29	11	2	71	45	22	10	.308	.418
Bucky Harris	2B128	R	30	128	475	98	127	20	3	1	55	66	33	18	.267	.328
Bobby Reeves	SS96, 3B12, 2B2	R	23	112	380	37	97	11	5	1	39	21	53	3	.255	.318
Ossie Bluege	3B146	R	26	146	503	71	138	21	10	1	66	57	47	15	.274	.362
Sam Rice	OF139	L	36	142	603	98	179	33	14	2	65	36	11	19	.297	.408
Tris Speaker	OF120, 1B17	L	39	141	523	71	171	43	6	2	73	55	8	9	.327	.444
Goose Goslin	OF148	L	26	148	581	96	194	37	15	13	120	50	28	21	.334	.516
Muddy Ruel	C128	R	31	131	428	61	132	16	5	1	52	63	18	9	.308	.376
Earl McNeely	OF47, 1B4	R	29	73	185	40	51	10	4	0	16	11	13	11	.276	.373
Bennie Tate	C39	L	25	61	131	12	41	5	1	1	24	8	4	0	.313	.389
Stuffy Stewart	2B37, 3B2	R	33	56	129	24	31	6	2	0	4	8	15	12	.240	.318
2 Topper Rigney	SS32, 3B6	R	30	45	132	20	36	5	4	0	13	22	10	1	.273	.371
Sloppy Thurston	P29	R	28	42	92	11	29	4	2	2	17	5	10	1	.315	.467
Sammy West	OF18	L	22	38	67	9	16	4	1	0	6	8	8	1	.239	.328
Ollie Tucker	OF5	L	25	20	24	1	5	2	0	0	8	4	2	0	.208	.292
1 Nick Cullop	OF5, 1B1	R	26	15	23	2	5	2	0	0	1	1	6	0	.217	.304
1 Buddy Myer	SS15	L	23	15	51	7	11	1	0	0	7	8	3	3	.216	.235
Babe Ganzel	OF13	R	26	13	48	7	21	4	2	1	13	7	3	0	.438	.667
Grant Gillis	SS10	R	26	10	36	8	8	3	1	0	2	2	0	0	.222	.361
Jackie Hayes	SS8, 3B1	R	20	10	29	2	7	0	0	0	2	1	2	0	.241	.241
Johnny Berger	C9	R	25	9	15	1	4	0	0	0	1	2	3	0	.267	.267
Eddie Onslow	1B5	L	34	9	18	1	4	1	0	0	1	1	0	0	.222	.278
1 Mickey O'Neil	C4	R	29	5	6	0	0	0	0	0	0	0	1	0	.000	.000
Red Barnes	OF3	L	23	3	11	5	4	1	0	0	0	1	3	0	.364	.455

Buddy Dear 21 R 0-1, Lefty Atkinson 23 L 0-1, Patsy Gharrity(DE)34

NAME	T	AGE	W	L	PCT	SV	G	GS	CG	IP	H	BB	SO	ShO	ERA
		31	110	44	.714	20	155	155	82	1390	1403	409	431	11	3.20
Waite Hoyt	R	26	22	7	.759	1	36	32	23	256	242	54	86	3	2.64
Wilcy Moore	R	30	19	7	.731	13	50	12	6	213	185	59	75	1	2.28
Herb Pennock	L	33	19	8	.704	2	34	26	18	210	225	48	51	1	3.00
Urban Shocker	R	36	18	6	.750	0	31	27	13	200	207	41	35	2	2.84
Dutch Ruether	L	33	13	6	.684	0	27	26	12	184	202	52	45	3	3.38
George Pipgras	R	27	10	3	.769	0	29	21	9	166	148	77	81	1	4.12
Myles Thomas	R	29	7	4	.636	0	21	9	1	89	111	43	25	0	4.85
Bob Shawkey	R	36	2	3	.400	4	19	2	0	44	44	16	23	0	2.86
Joe Giard	L	28	0	0	.000	0	16	0	0	27	38	19	10	0	8.00
Walter Beall	R	27	0	0	.000	0	1	0	0	1	1	0	0	0	9.00
		31	91	63	.591	25	155	155	66	1390	1467	442	553	8	3.95
Lefty Grove	L	27	20	13	.606	9	51	28	14	262	251	79	174	1	3.20
Rube Walberg	L	27	17	12	.586	4	46	34	15	249	257	91	136	0	3.98
Jack Quinn	R	43	15	10	.600	1	34	25	11	207	211	37	43	3	3.18
Howard Ehmke	R	33	12	10	.545	0	30	27	10	190	200	60	68	1	4.21
Eddie Rommel	R	29	11	3	.786	1	30	17	8	147	166	48	33	2	4.35
Sam Gray	R	29	8	6	.571	3	37	13	3	133	153	51	49	1	4.53
Jing Johnson	R	32	4	2	.667	0	17	3	2	52	42	16	16	0	3.46
Lefty Willis	L	21	3	1	.750	0	15	2	1	27	32	11	7	0	5.67
Ike Powers	R	21	1	1	.500	0	11	1	0	26	26	7	3	0	4.50
2 Guy Cantrell	R	23	0	2	.000	0	2	2	2	18	25	7	7	0	5.00
Joe Pate	L	35	0	3	.000	6	32	0	0	54	67	21	14	0	5.17
Neal Baker	R	23	0	0	.000	0	5	2	0	17	27	7	3	0	5.82
Jimmy Dykes	R	30	0	0	.000	1	2	0	0	2	2	1	0	0	4.50
Buzz Wetzel	R	32	0	0	.000	0	2	1	0	5	8	5	0	0	7.20
Carroll Yerkes	L	24	0	0	.000	0	1	0	0	1	0	1	0	0	0.00
		28	85	69	.552	23	157	157	62	1408	1444	491	497	10	3.95
Hod Lisenbee	R	28	18	9	.667	0	39	34	17	242	221	78	105	4	3.57
Bump Hadley	R	22	14	6	.700	0	30	27	13	199	177	86	60	0	2.85
Sloppy Thurston	R	28	13	13	.500	0	29	28	13	205	254	60	38	2	4.48
Firpo Marberry	R	28	10	7	.588	9	56	10	2	155	177	68	74	0	4.64
Garland Braxton	L	17	10	9	.526	13	59	2	0	156	144	33	96	0	2.94
Walter Johnson(BL)	R	39	5	6	.455	0	18	15	7	108	113	26	48	1	5.08
1 General Crowder	R	28	4	7	.364	0	15	11	4	67	58	42	22	2	4.57
2 Tom Zachary	R	31	4	7	.364	0	15	14	5	110	126	30	13	1	3.68
Bobby Burke	L	20	3	2	.600	0	35	6	1	99	91	32	20	0	4.00
Stan Coveleski	R	38	2	1	.667	0	5	4	0	14	13	8	3	0	3.21
Paul Hopkins	R	22	1	0	1.000	0	2	1	0	9	13	4	5	0	5.00
George Murray	R	28	1	1	.500	0	7	3	0	18	18	15	5	0	7.00
Dick Coffman	R	20	0	1	.000	0	5	2	0	16	20	2	5	0	3.37
Dick Jones	R	25	0	0	.000	0	2	0	0	3	8	5	1	0	24.00
Clay Van Alstyne	R	27	0	0	.000	0	2	0	0	3	3	0	0	0	3.00
Ralph Judd	R	16	0	0	.000	1	1	0	0	4	8	2	2	0	6.75

DETROIT 4th 82-71 .536 27.5 — GEORGE MORIARTY

NAME	G by POS	B	AGE	G	AB	R	H	2B	3B	HR	RBI	BB	SO	SB	BA	SA
TOTALS			28	156	5299	845	1533	282	100	51	755	587	420	141	.289	.409
Lu Blue	1B104	B	30	112	365	71	95	17	9	1	42	71	28	13	.260	.364
Charlie Gehringer	2B121	L	24	133	508	110	161	29	11	4	61	52	31	17	.317	.441
Jackie Tavener	SS114	L	29	116	419	60	115	22	9	5	59	36	38	20	.274	.406
Jack Warner	3B138	R	23	139	559	78	149	22	9	1	45	47	45	15	.267	.343
Harry Heilmann	OF135	R	32	141	505	106	201	50	9	14	120	72	16	11	.398	.616
Heinie Manush	OF150	L	25	152	593	102	177	31	18	6	80	47	29	12	.298	.442
Bob Fothergill	OF137	R	29	143	527	93	189	38	9	9	114	47	31	9	.359	.516
Larry Woodall	C86	R	32	88	246	28	69	8	6	0	39	37	9	9	.280	.362
Marty McManus	SS39, 2B35, 3B22, 1B6	R	27	108	369	60	99	19	7	9	69	34	38	8	.268	.431
Johnny Bassler	C67	L	32	81	200	19	57	7	0	0	24	45	9	1	.285	.320
Johnny Neun	1B53	B	26	79	204	38	66	9	4	0	27	35	13	22	.324	.407
Al Wingo	OF34	L	29	75	137	15	32	8	2	0	20	25	14	1	.234	.321
Art Ruble	OF43	L	24	56	91	16	15	4	2	0	11	14	15	2	.165	.253
Merv Shea	C31	R	26	34	85	5	15	6	3	0	9	7	15	0	.176	.318
Bernie deViveiros	SS14, 3B1	R	26	24	22	4	5	1	0	0	2	2	8	1	.227	.273
Clyde Manion		R	30	1	1	0	0	0	0	0	0	1	0	0	.000	.000

NAME	T	AGE	W	L	PCT	SV	G	GS	CG	IP	H	BB	SO	ShO	ERA
		27	82	71	.536	17	156	156	75	1391	1542	577	421	5	4.12
Earl Whitehill	L	27	16	14	.533	3	41	31	17	236	238	105	95	3	3.36
Rip Collins	R	31	13	7	.650	0	30	25	10	173	207	59	37	1	4.68
Ken Hollaway	R	29	11	12	.478	6	36	23	11	183	210	61	36	1	4.09
Sam Gibson	R	27	11	12	.478	0	33	26	11	190	201	86	76	0	3.70
Ownie Carroll	R	24	10	6	.625	0	31	15	8	172	186	73	41	0	3.98
Lil Stoner	R	28	10	13	.435	5	38	24	13	215	251	77	63	0	3.98
Haskell Billings	R	19	5	4	.556	0	10	9	5	67	64	39	18	0	4.84
George Smith	R	25	4	1	.800	0	29	0	0	71	62	50	32	0	3.93
Don Hankins	R	25	2	1	.667	2	20	1	0	40	67	13	10	0	6.43
Ed Wells	L	27	0	1	.000	1	8	1	0	20	28	5	5	0	6.75
Jess Doyle	R	29	0	0	.000	0	7	0	0	12	16	5	5	0	8.25
Jim Walkup	L	31	0	0	.000	0	2	0	0	2	3	0	0	0	4.50
Augie Johns	L	27	0	0	.000	0	1	0	0	1	1	1	1	0	9.00
Rufus Smith	L	22	0	0	.000	0	1	1	0	8	8	3	2	0	3.38

CHICAGO 5th 70-83 .458 39.5 — RAY SCHALK

NAME	G by POS	B	AGE	G	AB	R	H	2B	3B	HR	RBI	BB	SO	SB	BA	SA
TOTALS			28	153	5157	662	1433	285	61	36	610	493	389	90	.278	.378
Bud Clancy	1B123	L	26	130	464	46	139	21	2	3	53	24	24	4	.300	.373
Aaron Ward	2B138, 3B6	R	30	145	463	75	125	25	8	5	56	63	56	6	.270	.391
Bill Hunnefield	SS78, 2B17, 3B1	B	28	112	365	45	104	25	1	2	36	25	24	13	.285	.375
Willie Kamm	3B146	R	27	148	540	85	146	32	13	0	59	70	18	7	.270	.378
Bill Barrett	OF147	R	27	147	556	62	159	35	9	4	83	52	46	20	.286	.403
Alex Metzler	OF134	L	24	134	543	87	173	29	11	3	61	61	39	15	.319	.429
Bibb Falk	OF145	L	28	145	535	76	175	35	6	9	83	52	19	5	.327	.465
Harry McCurdy	C82	L	27	86	262	34	75	19	3	1	27	32	24	6	.286	.393
Buck Crouse	C81	L	30	85	222	22	53	11	0	0	20	21	10	4	.239	.288
Roger Peckinpaugh	SS60	R	36	68	217	23	64	6	3	0	23	21	6	2	.295	.350
2 Bernie Neis	OF21	B	31	45	76	9	22	5	0	0	11	10	9	1	.289	.355
Earl Sheely	1B36	R	34	45	129	11	27	3	0	2	16	20	5	1	.209	.279
Sarge Connally	P43	R	28	43	67	5	22	1	0	0	6	2	10	0	.328	.343
Moe Berg (RL)	2B10, C10, SS6, 3B3	R	25	35	69	4	17	4	0	0	4	4	10	0	.246	.304
Ike Boone (IL)	OF11	L	30	29	53	10	12	4	0	1	11	3	4	0	.226	.358
Ray Flaskamper	SS25	B	25	26	95	12	21	5	0	0	6	3	8	0	.221	.274
Ray Schalk	C15	R	34	16	26	2	6	2	0	0	2	2	1	0	.231	.308
Carl Reynolds	OF13	R	24	14	42	5	9	3	0	1	7	5	7	1	.214	.357
Johnny Mostil (IL)	OF6	R	31	13	16	3	2	0	0	0	1	0	1	1	.125	.125
Kid Willson	OF2	L	31	7	10	1	1	0	0	0	1	0	2	0	.100	.100
Jim Battle	3B4, SS2	R	26	6	8	1	3	0	1	0	0	0	1	0	.375	.625
Randy Moore	OF4	L	22	6	15	0	0	0	0	0	0	0	2	0	.000	.000
Bobby Way	2B1	R	21	5	3	3	1	0	0	0	1	0	1	0	.333	.333
Lena Blackburne		R	40	1	1	1	1	0	0	0	1	0	0	0	1.000	1.000

NAME	T	AGE	W	L	PCT	SV	G	GS	CG	IP	H	BB	SO	ShO	ERA
		29	70	83	.458	8	153	153	85	1367	1467	440	365	10	3.91
Ted Lyons	R	26	22	14	.611	2	39	34	30	308	291	67	71	2	2.84
Tommy Thomas	R	27	19	16	.543	1	40	36	24	308	271	94	107	3	2.97
Ted Blankenship	R	26	12	17	.414	0	37	34	11	237	280	74	51	3	5.05
Sarge Connally	R	28	10	15	.400	5	43	18	11	198	217	83	58	1	4.09
Red Faber (SA)	R	38	4	7	.364	0	18	15	6	111	131	41	39	0	4.54
Elmer Jacobs	R	34	2	4	.333	0	25	8	2	74	105	37	22	1	4.63
Bert Cole	L	29	1	4	.200	0	27	2	0	67	79	19	12	0	4.70
Frank Stewart	R	20	0	1	.000	0	1	1	0	4	5	4	0	0	9.00
Charlie Barnabe	L	27	0	5	.000	0	17	5	1	61	86	20	5	0	5.31
Joe Brown	R	26	0	0	.000	0	1	0	0	0	2	1	0	0	∞

CLEVELAND 6th 66-87 .431 43.5 — JACK McCALLISTER

NAME	G by POS	B	AGE	G	AB	R	H	2B	3B	HR	RBI	BB	SO	SB	BA	SA
TOTALS			28	153	5202	668	1471	321	52	26	616	381	366	64	.283	.379
George Burns	1B139	R	34	140	549	84	175	51	2	3	78	42	27	13	.319	.435
Lew Fonseca	2B96, 1B13	R	28	112	428	60	133	20	7	2	40	12	17	12	.311	.404
Joe Sewell	SS153	L	28	153	569	83	180	48	5	1	92	51	7	3	.316	.424
Rube Lutzke	3B98	R	29	100	311	35	78	12	3	0	41	22	29	2	.251	.309
Homer Summa	OF145	L	28	145	574	72	164	41	7	4	74	32	18	6	.286	.402
Fred Eichrodt	OF81	R	24	85	267	24	59	19	2	0	25	16	25	2	.221	.307
Charlie Jamieson	OF127	L	34	127	489	73	151	23	6	0	36	64	14	7	.309	.380
Luke Sewell	C126	R	26	128	470	52	138	27	6	0	53	20	23	4	.294	.377
Johnny Hodapp	3B67, 1B4	R	21	79	240	25	73	15	3	5	40	14	23	2	.304	.454
Freddie Spurgeon	2B52	R	25	57	179	30	45	6	1	1	19	18	14	8	.251	.313
Glenn Myatt	C26	L	29	55	94	15	23	6	0	2	8	12	7	1	.245	.372
Joe Shaute	P45	L	27	45	83	7	27	5	1	0	6	2	9	0	.325	.410
2 Nick Cullop	OF20, P1	R	26	32	68	9	16	2	3	1	8	9	19	0	.235	.397
2 Baby Doll Jacobson	OF31	R	36	32	103	13	26	5	0	0	13	6	4	0	.252	.301
1 Bernie Neis	OF29	B	31	32	96	17	29	9	0	4	18	18	9	0	.302	.521
Johnny Gill	OF17	L	22	21	60	8	13	3	0	1	4	7	13	1	.217	.317
Sam Langford	OF20	L	27	20	67	10	18	5	0	1	7	5	7	0	.269	.388
Pat McNulty	OF12	L	28	19	41	3	13	1	0	0	4	4	3	1	.317	.341
Johnny Burnett	2B2	L	22	17	8	5	0	0	0	0	0	0	3	1	.000	.000
Martin Autry	C14	R	24	16	43	5	11	4	1	0	7	0	6	0	.256	.395
Carl Lind	2B11, SS1	R	23	12	37	2	5	0	0	0	1	5	7	1	.135	.135
Ernie Padgett	2B4	R	28	7	7	1	2	0	0	0	0	0	2	0	.286	.286
George Gerken	OF5	R	23	6	14	1	3	0	0	0	2	1	3	0	.214	.214
Dutch Ussat	3B4	R	23	4	16	4	3	0	1	0	2	2	1	0	.188	.313

NAME	T	AGE	W	L	PCT	SV	G	GS	CG	IP	H	BB	SO	ShO	ERA
		28	66	87	.431	8	153	153	72	1353	1542	508	366	5	4.27
Willis Hudlin	R	21	18	12	.600	0	43	30	18	265	291	83	65	1	4.01
Jake Miller	L	29	10	8	.556	0	34	23	11	185	189	48	53	0	3.21
Garland Buckeye	L	29	10	17	.370	1	35	25	13	205	231	74	38	2	3.95
Joe Shaute	L	27	9	16	.360	2	45	28	14	230	255	75	63	0	4.23
George Uhle (SA)	R	28	8	9	.471	1	25	22	10	153	187	59	69	1	4.36
George Grant	R	24	4	6	.400	1	25	3	2	75	85	40	19	0	4.44
Benn Karr	R	33	3	3	.500	2	22	5	1	77	92	32	17	0	5.02
Emil Levsen (AJ)	R	29	3	7	.300	0	25	13	2	80	96	37	15	1	5.52
Sherry Smith	L	36	1	4	.200	1	11	2	1	38	53	14	8	0	5.44
Hal McKain	R	20	0	1	.000	0	2	1	0	11	18	4	5	0	4.09
Jumbo Brown (NJ)	R	20	0	2	.000	0	8	0	0	19	19	26	8	0	6.16
Willie Underhill	R	22	0	2	.000	0	4	1	0	8	12	11	4	0	10.13
Hap Collard	R	28	0	0	.000	0	4	0	0	5	8	3	2	0	5.40
2 Nick Cullop	R	26	0	0	.000	0	1	0	0	1	3	0	0	0	9.00
Wes Ferrell	R	19	0	0	.000	0	1	0	0	1	3	2	0	0	27.00

ST. LOUIS 7th 59-94 .386 50.5 — DAN HOWLEY

NAME	G by POS	B	AGE	G	AB	R	H	2B	3B	HR	RBI	BB	SO	SB	BA	SA
TOTALS			32	155	5220	724	1440	262	59	55	657	443	420	91	.276	.380
George Sisler	1B149	L	34	149	614	87	201	32	8	5	97	24	15	27	.327	.430
Oscar Melillo	2B101	R	27	107	356	45	80	18	2	0	26	25	28	3	.225	.287
Wally Gerber	SS141, 3B1	R	35	142	438	44	98	13	9	0	45	35	25	2	.224	.295
Frank O'Rourke	3B120, 2B16, 1B3	R	32	140	538	85	144	25	3	1	39	64	43	19	.268	.331
Harry Rice	OF130, 3B7	L	26	137	520	90	149	26	9	7	68	50	21	6	.287	.412
Bing Miller	OF126	R	32	143	492	83	160	32	7	5	75	30	26	9	.325	.449
Ken Williams	OF113	L	37	131	421	70	136	23	6	17	74	57	30	9	.323	.527
Wally Schang	C75	B	37	97	263	40	84	15	2	5	42	41	33	3	.319	.449
Herschel Bennett	OF55	L	30	93	256	40	68	12	2	3	30	14	21	6	.266	.363
Spencer Adams	2B54, 3B28	L	29	88	259	32	69	11	3	0	29	24	33	1	.266	.332
Steve O'Neill	C60	R	35	74	191	14	44	7	0	1	22	20	6	0	.230	.283
Fred Schulte (BW-CN)	OF49	R	26	60	189	32	60	16	5	3	34	20	14	5	.317	.503
Otto Miller	SS35, 3B11	R	26	51	76	8	17	5	0	0	8	8	5	0	.224	.289
Leo Dixon	C35	R	30	36	103	6	20	3	1	0	12	7	6	0	.194	.243
Red Kress	SS7	R	20	7	23	3	7	2	1	1	3	3	3	0	.304	.609
Guy Sturdy	1B5	L	27	5	21	5	9	1	0	0	5	1	0	1	.429	.476

NAME	T	AGE	W	L	PCT	SV	G	GS	CG	IP	H	BB	SO	ShO	ERA
		29	59	94	.386	8	155	155	80	1353	1592	604	385	4	4.95
Milt Gaston	R	31	13	17	.433	1	37	30	21	254	275	100	77	0	5.00
Elam Vangilder	R	31	10	12	.455	1	44	23	12	203	245	102	62	3	4.79
Lefty Stewart	L	26	8	11	.421	1	27	19	11	156	187	43	43	0	4.27
Sad Sam Jones	R	34	8	14	.364	0	30	26	11	190	211	102	72	0	4.31
Win Ballou	R	29	5	6	.455	0	21	11	4	90	105	46	17	0	4.80
1 Tom Zachary	R	31	4	6	.400	0	13	12	6	78	110	27	13	0	4.38
2 General Crowder	R	28	3	5	.373	3	21	8	2	74	71	42	30	1	4.99
Ernie Nevers	R	24	3	8	.273	2	27	5	2	95	105	35	22	0	4.92
Ernie Wingard	L	26	2	13	.133	0	38	17	7	156	213	79	28	0	6.58
Boom-Boom Beck	R	22	1	0	1.000	0	3	1	1	11	15	5	6	0	5.72
Chet Falk	L	22	1	0	1.000	0	9	0	0	16	25	10	2	0	5.62
Jiggs Wright	R	26	1	0	1.000	0	2	1	1	12	8	4	4	0	4.50
Stew Bolen	L	24	0	1	.000	0	3	1	1	10	14	5	7	0	8.10
George Blaeholder	R	23	0	1	.000	0	1	1	1	9	8	4	2	0	5.00

BOSTON 8th 51 103 .331 59 — BILL CARRIGAN

NAME	G by POS	B	AGE	G	AB	R	H	2B	3B	HR	RBI	BB	SO	SB	BA	SA
TOTALS			28	154	5207	597	1348	271	78	28	550	430	456	82	.259	.357
Phil Todt	1B139	R	25	140	516	55	122	22	6	6	52	28	23	6	.236	.337
Bill Regan	2B121	R	28	129	468	43	128	37	10	2	66	26	51	10	.274	.408
2 Buddy Myer	SS101, 3B14, OF10, 2B1	L	23	133	469	59	135	22	11	2	47	48	16	9	.288	.394
Billy Rogell	3B53, 2B2, OF2	B	22	82	207	35	55	14	6	2	28	24	28	3	.266	.420
Jack Tobin	OF93	L	35	111	374	52	116	18	3	2	40	36	9	5	.310	.390
Ira Flagstead	OF129	R	33	131	466	63	133	26	8	4	69	57	25	12	.285	.401
Wally Shaner	OF108, 1B1	R	27	122	406	54	111	33	6	3	49	21	35	11	.273	.406
Grover Hartley	C86	R	38	103	244	23	67	11	0	1	31	22	14	1	.275	.332
Jack Rothrock	SS40, 2B36, 3B20, 1B13	B	22	117	428	61	111	24	8	1	36	24	46	5	.259	.360
Cleo Carlyle	OF83	L	24	95	278	31	65	12	8	1	28	36	40	4	.234	.345
Fred Hofmann	C81	R	33	87	217	20	59	19	1	0	24	21	26	2	.272	.369
Red Rollings	3B44, 1B10, 2B2	L	23	82	184	19	49	4	1	0	9	12	10	3	.266	.299
1 Fred Haney	3B34, OF1	R	29	47	116	23	32	4	1	3	12	25	14	4	.276	.405
1 Baby Doll Jacobson	OF39	R	36	45	155	11	38	9	3	0	24	5	12	1	.245	.342
Bill Moore	C42	L	25	44	69	7	15	2	0	0	4	13	8	0	.217	.246
Arlie Tarbert	OF27	R	22	33	69	5	13	1	0	0	5	3	12	0	.188	.203
1 Pee Wee Wanninger	SS15	L	24	18	60	4	12	0	0	0	1	6	2	2	.200	.200
Frank Welch	OF6	R	29	15	28	2	5	2	0	0	4	5	1	0	.179	.250
1 Topper Rigney	3B4, SS1	R	30	8	18	0	2	1	0	0	0	1	2	0	.111	.167
Marty Karow	SS3, 3B2	R	22	6	10	0	2	1	0	0	0	0	2	0	.200	.300

Elmer Eggert 25 R 0-3, John Freeman 26 R 0-2, Fred Bratchi 35 R 0-1

NAME	T	AGE	W	L	PCT	SV	G	GS	CG	IP	H	BB	SO	ShO	ERA
		25	51	103	.331	7	154	154	63	1376	1603	558	381	6	4.68
Slim Harriss	R	30	14	21	.400	1	44	27	11	218	253	66	77	1	4.17
Hal Wiltse	L	23	10	18	.357	1	36	29	13	219	276	76	47	1	5.09
Tony Welzer	R	28	6	11	.353	1	37	19	8	182	214	71	56	0	4.45
Danny MacFayden	R	22	5	8	.385	2	34	16	6	160	176	59	42	1	4.27
Del Lundgren	R	26	5	12	.294	0	30	17	5	136	160	87	39	2	6.29
Red Ruffing	R	23	5	13	.278	2	26	18	10	158	160	87	77	0	4.67
Jack Russell	R	21	4	9	.308	0	34	15	4	147	172	40	25	1	4.10
Herb Bradley	R	24	1	1	.500	0	6	2	2	23	16	7	6	0	3.13
Ted Wingfield	R	27	1	7	.125	0	20	8	2	75	105	27	1	0	5.04
Frank Bennett	R	22	0	1	.000	0	4	1	0	12	15	6	1	0	3.00
John Wilson	R	22	0	2	.000	0	5	2	2	25	31	13	8	0	3.60
Rudy Sommers	L	38	0	0	.000	0	7	0	0	14	18	14	2	0	8.36
Bob Cremins	L	21	0	0	.000	0	4	0	0	5	5	3	0	0	5.40
Frank Bushey	R	20	0	0	.000	0	1	0	0	1	2	2	0	0	9.00

PITTSBURGH 1st 94-60 .610 — DONIE BUSH

NAME	G by POS	B	AGE	G	AB	R	H	2B	3B	HR	RBI	BB	SO	SB	BA	SA
TOTALS			28	156	5397	817	1648	258	78	54	759	437	355	65	.305	.412
Joe Harris	1B116, OF3	R	36	129	411	57	134	27	9	5	73	48	19	0	.326	.472
George Grantham	2B124, 1B29	L	27	151	531	96	162	33	11	8	66	74	39	9	.305	.454
Glenn Wright	SS143	R	26	143	570	78	160	26	4	9	105	39	46	4	.281	.388
Pie Traynor	3B143, SS9	R	27	149	573	93	196	32	9	5	106	22	11	11	.342	.455
Paul Waner	OF143, 1B14	L	24	155	623	113	237	40	17	9	131	60	14	5	.380	.543
Lloyd Waner	OF150, 2B1	L	21	150	629	133	223	17	6	2	27	37	23	14	.355	.410
Clyde Barnhart	OF94	R	31	108	360	66	115	25	5	3	54	37	19	2	.319	.442
Johnny Gooch	C91	B	29	101	291	22	75	17	2	2	48	19	21	0	.258	.351
Kiki Cuyler	OF73	R	27	85	285	60	88	13	7	3	31	37	36	20	.309	.435
Earl Smith (ST)	C61	L	30	66	189	16	51	3	1	5	25	21	11	0	.270	.376
Hal Rhyne (IL)	2B45, 3B10, SS7	R	28	62	168	21	46	5	0	0	17	14	9	0	.274	.304
Roy Spencer	C34	R	27	38	92	9	26	3	1	0	13	3	3	0	.283	.337
Fred Brickell	OF3	L	20	32	21	6	6	1	0	1	4	1	0	0	.286	.476
Adam Comorosky	OF16	R	22	18	61	5	14	1	0	0	4	3	1	0	.230	.246
Heinie Groh	3B12	R	37	14	35	2	10	1	0	0	3	2	2	0	.286	.314
Joe Cronin	2B7, SS4, 1B1	R	20	12	22	2	5	1	0	0	3	2	3	0	.227	.273
Herman Layne	OF2	R	26	11	6	3	0	0	0	0	0	1	0	0	.000	.000
Eddie Sicking	2B5	R	30	6	7	1	1	1	0	0	3	1	0	0	.143	.286
Dick Bartell	SS1	R	19	1	2	0	0	0	0	0	0	2	0	0	.000	.000

NAME	T	AGE	W	L	PCT	SV	G	GS	CG	IP	H	BB	SO	ShO	ERA
		31	94	60	.610	10	156	156	90	1385	1400	418	435	10	3.66
Carmen Hill	R	31	22	11	.667	3	43	31	22	278	260	80	95	2	3.24
Ray Kremer	R	34	19	8	.704	2	35	28	18	226	205	53	63	3	2.47
Lee Meadows	R	32	19	10	.655	0	40	38	25	299	315	66	84	2	3.40
Vic Aldridge	R	33	15	10	.600	1	35	34	17	239	248	74	86	1	4.26
Johnny Miljus	R	32	8	3	.727	0	19	6	3	76	62	17	24	2	1.89
Johnny Morrison (ST)	R	31	3	2	.600	3	21	2	1	54	63	21	21	0	4.17
Joe Dawson	R	29	3	7	.300	0	20	7	4	81	80	32	17	0	4.44
Mike Cvengros	L	25	2	1	.667	1	23	4	0	54	55	24	21	0	3.33
Roy Mahaffey	R	24	1	0	1.000	0	2	1	0	9	9	9	4	0	8.00
1 Bullet Joe Bush	R	34	1	2	.333	0	5	3	0	7	14	5	1	0	12.86
Emil Yde	L	27	1	3	.250	0	9	2	0	30	45	15	9	0	9.60
Chet Nichols	R	29	0	3	.000	0	8	0	0	28	34	17	9	0	5.79
1 Don Songer	L	28	0	0	.000	0	2	0	0	5	10	4	1	0	10.80
Red Peery	L	20	0	0	.000	0	1	0	0	1	0	1	0	0	0.00

ST. LOUIS 2nd 92-61 .601 1.5 — BOB O'FARRELL

NAME	G by POS	B	AGE	G	AB	R	H	2B	3B	HR	RBI	BB	SO	SB	BA	SA
TOTALS			27	153	5207	754	1450	264	79	84	700	484	511	110	.278	.408
Jim Bottomley	1B152	L	27	152	574	95	174	31	15	19	124	74	49	8	.303	.509
Frankie Frisch	2B153, SS1	B	28	153	617	112	208	31	11	10	78	43	10	48	.337	.472
Heinie Schuble (RL)	SS65	R	20	65	218	29	56	6	2	4	28	7	27	0	.257	.358
Les Bell	3B100, SS10	R	25	115	390	48	101	26	6	9	65	34	63	5	.259	.426
Wattie Holm	OF97, 3B9	R	25	110	419	55	120	27	8	3	66	24	29	4	.286	.411
Taylor Douthit	OF125	R	26	130	488	81	128	29	6	5	50	52	45	6	.262	.377
Chick Hafey (IL)	OF94	R	24	103	346	62	114	26	5	18	63	36	41	12	.329	.590
Frank Snyder	C62	R	34	63	194	7	50	5	0	1	30	9	18	0	.258	.299
Billy Southworth	OF83	L	34	92	306	52	92	15	5	2	39	23	7	10	.301	.402
Specs Toporcer	3B54, SS27, 2B2, 1B1	L	28	86	290	37	72	13	4	0	19	27	16	5	.248	.321
Johnny Schulte	C59	L	30	64	156	35	45	8	2	9	32	47	19	1	.288	.538
Ray Blades (KJ)	OF50	R	30	61	180	33	57	8	5	2	29	28	22	3	.317	.450
Bob O'Farrell	C53	R	30	61	178	19	47	10	1	0	18	23	22	3	.264	.331
Tommy Thevenow (BN)	SS59	R	23	59	191	23	37	6	1	0	4	14	8	2	.194	.236
Danny Clark	OF9	L	33	58	72	8	17	2	2	0	13	8	7	0	.236	.319
Ernie Orsatti	OF26	L	24	27	92	15	29	7	3	0	12	11	12	2	.315	.457
Rabbit Maranville	SS9	R	35	9	29	0	7	1	0	0	0	2	2	0	.241	.276
Wally Roettger	OF3	R	24	5	1	0	0	0	0	0	0	1	0	0	.000	.000
Bobby Schang	C3	R	40	3	5	0	1	0	0	0	0	0	0	0	.200	.200
Homer Peel	OF1	R	24	2	2	0	0	0	0	0	0	0	1	0	.000	.000

NAME	T	AGE	W	L	PCT	SV	G	GS	CG	IP	H	BB	SO	ShO	ERA
		31	92	61	.601	11	153	153	89	1367	1416	363	394	14	3.57
Jesse Haines	R	33	24	10	.706	1	38	36	25	301	273	77	89	6	2.72
Pete Alexander	R	40	21	10	.677	3	37	30	22	268	261	38	48	2	2.52
Bill Sherdel	L	30	17	12	.586	6	39	28	18	232	241	48	59	0	3.53
Flint Rhem	R	26	10	12	.455	0	27	26	9	169	189	54	51	2	4.42
Fred Frankhouse	R	23	5	1	.833	0	6	6	5	50	41	16	20	1	2.70
Art Reinhart	L	28	5	2	.714	1	21	9	4	82	82	36	15	2	4.17
2 Bob McGraw	R	32	4	5	.444	0	18	12	4	94	121	30	37	1	5.07
Carlisle Littlejohn	R	25	3	1	.750	0	14	2	1	42	47	14	16	0	4.50
Vic Keen	R	28	2	1	.667	0	21	0	0	34	39	8	12	0	4.76
Hi Bell (JJ)	R	29	1	3	.250	0	25	1	0	57	71	22	31	0	3.95
Jimmy Ring	R	32	0	4	.000	0	13	3	1	33	39	17	13	0	6.55
Syl Johnson	R	26	0	0	.000	0	2	0	0	3	3	0	2	0	6.00
Eddie Dyer	L	26	0	0	.000	0	1	0	0	2	5	2	1	0	18.00
3 Tony Kaufmann	R	26	0	0	.000	0	1	0	0	.1	4	1	0	0	81.00

NEW YORK 3rd 92-62 .597 2 — JOHN McGRAW

NAME	G by POS	B	AGE	G	AB	R	H	2B	3B	HR	RBI	BB	SO	SB	BA	SA
TOTALS			28	155	5372	817	1594	251	62	109	765	461	462	73	.297	.427
Bill Terry	1B150	L	28	150	580	101	189	32	13	20	121	46	53	1	.326	.529
Rogers Hornsby	2B155	R	31	155	568	133	205	32	9	26	125	86	38	9	.361	.586
Travis Jackson	SS124, 3B2	R	23	127	469	67	149	29	4	14	98	32	30	8	.318	.486
Fred Lindstrom	3B87, OF51	R	21	138	562	107	172	36	8	7	58	40	40	10	.306	.436
George Harper	OF142	L	35	145	483	85	160	19	6	16	87	84	27	7	.331	.495
Edd Roush	OF138	L	34	140	570	83	173	27	4	7	58	26	15	18	.304	.402
Heinie Mueller	OF56, 1B1	L	27	84	190	33	55	6	1	3	19	25	12	2	.289	.379
2 Zack Taylor	C81	R	28	83	258	18	60	7	3	0	21	17	20	2	.233	.283
Andy Reese	3B64, OF16, 1B1	R	23	97	355	43	94	14	2	4	21	13	52	5	.265	.349
Mel Ott	OF32	L	18	82	163	23	46	7	3	1	19	13	9	2	.282	.380
Al DeVormer	C54, 1B3	R	35	68	141	14	35	3	1	2	21	11	11	1	.248	.326
Jack Cummings	C34	R	23	43	80	8	29	6	1	2	14	5	10	0	.363	.538
Ty Tyson	OF41	R	35	43	159	24	42	7	2	1	17	10	19	5	.264	.352
1 Doc Farrell	SS36, 3B2	R	25	42	142	13	55	10	1	3	34	12	11	0	.387	.535
2 Les Mann	OF22	R	33	29	67	13	22	4	1	2	10	8	7	2	.328	.507
Sam Hamby	C19	R	29	21	52	6	10	0	1	0	5	7	7	1	.192	.231
2 Mickey O'Neill	C16	R	29	16	38	2	5	0	0	0	3	5	2	0	.132	.132
2 Herb Thomas	OF3, SS1	R	25	13	17	2	3	1	1	0	1	1	1	0	.176	.353
Tex Jeanes	OF6, P1	R	26	11	20	5	6	0	0	0	0	2	2	0	.300	.300
Buck Jordan		L	20	5	5	0	1	0	0	0	0	0	3	0	.200	.200
Joe Klinger	OF1	R	24	3	5	0	2	0	0	0	0	0	2	0	.400	.400

Red Smith 23 R 0-0, Ross Youngs (IL) 30

NAME	T	AGE	W	L	PCT	SV	G	GS	CG	IP	H	BB	SO	ShO	ERA
		28	92	62	.597	16	155	155	65	1382	1520	453	442	7	3.97
Burleigh Grimes	R	33	19	8	.704	2	39	34	15	260	274	87	102	2	3.53
Freddie Fitzsimmons	R	25	17	10	.630	3	42	31	14	245	260	67	78	1	3.71
Virgil Barnes	R	30	14	11	.560	2	35	29	12	229	251	51	66	2	3.97
2 Larry Benton	R	29	13	5	.722*	2	29	23	8	173	183	54	65	1	3.95
Dutch Henry	L	25	11	6	.647	4	45	15	7	164	184	31	40	1	4.22
1 Hugh McQuillan	R	29	5	4	.556	0	11	9	5	58	73	22	17	0	4.50
2 Don Songer	L	28	3	5	.375	1	22	1	0	50	48	31	9	0	2.88
Bill Clarkson	R	28	3	9	.250	2	26	7	2	87	92	52	28	0	4.34
1 Kent Greenfield	R	25	2	2	.500	0	12	1	0	20	39	13	4	0	9.45
Jim Faulkner	L	27	1	0	1.000	0	3	1	0	10	13	5	2	0	3.60
2 Norman Plitt	R	34	1	0	1.000	0	3	0	0	7	9	1	0	0	3.86
Mul Holland	R	24	1	0	1.000	0	2	0	0	2	0	3	0	0	0.00
Ben Cantwell	R	25	1	1	.500	0	5	2	1	20	26	2	6	0	4.05
2 Bullet Joe Bush	R	34	1	1	.500	0	3	2	1	12	18	5	6	0	7.50
Fay Thomas	R	22	0	0	.000	0	9	0	0	16	19	4	11	0	3.38
Jack Bentley	L	32	0	0	.000	0	4	0	0	10	7	10	3	0	2.70
Hank Boney	R	23	0	0	.000	0	3	0	0	4	4	2	0	0	2.25
Virgil Cheeves	R	26	0	0	.000	0	3	0	0	6	8	4	1	0	4.50
Bill Walker	L	23	0	0	.000	0	3	0	0	4	6	5	4	0	9.00
Tex Jeanes	R	26	0	0	.000	0	1	0	0	1	2	2	0	0	9.00
Art Johnson	L	30	0	0	.000	0	1	0	0	3	1	1	0	0	0.00
Ned Porter	R	22	0	0	.000	0	1	0	0	2	3	1	0	0	0.00

*Benton, also with Boston, league leader in PCT with .708

CHICAGO 4th 85-68 .556 8.5 — JOE McCARTHY

NAME	G by POS	B	AGE	G	AB	R	H	2B	3B	HR	RBI	BB	SO	SB	BA	SA
TOTALS			27	153	5303	750	1505	266	63	74	692	481	492	65	.284	.400
Charlie Grimm	1B147	L	28	147	543	68	169	29	6	2	74	45	21	3	.311	.398
Clyde Beck	2B99, 3B17, SS1	R	25	117	391	44	101	20	5	2	44	43	37	0	.258	.350
Woody English	SS84, 3B1	R	20	87	334	46	97	14	4	1	28	16	26	1	.290	.365
Sparky Adams	2B60, 3B53, SS40	R	32	146	647	100	189	17	7	0	49	42	26	26	.292	.340
Earl Webb	OF86	L	28	102	332	58	100	18	4	14	52	48	31	3	.301	.506
Hack Wilson	OF146	R	27	146	551	119	175	30	12	30	129	71	70	13	.318	.579
Riggs Stephenson	OF146, 3B6	R	29	152	579	101	199	46	9	7	82	65	28	8	.344	.491
Gabby Hartnett	C125	R	26	127	449	56	132	32	5	10	80	44	42	2	.294	.454
Cliff Heathcote	OF57	L	29	83	228	28	67	12	4	2	25	20	16	6	.294	.408
Pete Scott	OF36	R	28	71	156	28	49	18	1	0	21	19	18	1	.314	.442
Eddie Pick	3B49, 2B1, OF1	B	28	54	181	23	31	5	2	2	15	20	26	0	.171	.254
Mike Gonzalez	C36	R	36	39	108	15	26	4	1	1	15	10	8	1	.241	.324
Chuck Tolson	1B8	R	25	39	54	6	16	4	0	2	17	4	9	0	.296	.481
1 Jimmy Cooney	SS33	R	32	33	132	16	32	2	0	0	6	8	7	1	.242	.258
Howard Freigau	3B30	R	24	30	86	12	20	5	0	0	10	9	10	0	.233	.291
Elmer Yoter	3B11	R	27	13	27	2	6	1	1	0	5	4	4	0	.222	.333
2 Fred Haney		R	29	4	3	0	0	0	0	0	0	0	0	0	.000	.000
Harry Wilke	3B3	R	26	3	9	0	0	0	0	0	0	0	1	0	.000	.000
John Churry	C1	R	26	1	1	0	1	0	0	0	0	0	0	0	1.000	1.000
Tommy Sewell		L	21	1	1	0	0	0	0	0	0	0	0	0	.000	.000

NAME	T	AGE	W	L	PCT	SV	G	GS	CG	IP	H	BB	SO	ShO	ERA
		27	85	68	.556	5	153	153	75	1385	1439	514	465	11	3.65
Charlie Root	R	28	26	15	.634	2	48	36	21	309	296	117	145	4	3.76
Sheriff Blake	R	27	13	14	.481	0	32	27	13	224	238	82	64	2	3.29
2 Hal Carlson	R	33	12	8	.600	0	27	22	15	184	201	27	27	2	3.18
Guy Bush	R	25	10	10	.500	2	36	22	9	193	177	79	62	1	3.03
Percy Jones (EJ)	L	27	7	8	.467	0	30	11	5	113	123	72	37	1	4.06
Bob Osborn	R	24	5	5	.500	0	24	12	2	108	125	48	45	0	4.17
Jim Brillheart	L	23	4	2	.667	0	32	12	4	129	140	38	36	0	4.12
Luther Roy	R	24	3	1	.750	0	11	0	0	20	14	11	5	0	2.25
1 Tony Kaufmann	R	26	3	3	.500	0	9	6	3	53	75	19	21	0	6.45
2 Art Nehf	L	34	1	1	.500	1	8	2	2	26	25	9	12	1	1.38
Lefty Weinert	L	25	1	1	.500	0	5	3	1	20	21	6	5	0	4.50
2 Wayland Dean	R	25	0	0	.000	0	2	0	0	2	0	2	2	0	0.00
Hank Grampp	R	23	0	0	.000	0	2	0	0	3	4	1	3	0	9.00
Johnny Welch	R	20	0	0	.000	0	1	0	0	1	0	3	1	0	9.00

CINCINNATI 5th 75-78 .490 18.5 — JACK HENDRICKS

NAME	G by POS	B	AGE	G	AB	R	H	2B	3B	HR	RBI	BB	SO	SB	BA	SA
TOTALS			29	153	5185	643	1439	222	77	29	575	402	332	62	.278	.367
Wally Pipp	1B114	L	34	122	443	49	115	19	6	2	41	32	11	2	.260	.343
Hughie Critz	2B113	R	26	113	396	50	110	10	8	4	49	16	18	7	.278	.374
Hod Ford	SS104, 2B12	R	29	115	409	45	112	16	2	1	46	33	34	0	.274	.330
Chuck Dressen	3B142, SS2	R	28	144	548	78	160	36	10	2	55	71	32	7	.292	.405
Curt Walker	OF141	L	30	146	527	60	154	16	10	6	80	47	19	5	.292	.395
Ethan Allen	OF98	R	23	111	359	54	106	26	4	2	20	14	23	12	.295	.407
Rube Bressler	OF120	R	32	124	467	43	136	14	8	3	77	32	22	4	.291	.375
Bubbles Hargrave	C92	R	34	102	305	36	94	18	3	0	35	31	18	0	.308	.387
Billy Zitzmann	OF60, SS8, 3B3	R	29	88	232	47	66	10	4	0	24	20	18	9	.284	.362
Red Lucas	P37, 2B5, SS3, OF1	L	25	80	150	14	47	5	2	0	28	12	10	0	.313	.373
Val Picinich	C61	R	30	65	173	16	44	8	3	0	12	24	15	3	.254	.335
George Kelly	1B49, 2B13, OF2	R	31	61	222	27	60	16	4	5	21	11	23	1	.270	.446
Cuckoo Christenson	OF50	L	27	57	185	25	47	6	0	0	16	20	16	4	.254	.286
Clyde Sukeforth	C24	L	25	38	58	12	11	2	0	0	2	7	2	2	.190	.224
Pinky Pittinger	2B20, SS9, 3B2	R	28	31	84	17	23	5	0	1	10	2	5	4	.274	.369
Babe Pinelli	3B15, SS9, 2B5	R	31	30	76	11	15	2	0	1	4	6	7	2	.197	.263
2 Pee Wee Wanninger	SS28	L	24	28	93	14	23	2	2	0	8	6	7	0	.247	.312
Pid Purdy	OF16	L	23	18	62	15	22	2	4	1	12	4	3	0	.355	.565
Jack White	2B3, SS2	B	21	5	4	1	0	0	0	0	0	0	0	0	.000	.000
Ray Wolf	1B1	R	22	1	1	0	0	0	0	0	0	0	0	0	.000	.000

NAME	T	AGE	W	L	PCT	SV	G	GS	CG	IP	H	BB	SO	ShO	ERA
		31	75	78	.490	12	153	153	87	1368	1472	316	407	12	3.54
Red Lucas	R	25	18	11	.621	2	37	23	19	240	231	39	51	4	3.37
Jakie May	L	31	15	12	.556	1	44	28	17	236	242	70	121	2	3.51
Dolf Luque	R	36	13	12	.520	0	29	27	17	231	225	56	76	2	3.19
Eppa Rixey	L	36	12	10	.545	1	34	29	11	220	240	43	42	1	3.48
Pete Donohue	R	26	6	16	.273	1	33	24	12	191	253	32	48	1	4.10
Ray Kolp	R	32	3	3	.500	3	24	5	2	82	86	29	28	1	3.07
1 Art Nehf	L	34	3	5	.375	4	21	5	1	45	59	14	21	0	5.60
Carl Mays	R	35	3	7	.300	0	14	9	6	82	89	10	17	0	3.51
Pete Appleton	R	23	2	1	.667	0	6	2	2	30	29	17	3	1	1.80
Jim Beckman	R	22	0	1	.000	0	4	1	0	12	18	6	0	0	6.00

BROOKLYN 6th 65-88 .425 28.5 — WILBERT ROBINSON

NAME	G by POS	B	AGE	G	AB	R	H	2B	3B	HR	RBI	BB	SO	SB	BA	SA
TOTALS			30	154	5193	541	1314	195	74	39	499	368	494	106	.253	.342
Babe Herman	1B105, OF1	L	24	130	412	65	112	26	9	14	73	39	41	4	.272	.481
Jay Partridge	2B140	L	24	146	572	72	149	17	6	7	40	20	36	9	.260	.348
John Butler	SS90, 3B60	R	34	149	521	39	124	13	6	2	57	34	33	9	.238	.298
Bob Barrett	3B96	R	28	99	355	29	92	10	2	5	38	14	22	1	.259	.341
Max Carey	OF141	B	37	144	538	70	143	30	10	1	54	64	18	32	.266	.364
Jigger Statz	OF122, 2B1	R	29	130	507	64	139	24	7	1	21	26	43	10	.274	.355
Gus Felix	OF119	R	32	130	445	43	118	21	8	0	57	39	47	6	.265	.348
Hank DeBerry	C67	R	32	68	201	15	47	3	2	1	21	17	8	1	.234	.284
Harvey Hendrick	OF64, 1B53, 2B1	L	29	128	458	55	142	18	11	4	50	24	40	29	.310	.424
Jake Flowers	SS65, 2B1	R	25	67	231	26	54	5	5	2	20	21	25	3	.234	.325
Butch Henline	C60	R	32	67	177	12	47	10	3	1	18	17	10	1	.266	.373
Charlie Hargreaves	C44	R	30	46	133	9	38	3	1	0	11	14	7	1	.286	.323
Irish Meusel	OF17	R	34	42	74	7	18	3	1	1	7	11	5	0	.243	.351
Overton Tremper	OF18	R	21	26	60	4	14	0	0	0	4	0	2	0	.233	.233
Chuck Corgan (IL)	2B13, SS3	B	24	19	57	3	15	1	0	0	1	4	4	0	.263	.281
Merwin Jacobson	OF3	L	33	11	6	4	0	0	0	0	1	0	1	0	.000	.000
Bill Marriott	3B2	L	34	6	9	0	1	0	1	0	1	2	2	0	.111	.333
Oscar Roettger	OF1	R	27	5	4	0	0	0	0	0	0	1	1	0	.000	.000
Chick Fewster		R	31	4	1	1	0	0	0	0	0	0	0	0	.000	.000

NAME	T	AGE	W	L	PCT	SV	G	GS	CG	IP	H	BB	SO	ShO	ERA
		32	65	88	.425	10	154	154	74	1375	1382	418	**574**	7	**3.36**
Dazzy Vance	R	36	16	15	.516	1	34	32	**25**	273	242	69	**184**	2	2.70
Jesse Petty	L	32	13	18	.419	1	42	33	19	272	263	53	101	2	2.98
Bill Doak	R	36	11	8	.579	0	27	20	6	145	153	40	32	1	3.48
Watty Clark	L	25	7	2	.778	2	27	3	1	74	74	19	32	0	2.31
Jumbo Jim Elliott	L	26	6	13	.316	3	30	21	12	188	188	60	99	2	3.30
Doug McWeeney	R	30	4	8	.333	1	34	22	6	164	167	70	73	0	3.57
Rube Ehrhardt	R	32	3	7	.300	2	46	3	2	96	90	37	22	0	3.56
1 Norman Plitt	R	34	2	6	.250	0	19	8	1	62	73	36	9	0	4.93
Jesse Barnes	R	34	2	10	.167	0	18	10	2	79	106	25	14	0	5.70
Ray Moss	R	25	1	0	1.000	0	1	1	0	8	11	1	1	0	3.38
1 Bob McGraw	R	32	0	1	.000	0	1	1	0	4	5	2	2	0	9.00
1 Guy Cantrell	R	23	0	0	.000	0	6	0	0	10	10	6	5	0	2.70

BOSTON 7th 60-94 .390 34 — DAVE BANCROFT

NAME	G by POS	B	AGE	G	AB	R	H	2B	3B	HR	RBI	BB	SO	SB	BA	SA
TOTALS			29	155	5370	651	1498	216	61	37	582	346	363	100	.279	.363
Jack Fournier	1B102	L	34	122	374	55	106	18	2	10	53	44	16	4	.283	.422
Doc Gautreau	2B57	R	25	87	236	38	58	12	2	0	20	25	20	11	.246	.314
Dave Bancroft	SS104, 3B1	B	36	111	375	44	91	13	4	1	31	43	36	5	.243	.307
Andy High	3B89, 2B8, SS2	L	29	113	384	59	116	15	9	4	46	26	11	4	.302	.419
Lance Richbourg	OF110	L	29	115	450	57	139	12	9	2	34	22	30	24	.309	.389
Jim Welsh	OF129, 1B1	L	24	131	497	72	143	26	7	9	54	23	27	11	.288	.423
Eddie Brown	OF150, 1B1	R	35	155	558	64	171	35	6	2	75	28	20	11	.306	.401
Shanty Hogan	C61	R	21	71	229	24	66	17	1	3	32	9	23	2	.288	.410
Eddie Moore	3B52, 2B39, OF16, SS1	R	28	112	411	53	124	14	4	1	32	39	17	5	.302	.363
2 Doc Farrell	SS57, 2B40, 3B18	R	25	110	424	44	124	13	2	1	58	14	21	4	.292	.340
Jack Smith	OF48	L	32	84	183	27	58	6	4	1	24	16	12	8	.317	.410
Dick Burrus	1B61	L	29	72	220	22	70	8	3	0	32	17	10	3	.318	.382
Frank Gibson	C47	B	36	60	167	7	37	1	2	0	19	3	10	2	.222	.251
Luke Urban	C34	R	29	35	111	11	32	5	0	0	10	3	6	1	.288	.333
1 Zack Taylor	C27	R	28	30	96	8	23	2	1	1	14	8	5	0	.240	.313
1 Les Mann	OF24	R	33	29	66	8	17	3	1	0	6	8	3	2	.258	.333
1 Herb Thomas	2B17, SS2	R	25	24	74	11	17	6	1	0	6	3	9	2	.230	.338
Earl Clark	OF13	R	19	13	44	6	12	1	0	0	3	2	4	0	.273	.295
Dinny McNamara	OF3	L	21	11	9	3	0	0	0	0	0	0	3	0	.000	.000
Johnny Cooney		R	26	10	1	3	0	0	0	0	0	0	0	0	.000	.000
Sid Graves	OF5	R	25	7	20	5	5	1	1	0	2	0	1	1	.250	.400

NAME	T	AGE	W	L	PCT	SV	G	GS	CG	IP	H	BB	SO	ShO	ERA
		29	60	94	.390	11	155	155	52	**1390**	1602	468	402	3	4.22
Joe Genewich	R	30	11	8	.579	1	40	19	7	181	199	54	38	0	3.83
2 Kent Greenfield	R	25	11	14	.440	0	27	26	11	190	203	59	59	1	3.84
Bob Smith	R	29	10	18	.357	3	41	32	16	261	297	75	81	1	3.76
Charlie Robertson	R	31	7	17	.292	0	28	22	6	154	188	46	49	0	4.73
Geroge Mogridge	L	38	6	4	.600	5	20	1	0	49	48	15	26	0	3.67
1 Larry Benton	R	29	4	2	.667*	0	11	10	3	60	72	27	25	0	4.50
Johnny Wertz	R	29	4	10	.286	1	42	15	4	164	204	52	39	0	4.55
2 Hugh McQuillan	R	29	3	5	.375	0	13	11	2	78	109	24	17	0	5.54
Foster Edwards	R	23	2	8	.200	0	29	11	1	92	95	45	37	0	4.99
Guy Morrison	R	31	1	2	.333	0	11	3	1	34	40	15	6	0	4.50
Hal Goldsmith	R	28	1	3	.250	1	22	5	1	72	83	26	13	0	3.50
Art Mills	R	24	0	1	.000	0	15	1	0	38	41	18	7	0	3.79
Bunny Hearn	L	23	0	2	.000	0	8	0	0	13	16	9	5	0	4.15
Jack Knight	R	32	0	0	.000	0	3	0	0	3	6	2	0	0	15.00
Dick Rudolph	R	39	0	0	.000	0	1	0	0	1	1	1	0	0	0.00

*Benton, also with New York, league leader in PCT with .708

PHILADELPHIA 8th 51-103 .331 43 — STUFFY McINNIS

NAME	G by POS	B	AGE	G	AB	R	H	2B	3B	HR	RBI	BB	SO	SB	BA	SA
TOTALS			31	155	5317	678	1487	216	46	57	617	434	482	68	.280	.370
Russ Wrightstone	1B136, 2B1, 3B1	L	34	141	533	62	163	24	5	6	75	48	20	9	.306	.403
Fresco Thompson	2B153	R	25	153	597	78	181	32	14	1	70	34	36	19	.303	.409
Heinie Sand	SS86, 3B58	R	29	141	535	87	160	22	8	1	49	58	59	5	.299	.376
Barney Friberg	3B103, 2B5	R	27	111	335	31	78	8	2	1	28	41	49	3	.233	.278
Cy Williams	OF130	L	39	131	492	86	135	18	2	**30**	98	61	57	0	.274	.502
Freddy Leach	OF139	L	29	140	536	69	164	30	4	12	83	21	32	2	.306	.444
Dick Spalding	OF113	L	33	115	442	68	131	16	3	0	25	38	40	5	.296	.346
Jimmie Wilson	C124	R	26	128	443	50	122	15	2	2	45	34	15	13	.275	.332
Jack Scott	P48	L	35	83	114	6	33	6	0	1	17	9	9	0	.289	.368
2 Jimmy Cooney (JJ)	SS74	R	32	76	259	33	70	12	1	0	15	13	9	4	.270	.324
Johnny Mokan	OF63	R	31	74	213	22	61	13	2	0	33	25	21	5	.286	.366
Al Nixon	OF44	R	41	54	154	18	48	7	0	0	18	5	5	1	.312	.357
Bubber Jonnard	C41	R	27	53	143	18	42	6	0	0	14	7	7	0	.294	.336
Dick Attreau	1B26	L	30	44	83	17	17	1	1	1	11	14	18	1	.205	.277
Harry O'Donnell	C12	R	33	16	16	1	1	0	0	0	2	2	2	0	.063	.063
Bill Hohman	OF6	R	23	7	18	1	5	0	0	0	0	2	3	0	.278	.278
Henry Baldwin	SS3, 3B2	R	33	6	16	1	5	0	0	0	1	1	2	0	.313	.313
Bill Dietrick	SS5	R	25	5	6	1	1	0	0	0	0	0	0	0	.167	.167
Stuffy McInnis	1B1	R	36	1	0	0	0	0	0	0	0	0	0	0	.000	.000

NAME	T	AGE	W	L	PCT	SV	G	GS	CG	IP	H	BB	SO	ShO	ERA
		29	51	**103**	.331	6	155	155	81	1357	**1710**	462	377	5	5.35
Jack Scott	R	35	9	**21**	.300	1	**48**	25	17	233	304	69	69	1	5.10
Dutch Ulrich	R	27	8	11	.421	1	32	18	14	193	201	40	42	1	3.17
Alex Ferguson	R	30	8	16	.333	0	31	31	16	227	280	65	73	0	4.84
Hub Pruett	L	26	7	17	.292	1	31	28	12	186	238	89	90	1	6.05
Clarence Mitchell	L	36	6	3	.667	0	13	12	8	95	99	28	17	1	4.07
1 Hal Carlson	R	33	4	5	.444	1	11	9	4	64	80	18	13	0	5.20
Art Decatur	R	33	3	5	.375	0	29	3	0	97	130	20	27	0	7.24
Claude Willoughby	R	28	3	7	.300	2	35	6	1	98	126	53	14	1	6.52
Les Sweetland	L	25	2	10	.167	0	21	13	6	104	147	53	21	0	6.14
Russ Miller	R	27	1	1	.500	0	2	2	1	15	21	3	4	0	5.40
1 Wayland Dean	R	25	0	1	.000	0	2	0	0	3	6	2	1	0	12.00
Lefty Taber	L	27	0	1	.000	0	3	1	0	3	8	5	0	0	21.00
Ed Baecht	R	20	0	1	.000	0	1	1	0	6	12	2	0	0	12.00
Augie Walsh	R	22	0	1	.000	0	1	1	1	10	12	5	0	0	4.50
2 Tony Kaufmann	R	26	0	3	.000	0	5	5	1	19	37	8	4	0	10.42
Skinny O'Neal	R	28	0	0	.000	0	2	0	0	5	9	2	2	0	9.00

WORLD SERIES – NEW YORK (AL) 4 PITTSBURGH (NL) 0

LINE SCORES

TEAM	1	2	3	4	5	6	7	8	9	10	11	12	R	H	E
Game 1 October 5 at Pittsburgh															
NY (AL)	1	0	3	0	1	0	0	0	0				5	6	1
PIT (NL)	1	0	1	0	1	0	0	1	0				4	9	2
Hoyt, Moore (8) **Kremer**, Miljus (6)															
Game 2 October 6 at Pittsburgh															
NY	0	0	3	0	0	0	0	3	0				6	11	0
PIT	1	0	0	0	0	0	0	1	0				2	7	2
Pipgras **Aldridge**, Cvengros (8), Dawson (9)															
Game 3 October 7 at New York															
PIT	0	0	0	0	0	0	0	1	0				1	3	1
NY	2	0	0	0	0	0	6	0	X				8	9	0
Meadows, Cvengros (7) **Pennock**															
Game 4 October 8 at New York															
PIT	1	0	0	0	0	0	2	0	0				3	10	1
NY	1	0	0	0	2	0	0	0	1				4	12	2
Hill, **Miljus** (7) **Moore**															

COMPOSITE BATTING

NAME	POS	G	AB	R	H	2B	3B	HR	RBI	BA
New York (AL)										
Totals		4	136	23	38	6	2	2	19	.279
Koenig	SS	4	**18**	5	**9**	**2**	0	0	2	**.500**
Meusel	OF	4	17	1	2	0	0	0	1	.118
Combs	OF	4	16	**6**	5	0	0	0	2	.313
Ruth	OF	4	15	4	6	0	0	**2**	**7**	.400
Lazzeri	2B	4	15	1	4	1	0	0	2	.267
Dugan	3B	4	15	2	3	0	0	0	0	.200
Gehrig	1B	4	13	2	4	**2**	**2**	0	4	.308
Collins	C	2	5	0	3	1	0	0	0	.600
Moore	P	2	5	0	1	0	0	0	0	.200
Bengough	C	2	4	1	0	0	0	0	0	.000
Pennock	P	1	4	1	0	0	0	0	1	.000
Pipgras	P	1	3	0	1	0	0	0	0	.333
Hoyt	P	1	3	0	0	0	0	0	0	.000
Grabowski	C	1	2	0	0	0	0	0	0	.000
Durst	PH	1	1	0	0	0	0	0	0	.000
Pittsburgh (NL)										
Totals		4	130	10	29	6	1	0	10	.223
Barnhart	OF	4	16	0	5	1	0	0	4	.313
L. Waner	OF	4	15	5	6	1	1	0	0	.400
P. Waner	OF	4	15	0	5	1	0	0	3	.333
Harris	1B	4	15	0	3	0	0	0	1	.200
Traynor	3B	4	15	1	3	1	0	0	0	.200
Wright	SS	4	13	1	2	0	0	0	2	.154
Grantham	2B	3	11	0	4	1	0	0	0	.364
Smith	C	3	8	0	0	0	0	0	0	.000
Gooch	C	3	5	0	0	0	0	0	0	.000
Rhyne	2B	1	4	0	0	0	0	0	0	.000
Kremer	P	1	2	1	1	1	0	0	0	.500
Brickell	PH	2	2	1	0	0	0	0	0	.000
Aldridge	P	1	2	0	0	0	0	0	0	.000
Meadows	P	1	2	0	0	0	0	0	0	.000
Miljus	P	2	2	0	0	0	0	0	0	.000
Spencer	C	1	1	0	0	0	0	0	0	.000
Groh	PH	1	1	0	0	0	0	0	0	.000
Hill	P	1	1	0	0	0	0	0	0	.000
Yde	PR	1	0	1	0	0	0	0	0	.000
Cvengros	P	2	0	0	0	0	0	0	0	.000
Dawson	P	1	0	0	0	0	0	0	0	.000

COMPOSITE PITCHING

NAME	G	IP	H	BB	SO	W	L	SV	ERA
New York (AL)									
Totals	4	36	29	4	7	4	0	1	2.00
Moore	**2**	**10.2**	**11**	2	2	1	0	1	**0.84**
Pennock	1	9	3	0	1	1	0	0	1.00
Pipgras	1	9	7	1	2	1	0	0	2.00
Hoyt	1	7.1	8	1	2	1	0	0	4.91
Pittsburgh (NL)									
Totals	4	34.2	38	13	25	0	4	0	5.19
Aldridge	1	7.1	10	**4**	4	0	1	0	7.36
Miljus	**2**	6.2	4	**4**	**6**	0	1	0	1.35
Meadows	1	6.1	7	1	**6**	0	1	0	9.95
Hill	1	6	9	1	**6**	0	0	0	4.50
Kremer	1	5	5	3	1	0	1	0	3.60
Cvengros	**2**	2.1	3	0	2	0	0	0	3.86
Dawson	1	1	0	0	0	0	0	0	0.00

1928 That Near Eclipse Over the Bronx

Connie Mack's Athletics had not won a pennant since the Tall Tactician dismantled his powerhouse squad after the 1914 Series, but his rebuilt A's came extremely close in what proved to be the two team dog fight of 1928. The Yankees had bludgeoned their opposition into oblivion in 1927, and the first three months of the new season promised to be another Bronx runaway. Such was not the case, as a comfortable Yankee lead started to wilt under the heat of the Athletics' 25-8 record in July. The lead continued to melt off the Yankees' margin as the White Elephants stayed hot through August and then, with Al Simmons swinging a torrid bat and Lefty Grove pitching great ball, the Mackmen pulled even with the Yankees on September 7, and actually climbed into first with a win the next day. On the following day, Sunday, September 9, the Athletics came to the Bronx to face Babe Ruth, Lou Gehrig, and company in a double-header. The largest baseball crowd in history, 85,264, piled into Yankee Stadium to see the pivotal point in the pennant race, and left the park with full hearts as the Yankees captured both games, 3-0 and 7-3, to retake the league lead. The Athletics remained close on New York's heels, but they could never reach the top again as the Bronx Bombers clinched the flag on September 28, two days before the end of the season.

Both squads had star-studded rosters. The Yankees, with Ruth and Gehrig one-two in the league in home runs, were also one-two-three in the league in RBI's with Ruth, Gehrig, and Bob Meusel. Although Earle Combs and Tony Lazzeri added more fire to the best attack in the league, New York's pitching was not up to 1927 standards. But Waite Hoyt continued to win 20 games, and George Pipgras broke that barrier for the first time and led the pitchers with 24 wins. As Al Simmons, Jimmie Foxx, Mickey Cochrane, Bing Miller, Ty Cobb, and Max Bishop made the Athletic lineup a nightmare for pitchers, Grove provided the nightmare for batters as he tied Pipgras for the league lead in wins and led the circuit in strikeouts with 183.

Goose Goslin of the Senators, Heinie Manush of St. Louis, and Buddy Myer of Boston were the only American Leaguers to break the Yankees' and A's monopoly on the offensive statistical categories. Goslin won the batting crown with .379, Manush had the most hits with 241, and Myer was the best of the base stealers with 30.

The Giants won 25 games in September, but fell short of the National League pennant by finishing two games behind the champion St. Louis Cardinals. The steady Cards weathered the New York storm and clinched the flag on September 29. Sunny Jim Bottomley led the Cardinal's offense, pacing the loop in homers and runs batted in, and Chick Hafey and Frankie Frisch also chipped in with solid batting. Bill Sherdel and Jess Haines gave St. Louise two 20-game aces on the hill, enough to make new manger Bill McKechnie's first season a pleasant one. The New York lineup sported top hitters, Bill Terry, Freddy Lindstrom, and Mel Ott, and Larry Benton and Fat Freddy Fitzsimmons led a solid pitching staff with 20-win seasons.

The batting title went to Rogers Hornsby of Boston, who was playing with his third team in three years. Jim Bottomley was alone at the top with 136 RBI's, but shared the league lead with 31 home runs with Hack Wilson.

The Giants' Benton and Pittsburgh's spitballing Burleigh Grimes won 25 games apiece to pace the league's pitchers, as Brooklyn's Dazzy Vance used a blazing fast ball to win the E.R.A. title with a 2.09 mark.

The Series aped the 1927 Classic in that the Yankees again blasted their opposition out of the park in four games. The awesome duo of Ruth & Gehrig told the whole story, as Ruth hit .625 with three home runs, and Gehrig hit .545 with four homers. Game four best exemplified Yankee thunder as Ruth collected his entire Series output with three homers, and Gehrig hit his fourth round-tripper. Hoyt worked through the barrage and gave up 11 hits in the 7-3 contest enroute to his second victory and the clincher in what turned out to be the revenge for the Cardinal's 1926 Series win.

The year also saw several well-known ships pass in the night. Leo Durocher joined the Yankees as a utility infielder just in time to see Ty Cobb and Tris Speaker end their illustrious careers as part-time outfielders on Connie Mack's near-miss Athletics.

1928 AMERICAN LEAGUE

NAME	G by POS	B	AGE	G	AB	R	H	2B	3B	HR	RBI	BB	SO	SB	BA	SA
NEW YORK 1st 101-53 .656	**MILLER HUGGINS**															
TOTALS			28	154	5337	**894**	**1578**	269	79	**133**	**817**	**562**	**544**	51	**.296**	**.450**
Lou Gehrig	1B154	L	25	154	562	139	210	**47**	13	27	**142**	95	69	4	.374	.648
Tony Lazzeri(SJ)	2B110	R	24	116	404	62	134	30	11	10	82	43	50	15	.332	.535
Mark Koenig	SS125	L	25	132	533	89	170	19	10	4	63	32	19	3	.319	.415
Joe Dugan	3B91	R	31	94	312	33	86	15	0	6	34	16	15	1	.276	.381
Babe Ruth	OF154	L	33	154	536	**163**	173	29	8	**54**	**142**	**135**	**87**	4	.323	**.709**
Earle Combs	OF149	L	29	149	626	118	194	33	**21**	7	56	77	33	10	.310	.463
Bob Meusel(NJ)	OF131	R	31	131	518	77	154	45	5	11	113	39	56	6	.297	.467
Johnny Grabowski	C75	R	28	75	202	21	48	7	1	1	21	10	21	0	.238	.297
Leo Durocher	2B66, SS29	B	22	102	296	46	80	8	6	0	31	22	52	1	.270	.338
Gene Robertson	3B70, 2B3	L	28	83	251	29	73	9	0	1	36	14	6	2	.291	.339
Cedric Durst	OF33, 1B3	L	31	74	135	18	34	2	1	2	10	7	9	1	.252	.326
Pat Collins	C70	R	31	70	136	18	30	5	0	6	14	35	16	0	.221	.390
Ben Paschal	OF25	R	32	65	79	12	25	6	1	1	15	8	11	1	.316	.456
Benny Bengough(HJ)	C58	R	29	58	161	12	43	3	1	0	9	7	8	0	.267	.298
Mike Gazella	3B16, 2B4, SS3	R	31	32	56	11	13	0	0	0	2	6	7	2	.232	.232
Bill Dickey	C10	L	21	10	15	1	3	1	1	0	2	0	2	0	.200	.400
2 George Burns	1B2	R	35	4	4	1	2	0	0	0	0	0	1	0	.500	.500

NAME	T	AGE	W	L	PCT	SV	G	GS	CG	IP	H	BB	SO	ShO	ERA
		29	**101**	53	**.656**	**21**	154	154	82	1375	1466	452	487	13	3.74
George Pipgras	R	28	**24**	13	.649	3	46	**38**	22	**301**	**314**	103	139	4	3.38
Waite Hoyt	R	28	23	7	.767	**8**	42	31	19	273	279	60	67	3	3.36
Herb Pennock(IL)	L	34	17	6	.739	3	28	24	18	211	215	40	53	**5**	2.56
Hank Johnson	R	22	14	9	.609	0	31	22	10	199	188	**104**	110	1	4.30
Al Shealy	R	28	8	6	.571	2	23	12	3	96	124	42	39	0	5.06
Stan Coveleski	R	39	5	1	.833	0	12	8	2	58	72	20	5	0	5.74
Wilcy Moore	R	31	4	4	.500	2	35	2	0	60	71	31	18	0	4.20
2 Tom Zachary	L	32	3	3	.500	1	7	6	3	46	54	15	7	0	3.91
Fred Heimach	L	27	2	3	.400	0	13	9	5	68	66	16	25	0	3.31
Myles Thomas	R	30	1	0	1.000	0	12	1	0	32	33	9	10	0	3.38
Archie Campbell	R	24	0	1	.000	2	13	1	0	24	30	11	9	0	5.25
Rosy Ryan	R	30	0	0	.000	0	3	0	0	6	17	1	5	0	16.50
Urban Shocker(DD)	R	37	0	0	.000	0	1	0	0	2	3	0	0	0	0.00

NAME	G by POS	B	AGE	G	AB	R	H	2B	3B	HR	RBI	BB	SO	SB	BA	SA
PHILADELPHIA 2nd 98-55 .641 2.5	**CONNIE MACK**															
TOTALS			30	153	5226	829	1540	**323**	75	89	759	533	442	59	.295	.436
Joe Hauser	1B88	L	29	95	300	61	78	19	5	16	59	52	45	4	.260	.517
Max Bishop	2B125	L	28	126	472	104	149	27	5	6	50	97	36	9	.316	.432
Joe Boley	SS132	R	31	132	425	49	112	20	3	0	49	32	11	5	.264	.325
Sammy Hale	3B79	R	31	88	314	38	97	20	9	4	58	9	21	2	.309	.468
Ty Cobb	OF85	L	41	95	353	54	114	27	4	1	40	34	16	5	.323	.431
Bing Miller	OF133	R	33	139	510	76	168	34	7	8	85	27	24	10	.329	.471
Al Simmons(IL)	OF114	R	26	119	464	78	163	33	9	15	107	31	30	1	.351	.558
Mickey Cochrane	C130	L	25	131	468	92	137	26	12	10	57	76	25	7	.293	.464
Jimmie Foxx	3B60, 1B30, C19	R	20	118	400	85	131	29	10	13	79	60	43	3	.328	.548
Mule Haas	OF82	L	24	91	332	41	93	21	4	6	39	23	20	2	.280	.422
Jimmy Dykes	2B32, SS27, 3B20, 1B8, OF1	R	31	85	242	39	67	11	0	5	30	27	21	2	.277	.384
Tris Speaker	OF50	L	40	64	191	28	51	23	2	3	29	10	5	5	.267	.455
Ossie Orwoll	1B34, P27	L	27	64	170	28	52	13	2	0	22	16	24	3	.306	.406
Walt French	OF20	L	28	49	74	9	19	4	0	0	7	2	5	1	.257	.311
Eddie Collins	2B2, SS1	L	41	36	33	3	10	3	0	0	7	4	4	0	.303	.394
Joe Hassler	SS28	R	23	28	34	5	9	2	0	0	3	2	4	0	.265	.324
Cy Perkins	C19	R	32	19	29	1	5	0	0	0	1	1	1	0	.172	.172

NAME	T	AGE	W	L	PCT	SV	G	GS	CG	IP	H	BB	SO	ShO	ERA
		31	98	55	.641	16	153	153	81	1368	1349	424	**607**	**15**	**3.36**
Lefty Grove	L	28	**24**	8	.750	4	39	31	24	262	228	64	**183**	4	2.57
Jack Quinn	R	44	18	7	.720	1	31	28	18	211	239	34	43	4	2.90
Rube Walberg	L	28	17	12	.586	1	38	30	14	236	236	64	112	3	3.55
Eddie Rommel	R	30	13	5	.722	4	43	11	6	174	177	26	37	0	3.05
Howard Ehmke	R	34	9	8	.529	0	23	18	5	139	135	44	34	1	3.63
George Earnshaw	R	28	7	7	.500	1	26	22	7	158	143	100	117	3	3.82
Ossie Orwoll	L	27	6	5	.545	2	27	8	3	106	110	50	53	0	4.58
Bullet Joe Bush	R	35	2	1	.667	1	11	2	1	35	39	18	15	0	5.14
Ike Powers	R	22	1	0	1.000	2	9	0	0	12	8	10	4	0	4.50
Bill Shores	R	24	1	1	.500	0	3	2	1	14	13	7	5	0	3.21
Art Daney	R	23	0	0	.000	0	1	0	0	1	1	0	0	0	0.00
Jing Johnson	R	33	0	0	.000	0	3	0	0	11	13	5	3	0	4.91
Carroll Yerkes	L	25	0	1	.000	0	2	1	1	9	7	2	1	0	2.00

NAME	G by POS	B	AGE	G	AB	R	H	2B	3B	HR	RBI	BB	SO	SB	BA	SA
ST. LOUIS 3rd 82-72 .532 19	**DAN HOWLEY**															
TOTALS			28	154	5217	722	1431	276	76	63	707	548	479	76	.274	.393
Lu Blue	1B154	B	31	154	549	116	154	32	11	14	80	105	43	12	.281	.455
Otis Brannan	2B135	L	29	135	483	68	118	18	3	10	66	60	19	3	.244	.356
Red Kress	SS150	R	21	150	560	78	153	26	10	3	81	48	70	5	.273	.371
Frank O'Rourke(BG)	3B96, SS2	R	33	99	391	54	103	24	3	1	62	21	19	10	.263	.348
Earl McNeely	OF120	R	30	127	496	66	117	27	7	0	44	37	39	8	.236	.319
Fred Schulte	OF143	R	27	146	556	90	159	44	6	7	85	51	60	6	.286	.424
Heinie Manush	OF154	L	26	154	638	104	**241**	**47**	20	13	108	39	14	17	.378	.575
Wally Schang	C82	B	38	91	245	41	70	10	5	3	39	68	26	8	.286	.404
Clyde Manion	C71	R	31	76	243	25	55	5	1	2	31	15	18	3	.226	.280
Larry Bettencourt	3B41, OF2, C1	R	22	67	159	30	45	9	4	4	24	22	19	2	.283	.465
Guy Sturdy	1B1	L	28	54	45	3	10	1	0	1	8	8	4	1	.222	.311
Oscar Melillo	2B28, 3B19	R	28	51	132	9	25	2	0	0	9	9	11	2	.189	.205
Beauty McGowen	OF47	L	26	47	168	35	61	13	4	2	18	16	15	2	.363	.524
Ollie Sax	3B9	R	23	16	17	4	3	0	0	0	0	5	3	0	.176	.176
Billy Mullen(KJ)	3B6	R	33	15	18	2	7	1	0	0	2	3	4	0	.389	.444
Steve O'Neill(JJ)	C10	R	36	10	24	4	7	1	0	0	6	8	0	0	.292	.333
Fred Bennett	OF1	R	26	7	8	0	2	1	0	0	0	0	2	0	.250	.375
1 Wally Gerber	SS6	R	36	6	18	1	5	1	0	0	0	1	3	0	.278	.333
2 Frank Wilson	OF1	L	26	6	5	1	0	0	0	0	0	0	0	0	.000	.000
Ike Danning	C2	R	23	2	6	0	3	0	0	0	1	1	2	0	.500	.500

NAME	T	AGE	W	L	PCT	SV	G	GS	CG	IP	H	BB	SO	ShO	ERA
		26	82	72	.532	15	154	154	80	1374	1487	454	456	6	4.17
General Crowder	R	29	21	5	**.808**	2	41	31	19	244	238	91	99	1	3.69
Sam Gray	R	30	20	12	.625	3	35	31	21	263	256	86	102	2	3.19
Jack Ogden	R	30	15	16	.484	2	38	31	18	243	257	80	67	1	4.15
George Blaeholder	R	24	10	15	.400	3	38	26	9	214	235	52	87	1	4.37
Lefty Stewart	L	27	7	9	.438	3	29	17	7	143	173	32	25	1	4.65
Dick Coffman	R	21	4	5	.444	1	29	7	3	86	122	37	25	0	6.07
Boom-Boom Beck	R	23	2	3	.400	0	16	4	2	49	52	20	17	0	4.41
2 Hal Wiltse	L	24	2	5	.286	0	26	5	0	72	93	35	23	0	5.25
Ernie Nevers	R	25	1	0	1.000	0	6	0	0	9	9	2	1	0	3.00
Ed Strelecki	R	23	0	2	.000	1	22	2	1	50	49	17	8	0	4.32
Jiggs Wright	R	27	0	0	.000	0	2	0	0	2	3	2	2	0	13.50

WASHINGTON 4th 75-79 .487 26 — BUCKY HARRIS

NAME	G by POS	B	AGE	G	AB	R	H	2B	3B	HR	RBI	BB	SO	SB	BA	SA
TOTALS			27	155	5320	718	1510	277	93	40	681	481	390	110	.284	.393
Joe Judge	1B149	L	34	153	542	78	166	31	10	3	93	80	19	16	.306	.417
Bucky Harris	2B96, 3B1, OF1	R	31	99	358	34	73	11	5	0	28	27	26	5	.204	.263
Bobby Reeves	SS66, 2B22, 3B8, OF1	R	24	102	353	44	107	16	8	3	42	24	47	4	.303	.419
Ossie Bluege	3B144	R	27	146	518	78	154	33	7	2	75	46	27	18	.297	.400
Sam Rice	OF147	L	38	148	616	95	202	32	15	2	55	49	15	16	.328	.438
Red Barnes	OF104	L	24	114	417	82	126	22	15	6	51	55	38	7	.302	.470
Goose Goslin	OF125	L	27	135	456	80	173	36	10	17	102	48	19	16	**.379**	.614
Muddy Ruel	C101, 1B2	R	32	108	350	31	90	18	2	0	55	44	14	12	.257	.320
Sammy West	OF116	L	23	125	378	59	114	30	7	3	40	20	23	5	.302	.442
Joe Cronin	SS63	R	21	63	227	23	55	10	4	0	25	22	27	4	.243	.322
Jackie Hayes	2B41, SS15, 3B2	R	21	60	210	30	54	7	3	0	22	5	10	3	.257	.319
Bennie Tate	C30	L	26	57	122	10	30	6	0	0	15	10	4	0	.246	.295
Ed Kenna	C34	R	30	41	118	14	35	4	2	1	20	14	8	1	.297	.390
Grant Gillis	SS16, 2B5, 3B3	R	27	24	87	13	22	5	1	0	10	4	5	0	.253	.333
1 George Sisler	1B5, OF5	L	35	20	49	1	12	1	0	0	2	1	2	0	.245	.265
Dick Spaulding	OF11	L	34	16	23	1	8	0	0	0	0	0	4	0	.348	.348
Harley Boss	1B5	L	19	12	12	1	3	0	0	0	2	3	1	0	.250	.250
Babe Ganzel	OF7	R	27	10	26	2	2	1	0	0	4	1	4	0	.077	.115
Pelham Ballenger	3B3	R	34	3	9	0	1	0	0	0	0	0	1	0	.111	.111

Al Bool 30 R 1-7, Ed Crowley 21 R 0-1, Hugh McMullen 26 B 0-1, Patsy Gharrity (DE) 36

NAME	T	AGE	W	L	PCT	SV	G	GS	CG	IP	H	BB	SO	ShO	ERA
TOTALS		28	75	79	.487	10	155	155	77	1384	1420	466	462	**15**	3.88
Sad Sam Jones	R	35	17	7	.708	0	30	27	19	225	209	78	63	4	2.84
Garland Braxton	L	28	13	11	.542	6	38	24	15	218	177	44	94	2	**2.52**
Firpo Marberry	R	29	13	13	.500	3	**48**	11	7	161	160	42	76	1	3.86
Bump Hadley	R	23	12	13	.480	0	33	31	16	232	236	100	80	3	3.53
Milt Gaston	R	32	6	12	.333	0	28	22	8	149	179	53	45	3	5.50
1 Tom Zachary	L	32	6	9	.400	0	20	14	5	103	130	40	19	1	5.42
Lloyd Brown	L	23	4	4	.500	1	27	10	2	107	112	40	38	0	4.04
Bobby Burke	L	21	2	4	.333	0	26	7	2	85	87	18	27	1	3.92
Hod Lisenbee	R	29	2	6	.250	0	16	9	3	77	102	32	13	0	6.08
Clay Van Alstyne	R	28	0	0	.000	0	4	0	0	21	26	13	5	0	5.57
Jim Weaver	R	24	0	0	.000	0	3	0	0	6	2	6	2	0	1.50

CHICAGO 5th 72-82 .468 29 — RAY SCHALK 32-42 .432 LENA BLACKBURNE 40-40 .500

NAME	G by POS	B	AGE	G	AB	R	H	2B	3B	HR	RBI	BB	SO	SB	BA	SA
TOTALS			28	155	5207	656	1405	231	77	24	592	469	488	**144**	.270	.358
Bud Clancy	1B128	L	27	130	487	64	132	19	11	2	37	42	25	6	.271	.368
Bill Hunnefield	2B83, SS3, 3B1	B	29	94	333	42	98	8	3	2	24	26	24	16	.294	.354
Bill Cissell	SS123	R	24	125	443	66	115	22	3	1	60	29	41	18	.260	.330
Willie Kamm	3B155	R	28	155	552	70	170	30	12	1	84	73	22	17	.308	.411
Alex Metzler	OF134	L	25	139	464	71	141	18	14	3	55	77	30	16	.304	.422
Johnny Mostil	OF131	R	32	133	503	69	136	19	8	0	51	66	54	23	.270	.340
Bibb Falk	OF78	L	29	98	286	42	83	18	4	1	37	25	16	5	.290	.392
Moe Berg	C73	R	26	76	224	25	55	16	0	0	29	14	25	2	.246	.317
Buck Redfern	2B45, SS33, 3B1	R	26	86	261	22	61	6	3	0	35	12	19	8	.234	.280
Carl Reynolds	OF74	R	25	84	291	51	94	21	11	2	36	17	13	15	.323	.491
Buck Crouse	C76	L	31	78	218	17	55	5	2	2	20	19	14	3	.252	.321
Bill Barrett	OF37, 2B25	R	28	76	235	34	65	11	2	3	26	14	30	8	.277	.379
Harry McCurdy	C34	L	28	49	103	12	27	10	0	2	13	8	15	1	.262	.417
Art Shires	1B32	L	20	33	123	20	42	6	1	1	11	13	10	0	.341	.431
George Blackerby	OF20	R	24	30	83	8	21	0	0	0	12	4	10	2	.253	.253
Randy Moore	OF16	L	23	24	61	6	13	4	1	0	5	3	5	0	.213	.311
Karl Swanson	2B21	L	24	22	64	2	9	1	0	0	6	4	7	3	.141	.156
Johnny Mann	3B3	R	30	6	6	0	2	0	0	0	1	1	0	0	.333	.333
Ray Schalk	C1	R	35	2	1	0	1	0	0	0	1	0	0	1	1.000	1.000

NAME	T	AGE	W	L	PCT	SV	G	GS	CG	IP	H	BB	SO	ShO	ERA
TOTALS		28	72	82	.468	11	155	155	**88**	1378	1516	501	418	6	3.98
Tommy Thomas	R	28	17	16	.515	2	36	32	24	283	277	76	129	3	3.08
Ted Lyons	R	27	15	14	.517	6	39	27	21	240	276	68	60	0	3.98
Red Faber	R	29	13	9	.591	0	27	27	16	201	223	68	43	2	3.76
Grady Adkins	R	31	10	16	.385	1	36	27	14	225	233	89	54	0	3.72
Ted Blankenship	R	27	9	11	.450	0	27	22	8	158	186	80	36	0	4.61
Ed Walsh	R	23	4	7	.364	0	14	10	3	78	86	42	32	0	4.96
Sarge Connally	R	29	2	5	.286	2	28	5	1	74	89	29	28	0	4.87
George Cox	R	23	1	2	.333	0	26	2	0	89	110	39	22	0	5.26
Bob Weiland	L	22	1	0	1.000	0	1	1	1	9	7	5	9	1	0.00
Charlie Barnabe	L	28	0	2	.000	0	7	2	0	10	17	0	3	0	6.30
Dan Dugan	L	21	0	0	.000	0	1	0	0	.1	0	0	0	0	0.00
John Goodell	L	21	0	0	.000	0	2	0	0	3	6	2	0	0	18.00
Rudy Leopold	L	22	0	0	.000	0	2	0	0	2	3	0	0	0	4.50
Al Williamson	R	28	0	0	.000	0	1	0	0	2	1	0	0	0	0.00
Roy Wilson	L	31	0	0	.000	0	1	0	0	3	2	3	2	0	0.00

DETROIT 6th 68-86 .442 33 — GEORGE MORIARTY

NAME	G by POS	B	AGE	G	AB	R	H	2B	3B	HR	RBI	BB	SO	SB	BA	SA
TOTALS			29	154	5292	744	1476	265	**97**	62	686	469	438	113	.279	.401
Bill Sweeney	1B75, OF3	R	24	89	309	47	78	15	5	0	19	15	28	12	.252	.333
Charlie Gehringer	2B154	L	25	154	603	108	193	29	16	6	74	69	22	15	.320	.451
Jackie Tavener	SS131	L	30	132	473	59	123	24	15	5	52	33	51	13	.260	.406
Marty McManus	3B92, 1B45, SS1	R	28	139	500	78	144	37	5	8	73	51	32	11	.288	.430
Harry Heilmann	OF126, 1B25	R	33	151	558	83	183	38	10	14	107	57	45	7	.328	.507
Harry Rice	OF129, 3B2	L	27	131	510	87	154	21	12	6	81	44	27	20	.302	.425
Bob Fothergill	OF90	R	30	111	347	49	110	28	10	3	63	24	19	8	.317	.481
Pinky Hargrave	C88	B	32	121	321	38	88	13	5	10	63	32	28	4	.274	.439
Al Wingo	OF71	L	30	87	242	30	69	13	2	2	30	40	17	2	.285	.380
Jack Warner	3B52, SS7	R	24	75	206	33	44	4	4	0	13	16	15	4	.214	.272
Larry Woodall	C62	R	33	65	186	19	39	5	1	0	13	24	10	3	.210	.247
C. Galloway (PB)	SS22, 3B21, 1B1, OF1	R	31	53	148	17	39	5	2	1	17	15	3	7	.264	.345
Paul Easterling	OF34	R	22	43	114	17	37	7	1	3	12	8	24	2	.325	.482
Merv Shea	C30	R	27	39	85	8	20	2	3	0	9	9	11	2	.235	.329
Johnny Neun (IL)	1B25	B	27	36	108	15	23	3	1	0	5	7	10	2	.213	.259
John Stone	OF26	L	22	26	113	20	40	10	3	2	21	5	8	1	.354	.549

NAME	T	AGE	W	L	PCT	SV	G	GS	CG	IP	H	BB	SO	ShO	ERA
TOTALS		27	68	86	.442	16	154	154	65	1372	1481	**567**	451	5	4.32
Ownie Carroll	R	25	16	12	.571	2	34	28	19	231	219	87	51	2	3.27
Elam Vangilder	R	32	11	10	.524	5	38	11	7	156	163	68	43	0	3.92
Earl Whitehill	L	28	11	16	.407	0	31	30	12	196	214	78	93	1	4.32
Vic Sorrell	R	27	8	11	.421	0	29	23	8	171	182	83	67	0	4.79
Haskell Billings	R	20	5	10	.333	0	21	16	3	111	118	59	48	1	5.11
Sam Gibson	R	28	5	8	.385	0	20	18	5	120	155	52	29	1	5.40
Lil Stoner	R	29	5	8	.385	4	36	11	4	126	151	42	29	0	4.36
Ken Holloway	R	30	4	8	.333	2	30	11	5	120	137	32	32	0	4.35
Phil Page	L	22	2	0	1.000	0	3	2	2	22	21	10	3	0	2.45
George Smith	R	26	1	1	.500	3	39	2	0	106	103	50	54	0	4.42
Charlie Sullivan	R	25	0	2	.000	0	3	2	0	12	18	6	2	0	6.75

CLEVELAND 7th 62-92 .403 39 — ROGER PECKINPAUGH

NAME	G by POS	B	AGE	G	AB	R	H	2B	3B	HR	RBI	BB	SO	SB	BA	SA
TOTALS			28	155	**5386**	674	1535	299	61	34	611	377	426	50	.285	.382
Lew Fonseca (BL)	1B56, 3B15, SS4, 2B1	R	29	75	263	38	86	19	4	3	36	13	17	4	.327	.464
Carl Lind	2B154	R	24	154	**650**	102	191	42	4	1	54	36	48	8	.294	.375
Joe Sewell	SS137, 3B19	L	29	155	588	79	190	40	2	4	70	58	9	7	.323	.418
Johnny Hodapp	3B101, 1B13	R	22	116	449	51	145	31	6	2	73	20	20	2	.323	.432
Homer Summa	OF132	L	29	134	504	60	143	26	3	3	57	20	15	4	.284	.365
Sam Langford	OF107	L	28	110	427	50	118	17	8	4	50	21	35	3	.276	.382
Charlie Jamieson	OF111	L	35	112	433	63	133	18	4	1	37	56	20	3	.307	.374
Luke Sewell	C118	R	27	122	411	52	111	16	9	3	52	26	27	3	.270	.375
1 George Burns	1B53	R	35	82	209	29	52	12	1	5	30	17	11	2	.249	.388
Eddie Morgan	1B36, OF21, 3B14	R	24	76	265	42	83	24	6	4	54	21	17	5	.313	.494
Glenn Myatt	C30	L	30	58	125	9	36	7	2	1	15	13	13	0	.288	.400
George Uhle (SA)	P31	R	29	55	98	9	28	3	2	1	17	8	4	0	.286	.388
Luther Harvel	OF39	R	22	40	136	12	30	6	1	0	12	4	17	1	.221	.279
George Gerken	OF34	R	24	38	115	16	26	7	2	0	9	12	22	3	.226	.322
Ed Montague	SS15, 3B9	R	22	32	51	12	12	0	1	0	3	6	7	0	.235	.275
Red Dorman	OF24	R	22	25	77	12	28	6	0	0	11	9	6	1	.364	.442
Martin Autry	C18	R	25	22	60	6	18	6	1	1	9	1	7	0	.300	.483
Bruce Caldwell	OF10, 1B1	R	22	18	27	2	6	1	1	0	3	2	2	1	.222	.333
Ollie Tucker	OF14	L	26	14	47	5	6	0	0	1	2	7	3	0	.128	.191
Jonah Goldman	SS7	R	21	7	21	1	5	1	0	0	2	3	0	0	.238	.286
Aaron Ward	3B3, SS2, 2B1	R	31	6	9	0	1	0	0	0	0	1	2	0	.111	.111
Al VanCamp	1B5	R	24	5	17	0	4	1	0	0	2	0	1	1	.235	.294
Cecil Bolton	1B4	L	24	4	13	1	2	0	2	0	0	2	2	0	.154	.462
Johnny Burnett	SS2	L	23	3	10	3	5	0	0	0	1	0	1	0	.500	.500

Johnny Gill 23 L 0-2, Art Reinholz 25 R 1-3, 1 Frank Wilson 26 L 0-1, Grover Hartley (DP) 39

NAME	T	AGE	W	L	PCT	SV	G	GS	CG	IP	H	BB	SO	ShO	ERA
TOTALS		26	62	92	.403	15	155	155	70	1378	**1615**	511	416	4	4.47
Willis Hudlin	R	22	14	14	.500	7	42	26	10	220	231	90	62	0	4.05
Joe Shaute	L	28	13	17	.433	2	36	32	21	254	295	68	81	1	4.04
George Uhle (SA)	R	29	12	17	.414	1	31	28	18	214	252	48	74	2	4.08
George Grant	R	25	10	8	.556	0	28	18	6	155	196	76	39	1	5.05
Jake Miller	L	30	8	9	.471	0	25	23	7	158	203	43	37	0	4.44
Bill Bayne	L	29	2	5	.286	3	37	6	3	109	128	43	39	0	5.13
1 Garland Buckeye	L	30	1	5	.167	0	9	6	0	35	58	5	6	0	6.69
2 Johnny Miljus	R	33	1	4	.200	1	11	4	1	51	46	20	19	0	2.65
Willie Underhill	R	23	1	2	.333	0	11	3	1	28	33	20	16	0	4.50
Les Barnhart	R	23	0	1	.000	0	2	1	0	9	13	4	1	0	7.00
Clint Brown	R	24	0	1	.000	0	2	1	1	11	14	2	2	0	4.91
Jumbo Brown	R	21	0	1	.000	0	5	0	0	15	19	15	12	0	6.60
Hap Collard	R	29	0	0	.000	0	1	0	0	4	4	4	1	0	2.25
Wes Ferrell	R	20	0	2	.000	0	2	2	1	16	15	5	4	0	2.25
Mel Harder	R	18	0	2	.000	1	23	1	0	49	64	32	15	0	6.61
Emil Levsen	R	30	0	3	.000	0	11	3	0	41	39	31	7	0	5.49
Jim Moore	R	24	0	1	.000	0	1	1	1	9	5	5	1	0	2.00

BOSTON 8th 57-96 .373 43.5 — BILL CARRIGAN

NAME	G by POS	B	AGE	G	AB	R	H	2B	3B	HR	RBI	BB	SO	SB	BA	SA
TOTALS			29	154	5132	589	1356	260	62	38	544	389	512	99	.264	.361
Phil Todt	1B144	L	26	144	539	61	136	31	8	12	73	26	47	6	.252	.406
Bill Regan	2B137, OF1	R	29	138	511	53	135	30	6	7	75	21	40	9	.264	.387
2 Wally Gerber	SS103	R	36	104	300	21	64	6	1	0	28	32	31	6	.213	.240
Buddy Myer	3B144	L	24	147	536	78	168	26	6	1	44	53	28	**30**	.313	.390
Doug Taitt	OF139, P1	L	25	143	482	51	144	28	14	3	61	36	32	13	.299	.434
Ira Flagstead	OF135	R	34	140	510	84	148	41	4	1	39	60	23	12	.290	.392
Ken Williams	OF127	L	38	133	462	59	140	25	1	8	67	37	15	4	.303	.413
Fred Hofmann	C71	R	34	78	199	14	45	8	1	0	16	11	25	0	.226	.276
Rothrock	OF53, 3B17, 1B16, SS13, 2B2, C1, P1	B	23	117	344	52	92	9	4	3	22	33	40	12	.267	.343
Billy Rogell	SS67, 2B22, OF6, 3B3	B	23	102	296	33	69	10	4	0	29	22	47	2	.233	.294
Johnnie Heving	C62	R	32	82	158	11	41	7	2	0	11	11	10	1	.259	.329
Charlie Berry	C63	R	25	80	177	18	46	7	3	1	19	21	19	1	.260	.350
Red Ruffing	P42	R	24	60	121	12	38	13	1	2	19	3	12	0	.314	.488
Red Rollings	1B5, 2B4, OF4, 3B1	L	24	50	48	7	11	3	1	0	9	6	8	0	.229	.333
Carl Sumner	OF10	L	19	16	29	6	8	1	1	0	3	5	6	0	.276	.379
Denny Williams	OF6	L	28	16	18	1	4	0	0	0	1	1	1	0	.222	.222
George Loepp	OF14	R	26	15	51	6	9	3	1	0	3	5	12	0	.176	.275
Casper Asbjornson	C6	R	19	6	16	0	3	1	0	0	1	1	1	0	.188	.250
Arlie Tarbert	OF6	R	23	6	17	1	3	1	0	0	2	1	1	1	.176	.235
Paul Hinson		R	24	3	0	1	0	0	0	0	0	0	0	0	.000	.000
Freddie Moncewicz	SS2	R	24	3	1	0	0	0	0	0	0	0	1	0	.000	.000

NAME	T	AGE	W	L	PCT	SV	G	GS	CG	IP	H	BB	SO	ShO	ERA
TOTALS		25	57	**96**	.373	9	154	154	69	1352	1492	452	407	**5**	4.39
Ed Morris	R	28	19	15	.559	5	47	29	20	258	255	80	104	0	3.52
Jack Russell	R	22	11	14	.440	0	32	26	10	201	233	41	27	2	3.85
Red Ruffing	R	24	10	**25**	.286	2	42	34	25	289	303	96	118	1	3.90
Danny MacFayden	R	23	9	15	.375	0	33	28	9	195	215	78	61	0	4.75
Slim Harriss	R	31	8	11	.421	1	27	15	4	128	141	33	37	1	4.64
Frank Bennett	R	23	0	0	.000	0	1	0	0	1	1	0	0	0	0.00
Herb Bradley	R	25	0	3	.000	0	15	5	1	47	64	16	14	1	7.28
Cliff Garrison	R	21	0	0	.000	0	6	0	0	16	22	6	0	0	7.88
Marty Griffin	R	26	0	3	.000	0	11	3	0	38	42	17	9	0	4.97
Jack Rothrock	R	23	0	0	.000	0	1	0	0	1	0	0	0	0	0.00
Merle Settlemire	L	25	0	6	.000	0	30	9	0	82	116	34	12	0	5.49
John Shea	L	23	0	0	.000	0	1	0	0	1	1	1	0	0	18.00
Pat Simmons	R	19	0	2	.000	1	31	3	0	69	69	38	16	0	4.04
Steve Slayton	R	26	0	0	.000	0	3	0	0	7	6	3	2	0	3.86
Doug Taitt	R	25	0	0	.000	0	1	0	0	1	2	2	1	0	27.00
John Wilson	R	23	0	0	.000	0	2	0	0	5	6	6	1	0	9.00
1 Hal Wiltse	L	24	0	2	.000	0	2	2	1	12	16	1	5	0	9.00

ST. LOUIS 1st 95-59 .617 — BILL McKECHNIE

NAME	G by POS	B	AGE	G	AB	R	H	2B	3B	HR	RBI	BB	SO	SB	BA	SA
TOTALS			28	154	5357	807	1505	**292**	70	113	749	**568**	438	82	.281	.425
Jim Bottomley	1B148	L	28	149	576	123	187	42	**20**	**31**	**136**	71	54	10	.325	.628
Frankie Frisch	2B139	B	29	141	547	107	164	29	9	10	86	64	17	29	.300	.441
Rabbit Maranville	SS112, 2B2	R	36	112	366	40	88	14	10	1	34	36	27	3	.240	.342
Wattie Holm	3B83, OF7	R	26	102	386	61	107	24	6	3	47	32	17	1	.277	.394
2 George Harper	OF84	L	36	99	272	41	83	8	2	17	58	51	15	2	.305	.537
Taylor Douthit	OF154	R	27	154	648	111	191	35	3	3	43	84	36	11	.295	.372
Chick Hafey	OF133	R	25	138	520	101	175	46	6	27	111	40	53	8	.337	.604
2 Jimmie Wilson	C120	R	27	120	411	45	106	26	2	2	50	45	24	9	.258	.345
Andy High	3B73, 2B19	L	30	111	368	58	105	14	3	6	37	37	10	2	.285	.389
Tommy Thevenow	SS64, 3B3, 1B1	R	24	69	171	11	35	8	3	0	13	20	12	0	.205	.287
Wally Roettger (BL)	OF66	R	25	68	261	27	89	17	4	6	44	10	22	2	.341	.506
Ray Blades	OF19	R	31	51	85	9	20	7	1	1	19	20	26	0	.235	.376
Pepper Martin	OF4	R	24	39	13	11	4	0	0	0	0	1	2	2	.308	.308
Pete Alexander	P34	R	41	34	86	13	25	2	0	1	11	4	8	0	.291	.349
Ernie Orsatti	OF17, 1B5	L	25	27	69	10	21	6	0	3	15	10	11	0	.304	.522
2 Earl Smith	C18	L	31	24	58	3	13	2	0	0	7	5	4	0	.224	.259
1 Bob O'Farrell	C14	R	31	16	52	6	11	1	0	0	4	13	9	2	.212	.231
Gus Mancuso	C11	R	22	11	38	2	7	0	1	0	3	0	5	0	.184	.237
Howie Williamson		L	23	10	9	0	2	0	0	0	0	1	4	0	.222	.222
Specs Toporcer	1B1, 2B1	L	29	8	14	0	0	0	0	0	0	0	3	0	.000	.000
1 Spud Davis	C2	R	23	2	5	1	1	0	0	0	1	1	0	0	.200	.200

NAME	T	AGE	W	L	PCT	SV	G	GS	CG	IP	H	BB	SO	ShO	ERA
		31	**95**	59	**.617**	**21**	154	154	**83**	**1415**	1470	399	422	4	3.38
Bill Sherdel	L	31	21	10	.677	**5**	38	27	20	249	251	56	72	0	2.86
Jesse Haines	R	34	20	8	.714	0	33	28	20	240	238	72	77	1	3.19
Pete Alexander	R	41	16	9	.640	2	34	31	18	244	262	37	59	1	3.36
Flint Rhem	R	27	11	8	.579	3	28	22	9	170	199	71	47	0	4.13
Syl Johnson	R	27	8	4	.667	3	34	6	2	120	117	33	66	0	3.90
2 Clarence Mitchell	L	37	8	9	.471	0	19	18	9	150	149	38	31	1	3.30
Art Reinhart	L	29	4	6	.400	2	23	9	3	75	80	27	12	1	2.88
Fred Frankhouse	R	24	3	2	.600	1	21	10	1	84	91	36	29	0	3.96
Hal Haid	R	30	2	2	.500	**5**	27	0	0	47	39	11	21	0	2.30
Carlisle Littlejohn	R	26	2	1	.667	0	12	2	1	32	36	14	6	0	3.66
Tony Kaufmann	R	27	0	0	.000	0	4	1	0	5	8	4	2	0	9.00

NEW YORK 2nd 93-61 .604 2 — JOHN McGRAW

NAME	G by POS	B	AGE	G	AB	R	H	2B	3B	HR	RBI	BB	SO	SB	BA	SA
TOTALS			26	155	**5459**	807	1600	276	59	**118**	**758**	444	376	62	.293	**.430**
Bill Terry	1B149	L	29	149	568	100	185	36	11	17	101	64	36	7	.326	.518
Andy Cohen	2B126, SS3, 3B1	R	23	129	504	64	138	24	7	9	59	31	17	3	.274	.403
Travis Jackson	SS149	R	24	150	537	73	145	35	6	14	77	56	46	8	.270	.436
Fred Lindstrom	3B153	R	22	153	646	99	**231**	39	9	14	107	25	21	15	.358	.511
Mel Ott	OF115, 2B5, 3B1	L	19	124	435	69	140	26	4	18	77	52	36	3	.322	.524
Jim Welsh	OF117	L	25	124	476	77	146	22	5	9	54	29	30	4	.307	.431
Lefty O'Doul	OF94	L	31	114	354	67	113	19	4	8	46	30	8	9	.319	.463
Shanty Hogan	C124	R	22	131	411	48	137	25	2	10	71	42	25	0	.333	.477
Andy Reese	OF64, 2B26, 1B6, SS6, 3B6	R	24	109	406	61	125	18	4	6	44	13	24	7	.308	.416
Les Mann	OF68	R	34	82	193	29	51	7	1	2	25	18	9	2	.264	.342
2 Bob O'Farrell	C63	R	31	75	133	23	26	6	0	2	20	34	16	2	.195	.286
Edd Roush(IL)	OF39	L	35	46	163	20	41	5	3	2	13	14	8	1	.252	.356
Jack Cummings	C4	R	24	33	27	4	9	2	0	2	9	3	4	0	.333	.630
2 Russ Wrightstone	1B2	L	35	30	25	3	4	0	0	1	5	3	2	0	.160	.280
1 George Harper	OF18	L	36	19	57	11	13	1	0	2	7	10	4	1	.228	.351
Chick Fullis		R	24	11	1	5	0	0	0	0	0	1	1	0	.000	.000
1 Art Jahn	OF8	R	32	10	29	7	8	1	0	1	7	2	5	0	.276	.414
Ray Foley		L	22	2	1	1	0	0	0	0	0	1	1	0	.000	.000
Bill Haeffner	C2	R	33	2	1	0	0	0	0	0	0	0	0	0	.000	.000
1 Al Spohrer	C3	R	25	2	2	0	0	0	0	0	0	0	0	0	.000	.000
Joe Price	OF1	R	31	1	1	0	0	0	0	0	0	0	1	0	.000	.000
Pat Veltman	OF1	R	22	1	3	1	1	0	1	0	0	1	0	0	.333	1.000

NAME	T	AGE	W	L	PCT	SV	G	GS	CG	IP	H	BB	SO	ShO	ERA
		29	93	61	.604	16	155	155	79	1395	1454	405	399	7	3.66
Larry Benton	R	30	**25**	9	**.735**	4	42	35	**28**	310	299	71	90	2	2.73
Freddie Fitzsimmons	R	26	20	9	.690	1	40	32	16	261	264	65	67	1	3.69
2 Joe Genewich	R	31	11	4	.733	3	26	18	10	158	136	54	37	2	3.19
Carl Hubbell	L	25	10	6	.625	1	20	14	8	124	117	21	37	1	2.83
Jim Faulkner	L	28	9	8	.529	2	38	8	3	117	131	41	32	0	3.54
Vic Aldridge (HO)	R	34	4	7	.364	2	22	17	3	119	133	45	33	0	4.84
Jack Scott	R	36	4	1	.800	1	16	3	3	50	59	11	17	0	3.60
1 Virgil Barnes	R	31	3	3	.500	0	10	9	3	55	71	18	11	1	5.07
Dutch Henry (HJ-ST)	L	26	3	6	.333	1	17	8	4	64	82	25	23	0	3.80
Bill Walker	L	24	3	6	.333	0	22	8	1	76	79	31	39	0	4.74
1 Ben Cantwell	R	26	1	0	1.000	1	7	1	0	18	20	4	0	0	4.50
2 Garland Buckeye	L	30	0	0	.000	0	1	0	0	4	9	2	3	0	13.50
Tiny Chaplin	R	22	0	2	.000	0	12	1	0	24	27	8	5	0	4.50
1 Bill Clarkson	R	29	0	0	.000	0	4	0	0	6	10	1	3	0	7.50
Leo Mangum	R	32	0	0	.000	0	1	1	0	3	6	5	1	0	15.00
Chet Nichols	R	30	0	0	.000	0	3	0	0	3	11	3	1	0	21.00

CHICAGO 3rd 91-63 .591 4 — JOE McCARTHY

NAME	G by POS	B	AGE	G	AB	R	H	2B	3B	HR	RBI	BB	SO	SB	BA	SA
TOTALS			29	154	5260	714	1460	251	64	92	665	508	**517**	**83**	.278	.402
Charlie Grimm	1B147	L	29	147	547	67	161	25	5	5	62	39	20	7	.294	.386
Freddie Maguire	2B138	R	29	140	574	67	160	24	7	1	41	25	38	6	.279	.350
Woody English	SS114, 3B2	R	21	116	475	68	142	22	4	2	34	30	28	4	.299	.375
Clyde Beck	3B87, SS47, 2B1	R	26	131	483	72	124	18	4	3	52	58	58	3	.257	.329
Kiki Cuyler	OF127	R	28	133	499	92	142	25	9	17	79	51	61	**37**	.285	.473
Hack Wilson	OF143	R	28	145	520	89	163	32	9	**31**	120	77	**94**	4	.313	.588
Riggs Stephenson	OF135	R	30	137	512	75	166	36	9	8	90	68	29	8	.324	.477
Gabby Hartnett	C118	R	27	120	388	61	117	26	9	14	57	65	32	3	.302	.523
Cliff Heathcote	OF39	L	30	67	137	26	39	8	0	3	18	17	12	6	.285	.409
Johnny Butler	3B59, SS2	R	35	62	174	17	47	7	0	0	16	19	7	2	.270	.310
Earl Webb	OF31	L	23	62	140	22	35	7	3	3	23	14	17	0	.250	.407
Mike Gonzalez	C45	R	37	49	158	12	43	9	2	1	21	12	7	2	.272	.373
Norm McMillan	2B19, 3B18	R	32	49	123	11	27	2	2	1	12	13	19	0	.220	.293
Joe Kelly	1B10	L	28	32	52	3	11	1	0	1	7	1	3	0	.212	.288
Johnny Moore		L	26	4	4	0	0	0	0	0	0	0	0	0	.000	.000
Ray Jacobs		R	26	2	2	0	0	0	0	0	0	0	1	0	.000	.000
Elmer Yoter	3B1	R	28	1	0	0	0	0	0	0	0	0	0	0	.000	.000

NAME	T	AGE	W	L	PCT	SV	G	GS	CG	IP	H	BB	SO	ShO	ERA
		29	91	63	.591	14	154	154	75	1381	1383	508	531	12	3.39
Pat Malone	R	25	18	13	.581	2	42	25	16	251	218	99	155	2	2.83
Sheriff Blake	R	28	17	11	.607	1	34	29	16	241	209	101	78	4	2.46
Guy Bush	R	26	15	6	.714	2	42	24	9	204	229	86	61	2	3.84
Charlie Root	R	29	14	18	.438	2	40	30	13	237	214	73	122	1	3.57
Art Nehf	L	35	13	7	.650	0	31	21	10	177	190	52	40	2	2.64
Percy Jones	L	28	10	6	.625	3	39	18	9	154	167	56	41	1	4.03
Hal Carlson (IL)	R	34	3	2	.600	4	20	5	2	56	74	15	11	0	5.95
Lefty Weinert	L	26	1	0	1.000	0	10	1	0	17	24	9	8	0	5.29
Ed Holley	R	26	0	0	.000	0	13	1	0	31	31	16	10	0	3.77
Ben Tincup	R	37	0	0	.000	0	2	0	0	9	14	1	3	0	7.00
Johnny Welch	R	21	0	0	.000	0	3	0	0	4	13	0	2	0	15.75

PITTSBURGH 4th 85-67 .559 9 — DONIE BUSH

NAME	G by POS	B	AGE	G	AB	R	H	2B	3B	HR	RBI	BB	SO	SB	BA	SA
TOTALS			27	152	5371	**837**	**1659**	246	**100**	52	768	435	352	64	**.309**	.421
George Grantham	1B119, 2B1, 3B1	L	28	124	440	93	142	24	9	10	85	59	37	9	.323	.486
Sparky Adams	2B107, SS27, OF1	R	33	135	539	91	149	14	6	0	38	64	18	8	.276	.325
Glenn Wright	SS101, 1B1, OF1	R	27	108	407	63	126	20	8	8	66	21	53	3	.310	.457
Pie Traynor	3B144	R	28	144	569	91	192	38	12	3	124	28	10	12	.337	.462
Paul Waner	OF131, 1B24	L	25	152	602	**142**	223	**50**	19	6	86	77	16	6	.370	.547
Lloyd Waner	OF52	L	22	152	**659**	121	221	22	14	5	61	40	13	8	.335	.434
Fred Brickell	OF50	L	21	81	202	34	65	4	4	3	41	20	18	5	.322	.426
2 Charlie Hargreaves	C77	R	31	79	260	15	74	8	2	1	32	12	9	1	.285	.342
Dick Bartell	2B39, SS27, 3B1	R	20	72	233	27	71	8	4	1	36	21	18	4	.305	.386
Clyde Barnhart	OF48, 3B1	R	32	61	196	18	58	6	2	4	30	11	9	3	.296	.408
Pete Scott (CN)	OF42, 1B8	R	29	60	177	33	55	10	4	5	33	18	14	1	.311	.497
Adam Comorosky (AJ)	OF49	R	23	51	176	22	52	6	3	2	34	15	6	1	.295	.398
Rollie Hemsley	C49	R	21	50	133	14	36	2	3	0	18	4	10	1	.271	.331
Burleigh Grimes	P48	R	34	48	131	17	42	8	1	0	16	4	15	1	.321	.397
1 Earl Smith	C28	L	31	32	85	8	21	6	0	2	11	11	7	0	.247	.388
1 Johnny Gooch	C31	B	30	31	80	7	19	2	1	0	5	3	6	0	.238	.288
Eddie Mulligan	3B6, 2B4	R	33	27	43	4	10	2	0	0	1	3	4	0	.233	.279
1 Joe Harris	1B6	R	37	16	23	2	9	2	1	0	2	4	2	0	.391	.565
Mack Hillis	2B8, 3B1	R	26	11	36	6	9	2	3	1	7	0	6	1	.250	.556
Cobe Jones	SS1	B	22	1	2	0	1	0	0	0	0	0	0	0	.500	.500
John O'Connell	C1	R	24	1	1	0	0	0	0	0	0	0	0	0	.000	.000
Bill Windle	1B1	L	23	1	1	1	1	1	0	0	0	0	0	0	1.000	2.000

NAME	T	AGE	W	L	PCT	SV	G	GS	CG	IP	H	BB	SO	ShO	ERA
		31	85	67	.559	11	152	152	82	1354	1422	446	385	8	3.95
Burleigh Grimes	R	34	**25**	14	.641	3	**48**	**37**	**28**	**331**	311	77	97	**4**	2.99
Carmen Hill	R	32	16	10	.615	2	36	31	16	237	229	81	73	1	3.53
Ray Kremer	R	35	15	13	.536	0	34	31	17	219	253	68	61	1	4.64
Fred Fussell	L	32	8	9	.471	1	28	20	9	160	183	41	43	2	3.60
Erv Brame	R	26	7	4	.636	0	24	11	6	96	110	44	22	0	5.06
Joe Dawson	R	30	7	7	.500	3	31	7	1	129	116	56	36	0	3.28
1 Johnny Miljus	R	33	5	7	.417	1	21	10	3	70	90	33	26	0	5.27
Bill Burwell	R	33	1	0	1.000	0	4	1	0	21	18	8	2	0	5.14
Lee Meadows (SA)	R	33	1	1	.500	0	4	2	1	10	18	5	3	0	8.10
Less Bartholomew	L	25	0	0	.000	0	6	0	0	23	31	9	6	0	7.04
Homer Blankenship	R	25	0	2	.000	0	5	2	1	22	27	9	6	0	5.73
Glenn Spencer	R	22	0	0	.000	0	4	0	0	6	4	3	2	0	1.50
Walt Tauscher	R	26	0	0	.000	1	17	0	0	29	28	12	7	0	4.97
Elmer Tutwiler	R	22	0	0	.000	0	2	0	0	4	4	0	1	0	4.50

CINCINNATI 5th 78-74 .513 16 — JACK HENDRICKS

NAME	G by POS	B	AGE	G	AB	R	H	2B	3B	HR	RBI	BB	SO	SB	BA	SA
TOTALS			29	153	5184	648	1449	229	67	32	588	386	330	**83**	.280	.368
George Kelly	1B99, OF13	R	32	116	402	46	119	33	7	3	58	28	35	2	.296	.435
Hughie Critz	2B153	R	27	153	641	95	190	21	11	5	52	37	24	18	.296	.387
Hod Ford	SS149	R	30	149	506	49	122	17	4	0	54	47	31	1	.241	.291
Chuck Dressen	3B135	R	24	135	498	72	145	26	3	1	59	43	22	10	.291	.361
Curt Walker (FS)	OF122	L	31	123	427	64	119	15	12	6	73	49	14	19	.279	.412
Ethan Allen	OF129	R	24	129	485	55	148	30	7	1	62	27	29	6	.305	.402
Billy Zitzmann	OF78, 3B1	R	30	101	266	53	79	9	3	3	33	13	22	13	.297	.387
Val Picinich	C93	R	31	96	324	29	98	15	1	7	35	20	25	1	.302	.420
Wally Pipp	1B72	L	35	95	272	30	77	11	3	2	26	23	13	1	.283	.368
Marty Callaghan	OF69	L	28	81	238	29	69	11	4	0	24	27	10	5	.290	.370
Pid Purdy (BY)	OF61	L	24	70	223	32	69	11	1	0	25	23	13	1	.309	.368
Bubbles Hargrave	C57	R	35	65	190	19	56	12	3	0	23	13	14	4	.295	.389
Joe Stripp	OF21, 3B17, SS1	R	25	42	139	18	40	7	3	1	17	8	8	0	.288	.403
Pinky Pittinger	SS12, 2B4, 3B4	R	29	40	38	12	9	0	1	0	4	0	1	2	.237	.289
Red Lucas (BN)	P27	L	26	39	73	8	23	2	1	0	7	4	6	0	.315	.370
Clyde Sukeforth	C26	L	26	33	53	5	7	2	1	0	3	3	5	0	.132	.208
Jack White	2B1	B	22	1	3	0	0	0	0	0	0	0	1	0	.000	.000

NAME	T	AGE	W	L	PCT	SV	G	GS	CG	IP	H	BB	SO	ShO	ERA
		31	78	74	.513	11	153	153	68	1372	1516	410	355	11	3.94
Eppa Rixey	L	37	19	18	.514	2	43	**37**	17	291	**317**	67	58	3	3.43
Ray Kolp	R	33	13	10	.565	3	44	24	12	209	219	55	61	1	3.19
Red Lucas (BN)	R	26	13	9	.591	1	27	19	13	167	164	42	35	**4**	3.40
Dolf Luque	R	37	11	10	.524	1	33	29	11	234	254	84	72	1	3.58
Pete Donohue	R	27	7	11	.389	0	23	18	8	150	180	32	37	0	4.74
Carl Mays	R	36	4	1	.800	1	14	7	4	63	67	22	10	1	3.86
Ken Ash	R	26	3	3	.500	0	8	5	2	36	43	13	6	0	6.50
Pete Appleton	R	24	3	4	.429	0	31	1	0	83	101	22	20	0	4.66
Jakie May (IL)	L	32	3	5	.375	1	21	11	1	79	99	35	39	1	4.44
Jim Joe Edwards	L	33	2	2	.500	2	18	1	0	32	43	20	11	0	7.59
Jim Beckman	R	23	0	1	.000	0	6	0	0	15	19	9	4	0	6.00
Si Johnson	R	21	0	0	.000	0	3	0	0	10	9	5	1	0	4.50
Harlan Pyle	R	22	0	0	.000	0	2	1	0	1	1	4	1	0	21.00

BROOKLYN 6th 77-76 .503 17.5 — WILBERT ROBINSON

NAME	G by POS	B	AGE	G	AB	R	H	2B	3B	HR	RBI	BB	SO	SB	BA	SA
TOTALS			32	155	5243	665	1393	229	70	66	621	557	510	81	.266	.374
Del Bissonette	1B155	L	28	155	587	90	188	30	13	25	106	70	75	5	.320	.543
Jake Flowers	2B94, SS6	R	26	103	339	51	93	11	6	2	44	47	30	10	.274	.360
Dave Bancroft	SS149	B	37	149	515	47	127	19	5	0	51	59	20	7	.247	.303
Harvey Hendrick	3B91, OF17	L	30	126	425	83	135	15	10	11	59	54	34	16	.318	.478
Babe Herman	OF127	L	25	134	486	64	165	37	6	12	91	38	36	1	.340	.514
Max Carey	OF95	B	38	108	296	41	73	11	0	2	19	47	24	18	.247	.304
Rube Bressler	OF137	R	33	145	501	78	148	29	13	4	70	80	33	2	.295	.429
Hank DeBerry	C80	R	33	82	250	19	65	8	2	0	23	18	15	3	.252	.298
Harry Riconda	2B53, 3B21, SS16	R	31	92	281	22	63	15	4	3	35	20	28	6	.224	.338
Jigger Statz	OF52, 2B1	R	30	77	171	28	40	8	1	0	16	18	12	3	.234	.292
Ty Tyson	OF55	R	36	59	210	25	57	11	1	1	21	10	14	3	.271	.348
Butch Henline	C45	R	33	55	132	12	28	3	1	2	8	17	8	2	.212	.295
2 Joe Harris	OF16	R	37	55	89	8	21	6	1	1	8	14	4	0	.236	.360
2 Johnny Gooch	C38	B	30	42	101	9	32	1	2	0	12	7	9	0	.317	.366
Wally Gilbert	3B39	R	27	39	153	26	31	4	0	0	3	14	8	2	.203	.229
Jay Partridge	2B18, 3B2	L	25	37	73	18	18	0	1	0	12	13	6	2	.247	.274
1 Charlie Hargreaves	C20	R	31	20	61	3	12	2	0	0	5	6	6	1	.197	.230
1 Howard Freigau	3B10, SS1	R	25	17	34	6	7	2	0	0	3	1	3	0	.206	.265

Overton Tremper 22 R 6-31, Max West 23 R 6-21, Al Lopez 19 R 0-12, Chuck Corgan (DD) 25

NAME	T	AGE	W	L	PCT	SV	G	GS	CG	IP	H	BB	SO	ShO	ERA
TOTALS		31	77	76	.503	15	155	155	75	1396	1378	468	**551**	**16**	**3.25**
Dazzy Vance	R	37	22	10	.688	2	38	32	24	280	226	72	**200**	4	**2.09**
Jesse Petty	L	33	15	15	.500	1	40	31	15	234	264	56	74	2	4.04
Doug McWeeney	R	31	14	14	.500	1	42	32	12	244	218	**114**	79	**4**	3.17
Watty Clark	L	26	12	9	.571	3	40	19	10	195	193	50	85	2	2.68
Jumbo Jim Elliott	L	27	9	14	.391	1	41	21	7	192	194	64	74	2	3.89
Bill Doak	R	37	3	8	.273	3	28	12	4	99	104	35	12	1	3.27
Rube Ehrhardt	R	33	1	3	.250	2	28	2	1	54	74	27	12	0	4.67
Lou Koupal	R	29	1	0	1.000	1	17	1	1	37	43	15	10	0	2.43
Ray Moss	R	26	0	3	.000	1	27	5	1	60	62	35	5	1	4.95

BOSTON 7th 50-103 .327 44.5 — JACK SLATTERY 11-20 .355 — ROGERS HORNSBY 39-83 .320

NAME	G by POS	B	AGE	G	AB	R	H	2B	3B	HR	RBI	BB	SO	SB	BA	SA
TOTALS			31	153	5228	631	1439	241	41	52	577	477	377	60	.275	.367
2 George Sisler	1B118, P1	L	35	118	491	71	167	26	4	4	68	30	15	11	.340	.434
Rogers Hornsby	2B140	R	32	140	486	99	188	42	7	21	94	**107**	41	5	**.387**	**.632**
Doc Farrell	SS132, 2B1	R	26	134	483	36	104	14	2	3	43	26	26	3	.215	.271
Les Bell	3B153	R	26	153	591	58	164	36	7	10	91	40	45	1	.277	.413
Lance Richbourg	OF148	L	30	148	612	105	206	26	12	2	52	62	39	11	.337	.428
Jack Smith	OF65	L	33	96	254	30	71	9	2	1	32	21	14	6	.280	.343
Eddie Brown	OF129, 1B1	R	36	142	523	45	140	28	2	2	59	24	22	6	.268	.340
Zack Taylor	C124	R	29	125	399	36	100	15	1	2	30	33	29	2	.251	.308
Eddie Moore	OF54, 2B1	R	29	68	215	27	51	9	0	2	18	19	12	7	.237	.307
Dick Burrus	1B32	L	30	64	137	15	37	6	0	3	13	19	8	1	.270	.380
2 Howard Freigau	SS14, 2B11	R	25	52	109	11	28	8	1	1	17	9	14	1	.257	.376
2 Al Spohrer	C48	R	25	51	124	15	27	3	0	0	9	5	11	1	.218	.242
Heinie Mueller	OF41	L	28	42	151	25	34	3	1	0	19	17	9	1	.225	.258
Earl Clark	OF27	R	20	28	112	18	34	9	1	0	10	4	8	0	.304	.402
Doc Gautreau	2B4, SS1	R	26	23	18	3	5	0	1	0	1	4	3	1	.278	.389
Jimmy Cooney	SS11, 2B4	R	33	18	51	2	7	0	0	0	3	2	5	1	.137	.137
Luke Urban	C10	R	30	15	17	0	3	0	0	0	2	0	1	0	.176	.176
Dinny McNamera	OF3	L	22	9	4	2	1	0	0	0	0	0	1	0	.250	.250
Charlie Fitzberger		L	24	7	7	0	2	0	0	0	0	0	3	0	.286	.286
Dave Harris	OF6	R	28	7	17	2	2	1	0	0	0	2	6	0	.118	.176
Bill Cronin	C3	R	25	3	2	1	0	0	0	0	0	1	0	0	.000	.000
Earl Williams	C1	R	25	3	2	0	0	0	0	0	0	0	1	0	.000	.000

NAME	T	AGE	W	L	PCT	SV	G	GS	CG	IP	H	BB	SO	ShO	ERA
TOTALS		28	50	103	.327	6	153	153	54	1360	1596	524	343	1	4.83
Bob Smith	R	30	13	17	.433	2	38	25	14	244	274	74	59	0	3.87
Ed Brandt	L	23	9	**21**	.300	0	38	31	12	225	234	109	84	1	5.08
Art Delaney	R	33	9	17	.346	2	39	22	8	192	197	56	45	0	3.80
2 Ben Cantwell	R	26	3	3	.500	0	22	9	3	90	112	36	18	0	5.10
Johnny Cooney	L	27	3	7	.300	1	24	6	2	90	106	31	18	0	4.30
1 Joe Genewich	R	31	3	7	.300	0	13	11	4	81	88	18	15	0	4.11
Kent Greenfield	R	26	3	11	.214	0	32	23	5	144	173	60	30	0	5.31
2 Virgil Barnes	R	31	2	7	.222	0	16	10	1	60	86	26	7	0	5.85
Foster Edwards	R	24	2	1	.667	0	21	3	2	49	67	23	17	0	5.69
Charlie Robertson	R	32	2	5	.286	1	13	7	3	59	73	16	17	0	5.34
Bunny Hearn	L	24	1	0	1.000	0	7	0	0	10	6	8	8	0	6.30
Ray Boggs	L	23	0	0	.000	0	4	0	0	5	2	7	0	0	5.40
2 Bill Clarkson	R	29	0	2	.000	0	19	1	0	35	53	22	8	0	6.69
Hal Goldsmith	R	29	0	0	.000	0	4	0	0	8	14	1	1	0	3.38
Bonnie Hollingsworth	R	32	0	2	.000	0	7	2	0	22	30	13	10	0	5.32
Art Mills	R	25	0	0	.000	0	4	0	0	8	17	8	2	0	12.38
Guy Morrison	R	32	0	0	.000	0	1	0	0	3	4	3	0	0	12.00
Emilio Palmero	L	33	0	1	.000	0	3	1	0	7	14	2	0	0	5.14
2 George Sisler	L	35	0	0	.000	0	1	0	0	1	0	1	0	0	0.00
Clay Touchstone	R	25	0	0	.000	0	5	0	0	8	15	2	1	0	4.50
Johnny Wertz	R	30	0	2	.000	0	10	2	0	18	31	8	5	0	10.50

PHILADELPHIA 8th 43-109 .283 51 — BURT SHOTTON

NAME	G by POS	B	AGE	G	AB	R	H	2B	3B	HR	RBI	BB	SO	SB	BA	SA
TOTALS			27	152	5234	660	1396	257	47	85	606	503	510	53	.267	.382
Don Hurst	1B104	L	22	107	396	73	113	23	4	19	64	68	40	3	.285	.508
Fresco Thompson	2B152	R	26	152	634	99	182	34	11	3	50	42	27	19	.287	.390
Heinie Sand	SS137	R	30	141	426	38	90	26	1	0	38	60	47	1	.211	.277
Pinky Whitney	3B149	R	23	151	585	73	176	35	4	10	103	36	30	3	.301	.426
Chuck Klein	OF63	L	23	64	253	41	91	14	4	11	34	14	22	0	.360	.577
Denny Sothern	OF136	R	24	141	579	82	165	27	5	5	38	34	53	17	.285	.375
Freddy Leach	OF120, 1B25	L	30	145	588	83	179	36	11	13	96	30	30	4	.304	.469
Walt Lerian	C74	R	25	96	239	28	65	16	2	2	25	41	29	1	.272	.381
Cy Williams	OF69	L	40	99	238	31	61	9	0	12	37	54	34	0	.256	.445
2 Spud Davis	C49	R	23	67	163	16	46	2	0	3	18	15	11	0	.282	.350
Johnny Schulte	C34	L	31	65	113	14	28	2	2	4	17	15	12	0	.248	.407
Bill Deitrick (BL)	OF21, SS8	L	26	52	100	13	20	6	0	0	7	17	10	1	.200	.260
Barney Friberg	SS31, 3B5, 2B3, OF3, 1B2	R	28	52	94	11	19	3	0	1	7	12	16	0	.202	.266
2 Art Jahn	OF29	R	32	36	94	8	21	4	0	0	11	4	11	0	.223	.266
1 Russ Wrightstone	OF26, 1B4	L	35	33	91	7	19	5	1	1	11	14	5	0	.209	.319
Al Nixon	OF20	R	42	25	64	7	15	2	0	0	7	6	4	1	.234	.266
Bill Kelly	1B23	R	28	23	71	6	12	1	1	0	5	7	20	0	.169	.211
1 Jimmie Wilson	C20	R	27	21	70	11	21	4	1	0	13	9	8	3	.300	.386
Harvey MacDonald	OF2	L	30	13	16	0	4	0	0	0	2	2	3	0	.250	.250

Dutch Ulrich (IL) 28

NAME	T	AGE	W	L	PCT	SV	G	GS	CG	IP	H	BB	SO	ShO	ERA
TOTALS		29	43	**109**	.283	11	152	152	42	1353	**1654**	**671**	403	4	5.52
Ray Benge	R	26	8	18	.308	1	40	28	12	202	219	88	68	1	4.54
Bob McGraw	R	33	7	8	.467	1	39	3	0	132	150	56	28	0	4.64
Claude Willoughby	R	29	6	5	.545	1	35	13	5	131	180	83	26	1	5.29
Alex Ferguson	R	31	5	10	.333	2	34	19	5	132	162	48	50	1	5.66
Jimmy Ring	R	33	4	17	.190	1	35	25	4	173	214	103	72	0	6.40
Augie Walsh	R	23	4	9	.308	2	38	11	2	122	160	40	38	0	6.20
Les Sweetland	L	26	3	15	.167	2	37	18	5	135	163	97	23	0	6.60
John Milligan	L	24	2	5	.286	0	13	7	3	68	69	32	22	0	4.37
Hub Pruett	L	27	2	4	.333	0	13	9	4	71	78	49	35	0	4.56
Ed Baecht	R	21	1	1	.500	0	9	1	0	24	37	9	10	0	6.00
Earl Caldwell	R	23	1	4	.200	0	5	5	1	35	46	17	6	1	5.66
June Green	R	29	0	0	.000	0	1	0	0	2	5	0	0	0	9.00
Ed Lennon	R	30	0	0	.000	0	5	0	0	12	19	10	6	0	9.00
Russ Miller	R	28	0	12	.000	1	33	12	1	108	137	34	19	0	5.42
1 Clarence Mitchell	L	37	0	0	.000	0	3	0	0	6	13	2	0	0	9.00
Marty Walker	L	25	0	1	.000	0	1	1	0	0	2	3	0	0	∞

WORLD SERIES – NEW YORK (AL) 4 ST. LOUIS (NL) 0

LINE SCORES

TEAM	1	2	3	4	5	6	7	8	9	10	11	12	R	H	E
Game 1 October 4 at New York															
STL (NL)	0	0	0	0	0	0	1	0	0				1	3	1
NY (AL)	1	0	0	2	0	0	0	1	X				4	7	0
Sherdel, Johnson (8) — **Hoyt**															
Game 2 October 5 at New York															
STL	0	3	0	0	0	0	0	0	0				3	4	1
NY	3	1	4	0	0	0	1	0	X				9	8	2
Alexander, Mitchell (3) — **Pipgras**															
Game 3 October 7 at St. Louis															
NY	0	1	0	2	0	3	1	0	0				7	7	2
STL	2	0	0	0	1	0	0	0	0				3	9	3
Zachary — **Haines**, Johnson (7), Rhem (8)															
Game 4 October 9 at St. Louis															
NY	0	0	0	1	0	0	4	2	0				7	15	2
STL	0	0	1	1	0	0	0	0	1				3	11	0
Hoyt — **Sherdel**, Alexander (7)															

COMPOSITE BATTING

NAME	POS	G	AB	R	H	2B	3B	HR	RBI	BA
New York (AL) Totals		4	134	27	37	7	0	9	25	.276
Koenig	SS	4	**19**	1	3	0	0	0	0	.158
Ruth	OF	4	16	**9**	**10**	**3**	0	3	4	**.625**
Meusel	OF	4	15	5	3	1	0	1	3	.200
Bengough	C	4	13	1	3	0	0	0	1	.231
Lazzeri	2B	4	12	2	3	1	0	0	0	.250
Gehrig	1B	4	11	5	6	1	0	**4**	**9**	.545
Paschal	OF	3	10	0	2	0	0	0	1	.200
Durst	OF	4	8	3	3	0	0	1	2	.375
Robertson	3B	3	8	1	1	0	0	0	2	.125
Hoyt	P	2	7	0	1	0	0	0	0	.143
Dugan	3B	3	6	0	1	0	0	0	1	.167
Zachary	P	1	4	0	0	0	0	0	0	.000
Durocher	2B	4	2	0	0	0	0	0	0	.000
Pipgras	P	1	2	0	0	0	0	0	0	.000
Collins	C	1	1	0	1	1	0	0	0	1.000
Combs	PH	1	0	0	0	0	0	0	1	.000
St. Louis (NL) Totals		4	131	10	27	5	1	1	9	.207
High	3B	4	17	1	5	2	0	0	1	.294
Hafey	OF	4	15	0	3	0	0	0	0	.200
Bottomley	1B	4	14	1	3	0	1	1	3	.214
Maranville	SS	4	13	2	4	1	0	0	0	.308
Frisch	2B	4	13	1	3	0	0	0	1	.231
Douthit	OF	3	11	1	1	0	0	0	1	.091
Wilson	C	3	11	1	1	1	0	0	1	.091
Harper	OF	3	9	1	1	0	0	0	0	.111
Orsatti	OF	4	7	1	2	1	0	0	0	.286
Holm	OF	3	6	0	1	0	0	0	1	.167
Sherdel	P	2	5	0	0	0	0	0	0	.000
Smith	C	1	4	0	3	0	0	0	0	.750
Haines	P	1	2	0	0	0	0	0	0	.000
Mitchell	P	1	2	0	0	0	0	0	0	.000
Alexander	P	2	1	0	0	0	0	0	1	.000
Blades	PH	1	1	0	0	0	0	0	0	.000
Johnson	P	2	0	0	0	0	0	0	0	.000
Martin	PR	1	0	1	0	0	0	0	0	.000
Rhem	P	1	0	0	0	0	0	0	0	.000
Thevenow	SS	1	0	0	0	0	0	0	0	.000

COMPOSITE PITCHING

NAME	G	IP	H	BB	SO	W	L	SV	ERA
New York (AL) Totals	4	36	27	11	29	4	0	0	2.00
Hoyt	**2**	**18**	14	**6**	**14**	**2**	0	0	**1.50**
Pipgras	1	9	4	4	8	1	0	0	2.00
Zachary	1	9	9	1	7	1	0	0	3.00
St. Louis (NL) Totals	4	34	37	13	12	0	4	0	6.09
Sherdel	**2**	13.1	**15**	3	3	0	2	0	4.73
Haines	1	6	6	3	3	0	1	0	4.50
Mitchell	1	5.2	2	2	2	0	0	0	1.59
Alexander	**2**	5	10	4	2	0	1	0	19.80
Johnson	**2**	2	4	1	1	0	0	0	4.50
Rhem	1	2	0	0	1	0	0	0	0.00

1929 The Return from Exile

When Connie Mack dismantled his 1914 American League champions, he could not have foreseen the long wait he would have before returning to the throne. It took 15 years of wandering in the bush for the White Elephants and 104 victories in 1929 before Mack and his Athletics could claim clear superiority over the rest of the loop. Mack had slowly pieced together the elements of his current machine by plucking them one by one from the minor league ranks. Lefty Grove and George Earnshaw provided Mack with a pair of 20-win stoppers. Behind the two aces, four additional hurlers won in double figures, led by Rube Walberg's 18 victories. Al Simmons and Jimmie Foxx formed the heart of the lineup, as both hit over .350, swatted over 30 homers, and knocked in over 115 runs, and Bing Miller, Mule Haas, Mickey Cochrane, and Jimmy Dykes complemented the pair by each hitting over .310.

The Yankees were forced to rebuild in places and could not keep pace with the Athletics. Miller Huggins experimented on the left side of the infield, giving Leo Durocher a lot of time at shortstop, while coming up with a gem in rookie catcher Bill Dickey. Good years from Babe Ruth, Lou Gehrig, and Tony Lazzeri could carry the club no closer than a distant second, as Waite Hoyt and Herb Pennock fell off in their pitching and Bob Meusel no longer could provide the slugging threat of former years. To cap a poor season with tragedy, manager Miller Huggins took ill and died in September.

While the Athletics were reclaiming a crown they had held years ago, the Chicago Cubs were also picking up a scepter for the first time in 11 years. Joe McCarthy's squad had finished third in 1928, and additional punch was infused into the lineup by trading for Rogers Hornsby from Boston. Playing with his fourth club in as many years, the Rajah sparkled for the Bruins by hitting .380, belting 39 round-trippers, and propelling 149 runs across the plate. Hornsby was helped by the all-star outfield of Kiki Cuyler, Hack Wilson, and Riggs Stephenson, all of whom hit over .340 and together accounted for 371 RBI's. Even with star catcher Gabby Hartnett sidelined for the season with a sore arm, the Cubs managed an easy victory as Charlie Root, Guy Bush, and Pat Malone led a pitching staff which trailed only the Giants' in team E.R.A.

Connie Mack surprised everyone by naming 35-year-old Howard Ehmke, who appeared in only 11 games all year, as his opening game pitcher in the World Series. In passing up his ace, Lefty Grove, Mack came out smelling like a rose, as Ehmke used a variety of slow stuff to fan a record 13 Cubs and win the opener 3-1 over Charlie Root. George Earnshaw hurled the next two games, winning the first with relief help from Grove and losing the second. The Cubs appeared to be on the edge of evening the Series with an 8-0 lead in the seventh inning of game four. But lightning then struck, and Mackmen electrified the Philadelphia crowd by scoring an incredible 10 runs, greatly aided by Cub centerfielder Hack Wilson's losing two fly balls in the sun. The fans expected to see the A's quickly finish off a disheartened Cub squad in game five, but such did not prove to be the case as Cub pitcher Pat Malone held a 2-0 edge going into the last of the ninth with one out. But then, quick as another lightning bolt, Max Bishop singled and Haas homered to knot the score. After another out, Simmons belted a double to reignite the pandemonium. Bing Miller then capped the comeback, the season, and the pandemonium by doubling Simmons across the plate to once again make Mack and the White Elephants the toast of Philadelphia.

1929 AMERICAN LEAGUE

NAME	G by POS	B	AGE	G	AB	R	H	2B	3B	HR	RBI	BB	SO	SB	BA	SA
PHILADELPHIA 1st 104-46 .693		**CONNIE MACK**														
TOTALS			29	151	5204	901	1539	288	76	122	845	543	440	63	.296	.451
Jimmie Foxx	1B142, 3B7	R	21	149	517	123	183	23	9	33	117	103	**70**	9	.354	.625
Max Bishop	2B129	L	29	129	475	102	110	19	6	3	36	**128**	44	1	.232	.316
Joe Boley	SS88, 3B1	R	32	91	303	36	76	17	6	2	47	24	16	1	.251	.366
Sammy Hale	3B99, 2B1	R	32	101	379	51	105	14	3	1	40	12	18	6	.277	.338
Bing Miller	OF145	R	34	147	556	84	186	32	16	8	93	40	25	24	.335	.493
Mule Haas	OF139	L	25	139	578	115	181	41	9	16	82	34	38	0	.313	.498
Al Simmons	OF142	R	27	143	581	114	212	41	9	34	**157**	31	38	4	.365	.642
Mickey Cochrane	C135	L	26	135	514	113	170	37	8	7	95	69	8	7	.331	.475
Jimmy Dykes	SS60, 3B45, 2B12	R	32	119	401	76	131	34	6	13	79	51	25	8	.327	.539
Walt French	OF10	L	29	45	45	7	12	1	0	1	9	2	3	0	.267	.356
Cy Perkins	C38	R	33	38	76	4	16	4	0	0	9	5	4	0	.211	.263
Homer Summa	OF24	L	30	37	81	12	22	4	0	0	10	2	1	1	.272	.321
Ossie Orwoll	P12, OF9	L	28	30	51	6	13	2	1	0	6	2	11	0	.255	.333
2 George Burns	1B19	R	36	29	49	5	13	5	0	1	11	2	3	1	.265	.429
Jim Cronin	2B10, SS9, 3B4	B	23	25	56	7	13	2	1	0	4	5	7	0	.232	.304
Bevo LeBourveau	OF3	L	34	12	16	1	5	0	1	0	2	5	1	0	.313	.438
Eddie Collins		L	42	9	7	0	0	0	0	0	0	2	0	0	.000	.000
Bud Morse	2B8	L	24	8	27	1	2	0	0	0	0	0	2	0	.074	.074
Joe Hassler	SS2	R	24	4	4	1	0	0	0	0	0	0	2	0	.000	.000
Eric McNair	SS4	R	20	4	8	2	4	1	0	0	3	0	0	1	.500	.625
Cloy Mattox	C3	L	26	3	6	0	1	0	0	0	0	1	1	0	.167	.167
Doc Cramer	OF1	L	23	2	6	0	0	0	0	0	0	0	2	0	.000	.000
Rudy Miller	3B2	R	28	2	4	1	1	0	0	0	1	3	0	0	.250	.250
NEW YORK 2nd 88-66 .571 18		**MILLER HUGGINS (DD) 50 82-61 .573 ART FLETCHER 6-5 .545**														
TOTALS			27	154	5379	899	1587	262	74	**142**	828	554	**518**	51	.295	.450
Lou Gehrig	1B154	L	26	154	553	127	166	33	9	35	126	122	68	4	.300	.582
Tony Lazzeri	2B147	R	25	147	545	101	193	37	11	18	106	69	45	9	.354	.561
Leo Durocher	SS93, 2B12	B	23	106	341	53	84	4	5	0	32	34	33	3	.246	.287
1 Gene Robertson	3B77	L	29	90	309	45	92	15	6	0	35	28	6	3	.298	.385
Babe Ruth	OF133	L	34	135	499	121	172	26	6	**46**	154	72	60	5	.345	**.697**
Earl Combs	OF141	L	30	142	586	119	202	33	15	3	65	69	32	11	.345	.468
Bob Meusel	OF96	R	32	100	391	46	102	15	3	10	57	17	42	1	.261	.391
Bill Dickey	C127	L	22	130	447	60	145	30	6	10	65	14	16	4	.324	.485
Mark Koenig	SS61, 3B37, 2B1	B	26	116	373	44	109	27	5	3	41	23	17	1	.292	.416
Cedric Durst	OF72, 1B1	L	32	92	202	32	52	3	3	4	31	15	25	3	.257	.361
Lyn Lary	3B55, SS14, 2B2	R	23	80	236	48	73	9	2	5	26	24	15	4	.309	.428
Sammy Byrd	OF54	R	22	62	170	32	53	12	0	5	28	28	18	1	.312	.471
Ben Paschal	OF20	R	33	42	72	13	15	3	0	2	11	6	3	1	.208	.333
Benny Bengough (AJ)	C23	R	30	23	62	5	12	2	1	0	7	0	2	0	.194	.258
Johnny Grabowski	C22	R	29	22	59	4	12	1	0	0	2	3	6	1	.203	.220
Art Jorgens	C15	R	24	18	34	6	11	3	0	0	4	6	7	0	.324	.412
1 George Burns		R	36	9	9	0	0	0	0	0	0	0	4	0	.000	.000
Julie Wera	3B4	R	27	5	12	1	5	0	0	0	2	1	1	0	.417	.417
Liz Funk		L	24	1	0	0	0	0	0	0	0	0	0	0	.000	.000
CLEVELAND 3rd 81-71 .533 24		**ROGER PECKINPAUGH**														
TOTALS			28	152	5187	717	1525	294	79	62	684	453	363	75	.294	.417
Lew Fonseca	1B147	R	30	148	566	97	209	44	15	6	103	50	23	19	**.369**	.532
Johnny Hodapp	2B72	R	23	90	294	30	96	12	7	4	51	15	14	3	.327	.456
Jackie Tavener	SS89	L	31	92	250	25	53	9	4	2	26	26	28	1	.212	.304
Joe Sewell	3B152	L	30	152	578	90	182	38	3	7	73	48	4	6	.315	.427
Bibb Falk	OF121	L	30	126	430	66	133	30	7	13	94	42	14	4	.309	.502
Earl Averill	OF152	L	27	152	603	110	199	43	13	18	97	64	53	13	.330	.534
Charlie Jamieson	OF93	L	36	102	364	56	106	22	1	0	26	50	12	2	.291	.357
Luke Sewell	C123	R	28	124	406	41	96	16	3	1	39	29	26	6	.236	.298
Eddie Morgan	OF81	R	25	93	318	60	101	19	10	3	38	37	24	4	.318	.469
Ray Gardner	SS82	R	27	82	256	28	67	3	2	1	24	29	16	10	.262	.301
Dick Porter	OF30, 2B22	L	27	71	192	26	63	16	5	1	24	17	14	3	.328	.479
Carl Lind	2B64, 3B1	R	25	66	225	19	54	8	1	0	12	13	17	0	.240	.284
Glenn Myatt	C41	L	31	59	129	14	30	4	1	1	17	7	5	0	.233	.302
Joe Hauser	1B8	L	30	37	48	8	12	1	1	3	9	4	8	0	.250	.500
Grover Hartley	C13	R	40	24	33	2	9	0	1	0	8	2	1	0	.273	.333
Johnny Burnett	SS10, 2B4	L	24	19	33	2	5	1	0	0	2	1	2	0	.152	.182
Dan Jessee		L	28	1	0	0	0	0	0	0	0	0	0	0	.000	.000

NAME	T	AGE	W	L	PCT	SV	G	GS	CG	IP	H	BB	SO	ShO	ERA
		31	**104**	46	**.693**	**24**	151	151	72	1357	1371	487	**573**	8	**3.44**
George Earnshaw	R	29	**24**	8	.750	1	44	33	13	255	233	**125**	149	2	3.28
Lefty Grove	L	29	20	6	**.769**	4	42	**37**	21	275	278	81	**170**	2	**2.82**
Rube Walberg	L	29	18	11	.621	4	40	33	20	268	256	99	94	3	3.59
Eddie Rommel	R	31	12	2	.857	4	32	6	4	114	135	34	25	0	2.84
Jack Quinn	R	45	11	9	.550	2	35	18	7	161	182	39	41	0	3.97
Bill Shores	R	25	11	6	.647	7	39	13	5	153	150	59	49	1	3.59
Howard Ehmke	R	35	7	2	.778	0	11	8	2	55	48	15	20	0	3.27
Carroll Yerkes	L	26	1	0	1.000	1	19	2	0	37	47	13	11	0	4.62
Bill Breckinridge	R	23	0	0	.000	0	3	1	0	10	10	16	2	0	8.10
Ossie Orwoll	L	28	0	2	.000	1	12	0	0	30	32	6	12	0	4.80
		30	88	66	.571	18	154	154	64	1373	1475	485	484	12	4.18
George Pipgras	R	29	18	12	.600	0	39	33	13	225	229	95	125	3	4.24
Ed Wells	L	29	13	9	.591	0	31	23	10	193	179	81	78	3	4.34
Tom Zachary	L	33	12	0	1.000	2	26	11	7	120	131	30	35	2	2.47
Fred Heimach	L	28	11	6	.647	4	35	10	3	135	141	29	26	3	4.00
Waite Hoyt	R	29	10	9	.526	1	30	25	12	202	219	69	57	0	4.23
Herb Pennock	L	35	9	11	.450	2	27	23	8	158	205	28	49	1	4.90
Wilcy Moore	R	32	6	4	.600	8	41	0	0	62	64	19	21	0	4.06
Roy Sherid	R	21	6	6	.500	1	33	15	9	160	165	55	51	0	3.49
Hank Johnson (XJ)	R	23	3	3	.500	0	12	8	2	43	37	39	24	0	5.02
Bots Nekola	L	21	0	0	.000	0	9	1	0	19	21	15	2	0	4.26
Gordon Rhodes	R	21	0	4	.000	0	10	4	0	43	57	16	13	0	4.81
1 Myles Thomas	R	31	0	2	.000	0	5	1	0	15	27	9	3	0	10.80
		29	81	71	.533	10	152	152	80	1352	1570	488	389	8	4.05
Wes Ferrell	R	21	21	10	.677	5	43	25	18	243	256	109	100	1	3.59
Willis Hudlin	R	23	17	15	.531	1	40	33	22	280	299	73	60	2	3.34
Jake Miller	L	31	14	12	.538	0	29	29	14	206	227	60	58	2	3.58
Johnny Miljus	R	34	8	8	.500	2	34	15	4	128	174	64	42	0	5.20
Joe Shaute (SA)	R	29	8	8	.500	0	26	24	8	162	211	52	43	0	4.28
Ken Hollaway (HJ)	R	31	6	5	.545	0	25	11	6	119	118	37	32	2	3.02
Jimmy Zinn	R	34	4	6	.400	2	18	11	6	105	150	33	29	1	5.06
Milt Shoffner	L	23	2	3	.400	0	11	3	1	45	46	22	15	0	5.00
Mel Harder	R	19	1	0	1.000	0	11	0	0	18	24	5	4	0	5.50
Clint Brown	R	25	0	2	.000	0	3	1	1	16	18	6	1	0	3.38
George Grant	R	26	0	2	.000	0	12	0	0	24	41	23	5	0	10.50
Jim Moore	R	25	0	0	.000	0	2	0	0	6	6	4	0	0	9.00

ST. LOUIS 4th 79-73 .520 26 — DAN HOWLEY

NAME	G by POS	B	AGE	G	AB	R	H	2B	3B	HR	RBI	BB	SO	SB	BA	SA
TOTALS			30	154	5174	733	1426	276	63	46	672	**589**	431	72	.276	.380
Lu Blue	1B151	B	32	151	573	111	168	40	10	6	61	126	32	12	.293	.429
Oscar Mellilo	2B141	R	29	141	494	57	146	17	10	5	67	29	30	11	.296	.401
Red Kress	SS146	R	22	147	557	82	170	38	4	9	107	52	54	5	.305	.436
Frank O'Rourke	3B151, 2B3, SS2	R	34	154	585	81	147	23	9	2	62	41	28	14	.251	.332
Beuty McGowan	OF117	L	27	125	441	62	112	26	6	2	51	61	34	5	.254	.354
Fred Schulte	OF116	R	28	121	446	63	137	24	5	3	71	59	44	8	.307	.404
Heinie Manush	OF141	L	27	142	574	85	204	**45**	10	6	81	43	24	9	.355	.500
Wally Schang	C85	B	39	94	249	43	59	10	5	5	36	74	22	1	.237	.378
Earl McNeely	OF62	R	31	69	230	27	56	8	1	1	18	7	13	2	.243	.300
Rick Ferrell	C45	R	23	64	144	21	33	6	1	0	20	32	10	1	.229	.285
Red Badgrow	OF37	L	26	54	148	27	42	12	0	1	18	11	15	1	.284	.385
Clyde Manion	C34	R	32	35	111	16	27	2	0	0	11	15	3	1	.243	.261
Otis Brannan	2B19	L	30	23	51	4	15	1	0	1	8	4	4	0	.294	.373
Tom Jenkins	OF3	L	31	21	22	1	4	0	1	0	0	4	8	0	.182	.273
Len Dondero	3B10, 2B5	R	25	19	31	2	6	0	0	1	8	0	4	0	.194	.290
Ed Roetz	SS8, 1B5, 2B2, 3B1	R	23	16	45	7	11	4	1	0	5	4	6	0	.244	.378
Jimmy Austin	3B1	B	49	1	1	0	0	0	0	0	0	0	1	0	.000	.000

NAME	T	AGE	W	L	PCT	SV	G	GS	CG	IP	H	BB	SO	ShO	ERA
TOTALS		28	79	73	.520	10	154	154	83	1371	1474	462	415	**15**	4.08
Sam Gray	R	31	18	15	.545	1	43	**37**	23	**305**	**336**	96	109	4	3.72
General Crowder	R	30	17	15	.531	4	40	34	19	267	272	93	79	4	3.91
George Blaeholder	R	25	14	15	.483	2	42	24	13	222	237	61	72	4	4.18
Rip Collins	R	33	11	6	.647	1	26	20	10	155	162	73	47	1	4.00
Lefty Stewart	L	28	9	6	.600	0	23	18	8	150	137	49	47	1	3.24
Jack Ogden	R	31	4	8	.333	0	34	14	7	131	154	44	32	0	4.94
Chad Kimsey	R	22	3	6	.333	1	24	3	1	84	88	19	13	0	5.07
Dick Coffman	R	22	1	1	.500	1	27	3	1	53	61	14	11	1	5.94
Fred Stiely	L	28	1	0	1.000	0	1	1	1	9	11	3	2	0	0.00
Ed Strelecki	R	24	1	1	.500	0	7	0	0	11	12	6	2	0	4.91
Herb Cobb	R	24	0	0	.000	0	1	0	0	1	3	1	0	0	36.00
Oscar Estrada	L	25	0	0	.000	0	1	0	0	1	1	1	0	0	0.00
2 Paul Hopkins	R	24	0	0	.000	0	2	0	0	2	0	2	1	0	0.00

WASHINGTON 5th 71-81 .467 34 — WALTER JOHNSON

NAME	G by POS	B	AGE	G	AB	R	H	2B	3B	HR	RBI	BB	SO	SB	BA	SA
TOTALS			29	153	5237	730	1445	244	66	48	656	556	400	86	.276	.375
Joe Judge	1B142	L	35	143	543	83	171	35	8	6	71	73	33	12	.315	.442
Buddy Myer	2B88, 3B53	L	25	141	563	80	169	29	10	3	82	63	33	18	.300	.403
Joe Cronin	SS143, 2B1	R	22	145	492	72	139	29	8	8	60	85	37	5	.283	.423
Jackie Hayes	3B63, 2B56, SS2	R	22	123	424	52	117	20	3	2	57	24	29	4	.276	.351
Sam Rice	OF147	L	39	150	616	119	199	39	10	1	62	55	9	16	.323	.424
Sammy West	OF139	L	34	142	510	60	136	16	8	3	75	45	41	9	.267	.347
Goose Goslin	OF142	L	28	145	552	82	159	28	7	18	91	66	33	10	.288	.462
Bennie Tate	C74	L	27	81	265	26	78	12	3	0	30	16	8	2	.294	.362
Red Barnes	OF30	L	25	72	130	16	26	5	2	1	15	13	12	1	.200	.292
Muddy Ruel	C63	R	33	69	188	16	46	4	2	0	20	31	7	0	.245	.287
Ossie Bluege (KJ)	3B34, 2B14, SS10	R	28	64	220	35	65	6	0	5	31	19	15	6	.295	.391
Roy Spencer	C41	R	29	50	116	18	18	4	0	1	9	8	15	0	.155	.216
Charlie Gooch	1B7, 3B7, SS1	R	27	39	57	6	16	2	1	0	5	7	8	0	.281	.351
Harley Boss	1B18	L	20	28	66	9	18	2	1	0	6	2	6	0	.273	.333
Stuffy Stewart	2B3	R	35	22	6	10	0	0	0	0	0	1	0	0	.000	.000
2 Ira Flagstead	OF11	R	35	18	39	5	7	1	0	0	9	4	5	1	.179	.205
Spence Harris	OF4	L	28	6	14	1	3	1	0	0	1	0	3	1	.214	.286
Patsy Gharrity		R	37	3	2	0	0	0	0	0	0	1	2	0	.000	.000
Nick Altrock	OF1	B	52	1	1	0	1	0	0	0	0	0	0	0	1.000	1.000
Doc Land	OF1	L	26	1	3	0	0	0	0	0	0	1	0	0	.000	.000

NAME	T	AGE	W	L	PCT	SV	G	GS	CG	IP	H	BB	SO	ShO	ERA
TOTALS		27	71	81	.467	17	153	153	62	1354	1429	496	494	3	4.34
Firpo Marberry	R	30	19	12	.613	**11**	**49**	26	16	250	233	69	121	0	3.06
Garland Braxton	L	29	12	10	.545	4	37	20	9	182	219	51	59	0	4.85
Sad Sam Jones	R	36	9	9	.500	0	24	24	8	154	156	49	36	1	3.91
Lloyd Brown	L	24	8	7	.533	0	40	15	7	168	186	69	48	1	4.18
2 Myles Thomas	R	31	7	8	.467	2	22	14	7	125	139	48	33	0	3.53
Bobby Burke	L	22	6	8	.429	0	37	17	4	141	154	55	51	0	4.79
Bump Hadley	R	24	6	16	.273	0	37	27	7	195	196	85	98	1	5.63
Ad Liska (SA)	R	22	3	9	.250	0	24	10	4	94	87	42	33	0	4.79
Walter Beall	R	29	1	0	1.000	0	3	0	0	7	8	7	3	0	3.86
Archie Campbell	R	25	0	1	.000	0	4	0	0	4	10	5	1	0	15.75
1 Paul Hopkins	R	24	0	1	.000	0	7	0	0	16	15	9	5	0	2.25
Paul McCullough	R	30	0	0	.000	0	3	0	0	7	7	2	3	0	9.00
Don Savidge	R	20	0	0	.000	0	3	0	0	6	12	2	2	0	9.00
Ed Wineapple	L	22	0	0	.000	0	1	0	0	4	7	3	1	0	4.50

DETROIT 6th 70-84 .455 36 — BUCKY HARRIS

NAME	G by POS	B	AGE	G	AB	R	H	2B	3B	HR	RBI	BB	SO	SB	BA	SA
TOTALS			28	155	**5592**	**926**	**1671**	**339**	97	110	**851**	521	496	95	**.299**	**.453**
Dale Alexander	1B155	R	26	155	626	110	**215**	43	15	25	137	56	63	5	.343	.580
Charlie Gehringer	2B154	L	26	155	634	**131**	**215**	**45**	**19**	13	106	64	19	**27**	.339	.532
Heinie Schuble	SS86, 3B2	R	22	92	258	35	60	11	7	2	28	19	23	3	.233	.353
Marty McManus	3B150, SS9	R	29	154	599	99	168	32	8	18	90	60	52	16	.280	.451
Harry Heilmann	OF113, 1B1	R	34	125	453	86	156	41	7	15	120	50	39	5	.344	.565
Harry Rice	OF127, 3B3	L	28	130	536	97	163	33	7	6	69	61	23	6	.304	.425
Roy Johnson	OF146	L	26	148	**640**	128	201	**45**	14	10	69	67	60	20	.314	.475
Eddie Phillips	C63	R	28	68	221	24	52	13	1	2	21	20	16	0	.235	.330
Bob Fothergill	OF59	R	31	115	277	42	98	24	9	6	62	11	11	3	.354	.570
Pinky Hargrave	C48	B	33	76	185	26	61	12	0	3	26	20	24	2	.330	.443
Yats Wuestling	SS52, 2B1, 3B1	R	25	54	150	13	30	4	1	0	16	9	24	1	.200	.240
John Stone	OF36	L	23	51	150	23	39	11	2	2	15	11	13	1	.260	.400
Merv Shea	C50	R	28	50	162	23	47	6	0	3	24	19	18	2	.290	.383
George Uhle	P32	R	30	40	108	18	37	1	1	0	13	6	6	0	.343	.370
Bill Akers	SS24	R	24	24	83	15	22	4	1	1	9	10	9	2	.265	.373
Ray Hayworth	C14	R	25	14	43	5	11	0	0	0	4	3	8	0	.256	.256
1 Frank Sigafoos	3B6, SS5	R	25	14	23	3	4	1	0	0	2	5	4	0	.174	.217
Nolen Richardson	SS13	R	26	13	21	2	4	0	0	0	2	2	1	1	.190	.190
Bucky Harris	2B4, SS1	R	32	7	11	3	1	0	0	0	0	2	2	1	.091	.091
Larry Woodall		R	34	1	1	0	0	0	0	0	0	0	0	0	.000	.000

NAME	T	AGE	W	L	PCT	SV	G	GS	CG	IP	H	BB	SO	ShO	ERA
TOTALS		28	70	84	.455	9	155	155	82	**1390**	**1641**	**646**	467	5	4.96
George Uhle	R	30	15	11	.577	0	32	30	23	249	283	58	100	1	4.08
Vic Sorrell	R	28	14	15	.483	1	36	31	13	226	270	106	81	1	5.18
Earl Whitehill	L	29	14	15	.483	1	38	28	18	245	267	96	103	1	4.63
Ownie Carroll	R	26	9	17	.346	1	34	26	12	202	249	86	54	0	4.63
Emil Yde	L	29	7	3	.700	0	29	6	4	87	100	63	23	1	5.27
George Smith	R	27	3	2	.600	0	14	2	1	36	42	36	13	0	5.75
Lil Stoner	R	30	3	3	.500	4	24	3	1	53	57	31	12	0	5.26
Art Herring	R	22	2	1	.667	0	4	4	2	32	38	19	15	0	4.78
Kyle Graham	R	29	1	3	.250	1	13	6	2	52	70	33	7	0	5.53
Chief Hogsett	L	25	1	2	.333	0	4	4	2	29	34	9	9	1	2.79
Augie Prudhomme	R	26	1	6	.143	1	34	6	2	94	119	53	26	0	6.22
Frank Barnes	L	29	0	1	.000	0	4	1	0	5	10	3	0	0	7.20
Haskell Billings (XJ)	R	21	0	1	.000	0	8	0	0	19	27	9	1	0	5.21
Phil Page	L	23	0	2	.000	0	10	4	1	25	29	19	6	0	8.28
Elam Vangilder	R	33	0	1	.000	0	6	0	0	11	16	7	3	0	6.54
Whit Wyatt	R	21	0	1	.000	0	4	4	1	25	30	18	14	0	6.84

CHICAGO 7th 59-93 .388 46 — LENA BLACKBURNE

NAME	G by POS	B	AGE	G	AB	R	H	2B	3B	HR	RBI	BB	SO	SB	BA	SA
TOTALS			26	152	5248	627	1406	240	74	37	558	425	436	**112**	.268	.363
Art Shires	1B88, 2B2	L	21	100	353	41	110	20	7	3	41	32	20	4	.312	.433
John Kerr	2B122	R	30	127	419	50	108	20	4	1	39	31	24	9	.258	.332
Bill Cissell	SS152	R	25	152	618	83	173	27	12	5	62	28	53	26	.280	.387
Willie Kamm	3B145	R	29	147	523	72	140	33	6	3	63	75	23	12	.268	.371
Carl Reynolds	OF130	R	26	131	517	81	164	24	12	11	67	20	37	19	.317	.474
Dutch Hoffman	OF89	R	25	107	337	27	87	16	5	3	37	24	28	6	.258	.362
Alex Metzler	OF141	L	26	146	568	80	156	23	13	2	49	80	45	11	.275	.371
Moe Berg	C106	R	27	107	352	32	101	7	0	0	47	17	16	5	.287	.307
Bud Clancy	1B74	L	28	92	290	36	82	14	6	3	45	16	19	3	.283	.403
Johnny Watwood	OF77	L	22	85	278	33	84	12	6	2	28	22	21	6	.302	.410
Bill Hunnefield	2B26, 3B4, SS2	B	30	47	127	13	23	5	0	0	9	7	3	7	.181	.220
2 Doug Taitt	OF30	L	26	47	124	11	21	7	0	0	12	8	13	0	.169	.226
Buck Crouse	C40	L	32	45	107	11	29	7	0	2	12	5	7	2	.271	.393
Martin Autry	C30	R	26	43	96	7	20	6	0	1	12	1	8	0	.208	.302
Buck Redfern	2B11, 3B5, SS4	R	27	21	46	0	6	0	0	0	3	3	3	1	.130	.130
Johnny Mostil (BN)	OF11	R	33	12	35	4	8	3	0	0	3	6	2	1	.229	.314
2 Frank Sigafoos	2B6	R	25	7	3	1	1	0	0	0	1	2	1	0	.333	.333
1 Bill Barrett		R	29	3	1	0	0	0	0	0	0	2	0	0	.000	.000
Karl Swanson		L	25	2	1	0	0	0	0	0	0	0	0	0	.000	.000

NAME	T	AGE	W	L	PCT	SV	G	GS	CG	IP	H	BB	SO	ShO	ERA
TOTALS		28	59	93	.388	7	152	152	78	1358	1481	505	328	5	4.41
Tommy Thomas	R	29	14	18	.438	1	36	31	**24**	260	270	60	62	2	3.19
Ted Lyons	R	28	14	20	.412	2	37	31	21	259	276	76	57	1	4.10
Red Faber	R	40	13	13	.500	0	31	31	15	234	241	61	68	1	3.88
Hal McKain	R	22	6	9	.400	1	34	10	4	158	158	85	33	1	3.65
Ed Walsh	R	24	6	11	.353	0	24	20	7	129	156	64	31	0	5.65
Grady Adkins	R	32	2	11	.154	0	31	15	5	138	168	67	24	0	5.35
Bob Weiland	L	23	2	4	.333	1	15	9	1	62	62	43	25	0	5.81
Dan Dugan	L	22	1	4	.200	1	19	2	0	65	77	19	15	0	6.65
2 Dutch Henry	L	27	1	0	1.000	0	2	1	1	15	20	7	2	0	6.00
Lena Blackburne	R	42	0	0	.000	0	1	0	0	.1	1	0	0	0	0.00
Ted Blankenship (HO)	R	28	0	2	.000	0	8	1	0	18	28	9	7	0	9.00
Jerry Byrne	R	22	0	1	.000	0	3	1	0	7	11	6	1	0	7.71
Sarge Connally	R	30	0	0	.000	1	11	0	0	11	13	8	3	0	4.91

BOSTON 8th 58-96 .377 48 — BILL CARRIGAN

NAME	G by POS	B	AGE	G	AB	R	H	2B	3B	HR	RBI	BB	SO	SB	BA	SA
TOTALS			28	155	5160	605	1377	285	69	28	561	413	494	86	.267	.365
Phil Todt	1B153	L	27	153	534	49	140	38	10	4	63	31	28	6	.262	.393
Bill Regan	2B91, 3B10, 1B1	R	30	104	371	38	107	27	7	1	54	22	38	7	.288	.407
Hal Rhyne	SS114, 3B1, OF1	R	30	120	346	41	87	24	5	0	38	25	14	4	.251	.350
Bobby Reeves	3B132, 2B2, 1B1	R	25	140	460	66	114	19	2	2	28	60	57	7	.248	.311
2 Bill Barrett	OF109, 3B1	R	29	111	370	57	100	23	4	3	35	51	38	11	.270	.378
Jack Rothrock	OF128	B	24	143	473	70	142	19	7	6	59	43	47	23	.300	.408
Russ Scarritt	OF145	L	26	151	540	69	159	26	17	1	72	34	38	13	.294	.411
Charlie Berry	C72	R	26	77	207	19	50	11	4	1	21	15	29	2	.242	.348
Elliot Bigelow	OF58	L	30	100	211	23	60	16	0	1	26	23	18	1	.284	.374
Bill Narleski	SS51, 2B28, 3B10	R	30	96	260	30	72	16	1	0	25	21	22	4	.277	.346
Johnnie Heving	C55	R	33	76	188	26	60	4	3	0	23	8	7	1	.319	.372
Ken Williams	OF36, 1B2	L	30	74	139	21	48	14	2	3	22	15	7	1	.345	.540
Bob Barrett	3B34, 1B4, 2B2, OF1	R	39	68	126	15	34	10	0	0	19	10	6	3	.270	.349
Wally Gerber	SS30, 2B22	R	37	61	91	6	15	3	1	0	5	8	12	1	.165	.220
Red Ruffing	P35, OF2	R	25	60	114	9	35	9	0	2	17	2	13	0	.307	.439
Alex Gaston	C49	R	36	55	116	14	26	5	2	2	10	6	8	1	.224	.353
Grant Gillis	2B25	R	28	28	73	5	18	4	0	0	11	6	8	0	.247	.301
1 Doug Taitt	OF21	L	26	26	65	6	18	4	0	0	6	8	5	0	.277	.338
Jerry Standaert	1B10	R	27	19	18	1	3	2	0	0	4	3	2	0	.167	.278
Casper Asbjornson	C15	R	20	17	29	1	3	0	0	0	0	1	6	0	.103	.103
1 Ira Flagstead	OF13	R	35	16	36	9	11	2	0	0	3	5	1	1	.306	.361
Joe Cicero	OF7	R	18	10	32	6	10	2	2	0	4	0	2	0	.313	.500
Ed Connolly	C5	R	20	5	8	0	0	0	0	0	0	0	2	0	.000	.000
Jack Ryan	OF2	R	24	2	3	0	0	0	0	0	0	0	0	0	.000	.000
Denny Williams (DD) 29																

NAME	T	AGE	W	L	PCT	SV	G	GS	CG	IP	H	BB	SO	ShO	ERA
TOTALS		26	58	**96**	.377	5	155	155	**84**	1366	1537	496	416	9	4.43
Ed Morris	R	29	14	14	.500	1	33	26	17	208	227	95	73	2	4.45
Milt Gaston	R	33	12	19	.387	2	39	29	20	244	265	81	83	1	3.73
Danny MacFayden	R	24	10	18	.357	0	32	26	14	221	225	81	61	4	3.62
Red Ruffing	R	25	9	**22**	.290	1	35	30	18	244	280	118	109	1	4.87
Jack Russell	R	23	6	18	.250	0	35	32	13	227	263	40	37	0	3.92
Bill Bayne	L	30	5	5	.500	0	27	6	2	84	111	29	26	0	6.75
Ed Carroll	R	21	1	0	1.000	0	24	3	0	67	77	20	13	0	5.56
Ed Durham	R	21	1	0	1.000	0	14	1	0	22	34	14	6	0	9.41
Herb Bradley	R	26	0	0	.000	0	3	0	0	4	7	2	0	0	6.75
Ray Dobens	L	22	0	0	.000	0	11	2	0	28	32	9	4	0	3.86
Hod Lisenbee	R	30	0	0	.000	0	5	0	0	9	10	4	2	0	5.00
Pat Simmons	R	20	0	0	.000	1	2	0	0	7	6	3	2	0	0.00

CHICAGO 1st 98-54 .645 — JOE McCARTHY

NAME	G by POS	B	AGE	G	AB	R	H	2B	3B	HR	RBI	BB	SO	SB	BA	SA
TOTALS			30	156	5471	982	1655	310	46	139	933	589	567	103	.303	.452
Charlie Grimm (BW)	1B120	L	30	120	463	66	138	28	3	10	91	42	25	3	.298	.436
Rogers Hornsby	2B156	R	33	156	602	156	229	47	8	39	149	87	65	2	.380	.679
Woody English	SS144	R	22	144	608	131	168	29	3	1	52	68	50	13	.276	.339
Norm McMillan	3B120	R	33	124	495	77	134	35	5	5	55	36	43	13	.271	.392
Kiki Cuyler	OF129	R	29	139	509	111	183	29	7	15	102	66	56	43	.360	.532
Hack Wilson	OF150	R	29	150	574	135	198	30	5	39	159	78	83	3	.345	.618
Riggs Stephenson	OF130	R	31	136	495	91	179	36	6	17	110	67	21	10	.362	.562
2 Zack Taylor	C64	R	30	64	215	29	59	16	3	1	31	19	18	0	.274	.391
Cliff Heathcote	OF52	L	31	82	224	45	70	17	0	2	31	25	17	9	.313	.415
Mike Gonzalez	C60	R	38	60	167	15	40	3	0	0	18	18	14	1	.240	.257
Clyde Beck	3B33, SS14	R	27	54	190	28	40	7	0	0	9	19	24	3	.211	.247
Johnny Moore	OF15	L	27	37	63	13	18	1	0	2	8	4	6	0	.286	.397
Chuck Tolson	1B31	R	27	32	109	13	28	5	0	1	19	9	16	0	.257	.330
Johnny Schulte	C30	L	32	31	69	6	18	3	0	0	9	7	11	0	.261	.304
Earl Grace	C27	L	22	27	80	7	20	1	0	2	17	9	7	0	.250	.338
Footsie Blair	3B8, 1B7, 2B2	L	25	26	72	10	23	5	0	1	8	3	4	1	.319	.431
Gabby Hartnett (SA)	C1	R	28	25	22	2	6	2	1	1	9	5	5	1	.273	.591
Tom Angley	C5	L	24	5	16	1	4	1	0	0	6	2	2	0	.250	.313
Danny Taylor	OF1	R	28	2	3	0	0	0	0	0	0	1	1	0	.000	.000

NAME	T	AGE	W	L	PCT	SV	G	GS	CG	IP	H	BB	SO	ShO	ERA
TOTALS		30	98	54	.645	21	156	156	79	1399	1542	564	548	14	4.16
Pat Malone	R	26	22	10	.688	2	40	30	19	267	283	102	166	5	3.57
Charlie Root	R	30	19	6	.760	5	43	31	19	272	286	83	124	4	3.47
Guy Bush	R	27	18	7	.720	8	50	29	18	271	277	107	82	2	3.65
Sheriff Blake	R	29	14	13	.519	1	35	30	13	218	244	130	70	1	4.29
Hal Carlson	R	35	11	5	.688	2	31	14	6	112	131	31	35	2	5.14
Art Nehf	L	36	8	5	.615	1	32	15	4	121	148	39	27	0	5.58
Mike Cvengros	L	27	5	4	.556	2	32	2	0	64	82	29	23	0	4.64
Trader Horne	R	30	1	1	.500	0	11	1	0	23	24	21	6	0	5.09
Hank Grampp	R	25	0	1	.000	0	1	1	0	2	4	3	0	0	27.00
Claude Jonnard	R	32	0	1	.000	0	12	2	0	28	41	11	11	0	7.39
Bob Osborne	R	26	0	0	.000	0	3	1	0	9	8	2	1	0	3.00
Ken Penner	R	33	0	1	.000	0	5	0	0	13	14	6	3	0	2.77

PITTSBURGH 2nd 88-65 .575 10.5 — DONIE BUSH 67-51 .568 JEWEL ENS 21-14 .600

NAME	G by POS	B	AGE	G	AB	R	H	2B	3B	HR	RBI	BB	SO	SB	BA	SA
TOTALS			27	154	5490	904	1663	285	116	60	828	503	335	94	.303	.430
Earl Sheely	1B139	R	36	139	485	63	142	22	4	6	88	75	24	6	.293	.392
George Grantham	2B76, OF19, 1B12	L	29	110	349	85	107	23	10	12	90	93	38	10	.307	.533
Dick Bartell	SS97, 2B74	R	21	143	610	101	184	40	13	2	57	40	29	11	.302	.420
Pie Traynor	3B130	R	29	130	540	94	192	27	12	4	108	30	7	13	.356	.472
Paul Waner	OF143, 1B7	L	26	151	596	131	200	43	15	15	100	89	24	15	.336	.534
Lloyd Waner	OF151	L	23	151	662	134	234	28	20	5	74	37	20	6	.353	.479
Adam Comorosky	OF121	R	24	127	473	86	152	26	11	6	97	40	22	19	.321	.461
Charlie Hargreaves	C101	R	32	102	328	33	88	12	5	1	44	16	12	1	.268	.345
Rollie Hemsley	C80	R	22	88	235	31	68	13	7	0	37	11	22	1	.289	.404
Sparky Adams	SS30, 2B20, 3B15, OF2	R	34	74	196	37	51	8	1	0	11	15	5	3	.260	.311
Fred Brickell	OF27	L	22	60	118	13	37	4	2	0	17	7	12	3	.314	.381
Erv Brame	P37	L	27	59	116	9	36	8	1	4	25	2	7	0	.310	.500
Stu Clarke	SS41, 3B15, 2B1	R	23	57	178	20	47	5	7	2	21	19	21	3	.264	.404
Burleigh Grimes	P33	R	35	33	91	11	26	3	3	0	12	4	10	0	.286	.385
3 Ira Flagstead	OF9	R	35	26	50	8	14	2	1	0	6	4	2	1	.280	.360
Cobe Jones	SS15	B	23	25	63	6	16	5	1	0	4	1	5	1	.254	.365
Bob Linton	C8	L	27	17	18	0	2	0	0	0	1	1	2	0	.111	.111
Jim Mosolf	OF3	L	23	8	13	3	6	1	1	0	2	1	1	0	.462	.692
Harry Riconda	SS4	R	32	8	15	3	7	2	0	0	2	0	0	0	.467	.600
Jim Stroner	3B2	R	36	6	8	0	3	1	0	0	0	1	0	0	.375	.500
Mel Ingram		R	24	3	0	1	0	0	0	0	0	0	0	0	.000	.000
John O'Connell	C2	R	25	2	7	1	1	1	0	0	0	1	1	0	.143	.286
Ben Sankey	SS2	R	21	2	7	1	1	0	0	0	0	0	1	0	.143	.143
Bill Windle	1B2	L	24	2	1	0	0	0	0	0	0	0	1	0	.000	.000

NAME	T	AGE	W	L	PCT	SV	G	GS	CG	IP	H	BB	SO	ShO	ERA
TOTALS		31	88	65	.575	13	154	154	79	1379	1530	439	409	5	4.36
Kay Kremer	R	36	18	10	.643	0	34	27	14	222	226	60	66	0	4.26
Burleigh Grimes	R	35	17	7	.708	2	33	29	18	233	245	70	62	2	3.13
Erv Brame	R	27	16	11	.593	0	37	28	19	230	250	71	68	1	4.54
Jesse Petty	L	34	11	10	.524	0	36	25	12	184	197	42	58	1	3.72
Steve Swetonic	R	25	8	10	.444	5	41	12	3	144	172	50	35	0	4.81
Larry French	L	21	7	5	.583	1	30	13	6	123	130	62	49	0	4.90
Heinie Meine	R	33	7	6	.538	1	22	13	7	108	120	34	19	1	4.50
Fred Fussell	L	33	2	2	.500	1	21	3	0	40	68	8	18	0	8.55
1 Carmen Hill	R	33	2	3	.400	3	27	3	0	79	94	35	28	0	3.99
Leon Chagnon	R	26	0	0	.000	0	1	1	0	7	11	1	4	0	9.00
Joe Dawson	R	31	0	1	.000	0	4	0	0	9	13	3	2	0	8.00
Ralph Erickson	L	25	0	0	.000	0	1	0	0	1	2	2	0	0	27.00
Lee Meadows	R	34	0	0	.000	0	1	0	0	1	2	1	0	0	9.00

NEW YORK 3rd 84-67 .556 13.5 — JOHN McGRAW

NAME	G by POS	B	AGE	G	AB	R	H	2B	3B	HR	RBI	BB	SO	SB	BA	SA
TOTALS			27	152	5388	897	1594	251	47	136	829	482	405	85	.296	.436
Bill Terry	1B149, OF1	L	30	150	607	103	226	39	5	14	117	48	35	10	.372	.522
Andy Cohen	2B94, SS1, 3B1	R	24	101	347	40	102	12	2	5	47	11	15	3	.294	.383
Travis Jackson	SS149	R	25	149	551	92	162	21	12	21	90	64	56	10	.294	.490
Fred Lindstrom	3B128	R	23	130	549	99	175	23	6	15	91	30	28	10	.319	.464
Mel Ott	OF149, 2B1	L	20	150	545	138	179	37	2	42	151	113	38	6	.328	.635
Edd Roush	OF107	L	36	115	450	76	146	19	7	8	52	45	16	6	.324	.451
Freddy Leach	OF95	L	31	113	411	74	119	22	6	8	47	17	14	10	.290	.431
Shanty Hogan	C93	R	23	102	317	19	95	13	0	5	45	25	22	1	.300	.388
Bob O'Farrell	C84	R	32	91	248	35	76	14	3	4	42	28	30	3	.306	.435
Chick Fullis	OF78	R	25	86	274	67	79	11	1	7	29	30	26	7	.288	.412
Pat Crawford	1B7, 3B1	L	27	65	57	13	17	3	0	3	24	11	5	1	.298	.509
2 Doc Farrell	3B28, 2B25, SS4	R	27	63	178	18	38	6	0	0	16	9	17	2	.213	.247
Andy Reese (IL)	2B44, OF8, 3B4	R	25	58	209	36	55	11	3	0	21	15	19	8	.263	.344
Tony Kaufmann	OF16	R	28	39	32	18	1	0	0	0	1	6	4	3	.031	.031
1 Jim Welsh	OF35	L	26	38	129	25	32	7	0	2	8	9	3	3	.248	.349
Doc Marshall	2B5	R	23	5	15	6	6	2	0	0	2	1	0	0	.400	.533
Ray Schalk	C5	R	36	5	2	0	0	0	0	0	0	0	1	0	.000	.000
1 Jack Cummings	C1	R	25	3	3	0	1	0	0	0	0	0	0	0	.333	.333
Buck Jordan	1B1	L	22	2	2	1	1	1	0	0	0	0	0	0	.500	1.000
Pat Veltman	C1	R	23	2	1	1	0	0	0	0	0	2	0	0	.000	.000
Sam Leslie	OF1	L	23	1	1	0	0	0	0	0	1	0	0	0	.000	.000

NAME	T	AGE	W	L	PCT	SV	G	GS	CG	IP	H	BB	SO	ShO	ERA
TOTALS		30	84	67	.556	13	152	152	68	1372	1536	387	431	9	3.97
Carl Hubbell	R	26	18	11	.621	1	39	35	19	268	273	67	106	1	3.69
Freddie Fitzsimmons	R	27	15	11	.577	1	37	31	14	222	242	66	55	4	4.09
Bill Walker	L	25	14	7	.667	0	29	23	13	178	188	57	65	1	3.08
Larry Benton	R	31	11	17	.393	3	39	30	14	237	276	61	63	3	4.14
Carl Mays	R	37	7	2	.778	4	37	8	1	123	140	31	32	0	4.32
Jack Scott	R	37	7	6	.538	1	30	6	2	92	89	27	40	0	3.52
1 Dutch Henry	L	27	5	6	.455	1	27	9	4	101	129	31	27	0	3.83
Joe Genewich	R	32	3	7	.300	1	21	9	1	85	133	30	19	0	6.78
Ralph Judd	R	27	3	0	1.000	0	18	0	0	51	49	11	21	0	2.65
Roy Parmelee	R	22	1	0	1.000	0	2	1	0	7	13	3	1	0	9.00
Ray Lucas	R	20	0	0	.000	1	3	0	0	8	3	3	1	0	0.00
Jim Tennant	R	21	0	0	.000	0	1	0	0	1	1	0	1	0	0.00

ST. LOUIS 4th 78-74 .513 20 — BILLY SOUTHWORTH 43-45 .489 GABBY STREET 2-0 1.000 BILL McKECHNIE 33-29 .532

NAME	G by POS	B	AGE	G	AB	R	H	2B	3B	HR	RBI	BB	SO	SB	BA	SA
TOTALS			27	154	5364	831	1569	310	84	100	779	490	455	72	.293	.438
Jim Bottomley	1B145	L	29	146	560	108	176	31	12	29	137	70	54	3	.314	.568
Frankie Frisch	2B121, 3B13, SS1	B	30	138	527	93	176	40	12	5	74	53	12	24	.334	.484
Charlie Gelbert	SS146	R	23	146	512	60	134	29	8	3	65	51	46	8	.262	.367
Andy High	3B123, 2B22	L	31	146	603	95	178	32	4	10	63	38	18	7	.295	.411
Ernie Orsatti	OF77, 1B10	L	26	113	346	64	115	21	7	3	39	33	43	7	.332	.460
Taylor Douthit	OF150	R	28	150	613	128	206	42	7	9	62	79	49	8	.336	.471
Chick Hafey	OF130	R	26	134	517	101	175	47	9	29	125	45	42	7	.338	.632
Jimmie Wilson	C119	R	28	120	394	59	128	27	8	4	71	43	19	4	.325	.464
Wally Roettger	OF69	R	26	79	269	27	68	11	3	3	42	13	27	0	.253	.349
Wattie Holm	OF44, 3B1	R	27	64	176	21	41	5	6	0	14	12	8	1	.233	.330
Earl Smith	C50	L	32	57	145	9	50	8	0	1	22	18	6	0	.345	.421
Carey Selph (FJ)	2B16	R	27	25	51	8	12	1	1	0	7	6	4	1	.235	.294
Eddie Delker	SS9, 2B7, 3B3	R	22	22	40	5	6	0	1	0	3	2	12	0	.150	.200
Billy Southworth	OF5	L	36	19	32	1	6	2	0	0	3	2	4	0	.188	.250
Bubber Jonnard	C18	R	29	18	31	1	3	0	0	0	2	0	6	0	.097	.097
Johnny Butler	3B9, SS8	R	36	17	55	5	9	1	1	0	5	4	5	0	.164	.218
Fred Haney	3B6	R	31	10	26	4	3	1	1	0	2	1	2	0	.115	.231

NAME	T	AGE	W	L	PCT	SV	G	GS	CG	IP	H	BB	SO	ShO	ERA
TOTALS		32	78	74	.513	8	154	154	83	1360	1604	474	453	6	4.66
Syl Johnson	R	28	13	7	.650	3	42	19	12	182	186	56	80	3	3.61
Jesse Haines	R	35	13	10	.565	0	28	25	12	180	230	73	59	0	5.70
Bill Sherdel	L	32	10	15	.400	0	33	22	11	196	278	58	69	1	5.92
Pete Alexander (ST)	R	42	9	8	.529	0	22	19	8	132	149	23	33	0	3.89
Hal Haid	R	31	9	9	.500	4	38	12	8	155	171	66	41	0	4.06
Clarence Mitchell	L	38	8	11	.421	0	25	22	16	173	221	60	39	0	4.27
Fred Frankhouse	R	25	7	2	.778	1	30	12	6	133	149	43	37	0	4.13
Wild Bill Hallahan	L	26	4	4	.500	0	20	12	5	94	94	60	52	0	4.40
Al Grabowski	L	27	3	2	.600	0	6	6	4	50	44	8	22	2	2.52
Bill Doak	R	38	1	2	.333	0	3	2	0	9	17	5	3	0	12.00
Jim Lindsey	R	31	1	1	.500	0	2	2	1	16	20	2	8	0	5.63
Hi Bell (IL)	R	31	0	2	.000	0	7	0	0	13	19	4	4	0	6.92
Hal Goldsmith	R	30	0	0	.000	0	2	0	0	4	3	1	0	0	6.75
2 Carmen Hill	R	33	0	0	.000	0	3	1	0	9	10	8	1	0	8.00
Mul Holland	R	26	0	1	.000	0	8	0	0	14	13	7	5	0	9.64

PHILADELPHIA 5th 71-82 .464 27.5 — BURT SHOTTON

NAME	G by POS	B	AGE	G	AB	R	H	2B	3B	HR	RBI	BB	SO	SB	BA	SA
TOTALS			26	154	5484	897	1693	305	51	153	841	573	470	59	.309	.467
Don Hurst	1B154	L	23	154	589	100	179	29	4	31	125	80	36	10	.304	.525
Fresco Thompson	2B148	R	27	148	623	115	202	41	3	4	53	75	34	16	.324	.419
Tommy Thevenow (BJ)	SS90	R	25	90	317	30	72	11	0	0	35	25	25	3	.227	.262
Pinky Whitney	3B154	R	24	154	612	89	200	43	14	8	115	61	35	7	.327	.482
Chuck Klein	OF149	L	24	149	616	126	219	45	6	43	145	54	61	5	.356	.657
Denny Sothern	OF71	R	25	76	294	52	90	21	3	5	27	16	24	13	.306	.449
Lefty O'Doul	OF154	L	32	154	638	152	254	35	6	32	122	76	19	2	.398	.622
Walt Lerian	C103	R	26	105	273	28	61	13	2	7	25	53	37	0	.223	.363
Barney Friberg	SS73, OF40, 2B8, 1B2	R	29	128	455	74	137	21	10	7	55	49	54	1	.301	.437
Spud Davis	C89	R	24	98	263	31	90	18	0	7	48	19	17	1	.342	.490
Cy Williams	OF11	L	41	66	65	11	19	2	0	5	21	22	9	0	.292	.554
Homer Peel	OF39, 1B1	R	26	53	156	16	42	12	1	0	19	12	7	1	.269	.359
Les Sweetland	P43	R	27	53	89	14	26	2	0	0	12	3	18	0	.292	.315
Elmer Miller	P8, OF4	L	25	31	38	3	9	1	0	1	4	1	5	0	.237	.342
June Green	P5	L	30	21	19	1	4	1	0	0	0	2	4	0	.211	.263
George Susce	C11	R	20	17	17	5	5	3	0	1	1	1	2	0	.294	.647
Tripp Sigman	OF10	L	30	10	29	8	15	1	0	2	9	3	1	0	.517	.759
Joe O'Rourke		L	24	3	3	0	0	0	0	0	0	0	1	0	.000	.000
Terry Lyons	1B1	R	20	1	0	0	0	0	0	0	0	0	0	0	.000	.000
Dutch Ulrich (DD) 28																

NAME	T	AGE	W	L	PCT	SV	G	GS	CG	IP	H	BB	SO	ShO	ERA
TOTALS		28	71	82	.464	24	154	154	45	1348	1743	616	369	5	6.13
Claude Willoughby	R	30	15	14	.517	4	49	34	14	243	288	108	50	1	5.00
Les Sweetland	L	27	13	11	.542	2	43	25	10	204	255	87	47	2	5.12
Ray Benge	R	27	11	15	.423	4	38	27	9	199	255	77	78	2	6.29
Phil Collins	R	27	9	7	.563	5	43	11	3	153	172	83	61	0	5.77
2 Lou Koupal	R	30	5	5	.500	2	15	12	3	87	106	29	18	0	4.76
Bob McGraw	R	34	5	5	.500	4	41	4	0	86	113	43	22	0	5.76
Harry Smythe	L	24	4	6	.400	1	19	7	2	69	94	15	12	0	5.22
Hal Elliott	R	30	3	7	.300	2	40	8	2	114	146	59	32	0	6.08
1 Luther Roy	R	26	3	6	.333	0	21	12	1	89	137	37	16	0	8.39
Sam Dailey	R	24	2	2	.500	0	20	5	0	51	74	23	18	0	7.59
1 Alex Ferguson	R	32	1	2	.333	0	5	4	1	13	19	10	3	0	11.77
June Green	R	27	0	0	.000	0	5	0	0	14	33	9	3	0	19.29
Jim Holloway	R	20	0	0	.000	0	3	0	0	5	10	5	4	0	12.60
Elmer Miller	L	25	0	1	.000	0	8	2	0	11	12	21	5	0	11.45
John Milligan	L	25	0	1	.000	0	8	3	0	10	29	10	2	0	16.20

BROOKLYN 6th 70-83 .458 28.5 WILBERT ROBINSON

NAME	G by POS	B	AGE	G	AB	R	H	2B	3B	HR	RBI	BB	SO	SB	BA	SA
TOTALS			31	153	5273	755	1535	282	69	99	705	504	454	80	.291	.427
Del Bissonette (IL)	1B113	L	29	116	431	68	121	28	10	12	75	46	58	2	.281	.476
Eddie Moore	2B74, SS36, OF2, 3B1	R	30	111	402	48	119	18	6	0	48	44	16	3	.296	.371
Dave Bancroft	SS102	B	38	104	358	35	99	11	3	1	44	29	11	7	.277	.332
Wally Gilbert	3B142	R	28	143	569	88	173	31	4	3	58	42	29	7	.304	.388
Babe Herman	OF141, 1B2	L	26	146	569	105	217	42	13	21	113	55	45	21	.381	.612
Johnny Frederick	OF143	L	28	148	628	127	206	52	6	24	75	39	34	6	.328	.545
Rube Bressler	OF122	R	34	136	456	72	145	22	8	9	77	67	27	4	.318	.461
Val Picinich	C85	R	32	93	273	28	71	16	6	4	31	34	24	3	.260	.407
Harvey Hendrick	OF42, 1B39, 3B7, SS4	L	31	110	384	69	136	25	6	14	82	31	20	14	.354	.560
Billy Rhiel	2B47, 3B7, SS2	R	28	76	205	27	57	9	4	4	25	19	25	0	.278	.420
Hank DeBerry	C68	R	34	68	210	13	55	11	1	1	25	17	15	1	.262	.338
Jake Flowers (IL)	2B39	R	27	46	130	16	26	6	0	1	16	22	6	9	.200	.269
Butch Henline	C21	R	34	27	62	5	15	2	0	1	7	9	9	0	.242	.323
Glen Wright (AJ)	SS3	R	28	24	25	4	5	0	0	1	6	3	6	0	.200	.320
Max Carey	OF4	B	39	19	23	2	7	0	0	0	1	3	2	0	.304	.304
Jack Warner	SS17	R	25	17	62	3	17	2	0	0	4	7	6	3	.274	.306
Nick Cullop (BG)	OF11, 1B1	R	30	13	41	7	8	2	2	1	5	8	7	0	.195	.415

Max West 24 R 2-8, 1 Johnny Gooch 31 B 0-1

NAME	T	AGE	W	L	PCT	SV	G	GS	CG	IP	H	BB	SO	ShO	ERA
		30	70	83	.458	16	153	153	59	1358	1553	549	549	8	4.92
Watty Clark	L	27	16	19	.457	1	41	36	19	279	295	71	140	3	3.74
Dazzy Vance	R	38	14	13	.519	0	31	26	17	231	244	47	126	1	3.90
Johnny Morrison	R	33	13	7	.650	8	39	10	4	137	150	61	57	0	4.47
Ray Moss	R	27	11	6	.647	0	39	20	7	182	214	81	59	2	5.04
Clise Dudley	R	25	6	14	.300	0	35	21	8	157	202	64	33	1	5.68
Doug McWeeney	R	32	4	10	.286	1	36	24	4	146	167	93	59	0	6.10
Cy Moore	R	24	3	3	.500	2	32	4	0	68	87	31	17	0	5.56
Win Ballou	R	31	2	3	.400	0	25	1	0	58	69	38	20	0	6.67
Jumbo Jim Elliott	L	28	1	2	.333	0	6	3	0	19	21	16	7	0	6.63
Clarence Blethen	R	35	0	0	.000	0	2	0	0	2	4	3	0	0	9.00
Joe Bradshaw	R	31	0	0	.000	0	2	0	0	4	3	4	1	0	4.50
2 Alex Ferguson	R	32	0	1	.000	0	3	3	0	2	7	1	1	0	22.50
2 Kent Greenfield	R	27	0	0	.000	0	6	0	0	9	13	3	1	0	8.00
1 Lou Koupal	R	30	0	1	.000	4	18	3	0	40	49	25	17	0	5.40
Bobo Newsom	R	21	0	3	.000	0	3	2	0	9	15	5	6	0	11.00
Jimmy Pattison	L	20	0	1	.000	0	6	0	0	12	9	4	5	0	4.50
2 Luther Roy	R	26	0	0	.000	0	2	0	0	4	4	2	0	0	4.50

CINCINNATI 7th 66-88 .429 33 JACK HENDRICKS

NAME	G by POS	B	AGE	G	AB	R	H	2B	3B	HR	RBI	BB	SO	SB	BA	SA
TOTALS			29	155	5269	686	1478	258	79	34	618	412	347	134	.281	.379
George Kelly	1B147	R	33	147	577	73	169	45	9	5	103	33	61	7	.293	.428
Hughie Critz (KJ)	2B106, SS1	R	28	107	425	55	105	17	9	1	50	27	21	9	.247	.336
Hod Ford	SS108, 2B42	R	31	148	529	68	146	14	6	3	50	41	25	8	.276	.342
Chuck Dressen	3B98, 2B8	R	30	110	401	49	98	22	3	1	36	41	21	8	.244	.322
Curt Walker	OF138	L	32	141	492	76	154	28	15	7	83	85	17	17	.313	.474
Ethan Allen	OF137	R	25	143	538	69	157	27	11	6	64	20	21	21	.292	.416
Evar Swanson	OF142	R	26	148	574	100	172	35	12	4	43	41	47	33	.300	.423
2 Johnny Gooch	C86	B	31	92	287	22	86	13	5	0	34	24	10	4	.300	.380
Clyde Sukeforth	C76	L	27	84	237	31	84	16	2	1	33	17	6	8	.354	.451
Pid Purdy	OF42	L	25	82	181	22	49	7	5	1	16	19	8	2	.271	.381
Pinky Pittinger	SS50, 3B8, 2B4	R	30	77	210	31	62	11	0	0	27	5	4	8	.295	.348
Red Lucas	P32	L	27	76	140	15	41	6	0	0	13	13	15	1	.293	.336
Joe Stripp	3B55, 2B2	R	26	64	187	24	40	3	2	3	20	24	15	2	.214	.299
Billy Zitzmann	OF22, 1B5	R	31	47	84	18	19	3	0	0	6	9	10	4	.226	.262
Pete Donahue	P32	R	28	32	60	1	20	0	0	0	13	1	5	1	.333	.333
Leo Dixon	C14	R	32	14	30	0	5	2	0	0	2	3	7	0	.167	.233
Wally Shaner	1B8, OF2	R	29	13	28	5	9	0	0	1	4	4	5	1	.321	.429

Estel Crabtree 25 L 0-1, Hugh McMullen 27 B 0-1, Ivy Wingo 38 L 0-1

NAME	T	AGE	W	L	PCT	SV	G	GS	CG	IP	H	BB	SO	ShO	ERA
		32	66	88	.429	8	155	155	75	1369	1558	413	347	5	4.41
Red Lucas	R	27	19	12	.613	0	32	32	28	270	267	58	72	2	3.60
Pete Donahue	R	28	10	13	.435	0	32	24	7	178	243	51	30	0	5.41
Jakie May	L	33	10	14	.417	3	41	24	10	199	219	75	92	0	4.61
Eppa Rixey	L	38	10	13	.435	1	35	24	11	201	235	60	37	0	4.16
Ray Kolp	R	34	8	10	.444	0	30	16	4	145	151	39	27	1	4.03
Dolf Luque	R	38	5	16	.238	0	32	22	8	176	213	56	43	1	4.50
Ken Ash	R	27	1	5	.167	2	29	7	2	82	91	30	26	0	4.83
Rube Ehrhardt	R	34	1	2	.333	1	24	1	1	49	58	22	9	1	4.78
Benny Frey	R	23	1	2	.333	0	3	3	2	24	29	8	1	0	4.13
Marv Gudat	L	23	1	1	.500	0	7	2	2	27	29	4	0	0	3.33
Si Johnson	R	22	0	0	.000	0	1	0	0	2	2	1	0	0	4.50
Dutch Kemner	R	30	0	0	.000	1	9	0	0	15	19	8	10	0	7.80
Paul Zahniser	R	32	0	0	.000	0	1	0	0	1	2	1	0	0	27.00

BOSTON 8th 56-98 .364 43 JUDGE FUCHS

NAME	G by POS	B	AGE	G	AB	R	H	2B	3B	HR	RBI	BB	SO	SB	BA	SA
TOTALS			30	154	5291	657	1481	252	77	33	598	408	432	65	.280	.375
George Sisler	1B154	L	36	154	629	67	205	40	8	2	79	33	17	6	.326	.424
Freddie Maguire	2B138, SS1	R	30	138	496	54	125	26	8	0	41	19	40	8	.252	.337
Rabbit Maranville	SS145, 2B1	R	37	146	560	87	159	26	10	0	55	47	33	13	.284	.366
Les Bell	3B127, 2B1, SS1	R	27	139	483	58	144	23	5	9	72	50	42	4	.298	.422
Lance Richbourg	OF134	L	31	139	557	76	170	24	13	3	56	42	26	7	.305	.411
Earl Clark	OF74	R	21	84	279	43	88	13	3	1	30	12	30	6	.315	.394
George Harper	OF130	L	37	136	457	65	133	25	5	10	68	69	27	5	.291	.433
Al Spohrer	C109	R	26	114	342	42	93	21	8	2	48	26	35	1	.272	.398
Joe Dugan	3B24, SS5, 2B2, OF2	R	32	60	125	14	38	10	0	0	15	8	8	0	.304	.384
2 Jim Welsh	OF51	L	26	53	186	24	54	8	7	2	16	13	9	1	.290	.441
Bernie James	2B32, OF1	R	23	46	101	12	31	3	2	0	9	9	13	3	.307	.376
Heinie Mueller	OF24	L	29	46	93	10	19	2	1	0	11	12	12	2	.204	.247
Johnny Cooney	OF16, P14	R	28	41	72	10	23	4	1	0	6	3	3	1	.319	.403
Lou Legett	C28	R	28	39	81	7	13	2	0	0	6	3	18	2	.160	.185
1 Zack Taylor	C31	R	30	34	101	8	25	7	0	0	10	7	9	0	.248	.317
Socks Seibold	P33	R	33	33	70	6	20	2	0	0	9	6	6	0	.286	.314
Phil Noyles	OF20	L	29	20	68	9	16	0	2	0	14	6	8	0	.235	.292
Jack Smith	OF9	L	34	19	20	2	5	0	0	0	2	2	2	0	.250	.250
Buzz Boyle	OF17	L	21	17	57	8	15	2	1	1	2	6	11	2	.263	.386
Red Barron	OF6	R	29	10	21	3	4	1	0	0	1	1	4	2	.190	.238
Bill Dunlap	OF9	R	20	10	29	6	12	0	1	1	4	4	4	0	.414	.586
Hank Gowdy	C9	R	39	10	16	1	7	0	0	0	3	0	2	0	.438	.438
2 Gene Robertson	3B6, SS1	L	29	8	28	1	8	0	0	0	6	1	0	1	.286	.286

Pat Collins 32 R 0-5, Bill Cronin 26 R 1-9, Henry Peploski 23 L 2-10, 1 Doc Farrell 27 R 1-8, 2 Jack Cummings 25 R 1-6, Al Weston 23 R 0-3, Johnny Evers 47 L 0-0

NAME	T	AGE	W	L	PCT	SV	G	GS	CG	IP	H	BB	SO	ShO	ERA
		30	56	98	.364	12	154	154	78	1353	1604	530	366	4	5.12
Socks Seibold	R	33	12	17	.414	1	33	27	16	206	228	80	54	1	4.72
Bob Smith	R	31	11	17	.393	3	34	29	19	231	256	71	65	1	4.68
Ed Brandt	L	24	8	13	.381	0	26	21	13	168	196	83	50	0	5.52
Percy Jones	L	29	7	15	.318	0	35	22	11	188	219	84	69	1	4.64
Ben Cantwell	R	27	4	13	.235	2	27	20	8	157	171	52	25	0	4.47
Bruce Cunningham	R	23	4	6	.400	1	17	8	4	92	100	32	22	0	4.50
Art Delaney	R	34	3	5	.375	0	20	8	3	75	103	35	17	1	6.12
Dixie Leverett	R	35	3	7	.300	1	24	12	3	98	135	30	28	0	6.34
Johnny Cooney	L	28	2	3	.400	3	14	2	1	45	57	22	11	0	5.00
Bunny Hearn	L	25	2	0	1.000	0	10	1	0	18	18	9	12	0	4.50
Bill Clarkson	R	30	0	1	.000	0	2	1	0	7	16	4	0	0	10.29
1 Kent Greenfield	R	27	0	0	.000	0	6	2	0	16	33	15	7	0	10.69
Red Peery	L	22	0	1	.000	0	9	1	0	44	53	9	3	0	5.11
Clay Touchstone	R	26	0	0	.000	0	1	0	0	3	6	0	1	0	15.00
Johnny Wertz	R	31	0	0	.000	1	4	0	0	6	13	4	2	0	10.50

WORLD SERIES – PHILADELPHIA (AL) 4 CHICAGO (NL) 1

LINE SCORES

TEAM	1	2	3	4	5	6	7	8	9	10	11	12	R	H	E
Game 1 October 8 at Chicago															
PHI (AL)	0	0	0	0	0	0	1	0	2				3	6	1
CHI (NL)	0	0	0	0	0	0	0	0	1				1	8	2
Ehmke	Root, Bush (8)														
Game 2 October 9 at Chicago															
PHI	0	0	3	3	0	0	1	2	0				9	12	0
CHI	0	0	0	0	3	0	0	0	0				3	11	1
Earnshaw, Grove (5)	Malone, Blake (4), Carlson (6), Nehf (9)														
Game 3 October 11 at Philadelphia															
CHI	0	0	0	0	0	3	0	0	0				3	6	1
PHI	0	0	0	0	1	0	0	0	0				1	9	1
Bush	Earnshaw														
Game 4 October 12 at Philadelphia															
CHI	0	0	0	2	0	5	1	0	0				8	10	2
PHI	0	0	0	0	0	0	10	0	X				10	15	2
Root, Nehf (7) Blake (7), Malone (7), Carlson (8)	Quinn, Walberg (6), Rommel (7), Grove (8)														
Game 5 October 14 at Philadelphia															
CHI	0	0	0	2	0	0	0	0	0				2	8	1
PHI	0	0	0	0	0	0	0	0	3				3	6	0
Malone	Ehmke, Walberg (4)														

COMPOSITE BATTING

NAME	POS	G	AB	R	H	2B	3B	HR	RBI	BA
Philadelphia (AL) Totals		5	171	26	48	5	0	6	26	.281
Haas	OF	5	21	3	5	0	0	2	6	.238
Bishop	2B	5	21	2	4	0	0	0	1	.190
Foxx	1B	5	20	5	7	1	0	2	5	.350
Simmons	OF	5	20	6	6	1	0	2	5	.300
Dykes	3B	5	19	2	8	1	0	0	4	.421
Miller	OF	5	19	1	7	1	0	0	4	.368
Boley	SS	5	17	1	4	0	0	0	1	.235
Cochrane	C	5	15	5	6	1	0	0	0	.400
Ehmke	P	2	5	0	1	0	0	0	0	.200
Earnshaw	P	2	5	1	0	0	0	0	0	.000
Grove	P	2	2	0	0	0	0	0	0	.000
Burns	PH	1	2	0	0	0	0	0	0	.000
Quinn	P	1	2	0	0	0	0	0	0	.000
Walberg	P	2	1	0	0	0	0	0	0	.000
French	PH	1	1	0	0	0	0	0	0	.000
Summa	PH	1	1	0	0	0	0	0	0	.000
Rommel	P	1	0	0	0	0	0	0	0	.000
Chicago (NL) Totals		5	173	17	43	6	2	1	15	.249
Hornsby	2B	5	21	4	5	1	1	0	1	.238
English	SS	5	21	1	4	2	0	0	0	.190
Cuyler	OF	5	20	4	6	1	0	0	4	.300
McMillan	3B	5	20	0	2	0	0	0	0	.100
Stephenson	OF	5	19	3	6	1	0	0	3	.316
Grimm	1B	5	18	2	7	0	0	1	4	.389
Wilson	OF	5	17	2	8	0	1	0	0	.471
Taylor	C	5	17	0	3	0	0	0	3	.176
Root	P	2	5	0	0	0	0	0	0	.000
Malone	P	3	4	0	1	1	0	0	0	.250
Hartnett	PH	3	3	0	0	0	0	0	0	.000
Bush	P	2	3	1	0	0	0	0	0	.000
Blake	P	2	1	0	1	0	0	0	0	1.000
Gonzalez	C	2	1	0	0	0	0	0	0	.000
Blair	PH	1	1	0	0	0	0	0	0	.000
Heathcote	PH	1	1	0	0	0	0	0	0	.000
Tolson	PH	1	1	0	0	0	0	0	0	.000
Carlson	P	2	0	0	0	0	0	0	0	.000
Nehf	P	2	0	0	0	0	0	0	0	.000

COMPOSITE PITCHING

NAME	G	IP	H	BB	SO	W	L	SV	ERA
Philadelphia (AL) Totals	5	45	43	13	50	4	1	2	2.40
Earnshaw	2	13.2	14	6	17	1	1	0	2.63
Ehmke	2	12.2	14	3	13	1	0	0	1.42
Grove	2	6.1	3	1	10	0	0	2	0.00
Walberg	2	6.1	3	0	8	1	0	0	0.00
Quinn	1	5	7	2	2	0	0	0	9.00
Rommel	1	1	2	1	0	1	0	0	9.00
Chicago (NL) Totals	5	43.2	48	13	27	1	4	0	4.33
Root	2	13.1	12	2	8	0	1	0	4.73
Malone	3	13	12	7	11	0	2	0	4.16
Bush	2	11	12	2	4	1	0	0	0.82
Carlson	2	4	7	1	3	0	0	0	6.75
Blake	2	1.1	4	0	1	0	1	0	13.50
Nehf	2	1	1	1	0	0	0	0	18.00

⊜ ⊜ 1930 The Guns of Summer ⊜ ⊜

The barrage began in the spring, reached a deafening crescendo during the heat of summer, and subsided in the cool sanity of autumn. Never before had such an offensive been staged, and never again would the cannon fire of baseball bats strike so often and so effectively. With the depression in full bloom and pocketbooks near empty, baseball juiced up the ball to liven the attendance and the action. For the batters, it was a vision of heaven on earth. And for the pitchers, it was the fright and embarrassment that open season had been declared on them. Even the spitball, once the wet tool of a crafty artisan, was now gone. All that remained were frantic batting averages and over-inflated earned run averages.

Although all clubs enjoyed the glory of the hitter, and all suffered the agony of the pitcher, none matched the extremes of the Philadelphia Phillies. They rapped out hits at a .315 batting clip as five .300 hitters filled the lineup. Outfielders, Lefty O'Doul and powerful Chuck Klein, led the attack with plus .380 averages. Yet, instead of moving towards the top of the heap, the Phils dropped three slots into the National League basement on the dismal arms of a pitching staff which posted a monstrous 6.71 earned run average.

Beyond the Phillies, the proof of the shambles was as great. One team since 1937 has posted a team .300 batting average. In 1930, nine clubs reached that high plateau. The entire National League compiled a .303 average while American League swingers settled for a more reasonable .288 rate. The New York Giants boosted the senior circuit tally with a club .319 mark, tops in the majors, with first sacker Bill Terry hitting .401, the last National Leaguer to scale that sacred peak. Another stellar individual performance was delivered by the Cubs' Hack Wilson. The stumpy outfielder staged the first race on Babe Ruth's home run record by launching 56 circuit blasts and, in the process, driving in an all-time high of 190 runs. Of all clubs in the majors, only Washington managed to get a team E.R.A. below 4.00 from its pitching staff, as the bulk of hurlers merely stuck fingers in crumbling dams trying to hold back floods of runs.

In the National League, the mayhem was greater. Even with Wilson's fantastic season and the return of tomato-face Gabby Hartnett to full-time action, the Cubs failed to repeat as champions, though a foot injury to Rogers Hornsby understandably slowed them down. The pennant, instead, went to the St. Louis Cardinals, led by new manager Gabby Street. All eight St. Louis starters hit over .300, but Frankie Frisch and bespectacled Chick Hafey stood out for their excellence. Wild Bill Hallahan climbed out of a rut of mediocrity to win 15 games on the mound, and the mid-season acquisition of aging spit-baller Burleigh Grimes helped Street immensely. With hitting stars legion, Brooklyn's Dazzy Vance shined as the only hurler in the loop to post an E.R.A. under 3.00.

The Athletics' Lefty Grove filled the same slot as Vance in the American League, but did it in more spectacular fashion by winning 28 games and tallying up a 2.54 E.R.A. to combine with George Earnshaw to give Connie Mack the only pair of 20-win aces in the majors. With Al Simmons, Double-X Jimmie Foxx, and Mickey Cochrane swinging the timber, Mack's eighth pennant came easily. Only Washington, sparked by shortstop Joe Cronin, provided any competition for the A's.

When the World Series rolled around, the loud guns of summer quieted to an almost unrecognizable whimper as the Cardinals managed a robust .200 rate, while the Mackmen compiled a stirring .197 mark. The difference between the clubs proved to be the hurling of Grove and Earnshaw. It was a difference good enough for a six-game Philadelphia triumph and the last world's championship that Connie Mack would ever claim.

1930 AMERICAN LEAGUE

NAME	G by POS	B	AGE	G	AB	R	H	2B	3B	HR	RBI	BB	SO	SB	BA	SA
PHILADELPHIA 1st 102-52 .662		CONNIE MACK														
	TOTALS		28	154	5345	951	1573	319	74	125	895	599	531	50	.294	.452
Jimmie Foxx	1B153	R	22	153	562	127	188	33	13	37	156	93	**66**	7	.335	.637
Max Bishop	2B127	L	30	130	441	117	111	27	6	10	38	128	60	3	.252	.408
Joe Boley	SS120	R	33	121	420	41	116	22	2	4	55	32	26	0	.276	.367
Jimmy Dykes	3B123, OF1	R	33	125	435	69	131	28	4	6	73	74	53	3	.301	.425
Bing Miller	OF154	R	35	154	585	89	177	38	7	9	100	47	22	13	.303	.438
Mule Haas	OF131	L	26	132	532	91	159	33	7	2	68	43	33	2	.299	.398
Al Simmons	OF136	R	28	138	554	**152**	211	41	16	36	165	39	34	9	**.381**	.708
Mickey Cochrane	C130	L	27	130	487	110	174	42	5	10	85	55	18	5	.357	.526
Eric McNair	SS31, 3B29, 2B5, OF1	R	21	78	237	27	63	12	2	0	34	9	19	5	.266	.333
Dib Williams	2B39, SS19, 3B1	R	20	67	191	24	50	10	3	3	22	15	19	2	.262	.393
Wally Schang	C36	B	40	45	92	16	16	4	1	1	9	17	15	0	.174	.272
Doc Cramer	OF21, SS1	L	24	30	82	12	19	1	1	0	6	2	8	0	.232	.268
Homer Summa	OF15	L	31	25	54	10	15	2	1	1	5	4	1	0	.278	.407
Spence Harris	OF13	L	29	22	49	4	9	1	0	0	5	5	2	0	.184	.204
Cy Perkins	C19, 1B1	R	34	20	38	1	6	2	0	0	4	2	3	0	.158	.211
2 Jim Moore	OF13	R	27	15	50	10	19	3	0	2	12	2	4	1	.380	.560
Pinky Higgins	3B5, 2B2, SS1	R	21	14	24	1	6	2	0	0	0	4	5	0	.250	.333
Jim Keesey	1B3	R	27	11	12	2	3	1	0	0	2	1	2	0	.250	.333
Eddie Collins		L	43	3	2	1	1	0	0	0	0	0	0	0	.500	.500
WASHINGTON 2nd 94-60 .610 8		WALTER JOHNSON														
	TOTALS		29	154	5370	892	1620	300	98	57	819	537	438	**101**	.302	.426
Joe Judge	1B117	L	36	126	442	83	144	29	11	10	80	60	29	13	.326	.509
Buddy Myer	2B134, OF2	L	26	138	541	97	164	18	8	2	61	58	31	14	.303	.377
Joe Cronin	SS154	R	23	154	587	127	203	41	9	13	126	72	36	17	.346	.513
Ossie Bluege	3B134	R	29	134	476	64	138	27	7	3	69	51	40	15	.290	.395
Sam Rice	OF145	L	40	147	593	121	207	35	13	1	73	55	14	13	.349	.457
Sammy West	OF118	L	25	120	411	75	135	22	10	6	67	37	34	5	.328	.474
2 Heinie Manush	OF86	L	28	88	356	74	129	33	8	7	65	26	17	4	.362	.559
Roy Spencer	C93	R	30	93	321	32	82	11	4	0	36	18	27	3	.255	.315
2 Dave Harris	OF59	R	30	73	205	40	65	19	8	4	44	28	35	6	.317	.546
Muddy Ruel	C60	R	34	66	198	18	50	3	4	0	26	24	13	1	.253	.308
Jackie Hayes	2B29, 3B9, 1B8	R	23	51	166	25	47	7	2	1	20	7	8	2	.283	.367
George Loepp	OF48	R	28	50	134	23	37	7	1	0	14	20	9	0	.276	.343
1 Goose Goslin	OF47	L	29	47	188	34	51	11	5	7	38	19	19	3	.271	.495
2 Art Shires	1B21	L	22	38	84	11	31	5	0	1	19	5	5	1	.369	.464
Firpo Marberry	P33	R	31	33	73	9	24	4	0	0	14	4	7	0	.329	.384
Joe Kuhel	1B16	L	24	18	63	9	18	3	3	0	17	5	6	1	.286	.429
Jim McLeod	3B10, SS7	R	21	18	34	3	9	1	0	0	1	1	5	1	.265	.294
1 Bennie Tate	C9	L	28	14	20	1	5	0	0	0	2	0	1	0	.250	.250
1 Red Barnes		L	26	12	12	1	2	1	0	0	0	0	3	0	.167	.250
2 Pinky Hargrave	C9	B	34	10	31	3	6	2	2	1	7	3	1	1	.194	.484
2 Bill Barrett	OF1	R	30	6	4	0	0	0	0	0	0	1	2	0	.000	.000
Ray Treadaway	3B4	L	22	6	19	1	4	2	0	0	1	0	3	0	.211	.316
Harley Boss 21 L 0-3, Jake Powell 21 R 0-4, Patsy Gharrity 38 R 0-1																
NEW YORK 3rd 86-68 .558 16		BOB SHAWKEY														
	TOTALS		26	154	**5448**	**1062**	**1683**	298	**110**	**152**	**986**	**644**	**569**	91	**.309**	**.488**
Lou Gehrig	1B153	L	27	154	581	143	220	42	17	41	**174**	101	63	12	.379	.721
Tony Lazzeri	2B77, 3B60, SS8, 1B1, OF1	R	26	143	571	109	173	34	15	9	121	60	62	4	.303	.462
Lyn Lary	SS113	R	24	117	464	93	134	20	8	3	52	45	40	14	.289	.386
Ben Chapman	3B91, 2B45	R	21	138	513	74	162	31	10	10	81	43	58	14	.316	.474
Babe Ruth	OF144, P1	L	35	145	518	150	186	28	9	**49**	153	**136**	61	10	.359	**.732**
2 Harry Rice	OF87, 1B6, 3B1	L	29	100	346	62	103	17	5	7	74	31	21	3	.298	.436
Earle Combs	OF135	L	31	137	532	129	183	30	**22**	7	82	74	26	16	.344	.523
Bill Dickey	C101	L	23	109	366	55	124	25	7	5	65	21	14	7	.339	.486
Sammy Byrd	OF85	R	23	92	218	46	62	12	2	6	31	30	18	5	.284	.440
Dusty Cooke	OF73	L	23	92	216	43	55	12	3	6	29	32	61	4	.255	.421
Jimmy Reese	2B48, 3B5	L	25	77	188	44	65	14	2	3	18	11	8	1	.346	.489
2 Red Ruffing	P34	R	26	52	99	15	37	6	2	4	21	7	7	0	.374	.596
Bubbles Hargrave	C34	R	37	45	108	11	30	7	0	0	12	10	9	0	.278	.343
Benny Bengough	C44	R	31	44	102	10	24	4	2	0	12	3	8	1	.235	.314
2 Yats Wuestling	SS21, 3B3	R	26	25	58	5	11	0	1	0	3	4	14	0	.190	.224
1 Mark Koenig	SS19	B	27	21	74	9	17	5	0	0	0	6	5	0	.230	.297
Art Jorgens	C16	R	25	16	30	7	11	3	0	0	1	2	4	0	.367	.467
Cedric Durst	OF8	L	33	8	19	0	3	1	0	0	5	0	1	0	.158	.211
Bill Werber 22 R 4-14, Bill Karlon 21 R 0-5																

NAME	T	AGE	W	L	PCT	SV	G	GS	CG	IP	H	BB	SO	ShO	ERA
PHILADELPHIA		32	**102**	52	**.662**	**21**	154	154	72	1371	1457	488	**672**	**8**	4.28
Lefty Grove	L	30	**28**	5	**.848**	**9**	**50**	32	22	291	273	60	**209**	2	**2.54**
George Earnshaw	R	30	22	13	.629	2	49	**39**	20	296	299	**139**	193	**3**	4.44
Rube Walberg	L	30	13	12	.520	1	38	30	12	205	207	85	100	2	4.70
Bill Shores	R	26	12	4	.750	0	31	19	7	159	169	70	48	1	4.19
Eddie Rommel	R	32	9	4	.692	3	35	9	5	130	142	27	35	0	4.29
Roy Mahaffey	R	27	9	5	.643	0	33	16	6	153	186	53	38	0	5.00
Jack Quinn	R	46	9	7	.563	6	35	7	0	90	109	22	28	0	4.40
Glenn Liebhardt	R	19	0	1	.000	0	5	0	0	9	14	8	2	0	11.00
Howard Ehmke	R	36	0	1	.000	0	3	1	0	10	22	2	4	0	11.70
Charlie Perkins	L	24	0	0	.000	0	8	1	0	24	25	15	15	0	6.37
Al Mahon	L	19	0	0	.000	0	3	0	0	4	11	7	0	0	24.75
WASHINGTON		28	94	60	.610	14	154	154	**78**	1369	1367	504	524	4	**3.96**
Lloyd Brown	L	25	16	12	.571	0	38	22	10	197	220	65	59	1	4.25
Firpo Marberry	R	31	15	5	.750	1	33	22	9	185	190	53	56	2	4.09
Sad Sam Jones (SA)	R	37	15	7	.682	0	25	25	14	183	195	61	60	0	4.09
2 General Crowder	R	31	15	9	.625	1	27	25	20	202	191	69	65	0	3.61
Bump Hadley	R	25	15	11	.577	2	42	34	15	260	242	105	162	0	3.74
Ad Liska	R	23	9	7	.563	1	32	16	7	151	140	71	40	1	3.28
1 Garland Braxton	L	30	3	2	.600	5	15	0	0	27	22	9	7	0	3.33
Bobby Burke	L	23	3	4	.429	3	24	4	2	74	62	29	35	0	3.65
Myles Thomas	R	32	2	2	.500	0	12	2	0	34	49	15	12	0	8.21
Carl Fischer	L	24	1	1	.500	1	8	4	1	33	37	18	21	0	4.91
Harry Child	R	**25**	0	0	.000	0	5	0	0	10	10	5	5	0	6.30
Carlos Moore	R	23	0	0	.000	0	4	0	0	12	9	4	2	0	2.25
NEW YORK		28	86	68	.558	15	154	154	65	1368	1586	524	572	7	4.88
2 Red Ruffing	R	26	15	5	.750	1	34	25	12	198	220	62	117	2	4.14
George Pipgras	R	30	15	15	.500	4	44	30	15	221	230	70	111	**3**	4.11
Hank Johnson	R	24	14	11	.560	2	44	15	7	175	177	104	115	1	4.68
Ed Wells	L	30	12	3	.800	0	27	21	7	151	185	49	46	0	5.18
Roy Sherid	R	22	12	13	.480	4	37	21	8	184	214	87	59	0	5.23
Herb Pennock	L	36	11	7	.611	0	25	19	11	156	194	20	46	1	4.33
1 Waite Hoyt	R	30	2	2	.500	0	8	7	2	48	64	9	10	0	4.50
Lefty Gomez	L	21	2	5	.286	1	15	6	2	60	66	28	22	0	5.55
Babe Ruth	L	35	1	0	1.000	0	1	1	1	9	11	2	3	0	3.00
1 Tom Zachary	L	34	1	1	.500	0	3	3	0	17	18	9	1	0	6.35
Lou McEvoy	R	28	1	3	.250	3	28	1	0	52	64	29	14	0	6.75
2 Ownie Carroll	R	27	0	1	.000	0	10	1	0	33	49	18	8	0	6.54
Frank Barnes	L	30	0	1	.000	0	2	2	0	12	13	13	2	0	8.25
Sam Gibson	R	30	0	1	.000	0	2	2	0	6	14	6	3	0	15.00
2 Ken Hollaway	R	32	0	0	.000	0	16	0	0	34	52	8	11	0	5.29
Bill Henderson	R	28	0	0	.000	0	3	0	0	8	7	4	2	0	4.50
Gordon Rhodes	R	22	0	0	.000	0	3	0	0	2	3	4	1	0	9.00
Foster Edwards	R	26	0	0	.000	0	2	0	0	2	5	2	1	0	18.00

CLEVELAND 4th 81-73 .526 21 — ROGER PECKINPAUGH

NAME	G by POS	B	AGE	G	AB	R	H	2B	3B	HR	RBI	BB	SO	SB	BA	SA
TOTALS			28	154	5439	890	1654	358	59	72	830	490	461	51	.304	.431
Eddie Morgan	1B129, OF19	R	26	150	584	122	204	47	11	26	136	62	66	8	.349	.601
Johnny Hodapp	2B154	R	24	154	635	111	225	51	8	9	121	32	29	6	.354	.502
Jonah Goldman	SS93, 3B20	R	23	111	306	32	74	18	0	1	44	28	25	3	.242	.310
Joe Sewell	3B97	L	31	109	353	44	102	17	6	0	48	42	3	1	.289	.371
Dick Porter (PB)	OF118	L	28	119	480	100	168	43	8	4	57	55	31	3	.350	.498
Earl Averill	OF134	L	28	139	534	102	181	33	8	19	119	56	48	10	.339	.537
Charlie Jamieson	OF95	L	37	103	366	64	110	22	1	1	52	36	20	5	.301	.374
Luke Sewell (BG)	C76	R	29	76	292	40	75	21	2	1	43	14	9	5	.257	.353
Glenn Myatt	C71	L	32	86	265	30	78	23	2	2	37	18	17	2	.294	.419
Bob Seeds	OF70	R	23	85	277	37	79	11	3	3	32	12	22	1	.285	.379
Bibb Falk	OF42	L	31	82	191	34	62	12	1	4	36	23	8	2	.325	.461
Ed Montague	SS46, 3B13	R	24	58	179	37	47	5	2	1	16	37	38	1	.263	.330
Johnny Burnett	3B27, SS19	L	25	54	170	28	53	13	0	0	20	17	8	2	.312	.388
Wes Ferrell	P43	R	22	53	118	19	35	8	3	0	14	12	15	0	.297	.415
Lew Fonseca (BA)	1B28, 3B6	R	31	40	129	20	36	9	2	0	17	7	7	1	.279	.380
Ray Gardner	SS22	R	28	33	13	7	1	0	0	0	1	0	1	0	.077	.077
Carl Lind	SS22, 2B1	R	26	24	69	8	17	3	0	0	6	3	7	0	.246	.390
Joe Sprinz	C17	R	27	17	45	5	8	1	0	0	2	4	4	0	.178	.200

Joe Vosmik 20 R 6-26, Ralph Winegarner 20 R 10-22, George Detore 23 R 2-12, Grover Hartley 41 R 3-4

NAME	T	AGE	W	L	PCT	SV	G	GS	CG	IP	H	BB	SO	ShO	ERA
		25	81	73	.526	14	154	154	69	1360	1663	528	441	5	4.88
Wes Ferrell	R	22	25	13	.658	3	43	35	25	297	299	106	143	1	3.30
Willis Hudlin	R	24	13	16	.448	1	37	33	13	217	255	76	60	1	4.56
Mel Harder	R	20	11	10	.524	2	36	19	7	175	205	68	44	0	4.22
Clint Brown	R	26	11	13	.458	1	35	31	16	214	271	51	54	3	4.96
Pete Appleton	R	26	8	7	.533	1	39	7	2	119	122	53	45	0	4.01
Jake Miller	L	32	4	4	.500	0	24	9	1	88	147	38	31	0	7.16
Belve Bean	R	25	3	3	.500	2	23	3	2	74	99	32	19	0	5.47
Milt Shoffner	L	24	3	4	.429	0	24	10	1	86	129	50	17	0	7.94
Les Barnhart	R	25	1	0	1.000	0	1	1	0	8	12	4	1	0	6.75
1 Ken Hollaway	R	32	1	1	.500	2	12	2	0	30	49	14	8	0	8.40
Roxie Lawson	R	24	1	2	.333	0	7	4	2	34	46	23	10	0	6.09
Sal Gliatto	R	28	0	0	.000	2	8	0	0	15	21	9	7	0	6.60
Joe Shaute (SA)	L	30	0	0	.000	0	4	0	0	5	8	4	2	0	14.40

DETROIT 5th 75-79 .487 27 — BUCKY HARRIS

NAME	G by POS	B	AGE	G	AB	R	H	2B	3B	HR	RBI	BB	SO	SB	BA	SA
TOTALS			26	154	5297	783	1504	298	90	82	728	461	508	98	.284	.421
Dale Alexander	1B154	R	27	154	602	86	196	33	8	20	135	42	56	6	.326	.507
Charlie Gehringer	2B154	L	27	154	610	144	201	47	15	16	98	69	17	19	.330	.534
2 Mark Koenig	SS70, 3B2, P2, OF1	B	27	76	267	37	64	9	2	1	16	20	15	2	.240	.300
Marty McManus	3B130, SS3, 1B1	R	30	132	484	74	155	40	4	9	89	59	28	23	.320	.475
Roy Johnson	OF118	L	27	125	462	84	127	30	13	2	35	40	46	17	.275	.409
Liz Funk	OF129	L	25	140	527	74	145	26	11	4	65	29	39	12	.275	.389
John Stone	OF108	L	24	126	422	60	132	29	11	3	56	32	49	6	.313	.455
Ray Hayworth	C76	R	26	77	227	24	63	15	4	0	22	20	19	0	.278	.379
Bill Akers (JJ)	SS49, 3B26	R	25	85	233	36	65	8	5	9	40	36	34	5	.278	.472
George Uhle	P33	R	31	59	117	15	36	4	2	2	21	8	13	0	.308	.427
1 Pinky Hargrave	C40	B	34	55	137	18	39	8	0	5	18	20	12	2	.285	.453
1 Bob Fothergill	OF38	R	32	55	143	14	37	9	3	2	14	6	10	1	.259	.406
Bill Rogell	SS33, 3B13, OF1	B	25	54	144	20	24	4	2	0	9	15	23	1	.167	.222
Gene Desautels	C42	R	23	42	126	13	24	4	2	0	9	7	9	2	.190	.254
1 Harry Rice	OF35	L	29	37	128	16	39	6	0	2	24	19	8	0	.305	.398
Paul Easterling	OF25	R	24	29	79	7	16	6	0	1	14	6	18	0	.203	.316
Jimmy Shevlin	1B25	L	20	28	14	4	2	0	0	0	2	2	3	0	.143	.143
Frank Doljack	OF20	R	22	20	74	10	19	5	1	3	17	2	11	0	.257	.473
1 Tony Rensa	C18	R	28	20	37	6	10	2	1	1	3	6	7	1	.270	.459
Tom Hughes	OF16	L	22	17	59	8	22	2	3	0	5	4	8	0	.373	.508

Johnny Watson 22 L 3-12, 1 Yats Wuestling 26 R 0-9, Hughie Wise 24 R 2-6, Hank Greenberg 19 R 0-1

NAME	T	AGE	W	L	PCT	SV	G	GS	CG	IP	H	BB	SO	ShO	ERA
		27	75	79	.487	17	154	154	68	1352	1507	570	574	3	4.70
Earl Whitehill	L	30	17	13	.567	1	34	31	16	221	248	80	109	0	4.24
Vic Sorrell	R	29	16	11	.593	1	35	30	14	233	245	106	97	2	3.86
George Uhle	R	31	12	12	.500	3	33	29	18	239	239	75	117	1	3.65
Chief Hogsett	L	26	9	8	.529	1	33	17	4	146	174	63	54	0	5.42
2 Waite Hoyt	R	30	9	8	.529	4	26	20	8	136	176	47	25	0	4.76
Whit Wyatt (SA)	R	22	4	5	.444	2	21	7	2	86	76	35	68	0	3.56
Tommy Bridges	R	23	3	2	.600	0	8	5	2	38	28	23	17	0	4.03
Art Herring	R	23	3	3	.500	0	23	6	1	78	97	36	16	0	5.31
Charlie Sullivan	R	27	1	5	.167	5	40	3	2	94	112	53	38	0	6.51
Guy Cantrell	R	26	1	5	.167	0	16	2	1	35	38	20	20	0	5.66
Phil Page	L	24	0	1	.000	0	12	0	0	12	23	9	2	0	9.75
2 Mark Koenig	R	27	0	1	.000	0	2	1	0	9	11	8	6	0	11.00
1 Ownie Carroll	R	27	0	5	.000	0	6	3	0	20	30	9	4	0	10.80
Joe Samuels	R	25	0	0	.000	0	2	0	0	6	10	6	1	0	16.50

ST. LOUIS 6th 64-90 .416 38 — BILL KILLEFER

NAME	G by POS	B	AGE	G	AB	R	H	2B	3B	HR	RBI	BB	SO	SB	BA	SA
TOTALS			29	154	5278	751	1415	289	67	75	691	497	550	93	.268	.391
Lu Blue	1B111	B	33	117	425	85	100	27	5	4	42	81	44	12	.235	.351
Oscar Melillo	2B148	R	30	149	574	62	147	30	10	5	59	23	44	15	.256	.369
Red Kress	SS123, 3B31	R	23	154	614	94	192	43	8	16	112	50	56	3	.313	.487
Frank O'Rourke	3B84, SS23, 1B33	R	35	115	400	52	107	15	4	1	41	35	30	11	.268	.333
Ted Gullic	OF82, 1B3	R	23	92	308	39	77	7	5	4	44	27	43	4	.250	.344
Fred Schulte	OF98, 1B5	R	29	113	392	59	109	23	5	5	62	41	44	12	.278	.401
2 Goose Goslin	OF101	L	29	101	396	81	129	25	7	30	100	48	35	14	.326	.652
Rick Ferrell	C101	R	24	101	314	43	84	18	4	1	41	46	10	1	.268	.360
Red Badgro	OF61	L	27	89	234	30	56	18	3	1	27	13	27	3	.239	.355
Earl McNeely	OF38, 1B27	R	32	76	235	33	64	19	1	0	20	22	14	8	.272	.362
Sammy Hale	3B47	R	33	62	190	21	52	8	1	2	25	8	18	1	.274	.358
Chad Kimsey	P42	L	23	60	70	14	24	4	1	2	14	5	16	1	.343	.514
Clyde Manion	C56	R	33	57	148	12	32	1	0	1	11	24	17	0	.216	.243
2 Alex Metzler	OF56	L	27	56	209	30	54	6	3	1	23	21	12	5	.258	.330
1 Heinie Manush	OF48	L	28	49	198	26	65	16	4	2	29	5	7	3	.328	.480
Bernie Hungling	C10	R	34	10	31	4	10	2	0	0	2	5	3	0	.323	.387

Jack Burns 22 L 9-30, Jim Levey 23 B 9-28 Lin Storti 23 B 9-28, Jack Crouch 27 R 2-14, Joe Hassler 25 R 2-8, Tom Jenkins 32 L 2-8

NAME	T	AGE	W	L	PCT	SV	G	GS	CG	IP	H	BB	SO	ShO	ERA
		27	64	90	.416	10	154	154	68	1372	1639	449	470	5	5.07
Lefty Stewart	L	29	20	12	.625	0	35	33	23	271	281	70	79	1	3.45
George Blaeholder	R	26	11	13	.458	4	37	23	10	191	235	46	70	1	4.62
Rip Collins	R	34	9	7	.563	2	35	20	6	172	168	63	75	1	4.35
Dick Coffman	R	23	8	18	.308	1	38	30	12	196	250	69	54	1	5.14
Chad Kimsey	R	23	6	10	.375	1	42	4	1	113	139	45	32	0	6.37
Sam Gray	R	32	4	15	.211	0	27	24	7	168	215	52	51	0	6.26
Rollie Stiles	R	23	3	6	.333	0	20	7	3	102	136	41	25	0	5.91
1 General Crowder	R	31	3	7	.300	1	13	10	5	77	85	27	42	1	4.67
Herm Holshouser	R	23	0	1	.000	1	25	1	0	62	103	28	37	0	7.84
Fred Stiely	L	29	0	1	.000	0	4	2	1	19	27	8	5	0	8.53
Jack Ogden (VR) 32															

CHICAGO 7th 62-92 .403 40 — DONIE BUSH

NAME	G by POS	B	AGE	G	AB	R	H	2B	3B	HR	RBI	BB	SO	SB	BA	SA
TOTALS			27	154	5419	729	1496	256	90	63	675	389	479	74	.276	.391
Johnny Watwood	1B62, OF43	L	23	133	427	75	129	25	4	2	51	52	35	5	.302	.393
Bill Cissell	1B106, 3B24, SS10	R	26	141	561	82	152	28	9	2	48	28	32	16	.271	.364
Greg Mulleavy	SS73	R	24	77	289	27	76	14	5	0	28	20	23	5	.263	.346
Willie Kamm (HO)	3B105	R	30	111	331	49	89	21	6	3	47	51	20	5	.269	.396
Smead Jolley	OF151	L	28	152	616	76	193	38	12	16	114	28	52	3	.313	.492
2 Red Barnes	OF72	L	26	85	266	48	66	12	7	1	31	26	20	4	.248	.357
Carl Reynolds	OF132	R	27	138	563	103	202	25	18	22	104	20	39	16	.359	.584
2 Bennie Tate	C70	L	28	72	230	26	73	11	2	0	27	18	10	2	.317	.383
John Kerr	2B51, SS19	R	31	70	266	37	77	11	6	3	27	21	23	4	.289	.410
Bud Clancy (JJ)	1B60	L	29	68	234	28	57	8	3	3	27	12	18	3	.244	.342
Ted Lyons	P42	B	29	57	122	20	38	6	3	1	15	2	18	0	.311	.434
1 Alex Metzler	OF27	L	27	56	76	12	14	4	0	0	5	11	6	0	.184	.237
2 Bob Fothergill	OF30	R	32	51	131	10	40	9	0	0	24	4	8	0	.305	.374
Buck Crouse	C38	L	33	42	118	14	30	8	1	0	15	17	10	1	.254	.339
Irv Jeffries	3B20, SS13	R	24	40	97	14	23	3	0	2	11	3	2	1	.237	.330
1 Art Shires	1B33	L	22	37	128	14	33	5	1	1	18	6	6	2	.258	.336
Martin Autry	C29	R	27	34	71	1	18	1	1	0	5	4	8	0	.254	.296
1 Dave Harris	OF23, 2B1	R	30	33	86	16	21	2	1	5	13	7	22	0	.244	.465
Bill Hunnefield	SS22, 1B1	B	31	31	81	11	22	2	0	1	5	4	10	1	.272	.333
Blondy Ryan	3B23, SS2, 2B1	R	24	28	87	9	18	0	4	1	10	6	13	2	.207	.333
Johnny Riddle	C25	R	24	25	58	7	14	3	1	0	4	3	6	0	.241	.328
Ernie Smith	SS21	R	30	24	79	5	19	3	0	0	3	5	6	2	.241	.278
Moe Berg	C20	R	28	20	61	4	7	3	0	0	7	1	5	0	.115	.164
1 Jim Moore	OF9	R	27	16	39	4	8	2	0	0	2	6	3	0	.205	.256

Luke Appling 23 R 8-26, Bruce Campbell 20 L 5-10, Joe Klinger 27 R 3-8, Butch Henline 35 R 1-8, Hugh Willingham 22 R 1-4

NAME	T	AGE	W	L	PCT	SV	G	GS	CG	IP	H	BB	SO	ShO	ERA
		29	62	92	.403	10	154	154	67	1361	1629	407	471	2	4.71
Ted Lyons	R	29	22	15	.595	1	42	36	29	298	331	57	69	1	3.77
Pat Caraway	L	24	10	10	.500	1	38	21	9	193	194	57	83	1	3.87
Red Faber	R	41	8	13	.381	1	29	26	10	169	188	49	62	0	4.21
Hal McKain	R	23	6	4	.600	5	32	5	0	89	108	42	52	0	5.56
Tommy Thomas	R	30	5	13	.278	0	34	27	7	169	229	44	59	0	5.22
2 Garland Braxton	L	30	4	10	.286	1	19	10	2	91	127	33	44	0	6.43
Dutch Henry	L	28	2	17	.105	0	35	16	4	155	211	48	35	0	4.88
Jim Moore	R	25	2	1	.667	1	9	5	2	40	42	12	11	0	3.60
Ted Blankenship	R	29	2	1	.667	0	7	1	0	15	23	7	2	0	9.00
Ed Walsh	R	25	1	4	.200	0	37	4	4	104	131	30	37	0	5.36
Bob Wieland	L	24	0	4	.000	0	14	3	0	33	38	21	15	0	6.54
Biggs Wehde	R	23	0	0	.000	0	4	0	0	6	7	7	3	0	10.50

BOSTON 8th 52-102 .338 50 — HEINIE WAGNER

NAME	G by POS	B	AGE	G	AB	R	H	2B	3B	HR	RBI	BB	SO	SB	BA	SA
TOTALS			29	154	5286	612	1393	257	68	47	533	358	552	42	.264	.365
Phil Todt	1B104	L	28	111	383	49	103	22	5	11	62	24	33	4	.269	.439
Bill Regan	2B127, 3B2	R	31	134	507	54	135	35	10	3	53	25	60	4	.266	.393
Hal Rhyne	SS107	R	31	107	296	34	60	8	5	0	23	25	19	1	.203	.264
Otto Miller	3B83, 2B15	L	31	112	370	49	106	22	5	0	40	26	21	2	.286	.373
Earl Webb	OF116	L	31	127	449	61	145	30	6	16	66	44	56	2	.323	.523
Tom Oliver	OF154	R	27	154	646	86	189	34	2	0	46	42	25	6	.293	.351
Russ Scarritt	OF110	L	27	113	447	48	129	17	8	2	48	12	49	4	.289	.376
Charlie Berry	C85	R	27	88	256	31	74	9	6	6	35	16	22	2	.289	.441
2 Cedric Durst	OF75	L	33	102	302	29	74	19	5	1	24	17	24	3	.245	.351
Bobby Reeves (JJ)	3B62, SS15, 2B11	R	26	92	272	41	59	7	4	2	18	50	36	6	.217	.294
Bill Sweeney	1B56, 3B1	R	26	88	243	32	75	13	0	4	30	9	15	5	.309	.412
Johnnie Heving	C71	R	34	75	220	15	61	5	3	0	17	11	14	2	.277	.327
Rabbit Warstler	SS54	R	26	54	162	16	30	2	3	1	13	20	21	0	.185	.253
Jack Rothrock (BL)	OF9, 3B1	B	25	45	65	4	18	3	1	0	4	2	9	0	.277	.354
Bill Narleski	SS19, 3B14, 2B5	R	31	39	98	11	23	9	0	0	7	7	5	0	.235	.327
Ed Connolly	C26	R	21	27	48	1	9	2	0	0	7	4	3	0	.188	.229
Charlie Small	OF1	L	24	25	18	1	3	1	0	0	0	2	5	1	.167	.222
Joe Cicero	OF5, 3B2	R	19	18	30	5	5	1	2	0	4	1	5	0	.167	.333

1 Bill Barrett 30 R 3-18, Jim Galvin 22 R 0-2, Tom Winsett 20 L 0-1

NAME	T	AGE	W	L	PCT	SV	G	GS	CG	IP	H	BB	SO	ShO	ERA
		28	52	102	.338	5	154	154	78	1360	1505	488	356	4	4.70
Milt Gaston	R	34	13	20	.394	2	38	34	20	273	272	98	99	2	3.92
Danny MacFayden	R	25	11	14	.440	2	36	33	18	269	293	93	76	1	4.21
Hod Lisenbee	R	31	10	17	.370	0	37	31	15	237	254	86	47	0	4.40
Jack Russell	R	24	9	20	.310	0	35	30	15	230	302	53	35	0	5.44
Ed Morris (SJ)	R	30	4	9	.308	0	18	9	3	65	67	38	28	0	4.16
Ed Durham	R	22	4	15	.211	1	33	12	6	140	144	43	28	1	4.69
George Smith	R	28	1	2	.333	0	27	2	0	74	92	49	21	0	6.81
Frank Bushey	R	23	0	1	.000	0	11	0	0	30	34	15	4	0	6.30
Frank Mulroney	R	27	0	1	.000	0	2	0	0	3	3	0	2	0	3.00
1 Red Ruffing	R	26	0	3	.000	0	4	3	1	24	22	6	14	0	6.38
Ben Shields	L	27	0	0	.000	0	3	0	0	10	16	6	1	0	9.00
Bill Bayne	L	31	0	0	.000	0	1	0	0	4	5	1	1	0	4.50
Bob Kline	R	20	0	0	.000	0	1	0	0	1	1	0	0	0	0.00

ST. LOUIS 1st 92-62 .597 — GABBY STREET

NAME	G by POS	B	AGE	G	AB	R	H	2B	3B	HR	RBI	BB	SO	SB	BA	SA
TOTALS			29	154	5512	**1004**	1732	**373**	89	104	**942**	479	496	72	.314	.471
Jim Bottomley	1B124	L	30	131	487	92	148	33	7	15	97	44	36	5	.304	.493
Frankie Frisch	2B123, 3B10	B	31	133	540	121	187	46	9	10	114	55	16	15	.346	.520
Charlie Gelbert	SS139	R	24	139	513	92	156	39	11	3	72	43	41	6	.304	.441
Sparky Adams	3B104, 2B25, SS7	R	35	137	570	98	179	36	9	0	55	45	27	7	.314	.409
George Watkins	OF89, 1B13, 2B1	L	30	119	391	85	146	32	7	17	87	24	49	5	.373	.621
Taylor Douthit	OF154	R	29	154	**664**	109	201	41	10	7	93	60	38	4	.303	.426
Chick Hafey	OF116	R	27	120	446	108	150	39	12	26	107	46	51	12	.336	.652
Jimmie Wilson	C99	R	29	107	362	54	115	25	7	1	58	28	17	8	.318	.434
Showboat Fisher	OF67	L	31	92	254	49	95	18	6	8	61	25	21	4	.374	.587
Gus Mancuso	C61	R	24	76	227	39	83	17	2	7	59	18	16	1	.366	.551
Andy High	3B48, 2B3	L	32	72	215	34	60	12	2	2	29	23	6	1	.279	.381
Ernie Orsatti	1B22, OF11	L	27	48	131	24	42	8	4	1	15	12	18	1	.321	.466
Ray Blades	OF32	R	33	45	101	26	40	6	2	4	25	21	15	1	.396	.614
Homer Peel	OF21	R	27	26	73	9	12	2	0	0	10	3	4	0	.164	.192
1 Doc Farrell	SS15, 2B6, 1B1	R	28	23	61	3	13	1	1	0	6	4	2	1	.213	.262
George Puccinelli	OF3	R	23	11	16	5	9	1	0	3	8	0	1	0	.563	1.188
Earl Smith	C6	L	33	8	10	0	0	0	0	0	0	3	1	0	.000	.000
Pepper Martin		R	26	6	1	5	0	0	0	0	0	0	0	0	.000	.000

NAME	T	AGE	W	L	PCT	SV	G	GS	CG	IP	H	BB	SO	ShO	ERA
TOTALS		31	**92**	62	**.597**	**21**	154	154	63	1380	1595	477	**641**	5	4.40
Wild Bill Hallahan	L	27	15	9	.625	2	35	32	13	237	233	**126**	**177**	2	4.67
2 Burleigh Grimes	R	36	13	6	.684	0	22	19	10	152	174	43	58	1	3.02
Jesse Haines	R	36	13	8	.619	1	29	24	14	182	215	54	68	0	4.30
Flint Rhem	R	29	12	8	.600	0	26	19	9	140	173	37	47	0	4.44
Syl Johnson	R	29	12	10	.545	2	32	24	9	188	215	38	92	2	4.64
Jim Lindsey	R	32	7	5	.583	5	39	6	3	106	131	46	50	0	4.42
Al Grabowski	L	28	6	4	.600	1	33	8	1	106	121	50	45	0	4.84
Hi Bell	R	32	4	3	.571	8	39	9	2	115	143	23	42	0	3.91
Hal Haid	R	32	3	2	.600	2	20	0	0	33	38	14	13	0	4.09
1 Bill Sherdel	L	33	3	2	.600	0	13	7	1	64	86	13	29	0	4.64
1 Fred Frankhouse	R	26	2	3	.400	0	8	1	0	20	31	11	4	0	7.20
Dizzy Dean	R	19	1	0	1.000	0	1	1	1	9	3	3	5	0	1.00
1 Clarence Mitchell	L	39	1	0	1.000	0	1	1	0	3	5	2	1	0	6.00
Carmen Hill	R	34	0	1	.000	0	4	2	0	15	12	13	8	0	7.20
Tony Kaufmann	R	29	0	1	.000	0	2	1	0	10	15	4	2	0	8.10

CHICAGO 2nd 90-64 .584 2 — JOE McCARTHY 86-64 .573 ROGERS HORNSBY 4-0 1.000

NAME	G by POS	B	AGE	G	AB	R	H	2B	3B	HR	RBI	BB	SO	SB	BA	SA
TOTALS			29	156	5581	998	1722	305	72	**171**	940	**588**	**635**	70	.309	**.481**
Charlie Grimm	1B113	L	31	114	429	58	124	27	2	6	66	41	26	1	.289	.403
Footsie Blair	2B115, 3B13	L	26	134	578	97	158	24	12	6	59	20	58	9	.273	.388
Woody English	3B83, SS78	R	23	156	638	152	214	36	17	14	59	100	72	3	.335	.511
Les Bell	3B70, 1B2	R	28	74	248	35	69	15	4	5	47	24	27	1	.278	.431
Kiki Cuyler	OF156	R	30	156	642	155	228	50	17	13	134	72	49	**37**	.355	.547
Hack Wilson	OF155	R	30	155	585	146	208	35	6	**56**	**190**	**105**	**84**	3	.356	**.723**
Riggs Stephenson	OF80	R	32	109	341	56	125	21	1	5	68	32	20	2	.367	.478
Gabby Hartnett	C136	R	29	141	508	84	172	31	3	37	122	55	62	0	.339	.630
Clyde Beck	SS57, 2B24, 3B2	R	28	83	244	32	52	7	0	6	34	36	32	2	.213	.316
Danny Taylor	OF52	R	29	74	219	43	62	14	3	2	37	27	34	6	.283	.402
Cliff Heathcote	OF35	L	32	70	150	30	39	10	1	9	18	18	15	4	.260	.520
Guy Bush	P46	R	28	46	78	7	22	0	1	0	7	6	19	0	.282	.308
2 Doc Farrell	SS38, 2B1	R	28	46	113	21	33	6	0	1	16	9	5	0	.292	.372
Pat Malone	P45	L	27	45	105	12	26	0	0	4	10	7	19	0	.248	.362
Rogers Hornsby (FJ)	2B25	R	34	42	104	15	32	5	1	2	18	12	12	0	.308	.433
2 George Kelly	1B39	R	34	39	166	22	55	6	1	3	19	7	16	0	.331	.434
Zack Taylor	C28	R	31	32	95	12	22	2	1	1	11	2	12	0	.232	.305
Chuck Tolson	1B5	R	28	13	20	0	6	1	0	0	1	6	5	1	.300	.350

NAME	T	AGE	W	L	PCT	SV	G	GS	CG	IP	H	BB	SO	ShO	ERA
TOTALS		28	90	64	.584	12	156	156	67	**1404**	1642	528	601	6	4.80
Pat Malone	R	27	**20**	9	.690	4	45	35	**22**	272	290	96	142	2	3.94
Charlie Root	R	31	16	14	.533	3	37	30	15	220	247	63	124	**4**	4.34
Guy Bush	R	28	15	10	.600	3	46	25	11	225	291	86	75	0	6.20
Bud Teachout	L	26	11	4	.733	0	40	16	6	153	178	48	59	0	4.06
Bob Osborn	R	27	10	6	.625	1	35	13	3	127	147	53	42	0	4.96
Sheriff Blake	R	30	10	14	.417	0	34	24	7	187	213	99	80	0	4.81
Hal Carlson (DD)	R	36	4	2	.667	0	8	6	3	52	68	14	14	0	5.02
Lynn Nelson	R	25	3	2	.600	0	37	3	0	81	97	28	29	0	5.11
2 Jesse Petty	L	35	1	3	.250	0	9	3	0	39	51	6	18	0	3.00
Al Shealy	R	30	0	0	.000	0	24	0	0	27	37	14	14	0	8.00
Mal Moss	L	25	0	0	.000	1	12	1	0	19	18	14	4	0	6.16
Bill McAfee	R	22	0	0	.000	0	2	0	0	1	3	2	0	0	0.00
Lon Warneke	R	21	0	0	.000	0	1	0	0	1	2	5	0	0	45.00

NEW YORK 3rd 87-67 .565 5 — JOHN McGRAW

NAME	G by POS	B	AGE	G	AB	R	H	2B	3B	HR	RBI	BB	SO	SB	BA	SA
TOTALS			27	154	5553	959	1769	264	83	143	880	422	382	59	**.319**	.473
Bill Terry	1B154	L	31	154	633	139	**254**	39	15	23	129	57	33	8	**.401**	.619
2 Hughie Critz	2B124	R	29	124	558	93	148	17	11	4	50	24	26	7	.265	.357
Travis Jackson	SS115	R	26	116	431	70	146	27	8	13	82	32	25	6	.339	.529
Fred Lindstrom	3B148	R	24	148	609	127	231	39	7	22	106	48	33	15	.379	.575
Mel Ott	OF146	L	21	148	521	122	182	34	5	25	119	103	35	9	.349	.578
Wally Roettger	OF114	R	27	121	420	51	119	15	5	5	51	25	29	1	.283	.379
Freddy Leach	OF124	L	32	126	544	90	178	19	13	13	71	22	25	3	.327	.482
Shanty Hogan	C96	R	24	122	389	60	132	26	2	13	75	21	24	2	.339	.517
Bob O'Farrell	C69	R	33	94	249	37	75	16	4	4	54	31	21	1	.301	.446
Doc Marshall	SS45, 2B17, 3B5	R	24	78	223	33	69	5	3	0	21	13	9	0	.309	.359
2 Ethan Allen	OF62	R	26	76	238	48	73	9	2	7	31	12	23	5	.307	.450
Andy Reese	OF32, 3B10	R	26	67	172	26	47	4	2	4	25	10	12	1	.273	.390
1 Pat Crawford	2B18, 1B1	L	28	25	76	11	21	3	2	3	17	7	2	0	.276	.487
Chick Fullis	OF2	R	26	13	6	2	0	0	0	0	0	0	1	1	.000	.000
Dave Bancroft	SS8	B	39	10	17	0	1	1	0	0	0	2	1	0	.059	.118
Harry Rosenberg	OF3	R	31	9	5	1	0	0	0	0	0	1	4	0	.000	.000
Francis Healy	C1	R	20	7	2	2	0	0	0	0	0	0	0	0	.000	.000
Jo-Jo Moore	OF1	L	21	3	5	1	1	0	0	0	0	0	1	0	.200	.200
Sam Leslie		L	24	2	2	0	1	0	0	0	0	0	1	0	.500	.500
Ed Roush (HO) 37																

NAME	T	AGE	W	L	PCT	SV	G	GS	CG	IP	H	BB	SO	ShO	ERA
TOTALS		29	87	67	.565	19	154	154	64	1363	1546	439	522	6	4.60
Freddie Fitzsimmons	R	28	19	7	**.731**	1	41	29	17	224	230	59	76	1	4.26
Carl Hubbell	L	27	17	12	.586	2	37	32	17	242	263	58	117	3	3.87
Bill Walker	L	26	17	15	.531	1	39	34	13	245	258	88	105	2	3.93
2 Clarence Mitchell	L	39	10	3	.769	0	24	16	5	129	151	36	40	0	3.98
Joe Heving	R	29	7	5	.583	6	41	2	0	90	109	27	37	0	5.20
2 Pete Donohue	R	29	7	6	.538	1	18	11	4	87	135	18	26	0	6.10
Hub Pruett	L	29	5	4	.556	3	45	8	1	136	152	63	49	0	4.76
Joe Genewich	R	33	2	5	.286	3	18	9	3	61	71	20	13	0	5.61
Tiny Chaplin	R	24	2	6	.250	1	19	8	3	73	89	16	20	0	5.18
1 Larry Benton	R	32	1	3	.250	1	8	4	1	30	42	14	16	0	7.80
Roy Parmelee	R	23	0	1	.000	0	11	1	0	21	18	26	19	0	9.43
Ray Lucas	R	21	0	0	.000	0	6	0	0	10	9	10	1	0	7.20
Ralph Judd	R	28	0	0	.000	0	2	0	0	8	13	3	0	0	5.63
Bill Morrel	R	30	0	0	.000	0	2	0	0	8	6	1	3	0	1.13

BROOKLYN 4th 86-68 .558 6 — WILBERT ROBINSON

NAME	G by POS	B	AGE	G	AB	R	H	2B	3B	HR	RBI	BB	SO	SB	BA	SA
TOTALS			29	154	5433	871	1654	303	73	122	836	481	541	53	.304	.454
Del Bissonette	1B146	L	30	146	572	102	192	33	13	16	113	56	66	4	.336	.523
Neal Finn	2B81	R	28	87	273	42	76	13	0	3	30	26	18	3	.278	.359
Glenn Wright	SS134	R	29	135	532	83	171	28	12	22	126	32	70	2	.321	.543
Wally Gilbert	3B150	R	29	150	623	92	183	34	5	3	67	47	33	7	.294	.379
Babe Herman	OF153	L	27	153	614	143	241	48	11	35	130	66	56	18	.393	.678
Johnny Frederick	OF142	L	29	142	616	120	206	44	11	17	76	46	34	1	.334	.524
Rube Bressler	OF90, 1B7	R	35	109	335	53	100	12	8	3	52	51	19	4	.299	.409
Al Lopez	C126	R	21	128	421	60	130	20	4	6	57	33	35	3	.309	.418
Jake Flowers	2B65, OF1	R	28	89	253	37	81	18	3	2	50	21	18	5	.320	.439
Eddie Moore	2B23, OF23, SS17, 3B1	R	31	76	196	24	55	13	1	1	20	21	7	1	.281	.372
Harvey Hendrick	OF42, 1B7	L	32	68	167	29	43	10	1	5	28	20	19	2	.257	.419
Ike Boone	OF27	L	33	40	101	13	30	9	1	3	13	14	8	0	.297	.495
Hank DeBerry	C35	R	35	35	95	11	28	3	0	0	14	4	10	0	.295	.326
Gordon Slade	SS21	R	25	25	37	8	8	2	0	1	2	3	5	0	.216	.351
Val Picinich	C22	R	33	23	46	4	10	3	0	0	3	5	6	1	.217	.283
Hal Lee	OF12	R	25	22	37	5	6	0	0	1	4	4	5	0	.162	.243
Jack Warner	3B21	R	26	21	25	4	8	1	0	0	0	2	7	1	.320	.360

NAME	T	AGE	W	L	PCT	SV	G	GS	CG	IP	H	BB	SO	ShO	ERA
TOTALS		31	86	68	.558	15	154	154	74	1372	1480	394	526	**13**	**4.03**
Dazzy Vance	R	39	17	15	.531	0	35	31	20	259	241	55	173	**4**	**2.61**
Ray Phelps	R	26	14	7	.667	0	36	24	11	180	198	52	64	2	4.10
Dolf Luque	R	39	14	8	.636	2	31	24	16	199	221	58	62	2	4.30
Watty Clark	L	28	13	13	.500	6	44	24	9	200	209	38	81	1	4.19
Jumbo Jim Elliott	L	29	10	7	.588	1	35	21	6	198	204	70	59	2	3.95
Ray Moss	R	28	9	6	.600	1	36	11	5	118	127	55	30	0	5.11
Sloppy Thurston	R	31	6	4	.600	1	24	11	5	106	110	17	26	2	3.40
Clise Dudley	R	26	2	4	.333	1	21	7	2	67	103	27	18	0	6.31
Johnny Morrison	R	34	1	2	.333	1	16	0	0	35	47	16	11	0	5.40
Fred Heimach	L	29	0	2	.000	1	9	0	0	7	14	3	1	0	5.14
Jim Faulkner	L	30	0	0	.000	1	2	0	0	.1	2	1	0	0	81.00
Bobo Newsom	R	22	0	0	.000	0	2	0	0	3	2	2	1	0	6.00
Cy Moore	R	25	0	0	.000	0	1	0	0	0	2	0	0	0	0.00

PITTSBURGH 5th 80-74 .519 12 — JEWEL ENS

NAME	G by POS	B	AGE	G	AB	R	H	2B	3B	HR	RBI	BB	SO	SB	BA	SA
TOTALS			27	154	5346	891	1622	285	119	86	844	494	449	**76**	.303	.449
Gus Suhr	1B151	L	24	151	542	93	155	26	14	17	107	80	56	11	.286	.480
George Grantham	2B141, 1B4	L	30	146	552	120	179	34	14	18	99	81	66	5	.342	.534
Dick Bartell	SS126	R	22	129	475	69	152	32	13	4	75	39	34	8	.320	.467
Pie Traynor	3B130	R	30	130	497	90	182	22	11	9	119	48	19	7	.366	.509
Paul Waner	OF143	L	27	145	589	117	217	32	18	8	77	57	18	18	.368	.525
Lloyd Waner (IL)	OF65	L	24	68	260	32	94	8	3	1	36	5	5	3	.362	.427
Adam Comorosky	OF152	R	25	152	597	112	187	47	**23**	12	119	51	33	14	.313	.529
Rollie Hemsley	C98	R	23	104	324	45	82	19	6	2	45	22	21	3	.253	.367
Al Bool	C65	R	32	78	216	30	56	12	4	7	46	25	29	0	.259	.449
1 Fred Brickell	OF61	L	23	68	219	36	65	9	3	1	14	15	20	3	.297	.379
Charlie Engle	3B24, SS23, 2B10	R	26	67	216	34	57	10	1	0	15	22	20	1	.264	.319
Erv Brame	P32	L	28	50	116	20	41	5	0	3	22	0	2	0	.353	.474
Ira Flagstead	OF40	R	36	44	156	21	39	7	4	2	21	17	9	1	.250	.385
Jim Mosolf	OF12, P1	L	24	40	51	16	17	2	1	0	9	8	7	0	.333	.412
2 Denny Sothern	OF13	R	26	17	51	4	9	4	0	1	4	3	4	2	.176	.314
Ben Sankey	SS6, 2B4	R	22	13	30	6	5	0	0	0	0	2	3	0	.167	.167
Charlie Hargreaves	C11	R	33	11	31	4	7	1	0	0	2	2	1	0	.226	.258
Gus Dugas	OF9	L	23	9	31	8	9	2	0	0	1	7	4	0	.290	.355
Stu Clarke (NJ)	2B2	R	24	4	9	2	4	0	1	0	2	1	0	0	.444	.667
Howdie Groskloss	SS1	R	22	2	3	0	1	0	0	0	0	0	0	0	.333	.333

NAME	T	AGE	W	L	PCT	SV	G	GS	CG	IP	H	BB	SO	ShO	ERA
TOTALS		28	80	74	.519	13	154	154	**80**	1361	1730	438	393	5	5.24
Ray Kremer	R	37	**20**	12	.625	0	39	**38**	18	**276**	**366**	63	58	1	5.02
Erv Brame	R	28	17	8	.680	0	32	29	**22**	236	291	56	55	0	4.69
Larry French	L	22	17	**18**	.486	1	42	35	21	275	325	89	90	3	4.35
Glenn Spencer	R	24	8	9	.471	4	41	10	5	157	185	63	60	0	5.39
Steve Swetonic (IL)	R	26	6	6	.500	5	23	6	3	97	107	27	35	1	4.45
Heinie Meinie (IL)	R	34	6	8	.429	1	20	16	4	117	168	44	18	0	6.15
Spades Wood	L	21	4	3	.571	0	9	7	4	58	61	32	23	0	5.12
Ralph Erickson	L	26	1	0	1.000	0	7	0	0	14	21	10	2	0	7.07
1 Jesse Petty	L	35	1	6	.143	1	10	7	0	41	67	13	16	0	8.34
Percy Jones	L	30	0	1	.000	0	9	2	0	19	26	11	3	0	6.63
Leon Chagnon	R	27	0	3	.000	0	18	4	3	62	92	23	27	0	6.82
Lil Stoner	R	31	0	0	.000	0	5	0	0	6	7	3	1	0	4.50
Andy Bednar	R	**21**	0	0	.000	0	2	0	0	1	4	1	1	0	36.00
Marty Lang	L	24	0	0	.000	0	2	0	0	2	9	3	2	0	45.00
Bernie Walter	R	21	0	0	.000	0	1	0	0	1	0	0	1	0	0.00
Jim Mosolf	L	24	0	0	.000	0	1	0	0	.1	1	0	0	0	27.00

BOSTON 6th 70-84 .455 22 — BILL McKECHNIE

NAME	G by POS	B	AGE	G	AB	R	H	2B	3B	HR	RBI	BB	SO	SB	BA	SA
TOTALS			29	154	5356	693	1503	246	78	66	631	332	397	69	.281	.393
George Sisler	1B107	L	37	116	431	54	133	15	7	3	67	23	15	7	.309	.397
Freddie Maguire	2B146	R	31	146	516	54	138	21	5	0	52	20	22	4	.267	.328
Rabbit Maranville	SS138, 3B4	R	38	142	558	85	157	26	8	2	43	48	23	9	.281	.367
Buster Chatham	3B92, SS17	R	28	112	404	48	108	20	11	5	56	37	41	8	.267	.408
Lance Richbourg	OF128	L	32	130	529	81	161	23	8	3	54	19	31	13	.304	.395
Jim Welsh	OF110	L	27	113	422	51	116	21	9	3	36	29	23	5	.275	.389
Wally Berger	OF145	R	24	151	555	98	172	27	14	38	119	54	69	3	.310	.614
Al Spohrer	C108	R	27	112	356	44	113	22	8	2	37	22	24	3	.317	.441
Randy Moore	OF34, 3B13	L	25	83	191	24	55	9	0	2	34	10	13	3	.288	.366
Earl Clark	OF63	R	22	82	233	29	69	11	3	3	28	7	22	3	.296	.408
Johnny Neun	1B55	B	29	81	212	39	69	12	2	2	23	21	18	9	.325	.429
Bill Cronin	C64	R	27	66	178	19	45	9	1	0	17	4	8	0	.253	.315
Red Rollings	3B28, 2B10	L	26	52	123	10	29	6	0	0	10	9	5	2	.236	.285
Gene Robertson	3B17	L	30	21	59	7	11	1	0	0	7	5	3	0	.186	.203
Billy Rhiel	3B13, 2B2	R	29	20	47	3	8	4	0	0	4	2	5	0	.170	.255
Bill Dunlap	OF7	R	21	16	29	3	2	1	0	0	0	0	6	0	.069	.103
Hank Gowdy	C15	R	40	16	25	0	5	1	0	0	2	3	1	0	.200	.240
Bernie James	2B7	B	24	8	11	1	2	1	0	0	1	0	1	0	.182	.273
Buzz Boyle	OF1	L	22	1	1	0	0	0	0	0	0	0	0	0	.000	.000
Owen Kahm		R	25	1	0	1	0	0	0	0	0	0	0	0	.000	.000

NAME	T	AGE	W	L	PCT	SV	G	GS	CG	IP	H	BB	SO	ShO	ERA
		30	70	84	.455	11	154	154	71	1361	1624	475	424	6	4.91
Socks Seibold	R	34	15	16	.484	2	36	33	20	251	288	85	70	1	4.12
2 Tom Zachary	L	34	11	5	.688	0	24	22	10	151	192	50	57	1	4.59
Bob Smith	R	32	10	14	.417	5	38	24	14	220	247	85	84	2	4.25
Ben Cantwell	R	28	9	15	.375	2	31	21	10	173	213	45	43	0	4.89
2 Fred Frankhouse	R	26	7	6	.538	0	27	11	3	111	138	43	30	1	5.59
2 Bill Sherdel	L	33	6	5	.545	1	21	14	7	119	131	30	26	0	4.76
Bruce Cunningham	R	24	5	6	.455	0	36	6	2	107	121	41	28	0	5.47
Ed Brandt	L	25	4	11	.267	1	41	13	4	147	168	59	65	1	5.02
1 Burleigh Grimes	R	36	3	5	.375	0	11	9	1	49	72	22	15	0	7.35
Ken Jones	R	26	0	1	.000	0	8	1	0	20	28	4	4	0	5.85
Johnny Cooney	L	29	0	0	.000	0	2	0	0	7	16	3	1	0	18.00
Bob Brown	R	19	0	0	.000	0	3	0	0	6	10	8	1	0	10.50

CINCINNATI 7th 59-95 .383 33 — DAN HOWLEY

NAME	G by POS	B	AGE	G	AB	R	H	2B	3B	HR	RBI	BB	SO	SB	BA	SA
TOTALS			30	154	5245	665	1475	265	67	74	625	445	489	48	.281	.400
Joe Stripp	1B75, 3B48	R	27	130	464	74	142	37	6	3	64	51	37	15	.306	.431
Hod Ford	SS74, 2B66	R	32	132	424	36	98	16	7	1	34	24	28	2	.231	.309
Leo Durocher	SS103, 2B13	R	24	119	354	31	86	15	3	3	32	20	45	0	.243	.328
Tony Cuccinello	3B109, 2B15, SS4	R	22	125	443	64	138	22	5	10	78	47	44	5	.312	.451
Harry Heilmann	OF106, 1B19	R	35	142	459	79	153	43	6	19	91	64	50	2	.333	.577
Bob Meusel	OF112	R	33	113	443	62	128	30	8	10	62	26	63	9	.239	.460
Curt Walker	OF120	L	33	134	472	74	145	26	11	8	51	64	30	4	.307	.460
Clyde Sukeforth	C82	L	28	94	296	30	84	9	3	1	19	17	12	1	.284	.345
Evar Swanson	OF71	R	27	95	301	43	93	15	3	2	22	11	17	4	.309	.399
Johnny Gooch	C79	B	32	82	276	29	67	10	3	2	30	27	15	0	.243	.322
Red Lucas	P33	L	28	80	113	18	38	4	1	2	19	17	4	0	.336	.442
Marty Callaghan	OF54	L	30	79	225	28	62	9	2	0	16	19	25	1	.276	.333
2 Pat Crawford	2B54, 1B13	L	28	76	224	24	65	7	1	3	26	23	10	2	.290	.371
1 George Kelly	1B50	R	34	51	188	18	54	10	1	5	35	7	20	1	.287	.431
Benny Frey	P44	R	24	44	88	7	25	4	1	0	5	4	18	0	.284	.352
Chuck Dressen	3B10, 2B3	R	31	33	19	0	4	0	0	0	1	1	3	0	.211	.211
1 Hughie Critz	2B28	R	29	28	104	15	24	3	2	0	11	6	6	1	.231	.298
1 Ethan Allen	OF15	R	26	21	46	10	10	1	0	3	7	5	2	1	.217	.435
Nick Cullop	OF5	R	31	7	22	2	4	0	0	1	5	1	9	0	.182	.318
Lena Styles	C5, 1B1	R	30	7	12	2	3	0	1	0	1	1	2	0	.250	.417
Harry Riconda		R	33	1	1	0	0	0	0	0	0	0	0	0	.000	.000

NAME	T	AGE	W	L	PCT	SV	G	GS	CG	IP	H	BB	SO	ShO	ERA
		30	59	95	.383	11	154	154	61	1335	1650	394	361	6	5.08
Red Lucas	R	28	14	16	.467	1	33	28	18	211	270	44	53	1	5.37
Benny Frey	R	24	11	**18**	.379	1	44	28	14	245	295	62	43	2	4.70
Eppa Rixey	L	39	9	13	.409	0	32	21	5	164	207	47	37	0	5.10
Ray Kolp	R	35	7	12	.368	3	37	19	5	168	180	34	40	2	4.23
2 Larry Benton	R	32	7	12	.368	1	35	22	9	178	246	45	47	0	5.11
Si Johnson	R	23	3	1	.750	0	35	3	0	78	86	31	47	0	4.96
Jakie May	L	34	3	11	.214	0	26	18	5	112	147	41	44	1	5.79
Ken Ash	R	28	2	0	1.000	0	16	1	1	39	37	16	15	0	3.46
Archie Campbell	R	26	2	4	.333	4	23	3	1	58	71	31	19	0	5.43
1 Pete Donohue	R	29	1	3	.250	1	8	5	2	34	53	13	4	0	6.35
3 Ownie Carroll	R	27	0	1	.000	0	3	2	1	14	17	3	0	0	4.50
Al Eckert	L	24	0	1	.000	0	2	1	0	5	7	4	1	0	7.20
Biff Wysong	L	25	0	1	.000	0	1	1	0	2	6	3	1	0	22.50
Doug McWeeney	R	33	0	2	.000	0	8	2	0	26	28	20	10	0	7.27

PHILADELPHIA 8th 52-102 .338 40 — BURT SHOTTON

NAME	G by POS	B	AGE	G	AB	R	H	2B	3B	HR	RBI	BB	SO	SB	BA	SA
TOTALS			27	156	**5667**	944	**1783**	345	44	126	884	450	459	34	.315	.458
Don Hurst	1B96, OF7	L	24	119	391	78	128	19	3	17	78	46	22	6	.327	.522
Fresco Thompson	2B112	R	28	122	478	77	135	34	4	4	46	35	29	7	.282	.395
Tommy Thevenow	SS156	R	26	156	573	57	164	21	1	0	78	23	26	1	.286	.326
Pinky Whitney	3B148	R	25	149	606	87	207	41	5	8	117	40	41	3	.342	.465
Chuck Klein	OF156	L	25	156	648	**158**	250	**59**	8	40	170	54	50	4	.386	.687
1 Denny Sothern	OF84	R	26	90	347	66	97	26	1	5	36	22	37	6	.280	.403
Lefty O'Doul	OF131	L	33	140	528	122	202	37	7	22	97	63	21	3	.383	.604
Spud Davis	C96	R	25	106	329	41	103	16	1	14	65	17	20	1	.313	.495
Barney Friberg	2B44, OF35, SS12, 3B8	R	30	105	331	62	113	21	1	4	42	47	35	1	.341	.447
Monk Sherlock	1B70, 2B5, OF1	R	25	92	299	51	97	18	2	0	38	27	28	0	.324	.398
Harry McCurdy	C41	L	30	80	148	23	49	6	2	1	25	15	12	0	.331	.419
2 Tony Rensa	C49	R	28	54	172	31	49	11	2	3	31	10	18	0	.285	.424
2 Fred Brickell	OF53	L	23	53	240	33	59	12	6	0	17	13	21	1	.246	.346
Tripp Sigman	OF19	L	31	52	100	15	27	4	1	4	6	6	9	1	.270	.450
Cy Williams	OF3	L	42	21	17	1	8	2	0	0	2	4	3	0	.471	.588
Jim Spotts	C2	R	21	3	2	1	0	0	0	0	0	0	1	0	.000	.000
Walt Lerian (DD) 20																

NAME	T	AGE	W	L	PCT	SV	G	GS	CG	IP	H	BB	SO	ShO	ERA
		28	52	102	.338	7	156	156	54	1373	**1993**	**543**	384	2	6.71
Phil Collins	R	28	16	11	.593	3	47	25	17	239	287	86	87	1	4.78
Ray Benge	R	28	11	15	.423	1	38	29	14	226	305	81	70	0	5.69
Les Sweetland	L	28	7	15	.318	0	34	25	8	167	271	60	36	0	7.71
Hal Elliott	R	31	6	11	.353	0	**48**	11	2	117	191	58	37	0	7.69
Hap Collard	R	31	6	12	.333	0	30	15	4	127	188	39	25	0	6.80
Claude Willoughby	R	31	4	17	.190	1	41	24	5	153	241	68	38	1	7.59
Chet Nichols (HO)	R	32	1	2	.333	0	16	5	1	60	76	16	15	0	6.75
John Milligan	L	26	1	2	.333	0	9	2	1	28	26	21	7	0	3.21
Harry Smythe	L	25	0	3	.000	2	25	3	0	50	84	31	9	0	7.74
Pete Alexander	R	43	0	3	.000	0	9	3	0	22	40	6	6	0	9.00
Lou Koupal	R	31	0	4	.000	0	13	4	1	37	52	17	11	0	8.51
Snipe Hansen	L	23	0	7	.000	0	22	9	1	84	123	38	25	0	6.75
Buz Phillips	R	26	0	0	.000	0	14	1	0	44	68	18	9	0	7.98
By Speece	R	33	0	0	.000	0	11	0	0	20	41	4	9	0	13.05

WORLD SERIES – PHILADELPHIA (AL) 4 ST. LOUIS (NL) 2

LINE SCORES

TEAM	1	2	3	4	5	6	7	8	9	10	11	12	R	H	E
Game 1 October 1 at Philadelphia															
STL (NL)	0	0	2	0	0	0	0	0	0				2	9	0
PHI (AL)	0	1	0	1	0	1	1	1	X				5	5	0
Grimes / Grove															
Game 2 October 2 at Philadelphia															
STL	0	1	0	0	0	0	0	0	0				1	6	2
PHI	2	0	2	2	0	0	0	0	X				6	7	2
Rhem, Lindsey (4), Johnson (7) / Earnshaw															
Game 3 October 4 at St. Louis															
PHI	0	0	0	0	0	0	0	0	0				0	7	0
STL	0	0	0	1	1	0	2	1	X				5	10	0
Walberg, Shores (5), Quinn (7) / Hallahan															
Game 4 October 5 at St. Louis															
PHI	1	0	0	0	0	0	0	0	0				1	4	1
STL	0	0	1	2	0	0	0	0	X				3	5	1
Grove / Haines															
Game 5 October 6 at St. Louis															
PHI	0	0	0	0	0	0	0	0	2				2	5	0
STL	0	0	0	0	0	0	0	0	0				0	3	1
Earnshaw, Grove (8) / Grimes															
Game 6 October 8 at Philadelphia															
STL	0	0	0	0	0	0	0	0	1				1	5	1
PHI	2	0	1	2	1	1	0	0	X				7	7	0
Hallahan, Johnson (3), Lindsey (6), Bell (8) / Earnshaw															

COMPOSITE BATTING

NAME	POS	G	AB	R	H	2B	3B	HR	RBI	BA
Philadelphia (AL) Totals		6	178	21	35	10	2	6	21	.197
Simmons	OF	6	22	4	8	2	0	2	4	.364
Foxx	1B	6	21	3	7	2	1	1	3	.333
Miller	OF	6	21	0	3	2	0	0	3	.143
Boley	SS	6	21	1	2	0	0	0	1	.095
Dykes	3B	6	18	2	4	3	0	1	5	.222
Cochrane	C	6	18	5	4	1	0	2	4	.222
Bishop	2B	6	18	5	4	0	0	0	0	.222
Haas	OF	6	18	1	2	0	1	0	1	.111
Earnshaw	P	3	9	0	0	0	0	0	0	.000
Grove	P	3	6	0	0	0	0	0	0	.000
Moore	OF	3	3	0	1	0	0	0	0	.333
Walberg	P	1	2	0	0	0	0	0	0	.000
McNair	PH	1	1	0	0	0	0	0	0	.000
Quinn	P	1	0	0	0	0	0	0	0	.000
Shores	P	1	0	0	0	0	0	0	0	.000
St. Louis (NL) Totals		6	190	12	38	10	1	2	11	.200
Frisch	2B	6	24	0	5	2	0	0	0	.208
Douthit	OF	6	24	1	2	0	0	1	2	.083
Hafey	OF	6	22	2	6	5	0	0	2	.273
Bottomley	1B	6	22	1	1	1	0	0	0	.045
Adams	3B	6	21	0	3	0	0	0	1	.143
Gelbert	SS	6	17	2	6	0	1	0	2	.353
Wilson	C	4	15	0	4	1	0	0	2	.267
Watkins	OF	4	12	2	2	0	0	1	1	.167
Blades	OF	5	9	2	1	0	0	0	0	.111
Mancuso	C	2	7	1	2	0	0	0	0	.286
Grimes	P	2	5	0	2	0	0	0	0	.400
Haines	P	1	2	0	1	0	0	0	1	.500
Fisher	PH	2	2	0	1	1	0	0	0	.500
High	3B	1	2	1	1	0	0	0	0	.500
Hallahan	P	2	2	0	0	0	0	0	0	.000
Lindsey	P	2	1	0	1	0	0	0	0	1.000
Orsatti	PH	1	1	0	0	0	0	0	0	.000
Puccinelli	PH	1	1	0	0	0	0	0	0	.000
Rhem	P	1	1	0	0	0	0	0	0	.000
Bell	P	1	0	0	0	0	0	0	0	.000
Johnson	P	2	0	0	0	0	0	0	0	.000

COMPOSITE PITCHING

NAME	G	IP	H	BB	SO	W	L	SV	ERA
Philadelphia (AL) Totals	6	52	38	11	33	4	2	0	1.73
Earnshaw	3	25	13	7	19	2	0	0	0.72
Grove	3	19	15	3	10	2	1	0	1.42
Walberg	1	4.2	4	1	3	0	1	0	3.86
Quinn	1	2	3	0	1	0	0	0	4.50
Shores	1	1.1	3	0	0	0	0	0	13.50
St. Louis (NL) Totals	6	51	35	24	32	2	4	0	3.35
Grimes	2	17	10	6	13	0	2	0	3.71
Hallahan	2	11	9	8	8	1	1	0	1.64
Haines	1	9	4	4	2	1	0	0	1.00
Johnson	2	5	4	3	4	0	0	0	7.20
Lindsey	2	4.2	1	1	2	0	0	0	1.93
Rhem	1	3.1	7	2	3	0	1	0	10.80
Bell	1	1	0	0	0	0	0	0	0.00

1931 Adding Pepper to the Wounds

Cornelius Alexander McGillicuddy, more commonly know as Connie Mack, first broke in as a catcher with Washington in the National League in 1886. His playing career lasted until 1896 and was mediocre. But his managerial career, which began with Pittsburgh in 1894, was an event which would place his name high on the list whenever baseball history was discussed.

Mack's stay with Pittsburgh until 1896 was not the reason he would be remembered. Rather, it was the seed which led to his taking over the Philadelphia Athletics as owner and manager when the American League started in 1901. Now, thirty years later and still serving in the same dual capacity, Mack was on the threshold of an unprecedented event—three world championships in as many years. His courage and imagination had inspired him to lead other Athletics clubs to titles eight times before, only to tear his teams apart and almost start anew. In many instances the reason seemed to be economics, but it is almost certain that a strong pioneering spirit accompanied the moves.

The season of 1931 proved a cakewalk for Mack, finishing a strong 13½ games ahead of the Yankees and climaxing three years of winning over 100 games. In winning the pennant, the A's put two streaks together which devastated their rivals. The first was a 17-game stint in May, and the other came in July and lasted for 13 games. Mack's mainstay was MVP Lefty Grove, his pitching ace who compiled an amazing set of statistics—and probably one of the greatest records ever to stand. Grove won 31 and lost 4 for an amazing .886 percentage. He was low with a 2.05 E.R.A. and at one time reeled off 16 victories in a row. Grove's 1929-31 record of 79-15 was also unnerving.

The Cardinals had an easy time with the National League, winning by a full 13 games behind the MVP leadership of second baseman Frankie Frisch. Statistics in both leagues came closer to the norm, as some of the unnecessary juice was taken out of the baseballs. Chuck Klein of the Phillies, for instance, drove in 121 runs and won the title, while a year before he knocked in 170 runs and proved a poor second to Hack Wilson's 190.

In the World Series of 1929, Mack's forces had no trouble with the Cubs, easily winning four games to one. In 1930 the Cardinals also proved to be no problem, the Series going six games before Mack could claim victory. 1931 seemed to be the easiest Series in the last three years. The Cardinals were back and not that much stronger, and the Athletics were said to be the best team Mack had ever fielded, making them an odds-on choice to win their third straight title.

If the years had taught Mack anything, it was not to be overconfident. He wasn't. But what he did not take into account until it was too late was St. Louis' brash, young center fielder, Pepper Martin, whose career up to the Series deserved no special mention. Yet, suddenly Martin seemed blessed by divinity. After Grove brought Mack victory in the first game, Martin and Bill Hallahan beat the A's in the second game, 2-0. Martin contributed two hits in the third-game victory, and denied George Earnshaw a no-hitter in the Series evener by collecting the only two Cardinal hits.

In the fifth game, Martin got three hits and drove in four runs in a 5-1 victory. Grove evened matters in the sixth game, 8-1, but Martin, who wound up the Series with a .500 average, fittingly snuffed the final A's surge in the ninth inning of the finale with a two-out, two-on catch of Max Bishop's smoking line drive, which gave St. Louis a 4-2 win and the championship—an event Mack would never again witness from the dugout.

1931 AMERICAN LEAGUE

NAME	G by POS	B	AGE	G	AB	R	H	2B	3B	HR	RBI	BB	SO	SB	BA	SA
PHILADELPHIA 1st 107-45 .704		CONNIE MACK														
	TOTALS		28	153	5377	858	1544	311	64	118	798	526	543	27	.287	.435
Jimmie Foxx	1B112, 3B20, OF1	R	23	139	515	93	150	32	10	30	120	73	84	4	.291	.567
Max Bishop	2B130	L	31	130	497	115	146	30	4	5	37	112	51	3	.294	.400
Dib Williams	SS72, 2B10, OF1	R	21	86	294	41	79	12	2	6	40	19	21	2	.269	.384
Jimmy Dykes	3B87, SS15	R	34	101	355	48	97	28	2	3	46	49	47	1	.273	.389
Bing Miller	OF137	R	36	137	534	75	150	43	5	8	77	36	16	5	.281	.425
Mule Haas (BW)	OF102	L	27	102	440	82	142	29	7	8	56	30	29	0	.323	.475
Al Simmons	OF128	R	29	128	513	105	200	37	13	22	128	47	45	3	.390	.641
Mickey Cochrane	C117	L	28	122	459	87	160	31	6	17	89	56	21	2	.349	.553
Eric McNair	3B47, 2B16, SS13	R	22	79	280	41	76	10	1	5	33	11	19	1	.271	.368
Joe Boley	SS62, 2B1	R	34	67	224	26	51	9	3	0	20	15	13	1	.228	.295
Doc Cramer (BG)	OF55	L	25	65	223	37	58	8	2	2	20	11	15	2	.260	.341
Phil Todt	1B52	L	29	62	197	23	48	14	2	5	44	8	22	1	.244	.411
Jim Moore	OF36	R	28	49	143	18	32	5	1	2	21	11	13	0	.223	.315
Johnnie Heving	C40	R	35	42	113	8	27	3	2	1	12	6	8	0	.239	.327
Joe Palmisano	C16, 2B1	R	28	19	44	5	10	2	0	0	4	6	3	0	.227	.273
Lou Finney	OF8	L	20	9	24	7	9	0	1	0	3	6	1	0	.375	.458
NEW YORK 2nd 94-59 .614 13.5		JOE McCARTHY														
	TOTALS		28	155	5608	1067	1667	277	78	155	990	748	554	139	.297	.457
Lou Gehrig	1B154, OF1	L	28	155	619	163	211	31	15	46	184	117	56	17	.341	.662
Tony Lazzeri	2B90, 3B39	R	27	135	484	67	129	27	7	8	83	79	80	18	.267	.401
Lyn Lary	SS155	R	25	155	610	100	171	35	9	10	107	88	54	13	.280	.416
Joe Sewell	3B121, 2B1	L	32	130	484	102	146	22	1	6	64	62	8	1	.302	.388
Babe Ruth	OF142, 1B1	L	36	145	534	149	199	31	3	46	163	128	51	5	.373	.700
Earle Combs	OF129	L	32	138	563	120	179	31	13	5	58	68	34	11	.318	.446
Ben Chapman	OF137, 2B11	R	22	149	600	120	189	28	11	17	122	75	77	61	.315	.483
Bill Dickey	C125	L	24	130	477	65	156	17	10	6	78	39	20	2	.327	.442
Sammy Byrd	OF88	R	24	115	248	51	67	18	2	3	32	29	26	5	.270	.395
Jimmy Reese	2B61	L	26	65	245	41	59	10	2	3	26	17	10	2	.241	.335
Red Ruffing	P37, OF1	R	27	48	109	14	36	8	1	3	12	1	13	0	.330	.505
Art Jorgens	C40	R	26	46	100	12	27	1	2	0	14	9	3	0	.270	.320
Myril Hoag	OF23, 3B1	R	23	44	28	6	4	2	0	0	3	1	8	0	.143	.214
Dusty Cooke (SJ)	OF11	L	24	27	39	10	13	1	0	1	6	8	11	4	.333	.436
Cy Perkins	C16	R	35	16	47	3	12	1	0	0	7	1	4	0	.255	.277
Dixie Walker	OF2	L	20	2	10	1	3	2	0	0	1	0	4	0	.300	.500
Red Rolfe	SS1	L	22	1	0	0	0	0	0	0	0	0	0	0	.000	.000
WASHINGTON 3rd 92-62 .597 16		WALTER JOHNSON														
	TOTALS		29	156	5576	843	1588	308	93	49	788	481	459	72	.285	.400
Joe Kuhel	1B139	L	25	139	524	70	141	34	8	8	85	47	45	7	.269	.410
Buddy Myer	2B137	L	27	139	591	114	173	33	11	4	56	58	42	11	.293	.406
Joe Cronin	SS155	R	24	156	611	103	187	44	13	12	126	81	52	10	.306	.480
Ossie Bluege	3B152, SS1	R	30	152	570	82	155	25	7	8	98	50	39	16	.272	.382
Sam Rice	OF105	L	41	120	413	81	128	21	8	0	42	35	11	6	.310	.400
Sammy West	OF127	L	26	132	526	77	175	43	13	3	91	30	37	6	.333	.481
Heinie Manush	OF143	L	29	146	616	110	189	41	11	6	70	36	27	3	.307	.438
Roy Spencer	C145	R	31	145	483	48	133	16	3	1	60	35	21	0	.275	.327
Dave Harris	OF60	R	31	77	231	49	72	14	8	5	50	49	38	7	.312	.506
Harry Rice	OF42	L	30	47	162	32	43	5	6	0	15	12	10	2	.265	.370
Pinky Hargrave	C25	B	35	40	80	6	26	8	0	1	19	9	12	1	.325	.463
Jackie Hayes	2B19, 3B8, SS3	R	24	38	108	11	24	2	1	0	8	6	4	2	.222	.259
Joe Judge (IL)	1B15	L	37	35	74	11	21	3	0	0	9	8	8	0	.284	.324
Cliff Bolton	C13	L	24	23	43	3	11	1	1	0	6	1	5	0	.256	.326
Buck Jordan	1B7	L	24	9	18	3	4	2	0	0	1	1	3	0	.222	.333
Johnny Gill	OF8	L	26	8	30	2	8	2	1	0	5	1	6	0	.267	.400
Bill Andrus	3B2	R	23	3	7	0	0	0	0	0	1	0	1	0	.000	.000
Babe Phelps		L	23	3	3	0	1	0	0	0	0	0	0	0	.333	.333
Nick Altrock		B	54	1	0	0	0	0	0	0	0	1	0	0	.000	.000

NAME	T	AGE	W	L	PCT	SV	G	GS	CG	IP	H	BB	SO	ShO	ERA
		29	107	45	.704	16	153	153	97	1366	1342	457	574	12	3.47
Lefty Grove	L	31	31	4	.886	5	41	30	27	289	249	62	175	3	2.05
George Earnshaw	R	31	21	7	.750	6	43	30	23	282	255	75	152	3	3.67
Rube Walberg	L	31	20	12	.625	3	44	35	19	291	298	109	106	0	3.74
Roy Mafaffey	R	28	15	4	.789	2	30	20	8	162	161	82	59	0	4.22
2 Waite Hoyt	R	31	10	5	.667	0	16	14	9	111	130	37	30	2	4.22
Eddie Rommel	R	33	7	5	.583	0	25	10	8	118	136	27	18	1	2.97
Hank McDonald	R	20	2	4	.333	0	19	10	1	70	62	41	23	1	3.73
Lew Krausse	R	19	1	0	1.000	0	3	1	1	11	6	6	1	0	4.09
Jim Peterson	R	22	0	1	.000	0	6	1	1	13	18	4	7	0	6.23
Bill Shores	R	27	0	3	.000	0	6	2	0	16	26	10	2	0	5.06
Sol Carter	R	22	0	0	.000	0	2	0	0	2	1	4	1	0	22.50
		28	94	59	.614	17	155	155	78	1410	1461	543	686	4	4.20
Lefty Gomez	L	22	21	9	.700	3	40	26	17	243	206	85	150	0	2.63
Red Ruffing	R	27	16	14	.533	2	37	30	19	237	240	87	132	1	4.40
Hank Johnson	R	25	13	8	.619	4	40	23	8	196	176	102	106	0	4.73
Herb Pennock	L	37	11	6	.647	0	25	25	12	189	247	30	65	1	4.28
Ed Wells	L	31	9	5	.643	2	27	10	6	117	130	37	34	0	4.31
George Pipgras	R	31	7	6	.538	3	36	14	6	138	134	58	59	0	3.78
Gordon Rhodes	R	23	6	3	.667	0	18	11	4	87	82	52	36	0	3.41
Roy Sherid	R	23	5	5	.500	2	17	8	3	74	94	24	39	0	5.70
Ivy Andrews	R	24	2	0	1.000	0	7	3	1	34	36	8	10	0	4.23
Jim Weaver	R	27	2	1	.667	0	17	5	2	58	66	29	28	0	5.27
Lefty Weinert	L	29	2	2	.500	0	17	0	0	25	31	19	24	0	6.12
Lou McEvoy	R	29	0	0	.000	1	6	0	0	12	19	12	3	0	12.75
		29	92	62	.597	24	156	156	60	1394	1434	498	582	6	3.76
General Crowder	R	32	18	11	.621	2	44	26	13	234	255	72	85	1	3.89
Firpo Marberry	R	32	16	4	.800	7	45	25	11	219	211	63	88	1	3.45
Lloyd Brown	L	26	15	14	.517	0	42	32	15	259	256	79	79	1	3.20
Carl Fischer	L	25	13	9	.591	3	46	23	7	191	207	80	96	0	4.38
Bump Hadley	R	26	11	10	.524	8	55	11	2	180	145	92	124	0	3.05
Sad Sam Jones	R	38	9	10	.474	1	25	24	8	148	185	47	58	1	4.32
Bobby Burke	L	24	8	3	.727	2	30	13	3	129	124	50	38	1	4.26
Walt Tauscher	R	29	1	0	1.000	0	6	0	0	12	24	4	5	0	7.50
Monty Weaver	R	25	1	0	1.000	0	3	1	1	10	11	6	6	0	4.50
Ad Liska (SA)	R	24	0	1	.000	0	2	1	0	4	9	1	2	0	6.75
Walt Masters	R	24	0	0	.000	1	3	0	0	9	7	4	1	0	2.00

CLEVELAND 4th 78-76 .506 30 — ROGER PECKINPAUGH

NAME	G by POS	B	AGE	G	AB	R	H	2B	3B	HR	RBI	BB	SO	SB	BA	SA
TOTALS			28	155	5445	885	1612	**321**	69	71	812	555	433	63	.296	.419
Eddie Morgan	1B117, 3B3	R	27	131	462	87	162	33	4	11	86	83	46	4	.351	.511
Johnny Hodapp	2B121	R	25	122	468	71	138	19	4	2	56	27	23	1	.295	.365
Ed Montague	SS64	R	25	64	193	27	55	8	3	1	26	21	22	3	.285	.373
2 Willie Kamm	3B114	R	31	114	410	68	121	31	5	0	66	64	13	13	.295	.395
Dick Porter	OF109, 2B1	L	29	114	414	82	129	24	3	1	38	56	36	6	.312	.391
Earl Averill	OF155	L	29	155	**627**	140	209	36	10	32	143	68	38	9	.333	.576
Joe Vosmik	OF147	R	21	149	591	80	189	36	14	7	117	38	30	7	.320	.464
Luke Sewell	C105	R	30	108	375	45	103	30	4	1	53	36	17	1	.275	.384
Johnny Burnett	SS63, 2B35, 3B21, OF1	L	29	111	427	85	128	25	5	1	52	39	25	5	.300	.389
Bibb Falk	OF33	L	32	79	161	30	49	13	1	2	28	17	13	1	.304	.435
Glenn Myatt	C58	L	33	65	195	21	48	14	2	1	29	21	13	2	.246	.354
Wes Ferrell	P40	R	23	48	116	24	37	6	1	9	30	10	21	0	.319	.621
Bob Seeds	OF33, 1B2	R	24	48	134	26	41	4	1	1	10	11	11	1	.306	.373
George Detore	3B13, SS10, 2B3	R	24	30	56	3	15	6	0	0	7	8	2	0	.268	.375
Jonah Goldman	SS30	R	24	30	62	0	8	1	0	0	3	4	6	1	.129	.145
Charlie Jamieson	OF7	L	38	28	43	7	13	2	1	0	4	5	1	1	.302	.395
1 Lew Fonseca	1B26	R	32	26	108	21	40	9	1	1	14	8	7	3	.370	.500
Odell Hale	3B15, 2B10, SS1	R	22	25	92	14	26	2	4	1	5	8	8	2	.283	.424
1 Bill Hunnefield	SS21, 2B1	B	32	21	71	13	17	4	1	0	4	9	4	3	.239	.324
Bruce Connatser	1B12	R	28	12	49	5	14	3	0	0	4	2	3	0	.286	.347
Moe Berg	C8	R	29	10	13	1	1	1	0	0	0	1	1	0	.077	.154
Joe Sprinz	C1	R	28	1	3	0	0	0	0	0	0	0	0	0	.000	.000

NAME	T	AGE	W	L	PCT	SV	G	GS	CG	IP	H	BB	SO	ShO	ERA
		26	78	76	.506	9	155	155	76	1355	1577	561	470	6	4.63
Wes Ferrell	R	23	22	12	.647	3	40	35	**27**	276	276	**130**	123	2	3.75
Willis Hudlin	R	25	15	14	.517	4	44	34	15	254	313	88	83	1	4.61
Mel Harder	R	21	13	14	.481	1	40	24	9	194	229	72	63	0	4.36
Clint Brown	R	27	11	15	.423	0	39	33	12	233	284	55	50	1	4.72
Sarge Connally	R	32	5	5	.500	1	17	9	5	86	87	50	37	0	4.19
Pete Jablonowski	R	27	4	4	.500	0	29	4	3	80	100	29	25	0	4.62
Oral Hildebrand	R	24	2	1	.667	0	5	2	2	27	25	13	6	0	4.33
Jake Miller (AJ)	L	33	2	1	.667	0	10	5	1	41	45	19	17	1	4.39
Milt Shoffner	L	25	2	3	.400	0	12	4	1	41	55	26	12	0	7.24
Fay Thomas	R	26	2	4	.333	0	16	2	1	49	63	32	25	0	5.14
Belve Bean	R	26	0	1	.000	0	4	0	0	7	11	4	3	0	6.43
Howard Craighead	R	23	0	0	.000	0	4	0	0	6	8	2	2	0	6.00
2 Pete Donohue	R	30	0	0	.000	0	2	0	0	5	9	5	4	0	9.00
Roxie Lawson	R	25	0	2	.000	0	17	3	0	56	72	36	20	0	7.55

ST. LOUIS 5th 63-91 .409 45 — BILL KILLEFER

NAME	G by POS	B	AGE	G	AB	R	H	2B	3B	HR	RBI	BB	SO	SB	BA	SA
TOTALS			27	154	5374	722	1455	287	62	76	666	488	**580**	73	.271	.390
Jack Burns	1B143	L	23	144	570	75	148	27	7	4	70	42	58	19	.260	.353
Oscar Melillo	2B151	R	31	151	617	89	189	34	11	2	75	37	29	7	.306	.407
Jim Levey	SS139	R	24	139	498	53	104	19	2	5	38	35	83	13	.209	.285
Red Kress	3B84, OF40, SS38, 1B10	R	24	150	605	87	188	46	8	16	114	46	48	3	.311	.493
Tom Jenkins	OF58	L	33	81	230	20	61	7	2	3	25	17	25	1	.265	.352
Fred Schulte	OF134	R	30	134	553	100	168	32	7	9	65	56	49	6	.304	.436
Goose Goslin	OF151	L	30	151	591	114	194	42	10	24	105	80	41	9	.328	.555
Rick Ferrell	C108	R	25	117	386	47	118	30	4	3	57	56	12	2	.306	.427
Lin Storti	3B67, 2B7	B	24	86	273	32	60	15	4	3	26	15	50	0	.220	.337
Larry Bettencourt	OF58	R	25	74	206	27	53	9	2	3	26	31	35	4	.257	.364
Earl McNeely	OF36	R	33	49	102	12	23	4	0	0	15	9	5	4	.225	.265
Ed Grimes	3B22, 2B4, SS3	R	25	43	57	9	15	1	2	0	5	9	3	1	.263	.351
Benny Bengough	C37	R	32	40	140	6	35	4	1	0	12	4	4	0	.250	.293
Russ Young	C16	B	28	16	34	2	4	0	0	1	2	2	4	0	.118	.206
Frank Waddey	OF7	L	25	14	22	3	6	1	0	0	2	2	3	0	.273	.318
Buck Stanton	OF1	L	25	13	15	3	3	2	0	0	0	0	6	0	.200	.333
Jack Crouch	C7	R	28	8	12	0	0	0	0	0	1	0	4	0	.000	.000
Frank O'Rourke	SS2, 1B1	R	36	8	9	0	2	0	0	0	0	0	1	1	.222	.222
Nap Kloza	OF3	R	27	3	7	1	1	0	0	0	0	1	4	0	.143	.143

NAME	T	AGE	W	L	PCT	SV	G	GS	CG	IP	H	BB	SO	ShO	ERA
		26	63	91	.409	10	154	154	65	1362	**1623**	448	436	4	4.76
Lefty Stewart	L	30	14	17	.452	0	36	33	20	258	287	85	89	1	4.40
George Blaeholder	R	27	11	15	.423	0	35	32	13	226	280	56	79	1	4.54
Sam Gray	R	33	11	**24**	.314	2	43	**37**	13	258	**323**	54	88	0	5.09
Dick Coffman	R	24	9	13	.409	1	32	17	11	169	159	51	39	2	3.89
Wally Hebert	L	23	6	7	.462	0	23	13	5	103	128	43	26	0	5.07
Rip Collins	R	25	5	5	.500	0	17	14	2	107	130	38	34	0	3.79
Chad Kimsey	R	24	4	6	.400	7	42	1	0	94	121	27	27	0	4.40
Rollie Stiles	R	24	3	1	.750	0	34	2	0	81	112	60	32	0	7.22
2 Garland Braxton	L	31	0	0	.000	0	11	1	0	18	27	10	7	0	10.50
Bob Cooney	R	23	0	3	.000	0	5	4	1	39	46	20	13	0	4.15
Jess Doyle	R	33	0	0	.000	0	1	0	0	1	3	1	0	0	27.00
Fred Stiely	L	30	0	0	.000	0	4	0	0	7	7	3	2	0	6.43

BOSTON 6th 62-90 .408 45 — SHANO COLLINS

NAME	G by POS	B	AGE	G	AB	R	H	2B	3B	HR	RBI	BB	SO	SB	BA	SA
TOTALS			29	153	5379	625	1409	289	34	37	572	405	565	43	.262	.349
Bill Sweeney	1B124	R	27	131	498	48	147	30	3	1	58	20	30	5	.295	.373
Rabbit Warstler	2B42, SS19	R	27	66	181	20	44	5	3	0	10	15	27	2	.243	.304
Hal Rhyne	SS147	R	32	147	565	75	154	34	3	0	51	57	41	3	.273	.343
Otto Miller	3B75, 2B25	R	30	107	389	38	106	12	1	0	43	15	20	1	.272	.308
Earl Webb	OF151	L	32	151	589	96	196	**67**	3	14	103	70	51	2	.333	.528
Tom Oliver	OF148	R	28	148	586	52	162	35	5	0	70	25	17	4	.276	.353
J. Rothrock	OF79, 2B23, 1B8, 3B2, SS1	B	26	133	475	81	132	32	3	4	42	47	48	13	.278	.383
Charlie Berry	C102	R	28	111	357	41	101	16	2	6	49	29	38	4	.283	.389
Urban Pickering	3B74, 2B16	R	32	103	341	48	86	13	4	9	52	32	53	3	.252	.393
Al VanCamp	OF59, 1B25	R	27	101	324	34	89	15	4	0	33	20	24	3	.275	.346
Tom Winsett	OF8	L	21	64	76	6	15	1	0	1	7	4	21	0	.197	.250
Ed Connolly	C41	R	22	42	93	3	7	1	0	0	3	5	18	0	.075	.086
Bobby Reeves (BH)	2B29, P1	R	27	36	84	11	14	2	2	0	1	14	16	0	.167	.238
1 Muddy Ruel	C30	R	35	33	83	6	25	5	0	0	6	9	6	0	.301	.361
Ollie Marquardt	2B13	R	28	17	39	4	7	1	0	0	2	3	4	0	.179	.205
2 Marty McManus	3B11, 2B7	R	31	17	62	8	18	4	0	1	9	8	1	1	.209	.403
Gene Rye	OF10	L	24	17	39	3	7	0	0	0	1	2	5	0	.179	.179
Marv Olson	2B15	R	24	15	53	8	10	1	0	0	5	9	3	0	.189	.208
Russ Scarritt	OF9	L	28	10	39	2	6	1	0	0	1	2	2	0	.154	.179

George Stumpf 20 L 7-28, Howie Storie 20 R 2-17, Pat Creeden 25 L 0-8, John Smith 24 B 2-15, Johnny Lucas 28 R 0-2, Bill McWilliams 20 R 0-2, Bill Marshall 22 R 0-0

NAME	T	AGE	W	L	PCT	SV	G	GS	CG	IP	H	BB	SO	ShO	ERA
		28	62	90	.408	10	153	153	61	1367	1559	473	365	5	4.60
Danny MacFayden	R	26	16	12	.571	0	35	32	17	231	263	79	74	1	4.01
Wilcy Moore	R	34	11	13	.458	**10**	53	15	8	185	195	55	37	1	3.89
Jack Russell	R	25	10	18	.357	0	36	31	13	232	298	65	45	0	5.16
Ed Durham	R	23	8	10	.444	0	38	15	7	165	175	50	53	2	4.26
Bob Kline (IL)	R	21	5	5	.500	0	28	10	3	98	110	35	25	0	4.41
Hod Lisenbee	R	32	5	12	.294	0	41	17	6	165	190	49	42	0	5.18
Ed Morris	R	31	5	7	.417	0	37	14	3	131	131	74	46	0	4.74
Milt Gaston (SA)	R	35	2	13	.133	0	23	18	4	119	137	41	33	0	4.46
Jim Brillheart	L	27	0	0	.000	0	11	1	0	20	27	15	7	0	5.40
Walter Murphy	R	23	0	0	.000	0	2	0	0	2	4	1	0	0	9.00
Jud McLaughlin	L	19	0	0	.000	0	9	0	0	12	23	8	3	0	12.00
Bobby Reeves (BH)	R	27	0	0	.000	0	1	0	0	7	6	1	0	0	3.86

DETROIT 7th 61-93 .396 47 — BUCKY HARRIS

NAME	G by POS	B	AGE	G	AB	R	H	2B	3B	HR	RBI	BB	SO	SB	BA	SA
TOTALS			26	154	5430	651	1456	292	69	43	599	480	468	117	.268	.371
Dale Alexander	1B126, OF4	R	28	135	517	75	168	47	3	3	87	64	35	5	.325	.445
Charlie Gehringer (AJ)	2B78, 1B9	L	28	101	383	67	119	24	5	4	53	29	15	13	.311	.431
Billy Rogell	SS48	B	26	48	185	21	56	12	3	2	24	24	17	8	.303	.432
1 Marty McManus	3B79, 2B21, 1B1	R	31	107	362	39	98	17	3	3	53	49	22	7	.271	.359
Roy Johnson	OF150	L	28	151	621	107	173	37	**19**	8	55	72	51	33	.279	.438
Hub Walker	OF66	L	24	90	252	27	72	13	1	0	16	23	25	10	.286	.345
John Stone	OF147	L	25	147	584	86	191	28	11	10	76	56	48	13	.327	.464
Ray Hayworth	C88	R	27	88	273	28	70	10	3	0	25	19	27	0	.256	.315
Mark Koenig	2B55, SS35, P3	B	28	106	364	33	92	24	4	1	39	14	12	8	.253	.349
Marv Owen	SS37, 3B37, 1B27, 2B4	R	25	105	377	35	84	11	6	3	39	29	38	2	.223	.308
Frank Doljack	OF54	R	23	63	187	20	52	13	3	4	20	15	17	3	.278	.444
Gee Walker	OF44	R	23	59	189	20	56	17	2	1	28	14	21	10	.296	.423
George Uhle	P29	R	32	53	90	8	22	6	0	2	7	8	8	0	.244	.378
Johnny Grabowski	C39	R	31	40	136	9	32	7	1	1	14	6	19	0	.235	.324
Nolen Richardson	3B38	R	28	38	148	13	40	9	2	0	16	6	3	2	.270	.358
Wally Schang	C30	B	41	30	76	9	14	2	0	0	2	14	11	1	.184	.211
Bill Akers	SS21, 2B2	R	26	29	66	5	13	2	2	0	3	7	6	0	.197	.288
Lou Brower	SS20, 2B2	R	31	21	62	3	10	1	0	0	6	8	5	1	.161	.177
2 Muddy Ruel	C14	R	35	14	50	1	6	1	0	0	3	5	1	0	.120	.140

George Quellich 28 R 12-54, Joe Dugan 34 R 4-17, Bucky Harris 34 R 1-8, Gene Desautels 24 R 1-11, Ivey **Shiver 24 R 1-9**

NAME	T	AGE	W	L	PCT	SV	G	GS	CG	IP	H	BB	SO	ShO	ERA
		28	61	93	.396	6	154	154	86	1392	1549	**597**	511	5	4.56
Vic Sorrell	R	30	13	14	.481	1	35	32	19	247	267	114	99	1	4.12
Earl Whitehill	L	31	13	16	.448	0	34	34	22	272	287	118	81	0	4.07
George Uhle	R	32	11	12	.478	2	29	18	15	193	190	49	63	1	3.50
Tommy Bridges	R	24	8	16	.333	0	35	23	8	173	182	108	105	1	5.00
Art Herring	R	24	7	13	.350	1	35	16	9	165	186	67	64	0	4.31
Chief Hogsett	L	27	3	9	.250	2	22	12	5	112	150	33	47	0	5.97
1 Waite Hoyt	R	31	3	8	.273	0	16	12	5	92	124	32	10	0	5.87
Charlie Sullivan	R	**28**	3	2	.600	0	31	4	2	99	109	46	28	0	4.73
Orlin Collier	R	**24**	0	1	.000	0	2	2	0	10	17	7	3	0	8.10
Mark Koenig	R	28	0	0	.000	0	3	0	0	7	7	11	3	0	6.43
Whit Wyatt (SA)	R	23	0	2	.000	0	4	1	1	21	30	12	8	0	8.57

CHICAGO 8th 56-97 .366 51.5 — DONIE BUSH

NAME	G by POS	B	AGE	G	AB	R	H	2B	3B	HR	RBI	BB	SO	SB	BA	SA
TOTALS			28	156	5481	704	1423	238	69	27	649	483	445	94	.260	.343
Lu Blue	1B155	B	34	155	589	119	179	23	15	1	62	127	60	13	.304	.399
John Kerr	2B117, 3B7, SS1	R	32	128	444	51	119	17	2	2	50	35	22	9	.268	.329
Bill Cissell	SS83, 2B23, 3B1	R	27	109	409	42	90	13	5	1	46	16	26	18	.220	.284
Billy Sullivan	3B83, OF2, 1B1	L	20	92	363	48	100	16	5	2	33	20	14	4	.275	.364
Carl Reynolds	OF109	R	28	118	462	71	134	24	14	6	77	24	26	17	.290	.442
Johnny Watwood	OF102, 1B4	L	24	128	367	51	104	16	6	1	47	56	30	9	.283	.368
2 Lew Fonseca	OF95, 2B21, 1B2, 3B1	R	32	121	465	65	139	26	5	2	71	32	22	4	.299	.389
Bennie Tate	C85	L	29	89	273	27	73	12	3	0	22	26	10	1	.267	.333
Bob Fothergill	OF74	R	33	108	312	25	88	9	4	3	56	17	17	2	.282	.365
Luke Appling	SS76, 2B1	R	24	96	297	36	69	13	4	1	28	29	27	9	.232	.313
Frank Grube	C81	R	26	88	265	29	58	13	2	1	24	22	22	2	.219	.294
Irv Jeffries	3B61, 2B6, SS5	R	25	79	223	29	50	10	0	2	16	14	9	3	.224	.296
Mel Simons	OF59	L	31	68	189	24	52	9	0	0	12	12	17	1	.275	.323
Smead Jolley	OF23	L	29	54	110	5	33	11	0	3	28	7	4	0	.300	.482
Fred Eichrodt	OF32	R	28	34	117	9	25	5	1	0	15	1	8	0	.214	.274
Bill Norman	OF17	R	20	24	55	7	10	2	0	0	6	4	10	0	.182	.218
1 Willie Kamm	3B18	R	31	18	59	9	15	4	0	0	9	7	6	1	.254	.322
Butch Henline	C4	R	36	11	15	2	1	1	0	0	2	2	4	0	.067	.133
Hank Garrity	C7	R	23	8	14	0	3	1	0	0	2	1	2	0	.214	.286
Bruce Campbell	OF4	L	21	4	17	4	7	2	0	2	5	0	4	0	.412	.882

NAME	T	AGE	W	L	PCT	SV	G	GS	CG	IP	H	BB	SO	ShO	ERA
		29	56	**97**	.366	10	156	156	54	1387	1611	588	420	6	5.06
Vic Frasier	R	26	13	15	.464	4	46	29	13	254	258	127	87	2	4.46
Pat Caraway	L	25	10	**24**	.294	2	51	32	11	220	268	101	55	1	6.22
Red Faber	R	42	10	14	.417	1	44	19	5	184	210	57	49	1	3.82
Tommy Thomas	R	31	10	14	.417	2	42	36	11	242	296	69	71	2	4.80
Hal McKain (AJ)	R	24	6	9	.400	0	27	8	3	112	134	57	39	0	5.71
Ted Lyons	R	30	4	6	.400	0	22	12	7	101	117	33	16	0	4.01
Bob Weiland	L	25	2	7	.222	0	15	8	3	75	75	46	38	0	5.16
Biggs Wehde	R	24	1	0	1.000	0	8	0	0	16	19	10	3	0	6.75
Grant Bowler	R	23	0	1	.000	0	13	3	1	35	40	24	15	0	5.40
1 Garland Braxton	L	31	0	3	.000	1	17	3	0	47	71	23	28	0	6.89
Lou Garland	R	25	0	2	.000	0	7	2	0	17	30	14	4	0	10.06
Jim Moore	R	27	0	2	.000	0	33	4	0	84	93	27	15	0	4.93

ST. LOUIS 1st 101-53 .656 — GABBY STREET

	NAME	G by POS	B	AGE	G	AB	R	H	2B	3B	HR	RBI	BB	SO	SB	BA	SA
	TOTALS			29	154	5435	815	1554	**353**	74	60	751	432	475	**114**	.286	.411
	Jim Bottomley	1B93	L	31	108	382	73	133	34	5	9	75	34	24	3	.348	.534
	Frankie Frisch	2B129	B	32	131	518	96	161	24	4	4	82	45	13	**28**	.311	.396
	Charlie Gelbert	SS130	R	25	131	447	61	129	29	5	1	62	54	31	7	.289	.383
	Sparky Adams	3B138, SS6	R	36	143	608	97	178	**46**	5	1	40	42	24	16	.293	.390
	George Watkins	OF129	L	31	131	503	93	145	30	13	13	51	31	66	15	.288	.477
	Pepper Martin	OF110	R	27	123	413	68	124	32	8	7	75	30	40	16	.300	.467
	Chick Hafey	OF118	R	28	122	450	94	157	35	8	16	95	39	43	11	**.3489**	.569
	Jimmie Wilson	C110	R	30	115	383	45	105	20	2	0	51	28	15	5	.274	.337
	Ripper Collins	1B68, OF3	B	27	89	279	34	84	20	10	4	59	18	24	1	.301	.487
	Ernie Orsatti	OF45, 1B1	L	28	70	158	27	46	16	6	0	19	14	16	1	.291	.468
	Gus Mancuso	C56	R	25	67	187	13	49	16	1	1	23	18	13	2	.262	.374
	Andy High	3B23, 2B19	L	33	63	131	20	35	6	1	0	19	24	4	0	.267	.328
2	Jake Flowers	SS22, 2B20, 3B1	R	29	45	137	19	34	11	1	2	19	9	6	7	.248	.387
2	Wally Roettger	OF42	R	28	45	151	16	43	12	2	0	17	9	14	0	.285	.391
1	Taylor Douthit	OF36	R	30	36	133	21	44	11	2	1	21	11	9	1	.331	.466
	Ray Blades	OF20	R	34	35	67	10	19	4	0	1	5	10	7	1	.284	.388
	Mike Gonzalez	C12	R	40	15	19	1	2	0	0	0	3	0	3	0	.105	.105
	Joe Benes	SS6, 2B2, 3B1	R	30	10	12	1	2	0	0	0	0	2	1	0	.167	.167
	Joel Hunt	OF1	R	25	4	1	2	0	0	0	0	0	0	1	0	.000	.000
	Ray Cunningham	3B3	R	23	3	4	0	0	0	0	0	1	0	0	0	.000	.000
	Eddie Delker	3B1	R	24	1	2	0	1	1	0	0	2	0	0	0	.500	1.000
	Gabby Street	C1	R	48	1	1	0	0	0	0	0	0	0	0	0	.000	.000

	NAME	T	AGE	W	L	PCT	SV	G	GS	CG	IP	H	BB	SO	ShO	ERA
			31	**101**	53	**656**	**20**	154	154	80	1385	1470	449	**626**	**17**	3.45
	Wild Bill Hallahan	L	28	**19**	9	.679	4	37	30	16	249	242	**112**	**159**	3	3.29
	Paul Derringer	R	24	18	8	**.692**	2	35	23	15	212	225	65	134	4	3.35
	Burleigh Grimes	R	37	17	9	.654	0	29	28	17	212	240	59	67	3	3.65
	Jesse Haines	R	37	12	3	.800	0	19	17	8	122	134	28	27	2	3.02
	Syl Johnson	R	30	11	9	.550	2	32	24	12	186	186	29	82	2	3.00
	Flint Rhem	R	30	11	10	.524	1	33	26	10	207	214	60	72	2	3.57
	Jim Lindsey	R	33	6	4	.600	7	35	2	1	75	77	45	32	1	2.76
	Allyn Stout	R	26	6	0	1.000	3	30	3	1	73	87	34	40	0	4.19
	Tony Kaufmann	R	30	1	1	.500	1	15	1	0	49	65	17	13	0	6.06

NEW YORK 2nd 87-65 .572 13 — JOHN McGRAW

	NAME	G by POS	B	AGE	G	AB	R	H	2B	3B	HR	RBI	BB	SO	SB	BA	SA
	TOTALS			28	153	5372	768	1554	251	64	**101**	727	383	395	83	.289	.416
	Bill Terry	1B153	L	32	153	611	**121**	213	43	**20**	9	112	47	36	8	.3486	.529
	Hugh Critz (AJ)	2B54	R	30	66	238	33	69	7	2	4	17	8	17	4	.290	.387
	Travis Jackson	SS145	R	27	145	555	65	172	26	10	5	71	36	23	13	.310	.420
	Johnny Vergez	3B152	R	24	152	565	67	157	24	2	13	81	29	65	11	.278	.396
	Fred Lindstrom (BF)	OF73, 2B4	R	25	78	303	38	91	12	6	5	36	26	12	5	.300	.429
	Mel Ott	OF137	L	22	138	497	104	145	23	8	29	115	**80**	44	10	.292	.545
	Freddy Leach	OF125	L	33	129	515	75	159	30	5	6	61	29	9	4	.309	.421
	Shanty Hogan	C113	R	25	123	396	42	119	17	1	12	65	29	29	1	.301	.439
	Ethan Allen	OF77	R	27	94	298	58	98	18	2	5	43	15	15	6	.329	.453
	Chick Fullis	OF68, 2B9	R	27	89	302	61	99	15	2	3	28	23	13	13	.328	.421
	Bob O'Farrell	C80	R	34	85	174	11	39	8	3	1	19	21	23	0	.224	.322
	Doc Marshall	2B47, SS11, 3B3	R	25	68	194	15	39	6	2	0	10	8	8	1	.201	.253
3	Bill Hunnefield	2B56, SS5	B	32	64	196	23	53	5	0	1	17	9	16	3	.270	.311
	Sam Leslie	1B6	L	25	53	53	11	16	4	0	3	5	1	2	3	.302	.547
	Freddie Fitzsimmons	P35	R	29	35	92	16	21	3	1	4	18	7	18	0	.228	.413
	Francis Healy	C6	R	21	6	7	1	1	0	0	0	0	0	0	0	.143	.143
	Jo-Jo Moore	OF1	L	22	4	8	0	2	1	0	0	3	0	1	1	.250	.375
	Gil English	3B3	R	21	3	8	0	0	0	0	0	0	1	3	0	.000	.000

	NAME	T	AGE	W	L	PCT	SV	G	GS	CG	IP	H	BB	SO	ShO	ERA
			30	87	65	.572	12	153	153	90	1360	1341	422	**570**	**17**	**3.30**
	Freddie Fitzsimmons	R	29	18	11	.621	0	35	33	19	254	242	62	78	4	3.05
	Bill Walker	L	27	16	9	.640	3	37	38	19	239	212	64	121	**6**	**2.26**
	Carl Hubbell	L	28	14	12	.538	3	36	30	21	248	211	67	156	4	2.65
	Clarence Mitchell	L	40	13	11	.542	0	27	25	13	190	221	52	39	0	4.07
	Jack Berly	R	28	7	8	.467	0	27	11	4	111	114	51	45	1	3.89
	Jim Mooney	L	24	7	1	.875	0	10	8	6	72	71	16	38	2	2.00
	Bill Morrell	R	31	5	3	.625	1	20	7	2	66	83	27	16	0	4.36
	Tiny Chaplin	R	25	3	0	1.000	1	16	3	1	42	39	16	7	0	3.21
	Roy Parmelee	R	24	2	2	.500	0	13	5	4	59	47	33	30	0	3.66
	Joe Heving	R	30	1	6	.143	3	22	0	0	42	48	11	26	0	4.93
	Hal Schumacher	R	20	1	1	.500	1	8	2	1	18	31	14	11	0	11.00
1	Pete Donohue	R	30	0	1	.000	0	4	1	0	11	14	4	4	0	5.73
	Ray Lucas	R	22	0	0	.000	0	1	0	0	2	1	1	0	0	4.50
	Emil Planeta	R	22	0	0	.000	0	2	0	0	5	7	4	0	0	10.80

CHICAGO 3rd 84-70 .545 17 — ROGERS HORNSBY

	NAME	G by POS	B	AGE	G	AB	R	H	2B	3B	HR	RBI	BB	SO	SB	BA	SA
	TOTALS			29	156	**5451**	**828**	**1578**	340	67	84	**766**	**577**	**641**	49	**.289**	**.423**
	Charlie Grimm	1B144	L	32	146	531	65	176	33	11	4	66	53	29	1	.331	.458
	Rogers Hornsby	2B69, 3B26	R	35	100	357	64	118	37	1	16	90	56	23	1	.331	.574
	Woody English	SS138, 3B18	R	24	156	634	117	202	38	8	2	53	68	80	12	.319	.413
	Les Bell	3B70	R	29	75	252	30	71	17	1	4	32	19	22	0	.282	.405
	Kiki Cuyler	OF153	R	31	154	613	110	202	37	12	9	88	72	54	13	.330	.473
	Hack Wilson	OF103	R	31	112	395	66	103	22	4	13	61	63	69	1	.261	.435
	Danny Taylor	OF67	R	30	88	270	48	81	13	6	5	41	31	46	4	.300	.448
	Gabby Hartnett	C105	R	30	116	380	53	107	32	1	8	70	52	48	3	.282	.434
	Billy Jurges	3B54, 2B33, SS3	R	23	88	293	34	59	15	5	0	23	25	41	2	.201	.287
	Riggs Stephenson (BN)	OF66	R	33	80	263	34	84	14	4	1	52	37	14	1	.319	.414
	Footsie Blair	2B44, 1B23, 3B1	L	27	86	240	31	62	19	5	3	29	14	26	1	.258	.417
	Vince Barton	OF61	L	23	66	239	45	57	10	1	13	50	21	40	1	.238	.452
2	Rollie Hemsley	C53	R	24	66	204	28	63	17	4	3	31	17	30	4	.309	.475
	Johnny Moore	OF22	L	29	39	104	19	25	3	1	2	16	7	5	1	.240	.346
	Billy Herman	2B25	R	21	25	98	14	32	7	0	0	16	13	6	2	.327	.398
	Jimmy Adair	SS18	R	24	18	76	9	21	3	1	0	3	1	8	1	.276	.342
	Zack Taylor	C5	R	32	8	4	0	1	0	0	0	0	2	1	0	.250	.250
1	Earl Grace	C2	L	24	7	9	2	1	0	0	0	1	4	1	0	.111	.111
	Mike Kreevich	OF4	R	23	5	12	0	2	0	0	0	0	0	6	1	.167	.167

	NAME	T	AGE	W	L	PCT	SV	G	GS	CG	IP	H	BB	SO	ShO	ERA
			29	84	70	.545	8	156	156	80	1386	1448	**524**	541	8	3.97
	Charlie Root	R	32	17	14	.548	2	39	31	19	251	240	71	131	3	3.48
	Guy Bush	R	29	16	8	.667	2	39	24	14	180	190	66	54	1	4.50
	Pat Malone	R	28	16	9	.640	0	36	30	12	228	229	88	112	2	3.91
	Bob Smith	R	33	15	12	.556	2	36	29	18	240	239	62	63	2	3.23
	Les Sweetland	L	29	8	7	.533	0	26	14	9	130	156	61	32	0	5.05
	Jakie May (CN)	L	35	5	5	.500	2	31	4	1	79	81	43	38	0	3.87
	Ed Baecht	R	24	2	4	.333	0	22	6	2	67	64	32	34	0	3.76
	Lon Warneke	R	22	2	4	.333	0	20	7	3	64	67	37	27	0	3.23
	John Welch	R	24	2	1	.667	0	8	3	1	34	39	10	7	0	3.71
	Bud Treachout	L	27	1	2	.333	0	27	3	1	61	79	28	14	0	5.75
1	Sheriff Blake	R	31	0	4	.000	0	16	5	0	50	64	26	29	0	5.22

BROOKLYN 4th 79-73 .520 21 — WILBERT ROBINSON

	NAME	G by POS	B	AGE	G	AB	R	H	2B	3B	HR	RBI	BB	SO	SB	BA	SA
	TOTALS			29	153	5309	681	1464	240	**77**	71	633	409	512	45	.276	.390
	Del Bissonette	1B152	L	31	152	587	90	170	19	14	12	87	59	53	4	.290	.431
	Neal Finn	2B112	R	29	118	413	46	113	22	2	0	45	21	42	2	.274	.337
	Gordon Slade	SS82, 3B2	R	26	85	272	27	65	13	2	1	29	23	28	2	.239	.313
	Wally Gilbert	3B145	R	30	145	552	60	147	25	6	0	46	39	38	3	.266	.333
	Babe Herman	OF150	L	28	151	610	93	191	43	16	18	97	50	65	17	.313	.525
	Johnny Frederick	OF145	L	30	146	611	81	165	34	8	17	71	31	46	2	.270	.435
	Lefty O'Doul	OF132	L	34	134	512	85	172	32	11	7	75	48	16	5	.336	.482
	Al Lopez	C105	R	22	111	360	38	97	13	4	0	40	28	33	1	.269	.328
	Glenn Wright	SS75	R	30	77	268	36	76	9	4	9	32	14	35	1	.284	.448
	Fresco Thompson	2B43, SS10, 3B5	R	29	74	181	26	48	6	1	1	21	23	16	5	.265	.326
	Ernie Lombardi	C50	R	23	73	182	20	54	7	1	4	23	12	12	1	.297	.412
	Rube Bressler	OF35, 1B1	R	36	67	153	22	43	4	5	0	26	11	10	0	.281	.373
	Val Picinich	C15	R	34	24	45	5	12	4	0	1	4	4	9	1	.267	.422
1	Jake Flowers	2B6, SS1	R	29	22	31	3	7	0	0	0	1	7	4	1	.226	.226
	Denny Sothern	OF10	R	27	19	31	10	5	1	0	0	0	4	8	0	.161	.194
	Jack Warner (JJ)	SS2, 3B1	R	27	9	4	2	2	0	0	0	0	1	1	0	.500	.500
	Ike Boone		L	34	6	5	0	1	0	0	0	0	2	2	0	.200	.200
	Bobby Reis	3B6	R	22	6	17	3	5	0	0	0	2	2	0	0	.294	.294
	Max Rosenfeld	OF3	R	28	3	9	0	2	1	0	0	0	1	1	0	.222	.333
	Alta Cohen	OF1	L	22	1	3	1	2	0	0	0	0	0	0	0	.667	.667
1	Harvey Hendrick		L	33	1	1	0	0	0	0	0	0	0	0	0	.000	.000

	NAME	T	AGE	W	L	PCT	SV	G	GS	CG	IP	H	BB	SO	ShO	ERA
			33	79	73	.520	18	153	153	64	1356	1520	351	546	9	3.84
	Watty Clark	L	29	14	10	.583	1	34	28	16	233	243	52	96	3	3.21
	Joe Shaute	L	31	11	8	.579	0	25	19	6	129	162	32	50	0	4.81
	Dazzy Vance	R	40	11	13	.458	0	30	29	12	219	221	53	150	2	3.37
	Fred Heimach	L	30	9	7	.563	1	31	10	7	135	145	23	43	1	3.47
	Sloppy Thurston	R	32	9	9	.500	0	24	17	11	143	175	39	23	0	3.97
	Dolf Luque	R	40	7	6	.538	0	19	15	5	103	122	27	25	0	4.54
	Ray Phelps	R	27	7	9	.438	0	28	26	3	149	184	44	50	2	5.01
	Jack Quinn	R	47	5	4	.556	**15**	39	1	0	64	65	24	25	0	2.67
	Van Lingle Mungo	R	20	3	1	.750	0	5	4	2	31	27	13	12	1	2.32
	Pea Ridge Day	R	32	2	2	.500	1	22	2	1	57	75	13	30	0	4.58
	Cy Moore	R	26	1	2	.333	0	23	1	1	62	62	13	35	0	3.77
	Phil Gallivan	R	24	0	1	.000	0	6	1	0	15	23	7	1	0	5.40
	Earl Mattingly	R	26	0	1	.000	0	8	0	0	14	15	10	6	0	2.57
1	Ray Moss	R	29	0	0	.000	0	1	0	0	1	1	1	0	0	0.00

PITTSBURGH 5th 75-79 .487 26 — JEWEL ENS

	NAME	G by POS	B	AGE	G	AB	R	H	2B	3B	HR	RBI	BB	SO	SB	BA	SA
	TOTALS			27	155	5360	636	1425	243	70	41	597	493	454	59	.266	.360
	George Grantham	1B78, 2B51	L	31	127	465	91	142	26	6	10	46	71	50	5	.305	.452
	Tony Piet	2B44, SS1	R	24	44	167	22	50	12	4	0	24	13	24	10	.299	.419
	Tommy Thevenow	SS120	R	27	120	404	35	86	12	1	0	38	28	22	0	.213	.248
	Pie Traynor	3B155	R	31	155	615	81	183	37	15	2	103	54	28	6	.298	.416
	Paul Waner	OF138, 1B10	L	28	150	559	88	180	35	10	6	70	73	21	6	.322	.453
	Lloyd Waner	OF153, 2B1	L	25	154	**681**	90	**214**	25	13	4	57	39	16	7	.314	.407
	Adam Comorosky	OF90	R	26	99	350	37	85	12	1	1	48	34	28	11	.243	.291
	Eddie Phillips	C103	R	30	106	353	30	82	18	3	7	44	41	49	1	.232	.360
	Gus Suhr	1B76	L	25	87	270	26	57	13	4	4	32	38	25	4	.211	.333
	Woody Jensen	OF67	L	23	73	267	43	65	5	4	3	17	10	18	4	.243	.326
	Ben Sankey	SS49, 2B2, 3B2	R	23	57	132	14	30	2	5	0	14	14	10	0	.227	.318
	Howie Groskloss	2B39, SS3	R	23	53	161	13	45	7	2	0	20	11	16	1	.280	.348
	Erv Brame	P26	R	29	48	95	6	26	4	1	0	15	4	16	0	.274	.337
2	Earl Grace	C45	L	24	47	150	8	42	6	1	1	20	13	5	0	.280	.353
	Jim Mosolf	OF4	L	25	39	44	7	11	1	0	1	8	8	5	0	.250	.341
	Fred Bennett	OF21	R	29	32	89	6	25	5	0	1	7	7	4	0	.281	.371
	Bill Regan	2B28	R	32	28	104	8	21	8	0	1	10	5	19	2	.202	.308
	Hal Finney	C6	R	25	10	26	2	8	1	0	0	2	0	1	1	.308	.346
1	Rollie Hemsley	C9	R	24	10	35	3	6	3	0	0	1	3	3	0	.171	.257
	Pete McClanahan		R	24	7	4	2	2	0	0	0	0	2	0	0	.500	.500
	Bill Steinecke	C1	R	24	4	4	0	0	0	0	0	0	0	1	0	.000	.000

	NAME	T	AGE	W	L	PCT	SV	G	GS	CG	IP	H	BB	SO	ShO	ERA
			29	75	79	.487	5	155	155	89	**1390**	1489	442	345	9	3.66
	Heinie Meine	R	35	**19**	13	.594	0	36	**35**	22	**284**	278	87	58	3	2.98
	Larry French	L	23	15	13	.536	1	39	33	20	276	**301**	70	73	1	3.26
	Ray Kremer	R	38	11	15	.423	0	30	30	15	230	246	65	58	1	3.33
	Glenn Spencer	R	25	11	12	.478	3	38	18	11	187	180	65	51	1	3.42
	Erv Brame	R	29	9	13	.409	0	26	21	15	180	211	45	33	2	4.20
	Bob Osborn	R	28	6	1	.857	0	27	2	0	65	85	20	9	0	4.98
	Bill Harris	R	31	2	2	.500	0	4	4	3	31	21	9	10	1	0.87
	Spades Wood	L	22	2	6	.250	0	15	10	2	64	69	46	33	0	6.05
	Andy Bednar	R	**22**	0	0	.000	0	3	0	0	4	10	0	2	0	11.25
	George Grant	R	28	0	0	.000	0	11	0	0	17	28	7	6	0	7.41
	Steve Swetonic (SA)	R	27	0	2	.000	1	14	0	0	28	28	16	8	0	3.86
	Claude Willoughby	R	32	0	2	.000	0	9	2	1	26	32	12	4	0	6.23
	Gus Dugas (BJ) 24															

PHILADELPHIA 6th 66-88 .429 35 — BURT SHOTTON

NAME	G by POS	B	AGE	G	AB	R	H	2B	3B	HR	RBI	BB	SO	SB	BA	SA
TOTALS			26	155	5375	684	1502	299	52	81	649	437	492	42	.279	.400
Don Hurst	1B135	L	25	137	489	63	149	37	5	11	91	64	28	8	.305	.468
Les Mallon	2B97, 1B5, SS3, 3B3	R	25	122	375	41	116	19	2	1	45	29	40	0	.309	.379
Dick Bartell	SS133, 2B2	R	23	135	554	88	160	43	7	0	34	27	38	6	.289	.392
Pinky Whitney	3B128	R	26	130	501	64	144	36	5	9	74	30	38	6	.287	.433
Buzz Arlett	OF94, 1B13	B	32	121	418	65	131	26	7	18	72	45	39	3	.313	.538
Fred Brickell	OF122	L	24	130	514	77	130	14	5	1	31	42	39	5	.253	.305
Chuck Klein	OF148	L	26	148	594	**121**	200	34	10	**31**	**121**	59	49	7	.337	**.584**
Spud Davis	C114	R	26	120	393	30	128	32	1	4	51	36	28	0	.326	.443
Barney Friberg	2B64, 3B25, 1B5, SS3	R	31	103	353	33	92	19	5	1	26	33	25	1	.261	.351
Fred Koster	OF41	L	25	76	151	21	34	2	2	0	8	14	21	4	.225	.265
Harry McCurdy	C45	L	31	66	150	21	43	9	0	1	25	23	16	2	.287	.367
Hal Lee	OF38	R	26	44	131	13	29	10	0	2	12	10	18	0	.221	.344
Doug Taitt	OF38	L	28	38	151	13	34	4	2	1	15	4	14	0	.225	.298
Hugh Willingham	SS8, 3B2, OF1	R	23	23	35	5	9	2	1	1	3	2	9	0	.257	.457
Tony Rensa	C17	R	29	19	29	2	3	1	0	0	2	6	2	0	.103	.138
Bobby Stevens	SS10	L	24	12	35	3	12	0	0	0	4	2	2	0	.343	.343
Gene Connell	C6	R	25	6	12	1	3	0	0	0	0	0	3	0	.250	.250

NAME	T	AGE	W	L	PCT	SV	G	GS	CG	IP	H	BB	SO	ShO	ERA
		28	66	88	.429	16	155	155	60	1360	**1603**	511	499	6	4.58
Jumbo Jim Elliott	L	30	**19**	14	.576	5	**52**	30	12	249	288	83	99	2	4.27
Ray Benge	R	29	14	18	.438	2	38	31	16	247	251	61	117	2	3.17
Phil Collins	R	**29**	12	16	.429	4	42	27	16	240	268	83	73	2	3.86
Clise Dudley	R	27	8	14	.364	0	30	24	8	179	206	56	50	0	3.52
Frank Watt	R	28	5	5	.500	2	38	12	5	123	147	49	25	0	4.83
2 Sheriff Blake	R	31	4	5	.444	1	14	9	1	71	90	35	31	0	5.58
Stew Bolen	L	28	3	12	.200	0	28	16	2	99	117	63	55	0	6.36
Ben Shields	L	28	1	0	1.000	0	4	0	0	5	9	7	0	0	16.20
Bob Adams	R	24	0	1	.000	0	1	1	0	6	14	1	3	0	9.00
Hal Elliott	R	32	0	2	.000	2	16	4	0	33	46	19	8	0	9.55
Ed Fallenstein	R	22	0	0	.000	0	24	0	0	42	56	26	15	0	7.07
John Milligan	L	27	0	0	.000	0	3	0	0	8	11	4	6	0	3.38
Chet Nichols	R	33	0	1	.000	0	3	0	0	6	10	1	1	0	9.00
Dutch Schesler	R	31	0	0	.000	0	17	0	0	38	65	18	14	0	7.34
Lil Stoner	R	32	0	0	.000	0	7	1	0	14	22	5	2	0	6.43
Hal Wiltse	L	27	0	0	.000	0	1	0	0	1	3	0	0	0	9.00

BOSTON 7th 64-90 .416 37 — BILL McKECHNIE

NAME	G by POS	B	AGE	G	AB	R	H	2B	3B	HR	RBI	BB	SO	SB	BA	SA
TOTALS			30	156	5296	533	1367	221	59	34	490	368	430	46	.258	.341
Earl Sheely	1B143	R	38	147	538	30	147	15	2	1	77	34	21	0	.273	.314
Freddie Maguire	2B148	R	32	148	492	36	112	18	2	0	26	16	26	3	.228	.272
Rabbit Maranville	SS137, 2B11	R	39	145	562	69	146	22	5	0	33	56	34	9	.260	.317
Billy Urbanski	3B68, SS19	R	28	82	303	22	72	13	4	0	17	10	32	3	.238	.307
Wes Schulmerich	OF87	R	29	95	327	36	101	17	7	2	43	28	30	0	.309	.422
Wally Berger	OF156, 1B1	R	25	156	617	94	199	44	8	19	84	55	70	13	.323	.512
Red Worthington	OF124	R	25	128	491	47	143	25	10	4	44	26	38	1	.291	.407
Al Spohrer	C111	R	28	114	350	23	84	17	5	0	27	22	27	2	.240	.317
Lance Richbourg	OF71	L	33	97	286	32	82	11	6	2	29	19	14	9	.287	.388
Randy Moore	OF29, 3B22, 2B1	L	26	83	192	19	50	8	1	3	34	13	3	1	.260	.359
Johnny Neun	1B36	B	30	79	104	17	23	1	3	0	11	11	14	2	.221	.288
Bill Cronin	C50	R	28	51	107	8	22	6	1	0	10	7	5	0	.206	.280
Al Bool	C37	R	33	49	85	5	16	1	0	0	6	9	13	0	.188	.200
Bill Dreesen	3B47	L	26	48	180	38	40	10	4	1	10	23	23	1	.222	.339
Buster Chatham	SS6, 3B6	R	29	17	44	4	10	1	0	1	3	6	6	0	.227	.318
Earl Clark	OF14	R	23	16	50	8	11	2	0	0	4	7	4	1	.220	.260
Charlie Wilson	3B14	B	20	16	58	7	11	4	0	1	11	3	5	0	.190	.310
2 Bill Hunnefield	3B5, 2B4	B	32	11	21	2	6	0	0	0	1	0	2	0	.286	.286
Bucky Walters	3B6, 2B3	R	22	9	38	2	8	2	0	0	0	0	3	0	.211	.263
John Scalzi		R	24	2	1	0	0	0	0	0	0	0	1	0	.000	.000
Pat Veltman		R	25	1	1	0	0	0	0	0	0	0	0	0	.000	.000

NAME	T	AGE	W	L	PCT	SV	G	GS	CG	IP	H	BB	SO	ShO	ERA
		30	64	90	.416	9	156	156	78	1380	1465	406	419	12	3.90
Ed Brandt	L	26	18	11	.621	2	33	29	23	250	228	77	112	3	2.92
Tom Zachary	L	35	11	15	.423	2	33	28	16	229	243	53	64	3	3.10
Socks Seibold	R	35	10	18	.357	0	33	29	10	206	226	65	50	3	4.67
Fred Frankhouse	R	27	8	8	.500	1	26	15	6	127	125	43	50	0	4.04
Ben Cantwell	R	29	7	9	.438	2	33	16	9	156	160	34	32	2	3.63
Bill Sherdel	L	34	6	10	.375	0	27	16	8	138	163	35	34	0	4.24
Bruce Cunningham	R	25	3	12	.200	1	33	16	6	137	157	54	32	1	4.47
2 Ray Moss	R	29	1	3	.250	0	12	5	0	45	56	16	14	0	4.60
Bob Brown	R	20	0	1	.000	0	3	1	0	6	9	3	2	0	9.00
Hal Haid	R	33	0	2	.000	1	27	0	0	56	59	16	20	0	4.50
Bill McAfee	R	23	0	1	.000	0	18	1	0	30	39	10	9	0	6.30

CINCINNATI 8th 58-96 .377 43 — DAN HOWLEY

NAME	G by POS	B	AGE	G	AB	R	H	2B	3B	HR	RBI	BB	SO	SB	BA	SA
TOTALS			30	154	5343	592	1439	241	70	21	562	403	463	24	.269	.352
2 Harvey Hendrick	1B137	L	33	137	530	74	167	32	9	1	75	53	40	3	.315	.415
Tony Cuccinello	2B154	R	23	154	575	67	181	39	11	2	93	54	28	1	.315	.431
Leo Durocher	SS120	R	25	121	361	26	82	11	5	1	29	18	32	0	.227	.294
Joe Stripp	3B96, 1B9	R	28	105	426	71	138	26	2	3	42	21	31	5	.324	.415
Estel Crabtree	OF101, 3B4, 1B2	L	27	117	443	70	119	12	12	4	37	23	33	3	.269	.377
2 Taylor Douthit	OF95	R	30	95	374	42	98	9	1	0	24	42	24	4	.262	.291
Edd Roush	OF88	L	38	101	376	46	102	12	5	1	41	17	5	2	.271	.338
Clyde Sukeforth	C106	L	29	112	351	22	90	15	4	0	25	38	13	0	.256	.322
Nick Cullop	OF83	R	32	104	334	29	88	23	7	8	48	21	**86**	1	.263	.446
Red Lucas	P29	L	29	97	153	15	43	4	0	0	17	12	9	0	.281	.307
Cliff Heathcote	OF59	L	33	90	252	24	65	15	6	0	28	32	16	3	.258	.365
Hod Ford	SS73, 2B3, 3B1	R	33	84	175	18	40	8	1	0	13	13	13	0	.229	.286
Clyde Beck	3B38, SS6	R	29	53	136	17	21	4	2	0	19	21	14	1	.154	.213
Casper Asbjornson (BG)	C31	R	22	45	118	13	36	7	1	0	22	7	23	0	.305	.381
1 Wally Roettger	OF44	R	28	44	185	25	65	11	4	1	20	7	9	1	.351	.470
Lena Styles	C31	R	31	34	87	7	21	3	0	0	5	8	7	0	.241	.276
Frank Sigafoos	3B15, SS2	R	27	21	65	6	11	2	0	0	8	0	6	0	.169	.200
Mickey Heath	1B7	L	**27**	7	26	2	7	0	0	0	3	2	5	0	.269	.269
Chuck Dressen	3B4	R	32	5	15	0	1	0	0	0	0	1	1	0	.067	.067
Gene Moore	OF3	L	21	4	14	2	2	1	0	0	1	0	0	0	.143	.214
Ray Fitzgerald		R	26	1	1	0	0	0	0	0	0	0	0	0	.000	.000
Harry Heilmann (IL) 36																

NAME	T	AGE	W	L	PCT	SV	G	GS	CG	IP	H	BB	SO	ShO	ERA
		31	58	**96**	.377	6	154	154	70	1345	1545	399	317	7	4.22
Red Lucas	R	29	14	13	.519	0	29	29	**24**	238	261	39	56	3	3.59
Si Johnson	R	24	11	**19**	.367	0	42	33	14	262	273	74	95	0	3.78
Larry Benton	R	33	10	15	.400	2	38	23	12	204	240	53	35	2	3.35
Benny Frey	R	25	8	12	.400	2	34	17	7	134	166	36	19	1	4.90
Ray Kolp	R	36	4	9	.308	1	30	10	2	107	144	39	24	0	4.96
Jack Ogden	R	33	4	8	.333	1	22	9	3	89	79	32	24	1	2.93
Eppa Rixey	L	40	4	7	.364	0	22	17	4	127	143	30	22	0	3.90
Ownie Carroll	R	28	3	9	.250	0	29	12	4	107	135	51	24	0	5.55
Al Eckert	L	25	0	1	.000	0	14	1	0	19	26	9	5	0	9.00
Whitey Hilcher	R	22	0	1	.000	0	2	1	0	12	16	4	5	0	3.00
Ed Strelecki	R	26	0	0	.000	0	13	0	0	24	37	9	3	0	9.38
Biff Wylong	L	26	0	2	.000	0	12	2	0	22	25	23	5	0	7.77

WORLD SERIES – ST. LOUIS (NL) 4 PHILADELPHIA (AL) 3

LINE SCORES

TEAM	1	2	3	4	5	6	7	8	9	10	11	12	R	H	E
Game 1 October 1 at St. Louis															
PHI (AL)	0	0	4	0	0	0	2	0	0				6	11	0
STL (NL)	2	0	0	0	0	0	0	0	0				2	12	0
Grove — **Derringer**, Johnson (8)															
Game 2 October 2 at St. Louis															
PHI	0	0	0	0	0	0	0	0	0				0	3	0
STL	0	1	0	0	0	0	1	0	X				2	6	1
Earnshaw — **Hallahan**															
Game 3 October 5 at Philadelphia															
STL	0	2	0	2	0	0	0	0	1				5	12	0
PHI	0	0	0	0	0	0	0	0	2				2	2	0
Grimes — **Grove**, Mahaffey (9)															
Game 4 October 6 at Philadelphia															
STL	0	0	0	0	0	0	0	0	0				0	2	1
PHI	1	0	0	0	0	2	0	0	X				3	10	0
Johnson, Lindsey (6), Derringer (8) — **Earnshaw**															
Game 5 October 7 at Philadelphia															
STL	1	0	0	0	0	2	0	1	1				5	12	0
PHI	0	0	0	0	0	0	1	0	0				1	9	0
Hallahan — **Hoyt**, Walberg (7), Rommel (9)															
Game 6 October 9 at St. Louis															
PHI	0	0	0	0	4	0	4	0	0				8	8	1
STL	0	0	0	0	0	1	0	0	0				1	5	2
Grove — **Derringer**, Johnson (5), Lindsey (7), Rhem (9)															
Game 7 October 10 at St. Louis															
PHI	0	0	0	0	0	0	0	0	2				2	7	1
STL	2	0	2	0	0	0	0	0	X				4	5	0
Earnshaw, Walberg (8) — **Grimes**, Hallahan (9)															

COMPOSITE BATTING

NAME	POS	G	AB	R	H	2B	3B	HR	RBI	BA
St. Louis (NL)										
Totals		7	229	19	54	11	0	2	17	.236
Frisch	2B	7	**27**	2	7	2	0	0	1	.259
Bottomley	1B	7	25	2	4	1	0	0	2	.160
Martin	OF	7	24	**5**	**12**	**4**	0	1	5	**.500**
Hafey	OF	6	24	1	4	0	0	0	0	.167
Gelbert	SS	7	23	0	6	1	0	0	3	.261
Wilson	C	7	23	0	5	0	0	0	2	.217
High	3B	4	15	3	4	0	0	0	0	.267
Watkins	OF	5	14	4	4	1	0	1	2	.286
Roettger	OF	3	14	1	4	1	0	0	0	.286
Flowers	3B	5	11	1	1	1	0	0	0	.091
Grimes	P	2	7	0	2	0	0	0	2	.286
Hallahan	P	3	6	0	0	0	0	0	0	.000
Adams	3B	2	4	0	1	0	0	0	0	.250
Orsatti	OF	1	3	0	0	0	0	0	0	.000
Blades	PH	2	2	0	0	0	0	0	0	.000
Collins	PH	2	2	0	0	0	0	0	0	.000
Derringer	P	3	2	0	0	0	0	0	0	.000
Johnson	P	3	2	0	0	0	0	0	0	.000
Mancuso	C	2	1	0	0	0	0	0	0	.000
Lindsey	P	2	0	0	0	0	0	0	0	.000
Rhem	P	1	0	0	0	0	0	0	0	.000
Philadelphia (AL)										
Totals		7	227	22	50	5	0	3	20	.220
Simmons	OF	7	**27**	4	9	2	0	**2**	**8**	.333
Bishop	2B	7	**27**	4	4	0	0	0	0	.148
Miller	OF	7	26	3	7	1	0	0	1	.269
Williams	SS	7	25	2	8	1	0	0	1	.320
Cochrane	C	7	25	2	4	0	0	0	1	.160
Foxx	1B	7	23	3	8	0	0	1	3	.348
Haas	OF	7	23	1	3	1	0	0	2	.130
Dykes	3B	7	22	2	5	0	0	0	2	.227
Grove	P	3	10	0	0	0	0	0	0	.000
Earnshaw	P	3	8	0	0	0	0	0	0	.000
Moore	OF	2	3	0	1	0	0	0	0	.333
McNair	2B	2	2	1	0	0	0	0	0	.000
Cramer	PH	2	2	0	1	0	0	0	2	.500
Hoyt	P	1	2	0	0	0	0	0	0	.000
Boley	PH	1	1	0	0	0	0	0	0	.000
Heving	PH	1	1	0	0	0	0	0	0	.000
Walberg	P	2	0	0	0	0	0	0	0	.000
Mahaffey	P	1	0	0	0	0	0	0	0	.000

Rommel P 0-0, Todt PH 0-0

COMPOSITE PITCHING

NAME	G	IP	H	BB	SO	W	L	SV	ERA
St. Louis (NL)									
Totals	1	62	50	28	46	4	3	1	2.32
Hallahan	**3**	18.1	12	8	12	**2**	0	1	**0.49**
Grimes	2	17.2	**9**	**9**	11	**2**	0	0	2.04
Derringer	**3**	12.2	14	7	14	0	**2**	0	4.26
Johnson	**3**	9	10	**1**	6	0	1	0	3.00
Lindsey	2	3.1	4	3	2	0	0	0	**5.40**
Rhem	1	1	1	0	1	0	0	0	0.00
Philadelphia (AL)									
Totals	7	61	54	9	41	3	4	0	2.66
Grove	**3**	**26**	**28**	2	16	**2**	1	0	2.42
Earnshaw	**3**	24	12	4	**20**	1	**2**	0	1.88
Hoyt	1	6	7	0	1	0	1	0	4.50
Walberg	2	3	3	2	4	0	0	0	3.00
Mahaffey	1	1	1	1	0	0	0	0	9.00
Rommel	1	1	3	0	0	0	0	0	9.00

1932 Start with Hornsby and End with Ruth

With his Chicago Cubs in first place on August 2, a funny thing happened to manager Rogers Hornsby; he was bounced. Despite the lofty perch of his charges, Hornsby felt the axe after a severe disagreement in policy matters with president William Veeck, the father of baseball's daring promotion genius, Bill Veeck. When first baseman Charley Grimm was handed the reins, the press wondered if the Cubs could maintain their slight lead over the Pittsburgh Pirates.

As it turned out, the Bruins rallied under Jolly Cholly's leadership to stay out in front and wind up first by four games. Riggs Stephenson knocked in 85 runs in providing heart for the lineup, and player Grimm aided his managerial cause by driving 80 Cubs home. Billy Herman steadied the infield with his keystone play, and Gabby Hartnett tied all the loose ends together with his brainy receiving. A sore spot was eased late in the year when ex-Yankee Mark Koenig was brought to play shortstop. Rookie Lon Warneke proved to be the league pitching sensation by posting an E.R.A. of 2.37 to go with 22 victories, as Guy Bush, Pat Malone, and Charley Root provided veteran pitching talent to complement the rookie's performance.

Pittsburgh used the batting of Paul Waner, Lloyd Waner, Pie Traynor, and rookie Arky Vaughan to take second honors after a slow start. Brooklyn moved a notch up to third on the bat of Lefty O'Doul's .368 league-leading average, while Philadelphia could only manage fourth—despite the league's best offense led by Chuck Klein and Don Hurst. New York fell to sixth as manager John McGraw resigned early in the season for health reasons after 30 years at the helm. The defending champion Cardinals, despite 18 wins from rookie pitcher Dizzy Dean, collapsed into sixth place, due to age and the failure of several key personnel to perform at their previous year's level.

In the American League, the New York Yankees returned to the top after three years of Philadelphia Athletics' monopoly of the pennant penthouse. The Yankees' 107 wins were good enough for a 13-game bulge over the Mackmen, as Joe McCarthy won his first junior circuit pennant in an easy fashion. The schedule, which called for the Yankees to play the better teams in the first half and the weaker western teams as the major fare after June, gave way to an early Yankee lead and little doubt over the final outcome.

In New York's victory, Babe Ruth, at the ripe age of 37, still managed 41 homers, and Lou Gehrig rode the crest wave of his career with a .349 average and 151 RBI's. Tony Lazzeri and Ben Chapman each sent over 100 Yankees across the plate, and young Frank Crosetti filled the shortstop slot and went to his first World Series. Lefty Gomez and Red Ruffing provided a left-right pitching combination unmatched in the league while supported by Johnny Allen, who was 17-4 in his maiden season.

Although relegated to runner-ups, Philadelphia unseated the Yankees as the home run powerhouse of the league, directly as the result of Jimmie Foxx—who took the home run crown from the head of Ruth for the first time since 1925 by launching 58 clouts into the atmosphere. Foxx's 169 RBI's also paced the league, and his .364 average barely trailed Dale Alexander's for the batting crown. Al Simmons and Mickey Cochrane also contributed standout offensive years, but the Athletics' pitching fell off badly from its championship performances, as even Lefty Grove, with a 25-10 record, was not anywhere near his 1931 mark of 31-4. The Senators closely followed the A's in third on the strength of the batting of Heinie Manusch and Joe Cronin and the pitching of General Crowder's league-leading 26 wins.

For the third time in six years, the Yankees swept the Series in four games. The Yankees' attack completely destroyed the Cubs as Gehrig hit three home runs and Ruth and Lazzeri each contributed a pair. One of Ruth's home runs came in the third game and was a blast which became permanently lodged in baseball's folklore. There were bad feelings between the two teams, and Ruth supposedly responded to the Cubs' heckling by pointing to the center field bleachers with an 0-2 count and calling his home run shot. Charley Root, the pitcher who served up the legendary blast, went to his grave denying that Ruth ever called the home run which, ironically enough, turned out to be the Babe's final World Series round-tripper.

1932 AMERICAN LEAGUE

NAME	G by POS	B	AGE	G	AB	R	H	2B	3B	HR	RBI	BB	SO	SB	BA	SA
NEW YORK 1st 107-47 .695		JOE McCARTHY														
TOTALS			28	155	5477	**1002**	1564	279	82	160	**955**	**766**	527	77	.286	.454
Lou Gehrig	1B155	L	29	155	596	138	208	42	9	34	151	108	38	4	.349	.621
Tony Lazzeri	2B133, 3B5	R	28	141	510	79	153	28	16	15	113	82	64	11	.300	.506
Frankie Crosetti	SS83, 3B33, 2B1	R	21	115	398	47	96	20	9	5	57	51	51	3	.241	.374
Joe Sewell	3B122	L	33	124	503	95	137	21	3	11	68	56	3	0	.272	.392
Babe Ruth	OF127, 1B1	L	37	132	457	120	156	13	5	41	137	**130**	62	2	.341	.661
Earle Combs	OF138	L	33	143	591	143	190	32	10	9	65	81	16	3	.321	.455
Ben Chapman	OF149	R	23	150	581	101	174	41	15	10	107	71	55	**38**	.299	.473
Bill Dickey (SL)	C108	L	25	108	423	66	131	20	4	15	84	34	13	2	.310	.482
Sammy Byrd	OF90	R	25	104	209	49	62	12	1	8	30	30	20	1	.297	.478
Lyn Lary	SS80, 1B5, 2B2, 3B2, OF1	R	26	91	280	56	65	14	4	3	39	52	28	9	.232	.343
Art Jorgens	C55	R	27	55	151	13	33	7	1	2	19	14	11	0	.219	.318
Red Ruffing	P35	R	28	55	124	20	38	6	1	3	19	6	10	0	.306	.444
Myril Hoag	OF35, 1B1	R	24	46	54	18	20	5	0	1	7	7	13	1	.370	.519
Doc Farrell	2B16, SS5, 1B2, 3B1	R	30	26	63	4	11	1	1	0	4	2	8	0	.175	.222
Jack Saltzgaver	2B16	L	27	20	47	10	6	2	1	0	5	10	10	1	.128	.213
Eddie Phillips	C9	R	31	9	31	4	9	1	0	2	4	2	3	1	.290	.516
Joe Glenn	C5	R	23	6	16	0	2	0	0	0	0	1	0	5	.125	.125
Dusty Cooke (BL)		L	25	3	0	1	0	0	0	0	0	1	0	0	.000	.000
Roy Schalk	2B3	R	23	3	12	3	3	1	0	0	0	2	2	0	.250	.333
PHILADELPHIA 2nd 94-60 .610 13		CONNIE MACK														
TOTALS			30	154	**5537**	981	**1606**	303	52	**172**	923	647	**640**	38	**.290**	**.457**
Jimmie Foxx	1B141, 3B13	R	24	154	585	**151**	213	33	9	**58**	**169**	116	96	3	.364	**.749**
Max Bishop	2B106	L	32	114	409	89	104	24	2	5	37	110	43	2	.254	.359
Eric McNair	SS133	R	23	135	554	87	158	**47**	3	18	95	28	29	8	.285	.478
Jimmy Dykes	3B141, SS10, 2B1	R	35	153	558	71	148	29	5	7	90	77	65	8	.265	.373
Doc Cramer (BC)	OF86	L	26	92	384	73	129	27	6	3	46	17	27	3	.336	.461
Mule Haas	OF137	L	28	143	558	91	170	28	5	6	65	62	49	1	.305	.405
Al Simmons	OF154	R	30	154	**670**	144	**216**	28	9	35	151	47	76	4	.322	.548
Mickey Cochrane	C137, OF1	L	29	139	518	118	152	35	4	23	112	100	22	0	.293	.510
Bing Miller	OF84	R	37	95	305	40	90	17	4	7	58	20	11	7	.295	.446
Dib Williams	2B53, SS3	R	32	62	215	30	54	10	1	4	24	22	23	0	.251	.363
Lefty Grove	P44	L	32	44	107	10	18	1	0	4	12	5	51	0	.168	.290
George Earnshaw	P36	R	32	36	91	10	26	4	1	0	9	0	12	0	.286	.352
Johnnie Heving	C28	R	36	33	77	14	21	6	1	0	10	7	6	0	.273	.377
Ed Coleman (BN)	OF16	L	30	26	73	13	25	7	1	1	13	1	6	1	.342	.507
Oscar Roettger	1B15	R	32	26	60	7	14	1	0	0	6	5	4	0	.233	.250
Ed Madjeski	C8	R	22	17	35	4	8	0	0	0	3	3	6	0	.229	.229
1 Joe Boley	SS10	R	35	10	34	2	7	2	0	0	4	1	4	0	.206	.265
Al Reiss	SS6	B	33	9	5	0	1	0	0	0	1	1	1	0	.200	.200
John Jones	OF1	L	31	4	6	0	1	0	0	0	0	0	3	0	.167	.167
Ed Cihocki		R	25	1	1	0	0	0	0	0	0	0	0	0	.000	.000
WASHINGTON 3rd 93-61 .604 14		WALTER JOHNSON														
TOTALS			31	154	5515	840	1565	303	**100**	61	776	505	442	70	.284	.408
Joe Kuhel	1B85	L	26	101	347	52	101	21	5	4	52	32	19	5	.291	.415
Buddy Myer	2B139	L	28	143	577	120	161	38	16	5	52	69	33	12	.279	.426
Joe Cronin	SS141	R	25	143	557	95	177	43	**18**	6	116	66	45	7	.318	.492
Ossie Bluege	3B149	R	31	149	507	64	131	22	4	5	64	84	41	9	.258	.345
Carl Reynolds (BJ)	OF95	R	29	102	406	53	124	28	7	9	63	14	19	8	.305	.475
Sammy West	OF143	L	27	146	554	88	159	27	12	6	83	48	57	4	.287	.412
Heinie Manush	OF146	L	30	149	625	121	214	41	14	14	116	36	29	7	.342	.520
Roy Spencer	C98	R	32	102	317	28	78	9	0	1	41	24	17	0	.246	.284
Sam Rice	OF69	L	42	106	288	58	93	16	7	1	34	32	6	7	.323	.438
Joe Judge	1B78	L	38	82	291	45	75	16	3	3	29	37	19	3	.258	.364
Dave Harris	OF34	R	32	81	156	26	51	7	4	6	29	19	34	4	.327	.538
Moe Berg	C75	R	30	75	195	16	46	8	1	1	26	8	13	1	.236	.303
John Kerr	2B17, SS14, 3B8	R	33	51	132	14	36	6	1	0	15	13	3	3	.273	.333
Monty Weaver	P43	L	26	44	94	13	27	6	1	0	13	0	18	0	.287	.372
Howard Maple	C41	L	28	44	41	6	10	0	1	0	7	7	7	0	.244	.293
Wes Kingdon	3B8, SS4	R	31	18	34	10	11	3	1	0	3	5	2	0	.324	.471
Jim McLeod	SS1	R	23	7	0	1	0	0	0	0	0	1	0	0	.000	.000
Danny Musser	3B1	L	26	1	2	0	1	0	0	0	0	0	0	0	.500	.500

NAME	T	AGE	W	L	PCT	SV	G	GS	CG	IP	H	BB	SO	ShO	ERA
		29	**107**	47	**.695**	15	155	155	**95**	**1409**	1425	561	**780**	**11**	**3.98**
Lefty Gomez	L	23	24	7	.774	1	37	31	21	265	266	105	176	1	4.21
Red Ruffing	R	28	18	7	.720	2	35	29	22	259	219	115	**190**	3	3.09
Johnny Allen	R	27	17	4	**.810**	4	33	21	13	192	162	76	109	3	3.70
George Pipgras	R	32	16	9	.640	0	32	27	14	219	235	87	111	2	4.19
Herb Pennock	L	38	9	5	.643	0	22	21	9	147	191	38	54	1	4.59
2 Danny MacFayden	R	27	7	5	.583	1	17	14	8	121	137	37	33	0	3.94
Jumbo Brown	R	25	5	2	.714	1	19	3	3	56	58	30	31	1	4.50
Ed Wells	L	32	3	3	.500	2	22	0	0	32	38	12	13	0	4.22
2 Wilcy Moore	R	35	2	0	1.000	4	10	1	0	25	27	6	8	0	2.52
1 Ivy Andrews	R	25	2	1	.667	0	4	1	1	25	20	9	7	0	1.80
Hank Johnson (VR)	R	26	2	2	.500	0	5	4	2	31	34	15	27	0	4.93
Charlie Devens	R	22	1	0	1.000	0	1	1	1	9	6	7	4	0	2.00
1 Gordon Rhodes	R	24	1	2	.333	0	10	2	1	24	25	21	5	0	7.88
Johnny Murphy	R	23	0	0	.000	0	2	0	0	3	7	3	2	0	18.00
		29	94	60	.610	10	154	154	94	1386	1477	511	595	10	4.45
Lefty Grove	L	32	25	10	.714	7	44	30	**27**	292	269	79	188	**4**	**2.84**
George Earnshaw	R	32	19	13	.594	0	36	33	20	245	262	94	109	1	4.78
Rube Walberg	L	32	17	10	.630	1	41	34	19	272	305	103	96	3	4.73
Roy Mahaffey	R	29	13	13	.500	0	37	28	13	223	245	96	106	0	5.09
Tony Freitas	L	24	12	5	.706	0	23	18	10	150	150	48	31	1	3.84
Lew Krause	R	20	4	1	.800	0	20	3	2	57	64	24	16	1	4.58
Sugar Cain	R	25	3	4	.429	0	10	6	3	45	42	28	24	0	5.00
Eddie Rommel	R	34	1	2	.333	2	17	0	0	65	84	18	16	0	5.54
Joe Bowman	R	22	0	1	.000	0	7	0	0	11	14	6	4	0	8.18
Jim McKeithan	R	25	0	1	.000	0	4	2	0	13	18	5	0	0	6.93
Jimmie DeShong	R	22	0	0	.000	0	6	0	0	10	17	9	5	0	11.70
Irv Stein	R	21	0	0	.000	0	1	0	0	3	7	1	0	0	12.00
		29	93	61	.604	**22**	154	154	66	1384	1463	526	437	10	4.16
General Crowder	R	33	**26**	13	.667	1	50	**39**	21	**327**	**319**	77	103	3	3.33
Monty Weaver	R	26	22	10	.688	2	43	30	13	234	236	112	83	1	4.08
Lloyd Brown	L	27	15	12	.556	5	46	24	10	203	239	55	53	2	4.44
Firpo Marberry	R	33	8	4	.667	**13**	**54**	15	8	198	202	72	66	1	4.00
2 Tommy Thomas	R	32	8	7	.733	0	18	14	7	117	114	46	36	1	3.54
Bill McAfee	R	24	6	1	.857	0	8	5	2	41	47	22	10	0	3.95
1 Carl Fischer	L	26	3	2	.600	1	12	7	1	51	57	31	23	1	4.94
Bobby Burke	L	25	3	6	.333	0	22	10	2	91	98	44	32	0	5.14
Frank Ragland	R	28	1	0	1.000	0	12	1	0	38	54	21	11	0	7.34
2 Dick Coffman	R	25	1	6	.143	0	22	9	2	72	92	31	17	1	4.85
Ed Edelen	R	20	0	0	.000	0	2	0	0	1	0	6	0	0	27.00
Bob Friedrich	R	25	0	0	.000	0	2	0	0	4	4	7	2	0	11.25
Bud Thomas	R	21	0	0	.000	0	2	0	0	3	1	2	1	0	0.00

CLEVELAND 4th 87-65 .572 19 — ROGER PECKINPAUGH

NAME	G by POS	B	AGE	G	AB	R	H	2B	3B	HR	RBI	BB	SO	SB	BA	SA
TOTALS			29	153	5412	845	1544	310	74	78	778	556	454	52	.285	.413
Eddie Morgan	1B142	R	28	144	532	96	156	32	7	4	68	94	44	7	.293	.402
2 Bill Cissell	2B129, SS6	R	28	131	541	78	173	35	6	6	93	28	25	18	.320	.440
Johnny Burnett	SS103, 2B26	L	27	129	512	81	152	23	5	4	53	46	27	2	.297	.385
Willie Kamm	3B148	R	32	148	524	76	150	34	9	3	83	75	36	6	.286	.403
Dick Porter	OF145	L	30	146	621	106	191	42	8	4	60	64	43	2	.308	.420
Earl Averill	OF153	L	30	153	631	116	198	37	14	32	124	75	40	5	.314	.569
Joe Vosmik	OF153	R	22	153	621	106	194	39	12	10	97	58	42	2	.312	.462
Luke Sewell	C84	R	31	87	300	36	76	20	2	2	52	38	24	4	.253	.353
Glenn Myatt	C65	L	34	82	252	45	62	12	1	8	46	28	21	2	.246	.397
Ed Montague	SS57, 3B11	R	26	66	192	29	47	5	1	0	24	21	24	3	.245	.281
Bruce Connatser	1B14	R	29	23	60	8	14	3	1	0	4	4	8	1	.233	.317
Charlie Jamieson (CJ)	OF2	L	39	16	16	0	1	1	0	0	0	2	3	0	.063	.125
Mike Powers	OF8	L	26	14	33	4	6	4	0	0	5	2	2	0	.182	.303
Frankie Pytlak	C12	R	23	12	29	5	7	1	1	0	4	3	2	0	.241	.345
1 Johnny Hodapp	2B7	R	26	7	16	2	2	1	0	0	0	0	2	0	.125	.188
1 Bob Seeds	OF1	R	25	2	4	0	0	0	0	0	0	0	0	0	.000	.000

Boze Berger 22 R 0-1, 2 Joe Boley 35 R 1-4

NAME	T	AGE	W	L	PCT	SV	G	GS	CG	IP	H	BB	SO	ShO	ERA
		26	87	65	.572	8	153	153	93	1377	1506	446	439	6	4.12
Wes Ferrell	R	24	23	13	.639	1	38	34	26	288	299	104	105	3	3.65
Clint Brown	R	28	15	12	.556	1	37	32	21	263	298	50	59	1	4.07
Mel Harder	R	22	15	13	.536	0	39	32	17	255	277	68	90	1	3.74
Willis Hudlin	R	26	12	8	.600	2	33	21	11	182	204	59	65	0	4.70
Sarge Connally	R	33	8	6	.571	3	35	7	4	112	119	42	32	1	4.34
Oral Hildebrand	R	25	8	6	.571	0	27	15	7	129	124	62	49	0	3.70
2 Jack Russell	R	26	5	7	.375	1	18	11	6	113	146	27	27	0	4.70
Ralph Winegarner	R	22	1	0	1.000	0	5	1	1	17	7	13	5	0	1.06
Monte Pearson	R	22	0	0	.000	0	8	0	0	8	10	11	5	0	10.13
1 Pete Appleton	R	28	0	0	.000	0	4	0	0	5	11	3	1	0	16.20
Leo Moon	L	33	0	0	.000	0	1	0	0	6	11	7	1	0	10.50

DETROIT 5th 76-75 .503 29.5 — BUCKY HARRIS

NAME	G by POS	B	AGE	G	AB	R	H	2B	3B	HR	RBI	BB	SO	SB	BA	SA
TOTALS			27	152	5409	799	1479	291	80	80	742	486	523	**105**	.273	.401
Harry Davis	1B140	L	22	140	590	92	159	32	13	4	74	60	53	12	.269	.388
Charlie Gehringer	2B151	L	29	151	618	112	184	44	11	19	107	68	34	9	.298	.497
Billy Rogell	SS139, 3B4	B	27	143	554	88	150	29	6	9	61	50	38	14	.271	.394
Heinie Schuble	3B76, SS15	R	25	101	340	58	92	20	6	5	52	24	37	14	.271	.409
2 Earl Webb	OF84	L	33	87	338	49	97	19	8	3	51	39	18	1	.287	.417
Gee Walker	OF116	R	24	126	480	71	155	32	6	8	78	13	38	30	.323	.465
John Stone	OF141	L	26	144	582	106	173	35	12	17	108	58	64	2	.297	.486
Ray Hayworth	C105	R	28	108	338	41	99	20	2	2	44	31	22	1	.293	.382
Billy Rhiel	3B36, 1B12, OF8, 2B1	R	31	84	250	30	70	13	3	3	38	17	23	2	.280	.392
Jo-Jo White	OF47	L	23	79	208	25	54	6	3	2	21	22	19	6	.260	.346
Nolen Richardson	3B65, SS4	R	29	69	155	13	34	5	2	0	12	9	13	5	.219	.277
Muddy Ruel	C48	R	36	50	136	10	32	4	2	0	18	17	6	1	.235	.294
1 Roy Johnson	OF48	L	29	49	195	33	49	14	2	3	22	20	26	7	.251	.390
Gene Desautels	C24	R	25	28	72	8	17	2	0	0	2	13	11	0	.236	.264
Bill Lawrence	OF15	R	26	25	46	10	10	1	0	0	3	5	5	0	.217	.239
1 Dale Alexander	1B2	R	29	23	16	0	4	0	0	0	4	6	2	0	.250*	.250
Frank Doljack	OF6	R	24	8	26	5	10	1	0	1	7	2	2	1	.385	.538
George Susce	C2	R	23	2	0	0	0	0	0	0	0	0	0	0	.000	.000

NAME	T	AGE	W	L	PCT	SV	G	GS	CG	IP	H	BB	SO	ShO	ERA
		27	76	76	.500	17	152	152	66	1363	1421	592	521	9	4.30
Earl Whitehill	L	32	16	13	.552	0	32	31	17	244	255	93	81	3	4.54
Tommy Bridges	R	25	14	12	.538	1	34	26	10	201	174	119	108	**4**	3.36
Vic Sorrell	R	31	14	14	.500	0	32	31	13	234	234	77	84	1	4.04
Chief Hogsett	L	28	11	9	.550	7	47	15	7	178	201	66	56	0	3.54
Whit Wyatt	R	24	9	13	.409	1	43	22	10	206	228	102	82	0	5.02
George Uhle	R	33	6	6	.500	5	33	15	6	147	152	42	51	1	4.47
Izzy Goldstein	R	24	3	2	.600	0	16	6	2	56	63	41	14	0	4.50
Buck Marrow	R	22	2	5	.286	1	18	6	1	64	70	29	31	0	4.78
Art Herring	R	25	1	2	.333	2	12	0	0	22	25	15	12	0	5.32
2 Rip Sewell	R	25	0	0	.000	0	5	0	0	11	19	8	2	0	12.28

*Alexander, also with Boston, league leader in BA with .367

ST. LOUIS 6th 63-91 .409 44 — BILL KILLEFER

NAME	G by POS	B	AGE	G	AB	R	H	2B	3B	HR	RBI	BB	SO	SB	BA	SA
TOTALS			27	154	5449	736	1502	274	69	67	684	507	528	69	.276	.388
Jack Burns	1B150	L	24	150	617	111	188	33	8	11	70	61	43	17	.305	.438
Oscar Mellilo	2B153	R	32	154	612	71	148	19	11	3	66	36	42	6	.242	.324
Jim Levey	SS152	B	25	152	568	59	159	30	8	4	63	21	48	6	.280	.382
Art Scharein	3B77, SS3, 2B2	R	27	81	303	43	92	19	2	0	42	25	10	4	.304	.380
2 Bruce Campbell	OF137	L	22	137	585	83	169	35	11	14	85	40	100†	7	.289	.458
Fred Schulte	OF129, 1B5	R	31	146	565	106	166	35	6	9	73	71	44	5	.294	.425
Goose Goslin	OF149, 3B1	L	31	150	572	88	171	28	9	17	104	92	35	12	.299	.469
Rick Ferrell	C120	R	26	126	438	67	138	30	5	2	65	66	18	5	.315	.420
Benny Bengough	C47	R	33	54	139	13	35	7	1	0	15	12	4	0	.252	.317
Lin Storti (BF)	3B51	B	25	53	193	19	50	11	2	3	26	5	20	1	.259	.383
Debs Garms	OF33	L	24	34	134	20	38	7	1	1	8	17	7	4	.284	.373
Ed Grimes (JJ)	3B18, 2B2, SS1	R	26	31	68	7	16	0	1	0	13	6	12	0	.235	.265
Larry Bettencourt	OF4, 3B2	R	26	27	30	4	4	1	0	1	3	7	6	1	.133	.267
Tom Jenkins	OF12	L	34	25	62	5	20	1	0	0	5	1	6	0	.323	.339
Nap Kloza	OF3	R	28	19	13	4	2	0	1	0	2	4	4	0	.154	.308
Showboat Fisher	OF5	L	33	18	22	2	4	0	0	0	2	2	5	0	.182	.182
1 Johnny Schulte	C6	L	35	15	24	2	5	2	0	0	3	1	6	0	.208	.292
1 Red Kress	3B14	R	25	14	52	2	9	0	1	2	9	4	6	1	.173	.327
Jim McLaughlin	3B1	R	30	1	1	0	0	0	0	0	1	0	0	0	.000	.000

NAME	T	AGE	W	L	PCT	SV	G	GS	CG	IP	H	BB	SO	ShO	ERA
		27	63	91	.409	11	154	154	63	1377	**1592**	574	496	8	5.00
George Blaeholder	R	28	14	14	.500	0	42	36	16	258	304	76	80	1	4.71
Lefty Stewart	L	31	14	19	.424	1	41	32	18	260	269	99	86	2	4.61
2 Bump Hadley	R	27	13	**20**#	.394	1	40	33	12	230	244	**163**#	132	1	5.52
Sam Gray	R	34	8	12	.400	4	52	18	7	207	250	53	79	3	4.52
1 Dick Coffman	R	25	5	3	.625	0	9	6	3	61	66	21	14	1	3.10
1 Chad Kimsey	R	25	4	2	.667	3	33	0	0	78	85	33	13	0	4.04
1 Carl Fischer	L	26	3	7	.300	0	24	11	4	97	122	45	35	0	5.57
Bob Cooney	R	24	1	2	.333	1	23	3	1	71	94	36	23	0	6.98
Wally Hebert	L	24	1	12	.077	1	35	15	2	108	145	45	29	0	6.50
Lou Polli	R	30	0	0	.000	0	5	0	0	7	13	3	5	0	5.14

#Hadley, with St. Louis and Chicago, league leader in L(21) BB(171)

†Campbell, with St. Louis and Chicago, league leader in SO with 104

CHICAGO 7th 49-102 .325 56.6 — LEW FONSECA

NAME	G by POS	B	AGE	G	AB	R	H	2B	3B	HR	RBI	BB	SO	SB	BA	SA
TOTALS			27	152	5336	667	1426	274	56	36	607	459	386	89	.267	.360
Lu Blue	1B105	B	35	112	373	51	93	21	2	0	43	64	21	17	.249	.316
Jackie Hayes	2B97, SS10, 3B10	R	25	117	475	53	122	20	5	2	54	30	28	7	.257	.333
Luke Appling	SS85, 2B30, 3B14	R	25	139	489	66	134	20	10	3	63	40	36	9	.274	.374
Carey Selph	3B71, 2B26	R	30	116	396	50	112	19	8	0	51	31	9	7	.283	.371
2 Bob Seeds	OF112	R	25	116	434	53	126	18	6	2	45	31	37	5	.290	.373
Liz Funk	OF120	L	27	122	440	59	114	21	5	2	40	43	19	17	.259	.343
Bob Fothergill	OF86	R	34	116	346	36	102	24	1	7	50	27	10	4	.295	.431
Frank Grube	C92	R	27	93	277	36	78	16	2	0	31	33	13	6	.282	.354
2 Red Kress	OF64, SS53, 3B19	R	25	135	515	83	147	42	4	9	57	47	36	6	.285	.435
Billy Sullivan (RL)	1B52, 3B17, C5, OF3	L	21	93	307	31	97	16	1	1	45	20	9	1	.316	.384
2 Charlie Berry	C70	R	29	72	226	33	69	15	6	4	31	21	23	3	.305	.478
2 Johnny Hodapp	OF31, 2B5, 3B4	R	26	68	176	21	40	8	0	3	20	11	3	1	.227	.324
2 Jack Rothrock	OF19, 3B8, 1B1	B	27	39	64	8	12	2	1	0	6	5	9	1	.188	.250
Charlie English	3B13, SS1	R	22	24	63	7	20	3	1	1	8	3	7	0	.317	.444
Lew Fonseca	OF8, P1	R	33	18	37	0	5	1	0	0	6	1	7	0	.135	.162
1 Johnny Watwood	OF13	L	25	13	49	5	15	2	0	0	0	1	3	0	.306	.347
Evar Swanson	OF14	R	29	14	52	9	16	3	1	0	8	8	3	3	.308	.404
Bill Norman	OF13	R	21	13	48	6	11	3	1	0	2	2	3	0	.229	.333
1 Bill Cissell	SS12	R	28	12	43	7	11	1	1	1	5	1	0	0	.256	.395
1 Smead Jolley	OF11	L	30	12	42	3	15	3	0	0	7	3	0	1	.357	.429
Hal Anderson	OF9	R	28	9	32	4	8	0	0	0	2	0	1	0	.250	.250
1 Bruce Campbell	OF6	L	22	9	26	3	4	1	0	0	2	0	4†	0	.154	.192
Mel Simons	OF6	L	32	7	5	0	0	0	0	0	0	0	1	0	.000	.000

Fabian Kowalik 24 L 5-13, 1 Bennie Tate 30 L 1-10, Greg Mulleavy 26 R 0-3

NAME	T	AGE	W	L	PCT	SV	G	GS	CG	IP	H	BB	SO	ShO	ERA
		31	49	102	.325	12	152	152	50	1349	1550	579	377	2	4.82
Ted Lyons	R	31	10	15	.400	2	33	26	19	231	243	71	58	1	3.28
Sad Sam Jones	R	30	10	15	.400	0	30	28	10	200	217	75	64	0	4.23
Milt Gaston	R	36	7	17	.292	1	28	25	7	167	183	73	44	1	3.99
Paul Gregory	R	23	5	3	.625	0	33	9	3	118	125	51	39	0	4.50
1 Tommy Thomas	R	32	3	3	.500	0	12	3	1	44	55	15	11	0	6.14
Vic Frasier	R	27	3	13	.188	0	29	21	4	146	180	70	33	0	6.23
Pete Daglia	R	26	2	4	.333	0	12	5	2	50	67	20	16	0	5.76
Pat Caraway	L	26	2	6	.250	0	19	9	1	65	80	37	13	0	6.79
Red Faber	R	43	2	11	.154	6	42	5	0	106	123	38	26	0	3.74
Clarence Fieber	L	18	1	0	1.000	0	3	0	0	5	6	3	1	0	1.80
2 Chad Kimsey	R	25	1	1	.500	2	7	0	0	11	8	5	6	0	2.45
Charlie Biggs	R	25	1	1	.500	0	6	4	0	25	32	12	1	0	6.84
1 Bump Hadley	R	27	1	1#	.500	1	3	2	1	19	17	8#	13	0	3.79
Phil Gallivan	R	25	1	3	.250	0	13	3	1	33	49	24	12	0	7.63
Fabian Kowalik	R	24	0	1	.000	0	2	1	0	10	16	4	2	0	7.20
Art Smith	R	26	0	1	.000	0	3	2	0	7	17	4	1	0	11.57
Ed Walsh	R	27	0	2	.000	0	4	4	1	20	26	13	7	0	8.55
Bill Chamberlain	L	23	0	5	.000	0	12	5	0	41	39	25	11	0	4.61
Hal McKain	R	25	0	0	.000	0	8	0	0	11	17	5	7	0	11.46
Art Evans	L	20	0	0	.000	0	7	0	0	18	19	10	6	0	3.00
Bob Poser	R	22	0	0	.000	0	1	0	0	1	3	2	1	0	18.00
Grant Bowler	R	24	0	0	.000	0	4	0	0	6	15	3	2	0	16.50
Les Bartholomew	L	29	0	0	.000	0	3	0	0	5	5	6	1	0	5.40
Archie Wise	R	19	0	0	.000	0	2	0	0	7	8	5	2	0	5.14

Lew Fonseca 33 R 0-0, Jim Moore 28 R 0-0

BOSTON 8th 43-111 .279 64 — SHANO COLLINS 11-46 .193 — MARTY McMANUS 32-65 .330

NAME	G by POS	B	AGE	G	AB	R	H	2B	3B	HR	RBI	BB	SO	SB	BA	SA
TOTALS			29	154	5295	566	1331	253	57	53	530	469	539	46	.251	.351
2 Dale Alexander	1B101	R	29	101	376	58	140	27	3	8	56	55	19	4	.372*	.524
Marv Olson	2B106, 3B1	R	25	115	403	58	100	14	6	0	25	61	26	1	.248	.313
Rabbit Warstler	SS107	R	28	115	388	26	82	15	5	0	34	22	43	9	.211	.276
Urban Pickering	3B126, C1	R	33	132	457	47	119	28	5	2	40	39	71	3	.260	.357
2 Roy Johnson	OF85	L	29	94	348	70	104	24	4	11	47	44	41	13	.299	.486
Tom Oliver	OF116	R	29	122	455	39	120	23	3	0	37	25	12	1	.264	.327
2 Smead Jolley	OF126, C5	L	30	137	531	57	164	27	5	18	99	27	29	0	.309	.480
2 Bennie Tate	C76	L	30	81	273	21	67	12	5	2	26	20	6	0	.245	.348
Marty McManus	2B49, 3B30, SS2, 1B1	R	32	93	302	39	71	19	4	5	24	36	30	1	.235	.374
2 Johnny Watwood	OF46, 1B18	L	25	95	266	26	66	11	0	0	30	20	11	7	.248	.289
George Stumpf	OF51	L	21	79	169	18	34	2	2	1	18	18	21	1	.201	.254
Ed Connolly	C75	R	23	75	222	9	50	8	4	0	21	20	27	0	.225	.297
Hal Rhyne	SS55, 3B4, 2B1	R	33	71	207	26	47	12	5	0	14	23	14	3	.227	.333
1 Earl Webb	OF50, 1B2	L	33	52	192	23	54	9	1	5	27	25	15	0	.281	.417
Al Van Camp	1B25	R	28	34	103	10	23	4	2	0	6	4	17	0	.223	.301
Johnny Reder	1B10, 3B1	R	22	17	37	4	5	1	0	0	3	6	6	0	.135	.162
Andy Spognardi	2B9, SS3, 3B2	L	23	17	34	9	10	1	0	0	1	6	6	0	.294	.324
1 Jack Rothrock	OF12	B	27	12	48	3	10	1	0	0	0	5	5	3	.208	.229
1 Charlie Berry	C10	R	29	10	32	0	6	3	0	0	6	3	2	0	.188	.281
Howie Storie	C5	R	21	6	8	0	3	0	0	0	0	0	0	0	.375	.375
Otto Miller		R	31	2	2	0	0	0	0	0	0	0	0	0	.000	.000
Johnny Lucas		R	29	1	1	0	0	0	0	0	0	0	0	0	.000	.000
Hank Patterson	C1	R	24	1	1	0	0	0	0	0	0	0	0	0	.000	.000

NAME	T	AGE	W	L	PCT	SV	G	GS	CG	IP	H	BB	SO	ShO	ERA
		27	43	**111**	.279	7	154	154	42	1362	1574	**612**	365	2	5.02
Bob Kline	R	22	11	13	.458	2	47	19	4	172	203	76	31	1	5.28
2 Ivy Andrews	R	25	8	6	.571	0	25	19	8	142	144	53	30	0	3.80
Ed Durham	R	24	6	13	.316	0	34	22	4	175	187	49	52	0	3.81
Bob Weiland	L	26	6	16	.273	1	43	27	7	196	231	97	63	0	4.50
Johnny Welch	R	25	4	6	.400	0	20	8	3	72	93	38	26	1	5.25
1 Wilcy Moore	R	35	4	10	.286	4	37	2	0	84	98	42	28	0	5.25
1 Danny MacFayden	R	27	1	10	.091	0	12	11	6	78	91	33	29	0	5.08
John Michaels	L	24	1	6	.143	0	28	8	2	81	101	27	16	0	5.11
1 Jack Russell	R	26	1	7	.125	0	11	6	1	40	61	15	7	0	6.75
2 Gordon Rhodes	R	24	1	8	.111	0	12	11	4	79	79	31	22	0	5.13
Gordon McNaughton	R	21	0	1	.000	0	6	2	0	21	21	22	6	0	6.43
Pete Donohue	R	31	0	1	.000	0	4	2	0	13	18	6	1	0	7.61
2 Pete Appleton	R	28	0	3	.000	0	11	3	0	46	49	26	15	0	4.11
Ed Gallagher	L	21	0	3	.000	0	9	3	0	24	30	28	6	0	12.38
Larry Boerner	R	27	0	4	.000	0	21	5	0	61	71	37	19	0	5.02
Hod Lisenbee	R	33	0	4	.000	0	19	6	3	73	87	25	13	0	5.67
Regis Leheny	L	24	0	0	.000	0	2	0	0	3	5	3	1	0	15.00
Jud McLaughlin	L	20	0	0	.000	0	1	0	0	3	5	4	0	0	15.00

Ed Morris (DD)32

*Alexander, also with Detroit, league leader in BA with .367

CHICAGO 1st 90-64 .584 — ROGERS HORNSBY 53-44 .546 — CHARLIE GRIMM 37-20 .649

NAME	G by POS	B	AGE	G	AB	R	H	2B	3B	HR	RBI	BB	SO	SB	BA	SA
TOTALS			28	154	5462	720	1519	296	60	69	665	398	514	48	.278	.392
Charlie Grimm	1B149	L	33	149	570	66	175	42	2	7	80	35	22	2	.307	.425
Billy Herman	2B154	R	22	154	656	102	206	42	7	1	51	40	33	14	.314	.404
Billy Jurges	SS108, 3B5	R	24	115	396	40	100	24	4	2	52	19	26	1	.253	.348
Woody English	3B93, SS38	R	25	127	522	70	142	23	7	3	47	55	73	5	.272	.360
Kiki Cuyler (BF)	OF109	R	32	110	446	58	130	19	9	10	77	29	43	9	.291	.442
Johnny Moore	OF109	L	30	119	443	59	135	24	5	13	64	22	38	4	.305	.470
Riggs Stephenson	OF147	R	34	147	583	86	189	49	4	4	85	54	27	3	.324	.443
Gabby Hartnett	C117, 1B1	R	31	121	406	52	110	25	3	12	52	51	59	0	.271	.436
Stan Hack	3B51	L	22	72	178	32	42	5	6	2	19	17	16	5	.236	.365
Rollie Hemsley	C47, OF1	R	25	60	151	27	36	10	3	4	20	10	16	2	.238	.424
Marv Gudat	OF14, 1B8, P1	L	26	60	94	15	24	4	1	1	15	16	10	0	.255	.351
Lance Richbourg	OF33	L	34	44	148	22	38	2	2	1	21	8	4	0	.257	.318
Vince Barton	OF34	L	24	36	134	19	30	2	3	3	15	8	22	0	.224	.351
Mark Koenig	SS31	B	29	33	102	15	36	5	1	3	11	3	5	0	.353	.510
Frank Demaree	OF17	R	22	23	56	4	14	3	0	0	6	2	7	0	.250	.304
Zack Taylor	C14	R	33	21	30	2	6	1	0	0	3	1	4	0	.200	.233
Rogers Hornsby	OF10, 3B6	R	36	19	58	10	13	2	0	1	7	10	4	0	.224	.310
Harry Taylor	1B1	L	24	10	8	1	1	0	0	0	0	1	1	0	.125	.125
1 Danny Taylor	OF6	R	31	6	22	3	5	2	0	0	3	3	1	1	.227	.318

NAME	T	AGE	W	L	PCT	SV	G	GS	CG	IP	H	BB	SO	ShO	ERA
		31	90	64	.584	7	154	154	79	1401	1444	409	527	9	3.44
Lon Warneke	R	23	22	6	.786	0	35	32	25	277	247	64	106	4	2.37
Guy Bush	R	30	19	11	.633	0	40	30	15	239	262	70	73	1	3.20
Charlie Root	R	33	15	10	.600	3	39	23	11	216	211	55	96	0	3.58
Pat Malone	R	29	15	17	.469	0	37	33	17	237	222	78	120	2	3.38
Burleigh Grimes	R	38	6	11	.353	1	30	18	5	141	174	50	36	1	4.79
Bud Tinning	R	26	5	3	.625	0	24	7	2	93	93	24	30	0	2.81
Bob Smith	R	34	4	3	.571	2	34	11	4	119	148	36	35	1	4.61
Leroy Herrmann	R	26	2	1	.667	0	7	0	0	13	18	9	5	0	6.23
Jakie May	L	36	2	2	.500	1	35	0	0	54	61	19	20	0	4.33
Carroll Yerkes	L	29	0	0	.000	0	2	0	0	9	5	3	4	0	3.00
Ed Baecht	R	25	0	0	.000	0	1	0	0	1	1	1	0	0	0.00
Marv Gudat	L	26	0	0	.000	0	1	0	0	1	1	0	2	0	0.00
Bobo Newsom	R	24	0	0	.000	0	1	0	0	1	1	0	0	0	0.00

PITTSBURGH 2nd 86-68 .558 4 — GEORGE GIBSON

NAME	G by POS	B	AGE	G	AB	R	H	2B	3B	HR	RBI	BB	SO	SB	BA	SA
TOTALS			27	154	5421	701	1543	274	90	48	653	358	385	71	.285	.395
Gus Suhr	1B154	L	26	154	581	78	156	31	10	5	81	63	39	7	.263	.387
Tony Piet	2B154	R	25	154	574	66	162	25	8	7	85	46	56	19	.282	.390
Arky Vaughn	SS128	L	20	129	497	71	158	15	10	4	61	39	26	10	.318	.412
Pie Traynor	3B127	R	32	135	513	74	169	27	10	2	68	32	20	6	.329	.433
Paul Waner	OF154	L	29	154	630	107	215	62	10	8	82	56	24	13	.341	.510
Lloyd Waner	OF131	L	26	134	565	90	188	27	11	2	38	31	11	6	.333	.428
Adam Comorosky	OF92	R	27	108	370	54	106	18	4	4	46	25	20	7	.286	.389
Earl Grace	C114	L	25	115	390	41	107	17	5	8	55	14	23	0	.274	.405
Dave Barbee	OF78	R	27	97	327	37	84	22	6	5	55	18	38	1	.257	.407
Tommy Thevenow (BG)	SS29, 3B22	R	28	59	194	12	46	3	3	0	26	7	12	0	.237	.284
Gus Dugas	OF20	L	25	55	97	13	23	3	3	3	12	7	11	0	.237	.423
Tom Padden	C43	R	23	47	118	13	31	6	1	0	10	9	7	0	.263	.331
Hal Finney (EJ)	C11	R	26	31	33	14	7	3	0	0	4	3	4	0	.212	.303
Howdie Groskloss	SS1	R	24	17	20	1	2	0	0	0	0	0	3	0	.100	.100
Bill Brenzel	C9	R	22	9	24	0	1	1	0	0	2	0	4	0	.042	.083
Bill Brubaker	3B7	R	21	7	24	3	10	3	0	0	4	3	4	1	.417	.542
Woody Jensen	OF1	L	24	7	5	2	0	0	0	0	0	0	2	0	.000	.000

NAME	T	AGE	W	L	PCT	SV	G	GS	CG	IP	H	BB	SO	ShO	ERA
		29	86	68	.558	12	154	154	71	1377	1472	338	377	12	3.75
Larry French	L	24	18	16	.529	4	47	33	19	274	301	62	72	3	3.02
Bill Swift	R	24	14	10	.583	4	39	23	11	214	205	26	64	0	3.62
Heinie Meine	R	36	12	9	.571	1	28	25	13	172	193	45	32	1	3.87
Steve Swetonic	R	28	11	6	.647	0	24	19	11	163	134	55	39	4	2.82
Bill Harris	R	32	10	9	.526	2	37	17	4	168	178	38	63	0	3.64
Leon Chagnon	R	29	9	6	.600	0	30	10	4	128	140	34	52	1	3.94
Ray Kremer	R	39	4	3	.571	0	11	10	3	57	61	16	6	1	4.26
Glenn Spencer	R	26	4	8	.333	1	39	13	5	138	167	44	35	1	4.96
Erv Brame	R	30	3	1	.750	0	23	3	0	51	84	16	10	0	7.41
Hal Smith	R	30	1	0	1.000	0	2	1	1	12	9	2	4	1	0.75

BROOKLYN 3rd 81-73 .526 9 — MAX CAREY

NAME	G by POS	B	AGE	G	AB	R	H	2B	3B	HR	RBI	BB	SO	SB	BA	SA
TOTALS			30	154	5433	752	1538	296	59	110	703	388	574	61	.283	.420
George Kelly	1B62, OF1	R	36	64	202	23	49	9	1	4	22	22	27	0	.243	.356
Tony Cuccinello	2B154	R	24	154	597	76	168	32	6	12	77	46	47	5	.281	.415
Glenn Wright	SS122, 1B2	R	31	127	446	50	122	31	5	11	60	12	57	4	.274	.439
Joe Stripp	3B93, 1B43	R	29	138	534	94	162	36	9	6	64	36	30	14	.303	.438
Hack Wilson	OF125	R	32	135	481	77	143	37	5	23	123	51	85	2	.297	.538
2 Danny Taylor	OF96	R	31	105	395	84	128	22	7	11	48	33	41	13	.324	.499
Lefty O'Doul	OF148	L	35	148	595	120	219	32	8	21	90	50	20	11	.368	.555
Al Lopez	C125	R	23	126	404	44	111	18	6	1	43	34	35	3	.275	.356
Johnny Frederick	OF88	L	31	118	384	54	115	28	2	16	56	25	35	1	.299	.508
Gordon Slade	SS55, 3B23	R	27	79	250	23	60	15	1	1	23	11	26	3	.240	.320
Neal Finn	3B50, 2B2, SS1	R	30	65	189	22	45	5	2	0	14	11	15	2	.238	.286
Clyde Sukeforth	C36	L	30	59	111	14	26	4	4	0	12	6	10	1	.234	.342
Bud Clancy	1B53	L	31	53	196	14	60	4	2	0	16	6	13	0	.306	.347
Val Picinich	C24	R	35	41	70	8	18	6	0	1	11	4	8	0	.257	.386
Max Rosenfeld	OF30	R	29	34	39	8	14	3	0	2	7	0	10	2	.359	.590
Ike Boone	OF8	L	35	13	21	2	3	1	0	0	2	5	2	0	.143	.190
Alta Cohen	OF8	L	23	9	32	1	5	1	0	0	1	3	7	0	.156	.188
Bruce Caldwell	1B6	R	26	7	11	2	1	0	0	0	2	2	2	0	.091	.091
Dick Siebert	1B6	L	20	6	7	1	2	0	0	0	0	2	2	0	.286	.286
Paul Richards	C3	R	23	3	8	0	0	0	0	0	0	0	2	0	.000	.000
Fresco Thompson		R	30	3	1	0	0	0	0	0	0	0	0	0	.000	.000
Bobby Reis	3B1	R	23	1	4	0	1	0	0	0	0	0	1	0	.250	.250
Del Bissonnette (LJ)32																

NAME	T	AGE	W	L	PCT	SV	G	GS	CG	IP	H	BB	SO	ShO	ERA
		32	81	73	.526	16	154	154	61	1380	1538	403	497	7	4.27
Watty Clark	L	30	20	12	.625	0	40	36	19	273	282	49	99	2	3.49
Van Lingle Mungo	R	21	13	11	.542	2	39	33	11	223	224	115	107	1	4.44
Sloppy Thurston	R	33	12	8	.600	0	28	20	10	153	174	38	35	2	4.06
Dazzy Vance	R	41	12	11	.522	1	27	24	9	176	171	57	103	1	4.19
Fred Heimach	L	31	9	4	.692	0	36	15	7	168	203	28	30	0	3.96
Joe Shaute	L	32	7	7	.500	4	34	9	1	117	147	21	32	0	4.54
Ray Phelps	R	28	4	5	.444	0	20	8	4	79	101	27	21	1	5.92
Jack Quinn	R	48	3	7	.300	8	42	0	0	87	102	24	28	0	3.31
1 Waite Hoyt	R	32	1	3	.250	1	8	4	0	27	38	12	7	0	7.67
Fay Thomas	R	27	0	1	.000	0	7	2	0	17	22	8	9	0	7.41
Ed Pipgras	R	28	0	1	.000	0	5	1	0	10	16	6	5	0	5.40
Cy Moore	R	27	0	3	.000	0	20	2	0	49	56	17	21	0	4.78
Art Jones	R	25	0	0	.000	0	1	0	0	1	2	1	0	0	8.00

PHILADELPHIA 4th 78-76 .506 12 — BURT SHOTTON

NAME	G by POS	B	AGE	G	AB	R	H	2B	3B	HR	RBI	BB	SO	SB	BA	SA
TOTALS			27	154	5510	844	1608	330	67	122	780	446	547	71	.292	.442
Don Hurst	1B150	L	26	150	579	109	196	41	4	24	143	65	27	10	.339	.547
Les Mallon	2B88, 3B5	R	26	103	347	44	90	16	0	5	31	28	28	1	.259	.349
Dick Bartell	SS154	R	24	154	614	118	189	48	7	1	53	64	47	8	.308	.414
Pinky Whitney	3B151, 2B5	R	27	154	624	93	186	33	11	13	124	35	66	6	.298	.449
Chuck Klein	OF154	L	27	154	650	152	226	50	15	38	137	60	49	20	.348	.646
Kiddo Davis	OF133	R	30	137	576	100	178	39	6	5	57	44	56	16	.309	.424
Hal Lee	OF148	R	27	149	595	76	180	42	10	18	85	36	45	6	.303	.497
Spud Davis	C120	R	27	125	402	44	135	23	5	14	70	40	39	1	.336	.522
Harry McCurdy	C42	L	32	62	136	13	32	6	1	1	14	17	13	0	.235	.316
Barney Friberg	2B56	R	32	61	154	17	37	8	2	0	14	19	23	0	.240	.318
Fred Brickell	OF12	L	25	45	66	9	22	6	1	0	2	4	5	2	.333	.455
Al Todd	C25	R	28	33	70	8	16	5	0	0	9	1	9	1	.229	.300
2 Eddie Delker	2B27	R	25	30	62	7	10	1	1	1	7	6	14	0	.161	.258
2 Cliff Heathcote	1B7	L	34	30	39	7	11	2	0	1	5	3	3	0	.282	.410
1 Rube Bressler	OF18	R	37	27	83	9	19	6	1	0	6	2	5	0	.229	.325
Russ Scarritt	OF1	L	29	11	11	0	2	0	0	0	0	1	2	0	.182	.182
George Knothe	2B5	R	34	6	12	2	1	1	0	0	0	0	0	0	.083	.167
Doug Taitt		L	29	4	2	0	0	0	0	0	1	2	0	0	.000	.000
Hugh Willingham		R	24	4	2	0	0	0	0	0	0	0	0	0	.000	.000

NAME	T	AGE	W	L	PCT	SV	G	GS	CG	IP	H	BB	SO	ShO	ERA
		30	78	76	.506	17	154	154	69	1384	1589	450	459	4	4.47
Phil Collins	R	30	14	12	.538	3	43	21	6	184	231	65	66	0	5.28
Ray Benge	R	30	13	12	.520	6	41	28	13	222	247	58	89	2	4.05
2 Flint Rhem	R	31	11	7	.611	1	26	20	10	169	177	49	35	0	3.73
Jumbo Jim Elliott	L	31	11	10	.524	0	39	22	8	166	210	47	62	0	5.42
Ed Holley	R	30	11	14	.440	0	34	30	16	228	247	55	87	2	3.95
Snipe Hansen	L	25	10	10	.500	2	39	23	5	191	215	51	56	0	3.72
Ad Liska	R	25	2	0	1.000	1	8	0	0	27	22	10	6	0	1.67
Reggie Grabowski	R	24	2	2	.500	0	14	2	0	34	38	22	15	0	3.71
Hal Elliott	R	33	2	4	.333	0	16	7	0	58	70	38	13	0	5.74
Clise Dudley	R	28	1	1	.500	1	13	0	0	18	23	8	5	0	7.00
Jack Berly	R	29	1	2	.333	2	21	1	1	46	61	21	15	0	7.63
Chet Nichols	R	34	0	2	.000	1	11	0	0	19	23	14	5	0	7.11
Stew Bolen	L	29	0	0	.000	0	5	0	0	16	18	10	3	0	2.81
Bob Adams	R	25	0	0	.000	0	4	0	0	6	7	2	2	0	1.50

BOSTON 5th 77-77 .500 13 — BILL McKECHNIE

NAME	G by POS	B	AGE	G	AB	R	H	2B	3B	HR	RBI	BB	SO	SB	BA	SA
TOTALS			29	155	5506	649	1460	262	53	63	594	347	496	36	.265	.366
Art Shires (BK)	1B80	L	24	82	298	32	71	9	3	5	30	25	21	1	.238	.339
Rabbit Maranville	2B149	R	40	149	571	67	134	20	4	0	37	46	28	4	.235	.284
Billy Urbanski	SS136	R	29	136	563	80	153	25	8	8	46	28	60	8	.272	.387
Fritz Knothe	3B87	R	29	89	344	45	82	19	1	1	36	39	37	5	.238	.308
Wes Schulmerich	OF101	R	30	119	404	47	105	22	5	11	57	27	61	5	.260	.421
Wally Berger	OF134, 1B11	R	26	145	602	90	185	34	6	17	73	33	66	5	.307	.468
Red Worthington (BN)	OF104	R	26	105	435	62	132	35	8	8	61	15	24	1	.303	.476
Al Spohrer	C100	R	29	104	335	31	90	12	2	0	33	15	26	2	.269	.316
Randy Moore	OF41, 3B31, 1B22, C1	L	27	107	351	41	103	21	2	3	43	15	11	1	.293	.390
Freddy Leach	OF50	L	34	84	223	21	55	9	2	1	29	18	10	1	.247	.318
Pinky Hargrave (BN)	C73	B	36	82	217	20	57	14	3	4	33	24	18	1	.263	.410
Earl Clark	OF16	R	24	50	44	11	11	2	0	0	4	2	7	1	.250	.295
Buck Jordan	1B49	L	25	49	212	27	68	12	3	2	29	4	5	1	.321	.434
2 Hod Ford	2B20, SS16, 3B2	R	34	40	95	9	26	5	2	0	6	6	9	0	.274	.368
Dutch Holland	OF39	R	28	39	156	15	46	11	1	1	18	12	20	0	.295	.397
Bill Akers	3B20, 2B5, SS5	R	27	36	93	8	24	3	1	1	17	10	15	0	.258	.344
Bucky Walters	3B22	R	23	22	75	8	14	3	1	0	4	2	18	0	.187	.253
2 Johnny Schulte	C10	L	35	10	9	1	2	0	0	1	2	2	1	0	.222	.556
Ox Eckhardt		L	30	8	8	1	2	0	0	0	1	0	1	0	.250	.250

NAME	T	AGE	W	L	PCT	SV	G	GS	CG	IP	H	BB	SO	ShO	ERA
		30	77	77	.500	8	155	155	72	1414	1483	420	440	8	3.53
Ed Brandt	L	27	16	16	.500	1	35	31	19	254	271	57	79	2	3.97
Bob Brown	R	21	14	7	.667	1	35	28	9	213	187	104	110	0	3.30
Ben Cantwell	R	30	13	11	.542	5	37	9	3	146	133	33	33	1	2.96
Huck Betts	R	35	13	11	.542	1	31	27	16	222	229	35	32	3	2.80
Tom Zachary	L	36	12	11	.522	0	32	24	12	212	231	55	67	1	3.10
Fred Frankhouse	R	28	4	6	.400	0	37	6	3	109	113	45	35	0	3.55
Socks Seibold	R	36	3	10	.231	0	28	20	6	137	173	41	33	1	4.66
Bruce Cunningham	R	26	1	0	1.000	0	18	3	0	47	50	19	21	0	3.45
Hub Pruett (LJ)	L	31	1	5	.167	0	18	7	4	63	76	30	27	0	5.14
Leo Margum	R	36	0	0	.000	0	7	0	0	10	17	0	3	0	5.40
1 Bill Sherdel	L	35	0	0	.000	0	1	0	0	2	3	1	0	0	0.00

NEW YORK 6th (Tie) 72-82 .468 18 — JOHN McGRAW 17-23 .425 BILL TERRY 55-59 .482

NAME	G by POS	B	AGE	G	AB	R	H	2B	3B	HR	RBI	BB	SO	SB	BA	SA
TOTALS			25	154	**5530**	755	1527	263	54	116	718	348	391	31	.276	.406
Bill Terry	1B154	L	33	154	643	124	225	42	11	28	117	32	23	4	.350	.580
Hughie Critz	2B151	R	31	151	**659**	90	182	32	7	2	50	34	27	3	.276	.355
Doc Marshall	SS63	R	26	68	226	18	56	8	1	0	28	6	11	1	.248	.292
Johnny Vergez	3B111, SS1	R	25	118	376	42	98	21	3	6	43	25	36	1	.261	.380
Mel Ott	OF154	L	23	154	566	119	180	30	8	**38**	123	**100**	39	6	.318	.601
Fred Lindstrom	OF128, 3B15	R	26	144	595	83	161	26	5	15	92	27	28	6	.271	.407
Jo-Jo Moore	OF86	L	23	86	361	53	110	15	2	2	27	20	18	4	.305	.374
Shanty Hogan	C136	R	26	140	502	36	144	18	2	8	77	26	22	0	.287	.378
Chick Fullis	OF55, 2B1	R	28	96	235	35	70	14	3	1	21	11	12	1	.298	.396
Sam Leslie	1B2	L	26	77	75	5	22	4	0	1	15	2	5	0	.293	.387
Gil English	3B39, SS23	R	22	59	204	22	46	7	5	2	19	5	20	0	.225	.338
Ethan Allen	OF24	R	28	54	103	13	18	6	2	1	7	1	12	0	.175	.301
Travis Jackson (BK)	SS52	R	28	52	195	23	50	17	1	4	38	13	16	1	.256	.415
Bob O'Farrell	C41	R	35	50	67	7	16	3	0	0	8	11	10	0	.239	.284
Len Koenecke	OF35	L	28	42	137	33	35	5	0	4	14	11	13	3	.255	.380
Eddie Moore	SS21, 3B6, 2B5	R	33	37	87	9	23	3	0	1	6	9	6	1	.264	.333
Francis Healy	C11	R	22	14	32	5	8	2	0	0	4	2	8	0	.250	.313

Art McLarney 23 B 3-23, Pat Veltman 26 R 0-1, Jack Tobin 25 R 0-1

NAME	T	AGE	W	L	PCT	SV	G	GS	CG	IP	H	BB	SO	ShO	ERA
		30	72	82	.468	16	154	154	57	1375	1533	387	506	3	3.76
Carl Hubbell	L	29	18	11	.621	2	40	32	22	284	260	40	137	0	2.50
Freddie Fitzsimmons	R	30	11	11	.500	0	35	31	11	238	287	83	65	0	4.42
Hi Bell	R	34	8	4	.667	2	35	10	3	120	132	16	25	0	3.68
Bill Walker	L	28	8	12	.400	2	31	22	9	163	177	55	74	0	4.14
Dolf Luque	R	41	6	7	.462	5	38	5	1	110	128	32	32	0	4.01
Jim Mooney	L	25	6	10	.375	0	29	18	4	125	154	42	37	1	5.04
Hal Schumacher	R	21	5	6	.455	0	27	13	2	101	119	39	38	1	3.56
2 Waite Hoyt	R	32	5	7	.417	0	18	12	3	97	103	25	29	0	3.43
Sam Gibson	R	32	4	8	.333	3	41	5	1	82	107	30	39	1	4.83
Clarence Mitchell	L	41	1	3	.250	2	8	3	1	30	41	11	7	0	4.20
Roy Parmelee	R	25	0	3	.000	0	8	3	0	25	25	14	23	0	3.96

ST. LOUIS 6th (Tie) 72-82 .468 18 — GABBY STREET

NAME	G by POS	B	AGE	G	AB	R	H	2B	3B	HR	RBI	BB	SO	SB	BA	SA
TOTALS			30	156	5458	684	1467	307	51	76	626	420	514	**92**	.269	.385
Ripper Collins	1B81, OF60	B	28	149	549	82	153	28	8	21	91	38	67	4	.279	.474
Jimmy Reese	2B77	L	27	90	309	38	82	15	0	2	26	20	19	4	.265	.333
Charlie Gelbert	SS122	R	26	122	455	60	122	28	9	1	45	39	30	8	.268	.376
Jake Flowers	3B54, SS7, 2B2	R	30	67	247	35	63	11	1	2	18	31	18	7	.255	.332
George Watkins	OF120	L	32	127	458	67	143	35	3	9	63	45	46	18	.312	.461
Pepper Martin (BG)	OF69, 3B15	R	28	85	323	47	77	19	6	4	34	30	31	9	.238	.372
Ernie Orsatti (SJ)	OF96, 1B1	L	29	101	375	44	126	27	6	2	44	18	29	5	.336	.456
Gus Mancuso	C82	R	26	103	310	25	88	23	1	5	43	30	15	0	.284	.413
Frankie Frisch	2B75, 3B37, SS4	B	33	115	486	59	142	26	2	3	60	25	13	18	.292	.372
Jimmie Wilson	C75, 1B3, 2B1	R	31	92	274	36	68	16	2	2	28	15	18	9	.248	.343
Jim Bottomley	1B74	L	32	91	311	45	92	16	3	11	48	25	32	2	.296	.473
Ray Blades	OF62, 3B1	R	35	80	201	35	46	10	1	3	29	34	31	2	.229	.333
Sparky Adams (KJ)	3B30	R	37	31	127	22	35	3	1	0	13	14	5	0	.276	.315
George Puccinelli	OF30	R	25	31	108	17	30	8	0	3	11	12	13	1	.278	.435
1 Harvey Hendrick	3B12, OF5	L	34	28	72	8	18	2	0	1	5	5	9	0	.250	.319
Joe Medwick	OF26	R	20	26	106	13	37	12	1	2	12	2	10	3	.349	.538
Charlie Wilson	SS24	B	27	24	96	7	19	3	3	1	2	3	8	0	.198	.323
Ray Pepper	OF17	R	26	21	57	3	14	2	1	0	7	5	13	1	.246	.316
1 Eddie Delker	2B10, 3B5, SS4	R	25	20	42	1	5	4	0	0	2	8	7	0	.119	.214
Mike Gonzalez	C7	R	41	17	14	0	2	0	0	0	3	0	2	0	.143	.143
Joel Hunt	OF5	R	26	12	21	0	4	1	0	0	3	4	3	0	.190	.238
Ray Cunningham	3B8, 2B2	R	24	11	22	4	4	1	0	0	0	3	4	0	.182	.227
Wattie Holm	OF4	R	30	11	17	2	3	1	0	0	1	3	1	0	.176	.235

2 Rube Bressler 37 R 3-19, Bill DeLancey 20 L 5-26, 1 Hod Ford 34 R 0-2, Skeeter Webb 22 R 0-0

NAME	T	AGE	W	L	PCT	SV	G	GS	CG	IP	H	BB	SO	ShO	ERA
		29	72	82	.468	9	156	156	70	1396	1533	**455**	**681**	**13**	3.97
Dizzy Dean	R	21	18	15	.545	2	46	33	16	**286**	280	102	**191**	**4**	3.30
Wild Bill Hallahan	L	29	12	7	.632	1	25	22	13	176	169	69	198	1	3.12
Paul Derringer	R	25	11	14	.440	0	39	30	14	233	296	67	78	1	4.06
Tex Carleton	R	25	10	13	.435	0	44	22	9	196	198	70	113	3	4.09
Syl Johnson	R	31	5	14	.263	2	32	22	7	165	199	35	70	1	4.91
1 Flint Rhem	R	31	4	2	.667	0	6	6	5	50	48	10	18	1	3.06
Allyn Stout	R	27	4	5	.444	1	36	3	1	74	87	28	32	0	4.38
Jesse Haines	R	38	3	5	.375	0	20	10	4	85	116	16	27	1	4.76
Jim Lindsey	R	34	3	3	.500	3	33	5	0	89	96	38	31	0	4.96
Jim Winford	R	22	1	1	.500	0	4	1	0	8	9	5	4	0	6.75
Ray Starr	R	26	1	1	.500	0	3	2	1	20	19	10	6	1	2.70
1 Benny Frey	R	26	0	2	.000	0	2	0	0	3	6	2	0	0	12.00
2 Bill Sherdel	L	35	0	0	.000	0	3	0	0	6	7	1	1	0	4.50
Bud Teachout	L	28	0	0	.000	0	1	0	0	1	2	0	0	0	0.00
Dick Terwilliger	R	26	0	0	.000	0	1	0	0	3	1	2	2	0	0.00

CINCINNATI 8th 60-94 .390 30 — DAN HOWLEY

NAME	G by POS	B	AGE	G	AB	R	H	2B	3B	HR	RBI	BB	SO	SB	BA	SA
TOTALS			30	155	5443	575	1429	265	68	47	546	436	436	35	.263	.362
2 Harvey Hendrick	1B94	L	34	94	398	56	120	30	3	4	40	23	29	3	.302	.422
George Grantham	2B115, 1B10	L	32	126	493	81	144	29	6	6	39	56	40	4	.292	.412
Leo Durocher	SS142	R	26	143	457	43	99	22	5	1	33	36	40	3	.217	.293
Wally Gilbert	3B111	R	31	114	420	35	90	18	2	1	40	20	23	2	.214	.274
Babe Herman	OF146	L	29	148	577	87	188	38	**19**	16	87	60	45	7	.326	.541
Estel Crabtree	OF95	L	28	108	402	38	110	14	9	2	35	23	26	2	.274	.368
Wally Roettger	OF94	R	29	106	347	26	96	18	3	3	43	23	24	0	.277	.372
Ernie Lombardi	C110	R	24	118	413	43	125	22	9	11	68	41	19	0	.303	.479
Taylor Douthit	OF88	R	31	96	333	28	81	12	1	0	25	31	29	3	.243	.285
Jo-Jo Morrissey	SS45, 2B42, 3B12, OF1	R	28	89	269	15	65	10	1	0	13	14	15	2	.242	.286
Andy High	3B46, 2B12	L	34	84	191	16	36	4	2	0	12	23	6	1	.188	.230
Chick Hafey (IL)	OF65	R	29	83	253	34	87	19	3	2	36	22	20	4	.344	.466
Red Lucas	P31	L	30	76	150	13	43	11	2	0	19	10	9	0	.287	.387
Clyde Manion	C47	R	35	49	135	7	28	4	0	0	12	14	16	0	.207	.237
Mickey Heath	1B39	L	28	39	134	14	27	1	3	0	15	20	23	0	.201	.254
Casper Asbjornson	C16	R	23	29	58	5	10	2	0	1	4	0	15	0	.172	.259
Harry Heilmann	1B6	R	37	15	31	3	8	2	0	0	6	0	2	0	.258	.323

1 Cliff Heathcote 34 L 0-3, Jimmy Shevlin 22 L 5-24, Otto Bluege 22 R 0-0

NAME	T	AGE	W	L	PCT	SV	G	GS	CG	IP	H	BB	SO	ShO	ERA
		32	60	**94**	.390	6	155	155	**83**	1395	1505	276	359	6	3.79
Si Johnson	R	25	13	15	.464	2	42	27	14	245	246	57	94	2	3.27
Red Lucas	R	30	13	17	.433	0	31	31	**28**	269	261	35	63	0	2.94
Ownie Carroll	R	29	10	**19**	.345	1	32	26	15	210	245	44	55	0	4.50
Ray Kolp	R	37	6	10	.375	1	32	19	7	160	176	27	42	2	3.88
Larry Benton	R	34	6	13	.316	2	35	21	7	180	201	27	35	0	4.30
Eppa Rixey	L	41	5	5	.500	0	25	11	6	112	108	16	14	2	2.65
2 Benny Frey	R	26	4	10	.286	0	28	15	5	131	159	30	27	0	4.33
Jack Ogden	R	34	2	2	.500	0	24	3	1	57	72	22	20	0	5.21
Bipp Wysong	L	27	1	0	1.000	0	7	0	0	12	13	8	5	0	3.75
Whitey Hilcher	R	23	0	3	.000	0	11	2	0	19	24	10	4	0	7.58

WORLD SERIES – NEW YORK (AL) 4 CHICAGO (NL) 0

LINE SCORES

TEAM	1	2	3	4	5	6	7	8	9	10	11	12	R	H	E
Game 1 September 28 at New York															
CHI (NL)	2	0	0	0	0	0	2	2	0				6	10	1
NY (AL)	0	0	0	3	0	5	3	1	X				12	8	2
Bush, Grimes (6), Smith (8)				**Ruffing**											
Game 2 September 29 at New York															
CHI	1	0	1	0	0	0	0	0	0				2	9	0
NY	2	0	2	0	1	0	0	0	X				5	10	1
Warneke		**Gomez**													
Game 3 October 1 at Chicago															
NY	3	0	1	0	2	0	0	0	1				7	8	1
CHI	1	0	2	1	0	0	0	0	1				5	9	4
Pipgras, Pennock (9)				**Root**, Malone (5), May (8), Tinning (9)											
Game 4 October 2 at Chicago															
NY	1	0	2	0	0	2	4	0	4				13	19	4
CHI	4	0	0	0	0	1	0	0	1				6	9	1
Allen, **W. Moore** (1), Pennock (7)				Bush, Warneke (1), **May** (4), Tinning (7), Grimes (9)											

COMPOSITE BATTING

NAME	POS	G	AB	R	H	2B	3B	HR	RBI	BA
New York (AL)										
Totals		4	144	37	45	6	0	8	36	.313
Gehrig	1B	4	17	**9**	**9**	1	0	**3**	**8**	**.529**
Chapman	OF	4	17	1	5	**2**	0	0	6	.294
Lazzeri	2B	4	17	4	5	0	0	2	5	.294
Dickey	C	4	16	2	7	0	0	0	4	.438
Combs	OF	4	16	8	6	1	0	1	4	.375
Ruth	OF	4	15	6	5	0	0	2	6	.333
Sewell	3B	4	15	4	5	1	0	0	3	.333
Crosetti	SS	4	15	2	2	1	0	0	0	.133
Pipgras	P	1	5	0	0	0	0	0	0	.000
Ruffing	P	2	4	0	0	0	0	0	0	.000
W. Moore	P	1	3	0	1	0	0	0	0	.333
Gomez	P	1	3	0	0	0	0	0	0	.000
Pennock	P	2	1	0	0	0	0	0	0	.000
Byrd	OF	1	0	0	0	0	0	0	0	.000
Hoag	PR	1	0	1	0	0	0	0	0	.000
Allen	P	1	0	0	0	0	0	0	0	.000
Chicago (NL)										
Totals		4	146	19	37	8	2	3	16	.253
Stephenson	OF	4	**18**	2	8	1	0	0	4	.444
Cuyler	OF	4	**18**	2	5	1	1	1	2	.278
Herman	2B	4	**18**	5	4	1	0	0	1	.222
English	3B	4	17	2	3	0	0	0	1	.176
Hartnett	C	4	16	2	5	**2**	0	1	1	.313
Grimm	1B	4	15	2	5	**2**	0	0	1	.333
Jurges	SS	3	11	1	4	1	0	0	1	.364
Demaree	OF	2	7	1	2	0	0	1	4	.286
J. Moore	OF	2	7	1	0	0	0	0	0	.000
Koenig	SS	2	4	1	1	0	1	0	1	.250
Warneke	P	2	4	0	0	0	0	0	0	.000
Hemsley	C	3	3	0	0	0	0	0	0	.000
Gudat	PH	2	2	0	0	0	0	0	0	.000
May	P	2	2	0	0	0	0	0	0	.000
Root	P	1	2	0	0	0	0	0	0	.000
Bush	P	2	1	0	0	0	0	0	0	.000
Grimes	P	2	1	0	0	0	0	0	0	.000
Tinning	P	2	0	0	0	0	0	0	0	.000
Hack	PR	1	0	0	0	0	0	0	0	.000
Malone	P	1	0	0	0	0	0	0	0	.000
Smith	P	1	0	0	0	0	0	0	0	.000

COMPOSITE PITCHING

NAME	G	IP	H	BB	SO	W	L	SV	ERA
New York (AL)									
Totals	4	36	37	11	24	4	0	2	3.25
Gomez	1	9	9	1	8	1	0	0	**1.00**
Ruffing	1	9	10	**6**	**10**	1	0	0	4.00
Pipgras	1	8	9	3	1	1	0	0	4.50
W. Moore	1	5.1	2	0	1	1	0	0	0.00
Pennock	2	4	2	1	4	0	0	**2**	2.25
Allen	1	.2	5	0	0	0	0	0	40.50
Chicago (NL)									
Totals	4	34	45	23	26	0	4	0	9.26
Warneke	2	**10.2**	**15**	5	8	0	1	0	5.91
Bush	2	5.2	5	**6**	2	0	1	0	14.29
May	2	4.2	9	3	4	0	1	0	11.57
Root	1	4.1	6	3	4	0	1	0	10.38
Malone	1	2.2	1	4	4	0	0	0	0.00
Grimes	2	2.2	7	2	0	0	0	0	23.63
Tinning	2	2.1	0	0	3	0	0	0	0.00
Smith	1	1	2	0	1	0	0	0	9.00

1933 A Starry Conglomerate

John McGraw was there and so was Connie Mack. There was also Ruth, Gehrig, Simmons, Dykes, Cronin, Gomez, Grove, Frisch, Klein, Terry, Traynor, Hubbell, Hartnett, and Paul Waner. They didn't all belong to the same team or league, but nevertheless they, with several other of their prominent colleagues, were assembled at Comiskey Park in Chicago on July 6, for the first All-Star Game.

McGraw came out of retirement to pilot the Nationals. Mack, at 61, had been around even before the junior circuit dawned and was an obvious choice to lead the Americans. The idea for *the game* came from Grantland Rice, dean of sportswriters. Baseball fans endorsed the idyllic scheme by sending 49,000 of their breed to pay homage to the event.

It was a game which millions of fans throughout the country had long conceived in fantasy, never daring to hope beyond their imaginative scribbling of dream lineups that it would suddenly turn into disbelieving reality. But there it was—plunk in the middle of a depression—a mastermind of a promotion that pitted the best against the best. Fostered as a benefit to raise funds for the National Association of Professional Baseball Players, the game was an instant success.

McGraw regarded the "dream game" for what it simply seemed to be—a dream game. Mack had different notions and a better team. Once he got the lead in the second inning on Lefty Grove's single, he coldly decided to play baseball and not shuttle his players, save for the pitchers and Earl Averill, who pinch-hit for General Crowder in the sixth. Mack's other players, Jimmie Foxx, Tony Lazzeri, Bill Dickey, Oral Hildebrand, and Wes Ferrell, spent the game in the best seats in the house—the dugout. Matters were decided in the third inning when Babe Ruth, playing on 38-year-old legs, delivered a home run with Charlie Gehringer on board for what turned out to be the go-ahead run in a 4-2 game.

In the regular business at hand, Washington captured the American League pennant in easy fashion behind rookie manager Joe Cronin, who also spent the season at shortstop with a .309 average. Washington's drive to the pennant was strongly aided by several off-season trades which brought to the team Goose Goslin, Fred Schulte, Lefty Stewart, Luke Sewell, Jack Russell, and Earl Whitehill.

The Yankees gave up the chance to repeat due to poorer pitching and age beginning to catch up with Ruth. The A's traded away their pennant hopes when Al Simmons, Jimmy Dykes, and Mule Haas were sent to the White Sox. Only Lefty Grove, 24-8, and Jimmie Foxx, winner of the Triple Crown, saved Mack from a totally disgraceful season.

The Giants matched Washington's stunt of winning a pennant with a playing-manager in Bill Terry, who led the team with a .322 average and a five-game victory over Pittsburgh for the Jints' first National League flag since 1924. Terry was the main offensive threat on a squad which relied heavily on strong pitching by aces, Carl Hubbell and Hal Schumacher. Reversing the New York story, the hot-hitting Pirates were hurt by a weak mound staff. The Cubs looked like they would easily repeat when they got Babe Herman from Cincinnati, but despite taking the Reds' best hitter they could do no better than tie their season series with the tail-enders and finish third, six games off the pace. The Phillies, although finishing seventh, helped make history behind Chuck Klein's Triple Crown performance, which made Philadelphia the only city ever to produce in one year two men to lead their leagues in average, home runs, and runs batted in.

When it came to the World Series, Washington and Cronin were the favorite, but the spirit which Terry instilled in bringing the Giants from sixth in 1932, was enough for a five-game Series victory. Both playing-managers played well, but the hero's laurels went to Carl Hubbell, who pitched two complete game victories, and 24-year-old Mel Ott, who led both teams in batting and clouted a tenth-inning homer to wrap up the final game for New York.

In another of the interesting highlights of the season, an energetic young man, Tom Yawkey, purchased the Red Sox in February. Yawkey's determination to bring a winning team to Boston often culminated—as history would prove in the many years to come—in spending exorbitant dollars for veteran players and hot prospects alike. But as fate would have it, Yawkey's dollars, more often than not, fell far short of the value he received. In fact, Yawkey's misfortunes did not wait long to visit him. When he purchased aging, but brilliant Lefty Grove from Connie Mack for the 1934 season, the hard luck was well underway.

1933 AMERICAN LEAGUE

NAME	G by POS	B	AGE	G	AB	R	H	2B	3B	HR	RBI	BB	SO	SB	BA	SA
WASHINGTON 1st 99-53 .651		JOE CRONIN														
TOTALS			30	153	5524	850	1586	281	86	60	793	539	395	65	.287	.402
Joe Kuhel	1B153	L	27	153	602	89	194	34	10	11	107	59	48	17	.322	.467
Buddy Myer	2B129	L	29	131	530	95	160	29	15	4	61	60	29	6	.302	.436
Joe Cronin	SS152	R	26	152	602	89	186	45	11	5	118	87	49	5	.309	.445
Ossie Bluege	3B128	R	32	140	501	63	131	14	0	6	71	55	34	6	.261	.325
Goose Goslin	OF128	L	32	132	549	97	163	35	10	10	64	42	32	5	.297	.452
Fred Schulte	OF142	R	32	144	550	98	162	30	7	5	87	61	27	10	.295	.402
Heinie Manush	OF150	L	31	153	658	115	221	32	17	5	95	36	18	6	.336	.459
Luke Sewell	C141	R	32	141	474	64	125	30	4	2	61	48	24	7	.264	.357
Dave Harris	OF45, 1B6, 3B2	R	33	82	177	33	46	9	2	5	38	25	26	3	.260	.418
Sam Rice	OF39	L	43	73	85	19	25	4	3	1	12	3	7	0	.294	.447
Bob Boken	2B31, 3B19, SS10	R	25	55	133	19	37	5	2	3	26	9	16	0	.278	.414
Moe Berg	C35	R	31	40	65	8	12	3	0	2	9	4	5	0	.185	.323
Cliff Bolton	C9, OF1	L	26	33	39	4	16	1	1	0	6	6	3	0	.410	.487
John Kerr	2B16, 3B1	R	34	28	40	5	8	0	0	0	0	3	2	0	.200	.200
Cecil Travis	3B15	L	19	18	43	7	13	1	0	0	2	2	5	0	.302	.326
Nick Altrock		B	56	1	1	0	0	0	0	0	0	0	0	0	.000	.000
NEW YORK 2nd 91-59 .607 7		JOE McCARTHY														
TOTALS			29	152	5274	927	1495	241	75	144	849	700	506	74	.283	.440
Lou Gehrig	1B152	L	30	152	593	138	198	41	12	32	139	92	42	9	.334	.605
Tony Lazzeri	2B138	R	29	139	523	94	154	22	12	18	104	73	62	15	.294	.486
Frankie Crosetti	SS133	R	22	136	451	71	114	20	5	9	60	55	40	4	.253	.379
Joe Sewell	3B131	L	34	135	524	87	143	18	1	2	54	71	4	2	.273	.323
Babe Ruth	OF132, 1B1, P1	L	38	137	459	97	138	21	3	34	103	114	90	4	.301	.582
Earle Combs	OF104	L	34	122	419	86	125	22	16	5	60	47	19	6	.298	.463
Ben Chapman	OF147	R	24	147	565	112	176	36	4	9	98	72	45	27	.312	.437
Bill Dickey	C127	L	26	130	478	58	152	24	8	14	97	47	14	3	.318	.490
Dixie Walker	OF77	L	22	98	328	68	90	15	7	15	51	26	28	2	.274	.500
Sammy Byrd	OF71	R	26	85	107	26	30	6	1	2	11	15	12	0	.280	.411
Red Ruffing	P35	R	29	55	115	10	29	3	1	2	13	7	15	0	.252	.348
Lyn Lary	3B28, SS16, 1B3, OF1	R	27	52	127	25	28	3	3	0	13	28	17	2	.220	.291
Doc Farrell	SS22, 2B20	R	31	44	93	16	25	0	0	0	6	16	6	0	.269	.269
Art Jorgens	C19	R	28	21	50	9	11	3	0	2	13	12	3	1	.220	.400
Tony Rensa	C8	R	31	8	29	4	9	2	1	0	3	1	3	0	.310	.448
Joe Glenn	C5	R	24	5	21	1	3	0	0	0	1	0	3	0	.143	.143
1 Bill Werber	3B1	R	25	3	2	0	0	0	0	0	0	0	0	0	.000	.000
PHILADELPHIA 3rd 79-72 .523 19.5		CONNIE MACK														
TOTALS			27	152	5330	875	1519	299	56	139	829	625	618	33	.285	.440
Jimmie Foxx	1B149, SS1	R	25	149	573	125	204	37	9	48	163	96	93	2	.356	.703
Max Bishop	2B113	L	33	117	391	80	115	27	1	4	42	106	46	1	.294	.399
Dib Williams	SS84, 2B29, 1B2	R	23	115	408	52	118	20	5	11	73	32	35	1	.289	.444
Pinky Higgins	3B152	R	24	152	567	85	178	35	11	13	99	61	53	2	.314	.483
Ed Coleman	OF89	L	31	102	388	48	109	26	3	6	68	19	51	0	.281	.410
Doc Cramer	OF152	L	27	152	661	109	195	27	8	8	75	36	24	5	.295	.396
Bob Johnson	OF142	R	26	142	535	103	155	44	4	21	93	85	74	8	.290	.505
Mickey Cochrane	C128	L	30	130	429	104	138	30	4	15	60	106	22	8	.322	.515
Eric McNair	SS46, 2B28	R	24	89	310	57	81	15	4	7	48	15	32	2	.261	.403
Lou Finney	OF63	L	22	74	240	26	64	12	2	3	32	13	17	1	.267	.371
Bing Miller	OF30, 1B6	R	38	67	120	22	33	7	1	2	17	12	7	4	.275	.400
Ed Madjeski	C41	R	23	51	142	17	40	4	0	0	17	4	21	0	.282	.310
Ed Cihocki	SS28, 2B1, 3B1	R	26	33	97	6	14	2	3	0	9	7	16	0	.144	.227
Frankie Hayes	C3	R	18	3	5	0	0	0	0	0	0	0	2	0	.000	.000
Joe Zapustas	OF2	R	25	2	5	0	1	0	0	0	0	0	0	0	.200	.200

NAME	T	AGE	W	L	PCT	SV	G	GS	CG	IP	H	BB	SO	ShO	ERA
		30	99	53	.651	26	153	153	68	1390	1415	452	447	5	3.82
General Crowder	R	34	24	15	.615	4	52	35	17	299	311	81	110	0	3.97
Earl Whitehill	L	33	22	8	.733	1	39	37	19	270	271	100	96	2	3.33
Lefty Stewart	L	32	15	6	.714	0	34	31	11	231	227	60	69	1	3.82
Jack Russell	R	27	12	6	.667	13	50	3	2	124	119	32	28	0	2.69
Monty Weaver	R	27	10	5	.667	0	23	21	12	152	147	53	45	1	3.26
Tommy Thomas	R	33	7	7	.500	3	35	14	2	135	149	49	35	0	4.80
Bobby Burke	L	26	4	3	.571	0	25	6	4	64	64	31	28	1	3.23
Bill McAfee	R	25	3	2	.600	5	27	1	0	53	64	21	14	0	6.62
Alex McColl	R	39	1	0	1.000	0	4	1	1	17	13	7	5	0	2.65
Ed Linke	R	21	1	0	1.000	0	3	2	0	16	15	11	6	0	5.06
Ray Prim	L	26	0	1	.000	0	2	1	0	14	13	2	6	0	3.21
Ed Chapman	R	27	0	0	.000	0	6	1	0	9	10	0	4	0	8.00
Bud Thomas	R	22	0	0	.000	0	2	0	0	4	11	2	1	0	15.75
John Campbell	R	25	0	0	.000	0	1	0	0	1	1	1	0	0	0.00
		30	91	59	.607	22	152	152	70	1355	1426	612	711	8	4.36
Lefty Gomez	L	24	16	10	.615	2	35	30	14	235	218	106	163	4	3.18
Johnny Allen	R	28	15	7	.682	1	25	24	10	185	171	87	119	1	4.38
Russ VanAtta	L	27	12	4	.750	1	26	22	10	157	160	63	76	1	4.18
Red Ruffing	R	29	9	14	.391	3	35	28	18	235	230	93	122	0	3.91
Jumbo Brown	R	26	7	5	.583	0	21	8	1	74	78	52	55	0	5.23
Herb Pennock	L	39	7	4	.636	4	23	5	2	65	96	21	22	1	5.54
3 George Uhle	R	34	6	1	.857	0	12	6	4	61	63	20	26	0	5.16
Don Brennan	R	29	5	1	.833	3	18	10	3	85	92	47	46	0	4.98
Wilcy Moore	R	36	5	6	.455	8	35	0	0	62	92	20	17	0	5.52
Danny MacFayden	R	28	3	2	.600	0	25	6	2	90	120	37	28	0	5.90
Charlie Devens	R	23	3	3	.500	0	14	8	2	62	59	50	23	0	4.35
1 George Pipgras	R	33	2	2	.500	0	4	4	3	33	32	12	14	0	3.27
Babe Ruth	L	38	1	0	1.000	0	1	1	1	9	12	3	0	0	5.00
Pete Appleton	R	29	0	0	.000	0	1	0	0	2	3	1	0	0	0.00
		28	79	72	.523	14	152	152	69	1344	1523	644	423	6	4.81
Lefty Grove	L	33	24	8	.750	6	45	28	21	275	280	83	114	2	3.21
Roy Mahaffey	R	30	13	10	.565	0	33	23	9	179	198	74	66	0	5.18
Sugar Cain	R	26	13	12	.520	1	38	32	16	218	244	137	43	1	4.25
Rube Walberg	L	33	9	13	.409	4	40	20	10	201	224	95	68	1	4.88
George Earnshaw	R	33	5	10	.333	0	21	18	4	118	153	58	37	0	5.95
Dick Barrett	R	26	4	4	.500	0	15	7	3	70	74	49	26	0	5.79
Johnny Marcum	R	23	3	2	.600	0	5	5	4	37	28	20	14	2	1.95
Jim Peterson	R	24	2	5	.286	0	32	5	0	91	114	36	18	0	4.95
Tony Freitas	L	25	2	4	.333	1	19	9	2	64	90	24	15	0	7.31
Gowell Claset	L	25	2	0	1.000	0	8	1	0	11	23	11	1	0	9.82
1 Hank McDonald	R	22	1	1	.500	0	4	1	0	12	14	4	1	0	5.25
Tim McKeithan	R	26	1	0	1.000	0	3	1	0	9	10	4	3	0	4.00
Bobby Coombs	R	25	0	1	.000	2	21	0	0	31	47	20	8	0	7.55
Bill Dietrich	R	23	0	1	.000	0	8	1	0	17	13	19	4	0	5.82
Hank Winston	R	29	0	0	.000	0	1	0	0	7	7	6	2	0	6.43
Emile Roy	R	26	0	1	.000	0	1	1	0	2	4	4	3	0	31.50

CLEVELAND 4th 75-76 .497 23.5 — ROGER PECKINPAUGH 26-25 .510 WALTER JOHNSON 49-51 .490

NAME	G by POS	B	AGE	G	AB	R	H	2B	3B	HR	RBI	BB	SO	SB	BA	SA
TOTALS			27	151	5240	654	1366	218	77	50	611	448	426	36	.261	.360
Harley Boss	1B110	L	24	112	438	54	118	17	7	1	53	25	27	2	.269	.347
Odell Hale	2B73, 3B21	R	24	98	351	49	97	19	8	10	64	30	37	2	.276	.462
Bill Knickerbocker (JJ)	SS80	R	21	80	279	20	63	16	3	2	32	11	30	1	.226	.326
Willie Kamm	3B131	R	33	133	447	59	126	17	2	1	47	54	27	7	.282	.336
Dick Porter	OF124	L	31	132	499	73	133	19	6	0	41	51	42	4	.267	.329
Earl Averill	OF149	L	31	151	599	83	180	39	16	11	92	54	29	3	.301	.474
Joe Vosmik	OF113	R	23	119	438	53	115	20	10	4	56	42	13	0	.263	.381
Roy Spencer	C72	R	33	75	227	26	46	5	2	0	23	23	17	0	.203	.242
1 Bill Cissell	2B62, SS46, 3B1	R	29	112	409	53	94	21	3	6	33	31	29	6	.230	.340
John Burnett	SS41, 2B17, 3B12	L	28	83	261	39	71	11	2	1	29	23	14	3	.272	.341
Frankie Pytlak	C69	R	24	80	248	36	77	10	6	2	33	17	10	3	.310	.423
Wes Ferrell (SA)	P28, OF13	R	25	61	140	26	38	7	0	7	26	20	22	0	.271	.471
Milt Galatzer	OF40, 1B5	L	26	57	160	19	38	2	1	1	17	23	21	2	.238	.281
Glenn Myatt	C27	L	35	40	77	10	18	4	0	0	7	15	8	0	.234	.286
Eddie Morgan	1B32, OF1	R	29	39	121	10	32	3	3	1	13	7	9	1	.264	.364
Mike Powers	OF11	L	27	24	47	6	13	2	1	0	2	6	6	2	.277	.362
Johnny Oulliber	OF18	R	22	22	75	9	20	1	0	0	3	4	5	0	.267	.280
Hal Trosky	1B11	L	20	11	44	6	13	1	2	1	8	2	12	0	.295	.477

NAME	T	AGE	W	L	PCT	SV	G	GS	CG	IP	H	BB	SO	ShO	ERA
		27	75	76	.497	7	151	151	74	1350	1382	465	437	12	3.71
Oral Hildebrand	R	26	16	11	.593	0	36	31	15	220	205	88	90	6	3.76
Mel Harder	R	23	15	17	.469	4	43	31	14	253	254	67	81	2	2.95
Wes Ferrell (SA)	R	25	11	12	.478	0	28	26	16	201	225	70	41	1	4.21
Clint Brown	R	29	11	12	.478	1	33	23	10	185	202	34	47	2	3.41
Monte Pearson	R	23	10	5	.667	0	19	16	10	135	111	55	54	0	2.33
Willis Hudlin	R	27	5	13	.278	1	34	17	6	147	161	61	44	0	3.98
Sarge Connally	R	34	5	3	.625	1	41	3	1	103	112	49	30	0	4.89
Belve Bean	R	28	1	2	.333	0	27	2	0	70	80	20	41	0	5.27
Thornton Lee	L	26	1	1	.500	0	3	2	2	17	13	11	7	0	4.24
Howard Craghead	R	25	0	0	.000	0	11	0	0	17	19	10	2	0	6.35

DETROIT 5th 75-79 .487 25 — BUCKY HARRIS 73-79 .480 DEL BAKER 2-0 1.000

NAME	G by POS	B	AGE	G	AB	R	H	2B	3B	HR	RBI	BB	SO	SB	BA	SA
TOTALS			26	155	5502	722	1479	283	78	57	676	475	523	68	.269	.380
Hank Greenberg	1B117	R	22	117	449	59	135	33	3	12	87	46	78	6	.301	.468
Charlie Gehringer	2B155	L	30	155	628	103	204	42	6	12	105	68	27	5	.325	.468
Billy Rogell	SS155	B	28	155	587	67	173	42	11	0	57	79	33	6	.295	.404
Marv Owen	3B136	R	27	138	550	77	144	24	9	2	65	44	56	2	.262	.349
John Stone	OF141	L	27	148	574	86	161	33	11	11	80	54	37	1	.280	.434
Pete Fox	OF124	R	23	128	535	82	154	26	13	7	57	23	38	9	.288	.424
Gee Walker	OF113	R	25	127	483	68	135	29	7	9	64	15	49	26	.280	.424
Ray Hayworth	C133	R	29	134	425	37	104	14	3	1	45	35	28	0	.245	.299
Jo-Jo White	OF54	L	24	91	234	43	59	9	5	2	34	27	26	5	.252	.359
Harry Davis	1B44	L	23	66	173	24	37	8	2	0	14	22	8	2	.214	.283
Heinie Schuble	3B23, SS2, 2B1	R	26	49	96	12	21	4	1	0	6	5	17	2	.219	.281
Frank Doljack	OF37	R	25	42	147	18	42	5	2	0	22	14	13	2	.286	.347
Gene Desautels	C30	R	26	30	42	5	6	1	0	0	4	4	6	0	.143	.167
Johnny Pasek	C28	R	28	28	61	6	15	4	0	0	4	7	7	2	.246	.311
Billy Rhiel	OF1	R	32	19	17	1	3	0	1	0	1	5	4	0	.176	.294
Frank Reiber	C6	R	23	13	18	3	5	0	1	1	3	2	3	0	.278	.556
1 Earl Webb	OF2	L	34	6	11	1	3	0	0	0	3	3	0	0	.273	.273

NAME	T	AGE	W	L	PCT	SV	G	GS	CG	IP	H	BB	SO	ShO	ERA
		27	75	79	.487	17	155	155	69	1398	1415	561	575	6	3.96
Firpo Marberry	R	34	16	11	.593	2	37	32	15	238	232	61	84	1	3.29
Tommy Bridges	R	26	14	12	.538	2	33	28	17	233	192	110	120	2	3.09
Vic Sorrell	R	32	11	15	.423	1	36	28	13	233	233	78	75	1	3.79
Carl Fischer	L	27	11	15	.423	3	35	22	9	183	176	84	93	0	3.54
Schoolboy Rowe (SJ)	R	23	7	4	.636	0	19	15	8	123	129	31	75	1	3.59
Chief Hogsett	L	29	6	10	.375	9	45	2	0	116	137	56	39	0	4.50
2 Vic Frasier	R	28	5	5	.500	0	20	14	4	104	129	59	26	0	6.66
Eldon Auker	R	22	3	3	.500	0	15	6	2	55	63	25	17	1	5.24
Art Herring	R	26	1	2	.333	0	24	3	1	61	61	20	20	0	3.84
Luke Hamlin	R	28	1	0	1.000	0	3	3	0	17	20	10	10	0	4.76
1 Whit Wyatt	R	25	0	1	.000	0	10	0	0	17	20	9	9	0	4.24
Roxie Lawson	R	27	0	1	.000	0	4	2	0	16	17	17	6	0	7.31
1 George Uhle	R	34	0	0	.000	0	1	0	0	1	2	0	1	0	18.00
Buts Nekola	L	25	0	0	.000	0	2	0	0	1	4	1	0	0	36.00

CHICAGO 6th 67-83 .447 31 — LEW FONSECA

NAME	G by POS	B	AGE	G	AB	R	H	2B	3B	HR	RBI	BB	SO	SB	BA	SA
TOTALS			29	151	5318	683	1448	251	53	43	642	539	416	43	.272	.360
Red Kress	1B111, OF8	R	26	129	467	47	116	20	5	10	78	37	40	4	.248	.377
Jackie Hayes	2B138	R	26	138	535	65	138	23	5	2	47	55	36	2	.258	.331
Luke Appling	SS151	R	26	151	612	90	197	36	10	6	85	56	29	6	.322	.443
Jimmy Dykes	3B151	R	36	151	554	49	144	22	6	1	68	69	37	3	.260	.327
Evar Swanson	OF139	R	30	144	539	102	165	25	7	1	63	93	35	19	.306	.384
Mule Haas	OF146	L	29	146	585	97	168	33	4	1	51	65	41	0	.287	.362
Al Simmons	OF145	R	31	146	605	85	200	29	10	14	119	39	49	5	.331	.481
Frank Grube	C83	R	28	85	256	23	59	13	0	0	23	38	20	1	.230	.281
Charlie Berry	C83	R	30	86	271	25	69	8	3	2	28	17	16	0	.255	.328
2 Earl Webb	OF16, 1B10	L	34	58	107	16	31	5	0	1	8	16	13	0	.290	.364
Billy Sullivan (RL)	1B22, C8	L	22	54	125	9	24	0	1	0	13	10	5	0	.192	.208
Ted Lyons	P36	B	32	51	91	11	26	2	1	1	11	4	6	0	.286	.363
Hal Rhyne	2B19, 3B13, SS2	R	34	39	83	9	22	1	1	0	10	5	9	1	.265	.301
Lew Fonseca (NJ)	1B12	R	34	23	59	8	12	2	0	2	15	7	6	1	.203	.339
Milt Bocek	OF6	R	20	11	22	3	8	1	0	1	3	4	6	0	.364	.545
John Stoneham	OF9	L	24	10	25	4	3	0	0	1	3	2	2	0	.120	.240
Liz Funk	OF2	L	28	10	9	1	2	0	0	0	0	1	0	0	.222	.222
Charlie English	2B3	R	23	3	9	2	4	2	0	0	1	1	1	0	.444	.667
Mem Lovett		R	21	1	1	0	0	0	0	0	0	0	0	0	.000	.000

NAME	T	AGE	W	L	PCT	SV	G	GS	CG	IP	H	BB	SO	ShO	ERA
		32	67	83	.447	13	151	151	53	1371	1505	519	423	8	4.45
Ed Durham	R	25	10	6	.625	0	24	21	6	139	137	46	65	0	4.47
Sad Sam Jones	R	40	10	12	.455	0	27	25	11	177	181	65	60	2	3.36
Ted Lyons	R	32	10	21	.321	1	36	27	14	228	260	74	74	2	4.38
Milt Gaston	R	37	8	12	.400	0	30	25	7	167	177	60	39	1	4.85
Joe Heving	R	32	7	5	.583	6	40	6	3	118	113	27	47	1	2.67
Jake Miller	L	35	5	6	.455	0	26	14	4	106	130	47	30	2	5.60
Paul Gregory	R	24	4	11	.267	0	23	17	5	104	124	47	18	0	4.93
Chad Kimsey	R	26	4	1	.800	0	28	2	0	96	124	36	19	0	5.53
Red Faber	R	44	3	4	.429	5	36	2	0	86	92	28	18	0	3.45
2 Whit Wyatt	R	25	3	4	.429	1	26	7	2	88	91	45	31	0	4.60
Les Tietje	R	21	2	0	1.000	0	3	3	1	22	16	15	9	0	2.45
1 Vic Frasier	R	28	1	1	.500	0	10	1	0	20	32	11	4	0	9.00
Hal Haid	R	35	0	0	.000	0	6	0	0	15	18	13	7	0	7.80
Ira Hutchinson	R	22	0	0	.000	0	1	1	0	4	7	3	2	0	13.50
George Murray	R	34	0	0	.000	0	2	0	0	2	3	2	0	0	9.00

BOSTON 7th 63-86 .423 34.5 — MARTY McMANUS

NAME	G by POS	B	AGE	G	AB	R	H	2B	3B	HR	RBI	BB	SO	SB	BA	SA
TOTALS			28	149	5201	700	1407	294	56	50	647	519	464	62	.271	.377
Dale Alexander	1B79	R	30	94	313	40	88	14	1	5	40	25	22	0	.281	.380
Johnny Hodapp	2B101, 1B10	R	27	115	413	55	129	27	5	3	54	33	14	1	.312	.424
Rabbit Warstler	SS87	R	29	92	322	44	70	13	1	1	17	42	36	2	.217	.273
Marty McManus	3B76, 2B26, 1B4	R	33	106	366	51	104	30	4	3	36	49	21	3	.284	.413
Roy Johnson	OF125	L	30	133	483	88	151	30	7	10	95	55	36	13	.313	.466
Dusty Cooke	OF118	L	26	119	454	86	132	35	10	5	54	67	71	7	.291	.445
Smead Jolley	OF102	L	31	118	411	47	116	32	4	9	65	24	20	1	.282	.445
2 Rick Ferrell	C116	R	27	118	421	50	125	19	4	3	72	58	19	2	.297	.382
2 Bill Werber	SS71, 3B38, 2B2	R	25	108	425	64	110	30	6	3	39	33	39	15	.259	.379
Tom Oliver	OF86	R	30	90	244	25	63	9	1	0	23	13	7	1	.258	.303
Bob Seeds	1B41, OF32	R	26	82	230	26	56	13	4	0	23	21	20	1	.243	.335
Bucky Walters	3B43, 2B7	R	24	52	195	27	50	8	3	4	28	19	24	1	.256	.390
Johnny Gooch	C26	B	35	37	77	6	14	1	1	0	2	11	7	0	.182	.221
2 Joe Judge	1B28	L	39	34	104	20	30	8	1	0	22	13	4	2	.288	.385
Bob Fothergill	OF4	R	35	28	32	1	11	1	0	0	5	2	4	0	.344	.375
George Stumpf	OF15	L	22	22	41	8	14	3	0	0	5	4	2	4	.341	.415
Barney Friberg	2B6, 3B5, SS2	R	33	17	41	5	13	3	0	0	9	6	1	0	.317	.390
1 Merv Shea	C16	R	32	16	56	1	8	3	0	0	8	4	7	0	.143	.196
Freddie Muller	2B14	R	25	15	48	6	9	1	1	0	3	5	5	1	.188	.250
Mel Almada	OF13	L	20	14	44	11	15	0	0	1	3	11	3	3	.341	.409
Johnny Watwood	OF9	L	26	13	30	2	4	0	0	0	2	3	3	0	.133	.133
Lou Legett	C2	R	32	8	5	1	1	1	0	0	1	0	0	0	.200	.400
Tom Winsett	OF4	L	23	6	12	1	1	0	0	0	0	1	6	0	.083	.083
Marv Olson	2B1	R	26	3	1	1	0	0	0	0	0	0	1	0	.000	.000
Greg Mulleavy		R	27	1	0	1	0	0	0	0	0	0	0	0	.000	.000

NAME	T	AGE	W	L	PCT	SV	G	GS	CG	IP	H	BB	SO	ShO	ERA
		27	63	86	.423	14	149	149	60	1328	1396	591	473	4	4.34
Gordon Rhodes	R	25	12	15	.444	0	34	29	14	232	242	93	85	0	4.03
2 George Pipgras (EJ)	R	33	9	8	.529	1	22	17	9	128	140	45	56	2	4.08
Bob Weiland	R	27	8	14	.364	3	39	27	12	216	197	100	97	0	3.87
Hank Johnson	R	27	8	6	.571	1	25	21	7	155	156	74	65	0	4.06
2 Lloyd Brown	L	28	8	11	.421	1	33	21	9	163	180	64	37	2	4.03
Ivy Andrews	R	26	7	13	.350	1	34	17	5	140	157	61	37	0	4.95
Bob Kline	R	23	7	8	.467	4	46	8	1	127	127	67	16	0	4.54
Johnny Welch	R	26	4	9	.308	3	47	7	1	129	142	67	68	0	4.60
Curt Fullerton	R	34	0	2	.000	0	6	2	2	25	36	13	10	0	8.64
Jud McLaughlin	L	21	0	0	.000	0	6	0	0	9	14	5	1	0	6.00
Mike Meola	R	27	0	0	.000	0	3	0	0	2	5	2	1	0	27.00

ST. LOUIS 8th 55-96 .364 43.5 — BILL KILLEFER 34-59 .366 ALLAN SOTHORON 1-3 .250 ROGERS HORNSBY 20-39 .370

NAME	G by POS	B	AGE	G	AB	R	H	2B	3B	HR	RBI	BB	SO	SB	BA	SA
TOTALS			27	153	5285	669	1337	244	64	64	605	520	556	70	.253	.360
Jack Burns	1B143	L	25	144	556	89	160	43	4	7	71	56	51	11	.288	.417
Oscar Melillo	2B130	R	33	132	496	50	145	23	6	3	79	29	18	12	.292	.381
Jim Levey	SS138	B	26	141	529	43	103	10	4	2	36	26	68	4	.195	.240
Art Scharein	3B95, SS24, 2B7	R	28	123	471	49	96	13	3	0	26	41	27	7	.204	.244
Bruce Campbell	OF144	R	23	148	567	87	157	38	8	16	106	69	77	10	.277	.457
Sammy West	OF127	L	28	133	517	93	155	25	12	11	48	59	49	10	.300	.458
Carl Reynolds	OF124	R	30	135	475	81	136	26	14	8	71	50	25	5	.286	.451
2 Merv Shea	C85	R	32	94	279	26	73	11	1	1	27	43	26	2	.262	.319
Ted Gullic	OF36, 3B33, 1B14	R	26	104	304	34	74	18	3	5	35	15	38	3	.243	.372
Debs Garms	OF47	L	25	78	189	35	60	10	2	4	24	30	21	2	.317	.455
Lin Storti	3B32, 2B24	B	26	70	210	26	41	7	4	3	21	25	31	2	.195	.310
Muddy Ruel	C28	R	37	36	63	13	12	2	0	0	8	24	4	0	.190	.222
2 Rollie Hemsley	C27	R	26	32	95	7	23	2	1	1	15	11	12	0	.242	.316
1 Rick Ferrell	C21	R	27	22	72	8	18	2	0	1	5	12	4	2	.250	.319
1 Jack Crouch	C9	R	39	19	30	1	5	0	0	1	5	2	6	0	.167	.267
2 Rogers Hornsby		R	37	11	9	2	3	1	0	1	2	2	1	0	.333	.778

NAME	T	AGE	W	L	PCT	SV	G	GS	CG	IP	H	BB	SO	ShO	ERA
		28	55	96	.364	10	153	153	55	1361	1574	531	426	7	4.82
George Blaeholder	R	29	15	19	.441	0	38	36	14	256	283	69	63	3	4.71
Bump Hadley	R	28	15	20	.429	3	45	36	19	317	309	141	149	2	3.92
Sam Gray	R	35	7	4	.636	4	38	6	0	112	131	45	36	0	4.10
Ed Wells	L	33	6	14	.300	1	36	22	10	204	230	63	58	0	4.19
Wally Hebert	L	25	4	6	.300	0	33	10	3	88	114	35	19	0	5.32
Rollie Stiles	R	26	3	7	.300	1	31	9	6	115	154	47	29	1	5.01
Dick Coffman	R	26	3	7	.300	1	21	13	3	81	114	39	19	1	5.89
Jack Knott	R	26	1	8	.111	0	20	9	0	83	88	33	19	0	4.99
1 Lloyd Brown	L	28	1	6	.143	0	8	6	0	39	57	17	7	0	7.15
2 Hank McDonald	R	22	0	4	.000	0	25	5	0	58	83	34	22	0	8.69
Garland Braxton	L	33	0	1	.000	0	5	1	0	8	11	8	5	0	10.13

NEW YORK 1st 91-61 .599 — **BILL TERRY**

NAME	G by POS	B	AGE	G	AB	R	H	2B	3B	HR	RBI	BB	SO	SB	BA	SA
TOTALS			29	156	5461	636	1437	204	41	82	598	377	477	31	.263	.361
Bill Terry (BW)	1B117	L	34	123	475	68	153	20	5	6	58	40	23	3	.322	.423
Hughie Critz	2B133	R	32	133	558	68	137	18	5	2	33	23	24	4	.246	.306
Blondy Ryan	SS146	R	27	146	525	47	125	10	5	3	48	15	62	0	.238	.293
Johnny Vergez	3B123	R	26	123	458	57	124	21	6	16	72	39	66	1	.271	.448
Mel Ott	OF152	L	24	152	580	98	164	36	1	23	103	75	48	1	.283	.467
Kiddo Davis	OF120	R	31	126	434	61	112	20	4	7	37	25	30	10	.258	.371
Jo-Jo Moore	OF132	L	24	132	524	56	153	16	5	0	42	21	27	4	.292	.342
Gus Mancuso	C142	R	27	144	481	39	127	17	2	6	56	48	21	0	.264	.345
Homer Peel	OF45	R	30	84	148	16	38	1	1	1	12	14	10	0	.257	.297
2 Lefty O'Doul	OF63	L	36	78	229	31	70	9	1	9	35	29	17	1	.306	.472
Bernie James	2B26, SS6, 3B5	B	27	60	125	22	28	2	1	1	10	8	12	5	.224	.280
Travis Jackson	SS21, 3B21	R	29	53	122	11	30	5	0	0	12	8	11	2	.246	.287
Paul Richards	C36	R	24	51	87	4	17	3	0	0	10	3	12	0	.195	.230
1 Sam Leslie	1B35	L	27	40	137	21	44	12	3	3	27	12	9	0	.321	.518
Chuck Dressen	3B16	R	34	16	45	3	10	4	0	0	3	1	4	0	.222	.311
Joe Malay	1B8	L	27	8	24	0	3	0	0	0	2	0	0	0	.125	.125
Phil Weintraub	OF6	L	25	8	15	3	3	0	0	1	1	3	2	0	.200	.400
Hank Leiber	OF1	R	22	6	10	1	2	0	0	0	0	0	2	0	.200	.200
Harry Danning	C1	R	21	3	2	0	0	0	0	0	0	1	0	0	.000	.000

NAME	T	AGE	W	L	PCT	SV	G	GS	CG	IP	H	BB	SO	ShO	ERA
		31	91	61	.599	15	156	156	75	1409	1280	400	555	23	2.71
Carl Hubbell	L	30	23	12	.657	5	45	33	22	309	256	47	156	10	1.66
Hal Schumacher	R	22	19	12	.613	1	35	33	21	259	199	84	96	7	2.15
Freddie Fitzsimmons	R	31	16	11	.593	0	36	35	13	252	243	72	65	1	2.89
Roy Parmelee	R	26	13	8	.619	0	32	32	14	218	191	77	132	3	3.18
Dolf Luque	R	42	8	2	.800	4	35	0	0	80	75	19	23	0	2.70
Hi Bell	R	35	6	5	.545	5	38	7	1	105	100	20	24	1	2.06
2 Watty Clark	L	31	3	4	.429	0	16	5	0	44	58	11	11	0	4.70
Bill Shores	R	29	2	1	.667	0	8	3	1	37	41	14	20	0	3.89
2 George Uhle	R	34	1	1	.333	0	6	1	0	14	16	6	4	0	7.71
Glenn Spencer	R	27	0	2	.000	0	17	3	1	47	52	26	14	0	5.17
Jack Salveson	R	19	0	2	.000	0	8	2	2	31	30	14	8	0	3.77
1 Ray Starr	R	27	0	1	.000	0	6	2	0	13	19	10	2	0	5.54

PITTSBURGH 2nd 87-67 .565 5 — **GEORGE GIBSON**

NAME	G by POS	B	AGE	G	AB	R	H	2B	3B	HR	RBI	BB	SO	SB	BA	SA
TOTALS			27	154	5429	667	1548	249	84	39	618	366	334	34	.285	.383
Gus Suhr	1B154	L	27	154	566	72	151	31	11	10	75	72	52	2	.267	.413
Tony Piet	2B97	R	26	107	362	45	117	21	5	1	42	19	28	12	.323	.417
Arky Vaughan	SS152	L	21	152	573	85	180	29	19	9	97	64	23	3	.314	.478
Pie Traynor	3B154	R	33	154	624	85	190	27	6	1	82	35	24	5	.304	.372
Paul Waner	OF154	L	30	154	618	101	191	38	16	7	70	60	20	3	.309	.456
Fred Lindstrom	OF130	R	27	138	538	70	167	39	10	5	55	33	22	1	.310	.448
Lloyd Waner	OF114	L	27	121	500	59	138	14	5	0	26	22	8	3	.276	.324
Earl Grace	C88	L	26	93	291	22	84	13	1	3	44	26	23	0	.289	.371
Tommy Thevenow	2B61, SS3, 3B1	R	29	73	253	20	79	5	1	0	34	3	5	2	.312	.340
Woody Jensen	OF40	L	25	70	196	29	58	7	3	0	15	8	2	1	.296	.362
Adam Comorosky	OF30	R	28	64	162	18	46	8	1	1	15	4	9	2	.284	.364
Hal Finney	C47	R	27	56	133	17	31	4	1	1	18	3	19	0	.233	.301
Tom Padden	C27	R	24	30	90	5	19	2	0	0	8	2	6	0	.211	.233
Pep Young	2B1, SS1	R	25	25	20	3	6	1	1	0	0	0	5	0	.300	.450
2 Val Picinich	C16	R	36	16	52	6	13	4	0	1	7	5	10	0	.250	.385
Bill Brubaker	3B1	R	22	2	2	0	0	0	0	0	0	0	0	0	.000	.000
Red Nonnenkamp		L	21	1	1	0	0	0	0	0	0	0	1	0	.000	.000

NAME	T	AGE	W	L	PCT	SV	G	GS	CG	IP	H	BB	SO	ShO	ERA
		30	87	67	.565	12	154	154	70	1373	1417	313	401	16	3.27
Larry French	L	25	18	13	.581	1	47	35	21	291	290	55	88	5	2.72
Heinie Meine	R	37	15	8	.652	0	32	29	12	207	227	50	50	2	3.65
Bill Swift	R	25	14	10	.583	0	37	29	13	218	214	36	64	2	3.14
Steve Swetonic	R	29	12	12	.500	0	31	21	8	165	166	64	37	3	3.49
Hal Smith	R	31	8	7	.533	1	28	19	8	145	149	31	40	2	2.86
Leon Chagnon	R	30	6	4	.600	1	39	5	1	100	100	17	35	0	3.69
Waite Hoyt	R	33	5	7	.417	4	36	8	4	117	118	19	44	1	2.92
Bill Harris	R	33	4	4	.500	5	31	0	0	59	68	14	19	0	3.20
Ralph Birkofer	L	24	4	2	.667	0	9	8	3	51	43	17	20	1	2.29
Ray Kremer	R	40	1	0	1.000	0	7	0	0	20	36	9	4	0	10.35
Clise Dudley	R	29	0	0	.000	0	1	0	0	.1	6	1	0	0	135.00

CHICAGO 3rd 86-68 .558 6 — **CHARLIE GRIMM**

NAME	G by POS	B	AGE	G	AB	R	H	2B	3B	HR	RBI	BB	SO	SB	BA	SA
TOTALS			30	154	5255	646	1422	256	51	72	608	392	475	52	.271	.380
Charlie Grimm	1B104	L	34	107	384	38	95	15	2	3	37	23	15	1	.247	.320
Billy Herman	2B153	R	23	153	619	82	173	35	2	0	44	45	34	5	.279	.342
Billy Jurges	SS143	R	25	143	487	49	131	17	6	5	50	26	39	3	.269	.359
Woody English	3B103, SS1	R	26	105	398	54	104	19	2	3	41	53	44	5	.261	.342
Babe Herman	OF131	L	30	137	508	77	147	36	12	16	93	50	57	6	.289	.502
Frank Demaree	OF133	R	23	134	515	68	140	24	6	6	51	22	42	4	.272	.377
Riggs Stephenson	OF91	R	35	97	346	45	114	17	4	4	51	34	16	5	.329	.436
Gabby Hartnett	C140	R	32	140	490	55	135	21	4	16	88	37	51	1	.276	.433
Mark Koenig	3B37, SS26, 2B2	B	30	80	218	32	62	12	1	3	25	15	9	5	.284	.390
Kiki Cuyler (BN)	OF69	R	33	70	262	37	83	13	3	5	35	21	29	4	.317	.447
Harvey Hendrick	1B38, OF8, 3B1	L	35	69	189	30	55	13	3	4	23	13	17	4	.291	.455
Gilly Campbell	C20	L	25	46	89	11	25	3	1	1	10	7	4	0	.281	.371
Lon Warneke	P36	R	24	39	100	9	30	6	1	2	13	3	13	0	.300	.440
Jim Mosolf	OF22	L	27	31	82	13	22	5	1	1	9	5	8	0	.268	.390
2 Taylor Douthit	OF18	R	32	27	71	8	16	5	0	0	5	11	7	2	.225	.296
Stan Hack	3B17	L	23	20	60	10	21	3	1	1	2	8	3	4	.350	.483
Dolph Camilli	1B16	L	26	16	58	8	13	2	1	2	7	4	11	3	.224	.397
Zack Taylor	C12	R	34	16	11	0	0	0	0	0	0	0	1	0	.000	.000
Babe Phelps	C2	L	25	3	7	0	2	0	0	0	2	0	1	0	.286	.286

NAME	T	AGE	W	L	PCT	SV	G	GS	CG	IP	H	BB	SO	ShO	ERA
		29	86	68	.558	9	154	154	95	1361	1316	411	488	16	2.92
Guy Bush	R	31	20	12	.625	2	41	32	20	259	261	68	84	4	2.75
Lon Warneke	R	24	18	13	.581	1	36	34	26	287	262	75	133	4	2.01
Charlie Root	R	34	15	10	.600	0	35	30	20	242	232	61	86	2	2.60
Bud Tinning	R	27	13	6	.684	1	32	21	10	175	169	60	59	3	3.19
Pat Malone	R	30	10	14	.417	0	31	26	13	186	186	59	72	2	3.92
Lynn Nelson	R	28	5	5	.500	1	24	3	3	76	65	30	20	0	3.20
1 Burleigh Grimes	R	39	3	6	.333	3	17	7	3	70	71	29	12	1	3.47
Roy Henshaw	L	21	2	1	.667	0	21	0	0	39	32	20	16	0	4.15
Leroy Herrmann	R	27	0	1	.000	1	9	1	0	21	26	8	4	0	5.57
Beryl Richmond	L	25	0	0	.000	0	4	0	0	5	10	0	0	0	1.80
Carroll Yerkes	L	30	0	0	.000	0	1	0	0	2	2	1	0	0	4.50

BOSTON 4th 83-71 .539 9 — **BILL McKECHNIE**

NAME	G by POS	B	AGE	G	AB	R	H	2B	3B	HR	RBI	BB	SO	SB	BA	SA
TOTALS			29	156	5243	552	1320	217	56	54	511	326	428	25	.252	.345
Buck Jordan	1B150	L	26	152	588	77	168	29	9	4	46	34	22	4	.286	.386
Rabbit Maranville	2B142	R	41	143	478	46	104	15	4	0	38	36	34	2	.218	.266
Billy Urbanski	SS143	R	30	144	566	65	142	21	4	0	35	33	48	4	.251	.302
2 Pinky Whitney	3B85, 2B18	R	28	100	382	42	94	17	2	8	49	25	23	2	.246	.364
Randy Moore	OF122, 1B10	L	28	135	497	64	150	23	7	8	70	40	16	3	.302	.425
Wally Berger	OF136	R	27	137	528	84	165	37	8	27	106	41	77	2	.313	.566
2 Hal Lee	OF87	R	28	88	312	32	69	15	9	1	28	18	26	1	.221	.337
Shanty Hogan	C95	R	27	96	328	15	83	7	0	3	30	13	9	0	.253	.302
Joe Mowry	OF64	B	25	86	249	25	55	8	5	0	20	15	22	1	.221	.293
Al Spohrer	C65	R	30	67	184	11	46	6	1	1	12	11	13	3	.250	.310
Dick Gyselman	3B42, 2B5, SS1	R	25	58	155	10	37	6	2	0	12	7	21	0	.239	.303
Ed Brandt	P41	L	28	47	97	9	30	4	0	0	6	4	7	0	.309	.351
Pinky Hargrave	C25	B	37	45	73	5	13	0	0	0	6	5	7	1	.178	.178
1 Fritz Knothe	3B33, SS9	R	30	44	158	15	36	5	2	1	6	13	25	1	.228	.304
1 Wes Schulmerich	OF21	R	31	29	85	10	21	6	1	1	13	5	10	0	.247	.376
Tommy Thompson	OF24	L	23	24	97	6	18	1	0	0	6	4	6	0	.186	.196
Red Worthington	OF10	R	27	17	45	3	7	4	0	0	0	1	3	0	.156	.244
Dutch Holland	OF7	R	29	13	31	3	8	3	0	0	3	3	8	1	.258	.355
Earl Clark	OF7	R	25	7	23	3	8	1	0	0	1	2	1	0	.348	.391
Hod Ford	SS5	R	35	5	15	0	1	0	0	0	1	3	1	0	.067	.067
Al Wright	2B3	R	20	4	1	0	1	0	0	0	0	0	0	0	1.000	1.000

NAME	T	AGE	W	L	PCT	SV	G	GS	CG	IP	H	BB	SO	ShO	ERA
		33	83	71	.539	16	156	156	85	1403	1391	355	383	15	2.96
Ben Cantwell	R	31	20	10	.667	2	40	29	18	255	242	54	57	2	2.61
Ed Brandt	L	28	18	14	.563	4	41	32	23	288	256	77	104	3	2.59
Fred Frankhouse	R	29	16	15	.516	2	43	30	14	245	249	77	83	2	3.16
Huck Betts	R	36	11	11	.500	4	35	26	17	242	225	55	40	2	2.79
Tom Zachary	L	37	7	9	.438	2	26	20	6	125	134	35	22	2	3.53
Leo Mangum	R	37	4	3	.571	0	25	5	2	84	93	11	28	1	3.32
2 Bob Smith	R	35	4	3	.571	1	14	4	3	59	68	7	16	1	3.20
Ed Fallenstein	R	24	2	1	.667	0	9	4	1	35	43	13	5	1	3.60
Socks Seibold	R	37	1	4	.200	1	11	5	1	38	43	14	10	0	3.65
2 Ray Starr	R	27	0	1	.000	1	9	1	0	28	32	9	15	0	3.86
Bob Brown	R	22	0	0	.000	0	5	0	0	7	6	3	3	0	2.57

ST. LOUIS 5th 82-71 .536 9.5 — **GABBY STREET 46-45 .505 FRANKIE FRISCH 36-26 .581**

NAME	G by POS	B	AGE	G	AB	R	H	2B	3B	HR	RBI	BB	SO	SB	BA	SA
TOTALS			30	154	5387	687	1486	256	61	57	629	391	528	99	.276	.378
Ripper Collins	1B123	B	29	132	493	66	153	26	7	10	68	38	49	7	.310	.452
Frankie Frisch	2B132, SS15	B	34	147	585	74	177	32	6	4	66	48	16	18	.303	.398
2 Leo Durocher	SS123	R	27	123	395	45	102	18	4	2	41	26	32	3	.258	.339
Pepper Martin	3B145	R	29	145	599	122	189	36	12	8	57	67	46	26	.316	.456
George Watkins	OF135	L	33	138	525	66	146	24	5	5	62	39	62	11	.278	.371
Ernie Orsatti	OF101, 1B3	L	29	120	436	55	130	21	6	0	38	33	33	14	.298	.374
Joe Medwick	OF147	R	21	148	595	92	182	40	10	18	98	26	56	5	.306	.497
Jimmie Wilson	C107	R	32	113	369	34	94	17	0	1	45	23	33	6	.255	.309
Ethan Allen	OF67	R	29	91	261	25	63	7	3	0	36	13	22	3	.241	.291
Pat Crawford	1B29, 2B15, 3B7	L	31	91	224	24	60	8	2	0	21	14	9	1	.268	.321
Bob O'Farrell	C50	R	36	55	163	16	39	4	2	2	20	15	25	0	.239	.325
1 Rogers Hornsby	2B17	R	37	46	83	9	27	6	0	2	21	12	6	1	.325	.470
Gordon Slade	SS31, 2B1	R	28	39	62	6	7	1	0	0	3	6	7	1	.113	.129
Estel Crabtree	OF7	L	29	23	34	6	9	3	0	0	3	2	3	1	.265	.353
Bill Lewis	C8	R	28	15	35	8	14	1	0	1	8	2	3	0	.400	.514
Burgess Whitehead	SS9, 2B3	R	23	12	7	2	2	0	0	0	1	0	1	0	.286	.286
Gene Moore	OF10	R	23	11	38	6	15	3	2	0	8	4	10	1	.395	.579
1 Sparky Adams	SS5, 3B3	R	38	8	30	1	5	1	0	0	0	1	3	0	.167	.200
Ray Pepper	OF2	R	27	3	9	2	2	0	0	1	2	0	1	0	.222	.556
Joe Sprinz	C3	R	30	3	5	1	1	0	0	0	0	1	1	0	.200	.200
Charlie Wilson	SS1	R	28	1	1	0	0	0	0	0	0	0	1	0	.000	.000
Charlie Gelbert (LJ) 27																

NAME	T	AGE	W	L	PCT	SV	G	GS	CG	IP	H	BB	SO	ShO	ERA
		31	82	71	.536	16	154	154	73	1383	1391	452	635	11	3.37
Dizzy Dean	R	22	20	18	.526	4	48	34	26	293	279	64	199	3	3.04
Tex Carleton	R	26	17	11	.607	3	44	33	15	277	263	97	147	4	3.38
Wild Bill Hallahan	L	30	16	13	.552	0	36	32	16	244	245	98	93	2	3.50
Bill Walker	L	29	9	10	.474	0	29	20	6	158	168	67	41	2	3.42
Jesse Haines	R	39	9	6	.600	1	32	10	5	115	113	37	37	0	2.50
Dazzy Vance	R	42	6	2	.750	3	28	11	2	99	105	28	67	0	3.55
Syl Johnson	R	32	3	3	.500	3	35	1	0	84	89	16	28	0	4.29
Jim Mooney	L	26	2	5	.286	1	21	8	2	77	87	26	14	0	3.74
2 Burleigh Grimes	R	39	0	1	.000	1	4	3	0	14	15	8	4	0	5.14
1 Paul Derringer	R	26	0	2*	.000	0	3	2	1	17	24	9	3	0	4.24
1 Allyn Stout	R	28	0	0	.000	0	1	0	0	2	1	1	1	0	0.00
Jim Lindsey	R	35	0	0	.000	0	1	0	0	2	2	1	1	0	4.50

*Derringer, also with Cincinnati, league leader in L with 27

BROOKLYN 6th 65-88 .425 26.5 — MAX CAREY

NAME	G by POS	B	AGE	G	AB	R	H	2B	3B	HR	RBI	BB	SO	SB	BA	SA
TOTALS			29	157	5367	617	1413	224	51	62	566	397	453	82	.263	.359
2 Sam Leslie	1B95	L	27	96	364	41	104	11	4	5	46	23	14	1	.286	.379
Tony Cuccinello	2B120, 3B14	R	25	134	485	58	122	31	4	9	65	44	40	4	.252	.388
Glenn Wright	SS51, 1B9, 3B2	R	32	71	192	19	49	13	0	1	18	11	24	1	.255	.339
Joe Stripp	3B140	R	30	141	537	69	149	20	7	1	51	26	23	5	.277	.346
Johnny Frederick	OF138	L	32	147	556	65	171	22	7	7	64	36	14	9	.308	.410
Danny Taylor	OF91	R	32	103	358	75	102	21	9	9	40	47	45	11	.285	.469
Hack Wilson	OF90, 2B5	R	33	117	360	41	96	13	2	9	54	52	50	7	.267	.389
Al Lopez	C124, 2B1	R	24	126	372	39	112	11	4	3	41	21	39	10	.301	.376
Buzz Boyle	OF90	L	25	93	338	38	101	13	4	0	31	16	24	7	.299	.361
Chick Outen	C56	L	28	93	153	20	38	10	0	4	17	20	15	1	.248	.392
Jake Flowers	SS36, 2B19, 3B8, OF1	R	31	78	210	28	49	11	2	2	22	24	15	13	.233	.333
Jimmy Jordan (BH)	SS51, 2B11	R	25	70	211	16	54	12	1	0	17	4	6	3	.256	.322
Joe Hutcheson	OF45	L	28	55	184	19	43	4	1	6	21	15	13	1	.234	.364
1 Lefty O'Doul	OF41	R	36	43	159	14	40	5	1	5	21	15	6	2	.252	.390
1 Joe Judge	1B28	L	34	42	112	7	24	2	1	0	9	7	10	1	.214	.250
Del Bissonette	1B32	L	33	35	114	9	28	7	0	1	10	2	17	2	.246	.307
Lonny Frey	SS34	B	22	34	135	25	43	5	3	0	12	13	13	4	.319	.400
Clyde Sukeforth	C18	L	31	20	36	1	2	0	0	0	0	2	1	0	.056	.056
Bert Delmas	2B10	L	22	12	28	4	7	0	0	0	0	1	7	0	.250	.250
1 Val Picinich	C6	R	36	6	6	1	1	1	0	0	0	0	1	0	.167	.333
Max Rosenfeld	OF2	R	30	5	9	0	1	0	0	0	0	1	1	0	.111	.111
Lu Blue	1B1	B	36	1	1	0	0	0	0	0	0	0	0	0	.000	.000

NAME	T	AGE	W	L	PCT	SV	G	GS	CG	IP	H	BB	SO	ShO	ERA
		29	65	88	.425	10	157	157	71	1386	1502	374	415	9	3.73
Van Lingle Mungo	R	22	16	15	.516	0	41	28	18	248	223	84	110	3	2.72
Ownie Carroll	R	30	13	15	.464	0	33	31	11	226	248	54	45	0	3.78
Boom-Boom Beck	R	28	12	20	.375	1	43	35	15	257	270	69	89	3	3.54
Ray Benge	R	31	10	17	.370	1	37	30	16	229	238	55	74	2	3.42
Sloppy Thurston	R	34	6	8	.429	3	32	15	5	131	171	34	22	0	4.53
Joe Shaute	L	33	3	4	.429	2	41	4	0	108	125	31	26	0	3.50
Dutch Leonard	R	24	2	3	.400	0	10	3	2	40	42	10	6	0	2.93
1 Watty Clark (AJ)	L	31	2	4	.333	1	11	8	4	51	61	6	14	1	4.76
Rosy Ryan	R	35	1	1	.500	2	30	0	0	61	69	16	22	0	4.57
Fred Heimach (BN)	L	32	0	1	.000	0	10	3	0	30	49	11	7	0	9.90
Ray Lucas	R	24	0	0	.000	0	2	0	0	5	6	4	0	0	7.20

PHILADELPHIA 7th 60-92 .395 31 — BURT SHOTTON

NAME	G by POS	B	AGE	G	AB	R	H	2B	3B	HR	RBI	BB	SO	SB	BA	SA
TOTALS			28	152	5261	607	1439	240	41	60	570	381	479	55	.274	.369
Don Hurst	1B142	L	27	147	550	58	147	27	8	8	76	48	32	3	.267	.389
Jack Warner	2B71, 3B30, SS1	R	29	107	340	31	76	15	1	0	22	28	33	1	.224	.274
Dick Bartell	SS152	R	25	152	587	78	159	25	5	1	37	56	46	6	.271	.336
Jim McLeod	3B67, SS1	R	24	67	232	20	45	6	1	0	15	12	25	1	.194	.228
Chuck Klein	OF152	L	28	152	606	101	**223**	**44**	7	**28**	**120**	56	36	15	**.368**	**.602**
Chick Fullis	OF151, 3B1	R	29	151	**647**	91	200	31	6	1	45	36	34	18	.309	.380
2 Wes Schulmerich	OF97	R	31	97	365	53	122	19	4	8	59	32	45	1	.334	.474
Spud Davis	C132	R	28	141	495	51	173	28	3	9	65	32	24	2	.349	.473
Al Todd	C34, OF2	R	29	73	136	13	28	4	0	0	10	4	18	1	.206	.235
Harry McCurdy	C2	L	33	73	54	9	15	1	0	2	12	16	6	0	.278	.407
Neal Finn (DD)	2B51	R	31	51	169	15	40	4	1	0	13	10	14	2	.237	.272
1 Hal Lee	OF45	R	28	46	167	25	48	12	2	0	12	18	13	1	.287	.383
2 Fritz Knothe	3B32, 2B4	R	30	41	113	10	17	2	0	0	11	6	19	2	.150	.168
Gus Dugas	1B11, OF1	L	26	37	71	4	12	3	0	0	9	1	9	0	.169	.211
1 Pinky Whitney	3B30	R	28	31	121	12	32	4	0	3	19	8	8	1	.264	.372
Mickey Haslin	2B26	R	22	26	89	3	21	2	0	0	9	3	5	1	.236	.258
Eddie Delker	2B17, 3B4	R	26	25	41	6	7	3	1	0	1	0	12	0	.171	.293
Alta Cohen	OF7	L	24	19	32	6	6	1	0	0	1	6	4	0	.188	.219
Fred Brickell	OF4	L	26	8	13	2	4	1	1	0	1	1	0	0	.308	.538
Hugh Willingham		R	25	1	1	0	0	0	0	0	0	0	0	0	.000	.000

NAME	T	AGE	W	L	PCT	SV	G	GS	CG	IP	H	BB	SO	ShO	ERA
		29	60	92	.395	13	152	152	52	1338	**1563**	410	341	10	4.34
Ed Holley	R	31	13	15	.464	0	30	28	12	207	219	62	56	3	3.52
Cy Moore	R	28	8	9	.471	1	36	18	9	161	177	42	53	3	3.75
Phil Collins	R	31	8	13	.381	**6**	42	13	5	151	178	57	40	1	4.11
Spipe Hansen	L	26	6	14	.300	1	32	22	8	168	199	30	47	0	4.45
Jumbo Jim Elliott	L	32	6	10	.375	2	35	21	6	162	188	49	43	0	3.83
Flint Rhem	R	32	5	14	.263	2	28	19	3	125	182	33	27	0	6.62
Frank Pearce	R	28	5	4	.556	0	20	7	3	82	78	29	18	1	3.62
Ad Liska	R	26	3	1	.750	1	45	1	0	76	96	26	23	0	4.50
John Jackson	R	23	2	2	.500	0	10	7	1	54	74	35	11	0	6.00
Jack Berly	R	30	2	3	.400	0	13	6	1	50	62	22	4	1	5.04
Reggie Grabowski	R	25	1	3	.250	0	10	5	4	48	38	10	9	1	2.44
Clarence Pickrel	R	22	1	0	1.000	0	9	0	0	14	20	3	6	0	3.86
Frank Ragland	R	29	0	4	.000	0	11	5	0	38	51	10	4	0	6.87
Charlie Butler	L	28	0	0	.000	0	1	0	0	1	1	2	0	0	9.00

CINCINNATI 8th 58-94 .382 33 — DONIE BUSH

NAME	G by POS	B	AGE	G	AB	R	H	2B	3B	HR	RBI	BB	SO	SB	BA	SA
TOTALS			30	153	5156	496	1267	208	37	34	455	349	354	30	.246	.320
Jim Bottomley	1B145	L	33	145	549	57	137	23	9	13	83	42	28	3	.250	.395
Jo-Jo Morrissey	2B88, SS63, 3B15	R	29	148	534	43	123	20	0	0	26	20	22	5	.230	.268
Otto Bluege	SS95, 2B10, 3B1	R	23	108	291	17	62	6	2	0	18	26	29	0	.213	.247
2 Sparky Adams	3B132, SS8	R	38	137	538	59	141	21	1	1	22	44	30	3	.262	.310
Harry Rice	OF141, 3B1	L	32	143	510	44	133	19	6	0	54	35	24	4	.261	.322
Chick Hafey	OF144	R	30	144	568	77	172	34	6	7	62	40	44	3	.303	.421
Johnny Moore	OF132	L	31	135	514	60	135	19	5	1	44	29	16	4	.263	.325
Ernie Lombardi	C95	R	25	107	350	30	99	21	1	4	47	16	17	2	.283	.382
George Grantham (BL)	2B72, 1B17	L	33	87	260	32	53	14	3	4	28	38	21	4	.204	.327
Wally Roettger	OF55	R	30	84	209	13	50	7	1	1	17	8	10	0	.239	.297
Red Lucas	P29	L	31	75	122	14	35	6	1	1	15	12	6	0	.287	.377
1 Rollie Hemsley	C41	R	26	49	116	9	22	8	0	0	7	6	8	0	.190	.259
Clyde Manion	C34	R	36	36	84	3	14	1	0	0	3	8	7	0	.167	.179
Andy High	3B11, 2B2	L	35	24	43	4	9	2	0	1	6	5	1	0	.209	.326
1 Leo Durocher	SS16	R	27	16	51	6	11	1	0	1	3	4	5	0	.216	.294
Tommy Robello	2B11, 3B2	R	20	14	30	1	7	3	0	0	3	1	5	0	.233	.333
2 Jack Crouch	C6	R	30	10	16	5	2	0	0	0	1	0	0	1	.125	.125
Eddie Hunter		R	28	1	0	0	0	0	0	0	0	0	0	0	.000	.000
1 Taylor Douthit		R	32	1	0	1	0	0	0	0	0	0	0	0	.000	.000

NAME	T	AGE	W	L	PCT	SV	G	GS	CG	IP	H	BB	SO	ShO	ERA
		32	58	**94**	.382	8	153	153	74	1352	1470	257	310	13	3.42
Red Lucas	R	31	10	16	.385	0	29	29	21	220	248	18	40	3	3.40
Larry Benton	R	35	10	11	.476	2	34	19	7	153	160	36	33	2	3.71
2 Paul Derringer	R	26	7	**25***	.219	1	33	31	16	231	240	51	86	2	3.23
Si Johnson	R	26	7	18	.280	1	34	28	14	211	212	54	51	4	3.50
Ray Kolp	R	38	6	9	.400	3	30	14	4	150	168	23	28	0	3.54
Benny Frey	R	27	6	4	.600	0	37	9	1	132	144	21	12	1	3.82
Eppa Rixey	L	42	6	3	.667	0	16	12	5	94	118	12	10	1	3.16
1 Bob Smith	R	35	4	4	.500	0	16	6	4	74	75	11	18	0	2.19
2 Allyn Stout	R	28	2	3	.400	0	23	5	2	71	85	26	29	0	3.80
Jack Quinn	R	49	0	1	.000	1	14	0	0	16	20	5	3	0	3.94

*Derringer, also with St. Louis, league leader in L with 27

WORLD SERIES – NEW YORK (NL) 4 WASHINGTON (AL) 1

LINE SCORES

TEAM	1 2 3	4 5 6	7 8 9	10 11 12	R	H	E
Game 1 October 3 at New York							
WAS	0 0 0	1 0 0	0 0 1		2	5	3
NY (NL)	2 0 2	0 0 0	0 0 X		4	10	2
Stewart, Russell (3), Thomas (8)	**Hubbell**						
Game 2 October 4 at New York							
WAS	0 0 1	0 0 0	0 0 0		1	5	0
NY	0 0 0	0 0 6	0 0 X		6	10	0
Crowder, Thomas (6), McColl (7)	**Schumacher**						
Game 3 October 5 at Washington							
NY	0 0 0	0 0 0	0 0 0		0	5	0
WAS	2 1 0	0 0 0	1 0 X		4	9	1
Fitzsimmons, Bell (8)	**Whitehill**						
Game 4 October 6 at Washington							
NY	0 0 0	1 0 0	0 0 0	0 1	2	11	1
WAS	0 0 0	0 0 0	1 0 0	0 0	1	8	0
Hubbell	**Weaver**, Russell (11)						
Game 5 October 7 at Washington							
NY	0 2 0	0 0 1	0 0 0	1	4	11	1
WAS	0 0 0	0 0 3	0 0 0	0	3	10	0
Schumacher, **Luque** (6)	Crowder, **Russell** (6)						

COMPOSITE BATTING

NAME	POS	G	AB	R	H	2B	3B	HR	RBI	BA
New York (NL) Totals		5	176	16	47	5	0	3	16	.267
Terry	1B	5	**22**	**3**	6	1	0	1	1	.273
Moore	OF	5	**22**	1	5	1	0	0	1	.227
Critz	2B	5	**22**	2	3	0	0	0	0	.136
Davis	OF	5	19	1	**7**	1	0	0	0	.368
Ott	OF	5	18	**3**	**7**	0	0	**2**	**4**	**.389**
Jackson	3B	5	18	**3**	4	1	0	0	2	.222
Ryan	SS	5	18	0	5	0	0	0	1	.278
Mancuso	C	5	17	2	2	1	0	0	2	.118
Schumacher	P	2	7	0	2	0	0	0	3	.286
Hubbell	P	2	7	0	2	0	0	0	0	.286
Fitzsimmons	P	1	2	0	1	0	0	0	0	.500
Peel	OF	2	2	0	1	0	0	0	0	.500
O'Doul	PH	1	1	1	1	0	0	0	2	1.000
Luque	P	1	1	0	1	0	0	0	0	1.000
Bell	P	1	0	0	0	0	0	0	0	.000
Washington (AL) Totals		5	173	11	37	4	0	2	11	.214
Cronin	SS	5	**22**	1	**7**	0	0	0	2	.318
Schulte	OF	5	21	1	**7**	1	0	1	**4**	.333
Myer	2B	5	20	2	6	1	0	0	2	.300
Goslin	OF	5	20	2	5	1	0	1	1	.250
Kuhel	1B	5	20	1	3	0	0	0	1	.150
Manush	OF	5	18	2	2	0	0	0	0	.111
Sewell	C	5	17	1	3	0	0	0	1	.176
Bluege	3B	5	16	1	2	1	0	0	0	.125
Crowder	P	2	4	0	1	0	0	0	0	.250
Weaver	P	1	4	0	0	0	0	0	0	.000
Whitehill	P	1	3	0	0	0	0	0	0	.000
Bolton	PH	2	2	0	0	0	0	0	0	.000
Harris	OF	3	2	0	0	0	0	0	0	.000
Russell	P	3	2	0	0	0	0	0	0	.000
Rice	PH	1	1	0	1	0	0	0	0	1.000
Stewart	P	1	1	0	0	0	0	0	0	.000
Kerr	PR	1	0	0	0	0	0	0	0	.000
McColl	P	1	0	0	0	0	0	0	0	.000
Thomas	P	2	0	0	0	0	0	0	0	.000

COMPOSITE PITCHING

NAME	G	IP	H	BB	SO	W	L	SV	ERA
New York (NL) Totals	5	47	37	13	**24**	4	1	0	1.53
Hubbell	2	**20**	13	**6**	**15**	**2**	0	0	**0.00**
Schumacher	2	14.2	13	5	3	1	0	0	**2.45**
Fitzsimmons	1	7	9	0	1	0	1	0	5.14
Luque	1	4.1	2	2	5	1	0	0	0.00
Bell	1	1	0	0	0	0	0	0	0.00
Washington (AL) Totals	5	46	47	11	21	1	4	0	**2.74**
Crowder	2	11	**16**	5	7	0	1	0	7.36
Russell	**3**	10.1	8	0	7	0	1	0	0.87
Weaver	1	10.1	11	4	3	0	1	0	1.74
Whitehill	1	9	5	2	2	1	0	0	**0.00**
McColl	1	2	0	0	0	0	0	0	0.00
Stewart	1	2	6	0	0	0	1	0	9.00
Thomas	2	1.1	1	0	2	0	0	0	0.00

1934 Dizzy and Daffy and Dizzy

Giant fans had a taste of first place for 127 days during the season, while Cardinal fans had only 11 days alone in the hallowed spot in which to jump and shout. They were a very importat 11 days. The first nine days occurred during the period from May 28, to June 5. The playing of the Giants was such that it seemed the Cardinals would never get around to having those other two days.

But, on September 28, Dizzy Dean shut out Cincinnati, 4-0, to leave the Cardinals and Giants with identical 93-58 records. The next day brother Paul, or more affectionately known as Daffy to complement his brother's nickname, defeated Cincinnati, 6-1, while in New York the Dodgers' Van Lingle Mungo beat the Giants, 5-1. Dizzy returned the next day to again shut out the hapless Reds, this time by a 9-0 deficit, to clinch the flag as the fading Giants bowed to Brooklyn, 8-5.

In capturing the pennant, playing-manager Frankie Frisch was the recipient of a 21-7 September compared to a 14-13 showing for the Giants. The Dean brothers had produced 49 victories, with the older Dizzy winning a league high of 30 and capturing the MVP honors.

The Cardinals had five of their regulars who batted .300 or better. Detroit, in winning their pennant, went one better by producing six regular men in the .300 bracket, and the other two, Billy Rogell and Pete Fox, had respective .296 and .285 averages. Mickey Cochrane, the manager-catcher, was purchased from Connie Mack during the winter and installed a winning spirit which enabled the Tigers, a Western team, to finally uproot their Eastern rivals after 14 years. Cochrane was greatly aided by pitchers, Schoolboy Rowe and Tommy Bridges, the former winning 24 games, of which 16 were won consecutively from June 15, to August 25.

The runner-up Yankees, although victims of costly injuries in the stretch, overshadowed the Tigers when it came to gathering personal honors. Lefty Gomez led all American League pitchers with 26 wins and a 2.33 E.R.A., while first baseman Lou Gehrig swept the Triple Crown with 49 home runs, 165 runs batted in, and a .363 average – accomplishing a feat that had always eluded his fabled teammate, Babe Ruth. The one distinction Ruth did accomplish during the season was on July 13, when he briefly put the Yankees in first place with his 700th lifetime home run.

When it came to the World Series, the Dean brothers continued to provide the same one-two consistency which allowed the Cardinals entry into the fall classic. But the human interest story of the fracas did not come from the brotherly duo. Although both came away from the Series with two victories and impressive earned run averages, the historic spotlight found its way on Joe Medwick, the St. Louis leftfielder who managed to bring the wrath and the soiled fruit of the Detroit fans upon his head.

With the Tigers behind 7-0 in the top half of the sixth-inning of the final game, Medwick jumped on the ball and ended on third base after sliding hard into the bag. Medwick's aggressive running got him into a near-fight with third baseman Marv Owen. Although the umpires managed to quiet the two players, they could do nothing to hush the screaming of the Detroit crowd whose team entered the bottom of the sixth nine runs back. Medwick attempted to take his position three times but on each occasion oranges, apples, newspapers, and other assorted debris drove him back. Fortunately, for the good of Medwick, Commissioner Landis was at the game. After speaking to the umpires, Landis summoned Medwick and Owen to his box. A few moments later Medwick left the game for his own protection. It was a move which pacified the steaming crowd, and gave them the only victory they would have in what turned out to be a very long 11-0 afternoon.

1934 AMERICAN LEAGUE

NAME	G by POS	B	AGE	G	AB	R	H	2B	3B	HR	RBI	BB	SO	SB	BA	SA
DETROIT 1st 101-53 .656	MICKEY COCHRANE															
TOTALS			28	154	5475	958	1644	349	53	74	872	639	528	124	.300	.424
Hank Greenberg	1B153	R	23	153	593	118	201	63	7	26	139	63	93	9	.339	.600
Charlie Gehringer	2B154	L	31	154	601	134	214	50	7	11	127	99	25	11	.356	.517
Billy Rogell	SS154	B	29	154	592	114	175	32	8	3	100	74	36	13	.296	.392
Mary Owen	3B154	R	28	154	565	79	179	34	9	8	96	59	37	3	.317	.451
Pete Fox	OF121	R	24	128	516	101	147	31	2	2	45	49	53	25	.285	.364
Jo-Jo White	OF100	L	25	115	384	97	120	18	5	0	44	69	39	28	.313	.385
Goose Goslin	OF149	L	33	151	614	106	187	38	7	13	100	65	38	5	.305	.453
Mickey Cochrane	C124	L	31	129	437	74	140	32	1	2	76	78	26	8	.320	.412
Gee Walker	OF80	R	26	98	347	54	104	19	2	6	39	19	20	20	.300	.418
Frank Doljack	OF30, 1B3	R	26	56	120	15	28	7	1	1	19	13	15	2	.233	.333
Ray Hayworth	C54	R	30	54	167	20	49	5	2	0	27	16	22	0	.293	.347
Schoolboy Rowe	P45	R	24	51	109	15	33	8	1	2	22	6	20	0	.303	.450
Flea Clifton	3B4, 2B1	R	24	16	16	3	1	0	0	0	1	1	2	0	.063	.063
Heinie Schuble	SS3, 3B2, 2B1	R	27	11	15	2	4	2	0	0	2	1	4	0	.267	.400
Rudy York	C2	R	20	3	6	0	1	0	0	0	0	1	3	0	.167	.167
Frank Reiber		R	24	3	1	0	0	0	0	0	0	2	0	0	.000	.000
Cy Perkins		R	38	1	1	0	0	0	0	0	0	0	0	0	.000	.000
Icehouse Wilson		R	21	1	1	0	0	0	0	0	0	0	0	0	.000	.000
NEW YORK 2nd 94-60 .610 7	JOE McCARTHY															
TOTALS			28	154	5368	842	1494	226	61	135	791	700	597	71	.278	.419
Lou Gehrig	1B153, SS1	L	31	154	579	128	210	40	6	49	165	109	31	9	.363	.706
Tony Lazzeri	2B92, 3B30	R	30	123	438	59	117	24	6	14	67	71	64	11	.267	.445
Frankie Crosetti	SS119, 3B23, 2B1	R	23	138	554	85	147	22	10	11	67	61	58	5	.265	.401
Jack Saltzgaver	3B84, 1B4	L	29	94	350	64	95	8	1	6	36	48	28	8	.271	.351
Babe Ruth	OF111	L	39	125	365	78	105	17	4	22	84	103	63	1	.288	.537
Ben Chapman	OF149	R	25	149	588	82	181	21	13	5	86	67	68	26	.308	.413
Myril Hoag	OF86	R	26	97	251	45	67	8	2	3	34	21	21	1	.267	.351
Bill Dickey (BG)	C104	R	27	104	395	56	127	24	4	12	72	38	18	0	.322	.494
Sammy Byrd	OF104	R	27	106	191	32	47	8	0	3	23	18	22	1	.246	.335
Red Rolfe	SS46, 3B26	L	25	89	279	54	80	13	2	0	18	26	16	2	.287	.348
Don Heffner	2B68	R	23	72	241	29	63	8	3	0	25	25	18	1	.261	.320
Earle Combs (FS)	OF62	L	35	63	251	47	80	13	5	2	25	40	9	3	.319	.434
Art Jorgens	C56	R	29	58	183	14	38	6	1	0	20	23	24	2	.208	.251
George Selkirk	OF46	L	26	46	176	23	55	7	1	5	38	15	17	1	.313	.449
Dixie Walker	OF1	L	23	17	17	2	2	0	0	0	0	1	3	0	.118	.118
Zack Taylor	C3	R	35	4	7	0	1	0	0	0	0	0	1	0	.143	.143
1 Lyn Lary	1B1	R	28	1	0	0	0	0	0	0	0	1	0	0	.000	.000
CLEVELAND 3rd 85-69 .552 16	WALTER JOHNSON															
TOTALS			28	154	5396	814	1550	340	46	100	763	526	433	52	.287	.423
Hal Trosky	1B154	L	21	154	625	117	206	45	9	35	142	58	49	2	.330	.598
Odell Hale	2B137, 3B5	R	25	143	563	82	170	44	6	13	101	48	50	8	.302	.471
Bill Knickerbocker	SS146	R	22	146	593	82	188	32	5	4	67	25	40	6	.317	.408
Willie Kamm	3B118	R	34	121	386	52	104	23	3	0	42	62	38	7	.269	.345
Sam Rice	OF78	L	44	97	335	48	98	19	1	1	33	28	9	5	.293	.364
Earl Averill	OF154	L	32	154	598	128	187	48	6	31	113	99	44	4	.313	.569
Joe Vosmik	OF104	R	24	104	405	71	138	33	2	6	78	35	10	1	.341	.477
Frankie Pytlak	C88	R	25	91	289	46	75	12	4	0	35	36	11	11	.260	.329
John Burnett	3B42, SS9, 2B3, OF2	L	29	72	208	28	61	11	2	3	30	18	11	1	.293	.409
2 Bob Seeds	OF48	R	27	61	186	28	46	8	1	0	18	21	13	2	.247	.301
Dutch Holland	OF31	R	30	50	128	19	32	12	1	2	13	13	11	0	.250	.406
Milt Galatzer	OF49	L	27	49	196	29	53	10	2	0	15	21	8	3	.270	.342
Glenn Myatt (BN)	C34	L	36	36	107	18	34	6	1	0	12	13	5	1	.318	.393
2 Moe Berg	C28	R	32	29	97	4	25	3	1	0	9	1	7	0	.258	.309
Eddie Moore	2B18, 3B3, SS2	R	35	27	65	4	10	2	0	0	8	10	4	0	.154	.185
Bill Brenzel	C15	R	24	15	51	4	11	3	0	0	3	2	1	0	.216	.275
1 Dick Porter	OF10	L	32	13	44	9	10	2	1	1	6	4	5	0	.227	.386
Kit Carson	OF4	L	21	5	18	4	5	2	1	0	1	2	3	0	.278	.500
Bob Garbark	C5	R	24	5	11	1	0	0	0	0	0	1	3	0	.000	.000
Roy Spencer	C4	R	34	5	7	0	1	1	0	0	2	0	1	0	.143	.286

NAME	T	AGE	W	L	PCT	SV	G	GS	CG	IP	H	BB	SO	ShO	ERA
		28	101	53	.656	14	154	154	74	1370	1467	488	640	11	4.06
Schoolboy Rowe	R	24	24	8	.750	1	45	30	20	266	259	81	149	3	3.45
Tommy Bridges	R	27	22	11	.667	1	36	35	23	275	249	104	151	3	3.67
Firpo Marberry	R	35	15	5	.750	3	38	19	6	156	174	48	64	1	4.56
Eldon Auker	R	23	15	7	.682	1	43	18	10	205	234	56	86	2	3.42
Vic Sorrell	R	33	6	9	.400	2	28	19	6	130	146	45	46	0	4.78
Carl Fischer	L	24	6	4	.600	1	20	15	4	95	107	38	39	1	4.36
2 General Crowder	R	35	5	1	.833	0	9	9	3	67	81	20	30	1	4.16
Chief Hogsett	L	30	3	2	.600	3	26	0	0	50	61	19	23	0	4.32
Luke Hamlin	R	29	2	3	.400	1	20	5	1	75	87	44	30	0	5.40
Red Phillips	R	25	2	0	1.000	1	7	1	1	23	31	16	3	0	6.26
Vic Frasier	R	29	1	3	.250	0	8	2	0	23	30	12	11	0	5.87
Steve Larkin	R	23	0	0	.000	0	2	1	0	6	8	5	8	0	1.50
		26	94	60	.610	10	154	154	83	1383	1349	542	656	13	3.75
Lefty Gomez	L	25	26	5	.839	1	38	33	25	282	223	96	158	6	2.33
Red Ruffing	R	30	19	11	.633	0	36	31	19	256	232	104	149	5	3.94
Johnny Murphy	R	25	14	10	.583	4	40	20	10	208	193	76	70	0	3.12
Johnny Broaca	R	24	12	9	.571	0	26	24	13	177	203	65	74	1	4.17
Jimmie DeShong	R	24	6	7	.462	3	31	12	6	134	126	56	40	0	4.10
Johnny Allen (SA)	R	29	5	2	.714	0	13	10	4	72	62	32	54	0	2.88
Danny MacFayden	R	29	4	3	.571	0	22	11	4	96	110	31	41	0	4.50
Russ Van Atta	L	28	3	5	.375	0	28	9	0	88	107	46	39	0	6.34
George Uhle	R	35	2	4	.333	0	10	2	0	16	30	7	10	0	10.13
3 Burleigh Grimes	R	40	1	2	.333	1	10	0	0	18	22	14	5	0	5.50
Charlie Devens	R	24	1	0	1.000	0	1	1	1	11	9	5	4	0	1.64
Vito Tamulis	L	22	1	0	1.000	0	1	1	1	9	7	1	5	1	0.00
1 Harry Smythe	L	29	0	2	.000	1	8	0	0	15	24	8	7	0	7.80
Floyd Newkirk	R	25	0	0	.000	0	1	0	0	1	1	1	0	0	0.00
		27	85	69	.552	19	154	154	72	1367	1476	582	554	8	4.28
Mel Harder	R	24	20	12	.625	4	44	29	17	255	246	81	91	6	2.61
Monte Pearson	R	24	18	13	.581	2	39	33	19	255	257	130	140	0	4.52
Willis Hudlin	R	28	15	10	.600	4	36	26	15	195	210	65	58	1	4.75
Oral Hildebrand	R	27	11	9	.550	1	33	28	10	198	225	99	72	1	4.50
Lloyd Brown	L	29	5	10	.333	6	38	15	5	117	116	51	39	0	3.85
Ralph Winegarner	R	24	5	4	.556	0	22	6	4	78	91	39	32	0	5.54
Belve Bean	R	29	5	1	.833	0	21	1	0	51	53	21	20	0	3.88
Clint Brown (BW)	R	30	4	3	.571	1	17	2	0	50	83	14	15	0	5.94
Thornton Lee	L	27	1	1	.500	0	24	6	0	86	105	44	41	0	5.02
2 Bob Weiland	L	28	1	5	.167	0	16	7	2	70	71	30	42	0	4.11
Sarge Connally	R	35	0	0	.000	1	5	0	0	5	4	5	1	0	5.40
Bill Perrin	L	24	0	1	.000	0	1	1	0	5	13	2	3	0	14.40
Denny Galehouse	R	22	0	0	.000	0	1	0	0	1	2	1	0	0	18.00

BOSTON 4th 76-76 .500 24 — BUCKY HARRIS

NAME	G by POS	B	AGE	G	AB	R	H	2B	3B	HR	RBI	BB	SO	SB	BA	SA
TOTALS			30	153	5339	820	1465	287	70	51	756	610	535	116	.274	.383
Eddie Morgan	1B137	R	30	138	528	95	141	28	4	3	79	81	46	7	.267	.352
Bill Cissell	2B96, SS7, 3B2	R	30	102	416	71	111	13	4	4	44	28	23	11	.267	.346
2 Lyn Lary	SS129	R	28	129	419	58	101	20	4	2	54	66	51	12	.241	.322
Bill Werber	3B130, SS22	R	26	152	623	129	200	41	10	11	67	77	37	40	.321	.472
Moose Solters	OF89	R	28	101	365	61	109	25	4	7	58	18	50	9	.299	.447
Carl Reynolds	OF100	R	31	113	413	61	125	26	9	4	86	27	28	5	.303	.438
Roy Johnson	OF137	L	31	143	569	85	182	43	10	7	119	54	36	11	.320	.467
Rick Ferrell	C128	R	28	132	437	50	130	29	4	1	48	66	20	0	.297	.389
Max Bishop	2B57, 1B15	L	34	97	253	65	66	13	1	1	22	82	22	3	.261	.332
2 Dick Porter	OF75	L	32	80	265	30	80	13	6	0	56	21	15	5	.302	.396
Dusty Cooke	OF44	L	27	74	168	34	41	8	5	1	26	36	25	7	.244	.369
Wes Ferrell	P26	R	26	34	78	12	22	4	0	4	17	7	15	1	.282	.487
Gordie Hinkle	C26	R	29	27	75	7	13	6	1	0	9	7	23	0	.173	.280
Mel Almada	OF23	L	21	23	90	7	21	2	1	0	10	6	8	3	.233	.278
1 Bucky Walters	3B23	R	25	23	88	10	19	4	4	4	18	3	12	0	.216	.489
Lou Legett	C17	R	33	19	38	4	11	0	0	0	1	2	4	0	.289	.289
Skinny Graham	OF13	L	24	13	47	7	11	2	1	0	3	6	13	2	.234	.319
Joe Judge	1B2	L	40	10	15	3	5	2	0	0	2	2	1	0	.333	.467
Al Niemiec	2B9	R	23	9	32	2	7	0	0	0	3	3	4	0	.219	.219
Don Kellett	SS4, 2B2, 3B1	R	24	9	9	0	0	0	0	0	0	1	5	0	.000	.000

1 Bob Seeds 27 R 1-6, Freddie Muller 26 R 0-1

NAME	T	AGE	W	L	PCT	SV	G	GS	CG	IP	H	BB	SO	ShO	ERA
		30	76	76	.500	9	153	153	68	1361	1527	543	538	8	4.32
Wes Ferrell	R	26	14	5	.737	1	26	23	17	181	205	49	67	3	3.63
Johnny Welch	R	27	13	15	.464	0	41	22	8	206	223	76	91	1	4.50
Gordon Rhodes	R	26	12	12	.500	2	44	31	10	219	247	98	79	0	4.56
Fritz Ostermueller	L	26	10	13	.435	3	33	23	10	199	200	99	75	0	3.48
Lefty Grove (SA)	L	34	8	8	.500	0	22	12	5	109	149	32	43	0	6.52
Hank Johnson	R	28	6	8	.429	1	31	14	7	124	162	53	66	1	5.37
Rube Walberg	L	34	6	7	.462	1	30	10	2	105	118	41	38	0	4.03
Herb Pennock	L	40	2	0	1.000	1	30	2	1	62	68	16	16	0	3.05
George Hockette	L	26	2	1	.667	0	3	3	3	27	22	6	14	2	1.67
1 Bob Weiland	L	28	1	5	.167	0	11	7	2	56	63	27	29	0	5.46
Joe Mulligan	R	20	1	0	1.000	0	14	2	1	45	46	27	13	0	3.60
Spike Merena	L	24	1	2	.333	0	4	3	2	25	20	16	7	1	2.88
George Pipgras	R	34	0	0	.000	0	2	1	0	3	4	3	0	0	9.00

PHILADELPHIA 5th 68-82 .453 31 — CONNIE MACK

NAME	G by POS	B	AGE	G	AB	R	H	2B	3B	HR	RBI	BB	SO	SB	BA	SA
TOTALS			27	153	5317	764	1491	236	50	**144**	708	491	584	57	.280	**.425**
Jimmie Foxx	1B140, 3B9	R	26	150	539	120	180	28	6	44	130	**111**	75	11	.334	.653
Rabbit Warstler	2B107, SS2	R	30	117	419	56	99	19	3	1	36	51	30	9	.236	.303
Eric McNair	SS131	R	25	151	599	80	168	20	4	17	82	35	42	7	.280	.412
Pinky Higgins	3B144	R	25	144	543	89	179	37	6	16	90	56	70	9	.330	.508
Ed Coleman	OF86	L	32	101	329	53	92	14	6	14	60	29	34	0	.280	.486
Doc Cramer	OF152	L	28	153	**649**	99	202	29	9	6	46	40	35	1	.311	.411
Bob Johnson	OF139	R	27	141	547	111	168	26	6	34	92	58	60	12	.307	.563
Charlie Berry	C99	R	31	99	269	14	72	10	2	0	34	22	23	1	.268	.320
Lou Finney	OF54, 1B15	L	23	92	272	32	76	11	4	1	28	14	17	4	.279	.360
Frankie Hayes	C89	R	19	92	248	24	56	10	0	6	30	20	44	2	.226	.339
Bing Miller	OF46	R	39	81	177	22	43	10	2	1	22	16	14	1	.243	.339
Dib Williams	2B53, SS2	R	24	66	205	25	56	10	1	2	17	21	18	0	.273	.361
Johnny Marcum	P37	R	24	58	112	10	30	4	0	1	13	3	5	0	.268	.330
Charlie Moss	C6	R	23	10	10	3	2	0	0	0	1	0	0	0	.200	.200
1 Ed Madjeski	C1	R	24	8	8	1	3	1	0	0	2	0	1	0	.375	.500
Jerry McQuaig	OF6	R	22	7	16	2	1	0	0	0	1	2	4	0	.063	.063

NAME	T	AGE	W	L	PCT	SV	G	GS	CG	IP	H	BB	SO	ShO	ERA
		26	68	82	.453	8	153	153	68	1337	1429	**693**	480	8	5.01
Johnny Marcum	R	24	14	11	.560	0	37	31	17	232	257	88	92	2	4.52
Joe Cascarella	R	27	12	15	.444	1	42	22	9	194	214	104	71	2	4.69
Bill Dietrich	R	24	11	12	.478	3	39	23	14	208	201	114	88	4	4.67
Sugar Cain	R	27	9	17	.346	0	36	32	15	231	235	128	66	0	4.40
Al Benton	R	23	7	9	.438	1	32	21	7	155	145	88	58	0	4.88
Roy Mahaffey	R	31	6	7	.462	2	37	14	3	129	142	55	37	0	5.37
1 Bob Kline	R	24	6	2	.750	1	20	0	0	40	50	13	14	0	6.30
George Caster	R	26	3	2	.600	0	5	3	2	37	32	14	15	0	3.41
Mort Flohr	L	22	0	2	.000	0	14	3	0	31	34	33	6	0	5.81
Harry Matuzak	R	24	0	3	.000	0	11	0	0	24	28	10	9	0	4.88
Whitey Wilshere	L	21	0	1	.000	0	9	2	0	22	39	15	19	0	11.86
Ed Lagger	R	21	0	0	.000	0	8	0	0	18	27	14	2	0	11.00
Jack Wilson	R	22	0	1	.000	0	2	2	1	9	15	9	2	0	12.00
Tim McKeithan	R	27	0	0	.000	0	3	0	0	4	7	5	0	0	15.75
Roy Vaughn	R	22	0	0	.000	0	2	0	0	4	3	3	1	0	2.25

ST. LOUIS 6th 67-85 .441 33 — ROGERS HORNSBY

NAME	G by POS	B	AGE	G	AB	R	H	2B	3B	HR	RBI	BB	SO	SB	BA	SA
TOTALS			27	154	5288	674	1417	252	59	62	631	514	**631**	43	.268	.373
Jack Burns	1B154	L	26	154	612	86	157	28	8	13	73	62	47	9	.257	.392
Oscar Melillo	2B141	R	34	144	552	54	133	19	3	2	55	28	27	4	.241	.297
Alan Strange	SS125	R	24	127	430	39	100	17	2	1	45	48	28	3	.233	.288
Harlond Clift	3B141	R	21	147	572	104	149	30	10	14	56	84	**100**	7	.260	.421
Bruce Campbell	OF123	L	24	138	481	62	134	25	6	9	74	51	64	5	.279	.412
Sammy West	OF120	L	29	122	482	90	157	22	10	9	55	62	55	3	.326	.469
Ray Pepper	OF136	R	28	148	564	71	168	24	6	7	101	29	67	1	.298	.399
Rollie Hemsley	C114, OF6	R	27	123	431	47	133	31	7	2	52	29	37	6	.309	.427
Ollie Bejma	SS32, 2B14, 3B13, OF9	R	26	95	262	39	71	16	3	2	29	40	36	3	.271	.378
Debs Garms	OF56	L	26	91	232	25	68	14	4	0	31	27	19	0	.293	.388
Frank Grube	C55	R	29	65	170	22	49	10	0	0	11	24	11	2	.288	.347
Rogers Hornsby	3B1, OF1	R	38	24	23	2	7	2	0	1	11	7	4	0	.304	.522
Earl Clark	OF9	R	26	13	41	4	7	2	0	0	1	1	3	0	.171	.220
George Puccinelli	OF6	R	27	10	26	4	6	1	0	2	5	1	8	0	.231	.500
Grover Hartley	C2	R	45	5	3	0	1	1	0	0	0	1	0	0	.333	.667
Art Scharein		R	29	1	2	0	1	0	0	0	2	0	0	0	.500	.500
Charley O'Leary		R	52	1	1	1	1	0	0	0	0	0	0	0	1.000	1.000

NAME	T	AGE	W	L	PCT	SV	G	GS	CG	IP	H	BB	SO	ShO	ERA
		28	67	85	.441	**20**	154	154	50	1350	1499	632	499	6	4.49
Bobo Newsom	R	26	16	**20**	.444	5	47	32	15	262	259	**149**	135	2	4.02
George Blaeholder	R	30	14	18	.438	3	39	33	14	234	**276**	68	66	1	4.23
Bump Hadley	R	29	10	16	.385	1	39	32	7	213	212	127	79	2	4.35
Jack Knott	R	27	10	3	.769	4	45	10	2	138	149	67	56	0	4.96
Dick Coffman	R	27	9	10	.474	3	40	21	6	173	212	59	55	1	4.53
Ivy Andrews	R	27	4	11	.267	3	43	13	2	139	166	65	51	0	4.66
1 Jim Weaver	R	30	2	0	1.000	0	5	5	2	20	17	20	11	0	6.30
Ed Wells	L	34	1	7	.125	1	33	8	2	92	108	35	27	0	4.79
Bill McAfee	R	26	1	0	1.000	0	28	0	0	62	84	26	11	0	5.81
Lefty Mills	L	24	0	0	.000	0	4	0	0	9	10	11	2	0	4.00
Jim Walkup	R	24	0	0	.000	0	3	0	0	8	6	5	6	0	2.25
Sam Gray (IL) 36															

WASHINGTON 7th 66-86 .434 34 — JOE CRONIN

NAME	G by POS	B	AGE	G	AB	R	H	2B	3B	HR	RBI	BB	SO	SB	BA	SA
TOTALS			30	155	5448	729	1512	278	70	51	682	567	447	49	.278	.382
Joe Kuhel (BN)	1B63	L	28	63	263	49	76	12	3	3	25	30	14	2	.289	.392
Buddy Myer	2B135	L	30	139	524	103	160	33	8	3	57	102	32	6	.305	.416
Joe Cronin (BA)	SS127	R	27	127	504	68	143	30	9	7	101	53	28	8	.284	.421
Cecil Travis	3B99	L	20	109	392	48	125	22	4	1	53	24	37	1	.319	.403
John Stone (NJ)	OF112	L	28	113	419	77	132	28	7	7	67	52	26	1	.315	.465
Fred Schulte	OF134	R	33	136	524	72	156	32	6	3	73	53	34	3	.298	.399
Heinie Manush	OF131	L	32	137	556	88	194	42	11	11	89	36	23	7	.349	.523
Eddie Phillips	C53	R	33	56	169	6	33	6	1	2	16	26	24	1	.195	.278
Ossie Bluege	3B41, SS30, 2B5, OF5	R	33	99	285	39	70	9	2	0	11	23	15	2	.246	.291
Dave Harris	OF64, 3B5	R	34	97	235	28	59	14	3	2	37	39	40	2	.251	.362
Luke Sewell (BG)	C50, OF7, 1B6, 2B1, 3B1	R	33	72	207	21	49	7	3	2	21	22	10	0	.237	.329
Pete Susko	1B58	L	29	58	224	25	64	5	3	2	25	18	10	3	.286	.362
2 Red Kress	1B30, OF10, 2B6, SS1, 3B1	R	27	56	171	18	39	4	3	4	24	17	19	3	.228	.357
Cliff Bolton	C39	L	27	42	148	12	40	9	1	1	17	11	9	2	.270	.365
1 Moe Berg	C31	R	32	33	86	5	21	4	0	0	6	6	4	2	.244	.291
John Kerr	3B17, 2B13	R	35	31	103	8	28	4	0	0	12	8	13	1	.272	.311
Gus Dugas	OF2	L	27	24	19	2	1	1	0	0	1	3	3	0	.053	.105
Johnny Gill	OF13	L	29	13	53	7	13	3	0	2	7	2	3	0	.245	.415
Elmer Klumpp	C11	R	27	12	15	2	2	0	0	0	0	0	1	0	.133	.133
1 Bob Boken	3B6, 2B1	R	26	11	27	5	6	1	1	0	6	3	1	2	.222	.333
Jake Powell	OF9	R	25	9	35	6	10	2	0	0	1	4	2	1	.286	.343
Fred Sington	OF9	R	24	9	35	2	10	2	0	0	6	4	3	0	.286	.343

NAME	T	AGE	W	L	PCT	SV	G	GS	CG	IP	H	BB	SO	ShO	ERA
		32	66	86	.434	12	155	155	61	1381	**1622**	503	412	3	4.68
Earl Whitehill	L	34	14	11	.560	0	32	31	15	235	269	94	96	0	4.52
Monty Weaver	R	28	11	15	.423	0	31	31	11	205	255	63	51	0	4.79
Bobby Burke	L	27	8	8	.500	0	37	15	7	168	155	72	52	1	3.21
Tommy Thomas	R	34	8	9	.471	1	33	18	7	133	154	58	42	1	5.48
Lefty Stewart	L	33	7	11	.389	0	24	22	7	152	184	36	36	1	4.03
Jack Russell	R	28	5	10	.333	7	**54**	9	3	158	179	56	38	0	4.16
1 General Crowder	R	35	4	10	.286	3	29	13	4	101	142	38	39	0	6.77
Alex McColl	R	40	3	4	.429	1	42	2	1	112	129	36	29	0	3.86
Ed Linke	R	22	2	2	.500	0	7	4	2	35	38	9	9	0	4.11
Reese Diggs	R	18	1	2	.333	0	4	3	2	21	26	15	2	0	6.86
Sid Cohen	L	26	1	1	.500	0	3	2	2	18	25	6	6	0	7.50
2 Bob Kline	R	24	1	0	1.000	0	6	0	0	4	10	4	1	0	15.75
Orville Armbrust	R	24	1	0	1.000	0	3	2	0	13	10	3	3	0	2.08
Ray Prim	L	27	0	2	.000	0	8	1	0	15	19	8	3	0	6.60
Allen Benson	R	26	0	1	.000	0	2	2	0	10	19	5	4	0	11.70
John Milligan	L	30	0	0	.000	0	2	0	0	3	6	0	1	0	9.00
Marc Filley	R	22	0	0	.000	0	1	0	0	.1	2	0	0	0	27.00

CHICAGO 8th 53-99 .349 47 — LEW FONSECA 4-13 .235 JIMMY DYKES 49-86 .363

NAME	G by POS	B	AGE	G	AB	R	H	2B	3B	HR	RBI	BB	SO	SB	BA	SA
TOTALS			29	153	5301	704	1395	237	40	71	662	565	524	36	.263	.363
Zeke Bonura	1B127	R	25	127	510	86	154	35	4	27	110	64	31	0	.302	.545
Jackie Hayes (BG)	2B61	R	27	62	226	19	58	9	1	1	31	23	20	3	.257	.319
Luke Appling	SS110, 2B8	R	27	118	452	75	137	28	6	2	61	59	27	3	.303	.405
Jimmy Dykes	3B74, 1B27, 2B27	R	37	127	456	52	122	17	4	7	82	64	28	1	.268	.368
Evar Swanson	OF105	R	31	117	426	71	127	9	5	0	34	59	31	10	.298	.343
Mule Haas	OF89	L	30	106	351	54	94	16	3	2	22	47	22	1	.268	.348
Al Simmons	OF138	R	32	138	558	102	192	36	7	18	104	53	58	3	.344	.530
2 Ed Madjeski	C79	R	24	85	281	36	62	14	2	5	32	14	31	2	.221	.338
2 Bob Boken	2B57, SS22	R	26	81	297	30	70	9	1	3	40	15	32	2	.236	.303
2 Marty Hopkins	3B63	R	27	67	210	22	45	7	0	2	28	42	26	0	.214	.276
Jocko Conlan	OF54	L	34	63	225	35	56	11	3	0	16	19	7	2	.249	.324
Merv Shea	C60	R	33	62	176	8	28	3	0	0	5	24	19	0	.159	.176
Frenchy Uhalt	OF40	L	24	57	165	28	40	5	1	0	16	29	12	6	.242	.285
Ted Lyons	P30	R	33	50	97	9	20	4	0	1	16	3	19	0	.206	.278
Joe Chamberlain	SS26, 3B14	R	24	43	141	13	34	5	1	2	17	6	38	1	.241	.333
Frenchy Bordagaray	OF17	R	22	29	87	12	28	3	1	0	2	3	8	1	.322	.379
Muddy Ruel	C21	R	38	22	57	4	12	3	0	0	7	8	5	0	.211	.263
Milt Bocek	OF10	R	21	19	38	3	8	1	0	0	3	5	5	0	.211	.237
Charlie Uhlir	OF6	L	21	14	27	3	4	0	0	0	3	2	6	0	.148	.148
Rip Radcliff	OF14	L	28	14	56	7	15	2	1	0	5	0	2	1	.268	.339
Mark Mauldin	3B10	R	19	10	38	3	10	2	0	1	3	0	3	0	.263	.395
1 Red Kress	2B3	R	27	8	14	3	4	0	0	0	1	3	3	0	.286	.286
George Caithamer	C5	R	23	5	19	1	6	1	0	0	3	1	5	0	.316	.368
Johnny Pasek	C4	R	29	4	9	1	3	0	0	0	0	1	1	0	.333	.333
Bill Fehring	C1	B	22	1	1	0	0	0	0	0	0	0	1	0	.000	.000

NAME	T	AGE	W	L	PCT	SV	G	GS	CG	IP	H	BB	SO	ShO	ERA
		32	53	**99**	.349	8	153	153	72	1355	1599	628	506	4	5.41
George Earnshaw	R	34	14	11	.560	0	33	30	16	227	242	104	97	2	4.52
Ted Lyons	R	33	11	13	.458	1	30	24	21	205	249	66	53	0	4.87
Sad Sam Jones	R	41	8	12	.400	0	27	26	11	183	217	60	60	1	5.11
Milt Gaston	R	38	6	19	.240	0	29	28	10	194	247	84	48	1	5.85
Les Tietje	R	22	5	14	.263	0	34	22	6	176	174	96	81	0	4.81
Phil Gallivan	R	27	4	7	.364	1	35	7	3	127	155	64	55	0	5.60
Whit Wyatt	R	26	4	11	.267	2	23	6	2	68	83	37	36	0	7.15
Joe Heving	R	33	1	7	.125	4	33	2	0	88	133	48	40	0	7.26
Vern Kennedy	R	27	0	2	.000	0	3	3	1	19	21	9	7	0	3.79
Huggo Klaerner	R	25	0	2	.000	0	3	3	1	17	24	16	9	0	11.12
Harry Kinzy	R	23	0	1	.000	0	13	2	1	34	38	31	12	0	5.03
Lee Stine	R	20	0	0	.000	0	4	0	0	11	11	10	8	0	8.18
Monty Stratton	R	22	0	0	.000	0	1	0	0	3	4	1	0	0	6.00
John Pomorski	R	28	0	0	.000	0	3	0	0	2	1	2	0	0	4.50
Ed Durham (IL) 26															

ST. LOUIS 1st 95-58 .621 — FRANKIE FRISCH

NAME	G by POS	B	AGE	G	AB	R	H	2B	3B	HR	RBI	BB	SO	SB	BA	SA
TOTALS			28	154	5502	799	1582	294	75	104	748	392	535	69	.288	.425
Ripper Collins	1B154	B	30	154	600	116	200	40	12	35	128	57	50	2	.333	.615
Frankie Frisch	2B115, 3B25	B	35	140	550	74	168	30	6	3	75	45	10	11	.305	.398
Leo Durocher	SS146	B	28	146	500	62	130	26	5	3	70	33	40	2	.260	.350
Pepper Martin	3B107, P1	R	30	110	454	76	131	25	11	5	49	32	41	23	.289	.425
Jack Rothrock	OF154, 2B1	B	29	154	647	106	184	35	3	11	72	49	56	10	.284	.399
Ernie Orsatti	OF90	L	31	105	337	39	101	14	4	0	31	27	31	6	.300	.365
Joe Medwick	OF149	R	22	149	620	110	198	40	18	18	106	21	83	3	.319	.529
Spud Davis	C94	R	29	107	347	45	104	22	4	9	65	34	27	0	.300	.464
Burgess Whitehead	2B48, SS29, 3B28	R	24	100	332	55	92	13	5	1	24	12	19	5	.277	.355
Bill DeLancey	C77	L	22	93	253	41	80	18	3	13	40	41	37	1	.316	.565
2 Chick Fullis	OF56	R	30	69	199	21	52	9	1	0	26	14	11	4	.261	.317
Pat Crawford	3B9, 2B4	L	32	61	70	3	19	2	0	0	16	5	3	0	.271	.300
Buster Mills	OF18	R	25	29	72	7	17	4	1	1	8	4	11	0	.236	.361
1 Kiddo Davis	OF9	R	32	16	33	6	10	3	0	1	4	3	1	1	.303	.485
Francis Healy	C2, 3B1, OF1	R	24	15	13	1	4	1	0	0	1	0	2	0	.308	.385
Gene Moore	OF3	L	24	9	18	2	5	1	0	0	1	2	2	0	.278	.333
Lew Riggs		L	24	2	1	0	0	0	0	0	0	0	1	0	.000	.000
2 Red Worthington		R	28	1	1	0	0	0	0	0	0	0	1	0	.000	.000

Charley Gelbert (LJ) 28

NAME	T	AGE	W	L	PCT	SV	G	GS	CG	IP	H	BB	SO	ShO	ERA
		30	95	58	.621	16	154	154	78	1387	1463	411	689	15	3.69
Dizzy Dean	R	23	30	7	.811	7	50	33	24	312	288	75	195	7	2.65
Paul Dean	R	20	19	11	.633	2	39	26	16	233	225	52	150	5	3.44
Tex Carleton	R	27	16	11	.593	2	40	31	16	241	260	52	103	0	4.26
Bill Walker	L	30	12	4	.750	0	24	19	10	153	160	66	76	1	3.12
Wild Bill Hallahan	L	31	8	12	.400	0	32	26	10	163	195	66	70	2	4.25
Jesse Haines	R	40	4	4	.500	1	37	6	0	90	86	19	17	0	3.50
Jim Mooney	L	27	2	4	.333	1	32	7	1	82	114	49	27	0	5.49
1 Burleigh Grimes	R	42	2	1	.667	0	4	0	0	8	5	2	1	0	3.38
1 Flint Rhem	R	33	1	0	1.000	1	5	1	0	16	26	7	6	0	4.50
2 Dazzy Vance	R	43	1	1	.500	1	19	4	1	59	62	14	33	0	3.66
Jim Winford	R	24	0	2	.000	0	5	1	0	13	17	6	3	0	7.61
2 Jim Lindsey	R	36	0	1	.000	1	11	0	0	14	21	3	7	0	6.43
Clarence Heise	L	26	0	0	.000	0	1	0	0	2	3	0	1	0	4.50
Pepper Martin	R	30	0	0	.000	0	1	0	0	2	1	0	0	0	4.50

NEW YORK 2nd 93-60 .608 2 — BILL TERRY

NAME	G by POS	B	AGE	G	AB	R	H	2B	3B	HR	RBI	BB	SO	SB	BA	SA
TOTALS			30	153	5396	760	1485	240	41	126	716	406	526	19	.275	.405
Bill Terry	1B153	L	35	153	602	109	213	30	6	8	83	60	47	0	.354	.463
Hughie Critz	2B137	R	33	137	571	77	138	17	1	6	40	19	24	3	.242	.306
Travis Jackson	SS130, 3B9	R	30	137	523	75	140	26	7	16	101	37	71	1	.268	.436
Johnny Vergez	3B104	R	27	108	320	31	64	18	1	7	27	28	55	1	.200	.328
Mel Ott	OF153	L	25	153	582	119	190	29	10	35	135	85	43	0	.326	.591
George Watkins	OF81	L	34	105	296	38	73	18	3	6	33	24	34	2	.247	.389
Jo-Jo Moore	OF131	L	25	139	580	106	192	37	4	15	61	31	23	5	.331	.486
Gus Mancuso	C122	R	28	122	383	32	94	14	0	7	46	27	19	0	.245	.337
Blondy Ryan	3B65, SS30, 2B25	R	28	110	385	35	93	19	0	2	41	19	68	3	.242	.306
Lefty O'Doul	OF38	L	37	83	177	27	56	4	3	9	46	18	7	2	.316	.525
Hank Leiber	OF51	R	23	63	187	17	45	5	3	2	25	4	13	1	.241	.332
Harry Danning	C37	R	22	53	97	8	32	7	0	1	7	1	9	1	.330	.433
Hal Schumacher	P41	R	23	44	117	19	28	5	1	6	15	2	26	0	.239	.453
Paul Richards	C37	R	25	42	75	10	12	1	0	0	3	13	8	0	.160	.173
Phil Weintraub	OF20	L	26	31	74	13	26	2	0	0	15	15	10	0	.351	.378
George Grantham	1B4, 3B2	L	34	32	29	5	7	2	0	1	4	8	6	0	.241	.414
Homer Peel	OF10	R	31	21	41	7	8	0	0	1	3	1	2	0	.195	.268
Fresco Thompson		R	32	1	1	0	0	0	0	0	0	0	0	0	.000	.000

NAME	T	AGE	W	L	PCT	SV	G	GS	CG	IP	H	BB	SO	ShO	ERA
		30	93	60	.608	30	153	153	68	1370	1384	351	499	13	3.19
Hal Schumacher	R	23	23	10	.697	0	41	36	18	297	299	89	112	2	3.18
Carl Hubbell	L	31	21	12	.636	8	49	34	25	313	286	37	118	5	2.30
Freddie Fitzsimmons	R	32	18	14	.563	1	38	37	14	263	266	51	73	3	3.05
Roy Parmelee (IL)	R	27	10	6	.625	0	22	20	7	153	134	60	83	2	3.41
Joe Bowman	R	24	5	4	.556	3	30	10	3	107	119	36	36	0	3.62
Hi Bell	R	36	4	3	.571	6	22	2	0	54	72	12	9	0	3.67
Dolf Luque	R	43	4	3	.571	7	26	0	0	42	54	17	12	0	3.86
Al Smith	L	26	3	5	.375	5	30	5	0	67	70	21	27	0	4.30
Jack Salveson	R	20	3	1	.750	0	12	4	0	38	43	13	18	0	3.55
Slick Castleman	R	20	1	0	1.000	0	7	1	0	17	18	10	5	0	5.29
1 Watty Clark	L	32	1	2	.333	0	5	4	1	19	23	5	6	0	6.63

CHICAGO 3rd 86-65 .570 8 — CHARLIE GRIMM

NAME	G by POS	B	AGE	G	AB	R	H	2B	3B	HR	RBI	BB	SO	SB	BA	SA
TOTALS			28	152	5347	705	1494	263	44	101	664	375	630	59	.279	.402
Charlie Grimm	1B74	L	35	75	267	24	79	8	1	5	47	16	12	1	.296	.390
Billy Herman	2B111	R	24	113	456	79	138	21	6	3	42	34	31	6	.303	.395
Billy Jurges	SS98	R	26	100	358	43	88	15	2	8	33	19	34	1	.246	.366
Stan Hack	3B109	L	24	111	402	54	116	16	6	1	21	45	42	11	.289	.366
Babe Herman	OF113, 1B7	L	31	125	467	65	142	34	5	14	84	35	71	1	.304	.488
Kiki Cuyler	OF142	R	34	142	559	80	189	42	8	6	69	31	62	15	.338	.474
Chuck Klein	OF110	L	29	115	435	78	131	27	2	20	80	47	38	3	.301	.510
Gabby Hartnett	C129	R	33	130	438	58	131	21	1	22	90	37	46	0	.299	.502
Woody English	SS56, 3B46, 2B7	R	27	109	421	65	117	26	5	3	31	48	65	6	.278	.385
Tuck Stainback	OF96, 3B1	R	23	104	359	47	110	14	3	2	46	8	42	7	.306	.379
Augie Galan	2B43, 3B3, SS1	B	22	66	192	31	50	6	2	5	22	16	15	4	.260	.391
2 Don Hurst	1B48	L	28	51	151	13	30	5	0	3	12	8	18	0	.199	.291
Babe Phelps	C18	L	26	44	70	7	20	5	2	2	12	1	8	0	.286	.500
Riggs Stephenson	OF15	R	36	38	74	5	16	0	0	0	7	7	5	0	.216	.216
1 Dolph Camilli	1B32	L	27	32	120	17	33	8	0	4	19	5	25*	1	.275	.442
2 Bob O'Farrell	C22	R	37	22	67	3	15	3	0	0	5	3	11	0	.224	.269
Bennie Tate	C8	L	32	11	24	1	3	0	0	0	0	1	3	0	.125	.125
Phil Cavarretta	1B5	L	17	7	21	5	8	0	1	1	6	2	3	1	.381	.619

NAME	T	AGE	W	L	PCT	SV	G	GS	CG	IP	H	BB	SO	ShO	ERA
		29	86	65	.570	9	152	152	73	1361	1432	417	633	11	3.76
Lon Warneke	R	25	22	10	.688	3	43	35	23	291	273	66	143	3	3.22
Guy Bush	R	32	18	10	.643	2	40	27	15	209	213	54	75	1	3.83
Pat Malone	R	31	14	7	.667	0	34	21	8	191	200	55	111	1	3.53
Bill Lee	R	24	13	14	.481	1	35	29	16	214	218	74	104	4	3.41
2 Jim Weaver	R	30	11	9	.555	0	27	20	8	159	163	54	98	1	3.91
Bud Tinning	R	28	4	6	.400	3	39	7	1	129	134	46	44	1	3.35
Charlie Root	R	35	4	7	.364	0	34	9	2	118	141	53	46	0	4.27
Roy Joiner	L	27	0	1	.000	0	20	2	0	34	61	8	9	0	8.21
Charlie Wiedemeyer	R	19	0	0	.000	0	4	1	0	8	16	4	2	0	10.13
Dick Ward	R	25	0	0	.000	0	3	0	0	6	9	2	1	0	3.00
Lynn Nelson	R	29	0	1	.000	0	2	1	0	1	4	1	0	0	36.00

*Camilli, also with Philadelphia, league leader in SO with 94

BOSTON 4th 78-73 .517 16 — BILL McKECHNIE

NAME	G by POS	B	AGE	G	AB	R	H	2B	3B	HR	RBI	BB	SO	SB	BA	SA
TOTALS			29	152	5370	683	1460	233	44	83	649	375	440	30	.272	.378
Buck Jordan	1B117	L	27	124	489	68	152	26	9	2	58	35	19	3	.311	.413
Marty McManus	2B73, 3B37	R	34	119	435	56	120	18	0	8	47	32	42	5	.276	.372
Billy Urbanski	SS145	R	31	146	605	104	177	30	6	7	53	56	37	4	.293	.397
Pinky Whitney	3B111, 2B36, SS2	R	29	146	563	58	146	26	2	12	79	25	54	7	.259	.377
Tommy Thompson	OF82	L	24	105	343	40	91	12	3	0	37	13	19	2	.265	.318
Wally Berger	OF150	R	28	150	615	92	183	35	8	34	121	49	65	2	.298	.546
Hal Lee	OF128, 2B4	R	29	139	521	70	152	23	6	8	79	47	43	3	.292	.405
Al Spohrer	C98	R	31	100	265	25	59	15	0	0	17	14	18	1	.223	.279
Randy Moore	OF72, 1B37	L	29	123	422	55	120	21	2	7	64	40	16	2	.284	.393
Shanty Hogan	C90	R	28	92	279	20	73	5	2	4	34	16	13	0	.262	.337
Les Mallon	2B42	R	28	66	166	23	49	6	2	0	18	15	12	0	.295	.343
1 Red Worthington	OF11	R	28	41	65	6	16	5	0	0	6	6	5	0	.246	.323
Joe Mowry	OF20, 2B1	B	26	25	79	9	17	3	0	1	4	3	13	0	.215	.291
Dick Gyselman	3B15, 2B2	R	26	24	36	7	6	1	1	0	4	2	11	0	.167	.250
Elbie Fletcher	1B1	L	18	8	4	4	2	0	0	0	0	0	2	1	.500	.500
Dan McGee	SS7	R	20	7	22	2	3	0	0	0	1	3	6	0	.136	.136
Johnnie Tyler	OF1	B	27	3	6	0	1	0	0	0	1	0	3	0	.167	.167

Rabbit Maranville (BL) 42

NAME	T	AGE	W	L	PCT	SV	G	GS	CG	IP	H	BB	SO	ShO	ERA
		32	78	73	.517	20	152	152	62	1360	1512	405	462	13	4.11
Fred Frankhouse	R	30	17	9	.654	1	37	31	13	234	239	77	78	2	3.19
Huck Betts	R	37	17	10	.630	3	40	27	10	213	258	42	69	2	4.06
Ed Brandt	L	29	16	14	.533	5	40	28	20	255	249	83	106	3	3.53
2 Flint Rhem	R	33	8	8	.500	0	25	20	5	153	164	38	56	2	3.59
Bob Smith	R	36	6	9	.400	5	39	5	3	122	133	36	26	0	4.65
Ben Cantwell	R	32	5	11	.313	5	27	19	6	143	163	34	45	1	4.34
Leo Mangum	R	38	5	3	.625	1	29	3	1	94	127	23	28	0	5.74
Bob Brown	R	23	1	3	.250	0	16	8	2	58	59	36	21	1	5.74
1 Tom Zachary	L	38	1	2	.333	0	5	4	2	24	27	8	4	1	3.38
Dick Oliver	R		1	3	.250	0	15	3	0	32	50	12	14	0	6.75
2 Jumbo Jim Elliott	L	33	1	1	.500	0	7	3	0	15	19	9	6	0	6.00
Clarence Pickrel	R	23	0	0	.000	0	10	1	0	16	24	7	9	0	5.06

PITTSBURGH 5th 74-76 .493 19.5 — GEORGE GIBSON 27-24 .529 PIE TRAYNOR 47-52 .475

NAME	G by POS	B	AGE	G	AB	R	H	2B	3B	HR	RBI	BB	SO	SB	BA	SA
TOTALS			27	151	5361	735	1541	281	77	52	679	440	398	44	.287	.398
Gus Suhr	1B151	L	28	151	573	67	162	36	13	13	103	66	52	4	.283	.459
Cookie Lavagetto	2B83	R	21	87	304	41	67	16	3	3	46	32	39	6	.220	.322
Arky Vaughan	SS149	L	22	149	558	115	186	41	11	12	94	94	38	10	.333	.511
Pie Traynor	3B110	R	34	119	444	62	137	22	10	1	61	21	27	3	.309	.410
Paul Waner	OF145	L	31	146	599	122	217	32	16	14	90	68	24	8	.362	.539
Lloyd Waner	OF139	L	28	140	611	95	173	27	6	1	48	38	12	6	.282	.352
Fred Lindstrom	OF92	R	28	97	383	59	111	24	4	4	49	23	21	1	.290	.405
Earl Grace	C83, 1B1	L	27	95	289	27	78	17	1	4	24	20	19	0	.270	.377
Tommy Thevenow	2B75, 3B44, SS1	R	30	122	446	37	121	16	2	0	54	20	20	0	.271	.316
Woody Jensen	OF66	L	26	88	283	34	82	13	4	0	27	4	13	2	.290	.364
Tom Padden	C76	R	25	82	237	27	76	12	2	0	22	30	23	3	.321	.388
Red Lucas	P29	L	32	68	105	11	23	5	1	0	8	6	16	1	.219	.286
Wally Roettger	OF23	R	31	47	106	7	26	5	1	0	11	3	8	0	.245	.311
Pep Young	2B2, SS2	R	26	19	17	3	4	0	0	0	2	0	6	0	.235	.235
Pat Veltman	C11	R	28	12	28	1	3	0	0	0	2	0	1	0	.107	.107
Hal Finney	C5	R	28	5	0	3	0	0	0	0	2	0	0	0	.000	.000
Bill Brubaker	3B3	R	23	3	6	0	2	1	0	0	1	1	0	0	.333	.500

NAME	T	AGE	W	L	PCT	SV	G	GS	CG	IP	H	BB	SO	ShO	ERA
		31	74	76	.493	8	151	151	63	1330	1523	354	487	8	4.19
Waite Hoyt	R	34	15	6	.714	5	48	15	8	191	184	43	105	3	2.92
Larry French	L	26	12	18	.400	1	49	35	16	264	299	59	103	3	3.58
Bill Swift	R	26	11	13	.458	0	37	24	13	213	244	46	81	1	3.97
Ralph Birkofer	L	25	11	12	.478	1	41	24	11	204	227	66	71	0	4.10
Red Lucas	R	32	10	9	.526	0	29	21	12	173	198	40	44	1	4.37
Heinie Meine	R	38	7	6	.538	0	26	14	2	106	134	25	22	0	4.33
Leon Chagnon	R	31	4	1	.800	1	33	1	0	58	68	24	19	0	4.81
Hal Smith (IL)	R	32	3	4	.429	0	20	5	1	50	72	18	15	0	7.20
2 Burleigh Grimes	R	40	1	2	.667	0	8	4	0	27	36	10	9	0	7.33
Bill Harris	R	34	0	0	.000	0	11	2	0	19	28	7	8	0	6.63
2 Ed Holley	R	32	0	3	.000	0	5	4	0	9	20	6	2	0	16.00
Cy Blanton	R	25	0	1	.000	0	1	1	0	8	5	4	5	0	3.38
Steamboat Struss	R	25	0	1	.000	0	1	1	0	7	7	6	3	0	6.43
Lloyd Johnson	L	23	0	0	.000	0	1	0	0	1	1	0	0	0	0.00

BROOKLYN 6th 71-81 .467 23.5 — CASEY STENGEL

NAME	G by POS	B	AGE	G	AB	R	H	2B	3B	HR	RBI	BB	SO	SB	BA	SA
TOTALS			29	153	5427	748	1526	284	52	79	699	548	555	55	.281	.396
Sam Leslie	1B138	L	28	146	546	75	181	29	6	9	102	69	34	5	.332	.456
Tony Cuccinello	2B101, 3B43	R	26	140	528	59	138	32	2	14	94	49	45	0	.261	.409
Lonny Frey	SS109, 3B13	B	23	125	490	77	139	24	5	8	57	52	54	11	.284	.402
Joe Stripp (NJ)	3B96, 1B7, SS1	R	31	104	384	50	121	19	6	1	40	22	20	2	.315	.404
Buzz Boyle	OF121	L	26	128	472	88	144	26	10	7	48	51	44	8	.305	.447
Len Koenecke	OF121	L	30	123	460	79	147	31	7	14	73	70	38	8	.320	.509
Danny Taylor	OF108	R	33	120	405	62	121	24	6	7	57	63	47	12	.299	.440
Al Lopez	C137, 2B2, 3B2	R	25	140	439	58	120	23	2	7	54	49	44	2	.273	.383
Johnny Frederick	OF77, 1B1	L	33	104	307	51	91	20	1	4	35	33	13	4	.296	.407
Jimmy Jordon	SS51, 2B41, 3B9	R	26	97	369	34	98	17	2	0	43	9	32	1	.266	.322
1 Hack Wilson	OF43	R	34	67	172	24	45	5	0	6	27	40	33	0	.262	.395
Glenn Chapman	OF40, 2B14	R	28	67	93	19	26	5	1	1	10	7	19	1	.280	.387
Jim Bucher(BN)	2B20, 3B6	L	23	47	84	12	19	5	2	0	8	4	7	1	.226	.333
Ray Berres	C37	R	26	39	79	7	17	4	0	0	3	1	16	0	.215	.266
Clyde Sukeforth	C18	L	32	27	43	5	7	1	0	0	1	1	6	0	.163	.186
Johnny McCarthy	1B13	L	24	17	39	7	7	2	0	1	5	2	2	0	.179	.308
Nick Tremark	OF9	L	21	17	28	3	7	1	0	0	6	2	2	0	.250	.286
Wally Millies	C2	R	27	2	7	0	0	0	0	0	0	0	0	0	.000	.000
Bert Hogg	3B1	R	21	2	1	0	0	0	0	0	0	0	0	0	.000	.000

NAME	T	AGE	W	L	PCT	SV	G	GS	CG	IP	H	BB	SO	ShO	ERA
Totals		29	71	81	.467	12	153	153	66	1354	1540	475	520	6	4.48
Van Lingle Mungo	R	23	18	16	.529	3	45	38	22	315	300	104	184	3	3.37
Ray Benge	R	32	14	12	.538	0	36	32	14	227	252	61	64	1	4.32
Dutch Leonard	R	25	14	11	.560	5	44	20	11	184	210	33	58	2	3.28
Johnny Babich	R	21	7	11	.389	1	25	19	7	135	148	51	62	0	4.20
2 Tom Zachary	L	38	5	6	.455	2	22	12	4	102	122	21	28	0	4.41
Les Munns	R	25	3	7	.300	0	33	9	4	99	106	60	41	0	4.73
Boom-Boom Beck	R	29	2	6	.250	0	22	9	2	57	72	32	24	0	7.42
Art Herring	R	27	2	4	.333	0	14	4	2	49	63	29	15	0	6.24
2 Watty Clark	L	32	2	0	1.000	0	17	1	0	25	40	9	10	0	5.40
Ownie Carroll	R	31	1	3	.250	1	26	5	0	74	108	33	17	0	6.45
Ray Lucas	R	25	1	1	.500	0	10	2	0	31	39	14	3	0	6.68
2 Harry Smythe	L	29	1	1	.500	0	8	0	0	21	30	8	5	0	6.00
Phil Page	L	28	1	0	1.000	0	6	0	0	10	13	6	4	0	5.40
Charlie Perkins	L	28	0	3	.000	0	11	2	0	24	37	14	5	0	8.63

PHILADELPHIA 7th 56-93 .376 37 — JIMMIE WILSON

NAME	G by POS	B	AGE	G	AB	R	H	2B	3B	HR	RBI	BB	SO	SB	BA	SA
TOTALS			28	149	5218	675	1480	286	35	56	634	398	534	52	.284	.384
2 Dolph Camilli	1B102	L	27	102	378	52	100	20	3	12	68	48	69*	3	.265	.429
Lou Chiozza	2B85, 3B26, OF17	L	24	134	484	66	147	28	5	0	44	34	35	9	.304	.382
Dick Bartell	SS146	R	26	146	604	102	187	30	4	0	37	64	59	13	.310	.373
2 Bucky Walters	3B80, 2B3, P2	R	25	83	300	36	78	20	3	4	38	19	54	1	.260	.387
2 Johnny Moore	OF115	L	32	116	458	68	157	34	6	11	93	40	18	7	.343	.515
2 Kiddo Davis	OF100	R	32	100	393	50	115	25	5	3	48	27	28	1	.293	.405
Ethan Allen	OF145	R	30	145	581	87	192	42	4	10	85	33	47	6	.330	.468
Al Todd	C82	R	30	91	302	33	96	22	2	4	41	10	39	3	.318	.444
Jimmie Wilson	C77, 1B1, 2B1	R	33	91	277	25	81	11	0	3	35	14	10	1	.292	.365
Mickey Haslin	3B26, 2B21, SS4	R	23	72	166	28	44	8	2	1	11	16	13	1	.265	.355
Harvey Hendrick	OF12, 1B7, 3B7	L	36	59	116	12	34	8	0	0	19	9	15	0	.293	.362
Irv Jeffries	2B52, 3B1	R	28	56	175	28	43	6	0	4	19	15	10	2	.246	.349
Andy High	3B14, 2B2	L	36	47	68	4	14	2	0	0	7	9	3	1	.206	.235
1 Don Hurst	1B34	L	28	40	130	16	34	9	0	2	21	12	7	1	.262	.377
1 Chick Fullis	OF27	R	30	28	102	8	23	6	0	0	12	10	4	2	.225	.284
Bud Clancy	1B10	L	33	20	49	0	12	0	0	1	7	8	4	0	.245	.306
Art Ruble	OF14	L	31	19	54	7	15	4	0	0	8	7	3	0	.278	.352
1 Wes Schulmerich	OF13	R	32	15	52	2	13	1	0	0	1	4	8	0	.250	.269
1 Marty Hopkins	3B9	R	27	10	25	6	3	2	0	0	3	7	5	0	.120	.200
Joe Holden	C6	L	21	10	14	1	1	0	0	0	0	0	2	0	.071	.071

Ed Boland 26 L 9-30, 2 Hack Wilson 34 R 2-20, Prince Oana 26 R 5-21, Fred Frink 22 R 0-0

NAME	T	AGE	W	L	PCT	SV	G	GS	CG	IP	H	BB	SO	ShO	ERA
Totals		29	56	93	.376	15	149	149	52	1297	1501	437	416	8	4.76
Curt Davis	R	30	19	17	.528	5	51	31	18	274	283	60	99	3	2.96
Phil Collins	R	32	13	18	.419	1	45	32	15	254	277	87	72	0	4.18
Snipe Hansen	L	27	6	12	.333	3	50	16	5	151	194	61	40	2	5.42
2 Syl Johnson	R	33	5	9	.357	3	42	10	4	134	122	24	54	3	3.49
Euel Moore	R	26	5	7	.417	1	20	16	3	122	145	41	38	0	4.06
Cy Moore	R	29	4	9	.308	0	35	15	3	127	163	65	55	0	6.45
George Darrow	L	30	2	6	.250	1	17	8	2	49	57	28	14	0	5.51
1 Ed Holley	R	32	1	8	.111	0	15	13	2	73	85	31	14	0	7.15
Reggie Grabowski	R	26	1	3	.250	0	27	5	0	65	114	23	13	0	9.28
1 Ted Kleinhans	L	35	0	0	.000	0	5	0	0	6	11	3	2	0	9.00
Frank Pearce	L	29	0	2	.000	0	7	1	0	20	25	5	4	0	7.20
1 Jumbo Jim Elliott	L	33	0	1	.000	0	3	1	0	5	8	4	1	0	10.80
Bucky Walters	R	25	0	0	.000	0	2	1	0	7	8	2	7	0	1.29
Bill Lohrman	R	21	0	1	.000	1	4	0	0	6	5	1	2	0	4.50
Cy Malis	R	27	0	0	.000	0	1	0	0	4	4	2	1	0	4.50

*Camilli, also with Chicago, league leader in SO with 94

CINCINNATI 8th 52-99 .344 42 — BOB O'FARRELL 26-58 .310 BURT SHOTTON 1-0 1.000 CHUCK DRESSEN 25-41 .379

NAME	G by POS	B	AGE	G	AB	R	H	2B	3B	HR	RBI	BB	SO	SB	BA	SA
TOTALS			30	152	5361	590	1428	227	65	55	560	313	532	34	.266	.364
Jim Bottomley	1B139	L	34	142	556	72	158	31	11	11	78	33	40	1	.284	.439
Tony Piet	2B49, 3B51	R	27	106	421	58	109	20	5	1	38	23	44	6	.259	.337
Gordon Slade	SS97, 2B39	R	29	138	555	61	158	19	8	4	52	25	34	6	.285	.369
Mark Koenig	3B64, SS58, 2B26, 1B4	B	31	151	633	60	172	26	6	1	67	15	24	5	.272	.336
Adam Comorosky	OF122	R	29	127	446	46	115	12	6	0	40	34	23	1	.258	.312
Chick Hafey	OF140	R	31	140	535	75	157	29	6	18	67	52	63	4	.293	.471
Harlin Pool	OF94	L	26	99	358	38	117	22	5	2	50	17	18	3	.327	.433
Ernie Lombardi	C111	R	26	132	417	42	127	19	4	9	62	16	22	0	.305	.434
Sparky Adams	3B38, 2B29	R	39	87	278	38	70	16	1	0	14	20	10	2	.252	.317
2 Wes Schulmerich	OF56	R	32	74	209	21	55	8	3	5	19	22	43	1	.263	.402
1 Bob O'Farrell	C42	R	37	44	123	10	30	8	3	1	9	11	19	0	.244	.382
Link Blakely	OF28	R	22	34	102	11	23	1	1	0	10	5	14	1	.225	.255
Clyde Manion	C24	R	37	25	54	4	10	0	0	0	4	4	7	0	.185	.185
Alex Kampouris	2B16	R	21	19	66	6	13	1	0	0	3	3	18	2	.197	.212
Ivey Shiver	OF15	R	27	19	59	6	12	1	0	2	6	3	15	1	.203	.322
Jimmy Shevlin	1B10	L	24	18	39	6	12	2	0	0	6	6	5	0	.308	.359
1 Johnny Moore	OF10	L	32	16	42	5	8	1	1	0	5	3	2	0	.190	.262
Jake Flowers		R	32	13	9	1	3	0	0	0	0	1	1	1	.333	.333
Frankie McCormick	1B2	R	23	12	16	1	5	2	1	0	5	0	1	0	.313	.563
Ted Petoskey	OF2	R	23	6	7	0	0	0	0	0	1	0	5	0	.000	.000

Harry McCurdy 34 L 0-6, Tommy Robello 21 R 0-2, Bill Marshall

NAME	T	AGE	W	L	PCT	SV	G	GS	CG	IP	H	BB	SO	ShO	ERA
Totals		31	52	99	.344	19	152	152	51	1347	1645	389	438	3	4.37
Paul Derringer	R	27	15	21	.417	4	47	31	18	261	297	59	122	1	3.59
Benny Frey	R	28	11	16	.407	2	39	30	12	245	288	42	33	2	3.53
Si Johnson	R	27	7	22	.241	3	46	31	9	216	264	84	89	0	5.21
Tony Freitas	L	26	6	12	.333	1	30	18	5	153	194	25	37	0	4.00
Allyn Stout	R	29	6	8	.429	1	41	16	4	141	170	47	51	0	4.85
Don Brennan	R	30	4	3	.571	2	28	7	2	78	89	35	31	0	3.81
2 Ted Kleinhans	L	35	2	6	.250	0	24	9	0	80	107	38	23	0	5.74
Beryl Richmond	L	26	1	2	.333	0	6	2	1	19	23	10	9	0	3.79
Ray Kolp	R	39	0	2	.000	3	28	2	0	62	78	12	19	0	4.50
Larry Benton	R	36	0	1	.000	2	16	1	0	29	53	7	5	0	6.52
1 Dazzy Vance	R	43	0	2	.000	0	6	2	0	18	28	11	9	0	7.50
Joe Shaute	L	34	0	2	.000	1	8	1	0	17	19	3	2	0	4.23
1 Syl Johnson	R	33	0	0	.000	0	2	0	0	7	9	0	0	0	2.57
1 Jim Lindsey	R	36	0	0	.000	0	4	0	0	4	4	2	2	0	4.50
Whitey Wistert	R	22	0	1	.000	0	2	1	0	8	5	5	1	0	1.13
Lee Grissom	L	26	0	1	.000	0	4	1	0	7	13	7	4	0	15.43
Sherman Edwards	R	24	0	0	.000	0	1	0	0	3	4	1	1	0	3.00
Junie Barnes	L	22	0	0	.000	0	2	0	0	.1	0	1	0	0	0.00

WORLD SERIES – ST. LOUIS (NL) 4 DETROIT (AL) 3

LINE SCORES

TEAM	1	2	3	4	5	6	7	8	9	10	11	12	R	H	E
Game 1 October 3 at Detroit															
STL (NL)	0	2	1	0	1	4	0	0	0				8	13	2
DET (AL)	0	0	1	0	0	1	0	1	0				3	8	5
Game 2 October 4 at Detroit															
STL	0	1	1	0	0	0	0	0	0	0	0	0	2	7	3
DET	0	0	0	1	0	0	0	0	1	0	0	1	3	7	0
Game 3 October 5 at St. Louis															
DET	0	0	0	0	0	0	0	0	1				1	8	2
STL	1	1	0	0	2	0	0	0	X				4	9	1
Game 4 October 6 at St. Louis															
DET	0	0	3	1	0	0	1	5	0				10	13	1
STL	0	1	1	2	0	0	0	0	0				4	10	5
Game 5 October 7 at St. Louis															
DET	0	1	0	0	0	2	0	0	0				3	7	0
STL	0	0	0	0	0	0	1	0	0				1	7	1
Game 6 October 8 at Detroit															
STL	1	0	0	0	2	0	1	0	0				4	10	2
DET	0	0	1	0	0	2	0	0	0				3	7	1
Game 7 October 9 at Detroit															
STL	0	0	7	0	0	2	2	0	0				11	17	1
DET	0	0	0	0	0	0	0	0	0				0	6	3

Game 1 pitchers: **D. Dean** — Crowder, Marberry (6), Hogsett (6)

Game 2 pitchers: Hallahan, B. Walker (9) — **Rowe**

Game 3 pitchers: Bridges, Hogsett (5) — **P. Dean**

Game 4 pitchers: **Auker** — Carleton, Vance (3), B. Walker (6), Haines (8), Mooney (9)

Game 5 pitchers: **Bridges** — D. Dean, Carleton (9)

Game 6 pitchers: **P. Dean** — Rowe

Game 7 pitchers: **D. Dean** — Auker, Rowe (3), Hogsett (3), Bridges (3), Marberry (8), Crowder (9)

COMPOSITE BATTING

NAME	POS	G	AB	R	H	2B	3B	HR	RBI	BA
St. Louis (NL) Totals		7	262	34	73	14	5	2	32	.279
Martin	3B	7	31	8	11	3	1	0	4	.355
Frisch	2B	7	31	2	6	1	0	0	4	.194
Collins	1B	7	30	4	11	1	0	0	3	.367
Rothrock	OF	7	30	3	7	3	1	0	6	.233
Medwick	OF	7	29	4	11	0	1	1	5	.379
DeLancey	C	7	29	3	5	3	0	1	4	.172
Durocher	SS	7	27	4	7	1	1	0	0	.259
Orsatti	OF	7	22	3	7	0	1	0	2	.318
D. Dean	P	4	12	3	3	2	0	0	1	.250
P. Dean	P	2	6	0	1	0	0	0	2	.167
Fullis	OF	3	5	0	2	0	0	0	0	.400
Hallahan	P	1	3	0	0	0	0	0	0	.000
S. Davis	PH	2	2	0	2	0	0	0	1	1.000
Crawford	PH	2	2	0	0	0	0	0	0	.000
B. Walker	P	2	2	0	0	0	0	0	0	.000
Carleton	P	2	1	0	0	0	0	0	0	.000
Haines	P	1	0	0	0	0	0	0	0	.000
Mooney	P	1	0	0	0	0	0	0	0	.000
Vance	P	1	0	0	0	0	0	0	0	.000
Whitehead	SS	1	0	0	0	0	0	0	0	.000
Detroit (AL) Totals		7	250	23	56	12	1	2	20	.224
Gehringer	2B	7	29	5	11	1	0	1	2	.379
Rogell	SS	7	29	3	8	1	0	0	4	.276
Goslin	OF	7	29	2	7	1	0	0	2	.241
Owen	3B	7	29	0	2	0	0	0	1	.069
Greenberg	1B	7	28	4	9	2	1	1	7	.321
Fox	OF	7	28	1	8	6	0	0	2	.286
Cochrane	C	7	28	2	6	1	0	0	1	.214
White	OF	7	23	6	3	0	0	0	0	.130
Bridges	P	3	7	0	1	0	0	0	0	.143
Rowe	P	3	7	0	0	0	0	0	0	.000
Auker	P	2	4	0	0	0	0	0	0	.000
G. Walker	PH	3	3	0	1	0	0	0	1	.333
Hogsett	P	3	3	0	0	0	0	0	0	.000
Doljack	OF	2	2	0	0	0	0	0	0	.000
Crowder	P	2	1	0	0	0	0	0	0	.000
Hayworth	C	1	0	0	0	0	0	0	0	.000
Marberry	P	2	0	0	0	0	0	0	0	.000

COMPOSITE PITCHING

NAME	G	IP	H	BB	SO	W	L	SV	ERA
St. Louis (NL) Totals	7	65.1	56	25	43	4	3	0	2.34
D. Dean	3	26	20	5	17	2	1	0	1.73
P. Dean	2	18	15	7	11	2	0	0	1.00
Hallahan	1	8.1	6	4	6	0	0	0	2.16
B. Walker	2	6.1	6	6	2	0	2	0	7.11
Carleton	2	3.2	5	2	2	0	0	0	7.36
Vance	1	1.1	2	1	3	0	0	0	0.00
Mooney	1	1	1	0	0	0	0	0	0.00
Haines	1	.2	1	0	2	0	0	0	0.00
Detroit (AL) Totals	7	65	73	11	31	3	4	0	3.74
Rowe	3	21.1	19	0	12	1	1	0	2.95
Bridges	3	17.1	21	1	12	1	1	0	3.63
Auker	2	11.1	16	5	2	1	1	0	5.56
Hogsett	3	7.1	6	3	3	0	0	0	1.23
Crowder	2	6	6	1	2	0	1	0	1.50
Marberry	2	1.2	5	1	0	0	0	0	21.60

1935 A Last Hurrah and a First Championship

Two of the biggest stories of the season took place in the cellars of both leagues. Connie Mack's Athletics had Jimmie Foxx, who batted .346 and hit 36 homers to tie for home run honors with Detroit's Hank Greenberg. There was also Doc Cramer, .332; Bob Johnson, .299; Pinky Higgins, .296; and rookie Wally Moses, who hit .325 before being shelved with a broken arm. The pitching wasn't much, although Johnny Marcum managed to win 17 games. All in all, Mack had the distinction of fielding one of the strongest tail-enders in league history.

By contrast, Boston of the National League was not as strong. In fact, their 115 losses was the greatest number of league defeats since the Cleveland Spiders' 134 setbacks in 1899. But Boston started the season with Babe Ruth, who was beginning his National League career with 708 home runs. Ruth, released from the Yankees because of age, had an auspicious start in his first at bat with a home run off Giant ace, Carl Hubbell. The four-bagger, however, did not prove an omen of things to come and in June, with an anemic .181 average, Ruth removed himself from the lineup. He had managed to collect six home runs for a career total of 714 a number that would defy challenge for decades to come.

If Ruth supplied the dramatics in the early going, the Cubs more than equalled the excitement in the last month of the season. After spending most of the year watching the Giants and Cardinals fighting it out, the Cubs put on a drive in September; their 21 straight wins proved enough to carry them to a National League pennant. Their final victims in the streak were the runner-up Cardinals. The Cubs entered St. Louis on September 25, with 18 consecutive victories and a five-game series. They needed two wins to clinch the flag and had to face the Dean brothers who, at about the same time the previous year, put the Cards over the top. In the first game, Lon Warneke beat Paul Dean, 1-0 and, in the first game of a double-header a day later, Bill Lee beat Dizzy Dean, 6-2. The Cubs iced the cake by winning the next game for their streak—the best since the Giants won 26 in a row in 1916.

MVP honors went to the Cubs' catcher Gabby Hartnett, who hit .344. Cincinnati, although finishing sixth, made baseball history by putting lights in the stadium and playing seven night games.

Before the American League season got underway, Tom Yawkey of the Red Sox shelled out $250,000 to Washington for Joe Cronin. When the season ended, the Red Sox had two pitchers who shared 45 wins and an outstanding manager-shortstop in Cronin, all of which was good for three more wins than 1934 and the same fourth-place finish. But with Yawkey's money, Lefty Grove's comeback of 20 wins, the E.R.A. crown of 2.70, and Wes Farrell's league high of 25 wins, hopes remained high for the 1936 season ahead.

Mickey Cochrane, Detroit's manager-catcher, was more concerned with 1935 and proving that his 1934 pennant victory was no fluke. His Tigers began the season dismally and fell to the cellar before being able to put a drive together behind MVP Greenberg, second baseman Charlie Gehringer, out fielders, Pete Fox and Goose Goslin, and a fine pitching staff including Schoolboy Rowe, Tommy Bridges, General Crowder, and Eldon Auker. Detroit's pennant gave Cochrane an enviable record. In seven years and with two different teams, he had been a member of five pennant winning teams.

The red-hot Cubs started the World Series with a 3-0 win behind Warneke and looked as if they would easily beat the Tigers—especially after Greenberg broke his wrist in the second game which Detroit won, 8-3. But the Tigers would not quit, going on to win four games to two for their first championship ever.

1935 AMERICAN LEAGUE

NAME	G by POS	B	AGE	G	AB	R	H	2B	3B	HR	RBI	BB	SO	SB	BA	SA
DETROIT 1st 93-58 .616		**MICKEY COCHRANE**														
TOTALS			29	152	5423	**919**	1573	301	83	106	**837**	**627**	456	70	**.290**	**.435**
Hank Greenberg	1B152	R	24	152	619	121	203	46	16	**36**	**170**	87	91	4	.328	.628
Charlie Gehringer	2B149	L	32	150	610	123	201	32	8	19	108	79	16	11	.330	.502
Billy Rogell	SS150	B	30	150	560	88	154	23	11	6	71	80	29	3	.275	.388
Marv Owen	3B131	R	29	134	483	52	127	24	5	2	71	43	37	1	.263	.346
Pete Fox	OF125	R	25	131	517	116	166	38	8	15	73	45	52	14	.321	.513
Jo-Jo White	OF98	L	26	114	412	82	99	13	12	2	32	68	42	19	.240	.345
Goose Goslin	OF144	L	34	147	590	88	172	34	6	9	109	56	31	5	.292	.415
Mickey Cochrane	C110	L	32	115	411	93	131	33	3	5	47	96	15	5	.319	.450
Gee Walker	OF85	R	27	98	362	52	109	22	6	7	53	15	21	6	.301	.453
Ray Hayworth	C48	R	31	51	175	22	54	14	2	0	22	9	14	0	.309	.411
Schoolboy Rowe	P42	R	25	45	109	19	34	3	2	3	28	12	12	0	.312	.459
Flea Clifton	3B21, 2B5, SS4	R	25	43	110	15	28	5	0	0	9	5	13	2	.255	.300
Chet Morgan	OF4	L	25	14	23	2	4	1	0	0	1	5	0	0	.174	.217
Heinie Schuble	3B2, 2B1	R	28	11	8	3	2	0	0	0	0	1	0	0	.250	.250
Hub Walker	OF7	L	28	9	25	4	4	3	0	0	1	3	4	0	.160	.280
Frank Reiber	C5	R	25	8	11	3	3	0	0	0	1	3	3	0	.273	.273
Hugh Shelley	OF5	R	24	7	8	1	2	0	0	0	1	2	1	0	.250	.250
NEW YORK 2nd 89-60 .597 3		**JOE McCARTHY**														
TOTALS			29	149	5214	818	1462	255	70	104	755	604	469	68	.280	.416
Lou Gehrig	1B149	L	32	149	535	**125**	176	26	10	30	119	**132**	38	8	.329	.583
Tony Lazzeri	2B118, SS9	R	31	130	477	72	130	18	6	13	83	63	75	11	.275	.417
Frankie Crosetti	SS87	R	24	87	305	49	78	17	6	8	50	41	27	3	.256	.430
Red Rolfe	3B136, SS17	L	26	149	639	108	192	33	9	5	67	57	39	7	.300	.404
George Selkirk	OF127	L	27	128	491	64	153	29	12	11	94	44	36	2	.312	.487
Ben Chapman	OF138	R	26	140	553	118	160	38	8	8	74	61	39	17	.289	.430
Jesse Hill	OF94	R	28	107	392	69	115	20	3	4	33	42	32	14	.293	.390
Bill Dickey	C118	L	28	120	448	54	125	26	6	14	81	35	11	1	.279	.458
Earle Combs	OF70	L	36	89	298	47	84	7	4	3	35	36	10	1	.282	.362
Jack Saltzgaver	2B25, 3B18, 1B6	L	30	61	149	17	39	6	0	3	18	23	12	0	.262	.362
Red Ruffing	P30	R	31	50	109	13	37	10	0	2	18	3	9	0	.339	.486
Myril Hoag	OF37	R	27	48	110	13	28	4	1	1	13	12	19	4	.255	.336
Art Jorgens	C33	R	30	36	84	6	20	2	0	0	8	12	10	0	.238	.262
2 Blondy Ryan	SS30	R	29	30	105	12	25	1	3	0	11	3	10	0	.238	.305
Joe Glenn	C16	R	26	17	43	7	10	4	0	0	6	4	1	0	.233	.326
Nolen Richardson	SS12	R	32	12	46	3	10	1	1	0	5	3	1	0	.217	.283
Don Heffner	2B10	R	24	10	36	3	11	3	1	0	8	4	1	0	.306	.444
Dixie Walker (SJ)	OF2	L	24	8	13	1	2	1	0	0	1	0	1	0	.154	.231
CLEVELAND 3rd 82-71 .536 12		**WALTER JOHNSON 46-48 .489**						**STEVE O'NEILL 36-23 .610**								
TOTALS			27	156	5534	776	1573	**324**	77	93	737	460	567	63	.284	.421
Hal Trosky	1B153	L	22	154	632	84	171	33	7	26	113	46	60	1	.271	.468
Boze Berger	2B120, SS3, 1B2, 3B1	R	25	124	461	62	119	27	5	5	43	34	97	7	.258	.371
Bill Knickerbocker	SS128	R	23	132	540	77	161	34	5	0	55	27	31	2	.298	.380
Odell Hale	3B149, 2B1	R	26	150	589	80	179	37	11	16	101	52	55	15	.304	.486
Bruce Campbell (IL)	OF75	L	25	80	308	56	100	26	3	7	54	31	33	2	.325	.497
Earl Averill	OF139	L	33	140	563	109	162	34	13	19	79	70	58	8	.288	.496
Joe Vosmik	OF150	R	25	152	620	93	**216**	**47**	**20**	10	110	59	30	2	.348	.537
Eddie Phillips	C69	R	34	70	220	18	60	16	1	1	41	15	21	0	.273	.368
Milt Galatzer	OF81	L	28	93	259	45	78	9	3	0	19	35	8	4	.301	.359
Roy Hughes	2B40, SS29, 3B1	R	24	82	266	40	78	15	3	0	14	18	17	13	.293	.372
AB Wright	OF47	R	29	67	160	17	38	11	1	2	18	10	17	2	.238	.356
R. Winegarner (AJ)	P25, OF4, 3B3, 1B1	R	25	65	84	11	26	4	1	3	17	9	12	1	.310	.488
Frankie Pytlak	C48	R	26	55	149	14	44	6	1	1	12	11	4	3	.295	.369
Bill Brenzel	C51	R	25	52	142	12	31	5	1	0	14	6	10	2	.218	.268
Willis Hudlin	P36	R	29	37	86	10	24	7	0	1	8	6	19	0	.279	.395
Kit Carson	OF4	L	22	16	22	1	5	2	0	0	1	2	6	0	.227	.318
1 Glenn Myatt	C10	L	37	10	36	1	3	1	0	0	2	4	3	0	.083	.111
Bob Garbark	C6	R	25	6	18	4	6	1	0	0	4	5	1	0	.333	.389
Willie Kamm	3B4	R	35	6	18	2	6	0	0	0	1	0	1	0	.333	.333
Greek George	C1	R	22	2	0	0	0	0	0	0	0	0	0	0	.000	.000

NAME	T	AGE	W	L	PCT	SV	G	GS	CG	IP	H	BB	SO	ShO	ERA
		28	**93**	53	**.616**	11	152	152	**87**	1364	1440	522	584	**16**	3.82
Tommy Bridges	R	28	21	10	.677	1	36	34	23	274	277	113	**163**	4	3.51
Schoolboy Rowe	R	25	19	13	.594	3	42	34	21	276	272	68	140	**6**	3.68
Eldon Auker	R	24	18	7	**.720**	0	36	25	13	195	213	61	63	2	3.83
General Crowder	R	36	16	10	.615	0	33	32	16	241	269	67	59	2	4.26
Chief Hogsett	L	31	6	6	.500	5	40	0	0	97	109	49	39	0	3.53
Joe Sullivan	L	24	6	6	.500	0	25	12	5	126	119	71	53	0	3.50
Vic Sorrell	R	34	4	3	.571	0	12	6	4	51	65	25	22	0	4.06
Roxie Lawson	R	29	3	1	.750	2	7	4	4	40	34	24	16	2	1.58
Clyde Hatter	L	26	0	0	.000	0	8	2	0	33	44	30	15	0	7.64
Firpo Marberry	R	36	0	1	.000	0	5	2	1	19	22	9	7	0	4.26
1 Carl Fischer	L	29	0	1	.000	0	3	1	0	12	16	5	7	0	6.00
		27	89	60	.597	13	149	149	76	1331	1276	516	**594**	12	**3.60**
Red Ruffing	R	31	16	11	.593	0	30	29	19	222	201	76	81	1	3.12
Johnny Broaca	R	25	15	7	.682	0	29	27	14	201	199	79	78	2	3.58
Johnny Allen	R	30	13	6	.684	0	23	23	12	167	149	58	113	2	3.61
Lefty Gomez	L	26	12	15	.444	1	34	30	15	246	223	86	138	2	3.18
Vito Tamulis	L	23	10	5	.667	1	30	19	9	161	178	55	57	3	4.08
Johnny Murphy	R	26	10	5	.667	5	40	8	4	117	110	55	28	0	4.08
Jumbo Brown	R	28	6	5	.545	0	20	8	3	87	94	37	41	0	3.62
Jimmie DeShong	R	25	4	1	.800	3	29	3	0	69	64	33	30	0	3.26
Pat Malone	R	32	3	5	.375	3	29	2	0	56	53	33	25	0	5.46
1 Russ VanAtta	L	29	0	0	.000	0	**5***	0	0	5	5	4	3	0	3.60
		28	82	71	.536	**21**	156	156	67	**1396**	1527	457	498	11	4.15
Mel Harder	R	25	22	11	.667	2	42	35	17	287	313	53	95	3	3.29
Willis Hudlin	R	29	15	11	.577	5	36	29	14	232	252	61	45	3	3.69
Oral Hildebrand	R	28	9	8	.529	5	34	20	8	171	171	63	49	0	3.95
Monte Pearson	R	25	8	13	.381	0	30	24	10	182	199	103	90	1	4.90
Lloyd Brown	L	30	8	7	.533	4	42	8	4	122	123	37	45	2	3.61
Thorton Lee	L	28	7	10	.412	1	32	20	8	181	179	71	81	1	4.03
2 Lefty Stewart	L	34	6	6	.500	2	24	10	2	91	122	17	24	1	5.44
Clint Brown	R	31	4	3	.571	2	23	5	1	49	61	14	20	0	5.14
Ralph Winegarner (AJ)	R	25	2	2	.500	0	25	4	2	67	89	29	41	0	5.78
Denny Galehouse	R	23	1	0	1.000	0	5	1	1	13	16	9	8	0	9.00
1 Belve Bean	R	30	0	0	.000	0	1	0	0	1	2	0	0	0	9.00

***VanAtta, also with St. Louis, League leader in G with 58**

BOSTON 4th 78-75 .516 16 — JOE CRONIN

	NAME	G by POS	B	AGE	G	AB	R	H	2B	3B	HR	RBI	BB	SO	SB	BA	SA
	TOTALS			28	154	5288	718	1458	281	63	69	660	609	470	**91**	.276	.392
	Babe Dahlgren	1B149	R	23	149	525	77	138	27	7	9	63	56	67	6	.263	.392
2	Oscar Melillo	2B105	R	35	106	399	45	104	13	2	1	39	38	22	3	.261	.311
	Joe Cronin	SS139	R	28	144	556	70	164	37	14	9	95	63	40	3	.295	.460
	Bill Werber	3B123	R	27	124	462	84	118	30	3	14	61	69	41	**29**	.255	.424
	Dusty Cooke	OF82	L	28	100	294	51	90	18	6	3	34	46	24	6	.306	.439
	Mel Almada	OF149, 1B3	L	22	151	607	85	176	27	9	3	59	55	34	20	.290	.379
	Roy Johnson	OF142	L	32	145	553	70	174	33	9	3	66	74	34	11	.315	.423
	Rick Ferrell	C131	R	29	133	458	54	138	34	4	3	61	65	15	5	.301	.413
	Carl Reynolds	OF64	R	32	78	244	33	66	13	4	6	35	24	20	4	.270	.430
	Bing Miller	OF29	R	40	78	138	18	42	8	1	3	26	10	8	0	.304	.442
2	Dib Williams	3B30, 2B29, SS15, 1B1	R	25	75	251	26	63	12	0	3	25	24	23	2	.251	.335
	Wes Ferrell	P41	R	27	75	150	25	52	5	1	7	32	21	16	0	.347	.533
	Max Bishop	2B34, 1B11, SS2	L	35	60	122	19	28	3	1	1	14	28	14	0	.230	.295
	Moe Berg	C37	R	33	38	98	13	28	5	0	2	12	5	3	0	.286	.398
1	Moose Solters	OF21	R	29	24	79	15	19	6	1	0	8	2	7	1	.241	.342
	Skinny Graham	OF2	L	25	8	10	1	3	0	0	0	1	1	3	1	.300	.300
	George Dickey	C4	B	19	5	11	1	0	0	0	0	1	1	3	0	.000	.000
	Doc Farrell	2B4	R	33	4	7	1	2	1	0	0	1	1	0	0	.286	.429
	John Kroner	3B2	R	26	2	4	1	1	0	0	0	0	1	1	0	.250	.250
	Lou Legett		R	34	2	0	1	0	0	0	0	0	0	0	0	.000	.000

	NAME	T	AGE	W	L	PCT	SV	G	GS	CG	IP	H	BB	SO	ShO	ERA
			29	78	75	.516	11	154	154	82	1376	1520	520	470	6	4.05
	Wes Ferrell	R	27	**25**	14	.641	0	41	**38**	**31**	**322**	**336**	108	110	3	3.52
	Lefty Grove	L	35	20	12	.625	1	35	30	23	273	269	65	121	1	**2.70**
	Johnny Welch	R	28	10	9	.526	2	31	19	10	143	155	53	48	1	4.47
	Fritz Ostermueller	L	27	7	8	.467	1	22	19	10	138	135	78	41	0	3.91
	Rube Walberg	L	35	5	9	.357	3	44	10	4	143	152	54	44	0	3.90
	Jack Wilson	R	23	3	4	.429	1	23	6	2	64	72	36	19	0	4.22
	Gordon Rhodes	R	27	2	10	.167	2	34	19	1	146	195	60	44	0	5.42
	George Hockette	L	27	2	3	.400	0	23	4	0	61	83	12	11	0	5.16
	Hank Johnson	R	29	2	1	.667	1	13	2	0	31	41	14	14	0	5.52
	Stew Bowers	R	20	2	1	.667	0	10	2	1	24	26	17	5	0	3.38
2	Joe Cascarella	R	28	0	3	.000	0	6	4	0	17	25	11	9	0	6.88
	George Pipgras	R	35	0	1	.000	0	5	1	0	5	9	5	2	0	14.40
	Hy Vandenberg	R	28	0	0	.000	0	3	0	0	5	15	4	2	0	21.60
	Walt Ripley	R	18	0	0	.000	0	2	0	0	4	7	3	0	0	9.00

CHICAGO 5th 74-78 .487 19.5 — JIMMY DYKES

	NAME	G by POS	B	AGE	G	AB	R	H	2B	3B	HR	RBI	BB	SO	SB	BA	SA
	TOTALS			**30**	153	5314	738	1460	262	42	74	690	580	405	46	.275	.382
	Zeke Bonura	1B138	R	26	138	550	107	162	34	4	21	92	57	28	4	.295	.485
	Jackie Hayes	2B85	R	28	89	329	45	88	14	0	4	45	29	15	3	.267	.347
	Luke Appling	SS153	R	28	153	525	94	161	28	6	1	71	122	40	12	.307	.389
	Jimmy Dykes	3B98, 1B16, 2B3	R	38	117	403	45	116	24	2	4	61	59	28	4	.288	.387
	Mule Haas (WJ)	OF84	L	31	92	327	44	95	22	1	2	40	37	17	4	.291	.382
	Al Simmons	OF126	R	33	128	525	68	140	22	7	16	79	33	43	4	.267	.427
	Rip Radcliff	OF142	L	29	146	623	95	178	28	8	10	68	53	21	4	.286	.404
	Luke Sewell	C112	R	34	118	421	52	120	19	3	2	67	32	18	3	.285	.359
	George Washington	OF79	L	28	108	339	40	96	22	3	8	47	10	18	1	.283	.437
2	Tony Piet	2B59, 3B17	R	28	77	292	47	87	17	5	3	27	33	27	2	.298	.421
	Jocko Conlan	OF37	L	35	65	140	20	40	7	1	0	15	14	6	3	.286	.350
	Marty Hopkins	3B49, 2B5	R	28	59	144	20	32	3	0	2	17	36	23	1	.222	.285
	Merv Shea	C43	R	34	46	122	8	28	2	0	0	13	30	9	0	.230	.246
	Fred Tauby	OF7	R	29	13	32	5	4	1	0	0	2	2	3	0	.125	.156
	Glenn Wright	2B7	R	34	9	25	1	3	1	0	0	1	0	6	0	.120	.160
2	Frank Grube	C9	R	30	9	19	1	7	2	0	0	6	3	2	0	.368	.474
	Mike Kreevich	3B6	R	27	6	23	3	10	2	0	0	2	1	0	1	.435	.522
1	Bud Hafey		R	22	2	0	1	0	0	0	0	0	0	0	0	.000	.000

	NAME	T	AGE	W	L	PCT	SV	G	GS	CG	IP	H	BB	SO	ShO	ERA
			29	74	78	.487	8	153	153	80	1361	1443	574	436	8	4.38
	Ted Lyons	R	34	15	8	.652	0	23	22	19	191	194	56	54	3	3.02
	John Whitehead	R	26	13	13	.500	0	28	27	18	222	209	101	72	1	3.73
	Vern Kennedy	R	28	11	11	.500	1	31	25	16	212	211	95	65	2	3.91
	Les Tietje	R	23	9	15	.375	0	30	21	9	170	184	81	64	1	4.29
	Sad Sam Jones	R	42	8	7	.533	0	21	19	7	140	162	51	38	0	4.05
2	Carl Fischer	L	29	5	5	.500	0	24	11	3	89	102	39	31	1	6.17
	Ray Phelps	R	31	4	8	.333	1	27	17	4	125	126	55	38	0	4.82
	Whit Wyatt	R	27	4	3	.571	5	30	1	0	52	65	25	22	0	6.75
	Joe Vance	R		2	2	.500	0	10	0	0	31	36	21	12	0	6.68
2	Jack Salveson	R	21	1	2	.333	1	20	2	2	67	79	23	22	0	4.84
	Monty Stratton	R	23	1	2	.333	0	5	5	2	38	40	9	8	0	4.03
1	George Earnshaw	R	35	1	2	.333	0	3	3	0	18	26	11	8	0	9.00
1	Talo Chelini	L	20	0	0	.000	0	2	0	0	5	7	4	1	0	12.60
	Lee Stine	R	21	0	0	.000	0	1	0	0	2	2	3	1	0	9.00

Joe Heving (DP) 34

WASHINGTON 6th 67-86 .438 27 — BUCKY HARRIS

	NAME	G by POS	B	AGE	G	AB	R	H	2B	3B	HR	RBI	BB	SO	SB	BA	SA
	TOTALS			29	154	**5592**	823	**1591**	255	**95**	32	763	595	406	54	.285	.381
	Joe Kuhel	1B151	L	29	151	633	99	165	25	9	2	74	78	44	5	.261	.338
	Buddy Myer	2B151	L	31	151	616	115	215	36	11	5	100	96	40	7	**.349**	.468
	Ossie Bluege	SS58, 3B25, 2B4	R	34	100	320	44	84	14	3	0	34	37	21	2	.263	.325
	Cecil Travis	3B114, OF16	L	21	138	534	85	170	27	8	0	61	41	28	4	.318	.397
	John Stone	OF114	L	29	125	454	78	143	27	18	1	78	39	29	4	.315	.460
	Jake Powell	OF136, 2B2	R	26	139	551	88	172	26	10	6	98	37	37	15	.312	.428
	Heinie Manush	OF111	L	33	119	479	68	131	26	9	4	56	35	17	2	.273	.390
	Cliff Bolton	C106	L	28	110	375	47	114	18	11	2	55	56	13	0	.304	.427
	Red Kress	SS53, 1B5, P3, OF2, 2B1	R	28	84	252	32	75	13	4	2	42	25	16	3	.298	.405
	Fred Schulte	OF55	R	34	75	224	33	60	6	4	2	23	26	22	0	.268	.357
	Dee Miles	OF45	L	26	60	216	28	57	5	2	0	29	7	13	6	.264	.306
	Sammy Holbrook	C47	R	24	52	135	20	35	2	2	2	25	30	16	0	.259	.348
	Ed Linke	P40	R	23	40	68	14	20	4	0	1	9	7	6	0	.294	.397
1	Lyn Lary	SS30	R	29	39	103	8	20	4	0	0	7	12	10	3	.194	.233
	Jack Redmond	C15	L	24	22	34	8	6	1	0	1	7	3	1	0	.176	.294
2	Alan Strange	SS16	R	25	20	54	3	10	2	1	0	5	4	1	0	.185	.259
	Fred Sington	OF4	R	25	20	22	1	4	0	0	0	3	5	1	0	.182	.182
	Bobby Estalella	3B15	R	24	15	51	7	16	2	0	2	10	17	7	1	.314	.471
	Chick Starr	C12	R	24	12	24	1	5	0	0	0	1	0	1	0	.208	.208
	Buddy Lewis	3B6	L	18	8	28	0	3	0	0	0	2	0	5	0	.107	.107
	John Mihalic	SS6	R	23	6	22	4	5	3	0	0	6	2	3	1	.227	.364
	Red Marion	OF3	R	21	4	11	1	2	1	0	1	1	0	2	0	.182	.545

	NAME	T	AGE	W	L	PCT	SV	G	GS	CG	IP	H	BB	SO	ShO	ERA
			29	67	86	.438	12	154	154	67	1379	1672	613	456	5	5.25
	Earl Whitehill	L	35	14	13	.519	0	34	34	19	279	318	104	102	1	4.29
2	Bobo Newsom (BK)	R	27	11	**12†**	.478	2	28	23	17	198	222	84	65	2	4.45
	Ed Linke	R	23	11	7	.611	3	40	22	10	178	211	80	51	0	5.01
	Bump Hadley	R	30	10	15	.400	0	35	32	13	230	268	102	77	0	4.93
	Leon Pettit	L	33	8	5	.615	3	41	7	1	109	129	58	45	0	4.95
	Jack Russell	R	29	4	9	.308	3	43	7	2	126	170	37	30	0	5.71
	Henry Coppola	R	22	3	4	.429	0	19	5	2	59	72	29	19	1	5.95
2	Belve Bean	R	30	2	0	1.000	0	10	2	0	31	43	19	6	0	7.26
	Jim Hayes	R	22	2	4	.333	0	7	4	1	28	38	23	9	0	8.36
	Bobby Burke	L	28	1	8	.111	0	15	10	2	66	90	27	16	0	7.50
	Monty Weaver (IL-SA)	R	29	1	1	.500	0	5	2	0	12	16	6	4	0	5.25
	Dick Lanahan	L	23	0	3	.000	0	3	3	0	21	27	17	10	0	5.57
	Phil Hensiek	R	33	0	3	.000	1	6	1	0	13	21	9	6	0	9.69
	Buck Rogers	L	22	0	1	.000	0	2	1	0	10	16	6	7	0	7.20
	Al McLean	R	22	0	0	.000	0	4	0	0	9	12	5	3	0	7.00
	Red Kress	R	28	0	0	.000	0	3	0	0	6	8	5	5	0	12.00
1	Lefty Stewart	L	34	0	1	.000	0	1	1	0	3	8	2	1	0	12.00
1	Tommy Thomas	R	35	0	0	.000	0	1	0	0	.1	3	0	0	0	54.00

†Newsom, also with St. Louis, league leader in L with 18

ST. LOUIS 7th 65-87 .428 28.5 — ROGERS HORNSBY

	NAME	G by POS	B	AGE	G	AB	R	H	2B	3B	HR	RBI	BB	SO	SB	BA	SA
	TOTALS			28	155	5365	718	1446	291	51	73	675	593	561	45	.270	.384
	Jack Burns	1B141	L	27	143	549	77	157	28	1	5	67	68	49	3	.286	.368
	Tom Carey	2B76	R	26	76	296	29	86	18	4	0	42	13	11	0	.291	.378
2	Lyn Lary	SS93	R	29	93	371	78	107	25	7	2	35	64	43	25	.288	.410
	Harlond Clift	3B127, 2B6	R	22	137	475	101	140	26	4	11	69	83	39	0	.295	.436
2	Ed Coleman	OF102	L	33	108	397	66	114	15	9	17	71	53	41	0	.287	.499
	Sammy West	OF135	L	30	138	527	93	158	37	4	10	70	75	46	1	.300	.442
2	Moose Solters	OF127	R	29	127	552	79	182	39	6	18	104	34	35	10	.330	.520
	Rollie Hemsley	C141	R	28	144	504	57	146	32	7	0	48	44	41	3	.290	.381
	Ray Pepper	OF57	R	29	92	261	20	66	15	3	4	37	20	32	0	.253	.379
	Beau Bell	OF37, 1B15, 3B3	R	27	76	220	20	55	8	2	3	17	16	16	1	.250	.345
	John Burnett	3B31, SS18, 2B12	L	30	70	206	17	46	10	1	0	26	19	16	1	.223	.282
	Ollie Bejma	2B47, SS8, 3B2	R	27	64	198	18	38	8	2	2	26	27	21	1	.192	.283
1	Alan Strange	SS49	R	25	49	147	8	34	6	1	0	17	17	7	0	.231	.286
	Tommy Heath	C37	R	21	47	93	10	22	3	0	0	9	20	13	0	.237	.269
1	Oscar Melillo	2B18	R	35	19	63	8	13	3	0	0	5	8	4	0	.206	.254
	Heinie Mueller	1B3, OF2	L	35	16	27	0	5	1	0	0	1	1	4	0	.185	.222
	Mike Mazzera	OF10	L	21	12	30	4	7	2	0	1	2	4	9	0	.233	.400
	Rogers Hornsby	1B3, 2B2, 3B1	R	39	10	24	1	5	3	0	0	3	3	6	0	.208	.333
	Debs Garms	OF2	L	27	10	15	1	4	0	0	0	0	2	2	0	.267	.267
	Hal Warnock	OF2	L	23	6	7	1	2	2	0	0	0	0	3	0	.286	.571
1	Frank Grube	C3	R	30	3	6	3	2	1	0	0	0	0	1	0	.333	.500

	NAME	T	AGE	W	L	PCT	SV	G	GS	CG	IP	H	BB	SO	ShO	ERA
			28	65	87	.428	15	155	155	42	1380	1667	640	435	4	5.26
	Ivy Andrews	R	28	13	7	.650	1	50	20	10	213	231	53	43	0	3.55
	Jack Knott	R	28	11	8	.579	**7**	48	19	7	188	219	78	45	2	4.60
2	Russ Van Atta	L	29	9	16	.360	3	**53#**	17	1	170	201	86	87	0	5.35
2	Sugar Cain	R	28	9	8	.529	0	31	24	8	168	197	**104***	68	0	5.25
	Fay Thomas	R	30	7	15	.318	1	49	19	4	147	165	89	67	0	4.78
	Jim Walkup	R	25	6	9	.400	0	55	20	4	181	226	104	44	1	6.27
	Dick Coffman	R	28	5	11	.313	2	41	18	5	144	206	46	34	0	6.13
	Earl Caldwell	R	30	3	2	.600	0	6	5	2	37	34	17	5	1	3.65
1	George Blaeholder	R	31	1	1	.500	0	6	2	0	18	25	6	0	0	7.00
	Bob Poser	R	25	1	1	.500	0	4	1	0	14	26	4	1	0	9.00
1	Bobo Newsom	R	27	0	**6†**	.000	1	7	6	1	43	54	13	22	0	4.81
	Bob Weiland	L	29	0	2	.000	0	14	4	0	32	39	31	11	0	9.56
2	Snipe Hansen	L	28	0	1	.000	0	10	0	0	27	44	9	8	0	8.67

***Cain, also with Philadelphia, league leader in BB with 123**

#Van Atta, also with New York, league leader in G with 58

†Newsom, also with Washington, league leader in L with 18

PHILADELPHIA 8th 58-91 .389 34 — CONNIE MACK

	NAME	G by POS	B	AGE	G	AB	R	H	2B	3B	HR	RBI	BB	SO	SB	BA	SA
	TOTALS			27	149	5269	710	1470	243	44	**112**	671	475	**602**	42	.279	.406
	Jimmie Foxx	1B121, C26, 3B2	R	27	147	535	118	185	33	7	**36**	115	114	**99**	6	.346	**.636**
	Rabbit Warstler	2B136, 3B2	R	31	138	496	62	124	20	7	3	59	56	53	8	.250	.337
	Eric McNair	SS121, 3B11, 1B2	R	26	137	526	55	142	22	2	4	57	35	33	3	.270	.342
	Pinky Higgins	3B131	R	26	133	524	69	155	32	4	23	94	42	62	6	.296	.504
	Charlie Moses (BA)	OF80	L	24	85	345	60	112	21	3	5	35	25	18	3	.325	.446
	Doc Cramer	OF149	L	29	149	**644**	96	214	37	4	3	70	37	34	6	.332	.416
	Bob Johnson	OF147	R	28	147	582	103	174	29	5	28	109	78	76	2	.299	.510
2	Paul Richards	C79	R	26	85	257	31	63	10	1	4	29	24	12	0	.245	.339
	Lou Finney	OF76, 1B18	L	24	109	410	45	112	11	6	0	31	18	18	7	.273	.329
	Johnny Marcum	P39	L	25	64	119	13	37	2	1	2	17	9	5	0	.311	.395
	Charlie Berry	C56	R	32	62	190	14	48	7	3	3	29	10	20	0	.253	.368
	Skeeter Newsome	SS24, 2B13, 3B4, OF1	R	24	59	145	18	30	7	1	1	10	5	9	2	.207	.290
	Alex Hooks	1B10	L	28	15	44	4	10	3	0	0	4	3	10	0	.227	.295
	Bernie Snyder	2B5, SS4	R	21	10	32	5	11	1	0	0	3	1	2	0	.344	.375
	Jack Peerson	SS4	R	24	10	19	3	6	1	0	0	1	1	1	0	.316	.368
1	Ed Coleman	OF1	L	33	10	13	0	1	0	0	0	0	0	3	0	.077	.077
	Bill Patton	C3	R	22	9	10	1	3	1	0	0	2	2	3	0	.300	.400
1	Dib Williams	2B2	R	25	4	10	0	1	0	0	0	0	0	1	0	.100	.100
	Charlie Moss	C1	R	24	4	3	1	1	0	0	0	1	1	0	0	.333	.333

Jack Owens 27 2-8, Bill Conroy 20 R 1-4

	NAME	T	AGE	W	L	PCT	SV	G	GS	CG	IP	H	BB	SO	ShO	ERA
			26	58	**91**	.389	10	149	149	58	1326	1486	**704**	469	7	5.12
	Johnny Marcum	R	26	17	12	.586	3	39	27	19	243	256	83	99	2	4.07
	Whitey Wilshere	L	22	9	9	.500	1	27	18	7	142	136	78	80	3	4.06
	Roy Mahaffey	R	32	8	4	.667	0	27	17	5	136	153	42	39	0	3.90
	Bill Dietrich	R	25	7	13	.350	3	43	15	8	185	203	101	59	1	5.40
2	George Blaeholder	R	31	6	10	.375	0	23	22	10	149	173	49	22	1	3.99
	Al Benton	R	24	3	4	.429	0	27	9	0	78	110	47	42	0	7.73
	Carl Doyle	R	22	2	7	.222	0	14	9	3	80	86	72	34	0	5.96
	George Caster	R	27	1	4	.200	1	25	1	0	63	86	37	24	0	6.29
	Dutch Lieber	R	26	1	1	.500	2	18	1	0	47	45	19	14	0	3.06
1	Joe Cascarella	R	28	1	6	.143	0	9	3	1	32	29	22	15	0	5.34
	Vallie Eaves	R	23	1	2	.333	0	3	3	1	14	12	15	6	0	5.14
	Bill Ferrazzi	R	28	1	2	.333	0	3	2	0	7	7	5	0	0	5.14
	Earl Huckleberry	R	25	1	0	1.000	0	1	1	0	7	8	4	2	0	9.00
	George Turbeville	R	20	0	3	.000	0	19	6	2	64	74	69	20	0	7.59
1	Sugar Cain	R	28	0	5	.000	0	6	5	0	26	39	**19***	5	0	6.58
	Woody Upchurch	L	24	0	2	.000	0	3	3	1	21	23	12	2	0	5.14
	Herman Fink	R	23	0	3	.000	0	5	3	0	16	18	10	2	0	9.00
	Al Veach	R	25	0	2	.000	0	2	2	1	10	20	9	3	0	11.70
	Wedo Martini	R	22	0	2	.000	0	3	2	0	6	8	11	1	0	18.00

***Cain, also with St. Louis, league leader in BB with 123**

CHICAGO 1st 100-54 .649 — CHARLIE GRIMM

NAME	G by POS	B	AGE	G	AB	R	H	2B	3B	HR	RBI	BB	SO	SB	BA	SA
TOTALS			27	154	5486	**847**	1581	**303**	62	88	**782**	**464**	471	66	**.288**	.414
Phil Cavarretta	1B145	L	18	146	589	85	162	28	12	8	82	39	61	4	.275	.404
Billy Herman	2B154	R	25	154	666	113	**227**	**57**	6	7	83	42	29	6	.341	.476
Billy Jurges	SS146	R	27	146	519	69	125	33	1	1	59	42	39	3	.241	.314
Stan Hack	3B111, 1B7	L	25	124	427	75	133	23	9	4	64	65	17	14	.311	.436
Chuck Klein	OF111	L	30	119	434	71	127	14	4	21	73	41	42	4	.293	.488
Frank Demaree	OF98	R	25	107	385	60	125	19	4	2	66	26	23	6	.325	.410
Augie Galan	OF154	B	23	154	646	**133**	203	41	11	12	79	87	53	**22**	.314	.467
Gabby Hartnett	C110	R	34	116	413	67	142	32	6	13	91	41	46	1	.344	.545
Fred Lindstrom	OF50, 3B33	R	29	90	342	49	94	22	4	3	62	10	13	1	.275	.389
Ken O'Dea	C63	L	22	76	202	30	52	13	2	6	38	26	18	0	.257	.431
Tuck Stainback	OF28	R	24	47	94	16	24	4	0	3	11	0	13	1	.255	.394
1 Kiki Cuyler	OF42	R	35	45	157	22	42	5	1	4	18	10	16	3	.268	.389
Woody English	3B16, SS12	R	28	34	84	11	17	2	0	2	8	20	4	1	.202	.298
Walter Stephenson	C6	R	24	16	26	2	10	1	1	0	2	1	5	0	.385	.500
Johnny Gill		L	30	3	3	2	1	1	0	0	1	0	1	0	.333	.667
Charlie Grimm	1B2	L	36	2	8	0	0	0	0	0	0	0	1	0	.000	.000

NAME	T	AGE	W	L	PCT	SV	G	GS	CG	IP	H	BB	SO	ShO	ERA
		27	**100**	54	**.649**	14	154	154	**81**	1394	1417	400	589	12	**3.26**
Bill Lee	R	25	20	6	**769**	1	39	32	18	252	241	84	100	3	2.96
Lon Warneke	R	26	20	13	.606	4	42	30	20	262	257	50	120	1	3.06
Larry French	L	27	17	10	.630	2	42	30	16	246	279	44	90	**4**	2.96
Charlie Root	R	36	15	8	.652	2	38	18	11	201	193	47	94	1	3.09
Roy Henshaw	L	23	13	5	.722	1	31	18	7	143	135	68	53	3	3.27
Tex Carleton	R	28	11	8	.579	1	31	22	8	171	169	60	84	0	3.89
Fabian Kowalik	R	27	2	2	.500	1	20	2	1	55	60	19	20	0	4.42
Clay Bryant	R	23	1	2	.667	2	9	1	0	23	34	7	13	0	5.09
Clyde Shoun	L	23	1	0	1.000	0	5	1	0	13	14	5	5	0	2.77
Hugh Casey	R	21	0	0	.000	0	13	0	0	26	29	14	10	0	3.81
Roy Joiner	L	28	0	0	.000	0	2	0	0	3	6	2	0	0	6.00

ST. LOUIS 2nd 96-58 .623 4 — FRANKIE FRISCH

NAME	G by POS	B	AGE	G	AB	R	H	2B	3B	HR	RBI	BB	SO	SB	BA	SA
TOTALS			25	154	5457	829	1548	286	59	86	762	404	521	71	.284	.405
Ripper Collins	1B150	B	31	150	578	109	181	36	10	23	122	65	45	0	.313	.529
Frankie Frisch	2B88, 3B5	B	36	103	354	52	104	16	2	1	55	35	16	2	.294	.359
Leo Durocher	SS142	B	29	143	513	62	136	23	5	8	78	29	46	4	.265	.376
Pepper Martin	3B114, OF18	R	31	135	539	121	161	41	6	9	54	33	58	20	.299	.447
Jack Rothrock	OF127	B	30	129	502	76	137	18	5	3	56	57	29	7	.273	.347
Terry Moore	OF117	R	23	119	456	63	131	34	3	6	53	15	40	13	.287	.414
Joe Medwick	OF154	R	23	154	634	132	224	46	13	23	126	30	59	4	.353	.576
Bill DeLancey	C83	L	23	103	301	37	84	14	5	6	41	42	34	0	.279	.419
Burgess Whitehead	2B80, 3B8, SS6	R	25	107	338	45	89	10	2	0	33	11	14	5	.263	.305
Spud Davis	C81, 1B5	R	30	102	315	28	100	24	2	1	60	33	30	0	.317	.416
Ernie Orsatti	OF60	L	32	90	221	28	53	9	3	1	24	18	25	10	.240	.321
Charlie Gelbert	3B37, SS21, 2B3	R	29	62	168	24	49	7	2	2	21	17	18	0	.292	.393
Dizzy Dean	P50	R	24	53	128	18	30	4	0	2	21	1	16	2	.234	.313
Charlie Wilson	3B8	B	30	16	31	1	10	0	0	0	1	2	2	0	.323	.323
Bob O'Farrell	C8	R	38	14	10	0	0	0	0	0	0	2	0	0	.000	.000
Lynn King	OF6	L	27	8	22	6	4	0	0	0	0	4	1	2	.182	.182
Lyle Judy	2B5	R	21	8	11	2	0	0	0	0	0	2	2	2	.000	.000
Tom Winsett	OF2	L	25	7	12	2	6	1	0	0	2	2	3	0	.500	.500
Sam Narron	C1	R	21	4	7	0	3	0	0	0	0	0	0	0	.429	.429
Gene Moore		L	25	3	3	0	0	0	0	0	0	0	1	0	.000	.000

NAME	T	AGE	W	L	PCT	SV	G	GS	CG	IP	H	BB	SO	ShO	ERA
		30	96	58	.623	18	154	154	73	1384	1447	382	**594**	10	3.54
Dizzy Dean	R	24	**28**	12	.700	5	50	**36**	**29**	**324**	**326**	82	**182**	3	3.11
Paul Dean	R	21	19	12	.613	5	46	33	19	270	261	55	143	2	3.37
Wild Bill Hallahan	L	32	15	8	.652	1	40	23	8	181	196	57	73	2	3.43
Bill Walker	L	31	13	8	.619	1	37	25	8	193	222	78	79	2	3.82
2 Phil Collins	R	33	7	6	.538	2	26	8	2	83	96	26	18	0	4.55
Jesse Haines	R	41	6	5	.545	2	30	12	3	115	110	28	24	0	3.60
Ed Heusser	R	26	5	5	.500	2	33	11	2	123	125	27	39	0	2.93
Ray Harrell	R	23	1	1	.500	0	11	1	0	30	39	11	13	0	6.60
Mike Ryba	R	32	1	1	.500	0	2	1	1	16	15	1	6	0	3.38
Bill McGee	R	25	1	0	1.000	0	1	1	1	9	3	1	2	0	1.00
Nubs Kleinke	R	24	0	0	.000	0	4	2	0	13	19	3	5	0	4.85
Jim Winford	R	25	0	0	.000	0	2	1	0	11	13	5	7	0	4.09
Bud Tinning	R	29	0	0	.000	0	4	0	0	8	9	5	2	0	5.63
Tony Kaufmann	R	34	0	0	.000	0	3	0	0	4	4	1	0	0	2.25
Al Eckert	L	29	0	0	.000	0	2	0	0	3	7	1	1	0	12.00
Mays Copeland	R	21	0	0	.000	0	1	0	0	.2	2	0	0	0	13.50
Dick Ward	R	26	0	0	.000	0	1	0	0	0	0	1	0	0	0.00

NEW YORK 3rd 91-62 .595 8.5 — BILL TERRY

NAME	G by POS	B	AGE	G	AB	R	H	2B	3B	HR	RBI	BB	SO	SB	BA	SA
TOTALS			29	156	**5623**	770	**1608**	248	56	**123**	703	392	479	32	.286	**.416**
Bill Terry	1B143	L	36	145	596	91	203	32	8	6	64	41	55	7	.341	.451
Mark Koenig	2B64, SS21, 3B15	B	32	107	396	40	112	12	0	3	37	13	18	0	.283	.336
Dick Bartell	SS137	R	27	137	539	60	141	28	4	14	53	37	52	5	.262	.406
Travis Jackson	3B128	R	31	128	511	74	154	20	12	9	80	29	64	3	.301	.440
Mel Ott	OF137, 3B15	L	26	152	593	113	191	33	6	31	114	82	58	7	.322	.555
Hank Leiber	OF154	R	24	154	613	110	203	37	4	22	107	48	29	0	.331	.512
Jo-Jo Moore	OF155	L	26	155	**681**	108	201	28	9	15	71	53	24	5	.295	.429
Gus Mancuso	C126	R	29	128	447	33	133	18	2	5	56	30	16	1	.298	.380
Hughie Critz	2B59	R	34	65	219	19	41	0	3	2	14	3	10	2	.187	.242
Harry Danning	C44	R	23	65	152	16	37	11	1	2	20	9	16	0	.243	.368
Phil Weintraub	1B19, OF7	L	27	64	112	18	27	3	3	1	6	17	13	0	.241	.348
Al Cuccinello	2B48, 3B2	R	20	54	165	27	41	7	1	4	20	1	20	0	.248	.376
Kiddo Davis	OF21	R	33	47	91	16	24	7	1	2	6	10	4	2	.264	.429
Hal Schumacher	P33	R	24	38	107	8	21	3	0	2	21	1	25	0	.196	.280
2 Glenn Myatt	C4	L	37	13	18	2	4	0	1	1	6	0	3	0	.222	.500
1 Paul Richards	C4	R	26	7	4	0	1	0	0	0	0	2	1	0	.250	.250
Joe Malay		L	29	1	1	0	1	0	0	0	0	0	0	0	1.000	1.000

NAME	T	AGE	W	L	PCT	SV	G	GS	CG	IP	H	BB	SO	ShO	ERA
		27	91	62	.595	11	156	156	76	**1404**	1433	411	524	10	3.78
Carl Hubbell	L	32	23	12	.657	0	42	35	24	303	314	49	150	1	3.27
Hal Schumacher	R	24	19	9	.679	0	33	33	19	262	235	70	79	3	2.89
Slick Castleman	R	21	15	6	.714	0	29	25	9	174	186	64	64	1	4.09
Roy Parmelee	R	28	14	10	.583	0	34	31	13	226	214	**97**	79	0	4.22
Al Smith	L	27	10	8	.556	5	40	10	4	124	125	32	44	1	3.41
F. Fitzsimmons (AJ)	R	33	4	8	.333	0	18	15	6	94	104	22	23	**4**	4.02
Frank Gabler	R	23	2	1	.667	0	26	1	0	60	79	20	24	0	5.70
Allyn Stout	R	30	1	4	.200	5	40	2	0	88	99	37	29	0	4.91
Harry Gumbert	R	25	1	2	.333	0	6	3	1	24	35	10	11	0	6.00
2 Euel Moore	R	27	1	0	1.000	0	6	0	0	8	9	4	3	0	5.63
Dolf Luque	R	44	1	0	1.000	0	2	0	0	4	1	1	2	0	0.00
Leon Chagnon	R	32	0	2	.000	1	14	1	0	38	32	5	16	0	3.55

PITTSBURGH 4th 86-67 .562 13.5 — PIE TRAYNOR

NAME	G by POS	B	AGE	G	AB	R	H	2B	3B	HR	RBI	BB	SO	SB	BA	SA
TOTALS			28	153	5415	743	1543	255	**90**	66	682	457	437	30	.285	.402
Gus Suhr	1B149, OF2	L	29	153	529	68	144	33	12	10	81	70	54	6	.272	.437
Pep Young	2B107, 3B6, OF6, SS4	R	27	128	494	60	131	25	10	7	82	21	59	2	.265	.399
Arky Vaughan	SS137	L	23	137	499	108	192	34	10	19	99	**97**	18	4	**.385**	**.607**
Tommy Thevenow	3B82, SS13, 2B8	R	31	110	408	38	97	9	9	0	47	12	23	1	.238	.304
Paul Waner	OF136	L	32	139	549	98	176	29	12	11	78	61	22	2	.321	.477
Lloyd Waner	OF121	L	29	122	537	83	166	22	14	0	46	22	10	1	.309	.402
Woody Jensen	OF140	L	27	143	627	97	203	28	7	8	62	15	14	9	.324	.429
Tom Padden	C94	R	26	97	302	35	82	9	1	1	30	48	26	1	.272	.318
Cookie Lavagetto	2B42, 3B15	R	22	78	231	27	67	9	4	0	19	18	15	1	.290	.364
Earl Grace	C69	L	28	77	224	19	59	8	1	3	29	32	17	1	.263	.348
2 Bud Hafey	OF47	R	22	58	184	29	42	11	2	6	16	16	48	0	.228	.408
Pie Traynor (JJ)	3B49, 1B1	R	35	57	204	24	57	10	3	1	36	10	17	2	.279	.373
Red Lucas	P20	L	33	47	66	6	21	6	0	0	10	7	11	0	.318	.409
1 Babe Herman	OF15, 1B3	L	32	26	81	8	19	8	1	0	7	3	10	0	.235	.358
Earl Browne	1B9	L	24	9	32	6	8	2	0	0	6	2	8	0	.250	.313
Bill Brubaker	3B5	R	24	6	11	1	0	0	0	0	0	2	5	0	.000	.000
Aubrey Epps	C1	R	23	1	4	1	3	0	1	0	3	0	0	0	.750	1.250
Steve Swetonic		R	31	1	0	1	0	0	0	0	0	0	0	0	.000	.000

NAME	T	AGE	W	L	PCT	SV	G	GS	CG	IP	H	BB	SO	ShO	ERA
		30	86	67	.562	11	153	153	76	1366	1428	312	549	**15**	3.42
Cy Blanton	L	26	18	13	.581	1	35	31	23	254	220	55	142	**4**	**2.59**
Bill Swift	R	27	15	8	.652	1	39	21	11	204	193	37	74	3	2.69
Jim Weaver	R	31	14	8	.636	0	33	22	11	176	177	58	87	**4**	3.43
Guy Bush	R	33	11	11	.500	2	41	25	8	204	237	40	42	1	4.32
Ralph Birkofer	L	26	9	7	.563	1	37	18	8	150	173	42	80	1	4.08
Red Lucas	R	33	8	6	.571	0	20	19	8	126	136	23	29	2	3.43
Waite Hoyt	R	35	7	11	.389	6	39	11	5	164	187	27	63	0	3.40
Mace Brown	R	26	4	1	.800	0	18	5	2	73	84	22	28	0	3.58
1 Jack Salveson	R	21	0	1	.000	0	5	0	0	7	11	5	2	0	9.00
Claude Passeau	R	26	0	1	.000	0	1	1	0	3	7	2	1	0	12.00
Hal Smith	R	33	0	0	.000	0	1	0	0	3	2	1	0	0	3.00
Wayne Osborne	R	22	0	0	.000	0	2	0	0	1	1	0	1	0	9.00

BROOKLYN 5th 70-83 .458 29.5 — CASEY STENGEL

NAME	G by POS	B	AGE	G	AB	R	H	2B	3B	HR	RBI	BB	SO	SB	BA	SA
TOTALS			28	154	5410	711	1496	235	62	59	666	430	520	60	.277	.376
Sam Leslie	1B138	L	29	142	520	72	160	30	7	5	93	55	19	4	.308	.421
Tony Cuccinello	2B64, 3B36	R	27	102	360	49	105	20	3	8	53	40	35	3	.292	.431
Lonny Frey	SS127, 2B4	B	24	131	515	88	135	35	11	11	77	66	68	6	.262	.437
Joe Stripp	3B88, 1B15, OF1	R	32	109	373	44	114	13	5	3	43	22	15	2	.306	.391
Buzz Boyle	OF124	L	27	127	475	51	129	17	9	4	44	43	45	7	.272	.371
Frenchy Bordagaray	OF105	R	23	120	422	69	119	19	6	1	39	17	29	18	.282	.363
Danny Taylor	OF99	R	34	112	352	51	102	19	5	7	59	46	32	6	.290	.432
Al Lopez	C126	R	26	128	379	50	95	12	4	3	39	35	36	2	.251	.327
Jim Bucher	2B41, 3B39, OF37	L	24	123	473	72	143	22	1	7	58	10	33	4	.302	.397
Len Koenecke (DD)	OF91	L	31	100	325	43	92	13	2	4	27	43	45	0	.283	.372
Jimmy Jordan	2B46, SS28, 3B5	R	27	94	295	26	82	7	0	0	30	9	17	3	.278	.302
Bobby Reis	OF21, P14, 2B4, 1B1, 3B1	R	26	52	85	10	21	3	2	0	4	6	13	2	.247	.329
Babe Phelps	C34	L	27	47	121	17	44	7	2	5	22	9	10	0	.364	.579
Van Lingle Mungo	P37	R	24	44	90	9	26	3	0	0	19	1	10	0	.289	.322
Zack Taylor	C26	R	36	26	54	2	7	3	0	0	5	2	8	0	.130	.185
John McCarthy	1B19	L	25	22	48	9	12	1	1	0	4	2	9	1	.250	.313
Buster Mills	OF17	R	26	17	56	12	12	2	1	1	7	5	11	0	.214	.339
Johnny Cooney	OF10	R	34	10	29	3	9	0	1	0	1	3	2	0	.310	.379
Nick Tremark	OF4	L	22	10	13	1	3	1	0	0	3	1	1	0	.231	.308
Vince Sherlock	2B8	R	26	9	26	4	12	1	0	0	6	1	2	1	.462	.500
Frank Skaff	3B3	R	21	6	11	4	6	1	1	0	3	0	2	0	.545	.818
Raoul Dedeaux	SS2	R	20	2	4	0	1	0	0	0	1	0	0	0	.250	.250
Whitey Ock	C1	R	23	1	3	0	0	0	0	0	0	1	2	0	.000	.000
Curly Onis	C1	R	26	1	1	0	1	0	0	0	0	0	0	0	1.000	1.000

NAME	T	AGE	W	L	PCT	SV	G	GS	CG	IP	H	BB	SO	ShO	ERA
		31	70	83	.458	**20**	154	154	62	1358	1519	436	480	11	4.22
Van Lingle Mungo	R	24	16	10	.615	2	37	26	18	214	205	90	143	**4**	3.66
Watty Clark	L	33	13	8	.619	0	33	25	11	207	215	28	35	1	3.30
Ray Benge	R	33	9	9	.500	1	23	17	5	125	142	47	39	1	4.46
2 George Earnshaw	R	35	8	12	.400	0	25	22	6	166	175	53	72	2	4.12
Tom Zachary	L	39	7	12	.368	4	25	21	9	158	193	35	33	1	3.59
Johnny Babich	R	22	7	14	.333	0	37	24	7	143	191	52	55	2	6.67
Dazzy Vance	R	44	3	2	.600	2	20	0	0	51	55	16	28	0	4.41
Bobby Reis	R	26	3	2	.600	2	14	2	1	41	46	24	7	0	2.85
Dutch Leonard	R	26	2	9	.182	**8**	43	11	4	138	152	29	41	0	3.91
Les Munns	R	26	1	3	.250	1	21	5	0	58	74	33	13	0	5.59
Tom Baker	R	22	1	0	1.000	0	11	1	1	42	48	20	10	0	4.29
Harry Eisenstat	L	19	0	1	.000	0	2	0	0	5	9	2	2	0	12.60
Frank Lamanske	L	28	0	0	.000	0	2	0	0	4	5	1	1	0	6.75
Bob Logan	L	25	0	1	.000	0	2	0	0	3	2	1	1	0	3.00
Bob Barr	R	22	0	0	.000	0	2	0	0	2	5	2	0	0	4.25
Harvey Green	R	20	0	0	.000	0	2	0	0	1	2	3	0	0	9.00

CINCINNATI 6th 68-85 .444 31.5 — **CHUCK DRESSEN**

	NAME	G by POS	B	AGE	G	AB	R	H	2B	3B	HR	RBI	BB	SO	SB	BA	SA
	TOTALS			28	154	5296	646	1403	244	68	73	605	392	547	72	.265	.378
	Jim Bottomley	1B97	L	35	107	399	44	103	21	1	1	49	18	24	3	.258	.323
	Alex Kampouris	2B141, SS6	R	22	148	499	46	123	26	5	7	62	32	84	8	.246	.361
	Billy Myers	SS112	R	24	117	445	60	119	15	10	5	36	29	81	10	.267	.380
	Lew Riggs	3B135	L	25	142	532	73	148	26	8	5	46	43	32	8	.278	.385
1	Val Goodman	OF146	L	26	148	592	86	159	23	18	12	72	35	50	14	.269	.429
	Sammy Byrd	OF115	R	28	121	416	51	109	25	4	9	52	37	51	4	.262	.406
2	Babe Herman	OF76, 1B14	L	32	92	349	44	117	23	5	10	58	35	25	5	.335	.516
	Ernie Lombardi	C82	R	27	120	332	36	114	23	3	12	64	16	6	0	.343	.539
	Gilly Campbell	C66, 1B5, OF1	L	27	88	218	26	56	7	0	3	30	42	7	3	.257	.330
	Billy Sullivan	1B40, 3B15, 2B6	L	24	85	241	29	64	9	4	2	36	19	16	4	.266	.361
	Gordon Slade	Ss30, 2B19, OF8, 3B7	R	30	71	196	22	55	10	0	1	14	16	16	0	.281	.347
2	Kiki Cuyler	OF57	R	35	62	223	36	56	8	3	2	22	27	18	5	.251	.341
	Adam Comorosky	OF40	R	30	59	137	22	34	3	1	2	14	7	14	1	.248	.328
	Hank Erickson	C25	R	27	37	88	9	23	3	2	1	4	6	4	0	.261	.375
	Harlin Pool	OF18	L	27	28	68	8	12	6	2	0	11	2	2	0	.176	.324
	Chick Hafey(SJ)	OF15	R	32	15	59	10	20	6	1	1	9	4	5	1	.339	.525
	Calvin Chapman	SS12, 2B4	L	24	15	53	6	18	1	0	0	3	4	5	2	.340	.358
1	Tony Piet	OF1	R	28	6	5	2	1	1	0	0	2	0	0	0	.200	.400
	Les Scarsella	1B2	L	21	6	10	4	2	1	0	0	0	3	1	0	.200	.300
	Ted Petoskey	OF2	R	24	4	5	0	2	0	0	0	0	0	1	1	.400	.400
	Lee Gamble	OF2	L	25	2	4	2	2	1	0	0	2	1	0	1	.500	.750

	NAME	T	AGE	W	L	PCT	SV	G	GS	CG	IP	H	BB	SO	ShO	ERA
			28	68	85	.444	12	154	154	59	1356	1490	438	500	9	4.30
	Paul Derringer	R	28	22	13	.629	2	45	33	20	277	295	49	120	3	3.51
	Gene Schott	R	21	8	11	.421	0	33	19	9	159	153	64	49	1	3.91
	Al Hollingsworth	L	27	6	13	.316	0	38	22	8	173	165	76	89	0	3.90
	Benny Frey	R	29	6	10	.375	2	38	13	3	114	164	32	24	1	6.87
	Tony Freitas	L	27	5	10	.333	2	31	18	5	144	174	38	51	0	4.56
	Si Johnson	R	28	5	11	.313	0	30	20	4	130	155	59	40	1	6.23
	Don Brennan	R	31	5	5	.500	5	38	5	2	114	101	44	48	1	3.16
	Emmett Nelson	R	30	4	4	.600	1	19	7	3	80	70	23	14	1	4.35
	Leroy Herrmann	R	29	3	5	.375	0	29	8	2	108	124	31	30	0	3.58
	Whitey Hilcher	R	26	2	0	1.000	0	4	2	1	19	19	5	9	1	2.84
1	Danny MacFayden	R	30	1	2	.333	0	7	4	1	36	39	13	13	0	4.75
	Lee Grissom	L	27	1	1	.500	0	3	3	1	21	31	4	13	0	3.86

PHILADELPHIA 7th 64-89 .418 35.5 — **JIMMIE WILSON**

	NAME	G by POS	B	AGE	G	AB	R	H	2B	3B	HR	RBI	BB	SO	SB	BA	SA
	TOTALS			30	156	5442	685	1466	249	32	92	624	392	661	52	.269	.378
	Dolph Camilli	1B156	L	28	156	602	88	157	23	5	25	83	65	113	9	.261	.440
	Lou Chiozza	2B120, 3B2	L	25	124	472	71	134	26	6	3	47	33	44	5	.284	.383
	Mickey Haslin (IL)	SS87, 3B11, 2B9	R	24	110	407	53	108	17	3	3	52	19	25	5	.265	.344
	Johnny Vergez	3B148, SS2	R	28	148	546	56	136	27	4	9	63	46	67	8	.249	.363
	Johnny Moore	OF150	L	33	153	600	84	194	33	3	19	93	45	50	4	.323	.483
	Ethan Allen	OF156	R	31	156	645	90	198	46	1	8	63	43	54	5	.307	.419
	George Watkins	OF148	L	35	150	600	80	162	25	5	17	76	40	78	3	.270	.413
	Al Todd	C87	R	31	107	328	40	95	18	3	3	42	19	35	3	.290	.390
	Jimmie Wilson	C78, 2B1	R	34	93	290	38	81	20	0	1	37	19	19	4	.279	.359
	Chile Gomez	SS36, 2B32	R	26	67	222	24	51	3	0	0	16	17	34	2	.230	.243
	Bucky Walters	P24, OF5, 2B2, 3B1	R	26	49	96	14	24	2	1	0	6	9	12	0	.250	.292
1	Blondy Ryan	SS35, 2B1, 3B1	R	29	39	129	13	34	3	0	1	10	7	20	1	.264	.310
	Ed Boland	OF10	L	27	30	47	5	10	0	0	0	4	4	6	1	.213	.213
	Fred Lucas	OF10	R	32	20	34	1	9	0	0	0	2	3	6	0	.265	.265
	Joe Holden	C4	L	22	6	9	0	1	0	0	0	0	0	3	1	.111	.111
	Art Bramhall	SS1, 3B1	R	26	2	1	0	0	0	0	0	0	0	0	0	.000	.000
	Dino Chiozza	SS2	L	23	2	0	1	0	0	0	0	0	0	0	0	.000	.000
	Bubber Jonnard	C1	R	35	1	1	0	0	0	0	0	0	0	1	0	.000	.000

	NAME	T	AGE	W	L	PCT	SV	G	GS	CG	IP	H	BB	SO	ShO	ERA
			27	64	89	.418	15	156	156	53	1375	1652	505	475	8	4.76
	Curt Davis	R	31	16	14	.533	2	44	27	19	231	264	47	74	3	3.66
	Orville Jorgens	R	27	10	15	.400	2	53	24	6	188	216	96	57	0	4.84
	Syl Johnson	R	34	10	8	.556	6	37	18	8	175	182	31	89	1	3.55
	Bucky Walters	R	26	9	9	.500	0	24	22	8	151	168	68	40	2	4.17
	Joe Bowman	R	25	7	10	.412	1	33	17	6	148	157	56	58	1	4.26
	Pretzels Pezzullo	L	24	3	5	.375	1	41	7	2	84	115	45	24	0	6.43
	Ray Prim	L	28	3	4	.429	0	29	6	1	73	110	15	27	0	5.79
	Jim Bivin	R	25	2	9	.182	1	47	14	0	162	220	65	54	0	5.78
	Hal Kelleher	R	21	2	0	1.000	0	3	3	2	25	26	12	12	1	1.80
	Hugh Mulcahy	R	21	1	5	.167	1	18	5	0	53	62	25	11	0	4.75
1	Euel Moore	R	27	1	6	.143	1	15	8	1	40	63	20	15	0	7.88
1	Phil Collins	R	33	0	2	.000	0	3	3	0	15	24	9	4	0	11.40
	Frank Pearce	R	30	0	0	.000	0	5	0	0	13	22	6	7	0	8.31
2	Tommy Thomas	R	35	0	1	.000	0	4	1	0	12	15	5	3	0	5.25
1	Snipe Hansen	L	28	0	1	.000	0	2	1	0	4	8	5	0	0	13.50

BOSTON 8th 38-115 .248 61.5 — **BILL McKECHNIE**

	NAME	G by POS	B	AGE	G	AB	R	H	2B	3B	HR	RBI	BB	SO	SB	BA	SA
	TOTALS			29	153	5309	575	1396	233	33	75	544	353	436	20	.263	.362
	Buck Jordan	1B95, 3B8, OF2	L	28	130	470	62	131	24	5	5	35	19	17	3	.279	.383
	Les Mallon	2B73, 3B36, OF1	R	29	116	412	48	113	24	2	2	25	28	37	3	.274	.357
	Billy Urbanski	SS129	R	32	132	514	53	118	17	0	4	30	40	32	3	.230	.286
	Pinky Whitney	3B74, 2B49	R	30	126	458	41	125	23	4	4	60	24	36	2	.273	.367
	Randy Moore	OF78, 1B21	L	30	125	407	42	112	20	4	4	42	26	16	1	.275	.373
	Wally Berger	OF149	R	29	150	589	91	174	39	4	34	130	50	80	3	.295	.548
	Hal Lee	OF110	R	30	112	422	49	128	18	6	0	39	18	25	0	.303	.374
	Al Spohrer	C90	R	32	92	260	22	63	7	1	1	16	9	12	0	.242	.288
	Tommy Thompson	OF85	L	25	112	297	34	81	7	1	4	30	36	17	2	.273	.343
	Joe Coscarart	3B41, SS27, 2B15	R	25	86	284	30	67	11	2	1	29	16	28	2	.236	.299
	Joe Mowry	OF45	B	27	81	136	17	36	8	1	1	13	11	13	0	.265	.360
	Shanty Hogan	C56	R	29	59	163	9	49	8	0	2	25	21	8	0	.301	.387
	Ray Mueller	C40	R	23	42	97	10	22	5	0	3	11	3	11	0	.227	.371
	Elbie Fletcher	1B39	L	19	39	148	12	35	7	1	1	9	7	13	1	.236	.318
	Babe Ruth	OF26	L	40	28	72	13	13	0	0	6	12	20	24	0	.181	.431
	Rabbit Maranville	2B20	R	43	23	67	3	10	2	0	0	5	3	3	0	.149	.179
	Johnnie Tyler	OF11	L	28	13	47	7	16	2	1	2	11	4	3	0	.340	.553
	Ed Moriarty	2B8	R	22	8	34	4	11	2	1	1	1	0	6	0	.324	.529
	Bill Lewis	C1	R	30	6	4	1	0	0	0	0	0	1	1	0	.000	.000
	Art Doll	C3	R	23	3	10	0	1	0	0	0	0	0	1	0	.100	.100

	NAME	T	AGE	W	L	PCT	SV	G	GS	CG	IP	H	BB	SO	ShO	ERA
			33	38	115	.248	5	153	153	54	1330	1645	404	355	6	4.93
	Fred Frankhouse	R	31	11	15	.423	0	40	29	10	231	278	81	64	1	4.75
	Bob Smith	R	37	8	18	.308	5	46	20	8	203	232	61	58	2	3.95
	Ed Brandt	L	30	5	19	.208	0	29	25	12	175	224	66	61	0	4.99
2	Danny MacFayden	R	30	5	13	.278	0	28	20	7	152	200	34	46	1	5.09
	Ben Cantwell	R	33	4	25	.138	0	39	24	13	211	235	44	34	0	4.61
	Huck Betts	R	38	2	9	.182	0	44	19	2	160	213	40	40	1	5.46
	Larry Benton	R	37	2	3	.400	0	29	0	0	72	103	24	21	0	6.88
	Bob Brown	R	24	1	8	.111	0	15	10	2	65	79	36	17	1	6.37
	Flint Rhem	R	34	0	5	.000	0	10	6	0	40	61	11	10	0	5.40
	Al Blanche	R	25	0	0	.000	0	6	0	0	17	14	5	4	0	1.59
	Leo Mangum	R	39	0	0	.000	0	3	0	0	5	6	2	0	0	3.60

WORLD SERIES – DETROIT (AL) 4 CHICAGO (NL) 2

LINE SCORES

TEAM	1	2	3	4	5	6	7	8	9	10	11	12	R	H	E
Game 1 October 2 at Detroit															
CHI (NL)	2	0	0	0	0	0	0	0	0				3	7	0
DET (AL)	0	0	0	0	0	0	0	0	0				0	4	3
Warneke — Rowe															
Game 2 October 3 at Detroit															
CHI	0	0	0	0	1	0	2	0	0				3	6	1
DET	4	0	0	3	0	0	1	0	X				8	9	2
Root, Henshaw (1), Kowalik (4) — Bridges															
Game 3 October 4 at Chicago															
DET	0	0	0	0	1	0	0	4	0	0	1		6	12	2
CHI	0	2	0	0	1	0	0	0	2	0	0		5	10	3
Auker, Hogsett (7), Rowe (8) — Lee, Warneke (8), French (10)															
Game 4 October 5 at Chicago															
DET	0	0	1	0	0	1	0	0	0				2	7	0
CHI	0	1	0	0	0	0	0	0	0				1	5	2
Crowder — Carleton, Root (8)															
Game 5 October 6 at Chicago															
DET	0	0	0	0	0	0	0	0	1				1	7	1
CHI	0	0	2	0	0	0	1	0	X				3	8	0
Rowe — Warneke, Lee (7)															
Game 6 October 7 at Detroit															
CHI	0	0	1	0	2	0	0	0	0				3	12	0
DET	1	0	0	1	0	1	0	0	1				4	12	1
French — Bridges															

COMPOSITE BATTING

NAME	POS	G	AB	R	H	2B	3B	HR	RBI	BA
Detroit (AL)										
Totals		6	206	21	51	11	1	1	18	.248
Fox	OF	6	26	1	10	3	1	0	4	.385
Gehringer	2B	6	24	4	9	3	0	0	4	.375
Cochrane	C	6	24	3	7	1	0	0	1	.292
Rogell	SS	6	24	1	7	2	0	0	1	.292
Goslin	OF	6	22	2	6	1	0	0	3	.273
Owen	3B-1B	6	20	2	1	0	0	0	1	.050
White	OF	5	19	3	5	0	0	0	1	.263
Clifton	3B	4	16	1	0	0	0	0	0	.000
Rowe	P	3	8	0	2	1	0	0	0	.250
Bridges	P	2	8	1	1	0	0	0	1	.125
Greenberg	1B	2	6	1	1	0	0	1	2	.167
Walker	OF	3	4	1	1	0	0	0	0	.250
Crowder	P	1	3	1	1	0	0	0	0	.333
Auker	P	1	2	0	0	0	0	0	0	.000
Hogsett	P	1	0	0	0	0	0	0	0	.000
Chicago (NL)										
Totals		6	202	18	48	6	2	5	17	.238
Galan	OF	6	25	2	4	1	0	0	2	.160
Herman	2B	6	24	3	8	2	1	1	6	.333
Hartnett	C	6	24	1	7	0	0	1	2	.292
Demaree	OF	6	24	2	6	1	0	2	2	.250
Cavarretta	1B	6	24	1	3	0	0	0	0	.125
Hack	3B-SS	6	22	2	5	1	1	0	0	.227
Jurges	SS	6	16	3	4	0	0	0	1	.250
Lindstrom	OF-3B	4	15	0	3	1	0	0	0	.200
Klein	OF	5	12	2	4	0	0	1	2	.333
Warneke	P	3	5	0	1	0	0	0	0	.200
French	P	2	4	1	1	0	0	0	0	.250
Kowalik	P	1	2	1	1	0	0	0	0	.500
O'Dea	PH	1	1	0	1	0	0	0	1	1.000
Henshaw	P	1	1	0	0	0	0	0	0	.000
Lee	P	2	1	0	0	0	0	0	0	.000
Stephenson	PH	1	1	0	0	0	0	0	0	.000
Carleton	P	1	1	0	0	0	0	0	0	.000
Root	P	2	0	0	0	0	0	0	0	.000

COMPOSITE PITCHING

NAME	G	IP	H	BB	SO	W	L	SV	ERA
Detroit (AL)									
Totals	6	55	48	11	29	4	2	0	2.29
Rowe	3	21	19	1	14	1	2	0	2.57
Bridges	2	18	18	4	9	2	0	0	2.50
Crowder	1	9	5	3	5	1	0	0	1.00
Auker	1	6	6	2	1	0	0	0	3.00
Hogsett	1	1	0	1	0	0	0	0	0.00
Chicago (NL)									
Totals	6	54.2	51	25	27	2	4	1	2.96
Warneke	3	16.2	9	4	5	2	0	0	0.54
French	2	10.2	15	2	8	0	2	0	3.38
Lee	2	10.1	11	5	5	0	0	1	3.48
Carleton	1	7	6	7	4	0	1	0	1.29
Kowalik	1	4.1	3	1	1	0	0	0	2.10
Henshaw	1	3.2	2	5	2	0	0	0	7.36
Root	2	2	5	1	2	0	1	0	18.00

1936 Pains and Streaks and Tears

It was a memorable year, made up of a costly broken wrist, two 15-game winning streaks, one 16-game winning streak, two rookies of fantastic potential, $300,000 paid for the privilege of finishing sixth, and the Hall of Fame in Cooperstown, New York, which opened its doors to enshrine Ty Cobb, Babe Ruth, Honus Wagner, Christy Mathewson, and Walter Johnson.

Item No. 1 was Detroit. After winning two successive pennants, the Tigers finished a noble second, but a dismal 19½ games behind the New York Yankees. The Tigers' problems began early as their powerhouse first baseman, Hank Greenberg, broke his wrist after playing 12 games. Then in mid-season, manager-catcher Mickey Cochrane broke down and had to go to Wyoming to regain his health.

In winning their first pennant since 1932, the Yankees unveiled Joe DiMaggio, a 22-year-old from Martinez, California. Well primed in the Pacific Coast League before making his debut, he finished second on the club in batting to Bill Dickey and second in home runs to Lou Gehrig, who led the league with 49 and captured the MVP Award.

The other rookie news came out of Cleveland and was even more spectacular. Indian fans watched in disbelief as a 17-year-old kid from Van Meter, Iowa, struck out 15 Browns in his major league bow on August 23. Three weeks later, Bob Feller made believers of everyone as he tied an American League strikeout record by fanning 17 Athletics. In Chicago, Luke Appling helped the White Sox to third place behind his league-leading .388 average, thus becoming the first shortstop and the first White Sox player to win an American League batting title. In Boston, there were tears all over owner Tom Yawkey's bank book. After spending large sums in 1934 and 1935 to bolster the Red Sox, Yawkey shelled out $300,000 to Connie Mack and the A's to get Jimmie Foxx, Doc Cramer, Eric McNair, and John Marcum, only to finish a dismal sixth, 28½ games out.

The National League couldn't boast of the same rookie finds as the American League, but they did have several notable streaks and a three-team pennant struggle from the Giants, Cubs, and Cardinals. St. Louis broke on top and looked something like the Gashouse Gang of 1934, but when Paul Dean developed arm trouble and brother Dizzy discovered he could not keep up his winning pace of the last two years, the Cards found themselves a disappointing tie for second with the Cubs, five games off the Giants. Aside from the Dean brothers putting together only 29 wins, compared to 47 in 1935, St. Louis could not contend with last-place Boston, which took their season series, 13-9.

The Cubs had replaced St. Louis at the top after a great June which had included a 15-game winning streak and seemed to be out of reach until the Giants awakened in late July and also fashioned a 15-game winning streak. In going for their second straight pennant, the Cubs traded back Chuck Klein, their big disappointment of 1935, to the Phillies for Ethan Allen and Curt Davis. But the Giants, with MVP Carl Hubbell, who won his last 16 games of the season, proved too much—especially after the Giants took three out of four at the end of August and destroyed whatever morale Chicago had left.

The Giants' and Yankees' victory marked the first time since 1923 that two New York Clubs met in the Series. Hubbell continued his season form by beating the Yankees in the Series opener, 6-1, and allowing seven scattered hits and no fielding chances for his outfielders. The Yankees then recovered by blasting the Giants, 18-4, and going on to win the Series—the same as in 1923—four games to two.

1936 AMERICAN LEAGUE

NAME	G by POS	B	AGE	G	AB	R	H	2B	3B	HR	RBI	BB	SO	SB	BA	SA
NEW YORK 1st 102-51 .667	JOE McCARTHY															
TOTALS			28	155	5591	**1065**	1676	315	83	**182**	**995**	**700**	594	76	.300	**.483**
Lou Gehrig	1B155	L	33	155	579	**167**	205	37	7	**49**	152	**130**	46	3	.354	**.696**
Tony Lazzeri	2B148, SS2	R	32	150	537	82	154	29	6	14	109	97	65	8	.287	.441
Frankie Crosetti	SS151	R	25	151	632	137	182	35	7	15	78	90	83	18	.288	.437
Red Rolfe	3B133	L	27	135	568	116	181	39	**15**	10	70	68	38	3	.319	.493
George Silkirk	OF135	L	28	137	493	93	152	28	9	18	107	94	60	13	.308	.511
2 Jake Powell	OF84	R	27	87	324	62	99	13	3	7	48	33	30	16	.306	.429
Joe DiMaggio	OF138	R	21	138	637	132	206	44	**15**	29	125	24	39	4	.323	.576
Bill Dickey	C107	L	29	112	423	99	153	26	8	22	107	46	16	0	.362	.617
Roy Johnson	OF33	L	33	63	147	21	39	8	2	1	19	21	14	3	.265	.367
Red Ruffing	P33	R	32	53	127	14	37	5	0	5	22	11	12	0	.291	.449
Myril Hoag (YJ)	OF39	R	28	45	156	23	47	9	4	3	34	7	16	3	.301	.468
Joe Glenn	C44	R	27	44	129	21	35	7	0	1	20	20	10	1	.271	.349
1 Ben Chapman	OF36	R	27	36	139	19	37	14	3	1	21	15	20	1	.266	.432
Jack Saltzgaver	3B16, 2B6, 1B4	L	31	34	90	14	19	5	0	1	13	13	18	0	.211	.300
Monte Pearson	P33	R	26	33	91	12	23	4	0	1	20	8	13	0	.253	.330
Art Jorgens	C30	R	31	31	66	5	18	3	1	0	5	2	3	0	.273	.348
Don Heffner	3B8, 2B5, SS3	R	25	19	48	7	11	2	1	0	6	6	5	0	.229	.313
Bob Seeds	OF9, 3B3	R	29	13	42	12	11	1	0	4	10	5	3	3	.262	.571
1 Dixie Walker	OF5	L	25	6	20	3	7	0	2	1	5	1	3	1	.350	.700
DETROIT 2nd 83-71 .539 19.5	MICKEY COCHRANE															
TOTALS			31	154	5464	921	1638	326	55	94	847	640	462	76	.300	.431
2 Jack Burns	1B138	L	28	138	558	96	158	36	3	4	63	79	45	4	.283	.380
Charlie Gehringer	2B154	L	33	154	641	144	227	**60**	12	15	116	83	13	4	.354	.555
Billy Rogell	SS146, 3B1	B	31	146	585	85	160	27	5	6	68	73	41	14	.274	.368
Marv Owen	3B153, 1B2	R	30	154	583	72	172	20	4	9	105	53	41	9	.295	.389
Gee Walker	OF125	R	28	134	550	105	194	55	5	12	93	23	30	17	.353	.536
Al Simmons	OF138, 1B1	R	34	143	568	96	186	38	6	13	112	49	35	6	.327	.484
Goose Goslin	OF144	L	35	147	572	122	180	33	8	24	125	85	50	14	.315	.526
Ray Hayworth	C81	R	32	81	250	31	60	10	0	1	30	39	18	0	.240	.292
Pete Fox	OF55	R	26	73	220	46	67	12	1	4	26	34	23	1	.305	.423
Jo-Jo White	OF18	L	27	58	51	11	14	3	0	0	6	9	10	2	.275	.333
Mickey Cochrane (IL)	C42	L	33	44	126	24	34	8	0	2	17	46	15	1	.270	.381
Eldon Auker	P35	R	25	35	78	7	24	1	2	0	15	7	24	0	.308	.372
Glenn Myatt	C27	L	38	27	78	5	17	1	0	0	5	9	4	0	.218	.231
Frank Reiber	C17, OF1	R	26	20	55	7	15	2	0	1	5	5	7	0	.273	.364
Flea Clifton	SS6, 3B2, 2B1	R	26	13	26	5	5	1	0	0	1	4	3	0	.192	.231
Hank Greenberg (BW)	1B12	R	25	12	46	10	16	6	2	1	16	9	6	1	.348	.630
Salty Parker	SS7, 1B2	R	22	11	25	6	7	2	0	0	4	2	3	0	.280	.360
Birdie Tebbetts	C10	R	26	10	33	7	10	1	2	1	4	5	3	0	.303	.545
Gil English	3B1	R	26	1	1	0	0	0	0	0	0	0	1	0	.000	.000
CHICAGO 3rd 81-70 .536 20	JIMMY DYKES															
TOTALS			30	153	5466	920	1597	282	56	60	862	684	417	66	.292	.397
Zeke Bonura	1B146	R	27	148	587	120	194	39	7	12	138	94	29	4	.330	.482
Jackie Hayes	2B89, SS13, 3B2	R	29	108	417	53	130	34	3	5	84	35	25	4	.312	.444
Luke Appling	SS137	R	29	138	526	111	204	31	7	6	128	85	25	10	**.388**	.508
Jimmy Dykes	3B125	R	39	127	435	62	116	16	3	7	60	61	36	1	.267	.366
Mule Haas	OF96, 1B7	L	32	119	408	75	116	26	2	0	46	64	29	1	.284	.358
Mike Kreevich	OF133	R	28	137	550	99	169	32	11	5	69	61	46	10	.307	.433
Rip Radcliff	OF132	L	30	138	618	120	207	31	7	8	82	44	12	6	.335	.447
Luke Sewell	C126	R	35	128	451	59	113	20	5	5	73	54	16	11	.251	.350
Tony Piet	2B68, 3B32	R	29	109	352	69	96	15	2	7	42	66	48	15	.273	.386
Larry Rosenthal	OF80	L	24	85	317	71	89	15	8	3	46	59	37	2	.281	.407
Vern Kennedy	P35	L	29	36	113	12	32	8	0	0	11	1	13	0	.283	.354
Frank Grube	C32	R	31	33	93	6	15	2	1	0	11	9	15	1	.161	.204
2 Dixie Walker (SJ)	OF17	L	25	26	70	12	19	2	0	0	11	14	6	1	.271	.300
George Washington	OF12	L	29	20	49	6	8	2	0	1	5	1	4	0	.163	.265
Jo-Jo Morrissey (BY)	3B9, SS4, 2B1	R	32	17	38	3	7	1	0	0	6	2	3	0	.184	.211
Merv Shea	C14	R	35	14	24	3	3	0	0	0	2	6	5	0	.125	.125
George Stumpf	OF4	L	25	10	22	3	6	1	0	0	5	2	1	0	.273	.318
Les Rock	1B2	L	23	2	1	0	0	0	0	0	1	0	0	0	.000	.000

NAME	T	AGE	W	L	PCT	SV	G	GS	CG	IP	H	BB	SO	ShO	ERA
		30	**102**	51	**.667**	**21**	155	155	77	**1401**	1474	663	**624**	6	**4.17**
Red Ruffing	R	32	20	12	.625	0	33	33	25	271	274	90	102	3	3.85
Monte Pearson	R	26	19	7	**.731**	1	33	31	15	223	191	135	118	1	3.71
Bump Hadley	R	31	14	4	.778	1	31	17	8	174	194	89	74	1	4.34
Lefty Gomez	L	27	13	7	.650	0	31	30	10	189	184	122	105	0	4.38
Johnny Broaca	R	26	12	7	.632	3	37	27	12	206	235	66	84	1	4.24
Pat Malone	R	33	12	4	.750	**9**	35	9	5	135	144	60	72	0	3.80
Johnny Murphy (JJ)	R	27	9	3	.750	5	27	5	2	88	90	36	34	0	3.38
Jumbo Brown	R	29	1	4	.200	1	20	3	0	64	93	29	19	0	5.91
Ted Kleinhans	L	37	1	1	.500	1	19	0	0	29	36	23	10	0	5.90
Kemp Wicker	L	29	1	2	.333	0	7	0	0	20	31	11	5	0	7.65
Steve Sundra	R	26	0	0	.000	0	1	0	0	1	2	2	1	0	0.00
		28	83	71	.539	13	154	154	76	1360	1568	562	526	**13**	5.00
Tommy Bridges	R	29	**23**	11	.676	1	39	**38**	26	295	289	115	**175**	5	3.60
Schoolboy Rowe	R	26	19	10	.655	3	41	35	19	245	266	64	115	4	4.52
Eldon Auker	R	25	13	16	.448	0	35	31	14	215	263	83	66	2	4.90
Roxie Lawson	R	30	8	6	.571	3	41	8	3	128	139	71	34	0	5.48
Vic Sorrell	R	35	6	7	.462	3	30	14	5	131	153	64	37	1	5.29
General Crowder	R	37	4	3	.571	0	9	7	1	44	64	21	10	0	8.39
Jake Wade	L	24	4	5	.444	0	13	11	4	78	93	52	30	1	5.31
Chad Kimsey	R	29	2	3	.400	3	22	0	0	52	58	29	11	0	4.85
Red Phillips	R	27	2	4	.333	0	22	6	3	87	124	22	15	0	6.52
Joe Sullivan	L	25	2	5	.286	1	26	4	1	80	111	40	32	0	6.75
1 Chief Hogsett	L	32	0	1	.000	0	3	0	0	4	8	1	1	0	9.00
		29	81	70	.536	8	153	153	**80**	1365	1603	578	414	5	5.06
Vern Kennedy	R	29	21	9	.700	0	35	34	20	274	282	**147**	99	1	4.63
2 Sugar Cain	R	29	14	10	.583	0	30	26	14	195	228	75	42	1	4.75
John Whitehead	R	27	13	13	.500	1	34	32	15	231	254	98	70	1	4.64
Ted Lyons	R	35	10	13	.435	0	26	24	15	182	227	45	48	1	5.14
Clint Brown	R	32	6	2	.750	5	38	2	0	83	106	24	19	0	4.99
Monty Stratton	R	24	5	7	.417	0	16	14	3	95	117	46	37	0	5.21
Italo Chelini	L	21	4	3	.571	0	18	6	5	84	100	30	16	0	4.93
3 Bill Dietrich	R	26	4	4	.500	0	14	11	6	83	93	36	39	1	4.66
Ray Phelps	R	32	4	6	.400	0	15	4	2	69	91	42	17	0	6.00
Red Evans	R	29	0	3	.000	1	17	0	0	47	70	22	19	0	7.66
Bill Shores	R	32	0	0	.000	0	9	0	0	17	26	8	5	0	9.53
1 Les Tietje	R	24	0	0	.000	0	2	0	0	2	6	5	3	0	31.50
Whit Wyatt	R	28	0	0	.000	1	3	0	0	3	3	0	0	0	0.00

WASHINGTON 4th 82-71 .536 20 — BUCKY HARRIS

NAME	G by POS	B	AGE	G	AB	R	H	2B	3B	HR	RBI	BB	SO	SB	BA	SA
TOTALS			29	153	5433	889	1601	293	**84**	62	822	576	398	**103**	.295	.414
Joe Kuhel	1B149, 3B1	L	30	149	588	107	189	42	8	16	118	64	30	15	.321	.502
Ossie Bluege	2B52, SS23, 3B15	R	35	90	319	43	92	12	1	1	55	38	16	5	.288	.342
Cecil Travis	SS71, OF53, 2B4, 3B2	L	22	138	517	77	164	34	10	2	92	39	21	4	.317	.433
Buddy Lewis	3B139	L	19	143	601	100	175	21	13	6	67	47	46	6	.291	.399
Carl Reynolds	OF72	R	33	89	293	41	81	18	2	4	41	21	22	8	.276	.392
2 Ben Chapman	OF97	R	27	97	401	91	133	36	7	4	60	69	18	19	.332	.486
John Stone	OF114	L	30	123	437	95	149	22	11	15	90	60	26	8	.341	.545
Cliff Bolton	C83	L	29	86	289	41	84	18	4	2	51	25	12	1	.291	.401
Red Kress	SS64, 2B33, 1B5	R	29	109	391	51	111	20	6	8	51	39	25	6	.204	.427
Jesse Hill	OF60	R	29	85	233	50	71	19	5	0	34	29	23	11	.305	.429
Wally Millies	C72	R	29	74	215	26	67	10	2	0	25	11	8	1	.312	.377
1 Jake Powell	OF53	R	27	53	214	40	62	11	5	1	30	19	21	10	.290	.402
Buddy Myer(IL)	2B43	L	32	51	156	31	42	5	2	0	15	42	11	7	.269	.327
John Mihalic	2B25	R	24	25	88	15	21	2	1	0	8	14	14	2	.239	.284
Fred Sington	OF25	R	26	25	94	13	30	8	0	1	28	15	9	0	.319	.436
Dee Miles	OF10	L	27	25	59	8	14	1	2	0	7	1	5	0	.237	.322
Shanty Hogan	C19	R	30	19	65	8	21	4	0	1	7	11	2	0	.323	.431
Bobby Estalella		R	25	13	9	2	2	0	2	0	0	4	5	0	.222	.667
Alex Sabo	C4	R	26	4	8	1	3	0	0	0	1	0	2	0	.375	.375
Chick Starr	C1	R	25	1	0	0	0	0	0	0	0	0	0	0	.000	.000

NAME	T	AGE	W	L	PCT	SV	G	GS	CG	IP	H	BB	SO	ShO	ERA
		30	82	71	.536	14	153	153	78	1346	1484	588	462	8	4.58
Jimmie DeShong	R	26	18	10	.643	2	34	31	16	224	255	96	59	2	4.62
Bobo Newsom	R	28	17	15	.531	2	43	**38**	24	285	294	146	156	4	4.31
Pete Appleton	R	32	14	9	.609	3	38	20	12	202	199	77	77	1	3.52
Earl Whitehill	L	36	14	11	.560	0	28	28	14	212	252	89	63	0	4.88
2 Joe Cascarella	R	29	9	8	.529	1	22	16	7	139	147	54	34	1	4.08
Monty Weaver	R	30	6	4	.600	1	26	5	3	91	92	38	15	0	4.35
1 Jack Russell	R	30	3	2	.600	3	18	5	1	50	66	25	6	0	6.30
Ed Linke	R	24	1	6	.167	0	13	6	1	52	73	14	11	0	7.10
Joe Bokina	R	26	0	2	.000	0	5	1	0	8	15	6	5	0	9.00
Ken Chase	L	22	0	0	.000	0	1	0	0	2	2	4	1	0	13.50
Sid Cohen	L	28	0	2	.000	1	19	1	0	36	44	14	21	0	5.25
Henry Coppola	R	23	0	0	.000	1	6	0	0	14	17	12	2	0	4.50
2 Bill Dietrich	R	26	0	1	.000	0	5	0	0	8	13	6	4	0	10.13
2 Firpo Marberry	R	37	0	2	.000	0	5	1	0	14	11	3	4	0	3.86
Bill Phebus	R	26	0	0	.000	0	2	1	0	7	4	4	4	0	2.57

CLEVELAND 5th 80-74 .519 22.5 — STEVE O'NEILL

NAME	G by POS	B	AGE	G	AB	R	H	2B	3B	HR	RBI	BB	SO	SB	BA	SA
TOTALS			26	157	**5646**	921	**1715**	**357**	82	123	852	514	470	66	**.304**	.461
Hal Trosky	1B151, 2B1	L	23	151	629	124	216	45	9	42	**162**	36	58	6	.343	.644
Roy Hughes	2B152	R	25	152	638	112	188	35	9	0	63	57	40	20	.295	.378
Bill Knickerbocker	SS155	L	24	155	618	81	182	35	3	8	73	56	30	5	.294	.400
Odell Hale	3B148, 2B3	R	27	153	620	126	196	50	13	14	87	64	43	8	.316	.506
Roy Weatherly	OF84	L	21	84	349	64	117	28	6	8	53	16	29	3	.335	.519
Earl Averill	OF150	L	34	152	614	136	**232**	39	**15**	28	126	65	35	3	.378	.627
Joe Vosmik	OF136	R	26	138	506	76	145	29	7	7	94	79	21	5	.287	.413
Billy Sullivan	C72, 3B5, 1B3, OF1	L	25	93	319	39	112	32	6	2	48	16	9	5	.351	.508
Bruce Campbell (IL)	OF47	L	26	76	172	35	64	15	2	6	30	19	17	2	.372	.587
Frankie Pytlak (BJ)	C58	R	27	75	224	35	72	15	4	0	31	24	11	5	.321	.424
Milt Galatzer	OF42, 1B1, P1	L	29	49	97	12	23	4	1	0	6	13	8	1	.237	.299
Jim Gleeson	OF33	B	24	41	139	26	36	9	2	4	12	18	17	2	.259	.439
Boze Berger	1B8, SS8, 3B7, SS2	R	26	28	52	1	9	2	0	0	3	1	14	0	.173	.212
George Uhle	P7	R	37	24	21	1	8	1	0	1	4	2	0	0	.381	.571
Greek George	C22	R	23	23	77	3	15	3	0	0	5	9	16	0	.195	.234
Joe Becker (BG)	C15	R	28	22	50	5	9	3	1	1	11	5	4	0	.180	.340
Jeff Heath	OF12	L	21	12	41	6	14	3	3	1	8	3	4	1	.341	.634

NAME	T	AGE	W	L	PCT	SV	G	GS	CG	IP	H	BB	SO	ShO	ERA
		29	80	74	.519	12	157	157	74	1389	1604	607	619	5	4.83
Johnny Allen	R	31	20	10	.667	1	36	31	19	243	234	97	165	4	3.44
Mel Harder	R	26	15	15	.500	1	36	30	13	225	294	71	84	0	5.16
Orel Hildebrand	R	29	10	11	.476	4	36	21	9	175	197	83	65	0	4.89
George Blaeholder	R	32	8	4	.667	0	35	16	6	134	158	47	30	0	5.10
Denny Galehouse	R	24	8	7	.533	1	36	15	5	148	161	68	71	0	4.86
Lloyd Brown (IL)	L	31	8	10	.444	1	24	16	12	140	166	45	34	1	4.18
Bob Feller	R	17	5	3	.625	1	14	8	5	62	52	47	76	0	3.34
Thornton Lee	L	29	3	5	.375	3	43	8	2	127	138	67	49	0	4.89
Willis Hudlin	R	30	1	5	.167	0	27	7	1	64	112	31	20	0	9.00
Al Milnar	L	22	1	2	.333	0	4	3	1	22	26	18	9	0	7.36
Bill Zuber	R	23	1	1	.500	0	2	2	1	14	14	15	5	0	6.43
Milt Galatzer	L	29	0	0	.000	0	1	0	0	6	7	5	3	0	4.50
Paul Kardow	R	20	0	0	.000	0	2	0	0	2	1	2	0	0	4.50
George Uhle	R	37	0	1	.000	0	7	0	0	13	26	5	5	0	8.53
Ralph Winegarner	R	26	0	0	.000	0	9	0	0	15	18	6	3	0	4.80

BOSTON 6th 74-80 .481 28.5 — JOE CRONIN

NAME	G by POS	B	AGE	G	AB	R	H	2B	3B	HR	RBI	BB	SO	SB	BA	SA
TOTALS			29	155	5383	775	1485	288	62	86	718	584	465	54	.276	.400
Jimmie Foxx	1B139, OF16, 3B1	R	28	155	585	130	198	32	8	41	143	105	**119**	13	.338	.631
Oscar Melillo	2B93	R	36	98	327	39	74	12	4	0	32	28	16	0	.226	.287
Eric McNair	SS84, 2B35, 3B11	R	27	128	494	68	141	36	2	4	74	27	34	3	.285	.391
Bill Werber	3B101, OF45, 2B1	R	28	145	535	89	147	29	6	10	67	89	37	23	.275	.407
Mel Almada	OF81	L	23	96	320	40	81	16	4	1	21	24	15	2	.253	.338
Doc Cramer	OF154	L	30	154	643	99	188	31	7	0	41	49	20	4	.292	.362
Dusty Cooke	OF91	L	29	111	341	58	93	20	3	6	47	72	48	4	.273	.402
Rick Ferrell	C121	R	30	121	410	59	128	27	5	8	55	65	17	0	.312	.461
John Kroner	2B38, 3B28, SS18, OF1	R	27	84	298	40	87	17	8	4	62	26	24	2	.292	.443
Heinie Manush (BG)	OF72	L	34	82	313	43	91	15	5	0	45	17	11	1	.291	.371
Joe Cronin (BG)	SS60, 3B21	R	29	81	295	36	83	22	4	2	43	32	21	1	.281	.403
Wes Ferrell	P39	R	28	61	135	20	36	6	1	5	24	14	10	0	.267	.437
Moe Berg	C39	R	34	39	125	9	30	4	1	0	19	2	6	0	.240	.288
Bing Miller	OF13	R	41	30	47	9	14	2	1	1	6	5	5	0	.298	.447
Babe Dahlgren	1B16	R	24	16	57	6	16	3	1	1	7	7	1	2	.281	.421
Fabian Gaffke	OF15	R	22	15	55	5	7	2	0	1	3	4	5	0	.127	.218
George Dickey	C10	B	20	10	23	0	1	1	0	0	0	2	3	0	.043	.087

NAME	T	AGE	W	L	PCT	SV	G	GS	CG	IP	H	BB	SO	ShO	ERA
		29	74	80	.481	9	155	155	78	1373	1501	552	584	11	4.39
Wes Ferrell	R	28	20	15	.571	0	39	**38**	**28**	**301**	**330**	119	106	3	4.19
Lefty Grove	L	36	17	12	.586	2	35	30	22	253	237	65	130	**6**	**2.81**
Fritz Ostermueller	L	28	10	16	.385	2	43	23	7	181	210	84	90	1	4.87
Johnny Marcum	R	26	8	13	.381	1	31	23	9	174	194	52	57	1	4.81
Jack Wilson	R	24	6	8	.429	3	43	9	2	136	152	86	74	0	4.43
Jim Henry	R	26	5	1	.833	0	21	8	2	76	75	40	36	0	4.62
Rube Walberg	L	36	5	4	.556	0	24	9	5	100	98	36	49	0	4.41
1 Johnny Welch	R	29	2	1	.667	0	9	3	1	33	43	8	9	0	5.45
Ted Olson	R	23	1	1	.500	0	5	3	1	18	24	8	5	0	7.50
Stew Bowers	R	21	0	0	.000	0	5	0	0	6	10	2	0	0	9.00
Joe Cascarella	R	29	0	2	.000	0	10	1	0	21	27	9	7	0	6.86
Emerson Dickman	R	21	0	0	.000	0	1	0	0	1	2	1	2	0	9.00
2 Mike Meola	R	30	0	2	.000	1	6	3	1	21	29	10	8	0	5.57
Jennings Poindexter	L	25	0	2	.000	0	3	3	0	11	13	16	2	0	6.54
2 Jack Russell	R	30	0	3	.000	0	23	2	0	40	57	16	9	0	5.63

ST. LOUIS 7th 57-95 .375 44.5 — ROGERS HORNSBY

NAME	G by POS	B	AGE	G	AB	R	H	2B	3B	HR	RBI	BB	SO	SB	BA	SA
TOTALS			29	155	5391	804	1502	299	66	79	761	625	**627**	62	.279	.403
Jim Bottomley	1B140	L	36	140	544	72	162	39	11	12	95	44	55	0	.298	.476
Tom Carey	2B128, SS1	R	27	134	488	58	133	27	6	1	57	27	25	2	.273	.359
Lyn Lary	SS155	R	30	155	620	112	179	30	6	2	52	117	54	**37**	.289	.366
Harlond Clift	3B152	R	23	152	576	145	174	40	11	20	73	115	68	12	.302	.514
Beau Bell	OF142, 1B17	R	28	155	616	100	212	40	12	11	123	60	55	4	.344	.502
Sammy West	OF148	L	31	152	533	78	148	26	4	7	70	94	70	2	.278	.381
Moose Solters	OF147	R	30	152	628	100	183	45	7	17	134	41	76	3	.291	.467
Rollie Hemsley	C114	R	29	116	377	43	99	24	2	2	39	46	30	2	.263	.353
Ed Coleman	OF18	L	34	92	137	13	40	5	4	2	34	15	17	0	.292	.431
Ray Pepper	OF18	R	30	75	124	13	35	5	0	2	23	5	23	0	.282	.371
Tony Giuliani	C66	R	23	71	198	17	43	3	0	0	13	11	13	0	.217	.232
Ollie Bejma	2B32, 3B7, SS1	R	28	67	139	19	36	2	3	2	18	27	21	0	.259	.360
1 Jack Burns	1B2	L	28	9	14	2	3	1	0	0	1	3	1	0	.214	.286
Rogers Hornsby	1B1	R	40	2	5	1	2	0	0	0	2	1	0	0	.400	.400

NAME	T	AGE	W	L	PCT	SV	G	GS	CG	IP	H	BB	SO	ShO	ERA
		31	57	95	.375	13	154	154	54	1348	**1776**	609	399	3	6.24
2 Chief Hogsett	L	32	13	15	.464	1	39	29	10	215	278	90	67	0	5.53
Tommy Thomas	R	36	11	9	.550	0	36	21	8	180	219	72	40	1	5.25
Jack Knott	R	29	9	17	.346	6	47	23	9	193	272	93	60	0	7.27
Ivy Andrews	R	29	7	12	.368	1	36	25	11	191	221	50	33	0	4.85
Earl Caldwell	R	31	7	16	.304	2	41	25	10	189	252	83	59	2	6.00
Russ VanAtta	L	30	4	7	.364	2	**52**	9	2	123	164	68	59	0	6.59
2 Les Tietje	R	24	3	5	.375	0	14	7	2	50	65	30	16	0	6.66
Roy Mahaffey	R	33	2	6	.250	1	21	9	1	60	82	40	13	0	8.10
1 Sugar Cain	R	29	1	1	.500	0	4	3	1	16	20	9	8	0	6.75
Sig Jakucki	R	26	0	3	.000	0	7	2	0	21	32	12	9	0	8.57
Harry Kimberlin	R	27	0	0	.000	0	13	0	0	20	24	16	4	0	5.40
Glenn Liebhardt	R	25	0	0	.000	0	24	0	0	55	98	27	20	0	8.84
1 Mike Meola	R	30	0	1	.000	0	9	0	0	19	29	13	6	0	9.47
Jim Walkup	R	26	0	3	.000	0	5	2	0	16	20	6	5	0	7.88

PHILADELPHIA 8th 53-100 .346 49 — CONNIE MACK

NAME	G by POS	B	AGE	G	AB	R	H	2B	3B	HR	RBI	BB	SO	SB	BA	SA
TOTALS			26	154	5373	714	1443	240	60	72	663	524	590	59	.269	.376
Lou Finney	1B78, OF73	L	25	151	**653**	100	197	26	10	1	41	47	22	7	.302	.377
1 Rabbit Warstler	2B66	R	32	66	236	27	59	8	6	1	24	36	16	0	.250	.347
Skeeter Newsome	SS123, 2B2, 3B1, OF1	R	25	127	471	41	106	15	2	0	46	25	27	13	.225	.265
Pinky Higgins	3B145	R	27	146	550	89	159	32	2	12	80	67	61	7	.289	.420
George Puccinelli	OF117	R	29	135	457	83	127	30	3	11	78	65	70	2	.278	.429
Wally Moses	OF144	L	25	146	585	98	202	35	11	7	66	62	32	12	.345	.479
Bob Johnson	OF131, 2B22, 1B1	R	29	153	566	91	165	29	14	25	121	88	71	6	.292	.525
Frankie Hayes	C143	R	21	144	505	59	137	25	2	10	67	46	58	3	.271	.388
Chubby Dean	1B77	L	20	111	342	41	98	21	3	1	48	24	24	3	.287	.374
Al Niemiec	2B52, SS5	R	25	69	203	22	40	3	2	1	20	26	16	2	.197	.246
Rusty Peters	SS25, 3B10, OF2, 2B1	R	21	45	119	12	26	3	2	3	16	4	28	1	.218	.353
Charlie Moss	C19	R	25	33	44	2	11	1	1	0	10	6	5	1	.250	.318
Emil Mailho	OF1	L	26	21	18	5	1	0	0	0	0	5	3	0	.056	.056
Charlie Berry	C12	R	33	13	17	0	1	1	0	0	1	6	2	0	.059	.118
Bill Nicholson	OF1	L	21	11	12	2	0	0	0	0	0	0	5	0	.000	.000
Dick Culler	2B7, SS2	R	21	9	38	3	9	0	0	0	1	1	3	0	.237	.237
Hugh Luby	2B9	R	23	9	38	3	7	1	0	0	3	0	7	2	.184	.211
Jack Peerson	SS7, 2B1	R	25	8	34	7	11	1	1	0	5	0	3	0	.324	.412
Jim Oglesby	1B3	L	30	3	11	0	2	0	0	0	2	2	0	0	.182	.182
Bill Conroy	C1	R	21	1	2	0	1	0	0	0	0	0	1	0	.500	.500

NAME	T	AGE	W	L	PCT	SV	G	GS	CG	IP	H	BB	SO	ShO	ERA
		26	53	**100**	.346	12	154	154	68	1352	1645	**696**	405	3	6.08
Harry Kelley	R	30	15	12	.556	3	35	27	20	235	250	75	82	1	3.87
Gordon Rhodes	R	28	9	**20**	.310	1	35	28	13	216	266	102	61	1	5.75
Buck Ross	R	21	9	14	.391	0	30	27	12	201	253	83	47	1	5.82
Herman Fink	R	24	8	16	.333	3	34	24	9	189	222	78	53	0	5.38
1 Bill Dietrich	R	26	4	6	.400	3	21	4	0	72	91	40	34	0	6.50
Fred Archer	L	26	2	3	.400	0	6	5	2	37	41	15	9	0	6.32
George Turbeville	R	21	2	5	.286	0	12	6	2	44	42	32	10	0	6.34
Randy Gumpert	R	18	1	2	.333	2	22	3	2	62	74	32	9	0	4.79
Hod Lisenbee	R	37	1	7	.125	0	19	7	4	86	115	24	17	0	6.17
Eddie Smith	L	22	1	1	.500	0	2	2	2	19	22	8	7	0	1.89
Whitey Wilshere (AJ)	L	23	1	2	.333	0	5	3	0	18	21	19	4	0	7.00
Red Bullock	L	23	0	2	.000	0	12	2	0	17	19	37	7	0	13.76
Carl Doyle	R	23	0	3	.000	0	8	6	1	39	66	29	12	0	10.85
Stu Flythe	R	24	0	0	.000	0	17	3	0	39	49	61	14	0	13.15
Hank Johnson	R	30	0	2	.000	0	3	3	0	12	16	10	6	0	7.50
Dutch Lieber	R	26	0	1	.000	0	3	0	0	12	17	6	1	0	7.50
Harry Matuzak	R	26	0	1	.000	0	6	1	0	15	21	4	8	0	7.20
Pete Naktenis	L	22	0	1	.000	0	7	1	0	19	24	27	18	0	12.32
Woody Upchurch	L	25	0	2	.000	0	7	2	1	22	36	14	6	0	9.82

NEW YORK 1st 92-62 .597 — BILL TERRY

NAME	G by POS	B	AGE	G	AB	R	H	2B	3B	HR	RBI	BB	SO	SB	BA	SA
TOTALS			29	154	5449	742	1529	237	48	97	687	431	452	31	.281	.395
Sam Leslie	1B99	L	30	117	417	49	123	19	5	6	54	23	16	0	.295	.408
Burgess Whitehead	2B153	R	26	154	632	99	176	31	3	4	47	29	32	14	.278	.356
Dick Bartell	SS144	R	28	145	510	71	152	31	3	8	42	40	36	6	.298	.418
Travis Jackson	3B116, SS9	R	32	126	465	41	107	8	1	7	53	18	56	0	.230	.297
Mel Ott	OF148	L	27	150	534	120	175	28	6	33	135	111	41	6	.328	.588
Hank Leiber	OF86, 1B1	R	25	101	337	44	94	19	7	9	67	37	41	1	.279	.457
Jo-Jo Moore	OF149	L	27	152	649	110	205	29	9	7	63	37	27	2	.316	.421
Gus Mancuso	C138	R	30	139	519	55	156	21	3	9	63	39	28	0	.301	.405
Jimmy Ripple	OF76	B	26	96	311	42	95	17	2	7	47	28	15	1	.305	.441
Bill Terry (KJ)	1B56	L	37	79	229	36	71	10	5	2	39	19	19	0	.310	.424
Kiddo Davis	OF22	R	34	47	67	6	16	1	0	0	5	6	5	0	.239	.254
Eddie Mayo	3B40	L	26	46	141	11	28	4	1	1	8	11	12	0	.199	.262
Mark Koenig	SS10, 2B8, 3B3	B	33	42	58	7	16	4	0	1	7	8	4	0	.276	.397
Harry Danning	C24	R	24	32	69	3	11	2	2	0	4	1	5	0	.159	.246
Roy Spencer	C14	R	36	19	18	3	5	1	0	0	3	2	3	0	.278	.333
Joe Martin	3B7	R	24	7	15	0	4	1	0	0	2	0	4	0	.267	.333
Charlie English	2B1	R	26	6	1	0	0	0	0	0	0	0	0	0	.000	.000
Johnny McCarthy	1B4	L	26	4	16	1	7	0	0	1	2	0	1	1	.438	.625
Jim Sheehan	C1	R	23	1	4	0	0	0	0	0	0	0	2	0	.000	.000
Babe Young		L	21	1	1	0	0	0	0	0	0	0	0	0	.000	.000

NAME	T	AGE	W	L	PCT	SV	G	GS	CG	IP	H	BB	SO	ShO	ERA
		28	92	62	.597	22	154	154	60	1385	1458	401	500	12	3.46
Carl Hubbell	L	33	26	6	.813	3	42	34	25	304	265	57	123	3	2.31
Al Smith	L	28	14	13	.519	2	43	30	9	209	217	69	89	4	3.79
Harry Gumbert	R	26	11	3	.786	0	39	15	3	141	157	54	52	0	3.89
Hal Schumacher	R	24	11	13	.458	1	35	30	9	215	234	69	75	3	3.47
Freddie Fitzsimmons	R	34	10	7	.588	2	28	17	7	141	147	39	35	0	3.32
Frank Gabler	R	24	9	8	.529	6	43	14	5	162	170	34	46	0	3.11
Dick Coffman	R	29	7	5	.583	7	42	2	0	102	119	23	26	0	3.88
Slick Castleman	R	22	4	7	.364	1	29	12	2	112	148	56	54	1	5.63
1 Firpo Marberry	R	37	0	0	.000	0	1	0	0	.1	1	0	0	0	0.00

CHICAGO 2nd (Tie) 87-67 .565 5 — CHARLIE GRIMM

NAME	G by POS	B	AGE	G	AB	R	H	2B	3B	HR	RBI	BB	SO	SB	BA	SA
TOTALS			27	154	5409	755	1545	275	36	76	707	491	462	68	.286	.392
Phil Cavarretta	1B115	L	19	124	458	55	125	18	1	9	56	17	36	8	.273	.376
Billy Herman	2B153	R	26	153	632	101	211	57	7	5	93	59	30	5	.334	.470
Billy Jurges	SS116	R	28	118	429	51	120	25	1	1	42	23	25	4	.280	.350
Stan Hack	3B140, 1B11	L	26	149	561	102	167	27	4	6	78	89	39	17	.298	.392
Frank Demaree	OF154	R	26	154	605	93	212	34	3	16	96	49	30	4	.350	.496
Augie Galan	OF145	B	24	145	575	74	152	26	4	8	81	67	50	16	.264	.365
2 Ethan Allen	OF89	R	32	91	373	47	110	18	6	3	39	13	30	12	.295	.399
Gabby Hartnett	C114	R	35	121	424	49	130	25	6	7	64	30	36	0	.307	.443
Ken O'Dea	C55	L	23	80	189	36	58	10	3	2	38	38	18	0	.307	.423
Johnny Gill	OF41	L	31	71	174	20	44	8	0	7	28	13	19	0	.253	.420
Woody English	SS42, 3B17, 2B1	R	29	64	182	33	45	9	0	0	20	40	28	1	.247	.297
Tuck Stainback	OF26	R	25	44	75	13	13	3	0	1	5	6	14	1	.173	.253
Charlie Grimm	1B35	L	37	39	132	13	33	4	0	1	16	5	8	0	.250	.303
1 Chuck Klein	OF29	L	31	29	109	19	32	5	0	5	18	16	14	0	.294	.477
Gene Lillard	SS4, 3B3	R	22	19	34	6	7	1	0	0	2	3	8	0	.206	.235
Walter Stephenson	C4	R	25	6	12	0	1	0	0	0	1	0	5	0	.083	.083

NAME	T	AGE	W	L	PCT	SV	G	GS	CG	IP	H	BB	SO	ShO	ERA
		28	87	67	.565	10	154	154	77	1383	1413	434	597	18	3.53
Larry French	L	28	18	9	.667	3	43	28	10	252	262	54	104	4	3.39
Bill Lee	R	26	18	11	.621	1	43	33	20	259	238	93	102	4	3.30
Lon Warneke	R	27	16	13	.552	1	40	29	13	240	246	76	113	4	3.45
Tex Carleton	R	29	14	10	.583	1	35	26	12	197	204	67	88	4	3.65
2 Curt Davis	R	32	11	9	.550	1	24	20	10	153	146	31	52	0	3.00
Roy Henshaw	L	24	6	5	.545	1	39	14	6	129	152	56	69	0	3.98
Charlie Root	R	37	3	6	.333	1	33	4	0	74	81	20	32	0	4.14
Clay Bryant	R	24	1	2	.333	0	26	0	0	57	57	24	35	0	3.32
1 Fabian Kowalik	R	28	0	2	.000	1	6	0	0	16	24	7	1	0	6.75
Clyde Shoun	L	24	0	0	.000	0	4	0	0	4	3	6	1	0	13.50

ST. LOUIS 2nd (Tie) 87-67 .565 5 — FRANKIE FRISCH

NAME	G by POS	B	AGE	G	AB	R	H	2B	3B	HR	RBI	BB	SO	SB	BA	SA
TOTALS			28	155	5537	795	1554	332	60	88	733	422	577	69	.281	.410
Johnny Mize	1B97, OF8	L	23	126	414	76	136	30	8	19	93	50	32	1	.329	.577
Stu Martin	2B83, SS3	L	22	92	332	63	99	21	4	6	41	29	27	17	.298	.440
Leo Durocher	SS136	R	30	136	510	57	146	22	3	1	58	29	47	3	.286	.347
Charlie Gelbert	3B60, SS28, 2B8	R	30	93	280	33	64	15	2	3	27	25	26	2	.229	.329
Pepper Martin	OF127, 3B15, P1	R	32	143	572	121	177	36	11	11	76	58	66	23	.309	.469
Terry Moore	OF133	R	24	143	590	85	156	39	4	5	47	37	52	9	.264	.369
Joe Medwick	OF155	R	24	155	636	115	223	64	13	18	138	34	33	3	.351	.577
Spud Davis	C103, 3B2	R	31	112	363	24	99	26	2	4	59	35	34	0	.273	.388
Ripper Collins	1B61, OF9	B	32	103	277	48	81	15	3	13	48	48	30	1	.292	.509
Brusie Ogrodowski	C85	R	24	94	237	28	54	15	1	1	20	10	20	0	.228	.312
Frankie Frisch	2B61, 3B22, SS1	B	37	93	303	40	83	10	0	1	26	36	10	2	.274	.317
Lynn King	OF34	L	28	78	100	12	19	2	1	0	10	9	14	2	.190	.230
Art Garibaldi	3B46, 2B24	R	28	71	232	30	64	12	0	1	20	16	30	3	.276	.341
Chick Fullis	OF26	R	32	47	89	15	25	6	1	0	6	7	11	0	.281	.371
Don Gutteridge	3B23	R	24	23	91	13	29	3	4	3	16	1	14	3	.319	.538
Eddie Morgan	OF4	L	21	8	18	4	5	0	0	1	3	2	4	0	.278	.444
2 Johnny Vergez	3B8	R	29	8	18	1	3	1	0	0	1	1	3	0	.167	.222
Lou Scoffic	OF3	R	23	4	7	2	3	0	0	0	2	1	2	0	.429	.429
Heinie Schuble	3B1	R	29	2	0	0	0	0	0	0	0	0	0	0	.000	.000
Walt Alston	1B1	R	24	1	1	0	0	0	0	0	0	0	1	0	.000	.000
Pat Ankenman	SS1	R	23	1	3	0	0	0	0	0	0	0	3	0	.000	.000
Bill DeLancey (IL) 24																

NAME	T	AGE	W	L	PCT	SV	G	GS	CG	IP	H	BB	SO	ShO	ERA
		30	87	67	.565	24	155	155	65	1398	1610	434	559	5	4.47
Dizzy Dean	R	25	24	13	.649	11	51	34	28	315	310	53	195	2	3.17
Roy Parmelee	R	29	11	11	.500	2	37	28	9	221	226	107	79	0	4.56
Jim Winford	R	26	11	10	.524	3	39	23	10	192	203	68	72	1	3.80
Jesse Haines	R	42	7	5	.583	1	25	9	4	99	110	21	19	0	3.91
Ed Heusser	R	27	7	3	.700	3	42	3	0	104	130	38	26	0	5.45
Paul Dean (SA)	R	22	5	5	.500	1	17	14	5	92	113	20	28	0	4.60
2 Si Johnson	R	29	5	3	.625	0	12	9	3	62	82	11	21	1	4.35
Mike Ryba	R	33	5	1	.833	0	14	0	0	45	55	16	25	0	5.40
Bill Walker	L	32	5	6	.455	1	21	13	4	80	106	27	22	1	5.85
2 George Earnshaw	R	36	2	1	.667	1	20	6	1	58	80	20	28	0	6.36
1 Wild Bill Hallahan	L	33	2	2	.500	0	9	6	1	37	58	17	16	0	6.32
Flint Rhem	R	35	2	1	.667	0	10	4	0	27	49	9	7	0	6.67
Bill McGee	R	26	1	1	.500	0	7	2	0	16	23	4	8	0	7.88
Bill Cox	R	23	0	0	.000	0	2	0	0	3	4	1	1	0	6.00
Pepper Martin	R	32	0	0	.000	0	1	0	0	2	1	2	0	0	0.00
Les Munns	R	27	0	3	.000	1	7	1	0	24	23	12	4	0	3.00
Cotton Pippen	R	26	0	2	.000	0	6	3	0	21	37	8	8	0	7.71
Nels Potter	R	24	0	0	.000	0	1	0	0	1	0	0	0	0	0.00

PITTSBURGH 4th 84-70 .545 8 — PIE TRAYNOR

NAME	G by POS	B	AGE	G	AB	R	H	2B	3B	HR	RBI	BB	SO	SB	BA	SA
TOTALS			29	156	5586	804	1596	283	80	60	732	517	502	37	.286	.397
Gus Suhr	1B156	L	30	156	583	111	182	33	12	11	118	95	34	8	.312	.467
Pep Young	2B123	R	28	125	475	47	118	23	10	6	77	29	52	3	.248	.377
Arky Vaughan	SS156	L	24	156	568	122	190	30	11	9	78	118	21	6	.335	.474
Bill Brubaker	3B145	R	25	145	554	77	160	27	4	6	102	50	96	5	.289	.384
Paul Waner	OF145	L	33	148	585	107	218	53	9	5	94	74	29	7	.373	.520
Lloyd Waner	OF92	L	30	106	414	67	133	13	8	1	31	31	5	1	.321	.399
Woody Jensen	OF153	L	28	153	696	98	197	34	10	10	58	16	19	2	.283	.404
Tom Padden	C87	R	27	88	281	22	70	9	2	1	31	22	41	0	.249	.306
Al Todd (BG)	C70	R	32	76	267	28	73	10	5	2	28	11	24	4	.273	.371
Fred Schulte	OF55	R	35	74	238	28	62	7	3	1	17	20	20	1	.261	.328
Red Lucas	P27	L	34	69	108	11	26	4	1	0	14	8	17	0	.241	.296
Cookie Lavagetto	2B37, 3B13, SS1	R	23	60	197	21	48	15	2	2	26	15	13	0	.244	.371
Bill Swift	P45	R	28	45	105	6	31	10	0	2	15	2	16	0	.295	.448
Bud Hafey	OF29	R	23	39	118	19	25	6	1	4	13	10	27	0	.212	.381
Hal Finney	C14	R	30	21	35	3	0	0	0	0	3	0	8	0	.000	.000
Johnny Dickshot	OF1	R	26	9	9	2	2	0	0	0	1	1	2	0	.222	.222
Earle Browne	OF4, 1B1	L	25	8	23	7	7	1	2	0	3	1	4	0	.304	.522

NAME	T	AGE	W	L	PCT	SV	G	GS	CG	IP	H	BB	SO	ShO	ERA
		31	84	70	.545	12	156	156	67	1395	1475	379	559	5	3.89
Bill Swift	R	28	16	16	.500	2	45	31	17	262	275	63	92	0	4.02
Red Lucas	R	34	15	4	.789	0	27	22	12	176	178	26	53	0	3.17
Jim Weaver	R	32	14	8	.636	0	38	31	11	226	239	74	108	1	4.30
Cy Blanton	R	27	13	15	.464	3	44	32	15	236	235	55	127	4	3.51
Mace Brown	R	27	10	11	.476	3	47	10	3	165	178	55	56	0	3.87
Ralph Birkofer	L	27	7	5	.583	0	34	13	2	109	130	41	44	0	4.71
Waite Hoyt (IL)	R	36	7	5	.583	1	22	9	6	117	115	20	37	0	2.69
1 Guy Bush	R	34	1	3	.250	2	16	0	0	35	49	11	10	0	5.91
Jack Tising	R	32	1	3	.250	0	10	6	1	47	52	24	27	0	4.21
Russ Bauers	R	22	0	0	.000	0	1	1	0	1	2	4	0	0	45.00
2 Johnny Welch	R	29	0	0	.000	1	9	1	0	22	22	6	5	0	4.50

CINCINNATI 5th 74-80 .481 18 — CHUCK DRESSEN

NAME	G by POS	B	AGE	G	AB	R	H	2B	3B	HR	RBI	BB	SO	SB	BA	SA
TOTALS			28	154	5393	722	1476	224	73	82	674	410	584	68	.274	.388
Les Scarsella	1B115	L	22	115	485	63	152	21	9	3	65	14	36	6	.313	.412
Alex Kampouris	2B119, OF1	R	23	122	355	43	85	10	4	5	46	24	46	3	.239	.332
Billy Myers	SS98	R	25	98	323	45	87	9	6	6	27	28	56	6	.269	.390
Lew Riggs	3B140	L	26	141	538	69	138	20	12	6	57	38	33	5	.257	.372
Ival Goodman	OF120	L	27	136	489	81	139	15	14	17	71	38	53	6	.284	.476
Kiki Cuyler	OF140	R	36	144	567	96	185	29	11	7	74	47	67	16	.326	.453
Babe Herman	OF92, 1B14	L	33	119	380	59	106	25	2	13	71	39	36	4	.279	.458
Ernie Lombardi	C105	R	28	121	387	42	129	23	2	12	68	19	16	1	.333	.496
Tommy Thevenow	SS68, 2B33, 3B12	R	32	106	321	25	75	7	2	0	36	15	23	2	.234	.268
Calvin Chapman	OF31, 2B23, 3B1	L	25	96	219	35	54	7	3	1	22	16	19	5	.247	.320
Hub Walker	OF73, 1B1, C1	L	29	92	258	49	71	18	1	4	23	35	32	8	.275	.399
Gilly Campbell	C71, 1B1	L	28	89	235	28	63	13	1	1	40	43	14	2	.268	.345
Sammy Byrd	OF37	R	29	59	141	17	35	8	0	2	13	11	11	0	.248	.348
George McQuinn	1B38	L	27	38	134	5	27	3	4	0	13	10	22	0	.201	.284
Al Hollingsworth	P29	L	28	34	73	17	23	2	0	1	11	5	8	0	.315	.384
Lee Handley	2B16, 3B7	R	22	24	78	10	24	1	0	2	8	7	16	3	.308	.397
Eddie Joost	SS7, 2B5	R	20	13	26	1	4	1	0	0	1	2	5	0	.154	.192
Eddie Miller	SS4, 2B1	R	19	5	10	0	1	0	0	0	0	1	1	0	.100	.100
Chick Hafey (IL) 33																

NAME	T	AGE	W	L	PCT	SV	G	GS	CG	IP	H	BB	SO	ShO	ERA
		28	74	80	.481	23	154	154	50	1367	1576	418	459	6	4.22
Paul Derringer	R	29	19	19	.500	5	51	37	13	282	331	42	121	2	4.02
Gene Schott	R	22	11	11	.500	1	31	22	8	180	184	73	65	0	3.80
Benny Frey	R	30	10	8	.556	0	31	12	5	131	164	30	20	0	4.26
Al Hollingsworth	L	28	9	10	.474	0	29	25	9	184	204	66	76	0	4.16
Peaches Davis	R	31	8	8	.500	5	26	15	5	126	139	36	32	0	3.57
Don Brennan	R	32	5	2	.714	9	41	4	0	94	117	35	40	0	4.40
2 Wild Bill Hallahan	L	33	5	9	.357	0	23	19	5	135	150	57	32	2	4.33
Lee Stine	R	22	3	8	.273	2	40	13	5	122	157	41	26	0	5.02
Lee Grissom	L	28	1	1	.500	0	6	4	0	24	33	9	13	0	6.37
Whitey Hilcher	R	27	1	2	.333	0	14	1	0	35	44	14	10	0	6.17
Whitey Moore	R	24	1	0	1.000	0	1	0	0	5	3	3	4	0	5.40
Emmett Nelson	R	31	1	0	1.000	0	6	1	0	17	24	4	3	0	3.18
Tony Freitas	L	28	0	2	.000	0	4	0	0	7	6	2	1	0	1.29
1 Si Johnson	R	29	0	0	.000	0	2	0	0	4	7	0	2	0	13.50
Dee Moore	R	22	0	0	.000	0	2	1	0	7	3	2	3	0	0.00
Jake Mooty	R	23	0	0	.000	1	8	0	0	14	10	4	11	0	3.86

BOSTON 6th 71-83 .461 21 — BILL McKECHNIE

NAME	G by POS	B	AGE	G	AB	R	H	2B	3B	HR	RBI	BB	SO	SB	BA	SA
TOTALS			29	157	5478	631	1450	207	45	67	594	433	582	23	.265	.356
Buck Jordan	1B136	L	29	138	555	81	179	27	5	3	66	45	22	2	.323	.405
Tony Cuccinello	2B150	R	28	150	565	68	174	26	3	7	86	58	49	1	.308	.402
Billy Urbanski	SS80, 3B38	R	33	122	494	55	129	17	5	0	26	31	42	2	.261	.316
Joe Coscarart	3B97, SS6, 2B1	R	26	104	367	28	90	11	2	2	44	19	37	0	.245	.302
Gene Moore	OF151	L	26	151	637	91	185	38	12	13	67	40	80	6	.290	.449
Wally Berger	OF133	R	30	138	534	88	154	23	3	25	91	53	84	1	.288	.483
Hal Lee	OF150	R	31	152	565	46	143	24	7	3	64	52	50	4	.253	.336
Al Lopez	C127, 1B1	R	27	128	426	46	103	12	5	7	50	41	41	1	.242	.343
Tommy Thompson	OF39, 1B25	L	26	106	266	37	76	9	0	4	36	31	12	3	.286	.365
2 Rabbit Warstler	SS74	R	32	74	304	27	64	6	0	0	17	22	33	2	.211	.230
2 Mickey Haslin	3B17, 2B7	R	25	36	104	14	29	1	2	2	11	5	9	0	.279	.385
Bill Lewis	C21	R	31	29	62	11	19	2	0	0	3	12	7	0	.306	.339
Ray Mueller	C23	R	24	24	71	5	14	4	0	0	5	5	17	0	.197	.254
1 Pinky Whitney	3B10	R	31	10	40	1	7	0	0	0	5	2	4	0	.175	.175
Ed Moriarty		R	23	6	6	0	1	0	0	0	0	0	1	0	.167	.167
Swede Larsen	2B2	R	22	3	1	0	0	0	0	0	0	0	0	0	.000	.000
Andy Pilney		R	23	3	2	0	0	0	0	0	0	0	1	0	.000	.000

NAME	T	AGE	W	L	PCT	SV	G	GS	CG	IP	H	BB	SO	ShO	ERA
TOTALS		32	71	83	.461	13	157	157	61	**1413**	1566	451	421	7	3.94
Danny MacFayden	R	31	17	13	.567	0	37	31	21	267	266	66	86	2	2.87
Tiny Chaplin	R	30	10	15	.400	2	40	31	14	232	273	62	86	0	4.11
Ben Cantwell	R	34	9	9	.500	2	34	12	4	133	127	35	42	0	3.05
1 Ray Benge	R	34	7	9	.438	0	21	19	2	115	161	38	32	0	5.79
Johnny Lanning	R	25	7	11	.389	0	28	20	3	153	154	55	33	1	3.65
Bobby Reis	R	27	6	5	.545	0	35	5	3	139	152	74	25	0	4.47
Bob Smith	R	38	6	7	.462	8	35	11	5	136	142	35	36	2	3.77
2 Guy Bush	R	34	4	5	.444	0	15	11	5	90	90	20	28	0	3.40
Roy Weir	L	25	4	3	.571	0	12	7	3	57	53	24	29	2	2.84
Wayne Osborne	R	23	1	1	.500	0	5	3	0	20	31	9	8	0	5.85
Johnny Babich	R	23	0	0	.000	0	3	0	0	6	11	6	1	0	10.50
Al Blanche	R	26	0	1	.000	1	11	0	0	16	20	8	4	0	6.19
Bob Brown	R	25	0	2	.000	0	2	2	0	8	10	3	5	0	5.63
Art Doll	R	24	0	1	.000	0	1	1	0	8	11	2	2	0	3.38
Gene Ford	R	24	0	0	.000	0	2	1	0	2	2	3	0	0	13.50
3 Fabian Kowalik	R	28	0	1	.000	0	1	1	1	9	18	2	0	0	8.00
Amby Murray	L	23	0	0	.000	0	4	1	0	11	15	3	2	0	4.09
Irish McCloskey	L	24	0	0	.000	0	4	1	0	8	14	3	2	0	11.25
Hal Weafer	R	22	0	0	.000	0	1	0	0	3	6	3	0	0	12.00

BROOKLYN 7th 67-87 .435 25 — CASEY STENGEL

NAME	G by POS	B	AGE	G	AB	R	H	2B	3B	HR	RBI	BB	SO	SB	BA	SA
TOTALS			28	156	5574	662	1518	263	43	33	596	390	458	55	.273	.353
Buddy Hassett	1B156	L	24	156	635	79	197	29	11	3	82	35	17	5	.310	.405
Jimmy Jordan	2B98, 3B6, SS1	R	28	115	398	26	93	15	1	2	28	15	21	1	.234	.291
Lonny Frey	SS117, 2B30, OF1	B	25	148	524	63	146	29	4	4	60	71	56	7	.279	.372
Joe Stripp	3B106	R	33	110	439	51	139	31	1	1	60	22	12	2	.317	.399
Frenchy Bordagaray	OF92, 2B11	R	24	125	372	63	117	21	3	4	31	17	42	12	.315	.419
Johnny Cooney	OF130	R	35	130	507	71	143	17	5	0	30	24	15	3	.282	.335
2 George Watkins	OF98	L	36	105	364	54	93	24	6	4	43	38	34	5	.255	.387
Ray Berres	C105	R	28	105	267	16	64	10	1	1	13	14	35	1	.240	.296
Babe Phelps	C98, OF1	L	28	115	319	36	117	23	2	5	57	27	18	1	.367	.498
Jim Bucher	3B39, 2B32, OF30	L	25	110	370	49	93	12	8	2	41	29	27	5	.251	.343
Sid Gautreaux	C15	B	24	75	71	8	19	3	0	0	16	9	7	0	.268	.310
Eddie Wilson (IL)	OF47	L	26	52	173	28	60	8	1	3	25	14	25	3	.347	.457
Ben Geraghty	SS31, 2B9, 3B5	R	23	51	129	11	25	4	0	0	9	8	16	4	.194	.225
Danny Taylor	OF31	R	35	43	116	12	34	6	0	2	15	11	14	2	.293	.397
Randy Moore	OF21	L	31	42	88	4	21	3	0	0	14	8	1	0	.239	.273
Jack Radtke	2B14, 3B5, SS4	B	23	33	31	8	3	0	0	0	2	4	9	3	.097	.097
Fred Lindstrom (LJ)	OF26	R	30	26	106	12	28	4	0	0	10	5	7	1	.264	.302
Tom Winsett	OF21	L	26	22	85	13	20	7	0	1	18	11	14	0	.235	.353
Ox Eckhardt	OF10	L	34	16	44	5	8	1	0	1	6	5	2	0	.182	.273
Nick Tremark	OF8	L	23	8	32	6	8	2	0	0	1	3	2	0	.250	.313
Johnny Hudson	SS4, 2B1	R	24	6	12	1	2	0	0	0	0	2	1	0	.167	.167
Dick Siebert	OF1	L	24	2	2	0	0	0	0	0	0	0	0	0	.000	.000

NAME	T	AGE	W	L	PCT	SV	G	GS	CG	IP	H	BB	SO	ShO	ERA
TOTALS		28	67	87	.435	18	156	156	59	1403	1466	**528**	**651**	7	3.98
Van Lingle Mungo	R	25	18	19	.486	3	45	**37**	22	312	275	**118**	**238**	2	3.35
Fred Frankhouse	R	32	13	10	.565	2	41	31	9	234	236	89	84	1	3.65
Ed Brandt	L	31	11	13	.458	2	38	29	12	234	246	65	104	1	3.50
Watty Clark	L	34	7	11	.389	2	33	16	1	120	162	28	28	1	4.43
Max Butcher	R	25	6	6	.500	2	38	15	5	148	154	59	55	0	3.95
George Jeffcoat	R	22	5	6	.455	3	40	5	3	96	84	63	46	0	4.50
1 George Earnshaw	R	36	4	9	.308	1	19	13	4	93	113	30	40	1	5.32
Tom Baker	R	23	1	8	.111	2	35	8	2	88	98	48	35	0	4.70
Harry Eisenstat	L	20	1	2	.333	0	5	2	1	14	22	6	5	0	5.79
Hank Winston	R	32	1	3	.250	0	14	0	0	32	40	16	8	0	6.19
Dutch Leonard	R	27	0	0	.000	1	16	0	0	32	34	5	8	0	3.66
1 Tom Zachary	L	40	0	0	.000	0	1	0	0	.1	2	1	0	0	54.00

PHILADELPHIA 8th 54-100 .351 38 — JIMMIE WILSON

NAME	G by POS	B	AGE	G	AB	R	H	2B	3B	HR	RBI	BB	SO	SB	BA	SA
TOTALS			29	154	5465	726	1538	250	46	**103**	682	451	**586**	50	.281	.401
Dolph Camilli	1B150	L	29	151	530	106	167	29	13	28	102	116	84	5	.315	.577
Chile Gomez	2B71, SS40	R	27	108	332	24	77	4	1	0	28	14	32	0	.232	.250
Leo Norris	SS121, 2B38	R	28	154	581	64	154	27	4	11	76	39	79	4	.265	.382
2 Pinky Whitney	3B111, 2B1	R	31	114	411	44	121	17	3	6	59	37	33	2	.294	.394
2 Chuck Klein	OF117	L	31	117	492	83	152	30	7	20	86	33	45	6	.309	.520
Lou Chiozza	OF90, 2B33, 3B26	L	26	144	572	83	170	32	6	1	48	37	39	17	.297	.379
Johnny Moore	OF112	L	34	124	472	85	155	24	3	16	68	26	22	1	.328	.494
Earl Grace	C65	L	29	86	221	24	55	11	0	4	32	34	20	0	.249	.353
Ernie Sulik	OF105	L	25	122	404	69	116	14	4	6	36	40	22	4	.287	.386
Jimmie Wilson	C63, 1B1	R	35	85	230	25	64	12	0	1	27	12	21	5	.278	.343
Bill Atwood	C53	R	24	71	192	21	58	9	2	2	29	11	15	0	.302	.401
Bucky Walters	P40, 2B1, 3B1	R	27	64	121	12	29	10	1	1	16	7	15	0	.240	.364
Claude Passeau	P49	R	27	50	78	8	22	3	0	2	7	2	29	0	.282	.397
2 Fabian Kowalik	P22, OF3	B	28	42	57	2	13	1	0	0	7	2	8	0	.228	.246
Charlie Sheerin	2B17, 3B13, SS5	R	27	39	72	4	19	4	0	0	4	7	18	0	.264	.319
1 Ethan Allen	OF30	R	32	30	125	21	37	3	1	1	9	4	8	4	.296	.360
Stan Sperry	2B15	L	22	20	37	2	5	3	0	0	4	3	5	0	.135	.216
1 George Watkins	OF17	L	36	19	70	7	17	4	0	2	5	5	13	2	.243	.386
1 Mickey Haslin	2B12, 3B5	R	25	16	64	6	22	1	1	0	6	3	5	0	.344	.391
1 Johnny Vergez	3B12	R	29	15	40	4	11	2	0	1	5	3	11	0	.275	.400

Morrie Arnovich 25 R 15-48, Walt Bashore 26 R 2-10, Gene Corbett 22 L 3-21, Joe Holden 23 L 0-1

NAME	T	AGE	W	L	PCT	SV	G	GS	CG	IP	H	BB	SO	ShO	ERA
TOTALS		28	54	**100**	.351	14	154	154	51	1365	**1630**	515	454	7	4.64
Claude Passeau	R	27	11	15	.423	3	49	21	8	217	247	55	85	2	3.48
Bucky Walters	R	27	11	**21**	.344	0	40	33	15	258	284	115	66	**4**	4.26
Joe Bowman	R	26	9	20	.310	1	40	28	12	204	243	53	80	0	5.03
Orville Jorgens	R	28	8	8	.500	0	39	21	4	167	196	69	59	0	4.80
Syl Johnson	R	35	5	7	.417	7	39	8	1	111	129	29	48	0	4.30
Pete Sivess	R	22	3	4	.429	0	17	6	2	65	84	36	22	0	4.57
1 Curt Davis	R	32	2	4	.333	0	10	8	3	60	71	19	18	0	4.65
Fuel Moore	R	28	2	3	.400	1	20	5	1	54	76	12	19	0	7.00
2 Ray Benge	R	34	1	4	.200	1	15	6	0	46	70	19	13	0	4.70
2 Fabian Kowalik	R	28	1	5	.167	0	22	8	2	77	100	31	19	0	5.38
Hugh Mulcahy	R	22	1	1	.500	0	3	2	2	23	20	12	2	0	3.13
Lefty Bertrand	L	27	0	0	.000	0	1	0	0	2	3	2	1	0	9.00
Elmer Burkart	R	19	0	0	.000	0	2	2	0	8	4	12	2	0	3.38
Herb Harris	L	23	0	0	.000	0	4	0	0	7	14	5	0	0	10.29
Hal Kelleher	R	22	0	5	.000	0	14	4	1	44	60	29	13	0	5.32
Pretzels Pezzullo	L	25	0	0	.000	0	1	0	0	2	1	6	0	0	4.50
2 Tom Zachary	L	40	0	3	.000	1	7	2	0	20	28	11	8	0	8.10

WORLD SERIES – NEW YORK (AL) 4 NEW YORK (NL) 2

LINE SCORES

TEAM	1	2	3	4	5	6	7	8	9	10	11	12	R	H	E
Game 1 September 30 at New York (NL)															
NY (AL)	0	0	1	0	0	0	0	0	0				1	7	2
NY (NL)	0	0	0	0	1	1	0	4	X				6	9	1
Ruffing / **Hubbell**															
Game 2 October 2 at New York (NL)															
NY (AL)	2	0	7	0	0	1	2	0	6				18	17	0
NY (NL)	0	1	0	3	0	0	0	0	0				4	6	1
Gomez / Schumacher, Smith (3), Coffman (3), Gabler (5), Gumbert (9)															
Game 3 October 3 at New York (AL)															
NY (NL)	0	0	0	0	1	0	0	0	0				1	11	0
NY (AL)	0	1	0	0	0	0	0	1	X				2	4	0
Fitzsimmons / **Hadley**, Malone (9)															
Game 4 October 4 at New York (AL)															
NY (NL)	0	0	0	1	0	0	0	1	0				2	7	1
NY (AL)	0	1	3	0	0	0	0	1	X				5	10	1
Hubbell, Gabler (8) / **Pearson**															
Game 5 October 5 at New York (AL)															
NY (NL)	3	0	0	0	0	1	0	0	0	1			5	8	3
NY (AL)	0	1	1	0	0	2	0	0	0	0			4	10	1
Schumacher / Ruffing, Malone (7)															
Game 6 October 6 at New York (NL)															
NY (AL)	0	2	1	2	0	0	0	1	7				13	17	2
NY (NL)	2	0	0	0	1	0	1	1	0				5	9	1
Gomez, Murphy (7) / Fitzsimmons, Castleman (4), Coffman (9), Gumbert (9)															

COMPOSITE BATTING

NAME	POS	G	AB	R	H	2B	3B	HR	RBI	BA
New York (AL)										
Totals		6	215	43	65	8	1	7	41	.302
DiMaggio	OF	6	26	3	9	3	0	0	3	.346
Crosetti	SS	6	26	5	7	2	0	0	3	.269
Rolfe	3B	6	25	5	**10**	0	0	0	4	.400
Dickey	C	6	25	5	3	0	0	1	5	.120
Selkirk	OF	6	24	6	8	0	1	**2**	3	.333
Gehrig	1B	6	24	5	7	1	0	**2**	**7**	.292
Powell	OF	6	22	**8**	**10**	1	0	1	5	**.455**
Lazzeri	2B	6	20	4	5	0	0	1	**7**	.250
Gomez	P	2	8	1	2	0	0	0	3	.250
Ruffing	P	3	5	0	0	0	0	0	0	.000
Pearson	P	1	4	0	2	1	0	0	0	.500
Murphy	P	1	2	1	1	0	0	0	1	.500
Hadley	P	1	2	0	0	0	0	0	0	.000
Malone	P	2	1	0	1	0	0	0	0	1.000
Johnson	PR-PH	2	1	0	0	0	0	0	0	.000
Seeds	PR	1	0	0	0	0	0	0	0	.000
New York (NL)										
Totals		6	203	23	50	9	0	4	20	.246
Moore	OF	6	**28**	4	6	2	0	1	1	.214
Terry	1B	6	25	1	6	0	0	0	5	.240
Ott	OF	6	23	4	7	2	0	1	3	.304
Bartell	SS	6	21	5	8	3	0	1	3	.381
Jackson	3B	6	21	1	4	0	0	0	1	.190
Whitehead	2B	6	21	1	1	0	0	0	2	.048
Mancuso	C	6	19	3	5	2	0	0	1	.263
Ripple	OF	5	12	2	4	0	0	1	3	.333
Hubbell	P	2	6	0	2	0	0	0	0	.333
Leiber	OF	2	6	0	0	0	0	0	0	.000
Fitzsimmons	P	2	4	0	2	0	0	0	0	.500
Schumacher	P	2	4	0	0	0	0	0	0	.000
Leslie	PH	3	3	0	2	0	0	0	0	.667
Koenig	2B	3	3	0	1	0	0	0	0	.333
Castleman	P	1	2	0	1	0	0	0	0	.500
Davis	PR-PH	4	2	2	1	0	0	0	0	.500
Danning	C	2	2	0	0	0	0	0	0	.000
Mayo	3B	1	1	0	0	0	0	0	0	.000
Coffman	P	2	0	0	0	0	0	0	0	.000
Gabler	P	2	0	0	0	0	0	0	0	.000
Gumbert	P	2	0	0	0	0	0	0	0	.000
Smith	P	1	0	0	0	0	0	0	0	.000

COMPOSITE PITCHING

NAME	G	IP	H	BB	SO	W	L	SV	ERA
New York (AL)									
Totals	6	54	50	21	33	4	2	2	3.33
Gomez	2	15.1	14	**11**	9	**2**	0	0	4.70
Ruffing	2	14	**16**	5	**12**	0	1	0	4.50
Pearson	1	9	7	2	7	1	0	0	2.00
Hadley	1	8	10	1	2	1	0	0	**1.12**
Malone	2	5	2	1	2	0	1	1	1.80
Murphy	1	2.2	1	1	1	0	0	1	3.38
New York (NL)									
Totals	6	53	65	26	35	2	4	0	6.79
Hubbell	2	**16**	15	2	10	1	1	0	2.25
Schumacher	2	12	13	10	11	1	1	0	5.25
Fitzsimmons	2	11.2	13	2	6	0	**2**	0	5.40
Gabler	2	5	7	4	0	0	0	0	7.20
Castleman	1	4.1	3	2	5	0	0	0	2.08
Gumbert	2	2	7	4	2	0	0	0	36.00
Coffman	2	1.2	5	1	1	0	0	0	32.40
Smith	1	.1	2	1	0	0	0	0	81.00

1937 The Battery Trouble in Detroit

The Detroit Tigers had hoped to improve on their second-place finish of 1936 and, once again, claim the junior circuit crown. But battery trouble shorted out their acceleration before they began. Star right-hander Schoolboy Rowe, who had won 19 games in the previous year, spent all of 1937 on the sidelines with an ailing wing. With Rowe's career up in the air, Mickey Cochrane's came to a sudden, but definite end on May 25, when a pitched ball fractured the catcher-manager's skull and placed his life in doubt. He recovered in time to resume control of the team late in the season, but never again would the great backstop catch. Rookie Rudy York was thrown into the catching breach and responded with 35 homers and 103 runs batted in, offsetting his defensive limitations behind the plate. Hank Greenberg socked 40 homers and a league-leading 183 RBI's, Gee Walker drove in 113 runs, and Charlie Gehringer led the loop with a .371 batting average. But the Tigers finished 13 games behind New York, consigned to second place by a mediocre pitching staff which missed Rowe badly.

No one was surprised at the repeat of the Yankees as champions, but the development of Joe DiMaggio into the premier American League outfielder raised some eyebrows. In his second season, Joltin' Joe polled 46 homers, tops in the league, and drove 167 Yankees home with his .346 batting. In addition, his center fielding was flawless and his base running heads-up. Lou Gehrig and Bill Dickey both had big years in average and power, and the Yankee lineup proved just as potent as Detroit's. But unlike the Tigers, New York also had pitching and boasted of the league's only two 20-game winners in Lefty Gomez and Red Ruffing. Gomez, in addition, won the E.R.A. title with a 2.33 mark. The rest of the staff was plagued by injuries, but Johnny Murphy made manager Joe McCarthy's job easier with effective relief work behind his ten saves. Ex-Yankee Johnny Allen continued to shine in a Cleveland uniform as he experienced a sensational season, winning 15 games before losing his only game on the final day of the season to post the league's highest winning percentage of .938.

Manager Bill Terry led his charges to a third National League pennant in his sixth year at the rudder of the Giant ship, edging the Cubs by defeating them head-on in late September in a series in New York. The repeat pennant was engineered without any super heroics. Terry got consistently good seasons from the entire squad, while Mel Ott provided the offensive leadership with 31 home runs and 95 runs batted in. Additionally, Ott unselfishly consented to move to third base in mid-season to plug up a sore gap at the hot corner. While Dick Bartell held the infield together with his solid play at shortstop, the Jints flashed two left-handed aces in Carl Hubbell and rookie Cliff Melton. Hubbell used his screwball to rack up a league-high 22 wins, while Melton chalked up 20 victories in his maiden season.

The Cubs had enough hitting to finish only three games out, but they missed the pitching of Lou Warneke, whom they had traded to St. Louis during the winter. Pittsburgh finished third with the Waners, Big Poison and Little Poison, while the batting of Joe "Ducky" Medwick, who won the Triple Crown, and Johnny Mize, who followed close behind, brought the Cardinals home in the first division despite an injury to Dizzy Dean. The ace pitcher suffered a broken toe in the All-Star Game when hit by Earl Averill's line drive. When he tried to resume pitching before the toe fully healed, he strained his arm and his brilliant, but short, career was effectively finished. Boston had no attack but came up with two 30-year-old rookies who won 20 games in Lou Fette and Jim Turner, the last of whom captured the league E.R.A. title with a 2.38 performance.

Whereas the Yanks beat the Giants in six games in 1936, they needed only five games to turn the trick in 1937. Yankee thunder, as usual, drove home a plethora of runs, scoring 28 to the Giants' 12. While Lefty Gomez made two complete winning appearances, 34-year-old Tony Lazzeri starred offensively by hitting .400 in his final fling as a Yankee before joining the Cubs as a player-coach.

1937 AMERICAN LEAGUE

NAME	G by POS	B	AGE	G	AB	R	H	2B	3B	HR	RBI	BB	SO	SB	BA	SA
NEW YORK 1st 102-52 .662	JOE McCARTHY															
TOTALS			28	157	5487	**979**	1554	282	73	**174**	**922**	**709**	607	60	.283	**456**
Lou Gehrig	1B157	L	34	157	569	138	200	37	9	37	159	**127**	49	4	.351	.643
Tony Lazzeri	2B125	R	33	126	446	56	109	21	3	14	70	71	76	7	.244	.399
Frankie Crosetti	SS147	R	26	149	611	127	143	29	5	11	49	86	**105**	13	.234	.352
Red Rolfe	3B154	L	28	154	648	143	179	34	10	4	62	90	53	4	.276	.378
Myril Hoag	OF99	R	29	106	362	48	109	19	8	3	46	33	33	4	.301	.423
Joe DiMaggio	OF150	R	22	151	621	**151**	215	35	15	**46**	167	64	37	3	.346	**.673**
Jake Powell (IL)	OF94	R	28	97	365	54	96	22	3	3	45	25	36	7	.263	.364
Bill Dickey	C137	L	30	140	530	87	176	35	2	29	133	73	22	3	.332	.570
George Selkirk (BC)	OF69	L	29	78	256	49	84	13	5	18	68	34	24	8	.328	.629
Tommy Henrich (JJ)	OF59	L	24	67	206	39	66	14	5	8	42	35	17	4	.320	.553
Don Heffner	2B38, SS13, 3B3, 1B1, OF1	R	26	60	201	23	50	6	5	0	21	19	19	1	.249	.328
Red Ruffing	P31	R	33	54	129	11	26	3	0	1	10	13	24	0	.202	.248
Joe Glenn	C24	R	28	25	53	6	15	2	2	0	4	10	11	0	.283	.396
Jack Saltzgaver	1B4	L	32	17	11	6	2	0	0	0	0	3	4	0	.182	.182
Art Jorgens	C11	R	32	13	23	3	3	1	0	0	3	2	5	0	.130	.174
1 Roy Johnson	OF12	L	34	12	51	5	15	3	0	0	6	3	2	1	.294	.353
Babe Dahlgren		R	25	1	1	0	0	0	0	0	0	0	0	0	.000	.000
DETROIT 2nd 89-65 .578 13	MICKEY COCHRANE															
TOTALS			29	155	**5516**	935	**1611**	309	62	150	873	656	**711**	89	**.292**	.452
Hank Greenberg	1B154	R	26	154	594	137	200	49	14	40	**183**	102	101	8	.337	.668
Charlie Gehringer	2B142	L	34	144	564	133	209	40	1	14	96	90	25	11	**.371**	.520
Billy Rogell	SS146	B	32	146	536	85	148	30	7	8	64	83	48	5	.276	.403
Marv Owen	3B106	R	31	107	396	48	114	22	5	1	45	41	24	3	.288	.376
Pete Fox	OF143	R	27	148	628	116	208	39	8	12	82	41	43	12	.331	.476
Jo-Jo White	OF82	L	28	94	305	50	75	5	7	0	21	50	40	12	.246	.308
Gee Walker	OF151	R	29	151	635	105	213	42	4	18	113	41	74	23	.335	.499
Rudy York	C54, 3B41	R	23	104	375	72	115	18	3	35	103	41	52	3	.307	.651
Goose Goslin	OF40, 1B1	L	36	79	181	30	43	11	1	4	35	35	18	0	.238	.376
Chet Laabs	OF62	R	25	72	242	31	58	13	5	8	37	24	66	6	.240	.434
Birdie Tebbetts	C48	R	27	50	162	15	31	4	3	2	16	10	13	0	.191	.290
Ray Hayworth	C28	R	33	30	78	9	21	2	0	1	8	14	15	0	.269	.333
Mickey Cochrane (PB)	C27	L	34	27	98	27	30	10	1	2	12	25	4	0	.306	.490
Cliff Bolton	C13	L	30	27	57	6	15	2	0	1	7	8	6	0	.263	.351
2 Charlie Gelbert	SS16	R	31	20	47	4	4	2	0	0	1	4	11	0	.085	.128
1 Gil English	2B12, 3B6	R	27	18	65	6	17	1	0	1	6	6	4	1	.262	.323
Babe Herman	OF2	L	34	17	20	2	6	3	0	0	3	1	6	2	.300	.450
Flea Clifton	3B7, SS4, 2B3	R	27	15	43	4	5	1	0	0	2	7	10	3	.116	.140
CHICAGO 3rd 86-68 .558 16	JIMMY DYKES															
TOTALS			30	154	5277	780	1478	280	76	67	726	549	447	70	.280	.400
Zeke Bonura	1B115	R	28	116	447	79	154	41	2	19	100	49	24	5	.345	.573
Jackie Hayes	2B143	R	30	143	573	63	131	27	4	2	79	41	37	1	.229	.300
Luke Appling	SS154	R	30	154	574	98	182	42	8	4	77	86	28	18	.317	.439
Tony Piet	3B86, 2B13	R	30	100	332	34	78	15	1	4	38	32	36	14	.235	.322
Dixie Walker	OF154	L	26	154	593	105	179	28	**16**	9	95	78	26	1	.302	.449
Mike Kreevich	OF138	R	29	144	583	94	176	29	**16**	12	73	43	45	10	.302	.468
Rip Radcliff	OF139	L	31	144	584	105	190	38	10	4	79	53	25	6	.325	.445
Luke Sewell	C118	R	36	122	412	51	111	21	6	1	61	46	18	4	.269	.357
Larry Rosenthal (LJ)	OF25	L	25	58	97	20	28	5	3	0	9	9	20	1	.289	.402
Mule Haas	1B32, OF2	L	33	54	111	8	23	3	3	0	15	16	10	1	.207	.288
Boze Berger	3B40, 2B1, SS1	R	27	52	130	19	31	5	0	5	13	15	24	1	.238	.392
Jimmy Dykes	1B15, 3B11	R	40	30	85	10	26	5	0	1	23	9	7	0	.306	.400
Merv Connors	3B28	R	23	28	103	12	24	4	1	2	12	14	19	2	.233	.350
Tony Rensa	C23	R	35	26	57	10	17	5	1	0	5	8	6	3	.298	.421
Hank Steinbacher	OF15	L	24	26	73	13	19	4	1	1	9	4	7	2	.260	.384
Merv Shea	C25	R	36	25	71	7	15	1	0	0	5	15	10	1	.211	.225

NAME	T	AGE	W	L	PCT	SV	G	GS	CG	IP	H	BB	SO	ShO	ERA
		30	**102**	52	**.662**	**21**	157	157	**82**	1396	1417	506	652	**15**	**3.65**
Lefty Gomez	L	28	**21**	11	.656	0	34	34	25	278	233	93	**194**	**6**	**2.33**
Red Ruffing	R	33	20	7	.741	0	31	31	22	256	242	68	131	4	2.99
Johnny Murphy	R	28	13	4	.765	10	39	4	0	110	121	50	36	0	4.17
Bump Hadley	R	32	11	8	.579	0	29	25	6	178	199	83	70	0	5.31
Monte Pearson	R	27	9	3	.750	1	22	20	7	145	145	64	71	1	3.17
Kemp Wicker	L	30	7	3	.700	0	16	10	6	88	107	26	14	1	4.40
Spud Chandler	R	29	7	4	.636	0	12	10	6	82	79	20	31	2	2.85
Frank Makosky	R	25	5	2	.714	3	26	1	1	58	64	24	27	0	4.97
Pat Malone	R	34	4	4	.500	6	28	9	3	92	109	35	49	0	5.48
2 Ivy Andrews	R	30	3	2	.600	1	11	5	3	49	49	17	17	1	3.12
Joe Vance	R	31	1	0	1.000	0	2	2	0	15	11	9	3	0	3.00
Johnny Broaca (JT)	R	27	1	4	.200	0	7	6	3	44	58	17	9	0	4.70
		27	89*	65	.578	11	155	155	70	1378	1521	635	485	6	4.87
Roxie Lawson	R	31	18	7	.720	1	37	29	15	217	236	115	68	0	5.27
Eldon Auker	R	26	17	9	.654	1	39	32	19	253	250	97	73	1	3.88
Tommy Bridges	R	30	15	12	.556	0	34	31	18	245	267	91	138	3	4.08
George Gill	R	28	11	4	.733	1	31	10	4	128	146	42	40	1	4.50
Boots Poffenberger	R	22	10	5	.667	3	29	16	5	137	147	79	35	0	4.66
Slick Coffman	R	26	7	5	.583	0	28	5	1	101	121	39	22	0	4.37
Jake Wade	L	25	7	10	.412	0	33	25	7	165	160	107	69	1	5.40
Jack Russell	R	31	2	5	.286	4	25	0	0	40	63	20	10	0	7.65
Clyde Hatter	L	28	1	0	1.000	0	3	0	0	9	17	11	4	0	12.00
Schoolboy Rowe (AJ)	R	27	1	4	.200	0	10	2	1	31	49	9	6	0	8.71
Pat McLaughlin	R	26	0	2	.000	0	10	2	0	33	39	16	8	0	6.27
Vic Sorrell	R	36	0	2	.000	1	7	2	0	17	25	8	11	0	9.00
1 Bob Logan	L	27	0	0	.000	0	1	0	0	1	1	1	1	0	0.00
*1 win by forfeit															
		29	86	68	.558	**21**	154	154	70	1351	1435	532	533	**15**	4.17
Monte Stratton	R	25	15	5	.750	0	22	21	14	165	142	37	69	5	2.40
Vern Kennedy	R	30	14	13	.519	0	32	30	15	221	238	124	114	1	5.09
Ted Lyons	R	36	12	7	.632	0	22	22	11	169	182	45	45	0	4.15
Thornton Lee	L	30	12	10	.545	0	30	25	13	205	209	60	80	2	3.51
John Whitehead	R	28	11	8	.579	0	26	24	8	166	191	56	45	3	4.07
Bill Dietrich	R	27	8	10	.444	1	29	20	7	143	162	72	62	1	4.91
Clint Brown	R	33	7	7	.500	**18**	**53**	0	0	100	92	36	51	0	3.42
Sugar Cain	R	30	4	2	.667	0	18	6	1	69	88	51	17	0	6.13
Johnny Rigney	R	22	2	5	.286	1	22	4	0	91	107	46	38	0	4.95
Bill Cox	R	24	1	0	1.000	0	3	2	1	13	9	5	8	0	0.69
Italo Chelini	L	22	0	1	.000	0	4	0	0	9	15	0	3	0	10.00
George Gick	R	21	0	0	.000	1	1	0	0	2	0	0	1	0	0.00

CLEVELAND 4th 83-71 .539 19 — **STEVE O'NEILL**

NAME	G by POS	B	AGE	G	AB	R	H	2B	3B	HR	RBI	BB	SO	SB	BA	SA
TOTALS			28	156	5353	817	1499	304	76	103	754	570	551	76	.280	.423
Hal Trosky	1B152	L	24	153	601	104	179	36	9	32	128	65	60	3	.298	.547
John Kroner	2B64, 3B11	R	28	86	283	29	67	14	1	2	26	22	25	1	.237	.314
Lyn Lary	SS156	R	31	156	644	110	187	46	7	8	77	88	64	18	.290	.421
Odell Hale	3B90, 2B64	R	28	154	561	74	150	32	4	6	82	56	41	9	.267	.371
Bruce Campbell	OF123	L	27	134	448	82	135	42	11	4	61	67	49	4	.301	.471
Earl Averill	OF156	L	35	156	609	121	182	33	11	21	92	88	65	5	.299	.493
Moose Solters	OF149	R	31	152	589	90	190	42	11	20	109	42	56	6	.323	.533
Frankie Pytlak	C115	R	28	125	397	60	125	15	6	1	44	52	15	16	.315	.390
Roy Hughes	3B58, 2B32	R	26	104	346	57	96	12	6	1	40	40	22	11	.277	.355
Billy Sullivan	C38, 1B5, 3B1	L	26	72	168	26	48	12	3	3	22	17	7	1	.286	.446
Roy Weatherly	OF38, 3B1	L	22	53	134	19	27	4	0	5	13	6	14	1	.201	.343
Jeff Heath	OF14	L	22	20	61	8	14	1	4	0	8	0	9	0	.230	.377
Joe Becker	C12	R	29	18	33	3	11	2	1	0	2	3	4	0	.333	.455
Hugh Alexander	OF3	R	19	7	11	0	1	0	0	0	0	0	5	1	.091	.091
Blas Monaco	2B3	B	21	5	7	0	2	0	1	0	2	0	2	0	.286	.571
Ken Keltner	3B1	R	20	1	1	0	0	0	0	0	1	0	0	0	.000	.000
Bill Sodd		R	22	1	1	0	0	0	0	0	0	0	1	0	.000	.000

NAME	T	AGE	W	L	PCT	SV	G	GS	CG	IP	H	BB	SO	ShO	ERA
		30	83	71	.539	15	156	156	64	1365	1529	566	630	4	4.39
Johnny Allen (IL)	R	32	15	1	.938	0	24	20	14	173	157	60	87	0	2.55
Mel Harder	R	27	15	12	.556	2	38	30	13	234	269	86	95	0	4.27
Willis Hudlin	R	31	12	11	.522	2	35	23	10	176	213	43	31	2	4.09
Bob Feller (AJ)	R	18	9	7	.563	1	26	19	9	149	116	106	150	0	3.38
Denny Galehouse	R	25	9	14	.391	3	36	29	7	201	238	83	78	0	4.57
Joe Heving	R	36	8	4	.667	5	40	0	0	73	92	30	35	0	4.81
Earl Whitehill	L	37	8	8	.500	2	33	22	6	147	189	80	53	1	6.49
1 Ivy Andrews	R	30	3	4	.429	0	20	4	1	60	76	9	16	1	4.15
Whit Wyatt	R	29	2	3	.400	0	29	4	2	73	67	40	52	0	4.44
Lloyd Brown	L	32	2	6	.250	0	31	5	2	77	107	27	32	0	6.55
1 Carl Fischer	L	31	0	1	.000	0	2	0	0	1	2	1	1	0	18.00
Ken Jungels	R	21	0	0	.000	0	2	0	0	3	3	1	0	0	0.00

BOSTON 5th 80-72 .526 21 — **JOE CRONIN**

NAME	G by POS	B	AGE	G	AB	R	H	2B	3B	HR	RBI	BB	SO	SB	BA	SA
TOTALS			28	154	5354	821	1506	269	64	100	769	601	557	79	.281	.411
Jimmie Foxx	1B150, C1	R	29	150	569	111	162	24	6	36	127	99	96	10	.285	.538
Eric McNair	2B106, SS9, 3B4, 1B1	R	28	126	455	60	133	29	4	12	76	30	33	10	.292	.453
Joe Cronin	SS148	R	30	148	570	102	175	40	4	18	110	84	73	5	.307	.486
Pinky Higgins	3B152	R	28	153	570	88	172	33	5	9	106	76	51	2	.302	.425
2 Ben Chapman	OF112, SS1	R	28	113	423	76	130	23	11	7	57	57	35	27*	.307	.463
Doc Cramer	OF133	L	31	133	560	90	171	22	11	0	51	35	14	8	.305	.384
Buster Mills	OF120	R	28	123	505	85	149	25	8	7	58	46	41	11	.295	.418
Gene Desautels	C94	R	30	96	305	33	74	10	3	0	27	36	26	1	.243	.295
Dom Dallessandro	OF35	L	23	68	147	18	34	7	1	0	11	27	16	2	.231	.293
Bobby Doerr	2B47	R	19	55	147	22	33	5	1	2	14	18	25	2	.224	.313
Fabian Gaffke	OF50	R	23	54	184	32	53	10	4	6	34	15	25	1	.288	.484
Moe Berg	C47	R	35	47	141	13	36	3	1	0	20	5	4	0	.255	.291
1 Mel Almada	OF27, 1B4	L	24	32	110	17	26	6	2	1	9	15	6	0	.236	.355
Oscar Melillo	2B19, SS2, 3B2	R	37	26	56	8	14	2	0	0	6	5	4	0	.250	.286
1 Rick Ferrell	C18	R	31	18	65	8	20	2	0	1	4	15	4	0	.308	.385
Johnny Peacock	C9	L	27	9	32	3	10	2	1	0	6	1	0	0	.313	.438

Stew Bowers 22 R 0-1, Bob Daughters 22 R 0-0

NAME	T	AGE	W	L	PCT	SV	G	GS	CG	IP	H	BB	SO	ShO	ERA
		30	80	72	.526	14	154	154	74	1366	1520	597	682	5	4.48
Lefty Grove	L	37	17	9	.654	0	32	32	21	262	269	83	153	2	3.02
Jack Wilson	R	25	16	10	.615	7	51	21	14	221	209	119	137	1	3.71
2 Bobo Newsom	R	29	13	10	.565	0	30	27#	14	208	195	119#	127	1	4.37
Johnny Marcum	R	27	13	11	.542	3	37	23	9	184	230	47	59	1	4.84
Archie McKain	L	26	8	8	.500	2	36	18	3	137	152	64	66	0	4.66
Rube Walberg	L	37	5	7	.417	1	32	11	3	105	143	46	46	0	5.57
1 Wes Ferrell	R	29	3	6	.333	0	12	11	5†	73†	111†	34	31	0	7.64
Fritz Ostermueller	L	29	3	7	.300	1	25	7	2	87	101	44	29	0	4.97
Jim Henry	R	27	1	0	1.000	0	3	2	1	15	15	11	8	0	5.40
Joe Gonzales	R	22	1	2	.333	0	8	2	2	31	37	11	11	0	4.35
2 Tommy Thomas	R	37	0	2	.000	0	9	0	0	11	16	4	4	0	4.09
Ted Olson	R	24	0	0	.000	0	11	0	0	32	42	15	11	0	7.31

*Chapman, also with Washington, league leader in SB with 35

#Newsom, also with Washington, league leader in GS (37) and BB (167)

†Ferrell, also with Washington, league leader in CG (26) IP (281), and H (325)

WASHINGTON 6th 73-80 .477 28.5 — **BUCKY HARRIS**

NAME	G by POS	B	AGE	G	AB	R	H	2B	3B	HR	RBI	BB	SO	SB	BA	SA
TOTALS			29	158	5578	757	1559	245	84	47	691	591	503	61	.279	.379
Joe Kuhel	1B136	L	31	136	547	73	155	24	11	6	61	63	39	6	.283	.400
Buddy Myer	2B119, OF1	L	33	125	430	54	126	16	10	1	65	78	41	2	.293	.384
Cecil Travis	SS129	L	23	135	526	72	181	27	7	3	66	39	34	3	.344	.439
Buddy Lewis	3B156	L	20	156	668	107	210	32	6	10	79	52	44	11	.314	.425
John Stone	OF137	L	31	139	542	84	179	33	15	6	88	66	36	6	.330	.480
2 Mel Almada	OF100	L	24	100	433	74	134	21	4	4	33	38	21	12	.309	.404
Al Simmons	OF102	R	35	103	419	60	117	21	10	8	84	27	35	3	.279	.434
2 Rick Ferrell	C84	R	31	86	279	31	64	6	0	1	32	50	18	1	.229	.262
Fred Sington	OF64	R	27	78	228	27	54	15	4	3	36	37	33	1	.237	.377
Wally Millies	C56	R	30	59	179	21	40	7	1	0	28	9	15	1	.223	.274
2 Wes Ferrell	P25	R	29	53	106	7	27	5	0	0	16	9	18	0	.255	.302
Ossie Bluege	SS28, 1B2, 3B2	R	36	42	127	12	36	4	2	1	13	13	19	1	.283	.370
John Mihalic	2B28, SS3	R	25	38	107	13	27	5	2	0	8	17	9	2	.252	.336
1 Ben Chapman	OF32	R	28	35	130	23	34	7	1	0	12	26	7	8*	.262	.331
1 Jesse Hill	OF21	R	30	33	92	24	20	2	1	1	4	13	16	2	.217	.293
Jimmy Wasdell	1B21, OF7	L	23	32	110	13	28	4	4	2	12	7	13	0	.255	.418
George Case	OF22	R	21	22	90	14	26	6	2	0	11	3	5	2	.289	.400
Shanty Hogan	C21	R	31	21	66	4	10	4	0	0	5	6	8	0	.152	.212
Jimmy Bloodworth	2B14	R	19	15	50	3	11	2	1	0	8	5	8	0	.220	.300
1 Johnny Riddle	C8	R	31	8	26	2	7	0	0	0	3	0	2	0	.269	.269
Herb Crompton	C2	R	25	2	3	0	1	0	0	0	0	0	0	0	.333	.333
Milt Gray	C2	R	23	2	6	0	0	0	0	0	0	0	1	0	.000	.000
Mike Guerra	C1	R	24	1	3	0	0	0	0	0	0	0	2	0	.000	.000
Jerry Lynn	2B1	R	21	1	3	0	2	1	0	0	0	0	0	0	.667	1.000

Alex Sabo 27 R 0-0, Frank Trechock 21 R 2-4

NAME	T	AGE	W	L	PCT	SV	G	GS	CG	IP	H	BB	SO	ShO	ERA
		29	73	80	.477	14	158	158	75	1399	1498	676	535	5	4.57
Jimmy DeShong	R	27	14	15	.483	1	37	34	20	264	290	124	86	0	4.91
Monty Weaver	R	31	12	9	.571	0	30	26	9	189	197	70	44	0	4.19
2 Wes Ferrell	R	29	11	13	.458	0	25	24	21†	208†	214†	88	92	0	3.93
Pete Appleton	R	33	8	15	.348	2	35	18	7	168	167	72	62	4	4.39
Ed Linke	R	25	6	1	.857	3	36	7	0	129	158	59	61	0	5.58
Joe Krakauskas	L	22	4	1	.800	0	5	4	3	40	33	22	18	0	2.70
Ken Chase	L	23	4	3	.571	0	14	9	4	76	74	60	43	0	4.14
2 Carl Fischer	L	31	4	5	.444	2	17	11	2	72	74	31	30	0	4.38
Bill Phebus	R	27	3	2	.600	1	6	5	4	41	33	24	12	1	2.20
1 Bobo Newsom	R	29	3	4	.429	0	11	10#	3	68	76	48#	39	0	5.82
Sid Cohen	L	29	2	4	.333	4	33	0	0	55	64	7	22	0	3.11
Joe Kohlman	R	24	1	0	1.000	0	2	2	1	13	15	3	3	0	4.15
Bucky Jacobs	R	24	1	1	.500	0	11	1	0	22	26	11	8	0	4.91
Dick Lanahan	L	25	0	1	.000	0	6	2	0	11	16	13	2	0	13.10
Red Anderson	R	25	0	1	.000	0	2	1	0	11	11	11	3	0	6.54
1 Joe Cascarella	R	30	0	5	.000	1	10	4	1	32	50	23	10	0	8.15

*Chapman, also with Boston, league leader in SB with 35

#Newsom, also with Boston, league leader in GS (37) and BB (167)

†Ferrell, also with Boston, league leader in CG (26), IP (281), and H (325)

PHILADELPHIA 7th 54-97 .358 46.5 — **CONNIE MACK**

NAME	G by POS	B	AGE	G	AB	R	H	2B	3B	HR	RBI	BB	SO	SB	BA	SA
TOTALS			27	154	5228	699	1398	278	60	94	649	583	557	95	.267	.397
Chubby Dean	1B78, P2	L	21	104	309	36	81	14	4	2	31	42	10	2	.262	.353
Rusty Peters	2B70, 3B31, SS13	R	22	116	339	39	88	17	6	3	43	41	59	4	.260	.372
Skeeter Newsome	SS122	R	26	122	438	53	111	22	1	1	30	37	22	11	.253	.315
Bill Werber	3B125, OF3	R	29	128	493	85	144	31	4	7	70	74	39	35	.292	.414
Wally Moses	OF154	L	26	154	649	113	208	48	13	25	86	54	38	9	.320	.550
2 Jesse Hill	OF68	R	30	70	242	32	71	12	3	1	37	31	20	16	.293	.380
Bob Johnson	OF133, 2B2	R	30	138	477	91	146	32	6	25	108	98	56	9	.306	.556
Earle Brucker	C92	R	36	102	317	40	82	16	5	6	37	48	30	1	.259	.397
Lou Finney	1B50, OF39, 2B1	L	26	92	379	53	95	14	9	1	20	20	16	2	.251	.343
Jack Rothrock	OF58, 2B1	B	32	88	232	28	62	15	0	0	21	28	15	1	.267	.332
Lynn Nelson	P30, OF6	L	32	74	113	18	40	6	2	4	29	6	13	1	.354	.549
Frankie Hayes	C56	R	22	60	188	24	49	11	1	10	38	29	34	0	.261	.489
Wayne Ambler	2B56	R	21	56	162	3	35	5	0	0	11	13	8	1	.216	.247
Warren Huston	2B16, SS15, 3B2	R	23	38	54	5	7	3	0	0	3	2	9	0	.130	.185
Ace Parker	SS19, 2B9, OF5	R	25	38	94	8	11	0	1	2	13	4	17	0	.117	.202
Bill Cissell	2B33	R	33	34	117	15	31	7	0	1	14	17	10	0	.265	.350
Gene Hasson	1B28	L	21	28	98	12	30	6	3	3	14	13	14	0	.306	.520
Bill Conroy	C18, 1B1	R	22	26	60	4	12	1	1	0	3	7	9	1	.200	.250
Babe Barna	OF9, 1B1	L	22	14	36	10	14	2	0	2	9	2	6	1	.389	.611
Doyt Morris	OF3	R	20	6	13	0	2	0	0	0	0	0	3	0	.154	.154
Eddie Yount	OF2	R	20	4	7	1	2	0	0	0	1	0	1	0	.286	.286
Hal Wagner	C1	L	21	1	1	0	0	0	0	0	0	0	0	0	.000	.000

NAME	T	AGE	W	L	PCT	SV	G	GS	CG	IP	H	BB	SO	ShO	ERA
		26	54	97	.358	9	154	154	65	1335	1490	613	469	6	4.85
Harry Kelley	R	31	13	21	.382	0	41	29	14	205	267	79	68	0	5.36
George Caster	R	29	12	19	.387	0	34	33	19	232	227	107	100	3	4.42
Bud Thomas	R	26	8	15	.348	0	35	26	6	170	208	52	54	0	4.98
Buck Ross	R	22	5	10	.333	0	28	22	7	147	183	63	37	1	4.90
Al Williams	R	23	4	1	.800	1	16	8	2	75	88	49	27	0	5.40
Lynn Nelson	R	32	4	9	.308	2	30	4	1	116	140	51	49	0	5.90
Eddie Smith	L	23	4	17	.190	5	38	23	14	197	178	90	79	0	3.93
Herman Fink	R	25	2	1	.667	1	28	3	1	80	82	35	18	0	4.05
Bill Kalfass	L	21	1	0	1.000	0	3	1	1	12	10	10	9	0	3.00
Chubby Dean	L	21	1	0	1.000	0	2	1	0	9	7	6	4	0	4.00
George Turbeville	R	22	0	4	.000	0	31	3	0	77	80	56	17	0	4.79
Randy Gumpert	R	19	0	0	.000	0	10	1	0	12	16	15	5	0	12.00
Fred Archer	L	27	0	0	.000	0	1	0	0	3	4	0	2	0	6.00

Woody Upchurch (AA) 26

ST. LOUIS 8th 46-108 .299 56 — **ROGERS HORNSBY 25-50 .333** — **JIM BOTTOMLEY 21-58 .266**

NAME	G by POS	B	AGE	G	AB	R	H	2B	3B	HR	RBI	BB	SO	SB	BA	SA
TOTALS			28	156	5510	715	1573	327	44	71	682	514	510	30	.285	.399
Harry Davis	1B112, OF1	L	27	120	450	89	124	25	3	3	35	71	26	7	.276	.364
Tom Carey	2B87, SS44, 3B1	R	28	130	487	54	134	24	1	1	40	21	26	3	.275	.335
Bill Knickerbocker	SS115, 2B6	R	25	121	491	53	128	29	5	4	61	30	32	3	.261	.365
Harlond Clift	3B155	R	24	155	571	103	175	36	7	29	118	98	80	8	.306	.546
Beau Bell	OF131, 1B26, 3B2	R	29	156	642	82	218	51	8	14	117	53	54	2	.340	.509
Sammy West	OF105	L	32	122	457	68	150	37	4	7	58	46	28	1	.328	.473
Joe Vosmik	OF143	R	27	144	594	81	193	47	9	4	93	49	38	2	.325	.455
Rollie Hemsley	C94, 1B2	R	30	100	334	30	74	12	3	3	28	25	29	0	.222	.302
Ethan Allen	OF78	R	33	103	320	39	101	18	1	0	31	21	17	3	.316	.378
Ben Huffman	C42	R	22	76	176	18	48	9	0	1	24	10	7	1	.273	.341
Jim Bottomley	1B24	L	37	65	109	11	26	7	0	1	12	18	15	1	.239	.330
Jerry Lipscomb	2B27, P3, 3B1	R	26	36	96	11	31	9	1	0	8	11	10	0	.323	.438
Red Barkley	2B31	R	23	31	101	9	27	6	0	0	14	14	17	1	.267	.327
Eddie Silber	OF21	R	23	22	83	10	26	2	0	0	4	5	13	0	.313	.337
Rogers Hornsby	2B17	R	41	20	56	7	18	3	0	1	11	7	5	0	.321	.429
Tony Giuliani	C19	R	24	19	53	6	16	1	0	0	3	3	3	0	.302	.321
Tommy Heath	C14	R	23	17	43	4	10	0	2	1	3	10	3	0	.233	.395
Mike Mazzera		L	23	7	7	1	2	2	0	0	0	0	2	0	.286	.571
Sam Harshany	C4	R	27	5	11	0	1	1	0	0	0	3	0	0	.091	.182
Tom Cafego	OF1	L	25	4	4	1	0	0	0	0	0	0	1	0	.000	.000

NAME	T	AGE	W	L	PCT	SV	G	GS	CG	IP	H	BB	SO	ShO	ERA
		32	46	108	.299	8	156	156	55	1363	1770	653	468	2	6.00
Jim Walkup	R	27	9	12	.429	0	27	18	6	150	218	83	46	0	7.38
Oral Hildebrand	R	30	8	17	.320	1	30	27	12	201	228	87	75	1	5.15
Jack Knott	R	30	8	18	.308	2	38	22	8	191	220	91	74	0	4.90
Chief Hogsett	L	33	6	19	.240	2	37	26	8	177	245	75	68	1	6.31
Lou Koupal (BG)	R	38	4	9	.308	0	26	13	6	106	150	55	24	0	6.54
Julio Bonetti	R	25	4	11	.267	1	28	16	7	143	190	60	43	0	5.85
1 Sheriff Blake	R	37	2	2	.500	1	15	1	0	37	55	20	12	0	7.54
Bill Trotter	R	28	2	9	.182	1	34	12	3	122	150	50	37	0	5.83
Lefty Mills	L	27	1	1	.500	0	2	2	1	13	16	10	10	0	6.23
Russ Van Atta	L	31	1	2	.333	0	16	6	1	59	74	32	34	0	5.49
Les Tietje	R	25	1	2	.333	0	5	4	2	30	32	17	5	0	4.20
1 Tommy Thomas	R	37	0	1	.000	0	17	2	0	31	46	10	10	0	6.99
George Hennessey	R	26	0	1	.000	0	5	0	0	7	15	6	4	0	10.29
Emil Bildilli	L	24	0	1	.000	0	4	1	0	8	12	3	2	0	10.13
Bill Miller	R	27	0	1	.000	0	1	1	0	4	7	4	1	0	13.50
Harry Kimberlin	R	28	0	2	.000	0	3	2	1	15	16	9	5	0	2.40
Earl Caldwell	R	32	0	0	.000	0	9	2	0	29	39	13	8	0	6.83
Bill Strickland	R	29	0	0	.000	0	9	0	0	21	28	15	6	0	6.00
Ed Baecht	R	30	0	0	.000	0	3	0	0	6	13	6	3	0	13.50
Jerry Lipscomb	R	26	0	0	.000	0	3	0	0	10	13	5	1	0	6.30
Bob Muncrief	R	21	0	0	.000	0	1	1	0	2	3	2	0	0	4.50

NEW YORK 1st 95-57 .625 — **BILL TERRY**

NAME	G by POS	B	AGE	G	AB	R	H	2B	3B	HR	RBI	BB	SO	SB	BA	SA
TOTALS			28	152	5329	732	1484	251	41	111	677	412	492	45	.278	.403
Johnny McCarthy	1B110	L	27	114	420	53	117	19	3	10	65	24	37	2	.279	.410
Burgess Whitehead	2B152	R	27	152	574	64	164	15	6	5	52	28	20	7	.286	.359
Dick Bartell	SS128	R	29	128	516	91	158	38	2	14	62	40	38	5	.306	.469
Lou Chiozza	3B93, OF12, 2B2	L	27	117	439	49	102	11	2	4	29	20	30	6	.232	.294
Mel Ott	OF91, 3B60	L	28	151	545	99	160	28	2	31	95	102	69	7	.294	.523
Jimmy Ripple	OF111	L	27	121	426	70	135	23	3	5	66	29	20	3	.317	.420
Jo-Jo Moore	OF140	L	28	142	580	89	180	37	10	6	57	46	37	7	.310	.440
Harry Danning	C86	R	25	93	292	30	84	12	4	8	51	18	20	0	.288	.438
Gus Mancuso (BG)	C81	R	31	86	287	30	80	17	1	4	39	17	20	1	.279	.387
Sam Leslie	1B44	L	31	72	191	25	59	7	2	3	30	20	12	1	.309	.414
2 Wally Berger	OF52	R	31	59	199	40	58	11	2	12	43	18	30	3	.291	.548
1 Kiddo Davis	OF37	R	35	56	76	20	20	10	0	0	9	10	7	1	.263	.395
Hank Leiber (YJ)	OF46	R	26	51	184	24	54	7	3	4	32	15	27	1	.293	.429
Mickey Haslin	SS9, 2B4, 3B4	R	26	27	42	8	8	1	0	0	5	9	3	1	.190	.214
Blondy Ryan	SS19, 2B1, 3B1	R	31	21	75	10	18	3	1	1	13	6	8	0	.240	.347
2 Phil Weintraub	OF1	L	29	6	9	3	3	2	0	0	1	1	1	0	.333	.556
Ed Madjeski	C5	R	27	5	15	0	3	0	0	0	2	0	2	0	.200	.200

NAME	T	AGE	W	L	PCT	SV	G	GS	CG	IP	H	BB	SO	ShO	ERA
		28	95	57	.625	17	152	152	67	1361	1341	404	653	11	3.43
Carl Hubbell	L	34	22	8	.733	4	39	32	18	262	261	55	159	4	3.19
Cliff Melton	L	25	20	9	.690	7	46	27	14	248	216	55	142	2	2.61
Hal Schumacher	R	26	13	12	.520	1	38	29	10	218	222	89	100	1	3.59
Slick Castleman (AJ)	R	23	11	6	.647	0	23	23	10	160	148	33	78	2	3.32
Harry Gumbert	R	27	10	11	.476	1	34	24	10	200	194	62	65	1	3.69
Dick Coffman	R	30	8	3	.727	3	42	1	0	80	93	31	30	0	3.04
Al Smith	L	29	5	4	.556	0	33	9	2	86	91	30	41	0	4.19
1 Freddie Fitzsimmons	R	35	2	2	.500	0	6	4	1	27	28	8	13	1	4.67
2 Tom Baker	R	24	1	0	1.000	0	13	0	0	31	30	16	11	0	4.06
2 Don Brennan	R	33	1	0	1.000	0	6	0	0	9	12	9	1	0	7.00
2 Jumbo Brown	R	30	1	0	1.000	0	4	0	0	9	5	5	4	0	1.00
Bill Lohrman	R	24	1	0	1.000	1	2	1	1	10	5	2	3	0	0.90
1 Ben Cantwell	R	35	0	1	.000	0	1	1	0	4	6	1	1	0	9.00
Hy Vandenberg	R	30	0	1	.000	0	1	1	1	8	10	6	2	0	7.88
1 Frank Gabler	R	25	0	0	.000	0	6	0	0	9	20	2	3	0	10.00

CHICAGO 2nd 93-61 .604 3 — **CHARLIE GRIMM**

NAME	G by POS	B	AGE	G	AB	R	H	2B	3B	HR	RBI	BB	SO	SB	BA	SA
TOTALS			27	154	5349	811	1537	253	74	96	762	538	496	71	.287	.416
Ripper Collins (BN)	1B111	B	33	115	456	77	125	16	5	16	71	32	46	2	.274	.436
Billy Herman	2B137	R	27	138	564	106	189	35	11	8	65	56	22	2	.335	.479
Billy Jurges	SS128	R	29	129	450	53	134	18	10	1	65	42	41	2	.298	.389
Stan Hack	3B150, 1B4	L	27	154	582	106	173	27	6	2	63	83	42	16	.297	.375
Frank Demaree	OF154	R	27	154	615	104	199	36	6	17	115	57	31	6	.324	.485
Joe Marty	OF84	R	23	88	290	41	84	17	2	5	44	28	30	3	.290	.414
Augie Galan	OF140, 2B8, SS2	B	25	147	611	104	154	24	10	18	78	79	48	23	.252	.412
Gabby Hartnett	C103	R	36	110	356	47	126	21	6	12	82	43	19	0	.354	.548
Phil Cavarretta	OF55, 1B43	L	20	106	329	43	94	18	7	5	56	32	35	7	.286	.429
Ken O'Dea	C64	L	24	83	219	31	66	7	5	4	32	24	26	1	.301	.434
Lonny Frey	SS30, 2B13, 3B9, OF5	B	26	78	198	33	55	9	3	1	22	33	15	6	.278	.369
Tuck Stainback	OF49	R	26	72	160	18	37	7	1	0	14	7	16	3	.231	.288
John Bottarini	C18, OF1	R	28	26	40	3	11	3	0	1	7	5	10	0	.275	.425
Carl Reynolds	OF2	R	34	7	11	0	3	1	0	0	1	2	2	0	.273	.364
Bob Garbark		R	27	1	1	0	0	0	0	0	0	0	0	0	.000	.000
Dutch Meyer		R	21	1	0	0	0	0	0	0	0	0	0	0	.000	.000

NAME	T	AGE	W	L	PCT	SV	G	GS	CG	IP	H	BB	SO	ShO	ERA
		30	93	61	.604	13	154	154	73	1381	1434	502	596	11	3.98
Tex Carleton	R	30	16	8	.667	0	32	27	18	208	183	94	105	4	3.16
Larry French	L	29	16	10	.615	0	42	28	11	208	229	65	100	4	3.98
Bill Lee	R	27	14	15	.483	3	42	33	17	272	289	73	108	2	3.54
Charlie Root	R	38	13	5	.722	5	43	15	5	179	173	32	74	0	3.37
Curt Davis (IL)	R	33	10	5	.667	1	28	14	8	124	138	30	32	0	4.06
Clay Bryant	R	25	9	3	.750	3	38	10	4	135	117	78	75	1	4.27
Clyde Shoun	L	25	7	7	.500	0	37	9	2	93	118	45	43	0	5.61
Roy Parmelee	R	30	7	8	.467	0	33	18	8	146	165	79	55	0	5.12
Kirby Higbe	R	22	1	0	1.000	0	1	0	0	5	4	1	2	0	5.40
2 Bob Logan	L	27	0	0	.000	1	4	0	0	6	6	4	2	0	1.50
Newt Kimball	R	22	0	0	.000	0	2	0	0	5	12	1	0	0	10.80

PITTSBURGH 3rd 86-68 .558 10 — **PIE TRAYNOR**

NAME	G by POS	B	AGE	G	AB	R	H	2B	3B	HR	RBI	BB	SO	SB	BA	SA
TOTALS			29	154	5433	704	1550	223	86	47	649	463	480	32	.285	.384
Gus Suhr	1B151	L	31	151	575	69	160	28	14	5	97	83	42	2	.278	.402
Lee Handley	2B126, 3B1	R	23	127	480	59	120	21	12	3	37	37	40	5	.250	.363
Arky Vaughan	SS108, OF12	L	25	126	469	71	151	17	17	5	72	54	22	7	.322	.463
Bill Brubaker	3B115, SS3, 1B1	R	26	120	413	57	105	20	4	6	48	47	51	2	.254	.366
Paul Waner	OF150, 1B3	L	34	154	619	94	219	30	9	2	74	63	34	4	.354	.441
Lloyd Waner	OF123	L	31	129	537	80	177	23	4	1	45	34	12	3	.330	.393
Woody Jensen	OF120	L	29	124	509	77	142	23	9	5	45	15	29	2	.279	.389
Al Todd	C128	R	33	133	514	51	158	18	10	8	86	16	36	2	.307	.428
Pep Young	SS45, 3B39, 2B30	R	29	113	408	43	106	20	3	9	54	26	63	4	.260	.390
Johnny Dickshot	OF64	R	27	82	264	42	67	8	4	3	33	26	36	0	.254	.348
Red Lucas	P20	L	35	59	82	8	22	3	0	0	17	7	6	0	.268	.305
Tom Padden	C34	R	28	35	98	14	28	2	0	0	8	13	11	1	.286	.306
Fred Schulte	OF4	R	36	29	20	5	2	0	0	0	3	4	3	0	.100	.100
Pie Traynor	3B3	R	37	5	12	3	2	0	0	0	0	0	1	0	.167	.167
Bill Schuster	SS2	R	24	3	6	2	3	0	0	0	1	1	0	0	.500	.500
Ray Berres	C2	R	29	2	6	0	1	0	0	0	0	0	0	0	.167	.167

NAME	T	AGE	W	L	PCT	SV	G	GS	CG	IP	H	BB	SO	ShO	ERA
		29	86	68	.558	17	154	154	67	1367	1398	428	643	12	3.56
Cy Blanton	R	28	14	12	.538	0	36	34	14	243	250	76	143	4	3.30
Russ Bauers	R	23	13	6	.684	1	34	19	11	188	174	80	118	2	2.87
Ed Brandt	L	32	11	10	.524	2	33	25	7	176	177	67	74	3	3.12
Bill Swift	R	29	9	10	.474	3	36	17	9	164	160	34	84	0	3.95
Jim Weaver	R	33	8	5	.615	0	32	9	2	110	106	31	44	1	3.19
Joe Bowman	R	27	8	8	.500	1	30	19	7	128	161	35	38	0	4.57
Red Lucas	R	35	8	10	.444	0	20	20	9	126	150	23	20	1	4.29
Mace Brown	R	28	7	2	.778	7	50	2	0	108	109	45	60	0	4.17
Jim Tobin	R	24	6	3	.667	1	20	8	7	87	74	28	37	0	3.00
Ken Heintzelman	L	21	1	0	1.000	0	1	1	1	9	6	3	4	0	2.00
1 Waite Hoyt	R	37	1	2	.333	2	11	0	0	28	31	6	21	0	4.50

ST. LOUIS 4th 81-73 .526 15 — **FRANKIE FRISCH**

NAME	G by POS	B	AGE	G	AB	R	H	2B	3B	HR	RBI	BB	SO	SB	BA	SA
TOTALS			26	156	5476	789	1543	264	67	94	731	385	569	78	.282	.406
Johnny Mize	1B144	L	24	145	560	103	204	40	7	25	113	56	57	2	.364	.595
Jimmy Brown	2B112, SS25, 3B1	B	27	138	525	86	145	20	9	2	53	27	29	10	.276	.360
Leo Durocher	SS134	R	31	135	477	46	97	11	3	1	47	38	36	6	.203	.245
Don Gutteridge	3B105, SS8	R	25	119	447	66	121	26	10	7	61	25	66	12	.271	.421
Don Padgett	OF109	L	25	123	446	62	140	22	6	10	74	30	43	4	.314	.457
Terry Moore	OF106	R	25	115	461	76	123	17	3	5	43	32	41	13	.267	.349
Joe Medwick	OF156	R	25	156	633	111	237	56	10	31	154	41	50	4	.374	.641
Brusie Ogrodowski	C87	R	25	90	279	37	65	10	3	3	31	11	17	2	.233	.323
Pepper Martin	OF82, 3B5	R	33	98	339	60	103	27	8	5	38	33	50	9	.304	.475
Frenchy Bordagaray	3B50, OF28	R	25	96	300	43	88	11	4	1	37	15	25	11	.293	.367
Stu Martin	2B48, 1B9, SS1	L	23	90	223	34	58	6	1	1	17	32	18	3	.260	.309
Mickey Owen (JJ)	C78	R	21	80	234	17	54	4	2	0	20	15	13	1	.231	.265
Dick Siebert	1B7	L	25	22	38	3	7	2	0	0	2	4	8	1	.184	.237
Frankie Frisch	2B5	B	38	17	32	3	7	2	0	0	4	1	0	0	.219	.281
Herb Bremer	C10	R	23	11	33	2	7	1	0	0	3	2	4	0	.212	.242
2 Randy Moore	OF1	L	32	8	7	0	0	0	0	0	0	0	0	0	.000	.000
Bill Delancy (IL) 35																

NAME	T	AGE	W	L	PCT	SV	G	GS	CG	IP	H	BB	SO	ShO	ERA
		31	81*	73	.526	4	156	156	81	1402	1546	448	571	10	3.95
Lon Warneke	R	28	18	11	.621	0	36	33	18	239	280	69	87	2	4.52
Bob Weiland	L	31	15	14	.517	0	41	34	21	264	283	94	105	2	3.55
Dizzy Dean (BT)	R	26	13	10	.565	1	27	25	17	197	200	33	120	4	2.70
Si Johnson	R	30	12	12	.500	1	38	21	12	192	222	43	64	1	3.33
Mike Ryba	R	34	9	6	.600	0	38	8	5	135	152	40	57	0	4.13
Howie Krist	R	21	3	1	.750	0	6	4	1	28	34	10	6	0	4.18
Jesse Haines	R	43	3	3	.500	0	16	6	2	66	81	23	18	0	4.50
Ray Harrell	R	25	3	7	.300	1	35	15	1	97	99	59	41	1	5.85
Jim Winford	R	27	2	4	.333	0	16	4	0	46	56	27	17	0	5.87
Bill McGee	R	27	1	0	1.000	0	4	1	1	14	13	4	9	0	2.57
Nubs Kleinke	R	26	1	1	.500	0	5	2	1	21	25	7	9	0	4.72
Abe White	L	31	0	1	.000	0	5	0	0	9	14	3	2	0	7.00
2 Sheriff Blake	R	37	0	3	.000	0	14	2	2	44	45	18	20	0	3.68
Tom Sunkel	L	24	0	0	.000	1	9	1	0	29	24	11	9	0	2.79
Nate Andrews	R	23	0	0	.000	0	4	0	0	9	12	3	6	0	4.00
John Chambers	R	25	0	0	.000	0	2	0	0	2	5	2	1	0	18.00
Paul Dean (SA)	R	23	0	0	.000	0	1	0	0	0	1	2	0	0	∞

*1 win by forfeit

BOSTON 5th 79-73 .520 16 — **BILL McKECHNIE**

NAME	G by POS	B	AGE	G	AB	R	H	2B	3B	HR	RBI	BB	SO	SB	BA	SA
TOTALS			28	152	5124	579	1265	200	41	63	534	485	707	45	.247	.339
Elbie Fletcher	1B148	L	21	148	539	56	133	22	4	1	38	56	64	3	.247	.308
Tony Cuccinello	2B151	R	29	152	575	77	156	36	4	11	80	61	40	2	.271	.405
Rabbit Warstler	SS149	R	33	149	555	57	124	20	0	3	36	51	62	4	.223	.276
2 Gil English	3B71	R	27	79	269	25	78	5	2	2	37	23	27	3	.290	.346
Gene Moore	OF148	L	27	148	561	88	159	29	10	16	70	61	73	11	.283	.456
Vince DiMaggio	OF130	R	24	132	493	56	126	18	4	13	69	39	111	8	.256	.387
Debs Garms	OF81, 3B36	L	29	125	478	60	124	15	8	2	37	37	33	2	.259	.337
Al Lopez	C102	R	28	105	334	31	68	11	1	3	38	35	57	3	.204	.269
2 Roy Johnson	OF63, 3B1	L	34	85	260	24	72	8	3	3	22	38	29	5	.277	.365
Eddie Mayo	3B50	L	27	65	172	19	39	6	1	1	18	15	20	1	.227	.291
Ray Mueller	C57	R	25	64	187	21	47	9	2	2	26	18	36	1	.251	.353
Bobby Reis	OF18, 1B4, P4	R	28	45	86	10	21	5	0	0	6	13	12	2	.244	.302
1 Wally Berger	OF28	R	31	30	113	14	31	9	1	5	22	11	33	0	.274	.504
Tommy Thevenow	SS12, 3B6, 2B2	R	33	21	34	5	4	0	1	0	2	4	2	0	.118	.176
Beauty McGowan	OF2	L	35	9	12	0	1	0	0	0	0	1	2	0	.083	.083
1 Buck Jordan		L	30	8	8	1	2	0	0	0	0	0	0	0	.250	.250
2 Johnny Riddle	C2	R	31	2	3	0	0	0	0	0	0	1	0	0	.000	.000
Link Wasem	C2	R	26	2	1	0	0	0	0	0	0	0	0	0	.000	.000
Billy Urbanski (BN)		R	34	1	1	0	0	0	0	0	0	0	1	0	.000	.000

NAME	T	AGE	W	L	PCT	SV	G	GS	CG	IP	H	BB	SO	ShO	ERA
		31	79	73	.520	10	152	152	85	1359	1344	372	387	16	3.22
Lou Fette	R	30	20	10	.667	0	35	33	23	259	243	81	70	5	2.88
Jim Turner	R	33	20	11	.645	1	33	30	24	257	228	52	69	5	2.38
Danny MacFayden	R	32	14	14	.500	0	32	32	16	246	250	60	70	2	2.93
Guy Bush	R	35	8	15	.348	1	32	20	11	181	201	48	56	1	3.53
Johnny Lanning	R	26	5	7	.417	2	32	11	4	117	107	40	37	1	3.92
Ira Hutchinson	R	26	4	6	.400	0	31	8	1	92	99	35	29	0	3.72
2 Frank Gabler	R	25	4	7	.364	2	19	9	2	76	84	16	19	1	5.09
Milt Shoffner	L	31	3	1	.750	1	6	5	3	43	38	9	13	1	2.51
Roy Weir (SA)	L	26	1	1	.500	0	10	4	1	33	27	19	8	0	3.82
Bob Smith	R	39	0	1	.000	3	18	0	0	44	52	6	14	0	4.09
Bobby Reis	R	28	0	0	.000	0	4	0	0	5	3	5	0	0	1.80
Vic Frasier	R	32	0	0	.000	0	3	0	0	8	12	1	2	0	5.63

BROOKLYN 6th 62-91 .405 33.5 — BURLEIGH GRIMES

NAME	G by POS	B	AGE	G	AB	R	H	2B	3B	HR	RBI	BB	SO	SB	BA	SA
TOTALS			29	155	5295	616	1401	258	53	37	554	469	583	69	.265	.354
Buddy Hassett	1B131, OF7	L	25	137	556	71	169	31	6	1	53	20	19	13	.304	.387
Cookie Lavagetto	2B100, 3B45	R	24	149	503	64	142	26	6	8	70	74	41	13	.282	.406
Woody English	SS116, 2B11	R	30	129	378	45	90	16	2	1	42	65	55	4	.238	.299
Joe Stripp	3B66, 1B14, SS3	R	34	90	300	37	73	10	2	1	26	20	18	1	.243	.300
Heinie Manush	OF123	L	35	132	466	57	155	25	7	4	73	40	24	6	.333	.442
Johnny Cooney	OF111, 1B2	R	36	120	430	61	126	18	5	0	37	22	10	5	.293	.358
Gib Brack	OF101	R	29	112	372	60	102	27	9	5	38	44	93	9	.274	.435
Babe Phelps	C111	L	29	121	409	42	128	37	3	7	58	25	28	2	.313	.469
Jim Bucher	2B49, 3B43, OF6	L	26	125	380	44	96	11	2	4	37	20	18	5	.253	.324
Tom Winsett	OF101, PI	L	27	118	350	32	83	15	5	5	42	45	64	3	.237	.351
Roy Spencer	C45	R	37	51	117	5	24	2	2	0	4	8	17	0	.205	.256
Lindsay Brown	SS45	R	25	48	115	16	31	3	1	0	6	3	17	1	.270	.313
Eddie Wilson	OF21	L	27	36	54	11	12	4	1	1	8	17	14	1	.222	.389
Tony Malinosky	3B13, SS11	R	27	35	79	7	18	2	0	0	3	9	11	0	.228	.253
Eddie Morgan	1B7, OF7	L	22	31	48	4	9	3	0	0	5	9	7	0	.188	.250
Paul Chervinko	C26	R	26	30	48	1	7	0	1	0	2	3	16	0	.146	.188
Goody Rosen	OF21	L	24	22	77	10	24	5	1	0	6	6	6	2	.312	.403
George Cisar	OF13	R	24	20	29	8	6	0	0	0	4	2	6	3	.207	.207
Bert Haas	OF4, 1B3	R	23	16	25	2	10	3	0	0	2	1	1	0	.400	.520
Johnny Hudson	SS11, 2B1	R	25	13	27	3	5	4	0	0	2	3	9	0	.185	.333
1 Randy Moore	C10	L	32	13	22	3	3	1	0	0	2	3	2	0	.136	.182
Jake Daniel	1B7	L	25	12	27	3	5	1	0	0	3	3	4	0	.185	.222

Sid Gautreaux 25 B 1-10, Nick Polly 20 R 4-18, Art Parks 25 L 5-16, Elmer Klumpp 30 R 1-11, George Fallon 20 R 2-8

NAME	T	AGE	W	L	PCT	SV	G	GS	CG	IP	H	BB	SO	ShO	ERA
		30	62	91	.405	8	155	155	63	1363	1470	476	592	5	4.13
Luke Hamlin	R	32	11	13	.458	1	39	25	11	186	183	48	93	1	3.58
Max Butcher (JJ)	R	26	11	15	.423	0	39	24	8	192	203	75	57	1	4.27
Fred Frankhouse	R	33	10	13	.435	0	33	26	9	179	214	78	64	1	4.27
Van Lingle Mungo	R	26	9	11	.450	3	25	21	14	161	136	56	122	0	2.91
2 Waite Hoyte	R	37	7	7	.500	0	27	19	10	167	180	30	44	1	3.23
Roy Henshaw	L	25	5	12	.294	2	42	16	5	156	176	69	98	0	5.08
2 F. Fitzsimmons (BG)	R	35	4	8	.333	0	13	13	4	91	91	32	29	0	4.25
Harry Eisenstat	L	21	3	3	.500	0	13	4	0	48	61	11	12	0	3.94
Buck Marrow	R	27	1	2	.333	0	6	3	1	16	19	9	2	0	6.75
George Jeffcoat (IL)	R	23	1	3	.250	0	21	3	1	54	58	27	29	1	5.17
Jim Lindsey	R	39	0	1	.000	2	20	0	0	38	43	12	15	0	3.55
1 Tom Baker	R	24	0	1	.000	0	7	0	0	8	14	5	2	0	9.00
Ralph Birkofer	L	28	0	2	.000	0	11	1	0	30	45	9	9	0	6.60
2 Ben Cantwell	R	35	0	0	.000	0	13	0	0	27	32	8	12	0	4.67
Jim Peterson	R	28	0	0	.000	0	3	0	0	6	8	2	4	0	7.50
Watty Clark	L	35	0	0	.000	0	2	0	0	2	4	3	0	0	9.00
Tom Winsett	L	27	0	0	.000	0	1	0	0	1	3	2	0	0	18.00

PHILADELPHIA 7th 61-92 .399 34.5 — JIMMIE WILSON

NAME	G by POS	B	AGE	G	AB	R	H	2B	3B	HR	RBI	BB	SO	SB	BA	SA
TOTALS			28	154	5424	724	1482	258	37	103	668	478	640	66	.273	.391
Dolph Camilli	1B131	L	30	131	475	101	161	23	7	27	80	90	82	6	.339	.587
Del Young	2B108	B	25	109	360	36	70	9	2	0	24	18	55	6	.194	.231
George Scharein	SS146	R	22	146	511	44	123	20	1	0	57	36	47	13	.241	.284
Pinky Whitney	3B130	R	32	138	487	56	166	19	4	8	79	43	44	6	.341	.446
Chuck Klein	OF102	L	32	115	406	74	132	20	2	15	57	39	21	3	.325	.495
Hersh Martin	OF139	B	27	141	579	102	164	35	7	8	49	69	66	11	.283	.409
Morrie Arnovich	OF107	R	26	117	410	60	119	27	4	10	60	34	32	5	.290	.449
Bill Atwood	C80	R	25	87	279	27	68	15	1	2	32	30	27	3	.244	.326
Leo Norris	2B74, 3B24, SS20	R	29	116	381	45	98	24	3	9	36	21	53	3	.257	.407
Earl Brown	OF54, 1B32	L	26	105	332	42	97	19	3	6	52	21	41	4	.292	.422
Johnny Moore	OF72	L	35	96	307	46	98	16	2	9	59	18	18	2	.319	.472
Earl Grace	C64	L	30	80	223	19	47	10	1	6	29	33	15	0	.211	.345
Bucky Walters	P37, 3B8	R	28	56	137	15	38	6	0	1	16	5	16	1	.277	.343
Jimmie Wilson	C22, 1B2	R	36	39	87	15	24	3	0	1	8	6	4	1	.276	.345
Howie Gorman	OF7	L	24	13	19	3	4	1	0	0	1	1	1	1	.211	.263
Fred Tauby	OF7	R	31	11	20	2	0	0	0	0	3	0	5	1	.000	.000

Walter Stephenson 26 R 6-23, Gene Corbett 23 L 4-12, Bill Andrus 29 R 0-2

NAME	T	AGE	W	L	PCT	SV	G	GS	CG	IP	H	BB	SO	ShO	ERA
		28	61	92*	.399	15	154	154	59	1371	1629	501	529	6	5.06
Wayne LaMaster	L	30	15	19	.441	4	50	30	10	220	255	82	135	1	5.32
Bucky Walters	R	28	14	15	.483	0	37	34	15	246	292	86	87	3	4.76
Claude Passeau	R	28	14	18	.438	2	50	34	18	292	348	79	135	1	4.35
Hugh Mulcahy	R	23	8	18	.308	3	56	25	9	216	256	97	54	1	5.13
Syl Johnson	R	36	4	10	.286	3	32	15	4	138	155	22	46	0	5.02
Orville Jorgens	R	29	3	4	.429	3	52	11	1	141	159	68	34	0	4.40
Hal Kelleher	R	23	2	4	.333	0	27	2	1	58	72	31	20	0	6.67
Pete Sivess	R	23	1	1	.500	0	6	2	1	23	30	11	4	0	8.10
Bob Allen	R	22	0	1	.000	0	3	1	0	12	18	8	8	0	6.75
Leon Pettit	L	35	0	1	.000	0	3	1	0	4	6	4	0	0	11.25
Elmer Burkart	R	20	0	0	.000	0	7	0	0	16	20	9	4	0	6.19
Larry Crawford	L	23	0	0	.000	0	6	0	0	6	12	1	2	0	15.00
Bobby Burke	L	30	0	0	.000	0	2	0	0	0	1	2	0	0	∞
Walt Masters	R	30	0	0	.000	0	1	0	0	1	5	1	0	0	36.00

*1 loss by forfeit

CINCINNATI 8th 56-98 .364 40 — CHUCK DRESSEN 51-78 .342 — BOBBY WALLACE 5-20 .200

NAME	G by POS	B	AGE	G	AB	R	H	2B	3B	HR	RBI	BB	SO	SB	BA	SA
TOTALS			28	155	5230	612	1329	215	59	73	567	437	586	53	.254	.360
2 Buck Jordan	1B76	L	30	98	316	45	89	14	3	1	28	25	14	6	.282	.354
Alex Kampouris	2B146	R	24	146	458	62	114	21	4	17	71	60	65	2	.249	.424
Billy Myers	SS121, 2B6	R	26	124	335	35	84	13	3	7	43	44	57	0	.251	.370
Lew Riggs	3B100, 2B4, SS1	L	27	122	384	43	93	17	5	6	45	24	17	4	.242	.359
Ival Goodman	OF141	L	28	147	549	86	150	25	12	12	55	55	58	10	.273	.428
Chick Hafey	OF64	R	34	89	257	39	67	11	5	9	41	23	42	2	.261	.447
Kiki Cuyler	OF106	R	37	117	406	48	110	12	4	0	32	36	50	10	.271	.320
Ernie Lombardi	C90	R	29	120	368	41	123	22	1	9	59	14	17	1	.334	.473
Les Scarsella	1B65, OF14	L	23	110	329	35	81	11	4	3	34	17	26	5	.246	.331
Hub Walker	OF58, 2B3	L	30	78	221	33	55	9	4	1	19	34	24	7	.249	.339
Spud Davis	C59	R	32	76	209	19	56	10	1	3	33	23	15	0	.268	.368
1 Phil Weintraub	OF47	L	29	49	177	27	48	10	4	3	20	19	25	1	.271	.424
Jimmy Outlaw	3B41	R	24	49	165	18	45	7	3	0	11	3	31	2	.273	.352
1 Charlie Gelbert	SS37, 2B9, 3B1	R	31	43	114	12	22	4	0	1	13	15	12	1	.193	.254
2 Kiddo Davis	OF35	R	35	40	136	19	35	6	0	1	5	16	6	1	.257	.324
Eddie Miller	SS30, 3B4	R	20	36	60	3	9	3	1	0	5	3	8	0	.150	.233
Frank McCormick	1B20, 2B4, OF1	R	26	24	83	5	27	5	0	0	9	2	4	1	.325	.386
Charlie English	3B15, 2B2	R	27	17	63	1	15	3	1	0	4	0	2	0	.238	.317

Gilly Campbell 29 L 11-40, Double Joe Dwyer 33 L 3-11, Harry Craft 22 R 13-42, Dee Moore 23 R 1-13, Eddie Joost 21 R 1-12, Pinky Jorgensen 22 R 4-14, Dutch Mele 22 L 2-14, Arnie Moser 21 R 0-5, Gus Brittain 27 R 1-6, Harry Chozen 21 R 1-4

NAME	T	AGE	W	L	PCT	SV	G	GS	CG	IP	H	BB	SO	ShO	ERA
		28	56	98	.364	18	155	155	64	1358	1428	533	581	10	3.94
Lee Grissom	L	29	12	17	.414	6	50	30	14	224	193	93	149	5	3.25
Peaches Davis	R	32	11	13	.458	3	42	24	11	218	252	51	59	1	3.59
Paul Derringer	R	30	10	14	.417	1	43	26	12	223	240	55	94	1	4.04
Al Hollingsworth	L	29	9	15	.375	5	43	24	11	202	224	73	74	1	3.92
Gene Schott	R	23	4	13	.235	1	37	17	7	154	150	48	56	2	2.98
Johnny Vander Meer	L	22	3	5	.375	0	19	9	4	84	63	69	52	0	3.86
Wild Bill Hallahan	L	34	3	9	.250	0	21	9	2	63	90	29	18	0	6.14
1 Jumbo Brown	R	30	1	0	1.000	0	4	1	0	10	16	3	4	0	8.10
1 Don Brennan	R	33	1	1	.500	0	10	0	0	16	25	10	6	0	6.75
2 Joe Cascarella	R	30	1	2	.333	1	11	3	2	44	44	22	16	0	3.89
Ted Kleinhans	L	38	1	2	.333	0	7	3	1	27	29	12	13	0	2.33
Paul Gehrman	R	25	0	1	.000	0	2	1	0	9	11	5	1	0	3.00
Jake Mooty	R	24	0	3	.000	1	14	2	0	39	54	22	11	0	8.31
Whitey Moore	R	25	0	3	.000	0	13	6	0	39	32	39	27	0	4.85
Red Barrett	R	22	0	0	.000	0	1	0	0	6	5	2	1	0	1.50

WORLD SERIES – NEW YORK (AL) 4 NEW YORK (NL) 1

LINE SCORES

TEAM	1	2	3	4	5	6	7	8	9	10	11	12	R	H	E
Game 1 October 6 at Yankee Stadium															
NY (NL)	0	0	0	0	1	0	0	0	0				1	6	2
NY (AL)	0	0	0	0	0	7	0	1	X				8	7	0
Game 2 October 7 at Yankee Stadium															
NY (NL)	1	0	0	0	0	0	0	0	0				1	7	0
NY (AL)	0	0	0	0	2	4	2	0	X				8	12	0
Game 3 October 8 at Polo Grounds															
NY (AL)	0	1	2	1	1	0	0	0	0				5	9	0
NY (NL)	0	0	0	0	0	0	1	0	0				1	5	4
Game 4 October 9 at Polo Grounds															
NY (AL)	1	0	1	0	0	0	0	0	1				3	6	0
NY (NL)	0	6	0	0	0	0	1	0	X				7	12	3
Game 5 October 10 at Polo Grounds															
NY (AL)	0	1	1	0	2	0	0	0	0				4	8	0
NY (NL)	0	0	2	0	0	0	0	0	0				2	10	0

Game 1: **Hubbell**, Gumbert (6), Coffman (6), Smith (8) — **Gomez**

Game 2: **Melton**, Gumbert (5), Coffman (6) — **Ruffing**

Game 3: **Pearson**, Murphy (9) — **Schumacher**, Melton (7), Brennan (9)

Game 4: **Hadley**, Andrews (2), Wicker (8) — **Hubbell**

Game 5: **Gomez** — **Melton**, Smith (6), Brennan (8)

COMPOSITE BATTING

NAME	POS	G	AB	R	H	2B	3B	HR	RBI	BA
New York (AL) Totals		5	169	28	42	6	4	4	25	.249
DiMaggio	OF	5	22	2	6	0	0	1	4	.273
Crosetti	SS	5	21	2	1	0	0	0	0	.048
Hoag	OF	5	20	4	6	1	0	1	2	.300
Rolfe	3B	5	20	3	6	2	1	0	1	.300
Selkirk	OF	5	19	5	5	1	0	0	6	.263
Dickey	C	5	19	3	4	0	1	0	3	.211
Gehrig	1B	5	17	4	5	1	1	1	3	.294
Lazzeri	2B	5	15	3	6	0	1	1	2	.400
Gomez	P	2	6	2	1	0	0	0	1	.167
Ruffing	P	1	4	0	2	1	0	0	3	.500
Pearson	P	1	3	0	0	0	0	0	0	.000
Andrews	P	1	2	0	0	0	0	0	0	.000
Powell	PH	1	1	0	0	0	0	0	0	.000
Hadley	P	1	0	0	0	0	0	0	0	.000
Murphy	P	1	0	0	0	0	0	0	0	.000
Wicker	P	1	0	0	0	0	0	0	0	.000
New York (NL) Totals		5	169	12	40	6	0	1	12	.237
Moore	OF	5	23	1	9	1	0	0	1	.391
Bartell	SS	5	21	3	5	1	0	0	1	.238
Ott	3B	5	20	1	4	0	0	1	3	.200
McCarthy	1B	5	19	1	4	1	0	0	1	.211
Ripple	OF	5	17	2	5	0	0	0	0	.294
Whitehead	2B	5	16	1	4	2	0	0	0	.250
Danning	C	3	12	0	3	1	0	0	2	.250
Leiber	OF	3	11	2	4	0	0	0	2	.364
Mancuso	C	3	8	0	0	0	0	0	1	.000
Chiozza	OF	2	7	0	2	0	0	0	0	.286
Hubbell	P	2	6	1	0	0	0	0	1	.000
Berger	PH	3	3	0	0	0	0	0	0	.000
Melton	P	3	2	0	0	0	0	0	0	.000
Leslie	PH	2	1	0	0	0	0	0	0	.000
Coffman	P	2	1	0	0	0	0	0	0	.000
Ryan	PH	1	1	0	0	0	0	0	0	.000
Schumacher	P	1	1	0	0	0	0	0	0	.000
Brennan	P	2	0	0	0	0	0	0	0	.000
Gumbert	P	2	0	0	0	0	0	0	0	.000
Smith	P	2	0	0	0	0	0	0	0	.000

COMPOSITE PITCHING

NAME	G	IP	H	BB	SO	W	L	SV	ERA
New York (AL) Totals	5	44	40	11	21	4	1	1	2.45
Gomez	2	18	16	2	8	2	0	0	1.50
Ruffing	1	9	7	3	8	1	0	0	1.00
Pearson	1	8.2	5	2	4	1	0	0	1.04
Andrews	1	5.2	6	4	1	0	0	0	3.18
Hadley	1	1.1	6	0	0	0	1	0	33.75
Wicker	1	1	0	0	0	0	0	0	0.00
Murphy	1	.1	0	0	0	0	0	1	0.00
New York (NL) Totals	5	43	42	21	21	1	4	0	4.81
Hubbell	2	14.1	12	4	7	1	1	0	3.77
Melton	3	11	12	6	7	0	2	0	4.91
Schumacher	1	6	9	4	3	0	1	0	6.00
Coffman	2	4.1	2	5	1	0	0	0	4.15
Brennan	2	3	1	1	1	0	0	0	0.00
Smith	2	3	2	0	1	0	0	0	3.00
Gumbert	2	1.1	4	1	1	0	0	0	27.00

1938 The Struggle for Second Fiddle

The season, as so many others before it, consisted of winning spurts and losing streaks, as well as injuries, sore arms, bad breaks, an abundance of cheers and boos, new faces making good, and familiar and tried faces doing well enough to hang around for another year. Yet, when all the finery was cleared away, the 1938 season got down to seven games.

The highlights of the year included such grandeur and tragedy as Cincinnati's Johnny Vander Meer earning immortality with back-to-back no-hit performances, and Monty Stratton, the 26-year-old star of the White Sox pitching staff, blowing his leg off in a hunting accident after the season. The year also saw Brooklyn joining the night baseball scene, a $200,000 trade for a sore arm pitcher, and the fantastic return to form of the Red Sox's Jimmie Foxx—who went from a .285 batting average in 1937 to a league-leading .349 MVP performance. There was also Detroit's Hank Greenberg hitting 58 homers and the Reds' first baseman Frank McCormick who became the third modern player in his first full season to collect over 200 hits with his 209 tallies (Lloyd Waner turned the trick in 1927 with 223 and Johnny Frederick with 206 in 1929).

Injuries took their toll in both leagues and altered the outcome for several teams. The Giants' Carl Hubbell developed a sore arm and was shelved in August with a 13-10 record, losing his chance for a sixth straight 20-game season. Lefty Grove had 14 victories for the Red Sox when he was sidelined in mid-July, displaying a form which eventually earned him the American League's E.R.A. title with 3.07. The White Sox also suffered when Luke Appling broke his ankle in spring training and was lost for half the season and Clint Brown, their star reliever, chipped a bone in his pitching arm. Another victim of arm trouble was Cleveland's Johnny Allen, whose injury in the thick of the race finished whatever chance the Indians had for the pennant.

Of the seven games which capped the season, three took place between Pittsburgh and Chicago in late September to decide the National League pennant. Chicago, after replacing manager Charlie Grimm with catcher Gabby Hartnett, started a miraculous climb toward the Pirates and found themselves a game-and-a-half out when both clubs convened at Wrigley Field on September 27, for a three-game set. (The Giants and Reds had been eliminated two days before.)

Dizzy Dean, the sore arm pitcher for whom the Cubs paid the Cardinals $200,000, was picked to start the game—his first since August 20. Dean surprised everyone by lasting until two out in the ninth giving the Cubs and their 42,223 fans a 2-1 triumph. The next day Hartnett provided all the heroics in the ninth inning when, with two outs and darkness threatening to end the game, he hit a home run to break a 5-5 tie and put the Cubs in first place. On the 29th, the Cubs made it ten straight with a 10-1 win, which all but broke the back of the Pirates and earned them a final two-game pennant margin, capped by a sizzling finishing record of 21-4.

In the World Series, which made up those other four games of 1938, the Cubs welcomed the Yankees into Wrigley Field. Unlike the tough, senior circuit dogfight, New York easily won their third straight American League title by 9½ games over the Red Sox. In the first game the Cubs called on Bill Lee while the Yankees sent in their ace, 21-game winner Red Ruffing. With a brisk wind blowing in and preventing any home runs, the Yankees' infield sparkled and won, 3-1, on an attack paced by Bill Dickey's four singles. The next day, while the Yankees gave the nod to 18-game winner Lefty Gomez, the Cubs responded with sore-armed Dean who, mostly relying on pitching savvy and guts, took a 3-2 lead into the eight inning when he was greeted by a Frank Crosetti two-run homer. Joe DiMaggio applied the finishing touch in the ninth with another two-run shot which sent Dean out of the game and the Yankees to a final, 6-3 victory.

In the third game the action moved to New York where Joe Gordon provided most of the fireworks with a home run and bases-loaded single to give the Yankees a 5-2 victory. In the fourth and final game the Cubs used six pitchers to no avail as the Yankees scored eight times to sweep the Series and become the first team in baseball to win three straight world's championships.

1938 AMERICAN LEAGUE

NAME	G by POS	B	AGE	G	AB	R	H	2B	3B	HR	RBI	BB	SO	SB	BA	SA
NEW YORK 1st 99-53 .651	JOE McCARTHY															
TOTALS			28	157	5410	966	1480	283	63	174	917	749	616	91	.274	.446
Lou Gehrig	1B157	L	35	157	576	115	170	32	6	29	114	107	75	6	.295	.523
Joe Gordon	2B126	R	23	127	458	83	117	24	7	25	97	56	72	11	.255	.502
Frankie Crosetti	SS157	R	27	157	631	113	166	35	3	9	55	106	97	27	.263	.371
Red Rolfe	3B151	L	29	151	631	132	196	36	8	10	80	74	44	13	.311	.441
Tommy Henrich	OF130	L	25	131	471	109	127	24	7	22	91	92	32	6	.270	.490
Joe DiMaggio	OF145	R	23	145	599	129	194	32	13	32	140	59	21	6	.324	.581
George Selkirk	OF95	L	30	99	335	58	85	12	5	10	62	68	52	9	.254	.409
Bill Dickey	C126	L	31	132	454	84	142	27	4	27	115	75	22	3	.313	.568
Myril Hoag	OF70	R	30	85	267	28	74	14	3	0	48	25	31	4	.277	.352
Bill Knickerbocker	2B34, SS3	R	26	46	128	15	32	8	3	1	21	11	10	0	.250	.383
Jake Powell	OF43	R	29	45	164	27	42	12	1	2	20	15	20	3	.256	.378
Joe Glenn	C40	R	29	41	123	10	32	7	2	0	25	10	14	1	.260	.350
Babe Dahlgren	3B8, 1B6	R	26	27	43	8	8	1	0	0	1	1	7	0	.186	.209
Art Jorgens	C8	R	33	9	17	3	4	2	0	0	2	3	3	0	.235	.353
BOSTON 2nd 88-61 .591 9.5	JOE CRONIN															
TOTALS			28	150	5230	902	1566	298	56	98	860	650	463	55	.299	.434
Jimmie Foxx	1B149	R	30	149	565	139	197	33	9	50	175	119	76	5	.349	.704
Bobby Doerr	2B145	R	20	145	509	70	147	26	7	5	80	59	39	5	.289	.397
Joe Cronin	SS142	R	31	143	530	98	172	51	5	17	94	91	60	7	.325	.536
Pinky Higgins	3B138	R	29	139	524	77	159	29	5	5	106	71	55	10	.303	.406
Ben Chapman	OF126, 3B1	R	29	127	480	92	163	40	8	6	80	65	33	13	.340	.494
Doc Cramer	OF148, P1	L	32	148	658	116	198	36	8	0	71	51	19	4	.301	.380
Joe Vosmik	OF146	R	28	146	621	121	201	37	6	9	86	59	26	0	.324	.446
Gene Desautels	C108	R	31	108	333	47	97	16	2	2	48	57	31	1	.291	.369
Red Nonnenkamp	OF39, 1B5	L	26	87	180	37	51	4	1	0	18	21	13	6	.283	.317
Johnny Peacock	C57, 1B1, OF1	L	28	72	195	29	59	7	1	1	39	17	4	4	.303	.364
Erick McNair	SS15, 2B14, 3B3	R	29	46	96	9	15	1	1	0	7	3	6	0	.156	.188
Jim Tabor	3B11, SS2	R	24	19	57	8	18	3	2	1	8	1	6	0	.316	.491
Fabian Gaffke	OF2, C1	R	24	15	10	2	1	0	0	0	1	3	2	0	.100	.100
Moe Berg	C7, 1B1	R	36	10	12	0	4	0	0	0	0	0	1	0	.333	.333
CLEVELAND 3rd 86-66 .566 13	OSSIE VITT															
TOTALS			28	153	5356	847	1506	300	89	113	797	550	605	83	.281	.434
Hal Trosky	1B148	L	25	150	554	106	185	40	9	19	110	67	40	5	.334	.542
Odell Hale	2B127	R	29	130	496	69	138	32	2	8	69	44	39	8	.278	.399
Lyn Lary	SS141	R	32	141	568	94	152	36	4	3	51	88	65	23	.268	.361
Ken Keltner	3B149	R	21	149	576	86	159	31	9	26	113	33	75	4	.276	.497
Bruce Campbell	OF122	L	28	133	511	90	148	27	12	12	72	53	57	11	.290	.460
Earl Averill	OF131	L	36	134	482	101	159	27	15	14	93	81	48	5	.330	.535
Jeff Heath	OF122	L	23	126	502	104	172	31	18	21	112	33	55	3	.343	.602
Frankie Pytlak	C99	R	29	113	364	46	112	14	7	1	43	36	15	9	.308	.393
Roy Weatherly	OF55	L	23	83	210	32	55	14	3	2	18	14	14	8	.262	.386
Moose Solters	OF46	R	32	67	199	30	40	6	3	2	22	13	28	4	.201	.291
Rollie Hemsley	C58	R	31	66	203	27	60	11	3	2	28	23	14	1	.296	.409
John Kroner	2B31, 1B7, 3B3, SS1	R	29	51	117	13	29	16	0	1	17	19	6	0	.248	.410
Skeeter Webb	SS13, 3B3, 2B2	R	28	20	58	11	16	2	0	0	2	8	7	1	.276	.310
Hank Helf	C5	R	24	6	13	1	1	0	0	0	1	1	1	0	.077	.077
Oscar Grimes	2B2, 1B1	R	23	4	10	2	2	0	1	0	2	2	0	0	.200	.400
Tommy Irwin	SS3	R	25	3	9	1	1	0	0	0	0	3	1	0	.111	.111
Ray Mack	2B2	R	21	2	6	2	2	0	1	0	2	0	1	0	.333	.667
Lloyd Russell		R	25	2	0	0	0	0	0	0	0	0	0	0	.000	.000
Chuck Workman	OF1	L	23	2	5	1	2	0	0	0	0	0	0	0	.400	.400
Lou Boudreau	3B1	R	20	1	1	0	0	0	0	0	1	0	0	0	.000	.000

NAME	T	AGE	W	L	PCT	SV	G	GS	CG	IP	H	BB	SO	ShO	ERA
		30	99	53	.651	13	157	157	91	1382	1436	566	567	10	3.91
Red Ruffing	R	34	21	7	.750	0	31	31	22	247	246	82	127	3	3.32
Lefty Gomez	L	29	18	12	.600	0	32	32	20	239	239	99	129	3	3.35
Monte Pearson	R	28	16	7	.696	0	28	27	17	202	198	113	98	1	3.97
Spud Chandler	R	30	14	5	.737	0	23	23	14	172	183	47	36	2	4.03
Bump Hadley	R	33	9	8	.529	1	29	17	8	167	165	66	61	1	3.61
Johnny Murphy	R	29	8	2	.800	11	32	2	1	91	90	41	43	0	4.25
Steve Sundra	R	28	6	4	.600	0	25	8	3	94	107	43	33	0	4.79
Joe Beggs	R	27	3	2	.600	0	14	9	4	58	69	20	8	0	5.43
2 Wes Ferrell	R	30	2	2	.500	0	5	4	1	30	52	18	7	0	8.10
Ivy Andrews	R	31	1	3	.250	1	19	1	1	48	51	17	13	0	3.00
Kemp Wicker	L	31	1	0	1.000	0	1	0	0	1	0	1	0	0	0.00
Atley Donald	R	27	0	1	.000	0	2	2	0	12	7	14	6	0	5.25
Lee Stine	R	24	0	0	.000	0	4	0	0	9	9	1	4	0	1.00
Joe Vance	R	32	0	0	.000	0	3	1	0	11	20	4	2	0	7.36
		30	88	61	.591	15	150	150	67	1316	1472	528	484	10	4.46
Jim Bagby	R	21	15	11	.577	2	43	25	10	199	218	90	73	1	4.21
Jack Wilson	R	26	15	15	.500	1	37	27	11	195	200	91	96	3	4.29
Lefty Grove (SA)	L	38	14	4	.778	1	24	21	12	164	169	52	99	1	3.07
Fritz Ostermueller	L	30	13	5	.722	2	31	18	10	177	199	58	46	1	4.58
2 Joe Heving	R	37	8	1	.889	2	16	11	7	82	94	22	34	1	3.73
Archie McKain	L	27	5	4	.556	6	37	5	1	100	119	44	27	0	5.19
Emerson Dickman	R	23	5	5	.500	0	32	11	3	104	117	54	22	1	5.28
Bill Harris	R	38	5	5	.500	1	13	11	5	80	83	21	26	1	4.05
Johnny Marcum	R	28	5	6	.455	0	15	11	7	92	113	25	25	0	4.11
Dick Midkiff	R	23	1	1	.500	0	13	2	0	35	43	21	10	0	5.19
1 Lee Rogers	L	24	1	1	.500	0	14	2	0	28	32	18	7	0	6.43
Charlie Wagner	R	25	1	3	.250	0	13	6	1	37	47	24	14	0	8.27
Al Baker	R	32	0	0	.000	0	3	0	0	8	13	2	2	0	9.00
Doc Cramer	L	32	0	0	.000	0	1	0	0	4	3	3	1	0	4.50
Bill Humphrey	R	27	0	0	.000	0	2	0	0	2	5	1	0	0	9.00
Bill LeFebvre	L	22	0	0	.000	0	1	0	0	4	8	0	0	0	13.50
Ted Olson	R	25	0	0	.000	0	2	0	0	7	9	2	2	0	6.43
		28	86	66	.566	17	153	153	68	1353	1416	681	717	5	4.60
Bob Feller	R	19	17	11	.607	1	39	36	20	278	225	208	240	2	4.08
Mel Harder	R	28	17	10	.630	4	38	29	15	240	257	62	102	2	3.83
Johnny Allen (AJ)	R	33	14	8	.636	0	30	27	13	200	189	81	112	0	4.19
John Humphries	R	23	9	8	.529	6	45	6	1	103	105	63	56	0	5.24
Earl Whitehill	L	38	9	8	.529	0	26	23	4	160	187	83	60	0	5.57
Willis Hudlin	R	32	8	8	.500	1	29	15	8	127	158	45	27	0	4.89
Denny Galehouse	R	26	7	8	.467	3	36	12	5	114	119	65	66	1	4.34
Al Milnar	L	24	3	1	.750	1	23	5	2	68	90	26	29	0	5.03
1 Joe Heving	R	37	1	1	.500	0	3	0	0	6	10	5	0	0	9.00
Ken Jungels	R	22	1	0	1.000	0	9	0	0	15	21	18	7	0	9.00
Clay Smith	R	23	0	0	.000	0	4	0	0	11	18	2	3	0	6.55
Charley Suche	L	22	0	0	.000	0	1	0	0	1	4	3	1	0	36.00
Bill Zuber	R	25	0	3	.000	1	15	0	0	29	33	20	14	0	4.97

DETROIT 4th 84-70 .545 16 — MICKEY COCHRANE

NAME	G by POS	B	AGE	G	AB	R	H	2B	3B	HR	RBI	BB	SO	SB	BA	SA
TOTALS			28	155	5270	862	1434	219	52	137	804	695	581	76	.272	.411
Hank Greenberg	1B155	R	27	155	556	**144**	175	23	4	**58**	146	**119**	92	7	.315	.683
Charlie Gehringer	2B152	L	35	152	568	133	174	32	5	20	107	112	21	14	.306	.486
Billy Rogell	SS134	B	33	136	501	76	130	22	8	3	55	86	37	9	.259	.353
Don Ross	3B75	R	23	77	265	22	69	7	1	1	30	28	11	1	.260	.306
Pete Fox	OF154	R	28	155	634	91	186	35	10	7	96	31	39	16	.293	.413
Chet Morgan	OF74	L	28	74	306	50	87	6	1	0	27	20	12	5	.284	.310
Dixie Walker	OF114	L	27	127	454	84	140	27	6	6	43	65	32	5	.308	.434
Rudy York	C116, OF14, 1B1	R	24	135	463	85	138	27	2	33	127	92	74	1	.298	.579
Mark Christman	3B69, SS21	R	24	95	318	35	79	6	4	1	44	27	21	5	.248	.302
Jo-Jo White	OF55	L	29	78	206	40	54	6	1	0	15	29	15	3	.262	.301
Chet Laabs	OF53	R	26	64	211	26	50	7	3	7	37	15	52	3	.237	.398
Birdie Tebbetts	C53	R	28	53	143	16	42	6	2	1	25	12	13	1	.294	.385
Tony Piet	3B18, 2B1	R	31	41	80	9	17	6	0	0	14	15	11	2	.213	.288
Vern Kennedy	P33	L	31	37	79	10	23	3	0	0	8	1	11	0	.291	.329
Roy Cullenbine	OF17	B	22	25	67	12	19	1	3	0	9	12	9	2	.284	.388
1 Ray Hayworth	C7	R	34	8	19	1	4	0	0	0	5	3	4	1	.211	.211
Benny McKoy	2B6, 3B1	L	22	7	15	2	3	1	0	0	0	1	2	0	.200	.267
George Archie		R	24	3	2	0	0	0	0	0	0	0	1	0	.000	.000
Clyde Hatter (DD) 29																

NAME	T	AGE	W	L	PCT	SV	G	GS	CG	IP	H	BB	SO	ShO	ERA
		28	84	70	.545	11	155	155	75	1348	1532	608	435	2	4.79
Tommy Bridges	R	31	13	9	.591	1	25	20	13	151	171	58	101	0	4.59
George Gill	R	29	12	9	.571	0	24	23	13	164	195	50	30	1	4.12
Vern Kennedy (SA)	R	31	12	9	.571	2	33	26	11	190	215	113	53	0	5.07
Eldon Auker	R	27	11	10	.524	0	27	24	12	161	184	56	46	1	5.25
Harry Eisenstat	L	22	9	6	.600	4	32	9	5	125	131	29	37	0	3.74
Roxie Lawson	R	32	8	9	.471	1	27	16	5	127	154	82	39	0	5.46
Boots Poffenberger	R	23	6	7	.462	1	25	15	8	125	147	66	28	0	4.82
Al Benton	R	27	5	3	.625	0	19	10	6	95	93	39	33	0	3.32
Slick Coffman	R	27	4	4	.500	2	39	6	1	96	120	48	31	0	6.00
Jake Wade	L	26	3	2	.600	0	27	2	0	70	73	48	23	0	6.56
Bob Harris	R	22	1	0	1.000	0	3	1	1	10	14	4	7	0	7.20
Woody Davis	R	25	0	0	.000	0	2	0	0	6	3	4	1	0	1.50
Joe Rogalski	R	25	0	0	.000	0	2	0	0	7	12	2	4	0	2.57
Schoolboy Rowe (AJ)	R	28	0	2	.000	0	4	3	0	21	20	11	4	0	3.00

WASHINGTON 5th 75-76 .497 23.5 — BUCKY HARRIS

NAME	G by POS	B	AGE	G	AB	R	H	2B	3B	HR	RBI	BB	SO	SB	BA	SA
TOTALS			28	152	**5474**	814	**1602**	278	72	85	767	573	379	65	.293	.416
Zeke Bonura	1B129	R	29	137	540	72	156	27	3	22	114	44	29	2	.289	.472
Buddy Myer	2B121	L	34	127	437	79	147	22	8	6	71	93	32	9	.336	.465
Cecil Travis	SS143	L	24	146	567	96	190	30	5	5	67	58	22	6	.335	.432
Buddy Lewis	3B151	L	21	151	656	122	194	35	9	12	91	58	35	17	.296	.431
George Case	OF101	R	22	107	433	69	132	27	3	2	40	39	28	11	.305	.395
2 Sammy West	OF85	L	33	92	344	51	104	19	5	5	47	33	21	1	.302	.430
Al Simmons	OF117	R	36	125	470	79	142	23	6	21	95	30	40	2	.302	.511
Rick Ferrell	C131	R	32	135	411	55	120	24	5	1	58	75	17	1	.292	.382
Taffy Wright	OF60	L	26	100	263	37	92	18	10	2	36	13	17	1	.350	.517
Ossie Bluege	2B38, SS10, 1B1, 3B1	R	37	58	184	25	48	12	1	0	21	21	11	3	.261	.337
John Stone (IL)	OF53	L	32	56	213	24	52	12	4	3	28	30	16	2	.244	.380
Jimmy Wasdell	1B26, OF6	L	24	53	140	19	33	2	1	2	16	12	12	5	.236	.307
1 Mel Almada	OF47	L	25	47	197	24	48	7	4	1	15	8	16	4	.244	.335
Tony Giuliani	C46	R	25	46	115	10	25	4	0	0	15	8	3	1	.217	.252
Goose Goslin	OF13	L	37	38	57	6	9	3	0	2	8	8	5	0	.158	.316
Mickey Livingston	C2	R	23	2	4	0	3	2	0	0	1	0	1	0	.750	1.250

NAME	T	AGE	W	L	PCT	SV	G	GS	CG	IP	H	BB	SO	ShO	ERA
		30	75	76	.497	11	152	152	59	1360	1472	655	515	6	4.94
1 Wes Ferrell	R	30	13	8	.619	0	23	22	9	149	193	68	36	0	5.92
Dutch Leonard	R	29	12	15	.444	0	33	31	15	223	221	53	68	3	3.43
Ken Chase	L	24	9	10	.474	1	32	21	7	150	151	113	64	0	5.58
2 Harry Kelley	R	32	9	8	.529	1	38	14	7	148	162	46	44	2	4.50
Joe Krakauskas	L	23	7	5	.583	0	29	10	5	121	99	88	104	1	3.12
Monty Weaver	R	32	7	6	.538	0	31	18	7	139	157	74	43	0	5.24
Pete Appleton	R	34	7	9	.438	5	43	10	5	164	175	61	62	0	4.61
Jimmie DeShong	R	28	5	8	.385	0	31	14	1	131	160	83	41	0	6.60
Chief Hogsett	L	34	5	6	.455	3	31	9	1	91	107	36	33	0	6.03
Rene Monteagudo	L	22	1	1	.500	0	5	3	2	22	26	15	13	0	5.73
Joe Kohlman	R	25	0	0	.000	0	7	0	0	14	12	11	5	0	6.43
Bill Phebus	R	28	0	0	.000	1	5	0	0	6	9	7	2	0	12.00

CHICAGO 6th 65-83 .439 32 — JIMMY DYKES

NAME	G by POS	B	AGE	G	AB	R	H	2B	3B	HR	RBI	BB	SO	SB	BA	SA
TOTALS			31	149	5199	709	1439	239	55	67	657	514	489	56	.277	.383
Joe Kuhel	1B111	L	32	117	412	67	110	27	4	8	51	72	35	9	.267	.410
Jackie Hayes (KJ)	2B61	R	31	62	238	40	78	21	2	1	20	24	6	3	.328	.445
Luke Appling (BN)	SS78	R	31	81	294	41	89	14	0	0	44	42	17	1	.303	.350
Marv Owen	3B140	R	32	141	577	84	162	23	6	6	55	45	31	6	.281	.373
Hank Steinbacher	OF101	L	25	106	399	59	132	23	8	4	61	41	19	1	.331	.459
Mike Kreevich	OF127	R	30	129	489	73	145	26	12	6	73	55	23	13	.297	.436
Gee Walker	OF107	R	30	120	442	69	135	23	6	16	87	38	32	9	.305	.493
Luke Sewell	C65	R	37	65	211	23	45	4	1	0	27	20	20	0	.213	.242
Rip Radcliff	OF99, 1B23	L	32	129	503	64	166	23	6	5	81	36	17	5	.330	.429
Boze Berger	SS67, 2B42, 3B9	R	28	118	470	60	102	15	3	3	36	43	80	4	.217	.281
Larry Rosenthal	OF22	L	26	61	105	14	30	5	1	1	12	12	13	0	.286	.381
Tony Rensa	C57	R	36	59	165	15	41	5	0	3	19	25	16	1	.248	.333
Norm Schlueter	C34	R	21	35	118	11	27	5	1	0	7	4	15	1	.229	.288
Thornton Lee	P33	L	31	34	97	14	25	3	1	4	16	0	23	0	.258	.433
Jimmy Dykes	2B23, 3B1	R	41	26	89	9	27	4	2	2	13	10	8	0	.303	.461
Merv Connors	1B16	R	24	24	62	14	22	4	0	6	13	9	17	0	.355	.710
George Meyer	2B24	R	25	24	81	10	24	2	2	0	9	11	17	3	.296	.370
Tommy Thompson	1B1	L	28	19	18	2	2	0	0	0	2	1	2	0	.111	.111
Mike Tresh	C10	R	24	10	29	3	7	2	0	0	2	8	4	0	.241	.310
John Gerlach	SS8	R	21	9	25	2	7	0	0	0	1	4	2	0	.280	.280
Jesse Landrum	2B3	R	25	4	6	0	0	0	0	0	1	0	2	0	.000	.000
Joe Martin		R	26	1	0	0	0	0	0	0	0	0	0	0	.000	.000

NAME	T	AGE	W	L	PCT	SV	G	GS	CG	IP	H	BB	SO	ShO	ERA
		29	65	83	.439	9	149	149	83	1316	1449	550	432	5	4.36
Monty Stratton (LA)	R	26	15	9	.625	2	26	22	17	186	186	56	82	0	4.02
Thornton Lee	L	31	13	12	.520	1	33	30	18	245	252	94	77	1	3.49
John Whitehead	R	29	10	11	.476	2	32	24	10	183	218	80	38	1	4.77
Ted Lyons	R	37	9	11	.450	0	23	23	17	195	238	52	54	1	3.69
Johnny Rigney	R	23	9	9	.500	1	38	12	7	167	164	72	84	0	3.56
2 Jack Knott	R	31	5	10	.333	0	20	18	9	131	135	54	35	0	4.05
Bill Dietrich (AJ)	R	28	2	4	.333	0	8	7	1	48	49	31	11	0	5.44
Clint Brown (AJ)	R	34	1	3	.250	2	8	0	0	14	16	9	2	0	4.50
2 Frank Gabler	R	26	1	7	.125	0	18	7	3	69	101	34	17	0	9.13
Harry Boyles	R	26	0	4	.000	1	9	2	1	29	31	25	18	0	5.28
Sugar Cain	R	31	0	1	.000	0	5	3	0	20	26	18	6	0	4.50
1 Bill Cox	R	25	0	2	.000	0	7	1	0	12	11	13	5	0	6.75
Gene Ford	R	26	0	0	.000	0	4	0	0	14	21	12	2	0	10.29
George Gick	R	22	0	0	.000	0	1	0	0	1	0	1	0	0	0.00
Bob Uhle	L	24	0	0	.000	0	1	0	0	2	1	0	0	0	0.00

ST. LOUIS 7th 55-97 .362 44 — GABBY STREET

NAME	G by POS	B	AGE	G	AB	R	H	2B	3B	HR	RBI	BB	SO	SB	BA	SA
TOTALS			28	156	5333	755	1498	273	36	92	713	590	528	51	.281	.397
George McQuinn	1B148	L	29	148	602	100	195	42	7	12	82	58	49	4	.324	.477
Don Heffner	2B141	R	27	141	473	47	116	23	3	2	69	65	53	1	.245	.319
Red Kress	SS150	R	31	150	566	74	171	33	3	7	79	69	47	5	.302	.408
Harlond Clift	3B149	R	25	149	534	119	155	25	7	34	118	118	67	10	.290	.554
Beau Bell	OF132, 1B4	R	30	147	526	91	138	35	3	13	84	71	46	1	.262	.414
2 Mel Almada	OF101	L	25	102	436	77	149	22	2	3	37	38	22	9	.342	.422
Buster Mills	OF113	R	29	123	466	66	133	24	4	3	46	43	46	7	.285	.373
Billy Sullivan	C99, 1B6	R	27	111	375	35	104	16	1	7	49	20	10	8	.277	.381
Mike Mazzera	OF47	L	24	86	204	33	57	8	2	6	29	12	25	1	.279	.426
Tommy Heath	C65	R	24	70	194	22	44	13	0	2	22	35	24	0	.227	.325
Roy Hughes	2B21, 3B5, SS2	R	27	58	96	16	27	3	0	2	13	12	11	3	.281	.375
1 Sammy West	OF41	L	33	44	165	17	51	8	2	1	27	14	9	1	.309	.400
Glenn McQuillan	OF30	R	23	43	116	14	33	4	0	0	13	4	12	0	.284	.319
Ethan Allen	OF7	R	34	19	33	4	10	3	1	0	4	2	4	0	.303	.455
Joe Grace	OF12	L	24	12	47	7	16	1	0	0	4	2	3	0	.340	.362
Sam Harshany	C10	R	28	11	24	2	7	0	0	0	0	3	2	0	.292	.292
Sig Gryska	SS7	R	22	7	21	3	10	2	1	0	4	3	3	0	.476	.667
Johnny Lucadello	3B6	B	19	7	20	1	3	1	0	0	0	0	0	0	.150	.200

NAME	T	AGE	W	L	PCT	SV	G	GS	CG	IP	H	BB	SO	ShO	ERA
		29	55	97	.362	7	156	156	71	1345	**1584**	**737**	632	3	5.80
Bobo Newsom	R	30	20	16	.556	1	44	**40**	**31**	**330**	**334**	192	226	0	5.07
Lefty Mills	L	28	10	12	.455	0	30	27	15	210	216	116	134	1	5.31
Oral Hildebrand	R	31	8	10	.444	0	23	23	10	163	194	73	66	0	5.69
Russ VanAtta	L	32	4	7	.364	0	25	12	3	104	118	61	35	0	6.06
Fred Johnson	R	44	3	7	.300	3	17	6	3	69	91	27	24	0	5.61
Julio Bonetti	R	26	2	3	.400	0	17	0	0	28	41	13	7	0	6.43
Les Tietje	R	26	2	5	.286	0	17	8	2	62	83	38	15	1	7.55
Emil Bildilli	L	25	1	2	.333	0	5	3	2	22	33	11	11	0	6.95
Ed Cole	R	29	1	5	.167	3	36	6	1	89	116	48	26	0	5.16
2 Bill Cox	R	25	1	4	.200	0	22	7	1	63	81	35	16	0	7.00
1 Jack Knott	R	31	1	2	.333	0	7	4	0	30	35	15	8	0	4.80
Ed Linke	R	26	1	7	.125	0	21	2	0	40	60	33	18	0	7.88
Jim Walkup	R	28	1	12	.077	0	18	13	1	94	127	53	28	0	6.80
Harry Kimberlin	L	29	0	0	.000	0	1	1	1	8	8	3	1	0	3.38
Glenn Liebhardt	R	27	0	0	.000	0	2	0	0	3	4	0	1	0	6.00
1 Vito Tamulis	L	26	0	3	.000	0	3	2	0	15	26	10	11	0	7.80
Bill Trotter	R	29	0	1	.000	0	1	1	1	8	8	0	1	0	5.63
1 Jim Weaver	R	34	0	1	.000	0	1	1	0	7	9	9	4	0	9.00

PHILADELPHIA 8th 53-99 .349 46 — CONNIE MACK

NAME	G by POS	B	AGE	G	AB	R	H	2B	3B	HR	RBI	BB	SO	SB	BA	SA
TOTALS			26	154	5229	726	1410	243	62	98	686	605	590	65	.270	.396
Lou Finney	1B64, OF46	L	27	122	454	61	125	21	12	10	48	39	25	5	.275	.441
Dario Lodigiani	2B80	R	22	93	325	36	91	15	1	6	44	34	25	3	.280	.388
Wayne Ambler	SS116, 2B4	R	22	120	393	42	92	21	2	0	38	48	31	2	.234	.298
Bill Werber	3B134	R	30	134	499	92	129	22	7	11	69	93	37	19	.259	.397
Wally Moses	OF139	L	27	142	589	86	181	29	8	8	49	58	31	15	.307	.424
Bob Johnson	OF150, 2B3, 3B1	R	31	152	563	114	176	27	9	30	113	87	73	9	.313	.552
Sam Chapman	OF114	R	22	114	406	60	105	17	7	17	63	55	94	3	.259	.461
Frankie Hayes	C90	R	23	99	316	56	92	19	3	11	55	54	51	2	.291	.475
Lynn Nelson	P32	L	33	67	112	12	31	0	0	0	15	7	12	0	.277	.277
Stan Sperry	2B60	L	24	60	253	28	69	6	3	0	27	15	9	1	.273	.320
Ace Parker	SS26, 2B9, 3B9	R	26	56	113	12	26	5	0	0	12	10	16	1	.230	.274
Earle Brucker	C44, 1B1	R	37	53	171	26	64	21	1	3	35	19	16	1	.374	.561
2 Dick Siebert (KJ, AJ)	1B46	L	26	48	194	24	55	8	3	0	28	10	9	2	.284	.356
Mule Haas	OF12, 1B6	L	34	40	78	7	16	2	0	0	12	12	10	0	.205	.231
Hal Wagner	C30	L	22	33	88	10	20	2	1	0	8	8	9	0	.227	.273
Nick Etten	1B22	L	24	22	81	6	21	6	2	0	11	9	7	1	.259	.383
Gene Hasson	1B19	L	22	19	69	10	19	6	2	1	12	12	7	0	.275	.464
Skeeter Newsome (PB)	SS15	R	27	17	48	7	13	4	0	0	7	1	4	1	.271	.354
Chubby Dean	P6	L	22	16	20	3	6	2	0	0	1	1	4	0	.300	.400
Irv Bartling	SS13, 3B1	R	24	14	46	5	8	1	1	0	5	3	7	0	.174	.239
Babe Barna	OF7	L	23	9	30	4	4	0	0	0	2	3	5	0	.133	.133
Paul Easterling	OF1	R	32	4	7	1	2	0	0	0	0	1	2	0	.286	.286
Rusty Peters	SS2	R	23	2	7	0	0	0	0	0	0	0	1	0	.000	.000
Charlie Berry	C1	R	35	1	2	0	0	0	0	0	0	0	0	0	.000	.000

NAME	T	AGE	W	L	PCT	SV	G	GS	CG	IP	H	BB	SO	ShO	ERA
		26	53	**99**	.349	12	154	154	56	1324	1573	599	473	4	5.48
George Caster	R	30	16	**20**	.444	1	42	**40**	20	281	310	117	112	2	4.36
Lynn Nelson	R	33	10	11	.476	2	32	23	13	191	215	79	75	0	5.65
Buck Ross	R	23	9	16	.360	0	29	28	10	184	218	80	54	0	5.33
Bud Thomas	R	27	9	14	.391	0	42	29	7	212	259	62	48	0	4.92
Eddie Smith	L	24	3	10	.231	4	43	1	0	131	151	76	78	0	5.91
Chubby Dean	L	22	2	1	.667	0	6	1	0	23	22	15	3	0	3.52
Nels Potter	R	26	2	12	.143	5	35	9	4	111	139	49	43	0	6.49
Dave Smith	R	23	2	1	.667	0	21	0	0	44	50	28	13	0	5.11
Ralph Buxton	R	27	0	1	.000	0	5	0	0	9	12	5	9	0	5.00
Randy Gumpert	R	20	0	2	.000	0	4	2	0	12	24	10	1	0	11.25
1 Harry Kelley	R	32	0	2	.000	0	4	3	0	8	17	10	3	0	16.88
Jim Reninger	R	25	0	2	.000	0	4	4	1	23	28	14	9	0	7.04
Al Williams	R	24	0	7	.000	0	30	8	1	93	128	54	25	0	6.97

CHICAGO 1st 89-63 .586 — CHARLIE GRIMM 45-36 .556 GABBY HARTNETT 44-27 .620

NAME	G by POS	B	AGE	G	AB	R	H	2B	3B	HR	RBI	BB	SO	SB	BA	SA
TOTALS			29	154	5333	713	1435	242	70	65	673	522	476	49	.269	.377
Ripper Collins	1B135	B	34	143	490	78	131	22	8	13	61	54	48	1	.267	.424
Billy Herman	2B151	R	28	152	624	86	173	34	7	1	56	59	31	3	.277	.359
Billy Jurges	SS136	R	30	137	465	53	114	18	3	1	47	58	53	3	.245	.303
Stan Hack	3B152	L	28	152	609	109	195	34	11	4	67	94	39	**16**	.320	.432
Frank Demaree	OF125	R	28	129	476	63	130	15	7	8	62	45	34	1	.273	.384
Carl Reynolds	OF125	R	35	125	497	59	150	28	10	3	67	22	32	9	.302	.416
Augie Galan	OF103	B	26	110	395	52	113	16	9	6	69	49	17	8	.286	.418
Gabby Hartnett	C83	R	37	88	299	40	82	19	1	10	59	48	17	1	.274	.445
Phil Cavarretta	OF52, 1B28	L	21	92	268	29	64	11	4	1	28	14	27	4	.239	.321
Ken O'Dea	C71	L	25	86	247	22	65	12	1	3	33	12	18	1	.263	.356
Joe Marty	OF68	R	24	76	235	32	57	8	3	7	35	18	26	0	.243	.391
Tony Lazzeri	SS25, 3B7, 2B4, OF1	R	34	54	120	21	32	5	0	5	23	22	30	0	.267	.433
Bob Garbark	C20, 1B1	R	28	23	54	2	14	0	0	0	5	1	0	0	.259	.259
Jim Asbell	OF10	R	24	17	33	6	6	2	0	0	3	3	9	0	.182	.242
Coaker Triplett	OF9	R	26	12	36	4	9	2	1	0	2	0	1	0	.250	.361
Steve Mesner	SS1	R	20	2	4	2	1	0	0	0	0	1	1	0	.250	.250
Bobby Mattick	SS1	R	22	1	1	0	1	0	0	0	0	1	0	0	1.000	1.000

NAME	T	AGE	W	L	PCT	SV	G	GS	CG	IP	H	BB	SO	ShO	ERA
		31	**89**	63	**586**	**18**	154	154	67	**1397**	1414	454	**583**	**16**	**3.37**
Bill Lee	R	28	**22**	9	**.710**	2	44	**37**	19	291	281	74	121	**9**	**2.66**
Clay Bryant	R	26	19	11	.633	2	44	30	17	270	235	**125**	**135**	3	3.10
Tex Carleton	R	31	10	9	.526	0	33	24	9	168	213	74	80	0	5.41
Larry French	L	30	10	19	.345	0	43	27	10	201	210	62	83	3	3.81
Charlie Root	R	39	8	7	.533	8	44	11	5	161	163	30	70	0	2.85
Dizzy Dean (AJ)	R	27	7	1	.875	0	13	10	3	75	63	8	22	1	1.80
Jack Russell	R	32	6	1	.857	3	42	0	0	102	100	30	29	0	3.35
Vance Page	R	34	5	4	.556	1	13	9	3	68	90	13	18	0	3.84
Al Epperly	R	20	2	0	1.000	0	9	4	1	27	28	15	10	0	3.67
Kirby Higbe	R	23	0	0	.000	0	2	2	0	10	10	6	4	0	5.40
Newt Kimball	R	23	0	0	.000	0	1	0	0	1	3	1	1	0	9.00
Bob Logan	L	28	0	2	.000	2	14	0	0	23	18	17	10	0	2.74

PITTSBURGH 2nd 86-64 .573 2 — PIE TRAYNOR

NAME	G by POS	B	AGE	G	AB	R	H	2B	3B	HR	RBI	BB	SO	SB	BA	SA
TOTALS			30	152	5422	707	1511	265	66	65	659	485	409	47	.279	.388
Gus Suhr	1B145	L	32	145	530	82	156	35	14	3	64	87	37	4	.294	.430
Pep Young	2B149	R	30	149	562	58	156	36	5	4	79	40	64	7	.278	.381
Arky Vaughan	SS147	L	26	148	541	88	174	35	5	7	68	104	21	14	.322	.444
Lee Handley	3B136	R	24	139	570	91	153	25	8	6	51	53	31	7	.268	.372
Paul Waner	OF147	L	35	148	625	77	175	31	6	6	69	47	28	2	.280	.378
Lloyd Waner	OF144	L	32	147	619	79	194	25	7	5	57	28	11	5	.313	.401
Johnny Rizzo	OF140	R	25	143	555	97	167	31	9	23	111	54	61	1	.301	.514
Al Todd	C132	R	34	133	491	52	130	19	7	7	75	18	31	2	.265	.375
Woody Jensen	OF38	L	30	68	125	12	25	4	0	0	10	1	3	0	.200	.232
Bill Brubaker	3B18, 1B9, SS3, OF1	R	27	45	112	18	33	5	0	3	19	9	14	2	.295	.420
Ray Berres	C40	R	30	40	100	7	23	2	0	0	6	8	10	0	.230	.250
Red Lucas	P13	L	36	33	46	1	5	0	0	0	2	3	2	0	.109	.109
Johnny Dickshot	OF10	R	28	29	35	3	8	0	0	0	4	8	5	3	.229	.229
2 Heinie Manush		L	36	15	13	2	4	1	1	0	4	2	0	0	.308	.538
Tommy Thevenow	2B9, SS4, 3B1	R	34	15	25	2	5	0	0	0	2	4	0	0	.200	.200

NAME	T	AGE	W	L	PCT	SV	G	GS	CG	IP	H	BB	SO	ShO	ERA
		29	86	64	.573	15	152	152	57	1380	1406	432	557	8	3.46
Mace Brown	R	29	15	9	.625	5	**51**	2	0	133	155	44	55	0	3.79
Jim Tobin	R	25	14	12	.538	0	40	33	14	241	254	66	70	2	3.47
Russ Bauers	R	24	13	14	.481	3	40	34	12	243	207	99	117	3	3.07
Bob Klinger	R	30	12	5	.706	1	28	21	10	159	152	42	58	1	3.00
Cy Blanton	R	29	11	7	.611	0	29	25	10	173	190	46	80	1	[illegible]
Bill Swift	R	30	7	5	.583	4	36	9	2	150	155	40	77	0	3.24
Red Lucas	R	36	6	3	.667	0	13	13	4	84	90	16	19	0	3.54
Ed Brandt	L	33	5	4	.556	0	24	14	5	96	93	35	38	1	3.47
Joe Bowman (SA)	R	28	3	4	.429	1	17	1	0	60	68	20	25	0	4.65
Ken Heintzelman	L	22	0	0	.000	0	1	0	0	2	1	3	1	0	9.00
Rip Sewell	R	31	0	1	.000	1	17	0	0	38	41	21	17	0	4.26

NEW YORK 3rd 83-67 .553 5 — BILL TERRY

NAME	G by POS	B	AGE	G	AB	R	H	2B	3B	HR	RBI	BB	SO	SB	BA	SA
TOTALS			28	152	5255	705	1424	210	36	**125**	672	465	528	31	.271	.396
Johnny McCarthy	1B125	L	28	134	470	55	128	13	4	8	59	39	28	3	.272	.368
2 Alex Kampouris	2B79	R	25	82	268	35	66	9	1	5	37	27	50	0	.246	.343
Dick Bartell	SS127	R	30	127	481	67	126	26	1	9	49	55	60	4	.262	.376
Mel Ott	3B113, OF37	L	29	150	527	**116**	164	23	6	**36**	116	118	47	2	.311	.583
Jimmy Ripple	OF131	L	28	134	501	68	131	21	3	10	60	49	21	2	.261	.375
Hank Leiber	OF89	R	27	98	360	50	97	18	4	12	65	31	45	0	.269	.442
Jo-Jo Moore	OF114	L	29	125	506	76	153	23	6	11	56	22	27	2	.302	.437
Harry Danning	C114	R	26	120	448	59	137	26	3	9	60	23	40	1	.306	.438
Bob Seeds	OF76	R	31	81	296	35	86	12	3	9	52	20	33	0	.291	.443
Sam Leslie	1B32	L	32	76	154	12	39	7	1	1	16	11	6	0	.253	.331
Lou Chiozza (BL)	2B34, OF16, 3B1	L	28	57	179	15	42	7	2	3	17	12	7	5	.235	.346
Gus Mancuso	C44	R	32	52	158	19	55	8	0	2	15	17	13	0	.348	.437
George Myatt	SS24, 3B19	L	24	43	170	27	52	2	1	3	10	14	13	10	.306	.382
Bill Cissell	2B33, 3B6	R	34	38	149	19	40	6	0	2	18	6	11	1	.268	.349
Mickey Haslin	3B15, 2B13	R	27	31	102	13	33	3	0	3	15	4	4	0	.324	.441
1 Wally Berger	OF9	R	32	16	32	5	6	0	0	0	4	2	4	0	.188	.188
Blondy Ryan	2B5, 3B3, SS2	R	32	12	24	1	5	0	0	0	0	1	3	0	.208	.208
Les Powers		L	25	2	3	0	0	0	0	0	0	0	1	0	.000	.000
Burgess Whitehead (IL) 28																

NAME	T	AGE	W	L	PCT	SV	G	GS	CG	IP	H	BB	SO	ShO	ERA
		28	83	67	.553	**18**	152	152	59	1349	1370	389	497	8	3.62
Harry Gumbert	R	28	15	13	.536	0	38	33	14	236	238	84	84	0	4.00
Cliff Melton	L	26	14	14	.500	0	36	31	10	243	266	61	101	1	3.89
Carl Hubbell (SA)	L	35	13	10	.565	1	24	22	13	179	171	33	104	1	3.07
Hal Schumacher	R	27	13	8	.619	0	28	28	12	185	178	50	54	4	3.50
Bill Lohrman	R	25	9	6	.600	0	31	14	3	152	152	33	52	0	3.32
Dick Coffman	R	31	8	4	.667	**12**	**51**	3	1	111	116	21	21	1	3.49
Jumbo Brown	R	31	5	3	.625	5	43	0	0	90	65	28	42	0	1.80
Slick Castleman	R	24	4	5	.444	0	21	14	4	91	108	37	18	0	4.15
Johnnie Wittig	R	24	2	3	.400	0	13	6	2	39	41	26	14	0	4.85
Tom Baker	R	25	0	0	.000	0	2	0	0	4	5	3	0	0	6.75
Oscar Georgy	R	31	0	0	.000	0	1	0	0	1	2	1	0	0	18.00
Hy Vandenberg	R	31	0	1	.000	0	6	1	0	18	28	12	7	0	7.50

CINCINNATI 4th 82-68 .547 6 — BILL McKECHNIE

NAME	G by POS	B	AGE	G	AB	R	H	2B	3B	HR	RBI	BB	SO	SB	BA	SA
TOTALS			28	151	5391	723	1495	251	57	110	679	366	518	19	.277	.406
Frank McCormick	1B151	R	27	151	**640**	89	**209**	40	4	5	106	18	17	1	.327	.425
Lonny Frey	2B121, SS3	B	27	124	501	76	133	26	6	4	36	49	50	4	.265	.365
Billy Myers	SS123, 2B11	R	27	134	442	57	112	18	6	12	47	41	80	2	.253	.403
Lew Riggs	3B142	L	28	142	531	53	134	21	13	2	55	40	28	3	.252	.352
Ival Goodman	OF142	L	29	145	568	103	166	27	10	30	92	53	51	3	.292	.533
Harry Craft	OF151	R	23	151	612	70	165	28	9	15	83	29	46	3	.270	.418
2 Wally Berger	OF98	R	32	99	407	74	125	23	4	16	56	29	44	2	.307	.501
Ernie Lombardi	C123	R	30	129	489	60	167	30	1	19	95	40	14	0	**.342**	.524
Dusty Cooke	OF51	L	31	82	233	41	64	15	1	2	33	28	36	0	.275	.373
Lee Gamble	OF9	L	28	53	75	13	24	3	1	0	5	0	6	0	.320	.387
Willard Hershberger	C39, 2B1	R	**28**	49	105	12	29	3	1	0	12	5	6	1	.276	.324
Nolen Richardson	SS35	R	35	35	100	8	29	4	0	0	10	3	4	0	.290	.330
1 Alex Kampouris	2B21	R	25	21	74	13	19	1	0	2	7	10	13	0	.257	.351
Don Lang	3B15, 2B1, SS1	R	23	21	50	5	13	3	1	1	11	2	7	0	.260	.420
1 Spud Davis	C11	R	33	12	36	3	6	1	0	0	1	5	6	0	.167	.194
2 Justin Stein	SS7, 2B2	R	26	11	18	3	6	1	0	0	1	0	1	0	.333	.389
1 Buck Jordan		L	31	9	7	0	2	0	0	0	0	2	0	0	.286	.286
Kiddo Davis	OF5	R	36	5	18	3	5	1	0	0	0	1	4	0	.278	.333
Jimmy Outlaw		R	25	4	0	1	0	0	0	0	0	0	0	0	.000	.000
Nino Bongiovanni	OF2	L	26	2	7	0	2	1	0	0	0	0	0	0	.286	.429
Dick West		R	22	1	1	0	0	0	0	0	0	0	0	0	.000	.000

NAME	T	AGE	W	L	PCT	SV	G	GS	CG	IP	H	BB	SO	ShO	ERA
		29	82	68	.547	16	151	151	72	1362	1329	463	542	11	3.62
Paul Derringer	R	31	21	14	.600	3	41	**37**	**26**	**307**	**315**	49	132	4	2.93
Johnny Vander Meer	L	23	15	10	.600	0	32	29	16	225	177	103	125	3	3.12
2 Bucky Walters	R	29	11	6	.647	1	27	22	11	168	168	66	65	2	3.70
Peaches Davis	R	33	7	12	.368	1	29	19	11	168	193	40	28	1	3.96
Whitey Moore	R	26	6	4	.600	0	19	11	3	90	66	42	38	1	3.50
2 Jim Weaver	R	34	6	4	.600	3	30	15	2	129	109	54	64	0	3.14
Gene Schott	R	24	5	5	.500	2	31	4	0	83	89	32	21	0	4.45
Joe Cascarella	R	31	4	7	.364	4	33	1	0	61	66	22	30	0	4.57
Red Barrett	R	23	2	0	1.000	0	6	2	2	29	28	15	5	0	3.10
Lee Grissom (KJ)	L	30	2	3	.400	0	14	7	0	51	60	22	16	0	5.29
1 Al Hollingsworth	L	30	2	2	.500	0	9	4	1	34	43	12	13	0	7.15
Ray Benge	R	36	1	1	.500	2	9	0	0	15	13	6	5	0	4.20
Ted Kleinhans	L	39	0	0	.000	0	1	0	0	1	2	0	0	0	9.00

BOSTON 5th 77-75 .507 12 — CASEY STENGEL

NAME	G by POS	B	AGE	G	AB	R	H	2B	3B	HR	RBI	BB	SO	SB	BA	SA
TOTALS			29	153	5250	561	1311	199	39	54	519	424	548	49	.250	.333
Elbie Fletcher	1B146	L	22	147	529	71	144	24	7	6	48	60	40	5	.272	.378
Tony Cuccinello	2B147	R	30	147	555	62	147	25	2	9	76	52	32	4	.265	.366
Rabbit Warstler	SS135, 2B7	R	34	142	467	37	108	10	4	0	40	48	38	3	.231	.270
2 Joe Stripp	3B58	R	35	59	229	19	63	10	0	1	19	10	7	2	.275	.332
Johnny Cooney	OF110, 1B13	R	37	120	432	45	117	25	5	0	17	22	12	2	.271	.352
Vince DiMaggio	OF149, 2B1	R	25	150	540	71	123	28	3	14	61	65	**134**	11	.228	.369
Max West	OF109, 1B7	L	21	123	418	47	98	16	5	10	63	38	38	5	.234	.368
Ray Mueller	C75	R	26	83	274	23	65	8	6	4	35	16	28	3	.237	.354
Debs Garms	OF63, 3B54, 2B1	L	30	117	428	62	135	19	1	0	47	34	22	4	.315	.364
Al Lopez	C71	R	29	71	236	19	63	6	1	1	14	11	24	5	.267	.314
Harl Maggert	OF10, 3B8	R	24	66	89	12	25	3	0	3	19	10	20	0	.281	.416
Gene Moore	OF47	R	28	54	180	27	49	8	3	3	19	16	20	1	.272	.400
Gil English	3B43, OF3, 2B2, SS2	R	28	53	165	17	41	6	0	2	21	15	16	1	.248	.321
Bobby Reis	P16, OF10, SS3, 2B1, C1	R	29	34	49	6	9	0	0	0	4	1	3	1	.184	.184
Jim Hitchcock	SS24, 3B2	R	27	28	76	2	13	0	0	0	7	2	11	1	.171	.171
Johnny Riddle	C19	R	32	19	57	6	16	1	0	0	2	4	2	0	.281	.298
Bob Kahle		R	22	8	3	2	1	0	0	0	0	0	0	0	.333	.333
Eddie Mayo	3B6, SS2	L	28	8	14	2	3	0	0	1	4	1	0	0	.214	.429
Roy Johnson	OF7	L	35	7	29	2	5	0	0	0	1	1	5	1	.172	.172
Ralph McLeod	OF1	L	21	6	7	1	2	1	0	0	0	0	2	0	.286	.429
Butch Sutcliffe	C3	R	22	4	4	1	1	0	0	0	2	2	1	0	.250	.250
Joe Walsh	SS4	R	21	4	8	0	0	0	0	0	0	0	2	0	.000	.000
Tom Kane	2B2	R	31	2	2	0	0	0	0	0	0	2	0	0	.000	.000

NAME	T	AGE	W	L	PCT	SV	G	GS	CG	IP	H	BB	SO	ShO	ERA
		30	77	75	.507	12	153	153	**83**	1380	1375	465	413	15	3.40
Danny MacFayden	R	33	14	9	.609	0	29	29	19	220	208	64	58	5	2.95
Jim Turner	R	34	14	18	.438	0	35	34	22	268	267	54	71	3	3.46
Lou Fette	R	31	11	13	.458	1	33	32	17	240	235	79	83	3	3.15
Dick Errickson	R	24	9	7	.563	6	34	10	6	123	113	56	40	1	3.15
Ira Hutchinson	R	27	9	8	.529	4	36	12	4	151	150	61	38	1	2.74
Johnny Lanning	R	27	8	7	.533	0	32	18	4	138	146	52	39	1	3.72
Milt Shoffner	L	32	8	7	.533	1	26	15	9	140	147	36	49	1	3.54
Tom Earley	R	**21**	1	0	1.000	0	2	1	1	11	8	1	4	0	3.27
Johnny Niggerling	R	34	1	0	1.000	0	2	0	0	2	4	1	1	0	9.00
Bobby Reis	R	29	1	6	.143	0	16	2	1	58	61	41	20	0	4.97
Roy Weir	L	27	1	0	1.000	0	5	0	0	13	14	6	3	0	6.92
Mike Balas	R	28	0	0	.000	0	1	0	0	1	3	0	0	0	9.00
Art Doll	R	26	0	0	.000	0	3	0	0	4	4	3	1	0	2.25
1 Frank Gabler	R	26	0	0	.000	0	1	0	0	.1	3	1	0	0	81.00
Art Kenney	L	22	0	0	.000	0	2	0	0	2	3	8	2	0	18.00
Hiker Moran	R	26	0	0	.000	0	1	0	0	3	1	1	0	0	0.00
2 Tommy Reis	R	23	0	0	.000	0	4	0	0	6	8	1	4	0	7.50

ST. LOUIS 6th 71-80 .470 17.5 — FRANKIE FRISCH 62-72 .463 MIKE GONZALEZ 9-8 .529

NAME	G by POS	B	AGE	G	AB	R	H	2B	3B	HR	RBI	BB	SO	SB	BA	SA
TOTALS			26	156	5528	725	1542	288	74	91	680	412	492	55	.279	.407
Johnny Mize	1B140	L	25	149	531	85	179	34	16	27	102	74	47	0	.337	.614
Stu Martin	2B99	L	24	114	417	54	116	26	2	1	27	30	28	4	.278	.357
Lynn Myers	SS69	R	24	70	227	18	55	10	2	1	19	9	25	9	.242	.317
Don Gutteridge	3B73, SS68	R	26	142	552	61	141	21	15	9	64	29	49	14	.255	.397
Enos Slaughter	OF92	L	22	112	395	59	109	20	10	8	58	32	38	1	.276	.438
Terry Moore	OF75, 3B6	R	26	94	312	49	85	21	3	4	21	46	19	9	.272	.397
Joe Medwick	OF144	R	26	146	590	100	190	47	8	21	122	42	41	0	.322	.536
Mickey Owen	C116	R	22	122	397	45	106	25	2	4	36	32	14	2	.267	.370
Don Padgett	OF71, 1B16, C6	L	26	110	388	59	105	26	5	8	65	18	28	0	.271	.425
Jimmy Brown	2B49, SS30, 3B24	B	28	108	382	50	115	12	6	0	38	27	9	7	.301	.364
Pepper Martin	OF62, 3B4	R	34	91	269	34	79	18	2	2	38	18	34	4	.294	.398
Frenchy Bordagaray	OF29, 3B4	R	26	81	156	19	44	5	1	0	21	8	9	2	.282	.327
1 Joe Stripp	3B51	R	35	54	199	24	57	7	0	0	18	18	10	0	.286	.322
Herb Bremer	C50	R	24	50	151	14	33	5	1	2	14	9	36	1	.219	.305
Lon Warneke	P31	R	29	31	71	5	23	3	0	0	6	2	7	0	.324	.366
Jim Bucher	2B14, 3B1	L	27	17	57	7	13	3	1	0	7	2	2	0	.228	.316
Hal Epps	OF10	L	24	17	50	8	15	0	0	1	3	2	4	2	.300	.360
Creepy Crespi	SS7	R	20	7	19	2	5	2	0	0	1	2	7	0	.263	.368
1 Tuck Stainback	OF2	R	27	6	10	2	0	0	0	0	0	0	3	0	.000	.000
1 Dick Siebert		L	26	1	1	1	0	0	0	0	0	0	0	0	1.000	1.000

Bill DeLancey (IL) 26

NAME	T	AGE	W	L	PCT	SV	G	GS	CG	IP	H	BB	SO	ShO	ERA
TOTALS		27	71	80	.470	16	156	156	58	1384	1482	474	534	10	3.84
Bob Weiland	L	32	16	11	.593	1	35	29	11	228	248	67	117	1	3.59
Lon Warneke	R	29	13	8	.619	0	31	26	12	197	199	64	89	4	3.97
Curt Davis	R	34	12	8	.600	3	40	21	8	173	187	27	36	2	3.64
Bill McGee	R	28	7	12	.368	5	47	25	10	216	216	78	104	1	3.21
Clyde Shoun	L	26	6	6	.500	1	40	12	3	117	130	43	37	0	4.15
Roy Henshaw	L	26	5	11	.313	0	27	15	4	130	132	48	34	0	4.02
Max Macon	L	22	4	11	.267	2	38	12	5	129	133	61	39	1	4.12
Paul Dean	R	24	3	1	.750	0	5	4	2	31	37	5	14	1	2.61
Mort Cooper	R	25	2	1	.667	1	4	3	1	24	17	12	11	0	3.00
Ray Harrell	R	26	2	3	.400	2	32	3	1	63	78	29	32	0	4.86
Mike Ryba	R	35	1	1	.500	0	3	0	0	5	8	1	0	0	5.40
Guy Bush	R	36	0	1	.000	1	6	0	0	6	6	3	1	0	4.50
Si Johnson	R	31	0	3	.000	0	6	3	0	16	27	6	4	0	7.31
Howie Krist	R	22	0	0	.000	0	2	0	0	1	1	0	1	0	0.00
Max Lanier	L	22	0	3	.000	0	18	3	1	45	57	28	14	0	4.20
Preacher Roe	L	23	0	0	.000	0	1	0	0	3	6	2	1	0	12.00

BROOKLYN 7th 69-80 .463 17.5 — BURLEIGH GRIMES

NAME	G by POS	B	AGE	G	AB	R	H	2B	3B	HR	RBI	BB	SO	SB	BA	SA
TOTALS			29	151	5142	704	1322	225	79	61	647	611	615	66	.257	.367
Dolph Camilli	1B145	L	31	146	509	106	128	25	11	24	100	119	101	6	.251	.485
Johnny Hudson	2B132, SS3	R	26	135	498	59	130	21	5	2	37	39	76	7	.261	.335
Leo Durocher	SS141	R	32	141	479	41	105	18	5	1	56	47	30	3	.219	.284
Cookie Lavagetto	3B132, 2B4	R	25	137	487	68	133	34	6	6	79	68	31	15	.273	.405
Goody Rosen	OF113	L	25	138	473	75	133	17	11	4	51	66	43	0	.281	.389
Ernie Koy	OF135, 3B1	R	28	142	521	78	156	29	13	11	76	38	76	15	.299	.468
Buddy Hassett	OF71, 1B8	L	26	115	335	49	98	11	6	0	40	32	19	3	.293	.361
Babe Phelps	C55	L	30	66	208	33	64	12	2	5	46	23	15	2	.308	.457
Kiki Cuyler	OF68	R	38	82	253	45	69	10	8	2	23	34	23	6	.273	.399
Gilly Campbell	C44	L	30	54	126	10	31	5	0	0	11	19	9	0	.246	.286
Merv Shea	C47	R	37	48	120	14	22	5	0	0	12	28	20	1	.183	.225
1 Gib Brack	OF13	R	30	40	56	10	12	2	1	1	6	4	14	1	.214	.339
3 Tuck Stainback	OF23	R	27	35	104	15	34	6	3	0	20	2	4	1	.327	.442
Woody English	3B21, 2B3, SS3	R	31	34	72	9	18	2	0	0	7	8	11	2	.250	.278
Pete Coscarart	2B27	R	25	32	79	10	12	3	0	0	6	9	18	0	.152	.190
Packy Rogers	SS9, 3B8, 2B3, OF1	R	25	23	37	3	7	1	1	0	5	6	6	0	.189	.270
Oris Hockett	OF17	L	28	21	70	8	23	5	1	1	8	4	9	0	.329	.471
Woody Williams	SS18, 3B1	R	25	20	51	6	17	1	1	0	6	4	1	1	.333	.392

1 Heinie Manush 36 L 12-51, Fred Sington 28 R 19-53, Roy Spencer 38 R 12-45, Paul Chervinko 27 R 4-27, Tom Winsett 28 L 9-30
Greek George 25 R 4-20, 2 Ray Hayworth 34 R 0-4, Bert Haas 24 R 0-0, Ray Thomas 25 R 1-3

NAME	T	AGE	W	L	PCT	SV	G	GS	CG	IP	H	BB	SO	ShO	ERA
TOTALS		30	69	80	.463	14	151	151	56	1332	1464	446	469	12	4.07
Luke Hamlin	R	33	12	15	.444	6	44	30	10	237	243	65	97	0	3.68
2 Vito Tamulis	L	26	12	6	.667	2	38	18	9	160	181	40	70	0	3.83
Freddie Fitzsimmons	R	36	11	8	.579	0	27	26	12	203	205	43	38	1	3.01
Tot Pressnell	R	31	11	14	.440	3	43	19	6	192	209	56	57	1	3.56
Bill Posedel	R	31	8	9	.471	1	33	17	6	140	178	46	49	1	5.66
1 Max Butcher	R	27	5	4	.556	2	24	8	3	73	104	39	21	1	6.53
Van Lingle Mungo	R	27	4	11	.267	0	24	18	6	133	133	72	72	2	3.92
Fred Frankhouse	R	34	3	5	.375	0	30	8	2	94	92	44	32	1	4.02
John Gaddy	R	24	2	0	1.000	0	2	2	1	13	13	4	3	0	0.69
Sam Nahem	R	22	1	0	1.000	0	1	1	1	9	6	4	2	0	3.00
Waite Hoyt	R	38	0	3	.000	0	6	1	0	16	24	5	3	0	5.07
2 Wayne LeMaster	L	31	0	1	.000	0	3	0	0	11	17	3	3	0	4.91
Buck Marrow	R	28	0	1	.000	0	15	0	0	20	23	11	6	0	4.60
Dykes Potter	R	27	0	0	.000	0	2	0	0	2	4	0	1	0	4.50
2 Lee Rogers	L	24	0	2	.000	0	12	2	0	24	23	10	11	0	5.63
Jim Winford	R	28	0	1	.000	0	2	1	0	6	9	4	4	0	10.50

PHILADELPHIA 8th 45-105 .300 43 — JIMMIE WILSON 45-103 .304 HANS LOBERT 0-2 .000

NAME	G by POS	B	AGE	G	AB	R	H	2B	3B	HR	RBI	BB	SO	SB	BA	SA
TOTALS			28	151	5192	550	1318	233	29	40	503	423	507	38	.254	.333
Phil Weintraub	1B98	L	30	100	351	51	109	23	2	4	45	64	43	1	.311	.422
Emmett Mueller	2B111, 3B21	B	25	136	444	53	111	12	4	4	34	64	43	2	.250	.322
Del Young	SS87, 2B17	B	26	108	340	27	78	13	2	0	31	20	35	0	.229	.279
Pinky Whitney	3B75, 1B4, 2B2	R	33	102	300	27	83	9	1	3	38	27	22	0	.277	.343
Chuck Klein	OF119	L	33	129	458	53	113	22	2	8	61	38	30	7	.247	.356
Hersh Martin	OF116	B	28	120	466	58	139	36	6	3	39	34	48	8	.298	.421
Morrie Arnovich	OF133	R	27	139	502	47	138	29	0	4	72	42	37	2	.275	.357
Bill Atwood	C94	R	26	102	281	27	55	8	1	3	28	25	26	0	.196	.263
George Scharein	SS77, 2B39, 3B1	R	23	117	390	47	93	16	4	1	29	16	33	11	.238	.308
2 Buck Jordan	3B58, 1B17	L	31	87	310	31	93	18	1	0	18	17	4	1	.300	.365
2 Gib Brack	OF68	R	30	72	282	40	81	20	4	4	28	18	30	2	.287	.429
2 Spud Davis	C63	R	33	70	215	11	53	7	0	2	23	14	14	1	.247	.307
Cap Clark	C29	L	31	52	74	11	19	1	1	0	4	9	10	0	.257	.297
2 Tuck Stainback	OF25	R	27	30	81	9	21	3	0	1	11	3	3	1	.259	.333
Gene Corbett	1B22	L	24	24	75	7	6	1	0	2	7	6	11	0	.080	.173
Earl Browne	1B16, OF2	L	27	21	74	4	19	4	0	0	8	5	11	0	.257	.311
1 Justin Stein	3B7, 2B3	R	26	11	39	6	10	0	1	0	2	2	4	0	.256	.308
Eddie Feinberg	SS4, OF2	B	19	10	20	0	3	0	0	0	0	0	1	0	.150	.150
Ray Stoviak	OF4	L	23	10	10	1	0	0	0	0	0	0	3	0	.000	.000

Alex Pitko 23 R 6-19, Art Rebel 23 L 2-9, Jimmie Wilson 37 R 0-2, Howie Gorman 25 L 0-1

NAME	T	AGE	W	L	PCT	SV	G	GS	CG	IP	H	BB	SO	ShO	ERA
TOTALS			45	105	.300	6	151	151	68	1329	1516	582	492	3	4.93
Claude Passeau	R	29	11	18	.379	1	44	33	15	239	281	93	100	0	4.52
Hugh Mulcahy	R	24	10	20	.333	1	46	34	15	267	294	120	90	0	4.62
2 Al Hollingsworth	L	30	5	16	.238	0	24	21	11	174	177	77	80	1	3.83
2 Max Butcher	R	27	4	8	.333	0	12	12	11	98	94	31	29	0	2.94
1 Wayne LeMaster	L	31	4	7	.364	0	18	12	1	64	80	31	35	1	7.73
1 Bucky Walters	R	29	4	8	.333	0	12	12	9	83	91	42	28	1	5.20
Pete Sivess	R	24	3	6	.333	3	39	8	2	116	143	69	32	0	5.51
Syl Johnson	R	37	2	7	.222	0	22	6	2	83	87	11	21	0	4.23
Wild Bill Hallahan	L	35	1	8	.111	0	21	10	1	89	107	45	22	0	5.46
Al Smith	L	30	1	4	.200	1	37	1	0	86	115	40	46	0	6.28
Elmer Burkart	R	21	0	1	.000	0	2	1	1	10	12	3	1	0	4.50
Ed Heusser	R	29	0	0	.000	0	1	0	0	1	2	1	0	0	27.00
Hal Kelleher	R	24	0	0	.000	0	6	0	0	7	16	9	4	0	19.29
Tom Lanning	L	29	0	1	.000	0	3	1	0	7	9	2	2	0	6.43
Tommy Reis	R	23	0	1	.000	0	4	0	0	5	8	8	2	0	18.00

WORLD SERIES — NEW YORK (AL) 4 CHICAGO (NL) 0

LINE SCORES

TEAM	1 2 3	4 5 6	7 8 9	10 11 12	R	H	E
Game 1 October 5 at Chicago							
NY (AL)	0 2 0	0 0 0	1 0 0		3	12	1
CHI (NL)	0 0 1	0 0 0	0 0 0		1	9	1
Ruffing	Lee, Russell (9)						
Game 2 October 6 at Chicago							
NY	0 2 0	0 0 0	0 2 2		6	7	2
CHI	1 0 2	0 0 0	0 0 0		3	11	0
Gomez, Murphy (8)	Dean, French (9)						
Game 3 October 8 at New York							
CHI	0 0 0	0 1 0	0 1 0		2	5	1
NY	0 0 0	0 2 2	0 1 X		5	7	2
Bryant, Russell (6), French (7)	Pearson						
Game 4 October 9 at New York							
CHI	0 0 0	1 0 0	0 2 0		3	8	1
NY	0 3 0	0 0 1	0 4 X		8	11	1
Lee, Root (4), Page (7), French (8), Carleton (8), Dean (8)	Ruffing						

COMPOSITE BATTING

NAME	POS	G	AB	R	H	2B	3B	HR	RBI	BA
New York (AL)										
Totals		4	135	22	37	6	1	5	21	.274
Rolfe	3B	4	18	0	3	0	0	0	1	.167
Crosetti	SS	4	16	1	4	2	1	1	6	.250
Henrich	OF	4	16	3	4	1	0	1	1	.250
Dickey	C	4	15	2	6	0	0	1	2	.400
Gordon	2B	4	15	3	6	2	0	1	6	.400
DiMaggio	OF	4	15	4	4	0	0	1	2	.267
Gehrig	1B	4	14	4	4	0	0	0	0	.286
Selkirk	OF	3	10	0	2	0	0	0	1	.200
Ruffing	P	2	6	1	1	0	0	0	1	.167
Hoag	OF	2	5	3	2	1	0	0	1	.400
Pearson	P	1	3	1	1	0	0	0	0	.333
Gomez	P	1	2	0	0	0	0	0	0	.000
Murphy	P	1	0	0	0	0	0	0	0	.000
Powell	OF	1	0	0	0	0	0	0	0	.000
Chicago (NL)										
Totals		4	136	9	33	4	1	2	8	.243
Hack	3B	4	17	3	8	1	0	0	1	.471
Herman	2B	4	16	1	3	0	0	0	0	.188
Collins	1B	4	15	1	2	0	0	0	0	.133
Cavarretta	OF	4	13	1	6	1	0	0	0	.462
Jurges	SS	4	13	0	3	1	0	0	0	.231
Marty	OF	3	12	1	6	1	0	1	5	.500
Reynolds	OF	4	12	0	0	0	0	0	0	.000
Hartnett	C	3	11	0	1	0	1	0	0	.091
Demaree	OF	3	10	1	1	0	0	0	0	.100
O'Dea	C	3	5	1	1	0	0	1	2	.200
Dean	P	2	3	0	2	0	0	0	0	.667
Lee	P	2	3	0	0	0	0	0	0	.000
Galan	PH	2	2	0	0	0	0	0	0	.000
Lazzeri	PH	2	2	0	0	0	0	0	0	.000
Bryant	P	1	2	0	0	0	0	0	0	.000
French	P	3	0	0	0	0	0	0	0	.000
Russell	P	2	0	0	0	0	0	0	0	.000
Carleton	P	1	0	0	0	0	0	0	0	.000
Page	P	1	0	0	0	0	0	0	0	.000
Root	P	1	0	0	0	0	0	0	0	.000

COMPOSITE PITCHING

NAME	G	IP	H	BB	SO	W	L	SV	ERA
New York (AL)									
Totals	4	36	33	6	26	4	0	1	1.75
Ruffing	2	18	17	2	11	2	0	0	1.50
Pearson	1	9	5	2	9	1	0	0	1.00
Gomez	1	7	9	1	5	1	0	0	3.86
Murphy	1	2	2	1	1	0	0	1	0.00
Chicago (NL)									
Totals	4	34	37	11	16	0	4	0	5.03
Lee	2	11	15	1	8	0	2	0	2.45
Dean	2	8.1	6	1	2	0	1	0	6.48
Bryant	1	5.1	6	5	3	0	1	0	6.75
French	3	3.1	1	1	2	0	0	0	2.70
Root	1	3	3	0	1	0	0	0	3.00
Russell	2	1.2	1	1	0	0	0	0	0.00
Page	1	1.1	2	0	0	0	0	0	13.50
Carleton	1	0	1	2	0	0	0	0	∞

1939 McCarthy's Final Walk

For the first three days of the season, the rain accomplished what both leagues had failed to do for three years—stop the Yankees. It was not until April 20, that Joe McCarthy and his men could get their first game in. When they did, it was enough to catapult them from a cellar-dwelling zero percentage to a first-place tie. Then, after floating between first and second place until May 11, they cut themselves loose from the rest of the league.

Although the final standings of a 17-game margin over Boston gave the impression of a trouble-free season, there were some problems for a time from the Red Sox. In early July, on the brink of the All-Star break, the Bostonians came to Yankee Stadium and shocked McCarthy, his Yankees, and their fans with five straight triumphs—four of the wins occurring in a pair of doubleheaders. After the All-Star break the Yankees went to Detroit and lost their sixth straight. But then McCarthy pulled his forces together and won eight in a row, which was enough to offset Boston's 23-10 July record.

In spite of finishing a poor second, the Red Sox got the chance to unveil a 20-year-old Californian who would keep Boston on the map for many years to come. Ted Williams made his major league debut and batted .327, hit 31 home runs, and drove in 145 runs, the last of which was enough to lead the league. On the other end of the yardstick for Boston was Lefty Grove who, despite his 39 years of age, turned in a fine 15-4 performance behind his league-leading 2.54 E.R.A. While Cleveland's season was heightened by the hitting of Hal Trosky, Odell Hale, and Ken Keltner—all .300 hitters, and the brilliant pitching of 20-year-old Bob Feller, who led the league in wins with 24 and strikeouts with 246, the club could do no more than limp home a distant third, 20½ games back.

In the National League, the Cincinnati Reds finished first, a feat they had been unable to accomplish since 1919—the year they were unknowingly winning a "fixed" Series. The Rhinelanders' rise to the top was a dramatic one, considering their last-place finish in 1937. The only real challenge all year came from upstart St. Louis, who wound up sixth in 1938 and almost overtook the Reds at the wire, had it not been for the pitching of Paul Derringer—who clinched the pennant with a 5-3 win on September 29. It was Derringer, with 25 wins, and Bucky Walters, a former infielder with 27 wins, who spearheaded the Reds' success.

Dethroned Chicago suffered a collapse of their mound staff and finished fourth, the first time since 1927, mostly due to Dizzy Dean's being unable to regain his form. The Dodgers, after a six-year hiatus in the second division, began to show signs of life behind the presence of shortstop Leo Durocher, who took over the field leadership of the club and guided them to third place in his first managerial attempt. Durocher, while turning in a .277 average to help his own cause, got additional offensive help from Doug Camilli and Cookie Lavagetto, and good pitching out of 20-game winner Luke Hamlin. New York and Pittsburgh, both plagued with pitching problems and unable to get going, fell into the second division.

Bill McKechnie ushered his Reds into Yankee Stadium for the first Series game on October 4, and it was tied until the ninth inning when Bill Dickey's single drove in the winning run. McCarthy called on Monte Pearson to start the second game, and the Oakland native came within five outs of World Series history. Pearson had allowed one walk all day when Ernie Lombardi singled with one out in the eighth to spoil the no-hit bid. Then, in the ninth inning with two out, Werber, who had the only walk before Lombardi's clean hit, singled sharply to left to deny Pearson even a record performance one-hitter. The Yankees took the next two, running into a mild obstacle in the last game when they had to go to the tenth inning before wrapping up their second successive, four-game World Series sweep—thus giving Joe McCarthy the distinction of being the first man in baseball ever to win four straight championships. The Yankee victory also culminated in an impressive 16-3, four-year Series record.

The one Yankee tragedy for the year, a tragic footnote to all of baseball, was Lou Gehrig's voluntary retirement on May 2, after playing in only eight games. Gehrig quit the Yankees after playing in a miraculous 2,130 consecutive games and left behind a lifetime .340 batting average, 493 home runs, and a spirit of dedication hard to equal. On June 21, the Mayo Clinic announced that Gehrig was suffering from a rare neuromuscular disease, amyotrophic lateral sclerosis, that would claim his life two years later.

1939 AMERICAN LEAGUE

NAME	G by POS	B	AGE	G	AB	R	H	2B	3B	HR	RBI	BB	SO	SB	BA	SA
NEW YORK 1st 106-45 .702		JOE McCARTHY														
TOTALS			27	152	5300	**967**	1521	259	55	**166**	**903**	**701**	543	72	.287	**.451**
Babe Dahlgren	1B144	R	27	144	531	71	125	18	6	15	89	57	54	2	.235	.377
Joe Gordon	2B151	R	24	151	567	92	161	32	5	28	111	75	57	11	.284	.506
Frankie Crosetti	SS152	R	28	152	**656**	109	153	25	5	10	56	65	81	11	.233	.332
Red Rolfe	3B152	L	30	152	648	**139**	**213**	**46**	10	14	80	81	41	7	.329	.495
Charlie Keller	OF105	L	22	111	398	87	133	21	6	11	83	81	49	6	.334	.500
Joe DiMaggio	OF117	R	24	120	462	108	176	32	6	30	126	52	20	3	**.381**	.671
George Selkirk	OF124	L	31	128	418	103	128	17	4	21	101	103	49	12	.306	.517
Bill Dickey	C126	L	32	128	480	98	145	23	3	24	105	77	37	5	.302	.513
Tommy Henrich	OF88, 1B1	L	26	99	347	64	96	18	4	9	57	51	23	7	.277	.429
Red Ruffing	P28	R	35	44	114	12	35	1	0	1	20	7	18	1	.307	.342
Buddy Rosar	C35	R	24	43	105	18	29	5	1	0	12	13	10	4	.276	.343
Jake Powell	OF23	R	30	31	86	12	21	4	1	1	9	3	8	1	.244	.349
1 Joe Gallagher	OF12	R	25	14	41	8	10	0	1	2	9	3	8	1	.244	.439
Lou Gehrig (IL)	1B8	L	36	8	28	2	4	0	0	0	1	5	1	0	.143	.143
Bill Knickerbocker	2B2, SS2	R	27	6	13	2	2	1	0	0	1	0	0	0	.154	.231
Art Jorgens	C2	R	34	3	0	1	0	0	0	0	0	0	0	0	.000	.000
BOSTON 2nd 89-62 .589 17		JOE CRONIN														
TOTALS			28	152	5308	890	**1543**	287	57	124	833	591	505	42	**.291**	.436
Jimmie Foxx	1B123, P1	R	31	124	467	130	168	31	10	**35**	105	89	72	4	.360	**.694**
Bobby Doerr	2B126	R	21	127	525	75	167	28	2	12	73	38	32	1	.318	.448
Joe Cronin	SS142	R	32	143	520	97	160	33	3	19	107	87	48	6	.308	.492
Jim Tabor	3B148	R	25	149	577	76	167	33	8	14	95	40	54	16	.289	.447
Ted Williams	OF149	L	20	149	565	131	185	44	11	31	**145**	107	64	2	.327	.609
Doc Cramer	OF135	L	33	137	589	110	183	30	6	0	56	36	17	3	.311	.382
Joe Vosmik	OF144	R	29	145	554	89	153	29	6	7	84	66	33	4	.276	.388
Johnny Peacock	C84	L	29	92	274	33	76	11	4	0	36	29	11	1	.277	.347
2 Lou Finney	1B32, OF24	L	28	95	249	43	81	18	3	1	46	24	11	2	.325	.434
Gene Desautels	C73	R	32	76	226	26	55	14	0	0	21	33	13	3	.243	.305
Red Nonnenkamp	OF15	L	27	58	75	12	18	2	1	0	5	12	6	0	.240	.293
Tom Carey	2B35, SS10	R	30	54	161	17	39	6	2	0	20	3	9	0	.242	.304
Boze Berger	SS10, 3B5, 2B2	R	29	20	30	4	9	2	0	0	2	1	10	0	.300	.367
Moe Berg	C13	R	37	14	33	3	9	1	0	1	5	2	3	0	.273	.394
Fabian Gaffke		R	25	1	1	0	0	0	0	0	1	0	0	0	.000	.000
CLEVELAND 3rd 87-67 .565 20.5		OSSIE VITT														
TOTALS			27	154	5316	797	1490	291	**79**	85	730	557	574	72	.280	.413
Hal Trosky	1B118	L	26	122	448	89	150	31	4	25	104	52	28	2	.335	.589
Odell Hale	2B73, 3B2	R	30	108	253	36	79	16	2	4	48	25	18	4	.312	.439
Skeeter Webb	SS81	R	29	81	269	28	71	14	1	2	26	15	24	1	.264	.346
Ken Keltner	3B154	R	22	154	587	84	191	35	11	13	97	51	41	6	.325	.489
Bruce Campbell	OF115	L	29	130	450	84	129	23	13	8	72	67	48	7	.287	.449
Ben Chapman	OF146	R	30	149	545	101	158	31	9	6	82	87	30	18	.290	.413
Jeff Heath	OF108	L	24	121	431	64	126	31	7	14	69	41	64	8	.292	.494
Rollie Hemsley	C106	R	32	107	395	58	104	17	4	2	36	26	26	2	.263	.342
Oscar Grimes	2B48, 1B43, SS37	R	24	119	364	51	98	20	5	4	56	56	61	8	.269	.385
Roy Weatherly	OF76	L	24	95	323	43	100	16	6	1	32	19	23	7	.310	.406
Frankie Pytlak	C51	R	30	63	183	20	49	2	5	0	14	20	5	4	.268	.333
Lou Boudreau	SS53	R	21	53	225	42	58	15	4	0	19	28	24	2	.258	.360
1 Moose Solters	OF25	R	33	41	102	19	28	7	2	2	19	9	15	2	.275	.441
Ray Mack	2B34, 3B1	R	22	36	112	12	17	4	1	1	6	12	19	0	.152	.232
1 Jim Shilling	2B27, SS3	R	24	31	98	8	27	7	2	0	12	7	9	1	.276	.388
1 Earl Averill	OF11	L	37	24	55	8	15	8	0	1	7	6	12	0	.273	.473
Luke Sewell	C15, 1B1	R	38	16	20	1	3	1	0	0	1	3	1	0	.150	.200
1 Lyn Lary	SS2	R	33	3	2	0	0	0	0	0	0	0	1	0	.000	.000

NAME	T	AGE	W	L	PCT	SV	G	GS	CG	IP	H	BB	SO	ShO	ERA
		30	**106**	45	**.702**	**26**	152	152	**87**	1349	1208	567	565	**12**	**3.31**
Red Ruffing	R	35	21	7	.750	0	28	28	22	233	211	75	95	**4**	2.94
Atley Donald	R	28	13	3	.813	1	24	20	11	153	144	60	55	1	3.71
Lefty Gomez	L	30	12	8	.600	0	26	26	14	198	173	84	102	2	3.41
Bump Hadley	R	34	12	6	.667	2	26	18	7	154	132	85	65	1	2.98
Monte Pearson	R	29	12	5	.706	0	22	20	8	146	151	70	76	0	4.50
Steve Sundra	R	29	11	1	.917	0	24	11	8	121	110	56	27	1	2.75
Oral Hildebrand	R	32	10	4	.714	2	21	15	7	127	102	41	50	1	3.05
Marius Russo	L	24	8	3	.727	2	21	11	9	116	86	41	55	2	2.41
Spud Chandler (BL)	R	31	3	0	1.000	0	11	0	0	19	26	9	4	0	2.84
Johnny Murphy	R	30	3	6	.333	**19**	38	0	0	61	57	28	30	0	4.43
Wes Ferrell	R	31	1	2	.333	0	3	3	1	19	14	17	6	0	4.74
Marv Breuer	R	25	0	0	.000	0	1	0	0	1	2	1	0	0	9.00
		29	89	62	.589	20	152	152	52	1351	1533	543	539	4	4.56
Lefty Grove	L	39	15	4	**.789**	0	23	23	17	191	180	58	81	2	**2.54**
Joe Heving	R	38	11	3	.786	7	46	5	1	107	124	34	43	0	3.70
Fritz Ostermueller	L	31	11	7	.611	4	34	20	8	159	173	58	61	0	4.25
Jack Wilson	R	27	11	11	.500	2	36	22	6	177	198	75	80	0	4.68
Eldon Auker	R	28	9	10	.474	0	31	25	6	151	183	61	43	1	5.36
Denny Galehouse	R	27	9	10	.474	0	30	18	6	147	160	52	68	1	4.53
Emerson Dickman	R	24	8	3	.727	5	48	1	0	114	126	43	46	0	4.42
Jim Bagby	R	22	5	5	.500	0	21	11	3	80	119	36	35	0	7.09
Woody Rich (SA)	R	22	4	3	.571	1	21	12	3	77	78	35	24	0	4.91
Charlie Wagner	R	26	3	1	.750	0	9	5	0	38	49	14	13	0	4.26
Bill LeFebvre	L	23	1	1	.500	0	5	3	0	26	35	14	8	0	5.88
1 Jake Wade	L	27	1	4	.200	0	20	6	1	48	68	37	21	0	6.19
Monty Weaver	R	33	1	0	1.000	1	9	1	1	20	26	13	6	0	6.75
Jimmie Foxx	R	31	0	0	.000	0	1	0	0	1	1	0	1	0	0.00
Bill Sayles	R	21	0	0	.000	0	5	0	0	14	14	13	9	0	7.07
		27	87	67	.565	13	154	154	69	1365	1394	602	614	9	4.08
Bob Feller	R	20	**24**	9	.727	1	39	35	**24**	**297**	227	**142**	**246**	**4**	2.85
Mel Harder	R	29	15	9	.625	1	29	26	12	208	213	64	67	1	3.50
Al Milnar	L	25	14	12	.538	3	37	26	12	209	212	99	76	1	3.79
Johnny Allen	R	34	9	7	.563	0	28	26	9	175	199	56	79	2	4.58
Willis Hudlin	R	33	9	10	.474	3	27	20	7	143	175	42	28	0	4.91
2 Harry Eisenstat	L	23	6	7	.462	2	26	11	4	104	109	28	38	1	3.29
Johnny Broaca	R	29	4	2	.667	0	22	2	0	46	53	28	13	0	4.70
Joe Dobson	R	22	2	3	.400	1	35	3	0	78	87	51	27	0	5.88
Bill Zuber	R	26	2	0	1.000	0	16	1	0	32	41	19	16	0	5.91
John Humphries	R	24	2	4	.333	2	15	1	0	28	30	32	12	0	8.36
Tom Drake (AJ)	R	24	0	1	.000	0	8	1	0	15	23	19	1	0	9.00
Mike Naymick	R	21	0	1	.000	0	2	1	1	5	3	5	3	0	1.80
Floyd Stromme	R	22	0	1	.000	0	5	0	0	13	13	13	4	0	4.85
Lefty Sullivan	L	22	0	1	.000	0	7	1	0	13	9	9	4	0	4.15

CHICAGO 4th 85-69 .552 22.5 — **JIMMY DYKES**

NAME	G by POS	B	AGE	G	AB	R	H	2B	3B	HR	RBI	BB	SO	SB	BA	SA
TOTALS			31	155	5279	755	1451	220	56	64	681	579	502	113	.275	.374
Joe Kuhel	1B136	L	33	139	546	107	164	24	9	15	56	64	51	18	.300	.460
Ollie Bejma	2B81, SS1, 3B1	R	31	90	307	52	77	9	3	8	44	36	27	1	.251	.378
Luke Appling	SS148	R	32	148	516	82	162	16	6	0	56	105	37	16	.314	.368
Eric McNair	3B103, 2B19, SS9	R	30	129	479	62	155	18	5	7	82	38	41	17	.324	.426
Larry Rosenthal	OF93	L	27	107	324	50	86	21	5	10	51	53	46	6	.265	.454
Mike Kreevich	OF139, 3B4	R	31	145	541	85	175	30	8	5	77	59	40	23	.323	.436
Gee Walker	OF147	R	31	149	598	95	174	30	11	13	111	28	43	17	.291	.443
Mike Tresh	C119	R	25	119	352	49	91	5	2	0	38	64	30	3	.259	.284
Rip Radcliff	OF78, 1B20	L	33	113	397	49	105	25	2	2	53	26	21	6	.264	.353
Jackie Hayes	2B69	R	32	72	269	34	67	12	3	0	23	27	10	0	.249	.316
Hank Steinbacher	OF22	L	26	71	111	16	19	2	1	1	15	21	8	0	.171	.234
Marv Owen	3B55	R	33	58	194	22	46	9	0	0	15	16	15	4	.237	.284
Norm Schlueter	C32	R	22	34	56	5	13	2	1	0	8	1	11	2	.232	.304
Ken Silvestri	C20	B	23	22	75	6	13	3	0	2	5	6	13	0	.173	.293
Tony Rensa	C13	R	37	14	25	3	5	0	0	0	2	1	2	0	.200	.200
John Gerlach	3B1	R	22	3	2	0	2	0	0	0	0	0	0	0	1.000	1.000
Bob Kennedy	3B2	R	18	3	8	0	2	0	0	0	1	0	0	0	.250	.250
Jimmy Dykes	3B2	R	42	2	1	0	0	0	0	0	0	0	0	0	.000	.000
1 Tommy Thompson		L	29	1	0	0	0	0	0	0	1	0	0	0	.000	.000

NAME	T	AGE	W	L	PCT	SV	G	GS	CG	IP	H	BB	SO	ShO	ERA
		30	85	69	.552	21	155	155	62	1377	1470	454	535	5	4.31
Thornton Lee	L	32	15	11	.577	3	33	29	15	235	260	70	81	2	4.21
Johnny Rigney	R	24	15	8	.652	0	35	29	11	219	208	84	119	2	3.70
Ted Lyons	R	38	14	6	.700	0	21	21	16	173	162	26	65	0	2.76
Clint Brown	R	35	11	10	.524	18	61	0	0	118	127	27	41	0	3.89
Jack Knott	R	32	11	6	.647	0	25	23	8	150	157	41	56	0	4.14
2 Eddie Smith	L	25	9	11	.450	0	29	22	7	177	161	90	67	1	3.66
Bill Dietrich	R	24	7	8	.467	0	25	19	2	128	134	56	43	0	5.20
2 Johnny Marcum	R	29	3	3	.400	0	19	6	2	90	125	19	32	0	6.00
Harry Boyles	R	27	0	0	.000	0	2	0	0	3	4	6	1	0	12.00
Jess Dobernic	R	21	0	1	.000	0	4	0	0	3	3	6	1	0	15.00
Vallie Eaves	R	27	0	1	.000	0	2	1	1	12	11	8	5	0	4.50
Vic Frasier (PB)	R	34	0	1	.000	0	10	1	0	24	45	11	7	0	10.13
Art Herring	R	32	0	0	.000	0	7	0	0	14	13	5	8	0	5.79
1 John Whitehead	R	30	0	3	.000	0	7	4	0	32	60	5	9	0	8.16

DETROIT 5th 81-73 .526 26.5 — **DEL BAKER**

NAME	G by POS	B	AGE	G	AB	R	H	2B	3B	HR	RBI	BB	SO	SB	BA	SA
TOTALS			29	155	5326	849	1487	277	67	124	806	620	592	88	.279	.426
Hank Greenberg	1B136	R	28	138	500	112	156	42	7	33	112	91	**95**	8	.312	.622
Charlie Gehringer	2B107	L	36	118	406	86	132	29	6	16	86	68	16	4	.325	.544
Frank Croucher	SS93, 2B3	R	24	97	324	38	87	15	0	5	40	16	42	2	.269	.361
Pinky Higgins	3B130	R	30	132	489	57	135	23	2	8	76	56	41	7	.276	.380
Pete Fox	OF126	R	29	141	519	69	153	24	6	7	66	35	41	23	.295	.405
Barney McCosky	OF145	L	21	147	611	120	190	33	14	4	58	70	45	20	.311	.430
2 Earl Averill	OF80	L	37	87	309	58	81	20	6	10	58	43	30	4	.262	.463
Birdie Tebbetts	C100	R	29	106	341	37	89	22	2	4	53	25	20	2	.261	.372
Rudy York	C67, 1B19	R	25	102	329	66	101	16	1	20	68	41	50	5	.307	.544
Roy Cullenbine	OF46, 1B2	B	23	75	179	31	43	9	2	6	23	34	29	0	.240	.413
Billy Rogell	SS43, 3B21, 2B2	B	34	74	174	24	40	6	3	2	23	26	14	3	.230	.333
Johnny McCoy	2B34, SS16	L	23	55	192	38	58	13	6	1	33	29	26	3	.302	.448
2 Beau Bell	OF37	R	31	54	134	14	32	4	2	0	24	24	16	0	.239	.299
2 Red Kress (BL)	SS25, 2B16, 3B4	R	32	51	157	19	38	7	0	1	22	17	16	2	.242	.306
1 Dixie Walker	OF37	L	28	43	154	30	47	4	5	4	19	15	8	4	.305	.474
Les Fleming	OF3	L	23	8	16	0	0	0	0	0	1	0	4	0	.000	.000
1 Mark Christman	3B6	R	25	6	16	0	4	2	0	0	0	0	2	0	.250	.375
1 Chet Laabs	OF5	R	27	5	16	1	5	1	1	0	2	2	0	0	.313	.500
Dixie Parsons	C4	R	23	5	1	0	0	0	0	0	0	1	1	0	.000	.000
Merv Shea	C4	R	38	4	2	0	0	0	0	0	0	0	1	0	.000	.000

NAME	T	AGE	W	L	PCT	SV	G	GS	CG	IP	H	BB	SO	ShO	ERA
		29	81	73	.526	16	155	155	64	1367	1430	574	633	6	4.29
Tommy Bridges	R	32	17	7	.708	2	29	26	16	198	186	61	129	2	3.50
2 Bobo Newsom	R	31	17	10	.630	2	35	31†	21†	246	222	104	164	2	3.37
Schoolboy Rowe	R	29	10	12	.455	0	28	24	8	164	192	61	51	1	4.99
Dizzy Trout	R	24	9	10	.474	2	33	22	6	162	168	74	72	0	3.61
3 Bud Thomas	R	28	7	0	1.000	1	27	0	0	47	45	20	14	0	4.21
Al Benton	R	28	6	8	.429	5	37	16	3	150	182	58	67	0	4.56
Archie McKain	L	28	5	6	.455	4	32	11	4	130	120	54	49	1	3.67
Fred Hutchinson	R	19	3	6	.333	0	13	12	3	85	95	51	22	0	5.19
Slick Coffman	R	28	2	1	.667	0	23	1	0	42	51	22	10	0	6.43
1 Harry Eisenstat	L	23	2	2	.500	0	10	2	1	30	39	9	6	0	6.90
Floyd Giebell	R	29	1	1	.500	0	9	0	0	15	19	12	9	0	3.00
1 Bob Harris	R	23	1	1	.500	0	5	1	0	18	18	8	9	0	4.00
1 Roxie Lawson	R	33	1	1	.500	0	2	1	0	11	7	7	4	0	4.91
1 George Gill	R	30	0	1	.000	0	3	1	0	9	14	3	1	0	0.00
1 Vern Kennedy	R	32	0	3*	.000	0	4	4	1	21	25	9	9	0	6.43
1 Red Lynn	R	25	0	1	.000	0	4	0	0	8	11	3	3	0	9.00
Hal Newhouser	L	18	0	1	.000	0	1	1	1	5	3	4	4	0	5.40
2 Cotton Pippen	R	29	0	1	.000	0	3	2	0	14	18	6	5	0	7.07
2 Jim Walkup	R	29	0	1	.000	0	7	0	0	12	15	8	5	0	7.50

***Kennedy, also with St. Louis, league leader in L with 20**
†Newsom, also with St. Louis, league leader in GS(37) and CG(24)

WASHINGTON 6th 65-87 .428 41.5 — **BUCKY HARRIS**

NAME	G by POS	B	AGE	G	AB	R	H	2B	3B	HR	RBI	BB	SO	SB	BA	SA
TOTALS			27	153	5334	702	1483	249	**79**	44	648	547	460	94	.278	.379
Mickey Vernon	1B75	L	21	76	276	23	71	15	4	1	30	24	28	1	.257	.351
Jimmy Bloodworth	2B73, OF5	R	21	83	318	34	92	24	1	4	40	10	26	3	.289	.409
Cecil Travis	SS118	L	25	130	476	55	139	20	9	5	63	34	25	0	.292	.403
Buddy Lewis	3B134	L	22	140	536	87	171	23	**16**	10	75	72	27	10	.319	.478
George Case	OF123	R	23	128	530	103	160	20	7	2	35	56	36	**51**	.302	.377
Sammy West	OF89, 1B17	L	34	115	390	52	110	20	8	3	52	67	29	1	.282	.397
Taffy Wright	OF123	L	27	129	499	77	154	29	11	4	93	38	19	1	.309	.435
Rick Ferrell	C83	R	33	87	274	32	77	13	1	0	31	41	12	1	.281	.336
Buddy Myer	2B65	L	35	83	258	33	78	10	3	1	32	40	18	4	.302	.376
Bobby Estalella	OF74	R	28	82	280	51	77	18	6	8	41	40	27	2	.275	.468
Charlie Gelbert	SS28, 3B20, 2B1	R	33	68	188	36	48	7	5	3	29	30	11	2	.255	.394
Johnny Welaj	OF55	R	25	63	201	23	55	11	2	1	33	13	20	13	.274	.363
Tony Giuliani	C50	R	26	54	172	20	43	6	2	0	18	4	7	0	.250	.308
Jake Early	C24	L	22	32	84	8	22	7	2	0	14	5	14	0	.262	.393
Jimmy Wasdell	1B28	L	25	29	109	12	33	5	1	0	13	9	16	3	.303	.367
Bob Prichard	1B26	L	21	26	85	8	20	5	0	0	8	19	16	0	.235	.294
Ossie Bluege	1B11, 2B2, SS2, 3B2	R	38	18	59	5	9	0	0	0	3	7	2	1	.153	.153
Jim Quick	SS10	R	19	12	41	3	10	1	0	0	2	1	1	1	.244	.268
Ed Leip	2B8	R	28	9	32	4	11	1	0	0	2	2	4	0	.344	.375

Morrie Aderholt 23 L 5-25, Al Evans 22 R 7-21, Elmer Gedeon 22 R 3-15, Alex Pitko 24 R 1-8, Bobby Loane 24 R 0-9

NAME	T	AGE	W	L	PCT	SV	G	GS	CG	IP	H	BB	SO	ShO	ERA
		27	65	87	.428	10	153	153	72	1355	1420	602	521	4	4.60
Dutch Leonard	R	30	20	8	.714	0	34	34	21	269	**273**	59	88	2	3.55
Joe Krakauskas	L	24	11	17	.393	1	39	29	12	217	230	114	110	0	4.60
Ken Chase	L	25	10	19	.345	0	32	31	15	232	215	114	118	1	3.80
Joe Haynes	R	21	8	12	.400	0	27	20	10	173	186	78	64	1	5.36
Pete Appleton	R	35	5	10	.333	6	40	4	2	103	104	48	50	0	4.54
Alex Carrasquel	R	26	5	9	.357	2	40	17	7	159	165	68	41	0	4.70
Harry Kelley (KJ-GJ)	R	33	4	3	.571	1	15	3	2	54	69	14	20	0	4.67
Walt Masterson	R	19	2	2	.500	0	24	5	1	58	66	48	12	0	5.59
Dick Bass	R	32	0	1	.000	0	1	1	0	8	7	6	1	0	6.75
Jimmie DeShong	R	29	0	3	.000	0	7	6	1	41	56	31	12	0	8.56
Bill Holland	L	24	0	1	.000	0	3	0	0	4	6	5	2	0	11.25
Bucky Jacobs	R	26	0	0	.000	0	2	0	0	3	1	0	1	0	0.00
Mike Palagyi	R	21	0	0	.000	0	1	0	0	0	0	3	0	0	∞
2 Bud Thomas	R	28	0	0	.000	0	4	0	0	9	11	2	0	0	6.00
Lou Thuman	R	15	0	0	.000	0	3	0	0	4	5	2	1	0	9.00
Early Wynn	R	19	0	2	.000	0	3	3	1	20	26	10	1	0	5.85

PHILADELPHIA 7th 55-97 .362 51.5 — **CONNIE MACK**

NAME	G by POS	B	AGE	G	AB	R	H	2B	3B	HR	RBI	BB	SO	SB	BA	SA
TOTALS			27	153	5309	711	1438	282	55	98	666	503	532	60	.271	.400
Dick Siebert	1B99	L	27	101	402	58	118	28	3	6	47	21	22	4	.294	.423
Sep Gantenbein	2B76, 3B14, SS5	L	22	111	348	47	101	14	4	4	36	32	22	1	.290	.388
Skeeter Newsome	SS93, 2B2	R	28	99	248	22	55	9	1	0	17	19	12	5	.222	.266
Dario Lodigiani	3B89, 2B28	R	23	121	393	46	102	22	4	6	44	42	18	2	.260	.382
Wally Moses	OF103	L	28	115	437	68	134	28	7	3	33	44	23	7	.307	.423
Sam Chapman	OF117, 1B19	R	23	140	498	74	134	24	6	15	64	51	62	11	.269	.432
Bob Johnson	OF150, 2B1	R	32	150	544	115	184	30	9	23	114	99	59	15	.338	.553
Frankie Hayes	C114	R	24	124	431	66	122	28	5	20	83	40	55	4	.283	.510
Dee Miles	OF77	L	30	106	320	49	96	17	6	1	37	15	17	3	.300	.400
Bill Nagel	2B56, 3B43, P1	R	23	105	341	39	86	19	4	12	39	25	86	2	.252	.437
Wayne Ambler	SS77, 2B19	R	23	95	227	15	48	13	0	0	24	22	25	1	.211	.269
Chubby Dean	P54	L	23	80	77	12	27	4	0	0	19	8	4	0	.351	.403
Earle Brucker	C47	R	38	62	172	18	50	15	1	3	31	24	16	0	.291	.442
Eric Tipton	OF34	R	24	47	104	12	24	4	2	1	14	13	7	2	.231	.337
Nick Etten	1B41	L	25	43	155	20	39	11	2	3	29	16	11	0	.252	.406
Eddie Collins	OF6, 2B1	L	22	32	21	6	5	1	0	0	0	0	3	1	.238	.286
Al Brancato	3B20, SS1	R	20	21	68	12	14	5	0	1	8	8	4	1	.206	.324
Fred Chapman	SS15	R	22	15	49	5	14	1	1	0	1	1	3	1	.286	.347
1 Lou Finney	OF4	L	28	9	22	1	3	0	0	0	1	2	0	0	.136	.136

Bob McNamara 22 R 2-9, Bill Lillard 21 R 6-19, Hal Wagner 23 L 1-8, Harry O'Neill 22 R 0-0

NAME	T	AGE	W	L	PCT	SV	G	GS	CG	IP	H	BB	SO	ShO	ERA
		28	55	97	.362	12	153	153	50	1343	1687	579	397	5	5.79
Lynn Nelson	R	34	10	13	.435	1	35	24	12	198	233	64	75	1	4.77
George Caster (IL)	R	31	9	9	.500	0	28	17	7	136	144	45	59	1	4.90
Nels Potter	R	27	8	12	.400	2	41	25	9	196	258	88	60	0	6.61
Bill Beckman	R	31	7	11	.389	0	27	19	7	155	198	41	20	2	5.40
Bucky Ross	R	24	6	14	.300	0	29	28	6	174	216	95	43	1	6.00
Chubby Dean	L	23	5	8	.385	7	54	1	0	117	132	80	39	0	5.23
1 Cotton Pippin	R	29	4	11	.267	1	25	17	5	119	169	43	33	0	5.97
Bob Joyce	R	24	3	5	.375	0	30	6	1	108	156	37	25	0	6.67
Les McCrabb	R	24	1	2	.333	0	5	4	2	36	42	10	11	0	4.00
Roy Parmelee	R	32	1	6	.143	1	14	5	0	45	42	35	13	0	6.40
1 Eddie Smith	L	25	1	0	1.000	0	3	0	0	4	7	2	3	0	9.00
Walt Masters	R	32	0	0	.000	0	4	0	0	11	15	8	2	0	6.55
Bill Nagel	R	23	0	0	.000	0	1	0	0	3	7	1	0	0	12.00
Sam Page	R	23	0	3	.000	0	4	3	1	22	34	15	11	0	6.95
Jim Reninger	R	26	0	2	.000	0	4	2	0	16	24	12	3	0	7.88
Jim Schelle	R	22	0	0	.000	0	1	0	0	0	1	3	0	0	∞
Dave Smith	R	24	0	0	.000	0	1	0	0	0	1	2	0	0	0.00
1 Bud Thomas	R	28	0	1	.000	0	2	2	0	4	8	1	0	0	15.75

ST. LOUIS 8th 43-111 .279 64.5 — **FRED HANEY**

NAME	G by POS	B	AGE	G	AB	R	H	2B	3B	HR	RBI	BB	SO	SB	BA	SA
TOTALS			27	156	**5422**	733	1453	242	50	91	696	559	**606**	48	.268	.381
George McQuinn	1B154	L	30	154	617	101	195	37	13	20	94	65	42	6	.316	.515
Johnny Bernadino	2B114, 3B8, SS2	R	22	126	468	42	120	24	5	5	58	37	36	6	.256	.361
Don Heffner	SS73, 2B32	R	28	110	375	45	100	10	2	1	35	48	39	1	.267	.312
Harlond Clift	3B149	R	26	151	526	90	142	25	2	15	84	**111**	55	4	.270	.411
Myril Hoag	OF117, P1	R	31	129	482	58	142	23	4	10	75	24	35	9	.295	.421
2 Chet Laabs	OF79	R	27	95	317	52	95	20	5	10	62	33	62	4	.300	.489
2 Joe Gallagher	OF67	R	25	71	266	41	75	17	2	9	40	17	42	0	.282	.462
Joe Glenn	C82	R	30	88	286	29	78	13	1	4	29	31	40	4	.273	.367
Billy Sullivan	OF59, C19, 1B4	L	28	118	332	53	96	17	5	5	50	34	18	3	.289	.416
2 Mark Christman	SS64, 2B1	R	25	79	222	27	48	6	3	0	20	20	10	2	.216	.270
Joe Grace	OF53	L	25	74	207	35	63	11	2	3	22	19	24	3	.304	.420
Hal Spindel	C32	R	26	48	119	13	32	3	1	0	11	8	7	0	.269	.311
Sam Harshany	C36	R	29	42	145	15	35	2	0	0	15	9	8	0	.241	.255
1 Mel Almada	OF34	L	26	42	134	17	32	2	1	1	7	10	8	1	.239	.291
2 Moose Solters	OF30	R	33	40	131	14	27	6	1	0	14	10	20	1	.206	.267
Mike Mazzera	OF25	L	25	34	111	21	33	5	2	3	22	10	20	0	.297	.459
2 Tommy Thompson	OF23	L	29	30	86	23	26	5	0	1	7	23	7	0	.302	.395
Sig Gryska	SS14	R	23	18	49	4	13	2	0	0	8	6	10	3	.265	.306
1 Roy Hughes	2B6, SS1	R	28	17	23	6	2	0	0	0	1	4	4	0	.087	.087
1 Red Kress	SS13	R	32	13	43	5	12	1	0	0	8	6	2	1	.279	.302
1 Beau Bell	OF9	R	31	11	32	4	7	1	0	1	5	4	3	0	.219	.344

Johnny Lucadello 20 B 7-30, Bob Neighbors 21 R 2-11, Eddie Silber 25 R 0-1

NAME	T	AGE	W	L	PCT	SV	G	GS	CG	IP	H	BB	SO	ShO	ERA
		30	43	**111**	.279	3	156	156	56	1371	**1724**	**739**	516	3	6.01
2 Vern Kennedy	R	32	9	**17***	.346	0	33	27	12	192	229	115	55	1	5.72
Jack Kramer	R	31	9	16	.360	0	40	31	10	212	209	127	68	2	5.82
Bill Trotter	R	30	6	13	.316	0	41	13	4	157	205	54	61	0	5.33
Lefty Mills	L	29	4	11	.267	2	34	14	4	144	147	113	103	0	6.56
2 Bob Harris	R	23	3	12	.200	0	28	16	6	126	162	71	48	0	5.71
2 Roxie Lawson	R	33	3	7	.300	0	36	14	5	151	181	83	43	0	5.30
1 Bobo Newsom	R	31	3	1	.750	0	6	6†	3†	46	50	22	28	0	4.70
1 Johnny Marcum	R	29	2	5	.286	0	12	6	2	48	66	10	14	0	7.69
Emil Bildilli	L	26	1	1	.500	0	12	2	2	19	21	6	8	0	3.32
2 George Gill	R	30	1	12	.077	0	27	11	5	95	139	34	24	0	7.11
Harry Kimberlin	R	30	1	2	.333	0	17	3	0	41	59	19	11	0	5.49
2 John Whitehead	R	30	1	3	.256	1	26	4	0	66	88	17	9	0	5.86
Ed Cole	R	30	0	2	.000	0	6	0	0	6	8	6	5	0	7.50
Bill Cox	R	26	0	2	.000	0	4	2	1	9	10	8	8	0	10.00
Roy Hanning	R	21	0	1	.000	0	4	1	0	10	6	4	8	0	3.60
Myril Hoag	R	31	0	0	.000	0	1	0	0	1	0	0	0	0	0.00
Fred Johnson	R	45	0	1	.000	0	5	2	1	14	23	9	2	0	6.43
Bob Muncrief	R	23	0	0	.000	0	2	0	0	3	7	3	1	0	15.00
Ewald Pyle	L	28	0	2	.000	0	6	1	0	8	17	11	5	0	13.50
Russ VanAtta (SA)	L	33	0	0	.000	0	2	1	0	7	9	7	6	0	11.57
2 Jake Wade	L	27	0	2	.000	0	4	2	1	16	26	19	9	0	11.25
1 Jim Walkup	R	29	0	1	.000	0	1	0	0	1	2	1	0	0	0.00

***Kennedy and †Newsom (See Detroit)**

CINCINNATI 1st 97-57 .630 — BILL McKECHNIE

NAME	G by POS	B	AGE	G	AB	R	H	2B	3B	HR	RBI	BB	SO	SB	BA	SA
TOTALS			29	156	5378	767	1493	269	60	98	714	500	538	46	.278	.405
Frank McCormick	1B156	R	28	156	630	99	209	41	4	18	128	40	16	1	.332	.495
Lonny Frey	2B124	L	28	125	484	95	141	27	9	11	55	72	46	5	.291	.452
Billy Myers	SS151	R	28	151	509	79	143	18	6	9	56	71	90	4	.281	.393
Bill Werber	3B147	R	31	147	599	115	173	35	5	5	57	91	46	15	.289	.389
Ival Goodman	OF123	L	30	124	470	85	152	37	16	7	84	54	32	2	.323	.515
Harry Craft	OF134	R	24	134	502	58	129	20	7	13	67	27	54	5	.257	.402
Wally Berger	OF95	R	33	97	329	36	85	15	1	14	44	36	63	1	.258	.438
Ernie Lombardi	C120	R	31	130	450	43	129	26	2	20	85	35	19	0	.287	.487
Lee Gamble	OF56	L	29	72	221	24	59	7	2	0	14	9	14	5	.267	.317
Nino Bongiovanni	OF39	L	27	66	159	17	41	6	0	0	16	9	8	0	.258	.296
Willard Hershberger	C60	R	29	63	174	23	60	9	2	0	32	9	4	1	.345	.420
Frenchy Bordagaray	OF43, 2B2	R	27	63	122	19	24	5	1	0	12	9	10	3	.197	.254
Eddie Joost	2B32, SS6	R	23	42	143	23	36	6	3	0	14	12	15	1	.252	.336
Bucky Walters	P39	R	30	40	120	16	39	8	1	1	16	5	12	1	.325	.433
Lew Riggs	3B11	L	29	22	38	5	6	1	0	0	1	5	4	1	.158	.184
Les Scarsella (KJ)		L	25	16	14	0	2	0	0	0	2	0	2	0	.143	.143
2 Al Simmons	OF5	R	37	9	21	0	3	0	0	0	1	2	3	0	.143	.143
Vince DiMaggio	OF7	R	26	8	14	1	1	1	0	0	2	2	10	0	.071	.143
Dick West	OF5, C1	R	23	8	19	1	4	0	0	0	4	1	4	0	.211	.211
1 Bud Hafey	OF4	R	26	6	13	1	2	1	0	0	1	1	4	1	.154	.231
Jimmie Wilson	C1	R	38	4	3	0	1	0	0	0	0	0	1	0	.333	.333
Milt Galatzer	1B2	L	32	3	5	0	0	0	0	0	0	0	1	0	.000	.000
Nolen Richardson	SS1	R	36	1	3	0	0	0	0	0	0	0	0	0	.000	.000

NAME	T	AGE	W	L	PCT	SV	G	GS	CG	IP	H	BB	SO	ShO	ERA
TOTALS		29	97	57	.630	9	156	156	86	404	1340	499	637	13	3.27
Bucky Walters	R	30	27	11	.711	0	39	36	31	319	250	109	137	2	2.29
Paul Derringer	R	32	25	7	.781	0	38	35	28	301	321	35	128	5	2.93
Whitey Moore	R	27	13	12	.520	3	42	24	9	188	177	95	81	2	3.45
Junior Thompson	R	22	13	5	.722	2	42	11	5	152	130	55	87	3	2.55
Lee Grissom	L	31	9	7	.563	0	33	21	3	154	145	56	53	0	4.09
Johnny Vander Meer	L	24	5	9	.357	0	30	21	8	129	128	95	102	0	4.67
Johnny Niggerling	R	35	2	1	.667	0	10	5	2	40	51	13	20	1	5.85
2 Milt Shoffner	L	33	2	2	.500	0	10	3	0	38	43	11	6	0	3.32
Peaches Davis	R	34	1	0	1.000	2	20	0	0	31	43	11	4	0	6.39
Red Barrett	R	24	0	0	.000	0	2	0	0	5	5	1	1	0	1.80
Art Jacobs (SJ)	L	36	0	0	.000	1	1	0	0	1	2	1	0	0	9.00
Hank Johnson	R	33	0	3	.000	1	20	0	0	31	30	13	10	0	2.03
Wes Livengood	R	28	0	0	.000	0	5	0	0	6	9	3	4	0	9.00
Pete Naktenis	L	25	0	0	.000	0	3	0	0	4	2	0	1	0	2.25
Elmer Riddle	R	24	0	0	.000	0	1	0	0	2	1	0	0	0	0.00
Jim Weaver	R	35	0	0	.000	0	3	0	0	3	3	1	3	0	3.00

ST. LOUIS 2nd 92-61 .601 4.5 — RAY BLADES

NAME	G by POS	B	AGE	G	AB	R	H	2B	3B	HR	RBI	BB	SO	SB	BA	SA
TOTALS			27	155	5447	779	1601	332	62	98	732	475	566	44	.294	.432
Johnny Mize	1B152	L	26	153	564	104	197	44	14	28	108	92	49	0	.349	.626
Stu Martin	2B107	L	25	120	425	60	114	26	7	3	30	33	40	4	.268	.384
Jimmy Brown	SS104, 2B50	B	29	147	645	88	192	31	8	3	51	32	18	4	.298	.384
Don Gutteridge	3B143, SS2	R	27	148	524	71	141	27	4	7	54	27	70	5	.269	.376
Enos Slaughter	OF149	L	23	149	604	95	193	52	5	12	86	44	53	2	.320	.482
Terry Moore	OF121, P1	R	27	130	417	65	123	25	2	17	77	43	38	6	.295	.487
Joe Medwick	OF149	R	27	150	606	98	201	48	8	14	117	45	44	6	.332	.507
Mickey Owen	C126	R	23	131	344	32	89	18	2	3	35	43	28	6	.259	.349
Don Padgett	C61, 1B6	L	27	92	233	38	93	15	3	5	53	18	11	1	.399	.554
Lynn King	OF44	L	31	89	85	10	20	2	0	0	11	15	3	2	.235	.259
Pepper Martin	OF51, 3B22	R	35	88	281	48	86	17	7	3	37	30	35	6	.306	.448
Lynn Myers	SS36, 2B13, 3B5	R	25	74	117	24	28	6	1	0	10	12	23	1	.239	.308
Curt Davis	P49	R	35	63	105	10	40	5	0	1	17	3	22	0	.381	.457
3 Lyn Lary	SS30, 3B3	R	33	34	75	11	14	3	0	0	9	16	15	1	.187	.227
Herman Franks	C13	R	25	17	17	1	1	0	0	0	3	3	3	0	.059	.059
Creepy Crespi	2B6, SS4	R	21	15	29	3	5	1	0	0	6	3	6	0	.172	.207
Herb Bremer	C8	R	25	9	9	0	1	0	0	0	1	0	2	0	.111	.111
Joe Orengo	SS7	R	24	7	3	0	0	0	0	0	0	0	1	0	.000	.000
Johnny Hopp	1B1	L	22	6	4	1	2	1	0	0	2	1	1	0	.500	.750

Bob Repass 21 R 2-6, Buster Adams 24 R 0-1, Johnny Echols 22 R 0-0, Eddie Lake 23 R 1-4, Bill DeLancey (IL) 27

NAME	T	AGE	W	L	PCT	SV	G	GS	CG	IP	H	BB	SO	ShO	ERA
TOTALS		29	92	61	.601	32	155	155	45	1385	1377	498	603	18	3.59
Curt Davis	R	35	22	16	.579	7	49	31	13	248	279	48	70	3	3.63
Bob Bowman	R	28	13	5	.722	9	51	15	4	169	141	60	78	2	2.61
Lon Warneke	R	30	13	7	.650	2	34	21	6	162	160	49	59	3	3.78
Mort Cooper	R	26	12	6	.667	4	45	26	7	211	208	97	130	2	3.24
Bill McGee	R	29	12	5	.706	0	43	17	5	156	155	59	56	4	3.81
Bob Weiland	L	33	10	12	.455	1	32	23	6	146	146	50	63	3	3.58
Tom Sunkel	L	26	4	4	.500	0	20	11	2	85	79	56	54	1	4.24
Clyde Shoun	L	27	3	1	.750	9	53	2	0	103	98	42	50	0	3.76
Max Lanier	L	23	2	1	.667	0	7	6	2	38	29	13	14	0	2.37
Nate Andrews	R	25	1	2	.333	0	11	1	0	16	24	12	6	0	6.75
Frank Barrett	R	26	0	1	.000	0	1	0	0	2	1	1	3	0	4.50
Paul Dean	R	25	0	1	.000	0	16	2	0	43	54	10	16	0	6.07
Murry Dickson	R	22	0	0	.000	0	1	0	0	4	1	1	2	0	0.00
Terry Moore	R	27	0	0	.000	0	1	0	0	1	0	0	1	0	0.00
Ken Raffensberger	L	21	0	0	.000	0	1	0	0	1	2	0	1	0	0.00

BROOKLYN 3rd 84-69 .549 12.5 — LEO DUROCHER

NAME	G by POS	B	AGE	G	AB	R	H	2B	3B	HR	RBI	BB	SO	SB	BA	SA
TOTALS			28	157	5350	708	1420	265	57	78	653	564	631	59	.265	.380
Dolph Camilli	1B157	L	32	157	565	105	164	30	12	26	104	110	107	1	.290	.524
Pete Coscarart	2B107, 3B4, SS2	R	26	115	419	59	116	22	2	4	43	46	56	10	.277	.368
Leo Durocher	SS113, 3B1	R	33	116	390	42	108	21	6	1	34	27	24	2	.277	.369
Cookie Lavagetto	3B149	R	26	153	587	93	176	28	5	10	87	78	30	14	.300	.416
Art Parks	OF65	L	27	71	239	27	65	13	2	1	19	28	14	2	.272	.356
Gene Moore	OF86, 1B1	L	29	107	306	45	69	13	6	3	39	40	50	4	.225	.337
Ernie Koy	OF114	R	29	125	425	57	118	37	5	8	67	39	64	11	.278	.445
Babe Phelps	C92	L	31	98	323	33	92	21	2	6	42	23	24	0	.285	.418
Johnny Hudson	SS50, 2B45, 3B1	R	27	109	343	46	87	17	3	2	32	30	36	5	.254	.338
Al Todd	C73	R	35	86	245	28	68	10	0	5	32	13	16	1	.278	.380
Tuck Stainback	OF55	R	28	68	201	22	54	7	0	3	19	4	23	0	.269	.348
Dixie Walker (KJ)	OF59	L	28	61	225	27	63	6	4	2	38	20	10	1	.280	.369
Goody Rosen	OF47	L	26	54	183	22	46	6	4	1	12	23	21	4	.251	.344
2 Mel Almada	OF32	L	26	39	112	11	24	4	0	0	3	9	17	2	.214	.250
Fred Sington	OF22	R	29	32	84	13	23	5	0	1	7	15	15	0	.274	.369
2 Lyn Lary	SS12, 3B7	R	33	29	31	7	5	1	1	0	1	12	6	1	.161	.258
2 Jimmy Ripple	OF28	L	29	28	106	18	35	8	4	0	28	11	8	0	.330	.481
1 Ray Hayworth	C18	R	35	21	26	0	4	2	0	0	1	4	7	0	.154	.231
1 Tony Lazzeri	2B11, 3B2	R	35	14	39	6	11	2	0	3	6	10	7	1	.282	.564
Chris Hartje	C8	R	24	9	16	2	5	1	0	0	5	1	0	0	.313	.375
Oris Hockett	OF1	L	29	9	13	3	3	0	0	0	1	1	1	0	.231	.231

Lindsey Deal 27 L 0-7, Gene Schott 25 R 0-0

NAME	T	AGE	W	L	PCT	SV	G	GS	CG	IP	H	BB	SO	ShO	ERA
TOTALS		27	84	69	.549	13	157	157	69	1410	1431	399	528	9	3.64
Luke Hamlin	R	34	20	13	.606	0	40	36	19	270	255	54	88	2	3.63
Hugh Casey	R	25	15	10	.600	1	40	25	15	227	228	54	79	0	2.93
Tot Pressnell	R	32	9	7	.563	2	31	18	10	157	171	33	43	2	4.01
Vito Tamulis	L	27	9	8	.529	4	39	17	8	159	177	45	83	1	4.36
Whit Wyatt	R	31	8	3	.727	0	16	14	6	109	88	39	52	2	2.31
Freddie Fitzsimmons	R	37	7	9	.438	3	27	20	5	151	178	28	44	0	3.87
Ira Hutchinson	R	28	5	2	.714	1	41	1	0	106	103	51	46	0	4.33
Bill Crouch	R	28	4	0	1.000	0	6	3	3	38	37	14	10	0	2.60
Van Lingle Mungo (BL)	R	28	4	5	.444	0	14	10	1	77	70	33	34	0	3.27
Carl Doyle	R	26	1	2	.333	1	5	1	1	18	8	7	7	1	1.00
Red Evans	R	32	1	8	.111	1	24	6	0	64	74	26	28	0	5.20
2 Al Hollingsworth	L	31	1	2	.333	0	8	5	1	27	33	11	11	0	5.33
George Jeffcoat	R	25	0	0	.000	0	1	0	0	2	2	0	1	0	0.00
Boots Poffenberger (ST)	R	24	0	0	.000	0	3	1	0	5	7	4	2	0	5.40

CHICAGO 4th 84-70 .545 13 — GABBY HARTNETT

NAME	G by POS	B	AGE	G	AB	R	H	2B	3B	HR	RBI	BB	SO	SB	BA	SA
TOTALS			29	156	5293	724	1407	263	62	91	671	523	553	61	.266	.391
Rip Russell	1B143	R	24	143	542	55	148	24	5	9	79	36	56	2	.273	.386
Billy Herman	2B156	R	29	156	623	111	191	34	18	7	70	66	31	9	.307	.453
Dick Bartell	SS101, 3B1	R	31	105	336	37	80	24	2	3	34	42	25	6	.238	.348
Stan Hack	3B156	L	29	156	641	112	191	28	6	8	56	65	35	17	.298	.398
Jim Gleeson	OF91	B	27	111	332	43	74	19	6	4	45	39	46	7	.223	.352
Hank Leiber	OF98	R	28	112	365	65	113	16	1	24	88	59	42	1	.310	.556
Augie Galan	OF145	B	27	148	549	104	167	36	8	6	71	75	26	8	.304	.432
Gabby Hartnett	C86	R	38	97	306	36	85	18	2	12	59	37	32	0	.278	.467
Carl Reynolds	OF72	R	36	88	281	33	69	10	6	4	44	16	38	5	.246	.367
Gus Mancuso	C76	R	33	80	251	17	58	10	0	2	17	24	19	0	.231	.295
Bill Nicholson	OF58	L	24	58	220	37	65	12	5	5	38	20	29	0	.295	.464
Bobby Mattick	SS48	R	23	51	178	16	51	12	1	0	23	6	19	1	.287	.365
Bob Garbark	C21	R	24	24	21	1	3	0	0	0	0	0	3	0	.143	.143
1 Joe Marty	OF21	R	25	23	76	6	10	1	0	2	10	4	13	2	.132	.224
Phil Cavarretta (BN)	1B13, OF1	L	22	22	55	4	15	3	1	0	0	4	3	2	.273	.364
Steve Mesner	SS12, 2B1, 3B1	R	21	17	43	7	12	4	0	0	6	3	4	0	.279	.372

NAME	T	AGE	W	L	PCT	SV	G	GS	CG	IP	H	BB	SO	ShO	ERA
TOTALS		32	84	70	.545	13	156	156	72	1392	1504	430	584	8	3.80
Bill Lee	R	29	19	15	.559	0	37	36	20	282	295	85	105	1	3.45
Larry French	L	31	15	8	.652	1	36	21	10	194	205	50	98	2	3.29
2 Claude Passeau	R	30	13	9	.591	3	34	27	13	221	215	48	108*	1	3.05
Charlie Root	R	40	8	8	.500	4	35	16	8	167	189	34	65	0	4.04
Vance Page	R	35	7	7	.500	1	27	17	8	139	169	37	43	1	3.88
Dizzy Dean	R	28	6	4	.600	0	19	13	7	96	98	17	27	2	3.38
Jack Russell	R	33	4	3	.571	3	39	0	0	69	78	24	32	0	3.65
Earl Whitehill (BG)	L	39	4	7	.364	1	24	11	2	89	102	50	42	1	5.16
Gene Lillard	R	25	3	5	.375	0	20	7	2	55	68	36	31	0	6.55
Clay Bryant (SA)	R	27	2	1	.667	0	4	4	2	31	42	14	9	0	5.81
1 Kirby Higbe	R	24	2	1	.667	0	9	2	0	23	12	22	16	0	3.13
Vern Olsen	L	21	1	0	1.000	0	4	0	0	8	2	7	3	0	0.00
1 Ray Harrell	R	27	0	2	.000	0	4	2	0	17	29	6	5	0	8.47

*Passeau, also with Philadelphia, league leader in SO with 137

NEW YORK 5th 77-74 .510 18.5 — BILL TERRY

NAME	G by POS	B	AGE	G	AB	R	H	2B	3B	HR	RBI	BB	SO	SB	BA	SA
TOTALS			29	151	5129	703	1395	211	38	116	651	498	499	26	.272	.396
Zeke Bonura	1B122	R	30	123	455	75	146	26	6	11	85	46	22	1	.321	.477
Burgess Whitehead	2B91, SS4, 3B1	R	29	95	335	31	80	6	3	2	24	24	19	1	.239	.293
Billy Jurges	SS137	R	31	138	543	84	155	21	11	6	63	47	34	3	.285	.398
Tom Hafey	3B70	R	25	70	256	37	62	10	1	6	26	10	44	1	.242	.359
Mel Ott	OF96, 3B20	L	30	125	396	85	122	23	2	27	80	100	50	2	.308	.581
Frank Demaree	OF150	R	29	150	560	68	170	27	2	11	79	66	40	2	.304	.418
Jo-Jo Moore	OF136	L	30	138	562	80	151	23	2	10	47	45	17	5	.269	.370
Harry Danning	C132	R	27	135	520	79	163	28	5	16	74	35	42	4	.313	.479
Alex Kampouris	2B62, 3B1	R	26	74	201	23	50	12	2	5	29	30	41	0	.249	.403
1 Jimmy Ripple	OF23	L	29	66	123	10	28	4	0	1	6	8	7	0	.228	.285
Bob Seeds	OF50	R	32	63	173	33	46	5	1	5	26	22	31	1	.266	.393
Ken O'Dea	C30	L	26	52	97	7	17	1	0	3	11	10	16	0	.175	.278
Johnny McCarthy	1B12, OF4, P1	L	29	50	80	12	21	6	1	1	11	3	8	0	.263	.400
Lou Chiozza (BL)	3B30, SS8	L	29	40	142	19	38	3	1	3	12	9	10	3	.268	.366
George Myatt (KJ)	3B14	L	25	22	53	7	10	2	0	0	3	6	6	2	.189	.226
Babe Young	1B22	L	24	22	75	8	23	4	0	3	14	5	6	0	.307	.480
2 Tony Lazzeri	3B13	R	35	13	44	7	13	0	0	1	8	7	6	0	.295	.364
Skeeter Scalzi	SS5, 3B1	R	26	11	18	3	6	0	0	0	0	3	2	1	.333	.333
Johnny Dickshot	OF10	R	29	10	34	3	8	0	0	0	5	5	3	0	.235	.235

Al Glossop 26 B 6-32, 2 Ray Hayworth 35 R 3-13

NAME	T	AGE	W	L	PCT	SV	G	GS	CG	IP	H	BB	SO	ShO	ERA
TOTALS		29	77	74	.510	20	151	151	55	1319	1412	477	505	6	4.07
Harry Gumbert	R	29	18	11	.621	0	36	34	14	244	257	81	81	2	4.32
Hal Schumacher	R	28	13	10	.565	0	29	27	8	182	199	89	58	1	4.80
Bill Lohrman	R	26	12	13	.480	1	38	24	9	186	200	45	70	1	4.06
Cliff Melton	L	27	12	15	.444	5	41	23	9	207	214	65	95	2	3.57
Carl Hubbell	L	36	11	9	.550	2	29	18	10	154	150	24	62	0	2.75
Jumbo Brown	R	32	4	0	1.000	7	31	0	0	56	69	25	24	0	4.18
Manny Salvo	R	26	4	10	.286	1	32	18	4	136	150	75	69	0	4.63
Slick Castleman	R	25	1	2	.333	1	12	4	0	34	36	23	6	0	4.50
Dick Coffman	R	32	1	2	.333	3	28	0	0	38	50	6	9	0	3.08
2 Red Lynn	R	25	1	0	1.000	1	26	0	0	50	44	21	22	0	3.06
Tom Gorman	L	23	0	0	.000	0	4	0	0	5	7	1	2	0	7.20
Hy Vandenberg	R	32	0	0	.000	0	2	1	0	6	10	6	3	0	6.00
Johnnie Wittig	R	25	0	2	.000	0	5	2	1	17	18	14	4	0	7.41
Johnny McCarthy	L	29	0	0	.000	0	1	0	0	5	8	2	0	0	7.20

PITTSBURGH 6th 68-85 .444 28.5 — PIE TRAYNOR

NAME	G by POS	B	AGE	G	AB	R	H	2B	3B	HR	RBI	BB	SO	SB	BA	SA
TOTALS			29	153	5269	666	1453	261	60	63	617	477	420	44	.276	.384
2 Elbie Fletcher	1B101	L	23	102	370	49	112	23	4	12	71	48	28	3	.303	.484
Pep Young	2B84	R	31	84	293	34	81	14	3	3	29	23	29	1	.276	.375
Arky Vaughan	SS152	L	27	152	595	94	182	30	11	6	62	70	20	12	.306	.424
Lee Handley	3B100	R	25	101	376	43	107	14	5	1	42	32	20	17	.285	.356
Paul Waner	OF106	L	36	125	461	62	151	30	6	3	45	35	18	0	.328	.438
Lloyd Waner	OF92, 3B1	L	33	112	379	49	108	15	3	0	24	17	13	0	.285	.340
Johnny Rizzo	OF86	R	26	94	330	49	86	23	3	6	54	42	27	0	.261	.403
Ray Berres	C80	R	31	81	231	22	53	6	1	0	16	11	25	1	.229	.264
Bill Brubaker	2B65, 3B32, SS1	R	28	100	345	41	80	23	1	7	43	29	51	3	.232	.365
Ray Mueller	C81	R	27	86	180	14	42	8	1	2	18	14	22	0	.233	.322
2 Chuck Klein	OF66	L	34	85	270	37	81	16	4	11	47	26	17	1	.300	.511
Fern Bell	OF67, 3B1	R	26	83	262	44	75	5	8	2	34	42	18	2	.286	.389
Joe Bowman	P37	L	29	70	96	9	33	8	1	0	18	5	9	0	.344	.448
1 Gus Suhr	1B52	L	33	63	204	23	59	10	2	1	31	25	23	4	.289	.373
Bob Elliott	OF30	R	22	32	129	18	43	10	3	3	19	9	4	0	.333	.527
George Susce	1B31	R	30	31	75	8	17	3	1	1	4	12	5	0	.227	.333
Maurice Van Robays	OF25, 2B1	R	24	27	105	13	33	9	0	2	16	6	10	0	.314	.457
Frankie Gustine	3B22	R	19	22	70	5	13	3	0	0	3	9	4	0	.186	.229
Jack Juelich	2B10, 3B2	R	22	17	46	5	11	0	2	0	4	2	4	0	.239	.326

Woody Jensen 31 L 2-12, Heinie Manush 37 L 0-12, Joe Schultz 20 L 4-14, Eddie Yount 22 R 0-2

NAME	T	AGE	W	L	PCT	SV	G	GS	CG	IP	H	BB	SO	ShO	ERA
		28	68	85	.444	15	153	153	53	1354	1537	423	464	10	4.15
Bob Klinger	R	31	14	17	.452	0	37	33	10	225	251	81	64	2	4.36
Joe Bowman	R	29	10	14	.417	1	37	27	10	185	217	43	58	1	4.48
Rip Sewell	R	32	10	9	.526	2	52	12	5	176	177	73	69	1	4.09
Mace Brown	R	30	9	13	.409	7	47	19	8	200	232	52	71	1	3.38
Jim Tobin	R	26	9	9	.500	0	25	19	8	145	194	33	43	0	4.53
Bill Swift	R	31	5	7	.417	4	36	8	2	130	150	28	56	1	3.88
2 Max Butcher	R	28	4	4*	.500	0	14	12	5	87	104	23	21	2	3.41
Russ Bauers (SA)	R	25	2	4	.333	1	15	8	1	54	46	25	12	0	3.33
Cy Blanton (SA)	R	30	2	3	.400	0	10	6	1	42	45	10	11	0	4.29
Johnny Gee	L	23	1	2	.333	0	3	3	1	20	20	10	16	0	4.05
Ken Heintzelman	L	23	1	1	.500	0	17	2	1	36	35	18	18	1	5.00
Oad Swigart	R	24	1	1	.500	0	3	3	1	24	27	6	8	1	4.50
Bill Clemensen	R	20	0	1	.000	0	12	1	0	27	32	20	13	0	7.33
Pep Rambert	R	22	0	0	.000	0	2	0	0	4	7	1	4	0	9.00

*Butcher, also with Philadelphia, league leader in L with 17

BOSTON 7th 63-88 .417 32.5 — CASEY STENGEL

NAME	G by POS	B	AGE	G	AB	R	H	2B	3B	HR	RBI	BB	SO	SB	BA	SA
TOTALS			28	152	5286	572	1395	199	39	56	534	366	494	41	.264	.348
Buddy Hassett	1B23, OF23	L	27	147	590	72	182	15	3	2	60	29	14	13	.308	.354
Tony Cuccinello (NJ)	2B80	R	31	81	310	42	95	17	1	2	40	26	26	5	.306	.387
Eddie Miller (BL)	SS77	R	22	77	296	32	79	12	2	4	31	16	21	4	.267	.361
Hank Majeski	3B99	R	22	106	367	35	100	16	1	7	54	18	30	2	.272	.379
Debs Garms	OF96, 3B37	L	31	132	513	68	153	24	9	2	37	39	20	2	.298	.392
Johnny Cooney	OF116, 1B2	R	38	118	368	39	101	8	1	2	27	21	8	2	.274	.318
Max West	OF124	L	22	130	449	67	128	26	6	19	82	51	55	1	.285	.497
Al Lopez	C129	R	30	131	412	32	104	22	1	8	49	40	45	1	.252	.369
Rabbit Warstler	SS49, 2B43, 3B21	R	35	114	342	34	83	11	3	0	24	24	31	2	.243	.292
1 Al Simmons	OF82	R	37	93	330	39	93	17	5	7	43	22	40	0	.282	.427
Jimmy Outlaw	OF39, 3B2	R	26	65	133	15	35	2	0	0	5	10	14	1	.263	.278
Sibby Sisti	2B34, 3B17, SS10	R	18	63	215	19	49	7	1	1	11	12	38	4	.228	.284
Phil Masi	C42	R	22	46	114	14	29	7	2	1	14	9	15	0	.254	.377
1 Elbie Fletcher	1B31	L	23	35	106	14	26	2	0	0	6	19	5	1	.245	.264
Ralph Hodgin	OF9	L	23	32	48	4	10	1	0	0	4	3	4	0	.208	.229
Whitey Wietelmann	SS22, 2B1	R	20	23	69	2	14	1	0	0	5	2	9	1	.203	.217
Bama Rowell	OF16	L	23	21	59	5	11	2	2	0	6	1	4	0	.186	.288
Stan Andrews	C10	R	22	13	26	1	6	0	0	0	1	1	2	0	.231	.231
Red Barkley	SS7, 3B4	R	25	12	11	1	0	0	0	0	0	1	2	0	.000	.000

Otto Huber 25 R 6-22, Chet Ross 27 R 10-31, Chet Clemens 22 R 5-23, Oliver Hill 29 L 1-2, Bill Schuster 26 R 0-3

NAME	T	AGE	W	L	PCT	SV	G	GS	CG	IP	H	BB	SO	ShO	ERA
		31	63	88	.417	15	152	152	68	1358	1400	513	430	11	3.71
Bill Posedel	R	32	15	13	.536	0	33	29	18	221	221	78	73	5	3.91
Lou Fette	R	32	10	10	.500	0	27	26	11	146	123	61	35	6	2.96
Danny MacFayden	R	34	8	14	.364	2	33	28	8	192	221	59	46	0	3.89
Dick Errickson	R	25	6	9	.400	1	28	11	3	128	143	54	33	0	4.01
Joe Sullivan	L	28	6	9	.400	2	31	11	7	114	114	50	46	0	3.63
Johnny Lanning	R	28	5	6	.455	4	37	6	3	129	120	53	45	0	3.42
1 Milt Shoffner	L	33	4	6	.400	1	25	11	7	132	133	42	51	0	3.14
Jim Turner (BY)	R	35	4	11	.267	0	25	22	9	158	181	51	50	0	4.27
George Barnicle	R	21	2	2	.500	0	6	1	0	18	16	8	15	0	5.00
Joe Callahan	R	22	1	0	1.000	0	4	1	1	17	17	3	8	0	3.18
Tom Earley	R	22	1	4	.200	1	14	2	0	40	49	19	9	0	4.73
Hiker Moran	R	27	1	1	.500	0	6	2	1	20	21	11	4	0	4.50
Fred Frankhouse	R	35	0	2	.000	4	23	0	0	38	37	18	12	0	2.61
Al Veigel	R	22	0	1	.000	0	2	2	0	3	3	5	1	0	6.00
Roy Weir	L	28	0	0	.000	0	2	0	0	3	1	1	2	0	0.00

PHILADELPHIA 8th 45-106 .298 50.5 — DOC PROTHRO

NAME	G by POS	B	AGE	G	AB	R	H	2B	3B	HR	RBI	BB	SO	SB	BA	SA
TOTALS			28	152	5133	553	1341	232	40	49	510	421	486	47	.261	.351
2 Gus Suhr	1B60	L	33	60	198	21	63	12	2	3	24	34	14	1	.318	.444
2 Roy Hughes	2B65	R	28	65	237	22	54	5	1	1	16	21	18	4	.228	.270
George Scharein	SS117	R	24	118	399	35	95	17	1	1	33	13	40	4	.238	.293
Pinky May	3B132	R	28	135	464	49	133	27	3	2	62	41	20	4	.287	.371
2 Joe Marty	OF79, P1	R	25	91	299	32	76	12	6	9	44	24	27	1	.254	.425
Hersh Martin	OF95	B	29	111	393	59	111	28	5	1	22	42	27	4	.282	.387
Morrie Arnovich	OF132	R	28	134	491	68	159	25	2	5	67	58	28	7	.324	.413
Spud Davis	C85	R	34	87	202	10	62	8	1	0	23	24	20	0	.307	.356
Emmett Mueller	2B51, 3B17, OF17, SS1	B	26	115	341	46	95	19	4	9	43	33	34	4	.279	.437
Gib Brack	OF48, 1B19	R	31	91	270	40	78	21	4	6	41	26	49	1	.289	.468
Wally Millies	C84	R	32	84	205	12	48	3	0	0	12	9	5	0	.234	.249
Del Young	SS55, 2B17	B	27	77	217	22	57	9	2	3	20	8	24	1	.263	.364
LeGrant Scott	OF55	L	28	76	232	31	65	15	1	1	26	22	14	5	.280	.366
Jack Bolling	1B48	L	22	69	211	27	61	11	0	3	13	11	10	6	.289	.384
Pinky Whitney	1B12, 2B8, 3B2	R	34	34	75	9	14	0	1	1	6	7	4	0	.187	.253
1 Chuck Klein	OF11, 1B1	L	34	25	47	8	9	2	1	1	9	10	4	1	.191	.340
Les Powers	1B13	L	26	19	52	7	18	1	1	0	2	4	6	0	.346	.404
2 Bud Hafey	OF13, P2	R	26	18	51	3	9	1	0	0	3	3	12	1	.176	.196
Bennie Warren	C17	R	27	18	56	4	13	0	0	1	7	7	7	0	.232	.286

Bud Bates 27 R 15-58, Dave Coble 26 R 7-25, Stan Benjamin 25 R 7-50, Charlie Letchas 23 R 10-44, 2 Jim Shilling (LJ) 24 R 10-33, Eddie Feinberg 20 B 4-18, Len Gabrielson (JJ) 23 L 4-18, Joe Kracher 23 R 1-5, Bill Atwood 27 R 0-6, Johnny Watwood 32 L 1-6

NAME	T	AGE	W	L	PCT	SV	G	GS	CG	IP	H	BB	SO	ShO	ERA
		28	45	106	.298	12	152	152	67	1327	1502	579	447	3	5.17
2 Kirby Higbe	R	24	10	14	.417	2	34	26	14	187	208	101	79	1	4.86
Hugh Mulcahy	R	25	9	16	.360	4	38	31	14	226	246	93	59	1	4.98
Syl Johnson	R	38	8	8	.500	2	22	14	6	111	112	15	37	0	3.81
Boom-Boom Beck	R	34	7	14	.333	3	34	16	12	183	203	64	77	0	4.72
2 Ray Harrell	R	27	3	7	.300	0	22	10	4	95	101	56	35	0	5.40
1 Max Butcher	R	28	2	13*	.133	0	19	16	3	104	131	51	27	0	5.63
1 Claude Passeau	R	30	2	4	.333	0	8	8	4	53	54	25	29†	1	4.24
Ike Pearson	R	22	2	13	.133	0	26	13	4	125	144	56	29	0	5.76
Elmer Burkart	R	22	1	0	1.000	0	5	0	0	8	11	2	2	0	4.50
1 Al Hollingsworth	L	31	1	9	.100	0	15	10	3	60	78	27	24	0	5.85
Roy Bruner	R	22	0	4	.000	0	4	4	2	27	38	13	11	0	6.67
2 Bud Hafey	R	26	0	0	.000	0	2	0	0	1	7	1	1	0	45.00
Jim Henry	R	29	0	1	.000	1	9	1	0	23	24	8	7	0	5.09
Bill Hoffman	L	21	0	0	.000	0	3	0	0	6	8	7	1	0	13.50
Bill Kerksieck	R	25	0	2	.000	0	23	2	1	63	81	32	13	0	7.14
2 Joe Marty	R	25	0	0	.000	0	1	0	0	4	2	3	1	0	4.50
Jennings Poindexter	L	28	0	0	.000	0	11	1	0	30	29	15	12	0	4.20
1 Gene Schott	R	25	0	1	.000	0	4	0	0	11	14	5	1	0	4.91
Al Smith	L	31	0	0	.000	0	5	0	0	9	11	5	2	0	4.00

*Butcher (see Pittsburgh) †Passeau (see Chicago)

WORLD SERIES – NEW YORK (AL) 4 CINCINNATI (NL) 0

LINE SCORES

TEAM	1	2	3	4	5	6	7	8	9	10	11	12	R	H	E
Game 1 October 4 at New York															
CIN (NL)	0	0	0	1	0	0	0	0	0				1	4	0
NY (AL)	0	0	0	0	1	0	0	0	1				2	6	0
Derringer	Ruffing														
Game 2 October 5 at New York															
CIN	0	0	0	0	0	0	0	0	0				0	2	0
NY	0	0	3	1	0	0	0	0	X				4	9	0
Walters	Pearson														
Game 3 October 7 at Cincinnati															
NY	2	0	2	0	3	0	0	0	0				7	5	1
CIN	1	2	0	0	0	0	0	0	0				3	10	0
Gomez, Hadley (2)	Thompson, Grissom (5), Moore (7)														
Game 4 October 8 at Cincinnati															
NY	0	0	0	0	0	0	2	0	2	3			7	7	1
CIN	0	0	0	0	0	0	3	1	0	0			4	11	4
Hildebrand, Sundra (5), Murphy (7)	Derringer, Walters (8)														

COMPOSITE BATTING

NAME	POS	G	AB	R	H	2B	3B	HR	RBI	BA
New York (AL) Totals		4	131	20	27	4	1	7	18	.206
Keller	OF	4	16	8	7	1	1	3	6	.438
DiMaggio	OF	4	16	3	5	0	0	1	3	.313
Rolfe	3B	4	16	2	2	0	0	0	0	.125
Crosetti	SS	4	16	2	1	0	0	0	1	.063
Dickey	C	4	15	2	4	0	0	2	5	.267
Dahlgren	1B	4	14	2	3	2	0	1	2	.214
Gordon	2B	4	14	1	2	0	0	0	1	.143
Selkirk	OF	4	12	0	2	1	0	0	0	.167
Ruffing	P	1	3	0	1	0	0	0	0	.333
Hadley	P	1	3	0	0	0	0	0	0	.000
Murphy	P	1	2	0	0	0	0	0	0	.000
Pearson	P	1	2	0	0	0	0	0	0	.000
Gomez	P	1	1	0	0	0	0	0	0	.000
Hildebrand	P	1	1	0	0	0	0	0	0	.000
Sundra	P	1	0	0	0	0	0	0	0	.000
Cincinnati (NL) Totals		4	133	8	27	3	1	0	8	.203
Frey	2B	4	17	0	0	0	0	0	0	.000
Werber	3B	4	16	1	4	0	0	0	2	.250
McCormick	1B	4	15	1	6	1	0	0	1	.400
Goodman	OF	4	15	3	5	1	0	0	1	.333
Berger	OF	4	15	0	0	0	0	0	1	.000
Lombardi	C	4	14	0	3	0	0	0	2	.214
Myers	SS	4	12	2	4	0	1	0	0	.333
Craft	OF	4	11	0	1	0	0	0	0	.091
Derringer	P	2	5	0	1	0	0	0	0	.200
Simmons	OF	1	4	1	1	1	0	0	0	.250
Walters	P	2	3	0	0	0	0	0	0	.000
Hershberger	C	3	2	0	1	0	0	0	1	.500
Bongiovanni	PH	1	1	0	0	0	0	0	0	.000
Gamble	PH	1	1	0	0	0	0	0	0	.000
Moore	P	1	1	0	0	0	0	0	0	.000
Thompson	P	1	1	1	0	0	0	0	0	1.000
Bordagaray	PR	2	0	0	0	0	0	0	0	.000
Grissom	P	1	0	0	0	0	0	0	0	.000

COMPOSITE PITCHING

NAME	G	IP	H	BB	SO	W	L	SV	ERA
New York (AL) Totals	4	37	27	6	22	4	0	0	1.22
Pearson	1	9	2	1	8	1	0	0	0.00
Ruffing	1	9	4	1	4	1	0	0	1.00
Hadley	1	8	7	3	2	1	0	0	2.25
Hildebrand	1	4	2	0	3	0	0	0	0.00
Murphy	1	3.1	5	0	2	1	0	0	2.70
Sundra	1	2.2	4	1	2	0	0	0	0.00
Gomez	1	1	3	0	1	0	0	0	9.00
Cincinnati (NL) Totals	4	35.2	27	9	20	0	4	0	4.29
Derringer	2	15.1	9	3	9	0	1	0	2.35
Walters	2	11	13	1	6	0	2	0	4.91
Thompson	1	4.2	5	4	3	0	1	0	13.50
Moore	1	3	0	0	2	0	0	0	0.00
Grissom	1	1.2	0	1	0	0	0	0	0.00

1940 Baker's Shift and McKechnie's Dozen

Del Baker took over as manager of Detroit toward the end of the 1938 season and posted a 37-20 record. In 1939 he remained at the helm all season and won 81 while losing 73, enough for a slip from fourth to fifth place. Then, in the spring of 1940, Baker simply shifted Hank Greenberg from first to left field and Rudy York from a part-time backstop to a full-time first baseman. Presto—a pennant! Yet, for all the honors of being tops in the best race the junior circuit staged up to 1940, Baker and his Tigers were again overshadowed by the omnipotent presence of the Yankees, who found themselves floundering in the league's basement in May only to make a fantastic dash down the stretch to wind up in third place, two games off the leaders.

If the Yankees threw a giant shadow, the Indians projected an even more stifling silhouette.

Bob Feller no-hit the White Sox on opening day and then went on to notch a league high 27 wins and league low 2.61 E.R.A. Lou Boudreau knocked in 101 runs and hit .295, good enough to take Rookie of the Year honors. But the Indians also suffered from incompatibility, which was enough of a problem to shatter their day in the sun. In a time when the status quo was more a way of life than something to throw stones at, Cleveland players found the courageous audacity to present a petition to the owners for the release of manager Ossie Vitt. The Cleveland establishment, ignoring the majority of 25 for the minority of one, refused the demand and watched a dispirited team make a faint-hearted stretch drive to finish a frustrating one-game off the Tigers.

Regardless of Cleveland's morale and the Yankees' Joe DiMaggio, who put his second straight batting title together, the Tigers had the MVP in Greenberg and the kind of power which unnerved the league—smashing 26 homers in 17 games. Aside from Greenberg's 41 home runs and York's 33, there was also Schoolboy Rowe's return to form (16-3) after three years of arm misery, and Bobo Newsom, 21-5, who finally managed to land on a pennant winner after six teams in ten years.

In contrast to the American League pennant struggle, the National League winner reversed roles and had a cakewalk. But the senior circuit, always seeming to have a lock on baseball's theatrics, presented a winner which was made to wear both masks of the traditional theater. After the Dodgers got off in perfect form with nine straight wins climaxed by Ted Carelton's no-hitter over the Reds on April 30, Cincinnati began their pennant drive and, in early July, went in front to stay.

St. Louis, which had provided most of the competition in 1939, got off to a poor start and replaced manager Ray Blades with Billy Southworth. They also traded Joe Medwick and Curt Davis to the Dodgers for Ernie Koy, Carl Doyle, and Newt Kimball, plus picking up $100,000 in the swap. But the Dodgers' thrust to second was credited more to 38-year-old Freddie Fitzsimmons' 16-2 record than to the trades.

Whatever chance the Dodgers might have had was denied when rookie shortstop Pee Wee Reese broke his foot in mid-August and Cookie Lavagetto was sidelined at about the same time with appendicitis.

The Reds finished the season 12 games in front for manager Bill McKechnie. The statistics, though, tell little of the drama which unfolded at Cincinnati. While visiting Boston on August 2, catcher Willard Hershberger committed suicide. Then, in mid-September, starting catcher Ernie Lombardi sprained an ankle. It took 39-year-old coach Jimmie Wilson to rekindle the team's spirits. He took over the catching chores for the remainder of the season and turned in a fine job.

As the Reds entered the World Series, they still relied heavily on the catching of Wilson. In the first game Detroit routed Paul Derringer, one of Cincinnati's aces, in a five-run second-inning barrage and went on to win 7-2 behind Bobo Newsom. Bucky Walters, the other half of the Red's pitching power, evened matters the next day with a three-hit, 5-3 victory over Schoolboy Rowe. The Tigers got the upper hand in game three before Derringer returned in the fourth contest to knot up the Series with a 5-2 win. Newsom again gave the Tigers an edge in games, but after Walters bested Rowe—who didn't last through the first—the outcome came down to a second rematch between Derringer and Newsom. After Detroit got an unearned run in the third, Derringer held on and picked up two runs in the seventh to give the Reds a 2-1 win for their first championship in 21 years. In Wilson, who provided a steady hand behind the plate—especially in the important sixth-game shutout—there was no disappointment as he finished the Series with an impressive .353 batting average.

1940 AMERICAN LEAGUE

NAME	G by POS	B	AGE	G	AB	R	H	2B	3B	HR	RBI	BB	SO	SB	BA	SA
DETROIT 1st 90-64 .584		DEL BAKER														
TOTALS			30	155	5418	**888**	1549	**312**	65	134	**829**	**664**	556	66	**.286**	.442
Rudy York	1B155	R	26	155	588	105	186	46	6	33	134	89	88	3	.316	.583
Charlie Gehringer	2B138	L	37	139	515	108	161	33	3	10	81	101	17	10	.313	.447
Dick Bartell	SS139	R	32	139	528	76	123	24	3	7	53	76	53	12	.233	.330
Pinky Higgins	3B129	R	31	131	480	70	130	24	3	13	76	61	31	4	.271	.415
Pete Fox	OF85	R	30	93	350	49	101	17	4	5	48	21	30	7	.289	.403
Barney McCosky	OF141	L	22	143	589	123	**200**	39	**19**	4	57	67	41	13	.340	.491
Hank Greenberg	OF148	R	29	148	573	129	195	**50**	8	**41**	**150**	93	75	6	.340	**.670**
Birdie Tebbetts	C107	R	30	111	379	46	112	24	4	4	46	35	14	4	.296	.412
Bruce Campbell	OF74	L	30	103	297	56	84	15	5	8	44	45	28	2	.283	.448
Billy Sullivan	C57, 3B6	L	29	78	220	36	68	14	4	3	41	31	11	2	.309	.450
Earl Averill	OF22	L	38	64	118	10	33	4	1	2	20	5	14	0	.280	.381
Frank Croucher	SS26, 2B7, 3B1	R	25	37	57	3	6	0	0	0	2	4	5	0	.105	.105
Red Kress	3B17, SS12	R	33	33	99	13	22	3	1	1	11	10	12	0	.222	.303
Scat Metha	2B10, 3B6	R	26	26	37	6	9	0	1	0	3	2	8	0	.243	.297
Dutch Meyer	2B21	R	24	23	58	12	15	3	0	0	6	4	10	2	.259	.310
Tuck Stainback	OF9	R	29	15	40	4	9	2	0	0	1	1	9	0	.225	.275
Pat Mullin	OF1	L	22	4	4	0	0	0	0	0	0	0	0	0	.000	.000
Frank Secory		R	27	1	1	0	0	0	0	0	0	0	1	0	.000	.000
CLEVELAND 2nd 89-65 .578 1		OSSIE VITT														
TOTALS			27	155	5361	710	1422	287	61	101	660	519	597	53	.265	.398
Hal Trosky	1B139	L	27	140	522	85	154	39	4	25	93	79	45	1	.295	.529
Ray Mack	2B146	R	23	146	530	60	150	21	5	12	69	51	77	4	.283	.409
Lou Boudreau	SS155	R	22	155	627	97	185	46	10	9	101	73	39	6	.295	.443
Ken Keltner	3B148	R	23	149	543	67	138	24	10	15	77	51	56	10	.254	.418
Beau Bell	OF97, 1B14	R	32	120	444	55	124	22	2	4	58	34	41	2	.279	.365
Roy Weatherly	OF135	L	25	135	578	90	175	35	11	12	59	27	26	9	.303	.464
Ben Chapman	OF140	R	31	143	548	82	157	40	6	4	50	78	45	13	.286	.403
Rollie Hemsley	C117	R	33	119	416	46	111	20	5	4	42	22	25	1	.267	.368
Jeff Heath	OF90	L	25	100	356	55	78	16	3	14	50	40	62	5	.219	.399
Frankie Pytlak (IL)	C58, OF1	R	31	62	149	16	21	2	1	0	16	17	5	0	.141	.168
Odell Hale	3B3	R	31	48	50	3	11	3	1	0	6	5	7	0	.220	.320
Soup Campbell	OF16	L	25	35	62	8	14	1	0	0	2	7	12	0	.226	.242
Rusty Peters	2B9, SS6, 3B6, 1B1	R	25	30	71	5	17	3	2	0	7	4	14	1	.239	.338
Oscar Grimes (CJ)	1B4, 3B1	R	25	11	13	3	0	0	0	0	0	0	5	0	.000	.000
Hank Helf	C1	R	26	1	1	0	0	0	0	0	0	0	0	0	.000	.000
NEW YORK 3rd 88-66 .571 2		JOE McCARTHY														
TOTALS			28	155	5286	817	1371	243	66	**155**	757	648	606	59	.259	.418
Babe Dahlgren	1B155	R	28	155	568	51	150	24	4	12	73	46	54	1	.264	.384
Joe Gordon	2B155	R	25	155	616	112	173	32	10	30	103	52	57	18	.281	.511
Frankie Crosetti	SS145	R	29	145	546	84	106	23	4	4	31	72	77	14	.194	.273
Red Rolfe	3B138	L	31	139	588	102	147	26	6	10	53	50	48	4	.250	.366
Charlie Keller	OF136	L	23	138	500	102	143	18	15	21	93	**106**	65	8	.286	.508
Joe DiMaggio	OF130	R	25	132	508	93	179	28	9	31	133	61	30	1	**.352**	.626
George Selkirk	OF111	L	32	118	379	68	102	17	5	19	71	84	43	3	.269	.491
Bill Dickey	C102	L	33	106	372	45	92	11	1	9	54	48	32	0	.247	.355
Tommy Henrich	OF76, 1B2	L	27	90	293	57	90	28	5	10	53	48	30	1	.307	.539
Buddy Rosar	C63	R	25	73	228	34	68	11	3	4	37	19	11	7	.298	.425
Bill Knickerbocker	SS19, 3B17	R	28	45	124	17	30	8	1	1	10	14	8	1	.242	.347
Buster Mills	OF14	R	31	34	63	10	25	3	3	1	15	7	5	0	.397	.587
Jake Powell (CN)	OF7	R	31	12	27	3	5	0	0	0	2	1	4	0	.185	.185
Mike Chartak	OF3	L	24	11	15	2	2	1	0	0	3	5	5	0	.133	.200

NAME	T	AGE	W	L	PCT	SV	G	GS	CG	IP	H	BB	SO	ShO	ERA
		27	**90**	64	**.584**	**23**	155	155	59	1375	1425	570	**752**	10	4.01
Bobo Newsom	R	32	21	5	.808	0	36	34	20	264	235	100	164	3	2.83
Schoolboy Rowe	R	30	16	3	**.842**	0	27	23	11	169	170	43	61	1	3.46
Tommy Bridges	R	33	12	9	.571	0	29	28	12	198	171	88	133	2	3.36
Hal Newhouser	L	19	9	9	.500	0	28	20	7	133	149	76	89	0	4.87
Johnny Gorsica	R	25	7	7	.500	0	29	20	5	160	170	57	68	2	4.33
Al Benton	R	29	6	10	.375	**17**	42	0	0	79	93	36	50	0	4.44
Archie McKain	L	29	5	0	1.000	3	27	0	0	51	48	25	24	0	2.82
Dizzy Trout	R	25	3	7	.300	2	33	10	1	101	125	54	64	0	4.46
Fred Hutchinson	R	20	3	7	.300	0	17	10	1	76	85	26	32	0	5.68
Tom Seats	L	28	2	2	.500	1	26	2	0	56	67	21	25	0	4.66
Floyd Giebell	R	30	2	0	1.000	0	2	2	2	18	14	4	11	1	1.00
Clay Smith	R	25	1	1	.500	0	14	1	0	28	32	13	14	0	5.14
Cotton Pippen	R	30	1	2	.333	0	4	3	0	21	29	10	9	0	6.86
Lynn Nelson	R	35	1	1	.500	0	6	2	0	14	23	9	7	0	10.93
Dick Conger	R	19	1	0	1.000	0	2	0	0	3	2	3	1	0	3.00
Bud Thomas	R	29	0	1	.000	0	3	0	0	4	8	3	0	0	9.00
Bob Uhle	L	26	0	0	.000	0	1	0	0	0	4	2	0	0	∞
		27	89	65	.578	22	155	155	72	1375	1328	512	686	**13**	**3.63**
Bob Feller	R	21	**27**	11	.711	4	**43**	**37**	**31**	**320**	245	118	**261**	**4**	**2.62**
Al Milnar	L	26	18	10	.643	3	37	33	15	242	242	99	99	**4**	3.27
Al Smith	L	32	15	7	.682	2	31	24	11	183	187	55	46	1	3.44
Mel Harder	R	30	12	11	.522	0	31	25	5	186	200	59	76	0	4.06
Johnny Allen	R	35	9	8	.529	5	32	17	5	139	126	48	62	3	3.43
Joe Dobson	R	23	3	7	.300	3	40	7	2	100	101	48	57	1	4.95
1 Willis Hudlin	R	34	2	1	.667	0	4	4	2	24	31	2	8	0	4.88
Harry Eisenstat	L	24	1	4	.200	4	27	3	0	72	78	12	27	0	3.13
Mike Naymick	R	22	1	2	.333	0	13	4	0	30	36	17	15	0	5.10
Bill Zuber	R	27	1	1	.500	0	17	0	0	24	25	14	12	0	5.63
John Humphries	R	25	0	2	.000	1	19	1	1	34	35	29	17	0	8.21
Nate Andrews	R	26	0	1	.000	0	6	0	0	12	16	6	3	0	6.00
Dixie Howell	R	20	0	0	.000	0	3	0	0	5	2	4	2	0	1.80
Ken Jungels	R	24	0	0	.000	0	2	0	0	3	3	1	1	0	3.00
Cal Dorsett	R	27	0	0	.000	0	1	0	0	1	1	0	0	0	9.00
		30	88	66	.571	14	155	155	76	1373	1389	511	559	10	3.89
Red Ruffing	R	36	15	12	.556	0	30	30	20	226	218	76	97	3	3.38
Marius Russo	L	25	14	8	.636	1	30	24	15	189	181	55	87	0	3.29
Ernie Bonham	R	26	9	3	.750	0	12	12	10	99	83	13	37	3	1.91
Spud Chandler	R	32	8	7	.533	0	27	24	6	172	184	60	56	1	4.60
Marv Breuer	R	26	8	9	.471	0	27	22	10	164	175	61	71	0	4.55
Atley Donald	R	29	8	3	.727	0	24	11	6	119	113	59	60	1	3.03
Johnny Murphy	R	31	8	4	.667	9	35	1	0	63	58	15	23	0	3.71
Monte Pearson	R	30	7	5	.583	0	16	16	7	110	108	44	43	1	3.68
Steve Sundra	R	30	4	6	.400	2	27	8	2	99	121	42	26	0	5.55
Bump Hadley	R	35	3	5	.375	2	25	2	0	80	88	52	39	0	5.74
Lefty Gomez (SA)	L	31	3	3	.500	0	9	5	0	27	37	18	14	0	6.67
Oral Hildebrand	R	33	1	1	.500	0	13	0	0	19	19	14	5	0	1.89
1 Lee Grissom	L	32	0	0	.000	0	5	0	0	5	4	2	1	0	0.00

BOSTON 4th (Tie) 82-72 .532 8 — JOE CRONIN

NAME	G by POS	B	AGE	G	AB	R	H	2B	3B	HR	RBI	BB	SO	SB	BA	SA
TOTALS			28	154	**5481**	872	**1566**	301	**80**	145	810	590	597	55	**.286**	**.449**
Jimmie Foxx	1B95, C42, 3B1	R	32	144	515	106	153	30	4	36	119	101	87	4	.297	.581
Bobby Doerr	2B151	R	22	151	595	87	173	37	10	22	105	57	53	10	.291	.497
Joe Cronin	SS146, 3B2	R	33	149	548	104	156	35	6	24	111	83	65	7	.285	.502
Jim Tabor (IL)	3B120	R	26	120	459	73	131	28	6	21	81	42	58	14	.285	.510
Dom DiMaggio	OF94	R	23	108	418	81	126	32	6	8	46	41	46	7	.301	.464
Doc Cramer	OF149	L	34	150	**661**	94	**200**	27	12	1	51	36	29	3	.303	.384
Ted Williams	OF143, P1	L	21	144	561	**134**	193	43	14	23	113	96	54	4	.344	.594
Gene Desautels	C70	R	33	71	222	19	50	7	1	0	17	32	13	0	.225	.266
Lou Finney	OF69, 1B51	L	29	130	534	73	171	31	15	5	73	33	13	5	.320	.463
Johnny Peacock	C48	L	30	63	131	20	37	4	1	0	13	23	10	1	.282	.328
Stan Spence	OF15	L	25	51	68	5	19	2	1	2	13	4	9	0	.279	.426
Tom Carey	SS20, 2B4, 3B4	R	31	43	62	4	20	4	0	0	7	2	1	0	.323	.387
2 Charlie Gelbert	3B29, SS1	R	34	30	91	9	18	2	0	0	8	8	16	0	.198	.220
Joe Glenn	C19	R	31	22	47	3	6	1	0	0	4	5	7	0	.128	.149
Marv Owen	3B9, 1B8	R	34	20	57	4	12	0	0	0	6	8	4	0	.211	.211
Tony Lupien	1B8	L	23	10	19	5	9	3	2	0	4	1	1	0	.474	.842
Red Nonnenkamp		L	28	9	7	0	0	0	0	0	1	1	4	0	.000	.000

NAME	T	AGE	W	L	PCT	SV	G	GS	CG	IP	H	BB	SO	ShO	ERA
		29	82	72	.532	16	154	154	51	1380	1568	625	613	4	4.88
Jack Wilson	R	28	12	6	.667	5	41	16	9	158	170	87	102	0	5.07
Joe Heving	R	39	12	7	.632	3	39	7	4	119	129	42	55	0	4.01
Jim Bagby	R	23	10	16	.385	2	36	21	6	183	217	83	57	1	4.72
Emerson Dickman	R	25	8	6	.571	3	35	9	2	100	121	38	40	0	6.03
Lefty Grove	L	40	7	6	.538	0	22	21	9	153	159	50	62	1	4.00
Herb Hash	R	29	7	7	.500	3	34	12	3	120	123	84	36	1	4.95
Denny Galehouse	R	28	6	6	.500	0	25	20	5	120	155	41	53	0	5.18
Earl Johnson	L	21	6	2	.750	0	17	10	2	70	69	39	26	0	4.11
Fritz Ostermueller	L	32	5	9	.357	0	31	16	5	144	166	70	80	0	4.94
Mickey Harris	L	23	4	2	.667	0	13	9	3	68	83	26	36	0	5.03
Bill Fleming	R	26	1	2	.333	0	10	6	1	46	53	20	24	0	4.89
Charlie Wagner	R	27	1	0	1.000	0	12	1	0	29	45	8	13	0	5.59
Bill Butland	R	22	1	2	.333	0	3	3	1	21	27	10	5	0	5.57
Yank Terry	R	29	1	0	1.000	0	4	1	0	19	24	11	9	0	9.00
Woody Rich	R	23	1	0	1.000	0	3	1	1	12	9	1	8	0	0.75
Alex Mustalkis	R	31	0	1	.000	0	6	1	0	15	15	15	6	0	9.00
Ted Williams	R	21	0	0	.000	0	1	0	0	2	3	0	1	0	4.50

CHICAGO 4th (Tie) 82-72 .532 8 — JIMMY DYKES

NAME	G by POS	B	AGE	G	AB	R	H	2B	3B	HR	RBI	BB	SO	SB	BA	SA
TOTALS			30	155	5386	735	1499	238	63	73	671	496	569	52	.278	.387
Joe Kuhel	1B155	L	34	155	603	111	169	28	8	27	94	87	59	12	.280	.488
Skeeter Webb	2B74, SS7, 3B1	R	30	84	334	33	79	11	2	1	29	30	33	3	.237	.290
Luke Appling	SS150	R	33	150	566	96	197	27	13	0	79	69	35	3	.348	.442
Bob Kennedy	3B154	R	19	154	606	74	153	23	3	3	52	42	58	3	.252	.315
Taffy Wright	OF144	L	28	147	581	79	196	31	9	5	88	43	25	4	.337	.448
Mike Kreevich	OF144	R	32	144	582	86	154	27	10	8	55	34	49	15	.265	.387
Moose Solters	OF107	R	34	116	428	65	132	28	3	12	80	27	54	3	.308	.472
Mike Tresh	C135	R	26	135	480	62	135	15	5	1	64	49	40	3	.281	.340
Larry Rosenthal	OF92	L	28	107	276	46	83	14	5	6	42	64	32	2	.301	.453
Eric McNair	2B65, 3B1	R	31	66	251	26	57	13	1	7	31	12	26	1	.227	.371
Tom Turner	C29	R	23	37	96	11	20	1	2	0	6	3	12	1	.208	.260
Ken Silvestri	C1	B	24	28	24	5	6	2	0	2	10	4	7	0	.250	.583
Jackie Hayes	2B15	R	33	18	41	2	8	0	1	0	1	2	11	0	.195	.244
Don Kolloway	2B10	R	21	10	40	5	9	1	0	0	3	0	3	1	.225	.250
Dave Short		L	23	4	3	1	1	0	0	0	0	1	2	0	.333	.333

NAME	T	AGE	W	L	PCT	SV	G	GS	CG	IP	H	BB	SO	ShO	ERA
		32	82	72	.532	18	155	155	**83**	**1387**	1335	480	574	10	3.74
Johnny Rigney	R	25	14	18	.438	3	39	33	19	281	240	90	141	2	3.11
Eddie Smith	L	26	14	9	.609	0	32	28	12	207	179	95	119	0	3.22
Thornton Lee	L	33	12	13	.480	0	28	27	24	228	223	56	87	1	3.47
Ted Lyons	R	39	12	8	.600	0	22	22	17	186	188	37	72	**4**	3.24
Jack Knott	R	33	11	9	.550	0	25	23	4	158	166	52	44	2	4.56
Bill Dietrich	R	30	10	6	.625	0	23	17	6	150	154	65	43	1	4.02
Clint Brown	R	36	4	6	.400	10	37	0	0	66	75	16	23	0	3.68
Pete Appleton	R	36	4	0	1.000	5	25	0	0	58	54	28	21	0	5.59
Jack Hallett	R	26	1	1	.500	0	2	2	1	14	15	6	9	0	6.43
Vallie Eaves	R	28	0	2	.000	0	5	3	0	19	22	24	11	0	6.63
Ed Weiland	R	25	0	0	.000	0	5	0	0	14	15	7	3	0	9.00
Orval Grove	R	20	0	0	.000	0	3	0	0	6	4	4	1	0	3.00

ST. LOUIS 6th 67-87 .435 23 — FRED HANEY

NAME	G by POS	B	AGE	G	AB	R	H	2B	3B	HR	RBI	BB	SO	SB	BA	SA
TOTALS			29	156	5416	757	1423	278	58	118	716	556	642	51	.263	.401
George McQuinn	1B150	L	31	151	594	78	166	39	10	16	84	57	58	3	.279	.460
Don Heffner	2B125	R	29	126	487	52	115	23	2	3	53	39	37	5	.236	.310
Johnny Berardino	SS112, 2B13, 3B9	R	23	142	523	71	135	31	4	16	85	32	46	6	.258	.424
Harlond Clift	3B147	R	27	150	523	92	143	29	5	20	87	104	62	9	.273	.463
Chet Laabs	OF63	R	28	105	218	32	59	11	5	10	40	34	59	3	.271	.505
Walt Judnich	OF133	L	23	137	519	97	157	27	7	24	89	54	71	8	.303	.520
Rip Radcliff	OF139, 1B4	L	34	150	584	83	**200**	33	9	7	81	47	20	6	.342	.466
Bob Swift	C128	R	25	130	398	37	97	20	1	0	39	28	39	1	.244	.299
2 Roy Cullenbine	OF57, 1B6	B	24	86	257	41	59	11	2	7	31	50	34	0	.230	.370
Joe Grace	OF51, C12	L	26	80	229	45	59	14	2	5	25	26	23	2	.258	.402
Myril Hoag	OF46	R	32	76	191	20	50	11	0	3	26	13	30	2	.262	.366
George Susce	C61	R	31	61	113	6	24	4	0	0	13	9	9	1	.212	.248
Alan Strange	SS35, 2B4	R	30	54	167	26	31	8	3	0	6	22	12	2	.186	.269
Vern Kennedy	P34	L	33	35	84	12	25	3	1	2	12	3	13	0	.298	.429
Lyn Lary	SS12, 2B1	R	34	27	54	5	3	1	1	0	3	4	7	0	.056	.111
1 Joe Gallagher	OF15	R	26	23	70	14	19	3	1	2	8	4	12	2	.271	.429
Johnny Lucadello	2B16	B	21	17	63	15	20	4	2	2	10	6	4	1	.317	.540
Sam Harshany	C2	R	30	3	1	0	0	0	0	0	0	1	0	0	.000	.000
Fuzz White		L	22	2	2	0	0	0	0	0	0	0	0	0	.000	.000

NAME	T	AGE	W	L	PCT	SV	G	GS	CG	IP	H	BB	SO	ShO	ERA
		30	67	87	.435	9	156	156	64	1373	**1592**	**646**	439	4	5.13
Eldon Auker	R	29	16	11	.593	0	38	35	20	264	299	96	78	2	3.95
Vern Kennedy	R	33	12	17	.414	0	34	32	18	222	263	122	70	0	5.59
Bob Harris	R	24	11	15	.423	1	35	28	8	194	225	85	49	1	4.92
Johnny Niggeling	R	36	7	11	.389	0	28	20	10	154	148	69	82	0	4.44
Bill Trotter	R	31	7	6	.538	2	36	4	1	98	117	31	29	0	3.77
Roxie Lawson	R	34	5	3	.625	4	30	2	0	72	77	54	18	0	5.13
Jack Kramer	R	22	3	7	.300	0	16	9	1	65	86	26	12	0	6.23
Emil Bildilli	L	27	2	4	.333	1	28	11	3	97	113	52	32	0	5.57
Slick Coffman	R	29	2	2	.500	1	31	4	1	75	108	23	26	0	6.24
John Whitehead (NJ)	R	31	1	3	.250	0	15	4	1	40	46	14	11	1	5.40
Maury Newlin	R	26	1	0	1.000	0	1	1	0	6	4	2	3	0	6.00
Lefty Mills	L	30	0	6	.000	0	26	5	1	59	64	52	18	0	7.78
3 Willis Hudlin	R	34	0	1	.000	0	6	1	0	11	19	8	4	0	11.46
Bill Cox	R	27	0	1	.000	0	12	0	0	17	23	12	7	0	7.41

WASHINGTON 7th 64-90 .416 26 — BUCKY HARRIS

NAME	G by POS	B	AGE	G	AB	R	H	2B	3B	HR	RBI	BB	SO	SB	BA	SA
TOTALS			27	154	5365	665	1453	266	67	52	600	468	504	**94**	.271	.374
1 Zeke Bonura	1B79	R	31	79	311	41	85	16	3	3	45	40	13	2	.273	.373
Jimmy Bloodworth	2B96, 1B17, 3B6	R	22	119	469	47	115	17	8	11	70	16	71	3	.245	.386
Jimmy Pofahl	SS112, 2B4	R	23	119	406	34	95	23	5	2	36	37	55	2	.234	.330
Cecil Travis	3B113, SS23	L	26	136	528	60	170	37	11	2	76	48	23	0	.322	.445
Buddy Lewis	OF112, 3B36	L	23	148	600	101	190	38	10	6	63	74	36	15	.317	.443
George Case	OF154	R	24	154	656	109	192	29	5	5	56	52	39	**35**	.293	.375
Gee Walker	OF140	R	32	140	595	87	175	29	7	13	96	24	58	21	.294	.432
Rick Ferrell	C99	R	34	103	326	35	89	18	2	0	28	47	15	1	.273	.340
Johnny Welaj	OF53	R	26	88	215	31	55	9	0	3	21	19	20	8	.256	.340
Jake Early	C56	L	23	80	206	26	53	8	4	5	14	23	22	0	.257	.408
Buddy Myer	2B54	L	36	71	210	28	61	14	4	0	29	34	10	6	.290	.395
Sammy West	1B12, OF9	L	35	57	99	7	25	6	1	1	18	16	13	0	.253	.364
Jack Sanford	1B34	R	23	34	122	5	24	4	2	0	10	6	17	0	.197	.262
1 Charlie Gelbert	SS12, P2, 2B1	R	34	22	54	7	20	7	1	0	7	4	3	0	.370	.537
Al Evans	C9	R	23	14	25	1	8	2	0	0	7	6	7	1	.320	.400
1 Jimmy Wasdell	1B8	L	26	10	35	3	3	1	0	0	0	2	7	0	.086	.114
Sherry Robertson	SS10	R	21	10	33	4	7	0	1	0	0	5	6	0	.212	.273
Mickey Vernon	1B4	L	22	5	19	0	3	0	0	0	0	0	3	0	.158	.158
Jim Mallory	OF3	R	21	4	12	2	2	0	0	0	0	1	1	0	.167	.167
Dick Hahn	C1	R	23	1	3	0	0	0	0	0	0	0	0	0	.000	.000
Morrie Aderholt	2B1	L	24	1	2	0	0	0	0	0	0	0	0	0	.000	.000

NAME	T	AGE	W	L	PCT	SV	G	GS	CG	IP	H	BB	SO	ShO	ERA
		25	64	90	.416	7	154	154	74	1350	1494	618	618	6	4.59
Sid Hudson	R	25	17	16	.515	1	38	31	19	252	272	81	96	3	4.57
Ken Chase	L	26	15	17	.469	0	35	34	20	262	260	**143**	129	1	3.23
Dutch Leonard	R	31	14	**19**	.424	0	35	35	23	289	**328**	78	124	2	3.49
Alex Carrasquel	R	27	6	2	.750	0	28	0	0	48	42	29	19	0	4.88
Walt Masterson	R	20	3	13	.188	2	31	19	3	130	128	88	68	0	4.92
Joe Haynes	R	22	3	6	.333	0	22	7	1	63	85	34	23	0	6.57
Rene Monteagudo	L	24	2	6	.250	2	27	8	3	101	128	52	64	0	6.06
Joe Krakauskas	L	25	1	6	.143	2	32	10	2	109	137	73	68	0	6.44
2 Willis Hudlin	R	34	1	2	.333	0	8	6	1	37	50	5	9	0	6.57
Al Hollingsworth	L	32	1	0	1.000	0	3	2	0	18	18	11	7	0	5.50
Red Anderson	R	28	1	1	.500	0	2	2	2	14	12	5	3	0	3.86
Bucky Jacobs	R	27	0	1	.000	0	9	0	0	15	16	9	6	0	6.00
Lou Thuman	R	23	0	1	.000	0	2	0	0	5	10	7	0	0	14.40
1 Charlie Gelbert	R	34	0	0	.000	0	2	0	0	4	5	3	1	0	9.00
Gil Torres	R	24	0	0	.000	0	2	0	0	3	3	0	1	0	0.00

PHILADELPHIA 8th 54-100 .351 36 — CONNIE MACK

NAME	G by POS	B	AGE	G	AB	R	H	2B	3B	HR	RBI	BB	SO	SB	BA	SA
TOTALS			26	154	5304	703	1391	242	53	105	648	556	**656**	48	.262	.387
Dick Siebert	1B154	L	28	154	595	69	170	31	6	5	77	33	34	8	.286	.383
Benny McCoy	2B130, 3B1	L	24	134	490	56	126	26	5	7	62	65	44	2	.257	.373
Al Brancato	SS80, 3B25	R	21	107	298	42	57	11	2	1	23	28	36	3	.191	.252
Al Rubeling	3B98, 2B10	R	27	108	376	49	92	16	6	4	38	48	58	4	.245	.351
Wally Moses	OF133	L	29	142	537	91	166	41	9	9	50	75	44	6	.309	.469
Sam Chapman	OF129	R	24	134	508	88	140	26	3	23	75	46	**96**	2	.276	.474
Bob Johnson	OF136	R	33	138	512	93	137	25	4	31	103	83	64	8	.268	.514
Frankie Hayes	C134, 1B2	R	25	136	465	73	143	23	4	16	70	61	59	9	.308	.477
Dee Miles	OF50	L	31	88	236	26	71	9	6	1	23	8	18	1	.301	.403
Sep Gantenbein	3B45, 1B6, SS3, OF1	L	23	75	197	21	47	6	2	4	23	11	21	1	.239	.350
Bill Lillard	SS69, 2B1	R	22	73	206	26	49	8	2	1	21	28	28	0	.238	.311
Chubby Dean	P30, 1B1	L	24	67	90	6	26	2	0	0	6	16	9	0	.289	.311
Al Simmons	OF18	R	38	37	81	7	25	4	0	1	19	4	8	0	.309	.395
Hal Wagner (BG)	C28	L	24	34	75	9	19	5	1	0	10	11	6	0	.253	.347
Fred Chapman	SS25	R	23	26	69	6	11	1	0	0	4	6	10	1	.159	.174
Crash Davis	2B19, SS1	R	20	23	67	4	18	1	1	0	9	3	10	1	.269	.313
Earle Brucker	C13	R	39	23	46	3	9	1	1	0	2	6	3	0	.196	.261
Elmer Valo	OF6	L	19	6	23	6	8	0	0	0	6	0	3	2	.348	.348
Jack Wallaesa	SS6	R	20	6	20	0	3	0	0	0	2	0	2	0	.150	.150
Eric Tipton	OF2	R	25	2	8	2	1	0	1	0	0	1	1	0	.125	.375
Dario Lodigiani		R	24	1	1	0	0	0	0	0	0	0	0	0	.000	.000
Buddy Hancken	C1	R	25	1	0	0	0	0	0	0	0	0	0	0	.000	.000

NAME	T	AGE	W	L	PCT	SV	G	GS	CG	IP	H	BB	SO	ShO	ERA
		27	54	**100**	.351	12	154	154	72	1345	1543	534	488	4	5.22
Johnny Babich	R	27	14	13	.519	0	31	30	16	229	222	80	94	1	3.73
Nels Potter	R	28	9	14	.391	0	31	25	13	201	213	71	73	0	4.43
Bill Beckmann	R	32	8	4	.667	1	34	9	6	127	132	35	47	2	4.18
Chubby Dean	L	24	6	13	.316	1	30	19	8	159	220	63	38	1	6.62
Ed Heusser	R	31	6	13	.316	5	41	6	2	110	144	42	39	0	4.99
Buck Ross	R	25	5	10	.333	1	24	19	10	156	160	60	43	0	4.38
George Caster	R	32	4	**19**	.174	2	36	24	11	178	234	69	75	0	6.57
Porter Vaughan	L	21	2	9	.182	2	18	15	5	99	104	61	46	0	5.36
Herman Besse	L	28	0	3	.000	0	17	5	0	53	70	34	19	0	8.83
Les McCrabb	R	25	0	0	.000	0	4	0	0	12	19	2	4	0	6.75
Phil Marchildon	R	26	0	2	.000	0	2	2	1	10	12	8	4	0	7.20
Carl Miles	L	22	0	0	.000	0	2	0	0	8	9	8	6	0	13.50
Pat McLaughlin	R	29	0	0	.000	0	1	0	0	2	4	1	0	0	13.50

CINCINNATI 1st 100-53 .654 — BILL McKECHNIE

NAME	G by POS	B	AGE	G	AB	R	H	2B	3B	HR	RBI	BB	SO	SB	BA	SA
TOTALS			28	155	5372	707	1427	264	38	89	649	453	503	72	.266	.379
Frank McCormick	1B155	R	29	155	618	93	191	44	3	19	127	52	26	2	.309	.482
Lonny Frey	2B150	L	29	150	563	102	150	23	6	8	54	80	48	22	.266	.371
Billy Myers	SS88	R	29	90	282	33	57	14	2	5	30	30	56	0	.202	.319
Bill Werber	3B143	R	32	143	584	105	162	35	5	12	48	68	40	16	.277	.416
Ival Goodman	OF135	L	31	136	519	78	134	20	6	12	63	60	54	9	.258	.389
Harry Craft	OF109, 1B2	R	25	115	422	47	103	18	5	6	48	17	46	2	.244	.353
Mike McCormick	OF107	R	23	110	417	48	125	20	0	1	30	13	36	8	.300	.355
Ernie Lombardi	C101	R	32	109	376	50	120	22	0	14	74	31	14	0	.319	.489
Eddie Joost	SS78, 2B7, 3B4	R	24	88	278	24	60	7	2	1	24	32	40	4	.216	.266
2 Morrie Arnovich	OF60	R	29	62	211	17	60	10	2	0	21	13	10	1	.284	.351
Willard Hershberger (DD)	C37	R	30	48	123	6	38	4	2	0	26	6	6	0	.309	.374
Lew Riggs	3B11	L	30	41	72	8	21	7	1	1	9	2	4	0	.292	.458
Lew Gamble	OF10	L	30	38	42	12	6	1	0	0	0	0	1	0	.143	.167
2 Jimmy Ripple	OF30	L	30	32	101	15	31	10	0	4	20	13	5	1	.307	.525
2 Johnny Rizzo	OF30	R	27	31	110	17	31	6	0	4	17	14	14	1	.282	.445
Bill Baker	C24	R	29	27	69	5	15	1	1	0	7	4	8	2	.217	.261
Jimmie Wilson	C16	R	39	16	37	2	9	2	0	0	3	2	1	1	.243	.297
Mike Dejan	OF2	L	25	12	16	1	3	0	1	0	2	3	3	0	.188	.313
Dick West	C7	R	24	7	28	4	11	2	0	1	6	0	2	1	.393	.571
1 Wally Berger		R	34	2	2	0	0	0	0	0	0	0	1	0	.000	.000
1 Vince DiMaggio	OF1	R	27	2	4	2	1	0	0	0	0	1	0	0	.250	.250

NAME	T	AGE	W	L	PCT	SV	G	GS	CG	IP	H	BB	SO	ShO	ERA
TOTALS		29	100	53	.654	11	155	155	91	1408	1263	445	557	10	3.05
Bucky Walters	R	31	22	10	.688	0	36	36	29	305	241	92	115	3	2.48
Paul Derringer	R	33	20	12	.625	0	37	37	26	297	280	48	115	3	3.06
Junior Thompson	R	23	16	9	.640	0	33	31	17	225	197	96	103	3	3.32
Jim Turner	R	36	14	7	.667	0	24	23	11	187	187	32	53	0	2.89
Joe Beggs	R	29	12	3	.800	7	37	1	0	77	68	21	25	0	1.99
Whitey Moore	R	28	8	8	.500	1	25	15	5	117	100	56	60	1	3.62
Johnny Vander Meer	L	25	3	1	.750	1	10	7	2	48	38	41	41	0	3.75
Johnny Hutchings	R	24	2	1	.667	0	19	4	0	54	53	18	18	0	3.50
Milt Shoffner	L	34	1	0	1.000	0	20	0	0	54	56	18	17	0	5.67
Elmer Riddle	R	25	1	2	.333	2	15	1	1	34	30	17	9	0	1.85
Red Barrett	R	25	1	0	1.000	0	3	0	0	3	5	1	0	0	6.00
Witt Guise	L	31	0	0	.000	0	2	0	0	8	8	5	1	0	1.13

BROOKLYN 2nd 88-65 .575 12 — LEO DUROCHER

NAME	G by POS	B	AGE	G	AB	R	H	2B	3B	HR	RBI	BB	SO	SB	BA	SA
TOTALS			28	156	5470	697	1421	256	70	93	653	522	569	56	.260	.383
Dolph Camilli	1B140	L	33	142	512	92	147	29	13	23	96	89	83	9	.287	.529
Pete Coscarart	2B140	R	27	143	506	55	120	24	4	9	58	53	59	5	.237	.354
Pee Wee Reese (BF)	SS83	R	21	84	312	58	85	8	4	5	28	45	42	15	.272	.372
Cookie Lavagetto (IL)	3B116	R	27	118	448	56	115	21	3	4	43	70	32	4	.257	.344
Joe Vosmik	OF99	R	30	116	404	45	114	14	6	1	42	22	21	0	.282	.354
Dixie Walker	OF136	L	29	143	556	75	171	37	8	6	66	42	21	3	.308	.435
2 Joe Medwick	OF103	R	28	106	423	62	127	18	12	14	66	26	28	2	.300	.499
Babe Phelps	C99, 1B1	L	32	118	370	47	109	24	5	13	61	30	27	2	.295	.492
Johnny Hudson	SS38, 2B27, 3B1	R	28	85	179	13	39	4	3	0	19	9	26	2	.218	.274
2 Jimmy Wasdell	OF42, 1B17	L	26	77	230	35	64	14	4	3	37	18	24	4	.278	.413
Herman Franks	C43	R	26	65	131	11	24	4	0	1	14	20	6	2	.183	.237
Leo Durocher	SS53, 2B4	R	34	62	160	10	37	9	1	1	14	12	13	1	.231	.319
Gus Mancuso	C56	R	34	60	144	16	33	8	0	0	16	13	7	0	.229	.285
Pete Reiser	3B30, OF17, SS5	L	21	58	225	34	66	11	4	3	20	15	33	2	.293	.418
Charlie Gilbert	OF43	L	20	57	142	23	35	9	1	2	8	8	13	0	.246	.366
2 Joe Gallagher	OF31	R	26	57	110	10	29	6	1	3	16	2	14	1	.264	.418
1 Ernie Koy	OF19	R	30	24	48	9	11	2	1	1	8	3	3	1	.229	.375
1 Roy Cullenbine	OF19	B	24	22	61	8	11	1	0	1	9	23	11	2	.180	.246
Don Ross	3B10	R	25	10	38	4	11	2	0	1	8	3	3	1	.289	.421
1 Gene Moore	OF6	L	30	10	26	3	7	2	0	0	2	1	3	0	.269	.346
1 Jimmy Ripple	OF3	L	30	7	13	0	3	0	0	0	0	2	2	0	.231	.231
Tony Giuliani	C1	R	27	1	1	0	0	0	0	0	0	0	0	0	.000	.000

NAME	T	AGE	W	L	PCT	SV	G	GS	CG	IP	H	BB	SO	ShO	ERA
TOTALS		32	88	65	.575	14	156	156	65	1433	1366	393	639	17	3.50
Freddie Fitzsimmons	R	38	16	2	.889	1	20	18	11	134	120	25	35	4	2.82
Whit Wyatt	R	32	15	14	.517	0	37	34	16	239	233	62	124	5	3.46
Hugh Casey	R	26	11	8	.579	2	44	10	5	154	136	51	53	2	3.62
Luke Hamlin	R	35	9	8	.529	0	33	25	9	182	183	34	91	2	3.07
Vito Tamulis	L	28	8	5	.615	2	41	12	4	154	147	34	55	1	3.10
2 Curt Davis	R	36	8	7	.533	2	22	18	9	137	135	19	46	0	3.81
Tex Carleton	R	33	6	6	.500	2	34	17	4	149	140	47	88	1	3.81
Tot Pressnell	R	33	6	5	.545	2	24	4	1	68	58	17	21	1	3.71
1 Newt Kimball	R	25	3	1	.750	1	21	0	0	34	29	15	21	0	3.18
2 Lee Grissom	L	32	2	5	.286	0	14	10	3	74	59	34	56	1	2.80
Ed Head	R	22	1	2	.333	0	13	5	2	39	40	18	13	0	4.15
Van Lingle Mungo (AJ)	R	29	1	0	1.000	1	7	0	0	22	24	10	9	0	2.45
Wes Flowers	L	26	1	1	.500	0	5	2	0	21	23	10	8	0	3.43
Max Macon	L	24	1	0	1.000	0	2	0	0	2	5	0	1	0	22.50
1 Carl Doyle	R	27	0	0	.000	1	3	0	0	6	18	6	4	0	25.50
Steve Rachunok	R	23	0	1	.000	0	2	1	1	10	9	5	10	0	4.50
2 Lou Fette	R	33	0	0	.000	0	2	0	0	3	3	2	0	0	0.00
Wes Ferrell	R	32	0	0	.000	0	1	0	0	4	4	4	4	0	6.75

ST. LOUIS 3rd 84-69 .549 16 — RAY BLADES 15-24 .385 MIKE GONZALEZ 0-5 .000 BILLY SOUTHWORTH 69-40 .633

NAME	G by POS	B	AGE	G	AB	R	H	2B	3B	HR	RBI	BB	SO	SB	BA	SA
TOTALS			27	156	5499	747	1514	266	61	119	709	479	610	97	.275	.411
Johnny Mize	1B153	L	27	155	579	111	182	31	13	43	137	82	49	7	.314	.636
Joe Orengo	2B77, 3B34, SS19	R	25	129	415	58	119	23	4	7	56	65	90	9	.287	.412
Marty Marion	SS125	R	22	125	435	44	121	18	1	3	46	21	34	9	.278	.345
Stu Martin	3B73, 2B33	L	26	112	369	45	88	12	6	4	32	33	35	4	.238	.336
Enos Slaughter	OF132	L	24	140	516	96	158	25	13	17	73	50	35	8	.306	.504
Terry Moore	OF133	R	28	136	537	92	163	33	4	17	64	42	44	18	.304	.475
2 Ernie Koy	OF91	R	30	93	348	44	108	19	5	8	52	28	59	12	.310	.463
Mickey Owen	C113	R	24	117	307	27	81	16	2	0	27	34	13	4	.264	.329
Jimmy Brown	2B48, 3B41, SS28	B	30	107	454	56	127	17	4	0	30	24	15	9	.280	.335
Don Padgett	C72, 1B2	L	28	93	240	24	58	15	1	6	41	26	14	1	.242	.388
Pepper Martin	OF63, 3B2	R	36	86	228	28	72	15	4	3	39	22	24	6	.316	.456
Johnny Hopp	OF39, 1B10	L	23	80	152	24	41	7	4	1	14	9	21	3	.270	.388
Don Gutteridge	3B39	R	28	69	108	19	29	5	0	3	14	5	15	3	.269	.398
1 Joe Medwick	OF37	R	28	37	158	21	48	12	0	3	20	6	8	0	.304	.437
Eddie Lake	2B17, SS6	R	24	32	66	12	14	3	0	2	7	12	17	1	.212	.348
Bill DeLancey	C12	L	28	15	18	0	4	0	0	0	2	0	2	0	.222	.222
Red Jones	OF1	L	25	12	11	0	1	0	0	0	1	1	2	0	.091	.091
Hal Epps	OF3	L	26	11	15	6	3	0	0	0	1	0	3	0	.200	.200

Harry Walker 23 L 5-27, Carden Gillenwater 22 R 4-25, Walker Cooper 25 R 6-19, Creepy Crespi 22 R 3-11

NAME	T	AGE	W	L	PCT	SV	G	GS	CG	IP	H	BB	SO	ShO	ERA
TOTALS		29	84	69	.549	14	156	156	71	1395	1457	488	550	10	3.83
Bill McGee	R	30	16	10	.615	0	38	31	11	218	222	96	78	3	3.80
Lon Warneke	R	31	16	10	.615	0	33	31	17	232	235	47	85	1	3.14
Clyde Shoun	L	28	13	11	.542	5	54	19	13	197	193	46	82	1	3.93
Mort Cooper	R	27	11	12	.478	3	38	29	16	231	225	86	95	3	3.62
Max Lanier	L	24	9	6	.600	3	35	11	4	105	113	38	49	2	3.34
Bob Bowman	R	29	7	5	.583	0	28	17	7	114	118	43	43	0	4.34
Ira Hutchinson	R	29	4	2	.667	1	20	2	1	63	68	19	19	0	3.14
2 Carl Doyle (BW)	R	27	3	3	.500	0	21	5	1	81	99	41	44	0	5.89
Jack Russell	R	34	3	4	.429	1	26	0	0	54	53	26	16	0	2.50
Ernie White	L	23	1	1	.500	0	8	1	0	22	29	14	15	0	4.09
2 Newt Kimball	R	25	1	0	1.000	0	2	1	1	14	11	6	6	0	2.57
1 Curt Davis	R	36	0	4	.000	1	14	7	0	54	73	19	12	0	5.17
Gene Lillard	R	26	0	1	.000	0	2	1	0	5	8	4	2	0	12.60
Harry Brecheen	L	25	0	0	.000	0	3	0	0	3	2	2	4	0	0.00
Murry Dickson	R	23	0	0	.000	0	1	1	0	2	5	1	0	0	13.50
Bob Weiland	L	34	0	0	.000	0	1	0	0	1	3	0	0	0	27.00

PITTSBURGH 4th 78-76 .506 22.5 — FRANKIE FRISCH

NAME	G by POS	B	AGE	G	AB	R	H	2B	3B	HR	RBI	BB	SO	SB	BA	SA
TOTALS			29	156	5466	809	1511	276	68	76	740	553	494	69	.276	.394
Elbie Fletcher	1B147	L	24	147	510	94	139	22	7	16	104	119	54	5	.273	.437
Frankie Gustine	2B130	R	20	133	524	59	147	32	7	1	55	35	39	7	.281	.374
Arky Vaughan	SS155, 3B2	L	28	156	594	113	178	40	15	7	95	88	25	12	.300	.453
Lee Handley	3B80, 2B7	R	26	98	302	50	85	7	4	1	19	27	16	7	.281	.341
Bob Elliott	OF147	R	23	148	551	88	161	34	11	5	64	45	28	13	.292	.421
2 Vince DiMaggio	OF108	R	27	110	356	59	103	26	0	19	54	37	83	11	.289	.522
Maurice VanRobays	OF143, 1B1	R	25	145	572	82	156	27	7	11	116	33	58	2	.272	.402
Spud Davis	C87	R	35	99	285	23	93	14	1	5	39	35	20	0	.326	.435
Debs Garms	3B64, OF19	L	32	103	358	76	127	23	7	5	57	23	6	3	.355	.500
Paul Waner	OF45	L	37	89	238	32	69	16	1	1	32	23	14	0	.290	.378
Lloyd Waner	OF42	L	34	72	166	30	43	3	0	0	3	5	5	2	.259	.277
2 Al Lopez	C59	R	31	59	174	15	45	6	2	1	24	13	13	5	.259	.333
Joe Bowman	P32	L	30	57	90	11	22	5	1	1	14	14	14	0	.244	.356
Pep Young	2B33, SS7, 3B5	R	32	54	136	19	34	8	2	2	20	12	23	1	.250	.382
Bill Brubaker	3B19, SS8, 1B4	R	29	38	78	8	15	3	1	0	7	8	16	0	.192	.256
Ed Fernandes	C27	B	22	28	33	1	4	1	0	0	2	7	6	0	.121	.152
1 Ray Berres	C21	R	32	21	32	2	6	0	0	0	2	1	1	0	.188	.188
Joe Schultz	C13	L	21	16	36	2	7	0	1	0	4	2	1	0	.194	.250
1 Johnny Rizzo	OF7	R	27	9	28	1	5	1	0	0	2	5	5	0	.179	.214

Fern Bell 27 R 0-3, Ray Mueller 28 R 1-3, Ed Leip 29 R 1-5, Frank Kalin 22 R 0-3, Johnny Gee (SA) 24

NAME	T	AGE	W	L	PCT	SV	G	GS	CG	IP	H	BB	SO	ShO	ERA
TOTALS		30	78	76	.506	24	156	156	49	1388	1569	492	491	8	4.36
Rip Sewell	R	33	16	5	.762	1	33	23	14	190	169	67	60	2	2.79
Mace Brown	R	31	10	9	.526	7	48	17	5	173	181	49	73	2	3.49
Joe Bowman	R	30	9	10	.474	2	32	24	10	188	209	66	57	0	4.45
Ken Heintzelman	L	24	8	8	.500	3	39	16	5	165	193	65	71	2	4.47
Bob Klinger	R	32	8	13	.381	3	39	22	3	142	196	53	48	0	5.39
Max Butcher	R	29	8	9	.471	2	35	24	6	136	161	46	40	2	6.02
Johnny Lanning	R	29	8	4	.667	2	38	7	2	116	119	39	42	0	4.03
Dick Lanahan	L	28	6	8	.429	2	40	8	4	108	121	42	45	0	4.25
Danny MacFayden	R	35	5	4	.556	2	35	8	0	91	112	27	24	0	3.56
Russ Bauers	R	26	0	2	.000	0	15	2	0	31	42	18	11	0	7.55
Oad Swigart	R	25	0	2	.000	0	7	2	0	22	27	10	9	0	4.50
Dutch Dietz	R	28	0	1	.000	0	4	2	0	15	22	4	8	0	6.00
Pep Rambert	R	23	0	1	.000	0	3	1	0	8	12	4	0	0	7.88
Ray Harrell	R	28	0	0	.000	0	3	0	0	3	5	2	3	0	9.00

CHICAGO 5th 75-79 .487 25.5 — GABBY HARTNETT

NAME	G by POS	B	AGE	G	AB	R	H	2B	3B	HR	RBI	BB	SO	SB	BA	SA
TOTALS			29	154	5389	681	1441	272	48	86	627	482	566	63	.267	.384
Phil Cavarretta (JJ)	1B52	L	23	65	193	34	54	11	4	2	22	31	18	3	.280	.409
Billy Herman	2B135	R	30	135	558	77	163	24	4	5	57	47	30	1	.292	.376
Bobby Mattick	SS126, 3B1	R	24	128	441	30	96	15	0	0	33	19	33	5	.218	.252
Stan Hack	3B148, 1B1	L	30	149	603	101	191	38	6	8	40	75	24	21	.317	.439
Bill Nicholson	OF123	L	25	135	491	78	146	27	7	25	98	50	67	2	.297	.534
Hank Leiber	OF103, 1B12	R	29	117	440	68	133	24	2	17	86	45	68	1	.302	.482
Jim Gleeson	OF123	B	28	129	485	76	152	39	11	5	61	54	52	4	.313	.470
Al Todd	C104	R	36	104	381	31	97	13	2	6	42	11	29	1	.255	.346
Dom Dallessandro	OF74	L	26	107	287	33	77	19	6	1	36	34	13	4	.268	.387
Rip Russell (IL)	1B51, 3B3	R	25	68	215	15	53	7	2	5	33	8	23	1	.247	.367
Augie Galan (BK)	OF54, 2B2	B	28	68	209	33	48	14	2	3	22	37	23	9	.230	.359
2 Zeke Bonura	1B44	R	31	49	182	20	48	14	0	4	20	10	4	1	.264	.407
Bob Collins	C42	R	30	47	120	11	25	3	0	1	14	14	18	4	.208	.258
2 Rabbit Warstler	SS28, 2B17	R	36	45	159	19	36	4	1	1	18	8	19	1	.226	.283
Gabby Hartnett	C22, 1B1	R	39	37	64	3	17	3	0	1	12	8	7	0	.266	.359
Billy Rogell	SS14, 3B9, 2B3	B	35	33	59	7	8	0	0	1	3	2	8	1	.136	.186
Clyde McCullough	C7	R	23	9	26	4	4	1	0	0	1	5	5	0	.154	.192
Bobby Sturgeon	SS7	R	20	7	21	1	4	1	0	0	2	0	1	0	.190	.238

NAME	T	AGE	W	L	PCT	SV	G	GS	CG	IP	H	BB	SO	ShO	ERA
TOTALS		30	75	79	.487	14	154	154	69	1393	1418	430	564	12	3.54
Claude Passeau	R	31	20	13	.606	5	46	31	20	281	259	59	124	4	2.50
Larry French	R	32	14	14	.500	2	40	33	18	246	240	64	107	3	3.29
Vern Olsen	L	22	13	9	.591	0	34	20	9	173	172	62	71	4	2.97
Bill Lee	R	30	9	17	.346	0	37	30	9	211	246	70	70	1	5.03
Ken Raffensberger	L	22	7	9	.438	3	43	10	3	115	120	29	55	0	3.37
Jake Mooty	R	27	6	6	.500	1	20	12	6	114	101	49	42	0	2.92
Dizzy Dean (SA)	R	29	3	3	.500	0	10	9	3	54	68	20	18	0	5.17
Charlie Root	R	41	2	4	.333	1	36	8	1	112	118	33	50	0	3.86
Vance Page	R	36	1	3	.250	2	30	1	0	59	65	26	22	0	4.42
Clay Bryant (SA)	R	28	0	1	.000	0	8	0	0	26	26	14	5	0	4.85
Julio Bonetti	R	28	0	0	.000	0	1	0	0	1	3	4	0	0	27.00

NEW YORK 6th 72-80 .474 27.5 — BILL TERRY

	NAME	G by POS	B	AGE	G	AB	R	H	2B	3B	HR	RBI	BB	SO	SB	BA	SA
	TOTALS			29	152	5324	663	1423	201	46	91	614	453	478	45	.267	.374
	Babe Young	1B147	L	25	149	556	75	159	27	4	17	101	69	28	4	.286	.441
2	Tony Cuccinello	2B47, 3B37	R	32	88	307	26	64	9	2	5	36	16	42	1	.208	.300
	Mickey Witek	SS89,2B32	R	24	119	433	34	111	7	0	3	31	24	17	2	.256	.293
	Burgess Whitehead	3B74, 2B57, SS4	R	30	133	568	68	160	9	6	4	36	26	17	9	.282	.340
	Mel Ott	OF111, 3B42	L	31	151	536	89	155	27	3	19	79	100	50	6	.289	.457
	Frank Demaree	OF119	R	30	121	460	68	139	18	6	7	61	45	39	5	.302	.413
	Jo-Jo Moore	OF133	L	31	138	543	83	150	33	4	6	46	43	30	7	.276	.385
	Harry Danning	C131	R	28	140	524	65	157	34	4	13	91	35	31	3	.300	.454
	Johnny Rucker	OF57	L	23	86	277	38	82	7	5	4	23	7	32	4	.296	.401
	Billy Jurges (PB)	SS63	R	32	63	214	23	54	3	3	2	36	25	14	2	.252	.322
	Bob Seeds	OF40	R	33	56	155	18	45	5	2	4	16	17	19	0	.290	.426
	Johnny McCarthy	1B6	L	30	51	67	6	16	4	0	0	5	2	8	0	.239	.299
	Ken O'Dea (PB)	C31	L	27	48	96	9	23	4	1	0	12	16	15	0	.240	.302
1	Al Glossop	2B24	B	27	27	91	16	19	3	0	4	8	10	16	1	.209	.374
	Glen Stewart	3B6, SS5	R	27	15	29	1	4	1	0	0	0	1	2	0	.138	.172
	Buster Maynard	OF7	R	27	7	29	6	8	2	2	1	2	2	6	0	.276	.586
	Red Tramback	OF1	L	24	2	4	0	1	0	0	0	0	1	1	1	.250	.250

	NAME	T	AGE	W	L	PCT	SV	G	GS	CG	IP	H	BB	SO	ShO	ERA
	TOTALS		30	72	80	.474	18	152	152	57	1360	1383	473	606	11	3.79
	Hal Schumacher	R	29	13	13	.500	1	34	30	12	227	218	96	123	1	3.25
	Harry Gumbert	R	30	12	14	.462	2	35	30	14	237	230	81	77	2	3.76
	Carl Hubbell	L	37	11	12	.478	0	31	27	11	214	220	59	86	2	3.66
	Bill Lohrman	R	27	10	15	.400	1	31	28	11	195	200	43	73	**5**	3.78
	Cliff Melton	L	28	10	11	.476	2	37	21	4	167	185	68	91	1	4.90
	Paul Dean	R	26	4	4	.500	0	27	7	2	99	110	29	32	0	3.91
	Red Lynn	R	26	4	3	.571	3	33	0	0	42	40	24	25	0	3.86
	Roy Joiner	L	33	3	2	.600	1	30	2	0	53	66	17	25	0	3.40
	Jumbo Brown	R	33	2	4	.333	7	41	0	0	55	49	25	31	0	3.44
	Bob Carpenter	R	22	2	0	1.000	0	5	3	2	33	29	14	25	0	2.73
	Hy Vandenberg	R	33	1	1	.500	1	13	3	1	32	27	16	17	0	3.94
4	Willis Hudlin	R	34	0	1	.000	0	1	1	0	5	9	1	1	0	10.80

BOSTON 7th 65-87 .428 34.5 — CASEY STENGEL

	NAME	G by POS	B	AGE	G	AB	R	H	2B	3B	HR	RBI	BB	SO	SB	BA	SA
	TOTALS			27	152	5329	623	1366	219	50	59	558	402	581	48	.256	.349
	Buddy Hassett	1B98, OF13	L	28	124	458	59	107	19	4	0	27	25	16	4	.234	.293
	Bama Rowell	2B115, OF7	L	24	130	486	46	148	19	8	3	58	18	22	12	.305	.395
	Eddie Miller	SS151	R	23	151	569	78	157	33	3	14	79	41	43	8	.276	.418
	Sibby Sisti	3B102, 2B16	R	19	123	459	73	115	19	5	6	34	36	64	4	.251	.353
	Max West	OF102, 1B36	L	23	139	524	72	137	27	5	7	72	65	54	2	.261	.372
	Johnny Cooney	OF99, 1B7	R	39	108	365	40	116	14	3	0	21	25	9	4	.318	.373
	Chet Ross	OF149	R	23	149	569	84	160	23	14	17	89	59	**127**	4	.281	.460
2	Ray Berres	C85	R	32	85	229	12	44	4	1	0	14	18	19	0	.192	.218
2	Gene Moore	OF94	L	30	103	363	46	106	24	1	5	39	25	32	2	.292	.405
	Phil Masi	C52	R	23	63	138	11	27	4	1	1	14	14	14	0	.196	.261
2	Al Glossop	2B10, 3B18, SS10	B	27	60	148	17	35	2	1	3	14	17	22	1	.236	.324
1	Al Lopez	C36	R	31	36	119	20	35	3	1	2	17	6	8	1	.294	.387
	Whitey Wietelmann	2B15, 3B9, SS3	R	21	35	41	3	8	1	0	0	1	5	5	0	.195	.220
1	Tony Cuccinello	3B33	R	32	34	126	14	34	9	0	0	19	8	9	1	.270	.341
1	Rabbit Warstler	2B24, 3B2, SS1	R	36	33	57	6	12	0	0	0	4	10	5	0	.211	.211
	Stan Andrews	C14	R	23	19	33	1	6	0	0	0	2	0	3	1	.182	.182
	Les Scarsella	1B15	L	26	18	60	7	18	1	3	0	8	3	5	2	.300	.417
	Bobby Loane	OF10	R	25	13	22	4	5	3	0	0	1	2	5	2	.227	.364
	Mel Preibisch	OF11	R	25	11	40	3	9	2	0	0	5	2	4	0	.225	.275
	Siggy Broskie	C11	R	29	11	22	1	6	1	0	0	4	1	2	0	.273	.318

Claude Wilborn 27 L 0-7, Buddy Gremp 20 R 2-9, Don Manno 25 R 2-7, Hank Majeski 23 R 0-3

	NAME	T	AGE	W	L	PCT	SV	G	GS	CG	IP	H	BB	SO	ShO	ERA
	TOTALS		28	65	87	.428	12	152	152	76	1359	1444	**573**	435	9	4.36
	Dick Errickson	R	26	12	13	.480	4	34	29	17	236	241	90	34	3	3.17
	Bill Posedel	R	33	12	17	.414	1	35	32	18	233	263	81	86	0	4.13
	Joe Sullivan	L	29	10	14	.417	1	36	22	7	177	157	89	64	0	3.56
	Manny Salvo	R	27	10	9	.526	0	21	20	14	161	151	43	60	**5**	3.07
	Jim Tobin (KJ)	R	27	7	3	.700	0	15	11	9	96	102	24	29	0	3.84
	Nick Strincevich	R	25	4	8	.333	1	32	14	5	129	142	63	54	0	5.51
	Al Javery	R	22	2	4	.333	1	29	4	1	83	99	36	42	0	5.53
	Al Piechota	R	26	2	5	.286	0	21	8	2	61	68	41	18	0	5.75
	Tom Earley	R	23	2	0	1.000	0	4	1	1	16	16	3	5	1	3.94
	Dick Coffman	R	33	1	5	.167	3	31	0	0	48	63	11	11	0	5.44
	George Barnicle	R	22	1	0	1.000	0	13	2	1	33	28	31	11	0	7.36
	Frank LaManna	R	20	1	0	1.000	0	5	1	1	13	13	8	3	0	4.85
	Bill Swift	R	32	1	1	.500	1	4	0	0	9	12	7	7	0	3.00
1	Lou Fette	R	33	0	5	.000	0	7	5	0	32	38	18	2	0	5.63
	Joe Callahan	R	23	0	2	.000	0	6	2	0	15	20	13	3	0	10.20
	Ace Williams	L	23	0	0	.000	0	5	0	0	9	21	12	5	0	16.00
	Art Johnson	L	23	0	1	.000	0	2	1	0	6	10	3	1	0	10.50

PHILADELPHIA 8th 50-103 .327 50 — DOC PROTHRO

	NAME	G by POS	B	AGE	G	AB	R	H	2B	3B	HR	RBI	BB	SO	SB	BA	SA
	TOTALS			27	153	5137	494	1225	180	35	75	459	435	527	25	.238	.331
	Art Mahan	1B145, P1	L	27	146	544	55	133	24	5	2	39	40	37	4	.244	.318
	Ham Schulte	2B119, SS1	R	27	120	436	44	103	18	2	1	21	32	30	3	.236	.294
	Bobby Bragan	SS132, 3B2	R	22	132	474	36	105	14	1	7	44	28	34	2	.222	.300
	Pinky May	3B135, SS1	R	29	136	501	59	147	24	2	1	48	58	33	2	.293	.355
	Chuck Klein	OF96	L	35	116	354	39	77	16	2	7	37	44	30	2	.218	.333
	Joe Marty	OF118	R	26	123	455	52	123	21	8	13	50	17	50	2	.270	.437
3	Johnny Rizzo	OF91, 3B7	R	27	103	367	53	107	12	2	20	53	37	31	2	.292	.499
	Bennie Warren	C97, 1B1	R	28	106	289	33	71	6	1	12	34	40	46	1	.246	.398
	Emmett Mueller	2B34, OF31, 3B13, 1B2	B	27	97	263	24	65	13	2	3	28	37	23	2	.247	.346
	Bill Atwood	C69	R	28	78	203	7	39	9	0	0	22	25	18	0	.192	.236
	Mike Mazzera	OF42, 1B11	L	26	69	156	16	37	5	4	0	13	19	15	1	.237	.321
1	Morrie Arnovich	OF37	R	29	39	141	13	28	2	1	0	12	14	15	0	.199	.227
	Danny Litwhiler	OF34	R	23	36	142	10	49	2	2	5	17	3	13	1	.345	.493
	Hersh Martin	OF23	B	30	33	83	10	21	6	1	0	5	9	9	1	.253	.349
	Wally Millies	C24	R	33	26	43	1	3	0	0	0	0	4	4	0	.070	.070
2	Wally Berger	OF11, 1B1	R	34	20	41	3	13	2	0	1	5	4	8	1	.317	.439
	Al Monchak	SS9, 2B1	R	23	19	14	1	2	0	0	0	0	0	6	1	.143	.143
	Del Young	SS6, 2B5	B	28	15	33	2	8	0	1	0	1	2	1	0	.242	.303
	George Jumonville	SS10, 3B1	R	23	11	34	0	3	0	0	0	0	1	6	0	.088	.088
	Hal Marnie	2B11	R	21	11	34	4	6	0	0	0	4	4	2	0	.176	.176
	Neb Stewart	OF9	R	22	10	31	3	4	0	0	0	0	1	5	0	.129	.129
	Gus Suhr	1B7	L	34	10	25	4	4	0	0	2	5	5	5	0	.160	.400

Stan Benjamin 26 R 2-9, George Scharein 25 R 5-17, Sam File 18 R 1-13, Ed Levy 23 R 0-1, Roy Hughes 29 R 0-0

	NAME	T	AGE	W	L	PCT	SV	G	GS	CG	IP	H	BB	SO	ShO	ERA
	TOTALS		30	50	**103**	.327	8	153	153	66	1357	1429	475	485	5	4.40
	Kirby Higbe	R	25	14	19	.424	1	41	36	20	283	242	**121**	**137**	1	3.72
	Hugh Mulcahy	R	26	13	**22**	.371	0	36	36	21	280	**283**	91	82	3	3.60
	Si Johnson	R	33	5	14	.263	1	37	14	5	138	145	42	58	0	4.89
	Boom-Boom Beck	R	35	4	9	.308	0	29	15	4	129	147	41	38	0	4.33
	Cy Blanton	R	31	4	3	.571	0	13	10	5	77	82	21	24	0	4.32
	Ike Pearson	R	23	3	14	.176	1	29	20	5	145	160	57	43	1	5.46
	Lefty Smoll	L	26	2	8	.200	0	33	9	0	109	145	36	31	0	5.37
	Syl Johnson	R	39	2	2	.500	2	17	2	2	41	37	5	13	0	4.17
	Lloyd Brown	L	35	1	3	.250	3	18	2	0	38	58	16	16	0	6.16
	Johnny Podgajny	R	20	1	3	.250	0	4	4	3	35	33	1	12	0	2.83
	Frank Hoerst	L	22	1	0	1.000	0	6	0	0	12	12	8	3	0	5.25
	Charlie Frye	R	25	0	6	.000	0	15	5	1	50	58	26	18	0	4.68
	Maxie Wilson	L	24	0	0	.000	0	3	0	0	7	16	2	3	0	12.86
	Roy Bruner	R	23	0	0	.000	0	2	0	0	6	5	6	4	0	6.00
	Paul Masterson	L	24	0	0	.000	0	2	0	0	5	5	2	3	0	7.20
	Art Mahan	L	27	0	0	.000	0	1	0	0	1	1	0	0	0	0.00

WORLD SERIES – CINCINNATI (NL) 4 DETROIT (AL) 3

LINE SCORES

TEAM	1	2	3	4	5	6	7	8	9	10	11	12	R	H	E
Game 1 October 2 at Cincinnati															
DET (AL)	0	5	0	0	2	0	0	0	0				7	10	1
CIN (NL)	0	0	0	1	0	0	0	1	0				2	8	3
Newsom	**Derringer**, Moore (2), Riddle (9)														
Game 2 October 3 at Cincinnati															
DET	2	0	0	0	0	1	0	0	0				3	3	1
CIN	0	2	2	1	0	0	0	0	X				5	9	0
Rowe, Gorsica (4)	**Walters**														
Game 3 October 4 at Detroit															
CIN	1	0	0	0	0	0	0	1	2				4	10	1
DET	0	0	0	1	0	0	4	2	X				7	13	1
Turner, Moore (7), Beggs (8)	**Bridges**														
Game 4 October 5 at Detroit															
CIN	2	0	1	1	0	0	0	1	0				5	11	1
DET	0	0	1	0	0	1	0	0	0				2	5	1
Derringer	**Trout**, Smith (3), McKain (7)														
Game 5 October 6 at Detroit															
CIN	0	0	0	0	0	0	0	0	0				0	3	0
DET	0	0	3	4	0	0	0	1	X				8	13	0
Thompson, Moore (4), Vander Meer (5), Hutchings (8)	**Newsom**														
Game 6 October 7 at Cincinnati															
DET	0	0	0	0	0	0	0	0	0				0	5	0
CIN	2	0	0	0	0	1	0	1	X				4	10	2
Rowe, Gorsica (1), Hutchinson (8)	**Walters**														
Game 7 October 8 at Cincinnati															
DET	0	0	1	0	0	0	0	0	0				1	7	0
CIN	0	0	0	0	0	0	2	0	X				2	7	1
Newsom	**Derringer**														

COMPOSITE BATTING

NAME	POS	G	AB	R	H	2B	3B	HR	RBI	BA
Cincinnati (NL)										
Totals		7	232	22	58	14	0	2	21	.250
M. McCormick	OF	7	**29**	1	9	3	0	0	2	.310
Goodman	OF	7	**29**	**5**	8	2	0	0	5	.276
F. McCormick	1B	7	28	2	6	1	0	0	0	.214
Werber	3B	7	27	**5**	**10**	**4**	0	0	2	.370
Joost	2B	7	25	0	5	0	0	0	2	.200
Myers	SS	7	23	0	3	0	0	0	2	.130
Ripple	OF	7	21	3	7	2	0	1	**6**	.333
Wilson	C	6	17	2	6	0	0	0	0	.353
Walters	P	2	7	2	2	1	0	1	2	.286
Derringer	P	3	7	0	0	0	0	0	0	.000
Baker	C	3	4	1	1	0	0	0	0	.250
Lombardi	C	2	3	0	1	1	0	0	0	.333
Riggs	PH	3	3	1	0	0	0	0	0	.000
Frey	PH	3	2	0	0	0	0	0	0	.000
Moore	P	3	2	0	0	0	0	0	0	.000
Turner	P	1	2	0	0	0	0	0	0	.000
Arnovich	OF	1	1	0	0	0	0	0	0	.000
Craft	PH	1	1	0	0	0	0	0	0	.000
Thompson	P	1	1	0	0	0	0	0	0	.000

Beggs P 0-0, Hutchings P 0-0, Riddle P 0-0, Vander Meer P 0-0

NAME	POS	G	AB	R	H	2B	3B	HR	RBI	BA
Detroit (AL)										
Totals		7	228	28	56	9	3	4	24	.246
Greenberg	OF	7	28	**5**	**10**	2	1	1	**6**	.357
Gehringer	2B	7	28	3	6	0	0	0	1	.214
Bartell	SS	7	26	2	7	2	0	0	3	.269
York	1B	7	26	3	6	0	1	1	2	.231
Campbell	OF	7	25	4	9	1	0	1	5	.360
Higgins	3B	7	24	2	9	3	1	1	**6**	**.375**
McCosky	OF	7	23	**5**	7	1	0	0	1	.304
Sullivan	C	5	13	3	1	0	0	0	0	.077
Tebbetts	C	4	11	0	0	0	0	0	0	.000
Newsom	P	3	10	1	1	0	0	0	0	.100
Gorsica	P	2	4	0	0	0	0	0	0	.000
Averill	PH	3	3	0	0	0	0	0	0	.000
Bridges	P	1	3	0	0	0	0	0	0	.000
Fox	PH	1	1	0	0	0	0	0	0	.000
Rowe	P	2	1	0	0	0	0	0	0	.000
Smith	P	1	1	0	0	0	0	0	0	.000
Trout	P	1	1	0	0	0	0	0	0	.000
Croucher	SS	1	0	0	0	0	0	0	0	.000
Hutchinson	P	1	0	0	0	0	0	0	0	.000
McKain	P	1	0	0	0	0	0	0	0	.000

COMPOSITE PITCHING

NAME	G	IP	H	BB	SO	W	L	SV	ERA
Cincinnati (NL)									
Totals	7	61	56	30	30	4	3	0	3.68
Derringer	**3**	19.1	17	**10**	6	**2**	1	0	2.79
Walters	2	18	8	6	6	**2**	0	0	1.50
Moore	**3**	8.1	8	6	7	0	0	0	3.25
Turner	1	6	8	0	4	0	1	0	7.50
Thompson	1	3.1	8	4	2	0	1	0	16.22
Vander Meer	1	3	2	3	2	0	0	0	0.00
Beggs	1	1	3	0	1	0	0	0	9.00
Hutchings	1	1	2	1	0	0	0	0	9.00
Riddle	1	1	0	0	2	0	0	0	0.00
Detroit (AL)									
Totals	7	60	58	15	30	3	4	0	3.00
Newsom	**3**	**26**	**18**	4	**17**	**2**	1	0	1.38
Gorsica	2	11.1	6	4	4	0	0	0	**0.79**
Bridges	1	9	10	1	5	1	0	0	3.00
Smith	1	4	1	3	1	0	0	0	2.25
Rowe	2	3.2	12	1	1	0	**2**	0	17.17
McKain	1	3	4	0	0	0	0	0	3.00
Trout	1	2	6	1	1	0	1	0	9.00
Hutchinson	1	1	1	1	1	0	0	0	9.00

1941 That Magnificent Streak

When the season of 1941 is recalled, it is mostly because of one man and the incredible record he achieved. Records that are made or broken over a lifetime are significant, but hardly ever as dramatic or immediate as those records attained in a single season. In 1941, the Yankees' Joe DiMaggio hit safely in 56 consecutive games—a feat considered by most to be monumental in view of the pressures and the lack of consistency characteristic of baseball. DiMaggio started his streak on May 15, and continued it through the most stringent of official scoring decisions until July 17.

The highlight of the streak came when DiMaggio tied Willie Keeler's major league mark of 44 consecutive games, achieved in 1897, by getting a hit in the second inning of what turned out to be a rain-shortened, five-inning affair. The day after the 56 game streak was stopped on great plays by Ken Keltner and Lou Boudreau, DiMaggio started a new streak of 16 games. Earlier in his career, while in the Pacific Coast League in 1933, DiMaggio had hit safely in 61 straight games.

Aside from personal glory, the streak contributed to a rousing Yankee comeback and a pennant victory by 17 games over the Red Sox. Boston's own Ted Williams also had a miraculous year by winning the batting title with a .406 average—the first major league batter to turn the trick since Bill Terry's .401 in 1930—and the home run crown with 37 round-trippers. Williams' 120 RBI's fell five short of DiMaggio's league-leading 125 and cost him the Triple Crown. In fact, DiMaggio's performance was such that it overshadowed the Boston slugger in the MVP voting. Williams' one moment alone in the limelight away from DiMaggio came in the All-Star Game when, with two outs and two on in the ninth inning, he hit a home run to give the American League a 7-5 win.

The raging war in Europe had slowly started to exact its toll on baseball and was most noticeable with the 1940 pennant-winning Detroit Tigers. They lost Hank Greenberg, their 1940 MVP, after he played 19 games and wound up in a dismal tie for fourth, 26 games out.

Cincinnati was looking for its third straight pennant in the National League but got off to a poor start and could never recover well enough to catch the Dodgers and Cardinals, who fought it out until the close of the season when the Dodgers finally nailed down the flag in late September. The Dodgers' big men offensively, were Dolph Camilli and Pete Reiser. Camilli led the league in home runs, 34, and RBI's, 120, and was named MVP while Reiser, playing his first full year, took league batting honors with a .343 average. Kirby Higbe, and Whit Wyatt provided the bulk of Brooklyn's pitching as they shared league honors with 22 wins each. The pennant, which was the Dodgers' third but their first since 1920, brought great joy to the borough of Brooklyn. But the World Series proved another matter and brought nothing but tears.

In the first game of the Series, 68,540 fans showed up at Yankee Stadium—the largest Series crowd to that time—and the Yankees won 3-2, mostly because of Pee Wee Reese's trying to reach third on a foul out in front of the Yankee bench in the seventh inning. Game two uplifted Dodger hearts with a 3-2 win behind Wyatt, but the third game again sent Brooklyn's hopes scurrying as the old ace and favorite, Freddie Fitzsimmons, was struck by a savage line drive on the leg in the seventh inning and forced to leave a scoreless game, which the Yankees won in the eighth, 2-1.

All of the Dodger heartbreak that had occurred until the fourth game was infinitesimal when compared with the disastrous ninth inning. With Brooklyn leading 4-3 and two men out, Tommy Henrich swung and missed the low third strike, but Mickey Owen could not stop the ball and Henrich wound up on first, opening the door for four runs and a 7-4 Yankee victory.

The demoralized Dodgers collected four hits in the final 3-1 loss and gave the Yankees a happy winter send-off with a five-game Series victory.

1941 AMERICAN LEAGUE

NEW YORK 1st 101-53 .656 — JOE McCARTHY

NAME	G by POS	B	AGE	G	AB	R	H	2B	3B	HR	RBI	BB	SO	SB	BA	SA
TOTALS			27	156	5444	830	1464	243	60	151	774	616	565	51	.269	.419
Johnny Sturm	1B124	L	25	124	524	58	125	17	3	3	36	37	50	3	.239	.300
Joe Gordon	2B131, 1B30	R	26	156	588	104	162	26	7	24	87	72	80	10	.276	.466
Phil Rizzuto	SS128	R	23	133	515	65	158	20	9	3	46	27	36	14	.307	.398
Red Rolfe	3B134	L	32	136	561	106	148	22	5	8	42	57	38	3	.264	.364
Tommy Henrich	OF139	L	28	144	538	106	149	27	5	31	85	81	40	3	.277	.519
Joe DiMaggio	OF139	R	26	139	541	122	193	43	11	30	125	76	13	4	.357	.643
Charlie Keller	OF137	L	24	140	507	102	151	24	10	33	122	102	65	6	.298	.580
Bill Dickey	C104	L	34	109	348	35	99	15	5	7	71	45	17	2	.284	.417
George Selkirk	OF47	L	33	70	164	30	36	5	0	6	25	28	30	1	.220	.360
Buddy Rosar	C60	R	26	67	209	25	60	17	2	1	36	22	10	0	.287	.402
Jerry Priddy	2B31, 3B14, 1B10	R	21	56	174	18	37	7	0	1	26	18	16	4	.213	.270
Frankie Crosetti	SS32, 3B13	R	30	50	148	13	33	2	2	1	22	18	14	0	.223	.284
Red Ruffing	P23	R	37	38	89	10	27	8	1	2	22	4	12	0	.303	.483
Frenchy Bordagaray	OF19	R	29	36	73	10	19	1	0	0	4	6	8	1	.260	.274
Ken Silvestri (IL)	C13	B	25	17	40	6	10	5	0	1	4	7	6	0	.250	.450
Johnny Lindell		R	24	1	1	0	0	0	0	0	0	0	0	0	.000	.000

NAME	T	AGE	W	L	PCT	SV	G	GS	CG	IP	H	BB	SO	ShO	ERA
		29	101	53	.656	26	156	156	75	1396	1309	598	589	13	3.53
Lefty Gomez	L	32	15	5	.750	0	23	23	8	156	151	103	76	2	3.75
Red Ruffing	R	37	15	6	.714	0	23	23	13	186	177	54	60	2	3.53
Marius Russo	L	26	14	10	.583	1	28	27	17	210	195	87	105	3	3.09
Spud Chandler	R	33	10	4	.714	4	28	20	11	164	146	60	60	4	3.18
Atley Donald	R	30	9	5	.643	0	22	20	10	159	141	69	71	0	3.57
Ernie Bonham	R	27	9	6	.600	2	23	14	7	127	118	31	43	1	2.98
Marv Breuer	R	27	9	7	.563	2	26	18	7	141	131	49	77	1	4.09
Johnny Murphy	R	32	8	3	.727	15	35	0	0	77	68	40	29	0	1.99
Norm Branch	R	26	5	1	.833	2	27	0	0	47	37	26	28	0	2.87
Steve Peek	R	26	4	2	.667	0	17	8	2	80	85	39	18	0	5.06
Charley Stanceu	R	25	3	3	.500	0	22	2	0	48	58	35	21	0	5.60
George Washburn	R	26	0	1	.000	0	1	1	0	2	2	5	1	0	13.50

BOSTON 2nd 84-70 .545 17 — JOE CRONIN

NAME	G by POS	B	AGE	G	AB	R	H	2B	3B	HR	RBI	BB	SO	SB	BA	SA
TOTALS			29	155	5359	865	1517	304	55	124	805	683	567	67	.283	.430
Jimmie Foxx	1B124, 3B5, OF1	R	33	135	487	87	146	27	8	19	105	93	103	2	.300	.505
Bobby Doerr	2B132	R	23	132	500	74	141	28	4	16	93	43	43	1	.282	.450
Joe Cronin	SS119, 3B22, OF1	R	34	143	518	98	161	38	8	16	95	82	55	1	.311	.508
Jim Tabor	3B125	R	27	126	498	65	139	29	3	16	101	36	48	17	.279	.446
Lou Finney	OF92, 1B24	L	30	127	497	83	143	24	10	4	53	38	17	2	.288	.400
Dom DiMaggio	OF144	R	24	144	584	117	165	37	6	8	58	90	57	13	.283	.408
Ted Williams	OF133	L	22	143	456	135	185	33	3	37	120	145	27	2	.406	.735
Frankie Pytlak	C91	R	32	106	336	36	91	23	1	2	39	28	19	5	.271	.363
Skeeter Newsome	SS69, 2B23	R	30	93	227	28	51	6	0	2	17	22	11	10	.225	.278
Stan Spence	OF52, 1B1	L	26	86	203	22	47	10	3	2	28	18	14	1	.232	.340
Johnny Peacock	C70	L	31	79	261	28	74	20	1	0	27	21	3	2	.284	.368
Pete Fox	OF62	R	31	73	268	38	81	12	7	0	31	21	32	9	.302	.399
Tom Carey	2B9, SS8	R	32	24	20	7	4	0	0	0	2	0	2	0	.200	.200
1 Odell Hale	3B6, 2B1	R	32	12	24	5	5	2	0	1	1	3	4	0	.208	.417
Al Flair	1B8	L	24	10	30	3	6	2	1	0	2	1	1	1	.200	.333
Paul Campbell		L	23	1	0	0	0	0	0	0	0	0	0	0	.000	.000

NAME	T	AGE	W	L	PCT	SV	G	GS	CG	IP	H	BB	SO	ShO	ERA
		29	84*	70	.545	11	155	155	70	1372	1453	611	574	8	4.19
Dick Newsome	R	31	19	10	.655	0	36	29	17	214	235	79	58	2	4.12
Joe Dobson	R	24	12	5	.706	0	27	18	7	134	136	67	69	1	4.50
Charlie Wagner	R	28	12	8	.600	0	29	25	12	187	175	85	51	3	3.08
Mickey Harris	L	24	8	14	.364	1	35	22	11	194	189	86	111	1	3.25
Mike Ryba	R	38	7	3	.700	6	40	3	0	121	143	42	54	0	4.46
Lefty Grove	L	41	7	7	.500	0	21	21	10	134	155	42	54	0	4.37
Tex Hughson	R	25	5	3	.625	0	12	8	4	61	70	13	22	0	4.13
Earl Johnson	L	22	4	5	.444	0	17	12	4	94	90	51	46	0	4.50
Jack Wilson	R	29	4	13	.235	1	27	12	4	116	140	70	55	1	5.03
2 Nels Potter	R	29	2	0	1.000	0	10	0	0	20	21	16	6	0	4.50
Herb Hash	R	30	1	0	1.000	1	4	0	0	8	7	7	3	0	5.63
Bill Fleming	R	27	1	1	.500	1	16	1	0	41	32	24	20	0	3.95
Emerson Dickman (MS)	R	26	1	1	.500	0	9	3	1	31	37	17	16	0	6.39
Oscar Judd	L	33	0	0	.000	1	7	0	0	12	15	10	5	0	9.00
Woody Rich	R	24	0	0	.000	0	2	1	0	4	8	2	4	0	15.75

*1 win by forfeit

CHICAGO 3rd 77-77 .500 24 — JIMMY DYKES

NAME	G by POS	B	AGE	G	AB	R	H	2B	3B	HR	RBI	BB	SO	SB	BA	SA
TOTALS			30	156	5404	638	1376	245	47	47	569	510	476	91	.255	.343
Joe Kuhel	1B151	L	35	153	600	99	150	39	5	12	63	70	55	20	.250	.392
Bill Knickerbocker	2B88	R	29	89	343	51	84	23	2	7	29	41	27	6	.245	.385
Luke Appling	SS154	R	34	154	592	93	186	26	8	1	57	82	32	12	.314	.390
Dario Lodigiani	3B86	R	25	87	322	39	77	19	2	4	40	31	19	0	.239	.348
Taffy Wright	OF134	L	29	136	513	71	165	35	5	10	97	60	27	5	.322	.468
Mike Kreevich	OF113	R	33	121	436	44	101	16	8	0	37	35	26	17	.232	.305
2 Myril Hoag	OF99	R	33	106	380	30	97	13	3	1	44	27	29	6	.255	.313
Mike Tresh	C115	R	27	115	390	38	98	10	1	0	33	38	27	1	.251	.282
Bob Kennedy	3B71	R	20	76	257	16	53	9	3	1	29	17	23	5	.206	.276
Mose Solters (IJ)	OF63	R	35	76	251	24	65	9	4	4	43	18	31	3	.259	.375
Don Kolloway	2B62, 1B4	R	22	71	280	33	76	8	3	3	24	6	12	11	.271	.354
2 Ben Chapman	OF49	R	32	57	190	26	43	9	1	2	19	19	14	2	.226	.316
Tom Turner	C35	R	24	38	126	7	30	5	0	0	8	9	15	2	.238	.278
George Dickey	C17	B	25	32	55	6	11	1	0	2	8	5	7	0	.200	.327
Skeeter Webb	2B18, SS5, 3B3	R	31	29	84	7	16	2	0	0	6	3	9	1	.190	.214
1 Larry Rosenthal	OF18	L	29	20	59	9	14	4	0	0	1	12	5	0	.237	.305
Dave Philley	OF2	B	21	7	9	4	2	1	0	0	0	3	3	0	.222	.333
Stan Goletz		L	23	5	5	0	3	0	0	0	0	0	2	0	.600	.600
Jake Jones	1B3	R	20	3	11	0	0	0	0	0	0	0	4	0	.000	.000
Dave Short (MS)	OF2	L	44	3	8	0	0	0	0	0	0	2	1	0	.000	.000
Chet Hajduk		R	22	1	1	0	0	0	0	0	0	0	0	0	.000	.000

NAME	T	AGE	W	L	PCT	SV	G	GS	CG	IP	H	BB	SO	ShO	ERA
		30	77	77	.500	4	156	156	106	1416	1362	521	564	14	3.52
Thornton Lee	L	34	22	11	.667	1	35	34	30	300	258	92	130	3	2.37
Johnny Rigney	R	26	13	13	.500	0	30	29	18	237	224	92	119	3	3.84
Eddie Smith	L	27	13	17	.433	1	34	33	21	263	243	114	111	1	3.18
Ted Lyons	R	40	12	10	.545	0	22	22	19	187	199	37	63	2	3.71
Jack Hallett	R	27	5	5	.500	0	22	6	3	75	96	38	25	0	6.00
Bill Dietrich	R	31	5	8	.385	0	19	15	4	109	114	50	26	1	5.37
John Humphries (BT)	R	26	4	2	.667	1	14	6	4	73	63	22	25	4	1.85
2 Buck Ross	R	27	3	8	.273	0	20	11	7	108	99	43	30	0	3.17
Pete Appleton	R	37	0	3	.000	1	13	0	0	27	27	17	12	0	5.33
Joe Haynes	R	23	0	0	.000	0	8	0	0	28	30	11	18	0	3.86
Orval Grove	R	21	0	0	.000	0	2	0	0	7	9	5	5	0	10.29

CLEVELAND 4th (Tie) 75-79 .487 26

ROGER PECKINPAUGH

NAME	G by POS	B	AGE	G	AB	R	H	2B	3B	HR	RBI	BB	SO	SB	BA	SA
TOTALS			28	155	5283	677	1350	249	**84**	103	618	512	**605**	63	.256	.393
Hal Trosky (BG)	1B85	L	28	89	310	43	91	17	0	11	51	44	21	1	.294	.455
Ray Mack	2B145	R	24	145	501	54	114	22	4	9	44	54	69	8	.228	.341
Lou Boudreau	SS147	R	23	148	579	95	149	**45**	8	10	56	85	57	9	.257	.415
Ken Keltner	3B149	R	24	149	581	83	156	31	13	23	84	51	56	2	.269	.485
Jeff Heath	OF151	L	26	151	585	89	199	32	**20**	24	123	50	69	18	.340	.586
Roy Weatherly	OF88	L	26	102	363	59	105	21	5	3	37	32	20	2	.289	.399
Gee Walker	OF105	R	33	121	445	56	126	26	11	6	48	18	46	12	.283	.431
Rollie Hemsley	C96	R	34	98	288	29	69	10	5	2	24	18	19	2	.240	.330
Soup Campbell	OF78	L	26	104	328	36	82	10	4	3	35	31	21	1	.250	.332
Oscar Grimes	1B62, 2B13, 3B1	R	26	77	244	28	58	9	3	4	24	39	47	4	.238	.348
Gene Desautels (LJ)	C66	R	34	66	189	20	38	5	1	1	17	14	12	1	.201	.254
Beau Bell	OF14, 1B10	R	33	48	104	12	20	4	3	0	9	10	8	1	.192	.288
2 Larry Rosenthal	OF14, 1B1	L	29	45	75	10	14	3	1	1	8	9	10	1	.187	.293
Rusty Peters	SS11, 3B9, 2B3	R	26	29	63	6	13	2	0	0	2	7	10	0	.206	.238
Hank Edwards	OF16	L	22	16	68	10	15	1	1	1	6	2	4	0	.221	.309
Jim Hegan	C16	R	20	16	47	4	15	2	0	1	5	4	7	0	.319	.426
Red Howell		R	32	11	7	0	2	0	0	0	2	4	2	0	.286	.286
Chuck Workman		L	26	9	4	2	0	0	0	0	0	1	1	0	.000	.000
Buck Frierson	OF3	R	23	5	11	2	3	1	0	0	2	1	1	0	.273	.364
Bob Lemon	3B1	L	20	5	4	0	1	0	0	0	0	0	1	0	.250	.250
Fabian Gaffke	OF2	R	27	4	4	0	1	0	0	0	0	2	2	0	.250	.250

Jack Conway 21 R 1-2, Les Fleming 25 L 2-8, Vern Freiberger 17 R 1-8, Oris Hockett 31 L 2-6, Geroge Susce 32 R 0-0

NAME	T	AGE	W	L	PCT	SV	G	GS	CG	IP	H	BB	SO	ShO	ERA
TOTALS		30	75	79	.487	19	155	155	68	1377	1366	**660**	617	10	3.90
Bob Feller	R	22	**25**	13	.658	2	**44**	**40**	28	**343**	**284**	**194**	**260**	**6**	3.15
Al Smith	L	33	12	13	.480	0	29	27	13	207	204	75	76	2	3.83
Al Milnar	L	27	12	19	.387	0	35	30	9	229	236	116	82	1	4.36
Jim Bagby	R	24	9	15	.375	2	33	27	12	201	214	76	53	0	4.03
Joe Heving	R	40	5	2	.714	5	27	3	2	71	63	31	18	1	2.28
Mel Harder (SA)	R	31	5	4	.556	1	15	10	1	69	76	37	21	0	5.22
Clint Brown	R	37	3	3	.500	5	41	0	0	74	77	28	22	0	3.28
Harry Eisenstat	L	25	1	1	.500	2	21	0	0	34	43	16	11	0	4.24
Steve Gromek	R	21	1	1	.500	2	9	2	1	23	25	11	19	0	4.30
Joe Krakauskas	L	26	1	2	.333	0	12	5	0	42	39	29	25	0	4.07
2 Chubby Dean	L	25	1	4	.200	0	8	8	2	53	57	24	14	0	4.42
Cal Dorsett	R	28	0	1	.000	0	5	2	0	11	21	10	5	0	10.64
Red Embree	R	23	0	1	.000	0	1	1	0	4	7	3	4	0	6.75
Ken Jungels	R	25	0	0	.000	0	6	0	0	14	17	8	6	0	7.07
Nate Andrews	R	27	0	0	.000	0	2	0	0	2	3	2	1	0	13.50

DETROIT 4th (Tie) 75-79 .487 26

DEL BAKER

NAME	G by POS	B	AGE	G	AB	R	H	2B	3B	HR	RBI	BB	SO	SB	BA	SA
TOTALS			30	155	5370	686	1412	247	55	81	637	602	584	43	.263	.375
Rudy York	1B155	R	27	155	590	91	153	29	3	27	111	92	88	3	.259	.456
Charlie Gehringer	2B116	L	38	127	436	65	96	19	4	3	46	95	26	1	.220	.303
Frank Croucher	SS136	R	26	136	489	51	124	21	4	2	39	33	72	2	.254	.325
Pinky Higgins	3B145	R	32	147	540	79	161	28	3	11	73	67	45	5	.298	.422
Bruce Campbell	OF133	L	31	141	512	72	141	28	10	15	93	68	67	3	.275	.457
Barney McCoskey	OF122	L	23	127	494	80	160	26	8	3	55	61	33	8	.324	.425
2 Rip Radcliff	OF87	L	35	96	379	47	120	14	5	3	39	19	13	4	.317	.404
Birdie Tebbetts	C98	R	31	110	359	28	102	19	4	2	47	38	29	1	.284	.376
Tuck Stainback	OF80	R	30	94	200	19	49	8	1	2	10	3	21	6	.245	.325
Billy Sullivan	C63	L	30	85	234	29	66	15	1	3	29	35	11	0	.282	.393
Pat Mullin	OF51	L	23	54	220	42	76	11	5	5	23	18	18	5	.345	.509
Dutch Meyer	2B40	R	25	46	153	12	29	9	1	1	14	8	13	1	.190	.281
Boyd Perry	SS25, 2B11	R	27	36	83	9	15	5	0	0	11	10	9	1	.181	.241
Ned Harris	OF12	L	24	26	61	11	13	3	1	1	4	6	13	1	.213	.344
Eric McNair	3B11, SS3	R	32	23	59	5	11	1	0	0	3	4	4	0	.186	.203
Hank Greenberg (MS)	OF19	R	30	19	67	12	18	5	1	2	12	16	12	1	.269	.463
Murray Franklin	SS4, 3B1	R	27	13	10	1	3	1	0	0	0	2	2	0	.300	.400
Dick Wakefield	OF1	L	20	7	7	0	1	0	0	0	0	0	1	0	.143	.143
1 Dick Bartell	SS5	R	33	5	12	0	2	1	0	0	1	2	2	0	.167	.250
Bob Patrick	OF3	R	23	5	7	2	2	0	0	0	0	0	1	0	.286	.286

Fred Hutchinson 21 L 0-2, Hoot Evers 20 R 0-4

NAME	T	AGE	W	L	PCT	SV	G	GS	CG	IP	H	BB	SO	ShO	ERA
TOTALS		29	75	79	.487	16	155	155	52	1382	1399	645	**697**	8	4.18
Al Benton	R	30	15	6	.714	7	38	14	7	158	130	65	63	1	2.96
Bobo Newsom	R	33	12	**20**	.375	2	43	36	12	250	265	118	175	2	4.61
Dizzy Trout	R	26	9	9	.500	2	37	18	6	152	144	84	88	1	3.73
Johnny Gorsica	R	26	9	11	.450	2	33	21	8	171	193	55	59	1	4.47
Hal Newhouser	L	20	9	11	.450	0	33	27	5	173	166	137	106	1	4.79
Tommy Bridges	R	34	9	12	.429	0	25	22	10	148	128	70	90	1	3.41
Schoolboy Rowe	R	31	8	6	.571	1	27	14	4	139	155	33	54	0	4.14
1 Archie McKain	L	30	2	1	.667	0	15	0	0	43	58	11	14	0	5.02
Hal Manders	R	24	1	0	1.000	0	8	0	0	15	13	8	7	0	2.40
Bud Thomas	R	30	1	3	.250	2	26	1	0	73	74	22	17	0	4.19
Floyd Giebell	R	31	0	0	.000	0	17	2	0	34	45	26	10	0	6.09
Les Mueller	R	22	0	0	.000	0	4	0	0	13	9	10	8	0	4.85
Hal White	R	22	0	0	.000	0	4	0	0	9	11	6	2	0	6.00
Earl Cook	R	32	0	0	.000	0	1	0	0	2	4	0	1	0	4.50
Virgil Trucks	R	22	0	0	.000	0	1	0	0	2	4	0	3	0	9.00

ST. LOUIS 6th (Tie) 70-84 .455 31

FRED HANEY 15-29 .341 LUKE SEWELL 55-55 .500

NAME	G by POS	B	AGE	G	AB	R	H	2B	3B	HR	RBI	BB	SO	SB	BA	SA
TOTALS			27	157	5408	765	1440	281	58	91	729	**775**	552	50	.266	.390
George McQuinn	1B125	L	32	130	495	93	147	28	4	18	80	74	30	5	.297	.479
Don Heffner	2B105	R	30	110	399	48	93	14	2	0	17	38	27	5	.233	.278
Johnny Berardino	SS123, 3B1	R	24	128	469	48	127	30	4	5	89	41	27	3	.271	.384
Harlond Clift	3B154	R	28	154	584	108	149	33	9	17	84	113	93	6	.255	.430
Chet Laabs	OF100	R	29	118	392	64	109	23	6	15	59	51	59	5	.278	.482
Walt Judnich	OF140	L	24	146	546	90	155	40	6	14	83	80	45	5	.284	.456
Roy Cullenbine	OF120, 1B22	B	25	149	501	82	159	29	9	9	98	121	43	6	.317	.465
2 Rick Ferrell	C98	R	35	100	321	30	81	14	3	2	23	52	22	2	.252	.333
Joe Grace	OF88, C9	L	27	115	362	53	112	17	4	6	60	57	31	1	.309	.428
Johnny Lucadello	2B70, SS12, 3B6, OF1	B	22	107	351	58	98	22	4	2	31	48	23	5	.279	.382
Bob Swift	C58	R	26	63	170	13	44	7	0	0	21	22	11	2	.259	.300
Bobby Estalella	OF17	R	30	46	83	7	20	6	1	0	14	18	13	0	.241	.337
Alan Strange	SS32, 1B2, 3B1	R	31	45	112	14	26	4	0	0	11	15	5	1	.232	.268
1 Rip Radcliff	OF14, 1B3	L	35	19	71	12	20	2	2	2	14	10	1	1	.282	.451
Frank Grube	C18	R	36	18	39	1	6	2	0	0	1	2	4	0	.154	.205
2 George Archie	1B8	R	27	9	29	3	11	3	0	0	5	7	3	2	.379	.483
Glenn McQuillen	OF6	R	26	7	21	4	7	2	1	0	3	1	2	0	.333	.524
Chuck Stevens	1B4	B	22	4	13	2	2	0	0	0	2	0	1	0	.154	.154

Vern Stephens 20 R 1-2, 1 Myril Hoag 33 R 0-1

NAME	T	AGE	W	L	PCT	SV	G	GS	CG	IP	H	BB	SO	ShO	ERA
TOTALS		30	70	84	.455	10	157	157	65	1389	**1563**	549	454	7	4.72
Eldon Auker	R	30	14	15	.483	0	34	31	13	216	268	85	60	0	5.50
Bob Muncrief	R	25	13	9	.591	1	36	24	12	214	221	53	67	2	3.66
Bob Harris	R	25	12	14	.462	1	34	29	9	187	237	85	57	2	5.20
Denny Galehouse	R	29	9	10	.474	0	30	24	11	190	183	68	61	2	3.65
Johnny Niggeling	R	37	7	9	.438	0	24	20	13	168	168	63	68	1	3.80
Bill Trotter	R	32	4	2	.667	0	29	0	0	50	68	19	17	0	5.94
Jack Kramer	R	23	4	3	.571	2	29	3	0	59	69	40	20	0	5.19
George Caster	R	33	3	7	.300	3	32	9	3	104	105	37	36	0	5.02
1 Vern Kennedy	R	34	2	4	.333	0	6	6	2	45	44	27	6	0	4.40
1 Johnny Allen	R	36	2	5	.286	1	20	9	2	67	89	29	27	0	6.58
2 Archie McKain	L	30	0	1	.000	1	8	0	0	10	16	4	2	0	8.10
Maury Newlin	R	27	0	2	.000	1	14	0	0	28	43	12	10	0	6.43
Fritz Ostermueller	L	33	0	3	.000	0	15	2	0	46	45	23	20	0	4.50
Emil Bildilli	L	28	0	0	.000	0	2	0	0	2	5	3	2	0	13.50
Hooks Iott	L	21	0	0	.000	0	2	0	0	2	2	1	1	0	9.00

WASHINGTON 6th (Tie) 70-84 .455 31

BUCKY HARRIS

NAME	G by POS	B	AGE	G	AB	R	H	2B	3B	HR	RBI	BB	SO	SB	BA	SA
TOTALS			26	156	**5521**	728	1502	257	80	52	672	470	488	79	.272	.376
Mickey Vernon	1B132	L	23	138	531	73	159	27	11	9	93	43	51	9	.299	.443
Jimmy Bloodworth	2B132, 3B6, SS1	R	23	142	506	59	124	24	3	7	66	41	58	1	.245	.346
Cecil Travis	SS136, 3B16	L	27	152	608	106	**218**	39	19	7	101	52	25	2	.359	.520
1 George Archie	3B73, 1B23	R	27	105	379	45	102	20	4	3	48	30	42	8	.269	.367
Buddy Lewis	OF96, 3B49	L	24	149	569	97	169	29	11	9	72	82	30	10	.297	.434
Doc Cramer	OF152	L	35	154	**660**	93	180	25	6	2	66	37	15	4	.273	.338
George Case	OF151	R	25	153	649	95	176	32	8	2	53	51	37	**33**	.271	.354
Jake Early	C100	L	24	104	355	42	102	20	7	10	54	24	38	0	.287	.468
Al Evans	C51	R	24	53	159	16	44	8	4	1	19	9	18	0	.277	.396
Buddy Myer	2B24	L	37	53	107	14	27	3	1	0	9	18	10	2	.252	.299
Johnny Welaj	OF19	R	27	49	96	16	20	4	0	0	5	6	16	3	.208	.250
1 Ben Chapman	OF26	R	32	28	110	9	28	6	0	1	10	10	6	2	.255	.336
Sammy West	OF8	L	36	26	37	3	10	0	0	0	6	11	2	1	.270	.270
Roberto Ortiz	OF21	R	26	22	79	10	26	1	2	1	17	3	10	0	.329	.430
Jimmy Pofahl	SS21	R	24	22	75	9	14	3	2	0	6	10	11	1	.187	.280
1 Rick Ferrell	C21	R	35	21	66	8	18	5	0	0	13	15	4	1	.273	.348
Cliff Bolton	C3	L	34	14	11	0	0	0	0	0	1	1	2	0	.000	.000
Hilly Lane	3B13	R	23	13	50	8	14	2	0	0	6	4	5	1	.280	.320
Morrie Aderholt	2B2, 3B1	L	25	11	14	3	2	0	0	0	1	1	3	0	.143	.143

Jack Sanford 24 R 2-5, Charlie Letchas 25 R 1-8, Sherry Robertson 22 R 0-3

NAME	T	AGE	W	L	PCT	SV	G	GS	CG	IP	H	BB	SO	ShO	ERA
TOTALS		28	70	84*	.455	7	156	156	69	1389	1524	603	544	8	4.36
Dutch Leonard	R	32	18	13	.581	0	34	33	19	256	271	54	91	4	3.45
Sid Hudson	R	26	13	14	.481	0	33	33	17	250	242	97	108	3	3.46
Steve Sundra	R	31	9	13	.409	0	28	23	11	168	203	61	50	0	5.30
Alex Carrasquel	R	28	6	2	.750	2	35	5	4	97	103	49	30	0	3.43
Bill Zuber	R	28	6	4	.600	2	36	7	1	96	110	61	51	0	5.44
Ken Chase	L	27	6	18	.250	0	33	30	8	206	228	115	98	1	5.07
Walt Masterson	R	21	4	3	.571	3	34	6	1	78	101	53	40	0	6.00
Red Anderson	R	29	4	6	.400	0	32	6	1	112	127	53	34	0	4.18
Early Wynn	R	21	3	1	.750	0	5	5	4	40	35	10	15	0	1.58
2 Vern Kennedy	R	34	1	7	.125	0	17	7	2	66	77	39	22	0	5.73
Danny MacFayden	R	36	0	1	.000	0	5	0	0	7	12	5	3	0	10.29
Dick Mulligan	L	23	0	1	.000	0	1	1	1	9	11	2	2	0	5.00
Harry Dean	R	26	0	0	.000	0	2	0	0	2	2	3	0	0	4.50
Ronnie Miller	R	22	0	0	.000	0	1	0	0	2	2	1	0	0	4.50
Lou Thuman (MS)		24													

*1 loss by forfeit

PHILADELPHIA 8th 64-90 .416 37

CONNIE MACK

NAME	G by POS	B	AGE	G	AB	R	H	2B	3B	HR	RBI	BB	SO	SB	BA	SA
TOTALS			27	154	5336	713	1431	240	69	85	660	574	588	27	.268	.387
Dick Siebert	1B123	L	29	123	467	63	156	28	8	5	79	37	22	1	.334	.460
Benny McCoy	2B135	L	25	141	517	86	140	12	7	8	61	95	50	3	.271	.368
Al Brancato	SS139, 3B7	R	22	144	530	60	124	20	9	2	49	59	49	1	.234	.317
Pete Suder	3B136, SS3	R	25	139	531	45	130	20	9	4	52	19	47	1	.245	.339
Wally Moses	OF109	L	30	116	438	78	132	31	4	4	35	62	27	3	.301	.418
Sam Chapman	OF141	R	25	143	552	97	178	29	9	25	106	47	49	6	.322	.543
Bob Johnson	OF122, 1B28	R	34	149	552	98	152	30	8	22	107	95	75	6	.275	.478
Frankie Hayes	C126	R	26	126	439	66	123	27	4	12	63	62	56	2	.280	.442
Eddie Collins	OF50	L	24	80	219	29	53	6	3	0	12	20	24	2	.242	.297
Dee Miles	OF35	L	32	80	170	14	53	7	1	0	15	4	8	0	.312	.365
Hal Wagner	C42	L	25	46	131	18	29	8	2	1	15	19	9	1	.221	.336
Crash Davis	2B20, 1B12	R	21	39	105	8	23	3	0	0	8	11	16	0	.219	.248
Fred Chapman	SS28, 3B2, 2B1	R	24	35	69	1	11	1	0	0	4	4	15	1	.159	.174
Elmer Valo	OF10	L	20	15	50	13	21	0	1	2	6	4	2	0	.420	.580
Don Richmond	3B9	L	21	9	35	3	7	1	1	0	5	0	1	0	.200	.286
Al Simmons	OF5	R	39	9	24	1	3	1	0	0	1	1	2	0	.125	.167
Al Rubeling	3B6	R	28	6	19	0	5	0	0	0	2	2	1	0	.263	.263
Felix Mackiewicz	OF2	R	23	5	14	3	4	0	1	0	0	1	0	0	.286	.429

Ray Poole 21 L 0-2, John Leovich 23 R 1-2, Eric Tipton 26 R 2-4

NAME	T	AGE	W	L	PCT	SV	G	GS	CG	IP	H	BB	SO	ShO	ERA
TOTALS		29	64	**90**	.416	18	154	154	64	1365	1516	557	386	3	4.83
Jack Knott	R	34	13	11	.542	0	27	26	11	194	212	81	54	0	4.41
Phil Marchildon	R	27	10	15	.400	0	30	27	14	204	188	118	74	1	3.57
Les McCrabb	R	26	9	13	.409	2	26	23	11	157	188	49	40	1	5.50
Tom Ferrick	R	26	8	10	.444	7	36	4	2	119	130	33	30	1	3.78
Bill Beckmann	R	33	5	9	.357	1	22	15	4	130	141	33	28	0	4.57
Lum Harris	R	26	4	4	.500	2	33	10	5	132	134	51	49	0	4.77
2 Bump Hadley	R	36	4	6	.400	3	25	9	1	102	131	47	31	0	5.04
Herman Besse	L	29	2	0	1.000	0	6	2	1	20	28	12	8	0	9.90
Fred Caligiuri	R	22	2	2	.500	0	5	5	4	43	45	14	7	0	2.93
1 Chubby Dean	L	25	2	4	.333	0	18	7	2	76	90	35	22	0	6.16
Johnny Babich	R	28	2	7	.222	0	16	14	8	78	85	31	19	0	6.12
Rankin Johnson	R	24	1	0	1.000	0	7	0	0	10	14	3	0	0	3.60
1 Nels Potter	R	29	1	1	.500	2	10	3	1	23	35	16	7	0	9.39
Dick Fowler	R	20	1	2	.333	0	4	3	1	24	26	8	8	0	3.38
Tex Shirley	R	23	0	1	.000	1	5	0	0	7	8	6	1	0	2.57
1 Buck Ross	R	26	0	1	.000	0	1	1	0	4	10	2	0	0	18.00
Porter Vaughn	L	22	0	2	.000	0	5	3	1	23	32	12	6	0	7.83
Roger Wolff	R	30	0	2	.000	0	2	2	2	17	15	4	2	0	3.18
Pat Tobin	R	25	0	0	.000	0	1	0	0	1	4	2	0	0	36.00

BROOKLYN 1st 100-54 .649 — LEO DUROCHER

NAME	G by POS	B	AGE	G	AB	R	H	2B	3B	HR	RBI	BB	SO	SB	BA	SA
TOTALS			28	157	5485	800	1494	286	69	101	747	600	535	36	.272	.405
Dolph Camilli	1B148	L	34	149	529	92	151	29	6	34	120	104	115	3	.285	.556
2 Billy Herman	2B133	R	31	133	536	77	156	30	4	3	41	58	38	1	.291	.379
Pee-Wee Reese	SS151	R	22	152	595	76	136	23	5	2	46	68	56	10	.229	.294
Cookie Lavagetto	3B120	R	28	132	441	75	122	24	7	1	78	80	21	7	.277	.370
Dixie Walker	OF146	L	30	148	531	88	165	32	8	9	71	70	18	4	.311	.452
Pete Reiser	OF133	L	22	137	536	117	184	39	17	14	76	46	71	4	.343	.558
Joe Medwick	OF131	R	29	133	538	100	171	33	10	18	88	38	35	2	.318	.517
Mickey Owen	C128	R	25	128	386	32	89	15	2	1	44	34	14	1	.231	.288
Jimmy Wasdell	OF54, 1B15	L	27	94	265	39	79	14	3	4	48	16	15	2	.298	.419
Lew Riggs	3B43, 1B1, 2B1	L	31	77	197	27	60	13	4	5	36	16	12	1	.305	.487
Herman Franks	C54, OF1	L	27	57	139	10	28	7	0	1	11	14	13	0	.201	.273
Pete Coscarart	2B19, SS1	R	28	43	62	13	8	1	0	0	5	7	12	1	.129	.145
Whit Wyatt	P38	R	33	40	109	10	26	5	0	3	22	4	12	0	.239	.367
Joe Vosmik	OF18	R	31	25	56	0	11	0	0	0	4	4	4	0	.196	.196
Leo Durocher	SS12, 2B1	R	35	18	42	2	12	1	0	0	6	1	3	0	.286	.310
2 Augie Galan	OF6	B	29	17	27	3	7	3	0	0	4	3	1	0	.259	.370
Alex Kampouris (XJ)	2B15	R	28	16	51	8	16	4	2	2	9	11	8	0	.314	.588
Babe Phelps (ST)	C11	L	33	16	30	3	7	3	0	2	4	1	2	0	.233	.533
1 Paul Waner	OF9	L	38	11	35	5	6	0	0	0	4	8	0	0	.171	.171
Tommy Tatum	OF4	R	21	8	12	1	2	1	0	0	1	1	3	0	.167	.250

Tony Giuliani 28 R 0-2, George Pfister 22 R 0-2, Joe Gallagher (MS) 27

NAME	T	AGE	W	L	PCT	SV	G	GS	CG	IP	H	BB	SO	ShO	ERA
TOTALS		31	100	54	.649	22	157	157	66	1421	1236	495	603	17	3.14
Kirby Higbe	R	26	22	9	.710	3	48	39	19	298	244	132	121	2	3.14
Whit Wyatt	R	33	22	10	.688	1	38	35	23	288	223	82	176	7	2.34
Hugh Casey	R	27	14	11	.560	7	45	18	4	162	155	57	61	1	3.89
Curt Davis	R	37	13	7	.650	2	28	16	10	154	141	27	50	5	2.98
Luke Hamlin	R	36	8	8	.500	1	30	20	5	136	139	41	58	1	4.24
F. Fitzsimmons (AJ)	R	39	6	1	.857	0	13	12	3	83	78	26	19	1	2.06
2 Johnny Allen	R	36	3	0	1.000	0	11	4	1	57	38	12	21	0	2.53
Bill Swift	R	33	3	0	1.000	1	9	0	0	22	26	7	9	0	3.27
Newt Kimball	R	26	3	1	.750	1	15	5	1	52	43	29	17	0	3.63
2 Mace Brown (NJ)	R	32	3	2	.600	3	24	0	0	43	31	26	22	0	3.14
Bob Chipman	L	22	1	0	1.000	0	1	0	0	5	3	1	3	0	0.00
Tom Drake	R	26	1	1	.500	0	10	2	0	25	26	9	12	0	4.32
Kemp Wicker	L	34	1	2	.333	1	16	2	0	32	30	14	8	0	3.66
Ed Albasta	R	22	0	2	.000	0	2	2	0	13	11	8	5	0	6.23
2 Vito Tamulis	L	29	0	0	.000	1	12	0	0	22	21	10	8	0	3.68
2 Larry French	L	33	0	0	.000	0	6	1	0	16	16	4	8	0	3.38
1 Lee Grissom	L	33	0	0	.000	1	4	1	0	11	10	8	5	0	2.46
Van Lingle Mungo	R	30	0	0	.000	0	2	0	0	2	1	2	0	0	4.50

ST. LOUIS 2nd 97-56 .634 2.5 — BILLY SOUTHWORTH

NAME	G by POS	B	AGE	G	AB	R	H	2B	3B	HR	RBI	BB	SO	SB	BA	SA
TOTALS			28	155	5457	734	1482	254	56	70	664	540	543	47	.272	.371
Johnny Mize	1B122	L	28	126	473	67	150	39	8	16	100	70	45	4	.317	.535
Creepy Crespi	2B145	R	23	146	560	85	156	24	2	4	46	57	58	3	.279	.350
Marty Marion	SS155	R	23	155	547	50	138	22	3	3	58	42	48	8	.252	.320
Jimmy Brown	3B123, 2B11	B	31	132	549	81	168	28	9	3	56	45	22	2	.306	.406
Enos Slaughter (BC)	OF108	L	25	113	425	71	132	22	9	13	76	53	28	4	.311	.496
Terry Moore	OF121	R	29	122	493	86	145	26	4	6	68	52	31	3	.294	.400
Johnny Hopp	OF91, 1B39	L	24	134	445	83	135	25	11	4	50	50	63	15	.303	.436
Gus Mancuso	C105	R	35	106	328	25	75	13	1	2	37	37	19	0	.229	.293
Don Padgett	OF62, C18, 1B2	L	29	107	324	39	80	18	0	5	44	21	16	0	.247	.349
Estel Crabtree	OF50, 3B1	L	37	77	167	27	57	6	3	5	28	26	24	1	.341	.503
Coaker Triplett	OF46	R	29	76	185	29	53	6	3	3	21	18	27	0	.286	.400
Walker Cooper (BS)	C63	R	26	68	200	19	49	9	1	1	20	13	14	1	.245	.315
Eddie Lake	SS15, 3B15, 2B5	R	25	45	76	9	8	2	0	0	0	15	22	3	.105	.132
Steve Mesner	3B22	R	23	24	69	8	10	1	0	0	10	5	6	0	.145	.159
1 Ernie Koy	OF12	R	31	13	40	5	8	1	0	2	4	1	8	0	.200	.375
Stan Musial	OF11	L	20	12	47	8	20	4	0	1	7	2	1	1	.426	.574
Harry Walker	OF5	L	24	7	15	3	4	1	0	0	1	2	1	0	.267	.333
Erv Dusak	OF4	R	20	6	14	1	2	0	0	0	3	2	6	1	.143	.143
Whitey Kurowski	3B4	R	23	5	9	1	3	2	0	0	2	0	2	0	.333	.556

Walter Sessi 22 L 0-13, 2 Pep Young 33 R 0-2, Charlie Marshall 21 R 0-0

NAME	T	AGE	W	L	PCT	SV	G	GS	CG	IP	H	BB	SO	ShO	ERA
TOTALS		28	97	56	.634	20	155	155	64	1417	1289	502	659	15	3.19
Ernie White	L	24	17	7	.708	2	32	25	12	210	169	70	117	3	2.40
Lon Warneke	R	32	17	9	.654	0	37	30	12	246	227	82	83	4	3.15
Mort Cooper (EJ)	R	28	13	9	.591	0	29	25	12	187	175	69	118	0	3.90
2 Harry Gumbert	R	31	11	5	.688	1	33	17	8	144	139	30	53	3	2.75
Howie Krist	R	25	10	0	1.000	2	37	8	2	114	107	35	36	0	4.03
Max Lanier	L	25	10	8	.556	3	35	18	8	153	126	59	93	2	2.82
Sam Nahem	R	25	5	2	.714	1	26	8	2	82	76	38	31	0	2.96
Howie Pollet	L	20	5	2	.714	0	9	8	6	70	55	27	37	2	1.93
Clyde Shoun	L	29	3	5	.375	0	26	6	0	70	98	20	34	0	5.66
Johnny Grodzicki	R	24	2	1	.667	0	5	1	0	13	6	11	10	0	1.38
1 Hank Gornicki	R	30	1	0	1.000	0	4	1	1	11	6	9	6	1	3.28
Johnny Beazley	R	23	1	0	1.000	0	1	1	1	9	10	3	4	1	1.00
2 Bill Crouch	R	30	1	2	.333	6	18	4	0	45	45	14	15	0	3.00
Ira Hutchinson	R	30	1	5	.167	5	29	0	0	47	32	19	19	0	3.83
1 Bill McGee	R	31	0	1	.000	0	4	3	0	14	17	13	2	0	5.14
Hersh Lyons	R	25	0	0	.000	0	1	0	0	1	1	3	1	0	0.00

CINCINNATI 3rd 88-66 .571 12 — BILL McKECHNIE

NAME	G by POS	B	AGE	G	AB	R	H	2B	3B	HR	RBI	BB	SO	SB	BA	SA
TOTALS			29	154	5218	616	1288	213	33	64	567	477	428	68	.247	.337
Frank McCormick	1B154	R	30	154	603	77	162	31	5	17	97	40	13	2	.269	.421
Lonny Frey	2B145	R	30	146	543	78	138	29	5	6	59	72	37	16	.254	.359
Eddie Joost	SS147, 2B4, 1B2, 3B1	R	25	152	537	67	136	25	4	4	40	69	59	9	.253	.337
Bill Werber	3B107	R	33	109	418	56	100	9	2	4	46	53	24	14	.239	.299
Jim Gleeson	OF84	B	29	102	301	47	70	10	0	3	34	45	30	7	.233	.296
Harry Craft	OF115	R	26	119	413	48	103	15	2	10	59	33	43	4	.249	.368
Mike McCormick	OF101	R	24	110	369	52	106	17	3	4	31	30	24	4	.287	.382
Ernie Lombardi	C116	R	33	117	398	33	105	12	1	10	60	36	14	1	.264	.374
2 Ernie Koy	OF49	R	31	67	204	24	51	11	2	2	27	14	22	1	.250	.353
Dick West	C64	R	25	67	172	15	37	5	2	1	17	6	23	4	.215	.285
3 Lloyd Waner	OF44	L	35	55	164	17	42	4	1	0	6	8	0	0	.256	.293
Chuck Aleno	3B40, 1B2	R	24	54	169	23	41	7	3	1	18	11	16	3	.243	.337
Ival Goodman (IL)	OF40	L	32	42	149	14	40	5	2	1	12	16	15	1	.268	.349
Jimmy Ripple	OF25	L	31	38	102	10	22	6	1	1	9	9	4	0	.216	.324
Eddie Lukon	OF22	L	20	23	86	6	23	3	0	0	3	6	6	1	.267	.302
Bobby Mattick	SS12, 3B5, 2B1	R	25	20	60	8	11	3	0	0	7	8	7	1	.183	.233
Johnny Riddle	C10	R	35	10	10	2	3	0	0	0	0	0	1	0	.300	.300
Hank Sauer	OF8	R	22	9	33	4	10	4	0	0	5	1	4	0	.303	.424
Benny Zientara	2B6	R	21	9	21	3	6	0	0	0	2	1	3	0	.286	.286

1 Pep Young 33 R 2-12, 1 Bill Baker 30 R 0-1, Ray Lamanno 21 R 0-0, Eddie Shokes 21 L 0-1

NAME	T	AGE	W	L	PCT	SV	G	GS	CG	IP	H	BB	SO	ShO	ERA
TOTALS		30	88	66	.571	10	154	154	89	1387	1300	510	627	19	3.17
Elmer Riddle	R	26	19	4	.826	1	33	22	15	217	180	59	80	4	2.24
Bucky Walters	R	32	19	15	.559	2	37	35	27	302	292	88	129	5	2.83
Johnny Vander Meer	L	26	16	13	.552	0	33	32	18	226	172	126	202	6	2.83
Paul Derringer	R	34	12	14	.462	1	29	28	17	228	233	54	76	2	3.32
Jim Turner (NJ)	R	37	6	4	.600	0	23	10	3	113	120	24	34	0	3.11
Junior Thompson	R	24	6	6	.500	1	27	15	4	109	117	57	46	0	4.87
Joe Beggs	R	30	4	3	.571	5	37	0	0	57	57	27	19	0	3.79
Ray Starr	R	35	3	2	.600	0	7	4	3	34	28	6	11	2	2.65
Whitey Moore	R	29	2	1	.667	0	23	4	1	62	62	45	17	0	4.35
Monte Pearson	R	31	1	3	.250	0	7	4	1	24	22	15	8	0	5.25
Bob Logan	L	31	0	1	.000	0	2	0	0	3	5	5	0	0	9.00
1 Johnny Hutchings	R	25	0	0	.000	0	8	0	0	11	12	4	5	0	4.09

PITTSBURGH 4th 81-73 .526 19 — FRANKIE FRISCH

NAME	G by POS	B	AGE	G	AB	R	H	2B	3B	HR	RBI	BB	SO	SB	BA	SA
TOTALS			27	156	5297	690	1417	233	65	56	634	547	516	59	.268	.368
Elbie Fletcher	1B151	L	25	151	521	95	150	29	13	11	74	118	54	5	.288	.457
Frankie Gustine	2B104, 3B15	R	21	121	463	46	125	24	7	1	46	28	38	5	.270	.359
Arky Vaughan	SS97, 3B3	L	29	106	374	69	118	20	7	6	38	50	13	8	.316	.455
Lee Handley	3B114	R	27	124	459	59	132	18	4	0	33	35	22	16	.288	.344
Bob Elliott	OF139	R	24	141	527	74	144	24	10	3	76	64	52	6	.273	.374
Vince DiMaggio	OF151	R	28	151	528	73	141	27	5	21	100	68	100	10	.267	.456
Maurice Van Robays	OF121	R	26	129	457	62	129	23	5	4	78	41	29	0	.282	.381
Al Lopez	C114	R	32	114	317	33	84	9	1	5	43	31	23	0	.265	.347
Stu Martin	2B53, 3B2, 1B1	L	27	88	233	37	71	13	2	0	19	10	17	2	.305	.378
Debs Garms	3B29, OF24	L	33	83	220	25	58	9	3	3	42	22	12	0	.264	.373
Bud Stewart	OF41	R	25	73	172	27	46	7	0	0	10	12	17	3	.267	.308
Alf Anderson	SS58	R	27	70	223	32	48	7	2	1	10	14	30	2	.215	.278
Spud Davis	C49	R	36	57	107	3	27	4	1	0	6	11	11	0	.252	.308
Ripper Collins	1B11, OF3	B	37	49	62	5	13	2	2	0	11	6	14	0	.210	.306
2 Bill Baker	C33	R	30	35	67	5	15	3	0	0	6	11	0	0	.224	.269
Ed Leip	2B7, 3B1	R	30	15	25	1	5	0	2	0	3	1	2	1	.200	.360
Billy Cox	SS10	R	21	10	37	4	10	3	1	0	2	3	2	1	.270	.405
Vinnie Smith	C9	R	25	9	33	3	10	1	0	0	5	1	5	0	.303	.333
Culley Rikard	OF5	L	27	6	20	1	4	1	0	0	0	1	1	0	.200	.250

1 Lloyd Waner 35 L 1-4, Joe Schultz 22 L 1-2

NAME	T	AGE	W	L	PCT	SV	G	GS	CG	IP	H	BB	SO	ShO	ERA
TOTALS		30	81	73	.526	12	156	156	71	1374	1392	492	410	8	3.48
Max Butcher	R	30	17	12	.586	0	33	32	19	236	249	66	61	0	3.05
Rip Sewell	R	34	14	17	.452	2	39	32	18	249	225	84	76	2	3.72
Ken Heintzelman	L	25	11	11	.500	0	35	24	13	196	206	83	81	2	3.44
Johnny Lanning	R	30	11	11	.500	1	34	23	9	176	175	47	41	0	3.12
Bob Klinger	R	33	9	4	.692	4	35	9	3	117	127	30	36	0	3.92
Dutch Dietz	R	29	7	2	.778	1	33	6	4	100	88	33	22	1	2.34
2 Joe Sullivan	L	30	4	1	.800	1	16	4	0	39	40	22	10	0	3.00
Joe Bowman	R	31	3	2	.600	1	18	7	1	69	77	28	22	1	3.00
Lefty Wilkie	L	26	2	4	.333	2	26	6	2	79	90	40	16	1	4.56
Bill Clemensen	R	22	1	0	1.000	0	2	1	1	13	7	7	4	0	2.77
2 Nick Strincevich	R	26	1	2	.333	0	12	3	0	31	35	13	12	0	5.23
Russ Bauers	R	27	1	3	.250	0	8	5	1	37	40	25	20	0	5.59
Dick Lanahan	L	29	0	1	.000	0	7	0	0	12	13	3	5	0	5.25
Bill Brandt	R	26	0	1	.000	0	2	1	0	7	5	3	0	0	3.86
Johnny Gee	L	25	0	2	.000	0	3	2	0	7	10	5	2	0	6.43
Dick Conger	R	20	0	0	.000	0	2	1	0	4	3	3	2	0	0.00
1 Mace Brown	R	32	0	0	.000	0	1	0	0	1	2	0	0	0	0.00

Oad Swigert (MS) 26

NEW YORK 5th 74-79 .484 25.5 — BILL TERRY

NAME	G by POS	B	AGE	G	AB	R	H	2B	3B	HR	RBI	BB	SO	SB	BA	SA
TOTALS			30	156	5395	667	1401	248	35	95	625	504	518	36	.260	.371
Babe Young	1B150	L	26	152	574	90	152	28	5	25	104	66	39	1	.265	.462
Burgess Whitehead	2B104, 3B1	R	31	116	403	41	92	15	4	1	23	14	10	7	.228	.293
Billy Jurges	SS134	R	33	134	471	50	138	25	2	5	61	47	36	0	.293	.386
2 Dick Bartell	3B84, SS21	R	33	104	373	44	113	20	0	5	35	52	29	6	.303	.397
Mel Ott	OF145	L	32	148	525	89	150	29	0	27	90	100	68	5	.286	.495
Johnny Rucker	OF142	L	24	142	622	95	179	38	9	1	42	29	61	8	.288	.383
Jo-Jo Moore	OF116	L	32	121	428	47	117	16	2	7	40	30	15	4	.273	.369
Harry Danning	C116, 1B1	R	29	130	459	58	112	22	4	7	56	30	25	1	.244	.355
Morrie Arnovich	OF61	R	30	85	207	25	58	8	3	2	22	23	14	2	.280	.377
Joe Orengo	3B59, SS9, 2B6	R	26	77	252	23	54	11	2	4	25	28	49	1	.214	.321
Gabby Hartnett	C34	R	40	64	150	20	45	5	0	5	26	12	14	0	.300	.433
Ken O'Dea	C14	L	28	59	89	13	19	5	1	3	17	8	20	0	.213	.393
2 Odell Hale	2B29	R	32	41	102	13	20	3	0	0	9	18	13	1	.196	.225
Mickey Witek	2B23	R	25	26	94	11	34	5	0	1	16	4	2	0	.362	.447
John Davis	3B21	R	25	21	70	8	15	3	0	0	5	8	12	0	.214	.257
1 Frank Demaree	OF10	R	31	16	35	3	6	0	0	0	1	4	1	0	.171	.171
Johnny McCarthy	1B8, OF1	L	31	14	40	1	13	3	0	0	12	3	0	0	.325	.400
Babe Barna	OF10	L	26	10	42	5	9	3	0	1	5	2	6	0	.214	.357
Sid Gordon	OF9	R	23	9	31	4	8	1	1	0	4	6	1	0	.258	.355

Rae Blaemire 30 R 2-5, Jack Aragon 25 R 0-0

NAME	T	AGE	W	L	PCT	SV	G	GS	CG	IP	H	BB	SO	ShO	ERA
TOTALS		30	74	79	.484	18	156	156	55	1392	1455	539	566	12	3.94
Hal Schumacher	R	30	12	10	.545	1	30	26	12	206	187	79	63	3	3.36
Bob Carpenter	R	23	11	6	.647	2	29	19	8	132	138	42	42	1	3.82
Carl Hubbell	L	38	11	9	.550	1	26	22	11	164	169	53	75	1	3.57
Bill Lohrman	R	28	9	10	.474	3	33	20	6	159	184	40	61	2	4.02
Cliff Melton	L	29	8	11	.421	1	42	22	9	194	181	61	100	3	3.02
Bob Bowman	R	30	6	7	.462	1	29	6	2	80	100	36	25	0	5.74
Ace Adams	R	29	4	1	.800	1	38	0	0	71	84	35	18	0	4.82
Johnnie Wittig	R	27	3	5	.375	0	25	9	0	85	111	45	47	0	5.61
2 Bill McGee	R	31	2	9	.182	0	22	14	1	106	117	54	41	0	4.92
1 Bump Hadley	R	36	1	0	1.000	0	3	2	0	13	19	9	4	0	6.23
Rube Fischer	R	24	1	0	1.000	0	2	1	1	11	10	6	9	0	2.45
1 Harry Gumbert	R	31	1	1	.500	0	5	5	1	32	34	18	9	0	4.50
Harry Feldman	R	21	1	1	.500	0	3	3	1	20	21	6	9	1	4.05
Hugh East	R	21	1	1	.500	0	2	2	0	16	19	9	4	0	3.38
Tom Sunkel	L	28	1	1	.500	0	2	2	1	15	7	12	14	1	3.00
Dave Koslo	L	21	1	2	.333	0	4	3	2	24	17	10	12	0	1.88
Jumbo Brown	R	34	1	5	.167	8	31	0	0	57	49	21	30	0	3.32
Paul Dean	R	27	0	0	.000	0	5	0	0	6	8	3	3	0	3.00

CHICAGO 6th 70-84 .455 30 — JIMMIE WILSON

	NAME	G by POS	B	AGE	G	AB	R	H	2B	3B	HR	RBI	BB	SO	SB	BA	SA
	TOTALS			26	155	5230	666	1323	239	25	99	610	559	670	39	.253	.365
2	Babe Dahlgren	1B98	R	29	99	359	50	101	20	1	16	59	43	39	2	.281	.476
	Lou Stringer	2B137, SS7	R	24	145	512	59	126	31	4	5	53	59	86	3	.246	.352
	Bobby Sturgeon	SS126, 2B1, 3B1	R	21	129	433	45	106	15	3	0	25	9	30	5	.245	.293
	Stan Hack	3B150, 1B1	L	31	151	586	111	186	33	5	7	45	99	40	10	.317	.427
	Bill Nicholson	OF143	L	26	147	532	74	135	26	1	26	98	82	91	1	.254	.453
	Phil Cavarretta	OF66, 1B33	L	24	107	346	46	99	18	4	6	40	53	28	2	.286	.413
	Dom Dallessandro	OF131	L	27	140	486	73	132	36	2	6	85	68	37	3	.272	.391
	Clyde McCullough	C119	R	24	125	418	41	95	9	2	9	53	34	67	5	.227	.323
1	Augie Galan	OF31	B	29	65	120	18	25	3	0	1	13	22	10	0	.208	.258
	Lou Novikoff	OF54	R	25	62	203	22	49	8	0	5	24	11	15	0	.241	.355
	Hank Leiber (CN)	OF29, 1B15	R	30	53	162	20	35	5	0	7	25	16	25	0	.216	.377
	Bob Scheffing	C34	R	25	51	132	9	32	8	0	1	20	5	19	2	.242	.326
	Johnny Hudson	SS17, 2B13, 3B10	R	29	50	99	8	20	4	0	0	6	3	15	3	.202	.242
	Charlie Gilbert	OF22	L	21	39	86	11	24	2	1	0	12	11	6	1	.279	.326
	Greek George	C18	R	28	35	64	4	10	2	0	0	6	2	10	0	.156	.188
	Barney Olsen	OF23	R	21	24	73	13	21	6	1	1	4	4	11	0	.288	.438
	Billy Myers	SS19, 2B1	R	30	24	63	10	14	1	0	1	4	7	25	1	.222	.286
	Eddie Waitkus	1B9	L	21	12	28	1	5	0	0	0	0	0	3	0	.179	.179
1	Billy Herman	2B11	R	31	11	36	4	7	0	1	0	0	9	5	0	.194	.250

Lennie Merullo 24 R 6-17, Rip Russell 26 R 5-17, Al Todd 37 R 1-6, Frank Jelincich 21 R 1-8

	NAME	T	AGE	W	L	PCT	SV	G	GS	CG	IP	H	BB	SO	ShO	ERA
			32	70	84	.455	9	155	155	74	1365	1431	449	548	8	3.72
	Claude Passeau	R	32	14	14	.500	0	34	30	20	231	262	52	80	3	3.35
	Vern Olsen	L	23	10	8	.556	1	37	23	10	186	202	59	73	2	3.15
	Charlie Root	R	42	8	7	.533	0	19	15	6	107	133	37	46	0	5.38
	Jake Mooty	R	28	8	9	.471	4	33	14	7	153	143	56	45	1	3.35
	Bill Lee	R	31	8	14	.364	1	28	22	12	167	179	43	62	0	3.77
	Tot Pressnell	R	34	5	3	.625	1	29	1	0	70	69	23	27	0	3.09
	Paul Erickson	R	25	5	7	.417	1	32	15	7	141	126	64	85	1	3.70
1	Larry French	L	33	5	14	.263	0	26	18	6	138	161	43	60	1	4.63
	Vallie Eaves	R	29	3	3	.500	0	12	7	4	59	56	21	24	0	3.51
	Johnny Schmitz	L	20	2	0	1.000	0	5	3	1	21	12	9	11	0	1.29
	Vance Page	R	37	2	2	.500	1	25	3	1	48	48	30	17	0	4.31
	Ken Raffensberger	L	23	0	1	.000	0	10	1	0	18	17	7	5	0	4.50
	Walt Lanfranconi	R	24	0	1	.000	0	2	1	0	6	7	2	1	0	3.00
	Russ Meers	L	22	0	1	.000	0	1	1	0	8	5	0	5	0	1.13
	Wimpy Quinn	R	23	0	0	.000	0	3	0	0	5	3	3	2	0	7.20
	Emil Kush	R	24	0	0	.000	0	2	0	0	4	2	0	2	0	2.25
	Dizzy Dean (SA)	R	30	0	0	.000	0	1	1	0	1	3	0	1	0	18.00
2	Hank Gornicki	R	30	0	0	.000	0	1	0	0	2	3	0	2	0	4.50

BOSTON 7th 62-92 .403 38 — CASEY STENGEL

	NAME	G by POS	B	AGE	G	AB	R	H	2B	3B	HR	RBI	BB	SO	SB	BA	SA
	TOTALS			28	156	5414	592	1357	231	38	48	552	471	608	61	.251	.334
	Buddy Hassett	1B99	L	29	118	405	59	120	9	4	1	33	36	15	10	.296	.346
	Bama Rowell	2B112, OF14, 3B2	L	25	138	483	49	129	23	6	7	60	39	36	11	.267	.383
	Eddie Miller	SS154	R	24	154	585	54	140	27	3	6	68	35	72	8	.239	.326
	Sibby Sisti	3B137, 2B2, SS2	R	20	140	541	72	140	24	3	1	45	38	76	7	.259	.320
	Gene Moore	OF110	L	31	129	397	42	108	17	8	5	43	45	37	5	.272	.393
	Johnny Cooney	OF111, 1B4	R	40	123	442	52	141	25	2	0	29	27	15	3	.319	.385
	Max West	OF132	L	24	138	484	63	134	28	4	12	68	72	68	5	.277	.426
	Ray Berres	C120	R	33	120	279	21	56	10	0	1	19	17	20	2	.201	.247
2	Paul Waner	OF77, 1B1	L	38	95	294	40	82	10	2	2	46	47	14	1	.279	.347
	Phil Masi	C83	R	24	87	180	17	40	8	2	3	18	16	13	4	.222	.339
	Skippy Roberge	2B46, 3B5, SS2	R	24	55	167	12	36	6	0	0	15	9	18	0	.216	.251
2	Frank Demaree	OF28	R	31	48	113	20	26	5	2	2	15	12	5	2	.230	.363
1	Babe Dahlgren	1B39, 3B5	R	29	44	166	20	39	8	1	7	30	16	13	0	.235	.422
	Al Montgomery	C30	R	20	42	52	4	10	1	0	0	4	9	8	0	.192	.212
	Buddy Gremp	1B21, 2B6, C3	R	21	37	75	7	18	3	0	0	10	5	3	0	.240	.280
	Chet Ross (NJ)	OF12	R	24	29	50	1	6	1	0	0	4	9	17	0	.120	.140
	Don Manno	OF5, 3B3, 1B1	R	26	22	30	2	5	1	0	0	4	3	7	0	.167	.200
	Hank Majeski	3B11	R	24	19	55	5	8	5	0	0	3	1	13	0	.145	.236
2	Lloyd Waner	OF15	L	35	19	51	7	21	1	0	0	4	2	0	1	.412	.431
	Whitey Wietelmann	2B10, SS5, 3B2	R	22	16	33	1	3	0	0	0	0	1	2	0	.091	.091
	John Dudra	2B5, 3B5, 1B1, SS1	R	25	14	25	3	9	3	1	0	3	3	4	0	.360	.560

Earl Averill 39 L 2-17, Mel Preibisch 26 R 0-4, Buster Bray 28 L 1-11

	NAME	T	AGE	W	L	PCT	SV	G	GS	CG	IP	H	BB	SO	ShO	ERA
			26	62	92	.403	9	156	156	62	1386	1440	554	446	10	3.95
	Jim Tobin	R	28	12	12	.500	0	33	26	20	238	229	60	61	3	3.10
	Al Javery	R	23	10	11	.476	1	34	23	9	161	181	65	54	1	4.30
	Art Johnson	L	24	7	15	.318	1	43	18	6	183	189	71	70	0	3.54
	Manny Salvo	R	28	7	16	.304	0	35	27	11	195	192	93	67	2	4.06
	Tom Earley	R	24	6	8	.429	3	33	13	6	139	120	46	54	1	2.53
	Dick Errickson	R	27	6	12	.333	1	38	23	5	166	192	62	45	2	4.77
	Frank LaManna	R	21	5	4	.556	1	35	4	0	73	77	56	23	0	5.30
	Bill Posedel	R	34	4	4	.500	0	18	9	3	57	61	30	10	0	4.89
	Wes Ferrell	R	33	2	1	.667	0	4	3	1	14	13	9	10	0	5.14
1	Joe Sullivan	L	30	2	2	.500	0	16	2	0	52	60	26	11	0	4.16
2	Johnny Hutchings	R	25	1	6	.143	2	36	7	1	96	110	22	36	1	4.13
	George Barnicle	R	23	0	1	.000	0	1	1	0	7	5	4	2	0	6.43
1	Nick Strincevich	R	26	0	0	.000	0	3	0	0	3	7	6	1	0	12.00
	Eddie Carnett	L	24	0	0	.000	0	2	0	0	1	4	3	2	0	27.00
	Al Piechota	R	27	0	0	.000	0	1	0	0	1	0	1	0	0	0.00

PHILADELPHIA 8th 43-111 .279 57 — DOC PROTHRO

	NAME	G by POS	B	AGE	G	AB	R	H	2B	3B	HR	RBI	BB	SO	SB	BA	SA
	TOTALS			26	155	5233	501	1277	188	38	64	467	451	596	65	.244	.331
	Nick Etten	1B150	L	27	151	540	78	168	27	4	14	79	82	33	9	.311	.454
	Danny Murtaugh	2B85, SS1	R	23	85	347	34	76	8	1	0	11	26	31	18	.219	.248
	Bobby Bragan	SS154, 2B2, 3B1	R	23	154	557	37	140	19	3	4	69	26	29	7	.251	.318
	Pinky May	3B140	R	30	142	490	46	131	17	4	0	39	55	30	2	.267	.318
	Stan Benjamin	OF110, 1B8, 2B2, 3B1	R	27	129	480	47	113	20	7	3	27	20	81	17	.235	.325
	Joe Marty	OF132	R	27	137	477	60	128	19	3	8	39	51	41	6	.268	.371
	Danny Litwhiler	OF150	R	24	151	590	72	180	29	6	18	66	39	43	1	.305	.466
	Bennie Warren	C110	R	29	121	345	34	74	13	2	9	35	44	66	0	.214	.342
	Johnny Rizzo	OF62, 3B2	R	28	99	235	20	51	9	2	4	24	24	34	1	.217	.323
	Mickey Livingston	C71, 1B1	R	26	95	207	16	42	6	1	0	18	20	38	2	.203	.242
	Emmett Mueller (BG)	2B29, OF21, 3B19	B	28	93	233	21	53	11	1	1	22	22	24	2	.227	.296
	Hal Marnie	2B39, SS16, 3B3	R	22	61	158	12	38	3	3	0	11	13	25	0	.241	.297
	Chuck Klein	OF14	L	36	50	73	6	9	0	0	1	3	10	6	0	.123	.164
	Bill Nagel	2B12, OF2, 3B1	R	25	17	56	2	8	1	1	0	6	3	14	0	.143	.196
	Jim Carlin	OF9, 3B2	L	23	16	21	2	3	1	0	1	2	3	4	0	.143	.333
	Bill Harman	C5, P5	R	22	15	14	1	1	0	0	0	0	0	3	0	.071	.071
	Paul Busby	OF3	L	22	10	16	3	5	0	0	0	2	0	1	0	.313	.313

George Jumonville 24 R 3-7, Wally Millies 34 R 0-2

	NAME	T	AGE	W	L	PCT	SV	G	GS	CG	IP	H	BB	SO	ShO	ERA
			28	43	111	.279	9	155	155	35	1372	1499	606	552	4	4.50
	Johnny Podgajny	R	21	9	12	.429	0	34	24	8	181	191	70	53	0	4.62
	Tommy Hughes	R	21	9	14	.391	0	34	24	5	170	187	82	59	2	4.45
	Cy Blanton	R	32	6	13	.316	0	28	25	7	164	186	57	64	1	4.50
	Si Johnson	R	34	5	12	.294	2	39	21	6	163	207	54	80	1	4.53
	Ike Pearson	R	24	4	14	.222	6	46	10	0	136	139	70	38	0	3.57
	Frank Hoerst	L	23	3	10	.231	0	37	11	1	106	111	50	33	0	5.18
1	Bill Crouch	R	30	2	3	.400	1	20	5	1	59	65	17	26	0	4.42
2	Lee Grissom	L	33	2	13	.133	0	29	18	2	131	120	70	74	0	3.99
	Paul Masterson	L	25	1	0	1.000	0	2	1	1	11	11	6	8	0	4.91
	Rube Melton	R	24	1	5	.167	0	25	5	2	84	81	47	57	0	4.71
	Boom-Boom Beck	R	36	1	9	.100	0	34	7	2	95	104	35	34	0	4.64
1	Vito Tamulis	L	29	0	1	.000	0	6	1	0	12	21	7	5	0	9.00
	Dale Jones	R	22	0	1	.000	0	2	1	0	8	13	6	2	0	7.88
	Gene Lambert	R	20	0	1	.000	0	2	1	0	9	11	2	3	0	2.00
	Roy Bruner (MS)	R	24	0	3	.000	0	13	1	0	29	37	25	13	0	4.97
	Bill Harman	R	22	0	0	.000	0	5	0	0	13	15	8	3	0	4.85
	Hugh Mulcahy (MS) 27															

WORLD SERIES – NEW YORK (AL) 4 BROOKLYN (NL) 1

LINE SCORES

TEAM	1	2	3	4	5	6	7	8	9	10	11	12	R	H	E
Game 1 October 1 at New York															
BKN (NL)	0	0	0	0	1	0	1	0	0				2	6	0
NY (AL)	0	1	0	1	0	1	0	0	X				3	6	1
Davis, Casey (6), Allen (7) — **Ruffing**															
Game 2 October 2 at New York															
BKN	0	0	0	0	2	1	0	0	0				3	6	2
NY	0	1	1	0	0	0	0	0	0				2	9	1
Wyatt — **Chandler**, Murphy (6)															
Game 3 October 4 at Brooklyn															
NY	0	0	0	0	0	0	0	2	0				2	8	0
BKN	0	0	0	0	0	0	0	1	0				1	4	0
Russo — Fitzsimmons, **Casey** (8), French (8) Allen (9)															
Game 4 October 5 at Brooklyn															
NY	1	0	0	2	0	0	0	0	4				7	12	0
BKN	0	0	0	2	2	0	0	0	0				4	9	1
Donald, Breuer (5), **Murphy** (8) — Higbe, French (4) Allen (5), **Casey** (5)															
Game 5 October 6 at Brooklyn															
NY	0	2	0	0	1	0	0	0	0				3	6	0
BKN	0	0	1	0	0	0	0	0	0				1	4	1
Bonham — **Wyatt**															

COMPOSITE BATTING

NAME	POS	G	AB	R	H	2B	3B	HR	RBI	BA
New York (AL)										
Totals		5	166	17	41	5	1	2	16	.247
Sturm	1B	5	21	0	6	0	0	0	2	.286
Rolfe	3B	5	20	2	6	0	0	0	0	.300
DiMaggio	OF	5	19	1	5	0	0	0	1	.263
Keller	OF	5	18	5	7	2	0	0	5	.389
Henrich	OF	5	18	4	3	1	0	1	1	.167
Dickey	C	5	18	3	3	1	0	0	1	.167
Rizzuto	SS	5	18	0	2	0	0	0	0	.111
Gordon	2B	5	14	2	7	1	1	1	5	.500
Bonham	P	1	4	0	0	0	0	0	0	.000
Russo	P	1	4	0	0	0	0	0	0	.000
Ruffing	P	1	3	0	0	0	0	0	0	.000
Chandler	P	1	2	0	1	0	0	0	1	.500
Selkirk	PH	2	2	0	1	0	0	0	0	.500
Murphy	P	2	2	0	0	0	0	0	0	.000
Donald	P	1	2	0	0	0	0	0	0	.000
Breuer	P	1	1	0	0	0	0	0	0	.000
Rosar	C	1	0	0	0	0	0	0	0	.000
Bordagaray	PR	1	0	0	0	0	0	0	0	.000
Brooklyn (NL)										
Totals		5	159	11	29	7	2	1	11	.182
Reiser	OF	5	20	1	4	1	1	1	3	.200
Reese	SS	5	20	1	4	0	0	0	2	.200
Walker	OF	5	18	3	4	2	0	0	0	.222
Camilli	1B	5	18	1	3	1	0	0	1	.167
Medwick	OF	5	17	1	4	1	0	0	0	.235
Owen	C	5	12	1	2	0	1	0	2	.167
Lavagetto	3B	3	10	1	1	0	0	0	0	.100
Riggs	3B	3	8	0	2	0	0	0	1	.250
Herman	2B	4	8	0	1	0	0	0	0	.125
Coscarart	2B	3	7	1	0	0	0	0	0	.000
Wyatt	P	2	6	1	1	1	0	0	0	.167
Wasdell	OF	3	5	0	1	1	0	0	2	.200
Casey	P	3	2	0	0	0	0	0	0	.000
Galan	PH	2	2	0	0	0	0	0	0	.000
Davis	P	1	2	0	0	0	0	0	0	.000
Fitzsimmons	P	1	2	0	0	0	0	0	0	.000
Higbe	P	1	1	0	1	0	0	0	0	1.000
Franks	C	1	1	0	0	0	0	0	0	.000
Allen	P	3	0	0	0	0	0	0	0	.000
French	P	2	0	0	0	0	0	0	0	.000

COMPOSITE PITCHING

NAME	G	IP	H	BB	SO	W	L	SV	ERA
New York (AL)									
Totals	5	45	29	14	21	4	1	0	1.80
Bonham	1	9	4	2	2	1	0	0	1.00
Ruffing	1	9	6	3	5	1	0	0	1.00
Russo	1	9	4	2	5	1	0	0	1.00
Murphy	2	6	2	1	3	1	0	0	0.00
Chandler	1	5	4	2	2	0	1	0	3.60
Donald	1	4	6	3	2	0	0	0	9.00
Breuer	1	3	3	1	2	0	0	0	0.00
Brooklyn (NL)									
Totals	5	44	41	23	18	1	4	0	2.66
Wyatt	2	18	15	10	14	1	1	0	2.50
Fitzsimmons	1	7	4	3	1	0	0	0	0.00
Casey	3	5.1	9	2	1	0	2	0	3.38
Davis	1	5.1	6	3	1	0	1	0	5.06
Allen	3	3.2	1	3	0	0	0	0	0.00
Higbe	1	3.2	6	2	1	0	0	0	7.36
French	2	1	0	0	0	0	0	0	0.00

1942 Branch Rickey and His Victory Garden

Branch Rickey made his reputation at St. Louis by providing homegrown ball players to fill the Cardinal lineup. While other teams usually purchased young, but seasoned, talent from independent minor league clubs, Rickey decided to develop a farm system where green talent could be inexpensively signed by Cardinal scouts and then nurtured on St. Louis-owned farm clubs. The success of the Mahatma's scheme manifested itself in the bumper crop of young talent which arrived in St. Louis in this first war year. A 21-year-old left-hand batter, whose stance at the plate resembled a corkscrew, hit .315 while holding down the left field spot, his name, Stan Musial. Enos Slaughter and Terry Moore were established stars in the other two garden posts, but the main outfield reserve was another young batting student, Harry "the Hat" Walker. Whitey Kurowski came up to furnish another big bat in the lineup, and Johnny Beazley won 21 games as the farm system's representative on the mound staff. Marty Marion and the Cooper brothers, Walker and Mort, lent stability to the squad with Mort on the throwing end of the battery and brother combination, especially shining by winning 22 games and picking up the league's MVP Award.

The Brooklyn Dodgers, nevertheless, seemed sure to repeat as pennant winners when they held a 10½ game edge over the Birds in mid-August. But after sweeping a doubleheader from Brooklyn on August 4, the Cardinals caught fire, and the youthful squad went on to win 43 of its final 51 contests. Brooklyn held on as best it could in the face of the onslaught, yet soon found they were unable to keep pace. A St. Louis sweep of a two-game series at Ebbets Field in mid-September pulled the Cardinals into a first-place tie. The flying Redbirds then took the undisputed lead on September 13, and held it the rest of the way, despite a spirited fight from the Dodgers.

While Mort Cooper monopolized the league pitching honors, all the hitting awards went to players on also-ran teams. Boston's Ernie Lombardi, by hitting the ball harder than anyone else in captivity, won the batting title despite having a pair of cast iron legs. Giant skipper Mel Ott led the loop with 30 home runs, and new teammate Johnny Mize paced all sluggers with 110 runs batted in.

Joe McCarthy's Yankees served early notice on the American League that they planned to retain their crown, and proved it by seizing a quick lead that no one could whittle down all year. Finishing with a nine-game bulge over the runner-up Red Sox, the Yankees packed plenty of wallop as Joe DiMaggio, Charlie Keller, and Joe Gordon all knocked in over 100 tallies. The defense down the middle was impeccable, with DiMaggio in center field, Gordon and Phil Rizzuto around second, and veteran Bill Dickey behind the plate. As if that weren't enough, Tiny Bonham, Spud Chandler, and Hank Borowy gave the Bronx Bombers the best starting pitching in the loop, and Johnny Murphy the best relief pitching with a league-leading 11 saves.

The second-place Red Sox monopolized the individual honors, as Ted Williams followed up his .406 mark in 1941 by winning the Triple Crown with a .356 average, 36 homers, and 137 RBI's, and Tex Hughson led all pitchers with 22 wins. Despite Williams' marks, he was again denied the MVP Award, as it was given to the Yankees' Gordon for his "batting and fielding excellence".

The Yankees tabbed 37-year-old Red Ruffing to start the Series, and the veteran hurler did not allow a Cardinal hit until the eighth inning, as New York took the opener, 7-4. But the loss did nothing to dampen the Cardinals' spirit as they scored their four runs in the ninth inning and then swept the next four tilts behind the batting of Slaughter and Walker Cooper and Beazley's two complete games. This was to be the only Series loss McCarthy would suffer as manager of the Yankees.

After the season, more players started being drafted and began enlisting in the armed forces. Although the Cardinals, with a farm system chock-full of young talent, figured to weather the war-absences better than most clubs, the man most responsible for their success decided not to stick around to enjoy the fruits of his labor. During the winter, Branch Rickey jumped to a new challenge as general manager of the rival Brooklyn Dodgers—a move that would have vast repercussions on the game of baseball.

1942 AMERICAN LEAGUE

NAME	G by POS	B	AGE	G	AB	R	H	2B	3B	HR	RBI	BB	SO	SB	BA	SA
NEW YORK 1st 103-51 .669		JOE McCARTHY														
TOTALS			28	154	5305	**801**	1429	223	57	**108**	**744**	591	556	69	.269	.394
Buddy Hassett	1B132	L	30	132	538	80	153	16	6	5	48	32	16	5	.284	.364
Joe Gordon	2B147	R	27	147	538	88	173	29	4	18	103	79	**95**	12	.322	.491
Phil Rizzuto	SS144	R	24	144	553	79	157	24	7	4	68	44	40	22	.284	.374
Frankie Crosetti	3B62, SS8, 2B2	R	31	74	285	50	69	5	5	4	23	31	31	1	.242	.337
Tommy Henrich	OF119, 1B7	L	29	127	483	77	129	30	5	13	67	58	42	4	.267	.431
Joe DiMaggio	OF154	R	27	154	610	123	186	29	13	21	114	68	36	4	.305	.498
Charlie Keller	OF152	L	25	152	544	106	159	24	9	26	108	114	61	14	.292	.513
Bill Dickey (SJ)	C80	L	35	82	268	28	79	13	1	2	37	26	11	2	.295	.373
Red Rolfe	3B60	L	33	69	265	42	58	8	2	8	25	23	18	1	.219	.355
Buddy Rosar	C58	R	27	69	209	18	48	10	0	2	34	17	20	1	.230	.306
Jerry Priddy	3B35, 1B11, 2B8, SS3	R	22	59	189	23	53	9	2	2	28	31	27	0	.280	.381
George Selkirk	OF19	L	34	42	78	15	15	3	0	0	10	16	8	0	.192	.231
2 Rollie Hemsley	C29	R	35	31	85	12	25	3	1	0	15	5	9	1	.294	.353
3 Roy Cullenbine	OF19, 1B1	B	26	21	77	16	28	7	0	2	17	18	2	0	.364	.532
Tuck Stainback	OF3	R	31	15	10	0	2	0	0	0	0	0	2	0	.200	.200
Ed Levy	1B13	R	25	13	41	5	5	0	0	0	3	4	5	1	.122	.122
Ed Kearse	C11	R	26	11	26	2	5	0	0	0	2	3	1	1	.192	.192
1 Mike Chartak		L	26	5	5	0	0	0	0	0	0	0	0	0	.000	.000
BOSTON 2nd 93-59 .612 9		JOE CRONIN														
TOTALS			27	152	5248	761	**1451**	**244**	55	103	699	591	508	68	**.276**	**.403**
Tony Lupien	1B121	L	25	128	463	63	130	25	7	3	70	50	20	10	.281	.384
Bobby Doerr	2B142	R	24	144	545	71	158	35	5	15	102	67	55	4	.290	.455
Johnny Pesky	SS147	L	22	147	620	105	**205**	29	9	2	51	42	36	12	.331	.416
Jim Tabor	3B138	R	28	139	508	56	128	18	2	12	75	37	47	6	.252	.366
Lou Finney	OF95, 1B2	L	31	113	397	58	113	16	7	3	61	29	11	3	.285	.383
Dom DiMaggio	OF151	R	25	151	622	110	178	36	8	14	48	70	52	16	.286	.437
Ted Williams	OF150	L	23	150	522	**141**	186	34	5	**36**	**137**	**145**	51	3	**.356**	**.648**
Bill Conroy	C83	R	27	83	250	22	50	4	2	4	20	40	47	2	.200	.280
Johnny Peacock	C82	L	32	88	286	17	76	7	3	0	25	21	11	1	.266	.311
Pete Fox	OF71	R	32	77	256	42	67	15	5	3	42	20	28	8	.262	.395
Joe Cronin	3B11, 1B5, SS1	R	35	45	79	7	24	3	0	4	24	15	21	0	.304	.494
1 Jimmie Foxx	1B27	R	34	30	100	18	27	4	0	5	14	18	15	0	.270	.460
Skeeter Newsome	3B12, 2B10, SS7	R	31	29	95	7	26	6	0	0	9	9	5	2	.274	.337
Paul Campbell	OF4	L	24	26	15	4	1	0	0	0	0	1	5	1	.067	.067
Andy Gilbert	OF5	R	27	6	11	0	1	0	0	0	1	1	3	0	.091	.091
Tom Carey	2B1	R	33	1	1	0	1	0	0	0	1	0	0	0	1.000	1.000
ST. LOUIS 3rd 82-69 .543 19.5		LUKE SEWELL														
TOTALS			28	151	5229	730	1354	239	**62**	98	668	**609**	**607**	37	.259	.385
George McQuinn	1B144	L	33	145	554	86	145	32	5	12	78	60	77	1	.262	.403
Don Gutteridge	2B145, 3B2	R	30	147	616	90	157	27	11	1	50	59	54	16	.255	.339
Vern Stephens	SS144	R	21	145	575	84	169	26	6	14	92	41	53	1	.294	.433
Harlond Clift	3B141, SS1	R	29	143	541	108	148	39	4	7	55	106	48	6	.274	.399
Chet Laabs	OF139	R	30	144	520	90	143	21	7	27	99	88	88	0	.275	.498
Walt Judnich	OF122	L	25	132	457	78	143	22	6	17	82	74	41	3	.313	.499
Glenn McQuillen	OF77	R	27	100	339	40	96	15	12	3	47	10	17	1	.283	.425
Rick Ferrell	C95	R	36	99	273	20	61	6	1	0	26	33	13	0	.223	.253
Tony Criscola	OF52	L	26	91	158	17	47	9	2	1	13	8	13	2	.297	.399
3 Mike Chartak	OF64	L	26	73	237	37	59	11	2	9	43	40	27	3	.249	.426
2 Frankie Hayes	C51	R	27	56	159	14	40	6	0	2	17	28	39	0	.252	.327
1 Roy Cullenbine	OF23, 1B5	B	26	38	109	15	21	7	1	2	14	30	20	0	.193	.330
Johnny Berardino (MS)	SS6, 3B6, 1B5, 2B4	R	25	29	74	11	21	6	0	1	10	4	2	3	.284	.405
1 Bob Swift	C28	R	27	29	76	3	15	4	0	1	8	3	5	0	.197	.289
Don Heffner	2B6, 1B4	R	31	19	36	2	6	2	0	0	3	1	4	1	.167	.222
Alan Strange	3B10, SS3, 2B1	R	32	19	37	3	10	2	0	0	5	3	1	0	.270	.324
Luke Sewell	C6	R	41	6	12	1	1	0	0	0	0	1	5	0	.083	.083
2 Babe Dahlgren		R	30	2	2	0	0	0	0	0	0	0	0	0	.000	.000
Ray Hayworth		R	38	1	1	0	1	0	0	0	0	0	0	0	1.000	1.000

NAME	T	AGE	W	L	PCT	SV	G	GS	CG	IP	H	BB	SO	ShO	ERA
(New York totals)		30	**103**	51	**.669**	**17**	154	154	**88**	1375	1259	431	558	**18**	**2.91**
Ernie Bonham	R	28	21	5	**.808**	0	28	27	**22**	226	199	24	71	**6**	2.27
Spud Chandler	R	34	16	5	.762	0	24	24	17	201	176	74	74	3	2.37
Hank Borowy	R	26	15	4	.789	1	25	21	13	178	157	66	85	4	2.53
Red Ruffing	R	38	14	7	.667	0	24	24	16	194	183	41	80	4	3.20
Atley Donald	R	31	11	3	.786	0	20	19	10	148	133	45	53	1	3.10
Marv Breuer	R	28	8	9	.471	1	27	19	6	164	157	37	72	0	3.07
Lefty Gomez	L	33	6	4	.600	0	13	13	2	80	67	65	41	0	4.28
Marius Russo (SA)	L	27	4	1	.800	0	9	5	2	45	41	14	15	0	2.80
Johnny Murphy	R	33	4	10	.286	**11**	31	0	0	58	66	23	24	0	3.41
Johnny Lindell	R	25	2	1	.667	1	23	2	0	53	52	22	28	0	3.74
Mel Queen	R	24	1	0	1.000	0	4	0	0	6	6	3	0	0	0.00
2 Jim Turner	R	38	1	1	.500	1	5	0	0	7	4	1	2	0	1.29
Norm Branch (MS)	R	27	0	1	.000	2	10	0	0	16	18	16	13	0	6.19
(Boston totals)		30	93	59	.612	**17**	152	152	84	1359	1260	553	500	11	3.44
Tex Hughson	R	26	**22**	6	.786	4	38	30	**22**	**281**	258	75	**113**	4	2.59
Charlie Wagner	R	29	14	11	.560	0	29	26	17	205	184	95	52	2	3.29
Joe Dobson	R	25	11	9	.550	0	30	23	10	183	155	68	72	3	3.30
Mace Brown	R	33	9	3	.750	6	34	0	0	60	56	28	20	0	3.45
Oscar Judd	L	34	8	10	.444	2	31	19	11	150	135	90	70	0	3.90
Dick Newsome	R	32	8	10	.444	0	24	23	11	158	174	67	40	0	5.01
Bill Butland	R	24	7	1	.875	1	23	10	6	111	85	33	46	2	2.51
Yank Terry	R	31	6	5	.545	1	20	11	3	85	82	43	37	0	3.92
Ken Chase	L	28	5	1	.833	0	13	10	4	80	82	41	34	0	3.83
Mike Ryba	R	39	3	3	.500	3	18	0	0	44	49	13	16	0	3.89
(St. Louis totals)		32	82	69	.543	13	151	151	68	1363	1387	505	488	12	3.59
Johnny Niggeling	R	38	15	11	.577	0	28	27	16	206	173	93	107	3	2.67
Eldon Auker	R	31	14	13	.519	0	35	34	17	249	**273**	86	62	2	4.08
Denny Galehouse	R	30	12	12	.500	1	32	28	12	192	193	79	75	3	3.61
Al Hollingsworth	L	34	10	6	.625	4	33	18	7	161	173	52	60	1	2.96
George Caster	R	34	8	2	.800	5	39	0	0	80	62	39	34	0	2.81
2 Steve Sundra	R	32	8	3	.727	0	20	13	6	111	122	29	26	0	3.81
Bob Muncrief	R	26	6	8	.429	0	24	18	7	134	149	31	39	1	3.90
Fritz Ostermueller	L	34	3	1	.750	0	10	4	2	44	46	17	21	0	3.68
Stan Ferens	L	27	3	4	.429	0	19	3	1	69	76	21	23	0	3.78
2 Pete Appleton	R	38	1	1	.500	2	14	0	0	27	25	11	12	0	3.00
Loy Hanning	R	24	1	1	.500	0	11	0	0	17	26	12	9	0	7.94
1 Bob Harris	R	26	1	5	.167	0	6	6	0	34	37	17	9	0	5.56
Frank Biscan (MS)	L	22	0	1	.000	1	11	0	0	27	13	11	10	0	2.33
1 Bill Trotter	R	33	0	1	.000	0	3	0	0	2	5	2	0	0	18.00
John Whitehead	R	33	0	0	.000	0	4	0	0	4	8	1	0	0	6.75
Ewald Pyle	L	31	0	0	.000	0	2	0	0	5	6	4	1	0	7.20
Jack Kramer (VR) 24															

CLEVELAND 4th 75-79 .487 28 — LOU BOUDREAU

NAME	G by POS	B	AGE	G	AB	R	H	2B	3B	HR	RBI	BB	SO	SB	BA	SA
TOTALS			28	156	5317	590	1344	223	58	50	541	500	544	69	.253	.345
Les Fleming	1B156	L	26	156	548	71	160	27	4	14	82	106	57	6	.292	.432
Ray Mack	2B143	R	25	143	481	43	108	14	6	2	45	41	51	9	.225	.291
Lou Boudreau	SS146	R	24	147	506	57	143	18	10	2	58	75	39	7	.283	.370
Ken Keltner	3B151	R	25	152	624	72	179	34	4	6	78	20	36	4	.287	.383
Oris Hockett	OF145	L	32	148	601	85	150	22	7	7	48	45	45	12	.250	.344
Roy Weatherly	OF117	L	27	128	473	61	122	23	7	5	39	35	25	8	.258	.368
Jeff Heath	OF146	L	27	147	568	82	158	37	13	10	76	62	66	9	.278	.442
Otto Denning	C78, OF2	R	29	92	214	15	45	14	0	1	19	18	14	0	.210	.290
Buster Mills	OF53	R	33	80	195	19	54	4	2	1	26	23	18	5	.277	.333
Chubby Dean	P27	L	26	70	101	4	27	1	0	0	7	11	7	0	.267	.277
Jim Hegan	C66	R	21	68	170	10	33	5	0	0	11	11	31	1	.194	.224
Gene Desautels (BN)	C61	R	35	62	162	14	40	5	0	0	9	12	13	1	.247	.278
Oscar Grimes	2B24, 3B8, 1B1, SS1	R	27	51	84	10	15	2	0	0	2	13	17	3	.179	.202
Fabian Gaffke	OF16	R	28	40	67	4	11	2	0	0	3	6	13	1	.164	.194
Rusty Peters	SS24, 2B1, 3B1	R	27	34	58	6	13	5	1	0	2	2	14	0	.224	.345
Hank Edwards	OF12	L	23	13	48	6	12	2	1	0	7	5	8	2	.250	.333
Eddie Robinson	1B1	L	21	8	8	1	1	0	0	0	2	1	0	0	.125	.125
Bob Lemon	3B1	L	21	5	5	0	0	0	0	0	0	0	3	0	.000	.000
Ted Sepkowski	2B2	L	18	5	10	0	1	0	0	0	0	0	3	0	.100	.100
George Susce	C2	R	33	2	1	1	1	0	0	0	0	1	0	0	1.000	1.000

NAME	T	AGE	W	L	PCT	SV	G	GS	CG	IP	H	BB	SO	ShO	ERA
TOTALS		30	75	79	.487	11	156	156	61	1403	1353	560	448	12	3.59
Jim Bagby	R	25	17	9	.654	1	38	35	16	271	267	64	54	4	2.96
Mel Harder	R	32	13	14	.481	0	29	29	13	199	179	82	74	4	3.44
Al Smith	L	34	10	15	.400	0	30	24	7	168	163	71	66	1	3.96
Chubby Dean	L	26	8	11	.421	1	27	22	8	173	170	66	46	0	3.80
Al Milnar	L	28	6	8	.429	0	28	19	8	157	146	85	35	2	4.13
Joe Heving	R	41	5	3	.625	3	27	2	0	46	52	25	13	0	4.89
Vern Kennedy	R	35	4	8	.333	1	28	12	4	108	99	50	37	0	4.08
Tom Ferrick	R	27	3	2	.600	3	31	2	2	81	56	32	28	0	2.00
Red Embree	R	24	3	4	.429	0	19	6	2	63	58	31	44	0	3.86
Steve Gromek	R	22	2	0	1.000	0	14	0	0	44	46	23	14	0	3.68
Harry Eisenstat	L	26	2	1	.667	2	29	1	0	48	58	6	19	0	2.44
Clint Brown	R	38	1	1	.500	0	7	0	0	9	16	2	4	0	6.00
Ray Poat	R	24	1	3	.250	0	4	4	1	18	24	9	8	1	5.50
Joe Krakauskas	L	27	0	0	.000	0	3	0	0	7	7	4	2	0	3.86
Allie Reynolds	R	27	0	0	.000	0	2	0	0	5	5	4	2	0	0.00
Paul Calvert	R	24	0	0	.000	0	1	0	0	2	0	2	2	0	0.00
Pete Center	R	20	0	0	.000	0	1	0	0	3	7	4	0	0	18.00

Hal Trosky (IL) 29

DETROIT 5th 73-81 .474 30 — DEL BAKER

NAME	G by POS	B	AGE	G	AB	R	H	2B	3B	HR	RBI	BB	SO	SB	BA	SA
TOTALS			28	156	5327	589	1313	217	37	76	548	509	476	39	.246	.344
Rudy York	1B152	R	28	153	577	81	150	26	4	21	90	73	71	3	.260	.428
Jimmy Bloodworth	2B134, SS2	R	24	137	533	62	129	23	1	13	57	35	63	2	.242	.362
Billy Hitchcock	SS80, 3B1	R	25	85	280	27	59	8	1	0	29	26	21	2	.211	.246
Pinky Higgins	3B137	R	33	143	499	65	133	34	2	11	79	72	21	3	.267	.409
Ned Harris	OF104	L	25	121	398	53	108	16	10	9	45	49	35	5	.271	.430
Doc Cramer	OF150	L	36	151	630	71	166	26	4	0	43	43	18	4	.263	.317
Barney McCoskey	OF154	L	24	154	600	75	176	28	11	7	50	68	37	11	.293	.412
Birdie Tebbetts	C97	R	32	99	308	24	76	11	0	1	27	39	17	4	.247	.292
Don Ross	OF38, 3B20	R	27	87	226	29	62	10	2	3	30	36	16	2	.274	.376
Dixie Parsons	C62	R	26	63	188	8	37	4	0	2	11	13	22	1	.197	.250
Rip Radcliff	OF24, 1B4	L	36	62	144	13	36	5	0	1	20	9	6	0	.250	.306
Murray Franklin	SS32, 2B7	R	28	48	154	24	40	7	0	2	16	7	5	0	.260	.344
Charlie Gehringer (MS)	2B3	L	39	45	45	6	12	0	0	1	7	7	4	0	.267	.333
Johnny Lipon	SS34	R	19	34	131	5	25	2	0	0	9	7	7	1	.191	.206
1 Eric McNair	SS21	R	33	26	68	5	11	2	0	1	4	3	5	0	.162	.235
Dutch Meyer	2B14	R	26	14	52	5	17	3	0	2	9	4	4	0	.327	.500
Hank Riebe	C11	R	20	11	35	1	11	2	0	0	2	0	6	0	.314	.371
Bob Patrick (BK)	OF3	R	24	4	8	1	2	1	0	1	3	1	0	0	.250	.750
Al Unser	C4	R	29	4	8	2	3	0	0	0	0	0	2	0	.375	.375

NAME	T	AGE	W	L	PCT	SV	G	GS	CG	IP	H	BB	SO	ShO	ERA
TOTALS		27	73	81	.474	14	156	156	65	1399	1321	598	671	12	3.13
Virgil Trucks	R	23	14	8	.636	0	28	20	8	168	147	74	91	2	2.73
Hal White	R	23	12	12	.500	1	34	25	12	217	212	82	93	4	2.90
Dizzy Trout	R	27	12	18	.400	0	35	29	13	223	214	89	91	1	3.43
Tommy Bridges	R	35	9	7	.563	1	23	22	11	174	164	61	97	2	2.74
Hal Newhouser	L	21	8	14	.364	5	38	23	11	184	137	114	103	1	2.45
Al Benton	R	31	7	13	.350	2	35	30	9	227	210	84	110	1	2.89
Johnny Gorsica	R	27	3	2	.600	4	28	0	0	53	63	26	19	0	4.75
Charley Fuchs	R	28	3	3	.500	0	9	4	1	37	43	19	15	1	6.57
Hal Manders	R	25	2	0	1.000	0	18	0	0	33	39	15	14	0	4.09
Roy Henshaw	L	30	2	4	.333	1	23	2	0	62	63	27	24	0	4.06
1 Schoolboy Rowe	R	32	1	0	1.000	0	2	1	0	10	9	2	7	0	0.00
2 Jack Wilson	R	30	0	0	.000	0	9	0	0	13	20	5	7	0	4.85

CHICAGO 6th 66-82 .446 34 — JIMMY DYKES

NAME	G by POS	B	AGE	G	AB	R	H	2B	3B	HR	RBI	BB	SO	SB	BA	SA
TOTALS			30	148	4949	538	1215	214	36	25	487	497	427	114	.246	.318
Joe Kuhel	1B112	L	36	115	413	60	103	14	4	4	52	60	22	22	.249	.332
Don Kolloway	2B116, 1B33	R	23	147	601	72	164	40	4	3	60	30	39	16	.273	.368
Luke Appling	SS141	R	35	142	543	78	142	26	4	3	53	63	23	17	.262	.341
Bob Kennedy (MS)	3B96, OF16	R	21	113	412	37	95	18	5	0	38	22	41	11	.231	.299
Wally Moses	OF145	L	31	146	577	73	156	28	4	7	49	74	27	16	.270	.369
Myril Hoag	OF112	R	34	113	412	47	99	18	2	2	37	36	21	17	.240	.308
Taffy Wright	OF81	L	30	85	300	43	100	13	5	0	47	48	9	1	.333	.410
Mike Tresh	C72	R	28	72	233	21	54	8	1	0	15	28	24	2	.232	.275
Dario Lodigiani	3B43, 2B7	R	26	59	168	9	47	7	0	0	15	18	10	3	.280	.321
George Dickey (MS)	C29	B	26	59	116	6	27	3	0	1	17	9	11	0	.233	.284
Tom Turner	C54	R	25	56	182	18	44	9	1	3	21	19	15	0	.242	.352
Sammy West	OF45	L	37	49	151	14	35	5	0	0	25	31	18	2	.232	.265
Leo Wells	SS12, 3B6	R	24	35	62	8	12	2	0	1	4	4	5	1	.194	.274
Skeeter Webb	2B29	R	32	32	94	5	16	2	1	0	4	4	13	1	.170	.213
Bill Mueller	OF26	R	21	26	85	5	14	1	0	0	5	12	9	2	.165	.176
Val Heim (MS)	OF12	L	21	13	45	6	9	1	1	0	7	5	3	1	.200	.267
Bud Sketchley	OF12	L	23	13	36	1	7	1	0	0	3	7	4	0	.194	.222
Jimmy Grant	3B10	L	23	12	36	0	6	1	1	0	1	5	6	0	.167	.250
Jake Jones (MS)	1B5	R	21	7	20	2	3	1	0	0	0	2	2	1	.150	.200
Thurman Tucker	OF5	L	24	7	24	2	3	0	1	0	1	0	4	0	.125	.208

NAME	T	AGE	W	L	PCT	SV	G	GS	CG	IP	H	BB	SO	ShO	ERA
TOTALS		30	66	82	.446	8	148	148	86	1314	1304	473	432	8	3.58
Ted Lyons	R	41	14	6	.700	0	20	20	20	180	167	26	50	1	2.10
John Humphries	R	27	12	12	.500	0	28	28	17	228	227	59	71	2	2.68
Joe Haynes	R	24	8	5	.615	6	40	1	1	103	88	47	35	0	2.62
Eddie Smith	L	28	7	20	.259	1	29	28	18	215	223	86	78	2	3.98
Bill Dietrich	R	32	6	11	.353	0	26	23	6	160	173	70	39	0	4.89
Jake Wade	L	30	5	5	.500	0	15	10	3	86	84	56	32	0	4.08
Buck Ross	R	27	5	7	.417	1	22	14	4	113	118	39	37	2	5.02
Orval Grove (KJ)	R	22	4	6	.400	0	12	8	4	66	77	33	21	0	5.18
Johnny Rigney (MS)	R	27	3	3	.500	0	7	7	6	59	40	16	34	0	3.20
Thornton Lee	L	35	2	6	.250	0	11	8	6	76	82	31	25	1	3.32
Len Perme	L	24	0	1	.000	0	4	1	1	13	5	4	4	0	1.38
Ed Weiland	R	27	0	0	.000	0	5	0	0	10	18	3	4	0	7.20
1 Pete Appleton	R	38	0	0	.000	0	4	0	0	5	2	3	2	0	3.60

Moose Solters (VR) 36

WASHINGTON 7th 62-89 .411 39.5 — BUCKY HARRIS

NAME	G by POS	B	AGE	G	AB	R	H	2B	3B	HR	RBI	BB	SO	SB	BA	SA
TOTALS			26	151	5295	653	1364	224	49	40	593	581	536	98	.258	.341
Mickey Vernon	1B151	L	24	151	621	76	168	34	6	9	86	39	63	25	.271	.388
Ellis Clary	2B69, 3B2	R	25	76	240	34	66	9	0	0	16	45	25	2	.275	.313
John Sullivan	SS92	R	21	94	357	38	84	16	1	0	42	25	30	2	.235	.286
Bobby Estalella	3B78, OF36	R	31	133	429	68	119	24	5	8	65	85	42	5	.277	.413
Bruce Campbell (MS)	OF87	L	32	122	378	41	105	17	5	5	63	37	34	0	.278	.389
Stan Spence	OF149	L	27	149	629	94	203	27	15	4	79	62	16	5	.323	.432
George Case	OF120	R	26	125	513	101	164	26	2	5	43	44	30	44	.320	.407
Jake Early	C98	L	25	104	353	31	72	14	2	3	46	37	37	0	.204	.280
Jimmy Pofahl	SS49, 2B15, 3B14	R	25	84	283	22	59	7	2	0	28	29	30	4	.208	.247
Bob Repass	2B33, 3B29, SS11	R	24	81	259	30	62	11	1	2	23	33	30	6	.239	.313
Al Evans	C67	R	25	74	223	22	51	4	1	0	10	25	36	3	.229	.256
2 Roy Cullenbine	OF35, 3B28	B	26	64	241	30	69	19	0	2	35	44	18	1	.286	.390
Frank Croucher (SA)	2B18	R	27	26	65	2	18	1	1	0	5	3	9	0	.277	.323
Chile Gomez	2B23, 3B1	R	33	25	73	8	14	2	2	0	6	9	7	1	.192	.274
2 Mike Chartak	OF24	L	26	24	92	11	20	4	2	1	8	14	16	0	.217	.337
Roberto Ortiz	OF9	R	27	20	42	4	7	1	3	1	4	5	11	0	.167	.405
Stan Galle (MS)	3B3	R	23	13	18	3	2	0	0	0	1	1	0	0	.111	.111
Ray Hoffman	3B6	L	25	7	19	2	1	0	0	0	2	1	1	0	.053	.053
Al Kvashak (MS)	OF3	R	21	5	11	3	2	0	0	0	0	2	1	0	.182	.182
Gene Moore	OF1	L	32	1	2	0	0	0	0	0	0	0	1	0	.000	.000

NAME	T	AGE	W	L	PCT	SV	G	GS	CG	IP	H	BB	SO	ShO	ERA
TOTALS		28	62	89	.411	11	151	151	68	1347	1496	558	496	12	4.58
1 Bobo Newsom	R	34	11	17	.393	0	30	29	15	214	236	92	113	2	4.92
Early Wynn	R	22	10	16	.385	0	30	28	10	190	246	73	58	1	5.12
Sid Hudson	R	27	10	17	.370	2	35	31	19	239	266	70	72	1	4.37
Bill Zuber	R	29	9	9	.500	1	37	7	3	127	115	82	64	1	3.83
Alex Carrasquel	R	29	7	7	.500	4	35	15	7	152	161	53	40	1	3.43
Walt Masterson	R	22	5	9	.357	2	25	15	8	143	138	54	63	4	3.34
2 Bill Trotter	R	33	3	1	.750	0	17	0	0	41	52	14	13	0	5.71
Ray Scarborough	R	24	2	1	.667	0	17	5	1	63	68	32	16	1	4.14
Dutch Leonard (BN)	R	33	2	2	.500	0	6	5	1	35	28	5	15	1	4.11
Hardin Cathey	R	22	1	1	.500	0	12	2	0	30	44	16	8	0	7.50
1 Steve Sundra	R	32	1	3	.250	0	6	4	2	34	43	15	5	0	5.56
1 Jack Wilson	R	30	1	4	.200	0	12	6	1	42	57	23	18	0	6.64
Bill Kennedy	L	23	0	1	.000	2	8	2	1	18	21	10	4	0	8.00
Lou Bevil	R	20	0	1	.000	0	4	1	0	10	9	11	2	0	6.30
Dewey Adkins	R	24	0	0	.000	0	1	1	0	6	7	6	3	0	10.50
Phil McCullough	R	24	0	0	.000	0	1	0	0	3	5	2	2	0	6.00

PHILADELPHIA 8th 55-99 .357 48 — CONNIE MACK

NAME	G by POS	B	AGE	G	AB	R	H	2B	3B	HR	RBI	BB	SO	SB	BA	SA
TOTALS			29	154	5285	549	1315	213	46	33	517	440	490	44	.249	.325
Dick Siebert	1B152	L	30	153	612	57	159	25	7	2	74	24	17	4	.260	.333
Bill Knockerbocker (BG)	2B81, SS1	R	30	87	289	25	73	12	0	1	19	29	30	1	.253	.304
Pete Suder	SS69, 3B34, 2B31	R	26	128	476	46	122	20	4	4	54	24	39	4	.256	.340
Buddy Blair	3B126	L	31	137	484	48	135	26	8	5	66	30	30	1	.279	.397
Elmer Valo	OF122	L	21	133	459	64	115	13	10	2	40	70	21	13	.251	.336
Mike Kreevich	OF107	R	34	116	444	57	113	19	1	1	30	47	31	7	.255	.309
Bob Johnson	OF149	R	35	149	550	78	160	35	7	13	80	82	61	3	.291	.451
Hal Wagner	C94	L	26	104	288	26	68	17	1	1	30	24	29	1	.236	.313
Dee Miles	OF81	L	33	99	346	41	94	12	5	0	22	12	10	5	.272	.335
Crash Davis	2B57, SS26, 1B3	R	22	86	272	31	61	8	1	2	26	21	30	1	.224	.283
2 Bob Swift	C60	R	27	60	192	9	44	3	0	0	15	13	17	1	.229	.245
Jack Wallaesa	SS36	B	22	36	117	13	30	4	1	2	13	8	26	0	.256	.359
2 Eric McNair	SS29, 2B1	R	33	34	103	8	25	2	0	0	4	11	5	1	.243	.262
1 Frankie Hayes	C20	R	27	21	63	8	15	4	0	0	5	9	8	1	.238	.302
Eddie Collins (MS)	OF9	L	25	20	34	6	8	2	0	0	4	4	2	1	.235	.294
Jim Castiglia (MS)	C3	L	23	16	18	2	7	0	0	0	2	1	3	0	.389	.389
Larry Eschen	SS7, 2B1	R	21	12	11	0	0	0	0	0	0	4	6	0	.000	.000
Felix Mackiewicz	OF3	R	24	6	14	3	3	2	0	0	2	0	4	0	.214	.357
Ken Richardson	OF3, 1B1, 3B1	R	27	6	15	1	1	0	0	0	0	2	0	0	.067	.067
George Yankowski	C6	R	19	6	13	0	2	1	0	0	2	0	2	0	.154	.231
Bruce Konopka	1B3	L	22	5	10	2	3	0	0	0	1	1	0	0	.300	.300
Dick Adkins	SS3	R	22	3	7	2	1	0	0	0	0	2	2	0	.143	.143

NAME	T	AGE	W	L	PCT	SV	G	GS	CG	IP	H	BB	SO	ShO	ERA
TOTALS		27	55	99	.357	9	154	154	67	1375	1404	639	546	5	4.44
Phil Marchildon	R	28	17	14	.548	1	38	31	18	244	215	140	110	1	4.20
Roger Wolff	R	31	12	15	.444	3	32	25	15	214	206	69	94	2	3.32
Lum Harris	R	27	11	15	.423	0	26	20	10	166	146	70	60	1	3.74
Dick Fowler	R	21	6	11	.353	1	31	17	4	140	159	45	38	0	4.95
Russ Christopher	R	24	4	13	.235	1	30	18	10	165	154	99	58	0	3.82
Herman Besse	L	30	2	9	.182	1	30	14	4	133	163	69	78	0	6.16
Jack Knott (MS)	R	35	2	10	.167	0	20	14	4	95	127	36	31	0	5.59
2 Bob Harris	R	26	1	5	.167	0	16	8	2	78	77	24	26	1	2.88
Tex Shirley	R	24	0	1	.000	1	15	1	0	36	37	22	10	0	5.25
Bob Savage	R	20	0	1	.000	0	8	3	0	31	24	31	10	0	3.20
1 Bill Beckmann	R	34	0	1	.000	0	5	1	0	20	24	9	10	0	7.20
Joe Coleman	R	19	0	1	.000	0	1	0	0	6	8	1	0	0	3.00
Fred Caligiuri	R	23	0	3	.000	1	13	2	0	37	45	18	20	0	6.33
Tal Abernathy	L	20	0	0	.000	0	1	0	0	3	2	3	1	0	9.00
Sam Lowry	R	22	0	0	.000	0	1	0	0	3	3	1	0	0	6.00
Les McCrabb	R	27	0	0	.000	0	1	0	0	4	14	2	0	0	31.50

ST. LOUIS 1st 106-48 .688 — BILLY SOUTHWORTH

NAME	G by POS	B	AGE	G	AB	R	H	2B	3B	HR	RBI	BB	SO	SB	BA	SA
TOTALS			26	156	5421	755	1454	282	69	60	682	551	507	71	.268	.379
Johnny Hopp	1B88	L	25	95	314	41	81	16	7	3	37	36	40	14	.258	.382
Creepy Crespi	2B83, SS5	R	24	93	292	33	71	4	2	0	35	27	29	4	.243	.271
Marty Marion	SS147	R	24	147	485	66	134	38	5	0	54	48	50	8	.276	.375
Whitey Kurowski	3B104, SS1, OF1	R	24	115	366	51	93	17	3	9	42	33	60	7	.254	.391
Enos Slaughter	OF151	L	26	152	591	100	188	31	17	13	98	88	30	9	.318	.494
Terry Moore	OF126, 3B1	R	30	130	489	80	141	26	3	6	49	56	26	10	.288	.391
Stan Musial	OF135	L	21	140	467	87	147	32	10	10	72	62	25	6	.315	.490
Walker Cooper	C115	R	27	125	438	58	123	32	7	7	65	29	29	4	.281	.434
Jimmy Brown	2B82, 3B66, SS12	B	32	145	606	75	155	28	4	1	71	52	11	4	.256	.320
Ray Sanders	1B77	L	25	95	282	37	71	17	2	5	39	42	31	2	.252	.379
Harry Walker	OF56, 2B2	L	25	74	191	38	60	12	2	0	16	11	14	2	.314	.398
Coaker Triplett	OF46	R	30	64	154	18	42	7	4	1	23	17	15	1	.273	.390
Ken O'Dea	C49	L	29	58	192	22	45	7	1	5	32	17	23	0	.234	.359
Buddy Blattner	SS13, 2B3	R	22	19	23	3	1	0	0	0	1	3	6	0	.043	.043
Erv Dusak	OF8, 3B1	R	21	12	27	4	5	3	0	0	3	3	7	0	.185	.296
Sam Narron	C2	R	28	10	10	0	4	0	0	0	1	0	0	0	.400	.400
Estel Crabtree		L	38	10	9	1	3	2	0	0	2	1	3	0	.333	.556
1 Gus Mancuso	C3	R	36	5	13	0	1	0	0	0	1	0	0	0	.077	.077
Jeff Cross	SS1	R	23	1	4	0	1	0	0	0	1	0	0	0	.250	.250

NAME	T	AGE	W	L	PCT	SV	G	GS	CG	IP	H	BB	SO	ShO	ERA
TOTALS		26	106	48	.688	15	156	156	70	1409	1192	473	651	18	2.55
Mort Cooper	R	29	22	7	.759	0	37	35	22	279	207	68	152	10	1.77
Johnny Beazley	R	24	21	6	.778	3	43	23	13	215	181	73	91	3	2.14
Howie Krist	R	26	13	3	.813	1	34	8	3	118	103	43	47	0	2.52
Max Lanier	L	26	13	8	.619	2	34	20	8	161	137	60	93	2	2.96
Harry Gumbert	R	32	9	5	.643	5	38	19	5	163	156	59	52	0	3.26
Howie Pollet	L	21	7	5	.583	0	27	13	5	109	102	39	42	2	2.89
Ernie White (SA)	L	25	7	5	.583	2	26	19	7	128	113	41	67	1	2.53
Murry Dickson	R	25	6	3	.667	2	36	7	2	121	91	61	66	0	2.90
1 Lon Warneke	R	33	6	4	.600	0	12	12	5	82	76	15	31	0	3.29
2 Bill Beckmann	R	34	1	0	1.000	0	2	0	0	7	4	1	3	0	0.00
1 Bill Lohrman	R	29	1	1	.500	0	5	0	0	13	11	2	6	0	1.39
2 Whitey Moore	R	30	0	1	.000	0	9	0	0	12	10	11	1	0	4.50
1 Clyde Shoun	L	30	0	0	.000	0	2	0	0	2	1	0	0	0	0.00

BROOKLYN 2nd 104-50 .675 2 — LEO DUROCHER

NAME	G by POS	B	AGE	G	AB	R	H	2B	3B	HR	RBI	BB	SO	SB	BA	SA
TOTALS			29	155	5285	742	1398	263	34	62	678	572	484	79	.265	.362
Dolph Camilli	1B150	L	35	150	524	89	132	23	7	26	109	97	85	10	.252	.471
Billy Herman	2B153, 1B3	R	32	155	571	76	146	34	2	2	65	72	52	6	.256	.333
Pee Wee Reese	SS151	R	23	151	564	87	144	24	5	3	53	82	55	15	.255	.332
Arky Vaughan	3B119, SS5, 2B1	L	30	128	495	82	137	18	4	2	49	51	17	8	.277	.341
Dixie Walker	OF110	L	31	118	393	57	114	28	1	6	54	47	15	1	.290	.412
Pete Reiser (YJ)	OF125	L	23	125	480	89	149	33	5	10	64	48	45	20	.310	.463
Joe Medwick	OF140	R	30	142	553	69	166	37	4	4	96	32	25	2	.300	.403
Mickey Owen	C133	R	26	133	421	53	109	16	3	0	44	44	17	10	.259	.311
Johnny Rizzo	OF70	R	29	78	217	31	50	8	0	4	27	24	25	2	.230	.323
Lew Riggs	3B46, 1B1	L	32	70	180	20	50	5	0	3	22	13	9	0	.278	.356
Augie Galan	OF55, 1B4, 2B3	B	30	69	209	24	55	16	0	0	22	24	12	2	.263	.340
Frenchy Bordagaray	OF17	R	30	48	58	11	14	2	0	0	5	3	3	2	.241	.276
Billy Sullivan	C41	L	31	43	101	11	27	2	1	1	14	12	6	1	.267	.337
3 Babe Dahlgren	1B10	R	30	17	19	2	1	0	0	0	0	4	5	0	.053	.053
Alex Kampouris	2B9	R	29	10	21	3	5	2	1	0	3	0	4	0	.238	.429
Cliff Dapper	C8	R	22	8	17	2	8	1	0	1	9	2	2	0	.471	.706
Stan Rojek		R	23	1	0	1	0	0	0	0	0	0	0	0	.000	.000

NAME	T	AGE	W	L	PCT	SV	G	GS	CG	IP	H	BB	SO	ShO	ERA
TOTALS		31	104	50	.675	24	155	155	67	1399	1205	493	612	16	2.84
Whit Wyatt	R	34	19	7	.731	0	31	30	16	217	185	63	104	0	2.74
Kirby Higbe	L	27	16	11	.593	0	38	32	13	222	100	100	115	[illegible]	[illegible]
Larry French	L	34	15	4	.789	0	38	14	8	148	127	36	62	4	1.82
Curt Davis	R	38	15	6	.714	2	32	26	13	206	179	51	60	5	2.36
Ed Head	R	24	10	6	.625	4	36	15	5	137	118	47	78	1	3.55
Johnny Allen	R	37	10	6	.625	3	27	15	5	118	106	39	50	1	3.20
Hugh Casey	R	28	6	3	.667	13	50	2	0	112	91	44	54	0	2.25
Max Macon	L	26	5	3	.625	1	14	8	4	84	67	33	27	1	1.93
Les Webber	R	27	3	2	.600	1	19	3	1	52	46	22	23	0	2.94
Newt Kimball	R	27	2	0	1.000	0	14	1	0	29	27	19	8	0	3.72
2 Bobo Newsom	R	34	2	2	.500	0	6	5	2	32	28	14	21	1	3.38
2 Schoolboy Rowe	R	32	1	0	1.000	0	9	2	0	30	36	12	6	0	5.40
Chet Kehn	R	20	0	0	.000	0	3	1	0	8	8	4	3	0	6.75
Bob Chipman	L	23	0	0	.000	0	2	0	0	1	1	2	1	0	0.00
Freddie Fitzsimmons	R	40	0	0	.000	0	1	1	0	3	6	1	0	0	15.00

NEW YORK 3rd 85-67 .559 20 — MEL OTT

NAME	G by POS	B	AGE	G	AB	R	H	2B	3B	HR	RBI	BB	SO	SB	BA	SA
TOTALS			29	154	5210	675	1323	162	35	109	630	558	511	39	.254	.361
Johnny Mize	1B138	L	29	142	541	97	165	25	7	26	110	60	39	3	.305	.521
Mickey Witek	2B147	R	26	148	553	72	144	19	6	5	48	36	20	2	.260	.344
Billy Jurges	SS124	R	34	127	464	45	119	7	1	2	30	43	42	1	.256	.289
Bill Werber	3B93	R	34	98	370	51	76	9	2	1	13	51	22	9	.205	.249
Mel Ott	OF152	L	33	152	549	118	162	21	0	30	93	109	61	6	.295	.497
Willard Marshall	OF107	L	21	116	401	41	103	9	2	11	59	26	20	1	.257	.372
Babe Barna	OF89	L	27	104	331	39	85	8	7	6	58	38	48	3	.257	.378
Harry Danning	C116	R	30	119	408	45	114	20	3	1	34	34	29	3	.279	.350
Babe Young	OF54, 1B18	L	27	101	287	37	80	17	1	11	59	34	22	1	.279	.460
Dick Bartell	3B52, SS31	R	34	90	316	53	77	10	3	5	24	44	34	4	.244	.342
Buster Maynard	OF58, 3B10, 2B1	R	29	89	190	17	47	4	1	4	32	19	19	3	.247	.342
Hank Leiber	OF41, P1	R	31	58	147	11	32	6	0	4	23	19	27	0	.218	.340
2 Gus Mancuso	C38	R	36	39	109	4	21	1	1	0	8	14	7	1	.193	.220
Ray Berres	C12	R	34	12	32	0	6	0	0	0	1	2	3	0	.188	.188
Connie Ryan	2B11	R	22	11	27	4	5	0	0	0	2	4	3	1	.185	.185
Howie Moss	OF3	R	22	7	14	0	0	0	0	0	0	0	4	0	.000	.000
Sid Gordon	3B6	R	24	6	19	4	6	0	1	0	2	3	2	0	.316	.421
Charlie Fox	C3	R	20	3	7	1	3	0	0	0	1	1	2	0	.429	.429

NAME	T	AGE	W	L	PCT	SV	G	GS	CG	IP	H	BB	SO	ShO	ERA
TOTALS		29	85	67*	.559	13	154	154	70	1370	1299	493	497	12	3.31
2 Bill Lohrman	R	29	13	4	.765	0	26	19	12	158	143	33	41	2	2.56
Hal Schumacher	R	31	12	13	.480	0	29	29	12	216	208	82	49	3	3.04
Cliff Melton (EJ)	L	30	11	5	.688	1	23	17	12	144	122	33	61	2	2.63
Carl Hubbell	L	39	11	8	.579	0	24	20	11	157	158	34	61	0	3.96
Bob Carpenter	R	24	11	10	.524	0	28	25	12	186	192	51	53	2	3.15
Harry Feldman	R	22	7	1	.875	0	31	6	2	114	100	73	49	1	3.16
Ace Adams	R	30	7	4	.636	11	61	0	0	88	69	31	33	0	1.84
Bill McGee	R	32	6	3	.667	1	31	8	2	104	95	46	41	1	2.94
Dave Koslo	L	22	3	6	.333	0	19	11	3	78	79	32	42	1	5.08
Tom Sunkel	L	29	3	6	.333	0	19	11	3	64	65	41	29	0	4.78
Van Lingle Mungo	R	31	1	2	.333	0	9	5	0	36	38	21	27	0	6.00
Bill Voiselle	R	23	0	1	.000	0	2	1	0	9	6	4	5	0	2.00
Hank Leiber	R	31	0	1	.000	0	1	1	1	9	9	5	5	0	6.00
Hugh East	R	22	0	2	.000	0	4	1	0	7	15	7	2	0	10.29

***1 loss by forfeit**

CINCINNATI 4th 76-76 .500 29 — BILL McKECHNIE

NAME	G by POS	B	AGE	G	AB	R	H	2B	3B	HR	RBI	BB	SO	SB	BA	SA
TOTALS			31	154	5260	527	1216	198	39	66	488	483	549	42	.231	.321
Frank McCormick	1B144	R	31	145	564	58	156	24	0	13	89	45	18	1	.277	.388
Lonny Frey	2B140	L	31	141	523	66	139	23	6	2	39	87	38	9	.266	.344
Eddie Joost	SS130, 2B15	R	26	142	562	65	126	30	3	6	41	62	57	9	.224	.320
Bert Haas	3B146, 1B6, OF2	R	28	154	585	59	140	21	6	6	54	59	54	6	.239	.326
Max Marshall	OF129	L	28	131	530	49	135	17	6	7	43	34	38	4	.255	.349
Gee Walker	OF110	R	34	119	422	40	97	20	2	5	50	31	44	11	.230	.322
Eric Tipton	OF58	R	27	63	207	22	46	5	5	4	18	25	14	1	.222	.353
Ray Lamanno	C104	R	22	111	371	40	98	12	2	12	43	31	54	0	.264	.404
Ival Goodman	OF57	L	33	87	226	21	55	18	1	0	15	24	32	0	.243	.332
Mike McCormick (BL)	OF38	R	25	40	135	18	32	2	3	1	11	13	7	0	.237	.319
Frankie Kelleher	OF30	R	25	38	110	13	20	3	1	3	12	16	20	0	.182	.309
Harry Craft	OF33	R	27	37	113	7	20	2	1	0	6	3	11	0	.177	.212
1 Rollie Hemsley	C34	R	35	36	115	7	13	1	2	0	7	4	11	0	.113	.157
Dick West	C17, OF6	R	26	33	79	9	14	3	0	1	8	5	13	1	.177	.253
Damon Phillips	SS27	R	23	28	84	4	17	2	0	0	6	7	5	0	.202	.226
Al Lakeman	C17	R	23	20	38	0	6	1	0	0	2	3	10	0	.158	.184
Clyde Vollmer	OF11	R	20	12	43	2	4	0	0	1	4	1	5	0	.093	.163
Joe Abreu	3B6, 2B2	R	26	9	28	4	6	1	0	1	3	4	4	0	.214	.357
Jim Gleeson	OF5	B	30	9	20	3	4	0	0	0	2	2	2	0	.200	.200
Hank Sauer	1B4	R	23	7	20	4	5	0	0	2	4	2	2	0	.250	.550
Chuck Aleno	3B2, 2B1	R	25	7	14	1	2	1	0	0	0	3	3	0	.142	.214
Bobby Mattick	SS3	R	26	6	10	0	2	1	0	0	0	0	1	0	.200	.300
1 Ernie Koy		R	32	3	2	0	0	0	0	0	0	0	2	0	.000	.000
Frank Secory	OF2	R	29	2	5	1	0	0	0	0	1	3	2	0	.000	.000

NAME	T	AGE	W	L	PCT	SV	G	GS	CG	IP	H	BB	SO	ShO	ERA
TOTALS		31	76	76	.500	8	154	154	80	1412	1213	526	616	12	2.82
Johnny Vander Meer	L	27	18	12	.600	0	33	33	21	244	188	102	186	4	2.43
Ray Starr	R	36	15	13	.536	0	37	33	17	277	228	106	83	4	2.66
Bucky Walters	R	33	15	14	.517	0	34	32	21	254	223	73	109	2	2.66
Paul Derringer	R	35	10	11	.476	0	29	27	13	209	203	49	68	1	3.06
Elmer Riddle	R	27	7	11	.389	0	29	19	7	158	157	79	78	1	3.70
Joe Beggs	R	31	6	5	.545	8	38	0	0	89	65	33	24	0	2.12
Junior Thompson	R	25	4	7	.364	0	29	10	1	102	86	53	35	0	3.35
2 Clyde Shoun	L	30	1	3	.250	0	34	0	0	73	55	24	32	0	2.22
1 Jim Turner	R	38	0	0	.000	0	3	0	0	3	5	3	0	0	12.00
Ewell Blackwell	R	19	0	0	.000	0	2	0	0	3	3	3	1	0	6.00
1 Whitey Moore	R	30	0	0	.000	0	1	0	0	1	0	1	0	0	0.00

PITTSBURGH 5th 66-81 .449 36.5 — FRANKIE FRISCH

NAME	G by POS	B	AGE	G	AB	R	H	2B	3B	HR	RBI	BB	SO	SB	BA	SA
TOTALS			28	151	5104	585	1250	173	49	54	544	537	536	41	.245	.330
Elbie Fletcher	1B144	L	26	145	506	86	146	22	5	7	57	105	60	0	.289	.393
Frankie Gustine	2B108, SS2, 3B2, C1	R	22	115	388	34	89	11	4	2	35	29	27	5	.229	.294
Pete Coscarart	SS108, 2B25	R	29	133	487	57	111	12	4	3	29	38	56	2	.228	.287
Bob Elliott	3B142, OF1	R	25	143	560	75	166	26	7	9	89	52	35	2	.296	.416
Johnny Barrett	OF94	L	26	111	332	56	82	11	6	0	26	48	42	10	.247	.316
Vince DiMaggio	OF138	R	29	143	496	57	118	22	3	15	75	52	87	10	.238	.385
Jimmy Wasdell	OF97, 1B7	L	28	122	409	44	106	11	2	3	38	47	22	1	.259	.318
Al Lopez	C99	R	33	103	289	17	74	8	2	1	26	34	17	0	.256	.308
Maurice Van Robays	OF84	R	27	100	328	29	76	13	5	1	46	30	24	0	.232	.311
Babe Phelps	C72	L	34	95	257	21	73	11	1	9	41	20	24	2	.284	.440
Bud Stewart	OF34, 3B10, 2B6	L	26	82	183	21	40	8	4	0	20	22	16	2	.219	.306
Alf Anderson	SS48	R	28	54	166	24	45	4	1	0	7	18	19	4	.271	.307
Stu Martin (MM)	2B30, 1B1, SS1	L	28	42	120	16	27	4	2	1	12	8	10	1	.225	.317
Cully Rikard (BW)	OF16	L	28	38	52	6	10	2	1	0	5	7	8	0	.192	.269
Bill Baker (BH)	C11	R	31	18	17	1	2	0	0	0	2	1	0	0	.118	.118
Frank Colman	OF8	L	24	10	37	2	5	0	0	1	2	2	2	0	.135	.216
Johnny Wyrostek	OF8	L	22	9	35	0	4	0	1	0	3	3	2	0	.114	.171
Huck Geary (IL)	SS8	L	25	9	22	3	5	0	0	0	2	2	3	0	.227	.227
Jim Russell	OF3	B	23	5	14	2	1	0	0	0	0	1	4	0	.071	.071
Ed Leip (MS)		R	31	3	0	0	0	0	0	0	0	0	0	0	.000	.000
Lee Handley (SJ)28																

NAME	T	AGE	W	L	PCT	SV	G	GS	CG	IP	H	BB	SO	ShO	ERA
TOTALS		31	66	81	.449	11	151	151	64	1351	1376	435	426	13	3.58
Rip Sewell	R	35	17	15	.531	2	40	33	18	248	259	72	69	5	3.41
Bob Klinger	R	34	8	11	.421	1	37	19	8	153	151	45	58	1	3.24
Ken Heintzelman (EJ)	L	26	8	11	.421	0	27	18	5	130	143	63	39	3	4.57
Lefty Wilkie	L	27	6	7	.462	1	35	6	3	107	112	37	18	0	4.21
Johnny Lanning	R	31	6	8	.429	1	34	8	2	119	125	26	31	1	3.33
Dutch Dietz	R	30	6	9	.400	3	40	13	3	134	139	57	35	0	3.96
Hank Gornicki	R	31	5	6	.455	2	25	14	7	112	89	40	48	2	2.57
Max Butcher (SA)	R	31	5	8	.385	1	24	18	6	151	144	44	49	0	2.92
Luke Hamlin	R	37	4	4	.500	0	23	14	6	112	128	19	38	1	3.94
Bill Brandt	R	27	1	1	.500	0	3	3	1	16	23	5	4	0	5.06
Jack Hallett	R	28	0	1	.000	0	3	3	2	22	23	8	16	0	4.91
Ken Jungels	R	26	0	0	.000	0	6	0	0	14	12	4	7	0	6.43
Nick Strincevich	R	27	0	0	.000	0	7	1	0	22	19	9	10	0	2.86
Dick Conger	R	21	0	0	.000	0	2	1	0	8	9	5	3	0	2.25
Harry Shuman	R	26	0	0	.000	0	1	0	0	2	0	1	1	0	0.00
Johnny Gee (AJ)26															

CHICAGO 6th 68-86 .442 38 — JIMMIE WILSON

NAME	G by POS	B	AGE	G	AB	R	H	2B	3B	HR	RBI	BB	SO	SB	BA	SA
TOTALS			27	155	5352	591	1360	224	41	75	532	509	607	63	.254	.353
Phil Cavarretta	1B61, OF70	L	25	136	482	59	130	28	4	3	54	71	42	7	.270	.363
Lou Stringer	2B113, 3B1	R	25	121	406	45	96	10	5	9	41	31	55	3	.236	.352
Lennie Merullo	SS143	R	25	143	515	53	132	23	3	2	37	35	45	14	.256	.324
Stan Hack	3B139	L	32	140	553	91	166	36	3	6	39	94	40	9	.300	.409
Bill Nicholson	OF151	L	27	152	588	83	173	22	11	21	78	76	80	8	.294	.476
Dom Dallessandro	OF66	L	28	96	264	30	69	12	4	4	43	36	18	4	.261	.383
Lou Novikoff	OF120	R	26	128	483	48	145	25	5	7	64	24	28	3	.300	.416
Clyde McCullough	C97	R	25	109	337	39	95	22	1	5	31	25	47	7	.282	.398
Rip Russell	1B35, 2B24, 3B10, OF3	R	27	102	302	32	73	9	0	8	41	17	21	0	.242	.351
Charlie Gilbert	OF47	L	22	74	179	18	33	6	3	0	7	25	24	1	.184	.251
2 Jimmie Foxx (BR)	1B52, C1	R	34	70	205	25	42	8	0	3	19	22	55	1	.205	.288
Bobby Sturgeon (LJ)	2B32, SS29, 3B2	R	22	63	162	8	40	7	1	0	7	4	13	2	.247	.302
Chico Hernandez	C43	R	26	47	118	6	27	5	0	0	7	11	13	0	.229	.271
Bob Scheffing	C32	R	26	44	102	7	20	3	0	2	12	7	11	2	.196	.284
Peanuts Lowrey	OF19	R	23	27	58	4	11	0	0	1	4	4	4	0	.190	.241
1 Babe Dahlgren	1B14	R	30	17	56	4	12	1	0	0	6	4	2	0	.214	.232
Cy Block	3B8, 2B1	R	23	9	33	6	12	1	1	0	4	3	3	2	.364	.455
Marv Rickert	OF6	L	21	8	26	5	7	0	0	0	1	1	5	0	.269	.269
Paul Gillespie	C4	L	21	5	16	3	4	0	0	2	4	1	2	0	.250	.625
Whitey Platt	OF4	R	21	4	16	1	1	0	0	0	2	0	3	0	.063	.063
Marv Felderman	C2	R	24	3	6	0	1	0	0	0	0	1	4	0	.167	.167

NAME	T	AGE	W	L	PCT	SV	G	GS	CG	IP	H	BB	SO	ShO	ERA
		29	68	86	.442	14	155	155	71	1401	1447	525	507	10	3.60
Claude Passeau	R	33	19	14	.576	0	35	34	24	278	284	74	89	3	2.69
Bill Lee (AJ)	R	32	13	13	.500	0	32	30	18	220	221	67	75	1	3.85
Hi Bithorn	R	26	9	14	.391	2	38	16	9	171	191	81	65	0	3.68
Vern Olsen	L	24	6	9	.400	1	32	17	4	140	161	55	46	1	4.50
Bill Fleming	R	28	5	6	.455	2	33	14	4	134	117	63	59	2	3.02
2 Lon Warneke	R	33	5	7	.417	2	15	12	8	99	97	21	28	1	2.27
Johnny Schmitz	L	21	3	7	.300	2	23	10	1	87	70	45	51	0	3.41
Hank Wyse	R	24	2	1	.667	0	4	4	1	28	33	6	8	1	1.93
Jake Mooty	R	29	2	5	.286	1	19	10	1	84	89	44	20	0	4.71
Tot Pressnell	R	35	1	1	.500	4	27	0	0	39	40	5	9	0	5.54
2 Dick Errickson	R	28	1	1	.500	0	13	0	0	24	39	8	9	0	4.13
Ed Hanyzewski	R	21	1	1	.500	0	6	1	0	19	17	8	6	0	3.79
Paul Erickson	R	26	1	6	.143	0	18	7	1	63	70	41	26	0	5.43
Jesse Flores	R	27	0	1	.000	0	4	0	0	5	5	2	6	0	3.60
Joe Berry	R	37	0	0	.000	0	2	0	0	2	7	2	1	0	18.00
Vallie Eaves	R	30	0	0	.000	0	2	0	0	3	4	2	0	0	9.00
Bob Bowman	R	31	0	0	.000	0	1	0	0	1	1	0	0	0	0.00
Emil Kush	R	25	0	0	.000	0	1	0	0	2	1	1	1	0	0.00

BOSTON 7th 59-89 .399 44 — CASEY STENGEL

NAME	G by POS	B	AGE	G	AB	R	H	2B	3B	HR	RBI	BB	SO	SB	BA	SA
TOTALS			28	150	5077	515	1216	210	19	68	479	474	507	49	.240	.329
Max West	1B85, OF50	L	25	134	452	54	115	22	0	16	56	68	59	4	.254	.409
Sibby Sisti	2B124, OF1	R	21	129	407	50	86	11	4	4	35	45	55	5	.211	.287
Eddie Miller	SS142	R	25	142	534	47	130	28	2	6	47	22	42	11	.243	.337
Nanny Fernandez	3B98, OF44	R	23	145	577	63	147	29	3	6	55	38	61	15	.255	.347
Paul Waner	OF94	L	39	114	333	43	86	17	1	1	39	62	20	2	.258	.324
Tommy Holmes	OF140	L	25	141	558	56	155	24	4	4	41	64	10	2	.278	.357
Chet Ross	OF57	R	25	76	220	20	43	7	2	5	19	16	37	0	.195	.314
Ernie Lombardi	C85	R	34	105	309	32	102	14	0	11	46	37	12	1	.330	.482
Johnny Cooney	OF54, 1B23	R	41	74	198	23	41	6	0	0	7	23	5	2	.207	.237
Skippy Roberge	2B29, 3B27, SS6	R	25	74	172	10	37	7	0	1	12	9	19	1	.215	.273
Clyde Kluttz	C57	R	24	72	210	21	56	10	1	1	31	7	13	0	.267	.338
Buddy Gremp (MS)	1B62, 3B1	R	22	72	207	12	45	11	0	3	19	13	21	1	.217	.314
Frank Demaree	OF49	R	32	64	187	18	42	5	0	3	24	17	10	2	.225	.299
Phil Masi	C39, OF4	R	25	57	87	14	19	3	1	0	9	12	4	2	.218	.276
Jim Tobin	P37	R	29	47	114	14	28	2	0	6	15	16	23	0	.246	.421
Tony Cuccinello	3B20, 2B14	R	34	40	104	8	21	3	0	1	8	9	11	1	.202	.260
Whitey Wietelmann	SS11, 2B1	B	23	13	34	4	7	2	0	0	0	4	5	0	.206	.265
Ducky Detweiler	3B12	R	23	12	44	3	14	2	1	0	5	2	7	0	.318	.409

Frank McElyea 23 R 0-4, Mike Sandlock 26 B 1-1, Al Montgomery (DD) 21

NAME	T	AGE	W	L	PCT	SV	G	GS	CG	IP	H	BB	SO	ShO	ERA
		26	59*	89	.399	8	150	150	68	1334	1326	518	414	9	3.76
Al Javery	R	24	12	16	.429	0	42	37	19	261	251	78	85	5	3.03
Jim Tobin	R	29	12	21	.364	0	37	33	28	288	283	96	71	1	3.97
Lou Tost	L	31	10	10	.500	0	35	22	5	148	146	52	43	1	3.53
Manny Salvo	R	29	7	8	.467	0	25	14	6	131	129	41	25	1	3.02
Tom Earley	R	25	6	11	.353	1	27	18	6	113	120	55	28	0	4.70
Johnny Sain	R	24	4	7	.364	6	40	3	0	97	79	63	68	0	3.90
Bill Donovan	L	25	3	6	.333	0	31	10	2	89	97	32	23	1	3.44
1 Dick Errickson	R	28	2	5	.286	1	21	4	0	59	76	20	15	0	5.03
Johnny Hutchings	R	26	1	0	1.000	0	20	3	0	66	66	34	27	0	4.36
Lefty Wallace	L	20	1	3	.250	0	19	3	1	49	39	24	20	0	3.86
Frank LaManna	R	22	0	1	.000	0	5	0	0	7	5	3	2	0	5.14
Jim Hickey	R	21	0	1	.000	0	1	1	0	1	4	2	0	0	27.00
Art Johnson (MS)	L	25	0	0	.000	0	4	0	0	6	4	5	0	0	1.50
Warren Spahn	L	21	0	0	.000	0	4	2	1	16	25	11	7	0	5.63
George Diehl	R	24	0	0	.000	0	1	0	0	4	2	2	0	0	2.25

*1 win by forfeit

PHILADELPHIA 8th 42-109 .278 62.5 — HANS LOBERT

NAME	G by POS	B	AGE	G	AB	R	H	2B	3B	HR	RBI	BB	SO	SB	BA	SA
TOTALS			28	151	5060	394	1174	168	37	44	354	392	488	37	.232	.306
Nick Etten	1B135	L	28	139	459	37	121	21	3	8	41	67	26	3	.264	.375
Al Glossop	2B118, 3B1	B	29	121	454	33	102	15	1	4	40	29	35	3	.225	.289
Bobby Bragan	SS78, C22, 2B4, 3B3	R	24	109	335	17	73	12	2	2	15	20	21	0	.218	.284
Pinky May	3B107	R	31	115	345	25	82	15	0	0	18	51	17	3	.238	.281
Ron Northey	OF109	L	22	127	402	31	101	13	2	5	31	28	33	2	.251	.331
Lloyd Waner	OF75	L	36	101	287	23	75	7	3	0	10	16	6	1	.261	.307
Danny Litwhiler	OF151	R	25	151	591	59	160	25	9	9	56	27	42	2	.271	.389
Bennie Warren	C78, 1B1	R	30	90	225	19	47	6	3	7	20	24	36	0	.209	.356
Danny Murtaugh	SS60, 3B53, 2B32	R	24	144	506	48	122	16	4	0	27	49	39	13	.241	.289
2 Ernie Koy	OF78	R	32	91	258	21	63	9	3	4	26	14	50	0	.244	.349
Mickey Livingston	C78, 1B6	R	27	89	239	20	49	6	1	2	22	25	20	0	.205	.264
Stan Benjamin	OF45, 1B15	R	28	78	210	24	47	8	3	2	8	10	27	5	.224	.319
Earl Naylor	OF34, P20, 1B1	R	23	76	168	9	33	4	1	0	14	11	18	1	.196	.232
Bill Burich	SS19, 3B3	R	24	25	80	3	23	1	0	0	7	6	13	2	.288	.300
Hal Marnie	2B11, SS7, 3B1	R	23	24	30	3	5	0	0	0	0	1	2	1	.167	.167
Chuck Klein		L	37	14	14	0	1	0	0	0	0	0	2	0	.071	.071
Ed Freed	OF11	R	22	13	33	3	10	3	1	0	1	4	3	1	.303	.455
Ed Murphy	1B8	R	23	13	28	2	7	2	0	0	4	2	4	0	.250	.321
Bert Hodge	3B2	L	25	8	11	0	2	0	0	0	0	1	0	0	.182	.182

Benny Culp 28 R 0-0, Bill Peterman 21 R 1-1

NAME	T	AGE	W	L	PCT	SV	G	GS	CG	IP	H	BB	SO	ShO	ERA
		27	42	109	.278	6	151	151	51	1341	1328	605	472	2	4.12
Tommy Hughes	R	22	12	18	.400	1	40	31	19	253	224	99	77	0	3.06
Rube Melton	R	25	9	20	.310	4	42	29	10	209	180	114	107	1	3.70
Si Johnson	R	35	8	19	.296	0	39	26	10	195	198	72	78	1	3.69
Johnny Podgajny	R	22	6	14	.300	0	43	23	6	187	191	63	40	0	3.90
Frank Hoerst	L	24	4	16	.200	1	33	22	5	151	162	78	52	0	5.19
George Hennessey	R	31	1	1	.500	0	5	1	0	17	11	10	2	0	2.65
Sam Nahem	R	26	1	3	.250	0	35	2	0	75	72	40	38	0	4.92
Ike Pearson	R	25	1	6	.143	0	35	7	0	85	87	50	21	0	4.55
Boom-Boom Beck	R	37	0	1	.000	0	26	1	0	53	69	17	10	0	4.75
Andy Lapihuska	R	19	0	2	.000	0	3	2	0	21	17	13	8	0	5.14
Cy Blanton	R	33	0	4	.000	0	6	3	0	22	30	13	15	0	5.73
Earl Naylor	R	23	0	5	.000	0	20	4	1	60	68	29	19	0	6.15
Paul Masterson	L	26	0	0	.000	0	4	0	0	8	10	5	3	0	6.75
Hilly Flitcraft	L	18	0	0	.000	0	3	0	0	3	6	2	1	0	9.00
Gene Lambert	R	21	0	0	.000	0	1	0	0	1	3	0	1	0	9.00

WORLD SERIES — ST. LOUIS (NL) 4 NEW YORK (AL) 1

LINE SCORES

TEAM	1	2	3	4	5	6	7	8	9	10	11	12	R	H	E
Game 1 September 30 at St. Louis															
NY (AL)	0	0	0	1	1	0	0	3	2				7	11	0
STL (NL)	0	0	0	0	0	0	0	0	4				4	7	4
Game 2 October 1 at St. Louis															
NY	0	0	0	0	0	0	0	3	0				3	10	2
STL	2	0	0	0	0	0	1	1	X				4	6	0
Game 3 October 3 at New York															
STL	0	0	1	0	0	0	0	0	1				2	5	1
NY	0	0	0	0	0	0	0	0	0				0	6	1
Game 4 October 4 at New York															
STL	0	0	0	6	0	0	2	0	1				9	12	1
NY	1	0	0	0	0	5	0	0	0				6	10	1
Game 5 October 5 at New York															
STL	0	0	0	1	0	1	0	0	2				4	9	4
NY	1	0	0	1	0	0	0	0	0				2	7	1

Game 1 pitchers: Ruffing, Chandler (9) — M. Cooper, Gumbert (8), Lanier (9)
Game 2 pitchers: Bonham — Beazley
Game 3 pitchers: White — Chandler, Breuer (9), Turner (9)
Game 4 pitchers: M. Cooper, Gumbert (6), Pollet (6), Lanier (7) — Borowy, Donald (4), Bonham (7)
Game 5 pitchers: Beazley — Ruffing

COMPOSITE BATTING

NAME	POS	G	AB	R	H	2B	3B	HR	RBI	BA
St. Louis (NL)										
Totals		5	163	23	39	4	2	2	23	.239
W. Cooper	C	5	21	3	6	1	0	0	4	.286
Brown	2B	5	20	2	6	0	0	0	1	.300
Slaughter	OF	5	19	3	5	1	0	1	2	.263
Musial	OF	5	18	2	4	1	0	0	2	.222
Marion	SS	5	18	2	2	0	1	0	3	.111
T. Moore	OF	5	17	2	5	1	0	0	2	.294
Hopp	1B	5	17	3	3	0	0	0	0	.176
Kurowski	3B	5	15	3	4	0	1	1	5	.267
Beazley	P	2	7	0	1	0	0	0	0	.143
M. Cooper	P	2	5	1	1	0	0	0	2	.200
White	P	1	2	0	0	0	0	0	0	.000
Lanier	P	2	1	0	1	0	0	0	1	1.000
O'Dea	PH	1	1	0	1	0	0	0	1	1.000
Sanders	PH	2	1	1	0	0	0	0	0	.000
Walker	PH	1	1	0	0	0	0	0	0	.000
Crespi	PR	1	0	1	0	0	0	0	0	.000
Gumbert	P	2	0	0	0	0	0	0	0	.000
Pollet	P	1	0	0	0	0	0	0	0	.000
New York (AL)										
Totals		5	178	18	44	6	0	3	14	.247
Rizzuto	SS	5	21	2	8	0	0	1	1	.381
DiMaggio	OF	5	21	3	7	0	0	0	3	.333
Gordon	2B	5	21	1	2	1	0	0	0	.095
Keller	OF	5	20	2	4	0	0	2	5	.200
Cullenbine	OF	5	19	3	5	1	0	0	2	.263
Dickey	C	5	19	1	5	0	0	0	0	.263
Rolfe	3B	4	17	5	6	2	0	0	0	.353
Priddy	3B-1B	3	10	0	1	1	0	0	1	.100
Hassett	1B	3	9	1	3	1	0	0	2	.333
Ruffing	P	4	9	0	2	0	0	0	0	.222
Crosetti	3B	1	3	0	0	0	0	0	0	.000
Bonham	P	2	2	0	0	0	0	0	0	.000
Chandler	P	2	2	0	0	0	0	0	0	.000
Donald	P	1	2	0	0	0	0	0	0	.000
Rosar	PH	1	1	0	1	0	0	0	0	1.000
Selkirk	PH	1	1	0	0	0	0	0	0	.000
Borowy	P	1	1	0	0	0	0	0	0	.000
Stainback	PR	2	0	0	0	0	0	0	0	.000
Breuer	P	1	0	0	0	0	0	0	0	.000
Turner	P	1	0	0	0	0	0	0	0	.000

COMPOSITE PITCHING

NAME	G	IP	H	BB	SO	W	L	SV	ERA
St. Louis (NL)									
Totals	5	45	44	8	22	4	1	0	2.60
Beazley	2	18	17	3	6	2	0	0	2.50
M. Cooper	2	13	17	4	9	0	1	0	5.54
White	1	9	6	0	6	1	0	0	0.00
Lanier	2	4	3	1	1	1	0	0	0.00
Gumbert	2	.2	1	0	0	0	0	0	0.00
Pollet	1	.1	0	0	0	0	0	0	0.00
New York (AL)									
Totals	5	44	39	17	19	1	4	1	4.50
Ruffing	2	17.2	14	7	11	1	1	0	4.08
Bonham	2	11	9	3	3	0	1	0	4.09
Chandler	2	8.1	5	1	3	0	1	1	1.08
Donald	1	3	3	2	1	0	1	0	6.00
Borowy	1	3	6	3	1	0	0	0	18.00
Turner	1	1	0	1	0	0	0	0	0.00
Breuer	1	0	2	0	0	0	0	0	0.00

1943 The Lesser Struggle

As war raged throughout Europe and the Pacific, those remaining on the home front found their lives touched in a myriad of ways. As players, stars, and scrubs alike were drafted into the military in droves, baseball was forced to scramble to preserve the continuity it had enjoyed since 1876. Clubs had to operate with oldsters, youngsters, and draft deferred stars or not operate at all. When a Government order forbade the teams to conduct spring training below the Mason-Dixon line, such picturesque towns as Asbury Park, New Jersey, became the hosting ground for the spring sweat sessions. During the season itself, each club promoted the sales of war bonds, and sizeable contributions were handed over to various war charities. Although the National Pastime served as an escape from the violent overseas' headlines, the game itself became as altered as the other facets of American life.

The farm system which made the Cardinals into champions also served in the star-shortage year to make them pre-season favorites to cop the National League pennant, and the Redbirds waltzed through the circuit to an anticipated repeat championship. Enos Slaughter, Jimmy Brown, Terry Moore, and Johnny Beazley all had marched off into the armed forces, and Howie Pollet joined them after a sterling first half of the season. Harry Brecheen and Alpha Brazle appeared from the legendary Cardinal farm chain to shore up the pitching, while Lou Klein came to do an outstanding job at second base. Stan Musial grabbed his first batting title with a .357 mark, Walker Cooper swung a big stick, and Mort Cooper and Max Lanier starred on the pitching hill. Second-place Cincinnati finished 18 games back, and Branch Rickey suffered the frustration of having his new Brooklyn club limp home a distant 23½ lengths behind the Cardinal club he had largely put together. Chicago's Bill "Swish" Nicholson copped the home run and RBI crowns but lost out in MVP honors to the 22-year-old Musial.

The American League also produced a repeat pennant-winner as Joe McCarthy's New York Yankees pulled away from the Washington Senators after a close first half. Although the Yankees lost Joe DiMaggio, Phil Rizzuto, Tommy Henrich, Buddy Hassett, and Red Ruffing to Uncle Sam, their subs and veterans glowed bright enough with a steady competence that boosted the pinstripers to their seventh crown in eight years. After rookie Snuffy Stirnweiss failed to fill the shortstop gap, veteran Frank Crosetti plugged the hole in time for the club's spurt. The Yankee attack remained the class of the league, as 36-year-old Bill Dickey batted .351, Charlie Keller slugged 31 home runs, and Hassett's replacement, Nick Etten, knocked in 107 runs.

The Yankees also had the cream of the league's pitching in the arm of Spud Chandler, the winner of 20 out of 24 decisions and the owner of a 1.64 E.R.A., the lowest mark in the American League in 24 years—a performance which earned him the MVP Award. The 1942 Triple Crown winner, Ted Williams, was not faced with the frustration of post-season honors, as he spent the year in the cockpit of a fighter plane. Chicago's Luke Appling picked up the Splendid Splinter's batting title, and Detroit's Rudy York the other two pieces of the Triple Crown, with 34 homers and 118 runs batted in.

Both clubs in the World Series reached on a return ticket, but the result of the confrontation was a 360 degree reversal from 1942. The Yankees knocked out the Cardinals this time in five games by limiting them to nine runs for the entire Series.

1943 AMERICAN LEAGUE

NAME	G by POS	B	AGE	G	AB	R	H	2B	3B	HR	RBI	BB	SO	SB	BA	SA
NEW YORK 1st 98-56 .636	JOE McCARTHY															
TOTALS			29	155	5282	669	1350	218	59	100	635	624	562	46	.256	376
Nick Etten	1B154	L	29	154	583	78	158	35	5	14	107	76	31	3	.271	.420
Joe Gordon	2B152	R	28	152	543	82	135	28	5	17	69	98	75	4	.249	.413
Frankie Crosetti (SU)	SS90	R	32	95	348	36	81	8	1	2	20	36	47	4	.233	.279
Billy Johnson	3B155	R	24	155	592	70	166	24	6	5	94	53	30	3	.280	.367
Bud Metheny	OF91	L	28	103	360	51	94	18	2	9	36	39	34	2	.261	.397
Johnny Lindell	OF122	R	26	122	441	53	108	17	12	4	51	51	55	2	.245	.365
Charlie Keller	OF141	L	26	141	513	97	139	15	11	31	86	106	60	7	.271	.524
Bill Dickey	C71	L	36	85	242	29	85	18	2	4	33	41	12	2	.351	.492
Snuffy Stirnweiss	SS68, 2B4	R	24	83	274	34	60	8	4	1	25	47	37	11	.219	.288
Roy Weatherly	OF68	L	28	77	280	37	74	8	3	7	28	18	9	4	.264	.389
Tuck Stainback	OF61	R	32	71	231	31	60	11	2	0	10	7	16	3	.260	.325
Ken Sears	C50	L	25	60	187	22	52	7	0	2	22	11	18	1	.278	.348
Rollie Hemsley	C52	R	36	62	180	12	43	6	3	2	24	13	9	0	.239	.339
Oscar Grimes	SS3, 1B1	R	28	9	20	4	3	0	0	0	1	3	7	0	.150	.150
Aaron Robinson (MS)		L	28	1	1	0	0	0	0	0	0	0	1	0	.000	.000
WASHINGTON 2nd 84-69 .549 13.5	OSSIE BLUEGE															
TOTALS			27	153	5233	666	1328	245	50	47	617	605	579	142	.254	.347
Mickey Vernon	1B143	L	25	145	553	89	148	29	8	7	70	66	55	24	.268	.387
Jerry Priddy	2B134, SS15, 3B1	R	23	149	560	68	152	31	3	4	62	67	76	5	.271	.359
John Sullivan	SS133	R	22	134	456	49	95	12	2	1	55	57	59	6	.208	.250
1 Ellis Clary	3B68, SS1	R	26	73	254	36	65	19	1	0	19	43	31	8	.256	.339
George Case	OF140	R	27	141	613	102	180	36	5	1	52	40	27	61	.294	.374
Stan Spence	OF148	L	28	149	570	72	152	23	10	12	88	84	39	8	.267	.405
Bob Johnson	OF88, 3B19, 1B10	R	36	117	438	65	116	22	8	7	63	62	50	11	.265	.400
Jake Early	C122	L	26	126	423	37	109	23	3	5	60	52	43	5	.258	.362
Gene Moore	OF57, 1B1	L	33	92	254	41	68	14	3	2	39	19	29	0	.268	.370
Sherry Robertson	3B27, SS1	R	24	59	120	22	26	4	1	3	14	17	19	0	.217	.342
2 Alex Kampouris	3B33, 2B10, OF1	R	30	51	145	24	30	4	0	2	13	30	25	7	.207	.276
Tony Giuliani	C49	R	30	49	133	5	30	4	1	0	20	12	14	0	.226	.271
George Myatt	2B11, SS2, 3B2	L	29	42	53	11	13	3	0	0	3	13	7	3	.245	.302
Early Wynn	P37	R	23	38	98	6	29	3	1	1	11	1	11	0	.296	.378
Jake Powell	OF33	R	34	37	132	14	35	10	2	0	20	5	13	3	.265	.371
Red Marion	OF4	R	29	14	17	2	3	0	0	0	1	3	1	0	.176	.176
Red Roberts	SS6, 3B1	R	24	9	23	1	6	1	0	1	3	4	2	0	.261	.435
2 Harlond Clift	3B8	R	30	8	30	4	9	0	0	0	4	5	3	0	.300	.300
Ed Butka	1B3	R	27	3	9	0	3	1	0	0	1	0	3	0	.333	.444
2 Tom Padden	C2	R	34	3	3	1	0	0	0	0	0	1	1	0	.000	.000
Red Barbary		R	23	1	1	0	0	0	0	0	0	0	0	0	.000	.000
Robert Ortiz	OF1	R	28	1	4	0	1	0	0	0	0	0	0	0	.250	.250
CLEVELAND 3rd 82-71 .536 15.5	LOU BOUDREAU															
TOTALS			28	153	5265	600	1344	246	45	55	564	567	521	47	.255	.350
Mickey Rocco	1B108	L	27	108	405	43	97	14	4	5	46	51	40	1	.240	.331
Ray Mack	2B153	R	26	153	545	56	120	25	2	7	62	47	61	8	.220	.312
Lou Boudreau	SS152, C1	R	25	152	539	69	154	32	7	3	67	90	31	4	.286	.388
Ken Keltner	3B107	R	26	110	427	47	111	31	3	4	39	36	20	2	.260	.375
Roy Cullenbine	OF121, 1B13	B	27	138	488	66	141	24	4	8	56	96	58	3	.289	.404
Oris Hockett	OF139	L	33	141	601	70	166	33	4	2	51	45	45	13	.276	.354
Jeff Heath	OF111	L	28	118	424	58	116	22	6	18	79	63	58	5	.274	.481
Buddy Rosar	C114	R	28	115	382	53	108	17	1	1	41	33	12	0	.283	.340
Hank Edwards (MS)	OF74	L	24	92	297	38	82	18	6	3	28	30	34	4	.276	.407
Rusty Peters	3B46, SS14, 2B6, OF2	R	28	79	215	22	47	6	2	1	19	18	29	1	.219	.279
Gene Desautels	C66	R	36	68	185	14	38	6	1	0	19	11	16	2	.205	.249
Chubby Dean (MS)	P17	L	27	41	46	2	9	0	0	0	5	6	2	0	.196	.196
Otto Denning	1B34	R	30	37	129	8	31	6	0	0	13	5	1	3	.240	.287
Pat Seerey	OF16	R	20	26	72	8	16	3	0	1	5	4	19	0	.222	.306
2 Jimmy Grant	3B5	L	24	15	22	3	3	2	0	0	1	4	7	0	.136	.227
Eddie Turchin	3B4, SS2	R	26	11	13	4	3	0	0	0	1	3	1	0	.231	.231
Gene Woodling (MS)	OF6	L	20	8	25	5	8	2	1	1	5	1	3	0	.320	.600
Frank Doljack	OF3	R	35	3	7	0	0	0	0	0	0	1	2	0	.000	.000
George Susce (IJ)	C3	R	34	3	1	0	0	0	0	0	0	0	0	0	.000	.000
Jim McDonnell	C1	L	20	2	1	1	0	0	0	0	0	2	1	0	.000	.000

NAME	T	AGE	W	L	PCT	SV	G	GS	CG	IP	H	BB	SO	ShO	ERA
NEW YORK		31	98	56	.636	13	155	155	83	1415	1229	489	653	14	2.93
Spud Chandler	R	35	20	4	.833	0	30	30	20	253	197	54	134	5	1.64
Ernie Bonham	R	29	15	8	.652	1	28	26	17	226	197	52	71	4	2.27
Hank Borowy	R	27	14	9	.609	0	29	27	14	217	195	72	113	3	2.82
Butch Wensloff	R	27	13	11	.542	1	29	27	18	223	179	70	105	1	2.54
Johnny Murphy	R	34	12	4	.750	8	37	0	0	68	44	30	31	0	2.51
Bill Zuber	R	30	8	4	.667	1	20	13	7	118	100	74	57	0	3.89
Atley Donald	R	32	6	4	.600	0	22	15	2	119	134	38	57	0	4.61
Marius Russo	L	28	5	10	.333	1	24	14	5	102	89	45	42	1	3.71
Jim Turner	R	39	3	0	1.000	1	18	0	0	43	44	13	15	0	3.56
Tommy Bryne	R	23	2	1	.667	0	11	2	0	32	28	35	22	0	6.47
Marv Breuer	R	29	0	1	.000	0	5	1	0	14	22	6	6	0	8.36
WASHINGTON		28	84	69	.549	21	153	153	61	1388	1293	540	495	16	3.18
Early Wynn	R	23	18	12	.600	0	37	33	12	257	232	83	89	3	2.91
Dutch Leonard	R	34	11	13	.458	1	31	30	15	220	218	46	51	2	3.27
Alex Carrasquel	R	30	11	7	.611	5	39	13	4	144	160	54	48	1	3.69
Milo Candini	R	25	11	7	.611	1	28	21	8	166	144	65	67	3	2.49
Mickey Haefner	L	30	11	5	.688	6	36	13	8	165	126	60	65	1	2.29
Jim Mertz	R	26	5	7	.417	3	33	10	2	117	109	58	53	0	4.62
2 Johnny Niggeling	R	39	4	2	.667	0	6	6	5	51	27	17	24	3	0.88
Ray Scarborough (MS)	R	25	4	4	.500	3	24	6	2	86	93	46	43	0	2.83
Ewald Pyle	L	32	4	8	.333	1	18	11	2	73	70	45	25	1	4.07
3 Bobo Newsom	R	35	3	3	.500	0	6	6	2	40	38	21	11	0	3.83
Bill LeFebvre	L	27	2	0	1.000	0	6	3	1	32	33	16	10	0	4.50
Lefty Gomez	L	34	0	1	.000	0	1	1	0	5	4	5	0	0	5.40
Dewey Adkins	R	25	0	0	.000	0	7	0	0	10	9	5	1	0	2.70
Owen Scheetz	R	29	0	0	.000	1	6	0	0	9	16	4	5	0	7.00
Len Carpenter	R	29	0	0	.000	0	4	0	0	3	1	4	1	0	0.00
1 Ox Miller	R	28	0	0	.000	0	3	0	0	6	10	5	1	0	10.50
Vern Curtis	R	23	0	0	.000	0	2	0	0	4	3	6	1	0	6.75
CLEVELAND		30	82	71	.536	20	153	153	64	1406	1234	606	585	14	3.15
Al Smith	L	35	17	7	.708	1	29	27	14	208	186	72	72	3	2.55
Jim Bagby	R	26	17	14	.548	1	36	33	16	273	248	80	70	3	3.10
Allie Reynolds	R	28	11	12	.478	3	34	21	11	199	140	109	151	3	2.98
Vern Kennedy	R	36	10	7	.588	0	28	17	8	147	130	59	63	1	2.45
Mel Harder (BW)	R	33	8	7	.533	0	19	18	6	135	126	61	40	1	3.07
Jack Salveson	R	29	5	3	.625	3	23	11	4	86	87	26	24	3	3.35
Chubby Dean (MS)	L	27	5	5	.500	0	17	9	3	76	83	34	29	0	4.50
Mike Naymick	R	25	4	4	.500	2	29	4	0	63	32	47	41	0	2.29
Ray Poat	R	25	2	5	.286	0	17	4	1	45	44	20	31	0	4.40
Joe Heving	R	42	1	1	.500	9	30	1	0	72	58	34	34	0	2.75
Pete Center (MS)	R	21	1	2	.333	1	24	1	0	42	29	18	10	0	2.79
1 Al Milnar	L	29	1	3	.250	0	16	6	0	39	51	35	12	0	8.08
Eddie Kleiman	R	25	0	1	.000	0	1	1	1	9	8	5	2	0	1.00
Paul Calvert	R	25	0	0	.000	0	5	0	0	8	6	6	2	0	4.50
Steve Gromek	R	23	0	0	.000	0	3	0	0	4	6	0	4	0	9.00
Red Embree (VR) 25															
Hal Trosky (IL) 30															

CHICAGO 4th 82-72 .532 16 — JIMMY DYKES

NAME	G by POS	B	AGE	G	AB	R	H	2B	3B	HR	RBI	BB	SO	SB	BA	SA
TOTALS			30	155	5252	573	1297	193	46	33	509	561	581	173	.247	.320
Joe Kuhel	1B153	L	37	153	531	55	113	21	1	5	46	76	45	14	.213	.284
Don Kolloway (MS)	2B85	R	24	85	348	29	75	14	4	1	33	9	30	11	.216	.287
Luke Appling	SS155	R	36	155	585	63	192	33	2	3	80	90	29	27	**.328**	.407
Ralph Hodgin	3B56, OF42	L	27	117	407	52	128	22	8	1	50	20	24	3	.314	.415
Wally Moses	OF148	L	32	150	599	82	147	22	12	3	48	55	47	56	.245	.337
Thurman Tucker	OF132	L	25	139	528	81	124	15	6	3	39	79	72	29	.235	.303
Guy Curtright	OF128	R	30	138	488	67	142	20	7	3	48	69	60	13	.291	.379
Mike Tresh	C85	R	29	86	279	20	60	3	0	0	20	37	20	2	.215	.226
Skeeter Webb	2B54	R	33	58	213	15	50	5	2	0	22	6	19	5	.235	.277
1 Jimmy Grant	3B51	L	24	58	197	23	51	9	2	4	22	18	34	4	.259	.386
Dick Culler	3B26, 2B19, SS3	R	28	53	148	9	32	5	1	0	11	16	11	4	.216	.264
Tom Turner	C49	R	26	51	154	16	37	7	1	2	11	13	21	1	.240	.338
Moose Solters	OF21	R	37	42	97	6	15	0	0	1	8	7	5	0	.155	.186
2 Tony Cuccinello	3B30	R	35	34	103	5	28	5	0	2	11	13	13	3	.272	.379
Vince Castino	C30	R	25	33	101	14	23	1	0	2	16	12	11	0	.228	.297
John Humphries	P28	R	28	28	69	6	20	6	0	0	5	3	25	1	.290	.377
Don Hanski	1B5, P1	L	27	9	21	1	5	1	0	0	2	0	5	0	.238	.286
Frank Kalin (MS)		R	25	4	4	0	0	0	0	0	0	0	0	0	.000	.000
Cass Michaels	3B2	R	17	2	7	0	0	0	0	0	0	0	0	0	.000	.000

NAME	T	AGE	W	L	PCT	SV	G	GS	CG	IP	H	BB	SO	ShO	ERA
		30	82	72	.532	19	155	155	70	1400	1352	501	476	12	3.20
Orval Grove	R	23	15	9	.625	2	32	25	18	216	192	72	76	3	2.75
Bill Dietrich	R	33	12	10	.545	0	26	26	12	187	180	53	52	2	2.79
Buck Ross	R	28	11	7	.611	0	21	21	7	149	140	56	41	1	3.20
John Humphries	R	28	11	11	.500	0	28	27	8	188	198	54	51	2	3.30
Eddie Smith	L	29	11	11	.500	0	25	25	14	188	197	76	66	2	3.69
Joe Haynes	R	25	7	2	.778	2	35	2	1	109	114	32	37	0	2.97
Gordon Maltzberger	R	30	7	4	.636	**14**	37	0	0	99	86	24	48	0	2.45
Thornton Lee	L	36	5	9	.357	0	19	19	7	127	129	50	35	1	4.18
Jake Wade	L	31	3	7	.300	0	21	9	3	84	66	54	41	1	3.00
Bill Swift	R	35	0	2	.000	0	18	1	0	51	48	27	28	0	4.24
Don Hanski	L	27	0	0	.000	0	1	0	0	1	1	1	0	0	0.00
Floyd Speer	R	30	0	0	.000	0	1	0	0	1	1	2	1	0	9.00

DETROIT 5th 78-76 .506 20 — STEVE O'NEILL

NAME	G by POS	B	AGE	G	AB	R	H	2B	3B	HR	RBI	BB	SO	SB	BA	SA
TOTALS			29	155	5364	632	**1401**	200	47	77	571	483	553	40	**.261**	.116
Rudy York	1B155	R	29	155	571	90	155	22	11	**34**	**118**	84	88	5	.271	**.527**
Jimmy Bloodworth	2B129	R	25	129	474	41	114	23	4	6	52	29	59	4	.241	.344
Joe Hoover	SS144	R	28	144	575	78	140	15	8	4	38	36	101	6	.243	.318
Pinky Higgins	3B138	R	34	138	523	62	145	20	1	10	84	57	31	2	.277	.377
Ned Harris	OF96	L	26	114	354	43	90	14	3	6	32	47	29	6	.254	.362
Doc Cramer	OF138	L	37	140	606	79	182	18	4	1	43	31	13	4	.300	.348
Dick Wakefield	OF155	L	22	155	**633**	91	**200**	**38**	8	7	79	62	60	4	.316	.434
Paul Richards	C100	R	34	100	313	32	69	7	1	5	33	38	35	1	.220	.297
Don Ross	OF38, SS18, 2B7, 3B1	R	28	89	247	19	66	13	0	0	18	20	3	2	.267	.320
Rip Radcliff	OF19, 1B1	L	37	70	115	3	30	4	0	0	10	13	3	1	.261	.296
Joe Wood	2B22, 3B18	R	23	60	164	22	53	4	4	1	17	6	13	2	.323	.415
Charlie Metro	OF14	R	24	44	40	12	8	0	0	0	2	3	6	1	.200	.200
Dixie Parsons	C40	R	27	40	106	2	15	3	0	0	4	6	16	0	.142	.170
Al Unser	C37	R	30	38	101	14	25	5	0	0	4	15	15	0	.248	.297
Jimmy Outlaw	OF16	R	30	20	67	8	18	1	0	1	6	8	4	0	.269	.328
John McHale (MS)		L	21	4	3	0	0	0	0	0	0	1	1	0	.000	.000

NAME	T	AGE	W	L	PCT	SV	G	GS	CG	IP	H	BB	SO	ShO	ERA
		27	78	76	.506	20	155	155	67	1412	1226	549	**706**	**18**	3.00
Dizzy Trout	R	28	**20**	12	.625	6	44	30	18	247	204	101	111	**5**	2.48
Virgil Trucks	R	24	16	10	.615	2	33	25	10	203	170	52	118	2	2.84
Tommy Bridges	R	36	12	7	.632	0	25	22	11	192	159	61	124	3	2.39
Hal Newhouser	L	22	8	17	.320	1	37	25	10	196	163	**111**	144	1	3.03
Stubby Overmire	L	24	7	6	.538	1	29	18	8	147	135	38	48	3	3.18
Hal White	R	24	7	12	.368	2	32	24	7	178	150	71	58	2	3.39
Johnny Gorsica	R	28	4	5	.444	5	35	4	1	96	88	40	45	0	3.38
Prince Oana	R	35	3	2	.600	0	10	0	0	34	34	19	15	0	4.50
Rufe Gentry	R	25	1	3	.250	0	4	4	2	29	30	12	8	0	3.72
Roy Henshaw	L	31	0	2	.000	2	26	3	0	71	75	33	33	0	3.80
Joe Orrell	R	26	0	0	.000	1	10	0	0	19	18	11	2	0	3.79

ST. LOUIS 6th 72-80 .474 25 — LUKE SEWELL

NAME	G by POS	B	AGE	G	AB	R	H	2B	3B	HR	RBI	BB	SO	SB	BA	SA
TOTALS			30	153	5175	596	1269	229	36	78	552	569	**646**	37	.245	.349
George McQuinn	1B122	L	34	125	449	53	109	19	2	12	74	56	65	4	.243	.374
Don Gutteridge	2B132	R	31	132	538	77	147	35	6	1	36	50	46	10	.273	.366
Vern Stephens	SS123, OF11	R	22	137	512	75	148	27	3	22	91	54	73	3	.289	.482
1 Harlond Clift (IL)	3B104	R	30	105	379	43	88	11	3	3	25	54	37	5	.232	.301
Mike Chartak	OF77, 1B18	L	27	108	344	38	88	16	2	10	37	39	55	1	.256	.401
Milt Byrnes	OF114	L	26	129	429	58	120	28	7	4	50	54	49	1	.280	.406
Chet Laabs	OF150	R	31	151	580	83	145	27	7	17	85	73	**105**	5	.250	.409
Frankie Hayes	C76, 1B1	R	28	88	250	16	47	7	0	5	30	37	36	1	.188	.276
Mark Christman	3B37, SS24, 1B20, 2B14	R	29	98	336	31	91	11	5	2	35	19	19	0	.271	.351
Rick Ferrell	C70	R	37	74	209	12	50	7	0	0	20	34	14	0	.239	.273
Al Zarilla	OF60	L	24	70	228	27	58	7	1	2	17	17	20	1	.254	.320
Mike Kreevich	OF51	R	35	60	161	24	41	6	0	0	10	26	13	4	.255	.292
Joe Schultz	C26	L	24	46	92	6	22	5	0	0	8	9	8	0	.239	.393
Tony Criscola	OF13	L	27	29	52	4	8	0	0	0	1	8	7	0	.154	.154
2 Ellis Clary	3B14, 2B3	R	26	23	69	15	19	2	0	0	5	12	6	1	.275	.304
Floyd Baker	SS10, 3B1	L	26	22	46	5	8	2	0	0	4	6	4	0	.174	.217
1 Don Heffner	2B13, 1B1	R	32	18	33	2	4	1	0	0	2	2	2	0	.121	.152
Hal Epps	OF8	L	29	8	35	2	10	4	0	0	1	3	4	1	.286	.400
Hank Schmulbach		L	18	1	0	1	0	0	0	0	0	0	0	0	.000	.000

NAME	T	AGE	W	L	PCT	SV	G	GS	CG	IP	H	BB	SO	ShO	ERA
		33	72	80	.474	14	153	153	64	1385	1397	488	572	10	3.41
Steve Sundra	R	33	15	11	.577	0	32	29	13	208	212	66	44	3	3.26
Bob Muncrief	R	27	13	12	.520	1	35	27	12	205	211	48	80	3	2.81
Denny Galehouse	R	31	11	11	.500	1	31	28	14	224	217	74	114	2	2.77
Nels Potter	R	31	10	5	.667	1	33	13	8	168	146	54	80	0	2.79
George Caster	R	35	6	8	.429	8	35	0	0	76	69	41	43	0	2.13
1 Johnny Niggeling	R	39	6	8	.429	0	20	20	7	150	122	57	73	0	3.18
Al Hollingsworth	L	35	6	13	.316	3	35	20	9	154	169	51	63	1	4.21
Sid Peterson	R	25	2	0	1.000	0	3	0	0	10	15	3	0	0	2.70
Archie McKain	L	32	1	1	.500	0	10	0	0	16	16	6	6	0	3.94
2 Al Milnar	L	29	1	2	.333	0	3	2	1	15	23	9	7	0	5.40
2 Bobo Newsom	R	35	1	6	.143	0	10	9	0	52	69	35	37	0	7.44
Al LaMacchia	R	21	0	1	.000	0	1	1	0	4	9	2	2	0	11.25
1 Fritz Ostermueller	L	35	0	2	.000	0	11	3	0	29	36	13	4	0	4.97
2 Charley Fuchs	R	29	0	0	.000	0	13	0	0	36	42	11	9	0	4.00
Paul Dean	R	29	0	0	.000	0	3	1	0	13	16	3	1	0	3.46
Jack Kramer (MS)	R	25	0	0	.000	0	3	0	0	9	11	8	4	0	8.00
Fred Sanford	R	23	0	0	.000	0	3	0	0	9	7	4	2	0	2.00
2 Ox Miller	R	28	0	0	.000	0	2	0	0	6	7	3	3	0	12.00

BOSTON 7th 68-84 .447 29 — JOE CRONIN

NAME	G by POS	B	AGE	G	AB	R	H	2B	3B	HR	RBI	BB	SO	SB	BA	SA
TOTALS			27	155	**5392**	563	1314	223	42	57	510	486	591	86	.244	.332
Tony Lupien	1B153	L	26	154	608	65	155	21	9	4	47	54	23	16	.255	.339
Bobby Doerr	2B155	R	25	155	604	78	163	32	3	16	75	62	59	8	.270	.412
Skeeter Newsome	SS98, 3B15	R	32	114	449	48	119	21	2	1	22	21	21	5	.265	.327
Jim Tabor	3B133, OF2	R	29	137	537	57	130	26	3	13	85	43	54	7	.242	.374
Pete Fox	OF125	R	33	127	489	54	141	24	4	2	44	34	40	22	.288	.366
Catfish Metkovich	OF76, 1B2	L	21	78	321	34	79	14	4	5	27	19	38	1	.246	.361
Leon Culberson (NJ)	OF79	R	23	80	312	36	85	16	6	3	34	30	35	13	.272	.391
Roy Partee	C91	R	25	96	299	30	84	14	2	0	31	39	33	0	.281	.341
Johnny Lazor	OF63	L	30	83	208	21	47	10	2	0	13	21	25	5	.226	.293
Eddie Lake	SS63	R	27	75	216	26	43	10	0	3	16	47	35	3	.199	.287
Joe Cronin	3B10	R	26	59	77	8	24	4	0	5	29	11	4	0	.312	.558
Johnny Peacock	C32	L	33	48	114	7	23	3	1	0	7	10	9	1	.202	.246
Dee Miles	OF25	L	34	45	121	9	26	2	2	0	10	3	3	0	.215	.264
Al Simmons	OF33	R	41	40	133	9	27	5	0	1	12	8	21	0	.203	.263
Bill Conroy	C38	R	28	39	89	13	16	5	0	1	6	18	19	0	.180	.270
Ford Garrison	OF32	R	27	36	129	13	36	5	1	1	11	5	14	0	.279	.357
2 Babe Barna	OF29	L	28	30	112	19	19	4	1	2	10	15	24	2	.170	.277
Tom McBride	OF24	R	28	26	96	11	23	3	1	0	7	7	3	2	.240	.292
Danny Doyle	C13	R	26	13	43	2	9	1	0	0	6	7	9	0	.209	.233
Al Olsen		L	22	1	0	0	0	0	0	0	0	1	0	1	.000	.000
Lou Finney (VR) 32																

NAME	T	AGE	W	L	PCT	SV	G	GS	CG	IP	H	BB	SO	ShO	ERA
		31	68	84	.447	16	155	155	62	**1426**	1369	**615**	513	13	3.45
Tex Hughson	R	27	12	15	.444	2	35	32	**20**	266	242	73	114	4	2.64
Oscar Judd	L	35	11	6	.647	0	23	20	8	155	131	69	53	1	2.90
Dick Newsome	R	33	8	13	.381	0	25	22	8	154	166	68	40	2	4.50
Mike Ryba	R	40	7	5	.583	2	40	8	4	144	142	57	50	1	3.25
Yank Terry	R	32	7	9	.438	1	30	22	7	164	147	63	63	0	3.51
Joe Dobson	R	26	7	11	.389	0	25	20	9	164	144	57	63	3	3.13
Mace Brown	R	34	6	6	.500	9	**49**	0	0	93	71	51	40	0	2.13
Pinky Woods	R	28	5	6	.455	1	23	12	2	101	109	55	32	0	4.90
Lou Lucier	R	25	3	4	.429	0	16	9	3	74	94	33	23	0	3.89
1 Andy Karl	R	29	1	1	.500	1	11	0	0	26	31	13	6	0	3.46
Emmett O'Neill	R	25	1	4	.200	0	11	5	1	58	56	46	20	0	4.50
1 Ken Chase	L	29	0	4	.000	0	7	5	0	27	36	30	9	0	7.00

PHILADELPHIA 8th 49-105 .318 49 — CONNIE MACK

NAME	G by POS	B	AGE	G	AB	R	H	2B	3B	HR	RBI	BB	SO	SB	BA	SA
TOTALS			29	155	5244	497	1219	174	44	26	462	430	465	55	.232	.297
Dick Siebert	1B145	L	31	146	558	50	140	26	7	1	72	33	21	6	.251	.328
Pete Suder	2B95, 3B32, SS5	R	27	131	475	30	105	14	5	3	41	14	40	1	.221	.291
Irv Hall	SS148, 2B1, 3B1	R	24	151	544	37	139	15	4	0	54	22	42	10	.256	.298
Eddie Mayo	3B123	L	33	128	471	49	103	10	1	0	28	34	32	2	.219	.244
Johnny Welaj (MS)	OF72	R	29	93	281	45	68	16	1	0	15	15	17	12	.242	.306
Jo-Jo White	OF133	L	34	139	500	69	124	17	7	1	30	61	51	12	.248	.316
Bobby Estalella	OF97	R	32	117	367	43	95	14	4	11	63	52	44	1	.259	.409
Hal Wagner	C99	L	27	111	289	22	69	17	1	1	26	36	17	3	.239	.315
Bob Swift	C77	R	28	77	224	16	43	5	1	1	11	35	16	0	.192	.237
Elmer Valo (MS)	OF63	L	22	77	249	31	55	6	2	3	18	35	13	2	.221	.297
Jim Tyack	OF38	L	32	54	155	11	40	8	1	0	23	14	9	1	.258	.323
2 Don Heffner	2B47, 1B1	R	32	52	178	17	37	6	0	0	8	18	12	3	.208	.242
Jimmy Ripple	OF31	L	33	32	126	8	30	3	1	0	15	7	7	0	.238	.278
Frank Skaff	1B18, 3B3, SS1	R	29	32	64	8	18	2	1	1	8	6	11	0	.281	.391
George Staller	OF20	L	27	21	85	14	23	1	3	3	12	5	6	1	.271	.459
Bill Burgo	OF17	R	23	17	70	12	26	4	2	1	9	4	1	0	.371	.529
Joe Rullo	2B16	R	27	16	55	2	16	3	0	0	6	8	7	0	.291	.345
Felix Mackiewicz	OF3	R	25	9	16	1	1	0	0	0	0	2	8	0	.063	.063
Woody Wheaton	OF7	L	28	7	30	2	6	2	0	0	2	3	2	0	.200	.267
Tony Parisse	C5	R	32	6	17	0	3	0	0	0	1	2	2	0	.176	.176
Ed Busch	SS4	R	25	4	17	2	5	0	0	0	0	1	2	0	.294	.294
Vern Benson (MS)		L	18	2	2	0	0	0	0	0	0	0	0	0	.000	.000
Bruce Konopka (MS)		L	23	2	2	0	0	0	0	0	0	0	1	0	.000	.000
Earle Brucker		R	42	1	1	0	0	0	0	0	0	0	0	0	.000	.000
Lew Flick	OF1	L	28	1	5	2	3	0	0	0	0	0	0	0	.600	.600
George Kell	3B1	R	20	1	5	1	1	0	1	0	1	0	0	0	.200	.200

NAME	T	AGE	W	L	PCT	SV	G	GS	CG	IP	H	BB	SO	ShO	ERA
		28	49	**105**	.318	13	155	155	73	1394	**1421**	536	503	5	4.05
Jesse Flores	R	28	12	14	.462	0	31	27	13	231	208	70	113	0	3.12
Roger Wolff	R	32	10	15	.400	6	41	26	13	221	232	72	91	2	3.54
Lum Harris	R	28	7	**21**	.250	1	32	27	15	216	241	63	55	1	4.21
Don Black	R	26	6	16	.273	1	33	26	12	208	193	110	65	1	4.20
Russ Christopher	R	25	5	8	.385	2	24	15	5	133	120	58	56	0	3.45
Orie Arntzen	R	33	4	13	.235	0	32	20	9	164	172	69	66	0	4.23
Everett Fagan (MS)	R	25	2	6	.250	3	18	2	0	37	41	14	9	0	6.32
Herman Besse	L	31	1	1	.500	0	5	1	0	16	18	4	3	0	3.38
Charlie Bowles (MS)	R	26	1	1	.500	0	2	2	2	18	17	4	6	0	3.00
Lou Ciola	R	20	1	3	.250	0	12	3	2	44	48	22	7	0	5.52
Bert Kucyznski (MS)	R	23	0	1	.000	0	6	1	0	25	36	9	8	0	3.96
Carl Scheib	R	16	0	1	.000	0	6	0	0	19	24	3	3	0	4.26
1 John Burrows	L	29	0	1	.000	0	4	1	0	8	8	9	3	0	7.88
Bud Mains	R	21	0	1	.000	0	1	1	1	8	9	3	4	0	5.63
Tal Abernathy	L	21	0	3	.000	0	5	2	1	15	24	13	10	0	12.60
Sam Lowry	R	23	0	0	.000	0	5	0	0	18	18	9	3	0	5.00
Tom Clyde	R	19	0	0	.000	0	4	0	0	6	7	4	0	0	9.00
Norm Brown	R	24	0	0	.000	0	1	1	0	7	5	0	1	0	0.00

ST. LOUIS 1st 105-49 .682 — BILLY SOUTHWORTH

NAME	G by POS	B	AGE	G	AB	R	H	2B	3B	HR	RBI	BB	SO	SB	BA	SA
TOTALS			27	157	**5438**	679	**1515**	259	72	70	638	428	438	40	**.279**	**.391**
Ray Sanders	1B141	L	26	144	478	69	134	21	5	11	73	77	33	1	.280	.414
Lou Klein	2B126, SS51	R	24	154	627	91	180	28	14	7	62	50	70	9	.287	.410
Marty Marion	SS128	R	25	129	418	38	117	15	3	1	52	32	37	1	.280	.337
Whitey Kurowski	3B137, SS2	R	25	139	522	69	150	24	8	13	70	31	54	3	.287	.439
Stan Musial	OF155	L	22	157	617	108	**220**	**48**	**20**	13	81	72	18	9	**.357**	**.562**
Harry Walker	OF144, 2B1	L	26	148	564	76	166	28	6	2	53	40	24	5	.295	.376
2 Danny Litwhiler	OF70	R	26	80	258	40	72	14	3	7	31	19	31	1	.279	.438
Walker Cooper	C112	R	28	122	449	52	143	30	4	9	81	19	19	1	.319	.463
Johnny Hopp	OF52, 1B27	L	26	91	241	33	54	10	2	2	25	24	22	8	.224	.307
Debs Garms	OF47, 3B23, SS1	L	35	90	249	26	64	10	2	0	22	13	8	1	.257	.313
Ken O'Dea	C56	L	30	71	203	15	57	11	2	3	25	19	25	0	.281	.399
Frank Demaree	OF23	R	33	39	86	5	25	2	0	0	9	8	4	1	.291	.314
George Fallon	2B36	R	26	36	78	6	18	1	0	0	5	2	9	0	.231	.244
Jimmy Brown	2B19, 3B9, SS6	B	33	34	110	6	20	4	2	0	8	6	1	0	.182	.255
Sam Narron	C3	R	29	10	11	0	1	0	0	0	0	1	2	0	.091	.091
1 Coaker Triplett	OF6	R	31	9	25	1	2	0	0	1	4	1	6	0	.080	.200
1 Buster Adams	OF6	R	28	8	11	1	1	1	0	0	1	4	4	0	.091	.182

NAME	T	AGE	W	L	PCT	SV	G	GS	CG	IP	H	BB	SO	ShO	ERA
TOTALS		27	**105**	49	**.682**	15	157	157	**94**	**1427**	1241	477	**639**	**21**	**2.57**
Mort Cooper	R	30	**21**	8	**.724**	3	37	32	24	274	228	79	141	6	2.30
Max Lanier	L	27	15	7	.682	3	32	25	14	213	195	75	123	2	1.90
Howie Krist	R	27	11	5	.688	3	34	17	9	164	141	62	57	2	2.91
Harry Gumbert	R	33	10	5	.667	0	21	19	7	133	115	32	40	2	2.84
George Munger	R	24	9	5	.643	2	32	9	5	93	101	42	45	0	3.97
Harry Brecheen	L	28	9	6	.600	4	29	13	8	135	98	39	68	1	2.27
Murry Dickson	R	26	8	2	.800	0	31	7	2	116	114	49	44	0	3.57
Al Brazle	L	29	8	2	.800	0	13	9	8	88	74	29	26	1	1.53
Howie Pollet	L	22	8	4	.667	0	16	14	12	118	83	32	61	5	**1.75**
Ernie White (SA)	L	26	5	5	.500	0	14	10	5	79	78	33	28	1	3.76
Bud Byerly	R	22	1	0	1.000	0	2	2	0	13	14	5	6	0	3.46

CINCINNATI 2nd 87-67 .565 18 — BILL McKECHNIE

NAME	G by POS	B	AGE	G	AB	R	H	2B	3B	HR	RBI	BB	SO	SB	BA	SA
TOTALS			31	155	5329	608	1362	229	47	43	558	445	476	49	.256	.340
Frank McCormick	1B120	R	32	126	472	56	143	28	0	8	59	29	15	2	.303	.413
Lonny Frey	2B144	L	32	144	586	78	154	20	8	2	43	76	56	7	.263	.334
Eddie Miller	SS154	R	26	154	576	49	129	26	4	2	71	33	43	8	.224	.293
Steve Mesner	3B130	R	25	137	504	53	137	26	1	0	52	26	20	6	.272	.327
Max Marshall	OF129	L	29	132	508	55	120	11	8	4	39	34	52	8	.236	.313
Gee Walker	OF106	R	35	114	429	48	105	23	2	3	54	12	38	6	.245	.329
Eric Tipton	OF139	R	28	140	493	82	142	26	7	9	49	85	36	1	.288	.424
Ray Mueller	C140	R	31	141	427	50	111	19	4	8	52	56	42	1	.260	.379
Bert Haas	1B44, 3B23, OF18	R	29	101	332	39	87	17	6	4	44	22	26	6	.262	.386
Estel Crabtree	OF64	L	39	95	254	25	70	12	0	2	26	25	17	1	.276	.346
Dain Clay	OF33	R	23	49	93	19	25	2	4	0	9	8	14	1	.269	.376
Tony DePhillips	C35	R	30	35	20	0	2	1	0	0	2	1	5	0	.100	.150
Woody Williams	2B12, 3B7, SS5	R	30	30	69	8	26	2	1	0	11	1	3	0	.377	.435
Al Lakeman	C21	R	24	22	55	5	14	2	1	0	6	3	11	0	.255	.327
Frankie Kelleher	OF1	R	26	9	10	1	0	0	0	0	0	2	0	0	.000	.000
Chuck Aleno	OF2	R	26	7	10	0	3	0	0	0	1	2	1	0	.300	.300
1 Charlie Brewster	2B2	R	26	7	8	0	1	0	0	0	0	0	1	0	.125	.125
Lonnie Goldstein	1B2	L	25	5	5	1	1	0	0	0	0	2	1	0	.200	.200

Mike McCormick (MS) 26 R 2-15, Dick West 27 R 0-0, Junior Thompson (VR) 26

NAME	T	AGE	W	L	PCT	SV	G	GS	CG	IP	H	BB	SO	ShO	ERA
TOTALS		32	87	67	.565	17	155	155	78	1404	1298	581	498	18	3.13
Elmer Riddle	R	28	**21**	11	.656	3	36	33	19	260	235	107	69	5	2.63
Bucky Walters	R	34	15	15	.500	0	34	34	21	246	244	109	80	5	3.55
Johnny Vander Meer	L	28	15	16	.484	0	36	**36**	21	289	228	**162**	**174**	3	2.87
Clyde Shoun	L	31	14	5	.737	7	45	5	2	147	131	46	61	0	3.06
Ray Starr	R	37	11	10	.524	1	36	33	9	217	201	91	42	2	3.65
Joe Beggs	R	32	7	6	.538	0	39	4	4	115	120	25	28	2	2.35
Ed Heusser	R	34	4	3	.571	0	26	10	2	91	97	23	28	1	3.46
Rocky Stone	R	24	0	1	.000	0	13	0	0	25	23	8	11	0	4.32
Bob Malloy	R	25	0	0	.000	0	6	0	0	10	14	8	4	0	6.30
Jack Neimes	L	23	0	0	.000	0	3	0	0	3	5	2	1	0	6.00

BROOKLYN 3rd 81-72 .529 23.5 — LEO DUROCHER

NAME	G by POS	B	AGE	G	AB	R	H	2B	3B	HR	RBI	BB	SO	SB	BA	SA
TOTALS			30	153	5309	**716**	1444	**263**	35	39	**660**	**580**	422	58	.272	.357
Dolph Camilli (VR)	1B95	L	36	95	353	56	87	15	6	6	43	65	48	2	.247	.374
Billy Herman	2B117, 3B37	R	33	153	585	76	193	41	2	2	100	66	26	4	.330	.417
Arky Vaughan	SS99, 3B55	L	31	149	610	**112**	186	39	6	5	66	60	13	**20**	.305	.413
Frenchy Bordagaray	3B25, OF53	R	31	89	268	47	81	18	2	0	19	30	15	6	.302	.384
Dixie Walker	OF136	L	32	138	540	83	163	32	6	5	71	49	24	3	.302	.411
Augie Galan	OF124, 1B13	L	31	139	495	83	142	26	3	9	67	**103**	39	6	.287	.406
Luis Olmo	OF57	R	23	57	238	39	72	6	4	4	37	8	20	3	.303	.412
Mickey Owen	C100, 3B3, SS1	R	27	106	365	31	95	11	2	0	54	25	15	4	.260	.301
Al Glossop	SS33, 2B24, 3B17, OF1	B	30	87	217	28	37	9	0	3	21	28	27	0	.171	.253
Paul Waner	OF57	L	40	82	225	29	70	16	0	1	26	35	9	0	.311	.396
Bobby Bragan	C57, 3B12, SS5	R	25	74	220	17	58	7	2	2	24	15	16	0	.264	.341
1 Joe Medwick	OF42	R	31	48	173	13	47	10	0	0	25	10	8	1	.272	.329
Howie Schultz	1B45	R	20	45	182	20	49	12	0	1	34	6	24	3	.269	.352
Max Macon	P25, 1B3	L	27	45	55	7	9	0	0	0	6	0	1	1	.164	.164
Johnny Cooney	1B3, OF2	R	42	37	34	7	7	0	0	0	2	4	3	1	.206	.206
1 Dee Moore	C15, 3B9	R	29	37	79	8	20	3	0	0	12	11	8	1	.253	.291
Red Barkley	SS18	R	29	20	51	6	16	3	0	0	7	4	7	1	.314	.373
Gene Hermanski (MS)	OF17	L	23	18	60	6	18	2	1	0	12	11	7	1	.300	.367
1 Alex Kampouris	2B18	R	30	19	44	9	10	4	1	0	4	17	6	0	.227	.364
Boyd Bartley (MS)	SS9	R	23	9	21	0	1	0	0	0	1	1	3	0	.048	.048
Carden Gillenwater	OF5	R	25	8	17	1	3	0	0	0	2	2	3	0	.176	.176
Bill Hart	3B6, SS1	R	30	8	19	0	3	0	0	0	1	1	2	0	.158	.158
Al Campanis	2B7	B	26	7	20	3	2	0	0	0	0	4	5	0	.100	.100

2 Joe Orengo 28 R 3-15, Leo Durocher 37 R 4-18, Pat Ankenman (MS) 30 R 1-2, Gil Hodges 19 R 0-2, Hal Peck 26 L 0-1

NAME	T	AGE	W	L	PCT	SV	G	GS	CG	IP	H	BB	SO	ShO	ERA
TOTALS		31	81	72	.529	**22**	153	153	50	1370	1230	**637**	585	13	3.88
Whit Wyatt	R	35	14	5	.737	0	26	26	13	181	139	43	80	3	2.49
Kirby Higbe	R	28	13	10	.565	0	35	27	8	185	189	95	108	1	3.70
Curt Davis (BG)	R	39	10	13	.435	3	31	21	8	164	182	39	47	2	3.79
1 Bobo Newsom	R	35	9	4	.692	1	22	12	6	125	113	57	75	1	3.02
Ed Head	R	25	9	10	.474	6	47	18	7	170	166	66	83	3	3.65
Max Macon	L	27	7	5	.583	0	25	9	0	77	89	32	21	0	5.96
1 Johnny Allen (SU)	R	38	5	1	.833	1	17	1	0	38	42	25	15	0	4.26
Rube Melton	R	26	5	8	.385	0	30	17	4	119	102	79	63	2	3.93
Freddie Fitzsimmons	R	41	3	4	.429	0	9	7	1	45	50	21	12	1	5.40
Les Webber	R	28	2	2	.500	**10**	54	0	0	116	112	69	24	0	3.80
Rex Barney	R	18	2	2	.500	0	9	8	1	45	36	41	23	0	6.40
2 Fritz Ostermueller	L	35	1	1	.500	0	7	1	0	27	21	12	15	0	3.33
1 Newt Kimball	R	28	1	1	.500	1	5	0	0	11	9	5	2	0	1.64
Chris Haughey	R	17	0	1	.000	0	1	0	0	7	5	10	0	0	3.86
2 Bill Lohrman	R	30	0	2	.000	0	6	2	2	28	29	10	5	0	3.54
Hal Gregg	R	21	0	3	.000	0	5	4	0	19	21	21	7	0	9.47
2 Bill Sayles	R	25	0	0	.000	0	5	0	0	12	13	10	5	0	7.50
Bob Chipman	L	24	0	0	.000	0	1	0	0	2	2	2	0	0	0.00

PITTSBURGH 4th 80-74 .519 25 — FRANKIE FRISCH

NAME	G by POS	B	AGE	G	AB	R	H	2B	3B	HR	RBI	BB	SO	SB	BA	SA
TOTALS			28	157	5353	669	1401	240	**73**	42	623	573	566	**64**	.262	.357
Elbie Fletcher	1B154	L	27	154	544	91	154	24	5	9	70	95	49	1	.283	.395
Pete Coscarart	2B85, SS47, 3B1	R	30	133	491	57	119	19	6	0	48	46	48	4	.242	.305
Frankie Gustine	SS68, 2B40, 1B1	R	23	112	414	40	120	21	3	0	43	32	36	12	.290	.355
Bob Elliott	3B151, 2B2, SS1	R	26	156	581	82	183	30	12	7	101	56	24	4	.315	.444
Johnny Barrett	OF99	L	27	130	290	41	67	12	3	1	32	32	23	5	.231	.303
Vince DiMaggio	OF156, SS1	R	30	157	580	64	144	41	2	15	88	70	**126**	11	.248	.403
Jim Russell	OF134, 1B6	B	24	146	533	79	138	19	11	4	44	77	67	12	.259	.358
Al Lopez	C116, 3B1	R	34	118	372	40	98	9	4	1	39	44	25	2	.263	.317
Tommy O'Brien	OF48, 3B9	R	24	89	232	35	72	12	7	2	26	15	24	0	.310	.448
Maurice Van Robays	OF60	R	28	69	236	32	68	17	7	1	35	18	19	0	.288	.432
Bill Baker	C56	R	32	63	172	12	47	6	3	1	26	22	6	3	.273	.360
Johnny Wyrostek	OF20, 3B2, 1B1, 2B1	L	23	51	79	7	12	3	0	0	1	3	15	0	.152	.190
Al Rubeling	2B44, 3B1	R	30	47	168	23	44	8	4	0	9	8	17	0	.262	.357
Huck Geary	SS46	L	26	46	166	17	25	4	0	1	13	18	6	3	.151	.193
Rip Sewell	P35	R	36	41	105	9	30	4	1	0	17	2	21	7	.286	.343
Frank Colman	OF11	L	25	32	59	9	16	2	2	0	4	8	7	0	.271	.373

1 Jimmy Wasdell 29 L 1-2, Hank Camelli 28 R 0-3, Tony Ordenna 24 R 2-4, Bud Stewart (VR) 27

NAME	T	AGE	W	L	PCT	SV	G	GS	CG	IP	H	BB	SO	ShO	ERA
TOTALS		31	80	74	.519	12	157	157	74	1404	1424	421	396	11	3.04
Rip Sewell	R	36	**21**	9	.700	3	35	31	**25**	265	267	75	65	2	2.48
Bob Klinger	R	35	11	8	.579	0	33	25	14	195	185	58	65	3	2.72
Max Butcher	R	32	10	8	.556	1	33	21	10	194	191	57	45	2	2.60
Wally Hebert	L	35	10	11	.476	0	34	23	12	184	197	45	41	1	2.98
Hank Gornicki	R	32	9	13	.409	4	42	18	4	147	165	47	63	1	3.98
Xavier Rescigno	R	29	6	9	.400	2	37	14	5	133	125	45	41	1	3.05
Bill Brandt	R	28	4	1	.800	0	29	3	0	57	57	19	17	0	3.16
Johnny Lanning (MS)	R	[illegible]	4	1	.800	2	12	2	0	27	23	9	11	0	2.33
Johnny Gee	L	27	4	4	.500	0	15	10	2	82	89	27	18	0	4.28
Jack Hallett (MS)	R	29	1	2	.333	0	9	4	2	48	36	11	11	1	1.69
Cookie Cuccurullo	L	25	0	1	.000	0	1	1	0	7	10	3	3	0	6.43
1 Dutch Dietz	R	31	0	3	.000	0	8	0	0	9	12	4	4	0	6.00
2 Johnny Podgajny	R	23	0	4	.000	0	15	5	0	34	37	13	7	0	4.76
Harry Shuman	R	27	0	0	.000	0	11	0	0	22	30	8	5	0	5.32

CHICAGO 5th 74-79 .484 30.5 — JIMMIE WILSON

NAME	G by POS	B	AGE	G	AB	R	H	2B	3B	HR	RBI	BB	SO	SB	BA	SA
TOTALS			28	154	5279	632	1380	207	56	52	579	574	522	53	.261	.351
Phil Cavarretta	1B134, OF7	L	26	143	530	93	154	27	9	8	73	75	42	3	.291	.421
Eddie Stanky	2B131, SS12, 3B2	R	26	142	510	92	125	15	1	0	47	92	42	4	.245	.278
Lennie Merullo	SS125, 2B2, 3B1	R	26	129	453	37	115	18	3	1	25	26	42	7	.254	.313
Stan Hack	3B136	L	33	144	533	78	154	24	4	3	35	82	27	5	.289	.366
Bill Nicholson	OF154	L	28	154	608	95	188	30	9	**29**	**128**	71	86	4	.309	.531
Peanuts Lowrey	OF113, SS16, 2B3	R	24	130	480	59	140	25	12	1	63	35	24	13	.292	.400
Ival Goodman	OF61	L	34	80	225	31	72	10	5	3	45	24	20	4	.320	.449
Clyde McCullough (BN)	C81	R	26	87	266	20	63	5	2	2	23	24	33	6	.237	.293
Dom Dallessandro	OF45	L	29	87	176	13	39	8	3	1	31	40	14	1	.222	.318
Lou Novikoff (HO)	OF61	R	27	78	233	22	65	7	3	0	28	18	15	0	.279	.335
Stu Martin	2B22, 3B8, 1B2	L	29	64	118	13	26	4	0	0	5	15	10	1	.220	.254
Chico Hernandez	C41	R	27	43	126	10	34	4	0	0	9	9	9	0	.270	.302
2 Mickey Livingston	C31, 1B4	R	28	36	111	11	29	5	1	4	16	12	8	1	.261	.432
Heinz Becker	1B18	B	27	24	69	5	10	0	0	0	2	9	6	0	.145	.145
Al Todd	C17	R	39	21	45	1	6	0	0	0	1	1	5	0	.133	.133
Whitey Platt	OF14	R	22	20	41	2	7	3	0	0	2	1	7	0	.171	.244
Ed Sauer	OF13, 3B1	R	23	14	55	3	15	3	0	0	9	3	6	1	.273	.327
Andy Pafko	OF13	R	22	13	58	7	22	3	0	0	10	2	5	1	.379	.431
Bill Schuster	SS13	R	30	13	51	3	15	2	1	0	0	3	2	0	.294	.373
Don Johnson	2B10	R	31	10	42	5	8	2	0	0	1	2	4	0	.190	.238
John Ostrowski	OF5, 3B4	R	25	10	29	2	6	0	1	0	3	3	8	0	.207	.276
Pete Elko	3B9	R	25	9	30	1	4	0	0	0	0	4	5	0	.133	.133
Charlie Gilbert	OF6	L	23	8	20	1	3	0	0	0	0	3	3	1	.150	.150

Billy Holm 30 R 1-15, Mickey Kreitner 20 R 3-8

NAME	T	AGE	W	L	PCT	SV	G	GS	CG	IP	H	BB	SO	ShO	ERA
TOTALS		31	74	79	.484	14	154	154	67	1360	1378	394	513	13	3.24
Hi Bithorn	R	27	18	12	.600	2	39	30	19	250	226	65	86	**7**	2.59
Claude Passeau	R	34	15	12	.556	1	35	31	18	257	245	66	93	1	2.91
Paul Derringer	R	36	10	14	.417	3	32	22	10	174	184	39	75	2	3.57
Hank Wyse	R	25	9	7	.563	5	38	15	8	156	160	34	45	2	2.94
Ed Hanyzewski	R	22	8	7	.533	0	33	16	3	130	120	45	55	0	2.56
Ray Prim	L	36	4	3	.571	1	29	5	0	60	67	14	27	0	2.55
Lon Warneke	R	34	4	5	.444	0	21	10	4	88	82	18	30	0	3.17
1 Bill Lee	R	33	3	7	.300	0	13	12	4	78	83	27	18	0	3.58
Walter Signer	R	32	2	1	.667	0	4	2	1	25	24	4	5	0	2.88
Paul Erickson	R	27	1	3	.250	0	15	4	0	43	47	22	24	0	6.07
Bill Fleming	R	29	0	1	.000	0	11	0	0	32	40	12	12	0	6.47
Dale Alderson	R	25	0	1	.000	0	4	2	0	14	21	3	4	0	6.43
2 John Burrows	L	29	0	2	.000	2	23	1	0	33	25	16	18	0	3.82
1 Dick Barrett	R	36	0	4	.000	0	15	4	0	45	52	28	20	0	4.80
Jake Mooty	R	30	0	0	.000	0	2	0	0	1	2	1	1	0	0.00

BOSTON 6th 68-85 .444 36.5 — **CASEY STENGEL**

NAME	G by POS	B	AGE	G	AB	R	H	2B	3B	HR	RBI	BB	SO	SB	BA	SA
TOTALS			27	153	5196	465	1213	202	36	39	431	469	604	56	.233	.309
Johnny McCarthy (BN-MS)	1B78	L	33	78	313	32	95	24	6	2	33	10	19	1	.304	.438
Connie Ryan	2B100, 3B30	R	23	132	457	52	97	10	2	1	24	58	56	7	.212	.249
Whitey Wietelmann	SS153	B	24	153	534	33	115	14	1	0	39	46	40	9	.215	.245
Eddie Joost	3B67, 2B60, SS1	R	27	124	421	34	78	16	3	2	20	68	80	5	.185	.252
Chuck Workman	OF149, 1B3, 3B1	L	28	153	615	71	153	17	1	10	67	53	72	12	.249	.328
Tommy Holmes	OF152	L	26	152	629	75	170	33	10	5	41	58	20	7	.270	.378
Butch Nieman	OF93	L	25	101	335	39	84	15	8	7	46	39	39	4	.251	.406
Phil Masi	C73	R	26	80	238	27	65	9	1	2	28	27	20	7	.273	.345
Chet Ross	OF73	R	26	94	285	27	62	12	2	7	32	26	67	1	.218	.347
Kerby Farrell	1B69, P5	L	29	85	280	11	75	14	1	0	21	16	15	1	.268	.325
Clyde Kluttz	C55	R	25	66	207	13	51	7	0	0	20	15	9	0	.246	.280
Joe Burns	3B34, OF4	R	28	52	135	12	28	3	0	1	5	8	25	2	.207	.252
Jim Tobin	P33, 1B1	R	30	46	107	8	30	4	0	2	12	6	16	0	.280	.374
2 Hugh Poland	C38	L	30	44	141	5	27	7	0	0	13	4	11	0	.191	.241
Heinie Heltzel	3B29	R	29	29	86	6	13	3	0	0	5	7	13	0	.151	.186
Bill Brubaker	3B5, 1B3	R	32	13	19	3	8	3	0	0	1	2	2	0	.421	.579
1 Tony Cuccinello	3B4, 2B2, SS1	R	35	13	19	0	0	0	0	0	2	3	1	0	.000	.000
Buck Etchison	1B6	L	28	10	19	2	6	3	0	0	2	2	2	0	.316	.474
Sam Gentile		L	26	8	4	1	1	1	0	0	0	1	0	0	.250	.500
Ben Geraghty	2B1, SS1, 3B1	R	30	8	1	2	0	0	0	0	0	0	0	0	.000	.000
Connie Creeden		L	27	5	4	0	1	0	0	0	1	1	0	0	.250	.250

NAME	T	AGE	W	L	PCT	SV	G	GS	CG	IP	H	BB	SO	ShO	ERA
TOTALS		28	68	85	.444	4	153	153	87	1398	1361	440	409	13	3.25
Al Javery	R	25	17	16	.515	0	41	35	19	303	288	99	134	5	3.21
Jim Tobin	R	30	14	14	.500	0	33	30	24	250	241	69	52	1	2.63
Nate Andrews	R	29	14	20	.412	0	36	34	23	284	253	75	80	3	2.57
Red Barrett	R	28	12	18	.400	0	38	31	14	255	240	63	64	3	3.18
13 Manny Salvo	R	30	5	7	.417	0	21	14	5	99	99	31	26	1	3.46
Danny MacFayden	R	38	2	1	.667	0	10	1	0	21	31	9	5	0	6.00
Allyn Stout	R	38	1	0	1.000	1	9	0	0	9	17	4	3	0	7.00
Bill Donovan (MS)	L	26	1	0	1.000	0	7	0	0	15	17	9	1	0	1.80
John Dagenhard	R	26	1	0	1.000	0	2	1	1	11	9	4	2	0	0.00
George Jeffcoat	R	29	1	2	.333	0	8	1	0	18	15	10	10	0	3.00
Kerby Farrell	L	29	0	1	.000	0	5	0	0	23	24	9	4	0	4.30
Lou Tost	L	32	0	1	.000	0	3	1	0	7	10	4	3	0	5.14
Carl Lindquist	R	24	0	2	.000	0	2	2	0	13	17	4	1	0	6.23
Dave Odom	R	25	0	3	.000	2	22	3	1	55	54	30	17	0	5.24
Ben Cardoni	R	22	0	0	.000	1	11	0	0	28	38	14	5	0	6.43
Ray Martin (MS)	R	18	0	0	.000	0	2	0	0	3	3	1	1	0	9.00
George Diehl	R	25	0	0	.000	0	1	0	0	4	4	3	1	0	4.50
Roy Talcott	R	23	0	0	.000	0	1	0	0	1	1	2	0	0	18.00

PHILADELPHIA 7th 64-90 .416 41 — **BUCKY HARRIS 39-51 .433 FREDDIE FITZSIMMONS 25-39 .391**

NAME	G by POS	B	AGE	G	AB	R	H	2B	3B	HR	RBI	BB	SO	SB	BA	SA
TOTALS			28	157	5297	571	1321	186	36	66	529	499	556	29	.249	.335
2 Jimmy Wasdell	1B82, OF56	L	29	141	522	54	136	19	6	4	67	46	22	6	.261	.343
Danny Murtaugh (MS)	2B113	R	25	113	451	65	123	17	4	1	35	57	23	4	.273	.335
Glen Stewart	SS77, 2B18, 1B8, C1	R	30	110	336	23	71	10	1	2	24	32	41	1	.211	.265
Pinky May	3B132	R	32	137	415	31	117	19	2	1	48	56	21	2	.282	.345
Ron Northey	OF145	L	23	147	586	72	163	31	5	16	68	51	52	2	.278	.430
2 Buster Adams	OF107	R	28	111	418	48	107	14	7	4	38	39	67	2	.256	.352
2 Coaker Triplett	OF90	R	31	105	360	45	98	16	4	14	52	28	28	2	.272	.456
1 Mickey Livingston	C84, 1B2	R	28	84	265	25	66	9	2	3	18	19	18	1	.249	.332
Babe Dahlgren	1B73, 3B35, SS25, C1	R	31	136	508	55	146	19	2	5	56	50	39	2	.287	.362
Schoolboy Rowe	P27	R	33	82	120	14	36	7	0	4	18	15	21	0	.300	.458
2 Charlie Brewster	SS46	R	26	49	159	13	35	2	0	0	12	10	19	1	.220	.233
Ray Hamrick	2B31, SS12	R	21	44	160	12	32	3	1	0	9	8	28	0	.200	.231
2 Dee Moore	C21, OF6, 3B5, 1B1	R	29	37	113	13	27	4	1	1	8	15	8	0	.239	.319
1 Danny Litwhiler	OF34	R	26	36	139	23	36	6	0	5	17	11	14	1	.259	.410
Earl Naylor	OF33	R	24	33	120	12	21	2	0	3	14	12	16	1	.175	.267
Bob Finley	C24	R	27	28	81	9	21	2	0	1	7	4	10	0	.259	.321
Paul Busby	OF10	L	24	26	40	13	10	1	0	0	5	2	1	2	.250	.275
Andy Seminick	C22, OF1	R	22	22	72	9	13	2	0	2	5	7	22	0	.181	.292
1 Tom Padden	C16	R	34	17	41	5	12	0	0	0	1	2	6	0	.293	.293
Chuck Klein	OF2	L	38	12	20	0	2	0	0	0	3	0	3	1	.100	.100

Benny Culp 29 R 5-24, Garton Del Savio 29 R 1-11

NAME	T	AGE	W	L	PCT	SV	G	GS	CG	IP	H	BB	SO	ShO	ERA
TOTALS		31	64	90	.416	14	157	157	66	1393	1430	451	431	11	3.79
Schoolboy Rowe	R	33	14	8	.636	1	27	25	11	199	194	29	52	3	2.94
2 Dick Barrett	R	36	10	9	.526	1	23	20	10	169	137	51	65	2	2.40
Al Gerheauser	L	26	10	19	.345	0	38	31	11	215	222	70	92	2	3.60
Tex Kraus	L	25	9	15	.375	2	34	25	10	200	197	78	48	1	3.15
Si Johnson (MS)	R	36	8	3	.727	2	21	14	9	113	110	25	46	1	3.27
1 Johnny Podgajny	R	23	4	4	.500	0	13	5	3	64	77	16	13	0	4.22
1 Charley Fuchs	R	29	2	7	.222	1	17	9	4	78	76	34	12	1	4.27
Dick Conger	R	22	2	7	.222	0	13	10	2	55	72	24	18	0	6.05
Rogers McKee	L	16	1	0	1.000	0	4	1	1	13	12	5	1	0	6.23
2 Dutch Kietz	R	31	1	1	.500	2	21	0	0	36	42	15	10	0	6.50
2 Andy Karl	R	29	1	2	.333	0	9	2	0	27	44	11	4	0	7.00
2 Bill Lee	R	33	1	5	.167	3	13	7	2	61	70	21	17	0	4.57
2 Newt Kimball	R	28	1	6	.143	2	34	6	2	90	85	42	33	0	4.10
Ken Raffensberger	L	25	0	1	.000	0	1	1	1	8	7	2	3	0	1.13
Dale Matthewson	R	20	0	3	.000	0	11	1	0	26	26	8	8	0	4.85
George Eyrich (MS)	R	18	0	0	.000	0	9	0	0	19	23	9	5	0	3.32
Boom-Boom Beck	R	38	0	0	.000	0	4	0	0	14	24	5	3	0	9.64
Deacon Donahue	R	23	0	0	.000	0	2	0	0	4	4	1	1	0	4.50
Andy Lapihuska	R	20	0	0	.000	0	1	0	0	2	5	3	0	0	27.00
2 Manny Salvo	R	30	0	0	.000	0	1	0	0	.1	2	1	0	0	27.00
Bill Webb	R	29	0	0	.000	0	1	0	0	1	1	1	0	0	9.00

NEW YORK 8th 55-98 .359 49.5 — **MEL OTT**

NAME	G by POS	B	AGE	G	AB	R	H	2B	3B	HR	RBI	BB	SO	SB	BA	SA
TOTALS			31	156	5290	558	1309	153	33	81	517	480	470	35	.247	.335
1 Joe Orengo	1B82	R	28	83	266	28	58	8	2	6	29	36	46	1	.218	.331
Mickey Witek	2B153	R	27	153	622	68	195	17	0	6	55	41	23	1	.314	.370
Billy Jurges	SS99, 3B28	R	35	136	481	46	110	8	2	4	29	53	38	2	.229	.279
Dick Bartell	3B54, SS33	R	35	99	337	48	91	14	0	5	28	47	27	5	.270	.356
Mel Ott	OF111, 3B1	L	34	125	380	65	89	12	2	18	47	95	48	7	.234	.418
Johnny Rucker	OF117	L	26	132	505	56	138	19	4	2	46	22	44	4	.273	.339
2 Joe Medwick	OF74, 1B3	R	31	78	324	41	91	20	3	5	45	9	14	0	.281	.407
Gus Mancuso	C77	R	37	94	252	11	50	5	0	2	20	28	16	0	.198	.242
Sid Gordon	3B53, 1B41, OF28, 2B3	R	25	131	474	50	119	9	11	9	63	43	32	2	.251	.373
Buster Maynard	OF74, 3B22	R	30	121	393	43	81	8	2	9	32	24	27	3	.206	.305
Ernie Lombardi	C73	R	35	104	295	19	90	7	0	10	51	16	11	1	.305	.431
Nap Reyes	1B38, 3B1	R	23	40	125	13	32	4	2	0	13	4	12	2	.256	.320
1 Babe Barna	OF31	L	28	40	113	11	23	5	1	1	12	16	9	3	.204	.292
Charlie Mead	OF37	L	22	37	146	9	40	6	1	1	13	10	15	3	.274	.349
Buddy Kerr	SS27	R	20	27	98	14	28	3	0	2	12	8	5	1	.286	.378
Ray Berres	C17	R	35	20	28	1	4	1	0	0	0	1	2	0	.143	.179
Joe Stephenson	C6	R	22	9	24	4	6	1	0	0	1	0	5	0	.250	.292
Vic Bradford	OF1	R	28	6	5	1	1	0	0	0	1	1	1	0	.200	.200
1 Hugh Poland	C4	L	30	4	12	1	1	0	1	0	2	1	0	0	.083	.250

NAME	T	AGE	W	L	PCT	SV	G	GS	CG	IP	H	BB	SO	ShO	ERA
TOTALS		29	55	98	.359	19	156	156	35	1395	1473	626	588	6	4.08
Ace Adams	R	31	11	7	.611	9	70	3	1	140	121	55	46	0	2.83
Cliff Melton (EJ)	L	31	9	13	.409	0	34	28	6	186	184	69	55	2	3.19
1 Bill Lohrman	R	30	5	6	.455	1	17	12	3	80	110	25	16	0	5.11
Rube Fischer	R	26	5	10	.333	1	22	17	4	131	140	59	47	0	4.60
Johnnie Wittig	R	29	5	15	.250	4	40	22	4	164	171	76	56	1	4.23
Carl Hubbell (SA)	L	40	4	4	.500	0	12	11	3	66	87	24	31	0	4.91
Harry Feldman	R	23	4	5	.444	0	31	10	1	105	114	58	49	0	4.29
2 Ken Chase	L	29	4	12	.250	0	21	20	4	129	140	74	86	1	4.12
Van Lingle Mungo	R	32	3	7	.300	2	45	13	2	154	140	79	83	2	3.92
Bill Voiselle	R	24	1	2	.333	0	4	4	3	31	18	14	19	0	2.03
1 Bill Sayles	R	25	1	3	.250	0	18	3	1	53	60	23	38	0	4.75
Hugh East (MS)	R	23	1	3	.250	0	13	5	1	40	51	25	21	0	5.40
2 Johnny Allen	R	38	1	3	.250	2	15	0	0	41	37	14	24	0	3.07
Ken Trinkle	R	23	1	5	.167	0	11	6	1	46	51	15	10	0	3.72
Bobby Coombs	R	35	0	1	.000	0	9	0	0	16	33	8	5	0	12.94
Frank Seward	R	22	0	1	.000	0	1	1	1	9	12	5	2	0	3.00
Tom Sunkel	L	30	0	1	.000	0	1	1	0	3	4	3	0	0	9.00

WORLD SERIES – NEW YORK (AL) 4 ST. LOUIS (NL) 1

LINE SCORES

TEAM	1	2	3	4	5	6	7	8	9	10	11	12	R	H	E
Game 1 October 5 at New York															
STL (NL)	0	1	0	0	1	0	0	0	0				2	7	2
NY (AL)	0	0	0	2	0	2	0	0	X				4	8	2
Lanier, Brecheen (8) — **Chandler**															
Game 2 October 6 at New York															
STL	0	0	1	3	0	0	0	0	0				4	7	2
NY	0	0	0	1	0	0	0	0	2				3	6	0
M. Cooper — Bonham, Murphy (9)															
Game 3 October 7 at New York															
STL	0	0	0	2	0	0	0	0	0				2	6	4
NY	0	0	0	0	0	1	0	5	X				6	8	0
Brazle, Krist (8), Brecheen (8) — **Borowy**, Murphy (9)															
Game 4 October 10 at St. Louis															
NY	0	0	0	1	0	0	0	1	0				2	6	2
STL	0	0	0	0	0	0	1	0	0				1	7	1
Russo — Lanier, Brecheen (8)															
Game 5 October 11 at St. Louis															
NY	0	0	0	0	0	2	0	0	0				2	7	1
STL	0	0	0	0	0	0	0	0	0				0	10	1
Chandler — M. Cooper, Lanier (8), Dickson (9)															

COMPOSITE BATTING

NAME	POS	G	AB	R	H	2B	3B	HR	RBI	BA
New York (AL)										
Totals		5	159	17	35	5	2	2	14	.220
Johnson	3B	5	20	3	6	1	1	0	3	.300
Etten	1B	5	19	0	2	0	0	0	2	.105
Dickey	C	5	18	1	5	0	0	1	4	.278
Crosetti	SS	5	18	4	5	0	0	0	1	.278
Keller	OF	5	18	3	4	0	1	0	2	.222
Gordon	2B	5	17	2	4	1	0	1	2	.235
Stainback	OF	5	17	0	3	0	0	0	0	.176
Lindell	OF	4	9	1	1	0	0	0	0	.111
Metheny	OF	2	8	0	1	0	0	0	0	.125
Chandler	P	2	6	0	1	0	0	0	0	.167
Russo	P	1	3	1	2	2	0	0	0	.667
Borowy	P	1	2	1	1	1	0	0	0	.500
Bonham	P	1	2	0	0	0	0	0	0	.000
Stirnweiss	PH	1	1	1	0	0	0	0	0	.000
Weatherly	PH	1	1	0	0	0	0	0	0	.000
Murphy	P	2	0	0	0	0	0	0	0	.000
St. Louis (NL)										
Totals		5	165	9	37	5	0	2	8	.224
Klein	2B	5	22	0	3	0	0	0	0	.136
Musial	OF	5	18	2	5	0	0	0	0	.278
Kurowski	3B	5	18	2	4	1	0	0	1	.222
Walker	OF	5	18	0	3	1	0	0	0	.167
Sanders	1B	5	17	3	5	0	0	1	2	.294
W. Cooper	C	5	17	1	5	0	0	0	0	.294
Litwhiler	OF	5	15	0	4	1	0	0	2	.267
Marion	SS	5	14	1	5	2	0	1	2	.357
Garms	OF	2	5	0	0	0	0	0	0	.000
M. Cooper	P	2	5	0	0	0	0	0	0	.000
Lanier	P	3	4	0	1	0	0	0	1	.250
Hopp	OF	1	4	0	0	0	0	0	0	.000
O'Dea	C	2	3	0	2	0	0	0	0	.667
Brazle	P	1	3	0	0	0	0	0	0	.000
Demaree	PH	1	1	0	0	0	0	0	0	.000
Narron	PH	1	1	0	0	0	0	0	0	.000
Brecheen	P	3	0	0	0	0	0	0	0	.000
Dickson	P	1	0	0	0	0	0	0	0	.000
Krist	P	1	0	0	0	0	0	0	0	.000
White	PR	1	0	0	0	0	0	0	0	.000

COMPOSITE PITCHING

NAME	G	IP	H	BB	SO	W	L	SV	ERA
New York (AL)									
Totals	5	45	37	11	26	4	1	1	1.40
Chandler	2	18	17	3	10	2	0	0	0.50
Russo	1	9	7	1	2	1	0	0	0.00
Borowy	1	8	6	3	4	1	0	0	2.25
Bonham	1	8	6	3	9	0	1	0	4.50
Murphy	2	2	1	1	1	0	0	1	0.00
St. Louis (NL)									
Totals	5	43	35	12	30	1	4	0	2.51
M. Cooper	2	16	11	3	10	1	1	0	2.81
Lanier	3	15.1	13	3	13	0	1	0	1.76
Brazle	1	7.1	5	2	4	0	1	0	3.68
Brecheen	3	3.2	5	3	3	0	1	0	2.45
Dickson	1	0.2	0	1	0	0	0	0	0.00
Krist	1	0	0	0	0	0	0	0	0.00

1944 Meet Me in St. Louis, Louie . . .

Part of the story of 1944 was the war and the absentee stars. But there were more intricate parts to the tale than the war itself. The main theme was whether or not a 44-year-old tenant of the junior circuit would finally win a pennant. The protagonists in the affair were the St. Louis Browns. The Detroit Tigers assumed the role of antagonists, and the New York Yankees chose the part of catalyst. It was a perfect script with an outcome so exciting that if it hadn't unfolded before the eyes of the country, no one would have believed it.

The main characters included Detroit's Hal Newhouser and Dizzy Trout, and the Browns' Vern Stephens, Nels Potter, and Sig Jakucki, the last of whom pitched in seven games in 1936, went to the minors until 1938, and then voluntarily retired until showing up again in 1944 with a lifetime 0-3 major league record. Jakucki's return, if anything, was simply for the benefit of giving the Browns a full squad.

An indication of what September would bring began early in April as the Browns jumped off to a sudden start. It was so sudden, in fact, that the experts considered it a fluke. What the Browns did was to win their first nine games, a feat no other team in baseball had been able to accomplish.

Until late September, the American League race was a four-team flight among Boston, St. Louis, Detroit, and New York, but the Red Sox—after losing Tex Hughson and Bobby Doerr to the war—could not maintain the blistering pace. In the final week of the season, a blanket could literally be thrown over the other three contenders. Then, on the 27th, Detroit opened a little daylight by moving one game over the Browns and three over the Yankees. Rain washed out the games the next day and, on the 29th, the Yankees moved into St. Louis for a twin bill, while Detroit hooked up with Washington for two games. After the Browns came from behind to take the opener, Nels Potter pitched a brilliant six-hit, 1-0 shutout in the nightcap. Detroit could only manage a split and entered the final two days of the season with the same 87-65 record as St. Louis. On the 30th, Denny Galehouse blanked the Yankees, 2-0, while Newhouser kept the Tigers even with his 29th victory. On closing day, October 1, Detroit sent Trout after his 28th victory, but Washington and Dutch Leonard proved too much as the Tigers lost 4-1. At Sportsman's Park, the Browns gave the call to Jakucki, who was looking for his 13th victory. The Browns were behind, 2-0, in the fourth inning without a hit off Yankee rookie Mel Queen when Mike Kreevich got things started with a single and Chet Laabs followed with a homer. Then, in the fifth inning, Kreevich came up with two outs and again singled, followed by Laabs, who hit a 3-1 pitch into the bleachers. The Browns added another run in the eighth on Vern Stephens' homer and suddenly found themselves going to a World Series. Detroit's one consolation came when Newhouser won MVP honors—beating out Trout by four points.

Accompanying the Browns in the fall classic were their city rivals—the St. Louis Cardinals—who won their third pennant in a row in the most one-sided race in the National League in 40 years. In chalking up their 105 victories, the Cardinals proved untouchable. They spent only four days out of first place all season, won 73 of their first 100 games, and had more victories on September 1, (91), than the American League winner had at the close. The team also established an all-time record for fewest errors, with 112, and became the first National League team to win over 100 games three years in a row. To top it off, shortstop Marty Marion beat out Chicago's Bill Nicholson 190-189 in the MVP voting to give the Cardinals the distinction of capturing the honors for the third straight time.

The magic which carried the Browns to a pennant was not enough when it came to contending with the Cardinals. The Browns lost the World Series in six games, but for the fans of St. Louis it was not a difficult thing to swallow. After all, how could they get worked up when the final result showed St. Louis as champions of the world?

1944 AMERICAN LEAGUE

NAME	G by POS	B	AGE	G	AB	R	H	2B	3B	HR	RBI	BB	SO	SB	BA	SA
ST. LOUIS 1st 89-65 .578		LUKE SEWELL														
TOTALS			30	154	5269	684	1328	223	45	72	628	531	604	44	.252	.352
George McQuinn	1B146	L	35	146	516	83	129	26	3	11	72	85	74	4	.250	.376
Don Gutteridge	2B146	R	32	148	603	89	148	27	11	3	36	51	63	20	.245	.342
Vern Stephens	SS143	R	23	145	559	91	164	32	1	20	**109**	62	54	2	.293	.462
Mark Christman	3B145, 1B3	R	30	148	547	56	148	25	1	6	83	47	37	5	.271	.353
Gene Moore	OF98, 1B1	L	34	110	390	56	93	13	6	6	58	24	37	0	.238	.349
Milt Byrnes	OF122	L	27	128	407	63	120	20	4	4	45	68	50	1	.295	.393
Mike Kreevich	OF100	R	36	105	402	55	121	15	6	5	44	27	24	3	.301	.405
Red Hayworth	C86	R	29	89	269	20	60	11	1	1	25	10	13	0	.223	.283
Al Zarilla	OF79	L	25	100	288	43	86	13	6	6	45	29	33	1	.299	.448
Frank Mancuso	C87	R	26	88	244	19	50	11	0	1	24	20	32	1	.205	.262
Chet Laabs	OF55	R	32	66	201	28	47	10	2	5	23	29	33	3	.234	.378
Floyd Baker	2B17, SS16	L	27	44	97	10	17	3	0	0	5	11	5	2	.175	.206
Mike Chartak	1B12, OF7	L	28	35	72	8	17	2	1	1	7	6	9	0	.236	.333
Ellis Clary	3B11, 2B6	R	27	25	49	6	13	1	1	0	4	12	9	1	.265	.327
1 Hal Epps	OF18	L	30	22	62	15	11	1	1	0	3	14	14	0	.177	.226
Frank Demaree	OF16	R	34	16	51	4	13	2	0	0	6	6	3	0	.255	.294
2 Tom Turner	C11	R	27	15	25	2	8	1	0	0	4	2	5	0	.320	.360
Tom Hafey	OF4, 1B1	R	30	8	14	1	5	2	0	0	2	1	4	0	.357	.500
Joe Schultz	C3	L	25	3	8	1	2	0	0	0	0	0	1	0	.250	.250
Babe Martin	OF1	R	24	2	4	0	3	1	0	0	1	0	0	0	.750	1.000
Len Schulte		R	27	1	0	0	0	0	0	0	0	1	0	0	.000	.000
DETROIT 2nd 88-66 .571 1		STEVE O'NEILL														
TOTALS			32	156	5344	658	1405	220	44	60	591	**532**	500	61	.263	.354
Rudy York	1B151	R	30	151	583	77	161	27	7	18	98	68	73	5	.276	.439
Eddie Mayo	2B143, SS11	L	34	154	607	76	151	18	3	5	63	57	23	9	.249	.313
Joe Hoover	SS119, 2B1	R	29	120	441	67	104	20	2	0	29	35	66	7	.236	.290
Pinky Higgins	3B146	R	35	148	543	79	161	32	4	7	76	81	34	4	.297	.409
Jimmy Outlaw	OF137	R	31	139	535	69	146	20	6	3	57	41	40	7	.273	.350
Doc Cramer	OF141	L	38	143	578	69	169	20	9	2	42	37	21	6	.292	.369
Dick Wakefield (MS)	OF78	L	23	78	276	53	98	15	5	12	53	55	29	2	.355	.576
Paul Richards	C90	R	35	95	300	24	71	13	0	3	37	35	30	8	.237	.310
Chuck Hostetler	OF65	L	40	90	265	42	79	9	2	0	20	21	31	4	.298	.347
Bob Swift	C76	R	29	80	247	15	63	11	1	1	19	27	27	2	.255	.320
Don Ross	OF37, SS2, 1B1	R	29	66	167	14	35	5	0	2	15	14	9	2	.210	.275
Dizzy Trout	P49	R	29	51	133	18	36	4	1	5	24	9	28	2	.271	.429
Joe Orengo	SS29, 3B11, 1B5, 2B2	R	29	46	154	14	31	10	0	0	10	20	29	1	.201	.266
1 Charlie Hetro	OF20	R	25	38	78	8	15	0	1	0	5	3	10	1	.192	.218
Al Unser	2B5, C1	R	31	11	25	2	3	0	1	1	5	3	2	0	.120	.320
Red Borom	2B4, SS1	L	28	7	14	1	1	0	0	0	1	2	2	0	.071	.071
Don Heffner	2B5	R	33	6	19	0	4	1	0	0	1	5	1	0	.211	.263
Hack Miller	C5	R	33	5	5	1	1	0	0	1	3	1	1	0	.200	.800
Bubba Floyd	SS3	R	27	3	9	1	4	1	0	0	0	1	0	0	.444	.556
John McHale (MS) 22 L 0-1, Jack Sullivan 26 R 0-1																
NEW YORK 3rd 83-71 .539 6		JOE McCARTHY														
TOTALS			30	154	5331	674	1410	216	**74**	**96**	631	523	**627**	91	.264	**.387**
Nick Etten	1B154	L	30	154	573	88	168	25	4	**22**	91	**97**	29	4	.293	.466
Snuffy Stirnweiss	2B154	R	25	154	643	**125**	**205**	35	**16**	8	43	73	87	**55**	.319	.460
Mike Milosevich	SS91	R	29	94	312	27	77	11	4	0	32	30	37	1	.247	.308
Oscar Grimes	3B97, SS20	R	29	116	387	44	108	17	8	5	46	59	57	6	.279	.403
Bud Metheny	OF132	L	29	137	518	72	124	16	1	14	67	56	57	5	.239	.355
Johnny Lindell	OF149	R	27	149	594	91	178	33	**16**	18	103	44	56	5	.300	.500
Hersh Martin	OF80	B	34	85	328	49	99	12	4	9	47	34	26	5	.302	.445
Mike Garbark	C85	R	28	89	299	23	78	9	4	1	33	25	27	0	.261	.328
Rollie Hemsley (MS)	C76	R	37	81	284	23	76	12	5	2	26	9	13	0	.268	.366
Don Savage	3B60	R	25	71	239	31	63	7	5	4	24	20	41	1	.264	.385
Frankie Crosetti (VR)	SS55	R	33	55	197	20	47	4	2	5	30	11	21	3	.239	.355
Ed Levy	OF36	R	27	40	153	12	37	11	2	4	29	6	19	1	.242	.418
Russ Derry	OF28	L	27	38	114	14	29	3	0	4	14	20	19	1	.254	.386
1 Larry Rosenthal	OF26	L	32	36	101	9	20	3	0	0	9	19	15	1	.198	.228
Tuck Stainback	OF24	R	33	30	78	13	17	3	0	0	5	3	7	1	.218	.256
2 Johnny Cooney	OF2	R	43	10	8	1	1	0	0	0	1	1	0	0	.125	.125
2 Paul Waner		L	41	9	7	1	1	0	0	0	1	2	1	1	.143	.143
Bill Drescher	C1	L	23	4	7	0	1	0	0	0	0	0	0	0	.143	.143
Bob Collins	C3	R	34	3	3	0	1	0	0	0	0	1	0	0	.333	.333
Charlie Keller (MM) 27																

NAME	T	AGE	W	L	PCT	SV	G	GS	CG	IP	H	BB	SO	ShO	ERA
		31	**89**	65	**.578**	17	154	154	71	1397	1392	469	**581**	16	3.17
Nels Potter	R	32	19	7	.731	0	32	29	16	232	211	70	91	3	2.83
Jack Kramer	R	26	17	13	.567	0	33	31	18	257	233	75	124	1	2.49
Bob Muncrief	R	28	13	8	.619	1	33	27	12	219	216	50	88	3	3.08
Sig Jakucki	R	34	13	9	.591	3	35	24	12	198	211	54	67	4	3.55
Denny Galehouse	R	32	9	10	.474	0	24	19	6	153	162	44	80	2	3.12
George Caster	R	36	6	6	.500	**12**	42	0	0	81	91	33	46	0	2.44
Tex Shirley	R	26	5	4	.556	0	23	11	2	80	59	64	35	1	4.16
Al Hollingsworth	L	36	5	7	.417	1	26	10	3	93	108	37	22	2	4.45
Steve Sundra (MS)	R	34	2	0	1.000	0	3	3	2	19	15	4	1	0	1.42
Willis Hudlin (MS)	R	38	0	1	.000	0	1	0	0	2	3	0	1	0	4.50
Sam Zoldak	L	25	0	0	.000	0	18	0	0	39	49	19	15	0	3.69
Lefty West	L	28	0	0	.000	0	11	0	0	24	34	19	11	0	6.37
		29	88	66	.571	8	156	156	**87**	1400	1373	452	568	**20**	**3.09**
Hal Newhouser	L	23	**29**	9	.763	2	47	34	25	312	264	102	**187**	6	2.22
Dizzy Trout	R	29	27	14	.659	0	49	**40**	**33**	**352**	**314**	83	144	**7**	**2.12**
Rufe Gentry	R	26	12	14	.462	0	37	30	10	204	211	**108**	68	3	4.24
Stubby Overmire	L	25	11	11	.500	1	32	28	11	200	214	41	57	3	3.06
Johnny Gorsica	R	29	6	14	.300	4	34	19	8	162	192	32	47	1	4.11
Joe Orrell	R	27	2	1	.667	0	10	2	0	22	26	11	10	0	2.45
Boom-Boom Beck	R	39	1	2	.333	1	28	2	0	74	67	27	25	0	3.89
Bob Gillespie	R	25	0	1	.000	0	7	0	0	11	7	12	4	0	6.55
Jake Mooty	R	31	0	0	.000	0	15	0	0	28	35	18	7	0	4.50
Roy Henshaw	L	32	0	0	.000	0	7	1	0	12	17	6	10	0	9.00
Zeb Eaton	R	24	0	0	.000	0	6	0	0	16	19	8	4	0	5.63
Chief Hogsett	L	40	0	0	.000	0	3	0	0	6	7	4	5	0	0.00
		30	83	71	539	13	154	154	78	1390	1351	532	529	9	3.39
Hank Borowy	R	28	17	12	.586	2	35	30	19	253	224	88	107	3	2.63
Atley Donald	R	33	13	10	.565	0	30	19	9	159	173	59	48	0	3.34
Monk Dubiel	R	25	13	13	.500	0	30	28	19	232	217	86	79	3	3.38
Ernie Bonham	R	30	12	9	.571	0	26	25	17	214	228	41	54	1	2.99
Mel Queen	R	26	6	3	.667	0	10	10	4	82	68	34	30	1	3.29
Bill Zuber	R	31	5	7	.417	0	22	13	2	107	101	54	59	1	4.21
Joe Page	L	26	5	7	.417	0	19	16	4	103	100	52	63	0	4.54
Bill Bevens	R	27	4	1	.800	0	8	5	3	44	44	13	16	0	2.66
Steve Roser	R	26	4	3	.571	1	16	6	1	84	80	34	34	0	3.86
Jim Turner	R	40	4	4	.500	7	35	0	0	42	42	22	13	0	3.43
Johnny Johnson	L	29	0	2	.000	3	22	1	0	27	25	24	11	0	4.00
Al Lyons (MS)	R	25	0	0	.000	0	11	0	0	40	43	24	14	0	4.50
Spud Chandler (MS)	R	36	0	0	.000	0	1	1	0	6	6	1	1	0	4.50
Johnny Murphy (VR) 35															
Butch Wensloff (VR) 28															

BOSTON 4th 77-77 .500 12 — JOE CRONIN

NAME	G by POS	B	AGE	G	AB	R	H	2B	3B	HR	RBI	BB	SO	SB	BA	SA
TOTALS			30	156	5400	739	1456	277	56	69	691	522	505	60	.270	.380
Lou Finney(VR)	1B59, OF2	L	33	68	251	37	72	11	2	0	32	23	7	1	.287	.347
Bobby Doerr(MS)	2B125	R	26	125	468	95	152	30	10	15	81	58	31	5	.325	.528
Skeeter Newsome	SS126, 2B8, 3B1	R	33	136	472	41	114	26	3	0	41	33	21	4	.242	.309
Jim Tabor (MS)	3B114	R	30	116	438	58	125	25	3	13	72	31	38	4	.285	.445
Pete Fox	OF119	R	34	121	496	70	156	38	6	1	64	27	34	10	.315	.421
Catfish Metkovich	OF82, 1B50	L	22	134	549	94	152	28	8	9	59	31	57	13	.277	.406
Bob Johnson	OF142	R	37	144	525	106	170	40	8	17	106	95	67	2	.324	.528
Roy Partee	C85	R	26	89	280	18	68	12	0	2	41	37	29	0	.243	.307
Jim Bucher	3B44, 2B21	L	33	80	277	39	76	9	2	4	31	19	13	3	.274	.365
Joe Cronin	1B49	R	37	76	191	24	46	7	0	5	28	34	19	1	.241	.356
Leon Culberson	OF72	R	24	75	282	41	67	11	5	2	21	20	20	6	.238	.333
Tom McBride	OF57, 1B5	R	29	71	216	29	53	7	3	0	24	8	13	4	.245	.306
2 Hal Wagner (MS)	C64	L	28	66	223	21	74	13	4	1	38	29	14	1	.332	.439
Joe Bowman	P26	L	34	59	100	7	20	5	2	0	16	5	19	1	.200	.290
Eddie Lake	SS41, P6, 2B3, 3B1	R	28	57	126	21	26	5	0	0	8	23	22	5	.206	.246
Bill Conroy	C19	R	29	19	47	6	10	2	0	0	4	11	9	0	.213	.255
Johnny Lazor	OF6, C1	L	31	16	24	0	2	1	0	0	0	1	0	0	.083	.125
1 Ford Garrison	OF12	R	28	13	49	5	12	3	0	0	2	6	4	0	.245	.306
1 Johnny Peacock	C2	L	34	4	4	0	0	0	0	0	0	0	0	0	.000	.000

NAME	T	AGE	W	L	PCT	SV	G	GS	CG	IP	H	BB	SO	ShO	ERA
TOTALS		31	77	77	.500	17	156	156	58	1394	1404	592	524	5	3.82
Tex Hughson (MS)	R	28	18	5	.783	5	28	23	19	203	172	41	112	2	2.26
Mike Ryba	R	41	12	7	.632	2	42	7	2	138	119	39	50	0	3.33
Joe Bowman	R	34	12	8	.600	0	26	24	10	168	175	64	53	1	4.82
Frank Barrett	R	31	8	7	.533	8	38	2	0	90	93	42	40	0	3.70
Yank Terry	R	33	6	10	.375	0	27	17	3	133	142	65	30	0	4.20
Emmett O'Neill	R	26	6	11	.353	0	28	22	8	152	154	89	68	1	4.62
Rex Cecil	R	27	4	5	.444	0	11	9	4	61	72	33	33	0	5.16
Clem Hausmann	R	24	4	7	.364	2	32	12	3	137	139	69	43	0	3.42
Pinky Woods	R	29	4	8	.333	0	38	20	5	171	171	88	56	1	3.26
Clem Dreisewerd	L	28	2	4	.333	0	7	7	3	49	52	9	9	0	4.04
Oscar Judd	L	36	1	1	.500	0	9	6	1	30	30	15	9	0	3.60
Joe Wood	R	28	0	1	.000	0	3	1	0	10	13	3	5	0	6.30
Vic Johnson	L	23	0	3	.000	0	7	5	0	27	42	15	7	0	6.33
Eddie Lake	R	28	0	0	.000	0	6	0	0	19	20	11	7	0	4.26
1 Lou Lucier	R	26	0	0	.000	0	3	0	0	5	7	7	2	0	5.40
Stan Partenheimer	L	21	0	0	.000	0	1	1	0	1	3	2	0	0	18.00

CLEVELAND 5th (Tie) 72-82 .468 17 — LOU BOUDREAU

NAME	G by POS	B	AGE	G	AB	R	H	2B	3B	HR	RBI	BB	SO	SB	BA	SA
TOTALS			28	155	5481	643	1458	270	50	70	611	512	593	48	.266	.372
Mickey Rocco	1B155	L	28	155	653	87	174	29	7	13	70	56	51	4	.266	.392
Ray Mack	2B83	R	27	83	284	24	66	15	3	0	29	28	45	4	.232	.306
Lou Boudreau	SS149, C1	R	26	150	584	91	191	45	5	3	67	73	39	11	.327	.437
Ken Keltner	3B149	R	27	149	573	74	169	41	9	13	91	53	29	4	.295	.466
Roy Cullenbine	OF151	B	28	154	571	98	162	34	5	16	80	87	49	4	.284	.445
Oris Hockett	OF110	L	34	124	457	47	132	29	5	1	50	35	27	8	.289	.381
Pat Seerey	OF86	R	21	101	342	39	80	16	0	15	39	19	99	0	.234	.412
Buddy Rosar	C98	R	29	99	331	29	87	9	3	0	30	34	17	1	.263	.308
Rusty Peters	2B63, SS13, 3B8	R	29	88	282	23	63	13	3	1	24	15	35	2	.223	.301
Paul O'Dea	OF41, 1B3, P3	L	23	76	173	25	55	9	0	0	13	23	21	2	.318	.370
2 Myril Hoag	OF66	R	36	67	277	33	79	9	3	1	27	25	23	6	.285	.350
Jimmy Grant	2B20, 3B4	L	25	61	99	12	27	4	3	1	12	11	20	1	.273	.404
Jeff Heath	OF37	L	29	60	151	20	50	5	2	5	33	18	12	0	.331	.490
Norm Schlueter	C43	R	27	49	122	2	15	4	0	0	11	12	22	0	.123	.156
George Susce	C29	R	35	29	61	3	14	1	0	0	4	2	5	0	.230	.246
Jim McDonnell	C13	L	21	20	43	5	10	0	0	0	4	4	3	0	.233	.233
Russ Lyon	C3	R	31	7	11	1	2	0	0	0	0	1	1	0	.182	.182

Hank Ruszkowski 18 R 3-8, Steve Biras 22 R 2-2, Jim Devlin 21 L 0-1, Les Fleming (VR) 28

NAME	T	AGE	W	L	PCT	SV	G	GS	CG	IP	H	BB	SO	ShO	ERA
TOTALS		31	72	82	.468	18	155	155	48	1419	1428	621	524	7	3.65
Mel Harder	R	34	12	10	.545	0	30	27	12	196	211	69	64	2	3.72
Allie Reynolds	R	29	11	8	.579	1	28	21	5	158	141	91	84	1	3.30
Eddie Klieman	R	26	11	13	.458	5	47	19	5	178	185	70	44	1	3.39
Steve Gromek	R	24	10	9	.526	1	35	21	12	204	160	70	115	2	2.56
Joe Heving	R	43	8	3	.727	10	63	1	0	120	106	41	46	0	1.95
Al Smith	L	36	7	13	.350	0	28	26	7	182	197	69	44	1	3.41
Jim Bagby (MM)	R	27	4	5	.444	0	13	10	2	79	101	34	12	0	4.33
Ray Poat	R	26	4	8	.333	1	36	6	1	81	82	37	40	0	5.11
1 Vern Kennedy	R	37	2	5	.286	0	12	10	2	59	66	37	17	0	5.03
Earl Henry	L	27	1	1	.500	0	2	2	1	18	18	3	5	0	4.50
Hal Klein	L	21	1	2	.333	0	11	6	1	41	38	36	13	0	5.71
Paul Calvert	R	26	1	3	.250	0	35	4	0	77	89	38	31	0	4.56
Red Embree	R	26	0	1	.000	0	3	1	0	3	2	5	4	0	15.00
Bill Bonness	L	20	0	1	.000	0	2	1	0	7	11	5	1	0	7.71
1 Mike Naymick	R	26	0	0	.000	0	7	0	0	13	16	10	4	0	9.69
Paul O'Dea	L	23	0	0	.000	0	3	0	0	4	5	6	0	0	2.25

PHILADELPHIA 5th (Tie) 72-82 .468 17 — CONNIE MACK

NAME	G by POS	B	AGE	G	AB	R	H	2B	3B	HR	RBI	BB	SO	SB	BA	SA
TOTALS			29	155	5312	525	1364	169	47	36	475	422	490	42	.257	.327
Bill McGhee	1B75	L	35	77	287	27	83	12	0	1	19	21	20	2	.289	.341
Irv Hall	2B97, SS40, 1B4	R	25	143	559	60	150	20	8	0	45	31	46	2	.268	.333
Ed Busch	SS111, 2B27, 3B4	R	26	140	484	41	131	11	3	0	40	29	17	5	.271	.306
George Kell	3B139	R	21	139	514	51	138	15	3	0	44	22	23	5	.268	.309
1 Jo-Jo White	OF74, SS1	L	35	85	267	30	59	4	2	1	21	40	27	5	.221	.262
Bobby Estalella	OF128, 1B6	R	33	140	506	54	151	17	9	7	60	59	60	3	.298	.409
2 Ford Garrison	OF119	R	28	121	449	58	121	13	2	4	37	22	40	10	.269	.334
Frankie Hayes	C155, 1B1	R	29	155	581	62	144	18	6	13	78	57	59	2	.248	.367
Dick Siebert	1B74, OF58	L	32	132	468	52	143	27	5	6	52	62	17	2	.306	.423
2 Hal Epps	OF60	L	30	67	229	27	60	8	8	0	13	18	18	2	.262	.367
Joe Rullo	2B33, 1B1	R	28	35	96	5	16	0	0	0	5	6	19	1	.167	.167
2 Larry Rosenthal	OF19	L	32	32	54	5	11	2	0	1	6	5	9	0	.204	.296
Woody Wheaton	P11, OF8	L	29	30	59	1	11	2	0	0	5	5	3	1	.186	.220
Joe Burns	3B17, 2B9	R	29	28	75	5	18	2	0	1	8	4	8	0	.240	.307
Bill Burgo	OF22	R	24	27	88	6	21	2	0	1	3	7	3	1	.239	.295
2 Charlie Metro	OF11, 3B5, 2B2	R	25	24	40	4	4	0	0	0	1	7	6	0	.100	.100
Bobby Wilkins	SS9	R	21	24	25	7	6	0	0	0	3	1	4	0	.240	.240
Lew Flick	OF6	L	29	19	35	1	4	0	0	0	2	1	2	1	.114	.114
Bob Garbark	C15	R	34	18	23	2	6	2	0	0	2	1	0	0	.261	.348
Bill Mills	C1	R	23	5	4	0	1	0	0	0	0	1	1	0	.250	.250
1 Hal Wagner	C1	L	28	5	4	0	1	0	0	0	0	0	0	0	.250	.250

Tony Parisse 33 R 0-4, Al Simmons 42 R 3-6, Jim Pruett 26 R 1-4, Hal Peck 27 L 2-8

NAME	T	AGE	W	L	PCT	SV	G	GS	CG	IP	H	BB	SO	ShO	ERA
TOTALS		30	72	82	.468	14	155	155	72	1398	1345	390	534	9	3.26
Russ Christopher	R	26	14	14	.500	1	35	24	13	215	200	63	84	1	2.97
Bobo Newsom	R	36	13	15	.464	1	37	33	18	265	243	82	142	2	2.82
Joe Berry	R	39	10	8	.556	12	53	0	0	111	78	23	44	0	1.95
Lum Harris	R	29	10	9	.526	0	23	22	12	174	193	26	33	2	3.31
Don Black	R	27	10	12	.455	0	29	27	8	177	177	75	78	0	4.07
Jesse Flores	R	29	9	11	.450	0	27	25	11	186	172	49	65	2	3.39
Luke Hamlin	R	39	6	12	.333	0	29	23	9	190	204	38	58	2	3.74
Woody Wheaton	L	29	0	1	.000	0	11	1	1	38	36	20	15	0	3.55
Carl Scheib	R	17	0	0	.000	0	15	0	0	36	36	11	13	0	4.25
John McGillen	L	24	0	0	.000	0	2	0	0	1	1	2	0	0	18.00
Tal Abernathy	L	22	0	0	.000	0	1	0	0	3	5	1	2	0	3.00

CHICAGO 7th 71-83 .461 18 — JIMMY DYKES

NAME	G by POS	B	AGE	G	AB	R	H	2B	3B	HR	RBI	BB	SO	SB	BA	SA
TOTALS			31	154	5292	543	1307	210	55	23	495	439	448	66	.247	.320
Hal Trosky	1B130	L	31	135	497	55	120	32	2	10	70	62	30	3	.241	.374
Roy Schalk	2B142, SS5	R	35	146	587	47	129	14	4	1	44	45	52	5	.220	.262
Skeeter Webb	SS135, 2B5	R	34	139	513	44	108	19	6	0	30	20	39	7	.211	.271
Ralph Hodgin	3B82, OF33	L	28	121	465	56	137	25	7	1	51	21	14	3	.295	.385
Wally Moses	OF134	L	33	136	535	82	150	26	9	3	34	52	22	21	.280	.379
Thurman Tucker	OF120	L	26	124	446	59	128	15	6	2	46	57	40	13	.287	.361
Eddie Carnett	OF88, 1B25, P2	L	27	126	457	51	126	18	8	1	60	26	35	5	.276	.357
Mike Tresh	C93	R	30	93	312	22	81	8	1	0	25	37	15	0	.260	.292
Guy Curtright	OF51	R	31	72	198	22	50	8	2	2	23	23	21	4	.253	.343
Grey Clarke	3B45	R	31	63	169	14	44	10	1	0	27	22	6	0	.260	.331
Johnny Dickshot	OF40	L	34	62	162	18	41	8	5	0	15	13	10	2	.253	.364
Tony Cuccinello	3B30, 2B6	R	36	38	130	5	34	3	0	0	17	8	16	0	.262	.285
1 Tom Turner	C36	R	27	36	113	9	26	6	0	2	13	5	16	0	.230	.336
Ed Lopat	P27	L	26	30	81	8	25	1	1	0	6	5	5	0	.309	.346
Vince Castino	C26	R	26	29	78	8	18	5	0	0	3	10	13	0	.231	.295
Cass Michaels	SS21, 3B3	R	18	27	68	4	12	4	1	0	5	2	5	0	.176	.265
1 Myril Hoag	OF14	R	36	17	48	5	11	1	0	0	4	10	1	1	.229	.250
Tom Jordan	C14	R	24	14	45	2	12	1	1	0	3	1	0	0	.267	.333
Bill Metzig	2B5	R	25	5	16	1	2	0	0	0	1	1	4	0	.125	.125

NAME	T	AGE	W	L	PCT	SV	G	GS	CG	IP	H	BB	SO	ShO	ERA
TOTALS		30	71	83	.461	17	154	154	64	1391	1411	420	481	5	3.58
Bill Dietrich	R	34	16	17	.485	0	36	36	15	246	269	68	70	2	3.62
Orval Grove	R	24	14	15	.483	0	34	33	11	235	237	71	105	2	3.71
Ed Lopat	L	26	11	10	.524	0	27	25	13	210	217	59	75	1	3.26
G. Maltzberger (AJ)	R	31	10	5	.667	12	46	0	0	91	81	19	49	0	2.97
John Humphries	R	29	8	10	.444	1	30	20	8	169	170	57	42	0	3.67
Joe Haynes	R	26	5	6	.455	2	33	12	8	154	148	43	44	0	2.57
Thornton Lee (BA)	L	37	3	9	.250	0	15	14	6	113	105	25	39	0	3.03
Jake Wade	L	32	2	4	.333	2	19	5	1	75	75	41	35	0	4.80
Buck Ross	R	29	2	7	.222	0	20	9	2	90	97	35	20	0	5.20
Eddie Carnett	L	27	0	0	.000	0	2	0	0	2	3	0	1	0	9.00
Don Hanski	L	28	0	0	.000	0	2	0	0	3	5	2	0	0	12.00
Floyd Speer	R	31	0	0	.000	0	2	0	0	2	4	0	1	0	9.00

WASHINGTON 8th 64-90 .416 25 — OSSIE BLUEGE

NAME	G by POS	B	AGE	G	AB	R	H	2B	3B	HR	RBI	BB	SO	SB	BA	SA
TOTALS			31	154	5319	592	1386	186	42	33	531	470	477	127	.261	.330
Joe Kuhel	1B138	L	38	139	518	90	144	26	7	4	51	68	40	11	.278	.378
George Myatt	2B121, SS15, OF3	L	30	140	538	86	153	19	6	0	40	54	44	26	.284	.342
John Sullivan	SS138	R	23	138	471	49	118	12	1	0	30	52	43	3	.251	.280
Gil Torres	3B123, 2B10, 1B4	R	28	134	524	42	140	20	6	0	58	21	24	10	.267	.328
Jake Powell	OF90, 3B1	R	35	96	367	29	88	9	1	1	37	16	26	7	.240	.278
Stan Spence	OF150, 1B3	L	29	153	592	83	187	31	8	18	100	69	20	3	.316	.486
George Case	OF114	R	28	119	465	63	116	14	2	2	32	49	22	49	.249	.301
Rick Ferrell	C96	R	38	99	339	14	94	11	1	0	25	46	13	2	.277	.316
Roberto Ortiz	OF80	R	29	85	316	36	80	11	4	5	35	19	47	4	.253	.361
Mike Guerra	C58, OF1	R	31	75	210	29	59	7	2	1	29	13	14	8	.281	.348
Bill LeFebvre	P24, 1B2	L	28	60	62	4	16	2	2	0	8	12	9	0	.258	.355
Hilly Layne	3B18, 2B3	L	26	33	87	6	17	2	0	0	8	6	10	2	.195	.218
Fred Vaughn	2B26, 3B3	R	25	30	109	10	28	2	1	1	21	9	24	2	.257	.321
Ed Boland	OF14	L	36	19	69	4	16	4	0	0	14	0	6	0	.271	.339
Ed Butka	1B14	R	28	15	41	1	8	1	0	0	1	2	11	0	.195	.220
Al Evans (MS)	C8	R	27	14	22	5	2	0	0	0	0	2	6	0	.091	.091
Joe Vosmik	OF12	R	34	14	36	2	7	2	0	0	9	2	3	0	.194	.250
Harlond Clift	3B12	R	31	12	44	4	7	3	0	0	3	3	3	0	.159	.227
Rene Monteagudo	OF9	L	28	10	38	2	11	2	0	0	4	0	1	0	.289	.342
Preston Gomez	2B2, SS2	R	21	8	7	2	2	1	0	0	2	0	4	0	.286	.429
Eddie Yost	3B3 SS2	R	17	7	14	3	2	0	0	0	0	1	2	0	.143	.143
George Binks	OF3	L	29	5	12	0	3	0	0	0	0	0	1	0	.250	.250

Luis Suarez 27 R 0-2, Armando Valdes 22 R 0-1

NAME	T	AGE	W	L	PCT	SV	G	GS	CG	IP	H	BB	SO	ShO	ERA
TOTALS		31	64	90	.416	11	154	154	83	1381	1410	475	503	12	3.49
Dutch Leonard	R	35	14	14	.500	0	32	31	17	229	222	37	62	3	3.07
Mickey Haefner	L	31	12	15	.444	1	31	28	18	228	221	71	86	3	3.04
Johnny Niggeling	R	40	10	8	.556	0	24	24	14	206	164	88	121	2	2.32
Alex Carrasquel	R	31	8	7	.533	2	43	7	3	134	143	50	35	0	3.43
Early Wynn (MS)	R	24	8	17	.320	2	33	25	19	208	221	67	65	2	3.38
Milo Candini	R	26	6	7	.462	1	28	10	4	103	110	49	31	2	4.11
Roger Wolff	R	33	4	15	.211	2	33	21	5	155	186	60	73	0	4.99
Bill LeFebvre	L	28	2	4	.333	3	24	4	2	70	86	21	18	0	4.50
Vern Curtis (MS)	R	24	0	1	.000	0	3	1	0	10	8	3	2	0	2.70
Baby Ortiz	R	24	0	2	.000	0	2	2	1	13	13	6	4	0	6.23
Jug Thesenga	R	30	0	0	.000	0	5	1	0	12	18	12	2	0	5.25
Sandy Ullrich	R	22	0	0	.000	0	3	0	0	10	17	4	2	0	9.00
Bill Zinser	R	26	0	0	.000	0	2	0	0	1	1	5	1	0	18.00
Walt Holborow	R	30	0	0	.000	0	1	0	0	3	0	2	1	0	0.00

ST. LOUIS 1st 105-49 .682 — BILLY SOUTHWORTH

NAME	G by POS	B	AGE	G	AB	R	H	2B	3B	HR	RBI	BB	SO	SB	BA	SA
TOTALS			27	157	5475	772	1507	274	59	100	720	544	473	37	.275	.402
Ray Sanders	1B152	L	27	154	601	87	177	34	9	12	102	71	50	2	.295	.441
Emil Verban	2B146	R	28	146	498	51	128	14	2	0	43	19	14	0	.257	.293
Marty Marion	SS144	R	26	144	506	50	135	26	2	6	63	43	50	1	.267	.362
Whitey Kurowski	3B146, 2B9, SS1	R	26	149	555	95	150	25	7	20	87	58	40	2	.270	.449
Stan Musial	OF146	L	23	146	568	112	197	51	14	12	94	90	28	7	.347	.549
Johnny Hopp	OF131, 1B6	L	27	139	527	106	177	35	9	11	72	58	47	15	.336	.499
Danny Litwhiler	OF136	R	27	140	492	53	130	25	5	15	82	37	56	2	.264	.427
Walker Cooper	C97	R	29	112	397	56	126	25	5	13	72	20	19	4	.317	.504
Ken O'Dea	C69	L	31	85	265	35	66	11	2	6	37	37	29	1	.249	.374
Augie Bergamo	OF50, 1B2	L	26	80	192	35	55	6	3	2	19	35	23	0	.286	.380
Debs Garms	OF23, 3B21	L	36	73	149	17	30	3	0	0	5	13	8	0	.201	.221
George Fallon	2B38, SS24, 3B6	R	27	69	141	16	28	6	0	1	9	16	11	1	.199	.262
Pepper Martin	OF29	R	40	40	86	15	24	4	0	2	4	15	11	2	.279	.395
John Antonelli	1B3, 3B3, 2B2	R	28	8	21	0	4	1	0	0	1	0	4	0	.190	.238
Bob Keely	C1	R	34	1	0	0	0	0	0	0	0	0	0	0	.000	.000

NAME	T	AGE	W	L	PCT	SV	G	GS	CG	IP	H	BB	SO	ShO	ERA
		28	105	49	.682	12	157	157	89	1427	1228	468	637	26	2.67
Mort Cooper	R	31	22	7	.759	1	34	33	22	252	227	60	97	7	2.46
Ted Wilks	R	28	17	4	.810	0	36	21	16	208	173	49	70	4	2.64
Max Lanier	L	28	17	12	.586	0	33	30	16	224	192	71	141	5	2.65
Harry Brecheen	L	29	16	5	.762	0	30	22	13	189	174	46	88	3	2.86
George Munger	R	25	11	3	.786	2	21	12	7	121	92	41	55	2	1.34
Freddy Schmidt	R	28	7	3	.700	5	37	9	3	114	94	58	58	2	3.16
Al Jurisich	R	22	7	9	.438	1	30	14	5	130	102	65	53	2	3.39
1 Harry Gumbert	R	34	4	2	.667	1	10	7	3	61	60	19	16	0	2.51
Blix Donnelly	R	30	2	1	.667	2	27	4	2	76	61	34	45	1	2.13
Bud Byerly	R	23	2	2	.500	0	9	4	2	42	37	20	13	0	3.43
Bill Trotter	R	35	0	1	.000	0	2	1	0	6	14	4	0	0	13.50
2 Mike Naymick	R	26	0	0	.000	0	1	0	0	2	2	1	1	0	4.50

PITTSBURGH 2nd 90-63 .588 14.5 — FRANKIE FRISCH

NAME	G by POS	B	AGE	G	AB	R	H	2B	3B	HR	RBI	BB	SO	SB	BA	SA
TOTALS			28	158	5428	744	1441	248	80	70	706	573	616	87	.265	.379
Babe Dahlgren	1B158	R	32	158	599	67	173	28	7	12	101	47	56	2	.289	.419
Pete Coscarart	2B136, SS4, OF1	R	31	139	554	89	146	30	4	4	42	41	57	10	.264	.354
Frankie Gustine	SS116, 2B11, 3B1	R	24	127	405	42	93	18	3	2	42	33	41	8	.230	.304
Bob Elliott	3B140, SS1	R	27	143	538	85	160	28	16	10	108	75	42	9	.297	.465
Johnny Barrett	OF147	L	28	149	568	99	153	24	19	7	83	86	56	28	.269	.415
Vince DiMaggio	OF101, 3B1	R	31	109	342	41	82	20	4	9	50	33	83	6	.240	.401
Jim Russell	OF149	B	25	152	580	109	181	34	14	8	66	70	63	6	.312	.460
Al Lopez	C115	R	35	115	331	27	76	12	1	1	34	34	24	4	.230	.281
Frank Colman	OF53, 1B6	L	26	99	226	30	61	9	5	6	53	25	27	0	.270	.434
Al Rubeling	OF18, 2B17, 3B16	R	31	92	184	22	45	7	2	4	30	19	19	4	.245	.370
Frankie Zak	SS67	R	22	87	160	33	48	3	1	0	11	22	18	6	.300	.331
Tommy O'Brien	OF48, 3B1	R	25	85	156	27	37	6	2	3	20	21	12	1	.250	.372
Hank Camelli	C61	R	29	63	125	14	37	5	1	1	10	18	12	0	.296	.376
Spud Davis	C35	R	39	54	93	6	28	7	0	2	14	10	8	0	.301	.441
Lee Handley	2B19, 3B11, SS3	R	30	40	86	7	19	2	0	0	5	3	5	1	.221	.244
2 Lloyd Waner	OF7	L	38	19	14	2	5	0	0	0	2	2	0	0	.357	.357
Al Gionfriddo	OF1	L	22	4	6	0	1	0	0	0	0	1	1	0	.167	.167
Bill Rodgers	OF1	L	21	2	4	1	1	0	0	0	0	0	1	0	.250	.250

Vic Barnhart 21 R 1-2, Hank Sweeney 28 L 0-2, Bud Stewart (VR-MS) 28

NAME	T	AGE	W	L	PCT	SV	G	GS	CG	IP	H	BB	SO	ShO	ERA
		32	90	63	.588	19	158	158	77	1414	1466	435	452	10	3.44
Rip Sewell	R	37	21	12	.636	2	38	33	24	286	263	99	87	3	3.18
Nick Strincevich	R	29	14	7	.667	2	40	26	11	190	190	37	47	0	3.08
Preacher Roe	L	29	13	11	.542	1	39	25	7	185	182	59	88	1	3.11
Max Butcher	R	33	13	11	.542	1	35	27	13	199	216	46	43	5	3.12
2 Fritz Ostermueller	L	36	11	7	.611	1	28	24	14	205	201	65	80	1	2.72
Xavier Rescigno	R	30	10	8	.556	5	48	6	2	124	146	34	45	0	4.35
Ray Starr	R	38	6	5	.545	3	27	12	5	90	116	36	25	0	5.00
Cookie Cuccurullo	L	26	2	1	.667	4	32	4	0	100	110	41	31	0	4.09
Len Gilmore	R	26	0	1	.000	0	1	1	1	8	13	0	0	0	7.88
1 Johnny Gee	L	28	0	0	.000	0	4	0	0	11	20	5	3	0	7.36
Joe Vitelli	R	36	0	0	.000	0	4	0	0	7	5	7	2	0	2.57
Roy Wise	R	19	0	0	.000	0	2	0	0	3	4	3	1	0	9.00

CINCINNATI 3rd 89-65 .578 16 — BILL McKECHNIE

NAME	G by POS	B	AGE	G	AB	R	H	2B	3B	HR	RBI	BB	SO	SB	BA	SA
TOTALS			30	155	5271	573	1340	229	31	51	528	423	391	51	.254	.338
Frank McCormick	1B153	R	33	153	581	85	177	37	3	20	102	57	17	7	.305	.482
Woody Williams	2B155	R	31	155	653	73	157	23	3	1	35	44	24	7	.240	.289
Eddie Miller	SS155	R	27	155	536	48	112	21	5	4	55	41	41	9	.209	.289
Steve Mesner	3B120	R	26	121	414	31	100	17	4	1	47	34	20	1	.242	.309
Gee Walker	OF117	R	36	121	478	56	133	21	3	5	62	23	48	7	.278	.366
Dain Clay	OF98	R	24	110	356	51	89	15	0	0	17	17	18	8	.250	.292
Eric Tipton	OF139	R	29	140	479	62	144	28	3	3	36	59	32	5	.301	.390
Ray Mueller	C155	R	32	155	555	54	159	24	4	10	73	53	47	4	.286	.398
Max Marshall (MS)	OF59	L	30	66	229	36	56	13	2	4	23	21	10	3	.245	.371
Tony Criscola	OF35	L	28	64	157	14	36	3	2	0	14	14	12	0	.229	.274
Estel Crabtree	OF19, 1B2	L	40	58	98	7	28	4	1	0	11	13	3	0	.286	.347
Chuck Aleno	3B42, 1B3, SS3	R	27	50	127	10	21	3	0	1	15	15	15	0	.165	.213
Bucky Walters	P34	R	35	37	107	9	30	4	0	0	13	8	18	0	.280	.318
2 Jo-Jo White	OF23	L	35	24	85	9	20	2	0	0	5	10	7	0	.235	.259
Buck Fausett	3B6, P2	L	36	13	31	2	3	0	1	0	1	1	2	0	.097	.161
Joe Just	C10	R	28	11	11	0	2	0	0	0	0	0	2	0	.182	.182
Len Rice	C5	R	25	10	4	1	0	0	0	0	0	0	0	0	.000	.000
Chucho Ramos	OF3	R	26	4	10	1	5	1	0	0	0	0	0	0	.500	.600
Kermit Wahl	3B1	R	21	4	1	0	0	0	0	0	0	0	0	0	.000	.000
Jodie Beeler	2B1, 3B1	R	22	3	3	0	0	0	0	0	0	0	2	0	.000	.000
Mike Kosman		R	26	1	0	0	0	0	0	0	0	0	0	0	.000	.000
Al Lakeman		R	25	1	1	0	0	0	0	0	0	0	1	0	.000	.000
Johnny Riddle	C1	R	38	1	0	0	0	0	0	0	0	0	0	0	.000	.000

NAME	T	AGE	W	L	PCT	SV	G	GS	CG	IP	H	BB	SO	ShO	ERA
		31	89	65	.578	12	155	155	93	1398	1292	384	359	17	2.97
Bucky Walters	R	35	23	8	.742	1	34	32	27	285	233	87	77	6	2.40
Clyde Shoun	L	32	13	10	.565	2	38	21	12	203	193	42	55	1	3.01
Ed Heusser	R	35	13	11	.542	2	30	23	17	193	165	42	42	4	2.38
Arnold Carter	L	26	11	7	.611	3	33	18	9	149	143	40	33	3	2.60
Harry Gumbert	R	34	10	8	.556	2	24	19	11	155	157	40	40	2	3.31
Tommy de la Cruz	R	29	9	9	.500	1	34	20	9	191	170	45	65	0	3.25
Jim Konstanty	R	27	6	4	.600	0	20	12	5	113	113	33	19	1	2.79
Elmer Riddle (SJ)	R	29	2	2	.500	0	4	4	2	27	25	12	6	0	4.00
Joe Beggs (MS)	R	33	1	0	1.000	0	1	1	1	9	8	0	2	0	2.00
Bob Malloy (MS)	R	26	1	1	.500	0	9	0	0	23	22	11	4	0	3.13
Bob Katz	R	33	0	1	.000	0	6	2	0	18	17	7	4	0	4.00
2 Bill Lohrman	R	31	0	1	.000	0	2	1	0	2	5	2	0	0	22.50
Bob Ferguson	R	25	0	3	.000	1	9	2	0	16	24	10	9	0	9.00
Buck Fausett	R	36	0	0	.000	0	2	0	0	11	13	7	3	0	5.73
Howie Fox	R	23	0	0	.000	0	2	0	0	2	2	0	0	0	0.00
Jake Eisenhardt	L	21	0	0	.000	0	1	0	0	.1	0	1	0	0	0.00
Joe Nuxhall	L	15	0	0	.000	0	1	0	0	1	2	5	0	0	45.00
Kent Peterson	L	18	0	0	.000	0	1	0	0	1	0	0	0	0	0.00

CHICAGO 4th 75-79 .487 30 — JIMMIE WILSON 1-9 .100 ROY JOHNSON 0-1 .000 CHARLIE GRIMM 74-69 .517

NAME	G by POS	B	AGE	G	AB	R	H	2B	3B	HR	RBI	BB	SO	SB	BA	SA
TOTALS			29	157	5462	702	1425	236	46	71	639	520	521	53	.261	.360
Phil Cavarretta	1B139, OF13	L	27	152	614	106	197	35	15	5	82	67	42	4	.321	.451
Don Johnson	2B154	R	32	154	608	50	169	37	1	2	71	28	48	8	.278	.352
Lennie Merullo	SS56, 1B1	R	27	66	193	20	41	8	1	1	16	16	18	3	.212	.280
Stan Hack	3B75, 1B18	L	34	98	383	65	108	16	1	3	32	53	21	5	.282	.352
Bill Nicholson	OF156	L	29	156	582	116	167	35	8	33	122	93	71	3	.287	.545
Andy Pafko	OF123	R	23	128	469	47	126	16	2	6	62	28	23	2	.269	.350
Dom Dallessandro	OF106	L	30	117	381	53	116	19	4	8	74	61	29	1	.305	.438
Dewey Williams	C77	R	28	79	262	23	63	7	2	0	27	23	18	2	.240	.282
Roy Hughes	3B66, SS52	R	33	126	478	86	137	16	6	1	28	35	30	16	.287	.351
Lou Novikoff	OF29	R	28	71	139	15	39	4	2	3	19	10	11	1	.281	.403
Ival Goodman	OF35	L	35	62	141	24	37	8	1	1	16	23	15	0	.262	.355
Bill Schuster	SS38, 2B6	R	31	60	154	14	34	7	1	1	14	12	16	4	.221	.299
Billy Holm	C50	R	31	54	132	10	18	2	0	0	6	16	19	1	.136	.152
Mickey Kreitner	C39	R	21	39	85	3	13	2	0	0	1	8	16	0	.152	.176
Tony York	SS15, 3B12	R	31	28	85	4	20	1	0	0	7	4	11	0	.235	.247
Ed Sauer	OF12	R	24	23	50	3	11	4	0	0	5	2	6	0	.220	.300
Frank Secory	OF17	R	31	22	56	10	18	1	0	4	17	6	8	1	.321	.554
Roy Easterwood	C12	R	29	17	33	1	7	2	0	1	2	1	11	0	.212	.364
Jimmie Foxx	3B2, C1	R	36	15	20	0	1	1	0	0	2	2	5	0	.050	.100
1 Eddie Stanky	2B3, SS3, 3B3	R	27	13	25	4	6	0	1	0	0	2	2	1	.240	.320
Charlie Brewster	SS10	R	27	10	44	4	11	2	0	0	2	5	7	0	.250	.295
Paul Gillespie	C7	L	23	9	26	2	7	1	0	1	2	3	3	0	.269	.423
John Ostrowski	OF2	R	26	8	13	2	2	1	0	0	2	1	4	0	.154	.231
Pete Elko	3B6	R	26	7	22	2	5	1	0	0	0	0	0	0	.227	.273
Joe Stephenson (MS)	C3	R	23	4	8	1	1	0	0	0	0	1	3	1	.125	.125
Benn Mann		R	28	1	0	1	0	0	0	0	0	0	0	0	.000	.000

NAME	T	AGE	W	L	PCT	SV	G	GS	CG	IP	H	BB	SO	ShO	ERA
		31	75	79	.487	13	157	157	70	1401	1481	452	535	11	3.58
Hank Wyse	R	26	16	15	.516	1	41	34	14	257	277	57	86	3	3.15
Claude Passeau	R	35	15	9	.625	3	34	27	18	227	234	50	89	2	2.89
Bob Chipman	L	25	9	9	.500	2	26	21	8	129	147	40	41	1	3.49
Bill Fleming	R	30	9	10	.474	0	39	18	9	158	163	62	42	1	3.13
Hy Vandenberg	R	37	7	4	.636	2	35	9	2	126	123	51	54	0	3.64
Paul Derringer	R	37	7	13	.350	3	42	16	7	180	205	39	69	0	4.15
Red Lynn	R	30	5	4	.556	1	22	7	4	84	80	37	35	1	4.07
Paul Erickson	R	28	5	9	.357	1	33	15	5	124	113	67	82	3	3.56
Ed Hanyzewski (AJ)	R	23	2	5	.286	0	14	7	3	58	61	20	19	0	4.50
Charlie Gassaway	L	25	0	1	.000	0	2	2	0	12	20	10	7	0	7.50
Dale Alderson (MS)	R	26	0	0	.000	0	12	1	0	22	31	9	7	0	6.55
Mack Stewart	R	29	0	0	.000	0	8	0	0	12	11	4	3	0	1.50
John Burrows	L	30	0	0	.000	0	3	0	0	3	7	3	1	0	18.00
Hank Miklos	L	33	0	0	.000	0	2	0	0	7	9	3	0	0	7.71

NEW YORK 5th 67-87 .435 38 — MEL OTT

NAME	G by POS	B	AGE	G	AB	R	H	2B	3B	HR	RBI	BB	SO	SB	BA	SA
TOTALS			31	155	5306	682	1398	191	47	93	646	512	480	39	.263	.370
Phil Weintraub	1B99	L	36	104	361	55	114	18	9	13	77	59	59	0	.316	.524
George Hausmann	2B122	R	28	131	466	70	124	20	4	1	30	40	25	3	.266	.333
Buddy Kerr	SS149	R	21	150	548	68	146	31	4	9	63	37	32	14	.266	.387
Hugh Luby	3B65, 2B45, 1B1	R	31	111	323	30	82	10	2	2	35	52	15	2	.254	.316
Mel Ott	OF103, 3B4	L	35	120	399	91	115	16	4	26	82	90	47	2	.288	.544
Johnny Rucker	OF139	L	27	144	587	79	143	14	8	6	39	24	48	8	.244	.325
Joe Medwick	OF122	R	32	128	490	64	165	24	3	7	85	38	24	2	.337	.441
Ernie Lombardi	C100	R	36	117	373	37	95	13	0	10	58	33	25	0	.255	.370
Nap Reyes	1B63, 3B37, OF3	R	24	116	374	38	108	16	5	8	53	15	24	2	.289	.422
Billy Jurges	3B61, SS10, 2B1	R	36	85	246	28	52	2	1	1	23	23	20	4	.211	.240
Gus Mancuso	C72	R	38	78	195	15	49	4	1	1	25	30	20	0	.251	.297
Bruce Sloan	OF21	L	29	59	104	7	28	4	1	1	9	13	8	0	.269	.356
Red Treadway	OF38	L	24	50	170	23	51	5	2	0	5	13	11	2	.300	.353
Danny Gardella	OF25	L	24	47	112	20	28	2	2	6	14	11	13	0	.250	.464
Charlie Mead	OF23	L	23	39	78	5	14	1	0	1	8	5	7	0	.179	.231
Ray Berres	C12	R	36	16	17	4	8	0	0	1	2	1	0	0	.471	.647
Steve Filipowicz	OF10, C1	R	23	15	41	10	8	2	1	0	7	3	7	0	.195	.293
Roy Nichols	2B1, 3B1	R	23	11	9	3	2	1	0	0	0	2	2	0	.222	.333

NAME	T	AGE	W	L	PCT	SV	G	GS	CG	IP	H	BB	SO	ShO	ERA
		29	67	87	.435	21	155	155	47	1364	1413	587	499	4	4.29
Bill Voiselle	R	25	21	16	.568	0	43	41	25	313	276	118	161	1	3.02
Harry Feldman	R	24	11	13	.458	2	40	27	8	205	214	91	70	1	4.17
Ace Adams	R	32	8	11	.421	13	65	4	1	138	149	58	32	0	4.24
Ewald Pyle	L	33	7	10	.412	0	31	21	3	164	152	68	79	0	4.34
Rube Fischer	R	27	6	14	.300	2	38	18	2	129	128	87	39	1	5.16
Johnny Allen	R	39	4	7	.364	0	18	13	2	84	88	24	33	1	4.07
Frank Seward	R	23	3	2	.600	0	25	7	2	78	98	32	16	0	5.42
Andy Hansen	R	19	3	3	.500	1	23	4	0	53	63	32	15	0	6.45
Cliff Melton	L	32	2	2	.500	0	13	10	1	64	78	19	15	0	4.08
Bob Barthelson	R	19	1	1	.500	0	7	1	0	10	13	5	4	0	4.50
Jack Brewer	R	24	1	4	.200	0	14	7	2	55	66	16	21	0	5.56
Ken Brondell	R	22	0	1	.000	0	7	2	1	19	27	8	1	0	8.53
Ken Miller	R	29	0	1	.000	0	4	0	0	5	1	4	2	0	0.00
Lou Polli	R	42	0	2	.000	3	19	0	0	36	42	20	6	0	4.50
2 Johnny Gee	L	28	0	0	.000	0	4	0	0	5	5	0	3	0	0.00
Frank Rosso	R	23	0	0	.000	0	2	0	0	4	11	3	1	0	9.00
Walter Ockley	R	23	0	0	.000	0	2	0	0	3	2	2	1	0	3.00

BOSTON 6th 65-89 .422 40 — **BOB COLEMAN**

NAME	G by POS	B	AGE	G	AB	R	H	2B	3B	HR	RBI	BB	SO	SB	BA	SA
TOTALS			28	155	5282	593	1299	250	39	79	558	456	509	37	.246	.353
Buck Etchison	1B85	L	29	109	308	30	66	16	0	8	33	33	50	1	.214	.344
Connie Ryan (MS)	2B80, 3B14	R	24	88	332	56	98	18	5	4	25	36	40	13	.295	.416
Whitey Wietelman	SS103, 2B23, 3B1	B	25	125	417	46	100	18	1	2	32	33	25	0	.240	.302
Damon Phillips	3B90, SS60	R	25	140	489	35	126	30	1	1	53	28	34	1	.258	.329
Chuck Workman	OF103, 3B19	L	29	140	418	46	87	18	3	11	53	42	41	1	.208	.344
Tommy Holmes	OF155	L	27	155	631	93	195	42	6	13	73	61	11	4	.309	.456
Butch Nieman	OF126	L	26	134	468	65	124	16	6	16	65	47	47	5	.265	.427
Phil Masi	C63, 1B12, 3B2	R	27	89	251	33	69	13	5	3	23	31	20	4	.275	.402
Max Macon	1B72, OF22, P1	L	28	106	366	38	100	15	3	3	36	12	23	7	.273	.355
Clyde Kluttz	C58	R	26	81	229	20	64	12	2	2	19	13	14	0	.279	.376
Ab Wright	OF47	R	38	71	195	20	50	9	0	7	35	18	31	0	.256	.410
Stew Hofferth	C47	R	31	66	180	14	36	8	0	1	26	11	5	0	.200	.261
Chet Ross	OF38	R	27	54	154	20	35	9	2	5	26	12	23	1	.227	.409
Frank Drews	2B46	R	28	46	141	14	29	9	1	0	10	25	14	0	.206	.284
Warren Huston	3B20, 2B5, SS4	R	30	33	55	7	11	1	0	0	1	8	5	0	.200	.218
Mike Sandlock	3B22, SS7	L	28	30	30	1	3	0	0	0	2	5	3	0	.100	.100
Roland Gladu	3B15, OF3	L	31	21	66	5	16	2	1	1	7	3	8	0	.242	.348
Chet Clemens (MS)	OF7	R	27	19	17	7	3	1	1	0	2	2	2	0	.176	.353
Steve Shemo	2B16, 3B2	R	29	18	31	3	9	2	0	0	1	1	3	0	.290	.355
Ben Geraghty	2B4, 3B3	R	31	11	16	3	4	0	0	0	0	1	2	0	.250	.250

Dick Culler 29 R 2-28, Hugh Poland 31 L 3-23, Pat Capri 25 R 0-1, Gene Patton 17 L 0-0, Eddie Joost (VR) 28

NAME	T	AGE	W	L	PCT	SV	G	GS	CG	IP	H	BB	SO	ShO	ERA
TOTALS		29	65	89	.422	12	155	155	70	1388	1430	527	454	13	3.67
Jim Tobin	R	31	18	19	.486	3	43	36	28	299	271	97	83	5	3.01
Nate Andrews	R	30	16	15	.516	2	37	34	16	257	263	74	76	2	3.22
Al Javery	R	26	10	19	.345	3	40	33	11	254	248	118	137	3	3.54
Ira Hutchinson	R	33	9	7	.563	1	40	8	1	120	136	53	22	1	4.20
Red Barrett	R	29	9	16	.360	2	42	30	11	230	257	63	54	1	4.07
Woody Rich	R	27	1	1	.500	0	7	2	1	25	32	12	6	0	5.76
Stan Klopp	R	33	1	2	.333	0	24	0	0	46	47	33	17	0	4.30
Johnny Hutchings	R	28	1	4	.200	1	14	7	1	57	55	26	26	0	3.95
Ben Cardoni	R	23	0	6	.000	0	22	5	1	76	83	37	24	0	3.91
Jim Hickey (MS)	R	23	0	0	.000	0	8	0	0	9	15	5	3	0	5.00
Carl Lindquist	R	25	0	0	.000	0	5	0	0	9	8	2	4	0	3.00
George Woodend	R	26	0	0	.000	0	3	0	0	2	5	5	0	0	13.50
Max Macon	L	28	0	0	.000	0	1	0	0	3	10	1	1	0	21.00
Harry MacPherson	R	17	0	0	.000	0	1	0	0	1	0	1	1	0	0.00

BROOKLYN 7th 63-91 .409 42 — **LEO DUROCHER**

NAME	G by POS	B	AGE	G	AB	R	H	2B	3B	HR	RBI	BB	SO	SB	BA	SA
TOTALS			28	155	5393	690	1450	255	51	56	631	486	451	43	.269	.366
Howie Schultz	1B136	R	21	138	526	59	134	32	3	11	83	24	67	6	.255	.390
2 Eddie Stanky	2B58, SS35, 3B1	R	27	89	261	32	72	9	2	0	16	44	13	3	.276	.326
Bobby Bragan	SS51, C35, 3B6, 2B1	R	26	94	266	26	71	8	4	0	17	13	14	2	.267	.327
Frenchy Bordagaray	3B98, OF25	R	32	130	501	85	141	26	4	6	51	36	22	2	.281	.385
Dixie Walker	OF140	L	33	147	535	77	191	37	8	13	91	72	27	6	**.357**	.529
Goody Rosen	OF65	L	31	89	264	38	69	8	3	0	23	26	27	0	.261	.314
Augie Galan	OF147, 2B2	L	32	151	547	96	174	43	9	12	93	**101**	23	4	.318	.495
Mickey Owen	C125, 2B1	R	28	130	461	43	126	20	3	1	42	36	17	4	.273	.336
Luis Olmo	OF64, 2B42, 3B31	R	24	136	520	65	134	20	5	9	85	17	37	10	.258	.367
1 Paul Waner	OF32	L	41	83	136	16	39	4	1	0	16	27	7	0	.287	.331
Jack Bolling (MS)	1B27	L	27	56	131	21	46	14	1	1	25	14	4	0	.351	.496
Tommy Brown	SS46	R	16	46	146	17	24	4	0	0	8	8	17	0	.164	.192
Eddie Basinski	2B37, SS3	R	21	39	105	13	27	4	1	0	9	6	10	1	.257	.314
Barney Koch	2B29, SS1	R	21	33	96	11	21	2	0	0	1	3	9	0	.219	.240
Bill Hart	SS25, 3B2	R	31	29	90	8	16	4	2	0	4	9	7	1	.178	.267
Gil English	SS13, 3B11, 2B2	R	34	27	79	4	12	3	0	1	7	6	7	0	.152	.228
Eddie Miksis	3B15, SS10	R	17	26	91	12	20	2	0	0	11	6	11	4	.220	.242
Morrie Aderholt	OF13	L	28	17	59	9	16	2	3	0	10	4	4	0	.271	.407
1 Lloyd Waner	OF4	L	38	15	14	3	4	0	0	0	1	3	0	0	.286	.286
Pat Ankenman	2B11, SS2	R	31	13	24	1	6	1	0	0	3	0	2	0	.250	.292

Red Durrett 23 L 5-32, 1 Johnny Cooney 43 R 3-4, Ray Hayworth 40 R 0-10, Gene Mauch (MS) 18 R 2-15, Lou Rochelli (MS) 25 R 3-17, Clancy Smyres 22 B 0-2, Stan Andrews 27 R 1-8, Fats Dantonio 24 R 1-7, Roy Jarvis (MS) 18 R 0-1, Arky Vaughan (VR) 32

NAME	T	AGE	W	L	PCT	SV	G	GS	CG	IP	H	BB	SO	ShO	ERA
TOTALS		25	63	91	.409	13	155	155	50	1368	1471	**660**	487	4	4.68
Curt Davis	R	40	10	11	.476	4	31	23	12	194	207	39	49	1	3.34
Rube Melton	R	27	9	13	.409	0	37	23	6	187	178	96	91	1	3.47
Hal Gregg	R	22	9	16	.360	2	39	31	6	198	201	137	92	0	5.45
Les Webber	R	29	7	8	.467	3	48	9	1	140	157	64	42	0	4.95
Ben Chapman	R	35	5	3	.625	0	11	9	6	79	75	33	37	0	3.42
Ed Head (MS)	R	26	4	3	.571	0	9	8	5	63	54	19	17	1	2.71
1 Bob Chipman	L	25	3	1	.750	0	11	3	1	36	38	24	20	0	4.25
Art Herring	R	37	3	4	.429	1	12	6	3	55	59	17	19	1	3.44
Cal McLish	R	18	3	10	.231	0	23	13	3	84	110	48	24	0	7.82
Clyde King	R	19	2	1	.667	0	14	3	1	44	42	12	14	0	3.07
1 Fritz Ostermueller	L	36	2	1	.667	1	10	4	3	42	46	12	17	0	3.21
Whit Wyatt	R	36	2	6	.250	0	9	9	1	38	51	16	4	0	7.11
Charley Fuchs	R	30	1	0	1.000	0	8	0	0	16	25	9	5	0	5.63
Wes Flowers	L	30	1	1	.500	0	9	1	0	17	26	13	3	0	7.94
Tom Sunkel	L	31	1	3	.250	1	12	3	0	24	39	10	6	0	7.50
Tommy Warren	L	26	1	4	.200	0	22	4	2	69	74	40	18	0	4.96
Ralph Branca	R	18	0	2	.000	1	21	1	0	45	46	32	16	0	7.00
John Wells	R	21	0	2	.000	0	4	2	0	15	18	11	7	0	5.40
Chink Zachary	R	26	0	2	.000	0	4	2	0	10	10	7	3	0	9.58

1 Bill Lohrman 31 R 0-0, Claude Crocker 19 R 0-0, Jack Franklin 24 R 0-0, Charlie Osgood 17 R 0-0, Frank Wurm 20 L 0-0

PHILADELPHIA 8th 61-92 .399 43.5 — **FREDDIE FITZSIMMONS**

NAME	G by POS	B	AGE	G	AB	R	H	2B	3B	HR	RBI	BB	SO	SB	BA	SA
TOTALS			28	154	5301	539	1331	199	42	55	495	470	500	32	.251	.336
Tony Lupien	1B151	L	27	153	597	82	169	23	9	5	52	56	29	18	.283	.377
Moon Mullen	2B114, 3B1, C1	L	27	118	464	51	124	9	4	0	31	28	32	4	.267	.304
Ray Hamrick (MS)	SS74	R	22	74	292	22	60	10	1	1	23	23	34	1	.205	.257
Glen Stewart	3B83, SS32, 2B1	R	31	118	377	32	83	11	5	0	29	28	40	0	.220	.276
Ron Northey	OF151	L	24	152	570	72	164	35	9	22	104	67	51	1	.288	.496
Buster Adams	OF151	R	29	151	584	86	165	35	3	17	64	74	74	2	.283	.440
Jimmy Wasdell	OF121, 1B4	L	30	133	451	47	125	20	3	3	40	45	17	0	.277	.355
Bob Finley	C74	R	28	94	281	18	70	11	1	1	21	12	25	1	.249	.306
Charlie Letchas	2B47, 3B32, SS29	R	28	116	396	29	94	8	0	0	33	32	27	0	.237	.258
Ted Cieslak	3B48, OF5	R	27	85	220	18	54	10	0	2	11	21	17	1	.245	.318
Coaker Triplett	OF44	R	32	84	184	15	43	5	1	1	25	19	10	1	.234	.288
2 Johnny Peacock	C73, 2B1	L	34	83	253	21	57	9	3	0	21	31	5	1	.225	.285
Andy Seminick	C11, OF7	R	23	22	63	9	14	2	1	0	4	6	17	2	.222	.286
Granny Hamner	SS21	R	17	21	77	6	19	1	0	0	5	3	7	0	.247	.260
Heinie Heltzel	SS10	R	30	11	22	1	4	1	0	0	0	2	3	0	.182	.227

Merv Shea 43 R 4-15, Joe Antolik 28 R 2-6, Putsy Caballero 16 R 0-4, Benny Culp (MS) 30 R 0-2, Chuck Klein 39 L 1-7, Lee Riley 37 L 1-12, Nick Goulish 26 L 0-1, Turkey Tyson 29 L 0-1

NAME	T	AGE	W	L	PCT	SV	G	GS	CG	IP	H	BB	SO	ShO	ERA
TOTALS		29	61	**92**	.399	6	154	154	66	1395	1407	459	496	11	3.64
Charley Schanz	R	25	13	16	.448	3	40	30	13	241	231	103	84	1	3.32
Ken Raffensberger	L	26	13	**20**	.394	0	37	31	18	259	257	45	136	3	3.06
Dick Barrett	R	37	12	18	.400	0	37	27	11	221	223	88	74	1	3.87
Bill Lee	R	34	10	11	.476	1	31	28	11	208	199	57	50	3	3.16
Al Gerheauser	L	27	8	16	.333	0	30	29	10	183	210	65	66	2	4.57
Andy Karl	R	30	3	2	.600	2	38	0	0	89	76	21	26	0	2.32
Chet Covington	L	33	1	1	.500	0	19	0	0	39	46	8	13	0	4.62
2 Vern Kennedy	R	37	1	5	.167	0	12	7	3	55	60	20	23	0	4.25
Barney Mussill	L	24	0	1	.000	0	16	0	0	19	20	13	5	0	6.16
Deacon Donahue	R	**24**	0	2	.000	0	6	0	0	9	18	2	2	0	8.00
Harry Shuman	R	28	0	0	.000	0	18	0	0	27	26	11	4	0	4.00
Dale Matthewson	R	21	0	0	.000	0	17	1	0	32	27	16	8	0	3.94
John Fick	L	23	0	0	.000	0	4	0	0	5	3	3	2	0	3.60
2 Lou Lucier	R	26	0	0	.000	0	1	0	0	2	3	2	1	0	13.50
Rogers McKee	L	17	0	0	.000	0	1	0	0	2	2	1	0	0	4.50
Charlie Ripple	L	22	0	0	.000	1	1	1	0	2	6	4	2	0	18.00
Al Verdel	R	23	0	0	.000	0	1	0	0	1	0	0	0	0	0.00

WORLD SERIES — ST. LOUIS (NL) 4 ST. LOUIS (AL) 2

LINE SCORES

TEAM	1	2	3	4	5	6	7	8	9	10	11	12	R	H	E
Game 1 October 4 at Sportsman's Park															
STL (AL)	0	0	0	2	0	0	0	0	0				2	2	0
STL (NL)	0	0	0	0	0	0	0	0	1				1	7	0
Galehouse / **M. Cooper**, Donnelly (8)															
Game 2 October 5 at Sportsman's Park															
STL (AL)	0	0	0	0	0	0	2	0	0	0	0		2	7	4
STL (NL)	0	0	1	1	0	0	0	0	0	0	1		3	7	0
Potter, **Muncrief** (7) / Lanier, **Donnelly** (8)															
Game 3 October 6 at Sportsman's Park															
STL (NL)	1	0	0	0	0	0	1	0	0				2	7	0
STL (AL)	0	0	4	0	0	0	2	0	X				6	8	2
Wilks, Schmidt (3), Jurisch (7), Byerly (7) / **Kramer**															
Game 4 October 7 at Sportsman's Park															
STL (NL)	2	0	2	0	0	1	0	0	0				5	12	0
STL (AL)	0	0	0	0	0	0	0	1	0				1	9	1
Brecheen / **Jakucki**, Hollingsworth (4), Shirley (8)															
Game 5 October 8 at Sportsman's Park															
STL (NL)	0	0	0	0	0	1	0	1	0				2	6	1
STL (AL)	0	0	0	0	0	0	0	0	0				0	7	1
M. Cooper / **Galehouse**															
Game 6 October 9 at Sportsman's Park															
STL (AL)	0	1	0	0	0	0	0	0	0				1	3	2
STL (NL)	0	0	0	3	0	0	0	0	X				3	10	0
Potter, Muncrief (4), Kramer (7) / **Wilks**															

COMPOSITE BATTING

NAME	POS	G	AB	R	H	2B	3B	HR	RBI	BA
St. Louis (NL)										
Totals		6	204	16	49	9	1	3	15	.240
Hopp	OF	6	27	2	5	0	0	0	0	.185
Musial	OF	6	23	2	7	2	0	1	2	.304
Kurowski	3B	6	23	2	5	1	0	0	1	.217
W. Cooper	C	6	22	1	7	2	1	0	2	.318
Marion	SS	6	22	1	5	3	0	0	2	.227
Sanders	1B	6	21	5	6	0	0	1	1	.286
Litwhiler	OF	5	20	2	4	1	0	1	1	.200
Verban	2B	6	17	1	7	0	0	0	2	.412
Bergamo	OF	3	6	0	0	0	0	0	1	.000
Lanier	P	2	4	0	2	0	0	0	1	.500
M. Cooper	P	2	4	0	0	0	0	0	0	.000
Brecheen	P	1	4	0	0	0	0	0	0	.000
O'Dea	PH	3	3	0	1	0	0	0	2	.333
Fallon	2B	2	2	0	0	0	0	0	0	.000
Garms	PH	2	2	0	0	0	0	0	0	.000
Wilks	P	2	2	0	0	0	0	0	0	.000
Donnelly	P	2	1	0	0	0	0	0	0	.000
Schmidt	P	1	1	0	0	0	0	0	0	.000
Byerly	P	1	0	0	0	0	0	0	0	.000
Jurisch	P	1	0	0	0	0	0	0	0	.000
St. Louis (AL)										
Totals		6	197	12	36	9	1	1	9	.183
Kreevich	OF	6	26	0	6	3	0	0	0	.231
Stephens	SS	6	22	2	5	1	0	0	0	.227
Moore	OF	6	22	4	4	0	0	0	0	.182
Christman	3B	6	22	0	2	0	0	0	1	.091
Gutteridge	2B	6	21	1	3	1	0	0	0	.143
Hayworth	C	6	17	1	2	1	0	0	1	.118
McQuinn	1B	6	16	2	7	2	0	1	**5**	**.438**
Laabs	OF	5	15	1	3	1	1	0	0	.200
Zarilla	OF	4	10	1	1	0	0	0	1	.100
Galehouse	P	2	5	0	1	0	0	0	1	.200
Kramer	P	2	4	0	0	0	0	0	0	.000
Potter	P	2	4	0	0	0	0	0	0	.000
Mancuso	C	2	3	0	2	0	0	0	1	.667
Baker	2B	2	2	0	0	0	0	0	0	.000
Byrnes	PH	3	2	0	0	0	0	0	0	.000
Chartak	PH	2	2	0	0	0	0	0	0	.000
Muncrief	P	2	1	0	0	0	0	0	0	.000
Clary	PH	1	1	0	0	0	0	0	0	.000
Turner	PH	1	1	0	0	0	0	0	0	.000

Hollingsworth P 0-1, Shirley P 0-0, Jakucki P 0-0

COMPOSITE PITCHING

NAME	G	IP	H	BB	SO	W	L	SV	ERA
St. Louis (NL)									
Totals	6	55	36	23	49	4	2	0	1.96
M. Cooper	2	16	9	5	**16**	1	1	0	1.12
Lanier	2	12.1	8	**8**	11	1	0	0	2.18
Brecheen	1	9	9	4	4	1	0	0	1.00
Wilks	2	6.1	5	3	7	0	1	0	5.68
Donnelly	2	6	2	1	9	1	0	0	0.00
Schmidt	1	3.1	1	1	1	0	0	0	0.00
Byerly	1	1.1	0	0	1	0	0	0	0.00
Jurisch	1	.2	2	1	0	0	0	0	27.00
St. Louis (AL)									
Totals	6	54.1	49	19	43	2	4	0	1.49
Galehouse	2	**18**	**13**	5	15	1	1	0	1.50
Kramer	2	11	9	4	12	1	0	0	**0.00**
Potter	2	9.2	10	3	6	0	1	0	0.93
Muncrief	2	6.2	5	4	4	0	1	0	1.35
Hollingsworth	1	4	5	2	1	0	0	0	2.25
Jakucki	1	3	5	0	4	0	1	0	9.00
Shirley	1	2	2	1	1	0	0	0	0.00

1945 Greenberg's *Grand* Return

War-time travel restrictions cancelled the All-Star Game, the St. Louis Browns signed Pete Gray, a one-armed outfielder, and baseball had a new commissioner. Judge Kennesaw Mountain Landis, the only commissioner the game had known since 1920, died November 25, 1944. Although controversial and sometimes questioningly stern, Landis had given baseball the discipline necessary to survive the holocaust of 1919—a year when it was learned that the World Series could be fixed and the sport could not be isolated from the other pressures which comprised American life.

The club owners named Albert B. (Happy) Chandler, a U.S. Senator from Kentucky, to replace the iron-handed Judge. Chandler's first year was tinged with an even greater excitement than the Judge had enjoyed in 1944. Once again, the Detroit Tigers were involved in the nerve-splitting action. The outcome, happily for Tiger fans, was a reversal of the disappointment of the previous September. On the final day of the season, Detroit found themselves in front by one game over Washington, which had already finished its schedule. The Tigers had waited since September 26, to clinch the pennant, but could not compete with the rain, which brought their momentum to a grinding halt. They had two chances to put the flag away and, at the same time, revenge themselves against the Browns. But it started to rain again on the afternoon of the 30th, causing Detroit to wonder if the skies of St. Louis would ever permit another baseball game, let alone a doubleheader. Pitchers, Nels Potter of St. Louis, and Detroit's Virgil Trucks, who was released from the navy in time to pitch the first game, warmed up three times waiting for the skies to clear. They never did, but the rain stopped, and the game got underway.

In the sixth inning Trucks gave way to ace Hal Newhouser, who quelled a St. Louis rally with one out and the bases loaded to momentarily keep a 2-1 lead intact. Then in the seventh, the Browns got a run to tie the game and added another in the eighth to go ahead. Detroit found themselves against the wall in the ninth. With the skies getting darker, they loaded the bases with one out. Veteran Hank Greenberg, who had joined the team in mid-season after a four year military stint, found himself at the plate. The count was 1-1 when Greenberg met the next pitch head on and sent it into the left field bleachers to make the second game unnecessary and to give the Tigers the lowest percentage pennant winner (.575) in major league history. The victory was the 25th for Newhouser, who was again named MVP, thereby becoming the only man since Jimmie Foxx's 1932-33 performances to win the honors back-to-back.

The National League story was not as dramatic as the one the junior circuit offered. Brooklyn, led by Leo Durocher, surprised everyone and finished third, and the Chicago Cubs—led by field captain Phil Cavarretta's MVP performance—won the pennant by three games over the Cardinals, who lost Stan Musial to the army and the chance to make it four flags in a row. En route to their tenth flag in the twentieth century, the Cubs set a record by sweeping 20 doubleheaders and further helped themselves by taking 21 out of the 22 games with Cincinnati.

Cavaretta led his teammates into the World Series and batted a sizzling .423. Claude Passeau picked up a victory on a one-hitter over the Tigers, and Hank Borowy, who led the league with a 2.14 E.R.A., collected two wins. But it was not enough as Newhouser returned in the finale to win his second game of the Series over a tired Borowy—pitching on one day's rest—and giving the Tigers the championship.

1945 AMERICAN LEAGUE

NAME	G by POS	B	AGE	G	AB	R	H	2B	3B	HR	RBI	BB	SO	SB	BA	SA
DETROIT 1st 88-65 .575		**STEVE O'NEILL**														
TOTALS			33	155	5257	633	1345	**227**	47	77	588	517	533	60	.256	.361
Rudy York	1B155	R	31	155	595	71	157	25	5	18	87	59	85	6	.264	.413
Eddie Mayo	2B124	L	35	134	501	71	143	24	3	10	54	48	29	7	.285	.405
Skeeter Webb	SS104, 2B11	R	35	118	407	43	81	12	2	0	21	30	35	8	.199	.238
Bob Maier	3B124, OF5	R	29	132	486	58	128	25	7	1	34	37	32	7	.263	.350
2 Roy Cullenbine	OF146	B	29	146	523	80	145	27	5	18	93	**101***	36	2	.277	.451
Doc Cramer	OF140	L	39	141	541	62	149	22	8	6	58	35	21	2	.275	.379
Jimmy Outlaw	OF105, 3B21	R	32	132	446	56	121	16	5	0	34	45	33	6	.271	.330
Bob Swift	C94	R	30	95	279	19	65	5	0	0	24	25	22	1	.233	.251
Paul Richards	C83	R	36	83	234	26	60	12	1	3	32	19	31	4	.256	.355
Hank Greenberg (MS)	OF72	R	34	78	270	47	84	20	2	13	60	42	40	3	.311	.544
Joe Hoover	SS68	R	30	74	222	33	57	10	5	1	17	21	35	6	.257	.360
Red Borum	2B28, 3B4, SS2	L	29	55	130	19	35	4	0	0	9	7	8	4	.269	.300
Chuck Hostetler	OF8	L	41	42	44	3	7	3	0	0	2	7	8	0	.159	.227
Hub Walker	OF7	L	38	28	23	4	3	0	0	0	1	9	4	1	.130	.130
John McHale	1B3	L	23	19	14	0	2	0	0	0	1	1	4	0	.143	.143
Ed Mierkowicz	OF6	R	21	10	15	0	2	2	0	0	2	1	3	0	.133	.267
1 Don Ross	3B8	R	30	8	29	3	11	4	0	0	4	5	1	2	.379	.517
Hack Miller	C2	R	34	2	4	0	3	0	0	0	1	0	0	0	.750	.750
Russ Kerns		L	24	1	1	0	0	0	0	0	0	0	0	0	.000	.000
Carl McNabb		R	28	1	1	0	0	0	0	0	0	0	1	0	.000	.000
Milt Welch	C1	R	20	1	2	0	0	0	0	0	0	0	1	0	.000	.000
WASHINGTON 2nd 87-67 .565 1.5		**OSSIE BLUEGE**														
TOTALS			32	156	5326	622	1375	197	**63**	27	570	545	489	**110**	.258	.334
Joe Kuhel	1B141	L	39	142	533	73	152	29	13	2	75	79	31	10	.285	.400
George Myatt	2B94, OF32, 3B6, SS1	L	31	133	490	81	145	17	7	1	39	63	43	30	.296	.365
Gil Torres	SS145, 3B2	R	29	147	562	39	133	12	5	0	48	21	29	7	.237	.276
Harlond Clift	3B111	R	32	119	375	49	79	12	0	8	53	76	58	2	.211	.307
Buddy Lewis (MS)	OF69	L	28	69	258	42	86	14	7	2	37	37	15	1	.333	.465
George Binks	OF128, 1B20	L	30	145	550	62	153	32	6	6	81	34	52	11	.278	.391
George Case	OF123	R	29	123	504	72	148	19	5	1	31	49	27	30	.294	.357
Rick Ferrell	C83	R	39	91	286	33	76	12	1	1	38	43	13	2	.266	.325
Fred Vaughn	2B76, SS1	R	26	80	268	28	63	7	4	1	25	23	48	0	.235	.302
Hilly Layne	3B33	L	27	61	147	23	44	5	4	1	14	10	7	0	.299	.408
Mike Guerra	C38	R	32	56	138	11	29	1	1	1	15	10	12	4	.210	.254
Jose Zardon	OF43	R	22	54	131	13	38	5	3	0	13	7	11	3	.290	.374
Al Evans	C41	R	28	51	150	19	39	11	2	2	19	17	22	2	.260	.400
2 Mike Kreevich	OF40	R	37	45	158	22	44	8	2	1	23	21	11	7	.278	.373
1 Jake Powell	OF27	R	36	31	98	4	19	2	0	0	3	8	8	1	.194	.214
Dick Kimble	SS15	L	29	20	49	5	12	1	1	0	1	5	2	0	.245	.306
Vince Ventura	OF15	R	28	18	58	4	12	0	0	0	2	4	4	0	.207	.207
Walt Chipple	OF13	R	26	18	44	4	6	0	0	0	5	5	6	0	.136	.136
Cecil Travis (MS)	3B14	L	31	15	54	4	13	2	1	0	10	4	5	0	.241	.315
Howie McFarland	OF3	R	34	6	11	0	1	0	0	0	2	0	3	0	.091	.091
Roberto Ortiz (VR) 30																
ST. LOUIS 3rd 81-70 .536 6		**LUKE SEWELL**														
TOTALS			30	154	5227	597	1302	215	37	63	557	500	555	25	.249	.341
George McQuinn	1B136	L	26	139	483	69	134	31	3	7	61	65	51	1	.277	.398
Don Gutteridge	2B128, OF14	R	33	143	543	72	129	24	3	2	49	43	46	9	.238	.304
Vern Stephens	SS144, 3B4	R	24	149	571	90	165	27	3	**24**	89	55	70	2	.289	.473
Mark Christman	3B77	R	31	78	289	32	80	7	4	4	34	19	19	1	.277	.370
Gene Moore	OF100	L	35	110	354	48	92	16	2	5	50	40	26	1	.260	.359
1 Mike Kreevich	OF81	R	37	84	295	34	70	11	1	2	21	37	27	4	.237	.302
Milt Byrnes	OF125, 1B2	L	28	133	442	53	110	29	4	8	59	78	84	1	.249	.387
Frank Mancuso	C115	R	27	119	365	39	98	13	3	1	38	46	44	0	.268	.329
Len Schulte	3B71, 2B37, SS14	R	28	119	430	37	106	16	1	0	36	24	35	0	.247	.288
Pete Gray	OF61	L	28	77	234	26	51	6	2	0	13	13	11	5	.218	.261
2 Lou Finney	OF36, 1B22, 3B1	L	34	57	213	24	59	8	4	2	22	21	6	0	.277	.380
Red Hayworth	C55	R	30	56	160	7	31	4	0	0	17	7	6	0	.194	.219
Babe Martin	OF48, 1B6	R	25	54	185	13	37	5	2	2	16	11	24	0	.200	.281
Tex Shirley	P32	B	27	43	70	7	20	1	0	0	8	0	11	1	.286	.300
Joe Schultz	C4	L	26	41	44	1	13	2	0	0	8	3	1	0	.295	.341
Chet Laabs (MS)	OF35	R	33	35	109	15	26	4	3	1	8	16	17	0	.239	.358
Nels Potter	P32	L	33	32	92	3	28	2	0	0	5	2	7	0	.304	.326
Ellis Clary	3B16, 2B3	R	28	26	38	6	8	1	0	1	2	2	3	0	.211	.316

NAME	T	AGE	W	L	PCT	SV	G	GS	CG	IP	H	BB	SO	ShO	ERA
		29	**88**	65	**.575**	**16**	155	155	78	1394	1305	538	**588**	**19**	2.99
Hal Newhouser	L	24	**25**	9	**.735**	2	40	**36**	**29**	**313**	239	110	**212**	**8**	**1.81**
Dizzy Trout	R	30	18	15	.545	2	41	31	18	246	252	79	97	4	3.15
Al Benton (BN)	R	34	13	8	.619	3	31	27	12	192	175	63	76	5	2.02
Stubby Overmire	L	26	9	9	.500	4	31	22	9	162	189	42	36	0	3.89
Les Mueller	R	26	6	8	.429	1	26	18	6	135	117	58	42	2	3.67
2 George Caster	R	37	5	1	.833	2	22	0	0	51	47	27	23	0	3.88
Zeb Eaton	R	25	4	2	.667	0	17	3	0	53	48	40	15	0	4.08
2 Jim Tobin	R	32	4	5	.444	1	14	6	2	58	61	28	14	0	3.57
Joe Orrell	R	28	2	3	.400	0	12	5	1	48	46	24	14	0	3.00
Tommy Bridges (MS)	R	38	1	0	1.000	0	4	1	0	11	14	2	6	0	3.27
Walter Wilson	R	31	1	3	.250	0	25	4	1	70	76	35	28	0	4.63
Art Houtteman	R	17	0	2	.000	0	13	0	0	25	27	11	9	0	5.40
Billy Pierce	L	18	0	0	.000	0	5	0	0	10	6	10	10	0	1.80
Prince Oana	R	37	0	0	.000	1	3	1	0	11	3	7	3	0	1.64
Pat McLaughlin	R	34	0	0	.000	0	1	0	0	1	2	0	0	0	9.00
Virgil Trucks (MS)	R	26	0	0	.000	0	1	1	0	5	3	2	3	0	1.80
Rufe Gentry (HO) 27															

***Cullenbine, also with Cleveland, league leader in BB with 112**

NAME	T	AGE	W	L	PCT	SV	G	GS	CG	IP	H	BB	SO	ShO	ERA
		32	87	67	.565	11	156	156	82	**1413**	1307	440	550	**19**	**2.92**
Roger Wolff	R	34	20	10	.667	2	33	29	21	250	200	53	108	4	2.12
Dutch Leonard	R	36	17	7	.708	1	31	29	12	216	208	35	96	4	2.13
Mickey Haefner	L	32	16	14	.533	3	37	28	19	238	226	69	83	1	3.48
Marino Pieretti	R	24	14	13	.519	2	44	27	14	233	235	91	66	3	3.32
Alex Carrasquel	R	32	7	5	.583	1	35	7	5	123	105	40	38	2	2.71
Johnny Niggeling	R	41	7	12	.368	0	26	25	8	177	161	73	90	2	3.15
Sandy Ullrich	R	23	3	3	.500	1	28	6	0	81	91	34	26	0	4.56
2 Pete Appleton	R	41	1	0	1.000	1	6	2	1	21	16	11	12	0	3.43
Walt Holborow	R	31	1	1	.500	0	15	1	1	31	20	16	14	1	2.32
Walt Masterson (MS)	R	25	1	2	.333	0	4	2	1	25	21	10	14	1	1.08
Dick Stone	L	33	0	0	.000	0	3	0	0	5	6	2	0	0	0.00
Armando Roche	R	18	0	0	.000	0	2	0	0	6	10	2	0	0	6.00
Joe Cleary	R	24	0	0	.000	0	1	0	0	.1	5	3	1	0	189.00
Bert Shepard	L	25	0	0	.000	0	1	0	0	5	3	1	2	0	1.80

NAME	T	AGE	W	L	PCT	SV	G	GS	CG	IP	H	BB	SO	ShO	ERA
		30	81	70	.536	8	154	154	**91**	1383	1307	506	570	10	3.14
Nels Potter	R	33	15	11	.577	0	32	32	21	255	212	68	129	3	2.47
Bob Muncrief	R	29	13	4	.765	1	27	15	10	146	132	44	54	0	2.71
Al Hollingsworth	L	37	12	9	.571	1	26	22	15	173	164	68	64	1	2.71
Sig Jakucki	R	35	12	10	.545	2	30	24	15	192	188	65	55	1	3.52
Jack Kramer	R	27	10	15	.400	2	29	25	15	193	190	73	99	3	3.36
Tex Shirley	R	27	8	12	.400	0	32	24	10	184	191	93	77	2	3.62
Sam Zoldak	L	26	3	2	.600	0	26	1	1	70	74	18	19	0	3.34
Lefty West	L	29	3	4	.429	0	24	8	1	74	71	31	38	0	3.65
Al LaMacchia	R	23	2	0	1.000	0	5	0	0	9	6	3	2	0	2.00
Ox Miller	R	30	2	1	.667	0	4	3	3	28	23	5	4	0	1.61
1 George Caster	R	37	1	2	.333	1	10	0	0	16	20	7	9	0	6.75
Earl Jones	L	26	0	0	.000	1	10	0	0	28	18	18	13	0	2.57
Cliff Fannin	L	21	0	0	.000	0	5	0	0	10	8	5	5	0	2.70
Dee Sanders	R	24	0	0	.000	0	2	0	0	1	7	1	1	0	54.00
1 Pete Appleton (MS)	R	41	0	0	.000	0	2	0	0	2	3	7	1	0	18.00

NEW YORK 4th 81-71 .533 6.5 — JOE McCARTHY

NAME	G by POS	B	AGE	G	AB	R	H	2B	3B	HR	RBI	BB	SO	SB	BA	SA
TOTALS			30	152	5176	**676**	1343	189	61	**93**	**639**	**618**	567	64	.259	.373
Nick Etten	1B152	L	31	152	565	77	161	24	4	18	**111**	90	23	2	.285	.437
Snuffy Stirnweiss	2B152	R	26	152	**632**	**107**	**195**	32	**22**	10	64	78	62	**33**	**.309**	**.476**
Frankie Crosetti	SS126	R	34	130	441	57	105	12	0	4	48	59	65	7	.238	.293
Oscar Grimes	3B141, 1B1	R	30	142	480	64	127	19	7	4	45	97	73	7	.265	.358
Bud Metheny	OF128	L	30	133	509	64	126	18	2	8	53	54	31	5	.248	.338
Tuck Stainback	OF83	R	34	95	327	40	84	12	2	5	32	13	20	0	.257	.352
Hersh Martin	OF102	B	35	117	408	53	109	18	6	7	53	65	31	4	.267	.392
Mike Garbark	C59	R	29	60	176	23	38	5	3	1	26	23	12	0	.216	.295
Russ Derry	OF60	L	28	78	253	37	57	6	2	13	45	31	49	1	.225	.419
Aaron Robinson (MS)	C46	L	30	50	160	19	45	6	1	8	24	21	23	0	.281	.481
Bill Drescher	C33	L	24	48	126	10	34	3	1	0	15	8	5	0	.270	.310
Charlie Keller (MM)	OF44	L	28	44	163	26	49	7	4	10	34	31	21	0	.301	.577
Johnny Lindell (MS)	OF41	R	28	41	159	26	45	6	3	1	20	17	10	2	.283	.377
Herb Crompton	C33	R	33	36	99	6	19	3	0	0	12	2	7	0	.192	.222
Don Savage	3B14, OF2	R	26	34	58	5	13	1	0	0	3	3	14	1	.224	.241
Joe Buzas	SS12	R	25	30	65	8	17	2	1	0	6	2	5	2	.262	.323
Mike Milosevich	SS22, 2B1	R	30	30	69	5	15	2	0	0	7	6	6	0	.217	.246
Paul Waner (MS)		L	42	1	0	0	0	0	0	0	0	0	0	0	.000	.000

NAME	T	AGE	W	L	PCT	SV	G	GS	CG	IP	H	BB	SO	ShO	ERA
TOTALS		30	81	71	.533	14	152	152	78	1355	1277	485	474	9	3.45
Bill Bevens	R	28	13	9	.591	0	29	25	14	184	174	68	76	2	3.67
1 Hank Borowy	R	29	10	5	.667	0	18	18	7	132	107	58	35	1	3.14
Monk Dubiel	R	26	10	9	.526	0	26	20	9	151	157	62	45	1	4.65
Al Gettel	R	27	9	8	.529	3	27	17	9	155	141	53	67	0	3.89
Ernie Bonham	R	31	8	11	.421	0	23	23	12	181	186	22	42	0	3.28
Red Ruffing	R	41	7	3	.700	0	11	11	8	87	85	20	24	1	2.90
Joe Page	L	27	6	3	.667	0	20	9	4	102	95	46	50	0	2.82
Atley Donald (IJ-EJ)	R	34	5	4	.556	0	9	9	6	64	62	25	19	2	2.95
Bill Zuber	R	32	5	11	.313	1	21	14	7	127	121	56	50	0	3.19
Ken Holcombe	R	26	3	3	.500	0	23	2	0	55	43	27	20	0	1.80
Jim Turner	R	41	3	4	.429	**10**	30	0	0	54	45	31	22	0	3.67
Spud Chandler (MS)	R	37	2	1	.667	0	4	4	2	31	30	7	12	1	4.65
Steve Roser	R	27	0	0	.000	0	11	0	0	27	27	8	11	0	3.67
Paul Schreiber	R	42	0	0	.000	0	2	0	0	4	4	2	1	0	4.50

Johnny Murphy (VR)36

CLEVELAND 5th 73-72 .503 11 — LOU BOUDREAU

NAME	G by POS	B	AGE	G	AB	R	H	2B	3B	HR	RBI	BB	SO	SB	BA	SA
TOTALS			27	147	4898	557	1249	216	48	65	519	505	**578**	19	.255	.359
Mickey Rocco	1B141	L	29	143	565	81	149	28	6	10	56	52	40	0	.264	.388
Dutch Meyer	2B130	R	29	130	524	71	153	29	8	7	48	40	32	2	.292	.418
Lou Boudreau (BN)	SS97	R	27	97	346	50	106	24	1	3	48	35	20	0	.306	.408
2 Don Ross	3B106	R	30	106	363	26	95	15	1	2	43	42	15	0	.262	.325
Pat Seerey	OF117	R	22	126	414	56	98	22	2	14	56	66	**97**	1	.237	.401
Felix Mackiewicz	OF112	R	27	120	359	42	98	14	7	2	37	44	41	5	.273	.368
Jeff Heath (KJ)	OF101	L	30	102	370	60	113	16	7	15	61	56	39	3	.305	.508
2 Frankie Hayes	C119	R	30	119	385	39	91	15	6	6	43	53	52	1	.236	.353
Al Cihocki	SS41, 3B29, 2B23	R	21	92	283	21	60	9	3	0	24	11	48	2	.212	.265
Paul O'Dea	OF53, P1	L	24	87	221	21	52	2	2	1	21	20	26	3	.235	.276
Ed Wheeler	3B14, SS11, 2B3	R	28	46	72	12	14	2	0	0	2	8	13	1	.194	.222
Les Fleming	OF33, 1B5	L	29	42	140	18	46	10	2	3	22	11	5	0	.329	.493
Myril Hoag	OF33, P2	R	37	40	128	10	27	5	3	0	3	11	18	1	.211	.297
Eddie Carnett (MS)	OF16, P2	L	28	30	73	5	16	7	0	0	7	2	9	0	.219	.315
Jim McDonnell	C23	L	22	28	51	3	10	2	0	0	8	2	4	0	.196	.235
Elmer Weingartner	SS20	R	26	20	39	5	9	1	0	0	1	4	11	0	.231	.256
Pop Williams	1B3	R	31	16	19	0	4	0	0	0	0	1	2	0	.211	.211
Hank Ruszkowski (MS)	C14	R	19	14	49	2	10	0	0	0	5	4	9	0	.204	.204
Stan Benjamin	OF4	R	31	14	21	1	7	2	0	0	3	0	0	0	.333	.429
1 Red Steiner	C11	L	30	12	20	0	3	0	0	0	2	1	4	0	.150	.150
Gene Desautels (MS)	C10	R	38	10	9	1	1	0	0	0	0	1	0	0	.111	.111

1 Roy Cullenbine 29 B 1-13*, Bob Rothel 21 R 2-10

NAME	T	AGE	W	L	PCT	SV	G	GS	CG	IP	H	BB	SO	ShO	ERA
TOTALS		29	73	72	.503	12	147	147	76	1302	1269	501	497	14	3.31
Steve Gromek	R	25	19	9	.679	1	33	30	21	251	229	66	101	3	2.55
Allie Reynolds	R	30	18	12	.600	4	44	30	16	247	227	**130**	112	2	3.21
Jim Bagby	R	28	8	11	.421	1	25	19	11	159	171	59	38	3	3.74
Pete Center	R	23	6	3	.667	1	31	8	2	86	89	28	34	0	3.98
Bob Feller (MS)	R	26	5	3	.625	0	9	9	7	72	50	35	59	1	2.50
Eddie Klieman	R	27	5	8	.385	4	38	12	4	126	123	49	33	1	3.86
Al Smith	L	37	5	12	.294	1	21	19	8	134	141	48	34	3	3.83
Red Embree (MS)	R	27	4	4	.500	0	8	8	5	70	56	26	42	1	1.93
Mel Harder	R	35	3	7	.300	0	11	11	2	76	93	23	16	0	3.67
Earl Henry	L	28	0	3	.000	0	15	1	0	22	20	20	10	0	5.32
Jack Salveson	R	31	0	0	.000	0	19	0	0	44	52	6	11	0	3.68
Hal Klein	L	22	0	0	.000	0	3	0	0	7	8	7	5	0	3.86
Eddie Carnett (MS)	L	28	0	0	.000	0	2	0	0	2	0	0	1	0	0.00
Myril Hoag	R	37	0	0	.000	0	2	0	0	3	3	1	0	0	0.00
Paul Calvert	R	27	0	0	.000	0	1	0	0	1	3	1	1	0	18.00
Paul O'Dea	L	24	0	0	.000	0	1	0	0	2	4	2	0	0	13.50

Ray Poat (VR) 27

***Cullenbine, also with Detroit, league leader in BB with 112**

CHICAGO 6th 71-78 .477 15 — JIMMY DYKES

NAME	G by POS	B	AGE	G	AB	R	H	2B	3B	HR	RBI	BB	SO	SB	BA	SA
TOTALS			32	150	5077	596	1330	204	55	22	545	470	467	78	**.262**	.337
Kerby Farrell	1B97	L	31	103	396	44	102	11	3	0	34	24	18	4	.258	.301
Roy Schalk	2B133	R	36	133	513	50	127	23	1	1	65	32	41	3	.248	.302
Cass Michaels	SS126, 2B1	R	19	129	445	47	109	8	5	2	54	37	28	8	.245	.299
Tony Cuccinello	3B112	R	37	118	402	50	124	25	3	2	49	45	19	6	.308	.400
Wally Moses	OF139	L	34	140	569	79	168	**35**	15	2	50	69	33	11	.295	.420
Oris Hockett	OF106	L	35	106	417	46	122	23	4	2	55	27	30	10	.293	.381
Johnny Dickshot	OF124	R	35	130	486	74	147	19	10	4	58	48	41	18	.302	.407
Mike Tresh	C150	R	31	150	458	50	114	11	0	0	47	65	37	6	.249	.273
Guy Curtright	OF84	R	32	98	324	51	91	15	7	4	32	39	29	3	.281	.407
Floyd Baker	3B58, 2B11	L	28	82	208	22	52	8	0	0	19	23	12	3	.250	.288
Bill Nagel	1B57, 3B1	R	29	67	220	21	46	10	3	3	27	15	41	3	.209	.323
Ed Lopat	P26	L	27	32	82	13	24	4	0	1	13	2	9	0	.293	.378
Danny Reynolds	SS14, 2B11	R	25	29	72	6	12	2	1	0	4	3	8	1	.167	.222
Vince Castino	C25	R	27	26	37	2	8	1	0	0	4	3	7	0	.216	.243
Luke Appling (MS)	SS17	R	38	18	58	12	21	2	2	1	10	12	7	1	.362	.517
Joe Orengo	3B7, 2B1	R	30	17	15	5	1	0	0	0	1	3	2	0	.067	.067
Bill Mueller (MS)	OF7	R	24	13	9	3	0	0	0	0	0	2	1	1	.000	.000

Hal Trosky (IL) 32

NAME	T	AGE	W	L	PCT	SV	G	GS	CG	IP	H	BB	SO	ShO	ERA
TOTALS		32	71	78	.477	13	150	150	84	1331	**1400**	448	486	13	3.69
Thornton Lee	L	38	15	12	.556	0	29	28	19	228	208	76	108	1	2.45
Orval Grove	R	25	14	12	.538	1	33	30	16	217	233	68	54	4	3.44
Ed Lopat	L	27	10	13	.435	1	26	24	17	199	226	56	74	1	4.12
Bill Dietrich (EJ)	R	35	7	10	.412	0	18	16	6	122	136	36	43	3	4.20
Earl Caldwell	R	40	6	7	.462	4	27	11	5	105	108	37	45	1	3.60
John Humphries	R	30	6	14	.300	1	22	21	10	153	172	48	33	1	4.24
Joe Haynes (BL)	R	27	5	5	.500	1	14	13	8	104	92	29	34	1	3.55
Frank Papish	L	27	4	4	.500	1	19	5	3	84	75	40	45	0	3.75
Johnny Johnson	L	30	3	0	1.000	4	29	0	0	70	85	35	38	0	4.24
Buck Russ	R	30	1	1	.500	0	13	2	0	37	51	17	8	0	5.84
Clay Touchstone	R	42	0	0	.000	0	6	0	0	10	14	6	4	0	5.40

BOSTON 7th 71-83 .461 17.5 — JOE CRONIN

NAME	G by POS	B	AGE	G	AB	R	H	2B	3B	HR	RBI	BB	SO	SB	BA	SA
TOTALS			30	157	**5367**	599	**1393**	225	44	60	561	541	534	72	.260	.346
Catfish Metkovich	1B97, OF42	L	23	138	539	65	140	26	3	5	62	51	70	19	.260	.347
Skeeter Newsome	2B82, SS33, 3B11	R	34	125	438	45	127	30	1	1	48	20	15	6	.290	.370
Eddie Lake	SS130, 2B1	R	29	133	473	81	132	27	1	11	51	106	37	9	.279	.410
Johnny Tobin	3B72, 2B5, OF1	L	24	84	278	25	70	6	2	0	21	26	24	2	.252	.288
Johnny Lazor	OF81	L	32	101	335	35	104	19	2	5	45	18	17	3	.310	.424
Leon Culberson	OF91	R	25	97	331	26	91	21	6	6	45	20	37	4	.275	.429
Bob Johnson	OF140	R	38	143	529	71	148	27	7	12	74	63	56	5	.280	.425
Bob Garbark	C67	R	35	68	199	21	52	6	0	0	17	18	10	0	.261	.291
Tom McBride	OF81, 1B11	R	30	100	344	38	105	11	7	1	47	26	17	2	.305	.387
Ben Steiner	2B77	L	23	78	304	39	78	8	3	3	20	31	29	10	.257	.332
Pete Fox	OF57	R	35	66	208	21	51	4	1	0	20	11	18	2	.245	.275
Dolph Camilli (MS)	1B54	L	38	63	198	24	42	5	2	2	19	35	38	2	.212	.288
Boo Ferriss	P35	L	23	61	120	16	32	7	1	1	19	19	11	0	.267	.367
Billy Holm	C57	R	32	58	135	12	25	2	1	0	9	23	17	1	.185	.215
Ty LaForest	3B45, OF5	R	26	52	204	25	51	7	4	2	16	10	35	4	.250	.353
Jim Bucher	3B32, 2B2	L	34	52	151	19	34	4	3	0	11	7	13	1	.225	.291
Fred Walters	C38	R	32	40	93	2	16	2	0	0	5	10	9	1	.172	.194
2 Red Steiner	C24	L	30	26	59	6	12	1	0	0	4	14	2	0	.203	.220
Frankie Pytlak (MS)	C6	R	36	9	17	1	2	0	0	0	0	3	0	0	.118	.118
1 Lloyd Christopher	OF3	R	25	8	14	4	4	0	0	0	4	3	2	0	.286	.286

Nick Polly 28 R 1-7, Joe Cronin (BL) 38 R 3-8, 1 Lou Finney (VR) 34 L 0-2

NAME	T	AGE	W	L	PCT	SV	G	GS	CG	IP	H	BB	SO	ShO	ERA
TOTALS		28	71	83	.461	13	157	157	71	1391	1389	**656**	490	15	3.80
Boo Ferriss	R	23	21	10	.677	2	35	31	26	265	**263**	85	94	5	2.95
Emmett O'Neill	R	27	8	11	.421	0	24	22	10	142	134	117	55	1	5.13
Mike Ryba	R	42	7	6	.538	2	34	9	4	123	122	33	44	1	2.49
Vic Johnson	L	24	6	4	.600	2	26	9	4	85	90	46	21	1	4.02
Jim Wilson (FS)	R	23	6	8	.429	0	23	21	8	144	121	88	50	2	3.31
Clem Hausmann	R	25	5	7	.417	2	31	13	4	125	131	60	30	2	5.04
Frank Barrett	R	32	4	3	.571	3	37	0	0	86	77	29	35	0	2.62
Otie Clark	R	27	4	4	.500	0	12	9	4	82	86	19	20	1	3.07
Pinky Woods (JJ)	R	30	4	7	.364	2	24	12	3	107	108	63	36	0	4.21
Randy Heflin	R	26	4	10	.286	0	20	14	6	102	102	61	39	2	4.06
Rex Cecil	R	28	2	5	.286	0	7	7	1	45	46	27	30	0	5.20
Clem Dreisewerd (MS)	L	29	0	1	.000	0	2	2	0	10	13	2	3	0	4.50
1 Oscar Judd	L	37	0	1	.000	0	2	1	0	6	10	3	5	0	9.00
1 Joe Bowman	R	35	0	2	.000	0	3	3	0	12	18	9	0	0	9.00
Yank Terry	R	34	0	4	.000	0	12	4	1	57	68	14	28	0	4.11

PHILADELPHIA 8th 52-98 .347 34.5 — CONNIE MACK

NAME	G by POS	B	AGE	G	AB	R	H	2B	3B	HR	RBI	BB	SO	SB	BA	SA
TOTALS			29	153	5296	494	1297	201	37	33	440	449	463	25	.245	.316
Dick Siebert	1B147	L	33	147	573	62	153	29	1	7	51	50	33	2	.267	.358
Irv Hall	2B151	R	26	151	616	62	161	17	5	0	50	35	42	3	.261	.305
Ed Busch	SS116, 3B5, 2B2, 1B1	R	27	126	416	37	104	10	3	0	35	32	9	2	.250	.288
George Kell	3B147	R	22	147	567	50	154	30	3	4	56	27	15	2	.272	.356
Hal Peck	OF110	L	28	112	449	51	124	22	9	5	39	37	28	5	.278	.399
Bobby Estalella	OF124	R	34	126	451	45	135	25	6	8	52	74	46	1	.299	.435
Mayo Smith	OF65	L	30	73	203	18	43	5	0	0	11	36	13	0	.212	.236
Buddy Rosar(VR)	C85	R	30	92	300	23	63	12	1	1	25	20	16	2	.210	.267
Bill McGhee	OF48, 1B8	L	36	93	250	24	63	6	1	0	19	24	16	3	.252	.284
Charlie Metro	OF57	R	26	65	200	18	42	10	1	3	15	23	33	1	.210	.315
Bobby Wilkins	SS40, OF4	R	22	62	154	22	40	6	0	0	4	10	17	2	.260	.299
Greek George	C46	R	32	51	138	8	24	4	1	0	11	17	29	0	.174	.217
Ernie Kish	OF30	L	27	43	110	10	27	5	1	0	10	9	9	0	.245	.309
1 Frankie Hayes	C32	R	30	32	110	12	25	2	1	3	14	18	14	1	.227	.345
Joe Burns	OF19, 3B5, 1B1	R	30	31	90	7	23	1	1	0	3	4	17	0	.256	.289
Larry Rosenthal	OF21	L	33	28	75	6	15	3	2	0	5	9	8	0	.200	.293
Joe Cicero	OF7	R	34	12	19	3	3	0	0	0	0	1	6	0	.158	.158
Joe Astroth	C8	R	22	10	17	1	1	0	0	0	1	0	1	0	.059	.059
Al Brancato (MS)	SS10	R	26	10	34	3	4	1	0	0	0	1	3	0	.118	.147
Sam Chapman (MS)	OF8	R	29	9	30	3	6	2	0	0	1	2	4	0	.200	.267
Ford Garrison (MS)	OF5	R	29	6	23	3	7	1	0	1	6	4	3	1	.304	.478

Jim Pruett 27 R 2-9, Larry Drake 24 L 0-2

NAME	T	AGE	W	L	PCT	SV	G	GS	CG	IP	H	BB	SO	ShO	ERA
TOTALS		30	52	**98**	.347	8	153	153	65	1381	1380	571	531	11	3.62
Russ Christopher	R	27	13	13	.500	2	33	27	17	227	213	75	100	2	3.17
Joe Berry	R	40	8	7	.533	5	**52**	0	0	130	114	38	51	0	2.35
Bobo Newsom	R	37	8	**20**	.286	0	36	34	16	257	255	103	177	3	3.29
Jesse Flores	R	30	7	10	.412	1	29	24	9	191	180	63	52	4	3.44
Lou Knerr	R	23	5	11	.313	0	27	17	5	130	142	74	41	0	4.22
Don Black (ST)	R	28	5	11	.313	0	26	18	8	125	154	69	47	0	5.18
Charlie Gassaway	L	26	4	7	.364	0	24	11	4	118	114	55	50	0	3.74
Bill Connelly	R	20	1	1	.500	0	2	1	0	8	7	8	0	0	4.50
Dick Fowler (MS)	R	24	1	2	.333	0	7	3	2	37	41	18	21	1	4.86
Phil Marchildon (MS)	R	31	0	1	.000	0	3	2	0	9	5	11	2	0	4.00
Charlie Bowles (MS)	R	28	0	3	.000	0	8	4	1	33	35	23	11	0	5.18
Steve Gerkin	R	29	0	12	.000	0	21	12	3	102	112	27	25	0	3.62
Carl Scheib (MS)	R	18	0	0	.000	0	4	0	0	9	6	4	2	0	3.00
Woody Crowson	R	26	0	0	.000	0	1	0	0	3	2	3	2	0	6.00

CHICAGO 1st 98-56 .636 — **CHARLIE GRIMM**

NAME	G by POS	B	AGE	G	AB	R	H	2B	3B	HR	RBI	BB	SO	SB	BA	SA
TOTALS			29	155	5298	735	1465	229	52	57	674	554	462	69	.277	.372
Phil Cavarretta	1B120, OF11	L	28	132	498	94	177	34	10	6	97	81	34	5	.355	.500
Don Johnson	2B138	R	33	138	557	94	168	23	2	2	58	32	34	9	.302	.361
Lennie Merullo	SS118	R	28	121	394	40	94	18	0	2	37	31	30	7	.239	.299
Stan Hack	3B146, 1B5	L	35	150	597	110	193	29	7	2	43	99	30	12	.323	.405
Bill Nicholson	OF151	L	30	151	559	82	136	28	4	13	88	92	73	4	.243	.377
Andy Pafko	OF140	R	24	144	534	64	159	24	12	12	110	45	36	5	.298	.455
Peanuts Lowrey	OF138, SS2	R	26	143	523	72	148	22	7	7	89	48	27	11	.283	.392
Mickey Livingston	C68, 1B1	R	30	71	224	19	57	4	2	2	23	19	6	2	.254	.317
Paul Gillespie	C45, OF1	L	24	75	163	12	47	6	0	3	25	18	9	2	.288	.380
Roy Hughes (KJ)	SS36, 2B21, 3B9, 1B2	R	34	69	222	34	58	8	1	0	8	16	18	6	.261	.306
Heinz Becker	1B28	B	29	67	133	25	38	8	2	2	27	17	16	0	.286	.421
Dewey Williams	C54	R	29	59	100	16	28	2	2	2	5	13	13	0	.280	.400
Ed Sauer	OF26	R	25	49	93	8	24	4	1	2	11	8	23	2	.258	.387
Bill Schuster	SS22, 2B3, 3B1	R	32	45	47	8	9	2	1	0	2	7	4	2	.191	.277
Frank Secory	OF12	R	32	35	57	4	9	1	0	0	6	2	7	0	.158	.175
Len Rice (CN)	C29	R	26	32	99	10	23	3	0	0	7	5	8	2	.232	.263
Reggie Otero	1B8	L	29	14	23	1	9	0	0	0	5	2	2	0	.391	.391
Johnny Moore		L	43	7	6	0	1	0	0	0	2	1	1	0	.167	.167

John Ostrowski 27 R 3-10, Cy Block (MS) 26 R 1-7, 2 Loyd Christopher 25 R 0-0

NAME	T	AGE	W	L	PCT	SV	G	GS	CG	IP	H	BB	SO	ShO	ERA
TOTALS		32	98	56	.636	14	155	155	86	1366	1301	385	541	15	2.98
Hank Wyse	R	27	22	10	.688	0	38	34	23	278	272	55	77	2	2.69
Claude Passeau	R	36	17	9	.654	1	34	27	19	227	205	59	98	5	2.46
Paul Derringer	R	38	16	11	.593	4	35	30	15	214	223	51	86	1	3.45
Ray Prim	L	38	13	8	.619	2	34	19	9	165	142	23	88	2	2.40
Hank Borowy	R	29	11	2	.846	1	15	14	11	122	105	47	47	1	2.14
Hy Vandenberg	R	38	7	3	.700	2	30	7	3	95	91	33	35	1	3.51
Paul Erickson	R	29	7	4	.636	3	28	9	3	108	94	48	53	0	3.33
Bob Chipman	L	26	4	5	.444	0	25	10	3	72	63	34	29	1	3.50
2 Ray Starr	R	39	1	0	1.000	0	9	1	0	13	17	7	5	0	7.62
Mack Stewart	R	30	0	1	.000	0	16	1	0	28	37	14	9	0	4.82
Lon Warneke	R	35	0	1	.000	0	9	1	0	14	16	1	6	0	3.86
Jorge Comellas	R	28	0	2	.000	0	7	1	0	12	11	6	6	0	4.50
Walter Signer	R	34	0	0	.000	1	6	0	0	8	11	5	0	0	3.38
Ed Hanyzewski	R	24	0	0	.000	0	2	1	0	5	7	1	0	0	5.40
George Hennessey	R	34	0	0	.000	0	2	0	0	4	7	1	2	0	6.75

ST. LOUIS 2nd 95-59 .617 3 — **BILLY SOUTHWORTH**

NAME	G by POS	B	AGE	G	AB	R	H	2B	3B	HR	RBI	BB	SO	SB	BA	SA
TOTALS			27	155	5487	756	1498	256	44	64	698	515	488	55	.273	.371
Ray Sanders	1B142	L	28	143	537	85	148	29	3	8	78	83	55	3	.276	.385
Emil Verban	2B155	R	29	155	597	59	166	22	8	0	72	19	15	4	.278	.342
Marty Marion	SS122	R	27	123	430	63	119	27	5	1	59	39	39	2	.277	.370
Whitey Kurowski	3B131, SS6	R	27	133	511	84	165	27	3	21	102	45	45	1	.323	.511
Johnny Hopp	OF104, 1B15	L	28	124	446	67	129	22	8	3	44	49	24	14	.289	.395
2 Buster Adams	OF140	R	30	140	578	98	169	26	0	20	101	57	75	3	.292	.441
Red Schoendienst	OF118, SS10, 2B1	B	22	137	565	89	157	22	6	1	47	21	17	26	.278	.343
Ken O'Dea	C91	L	32	100	307	36	78	18	2	4	43	50	31	0	.254	.365
Augie Bergamo	OF77, 1B2	L	27	94	304	51	96	17	2	3	44	43	21	0	.316	.414
Del Rice	C77	R	22	83	253	27	66	17	3	1	28	16	33	0	.261	.364
Debs Garms	3B32, OF10	L	37	74	146	23	49	7	2	0	18	31	3	0	.336	.411
Pep Young	SS11, 3B9, 2B3	R	37	27	47	5	7	1	0	1	4	1	8	0	.149	.234
Art Rebel	OF18	L	30	26	72	12	25	4	0	0	5	6	4	1	.347	.403
Dave Bartosch	OF11	R	28	24	47	9	12	1	0	0	1	6	3	0	.255	.277
George Fallon	SS20, 2B4	R	28	24	55	4	13	2	1	0	7	6	6	1	.236	.309
Lou Klein (MS)	SS7, OF7, 3B4, 2B2	R	26	19	57	12	13	4	1	1	6	14	9	0	.228	.386
1 Jim Mallory	OF11	R	26	13	43	3	10	2	0	0	5	0	2	0	.233	.279
Gene Crumling	C6	R	23	6	12	0	1	0	0	0	1	0	1	0	.083	.083

1 Glenn Crawford 31 L 0-3, Walker Cooper (MS) 30 R 7-18, 1 John Antonelli 29 R 0-3, Bob Keely 35 R 0-1

NAME	T	AGE	W	L	PCT	SV	G	GS	CG	IP	H	BB	SO	ShO	ERA
TOTALS		28	95	59	.617	9	155	155	77	1409	1351	497	510	18	3.24
2 Red Barrett	R	30	21*	9	.700	0	36	29	22*	247*	244*	38	63	3	2.73
Ken Burkhart	R	28	18	8	.692	2	42	22	12	217	206	66	67	4	2.90
Harry Brecheen	L	30	15	4	.789	2	24	18	13	157	136	44	63	3	2.52
George Dockins	L	28	8	6	.571	0	31	12	5	126	132	38	33	2	3.21
Blix Donnelly	R	31	8	10	.444	2	31	23	9	166	157	87	76	1	3.52
Jack Creel	R	29	5	4	.556	2	26	8	2	87	78	45	34	0	4.14
Bud Byerly	R	24	4	5	.444	0	33	8	2	95	111	41	39	0	4.74
Ted Wilks (SA)	R	29	4	7	.364	0	18	16	4	98	103	29	28	1	2.94
Glenn Gardner	R	29	3	1	.750	1	17	4	2	55	50	27	20	1	3.27
Al Jurisich	R	23	3	3	.500	0	27	6	1	72	61	41	42	0	5.13
1 Mort Cooper (EJ)	R	32	2	0	1.000	0	4	3	1	24	20	7	14	0	1.50
Max Lanier (MS)	L	29	2	2	.500	0	4	3	3	26	22	8	16	0	1.73
Bill Crouch	R	34	1	0	1.000	0	6	0	0	13	12	7	4	0	3.46
Art Lopatka	L	25	1	0	1.000	0	4	1	1	12	7	3	5	0	1.50
Stan Partenheimer	L	22	0	0	.000	0	8	2	0	13	12	16	6	0	6.23

*Barrett, also with Boston, league leader in W (23), CG (24), IP (285), H (287)

BROOKLYN 3rd 87-67 .565 11 — **LEO DUROCHER**

NAME	G by POS	B	AGE	G	AB	R	H	2B	3B	HR	RBI	BB	SO	SB	BA	SA
TOTALS			28	155	5418	795	1468	257	71	57	720	629	434	75	.271	.376
Augie Galan	1B66, OF49, 3B40	L	33	152	576	114	177	36	7	9	92	114	27	13	.307	.441
Eddie Stanky	2B153, SS1	R	28	153	555	128	143	29	5	1	39	148	42	6	.258	.333
Eddie Basinski	SS101, 2B6	R	22	108	336	30	88	9	4	0	33	11	33	0	.262	.313
Frenchy Bordagaray	3B57, OF22	R	35	113	273	32	70	9	6	2	49	29	15	7	.256	.355
Dixie Walker	OF153	L	34	154	607	102	182	42	9	8	124	75	16	6	.300	.438
Goody Rosen	OF141	L	32	145	606	126	197	24	11	12	75	50	36	4	.325	.460
Luis Olmo	OF106, 3B31, 2B1	R	25	141	556	62	174	27	13	10	110	36	33	15	.313	.462
Mike Sandlock	C47, SS22, 2B4, 3B2	B	29	80	195	21	55	14	2	2	17	18	19	2	.282	.405
Bill Hart	3B39, SS8	R	32	58	161	27	37	6	2	3	27	14	21	7	.230	.348
Tommy Brown	2B55, OF1	R	17	57	196	13	48	3	4	2	19	6	16	3	.245	.332
Ed Stevens	1B55	L	20	55	201	29	55	14	3	4	29	32	20	0	.274	.433
2 Johnny Peacock	C38	L	35	48	110	11	28	5	1	0	14	24	10	2	.255	.318
Fats Dantonio	C45	R	25	47	128	12	32	6	1	0	12	11	6	3	.250	.313
Howie Schultz	1B38	R	22	39	142	18	34	8	2	1	19	10	14	2	.239	.345
1 Morrie Aderholt	OF8	L	29	39	60	4	13	1	0	0	6	3	10	0	.217	.233
Babe Herman	OF3	L	42	37	34	6	9	1	0	1	9	5	7	0	.265	.382
Mickey Owen (MS)	C24	R	29	24	84	5	24	9	0	0	11	10	2	0	.286	.393
1 Stan Andrews	C21	R	28	21	49	5	8	0	1	0	2	5	4	0	.163	.204
Clyde Sukeforth	C13	L	43	18	51	2	15	1	0	0	1	4	1	0	.294	.314
Red Durrett	OF4	L	24	8	16	2	2	0	0	0	0	3	3	0	.125	.125
John Douglas	1B4	L	27	5	9	0	0	0	0	0	0	2	4	0	.000	.000

Don Lund 22 R 0-3, Bill White 21 R 0-1, Claude Corbitt 29 R 2-4, Leo Durocher 39 R 1-5, Ray Hayworth 28 R 0-2, Erv Palica 17 R 0-0, Arky Vaughan (VR) 33

NAME	T	AGE	W	L	PCT	SV	G	GS	CG	IP	H	BB	SO	ShO	ERA
TOTALS		28	87	67	.565	18	155	155	61	1392	1357	586	557	7	3.70
Hal Gregg	R	23	18	13	.581	2	42	34	13	254	221	120	139	2	3.47
Tom Seats	L	33	10	7	.588	0	31	18	6	122	127	37	44	2	4.35
Curt Davis	R	41	10	10	.500	0	24	18	10	150	171	21	39	0	3.24
Vic Lombardi	L	22	10	11	.476	4	38	24	9	204	195	86	64	0	3.31
Cy Buker	R	26	7	2	.778	5	42	4	0	87	90	45	48	0	3.31
Les Webber	R	30	7	3	.700	0	17	7	5	75	69	25	30	0	3.60
Art Herring	R	38	7	4	.636	2	22	15	7	124	103	43	34	2	3.48
Clyde King	R	20	5	5	.500	3	42	2	0	112	131	48	29	0	4.10
Ralph Branca	R	19	5	6	.455	1	16	15	7	110	73	79	69	0	3.03
Lee Pfund	R	25	3	2	.600	0	15	10	2	62	69	35	27	0	5.22
1 Ben Chapman	R	36	3	3	.500	0	10	7	2	54	64	32	23	0	5.50
Nick Nitcholas	R	36	1	0	1.000	0	7	0	0	19	19	1	4	0	5.21
Ernie Rudolph	R	35	1	0	1.000	0	7	0	0	9	12	7	3	0	5.00
Ray Hathaway	R	28	0	1	.000	0	4	1	0	9	11	6	3	0	4.00
Claude Crocker	R	20	0	0	.000	1	1	0	0	2	2	1	1	0	0.00

PITTSBURGH 4th 82-72 .532 16 — **FRANKIE FRISCH**

NAME	G by POS	B	AGE	G	AB	R	H	2B	3B	HR	RBI	BB	SO	SB	BA	SA
TOTALS			28	155	5343	753	1425	259	56	72	695	590	480	81	.267	.377
Babe Dahlgren	1B144	R	33	144	531	57	133	24	8	5	75	51	51	1	.250	.354
Pete Coscarart	2B122, SS1	R	32	123	392	59	95	17	2	8	38	55	55	2	.242	.357
Frankie Gustine	SS104, 2B29, C1	R	25	128	478	67	134	27	5	2	66	37	33	8	.280	.370
Bob Elliott	3B81, OF61	R	28	144	541	80	157	36	6	8	108	64	38	5	.290	.423
Johnny Barrett	OF132	L	29	142	507	97	130	29	4	15	67	79	68	25	.256	.432
Al Gionfriddo	OF106	L	23	122	409	74	116	18	9	2	42	60	22	12	.284	.386
Jim Russell	OF140	B	26	146	510	88	145	24	8	12	77	71	40	15	.284	.433
Al Lopez	C91	R	36	91	243	22	53	8	0	0	18	35	12	1	.218	.251
Lee Handley	3B79	R	31	98	312	39	93	16	2	1	32	20	16	7	.298	.372
Bill Salkeld	C86	L	28	95	267	45	83	16	1	15	52	50	16	2	.311	.547
Frank Colman	1B22, OF12	L	27	77	153	18	32	11	1	4	30	9	16	0	.209	.373
Vic Barnhart	SS60, 3B4	R	22	71	201	21	54	7	0	0	19	9	11	2	.269	.303
Tommy O'Brien (IL)	OF45	R	26	58	161	23	54	6	5	0	18	9	13	0	.335	.435
Jack Saltzgaver	2B31, 3B1	L	40	52	117	20	38	5	3	0	10	8	8	0	.325	.419
Rip Sewell	P33	R	38	35	64	10	20	3	0	0	6	7	11	1	.313	.359
Spud Davis	C13	R	40	23	33	2	8	2	0	0	6	2	2	0	.242	.303
Lloyd Waner	OF3	L	39	23	19	5	5	0	0	0	1	1	3	0	.263	.263
Frankie Zak	SS10, 2B1	R	23	15	28	2	4	2	0	0	3	3	5	0	.143	.214

Hank Camelli 30 R 0-2, Bill Rodgers (MS) 22 L 1-1, Joe Vitelli 37 R 0-0

NAME	T	AGE	W	L	PCT	SV	G	GS	CG	IP	H	BB	SO	ShO	ERA
TOTALS		31	82	72	.532	16	155	155	73	1387	1477	455	518	8	3.76
Nick Strincevich	R	30	16	10	.615	2	36	29	18	228	235	49	74	1	3.32
Preacher Roe	L	30	14	13	.519	1	33	31	15	235	228	46	148	3	2.87
Ken Gables	R	26	11	7	.611	1	29	16	6	139	139	46	49	0	4.14
Rip Sewell	R	38	11	9	.550	1	33	24	9	188	212	91	60	1	4.07
Max Butcher	R	34	10	8	.556	0	28	20	12	169	184	46	37	2	3.04
2 Boom-Boom Beck	R	40	6	1	.857	0	14	5	4	63	54	14	20	0	2.14
F. Ostermueller (MS)	L	37	5	4	.556	0	14	11	4	81	74	37	29	1	4.56
Al Gerheauser	L	28	5	10	.333	1	32	14	5	140	170	54	55	0	3.92
Xavier Rescigno	R	31	3	5	.375	9	44	1	0	79	95	34	29	0	5.70
Cookie Cuccurullo	L	27	1	3	.250	1	29	4	0	57	68	34	17	0	5.21
1 Ray Starr	R	39	0	2	.000	0	4	0	0	7	10	4	0	0	9.00
Johnny Lanning (MS)	R	34	0	0	.000	0	1	0	0	2	8	0	0	0	36.00

NEW YORK 5th 78-74 .513 19 — **MEL OTT**

NAME	G by POS	B	AGE	G	AB	R	H	2B	3B	HR	RBI	BB	SO	SB	BA	SA
TOTALS			30	154	5350	668	1439	175	35	114	626	501	457	38	.269	.379
Phil Weintraub	1B77	L	37	82	283	45	77	9	1	10	42	54	29	2	.272	.417
George Hausmann	2B154	R	29	154	623	98	174	15	8	2	45	73	46	7	.279	.339
Buddy Kerr	SS148	R	22	149	546	53	136	20	3	4	40	41	34	5	.249	.319
Nap Reyes	3B115, 1B5	R	25	122	431	39	124	15	4	5	44	25	26	1	.288	.376
Mel Ott	OF118	L	36	135	451	73	139	23	0	21	79	71	41	1	.308	.499
Johnny Rucker	OF98	L	28	105	429	58	117	19	11	7	51	20	36	7	.273	.417
Danny Gardella	OF94, 1B15	L	25	121	430	54	117	10	1	18	71	46	55	2	.272	.426
Ernie Lombardi	C96	R	37	115	368	46	113	7	1	19	70	43	11	0	.307	.486
Red Treadway	OF60	L	25	88	224	31	54	4	2	4	23	20	13	3	.241	.330
2 Clyde Kluttz	C57	R	27	73	222	25	62	14	0	4	21	15	10	1	.279	.396
Billy Jurges	3B44, SS8	R	37	61	176	22	57	3	1	3	24	24	11	2	.324	.403
2 Jim Mallory	OF21	R	26	37	94	10	28	1	0	0	9	6	7	1	.298	.309
Steve Filipowicz	OF31	R	24	35	112	14	23	5	0	2	16	4	13	0	.205	.304
Whitey Lockman (MS)	OF32	L	18	32	129	16	44	9	0	3	18	13	10	1	.341	.481
Mike Schemer	1B27	L	27	31	108	10	36	3	1	1	10	6	1	2	.333	.407
Johnny Hudson	3B5, 2B2	R	33	28	11	8	0	0	0	0	0	1	1	0	.000	.000
Roy Zimmerman	1B25, OF1	L	28	27	98	14	27	1	0	5	15	5	16	1	.276	.439
1 Joe Medwick	OF23	R	33	26	92	14	28	4	0	3	11	2	2	2	.304	.446
Ray Berres	C20	R	37	20	30	4	5	0	0	0	2	2	3	0	.167	.167
Al Gardella	1B9, OF1	L	27	16	26	2	2	0	0	0	1	4	3	0	.077	.077
Charlie Mead	OF11	L	24	11	37	4	10	1	0	1	6	5	2	0	.270	.378
Bill DeKoning	C2	R	25	3	1	0	0	0	0	0	0	0	1	0	.000	.000

NAME	T	AGE	W	L	PCT	SV	G	GS	CG	IP	H	BB	SO	ShO	ERA
TOTALS		27	78	74	.513	21	154	154	53	1375	1401	529	530	13	4.06
Van Lingle Mungo	R	34	14	7	.667	0	26	26	7	183	161	71	101	2	3.20
Bill Voiselle	R	26	14	14	.500	0	41	35	14	232	249	97	115	4	4.50
Harry Feldman	R	25	12	13	.480	1	35	30	10	218	213	69	74	3	3.26
Ace Adams	R	33	11	9	.550	15	65	0	0	113	109	44	39	0	3.42
Jack Brewer	R	25	8	6	.571	0	28	21	8	160	162	58	49	0	3.83
Sal Maglie	R	28	5	4	.556	0	13	10	7	84	72	22	32	3	2.36
Andy Hansen (MS)	R	20	4	3	.571	3	23	13	4	93	98	28	37	0	4.65
Slim Emmerich	R	25	4	4	.500	0	31	7	1	100	111	33	27	0	4.86
Rube Fischer	R	28	3	8	.273	1	31	4	0	77	90	49	27	0	5.61
Adrian Zabala	L	28	2	4	.333	0	11	5	1	43	46	20	14	0	4.81
Don Fisher	R	29	1	0	1.000	0	2	1	1	18	12	7	4	1	2.00
Roy Lee	L	27	0	2	.000	0	3	1	0	7	8	3	0	0	11.57
Ray Harrell	R	33	0	0	.000	0	12	0	0	25	34	14	7	0	5.04
1 Ewald Pyle	L	34	0	0	.000	0	6	1	0	6	16	4	2	0	18.00
Loren Bain	R	22	0	0	.000	0	3	0	0	8	10	4	1	0	7.88
Johnny Gee (VR)	L	29	0	0	.000	1	2	0	0	3	5	2	1	0	9.00
John Phillips	R	26	0	0	.000	0	1	0	0	4	5	4	0	0	11.25
Cliff Milton (ST) 33															

BOSTON 6th 67-85 .441 30 — BOB COLEMAN 42-49 .462 — DEL BISSONETTE 25-36 .410

NAME	G by POS	B	AGE	G	AB	R	H	2B	3B	HR	RBI	BB	SO	SB	BA	SA
TOTALS			29	154	5441	721	1453	229	25	101	668	520	510	**82**	.267	.374
Vince Shupe	1B77	L	23	78	283	22	76	8	0	0	15	17	16	3	.269	.297
Whitey Wietelmann	2B87, SS39, 3B2, P1	B	26	123	428	53	116	15	3	4	33	39	27	4	.271	.348
Dick Culler	SS126, 3B6	R	30	136	527	87	138	12	1	2	30	50	35	7	.262	.300
Chuck Workman	3B107, OF24	L	30	139	514	77	141	16	2	25	87	51	58	9	.274	.459
Tommy Holmes	OF154	L	28	154	636	125	**224**	**47**	6	**28**	117	70	9	15	.352	**.577**
Carden Gillenwater	OF140	R	27	144	517	74	149	20	2	7	72	73	70	13	.288	.375
Butch Nieman	OF57	L	27	97	247	43	61	15	0	14	56	43	33	11	.247	.478
Phil Masi	C95, 1B7	R	28	114	371	55	101	25	4	7	46	42	32	9	.272	.418
Bill Ramsey	OF43	R	24	78	137	16	40	8	0	1	12	4	22	1	.292	.372
Joe Mack	1B65	B	33	66	260	30	60	13	1	3	44	34	39	1	.231	.323
2 Joe Medwick	OF38, 1B5	R	33	66	218	17	62	13	0	0	26	12	12	3	.284	.344
Stew Hofferth	C45	R	32	50	170	13	40	2	0	3	15	14	11	1	.235	.300
Frank Drews	2B48	R	29	49	147	13	30	4	1	0	19	16	18	0	.204	.245
Tom Nelson	3B20, 2B12	R	28	40	121	6	20	2	0	0	6	4	13	1	.165	.182
Eddie Joost (BT-BW)	2B19, 3B16	R	29	35	141	16	35	7	1	0	9	13	7	0	.248	.312
2 Morrie Aderholt	OF24, 2B1	L	29	31	102	15	34	4	0	2	11	9	6	0	.333	.431
1 Clyde Kluttz	C19	R	27	25	81	9	24	4	1	0	10	2	6	0	.296	.370
Steve Shemo	2B12, 3B3, SS1	R	30	17	46	4	11	1	0	0	7	1	3	0	.239	.261

Mike Ulisney 27 R 7-18, Norm Wallen 28 R 2-15, Stan Wentzel 28 R 4-19

NAME	T	AGE	W	L	PCT	SV	G	GS	CG	IP	H	BB	SO	ShO	ERA
TOTALS		31	67	85	.441	13	154	154	57	1392	1474	557	404	7	4.03
1 Jim Tobin	R	32	9	14	.391	0	27	25	16	197	220	56	38	0	3.84
Ed Wright	R	26	8	3	.727	0	15	12	7	111	104	33	24	1	2.51
2 Mort Cooper	R	32	7	4	.636	1	20	11	4	78	77	27	45	1	3.35
Johnny Hutchings	R	29	7	6	.538	3	57	12	3	185	173	75	99	2	3.75
Bob Logan	L	35	7	11	.389	1	34	25	5	187	213	53	53	1	3.18
Nate Andrews	R	31	7	12	.368	0	21	19	8	138	160	52	26	0	4.57
2 Bill Lee	R	35	6	3	.667	0	16	13	6	106	112	36	12	1	2.80
Don Hendrickson	R	29	4	8	.333	5	37	2	1	73	74	39	14	0	4.93
Tom Earley	R	**28**	2	1	.667	0	11	2	1	41	36	19	4	0	4.61
1 Red Barrett	R	30	**2***	3	.400	2	9	5	**2***	**38***	**43***	16	13	0	4.74
Ira Hutchinson	R	34	2	3	.400	1	11	0	0	29	33	8	4	0	4.97
Al Javery (CJ)	R	27	2	7	.222	0	17	14	2	77	92	51	18	1	6.31
Lefty Wallace	L	23	1	0	1.000	0	5	3	1	20	18	9	4	0	4.50
Charlie Cozart	L	25	1	0	1.000	0	5	0	0	8	10	15	4	0	10.13
Joe Heving	R	44	1	0	1.000	0	3	0	0	5	5	3	1	0	3.60
Elmer Singleton	R	27	1	4	.200	0	7	5	1	37	35	14	14	0	4.86
Hal Schacker	R	20	0	1	.000	0	6	0	0	15	14	9	6	0	5.40
2 Ewald Pyle	L	34	0	1	.000	0	4	2	0	14	16	18	10	0	7.07
Bob Whitcher	L	28	0	2	.000	0	6	3	0	16	12	12	6	0	2.81

Lou Fette 38 R 0-2, Ben Cardoni 24 R 0-0, Whitey Wietelmann 26 R 0-0 ***Barrett (see STL)**

CINCINNATI 7th 61-93 .396 37 — BILL McKECHNIE

NAME	G by POS	B	AGE	G	AB	R	H	2B	3B	HR	RBI	BB	SO	SB	BA	SA
TOTALS			29	154	5283	536	1317	221	26	56	498	392	**532**	71	.249	.333
Frank McCormick	OF151	R	34	152	580	68	160	33	0	10	81	56	22	6	.276	.384
Woody Williams	2B133	R	32	133	482	46	114	14	0	0	27	39	24	6	.237	.266
Eddie Miller (BK)	SS115	R	28	115	421	46	100	27	2	13	49	18	38	4	.238	.404
Steve Mesner	3B148, 2B3	R	27	150	540	52	137	19	1	1	52	52	18	4	.254	.298
Al Libke	OF108, P4, 1B2	L	27	130	449	41	127	23	5	4	53	34	62	6	.283	.383
Dain Clay	OF152	R	25	153	**656**	81	184	29	2	1	50	37	58	19	.280	.335
Eric Tipton	OF83	R	30	108	331	32	80	17	1	5	34	40	37	11	.242	.344
Al Lakeman	C74	R	26	76	258	22	66	9	4	8	31	17	45	0	.256	.415
Gee Walker	OF67, 3B3	R	37	106	316	28	80	11	2	2	21	16	38	8	.253	.320
Dick Sipek	OF31	L	22	82	156	14	38	6	2	0	13	9	15	0	.244	.308
Kermit Wahl	2B32, SS31, 3B7	R	22	71	194	18	39	8	2	0	10	23	22	2	.201	.263
Al Unser	C61	R	32	67	204	23	54	10	3	3	21	14	24	0	.265	.387
Hank Sauer (MS)	OF28, 1B3	R	26	31	116	18	34	1	0	5	20	6	16	2	.293	.431
Johnny Riddle	C23	R	39	23	45	0	8	0	0	0	2	4	6	0	.178	.178
1 Wally Flager	SS15	L	23	21	52	5	11	1	0	0	6	8	5	0	.212	.231
Joe Just	C14	R	29	14	34	2	5	0	0	0	2	4	7	0	.147	.147

Eddie Lukon (MS) 24 L 1-8, Ray Mederios 19 R 0-0

NAME	T	AGE	W	L	PCT	SV	G	GS	CG	IP	H	BB	SO	ShO	ERA
TOTALS		33	61	93	.396	6	154	154	77	1366	1439	534	372	11	4.00
2 Joe Bowman	R	35	11	13	.458	0	25	24	15	186	198	68	71	1	3.58
Ed Huesser	R	36	11	16	.407	1	31	30	18	223	248	60	56	4	3.71
Bucky Walters (AJ)	R	36	10	10	.500	0	22	22	12	168	166	51	45	3	2.68
Howie Fox	R	24	8	13	.381	0	45	15	7	164	169	77	54	0	4.94
2 Vern Kennedy	R	38	5	12	.294	1	24	20	11	158	170	69	38	1	3.99
Frank Dasso	R	27	4	5	.444	0	16	12	6	96	89	53	39	0	3.66
Mel Bosser	R	25	2	0	1.000	0	7	2	0	16	9	17	3	0	3.38
Arnold Carter	L	27	2	4	.333	0	13	6	2	47	54	13	4	1	3.06
Earl Harrist	R	25	2	4	.333	0	14	5	1	62	60	27	15	0	3.63
1 Boom-Boom Beck	R	40	2	4	.333	1	11	5	2	48	42	12	9	0	3.38
Mike Modak	R	23	1	2	.333	1	20	3	1	42	52	23	7	1	5.79
Johnny Hetki	R	23	1	2	.333	0	5	2	2	33	28	11	9	0	3.55
Hod Lisenbee	R	46	1	3	.250	1	31	3	0	80	97	16	14	0	5.51
Elmer Riddle (ST)	R	30	1	4	.200	0	12	3	0	30	39	27	5	0	8.10
Herm Wehmeier	R	18	0	1	.000	0	2	2	0	5	10	4	0	0	12.60
Guy Bush	R	43	0	0	.000	1	4	0	0	4	5	3	1	0	9.00
Al Libke	R	27	0	0	.000	0	4	0	0	4	3	3	2	0	0.00

PHILADELPHIA 8th 46-108 .299 52 — FREDDIE FITZSIMMONS 17-50 .254 — BEN CHAPMAN 29-58 .333

NAME	G by POS	B	AGE	G	AB	R	H	2B	3B	HR	RBI	BB	SO	SB	BA	SA
TOTALS			30	154	5203	548	1278	197	27	56	503	449	501	54	.246	.326
Jimmy Wasdell	1B63, OF65	L	31	134	500	65	150	19	8	7	60	32	11	7	.300	.412
Fred Daniels	2B75, 3B1	R	20	76	230	15	46	3	2	0	10	12	22	1	.200	.230
Bitsy Mott	SS63, 2B27, 3B7	R	27	90	289	21	64	8	0	0	22	27	25	2	.221	.249
2 John Antonelli	3B108, 2B23, 1B1, SS1	R	29	125	504	50	129	27	2	1	28	24	24	1	.256	.323
Vance Dinges	OF65, 1B42	L	30	109	397	46	114	15	4	1	36	35	17	5	.287	.353
Vince DiMaggio	OF121	R	32	127	452	64	116	25	3	19	84	43	**91**	12	.257	.451
Coaker Triplett	OF92	R	33	120	363	36	87	11	1	7	46	40	27	6	.240	.333
Andy Seminick	C70, 3B4, OF1	R	24	80	188	18	45	7	2	6	26	18	38	3	.239	.394
Rene Monteagudo	OF35, P14	L	29	114	193	26	58	6	0	0	15	28	7	2	.301	.332
Jimmie Foxx	1B40, 3B14, P9	R	37	89	224	30	60	11	1	7	38	23	39	0	.268	.420
2 Glenn Crawford	OF38, SS34, 2B14	L	31	82	302	41	89	13	2	2	24	36	15	5	.295	.371
Gus Mancuso	C70	R	39	70	176	11	35	5	0	0	16	28	10	2	.199	.227
2 Wally Flager	SS48, 2B1	L	23	49	168	21	42	4	1	2	15	17	15	1	.250	.321
2 Jake Powell	OF44	R	36	48	173	13	40	5	0	1	14	8	13	1	.231	.277
Nick Picciuto	3B30, 2B4	R	23	36	89	7	12	6	0	0	6	6	17	0	.135	.202
Hal Spindel	C31	R	32	36	87	7	20	3	0	0	8	6	7	0	.230	.264
1 Johnny Peacock	C23	L	35	33	74	6	15	6	0	0	6	6	0	1	.203	.284
Garvin Hamner	2B21, SS9, 3B1	R	21	32	101	12	20	3	0	0	5	7	9	2	.198	.228
2 Ben Chapman	OF10, 3B4, P3	R	36	24	51	4	16	2	0	0	4	2	1	0	.314	.353
Ed Walczak	2B17, SS2	R	29	20	57	6	12	3	0	0	2	6	9	0	.211	.263
Tony Lupien (MS)	1B15	L	28	15	54	1	17	1	0	0	3	6	0	2	.315	.333
1 Buster Adams	OF14	R	30	14	56	6	13	3	1	2	8	5	5	0	.232	.429
Granny Hamner (MS)	SS13	R	18	14	41	3	7	2	0	0	6	1	3	0	.171	.220

2 Stan Andrews 28 R 11-33, Nick Goulish 27 L 3-11, Putsy Caballero 17 R 0-1, Don Hasenmayer (MS) 18 R 2-18

NAME	T	AGE	W	L	PCT	SV	G	GS	CG	IP	H	BB	SO	ShO	ERA
TOTALS		30	46	**108**	.299	**26**	154	154	31	1353	**1545**	**608**	433	4	4.64
Andy Karl	R	31	8	8	.500	**15**	**67**	2	1	181	175	50	51	0	2.98
Dick Barrett	R	38	8	**20**	.286	1	36	30	8	191	**216**	92	72	0	5.42
Dick Mauney	R	25	6	10	.375	1	20	16	6	123	127	27	35	2	3.07
2 Oscar Judd	L	37	5	4	.556	2	23	9	3	83	80	40	36	1	3.80
Tex Kraus	L	27	4	9	.308	0	19	13	0	82	96	40	28	0	5.38
Charlie Sproull	R	26	4	10	.286	1	34	19	2	130	158	80	47	0	5.95
Charley Schanz (IL)	R	26	4	15	.211	5	35	21	5	145	165	87	56	1	4.34
1 Bill Lee	R	35	3	6	.333	0	13	13	2	77	107	30	13	0	4.68
Dick Coffman	R	38	2	1	.667	0	14	0	0	26	39	2	2	0	5.19
Jimmie Foxx	R	37	1	0	1.000	0	9	2	0	23	13	14	10	0	1.57
Hugh Mulcahy (MS)	R	31	1	3	.250	0	5	4	1	28	33	9	2	0	3.86
Lou Lucier	R	27	0	1	.000	1	13	0	0	20	14	5	5	0	2.25
Don Grate	R	21	0	1	.000	0	4	2	0	8	18	12	6	0	18.00
Charlie Ripple	L	23	0	1	.000	0	4	0	0	8	7	10	5	0	6.75
Lefty Scott	L	29	0	2	.000	0	8	2	0	22	29	12	5	0	4.50
1 Vern Kennedy	R	38	0	3	.000	0	12	3	0	36	43	14	13	0	5.50
Ken Raffensberger (MS)	L	27	0	3	.000	0	5	4	1	24	28	14	6	0	4.50
Izzy Leon	R	**34**	0	4	.000	0	14	4	0	39	49	19	11	0	5.31
Whit Wyatt	R	37	0	7	.000	0	10	10	2	51	72	14	10	0	5.29
Rene Monteagudo	L	29	0	0	.000	0	14	0	0	46	67	28	16	0	7.43
Mitch Chetkovich	R	27	0	0	.000	0	4	0	0	3	2	3	0	0	0.00
2 Ben Chapman	R	36	0	0	.000	0	3	0	0	7	7	6	4	0	7.71

WORLD SERIES – DETROIT (AL) 4 CHICAGO (NL) 3

LINE SCORES

TEAM	1	2	3	4	5	6	7	8	9	10	11	12	R	H	E
Game 1 October 3 at Detroit															
CHI (NL)	4	0	3	0	0	0	2	0	0				9	13	0
DET	0	0	0	0	0	0	0	0	0				0	6	0
Borowy — **Newhouser**, Benton (3), Tobin (5), Mueller (8)															
Game 2 October 4 at Detroit															
CHI	0	0	0	1	0	0	0	0	0				1	7	0
DET	0	0	0	0	4	0	0	0	X				4	7	0
Wyse, Erickson (7) — **Trucks**															
Game 3 October 5 at Detroit															
CHI	0	0	0	2	0	0	1	0	0				3	8	0
DET	0	0	0	0	0	0	0	0	0				0	1	2
Passeau — **Overmire**, Benton (7)															
Game 4 October 6 at Chicago															
DET	0	0	0	4	0	0	0	0	0				4	7	1
CHI	0	0	0	0	0	1	0	0	0				1	5	1
Trout — **Prim**, Derringer (4), Vandenberg (6), Erickson (8)															
Game 5 October 7 at Chicago															
DET	0	0	1	0	0	4	1	0	2				8	11	0
CHI	0	0	1	0	0	0	2	0	1				4	7	2
Newhouser — **Borowy**, Vandenberg (6), Chipman (6), Derringer (7), Erickson (9)															
Game 6 October 8 at Chicago															
DET	0	1	0	0	0	0	2	4	0	0	0	0	7	13	1
CHI	0	0	0	0	4	1	2	0	0	0	0	1	8	15	3
Trucks, Caster (5), Bridges (6), Benton (7), **Trout** (8) — Passeau, Wyse (7), Prim (8), **Borowy** (9)															
Game 7 October 10 at Chicago															
DET	5	1	0	0	0	0	1	2	0				9	9	1
CHI	1	0	0	1	0	0	0	1	0				3	10	0
Newhouser — **Borowy**, Derringer (1), Vandenberg (2), Erickson (6), Passeau (8), Wyse (9)															

COMPOSITE BATTING

NAME	POS	G	AB	R	H	2B	3B	HR	RBI	BA
Detroit (AL)										
Totals		7	242	32	54	10	0	2	32	.223
Cramer	OF	7	29	**7**	**11**	0	0	0	4	.379
Mayo	2B	7	28	4	7	1	0	0	2	.250
Outlaw	3B	7	28	1	5	0	0	0	3	.179
York	1B	7	28	1	5	1	0	0	3	.179
Webb	SS	7	27	4	5	0	0	0	1	.185
Greenberg	OF	7	23	**7**	7	**3**	0	**2**	7	.304
Cullenbine	OF	7	22	5	5	2	0	0	4	.227
Richards	C	7	19	0	4	2	0	0	6	.211
Newhouser	P	3	8	0	0	0	0	0	1	.000
Trout	P	2	6	0	1	0	0	0	0	.167
Swift	C	3	4	1	1	0	0	0	0	.250
Trucks	P	2	4	0	0	0	0	0	0	.000
Hoover	SS	1	3	1	1	0	0	0	1	.333
Hostetler	PH	3	3	0	0	0	0	0	0	.000
McHale	PH	3	3	0	0	0	0	0	0	.000
Walker	PH	2	2	1	1	1	0	0	0	.500
Maier	PH	1	1	0	1	0	0	0	0	1.000
Borom	PH	2	1	0	0	0	0	0	0	.000
Eaton	PH	1	1	0	0	0	0	0	0	.000

Overmire P 0-1, Tobin P 0-1, Mierkowicz OF 0-0,
Benton P 0-0, Bridges P 0-0, Caster P 0-0, Mueller P 0-0

NAME	POS	G	AB	R	H	2B	3B	HR	RBI	BA
Chicago (NL)										
Totals		7	247	29	65	16	3	1	27	.263
Hack	3B	7	**30**	1	**11**	**3**	0	0	4	.367
Lowrey	OF	7	29	4	9	1	0	0	0	.310
Johnson	2B	7	29	4	5	2	1	0	0	.172
Nicholson	OF	7	28	1	6	1	1	0	**8**	.214
Pafko	OF	7	28	5	6	2	1	0	2	.214
Cavarretta	1B	7	26	**7**	**11**	2	0	1	5	**.423**
Livingston	C	6	22	3	8	**3**	0	0	4	.364
Hughes	SS	6	17	1	5	1	0	0	3	.294
Passeau	P	3	7	1	0	0	0	0	1	.000
Borowy	P	4	6	1	1	1	0	0	0	.167
Gillespie	C	3	6	0	0	0	0	0	0	.000
Secory	PH	5	5	0	2	0	0	0	0	.400
Wyse	P	3	3	0	0	0	0	0	0	.000
Becker	PH	3	2	0	1	0	0	0	0	.500
Merullo	SS	3	2	0	0	0	0	0	0	.000
Sauer	PH	2	2	0	0	0	0	0	0	.000
Williams	C	2	2	0	0	0	0	0	0	.000

Schuster SS 0-1, Vandenberg P 0-1, McCullough PH 0-1, Erickson P 0-0,
Derringer P 0-0, Prim P 0-0, Block PR 0-0, Chipman P 0-0

COMPOSITE PITCHING

NAME	G	IP	H	BB	SO	W	L	SV	ERA
Detroit (AL)									
Totals	7	65.2	65	19	48	4	3	0	3.83
Newhouser	3	**20.2**	**25**	4	**22**	**2**	1	0	6.10
Trout	2	13.2	9	3	9	1	1	0	**0.65**
Trucks	2	13.1	14	5	7	1	0	0	3.38
Overmire	1	6	4	2	2	0	1	0	3.00
Benton	3	4.2	6	0	5	0	0	0	1.93
Tobin	1	3	4	1	0	0	0	0	6.00
Mueller	1	2	0	1	1	0	0	0	0.00
Bridges	1	1.2	3	3	1	0	0	0	16.20
Caster	1	.2	0	0	1	0	0	0	0.00
Chicago (NL)									
Totals	7	65	54	33	22	3	4	0	4.15
Borowy	**4**	18	21	6	8	**2**	**2**	0	4.00
Passeau	3	16.2	7	**8**	3	1	0	0	2.70
Wyse	3	7.2	8	4	1	0	1	0	7.04
Erickson	**4**	7	8	3	5	0	0	0	3.86
Vandenberg	3	6	1	3	3	0	0	0	0.00
Derringer	3	5.1	5	7	1	0	0	0	6.75
Prim	2	4	4	1	1	0	1	0	9.00
Chipman	1	.1	0	1	0	0	0	0	0.00

WORLD WAR II MILITARY SERVICE — AMERICAN LEAGUE

Full seasons missed by active players who played in at least one major league game before entering military service.

BOSTON

Pitchers

		44	45	Mace Brown
	43	44	45	Bill Butland
42				Emerson Dickman
		44	45	Joe Dobson
42	43	44	45	Mickey Harris
			45	Tex Hughson
42	43	44	45	Earl Johnson
	43	44	45	Charlie Wagner

Catchers

			45	Bill Conroy
		44	45	Danny Doyle
			45	Roy Partee
42	43	44		Frankie Pytlak
			45	Hal Wagner

Infielders

	43	44	45	Paul Campbell
	43	44	45	Tom Carey
			45	Bobby Doerr
42	43	44	45	Al Flair
	43	44	45	Johnny Pesky
			45	Jim Tabor

Outfielders

	43	44	45	Dom DiMaggio
	43	44	45	Andy Gilbert
	43	44	45	Ted Williams

CHICAGO

Pitchers

42	43	44	45	Stan Goletz
			45	Don Hanski
	43	44	45	Ted Lyons
			45	Gordon Maltzberger
	43	44	45	Len Perme
	43	44	45	Johnny Rigney
		44	45	Eddie Smith
	43	44	45	Ed Weiland

Catchers

	43	44	45	George Dickey
			45	Ed Fernandes

Infielders

		44		Luke Appling
	43	44	45	Jake Jones
	43	44	45	Bob Kennedy
		44	45	Don Kolloway
	43	44	45	Dario Lodigiani
			45	Bill Metzig
	43			Roy Schalk
	43	44	45	Leo Wells

Outfielders

	43	44	45	Val Heim
	43			Myril Hoag
			45	Ralph Hodgin
		44	45	Frank Kalin
	43	44		Bill Mueller
	43	44	45	Dave Philley
42	43	44	45	Dave Short
			45	Thurman Tucker
	43	44	45	Sammy West
	43	44	45	Taffy Wright

CLEVELAND

Pitchers

		44		Pete Center
		44	45	Chubby Dean
42	43	44	45	Cal Dorsett
	43	44	45	Harry Eisenstat
42	43	44		Bob Feller
	43	44	45	Tom Ferrick
	43	44	45	Joe Krakauskas

Catchers

		44		Gene Desautels
	43	44	45	Jim Hegan

Infielders

42	43	44	45	Jack Conway
			45	Ken Keltner
	43	44	45	Bob Lemon
			45	Ray Mack
			45	Rusty Peters
	43	44	45	Eddie Robinson
		44	45	Ted Sepkowski

Outfielders

42	43	44	45	Soup Campbell
		44	45	Hand Edwards
	43	44	45	Buster Mills
		44	45	Gene Woodling

DETROIT

Pitchers

	43	44		Al Benton
		44		Tommy Bridges
			45	Johnny Gorsica
42	43	44	45	Fred Hutchinson
42	43	44		Les Mueller
		44		Virgil Trucks
		44	45	Hal White

Catchers

	43	44	45	Hank Riebe
	43	44	45	Birdie Tebbetts

Infielders

		44	45	Jimmy Bloodworth
	43	44	45	Murray Franklin
	43	44	45	Charlie Gehringer
			45	Pinky Higgins
	43	44	45	Billy Hitchcock
	43	44	45	Johnny Lipon
	43	44		Dutch Meyer
		44	45	Joe Wood

Outfielders

	43	44	45	Hoot Evers
42	43	44		Hank Greenberg
		44	45	Ned Harris
	43	44		Barney McCosky
42	43	44	45	Pat Mullin
	43	44	45	Bob Patrick
		44	45	Rip Radcliff (also 46)
			45	Dick Wakefield
42	43	44		Hub Walker

NEW YORK

Pitchers

	43	44	45	Norm Branch
		44	45	Tommy Byrne
	43	44	45	Randy Gumpert
			45	Al Lyons
42	43	44	45	Steve Peek
			45	Mel Queen
	43	44		Red Ruffing
		44	45	Marius Russo
42	43	44	45	Charley Stanceau
			45	Jake Wade
			45	Butch Wensloff (also 46)

Catchers

		44	45	Bill Dickey
			45	Rollie Hemsley
		44		Aaron Robinson
		44	45	Ken Sears
42	43	44	45	Ken Silvestri

Infielders

		44	45	Joe Gordon
	43	44	45	Buddy Hassett
		44	45	Billy Johnson
	43	44	45	Hank Majeski
	43	44	45	Phil Rizzuto
42	43	44	45	Johnny Sturm

Outfielders

	43	44	45	Joe DiMaggio
	43	44	45	Tommy Henrich
	43	44	45	George Selkirk
		44	45	Roy Weatherly

PHILADELPHIA

Pitchers

		44	45	Herman Besse
		44		Charlie Bowles
		44	45	Norm Brown
	43	44	45	Fred Caligiuri (also 46)
		44	45	Lou Ciola (also 46)
		44	45	Tom Clyde (also 46)
	43	44	45	Joe Coleman
		44	45	Everett Fagan
	43	44		Dick Fowler
	43	44	45	Bob Harris
			45	Lum Harris
42	43	44	45	Rankin Johnson
	43	44	45	Jack Knott
		44	45	Bert Kuczynski (also 46)
		44	45	Sam Lowry (also 46)
	43	44		Phil Marchildon
	43	44	45	Bob Savage
42	43	44	45	Porter Vaughan

Catchers

	43	44	45	Jim Castiglia
	43	44	45	George Yankowski (also 46)

Infielders

	43	44	45	Buddy Blair
42	43	44		Al Brancato
	43	44	45	Crash Davis
		44	45	Bruce Konopka
42	43	44	45	Benny McCoy
42	43	44	45	Don Richmond
		44	45	Pete Suder
	43	44	45	Jack Wallaesa

Outfielders

		44	45	Vern Benson
42	43	44		Sam Chapman
	43	44	45	Eddie Collins
			45	Hal Epps
42	43	44	45	Ray Poole
		44	45	George Staller
		44	45	Elmer Valo
		44	45	Johnny Welaj

ST. LOUIS

Pitchers

	43	44		Pete Appleton
	43	44	45	Frank Biscan
			45	Denny Galehouse
	43	44	45	Hooks Iott
		44	45	Al Milnar
42	43	44	45	Maury Newlin
		44	45	Fred Sanford
			45	Steve Sundra

Catchers

		44	45	Hank Helf
			45	Tom Turner

Infielders

42	43	44	45	George Archie
	43	44	45	Johnny Berardino
42	43	44	45	Johnny Lucadello
		44	45	Hank Schmulbach (also 46)
	43	44	45	Chuck Stevens

Outfielders

42	43	44	45	Joe Grace
	43	44	45	Walt Judnich
	43	44	45	Glenn McQuillen
			45	Al Zarilla

WASHINGTON

Pitchers

42				Red Anderson
	43	44	45	Lou Bevil
			45	Milo Candini
			45	Vern Curtis
	43	44	45	Sid Hudson
	43	44	45	Bill Kennedy
			45	Bill LeFebvre
	43	44		Walt Masterson
	43	44	45	Phil McCullough
		44	45	Jim Mertz (also 46)
42	43	44	45	Ronnie Miller
		44	45	Ray Scarborough
42	43	44	45	Lou Thuman (also 41)
	43	44	45	Maxie Wilson
			45	Early Wynn

Catchers

		44	45	Jake Early
	43			Al Evans

Infielders

	43	44	45	Frank Croucher
	43	44	45	Stan Galle
		44	45	Alex Kampouris
42	43			Hilly Layne
		44	45	Jerry Priddy
		44	45	Sherry Robertson
42	43	44	45	Jack Sanford
			45	John Sullivan (also 46)
42	43	44		Cecil Travis
		44	45	Mickey Vernon
			45	Eddie Yost

Outfielders

	43	44	45	Bruce Campbell
	43	44	45	Al Kvasnak
42	43	44		Buddy Lewis
42	43	44		Jim Mallory
			45	Stan Spence

Total American League: 1942=40 1943=119 1944=168 1945=180

WORLD WAR II MILITARY SERVICE — NATIONAL LEAGUE

Full seasons missed by active players who played in at least one major league game before entering military service

BOSTON

Pitchers

- 44 45 Bill Donovan
- 43 44 Tom Earley
- 43 44 45 Art Johnson
- 43 44 45 Frank LaManna
- 44 45 Ray Martin (also 46)
- 42 43 44 45 Bill Posedel
- 45 Woody Rich
- 43 44 45 Johnny Sain
- 43 44 45 Warren Spahn
- 44 45 Lou Tost
- 43 44 45 Ace Williams

Catchers

- 45 Hugh Poland

Infielders

- 43 44 45 Ducky Detweiler
- 42 43 44 45 John Dudra
- 43 44 45 Nanny Fernandez
- 43 44 45 Buddy Gremp
- 45 Max Macon (also 46)
- 44 45 Johnny McCarthy
- 45 Gene Patton
- 45 Damon Phillips
- 43 44 45 Skippy Roberge
- 42 43 44 45 Bama Rowell
- 45 Connie Ryan
- 43 44 45 Sibby Sisti
- 45 Tom York

Outfielders

- 45 Chet Clemens
- 44 45 Sam Gentile
- 43 44 45 Frank McElyea
- 45 Chet Ross
- 43 44 45 Max West

BROOKLYN

Pitchers

- 44 45 Rex Barney
- 43 44 45 Hugh Casey
- 44 45 Dutch Dietz
- 43 44 45 Larry French
- 44 45 Chris Haughey
- 45 Ed Head
- 44 45 Kirby Higbe
- 43 44 45 Chet Kehn
- 45 Cal McLish
- 45 Rube Melton
- 44 45 Bill Sayles

Catchers

- 43 44 45 Cliff Dapper
- 42 43 44 45 Herman Franks
- 44 45 Gil Hodges
- 42 43 44 45 Don Padgett

Infielders

- 44 45 Boyd Bartley
- 45 Jack Bolling
- 45 Bobby Bragan (also 46)
- 44 Dolf Camilli
- 44 45 Alex Campanis
- 44 45 Billy Herman
- 42 43 44 45 Cookie Lavagetto
- 45 Gene Mauch
- 45 Eddie Miksis
- 43 44 45 Pee Wee Reese
- 43 44 45 Lew Riggs
- 45 Lou Rochelli (also 46)
- 43 44 45 Stan Rojek

Outfielders

- 42 43 44 45 Joe Gallagher (also 41)
- 44 45 Gene Hermanski
- 43 44 45 Pete Reiser
- 43 44 45 Johnny Rizzo
- 42 43 44 45 Tommy Tatum

CHICAGO

Pitchers

- 45 Dale Alderson
- 44 45 Hi Bithorn
- 45 Bill Fleming
- 43 44 45 Emil Kush
- 42 43 44 45 Walt Lanfranconi
- 45 Red Lynn
- 42 43 44 45 Russ Meers
- 43 44 45 Vern Olsen
- 43 44 45 Johnny Schmitz
- 44 Lon Warneke

Catchers

- 43 44 45 Marv Felderman
- 44 Mickey Livingston
- 44 45 Clyde McCullough
- 43 44 45 Bob Scheffing
- 45 Joe Stephenson
- 43 44 45 Bennie Warren

Infielders

- 43 44 Cy Block
- 44 45 Al Glossop
- 43 44 45 Lou Stringer
- 43 44 45 Bobby Sturgeon
- 42 43 44 45 Eddie Waitkus

Outfielders

- 45 Dom Dallessandro
- 44 45 Charlie Gilbert
- 44 Peanuts Lowrey
- 45 Lou Novikoff
- 44 45 Whitey Platt
- 43 44 45 Marv Rickert

CINCINNATI

Pitchers

- 45 Joe Beggs
- 43 44 45 Ewell Blackwell
- 45 Harry Gumbert
- 45 Jim Konstanty
- 45 Bob Malloy
- 44 45 Jack Niemes
- 45 Kent Peterson (also 46)
- 45 Clyde Shoun
- 44 45 Junior Thompson
- 44 45 Johnny Vander Meer

Catchers

- 43 44 45 Ray Lamanno
- 45 Ray Mueller
- 44 45 Dick West

Infielders

- 44 45 Lonny Frey
- 45 Lonnie Goldstein
- 44 45 Bert Haas
- 44 Hank Sauer
- 43 44 45 Eddie Shokes
- 42 43 44 45 Benny Zientara

Outfielders

- 44 45 Frankie Kelleher
- 43 44 Eddie Lukon
- 45 Max Marshall
- 44 45 Mike McCormick
- 43 44 45 Howie Moss
- 43 44 45 Clyde Vollmer

NEW YORK

Pitchers

- 43 44 45 Bob Carpenter
- 44 45 Hugh East
- 43 44 45 Dave Koslo
- 43 44 45 Hal Schumacher
- 44 45 Ken Trinkle
- 44 45 Johnnie Wittig

Catchers

- 42 43 44 Jack Aragon
- 43 44 45 Harry Danning
- 43 44 45 Charlie Fox

Infielders

- 44 45 Dick Bartell
- 43 44 45 Buddy Blattner
- 42 43 44 45 John Davis
- 44 45 Sid Gordon
- 45 Hugh Luby
- 43 44 45 Johnny Mize
- 44 45 Mickey Witek
- 43 44 45 Babe Young

Outfielders

- 42 43 44 45 Morrie Arnovich
- 44 45 Vic Bradford (also 46)
- 43 44 45 Willard Marshall
- 44 45 Buster Maynard

PHILADELPHIA

Pitchers

- 42 43 44 45 Roy Bruner
- 44 45 Dick Conger
- 44 45 George Eyrich (also 46)
- 42 43 44 45 Lee Grissom
- 42 Bill Harman
- 43 44 45 Frank Hoerst
- 43 44 45 Tommy Hughes
- 44 45 Si Johnson
- 42 43 44 45 Dale Jones
- 44 Tex Kraus
- 43 44 45 Gene Lambert
- 44 45 Andy Lapihuska
- 45 Rogers McKee (also 46)
- 42 43 44 Hugh Mulcahy (also 41)
- 42 43 44 45 Dick Mulligan
- 43 44 45 Sam Nahem
- 43 44 45 Ike Pearson
- 44 45 Schoolboy Rowe

Catchers

- 45 Benny Culp
- 44 45 Dee Moore
- 43 44 45 Bill Peterman

Infielders

- 43 44 45 Bill Burich
- 45 Ray Hamrick (also 46)
- 45 Charlie Letchas
- 43 44 45 Hal Marnie
- 44 45 Pinky May
- 42 43 44 45 Emmett Mueller
- 45 Moon Mullen (also 46)
- 43 44 45 Ed Murphy
- 44 45 Danny Murtaugh

Outfielders

- 42 43 44 45 Jim Carlin
- 43 44 45 Ed Freed
- 43 44 45 Ernie Koy
- 42 43 44 45 Joe Marty
- 45 Ron Northey

PITTSBURGH

Pitchers

- 43 44 45 Ed Albosta
- 44 45 Russ Bauers
- 44 45 Bill Brandt
- 42 43 44 45 Bill Clemensen
- 44 45 Hank Gornicki
- 44 45 Jack Hallett
- 43 44 45 Ken Heintzelman
- 44 45 Bob Klinger
- 44 Johnny Lanning
- 42 43 44 45 Oad Swigert (also 41)
- 43 44 45 Lefty Wilkie

Catchers

- 44 45 Bill Baker
- 45 Roy Jarvis
- 42 43 44 45 Vinnie Smith
- 44 45 Billy Sullivan (also 46)

Infielders

- 44 45 Alf Anderson
- 42 43 44 45 Billy Cox
- 44 45 Elbie Fletcher
- 44 45 Huck Geary
- 43 44 45 Ed Leip
- 42 43 44 45 Burgess Whitehead

Outfielders

- 43 44 45 Culley Rikard
- 44 45 Bud Stewart
- 44 45 Maurice Van Robays

ST. LOUIS

Pitchers

- 43 44 45 Johnny Beazley
- 44 45 Al Brazle
- 44 45 Murry Dickson
- 42 43 44 45 Johnny Grodzicki
- 44 45 Howie Krist
- 43 44 45 Whitey Moore
- 45 George Munger
- 44 45 Howie Pollet
- 45 Freddy Schmidt
- 44 45 Ernie White

Catchers

none

Infielders

- 44 45 Jimmy Brown
- 43 44 45 Creepy Crespi (also 46)
- 43 44 45 Jeff Cross
- 44 Lou Klein

Outfielders

- 43 44 45 Erv Dusak
- 45 Danny Litwhiler
- 43 44 45 Terry Moore
- 45 Stan Musial
- 44 45 Earl Naylor
- 42 43 44 45 Walter Sessi
- 43 44 45 Enos Slaughter
- 44 45 Harry Walker
- 44 45 Johnny Wyrostek

Total National League: 1942=31 1943=100 1944=174 1945=204

USE NAME – GIVEN NAMES (NICKNAMES)	TEAM BY YEAR	BIRTH DATE	BIRTH PLACE	DEATH DATE	LIFETIME BATTING TOTALS																
					B	T	HGT	WGT	G	AB	R	H	2B	3B	HR	RBI	BB	SO	SB	BA	SA
Abreu, Joe-Joseph Lawrence (The Magician)	42CinN	5-24-16	Oakland, Cal.		R	R	5'8	160	9	28	4	6	1	0	1	3	4	4	0	.214	.357
Adair, Jimmy-James Audrey (Choppy)	31ChiN	1-25-07	Waxahachie, Tex.		R	R	5'10	154	18	76	9	21	3	1	0	3	1	8	1	.276	.342
Adams, Buster-Elvin Clark	39,43StLN 43-45PhiN 45-46StLN 47PhiN	6-24-15	Trinidad, Colo.		R	R	6'	180	576	2003	282	532	96	12	50	249	234	281	12	.266	.400
Adams, Sparky-Earl John	23-27ChiN 28-29PitN 30-33StLN 33-34CinN	8-26-94	Newtown, Pa.		R	R	5'6	151	1424	5557	844	1588	249	48	9	394	453	223	154	.286	.353
Adams, Spencer (Sparky)	23PitN 25WasA 26NYA 27StLA	6-21-98	Layton, Utah	11-24-70	L	R	5'9	165	180	395	61	101	16	5	0	38	38	50	5	.256	.322
Aderholt, Morrie-Morris Woodrow	39-41WasA 44-45BknN 45BosN	9-13-15	Mt. Olive, N.C.	3-18-55	L	R	6'1	188	106	262	36	70	7	3	3	32	19	29	3	.267	.351
Adkins, Dick-Richard Earl	42PhiA	3- 3-20	Electra, Tex.	9-12-55	R	R	5'10	165	3	7	2	1	0	0	0	0	0	2	0	.143	.143
Akers, Bill-William G. (Bump)	29-31DetA 32BosN	12-25-04	Chattanooga, Tenn.	4-13-62	R	R	5'11	178	174	475	64	124	17	9	11	69	63	64	7	.261	.404
Aleno, Chuck-Charles	41-44CinN	2-19-17	St. Louis, Mo.		R	R	6'2	215	118	320	34	67	11	3	2	34	31	35	3	.209	.281
Alexander, Dale-David Dale (Moose)	29-32DetA 32-33BosA	4-26-03	Greenville, Tenn.		R	R	6'3	210	662	2450	369	811	164	30	61	459	248	197	20	.331	.497
Alexander, Hugh-Hugh	37CleA	7-10-17	Buffalo, Mo.		R	R	6'	190	7	11	0	1	0	0	0	0	0	5	1	.091	.091
Allen, Ethan-Ethan Nathan	26-30CinN 30-32NYN 33StLN 34-36PhiN 36ChiN 37-38StLA	1- 1-04	Cincinnati, Ohio		R	R	6'1	180	1281	4418	623	1325	255	45	47	501	223	310	84	.300	.410
Almada, Mel-Baldomero Melo	33-37BosA 37-38WasA 38-39StLA 39BknN	2- 7-13	Hwatabampo, Mexico		L	L	6'	170	646	2483	363	706	107	27	15	197	214	150	56	.284	.367
Alston, Walt-Walter Emmons (Smokey)	36StLN M54-57BknN M58-75LAN	12- 1-11	Venice, Ohio		R	R	6'2	195	1	1	0	0	0	0	0	0	0	1	0	.000	.000
Ambler, Wayne-Wayne Harper	37-39PhiA	11- 8-15	Abington, Pa.		R	R	5'9	165	271	782	60	175	39	2	0	73	83	64	4	.224	.279
Anderson, Hal-Harold	32ChiA	2-10-04	St. Louis, Mo.	5- 1-74	R	R	5'11	160	9	32	4	8	0	0	0	2	0	1	0	.250	.250
Andrews (Andruskewicz), Stan-Stanley Joseph (Polo)	39-40BosN 44-45BknN 45PhiN	4-17-17	Lynn, Mass.		R	R	5'11	178	70	149	11	32	2	1	1	12	8	16	2	.215	.262
Andrus, Bill-William Morgan	31WasA 37PhiN	7-25-07	Beaumont, Tex.		R	R	6'	185	6	9	0	0	0	0	0	1	0	3	0	.000	.000
Angley, Tom-Thomas Samuel	29ChiN	10- 2-04	Baltimore, Md.	10-26-52	L	R	5'8	190	5	16	1	4	1	0	0	6	2	2	0	.250	.313
Ankenman, Pat-Fred Norman	36StLN 43-44BknN	12-23-12	Houston, Tex.		R	R	5'4	125	15	29	2	7	1	0	0	3	0	5	0	.241	.276
Antolick, Joe-Joseph	44PhiN	4-11-16	Hokendaugua, Pa.		R	R	6'	185	4	6	1	2	0	0	0	0	1	0	0	.333	.333
Antonelli, John-John Lawrence	44-45StLN 45PhiN	7-15-15	Memphis, Tenn.		R	R	5'10	165	135	528	50	133	28	2	1	29	24	29	1	.252	.318
Appling, Luke, Lucius Benjamin (Old Aches and Pains)	30-43ChiA 44MS 45-50ChiA M67KCA	2- 2-07	High Point, N.C.		R	R	5'10	183	2422	8857	1319	2749	440	102	45	1116	1302	528	179	.310	.398
Aragon, Jack-Angel Valdez Jr.	41NYN 42-44MS	11-20-15	Havana, Cuba		R	R	5'10	176	1	0	0	0	0	0	0	0	0	0	0	–	–
Archdeacon, Maurice-Maurice John (Flash)	23-25ChiA	12-14-98	St. Louis, Mo.	9- 5-54	L	L	5'8	153	127	384	84	128	14	4	0	[illegible]	40	[illegible]	13	[illegible]	.391
Archie, George-George Albert	38DetA 41WasA 41,46StLA 42-45MS	4-27-14	Nashville, Tenn.		R	R	6'	170	121	421	49	115	24	4	3	53	37	47	10	.273	.371
Arlett, Buzz-Russell Loris	31PhiN	1- 3-99	Elmhurst, Cal.	5-16-64	B	R	6'3	225	121	418	65	131	26	7	18	72	45	39	3	.313	.538
Arnovich, Morrie-Morris (Snooker)	36-40PhiN 40CinN 41NYN 42-45MS 46NYN	1-20-10	Superior, Wis.	7-20-59	R	R	5'10	168	590	2013	234	577	104	12	22	261	185	139	17	.287	.383
Asbell, Jim-James Marion (Big Jim)	38ChiN	6-22-14	Dallas, Tex.	7- 6-67	R	R	6'	210	17	33	6	6	2	0	0	3	3	9	0	.182	.242
Asbjornson, Casper-Robert Anthony	29-29BosA 31-32CinN	6-19-09	Concord, Mass.	1-21-70	R	R	6'1	196	97	221	19	52	10	1	1	27	9	45	0	.235	.303
Atkinson, Lefty-Hubert Burley	27WasA	6- 4-04	Chicago, Ill.	2-12-61	L	L	5'7	149	1	1	1	0	0	0	0	0	0	0	0	.000	.000
Attreau, Dick-Richard Gilbert	26-27PhiN	4- 8-97	Chicago, Ill.	7- 5-64	L	L	6'	160	61	144	26	31	2	2	1	16	20	23	1	.215	.278
Atwood, Bill-William Franklin	36-40PhiN	9-25-11	Rome, Ga.		R	R	6'	190	342	961	82	220	41	4	7	112	93	89	4	.229	.302
Autry, Martin-Martin Gordon (Chick)	24NYA 26-28CleA 29-30ChiA	3- 5-03	Martindale, Tex.	1-26-50	R	R	6'	180	120	277	21	68	17	3	2	25	15	29	0	.245	.350
Averill, Earl-Howard Earl	29-39CleA 39-40DetA 41BosN	5-21-02	Snohomish, Wash.		L	R	5'10	172	1669	6358	1224	2020	401	128	238	1165	775	518	69	.318	.533
Badgro, Red-Morris Hiram 27-28, 30-36 played in N.F.L.	29-30StLA	12- 1-02	Orilla, Wash.		L	R	6'	190	143	382	57	98	30	3	2	45	24	42	4	.257	.366
Bagwell, Bill-William Mallory (Big Bill)	23BosN 25PhiA	2-24-96	Choudrant, La.		L	L	6'1	175	92	143	12	42	6	3	2	20	8	14	0	.294	.420
Bailey, Gene-Arthur Eugene	17PhiA 18MS 19-20BosN 20BosA 23-24BknN	11-25-93	Pearsall, Tex.	11-14-73	R	R	5'8	160	213	634	95	156	16	7	2	52	63	61	13	.246	.303
Baker, Bill-William Presley	40-41CinN 41-43,46PitN 44-45MS 48-49StLN	2-21-11	Paw Creek, N.C.		R	R	6'	200	263	588	45	145	25	5	2	68	68	30	6	.247	.316
Baldwin, Henry-Henry Clay (Ted)	27PhiN	6-13-94	Chadds Ford, Pa.		R	R	5'11	180	6	16	1	5	0	0	0	1	1	2	0	.313	.313
Ballenger, Pelham-Pelham Ashby	28WasA	2- 6-94	Gilreath Mill, S.C.	12- 8-48	R	R	5'11	160	3	9	0	1	0	0	0	0	0	1	0	.111	.111
Bancroft, Dave-David James (Beauty)	15-20PhiN 20-23NYN 24-27BosN 28-29BknN 30NYN M24-27BosN	4-20-91	Sioux City, Iowa	10- 9-72	B	R	5'9	160	1913	7182	1048	2004	320	77	32	591	827	487	145	.279	.358
Barbare, Walter-Walter Lawrence (Dinty)	14-16CleA 18BosA 19-20PitN 21-22BosN	8-11-91	Greenville, S.C.	10-28-65	R	R	6'	162	500	1777	173	462	52	21	1	156	88	121	37	.260	.315
Barbary, Red-Donald Odell	43WasA	6-20-20	Simpsonville, S.C.		R	R	6'3	190	1	1	0	0	0	0	0	0	0	0	0	.000	.000
Barbee, Dave-David Monroe	26PhiA 32PitN	5- 7-05	Greensboro, N.C.	7- 1-68	R	R	6'	178	116	374	44	92	23	7	6	60	20	42	1	.246	.393
Barber, Turner-Tyrus Turner	15-16WasA 17-22ChiN 23BknN	7- 9-93	Lavinia, Tenn.	10-20-68	L	R	5'11	170	491	1531	189	442	47	21	2	185	115	112	28	.289	.351
Barkley, Red-John Duncan	37StLA 39BosN 43BknN	9-19-13	Childress, Tex.		R	R	5'11	160	63	163	16	43	9	0	0	21	19	26	2	.264	.319
Barna, Babe-Herbert Paul	37-38PhiA 41-43NYN 43BosA	3- 2-15	Clarksburg, W.Va.	5-18-72	L	R	6'2	210	207	664	88	154	22	9	12	96	76	98	9	.232	.346
Barnes, Eppie-Everett Duane	23-24PitN	12- 1-00	Ossining, N.Y.		L	R	5'9	175	4	7	0	1	0	0	0	0	0	2	0	.143	.143
Barnes, Honey-John Francis	26NYA	1-31-00	Fulton, N.Y.		L	R	5'10	175	1	0	0	0	0	0	0	0	1	0	0	–	–
Barnes, Red-Emile Deering	27-30WasA 30ChiA	12-25-03	Suggsville, Ala.	7- 3-59	L	R	5'10	158	286	836	152	224	41	24	8	97	95	76	12	.268	.403
Barnes, Sam-Samuel Thomas	21DetA	12-18-99	Suggsville, Ala.		L	R	5'8	150	7	11	2	2	1	0	0	0	2	1	0	.182	.273
Barnhart, Clyde-Clyde Lee (Pooch)	20-28PitN	12-29-95	Buck Valley, Pa.		R	R	5'10	155	814	2673	405	788	123	62	27	436	265	149	35	.295	.418
Barnhart, Vic-Victor Dee	44-46PitN	9- 1-22	Hagerstown, Md.		R	R	6'	188	74	204	21	55	7	0	0	19	10	12	2	.270	.304
Barrett, Bill-William Joseph (Whispering Bill)	21PhiA 23-29ChiA 29-30BosA 30WasA	5-28-00	Cambridge, Mass.	1-26-51	R	R	6'	175	718	2395	318	690	151	30	23	328	211	239	80	.288	.405
Barrett, Bob-Robert Schley (Jumbo)	23-25ChiN 25,27BknN 29BosA	1-27-99	Atlanta, Ga.		R	R	5'11	175	239	650	57	169	23	5	10	86	32	61	6	.260	.357
Barrett, Johnny-John Joseph	42-46PitN 46BosN	12-18-15	Lowell, Mass.	8-17-74	L	L	5'10	170	588	1811	303	454	82	32	23	220	265	201	69	.251	.369
Barron, Red-David Irenus	29BosN	6-21-00	Clarksville, Ga.		R	R	6'	185	10	21	3	4	1	0	0	1	1	4	2	.190	.238
Bartell, Dick-Richard William (Rowdy Richard)	27-30PitN 31-34PhiN 35-38NYN 39ChiN 40-41DetA 41-43,46NYN 44-45MS	11-22-07	Chicago, Ill.		R	R	5'9	160	2016	7629	1130	2165	442	71	79	710	748	627	109	.284	.391
Bartley, Boyd-Boyd Owen	43BknN 44-46MS	2-11-20	Chicago, Ill.		R	R	5'9	165	9	21	0	1	0	0	0	1	1	3	0	.048	.048
Bartling, Irv-Irving Henry	38PhiA	6-27-14	Bay City, Mich.	6-12-73	R	R	6'	175	14	46	5	8	1	1	0	5	3	7	0	.174	.239
Barton, Vince-Vincent David	31-32ChiN	2- 1-08	Edmonton, Canada		L	R	6'	180	102	373	64	87	12	4	16	65	29	62	1	.233	.416
Bartosch, Dave-David Robert	45StLN	3-24-17	St. Louis, Mo.		R	R	6'1	190	24	47	9	12	1	0	0	1	6	3	0	.255	.277
Bashore, Walt-Walter Franklin	36PhiN	10- 6-09	Harrisburg, Pa.		R	R	6'	170	10	10	1	2	0	0	0	0	1	3	0	.200	.200
Basinski, Eddie-Edwin Frank (Fiddler)	44-45BknN 47PitN	11- 4-22	Buffalo, N.Y.		R	R	6'1	172	203	602	58	147	19	7	4	59	35	70	1	.244	.319
Bassler, Johnny-John Landis	13-14CleA 21-27DetA	6- 3-95	Lancaster, Pa.		L	R	5'9	170	811	2319	250	704	99	16	1	318	437	81	13	.304	.361
Bates, Bud-Hubert Edgar	39PhiN	3-16-12	Los Angeles, Cal.		R	R	6'	165	15	58	8	15	2	0	1	2	2	8	1	.259	.345
Bates, Charlie-Charles William	27PhiA	9-17-05	Philadelphia, Pa.		R	R	5'10	165	9	38	5	9	2	2	0	2	3	5	3	.237	.395
Battle, Jim-James Milton	27ChiA	3-26-01	Bailer, Tex.		R	R	6'1	170	6	8	1	3	0	1	0	0	0	1	0	.375	.625
Beck, Clyde-Clyde Eugene (Jersey)	26-30ChiN 31CinN	1- 6-02	Bassett, Cal.		R	R	5'10	150	468	1525	203	354	56	11	12	162	184	180	9	.232	.307
Becker, Heinz-Heinz Reinhard (Dutch)	43,45-46ChiN 46-47CleA	8-26-15	Berlin, Germany		B	R	6'2	200	152	358	45	94	18	3	2	47	50	42	1	.263	.346
Becker, Joe-Joseph Edward	36-37CleA	6-25-08	St. Louis, Mo.		R	R	6'1	180	40	83	8	20	5	2	1	13	8	8	0	.241	.386
Bedford, Jim-James Eldred	25CleA	5-25-04	Hudson, N.Y.	6-27-62	R	R	5'8	155	2	3	1	0	0	0	0	0	0	1	0	.000	.000
Beeler, Jodie-Joseph Sam	44CinN	11-26-21	Dallas, Tex.		R	R	6'	170	3	3	0	0	0	0	0	0	0	2	0	.000	.000
Begley, Jim-James Lawrence (Imp)	24CinN	9-13-02	San Francisco, Cal.	2-22-57	R	R	5'6	140	2	5	1	1	0	0	0	0	2	0	0	.200	.200
Bejma, Ollie-Aloysius Frank	34-36StLA 39ChiA	9-12-07	South Bend, Ind.		R	R	5'10	165	316	906	128	222	35	11	14	117	130	105	5	.245	.354
Bell, Beau-Roy Chester	35-39StLA 39DetA 40-41CleA	8-20-07	Bellville, Tex.		R	R	6'2	185	767	2718	378	806	165	32	46	437	272	239	11	.297	.432
Bell, Fern-Fern Lee (Danny)	39-40PitN	1-21-13	Ada, Okla.		R	R	6'	180	89	265	44	75	5	8	2	35	43	19	2	.283	.385
Bell, Les-Lester Rowland	23-27StLN 28-29BosN 30-31ChiN	12-14-01	Harrisburg, Pa.		R	R	5'11	165	896	3239	404	938	184	49	66	509	276	322	25	.290	.438
Benes, Joe-Joseph Anthony (Bananas)	31StLN	1- 1-01	Queens, N.Y.		R	R	5'8	158	10	12	1	2	0	0	0	0	2	1	0	.167	.167
Bengough, Benny-Bernard Oliver	23-30NYA 31-32StLA	7-27-98	Niagara Falls, N.Y.	12-22-68	R	R	5'7	168	411	1125	83	287	46	12	0	108	62	45	2	.255	.317
Benjamin, Stan-Alfred Stanley	39-42PhiN 45CleA	5-20-14	Framingham, Mass.		R	R	6'2	194	241	770	77	176	32	11	5	41	32	115	23	.229	.318
Bennett, Fred-James Fred (Red)	28StLA 31PitN	3-15-02	Atkins, Ark.	5-12-57	R	R	5'9	185	39	97	6	27	6	0	1	7	7	6	0	.278	.371
Bennett, Herschel-Herschel Emmett	23-27StLA	9-21-96	Elwood, Mo.	9- 9-64	L	R	5'9	160	312	877	135	242	41	13	7	104	58	65	13	.276	.376
Bennett, Joe-Joseph Rosenblum	23PhiN	7- 2-00	New York, N.Y.		R	R	5'9	168	1	0	0	0	0	0	0	0	0	0	0	–	–
Bentley, Jack-John Needles (See P20-45)	13-16WasA 23-25NYN 26PhiN 26-27NYN	3- 8-95	Sandy Spring, Md.	10-24-69	L	L	6'	200	287	584	58	170	30	8	7	71	21	39	0	.291	.406
Benton, Stan-Stanley W.	22PhiN	9-29-01	Canal City, Ky.		L	R	5'7	150	6	19	1	4	1	0	0	3	2	1	0	.211	.263
Berg, Moe-Morris	23BknN 26-30ChiA 31CleA 32-34WasA 34CleA 35-39BosA	3- 2-02	New York, N.Y.	5-29-72	R	R	6'1	185	663	1812	150	441	71	6	6	206	78	117	11	.243	.299
Bergamo, Augie-August Samuel	44-45StLN	2-14-18	Detroit, Mich.		L	L	5'9	165	174	496	86	151	23	5	5	63	78	44	0	.304	.401
Berger, Boze-Louis William	32,35-36CleA 37-38ChiA 39BosA	5-13-10	Baltimore, Md.		R	R	6'2	180	343	1144	146	270	51	8	13	97	94	226	12	.236	.329

USE NAME – GIVEN NAMES (NICKNAMES)	TEAM BY YEAR	BIRTH DATE	BIRTH PLACE	DEATH DATE	B	T	HGT	WGT	G	AB	R	H	2B	3B	HR	RBI	BB	SO	SB	BA	SA
									LIFETIME BATTING TOTALS												
Berger, Johnny-John Henne	22PhiA 27WasA	8-27-01	Philadelphia, Pa.		R	R	5'9	165	11	16	1	5	0	0	0	1	2	3	1	.313	.313
Berger, Wally-Walter Antone	30-37BosN 37-38NYN 38-40CinN 40PhiN	10-10-05	Chicago, Ill.		R	R	6'2	198	1350	5163	809	1550	299	59	242	898	435	694	36	.300	.522
Berres, Ray-Raymond Frederick	34,36BknN 37-40PitN 40-41BosN 42-45NYN	8-31-07	Kenosha, Wis.		R	R	5'9	170	561	1330	96	287	37	3	3	78	76	134	4	.216	.255
Berry, Charlie-Charles Francis	25PhiA 28-32BosA 32-33ChiA 34-36,38PhiA	10-18-02	Phillipsburg, N.J.	9- 6-72	R	R	6'	185	709	2018	196	539	88	29	23	256	160	196	13	.267	.374
25-26 played in N.F.L.																					
Berry, Howard-Joseph Howard Jr. (Nig)	21-22NYN	12-31-94	Philadelphia, Pa.		B	R	5'11	165	15	6	0	2	0	1	0	2	1	1	0	.333	.667
21-22 played in N.F.L.																					
Bettencourt, Larry-Lawrence Joseph 33 played in N.F.L.	28,31-32StLA	9-22-05	Newark, Cal.		R	R	5'11	195	168	395	61	102	19	6	8	53	60	60	7	.258	.397
Bigbee, Carson-Carson Lee (Skeeter)	16-26PitN	3-31-95	Waterloo, Ore.	10-17-64	L	R	5'9	157	1147	4192	629	1205	139	75	17	324	344	161	182	.287	.369
Bigelow, Elliot-Elliot Allardice (Babe, Gilly)	29BosA	10-13-98	Tarpon Springs, Fla.	8-10-33	L	L	5'11	185	100	211	23	60	16	0	1	26	23	18	1	.284	.374
Biras, Steve-Stephen Alexander	44CleA	2-26-22	East St. Louis, Ill.	4-21-65	R	R	5'11	185	2	2	0	2	0	0	0	2	0	0	0	1.000	1.000
Bischoff, George-John George (Smiley)	25ChiA 25-26BosA	10-28-94	Edwardsville, Ill.		R	R	5'8	160	107	271	20	71	20	3	1	35	22	32	2	.262	.369
Bishop, Max-Max Frederick (Tilly, Camera Eye)	24-33PhiA 34-35BosA	9- 5-99	Waynesboro, Pa.	2-24-62	L	R	5'8	165	1338	4494	966	1216	236	35	41	379	1153	452	43	.271	.366
Bissonette, Del-Adelphia Louis	28-31BknN 32LJ 33BknN M45BosN	9- 6-99	Winthrop, Me.	6- 9-72	L	L	5'11	180	604	229	359	699	117	50	65	391	233	269	17	.305	.485
Black, Bill-John William (Jiggy)	24ChiA	8-12-99	Philadelphia, Pa.	1-14-68	L	R	5'11	168	6	5	0	1	1	0	0	0	0	0	0	.200	.200
Blackerby, George-George Franklin	28ChiA	11-10-03	Gluther, Okla.		R	R	6'1	176	30	83	8	21	21	0	0	12	4	10	2	.253	.253
Blades, Ray-Francis Raymond	22-28,30-32,M39-40StLN	8- 6-96	Mt. Vernon, Ill.		R	R	5'8	163	767	2415	467	726	133	51	50	340	331	310	33	.301	.460
Blaemire, Rae-Rae Bertram	41NYN	2- 8-11	Gary, Ind.		R	R	6'	178	2	5	0	2	0	0	0	0	0	0	0	.400	.400
Blair, Buddy-Louis Nathan	42PhiA 43-45MS	9-10-10	Columbia, Miss.		L	R	6'	186	137	484	48	135	26	8	5	66	30	30	1	.279	.397
Blair, Footsie-Clarence Vick	29-31ChiN	7-13-03	Pryor, Okla.		L	R	6'1	180	246	890	138	243	48	17	10	96	37	88	11	.273	.399
Blakely, Link-Lincoln Howard	34CinN	2-12-12	Oakland, Cal.		R	R	6'	180	34	102	11	23	1	1	0	10	5	14	1	.225	.255
Block, Cy-Seymour	42ChiN 43-44MS 45-46ChiN	5- 4-19	Brooklyn, N.Y.		R	R	6'	180	17	53	9	16	1	1	0	5	7	3	2	.302	.358
Bloodworth, Jimmy-James Henry	37,39-41WasA 42-43DetA 44-45MS 46DetA 47PitN 49-50CinN 50-51PhiN	7-26-17	Tallahassee, Fla.		R	R	5'11	180	1002	3519	347	874	160	20	62	451	202	407	19	.248	.358
Blott, Jack-John Leonard	24CinN	8-24-02	Girard, Ohio	6-11-64	R	R	6'	210	2	1	0	0	0	0	0	0	0	0	0	.000	.000
Blue, Lu-Luzerne Atwell	21-27DetA 28-30StLA 31-32ChiA 33BknN	3- 5-97	Washington, D.C.	7-28-58	B	L	5'10	165	1615	5904	1151	1696	319	109	44	692	1092	436	150	.287	.401
Bluege, Ossie-Oswald Louis	22-39,M43-47WasA	10-24-00	Chicago, Ill.		R	R	5'11	162	1867	6440	883	1751	276	67	43	848	724	525	140	.272	.356
Bluege, Otto-Otto Adam (Squeaky)	32-33CinN	7-20-09	Chicago, Ill.		R	R	5'10	154	109	291	18	62	6	2	0	18	26	29	0	.213	.247
Bocek, Milt-Milton Frank	33-34ChiA	7-16-12	Chicago, Ill.		R	R	6'1	185	30	60	6	16	2	0	1	6	9	11	0	.267	.350
Boeckel, Tony-Norman Doxie	17PitN 18MS 19PitN 19-23BosN	8-25-92	Los Angeles, Cal.	2-16-24	R	R	5'10	175	777	2880	372	813	130	36	27	337	237	218	90	.282	.381
Bohne (Cohen), Sammy-Samuel Arthur	16StLN 21-26CinN 26BknN	10-22-96	San Francisco, Cal.		R	R	5'9	175	663	2315	309	605	87	45	16	228	193	154	75	.261	.359
Boken, Bob-Robert Anthony	33-34WasA 34ChiA	2-23-08	Maryville, Ill.		R	R	6'2	165	147	457	54	113	15	4	6	72	27	49	4	.247	.337
Boland, Ed-Edward John	34-35PhiN 44WasA	4-18-08	Queens, N.Y.		L	L	5'10	165	57	136	11	35	5	1	0	23	4	14	2	.257	.309
Boley (Bolinsky), Joe-John Peter	27-32PhiA 32CleA	7-19-96	Mahanoy City, Pa.	12-30-62	R	R	5'11	170	540	1780	203	478	88	22	7	227	130	84	15	.269	.354
Bolling, Jack-John Edward	39PhiN 44BknN 45-46MS	2-20-17	Mobile, Ala.		L	L	5'11	168	125	342	48	107	25	1	4	38	25	14	6	.313	.427
Bolton, Cliff-William Clifton	31,33-36WasA 37DetA 41WasA	4-10-07	High Point, N.C.		L	R	5'9	160	335	962	113	280	49	18	6	143	108	50	3	.291	.398
Bolton, Glenn-Cecil Glenford (Lefty)	28CleA	2-13-04	Booneville, Miss.		L	L	6'4	195	4	13	1	2	0	2	0	0	2	2	0	.154	.462
Bongiovanni, Nino-Anthony Thomas	38-39CinN	12-21-11	Pike's Peak, La.		L	L	5'10	175	68	166	17	43	7	0	0	16	9	8	0	.259	.301
Bonura, Zeke-Henry John	34-37ChiA 38WasA 39NYN 40WasA 40ChiN	9-20-08	New Orleans, La.		R	R	6'	210	917	3582	600	1099	232	29	119	704	404	180	19	.307	.487
Bool, Al-Albert J.	28WasA 30PitN 31BosN	8-24-97	Lincoln, Neb.		R	R	6'	185	129	308	35	73	13	4	7	53	34	42	0	.237	.373
Boone, Ike-Isaac Morgan	22NYN 23-25BosA 27ChiA 30-32BknN	2-17-97	Samantha, Ala.	8- 1-58	L	R	6'	195	356	1159	176	370	78	11	26	192	140	68	3	.319	.473
Bordagaray, Frenchy-Stanley George	34ChiA 35-36BknN 37-38StLN 39CinN 41NYA 42-45BknN	1- 3-12	Coalinga, Cal.		R	R	5'8	175	930	2632	410	745	120	28	14	270	173	186	65	.283	.366
Borom, Red-Edward Jones	44-45DetA	10-30-15	Spartanburg, S.C.		L	R	5'11	180	62	144	20	36	4	0	0	10	9	10	4	.250	.278
Boss, Harley-Elmer Harley (Lefty)	28-30WasA 33CleA	11-19-08	Hodge, La.	5-15-64	L	L	5'11	185	155	519	64	139	19	8	1	61	30	34	2	.268	.341
Bottarini, John-John Charles	37ChiN	9-14-08	Crockett, Cal.		R	R	6'	190	26	40	3	11	3	0	1	7	5	10	0	.275	.425
Bottomley, Jim-James LeRoy (Sunny Jim)	22-32StLN 33-35CinN 36-37,M37StLA	4-23-00	Oglesby, Ill.	12-11-59	L	L	6'	180	1991	7471	1177	2313	465	151	219	1422	664	591	58	.310	.500
Boudreau, Lou-Louis	38-50,M42-50CleA 51-52,M52-54BosA M55-57KCA M60ChiN	7-17-17	Harvey, Ill.		R	R	5'11	185	1646	6030	861	1779	385	66	68	789	796	309	51	.295	.415
38-39 played in N.B.L., 39-40 head coach in N.B.L.																					
Bowman, Elmer-Elmari Wilhelm	20WasA	3-19-97	Proctor, Vt.		R	R	6'	193	2	1	1	0	0	0	0	0	1	0	0	.000	.000
Bowman, Joe-Joseph Emil (See P20-45)	32PhiA 34NYN 35-36PhiN 37-41PitN 44-45BosA 45CinN	6-17-10	Argentine, Kans.		L	R	6'2	190	430	639	62	141	24	8	2	75	46	90	3	.221	.293
Boyle, Buzz-Ralph Francis	29-30BosN 33-35BknN	2- 9-08	Cincinnati, Ohio		L	L	5'11	170	366	1343	185	389	58	24	12	125	116	125	24	.290	.395
Boyle, Jim-James John	26NYN	1-19-04	Cincinnati, Ohio	12-24-58	R	R	6'	180	1	0	0	0	0	0	0	0	0	0	0	–	–
Brack, Gib-Gilbert Herman (Gibby)	37-38BknN 38-39PhiN	3-29-08	Chicago, Ill.	1-20-60	R	R	5'9	170	315	980	150	273	70	18	16	113	92	186	13	.279	.436
Bradford, Vic-Henry Victor	43NYN 44-46MS	3- 5-15	Brownsville, Tenn.		R	R	6'2	190	6	5	1	1	0	0	0	1	1	1	0	.200	.200
Brady, Cliff-Clifford Francis	20BosA	3- 6-97	St. Louis, Mo.	9-25-74	R	R	5'6	140	53	180	16	41	5	1	0	12	13	12	0	.228	.267
Bragan, Bobby-Robert Randall	40-42PhiN 43-44BknN 45-46MS 47-48BknN M56-57PitN M58CleA M63-65MilN M66AtLN	10-30-17	Birmingham, Ala.		R	R	5'10	175	597	1900	136	456	62	12	15	172	110	117	12	.240	.309
Bramhall, Art-Arthur Washington	35PhiN	2-22-09	Chicago, Ill.		R	R	5'11	170	2	1	0	0	0	0	0	0	0	0	0	.000	.000
Brancato, Al-Albert	39-41PhiA 42-44MS 45PhiA	5-29-19	Philadelphia, Pa.		R	R	5'10	188	282	930	117	199	37	11	4	80	96	92	5	.214	.290
Brannan, Otis-Otis Owen	28-29StLA	3-13-99	Greenbrier, Ark.	6- 6-67	L	R	5'9	160	158	534	72	133	19	3	11	74	64	23	3	.249	.358
Branom, Dud-Edgar Dudley	27PhiA	11-30-97	Sulphur Springs, Tex.		L	L	6'1	190	30	94	8	22	1	0	0	13	2	5	2	.234	.254
Bratcher, Joe-Joseph Warlick (Goobers)	24StLN	7-22-98	Grand Saline, Tex.		L	R	5'8	140	4	1	1	0	0	0	0	0	0	0	0	.000	.000
Bratschi, Fred-Frederick Oscar (Fritz)	21ChiA 26-27BosA	1-16-92	Alliance, Ohio	1-10-62	R	R	5'10	170	89	196	12	54	11	1	0	22	14	17	0	.276	.342
Bray, Buster-Clarence Wilbur	41BosN	4- 1-13	Birmingham, Ala.		L	L	6'	170	4	11	2	1	1	0	0	1	1	2	0	.091	.182
Brazill, Frank-Frank Leo	21-22PhiA	8-11-99	Spangler, Pa.		L	L	5'11	175	72	190	17	49	3	1	0	20	23	22	2	.258	.284
Bremer, Herb-Herbert Frederick	37-39StLN	10-25-13	Chicago, Ill.		R	R	6'	195	70	193	16	41	6	1	2	18	11	42	1	.212	.285
Brenzel, Bill-William Richard	32PitN 34-35CleA	3- 3-10	Oakland, Cal.		R	R	5'10	173	76	217	16	43	9	1	0	19	8	15	2	.198	.249
Bressler, Rube-Raymond Bloom (See P01-19)	14-16PhiA 17-27CinN 28-31BknN 32PhiN 32StLN	10-23-94	Coder, Pa.	11- 7-66	R	L	6'	187	1305	3881	544	1171	164	87	32	586	449	246	47	.302	.414
Brewster, Charlie-Charles Lawrence	43CinN 43PhiN 44ChiN 46CleA	12-27-16	Marthaville, La.		R	R	5'9	175	69	213	17	47	4	0	0	14	16	28	1	.221	.239
Brickell, Fred-George Frederick	26-30PitN 30-33PhiN	11- 9-06	Saffordville, Kans.	4- 8-61	L	R	5'7	160	501	1448	221	407	54	23	6	131	106	121	19	.281	.363
Brittain, Gus-August Schuster	37CinN	11-29-09	Wilmington, N.C.	2-16-74	R	R	5'10	192	3	6	0	1	0	0	0	0	0	3	0	.167	.167
Brooks (Brozek), Mandy-Jonathan Joseph	25-26ChiN	8-18-98	Milwaukee, Wis.	6-17-62	R	R	5'9	165	116	397	62	107	26	7	15	78	24	33	10	.270	.484
Broskie, Siggy-Sigmund Theodore (Chaps)	40BosN	3-23-11	Iselin, Pa.	5-17-75	R	R	5'11	200	11	22	1	6	1	0	0	4	1	2	0	.273	.318
Brottem, Tony-Anton Christian	16,18StLN 21WasA 21PitN	4-30-92	Halstead, Minn.	8- 5-29	R	R	6'	176	62	135	10	29	3	0	0	13	9	22	1	.215	.237
Brower, Frank-Frank Willard (Turkeyfoot)	20-22WasA 23-24CleA	3-26-93	Gainesville, Va.	11-20-60	L	R	6'2	180	450	1297	206	371	74	20	30	205	168	84	17	.286	.443
Brower, Lou-Louis Lester	31DetA	7- 1-00	Cleveland, Ohio		R	R	5'10	155	21	62	3	10	1	0	0	6	8	5	1	.161	.177
Brown, Eddie-Edward William (Glass Arm Eddie)	20-21NYN 24-25BknN 26-28BosN	7-17-91	Milligan, Neb.	9-10-56	R	R	6'3	190	790	2902	341	878	170	33	16	407	127	109	29	.303	.400
Brown, Jimmy-James Roberson	37-43StLN 44-45MS 46PitN	4-25-10	Jamesville, N.C.		B	R	5'8	165	890	3512	465	980	146	42	9	319	231	110	39	.279	.352
Brown, Lindsay-John Lindsay (Red)	37BknN	7-22-11	Mason, Tex.	1- 1-67	R	R	5'10	160	48	115	16	31	3	1	0	6	3	17	1	.270	.313
Browne, Earl-Earl James (Snitz)	35-36PitN 37-38PhiN	3- 5-11	Louisville, Ky.		L	L	6'	175	143	461	59	131	26	5	6	69	29	64	4	.284	.401
Brubaker, Bill-Wilbur Lee	32-40PitN 43BosN	11- 7-10	Cleveland, Ohio		R	R	6'2	190	479	1564	208	413	85	10	22	225	151	239	13	.264	.373
Brucker, Earle-Earle Francis Sr.	37-40,43PhiA M52CinN	5- 6-01	Albany, N.Y.		R	R	5'11	175	241	707	87	205	53	8	12	105	97	65	2	.290	.438
Bruggy, Frank-Frank Leo	21PhiN 22-24PhiA 25CinN	5- 4-91	Elizabeth, N.J.	4- 5-59	R	R	5'11	195	259	620	53	172	27	2	6	52	43	72	12	.277	.356
Bubser, Hal-Harold Fred	22ChiA	9-28-95	Chicago, Ill.		R	R	5'11	170	3	3	0	0	0	0	0	0	0	2	0	.000	.000
Bucher, Jim-James Quinter	34-37BknN 38StLN 44-45BosA	3-11-11	Manassas, Va.		L	R	5'11	170	554	1792	242	474	66	19	17	193	91	113	19	.265	.351
Burgo, Bill-William Ross	43-44PhiA	11-15-19	Johnstown, Pa.		R	R	5'8	185	44	158	18	47	6	2	2	12	11	4	1	.297	.399
Burich, Bill-William Max	42PhiN 43-45MS 46PhiN	5-29-18	Calumet, Mich.		R	R	6'	180	27	81	4	23	1	0	0	7	6	13	2	.284	.296
Burke, Les-Leslie Kingston (Buck)	23-26DetA	12-18-02	Lynn, Mass.		L	R	5'9	168	194	506	73	131	17	7	0	47	46	32	7	.259	.320
Burke, Pat-Patrick Edward	24StLA	5-13-01	St. Louis, Mo.	7- 7-65	R	R	5'11	170	1	3	0	0	0	0	0	1	0	0	0	.000	.000
Burnett, Johnny-John Henderson	27-34CleA 35StLA	11- 1-04	Bartow, Fla.	8-13-59	L	R	5'11	175	558	1835	288	521	94	15	9	213	163	107	15	.284	.366
Burns, George-George Henry (Tioga George)	14-17DetA 18-20PhiA 20-21CleA 22-23BosA 24-28CleA 28-29NYA 29PhiA	1-31-93	Niles, Ohio		R	R	6'1	180	1866	6573	901	2018	444	72	72	948	363	433	153	.307	.429
Burns, Jack-John Irving (Slug)	30-36StLA 36-DetA	8-31-07	Cambridge, Mass.	4-18-75	L	L	6'1	175	890	3506	541	980	199	31	44	417	376	299	63	.280	.392
Burns, Joe-Joseph Francis	24ChiA	2-25-00	Trenton, N.J.		R	R	6'	175	8	19	1	2	0	0	0	0	0	2	0	.105	.105

USE NAME – GIVEN NAMES (NICKNAMES)	TEAM BY YEAR	BIRTH DATE	BIRTH PLACE	DEATH DATE	B	T	HGT	WGT	G	AB	R	H	2B	3B	HR	RBI	BB	SO	SB	BA	SA
									LIFETIME BATTING TOTALS												
Burns, Joe-Joseph James	43BosN 44-45PhiA	6-17-15	Bryn Mawr, Pa.		R	R	5'10	175	111	300	24	69	6	1	2	16	16	50	2	.230	.277
Burrus, Dick-Maurice Lennon	20-21PhiA 25-28BosN	1-29-98	Hatteras, N.C.	2- 2-72	L	L	5'11	175	1760	513	206	513	87	12	11	211	138	95	18	.291	.373
Busby, Paul-Paul Miller (Red)	41,43PhiN	8-25-18	Waynesboro, Miss.		L	R	6'1	175	36	56	16	15	1	0	0	7	2	2	2	.268	.286
Busch, Ed-Edgar John	43-45PhiA	11-16-17	Lebanon, Ill.		R	R	5'10	175	270	917	80	240	21	6	0	75	62	28	7	.262	.298
Buskey, Joe-Joseph Henry (Jazzbow)	26PhiN	12-18-02	Cumberland, Md.	4-11-49	R	R	5'10	175	5	8	1	0	0	0	0	0	1	1	0	.000	.000
Butka, Ed-Edward Luke (Babe)	43-44WasA	1- 7-16	Canonsburg, Pa.		R	R	6'3	193	18	50	1	11	2	0	0	2	2	14	0	.220	.260
Butler, Johnny-John Stephen (Trolley Line)	26-27BknN 28ChiN 29StLN	3-20-93	Fall River, Kans.	4-29-67	R	R	6'	175	375	1251	115	315	48	12	3	146	111	89	17	.252	.317
Buzas, Joe-Joseph John	45NYA	10- 2-19	Alpha, N.J.		R	R	6'1	180	30	65	8	17	2	1	0	6	2	5	2	.262	.323
Byrd, Sammy-Samuel Dewey (Babe Ruth's Legs)	29-34NYA 35-36CinN	10-15-06	Bremen, Ga.		R	R	5'10	175	745	1700	304	465	101	10	38	220	198	178	17	.274	.412
Byrnes, Milt-Milton John (Skippy)	43-45StLA	11-15-16	St. Louis, Mo.		L	L	5'10	170	390	1278	174	350	77	15	16	154	200	183	3	.274	.395
Cafego, Tom-Thomas	37StLA	8-21-11	Whipple, W.Va.	10-29-61	L	R	5'10	160	4	4	1	0	0	0	0	0	0	1	0	.000	.000
Caithamer, George-George Theodore	34ChiA	7-22-10	Chicago, Ill.	6- 1-54	R	R	5'8	160	5	19	1	6	1	0	0	3	1	5	0	.316	.368
Caldwell, Bruce-Bruce 28 played in N.F.L.	28CleA 32BknN	2- 8-06	Ashton, R.I.	2-15-59	R	R	6'	195	25	38	4	7	1	1	0	5	4	4	1	.184	.263
Callaghan, Marty-Martin Francis	22-23ChiN 28,30CinN	6- 9-00	Norwood, Mass.	6-24-75	L	L	5'10	157	295	767	106	205	28	13	0	74	71	70	10	.267	.338
Callaway, Frank-Frank Burnett	21-22PhiA	2-26-98	Knoxville, Tenn.		R	R	6'	170	43	98	12	25	1	3	0	6	2	24	1	.255	.327
Camilli, Dolph-Adolph Louis	33-34ChiN 34-37PhiN 38-43BknN 44MS 45BosA	4-23-07	San Francisco, Cal.		L	L	5'10	185	1490	5353	936	1482	261	86	239	950	947	961	60	.277	.492
Campanis, Al-Alexander Sebastian	43BknN 44-45MS	11- 2-16	Kos, Greece		B	R	6'	185	7	20	3	2	0	0	0	0	4	5	0	.100	.100
Campbell, Bruce-Bruce Douglas	30-32ChiA 32-34StLA 35-39CleA 40-41DetA	10-20-09	Chicago, Ill.		L	R	6'1	185	1360	4762	759	1382	295	87	106	766	548	584	53	.290	.455
	42WasA 43-45MS																				
Campbell, Gilly-William Gilthorpe	33ChiN 35-37CinN 38BknN	2-13-08	Kansas City, Kans.	2-21-73	L	R	5'11	176	295	708	78	186	30	2	5	93	116	35	5	.263	.332
Campbell, Soup-Clarence	40-41CleA 42-46MS	3- 7-15	Sparta, Va.		L	R	6'1	188	139	390	44	96	11	4	3	37	38	33	1	.246	.318
Capri, Pat-Patrick Nicholas	44BosN	11-27-18	New York, N.Y.		R	R	6'	170	7	1	1	0	0	0	0	0	0	1	0	.000	.000
Carey (Carnarius), Max (Maximilan)-Max George (Scoops)	10-26PitN 26-29,M32-33BknN	1-11-90	Terre Haute, Ind.		B	R	5'11	170	2476	9363	1545	2665	419	159	69	800	1040	695	738	.285	.385
Carey, Tom-Thomas Francis Aloysious (Scoops)	35-37StLA 39-42,46BosA 43-45MS	10-11-08	Hoboken, N.J.	2-21-70	R	R	5'8	175	465	1520	169	418	79	13	2	169	66	75	3	.275	.348
Carlin, Jim-James Arthur	41PhiN 42-45MS	2-23-18	Wylam, Ala.		L	R	5'11	165	16	21	2	3	1	0	1	2	3	4	0	.143	.333
Carlyle, Cleo-Hiram Cleo	27BosA	9- 7-02	Fairburn, Ga.	11-12-67	L	R	6'	170	95	278	31	65	12	8	1	28	36	40	4	.234	.345
Carlyle, Roy-Roy Edward (Dizzy)	25WasA 25-26BosA 26NYA	12-10-00	Buford, Ga.	11-22-56	L	R	6'2	195	174	494	61	157	31	6	9	76	24	57	1	.318	.460
Carnett, Eddie-Edwin Elliott (Lefty) (See P20-45)	41BosN 44ChiA 45CleA 46MS	10-21-16	Springfield, Mo.		L	L	6'	185	158	530	56	142	25	8	1	67	28	44	5	.268	.351
Carson, Kit-Walter Lloyd	34-35CleA	11-15-12	Colton, Cal.		L	L	6'	180	21	40	5	10	4	1	0	2	4	9	0	.250	.400
Carter, Blackie-Otis Leonard	25-26NYN	9-30-02	Langley, S.C.		R	R	5'10	175	6	21	4	4	1	0	1	1	1	1	0	.190	.381
Carter, Howard-John Howard (Nick)	26CinN	10-13-04	New York, N.Y.		R	R	5'10	154	5	1	0	0	0	0	0	0	0	0	0	.000	.000
Case, George-George Washington	37-45WasA 46CleA 47WasA	11-11-15	Trenton, N.J.		R	R	6'	183	1226	5017	785	1415	233	43	21	377	425	297	349	.282	.358
Castiglia, Jim-James Vincent	42PhiA 43-45MS	9-30-18	Passaic, N.J.		L	R	5'11	200	16	18	2	7	0	0	0	2	1	3	0	.389	.389
41,45-48 played in N.F.L. 47 played in A.A.F.C.																					
Castino, Vince-Vincent Charles	43-45ChiA	10-11-17	Willisville, Ill.	3- 6-67	R	R	5'9	175	88	216	24	49	7	0	2	23	25	31	0	.227	.287
Cather, Ted-Theodore P	12-14StLN 14-15BosN	5-20-89	Chester, Pa.	4- 9-45	R	R	5'10	178	201	548	60	138	30	8	2	72	34	90	21	.252	.347
Cavarretta, Phil-Philip Joseph	34-53,M51-53ChiN 54-55ChiA	7-19-16	Chicago, Ill.		L	L	5'11	175	2030	6754	990	1977	347	99	95	920	820	598	65	.293	.416
Caveney, Ike-James Christopher	22-25CinN	12-10-94	San Francisco, Cal.	7- 6-49	R	R	5'9	168	466	1577	173	410	61	24	13	196	97	126	15	.260	.354
Chamberlain, Joe-Joseph Jeremiah	34ChiA	5-10-10	San Francisco, Cal.		R	R	6'1	175	43	141	13	34	5	1	2	17	6	38	1	.241	.333
Chaplin (Chapman), Bert-Bert Edgar (Chappy)	20-22BosA	9-25-93	Pelzer, S.C.		L	R	5'7	158	35	76	10	14	2	1	0	7	13	11	2	.184	.237
Chapman, Ben-William Benjamin (See P20-45)	30-36NYA 36-37WasA 37-38BosA	12-25-08	Nashville, Tenn.		R	R	6'	190	1716	6478	1144	1958	407	107	90	977	824	556	287	.302	.440
	39-40CleA 41WasA 41ChiA 44-45BknN 45-46,M45-48PhiN																				
Chapman, Calvin-Calvin Louis	35-36CinN	12-20-10	Courtland, Miss.		L	R	5'9	160	111	272	41	72	8	3	1	25	20	24	7	.265	.327
Chapman, Fred-William Fred (Chappie)	39-41PhiA 42-45MS	7-17-16	Liberty, S.C.		R	R	6'1	185	76	187	12	36	3	1	0	9	11	28	3	.193	.219
Chapman, Glenn-Glenn Justice (Pete)	34BknN	1-21-06	Cambridge City, Ind.		R	R	5'11	170	67	93	19	26	5	1	1	10	7	19	1	.280	.387
Chapman, John-John Joseph	24PhiA	10-15-00	Centralia, Pa.	11- 3-53	R	R	5'10	175	19	71	7	20	4	1	0	6	3	3	0	.282	.366
Chartak, Mike-Michael George (Shotgun)	40,42NYA 42WasA 42-44StLA	4-28-16	Brooklyn, N.Y.	7-25-67	L	L	6'2	180	256	765	96	186	34	7	21	98	104	112	4	.243	.388
Chatham, Buster-Charles L.	30-31BosN	12-25-01	West, Tex.		R	R	5'5	150	129	448	52	118	21	11	6	59	43	47	8	.263	.400
Chervinko, Paul-Paul	37-38BknN	7-23-10	Trauger, Pa.		R	R	5'8	185	42	75	1	11	0	1	0	5	5	16	0	.147	.173
Chiozza, Dino-Dino Joseph (Dynamo)	35PhiN	6-30-12	Memphis, Tenn.	4-23-72	L	R	6'	170	2	0	1	0	0	0	0	0	0	0	0	–	–
Chiozza, Lou-Louis Peo	34-36PhiN 37-39NYN	5-11-10	Tallulah, La.	2-28-71	L	R	6'	172	616	2288	303	633	107	22	14	197	145	165	45	.277	.361
Chipple (Chlipala), Walt-Walter John	45WasA	9-26-18	Utica, N.Y.		R	R	6'	168	18	44	4	6	0	0	0	5	5	6	0	.136	.136
Chozen, Harry-Harry Kenneth	37CinN	9-27-15	Winnebago, Minn.		R	R	5'10	190	1	4	0	1	0	0	0	0	0	0	0	.250	.250
Christenbury, Lloyd-Lloyd Reid (Low)	19-22BosN	10-19-93	Mecklenburg Co., N.C.	12-13-44	L	R	5'7	165	205	414	78	113	14	6	4	47	54	32	5	.273	.365
Christensen, Cuckoo-Walter Neils (Seacap)	26-27CinN	10-24-99	San Francisco, Cal.		L	L	5'6	156	171	514	66	162	21	7	0	57	60	34	12	.315	.383
Christman, Mark-Marquette Joseph	38-39DetA 39,43-46StLA 47-49WasA	10-21-13	Maplewood, Mo.		R	R	5'11	175	911	3081	294	781	113	23	19	348	220	179	17	.253	.324
Churry, John-John	24-27ChiN	11-26-00	Johnstown, Pa.	2- 8-70	R	R	5'9	172	12	18	1	5	1	0	0	1	3	2	0	.278	.333
Cicero, Joe-Joseph Francis (Dode)	29-30BosA 45PhiA	11-18-10	Atlantic City, N.J.		R	R	5'8	167	40	81	14	18	3	4	0	8	2	13	0	.222	.358
Cieslak, Ted-Thaddeus Walter	44PhiN	11-22-16	Milwaukee, Wis.		R	R	5'10	175	85	220	18	54	10	0	2	11	21	17	1	.245	.318
Cihocki, Al-Albert Joseph	45CleA	5- 7-24	Nanticoke, Pa.		R	R	5'11	185	92	283	21	60	9	3	0	24	11	48	2	.212	.265
Cihocki, Ed-Edward Joseph (Cy)	32-33PhiA	5- 9-07	Wilmington, Del.		R	R	5'8	163	34	98	6	14	2	3	0	9	7	16	0	.143	.224
Cisar, George-George Joseph	37BknN	8-25-12	Chicago, Ill.		R	R	6'	175	20	29	8	6	0	0	0	4	2	6	3	.207	.207
Cissell, Bill-Chalmer William	28-32ChiA 32-33CleA 34BosA 37PhiA 38NYN	1- 3-04	Perryville, Mo.	3-15-49	R	R	5'11	170	956	3706	516	990	173	43	29	423	212	250	114	.267	.360
Clabaugh, Moose-John William	26BknN	11-13-01	Albany, Mo.		L	R	6'	185	11	14	2	1	1	0	0	1	0	1	0	.071	.143
Claire, Dave-David Matthew	20DetA	11-17-97	Ludington, Mich.	1- 7-56	R	R	5'7	170	3	7	1	1	0	0	0	0	0	0	0	.143	.143
Clancy, Bud-John William	24-30ChiA 32BknN 34PhiN	9-15-00	Odell, Ill.	9-27-68	L	L	6'	170	522	1796	204	504	69	26	12	198	111	106	19	.281	.368
Clanton, Uke-Ucal (Cat)	22CleA	2-19-98	Powell, Mo.	2-24-60	L	L	5'8	160	1	1	0	0	0	0	0	0	0	1	0	.000	.000
Clark, Cap-John Carrol	38PhiN	9-19-06	Snow Camp, N.C.	2-16-57	L	R	5'11	180	52	74	11	19	1	1	0	4	9	10	0	.257	.297
Clark, Danny-Daniel Curran	22DetA 24BosA 27StLN	1-18-94	Meridian, Miss.	5-23-37	L	R	5'9	167	245	582	75	161	36	8	5	93	74	37	5	.277	.392
Clark, Earl-Bailey Earl	27-33BosN 34StLA	11- 6-07	Washington, D.C.	1-16-38	R	R	5'10	160	293	826	122	240	41	7	4	81	37	79	11	.291	.372
Clarke, Grey-Richard Grey (Noisy)	44ChiA	9-26-12	Fulton, Ala.		R	R	5'9	183	63	169	14	44	10	1	0	27	22	6	0	.260	.331
Clarke, Stu-William Stuart	29-30PitN	1-24-06	San Francisco, Cal.		R	R	5'8	160	61	187	22	51	5	8	2	23	20	21	3	.273	.417
Clarke, Sumpter-Sumpter Mills	20ChiN 23-24CleA	10-18-97	Savannah, Ga.	3-16-62	R	R	5'11	170	37	110	17	25	6	1	0	11	6	13	0	.227	.300
Clary, Ellis-Ellis (Cat)	42-43WasA 43-45StLA	9-11-16	Valdosta, Ga.		R	R	5'8	160	223	650	97	171	32	2	1	46	114	74	12	.263	.323
Clay, Dain-Dain Elmer (Ding-a-Ling)	43-46CinN	7-10-19	Hicksville, Ohio		R	R	5'10	160	433	1540	203	397	63	6	3	98	115	130	39	.258	.312
Clemens, Chet-Chester Spurgeon	39,44BosN 45-46MS	5-10-17	San Fernando, Cal.		R	R	6'	175	28	40	9	8	1	1	0	3	3	5	1	.200	.275
Clemons, Vern-Verne James (Fats, Tubby, Stinger)	16StLA 19-24StLN	9- 8-91	Clemons, Iowa	5- 5-59	R	R	5'10	190	474	1271	78	364	56	11	5	140	119	62	6	.286	.360
Clift, Harlond-Harlond Benton (Darkie)	34-43StLA 43-45WasA	8-12-12	El Reno, Okla.		R	R	5'11	180	1582	5730	1070	1558	309	62	178	829	1070	713	69	.272	.441
Clifton, Flea-Herman Earl	34-37DetA	12-12-09	Cincinnati, Ohio		R	R	5'10	160	87	195	27	39	7	0	0	13	17	28	5	.200	.236
Clough, Ed-Edgar George (Spec) (See P20-45)	24-26StLN	10-28-06	Wiconisco, Pa.	1-30-44	L	L	6'2	188	11	19	0	2	0	0	0	1	0	3	0	.105	.105
Coble, Dave-David Lamar	39PhiN	12-24-12	Monroe, N.C.	10-15-71	R	R	6'1	183	15	25	2	7	1	0	0	0	0	3	0	.280	.320
Cochrane, Mickey-Gordon Stanley (Black Mike)	25-33PhiA 34-37,M34-38DetA	4- 6-03	Bridgewater, Mass.	6-28-62	L	R	5'10	180	1482	5169	1041	1652	333	64	119	832	857	217	64	.320	.478
Cohen, Alta-Alta Albert	31-32BknN 33PhiN	12-25-08	New York, N.Y.		L	L	5'10	170	29	67	8	13	2	0	0	2	9	11	0	.194	.224
Cohen, Andy-Andrew Howard	26,28-29NYN M60PhiN	10-25-04	Baltimore, Md.		R	R	5'8	155	262	886	108	249	36	10	14	114	43	34	6	.281	.392
Coleman, Ed-Parke Edward	32-35PhiA 35-36StLA	12- 1-01	Canby, Ore.	8- 5-64	L	R	6'2	200	439	1337	193	381	67	23	40	246	117	152	1	.285	.459
Collins, Bob-Robert Joseph (Rip)	40ChiN 44NYA	9-18-09	Pittsburgh, Pa.	4-19-69	R	R	5'11	176	50	123	11	26	3	0	1	14	15	18	4	.211	.260
Collins, Eddie-Edward Trowbridge Jr.	39,41-42PhiA 43-45MS	11-23-16	Lansdowne, Pa.		L	R	5'10	175	132	274	41	66	9	3	0	16	24	29	4	.241	.296
Collins, Pat-Tharon Patrick	19-24StLA 26-28NYA 29BosN	9-13-96	Sweet Springs, Mo.	5-20-60	R	R	5'9	178	542	1203	146	306	46	6	33	168	235	200	4	.254	.385
Collins, Ripper-James Anthony	31-36StLN 37-38ChiN 41PitN	3-30-04	Altoona, Pa.	4-16-70	B	L	5'9	165	1084	3784	615	1121	205	65	135	659	356	373	18	.296	.492
Colman, Frank-Frank Lloyd	42-46PitN 46-47NYA	3- 2-18	London, Canada		L	L	5'11	186	271	571	66	130	25	8	15	106	49	66	0	.228	.378
Combs, Earle-Earle Bryan (The Kentucky Colonel)	24-35NYA	5- 4-99	Pebworth, Ky.		L	R	6'	185	1455	5748	1186	1866	309	154	58	629	670	278	96	.325	.462
Comorosky, Adam-Adam Anthony	26-33PitN 34-35CinN	12- 9-04	Swoyersville, Pa.	3- 2-51	R	R	5'10	167	813	2787	404	795	134	51	28	417	214	158	57	.285	.400
Conlan, Jocko-John Bertrand	34-35ChiA	12- 6-99	Chicago, Ill.		L	L	5'7	165	128	365	55	96	18	4	0	31	33	13	5	.263	.334
Conlon, Art-Arthur Joseph (Jocko)	23BosN	12-10-97	Woburn, Mass.		R	R	5'7	145	59	147	23	32	3	0	0	17	11	11	0	.218	.238

USE NAME – GIVEN NAMES (NICKNAMES)	TEAM BY YEAR	BIRTH DATE	BIRTH PLACE	DEATH DATE	B	T	HGT	WGT	G	AB	R	H	2B	3B	HR	RBI	BB	SO	SB	BA	SA
Connatser, Bruce-Broadus Milburn	31-32CleA	9-19-02	Sevierville, Tenn.	1-27-71	R	R	5'11	170	35	109	13	28	6	1	0	8	6	11	1	.257	.330
Connell, Gene-Eugene Joseph	31PhiN	5-10-06	Hazelton, Pa.	8-31-37	R	R	6'	180	6	12	1	3	0	0	0	0	0	3	0	.250	.250
Connell, Joe-Joseph Bernard	26NYN	1-16-02	Bethlehem, Pa.		L	L	5'8	165	2	1	1	0	0	0	0	0	0	0	0	.000	.000
Connelly, Tom-Thomas Martin	20-21NYA	10-20-98	Chicago, Ill.		L	R	5'11	165	5	6	0	1	0	0	0	0	1	0	0	.167	.167
Connolly, Bud-Mervin Thomas (Mike)	25BosA	5-25-01	San Francisco, Cal.	6-12-64	R	R	5'8	154	43	107	12	28	7	1	0	21	23	9	0	.262	.346
Connolly, Ed-Edward Joseph Sr.	29-32BosA	7-17-08	Brooklyn, N.Y.	11-12-63	R	R	5'9	180	149	371	13	66	11	4	0	31	29	50	0	.178	.229
Connolly, Joe-Joseph George (Coaster Joe)	21NYN 22-23CleA 24BosA	6- 4-96	San Francisco, Cal.	3-30-60	R	R	6'	170	80	168	32	45	12	2	3	32	21	18	2	.268	.417
Connors, Merv-Mervyn James	37-38ChiA	1-23-14	Berkeley, Cal.		R	R	6'2	192	52	165	26	46	8	1	8	25	23	36	2	.279	.485
Conroy, Bill-William Gordon	35-37PhiA 42 44BosA 45MS	2-26-15	Bloomington, Ill.		R	R	6'	185	169	452	45	90	13	3	5	33	77	85	3	.199	.274
Conroy, Pep-William Frederick	23WasA	1- 9-99	Chicago, Ill.		R	R	5'8	160	18	60	6	8	2	2	0	2	4	9	0	.133	.233
Cooke, Dusty-Allen Lindsey	30-32NYA 33-36BosA 38CinN M48PhiN	6-23-07	Swepsonville, N.C.		L	R	6'1	205	608	1745	324	488	109	28	24	229	290	276	32	.280	.415
Cooney, Jimmy-James Edward (Scoops)	17BosA 18MS 19NYN 24-25StLN 26-27ChiN 27PhiN 28BosN	8-24-94	Cranston, R.I.		R	R	5'11	160	448	1575	181	413	64	16	2	150	76	58	30	.262	.327
Cooney, Johnny-John Walter (See P20-45)	21-30,38-42BosN 35-37,43-44BknN 44NYA	3-18-01	Cranston, R.I.		R	L	5'10	165	1172	3372	408	965	130	26	2	219	208	107	30	.286	.342
Corbett, Gene-Eugene Louis	36-38PhiN	10-25-13	Winona, Minn.		L	R	6'2	190	37	108	12	13	3	0	2	10	8	14	0	.120	.204
Corgan, Chuck-Charles Howard 24-27 played in N.F.L.	25,27BknN	12-04-02	Wagoner, Okla.	6-13-28	B	R	6'	185	33	104	7	23	2	1	0	1	7	13	0	.221	.260
Cortazzo, Shine-John Francis	23ChiA	9-26-04	Wilmerding, Pa.	3- 4-63	R	R	5'4	142	1	1	0	0	0	0	0	0	0	0	0	.000	.000
Coscarart, Joe-Joseph Marvin	35-36BosN	11-18-09	Escondido, Cal.		R	R	6'	185	190	651	58	157	22	4	3	73	35	65	2	.241	.301
Coscarart, Pete-Pete Joseph	38-41BknN 42-46PitN	6-16-13	Escondido, Cal.		R	R	5'11	175	864	2992	399	728	129	22	28	269	295	361	34	.243	.329
Cote, Pete-Warren Peter	26NYN	8-30-02	Cambridge, Mass.		R	R	5'6	148	2	1	0	0	0	0	0	0	0	0	0	.000	.000
Cotter, Ed-Edward Christopher	26PhiN	7- 4-04	Hartford, Conn.	6-14-59	R	R	6'	185	17	26	3	8	0	1	0	1	1	4	1	.308	.385
Cotter, Harvey-Harvey Louis (Hooks)	22,24ChiN	5-22-00	Holden, Mo.	8- 6-55	L	L	5'10	160	99	311	39	82	17	4	4	33	36	31	3	.264	.383
Cousineau, Dee-Edward Thomas (Ed)	23-25BosN	12-16-98	Watertown, Mass.	7-14-51	R	R	6'	170	5	4	1	2	0	0	0	2	0	0	0	.500	.500
Cox, Dick-Elmer Joseph	25-26BknN	9-30-97	Pasadena, Cal.		R	R	5'7	158	246	832	121	261	40	14	8	109	83	49	10	.314	.424
Crabtree, Estel-Estel Crayton (Crabby)	29,31-32CinN 33,41-42StLN 43-44CinN	8-19-03	Crabtree, Ohio	1- 4-67	L	R	6'	168	489	1408	174	396	53	25	13	142	113	109	8	.281	.382
Craft, Harry-Harry Francis	37-42CinN M57-59KCA M61ChiN M62-64HouN	4-19-15	Ellisville, Miss.		R	R	6'1	185	566	2104	237	533	85	25	44	267	110	203	14	.253	.380
Cramer, Doc-Roger Maxwell (Flit)	29-35PhiA 36-40BosA 41WasA 42-48DetA	7-22-05	Beach Haven, N.J.		L	R	6'2	185	2239	9140	1357	2705	396	109	37	842	571	345	62	.296	.375
Crawford, Glenn-Glenn Martin (Shorty)	45StLN 45-46PhiN	12- 2-13	North Branch, Mich.	1- 2-72	L	R	5'9	165	87	306	41	89	13	2	2	24	37	15	5	.291	.366
Crawford, Pat-Clifford Rankin	29-30NYN 30CinN 33-34StLN	1-28-02	Society Hill, S.C.		L	R	5'11	170	318	651	75	182	23	5	9	104	60	29	4	.280	.372
Creeden, Connie-Cornelius Stephen	43BosN	7-21-15	Danvers, Mass.		L	R	6'	190	5	4	0	1	0	0	0	1	1	0	0	.250	.250
Creeden, Pat-Patrick Francis (Whoops)	31BosA	5-23-06	Newburyport, Mass.		L	R	5'8	175	5	8	0	0	0	0	0	0	1	3	0	.000	.000
Crespi, Creepy-Frank Angelo Joseph	38-42StLN 43-46MS	2-16-18	St. Louis, Mo.		R	R	5'9	175	264	911	125	240	32	4	4	88	90	102	8	.263	.321
Criscola, Tony-Anthony Paul	42-43StLA 44CinN	7- 9-15	Walla Walla, Wash.		L	R	5'11	180	184	367	35	91	12	4	1	28	30	32	2	.248	.311
Critz, Hughie-Hugh Melville	24-30CinN 30-35NYN	9-17-00	Starkville, Miss.		R	R	5'8	147	1478	5930	832	1591	195	95	38	531	289	257	97	.268	.352
Crompton, Herb-Herbert Bryan (Workhorse)	37WasA 45NYA	11- 7-11	Taylor Ridge, Ill.	8- 5-63	R	R	6'	185	38	102	6	20	3	0	0	12	2	7	0	.196	.225
Cronin, Bill-William Patrick (Crungy)	28-31BosN	12-26-02	West Newton, Mass.	10-26-66	R	R	5'9	167	126	296	28	68	15	2	0	27	12	13	0	.230	.294
Cronin, Jim-James John	29PhiA	8- 7-05	Richmond, Cal.		B	R	5'10	150	25	56	7	13	2	1	0	4	5	7	0	.232	.304
Cronin, Joe-Joseph Edward	26-27PitN 28-34,M33-34WasA 35-45,M35-47BosA	10-12-06	San Francisco, Cal.		R	R	5'11	180	2124	7577	1233	2285	514	118	170	1423	1059	700	87	.302	.468
Crosetti, Frankie-Frank Peter Joseph (The Crow)	32-48NYA	10- 4-10	San Francisco, Cal.		R	R	5'10	165	1683	6277	1006	1541	260	65	98	649	792	799	113	.245	.354
Crouch, Jack-Jack Albert (Roxy)	30-31,33StLA 33CinN	6-12-03	Salisbury, N.C.		R	R	5'9	165	43	72	7	9	1	0	1	8	3	13	1	.125	.181
Croucher, Frank-Frank Donald (Dingle)	39-41DetA 42WasA 43-45MS	7-23-14	San Antonio, Tex.		R	R	5'11	165	296	935	94	235	37	5	7	86	56	128	4	.251	.324
Crouse, Buck-Clyde Elsworth	23-30ChiA	1- 6-97	Anderson, Ind.		L	R	5'8	158	470	1306	128	342	54	6	8	160	114	68	14	.262	.331
Crowley, Ed-Edgar Jewel	28WasA	8- 6-06	Watkinsville, Ga.	4-14-70	R	R	6'1	180	2	1	0	0	0	0	0	0	0	0	0	.000	.000
Crumling, Gene-Eugene Leon	45StLN	4- 5-22	Wrightsville, Pa.		R	R	6'	180	6	12	0	1	0	0	0	1	0	1	0	.083	.083
Crump, Buddy-Arthur Elliott	24NYN	11-29-01	Norfolk, Va.		L	L	5'10	156	1	4	0	0	0	0	0	1	0	1	0	.000	.000
Cuccinello, Al-Alfred Edward	35NYN	11-26-14	Queens, N.Y.		R	R	5'10	165	54	165	27	41	7	1	4	20	1	20	0	.248	.376
Cuccinello, Tony-Anthony Francis	30-31CinN 32-35BknN 36-40BosN 40NYN 42-43BosN 43-45ChiA	11- 8-07	Queens, N.Y.		R	R	5'7	160	1704	6184	730	1729	334	46	94	884	579	497	42	.280	.394
Culberson, Leon-Delbert Leon	43-47BosA 48WasA	8- 6-19	Hall's Station, Ga.		R	R	5'11	180	370	1217	148	324	59	18	14	131	106	126	27	.266	.379
Cullenbine, Roy-Roy Joseph	38-39DetA 40BknN 40-42StLA 42WasA 42NYA 43-45CleA 45-47DetA	10-18-15	Nashville, Tenn.		B	R	6'1	195	1181	3879	627	1072	209	32	110	599	852	399	26	.276	.432
Cullop, Nick-Henry Nicholas	26NYA 27WasA 27CleA 29BknN 30-31CinN	10-16-00	St. Louis, Mo.		R	R	6'	200	173	490	49	122	29	12	11	67	40	128	1	.249	.424
Culp, Benny-Benjamin Baldy	42-44PhiN 45MS	1-19-14	Philadelphia, Pa.		R	R	5'9	175	15	26	5	5	1	0	0	2	3	3	0	.192	.231
Cummings, Jack-John William	26-29NYN 29BosN	4- 1-04	Pittsburgh, Pa.	10- 5-62	R	R	6'	195	89	132	15	45	11	1	4	28	12	18	0	.341	.530
Cunningham, Bill-William Aloysius	21-23NYN 24BosN	7-30-95	San Francisco, Cal.	9-26-53	R	R	5'8	155	318	945	113	270	39	12	9	112	52	48	17	.286	.381
Cunningham, Ray-Raymond Lee	31-32StLN	1-17-08	Mesquite, Tex.		R	R	5'7	150	14	26	4	4	1	0	0	1	3	4	0	.154	.192
Curtright, Guy-Guy Paxton	43-46ChiA	10-18-12	Holliday, Mo.		R	R	5'11	200	331	1065	147	294	45	16	9	108	142	124	20	.276	.374
Cuyler, Kiki-Hazen Shirley	21-27PitN 28-35ChiN 35-37CinN 38BknN	8-30-99	Harrisville, Mich.	2-11-50	R	R	5'11	180	1879	7161	1305	2299	394	157	128	1065	676	752	328	.321	.474
Dahlgren, Babe-Ellsworth Tenney	35-36BosA 37-40NYA 41BosN 41-42ChiN 42StLA 42BknN 43PhiN 44-45PitN 46StLA	6-15-12	San Francisco, Cal.		R	R	6'	190	1137	4045	470	1056	174	37	82	569	381	401	18	.261	.383
Dallessandro, Dom-Nicholas Dominic (Dim Dom)	37BosA 40-44ChiN 45MS 46-47ChiN	10- 3-13	Reading, Pa.		L	L	5'6	168	746	1945	242	520	110	23	22	303	310	150	16	.267	.381
Daniel, Jake-Handley Jacob	37BknN	4-22-12	Roanoke, Ala.		L	L	5'11	175	12	27	3	5	1	0	0	3	3	4	0	.185	.222
Daniels, Fred-Fred Clinton (Tony)	45PhiN	12-28-24	Gastonia, N.C.		R	R	5'10	185	76	230	15	46	3	2	0	10	12	22	1	.200	.230
Danning, Harry-Harry (Harry the Horse)	33-42NYN 43-45MS	9- 6-11	Los Angeles, Cal.		R	R	6'1	190	890	2971	363	847	162	26	57	397	187	217	13	.285	.415
Danning, Ike-Ike	28StLA	1-20-05	Los Angeles, Cal.		R	R	5'10	160	2	6	0	3	0	0	0	1	1	2	0	.500	.500
Dantonio, Fats-John James	44-45BknN	12-31-19	New Orleans, La.		R	R	5'8	165	50	135	12	33	6	1	0	12	11	7	3	.244	.304
Dapper, Cliff-Clifford Roland	42BknN 43-45MS	1- 2-20	Los Angeles, Cal.		R	R	6'2	190	8	17	2	8	1	0	1	9	2	2	0	.471	.706
Dashiell, Wally-John Wallace	24ChiA	5- 9-02	Jewett, Tex.	5-20-72	R	R	5'9	170	1	2	0	0	0	0	0	0	0	0	0	.000	.000
Daughters, Bob-Robert Francis (Red)	37BosA	8- 5-14	Cincinnati, Ohio		R	R	6'2	185	1	0	1	0	0	0	0	0	0	0	0	–	–
Davis, Crash-Lawrence Columbus	40-42PhiA 43-45MS	7-14-19	Canon, Ga.		R	R	6'	173	148	444	43	102	12	2	2	43	35	56	2	.230	.279
Davis, Harry-Harry Albert (Stinky)	32-33DetA 37StLA	5- 7-10	Shreveport, La.		L	L	5'10	160	327	1213	205	320	65	18	7	123	153	87	21	.264	.364
Davis, Ike-Isaac Marion	19WasA 24-25ChiA	6-14-95	Pueblo, Colo.		R	R	5'7	155	164	609	110	143	32	10	0	65	73	69	19	.235	.320
Davis, John-John Humphrey (Red)	41NYN 42-45MS	7-15-15	Laurel Run, Pa.		R	R	5'11	172	21	70	8	15	3	0	0	5	8	12	0	.214	.257
Davis, Kiddo-George Willis	26NYA 32PhiN 33,35-37NYN 34StL-PhiN 37-38CinN	2-12-02	Bridgeport, Conn.		R	R	5'11	178	575	1824	281	515	112	16	19	171	142	141	32	.282	.393
Davis, Spud-Virgil Lawrence	28StLN 28-33PhiN 34-36StLN 37-38CinN 38-39PhiN 40-41,44-45,M46PitN	12-20-04	Birmingham, Ala.		R	R	6'1	197	1458	4255	388	1312	244	22	77	647	386	326	6	.308	.430
Deal, Lindsay-Lindsay Fred	39BknN	9- 3-11	Lenoir, N.C.		L	R	6'	175	4	7	0	0	0	0	0	0	0	2	0	.000	.000
Dean, Chubby-Alfred Lovill (See P20-45)	36-41PhiA 41-43CleA 44-46MS	8-24-15	Mt. Airy, N.C.	12-21-70	L	L	5'11	188	533	1047	106	287	47	7	3	128	115	65	5	.274	.341
Dear, Buddy-Paul Stanford	27WasA	12- 1-05	Norfolk, Va.		R	R	5'8	143	2	1	1	0	0	0	0	0	0	0	0	.000	.000
DeBerry, Hank-John Herman	16-17CleA 18MS 22-30BknN	12-29-94	Savannah, Tenn.	9-10-51	R	R	5'11	195	648	1850	170	494	81	16	11	234	148	119	13	.267	.346
Dedeaux, Rod-Raoul	35BknN	2-17-15	New Orleans, La.		R	R	5'11	160	2	4	0	1	0	0	0	1	0	0	0	.250	.250
Deitrick, William Alexander	27-28PhiN	4-30-02	Hanover Co., Va.	5- 6-46	R	R	5'10	160	57	106	14	21	6	0	0	7	17	10	1	.198	.255
Dejan, Mike-Mike Dan	40CinN	1-13-15	Cleveland, Ohio	2- 2-53	L	L	6'1	185	12	16	1	3	0	1	0	2	3	3	0	.188	.313
DeKoning, Bill-William Callahan	45NYN	12-19-19	Brooklyn, N.Y.		R	R	5'11	185	3	1	0	0	0	0	0	0	0	1	0	.000	.000
DeLancey, Bill-William Pinkney	32,34-35,40StLN 36-39IL	11-28-11	Greensboro, N.C.	11-28-46	L	R	5'11	185	219	598	79	173	32	10	19	85	85	74	1	.289	.472
Delker, Eddie-Edward Alberts	29,31-32StLN 32-33PhiN	4-17-07	Palo Alto, Pa.		R	R	5'10	170	98	187	19	29	9	3	1	15	16	45	0	.155	.251
Delmas, Bert-Albert Charles	33BknN	5-20-11	San Francisco, Cal.		L	R	5'11	165	12	28	4	7	0	0	0	0	1	7	0	.250	.250
Del Savio, Garton-Garton Orville	43PhiN	11-26-13	New York, N.Y.		R	R	5'9	165	4	11	0	1	0	0	0	0	1	0	0	.091	.091
Demaree (Dimaria), Frank-Joseph Franklin	32-33,35-38ChiN 39-41NYN 41-42BosN 43StLN 44StLA	6-10-10	Winters, Cal.	8-30-58	R	R	5'11	185	1155	4144	578	1241	190	36	72	591	359	269	33	.299	.415
Dennehy, Tod-Thomas Francis	23PhiN	5-12-99	Philadelphia, Pa.		L	L	5'11	175	9	24	4	7	2	0	0	2	1	3	0	.292	.375
Denning, Otto-Otto George (Dutch)	42-43CleA	12-28-12	Hays, Kans.		R	R	6'	180	129	343	23	76	20	0	1	32	23	15	3	.222	.287
DePhillips, Tony-Anthony Andrew	43CinN	9-20-12	New York, N.Y.		R	R	6'2	185	35	20	0	2	1	0	0	2	1	5	0	.100	.150
Derry, Russ-Alva Russell	44-45NYA 46PhiA 49StLN	10- 7-16	Princeton, Mo.		L	R	6'1	180	187	553	68	124	17	7	17	73	78	124	2	.224	.373

USE NAME – GIVEN NAMES (NICKNAMES)	TEAM BY YEAR	BIRTH DATE	BIRTH PLACE	DEATH DATE	B	T	HGT	WGT	G	AB	R	H	2B	3B	HR	RBI	BB	SO	SB	BA	SA
									LIFETIME BATTING TOTALS												
Desautels, Gene-Eugene Abraham (Red)	30-33DetA 37-40BosA 41-43CleA 44MS 45CleA 46PhiA	6-13-07	Worcester, Mass.		R	R	5'11	170	712	2012	211	469	73	11	3	186	233	167	12	.233	.285
Detore, George-George Francis	30-31CleA	11-11-06	Utica, N.Y.		R	R	5'8	170	33	68	3	17	7	0	0	9	8	2	2	.250	.353
Detweiler, Ducky-Robert Sterling	42BosN 43-45MS 46BosN	2-15-19	Trumbauersville, Pa.		R	R	5'11	178	13	45	3	14	2	1	0	5	2	7	0	.311	.400
Devine, Mickey-William Patrick	18PhiN 20BosA 25NYN	5- 9-92	Albany, N.Y.	10- 1-37	R	R	5'10	165	33	53	7	12	4	0	0	4	3	6	1	.226	.302
deViveiros, Bernie-Bernard John	24ChiA 27DetA	4-19-01	Oakland, Cal.		R	R	5'7	160	25	23	4	5	1	0	0	2	2	8	1	.217	.261
Devlin, Jim-James Raymond	44CleA	8-25-22	Plains, Pa.		L	R	5'11	165	1	1	0	0	0	0	0	0	0	0	0	.000	.000
DeVormer, Al-Albert E.	18ChiA 21-22NYA 23BosA 27NYN	8-19-91	Grand Rapids, Mich.	8-29-66	R	R	6'	175	196	477	50	123	20	5	2	57	20	46	7	.258	.333
Dickey, Bill-William Malcolm	28-43NYA 44-45MS 46,M46NYA	6- 6-07	Bastrop, La.		L	R	6'1	185	1789	6300	930	1969	343	72	202	1209	678	289	36	.313	.486
Dickshot (Dicksus), Johnny-John Oscar	36-38PitN 39NYN 44-45ChiA	1-24-10	Waukegan, Ill.		R	R	6'	195	322	990	142	273	35	19	7	116	101	97	23	.276	.371
Dillhoefer, Pickles-William Martin	17ChiN 18PhiN 19-21StLN	10-13-94	Cleveland, Ohio	2-22-22	R	R	5'7	154	247	600	59	134	16	10	0	48	35	30	12	.223	.283
DiMaggio, Joe-Joseph Paul	36-42NYA 43-45MS 46-51NYA	11-25-14	Martinez, Cal.		R	R	6'2	193	1736	6821	1390	2214	389	131	361	1537	790	369	30	.325	.579
DiMaggio, Vince-Vincent Paul	37-38BosN 39-40CinN 40-44PitN 45-46PhiN 46NYN	9- 6-12	Martinez, Cal.		R	R	5'11	183	1110	3849	491	959	209	24	125	584	412	837	79	.249	.413
Dinges, Vance-Vance (George)	45-46PhiN	5-29-15	Elizabeth, N.J.		L	L	6'2	175	159	501	53	146	20	5	2	46	44	29	7	.291	.363
Dixon, Leo-Leo Michael	25-27StLA 29CinN	9- 6-96	Chicago, Ill.		R	R	5'11	170	159	427	40	88	19	3	1	41	45	69	4	.206	.272
Doerr, Bobby-Robert Pershing	37-44BosA 45MS 46-51BosA	4- 7-18	Los Angeles, Cal.		R	R	5'11	175	1865	7093	1094	2042	381	89	223	1247	809	608	54	.288	.461
Doljack, Frank-Frank Joseph (Dolie)	30-34DetA 43CleA	10- 5-07	Cleveland, Ohio	1-23-48	R	R	5'11	185	192	561	68	151	31	7	9	85	47	60	8	.269	.398
Doll, Art-Arthur James (Moose) (See P20-45)	35-36,38BosN	5- 7-12	Chicago, Ill.		R	R	6'	200	7	13	0	2	0	0	0	0	0	3	0	.154	.154
Donahue, John-John Frederick (Jiggs)	23BosA	4-19-94	Roxbury, Mass.	10- 3-49	B	R	5'8	170	10	36	5	10	4	0	0	1	4	5	0	.278	.389
Dondero, Len-Leonard Peter (Mike)	29StLA	9-12-03	Newark, Cal.		R	R	5'11	178	19	31	2	6	0	0	1	8	0	4	0	.194	.290
Doran, Bill-William James	22CleA	6-14-00	San Francisco, Cal.		L	R	5'11	175	3	2	0	1	0	0	0	0	1	0	0	.500	.500
Dorman, Charlie-Charles William	23ChiA	4-23-98	San Francisco, Cal.	11-15-28	R	R	6'	179	1	2	0	1	0	0	0	0	0	0	0	.500	.500
Dorman, Red-Charles Dwight	28CleA	10- 3-05	Jacksonville, Ill.		R	R	5'11	180	23	77	10	28	6	0	0	11	9	6	1	.364	.442
Douglas, John-John Franklin	45BknN	9-14-17	Thayer, W.Va.		L	L	6'2	195	5	9	0	0	0	0	0	0	2	4	0	.000	.000
Douglass, Astyanax-Astyanax Saunders	21,25CinN	9-19-97	Covington, Tex.	1-26-75	L	R	6'1	190	11	24	2	4	0	0	0	1	1	4	0	.167	.167
Douthit, Taylor-Taylor Lee	23-31StLN 31-33CinN 33ChiN	4-22-01	Little Rock, Ark.		R	R	5'11	175	1074	4127	665	1201	220	38	29	396	443	312	67	.291	.384
Doyle, Danny-Howard James	43BosA 44-45MS	1-24-17	McLoud, Okla.		R	R	6'1	195	13	43	2	9	1	0	0	6	7	9	0	.209	.233
Dreesen, Bill-William Richard	31BosN	7-26-04	New York, N.Y.	11- 9-71	L	R	5'7	160	48	180	38	40	10	4	1	10	23	23	1	.222	.339
Drescher, Bill-William Clayton (Dutch, Moose)	44-46NYA	5-23-21	Congers, N.Y.	5-15-68	L	R	6'2	190	57	139	10	37	4	1	0	16	8	5	0	.266	.309
Dressen, Chuck-Charles Walter 20,22-23 played in N.F.L.	25-31CinN 33NYN M34-37CinN M52-53BknN M55-57WasA M60-61MilN M63-66DetA	9-20-98	Decatur, Ill.	8-10-66	R	R	5'6	146	646	2215	313	603	123	29	11	221	219	118	30	.272	.369
Drews, Frank-Frank John	44-45BosN	5-25-16	Buffalo, N.Y.	4-22-72	R	R	5'10	175	95	288	27	59	13	2	0	29	41	32	0	.205	.264
Dudley, Dud (See Dud Lee)	20StLA																				
Dudra, John-John Joseph	41BosN 42-45MS	5-27-16	Assumption, Ill.	10-24-65	R	R	5'11	175	14	25	3	9	3	1	0	3	3	4	0	.360	.560
Dugan, Joe-Joseph Anthony (Jumping Joe)	17-21PhiA 22BosA 22-28NYA 29BosN 31DetA	5-12-97	Mahanoy City, Pa.		R	R	5'11	160	1446	5405	664	1515	277	46	42	571	250	418	37	.280	.372
Dugas, Gus-Augustin Joseph	30PitN 31BJ 32PitN 33PhiN 34WasA	3-24-07	St. Jean-de-Matha, Can.		L	L	5'9	165	125	218	27	45	9	3	3	23	18	27	0	.206	.317
Duncan, Pat-Louis Baird	15PitN 18MS 19-24CinN	10- 6-93	Coalton, Ohio	7-17-60	R	R	5'10	170	727	2695	361	827	137	50	23	374	184	164	55	.307	.420
Dunham, Lee-Leland Huffield	26PhiN	6- 9-02	Atlanta, Ill.		L	L	5'11	185	5	4	0	1	0	0	0	1	0	1	0	.250	.250
Dunlap, Bill-William James	29-30BosN	5- 1-09	Three Rivers, Mass.		R	L	5'11	170	26	58	9	14	1	1	1	4	4	10	0	.241	.345
Durning, George-George Warren	25PhiN	5- 9-02	Philadelphia, Pa.		R	R	5'11	175	5	14	3	5	0	0	0	1	2	1	0	.357	.357
Durocher, Leo-Leo Ernest (The Lip)	25,28-29NYA 30-33CinN 33-37StLN 38,41,43,45,M39-46BknN 47SL M48BknN M48-55NYN M66-72ChiN M72-73HouN	7-27-05	W. Springfield, Mass.		R	R	5'10	160	1637	5350	575	1320	210	56	24	567	377	480	31	.247	.320
					Bats Both 28-29																
Durrett, Red-Elmer Charles	44-45BknN	2- 3-21	Sherman, Tex.		L	L	5'10	170	19	48	5	7	1	0	1	1	10	13	0	.146	.229
Durst, Cedric-Cedric Montgomery	22-23,26StLA 27-30NYA 30BosA	8-23-96	Austin, Tex.	2-16-71	L	L	5'11	160	481	1103	146	269	39	17	15	122	75	100	7	.244	.351
Dwyer, Double Joe-Joseph Michael	37CinN	3-27-04	Orange, N.J.		L	L	5'9	186	12	11	2	3	0	0	0	1	1	0	0	.273	.273
Dykes, Jimmy-James Joseph	18-32PhiA 33-39,M34-46ChiA M51-53PhiA M54BalA M58CinN M59-60DetA M60-61CleA	11-10-96	Philadelphia, Pa.		R	R	5'9	185	2282	8046	1108	2256	453	90	108	1071	955	849	70	.280	.399
Early, Jake-Jacob Willard	39-43WasA 44-45MS 46WasA 47StLA 48-49WasA	5-19-17	King's Mountain, N.C.		L	R	5'11	168	747	2208	216	532	98	23	32	264	280	259	7	.241	.350
East, Carl-Carlton William (See P01-19)	15StLA 24WasA	8-27-94	Rome, Ga.	1-15-53	L	R	6'2	178	3	7	1	2	1	0	0	2	2	1	0	.286	.429
Easterling, Paul-Paul	28,30DetA 38PhiA	9-28-05	Reidsville, Ga.		R	R	5'11	180	76	200	25	55	13	1	4	26	15	44	2	.275	.410
Easterwood, Roy-Roy Charles (Shag)	44ChiN	1-12-15	Waxahachie, Tex.		R	R	6'	196	17	33	1	7	2	0	1	2	1	11	0	.212	.364
Eayrs, Eddie-Edwin (See P20-45)	13PitN 20-21BosN 21BknN	11-10-90	Blackstone, Mass.	11-30-69	L	L	5'7	160	114	271	32	83	5	2	1	26	32	23	4	.306	.351
Echols, Johnny-John Gresham	39StLN	1- 9-17	Atlanta, Ga.	11-13-72	R	R	5'10	175	2	0	0	0	0	0	0	0	0	0	0	–	–
Eckhardt, Ox-Oscar George 28 played in N.F.L.	32BosN 36BknN	12-23-01	Yorktown, Tex.	4-22-51	L	R	6'1	185	24	52	6	10	1	0	1	7	5	3	0	.192	.269
Eggert, Elmer-Elmer Albert (Mose)	27BosA	1-29-02	Rochester, N.Y.	4- 9-71	R	R	5'9	160	5	3	0	0	0	0	0	0	1	1	0	.000	.000
Eibel, Hack-Henry Hack	12CleA 20BosA	12- 6-93	Brooklyn, N.Y.	10-16-45	L	L	5'11	220	30	46	4	8	2	0	0	6	3	6	1	.174	.217
Eichrodt, Fred-Frederick George (Ike)	25-27CleA 31ChiA	1- 6-03	Chicago, Ill.	7-14-65	R	R	5'11	167	171	516	51	121	34	5	0	51	21	51	3	.234	.320
Elko, Pete-Peter (Piccolo Pete)	43-44ChiN	6-17-18	Wilkes-Barre, Pa.		R	R	5'11	185	16	52	3	9	1	0	0	0	4	6	0	.173	.192
Ellerbe, Frank-Francis Rogers (Governor)	19-21WasA 21-24StLA 24CleA	12-25-95	Marion, S.C.		R	R	5'10	165	420	1453	179	389	58	22	4	152	72	136	12	.268	.346
Elliott, Allen-Allen Clifford (Ace)	23-24ChiN	12-25-97	St. Louis, Mo.		L	R	6'	170	63	182	21	44	8	2	2	29	2	13	3	.242	.341
Elliott, Carter-Carter Ward	21ChiN	11-29-93	Atchison, Kans.	5-21-59	L	R	5'11	165	12	28	5	7	2	0	0	0	5	3	0	.250	.321
Elmore, Ellie-Verdo Wilson	24StLA	12-10-99	Gordo, Ala.	8- 5-69	L	R	6'	190	7	17	2	3	3	0	0	0	1	3	0	.176	.353
Elsh, Roy-Eugene Roy	23-25ChiA	3- 1-96	Pennsgrove, N.J.		R	R	5'9	165	173	404	55	106	17	3	0	39	31	44	23	.262	.319
Emery, Spoke-Herrick Smith	24PhiN	12-10-98	Bay City, Mich.	6- 2-75	R	L	5'9	165	5	3	3	2	0	0	0	0	0	0	0	.667	.667
Emmer, Frank-Frank William	16,26CinN	2-17-96	Crestline, Ohio	10-18-63	R	R	5'8	150	122	313	30	57	10	7	0	20	20	57	2	.182	.259
Emmerich, Bob-Robert G.	23BosN	8- 1-97	New York, N.Y.	11-23-48	R	R	5'3	155	13	24	3	2	0	0	0	0	2	3	1	.083	.083
Engle, Charlie-Charles	25-26PhiA 30PitN	8-27-03	Brooklyn, N.Y.		R	R	5'7	155	87	235	41	59	10	1	0	15	32	26	1	.251	.302
English, Charlie-Charles Dewie	32-33ChiA 36NYN 37CinN	4- 8-10	Darlington, S.C.		R	R	5'9	160	50	136	10	39	8	2	1	13	4	10	0	.287	.397
English, Gil-Gilbert Raymond	31-32NYN 36-37DetA 37-38BosN 44BknN	7- 2-09	Glenola, N.C.		R	R	5'11	180	240	791	74	194	22	7	8	90	56	78	5	.245	.321
English, Woody-Elwood George	27-36ChiN 37-38BknN	3- 2-07	Fredonia, Ohio		R	R	5'10	155	1261	4746	801	1356	236	52	32	422	571	536	57	.286	.378
Ennis, Russ-Russell Elwood (Hack)	26WasA	3-10-97	Superior, Wis.	1-29-49	R	R	5'11	160	1	0	0	0	0	0	0	0	0	0	0	–	–
Ens, Jewel-Jewel Winklemeyer	22-25,M29-31PitN	8-24-89	St. Louis, Mo.	1-17-50	R	R	6'	172	67	186	25	54	8	4	1	24	7	16	5	.290	.392
Epps, Aubrey-Aubrey Lee (Yo-Yo)	35PitN	3- 3-12	Memphis, Tenn.		R	R	5'10	170	1	4	1	3	0	1	0	3	0	0	0	.750	1.250
Epps, Hal-Harold Franklin	38,40StLN 43-44StLA 44PhiA 45-46MS	3-26-14	Athens, Ga.		L	L	6'	175	125	391	58	99	13	9	1	21	37	43	5	.253	.340
Erickson, Hank-Henry Nels (Popeye)	35CinN	11-11-07	Chicago, Ill.	12-19-64	R	R	6'1	185	37	88	9	23	3	2	1	4	6	4	0	.261	.375
Eschen, Larry-Lawrence Edward	42PhiA	9-22-20	Suffern, N.Y.		R	R	6'	180	12	11	0	0	0	0	0	0	4	6	0	.000	.000
Estalella, Bobby-Roberto [Mendez]	35-36,39WasA 41StLA 42WasA 43-45PhiA 46-48SM 49PhiA	4-25-11	Cardenas, Cuba		R	R	5'6	185	680	2196	279	620	106	33	44	308	350	246	13	.282	.421
Etchison, Buck-Clarence Hampton	43-44BosN	1-27-15	Baltimore, Md.		L	L	6'1	190	119	327	32	72	19	0	8	35	35	52	1	.220	.352
Etten, Nick-Nicholas Raymond Thomas	38-39PhiA 41-42PhiN 43-46NYA 47PhiN	9-19-13	Spring Grove, Ill.		L	L	6'2	198	937	3320	426	921	167	25	89	526	480	199	22	.277	.423
Evans, Joe-Joseph Patton (Doc)	15-22CleA 23WasA 24-25StLA	5-15-95	Meridian, Miss.	8- 8-53	R	R	5'9	160	733	2043	306	529	71	31	3	210	212	152	64	.259	.328
Ewing (Cohen), Reuben-Reuben	21StLN	11-30-99	Odessa, Russia	10- 5-70	R	R	5'5	150	3	1	0	0	0	0	0	0	0	1	0	.000	.000
Ezzell, Homer-Homer Estell	23StLA 24-25BosA	2-28-96	Victoria, Tex.		R	R	5'10	158	236	734	104	196	20	8	0	61	47	58	25	.267	.316
Falk, Bibb-Bibb August (Jockey)	20-28ChiA 29-31CleA	1-27-99	Austin, Tex.		L	L	6'	175	1354	4656	656	1463	300	59	69	785	412	279	46	.314	.448
Fallon, George-George Decatur (Flash)	37BknN 43-45StLN	7- 8-16	Jersey City, N.J.		R	R	5'9	155	133	282	26	61	10	1	1	21	25	26	2	.216	.270
Farrell, Doc-Edward Stephen	25-27NYN 27-29BosN 29NYN 30StLN 30ChiN 32-33NYA 35BosA	12-26-01	Johnson City, N.Y.	12-20-66	R	R	5'8	160	591	1799	181	467	63	8	10	213	109	120	14	.260	.320
Farrell, Kerby-Major Kerby	43BosN 45ChiA M57CleA	9- 3-13	Leapwood, Tenn.		L	L	5'11	172	188	676	55	177	25	4	0	55	40	33	5	.262	.311
Fausett, Buck-Robert Shaw (Leaky)	44CinN	4- 8-08	Sheridan, Ark.		L	R	5'10	170	13	31	2	3	0	1	0	1	1	2	0	.097	.161
Fehring, Bill-William Paul (Dutch)	34ChiA	5-31-12	Columbus, Ind.		B	R	6'	195	1	1	0	0	0	0	0	0	0	1	0	.000	.000
Feinberg, Eddie-Edward (Itzy)	38-39PhiN	9-29-18	Philadelphia, Pa.		B	R	5'9	165	16	38	2	7	1	0	0	0	2	1	0	.184	.211
Felderman, Marv-Marvin Wilfred	42ChiN 43-45MS	12-17-17	Bellevue, Iowa		R	R	6'1	187	3	6	0	1	0	0	0	0	1	4	0	.167	.167
Felix, Gus-August Guenther	23-25BosN 26-27BknN	5-24-95	Cincinnati, Ohio	5-12-60	R	R	6'	180	583	2046	256	561	91	25	12	230	189	194	28	.274	.361
Fernandes, Ed-Edward Paul	40PitN 45MS 46ChiA	3-11-18	Oakland, Cal.	11-27-68	B	R	5'9	185	42	65	5	12	3	0	0	6	15	13	0	.185	.231
Ferrell, Rick-Richard Benjamin	29-33StLA 33-37BosA 37-41WasA 41-43StLA 44-45,47WasA	10-12-05	Durham, N.C.		R	R	5'10	160	1884	6028	687	1692	324	45	28	734	931	277	29	.281	.363

USE NAME – GIVEN NAMES (NICKNAMES)	TEAM BY YEAR	BIRTH DATE	BIRTH PLACE	DEATH DATE	B	T	HGT	WGT	G	AB	R	H	2B	3B	HR	RBI	BB	SO	SB	BA	SA
					LIFETIME BATTING TOTALS																
Ferrell, Wes-Wesley Cheek (See P20-45)	27-33CleA 34-37BosA 37-38WasA 38-39NYA 40BknN 41BosN	2- 2-08	Greensboro, N.C.		R	R	6'2	195	548	1176	175	329	57	12	38	208	129	185	2	.280	.446
Fewster, Chick-Wilson Lloyd	17-22NYA 22-23BosA 24-25CleA 26-27BknN	11-10-95	Baltimore, Md.	4-16-45	R	R	5'11	160	644	1963	282	506	91	12	6	167	240	264	57	.258	.326
File, Sam-Lawrence Samuel	40PhiN	5-18-22	Chester, Pa.		R	R	5'11	160	7	13	0	1	0	0	0	1	0	2	0	.077	.077
Filipowicz, Steve-Stephen Charles (Flip) 45-46 played in N.F.L.	44-45NYN 48CinN	6-28-21	Donora, Pa.	2-21-75	R	R	5'8	195	57	179	24	40	7	2	2	26	9	21	0	.223	.318
Finley, Bob-Robert Edward	43-44PhiN	11-25-15	Ennis, Tex.		R	R	6'1	200	122	362	27	91	13	1	2	28	16	35	1	.251	.309
Finn, Neal-Cornelius Francis (Mickey)	30-32BknN 33PhiN	1-24-02	New York, N.Y.	7- 7-33	R	R	5'11	168	321	1044	125	274	44	5	3	102	68	89	9	.262	.323
Finney, Hal-Harold Wilson	31-34,36PitN	7- 7-05	Lafayette, Ala.		R	R	5'11	170	123	227	39	46	8	1	1	27	6	32	1	.203	.260
Finney, Lou-Louis Klopsche	31,33-39PhiA 39-42BosA 43VR 44-45BosA 45-46StLA 47PhiN	8-13-10	Buffalo, Ala.	4-22-66	L	R	6'	180	1270	4631	643	1329	203	85	31	494	329	186	39	.287	.388
Fisher, Showboat-George Aloys	23-24WasA 30StLN 32StLA	1-16-99	Jennings, Iowa		L	R	5'10	170	138	340	62	114	21	6	8	71	37	35	6	.335	.503
Fitzberger, Charlie-Charles Casper (Hon)	28BosN	2-13-04	Baltimore, Md.	1-25-65	L	L	6'1	170	7	7	0	2	0	0	0	0	0	3	0	.286	.286
Fitzgerald, Howie-Howard Chumney (Lefty)	22,24ChiN 26BosA	5-16-02	Eagle Lake, Tex.	2-27-59	L	L	5'11	163	48	140	15	36	3	0	0	14	8	11	2	.257	.279
Fitzgerald, Ray-Raymond Francis	31CinN	12- 5-04	Chicopee, Mass.		R	R	5'9	168	1	1	0	0	0	0	0	0	0	0	0	.000	.000
Flager, Wally-Walter Leonard	45CinN 45PhiN	11- 3-21	Chicago Heights, Ill.		L	R	5'11	160	70	220	26	53	5	1	2	21	25	20	1	.241	.300
Flagstead, Ira-Ira James (Pete)	17DetA 18MS 19-23DetA 23-29BosA 29WasA 29-30PitN	9-22-93	Montague, Mich.	3-13-40	R	R	5'9	165	1218	4139	644	1201	261	49	40	450	467	288	71	.290	.460
Flair, Al-Albert Dell (Broadway)	41BosA 42-45MS	7-24-16	New Orleans, La.		L	L	6'4	195	10	30	3	6	2	1	0	2	1	1	1	.200	.333
Flaskamper, Ray-Raymond Harold (Flash)	27ChiA	10-31-01	St. Louis, Mo.		B	R	5'7	140	26	95	12	21	5	0	0	6	3	8	0	.221	.274
Fletcher, Elbie-Elburt Preston	34-35,37-39BosN 39-43PitN 45MS 46-47PitN 49BosN	3-18-16	Milton, Mass.		L	L	6'	180	1415	4879	723	1323	228	58	79	616	851	495	32	.271	.390
Flick, Lew-Lewis Miller	43-44PhiA	2-18-15	Bristol, Tenn.		L	L	5'9	155	20	40	3	7	0	0	0	2	1	2	1	.175	.175
Florence, Paul-Paul Robert (Pep) 20 played in N.F.L.	26NYN	4-22-00	Chicago, Ill.		L	R	6'1	185	76	188	19	43	4	3	2	14	23	12	2	.229	.314
Flowers, Jake-D'Arcy Raymond	23,26StLN 27-31BknN 31-32StLN 33BknN 34CinN	3-16-02	Cambridge, Md.	12-27-62	R	R	5'11	170	583	1693	229	433	75	18	16	201	190	139	58	.256	.350
Floyd, Bubba-Leslie Roe	44DetA	6-23-17	Dallas, Tex.		R	R	5'11	160	3	9	1	4	1	0	0	0	1	0	0	.444	.556
Foley, Ray-Raymond Kirwin	28NYN	6-23-06	Naugatuck, Conn.		L	R	5'11	173	2	1	1	0	0	0	0	0	1	1	0	.000	.000
Fonseca, Lew-Lewis Albert	21-24CinN 25PhiN 27-31CleA 31-33,M32-34ChiA	1-21-99	Oakland, Cal.		R	R	5'11	180	937	3404	518	1075	203	50	31	485	186	199	64	.316	.432
Ford, Hod-Horace Hills	19-23BosN 24PhiN 25BknN 26-31CinN 32StLN 32-33BosN	7-23-97	New Haven, Conn.		R	R	5'10	165	1446	4833	484	1269	200	55	16	494	351	354	21	.263	.337
Foss, George-George Dueward (Deeby)	21WasA	6-13-97	Register, Ga.	11-10-69	R	R	5'10	170	4	7	0	0	0	0	0	0	0	1	0	.000	.000
Fothergil, Bob-Robert Roy (Fats)	22-30DetA 30-32ChiA 33BosA	8-16-97	Massillon, Ohio	3-20-38	R	R	5'10	230	1105	3265	453	1064	225	52	36	582	202	177	40	.326	.460
Fournier, Jack-Jacques Frank	12-17ChiA 18NYA 20-22StLN 23-26BknN 27BosN	9-28-92	Au Sable, Mich.	9- 5-73	L	R	6'	195	1530	5207	821	1631	252	113	136	859	587	408	145	.313	.483
Fowler, Boob-Joseph Chester	23-25CinN 26BosA	11-11-00	Waco, Tex.		L	R	5'11	180	78	175	30	57	7	2	1	18	6	19	3	.326	.406
Fox, Charlie-Charles Francis (Irish)	42NYN 43-45MS M70-74SFN	10- 7-21	New York, N.Y.		R	R	5'11	180	3	7	1	3	0	0	0	1	1	2	0	.429	.429
Fox, Pete-Ervin	33-40DetA 41-45BosA	3- 8-09	Evansville, Ind.	7- 5-66	R	R	5'11	165	1461	5636	895	1678	315	75	65	694	392	471	158	.298	.415
Foxx, Jimmie-James Emory (Double X, The Beast) (See P20-45)	25-35PhiA 36-42BosA 42,44ChiN 45PhiN	10-22-07	Sudlersville, Md.	7-21-67	R	R	6'	195	2317	8134	1751	2646	458	125	534	1921	1452	1311	87	.325	.609
Franklin, Murray-Murray Asher (Moe)	41-42DetA 43-45MS 46-49SM	4- 1-14	Chicago, Ill.		R	R	6'	175	61	164	25	43	8	0	2	16	9	7	0	.262	.348
Franks, Herman-Herman Louis	39StLN 40-41BknN 42-45MS 47-48PhiA 49NYN M65-68SFN	1- 1-14	Price, Utah		L	R	5'10	187	188	403	35	80	18	2	3	43	57	37	2	.199	.275
Frederick, Johnny-John Henry	29-34BknN	1-26-01	Denver, Colo.		L	L	5'11	165	805	3102	498	954	200	35	85	377	210	176	23	.308	.477
Freed, Ed-Edwin Charles	42PhiN 43-45MS	8-22-19	Centre Valley, Pa.		R	R	5'6	165	13	33	3	10	3	1	0	1	4	3	1	.303	.455
Freeman, John-John Edward (Buck)	27BosA	1-24-01	Boston, Mass.	4-14-58	R	R	5'8	160	4	2	0	0	0	0	0	0	0	0	0	.000	.000
Freiberger, Vern-Vern Donald	41CleA	12-19-23	Detroit, Mich.		R	L	6'1	175	2	8	0	1	0	0	0	1	0	2	0	.125	.125
Freigau, Howard-Howard Earl (Ty)	22-25StLN 25-27ChiN 28BknN 28BosN	8- 1-02	Dayton, Ohio	7-18-32	R	R	5'10	160	579	1974	224	537	99	25	15	226	138	161	32	.272	.370
French, Ray-Raymond Edward	20NYA 23BknN 24ChiA	1- 9-95	Alameda, Cal.		R	R	5'9	158	82	187	29	36	6	1	0	19	14	21	3	.193	.235
French, Walt-Walter Edward (Fitz) 22,25 played in N.F.L.	23,25-29PhiA	7-12-99	Moorestown, N.J.		L	R	5'8	155	398	981	142	297	45	12	2	109	44	62	13	.303	.379
Frey, Lonny-Linus Reinhard (Junior)	33-36BknN 37ChiN 38-43CinN 44-45MS 46CinN 47ChiN 47-48NYA 48NYN	8-23-10	St. Louis, Mo.		L	R	5'10	160	1535	5517	848	1482	263	69	61	549	752	525	105	.269	.374
					Bats Both 33-38																
Friberg, Barney-Augustaf Bernhardt	19-20,22-25ChiN 25-32PhiN 33BosA	8-18-99	Manchester, N.H.	12- 8-58	R	R	5'11	178	1299	4169	544	1170	181	44	38	471	471	498	51	.281	.373
Frierson, Buck-Robert Lawrence	41CleA	7-29-17	Chicota, Tex.		R	R	6'3	195	5	11	2	3	1	0	0	2	1	1	0	.273	.364
Frink, Fred-Frederink Ferdinand	34PhiN	8-25-11	Macon, Ga.		R	R	6'1	180	2	0	0	0	0	0	0	0	0	0	0	–	–
Frisch, Frankie-Frank Francis (The Fordham Flash)	19-26NYN 27-37,M33-38StLN M40-46PitN M49-51ChiN	9- 9-98	Queens, N.Y.	3-12-73	B	R	5'11	165	2310	9112	1532	2880	466	138	105	1244	730	272	419	.316	.432
Fuhrman, Ollie-Alfred J.	22PhiA	7-20-96	Jordan, Minn.	1-11-69	B	R	5'11	185	6	6	1	2	1	0	0	0	0	0	0	.333	.500
Fulghum, Dot-James Lavoisier	21PhiA	7- 4-00	Valdosta, Ga.	11-11-67	R	R	5'10	170	2	2	0	0	0	0	0	0	1	1	0	.000	.000
Fullis, Chick-Charles Philip	28-32NYN 33-34PhiN 34,36StLN	2-27-04	Girardville, Pa.	3-28-46	R	R	5'9	170	590	1855	305	548	92	14	12	167	132	113	46	.295	.380
Funk, Liz-Elias Calvin	29NYA 30DetA 32-33ChiA	10-28-04	La Cygne, Kans.	1-16-68	L	L	5'9	160	273	976	134	261	47	16	6	105	73	58	29	.267	.367
Gabrielson, Len-Leonard Hilborne	39PhiN	9- 8-15	Oakland, Cal.		L	L	6'3	210	5	18	3	4	0	0	0	1	2	3	0	.222	.222
Gaffke, Fabian-Fabian Sebastian	36-39BosA 41-42CleA	8- 5-13	Milwaukee, Wis.		R	R	5'10	185	129	321	43	73	14	4	7	42	30	47	2	.227	.361
Gagnon, Chick-Harold Dennis	22DetA 24WasA	9-27-97	Milbury, Mass.	4-30-70	R	R	5'8	158	13	9	3	2	0	0	0	1	0	2	0	.222	.222
Galan, Augie-August John	34-40ChiN 41-46BknN 47-48CinN 49NYN 49PhiA	5-25-12	Berkeley, Cal.		B	R	6'	175	1742	5937	1004	1706	336	74	100	830	979	393	123	.287	.419
					Bats Left 43-49																
Galatzer, Milt-Milton	33-36CleA 39CinN	5- 4-07	Chicago, Ill.		L	L	5'10	168	251	717	105	192	25	7	1	57	92	46	10	.268	.326
Gallagher, Gil-Lawrence Kirby	22BosN	9- 5-96	Washington, D.C.	1- 6-57	B	R	5'8	155	7	22	1	1	1	0	0	2	1	7	0	.045	.091
Gallagher, Jackie-John Laurence	23CleA	1-28-02	Providence, R.I.		L	L	5'10	175	1	1	0	1	0	0	0	1	0	0	0	1.000	1.000
Gallagher, Joe-Joseph Emmett (Muscles)	39NYA 39-40StLA 40BknN 41-45MS	3- 7-14	Buffalo, N.Y.		R	R	6'2	210	165	487	73	133	26	5	16	73	26	76	4	.273	.446
Galle (Galezewski), Stan-Stanley Joseph	42WasA 43-45MS	2- 7-19	Milwaukee, Wis.		R	R	5'7	165	13	18	3	2	0	0	0	1	1	0	0	.111	.111
Galloway, Chick-Clarence Edward	19-27PhiA 28DetA	8- 4-96	Manning, S.C.	11- 7-69	R	R	5'8	160	1076	3583	381	946	136	46	17	407	274	224	79	.264	.342
Galvin, Jim-James Joseph	30BosA	8-11-07	Somerville, Mass.	9-30-69	R	R	6'1	180	2	2	0	0	0	0	0	0	0	0	0	.000	.000
Gamble, Lee-Lee Jesse	35,38-40CinN	6-28-10	Renovo, Pa.		L	R	6'1	170	165	342	51	91	12	3	0	21	10	21	6	.266	.319
Gantenbein, Sep-Joseph Steven	39-40PhiA	8-25-16	San Francisco, Cal.		L	R	5'9	168	186	545	68	148	20	6	8	59	43	43	2	.272	.374
Ganzel, Babe-Foster Pirie	27-28WasA	5-22-01	Malden, Mass.		R	R	5'10	172	23	74	9	23	5	2	1	17	8	7	0	.311	.473
Garbark, Bob-Robert Michael	34-35CleA 37-39ChiN 44PhiA 45BosA	11-13-09	Houston, Tex.		R	R	5'11	178	145	327	31	81	9	0	0	28	26	17	0	.248	.275
Garbark, Mike-Michael Nathaniel	44-45NYA	2- 2-16	Houston, Tex.		R	R	6'	200	149	475	46	116	14	7	2	59	48	39	0	.244	.316
Gardella, Al-Alfred Stephan	45NYN	1-11-18	New York, N.Y.		L	L	5'10	172	16	26	2	2	0	0	0	1	4	3	0	.077	.077
Gardella, Danny-Daniel Lewis	44-45NYN 46-49SM 50StLN	2-26-20	New York, N.Y.		L	L	5'8	160	169	543	74	145	12	3	24	85	57	68	2	.267	.433
Gardner, Ray-Raymond Vincent	29-30CleA	10-25-01	Frederick, Md.	5- 3-68	R	R	5'8	145	115	269	35	68	3	2	1	25	29	17	10	.253	.290
Garibaldi, Art-Arthur Edward	36StLN	8-20-07	San Francisco, Cal.	10-19-67	R	R	5'8	175	71	232	30	64	12	0	1	20	16	30	3	.276	.341
Garms, Debs-Debs C.	32-35StLA 37-39BosN 40-41PitN 43-45StLN	6-26-08	Bangs, Tex.		L	R	5'9	165	1010	3111	438	910	141	39	17	328	288	161	18	.293	.379
Garrison, Ford-Robert Ford (Snapper, Rocky)	43-44BosA 44-46PhiA	8-29-15	Greenville, S.C.		R	R	5'10	180	185	687	80	180	22	3	6	56	37	67	11	.262	.329
Garrity, Hank-Francis Joseph	31ChiA	2- 4-08	Boston, Mass.	9- 1-62	R	R	6'1	185	8	14	0	3	1	0	0	2	1	2	0	.214	.286
Gaston, Alex-Alexander Nathaniel	20-23NYN 26,29BosA	3-12-93	New York, N.Y.		R	R	5'9	170	215	514	58	112	13	6	3	41	29	56	5	.218	.284
Gautreau, Doc-Walter Paul (Punk)	25PhiA 25-28BosN	7-26-01	Cambridge, Mass.	8-23-70	R	R	5'4	130	261	806	122	207	34	10	0	52	99	63	40	.257	.324
Gautreaux, Sid-Sidney Allen (Pudge)	36-37BknN	5- 4-12	Schriever, La.		B	R	5'8	190	86	81	8	20	4	0	0	18	10	8	0	.247	.296
Gazella, Mike-Michael	23,26-28NYA	10-13-96	Olyphant, Pa.		R	R	5'7	165	160	352	51	85	14	4	0	33	56	50	8	.241	.304
Geary, Huck-Eugene Francis Joseph	42-43PitN 44-45MS	1-22-17	Buffalo, N.Y.		L	R	5'10	170	55	188	20	30	4	0	1	15	20	9	3	.160	.197
Gedeon, Elmer-Elmer John	39WasA	4-15-17	Cleveland, Ohio	4-15-44	R	R	6'4	196	5	15	1	3	0	0	0	1	2	5	0	.200	.200
Gehrig, Lou-Henry Louis (The Iron Horse, Columbia Lou)	23-39NYA	6-19-03	New York, N.Y.	6- 2-41	L	L	6'	200	2164	8001	1888	2721	535	162	493	1991	1510	788	102	.340	.632
Gehringer, Charlie-Charles Leonard (The Mechanical Man)	24-42DetA 43-45MS	5-11-03	Fowlerville, Mich.		L	R	5'11	180	2323	8860	1774	2839	574	146	184	1427	1185	372	181	.320	.480
Gelbert, Charley-Charles Magnus	29-32StLN 33-34LJ 35-36StLN 37CinN 35DetA 39-40WasA 40BosA	1-26-06	Scranton, Pa.	1-13-67	R	R	5'11	170	876	2869	398	766	169	43	17	350	290	245	34	.267	.374
Gentile, Sam-Samuel Christopher	43BosN 44-45MS	10-12-16	Charlestown, Mass.		L	R	5'11	180	8	4	1	1	1	0	0	0	1	0	0	.250	.500
George, Greek-Charles Peter	35-36CleA 38BknN 41ChiN 45PhiA	12-25-12	Waycross, Ga.		R	R	6'2	200	118	299	15	53	9	2	0	24	28	59	0	.177	.221
Geraghty, Ben-Benjamin Raymond	36BknN 43-44BosN	7-19-12	Jersey City, N.J.	6-18-63	R	R	5'11	175	70	146	16	29	4	0	0	9	9	18	4	.199	.226
Gerber, Wally-Walter (Spooks)	14-15PitN 17-28StLA 28-29BosA	8-18-91	Columbus, Ohio	6-19-51	R	R	5'10	152	1522	5099	558	1309	172	46	7	476	465	357	41	.257	.313
Gerken, George-George Herbert (Pickles)	27-28CleA	7-28-03	Chicago, Ill.		R	R	5'11	175	44	129	17	29	7	2	0	11	13	25	3	.225	.310
Gerlach, John John Glenn	38-39ChiA	5-11-17	Shullsburg, Wis.		R	R	5'9	165	12	27	2	9	0	0	0	1	4	2	0	.333	.333

USE NAME – GIVEN NAMES (NICKNAMES)	TEAM BY YEAR	BIRTH DATE	BIRTH PLACE	DEATH DATE	B	T	HGT	WGT	G	AB	R	H	2B	3B	HR	RBI	BB	SO	SB	BA	SA
					LIFETIME BATTING TOTALS																
Geygan, Chappie, James Edward	24-26BosA	6- 3-03	Ironton, Ohio	3-15-66	R	R	5'11	170	40	103	7	26	5	2	0	4	5	19	0	.252	.340
Gharrity, Patsy-Edward Patrick	16-23WasA 24-28DE 29-30WasA	3-13-92	Parnell, Iowa	10-10-66	R	R	5'10	170	676	1961	237	513	92	26	20	249	188	231	32	.262	.366
Gibson, Charlie-Charles Griffin	24PhiA	11-21-99	LaGrange, Ga.		R	R	5'8	160	12	15	1	2	0	0	0	1	0	0	0	.133	.133
Gibson, Frank-Frank Gilbert	13DetA 21-27BosN	9-27-90	Omaha, Neb.	4-27-61	B	R	6'1	172	468	1155	121	317	57	19	8	146	55	127	12	.274	.377
					Bats Left 13,21-22,24																
Gilbert, Andy-Andrew	42BosA 43-45MS 46BosA	7-18-14	Latrobe, Pa.		R	R	6'1	203	8	12	1	1	0	0	0	1	1	3	0	.083	.083
Gilbert, Charlie-Charles Mader	40BknN 41-43ChiN 44-45MS 46ChiN 46-47PhiN	7- 8-19	New Orleans, La.		L	L	5'9	165	364	852	109	195	27	9	5	55	86	82	7	.229	.299
Gilbert, Wally-Walter John 23-27 played in N.F.L.	28-31BknN 32CinN	12-19-00	Oscoda, Mich.	9- 8-58	R	R	6'1	190	591	2317	301	624	112	17	7	214	162	131	21	.269	.341
Gilham, George-George Lewis	20-21StLN	9- 8-99	Shamokin, Pa.	4-25-37	R	R	5'11	164	2	4	0	0	0	0	0	0	0	1	0	.000	.000
Gill, Johnny-John Wesley (Patcheye)	27-28CleA 31,34WasA 35-36ChiN	3-27-05	Nashville, Tenn.		L	R	6'2	190	118	322	39	79	17	1	10	45	23	43	1	.245	.398
Gillenwater, Carden-Carden Edison	40StLN 43BknN 45-46BosN 48WasA	5-13-18	Riceville, Tenn.		R	R	6'1	175	335	1004	129	261	41	7	11	114	153	138	20	.260	.348
Gillespie, Paul-Paul Allen	42,44-45ChiN	9-18-20	Cartersville, Ga.		L	R	6'3	195	89	205	17	58	7	0	6	31	22	14	2	.283	.405
Gillis, Grant-Grant	27-28WasA 29BosA	1-24-01	Grove Hill, Ala.		R	R	5'10	165	62	196	26	48	12	2	0	23	12	13	0	.245	.327
Gionfriddo, Al-Albert Francis	44-47PitN 47BknN	3- 8-22	Dysart, Pa.		L	L	5'6	165	228	580	95	154	22	12	2	58	91	39	15	.266	.355
Giuliani, Tony-Angelo John	36-37StLA 38-39WasA 40-41BknN 43WasA	11-24-12	St. Paul, Minn.		R	R	5'11	175	243	674	58	157	18	3	0	69	38	40	1	.233	.269
Gladu, Roland-Roland Edouard	44BosN	5-10-13	Montreal, Canada		L	R	5'9	185	21	66	5	16	2	1	1	7	3	8	0	.242	.348
Gleason, Billy-William Patrick	16-17PitN 21StLA	9- 6-94	Chicago, Ill.	1- 9-57	R	R	5'6	157	40	118	9	26	1	1	0	8	11	11	1	.220	.246
Gleeson, Jim-James Joseph (Gee Gee)	36CleA 39-40ChiN 41-42CinN	3- 5-12	Kansas City, Mo.		B	R	6'1	191	392	1277	195	336	77	19	16	154	158	147	20	.263	.391
Gleich, Frank-Frank Elmer (Inch)	19-20NYA 21IL	3- 7-94	Columbus, Ohio	3-27-49	L	R	5'11	175	29	45	6	6	0	0	0	4	7	10	0	.133	.133
Glenn (Gurzensky), Joe-Joseph Charles (Gabber)	32-33,35-38NYA 39StLA 40BosA	11-19-08	Dickson City, Pa.		R	R	5'11	175	248	718	77	181	34	5	5	89	81	91	6	.252	.334
Glossop, Al-Alban	39-40NYN 40BosN 42PhiN 43BknN 44-45MS 46ChiN	7-23-12	Christopher, Ill.		B	R	6'	170	309	952	99	199	29	2	15	86	89	105	5	.209	.291
Goebel, Ed-Edwin	22WasA	9- 1-99	Brooklyn, N.Y.		R	R	5'11	170	37	59	13	16	1	0	1	3	8	16	1	.271	.339
Goldman, Jonah-Jonah John	[illegible]	[illegible]	New York, N.Y.		R	R	5'7	170	148	389	33	87	20	0	1	49	35	31	4	.224	.283
Goldstein, Lonnie-Leslie Elmer	43CinN 45MS 46CinN	5-13-18	Austin, Tex.		L	L	6'2	190	11	10	2	1	0	0	0	0	0	0	0	.100	.100
Goletz, Stan-Stanley (Stash)	41ChiA 42-45MS	5-21-18	Crescent, Ohio		L	L	6'3	200	5	5	0	3	0	0	0	0	0	2	0	.600	.600
Golvin, Walt-Walter George	22ChiN	2- 1-94	Hershey, Neb.	6-11-73	L	L	6'	165	2	2	0	0	0	0	0	1	0	0	0	.000	.000
Gomez, Chile-Jose Luis [Rodriguez]	35-36PhiN 42WasA	5-23-09	Villa Union, Mexico		R	R	5'10	165	200	627	56	142	9	3	0	50	40	73	3	.226	.250
Gomez, Preston (Pedro)-Preston [Martinez]	44WasA M69-72SDN M74-75HouN	4-20-23	Preston, Cuba		R	R	5'11	170	8	7	2	2	1	0	0	2	0	4	0	.286	.429
Gonzalez, Mike-Miguel Angel [Cordero]	12BosN 14CinN 15-18StLN 19-21NYN	9-24-90	Havana, Cuba		R	R	6'1	200	1042	2829	283	717	123	19	13	263	231	198	52	.253	.324
	24-25StLN 25-29ChiN 31-32,M38,40StLN																				
Gooch, Charlie-Charles Purman	29WasA	6- 5-02	Smyrna, Tenn.		R	R	5'9	170	39	57	6	16	2	1	0	5	7	8	0	.281	.351
Gooch, Johnny-John Beverley	21-28PitN 28-29BknN 29-30CinN 33BosA	11- 9-97	Smyrna, Tenn.	5-15-75	B	R	5'11	175	805	2363	227	662	98	29	7	293	206	141	11	.280	.355
Goodman, Ival-Ival Richard (Goodie)	35-42CinN 43-44ChiN	7-23-08	Northview, Mo.		L	R	5'11	170	1107	3928	609	1104	188	85	95	525	382	380	49	.281	.445
Gordon, Joe-Joseph Lowell (Flash)	38-43NYA 44-45MS 46NYA 47-50,M58-60CleA	2-18-15	Los Angeles, Cal.		R	R	5'10	180	1566	5707	914	1530	264	52	253	975	759	702	89	.268	.466
	M60DetA M61KCA M69KCA																				
Gorman, Howie-Howard Paul (Lefty)	37-38PhiN	5-14-13	Pittsburgh, Pa.		L	L	6'2	160	14	20	3	4	1	0	0	1	1	1	1	.200	.250
Goslin, Goose-Leon Allen	21-30WasA 30-32StLA 33WasA 34-37DetA 38WasA	10-16-00	Salem, N.J.	5-15-71	L	R	5'11	185	2287	8654	1483	2735	500	173	248	1609	948	585	175	.316	.500
Goulish, Nick-Nicholas Edward	44-45PhiN	11-13-17	Punxsutawney, Pa.		L	L	6'1	179	14	12	4	3	0	0	0	2	1	3	0	.250	.250
Grabowski, Johnny-John Patrick (Nig)	24-26ChiA 27-29NYA 31DetA	1- 7-00	Ware, Mass.	5-23-46	R	R	5'10	185	296	816	84	206	25	8	3	86	47	84	1	.252	.314
Grace, Earl-Robert Earl	29,31ChiN 31-35PitN 36-37PhiN	2-24-07	Barlow, Ky.		L	R	6'	175	627	1877	169	493	83	10	31	251	185	130	1	.263	.367
Grace, Joe-Joseph LaVerne	38-41StLA 42-45MS 46StLA 46-47WasA	1- 5-14	Gorham, Ill.	9-18-69	L	R	6'1	180	484	1561	225	442	76	18	20	172	179	135	9	.283	.393
Graham, Roy-Roy Vincent	22-23ChiA	2-22-95	San Francisco, Cal.	4-26-33	R	R	5'10	175	41	85	3	16	2	0	0	6	9	6	0	.188	.212
Graham, Skinny-Arthur William	34-35BosA	8-12-09	Somerville, Mass.	7-10-67	L	R	5'7	162	21	57	8	14	2	1	0	4	7	16	3	.246	.316
Grant, Jimmy-James Charles	42-43ChiA 43-44CleA	10- 6-18	Racine, Wis.	7- 8-70	L	R	5'8	166	146	354	38	87	16	6	5	36	38	67	5	.246	.367
Grantham, George-George Farley (Boots)	22-24ChiN 25-31PitN 32-33CinN 34NYN	5-20-00	Galena, Kans.	3-16-54	L	R	5'10	170	1444	4989	912	1508	292	93	105	712	717	526	132	.302	.461
Graves, Joe-Joseph Ebenezer	26ChiN	2-27-06	Marblehead, Mass.		L	R	5'10	160	2	5	0	0	0	0	0	0	0	1	0	.000	.000
Graves, Sid-Samuel Sidney (Whitey)	27BosN	11-30-01	Marblehead, Mass.		R	R	6'	170	7	20	5	5	1	1	0	2	0	1	1	.250	.400
Gray, Milt-Milton Marshall	37WasA	2-21-14	Louisville, Ky.	6-30-69	R	R	6'1	180	2	6	0	0	0	0	0	0	0	1	0	.000	.000
Gray (Wyshner), Pete-Peter J.	45StLA	3- 6-17	Nanticoke, Pa.		L	L	6'1	169	77	234	26	51	6	2	0	13	13	11	5	.218	.261
Greene (Green), Joe-Joseph Henry (Tilly)	24PhiA	9-17-97	Philadelphia, Pa.	2- 4-72	R	R	6'2	170	1	1	0	0	0	0	0	0	0	0	0	.000	.000
Greenberg, Hank-Henry Benjamin (Hammerin' Hank)	30,33-41DetA 42-44MS	1- 1-11	New York, N.Y.		R	R	6'4	210	1394	5193	1051	1628	379	71	331	1276	852	844	58	.313	.605
	45-46DetA 47PitN																				
Gremp, Buddy-Louis Edward	40-42BosN 43-45MS	8- 5-19	Denver, Colo.		R	R	6'1	175	113	291	19	65	14	0	3	31	18	24	1	.223	.302
Griesenbeck, Tim-Carlos Phillippe Timothy	20StLN	12-10-97	San Antonio, Tex.	3-25-53	R	R	5'11	185	5	3	1	1	0	0	0	0	0	0	0	.333	.333
Griffin, Ivy-Ivy Moore	19-21PhiA	1-16-96	Thomasville, Ala.	8-25-57	L	R	5'11	180	185	638	65	164	21	5	0	39	23	65	4	.257	.306
Griffith, Bert-Bartholomew Joseph (Buck)	22-23BknN 24WasA	3-30-96	St. Louis, Mo.	5- 5-73	R	R	6'	188	191	581	69	174	30	12	4	72	18	28	6	.299	.413
Grigsby, Denver-Denver Clarence	23-25ChiN	3-24-01	Jackson, Ky.	11-10-73	L	R	5'9	155	199	620	86	179	28	4	3	73	57	64	12	.289	.361
Grimes, Bummer-Austin Roy	20NYN	9-11-93	Bergholz, Ohio	9-13-54	R	R	6'1	185	26	57	5	9	1	0	0	3	3	8	1	.158	.175
Grimes, Ed-Edward Adelbert	31-32StLA	9- 8-05	Chicago, Ill.	10- 4-74	R	R	5'10	165	74	125	16	31	1	3	0	18	15	15	1	.248	.304
Grimes, Oscar-Oscar Ray Jr.	38-42CleA 43-46NYA 46PhiA	4-13-15	Minerva, Ohio		R	R	5'11	178	602	1832	235	469	73	24	18	200	297	303	30	.256	.352
Grimes, Ray-Oscar Ray Sr.	20BosA 21-24ChiN 26PhiN	9-11-93	Bergholz, Ohio	5-25-53	R	R	6'	175	433	1537	269	505	101	25	27	263	204	133	21	.329	.480
Grimm, Charlie-Charles John (Jolly Cholly)	16PhiA 18StLN 19-24PitN	8-28-98	St. Louis, Mo.		L	L	5'11	173	2164	7917	908	2299	394	108	79	1078	578	410	57	.290	.397
	25-36,M32-38,44-49ChiN M52BosN M53-56MilN M60ChiN																				
Groskloss, Howdie-Howard Hoffman	30-32PitN	4-10-08	Pittsburgh, Pa.		R	R	5'9	176	72	184	14	48	7	2	0	21	11	19	1	.261	.321
Gross, Turkey-Ewell	25BosA	2-21-96	Mesquite, Tex.	1-11-36	R	R	6'	165	9	32	2	3	0	1	0	2	2	2	0	.094	.156
Grube, Frank-Franklin Thomas (Hans)	31-33ChiA 34-35StLA 35-36ChiA 41StLA	1- 7-05	Easton, Pa.	7- 2-45	R	R	5'9	190	394	1125	121	274	59	5	1	107	131	88	12	.244	.308
28 played in N.F.L.																					
Gryska, Sig-Sigmund Stanley	38-39StLA	11- 4-15	Chicago, Ill.		R	R	5'11	173	25	70	7	23	4	1	0	12	9	13	3	.329	.414
Gudat, Marv-Marvin John (See P20-45)	29CinN 32ChiN	8-27-05	Goliad, Tex.	3- 1-54	L	L	5'11	176	69	104	15	26	4	1	1	15	16	10	0	.250	.337
Guisto, Lou-Louis Joseph	16-17CleA 18MS 21-23CleA	1-16-94	Napa, Cal.		R	R	5'11	193	156	449	35	88	19	3	0	59	46	44	5	.196	.252
Gulley, Tom-Thomas Jefferson	23-24CleA 26ChiA	12-25-99	Garner, N.C.	11-24-66	L	R	5'11	178	26	58	10	12	4	2	0	9	8	4	0	.207	.345
Gullic, Ted-Theodore Jasper	30,33StLA	1- 2-07	Koshkonong, Mo.		R	R	6'2	175	196	612	73	151	25	8	9	79	42	81	7	.247	.358
Gustine, Frankie-Frank William	39-48PitN 49ChiN 50StLA	2-20-20	Hoopeston, Ill.		R	R	6'	175	1261	4582	553	1214	222	47	38	480	369	427	60	.265	.359
Gutteridge, Don-Donald Joseph	36-40StLN 42-45StLA 46-47BosA 48PitN	6-19-12	Pittsburg, Kans.		R	R	5'10	165	1151	4202	586	1075	200	64	39	391	309	444	95	.256	.362
	M69-70ChiA																				
Gyselman, Dick-Richard Renald	33-34BosN	4- 6-08	San Francisco, Cal.		R	R	6'2	170	82	191	17	43	7	3	0	16	9	32	0	.225	.293
Haas, Mule-George William	25PitN 28-32PhiA 33-37ChiA 38PhiA	10-15-03	Montclair, N.J.	6-30-74	L	R	6'1	175	1168	4303	706	1257	254	45	43	496	433	299	12	.292	.402
Hack, Stan-Stanley Camfield (Smiling Stan)	32-47,M54-56ChiN M58StLN	12- 6-09	Sacramento, Cal.		L	R	6'	170	1938	7278	1239	2193	363	81	57	642	1092	466	165	.301	.397
Haeffner, Bill-William Bernhard	15PhiA 20PitN 28NYN	7-18-94	Philadelphia, Pa.		R	R	5'9	165	59	180	8	35	4	1	0	14	8	15	1	.194	.228
Hafey, Bud-Daniel Albert	35ChiA 35-36PitN 39CinN 39PhiN	8- 6-12	Berkeley, Cal.		R	R	6'	185	123	366	53	78	19	3	10	33	30	91	2	.213	.363
Hafey, Chick-Charles James	24-31StLN 32-35CinN 36IL 37CinN	2-12-03	Berkeley, Cal.	7- 2-73	R	R	6'	185	1283	4625	777	1466	341	67	164	833	372	477	70	.317	.526
Hafey, Tom-Thomas Francis (The Arm)	39NYN 44StLA	7-12-13	Berkeley, Cal.		R	R	6'1	180	78	270	38	67	12	1	6	28	11	48	1	.248	.367
Hahn, Dick-Richard Frederick	40WasA	7-24-16	Canton, Ohio		R	R	5'11	176	1	3	0	0	0	0	0	0	0	0	0	.000	.000
Haines, Hinkey-Henry Luther 25-29,31 played in N.F.L.	23NYA	12-23-98	Red Lion, Pa.		R	R	5'10	170	28	25	9	4	2	0	0	3	4	5	3	.160	.240
Hajduk, Chet-Chester	41ChiA	7-21-18	Chicago, Ill.		R	R	6'	195	1	1	0	0	0	0	0	0	0	0	0	.000	.000
Hale, Odell-Arvel Odell (Bad News)	31,33-40CleA 41BosA 41NYN	8-10-08	Hosston, La.		R	R	5'10	175	1062	3701	551	1071	240	51	73	573	353	315	57	.289	.441
Hale, Sammy-Samuel Douglas	20-21DetA 23-29PhiA 30StLA	9-10-96	Glen Rose, Tex.	9- 6-74	R	R	5'9	160	883	2915	422	880	157	54	30	392	130	218	41	.302	.424
Hall, Irv-Irvin Gladstone	43-46PhiA	10- 7-18	Alberton, Md.		R	R	5'10	160	508	1904	178	496	58	19	0	168	97	148	16	.261	.311
Hamby, Sam-James Sanford (Cracker)	26-27NYN	7-29-97	Wilkesboro, N.C.		R	R	6'	170	22	55	6	10	0	1	0	5	7	7	1	.182	.218
Hamner, Garvin-Wesley Garvin (Wes)	45PhiN	3-18-24	Richmond, Va.		R	R	5'11	172	32	101	12	20	3	0	0	5	7	9	2	.198	.228
Hamrick, Ray-Raymond Bernard	43-44PhiN 45-46MS	8- 1-21	Nashville, Tenn.		R	R	5'11	160	118	452	34	92	13	2	1	32	31	62	1	.204	.248
Hancken, Buddy-Morris Medlock	40PhiA	8-30-14	Birmingham, Ala.		R	R	6'1	175	1	0	0	0	0	0	0	0	0	0	0	–	–
Handley, Lee-Lee Elmer (Jeep)	36CinN 37-41,44-46PitN 47PhiN	7-31-13	Clarion, Iowa	4- 8-70	R	R	5'7	160	968	3356	418	902	122	45	15	297	267	204	68	.269	.345
Haney, Fred-Fred Girard (Pudge)	22-25DetA 26-27BosA 27ChiN 29StLN M39-41StLA	4-25-98	Albuquerque, N.M.		R	R	5'6	170	622	1977	338	544	66	21	8	228	282	123	50	.275	.342
	M53-55PitN M56-59MilN																				
Hanski (Hanyzewski), Don-Donald Thomas	43-44ChiA 45MS	2-27-16	La Porte, Ind.	9- 2-57	L	L	5'11	180	11	22	1	5	1	0	0	2	0	5	0	.227	.273
Happenny, John Clifford (Cliff)	23ChiA	5-18-01	Waltham, Mass.		R	R	5'11	165	32	86	7	19	5	0	0	10	3	13	0	.221	.279

USE NAME – GIVEN NAMES (NICKNAMES)	TEAM BY YEAR	BIRTH DATE	BIRTH PLACE	DEATH DATE	B	T	HGT	WGT	G	AB	R	H	2B	3B	HR	RBI	BB	SO	SB	BA	SA
									LIFETIME BATTING TOTALS												
Hargrave, Bubbles-Eugene Franklin	13-15ChiN 21-28CinN 30NYA	7-15-92	New Haven, Ind.	2-23-69	R	R	5'10	174	852	2533	314	786	155	58	29	376	217	165	29	.310	.452
Hargrave, Pinky-William McKinley	23-25WasA 25-26StLA 28-30DetA 30-31WasA 32-33BosN	1-31-96	New Haven, Ind.	10- 3-42	B	R	5'9	180	650	1602	177	445	91	16	39	265	140	165	17	.278	.428
					Bats Right 23-26																
Hargreaves, Charlie-Charles Russell	23-28BknN 28-30PitN	12-14-96	Trenton, N.J.		R	R	6'	170	423	1188	96	321	44	11	4	139	77	49	6	.270	.336
Harper, George-George Washington	16-18DetA 22-24CinN 24-26PhiN 27-28NYN 28StLN 29BosN	6-24-92	Arlington, Ky.		L	R	5'8	167	1073	3398	505	1030	158	43	91	528	389	208	58	.303	.455
Harrington, Andy-Andrew Matthew	25DetA	2-12-03	Mountain View, Cal.		R	R	5'11	170	1	1	0	0	0	0	0	0	0	0	0	.000	.000
Harris, Bucky-Stanley Raymond	19-28,M24-28WasA 29,31,M29-33DetA M34BosA M35-42WasA M43PhiN M47-48NYA M50-54WasA M55-56DetA	11- 8-96	Port Jervis, N.Y.		R	R	5'9	156	1264	4736	722	1297	224	64	9	506	472	310	166	.274	.354
Harris, Dave-David Stanley (Sheriff)	25,28BosN 30ChiA 30-34WasA	6-14-00	Summerfield, N.C.	9-18-73	R	R	5'11	190	542	1477	243	406	74	33	32	247	196	245	28	.281	.444
Harris, Joe-Joseph (Moon)	14NYA 17CleA 18MS 19CleA 20-21DO 22-25BosA 25-26WasA 27-28PitN 28BknN	5-20-91	Coulters, Pa.	12-10-59	R	R	5'9	170	970	3035	461	963	201	64	47	517	418	188	35	.317	.472
Harris, Ned-Robert Ned	41-43DetA 44-45MS 46DetA	7- 9-16	Ames, Iowa		L	L	5'11	175	262	814	107	211	33	14	16	81	102	77	12	.259	.393
Harris, Spence-Spencer Anthony	25-26ChiA 29WasA 30PhiA	8-12-00	Duluth, Minn.		L	L	5'9	160	164	377	53	94	15	3	3	46	39	33	10	.249	.329
Harshany, Sam-Samuel	37-40StLA	5- 1-10	Madison, Ill.		R	R	6'	180	61	181	17	43	3	0	0	15	16	10	0	.238	.254
Hart, Bill-William Woodrow	43-45BknN	3- 4-13	Wisconisco, Pa.	7-29-68	R	R	6'	175	95	270	35	56	10	4	3	32	24	30	8	.207	.307
Hartje, Chris-Christian Henry	39BknN	3-25-15	San Francisco, Cal.	6-26-46	R	R	5'11	180	9	16	2	5	1	0	0	5	1	0	0	.313	.375
Hartnett, Gabby-Charles Leo (Old Tomato Face)	22-40,M38-40ChiN 41NYN	12-20-00	Woonsocket, R.I.	12-20-72	R	R	6'1	195	1995	6432	867	1912	396	64	236	1179	703	697	28	.297	.489
Harvel, Luther-Luther Raymond (Red)	28CleA	9-30-05	Cambria, Ill.		R	R	5'11	180	40	136	12	30	6	1	0	12	4	17	1	.221	.279
Hasenmayer, Don-Donald Irvin	45-46PhiN	4- 4-27	Roslyn, Pa.		R	R	5'10	180	11	30	1	3	1	0	0	1	2	3	0	.100	.133
Haslin, Mickey-Michael Joseph	33-36PhiN 36BosN 37-38NYN	10-31-10	Wilkes-Barre, Pa.		R	R	5'8	165	318	974	125	265	33	8	9	109	59	64	8	.272	.350
Hassett, Buddy-John Aloysius	36-38BknN 39-41BosN 42NYA 43-46MS	9- 5-11	New York, N.Y.		L	L	5'11	180	929	3517	469	1026	130	40	12	343	209	116	53	.292	.362
Hassler, Joe-Joseph Frederick	28-29PhiA 30StLA	4- 7-05	Fort Smith, Ark.	9- 4-71	R	R	6'	165	37	46	9	11	2	0	0	4	2	7	0	.239	.283
Hasson, Gene-Charles Eugene	37-38PhiA	7-20-15	Connellsville, Pa.		L	L	6'	197	47	167	22	49	12	5	4	26	25	21	0	.293	.497
Hauser, Joe-Joseph John (Unser Choe)	22-24,26,28PhiA 25BK 27JJ 29CleA	1-12-99	Milwaukee, Wis.		L	L	5'10	175	629	2044	351	580	103	29	79	356	250	228	19	.284	.478
Hausmann, George-George John	44-45NYN 46-48SM 49NYN	2-11-16	St. Louis, Mo.		R	R	5'5	145	301	1136	173	304	35	13	3	78	120	77	10	.268	.329
Hawks, Chicken-Nelson Louis	21NYA 25PhiN	2- 3-96	San Francisco, Cal.	5-26-73	L	L	5'11	167	146	393	68	124	17	8	7	60	37	45	3	.316	.453
Hayes, Frankie-Franklin Whitman (Blimp)	33-34,36-42PhiA 42-43StLA 44-45PhiA 45-46CleA 46ChiA 47BosA	10-13-14	Jamesburg, N.J.	6-22-55	R	R	6'1	200	1364	4493	545	1164	213	32	119	628	564	627	30	.259	.400
Hayes, Jackie-Minter Carney	27-31WasA 32-40ChiA	7-19-06	Clanton, Ala.		R	R	5'10	165	1091	4040	494	1069	196	33	20	493	309	241	34	.265	.344
Hayworth, Ray-Raymond Hall	26,29-38DetA 38-39BknN 39NYN 42StLA 44-45BknN	1-29-04	High Point, N.C.		R	R	6'	180	699	2062	221	546	92	16	5	238	198	188	2	.265	.332
Hayworth, Red-Myron Claude	44-45StLA 46-49SM	5-14-15	High Point, N.C.		R	R	6'1	200	145	429	27	91	15	1	1	42	17	19	0	.212	.259
Healy, Francis-Francis Paul	30-32NYN 34StLN	6-29-10	Holyoke, Mass.		R	R	5'10	175	42	54	9	13	3	0	0	5	2	10	0	.241	.296
Heath, Jeff-John Geoffrey	36-45CleA 46WasA 46-47StLA 48-49BosN	4- 1-15	Fort William, Canada		L	R	5'11	200	1383	4937	777	1447	279	102	194	887	593	670	56	.293	.509
Heath, Mickey-Minor Wilson	31-32CinN	10-30-03	Toledo, Ohio		L	L	5'11	175	46	160	16	34	1	3	0	18	22	28	0	.213	.256
Heath, Tommy-Thomas George	35,37-38StLA	8-18-13	Akron, Ohio	2-26-67	R	R	5'11	185	134	330	36	76	16	2	3	34	65	40	0	.230	.318
Heathcote, Cliff-Clifton Earl	18-22StLN 22-30ChiN 31-32CinN 32PhiN	1-24-98	Glen Rock, Pa.	1-19-39	L	L	5'10	160	1415	4443	643	1222	206	55	42	448	367	325	190	.275	.375
Heffner, Don-Donald Henry (Jeep)	34-37NYA 38-43StLA 43PhiA 44DetA M66CinN	2- 8-11	Rouzerville, Pa.		R	R	5'10	155	743	2526	275	610	99	19	6	248	270	218	18	.241	.303
Heilmann, Harry-Harry Edwin (Slug)	14,16-29DetA 30CinN 31IL 32CinN	8- 3-94	San Francisco, Cal.	7- 9-51	R	R	6'1	200	2146	7787	1291	2660	542	151	183	1537	856	550	112	.342	.520
Heim, Val-Val Raymond	42ChiA 43-45MS	11- 4-20	Plymouth, Wis.		L	R	5'11	170	13	45	6	9	1	1	0	7	5	3	1	.200	.267
Heine, Bud-William Henry	21NYN	9-22-00	Elmira, N.Y.		L	R	5'8	145	1	2	0	0	0	0	0	0	0	0	0	.000	.000
Heltzel, Heinie-William Wade	43BosN 44PhiN	12-21-13	York, Pa.		R	R	5'11	150	40	108	7	17	4	0	0	5	9	16	0	.157	.194
Hemsley, Rollie-Ralston Burdett	28-31PitN 31-32ChiN 33CinN 33-37StLA 38-41CleA 42CinN 42-44NYA 45MS 46-47PhiN	6-24-07	Syracuse, Ohio	7-31-72	R	R	5'10	180	1593	5047	562	1321	257	72	31	555	357	395	29	.262	.360
Hendrick, Harvey-Harvey Lee (Gink)	23-24NYA 25CleA 27-31BknN 31CinN 32StLN 32CinN 33ChiN 34PhiN	11- 9-97	Mason, Tenn.	10-29-41	L	R	6'2	190	922	2910	434	896	157	46	48	413	239	243	75	.308	.443
Henline, Butch-Walter John	21NYN 21-26PhiN 27-29BknN 30-31ChiA	12-20-94	Fort Wayne, Ind.	10- 9-57	R	R	5'10	175	740	2101	58	611	96	21	40	268	192	156	18	.291	.414
Henrich, Fritz-Frank Wilde	24PhiN	5- 8-99	Cincinnati, Ohio	5- 1-59	L	L	5'10	160	36	90	4	19	4	0	0	4	2	12	0	.211	.256
Henrich, Tommy-Thomas David (Old Reliable)	37-42NYA 43-45MS 46-50NYA	2-20-13	Masillon, Ohio		L	L	6'	180	1284	4603	901	1297	269	73	183	795	712	383	37	.282	.491
Henry, Snake-Frederick Marshall	22-23BosN	7-19-95	Waynesville, N.C.		L	L	6'	170	29	75	6	14	4	1	0	7	3	9	2	.187	.267
Herman, Babe-Floyd Caves	26-31BknN 32CinN 33-34ChiN 35PitN 35-36CinN 35DetA 45BknN	6-26-03	Buffalo, N.Y.		L	L	6'4	190	1552	5603	882	1818	399	110	181	997	520	553	94	.324	.532
Herman, Billy-William Jennings Bryan	31-41ChiN 41-43BknN 44-45MS 46BknN 46BosN 47,M47PitN M64-66BosA	7- 7-09	New Albany, Ind.		R	R	5'11	180	1922	7707	1163	2345	486	82	47	839	737	428	67	.304	.407
Hermann, Al-Albert Bartel	23-24BosN	3-28-01	Milltown, N.J.		R	R	6'	180	32	94	2	22	4	0	0	11	0	8	3	.234	.277
Hernandez, Chico-Salvador Jose [Ramos]	42-43ChiN	1- 3-16	Havana, Cuba		R	R	6'	195	90	244	16	61	9	0	0	16	20	22	0	.250	.287
Herrara, Mike-Ramon	25-26BosA	12-19-97	Havana, Cuba		R	R	5'6	147	84	276	22	76	14	1	0	27	17	15	1	.275	.333
Hershberger, Willard-Willard McKee	38-40CinN	5-28-10	Lemon Cove, Cal.	8- 3-40	R	R	5'10	167	160	402	41	127	16	5	0	70	20	16	2	.316	.381
Heving, Johnnie-John Aloys	20StLA 24-25,28-30BosA 31-32PhiA	4-29-96	Covington, Ky.	12-24-68	R	R	6'	175	399	985	103	261	37	12	1	90	65	59	4	.265	.330
Higbe, Mahlon-Mahlon Jesse	22NYN	8-16-01	Louisville, Ky.	4- 7-68	R	R	5'11	165	3	10	2	4	0	0	1	5	0	2	0	.400	.700
Higgins, Pinky-Michael Franklin	30,33-36PhiA 37-38BosA 39-44DetA 45MS 46DetA 46,M55-59,M60-62BosA	5-27-09	Red Oak, Tex.	3-21-69	R	R	6'1	185	1802	6636	930	1941	375	50	140	1075	800	590	61	.292	.427
High, Andy Andrew Aird (Handy Andy)	22-25BknN 25-27BosN 28-31StLN 32-33CinN 34PhiN	11-21-97	Ava, Ill.		L	R	5'6	155	1314	4400	618	1250	195	65	44	482	426	130	33	.284	.388
High, Charlie-Charles Edwin	19-20PhiA	12- 1-98	Ava, Ill.	9-11-60	L	R	5'9	170	28	94	9	22	2	1	1	7	6	10	2	.234	.309
Hill, Jesse-Jesse Terrill	35NYA 36-37WasA 37PhiA	1-20-07	Yates, Mo.		R	R	5'9	165	295	959	175	277	53	12	6	108	115	91	43	.289	.388
Hill, Oliver-Oliver Clinton	39BosN	10-16-09	Powder Springs, Ga.	9-20-70	L	R	5'11	178	2	2	1	1	1	0	0	0	0	0	0	.500	1.000
Hiller, Hob-Harvey Max	20-21BosA	5-12-93	E. Mauch Chunk, Pa.	12-27-56	R	R	5'8	162	18	30	4	5	1	1	0	2	2	5	0	.167	.267
Hillis, Mack-Malcolm David	24NYA 28PitN	7-23-01	Cambridge, Mass.	6-16-61	R	R	5'10	165	12	37	7	9	2	3	1	7	0	6	1	.243	.541
Hinkle, Gordie-Daniel Gordon	34BosA	4- 3-05	Toronto, Ohio	3-18-71	R	R	6'	185	27	75	7	13	6	1	0	9	7	23	0	.173	.280
Hinson, Paul-James Paul	28BosA	5- 9-04	Van Leer, Tenn.	9-23-60	R	R	5'10	150	3	0	1	0	0	0	0	0	0	0	0	–	–
Hitchcock, Jim-James Franklin	38BosN	6-28-11	Inverness, Ala.	6-23-59	R	R	5'11	175	28	76	2	13	0	0	0	7	2	11	1	.171	.171
Hoag, Myril-Myril Oliver	31-32,34-38NYA 39-41StLA 41-42ChiA 43MS 44ChiA 44-45CleA	3- 9-08	Davis, Cal.	7-28-71	R	R	5'11	180	1020	3147	384	854	141	33	28	401	252	298	59	.271	.364
Hock, Ed-Edward Francis	20StLN 23-24CinN	3-27-99	Franklin Furnace, O.	11-21-63	L	R	5'10	165	19	10	7	1	0	0	0	0	0	2	0	.100	.100
Hockett, Oris-Oris Leon (Brown)	38-39BknN 41-44CleA 45ChiA	9-29-09	Amboy, Ind.	3-23-69	L	R	5'9	182	551	2165	259	598	112	21	13	214	159	157	43	.276	.365
Hodapp, Johnny-Urban John	25-32CleA 32ChiA 33BosA	9-26-05	Cincinnati, Ohio		R	R	6'	185	791	2826	378	880	169	34	28	429	163	136	18	.311	.425
Hodge, Bert-Edward Burton	42PhiN	5-25-17	Knoxville, Tenn.		L	R	5'11	170	8	11	0	2	0	0	0	0	1	0	0	.182	.182
Hodgin, Ralph-Elmer Ralph	39BosN 43-44ChiA 45MS 46-48ChiA	2-10-16	Greensboro, N.C.		L	R	5'10	167	530	1689	198	481	79	24	4	188	97	63	7	.285	.367
Hofferth, Stew-Stewart Edward	44-46BosN	1-27-13	Logansport, Ind.		R	R	6'2	195	136	408	30	88	11	1	4	51	28	22	1	.216	.277
Hoffman, Dutch-Clarence Casper	29ChiA	1-28-04	Freeburg, Ill.	12- 6-62	R	R	6'	175	107	337	27	87	16	5	3	37	24	28	6	.258	.362
Hoffman, Ray-Raymond Lamont	42WasA	6- 4-17	Detroit, Mich.		L	R	6'	175	7	19	2	1	0	0	0	2	1	1	0	.053	.053
Hofmann, Fred-Fred (Bootnose)	19-25NYA 27-28BosA	6-10-94	St. Louis, Mo.	11-19-64	R	R	5'11	175	378	1000	98	247	49	11	7	93	77	120	6	.247	.339
Hogan, Kenny-Kenneth Timothy	21CinN 23-24CleA	10- 9-02	Cleveland, Ohio		L	R	5'9	145	4	3	0	0	0	0	0	0	0	1	0	.000	.000
Hogan, Shanty-James Francis	25-27BosN 28-32NYN 33-35BosN 36-37WasA	3-21-06	Somerville, Mass.	4- 7-67	R	R	6'1	240	989	3180	288	939	146	12	61	474	220	188	6	.295	.406
Hogg, Bert-Wilbert George	34BknN	4-21-13	Detroit, Mich.		R	R	5'11	162	2	1	0	0	0	0	0	0	0	0	0	.000	.000
Hohman, Bill-William Henry	27PhiN	11-27-03	Brooklyn, Md.	10-29-68	R	R	6'	178	7	18	1	5	0	0	0	0	2	3	0	.278	.278
Holbrook, Sammy-James Marbury	35WasA	7-17-10	Meridian, Miss.		R	R	5'11	189	52	135	20	35	2	2	2	25	30	16	0	.259	.348
Holden, Joe-Joseph Francis (Socks)	34-36PhiN	6- 4-13	St. Clair, Pa.		L	R	5'11	175	17	24	1	2	0	0	0	0	0	5	1	.083	.083
Holke, Walter-Walter Henry (Union Man)	14,16-18NYN 19-22BosN 23-25PhiN 25CinN	12-25-92	St. Louis, Mo.	10-12-54	B	L	6'2	185	1212	4456	464	1278	153	58	24	487	191	304	81	.287	.363
Hollahan, Bill-Willis James (Happy)	20WasA	11-22-96	New York, N.Y.	11-27-65	R	R	5'9	165	3	4	0	1	0	0	0	1	1	2	1	.250	.250
Holland, Dutch-Robert Clyde	32-33BosN 34CleA	10-12-03	Middlesex, N.C.	6-16-67	R	R	6'1	190	102	315	37	86	26	2	3	34	28	39	1	.273	.397
Hollocher, Charlie-Charles Jacob	18-24ChiN	6-11-96	St. Louis, Mo.	8-14-40	L	R	5'7	154	760	2936	411	894	145	35	14	241	277	94	99	.304	.392
Holm, Billy-William Fred	43-44ChiN 45BosA	7-21-12	Chicago, Ill.		R	R	5'10	168	119	282	22	44	4	1	0	15	41	40	2	.156	.177
Holm, Wattie-Roscoe Albert	24-29,32StLN	12-28-01	Peterson, Iowa	5-19-50	R	R	5'9	160	436	1493	207	410	73	26	6	174	100	86	11	.275	.370
Holt, Red-James Emmett Madison	25PhiA	7-25-94	Dayton, Tenn.	2- 2-61	L	L	5'11	175	27	88	13	24	7	0	1	8	12	9	0	.273	.386
Hood, Abe-Aubrey Lincoln	25BosN	1-31-03	Comnock, N.C.		L	R	5'7	152	5	21	2	6	2	0	1	2	1	0	0	.286	.524

USE NAME – GIVEN NAMES (NICKNAMES)	TEAM BY YEAR	BIRTH DATE	BIRTH PLACE	DEATH DATE	B	T	HGT	WGT	G	AB	R	H	2B	3B	HR	RBI	BB	SO	SB	BA	SA
					LIFETIME BATTING TOTALS																
Hood, Wally-Wallace James Sr.	20PitN 20-22BknN	2- 9-95	Whittier, Cal.	5- 2-65	R	R	5'11	160	67	80	23	19	2	2	1	5	14	18	5	.238	.350
Hooks, Alex-Alexander Marcus	35PhiA	8-29-06	Edgewood, Tex.		L	L	6'1	183	15	44	4	10	3	0	0	4	3	10	0	.227	.295
Hoover, Joe-Robert Joseph	43-45DetA	4-15-15	Brawley, Cal.	9- 2-65	R	R	5'11	175	338	1238	178	301	45	15	5	84	92	202	19	.243	.316
Hopkins, Marty-Meredith Hilliard	34PhiN 34-35ChiA	2-22-07	Wolfe City, Tex.	11-20-63	R	R	5'11	175	136	379	48	80	12	0	4	48	85	54	1	.211	.274
Horan, Shags-Joseph Patrick	24NYA	9- 6-95	St. Louis, Mo.	2-13-69	R	R	5'10	170	22	31	4	9	1	0	0	7	1	5	0	.290	.323
Hornsby, Rogers-Rogers (Rajah)	15-26,M25-26StLN 27NYN 28,M28BosN	4-27-96	Winters, Tex.	1- 5-63	R	R	5'11	175	2259	8173	1579	2930	541	169	301	1584	1038	679	135	.358	.577
	29-32,M30-32ChiN 33StLN 33-37,M33-37,52StLA M52-53CinN																				
Hostetler, Chuck-Charles Cloyd	44-45DetA	9-22-03	McClellandtown, Pa.	2-18-71	L	R	6'	175	132	309	45	86	12	2	0	22	28	39	4	.278	.330
Howell, Red-Murray Donald (Porky)	41CleA	1-29-09	Atlanta, Ga.	10- 1-50	R	R	6'	215	11	7	0	2	0	0	0	2	4	2	0	.286	.286
Huber, Clarence-Clarence Bill (Gilly)	20-21DetA 25-26PhiN	10-28-96	Tyler, Tex.	2-22-65	R	R	5'10	165	254	854	95	225	47	13	6	93	59	67	12	.263	.370
Huber, Otto-Otto	39BosN	3-12-14	Garfield, N.J.		R	R	5'10	165	11	22	2	6	1	0	0	3	0	1	0	.273	.318
Hudgens, Jimmy-James Price	23StLN 25-26CinN	8-24-02	Newburg, Mo.	8-26-55	L	L	6'	180	26	39	4	11	3	1	0	1	5	4	0	.282	.410
Hudson, Johnny-John Wilson (Mr. Chips)	36-40BknN 41ChiN 45NYN	6-30-12	Bryan, Tex.	11- 7-70	R	R	5'10	165	426	1169	138	283	50	11	4	96	87	164	17	.242	.314
Huffman, Ben-Benjamin Franklin	37StLA	7-18-14	Rileyville, Va.		L	R	5'11	175	76	176	18	48	9	0	1	24	10	7	1	.273	.341
Hughes, Roy-Roy John (Jeep, Sage)	35-37CleA 38-39StLA 39-40PhiN 44-45ChiN 46PhiN	1-11-11	Cincinnati, Ohio		R	R	5'10	167	763	2582	396	705	105	27	5	205	222	175	80	.273	.340
Hughes, Tom-Thomas Franklin	30DetA	8- 6-07	Emmet, Ark.		L	R	6'1	190	17	59	8	22	2	3	0	5	4	8	0	.373	.508
Hungling, Bernie-Bernard Herman (Bud)	22-23BknN 30StLA	3- 5-96	Dayton, Ohio	3-30-68	R	R	6'2	180	51	137	13	33	3	2	1	15	11	25	2	.241	.314
Hunnefield, Bill-William Fenton (Wild Bill)	26-30ChiA 31CleA 31BosN 31NYN	1- 5-99	Dedham, Mass.		B	R	5'10	165	511	1664	230	452	75	9	9	144	117	111	67	.272	.344
Hunt, Joel-Oliver Joel (Jodie)	31-32StLN	10-11-05	Texico, N.M.		R	R	5'10	165	16	22	2	4	1	0	0	3	4	4	0	.182	.227
Hunter, Eddie-Edison Franklin	33CinN	2- 6-05	Bellevue, Ky.	3-14-67	R	R	5'8	150	1	0	0	0	0	0	0	0	0	0	0	–	–
Hurst, Don-Frank O'Donnell	28-34PhiN 34ChiN	8-12-05	Maysville, Ky.	12- 6-52	L	L	6'	215	905	3275	510	976	190	28	115	610	391	210	41	.298	.478
Husta, Carl-Carl Lawrence (Sox) 25-31 played in A.B.L.	25PhiA	4- 8-02	Egg Harbor, N.J.	11- 6-51	R	R	5'11	176	6	22	2	3	0	0	0	2	2	3	0	.136	.136
Huston, Warren-Warren Llewellyn	37PhiA 44BosN	10-31-13	Newtonville, Mass.		R	R	6'	170	71	103	12	10	4	0	0	1	10	11	0	.166	.202
Hutcheson, Joe-Joseph Johnson (Poodles)	33BknN	2- 5-05	Springtown, Tex.		L	R	6'2	200	55	184	19	43	4	1	6	21	15	13	1	.234	.364
Hutson, Roy-Roy Lee	25BknN	2-27-02	Luray, Mo.	5-20-57	L	R	5'9	165	7	8	1	4	0	0	0	1	1	1	0	.500	.500
Ingram, Mel-Melvin David	29PitN	7- 4-04	Asheville, N,C,		R	R	5'11	175	3	0	1	0	0	0	0	0	0	0	0	–	–
Irwin, Tommy-Thomas Andrew	38CleA	12-20-12	Altoona, Pa.		R	R	5'11	165	3	9	1	1	0	0	0	0	3	1	0	.111	.111
Irwin, Walt-Walter Kingsley (Lightning)	21StLN	9-23-97	Henrietta, Pa.		R	R	5'10	170	4	1	1	0	0	0	0	0	0	1	0	.000	.000
Jackson, Travis-Travis Calvin (Stonewall)	22-36NYN	11- 2-03	Waldo, Ark.		R	R	5'10	160	1656	6086	833	1768	291	86	135	929	412	565	71	.291	.433
Jacobs, Ray-Raymond F.	28ChiN	1- 2-02	Salt Lake City, Utah	4- 4-52	R	R	6'	160	2	2	0	0	0	0	0	0	0	1	0	.000	.000
Jacobson, Baby Doll-William Chester	15DetA 15,17StLA 18MS 19-26StLA	8-16-90	Cable, Ill.		R	R	6'3	215	1472	5507	787	1714	328	94	83	819	355	410	86	.311	.450
	26-27BosA 27CleA 27PhiA																				
Jacobson, Merwin-Merwin John William (Jake)	15NYN 16ChiN 26-27BknN	3- 7-94	New Britain, Conn.		L	L	5'11	165	133	331	47	76	9	2	0	24	38	34	7	.230	.269
Jahn, Art-Arthur Charles	25ChiN 28NYN 28PhiN	12- 2-95	Struble, Iowa	1- 9-48	R	R	6'	180	104	349	45	97	15	8	1	55	17	36	2	.278	.375
James, Bernie-Robert Byrne	29-30BosN 33NYN	9- 2-05	Angleton, Tex.		B	R	5'9	150	114	237	35	61	6	3	1	20	17	26	8	.257	.321
					Bats Right 29																
Jamieson, Charlie-Charles Devine (See P01-19)	15-17WasA 17-18PhiA 19-32CleA	2- 7-93	Paterson, N.J.	10-27-69	L	L	5'9	165	1779	6564	1062	1990	322	80	18	550	748	345	132	.303	.385
Jeanes, Tex-Ernest Lee	21-22CleA 25-26WasA 27NYN	12-19-00	Maypearl, Tex.	4- 5-73	R	R	6'	176	52	72	15	19	3	0	1	9	7	7	1	.264	.347
Jeffries, Irv-Irvine Franklin	30-31ChiA 34PhiN	9-10-05	Louisville, Ky.		R	R	5'10	175	175	495	71	116	19	0	8	46	32	21	6	.234	.321
Jelincich, Frank-Frank Anthony (Jelly)	41ChiN 42-45MS	9- 3-19	San Jose, Cal.		R	R	6'2	198	4	8	0	1	0	0	0	1	0	2	0	.125	.125
Jenkins, John-John Robert	22ChiA	7- 7-96	Bosworth, Mo.	8- 3-68	R	R	5'8	160	5	3	0	0	0	0	0	1	0	2	0	.000	.000
Jenkins, Tom-Thomas Griffin (Tut)	25-26BosA 26PhiA 29-32StLA	4-10-98	Camden, Ala.		L	R	6'1	174	171	459	42	119	14	6	3	44	28	53	1	.259	.336
Jensen, Woody-Forrest Docenus	31-39PitN	8-11-07	Bremerton, Wash.		L	L	5'10	160	738	2720	392	774	114	37	26	235	69	100	20	.285	.382
Jessee, Dan-Daniel Edward	29CleA	2-22-01	Olive Hill, Ky.	4-30-70	L	R	5'10	165	1	0	0	0	0	0	0	0	0	0	0	–	–
Johnson, Bob-Robert Lee (Indian Bob)	33-42PhiA 43WasA 44-45BosA	11-26-06	Pryor, Okla.		R	R	6'	180	1863	6920	1239	2051	396	95	288	1283	1073	851	96	.296	.506
Johnson, Don-Donald Spore (Pep)	43-48ChiN	12- 7-11	Chicago, Ill.		R	R	6'	170	511	1935	219	528	89	6	8	175	112	171	26	.273	.337
Johnson, Ed-Edwin Cyril	20WasA	3-31-99	Morganfield, Ky.		L	R	5'9	160	2	8	0	2	0	0	0	1	0	0	0	.250	.250
Johnson, Ernie-Ernest Rudolph	12ChiA 15StLF 16-18StLA 21-23ChiA 23-25NYA	4-29-88	Chicago, Ill.	5- 1-52	L	R	5'9	151	811	2619	372	697	91	36	19	256	181	118	114	.266	.350
Johnson, Paul-Paul Oscar	18BosN 20-21PhiA	9- 2-96	N. Grosvenordale, Conn.	2-14-73	R	R	5'8	160	67	199	23	55	6	2	1	15	13	25	2	.276	.342
Johnson, Roy-Roy Cleveland	29-32DetA 32-35BosA 36-37NYA 37-38BosN	2-23-03	Pryor, Okla.	9-11-73	L	R	5'9	175	1153	4358	717	1292	275	83	58	556	489	380	135	.296	.438
Johnston, Fred-Wilfred Ivey (Red Top)	24BknN	7- 9-99	Charlotte, N.C.	5-14-59	R	R	5'11	170	4	4	1	1	0	0	0	0	0	1	0	.250	.250
Johnston, Jimmy-James Harle	11ChiA 14ChiN 16-25BknN 26BosN 26NYN	12-10-89	Cleveland, Tenn.	2-14-67	R	R	5'10	160	1377	5070	754	1493	185	75	22	410	391	246	169	.294	.374
Jolley, Smead-Smead Powell (Smudge)	30-32ChiA 32-33BosA	1-14-02	Wesson, Ark.		L	R	6'3	210	473	1710	188	521	111	21	46	313	89	105	5	.305	.475
Jones, Binky-John Joseph	24BknN	7-11-99	St. Louis, Mo.	5-13-61	R	R	5'9	154	10	37	0	4	1	0	0	2	0	3	0	.108	.135
Jones, Bob-Robert Walter (Ducky)	17-25DetA	12- 2-89	Clayton, Cal.	8-30-64	L	R	6'	170	853	2990	399	791	120	38	7	316	208	156	49	.265	.337
Jones, Cobe-Dyas Coburn	28-29PitN	8-21-05	Denver, Colo.	6- 3-69	B	R	5'7	155	27	65	6	17	5	1	0	4	1	5	1	.262	.369
Jones, Howie-Howard	21StLN	3- 1-97	Irwin, Pa.	7-15-72	L	L	5'11	165	3	2	0	0	0	0	0	0	0	1	0	.000	.000
Jones, John-John William (Skins)	23,32PhiA	5-13-01	Coatsville, Pa.	11- 3-56	L	L	5'11	185	5	10	0	2	0	0	0	1	0	4	0	.200	.200
Jones, Red-Maurice Morris	40StLN	11- 2-14	Timpson, Tex.		L	R	6'3	190	12	11	0	1	0	0	0	1	1	2	0	.091	.091
Jonnard, Bubber-Clarence James	20ChiA 22PitN 26-27PhiN 29StLN 35PhiN	11-23-97	Nashville, Tenn.		R	R	6'1	185	103	235	26	54	7	1	0	20	12	23	0	.230	.268
Jordan, Buck-Baxter Byerly	27,29NYN 31WasA 32-37BosN 37-38CinN 38PhiN	1-16-07	Cooleemee, N.C.		L	R	6'	170	811	2980	396	890	153	35	17	281	182	109	20	.299	.391
Jordan, Jimmy-James William (Lord)	33-36BknN	1-13-08	Tucapau, S.C.	12- 4-57	R	R	5'9	157	376	1273	102	327	51	4	2	118	37	76	8	.257	.308
Jorgens, Art-Arndt Ludwig	29-39NYA	5-18-05	Modum, Norway		R	R	5'9	160	307	738	79	176	31	5	4	89	85	73	3	.238	.310
Jorgensen, Pinky-Carl	37CinN	11-21-14	Laton, Cal.		R	R	6'1	195	6	14	1	4	0	0	0	1	1	2	0	.286	.286
Jourdan, Ted-Theodore Charles	16-18,20ChiA	9- 5-95	New Orleans, La.	9-23-61	L	L	6'	175	75	196	19	42	6	2	0	11	19	21	5	.214	.265
Judge, Joe-Joseph Ignatius	15-32WasA 33BknN 33-34BosA	5-25-94	Brooklyn, N.Y.	3-11-63	L	L	5'8	155	2170	7894	1184	2350	433	159	71	1034	965	478	213	.298	.420
Judnich, Walt-Walter Franklin	40-42StLA 43-45MS 46-47StLA 48CleA 49PitN	1-24-17	San Francisco, Cal.	7-12-71	L	L	6'1	205	790	2786	424	782	150	29	90	420	385	298	20	.281	.452
Judy, Lyle-Lyle LeRoy (Punch)	35StLN	11-15-13	Lawrenceville, Ill.		R	R	5'10	150	8	11	2	0	0	0	0	0	2	2	2	.000	.000
Juelich, Jack-John Samuel (Red)	39PitN	9-20-16	St. Louis, Mo.	12-25-70	R	R	5'11	180	17	46	5	11	0	2	0	4	2	4	0	.239	.326
Jumonville, George-George Benedict	40-41PhiN	5-16-17	Mobile, Ala.		R	R	6'	175	17	41	1	6	0	0	1	2	1	6	0	.146	.220
Jurges, Billy-William Frederick	31-38ChiN 39-45NYN 46-47ChiN M59-60BosA	5- 9-08	Bronx, N.Y.		R	R	5'11	175	1816	6253	721	1613	245	55	43	656	568	530	36	.258	.335
Just (Juszczak), Joe-Joseph Erwin	44-45CinN	1- 8-16	Milwaukee, Wis.		R	R	5'11	185	25	45	2	7	0	0	0	2	4	9	0	.156	.156
Kahdot, Ike-Isaac Leonard (Chief)	22CleA	10-22-01	Georgetown, Okla.		R	R	5'6	160	4	2	0	0	0	0	0	0	0	1	0	.000	.000
Kahle, Bob-Robert Wayne	38BosN	11-23-15	Newcastle, Ind.		R	R	6'	170	8	3	2	1	0	0	0	0	0	0	0	.333	.333
Kahn, Owen-Owen Earle (Jack)	30BosN	6- 5-05	Richmond, Va.		R	R	5'11	160	1	0	1	0	0	0	0	0	0	0	0	–	–
Kalin (Kalinkiewicz), Frank-Frank Bruno (Fats)	40PitN 43ChiA 44-45MS	10- 3-17	Steubenville, Ohio		R	R	6'	200	7	7	0	0	0	0	0	1	2	0	0	.000	.000
Kamm, Willie-William Edward	23-31ChiA 31-35CleA	2- 2-00	San Francisco, Cal.		R	R	5'10	170	1692	5851	802	1643	348	85	29	826	824	405	126	.281	.384
Kampouris, Alex-Alex William	34-38CinN 38-39NYN 41-43BknN 43WasA 44-45MS	11-13-12	Sacramento, Cal.		R	R	5'8	155	708	2182	272	531	94	20	45	284	244	360	22	.243	.367
Kane, John-John Francis	25ChiA	2-19-00	Chicago, Ill.		B	R	5'10	162	14	56	6	10	1	0	0	3	0	3	0	.179	.196
Kane, Tom-Thomas Joseph (Sugar)	38BosN	12-15-06	Chicago, Ill.		R	R	5'10	160	2	2	0	0	0	0	0	0	2	0	0	.000	.000
Karlon, Bill-William John (Hank)	30NYA	1-21-09	Palmer, Mass.	12- 7-64	R	R	6'1	190	2	5	0	0	0	0	0	0	0	1	0	.000	.000
Karow, Marty-Martin Gregory	27BosA	7-18-04	Braddock, Pa.		R	R	5'10	170	6	10	0	2	1	0	0	0	0	2	0	.200	.300
Kaufmann, Tony-Anthony Charles (See P20-45)	21-27ChiN 27PhiN 27-28StLN 29NYN	12-16-00	Chicago, Ill.		R	R	5'11	165	260	414	62	91	19	1	9	57	28	82	4	.220	.336
	30-31,35StLN																				
Kearns, Ted-Edward Joseph 25-30 played in A.B.L.	24-25ChiN	1- 1-00	Trenton, N.J.	12-21-49	R	R	5'11	180	7	18	0	5	0	1	0	1	1	1	0	.278	.389
Kearse, Ed-Edward Paul (Trick)	42NYA	2-23-16	San Francisco, Cal.	7-15-68	R	R	6'1	195	11	26	2	5	0	0	0	2	3	1	1	.192	.192
Keely, Bob-Robert William	44-45StLN	8-22-09	St. Louis, Mo.		R	R	6'	175	2	1	0	0	0	0	0	0	0	0	0	.000	.000
Keesey, Jim-James Ward	25,30PhiA	10-27-02	Perryville, Md.	9- 5-51	R	R	6'	170	16	17	3	5	1	0	0	3	1	4	0	.294	.353
Kelleher, Frankie-Francis Eugene	42-43CinN 44-45MS	8-22-16	San Francisco, Cal.		R	R	6'1	195	47	120	14	20	3	1	3	12	18	20	0	.167	.283
Kelleher, John-John Patrick	12StLN 16BknN 21-23ChiN 24BosN	9-13-93	Brookline, Mass.	8-21-60	R	R	5'11	150	235	703	81	206	29	8	10	89	45	42	9	.293	.400
Keller, Charlie-Charles Ernest (King Kong)	39-43NYA 44MM 45-49NYA 50-51DetA 52NYA	9-12-16	Middletown, Md.		L	R	5'10	185	1170	3791	725	1085	166	72	189	760	784	499	45	.286	.518
Kellett, Don-Donald Stafford (Red)	34BosA	7-15-09	Brooklyn, N.Y.		R	R	6'	185	9	9	0	0	0	0	0	0	1	5	0	.000	.000
Kelly, Bill-William Henry (Big Bill)	20PhiA 28PhiN	12-28-99	Syracuse, N.Y.		R	R	6'	190	32	84	6	15	2	1	0	5	7	22	0	.179	.226
Kelly, George-George Lange (Highpockets)	15-17NYN 17PitN 18MS 19-26NYN	9-10-95	San Francisco, Cal.		R	R	6'4	190	1622	5993	819	1778	337	76	148	1020	386	694	65	.297	.452
	27-30CinN 30ChiN 32BknN																				
Kelly, Joe-Joseph James	26,28ChiN	4-23-00	New York, N.Y.	11-24-67	L	L	6'	180	97	228	19	70	16	3	1	39	8	14	0	.307	.417

USE NAME – GIVEN NAMES (NICKNAMES)	TEAM BY YEAR	BIRTH DATE	BIRTH PLACE	DEATH DATE	B	T	HGT	WGT	G	AB	R	H	2B	3B	HR	RBI	BB	SO	SB	BA	SA
									LIFETIME BATTING TOTALS												
Keltner, Ken-Kenneth Frederick	37-44CleA 45MS 46-49CleA 50BosA	10-31-16	Milwaukee, Wis.		R	R	6'	190	1526	5683	737	1570	308	69	163	852	514	480	39	.276	.441
Kenna, Ed-Edward Aloysius (Scrap Iron)	28WasA	9-30-97	San Francisco, Cal.	8-21-72	R	R	5'8	145	41	118	14	35	4	2	1	20	14	8	1	.297	.390
Kerns, Dan-Daniel P.	20PhiA		Philadelphia, Pa.						1	1	0	0	0	0	0	0	0	0	0	.000	.000
Kerns, Russ-Russell Eldon	45DetA	11-10-20	Fremont, Ohio		L	R	6'	188	1	1	0	0	0	0	0	0	0	0	0	.000	.000
Kerr, John-John Francis	23-24DetA 29-31ChiA 32-34WasA	11-26-98	San Francisco, Cal.		R	R	5'8	158	471	1457	172	388	59	13	6	145	115	92	26	.266	.337
					Bats Both 23-24																
Kerr, Mel-John Melville	25ChiN	5-22-03	Souris, Canada		L	L	5'11	155	1	0	1	0	0	0	0	0	0	0	0	–	–
Kibbie, Hod-Horace Kent	25BosN	7-18-03	Fort Worth, Tex.		R	R	5'10	150	11	41	5	11	2	0	0	2	5	6	0	.268	.317
Kilduff, Pete-Peter John	17NYN 17-19ChiN 19-21BknN	4- 4-93	Weir City, Kans.	2-14-30	R	R	5'7	155	428	1384	163	374	62	28	4	159	134	132	28	.270	.364
Kimble, Dick-Richard Louis	45WasA	7-27-15	Buchtel, Ohio		L	R	5'9	180	20	49	5	12	1	1	0	1	5	7	0	.245	.306
Kimmick, Wally-Wally Lyons	19StLN 21-23CinN 25-26PhiN	5-30-97	Turtle Creek, Pa.		R	R	5'11	174	163	345	39	90	9	5	1	31	34	61	4	.261	.325
King, Lee-Edward Lee	16-18PitN 19-21NYN 21-22PhiN 22NYN	12-26-92	Hundred, W.Va.	9-16-67	R	R	5'10	175	411	1189	134	294	60	18	15	144	82	175	16	.247	.366
King, Lynn-Lynn Paul (Dig)	35-36,39StLN	11-28-07	Villisca, Iowa	5-11-72	L	R	5'9	165	175	207	28	43	4	1	0	21	28	18	6	.208	.237
Kingdon, Wes-Wescott William	32WasA	7- 4-00	Los Angeles, Cal.	4-19-75	R	R	5'8	148	18	34	10	11	3	1	0	3	5	2	0	.324	.471
Kish, Ernie-Ernest Alexander	45PhiA	2- 6-18	Washington, D.C.		L	R	5'10	170	43	110	10	27	5	1	0	10	9	9	0	.245	.309
Klee, Ollie-Ollie Chester (Babe)	25CinN	5-20-00	Piqua, Ohio		L	R	5'9	160	3	1	0	0	0	0	0	0	0	1	0	.000	.000
Klein, Chuck-Charles Herbert	28-33PhiN 34-36ChiN 37-39PhiN 39PitN 40-44PhiN	10- 7-04	Indianapolis, Ind.	3-28-58	L	R	6'	185	1753	6486	1168	2076	398	74	300	1201	601	521	79	.320	.543
Klein, Lou-Louis Frank	43StLN 44MS 45-46StLN 47-48SM 49StLN 51CleA 51PhiA	10-22-18	New Orleans, La.		R	R	5'11	167	305	1037	162	269	48	15	16	101	105	119	10	.259	.381
	M61-62,65ChiN																				
Klinger, Joe-Joseph John	27NYN 30ChiA	8- 2-02	Canonsburg, Pa.	7-31-60	R	R	6'	190	7	13	0	5	0	0	0	1	0	2	0	.385	.385
Kloza, Nap-John Clarence	31-32StLA	9- 7-03	Poland	6-11-62	R	R	5'11	180	22	20	5	3	0	1	0	2	5	8	0	.150	.250
Klugmann, Joe-Joe	21-22ChiN 24BknN 25CleA	3-26-95	St. Louis, Mo.	7-18-51	R	R	5'11	175	77	187	22	47	11	3	0	17	11	15	3	.251	.342
Klumpp, Elmer-Elmer Edward	34WasA 37BknN	8-26-06	St. Louis, Mo.		R	R	6'	184	17	26	2	3	0	0	0	2	1	5	0	.115	.115
Knickerbocker, Bill-William Hart	33-36CleA 37StLA 38-40NYA 41ChiA 42PhiA	12-29-11	Los Angeles, Cal.		R	R	5'11	170	907	3418	423	943	198	27	28	368	244	238	25	.276	.374
Knode, Mike-Kenneth Thomson	20StLN	11- 8-95	Westminister, Md.		L	R	5'10	160	42	65	11	15	1	1	0	12	5	6	0	.231	.277
Knode, Ray-Robert Traxell (Bob)	23-26CleA	1-28-01	Westminister, Md.		L	L	5'10	160	109	207	32	55	7	1	2	21	17	11	6	.266	.338
Knothe, Fritz-Wilfred Edgar	32-33BosN 33PhiN	5- 1-03	Passaic, N.J.	3-27-63	R	R	5'10	180	174	615	70	135	26	3	2	53	58	81	8	.220	.281
Knothe, George-George Bertram (Whitey)	32PhiN	1-12-98	Bayonne, N.J.		R	R	5'10	165	6	12	2	1	1	0	0	0	0	0	0	.083	.167
Knox, Cliff-Clifford Hiram (Bud)	24PitN	1- 7-02	Coalville, Iowa	9-24-65	B	R	5'11	178	6	18	1	4	0	0	0	2	2	0	0	.222	.222
Koch, Barney-Barnett	44BknN	3-23-23	Campbell, Neb.		R	R	5'8	140	33	96	11	21	2	0	0	1	3	9	0	.219	.240
Koehler, Pip-Horace Levering 27-28,30-31 played in A.B.L.	25NYN	1-16-02	Gilbert, Pa.		R	R	5'10	165	12	2	1	0	0	0	0	0	0	1	0	.000	.000
Koenecke, Len-Leonard George	32NYN 34-35BknN	1-18-04	Baraboo, Wis.	9-17-35	L	R	5'11	190	265	922	155	274	49	9	22	114	124	96	11	.297	.441
Koenig, Mark-Mark Anthony	25-30NYA 30-31DetA 32-33ChiN 34CinN 35-36NYN	7-19-02	San Francisco, Cal.		B	R	6'	180	1162	4271	572	1190	195	49	28	443	222	190	31	.279	.367
Kopf, Wally-Walter Henry	21NYN	7-10-99	Stonington, Conn.		B	R	5'11	168	2	3	0	1	0	0	0	0	1	1	0	.333	.333
Kopshaw, George-George Karl	23StLN	7- 5-95	Passaic, N.J.	12-26-34	R	R	5'11	176	2	5	1	1	1	0	0	0	0	1	0	.200	.400
Kosman, Mike-Michael Thomas	44CinN	12-10-17	Hamtramck, Mich.		R	R	5'9	160	1	0	0	0	0	0	0	0	0	0	0	–	–
Koster, Fred-Frederick Charles (Fritz)	31PhiN	12-21-05	Louisville, Ky.		L	L	5'10	165	76	151	21	34	2	2	0	8	14	21	4	.225	.265
Koy, Ernie-Ernest Anyz (Chief)	38-40BknN 40-41StLN 41-42CinN 42PhiN 43-45MS	9-17-09	Sealy, Tex.		R	R	6'	200	558	1846	238	515	108	29	36	260	137	284	40	.279	.427
Kracher, Joe-Joseph Peter (Jug)	39PhiN	11- 4-15	Philadelphia, Pa.		R	R	5'11	185	5	5	1	1	0	0	0	0	2	1	0	.200	.200
Kreevich, Mike-Michael Andreas	31ChiN 35-41ChiA 42PhiA 43-45StLA 45WasA	6-10-08	Mount Olive, Ill.		R	R	5'8	168	1241	4676	676	1321	221	75	45	514	446	341	115	.283	.391
Kreitner, Mickey-Albert Joseph	43-44ChiN	10-10-22	Nashville, Tenn.		R	R	6'3	190	42	93	3	16	2	0	0	3	9	18	0	.172	.194
Kress, Red-Ralph (See P20-45)	27-31StLA 32-34ChiA 34-36WasA 38-39StLA	1- 2-07	Columbia, Cal.	11-29-62	R	R	5'11	165	1391	5087	690	1454	298	58	89	799	474	453	47	.286	.420
	40DetA 46NYN																				
Kroner, John-John Harold	35-36BosA 37-38CleA	11-13-08	St. Louis, Mo.	8-26-68	R	R	6'	165	223	702	83	184	47	9	7	105	68	56	3	.262	.385
Krug, Marty-Martin John	12BosA 22ChiN	9-10-88	Coblenz, Germany	6-27-66	R	R	5'9	165	143	489	73	136	25	5	4	67	48	43	9	.278	.374
Kuhel, Joe-Joseph Anthony	30-37WasA 38-43ChiA 44-46WasA 46-47ChiA M48-49WasA	6-25-06	Cleveland, Ohio		L	L	6'	180	2105	7985	1236	2212	412	111	131	1049	980	612	178	.277	.406
Kurowski, Whitey-George John	41-49StLN	4-19-18	Reading, Pa.		R	R	5'11	193	916	3229	518	925	162	32	106	529	369	332	19	.286	.455
Kvasnak, Al-Alexander	42WasA 43-45MS	1-11-21	Sagamore, Pa.		R	R	6'1	170	5	11	3	2	0	0	0	0	2	1	0	.182	.182
Laabs, Chet-Chester Peter	37-39DetA 39-46StLA 47PhiA	4-30-12	Milwaukee, Wis.		R	R	5'8	175	950	3102	467	813	151	44	117	509	389	595	32	.262	.452
Lacy, Guy-Osceola Guy	26CleA	6-12-97	Cleveland, Tenn.		L	R	5'11	170	13	24	2	4	0	0	1	2	2	2	0	.167	.292
LaForest, Ty-Byron Joseph	45BosA	4-18-19	Edmundston, Canada	5- 5-47	R	R	5'9	165	52	204	25	51	7	4	2	16	10	35	4	.250	.353
Lakeman, Al-Albert Wesley (Moose)	42-47CinN 47-48PhiN 49BosN 54DetA	12-31-18	Cincinnati, Ohio		R	R	6'2	195	239	646	40	131	17	5	15	66	36	137	0	.203	.314
Lamar, Bill-William Harmong (Good Time Bill)	17-19NYA 19BosA 20-21BknN	3-21-97	Rockville, Md.	5-24-70	L	R	6'1	185	550	2040	303	633	114	23	19	245	86	78	25	.310	.417
	24-27PhiA																				
Lamb, Lyman-Laymon Raymond	20-21StLA	3-17-95	Lincoln, Neb.	10- 5-55	R	R	5'7	150	54	158	22	43	11	2	1	21	4	19	2	.272	.386
LaMotte, Bobby-Robert Eugene	20-22WasA 25-26StLA	2-15-98	Savannah, Ga.	11- 2-70	R	R	5'11	160	221	693	99	175	34	9	3	85	66	50	11	.253	.341
Land, Doc-William Gilbert	29WasA	5-14-03	Binnsville, Mass.		L	L	5'11	165	1	3	0	0	0	0	0	0	1	0	0	.000	.000
Landrum, Jesse-Jesse Glenn	38ChiA	7-31-12	Crockett, Tex.		R	R	5'11	175	4	6	0	0	0	0	0	1	0	2	0	.000	.000
Lane, Hunter-James Hunter (Dodo)	24BosN	7-20-00	Pulaski, Tenn.		R	R	5'11	165	7	15	0	1	0	0	0	0	1	1	0	.067	.067
Langford, Sam-Elton J.	26BosA 27-28CleA	5-21-00	Briggs, Tex.		L	R	6'	180	131	495	61	136	22	8	5	57	26	42	3	.275	.382
Lapan, Pete-Peter Nelson	22-23WasA	6-25-91	Easthampton, Mass.	1- 5-53	R	R	5'7	165	13	36	7	11	1	0	1	6	3	4	1	.306	.417
Larsen, Swede-Erling Adeli	36BosN	11-15-13	Jersey City, N.J.		R	R	5'11	170	3	1	0	0	0	0	0	0	0	0	0	.000	.000
Lary, Lyn-Lynford Hobart (Broadway)	29-34NYA 34BosA 35WasA 35-36StLA 37-39CleA	1-28-06	Armona, Cal.	1- 9-73	R	R	6'	165	1302	4604	805	1239	247	66	38	526	705	470	162	.269	.372
	39BknN 39StLN 40StLA																				
Lavagetto, Cookie-Harry Arthur	34-36PitN 37-41BknN 42-45MS 46-47BknN	12- 1-12	Oakland, Cal.		R	R	6'	170	1043	3509	487	945	183	37	40	486	485	244	63	.269	.377
	M57-60WasA M61MinA																				
Lawrence, Bill-William Henry	32DetA	3-11-06	San Mateo, Cal.		R	R	6'4	194	25	46	10	10	1	0	0	3	5	5	0	.217	.239
Layne, Herman-Herman	27PitN	2-13-01	New Haven, W.Va.	8-27-73	R	R	5'11	165	11	6	3	0	0	0	0	0	1	0	0	.000	.000
Layne, Hilly-Ivoria Hillis	41WasA 42-43MS 44-45WasA	2-23-18	Whitewell, Tenn.		L	R	6'	170	107	284	37	75	9	4	1	28	20	22	3	.264	.335
Lazor, Johnny-John Paul	43-46BosA	9- 9-12	Taylor, Wash.		L	R	5'10	180	223	596	57	157	30	4	6	62	40	53	8	.263	.357
Lazzeri, Tony-Anthony Michael (Poosh 'Em Up)	26-37NYA 38ChiN 39BknN 39NYN	12- 6-03	San Francisco, Cal.	8- 6-46	R	R	5'11	170	1740	6297	986	1840	334	115	178	1191	870	864	148	.292	.467
Leach, Freddy-Frederick M.	23-28PhiN 29-31NYN 32BosN	11-23-97	Springfield, Mo.		L	R	5'11	183	991	3733	543	1147	196	53	72	509	163	189	32	.307	.446
Leathers, Hal-Harold Langford	20ChiN	12- 2-98	Los Angeles, Cal.		L	R	5'7	152	9	23	3	7	1	0	1	1	1	1	1	.304	.478
LeBourveau, Bevo-DeWitt Wiley	19-22PhiN 29PhiA	8-24-94	Dana, Cal.	12- 9-47	L	R	5'11	175	280	788	100	217	27	11	11	70	79	125	15	.275	.379
Lee, Cliff-Clifford Walker	19-20PitN 21-24PhiN 24CinN 25-26CleA	8- 4-96	Lexington, Neb.		R	R	6'1	175	521	1583	216	475	87	28	38	216	104	186	14	.300	.462
Lee, Dud-Ernest Dudley (played as Dud Dudley 1920)	20-21StLA 24-26BosA	8-22-99	Denver, Colo.	1- 7-71	L	R	5'9	150	253	732	80	163	20	9	0	60	88	70	12	.223	.275
Lee, Hal-Harold Burnham (Sheriff)	31-33PhiN 33-36BosN	2-15-05	Ludlow, Miss.		R	R	5'11	180	752	2750	316	755	144	40	33	323	203	225	15	.275	.392
Lees, George-George Edward	21ChiA	2- 2-95	Bethlehem, Pa.		R	R	5'9	150	20	42	3	9	2	0	0	4	0	3	0	.214	.262
LeFevre, Al-Alfredo Modesto	20NYN	9-16-98	New York, N.Y.		L	R	5'10	160	17	27	5	4	0	1	0	0	0	13	0	.148	.222
Lefler, Wade-Wade Hampton	24BosN 24WasA	6- 5-96	Cooleemee, N.C.		L	R	5'11	162	6	9	0	5	3	0	0	4	0	1	0	.556	.889
Legett, Lou-Louis Alfred (Doc)	29BosN 33-35BosA	6- 1-01	New Orleans, La.		R	R	5'10	166	68	124	13	25	3	0	0	8	5	22	2	.202	.226
Leiber, Hank-Henry Edward	33-38NYN 39-41ChiN 42NYN	1-17-11	Phoenix, Ariz.		R	R	6'1	205	813	2805	410	808	137	24	101	518	274	319	5	.288	.462
Leifer, Elmer-Elmer Edwin	21ChiA	5-23-93	Clarington, Ohio	9-26-48	L	R	5'9	170	9	10	0	3	0	0	0	1	0	4	0	.300	.300
Leip, Ed-Edgar Ellsworth	39WasA 40-42PitN 43-45MS	11-29-10	Trenton, N.J.		R	R	5'9	160	30	62	7	17	1	2	0	5	3	6	1	.274	.355
Leovich, John-John Joseph	41PhiA	5- 5-18	Portland, Ore.		R	R	6'	200	1	2	0	1	1	0	0	0	0	0	0	.500	1.000
Lerian, Walt-Walter Irvin (Peck)	28-29PhiN	3- 3-03	Baltimore, Md.	10-22-29	R	R	5'11	170	201	512	56	126	29	4	8	50	94	66	1	.246	.365
Leslie, Roy-Roy Reid	17ChiN 19StLN 22PhiN	8-23-94	Bailey, Tex.	4- 9-72	R	R	6'1	190	160	556	47	148	24	2	6	55	42	57	4	.266	.349
Leslie, Sam-Samuel Andrew (Sambo)	29-33NYN 33-35BknN 36-38NYN	7-26-05	Moss Point, Miss.		L	L	6'	192	822	2460	311	749	123	28	36	389	216	118	14	.304	.421
Letchas, Charlie-Charlie	39PhiN 41WasA 44PhiN 45MS 46PhiN	10- 3-15	Thomasville, Ga.		R	R	5'10	150	136	461	32	108	10	0	1	37	35	31	0	.234	.262
Levey, Jim-James Julius 34-36 played in N.F.L.	30-33StLA	9-13-06	Pittsburgh, Pa.	3-14-70	B	R	5'10	154	440	1632	162	375	61	14	11	140	85	201	23	.230	.305
					Bats Right 30-31																
Levy (Whitner), Ed-Edward Clarence	40PhiN	10-28-16	Birmingham, Ala.		R	R	6'5	190	1	1	0	0	0	0	0	0	0	0	0	.000	.000
Lewis, Bill-William Henry (Buddy)	33StLN 35-36BosN	10-15-04	Ripley, Tenn.		R	R	5'9	165	50	101	20	33	3	0	1	11	15	11	0	.327	.386
Lewis, Buddy-John Kelly	35-41WasA 42-44MS 45-47,49WasA	8-10-16	Gastonia, N.C.		L	R	6'1	175	1349	5261	830	1563	249	93	71	607	573	303	83	.297	.420
Libke, Al-Albert Walter (Big Al)	45-46CinN	9-12-18	Tacoma, Wash.		L	R	6'4	215	254	880	73	236	45	6	9	95	77	112	6	.268	.364
Lillard, Bill-William Beverley	39-40PhiA	1-10-18	Goleta, Cal.		R	R	5'10	170	80	225	30	55	9	2	1	22	31	29	0	.244	.316
Lillard, Gene-Robert Eugene (See P20-45)	36,39ChiN 40StLN	11-12-13	Santa Barbara, Cal.		R	R	5'10	178	44	44	9	8	1	0	0	2	9	11	0	.182	.205
Lind, Carl-Henry Carl (Hooks)	27-30CleA	9-19-03	New Orleans, La.	8- 2-46	R	R	6'	170	256	981	131	267	53	5	1	73	57	79	9	.272	.340
Lindstrom, Fred-Frederick Charles (Lindy)	24-32NYN 33-34PitN 35ChiN 36BknN	11-21-05	Chicago, Ill.		R	R	5'11	170	1438	5611	895	1747	301	81	103	779	334	276	84	.311	.449

USE NAME – GIVEN NAMES (NICKNAMES)	TEAM BY YEAR	BIRTH DATE	BIRTH PLACE	DEATH DATE	B	T	HGT	WGT	G	AB	R	H	2B	3B	HR	RBI	BB	SO	SB	BA	SA
									LIFETIME BATTING TOTALS												
Linton, Bob-Claude C.	29PitN	4-18-02	Emerson, Ark.		L	R	6'	185	17	18	0	2	0	0	0	1	1	2	0	.111	.111
Lipscomb, Jerry-Gerald (Nig)	37StLA	2-24-11	Rutherfordton, N.C.		R	R	6'	175	36	96	11	31	9	1	0	8	11	10	0	.323	.438
Litwhiler, Danny-Daniel Webster	40-43PhiN 43-44StLN 45MS 46StLN 47-48BosN 48-51CinN	8-31-16	Ringtown, Pa.		R	R	5'10	198	1057	3494	428	982	162	32	107	451	299	377	11	.281	.438
Livingston, Mickey-Thompson Orville	38WasA 41-43PhiN 43ChiN 44MS 45-47ChiN 47-49NYN 49BosN 51BknN	11-15-14	Newberry, S.C.		R	R	6'1	185	561	1490	128	354	56	9	19	153	144	141	7	.238	.326
Loane, Bobby-Robert Kenneth	39WasA 40BosN	8- 6-14	Berkeley, Cal.		R	R	6'	190	16	31	6	5	3	0	0	2	6	9	2	.161	.258
Lodigiani, Dario-Dario Joseph (Lodi)	38-40PhiA 41-42ChiA 43-45MS 46ChiA	6- 6-16	San Francisco, Cal.		R	R	5'8	150	405	1364	142	355	71	7	16	156	141	86	12	.260	.358
Loepp, George-George Herbert	28BosA 30WasA	9-11-01	Detroit, Mich.	9- 4-67	R	R	5'11	170	65	185	29	46	10	2	0	17	25	21	0	.249	.324
Loftus, Dick-Richard Joseph	24-25BknN	3- 7-01	Concord, Mass.	1-21-72	L	R	6'	155	97	212	34	53	12	0	0	21	12	7	3	.250	.307
Lombardi, Ernie-Ernesto Natali (Schnozz)	31BknN 32-41CinN 42BosN 43-47NYN	4- 6-08	Oakland, Cal.		R	R	6'3	230	1853	5855	601	1792	277	27	190	990	430	262	8	.306	.460
Long, Jimmie-James Albert	22ChiA	6-29-98	Fort Dodge, Iowa	9-14-70	R	R	5'11	160	3	3	0	0	0	0	0	0	1	0	0	.000	.000
Lopez, Al-Alfonso Ramon	28,30-35BknN 36-40BosN 40-46PitN 47,M51-56CleA M57-65,68-69ChiA	8-20-08	Tampa, Fla.		R	R	5'11	165	1950	5916	613	1547	206	43	51	652	556	538	46	.261	.337
Lord, Carl-William Carlton	23PhiN	1- 7-00	Philadelphia, Pa.	8-15-47	R	R	5'11	170	17	47	3	11	2	0	0	2	2	3	0	.234	.277
Lovelace, Grover-Grover Thomas	22PitN	9- 8-98	Wolfe City, Tex.		R	R	5'11	167	1	1	0	0	0	0	0	0	0	0	0	.000	.000
Lovett, Mem-Merritt Marwood	33ChiA	6-15-12	Chicago, Ill.		R	R	5'9	165	1	1	0	0	0	0	0	0	0	0	0	.000	.000
Luby, Hugh-Hugh Max (Hal)	36PhiA 44NYN 45MS	6-13-13	Blackfoot, Ida.		R	R	5'10	185	120	361	33	89	11	2	2	38	52	22	4	.247	.305
Lucadello, Johnny-John	38-41StLA 42-45MS 46StLA 47NYA	2-22-19	Thurber, Tex.		B	R	5'11	160	239	686	95	181	36	7	5	60	93	56	6	.264	.359
Lucas, Fred-Frederick Warrington	35PhiN	1-19-03	Vineland, N.J.		R	R	5'10	165	20	34	1	9	0	0	0	2	3	6	0	.265	.265
Lucas, Johnny-John Charles (Buster)	31-32BosA	2-10-03	Glen Carbon, Ill.	10-31-70	R	L	5'10	186	4	3	0	0	0	0	0	0	0	1	0	.000	.000
Lucas, Red-Charles Frederick (See P20-45)	23NYN 24-25BosN 26-33CinN 34-38PitN	4-28-02	Columbia, Tenn.		L	R	5'10	170	907	1439	155	404	61	13	3	190	124	133	2	.281	.347
Luce, Frank-Frank Edward	23PitN	12- 6-96	Spencer, Ohio	2- 3-42	L	R	5'11	180	9	12	2	6	0	0	0	3	2	2	2	.500	.500
Lucey, Joe-Joseph Earl (Scootch) (See P20-45)	20NYA 25BosA	3-27-97	Holyoke, Mass.		R	R	6'	168	13	18	0	2	0	0	0	0	0	4	0	.111	.111
Luebbe, Roy-Roy John	25NYA	9-17-00	Parkersburg, Iowa		B	R	6'1	183	8	15	1	0	0	0	0	3	2	6	0	.000	.000
Lupien, Tony-Ulysses John	40,42-43BosA 44-45PhiN 48ChiA	4-23-17	Chelmsford, Mass.		L	L	5'10	185	614	2358	285	632	92	30	18	230	241	111	57	.268	.355
Lutz, Red-Louis William	22CinN	12-17-98	Cincinnati, Ohio		R	R	5'11	170	1	1	0	1	1	0	0	0	0	0	0	1.000	2.000
Lutzke, Rube-Walter John	23-27CleA	11-17-97	Milwaukee, Wis.	3- 6-38	R	R	5'11	175	572	1876	216	468	87	18	4	223	179	196	24	.249	.321
Lynch, Walt-Walter Edward	22BosA	4-15-97	Buffalo, N.Y.		R	R	6'	176	3	2	1	1	0	0	0	0	0	0	0	.500	.500
Lynn, Jerry-Jerome Edward	37WasA	4-14-16	Scranton, Pa.	9-25-72	R	R	5'10	164	1	3	0	2	1	0	0	0	0	0	0	.667	1.000
Lyon, Russ-Russell Mayo	44CleA	6-26-13	Ball Ground, Ga.		R	R	6'1	230	7	11	1	2	0	0	0	0	1	1	0	.182	.182
Lyons, Terry-Terence Hilbert	29PhiN	12-14-08	New Holland, Ohio	9- 9-59	R	R	6'	165	1	0	0	0	0	0	0	0	0	0	0	–	–
MacDonald, Harvey-Harvey Forsyth	28PhiN	5-18-98	New York, N.Y.	10- 4-65	L	L	5'11	170	13	16	0	4	0	0	0	2	2	3	0	.250	.250
Mack (Maciarz), Joe-Joe John	45BosN	1- 4-12	Chicago, Ill.		B	L	5'11	185	66	260	30	60	13	1	3	44	34	39	1	.231	.323
Mack (Mlckovsky), Ray-Raymond James	38-44CleA 45MS 46CleA 47NYA 47ChiN	8-31-16	Cleveland, Ohio	5- 7-69	R	R	6'	200	791	2708	273	629	113	24	34	278	261	365	35	.232	.329
Mackiewicz, Felix-Felix Thaddeus	41-43PhiA 45-47CleA 47WasA	11-20-17	Chicago, Ill.		R	R	6'2	197	223	672	85	174	32	12	2	55	63	88	10	.259	.351
Macon, Max-Max Cullen (See P20-45)	38StLN 40,42-43BknN 44BosN 45-46MS 47BosN	10-14-15	Pensacola, Fla.		L	L	6'3	175	226	502	54	133	17	4	3	46	16	32	9	.265	.333
MacPhee, Waddy-Walter Scott	22NYN	12-23-99	Brooklyn, N.Y.		R	R	5'8	155	2	7	2	2	0	1	0	0	1	0	0	.286	.571
Madjeski (Majewski), Ed-Edward William	32-34PhiA 34ChiA 37NYN	7-24-09	Queens, N.Y.		R	R	5'11	178	166	481	58	116	19	2	5	56	21	61	2	.241	.320
Maggert, Harl-Harl Warren	38BosN	5- 4-14	Los Angeles, Cal.		R	R	6'	190	66	89	12	25	3	0	3	19	10	20	0	.281	.416
Maguire, Freddie-Fred Edward	22-23NYN 28ChiN 29-31BosN	5-10-99	Roxbury, Mass.	11- 3-61	R	R	5'11	155	618	2120	226	545	90	22	1	163	82	131	23	.257	.322
Mahady, Jim-James Bernard	21NYN	4-22-01	Cortland, N.Y.	8- 9-36	R	R	5'11	170	1	0	0	0	0	0	0	0	0	0	0	–	–
Mahan, Art-Arthur Leo	40PhiN	6- 8-13	Somerville, Mass.		L	L	5'11	178	146	544	55	133	24	5	2	39	40	37	4	.244	.318
Maier, Bob-Robert Phillip	45DetA	9- 5-15	Dunellen, N.J.		R	R	5'8	180	132	486	58	128	25	7	1	34	37	32	7	.263	.350
Mailho, Emil-Emil Pierre (Lefty)	36PhiA	12-16-09	Berkeley, Cal.		L	L	5'10	165	21	18	5	1	0	0	0	0	5	3	0	.056	.056
Maisel, George-George John	13StLA 16DetA 21-22ChiN	3-12-92	Catonsville, Md.	11-20-68	R	R	5'10	180	167	500	67	141	10	3	0	50	20	24	18	.282	.314
Malay, Joe-Joseph Charles	33,35NYN	10-25-05	Brooklyn, N.Y.		L	L	6'	175	9	25	0	4	0	0	0	2	0	0	0	.160	.160
Malinosky, Tony-Anthony Francis	37BknN	10- 5-09	Collinsville, Ill.		R	R	5'10	165	35	79	7	18	2	0	0	3	9	11	0	.228	.253
Mallon, Les-Leslie Clyde	31-32PhiN 34-35BosN	11-21-05	Sweetwater, Tex.		R	R	5'8	160	383	1300	156	368	65	5	8	119	100	117	4	.283	.359
Mallonee, Ben-Howard Bennett (Lefty)	21PhiA	3-31-94	Baltimore, Md.		L	L	5'6	150	7	24	2	6	1	0	0	0	1	1	0	.250	.292
Mallonee, Jule-Julius Norris	25ChiA	4- 4-00	Charlotte, N.C.	12-26-34	L	R	6'2	180	2	3	1	0	0	0	0	0	1	0	0	.000	.000
Mallory, Jim-James Baugh (Sunny Jim)	40WasA 42-44MS 45StLN 45NYN	9- 1-18	Lawrenceville, Va.		R	R	6'1	170	54	149	15	40	3	0	0	14	7	10	1	.268	.289
Mancuso, Frank-Frank Octavius	44-46StLA 47WasA	5-23-18	Houston, Tex.		R	R	6'	195	337	1002	85	241	37	7	5	98	101	118	2	.241	.306
Mancuso, Gus-August Rodney (Blackie)	28,30-32StLN 33-38NYN 39ChiN 40BknN 41-42StLN 42-44NYN 45PhiN	12- 5-05	Galveston, Tex.		R	R	5'10	185	1460	4505	386	1194	197	16	53	543	418	264	8	.265	.351
Manion, Clyde-Clyde Jennings (Pete)	20-24,26-27DetA 28-30StLA 32-34CinN	10-30-96	Jefferson City, Mo.		R	R	5'11	175	477	1145	96	250	25	3	3	112	118	102	5	.218	.253
Mann, Ben-Ben Garth (Red)	44ChiN	11-16-15	Brandon, Tex.		R	R	6'	155	1	0	1	0	0	0	0	0	0	0	0	–	–
Mann, Johnny-John Leo	28ChiA	2- 4-98	Fontanet, Ind.		R	R	5'11	160	6	6	0	2	0	0	0	1	1	0	0	.333	.333
Manno, Don-Donald D.	40-41BosN	5-15-15	Williamsport, Pa.		R	R	6'1	190	25	37	3	7	1	0	1	8	3	9	0	.189	.297
Manush, Heinie-Henry Emmett	23-27DetA 28-30StLA 30-35WasA 36BosA 37-38BknN 38-39PitN	7-20-01	Tuscumbia, Ala.	5-12-71	L	L	6'1	200	2009	7653	1287	2524	491	160	110	1173	506	345	114	.330	.479
Maple, Howard-Howard Albert	32WasA	7-20-03	Adrian, Mo.	11- 9-70	L	R	5'7	175	44	41	6	10	0	1	0	7	7	7	0	.244	.293
Maranville, Rabbit-Walter James Vincent	12-20BosN 21-24PitN 25,M25ChiN 26BknN 27-28StLN 29-33BosN 34BL 35BosN	11-11-91	Springfield, Mass.	1- 5-54	R	R	5'5	155	2670	10078	1255	2605	380	177	28	884	839	756	291	.258	.340
Marion, Marty-Martin Whitford (Slats, The Octopus)	40-50StLN M51StLN 51XJ 52-53,M52-53StLA M54-56ChiA	12- 1-17	Richburg, S.C.		R	R	6'2	170	1572	5506	602	1448	272	37	36	624	470	537	35	.263	.345
Marion, Red-John Wyeth	35,43WasA	3-14-14	Richburg, S.C.	3-13-75	R	R	6'2	175	18	28	3	5	1	0	1	2	3	3	0	.179	.321
Marnie, Hal-Harry Sylvester	40-42PhiN 43-45MS	7- 6-18	Philadelphia, Pa.		R	R	6'1	178	96	222	19	49	3	3	0	15	18	29	1	.221	.261
Marquardt, Ollie-Albert Ludwig	31BosA	9-22-02	Toledo, Ohio	2- 7-68	R	R	5'9	160	17	39	4	7	1	0	0	2	3	4	0	.179	.205
Marriott, Bill-William Earl	17ChiN 18MS 20-21ChiN 25BosN 26-27BknN	4-18-93	Pratt, Kans.	8-11-69	R	R	6'	170	264	826	86	220	27	14	4	95	57	55	16	.266	.347
Marshall, Bill-William Henry	31BosA 34CinN	2-14-09	Dorchester, Mass.		R	R	5'8	156	7	8	1	1	0	0	0	0	0	2	0	.125	.125
Marshall (Marczlewicz), Charlie-Charles Anthony	41StLN	8-28-19	Wilmington, Del.		R	R	5'10	178	1	0	0	0	0	0	0	0	0	0	0	–	–
Marshall, Doc-Edward Herbert	29-32NYN	6- 4-06	New Albany, Miss.		R	R	5'11	150	219	658	72	170	21	6	0	61	28	28	2	.258	.309
Marshall, Max-Milo Max	42-44CinN 45MS	9-18-13	Shenandoah, Iowa		L	R	6'1	180	329	1267	140	311	41	16	15	105	89	100	15	.245	.339
Martin (Martinovich), Babe-Boris Michael	44-46StLA 48-49BosA 53StLA	3-28-20	Seattle, Wash.		R	R	5'11	194	69	206	13	44	6	2	2	18	13	27	0	.214	.291
Martin, Hersh-Herschel Ray	37-40PhiN 44-45NYA	9-19-09	Birmingham, Ala.		B	R	6'2	190	607	2257	331	643	135	29	28	215	253	207	33	.285	.408
Martin, Joe-William Joseph (Smokey Joe)	36NYN 38ChiA	8-28-11	Seymour, Mo.	9-28-60	R	R	5'11	181	8	15	0	4	1	0	0	2	0	4	0	.267	.333
Martin, Pepper-Johnny Leonard Roosevelt (The Wild Hoss of the Osage)	28,30-40,44StLN	2-29-04	Temple, Okla.	3- 5-65	R	R	5'8	170	1189	4117	756	1227	270	75	59	501	369	438	146	.298	.443
Martin, Stu-Stuart McGuire	36-40StLN 41-42PitN 43ChiN	11-17-13	Rich Square, N.C.		L	R	6'	155	722	2237	322	599	112	24	16	183	190	185	36	.268	.361
Marty, Joe-Joseph Anton	37-39ChiN 39-41PhiN 42-45MS	9- 1-13	Sacramento, Cal.		R	R	6'	182	538	1832	223	478	78	22	44	222	142	187	14	.261	.400
Matthews, Wid-Wid Curry	23PhiA 24-25WasA	10-20-96	Raleigh, Ill.	10- 5-65	L	L	5'8	140	192	663	79	188	21	10	1	39	61	32	19	.284	.350
Mattick, Bobby-Robert James	38-40ChiN 41-42CinN	12- 5-15	Sioux City, Iowa		R	R	5'11	178	206	690	54	161	31	1	0	64	33	60	7	.233	.281
Mattox, Cloy-Cloy Mitchell (Monk)	29PhiA	11-21-02	Leesville, Va.		L	R	5'8	168	3	6	0	1	0	0	0	0	1	1	0	.167	.167
Mattox, Jim-James Powell	22-23PitN	12-17-96	Leesville, Va.		L	R	5'9	168	51	83	15	21	2	2	0	4	1	8	0	.253	.325
Mauldin, Mark-Marshall Reese	34ChiA	11- 5-14	Atlanta, Ga.		R	R	5'11	170	10	38	3	10	2	0	1	3	0	3	0	.263	.395
May, Pinky-Merrill Glend	39-43PhiN 44-45MS	1-18-11	Laconia, Ind.		R	R	5'11	165	665	2215	210	610	102	11	4	215	261	121	13	.275	.337
Maynard, Buster-James Walter	40,42-43NYN 44-45MS 46NYN	3-25-13	Henderson, N.C.		R	R	5'11	170	224	616	68	136	14	5	14	66	46	53	6	.221	.328
Maynard, Chick-Leroy Evans	22BosA	11- 2-96	Turner Falls, Mass.	1-31-57	L	R	5'9	150	12	24	1	3	0	0	0	0	3	2	0	.125	.125
Mayo (Mayoski), Eddie-Edward Joseph	36NYN 37-38BosN 43PhiA 44-48DetA	4-15-10	Holyoke, Mass.		L	R	5'11	178	834	3013	350	759	119	16	26	287	258	175	29	.252	.328
Mazzera, Mike-Melvin Leonard	35,37-39StLA 40PhiN	1-31-14	Stockton, Cal.		L	L	5'11	180	208	508	75	136	22	8	10	66	45	71	2	.268	.402
McBride, Tom-Thomas Raymond	43-47BosA 47-48WasA	11- 2-14	Bonham, Tex.		R	R	6'1	188	408	1186	140	326	39	16	2	141	93	63	13	.275	.340
McCann, Emmett-Robert Emmett	20-21PhiA 26BosA	3- 4-02	Philadelphia, Pa.	4-15-37	R	R	5'11	150	71	194	19	44	6	1	0	18	8	8	2	.227	.268
McCarren, Bill-William Joseph	23BknN	11- 4-95	Fortenia, Pa.		R	R	5'11	170	69	216	28	53	10	1	3	27	22	39	0	.245	.343
McCarthy, Johnny-John Joseph	34-35BknN 36-41NYN 43BosN 44-45MS 46BosN 48NYN	1- 7-10	Chicago, Ill.	9-13-73	L	L	6'2	185	542	1557	182	432	72	16	25	209	90	114	8	.277	.392

USE NAME – GIVEN NAMES (NICKNAMES)	TEAM BY YEAR	BIRTH DATE	BIRTH PLACE	DEATH DATE	B	T	HGT	WGT	G	AB	R	H	2B	3B	HR	RBI	BB	SO	SB	BA	SA
McClanahan, Pete-Peter	31PitN	10-24-06	Coldspring, Tex.		R	R	5'9	170	7	4	2	2	0	0	0	0	2	0	0	.500	.500
McClellan, Hervey-Hervey McDowell	19-24ChiA 25IL	12-22-94	Cynthiana, Ky.	11- 6-25	R	R	5'10	150	344	1162	130	257	54	8	4	98	68	103	23	.221	.292
McCormick, Frank-Frank Andrew (Buck)	34,37-45CinN 46-47PhiN 47-48BosN	6- 9-11	New York, N.Y.		R	R	6'4	205	1534	5723	722	1711	334	26	128	954	399	189	27	.299	.434
McCoy, Benny-Benjamin Jenison	38-39DetA 40-41PhiA 42-45MS	11- 9-15	Jenison, Mich.		L	R	5'9	170	337	1214	182	327	52	18	16	156	190	122	8	.269	.381
McCrea, Frank-Francis William	25CleA	9- 6-96	Jersey City, N.J.		R	R	5'9	155	1	5	1	1	0	0	0	0	0	0	0	.200	.200
McCue, Frank-Frank Aloysius	22PhiA	10- 4-98	Chicago, Ill.	7- 5-53	B	R	5'9	150	2	5	0	0	0	0	0	0	0	0	0	.000	.000
McCurdy, Harry-Harry Henry (Hank)	22-23StLN 26-28ChiA 30-33PhiN 34CinN	9-15-99	Stevens Point, Wis.	7-21-72	L	R	5'11	187	543	1157	148	326	71	12	9	148	129	108	12	.282	.387
McDonnell, Jim-James William (Mack)	43-45CleA	8-15-22	Gagetown, Mich.		L	R	5'11	165	50	95	9	20	2	0	0	12	8	8	0	.211	.232
McElyea, Frank-Frank	42BosN 43-45MS	8- 4-18	Carmi, Ill.		R	R	6'6	220	7	4	0	0	0	0	0	0	0	0	0	.000	.000
McFarland, Howie-Howard Alexander	45WasA	3- 7-11	El Reno, Okla.		R	R	6'	175	6	11	0	1	0	0	0	2	0	3	0	.091	.091
McGee, Dan-Daniel Aloysius	34BosN	9-29-13	New York, N.Y.		R	R	5'8	152	7	22	2	3	0	0	0	1	3	6	0	.136	.136
McGee, Tubby-Francis D.	25WasA	4-28-99	Columbus, Ohio	1-30-34	R	R	5'11	175	2	3	0	0	0	0	0	0	0	1	0	.000	.000
McGhee, Bill-William Mac (Fibber)	44-45PhiA	9- 5-08	Shawmut, Ala.		L	L	5'11	185	170	537	51	146	18	1	1	38	45	36	5	.272	.315
McGowan, Beauty-Frank Bernard	22-23PhiA 28-29StLA 37BosN	11- 8-01	Branford, Conn.		L	R	5'11	190	375	1208	174	316	58	16	6	108	154	122	17	.262	.351
McHenry, Austin-Austin Bush	18-22StLN	9-22-95	Stout, Ohio	11-27-22	R	R	5'11	152	543	1959	262	592	105	39	34	286	117	229	35	.302	.448
McLarney, Art-Arthur James	32NYN	12-20-08	Fort Worden, Wash.		B	R	6'	168	9	23	2	3	1	0	0	3	1	3	0	.130	.174
McLaughlin, Jim-James Robert	32StLA	1- 3-02	St. Louis, Mo.		R	R	5'8	168	1	1	0	0	0	0	0	1	0	0	0	.000	.000
McLeod, Jim-Soule James	30,32WasA 33PhiN	9-12-08	Jones, La.		R	R	6'	187	92	266	24	54	7	1	0	16	14	30	2	.203	.237
McLeod, Ralph-Ralph Alton	38BosN	10-19-16	North Quincy, Mass.		L	L	6'	170	6	7	1	2	1	0	0	0	0	2	0	.286	.429
McManus, Marty-Martin Joseph	20-26StLA 27-31DetA 31-33,M32-33BosA 34BosN	3-14-00	Chicago, Ill.	2-18-66	R	R	5'10	160	1831	6660	1008	1926	401	88	120	996	675	558	126	.289	.430
McMillan, Norm-Norman Alexis (Bub)	22NYA 23BosA 24StLA 28-29ChiN	10- 5-95	Latta, S.C.	9-28-69	R	R	6'	175	413	1356	157	353	74	16	6	147	95	133	36	.260	.352
McMullen, Hugh-Hugh Raphael	25-26NYN 28WasA 29CinN	12-16-01	La Cygne, Kans.		B	R	6'1	180	64	108	6	19	3	0	0	6	2	22	1	.176	.204
McNabb, Carl-Carl Mac (Skinny)	45DetA	1-25-17	Stevenson, Ala.		R	R	5'9	155	1	1	0	0	0	0	0	0	0	1	0	.000	.000
McNair, Eric-Donald Eric (Boob)	29-35,42PhiA 36-38BosA 39-40ChiA 41-42DetA	4-12-09	Meridian, Miss.	3-11-49	R	R	5'8	160	1251	4519	592	1240	229	29	82	633	261	328	59	.274	.392
McNally, Mike-Michael Joseph	15-17BosA 18MS 19-20BosA 21-24NYA 25WasA	9-13-93	Minooka, Pa.	5-29-65	R	R	5'11	150	492	1078	169	257	16	6	1	85	92	97	39	.238	.267
McNamara, Bob-Robert Maxey	39PhiA	9-19-16	Denver, Colo.		R	R	5'10	170	9	9	0	2	1	0	0	3	1	1	0	.222	.333
McNamara, Dinny-John Raymond	27-28BosN	9-16-05	Lexington, Mass.	12-20-63	L	R	5'9	165	20	13	5	1	0	0	0	0	0	4	0	.077	.077
McNamara, George-George Francis	22WasA	1-11-03	Chicago, Ill.		L	R	6'	175	3	11	3	3	0	0	0	1	1	2	0	.273	.273
McNamara, Tom-Thomas Henry	22PitN	11- 5-95	Roxbury, Mass.	12-20-63	R	R	6'2	200	1	1	0	0	0	0	0	0	0	0	0	.000	.000
McNeely, Earl-George Earl	24-27WasA 28-31StLA	5-12-98	Sacramento, Cal.	7-16-71	R	R	5'9	140	683	2254	369	614	107	33	4	213	183	187	68	.272	.354
McNulty, Pat-Patrick Howard	22,24-27CleA	2-27-99	Cleveland, Ohio	5- 4-63	L	R	5'11	160	308	820	132	238	36	9	6	84	98	62	22	.290	.378
McQuaig, Jerry-Gerald Joseph	34PhiA	1-31-12	Douglas, Ga.		R	R	5'11	183	7	16	2	1	0	0	0	1	2	4	0	.063	.063
McQuillen, Glenn-Glenn Richard (Red)	38,41-42StLA 43-45MS 46-47StLA	4-19-15	Strasburg, Va.		R	R	6'	198	210	643	82	176	24	16	4	75	34	49	1	.274	.379
McQuinn, George-George Hartley	36CinN 38-45StLA 46PhiA 47-48NYA	5-29-09	Arlington, Va.		L	L	5'11	165	1550	5747	832	1588	315	64	135	794	712	634	32	.276	.424
McWilliams, Bill-William Henry	31BosA	11-28-10	Dubuque, Iowa		R	R	6'	185	2	2	0	0	0	0	0	0	0	1	0	.000	.000
Mead, Charlie-Charles Richard	43-45NYN	4- 9-21	Vermilion, Canada		L	R	6'2	185	87	261	18	64	8	1	3	27	20	24	3	.245	.318
Medeiros, Ray-Ray Antone (Pep)	45CinN	5- 9-26	Oakland, Cal.		R	R	5'10	163	1	0	0	0	0	0	0	0	0	0	0	–	–
Medwick, Joe-Joseph Michael (Ducky, Muscles)	32-40StLN 40-43BknN 43-45NYN 45BosN 46BknN 47-48StLN	11-24-11	Carteret, N.J.	3-21-75	R	R	5'10	187	1984	7635	1198	2471	540	113	205	1383	437	551	42	.324	.505
Mele, Dutch-Albert Ernest	37CinN	1-11-15	New York, N.Y.	2-12-75	L	L	6'1	195	6	14	1	2	1	0	0	1	1	1	0	.143	.214
Melillo, Oscar-Oscar Donald (Ski, Spinach)	26-35StLA 35-37BosA	4- 4-99	Chicago, Ill.	11-14-63	R	R	5'8	150	1377	5063	591	1316	210	64	22	548	327	306	69	.260	.340
Mellana, Joe-Joseph Peter	27PhiA	3-11-05	Oakland, Cal.	11- 1-69	R	R	5'11	180	4	7	1	2	0	0	0	2	0	1	0	.286	.286
Menosky, Mike-Michael William (Leaping Mike)	14-15PitF 16-17WasA 18MS 19WasA 20-23BosA	10-16-94	Glen Campbell, Pa.		L	R	5'10	163	809	2465	382	685	98	38	18	250	295	260	90	.278	.370
Merewether, Art-Arthur Francis (Merry)	22PitN	7- 7-02	E. Providence, R.I.		R	R	5'9	155	1	1	0	0	0	0	0	0	0	0	0	–	–
Merritt, Herm-Herman G.	21DetA	11-12-00	Independence, Kan.	5-26-27	R	R			20	46	3	17	1	2	0	6	1	5	1	.370	.478
Merullo, Lennie-Leonard Richard	41-47ChiN	5- 5-17	Boston, Mass.		R	R	5'11	166	639	2071	191	497	92	8	6	152	136	174	38	.240	.301
Mesner, Steve-Stephan Mathias	38-39ChiN 41StLN 43-45CinN	1-13-18	Los Angeles, Cal.		R	R	5'9	178	451	1574	153	397	67	6	2	167	121	69	11	.252	.306
Metha, Scat-Frank Joseph	40DetA	12-13-13	Los Angeles, Cal.		R	R	5'11	165	26	37	6	9	0	1	0	3	2	8	0	.243	.297
Metheny, Bud-Arthur Beauregard	43-46NYA	6- 1-15	St. Louis, Mo.		L	L	5'11	190	376	1390	187	344	52	5	31	156	149	122	12	.247	.359
Metro (Moreskonich), Charlie-Charles	43-44DetA 44-45PhiA M62ChiN M70KCA	4-28-19	Nanty-Glo, Pa.		R	R	5'11	178	171	358	42	69	10	2	3	23	36	55	3	.193	.257
Metz, Lenny-Leonard Raymond	23-25PhiN	7- 6-99	Louisville, Colo.	2-24-53	R	R	5'11	175	30	58	6	10	0	0	0	4	5	5	0	.172	.172
Metzig, Bill-William Andrew	44ChiA	12- 4-18	Fort Dodge, Iowa		R	R	6'1	180	5	16	1	2	0	0	0	1	1	4	0	.125	.125
Metzler, Alex-Alexander	25ChiN 26PhiA 27-30ChiA 30StLA	1- 4-03	Fresno, Cal.	11-30-73	L	R	5'9	167	560	1965	290	561	85	41	9	207	260	144	48	.285	.384
Meusel, Bob-Robert William (Long Bob)	20-29NYA 30CinN	7-19-96	San Jose, Cal.		R	R	6'3	190	1407	5475	826	1693	368	95	156	1067	375	619	139	.309	.497
Meusel, Irish-Emil Frederick	14WasA 18-21PhiN 21-26NYN 27BknN	6- 9-93	Oakland, Cal.	3- 1-63	R	R	5'11	178	1289	4900	700	1521	250	93	106	819	269	199	113	.310	.464
Meyer, Dutch-Lambert Daniel	37ChiN 40-42DetA 43-44MS 45-46CleA	10- 6-15	Waco, Tex.		R	R	5'10	181	286	994	113	262	49	12	10	93	82	75	5	.264	.367
Meyer, George-George Francis	38ChiA	8-22-12	Chicago, Ill.		R	R	5'11	165	24	81	10	24	2	2	0	9	11	17	3	.296	.370
Michaels, Ralph-Ralph Joseph	24-26ChiN	5- 3-02	Etna, Pa.		R	R	5'10	178	32	61	11	18	1	0	0	8	6	10	1	.295	.311
Mihalic, John-John Michael	35-37WasA	11-13-11	Cleveland, Ohio		R	R	5'11	172	69	217	32	53	10	3	0	22	33	26	5	.244	.318
Miles, Dee-Wilson Daniel	35-36WasA 39-42PhiA 43BosA	2-15-09	Kellerman, Ala.		L	L	6'	175	503	1468	175	411	53	24	2	143	50	74	15	.280	.353
Miller, Bing-Edmund John	21WasA 22-26PhiA 26-27StLA 28-34PhiA 35-36BosA	8-30-94	Vinton, Iowa	5- 7-66	R	R	6'	185	1821	6212	946	1937	389	96	116	990	383	340	128	.312	.461
Miller, Eddie-Edward Robert (Eppie)	36-37CinN 39-42BosN 43-47CinN 48-49PhiN 50StLN	11-26-16	Pittsburgh, Pa.		R	R	5'9	180	1510	5337	539	1270	263	28	97	640	351	465	64	.238	.352
Miller, Hack-James Eldridge	44-45DetA	2-13-11	Celeste, Tex.	11-21-66	R	R	5'11	215	7	9	1	4	0	0	1	4	1	1	0	.444	.778
Miller, Hack-Lawrence H.	16BknN 18BosA 22-25ChiN	1- 1-94	New York, N.Y.	9-17-71	R	R	5'9	195	349	1200	164	387	65	11	38	205	64	103	10	.323	.490
Miller, Jake-Jacob George	22PitN	2- 5-97	Baltimore, Md.		R	R	5'10	170	3	11	0	1	0	0	0	0	2	0	1	.091	.091
Miller, Otto-Otis Louis	27StLA 30-32BosA	2- 2-01	Belleville, Ill.	7-26-59	R	R	5'10	168	272	837	95	229	39	6	0	91	49	46	3	.274	.335
Miller, Ralph-Ralph Joseph 25-31 played in A.B.L.	20-21PhiN 24WasA	2-29-96	Fort Wayne, Ind.	3-18-39	R	R	6'	190	163	557	48	138	24	1	3	54	18	43	6	.248	.311
Miller, Rudy-Rudel Charles	29PhiA	7-12-00	Kalamazoo, Mich.		R	R	6'1	180	2	4	1	1	0	0	0	1	3	0	0	.250	.250
Millies, Wally-Walter Louis	34BknN 36-37WasA 39-41PhiN	10-18-06	Chicago, Ill.		R	R	5'10	170	246	651	60	158	20	3	0	65	33	32	2	.243	.283
Mills, Bill-William Henry	44PhiA																				
Mills, Buster-Colonel Buster	34StLN 35BknN 37BosA 38StLA 40NYA 42CleA 43-45MS 46CleA	9-16-08	Ranger, Tex.		R	R	5'11	195	415	1379	200	396	62	19	14	163	131	137	23	.287	.390
Milosevich, Mike-Michael (Mollie)	44-45NYA	1-13-15	Ziegler, Ill.	2- 3-66	R	R	5'10	172	124	381	32	92	13	4	0	39	36	43	1	.241	.297
Mitchell, Clarence-Clarence Elmer (See P20-45)	11DetA 16-17CinN 18-22BknN 23-28PhiN 28-30StLN 30-32NYN	2-22-91	Frankin, Neb.	11- 6-63	L	L	5'11	190	650	1287	138	324	41	10	7	133	72	92	9	.252	.315
Mitchell, Johnny-John Franklin	21-22NYA 22-23BosA 24-25BknN	8- 9-94	Detroit, Mich.	11- 4-65	B	R	5'8	155	329	1175	152	288	38	8	2	63	119	81	14	.245	.296
Mize, Johnny-John Robert (Big Jawn, The Big Cat)	36-41StLN 42NYN 43-45MS 46-49NYN 49-53NYA	1- 7-13	Demorest, Ga.		L	R	6'2	215	1884	6443	1118	2011	367	83	359	1337	856	524	28	.312	.562
Mizeur, Bill-William Francis (Bad Bill)	23-24StLA	6-22-00	Nokomis, Ill.		L	R	6'2	190	2	2	0	0	0	0	0	0	0	0	0	.000	.000
Mohardt, John-John Henry 21-25 played in N.F.L.	22DetA	1-21-98	Pittsburgh, Pa.	11-24-61	R	R	5'10	165	5	1	2	1	0	0	0	0	1	0	0	1.000	1.000
Mokan, Johnny-John Leo	21-22PitN 22-27PhiN	9-23-95	Buffalo, N.Y.		R	R	5'7	165	582	1936	282	563	98	17	32	273	206	150	26	.291	.409
Monaco, Blas-Blas	37,46CleA	11-16-15	San Antonio, Tex.		B	R	5'11	170	17	13	2	2	0	1	0	2	1	3	0	.154	.308
Moncewicz, Freddie-Frederick Alfred	28BosA	9- 1-03	Brockton, Mass.	4-23-69	R	R	5'9	175	3	1	0	0	0	0	0	0	0	1	0	.000	.000
Monchak, Al-Alex	40PhiN	3- 5-17	Bayonne, N.J.		R	R	6'	180	19	14	1	2	0	0	0	0	0	6	1	.143	.143
Monroe, John-John Allen	21NYN 21PhiN	8-24-98	Farmersville, Tex.	6-19-56	L	R	5'8	160	60	154	17	41	4	2	2	11	14	15	2	.266	.357
Montague, Ed-Edward Francis	28,30-32CleA	7-24-05	San Francisco, Cal.		R	R	5'10	165	220	615	105	161	18	7	2	69	85	91	7	.262	.324
Monteagudo, Rene-Rene (Miranda) (See P20-45)	38,40,44WasA 45PhiN	3-12-16	Havana, Cuba	9-14-73	L	L	5'7	165	156	270	32	78	9	1	0	21	29	12	2	.289	.330
Montgomery, Al-Alvin Atlas	41BosN	7- 3-20	Loving, N.M.	4-26-42	R	R	5'10	185	42	52	4	10	1	0	0	4	9	8	0	.192	.212
Moore, Al-Albert James	25-26NYN	8- 4-02	Brooklyn, N.Y.	11-29-74	R	R	5'10	174	30	89	12	19	4	0	0	10	6	9	2	.213	.258
Moore, Bill-William Henry (Willie)	26-27BosA	12-12-01	Kansas City, Mo.	5-24-72	L	R	6'	180	49	87	9	18	2	0	0	4	13	12	0	.207	.230
Moore, Dee-D C	36-37CinN 43BknN 43PhiN 44-45MS 46PhiN	4- 6-14	Amarillo, Tex.		R	R	5'11	190	98	228	29	53	9	2	1	22	34	24	1	.232	.303
Moore, Eddie-Graham Edward	23-26PitN 26-28BosN 29-30BknN 32NYN 34CleA	1-18-99	Barlow, Ky.		R	R	5'7	165	748	2474	360	706	108	26	13	257	272	121	52	.285	.366
Moore, Gene-Eugene Jr. (Rowdy)	31CinN 33-35StLN 36-38BosN 39-40BknN 40-41BosN 42-43WasA 44-45StLA	8-26-09	Lancaster, Tex.		L	L	5'11	175	1042	3543	497	958	179	53	58	436	317	401	31	.270	.400

USE NAME – GIVEN NAMES (NICKNAMES)	TEAM BY YEAR	BIRTH DATE	BIRTH PLACE	DEATH DATE	B	T	HGT	WGT	G	AB	R	H	2B	3B	HR	RBI	BB	SO	SB	BA	SA
					LIFETIME BATTING TOTALS																
Moore, Jim-James William	30ChiA 30-31PhiA	4-24-03	Paris, Tenn.		R	R	6'	187	80	232	32	59	10	1	4	35	19	20	1	.254	.358
Moore, Johnny-John Francis	28-29,31-32ChiN 33-34CinN 34-37PhiN 45ChiN	3-23-02	Waterville, Conn.		L	R	5'11	175	846	3013	439	926	155	26	73	452	195	176	23	.307	.449
Moore, Jo-Jo-Joseph Gregg (The Gause Ghost)	30-41NYN	12-25-08	Gause, Tex.		L	R	5'11	155	1335	5427	809	1615	258	53	79	513	348	247	46	.298	.408
Moore, Randy-Randolph Edward	27-28ChiA 30-35BosN 36-37BknN 37StLN	6-21-05	Naples, Tex.		L	R	6'	185	749	2253	258	627	110	17	27	308	158	85	11	.278	.378
Moore, Terry-Terry Bluford	35-42StLN 43-45MS 46-48StLN M54PhiN	5-27-12	Vernon, Ala.		R	R	5'11	195	1298	4700	719	1318	263	28	80	513	406	368	82	.280	.399
Morehart, Ray-Raymond Anderson	24,26ChiA 27NYA	12- 2-99	Abner, Tex.		L	R	5'9	157	177	487	82	131	21	7	1	49	57	40	10	.269	.347
Morgan, Chet-Chester Collins (Chick)	35,38DetA	6- 6-10	Cleveland, Miss.		L	R	5'9	160	88	329	52	91	7	1	0	28	25	12	5	.277	.304
Morgan, Eddie-Edward Carre	28-33CleA 34BosA	5-22-04	Cairo, Ill.		R	R	6'	180	771	2810	512	879	186	45	52	474	385	252	36	.313	.467
Morgan, Eddie-Edwin Willis (Pepper)	36StLN 37BknN	11-19-14	Brady Lake, Ohio		L	L	5'10	160	39	66	8	14	3	0	1	8	11	11	0	.212	.303
Moriarty, Ed-Edward Jerome	35-36BosN	10-12-12	Holyoke, Mass.		R	R	5'10	180	14	40	4	12	2	1	1	1	0	7	0	.300	.475
Morris, Doyt-Doyt Theodore	37PhiA	7-15-16	Stanley, N.C.		R	R	6'4	195	6	13	0	2	0	0	0	0	0	3	0	.154	.154
Morrissey, Jo-Jo-Joseph Anselm	32-33CinN 36ChiA	1-16-04	Warren, R.I.	5- 2-50	R	R	6'1	178	254	841	61	195	31	1	0	45	36	40	7	.232	.271
Morse, Bud-Newell Obediah	29PhiA	9- 4-04	Berkeley, Cal.		L	R	5'9	150	8	27	1	2	0	0	0	0	0	2	0	.074	.074
Moser, Arnie-Arnold Robert	37CinN	8- 9-15	Houston, Tex.		R	R	5'11	165	5	5	0	0	0	0	0	0	0	2	0	.000	.000
Moses, Wally-Wallace	35-41PhiA 42-46ChiA 46-48BosA 49-51PhiA	10- 8-10	Uvalda, Ga.		L	L	5'10	160	2012	7356	1114	2138	435	110	89	679	821	457	174	.291	.416
Mosolf, Jim-James Frederick	29-31PitN 33ChiN	8-21-05	Puyallup, Wash.		L	R	5'10	186	118	190	39	56	9	3	2	28	22	21	0	.295	.405
Moss, Charlie-Charles Crosby	34-36PhiA	3-20-11	Meridian, Miss.		R	R	5'10	160	47	57	6	14	1	1	0	12	7	5	1	.246	.298
Mostil, Johnny-John Anthony	18,21-29ChiA	6- 1-96	Chicago, Ill.	12-10-70	R	R	5'9	168	972	3507	618	1054	209	82	23	376	415	336	176	.301	.427
Mott, Bitsy-Elisha Matthew	45PhiN	6-12-18	Arcadia, Fla.		R	R	5'8	155	90	289	21	64	8	0	0	22	27	25	2	.221	.249
Mowry, Joe-Joseph Aloysius	33-35BosN	4- 6-08	St. Louis, Mo.		B	R	6'	198	192	464	51	108	19	6	2	37	29	48	1	.233	.313
Mueller, Bill-William Lawrence (Hawk)	42ChiA 43-44MS 45ChiA	11- 9-20	Bay City, Mich.		R	R	6'2	180	39	94	8	14	1	0	0	5	14	10	3	.149	.160
Mueller, Emmett-Emmett Jerome (Heinie)	38-41PhiN 42-45MS	7-20-12	St. Louis, Mo.		B	R	5'6	167	441	1281	144	324	55	11	17	127	156	124	10	.253	.353
Mueller, Heinie-Clarence Francis	20-26StLN 26-27NYN 28-35BosN 35StLA	9 10 00	Creve Coeur, Mo.	1-23-75	L	L	5'8	158	693	2118	296	597	87	37	22	272	168	147	37	.282	.389
Mueller, Ray-Ray Coleman (Iron Man)	35-38BosN 39-40PitN 43-44CinN 45MS	3- 8-12	Pittsburg, Kans.		R	R	5'9	175	985	2911	281	733	123	23	56	373	250	322	11	.252	.369
	46-49CinN 49-50NYN 50PitN 51BosN																				
Mueller, Walter-Walter John	22-24,26PitN	12- 6-94	Central, Mo.	8-16-71	R	R	5'8	160	121	345	46	95	10	7	2	49	13	19	4	.275	.362
Mulleavy, Greg-Gregory Thomas (Moe)	30,32ChiA 33BosA	9-25-05	Detroit, Mich.		R	R	5'9	167	79	292	28	76	14	5	0	28	20	23	5	.260	.342
Mullen, Billy-William John	20-21StLA 23BknN 26DetA 28StLA	1-23-96	St. Louis, Mo.	5- 4-71	R	R	5'8	160	35	47	5	11	1	0	0	2	10	6	1	.234	.255
Mullen, Moon-Ford Parker	44PhiN 45-46MS	2- 9-17	Olympia, Wash.		R	R	5'9	165	118	464	51	124	9	4	0	31	28	32	4	.267	.304
Muller, Freddie-Frederick William	33-34BosA	12-21-07	Newark, Cal.		R	R	5'10	170	17	49	7	9	1	1	0	3	6	5	1	.184	.245
Mulligan, Eddie-Edward Joseph	15-16ChiN 21-22ChiA 28PitN	8-27-94	St. Louis, Mo.		R	R	5'9	152	351	1235	143	287	41	24	1	88	70	120	23	.232	.307
Munson (Carlson), Joe-Joseph Martin Napoleon	25-26ChiN	11- 6-99	Renovo, Pa.		L	R	5'9	184	42	136	22	39	5	3	3	18	11	5	1	.287	.434
Murphy, Ed-Edward Joseph	42PhiN 43-45MS	8-23-18	Joliet, Ill.		R	R	5'11	190	13	28	2	7	2	0	0	4	2	4	0	.250	.321
Murray, Bobby-Robert Hayes	23WasA	7- 4-98	St. Albans, Vt.		L	R	5'7	155	10	39	2	7	1	0	0	2	1	4	1	.179	.205
Murray, Tony-Anthony Joseph	23ChiN	4-30-04	Chicago, Ill.	3-19-74	R	R	5'10	154	2	4	0	1	0	0	0	0	0	0	0	.250	.250
Muser, Danny-William Daniel	32WasA	9- 5-05	Zion, Pa.		L	R	5'9	160	1	2	0	1	0	0	0	0	0	0	0	.500	.500
Myatt, George-George Edward (Mercury, Foghorn)	38-39NYN 43-47WasA M68-69PhiN	6-14-14	Denver, Colo.		L	R	5'11	167	407	1345	220	381	44	14	4	99	156	120	72	.283	.346
Myatt, Glenn-Glenn Calvin	20-21PhiA 23-35CleA 35NYN 36DetA	7- 9-97	Argenta, Ark.	8- 9-69	L	R	5'11	165	1004	2678	346	722	137	37	38	387	249	195	18	.270	.391
Myer, Buddy-Charles Solomon	25-27WasA 27-28BosA 29-41WasA	3-16-04	Ellisville, Miss.	10-31-74	L	R	5'10	150	1923	7038	1174	2131	353	130	38	850	965	428	156	.303	.406
Myers, Billy-William Harrison	35-40CinN 41ChiN	8-14-10	Enola, Pa.		R	R	5'8	168	738	2399	319	616	88	33	45	243	250	445	23	.257	.377
Myers, Lynn-Linwood Lincoln	38-39StLN	2-23-14	Enola, Pa.		R	R	5'6	145	144	344	42	83	16	3	1	29	21	48	10	.241	.314
Nagel, Bill-William Taylor	39PhiA 41PhiN 45ChiA	8-19-15	Memphis, Tenn.		R	R	6'	190	189	617	62	140	30	8	15	72	43	141	5	.227	.374
Naleway, Frank-Frank (Chick)	24ChiA	7- 4-01	Chicago, Ill.	1-28-49	R	R	5'9	165	1	2	0	0	0	0	0	0	1	0	0	.000	.000
Narleski, Bill-William Edward (Cap)	29-30BosA	6- 9-99	Perth Amboy, N.J.	7-22-64	R	R	5'9	160	135	358	41	95	25	1	0	32	28	27	4	.265	.341
Narron, Sam-Samuel	35,42-43StLN	8-25-13	Middlesex, N.C.		R	R	5'10	180	24	28	0	8	0	0	0	1	1	2	0	.286	.286
Naylor, Earl-Earl Eugene (See P20-45)	42-43PhiN 44-45MS 46BknN	5-19-19	Kansas City, Mo.		R	R	6'	190	112	290	22	54	6	1	3	28	23	35	2	.186	.245
Neighbors, Bob-Robert Otis	39StLA	11- 9-17	Talahina, Okla.	8- 8-52	R	R	5'11	165	7	11	3	2	0	0	1	1	0	1	0	.182	.455
Neis, Bernie-Bernard Edmund	20-24BknN 25-26BosN 27CleA 27ChiA	9-26-95	Bloomington, Ill.	11-29-72	B	R	5'7	160	677	1825	297	496	84	18	25	210	201	186	46	.272	.379
					Bats Right 20-21																
Neitzke, Ernie-Ernest Fred	21BosA	11-13-94	Toledo, Ohio		R	R	5'10	180	11	25	3	6	0	0	0	1	4	4	0	.240	.240
Nelson, Tom-Thomas Cousineau (Hollywood)	45BosN	5- 1-17	Chicago, Ill.	9-24-73	R	R	5'11	180	40	121	6	20	2	0	0	6	4	13	1	.165	.182
Neun, Johnny-John Henry	25-28DetA 30-31BosN M46NYA M47-48CinN	10-28-00	Baltimore, Md.		B	L	5'10	175	432	945	171	273	42	17	2	85	110	93	41	.289	.376
Newsome, Skeeter-Lamar Ashby	35-39PhiA 41-45BosA 46-47PhiN	10-18-10	Phenix City, Ala.		R	R	5'9	155	1128	3716	381	910	164	15	9	292	246	194	67	.245	.304
Nichols, Roy-Roy	44NYN	3- 3-21	Little Rock, Ark.		R	R	5'11	155	11	9	3	2	1	0	0	0	2	2	0	.222	.333
Nicholson, Bill-William Beck (Swish)	36PhiA 39-48ChiN 49-53PhiN	12-11-14	Chestertown, Md.		L	R	6'	205	1677	5546	837	1484	272	60	235	948	800	828	27	.268	.465
Nicholson, Fred-Frederick	17DetA 18MS 19-20PitN 21-22BosN	9- 1-94	Honey Grove, Tex.		R	R	5'10	173	303	794	112	247	34	21	12	105	65	97	21	.311	.452
Niebergall, Charlie-Charles Arthur (Nig)	21,23-24StLN	5-23-99	New York, N.Y.		R	R	5'10	160	54	92	9	21	7	0	0	8	5	11	0	.228	.304
Niehaus, Al-Albert Bernard	25PitN 25CinN	6- 1-99	Cincinnati, Ohio	10-14-31	R	R	5'11	175	68	211	23	58	18	2	0	21	14	15	1	.275	.379
Nieman, Butch-Elmer LeRoy	43-45BosN	2- 8-18	Herkimer, Kans.		L	L	6'2	195	332	1050	147	269	46	14	37	167	129	119	20	.256	.432
Niemiec, Al-Alfred Joseph	34BosA 36PhiA	5-18-11	Meriden, Conn.		R	R	5'11	158	78	235	24	47	3	2	1	23	29	20	2	.200	.243
Nixon, Al-Albert Richard	15-16,18BknN 21-23BosN 26-28PhiN	4-11-86	Atlantic City, N.J.	11- 9-60	R	L	5'8	164	422	1345	180	372	60	13	7	118	66	77	19	.277	.356
Nonnenkamp, Red-Leo William	33PitN 38-40BosA	7- 7-11	St. Louis, Mo.		L	L	5'11	165	155	263	49	69	6	2	0	24	34	24	6	.262	.300
Norman, Bill-Henry Willis Patrick	31-32ChiA M58-59DetA	7-16-10	St. Louis, Mo.	4-21-62	R	R	6'2	190	37	103	13	21	5	1	0	8	6	13	0	.204	.272
Norris, Leo-Leo John	36-37PhiN	5-17-08	Bay St. Louis, Miss.		R	R	5'11	165	270	962	109	252	51	7	20	112	60	132	7	.262	.392
Novikoff, Lou-Louis Alexander (The Mad Russian)	41-44ChiN 45MS 46PhiN	10-12-15	Glendale, Ariz.	9-30-70	R	R	5'10	185	356	1081	107	305	45	10	15	138	64	71	4	.282	.384
Oana, Prince-Henry Kauhane (See P20-45)	34PhiN 43,45DetA	1-22-08	Waipahu, Hawaii		R	R	6'2	193	30	52	8	16	3	1	1	10	1	3	0	.308	.462
O'Brien, Mickey-Frank Andrew	23PhiN	9-13-94	San Francisco, Cal.		R	R	5'8	160	15	21	3	7	2	0	0	0	2	1	0	.333	.429
O'Brien, Tommy-Thomas Edward (Obie)	43-45PitN 49-50BosA 50WasA	12-19-18	Anniston, Ala.		R	R	5'11	195	293	714	110	198	30	14	8	78	70	66	2	.277	.392
Ock, Whitey-Harold David	35BknN	3-17-12	Brooklyn, N.Y.	3-18-75	R	R	5'11	180	1	3	0	0	0	0	0	0	1	2	0	.000	.000
O'Connell, Jimmy-James Joseph	23-24NYN 24DL	2-11-01	Sacramento, Cal.		L	R	5'10	175	139	356	66	96	13	4	8	57	45	48	9	.270	.396
O'Connell, John-John Charles	28-29PitN	6-13-04	Pittsburgh, Pa.		R	R	6'	175	3	8	1	1	1	0	0	0	1	1	0	.125	.250
O'Dea, Ken-James Kenneth	35-38ChiN 39-41NYN 42-46StLN 46BosN	3-16-13	Lima, N.Y.		L	R	6'	180	832	2195	262	560	101	20	40	323	273	251	3	.255	.374
O'Dea, Paul-Paul (Lefty)	44-45CleA	7- 3-20	Cleveland, Ohio		L	L	6'	200	163	394	46	107	11	2	1	34	43	47	5	.272	.317
Odom, Heinie-Herman Boyd	25NYA	10-13-00	Rusk, Tex.	8-31-70	B	R	6'	170	1	1	0	1	0	0	0	0	0	0	0	1.000	1.000
O'Donnell, Harry-Harry Herman (Butch)	27PhiN	4- 2-94	Philadelphia, Pa.	1-31-58	R	R	5'10	180	16	16	1	1	0	0	0	2	2	2	0	.063	.063
O'Doul, Lefty-Francis Joseph	19-20,22NYA 23BosA 28NYN 29-30PhiN 31-33BknN	3- 4-97	San Francisco, Cal.	12- 7-69	L	L	6'	180	970	3264	624	1140	175	41	113	542	333	122	36	.349	.532
	33-34NYN																				
O'Farrell, Bob-Robert Arthur	15-25ChiN 25-28,M27StLN 28-32NYN 33StLN	10-19-96	Waukegan, Ill.		R	R	5'9	180	1492	4101	517	1120	201	58	51	549	547	408	35	.273	.388
	34,M34CinN 34ChiN 35StLN																				
Oglesby, Jim-James Dorn	36PhiA	8-10-05	Schofield, Mo.	9- 1-55	L	L	6'	190	3	11	0	2	0	0	0	2	2	0	0	.182	.182
Ogrodowski, Brusie-Ambrose Francis	36-37StLN	2-17-12	Hoytville, Pa.	3- 5-56	R	R	5'11	175	184	516	65	119	25	4	4	51	21	37	2	.231	.318
Oliver, Tom-Thomas Noble (Rebel)	30-33BosA	1-15-03	Montgomery, Ala.		R	R	6'	168	514	1931	202	534	101	11	0	176	105	61	12	.277	.340
Olmo, Luis-Luis Francisco Rodriguez (Jibaro)	43-45,49BknN 46-48SM 50-51BosN	8-11-19	Arecibo, P.R.		R	R	5'11	185	462	1629	208	458	65	25	29	272	88	128	33	.281	.405
Olsen, Al-Albert William (Ole)	43BosA	3-30-21	San Diego, Cal.		L	L	6'	165	1	0	0	0	0	0	0	0	1	0	0	–	–
Olsen, Barney-Bernard Charles	41ChiN	9-11-19	Everett, Mass.		R	R	5'11	180	24	73	13	21	6	1	1	4	4	11	0	.288	.438
Olson, Marv-Marvin Clement (Sparky)	31-33BosA	5-28-07	Gaysville, S.D.		R	R	5'7	160	133	457	67	110	15	6	0	30	70	30	1	.241	.300
O'Neil, Mickey-George Michael	19-25BosN 26BknN 27WasA 27NYN	4-12-98	St. Louis, Mo.	4- 8-64	R	R	5'10	185	672	1995	177	475	41	23	4	179	139	127	18	.238	.288
O'Neill, Harry-Harry Mink	39PhiA	5- 8-17	Philadelphia, Pa.	3- 6-45	R	R	6'3	205	1	0	0	0	0	0	0	0	0	0	0	–	–
O'Neill, Jim-James Leo	20,23WasA	2-23-93	Minooka, Pa.		R	R	5'10	165	109	327	33	94	18	7	1	43	14	33	7	.287	.394
Onis, Curly-Manuel Dominguez (Ralph)	35BknN	10-24-08	Tampa, Fla.		R	R	5'9	180	1	1	0	1	0	0	0	0	0	0	0	1.000	1.000
Ordenana, Tony-Antonio [Rodriguez] (Mosquito)	43PitN	10-30-18	Guanabacoa, Cuba		R	R	5'9	158	1	4	0	2	0	0	0	3	0	0	0	.500	.500
Orengo, Joe-Joseph Charles	39-40StLN 41,43NYN 43BknN 44DetA 45ChiA	11-29-14	San Francisco, Cal.		R	R	6'	185	366	1120	129	266	54	8	17	122	156	219	12	.238	.346
Orme, George-George William	20BosA	9-16-91	Lebanon, Ind.	3-16-62	R	R	5'10	160	4	6	4	2	0	0	0	1	3	0	0	.333	.333
O'Rourke, Frank-Francis James (Blackie)	12BosN 17-18BknN 20-21WasA 22BosA	11-28-94	Hamilton, Canada		R	R	5'10	165	1131	4069	547	1032	196	42	15	430	314	377	101	.254	.333
	24-26DetA 27-31StLA																				

USE NAME – GIVEN NAMES (NICKNAMES)	TEAM BY YEAR	BIRTH DATE	BIRTH PLACE	DEATH DATE	B	T	HGT	WGT	G	AB	R	H	2B	3B	HR	RBI	BB	SO	SB	BA	SA
									LIFETIME BATTING TOTALS												
O'Rourke, Joe-Joseph Leo Jr.	29PhiN	10-28-04	Philadelphia, Pa.		L	R	5'7	145	3	3	0	0	0	0	0	0	0	1	0	.000	.000
Orsatti, Ernie-Ernest Ralph	27-35StLN	9- 8-02	Los Angeles, Ca.	9- 4-68	L	L	5'8	154	701	2165	306	663	129	39	10	237	176	218	46	.306	.416
Ortiz, Roberto-Roberto Gonzalo [Nunez]	41-44WasA 45VR 46-48SM 49-50WasA 50PhiA	6-30-15	Camaguey, Cuba	9-15-71	R	R	6'4	210	213	659	67	168	18	10	8	78	43	95	4	.255	.349
Orwoll, Ossie-Oswald Christian (See P20-45) 26 played in N.F.L.	28-29PhiA	11-17-00	Portland, Ore.	5- 8-67	L	L	6'	174	94	221	34	65	15	3	0	28	18	35	3	.294	.389
Ostergard, Red-Robert Lund	21ChiA	5-11-98	Galveston, Tex.		L	R	5'10	175	12	11	2	4	0	0	0	0	0	2	0	.364	.364
Otero, Reggie-Regino Joseph [Gomez]	45ChiN	9- 7-15	Havana, Cuba		L	R	5'11	160	14	23	1	9	0	0	0	5	2	2	0	.391	.391
Ott, Mel-Melvin Thomas (Master Melvin)	26-47,M42-48NYN	3- 2-09	Gretna, La.	11-21-58	L	R	5'9	170	2730	9456	1859	2876	488	72	511	1860	1708	896	89	.304	.533
Oulliber, Johnny-John Andrew	33CleA	2-24-11	New Orleans, La.		R	R	5'11	165	22	75	9	20	1	0	0	3	4	5	0	.267	.280
Outen, Chick-William Austin	33BknN	6-17-05	Mount Holly, N.C.	9-11-61	L	R	6'	200	93	153	20	38	10	0	4	17	20	15	1	.248	.392
Outlaw, Jimmy-James Paulus	37-38CinN 39BosN 43-49DetA	1-20-13	Orme, Tenn.		R	R	5'8	165	650	1974	257	529	79	17	6	184	188	176	24	.268	.334
Owen, Marv-Marvin James (Freck)	31,33-37DetA 38-39ChiA 40BosA	3-22-06	Agnew, Cal.		R	R	6'1	175	1011	3782	473	1040	167	44	31	497	338	283	30	.275	.367
Owen, Mickey-Arnold Malcolm	37-40StLN 41-45BknN 46-48SM 49-51ChiN 54BosA	4-14-16	Nixa, Mo.		R	R	5'10	190	1209	3649	338	929	163	21	14	378	326	181	36	.255	.322
Owens, Jack-Furman Lee	35PhiA	5- 6-08	Converse, S.C.	11-14-58	R	R	5'10	210	2	8	0	2	0	0	0	1	0	1	0	.250	.250
Padden, Tom-Thomas Francis	32-37PitN 43PhiN 43WasA	10- 6-08	Manchester, N.H.	6-11-73	R	R	6'	183	399	1170	122	318	40	6	2	110	127	121	5	.272	.321
Padgett, Don-Don Wilson	37-41StLN 42-45MS 46BknN 46BosN 47-48PhiN	12- 5-11	Caroleen, N.C.		L	R	6'	190	699	1991	247	573	111	16	37	338	141	130	6	.288	.415
Padgett, Ernie-Ernest Kitchen (Red)	23-25BosN 26-27CleA	3- 1-99	Philadelphia, Pa.	4-15-57	R	R	5'8	155	271	838	84	223	34	17	1	81	61	75	8	.266	.351
Palmisano, Joe-Joseph A.	31PhiA	11-19-02	West Point, Ga.	11- 5-71	R	R	5'8	160	19	44	5	10	2	0	0	4	6	3	0	.227	.273
Parisse, Tony-Louis Peter	43-44PhiA	6-25-11	Philadelphia, Pa.	6- 2-56	R	R	5'10	165	10	21	0	3	0	0	0	1	2	3	0	.143	.143
Parker, Ace-Clarence McKoy 37-41,45 played in N.F.L. 46 played in A.A.F.C.	37-38PhiA	5-17-12	Portsmouth, Va.		R	R	6'	180	94	207	20	37	5	1	2	25	14	33	1	.179	.242
Parker, Dixie-Douglas Woolley	23PhiN	4-24-95	Forest Home, Ala.	5-15-72	L	R	5'11	160	4	5	0	1	0	0	0	1	0	1	0	.200	.200
Parker, Salty-Francis James	36DetA M67NYN	7- 8-13	East St. Louis, Ill.		R	R	6'	173	11	25	6	7	2	0	0	4	2	3	0	.280	.360
Parkinson, Frank-Frank Joseph (Parky)	21-24PhiN	3-23-95	Dickson City, Pa.	7- 4-60	R	R	6'	180	378	1311	157	335	57	8	24	149	95	233	9	.256	.336
Parks, Art-Artie William	37,39BknN	1- 1-11	Paris, Ark.		L	R	5'9	170	78	255	29	70	15	2	1	19	30	16	2	.275	.361
Parsons, Dixie-Edward Dixon	39,42-43DetA	5-12-16	Talladega, Ala.		R	R	6'2	180	108	295	10	52	7	0	2	15	20	39	1	.176	.220
Partee, Roy-Roy Robert	43-44BosA 45MS 46-47BosA 48StLA	9-17-17	Los Angeles, Cal.		R	R	5'10	180	367	1090	89	273	41	5	2	114	132	120	2	.250	.303
Partridge, Jay-James Bugg	27-28BknN	11-15-02	Mountville, Ga.	1-14-74	L	R	5'11	160	183	645	90	167	17	7	7	52	33	42	11	.259	.340
Paschal, Ben-Benjamin Edwin	15CleA 20BosA 24-29NYA	10-13-95	Enterprise, Ala.	11-10-74	R	R	5'11	185	364	787	143	243	47	11	24	139	72	93	24	.309	.488
Pasek, Johnny-John Paul	33DetA 34ChiA	6-25-05	Niagara Falls, N.Y.		R	R	5'10	175	32	70	7	18	4	0	0	4	8	8	2	.257	.314
Patrick, Bob-Robert Lee	41-42DetA 43-45MS	10-27-17	Fort Smith, Ark.		R	R	6'2	190	9	15	3	4	1	0	1	3	1	1	0	.267	.533
Patterson, Bill-William Jennings Bryan (Pat)	21NYN	1-29-97	Belleville, Ill.		R	R	6'1	175	23	35	5	14	0	0	1	5	2	5	0	.400	.486
Patterson, Hank-Henry Joseph Colquit	32BosA	7-17-07	San Francisco, Cal.	9-30-70	R	R	5'11	170	1	1	0	0	0	0	0	0	0	0	0	.000	.000
Patton, Bill-George William	35PhiA	10- 7-12	Cornwall, Pa.		R	R	6'2	180	9	10	1	3	1	0	0	2	2	3	0	.300	.400
Patton, Gene-Gene Tunney	44BosN 45MS	7- 8-26	Coatesville, Pa.		L	R	5'10	165	1	0	0	0	0	0	0	0	0	0	0	–	–
Peacock, Johnny-John Gaston	37-44BosA 44-45PhiN 45BknN	1-10-10	Fremont, N.C.		L	R	5'11	165	619	1734	175	455	74	16	1	194	183	63	14	.262	.325
Peel, Homer-Homer Hefner	27StLN 29PhiN 30StLN 33-34NYN	10-10-02	Port Sullivan, Tex.		R	R	5'9	170	186	420	48	100	15	2	2	44	30	24	1	.238	.298
Peerson, Jack-Jack Chiles	35-36PhiA	8-28-10	Brunswick, Ga.	10-23-66	R	R	5'10	165	18	53	10	17	2	1	0	6	1	4	0	.321	.396
Pence, Elmer-Elmer Clair	22ChiA	8-17-00	Valley Springs, Cal.	9-17-68	R	R	6'	185	1	0	0	0	0	0	0	0	0	0	0	–	–
Peploski, Henry-Henry Stephen	29BosN	9-15-05	Garlin, Poland		L	R	5'9	155	6	10	1	2	0	0	0	1	1	3	0	.200	.200
Pepper, Ray-Raymond Watson	32-33StLN 34-36StLA	8- 5-05	Decatur, Ala.		R	R	6'2	195	339	1015	109	285	46	10	14	170	59	136	2	.281	.387
Perkins, Cy-Ralph Foster	15,17-30PhiA 31NYA 34DetA	2-27-96	Gloucester, Mass.	10- 2-63	R	R	5'10	158	1171	3604	329	933	175	35	30	409	301	221	18	.259	.352
Perrin, Jack-John Stephenson	21BosA	2- 4-98	Escanaba, Mich.	6-24-69	L	R	5'9	160	4	13	3	3	0	0	0	1	0	3	0	.231	.231
Perry, Boyd-Boyd Glenn	41DetA	3-21-14	Snow Camp, N.C.		R	R	5'10	158	36	83	9	15	5	0	0	11	10	9	1	.181	.241
Peterman, Bill-William David	42PhiN 43-45MS	4-20-21	Philadelphia, Pa.		R	R	6'2	185	1	1	0	1	0	0	0	0	0	0	0	1.000	1.000
Peters, John-John William (Shotgun)	15DetA 18CleA 21-22PhiN	7-14-93	Kansas City, Kans.	2-21-32	R	R	6'	192	112	302	22	80	13	1	7	47	16	33	1	.265	.384
Peters, Rusty-Russell Dixon	36-38PhiA 40-44CleA 45MS 46CleA 47StLA	12-14-14	Roanoke, Va.		R	R	5'11	170	471	1222	123	289	53	16	8	117	98	199	9	.236	.326
Petoskey, Ted-Fred Lee	34-35CinN	1- 5-11	St. Charles, Mich.		R	R	5'11	183	10	12	0	2	0	0	0	1	0	6	1	.167	.167
Pfister, George-George Edward	41BknN	9- 4-18	Bound Brook, N.J.		R	R	6'	200	1	2	0	0	0	0	0	0	0	0	0	.000	.000
Phelps, Babe-Ernest Gordon (Blimp)	31WasA 33-34ChiN 35-41BknN 42PitN	4-19-08	Odenton, Md.		L	R	6'2	225	726	2117	239	657	143	19	54	345	159	157	9	.310	.472
Phillips, Damon-Damon Ruswell (Dee)	42CinN 44BosN 45MS 46BosN	6- 8-19	Corsicana, Tex.		R	R	6'	176	170	575	39	144	32	1	1	59	35	39	1	.250	.315
Phillips, Eddie-Edward David	24BosN 29DetA 31PitN 32NYA 34WasA 35CleA	2-17-01	Worcester, Mass.	1-26-68	R	R	6'	178	312	997	82	236	54	6	14	126	104	115	3	.237	.345
Picciuto, Nick-Nicholas Thomas	45PhiN	8-27-21	Newark, N.J.		R	R	5'8	165	36	89	7	12	6	0	0	6	6	17	0	.135	.202
Picinich, Val-Valentine John	16-17PhiA 18-22WasA 23-25BosA 26-28CinN 29-33BknN 33PitN	9- 8-96	New York, N.Y.	12- 5-42	R	R	5'9	165	1037	2877	298	743	166	25	27	298	314	382	31	.258	.361
Pick, Eddie-Edgar Everett	23-24CinN 27ChiN	5- 7-99	Attleboro, Mass.	5-13-67	B	R	6'	185	66	191	25	34	5	2	2	17	23	30	0	.178	.257
Pickering, Urban-Urbane Henry (Pick)	31-32BosA	6- 3-99	Hoxie, Kans.	5-13-70	R	R	5'11	175	235	798	95	205	41	9	11	92	72	124	6	.257	.372
Piet (Pietruszka), Tony-Anthony Francis	31-33PitN 34-35CinN 35-37ChiA 38DetA	12- 7-06	Berwick, Pa.		R	R	6'	175	744	2585	352	717	132	30	23	312	247	274	80	.277	.378
Pilney, Anoy-Antone James	36BosN	1-19-13	Frontenac, Kans.		R	R	5'11	174	3	2	0	0	0	0	0	0	0	1	0	.000	.000
Pinelli (Paolinelli), Babe-Ralph Arthur (Rinaldo Angelo)	18ChiA 20DetA 22-27CinN	10-18-95	San Francisco, Cal.		R	R	5'9	165	774	2617	327	723	101	33	5	298	182	162	71	.276	.346
Pipp, Wally-Walter Clement	13DetA 15-25NYA 26-28CinN	2-17-93	Chicago, Ill.	1-11-65	L	L	6'1	180	1872	6914	974	1941	311	148	90	996	596	551	125	.281	.408
Pitko, Alex-Alexander (Spunk)	38PhiN 39WasA	1-22-14	Burlington, N.J.		R	R	5'10	180	11	27	2	7	1	0	0	3	4	6	1	.259	.296
Pittenger, Pinky-Clarke Alonzo	21-23BosA 25ChiN 27-29CinN	2-24-99	Hudson, Mich.		R	R	5'10	160	373	959	118	252	32	3	1	83	37	50	27	.263	.306
Pofahl, Jimmy-James Willard	40-42WasA	6-18-17	Faribault, Minn.		R	R	5'11	173	225	764	65	168	33	9	2	70	76	96	7	.220	.295
Poland, Hugh-Hugh Reid	43NYN 43-44BosN 45MS 46BosN 47PhiN 47-48CinN	1-19-13	Tompkinsville, Ky.		L	R	5'11	185	83	211	8	39	10	1	0	19	6	16	0	.185	.242
Polly (Polachanin), Nick-Nicholas Joseph	37BknN 45BosA	4-18-17	Chicago, Ill.		R	R	5'11	190	14	25	2	5	0	0	0	3	0	2	0	.200	.200
Pool, Harlin-Harlin Welty (Samson)	34-35CinN	3-12-08	Lakeport, Cal.	2-15-63	L	R	5'10	195	127	426	46	129	28	7	2	61	19	20	3	.303	.415
Poole, Jim-James Robert (Easy)	25-27PhiA	5-12-95	Taylorsville, N.C.	1- 2-75	L	R	6'	175	283	940	118	271	54	13	13	140	59	68	9	.288	.415
Porter, Dick-Richard Twilley (Twitchy)	29-34CleA 34BosA	12-30-01	Princess Anne, Md.	9-24-74	L	R	5'10	170	675	2515	426	774	159	37	11	282	268	186	23	.308	.414
Post, Sam-Samuel Gilbert	22BknN	11-17-96	Richmond, Va.	3-31-71	L	L	6'1	170	9	25	3	7	0	0	0	4	1	4	1	.280	.280
Powell, Jake-Alvin Jacob	30,34-36WasA 36-40NYA 43-45WasA 45PhiN	7-15-08	Silver Spring, Md.	11- 4-48	R	R	5'11	180	688	2540	353	689	116	26	22	327	174	219	65	.271	.363
Powell, Ray-Raymond Reath (Rabbit)	13DetA 17-24BosN	11-20-88	Siloam Springs, Ark.	10-16-62	L	R	5'9	160	875	3324	467	890	117	67	35	276	321	461	51	.268	.375
Powers, Les-Leslie Edwin	38NYN 39PhiN	11- 5-12	Seattle, Wash.		L	L	6'	175	21	55	7	18	1	1	0	2	4	7	0	.327	.382
Powers, Mike-Ellis Foree	32-33CleA	3- 2-06	Crestwood, Ky.		L	L	6'1	185	38	80	10	19	6	1	0	7	8	8	2	.238	.338
Pratt, Frank-Francis Bruce (Truckhorse)	21ChiA	8-24-97	Blockton, Ala.	3- 8-74	L	R	5'9	155	1	1	0	0	0	0	0	0	0	0	0	.000	.000
Preibisch, Mel-Melvin Adolphus (Primo)	40-41BosN	11-23-14	Sealy, Tex.		R	R	5'11	185	16	44	3	9	2	0	0	5	3	6	0	.205	.250
Price, Joe-Joseph Preston (Lumber)	28NYN	4-10-97	Milligan Coll., Tenn.	1-15-61	R	R	6'2	187	1	1	0	0	0	0	0	0	0	1	0	.000	.000
Prichard, Bob-Robert Alexander	39WasA	10-21-17	Paris, Tex.		L	L	6'1	195	26	85	8	20	5	0	0	8	19	16	0	.235	.294
Propst, Jake-William Jacob	23WasA	3-10-95	Kennedy, Ala.	2-24-67	L	R	5'10	165	1	1	0	0	0	0	0	0	0	0	0	.000	.000
Prothro, Doc-James Thompson	20,23-24WasA 25BosA 26CinN M39-41PhiN	7-16-93	Memphis, Tenn.	10-14-71	R	R	5'10	175	180	600	66	191	34	10	0	81	69	40	13	.318	.408
Pruess, Earl-Earl Henry (Gibby)	20StLA	4- 2-95	Chicago, Ill.		R	R	5'10	170	1	0	1	0	0	0	0	0	1	0	1	–	–
Pruett, Jim-James Calvin	44-45PhiA	12-16-17	Nashville, Tenn.		R	R	5'10	178	9	13	2	3	0	0	0	0	2	2	0	.231	.231
Puccinelli, George-George Lawrence (Count, Pooch)	30,32StLN 34StLA 36PhiA	6-22-07	San Francisco, Cal.	4-16-56	R	R	6'	190	187	607	109	172	40	3	19	102	78	92	3	.283	.453
Purdy, Pid-Everett Virgil 26-27 played in N.F.L.	26ChiA 27-29CinN	6-15-04	Beatrice, Neb.	1-16-51	L	R	5'6	150	181	499	74	146	22	11	2	59	48	25	3	.293	.393
Pytlak, Frankie-Frank Anthony	32-40CleA 41BosA 42-44MS 45-46BosA	7-30-08	Buffalo, N.Y.		R	R	5'7	160	795	2399	316	677	100	36	7	272	247	97	56	.282	.363
Quellich, George-George William	31DetA	2-10-03	Johnsville, Cal.	8-21-58	R	R	6'1	180	13	54	6	12	5	0	1	11	3	4	1	.222	.370
Quick, Jim-James Harold	39WasA	10- 4-19	Rome, Ga.		R	R	5'10	163	12	41	3	10	1	0	0	2	1	1	1	.244	.268
Rabbitt, Joe-Joseph Patrick	22CleA	1-16-00	Frontenac, Kans.	12- 5-69	L	R	5'9	156	2	3	1	1	0	0	0	0	0	0	0	.333	.333
Radcliff, Rip-Raymond Allen	34-39ChiA 40-41StLA 41-43DetA 44-46MS	1-19-06	Kiowa, Okla.	5-23-62	L	L	5'10	170	1081	4074	598	1267	205	50	42	532	310	141	40	.311	.417
Rader, Don-Donald Russell	13ChiA 21PhiN	9- 5-93	Wolcott, Ind.		L	R	5'10	164	11	35	5	10	3	0	0	3	3	5	0	.286	.371
Radtke, Jack-Jack William	36BknN	4-14-13	Denver, Colo.		B	R	5'7	160	33	31	8	3	0	0	0	2	4	9	3	.097	.097
Ramos, Chucho-Jesus Manuel [Garcia]	44CinN	4-12-18	Maturin, Venezuela		R	L	5'10	167	4	10	1	5	1	0	0	0	0	0	0	.500	.600
Ramsey, Bill-William Thrace (Square Jaw)	45BosN	2-20-21	Osceola, Ark.		R	R	6'1	190	78	137	16	40	8	0	1	12	4	22	1	.292	.372

USE NAME – GIVEN NAMES (NICKNAMES)	TEAM BY YEAR	BIRTH DATE	BIRTH PLACE	DEATH DATE	B	T	HGT	WGT	G	AB	R	H	2B	3B	HR	RBI	BB	SO	SB	BA	SA
									LIFETIME BATTING TOTALS												
Rapp, Goldie-Joseph Aloysius	21-23PhiN	2- 6-92	Cincinnati, Ohio		B	R	5'10	165	276	1064	134	269	47	5	2	73	75	64	16	.253	.312
Rawlings, Johnny-John William (Red)	14CinN 14-15KCF 17-20BosN 20-21PhiN 21-22NYN 23-26PitN	8-17-92	Bloomfield, Iowa	10-16-72	R	R	5'8	158	1080	3721	408	927	122	28	14	302	257	210	92	.249	.308
Rebel, Art-Arthur Anthony	38PhiN 45StLN	3- 4-15	Cincinnati, Ohio		L	L	5'8	180	33	81	14	27	4	0	0	6	7	5	1	.333	.383
Reder, Johnny-John Anthony	32BosA	9-24-09	Lublin, Poland		R	R	6'	184	17	37	4	5	1	0	0	3	6	6	0	.135	.162
Redfern, Buck-George Howard	28-29ChiA	4- 7-02	Asheville, N.C.	9- 8-64	R	R	5'11	165	107	307	22	67	6	3	0	38	15	22	9	.218	.257
Redmond, Jack-John McKittrick (Red)	35WasA	9- 3-10	Florence, Ariz.	7-27-68	L	R	5'11	185	22	34	8	6	1	0	1	7	3	1	0	.176	.294
Reese, Andy-Andrew Jackson	27-30NYN	2- 7-04	Tupelo, Miss.	1-10-66	R	R	5'11	180	331	1142	166	321	47	11	14	111	51	107	21	.281	.378
Reese (Soloman), Jimmie-James Herman	30-31NYA 32StLN	10- 1-04	Los Angeles, Cal.		L	R	5'11	165	232	742	123	209	39	4	8	70	48	37	7	.278	.373
Reeves, Bobby-Robert Edwin (Gunner)	26-28WasA 29-31BosA	6-24-04	Hill City, Tenn.		R	R	5'11	170	502	1598	203	402	55	22	8	135	175	218	21	.252	.329
Regan, Bill-William Wright	26-30BosA 31PitN	1-23-99	Pittsburgh, Pa.	6-11-68	R	R	5'10	155	641	2364	236	632	158	36	18	292	122	245	38	.267	.387
Rego (DoRego), Tony-Antone (Mighty Midget)	24-25StLA	10-31-97	Wailuku, Hawaii		R	R	5'5	140	44	91	10	26	3	1	0	8	4	5	0	.286	.341
Reiber, Frank-Frank Bernard (Tubby)	33-36DetA	9-19-09	Huntington, W.Va.		R	R	5'8	170	44	85	13	23	2	1	2	9	12	13	0	.271	.388
Reichle, Dick-Richard Wendell 23 played in N.F.L.	22-23BosA	11-23-96	Lincoln, Ill.	6-13-67	L	R	6'	185	128	385	43	99	18	3	1	39	22	36	3	.257	.327
Reinholz, Art-Arthur August	28CleA	1-27-03	Detroit, Mich.		R	R	5'10	175	2	3	0	1	0	0	0	0	1	0	0	.333	.333
Reis, Bobby-Robert Joseph Thomas (See P20-45)	31-32,35BknN 36-38BosN	1- 2-09	Queens, N.Y.	5- 1-73	R	R	6'1	190	175	301	32	70	10	2	0	21	25	35	5	.233	.279
Reiss, Al-Albert Allen	32PhiA	1- 8-09	Elizabeth, N.J.		B	R	5'10	165	9	5	0	1	0	0	0	1	1	1	0	.200	.200
Rensa, Tony-Tony George (Pug)	30DetA 30-31PhiN 33NYA 37-39ChiA	9-29-01	Parsons, Pa.		R	R	5'10	180	200	514	71	134	26	5	7	65	57	54	5	.261	.372
Repass, Bob-Robert Willis	39StLN 42WasA	11- 6-17	West Pittston, Pa.		R	R	6'1	185	84	265	30	64	12	1	2	24	33	32	6	.242	.317
Reyes, Nap-Napoleon Aguilera	43-45NYN 46-49SM 50NYN	11-24-19	San Luis, Cuba		R	R	6'1	205	279	931	90	264	35	11	13	110	44	62	5	.284	.387
Reynolds, Carl-Carl Nettles	27-31ChiA 32,36WasA 33StLA 34-35BosA 37-39ChiN	2- 1-03	La Rue, Tex.		R	R	6'	194	1222	4495	672	1357	247	107	80	699	262	308	112	.302	.458
Reynolds, Danny-Daniel Vance (Squirrel)	45ChiA	11-27-19	Stony Point, N.C.		R	R	5'11	158	29	72	6	12	2	1	0	4	3	8	1	.167	.222
Rhiel, Billy-William Joseph	29BknN 30BosN 32-33DetA	8-16-00	Youngstown, Ohio	8-16-46	R	R	5'11	175	200	519	61	138	26	8	7	68	43	57	2	.266	.387
Rhyne, Hal-Harold J.	26-27PitN 29-32BosA 33ChiA	3-30-99	Paso Robles, Cal.	1- 7-71	R	R	5'8	163	655	2031	252	508	98	22	2	192	184	127	13	.250	.323
Rice, Bob-Robert Turnbull	26PhiN	5-28-99	Philadelphia, Pa.		R	R	5'10	170	19	54	3	8	0	1	0	10	3	4	0	.195	.245
Rice, Harry-Harry Francis	23-27StLA 28-30DetA 30NYA 31WasA 33CinN	11-22-00	Ware Station, Ill.	1- 1-71	L	R	5'9	185	1024	3740	620	1118	186	63	48	506	376	194	60	.299	.421
Rice, Len-Leonard Oliver	44CinN 45ChiN	9- 2-18	Lead, S.D.		R	R	6'	175	42	103	11	23	3	0	0	7	5	8	2	.223	.252
Rice, Sam-Edgar Charles (See P01-19)	15-33WasA 34CleA	2-20-90	Morocco, Ind.	10-13-74	L	R	5'9	150	2404	9269	1514	2987	497	184	34	1078	709	275	351	.322	.427
Richards, Paul-Paul Rapier	32BknN 33-35NYN 35PhiA 43-46DetA M51-54ChiA M55-61BalA	11-21-08	Waxahachie, Tex.		R	R	6'2	180	523	1417	140	321	51	5	15	155	157	149	15	.227	.301
Richardson, Nolen-Clifford Nolen	29,31-32DetA 35NYA 38-39CinN	1-18-03	Chattanooga, Tenn.	9-25-51	R	R	6'1	170	168	473	39	117	19	5	0	45	23	22	8	.247	.309
Richbourg, Lance-Lancelot Clayton	21PhiN 24WasA 27-31BosN 32ChiN	12-18-97	DeFuniak Spr., Fla.	9-10-75	L	R	5'10	160	698	2619	378	806	101	51	13	247	174	153	65	.308	.400
Riconda, Harry-Henry Paul 26-27,28-30 played in A.B.L.	23-24PhiA 26BosN 28BknN 29PitN 30CinN	3-17-97	New York, N.Y.	11-15-58	R	R	5'10	175	243	765	83	189	44	11	4	70	61	91	13	.247	.349
Riddle, Johnny-John Ludy (Mutt)	30ChiA 37WasA 37-38BosN 41,44-45CinN 48PitN	10- 3-05	Clinton, S.C.		R	R	5'11	190	98	214	18	51	4	1	0	11	13	19	0	.238	.266
Riggs, Lew-Lewis Sidney	34StLN 35-40CinN 41-43BknN 43-45MS 46BknN	4-22-10	Mebane, N.C.		L	R	6'	175	760	2477	298	650	110	43	28	271	181	140	22	.262	.375
Rigney, Topper-Emory Elmo	22-25DetA 26-27BosA 27WasA	1- 7-97	Groveton, Tex.	1- 6-72	R	R	5'9	150	694	2326	324	669	113	39	13	314	377	176	44	.288	.387
Riley, Jim-James Norman	21StLA 23WasA	5-25-95	Bayfield, Canada	5-25-69	L	R	5'10	185	6	14	1	0	0	0	0	0	3	3	0	.000	.000
Riley, Lee-Leon Francis	44PhiN	8-20-06	Princeton, Neb.	9-13-70	L	R	6'1	185	4	12	1	1	1	0	0	1	0	0	0	.083	.167
Ripple, Jimmy-James Albert	36-39NYN 39-40BknN 40-41CinN 43PhiA	10-14-09	Export, Pa.	7-16-59	L	R	5'10	170	554	1809	241	510	92	14	28	251	156	89	7	.282	.395
Rizzo, Johnny-John Costa	38-40PitN 40CinN 40-41PhiN 42BknN 43-46MS	7-30-12	Houston, Tex.		R	R	6'	190	557	1842	268	497	90	16	61	288	200	197	7	.270	.435
Robello, Tommy-Thomas Vardasco (Tony)	33-34CinN	2- 9-13	San Leandro, Cal.		R	R	5'10	175	16	32	1	7	3	0	0	3	1	6	0	.219	.313
Roberge, Skippy-Joseph Albert Armand	41-42BosN 43-45MS 46BosN	5-19-17	Lowell, Mass.		R	R	5'11	185	177	508	35	112	19	2	3	47	25	49	2	.220	.283
Roberts, Red-Charles Emory	43WasA 44-45MS	8- 8-18	Carrollton, Ga.		R	R	6'	170	9	23	1	6	1	0	1	3	4	2	0	.261	.435
Robertson, Gene-Eugene Edward	19,22-26StLA 28-29NYA 29-30BosN	12-25-99	St. Louis, Mo.		L	R	5'7	152	656	2200	311	615	101	23	20	249	205	79	29	.280	.374
Rocco, Mickey-Michael Dominick	43-46CleA	3- 2-16	St. Paul, Minn.		L	L	5'11	188	440	1721	219	444	73	17	30	186	174	146	6	.258	.372
Rochelli, Lou-Louis Joseph	44BknN 45-46MS	1-11-19	Williamson, Ill.		R	R	6'1	175	5	17	0	3	0	1	0	2	2	6	0	.176	.294
Rock (Schwarzrock), Les-Lester Henry	36ChiA	8-19-12	Springfield, Minn.		L	R	6'2	184	2	1	0	0	0	0	0	1	0	0	0	.000	.000
Rodgers, Bill-William Sherman	44-45PitN	12- 5-22	Harrisburg, Pa.		L	L	6'	162	3	5	1	2	0	0	0	0	0	1	0	.400	.400
Roettger, Oscar-Oscar Frederick Louis (See P20-45)	23-24NYA 27BknN 32PhiA	2-19-00	St. Louis, Mo.		R	R	6'	170	37	66	7	14	1	0	0	6	6	5	0	.212	.227
Roettger, Wally-Walter Henry	27-29StLN 30NYN 31CinN 31StLN 32-33CinN 34PitN	8-28-02	St. Louis, Mo.		R	R	6'2	190	599	1949	192	556	96	23	19	245	99	143	4	.285	.387
Roetz, Ed-Edward Bernard	29StLA	8- 6-05	Philadelphia, Pa.	3-16-65	R	R	5'10	160	16	45	7	11	4	1	0	5	4	6	0	.244	.378
Rogell, Billy-William George	25,27-28BosA 30-39DetA 40ChiN	11-24-04	Springfield, Ill.		B	R	5'10	163	1482	5149	755	1375	256	75	42	609	649	416	82	.267	.370
Rogers (Hazinski), Packy-Stanley Frank	38BknN	4-26-13	Swoyersville, Pa.		R	R	5'8	175	23	37	3	7	1	1	0	5	6	6	0	.189	.270
Rohwer, Ray-Ray	21-22PitN	6- 5-95	Dixon, Cal.		L	L	5'10	155	83	169	25	48	9	5	3	28	14	25	1	.284	.450
Rolfe, Red-Robert Abial 46-47 head coach in B.A.A.	31,34-42NYA M49-52DetA	10-17-08	Penacook, N.H.	7- 8-69	L	R	5'11	170	1175	4827	942	1394	257	67	69	497	526	335	44	.289	.413
Rollings, Red-William Russell	27-28BosA 30BosN	3-31-04	Mobile, Ala.	12-31-64	L	R	5'11	167	184	355	36	89	13	2	0	28	27	23	5	.251	.299
Rosar, Buddy-Warren Vincent	39-42NYA 43-44CleA 45-49PhiA 50-51BosA	7- 3-14	Buffalo, N.Y.		R	R	5'9	190	988	3198	335	836	147	15	18	367	315	161	17	.261	.334
Rosen, Goody-Goodwin George	37-39,44-46BknN 46NYN	8-28-12	Toronto, Canada		L	L	5'10	155	551	1916	310	557	71	34	22	197	218	166	12	.291	.398
Rosenberg, Harry-Harry	30NYN	6-22-09	San Francisco, Cal.		R	R	5'10	180	9	5	1	0	0	0	0	0	1	4	0	.000	.000
Rosenberg, Lou-Louis C.	23ChiA	3- 5-03	San Francisco, Cal.		R	R	5'7	155	3	4	0	1	0	0	0	0	0	1	0	.250	.250
Rosenfeld, Max-Max	31-33BknN	12-23-02	New York, N.Y.	3-10-69	R	R	5'8	175	42	57	8	17	4	0	2	7	2	12	2	.298	.474
Rosenthal, Larry-Lawrence John	36-41ChiA 41CleA 44NYA 44-45PhiA	5-21-12	St. Paul, Minn.		L	L	6'	190	579	1483	240	390	75	25	22	189	251	195	13	.263	.392
Rosenthal, Si-Simon	25-26BosA	11-13-03	Boston, Mass.	4- 7-69	L	L	5'9	165	126	357	40	95	17	5	4	42	26	21	5	.266	.375
Roser, Bunny-John William Joseph (Jack)	22BosN	11-15-01	St. Louis, Mo.		L	L	5'11	175	32	113	13	27	3	4	0	16	10	19	2	.239	.336
Ross, Chet-Chester James	39-44BosN 45MS	4- 1-17	Buffalo, N.Y.		R	R	6'1	195	413	1309	156	316	53	21	34	170	124	281	6	.241	.392
Ross, Don-Donald Raymond	38DetA 40BknN 42-45DetA 45-46CleA	7-16-14	Pasadena, Cal.		R	R	6'1	185	498	1488	129	390	63	4	12	162	165	70	10	.262	.334
Rothel, Bob-Robert Burton	45CleA	9-17-23	Columbia Sta., Ohio		R	R	5'10	170	4	10	0	2	0	0	0	0	3	1	0	.200	.200
Rothrock, Jack-John Houston	25-32BosA 32ChiA 34-35StLN 37PhiA	3-14-05	Long Beach, Cal.		B	R	5'11	165	1014	3350	498	924	162	35	28	327	299	312	75	.276	.370
Roush, Edd-Edd J.	13ChiA 14IndF 15NwkF 16NYN 16-26CinN 27-29NYN 30HO 31CinN	5- 8-93	Oakland City, Ind.		L	L	5'11	170	1967	7361	1099	2377	339	182	68	981	484	215	268	.323	.446
Rowe, Schoolboy-Lynwood Thomas (See P20-45)	33-42DetA 42BknN 43PhiN 44-45MS 46-49PhiN	1-11-10	Waco, Tex.	1- 8-61	R	R	6'4	210	491	909	116	239	36	9	18	153	86	157	3	.263	.382
Rowell, Bama-Carvel William	39-41BosN 42-45MS 46-47BosN 48PhiN	1-13-16	Citronelle, Ala.		L	R	5'11	185	574	1901	200	523	95	26	19	217	113	105	37	.275	.382
Rowland, Chuck-Charles Leland	23PhiA	7-23-99	Warrenton, N.C.		R	R	6'1	185	5	6	0	0	0	0	0	0	0	2	0	.000	.000
Rubeling, Al-Albert William	40-41PhiA 43-44PitN	5-10-13	Baltimore, Md.		R	R	6'	185	253	747	94	186	31	12	8	79	77	95	8	.249	.355
Ruble, Art-William Arthur (Speedy)	27DetA 34PhiN	3-11-03	Knoxville, Tenn.		L	R	5'10	168	75	145	23	30	8	2	0	19	21	18	2	.207	.290
Rucker, Johnny-John Joel (The Crabapple Comet)	40-46NYN	1-15-17	Crabapple, Ga.		L	R	6'2	175	705	2617	354	711	105	39	21	214	109	248	35	.272	.366
Ruel, Muddy-Harold Dominic	15StLA 17-20NYA 21-22BosA 23-30WasA 31BosA 31-32DetA 33StLA 34ChiA M47StLA	2-20-96	St. Louis, Mo.	11-13-63	R	R	5'9	150	1470	4514	494	1242	187	29	4	532	606	238	61	.275	.332
Ruether, Dutch-Walter Henry (See P20-45)	17ChiN 17-20CinN 21-24BknN 25-26WasA 26-27NYA	9-13-93	Alameda, Cal.	5-16-70	L	L	6'1	180	487	969	83	250	30	12	7	111	77	129	3	.258	.335
Ruffing, Red-Charles Herbert (See P20-45)	24-30BosA 30-42NYA 43-44MS 45-46NYA 47ChiA	5- 3-04	Granville, Ill.		R	R	6'2	205	882	1937	207	521	98	13	36	273	97	266	1	.269	.389
Rullo, Joe-Joseph Vincent	43-44PhiA	6-16-16	New York, N.Y.	10-28-69	R	R	5'11	168	51	151	7	32	3	0	0	11	14	26	1	.212	.232
Russell, Lloyd-Lloyd Opal (Tex)	38CleA	4-10-13	Atoka, Okla.	5-24-68	R	R	5'11	166	2	0	0	0	0	0	0	0	0	0	0	–	–
Russell, Reb-Ewell Albert (See P01-19)	13-19ChiA 22-23PitN	4-12-89	Jackson, Miss.	9-30-73	L	L	5'11	185	417	976	142	262	48	25	21	172	42	130	9	.268	.433
Russell, Rip-Glen David	39-42ChiN 46-47BosA	1-26-15	Los Angeles, Cal.		R	R	6'1	180	425	1402	133	344	52	8	29	192	83	142	4	.245	.356
Ruszkowski, Hank-Henry Alexander	44-45CleA 46MS 47CleA	11-10-25	Cleveland, Ohio		R	R	6'	190	40	84	8	20	2	0	3	10	6	16	0	.238	.369
Ruth, Babe-George Herman (See P01-19)	14-19BosA 20-34NYA 35BosN	2- 6-95	Baltimore, Md.	8-16-48	L	L	6'2	215	2503	8399	2174	2873	506	136	714	2207	2056	1330	123	.342	.690
Ryan, Blondy-John Collins	30ChiA 33-34NYN 35PhiN 35NYA 37-38NYN	1- 4-06	Lynn, Mass.	11-28-59	R	R	6'1	178	386	1330	127	318	36	13	8	133	57	184	6	.239	.304
Ryan, Jack-John Francis	29BosA	5- 5-05	Mineral, Kans.	9- 2-67	R	R	6'	185	2	3	0	0	0	0	0	0	0	0	0	.000	.000
Rye (Mercantelli), Gene-Eugene Rudolph (Half-Pint)	31BosA	11-15-06	Chicago, Ill.		L	R	5'6	165	17	39	3	7	0	0	0	1	2	5	0	.179	.179
Sabo (Szabo), Alex-Alexander (Giz)	36-37WasA	2-14-10	New Brunswick, N.J.		R	R	6'	192	5	8	1	3	0	0	0	1	0	2	0	.375	.375
Saltzgaver, Jack-Otto Hamlin	32,34-37NYA 45PitN	1-23-05	Croton, Iowa		L	R	5'11	165	278	764	131	199	26	5	10	82	105	80	9	.260	.347
Sanberg, Gus-Gustave E.	23-24CinN	2-23-96	Queens, N.Y.	2- 3-30	R	R	6'1	189	31	69	2	12	1	0	0	4	3	8	0	.174	.188

USE NAME – GIVEN NAMES (NICKNAMES)	TEAM BY YEAR	BIRTH DATE	BIRTH PLACE	DEATH DATE	B	T	HGT	WGT	G	AB	R	H	2B	3B	HR	RBI	BB	SO	SB	BA	SA
									LIFETIME BATTING TOTALS												
Sand, Heinie-John Henry	23-28PhiN	7- 3-97	San Francisco, Cal.	11- 3-58	R	R	5'8	160	848	3033	457	781	145	32	18	251	382	340	21	.258	.344
Sanders, Ray-Raymond Floyd	42-45StLN 46BosN 47BA 48-49BosN	12- 4-16	Bonne Terre, Mo.		L	R	6'2	185	630	2182	321	597	114	19	42	329	328	216	8	.274	.401
Sandlock, Mike-Michael Joseph	42,44BosN 45-46BknN 53PitN	10-17-15	Old Greenwich, Conn.		B	R	6'1	180	195	446	34	107	19	2	2	31	38	45	2	.240	.305
					Bats Left 44																
Sanford, Jack-John Doward	40-41WasA 42-45MS 46WasA	6-23-17	Chatham, Va.		R	R	6'3	195	47	153	13	32	4	4	0	11	9	24	0	.209	.288
Sankey, Ben-Benjamin Turner	29-31PitN	9- 2-07	Nauvoo, Ala.		R	R	5'10	155	72	169	21	36	2	5	0	14	16	14	0	.213	.284
Sargent, Joe-Joseph Alexander (Horse Belly)	21DetA	9-24-93	Rochester, N.Y.	7- 5-50	R	R	5'10	165	66	178	21	45	8	5	2	22	24	26	2	.253	.388
Saunders, Rusty-Russell Collier 25-31 played in A.B.L.	27PhiA	3-12-06	Trenton, N.J.		R	R	6'2	205	5	15	2	2	1	0	0	2	3	2	0	.133	.200
40-41,45-46 played in N.B.L.																					
Savage, Don-Donald Anthony	44-45NYA	3- 5-19	Bloomfield, N.J.	12-25-61	R	R	6'	180	105	297	36	76	8	5	4	27	23	55	2	.256	.357
Sax, Ollie-Erik Oliver	28StLA	11- 5-04	Branford, Conn.		R	R	5'8	164	16	17	4	3	0	0	0	0	5	3	0	.176	.176
Scalzi, Johnny-John Anthony 31 played in N.F.L.	31BosN	3-22-07	Stamford, Conn.	9-27-62	R	R	5'7	170	2	1	0	0	0	0	0	0	0	1	0	.000	.000
Scalzi, Skeeter-Frank Joseph	39NYN	6-16-13	Lafferty, Ohio		R	R	5'6	160	11	18	3	6	0	0	0	0	3	2	1	.333	.333
Scaritt, Russ-Russell Mallory	29-31BosA 32PhiN	1-14-03	Pensacola, Fla.		L	R	5'10	165	285	1037	119	296	44	25	3	121	49	91	17	.285	.385
Scarsella, Les-Leslie George	35-37,39CinN 40BosN	11-23-13	Santa Cruz, Cal.	12-17-58	L	L	5'11	185	265	898	109	255	34	16	6	109	37	70	13	.284	.378
Schalk, Roy-LeRoy John	32NYA 43MS 44-45ChiA	11- 9-08	Chicago, Ill.		R	R	5'10	168	282	1112	100	259	38	5	2	109	79	95	8	.233	.281
Schang, Wally-Walter Henry	13-17PhiA 18-20BosA 21-25NYA 26-29StLA 30PhiA 31DetA	8-22-89	South Wales, N.Y.	3- 6-65	B	R	5'10	180	1839	5306	769	1506	264	90	59	710	849	573	120	.284	.401
Scharein, Art-Arthur Otto (Scoop)	32-34StLA	6-30-05	Decatur, Ill.	7- 2-69	R	R	6'	170	205	776	92	189	32	5	0	70	66	31	11	.244	.298
Scharein, George-George Albert (Tom)	37-40PhiN	11-21-14	Decatur, Ill.		R	R	6'1	174	388	1317	126	316	53	6	2	119	65	123	28	.240	.294
Scheer, Heinie-Henry William	22-23PhiA	6-23-00	New York, N.Y.		R	R	5'8	146	120	345	36	73	11	1	6	33	20	66	4	.212	.301
Schemer, Mike-Michael	45-46NYN	11-20-17	Baltimore, Md.		L	L	6'	195	32	109	10	36	3	1	1	10	6	1	2	.330	.404
Schindler, Bill-William Gibbons	20StLN	7-10-96	Perryville, Mo.		R	R	5'11	160	1	2	0	0	0	0	0	0	0	1	0	.000	.000
Schliebner, Dutch-Frederick Paul	23BknN 23StLA	5-19-91	Charlottenburg, Germ.	4-15-75	R	R	5'8	180	146	520	61	141	23	6	4	56	44	67	4	.271	.362
Schlueter, Norm-Norman John	38-39ChiA 44CleA	9-25-16	Belleville, Ill.		R	R	5'10	175	118	296	18	55	11	2	0	26	17	48	3	.186	.236
Schmandt, Ray-Raymond Henry	15StLA 18-22BknN	1-25-96	St. Louis, Mo.	2- 1-69	R	R	6'1	175	317	1054	122	284	36	13	3	122	46	75	11	.269	.337
Schmidt, Walter-Walter Joseph	16-24PitN 25StLN	3-20-87	Coal Hill, Ark.	7- 4-73	R	R	5'9	160	766	2411	213	619	63	20	3	234	137	105	57	.257	.303
Schmulbach, Hank-Henry Alrives	43StLA 44-46MS	1-17-25	East St. Louis, Ill.		L	R	5'11	165	1	0	1	0	0	0	0	0	0	0	0	–	–
Schuble, Heinie-Henry George	27StLN 29,32-35DetA 36StLN	11- 1-06	Houston, Tex.		R	R	5'8	160	332	935	139	235	43	16	11	116	57	108	19	.251	.367
Schulmerich, Wes-Edward Wesley	31-33BosN 33-34PhiN 34CinN	8-21-01	Hillsboro, Ore.		R	R	5'11	210	429	1442	169	417	73	20	27	192	118	197	7	.289	.424
Schulte (Schult), Fred-Fred William (Fritz)	33-35WasA 36-37PitN	1-13-01	Belvidere, Ill.		R	R	6'1	183	1178	4257	686	1241	249	54	47	593	462	361	56	.292	.409
Schulte (Schultenhenrich), Ham-Herman Joseph	40PhiN	9- 1-12	St. Charles, Mo.		R	R	5'8	158	120	436	44	103	18	2	1	21	32	30	3	.236	.294
Schulte, Johnny-John Clement	23StLA 27StLN 28PhiN 29ChiN 32StLA 32BosN	9- 8-96	Fredericktown, Mo.		L	R	5'11	190	192	374	59	98	15	4	14	64	76	49	1	.262	.436
Schulte (Schultenhenrich), Len-Leonard William	44-46StLA	12- 5-16	St. Charles, Mo.		R	R	5'10	160	124	435	38	108	16	1	0	38	25	35	0	.248	.290
Schultz, Howie-Howard Henry (Stretch, Steeple)	43-47BknN 47-48PhiN 48CinN	7- 3-22	St. Paul, Minn.		R	R	6'6	200	470	1588	163	383	85	7	24	208	82	218	15	.241	.349
46-49 played in N.B.L., 49-50, 51-53 played in N.B.A.																					
Schultz, Joe-Joseph Charles Sr. (Germany)	12-13BosN 15BknN 15ChiN 16PitN 19-24StLN 24-25PhiN 25CinN	7-24-93	Pittsburgh, Pa.	4-13-41	R	R	5'11	172	703	1959	235	558	83	19	15	249	116	102	35	.285	.370
Schultz, Joe-Joseph Charles Jr. (Dode)	39-41PitN 43-48StLA M69SeaA M73DetA	8-29-18	Chicago, Ill.		L	R	5'11	180	240	328	18	85	13	1	1	46	37	21	0	.259	.314
Schuster, Bill-William Charles (Broadway)	37PitN 39BosN 43-45ChiN	8- 4-12	Buffalo, N.Y.		R	R	5'9	164	123	261	27	61	11	3	1	17	23	23	6	.234	.310
Scoffic, Lou-Louis (Weaser)	36StLN	5-20-13	Herrin, Ill.		R	R	5'10	182	4	7	2	3	0	0	0	2	1	2	0	.429	.429
Scott, Everett-Lewis Everett (Deacon)	14-21BosA 22-25NYA 25WasA 26ChiA 26CinN	11-19-92	Bluffton, Ind.	11- 2-60	R	R	5'8	142	1654	5837	552	1455	208	58	20	549	243	282	69	.249	.315
Scott, LeGrant-LeGrant Edward	39PhiN	7-25-10	Cleveland, Ohio		L	L	5'9	170	76	232	31	65	15	1	1	26	22	14	5	.280	.366
Scott, Pete-Floyd John	26-27ChiN 28PitN	12-21-98	Woodland, Cal.	5- 3-53	R	R	5'11	175	208	522	95	158	41	6	8	88	59	63	5	.303	.450
Sears, Ken-Kenneth Eugene (Ziggy)	43NYA 44-45MS 46StLA	7- 6-17	Streator, Ill.	7-17-68	L	R	6'1	200	67	202	23	57	7	0	2	23	14	18	1	.282	.347
Secory, Frank-Frank Edward	40DetA 42CinN 44-46ChiN	8-24-12	Mason City, Iowa		R	R	6'1	200	93	162	21	37	5	0	7	36	17	24	1	.228	.389
See, Charlie-Charles Henry (Chad)	19-21CinN	10-13-96	Pleasantville, N.Y.	7-19-48	L	R	5'10	175	92	202	21	55	9	1	1	23	9	12	5	.272	.342
Seeds, Bob-Robert Ira (Suitcase Bob)	30-32CleA 32ChiA 33-34BosA 34CleA 36NYA 38-40NYN	2-24-07	Ringgold, Tex.		R	R	6'	180	615	1937	268	537	77	21	28	233	160	190	14	.277	.382
Siebold, Socks-Harry (See P20-45)	15-17PhiA 18MS 19PhiA 29-33BosN	5-31-96	Philadelphia, Pa.	9-21-65	R	R	5'8	162	207	395	27	76	7	1	1	27	25	43	1	.192	.223
Selkirk, George-George Alexander (Twinkletoes)	34-42NYA 43-45MS	1- 4-08	Huntsville, Canada		L	R	6'1	182	846	2790	503	810	131	41	108	576	486	319	49	.290	.483
Selph, Carey-Carey Isom	29StLN 32ChiA	12- 5-01	Donaldson, Ark.		R	R	5'9	175	141	447	58	124	20	9	0	58	37	13	8	.277	.362
Severeid, Hank-Henry Levai	11-13CinN 15-25StLA 25-26WasA 26NYA	6- 1-91	Story City, Iowa	12-17-68	R	R	6'	175	1390	4312	408	1245	204	42	17	539	329	169	35	.289	.367
Sewell, Joe-Joseph Wheeler	20-30CleA 31-33NYA	10- 9-98	Titus, Ala.		L	R	5'7	155	1903	7132	1141	2226	436	68	49	1051	844	114	74	.312	.413
Sewell, Luke-James Luther	21-32CleA 33-34WasA 35-38ChiA 39CleA 42,M41-46StLA M49-52CinN	1- 5-01	Titus, Ala.		R	R	5'9	160	1630	5383	653	1393	272	56	20	696	486	307	65	.259	.341
Sewell, Tommy-Thomas Wesley	27ChiN	4-16-06	Titus, Ala.	7-30-56	L	R	5'7	155	1	1	0	0	0	0	0	0	0	0	0	.000	.000
Shaner, Wally-Walter Dedaker (Skinny)	23CleA 26-27BosA 29CinN	5-24-00	Lynchburg, Va.		R	R	6'2	195	207	629	80	175	45	8	4	74	43	54	13	.278	.394
Shay, Marty-Arthur Joseph	16ChiN 24BosN	4-25-98	Boston, Mass.	2-20-51	R	R	5'7	148	21	75	4	18	3	1	0	2	5	6	2	.240	.307
Shea, Merv-Mervin David John	27-29DetA 33BosA 33StLA 34-37ChiA 38BknN 39DetA 44PhiN	9- 5-00	San Francisco, Cal.	1-27-53	R	R	5'11	175	439	1197	105	263	39	7	5	115	189	145	8	.220	.277
Sheehan, Jack-John Thomas	20-21BknN	4-15-93	Chicago, Ill.		B	R	5'8	165	8	17	2	2	1	0	0	0	1	1	0	.118	.176
Sheehan, Jim-James Thomas (Big Jim)	36NYN	6- 3-13	New Haven, Conn.		R	R	6'2	196	1	4	0	0	0	0	0	0	0	2	0	.000	.000
Sheely, Earl-Earl Homer (Whitey)	21-27ChiA 29PitN 31BosN	2-12-93	Bushnell, Ill.	9-16-52	R	R	6'3	195	1234	4471	572	1340	244	27	48	747	563	205	33	.300	.399
Sheerin, Charlie-Charles Joseph	36PhiN	4-17-09	Brooklyn, N.Y.		R	R	6'	188	39	72	4	19	4	0	0	4	7	18	0	.264	.319
Sheeley, Hugh-Hubert Leneirre	35DetA	10-26-10	Rogers, Tex.		R	R	6'	170	7	8	1	2	0	0	0	1	2	1	0	.250	.250
Shemo, Steve-Stephen Michael	44-45BosN	4- 9-15	Swoyersville, Pa.		R	R	5'11	175	35	77	7	20	3	0	0	8	2	6	0	.260	.299
Shepardson, Ray-Raymond Francis	24StLN	5- 3-97	Little Falls, N.Y.		R	R	5'11	170	3	6	1	0	0	0	0	0	0	3	0	.000	.000
Sherling, Ed-Edward Creech Shine	24PhiA	7-17-97	Coalburg, Ala.	11-16-65	R	R	6'1	185	4	2	2	1	1	0	0	0	0	0	0	.500	1.000
Sherlock, Monk-John Clinton	30PhiN	10-26-04	Buffalo, N.Y.		R	R	5'10	175	92	299	51	97	18	2	0	38	27	28	0	.324	.398
Sherlock, Vince-Vincent Thomas	35BknN	3-27-09	Buffalo, N.Y.		R	R	6'	180	9	26	4	12	1	0	0	6	1	2	1	.462	.500
Shevlin, Jimmy-James Cornelius	30DetA 32,34CinN	7- 9-09	Cincinnati, Ohio		L	L	5'10	155	53	77	13	19	4	0	0	12	12	8	4	.247	.299
Shilling, Jim-James Robert	39CleA 39PhiN	5-14-15	Tulsa, Okla.		R	R	5'11	175	42	131	11	37	8	5	0	16	8	13	1	.282	.420
Shinault, Ginger-Enoch Erskine	21-22CleA	9- 7-92	Benton, Ark.	12-29-30	R	R	6'1	168	35	44	6	13	2	0	0	3	6	7	1	.295	.341
Shinners, Ralph-Ralph Peter	22-23NYN 25StLN	10- 4-95	Monches, Wis.	7-23-62	R	R	6'	180	163	399	60	110	14	4	7	51	19	42	11	.276	.383
Shires, Art-Charles Arthur (Art the Great)	28-30ChiA 30WasA 32BosN	8-13-07	Italy, Tex.	7-13-67	L	R	6'2	190	290	986	118	287	45	12	11	119	81	62	8	.291	.395
Shirley, Mule-Ernest Raeford	24-25WasA	5-24-01	Snow Hill, N.C.	8- 4-55	L	L	5'11	180	44	100	14	21	3	2	0	18	4	14	0	.210	.280
Shiver, Ivey-Ivey Merwin (Chick)	31DetA 34CinN	1-22-07	Sylvester, Ga.	8-31-72	R	R	6'2	200	21	68	8	13	1	0	2	6	3	18	1	.191	.294
Short, Dave-David Orvis	40-41ChiA 42-45MS	5-11-17	Magnolia, Ark.		L	R	5'11	162	7	11	1	1	0	0	0	0	3	3	0	.091	.091
Shorten, Chick-Charles Henry	15-17BosA 18MS 19-21DetA 22StLA 23VR 24CinN	4-19-92	Scranton, Pa.	10-23-65	L	L	6'	175	527	1345	161	370	51	20	3	134	110	68	12	.275	.349
Shupe, Vince-Vincent William	45BosN	9- 5-21	East Canton, Ohio	4- 5-62	L	L	5'11	180	78	283	22	76	8	0	0	15	17	16	3	.269	.297
Siebert, Dick-Richard Walther	32,36BknN 37-38StLN 38-45PhiA	2-19-12	Fall River, Mass.		L	L	6'	170	1035	3917	439	1104	204	40	32	482	276	185	30	.282	.379
Siemer, Oscar-Oscar Sylvester (Cotton)	25-26BosN	8-14-01	St. Louis, Mo.	12- 5-59	R	R	5'9	162	47	119	8	29	1	1	1	11	3	7	0	.244	.294
Sigafoos, Frank-Francis Leonard	26PhiA 29DetA 29ChiA 31CinN	3-21-04	Easton, Pa.	4-12-68	R	R	5'9	170	55	134	14	27	3	0	0	13	7	14	0	.201	.224
Sigman, Tripp-Wesley Triplett	29-30PhiN	1-17-99	Mooresville, N.C.	3- 8-71	L	R	6'	180	62	129	23	42	5	1	6	15	9	10	1	.326	.519
Silber, Eddie-Edward James	37,39StLA	6- 6-14	Philadelphia, Pa.		R	R	5'11	170	23	84	10	26	2	0	0	4	5	14	0	.310	.333
Silverstri, Ken-Kenneth Joseph (Hawk)	39-40ChiA 41,46-47NYA 42-45MS 49-51PhiN	5- 3-16	Chicago, Ill.		B	R	6'1	200	102	203	26	44	11	1	5	25	31	41	0	.217	.355
Simmons (Szymanski), Al (Alois)-Aloysius Harry	24-32PhiA 33-35ChiA 36DetA 37-38WasA 39BosN 39CinN 40-41PhiA 43BosA 44PhiA	5-22-02	Milwaukee, Wis.	5-26-56	R	R	5'11	190	2215	8761	1507	2927	539	149	307	1827	615	737	87	.334	.535
Simon, Syl-Sylvester Adam	23-24StLA	12-14-97	Chandler, Ind.	2-28-73	R	R	5'10	170	24	33	5	8	1	1	0	6	3	5	0	.242	.333
Simons, Mel-Melbern Ellis (Butch)	31-32ChiA	7- 1-00	Carlyle, Ill.	11-10-74	L	R	5'10	175	75	194	24	52	9	0	0	12	12	18	1	.268	.314
Sington, Fred-Frederick William	34-37WasA 38-39BknN	2-24-10	Birmingham, Ala.		R	R	6'2	215	181	516	66	140	36	5	7	85	89	66	2	.271	.401
Sipek, Dick-Richard Francis	45CinN	1-16-23	Chicago, Ill.		L	R	5'9	170	82	156	14	38	6	2	0	13	9	15	0	.244	.308
Sisler, George-George Harold (Gorgeous George) (See P01-19)	15-22StLA 23IJ 24-27,M24-26StLA 28WasA 28-30BosN	3-24-93	Manchester, Ohio	3-26-73	L	L	5'11	170	2055	8267	1284	2812	425	164	102	1175	472	327	375	.340	.468
Skaff, Frank-Francis Michael	35BknN 43PhiA M66DetA	9-30-13	LaCrosse, Wis.		R	R	5'10	185	38	75	12	24	3	2	1	11	6	13	0	.320	.453
Sketchley, Bud-Harry Clement	42ChiA	3-30-19	Virden, Canada		L	L	5'10	180	13	36	1	7	1	0	0	3	7	4	0	.194	.222

USE NAME – GIVEN NAMES (NICKNAMES)	TEAM BY YEAR	BIRTH DATE	BIRTH PLACE	DEATH DATE	B	T	HGT	WGT	G	AB	R	H	2B	3B	HR	RBI	BB	SO	SB	BA	SA
					LIFETIME BATTING TOTALS																
Skiff, Bill-William Franklin	21PitN 26NYA	10-16-95	New Rochelle, N.Y.		R	R	5'10	170	22	56	7	14	2	0	0	11	0	5	1	.250	.286
Skinner, Camp-Elisha Harrison	22NYA 23BosA	6-25-97	Douglasville, Ga.	8- 4-44	L	R	5'11	165	34	46	2	9	2	0	0	3	0	4	1	.196	.239
Slade, Gordon-Gordon Leigh (Oskie)	30-32BknN 33StLN 34-35CinN	10- 9-04	Salt Lake City, Utah	1- 2-74	R	R	5'10	160	437	1372	147	353	60	11	8	123	84	116	12	.257	.335
Slayback, Scottie-Elbert	26NYN	10- 5-01	Paducah, Ky.		R	R	5'8	165	2	8	0	0	0	0	0	0	0	0	0	.000	.000
Sloan, Bruce-Bruce Adams (Fatso)	44NYN	10- 4-14	McAlester, Okla.	9-24-73	L	L	5'9	195	59	104	7	28	4	1	1	9	13	8	0	.269	.356
Small, Charlie-Charles Albert	30BosA	10-24-05	Auburn, Me.	1-14-53	L	R	5'11	180	25	18	1	3	1	0	0	0	2	5	1	.167	.222
Smith, Bob-Robert Eldridge (See P20-45)	23-30BosN 31-33ChiN 33CinN 33-37BosN	4-22-98	Rogersville, Tenn.		R	R	5'10	175	742	1689	154	409	64	17	5	166	52	110	16	.242	.309
Smith, Carr-Carr E.	23-24WasA	4- 8-01	Kernersville, N.C.		R	R	6'	175	10	19	1	3	1	0	0	1	0	3	0	.158	.211
Smith, Earl-Earl Leonard (Sheriff)	16ChiN 17-20StLA 21-22WasA	1-20-91	Oak Hill, Ohio	3-14-43	B	R	6'	175	495	1580	176	429	72	32	9	186	82	127	36	.272	.375
					Bats Left 20-22																
Smith, Earl-Earl Sutton (Oil)	19-23NYN 23-24BosN 24-27PitN 28-30StLN	2-14-97	Sheridan, Ark.	6- 9-63	L	R	5'10	180	860	2264	225	686	115	19	46	355	247	106	18	.303	.432
Smith, Elmer-Elmer John	14-16CleA 16-17WasA 17CleA 18MS 19-21CleA 22BosA 22-23NYA 25CinN	9-21-92	Sandusky, Ohio		L	R	5'10	165	1012	3195	469	881	181	62	70	540	319	359	54	.276	.437
Smith (Schmidt), Ernie-Ernest Henry (The Kansas City Kid)	30ChiA	10-11-01	Totowa, N.J.	4- 6-73	R	R	5'9	165	24	79	5	19	3	0	0	3	5	6	2	.241	.278
Smith (Smadt), Jack-John (Jan)	15-26StLN 26-29BosN	6-23-95	Chicago, Ill.	5- 2-72	L	L	5'8	165	1406	4532	783	1301	182	71	40	382	334	348	228	.287	.385
Smith, John-John Marshall	31BosA	9-27-06	Washington, D.C.		B	R	6'1	165	4	15	2	2	0	0	0	1	2	1	1	.133	.133
Smith, Mayo-Edward Mayo	45PhiA M55-58PhiN M59CinN M67-70DetA	1-17-15	New London, Mo.		L	R	6'	183	73	203	18	43	5	0	0	11	36	13	0	.212	.236
Smith, Mike-Elwood Hope	26NYN	11-16-04	Norfolk, Va.		L	R	5'11	170	4	7	0	1	0	0	0	0	0	2	0	.143	.143
Smith, Paddy-Lawrence Patrick	20BosA	5-16-94	Pelham, N.Y.		L	R	6'	195	2	2	0	0	0	0	0	0	0	1	0	.000	.000
Smith, Red-Marvin Harold	25PhiA	7-17-00	Ashley, Ill.	2-19-61	L	R	5'7	165	20	14	1	4	0	0	0	1	2	5	0	.286	.286
Smith, Red-Richard Paul 27-31 played in N.F.L.	27NYN	5-18-04	Brokaw, Wis.		R	R	5'10	185	1	0	0	0	0	0	0	0	0	0	0	–	–
Smith, Vinnie-Vincent Ambrose	41PitN 42-45MS 46PitN	12- 7-15	Richmond, Va.		R	R	6'1	176	16	54	5	14	1	0	0	5	2	10	0	.259	.278
Smyres, Clancy-Clarence Melvin	44BknN	5-24-22	Culver City, Cal.		B	L	5'11	175	5	2	1	0	0	0	0	0	0	0	0	.000	.000
Snipes, Roxy-Wyatt Eure (Rock)	23ChiA	10-28-96	Marion, S.C.	5- 1-41	L	R	6'	185	1	1	0	0	0	0	0	0	0	0	0	.000	.000
Snyder, Bernie-Bernard Austin	35PhiA	8-25-13	Philadelphia, Pa.		R	R	6'	165	10	32	5	11	1	0	0	3	1	2	0	.344	.375
Snyder, Frank-Frank Elton (Pancho)	12-19StLN 19-26NYN 27StLN	5-27-93	San Antonio, Tex.	1- 5-62	R	R	6'2	185	1392	4229	331	1122	170	44	47	525	281	416	37	.265	.360
Sodd, Bill-William	37CleA	9-18-14	Fort Worth, Tex.		R	R	6'2	210	1	1	0	0	0	0	0	0	0	1	0	.000	.000
Solomon, Moe-Moses H. (The Rabbi of Swat, Hickory)	23NYN	12- 8-00	New York, N.Y.	6-25-66	L	L	5'10	180	2	8	0	3	1	0	0	1	0	1	0	.375	.500
Solters (Soltesz), Moose-Julius Joseph	34-35BosA 35-36StLA 37-39CleA 39StLA 40-41ChiA 42VR 43ChiA	3-22-06	Pittsburgh, Pa.	9-28-75	R	R	6'	190	938	3421	503	990	213	42	83	599	221	377	42	.289	.449
Sorrells, Chick-Raymond Edwin (Red)	22CleA	7-31-96	Stringtown, Okla.		R	R	5'9	155	2	1	0	0	0	0	0	0	0	0	0	.000	.000
Sothern, Denny-Dennis Elwood	26,28-30PhiN 30PitN 31BknN	1-20-04	Washington, D.C.		R	R	5'11	175	357	1355	219	379	80	9	19	115	83	136	38	.280	.394
Southworth, Billy-William Harrison	13,15CleA 18-20PitN 21-23BosN 24-26NYN 26-27,29,M29,40-45StLN M46-51BosN	3- 9-93	Harvard, Neb.	11-15-69	L	R	5'9	170	1192	4359	661	1296	173	91	52	561	402	148	138	.297	.415
Spalding, Dick-Charles Harry	27PhiN 28WasA	10-13-93	Philadelphia, Pa.	2- 3-50	L	L	5'11	185	131	465	69	139	16	3	0	25	38	44	5	.299	.346
Spence, Stan-Stanley Orvil	40-41BosA 42-44WasA 45MS 46-47WasA 48-49BosA 49StLA	3-20-15	S. Portsmouth, Ky.		L	L	5'10	180	1112	3871	541	1090	196	60	95	575	520	248	21	.282	.437
Spencer, Roy-Roy Hampton	25-27PitN 29-32WasA 33-34CleA 36NYN 37-38BknN	2-22-00	Scranton, Pa.	2- 8-73	R	R	5'10	168	636	1814	177	448	57	13	3	203	128	130	4	.247	.298
Spencer, Vern-Vernon Murray	20NYN	2-24-96	Wixom, Mich.		L	R	5'7	165	45	140	15	28	2	3	0	19	11	17	4	.200	.257
Speraw, Paul-Paul Bachman (Polly, Birdie)	20StLA	10- 5-93	Annville, Pa.	2-22-62	R	R	5'8	145	1	2	0	0	0	0	0	0	0	0	0	.000	.000
Sperber, Ed-Edwin George	24-25BosN	1-21-95	Cincinnati, Ohio		L	L	5'11	175	26	61	8	17	2	0	1	12	10	9	3	.279	.361
Sperry, Stan-Stanley Kenneth	36PhiN 38PhiA	2-19-14	Evansville, Wis.	9-27-62	L	R	5'10	164	80	290	30	74	9	3	0	31	18	14	1	.255	.307
Spindel, Hal-Harold Stewart	39StLA 45-46PhiN	5-27-13	Chandler, Okla.		R	R	6'	185	85	209	20	53	6	1	0	20	14	14	0	.254	.292
Spognardi, Andy-Andrea Ettore	32BosA	10-18-08	Boston, Mass.		L	R	5'9	160	17	34	9	10	1	0	0	1	6	6	0	.294	.324
Spohrer, Al-Alfred Ray	28NYN 28-35BosN	12- 3-02	Philadelphia, Pa.	7-17-72	R	R	5'10	175	756	2218	213	575	103	25	6	199	124	166	13	.259	.336
Spotts, Jim-James Russell	30PhiN	4-10-09	Honeybrook, Pa.	6-15-64	R	R	5'10	175	3	2	1	0	0	0	0	0	0	1	0	.000	.000
Sprinz, Joe-Joseph Conrad (Mule)	30-31CleA 33StLN	8- 3-02	St. Louis, Mo.		R	R	5'11	185	21	53	6	9	1	0	0	2	5	5	0	.170	.189
Spurgeon, Freddie-Fred	24-27CleA	10- 9-01	Wabash, Ind.	11- 5-70	R	R	5'11	160	316	1177	181	335	47	7	1	100	60	71	23	.285	.339
Stainback, Tuck-George Tucker	34-37ChiN 38StLN 38PhiN 38-39BknN 40-41DetA 42-45NYA 46PhiA	8- 4-10	Los Angeles, Cal.		R	R	5'11	175	817	2261	284	585	90	14	17	204	64	213	27	.259	.333
Staley, Gale-George Gaylord	25ChiN	5- 2-99	De Pere, Wis.		L	R	5'8	167	7	26	2	11	2	0	0	3	2	1	0	.423	.500
Staller, George-George Walborn (Stopper)	43PhiA 44-45MS	4- 1-16	Rutherford Hgts, Pa.		L	L	5'11	190	21	85	14	23	1	3	3	12	5	6	1	.271	.459
Standaert, Jerry-Jerome John	25-26BknN 29BosA	11- 2-01	Chicago, Ill.	8- 4-64	R	R	5'10	168	86	132	14	42	10	2	0	18	8	10	0	.318	.424
Stanton, Buck-George Washington	31StLA	6-19-06	Stantonsburg, N.C.		L	L	5'10	150	13	15	3	3	2	0	0	0	0	6	0	.200	.333
Starr, Chick-William	35-36WasA	2-26-11	Brooklyn, N.Y.		R	R	6'1	175	13	24	1	5	0	0	0	1	0	1	0	.208	.208
Statz, Jigger-Arnold John	19-20NYN 20BosA 22-25ChiN 27-28BknN	10-20-97	Waukegan, Ill.		R	R	5'7	150	683	2585	376	737	114	31	17	215	194	211	77	.285	.373
					Bats Both 22																
Stein, Justin-Justin Marion (Ott)	38PhiN 38CinN	8- 9-11	St. Louis, Mo.		R	R	5'11	180	22	57	9	16	1	1	0	3	2	5	0	.281	.333
Steinbacher, Hank-Henry John	37-39ChiA	3-22-13	Sacramento, Cal.		L	R	5'11	180	203	583	88	170	29	10	6	85	66	34	3	.292	.407
Steinecke, Bill-William Robert	31PitN	2- 7-07	Cincinnati, Ohio		R	R	5'8	175	4	4	0	0	0	0	0	0	0	1	0	.000	.000
Steiner, Ben-Benjamin Saunders	45-46BosA 47DetA	7-28-21	Alexandria, Va.		L	R	5'11	165	82	308	41	79	8	3	3	20	31	29	10	.256	.331
Steiner, Red-James Harry	45CleA 45BosA 46-49SM	1- 7-15	Los Angeles, Cal.		L	R	5'11	175	38	79	6	15	1	0	0	6	15	6	0	.190	.203
Stephenson, Riggs-Jackson Riggs (Old Hoss)	21-25CleA 26-34ChiN	1- 5-98	Akron, Ala.		R	R	5'10	185	1310	4508	714	1515	321	54	63	773	494	247	54	.336	.473
Stephenson, Walter-Walter McQueen (Tarzan)	35-36ChiN 37PhiN	3-27-11	Saluda, N.C.		R	R	6'	180	32	61	3	17	1	1	0	5	3	13	0	.279	.328
Stevens, Bobby-Robert Jordan	31PhiN	4-17-07	Chevy Chase, Md.		L	R	5'8	149	12	35	3	12	0	0	0	4	2	2	0	.343	.343
Stewart, Glen-Glen Weldon (Gabby)	40NYN 43-44PhiN	9-29-12	Tullahoma, Tenn.		R	R	6'	175	243	742	56	158	22	6	2	53	61	83	1	.213	.267
Stewart, Neb-Walter Nesbitt	40PhiN	5-21-18	S. Charleston, Ohio		R	R	6'1	195	10	31	3	4	0	0	0	0	1	5	0	.129	.129
Stewart, Stuffy-John Franklin	16-17StLN 22PitN 23BknN 25-27,29WasA	1-31-94	Jasper, Fla.		R	R	5'9	160	176	265	74	63	14	3	1	18	17	32	21	.238	.325
Stock, Milt-Milton Joseph	13-14NYN 15-18PhiN 19-23StLN 24-26BknN	7-11-93	Chicago, Ill.		R	R	5'8	154	1628	6249	839	1806	270	58	22	696	455	321	155	.289	.361
Stokes (Stacek), Al-Albert John	25-26BosA	1- 1-00	Chicago, Ill.	Deceased	R	R	5'10	170	47	138	14	25	3	4	0	7	12	36	0	.181	.261
Stone, John-John Thomas (Rocky)	28-33DetA 34-38WasA	10-10-05	Lynchburg, Tenn.	11-11-55	L	R	6'1	178	1199	4490	739	1391	268	105	77	707	463	352	45	.310	.468
Stone, Tige-William Arthur	23StLN	9-18-01	Macon, Ga.	1- 1-60	R	R	5'8	145	5	1	0	1	0	0	0	0	2	0	0	1.000	1.000
Stoneham, John-John Andrew	33ChiA	11- 8-08	Wood River, Ill.		L	R	5'9	168	10	25	4	3	0	0	1	3	2	2	0	.120	.240
Storie, Howie-Howard Edward	31-32BosA	5-15-11	Pittsfield, Mass.	7-27-68	R	R	5'10	175	12	25	2	5	0	0	0	0	3	2	0	.200	.200
Storti, Lin-Lindo Ivan	30-33StLA	12- 5-06	Santa Monica, Cal.		B	R	5'10	162	216	704	83	160	34	11	9	75	47	107	3	.227	.345
Stoviak, Ray-Raymond Thomas	38PhiN	6- 6-15	Scottdale, Pa.		L	L	6'1	195	10	10	1	0	0	0	0	0	0	3	0	.000	.000
Strand, Paul-Paul Edward (See P01-19)	13-15BosN 24PhiA	12-19-93	Carbonado, Wash.	7- 2-74	R	L	6'	190	96	219	20	49	11	4	0	18	5	18	3	.224	.311
Strange, Alan-Alan Cochrane (Inky)	34-35StLA 35WasA 40-42StLA	11- 7-09	Philadelphia, Pa.		R	R	5'9	162	314	947	93	211	39	7	1	89	109	54	6	.223	.282
Stringer, Lou-Louis Bernard	41-42ChiN 43-45MS 46ChiN 48-50BosA	5-13-17	Grand Rapids, Mich.		R	R	5'11	173	409	1196	148	290	49	10	19	122	121	192	7	.242	.348
Stripp, Joe-Joseph Valentine (Jersey Joe)	28-31CinN 32-37BknN 38StLN 38BosN	2- 3-03	Harrison, N.J.		R	R	5'11	175	1146	4211	575	1238	219	43	24	464	280	226	50	.294	.384
Stroner, Jim-James M.	29PitN	9-26-92	Chicago, Ill.	11-16-71	R	R	5'10	175	6	8	0	3	1	0	0	0	1	0	0	.375	.500
Stuart, Luke-Luther Lane	21StLA	5-23-92	Alamance County, N.C.	6-15-47	R	R	5'8	165	3	3	2	1	0	0	1	2	0	1	0	.333	1.333
Stumpf, George-George Frederick	31-33BosA 36ChiA	12-15-10	New Orleans, La.		L	L	5'8	155	118	260	31	61	7	3	1	32	25	26	5	.235	.296
Sturdy, Guy-Guy R.	27-28StLA	8- 7-99	Sherman, Tex.	5- 4-65	L	L	6'	180	59	66	8	19	2	0	1	13	9	4	2	.288	.364
Sturgeon, Bobby-Robert Harwood	40-42ChiN 43-45MS 46-47ChiN 48BosN	8- 6-19	Clinton, Ind.		R	R	6'	175	420	1220	106	313	48	12	1	80	34	79	7	.257	.318
Sturm, Johnny-John Peter Joseph	41NYA 42-45MS	1-23-16	St. Louis, Mo.		L	L	6'1	185	124	524	58	125	17	3	3	36	37	50	3	.239	.300
Stutz, George-George (Kid)	26PhiN	2-12-93	Philadelphia, Pa.	12-29-30	R	R	5'5	150	6	9	0	0	0	0	0	0	0	2	0	.000	.000
Styles, Lena-William Graves	19-21PhiA 30-31CinN	11-27-99	Gurley, Ala.	3-14-56	R	R	6'1	185	77	176	14	44	7	2	0	16	16	24	1	.250	.313
Suarez, Luis-Luis Abelardo	44WasA	8-24-16	Alto Songo, Cuba		R	R	5'11	170	1	2	0	0	0	0	0	0	0	0	0	.000	.000
Suhr, Gus-August Richard	30-39PitN 39-40PhiN	1- 3-06	San Francisco, Cal.		L	R	6'	180	1435	5176	714	1446	288	114	84	818	718	433	53	.279	.428
Sukeforth, Clyde-Clyde LeRoy (Sukey)	26-31CinN 32-34,45,M47BknN	11-30-01	Washington, Me.		L	R	5'10	155	486	1237	122	326	50	14	2	96	95	57	12	.264	.331
Sulik, Ernie-Ernest Richard	36PhiN	7- 7-10	San Francisco, Cal.	5-31-63	L	L	5'10	178	122	404	69	116	14	4	6	36	40	22	4	.287	.386
Sullivan, Billy-William Joseph Jr.	31-33ChiA 35CinN 36-37CleA 38-39StLA 44-46MS47PitN	10-23-10	Chicago, Ill.		L	R	6'	170	962	2840	347	820	152	32	29	388	240	119	30	.289	.395
Sullivan, Jack-Carl Mancel	44DetA	2-22-18	Princeton, Tex.		R	R	5'11	172	1	1	0	0	0	0	0	0	0	0	0	.000	.000
Sullivan, John-John Lawrence	20-21BosN 21ChiN	3-21-90	Williamsport, Pa.	4- 1-66	R	R	5'11	180	162	495	64	153	28	8	5	69	48	55	6	.309	.428
Sullivan, John-John Paul	42-44WasA 45-46MS 47-48WasA 49StLA	11- 2-20	Chicago, Ill.		R	R	5'10	170	605	1833	203	422	52	9	1	162	216	206	18	.230	.270
Sullivan, Tom-Thomas Brandon	25CinN	12-19-06	Nome, Alaska	8-16-44	R	R	6'	190	1	1	0	0	0	0	0	0	0	0	0	.000	.000
Summa, Homer-Homer Wayne	20PitN 22-28CleA 29-30PhiA	11- 3-98	Gentry, Mo.	1-29-66	L	R	5'10	170	840	3001	413	905	166	34	18	361	166	88	44	.302	.398
Sumner, Carl-Carl Rinedahl	28BosA	9-28-08	Cambridge, Mass.		L	L	5'8	170	16	29	6	8	1	1	0	3	5	6	0	.276	.379
Susce, George-George Cyril Methodius (Good Kid)	29PhiN 32DetA 39PitN 40StLA 41-44CleA	8-13-08	Pittsburgh, Pa.		R	R	5'11	200	146	268	23	61	11	1	2	22	25	21	1	.228	.299

USE NAME – GIVEN NAMES (NICKNAMES)	TEAM BY YEAR	BIRTH DATE	BIRTH PLACE	DEATH DATE	B	T	HGT	WGT	G	AB	R	H	2B	3B	HR	RBI	BB	SO	SB	BA	SA
					LIFETIME BATTING TOTALS																
Susko, Pete-Peter Jonathan	34WasA	7- 2-04	Laura, Ohio		L	L	5'11	172	58	224	25	64	5	3	2	25	18	10	3	.286	.362
Sutcliffe, Butch-Charles Inigo	38BosN	7-22-15	Fall River, Mass.		R	R	5'9	165	4	4	1	1	0	0	0	2	2	1	0	.250	.250
Swanson, Evar-Ernest Evar 24-27 played in N.F.L.	29-30CinN 32-34ChiA	10-15-02	DeKalb, Ill.	7-17-73	R	R	5'9	170	518	1892	325	573	87	28	7	170	212	133	69	.303	.390
Swanson, Karl-Karl Edward	28-29ChiA	12-17-03	N. Henderson, Ill.		L	R	5'10	155	24	65	2	9	1	0	0	6	4	7	3	.138	.154
Sweeney, Bill-William Joseph	28DetA 30-31BosA	12-29-03	Cleveland, Ohio	4-18-57	R	R	5'11	185	308	1050	127	300	58	8	5	107	44	73	22	.286	.370
Sweeney, Hank-Henry Leon	44PitN	12-28-15	Franklin, Tenn.		L	L	6'	185	1	2	0	0	0	0	0	0	0	1	0	.000	.000
Swentor, Augie-August William	22ChiA	11-21-99	Seymour, Conn.	11-10-69	R	R	6'	185	1	1	0	0	0	0	0	0	0	1	0	.000	.000
Swift, Bob-Robert Virgil	42-43PhiA 44-53,M66DetA	3- 6-15	Salina, Kans.	10- 7-66	R	R	5'11	180	1001	2750	212	635	86	3	14	238	323	233	10	.231	.280
Tabor, Jim-James Reubin (Rawhide)	38-44BosA 45MS 46-47PhiN	11- 5-13	Owens Crossroads, Ala.	8-22-53	R	R	6'2	175	1005	3788	473	1021	191	29	104	598	286	377	69	.270	.418
Taitt, Doug-Douglas John (Poco)	28-29BosA 29ChiA 31-32PhiN	8- 3-02	Bay City, Mich.	12-12-70	L	R	6'	176	258	824	81	217	43	16	4	95	58	64	13	.263	.369
Tankersley, Leo-Lawrence William (Tank)	25ChiA	6- 8-01	Terrell, Tex.		R	R	6'	180	1	3	0	0	0	0	0	0	0	0	0	.000	.000
Tarbert, Arlie-Wilber Arlington	27-28BosA	9-10-04	Cleveland, Ohio	11-27-46	R	R	6'	160	39	86	6	16	2	0	0	7	4	13	1	.186	.209
Tate, Bennie-Henry Bennett	24-30WasA 30-32ChiA 32BosA 34ChiN	12- 3-01	Whitwell, Tenn.	10-27-73	L	R	5'8	165	566	1560	144	435	68	16	4	173	118	51	5	.279	.351
Tauby (Taubensee), Fred-Fred Joseph	35ChiA 37PhiN	3-27-06	Canton, Ohio	11-23-55	R	R	5'9	168	24	52	7	4	1	0	0	5	2	8	1	.077	.096
Tavener, Jackie-John Adam	21,25-28DetA 29CleA	12-27-97	Celina, Ohio	9-14-69	L	R	5'5	138	632	2131	254	543	88	53	13	242	186	231	47	.255	.364
Taylor, Chink-C L	25ChiN	2- 9-98	Burnet, Tex.		R	R	5'9	160	8	6	2	0	0	0	0	0	0	0	0	.000	.000
Taylor, Danny-Daniel Turney	26WasA 29-32ChiN 32-36BknN	12-23-00	Lash, Pa.	10-11-72	R	R	5'10	190	674	2190	388	650	121	37	44	305	267	268	56	.297	.446
Taylor, Eddie-Edward James	26BosN	11-17-01	Chicago, Ill.		R	R	5'6	160	92	272	37	73	8	2	0	33	38	26	4	.268	.313
Taylor, Harry-Harry Warren (Handsome Harry)	32ChiN	12-26-07	McKeesport, Pa.		L	L	6'1	185	10	8	1	1	0	0	0	0	1	1	0	.125	.125
Taylor, Leo-Leo Thomas	23ChiA	5-13-01	Walla Walla, Wash.		R	R	5'10	150	1	0	0	0	0	0	0	0	0	0	0	–	–
Taylor, Tommy-Thomas Livingston Carlton	24WasA	9-17-92	Mexia, Tex.	4- 5-56	R	R	5'10	176	26	73	11	19	3	1	0	10	2	8	2	.260	.329
Taylor, Zack-James Wren	20-25BknN 26-27BosN 27NYN 28-29BosN 29-33ChiN 34NYA 35BknN M46,48-51StLA	7-27-98	Yulee, Fla.	9-19-74	R	R	5'11	180	918	2865	258	748	113	28	9	311	161	192	9	.261	.329
Terry, Bill-William Harold (Memphis Bill)	23-36,M32-41NYN	10-30-98	Atlanta, Ga.		L	L	6'1	200	1721	6428	1120	2193	373	112	154	1078	537	449	56	.341	.506
Terry, Zeb-Zebulon Alexander	16-17ChiA 18BosN 19PitN 20-22ChiN	6-17-91	Denison, Tex.		R	R	5'8	130	640	2327	254	605	90	24	2	216	179	133	32	.260	.322
Thevenow, Tommy-Thomas Joseph	24-28StLN 29-30PhiN 31-35PitN 36CinN 37BosN 38PitN	9- 6-03	Madison, Ind.	7-29-57	R	R	5'10	155	1229	4164	380	1030	124	32	2	456	210	222	23	.247	.294
Thomas, Herb-Herbert Mark	24-25,27BosN 27NYN	5-26-02	Sampson City, Fla.		R	R	5'5	157	74	235	27	52	11	4	1	15	15	18	7	.221	.315
Thomas, Ray-Raymond Joseph	38BknN	7- 8-12	Dover, N.H.		R	R	5'10	175	1	3	1	1	0	0	0	0	0	0	0	.333	.333
Thomas, Red-Robert William	21ChiN	4-25-98	Hargrove, Ala.	3-29-62	R	R	5'11	165	8	30	5	8	3	0	1	5	4	5	0	.267	.467
Thompson, Frank-Frank E	20StLA	7- 4-93	Springfield, Mo.	6-27-40	R	R	5'8	155	22	53	7	9	0	0	0	5	13	10	1	.170	.170
Thompson, Fresco-Lafayette Fresco (Tommy)	25PitN 26NYN 27-30PhiN 31-32BknN 34NYN	6- 6-02	Centreville, Ala.	11-20-68	R	R	5'8	150	669	2560	400	762	149	34	13	249	215	143	69	.298	.398
Thompson, Tommy-Rupert Luckhart	33-36BosN 38-39ChiA 39StLA	5-19-10	Elkhart, Ill.	5-24-71	L	R	5'11	175	397	1107	142	294	34	4	9	119	108	63	7	.266	.328
Tierney, Cotton-James Arthur	20-23PitN 23PhiN 24BosN 25BknN	2-10-94	Kansas City, Kans.	4-18-53	R	R	5'8	175	630	2299	266	681	119	30	31	331	109	187	28	.296	.415
Tipton, Eric-Eric Gordon (Dukie, Blue Devil)	39-41PhiA 42-45CinN	4-20-15	Petersburg, Va.		R	R	5'11	190	501	1626	212	439	80	19	22	151	223	127	20	.270	.383
Tobin, Jack-John Martin (Tip)	32NYN	9-15-06	Jamaica Plain, Mass.		R	R	6'3	187	1	1	0	0	0	0	0	0	0	0	0	.000	.000
Tobin, Jack-John Thomas	14-15StLF 16,18-25StLA 26WasA 26-27BosA	5- 4-92	St. Louis, Mo.	12-10-69	L	L	5'9	150	1617	6173	934	1908	297	101	64	581	498	172	147	.309	.421
Tobin, Johnny-John Patrick (Jackie)	45BosA	1- 8-21	Oakland, Cal.		L	R	6'	165	84	278	25	70	6	2	0	21	26	24	2	.252	.288
Todd, Al-Alfred Chester	32-35PhiN 36-38PitN 39BknN 40-41,43ChiN	1- 7-04	Troy, N.Y.		R	R	6'1	198	863	2785	286	768	119	29	35	366	104	243	18	.276	.377
Todt, Phil-Philip Julius	24-30BosA 31PhiA	8- 9-01	St. Louis, Mo.	11-15-73	L	L	6'	175	957	3415	372	880	183	58	57	452	207	229	29	.258	.395
Tolson, Chick-Chester Julius (Slug)	25CleA 26-27,29-30ChiN	11- 6-01	Washington, D.C.		R	R	6'	185	144	275	23	78	16	1	4	45	26	39	1	.284	.393
Toporcer, Specs-George	21-28StLN	2- 9-99	New York, N.Y.		L	R	5'10	165	546	1566	223	437	76	22	9	151	150	93	22	.279	.373
Torphy, Red-Walter Anthony	20BosN	11- 6-91	Fall River, Mass.		R	R	5'11	169	3	15	1	3	2	0	0	2	0	1	0	.200	.333
Torres, Gil-Don Gilberto [Nunez] (See P20-45)	40,44-46WasA	8-23-15	Regla, Cuba		R	R	6'	155	346	1271	99	320	40	11	0	119	53	65	20	.252	.301
Torres, Ricardo-Ricardo J.	20-22WasA	-94	Cuba		R	R	5'11	160	22	37	9	11	1	0	0	3	2	6	0	.297	.324
Tromback, Red-Stephen Joseph	40NYN	10- 1-15	Iselin, Pa.		R	R	6'	175	2	4	0	1	0	0	0	0	1	1	1	.250	.250
Travis, Cecil-Cecil Howell	33-41WasA 42-44MS 45-47WasA	8- 8-13	Riverdale, Ga.		L	R	6'1	185	1328	4914	665	1544	266	77	27	657	402	291	23	.314	.416
Traynor, Pie-Harold Joseph	20-35,37,M34-39PitN	11-11-99	Framingham, Mass.	3-16-72	R	R	6'	170	1941	7559	1183	2416	371	164	58	1273	472	278	158	.320	.435
Treadway, Ray-Edgar Raymond	30WasA	10-31-07	Ragland, Ala.	10-12-35	L	R	5'7	150	6	19	1	4	2	0	0	1	0	3	0	.211	.316
Treadway, Red-Thadford Leon	44-45NYN	4-28-20	Athalone, N.C.		L	L	5'10	175	138	394	54	105	9	4	4	28	33	24	5	.266	.340
Trechock, Frank-Frank Adam	37WasA	12-24-15	Windber, Pa.		R	R	5'10	175	1	4	0	2	0	0	0	0	0	1	0	.500	.500
Tremark, Nick-Nicholas Joseph	34-36BknN	10-15-12	Yonkers, N.Y.		L	L	5'5	150	35	73	10	18	4	0	0	10	6	5	0	.247	.301
Tremper, Overton-Carlton Overton	27-28BknN	3-22-06	Brooklyn, N.Y.		R	R	5'10	163	36	91	5	20	2	1	0	5	0	3	0	.220	.264
Tresh, Mike-Michael	38-48ChiA 49CleA	2-23-14	Hazelton, Pa.	10- 4-66	R	R	5'11	170	1027	3169	326	788	74	14	2	297	402	263	19	.249	.283
Triplett, Coaker, Herman Coaker	38ChiN 41-43StLN 43-45PhiN	12-18-11	Boone, N.C.		R	R	5'11	185	470	1307	148	334	47	14	27	173	123	114	10	.256	.375
Trosky (Troyavesky), Hal-Harold Arthur Sr.	33-41CleA 42-43IL 44ChiA 45IL 46ChiA	11-11-12	Norway, Iowa		L	R	6'2	207	1347	5161	835	1561	331	58	228	1012	545	440	28	.302	.522
Tucker, Ollie-Oliver Dinwiddie	27WasA 28CleA	1-27-02	Radiant, Va.	7-13-40	L	R	5'11	180	34	71	6	11	2	0	1	10	11	5	0	.155	.225
Turchin, Eddie-Edward Lawrence (Smiley)	43CleA	2-10-17	New York, N.Y.		R	R	5'10	165	11	13	4	3	0	0	0	1	3	1	0	.231	.231
Turgeon, Pete-Eugene Joseph	23ChiN	1- 3-97	Minneapolis, Minn.		R	R	5'6	145	3	6	1	1	0	0	0	0	0	0	0	.167	.167
Turner, Tom-Thomas Richard	40-44ChiA 44StLA 45MS	9-18-16	Custer, Okla.		R	R	6'2	195	233	696	63	165	29	4	7	63	51	84	4	.237	.320
Twombly, Babe-Clarence Edward	20-21ChiN	1-18-96	Jamaica Plain, Mass.		L	R	5'10	165	165	358	47	109	9	2	3	32	28	30	9	.304	.366
Tyack, Jim-James Fred	43PhiA	1- 9-11	Florence, Mont.		L	R	6'2	195	54	155	11	40	8	1	0	23	14	9	1	.258	.323
Tyler (Tylka), Johnnie-John Anthony (Ty Ty)	34-35BosN	7-30-06	Mt. Pleasant, Pa.	7-11-72	L	R	6'	175	16	53	7	17	2	1	2	12	4	6	0	.321	.509
					Bats Both 34																
Tyson, Turkey-Cecil Washington	44PhiN	12- 6-14	Elm City, N.C.		L	R	6'5	225	1	1	0	0	0	0	0	0	0	0	0	.000	.000
Tyson, Ty-Albert Thomas	26-27NYN 28BknN	6- 1-92	Wilkes-Barre, Pa.	8-16-53	R	R	5'11	169	199	704	89	197	34	4	5	73	35	61	14	.280	.361
Uhalt, Frenchy-Bernard Bartholomew	34ChiA	4-27-10	Bakersville, Cal.		L	R	5'10	180	57	165	28	40	5	1	0	16	29	12	6	.242	.285
Uhle, George-George Ernest (Bull) (See P20-45)	19-28CleA 29-33DetA 33NYN 33-34NYA 36CleA	9-18-98	Cleveland, Ohio		R	R	6'	190	722	1360	172	393	60	21	9	187	98	112	6	.289	.384
Uhlir, Charlie-Charles	34ChiA	7-30-12	Chicago, Ill.		L	L	5'7	150	14	27	3	4	0	0	0	3	2	6	0	.148	.148
Ulisney, Mike-Michael Edward (Slugs)	45BosN	9-28-17	Greenwald, Pa.		R	R	5'9	165	11	18	4	7	1	0	1	4	1	0	0	.389	.611
Unser, Al-Albert Bernard	42-44DetA 45CinN	10-12-12	Morrisonville, Ill.		R	R	6'1	175	120	338	41	85	15	4	4	30	32	43	0	.251	.355
Urban, Luke-Louis John 21-24 played in N.F.L.	27-28BosN	3-22-98	Fall River, Mass.		R	R	5'8	168	50	128	11	35	5	0	0	12	3	7	1	.273	.313
Urbanski, Billy-William Michael	31-37BosN	6- 5-03	Staten Island, N.Y.	7-12-73	R	R	5'8	165	763	3046	379	791	123	27	19	207	198	252	24	.260	.337
Ussat, Dutch-William August	25,27CleA	4-11-04	Dayton, Ohio	5-29-59	R	R	6'1	170	5	17	4	3	0	1	0	2	2	1	0	.176	.294
Vache, Tex-Ernest Lewis	25BosA	11-17-95	Santa Monica, Cal.	6-11-53	R	R	6'1	195	110	252	41	79	15	7	3	48	21	33	2	.313	.464
Valdes, Armando-Armando Viera	44WasA	5- 2-22	Cardenas, Cuba		R	R	6'	175	1	1	0	0	0	0	0	0	0	0	0	.000	.000
Van Camp, Al-Albert Joseph	28CleA 31-32BosA	9- 7-03	Moline, Ill.		R	R	5'11	175	140	444	44	116	20	6	0	41	24	42	4	.261	.333
Van Robays, Maurice-Maurice Rene (Bomber)	39-43PitN 44-45MS 46PitN	11-15-14	Detroit, Mich.	3- 1-65	R	R	6'	190	529	1844	232	493	94	27	20	303	139	155	2	.267	.380
Vaughan, Arky-Joseph Floyd	32-41PitN 42-43BknN 44-46VR 47-48BknN	3- 9-12	Clifty, Ark.	8-30-52	L	R	5'10	175	1817	6622	1173	2103	356	128	96	926	937	276	118	.318	.453
Vaughn, Fred-Frederick Thomas (Muscles)	44-45WasA	10-18-18	Coalinga, Cal.	3- 3-64	R	R	5'10	185	110	377	38	91	9	5	2	46	32	72	2	.241	.308
Veltman, Pat-Arthur Patrick	26ChiA 28-29NYN 31BosN 32NYN 34PitN	3-24-06	Mobile, Ala.		R	R	6'	175	23	38	4	5	0	1	0	2	4	3	0	.132	.184
Ventura, Vince-Vincent	45WasA	4-18-17	New York, N.Y.		R	R	6'1	190	18	58	4	12	0	0	0	2	4	4	0	.207	.207
Vergez, Johnny-John Lewis	31-34NYN 35-36PhiN 36StLN	7- 9-06	Oakland, Cal.		R	R	5'8	165	672	2323	258	593	114	16	52	292	171	303	22	.255	.385
Vick, Ernie-Henry Arthur 25,27-28 played in N.F.L.	22,24-26StLN	7- 2-00	Toledo, Ohio		R	R	5'10	185	57	112	12	26	7	1	0	7	9	8	0	.232	.313
Vogel, Otto-Otto Henry	23-24ChiN	10-26-99	Mendota, Ill.	7-19-69	R	R	6'	195	111	253	38	63	11	3	2	30	17	37	6	.249	.340
Vosmik, Joe-Joseph Franklin	30-36CleA 37StLA 38-39BosA 40-41BknN 44WasA	4- 4-10	Cleveland, Ohio	1-27-62	R	R	6'	185	1414	5472	818	1682	335	92	65	874	514	272	23	.307	.438
Voyles, Phil-Philip Vance	29BosN	5-12-00	Murphy, N.C.	11- 3-72	L	R	5'11	175	20	68	9	16	0	2	0	4	6	8	0	.235	.294
Waddey, Frank-Frank Orum	31StLA	8-21-05	Memphis, Tenn.		L	L	5'10	185	14	22	3	6	1	0	0	2	2	3	0	.273	.318
Wade, Rip-Richard Frank	23WasA	1-12-98	Duluth, Minn.	6-16-57	L	R	5'11	174	33	69	8	16	2	2	2	14	5	10	0	.232	.406
Wagner, Hal-Harold Edward	37-44PhiA 44,46-47BosA 45MS 47-48DetA 48-49PhiN	7- 2-15	East Riverton, N.J.		L	R	6'	165	672	1849	179	458	90	12	15	227	253	152	10	.248	.334
Walczak, Ed-Edwin Joseph (Husky)	45PhiN	9-21-15	Arctic, R.I.		R	R	5'11	180	20	57	6	12	3	0	0	2	6	9	0	.211	.263
Walker, Curt-William Curtis	19NYA 20-21NYN 21-24PhiN 24-30CinN	7- 3-96	Beeville, Tex.	12- 9-55	L	R	5'9	170	1359	4858	718	1475	235	117	64	688	535	254	96	.304	.440
Walker, Dixie-Fred (The People's Cherce)	31,33-36NYA 36-37ChiA 38-39DetA 39-47BknN 48-49PitN	9-24-10	Villa Rica, Ga.		L	R	6'1	175	1905	6740	1037	2064	376	96	105	1023	817	325	59	.306	.437
Walker, Frank-Charles Franklin	17-18DetA 20-21PhiA 25NYN	9-22-94	Enoree, S.C.	9-16-74	R	R	5'11	165	139	407	38	87	16	5	3	41	29	66	5	.214	.300
Walker, Gee-Gerald Holmes	31-37DetA 38-39ChiA 40WasA 41CleA 42-45CinN	3-19-08	Gulfport, Miss.		R	R	5'11	188	1784	6771	954	1991	399	76	124	997	330	600	223	.294	.430
Walker, Hub-Harvey Willos	31,35DetA 36-37CinN 42-44MS 45DetA	8-17-06	Gulfport, Miss.		L	R	5'10	175	297	779	117	205	43	6	5	60	104	89	26	.263	.353
Walker, Johnny-John Miles	19-21PhiA	12-11-96	Toulon, Ill.		R	R	6'	175	125	454	41	114	15	5	2	50	9	32	5	.251	.319
Walker, Speed-Joseph Richard	23StLN	1-23-98	Munhall, Pa.	6-20-59	R	R	6'	175	2	7	1	2	0	0	0	0	0	1	0	.286	.286

USE NAME – GIVEN NAMES (NICKNAMES)	TEAM BY YEAR	BIRTH DATE	BIRTH PLACE	DEATH DATE	B	T	HGT	WGT	G	AB	R	H	2B	3B	HR	RBI	BB	SO	SB	BA	SA
									LIFETIME BATTING TOTALS												
Wallen (Walentoski), Norm-Norman Edward	45BosN	2-13-17	Milwaukee, Wis.		R	R	5'11	175	4	15	1	2	0	1	0	1	1	1	0	.133	.267
Walsh, Joe-Joseph Patrick (Tweet)	38BosN	3-13-17	Roxbury, Mass.		R	R	5'10	165	4	8	0	0	0	0	0	0	0	2	0	.000	.000
Walsh, Walt-Walter William	20PhiN	4-30-97	Newark, N.J.	1-15-66	R	R	5'11	170	2	0	0	0	0	0	0	0	0	0	0	–	–
Walters, Bucky-William Henry (See P20-45)	31-32BosN 33-34BosA 34-38PhiN 38-48,M48-49CinN 50BosN	4-19-09	Philadelphia, Pa.		R	R	6'1	180	715	1966	227	477	99	16	23	234	114	303	12	.243	.344
Walters, Fred-Fred James (Whale)	45BosA	9- 4-12	Laurel, Miss.		R	R	6'1	210	40	93	2	16	2	0	0	5	10	9	1	.172	.194
Walters, Roxy-Alfred John	15-18NYA 19-23BosA 24-25CleA	11- 5-92	San Francisco, Cal.	6- 3-56	R	R	5'8	160	498	1426	119	317	41	6	0	115	97	151	13	.222	.259
Wambsganss, Bill-William Adolph	14-23CleA 24-25BosA 26PhiA	3-19-94	Garfield Hts., Ohio		R	R	5'11	175	1492	5241	710	1359	215	59	7	519	490	357	142	.259	.327
Waner, Lloyd-Lloyd James (Little Poison)	27-41PitN 41BosN 41CinN 42PhiN 44BknN 44-45PitN	3-16-06	Harrah, Okla.		L	R	5'9	150	1993	7772	1201	2459	281	118	27	598	420	173	67	.316	.393
Waner, Paul-Paul Glee (Big Poison)	26-40PitN 41BknN 41-42BosN 43-44BknN 44-45NYA	4-16-03	Harrah, Okla.	8-29-65	L	R	5'9	153	2549	9459	1626	3152	603	190	113	1309	1090	376	104	.333	.473
Wanninger, Pee Wee-Paul Louis	25NYA 27BosA 27CinN	12-12-02	Birmingham, Ala.		L	R	5'7	150	163	556	53	130	15	8	1	31	23	43	5	.234	.295
Ward, Aaron-Aaron Lee	17-26NYA 27ChiA 28CleA	8-28-96	Booneville, Ark.	1-30-61	R	R	5'10	160	1059	3611	457	966	158	54	50	446	339	457	37	.268	.383
Warner, Jack-John Ralph	25-28DetA 29-31BknN 33PhiN	8-29-03	Evansville, Ind.		R	R	5'9	165	478	1546	199	387	52	20	1	120	142	137	32	.250	.312
Warnock, Hal-Harold Charles	35StLA	1- 6-12	New York, N.Y.		L	R	6'2	180	6	7	1	2	2	0	0	0	0	3	0	.286	.571
Warren, Bennie-Bennie Louis	39-42PhiN 43-45MS 46-47NYN	3- 2-12	Elk City, Okla.		R	R	6'1	184	377	989	97	217	26	7	33	104	129	177	1	.219	.360
Warstler, Rabbit-Harold Burton	30-33BosA 34-36PhiA 36-40BosN 40ChiN	9-13-03	North Canton, Ohio	5-31-64	R	R	5'7	150	1205	4088	431	935	133	36	11	332	405	414	42	.229	.287
Warwick, Bill-Firman Newton	21PitN 25-26StLN	11-26-97	Philadelphia, Pa.		R	R	6'	180	23	56	8	17	1	2	1	8	5	7	0	.304	.446
Wasdell, Jimmy-James Charles	37-40WasA 40-41BknN 42-43PitN 43-46PhiN 46-47CleA	5-15-14	Cleveland, Ohio		L	L	5'11	185	888	2866	339	782	109	34	29	341	243	165	29	.273	.365
Wasem, Link-Lincoln William	37BosN	1-30-11	Birmingham, Ohio		R	R	5'9	180	2	1	0	0	0	0	0	0	0	0	0	.000	.000
Washington, George-Sloane Vernon	35-36ChiA	6- 7-07	Linden, Tex.		L	R	5'11	190	128	388	46	104	24	3	9	52	11	22	1	.268	.415
Watkins, George-George Archibald (Watty)	30-33StLN 34NYN 35-36PhiN 36BknN	6- 4-00	Palestine, Tex.	6- 1-70	L	R	5'11	170	894	3207	490	925	192	42	73	420	246	382	61	.288	.443
Watson, Johnny-John Thomas	30DetA	1-16-08	Tazewell, Va.	4-29-65	L	R	6'	175	4	12	1	3	2	0	0	3	1	2	0	.250	.417
Watt, Allie-Albert Bailey	20WasA	12-12-99	Philadelphia, Pa.	3-15-68	R	R	5'8	154	1	1	0	1	1	0	0	1	0	0	0	1.000	2.000
Watwood, Johnny-John Clifford	29-32ChiA 32-33BosA 39PhiN	8-17-06	Alexander City, Ala.		L	L	6'1	186	469	1423	192	403	66	16	5	158	134	100	37	.283	.363
Way, Bobby-Robert Clinton	27ChiA	4- 2-06	Emlenton, Pa.	6-20-74	R	R	5'10	168	5	3	3	1	0	0	0	1	0	1	0	.333	.333
Weatherly, Roy-Cyril Roy (Stormy)	36-42CleA 43NYA 44-45MS 46NYA 50NYN	2-25-15	Warren, Tex.		L	R	5'7	170	811	2781	415	794	152	44	43	290	180	170	42	.286	.418
Webb, Earl-William Earl	25NYN 27-28ChiN 30-32BosA 32-33DetA 33ChiA	9-17-98	Bon Air, Tenn.	5-23-65	L	R	6'1	185	650	2161	326	661	155	25	56	333	260	202	8	.306	.478
Webb, Skeeter-James Laverne	32StLN 38-39CleA 40-44ChiA 45-47DetA 48PhiA	11- 4-09	Meridian, Miss.		R	R	5'9	150	699	2274	216	498	73	15	3	166	132	215	33	.219	.268
Weingartner, Elmer-Elmer William (Dutch)	45CleA	8- 3-18	Cleveland, Ohio		R	R	5'11	178	20	39	5	9	1	0	0	1	4	11	0	.231	.256
Weintraub, Phil-Philip (Mickey)	33-35NYN 37CinN 37NYN 38PhiN 44-45NYN	10-12-07	Chicago, Ill.		L	L	6'1	195	444	1382	215	407	67	19	32	207	232	182	4	.295	.440
Weis, Butch-Arthur John	22-25ChiN	3- 2-03	St. Louis, Mo.		L	L	5'11	180	128	341	39	92	14	4	2	50	43	44	6	.270	.352
Welaj, Johnny-John Ludwig	39-41WasA 43PhiA 44-45MS	5-27-14	Moss Creek, Pa.		R	R	6'	164	293	793	115	198	40	3	4	74	53	73	36	.250	.323
Welch, Frank-Frank Tiguer (Bugger)	19-26PhiA 27BosA	8-10-97	Birmingham, Ala.	7-25-57	R	R	5'9	175	738	2310	310	634	100	31	41	295	250	225	18	.274	.398
Welch, Herb-Herbert M. (Dutch)	25BosA	10-19-00	Dyersburg, Tenn.	4-15-67	L	R	5'6	154	13	38	2	11	0	1	0	2	0	6	0	.289	.342
Welch, Milt-Milton Edward	45DetA	7-26-24	Farmersville, Ill.		R	R	5'10	175	1	2	0	0	0	0	0	0	0	1	0	.000	.000
Welsh, Jim-James Daniel	25-27BosN 28-29NYN 29-30BosN	10- 9-02	Denver, Colo.	10-30-70	L	R	6'1	170	715	2684	387	778	127	47	35	288	156	144	37	.290	.411
Wendell, Lew-Louis Charles	15-16NYN 24-26PhiN	3-22-92	New York, N.Y.	7-11-53	R	R	5'11	178	62	100	3	18	2	1	0	10	6	17	0	.180	.220
Wentzel, Stan-Stanley Aaron	45BosN	1- 3-17	Lorain, Pa.		R	R	6'1	200	4	19	3	4	0	1	0	6	0	3	1	.211	.316
Wera, Julie-Julian Valentine	27,29NYA	2- 9-02	Winona, Minn.		R	R	5'8	164	43	54	8	15	3	0	1	10	2	6	0	.278	.389
Werber, Bill-William Murray	30,33NYA 33-36BosA 37-38PhiA 39-41CinN 42NYN	6-20-08	Berwyn, Md.		R	R	5'10	170	1295	5024	875	1363	271	50	78	539	701	363	215	.271	.392
West, Dick-Richard Thomas	38-43CinN 44-45MS	11-24-15	Louisville, Ky.		R	R	6'2	180	119	299	30	66	10	2	3	35	12	42	6	.221	.298
West, Max-Max Edward	38-42BosN 43-45MS 46BosN 46CinN 48PitN	11-28-16	Dexter, Mo.		L	R	6'1	182	824	2676	338	681	136	20	77	380	353	340	19	.254	.407
West, Max-Maxwell Walter	28-29BknN	7-14-04	Sunset, Tex.	4-25-71	R	R	5'11	175	12	29	5	8	2	1	0	2	5	1	0	.276	.414
West, Sammy-Samuel Filmore	27-32WasA 33-38StLA 38-41WasA 42ChiA 43-45MS	10- 5-04	Longview, Tex.		L	L	5'11	165	1753	6148	934	1838	347	101	75	838	696	540	53	.299	.425
Weston, Al-Alfred John	29BosN	12-11-05	Lynn, Mass.		R	R	6'	195	3	3	0	0	0	0	0	0	0	2	0	.000	.000
Wetzel, Dutch-Franklin Burton	20-21StLA	7- 7-93	Columbus, Ind.	3- 5-42	R	R	5'9	177	67	138	21	34	3	1	2	15	13	21	0	.246	.326
Whaley, Bill-William Carl	23StLA	2-10-99	Indianapolis, Ind.	3- 3-43	R	R	5'11	178	23	50	5	12	2	1	0	1	4	2	0	.240	.320
Wheaton, Woody-Elwood Pierce (See P20-45)	43-44PhiA	10- 3-14	Philadelphia, Pa.		L	L	5'8	160	37	89	3	17	4	0	0	7	8	5	1	.191	.236
Wheeler, Ed-Edward Raymond	45CleA	5-24-17	Los Angeles, Cal.		R	R	5'8	160	46	72	12	14	2	0	0	2	8	13	1	.194	.222
Whelan, Tom-Thomas Joseph	20BosN	1- 3-94	Lynn, Mass.	6-26-57	R	R	5'10	180	1	1	0	0	0	0	0	0	1	1	0	.000	.000
White, Bill-William Barney	45BknN	6-25-24	Paris, Tex.		R	R	5'11	190	4	1	2	0	0	0	0	0	1	1	0	.000	.000
White, Jack-John Peter	27-28CinN	8-31-05	New York, N.Y.	6-19-71	B	R	5'7	135	6	7	1	0	0	0	0	0	0	1	0	.000	.000
White, Jo-Jo Joyner Clifford	32-38DetA 43-44PhiA 44CinN M60CleA	6- 1-09	Red Oak, Ga.		L	R	5'11	165	877	2652	456	678	83	42	8	229	384	276	92	.256	.328
Whitehead, Burgess-Burgess Urquhart (Whitey)	33-35StLN 36-37NYN 38IL 39-41NYN 42-45MS 46PitN	6-29-10	Tarboro, N.C.		R	R	5'10	160	924	3316	415	883	100	31	17	245	150	138	51	.266	.331
Whitney, Pinky-Arthur Carter	28-33PhiN 33-36BosN 36-39PhiN	1- 2-05	San Antonio, Tex.		R	R	5'10	165	1539	5765	696	1701	303	56	93	927	400	438	45	.295	.415
Wietelmann, Whitey-William Frederick	39-46BosN 47PitN	3-15-19	Zanesville, Ohio		B	R	6'	170	580	1762	170	409	55	6	7	122	156	131	14	.232	.282
					Bats Right 39-41																
Wilborn, Claude-Claude Edward	40BosN	9- 1-12	Woodsdale, N.C.		L	R	6'1	180	5	7	0	0	0	0	0	0	0	1	0	.000	.000
Wilke, Harry-Henry Joseph	27ChiN	12-14-00	Cincinnati, Ohio		R	R	5'10	171	3	9	0	0	0	0	0	0	0	1	0	.000	.000
Wilkins, Bobby-Robert Linwood	44-45PhiA	8-11-22	Denton, N.C.		R	R	5'9	165	86	179	29	46	6	0	0	7	11	21	2	.257	.291
Williams, Cy-Fred	12-17ChiN 18-30PhiN	12-21-87	Wadena, Ind.	4-23-74	L	R	6'2	180	2002	6780	1024	1981	306	74	251	1005	690	721	115	.292	.470
Williams, Denny-Evon Daniel	21CinN 24-25,28BosA	12-13-99	Portland, Ore.	3-24-29	L	R	5'8	150	119	328	46	85	4	3	0	18	28	19	5	.259	.290
Williams, Dewey-Dewey Edgar (Dee)	44-47ChiN 48CinN	2- 5-16	Durham, N.C.		R	R	6'	160	193	464	48	108	11	4	3	37	46	52	2	.233	.293
Williams, Dib-Edwin Dibrell	30-35PhiA 35BosA	1-19-10	Greenbrier, Ark.		R	R	5'11	175	475	1574	198	421	74	12	29	201	133	140	7	.267	.385
Williams, Earl-Earl Baxter	28BosN	1-27-03	Cumberland Gap, Tenn.	3-10-58	R	R	6'	185	3	2	0	0	0	0	0	0	0	1	0	.000	.000
Williams, Ken-Kenneth Roy	15-16CinN 18-27StLA 28-29BosA	6-28-90	Grant's Pass, Ore.	1-22-59	L	R	6'	170	1397	4860	860	1552	285	77	196	914	566	287	154	.319	.531
Williams, Pap-Fred	45CleA	7-17-13	Meridian, Miss.		R	R	6'1	200	16	19	0	4	0	0	0	0	1	2	0	.211	.211
Williams, Woody-Woodrow Wilson	38BknN 43-45CinN	8-22-12	Pamplin, Va.		R	R	5'11	175	338	1255	133	314	40	5	1	79	88	52	14	.250	.292
Williamson, Howie-Nathaniel Howard	28StLN	12-23-04	Little Rock, Ark.		L	L	6'	170	10	9	0	2	0	0	0	0	1	4	0	.222	.222
Willingham, Hugh-Thomas Hugh	30ChiA 31-33PhiN	5-30-08	Dalhart, Tex.		R	R	6'	180	31	42	7	10	2	1	1	3	4	10	0	.238	.405
Willson, Kid-Frank Hoxie	18,27ChiA	11- 3-95	Bloomington, Neb.	4-17-64	L	R	6'1	190	11	11	3	1	0	0	0	1	1	3	0	.091	.091
Wilson, Charlie-Charles Woodrow (Swamp Baby)	31BosN 32-33,35StLN	1-13-05	Clinton, S.C.	12-19-70	B	R	5'10	178	57	186	15	40	7	3	2	14	8	16	0	.215	.317
Wilson, Eddie-Edward Francis	36-37BknN	9- 7-09	Hamden, Conn.		L	L	5'11	165	88	227	39	72	12	2	4	33	31	39	4	.317	.441
Wilson, Frank-Francis Edward (Squash)	24-26BosN 28CleA 28StLA	4-20-02	Medford, Mass.	11-25-74	L	R	6'	185	168	489	46	120	19	4	1	38	48	44	8	.245	.307
Wilson, Hack-Lewis Robert	23-25NYN 26-31ChiN 32-34BknN 34PhiN	4-26-00	Ellwood City, Pa.	11-23-48	R	R	5'6	190	1348	4760	884	1461	266	67	244	1062	674	713	52	.307	.545
Wilson, Icehouse-George Peacock	34DetA	9-14-12	Maricopa, Cal.	10-13-73	R	R	6'	186	1	1	0	0	0	0	0	0	0	0	0	.000	.000
Wilson, Jimmie-James (Ace)	23-28PhiN 28-33StLN 34-38,M34-38PhiN 39-40CinN M41-44ChiN	7-23-00	Philadelphia, Pa.	5-31-47	R	R	6'1	200	1525	4778	580	1358	252	32	32	621	356	280	86	.284	.370
Wilson, Mike-Samuel Marshall 23-25 played in N.F.L.	21PitN	12- 2-96	Edge Hill, Pa.		R	R	5'10	160	5	4	1	0	0	0	0	0	1	2	0	.000	.000
Windle, Bill-Willis Brewer	28-29PitN	12-13-04	Galena, Kans.		L	L	5'11	170	3	2	1	1	1	0	0	0	0	1	0	.500	1.000
Winegarner, Ralph-Ralph Lee (see P20-45)	30,32,34-36CleA 49StLA	10-29-09	Benton, Kans.		R	R	6'	182	136	185	28	51	7	1	5	28	15	43	1	.276	.405
Wingo, Al-Absalom Holbrook (Red)	19PhiA 24-28DetA	5- 6-98	Norcross, Ga.	10- 9-64	L	R	5'11	180	493	1326	224	409	87	19	9	191	211	119	23	.308	.423
Wingo (LaRiviere), Ed-Edmond Armand	20PhiA	10- 8-95	Ste. Anne, Canada	12- 5-64	R	R	5'5	160	1	4	0	1	0	0	0	1	0	0	0	.250	.250
Winsett, Tom-John Thomas (Long Tom)	30-31,33BosA 35StLN 36-38BknN	11-24-09	McKenzie, Tenn.		L	R	6'2	190	230	566	60	134	25	5	8	76	69	113	3	.237	.341
Wirts, Kettle-Elwood Vernon	21-23ChiN 24ChiA	10-31-97	Consumnes, Cal.	7-12-68	R	R	5'11	170	49	86	9	14	2	0	1	8	16	20	1	.163	.221
Wise, Hughie-Hugh Edward	30DetA	3- 9-06	Campbellsville, Ky.		B	R	6'	178	2	6	0	2	0	0	0	0	0	0	0	.333	.333
Witek, Mickey-Nicholas Joseph	40-43NYN 44-45MS 46-47NYN 49NYA	12-19-15	Luzerne, Pa.		R	R	5'10	170	580	2147	239	595	65	9	22	196	148	84	7	.277	.347
Withrow, Frank-Frank Blaine (Kid)	20,22PhiN	6-14-91	Greenwood, Mo.	9- 5-66	R	R	5'11	187	58	153	11	31	6	1	0	15	11	31	0	.203	.255
Witt (Wittkowski), Whitey (Ladislaw Waldemar)-Lawton Walter	16-17PhiA 18MS 19-21PhiA 22-25NYA 26BknN	9-28-95	Orange, Mass.		L	R	5'7	150	1139	4171	632	1195	144	62	18	302	489	309	78	.287	.364
Woehr, Andy-Andrew Emil	23-24PhiN	2- 4-96	Fort Wayne, Ind.		R	R	5'11	165	63	193	14	47	6	5	0	20	6	9	2	.244	.326
Wolf, Ray-Raymond Bernard	27CinN	7-15-04	Chicago, Ill.		R	R	5'11	175	1	1	0	0	0	0	0	0	0	0	0	.000	.000
Womack, Sid-Sidney Kirk (Tex)	26BosN	10- 2-96	Greensburg, La.	8- 8-58	R	R	5'10	185	1	3	0	0	0	0	0	1	0	0	0	.000	.000
Wood, Doc-Charles Spencer	23PhiA	2-28-00	Batesville, Miss.	11- 3-74	R	R	5'10	150	3	3	0	1	0	0	0	0	0	0	0	.333	.333
Wood, Joe-Joseph Perry	43DetA 44-45MS	10- 3-19	Houston, Tex.		R	R	5'9	160	60	164	22	53	4	4	1	17	6	13	2	.323	.415
Woodall, Larry-Charles Lawrence	20-29DetA	7-26-94	Staunton, Va.	5- 6-63	R	R	5'9	165	548	1317	161	353	50	15	1	160	159	67	16	.268	.331

USE NAME – GIVEN NAMES (NICKNAMES)	TEAM BY YEAR	BIRTH DATE	BIRTH PLACE	DEATH DATE	LIFETIME BATTING TOTALS B	T	HGT	WGT	G	AB	R	H	2B	3B	HR	RBI	BB	SO	SB	BA	SA
Workman, Chuck-Charles Thomas	38,41CleA 43-46BosN 46PitN	1- 6-15	Leeton, Mo.	1- 3-53	L	R	6'	175	526	1749	213	423	57	7	50	230	161	202	24	.242	.368
Worthington, Red-Robert Lee (Bob)	31-34BosN 34StLN	4-24-06	Alhambra, Cal.	12- 8-63	R	R	5'11	170	292	1037	118	298	69	18	12	111	48	71	2	.287	.423
Wright, Ab-Albert Owen 30 played in N.F.L.	35CleA 44BosN	11-16-05	Terlton, Okla.		R	R	6'1	190	138	355	37	88	20	1	9	53	28	48	2	.248	.386
Wright, Al-Albert Edgar (A-1)	33BosN	11-11-12	San Francisco, Cal.		R	R	6'1	170	4	1	0	1	0	0	0	0	0	0	0	1.000	1.000
Wright, Glenn-Forrest Glenn (Buckshot)	24-28PitN 29-33BknN 35ChiA	2- 6-01	Archie, Mo.		R	R	5'11	170	1119	4153	584	1219	203	76	94	723	209	407	38	.294	.447
Wright, Taffy-Taft Shedron	38-39WasA 40-42ChiA 43-45MS 46-48ChiA 49PhiA	8-10-11	Tabor City, N.C.		L	R	5'10	180	1029	3583	465	1115	175	55	38	553	347	155	32	.311	.423
Wrightstone, Russ-Russell Guy	20-28PhiN 28NYN	3-18-93	Bowmansdale, Pa.	2-25-69	L	R	5'10	176	929	2992	427	889	152	34	60	425	215	152	35	.297	.431
Wuestling, Yats-George	29-30DetA 30NYA	10-18-03	St. Louis, Mo.	4-26-70	R	R	5'11	167	83	217	18	41	4	2	0	19	15	41	0	.189	.226
Wyatt, Joe-Loral John	24CleA	4- 6-01	Petersburg, Ind.	12- 5-70	R	R	6'1	175	4	11	1	2	0	0	0	1	2	1	0	.182	.182
Yaryan, Yam-Clarence Everett	21-22ChiA	11 5 92	Knowlton, Iowa	11-16-64	R	R	5'10	180	81	173	20	45	10	2	2	24	15	26	1	.260	.376
York, Rudy-Rudolph Preston	34,37-45DetA 46-47BosA 47ChiA 48PhiA M59BosA	8-17-13	Ragland, Ala.	2- 5-70	R	R	6'1	220	1603	5891	876	1621	291	52	277	1152	791	867	38	.275	.483
York, Tony-Anthony Batton	44ChiN 45MS	11-27-12	Irene, Tex.	4-18-70	R	R	5'10	165	28	85	4	20	1	0	0	7	4	11	0	.235	.247
Yoter, Elmer-Elmer Ellsworth	21PhiA 24CleA 27-28ChiN	6-26-00	Plainfield, Pa.	7-26-66	R	R	5'7	155	36	96	5	24	2	2	0	12	9	13	0	.250	.313
Young, Babe-Norman Robert	36,39-42NYN 43-45MS 46-47NYN 47-48CinN 48StLN	7- 1-15	Queens, N.Y.		L	L	6'2	185	728	2403	320	656	121	17	79	415	274	161	9	.273	.436
Young, Del-Delmer Edward	37-40PhiN	5-11-12	Cleveland, Ohio		B	R	5'11	168	309	950	87	213	31	7	3	76	48	115	7	.224	.281
Young, Pep-Lemuel Floyd	33-40PitN 41CinN 41,45StLN	8-29-07	Jamestown, N.C.	1-14-62	R	R	5'9	162	730	2466	274	645	128	34	32	347	152	312	18	.262	.380
Young, Russ-Russell Charles 25-26 played in N.F.L.	31StLA	9-15-02	Bryan, Ohio		B	R	6'	190	16	34	2	4	0	0	1	2	2	4	0	.118	.206
Youngs, Ross (Royce)-Ross Middlebrook (Pep)	17-26NYN	4-10-97	Shiner, Tex.	10-22-27	L	R	5'8	162	1211	4627	812	1491	236	93	42	592	550	390	153	.322	.441
					Bats Both 17																
Yount, Eddie-Floyd Edwin	37PhiA 39PitN	12-19-16	Newton, N.C.		R	R	6'1	185	6	9	1	2	0	0	0	1	0	3	0	.222	.222
Zak, Frankie-Frank Thomas	44-46PitN	2-22-22	Passaic, N.J.	2- 6-72	R	R	5'10	150	123	208	43	56	5	1	0	14	26	23	6	.269	.303
Zapustas, Joe-Joseph John	33PhiA	7-25-07	Boston, Mass.		R	R	6'1	185	2	5	0	1	0	0	0	0	0	0	0	.200	.200
Zardon, Jose-Jose Antonio [Valdes] (Guineo)	45WasA	5-20-23	Havana, Cuba		R	R	6'	150	54	131	13	38	5	3	0	13	7	11	3	.290	.374
Zimmerman, Roy-Roy Franklin (Dutch)	45NYN 46-49SM	9-13-16	Pine Grove, Pa.		L	L	6'2	187	27	98	14	27	1	0	5	15	5	16	1	.276	.439
Zitzman, Billy-William Arthur	19PitN 19,25-29CinN	11-19-97	Queens, N.Y.		R	R	5'10	175	406	1004	197	268	38	11	3	89	83	85	42	.267	.336

					LIFETIME PITCHING TOTALS																	BATTING TOTALS			
USE NAME – GIVEN NAMES (NICKNAMES)	TEAM BY YEAR	BIRTH DATE	BIRTH PLACE	DEATH DATE	B	T	HGT	WGT	W	L	PCT	SV	G	GS	CG	IP	H	BB	SO	ShO	ERA	AB	H	HR	BA
Abernathy, Tal-Talmadge Lafayette	42-44PhiA	10-30-21	Bynum, N.C.		R	L	6'2	210	0	3	.000	0	7	2	1	20	31	17	13	0	11.07	5	1	0	.200
Abrams, George-George Allen	23CinN	11- 9-97	Seattle, Wash.		R	R	5'9	170	0	0	–	0	3	0	0	5	10	3	1	0	9.00	1	1	0	1.000
Acosta, Jose-Jose (Acostica)	20-21WasA 22ChiA	3- 4-91	San Antonio del Rio Blanco, Cuba		R	R	5'6	134	10	10	.500	4	55	13	6	213	265	68	45	1	4.51	60	9	0	.150
Adams, Ace-Ace Townsend	41-46NYN	3- 2-12	Willows, Cal.		R	R	5'11	182	41	33	.554	49	302	7	2	553	541	224	171	0	3.47	99	12	0	.121
Adams, Bob-Robert Andrew	31-32PhiN	1-20-07	Birmingham, Ala.	3- 6-70	R	R	6'2	165	0	1	.000	0	5	1	0	12	21	3	5	0	5.25	3	0	0	.000
Adams, Bob-Robert Burdette	25BosA	7-24-01	Holyoke, Mass.		R	R	5'11	168	0	0	–	0	2	0	0	6	10	3	1	0	7.50	3	1	0	.333
Adkins, Grady-Grady Emmett (Butcher Boy)	28-29ChiA	6-29-97	Jacksonville, Ark.	3-31-66	R	R	5'11	175	12	27	.308	1	67	42	19	363	401	156	78	0	4.34	116	21	0	.181
Alderson, Dale-Dale Leonard	43-44ChiN 45MS	3- 9-18	Belden, Neb.		R	R	5'10	190	0	1	.000	0	16	3	0	36	52	12	11	0	6.56	7	0	0	.000
Aldridge, Vic-Victor Eddington	17-18,22-24ChiN 25-27PitN 28NYN	10-25-93	Indian Springs, Ind.	4-17-73	R	R	5'10	175	97	80	.548	6	248	205	102	1601	1671	512	526	8	3.76	581	133	2	.229
Allen, Bob-Robert Earl (Thin Man)	37PhiN	7- 2-14	Smithville, Tenn.		R	R	6'1	165	0	1	.000	0	3	1	0	12	18	8	8	0	6.75	3	1	0	.333
Allen, Johnny-John Thomas	32-35NYA 36-40CleA 41StLA 41-43BknN 43-44NYN	9-30-04	Lenoir, N.C.	3-29-59	R	R	6'	180	142	75	.654	18	352	241	109	1950	1849	738	1070	17	3.75	716	124	4	.173
Alten, Ernie-Ernest Matthias (Lefty)	20DetA	12- 1-94	Avon, Ohio		R	L	6'	175	0	1	.000	0	14	1	0	23	40	9	4	0	9.00	3	0	0	.000
Anderson, Bill-William Edward (Lefty)	25BosN	12- 3-95	Boston, Mass.		R	L	6'1	165	0	0	–	0	2	0	0	3	5	2	1	0	9.00	1	0	0	.000
Anderson, Red-Arnold Revola	37,40-41WasA 42MS	6-19-12	Lawton, Iowa	8- 7-72	R	R	6'3	210	5	8	.385	0	36	9	3	137	150	69	40	0	4.35	39	11	0	.282
Andrews, Elbert-Elbert Devore	25PhiA	12-11-01	Greenwood, S.C.		L	R	6'	175	0	0	–	0	6	0	0	8	12	11	0	0	10.13	0	0	0	–
Andrews, Ivy-Ivy Paul (Poison)	31-32NYA 32-33BosA 34-36StLA 37CleA 37-38NYA	5- 6-07	Dora, Ala.	11-24-70	R	R	6'3	210	50	59	.459	8	249	108	43	1041	1151	342	257	2	4.14	319	59	0	.185
Andrews, Nate-Nathan Hardy	37,39StLA 40-41CleA 43-45BosN 46CinN 46NYN	9-30-13	Pembroke, N.C.		R	R	6'	195	41	54	.432	5	127	98	51	773	798	236	216	5	3.46	240	35	0	.146
Appleton, Pete-Peter William	27-28CinN 30-32CleA 32BosA 33NYA 36-39WasA 40-42ChiA 42,45StLA 43-44MS 45WasA	5-20-04 (Played as Pete Jablonowski 27-33)	Terryville, Conn.	1-18-74	R	R	5'11	180	57	66	.463	26	341	71	34	1141	1187	486	420	6	4.30	374	87	0	.233
Archer, Fred-Frederick Marvin (Lefty)	36-37PhiA	3- 7-10	Johnson City, Tenn.		L	L	6'	193	2	3	.400	0	7	5	2	40	45	15	11	0	6.35	15	4	0	.267
Armbrust, Orville-Orville Martin	34WasA	3- 3-10	Beirne, Ark.	10- 2-67	R	R	5'10	195	1	0	1.000	0	3	2	0	13	10	3	3	0	2.08	4	0	0	.000
Arntzen, Orie-Orie Edgar (Old Folks)	43PhiA	10-18-09	Beverly, Ill.	1-28-70	R	R	6'1	200	4	13	.235	0	32	20	0	164	172	69	66	0	4.23	50	8	0	.160
Ash, Ken-Kenneth Lowther	28-30CinN	9-16-01	Anmoore, W.Va.		R	R	5'11	165	6	8	.429	2	55	13	5	161	178	59	47	0	4.96	46	6	0	.130
Auker, Eldon LeRoy (Big Six)	33-38DetA 39BosA 40-42StLA	9-21-10	Norcatur, Kans.		R	R	6'2	194	130	101	.563	2	333	261	126	1963	2230	706	594	14	4.42	700	131	6	.187
Babich, Johnny-John Charles	34-35BknN 36BosN 40-41PhiA	5-14-13	Albion, Cal.		R	R	6'1	180	30	45	.400	1	112	87	34	592	657	220	231	3	4.93	211	36	0	.171
Baecht, Ed-Edward Joseph	26-28PhiN 31-32ChiN 37StLA	5-15-07	Baden, Okla.	8-15-57	R	R	6'2	195	5	6	.455	0	64	9	3	160	200	78	61	0	5.56	42	8	0	.190
Bagby, Jim-James Charles Jacob Jr.	38-40BosA 41-45CleA 46BosA 47PitN	9-18-16	Cleveland, Ohio		R	R	6'2	170	97	96	.503	9	303	198	84	1666	1815	608	431	13	3.96	619	140	3	.226
Bailey, Sweetbreads-Abraham Lincoln	19-21ChiN 21BknN	2-12-95	Joliet, Ill.	9-27-39	R	R	6'	184	4	7	.364	0	52	6	0	137	154	40	35	0	4.59	30	8	0	.267
Bain, Loren-Herbert Loren	45NYN	7- 4-22	Staples, Minn.		R	R	6'	190	0	0	–	0	3	0	0	8	10	4	1	0	7.88	3	1	0	.333
Baker, Al-Albert Jones	38BosA	2-28-06	Batesville, Miss.		R	R	5'11	170	0	0	–	0	3	0	0	8	13	2	2	0	9.00	4	0	0	.000
Baker, Neal-Neal Vernon	27PhiA	4-30-04	La Porte, Tex.		R	R	6'1	175	0	0	–	0	5	2	0	17	27	7	3	0	5.82	6	1	0	.167
Baker, Tom-Thomas Calvin (Rattlesnake)	35-37BknN 37-38NYN	6-11-13	Nursery, Tex.		R	R	6'1	180	3	9	.250	2	68	9	3	173	195	92	58	0	4.73	58	18	0	.310
Balas (Balaski), Mike-Mitchell Francis	38BosN	5-17-10	Lowell, Mass.		R	R	6'	195	0	0	–	0	1	0	0	1	3	0	0	0	9.00	0	0	0	–
Baldwin, Harry-Howard Edward	24-25NYN	6- 3-00	Baltimore, Md.	1-23-58	R	R	5'11	160	3	1	.750	0	11	2	1	35	45	12	5	0	4.37	11	4	0	.364
Ballou, Win-Noble Winfield (Old Pard)	25WasA 26-27StLA 29BknN	11-30-97	Mount Morgan, Ky.	1-30-63	R	R	5'10	170	19	20	.487	2	99	26	10	330	398	168	109	0	5.10	93	5	1	.054
Barfoot, Clyde-Clyde Raymond	22-23StLN 26DetA	7- 8-91	Richmond, Va.	3-11-71	R	R	6'	170	8	10	.444	5	86	5	2	250	293	66	49	1	4.10	76	20	0	.263
Barnabe, Charlie-Charles Edward	27-28ChiA	6-12-00	Russell Gulch, Colo.		L	L	5'11	164	0	7	.000	0	24	7	1	71	103	20	8	0	5.48	27	7	1	.259
Barnes, Bob-Robert Avery (Lefty)	24ChiA	1- 6-02	Washburn, Ill.		L	L	5'11	150	0	0	–	0	2	0	0	5	14	0	1	0	19.80	2	0	0	.000
Barnes, Frank-Frank Samuel (Lefty)	29DetA 30NYA	1- 9-00	Dallas, Tex.	9-27-67	L	L	6'3	195	0	2	.000	0	6	3	0	17	23	16	2	0	7.79	7	2	0	.286
Barnes, Jesse-Jesse Lawrence (Nubby)	15-17BosN 18-22NYN 23-25BosN 26-27BknN	8-26-92	Perkins, Okla.	9- 9-61	L	R	6'	170	153	149	.507	13	422	314	180	2570	2686	515	653	26	3.22	913	195	1	.214
Barnes, Junie-Junie Shoaf (Lefty)	34CinN	12- 1-11	Linwood, N.C.	12-31-63	L	L	6'	170	0	0	–	0	2	0	0	.1	0	1	0	0	0.00	0	0	0	–
Barnes, Virgil-Virgil Jennings (Zeke)	19-20,22-28NYN 28BosN	3- 5-97	Ontario, Kans.	7-24-58	R	R	6'	165	61	59	.508	11	205	135	58	1094	1192	293	275	7	3.66	371	40	0	.108
Barnhart, Ed-Edgar Vernon	24StLA	9-16-04	Providence, Mo.		L	R	5'10	160	0	0	–	0	1	0	0	1	0	2	0	0	0.00	0	0	0	–
Barnhart, Les-Leslie Earl (Barney)	28,30CleA	2-23-05	Hoxie, Kans.	10-11-71	R	R	6'	180	1	1	.500	0	3	2	0	17	25	8	2	0	6.75	5	1	0	.200
Barnicle, George-George Bernard	39-41BosN	8-26-17	Fitchburg, Mass.		R	R	6'2	175	3	3	.500	0	20	4	1	58	49	43	28	0	6.55	18	0	0	.000
Barr, Bob-Robert Alexander	35BknN	3-12-08	Newton, Mass.		R	R	6'	175	0	0	–	0	2	0	0	2	5	2	0	0	4.50	0	0	0	–
Barrett, Dick-Tracey Souter (Kewpie) (Played as Dick Oliver 33-34)	33PhiA 34BosN 43ChiN 43-45PhiN	9-28-06	Montoursville, Pa.	10-30-66	R	R	5'9	175	35	58	.376	2	141	91	32	729	752	320	271	3	4.30	222	40	0	.180
Barrett, Frank-Francis Joseph	39StLN 44-45BosA 46BosN 50PitN	7- 1-13	Ft. Lauderdale, Fla.		R	R	6'2	173	15	17	.469	12	104	2	0	218	211	90	90	0	3.51	54	9	0	.167
Barrett, Red-Charles Henry	37-40CinN 43-45BosN 45-46StLN 47-49BosN	2-14-15	Santa Barbara, Cal.		R	R	5'11	183	69	69	.500	7	253	149	67	1263	1292	312	333	11	3.53	398	54	0	.136
Barthelson, Bob-Robert Edward	44NYN	7-15-24	New Haven, Conn.		R	R	6'	185	1	1	.500	0	7	1	0	10	13	5	4	0	4.50	0	0	0	–
Bartholomew, Les-Lester Justin	28PitN 32ChiA	4- 4-03	Madison, Wis.	9-19-72	R	L	6'	195	0	0	–	0	9	0	0	28	36	15	7	0	6.75	8	1	0	.125
Bass, Dick-Richard William	39WasA	7- 7-06	Rogersville, Tenn.		R	R	6'2	175	0	1	.000	0	1	1	0	8	7	6	1	0	6.75	2	0	0	.000
Batchelder, Joe-Joseph Edmund (Win)	23-25BosN	7-11-98	Wenham, Mass.		R	L	5'7	165	1	0	1.000	0	11	1	1	21	26	4	6	0	5.66	3	0	0	.000
Bauers, Russ-Russell Lee	36-41PitN 44-45MS 46ChiN 50StLA	5-10-14	Townsend, Wis.		L	R	6'3	195	31	30	.508	6	129	71	27	599	562	271	300	5	3.53	207	50	0	.242
Baumgartner, Harry-Harry E	20DetA	10- 8-92	S. Pittsburg, Tenn.	12- 3-30	R	R	5'11	175	0	1	.000	0	9	0	0	18	18	6	7	0	4.00	4	1	0	.250
Baumgartner, Stan-Stanwood Fulton	14-16,21-22PhiN 17-20VR 24-26PhiA	12-14-92	Houston, Tex.	10- 4-55	L	L	6'1	185	27	21	.563	7	143	40	18	506	553	185	129	3	3.70	158	30	0	.190
Bayne, Bill-William Lear (Beverly)	19-24StLA 28CleA 29-30BosA	4-18-99	Pittsburgh, Pa.		L	L	5'9	160	31	32	.492	8	198	55	22	661	710	296	259	2	4.82	214	62	1	.290
Beall, Walter-Walter Esau	24-27NYA 29WasA	7-29-99	Washington, D.C.	1-28-59	R	R	5'10	178	5	5	.500	1	36	12	1	124	110	111	85	0	4.43	35	4	0	.114
Bean, Belve-Beveric Benton (Bill)	30-31,33-35CleA 35WasA	4-23-05	Mullin, Tex.		R	R	6'2	197	11	7	.611	2	86	8	2	235	288	96	89	0	5.32	72	19	1	.264
Beazley, Johnny-John Andrew	41-42,46StLN 43-45MS 47-49BosN	5-25-18	Nashville, Tenn.		R	R	6'2	190	31	12	.721	3	76	46	21	374	349	157	147	3	3.01	120	18	0	.150
Beck, Boom-Boom-Walter William	24,27-28StLA 33-34BknN 39-43PhiN 44DetA 45CinN 45PitN	10-16-04	Decatur, Ill.		R	R	6'2	200	38	69	.355	6	265	101	44	1034	1121	342	352	3	4.30	327	61	0	.187
Beckman, Jim-James Joseph	27-28CinN	3- 1-05	Cincinnati, Ohio		R	R	5'10	172	0	2	.000	0	10	1	0	28	37	15	4	0	5.86	4	0	0	.000
Beckmann, Bill-William Aloys	39-42PhiA 42StLN	12- 8-07	Clayton, Mo.		R	R	6'	175	21	25	.457	2	90	44	17	440	499	119	108	4	4.79	143	32	0	.224
Bedgood, Phil-Phillip Burlette	22-23CleA	3- 8-99	Harrison, Ga.	5- 8-27	R	R	6'3	218	1	2	.333	0	10	3	1	28	23	18	12	0	4.88	6	1	0	.167
Bednar, Andy-Andrew Jackson	30-31PitN	8-16-08	Streator, Ill.	11-25-37	R	R	5'11	180	0	0	–	0	5	0	0	5	14	1	3	0	15.19	0	0	0	–
Beggs, Joe-Joseph Stanley	38NYA 40-44,46-47CinN 45MS 47-48NYN	11- 4-10	Rankin, Pa.		R	R	6'1	182	48	35	.578	29	238	41	23	694	687	189	178	4	2.96	198	33	0	.167
Behan, Petie-Charles Frederick	21-23PhiN	12-11-87	Dallas City, Pa.	1-22-57	R	R	5'10	160	7	15	.318	2	40	24	9	189	248	72	43	1	4.76	67	13	0	.194
Bill, Hi-Herman S	24,26-27,29-30StLN 32-34NYN	7-16-97	Mt. Sherman, Ky.	6- 7-49	R	R	6'	185	32	34	.485	24	221	48	14	663	743	143	191	1	3.69	178	17	0	.096
Benge, Ray-Raymond Adelphia (Silent Cal)	25-26CleA 28-32PhiN 33-35BknN 36BosN 36PhiN 38CinN	4-22-02	Jacksonville, Tex.		R	R	5'9	160	101	130	.437	19	346	248	102	1875	2177	598	655	12	4.52	659	124	1	.188
Bennett, Bugs-Joseph Harley (Played as Bugs Morris 21)	18,21StLA 21ChiA	4-19-92	Kansas City, Mo.	11-21-57	R	R	5'9	163	0	5	.000	0	10	5	1	34	42	29	5	0	6.68	11	4	0	.364
Bennett, Frank-Francis Allen (Chip)	27-28BosA	10-27-04	Mardela Spr's., Md.	3-18-66	R	R	5'10	163	0	1	.000	0	5	1	0	13	16	6	1	0	2.70	3	0	0	.000
Benson, Allen-Allen Wilbert (Bullet Ben)	34WasA	3-28-08	Hurley, S.D.		R	R	6'1	185	0	1	.000	0	2	2	0	10	19	5	4	0	11.70	3	0	0	.000
Bentley, Jack-John Needles	13-16WasA 23-25NYN 26PhiN 26-27NYN	3- 8-95	Sandy Spring, Md.	10-24-69	L	L	6'	200	46	34	.575	9	138	90	39	714	761	263	259	4	4.01	(See B20-45)			
Benton, Al-John Alton	34-35PhiA 38-42,45-48DetA 43-44MS 49-50CleA 52BosA	3-18-11	Noble, Okla.	4-14-68	R	R	6'5	220	98	88	.527	66	455	167	58	1689	1672	733	697	10	3.66	512	50	0	.098
Benton, Larry-Lawrence James	23-27,35BosN 27-30NYN 30-34CinN	11-20-97	St. Louis, Mo.	4- 3-53	R	R	5'11	165	127	128	.498	22	455	258	123	2297	2559	691	670	13	4.03	738	122	2	.165
Benton, Sid-Sidney Wright	22StLN	8- 4-95	Buckner, Ark.		R	R	6'1	170	0	0	–	0	1	0	0	0	0	2	0	0	0.00	0	0	0	–
Berly, Jack-John Chambers	24StLN 31NYN 32-33PhiN	5-24-03	Natchitoches, La.		R	R	6'	190	10	13	.435	2	65	18	6	215	245	98	66	2	5.02	60	10	0	.167
Berry, Joe-Jonas Arthur (Jittery Joe)	42ChiN 44-46PhiA 46CleA	12-16-04	Huntsville, Ark.	9-27-58	R	R	5'10	145	21	22	.488	18	133	0	0	294	246	87	117	0	2.45	70	11	0	.157
Bertrand, Lefty-Roman Mathias	36PhiN	2-28-09	Cobden, Minn.		R	L	6'	180	0	0	–	0	1	0	0	2	3	2	1	0	9.00	0	0	0	–
Besse, Herman A.-Herman (Long Herm)	40-43,46PhiA 44-45MS	8-16-11	St. Louis, Mo.	8-13-72	L	L	6'2	190	5	15	.250	2	65	25	5	243	298	128	118	0	6.97	90	18	0	.200
Betts, Huck-Walter Martin	20-25PhiN 32-35BosN	2-18-97	Millsboro, Del.		L	R	5'11	170	61	68	.473	16	307	125	53	1366	1581	321	323	8	3.93	437	86	0	.197
Bevil (Bevilacqua), Lou-Louis Eugene	42WasA 43-45MS	11-27-22	Nelson, Ill.	2- 1-73	B	R	6'	190	0	1	.000	0	4	1	0	10	9	11	2	0	6.30	3	0	0	.000
Biemiller, Harry-Harry Lee	20WasA 25CinN	10- 9-97	Baltimore, Md.	5-25-65	R	R	6'1	171	1	1	.500	2	28	3	1	64	66	34	19	0	4.22	13	0	0	.000
Bigbee, Lyle-Lyle Randolph (Al)	20PhiA 21PitN	8-22-93	Sweet Home, Ore.	8- 5-42	L	R	6'	180	0	3	.000	0	17	0	0	53	70	29	13	0	6.96	72	13	1	.181
Biggs, Charlie-Charles Orval	32ChiA	9-15-06	French Lick, Ind.	5-24-54	R	R	6'1	185	1	1	.500	0	6	4	0	25	32	12	1	0	6.84	9	1	0	.111
Bildilli, Emil-Emil (Hill Billy)	37-41StLA	9-16-12	Diamond, Ind.	9-16-46	R	L	5'10	170	4	8	.333	1	41	17	7	148	184	75	55	0	5.84	45	8	0	.178
Billings, Haskell-Haskell Clark	27-29DetA	9-27-07	New York, N.Y.		R	R	5'11	180	10	15	.400	0	39	25	8	197	209	107	67	1	5.03	68	17	0	.250
Bird, Red-James Edward	21WasA	4-25-90	Stephenville, Tex.	3-23-72	L	L	5'11	170	0	0	–	0	1	0	0	5	5	1	2	0	5.40	1	0	0	.000
Birkofer, Ralph-Ralph Joseph (Lefty)	33-36PitN 37BknN	11- 5-08	Cincinnati, Ohio	3-16-71	L	L	5'11	213	31	28	.525	2	132	64	24	544	618	175	224	2	4.19	207	50	0	.242

USE NAME – GIVEN NAMES (NICKNAMES)	TEAM BY YEAR	BIRTH DATE	BIRTH PLACE	DEATH DATE	LIFETIME PITCHING TOTALS																	BATTING TOTALS			
					B	T	HGT	WGT	W	L	PCT	SV	G	GS	CG	IP	H	BB	SO	ShO	ERA	AB	H	HR	BA
Bishop, Bill-William Henry (Lefty)	21PhiA	10-22-00	Houtzdale, Pa.	2-14-56	L	L	5'9	185	0	0	–	0	2	0	0	7	8	10	4	0	9.00	3	0	0	.000
Bishop, Jim-James Morton	23-24PhiN	1-28-98	Montgomery City, Mo.	9-17-73	R	R	6'	185	0	4	.000	1	22	1	0	50	72	18	8	0	6.30	15	1	0	.067
Bithorn, Hi-Hiram Gabriel	42-43ChiN 44-45MS 46ChiN 47ChiA	3-18-16	Santurce, P.R.	1- 1-52	R	R	6'1	200	34	31	.523	5	105	53	30	510	516	171	185	8	3.16	177	28	0	.158
Bivin, Jim-James Nathaniel	35PhiN	12-11-09	Jackson, Miss.		R	R	6'	155	2	9	.182	1	47	14	0	162	220	65	54	0	5.78	48	7	0	.146
Black, Don-Donald Paul	43-45PhiA 46-48CleA	7-20-16	Salix, Iowa	4-21-59	R	R	6'	185	34	55	.382	1	154	113	37	797	803	400	293	4	4.35	256	47	0	.184
Blackburne, Lena-Russell Aubrey (Slats)	29,M28-29ChiA	10-23-86	Clifton Hts., Pa.	2-29-68	R	R	5'11	160	0	0	–	0	1	0	0	.1	1	0	0	0	0.00	(See B01-19)			
Blaeholder, George-George Franklin	27,27-35StLA 35PhiA 36CleA	1-26-04	Orange, Cal.	12-29-47	R	R	5'11	175	104	125	.454	12	338	251	106	1913	2220	535	572	13	4.54	626	89	3	.142
Blake, Sheriff-John Frederick	20PitN 24-31ChiN 31PhiN 37StLA	9-17-99	Ansted, W.Va.		L	R	6'	180	87	102	.460	8	304	196	81	1619	1766	767	621	11	4.14	558	118	0	.211
	37StLN				Bats Right 20,25-27																				
Blanche (Belangio), Al-Prosper Albert	35-36BosN	9-21-09	Somerville, Mass.		R	R	6'	178	0	1	.000	1	17	0	0	33	34	13	8	0	3.82	10	2	0	.200
Blankenship, Homer-Homer (Si)	22-23ChiA 28PitN	8- 4-02	Bonham, Tex.	6-22-74	R	R	6'	185	1	3	.250	1	13	2	1	40	57	15	10	0	5.18	12	3	0	.250
Blankenship, Ted-Theodore	22-30ChiA	5-10-01	Bonham, Tex.	1-14-45	R	R	6'1	170	77	79	.494	4	241	156	73	1321	1462	489	378	8	4.32	475	93	9	.196
Blanton, Cy-Darrell Elijah	34-39PitN 40-42PhiN	7- 6-08	Waurika, Okla.	9-13-45	L	R	5'11	180	68	71	.489	4	202	167	75	1219	1243	337	611	14	3.55	428	66	0	.154
Blethen, Clarence-Clarence Waldo (Climax)	23BosA 29BknN	7-11-93	Dover-Foxcroft, Me.	4-11-73	L	R	5'11	165	0	0	–	0	7	0	0	20	33	10	2	0	7.20	6	0	0	.000
Blume, Clint-Clinton Willis	22-23NYN	10-17-98	Brooklyn, N.Y.	6-12-73	R	R	5'11	175	3	0	1.000	0	13	2	1	33	29	21	4	0	3.00	7	1	0	.143
Boerner, Larry-Lawrence Hyer	32BosA	1-21-05	Staunton, Va.	10-16-69	R	R	6'4	175	0	4	.000	0	21	5	0	61	71	37	19	0	5.02	17	0	0	.000
Bogart, John-John Renzie (Big John)	20DetA	9-21-00	Bloomsburg, Pa.		R	R	6'2	195	2	1	.667	0	4	3	0	24	16	18	5	0	3.00	8	2	0	.250
Boggs, Ray-Raymond Joseph (Lefty)	28BosN	12-12-04	Reamsville, Kans.		L	L	6'	170	0	0	–	0	4	0	0	5	2	7	0	0	5.40	0	0	0	–
Bokina, Joe-Joseph	36WasA	4- 4-10	Northampton, Mass.		R	R	6'	184	0	2	.000	0	5	1	0	8	15	6	5	0	9.00	1	0	0	.000
Bolen, Stew-Stewart O'Neal	26-27StLA 31-32PhiN	10-12-02	Jackson, Ala.	8-30-69	L	L	5'11	180	3	13	.188	0	41	17	3	140	170	84	72	0	6.04	46	9	0	.196
Bonetti, Julio-Julio G.	37-38StLA 40ChiN	7-14-11	Genoa, Italy	6-18-52	R	R	6'	180	6	14	.300	1	46	16	7	172	234	77	50	0	6.07	55	7	0	.127
Boney, Hank-Henry Tate	27NYN	10-28-03	Wallace, N.C.		L	R	5'11	176	0	0	–	0	3	0	0	4	4	2	0	0	2.25	0	0	0	–
Bonham, Ernie-Ernest Edward (Tiny)	40-46NYA 47-49PitN	8-16-13	Ione, Cal.	9-15-49	R	R	6'2	215	103	72	.589	9	231	193	110	1553	1501	287	478	21	3.06	522	84	0	.161
Bonness, Bill-William John (Lefty)	44CleA	12-15-23	Cleveland, Ohio		R	L	6'4	200	0	1	.000	0	2	1	0	7	11	5	1	0	7.71	3	0	0	.000
Bono, Gus-Adlai Wendell	20WasA	8-29-94	Doe Run, Mo.	12- 3-48	R	R	5'11	175	0	2	.000	0	4	1	0	12	17	6	4	0	9.00	3	0	0	.000
Boone, Danny-James Albert	19PhiA 21DetA 22-23CleA	1-19-95	Samantha, Ala.	5-11-68	R	R	6'2	190	8	13	.381	1	42	16	6	162	205	62	25	2	5.11	50	9	0	.180
Borowy, Hank-Henry Ludwig	42-45NYA 45-48ChiN 49-50PhiN 50PitN	5-12-16	Bloomfield, N.J.		R	R	6'	175	108	82	.568	7	314	214	94	1715	1660	623	690	17	3.50	571	99	0	.173
	50-51DetA																								
Bosser, Mel-Melvin Edward	45CinN	2- 8-20	Johnstown, Pa.		R	R	6'	173	2	0	1.000	0	7	2	0	16	9	17	3	0	3.38	4	0	0	.000
Bowers, Stew-Stewart Cole (Doc)	35-37BosA	2-26-15	New Freedom, Pa.		B	R	6'	170	2	1	.667	0	15	2	1	30	36	19	5	0	4.50	5	1	0	.200
Bowler, Grant-Grant Tierney (Moose)	31-32ChiA	10-24-07	Denver, Colo.	6-25-68	R	R	6'	190	0	1	.000	0	17	3	1	41	55	27	17	0	7.02	12	1	0	.083
Bowles, Charlie-Charles James	43PhiA 44MS 45PhiA	3-15-17	Norwood, Mass.		R	R	6'3	180	1	4	.200	0	10	6	3	51	52	27	17	0	4.41	29	6	0	.207
Bowles, Emmett-Emmett Jerome (Chief)	22ChiA	8- 2-98	Wanette, Okla.	9- 3-59	R	R	6'	180	0	0	–	0	1	0	0	1	2	1	0	0	27.00	0	0	0	–
Bowman, Bob-Robert James	39-40StLN 41NYN 42ChiN	10- 3-10	Keystone, W. Va.	9- 4-72	R	R	5'10	160	26	17	.605	10	109	38	13	364	360	139	146	2	3.83	101	7	1	.069
Bowman, Joe-Joseph Emil	32PhiA 34NYN 35-36PhiN 37-41PitN	6-17-10	Argentine, Kans.		L	R	6'2	190	77	96	.445	11	298	184	74	1465	1656	484	502	5	4.40	(See B20-45)			
	44-45BosA 45CinN																								
Boyles, Harry-Harry (Stretch)	38-39ChiA	11-29-11	Granite City, Ill.		R	R	6'5	185	0	4	.000	1	11	2	1	32	35	31	19	0	5.91	9	1	0	.111
Bradley, Herb-Herbert Theodore	27-29BosA	1- 3-03	Agenda, Kans.	10-16-59	R	R	6'	170	1	4	.200	0	24	7	3	74	87	25	20	1	5.96	21	5	0	.238
Bradshaw, Joe-Joe Siah	29BknN	8-17-97	Roellen, Tenn.		R	R	6'4	200	0	0	–	0	2	0	0	4	3	4	1	0	4.50	0	0	0	–
Brady, Neal-Cornelius Joseph	15,17NYA 18MS 25CinN	3- 4-97	Covington, Ky.	6-19-47	R	R	6'	197	2	3	.400	1	24	5	2	82	88	32	22	0	4.17	31	7	0	.226
Brame, Erv-Ervin Beckham	28-32PitN	10-12-01	Big Rock, Tenn.	11-22-49	L	R	6'2	190	52	37	.584	1	142	92	62	793	946	232	188	3	4.76	396	121	8	.306
Branch, Norm-Norman Downs (Red)	41-42NYA 43-45MS	3-22-15	Spokane, Wash.		R	R	6'3	200	5	2	.714	4	37	0	0	63	55	42	41	0	3.71	13	1	0	.077
Brandt, Bill-William George	41-43PitN 44-45MS	3-21-15	Aurora, Ind.	5-16-68	R	R	5'8	170	5	3	.625	0	34	7	1	80	85	27	21	0	3.60	15	2	0	.133
Brandt, Ed-Edward Arthur	28-35BosN 36BknN 37-38PitN	2-17-05	Spokane, Wash.	11- 1-44	L	L	6'1	190	121	146	.453	17	378	278	150	2268	2342	778	877	18	3.86	793	187	0	.236
Braxton, Garland-Edgar Garland	21-22BosN 25-26NYA 27-30WasA	6-10-00	Snow Camp, N.C.	2-25-66	L	L	5'11	152	50	53	.485	32	283	70	28	938	1014	276	412	2	4.13	257	40	0	.156
	30-31ChiA 31,33StLA				Bats Both 25-26,33–Bats Right 21-22																				
Breckinridge, Bill-William Robertson	29PhiA	10-27-05	Tulsa, Okla.	8-23-58	R	R	5'11	175	0	0	–	0	3	1	0	10	10	16	2	0	8.10	4	0	0	.000
Brennan, Don-James Donald	33NYA 34-37CinN 37NYN	12- 2-03	Augusta, Me.	4-26-53	R	R	6'	210	21	12	.636	19	141	26	7	396	436	180	172	1	4.20	110	17	0	.155
Brenton, Lynn-Lynn Davis (Buck, Herb)	13,15CleA 20-21CinN	10- 7-90	Peoria, Ill.	10-14-68	R	R	5'10	165	5	12	.294	2	34	15	4	131	161	41	52	1	3.98	40	6	0	.150
Brett, Herb-Herbert James (Duke)	24-25ChiN	5-23-00	Lawrenceville, Va.	11-25-74	R	R	6'	175	1	1	.500	0	11	2	0	22	18	10	7	0	4.09	3	0	0	.000
Breuer, Marv-Marvin Howard (Baby Face)	39-43NYA	4-29-14	Rolla, Mo.		R	R	6'2	185	25	26	.490	3	86	60	23	484	487	154	226	1	4.04	157	10	0	.064
Brewer, Jack-John Herndon (Buddy)	44-46NYN	7-21-19	Los Angeles, Cal.		R	R	6'2	170	9	10	.474	0	43	28	10	217	231	76	73	0	4.35	75	14	0	.187
Bridges, Tommy-Thomas Jefferson Davis	30-43DetA 44MS 45-46DetA	12-28-06	Gordonville, Tenn.	4-19-68	R	R	5'10	155	194	138	.584	10	424	362	200	2827	2675	1192	1674	32	3.57	1003	181	0	.180
Brillheart, Jim-James Benson (Buck)	22-23WasA 27ChiN 31BosA	9-28-03	Dublin, Va.	9- 2-72	R	L	5'11	170	8	9	.471	1	86	23	7	287	314	137	98	0	4.17	86	6	1	.070
Broaca, Johnny-John Joseph	34-37NYA 39CleA	10- 3-09	Lawrence, Mass.		R	R	5'11	190	44	29	.603	3	121	86	42	674	748	255	258	4	4.09	254	23	0	.091
Brondell, Ken-Kenneth LeRoy	44NYN	10-17-21	Bradshaw, Neb.		R	R	6'1	195	0	1	.000	0	7	2	1	19	27	8	1	0	8.53	4	0	0	.000
Brown, Bob-Robert Murray	30-36BosN	4- 1-11	Ashmont, Mass.		R	R	6'	190	16	21	.432	1	79	49	13	363	360	193	159	2	4.49	115	21	0	.183
Brown, Clint-Clinton Harold	28-35CleA 36-40ChiA 41-42CleA	7- 8-03	Blackash, Pa.	12-31-55	L	R	6'1	190	89	93	.489	64	434	130	62	1485	1740	368	410	6	4.27	457	91	2	.199
Brown, Joe-Joseph Henry	27ChiA	7- 3-00	Little Rock, Ark.		R	R	6'	176	0	0	–	0	1	0	0	0	2	1	0	0	∞	0	0	0	–
Brown, Jumbo-Walter George	25ChiN 27-28CleA 32-33,35-36NYA	4-30-07	Greene, R.I.	10- 2-66	R	R	6'4	295	33	31	.516	29	249	23	7	598	619	300	301	1	4.06	157	32	0	.204
	37CinN 37-41NYN																								
Brown, Lloyd-Lloyd Andrew (Gimpy)	25BknN 20-32WasA 33StLA 33BosA	12-25-04	Beeville, Tex.	1-14-74	L	L	5'9	170	91	105	.464	21	404	181	77	1693	1899	590	510	10	4.20	552	106	4	.192
	34-37CleA 40PhiN																								
Brown, Mace-Mace Stanley	35-41PitN 41BknN 42-43,46BosA 44-45MS	5-21-09	N. English, Iowa		R	R	6'1	190	76	57	.571	48	387	55	18	1075	1125	388	435	3	3.47	313	43	0	.137
Brown, Myrl-Myrl Lincoln	22PitN	10-10-94	Waynesboro, Pa.		R	R	5'11	172	3	1	.750	0	7	5	2	35	42	13	9	0	5.91	11	3	0	.273
Bruner, Roy-Walter Roy	39-41PhiN 42-45MS	2-10-17	Cecilia, Ky.		R	R	6'	165	0	7	.000	0	19	5	2	62	80	44	28	0	5.81	17	2	0	.118
Bryant, Clay-Claiborne Henry	35-40ChiN	11-16-11	Madison Hts., Va.		R	R	6'2	195	32	20	.615	7	129	45	23	542	511	262	272	4	3.74	192	51	5	.266
Buckeye, Garland-Garland Maiers (Gob)	18WasA 25-28CleA 28NYN	10-16-97	Heron Lake, Minn.		L	L	6'	260	30	39	.435	1	108	67	29	565	622	214	134	4	3.90	204	47	5	.230
20-24 played in N.F.L.					Bats Both 18,27																				
Buker, Cy-Cyril Owen	45BknN	2- 5-19	Greenwood, Wis.		L	R	5'11	190	7	2	.778	5	42	4	1	87	90	45	48	0	3.31	16	3	0	.188
Bullock, Red-Malton Joseph	36PhiA	10-12-12	Biloxi, Miss.		L	L	6'1	192	0	2	.000	0	12	2	0	17	19	37	7	0	13.76	4	0	0	.000
Burkart, Elmer-Elmer Robert (Swede)	36-39PhiN	2- 1-17	Torresdale, Pa.		R	R	6'2	190	1	1	.500	0	16	3	1	42	47	26	9	0	4.93	12	1	0	.083
Burke, Bobby-Robert James (Lefty)	27-35WasA 37PhiN	1-23-07	Joliet, Ill.	2- 8-71	L	L	6'2	150	38	46	.452	5	253	88	27	917	926	360	299	4	4.30	278	54	0	.194
Burns, Denny-Dennis	23-24PhiA	5-24-98	Tiff City, Mo.	5-21-69	R	R	5'10	180	8	9	.471	1	41	20	9	181	212	75	34	0	4.62	51	7	0	.137
Burrows, John-John	43PhiA 43-44ChiN	10-30-13	Winnfield, La.		R	L	5'10	200	0	3	.000	2	30	2	0	43	40	28	22	0	5.65	4	2	0	.500
Burwell, Bill-William Edwin	20-21StLA 28,M47PitN	3-27-95	Jarbalo, Kans.	6-11-73	L	R	5'11	175	9	8	.529	6	70	6	1	218	253	79	49	0	4.38	76	15	0	.197
Bush, Guy-Guy Terrell (The Mississippi Mudcat)	23-34ChiN 35-36PitN 36-37BosN	8-23-01	Aberdeen, Miss.		R	R	6'	175	176	136	.564	34	542	308	151	2726	2950	859	850	16	3.86	888	143	0	.161
	38StLN 45CinN																								
Bush, Bullet Joe-Leslie Ambrose	12-17PhiA 18-21BosA 22-24NYA	11-27-92	Brainerd, Minn.	11- 1-74	R	R	5'9	173	195	183	516	18	489	364	224	3093	3001	1263	1319	35	3.51	1239	313	7	.253
	25StLA 26WasA 26-27PitN 27NYN 28PhiA																								
Bushey, Frank-Francis Clyde	27,30BosA	8- 1-06	Wheaton, Kans.	3-18-72	R	R	6'	180	0	1	.000	0	12	0	0	31	36	17	4	0	6.39	9	1	0	.111
Butcher, Max-Albert Maxwell	36-38BknN 38-39PhiN 39-45PitN	9-21-10	Holden, W.Va.	9-15-57	R	R	6'2	220	95	106	.473	9	334	229	104	1787	1935	583	485	15	3.73	598	110	1	.184
Butland, Bill-Wilburn Rue	40,42BosA 43-45MS 46-47BosA	3-22-18	Terre Haute, Ind.		R	R	6'5	185	9	3	.750	1	32	15	7	150	138	56	62	2	3.90	39	2	0	.051
Butler, Charlie-Charles Thomas (Lefty)	33PhiN	5-12-05	Green Cove Spr., Fla.	5-10-64	R	L	6'1	210	0	0	–	0	1	0	0	1	1	2	0	0	9.00	0	0	0	–
Byrne, Jerry-Gerald Wilford	29ChiA	2- 2-07	Parnell, Mich.	8-11-55	R	R	6'	170	0	1	.000	0	3	1	0	7	11	6	1	0	7.71	2	0	0	.000
Cadore, Leon-Leon Joseph	15-23BknN 23ChiN 24NYN	11-20-90	Chicago, Ill.	3-16-58	R	R	6'1	190	68	72	.486	3	192	147	83	1257	1273	289	445	10	3.14	442	92	5	.208
Cain, Sugar-Merritt Patrick	32-35PhiA 35-36StLA 36-38ChiA	4- 5-07	Macon, Ga.	4- 3-75	L	R	5'11	190	53	60	.469	1	178	137	58	989	1119	569	279	2	4.82	344	56	0	.163
					Bats Both 32-33																				
Caldwell, Charlie-Charles William	25NYA	8- 2-01	Bristol, Va.	11- 1-57	R	R	5'11	190	0	0	–	0	3	0	0	3	7	3	1	0	15.00	1	0	0	.000
Caldwell, Earl-Earl Welton (Teach)	28PhiN 35-37StLA 45-48ChiA 48BosA	4- 9-05	Sparks, Tex.		R	R	6'1	178	33	43	.434	25	200	49	18	582	656	259	202	5	4.68	157	28	1	.178
Caligiuri, Fred-Frederick John	41-42PhiA 43-46MS	10-22-18	West Hickory, Pa.		R	R	6'	190	2	5	.286	1	18	7	4	80	90	32	27	0	4.50	32	5	0	.156
Callahan, Joe-Joseph Thomas	39-40BosN	10- 8-16	Boston, Mass.	5-24-49	R	R	6'2	170	1	2	.333	0	10	3	1	32	37	16	11	0	6.47	9	0	0	.000
Campbell, Archie-Archibald Stewart (Iron Man)	28NYA 29WasA 30CinN	10-20-03	Maplewood, N.J.		R	R	6'	180	2	6	.250	6	40	4	1	86	111	47	29	0	5.86	19	5	0	.263
Campbell, John-John Millard	33WasA	9-13-07	Washington, D.C.		R	R	6'1	184	0	0	–	0	1	0	0	1	1	1	0	0	0.00	0	0	0	–
Cantrell, Guy-Guy Dewey (Gunner)	25BknN	4- 9-04	Clarita, Okla.	1-31-61	R	R	6'	190	2	7	.222	0	38	7	4	99	115	47	45	0	4.27	9	0	0	.000
Cantwell, Ben-Benjamin Caldwell	27-28NYN 28-36BosN 37-NYN 37BknN	4-13-02	Milan, Tenn.	12- 4-62	R	R	6'1	168	76	108	.413	21	316	163	75	1533	1640	382	348	6	3.91	503	116	0	.231
Caraway, Pat-Cecil Bradford Patrick	30-32ChiA	9-26-05	Gordon, Tex.	6- 9-74	L	L	6'4	180	22	40	.355	3	108	62	21	478	542	195	151	2	5.35	157	28	0	.178
Cardoni, Ben-Armond Joseph (Big Ben)	43-45BosN	8-21-20	Jessup, Pa.	4- 2-69	R	R	6'3	195	0	6	.000	1	36	5	1	108	127	54	34	0	4.75	24	4	0	.167
Carleton, Tex-James Otto	32-34StLN 35-38ChiN 40BknN	8-19-06	Comanche, Tex.		B	R	6'1	180	100	76	.568	9	293	202	91	1607	1630	561	808	16	3.91	540	100	6	.185
Carlson, Hal-Harold Gust	17-23PitN 24-27PhiN 27-30ChiN	5-17-94	Rockford, Ill.	5-28-30	R	R	6'	180	114	120	.487	19	377	238	121	2002	2256	498	590	17	3.97	712	159	5	.223
Carlson, Leon-Leon Alton (Swede)	20WasA	2-17-95	Jamestown, N.Y.	9-15-61	R	R	6'3	195	0	0	–	0	3	0	0	12	14	2	3	0	3.75	6	1	0	.167

USE NAME – GIVEN NAMES (NICKNAMES)	TEAM BY YEAR	BIRTH DATE	BIRTH PLACE	DEATH DATE	B	T	HGT	WGT	W	L	PCT	SV	G	GS	CG	IP	H	BB	SO	ShO	ERA	AB	H	HR	BA
									LIFETIME PITCHING TOTALS													BATTING TOTALS			
Carnett, Eddie-Edwin Elliott (Lefty)	41BosN 44ChiA 45CleA 46MS	10-21-16	Springfield, Mo.		L	L	6′	185	0	0	–	0	6	0	0	5	7	3	4	0	9.00	(See B20-45)			
Carpenter, Bob-Robert Louis	40-42NYN 43-45MS 46-47NYN 47ChiN	12-12-17	Chicago, Ill.		R	R	6′3	195	25	20	.556	2	80	54	23	400	411	132	134	4	3.60	131	22	0	.168
Carpenter, Lew-Lewis Emmett	43WasA	8-16-13	Woodstock, Ga.		R	R	6′2	195	0	0	–	0	4	0	0	3	1	4	1	0	0.00	0	0	0	–
Carrasquel, Alex-Alejandro Alexander Aparicio Elroy	39-45WasA 46-48SM 49ChiA	7-24-12	Caracas, Venezuela	8-19-69	R	R	6′1	182	50	39	.562	16	258	64	30	861	887	347	252	4	3.73	229	33	1	.144
Carroll, Ed-Edgar Fleischer	29BosA	7-27-07	Baltimore, Md.		R	R	6′3	185	1	0	1.000	0	24	3	0	67	77	20	13	0	5.64	16	1	0	.063
Carroll, Ownie-Owen Thomas	25,27-30DetA 30NYA 30-32CinN 33-34BknN	11-11-02	Kearny, N.J.	6- 8-75	R	R	5′10	165	65	89	.422	5	248	153	71	1330	1532	486	311	2	4.43	489	98	0	.200
Carter, Arnold-Arnold Lee (Lefty, Hook)	44-45CinN	3-14-18	Rainelle, W.Va.		L	L	5′10	170	13	11	.542	3	46	24	11	195	197	53	37	4	2.72	65	15	2	.231
Carter, Sol-Solomon Mobley (Buck)	31PhiA	12-23-08	Picayune, Miss.		R	R	6′	178	0	0	–	0	2	0	0	2	1	4	1	0	22.50	0	0	0	–
Cascarella, Joe-Joseph Thomas (Crooning Joe)	34-35PhiA 35-36BosA 36-37WasA 37-38CinN	6-28-07	Philadelphia, Pa.		R	R	5′10	175	27	48	.360	8	143	54	20	540	602	267	192	3	4.85	165	20	0	.121
Casey, Hugh-Hugh Thomas	35ChiN 39-42BknN 43-45MS 46-48BknN 49PitN 49NYA	10-14-13	Atlanta, Ga.	7- 3-51	R	R	6′1	207	75	42	.641	55	343	56	24	940	935	321	349	3	3.45	244	40	0	.164
Caster, George-George Jasper	34-35,37-40PhiA 41-45StLA 45-46DetA	8- 4-07	Colton, Cal.	12-18-55	R	R	6′1	180	76	100	.432	39	376	127	62	1376	1469	597	595	6	4.55	440	81	0	.184
Castleman, Slick-Clydell	34-39NYN	9- 8-13	Donelson, Tenn.		R	R	6′	185	36	26	.581	1	121	79	25	588	644	223	225	4	4.24	207	28	2	.135
Castner, Paul-Paul Henry (Lefty)	23ChiA	2-16-97	St. Paul, Minn.		L	L	5′11	187	0	0	–	0	6	0	0	10	14	5	0	0	6.30	3	0	0	.000
Cathey, Hardin-Hardin (Abner)	42WasA	7-16-19	Burns, Tenn.		R	R	6′	190	1	1	.500	0	12	2	0	30	44	16	8	0	7.50	8	3	0	.375
Causey, Red-Cecil Algernon	18-19NYN 19BosN 20-21PhiN 21-22NYN	8-11-93	Georgetown, Fla.	11-11-60	L	R	6′2	190	39	35	.527	6	131	80	35	649	666	230	139	3	3.59	210	33	0	.157
Cecil, Rex-Rex Holston	44-45BosA	10- 8-16	Lindsay, Okla.	10-30-66	L	R	6′3	195	6	10	.375	0	18	16	5	106	118	60	63	0	5.18	38	11	0	.289
Center, Pete-Marvin Earl	42-43CleA 44MS 45-46CleA	4-22-12	Hazel Green, Ky.		R	R	6′4	205	7	7	.500	3	77	9	2	160	154	70	50	0	4.11	31	2	0	.065
Chagnon, Leon-Leon Wilbur (Shag)	29-30,32-34PitN 35NYN	9-28-02	Pittsfield, N.H.	7-30-53	R	R	6′	182	19	16	.543	3	135	22	8	393	443	104	153	1	4.51	105	17	0	.162
Chamberlain, Bill-William Vincent	32ChiA	4-21-09	Stoughton, Mass.		R	L	5′10	173	0	5	.000	0	12	5	0	41	39	25	11	0	4.61	10	1	0	.100
Chambers, John-John Monroe	37StLN	9-10-11	Copperhill, Tenn.		L	R	6′	185	0	0	–	0	2	0	0	2	5	2	1	0	18.00	0	0	0	–
Chandler, Spud-Spurgeon Ferdinand	37-47NYA	9-12-07	Commerce, Ga.		R	R	6′	181	109	43	.717	6	211	184	109	1485	1327	463	614	26	2.84	540	110	0	.201
Chaplin, Tiny-James Bailey	28,30-31NYN 36BosN	7-13-05	Los Angeles, Cal.	3-25-39	R	R	6′1	195	15	23	.395	4	87	43	18	371	428	102	118	0	4.25	119	21	1	.176
Chapman, Ben-William Benjamin	44-45BknN 45-46, M45-48PhiN	12-25-08	Nashville, Tenn.		R	R	6′	190	8	6	.571	0	25	16	8	141	147	71	65	0	4.40	(See B20-45)			
Chapman, Ed-Edwin Volney	33WasA	11-28-05	Courtland, Miss.		B	R	6′1	185	0	0	–	0	6	1	0	9	10	2	4	0	8.00	3	0	0	.000
Chase, Ken-Kendall Fay (Lefty)	36-41WasA 42-43BosA 43NYN	10- 6-13	Oneonta, N.Y.		R	L	6′2	210	53	84	.387	1	188	160	62	1165	1188	694	582	4	4.27	419	69	1	.165
Cheeves, Virgil-Virgil Earl (Chief)	20-23ChiN 24CleA 27NYN	2-12-01	Oklahoma City, Okla.		R	R	6′	175	26	27	.491	2	111	56	18	458	526	188	98	2	4.74	141	26	1	.184
Chelini, Italo-Italo Vincent (Lefty)	35-37ChiA	10-10-14	San Francisco, Cal.	8-25-72	L	L	5′10	175	4	4	.500	0	24	6	5	98	122	34	20	0	5.79	35	6	0	.171
Chetkovich, Mitch-Mitchell	45PhiN	7-21-17	Fairpoint, Ohio	8-24-71	R	R	6′4	225	0	0	–	0	4	0	0	3	2	3	0	0	0.00	0	0	0	–
Child, Harry-Harry Patrick	30WasA	5-23-05	Baltimore, Md.	11- 8-72	B	R	5′11	175	0	0	–	0	5	0	0	10	10	5	5	0	6.30	4	1	0	.250
Christopher, Russ-Russell Ormand	42-47PhiA 48CleA 49IL	9-12-17	Richmond, Cal.	12- 5-54	R	R	6′3	170	54	64	.458	35	241	97	46	999	931	399	424	3	3.37	316	50	2	.158
Ciola, Lou-Louis Alexander	43PhiA 44-45MS	9- 6-22	Norfolk, Va.		R	R	5′9	175	1	3	.250	0	12	3	2	44	48	22	7	0	5.52	18	3	0	.167
Clark, Bob-Robert William	20-21CleA	8-22-97	Newport, Pa.	5-18-44	R	R	6′3	188	1	2	.333	0	16	2	2	51	82	19	10	1	5.47	13	2	0	.154
Clark, Otie-William Otis	45BosA	5-22-18	Boscobel, Wis.		R	R	6′1	190	4	4	.500	0	12	9	4	82	86	19	20	1	3.07	24	5	0	.208
Clark, Watty-William Watson (Lefty)	24CleA 27-33BknN 33-34NYN 34-37BknN	5-16-02	St. Joseph, La.	3- 4-72	L	L	6′	175	111	97	.534	16	355	206	91	1748	1897	383	643	14	3.66	598	117	1	.196
Clarke, Alan-Alan Thomas (Lefty)	21CinN	3- 8-96	Clarksville, Md.	3-11-75	B	L	5′11	180	0	1	.000	0	1	1	1	5	7	2	1	0	5.40	1	0	0	.000
Clarke, Rufe-Rufus Rivers	23-24DetA	4-13-00	Estill, S.C.		R	R	6′1	203	1	1	.500	0	7	0	0	11	9	11	3	0	4.09	1	0	0	.000
Clarkson, Bill-William Henry (Blackie)	27-28NYN 28-29BosN	9-27-98	Portsmouth, Va.	8-27-71	R	R	5′11	160	3	12	.200	2	51	9	2	134	171	79	39	0	5.44	25	2	0	.080
Claset, Gowell-Gowell Sylvester (Lefty)	33PhiA	11-16-07	Battle Creek, Mich.		B	L	6′3	210	2	0	1.000	0	8	1	0	11	23	11	1	0	9.82	2	1	0	.500
Cleary, Joe-Joseph Christopher (Fire)	45WasA	12- 3-20	Cork, Ireland		R	R	5′10	160	0	0	–	0	1	0	0	.1	5	3	1	0	189.00	0	0	0	–
Clemensen, Bill-William Melville	39,41PitN 42-45MS 46PitN	6-20-19	New Brunswick, N.J.		R	R	6′1	193	1	1	.500	0	15	2	1	42	39	27	19	0	5.57	10	2	0	.200
Clough, Ed-Edgar George (Spec)	25-26StLN	10-28-06	Wiconisco, Pa.	1-30-44	L	L	6′2	188	0	1	.000	0	4	1	0	12	16	8	3	0	10.50	(See B20-45)			
Clowers, Bill-William P.	26BosA	8-14-97	San Antonio, Tex.		L	L	5′11	175	0	0	–	0	2	0	0	2	2	0	0	0	0.00	0	0	0	–
Clyde, Tom-Thomas Knox	43PhiA 44-45MS	8-17-23	Wachapreague, Va.		R	R	6′3	195	0	0	–	0	4	0	0	6	7	4	0	0	9.00	2	0	0	.000
Cobb, Herm-Herbert Edward	29StLA	8- 6-04	Pinetops, N.C.		R	R	5′11	150	0	0	–	0	1	0	0	1	3	1	0	0	36.00	0	0	0	–
Coffman, Dick-Samuel Richard	27WasA 28-32StLA 32WasA 33-35StLA 36-39NYN 40BosN 45PhiN	12-18-06	Veto, Ala.	3-24-72	R	R	6′2	195	72	95	.431	38	472	132	47	1460	1782	463	372	9	4.65	400	51	0	.128
Coffman, Slick-George David	37-39DetA 40StLA	12-11-10	Veto, Ala.		R	R	5′11	160	15	12	.556	3	121	16	3	314	400	132	89	0	5.59	73	12	0	.164
Cohen, Sid-Sydney Harry	34,36-37WasA	5- 7-08	Baltimore, Md.		B	L	5′11	180	3	7	.300	5	55	3	2	109	133	37	49	0	4.54	33	5	0	.152
Cole, Bert-Albert George	21-25DetA 25CleA 27ChiA	7- 1-98	San Francisco, Cal.	5-30-75	L	L	6′1	180	28	32	.467	10	176	46	17	605	734	230	119	4	4.67	205	49	1	.239
Cole (Kisleauskas), Ed-Edward William	38-39StLA	3-22-09	Wilkes-Barre, Pa.		R	R	5′11	170	1	7	.125	3	42	6	1	95	124	54	31	0	5.31	22	3	0	.136
Collard, Hap-Earl Clinton	27-28CleA 30PhiN	8-29-98	Williams, Ariz.	7- 7-68	R	R	6′	170	6	12	.333	0	35	15	4	136	200	46	28	0	6.62	45	10	0	.222
Collier, Orlin-Orlin Edward	31DetA	2-17-07	East Prairie, Mo.	9- 9-44	R	R	5′11	180	0	1	.000	0	2	2	0	10	17	7	3	0	8.10	3	0	0	.000
Collins, Phil-Philip Eugene (Fidgety Phil)	23ChiN 29-35PhiN 35StLN	8-27-01	Chicago, Ill.	8-14-48	R	R	5′11	175	80	85	.485	24	292	141	64	1323	1541	497	423	4	4.67	482	93	4	.193
Collins, Rip-Harry Warren	20-21NYA 22BosA 23-27DetA 29-31StLA	2-26-96	Weatherford, Tex.	5-27-68	R	R	6′1	205	108	82	.568	5	311	220	86	1712	1795	674	569	15	3.99	582	96	1	.165
					Bats Both 20-23																				
Comellas, Jorge-Jorge (Pancho)	45ChiN	12- 7-16	Havana, Cuba		R	R	6′	185	0	2	.000	0	7	1	0	12	11	6	6	0	4.50	3	0	0	.000
Conger, Dick-Richard	40DetA 41-42PitN 43PhiN 44-46MS	4- 3-21	Los Angeles, Cal.	2-16-70	R	R	6′	185	3	7	.300	0	19	12	2	70	86	35	24	0	5.14	19	1	0	.053
Conkwright, Allen-Allen Howard (Red)	20DetA	12- 4-96	Sedalia, Mo.		R	R	5′10	170	2	1	.667	1	5	2	0	19	29	16	4	0	7.11	4	1	0	.250
Connally, Sarge-George Walter	21,23-29ChiA 31-34CleA	8-31-98	McGregor, Tex.		R	R	5′11	170	49	60	.450	31	303	67	33	996	1108	453	346	2	4.30	301	70	1	.233
Conway, Jerry-Jerome Patrick	20WasA	6- 7-01	Holyoke, Mass.		L	L	6′2	190	0	0	–	0	1	0	0	2	1	1	0	0	0.00	0	0	0	–
Cook, Earl-Earl Davis	41DetA	12-10-08	Stouffville, Canada		R	R	6′	195	0	0	–	0	1	0	0	2	4	0	1	0	4.50	0	0	0	–
Coombs, Bobby-Raymond Franklin	33PhiA 43NYN	2- 2-08	Goodwins Mills, Me.		R	R	5′9	160	0	2	.000	2	30	0	0	47	80	28	13	0	9.38	7	2	0	.286
Cooney, Bob-Robert Daniel	31-32StLA	7-12-07	Glens Falls, N.Y.		R	R	5′11	160	1	5	.167	1	28	7	2	110	140	56	36	0	5.97	35	5	0	.143
Cooney, Johnny-John Walter	21-26,28,30BosN	3-18-01	Cranston, R.I.		R	L	5′10	165	34	44	.436	6	159	76	44	796	858	223	224	7	3.72	(See B20-45)			
Cooper, Mort-Morton Cecil	38-45StLN 45-47BosN 47NYN 49ChiN	3- 2-13	Atherton, Mo.	11-17-58	R	R	6′2	210	128	75	.631	14	295	239	128	1802	1666	571	913	32	2.97	654	127	6	.194
Copeland, Mays-Mays	35StLN	8-31-13	Mt. View, Ark.		R	R	6′	180	0	0	–	0	1	0	0	1	2	0	0	0	9.00	0	0	0	–
Coopola, Henry-Henry Peter	35-36WasA	8- 6-12	East Douglas, Mass.		R	R	5′11	175	3	4	.429	1	25	5	2	73	89	41	21	1	5.67	17	2	0	.118
Couch, Johnny-John Daniel	17DetA 18MS 22-23CinN 23-25PhiN	3-31-91	Vaughn, Mont.		L	R	6′	180	29	34	.460	6	147	62	26	642	785	171	112	3	4.64	222	37	3	.167
Courtney, Harry-Harry Seymour	19-22WasA 22ChiA	11-19-98	Asheville, N.C.		L	L	6′4	185	22	27	.449	1	94	53	21	444	518	213	112	2	4.91	163	41	1	.252
Coveleski (Kowalewski), Stan (Stanislaus)-Stanley Anthony	12PhiA 16-24CleA 25-27WasA 28NYA	7-13-89	Shamokin, Pa.		R	R	5′11	166	216	143	.602	20	450	384	226	3092	3055	802	981	38	2.88	1058	168	1	.159
Covington, Chet-Chester Rogers (Chesty)	44PhiN	11- 6-10	Cairo, Ill.		B	L	6′2	225	1	1	.500	0	19	0	0	39	46	8	13	0	4.62	6	0	0	.000
Cox, Bill-William Donald	36StLN 37-38ChiA 38-40StLA	6-23-13	Ashmore, Ill.		R	R	6′1	185	2	9	.182	0	50	12	3	117	138	74	45	0	6.54	25	2	0	.080
Cox, Ernie-Ernest Thompson (Elmer)	22ChiA	2-19-94	Birmingham, Ala.		L	R	6′1	180	0	0	–	0	1	0	0	1	1	2	0	0	18.00	0	0	0	–
Cox, George-George Melvin	28ChiA	11-15-04	Sherman, Tex.		R	R	6′1	170	1	2	.333	0	26	2	0	89	110	39	22	0	5.26	26	2	0	.077
Cox, Les-Leslie Warren	26ChiA	8-14-05	Junction, Tex.	10-12-34	R	R	6′	164	0	1	.000	0	2	0	0	5	6	5	3	0	5.40	2	1	0	.500
Cox, Red-Plateau Rex	20DetA	2-16-95	Laurel Springs, N.C.		L	R	6′2	190	0	0	–	0	3	0	0	5	9	3	1	0	5.40	1	0	0	.000
Cozart, Charlie-Charles Rhubin	45BosN	10-17-19	Lenoir, N.C.		R	L	6′2	190	1	0	1.000	0	5	0	0	8	10	15	4	0	10.13	2	0	0	.000
Craghead, Howard-Howard Oliver (Judge)	31,33CleA	5-25-08	Selma, Cal.	7-15-62	R	R	6′2	200	0	0	–	0	15	0	0	23	27	12	4	0	6.26	3	0	0	.000
Crawford, Larry-Charles Lowrie	37PhiN	4-27-14	Swissvale, Pa.		L	L	6′1	165	0	0	–	0	6	0	0	6	12	1	2	0	15.00	0	0	0	–
Creel, Jack-Jack Dalton (Tex)	45StLN	4-23-16	Kyle, Tex.		R	R	6′	165	5	4	.556	2	26	8	2	87	78	45	34	0	4.14	26	2	0	.077
Cremins, Bob-Robert Anthony (Lefty)	27BosA	2-15-06	Pelham Manor, N.Y.		L	L	5′11	160	0	0	–	0	4	0	0	5	5	3	0	0	5.40	0	0	0	–
Crocker, Claude-Claude Arthur	44-45BknN	7-20-24	Caroleen, N.C.		R	R	6′2	185	0	0	–	1	3	0	0	5	8	6	2	0	7.20	1	1	0	1.000
Crouch, Bill-William Elmer	39BknN 41PhiN 41,45StLN	8-20-10	Wilmington, Del.		B	R	6′1	180	8	5	.615	7	50	12	4	155	159	52	55	0	3.48	41	3	0	.073
Crowder, General-Alvin Floyd	26-27,30-34WasA 27-30StLA 34-36DetA	1-11-99	Winston-Salem, N.C.	4- 3-72	L	R	5′10	170	167	115	.592	22	402	292	150	2344	2453	800	799	16	4.12	847	164	0	.194
Crowson, Woody-Thomas Woodrow	45PhiA	9-19-18	Fuquay Springs, N.C.	8-14-47	R	R	6′2	185	0	0	–	0	1	0	0	3	2	3	2	0	6.00	1	0	0	.000
Crumpler, Roy-Roy Maxton	20DetA 25PhiN	7- 8-96	Clinton, N.C.	10- 6-69	L	L	6′1	195	1	0	1.000	0	5	3	1	18	25	13	3	0	6.00	11	3	0	.273
Cuccurullo, Cookie-Arthur Joseph	43-45PitN	2- 8-18	Asbury Park, N.J.		L	L	5′10	168	3	5	.375	5	62	9	0	170	188	81	51	0	4.55	52	17	0	.327
Culloton, Bud-Bernard Aloysius	25-26PitN	5-19-96	Kingston, N.Y.		R	R	5′11	180	0	1	.000	0	13	1	0	25	22	7	4	0	3.24	3	0	0	.000
Cunningham, Bruce-Bruce Lee	29-32BosN	9-29-05	San Francisco, Cal.		R	R	5′10	165	13	24	.351	2	104	33	12	383	428	146	103	1	4.63	109	15	0	.138
Curtis, Vern-Vernon Eugene (Turk)	43-44WasA 45MS 46WasA	5-24-20	Cairo, Ill.		R	R	6′	170	0	1	.000	0	16	1	0	30	30	19	10	0	5.70	4	0	0	.000
Cvengros, Mike-Michael John	22NYN 23-25ChiA 27PitN 29ChiN	12- 1-01	Pana, Ill.	8- 2-70	L	L	5′8	160	25	40	.385	6	145	59	21	553	587	285	201	0	4.57	174	35	0	.201
Dagenhard, John-John Douglas	43BosN	4-25-17	Magnolia, Ohio		R	R	6′2	195	1	0	1.000	0	2	1	1	11	9	4	2	0	0.00	3	0	0	.000
Daglia, Pete-Peter George	32ChiA	2-28-06	Napa, Cal.	3-11-52	R	R	6′1	200	2	4	.333	0	12	5	2	50	67	20	16	0	5.76	13	1	0	.077
Dailey, Sam-Samuel L.	29PhiN	3-31-05	Kansas City, Kans.		R	R	5′11	168	2	2	.500	0	20	5	0	51	74	23	18	0	7.59	17	1	0	.059

USE NAME – GIVEN NAMES (NICKNAMES)	TEAM BY YEAR	BIRTH DATE	BIRTH PLACE	DEATH DATE	B	T	HGT	WGT	W	L	PCT	SV	G	GS	CG	IP	H	BB	SO	ShO	ERA	AB	H	HR	BA
									LIFETIME PITCHING TOTALS													BATTING TOTALS			
Daney, Art-Arthur Lee (Whitehorn)	28PhiA	7- 9-04	Talihina, Okla.		R	R	5'11	165	0	0	–	0	1	0	0	1	1	0	0	0	0.00	0	0	0	–
Danforth, Dave-David Charles (Dauntless Dave)	11-12PhiA 16-19ChiA 22-25StLA	3- 7-90	Granger, Tex.	9-19-70	L	L	6'	167	71	67	.514	24	286	114	44	1187	1235	455	484	3	3.88	350	56	0	.160
Darrow, George-George Oliver (Lefty)	34PhiN	7-12-03	Beloit, Kans.		L	L	6'	180	2	6	.250	1	17	8	2	49	57	28	14	0	5.51	15	2	0	.133
Dasso, Frank-Francis Joseph Nicholas	45-46CinN	8-31-17	Chicago, Ill.		R	R	5'11	185	4	5	.444	0	18	12	6	97	91	55	40	0	3.90	31	5	0	.161
Davenport, Claude-Claude Edwin	20NYN	5-28-98	Runge, Tex.		R	R	6'6	193	0	0	–	0	1	0	0	2	2	1	0	0	4.50	1	0	0	.000
Davenport, Lum-Joubert Lum	21-24ChiA	6-27-00	Tucson, Ariz.	4-21-61	L	L	6'1	165	1	4	.200	0	25	3	0	58	63	51	20	0	7.76	21	8	0	.381
Davies, Chick-Lloyd Garrison	14-15PhiA 25-26NYN	3- 6-92	Peabody, Mass.	9- 5-73	L	L	5'8	145	4	6	.400	6	45	5	1	120	137	54	38	0	4.50	(See B01-19)			
Davis, Curt-Curtis Benton (Coonskin)	34-36PhiN 36-37ChiN 38-40StLN 40-46BknN	9 7-03	Greenfield, Mo.	10-13-65	R	R	6'2	185	158	131	.547	33	429	281	141	2324	2459	479	684	24	3.42	813	165	11	.203
Davis, Dixie-Frank Talmadge	12CinN 15ChiA 18PhiN 20-26StLA	10-12-90	Wilson Mills, N.C.	2- 4-44	R	R	5'11	155	75	71	.514	2	239	165	77	1317	1311	688	460	10	3.97	441	87	0	.197
Davis, Peaches-Ray Thomas	36-39CinN	5-31-05	Glen Rose, Tex.		L	R	6'3	190	27	33	.450	11	117	58	27	543	627	138	123	2	3.86	185	33	0	.178
Davis, Woody-Woodrow Wilson (Babe)	38DetA	4-25-13	Nicholas, Ga.		L	R	6'1	200	0	0	–	0	2	0	0	6	3	4	1	0	1.50	1	0	0	.000
Dawson, Joe-Ralph Fenton	24CleA 27-29PitN	3- 9-98	Bow, Wash.		R	R	5'11	182	11	17	.393	3	59	18	5	239	233	112	62	0	4.14	77	20	0	.260
Day, Pea Ridge-Clyde Henry	24-25StLN 26CinN 31BknN	8-26-99	Pea Ridge, Ark.	3-22-34	R	R	6'	190	5	7	.417	2	46	9	3	122	163	28	48	0	5.31	41	7	0	.171
Dean, Chubby-Alfred Lovill	37-41PhiA 41-43CleA 44-46MS	8-24-15	Mt. Airy, N.C.	12-21-70	L	L	5'11	188	30	46	.395	9	162	68	23	686	781	323	195	1	5.08	(See B20-45)			
Dean, Dizzy-Jay Hanna	30,32-37StLN 38-41ChiN 47StLA	1-16-11	Lucas, Ark.	7-17-74	R	R	6'2	182	150	83	.644	30	317	230	154	1966	1921	458	1155	26	3.04	717	161	8	.225
Dean, Harry-James Harry	41WasA	5-12-15	Rockmart, Ga.	6- 1-60	R	R	6'4	185	0	0	–	0	2	0	0	2	2	3	0	0	4.50	0	0	0	–
Dean, Paul-Paul Dee (Daffy)	34-39StLN 40-41NYN 43StLA	8-14-13	Lucas, Ark.		R	R	6'	175	50	34	.595	8	159	87	44	787	825	179	387	8	3.75	256	40	0	.156
Dean, Wayland-Wayland Ogden	24-25NYN 26-27PhiN 27ChiN	6-20-02	Richwood, W.Va.	4-10-30	B	R	6'2	180	24	36	.400	1	96	60	27	446	559	188	147	2	5.31	196	49	6	.250
DeBerry, Joe-Joseph Gaddy	20-21StLA	11-29-96	Mt. Gilead, N.C.	10- 9-44	L	R	6'1	175	2	5	.286	0	20	8	3	67	80	30	13	1	5.24	20	3	0	.150
Decatur, Art-Arthur Rue	22-25BknN 25-27PhiN	1-14-94	Cleveland, Ohio	4-25-66	R	R	6'	190	23	34	.404	7	153	36	11	550	669	148	155	0	4.47	159	15	0	.094
de la Cruz, Tommy-Tomas	44CinN	9-18-14	Marianao, Cuba	9- 6-58	R	R	6'1	168	9	9	.500	1	34	20	9	191	170	45	65	0	3.25	58	9	0	.155
Delaney (Helenius), Art-Arthur Dewey	24StLN 28-29BosN	1- 5-95	Chicago, Ill.	5- 2-70	R	R	5'10	178	13	22	.371	2	67	31	12	287	319	97	64	1	4.26	91	14	1	.154
Derringer, Paul-Samuel Paul (Duke, 'Oom Paul)	31-33StLN 33-42CinN 43-45ChiN	10-17-06	Springfield, Ky.		R	R	6'3	205	223	212	.513	29	579	445	251	3646	3912	761	1507	32	3.46	1260	220	2	.175
DeShong, Jimmie-James Brooklyn	32PhiA 34-35NYA 36-39WasA	11-30-09	Harrisburg, Pa.		R	R	5'11	165	47	44	.516	9	175	100	44	873	968	432	273	2	5.08	293	58	0	.198
Devens, Charlie-Charles	32-34NYA	1- 1-10	Milton, Mass.		R	R	6'1	180	5	3	.625	0	16	10	4	82	74	62	31	0	3.73	25	3	0	.120
Deviney, Hal-John Harold	20BosA	4-11-93	Newton, Mass.		R	R			0	0	–	0	1	0	0	3	7	2	0	0	15.00	2	2	0	1.000
Dibut, Pedro-Pedro	24-25CinN	11-18-92	Cienfuegos, Cuba	Deceased	R	R	5'8	190	3	0	1.000	0	8	2	2	37	27	12	15	0	2.68	11	3	0	.273
Dickerman, Leo-Leo Louis	23-24BknN 24-25StLN	10-31-96	DeSoto, Mo.		R	R	6'4	192	19	27	.413	1	89	55	22	436	448	217	134	4	3.94	141	28	2	.199
Dickman, Emerson-George Emerson	36,38-41BosA 42MS	11-12-14	Buffalo, N.Y.		R	R	6'2	175	22	15	.595	8	125	24	6	350	403	153	126	1	5.32	110	16	1	.145
Diehl, George-George Krause	42-43BosN	2-25-18	Allentown, Pa.		R	R	6'2	196	0	0	–	0	2	0	0	8	6	5	1	0	3.38	2	0	0	.000
Dietrich, Bill-William John (Bullfrog)	33-36PhiA 36WasA 36-46ChiA 47-48PhiA	3-29-10	Philadelphia, Pa.		R	R	6'	200	108	128	.458	11	366	253	92	2004	2117	890	660	17	4.48	627	94	5	.150
Dietz, Dutch-Lloyd Arthur	40-43PitN 43PhiN	2-19-12	Cincinnati, Ohio	10-29-72	R	R	6'	180	14	16	.467	6	106	21	7	294	303	113	79	1	3.89	73	13	0	.178
Diggs, Reese-Reese Wilson (Diggsy)	34WasA	9-22-15	Mathews, Va.		B	R	6'2	175	1	2	.333	0	4	3	2	21	26	15	2	0	6.86	8	2	0	.250
Dobb, John-John Kenneth (Lefty)	24ChiA	11-15-01	Muskegon, Mich.		R	L	6'2	180	0	0	–	0	2	0	0	2	4	1	2	0	9.00	0	0	0	–
Dobens, Ray-Raymond Joseph (Lefty)	29BosA	7-28-06	Nashua, N.H.		L	L	5'8	165	0	0	–	0	11	2	0	28	32	0	4	0	3.86	8	3	0	.375
Dockins, George-George Woodrow (Lefty)	45StLN 47BknN	5- 5-17	Clyde, Kans.		L	L	6'	175	8	6	.571	0	35	12	5	131	142	40	34	2	3.57	35	6	0	.171
Dodge, Sam-Samuel Edward	21-22BosA	12-19-89	Philadelphia, Pa.		R	R	6'1	170	0	0	–	0	4	0	0	7	12	4	3	0	5.14	2	0	0	.000
Doll, Art-Arthur James (Moose)	36,38BosN	5- 7-12	Chicago, Ill.		R	R	6'	200	0	1	.000	0	4	1	0	12	15	5	3	0	3.00	(See B20-45)			
Donahue, Deacon-John Stephen Michael	43-44PhiN	6-23-20	Chicago, Ill.		R	R	6'	180	0	2	.000	0	8	0	0	13	22	3	3	0	6.92	1	0	0	.000
Donald, Atley-Richard Atley (Swampy)	38-45NYA	8-19-10	Morton, Miss.		L	R	6'1	186	65	33	.663	1	153	115	54	953	907	369	369	5	3.52	356	57	1	.160
Donohue, Pete-Peter Joseph	21-30CinN 30-31NYN 31CleA 32BosA	11- 5-00	Athens, Tex.		R	R	6'2	185	134	118	.532	12	344	270	137	2112	2439	422	571	16	3.87	732	180	6	.246
Donovan, Bill-Willard Earl	42-43BosN 44-45MS	7- 6-16	Maywood, Ill.		R	L	6'2	198	4	6	.400	0	38	10	2	104	114	41	24	1	3.20	28	7	0	.250
Dorsett, Cal-Calvin Leavelle (Preacher)	40-41CleA 42-45MS 45CleA	6-10-13	Lone Oak, Tex.	10-22-70	R	R	6'	185	0	1	.000	0	8	2	0	13	25	13	6	0	12.46	2	0	0	.000
Doyle, Carl-William Carl	35-36PhiA 39-40BknN 40StLN	7-30-12	Knoxville, Tenn.	9- 4-51	R	R	6'1	185	6	15	.286	2	51	21	6	224	277	155	101	1	6.91	82	16	1	.195
Doyle, Jess-Jesse Herbert	25-27DetA 31StLA	4-14-98	Knoxville, Tenn.	4-15-61	R	R	5'11	175	4	7	.364	9	55	3	0	135	183	57	38	0	6.27	37	10	2	.270
Drake, Logan-Logan Gaffney (L.G.)	22-24CleA	12-26-00	Spartanburg, S.C.	6- 1-40	R	R	5'10	165	0	1	.000	0	10	1	0	18	24	17	11	0	8.00	2	0	0	.000
Drake, Tom-Thomas Kendall	39CleA 41BknN	8- 7-14	Birmingham, Ala.		R	R	6'1	185	1	2	.333	0	18	3	0	40	49	28	13	0	6.08	7	2	0	.286
Dudley, Clise-Elzie Clise	29-30BknN 31-32PhiN 33PitN	8- 8-03	Graham, N.C.		L	R	6'1	195	17	33	.340	2	100	52	18	421	540	156	106	1	5.02	173	32	3	.185
Duff, Larry-Cecil Elba	22ChiA	11-30-97	Radersburg, Mont.	11-10-69	L	R	6'1	175	1	1	.500	0	3	1	0	13	16	3	7	0	4.85	5	2	0	.400
Dugan, Dan-Daniel Phillip	28-29ChiA	2-22-07	Plainfield, N.J.	6-25-68	L	L	6'1	187	1	4	.200	1	20	2	0	65	77	19	15	0	6.65	20	3	0	.150
Dumovich, Nick-Nicholas	23ChiN	1- 2-02	Sacramento, Cal.		L	L	6'	170	3	5	.375	1	28	8	1	94	118	45	23	0	4.60	29	7	0	.241
Durham, Ed-Edward Fant (Bull)	29-32BosA 33ChiA	8-17-07	Chester, S.C.		L	R	5'11	170	29	44	.397	1	143	71	23	641	677	202	204	3	4.45	202	24	0	.119
Dyer, Eddie-Edwin Hawley	22-27,M46-50StLN	10-11-00	Morgan City, La.	4-20-64	L	L	5'11	168	15	15	.500	3	69	23	10	256	316	96	63	2	4.75	157	35	2	.223
Earley, Tom-Thomas Francis Aloysius (Chick)	38-42BosN 43-44MS 45BosN	2-19-17	Roxbury, Mass.		R	R	6'	180	18	24	.429	5	91	37	15	360	349	143	104	2	3.78	114	23	0	.202
Earnshaw, George-George Livingston (Moose)	28-33PhiA 34-35ChiA 35-36BknN 36StLN	2-15-00	New York, N.Y.		R	R	6'4	210	127	93	.577	12	319	249	114	1916	1981	809	1002	17	4.38	704	162	3	.230
East, Hugh-Gordon Hugh	41-43NYN 44-45MS	7- 7-19	Birmingham, Ala.		R	R	6'2	185	2	6	.250	0	19	8	1	63	85	41	27	0	5.43	24	4	1	.167
Eaton, Zeb-Zebulon Vance (Red)	44-45DetA	2- 2-20	Cooleemee, N.C.		R	R	5'10	185	4	2	.667	0	23	3	0	69	67	48	19	0	4.43	42	9	2	.214
Eaves, Vallie-Vallie Ennis (Chief)	35PhiA 39-40ChiA 41-42ChiN	9- 6-11	Allen, Okla.	4-19-60	R	R	6'2	180	4	8	.333	0	24	14	6	107	105	70	46	0	4.54	35	4	0	.114
Eayrs, Eddie-Edwin	13PitN 20-21BosN	11-10-90	Blackstone, Mass.	11-30-69	L	L	5'7	160	1	2	.333	0	11	3	0	39	53	27	13	0	6.23	(See B20-45)			
Eckert, Al-Albert George (Obbie)	30-31CinN 35StLN	5-17-06	Milwaukee, Wisc.	4-20-74	L	L	5'10	174	0	2	.000	0	18	2	0	27	40	14	7	0	9.00	4	1	0	.250
Eckert, Charlie-Charles William (Buzz)	19-20,22PhiA	8- 8-98	Philadelphia, Pa.		R	R	5'10	165	0	3	.000	0	25	1	1	72	86	27	22	0	4.50	18	2	0	.111
Edelen, Ed-Edward Joseph (Doc)	32WasA	3-16-12	Bryantown, Md.		R	R	6'	191	0	0	–	0	2	0	0	1	0	6	0	0	27.00	0	0	0	–
Edmondson, George-George Henderson	22-24CleA	5-18-96	Waxahachie, Tex.	7-11-73	R	R	6'1	179	0	0	–	0	8	1	0	14	22	8	3	0	9.64	4	1	0	.250
Edwards, Foster-Foster Hamilton (Eddie)	25-28BosN 30NYA	9- 1-03	Holstein, Iowa		R	R	6'3	175	6	9	.400	0	56	17	4	170	193	84	60	0	4.76	42	2	0	.248
Edwards, Jim Joe-James Corbette	22-25CleA 25-26ChiA 28CinN	12-14-94	Banner, Miss.	1-19-65	R	L	6'2	185	26	37	.413	4	145	59	23	579	666	278	211	6	4.41	184	24	0	.130
Edwards, Sherman-Sherman Stanley	34CinN	7-25-09	Mt. Ida, Ark.		R	R	6'	165	0	0	–	0	1	0	0	3	4	1	1	0	3.00	1	0	0	.000
Ehmke, Howard-Howard Jonathan (Bob)	15BufF 16-17DetA 18MS 19-22DetA 23-26BosA 26-30PhiA	4-24-94	Silver Creek, N.Y.	3-17-59	R	R	6'3	190	166	166	.500	14	427	339	199	2822	2873	1042	1030	19	3.75	1009	210	0	.208
Ehrhardt, Rube-Welton Claude	24-28BknN 29CinN	11-20-94	Beecher, Ill.		R	R	6'2	190	22	34	.393	10	193	40	22	588	633	200	128	3	4.15	173	37	1	.214
Eisenhardt, Jake-Jacob Henry (Hank)	44CinN	10- 3-22	Perkasie, Pa.		L	L	6'3	195	0	0	–	0	1	0	0	.1	0	1	0	0	0.00	0	0	0	–
Eisenstat, Harry-Harry	35-37BknN 38-39DetA 39-42CleA 43-46MS	10-10-15	Brooklyn, N.Y.		L	L	5'11	180	25	27	.481	14	165	32	11	479	550	114	157	1	3.83	123	26	0	.211
Elliott, Hal-Harold William (Ace)	29-32PhiN	5-29-99	Mt. Clemens, Mich.	4-25-63	R	R	6'1	170	11	24	.314	4	120	30	4	322	453	174	90	0	6.96	89	12	0	.135
Elliott, Jumbo Jim-James Thompson	23StLA 25,27-30BknN 31-34PhiN 34BosN	10-22-00	St. Louis, Mo.	1- 7-70	L	L	6'3	235	63	74	.460	12	252	144	51	1207	1338	414	453	8	4.24	416	68	4	.163
Ellison, George-George Russell	20CleA	-97			R	R	6'3	185	0	0	–	0	1	0	0	1	0	2	1	0	0.00	0	0	0	–
Embry, Slim-Charles Akin	23ChiA	8-17-01	Columbia, Tenn.	10-10-47	R	R	6'2	184	0	0	–	0	1	0	0	3	7	2	1	0	9.00	0	0	0	–
Emmerich, Slim-William Peter	45-46NYN	9-29-19	Allentown, Pa.		R	R	6'1	170	4	4	.500	0	33	7	1	104	117	33	28	0	4.85	25	3	0	.120
Epperly, Al-Albert Paul (Pard)	38ChiN 50BknN	5- 7-18	Glidden, Iowa		L	R	6'2	194	2	0	1.000	0	14	4	1	36	42	20	13	0	4.00	8	2	0	.250
Erickson, Eric-Eric George Adolph	14NYN 16,18-19DetA 19-22WasA	3-13-92	Goteborg, Sweden	5-19-65	R	R	6'2	190	34	56	.378	4	145	94	42	822	805	379	367	3	3.85	279	50	1	.179
Erickson, Paul-Paul Walford (Li'l Abner)	41-48ChiN 48PhiN 48NYN	12-14-15	Zion, Ill.		R	R	6'2	200	37	48	.435	6	207	86	27	814	774	425	432	5	3.86	258	38	3	.147
Erickson, Ralph-Ralph Lief	29-30PitN	6-25-04	Dubois, Idaho		L	L	6'1	175	1	0	1.000	0	8	0	0	15	23	12	2	0	8.40	4	1	0	.250
Errickson, Dick-Ricahrd Merriwell (Lief)	38-42BosN 42ChiN	3- 4-14	Vineland, N.J.		R	R	6'1	175	36	47	.434	13	168	77	31	736	804	290	176	6	3.85	228	37	0	.162
Estrada, Oscar-Oscar	29StLA	2-15-04	Havana, Cuba		L	L	5'8	160	0	0	–	0	1	0	0	1	1	1	0	0	0.00	0	0	0	–
Eubanks, Uel-Uel Melvin (Poss)	22ChiN	2-14-02	Quinlan, Tex.	11-22-54	R	R	6'3	175	0	0	–	0	2	0	0	2	5	4	1	0	22.50	1	1	0	1.000
Evans, Art-William Arthur	32ChiA	8- 3-11	Elvins, Mo.	1- 8-52	B	L	6'1	181	0	0	–	0	7	0	0	18	19	10	6	0	3.00	5	0	0	.000
Evans, Red-Russell Earl	36ChiA 39BknN	11-12-06	Chicago, Ill.		R	R	5'11	168	1	11	.083	2	41	6	0	111	144	48	47	0	6.24	28	6	0	.214
Eyrich, George-George Lincoln	43PhiN 44-46MS	3- 3-25	Reading, Pa.		R	R	5'11	175	0	0	–	0	9	0	0	19	23	9	5	0	3.32	2	0	0	.000
Faber, Red-Urban Clarence	14-33ChiA	9- 6-88	Cascade, Iowa		B	R	6'2	180	254	212	.545	28	669	484	275	4087	4106	1213	1471	29	3.15	1269	170	3	.134
Faeth, Tony-Anthony Joseph	19-20CleA	7- 9-93	Aberdeen, S.D.		R	R	6'	180	0	0	–	0	19	0	0	43	44	30	21	0	2.72	9	0	0	.000
Falk, Chet-Chester Emanuel (Spot)	25-27StLA	5-15-05	Austin, Tex.		L	L	6'2	170	5	4	.556	0	40	8	3	115	158	54	16	0	6.03	44	12	0	.273
Fallenstein (Valestin), Ed-Edward Joseph (Jack)	31PhiN 33BosN	12-22-08	Newark, N.J.	11-24-71	R	R	6'3	180	2	1	.667	0	33	4	1	77	99	39	20	1	5.49	13	4	0	.308
Faulkner, Jim-James LeRoy (Lefty)	27-28NYN 30BknN	7-27-99	Beatrice, Neb.	6- 1-62	R	L	6'3	190	10	8	.556	3	43	10	3	127	146	47	34	0	3.76	41	10	0	.244
					Bats Left 27																				
Feldman, Harry-Harry	41-46NYN 47-49SM	11-10-19	New York, N.Y.	3-16-62	R	R	6'	175	35	35	.500	3	143	78	22	666	671	300	254	6	3.80	221	38	2	.172
Fenner, Hod-Horace Alfred	21ChiA	7-12-97	Martin, Mich.	11-20-54	R	R	5'10	165	0	0	–	0	2	1	0	7	14	3	1	0	7.71	2	0	0	.000
Ferguson, Alex-James Alexander	18,21NYA 22-25BosA 25NYA 25-26WasA 27-29PhiN 29BknN	2-16-97	Montclair, N.J.		R	R	6'	180	61	85	.418	10	257	166	62	1239	1449	478	396	2	4.90	397	42	0	.106

USE NAME – GIVEN NAMES (NICKNAMES)	TEAM BY YEAR	BIRTH DATE	BIRTH PLACE	DEATH DATE	B	T	HGT	WGT	W	L	PCT	SV	G	GS	CG	IP	H	BB	SO	ShO	ERA	AB	H	HR	BA
					LIFETIME PITCHING TOTALS																	BATTING TOTALS			
Ferguson, Bob-Robert Lester	44CinN	4-18-19	Birmingham, Ala.		R	R	6'1	180	0	3	.000	1	9	2	0	16	24	10	9	0	9.00	3	1	0	.333
Ferrazzi, Bill-William Joseph	35PhiA	4-19-07	West Quincy, Mass.		R	R	6'2	200	1	2	.333	0	3	2	0	7	7	5	0	0	5.14	1	0	0	.000
Ferrell, Wes-Wesley Cheek	27-33CleA 34-37BosA 37-38WasA 38-39NYA 40BknN 41BosN	2- 2-08	Greensboro, N.C.		R	R	6'2	195	193	128	.601	13	374	323	227	2623	2845	1040	985	17	4.04	(See B20-45)			
Fette, Lou-Louis Henry William	37-40BosN 40BknN 45BosN	3-15-07	Alma, Mo.		R	R	6'1	200	41	40	.506	1	109	97	51	691	658	248	194	14	3.15	236	44	0	.186
Fick, John-John Ralph	44PhiN	5-18-21	Baltimore, Md.	6- 9-58	L	L	5'10	150	0	0	–	0	4	0	0	5	3	3	2	0	3.60	0	0	0	–
Fieber, Clarence-Clarence Thomas (Lefty)	32ChiA	9- 4-13	San Francisco, Cal.		L	L	6'4	187	1	0	1.000	0	3	0	0	5	6	3	1	0	1.80	0	0	0	–
Filley, Marc-Marcus Lucius	34WasA	2-28-12	Troy, N.Y.		R	R	5'11	172	0	0	–	0	1	0	0	.1	2	0	0	0	27.00	0	0	0	–
Fillingim, Dana-Dana	15PhiA 18-23BosN 25PhiN	11- 6-93	Columbus, Ga.	2- 3-61	L	R	5'10	175	47	72	.395	5	200	113	59	1076	1170	313	270	10	3.56	368	77	2	.209
Fink, Herman-Herman Adam	35-37PhiA	8-22-11	Concord, N.C.		R	R	6'2	198	10	20	.333	4	67	30	10	285	322	123	73	0	5.21	93	14	0	.151
Fischer, Carl-Charles William	30-32WasA 32StLA 33-35DetA 35ChiA 37CleA 37WasA	11- 5-05	Medina, N.Y.	12-10-63	R	L	6'	180	46	50	.479	11	191	105	31	824	900	372	376	3	4.62	262	38	0	.145
Fischer, Rube-Reuben Walter	41,43-46NYN	9-19-16	Carlock, S.D.		R	R	6'4	190	16	34	.320	4	108	41	7	384	416	222	136	1	5.09	114	22	2	.193
Fisher, Clarence-Clarence Henry	19-20WasA	8-27-98	Letart, W.Va.	11- 2-65	R	R	6'	174	0	1	.000	0	4	0	0	8	13	8	1	0	11.25	1	0	0	.000
Fisher, Don-Donald Raymond	45NYN	2- 6-16	Cleveland, Ohio	7-29-73	R	R	6'	210	1	0	1.000	0	2	1	1	18	12	7	4	1	2.00	7	1	0	.143
Fitzke, Bob (Paul Frederick Herman)-Paul Robert	24CleA	7-30-00	La Crosse, Wis.	6-30-50	R	R	5'11	185	0	0	–	0	1	0	0	4	5	3	1	0	4.50	1	0	0	.000
Fitzsimmons, Freddie-Frederick Landis (Fat Freddie)	25-37NYN 37-43BknN M43-45PhiN	7-28-01	Mishawaka, Ind.		R	R	5'11	195	217	146	.598	13	513	426	186	3225	3335	846	870	30	3.51	1155	231	14	.200
Fleming, Bill-Leslie Fletchard	40-41BosA 42-44ChiN 45MS 46ChiN	7-31-13	Rowland, Cal.		R	R	6'	190	16	21	.432	3	123	40	14	440	442	193	167	3	3.80	125	13	0	.104
Flitcraft, Hilly-Hildreth Milton	42PhiN	8-21-23	Woodstown, N.J.		L	L	6'2	180	0	0	–	0	3	0	0	3	6	2	1	0	9.00	0	0	0	–
Flohr, Mort-Moritz Herman (Dutch)	34PhiA	8-15-11	Canisteo, N.Y.		L	L	6'	173	0	2	.000	0	14	3	0	31	34	33	6	0	5.81	12	4	0	.333
Flores, Jesse-Jesse Sandoval	42ChiN 43-47PhiA 50CleA	11- 2-14	Guadalajara, Mex.		R	R	5'10	175	44	59	.427	6	176	113	46	972	904	306	352	11	3.19	304	55	0	.181
Flowers, Wes-Charles Wesley	40,44BknN	8-13-13	Vanndale, Ark.		L	L	6'1	190	2	2	.500	0	14	3	0	38	49	23	11	0	5.45	10	4	0	.400
Flythe, Stu-Stuart McGuire	36PhiA	12- 5-11	Conway, N.C.	10-18-63	R	R	6'2	175	0	0	–	0	17	3	0	39	49	61	14	0	13.15	15	4	0	.267
Ford, Gene-Eugene Matthew	36BosN 38ChiA	[illegible]	Fort Dodge, Iowa	9- 7-70	R	R	6'2	195	0	0	–	0	6	1	0	16	23	15	2	0	10.69	6	1	0	.167
Foreman, Happy-August	24ChiA 26BosA	7-20-97	Memphis, Tenn.	2-13-53	L	L	5'7	160	0	0	–	0	0	0	0	11	10	9	4	0	3.27	4	0	0	.000
Fortune, Gary-Garrett Reese	16,18PhiN 20BosA	10-11-94	High Point, N.C.	9-23-55	B	R	5'11	176	0	5	.000	0	20	6	2	78	89	46	23	0	6.58	24	4	0	.107
Fowler, Jesse-Jesse Peter (Pete)	24StLN	10-30-98	Spartanburg, S.C.	9-23-73	R	L	5'10	158	1	1	.500	0	13	3	0	33	28	18	5	0	4.36	9	2	0	.222
Foxx, Jimmie-James Emory (Double X, The Beast)	39BosA 45PhiN	10-22-07	Sudlersville, Md.	7-21-67	R	R	6'	195	1	0	1.000	0	10	2	0	24	13	14	11	0	1.50	(See B20-45)			
Francis, Ray-Ray James	22WasA 23DetA 25NYA 25BosA	3- 8-93	Sherman, Tex.	7- 6-34	L	L	6'1	182	12	28	.300	3	82	36	15	337	409	110	96	2	4.65	107	17	0	.159
Frankhouse, Fred-Frederick Meloy	27-30StLN 30-35BosN 36-38BknN 39BosN	4- 9-04	Port Royal, Pa.		R	R	5'11	175	106	97	.522	12	402	216	81	1888	2033	701	622	10	3.92	636	132	1	.208
Franklin, Jack-James Wilford	44BknN	10-20-19	Paris, Ill.		R	R	5'11	170	0	0	–	0	1	0	0	2	2	4	0	0	13.50	0	0	0	–
Frasier, Vic-Victor Patrick	31-33ChiA 33-34DetA 37BosN 39ChiA	8- 5-04	Ruston, La.		R	R	6'	182	23	38	.377	4	126	68	21	580	686	291	170	2	5.76	186	33	0	.177
Freeman, Buck-Alexander Vernon	21-22ChiN	7- 5-96	Mart, Tex.	Deceased	B	R	5'10	167	9	11	.450	4	49	21	6	203	236	80	52	0	4.70	61	12	0	.197
Freeman, Harvey-Harvey Bayard (Buck)	21PhiA	12-22-97	Mottville, Mich.	1-10-70	R	R	5'10	145	1	4	.200	0	18	4	2	51	65	35	5	0	7.24	12	1	0	.083
Freeze, Jake-Carl Alexander	25ChiA	4-25-00	Huntingdon, Ark.		R	R	5'8	165	0	0	–	0	2	0	0	4	5	3	1	0	2.25	1	0	0	.000
Freitas, Tony-Antonio	32-33PhiA 34-36CinN	5- 5-08	Mill Valley, Cal.		R	L	5'8	161	25	33	.431	4	107	63	22	518	614	137	135	1	4.48	165	24	0	.145
French, Larry-Lawrence Herbert	29-34PitN 35-41ChiN 41-42BknN 43-45MS	11- 1-07	Visalia, Cal.		R	L	6'1	195	197	171	.535	17	570	384	198	3152	3375	819	1187	40	3.44	1057	199	1	.188
					Bats Both 34,40-42																				
Frey, Benny-Benjamin Rudolph	29-31CinN 32StLN 32-36CinN	4- 6-06	Dexter, Mich.	11- 1-37	R	R	5'10	165	57	82	.410	7	256	127	49	1159	1415	263	179	7	4.50	385	98	0	.255
Friday, Skipper-Grier William	23WasA	10-26-97	Gastonia, N.C.	8-25-62	R	R	5'11	170	0	1	.000	0	7	2	1	30	35	22	9	0	6.90	9	2	0	.222
Fried, Cy-Arthur Edwin	20DetA	7-23-97	San Antonio, Tex.	10-10-70	L	L	5'11	150	0	0	–	0	2	0	0	2	3	4	0	0	13.50	0	0	0	.000
Friedrich, Bob-Robert George	32WasA	8-30-06	Cincinnati, Ohio		R	R	5'11	165	0	0	–	0	2	0	0	4	4	7	2	0	11.25	1	0	0	–
Fry, Johnson-Johnson (Jay)	23CleA	11-21-01	Huntington, W.Va.	4- 7-59	R	R	6'1	150	0	0	–	0	1	0	0	4	6	4	0	0	11.25	1	1	0	1.000
Frye, Charlie-Charles Andrew	40PhiN	7-17-14	Hickory, N.C.	5-25-45	R	R	6'1	175	0	6	.000	0	15	5	1	50	58	26	18	0	4.68	19	5	0	.263
Fuchs, Charley-Charles Thomas	42DetA 43PhiN 43StLA 44BknN	11-18-13	Union Hill, N.J.	6-10-69	B	R	5'10	175	6	10	.375	1	47	13	5	166	186	73	41	2	4.88	43	3	0	.070
Fuhr, Oscar-Oscar Lawrence	21ChiN 24-25BosA	8-22-93	Defiance, Mo.	Deceased	L	L	6'	176	3	12	.200	0	63	16	4	175	249	69	59	1	6.38	43	9	0	.209
Fullerton, Curt-Curtis Hooper	21-25,33BosA	9-13-98	Ellsworth, Me.	1- 2-75	L	R	6'	162	10	37	.213	3	115	44	19	421	483	211	104	0	5.13	110	20	0	.182
Fussell, Fred-Frederick Morris (Moonlight Ace)	22-23ChiN 28-29PitN	10- 7-95	Sheridan, Mo.	10-23-66	L	L	5'10	155	14	17	.452	5	80	27	11	295	365	88	103	2	4.85	100	15	2	.150
Gabler, Frank-Frank Harold (The Great Gabbo)	35-37NYN 37-38BosN 38ChiA	11- 6-11	E. Highlands, Cal.	11- 1-67	R	R	6'1	175	16	23	.410	8	113	31	10	377	457	107	109	1	5.25	107	21	0	.196
Gables, Ken-Kenneth Harlin (Coral)	40-47PitN	1-21-19	Walnut Grove, Mo.	1- 2-60	R	R	5'11	210	13	11	.542	2	62	23	6	240	255	98	88	0	4.69	63	10	0	.159
Gaddy, John-John Wilson (Sheriff)	38BknN	2-15-14	Wadesboro, N.C.	5- 3-66	R	R	6'	182	2	0	1.000	0	2	2	1	13	13	4	3	0	0.69	6	0	0	.000
Gaines, Nemo-Willard Roland	21WasA	12-23-97	Alexandria, Va.		L	L	6'	180	0	0	–	0	4	0	0	5	5	2	1	0	0.00	1	0	0	.000
Galehouse, Denny-Dennis Ward	34-38CleA 39-40BosA 41-44StLA 45MS 46-47StLA 47-49BosA	12- 7-11	Marshallville, Ohio		R	R	6'1	195	109	118	.480	13	375	258	100	2003	2148	735	851	17	3.98	665	92	0	.138
Gallagher, Ed-Edward Michael (Lefty)	32BosA	11-28-10	Dorchester, Mass.		B	L	6'2	197	0	3	.000	0	9	3	0	24	30	28	6	0	12.38	5	0	0	.000
Gallivan, Phil-Philip Joseph	31BknN 32,34ChiA	5-29-07	Seattle, Wash.	11-24-69	R	R	6'	180	5	11	.313	1	54	11	4	175	227	95	68	0	5.97	51	12	0	.235
Gardiner, Art-Arthur Cecil	23PhiN	12-26-99	Brooklyn, N.Y.		R	R			0	0	–	0	1	0	0	0	1	1	0	0	0.00	0	0	0	–
Gardner, Glenn-Miles Glenn	45StLN	1-25-16	Burnsville, N.C.	7- 7-64	R	R	5'11	180	3	1	.750	1	17	4	2	55	50	27	20	1	3.27	21	7	0	.333
Garland, Lou-Louis Lyman	31ChiA	7-16-05	Archie, Mo.		R	R	6'2	200	0	2	.000	0	7	2	0	17	30	14	0	0	10.06	3	0	0	.000
Garrison, Cliff-Clifford Garry	28BosA	8-13-06	Meeker, Okla.		R	R	6'	180	0	0	–	0	6	0	0	16	22	6	0	0	7.88	3	0	0	.000
Gassaway, Charlie-Charles Cason (Sheriff)	44ChiN 45PhiA 46CleA	8-12-18	Gassaway, Tenn.		L	L	6'2	210	5	9	.357	0	39	19	4	181	188	91	80	0	4.03	58	8	0	.138
Gaston, Milt-Nathaniel Milton	24NYA 25-27StLA 28WasA 29-31BosA 32-34ChiA	1-27-96	Ridgefield Pk., N.J.		R	R	6'1	185	97	164	.372	8	355	271	127	2106	2338	836	615	10	4.55	724	145	6	.200
					Bats Both 33																				
Gaw, Chippy-George Joseph	20ChiN	3-13-92	West Newton, Mass.	5-26-68	R	R	5'11	180	1	1	.500	0	6	1	0	13	16	3	4	0	4.85	4	1	0	.250
Gearin, Dinty-Dennis John	23-24NYN 24BosN	10-15-97	Providence, R.I.	3-11-59	L	L	5'4	148	2	4	.333	0	13	6	3	53	56	28	13	0	3.74	16	5	0	.313
Gee, Johnny-John Alexander (Whiz) 46-47 played in N.B.L.	39PitN 40SA 41PitN 42AJ 43-44PitN 44-46NYN	12- 7-15	Syracuse, N.Y.		L	L	6'9	225	7	12	.368	1	44	21	4	175	209	64	65	0	4.42	51	8	0	.157
Gehrman, Paul-Paul Arthur (Dutch)	37CinN	5- 3-12	Mt. Angel, Ore.		R	R	6'	195	0	1	.000	0	2	1	0	9	11	5	1	0	3.00	3	0	0	.000
Genewich, Joe-Joseph Edward	22-28BosN 28-30NYN	1-15-97	Elmira, N.Y.		R	R	6'	174	73	92	.442	12	272	166	71	1401	1610	402	316	8	4.29	464	96	0	.207
Gentry, Rufe-James Ruffus	43-44DetA 45HO 46-48DetA	5-18-18	Winston-Salem, N.C.		R	R	6'1	180	13	17	.433	0	48	34	12	243	251	134	78	3	4.37	87	16	0	.184
Georgy, Oscar-Oscar John	38NYN	11-25-16	New Orleans, La.		R	R	6'3	180	0	0	–	0	1	0	0	1	2	1	0	0	18.00	0	0	0	–
Gerheauser, Al-Albert (Lefty)	43-44PhiN 45-46PitN 48StLA	6-24-17	St. Louis, Mo.	5-28-72	L	L	6'3	190	25	50	.333	1	149	79	27	643	726	224	255	4	4.13	211	44	1	.209
Gerkin, Steve-Stephen Paul (Splinter)	45PhiA	11-19-15	Grafton, W.Va.		R	R	6'1	162	0	12	.000	0	21	12	3	102	112	27	25	0	3.62	34	2	0	.059
Giard, Joe-Joseph Oscar (Peco)	25-26StLA 27NYA	10- 7-98	Ware, Mass.	7-10-56	L	L	5'10	170	13	15	.464	0	68	37	11	278	330	173	71	4	5.96	89	13	0	.146
Gibson, Sam-Samuel Braxton	26-28DetA 30NYA 32NYN	8- 5-99	King, N.C.		L	R	6'2	198	32	38	.457	5	131	75	33	594	676	249	208	4	4.24	202	50	0	.248
Gick, George-George Edward	37-38ChiA	10-18-15	Dunnington, Ind.		B	R	6'	190	0	0	–	1	2	0	0	3	0	0	2	0	0.00	0	0	0	–
Giebell, Floyd-Floyd George	39-41DetA	12-10-09	Pennsboro, W.Va.		L	R	6'2	172	3	1	.750	0	28	4	2	67	78	42	30	1	4.03	14	2	0	.143
Gill, George-George Lloyd	37-39DetA 39StLA	2-13-09	Catchings, Miss.		R	R	6'1	185	24	26	.480	1	85	45	22	396	494	129	95	2	5.05	135	17	0	.126
Gill, Haddie-Harold Edmund	23CinN	1-23-99	Brockton, Mass.	8- 1-32	L	L	5'10	145	0	0	–	0	1	0	0	1	1	1	1	0	0.00	0	0	0	–
Gillenwater, Claral-Claral Lewis	23ChiA	5-20-00	Simes, Ind.		R	R	6'	187	1	3	.250	0	5	3	1	21	28	6	2	1	5.57	6	0	0	.000
Gillespie, John-John Patrick (Silent John)	22CinN	2-25-00	Oakland, Cal.	2-15-54	R	R	5'11	172	3	3	.500	0	31	4	1	78	84	29	21	0	4.50	15	2	0	.133
Gilmore, Len-Leonard Preston (Meow)	44PitN	11- 3-17	Clinton, Ind.		R	R	6'3	175	0	1	.000	0	1	1	1	8	13	0	0	0	7.88	2	0	0	.000
Glaiser, John-John Burke (Bert)	20DetA	7-28-94	Yoakum, Tex.	3- 7-59	R	R	5'8	165	0	0	–	1	9	1	0	17	23	8	3	0	6.35	3	0	0	.000
Glass, Tom-Thomas Joseph	25PhiA	4-29-98	Greensboro, N.C.		R	R	6'3	170	1	0	1.000	0	2	0	0	5	9	0	2	0	5.40	2	0	0	.000
Glazner, Whitey-Charles Franklin	20-23PitN 23-24PhiN	9-17-92	Sycamore, Ala.		R	R	5'9	165	41	48	.461	4	142	102	46	784	895	249	266	6	4.21	260	47	2	.181
Gleason, Joe-Joseph Paul	20,22WasA	7- 9-95	Phelps, N.Y.		R	R	5'10	175	2	2	.500	0	11	5	3	49	67	24	14	0	6.06	16	2	0	.125
Glenn, Bob-Burdette	20StLN	6-16-94	West Sunbury, Pa.						0	0	–	0	2	0	0	2	2	0	0	0	0.00	0	0	0	–
Gliatto, Sal-Salvador Michael	30CleA	5- 7-02	Chicago, Ill.		B	R	5'8	150	0	0	–	2	8	0	0	15	21	9	7	0	6.60	2	0	0	.000
Goldsmith, Hal-Harold Eugene	26-28BosN 29StLN	8-18-98	Peconic, N.Y.		R	R	6'	174	6	10	.375	1	47	20	6	185	235	56	30	0	4.04	62	13	0	.210
Goldstein, Izzy-Isadore	32DetA	6- 6-08	New York, N.Y.		B	R	6'	160	3	2	.600	0	16	6	2	56	63	41	14	0	4.50	17	5	0	.294
Gomez, Lefty-Vernon Louis (Goofy, The Gay Castillion)	30-42NYA 43WasA	11-26-08	Rodeo, Cal.		L	L	6'2	173	189	102	.649	9	368	320	173	2503	2290	1095	1468	26	3.34	904	133	0	.147
Gonzales, Joe-Joe Madrid	37BosA	3-19-15	San Francisco, Cal.		R	R	5'9	175	1	2	.333	0	8	2	2	31	37	11	11	0	4.35	10	0	0	.000
Goodell, John-John Henry William (Lefty)	28ChiA	4- 5-07	Muskogee, Okla.		R	L	5'10	165	0	0	–	0	2	0	0	3	6	2	0	0	18.00	0	0	0	–
Gordinier, Ray-Raymond Cornelius	21-22BknN	4-11-92	Rochester, N.Y.	11-15-60	B	R	5'8	170	1	0	1.000	0	8	3	0	23	23	16	9	0	7.04	6	1	0	.167
Gorman, Tom-Thomas David (Big Tom)	39NYN	3-16-16	New York, N.Y.		R	L	6'2	200	0	0	–	0	4	0	0	5	7	1	2	0	7.20	1	0	0	.000
Gornicki, Hank-Frank Ted	41StLN 41ChiN 42-43PitN 44-45MS 46PitN	1-14-11	Niagara Falls, N.Y.		R	R	6'1	180	15	19	.441	6	79	33	12	285	275	107	123	4	3.38	82	12	1	.146
Gorsica (Gorczyca), Johnny-John Joseph Perry	40-44,46-47DetA 45MS	3-29-15	Bayonne, N.J.		R	R	6'2	180	31	39	.443	17	204	64	22	724	778	247	272	4	4.18	217	45	1	.207
Grabowski, Al-Alfons Francis (Hook)	29-30StLN	9- 4-01	Syracuse, N.Y.	10-29-66	L	L	5'11	175	9	6	.600	1	39	14	5	156	165	58	67	2	4.10	49	16	0	.327

USE NAME – GIVEN NAMES (NICKNAMES)	TEAM BY YEAR	BIRTH DATE	BIRTH PLACE	DEATH DATE	B	T	HGT	WGT	W	L	PCT	SV	G	GS	CG	IP	H	BB	SO	ShO	ERA	AB	H	HR	BA
					LIFETIME PITCHING TOTALS																	BATTING TOTALS			
Grabowski, Reggie-Reginald John	32-34PhiN	7-16-07	Syracuse, N.Y.	4- 2-55	R	R	6'	185	4	8	.333	0	51	12	4	147	190	55	37	1	5.76	40	3	0	.075
Graham, Kyle-Kyle B	24-26BosN 29DetA	8-14-99	Bessemer, Ala.	12- 1-73	R	R	6'2	172	11	22	.333	2	67	37	9	278	334	125	61	0	5.02	82	10	1	.122
Grampp, Hank-Henry Erchardt	27,29ChiN	9-28-03	New York, N.Y.		R	R	6'1	175	0	1	.000	0	3	1	0	5	8	4	3	0	16.20	0	0	0	–
Grant, George-George Addison	23-25StLA 27-29CleA 31PitN	1- 6-03	E. Tallassee, Ala.		R	R	5'11	175	15	20	.429	1	114	23	8	347	460	182	89	1	5.65	104	14	0	.135
Grant, Jim-James Ronald	23PhiN	8- 4-94	Coalville, Iowa		R	L	5'11	180	0	0	–	0	2	0	0	4	10	4	0	0	13.50	1	0	0	.000
Grate, Don-Donald (Buckeye)	45-46PhiN	8-27-23	Greenfield, Ohio		R	R	6'2	180	1	1	.500	0	7	2	0	16	22	14	8	0	9.56	4	0	0	.000
Gray, Sam-Samuel David (Sad Sam)	24-27PhiA 28-33StLA	10-15-97	Van Alstyne, Tex.	4-16-53	R	R	5'10	175	110	115	.489	22	379	231	101	1945	2196	639	730	15	4.19	648	124	2	.191
Green, Harvey-Harvey George	35BknN	2- 9-15	Kenosha, Wis.	7-24-70	B	R	6'2	185	0	0	–	0	2	0	0	1	2	3	0	0	9.00	0	0	0	–
Greene, June-June Foust	28-29PhiN	6-25-99	Ramseur, N.C.		L	R	6'	185	0	0	–	0	6	0	0	16	38	9	4	0	18.00	25	7	0	.280
Greene, Nelson-Nelson George (Lefty)	24-25BknN	9-20-00	Philadelphia, Pa.		L	L	6'	185	2	1	.667	1	15	1	0	31	59	9	7	0	8.71	8	2	0	.250
Greenfield, Kent-Kent	24-27NYN 27-29BosN 29BknN	7- 1-02	Guthrie, Ky.		R	R	6'1	180	41	48	.461	1	152	102	36	776	871	297	242	2	4.53	237	24	0	.101
Gregg, Hal-Harold Dana	43-47BknN 48-50PitN 52NYN	7-11-21	Anaheim, Cal.		R	R	6'3	195	40	48	.455	9	200	115	27	826	805	443	401	5	4.54	263	54	2	.205
Gregory, Paul-Paul Edwin (Pop)	32-33ChiA	7- 9-08	Tomnolen, Miss.		R	R	6'2	180	9	14	.391	0	56	26	8	222	249	98	57	0	4.70	73	8	0	.110
Griffin, Marty-Martin John	28BosA	9- 2-01	San Francisco, Cal.	11-19-51	R	R	6'2	200	0	3	.000	0	11	3	0	38	42	17	9	0	4.97	13	4	0	.308
Grimes, Burleigh-Burleigh Arland (Ol'Stubblebeard)	16-17PitN 18-26BknN 27NYN 28-29PitN 30BosN 30-31StLN 32-33ChiN 33-34StLN 34PitN 34NYA M37-38BknN	8-18-93	Clear Lake, Wis.		R	R	5'10	175	270	212	.560	18	615	495	314	4177	4406	1295	1512	35	3.52	1535	380	2	.248
Grissom, Lee-Lee Theo	34-39CinN 40NYA 40-41BknN 41PhiN 42-45MS	10-23-07	Sherman, Tex.		B (Bats Right 34,37)	L	6'3	200	29	48	.377	7	162	95	23	702	668	305	384	6	3.88	205	26	0	.127
Grove, Lefty-Robert Moses (Mose)	25-33PhiA 34-41BosA	3- 6-00	Lonaconing, Md.	5-22-75	L	L	6'3	190	300	141	.680	55	616	457	300	3940	3849	1187	2266	32	3.06	1369	202	15	.148
Grove, Orval-Orval LeRoy	40-49ChiA	8-29-19	Mineral, Kans.		R	R	6'3	196	63	73	.463	4	207	152	66	1177	1237	444	374	11	3.78	373	48	1	.129
Grubbs, Tom-Thomas Dillard (Judge)	20NYN	2-22-94	Mt. Sterling, Ky.		R	R	6'2	165	0	1	.000	0	1	1	0	5	9	0	0	0	7.20	1	0	0	.000
Gudat, Marv-Marvin John	29CinN 32ChiN	8-27-05	Goliad, Tex.	3- 1-54	L	L	5'11	176	1	1	.500	0	8	2	2	28	30	4	2	0	3.21	(See B20-45)			
Guise, Witt-Witt Orison (Lefty)	40CinN	9-18-08	Driggs, Ark.	8-13-68	L	L	6'2	172	0	0	–	0	2	0	0	8	8	5	1	0	1.13	3	1	0	.333
Gumbert, Harry-Harry Edward (Gunboat)	35-41NYN 41-44StLN 44CinN 45MS 46-49CinN 49-50PitN	11- 5-09	Elizabeth, Pa.		R	R	6'2	185	143	113	.559	48	508	235	96	2158	2186	721	709	12	3.68	708	130	5	.184
Hadley, Bump-Irving Darius	26-31WasA 32ChiA 32-34StLA 35WasA 36 40NYA 41NYN 41PhiA	7- 5-04	Lynn, Mass.	2-15-63	R	R	5'11	190	161	165	.494	25	528	355	135	2945	2980	1442	1318	12	4.25	1004	190	0	.189
Haid, Hal-Harold Augustine	19StLA 28-30StLN 31BosN 33ChiA	12-21-97	Barberton, Ohio	8-13-52	R	R	5'10	150	14	15	.483	12	119	12	8	308	330	123	103	0	4.15	72	9	0	.125
Haines, Jesse-Jesse Joseph (Pop)	18CinN 20-37StLN	7-22-93	Clayton, Ohio		R	R	6'	190	210	158	.571	10	555	388	208	3208	3460	871	981	23	3.64	1124	209	3	.186
Hallahan, Wild Bill-William Anthony	25-26,29-36StLN 36-37CinN 38PhiN	8- 4-02	Binghamton, N.Y.		R	L	5'10	170	102	94	.520	8	324	224	90	1740	1838	777	856	13	4.03	557	90	2	.162
Hallett, Jack-Jack Price	40-41ChiA 42-43,46PitN 44-45MS 48NYN	11-13-13	Toledo, Ohio		R	R	6'4	215	12	16	.429	0	73	24	11	278	280	106	128	2	4.05	80	19	1	.238
Hamann, Doc-Elmer Joseph	22CleA	12-21-00	New Ulm, Minn.	1-11-73	R	R	6'1	180	0	0	–	0	1	0	0	0	3	3	0	0	∞	0	0	0	–
Hamlin, Luke-Luke Daniel (Hot Potato)	33-34DetA 37-41BknN 42PitN 44PhiA	7- 3-04	Ferris Cen., Mich.		L	R	6'2	168	73	76	.490	9	261	181	70	1405	1442	353	563	9	3.77	463	76	1	.164
Hankins, Don-Donald Wayne	27DetA	2- 9-02	Pendleton, Ind.	5-16-63	R	R	6'3	183	2	1	.667	2	20	1	0	40	67	13	10	0	6.75	7	1	0	.143
Hanning, Loy-Loy Vernon	39,42StLA	10-18-17	Bunker, Mo.		R	R	6'2	175	1	2	.333	0	15	1	0	27	32	16	17	0	6.33	5	1	0	.200
Hansen, Snipe-Roy Emil	30,32-35PhiN 35StLA	2-21-07	Chicago, Ill.		B (Bats Left 30)	L	6'3	195	22	45	.328	6	155	71	19	625	783	194	176	2	5.01	200	31	0	.155
Hanski (Hanyzewski), Don-Donald Thomas	43-44ChiA 45MS	2-27-16	LaPorte, Ind.	9- 2-57	L	L	5'11	180	0	0	–	0	3	0	0	4	6	3	0	0	9.00	(See B20-45)			
Hanson, Ollie-Earl Sylvester	21ChiN	1-19-96	Holbrook, Mass.	8-19-51	R	R	5'9	178	0	2	.000	0	2	2	1	9	9	6	2	0	7.00	3	0	0	.000
Hanyzewski, Ed-Edward Michael	42-46ChiN	9-18-20	Union Mills, Ind.		R	R	6'1	200	12	13	.480	0	58	25	6	218	213	79	81	0	3.30	65	4	0	.062
Harder, Mel-Melvin LeRoy (Wimpy, Chief)	28-47,M61CleA	10-15-09	Beemer, Neb.		R	R	6'1	195	223	186	.545	23	582	433	181	3426	3706	1118	1160	24	3.80	1203	199	4	.165
Harman, Bill-William Bell	41PhiN 42MS	1- 2-19	Bridgewater, Va.		R	R	6'4	200	0	0	–	0	5	0	0	13	15	8	3	0	4.85	14	1	0	.071
Harrell, Ray-Raymond James (Cowboy)	35,37-38StLN 39ChiN 39PhiN 40PitN 45NYN	2-16-12	Petrolia, Tex.		R	R	6'1	185	9	20	.310	3	119	31	6	330	385	177	136	1	5.70	72	5	0	.069
Harris, Bill-William Milton	23-24CinN 31-34PitN 38BosA	6-23-00	Wylie, Tex.	8-21-65	R	R	6'1	180	24	22	.522	8	121	37	13	434	467	109	149	2	3.92	123	25	0	.203
Harris, Bob-Robert Arthur	38-39DetA 39-42StLA 42PhiA 43-45MS	5- 1-16	Gillette, Wyo.		R	R	6'	185	30	52	.366	2	127	89	26	647	770	294	205	4	4.95	202	39	0	.193
Harris, Herb-Herbert (Hub)	36PhiN	4-24-13	Whiting, Ind.		L	L	6'1	175	0	0	–	0	4	0	0	7	14	5	0	0	10.29	1	0	0	.000
Harris, Lum-Chalmer Luman	41-44PhiA 45MS 46PhiA 47WasA M61BalA M64-65HouN M68-72AtlN	1-17-15	New Castle, Ala.		R	R	6'1	180	35	63	.357	3	151	91	46	819	874	265	232	4	4.16	268	51	1	.190
Harriss, Slim-William Jennings Bryan	20-26PhiA 26-28BosA	12-11-96	Brownwood, Tex.	9-19-63	R	R	6'6	180	95	135	.413	16	349	228	89	1750	1963	630	644	6	4.25	565	82	1	.145
Hash, Herb-Herbert Howard	40-41BosA	2-13-11	Woolwine, Va.		R	R	6'1	180	8	7	.533	4	38	12	3	128	130	91	39	1	4.99	42	7	0	.167
Hasty, Bob-Robert Keller	19-24PhiA	5- 3-96	Canton, Ga.	5-28-72	R	R	6'3	210	29	53	.354	1	146	94	35	751	900	215	167	2	4.64	271	60	1	.221
Hathaway, Ray-Ray Wilson	45BknN	10-13-16	Greenville, Ohio		R	R	6'	165	0	1	.000	0	4	1	0	9	11	6	3	0	4.00	2	0	0	.000
Hatter, Clyde-Clyde Melnow (Mad)	35,37DetA	8- 7-08	Poplar Hill, Ky.	10-16-37	R	L	5'11	170	1	0	1.000	0	11	2	0	42	61	41	19	0	8.57	13	3	0	.231
Haughey, Chris-Christopher Francis (Bud)	43BknN 44-45MS	10- 3-25	Queens, N.Y.		R	R	6'1	180	0	1	.000	0	1	0	0	7	5	10	0	0	3.86	3	0	0	.000
Hausmann, Clem-Clemens Raymond	44-45BosA 49PhiA	8-17-19	Houston, Tex.		R	R	5'9	165	9	14	.391	4	64	25	7	263	270	131	73	2	4.21	77	7	0	.091
Hayes, Jim-James Millard	35WasA	2-11-13	Montevallo, Ala.		L	R	6'1	168	2	4	.333	0	7	4	1	28	38	23	9	0	8.36	8	2	0	.250
Head, Ed-Edward Marvin	40,42-44BknN 45MS 46BknN	1-25-18	Selma, Ala.		R	R	6'1	175	27	23	.540	11	118	53	22	465	434	174	208	5	3.48	131	32	0	.244
Head, Ralph-Ralph	23PhiN	8-30-93	Tallapoosa, Ga.	10- 8-62	R	R	5'10	175	2	9	.182	0	35	13	5	132	185	57	24	0	6.68	42	3	0	.071
Hearn, Bunny-Elmer Lafayette	26-29BosN	1-13-04	Brooklyn, N.Y.	3-31-74	L	L	5'8	180	7	11	.389	2	59	13	3	158	161	82	65	0	4.39	38	5	0	.132
Heath, Spencer-Spencer Paul	20ChiA	11- 5-94	Chicago, Ill.	1-25-30	B	R	6'	170	0	0	–	0	4	0	0	7	19	2	0	0	15.43	3	0	0	.000
Hebert, Wally-Wallace Andrew (Preacher)	31-33StLA 43PitN	8-21-07	Lake Charles, La.		L	L	6'1	195	21	36	.368	1	125	61	22	483	584	168	115	1	4.64	159	43	0	.270
Heflin, Randy-Randolph Rutherford	45-46BosA	9-11-18	Fredericksburg, Va.		L	R	6'	185	4	11	.267	0	25	15	6	117	118	73	45	2	3.85	38	5	0	.132
Heimach, Fred-Fred Amos (Lefty)	20-26PhiA 26BosA 28-29NYA 30-33BknN	1-27-01	Camden, N.J.	6- 1-73	L	L	6'	175	62	69	.473	7	296	127	56	1289	1510	360	334	5	4.46	542	128	3	.236
Heise, Clarence-Clarence Edward (Lefty)	34StLN	8- 7-07	Topeka, Kans.		L	L	5'10	172	0	0	–	0	1	0	0	2	3	0	1	0	4.50	0	0	0	–
Henderson, Bernie-Bernard (Barnyard)	21CleA	4-12-99	Douglassville, Tex.	6- 6-66	L	R	5'9	175	0	1	.000	0	2	1	0	3	5	0	1	0	9.00	1	0	0	.000
Henderson, Bill-William Maxwell	30NYA	11- 4-01	Altha, Fla.	10- 6-66	R	R	6'	185	0	0	–	0	3	0	0	8	7	4	2	0	4.50	2	1	0	.500
Hendrickson, Don-Donald Williamson	45-46BosN	7-14-15	Kewanna, Ind.		R	R	6'2	195	4	9	.308	5	39	2	1	75	78	41	16	0	4.92	19	3	0	.158
Hennessey, George-George (Three Star)	37StLA 42PhiN 45ChiN	10-28-07	Slatington, Pa.		R	R	5'10	168	1	2	.333	0	12	1	0	28	33	17	8	0	5.14	5	0	0	.000
Henry, Dutch-Frank John	21-22StLA 23-24BknN 27-29NYN 29-30ChiA	5-12-02	Cleveland, Ohio	8-23-68	L	L	6'1	173	27	43	.386	6	164	62	25	646	809	190	170	3	4.39	216	50	0	.231
Henry, Earl-Earl Clifford (Hook)	44-45CleA	6-10-17	Roseville, Ohio		L	L	5'11	172	1	4	.200	0	17	3	1	40	38	23	15	0	4.95	9	2	0	.222
Henry, Jim-James Francis	36-37BosA 39PhiN	6-26-10	Danville, Va.		R	R	6'2	175	6	2	.750	1	33	11	3	114	114	59	51	0	4.82	36	3	0	.083
Henshaw, Roy-Roy K	33,35-36ChiN 37BknN 38StLN 42-44DetA	7-29-11	Chicago, Ill.		R	L	5'8	155	33	40	.452	7	216	69	22	742	782	327	337	3	4.16	229	41	0	.179
Hensiek, Phil-Philip Frank (Sid)	35WasA	10-13-01	St. Louis, Mo.	2-21-72	R	R	6'	160	0	3	.000	1	6	1	0	13	21	9	6	0	9.69	3	2	0	.667
Herring, Art-Arthur L (Sandy)	29-33DetA 34BknN 39ChiA 44-46BknN 47PitN	3-10-07	Altus, Okla.		R	R	5'7	168	34	38	.472	13	199	56	25	697	754	284	243	3	4.33	208	31	0	.149
Herrmann, Leroy-Leroy George	32-33ChiN 35CinN	2-27-06	Steward, Ill.	7- 3-72	R	R	5'10	185	5	7	.417	1	45	9	2	142	168	48	39	0	4.12	38	10	0	.263
Heusser, Ed-Edward Burlton (The Wild Elk of the Wasatch)	35-36StLN 38PhiN 40PhiA 43-46CinN 48PhiN	5- 7-09	Mill Creek, Utah	3- 1-56	B (Bats Right 35-38)	R	6'	187	56	67	.455	18	266	104	50	1087	1167	300	299	10	3.69	335	69	3	.206
Heving, Joe-Joseph William	30-31NYN 33-34ChiA 35DP 37-38CleA 38-40BosA 41-44CleA 45BosN	9- 2-00	Covington, Ky.	4-11-70	R	R	6'1	185	76	48	.613	63	430	40	17	1039	1136	380	429	3	3.90	276	47	0	.170
Hickey, Jim-James Robert (Sid)	42,44BosN 45MS	8-22-20	N. Abington, Mass.		R	R	6'1	204	0	1	.000	0	9	1	0	10	9	7	3	0	7.20	2	0	0	.000
Higbe, Kirby-Walter Kirby	37-39ChiN 39-40PhiN 41-43BknN 44-45MS 46-47BknN 47-49PitN 49-50NYN	4- 8-15	Columbia, S.C.		R	R	5'11	190	118	101	.539	24	418	238	98	1954	1763	979	971	11	3.68	660	101	3	.153
Hilcher, Whitey-Walter Frank	31-32,35-36CinN	2-28-09	Chicago, Ill.	11-21-62	R	R	6'	174	3	6	.333	0	31	6	1	85	103	33	28	1	5.29	21	2	0	.095
Hildebrand, Oral-Oral Clyde	31-36CleA 37-38StLA 39-40NYA	4- 7-07	Bridgeport, Ind.		R	R	6'3	175	83	78	.516	13	258	182	80	1430	1490	623	527	9	4.36	513	96	0	.187
Hill, Carmen-Carmen Proctor (Specs)	15-16,18-19PitN 22NYN 26-29PitN 29-30StLN	10- 1-95	Royalton, Minn.		R	R	6'1	180	49	33	.598	8	147	85	47	788	769	267	264	5	3.44	277	53	0	.191
Hockette, George-George Edward (Lefty)	34-35BosA	4- 7-08	Perth, Miss.		L	L	6'	174	4	4	.500	0	26	7	3	88	105	18	25	2	4.09	25	5	0	.200
Hodge, Shovel-Clarence Clement	20-22ChiA	7- 6-93	Mt. Andrew, Ala	12-31-67	L	R	6'4	190	14	15	.483	3	75	21	9	302	360	131	67	0	5.16	116	29	0	.250
Hoerst, Frank-Francis Joseph (Lefty)	40-42PhiN 43-45MS 46-47PhiN	8-11-17	Philadelphia, Pa.		L	L	6'3	192	10	33	.233	1	98	41	8	348	381	175	105	0	5.17	91	14	0	.154
Hoffman, Bill-William Joseph	39PhiN	3- 3-18	Philadelphia, Pa.		L	L	5'9	170	0	0	–	0	3	0	0	6	8	7	1	0	13.50	1	0	0	.000
Hogsett, Chief-Elon Chester	29-36DetA 36-37StLA 38WasA 44DetA	11- 2-03	Brownell, Kans.		L	L	6'	190	63	87	.420	33	330	114	37	1221	1511	501	441	2	5.03	403	91	6	.226
Holborow, Walt-Walter Albert	44-45WasA 48PhiA	11-30-13	New York, N.Y.		R	R	5'11	187	2	3	.400	0	21	2	2	51	52	25	18	1	3.35	6	2	0	.333
Holland, Bill-William David	39WasA	6- 4-15	Varina, N.C.		L	L	6'1	190	0	1	.000	0	3	0	0	4	6	5	2	0	11.25	0	0	0	–
Holland, Mul-Howard Arthur	26CinN 27NYN 29StLN	1- 6-03	Franklin, Va.	2-16-69	R	R	6'4	185	1	1	.500	0	13	0	0	23	16	15	5	0	6.26	6	2	0	.333
Hollaway, Ken-Kenneth Eugene	22-28DetA 29-30CleA 30NYA	8- 8-97	Barwick, Ga.	9-25-68	R	R	6'	185	64	52	.552	18	285	111	43	1159	1370	397	293	4	4.40	378	63	0	.167
Holley, Ed-Edward Edgar	28ChiN 32-34PhiN 34PitN	7-23-01	Benton, Ky.		R	R	6'1	195	25	40	.385	0	97	76	30	548	602	170	169	5	4.40	196	31	0	.158
Holling, Carl-Carl	21-22DetA	7- 9-96	Dana, Cal.	7-18-62	R	R	6'1	172	4	8	.333	4	40	12	4	145	183	63	40	0	5.03	50	13	0	.260
Hollingsworth, Al-Albert Wayne (Boots)	35-38CinN 38-39PhiN 39BknN 40WasA 42-46StLA 46ChiA	2-25-08	St. Louis, Mo.		L	L	6'2	185	70	104	.402	15	315	185	78	1519	1642	587	608	7	3.99	525	103	2	.196

USE NAME – GIVEN NAMES (NICKNAMES)	TEAM BY YEAR	BIRTH DATE	BIRTH PLACE	DEATH DATE	B	T	HGT	WGT	W	L	PCT	SV	G	GS	CG	IP	H	BB	SO	ShO	ERA	AB	H	HR	BA
					LIFETIME PITCHING TOTALS																	BATTING TOTALS			
Hollingsworth, Bonnie-John Burnett	22PitN 23WasA 24BknN 28BosN	12-26-95	Jacksboro, Tenn.		R	R	5'10	170	4	9	.308	0	36	11	2	117	126	80	49	0	4.92	31	3	0	.097
Holloway, Jim-James Madison	29PhiN	9-22-08	Plaquemine, La.		R	R	6'1	165	0	0	–	0	3	0	0	5	10	5	1	0	12.60	1	1	0	1.000
Holshouser, Herm-Herman Alexander	30StLA	1-20-07	Rockwell, N.C.		R	R	6'	170	0	1	.000	1	25	1	0	62	103	28	37	0	7.84	16	2	0	.125
Hopkins, Paul-Paul Henry	27,29WasA 29StLA	9-25-04	Chester, Conn.		R	R	6'	175	1	1	.500	0	11	1	0	27	28	15	11	0	3.00	6	2	0	.333
Horne, Trader-Berlyn Dale (Sonny)	29ChiN	4-12-99	Bachman, Ohio		R	R	5'9	155	1	1	.500	0	11	1	0	23	24	21	6	0	5.09	5	2	0	.400
					Bats Both part of 29																				
Howe, Les-Lester Curtis (Lucky)	23-24BosA	8-24-95	Brooklyn, N.Y.		R	R	5'11	170	2	0	1.000	0	16	2	0	37	34	9	10	0	3.41	8	1	0	.125
Hoyt, Waite-Waite Charles (Schoolboy) 25-26 played in A.B.L.	18NYN 19-20BosA 21-30NYA 30-31DetA 31PhiA 32BknN 32NYN 33-37PitN 37-38BknN	9-9-99	Brooklyn, N.Y.		R	R	6'	180	237	182	.566	52	675	422	226	3762	4037	1003	1206	25	3.59	1287	255	0	.198
Hubbell, Bill-Wilbert William	19-20NYN 20-25PhiN 25-BknN	6-17-97	Henderson, Colo.		R	R	6'1	195	40	63	.388	10	204	108	50	930	1207	225	167	5	4.68	308	53	1	.172
Hubbell, Carl-Carl Owen (The Meal Ticket, King Carl)	28-43NYN	6-22-03	Carthage, Mo.		R	L	6'	170	253	154	.622	33	535	431	260	3591	3461	725	1677	36	2.98	1288	246	4	.191
					Bats Both 31-32																				
Huckleberry, Earl-Earl Eugene	35PhiA	5-23-10	Konawa, Okla.		R	R	5'11	165	1	0	1.000	0	1	1	0	7	8	4	2	0	9.00	3	0	0	.000
Hudlin, Willis-George Willis (Ace)	26-40CleA 40WasA 40StLA 40NYN 44StLA	5-23-06	Wagoner, Okla.		R	R	6'	190	158	156	.503	31	491	328	154	2613	3011	843	677	11	4.41	894	180	5	.201
Hughes, Bill-William Nesbert	21PitN	11-18-96	Philadelphia, Pa.	2-25-63	R	R	5'10	155	0	0	–	0	1	0	0	2	3	1	2	0	4.50	0	0	0	–
Hughson, Tex-Cecil Carlton	41-44BosA 45MS 46-49BosA	2-9-16	Kyle, Tex.		R	R	6'3	198	96	54	.640	17	225	156	99	1375	1270	372	693	15	2.95	447	53	0	.119
Hulihan, Harry-Harry Joseph	22BosN	4-18-99	Rutland, Vt.		R	L	5'11	170	2	3	.400	0	7	6	2	40	40	26	16	0	3.15	13	2	0	.154
Hulvey, Hank-James Hensel	23PhiA	7-18-97	Mt. Sidney, Va.		B	R	6'	180	0	1	.000	0	1	1	0	7	10	2	2	0	7.71	2	1	0	.500
Humphrey, Bill-Bryon William	38BosA	6-17-11	Vienna, Mo.		R	R	6'	180	0	0	–	0	2	0	0	2	5	1	0	0	9.00	0	0	0	–
Humphries, John-John William	38-40CleA 41-45ChiA 46PhiN	6-23-15	Clifton Forge, Va.	6-24-65	R	R	6'1	185	52	63	.452	12	211	111	49	1001	1024	373	317	9	3.79	329	63	0	.191
Huntzinger, Walter-Walter Henry (Shakes)	23-25NYN 26StLN 26ChiN	2-6-99	Pottsville, Pa.		R	R	6'	150	7	8	.467	3	60	8	2	167	179	49	40	0	3.61	36	6	0	.167
Hutchings, Johnny-John Richard Joseph	40-41CinN 41-42,44-46BosN	4-14-16	Chicago, Ill.	4-27-63	B	R	6'2	250	12	18	.400	6	155	34	5	472	474	180	212	3	3.95	130	21	0	.162
Hutchinson, Ira-Ira Kendall	33ChiA 37-38BosN 39BknN 40-41StLN 44-45BosN	8-31-10	Chicago, Ill.	8-21-73	R	R	5'10	180	34	33	.507	13	209	32	7	612	628	249	179	2	3.75	171	24	0	.140
Jablonowski, Pete (See Pete Appleton)																									
Jackson, John-John Lewis	33PhiN	7-15-09	Wynnefield, Pa.	10-24-56	R	R	6'2	180	2	2	.500	0	10	7	1	54	74	35	11	0	6.00	21	3	0	.143
Jacobs, Art-Arthur Edward (Lefty)	39CinN	8-28-02	Luckey, Ohio	6-8-67	L	L	5'10	170	0	0	–	1	1	0	0	1	2	1	0	0	9.00	0	0	0	–
Jacobs, Bucky-Newton Smith	37,39-40WasA	3-21-13	Altavista, Va.		R	R	5'11	150	1	2	.333	0	22	1	0	40	43	20	15	0	4.95	6	0	0	.000
Jaeger, Joe-Joseph Peter (Zip)	20ChiN	3-3-95	St. Cloud, Minn.	12-13-63	R	R	6'1	190	0	0	–	0	2	0	0	3	6	4	0	0	12.00	1	0	0	.000
Jakucki, Sig-Sigmund (Jack)	36,44-45StLA	8-20-09	Camden, N.J.		R	R	6'2	198	25	22	.532	5	72	50	27	411	431	131	131	5	3.79	149	24	3	.161
Jamerson, Charley-Charles Dewey (Lefty)	24BosA	1-26-00	Enfield, Ill.		L	L	6'1	195	0	0	–	0	1	0	0	1	1	3	0	0	18.00	0	0	0	–
Javery, Al-Alva William (Bear Tracks)	40-46BosN	6-5-18	Worcester, Mass.		R	R	6'3	183	53	74	.417	5	205	147	61	1142	1164	452	470	15	3.81	380	52	0	.137
Jeffcoat, George-George Edward	36-37,39BknN 43BosN	12-24-13	New Brookland, S.C.		R	R	5'11	175	7	11	.389	3	70	9	4	170	159	100	86	1	4.50	39	5	0	.128
Johns, Augie-Augustus Francis (Lefty)	26-27DetA	9-10-99	St. Louis, Mo.		L	L	5'9	170	6	4	.600	1	36	14	3	114	118	70	41	1	5.37	28	4	0	.143
Johnson, Art-Arthur Gilbert	27NYN	2-15-97	Warren, Pa.		B	L	6'1	167	0	0	–	0	1	0	0	3	1	1	0	0	0.00	0	0	0	–
Johnson, Art-Arthur Henry (Lefty)	40-42BosN 43-45MS	7-16-16	Winchester, Mass.		L	L	6'2	185	7	16	.304	1	49	19	6	195	203	79	71	0	3.69	57	8	0	–
Johnson, Fred-Frederick Edward (Cactus, Deacon)	22-23NYN 38-39StLA	3-10-94	Hanley, Tex.	6-14-73	R	R	5'11	180	5	10	.333	3	27	12	6	118	145	44	39	0	5.26	39	6	0	.154
Johnson, Hank-Henry Ward	25-26,28-32NYA 33-35BosA 36PhiA 39CinN	5-21-06	Bradenton, Fla.		R	R	5'11	175	63	56	.529	11	249	116	45	1065	1107	567	568	4	4.76	376	81	2	.215
					Bats Both 33																				
Johnson, Johnny-John Clifford (Swede)	44NYA 45ChiA 46AJ	9-29-14	Belmore, Ohio		L	L	6'	182	3	2	.600	7	51	1	0	97	110	59	49	0	4.18	20	7	0	.350
Johnson, Lloyd-Lloyd William (Eppa)	34PitN	12-24-10	Santa Rosa, Cal.		L	L	6'4	220	0	0	–	0	1	0	0	1	1	0	0	0	0.00	0	0	0	–
Johnson, Rankin-Adam Rankin Jr.	41PhiA 42-45MS	3-1-17	Hayden, Ariz.		R	R	6'3	177	1	0	1.000	0	7	0	0	10	14	3	0	0	3.60	1	0	0	.000
Johnson, Si-Silas Kenneth	28-36CinN 36-38StLN 40-43PhiN 44-45MS 46PhiN 46-47BosN	10-5-06	Marseilles, Ill.		R	R	5'11	185	101	165	.380	15	492	272	108	2280	2510	687	840	13	4.09	709	87	0	.123
Johnson, Syl-Sylvester W.	22-25DetA 26-33StLN 34CinN 34-40PhiN	12-31-00	Portland, Ore.		R	R	5'11	180	112	117	.489	43	542	210	82	2166	2290	488	920	13	4.06	702	127	4	.181
Johnson, Vic-Victor Oscar	44-45BosA 46CleA	8-3-20	Eau Claire, Wis.		R	L	6'	160	6	8	.429	2	42	15	4	126	152	69	31	1	5.07	42	5	0	.119
Joiner, Roy-Roy Merrill (Pop)	34-35ChiN 40NYN	10-30-06	Red Bluff, Cal.		L	L	6'	170	3	3	.500	1	52	4	0	90	133	27	34	0	5.30	22	5	0	.227
Jones, Art-Arthur Lenox	32BknN	2-7-07	Kershaw, S.C.		R	R	6'	165	0	0	–	0	1	0	0	1	2	1	0	0	18.00	0	0	0	–
Jones, Broadway-Jesse Frank	23PhiN	11-15-98	Millsboro, Del.		R	R	5'9	154	0	0	–	0	3	0	0	8	5	7	1	0	9.00	2	1	0	.500
Jones, Dale-Dale Eldon (Nubs)	41PhiN 42-45MS	12-17-18	Marquette, Neb.		R	R	6'1	172	0	1	.000	0	2	1	0	8	13	6	2	0	7.88	3	1	0	.333
Jones, Dick-Decatur Poindexter	26-27WasA	5-22-02	Meadville, Miss.		L	R	6'	184	2	1	.667	0	6	3	1	24	28	16	4	0	6.75	10	2	0	.200
Jones, Earl-Earl Leslie (Lefty)	45StLA	6-11-19	Fresno, Cal.		L	L	5'10	190	0	0	–	1	10	0	0	28	18	18	13	0	2.57	10	2	1	.200
Jones, Johnny-John Paul (Admiral)	19NYN 20BosN	8-25-92	Arcadia, La.		R	R	6'1	150	1	0	1.000	1	5	1	0	17	25	8	9	0	5.82	7	1	0	.143
Jones, Ken-Kenneth Frederick (Broadway)	24DetA 30BosN	4-13-04	Dover, N.J.		R	R	6'3	193	0	1	.000	0	9	1	0	22	29	5	4	0	5.32	5	1	0	.200
Jones, Percy-Percy Lee	20-22,25-28ChiN 29BosN 30PitN	10-28-99	Harwood, Tex.		R	L	5'11	175	53	57	.482	6	251	117	49	1026	1137	494	381	8	4.34	324	63	0	.194
Jones, Sad Sam-Samuel Pond	14-15CleA 16-21BosA 22-26NYA 27StLA 28-31WasA 32-35ChiA	7-26-92	Woodsfield, Ohio	7-6-66	R	R	6'	170	228	216	.514	31	647	487	250	3884	4084	1396	1223	35	3.84	1243	245	6	.197
Jonnard, Claude-Claude Alfred	21-24NYN 26StLA 29ChiN	11-23-96	Nashville, Tenn.	8-27-59	R	R	6'2	185	14	12	.538	17	137	9	2	350	372	122	160	0	3.78	90	5	0	.056
Jorgens, Orville-Orville Edward	35-37PhiN	6-4-08	Rockford, Ill.		R	R	6'1	180	21	27	.438	5	144	56	11	496	571	233	149	0	4.70	157	23	0	.146
Joyce, Bob-Robert Emmett	39PhiA 46NYN	1-14-15	Stockton, Cal.		R	R	6'1	180	6	9	.400	0	44	13	3	169	235	57	49	0	6.18	54	6	1	.111
Judd, Oscar-Thomas William Oscar (Ossie)	41-45BosA 45-48PhiN	2-14-08	Rebecca, Canada		L	L	6'	180	40	51	.440	7	161	99	43	770	744	397	304	4	3.90	317	83	3	.262
Judd, Ralph-Ralph Wesley	27WasA 29-30NYN	12-7-01	Perrysburg, Ohio	5-6-57	L	R	5'10	170	3	0	1.000	1	21	0	0	63	70	16	23	0	3.29	18	0	0	.000
Jungels, Ken-Kenneth Peter (Curly)	37-38,40-41CleA 42PitN	6-23-16	Aurora, Ill.	9-9-75	R	R	6'1	180	1	0	1.000	0	25	0	0	49	56	32	21	0	6.80	10	1	0	.100
Jurisich, Al-Alvin Joseph	44-45StLN 46-47PhiN	8-25-21	New Orleans, La.		R	R	6'2	193	15	22	.405	5	104	42	13	388	344	189	177	3	4.24	122	14	0	.115
Kalfass, Bill-William Phillip (Lefty)	37PhiA	3-3-16	New York, N.Y.	9-8-68	R	L	6'3	190	1	0	1.000	0	3	1	1	12	10	10	9	0	3.00	4	0	0	.000
Kamp, Ike-Alphonse Francis	24-25BosN	9-5-00	Roxbury, Mass.	2-26-55	B	L	6'	170	2	5	.286	0	25	5	1	65	77	40	24	0	5.12	13	2	0	.154
Kardow, Paul-Paul Otto (Tex)	36CleA	9-19-15	Humble, Tex.	4-27-68	R	R	6'6	210	0	0	–	0	2	0	0	2	1	2	0	0	4.50	0	0	0	–
Karl, Andy-Anton Andrew	43BosA 43-46PhiN 47BosN	4-8-14	Mt. Vernon, N.Y.		R	R	6'1	175	18	23	.439	26	191	4	1	423	451	130	107	0	3.51	95	16	0	.168
Karr, Benn-Benjamin Joyce (Baldy)	20-22BosA 25-27CleA	11-28-93	Mt. Pleasant, Miss.	12-8-68	L	R	6'	175	35	48	.422	5	177	58	29	781	921	260	180	1	4.60	392	96	2	.245
Katz, Bob-Robert Clyde	44CinN	1-30-11	Lancaster, Pa.		R	R	5'11	190	0	1	.000	0	6	2	0	18	17	7	4	0	4.00	4	0	0	.000
Kaufmann, Tony-Anthony Charles	21-27ChiN 27PhiN 27-28,30-31,35StLN	12-16-00	Chicago, Ill.		R	R	5'11	165	64	62	.508	12	202	118	74	1086	1198	368	345	9	4.18	(See B20-45)			
Keck, Cactus-Frank Joseph	22-23CinN	1-13-99	St. Louis, Mo.		R	R	5'11	170	10	12	.455	3	62	21	6	218	222	61	43	1	3.51	61	8	0	.131
Keefe, Dave-David Edwin	17PhiA 18MS 19-21PhiA 22CleA	1-9-97	Williston, Vt.		L	R	5'9	165	9	17	.346	1	97	27	12	353	403	113	126	1	4.16	107	22	0	.206
Keen, Vic-Howard Victor	18PhiA 21-25ChiN 26-27StLN	3-16-99	Belair, Md.		R	R	5'9	165	42	44	.488	6	165	82	41	749	888	248	202	1	4.11	230	34	0	.148
Keenan, Jimmie-James William (Sparkplug)	20-21PhiN	5-25-89	Avon, N.Y.		L	L	5'6	155	1	2	.333	0	16	2	0	35	51	16	9	0	6.43	10	0	0	.000
Kehn, Chet-Chester Lawrence	42BknN 43-45MS	10-30-21	San Diego, Cal.		R	R	5'11	168	0	0	–	0	3	1	0	8	8	4	3	0	6.75	2	2	0	1.000
Kelleher, Hal-Harold Joseph	35-38PhiN	6-24-14	Philadelphia, Pa.		R	R	6'	165	4	9	.308	0	50	9	4	134	174	81	49	1	5.98	39	9	0	.231
Kellett, Al-Alfred Henry	26-31 played in A.B.L. 23PhiA 24BosA	10-30-01	Red Bank, N.J.	7-14-60	R	R	6'3	200	0	1	.000	0	6	0	0	10	11	10	1	0	8.10	3	1	0	.333
Kelley, Harry-Harry Leroy	25-26WasA 36-38PhiA 38-39WasA	2-13-06	Parkin, Ark.	3-23-58	R	R	5'9	170	42	47	.472	5	146	78	43	676	812	244	230	3	4.86	232	50	0	.216
Kelly, Mike-Michael J.	26PhiN	11-9-02	St. Louis, Mo.		R	R	6'1	178	0	0	–	0	4	0	0	7	9	4	2	0	9.00	3	0	0	.000
Kelly, Ren-Reynolds Joseph	23PhiA	11-18-99	San Francisco, Cal.	8-24-63	R	R	6'	183	0	0	–	0	1	0	0	7	7	4	1	0	2.57	3	0	0	.000
Kemner, Dutch-Herman John	29CinN	3-4-99	Quincy, Ill.		R	R	5'10	175	0	0	–	1	9	0	0	15	19	8	10	0	7.80	4	1	0	.250
Kennedy, Vern-Lloyd Vernon	34-37ChiA 38-39DetA 39-41StLA 41WasA 42-44CleA 44-45PhiN 45CinN	3-20-07	Kansas City, Mo.		L	R	6'	175	104	132	.441	5	344	263	126	2025	2173	1049	691	7	4.68	743	181	4	.244
Kenney, Art-Arthur Joseph	38BosN	4-29-16	Milford, Mass.		L	L	6'	175	0	0	–	0	2	0	0	2	3	8	2	0	18.00	0	0	0	–
Kirksieck, Bill-Wayman William	39PhiN	12-6-13	Ulm, Ark.	3-11-70	R	R	6'1	183	0	2	.000	0	23	2	1	63	81	32	13	0	7.14	12	1	0	.083
Kerr, Dickie-Richard Henry	19-21ChiA 22-24SL 25ChiA	7-3-93	St. Louis, Mo.	5-4-63	L	L	5'7	155	53	35	.602	6	140	84	55	812	876	250	235	7	3.83	275	60	0	.218
Ketchum, Gus-Agustus Franklin	22PhiA	3-21-97	Royce City, Tex.		R	R	5'9	170	0	1	.000	0	6	0	0	16	19	8	4	0	5.63	4	0	0	.000
Kiefer, Joe-Joseph William (Smoke, Harlem Joe)	20ChiA 25-26BosA	7-19-99	West Leyden, N.Y.		R	R	5'11	190	0	5	.000	0	15	4	0	50	56	30	9	0	6.12	13	1	0	.077
Kimball, Newt-Newell W.	37-38ChiN 40StLN 40-43BknN 43PhiN	3-27-15	Logan, Utah		R	R	6'2	190	11	9	.550	5	94	13	4	236	219	117	88	0	3.78	50	9	0	.180
Kimberlin, Harry-Harry Lydle (Murphy)	36-39StLA	3-13-09	Sullivan, Mo.		R	R	6'3	175	1	4	.200	0	34	6	2	84	107	47	21	0	4.71	16	4	0	.250
Kime, Hal-Harold Lee (Lefty)	20StLN	3-15-99	West Salem, Ohio	5-16-39	L	L	5'9	160	0	0	–	0	4	0	0	7	9	2	1	0	2.57	1	0	0	.000
Kimsey, Chad-Clyde Elias	29-32StLA 32-33ChiA 36DetA	8-6-06	Copperhill, Tenn.	12-3-42	L	R	6'3	200	24	29	.453	17	198	10	2	508	623	194	121	0	5.08	206	58	6	.282
Kinzy, Harry-Henry Hersel (Slim)	34ChiA	7-19-10	Hallsville, Tex.		R	R	6'4	185	0	1	.000	0	13	2	1	34	38	31	12	0	5.03	10	3	0	.300
Kircher (Kerscher), Mike (Wolfgang)-Michael Andrew	19PhiA 20-21StLN	9-30-97	Rochester, N.Y.	6-26-72	B	R	6'1	185	2	2	.500	0	14	3	1	48	69	9	9	0	6.00	14	3	0	.214
Klaerner, Hugo-Hugo Emil (Dutch)	34ChiA	10-15-08	Fredericksburg, Tex.		R	R	5'11	190	0	2	.000	0	3	3	1	17	24	16	9	0	11.12	6	2	0	.333
Kleine, Hal-Harold John	44-45CleA	6-8-23	St. Louis, Mo.	12-10-57	L	L	6'2	193	1	2	.333	0	14	6	1	48	46	43	18	0	5.44	17	3	0	.176
Kleinhans, Ted-Theodore Otto	34PhiN 34CinN 36NYA 37-38CinN	4-8-99	Deer Park, Wis.		R	L	6'	170	4	9	.308	1	56	12	1	143	185	76	48	0	5.29	38	6	0	.158
Kleinke, Nubs-Norbert George	35,37StLN	5-19-11	Fond du Lac, Wis.	3-16-50	R	R	6'1	170	1	1	.500	0	9	4	1	34	44	10	14	0	4.76	10	0	0	.000

USE NAME – GIVEN NAMES (NICKNAMES)	TEAM BY YEAR	BIRTH DATE	BIRTH PLACE	DEATH DATE	B	T	HGT	WGT	W	L	PCT	SV	G	GS	CG	IP	H	BB	SO	ShO	ERA	AB	H	HR	BA
									LIFETIME PITCHING TOTALS													BATTING TOTALS			
Kline, Bob-Robert George (Junior)	30-33BosA 34PhiA 34WasA	12- 9-09	Enterprise, Ohio		R	R	6'3	200	30	28	.517	7	148	37	8	442	501	195	87	1	5.05	124	25	0	.202
Klinger, Bob-Robert Harold	38-43PitN 44-45MS 46-47BosA	6- 4-08	Allenton, Mo.		R	R	6'	180	66	61	.520	23	265	130	48	1090	1153	358	357	7	3.68	348	71	0	.204
Klopp, Stan-Stanley Harold (Betz)	44BosN	12-22-10	Womelsdorf, Pa.		R	R	6'1	180	1	2	.333	0	24	0	0	46	47	33	17	0	4.30	7	2	0	.286
Kneisch, Rudy-Rudolph Frank	26DetA	4-10-99	Baltimore, Md.	4- 6-65	R	L	5'10	175	0	1	.000	0	2	2	1	17	18	6	4	0	2.65	5	0	0	.000
Knight, Jack-Elma Russell	22StLN 25-26PhiN 27BosN	1-12-95	Pittsboro, Miss.		L	R	6'	175	10	18	.357	5	72	27	9	255	382	89	49	0	6.85	102	22	2	.216
Knott, Jack-John Henry	33-38StLA 38-40ChiA 41-42,46PhiA 43-45MS	3- 2-07	Dallas, Tex.		R	R	6'2	200	82	103	.443	19	325	192	62	1557	1787	642	484	4	4.97	482	58	0	.120
Knowlton, Bill-William Young	20PhiA	8-18-92	Philadelphia, Pa.	2-25-44	R	R			0	1	.000	0	1	1	0	6	9	3	5	0	4.50	2	0	0	.000
Kohlman, Joe-Joseph James (Blackie)	37-38WasA	1-28-13	Philadelphia, Pa.		R	R	5'11	172	1	0	1.000	0	9	2	1	27	27	14	8	0	5.33	8	1	0	.125
Kolp, Ray-Raymond Carl (Jockey)	21-24StLA 27-34CinN	10- 1-94	New Berlin, Ohio	7-29-67	R	R	5'10	187	79	95	.454	18	383	174	66	1688	1918	424	439	11	4.08	532	98	2	.184
Koupal, Lou-Louis Laddie	25-26PitN 28-29BknN 29-30PhiN 37StLA	12-19-98	Tabor, S.D.	12- 8-61	R	R	5'11	175	10	21	.323	7	101	35	12	336	436	156	87	0	5.57	104	11	0	.106
Kowalik, Fabian-Fabian Lorenz	32ChiA 35-36ChiN 36PhiN 36BosN	4-22-08	Falls City, Tex.	8-14-54	B	R	5'11	185	3	11	.214	2	51	12	4	167	218	63	42	0	5.44	95	23	0	.242
					Bats Right 36																				
Krakauskas, Joe-Joseph Victor Lawrence	37-40WasA 41-42CleA	3-28-15	Montreal, Canada	7- 8-60	L	L	6'1	203	26	36	.419	4	149	63	22	583	605	355	347	1	4.54	183	33	0	.180
	43-45MS 46CleA																								
Kraus, Tex-John William (Texas Jack)	43PhiN 44MS 45PhiN 46NYN	4-26-18	San Antonio, Tex.		R	L	6'4	190	15	25	.375	2	70	39	10	307	318	133	83	1	3.99	88	7	0	.080
Krausse, Lew-Lewis Bernard Sr.	31-32PhiA	6- 8-12	Media, Pa.		R	R	6'	167	5	1	.833	0	23	4	3	68	70	30	17	1	4.50	17	2	0	.118
Kremer, Ray-Remy Peter (Wiz)	24-33PitN	3-23-93	Oakland, Cal.	2- 8-65	R	R	6'	190	143	85	.627	10	308	247	134	1955	2108	483	516	14	3.77	687	122	5	.178
Kress, Red-Ralph	35WasA 46NYN	1- 2-07	Columbia, Cal.	11-29-62	R	R	5'11	165	0	0	–	0	4	0	0	10	13	6	6	0	11.70	(See B20-45)			
Krist, Howie-Howard Wilbur (Spud)	37-38,41-43StLN 44-45MS 46StLN	2-28-16	W. Henrietta, N.Y.		L	R	6'1	175	37	11	.771	6	128	37	15	444	408	158	150	2	3.32	149	25	0	.168
Kuczynski, Bert-Bernard Carl	43PhiA 44-46MS	1- 8-20	Philadelphia, Pa.		R	R	6'	195	0	1	.000	0	6	1	0	25	36	9	8	0	3.96	6	0	0	.000
43,46 played in N.F.L.																									
Kuhn, Bob-Bernard Daniel	24CleA	10-12-99	Vicksburg, Mich.	11-20-56	L	R	6'1	182	0	1	.000	0	1	0	0	1	4	0	0	0	27.00	0	0	0	–
Kunz, Earl-Earl Dewey (Pinch)	23PitN	12-25-99	Sacramento, Cal.	4-14-63	R	R	5'10	170	1	2	.333	1	21	2	1	46	48	24	12	0	5.48	12	1	0	.083
Lagger, Ed-Edwin Joseph	34PhiA	7-14-12	Joliet, Ill.		R	R	6'3	200	0	0	–	0	8	0	0	18	27	14	2	0	11.00	6	0	0	.000
LaManna, Frank-Frank (Hank)	40-42BosN 43-45MS	8-22-19	Watertown, Pa.		R	R	6'2	195	6	5	.545	1	45	5	1	93	95	67	28	0	5.23	39	10	0	.256
Lamanske, Frank-Frank James (Lefty)	35BknN	9-30-06	Oglesby, Ill.	8- 4-71	L	L	5'11	170	0	0	–	0	2	0	0	4	5	1	1	0	6.75	1	0	0	.000
LaMaster, Wayne-Wayne Lee	37-38PhiN 38BknN	2-13-07	Speed, Ind.		L	L	5'8	170	19	27	.413	4	71	42	11	295	352	116	173	2	5.83	107	25	0	.234
Lambert, Gene-Eugene Marion	41-42PhiN 43-45MS	4-26-21	Crenshaw, Miss.		R	R	5'11	175	0	1	.000	0	3	1	0	10	14	2	4	0	2.70	2	0	0	.000
Lanahan, Dick-Richard Anthony	35-37WasA 40-41PitN	9-27-11	Washington, D.C.		L	L	6'1	170	6	13	.316	2	56	13	4	152	177	75	62	0	5.15	42	5	0	.119
Lang, Marty-Martin John (Lefty)	30PitN	9-27-05	Hooper, Neb.	1-13-68	R	L	5'11	160	0	0	–	0	2	0	0	2	9	3	2	0	45.00	0	0	0	–
Lanier, Max-Hubert Max	38-46,49-51StLN 47-48SM 52-53NYN 53StLA	8-18-15	Denton, N.C.		R	L	5'11	190	108	82	.568	17	327	204	91	1619	1490	611	821	21	3.01	535	99	0	.185
Lanning, Johnny-John Young (Tobacco Chewin' Johnny)	36-39BosN	9- 6-10	Asheville, N.C.		R	R	6'1	185	58	60	.492	13	278	104	30	1072	1078	358	295	4	3.58	322	47	1	.146
	40-43PitN 44MS 45-46PitN 47BosN																								
Lanning, Tom-Thomas Newton	38PhiN	4-22-09	Biltmore, N.C.	11- 4-67	L	L	6'1	165	0	1	.000	0	3	1	0	7	9	2	2	0	6.43	1	1	0	1.000
Lansing, Gene-Eugene Hewitt (Jigger)	22BosN	1-11-98	Albany, N.Y.	1-18-45	R	R	6'1	185	0	1	.000	0	15	1	0	41	46	22	14	0	5.93	11	0	0	.000
Lapihuska, Andy-Andrew (Apples)	42-43PhiN 44-45MS	11- 1-22	Delmont, N.J.		L	R	5'10	175	0	2	.000	0	4	2	0	23	22	16	8	0	7.04	9	2	0	.222
Larkin, Steve-Stephen Patrick	34DetA	12- 9-10	Cincinnati, Ohio	5- 2-69	R	R	6'1	195	0	0	–	0	2	1	0	6	8	5	8	0	1.50	3	1	0	.333
Lasley, Bill-Willard Almond	24StLA	7-13-02	Marietta, Ohio		B	R	6'	175	0	0	–	0	2	0	0	4	7	2	0	0	6.75	1	0	0	.000
Lawrence, Bob-Robert Andrew (Larry)	24ChiA	12-14-99	Brooklyn, N.Y.		R	R	5'11	180	0	0	–	0	1	0	0	1	1	1	1	0	9.00	0	0	0	–
Lawson, Roxie-Alfred Voyle	30-31CleA 33,35-39DetA 39-40StLA	4-13-06	Donnellson, Iowa		R	R	6'	170	47	39	.547	11	208	83	34	852	963	512	258	2	5.37	283	49	0	.173
Lee, Bill-William Crutcher (Big Bill)	34-43ChiN 43-45PhiN	10-21-09	Plaquemine, La.		R	R	6'3	195	169	157	.518	13	462	378	182	2863	2953	893	998	29	3.54	980	165	5	.168
	45-46BosN 47ChiN																								
Lee, Ray-Roy Edwin	45NYN	9-28-17	Elmira, N.Y.		L	L	5'11	175	0	2	.000	0	3	1	0	7	8	3	0	0	11.57	1	0	0	.000
Lee, Thornton-Thornton Starr (Lefty)	33-36CleA 37-47ChiA 48NYN	9-13-06	Sonoma, Cal.		L	L	6'3	205	117	124	.485	10	374	272	155	2331	2327	838	937	14	3.56	835	167	4	.200
LeFebvre, Bill-Wilfrid Henry (Lefty)	38-39BosA 43-44WasA 45MS	11-11-15	Natick, R.I.		L	L	5'11	180	5	5	.500	3	36	10	3	132	162	51	36	0	5.05	87	24	1	.276
Leheny, Regis-Regis Francis	32BosA	1- 5-08	Pittsburgh, Pa.		L	L	6'	180	0	0	–	0	2	0	0	3	5	3	1	0	15.00	1	0	0	.000
Lehr, Norm-Norman Carl Michael (King)	26CleA	5-28-01	Rochester, N.Y.	7-17-68	R	R	6'	168	0	0	–	0	4	0	0	15	11	4	4	0	3.00	4	0	0	.000
Lennon, Ed-Edward Francis	28PhiN	8-17-97	Philadelphia, Pa.	9-13-47	R	R	5'11	170	0	0	–	0	5	0	0	12	19	10	6	0	9.00	4	0	0	.000
Leon, Izzy-Isidoro [Becerra]	45PhiN	1- 4-11	Cruces, Cuba		R	R	5'10	175	0	4	.000	0	14	4	0	39	49	19	11	0	5.31	9	1	0	.111
Leonard, Dutch-Emil John	33-36BknN 38-46WasA 47-48PhiN 49-53ChiN	3-25-09	Auburn, Ill.		R	R	6'	185	191	181	.513	44	640	375	192	3220	3304	737	1170	30	3.25	1054	177	0	.168
Leopold, Rudy-Rudolph Matas	28ChiA	7-27-05	Grand Cane, La.	9- 3-65	L	L	6'	160	0	0	–	0	2	0	0	2	3	0	0	0	4.50	1	0	0	.000
Leverett, Dixie-Gorham Vance	22-24,26ChiA 29BosN	3-29-94	Georgetown, Tex.	2-20-57	R	R	5'11	190	29	34	.460	6	122	77	33	639	725	221	193	4	4.49	214	50	0	.234
Leverette, Hod-Horace Wilbur (Levy)	20StLA	2- 4-89	Shreveport, La.	4-10-58	R	R	6'	200	0	2	.000	0	3	2	0	10	9	12	0	0	5.40	3	0	0	.000
Levsen, Emil-Emil Henry (Dutch)	23-28CleA	4-29-98	Wyoming, Iowa	3-12-72	R	R	6'	180	21	26	.447	0	80	51	23	402	426	173	88	3	4.19	135	24	0	.178
Lewis, Bert-William Burton	24PhiN	10- 3-95	Tonawanda, N.Y.	3-24-50	R	R	6'2	176	0	0	–	0	12	0	0	18	23	7	3	0	6.00	5	0	0	.000
Lieber, Dutch-Charles Edwin	35-36PhiA	2- 1-10	Alameda, Cal.	12-31-61	R	R	6'	180	1	2	.333	2	21	1	0	59	62	25	15	0	3.97	17	2	0	.118
Liebhardt, Glenn-Glenn Ignatius (Sandy)	30PhiA 36,38StLA	7-31-10	Cleveland, Ohio		R	R	5'10	170	0	1	.000	0	31	0	0	67	116	35	23	0	9.00	13	0	0	.000
Lillard, Gene-Robert Eugene	39ChiN 40StLN	11-12-13	Santa Barbara, Cal.		R	R	5'10	178	3	6	.333	0	22	8	2	60	76	40	33	0	7.05	(See B20-45)			
Lindquist, Carl-Carl Emil (Lindy)	43-44BosN	5- 9-19	Morris Run, Pa.		R	R	6'2	185	0	2	.000	0	7	2	0	22	25	6	5	0	4.91	5	0	0	.000
Lindsey, Jim-James Kendrick	22,24CleA 29-33StLN 34CinN 34StLN 37BknN	1-24-98	Greensburg, La.	10-25-63	R	R	6'1	175	21	20	.512	19	177	20	5	431	507	176	175	1	4.70	94	18	0	.191
Linke, Ed-Edward Karl	33-37WasA 38StLA	11- 9-11	Chicago, Ill.		R	R	5'11	180	22	22	.500	6	120	43	13	450	555	206	156	0	5.60	156	41	2	.263
Lisenbee, Hod-Horace Milton	27-28WasA 29-32BosA 36PhiA 45CinN	9-23-98	Clarksville, Tenn.		R	R	5'11	170	37	58	.389	1	207	107	48	969	1076	314	253	4	4.81	301	51	0	.169
Liska, Ad-Adolph James	29-31WasA 32-33PhiN	7-10-06	Dwight, Neb.		R	R	5'11	160	17	18	.486	3	111	28	11	352	354	150	104	1	3.86	103	11	0	.107
Littlejohn, Carlisle-Charles Carlisle	27-28StLN	10- 6-01	Mertens, Tex.		R	R	5'10	175	5	2	.714	0	26	4	2	74	83	28	22	0	4.14	23	5	0	.217
Livengood, Wes-Wesley Amos	39CinN	7-18-10	Salisbury, N.C.		R	R	6'2	172	0	0	–	0	5	0	0	6	9	3	4	0	9.00	0	0	0	–
Llewellyn, Clem-Clement Manly (Lew)	22NYA	8- 1-95	Dobson, N.C.	11-27-69	L	R	6'2	195	0	0	–	0	1	0	0	1	1	0	0	0	0.00	0	0	0	–
Loftus, Frank-Francis Patrick	26WasA	3-10-98	Scranton, Pa.		R	R	5'9	190	0	0	–	0	1	0	0	1	3	2	0	0	9.00	0	0	0	–
Logan, Bob-Robert Dean (Lefty)	35BknN 37DetA 37-38ChiN 41CinN 45BosN	2-10-10	Thompson, Neb.		R	L	5'10	170	7	15	.318	4	57	25	5	223	245	81	67	1	3.15	65	13	0	.200
Lohrman, Bill-William LeRoy	34PhiN 37-41NYN	5-22-13	Brooklyn, N.Y.		R	R	6'1	185	60	59	.504	8	198	121	47	991	1048	240	330	10	3.69	321	49	2	.153
	43-44BknN 44CinN																								
Long, Tommy-Thomas Francis (Little Hawk)	24BknN	4-22-98	Memphis, Tenn.	9-16-73	L	L	5'7	140	0	0	–	0	1	0	0	2	2	2	0	0	9.00	0	0	0	–
Lopatka, Art-Arthur Joseph	45StLN 46PhiN	5-20-20	Chicago, Ill.		B	L	5'10	170	1	1	.500	0	8	2	1	17	20	7	9	0	6.35	4	1	0	.250
Lowe, George-George Wesley	20CinN	4-25-95	Ridgefield Pk., N.J.		R	R	6'2	180	0	0	–	0	1	0	0	2	1	1	0	0	0.00	0	0	0	–
Lowry, Sam-Samuel Joseph (Mose)	42-43PhiA 44-46MS	3-25-20	Philadelphia, Pa.		R	R	5'11	170	0	0	–	0	6	0	0	21	21	10	3	0	5.14	7	1	0	.143
Lucas, Ray-Ray Wesley (Luke)	29-31NYN 33-34BknN	10- 2-08	Springfield, Ohio	10- 9-69	R	R	6'2	175	1	1	.500	1	22	2	0	56	58	32	5	0	5.79	9	3	0	.333
Lucas, Red-Charles Frederick	23NYN 24BosN 26-33CinN 34-38PitN	4-28-02	Columbia, Tenn.		L	R	5'10	170	157	135	.538	7	396	301	204	2543	2736	455	602	22	3.72	(See B20-45)			
Lucey, Joe-Joseph Earl (Scootch)	25BosA	3-27-97	Holyoke, Mass.		R	R	6'	168	0	1	.000	0	7	2	0	11	18	14	2	0	9.00	(See B20-45)			
Lucier, Lou-Louis Joseph	43-44BosA 44-45PhiN	3-23-18	Northbridge, Mass.		R	R	5'8	160	3	5	.375	1	33	9	3	101	118	47	31	0	3.83	25	5	0	.200
Ludolph, Willie-William Francis (Wee Willie)	24DetA	1-21-00	San Francisco, Cal.	4- 7-52	R	R	6'1	170	0	0	–	0	3	0	0	6	5	2	1	0	4.50	1	0	0	.000
Lundgren, Del-Ebin Delmar	24PitN 26-27BosA	9-21-00	Lindsborg, Kans.		R	R	5'8	160	5	15	.250	0	55	19	5	182	220	114	53	2	6.58	51	7	0	.137
Luque, Dolf-Adolfo (The Pride of Havana)	14-15BosN 18-29CinN	8- 4-90	Havana, Cuba	7- 3-57	R	R	5'7	160	193	179	.519	28	550	365	206	3221	3231	918	1130	26	3.24	1043	237	5	.227
	30-31BknN 32-35NYN																								
Lyle, Jim-James Charles	25WasA	7-24-02	Lake, Miss.		R	R	6'1	180	0	0	–	0	1	0	0	3	5	1	3	0	6.00	1	0	0	.000
Lynch, Adrian-Adrian Ryan	20StLA	2- 9-97	Laurens, Iowa	3-16-34	R	R			2	0	1.000	0	5	3	1	22	23	17	8	0	5.32	9	2	0	.222
Lynn, Red-Japhet Monroe	39DetA 39-40NYN 44ChiN 45MS	12-27-13	Kenney, Tex.		R	R	6'	162	10	8	.556	5	85	7	4	184	175	85	85	1	3.96	41	6	0	.146
Lyons, George-George Tony (Smooth)	20StLN 24StLA	1-25-91	Bible Grove, Ill.		R	R	5'11	180	5	3	.625	0	33	8	3	101	118	54	30	0	4.72	27	6	0	.222
Lyons, Hersh-Hershel Englebert	41StLN	7-23-15	Fresno, Cal.		R	R	5'11	195	0	0	–	0	1	0	0	1	1	3	1	0	0.00	0	0	0	–
Lyons, Ted-Theodore Amar	23-42ChiA 43-45MS 46,M46-48ChiA	12-28-00	Lake Charles, La.		B	R	5'11	200	260	230	.531	23	594	484	356	4162	4489	1121	1073	27	3.67	1563	364	5	.233
MacFayden, Danny-Daniel Knowles (Deacon Danny)	26-32BosA 32-34NYA	6-10-05	North Truro, Mass.	8-26-72	R	R	5'11	170	132	159	.454	9	465	332	157	2706	2981	872	797	17	3.96	910	129	1	.142
	35CinN 35-39BosN 40PitN 41WasA 43BosN																								
Mack, Frank-Frank George (Stubby)	22-23,25ChiA	2- 2-00	Oklahoma City, Okla.		R	R	6'1	180	2	3	.400	0	27	4	1	70	83	40	23	1	5.01	21	4	0	.190
Macon, Max-Max Cullen	38StLN 40,42-43BknN 44BosN 45-46MS 47BosN	10-14-15	Pensacola, Fla.		L	L	6'3	175	17	19	.472	3	81	29	9	297	305	128	90	2	4.24	(See B20-45)			
MacPherson, Harry-Harry William	44BosN	7-10-26	N. Andover, Mass.		R	R	5'10	150	0	0	–	0	1	0	0	1	0	1	1	0	0.00	0	0	0	–
Mahaffey, Roy-Lee Roy (Popeye)	26-27PitN 30-35PhiA 36StLA	2- 9-03	Belton, S.C.	7-23-69	R	R	6'	180	67	49	.578	5	224	128	45	1056	1181	452	365	0	5.01	396	73	4	.184
Mahon, Al-Alfred Gwin (Lefty)	30PhiA	9-23-10	Albion, Neb.		L	L	5'11	170	0	0	–	0	3	0	0	4	11	7	0	0	24.75	1	0	0	.000
Mails, Duster-John Walter (The Great)	15-16BknN 17-18MS 20-22CleA	10- 1-95	San Quentin, Cal.	7- 5-74	L	L	6'	195	32	25	.561	2	104	59	29	515	554	220	232	5	4.11	165	22	0	.133
	25-26StLN																								

USE NAME – GIVEN NAMES (NICKNAMES)	TEAM BY YEAR	BIRTH DATE	BIRTH PLACE	DEATH DATE	B	T	HGT	WGT	W	L	PCT	SV	G	GS	CG	IP	H	BB	SO	ShO	ERA	AB	H	HR	BA
									LIFETIME PITCHING TOTALS													BATTING TOTALS			
Mains, Bud-James Royal	43PhiA	6-12-22	Bridgton, Me.	3-17-69	R	R	6'2	190	0	1	.000	0	1	1	1	8	9	3	4	0	5.63	2	0	0	.000
Makosky, Frank-Frank	37NYA	1-20-12	Boonton, N.J.		R	R	6'1	185	5	2	.714	3	26	1	1	58	64	24	27	0	4.97	16	5	0	.313
Malis, Cy-Cyrus Sol	34PhiN	2-26-07	Philadelphia, Pa.	1-12-71	R	R	5'11	175	0	0	–	0	1	0	0	4	4	2	1	0	4.50	0	0	0	–
Malone, Pat-Perce Leigh	28-34ChiN 35-37NYA	9-25-02	Altoona, Pa.	5-13-43	L	R	6'2	200	134	92	.593	26	357	220	115	1915	1934	705	1024	16	3.74	688	129'	9	.188
					Bats Both 35-37																				
Maltzberger, Gordon-Gordon Ralph (Maltzy)	43-44,46-47ChiA 45MS	9-4-12	Utopia, Tex.	12-11-74	R	R	6'	170	20	13	.606	33	135	0	0	294	258	75	136	0	2.69	60	7	0	.117
Manders, Hal-Harold Carl	41-42,46DetA 46ChiN	6-14-17	Waukee, Iowa		R	R	6'	187	3	1	.750	0	30	1	0	60	71	28	28	0	4.80	12	2	0	.167
Mangum, Leo-Leo Allan (Blackie)	24-25ChiA 28NYN 32-35BosN	5-24-96	Durham, N.C.	7-9-74	R	R	6'1	187	11	10	.524	1	85	16	4	258	343	72	78	1	5.37	75	15	0	.200
Marberry, Firpo-Frederick	23-32WasA 33-35DetA 36NYN 36WasA	11-30-98	Streetman, Tex.		R	R	6'1	190	147	89	.623	101	551	187	86	2066	2049	686	822	7	3.63	669	128	1	.191
Marcum, Johnny-John Alfred (Footsie)	33-35PhiA 36-38BosA 39StLA 39ChiA	9-9-09	Campbellsburg, Ky.		L	R	5'11	197	65	63	.508	7	195	132	69	1100	1269	344	392	8	4.66	533	141	5	.265
Markle, Cliff-Clifford Monroe	15-16NYA 21-22CinN 24NYA	5-3-94	Dravosburg, Pa.	5-24-74	R	R	5'9	163	12	17	.414	0	56	21	12	235	235	110	90	2	4.10	69	6	0	.087
Marquis, Jim-James Milburn	25NYA	11-18-00	Yoakum, Tex.		R	R	5'11	174	0	0	–	0	2	0	0	7	12	6	0	0	10.29	1	0	0	.000
Marrow, Buck-Charles Kennon	32DetA 37-38BknN	8-29-09	Tarboro, N.C.		R	R	6'4	200	3	8	.273	1	39	9	2	100	112	49	39	0	5.04	25	3	0	.120
Martin, Pat-Patrick Francis	19-20PhiA	4-13-94	Brooklyn, N.Y.		L	L	5'11	170	1	6	.143	0	10	7	3	43	59	33	20	0	5.65	13	4	0	.308
Martin, Speed-Elwood Good	17StLA 18-22ChiN	9-15-93	Wawawai, Wash.		R	R	6'	165	29	43	.403	6	126	63	30	593	645	191	207	4	3.78	180	35	1	.194
Martina, Joe-Joseph John (Oyster Joe)	24WasA	7-8-89	New Orleans, La.	3-22-62	R	R	6'	183	6	8	.429	0	24	13	8	125	129	56	57	0	4.68	43	14	0	.326
Martini, Wedo-Guido Joe (Southern)	35PhiA	7-1-13	Birmingham, Ala.	10-28-70	R	R	5'10	165	0	2	.000	0	3	2	0	6	8	11	1	0	18.00	2	0	0	.000
Masters, Walt-Walter Thomas	31WasA 37PhiN 39PhiA	3-28-07	Pen Argyle, Pa.		R	R	5'10	180	0	0	–	1	8	0	0	21	27	13	3	0	6.00	4	0	0	.000
36,43-44 played in N.F.L.																									
Masterson, Paul-Paul Nickalis	40-42PhiN	10-16-15	Chicago, Ill.		L	L	5'11	165	1	0	1.000	0	8	1	1	24	26	13	14	0	6.00	5	0	0	.000
Matthews, Jim-James Vincent	22BosN	9-29-99	Baltimore, Md.		R	L	6'	170	0	1	.000	0	3	1	0	10	5	6	0	0	3.60	2	0	0	.000
Matthewson, Dale-Dale Wesley	43-44PhiN	5-15-23	Catasauqua, Pa.		R	R	5'11	145	0	3	.000	0	28	2	0	58	53	24	16	0	4.34	5	1	0	.200
Mattingly, Earl-Laurence Earl	31BknN	11-4-04	Newport, Md.		R	R	5'10	164	0	1	.000	0	8	0	0	14	15	10	6	0	2.57	3	0	0	.000
Matuzak, Harry-Harry George (Matty)	34,36PhiA	1-27-10	Omer, Mich.		R	R	5'11	185	0	4	.000	0	17	1	0	39	49	14	17	0	5.77	9	1	0	.111
Maun, Ernie-Ernest Gerald	24NYN 26PhiN	2-3-01	Clearwater, Kans.		L	R	6'	165	2	5	.286	1	36	5	0	73	103	28	14	0	6.16	15	5	0	.333
Mauney, Dick-Richard	45-47PhiN	1-26-20	Concord, N.C.	2-6-70	R	R	5'11	164	12	14	.462	4	53	24	9	229	240	52	72	3	2.99	[illegible]	10	0	.110
May, Buckshot-William Herbert	24PitN	12-13-99	Bakersfield, Cal.		L	R	6'2	170	0	0	–	0	1	0	0	1	2	0	1	0	0.00	0	0	0	–
May, Jakie-Frank Spruiell	17-21StLN 24-30CinN 31-32ChiN	11-25-95	Youngville, N.C.	6-3-70	R	L	5'8	178	72	95	.431	19	410	162	70	1563	1645	617	765	7	3.88	468	80	2	.171
Mays, Carl-Carl William (Sub)	15-19BosA 19-23NYA 24-28CinN 29NYN	11-12-91	Liberty, Ky.	4-4-71	L	R	5'11	195	207	127	.620	29	490	326	228	3021	2912	734	862	29	2.92	1085	291	5	.268
McAfee, Bill-William Fort	30ChiN 31BosN 32-33WasA 34StLA	9-7-07	Smithville, Ga.	7-8-58	R	R	6'2	186	10	4	.714	5	83	7	2	187	237	81	44	0	5.68	52	9	1	.173
McBee, Pryor-Pryor Edward (Lefty)	26ChiA	6-20-01	Blanco, Okla.	4-19-65	R	L	6'1	190	0	0	–	0	1	0	0	1	1	3	1	0	9.00	0	0	0	–
McCloskey, Irish-James Ellwood	36BosN	5-26-10	Danville, Pa.	8-18-71	L	L	5'10	180	0	0	–	0	4	1	0	8	14	3	2	0	11.25	1	0	0	.000
McColl, Alex-Alexander Boyd (Red)	33-34WasA	3-29-94	Eagleville, Ohio		B	R	6'1	178	4	4	.500	1	46	3	2	129	142	43	34	0	3.70	37	5	0	.135
McCrabb, Les-Lester William (Buster)	39-42,50PhiA	11-4-14	Wakefield, Pa.		R	R	5'11	175	10	15	.400	2	38	27	13	210	270	63	57	1	5.96	74	9	0	.122
McCullough, Paul-Paul Willard	29WasA	7-28-98	New Castle, Pa.	11-7-70	R	R	5'10	190	0	0	–	0	3	0	0	7	7	2	3	0	9.00	1	0	0	.000
McCullough, Phil-Pinson Lamar	42WasA 43-45MS	7-22-17	Stockbridge, Ga.		R	R	6'4	204	0	0	–	0	1	0	0	3	5	2	2	0	6.00	1	0	0	.000
McDonald, Hank-Henry Monroe	31,33PhiA 33StLA	1-16-11	Santa Monica, Cal.		R	R	6'3	200	3	9	.250	0	48	16	1	141	159	79	46	1	5.87	39	4	0	.103
McEvoy, Lou-Louis Anthony	30-31NYA	5-30-02	Williamsburg, Kan.	12-17-53	R	R	6'2	203	1	3	.250	4	34	1	0	64	83	41	17	0	7.88	20	2	0	.100
McGee, Bill-William Henry (Fiddler Bill)	35-41StLN 41-42NYN	11-16-09	Batchtown, Ill.		R	R	6'1	215	1	0	1.000	0	1	1	1	9	3	1	2	0	1.00	271	46	0	.170
McGillen, John-John Joseph	44PhiA	8-6-19	Eddystone, Pa.		L	L	6'1	175	0	0	–	0	2	0	0	1	1	2	0	0	18.00	0	0	0	–
McGraw, Bob-Robert Emmett	17-19NYA 19BosA 20NYA 25-27BknN	4-10-95	La Veto, Colo.		R	R	6'2	160	26	38	.406	6	168	47	17	591	677	265	164	1	4.89	174	24	1	.138
	27StLN 28-29PhiN																								
McGrew, Slim-Walter Howard	22-24WasA	8-5-99	Yoakum, Tex.	8-21-67	R	R	6'7	235	0	1	.000	0	10	2	0	30	40	17	10	0	6.60	10	0	0	.000
McIlree, Vance-Vance Elmer	21WasA	10-14-97	Riverside, Iowa	5-6-59	R	R	6'	160	0	0	–	0	1	0	0	1	1	0	0	0	9.00	0	0	0	–
McKain, Archie-Archie Richard (Happy)	37-38BosA 39-41DetA 41,43StLA	5-12-11	Delphos, Kans.		B	L	5'10	175	26	21	.553	16	165	34	8	487	529	208	188	1	4.25	142	25	2	.176
					Bats Left 41,43																				
McKain, Hal-Harold Leroy	27CleA 29-32ChiA	7-10-06	Logan, Iowa	1-24-70	L	R	5'11	185	18	23	.439	6	103	24	7	381	435	193	136	1	4.94	122	28	0	.230
McKee, Rogers-Rogers Hornsby	43-44PhiN 45-46MS	9-16-26	Shelby, N.C.		L	L	6'1	160	1	0	1.000	0	5	1	1	15	14	6	1	0	6.00	5	1	0	.200
McKeithan, Tim-Emmett James	32-34PhiA	11-2-06	Lawndale, N.C.	8-30-69	R	R	6'2	182	1	1	.500	0	10	3	0	26	35	14	3	0	7.27	7	1	0	.143
McLaughlin, Jud-Justin Theodore	31-33BosA	3-24-12	Brighton, Mass.	9-27-64	L	L	5'11	155	0	0	–	0	16	0	0	24	42	17	4	0	10.13	1	0	0	.000
McLaughlin, Pat-Patrick Elmer	37DetA 40PhiA 45DetA	8-17-10	Taylor, Tex.		R	R	6'2	175	0	2	.000	0	12	3	0	36	45	17	8	0	6.75	10	1	0	.100
McLean, Elrod-Albert Elrod	35WasA	9-20-12	Chicago, Ill.		R	R	5'11	165	0	0	–	0	4	0	0	9	12	5	3	0	7.00	2	0	0	.000
McNamara, Tim-Timothy Augustine	22-25BosN 26NYN	11-20-98	Millville, Mass.		R	R	5'11	170	14	29	.326	0	98	42	13	396	495	92	88	4	4.77	99	15	0	.152
McNaughton, Gordon-Gordon Joseph	32BosA	7-31-10	Chicago, Ill.	8-6-42	R	R	6'1	190	0	1	.000	0	6	2	0	21	21	22	6	0	6.43	8	2	0	.250
McQuaid, Herb-Herbert George	23CinN 26NYA	3-29-99	San Francisco, Cal.	4-4-66	R	R	6'2	185	2	0	1.000	0	29	2	0	72	79	23	15	0	4.38	14	0	0	.000
McQuillan, Hugh-Hugh A. (Handsome Hugh)	18-22BosN 22-27NYN 27BosN	9-15-97	New York, N.Y.	8-26-47	R	R	6'	170	88	94	.484	16	279	204	95	1562	1703	489	446	10	3.83	527	103	2	.195
McWeeny, Doug-Douglas Lawrence (Buzz)	21-22ChiA 23ST 24ChiA	8-17-96	Chicago, Ill.	1-1-53	R	R	6'2	180	37	57	.394	6	206	119	38	948	980	450	386	5	4.17	288	30	0	.104
	26-29BknN 30CinN																								
Meador, Johnny-John Davis	20PitN	12-4-92	Madison, N.C.	4-11-70	R	R	5'10	165	0	2	.000	0	12	2	0	36	48	7	5	0	4.25	6	1	0	.167
Meadows, Lee-Henry Lee (Specs)	15-19StLN 19-23PhiN 23-29PitN	7-12-94	Oxford, N.C.	1-29-63	L	R	5'9	190	188	180	.511	7	490	403	219	3150	3280	956	1063	25	3.38	1117	201	5	.180
					Bats Both 20-21,26,29																				
Meadows, Rufe-Rufus Rivers	26CinN	8-25-07	Chase City, Va.	5-10-70	L	L	5'11	175	0	0	–	0	1	0	0	.1	0	0	0	0	0.00	1	0	0	.000
Meeker, Roy-Charles Roy	23-24PhiA 26CinN	9-15-00	Lead Mines, Mo.	3-25-29	L	L	5'8	150	8	14	.364	0	42	17	8	192	214	103	54	1	4.73	63	12	0	.190
Meine, Heinie-Henry William (The Count of Luxembourg)	22StLA 29-34PitN	5-1-96	St. Louis, Mo.	3-18-68	R	R	5'11	180	66	50	.569	3	165	132	60	998	1125	287	199	7	3.96	341	40	0	.144
Melton, Cliff-Clifford George (Mountain Music)	37-44NYN 45ST	1-3-12	Brevard, N.C.		L	L	6'5	203	86	80	.518	16	272	179	65	1453	1446	431	660	13	3.42	469	77	0	.164
Melton, Rube-Reuben Franklin	41-42PhiN 43-44BknN 45MS 46-47BknN	2-27-17	Cramerton, N.C.	9-11-71	R	R	6'5	205	30	50	.375	5	162	87	25	704	620	395	363	6	3.62	208	25	1	.120
Meola, Mike-Emile Michael	33BosA 36StLA 36BosA	10-19-05	New York, N.Y.		R	R	5'11	175	0	3	.000	1	18	3	1	43	63	25	15	0	8.16	9	2	0	.222
Merena, Spike-John Joseph	34BosA	11-18-09	Paterson, N.J.		L	L	6'	185	1	2	.333	0	4	3	2	25	20	16	7	1	2.88	7	1	0	.143
Mertz, Jim-James Verlin	43WasA 44-46MS	8-10-16	Lima, Ohio		R	R	5'10	170	5	7	.417	3	33	10	2	117	109	58	53	0	4.62	38	7	0	.184
Messenger, Bud-Andrew Warren	24CleA	2-1-98	Grand Blanc, Mich.	11-4-71	R	R	6'	175	2	0	1.000	0	5	2	1	25	28	14	4	0	4.32	8	1	0	.125
Metivier, Dewey-George Dewey	22-24CleA	5-6-98	Cambridge, Mass.	3-2-47	L	R	5'11	175	7	7	.500	4	54	13	4	167	239	75	24	0	5.77	50	7	0	.140
Michaels, John-John Joseph	32BosA	7-10-07	Bridgeport, Conn.		L	L	5'10	154	1	6	.143	0	28	8	2	81	101	27	16	0	5.11	21	3	0	.143
Michaelson, John-John August (Mike)	21ChiA	8-12-93	Tivalkoski, Finland	4-16-68	R	R	5'9	165	0	0	–	0	2	0	0	3	4	1	1	0	9.00	0	0	0	–
Middleton, Jim-James Blaine (Rifle Jim)	17NYN 21DetA	5-28-89	Argos, Ind.	1-12-74	R	R	5'11	165	7	12	.368	8	51	10	2	158	184	52	40	0	4.50	42	5	0	.119
Middleton, John-John Wayne (Lefty)	22CleA	4-11-00	Mt. Calm, Tex.		L	L	6'1	185	0	1	.000	0	2	1	0	7	8	6	2	0	7.71	3	1	0	.333
Midkiff, Dick-Richard	38BosA	9-28-14	Gonzales, Tex.	10-30-56	R	R	6'2	195	1	1	.500	0	13	2	0	35	43	21	10	0	5.14	10	2	0	.200
Miklos, Hank-John Joseph	44ChiN	11-27-10	Chicago, Ill.		R	L	5'11	185	0	0	–	0	2	0	0	7	9	3	0	0	7.71	2	0	0	.000
Miles, Carl-Carl Thomas	40PhiA	3-22-18	Trenton, Mo.		B	L	5'11	178	0	0	–	0	2	0	0	8	9	8	6	0	13.50	4	3	0	.750
Miljus, Johnny-John Kenneth (Big Serb)	15PitF 17BknN 18MS	6-30-95	Pittsburgh, Pa.		R	R	6'1	178	29	26	.527	5	127	45	15	457	526	173	166	2	3.92	153	34	0	.222
	20-21BknN 27-28PitN 28-29CleA																								
Miller, Bill-William Francis (Wild Bill)	37StLA	4-12-10	Hannibal, Mo.		R	R	6'	180	0	1	.000	0	1	1	0	4	7	4	1	0	13.50	1	0	0	.000
Miller, Elmer-Elmer LeRoy	29PhiN	4-17-04	Detroit, Mich.		L	L	5'11	185	0	1	.000	0	8	2	0	11	12	21	5	0	11.45	38	9	1	.237
Miller, Jake-Walter Jacob	24-31CleA 33ChiA	2-28-98	Wagram, Ohio	8-20-75	L	L	6'1	185	60	58	.508	3	200	138	57	1069	1260	340	305	8	4.09	368	63	0	.171
Miller, Ken-Kenneth Albert (Whitey)	44NYN	5-2-15	St. Louis, Mo.		R	R	6'1	195	0	1	.000	0	4	0	0	5	1	4	2	0	0.00	1	0	0	.000
Miller, Ralph-Ralph Henry (Lefty)	21WasA	1-14-99	Vinton, Iowa	2-18-67	R	L	6'1	190	0	0	–	0	1	0	0	1	0	0	0	0	0.00	0	0	0	–
Miller, Red-Leo Alphonso	23PhiN	2-11-97	Philadelphia, Pa.		R	R	5'11	195	0	0	–	0	1	0	0	2	6	1	0	0	27.00	1	0	0	.000
Miller, Ronnie-Roland Arthur	41WasA 42-45MS	8-28-18	Mason City, Iowa		B	R	5'11	167	0	0	–	0	1	0	0	2	2	1	0	0	4.50	0	0	0	–
Miller, Russ-Russell Lewis	27-28PhiN	3-25-00	Etna, Ohio	4-30-62	R	R	5'11	165	1	13	.071	1	35	14	2	123	158	37	23	0	5.41	30	5	0	.167
Milligan, John-John Alexander	28-31PhiN 34WasA	1-22-04	Schuylerville, N.Y.	5-15-72	R	L	5'10	172	3	8	.273	0	35	12	4	117	141	67	38	0	5.15	34	3	0	.088
Mills, Art-Arthur Grant	27-28BosN	3-2-03	Utica, N.Y.	7-23-75	R	R	5'10	155	0	1	.000	0	19	1	0	46	58	26	7	0	5.28	8	0	0	.000
Mills, Lefty-Howard Robinson	34,37-40StLA	5-12-10	Dedham, Mass.		L	L	6'1	187	15	30	.333	2	96	48	21	435	453	302	267	1	6.06	134	20	1	.149
Milnar, Al-Albert Joseph (Happy)	36,38-43CleA 43StLA 44-45MS	12-26-13	Cleveland, Ohio		L	L	6'2	195	57	58	.496	7	188	127	49	996	1043	495	350	9	4.22	390	79	4	.203
	46StLA 46PhiN																								
Milstead, George-George Earl (Cowboy, Lefty)	24-26ChiN	6-26-03	Cleburne, Tex.		L	L	5'9	142	3	7	.300	2	36	9	2	106	130	45	27	0	4.16	32	2	0	.063
Miner, Ray-Raymond Theodore (Lefty)	21PhiA	4-4-97	Glens Falls, N.Y.	9-15-63	R	L	5'11	160	0	0	–	0	1	0	0	1	2	3	0	0	36.00	0	0	0	–
Mitchell, Clarence-Clarence Elmer	11DetA 16-17CinN 18-22BknN	2-22-91	Franklin, Neb.	11-6-63	L	L	5'11	190	125	139	.473	9	390	278	145	2217	2613	624	543	12	4.12	(See B20-45)			
	23-28PhiN 28-30StLN 30-32NYN																								
Mitchell, Monroe-Monroe Barr	23WasA	9-11-01	Starkville, Miss.		R	R	6'1	170	2	4	.333	2	10	6	3	42	57	22	8	1	6.43	12	3	0	.250
Modak, Mike-Michael Joseph Aloysius	45CinN 46MS	5-18-22	Campbell, Ohio		R	R	5'10	195	1	2	.333	1	20	3	1	42	52	23	7	1	5.79	10	2	0	.100
Mogridge, George-George Anthony	11-12ChiA 15-20NYA 21-25WasA	2-18-89	Rochester, N.Y.	3-4-62	L	L	6'2	165	133	130	.506	18	399	259	138	2275	2350	565	679	19	3.20	754	137	1	.182
	25StLA 26-27BosN																								
Mohart, George-George Benjamin	20-21BknN	3-6-92	Buffalo, N.Y.	10-2-70	R	R	5'9	165	0	1	.000	0	15	1	0	43	41	8	14	0	2.09	10	2	0	.200

					LIFETIME PITCHING TOTALS																	BATTING TOTALS			
USE NAME – GIVEN NAMES (NICKNAMES)	TEAM BY YEAR	BIRTH DATE	BIRTH PLACE	DEATH DATE	B	T	HGT	WGT	W	L	PCT	SV	G	GS	CG	IP	H	BB	SO	ShO	ERA	AB	H	HR	BA
Monteagudo, Rene-Rene [Miranda]	38,40WasA 45PhiN	3-12-16	Havana, Cuba	9-14-73	L	L	5'7	165	3	7	.300	2	46	11	5	169	221	95	93	0	6.39	(See B20-45)			
Moon, Leo-Leo (Lefty)	32CleA	6-22-99	Sweptsonville, N.C.	8-25-70	R	L	6'	175	0	0	–	0	1	0	0	6	11	7	1	0	10.50	2	1	0	.500
Mooney, Jim-Jim Irving	31-32NYN 33-34StLN	9- 4-06	Mooresburg, Tenn.		R	L	5'11	168	17	20	.459	2	92	41	13	356	426	133	116	3	4.25	105	11	0	.105
Moore, Bill-William Christopher	25DetA	9- 3-02	Corning, N.Y.		R	R	6'3	195	0	0	–	0	1	0	0	0	0	3	0	0	∞	0	0	0	–
Moore, Carlos-Carlos Whitman	30WasA	8- 3-06	Clinton, Tenn.	7- 2-58	R	R	6'1	180	0	0	–	0	4	0	0	12	9	4	2	0	2.25	4	0	0	.000
Moore, Cy-William Austin	29-32BknN 33-34PhiN	2- 7-05	Elberton, Ga.	3-28-72	R	R	6'1	190	16	26	.381	3	147	40	13	467	547	168	181	3	4.86	133	17	0	.128
Moore, Euel-Euel Walton (Chief)	34-35PhiN 35NYN 36PhiN	5-27-08	Reagan, Okla.		R	R	6'2	185	9	16	.360	3	61	29	5	224	293	77	75	0	5.50	81	15	0	.185
Moore, Jim-James Stanford	28-29CleA 30-32ChiA	12-14-03	Prescott, Ark.	5- 8-73	R	R	6'	165	2	4	.333	1	46	10	3	140	147	49	29	0	4.50	35	4	0	.114
Moore, Roy-Roy Daniel	20-22PhiA 22-23DetA	10-21-98	Austin, Tex.	4- 5-51	B	L	6'	185	11	26	.297	3	80	48	19	407	476	239	154	0	4.98	155	37	4	.239
Moore, Whitey-Lloyd Albert	36-42CinN 42StLN 43-45MS	6-10-12	Tuscarawas, Ohio		R	R	6'1	195	30	29	.508	4	133	60	18	514	450	292	228	4	3.75	156	16	0	.103
Moore, Wilcy-William Wilcy (Cy)	27-29NYA 31-32BosA 32-33NYA	5-20-97	Bonita, Tex.	3-29-63	R	R	6'	195	51	44	.537	49	261	32	14	691	732	232	204	2	3.69	205	21	1	.102
Mooty, Jake-J T	36-37CinN 40-43ChiN 44DetA	4-13-13	Bennett, Tex.	4-20-70	R	R	5'10	170	16	23	.410	8	111	38	14	433	434	194	145	1	4.03	132	27	0	.205
Moran, Hiker-Albert Thomas	38-39BosN	1- 1-12	Rochester, N.Y.		R	R	6'4	185	1	1	.500	0	7	2	1	23	22	12	4	0	3.91	5	1	0	.200
Morgan, Cy-Cyril Arlon	21-22BosN	12-11-96	Lakeville, Mass.	9-11-46	R	R	6'	170	1	1	.500	1	19	0	0	31	45	19	8	0	7.55	5	0	0	.000
Morrell, Bill-Willard Blackmer	26WasA 30-31NYN	4- 9-00	Boston, Mass.	8- 5-75	L	R	6'	172	8	6	.571	2	48	9	3	144	172	57	35	0	4.63	37	6	0	.162
					Bats Right 26																				
Morris, Bugs (See Bugs Bennett)																									
Morris, Ed-Walter Edward	22ChiN 28-31BosA	12- 7-99	Foshee, Ala.	3- 3-32	R	R	6'2	185	42	45	.483	6	140	78	43	674	702	293	256	2	4.19	221	43	1	.195
Morrisette, Bill-William Lee	15-16PhiA 20DetA	1-17-93	Baltimore, Md.	3-25-66	R	R	6'	176	3	1	.750	0	13	4	2	51	46	29	28	0	3.35	16	2	0	.125
Morrison, Guy-Walter Guy	27-28BosN	8-29-95	Hinton, W.Va.	8-14-34	R	R	5'11	185	1	2	.333	0	12	3	1	37	44	18	6	0	5.11	8	1	0	.125
Morrison, Johnny-John Dewey (Jughandle Johnny)	20-27PitN 29-30BknN	10-22-95	Pelleville, Ky.	3-20-66	R	R	5'11	188	103	80	.563	23	297	164	90	1536	1574	506	546	13	3.64	511	84	0	.164
Morrison, Phil-Philip Melvin	21PitN	10-18-94	Rockport, Ind.	1-18-55	B	R	6'2	190	0	0	–	0	1	0	0	1	1	0	1	0	0.00	0	0	0	–
Moss, Mal-Charles Malcolm	30ChiN	4-18-05	Sullivan, Ind.		R	L	6'	175	0	0	–	1	12	1	0	19	18	14	4	0	6.16	11	3	0	.273
Moss, Ray-Raymond Earl	26-31BknN 31BosN	12- 5-01	Chattanooga, Tenn.		R	R	6'1	185	22	18	.550	2	112	42	13	415	474	189	109	3	4.97	149	22	0	.148
Mueller, Les-Leslie Clyde	41DetA 42-44MS 45DetA	3- 4-19	Belleville, Ill.		R	R	6'3	190	6	8	.429	1	30	18	6	148	126	68	50	2	3.77	47	8	1	.170
Muich, Joe-Ignatius Andrew	24BosN	11-23-03	St. Louis, Mo.		R	R	6'2	175	0	0	–	0	3	0	0	9	19	5	1	0	11.00	3	0	0	.000
Mulcahy, Hugh-Hugh Noyes (Losing Pitcher)	35-40PhiN 41-44MS	9- 9-13	Brighton, Mass.		R	R	6'2	190	45	89	.336	9	220	143	63	1163	1271	487	314	5	4.48	388	64	0	.165
	45-46PhiN 47PitN																								
Mulligan, Joe-Joseph Ignatius (Big Joe)	34BosA	7-31-13	E. Weymouth, Mass.		R	R	6'4	210	1	0	1.000	0	14	2	1	45	46	27	13	0	3.60	12	0	0	.000
Mulrenan, Dominic-Dominic Joseph	21ChiA	12-18-93	Woburn, Mass.	7-27-64	R	R	5'11	170	2	8	.200	0	12	10	3	56	84	36	10	0	7.23	20	3	0	.150
Mulroney, Frank-Francis Joseph	30BosA	4- 8-03	Mallard, Iowa		R	R	6'	170	0	1	.000	0	2	0	0	3	3	0	2	0	3.00	0	0	0	–
Murcrief, Bob-Robert Cleveland	37,39,41-47StLA 48CleA 49PitN	1-28-16	Madill, Okla.		R	R	6'2	190	80	82	.494	9	288	165	67	1400	1503	392	525	11	3.81	438	68	0	.155
	49ChiN 51NYA																								
Mungo, Van Lingle-Van Lingle (Vandy)	31-41BknN 42-43,45NYN	6- 8-11	Pageland, S.C.		R	R	6'2	185	120	115	.511	16	364	259	123	2111	1957	862	1242	20	3.47	787	174	0	.221
Munns, Les-Leslie Ernest (Nemo)	34-35BknN 36StLN	11- 1-08	Fort Bragg, Cal.		R	R	6'5	212	4	13	.235	2	61	15	4	181	203	105	58	0	4.77	54	11	0	.204
Murchison, Tim-Thomas Malcolm	17StLN 20CleA	10- 8-96	Liberty, N.C.	10-20-62	R	L	6'	185	0	0	–	0	3	0	0	6	3	6	2	0	0.00	1	0	0	.000
Murphy, Johnny-John Joseph (Fireman, Grandma, Fordham Johnny)		7-14-08	New York, N.Y.	1-14-70	R	R	6'2	190	93	53	.637	107	415	40	17	1044	985	444	378	0	3.50	298	46	0	.154
	32,34-43NYA 44-45MS 46NYA 47BosA																								
Murphy, Walter-Walter Joseph	31BosA	9-27-07	New York, N.Y.		R	R	6'1	180	0	0	–	0	2	0	0	2	4	1	0	0	9.00	0	0	0	–
Murray, Amby-Ambrose Joseph	36BosN	6- 4-13	Fall River, Mass.		L	L	5'7	150	0	0	–	0	4	1	0	11	15	3	2	0	4.09	4	1	0	.250
Murray, George-George King (Smiler)	22NYA 23-24BosA 26-27WasA 33ChiA	9-23-98	Charlotte, N.C.	10-18-55	R	R	6'	200	20	26	.435	0	110	43	10	416	450	199	114	0	5.39	137	24	1	.175
Murray, Jim-James Francis (Big Jim)	22BknN	12-31-00	Scranton, Pa.	7-15-73	B	L	6'2	200	0	0	–	1	4	0	0	6	8	3	3	0	4.50	2	1	0	.500
Mussill, Barney-Bernard James	44PhiN	10- 1-19	Woodville, Pa.		R	L	6'1	200	0	1	.000	0	16	0	0	19	20	13	5	0	6.16	1	0	0	.000
Mustaikis, Alex-Alexander Dominick	40BosA	3-26-09	Chelsea, Mass.	1-17-70	R	R	6'4	196	0	1	.000	0	6	1	0	15	15	15	6	0	9.00	6	2	0	.333
Nahem, Sam-Samuel Ralph	38BknN 41StLN 42PhiN 43-45MS 48PhiN	10-19-15	New York, N.Y.		R	R	6'1	190	10	8	.556	1	90	12	3	225	222	127	101	0	4.68	61	10	0	.164
Naktenis, Pete-Peter Ernest	36PhiA 39CinN	2-12-14	Aberdeen, Wash.		L	L	6'1	185	0	1	.000	0	10	1	0	23	26	27	19	0	10.57	5	1	0	.200
Napier, Buddy-Skelton LeRoy	12StLA 18ChiN 20-21CinN	12-18-89	Byronville, Ga.	3-29-68	R	R	6'	180	4	6	.400	2	39	13	6	138	162	29	43	1	3.91	38	6	0	.158
Naylor, Earl-Earl Eugene	42PhiN	5-19-19	Kansas City, Mo.		R	R	6'	190	0	5	.000	0	20	4	1	60	68	29	19	0	6.15	(See B20-45)			
Naylor, Rollie-Roleine Cecil	17,19-24PhiA	2- 4-92	Crum, Tex.	6-18-66	R	R	6'1	180	42	83	.336	0	181	136	67	1010	1174	346	282	2	3.94	328	58	1	.177
Naymick, Mike-Michael John	39-40,43-44CleA 44StLN	9-16-17	Berlin, Pa.		R	R	6'8	225	5	7	.417	2	52	9	1	113	89	80	64	0	3.90	26	4	0	.154
Nehf, Art-Arthur Neukom	15-19BosN 19-26NYN 26-27CinN 27-29ChiN	7-31-92	Terre Haute, Ind.	12-18-60	L	L	5'9	176	184	120	.605	13	451	319	182	2708	2715	640	844	30	3.20	915	192	8	.210
Nekola, Bots-Francis Joseph	29NYA 33DetA	12-10-07	New York, N.Y.		L	L	5'11	175	0	0	–	0	11	1	0	20	25	16	2	0	5.85	4	2	0	.500
Nelson, Emmett-George Emmett (Ramrod)	35-36CinN	2-26-05	Viborg, S.D.	8-25-67	R	R	6'3	180	5	4	.556	1	25	8	3	77	94	27	17	1	4.09	21	3	0	.143
Nelson, Lynn-Lynn Bernard (Line Drive)	30,33-34ChiN 37-39PhiA 40DetA	2-24-05	Sheldon, N.D.	2-15-55	L	R	5'10	170	33	42	.440	6	166	60	29	677	777	262	255	1	5.25	367	103	5	.281
Neubauer, Hal-Harold Charles	25BosA	5-13-02	Hoboken, N.J.	9- 9-49	R	R	6'1	190	1	0	1.000	0	7	0	0	10	17	11	4	0	12.60	0	0	0	–
Nevers, Ernie-Ernest Alonzo	26-28StLA	6-11-03	Willow River, Minn.		R	R	6'	205	6	12	.333	2	44	12	6	179	196	61	39	0	4.63	60	12	0	.200
26-27,29-31 played in N.F.L.																									
Newkirk, Floyd-Floyd Elmo (Three Finger)	34NYA	7-16-08	Norris City, Ill.		R	R	5'11	178	0	0	–	0	1	0	0	1	1	1	0	0	0.00	0	0	0	–
Newkirk, Joel-Joel Ivan	19-20ChiN	5- 1-96	Kyana, Ind.		R	R	6'	180	0	1	.000	0	3	1	0	9	10	9	3	0	7.00	4	0	0	.000
Newlin, Maury-Maurice Milton (Mickey)	40-41StLA 42-45MS	6-22-14	Bloomingdale, Ind.		R	R	6'	176	1	2	.333	1	15	1	0	34	47	14	13	0	6.35	8	1	0	.125
Newsom, Bobo Louis-Norman (Buck)	29-30BknN 32ChiN 34-35StLA	8-11-07	Hartsville, S.C.	12- 7-62	R	R	6'3	210	211	222	.487	21	600	483	246	3758	3771	1732	2082	30	3.99	1337	253	1	.189
	35-37WasA 37BosA 38-39StLA 39-41DetA 42WasA 42-43BknN 43StLA																								
	43WasA 44-46PhiA 46-47WasA 47NYA 48NYN 52WasA 52-53PhiA																								
Newsome, Dick-Heber Hampton	41-43BosA	12-13-09	Ahoskie, N.C.	12-15-65	R	R	6'	185	35	33	.515	0	85	74	36	526	575	214	138	4	4.50	181	39	0	.215
Nichols, Chet-Chester Raymond Sr.	26-27PitN 28NYN 30-32PhiN	7- 2-97	Woonsocket, R.I.		R	R	5'11	160	1	8	.111	1	44	5	1	124	167	56	33	0	7.11	38	8	0	.211
Niemes, Jack-Jacob Leland	43CinN 44-46MS	10-19-19	Cincinnati, Ohio	3- 4-66	R	L	6'1	180	0	0	–	0	3	0	0	3	5	2	1	0	6.00	0	0	0	–
Niggeling, Johnny-John Arnold	38BosN 39CinN 40-43StLA 43-46WasA 46BosN	7-10-03	Remsen, Iowa	9-16-63	R	R	6'	170	64	69	.481	0	184	161	81	1250	1111	516	620	12	3.22	420	59	0	.140
Nitcholas, Nick-Otho James	45BknN	9-13-08	McKinney, Tex.		R	R	6'	195	1	0	1.000	0	7	0	0	19	19	1	4	0	5.21	4	1	0	.250
North, Lou-Louis Alexander	13DetA 17StLN 18MS 20-24StLN 24BosN	6-15-91	Elgin, Ill.	5-16-74	R	R	5'11	175	21	16	.568	13	172	25	8	463	509	200	199	0	4.43	137	27	1	.197
Oana, Prince-Henry Kauhane	43-45DetA	1-22-08	Waipahu, Hawaii		R	R	6'2	193	3	2	.600	1	13	1	0	45	37	26	18	0	3.80	(See B20-45)			
Ockey (Okypch), Walter-Walter Andrew (Footie)	44NYN	7- 4-20	New York, N.Y.	12- 4-71	R	R	6'	175	0	0	–	0	2	0	0	3	2	2	1	0	3.00	0	0	0	–
Odenwald, Ted-Theodore Joseph (Lefty)	21-22CleA	1- 4-02	Hudson, Wis.	10-23-65	R	L	5'10	147	1	0	1.000	0	11	0	0	18	22	8	6	0	4.50	3	0	0	.000
Odom, Dave-David Everett (Porky)	43BosN	6- 5-18	Dinuba, Cal.		R	R	5'10	185	0	3	.000	2	22	3	1	55	54	30	17	0	5.24	12	0	0	.000
O'Doul, Lefty-Francis Joseph	19-20, 22NYA 23BosA	3- 4-97	San Francisco, Cal.	12- 7-69	L	L	6'	180	1	1	.500	0	34	0	0	78	104	49	19	0	4.85	(See B20-45)			
Oeschger, Joe-Joseph Carl	14-19PhiN 19NYN 19-23BosN 24NYN	5-24-91	Chicago, Ill.		R	R	6'	190	82	116	.414	8	365	197	99	1818	1936	651	535	18	3.81	599	99	0	.165
	24PhiN 25BknN																								
Ogden, Curly-Warren Harvey	22-24PhiA 24-26WasA	1-24-01	Ogden, Pa.	8- 6-64	R	R	6'1	180	18	19	.486	0	93	38	19	377	378	186	88	4	3.80	135	33	0	.244
Ogden, Jack-John Mahlon	18NYN 28-29StLA 31-32CinN	11- 5-97	Ogden, Pa.		R	R	6'	190	25	34	.424	3	123	57	29	529	570	181	144	2	4.24	170	34	0	.200
Ogrodowski, Joe-Joseph Anthony	25BosN	2-17-12	Hoytville, Pa.	6-24-59	R	R	5'11	165	0	0	–	0	1	0	0	1	6	3	0	0	54.00	0	0	0	–
Okrie, Frank-Frank Anthony (Lefty)	20DetA	10-28-96	Detroit, Mich.	10-16-59	L	L	5'11	175	1	2	.333	0	21	1	1	41	44	18	9	0	5.27	5	1	0	.200
Oldham, Red-John Cyrus	14-15,20-22DetA 25-26PitN	7-15-93	Zion, Md.	1-28-61	B	L	6'	176	39	48	.448	12	176	93	39	854	978	292	267	2	4.15	283	64	2	.226
					Bats Left 22,25-26																				
Oliver, Dick (See Dick Barrett)																									
Olsen, Ole-Arthur	22-23DetA	9-12-94	S. Norwalk, Conn.		R	R	5'10	163	8	7	.533	3	54	17	6	178	189	57	64	0	4.96	47	8	0	.170
Olsen, Vern-Vern Jarl	39-42ChiN 43-45MS 47ChiN	3-16-18	Hillsboro, Ore.		R	L	6'	175	30	26	.536	2	112	60	23	517	547	192	201	7	3.39	169	39	1	.231
Olson, Ted-Theodore Otto	36-38BosA	8-27-12	Quincy, Mass.		R	R	6'	185	1	1	.500	0	18	3	1	57	75	25	18	0	7.26	18	4	0	.222
O'Neal, Skinny-Oran Herbert	25,27PhiN	5- 2-99	Gatewood, Mo.		R	R	5'8	140	0	0	–	0	13	1	0	25	44	14	8	0	9.36	7	1	0	.143
O.Neill, Emmett-Robert Emmett (Pinky)	43-45BosA 46ChiN 46ChiA	1-13-18	San Mateo, Cal.		R	R	6'3	185	15	26	.366	0	66	49	19	357	348	260	144	2	4.74	122	22	1	.180
O'Neill, Harry-Joseph Henry	22-23PhiA	2-20-97	Ridgetown, Canada	9- 5-69	R	R	6'	180	0	0	–	0	4	0	0	5	3	4	2	0	1.80	1	0	0	.000
Orrell, Joe-Forrest Gordon	43-45DetA	3- 6-17	National City, Cal.		R	R	6'4	210	4	4	.500	1	32	7	1	89	90	46	26	0	3.03	23	4	0	.174
Ortiz, Baby-Oliverio [Nunez]	44WasA	12- 5-19	Camaguey, Cuba		R	R	6'	190	0	2	.000	0	2	2	1	13	13	6	4	0	6.23	6	1	0	.167
Orwoll, Ossie-Oswald Christian 26 played in N.F.L.	28-29PhiA	11-17-00	Portland, Ore.	5- 8-67	L	L	6'	174	6	7	.462	3	39	8	3	136	142	56	65	0	4.63	(See B20-45)			
Osborn, Bob-John Bode	25-27,29-30ChiN 31PitN	4-17-03	San Diego, Tex.	4-19-60	R	R	6'1	175	27	17	.614	2	121	43	11	447	528	181	140	0	4.31	144	22	0	.153
Osborne, Tiny-Earnest Preston	22-24ChiN 24-25BknN	4- 9-93	Porterdale, Ga.	1- 5-69	L	R	6'4	215	31	40	.437	6	142	74	31	646	693	315	263	2	4.72	220	44	0	.200
Osborne, Wayne-Wayne Harold (Ossie)	35PitN 36BosN	10-11-12	Watsonville, Cal.		L	R	6'2	172	1	1	.500	0	7	3	1	21	32	9	9	0	6.00	8	2	0	.250
Osgood, Charlie-Charles Benjamin	44BknN	11-23-26	Somerville, Mass.		R	R	5'10	180	0	0	–	0	1	0	0	3	2	3	0	0	3.00	0	0	0	–
Ostermueller, Fritz-Frederick Raymond	34-40BosA 41-43StLA	9-15-07	Quincy, Ill.	12-17-57	L	L	5'11	175	114	115	.498	15	390	246	113	2068	2170	835	774	11	3.99	749	175	0	.234
	43-44BknN 44-48PitN																								
Ozmer, Doc-Horace Robert	23PhiA	5-25-01	Atlanta, Ga.	12-28-70	R	R	5'10	185	0	0	–	0	1	0	0	2	1	1	1	0	4.50	0	0	0	–
Page, Phil-Philip Rausac	28-30DetA 34BknN	8-23-05	Springfield, Mass.	6-26-58	R	L	6'2	175	3	3	.500	0	31	6	3	69	86	44	15	0	6.26	18	3	0	.167
Page, Sam-Samuel Walter	39PhiA	2-11-16	Woodruff, S.C.		L	R	6'	172	0	3	.000	0	4	3	1	22	34	15	11	0	6.95	7	3	0	.429
Page, Vance-Vance Linwood	38-41ChiN	9-15-03	Elm City, N.C.	7-14-51	R	R	6'1	185	15	16	.484	5	95	30	12	314	372	106	100	1	4.04	93	22	0	.237

USE NAME – GIVEN NAMES (NICKNAMES)	TEAM BY YEAR	BIRTH DATE	BIRTH PLACE	DEATH DATE	B	T	HGT	WGT	W	L	PCT	SV	G	GS	CG	IP	H	BB	SO	ShO	ERA	AB	H	HR	BA
									LIFETIME PITCHING TOTALS													BATTING TOTALS			
Palagyi, Mike-Michael Raymond	39WasA	7- 4-17	Conneaut, Ohio		R	R	6'2	185	0	0	–	0	1	0	0	0	0	3	0	0	∞	0	0	0	–
Palmero, Emilio-Emilio Antonio (Pal)	15-16NYN 21StLA 26WasA 28BosN	6-13-95	Guanabacoa, Cuba	7-15-70	L	L	5'11	157	6	15	.286	0	41	16	5	142	172	83	48	0	5.13	48	10	0	.208
					Bats Both 15-16																				
Parks, Slicker-Vernon Henry	21DetA	11-10-95	Fowler, Mich.		R	R	5'9	168	3	2	.600	0	10	1	0	25	33	16	10	0	5.76	9	1	0	.111
Parmalee, Roy-LeRoy Earl (Tarzan)	29-35NYN 36StLN 37ChiN 39PhiA	4-25-07	Lambertville, Mich.		R	R	6'1	190	59	55	.518	3	206	144	55	1121	1075	531	514	5	4.27	396	82	5	.207
Partenheimer, Stan-Stanwood Wendell (Party)	44BosA 45StLN	10-21-22	Chicopee Falls, Mass.		B	L	5'11	175	0	0	–	0	9	3	0	14	15	18	6	0	7.07	4	0	0	.000
Passeau, Claude-Claude William	35PitN 36-39PhiN 39-47ChiN	4- 9-09	Waynesboro, Miss.		R	R	6'3	198	162	150	.519	21	444	331	188	2718	2856	728	1104	26	3.32	982	189	15	.192
Pate, Joe-Joseph William	26-27PhiA	6- 6-92	Alice, Tex.	12-26-48	L	L	5'10	184	9	3	.750	12	79	2	0	167	176	72	38	0	3.50	37	7	0	.189
Pattison, Jimmy-James Wells	29BknN	12-18-08	Brooklyn, N.Y.		L	L	6'	185	0	1	.000	0	6	0	0	12	9	4	5	0	4.50	2	1	0	.500
Paulsen, Gil-Guilford Paul Hans	25StLN	11-14-02	Graettinger, Iowa		R	R	6'2	190	0	0	–	0	1	0	0	2	1	0	1	0	0.00	0	0	0	–
Payne, George-George Washington	20ChiA	5-23-94	Mt. Vernon, Ky.	1-24-59	R	R	5'11	172	1	1	.500	0	12	0	0	30	39	9	7	0	5.40	8	1	0	.125
Pearce, Frank-Franklin Thomas	33-35PhiN	8-31-05	Middletown, Ky.	9- 3-50	R	R	6'	170	5	6	.455	0	32	8	3	115	125	40	29	1	4.77	33	9	0	.273
Pearson, Ike-Isaac Overton	39-42PhiN 43-45MS 46PhiN 48ChiA	3- 1-17	Grenada, Miss.		R	R	6'1	180	13	50	.206	8	165	54	10	558	611	268	149	2	4.84	159	20	1	.126
Pearson, Monte- Montgomery Marcellus	32-35CleA 36-40NYA 41CinN	9- 2-09	Oakland, Cal.		R	R	6'	175	100	62	.617	4	224	191	94	1430	1392	740	703	5	4.00	513	117	2	.228
Peek, Steve-Stephen George	41NYA 42-45MS	7-30-14	Springfield, Mass.		B	R	6'2	195	4	2	.667	0	17	8	2	80	85	39	18	0	5.06	28	1	0	.036
Peery, Red-George A.	27PitN 29BosN	8-15-06	Payson, Utah		L	L	5'11	160	0	1	.000	0	10	1	0	45	53	10	3	0	5.00	14	3	0	.214
Pence, Rusty-Russell William	21ChiA	3-11-00	Marine, Ill.	8-11-71	R	R	6'	185	0	0	–	0	4	0	0	5	6	7	2	0	9.00	1	0	0	.000
Penner, Ken-Kenneth William	16CleA 29ChiN	4-24-96	Booneville, Ind.	5-28-59	L	R	5'11	170	0	1	.000	0	9	2	0	26	28	10	8	0	3.46	6	1	0	.167
Pennock, Herb-Herbert Jefferis (The Knight of Kennett Square)		2-10-94	Kennett Sq., Pa.	1-30-48	B	L	6'	160	240	161	.599	33	617	421	247	3558	3900	916	1227	35	3.61	1214	232	4	.191
	12-15PhiA 15-17BosA 18MS 19-22BosA 23-33NYA 34BosA																								
Perkins, Charlie-Charles Sullivan (Lefty)	30PhiA 34BknN	9- 9-05	Birmingham, Ala.		R	L	6'	175	0	3	.000	0	19	3	0	48	62	29	20	0	7.50	15	3	0	.200
Perme, Len-Leonard John	42ChiA 43-45MS 46ChiA	11-25-17	Cleveland, Ohio		L	L	6'	170	0	1	.000	0	8	1	1	17	11	11	6	0	3.18	3	1	0	.333
Perrin, Bill-William Joseph (Lefty)	34CleA	6-23-10	New Orleans, La.	6-30-74	R	L	5'11	172	0	1	.000	0	1	1	0	5	13	2	3	0	14.40	2	0	0	.000
[illegible]	18BosA 21-23StLN	3- 5-97	Santa Barbara, Cal.	12-28-67	R	R	5'9	165	22	18	.550	2	74	46	17	330	370	138	98	2	4.28	105	16	0	.152
Peterson, Jim-James Niels	31,33PhiA 37BknN	[illegible]	Philadelphia, Pa.	[illegible]	R	R	[illegible]	[illegible]	[illegible]	[illegible]	[illegible]	0	11	[illegible]	1	110	140	[illegible]	79	0	5.74	29	5	0	.172
Peterson, Sid-Sidney Herbert	43StLA	1-31-18	Havelock, N.D.		R	R	6'3	200	2	0	1.000	0	3	0	0	10	15	3	0	0	2.70	2	0	0	.000
Pettit, Leon-Leon Arthur (Lefty)	35WasA 37PhiN	6-23-02	Waynesburg, Pa.	11-21-74	L	L	5'10	180	8	6	.571	3	44	8	1	113	135	62	45	0	5.18	25	2	0	.080
Petty, Jess-Jesse Lee	21CleA 25-28BknN 29-30PitN 30ChiN	11-23-94	Orr, Okla.	10-23-71	R	L	6'	195	67	78	.462	4	207	154	76	1209	1286	296	407	6	3.68	413	53	0	.128
Pezzullo, Pretzels-John	35-36PhiN	12-10-10	Bridgeport, Conn.		L	L	5'11	180	3	5	.375	1	42	7	2	86	116	51	24	0	6.38	24	6	0	.250
Pfund, Lee-LeRoy Herbert	45BknN	10-10-19	Oak Park, Ill.		R	R	6'	185	3	2	.600	0	15	10	2	62	69	35	27	0	5.23	22	4	0	.182
Phebus, Bill-Raymond William	36-38WasA	8- 9-09	Cherryvale, Kans.		R	R	5'9	170	3	2	.600	2	13	6	4	54	46	35	18	1	3.33	10	0	0	.000
Phelps, Ray-Raymond Clifford	30-32BknN 35-36ChiA	12-11-03	Dunlap, Tenn.	7- 7-71	R	R	6'2	200	33	35	.485	1	126	79	24	602	700	220	190	5	4.93	209	31	1	.148
Phillips, Buz-Albert Abernathy	30PhiN	5-25-04	Newton, N.C.	11- 6-64	R	R	5'11	185	0	0	–	0	14	1	0	44	68	18	9	0	7.98	13	6	1	.462
Phillips, John-John Stephen (Jack)	45NYN	5-24-19	St. Louis, Mo.	6-16-58	R	R	6'1	185	0	0	–	0	1	0	0	4	5	4	0	0	11.25	2	1	0	.500
Phillips, Red-Clarence Lemuel	34,36DetA	11- 3-08	Pauls Valley, Okla.		R	R	6'3	195	4	4	.500	1	29	7	4	110	155	38	18	0	6.46	45	13	0	.289
Phillips, Tom-Thomas Gerald	15StLA 19CleA 21-22WasA	4- 1-89	Philipsburg, Pa.	4-12-29	R	R	6'2	190	8	12	.400	0	45	15	6	161	164	71	44	1	3.75	43	8	0	.186
Pickrel, Clarence-Clarence Douglas	33PhiN 34BosN	3-28-11	Gretna, Va.		R	R	6'1	180	1	0	1.000	0	19	1	0	30	44	10	15	0	4.50	3	0	0	.000
Piechota, Al-Aloysius Edward	40-41BosN	1-19-14	Chicago, Ill.		R	R	6'	195	2	5	.286	0	22	8	2	62	68	42	18	0	5.66	20	4	0	.200
Pierce, Ray-Raymond Lester (Lefty)	24ChiN 25-26PhiN	6- 6-97	Emporia, Kans.	5- 4-63	L	L	5'7	156	7	11	.389	0	66	15	5	182	269	63	38	0	5.64	52	8	0	.154
Piercy, Bill-William Benton (Wild Bill)	17,21NYA 22-24BosA 26ChiN	5- 2-96	El Monte, Cal.	8-28-51	R	R	6'1	170	27	43	.386	0	116	70	28	611	677	268	165	2	4.26	191	33	0	.173
Pierotti, Al-Albert Felix	20-21BosN	10-24-95	Boston, Mass.	2-12-64	R	R	5'10	195	1	2	.333	0	8	2	2	27	26	12	13	0	4.00	9	2	0	.222
20,22-24,27-29 played in N.F.L.																									
Pillette, Herman-Herman Polycarp (Old Folks)	17CinN 22-24DetA	12-26-95	St. Paul, Ore.	4-30-60	R	R	6'2	190	34	32	.515	3	107	77	33	564	600	192	148	4	3.45	195	42	0	.215
Pinto, Lerton-William Lerton	22,24PhiN	4- 8-98	Chillicothe, Ohio		L	L	6'	190	0	1	.000	0	12	0	0	29	38	14	5	0	5.59	10	1	0	.100
Pipgras, Ed-Edward John (Pip)	32BknN	6-15-04	Schleswig, Iowa	4-13-64	R	R	6'2	175	0	1	.000	0	5	1	0	10	16	6	5	0	5.40	2	0	0	.000
Pipgras, George-George William	23-24,27-33NYA 33-35BosA	12-20-99	Ida Grove, Iowa		R	R	6'1	185	102	73	.583	12	276	189	93	1487	1529	598	714	15	4.10	539	88	2	.163
Pippen, Cotton-Henry Harold	36StLN 39PhiA 39-40DetA	4- 2-10	Cisco, Tex.		R	R	6'2	180	5	16	.238	1	38	25	5	175	253	64	55	0	6.38	54	6	0	.111
Planeta, Emil-Emil Joseph	31NYN	1-13-09	Higganum, Conn.	2- 2-63	R	R	6'	190	0	0	–	0	2	0	0	5	7	4	0	0	10.80	1	0	0	.000
Plitt, Norman-Norman William	18,27BknN 27NYN	2-21-93	York, Pa.	2- 1-54	R	R	5'11	170	3	6	.333	0	23	8	1	72	85	38	9	0	4.75	20	5	0	.250
Podgajny, Johnny-John Sigmund (Specs)	40-43PhiN 43PitN 46CleA	6-10-20	Chester, Pa.	3- 2-71	R	R	6'2	173	20	37	.351	0	115	61	20	510	542	165	129	0	4.20	161	27	0	.168
Poetz, Joe-Joseph Frank	26NYN	6-22-00	St. Louis, Mo.	2- 7-42	R	R	5'10	175	0	1	.000	0	2	1	0	8	5	8	0	0	3.38	1	0	0	.000
Poffenberger, Boots-Cletus Elwood	37-38DetA 39BknN	7- 1-15	Williamsport, Md.		R	R	5'10	178	16	12	.571	4	57	32	13	267	301	149	65	0	4.75	96	19	0	.198
Poindexter, Jennings-Chester Jennings (Jinx)	36BosA 39PhiN	9-30-10	Pauls Valley, Okla.		L	L	5'10	165	0	2	.000	0	14	4	0	41	42	31	14	0	4.83	14	2	0	.143
Polli, Lou-Louis Americo (Crip)	32StLA 44NYN	7- 9-01	Barre, Vt.		R	R	5'10	165	0	2	.000	3	24	0	0	43	55	23	11	0	4.60	8	1	0	.125
Pomorski, John-John Leon	34ChiA	12-30-05	Brooklyn, N.Y.		R	R	6'	178	0	0	–	0	3	0	0	2	1	2	0	0	4.50	0	0	0	–
Ponder, Elmer-Charles Elmer	17PitN 18MS 19-21PitN 21ChiN	6-26-93	Reed, Okla.	4-20-74	R	R	6'	178	17	27	.386	0	69	42	20	378	395	72	113	3	3.21	124	13	0	.105
Porter, Ned-Ned Swindell	26-27NYN	5- 6-05	Apalachicola, Fla.	6-30-68	R	R	6'	173	0	0	–	0	3	0	0	4	5	1	1	0	2.25	0	0	0	–
Posedel, Bill-William John (Barnacle Bill)	38BknN 39-41BosN	8- 2-06	San Francisco, Fla.		R	R	5'11	175	41	43	.488	6	138	87	45	679	757	248	227	6	4.56	227	40	0	.176
	42-45MS 46BosN																								
Poser, Bob-John Falk	32ChiA 35StLA	3-16-10	Columbus, Wis.		L	R	6'	173	1	1	.500	0	5	1	0	15	29	6	2	0	9.60	7	1	0	.143
Pott, Nellie-Nelson Adolph (Lefty)	22CleA	7-16-99	Cincinnati, Ohio	12- 3-63	L	L	6'	185	0	0	–	0	2	0	0	2	7	2	0	0	31.50	0	0	0	–
Potter, Bob-Robert H. (Squire)	23WasA	3-18-02	Flatwoods, Ky.		R	R	6'1	185	0	0	–	0	1	0	0	3	11	4	1	0	21.00	0	0	0	–
Potter, Dykes-Marland Dykes	38BknN	9- 7-10	Ashland, Ky.		R	R	6'	185	0	0	–	0	2	0	0	2	4	0	1	0	4.50	0	0	0	–
Potter, Nels-Nelson Thomas	36StLN 38-41PhiA 41BosA 43-48StLA	8-23-11	Mt. Morris, Ill.		L	R	5'11	180	92	97	.487	22	349	177	89	1685	1721	582	747	6	4.00	562	128	0	.228
	48PhiA 48-49BosN																								
Powers, Ike-John Lloyd	27-28PhiA	3-13-06	Hancock, Md.	12-22-68	R	R	6'	188	2	1	.667	2	20	1	0	38	34	17	7	0	4.50	5	2	0	.400
Pressnell, Tot-Forest Charles	38-40BknN 41-42ChiN	8- 8-06	Findlay, Ohio		R	R	5'10	175	32	30	.516	12	154	42	17	526	547	134	157	4	3.80	149	24	0	.161
Prim, Ray-Raymond Lee (Pop)	33-34WasA 35PhiN 43,45-46ChiN	12-30-06	Salitpa, Ala.		R	L	6'	178	22	21	.512	4	116	34	10	350	379	72	161	2	3.57	100	18	0	.180
Proctor, Red-Noah Richard	23ChiA	10-27-00	Williamburg, Va.	12-17-54	R	R	6'1	165	0	0	–	0	2	0	0	4	11	2	0	0	13.50	0	0	0	–
Prudhomme, Augie-John Olgus	29DetA	11-20-02	Frierson, La.		R	R	6'2	186	1	6	.143	1	34	6	2	94	119	53	26	0	6.22	21	5	0	.238
Pruett, Hub-Hubert Shelby (Shucks)	22-24StLA 27-28PhiN 30NYN 32BosN	9- 1-00	Malden, Mo.		R	L	5'10	165	29	48	.377	13	211	69	28	745	816	396	357	1	4.63	212	36	0	.170
Pumpelly, Spence-Spencer Armstrong	25WasA	4-11-93	Owego, N.Y.	12- 5-73					0	0	–	0	1	0	0	1	1	1	0	0	9.00	0	0	0	–
Pyle, Ewald-Herbert Ewald (Lefty)	39,42StLA 43WasA 44-45NYN 45BosN	8-27-10	St. Louis, Mo.		L	L	6'	175	11	21	.344	1	67	36	5	270	277	150	122	1	5.03	84	12	0	.143
Pyle, Harlan-Harlan Albert (Firpo)	28CinN	11-29-05	Burchard, Neb.		R	R	6'2	180	0	0	–	0	2	1	0	1	1	4	1	0	27.00	1	0	0	.000
Quinn (Picus), Jack (John Quinn)-John Picus	09-12NYA 13BosN	7- 5-83	Janesville, Pa.	4-17-46	R	R	6'	196	248	219	.531	59	757	444	243	3947	4243	863	1331	28	3.27	1349	248	8	.184
	14-15BalF 18ChiA 19-21NYA 22-25BosA 25-30PhiA 31-32BknN 33CinN																								
Quinn, Wimpy-Wellington Hunt	41ChiN	5-12-18	Birmingham, Ala.	9- 1-54	R	R	6'2	187	0	0	–	0	3	0	0	5	3	3	2	0	7.20	2	1	0	.500
Rachunok, Steve-Stephen Stepanovich (The Mad Russian)	40BknN	12- 5-16	Rittman, Ohio		R	R	6'4	200	0	1	.000	0	2	1	1	10	9	5	10	0	4.50	2	0	0	.000
Rader, Drew-Drew Leon (Lefty)	21PitN	5-14-01	Elmira, N.Y.		R	L	6'2	187	0	0	–	0	1	0	0	2	2	0	0	0	0.00	1	0	0	.000
Ragland, Frank-Frank Roland	32WasA 33PhiN	5-26-04	Water Valley, Miss.	7-28-59	R	R	6'1	186	1	4	.200	0	23	6	0	76	105	31	15	0	7.11	21	5	0	.238
Rambert, Pep-Elmer Donald	39-40PitN	8- 1-16	Cleveland, Ohio		R	R	6'	195	0	1	.000	0	5	1	0	12	19	5	4	0	8.25	2	0	0	.000
Rambo, Pete-Warren Dawson	26PhiN	11- 1-06	Thoroughfare, N.J.		R	R	5'9	150	0	0	–	0	1	0	0	4	6	4	4	0	13.50	1	1	0	1.000
Reinhart, Art-Arthur Conrad	19,25-28StLN	5-29-99	Ackley, Iowa	11-11-46	L	L	6'1	170	30	18	.625	3	92	45	31	445	470	157	79	4	3.60	186	56	0	.301
Reis, Bobby-Robert Joseph Thomas	35BknN 36-38BosN	1- 2-09	Queens, N.Y.	5- 1-73	R	R	6'1	190	10	13	.435	2	69	9	5	243	262	144	52	0	4.26	(See B20-45)			
Reis, Tommy-Thomas Edward	38PhiN 38BosN	8- 6-14	Newport, Ky.		R	R	6'2	180	0	1	.000	0	8	0	0	11	16	9	6	0	12.27	2	0	0	.000
Reninger, Jim-James David	38-39PhiA	3- 7-13	Aurora, Ill.		R	R	6'3	210	0	4	.000	0	8	6	1	39	52	26	12	0	7.38	13	1	0	.077
Rescigno, Xavier-Xavier Frederick (Mr. X)	43-45PitN	10-13-13	New York, N.Y.		R	R	5'10	175	19	22	.463	16	129	21	7	336	366	113	115	1	4.15	72	9	0	.125
Rettig, Otto-Adolph John	22PhiA	1-29-94	New York, N.Y.		R	R	5'11	165	1	2	.333	0	4	4	1	18	18	12	3	0	5.00	6	0	0	.000
Rhem, Flint-Charles Flint (Shad)	24-28,30-32StLN 32-33PhiN 34StLN	1-24-01	Georgetown, S.C.	7-30-69	R	R	6'2	190	105	97	.520	10	294	229	91	1726	1958	529	534	9	4.20	610	88	3	.144
	34-35BosN 36StLN																								
Rhodes, Gordon-John Gordon (Dusty)	29-32NYA 32-35BosA 36PhiA	8-11-07	Winnemucca, Nev.	3-24-60	R	R	6'	187	43	74	.368	5	200	135	47	1048	1196	477	346	1	4.85	356	69	2	.194
Rich, Woody-Woodrow Earl	39-41BosA 44BosN 45MS	3- 9-17	Morganton, N.C.		L	R	6'2	185	6	4	.600	1	33	16	5	118	127	50	42	0	5.03	39	8	0	.205
Richmond, Beryl-Beryl Justice	33ChiN 34CinN	8-24-07	Glen Easton, W.Va.		B	L	6'1	185	1	2	.333	0	10	2	1	24	33	12	11	0	3.38	6	0	0	.000
					Bats Right 33																				
Richmond, Ray-Raymond Sinclair (Bud)	20-21StLA	6- 5-96	Fillmore, Ill.	10-21-69	R	R	6'	170	2	1	.667	0	9	3	1	32	41	23	11	0	8.72	10	1	0	.100
Riddle, Elmer-Elmer Ray	39-45CinN 46VR 47CinN 48-49PitN	7-31-14	Columbus, Ga.		R	R	5'11	170	65	52	.556	8	190	124	57	1023	974	458	342	13	3.40	339	69	1	.204
Rigney, Johnny-John Duncan	37-42ChiA 43-45MS 46-47ChiA	10-28-14	Oak Park, Ill.		R	R	6'2	190	64	64	.500	5	197	132	66	1188	1101	450	605	9	3.58	401	71	0	.177
Ring, Jimmy-James Joseph	17-20CinN 21-25PhiN 26NYN 27StLN 28PhiN	2-15-95	Brooklyn, N.Y.	7- 6-65	R	R	6'1	170	118	149	.442	11	389	294	154	2388	2545	953	835	9	4.07	817	120	4	.147
Ripley, Walt-Walter Franklin	35BosA	11-26-16	Worcester, Mass.		R	R	6'	168	0	0	–	0	2	0	0	4	7	3	0	0	9.00	0	0	0	–
Ripple, Charlie-Charles Dawson	44-46PhiN	12- 1-21	Bolton, N.C.		L	L	6'2	210	1	1	.500	0	11	1	0	13	18	20	10	0	9.69	2	1	0	.500
Riviere, Tink-Arthur Bernard	21StLN 25ChiA	8- 2-99	Liberty, Tex.	9-27-65	R	R	5'10	167	1	0	1.000	0	20	2	0	40	51	27	16	0	7.65	9	3	0	.333

USE NAME – GIVEN NAMES (NICKNAMES)	TEAM BY YEAR	BIRTH DATE	BIRTH PLACE	DEATH DATE	LIFETIME PITCHING TOTALS																	BATTING TOTALS			
					B	T	HGT	WGT	W	L	PCT	SV	G	GS	CG	IP	H	BB	SO	ShO	ERA	AB	H	HR	BA
Rixey, Eppa-Eppa (Eppa Jeptha)	12-17,19-20PhiN 18MS 21-33CinN	5- 3-91	Culpeper, Va.	2-28-63	R	L	6'5	210	266	251	.515	14	692	552	290	4494	4633	1082	1350	39	3.15	1522	291	3	.191
Roberts, Jim-James Newson (Big Jim)	24-25BknN	10-13-95	Artesia, Miss.		R	R	6'3	205	0	3	.000	0	12	5	0	26	42	8	10	0	7.27	7	1	0	.143
Robertson, Charlie-Charles Culbertson	19,22-25ChiA 26StLA 27-28BosN	1-31-96	Dexter, Tex.		L	R	6'	175	49	80	.380	1	166	142	60	1004	1149	377	310	6	4.45	327	68	0	.208
Roche, Armando-Armando (Baez)	45WasA	12- 7-26	Havana, Cuba		R	R	6'	190	0	0	–	0	2	0	0	6	10	2	0	0	6.00	1	0	0	.000
Roe-Clay-James Clay (Shad)	23WasA	1- 7-04	Green Brier, Tenn.	4- 4-56	L	L	6'2	180	0	1	.000	0	1	1	0	2	0	6	2	0	0.00	0	0	0	–
Roettger, Oscar-Oscar Frederick Louis	23-24NYA	2- 9-00	St. Louis, Mo.		R	R	6'	170	0	0	–	1	6	0	0	12	17	14	7	0	8.25	(See B20-45)			
Rogalski, Joe-Joseph Anthony	38DetA	7-16-12	Ashland, Wis.	11-20-51	R	R	6'1	187	0	0	–	0	2	0	0	7	12	0	2	0	2.57	2	0	0	.000
Rogers, Buck-Orlin Woodrow (Lefty)	35WasA	11- 5-12	Spring Garden, Va.		R	L	5'8	164	0	1	.000	0	2	1	0	10	16	6	7	0	7.20	3	0	0	.000
Rogers, Lee-Lee Otis (Buck, Lefty)	38BosA 38BknN	10- 8-13	Tuscaloosa, Ala.		R	L	5'11	170	1	3	.250	0	26	4	0	51	55	28	18	0	6.18	7	0	0	.000
Rommel, Eddie-Edwin Americus	20-32PhiA	9-13-97	Baltimore, Md.	8-26-70	R	R	6'2	197	171	119	.590	29	500	249	147	2557	2729	724	599	18	3.54	826	164	1	.199
Root, Charlie-Charles Henry (Chinski)	23StLA 26-41ChiN	3-17-99	Middletown, Ohio	11- 5-70	R	R	5'10	190	201	160	.557	40	632	341	177	3197	3252	889	1459	21	3.59	1086	196	11	.180
Roser, Steve-Emerson Corey	44-46NYA 46BosN	1-25-18	Rome, N.Y.		R	R	6'4	220	6	5	.545	2	45	8	1	149	147	64	64	0	4.05	43	4	0	.093
Ross, Buck-Lee Ravon	36-41PhiA 41-45ChiA	2- 3-15	Norwood, N.C.		R	R	6'2	170	56	95	.371	2	237	182	65	1363	1545	573	360	6	4.95	448	69	3	.154
Ross, Buster-Chester Franklin	24-26BosA	3-11-03	Kuttawa, Ky.		L	L	5'8	150	7	12	.368	1	64	10	1	190	233	74	31	1	5.02	50	8	0	.160
Rosso, Frank-Francis James	44NYN	3- 1-21	Agawam, Mass.		R	R	5'11	180	0	0	–	0	2	0	0	4	11	3	1	0	9.00	0	0	0	–
Rowe, Schoolboy-Lynwood Thomas	33-42DetA 42BknN 43PhiN 44-45MS	1-11-10	Waco, Tex.	1- 8-61	R	R	6'4	210	158	101	.610	12	382	278	137	2219	2330	558	913	22	3.87	(See B20-45)			
	46-49PhiN																								
Roy, Emile-Emile Arthur	33PhiA	3-26-07	Brighton, Mass.		R	R	5'11	180	0	1	.000	0	1	1	0	2	4	4	3	0	31.50	0	0	0	–
Roy, Luther-Luther Franklin	24-25CleA 27ChiN 29PhiN 29BknN	7-29-02	Ooltewah, Tenn.	7-24-63	R	R	5'10	161	6	12	.333	0	56	18	3	171	231	92	36	0	7.16	53	14	0	.264
Rudolph, Ernie-Ernest William	45BknN	2-13-10	Black R. Falls, Wis.		L	R	5'8	165	1	0	1.000	0	7	0	0	9	12	7	3	0	5.00	0	0	0	–
Ruether, Dutch-Walter Henry	17ChiN 17-20CinN 21-24BknN	9-13-93	Alameda, Cal.	5-16-70	L	L	6'1	180	137	95	.591	8	309	272	154	2123	2243	739	708	17	3.50	(See B20-45)			
	25-26WasA 26-27NYA																								
Ruffing, Red-Charles Herbert	24-30BosA 30-42NYA 43-44MS	5- 3-04	Granville, Ill.		R	R	6'2	205	273	225	.548	16	624	536	335	4342	4294	1541	1987	42	3.80	(See B20-45)			
	45-46NYA 47ChiA																								
Rush, Andy-Jesse Howard	25BknN	12-26-89	Longton, Kans.	3-16-69	R	R	6'3	180	0	1	.000	0	4	2	0	10	16	5	4	0	9.00	3	0	0	.000
Russell, Allan-Allan E.	15-19NYA 19-22BosA 23-25WasA	7-31-93	Baltimore, Md.		B	R	5'11	165	70	76	.479	41	345	112	55	1393	1382	610	603	5	3.52	415	65	0	.157
Russell, Jack-Jack Erwin	26-32BosA 32CleA 33-36WasA 36BosA	10-24-05	Paris, Tex.		R	R	6'1	178	85	141	.376	38	557	182	71	2051	2454	571	418	3	4.47	617	103	1	.167
	37DetA 38-39ChiN 40StLN																								
Russell, Jack-John Albert	17-18BknN 21-22ChiA	10-20-95	San Mateo, Cal.	11-20-30	L	L	6'2	195	2	7	.222	1	21	10	5	90	103	46	19	0	5.40	30	11	0	.367
Russo, Marius-Marius Ugo (Lefty)	39-43NYA 44-45MS 46NYA	7-19-14	Brooklyn, N.Y.		L	L	6'1	190	45	34	.570	5	120	84	48	681	618	253	311	6	3.13	235	50	0	.213
Ryan, Rosy-Wilfred Patrick Dolan	19-24NYN 25-26BosN 28NYA 33BknN	3-15-98	Worcester, Mass.		L	R	6'	185	52	47	.525	19	248	73	29	881	941	278	315	1	4.14	268	51	1	.190
Ryba, Mike-Dominic Joseph	35-38StLN 41-46BosA	6- 9-03	DeLancey, Pa.	12-13-71	R	R	5'11	180	52	34	.605	16	240	36	16	784	817	247	307	2	3.66	247	58	0	.235
Sale, Freddy-Frederick Link	24PitN	5- 2-02	Chester, S.C.	5-27-56	R	R	5'9	160	0	0	–	0	1	0	0	1	2	0	0	0	0.00	0	0	0	–
Salveson, Jack-John Theodore	33-34NYN 35PitN 35ChiA 43,45CleA	1- 5-14	Fullerton, Cal.	12-28-74	R	R	6'	180	9	9	.500	4	87	19	8	273	302	87	85	3	3.99	77	20	3	.260
Salvo, Manny-Manuel (Gyp)	39NYN 40-43BosN 43PhiN 43BosN	6-30-13	Sacramento, Cal.		R	R	6'4	210	33	50	.398	1	135	93	40	722	723	284	247	9	3.69	232	30	1	.129
Samuels, Joe-Joseph Jonas (Skabotch)	30DetA	3-21-05	Scranton, Pa.		R	R	6'1	196	0	0	–	0	2	0	0	6	10	6	1	0	16.50	1	0	0	.000
Sanders, Dee-Dee Wilma	45StLA	4- 8-21	Quitman, Tex.		R	R	6'3	195	0	0	–	0	2	0	0	1	7	1	1	0	54.00	0	0	0	–
Savidge, Don-Donald Snyder	29WasA	8-28-08	Berwick, Pa.		R	R	6'1	180	0	0	–	0	3	0	0	6	12	2	2	0	9.00	0	0	0	–
Sayles, Bill-William Nisbeth	39BosA 43NYN 43BknN 44-45MS	7-27-17	Portland, Ore.		R	R	6'2	175	1	3	.250	0	28	3	1	79	87	46	52	0	5.58	22	6	0	.273
Schacht, Al-Alexander (The Clown Prince of Baseball)	19-21WasA	11-11-92	New York, N.Y.		R	R	5'11	142	14	10	.583	2	53	18	8	197	254	61	38	1	4.48	52	10	0	.192
Schacker, Hal-Harold	45BosN	4- 6-25	Brooklyn, N.Y.		R	R	6'	190	0	1	.000	0	6	0	0	15	14	9	6	0	5.40	2	0	0	.000
Schanz, Charley-Charley Murrell	44-47PhiN 50BosA	6- 8-19	Anacortes, Wash.		R	R	6'3	215	28	43	.394	14	155	72	23	627	658	332	243	2	4.33	194	26	1	.134
Scheetz, Owen-Owen Franklin	43WasA	12-24-13	New Bedford, Ohio		R	R	6'	190	0	0	–	1	6	0	0	9	16	4	5	0	7.00	2	0	0	.000
Schelle, Jim-Gerald Anthony	39PhiA	4-13-17	Baltimore, Md.		R	R	6'3	204	0	0	–	0	1	0	0	0	1	3	0	0	∞	0	0	0	–
Schemanske, Fred-Frederick George (Buck)	23WasA	4-28-03	Detroit, Mich.	2-18-60	R	R	6'2	190	0	0	–	0	1	0	0	1	3	0	0	0	27.00	2	2	0	1.000
Schesler, Dutch-Charles	31PhiN	6- 1-00	Frankfurt, Germany	11-19-53	R	R	6'2	180	0	0	–	0	17	0	0	38	65	18	14	0	7.34	9	1	0	.111
Schillings, Red-Elbert Isaiah	22PhiA	3-29-00	Deport, Tex.	1- 7-54	R	R	5'10	180	0	0	–	0	4	0	0	8	10	11	4	0	6.75	2	0	0	.000
Schmidt, Freddy-Frederick Albert	44,46-47StLN 45MS 45ChiN 47PhiN	2- 9-16	Hartford, Conn.		R	R	6'1	185	13	11	.542	5	85	15	3	225	206	122	98	2	3.76	57	8	0	.140
Schnell, Karl-Karl Otto	22-23CinN	9-20-99	Los Angeles, Cal.		R	R	6'1	176	0	0	–	0	11	0	0	21	23	20	5	0	4.29	4	1	0	.250
Schott, Gene-Eugene Arthur	35-38CinN 39PhiN 39BknN	7-14-13	Batavia, Ohio		R	R	6'2	185	28	41	.406	4	136	62	24	587	590	222	192	3	3.73	199	42	1	.211
Schreiber, Paul-Paul Frederick (Von)	22-23BknN 45NYA	10- 8-02	Jacksonville, Fla.		R	R	6'2	180	0	0	–	1	12	0	0	20	22	10	5	0	4.05	3	0	0	.000
Schultz, Webb-Webb Carl	24ChiA	1-31-98	Wautoma, Wis.		R	R	5'11	172	0	0	–	0	1	0	0	1	1	0	0	0	9.00	0	0	0	–
Schulz, Walt-Walter-Frederick	20StLN	4-16-00	St. Louis, Mo.	2-27-28	R	R	6'	170	0	0	–	0	2	0	0	6	10	2	0	0	6.00	2	0	0	.000
Schumacher, Hal-Harold Henry (Prince Hal)	31-42NYN 43-45MS 46NYN	11-23-10	Hinckley, N.Y.		R	R	6'	190	158	121	.566	7	391	329	138	2482	2424	902	906	29	3.36	896	181	15	.202
Scott, George-George William	20StLN	11-17-96	Trenton, Mo.		R	R	6'1	175	0	0	–	0	2	0	0	6	4	3	1	0	4.50	1	0	0	.000
Scott, Jack-John William	16PitN 17,19-21BosN 22CinN 22-23, 25-26NYN	4-18-92	Ridgeway, N.C.	11-30-59	L	R	6'2	215	103	109	.486	19	356	195	115	1816	1969	493	657	11	3.85	680	187	5	.275
	27PhiN 28-29NYN																								
Scott, Lefty-Marshall	45PhiN	7-15-15	Roswell, N.M.	3- 3-64	R	L	6'	165	0	2	.000	0	8	2	0	22	29	12	5	0	4.50	3	0	0	.000
Seats, Tom-Thomas Edward	40DetA 45BknN	9-24-11	Farmington, N.C.		R	L	5'11	190	12	9	.571	1	57	20	6	178	194	58	69	2	4.45	55	10	0	.182
					Bats Both 40																				
Sedgwick, Duke-Henry Kenneth	21PhiN 23WasA	6- 1-99	Martins Ferry, Ohio		R	R	6'	175	1	4	.200	0	21	7	2	87	108	38	25	0	5.48	29	5	0	.172
Seibold, Socks-Harry	16-17PhiA 18MS 19PhiA 29-33BosN	5-31-96	Philadelphia, Pa.	9-21-65	R	R	5'8	162	48	86	.368	5	191	135	64	1065	1179	405	296	8	4.42	(See B20-45)			
Sell, Epp-Elwood Lester	22-23StLN	4-26-07	Llewellyn, Pa.	2-19-61	R	R	6'	175	4	3	.571	0	12	6	0	48	63	14	7	0	6.56	19	4	0	.211
Settlemire, Merle-Edgar Merle (Lefty)	28BosA	1-19-03	Santa Fe, Ohio		L	L	5'9	156	0	6	.000	0	30	9	0	82	116	34	12	0	5.49	17	3	0	.176
Seward, Frank-Frank Martin	43-44NYN	4- 7-21	Pennsauken, N.J.		R	R	6'3	200	3	3	.500	0	26	8	3	87	110	37	18	0	5.17	28	2	0	.071
Sewell, Rip-Truett Banks	32DetA 38-49PitN	5-11-07	Decatur, Ala.		R	R	6'1	180	143	97	.596	15	390	243	137	2119	2101	748	636	18	3.48	750	152	6	.203
Shanner, W. W.-W. W.	20PhiA					R			0	0	–	0	1	0	0	4	6	1	1	0	6.75	1	0	0	.000
Shaute, Joe-Joseph Benjamin (Lefty)	22-30CleA 31-33BknN 34CinN	8- 1-99	Peckville, Pa.	2-21-70	L	L	6'	190	99	109	.476	18	360	209	103	1819	2097	534	512	5	4.15	660	170	1	.258
Shawkey, Bob-James Robert	13-15PhiA 15-27,M30NYA	12- 4-90	Sigel, Pa.		R	R	5'11	168	198	150	.569	29	488	333	194	2938	2722	1018	1360	31	3.09	1049	225	3	.214
Shea, John-John Michael Joseph (Lefty)	28BosA	12-27-04	Everett, Mass.	12- 1-56	L	L	5'10	170	0	0	–	0	1	0	0	1	1	1	0	0	18.00	0	0	0	–
Shea, Red-Patrick Henry	18PhiA 21-22NYN	11-29-98	Ware, Mass.		R	R	6'	165	5	5	.500	0	23	4	1	64	64	15	17	0	3.80	19	1	0	.053
Shealy, Al-Albert Berley	28NYA 30ChiN	5-20-00	Chapin, S.C.	3- 7-67	R	R	5'11	175	8	6	.571	2	47	12	3	123	161	56	53	0	5.71	43	12	1	.279
Sheehan, Tom-Thomas Clancy	15-16PhiA 21NYA 24-25CinN 25-26PitN	3-31-94	Grand Ridge, Ill.		R	R	6'2	190	17	37	.315	5	146	54	26	607	677	242	169	3	4.00	190	39	0	.205
	M60SFN																								
Shepard, Bert-Robert Earl	45WasA	6-28-20	Dana, Ind.		L	L	5'11	185	0	0	–	0	1	0	0	5	3	1	2	0	1.80	3	0	0	.000
Sherdel, Bill-William Henry (Wee Willie)	18-30,32StLN 30-32BosN	8-15-96	McSherrystown, Pa.	11-14-68	L	L	5'10	160	165	146	.531	26	514	273	159	2709	3018	661	839	11	3.72	960	214	9	.223
Sherid, Roy-Roydan Richard	29-31NYA	1-25-08	Norristown, Pa.		R	R	6'2	185	23	24	.489	7	87	44	20	418	473	166	149	0	4.65	149	26	0	.174
Shields, Ben-Benjamin Cowan (Lefty)	24-25NYA 30BosA 31PhiN	6-17-03	Huntersville, N.C.		B	L	6'1	195	4	0	1.000	0	13	2	2	41	55	27	9	0	8.34	13	1	0	.077
Shields, Vince-Vincent William	24StLN	11-18-00	Fredericton, Can.	10-17-52	L	R	5'11	185	1	1	.500	0	2	1	0	12	10	3	4	0	3.00	5	2	0	.400
Shirey, Duke-Clair Lee	20WasA	6-20-98	Jersey Shore, Pa.	9- 1-62	R	R	6'1	175	0	1	.000	0	2	1	0	4	5	2	0	0	6.75	1	0	0	.000
Shirley, Tex-Alvis Newman	44-46StLA	4-25-18	Birthright, Tex.		B	R	6'1	175	19	30	.388	2	102	54	19	447	443	290	168	3	4.25	159	34	0	.214
					Bats Right 41-42																				
Shocker (Shockcor), Urban (Urbain Jacques)-Urban James	16-17NYA	8-22-90	Cleveland, Ohio	9- 9-28	R	R	5'10	180	188	117	.616	25	412	319	202	2681	2709	659	983	28	3.17	798	167	1	.209
	18-24StLA 25-28NYA																								
Shoffner, Milt-Milburn James	29-31CleA 37-39BosN 39-40CinN	11-13-05	Sherman, Tex.		L	L	6'1	184	25	26	.490	3	134	51	22	578	647	214	180	2	4.58	205	32	2	.156
Shores, Bill-William David	28-31PhiA 33NYN 36ChiA	5-26-04	Abilene, Tex.		R	R	6'	210	26	15	.634	7	96	39	14	396	425	168	129	2	4.16	121	21	0	.174
Shoun, Clyde-Clyde Mitchell (Hardrock)	35-37ChiN 38-42StLN 42-44CinN 45MS	3-20-12	Mountain City, Tenn.	3-20-68	L	L	6'1	188	73	59	.553	29	454	85	34	1286	1325	404	483	3	3.91	362	73	0	.202
	46-47CinN 47-49BosN 49ChiA																								
Shriver, Harry-Harry Graydon (Pop)	22-23BknN	9- 2-96	Wadestown, W.Va.	11-21-70	R	R	6'2	180	4	6	.400	0	26	15	4	112	122	48	39	2	3.13	28	1	0	.036
Shuman, Harry-Harry	42-43PitN 44PhiN	3- 5-16	Philadelphia, Pa.		R	R	6'2	195	0	0	–	0	30	0	0	51	56	20	10	0	4.41	3	0	0	.000
Signer, Walter-Walter Donald Aloyisius	43,45ChiN	10-12-10	New York, N.Y.	7-23-74	R	R	6'	165	2	1	.667	1	10	2	1	33	35	9	5	0	3.00	9	2	0	.222
Simmons (Simoni), Pat-Patrick Clement	28-29BosA	11-29-08	Watervliet, N.Y.	7- 3-68	R	R	5'11	172	0	2	.000	2	33	3	0	76	75	41	18	0	3.67	16	2	0	.125
Singleton, John-John Edward (Sheriff)	22PhiN	11-27-96	Gallipolis, Ohio	10-24-37	R	R	5'11	171	1	10	.091	0	22	9	3	93	127	38	27	1	5.90	36	5	0	.139
Sivess, Pete-Peter	36-38PhiN	9-23-13	South River, N.J.		R	R	6'3	195	7	11	.389	3	62	16	5	201	257	116	58	0	5.46	63	9	0	.143
Slappey, John-John Henry	20PhiA	8- 8-98	Albany, Ga.	6-10-57	L	L	6'4	170	0	1	.000	0	3	1	0	6	15	4	1	0	7.50	2	1	0	.500
Slayton, Steve-Foster Herbert	28BosA	4-26-02	Barre, Vt.		R	R	6'	163	0	0	–	0	3	0	0	7	6	3	2	0	3.86	2	0	0	.000
Smith, Al-Alfred John	34-37NYN 38-39PhiN 40-45CleA	10-12-07	Belleville, Ill.		L	L	5'11	180	99	101	.495	17	356	202	75	1663	1707	587	587	16	3.72	535	102	2	.191
Smith, Al-Alfred Kendricks	26NYN	12-13-03	Norristown, Pa.		R	R	6'	170	0	0	–	0	1	0	0	2	4	2	0	0	9.00	0	0	0	–
Smith, Art-Arthur Laird	32ChiA	6-21-06	Boston, Mass.		R	R	6'	175	0	1	.000	0	3	2	0	7	17	4	1	0	11.57	1	0	0	.000
Smith, Bob-Robert Eldridge	25-30BosN 31-32ChiN 33CinN 33-37BosN	4-22-98	Rogersville, Tenn.		R	R	5'10	175	106	139	.433	40	435	229	128	2238	2472	670	618	16	3.95	(See B20-45)			
Smith, Clay-Clay Jamieson	38CleA 40DetA	9-11-14	Cambridge, Kans.		R	R	6'2	190	1	1	.500	0	18	1	0	39	50	15	17	0	5.54	11	0	0	.000
Smith, Dave-David Merwin	38-39PhiA	12-17-14	Sellers, S.C.		R	R	5'10	170	2	1	.667	0	22	0	0	44	51	30	13	0	5.11	12	0	0	.000
Smith, Eddie-Edgar	36-39PhiA 39-43ChiA 44-45MS 46-47ChiA 47BosA	12-14-13	Columbus, N.J.		B	L	5'10	174	73	113	.392	12	282	197	91	1595	1554	739	694	7	3.82	531	100	1	.188

USE NAME – GIVEN NAMES (NICKNAMES)	TEAM BY YEAR	BIRTH DATE	BIRTH PLACE	DEATH DATE	B	T	HGT	WGT	W	L	PCT	SV	G	GS	CG	IP	H	BB	SO	ShO	ERA	AB	H	HR	BA
					LIFETIME PITCHING TOTALS																	BATTING TOTALS			
Smith, George-George Allen (Columbia George)	16-17NYN 18CinN	5-31-92	Byram, Conn.	1- 7-65	R	R	6'2	163	41	81	.336	4	229	118	52	1144	1321	255	263	6	3.89	349	34	0	.097
	18NYN 18BknN 19NYN 19-22PhiN 23BknN																								
Smith, George-George Shelby	26-29DetA 30BosA	10-17-01	Louisville, Ky.		R	R	6'2	175	10	8	.556	3	132	7	1	331	354	218	135	0	5.33	87	23	2	.264
Smith, Hal-Harold Lavern	32-35PitN	6-30-02	Creston, Iowa		R	R	6'3	195	12	11	.522	1	51	25	10	210	232	52	59	3	3.77	67	7	0	.104
Smith, Rufus-Rufus Frazier (Shirt)	27DetA	1-24-05	Guilford Coll., N.C.		R	L	5'8	180	0	0	–	0	1	1	0	8	8	3	2	0	3.38	3	0	0	.000
Smith, Sherry-Sherrod Malone	11-12PitN 15-17BknN 18MS 19-22BknN	2-18-91	Monticello, Ga.	9-12-49	L	L	6'1	170	114	118	.491	21	373	224	142	2052	2234	440	428	16	3.32	709	165	6	.233
	22-27CleA																								
Smoll, Lefty-Clyde Hetrick	40PhiN	4-17-14	Quakertown, Pa.		B	L	5'10	175	2	8	.200	0	33	9	0	109	145	36	31	0	5.37	31	5	0	.161
Smythe, Harry-William Henry	29-30PhiN 34NYA 34BknN	10-24-04	Augusta, Ga.		L	L	5'10	179	5	12	.294	4	60	10	2	155	232	62	33	0	6.39	54	13	0	.241
Snyder, Bill-William Nichols	19-20WasA	1-28-98	Mansfield, Ohio	10- 8-34	R	R			2	2	.500	1	18	5	1	62	65	31	22	0	3.77	21	6	0	.286
Songer, Don-Don	24-27PitN 27NYN	1-31-99	Walnut, Kans.	10- 3-62	L	L	6'	165	10	14	.417	4	71	16	5	202	204	98	44	1	3.39	53	7	0	.132
Sorrell, Vic-Victor Garland	28-37DetA	4- 9-01	Morrisville, N.C.	5- 4-72	R	R	5'10	180	92	101	.477	10	280	216	95	1673	1820	706	619	7	4.43	553	77	0	.139
Sothoron, Allan-Allan Sutton	14-15,17-21StLA 21BosA 21-22CleA	4-27-93	Laura, Ohio	6-17-39	B	R	5'11	182	92	100	.479	9	264	195	102	1583	1583	596	576	17	3.31	545	112	0	.206
	24-26StLN M33StLA				Bats Right 24-26																				
Speece, By-Byron Franklin	24WasA 25-26CleA 30PhiN	1- 6-97	West Baden, Ind.		R	R	5'11	170	5	6	.455	1	62	4	3	167	208	61	51	0	4.74	54	9	0	.167
Speer, Floyd-Floyd Vernie	43-44ChiA	1-27-13	Booneville, Ark.	3-22-69	R	R	6'	180	0	0	–	0	3	0	0	3	5	2	2	0	9.00	0	0	0	–
Spencer, Glenn-Glenn Edward	28,30-32PitN 33NYN	9-11-05	Corning, N.Y.	12-30-58	R	R	5'11	155	23	31	.426	8	139	44	22	535	588	201	162	2	4.53	155	19	0	.123
Springer, Brad-Bradford Louis	25StLA 26CinN	5- 9-04	Detroit, Mich.	1- 4-70	L	L	6'	155	0	0	–	0	3	0	0	4	3	9	1	0	4.50	1	0	0	.000
Sproull, Charlie-Charles William	45PhiN	1- 9-19	Taylorsville, Ga.		R	R	6'3	185	4	10	.286	1	34	19	2	130	158	80	47	0	5.95	35	5	0	.143
Starr, Ray-Raymond Francis (Iron Man)	32StLN 33NYN 33BosN	4-23-06	Nowata, Okla.	2- 9-63	R	R	6'1	178	37	35	.514	4	138	88	35	699	670	279	189	9	3.53	212	26	0	.123
	41-43CinN 44-45PitN 45ChiN																								
Stauffer, Ed-Charles Edward	23ChiN 25StLA	1-10-98	Emsworth, Pa.		R	R	5'11	185	0	1	.000	0	21	1	0	32	39	22	13	0	5.91	4	1	0	.250
Steengrafe, Milt-Milton Henry	24,26ChiA	5-26-00	San Francisco, Cal.		R	R	6'	170	1	1	.500	0	16	1	0	44	58	23	13	0	5.11	15	0	0	.000
Stein, Irv-Irvin Michael	32PhiA	5-21-11	Madisonville, La.		R	R	6'2	170	0	0	–	0	1	0	0	3	7	1	0	0	12.00	1	0	0	.000
Steineder, Ray-Raymond J.	23-24PitN 24PhiN	11-17-95	Salem, N.J.		R	R	6'	160	3	2	.600	0	29	2	1	86	95	39	34	0	4.92	25	10	0	.400
Stewart, Frank-Frank	27ChiA	9- 8-06	Minneapolis, Minn.		R	R	6'	170	0	1	.000	0	1	1	0	4	5	4	0	0	9.00	1	0	0	.000
Stewart, Lefty-Walter Cleveland	21DetA 27-32StLA 33-35WasA 35CleA	9-23-00	Sparta, Tenn.	9-26-74	R	L	5'10	160	100	98	.505	8	279	216	107	1724	1895	498	503	9	4.19	565	115	0	.204
Stewart, Mack-William Macklin	44-45ChiN	9-23-14	Stevenson, Ala.	3-21-60	R	R	6'	167	0	1	.000	0	24	1	0	40	48	18	12	0	3.83	4	1	0	.250
Stiely, Fred-Frederick Warren	29-31StLA	6- 1-01	Valley View, Pa.		L	L	5'8	170	1	1	.500	0	9	3	2	35	45	14	9	0	5.91	10	5	0	.500
Stiles, Rollie-Rolland Mays (Lena)	30-31,33StLA	11-17-06	Ratcliff, Ark.		R	R	6'1	180	9	14	.391	1	85	18	9	298	402	148	86	1	5.92	92	13	0	.141
Stimson, Carl-Carl Remus	23BosA	7-18-94	Hamburg, Iowa	11- 9-36	B	R	6'5	190	0	0	–	0	2	0	0	4	12	5	1	0	22.50	2	0	0	.000
Stine, Lee-Lee Elbert	34-35ChiA 36CinN 38NYA	11-17-13	Stillwater, Okla.		R	R	6'	180	3	8	.273	2	49	13	5	144	179	55	39	0	5.06	30	9	0	.300
Stokes, Art-Arthur Milton	25PhiA	9-13-96	Emmitsburg, Md.	6- 3-62	R	R	5'10	155	1	1	.500	0	12	0	0	24	24	10	7	0	4.13	4	0	0	.000
Stone, Arnie-Edwin Arnold	23-24PitN	12-19-92	North Creek, N.Y.	7-29-48	R	L	6'	180	4	3	.571	0	35	2	1	76	76	19	9	0	3.79	16	2	0	.125
Stone, Dick-Charles Richard	45WasA	12- 5-11	Oklahoma City, Okla.		L	L	5'9	153	0	0	–	0	3	0	0	5	6	2	0	0	0.00	0	0	0	–
Stone, Rocky-John Vernon	43CinN	8-23-18	Redding. Cal.		R	R	6'	200	0	1	.000	0	13	0	0	25	23	8	11	0	4.32	4	1	0	.250
Stoner, Lil-Ulysses Simpson Grant	24,24-29DetA 30PitN 31PhiN	2-28-99	Bowie, Tex.	6-26-66	R	R	5'10	180	50	58	.463	14	229	111	45	1005	1180	374	298	1	4.76	338	58	2	.172
Stout, Allyn-Allyn McClelland (Fish Hook)	31-33StLN 33-34CinN	10-31-04	Peoria, Ill.	12-22-74	R	R	5'10	167	20	20	.500	11	180	29	8	458	546	177	185	0	4.54	121	18	1	.149
	35NYN 43BosN																								
Stratton, Monty-Monty Franklin Pierce (Gander)	34-38ChiA 38LA	5-21-12	Celeste, Tex.		R	R	6'5	180	36	23	.610	2	70	62	36	487	489	149	196	5	3.71	192	43	4	.224
Strelecki, Ed-Edward Henry	28-29StLA 31CinN	4-10-05	Newark, N.J.	1- 9-68	R	R	5'11	180	1	3	.250	1	42	2	1	85	98	32	13	0	5.82	17	3	0	.176
Strickland, Bill-William Goss	37StLA	3-29-08	Nashville, Ga.		R	R	6'2	170	0	0	–	0	9	0	0	21	28	15	6	0	6.00	6	1	0	.167
Strincevich, Nick-Nicholas Mihailovich (Jumbo)	40-41BosN	3- 1-15	Gary, Ind.		R	R	6'1	180	46	49	.484	6	203	103	46	889	958	270	274	4	4.05	272	43	0	.158
	41-42,44-48PitN 48PhiN																								
Stromme, Floyd-Floyd Marvin (Rock)	39CleA	8- 1-16	Cooperstown, N.D.		R	R	5'11	170	0	1	.000	0	5	0	0	13	13	13	4	0	4.85	3	1	0	.333
Struss, Steamboat-Clarence Herbert	34PitN	2-24-09	Riverdale, Ill.		R	R	5'11	163	0	1	.000	0	1	1	0	7	7	6	3	0	6.43	3	1	0	.333
Stryker, Dutch-Sterling Alpa	24BosN 26BknN	7-29-95	Atl. Highlands, N.J.	11- 5-64	R	R	5'11	180	3	8	.273	0	22	10	2	75	98	23	22	0	6.60	23	5	0	.217
Stuart, Johnny-John Davis (Stud)	22-25StLN	4-27-01	Clinton, Tenn.	5-13-70	R	R	5'11	170	20	18	.526	3	82	34	21	358	360	156	124	1	4.75	127	29	0	.228
Stueland, George-George Anton	21-23,25ChiN	3- 2-99	Algona, Iowa	9- 9-64	B	R	6'1	174	9	6	.600	0	44	13	4	135	153	64	52	0	5.73	35	6	0	.171
Suche, Charley-Charles Morris	38CleA	8- 5-15	Cranes Mill, Tex.		R	L	6'2	190	0	0	–	0	1	0	0	1	4	3	1	0	36.00	1	1	0	1.000
Sullivan, Charlie-Charles Edward	28,30-31DetA	5-23-03	Yadkin Valley, N.C.	5-28-35	L	R	6'1	185	4	9	.308	5	74	9	4	205	239	105	68	0	5.66	52	11	0	.212
Sullivan, Jim-James Richard	21-22PhiA 23CleA	4- 5-94	Mine Run, Va.	2-12-72	R	R	5'11	165	0	5	.000	0	25	4	3	73	106	37	27	0	5.55	19	1	0	.053
Sullivan, Joe-Joe	35-36DetA 39-41BosN 41PitN	9-26-10	Mason City, Ill.		L	L	5'11	175	30	37	.448	5	150	55	20	589	601	298	216	0	4.00	208	43	0	.207
Sullivan, Lefty-Paul Thomas	39CleA	9- 7-16	Nashville, Tenn.		L	L	6'3	204	0	1	.000	0	7	1	0	13	9	9	4	0	4.15	3	0	0	.000
Sullivan, Tom-Thomas A.	22PhiN	10-18-95	Boston, Mass.	9-23-62	L	L	5'11	178	0	0	–	0	3	0	0	8	16	5	2	0	11.25	4	1	0	.250
Sundra, Steve-Stephen Richard (Smokey)	36,38-40NYA 41-42WasA	3-27-10	Luxor, Pa.	3-23-52	B	R	6'1	185	56	41	.577	2	168	99	47	858	944	321	214	4	4.17	302	63	2	.209
	42-44StLA 45MS 46StLA				Bats Right 41-43																				
Sunkel, Tom-Thomas Jacob (Lefty)	37,39StLN 41-43NYN 44BknN	8- 9-12	Paris, Ill.		L	L	6'1	190	9	15	.375	2	63	29	6	230	218	133	112	2	4.34	66	14	0	.212
Sutherland, Suds-Harvey Scott	21DetA	2-20-94	Coburg, Ore.		R	R	6'	180	6	2	.750	0	13	8	3	58	80	18	18	0	4.97	27	11	0	.407
Swartz, Dazzy-Monroe (Monty)	20CinN	1- 1-97	Farmersville, Ohio		R	R	5'11	182	0	1	.000	0	1	1	1	12	17	2	2	0	4.50	4	2	0	.500
Sweetland, Les-Leo	27-30PhiN 31ChiN	8-14-01	St. Ignace, Mich.	3- 4-74	R	L	5'11	155	33	58	.363	4	161	95	38	740	992	358	159	2	6.11	287	78	0	.272
					Bats Both 30-31																				
Swetonic, Steve-Stephen Albert	29-33,35PitN	8-13-03	Mt. Pleasant, Pa.	4-22-74	R	R	5'11	185	37	36	.507	11	133	58	25	597	607	212	154	8	3.80	200	34	0	.170
Swift, Bill-William Vincent	32-39PitN 40BosN 41BknN 43ChiA	1-10-08	Elmira, N.Y.	2-23-69	R	R	6'1	192	95	82	.537	20	336	163	78	1637	1682	351	636	7	3.58	591	134	3	.227
Swigart, Oad-Oadis Vaughn	39-40PitN 41-45MS	2-13-15	Archie, Mo.		L	R	6'	175	1	3	.250	0	10	5	1	46	54	16	17	1	4.50	13	3	0	.231
Taber, Lefty-Edward Timothy	26-27PhiN	1-11-00	Rock Island, Ill.		L	L	6'	180	0	1	.000	0	9	1	0	11	16	10	0	0	11.36	2	0	0	.000
Talcott, Roy-LeRoy Everett	43BosN	1-16-20	Brookline, Mass.		R	R	6'1	175	0	0	–	0	1	0	0	1	1	2	0	0	18.00	0	0	0	–
Tamulis, Vito-Vitautis Casimirus	34-35NYA 38StLA 38-40BknN	7-11-11	Cambridge, Mass.	5- 5-74	L	L	5'9	170	40	28	.588	10	170	70	31	692	758	202	294	6	3.97	229	40	1	.175
	41PhiN 41BknN																								
Tauscher, Walt-Walter Edward	28PitN 31WasA	11-22-01	LaSalle, Ind.		R	R	6'1	186	1	0	1.000	1	23	0	0	41	52	16	12	0	5.71	6	1	0	.167
Taylor, Arliss-Arliss W.	21PhiA		Clearfield, Pa.						0	1	.000	0	1	1	0	2	7	2	0	0	22.50	0	0	0	–
Teachout, Bud-Arthur John	30-31ChiN 32StLN	2-27-04	Los Angeles, Cal.		R	L	6'2	183	12	6	.667	0	68	19	7	215	259	76	73	0	4.52	84	22	0	.262
Tennant, Jim-James McDonnell	29NYN	3- 3-08	Shepherdstown, W.Va.	4-16-67	R	R	6'1	190	0	0	–	0	1	0	0	1	1	0	1	0	0.00	0	0	0	–
Terry, Yank-Lancelot Yank	40,42-45BosA	2-11-11	Bedford, Ind.		R	R	6'1	180	20	28	.417	2	93	55	14	458	463	196	167	0	4.09	145	21	0	.145
Terwilliger, Dick-Richard Martin	32StLN	6-27-06	Sand Lake, Mich.	1-21-69	R	R	5'11	178	0	0	–	0	1	0	0	3	1	2	2	0	0.00	1	0	0	.000
Theis, Jack-John Lewis	20CinN	7-23-91	Georgetown, Ohio	7- 6-41	R	R	6'	190	0	0	–	0	1	0	0	2	1	3	0	0	0.00	0	0	0	–
Thesenga, Jug-Arnold Joseph	44WasA	4-27-14	Jefferson, S.D.		R	R	6'	200	0	0	–	0	5	1	0	12	18	12	2	0	5.25	2	0	0	.000
Thomas, Bud-Luther Baxter	32-33WasA 37-39PhiA 39WasA 39-41DetA	9- 9-10	Faber, Va.		R	R	6'	180	25	34	.424	3	143	58	13	526	625	166	135	0	4.96	150	18	1	.120
Thomas, Fay-Fay Wesley (Scow)	27NYN 31CleA 32BknN 35StLA	10-10-04	Holyrood, Kans.		R	R	6'2	195	9	20	.310	1	81	23	5	229	269	133	112	0	4.95	56	6	0	.107
Thomas, Lefty-Clarence Fletcher	25-26WasA	10- 4-03	Glade Springs, Va.	3-21-52	L	L	6'2	190	0	2	.000	0	8	2	1	22	22	17	13	0	3.27	7	0	0	.000
Thomas, Myles-Myles Lewis	26-29NYA 29-30WasA	10-22-97	State College, Pa.	12-12-63	R	R	5'9	170	23	22	.511	2	105	40	11	435	499	189	121	0	4.64	146	35	0	.240
Thomas, Tommy-Alphonse	26-32ChiA 32-35WasA 35PhiN 36-37StLA 37BosA	12-23-99	Baltimore, Md.		R	R	5'10	175	117	128	.478	12	397	267	128	2174	2339	712	735	15	4.12	722	141	3	.195
Thompson, Junior-Eugene Earl	39-42CinN 43VR 44-45MS 46-47NYN	6- 7-17	Latham, Ill.		R	R	6'1	185	47	35	.573	7	185	68	27	687	602	328	315	6	3.26	200	45	0	.225
Thompson, Lee-John Dudley (Lefty)	21ChiA	2-26-98	Smithfield, Utah	2-17-63	L	L	6'1	185	0	3	.000	0	4	4	0	21	32	6	4	0	8.14	7	2	0	.286
Thuman, Lou-Louis Charles Frank	39-40WasA 41-45MS	12-13-16	Baltimore, Md.		R	R	6'2	185	0	1	.000	0	5	0	0	9	15	9	1	0	12.00	2	0	0	.000
Thurston, Sloppy-Hollis John	23StLA 23-26ChiA 27WasA 30-33BknN	6- 2-99	Fremont, Neb.	9-14-73	R	R	5'11	165	89	86	.509	13	288	178	95	1534	1859	369	306	8	4.26	648	175	5	.270
Tietje, Les-Leslie William (Toots)	33-36ChiA 36-38StLA	9-11-11	Summer, Iowa		R	R	6'	178	22	41	.349	0	105	65	22	513	560	282	193	2	5.11	171	17	0	.099
Tinning, Bud-Lyle Forrest	32-34ChiN 35StLN	3-12-06	Pilger, Neb.	1-17-61	B	R	5'11	198	22	55	.595	4	99	35	13	405	405	135	135	4	3.20	130	23	0	.177
					Bats Right 34-35																				
Tising, Jack-Johnnie Joseph	36PitN	10- 9-03	High Point, Mo.	9- 5-67	L	R	6'2	180	1	3	.250	0	10	6	1	47	52	24	27	0	4.21	11	3	0	.273
Tobin, Jim-James Anthony (Abba Dabba)	37-39PitN 40-45BosN 45DetA	12-27-12	Oakland, Cal.	5-19-69	R	R	6'	185	105	112	.484	5	287	227	156	1899	1929	557	498	12	3.44	796	183	17	.230
Tobin, Pat-Marion Brooks	41PhiA	1-28-16	Hermitage, Ark.	1-21-75	R	R	6'1	198	0	0	–	0	1	0	0	1	4	2	0	0	36.00	0	0	0	–
Torres, Gil-Don Gilberto Nunez	40,46WasA	8-23-15	Regla, Cuba		R	R	6'	155	0	0	–	1	5	0	0	10	12	3	3	0	5.40	(See B20-45)			
Tost, Lou-Louis Eugene	42-43BosN 44-45MS 47PitN	6- 1-11	Cumberland, Wash.	2-22-67	L	L	6'	175	10	11	.476	0	39	23	5	156	159	56	46	1	3.63	52	9	0	.173
Touchstone, Clay-Clayton Maffitt	28-29BosN 45ChiA	1-24-03	Moore, Pa.	4-28-49	R	R	5'11	175	0	0	–	0	12	0	0	21	35	8	6	0	6.43	4	1	0	.250
Townsend, Ira-Ira Dance (Pat)	20-21BosN	1- 9-94	Weimar, Tex.	7-21-65	R	R	6'1	180	0	0	–	0	8	1	0	14	21	6	1	0	3.86	4	0	0	.000
Townsend, Leo-Leo Alphonse (Lefty)	20-21BosN	1-15-91	Mobile, Ala.		L	L	5'10	160	2	3	.400	0	8	2	1	25	20	5	0	0	2.88	6	1	0	.167
Trotter, Bill-William Felix	37-42StLA 42WasA 44StLN	8-10-08	Cisne, Ill.		R	R	6'2	195	22	34	.393	3	163	31	9	484	619	174	158	0	5.39	109	6	0	.055
Trout, Dizzy-Paul Howard	39-52DetA 52BosA 57BalA	6-29-15	Sandcut, Ind.	2-28-72	R	R	6'2	205	170	161	.514	35	521	322	158	2726	2641	1046	1256	28	3.23	961	205	20	.213
Turbeville, George-George Elkins	35-37PhiA	8-24-14	Turbeville, S.C.		R	R	6'1	175	2	12	.143	0	62	15	4	185	196	157	47	0	6.13	59	10	0	.169
Turk, Lucas-Lucas Newton (Chief)	22WasA	5- 2-98	Homer, Ga.		R	R	6'	165	0	0	–	0	5	0	0	12	16	5	1	0	6.75	4	1	0	.250

USE NAME – GIVEN NAMES (NICKNAMES)	TEAM BY YEAR	BIRTH DATE	BIRTH PLACE	DEATH DATE	LIFETIME PITCHING TOTALS																	BATTING TOTALS			
					B	T	HGT	WGT	W	L	PCT	SV	G	GS	CG	IP	H	BB	SO	ShO	ERA	AB	H	HR	BA
Turner, Jim-James Riley (Milkman)	37-39BosN 40-42CinN 42-45NYA	8- 6-03	Antioch, Tenn.		L	R	6'	185	69	60	.535	20	231	119	69	1132	1123	283	329	8	3.22	399	87	1	.218
Turner, Ted-Theodore Holhot	20ChiN	5- 4-92	Lawrenceburg, Ky.	2- 4-58	R	R	6'	180	0	0	–	0	1	0	0	1	2	1	0	0	18.00	1	0	0	.000
Tutwiler, Elmer-Elmer Strange	28PitN	11- 9-05	Carbon Hill, Ala.		R	R	5'11	158	0	0	–	0	2	0	0	4	4	0	1	0	4.50	1	0	0	.000
Twombly, Cy-Edwin Parker	21ChiA	6-15-97	Groveland, Mass.	12- 3-74	R	R	5'10	170	1	2	.333	0	7	4	0	28	26	25	7	0	5.79	10	0	0	.000
Uchrinscko, Jimmie-James Emerson	26WasA	10-20-00	West Newton, Pa.		L	R	6'	185	0	0	–	0	3	0	0	8	13	8	0	0	10.13	2	0	0	.000
Uhle, Bob-Robert Ellwood (Lefty)	38ChiA 40DetA	9-17-13	San Francisco, Cal.		B	L	5'11	175	0	0	–	0	2	0	0	2	5	2	0	0	18.00	0	0	0	–
Uhle, George-George Ernest (Bull)	19-28CleA 29-33DetA 33NYN	9-18-98	Cleveland, Ohio		R	R	6'	190	200	166	.546	25	513	368	232	3120	3417	966	1135	20	3.99	(See B20-45)			
	33-34NYA 36CleA																								
Ullrich, Sandy-Carlos Santiago (Castello)	44-45WasA	7-25-21	Havana, Cuba		R	R	6'	175	3	3	.500	1	31	6	0	91	108	38	28	0	5.04	25	7	0	.280
Ulrich, Dutch-Frank W.	25-27PhiN 28IL	11-18-99	Baltimore, Md.	2-12-29	R	R	6'2	195	19	27	.413	2	98	39	24	406	452	89	123	3	3.48	138	23	0	.167
Underhill, Willie-Willie Vern	27-28CleA	9- 6-04	Yowell, Tex.	10-26-70	R	R	6'2	185	1	4	.200	0	15	4	1	36	45	31	20	0	5.75	12	4	0	.333
Upchurch, Woody-Jefferson Woodrow	35-36PhiA 37AA	4-13-11	Buies Creek, N.C.	10-23-71	R	L	6'	180	0	4	.000	0	10	5	2	43	59	26	8	0	7.53	14	3	0	.214
Van Alstyne, Clay-Clayton Emery (Spike)	27-28WasA	5-24-00	Stuyvesant, N.Y.	1- 5-60	R	R	5'11	180	0	0	–	0	6	0	0	24	29	13	5	0	5.25	8	2	1	.250
Van Atta, Russ-Russell (Sheriff)	33-35NYA 35-39StLA	6-21-06	Augusta, N.J.		L	L	6'	184	33	41	.446	6	207	76	17	713	838	367	339	1	5.59	206	47	2	.228
Vance, Dazzy-Charles Arthur	15PitN 15,18NYA 22-32BknN 33StLN	3- 4-91	Orient, Iowa	2-16-61	R	R	6'2	200	197	140	.585	11	442	347	216	2967	2809	840	2045	30	3.24	971	146	7	.150
	34CinN 34StLN 35BknN																								
Vance, Joe-Joseph Albert (Sandy)	35ChiA 37-38NYA	9-16-05	Devine, Tex.		R	R	6'1	190	3	2	.600	0	15	3	0	57	67	34	17	0	5.84	20	5	0	.250
31 played in N.F.L.																									
Vandenberg, Hy-Harold Harris	35BosA 37-40NYN 44-45ChiN	3-17-07	Abilene, Kans.		R	R	6'2	190	15	10	.600	5	90	22	7	290	304	128	120	1	4.34	89	15	0	.169
Vander Meer, Johnny-John Samuel (Double No-Hit, The Dutch Master)		11- 2-14	Prospect Park, N.J.		B	L	6'1	190	119	121	.496	2	346	285	131	2104	1799	1132	1294	30	3.44	685	104	1	.152
	37-43CinN 44-45MS 46-49CinN 50ChiN 51CleA																								
Vangilder, Elam-Elam Russell	19-27StLA 28-29DetA	4-23-96	Cape Girardeau, Mo.		R	R	6'1	192	100	102	.495	19	367	187	90	1714	1894	700	474	13	4.29	601	146	8	.243
Vargus, Bill-William Fay	25-26BosN	11-11-99	N. Scituate, Mass.		L	L	6'	165	1	1	.500	0	15	2	1	39	49	14	5	0	3.92	12	3	0	.250
Vaughan, Porter-Cecil Porter (Lefty)	40-41PhiA 42-45MS 46PhiA	5-11-19	Stevensville, Va.		R	L	6'1	178	2	11	.154	2	24	18	6	122	137	74	52	0	5.83	41	9	0	.220
Vaughn, Roy-Clarence LeRoy	34PhiA	9- 4-11	Sedalia, Mo.	3- 1-37	B	R	6'2	178	0	0	–	0	2	0	0	4	3	3	1	0	2.25	2	0	0	.000
Veach, Al-Alvis Lindell	35PhiA	8- 6-09	Maylene, Ala.		R	R	5'11	178	0	2	.000	0	2	2	1	10	20	9	3	0	11.70	4	0	0	.000
Vedder, Lou-Louis Edward	20DetA	4-20-97	Oakville, Mich.		R	R	5'10	175	0	0	–	0	1	0	0	2	0	0	1	0	0.00	0	0	0	–
Veigel, Al-Allen Francis	39BosN	1-30-17	Dover, Ohio		R	R	6'1	180	0	1	.000	0	2	2	0	3	3	5	1	0	6.00	1	0	0	.000
Verdel, Al-Albert Alfred (Stumpy)	44PhiN	6-10-21	Punxsutawney, Pa.		R	R	5'9	186	0	0	–	0	1	0	0	1	0	0	0	0	0.00	0	0	0	–
Vines, Bob-Robert Earl	24StLN 25PhiN	2-25-97	Waxahachie, Tex.		R	R	6'4	184	0	0	–	0	5	0	0	15	32	3	0	0	9.60	4	0	0	.000
Vitelli, Joe-Antonio Joseph	44-45PitN	4-12-08	McKees Rocks, Pa.	2- 7-67	R	R	6'1	195	0	0	–	0	4	0	0	7	5	7	2	0	2.57	3	0	0	.000
Voigt, Ollie-Olen Edward	24StLA	1-29-00	Wheaton, Ill.	4- 7-70	R	R	6'1	170	1	0	1.000	0	8	1	0	16	21	13	4	0	5.63	4	1	0	.250
Wade, Jake-Jacob Fields (Whistlin' Jake)	36-38DetA 39BosA 39StLA	4- 1-12	Morehead City, N.C.		L	L	6'2	175	27	40	.403	3	171	71	20	669	690	440	291	3	4.99	216	36	0	.167
	42-44ChiA 45MS 46NYA 46WasA																								
Wagner, Charlie-Charles Thomas (Broadway)	38-42, 46BosA 43-45MS	12- 3-12	Reading, Pa.		R	R	5'11	170	32	23	.582	0	100	67	30	527	532	245	157	5	3.91	170	20	0	.118
Walberg, Rube-George Elvin	23NYN 23-33PhiA 34-37BosA	7-27-99	Seattle, Wash.		L	L	6'1	190	156	141	.525	32	544	307	140	2645	2795	1031	1085	14	4.17	905	162	4	.179
Walker, Bill-William Henry	27-32NYN 33-36StLN	10- 7-03	E. St. Louis, Ill.	6-14-66	R	L	6'	175	97	77	.557	8	272	192	83	1489	1576	538	626	15	3.59	489	62	4	.127
Walker, Marty-Martin Van Buren	28PhiN	3-27-03	Philadelphia, Pa.		L	L	6'	170	0	1	.000	0	1	1	0	0	2	3	0	0	∞	0	0	0	–
Walker, Roy-James Roy (Dixie)	12,15CleA 17-18ChiN 21-22StLN	4-13-93	Lawrenceburg, Tenn.	2-10-62	R	R	6'1	180	18	27	.400	5	92	49	17	387	408	156	148	0	3.98	111	17	0	.153
					Bats Both 22																				
Walkup, Jim-James Elton	34-39StLA 39DetA	12-14-09	Havana, Ark.		R	R	6'1	170	16	38	.296	0	116	53	11	462	614	260	134	1	6.74	143	26	0	.182
Walkup, Jim-James Huey	27DetA	11- 3-95	Havana, Ark.		R	L	5'8	150	0	0	–	0	2	0	0	2	3	0	0	0	4.50	1	0	0	.000
Wallace, Lefty-James Harold	42BosN 43-44MS 45-46BosN	8-12-21	Evansville, Ind.		L	L	5'11	160	5	6	.455	0	51	14	4	144	133	64	51	0	4.13	38	3	0	.079
Walsh, Augie-August S.	27-28PhiN	8- 9-04	Wilmington, Del.		R	R	6'	175	4	10	.286	2	39	12	3	132	172	45	38	0	6.07	43	11	1	.256
Walsh, Ed-Edward Arthur	28-30,32ChiA	2-11-05	Meriden, Conn.	10-31-37	R	R	6'1	180	11	24	.314	0	79	38	15	331	399	149	107	0	5.57	111	24	0	.216
Walsh, Jim-James Thomas	21DetA	7-10-94	Roxbury, Mass.	5-13-67	L	L	5'11	175	0	0	–	0	3	0	0	4	2	1	3	0	2.25	0	0	0	–
Walter, Bernie-James Bernard	30PitN	8-15-08	Dover, Tenn.		R	R	6'1	175	0	0	–	0	1	0	0	1	0	0	1	0	0.00	0	0	0	–
Walters, Bucky-William Henry	34-38PhiN 38-48,M48-49CinN 50BosN	4-19-09	Philadelphia, Pa.		R	R	6'1	180	198	160	.553	4	428	398	242	3104	2990	1121	1107	42	3.30	(See B20-45)			
Walton, Zack (See Tom Zachary)																									
Ward, Dick-Richard O. (Ole)	34ChiN 35StLN	5-21-09	Herrick, S.D.	5-30-66	R	R	6'1	198	0	0	–	0	4	0	0	6	9	3	1	0	3.00	1	0	0	.000
Warmoth, Cy-Wallace Walter	16StLN 22-23WasA	2- 2-93	Bone Gap, Ill.	6-20-57	L	L	5'11	158	8	5	.615	0	29	14	5	129	130	89	54	0	4.26	45	9	0	.200
Warneke, Lon-Lonnie (The Arkansas Humming Bird)	30-36ChiN 37-42StLN	3-28-09	Mount Ida, Ark.		R	R	6'2	185	192	121	.613	13	445	343	192	2781	2726	739	1140	31	3.18	962	215	4	.223
	42-43ChiN 44MS 45ChiN																								
Warren, Tommy-Thomas Gentry	44BknN	7- 5-17	Tulsa, Okla.	1- 2-68	B	L	6'1	180	1	4	.200	0	22	4	2	69	74	40	18	0	4.96	43	11	0	.256
Washburn, George-George Edward	41NYA	10- 6-14	Solon, Me.		L	R	6'1	175	0	1	.000	0	1	1	0	2	2	5	1	0	13.50	1	0	0	.000
Watson, Mule-John Reeves	18-19PhiA 20PitN 20BosN 20PitN	10-15-96	Homer, La.	8-25-49	R	R	6'1	185	49	53	.480	4	178	126	53	940	1062	256	208	8	4.04	327	54	2	.165
	21-23BosN 23-24NYN																								
Watt, Frank-Frank Marion (Kilo)	31PhiN	12-15-02	Washington, D.C.	8-31-56	R	R	6'1	205	5	5	.500	2	38	12	5	123	147	49	25	0	4.83	39	8	0	.205
Wayenberg, Frank-Frank	24CleA	8-27-98	Franklin, Kans.	4-16-75	R	R	6'	170	0	0	–	0	2	1	0	7	7	5	3	0	5.14	2	1	0	.500
Weafer, Hal-Kenneth Albert (Al)	36BosN	2- 6-14	Woburn, Mass.		R	R	6'	183	0	0	–	0	1	0	0	3	6	3	0	0	12.00	1	0	0	.000
Weaver, Jim-James Dement (Big Jim)	28WasA 31NYA 34StLA 34ChiN	11-25-03	Fulton, Ky.		R	R	6'6	230	57	36	.613	3	189	108	38	894	891	336	449	7	3.88	289	30	0	.104
	35-37PitN 38StLA 38-39CinN																								
Weaver, Monte-Montgomery Morton (Prof)	31-38WasA 39BosA	6-15-06	Hilton, N.C.		L	R	6'	170	71	50	.587	4	201	135	57	1052	1137	435	297	2	4.36	378	79	0	.209
Webb, Bill-William Frederick	43PhiN	12-12-13	Atlanta, Ga.		R	R	6'2	180	0	0	–	0	1	0	0	1	1	1	0	0	9.00	0	0	0	–
Webber, Les-Lester Elmer	42-46BknN 46,48CleA	5- 6-15	Lakeport, Cal.		R	R	6'	185	23	19	.548	14	154	25	7	432	434	201	141	0	4.19	111	15	1	.135
Wehde, Biggs-Wilbur	30-31ChiA	11-23-06	Holstein, Iowa	9-21-70	R	R	5'10	180	1	0	1.000	0	12	0	0	22	26	17	6	0	7.78	4	0	0	.000
Weiland, Bob-Robert George (Lefty)	28-31ChiA 32-34BosA 34CleA	12-14-05	Chicago, Ill.		L	L	6'4	215	62	94	.397	7	277	179	66	1388	1463	611	614	7	4.24	443	57	3	.129
	35StLA 37-40StLN																								
Weiland, Ed-Edwin Nicholas	40,42ChiA 43-45MS	11-26-14	Evanston, Ill.	7-12-71	L	R	5'11	180	0	0	–	0	10	0	0	24	33	10	7	0	8.25	7	1	0	.143
Weinert, Lefty-Philip Walter	19-24PhiN 27-28ChiN 31NYA	4-21-02	Philadelphia, Pa.	4- 7-73	L	L	6'1	195	18	33	.353	2	131	49	19	438	528	222	160	0	4.58	142	37	0	.261
Weir, Roy-William Frank (Bill)	36-39BosN	2-25-11	Portland, Me.		L	L	5'8	170	6	4	.600	0	29	11	4	106	95	50	42	2	3.57	32	6	0	.188
Welch, Johnny-John Vernon	26-28,31ChiN 32-36BosA 36PitN	12- 2-06	Washington, D.C.	9- 2-40	L	R	6'3	184	35	41	.461	6	172	63	24	648	735	262	257	3	4.66	228	50	1	.219
Wells, Ed-Edwin Lee	23-27DetA 29-32NYA 33-34StLA	6- 7-00	Ashland, Ohio		L	L	6'1	183	68	69	.496	13	291	140	54	1233	1417	468	403	7	4.65	433	93	0	.215
Wells, John-John Frederick	44BknN	11-25-22	Junction City, Kan.		R	R	5'11	180	0	2	.000	0	4	2	0	15	18	11	7	0	5.40	4	1	0	.250
Welzer, Tony-Anton Frank	26-27BosA	4- 5-99	Germany	3-18-71	R	R	5'11	160	10	14	.417	1	77	25	9	323	381	128	86	1	4.60	80	12	0	.150
Wensloff, Butch-Charles William	43NYA 44VR 45-46MS 47NYA 48CleA	12- 3-15	Sausalito, Cal.		R	R	5'11	185	16	13	.552	1	41	32	19	277	222	95	125	1	2.60	98	19	0	.194
Wertz, Johnny-Henry Levi	26-29BosN	4-20-98	Pomaria, S.C.		R	R	5'10	180	15	21	.417	2	88	40	11	377	460	111	111	1	4.30	111	26	1	.234
West, Lefty-Weldon Edison	44-45StLA	9- 3-15	Gibsonville, N.C.		R	L	6'	165	3	4	.429	0	35	8	1	98	105	50	49	0	4.32	34	3	0	.088
Wetzel, Buzz-Charles Edward	27PhiA	8-25-94	Jay, Okla.	3- 7-41	R	R	6'1	162	0	0	–	0	2	1	0	5	8	5	0	0	7.20	1	1	0	1.000
Wheaton, Woody-Elwood Pierce	44PhiA	10- 3-14	Philadelphia, Pa.		L	L	5'8	160	0	1	.000	0	11	1	1	38	36	20	15	0	3.55	(See B20-45)			
Wheeler, Rip-Floyd Clark	21-22PitN 23-24ChiN	3- 2-98	Marion, Ky.	9-18-68	R	R	6'	180	4	8	.333	0	34	7	1	129	138	29	21	0	4.19	42	8	0	.190
Whitcher, Bob-Robert Arthur	45BosN	4-29-17	Berlin, N.H.		L	L	5'8	165	0	2	.000	0	6	3	0	16	12	12	6	0	2.81	3	1	0	.333
White, Abe-Adel	37StLN	5-16-06	Winder, Ga.		R	L	6'	185	0	1	.000	0	5	0	0	9	14	3	2	0	6.30	1	1	0	1.000
White, Ernie-Ernest Daniel	40-43StLN 44-45MS 46-48BosN	9- 5-16	Pacolet Mills, S.C.	5-22-74	R	L	5'11	175	30	21	.588	6	108	57	24	490	425	188	244	5	2.77	163	94	0	.209
Whitehead, John-John Henderson (Silent John)	35-39ChiA 39-40,42StLA	4-27-09	Coleman, Tex.	10-20-64	R	R	6'2	195	49	54	.476	4	172	119	52	944	1074	372	254	7	4.60	325	55	0	.169
Whitehill, Earl-Earl Oliver	23-32DetA 33-36WasA 37-38CleA 39ChiN	2- 7-00	Cedar Rapids, Iowa	10-22-54	L	L	5'9	174	218	185	.541	11	541	473	227	3563	3917	1431	1350	17	4.36	1291	264	4	.204
Wicker (Whicker), Kemp-Kemp Caswell	36-38NYA 41BknN	8-13-06	Kernsville, N.C.	6-11-73	R	L	5'11	182	10	7	.588	1	40	12	6	141	168	52	27	1	4.66	46	6	0	.130
Wiedemeyer, Charlie-Charles John	34ChiN	1-31-15	Chicago, Ill.		R	R	6'1	180	0	0	–	0	4	1	0	8	16	4	2	0	10.13	1	0	0	.000
Wieneke, Jack-John	21ChiA	3-10-94	Saltsburg, Pa.	3-16-33	R	L	6'	182	0	1	.000	0	10	3	0	25	39	17	10	0	8.28	9	1	1	.111
Wiginton, Fred-Frederick Thomas	23StLN	12-16-97	Rogers, Neb.		R	R	5'10	168	0	0	–	0	4	0	0	8	11	5	2	0	3.38	1	0	0	.000
Wilkie, Lefty-Aldon Jay	41-42PitN 43-45MS 46PitN	10-30-14	Zealandia, Canada		L	L	5'11	175	8	11	.421	3	68	12	5	194	215	80	37	1	4.59	62	17	0	.274
Wilkinson, Roy-Roy Hamilton	18CleA 19-22ChiA	5- 8-94	Canandaigua, N.Y.		R	R	6'1	170	12	31	.279	6	79	35	21	380	466	142	88	1	4.67	124	18	0	.145
Williams, Ace-Robert Fulton	40BosN 43-45MS 46BosN	3- 8-17	Montclair, N.J.		R	L	6'2	174	0	0	–	0	6	0	0	9	22	13	5	0	16.00	2	0	0	.000
Williams, Al-Almon Edward	37-38PhiA	5-11-14	Valhermosa Spr., Ala.	7-19-69	R	R	6'3	200	4	8	.333	1	46	16	3	169	216	103	52	0	6.23	49	3	0	.061
Williams, Leon-Leon Theo	26BknN	12- 2-05	Macon, Ga.		L	L	5'10	154	0	0	–	0	8	0	0	8	16	2	3	0	5.63	5	1	0	.200
Williamson, Al-Silas Albert	28ChiA	2-20-00	Buckville, Ark.		R	R	5'11	160	0	0	–	0	1	0	0	2	1	0	0	0	0.00	0	0	0	–
Willis, Lefty-Charles William	25-27PhiA	11- 4-05	Leetown, W.Va.	5-10-62	L	L	6'1	175	3	1	.750	1	28	4	1	64	72	25	23	0	3.94	18	2	0	.111
					Bats Right 25																				
Willoughby, Claude-Claude William (Weeping Willie)	25-30PhiN 31PitN	11-14-98	Fredonia, Kans.	8-14-73	R	R	5'9	165	38	58	.396	9	219	100	33	842	1111	406	175	4	5.84	272	39	0	.143
Wilshere, Whitey-Vernon Sprague	34-36PhiA	8- 3-12	Poplar Ridge, N.J.		L	L	6'	180	10	12	.455	1	41	23	7	182	196	112	103	3	5.29	50	4	0	.080
Wilson, Jack-John Francis (Black Jack)	34PhiA 35-41BosA 42WasA	4-12-12	Portland, Ore.		R	R	5'11	210	68	72	.486	20	281	121	50	1131	1233	601	590	5	4.59	413	82	3	.199
	42DetA																								

USE NAME – GIVEN NAMES (NICKNAMES)	TEAM BY YEAR	BIRTH DATE	BIRTH PLACE	DEATH DATE	LIFETIME PITCHING TOTALS																	BATTING TOTALS			
					B	T	HGT	WGT	W	L	PCT	SV	G	GS	CG	IP	H	BB	SO	ShO	ERA	AB	H	HR	BA
Wilson, John-John Samuel	27-28BosA	4-25-05	Coal City, Ala.		R	R	6'2	164	0	2	.000	0	3	0	0	4	4	3	1	0	4.50	10	1	0	.100
Wilson, Mutt-William Clarence	20DetA	7-20-96	Kiser, N.C.	8-31-62	R	R	6'3	167	1	1	.500	0	3	2	1	13	12	5	4	0	3.46	4	1	0	.250
Wilson, Roy-Roy Edward (Lefty)	28ChiA	9-13-96	Foster, Iowa	12- 3-69	L	L	6'	175	0	0	–	0	1	0	0	3	2	3	2	0	0.00	1	0	0	.000
Wilson, Tex-Gomer Russell	24BknN	7- 8-01	Trenton, Tex.	9-15-46	R	L	5'10	170	0	0	–	0	2	0	0	4	7	1	1	0	13.50	1	0	0	.000
Wilson, Walter-Walter Wood	45DetA	11-24-13	Glenn, Ga.		L	R	6'4	190	1	3	.250	0	25	4	1	70	76	35	28	0	4.63	19	1	0	.053
Wiltse, Hal-Harold James (Whitey)	26-28BosA 28StLA 31PhiN	8- 6-03	Clay City, Ill.		L	L	5'9	168	20	40	.333	1	102	65	23	500	589	211	134	2	4.88	162	26	0	.160
Wineapple, Ed-Edward (Lefty) 29-30 played in A.B.L.	29WasA	8-10-06	Boston, Mass.		L	L	6'	195	0	0	–	0	1	0	0	4	7	3	1	0	4.50	2	0	0	.000
Winegarner, Ralph-Ralph Lee	32,34-36CleA 49StLA	10-29-09	Benton, Kans.		R	R	6'	182	8	6	.571	0	70	11	7	194	229	89	89	0	5.34	(See B20-45)			
Winford, Jim-James Head (Cowboy)	32,34-37StLN 38BknN	10- 9-09	Shelbyville, Tenn.	12-16-70	R	R	6'1	180	14	18	.438	3	68	31	10	276	307	115	107	1	4.57	74	8	0	.108
Wingard, Ernie-Ernest James (Jim)	24-27StLA	10-17-00	Prattville, Ala.		L	L	6'2	176	29	43	.403	4	145	77	36	696	800	317	101	0	4.55	246	57	7	.232
Wingfield, Ted-Frederick Davis	23-24WasA 24-27BosA	8- 7-99	Bedford, Va.	7-18-75	R	R	5'11	168	24	44	.353	5	113	57	31	554	624	181	68	3	4.18	192	45	1	.234
Winn, George-George Benjamin (Breezy, Lefty)	19BosA 22-23CleA	10-26-97	Perry, Ga.	11- 1-69	L	L	5'11	170	1	2	.333	0	12	3	1	41	50	7	7	0	4.61	10	3	0	.300
Winston, Hank-Henry Rudolph	33PhiA 36BknN	6-15-04	Youngsville, N.C.	2- 7-74	L	R	6'3	226	1	3	.250	0	15	0	0	39	47	22	10	0	6.23	14	1	0	.071
Winters, Clarence-Clarence John	24BosA	9- 7-98	Detroit, Mich.	6-29-45					0	1	.000	0	4	2	0	7	22	4	3	0	20.57	3	1	0	.333
Winters, Jesse-Jesse Franklin (T-Bone)	19-20NYN 21-23PhiN	12-22-93	Stephenville, Tex.		L	R	6'1	165	13	24	.351	6	110	31	15	404	510	164	94	0	5.06	117	20	0	.171
Wise, Archie-Archibald Edwin	32ChiA	7-31-12	Waxahachie, Tex.		R	R	6'	165	0	0	–	0	2	0	0	7	8	5	2	0	5.14	4	0	0	.000
Wise, Roy-Roy Ogden	44PitN	11-18-24	Springfield, Ill.		B	R	6'2	170	0	0	–	0	2	0	0	3	4	3	1	0	9.00	0	0	0	–
Wisner, John-John Henry	19-20PitN 25-26NYN	11- 5-99	Grand Rapids, Mich.		R	R	6'3	195	4	5	.444	0	51	6	4	132	112	41	35	0	3.20	31	2	0	.065
Wistert, Whitey-Francis Michael	34CinN	2-20-12	Chicago, Ill.		R	R	6'4	210	0	1	.000	0	2	1	0	8	5	5	1	0	1.13	3	0	0	.000
Wittig, Johnnie-John Carl (Hans)	38-39,41,43NYN 44-45MS 49BosA	6-16-14	Baltimore, Md.		R	R	6'	180	10	25	.286	4	84	39	7	307	341	163	121	1	4.90	91	10	0	.110
Wolf, Lefty-Walter Francis	21PhiA	6-10-00	Hartford, Conn.	9-25-71	R	L	5'10	163	0	0	–	0	8	0	0	15	15	16	12	0	7.20	4	1	0	.250
Wolfe, Chuck-Charles Hunt	23PhiA	2-15-97	Wolfsburg, Pa.	11-27-57	L	R	5'7	175	0	0	–	0	3	0	0	10	6	8	1	0	3.60	3	1	0	.333
Wolff, Roger-Roger Francis	41-43PhiA 44-46WasA 47CleA 47PitN	1-10-11	Evansville, Ill.		R	R	6'1	208	52	69	.430	13	182	128	63	1025	1018	316	430	8	3.41	337	41	0	.122
Wood, Joe-Joseph Frank	44BosA	5-20-16	Shohola, Pa.		R	R	6'	190	0	1	.000	0	3	1	0	10	13	3	5	0	6.30	2	0	0	.000
Wood, Spades-Charles Asher	30-31PitN	1-13-09	Spartanburg, S.C.		L	L	5'10	150	6	9	.400	0	24	17	6	122	130	78	56	0	5.01	42	10	0	.238
Woodend, George-George Anthony	44BosN	12- 9-17	Hartford, Conn.		R	R	6'	200	0	0	–	0	3	0	0	2	5	5	0	0	13.50	0	0	0	–
Woods, John-John Fulton (Abe)	24BosA	1-18-98	Princeton, W.Va.	10- 4-46	R	R	5'11	150	0	0	–	0	1	0	0	1	0	3	0	0	0.00	0	0	0	–
Woods, Pinky-George Rowland	43-45BosA	5-22-15	Waterbury, Conn.		R	R	6'5	225	13	21	.382	3	85	44	10	379	388	206	124	1	3.97	126	24	0	.190
Workman, Hoge-Harry Hall	24BosA	9-25-99	Huntington, W.Va.	5-20-72	R	R	5'11	170	0	0	–	0	11	0	0	18	25	11	7	0	8.50	2	0	0	.000
Wright, Jiggs-James	27-28StLA	9-19-00	Hyde, England	4-10-63	R	R	6'3	195	1	0	1.000	0	4	1	1	14	11	6	6	0	5.79	4	0	0	.000
Wright, Rasty-Wayne Bromley	17-19,22-23StLA	11- 5-95	Ceredo, W.Va.	6-12-48	R	R	5'11	160	24	18	.571	5	109	43	17	451	481	132	114	1	4.05	133	26	0	.195
Wurm, Frank-Frank James	44BknN	4-27-24	Cambridge, N.Y.		B	L	6'1	175	0	0	–	0	1	1	0	.1	1	5	1	0	108.00	0	0	0	–
Wyatt, Whit-John Whitlow	29-33DetA 33-36ChiA 37CleA 39-44BknN	9-27-07	Kensington, Ga.		R	R	6'1	185	106	95	.527	13	360	210	97	1762	1684	642	872	17	3.78	607	133	7	.219
	45PhiN																								
Wyse, Hank-Henry Washington (Hooks)	42-47ChiN 50-51PhiA 51WasA	3- 1-18	Lunsford, Ark.		R	R	5'11	185	79	70	.530	8	251	159	67	1257	1339	373	362	11	3.52	435	71	0	.163
Wysong, Biff-Harlin	30-32CinN	4-13-05	Clarksville, Ohio	8- 8-51	L	L	6'3	195	1	3	.250	0	20	3	0	36	44	34	11	0	7.25	6	1	0	.167
Yarnell, Rusty-Waldo William	26PhiN	10-22-02	Chicago, Ill.		R	R	6'	175	0	1	.000	0	1	0	0	1	3	1	0	0	18.00	1	0	0	.000
Yarrison, Rube-Byron Wordsworth	22PhiA 24BknN	3- 9-96	Montgomery, Pa.		R	R	5'11	165	1	4	.200	0	21	3	0	45	62	15	12	0	7.80	8	1	0	.125
Yde, Emil-Emil Ogden	24-27PitN 29DetA	1-28-00	Great Lakes, Ill.	12- 5-68	B	L	5'11	165	49	25	.662	0	141	80	43	705	751	296	160	6	4.02	317	74	1	.233
					Bats Left 25																				
Yeargin, Al-James Almond (Grapefruit)	22,24BosN	10-16-01	Mauldin, S.C.	5- 8-37	R	R	6'2	175	1	12	.077	0	33	13	7	148	167	44	35	0	4.93	45	6	0	.133
Yellowhorse, Chief-Moses J.	21-22PitN	1-28-98	Pawnee, Okla.	4-10-64	R	R	5'10	180	8	4	.667	1	38	9	3	126	137	33	43	0	3.93	36	6	0	.167
Yerkes, Carroll-Charles Carroll (Lefty)	27-29PhiA 32-33ChiN	6-13-03	McSherrystown, Pa.	12-20-50	R	L	5'11	162	1	1	.500	1	25	3	1	58	61	20	16	0	3.88	16	1	0	.063
York, Lefty-James E.	19PhiA 21ChiN	11- 1-95	Tuskegee, Ala.	4- 9-61	L	L	5'10	185	5	11	.313	1	42	12	4	143	183	68	59	1	5.35	40	5	0	.125
Youngblood, Chief-Albert Clyde	22WasA	6-13-00	Hillsboro, Tex.	7- 6-68	R	R	6'3	202	0	0	–	0	2	0	0	4	9	7	0	0	15.75	2	0	0	.000
Yowell, Carl-Carl Columbus (Sundown)	24-25CleA	12-20-02	Madison, Va.		L	L	6'4	180	3	4	.429	0	16	6	3	63	77	30	20	0	5.43	19	3	0	.158
Zabala, Adrian-Adrian [Rodriguez]	45NYN 46-48SM 49NYN	8-26-16	San Antonio, Cuba		L	L	5'11	165	4	7	.364	1	26	9	3	84	90	30	27	1	5.04	26	4	0	.154
Zachary, Chink-Albert Myron	44BknN	10-19-17	Brooklyn, N.Y.		R	R	5'11	182	0	2	.000	0	4	2	0	10	10	7	3	0	9.90	3	0	0	.000
Zachary, Tom-Jonathan Thompson Walton	18PhiA 19-25WasA	5- 7-96	Graham, N.C.	1-24-69	L	L	6'1	187	185	191	.492	22	533	408	185	3136	3580	914	720	23	3.72	1122	254	6	.226
	26-27StLA 27-28WasA 28-30NYA 30-34BosN 34-36BknN 36PhiN																								
(Played as Zach Walton 18)																									
Zahniser, Paul-Paul Vernon	23-24WasA 25-26BosA 29CinN	9- 6-96	Sal City, Iowa	9-26-64	R	R	5'10	170	25	47	.347	1	125	80	29	619	746	284	145	4	4.66	189	25	0	.132
Zink, Walt-Walter Noble	21NYN	11-21-99	Pittsfield, Mass.	6-12-64	R	R	6'	165	0	0	–	0	2	0	0	4	4	3	1	0	2.25	1	0	0	.000
Zinn, Jimmy-James Edward	19PhiA 20-22PitN 29CleA	1-31-95	Benton, Ark.		L	R	6'	195	13	16	.448	7	66	26	15	299	390	80	108	2	4.30	120	34	2	.283
					Bats Right 29																				
Zinser, Bill-William Francis	44WasA	1- 6-18	Queens, N.Y.		R	R	6'1	185	0	0	–	0	2	0	0	1	1	5	1	0	18.00	0	0	0	–
Zuber, Bill-William Henry (Goober)	36,38-40CleA 41-42WasA	3-26-13	Middle Amana, Iowa		R	R	6'2	195	43	42	.506	6	224	65	23	785	767	468	383	3	4.29	229	31	0	.135
	43-46NYA 46-47BosA																								

1946-1960
Goin' for the Pump

In the age where the home run ball became the shortest distance between anonymity and newspaper headlines, baseball's ethnic imbalance was finally corrected. The racial mix began in 1947 when 28-year-old Jackie Robinson stepped on the playing field for the Brooklyn Dodgers. This was the doing of Branch Rickey, the team's imaginative general manager. Before coming to the parent club, Robinson spent the 1946 season with Montreal—the Dodgers' farm club, in a move more for "transitional" purposes of bringing a black man to baseball than to sharpen Robinson's skills. The fleet-footed Georgia native spent the first year of his life in the majors at first base, not his ordinary position, and led the National League in stolen bases. He also led the Dodgers to a pennant while taking home Rookie of the Year honors.

The entry of black athletes into baseball, while proving the most historic highlight of the period, also signalled the start of many changes. The pitcher's plight, as it had begun in 1920, did not improve. Instead, it only got worse as light bats became the mainstay of the batter's arsenal. Armed with a light weapon that responded to a good pair of wrists and could help negate the blazing fastball, the batter was able to continue his dominance over the pitcher. The result was that choking up on the bat became a rarity and nearly everyone went for the pump, or home run. Even a scuffed ball, which gave the pitcher some advantage, was no longer allowed. All this new-found power was sharply reflected in stolen base and home run totals, which seemed to be going in opposite directions. While stolen bases per game for both teams continued their downward spiral of less than one theft per game for both teams, home runs climbed to nearly two per game. Home run status also culminated in a healthier paycheck, and such were the state of affairs that they led to hardy power men driving Cadillacs while their counterparts on the mound had to find less expensive means of transportation.

Yet, what the home run ball did for the batter's prestige, it did not do for his batting average. Going for the long ball, while increasing strikeouts to almost five per nine innings, also lowered batting averages to below the .260 mark. Another factor that contributed to a reduction in base hits, was night baseball, which began in Cincinnati in 1935 and became a major part of most team schedules during the fifties. Only the Chicago Cubs, with the help of owner Bill Wrigley, managed to stave off the intrusion of the twentieth century.

Beyond the effects of a changing strategy, there was even a more profound upheaval taking place at the core of the game itself. Until the late forties, the only way to see a ball game was by going out to the ball park. If that was not possible, there was also the option of keeping an ear to the radio. It was these limited accesses that helped preserve the structure of the two eight-team circuits, as well as keeping baseball locked in the same geographical pattern it had chosen at the turn of the century. In fact, not since the Baltimore franchise transplanted itself as the American League's entry into New York for the start of the 1903 season had there been any franchise activity.

But a new technological giant—television—was on the rise and the tranquility of five decades slowly began to disintegrate. Also, as television evolved as a major force in the affairs of American life, so did the airplane. As radio had served to protect a franchise structure that extended no further than the Mississippi River, so did train travel, which was often long, tedious, and tiring. But as the country entered the fifties it was evident how quickly life was changing and baseball, always parallel to the events outside its domain, was no exception. Suddenly, those franchises that had been previously locked in and forced to accept low attendance found there was a means of escape.

The first of the franchise shifts took place in the National League in 1953 when the Boston Braves, unable to compete with Ted Williams and the neighboring Red Sox, moved to Milwaukee, which oddly enough had first hosted a National League club for the 1878 season. The Braves also held the distinction, along with the Chicago Cubs, of being original tenants of the National League and remaining in their respective cities without any interruption or changes in franchise since 1876. A year after the Braves changed homes, the hapless St. Louis Browns moved to Baltimore—a city that had lost its major league representation in 1902. The year after the Browns departed, the Philadelphia Athletics, once American League powerhouses, picked up and moved to Kansas City for the start of the 1955 season.

The next and last changes that occurred in the period took place three years later in the National League stronghold of New York, and were perhaps the most dramatic of any of the franchise shifts. The Brooklyn Dodgers and New York Giants, teams which had more emotional and historic ties with their patrons than any other clubs, shocked the baseball world and their followers alike by moving to California. While the Dodgers took residency in Los Angeles, the Giants moved to the northern reaches of San Francisco. Although the Giants' sliding attendance gave some justification for their departure, there seemed to be none for the Dodgers, who had enjoyed a near-fanatical following. Walter O'Malley, the Dodgers' president, claimed that insufficient parking and an aging stadium—Ebbets Field—as his reasons for the move. But even if New York politicians would have granted a new stadium—which they did not—it was doubtful that O'Malley would have turned down the potential awaiting him three thousand miles away.

Suddenly, in the course of five years, from 1953-1958, baseball found itself drastically altered. In three cities that had been represented by two teams each—St. Louis, Boston, and Philadelphia—there was now only one tenant per city. And New York, which had been able to support three teams, found itself with only the Yankees, which did neither the economics of the city nor the heart of National League fans any good. Although the tremors of such abrupt change would seem to have repercussions that would take another lifetime to heal, they proved only a tiny glimpse of what was to take place when the 1960's first dawned.

1946-1960 SINGLE SEASON LEADERS

BATTING

Batting Average

1	Ted Williams-Bos. (A)	1957	.388
2	Stan Musial-St.L. (N)	1948	.376
3	Ted Williams-Bos. (A)	1948	.369
4	Stan Musial-St.L. (N)	1946	.365
	Mickey Mantle-N.Y. (A)	1957	.365
6	Harry Walker-St.L. + Phi. (N)	1947	.363
7	Lou Boudreau-Cle. (A)	1948	.355
	Stan Musial-St.L. (N)	1951	.355
	Hank Aaron-Mil. (N)	1959	.355
10	Billy Goodman-Bos. (A)	1950	.354

Hits

1	Stan Musial-St.L. (N)	1948	230
2	Stan Musial-St.L. (N)	1946	228
3	Hank Aaron-Mil. (N)	1959	223
4	Richie Ashburn-Phi. (N)	1951	221
5	George Kell-Det. (A)	1950	218
6	Richie Ashburn-Phi. (N)	1958	215
7	Don Mueller-N.Y. (N)	1954	212
8	Harvey Kuenn-Det. (A)	1953	209
9	Johnny Pesky-Bos. (A)	1946	208
	Willie Mays-S.F. (N)	1950	208

lugging Average

1	Ted Williams-Bos. (A)	1957	.731
2	Mickey Mantle-N.Y. (A)	1956	.705
3	Stan Musial-St.L. (N)	1948	.702
4	Ted Williams-Bos. (A)	1946	.667
	Willie Mays-N.Y. (N)	1954	.667
6	Mickey Mantle-N.Y. (A)	1957	.665
7	Willie Mays-N.Y. (N)	1955	.659
8	Ralph Kiner-Pit. (N)	1949	.658
9	Ted Williams-Bos. (A)	1949	.650
10	Duke Snider-Bkn. (N)	1954	.647

Doubles

1	George Kell-Det. (A)	1950	56
2	Stan Musial-St.L. (N)	1953	53
3	Mickey Vernon-Was. (A)	1946	51
4	Stan Musial-St.L. (N)	1946	50
	Stan Spence-Was. (A)	1946	50
6	Vada Pinson-Cin. (N)	1959	47
7	Stan Musial-St.L. (N)	1948	46
	Hank Aaron-Mil. (N)	1959	46
9	Lou Boudreau-Cle. (A)	1947	45
10	Ted Williams-Bos. (A)	1948	44

Runs Batted In

1	Vern Stephens-Bos. (A)	1949	159
	Ted Williams-Bos. (A)	1949	159
3	Joe DiMaggio-N.Y. (A)	1948	155
4	Al Rosen-Cle. (A)	1953	145
5	Walt Dropo-Bos. (A)	1950	144
	Vern Stephens-Bos. (A)	1950	144
7	Ernie Banks-Chi. (N)	1959	143
8	Roy Campanella-Bkn. (N)	1953	142
9	Ted Kluszewski-Cin. (N)	1954	141
10	Johnny Mize-N.Y. (N)	1947	138

Triples

1	Dale Mitchell-Cle. (A)	1949	23
2	Stan Musial-St.L. (N)	1946	20
	Willie Mays-N.Y. (N)	1957	20
4	Stan Musial-St.L. (N)	1948	18
	Minnie Minoso-Chi. (A)	1954	18
6	Jim Gilliam-Bkn. (N)	1953	17
7	Hank Edwards-Cle. (A)	1946	16
	Harry Walker-St.L. + Phi. (N)	1947	16
	Jim Rivera-Chi. (A)	1953	16
10	Pete Runnels-Bos. (A)	1954	15
	Bill Bruton-Mil. (N)	1956	15

Runs

1	Ted Williams-Bos. (A)	1949	150
2	Ted Williams-Bos. (A)	1946	142
3	Tommy Henrich-N.Y. (A)	1948	138
4	Johnny Mize-N.Y. (N)	1947	137
5	Stan Musial-St.L. (N)	1948	135
6	Pee Wee Reese-Bkn. (N)	1949	132
	Duke Snider-Bkn. (N)	1953	132
	Mickey Mantle-N.Y. (A)	1956	132
9	Dom DiMaggio-Bos. (A)	1950	131
	Vada Pinson-Cin. (N)	1959	131

Home Runs

1	Ralph Kiner-Pit. (N)	1949	54
2	Mickey Mantle-N.Y. (A)	1956	52
3	Johnny Mize-N.Y. (N)	1947	51
	Ralph Kiner-Pit. (N)	1947	51
	Willie Mays-N.Y. (N)	1955	51
6	Ted Kluszewski-Cin. (N)	1954	49
7	Ralph Kiner-Pit. (N)	1950	47
	Eddie Mathews-Bos. (N)	1953	47
	Ted Kluszewski-Cin. (N)	1955	47
	Ernie Banks-Chi. (N)	1958	47

Bases on Balls

1	Ted Williams-Bos. (A)	1947	162
	Ted Williams-Bos. (A)	1949	162
3	Ted Williams-Bos. (A)	1946	156
4	Eddie Yost-Was. (A)	1956	151
5	Eddie Joost-Phi. (A)	1949	149
6	Mickey Mantle-N.Y. (A)	1957	146
7	Eddie Stanky-N.Y. (N)	1950	144
8	Ted Williams-Bos. (N)	1951	143
9	Eddie Yost-Was. (A)	1950	141
10	Eddie Stanky-Bkn. (N)	1946	137
	Roy Cullenbine-Det. (A)	1947	137
	Ralph Kiner-Pit. (N)	1951	137

Stolen Bases

1	Luis Aparicio-Chi. (A)	1959	56
2	Luis Aparicio-Chi. (A)	1960	51
3	Maury Wills-L.A. (N)	1960	50
4	Willie Mays-N.Y. (N)	1956	40
5	Willie Mays-N.Y. (N)	1957	38
6	Jackie Robinson-Bkn. (N)	1949	37
7	Sam Jethro-Bos. (N)	1950	35
	Sam Jethroe-Bos. (N)	1951	35
9	Pete Reiser-Bkn. (N)	1946	34
	Bill Bruton-Mil. (N)	1954	34

Strikeouts

1	Jim Lemon-Was. (A)	1956	138
2	Pancho Herrara-Phi. (N)	1960	136
3	Mickey Mantle-N.Y. (A)	1959	126
4	Steve Bilko-St.L. (N)	1953	125
	Mickey Mantle-N.Y. (A)	1960	125
6	Wally Post-Cin. (N)	1956	124
7	Larry Doby-Cle. (A)	1953	121
8	Jim Lemon-Was. (A)	1958	120
	Mickey Mantle-N.Y. (A)	1958	120
10	Woodie Held-Cle. (A)	1959	118

At Bats

1	Harvey Kuenn-Det. (A)	1953	679
2	Carl Furillo-Bkn. (N)	1951	667
3	Richie Ashburn-Phi. (N)	1949	662
	Granny Hamner-Phi. (N)	1949	662
5	Red Schoendienst-St.L. (N)	1947	659
6	Harvey Kuenn-Det. (A)	1954	656
7	Vada Pinson-Cin. (N)	1960	652
8	Don Blasingame-St.L. (N)	1957	650
9	Nellie Fox-Chi. (A)	1956	649
10	Dom DiMaggio-Bos. (A)	1948	648
	Nellie Fox-Chi. (A)	1952	648
	Vada Pinson-Cin. (N)	1959	648

PITCHING

Wins

1	Robin Roberts-Phi. (N)	1952	28
2	Don Newcombe-Bkn. (N)	1956	27
3	Bob Feller-Cle. (A)	1946	26
	Hal Newhouser-Det. (A)	1946	26
5	Boo Ferriss-Bos. (A)	1946	25
	Mel Parnell-Bos. (A)	1949	25
7	Johnny Sain-Bos. (N)	1948	24
	Bobby Shantz-Phi. (A)	1952	24
9	Ellis Kinder-Bos. (A)	1949	23
	Bob Lemon-Cle. (A)	1950	23
	Larry Jansen-N.Y. (N)	1951	23
	Sal Maglie-N.Y. (N)	1951	23
	Early Wynn-Cle. (A)	1952	23
	Robin Roberts-Phi. (N)	1953	23
	Warren Spahn-Mil. (N)	1953	23
	Bob Lemon-Cle. (A)	1954	23
	Robin Roberts-Phi. (N)	1954	23
	Early Wynn-Cle. (A)	1954	23
	Robin Roberts-Phi. (N)	1955	23

Winning Percentage

1	Roy Face-Pit. (N)	1959	.947
2	Preacher Roe-Bkn. (N)	1951	.880
3	Sandy Consuegra-Chi. (A)	1954	.842
4	Hoyt Wilhelm-N.Y. (N)	1952	.833
5	Sal Maglie-N.Y. (N)	1950	.818
6	Larry Jansen-N.Y. (N)	1947	.808
7	Boo Ferriss-Bos. (A)	1946	.806
8	Robin Roberts-Phi. (N)	1952	.800
	Eddie Lopat-N.Y. (A)	1953	.800
	Don Newcombe-Bkn. (N)	1955	.800

Losses

1	Art Ditmar-K.C. (A)	1956	22
	Robin Roberts-Phi. (N)	1957	22
3	Fred Sanford-St.L. (A)	1948	21
	Murry Dickson-Pit. (N)	1952	21
	Don Larsen-Bal. (A)	1954	21
6	Bill Wight-Chi. (A)	1948	20
	Alex Kellner-Phi. (A)	1950	20
	Bob Rush-Chi. (N)	1950	20
	Art Houtteman-Det. (A)	1952	20
	Harry Byrd-Phi. (A)	1953	20
	Murry Dickson-Phi. (N)	1954	20
	Sam Jones-Chi. (N)	1955	20
	Chuck Stobbs-Was. (A)	1957	20
	Glenn Hobbie-Chi. (N)	1960	20

Earned Run Average

1	Hal Newhouser-Det. (A)	1946	1.94
2	Billy Pierce-Chi. (A)	1955	1.97
3	Whitey Ford-N.Y. (A)	1958	2.01
4	Allie Reynolds-N.Y. (A)	1952	2.07
5	Spud Chandler-N.Y. (A)	1946	2.10
	Howie Pollet-St.L. (N)	1946	2.10
	Warren Spahn-Mil. (N)	1953	2.10
8	Bob Feller-Cle. (A)	1946	2.18
9	Hoyt Wilhelm-Bal. (A)	1959	2.19
10	Johnny Sain-Bos. (N)	1946	2.21

Saves

1	Joe Page-N.Y. (A)	1949	27
	Ellis Kinder-Bos. (A)	1953	27
3	Lindy McDaniel-St.L. (N)	1960	26
4	Jim Hughes-Bkn. (N)	1954	24
	Roy Face-Pit. (N)	1960	24
6	Jim Konstanty-Phi. (N)	1950	22
	Johnny Sain-N.Y. (A)	1954	22
8	Frank Smith-Cin. (N)	1954	20
	Ryne Duren-N.Y. (A)	1958	20
	Roy Face-Pit. (N)	1958	20

Bases on Balls

1	Sam Jones-Chi. (N)	1955	185
2	Bob Turley-Bal. (A)	1954	181
3	Tommy Byrne-N.Y. (A)	1949	179
4	Bob Turley-N.Y. (A)	1955	177
5	Tommy Byrne-N.Y. (A)	1950	160
6	Herb Score-Cle. (A)	1955	154
7	Bob Feller-Cle. (A)	1946	153
8	Tommy Byrne-N.Y. + St.L. (A)	1951	150
9	Bob Lemon-Cle. (A)	1950	146
10	Paul Foytack-Det. (A)	1956	142

Games Pitched

1	Jim Konstanty-Phi. (N)	1950	74
2	Hoyt Wilhelm-N.Y. (N)	1952	71
3	Mike Fornieles-Bos. (A)	1960	70
4	Ellis Kinder-Bos (A)	1953	69
	Don Elston-Chi. (N)	1958	69
6	Hoyt Wilhelm-N.Y. (N)	1953	68
	Roy Face-Pit. (N)	1956	68
	Roy Face-Pit. (N)	1960	68
9	Turk Lown-Chi. (N)	1957	67
	Gerry Staley-Chi. (A)	1959	67

Strikeouts

1	Bob Feller-Cle. (A)	1946	348
2	Hal Newhouser-Det. (A)	1946	275
3	Herb Score-Cle. (A)	1956	263
4	Don Drysdale-L.A. (N)	1960	246
5	Herb Score-Cle. (A)	1955	245
6	Don Drysdale-L.A. (N)	1959	242
7	Sam Jones-St.L. (N)	1958	225
8	Bub Turley-N.Y. (A)	1955	210
9	Sam Jones-S.F. (N)	1959	209
10	Jim Bunning-Det. (A)	1959	201
	Jim Bunning-Det. (A)	1960	201

Games Started

1	Bob Feller-Cle. (A)	1946	42
	Bob Friend-Pit. (N)	1956	42
3	Robin Roberts-Phi. (N)	1953	41
4	Johnny Sain-Bos. (N)	1947	39
	Vern Bickford-Bos. (N)	1950	39
	Robin Roberts-Phi. (N)	1950	39
	Warren Spahn-Bos. (N)	1950	39
	Robin Roberts-Phi. (N)	1951	39
	Ron Kline-Pit. (N)	1956	39
	Lew Burdette-Mil. (N)	1958	39

Shutouts

1	Bob Feller-Cle. (A)	1946	10
2	Bob Lemon-Cle. (A)	1948	10
3	Bob Porterfield-Was. (A)	1953	9
4	Warren Spahn-Bos. (N)	1947	7
	Harry Brecheen-St.L. (N)	1948	7
	Allie Reynolds-N.Y. (A)	1951	7
	Warren Spahn-Bos. (N)	1951	7
	Billy Pierce-Chi. (A)	1953	7
	Billy Hoeft-Det. (A)	1955	7
	Whitey Ford-N.Y. (A)	1958	7

Complete Games

1	Bob Feller-Cle. (A)	1946	36
2	Robin Roberts-Phi. (N)	1953	33
3	Robin Roberts-Phi. (N)	1952	30
4	Hal Newhouser-Det. (A)	1946	29
	Robin Roberts-Phi. (N)	1954	29
6	Johnny Sain-Bos. (N)	1947	28
	Bob Lemon-Cle. (A)	1952	28
8	Mel Parnell-Bos. (A)	1949	27
	Vern Bickford-Bos. (N)	1950	27
	Bobby Shantz-Phi. (A)	1952	27

Innings Pitched

1	Bob Feller-Cle. (A)	1946	371
2	Robin Roberts-Phi. (N)	1953	347
3	Robin Roberts-Phi. (N)	1954	337
4	Robin Roberts-Phi. (N)	1952	330
5	Johnny Sain-Bos. (N)	1947	315
	Robin Roberts-Phi. (N)	1951	315
7	Bob Friend-Pit. (N)	1956	314
8	Vern Bickford-Bos. (N)	1950	312
9	Warren Spahn-Bos. (N)	1951	311
10	Bob Lemon-Cle. (A)	1952	310

1946—1960 PERIOD LEADERS

BATTING

Batting Average
(Minimum 1000 Games or 4000 At Bats)

1	Ted Williams	1946-60	.340
2	Stan Musial	1946-60	.333
3	Hank Aaron	1954-60	.318
4	Willie Mays	1951-60	.317
5	George Kell	1946-57	.314
6	Harvey Kuenn	1952-60	.313
7	Dale Mitchell	*1946-56	.312
8	Jackie Robinson	*1947-56	.311
9	Richie Ashburn	1948-60	.310
10	Mickey Mantle	1951-60	.307

Hits

1	Stan Musial	1946-60	2710
2	Richie Ashburn	1948-60	2376
3	Red Schoendienst	1946-60	2292
4	Al Dark	*1946-60	2089
5	Nellie Fox	1947-60	2077
6	Del Ennis	*1946-59	2063
7	Mickey Vernon	1946-60	1946
	Yogi Berra	1946-60	1946
9	Carl Furillo	*1946-60	1910
10	Ted Williams	1946-60	1905

Slugging Average
(Minimum 1000 Games or 4000 At Bats)

1	Ted Williams	1946-60	.631
2	Willie Mays	1951-60	.585
3	Stan Musial	1946-60	.576
4	Mickey Mantle	1951-60	.568
5	Hank Aaron	1954-60	.560
6	Ernie Banks	1953-60	.557
7	Duke Snider	1947-60	.554
8	Eddie Mathews	1952-60	.549
9	Ralph Kiner	*1946-55	.548
10	Roy Campanella	*1948-57	.500

Home Runs

1	Ted Williams	1946-60	394
2	Stan Musial	1946-60	393
3	Ralph Kiner	*1946-55	369
4	Duke Snider	1947-60	368
5	Gil Hodges	1947-60	353
6	Eddie Mathews	1952-60	338
7	Mickey Mantle	1951-60	320
8	Yogi Berra	1946-60	318
9	Del Ennis	*1946-59	288
10	Hank Sauer	1948-59	281

Runs Batted In

1	Stan Musial	1946-60	1487
2	Ted Williams	1946-60	1324
3	Yogi Berra	1946-60	1306
4	Del Ennis	*1946-59	1284
5	Gil Hodges	1947-60	1223
6	Duke Snider	1947-60	1185
7	Vic Wertz	1947-60	1092
8	Carl Furillo	*1946-60	1058
9	Mickey Vernon	1946-60	1032
10	Yogi Berra	1946-60	1026

Triples

1	Stan Musial	1946-60	126
2	Richie Ashburn	1948-60	102
3	Enos Slaughter	1946-59	94
	Nellie Fox	1947-60	94
5	Willie Mays	1951-60	91
	Mickey Vernon	1946-60	91
7	Bill Bruton	1953-60	79
8	Minnie Minoso	1949-60	78
9	Duke Snider	1947-60	76
10	Bobby Thomson	*1946-60	74

Runs

1	Stan Musial	1946-60	1497
2	Ted Williams	1946-60	1257
3	Richie Ashburn	1948-60	1213
4	Eddie Yost	1946-60	1161
5	Duke Snider	1947-60	1136
6	Red Schoendienst	1946-60	1134
7	Pee Wee Reese	1946-58	1117
8	Mickey Mantle	1951-60	1113
9	Al Dark	*1946-60	1064
10	Yogi Berra	1946-60	1063
	Gil Hodges	1947-60	1063

Doubles

1	Stan Musial	1946-60	540
2	Red Schoendienst	1946-60	405
3	Mickey Vernon	1946-60	385
4	Ted Williams	1946-60	371
5	Al Dark	*1946-60	358
	Del Ennis	*1946-59	358
7	George Kell	1946-57	340
8	Duke Snider	1947-60	324
	Eddie Yost	1946-60	324
	Carl Furillo	*1946-60	324

Bases on Balls

1	Eddie Yost	1946-60	1533
2	Ted Williams	1946-60	1525
3	Stan Musial	1946-60	1222
4	Richie Ashburn	1948-60	1062
5	Pee Wee Reese	1946-58	1015
6	Ralph Kiner	*1946-55	1011
7	Mickey Mantle	1951-60	1004
8	Earl Torgeson	1947-60	969
9	Ferris Fain	*1947-55	903
10	Gil Hodges	1947-60	900

Stolen Bases

1	Richie Ashburn	1948-60	215
2	Willie Mays	1951-60	204
3	Jackie Robinson	*1947-56	197
4	Pee Wee Reese	1946-58	192
5	Luis Aparicio	1956-60	185
6	Minnie Minoso	1949-60	184
7	Jim Rivera	1952-60	157
8	Bill Bruton	1953-60	143
9	Earl Torgeson	1947-60	133
10	Phil Rizzuto	1946-56	113

Strikeouts

1	Gil Hodges	1947-60	1063
2	Duke Snider	1947-60	1048
3	Mickey Mantle	1951-60	1024
4	Larry Doby	*1947-59	1011
5	Eddie Yost	1946-60	849
6	Bobby Thomson	*1946-60	804
7	Eddie Mathews	1952-60	791
8	Vic Wertz	1947-60	779
9	Gus Zernial	*1949-59	755
10	Ralph Kiner	*1946-55	749

*—Entire major league career

PITCHING

Wins

1	Warren Spahn	1946-60	288
2	Early Wynn	1946-60	245
3	Robin Roberts	1948-60	233
4	Bob Lemon	*1946-58	207
5	Billy Pierce	1948-60	179
6	Murry Dickson	1946-59	158
7	Bob Feller	1946-56	154
8	Don Newcombe	*1949-60	149
9	Virgil Trucks	1946-58	147
10	Lew Burdette	1950-60	145
	Eddie Lopat	1946-55	145

Winning Percentage
(Minimum 100 Wins)

1	Whitey Ford	1950-60	.693
2	Vic Raschi	*1946-55	.667
3	Sal Maglie	1950-58	.663
4	Allie Reynolds	1946-54	.654
5	Preacher Roe	1946-54	.625
6	Don Newcombe	*1949-60	.623
7	Mel Parnell	*1947-56	.621
8	Bob Buhl	1953-60	.621
9	Eddie Lopat	1946-55	.620
10	Bob Lemon	*1946-58	.618

Losses

1	Robin Roberts	1948-60	189
2	Warren Spahn	1946-60	182
3	Early Wynn	1946-60	177
4	Murry Dickson	1946-59	176
5	Ned Garver	1948-60	154
6	Bob Rush	*1948-60	152
7	Billy Pierce	1948-60	143
8	Bob Friend	1951-60	139
9	Bob Lemon	*1946-58	128
10	Chuck Stobbs	1947-60	127

Earned Run Average
(Minimum 1500 Innings Pitched or 100 Wins)

1	Whitey Ford	1950-60	2.70
2	Warren Spahn	1946-60	2.98
3	Eddie Lopat	1946-55	3.12
4	Hal Newhouser	1946-55	3.18
5	Sal Maglie	1950-58	3.19
6	Billy Pierce	1948-60	3.21
7	Bob Lemon	*1946-58	3.23
8	Johnny Antonelli	1948-60	3.24
9	Mike Garcia	1948-60	3.25
10	Bob Feller	1946-56	3.32

Saves

1	Ellis Kinder	*1946-57	102
2	Clem Labine	1950-60	88
3	Joe Page	1946-54	76
4	Roy Face	1953-60	75
5	Jim Konstanty	1946-56	74
6	Hoyt Wilhelm	1952-60	65
7	Al Brazle	1946-54	60
8	Marv Grissom	*1946-59	58
	Ray Narleski	*1954-59	58
10	Gerry Staley	1947-60	57

Strikeouts

1	Warren Spahn	1946-60	2073
2	Early Wynn	1946-60	1922
3	Robin Roberts	1948-60	1817
4	Billy Pierce	1948-60	1726
5	Virgil Trucks	1946-58	1319
6	Bob Feller	1946-56	1289
7	Bob Lemon	*1946-58	1277
8	Bob Rush	*1948-60	1244
9	Harvey Haddix	1952-60	1194
10	Sam Jones	1951-60	1184

Games Pitched

1	Gerry Staley	1947-60	588
2	Warren Spahn	1946-60	567
3	Murry Dickson	1946-59	556
4	Early Wynn	1946-60	519
5	Robin Roberts	1948-60	503
6	Ellis Kinder	*1946-57	484
7	Hoyt Wilhelm	1952-60	473
8	Bob Lemon	*1946-58	460
9	Virgil Trucks	1946-58	454
	Clem Labine	1950-60	454

Shutouts

1	Warren Spahn	1946-60	51
2	Early Wynn	1946-60	40
3	Robin Roberts	1948-60	35
4	Billy Pierce	1948-60	34
5	Bob Lemon	*1946-58	31
6	Allie Reynolds	1946-54	30
7	Virgil Trucks	1946-58	29
8	Whitey Ford	1950-60	28
9	Bob Feller	1946-56	27
	Murry Dickson	1946-59	27
	Mike Garcia	1948-60	27

Games Started

1	Warren Spahn	1946-60	507
2	Early Wynn	1946-60	471
3	Robin Roberts	1948-60	454
4	Billy Pierce	1948-60	367
5	Bob Lemon	*1946-58	350
6	Ned Garver	1948-60	328
7	Murry Dickson	1946-59	323
8	Bob Rish	*1948-60	321
9	Bob Feller	1946-56	300
10	Bob Friend	1951-60	299

Innings Pitched

1	Warren Spahn	1946-60	4066
2	Robin Roberts	1948-60	3623
3	Early Wynn	1946-60	3518
4	Bob Lemon	*1946-58	2849
5	Murry Dickson	1946-59	2810
6	Billy Pierce	1948-60	2795
7	Ned Garver	1948-60	2448
8	Bob Rush	*1948-60	2409
9	Bob Feller	1946-56	2307
10	Virgil Trucks	1946-58	2306

Complete Games

1	Warren Spahn	1946-60	304
2	Robin Roberts	1948-60	270
3	Early Wynn	1946-60	227
4	Bob Lemon	*1946-58	188
5	Billy Pierce	1948-60	178
6	Bob Feller	1946-56	155
7	Ned Garver	1948-60	153
8	Murry Dickson	1946-59	145
9	Johnny Sain	1946-55	140
10	Don Newcombe	*1949-60	136

Complete Game Percentage
(Complete Games as a percentage of Games Started - minimum 175 Games Started)

1	Warren Spahn	1946-60	60.0
2	Hal Newhouser	1946-55	59.6
3	Robin Roberts	1948-60	59.5
4	Johnny Sain	1946-55	57.9
5	Bob Lemon	*1946-58	53.7
6	Bob Feller	1946-56	51.7
7	Eddie Lopat	1946-55	49.8
8	Mel Parnell	*1947-56	48.7
9	Billy Pierce	1948-60	48.5
10	Early Wynn	1946-60	48.2

1946 South of the Border

Although World War II was officially over and baseball's finest were back in their familiar ranks, tranquility no longer had a place in the major leagues. What had happened was that the new Mexican League, headed by millionaire Jorge Pasquel, had lured a cluster of players from the majors. The Cardinals lost pitchers, Max Lanier and Freddie Martin, and second baseman Lou Klein. Mickey Owen jumped from the Dodgers, along with Luis Olmo. Vern Stephens of the Browns also joined the exodus but immediately returned before the season started to escape Commissioner Chandler's decree that all jumpers would be barred from organized ball for five years. The first player to learn of Chandler's seriousness was Mickey Owen, who returned in August, asked for clemency, and was refused.

There were other players of marginal significance that fled to Mexico, making it almost impossible to predict how the balance of the pennant race would be upset. The one clear case of imbalance was the New York Giants, who lost eight players—four of them pitchers—and wound up in last place, although leading the league with 121 home runs, 40 ahead of their nearest rival. Those leaving the Giants included pitchers, Sal Maglie, Harry Feldman, and Ace Adams, and outfielder Danny Gardella.

Yet, regardless of the defectors, the show went on. The victorious Cubs of 1945 were plagued by slumps, as well as injuries to Andy Pafko, Stan Hack, and Don Johnson, and finished a poor third to both the Cardinals and Dodgers who, for the first time in major league history, forced a play-off to decide the National League winner.

Both clubs entered the final day of the season with 96-57 records but could not avert the deadlock as the Cubs thrashed the Cardinals 8-3, while Boston's Mort Cooper was shutting out the Dodgers, 4-0. The Dodgers journeyed to St. Louis for the first of three play-off games without the services of their most exciting player, Pete Reiser, who broke an ankle three weeks before. Brooklyn lost, 4-2, to the pitching arm of Howie Pollet. The Cardinals then came East for the second game and won the pennant, 8-4.

In Boston, the Red Sox finally made it to the altar after finishing second to the Yankees in 1938, 1939, 1941, and 1942 due mainly to the return of Ted Williams. A bit rusty from his three-year wartime layoff, he finished second in the Triple Crown categories, but won the praise of the sportswriters and was named MVP.

The World Series began with Ted Williams and Stan Musial as the men most likely to succeed. When it was over, after seven hectic games, Williams had a .200 average and Musial a .222 mark. Even Howie Pollet, the leagues' biggest winner, failed to win a game. The honors, instead, went to Harry Brecheen, a regular season .500 pitcher who picked up three victories, and Enos Slaughter, who proved victory could outweigh pain.

Early in the fifth game Slaughter was clipped on the elbow by a pitch and later forced to leave the game for what turned out to be a broken elbow. On the return train trip to St. Louis, where the Series resumed the next day, Slaughter got his elbow patched and played in the Cardinals' 4-1 series evener. The next day Slaughter played again but did not manage a hit until the bottom of the eighth with the score at 3-3.

In Boston's part of the inning, they had managed to score the tying runs although losing Dom DiMaggio because of a sprained ankle. Leon Culberson took DiMaggio's place in center. Slaughter was still on first base with two outs when Harry Walker hit a line drive over Johnny Pesky's head. Slaughter continued to circle the bases as Culberson's throw came into Pesky. The Boston shortstop was either not believing his eyes or thinking of things other than baseball. But whatever his thoughts were, they were enough to cause him to hesitate for a moment in relaying the throw to the plate as Slaughter slid home with what turned out to be the world's championship.

1946 AMERICAN LEAGUE

NAME	G by POS	B	AGE	G	AB	R	H	2B	3B	HR	RBI	BB	SO	SB	BA	SA
BOSTON 1st 104-50 .675			JOE CRONIN													
TOTALS			30	156	5318	**792**	**1441**	**268**	50	109	**736**	**687**	661	45	**.271**	**.402**
Rudy York	1B154	R	32	154	579	78	160	30	6	17	119	86	93	3	.276	.437
Bobby Doerr	2B151	R	28	151	583	95	158	34	9	18	116	66	67	5	.271	.453
Johnny Pesky	SS153	L	26	153	**621**	115	**208**	43	4	2	55	65	29	9	.335	.427
Rip Russell	3B70, 2B3	R	31	80	274	22	57	10	1	6	35	13	30	1	.208	.318
Catfish Metkovich	OF81	L	24	86	281	42	69	15	2	4	25	36	39	8	.246	.356
Dom DiMaggio	OF142	R	29	142	534	85	169	24	7	7	73	66	58	10	.316	.427
Ted Williams	OF150	L	27	150	514	**142**	176	37	8	38	123	**156**	44	0	.342	**.667**
Hal Wagner	C116	L	30	117	370	39	85	12	2	6	52	69	32	3	.230	.322
2 Pinky Higgins	3B59	R	37	64	200	18	55	11	1	2	28	24	24	0	.275	.370
Tom McBride	OF43	R	31	61	153	21	46	5	2	0	19	9	6	0	.301	.359
Leon Culberson	OF49, 3B4	R	26	59	179	34	56	10	1	3	18	16	19	3	.313	.430
2 Wally Moses	OF44	L	35	48	175	13	36	11	3	2	17	14	15	2	.206	.337
Roy Partee	C38	R	28	40	111	13	35	5	2	0	9	13	14	0	.315	.396
Paul Campbell	1B5	L	28	28	26	3	3	1	0	0	0	2	7	0	.115	.154
Johnny Lazor	OF7	L	33	23	29	1	4	0	0	1	4	2	11	0	.138	.241
Eddie Pellagrini	3B14, SS9	R	28	22	71	7	15	3	1	2	4	3	18	1	.211	.366
Don Gutteridge	2B9, 3B8	R	34	22	47	8	11	3	0	1	6	2	7	0	.234	.362
Ernie Andres	3B15	R	28	15	41	0	4	2	0	0	1	3	5	0	.098	.146
Ed McGah	C14	R	24	15	37	2	8	1	1	0	1	7	7	0	.216	.297

Frankie Pytlak 37 R 2-14, Tom Carey 37 R 1-5, Ben Steiner 24 L 1-4, Andy Gilbert 31 R0-1

NAME	T	AGE	W	L	PCT	SV	G	GS	CG	IP	H	BB	SO	ShO	ERA
		31	**104**	50	**.675**	**20**	156	156	79	1397	1359	501	667	15	3.38
Boo Ferriss	R	24	25	6	**.806**	3	40	35	26	274	274	71	106	6	3.25
Tex Hughson	R	30	20	11	.645	3	39	35	21	278	252	51	172	6	2.75
Mickey Harris	L	29	17	9	.654	0	34	30	15	223	236	76	131	0	3.63
Joe Dobson	R	29	13	7	.650	0	32	24	9	167	148	68	91	1	3.23
Jim Bagby	R	29	7	6	.538	0	21	11	6	107	117	49	16	1	3.70
2 Bill Zuber	R	33	5	1	.833	0	15	7	2	57	37	39	29	1	2.53
Earl Johnson	L	27	5	4	.556	3	29	5	0	80	78	39	40	0	3.71
Clem Dreisewerd	L	30	4	1	.800	0	20	1	0	47	50	15	19	0	4.21
Mace Brown	R	37	3	1	.750	1	18	0	0	26	26	16	10	0	2.08
Bob Klinger	R	38	3	2	.600	**9**	28	1	0	57	49	25	16	0	2.37
Charlie Wagner	R	33	1	0	1.000	0	8	4	0	31	32	19	14	0	5.81
Bill Butland	R	28	1	0	1.000	0	5	2	0	16	23	13	10	0	11.25
Mike Ryba	R	43	0	1	.000	1	9	0	0	13	12	5	5	0	3.46
Randy Heflin	R	27	0	1	.000	0	5	1	0	15	16	12	6	0	2.40
Mel Deutsch	R	30	0	0	.000	0	3	0	0	6	7	3	2	0	6.00
Tim Wilson	R	24	0	0	.000	0	1	0	0	1	2	0	0	0	18.00

NAME	G by POS	B	AGE	G	AB	R	H	2B	3B	HR	RBI	BB	SO	SB	BA	SA
DETROIT 2nd 92-62 .597 12			STEVE O'NEILL													
TOTALS			31	155	5318	704	1373	212	41	108	644	622	616	65	.258	.374
Hank Greenberg	1B140	R	35	142	523	91	145	29	5	**44**	**127**	80	88	5	.277	.604
Jimmy Bloodworth (MS)	2B71	R	28	76	249	26	61	8	1	5	36	12	26	3	.245	.345
Eddie Lake	SS155	R	30	155	587	105	149	24	1	8	31	103	69	15	.254	.339
2 George Kell	3B105, 1B1	R	23	105	434	67	142	19	9	4	41	30	14	3	.327	.440
Roy Cullenbine	OF81, 1B21	B	30	113	328	63	110	21	0	15	56	88	39	3	.335	.537
Hoot Evers (BN)	OF76	R	25	81	304	42	81	8	4	4	33	34	43	7	.266	.359
Dick Wakefield	OF104	L	25	111	396	64	106	11	5	12	59	59	55	3	.268	.412
Birdie Tebbetts	C87	R	36	87	280	20	68	11	2	1	34	28	23	1	.243	.307
Pat Mullin	OF75	L	28	93	276	34	68	13	4	3	35	25	36	3	.246	.355
Jimmy Outlaw	OF43, 3B38	R	33	92	299	36	78	14	2	2	31	29	24	5	.261	.341
Doc Cramer	OF50	L	40	68	204	26	60	8	2	1	26	15	8	3	.294	.368
Skeeter Webb	2B50, SS8	R	36	64	169	12	37	1	1	0	17	9	18	3	.219	.237
Paul Richards	C54	R	37	57	139	13	28	5	2	0	11	23	18	2	.201	.266
Eddie Mayo (TJ)	2B49	L	36	51	202	21	51	9	2	0	22	14	12	6	.252	.317
Anse Moore	OF32	L	28	51	134	16	28	4	0	1	8	12	9	1	.209	.261
Bob Swift	C42	R	31	42	107	13	25	2	0	2	10	14	7	0	.234	.308
Fred Hutchinson	P28	L	26	40	89	11	28	4	0	0	13	6	1	0	.315	.360
1 Barney McCoskey	OF24	L	28	25	91	11	18	5	0	1	11	17	9	0	.198	.286
1 Pinky Higgins	3B17	R	37	18	60	2	13	3	1	0	8	5	6	0	.217	.300
Johnny Lipon	SS8, 3B1	R	23	14	20	4	6	0	0	0	1	5	3	0	.300	.300

Johnny Groth 19 R 0-9, 1 Billy Hitchock 29 R 0-3, Ned Harris 29 L 0-1, Rip Radcliff (MS) 40

NAME	T	AGE	W	L	PCT	SV	G	GS	CG	IP	H	BB	SO	ShO	ERA
		30	92	62	.597	15	155	155	**94**	**1402**	1277	497	**896**	**18**	3.22
Hal Newhouser	L	25	**26**	9	.743	1	37	34	29	293	215	98	275	6	**1.94**
Dizzy Trout	R	31	17	13	.567	3	38	32	23	276	244	97	151	5	2.35
Virgil Trucks	R	27	14	9	.609	0	32	29	15	237	217	75	161	2	3.23
Fred Hutchinson	R	26	14	11	.560	2	28	26	16	207	184	66	138	3	3.09
Al Benton	R	35	11	7	.611	1	28	15	6	141	132	58	60	1	3.64
Stubby Overmire	L	27	5	7	.417	1	24	13	3	97	106	29	34	0	4.64
George Caster	R	38	2	1	.667	4	26	0	0	41	42	24	19	0	5.71
Lou Kretlow	R	23	1	0	1.000	0	1	1	1	9	7	2	4	0	3.00
Hal White	R	27	1	1	.500	0	11	1	1	27	34	15	12	0	5.67
Tommy Bridges	R	39	1	1	.500	1	9	1	0	21	24	8	17	0	6.00
Art Houtteman	R	18	0	1	.000	0	1	1	0	8	15	0	2	0	9.00
Ted Gray	L	21	0	2	.000	1	3	2	0	12	17	5	5	0	8.25
Johnny Gorsica (MS)	R	31	0	0	.000	1	14	0	0	24	28	11	14	0	4.50
Rufe Gentry	R	28	0	0	.000	0	2	0	0	3	4	7	1	0	15.00
1 Hal Manders	R	29	0	0	.000	0	2	0	0	6	8	2	3	0	10.50

NAME	G by POS	B	AGE	G	AB	R	H	2B	3B	HR	RBI	BB	SO	SB	BA	SA
NEW YORK 3rd 87-67 .565 17			JOE McCARTHY 22-13 .629 BILL DICKEY 57-48 .543 JOHNNY NEUN 8-6 .571													
TOTALS			30	154	5139	684	1275	208	50	**136**	649	627	706	48	.248	.387
Nick Etten	1B84	L	32	108	323	37	75	14	1	9	49	38	35	0	.232	.365
Joe Gordon	2B108	R	31	112	376	35	79	15	0	11	47	49	72	2	.210	.338
Phil Rizzuto	SS125	R	28	126	471	53	121	17	1	2	38	34	39	14	.257	.310
Snuffy Stirnweiss	3B79, 2B46, SS4	R	27	129	487	75	122	19	7	0	37	66	58	18	.251	.318
Tommy Henrich	OF111, 1B41	L	33	150	565	92	142	25	4	19	83	87	63	5	.251	.411
Joe DiMaggio	OF131	R	31	132	503	81	146	20	8	25	95	59	24	1	.290	.511
Charlie Keller	OF149	L	29	150	538	98	148	29	10	30	101	113	**101**	1	.275	.533
Aaron Robinson	C95	L	31	100	330	32	98	17	2	16	64	48	39	0	.297	.506
Johnny Lindell	OF74, 1B14	R	29	102	332	41	86	10	5	10	40	32	47	4	.259	.410
Billy Johnson (MS)	3B74	R	27	85	296	51	77	14	5	4	35	31	42	1	.260	.382
Bill Dickey	C39	L	39	54	134	10	35	8	0	2	10	19	12	0	.261	.366
Steve Souchock	1B20	R	27	47	86	15	26	3	3	2	10	7	13	0	.302	.477
Gus Niarhos	C29	R	25	37	40	11	9	1	1	0	2	11	2	1	.225	.300
Frankie Crosetti	SS24	R	35	28	59	4	17	3	0	0	3	8	2	0	.288	.339
Tommy Byrne	P4	L	26	14	9	2	2	0	0	0	0	1	0	0	.222	.222
1 Oscar Grimes	SS7, 2B5	R	31	14	39	1	8	1	0	0	4	1	7	0	.205	.231
Ken Silvestri	C12	B	30	13	21	4	6	1	0	0	1	3	7	0	.286	.333
1 Hank Majeski	3B2	R	29	8	12	1	1	0	1	0	0	0	3	0	.083	.250
Yogi Berra	C6	L	21	7	22	3	8	1	0	2	4	1	1	0	.364	.682

Bobby Brown 21 L 8-24, 2 Frank Colman 28 L 4-15, Bill Drescher 25 L2-6, Eddie Bockman 25 R 1-12,
Bud Metheny 31 L 0-3, Roy Weatherly 31 L 1-2, Butch Wensloff (MS) 30

NAME	T	AGE	W	L	PCT	SV	G	GS	CG	IP	H	BB	SO	ShO	ERA
		30	87	67	.565	17	154	154	68	1361	1232	552	653	17	3.13
Spud Chandler	R	38	20	8	.714	2	34	32	20	257	200	90	138	6	2.10
Bill Bevens	R	29	16	13	.552	0	31	31	18	250	213	78	120	3	2.23
Randy Gumpert	R	28	11	3	.786	1	33	12	4	133	113	32	63	0	2.30
Joe Page	L	28	9	8	.529	3	31	17	6	136	126	72	77	1	3.57
Al Gettel	R	28	6	7	.462	0	26	11	5	103	89	40	54	2	2.97
Red Ruffing	R	42	5	1	.833	0	8	8	4	61	37	23	19	2	1.77
Ernie Bonham	R	32	5	8	.385	3	18	14	6	105	97	23	30	2	3.69
Johnny Murphy	R	37	4	2	.667	7	27	0	0	45	40	19	19	0	3.40
Cuddles Marshall	R	21	3	4	.429	0	23	11	1	81	96	56	32	0	5.33
Vic Raschi	R	27	2	0	1.000	0	2	2	2	16	14	5	11	0	3.94
1 Jake Wade	L	34	2	1	.667	1	13	1	0	35	33	14	22	0	2.31
Bill Wight	L	24	2	2	.500	0	14	4	1	40	44	30	11	0	4.50
Mel Queen (MS)	R	28	1	1	.500	0	14	3	1	30	40	21	26	0	6.60
1 Steve Roser	R	28	1	1	.500	0	4	1	0	3	7	4	1	0	18.00
Tommy Byrne	L	26	0	1	.000	0	4	1	0	9	7	8	5	0	6.00
Karl Drews	R	26	0	1	.000	0	3	1	0	6	6	6	4	0	9.00
1 Bill Zuber	R	33	0	1	.000	0	3	0	0	6	10	3	3	0	12.00
Al Lyons	R	27	0	1	.000	0	2	1	0	8	11	6		0	5.40
Marius Russo	L	31	0	2	.000	0	8	3	0	19	26	11		0	4.34
Frank Hiller	R	25	0	2	.000	0	3	1	0	11	13	6		0	4.76

1 Charley Stanceu 30 R 0-0, Herb Karpel 28 L 0-0

WASHINGTON 4th 76-78 .494 28

OSSIE BLUEGE

NAME	G by POS	B	AGE	G	AB	R	H	2B	3B	HR	RBI	BB	SO	SB	BA	SA
TOTALS			29	155	5337	608	1388	260	63	60	553	511	641	51	.260	.366
Mickey Vernon	1B147	L	28	148	587	88	207	51	8	8	85	49	64	14	.353	.508
Jerry Priddy	2B138	R	26	138	511	54	130	22	8	6	58	57	73	9	.254	.364
Cecil Travis	SS75, 3B56	L	32	137	465	45	117	22	3	5	56	45	47	2	.252	.318
2 Billy Hitchcock	SS53, 3B46	R	29	98	354	27	75	8	3	0	25	26	52	2	.212	.251
Buddy Lewis	OF145	L	29	150	582	82	170	28	13	7	45	59	26	5	.292	.421
Stan Spence	OF150	L	31	152	578	83	169	50	10	16	87	62	31	1	.292	.497
2 Joe Grace	OF74	L	32	77	321	39	97	17	4	2	31	24	19	1	.302	.399
Al Evans	C81	R	29	88	272	30	69	10	4	2	30	30	28	1	.254	.342
S. Robertson	3B38, 2B14, SS12, OF1	R	27	74	230	30	46	6	3	6	19	30	42	6	.200	.330
George Binks	OF28	L	31	65	134	13	26	3	0	0	12	6	16	1	.194	.216
Jake Early	C64	L	29	64	189	13	38	6	0	4	18	23	27	0	.201	.296
Gil Torres	SS31, 3B18, 2B7, P3	R	30	63	185	18	47	8	0	0	13	11	12	3	.254	.297
Gil Coan	OF29	L	24	59	134	17	28	3	2	3	9	7	37	2	.209	.328
1 Jeff Heath	OF47	L	31	48	166	23	47	12	3	4	27	36	36	0	.283	.464
Mike Guerra	C27	R	33	41	83	3	21	2	1	0	4	5	6	1	.253	.301
George Myatt	3B7, 2B2	L	32	15	34	7	8	1	0	0	4	2	3	1	.235	.265
1 Joe Kuhel	1B6	L	40	14	20	2	3	0	0	0	2	5	2	0	.150	.150

Jack Sanford 29 R 6-26, Eddie Yost (MS) 19 R 2-25, Ray Goolsby 26 R 0-4, Roberto Ortiz (SM) 31, John Sullivan (MS) 25

NAME	T	AGE	W	L	PCT	SV	G	GS	CG	IP	H	BB	SO	ShO	ERA
		31	76	78	.494	10	155	155	71	1396	1459	547	537	8	3.74
Mickey Haefner	L	33	14	11	.560	1	33	27	17	228	220	80	85	2	2.84
2 Bobo Newsom	R	38	11	8	.579	1	24	22	14	178	163	60	82	2	2.78
Dutch Leonard	R	37	10	10	.500	0	26	23	7	162	182	36	62	2	3.56
Early Wynn (MS)	R	26	8	5	.615	0	17	12	9	107	112	33	36	0	3.11
Sid Hudson	R	31	8	11	.421	1	31	15	6	142	160	37	35	1	3.61
Ray Scarborough	R	28	7	11	.389	1	32	20	6	156	176	74	46	1	4.04
Walt Masterson	R	26	5	6	.455	1	29	9	2	91	105	67	61	0	6.03
Roger Wolff	R	35	5	8	.385	0	21	17	6	122	115	30	50	0	2.58
1 Johnny Niggeling	R	42	3	2	.600	0	8	6	3	38	39	21	10	0	4.03
Milo Candini	R	28	2	0	1.000	1	9	0	0	22	15	4	6	0	2.04
Marino Pieretti	R	25	2	2	.500	0	30	2	1	62	70	40	20	0	5.95
Bill Kennedy	L	27	1	2	.333	3	21	2	0	39	40	29	18	0	6.00
Maxie Wilson	L	30	0	1	.000	0	9	0	0	13	16	9	8	0	6.92
2 Al LaMacchia	R	24	0	1	.000	0	2	0	0	3	6	2	0	0	15.00
Vern Curtis	R	26	0	0	.000	0	11	0	0	16	19	10	7	0	7.31
2 Jake Wade	L	34	0	0	.000	0	6	0	0	11	12	12	9	0	4.91
Gil Torres	R	30	0	0	.000	1	3	0	0	7	9	3	2	0	7.71

Alex Carrasquel (SM) 33, Jim Mertz (MS) 30

CHICAGO 5th 74-80 .481 30

JIMMY DYKES 10-20 .333 TED LYONS 64-60 .516

NAME	G by POS	B	AGE	G	AB	R	H	2B	3B	HR	RBI	BB	SO	SB	BA	SA
TOTALS			31	155	5312	562	1364	206	44	37	515	501	600	78	.257	.333
Hal Trosky	1B80	L	33	88	299	22	76	12	3	2	31	34	37	4	.254	.334
Don Kolloway	2B90, 3B31	R	27	123	482	45	135	23	4	3	53	9	29	14	.280	.363
Luke Appling	SS149	R	39	149	582	59	180	27	5	1	55	71	41	6	.309	.378
Dario Lodigiani (EJ)	3B44	R	30	44	155	12	38	8	0	0	13	16	14	4	.245	.297
Taffy Wright (IL)	OF107	L	34	115	422	46	116	19	4	7	52	42	17	10	.275	.389
Thurman Tucker	OF110	L	28	121	438	62	126	20	3	1	36	54	45	9	.288	.354
Bob Kennedy	OF75, 3B29	R	25	113	411	43	106	13	5	5	34	24	42	6	.258	.350
Mike Tresh	C79	R	30	80	217	28	47	5	2	0	21	36	24	0	.217	.258
Cass Michaels	2B66, 3B13, SS6	R	20	91	291	37	75	8	0	1	22	29	36	9	.258	.296
Ralph Hodgin	OF57	L	30	87	258	32	65	10	1	0	25	19	6	0	.252	.298
Whitey Platt	OF61	R	25	84	247	28	62	8	5	3	32	17	34	1	.251	.360
2 Joe Kuhel	1B62	L	40	64	238	24	65	9	3	4	20	21	24	4	.273	.387
1 Wally Moses	OF36	L	35	56	168	20	46	9	1	4	16	17	20	2	.274	.411
2 Frankie Hayes	C50	R	31	53	179	15	38	6	0	2	16	29	33	1	.212	.279
Leo Wells	3B38, SS2	R	28	45	127	11	24	4	1	1	11	12	34	3	.189	.260
George Dickey	C30	B	30	37	78	8	15	1	0	0	1	12	13	0	.192	.205
Jake Jones (BW)	1B20	R	25	24	79	10	21	5	1	3	13	2	13	0	.266	.468
Guy Curtright	OF15	R	33	23	55	7	11	2	0	0	5	11	14	0	.200	.236
Dave Philley	OF17	B	26	17	68	10	24	2	3	0	17	4	4	5	.353	.471
Frank Whitman	SS6, 2B1, 1B1	R	21	17	16	7	1	0	0	0	1	2	6	0	.063	.063
Ed Fernandes	C12	B	28	14	32	4	8	2	0	0	4	8	7	0	.250	.313

1 Tom Jordan (AJ) 26 R 4-15, Floyd Baker 29 L 6-24, Joe Smaza 22 L 1-5

NAME	T	AGE	W	L	PCT	SV	G	GS	CG	IP	H	BB	SO	ShO	ERA
		31	74	80	.481	16	155	155	62	1392	1348	508	550	9	3.10
Earl Caldwell	R	41	13	4	.765	8	39	0	0	91	60	29	42	0	2.08
Ed Lopat	L	28	13	13	.500	0	29	29	20	231	216	48	89	2	2.73
Eddie Smith	L	32	8	11	.421	1	24	21	3	145	135	60	59	1	2.86
Orval Grove	R	26	8	13	.381	0	33	26	10	205	213	78	60	1	3.03
Frank Papish	L	28	7	5	.583	0	31	15	6	138	122	63	66	2	2.74
Joe Haynes	R	28	7	9	.438	2	32	23	9	177	203	60	60	0	3.76
Johnny Rigney (SJ)	R	31	5	5	.500	0	15	11	3	83	76	35	51	2	4.01
2 Al Hollingsworth	L	38	3	2	.600	1	21	2	0	55	63	22	22	0	4.58
Bill Dietrich (BG)	R	36	3	3	.500	1	11	9	3	62	63	24	20	0	2.61
G. Maltzberger (MS)	R	33	2	0	1.000	2	19	0	0	40	30	6	17	0	1.58
Thornton Lee (EJ)	L	39	2	4	.333	0	7	7	2	43	39	23	23	0	3.56
Ralph Hamner	R	29	2	7	.222	1	25	7	1	71	80	39	29	0	4.44
Ted Lyons	R	45	1	4	.200	0	5	5	5	43	38	9	10	0	2.30
Len Perme	L	28	0	0	.000	0	4	0	0	4	6	7	2	0	9.00
2 Emmett O'Neill	R	28	0	0	.000	0	2	0	0	4	4	5	0	0	0.00

Johnny Johnson (AJ) 31

CLEVELAND 6th 68-86 .442 36

LOU BOUDREAU

NAME	G by POS	B	AGE	G	AB	R	H	2B	3B	HR	RBI	BB	SO	SB	BA	SA
TOTALS			28	156	5242	537	1285	233	56	79	496	506	697	57	.245	.356
Les Fleming	1B80, OF1	L	30	99	306	40	85	17	5	8	42	50	42	1	.278	.444
Dutch Meyer	2B64	R	30	72	207	13	48	5	3	0	16	26	16	0	.232	.285
Lou Boudreau	SS139	R	28	140	515	51	151	30	6	6	62	40	14	6	.293	.410
Ken Keltner	3B112	R	29	116	398	47	96	17	1	13	45	30	38	0	.241	.387
Hank Edwards	OF123	L	27	124	458	62	138	33	16	10	54	43	48	1	.301	.509
Pat Seerey	OF115	R	23	117	404	57	91	17	2	26	62	65	101	2	.225	.470
George Case	OF118	R	30	118	484	46	109	23	4	1	22	34	38	28	.225	.295
Jim Hegan	C87	R	25	88	271	29	64	11	5	0	17	17	44	1	.236	.314
Felix Mackiewicz	OF72	R	28	78	258	35	67	15	4	0	16	16	32	5	.260	.349
Jack Conway	2B50, SS14, 3B3	R	26	68	258	24	58	6	2	0	18	20	36	2	.225	.264
Ray Mack	2B61	R	29	61	171	13	35	6	2	1	9	23	27	2	.205	.281
Gene Woodling	OF37	L	23	61	133	8	25	1	4	0	9	16	13	1	.188	.256
Don Ross	3B41, OF2	R	31	55	153	12	41	7	0	3	14	17	12	0	.268	.373
Bob Lemon	P32, OF12	L	25	55	89	9	16	3	0	1	4	7	18	0	.180	.247
1 Frankie Hayes	C50	R	31	51	156	11	40	12	0	3	18	21	26	1	.256	.391
2 Heinz Becker	1B44	B	30	50	147	15	44	10	1	0	17	23	18	1	.299	.381
Mickey Rocco	1B27	L	30	34	98	8	24	2	0	2	14	15	15	1	.245	.327
2 Jimmy Wasdell	1B4, OF3	L	32	32	41	1	11	0	0	0	4	4	4	1	.268	.268
Sherm Lollar	C24	R	21	28	62	7	15	6	0	1	9	5	9	0	.242	.387

2 Tom Jordan 26 R 7-35, Blas Monaco 30 B 0-6, Dale Mitchell 24 L 19-44, Buster Mills 37 R 6-22, Rusty Peters (MS) 31 R 6-21, 2 Howie Moss 26 R 2-32, Johnny Price 33 L 3-13, Eddie Robinson 25 L 11-27, Ralph Weigel 24 R 2-12, Charlie Brewster 29 R 0-2, Ted Sepkowski 22 L 4-8, Eddie Carnett (MS) 29, Hank Ruszkowski (MS) 20

NAME	T	AGE	W	L	PCT	SV	G	GS	CG	IP	H	BB	SO	ShO	ERA
		29	68	86	.442	13	156	156	63	1389	1282	649	789	16	3.62
Bob Feller	R	27	26	15	.634	4	48	42	36	371	277	153	348	10	2.18
Allie Reynolds	R	31	11	15	.423	0	31	28	9	183	180	108	107	3	3.89
Red Embree (MS)	R	28	8	12	.400	0	28	26	8	200	170	79	87	0	3.47
Mel Harder (HJ)	R	36	5	4	.556	0	13	12	4	92	85	31	21	1	3.42
Steve Gromek	R	26	5	15	.250	4	29	21	5	154	159	47	75	0	4.33
Bob Lemon	R	25	4	5	.444	1	32	5	1	94	77	68	39	0	2.49
2 Joe Berry	R	41	3	6	.333	1	21	0	0	37	32	21	16	0	3.41
Joe Krakauskas	L	31	2	5	.286	1	29	5	0	47	60	25	20	0	5.55
Bob Kuzava	L	23	1	0	1.000	0	2	2	0	12	9	11	4	0	3.00
Charlie Gassaway	L	27	1	1	.500	0	13	6	0	51	54	26	23	0	3.88
2 Les Webber	R	31	1	1	.500	0	4	2	0	5	13	5	5	0	25.20
Don Black	R	29	1	2	.333	0	18	4	0	44	45	21	15	0	4.50
Vic Johnson	L	25	0	1	.000	0	9	1	0	14	20	8	3	0	9.00
Ray Flanigan	R	23	0	1	.000	0	3	1	0	9	11	8	2	0	11.00
Ralph McCabe	R	27	0	1	.000	0	1	1	0	4	5	2	3	0	11.25
Pete Center	R	24	0	2	.000	1	21	0	0	29	29	20	6	0	4.97
Tom Ferrick	R	31	0	0	.000	1	9	0	0	18	25	4	9	0	5.00
Eddie Klieman	R	28	0	0	.000	0	9	0	0	15	18	10	2	0	6.60
Johnny Podgajny	R	26	0	0	.000	0	6	0	0	9	13	2	4	0	5.00

ST. LOUIS 7th 66-88 .429 38

LUKE SEWELL 53-71 .427 ZACK TAYLOR 13-17 .433

NAME	G by POS	B	AGE	G	AB	R	H	2B	3B	HR	RBI	BB	SO	SB	BA	SA
TOTALS			29	156	5373	621	1350	220	46	84	576	465	713	23	.251	.356
Chuck Stevens	1B120	B	27	122	432	53	107	17	4	3	27	47	62	4	.248	.326
Johnny Berardino	2B143	R	29	144	582	70	154	29	5	5	68	34	58	2	.265	.357
Vern Stephens	SS112	R	25	115	450	67	138	19	4	14	64	35	49	0	.307	.460
Mark Christman	3B77, SS47	R	32	128	458	40	118	22	2	1	41	22	29	0	.258	.321
Al Zarilla	OF107	L	27	125	371	46	96	14	9	4	43	27	37	3	.259	.377
Walt Judnich	OF137	L	28	142	511	60	134	23	4	15	72	60	54	0	.262	.411
2 Jeff Heath	OF83	L	31	86	316	46	87	20	4	12	57	37	37	0	.275	.478
Frank Mancuso	C85	R	28	87	262	22	63	8	3	3	23	30	31	1	.240	.328
Johnny Lucadello	3B37, 2B19	B	27	87	210	21	52	7	1	1	15	36	20	0	.248	.305
Bob Dillinger	3B54, SS1	R	27	83	225	33	63	6	3	0	11	19	32	8	.280	.333
Chet Laabs	OF72	R	34	80	264	40	69	13	0	16	52	20	50	3	.261	.492
Hank Helf	C69	R	32	71	182	17	35	11	0	6	21	9	40	0	.192	.352
Glenn McQuillen	OF48	R	31	59	166	24	40	3	3	1	12	19	18	0	.241	.313
1 Joe Grace	OF43	L	32	48	161	21	37	7	2	1	13	16	20	1	.230	.317
Joe Schultz	C17	L	27	42	57	1	22	4	0	0	14	11	2	0	.386	.456
Babe Dahlgren	1B24	R	34	28	80	2	14	1	0	0	9	8	13	0	.175	.188
Jerry Witte	1B18	R	30	18	73	7	14	2	0	2	4	0	18	0	.192	.301
Lou Finney	OF7	L	35	16	30	0	9	0	0	0	3	2	4	0	.300	.300
Paul Lehner	OF12	L	26	16	45	6	10	1	2	0	5	1	5	0	.222	.333

Les Moss 21 R 13-35, Ken Sears 28 L 5-15, George Archie 32 R 2-11, George Bradley 32 R 2-12, Len Schulte 29 R 2-5, Babe Martin 26 R 2-9, Hank Schmulbach (MS) 21

NAME	T	AGE	W	L	PCT	SV	G	GS	CG	IP	H	BB	SO	ShO	ERA
		29	66	88	.429	12	156	156	63	1382	1465	573	574	13	3.95
Jack Kramer	R	28	13	11	.542	0	31	28	13	195	190	68	69	3	3.18
Sam Zoldak	L	27	9	11	.450	2	35	21	9	170	166	57	51	2	3.44
Nels Potter	R	34	8	9	.471	0	23	19	10	145	152	59	72	0	3.72
Denny Galehouse	R	34	8	12	.400	0	30	24	11	180	194	52	90	2	3.65
Tex Shirley	R	28	6	12	.333	0	27	18	7	140	148	105	45	0	4.95
Cliff Fannin	L	22	5	2	.714	2	27	7	4	87	76	42	52	1	3.00
2 Tom Ferrick	R	31	4	1	.800	5	25	1	0	32	26	5	13	0	2.81
Ellis Kinder	R	31	3	3	.500	1	33	7	1	87	78	36	59	0	3.31
Bob Muncrief	R	30	3	12	.200	0	29	14	4	115	149	31	49	1	5.01
Fred Sanford	R	26	2	1	.667	0	3	3	2	22	19	9	8	2	2.05
Stan Ferens	L	31	2	9	.182	0	34	6	1	88	100	38	28	0	4.50
Frank Biscan	L	26	1	1	.500	1	16	0	0	23	28	22	9	0	5.09
1 Al Milnar	L	32	1	1	.500	0	4	2	1	15	15	6	1	1	2.40
Ox Miller	R	31	1	3	.250	1	11	3	0	35	52	15	12	0	6.94
1 Al LaMacchia	R	24	0	0	.000	0	8	0	0	15	17	7	3	0	6.00
1 Al Hollingsworth	L	38	0	0	.000	0	5	0	0	11	23	4	3	0	6.55
Chet Johnson	L	28	0	0	.000	0	5	3	0	18	20	13	8	0	5.00
Steve Sundra	R	36	0	0	.000	0	2	0	0	4	9	3	1	0	11.25
Ray Shore	R	25	0	0	.000	0	1	0	0	1	3	1	1	0	18.00

PHILADELPHIA 8th 49-105 .318 55

CONNIE MACK

NAME	G by POS	B	AGE	G	AB	R	H	2B	3B	HR	RBI	BB	SO	SB	BA	SA
TOTALS			30	155	5200	529	1317	220	51	40	481	482	594	39	.253	.338
George McQuinn	1B134	L	37	136	484	47	109	23	6	3	35	64	62	4	.225	.316
Gene Handley	2B68, 3B4, SS1	R	31	89	251	31	63	8	5	0	21	22	25	8	.251	.323
Pete Suder	SS67, 3B33, 2B12, 1B3, OF2	R	30	128	455	38	128	20	3	2	50	18	37	1	.281	.352
2 Hank Majeski	3B72	R	29	78	264	25	66	14	3	1	25	26	13	3	.250	.337
Elmer Valo	OF90	L	25	108	348	59	107	21	6	1	31	60	18	9	.307	.411
2 Barney McCosky	OF85	L	28	92	308	33	109	17	4	1	34	43	13	2	.354	.445
Sam Chapman	OF145	R	30	146	545	77	142	22	5	20	67	54	66	1	.261	.429
Buddy Rosar	C117	R	31	121	424	34	120	22	2	2	47	36	17	1	.283	.358
Tuck Stainback	OF66	R	35	91	291	35	71	10	2	0	20	7	20	3	.244	.292
Russ Derry	OF50	L	29	69	184	17	38	8	5	0	14	27	54	0	.207	.304
Irv Hall	2B40, SS7	R	27	63	185	19	46	6	2	0	19	9	18	1	.249	.303
Jack Wallaesa	SS59	B	26	63	194	16	38	4	2	5	11	14	47	1	.196	.314
2 Oscar Grimes	2B43, 3B6, SS4	R	31	59	191	28	50	5	0	1	20	27	29	2	.262	.304
Gene Desautels	C52	R	39	52	130	10	28	3	1	0	13	12	16	1	.215	.254
Hal Peck (AJ)	OF35	L	29	48	150	14	37	8	2	2	11	16	14	1	.247	.367
John Caulfield	SS31, 3B1	R	27	44	94	13	26	8	0	0	10	4	11	0	.277	.362
Bruce Konopka	1B20, OF1	L	26	38	93	7	22	4	1	0	9	4	8	0	.237	.301
1 George Kell	3B26	R	23	26	87	3	26	6	1	0	11	10	6	0	.299	.391
Don Richmond	3B16	L	26	16	62	3	18	3	0	1	9	0	10	1	.290	.387

Ford Garrison 30 R 4-37, George Armstrong 22 R 1-6, Vern Benson 21 L 0-5, Joe Astroth 23 R 1-7, Bobby Estalella (SM) 35, George Yankowski (MS) 23

NAME	T	AGE	W	L	PCT	SV	G	GS	CG	IP	H	BB	SO	ShO	ERA
		28	49	105	.318	5	155	155	61	1343	1371	577	562	10	3.90
Phil Marchildon	R	32	13	16	.448	1	36	29	16	227	197	114	95	1	3.49
Jesse Flores	R	31	9	7	.563	1	29	15	8	155	147	38	48	4	2.32
Dick Fowler	R	25	9	16	.360	0	32	28	14	206	213	75	89	1	3.28
Russ Christopher	R	28	5	7	.417	0	30	13	1	119	119	44	79	0	4.31
1 Bobo Newsom	R	38	3	5	.375	0	10	9	3	59	61	30	32	1	3.36
Lum Harris	R	31	3	14	.176	0	34	12	4	125	153	48	33	0	5.26
Bob Savage	R	24	3	15	.167	2	40	19	7	164	164	93	78	1	4.06
Lou Knerr	R	24	3	16	.158	0	30	22	6	148	171	67	58	0	5.41
Bill McCahan	R	25	1	1	.500	0	4	2	2	18	16	9	6	1	1.00
Everett Fagan (MS)	R	28	0	1	.000	0	20	0	0	45	47	24	12	0	4.80
1 Joe Berry	R	41	0	1	.000	0	5	0	0	13	15	3	5	0	2.77
Norm Brown	R	27	0	1	.000	0	4	0	0	7	8	6	3	0	6.43
Jack Knott	R	39	0	1	.000	0	3	1	0	6	7	1	2	0	6.00
Herman Besse	L	34	0	2	.000	1	7	3	0	21	19	9	10	0	5.14
Joe Coleman	R	23	0	2	.000	0	4	2	0	13	19	8	8	0	5.54
Lee Griffeth	L	21	0	0	.000	0	10	0	0	15	13	6	4	0	3.00
Pat Cooper	R	28	0	0	.000	0	1	0	0	1	1	1	0	0	0.00
Porter Vaughan	L	27	0	0	.000	0	1	0	0	1	0	1	0	0	0.00

Fred Caligiuri (MS) 27, Lou Ciola (MS) 23, Tom Clyde (MS) 22, Burt Kuczynski (MS) 26, Sam Lowry (MS) 26, Carl Scheib (MS) 19

ST. LOUIS 1st 98-58 .628 — EDDIE DYER (Defeated Brooklyn in playoff 2 games to 0)

NAME	G by POS	B	AGE	G	AB	R	H	2B	3B	HR	RBI	BB	SO	SB	BA	SA
TOTALS			27	156	5372	712	1426	265	56	81	665	530	537	58	.265	.381
Stan Musial	1B114, OF42	L	25	156	624	124	228	50	20	16	103	73	31	7	.365	.587
Red Schoendienst	2B128, 3B12, SS4	B	23	142	606	94	170	28	5	0	34	37	27	12	.281	.343
Marty Marion	SS145	R	28	146	498	51	116	29	4	3	46	59	53	1	.233	.325
Whitey Kurowski	3B138	R	28	142	519	76	156	32	5	14	89	72	47	2	.301	.462
Enos Slaughter	OF156	L	30	156	609	100	183	30	8	18	130	69	41	9	.300	.465
Terry Moore (KJ)	OF66	R	34	91	278	32	73	14	1	3	28	18	26	0	.263	.353
Harry Walker	OF92, 1B8	L	29	112	346	53	82	14	6	3	27	30	29	12	.237	.338
Joe Garagiola	C70	L	20	74	211	21	50	4	1	3	22	23	25	0	.237	.308
Erv Dusak	OF77, 3B11, 2B2	R	25	100	275	38	66	9	1	9	42	33	63	7	.240	.378
Dick Sisler	1B37, OF29	L	25	83	235	17	61	11	2	3	42	14	28	0	.260	.362
Buster Adams	OF58	R	31	81	173	21	32	6	0	5	22	29	27	3	.185	.306
Del Rice	C53	R	23	55	139	10	38	8	1	1	12	8	16	0	.273	.367
2 Clyde Kluttz	C49	R	28	52	136	8	36	7	0	0	14	10	10	0	.265	.316
Jeff Cross	SS17, 2B8, 3B1	R	27	49	69	17	15	3	0	0	6	10	8	4	.217	.261
Lou Klein(SM)	2B23	R	27	23	93	12	18	3	0	1	4	9	7	1	.194	.258
1 Ken O'Dea	C22	L	33	22	57	2	7	2	0	1	3	8	8	0	.123	.211
Bill Endicott	OF2	L	27	20	20	2	4	3	0	0	3	4	4	0	.200	.350
Nippy Jones	2B3	R	21	16	12	3	4	0	0	0	1	2	2	0	.333	.333
Walter Sessi		L	27	15	14	2	2	0	0	1	2	1	4	0	.143	.357

1 Danny Litwhiler (MS) 29 R 0-5, Del Wilbur 27 R 0-4, 1 Emil Verban 30 R 0-1, Creepy Crespi (MS) 28

NAME	T	AGE	W	L	PCT	SV	G	GS	CG	IP	H	BB	SO	ShO	ERA
		30	98	58	.628	15	156	156	75	1397	1326	493	607	18	3.01
Howie Pollet	L	25	21	10	.677	5	40	32	22	266	228	86	107	4	2.10
Murray Dickson	R	29	15	6	.714	1	47	19	12	184	160	56	82	2	2.89
Harry Brecheen	L	31	15	15	.500	3	36	30	14	231	212	67	117	5	2.49
Al Brazle	L	32	11	10	.524	0	37	15	6	153	152	55	58	2	3.29
Ted Wilks	R	30	8	0	1.000	1	40	4	0	95	88	38	40	0	3.41
Johnny Beazley	R	28	7	5	.583	0	19	18	5	103	109	55	36	0	4.46
Max Lanier (SM)	L	30	6	0	1.000	0	6	6	6	56	45	19	36	2	1.93
Ken Burkhart	R	29	6	3	.667	2	25	13	5	100	111	36	32	2	2.88
Red Barrett	R	31	3	2	.600	2	23	9	1	67	75	24	22	1	4.03
Freddie Martin (SM)	R	31	2	1	.667	0	6	3	2	29	29	8	19	0	4.03
George Munger (MS)	R	27	2	2	.500	1	10	7	2	49	47	12	28	0	3.31
Freddy Schmidt	R	30	1	0	1.000	0	16	0	0	27	27	15	14	0	3.33
1 Blix Donnelly	R	32	1	2	.333	0	13	0	0	14	17	10	11	0	3.86
Howie Krist	R	30	0	2	.000	0	15	0	0	19	22	8	3	0	6.63
Johnny Grodzicki	R	29	0	0	.000	0	3	0	0	4	4	4	2	0	9.00

BROOKLYN 2nd 96-60 .615 2 — LEO DUROCHER (Defeated by St. Louis in playoff 2 games to 0)

NAME	G by POS	B	AGE	G	AB	R	H	2B	3B	HR	RBI	BB	SO	SB	BA	SA
TOTALS			28	157	5285	701	1376	233	66	55	642	691	575	100	.260	.361
Ed Stevens	1B99	L	21	103	310	34	75	13	7	10	60	27	44	2	.242	.426
Eddie Stanky	2B141	R	29	144	483	98	132	24	7	0	36	137	56	8	.273	.352
Pee Wee Reese	SS152	R	27	152	542	79	154	16	10	5	60	87	71	10	.284	.378
Cookie Lavagetto	3B67	R	33	88	242	36	57	9	1	3	27	38	17	3	.236	.318
Dixie Walker	OF149	L	35	150	576	80	184	29	9	9	116	67	28	14	.319	.448
Carl Furillo	OF112	R	24	117	335	29	95	18	6	3	35	31	20	6	.284	.400
Pete Reiser (BN)	OF97, 3B15	L	27	122	423	75	117	21	5	11	73	55	58	34	.277	.428
Bruce Edwards	C91	R	22	92	292	24	78	13	5	1	25	34	20	1	.267	.356
Dick Whitman	OF85	L	25	104	265	39	69	15	3	2	31	22	19	5	.260	.362
Augie Galan	OF60, 3B19, 1B12	L	34	99	274	53	85	22	5	3	38	68	21	8	.310	.460
Howie Schultz	1B87	R	23	90	249	27	63	14	1	3	27	16	34	2	.253	.353
Ferrell Anderson	C70	R	28	79	199	19	51	10	0	2	14	18	21	1	.256	.337
Gene Hermanski	OF34	L	26	64	110	15	22	2	2	0	8	17	10	2	.200	.255
Bob Ramazotti	3B30, 2B16	R	29	62	120	10	25	4	0	0	7	9	13	0	.208	.242
1 Billy Herman	3B29, 2B16	R	36	47	184	24	53	8	4	0	28	26	10	2	.288	.375
Stan Rojek	SS15, 2B6, 3B4	R	27	45	47	11	13	2	1	0	2	4	1	1	.277	.362
Joe Medwick	OF18, 1B1	R	34	41	77	7	24	4	0	2	18	6	5	0	.312	.442
Eddie Miksis (MS)	3B13, 2B1	R	19	23	48	3	7	0	0	0	5	3	3	0	.146	.146
1 Don Padgett	C10	L	34	19	30	2	5	1	0	1	9	4	4	0	.167	.300
Mike Sandlock	C17, 3B1	B	30	19	34	1	5	0	0	0	0	3	4	0	.147	.147

Joe Tepsic 22 R 0-5, Earl Naylor 27 R 0-2, 1 Goody Rosen 33 L 1-3, 1 Jack Graham 29 L 1-5, John Corriden 27 B 0-0, Tommy Brown (MS) 18,
Otis Davis 25 L 0-0, Lew Riggs 36 L 0-4, Luis Olmo (SM) 26, Mickey Owen (SM) 30, Arky Vaughan (VR) 30, Bobby Bragan (MS) 28, Lou Rochelli (MS) 27

NAME	T	AGE	W	L	PCT	SV	G	GS	CG	IP	H	BB	SO	ShO	ERA
		27	96	60	.615	28	157	157	52	1416	1280	671	647	14	3.05
Kirby Higbe	R	31	17	8	.680	1	42	29	11	211	178	107	134	3	3.03
Joe Hatten	L	29	14	11	.560	2	42	30	13	222	207	110	85	0	2.84
Vic Lombardi	L	23	13	10	.565	0	41	25	13	193	170	84	60	2	2.89
Hank Behrman	R	25	11	5	.688	4	47	11	2	151	138	69	78	0	2.92
Hugh Casey	R	32	11	5	.688	5	46	1	0	100	101	33	31	0	1.98
Art Herring	R	39	7	2	.778	5	35	2	0	86	91	29	34	0	3.35
Rube Melton (MS)	R	29	6	3	.667	1	24	12	3	100	72	52	44	2	1.98
Hal Gregg	R	24	6	4	.600	2	26	16	4	117	103	44	54	2	3.00
Ralph Branca	R	20	3	1	.750	3	24	10	2	67	62	41	42	2	3.90
Ed Head (SA)	R	28	3	2	.600	1	13	7	3	56	56	24	17	1	3.21
1 Les Webber	R	31	3	3	.500	0	11	4	0	43	34	15	16	0	2.30
Rex Barney	R	21	2	5	.286	0	16	9	1	54	46	51	36	0	5.83
Paul Minner (SJ)	L	22	0	1	.000	0	3	0	0	4	6	3	3	0	6.75
Harry Taylor	R	27	0	0	.000	1	4	0	0	5	5	1	6	0	3.60
Jean Pierre Roy	R	26	0	0	.000	0	3	1	0	6	5	5	6	0	10.50
Curt Davis	R	42	0	0	.000	0	1	0	0	2	3	2	0	0	13.50
Glen Moulder	R	28	0	0	.000	0	1	0	0	2	2	1	1	0	4.50
Cal McLish (MS)	R	20	0	0	.000	0	1	0	0	0	1	0	0	0	∞

CHICAGO 3rd 82-71 .536 14.5 — CHARLIE GRIMM

NAME	G by POS	B	AGE	G	AB	R	H	2B	3B	HR	RBI	BB	SO	SB	BA	SA
TOTALS			30	155	5298	626	1344	223	50	56	566	586	599	43	.254	.346
Eddie Waitkus	1B106	L	26	113	441	50	134	24	5	4	55	23	14	3	.304	.408
Don Johnson (BH)	2B83	R	34	83	314	37	76	10	1	1	19	26	39	6	.242	.290
Billy Jurges	SS73, 3B7, 2B2	R	38	82	221	26	49	9	2	0	17	43	28	3	.222	.281
Stan Hack (BG)	3B90	L	36	92	323	55	92	13	4	0	26	83	32	3	.285	.350
Phil Cavarretta	OF86, 1B51	L	29	130	510	89	150	28	10	8	78	88	54	2	.294	.435
Peanuts Lowrey	OF126, 3B20	R	27	144	540	75	139	24	5	4	54	56	22	10	.257	.343
Marv Rickert	OF104	L	25	111	392	44	103	18	3	7	47	28	54	3	.263	.378
Clyde McCullough	C89	R	29	95	307	38	88	18	5	4	34	22	39	2	.287	.417
Bill Nicholson	OF80	L	31	105	296	36	65	13	2	8	41	44	44	1	.220	.358
Bobby Sturgeon	SS72, 2B21	R	26	100	294	26	87	12	2	1	21	10	18	0	.296	.361
Lou Stringer	2B62, SS1, 3B1	R	29	80	209	26	51	3	1	3	19	26	34	0	.244	.311
Mickey Livingston (NJ)	C56	R	31	66	176	14	45	14	0	2	20	20	19	0	.256	.369
Andy Pafko (BN-BA)	OF64	R	25	65	234	18	66	6	4	3	30	27	15	4	.282	.380
Lennie Merullo	SS44	R	29	65	126	14	19	8	0	0	7	11	13	2	.151	.214
Dom Dallessandro	OF20	L	32	65	89	4	20	2	2	1	9	23	12	1	.225	.326
John Ostrowski	3B50, 2B1	R	30	64	160	20	34	4	2	3	12	20	31	1	.213	.319
Bob Scheffing	C43	R	33	63	115	8	32	4	1	0	18	12	18	0	.278	.330
Frank Secory	OF9	R	33	33	43	6	10	3	0	3	12	6	6	0	.233	.512

1 Charlie Gilbert 26 L 1-13, 1 Heinz Becker 30 B 2-7, Cy Block 27 R 3-13, Rabbit Garriott 29 L 0-5, Hank Schenz 27 R 2-11,
Al Glossop 33 B 0-10, Ted Pawelek 26 L 1-4, Dewey Williams 30 R 1-5, Clarence Maddern 24 R 0-3

NAME	T	AGE	W	L	PCT	SV	G	GS	CG	IP	H	BB	SO	ShO	ERA
		30	82	71	.536	11	155	155	59	1393	1370	527	609	15	3.24
Hank Wyse	R	28	14	12	.538	1	40	27	12	201	206	52	52	2	2.69
Hank Borowy	R	30	12	10	.545	0	32	28	8	201	220	61	95	1	3.76
Johnny Schmitz	L	25	11	11	.500	2	41	31	14	224	184	94	135	2	2.61
Emil Kush	R	29	9	2	.818	2	40	6	1	130	120	43	50	1	3.05
Paul Erickson	R	30	9	7	.563	0	32	14	5	137	119	65	70	1	2.43
Claude Passeau	R	37	9	8	.529	0	21	21	10	129	118	42	47	2	3.14
Bob Chipman	L	27	6	5	.545	2	34	10	5	109	103	54	42	3	3.14
Hi Bithorn	R	30	6	5	.545	1	26	7	2	87	97	25	34	1	3.83
Rus Bauers	R	32	2	1	.667	1	15	2	2	43	45	19	22	0	3.56
Ray Prim (AJ)	L	39	2	3	.400	1	14	2	0	23	28	10	10	0	5.87
Ed Hanyzewski	R	25	1	0	1.000	0	3	0	0	6	8	5	1	0	4.50
Russ Meers	L	27	1	2	.333	0	7	2	0	11	10	10	2	0	3.27
Bill Fleming	R	32	0	1	.000	0	14	1	0	29	37	12	10	0	6.21
Red Adams	R	24	0	1	.000	0	8	0	0	12	18	7	8	0	8.25
2 Hal Manders	R	29	0	1	.000	0	2	1	0	6	11	3	4	0	9.00
Doyle Lade	R	25	0	2	.000	0	3	2	0	15	15	3	8	0	4.20
Vern Olsen	L	28	0	0	.000	0	5	0	0	10	10	9	8	0	2.70
Russ Meyer	R	22	0	0	.000	1	4	1	0	17	21	10	10	0	3.18
1 Emmett O'Neill	R	28	0	0	.000	0	1	0	0	1	0	3	1	0	0.00

BOSTON 4th 81-72 .529 15.5 — BILLY SOUTHWORTH

NAME	G by POS	B	AGE	G	AB	R	H	2B	3B	HR	RBI	BB	SO	SB	BA	SA
TOTALS			29	154	5225	630	1377	238	48	44	596	558	468	60	.264	.353
Ray Sanders	1B77	L	29	80	259	43	63	12	0	6	35	50	38	0	.243	.359
Connie Ryan	2B120, 3B24	R	26	143	502	55	121	28	8	1	48	55	63	7	.241	.335
Dick Culler	SS132	R	31	134	482	70	123	15	3	0	33	62	18	7	.255	.299
Nanny Fernandez	3B81, SS18, OF14	R	27	115	372	37	95	15	2	2	42	30	44	1	.255	.323
Tommy Holmes	OF146	L	29	149	568	80	176	35	6	6	79	58	14	7	.310	.424
Carden Gillenwater	OF78	R	28	99	224	30	51	10	1	1	14	39	27	3	.228	.295
Bama Rowell	OF85	L	30	95	293	37	82	12	6	3	31	29	15	5	.280	.392
Phil Masi	C124	R	29	133	397	52	106	17	5	3	62	55	41	5	.267	.358
Johnny Hopp	1B68, OF58	L	29	129	445	71	148	23	8	3	48	34	34	21	.333	.440
2 Danny Litwhiler	OF65, 3B2	R	29	79	247	29	72	12	2	8	38	19	23	1	.291	.453
2 Billy Herman	2B44, 1B22, 3B5	R	36	75	252	32	77	23	1	3	22	43	13	1	.306	.440
2 Mike McCormick	OF48	R	29	59	164	23	43	6	2	1	16	11	7	0	.262	.341
Skippy Roberge	3B48	R	29	48	169	13	39	6	2	2	20	7	12	1	.231	.325
2 Don Padgett	C26	L	34	44	98	6	25	3	0	2	21	5	7	1	.255	.347
Whitey Wietelmann	SS16, 3B8, 2B4, P3	B	27	44	78	7	16	0	0	0	5	14	8	0	.205	.205
Johnny Sain	P37	R	28	40	94	6	28	2	1	0	17	0	0	0	.298	.340
1 Chuck Workman	OF12	L	31	25	48	5	8	2	0	2	7	3	11	0	.167	.333
2 Johnny Barrett	OF17	L	30	24	43	3	10	3	0	0	6	12	1	0	.233	.302
Stew Hofferth	C15	R	33	20	58	3	12	1	1	0	10	3	6	0	.207	.259

Al Dark 24 R 3-13, Tommy Neill 26 L 12-45, 2 Ken O'Dea 33 L 7-32, Hugh Poland 33 L 1-6, Bob Brady 23 L 1-5,
Johnny McCarthy 36 L 1-7, Damon Phillips 27 R 1-2, Ducky Detweiler 26 R 0-1, Sibby Sisti 25 R 0-0, 1 Max West 29 L 0-1, Max Macon (MS) 30

NAME	T	AGE	W	L	PCT	SV	G	GS	CG	IP	H	BB	SO	ShO	ERA
		31	81	72	.529	12	154	154	74	1371	1291	478	531	10	3.37
Johnny Sain	R	28	20	14	.588	2	37	34	24	265	225	87	129	3	2.21
Mort Cooper	R	33	13	11	.542	1	28	27	15	199	181	39	83	3	3.12
Ed Wright	R	27	12	9	.571	0	36	21	9	176	164	71	44	2	3.53
Bill Lee	R	36	10	9	.526	0	25	21	8	140	148	45	32	0	4.18
Warren Spahn	L	25	8	5	.615	1	24	16	8	126	107	36	67	0	2.93
2 Si Johnson	R	39	6	5	.545	1	28	12	5	127	134	35	41	1	2.76
Lefty Wallace	L	24	3	3	.500	0	27	8	2	75	76	31	27	0	4.20
Bill Posedel	R	39	2	0	1.000	4	19	0	0	28	34	13	9	0	7.07
Frank Barrett	R	33	2	4	.333	1	23	0	0	35	35	17	12	0	5.14
Johnny Niggeling	R	42	2	5	.286	0	8	8	3	58	54	21	24	0	3.26
Dick Mulligan	L	28	1	0	1.000	0	4	0	0	15	6	9	4	0	2.40
Earl Reid	R	33	1	0	1.000	0	2	0	0	3	4	3	2	0	3.00
Steve Roser	R	28	1	1	.500	1	14	1	0	35	33	18	18	0	3.60
Elmer Singleton	R	28	0	1	.000	1	15	2	0	34	27	21	17	0	3.71
Ernie White	L	29	0	1	.000	0	12	1	0	24	22	12	8	0	4.13
Jim Konstanty	R	29	0	1	.000	0	10	1	0	15	17	7	9	0	5.40
Dan Hendrickson	R	30	0	1	.000	0	2	0	0	2	4	2	2	0	4.50
Al Javery	R	28	0	1	.000	0	2	1	0	3	5	5	0	0	15.00
Johnny Hutchings	R	30	0	1	.000	0	1	1	0	3	5	1	1	0	9.00

Whitey Wietelmann 27 R 0-0, Ace Williams 29 L 0-0, Ray Martin (MS) 21

PHILADELPHIA 5th 69-85 .448 28 — BEN CHAPMAN

NAME	G by POS	B	AGE	G	AB	R	H	2B	3B	HR	RBI	BB	SO	SB	BA	SA
TOTALS			29	155	5233	560	1351	209	40	80	517	417	590	41	.258	.359
Frank McCormick	1B134	R	35	135	504	46	143	20	2	11	66	36	21	2	.284	.397
2 Emil Verban	2B138	R	30	138	473	44	130	17	5	0	34	21	18	5	.275	.332
Skeeter Newsome	SS107, 2B3, 3B2	R	35	112	375	35	87	10	2	1	23	30	23	4	.232	.277
Jim Tabor	3B124	R	32	124	463	53	124	15	2	10	50	36	51	3	.268	.374
Ron Northey	OF111	L	26	128	438	55	109	24	6	16	62	39	59	1	.249	.441
Johnny Wyrostek	OF142	L	26	145	545	73	153	30	4	6	45	70	42	7	.281	.383
Del Ennis	OF138	R	21	141	540	70	169	30	6	17	73	39	65	5	.313	.485
Andy Seminick	C118	R	25	124	406	55	107	15	5	12	52	39	86	2	.264	.414
Roy Hughes	SS34, 3B31, 2B7, 1B1	R	35	89	276	23	65	11	1	0	22	19	15	7	.236	.283
2 Charlie Gilbert	OF69	L	26	88	260	34	63	5	2	1	17	25	18	3	.242	.288
Vance Dinges	1B26, OF1	L	31	50	104	7	32	5	1	1	10	9	12	2	.308	.404
Rollie Hemsley (BW)	C45	R	39	49	139	7	31	4	1	0	11	9	10	0	.223	.266
Oscar Judd	P30	L	38	46	79	7	25	2	1	1	8	4	4	0	.316	.405
John O'Neil	SS32	R	26	46	94	12	25	3	0	0	9	5	12	0	.266	.298
1 Jimmy Wasdell	OF11, 1B2	L	32	26	51	7	13	0	2	1	5	3	2	0	.255	.392
Lou Novikoff	OF3	R	30	17	23	0	7	1	0	0	3	1	2	0	.234	.348

Dee Moore 32 R 1-13, 1 Vince DiMaggio 33 R 4-19, Don Hasenmayer 19 R 1-12, Charlie Letchas (MS) 30 R 3-13, Danny Murtaugh 28 R 4-19,
Ken Richardson 31 R 3-20, Bill Burich (MS) 28 R 0-1, Granny Hamner 19 R 1-7, Glenn Crawford 32 L 0-1, Hal Spindel 33 R 1-3, Ray Hamrick (MS) 24, Moon Mullen (MS) 29

NAME	T	AGE	W	L	PCT	SV	G	GS	CG	IP	H	BB	SO	ShO	ERA
		30	69	85	.448	23	155	155	55	1369	1442	542	490	11	3.99
Schoolboy Rowe	R	36	11	4	.733	0	17	16	9	136	112	21	51	2	2.12
Oscar Judd	L	38	11	12	.478	2	30	24	12	173	169	90	65	1	3.54
Ken Raffensberger	L	28	8	15	.348	6	39	23	14	196	203	39	73	2	3.63
Dick Mauney	R	26	6	4	.600	2	24	7	3	90	98	18	31	1	2.70
Charley Schanz	R	27	6	6	.500	4	32	15	4	116	130	71	47	0	5.82
Tommy Hughes	R	26	6	9	.400	1	29	13	3	111	123	44	34	2	4.38
Al Jurisich	R	24	4	3	.571	1	13	10	2	68	71	31	34	1	3.71
2 Blix Donnelly	R	32	3	4	.429	1	12	8	2	76	64	24	38	0	2.96
Andy Karl	R	32	3	7	.300	5	39	0	0	65	84	22	15	0	4.98
1 Dick Mulligan	L	28	2	2	.500	1	19	5	1	55	61	27	16	0	4.75
Hugh Mulcahy	R	32	2	4	.333	0	16	5	1	63	69	33	12	0	4.43
2 Charley Stanceu	R	30	2	4	.333	0	14	11	1	70	71	39	23	0	4.24
Charlie Ripple	L	24	1	0	1.000	0	6	0	0	3	5	6	3	0	12.00
Ike Pearson	R	29	1	0	1.000	0	5	2	1	14	19	8	6	1	3.86

Don Grate 22 R 1-0, Lou Possehl 20 R 1-2, Frank Hoerst 28 L 1-6, Art Lopatka 26 L 0-1,
Eli Hodkey 28 L 0-1, Dick Koecher 20 L 0-1, John Humphries 31 R 0-0, Ben Chapman 37 R 0-0,
1 Si Johnson 39 R 0-0, 2 Al Milnar 32 L 0-0, George Eyrich (MS) 21, Rogers McKee (MS) 19

CINCINNATI 6th 67-87 .435 30 — **BILL McKECHNIE**

NAME	G by POS	B	AGE	G	AB	R	H	2B	3B	HR	RBI	BB	SO	SB	BA	SA
TOTALS			28	156	5291	523	1262	206	33	65	481	493	604	82	.239	.327
Bert Haas	1B131, 3B6	R	32	140	535	57	141	24	7	3	50	33	42	22	.264	.351
Bobby Adams	2B74, OF2, 3B1	R	24	94	311	35	76	13	3	4	24	18	32	16	.244	.344
Eddie Miller	SS88	R	29	91	299	30	58	10	0	6	36	25	34	5	.194	.288
Grady Hatton	3B116, OF2	L	23	116	436	56	118	18	3	14	69	66	53	6	.271	.422
Al Libke	OF115, P1	L	28	124	431	32	109	22	1	5	42	43	50	0	.253	.343
Dain Clay	OF120	R	26	121	435	52	99	17	0	2	22	53	40	11	.228	.280
Eddie Lukon	OF83	L	25	102	312	31	78	8	8	12	34	26	29	3	.250	.442
Ray Mueller	C100	R	34	114	378	35	96	18	4	8	48	27	37	0	.254	.386
Lonny Frey	2B65, OF28	L	35	111	333	46	82	10	3	3	24	63	31	5	.246	.321
Bob Usher	OF80, 3B1	R	21	92	152	16	31	5	1	1	14	13	27	2	.204	.270
Ray Lamanno	C61	R	26	85	239	18	58	12	0	1	30	11	26	0	.243	.305
Claude Corbitt	SS77	R	30	82	274	25	68	10	1	1	16	23	13	3	.248	.303
Benny Zientara	2B39, 3B36	R	26	78	280	26	81	10	2	0	16	14	11	3	.289	.339
2 Max West	OF58	L	29	72	202	16	43	13	0	5	18	32	36	1	.213	.351
Eddie Shokes	1B29	L	26	31	83	3	10	1	0	0	5	18	21	1	.120	.133
Al Lakeman	C6	R	27	23	30	0	4	0	0	0	4	2	7	0	.133	.133
1 Mike McCormick	OF21	R	29	23	74	10	16	2	0	0	5	8	4	0	.216	.243

Clyde Vollmer 24 R 4-22, 1 Howie Moss 26 R 5-26, Lonnie Goldstein (MS) 28 L 0-5, 1 Garland Lawing 26 R 0-3

NAME	T	AGE	W	L	PCT	SV	G	GS	CG	IP	H	BB	SO	ShO	ERA
		31	67	87	.435	11	156	156	69	1414	1334	467	506	17	3.07
Joe Beggs	R	35	12	10	.545	1	28	22	14	190	175	39	38	3	2.32
Bucky Walters	R	37	10	7	.588	0	22	22	10	151	146	64	60	2	2.56
Johnny Vander Meer	L	31	10	12	.455	0	29	25	11	204	175	78	94	5	3.18
Ewell Balckwell	R	23	9	13	.409	0	33	25	10	194	160	79	100	6	2.46
Ed Heusser	R	37	7	14	.333	2	29	21	9	168	167	39	47	1	3.21
Johnny Hetki	R	24	6	6	.500	1	32	11	4	126	121	31	41	0	3.00
Harry Gumbert	R	36	6	8	.429	4	36	10	5	119	112	42	44	0	3.25
Clay Lambert	R	29	2	2	.500	1	23	4	2	53	48	20	20	0	4.25
1 Nate Andrews	R	32	2	4	.333	0	7	7	3	43	50	8	13	0	3.98
Bob Malloy (MS)	R	28	2	5	.286	2	27	3	1	72	71	28	24	0	2.75
Clyde Shoun	L	34	1	6	.143	0	27	5	0	79	87	26	20	0	4.10
Howie Fox	R	25	0	0	.000	0	4	0	0	5	12	5	1	0	18.00
George Burpo	L	24	0	0	.000	0	2	0	0	2	4	5	1	0	18.00
Frank Dasso	R	28	0	0	.000	0	2	0	0	1	2	2	1	0	27.00
Al Libke	R	28	0	0	.000	0	1	1	0	5	4	3	2	0	3.60

Elmer Riddle (VR) 31, Mike Modak (MS) 24, Kent Peterson (MS) 20

PITTSBURGH 7th 63-91 .409 34 — **FRANKIE FRISCH 62-89 .411** — **SPUD DAVIS 1-2 .333**

NAME	G by POS	B	AGE	G	AB	R	H	2B	3B	HR	RBI	BB	SO	SB	BA	SA
TOTALS			29	155	5199	552	1300	202	52	60	508	592	555	48	.250	.344
Elbie Fletcher	1B147	L	30	148	532	72	136	25	8	4	66	111	37	4	.256	.355
Frankie Gustine	2B113, SS13, 3B7	R	26	131	495	60	128	23	6	8	52	40	52	2	.259	.378
Billy Cox	SS114	R	26	121	411	32	119	22	6	2	36	26	15	4	.290	.387
Lee Handley	3B102, 2B3	R	32	116	416	43	99	8	7	1	28	29	20	4	.238	.298
Bob Elliott	OF92, 3B43	R	29	140	486	50	128	25	3	5	68	64	44	6	.263	.358
Jim Russell	OF134, 1B5	B	27	146	516	68	143	29	6	8	50	67	54	11	.277	.403
Ralph Kiner	OF140	R	23	144	502	63	124	17	3	23	81	74	109	3	.247	.430
Al Lopez(BH)	C56	R	37	56	150	13	46	2	0	1	12	23	14	1	.307	.340
Jimmy Brown	SS30, 2B21, 3B9	B	36	79	241	23	58	6	0	0	12	18	5	3	.241	.266
Bill Salkeld	C51	L	29	69	160	18	47	8	0	3	19	39	16	2	.294	.400
Al Gionfriddo (IL)	OF33	L	24	64	102	11	26	2	2	0	10	14	5	1	.255	.314
Maurice Van Robays	OF37, 1B2	R	31	59	146	14	31	5	3	1	12	11	15	0	.212	.308
2 Chuck Workman	OF40, 3B1	L	31	58	145	11	32	4	1	2	16	11	19	2	.221	.303
Burgess Whitehead	2B30, 3B4, SS1	R	36	55	127	10	28	1	2	0	5	6	6	3	.220	.260
Bill Baker	C41, 1B1	R	35	53	113	7	27	4	0	1	8	12	6	0	.239	.301
Hank Camelli	C39	R	31	42	96	8	20	2	2	0	5	8	9	0	.208	.271
1 Johnny Barrett	OF21	L	30	32	71	7	12	3	0	0	6	8	11	1	.169	.211
Fritz Ostermueller	P27	L	38	28	64	7	21	3	0	0	2	5	8	0	.328	.375
1 Frank Colman	OF8, 1B2	L	28	26	53	3	9	3	0	1	6	2	7	0	.170	.283
Frankie Zak	SS10	R	24	21	20	8	4	0	0	0	0	1	0	0	.200	.200

Vinnie Smith (KJ) 30 R 4-21, Pete Coscarart 33 R 1-2, Alf Anderson 32 R 0-1, Vic Barnhart 23 R 0-1, Ben Guintini 26 R 0-3, Roy Jarvis (MS) 20 R 1-4, Billy Sullivan (MS) 35

NAME	T	AGE	W	L	PCT	SV	G	GS	CG	IP	H	BB	SO	ShO	ERA
		31	63	91	.409	6	155	155	61	1370	1406	541	458	10	3.72
Fritz Ostermueller	L	38	13	10	.565	0	27	25	16	193	193	56	57	2	2.84
Nick Strincevich	R	31	10	15	.400	1	32	22	11	176	185	44	49	3	3.58
Ed Bahr	R	26	8	6	.571	0	27	14	7	137	128	52	44	0	2.63
Ken Heintzelman	L	30	8	12	.400	1	32	24	6	158	165	86	57	2	3.76
Rip Sewell	R	39	8	12	.400	0	25	20	11	149	140	53	33	0	3.68
Jack Hallett	R	32	5	7	.417	0	35	9	3	115	107	39	64	1	3.29
Johnny Lanning	R	35	4	5	.444	1	27	9	3	91	97	31	16	0	3.07
Preacher Roe	L	31	3	8	.273	2	21	10	1	70	83	25	28	0	5.14
Al Gerheauser	L	29	2	2	.500	0	35	3	1	82	92	25	32	0	3.95
Ken Gables	R	27	2	4	.333	1	32	7	0	101	113	52	39	0	5.26
Junior Walsh	R	27	0	1	.000	0	4	2	0	10	9	10	2	0	5.40
Lee Howard	L	22	0	1	.000	0	3	2	1	13	14	9	6	0	2.08
Jim Hopper	R	27	0	1	.000	0	2	1	0	4	6	3	1	0	11.25
Al Tate	R	28	0	1	.000	0	2	1	1	9	8	7	2	0	5.00
Ed Albosta	R	27	0	6	.000	0	17	6	0	40	41	35	19	0	6.08
Hank Gornicki	R	35	0	0	.000	0	7	0	0	13	12	11	4	0	3.46
Lefty Wilkie	L	31	0	0	.000	0	7	0	0	8	13	3	3	0	10.13
Bill Clemensen	R	27	0	0	.000	0	1	0	0	2	0	0	2	0	0.00

NEW YORK 8th 61-93 .396 36 — **MEL OTT**

NAME	G by POS	B	AGE	G	AB	R	H	2B	3B	HR	RBI	BB	SO	SB	BA	SA
TOTALS			29	154	5191	612	1326	176	37	121	576	532	546	46	.255	.374
Johnny Mize (BH)	1B101	L	33	101	377	70	127	18	3	22	70	62	26	3	.337	.576
Buddy Blattner	2B114, 1B1	R	26	126	420	63	107	18	6	11	49	56	52	12	.255	.405
Buddy Kerr	SS126, 3B18	R	23	145	497	50	124	20	3	6	40	53	31	7	.249	.338
Bill Rigney	3B73, SS33	R	27	110	360	38	85	9	1	3	31	36	29	9	.236	.292
2 Goody Rosen	OF84	L	33	100	310	39	87	11	4	5	30	48	32	2	.281	.390
Willard Marshall	OF125	L	25	131	510	63	144	18	3	13	48	33	29	3	.282	.406
Sid Gordon	OF101, 3B30	R	28	135	450	64	132	15	4	5	45	60	27	1	.293	.378
Walker Cooper (EJ)	C73	R	31	87	280	29	75	10	1	8	46	17	12	0	.268	.396
Babe Young	1B49, OF24	L	31	104	291	30	81	11	0	7	33	30	21	3	.278	.388
2 Jack Graham	OF62, 1B7	L	29	100	270	34	59	6	4	14	47	23	37	1	.219	.426
Johnny Rucker	OF54	L	29	95	197	28	52	8	2	1	13	7	27	4	.264	.340
Ernie Lombardi	C63	R	38	88	238	19	69	4	1	12	39	18	24	0	.290	.466
Mikey Witek (JJ)	2B42, 3B35	R	30	82	284	32	75	13	2	4	29	28	10	1	.264	.366
Bennie Warren	C30	R	34	39	69	7	11	1	1	4	8	14	21	0	.159	.377
Mel Ott	OF16	L	37	31	68	2	5	1	0	1	4	8	15	0	.074	.132
Bobby Thomson	3B16	R	22	18	54	8	17	4	1	2	9	4	5	0	.315	.537
Jess Pike	OF10	L	29	16	41	4	7	1	1	1	6	6	9	0	.171	.317
2 Vince DiMaggio	OF13	R	33	15	25	2	0	0	0	0	0	2	5	0	.000	.000
2 Garland Lawing	OF4	R	26	8	12	2	2	0	0	0	0	0	3	0	.167	.167

Mickey Grasso 26 R 3-22, Buster Maynard 33 R 0-4, Dick Lajeskie 20 R 2-10, Dick Bartell 38 R 0-2, 1 Clyde Kluttz 28 R 3-8, Jim Gladd 23 R 1-11,
Morrie Arnovich 35 R 0-3, Mike Schemer 28 L 0-1, Danny Gardella (SM) 26, George Hausmann (SM) 30, Nap Reyes (SM) 28, Vic Bradford (MS) 31, Whitey Lockman (MS) 19

NAME	T	AGE	W	L	PCT	SV	G	GS	CG	IP	H	BB	SO	ShO	ERA
		28	61	93	.396	13	154	154	48	1353	1299	660	581	8	3.92
Dave Koslo	L	26	14	19	.424	1	40	35	17	265	251	101	121	3	3.63
Monte Kennedy	L	24	9	10	.474	1	38	27	10	187	153	116	71	1	3.42
Bill Voiselle	R	27	9	15	.375	0	36	25	10	178	171	85	89	2	3.74
Ken Trinkle	R	26	7	14	.333	2	48	13	2	151	146	74	49	0	3.87
Hal Schumacher	R	35	4	4	.500	1	24	13	2	97	95	52	48	0	3.90
Junior Thompson	R	29	4	6	.400	4	39	1	0	63	36	40	31	0	1.29
Bob Joyce	R	31	3	4	.429	0	14	7	2	61	79	20	24	0	5.31
Tex Kraus	L	28	2	1	.667	0	17	1	0	25	25	15	7	0	6.12
Mike Budnick	R	26	2	3	.400	3	35	7	1	88	75	48	36	1	3.17
Johnny Gee	L	30	2	4	.333	0	13	6	1	47	60	15	22	0	4.02
2 Nate Andrews	R	32	1	0	1.000	0	3	2	1	12	17	4	5	0	6.00
Woody Abernathy	L	31	1	1	.500	1	15	1	0	40	32	10	6	0	3.38
Rube Fischer	R	29	1	2	.333	0	15	1	0	36	48	21	14	0	6.25
Sheldon Jones	R	24	1	2	.333	0	6	4	1	28	21	17	24	0	3.21
Bob Carpenter (JJ)	R	28	1	3	.250	0	12	6	1	39	37	18	13	1	4.85
Ace Adams (SM)	R	34	0	1	.000	0	3	0	0	3	9	1	3	0	15.00
Marv Grissom	R	28	0	2	.000	0	4	3	0	19	17	13	9	0	4.26
Harry Feldman (SM)	R	26	0	2	.000	0	3	2	0	4	9	3	3	0	18.00

Slim Emmerich 26 R 0-0, Jack Breuer 26 R 0-0, John Carden 25 R 0-0, Red Kress 39 R 0-0,
Sal Maglie (SM) 29, Adrian Zabala (SM) 29, Andy Hansen (MS) 21

WORLD SERIES – ST. LOUIS (NL) 4 BOSTON (AL) 3

LINE SCORES

TEAM	1	2	3	4	5	6	7	8	9	10	11	12	R	H	E
Game 1 October 6 at St. Louis															
BOS (AL)	0	1	0	0	0	0	0	0	1	1			3	9	2
STL (NL)	0	0	0	0	0	1	0	1	0	0			2	7	0
Hughson, Johnson (9) — Pollet															
Game 2 October 7 at St. Louis															
BOS	0	0	0	0	0	0	0	0	0				0	4	1
STL	0	0	1	0	2	0	0	0	X				3	6	0
Harris, Dobson (8) — Brecheen															
Game 3 October 9 at Boston															
STL	0	0	0	0	0	0	0	0	0				0	6	1
BOS	3	0	0	0	0	0	0	1	X				4	8	0
Dickson, Wilks (8) — Ferriss															
Game 4 October 10 at Boston															
STL	0	3	3	0	1	0	1	0	4				12	20	1
BOS	0	0	0	1	0	0	0	2	0				3	9	4
Munger — Hughson, Bagby (3), Zuber (6), Brown (8), Ryba (9), Dreisewerd (9)															
Game 5 October 11 at Boston															
STL	0	1	0	0	0	0	0	0	2				3	4	1
BOS	1	1	0	0	0	1	3	0	X				6	11	3
Pollet, Brazle (1), Beazley (8) — Dobson															
Game 6 October 13 at St. Louis															
BOS	0	0	0	0	0	0	1	0	0				1	7	0
STL	0	0	3	0	0	0	0	1	X				4	8	0
Harris, Hughson (3), Johnson (8) — Brecheen															
Game 7 October 15 at St. Louis															
BOS	1	0	0	0	0	0	0	2	0				3	8	0
STL	0	1	0	0	2	0	0	1	X				4	9	1
Ferriss, Dobson (5), Klinger (8), Johnson (8) — Dickson, Brecheen (8)															

COMPOSITE BATTING

NAME	POS	G	AB	R	H	2B	3B	HR	RBI	BA
St. Louis (NL)										
Totals		7	232	28	60	19	2	1	27	.259
Schoendienst	2B	7	30	3	7	1	0	0	1	.233
Kurowski	3B	7	27	5	8	3	0	0	2	.296
Musial	1B	7	27	3	6	4	1	0	4	.222
Moore	OF	7	27	1	4	0	0	0	2	.148
Slaughter	OF	7	25	5	8	1	1	1	2	.320
Marion	SS	7	24	1	6	2	0	0	4	.250
Garagiola	C	5	19	2	6	2	0	0	4	.316
Walker	OF	7	17	3	7	2	0	0	6	.412
Brecheen	P	3	8	2	1	0	0	0	1	.125
Rice	C	3	6	2	3	1	0	0	0	.500
Dickson	P	2	5	1	2	2	0	0	1	.400
Dusak	OF	4	4	0	1	1	0	0	0	.250
Munger	P	1	4	0	1	0	0	0	0	.250
Pollet	P	2	4	0	0	0	0	0	0	.000
Sisler	PH	2	2	0	0	0	0	0	0	.000
Brazle	P	1	2	0	0	0	0	0	0	.000
Jones	PH	1	1	0	0	0	0	0	0	.000
Beazley	P	1	0	0	0	0	0	0	0	.000
Wilks	P	1	0	0	0	0	0	0	0	.000
Boston (AL)										
Totals		7	233	20	56	7	1	4	18	.240
Pesky	SS	7	30	2	7	0	0	0	0	.233
DiMaggio	OF	7	27	2	7	3	0	0	3	.259
Williams	OF	7	25	2	5	0	0	0	1	.200
Higgins	3B	7	24	1	5	1	0	0	2	.208
York	1B	7	23	6	6	1	1	2	5	.261
Doerr	2B	6	22	1	9	1	0	1	3	.409
H. Wagner	C	5	13	0	0	0	0	0	0	.000
Moses	OF	4	12	1	5	0	0	0	0	.417
McBride	OF	5	12	0	2	0	0	0	1	.167
Partee	C	5	10	1	1	0	0	0	1	.100
Culberson	OF	5	9	1	2	0	0	1	1	.222
Ferriss	P	2	6	0	0	0	0	0	0	.000
Gutteridge	2B	3	5	1	2	0	0	0	1	.400
Harris	P	3	3	0	1	0	0	0	0	.333
Hughson	P	3	3	0	1	0	0	0	0	.333
Dobson	P	3	3	0	0	0	0	0	0	.000
Russell	3B	2	2	1	2	0	0	0	0	1.000
Metkovich	PH	2	2	1	1	1	0	0	0	.500
Johnson	P	3	1	0	0	0	0	0	0	.000
Bagby	P	1	1	0	0	0	0	0	0	.000

Brown P 0-0, Campbell PR 0-0, Dreisewerd P 0-0, Klinger P 0-0, Ryba P 0-0, Zuber P 0-0

COMPOSITE PITCHING

NAME	G	IP	H	BB	SO	W	L	SV	ERA
St. Louis (NL)									
Totals	7	62	56	22	28	4	3	0	2.32
Brecheen	3	20	14	5	11	3	0	0	0.45
Dickson	2	14	11	4	7	0	1	0	3.86
Pollet	2	10.1	12	4	3	0	1	0	3.48
Munger	1	9	9	3	2	1	0	0	1.00
Brazle	1	6.2	7	6	4	0	1	0	5.40
Beazley	1	1	1	0	1	0	0	0	0.00
Wilks	1	1	2	1	0	0	0	0	0.00
Boston (AL)									
Totals	7	61	60	19	30	3	4	0	2.95
Hughson	3	14.1	14	3	8	0	1	0	3.14
Ferriss	2	13.1	13	2	4	1	0	0	2.02
Dobson	3	12.2	4	3	10	1	0	0	0.00
Harris	2	9.2	11	4	5	0	2	0	4.82
Johnson	3	3.1	1	2	1	1	0	0	2.70
Bagby	1	3	6	1	1	0	0	0	3.00
Zuber	1	2	3	1	1	0	0	0	4.50
Brown	1	1	4	1	0	0	0	0	27.00
Ryba	1	.2	2	1	0	0	0	0	0.00
Klinger	1	.2	2	1	0	0	1	0	13.50
Dreisewerd	1	.1	0	0	0	0	0	0	0.00

1947 Never a Dull Moment

Before the season got underway, it seemed to at least promise some good races and the usual array of dramatics. Certainly no one expected anything unusual before the season started.

One of the Yankee owners, Larry MacPhail, made the mistake of luring Charlie Dressen away from a Brooklyn coaching spot. Brooklyn manager Leo Durocher and general manager Branch Rickey then made the greater mistake of criticizing MacPhail publicly and compounded the mistake by accusing the Yankee executive of having alleged gamblers in his box at an exhibition game between the Yankees and Dodgers at Havana, Cuba, in March. As part of Durocher's communication program, he used his column in *The Brooklyn Eagle,* ghost-written by road secretary Harold Parrott.

MacPhail denied any gambler connections and filed libel charges with Commissioner Happy Chandler. The results: Durocher suspended for entire season for "conduct detrimental to baseball"; Dressen suspended for 30 days for "violating a verbal agreement to coach with Brooklyn"; Parrott fined $5,000 for "the statement in the *Eagle* column"; and the Yankees and Dodgers each fined $2,000 for "engaging in public feuding".

The Yankee-Dodger feud, while having its lighter side, was by no means an historic footnote to baseball. But there was another event underway in Brooklyn which was to have as much historical impact as the beginning of baseball itself. And for many, 1947 marked the *real* beginning of baseball—at least on a national level—as the doors were finally opened to the black athlete. The man responsible for the initiative was Branch Rickey, and the first black player was a 28-year-old infielder by the name of Jackie Robinson. Later in the year, the Dodgers repeated the experiment with Dan Bankhead, while Cleveland added Larry Doby, and the St. Louis Browns took on Hank Thompson and Willard Brown.

At the end of 1947, baseball found that it no longer had to *experiment* with the black man. Jackie Robinson firmly convinced one and all that talent was too great an asset to hide behind the excuse of dark skin pigmentation, as he hit .297, was named Rookie of the Year, and led the Dodgers to a five-game pennant victory over St. Louis.

The Boston Red Sox installed lights in Fenway Park, produced the second man in baseball history to win a second Triple Crown in Ted Williams, and finished third because of arm trouble to pitchers, Tex Hughson, Mickey Harris, and Dave Ferris. The Yankees obtained pitcher Bobo Newsom from Washington, recalled Vic Raschi from the minors, and returned to the pennant after a four-year layoff. Joe DiMaggio supplied the offensive muscle as he again beat out Williams for MVP honors, despite being well bathed in the shadow of the Boston slugger's statistics.

The Yankees and Dodgers provided a treat in the fall classic, which was filled with enough dramatics to guarantee them a place in World Series history. After winning the first two games without too much trouble, the Yankees lost the third, 9-8, despite the first pinch-hit homer in Series history—hit by rookie catcher-outfielder Yogi Berra.

The fourth game caused adrenaline to overflow, as Yankee pitcher Bill Bevans went into the bottom of the ninth with two outs and two on, needing only to retire pinch hitter Cookie Lavagetto to become the first man ever in post-season play to hurl a no-hitter. Such was not destined to be, as Lavagetto doubled off the right field wall to not only break the no-hitter, but also drive in two runs to give the Dodgers a 3-2 Series equalizer.

New York took the fifth game, and might have won the sixth, save for Al Gionfriddo's great catch of a DiMaggio clout ear-marked home run with two on in the sixth and the score 8-5. Joe Page, who saved a league high 17 games for the Yankees during the season, came out of the bullpen in the fifth inning of the seventh game to preserve a 5-2 Series victory.

1947 AMERICAN LEAGUE

NAME	G by POS	B	AGE	G	AB	R	H	2B	3B	HR	RBI	BB	SO	SB	BA	SA
NEW YORK 1st 97-57 .630		**BUCKY HARRIS**														
TOTALS			30	155	5308	**794**	**1439**	230	**72**	**115**	**746**	610	581	27	**.271**	**.407**
George McQuinn	1B142	L	38	144	517	84	157	24	3	13	80	78	66	0	.304	.437
Snuffy Stirnweiss	2B148	R	28	148	571	102	146	18	8	5	41	89	47	5	.256	.342
Phil Rizzuto	SS151	R	29	153	549	78	150	26	9	2	60	57	31	11	.273	.364
Billy Johnson	3B132	R	28	132	494	67	141	19	8	10	95	44	43	1	.285	.417
Tommy Henrich	OF132, 1B6	L	34	142	550	109	158	35	**13**	16	98	71	54	3	.287	.485
Joe DiMaggio	OF139	R	32	141	534	97	168	31	10	20	97	64	32	3	.315	.522
Johnny Lindell	OF118	R	30	127	476	66	131	18	7	11	67	32	70	1	.275	.412
Aaron Robinson	C74	L	32	82	252	23	68	11	5	5	36	40	26	0	.270	.413
Yogi Berra	C51, OF25	L	22	83	293	41	82	15	3	11	54	13	12	0	.280	.464
Bobby Brown	3B27, SS11, OF3	L	22	69	150	21	45	6	1	1	18	21	9	0	.300	.373
Charlie Keller (XJ)	OF43	L	30	45	151	36	36	6	1	13	36	41	18	0	.238	.550
Ralph Houk	C41	R	27	41	92	7	25	3	1	0	12	11	5	0	.272	.326
Allie Clark	OF16	R	24	24	67	9	25	5	0	1	14	5	2	0	.373	.493
2 Lonny Frey	2B8	L	36	24	28	10	5	2	0	0	2	10	1	3	.179	.250
Frank Colman	OF6	L	29	22	28	2	3	0	0	2	6	2	6	0	.107	.321
Jack Phillips	1B10	R	25	16	36	5	10	0	1	1	2	3	5	0	.278	.417
Johnny Lucadello	2B5	B	28	12	12	0	1	0	0	0	0	1	5	0	.083	.083
Sherm Lollar	C9	R	22	11	32	4	7	0	1	1	6	1	5	0	.219	.375
Frankie Crosetti 36 R 0-1, Ken Silvestri 31 B 2-10, 2 Ted Sepkowski 23 L 0-0 1 Ray Mack 30 R 0-0																
DETROIT 2nd 85-69 .552 12		**STEVE O'NEILL**														
TOTALS			29	158	5276	714	1363	**234**	42	103	657	**762**	565	52	.258	.377
Roy Cullenbine	1B138	B	31	142	464	82	104	18	1	24	78	137	51	3	.224	.422
Eddie Mayo	2B142	L	37	142	535	66	149	28	4	6	48	48	28	3	.279	.379
Eddie Lake	SS158	R	31	158	602	96	127	19	6	12	46	120	54	11	.211	.322
George Kell	3B152	R	24	152	588	75	188	29	5	5	93	61	16	9	.320	.412
Pat Mullin	OF106	L	29	116	398	62	102	28	6	15	62	63	66	3	.256	.470
Hoot Evers	OF123	R	26	126	460	67	136	24	5	10	67	45	49	8	.296	.435
Dick Wakefield	OF101	L	26	112	368	59	104	15	5	8	51	80	44	1	.283	.416
Bob Swift	C97	R	32	97	279	23	70	11	0	1	21	33	16	2	.251	.301
Vic Wertz	OF82	L	22	102	333	60	96	22	4	6	44	47	66	2	.288	.432
Doc Cramer	OF35	L	41	73	157	21	42	2	2	2	30	20	5	0	.268	.344
2 Hal Wagner	C71	L	31	71	191	19	55	10	0	5	32	28	16	0	.288	.419
Jimmy Outlaw	OF37, 3B9	R	34	70	127	20	29	7	1	0	15	21	14	3	.228	.299
Fred Hutchinson	P33	L	27	56	106	8	32	5	2	2	15	6	6	2	.302	.443
Skeeter Webb	2B30, SS6	R	37	50	79	13	16	3	0	0	6	7	9	3	.203	.241
John McHale	1B25	L	25	39	95	10	20	1	0	3	11	7	24	1	.211	.316
Ed Mierkowicz	OF10	R	23	21	42	6	8	1	0	1	1	1	12	1	.190	.286
1 Birdie Tebbetts	C20	R	37	20	53	1	5	1	0	0	2	3	3	0	.094	.113
Hank Riebe	C3	R	25	8	7	0	0	0	0	0	2	0	2	0	.000	.000
Johnny Groth 20 R 1-4, Ben Steiner 25 L 0-0																
BOSTON 3rd 83-71 .539 14		**JOE CRONIN**														
TOTALS			29	157	5322	720	1412	206	54	103	674	666	590	41	.265	.382
2 Jake Jones	1B109	R	26	109	404	50	95	14	3	16	76	41	60	5	.235	.403
Bobby Doerr	2B146	R	29	146	561	79	145	23	10	17	95	59	47	3	.258	.426
Johnny Pesky	SS133, 3B22	L	27	155	**638**	106	**207**	27	8	0	39	72	22	12	.324	.392
Sam Dente	3B46	R	25	46	168	14	39	4	2	0	11	19	15	0	.232	.280
Sam Mele	OF115, 1B1	R	24	123	453	71	137	14	8	12	73	37	35	0	.302	.448
Dom DiMaggio	OF134	R	30	136	513	75	145	21	5	8	71	74	62	10	.283	.390
Ted Williams	OF156	L	28	156	528	**125**	181	40	9	**32**	**114**	**162**	47	0	**.343**	**.634**
2 Birdie Tebbetts	C89	R	37	90	291	22	87	10	0	1	28	21	30	2	.299	.344
Wally Moses	OF58	L	36	90	255	32	70	18	2	2	27	27	16	3	.275	.384
Eddie Pellegrini (FJ)	3B42, SS26	R	29	74	231	29	47	8	1	4	19	23	35	2	.203	.299
Roy Partee	C54	R	29	60	169	14	39	2	0	0	16	18	23	0	.231	.243
Don Gutteridge	2B20, 3B19	R	35	54	131	20	22	2	0	2	5	17	13	3	.168	.229
1 Rudy York	1B48	R	33	48	184	16	39	7	0	6	27	22	32	0	.212	.348
Leon Culberson	OF25, 3B4	R	27	47	84	10	20	1	0	0	11	12	10	1	.238	.250
Rip Russell	3B13	R	32	26	52	8	8	1	0	1	3	8	7	0	.154	.231
1 Hal Wagner	C21	L	31	21	65	5	15	3	0	0	6	9	5	0	.231	.277
Merrill Combs	3B17	L	27	17	68	8	15	1	0	1	6	9	9	0	.221	.279
Billy Goodman	OF1	L	21	12	11	1	2	0	0	0	1	1	2	0	.182	.182
Ed McGah	C7	R	25	9	14	1	0	0	0	0	2	3	0	0	.000	.000
Matt Batts	C6	R	25	7	16	3	8	1	0	1	5	1	1	0	.500	.750
Frankie Hayes	C4	R	32	5	13	0	2	0	0	0	1	0	1	0	.154	.154
Strick Shafner	3B4	L	27	5	13	1	2	0	1	0	0	0	3	0	.154	.308
Doyle Aulds 26 R 1-4, 1 Tom McBride 32 R 1-5																

NAME	T	AGE	W	L	PCT	SV	G	GS	CG	IP	H	BB	SO	ShO	ERA
		30	**97**	57	**.630**	21	155	155	73	1374	1221	**628**	**691**	14	**3.39**
Allie Reynolds	R	32	19	8	**.704**	2	34	30	17	242	207	123	129	4	3.20
Spec Shea	R	26	14	5	.737	1	27	23	13	179	127	89	89	3	3.07
Joe Page	L	29	14	8	.636	**17**	56	2	0	141	105	72	116	0	2.49
Spud Chandler	R	39	9	5	.643	0	17	16	13	128	100	41	68	2	**2.46**
Vic Raschi	R	28	7	2	.778	0	15	14	6	105	89	38	51	1	3.86
2 Bobo Newsom	R	39	7	5	.583	0	17	15	6	116	109	30	42	2	2.79
Bill Bevens	R	30	7	13	.350	0	28	23	11	165	167	77	77	1	3.82
Karl Drews	R	27	6	6	.500	1	30	10	0	92	92	55	45	0	4.89
Randy Gumpert	R	29	4	1	.800	0	24	6	2	56	71	28	25	0	5.46
Don Johnson	R	20	4	3	.571	0	15	8	2	54	57	23	16	0	3.67
Butch Wensloff	R	31	3	1	.750	0	11	5	1	52	41	22	18	0	2.60
1 Al Lyons	R	28	1	0	1.000	0	6	0	0	11	18	9	7	0	9.00
Dick Starr	R	26	1	0	1.000	0	4	1	1	12	12	8	1	0	1.50
Bill Wight	L	25	1	0	1.000	0	1	1	1	9	8	2	3	0	1.00
1 Mel Queen	R	29	0	0	.000	0	5	0	0	7	9	4	2	0	9.00
Tommy Byrne	L	27	0	0	.000	0	4	1	0	4	5	6	2	0	4.50
Rugger Ardizoia	R	27	0	0	.000	0	1	0	0	1	4	1	0	0	18.00
		28	85	69	.552	18	158	158	**77**	1399	1382	531	648	**15**	3.57
Fred Hutchinson	R	27	18	10	.643	2	33	25	18	220	211	61	113	3	3.03
Hal Newhouser	L	26	17	**17**	.500	2	40	36	**24**	285	**268**	110	176	3	2.87
Stubby Overmire	L	28	11	5	.688	0	28	17	7	141	142	44	33	3	3.77
Dizzy Trout	R	32	10	11	.476	2	32	26	9	186	186	65	74	2	3.48
Virgil Trucks	R	28	10	12	.455	2	36	26	8	181	186	79	108	2	4.52
Art Houtteman	R	19	7	2	.778	0	23	9	7	111	106	36	58	2	3.41
Al Benton	R	36	6	7	.462	7	36	14	4	133	147	61	33	0	4.40
Hal White	R	28	4	5	.444	2	35	5	0	85	91	47	33	0	3.60
Johnny Gorsica	R	32	2	0	1.000	1	31	0	0	58	44	26	20	0	3.72
Rufe Gentry	R	29	0	0	.000	0	1	0	0	.1	1	2	0	0	81.00
		31	83	71	.539	19	157	157	64	1392	1383	575	586	13	3.81
Joe Dobson	R	30	18	8	.692	1	33	31	15	229	203	73	110	1	2.95
Earl Johnson	L	28	12	11	.522	8	45	17	6	142	129	62	65	3	2.98
Boo Ferriss	R	25	12	11	.522	0	33	28	14	218	241	92	64	1	4.05
Tex Hughson (RJ)	R	31	12	11	.522	0	29	26	13	189	173	71	119	3	3.33
2 Denny Galehouse	R	35	11	7	.611	0	21	21	11	149	150	34	38	3	3.32
Harry Dorish	R	25	7	8	.467	2	41	9	2	136	149	54	50	0	4.70
Mickey Harris (SJ)	L	30	5	4	.556	0	15	6	1	52	42	23	35	0	2.42
Mel Parnell	L	25	2	3	.400	0	15	5	1	51	60	27	23	0	6.35
Bill Zuber	R	34	1	0	1.000	0	20	1	0	51	60	31	23	0	5.29
Bob Klinger	R	39	1	1	.500	5	28	0	0	42	42	24	12	0	3.86
Tommy Fine	R	32	1	2	.333	0	9	7	1	36	41	19	10	0	5.50
2 Eddie Smith	L	33	1	3	.250	0	8	3	0	17	18	18	15	0	7.41
Cot Deal	R	24	0	1	.000	0	5	2	0	13	20	7	6	0	9.00
Chuck Stobbs	L	17	0	1	.000	0	4	1	0	9	10	10	5	0	6.00
Johnny Murphy	R	38	0	0	.000	3	32	0	0	55	41	28	9	0	2.78
Al Widmar	R	22	0	0	.000	0	2	0	0	1	1	2	1	0	18.00
Bill Butland	R	29	0	0	.000	0	1	0	0	2	3	0	1	0	4.50

CLEVELAND 4th 80-74 .519 17

LOU BOUDREAU

NAME	G by POS	B	AGE	G	AB	R	H	2B	3B	HR	RBI	BB	SO	SB	BA	SA
TOTALS			28	157	5367	687	1392	234	51	112	646	502	609	29	.259	.385
Eddie Robinson	1B87	L	26	95	318	52	78	10	1	14	52	30	18	1	.245	.415
Joe Gordon	2B155	R	32	155	562	89	153	27	6	29	93	62	49	7	.272	.496
Lou Boudreau	SS148	R	29	150	538	79	165	45	3	4	67	67	10	1	.307	.424
Ken Keltner	3B150	R	30	151	541	49	139	29	3	11	76	59	45	5	.257	.383
Hank Edwards (SJ)	OF100	L	28	108	393	54	102	12	3	15	59	31	55	1	.260	.420
Catfish Metkovich	OF119, 1B1	L	25	126	473	68	120	22	7	5	40	32	51	5	.254	.362
Dale Mitchell	OF115	L	25	123	493	69	156	16	10	1	34	23	14	2	.316	.396
Jim Hegan	C133	R	26	135	378	38	94	14	5	4	42	41	49	3	.249	.344
Hal Peck	OF97	L	30	114	392	58	115	18	2	8	44	27	31	3	.293	.411
Les Fleming	1B77	L	31	103	281	39	68	14	2	4	43	53	42	0	.242	.349
Pat Seerey	OF68	R	24	82	216	24	37	4	1	11	29	34	66	0	.171	.352
Al Lopez	C57	R	38	61	126	9	33	1	0	0	14	9	13	1	.262	.270
Eddie Bockman	3B12, 2B4, SS1, OF1	R	26	46	66	8	17	2	2	1	14	5	17	0	.258	.394
Jack Conway	SS24, 2B5, 3B1	R	27	34	50	3	9	2	0	0	5	3	8	0	.180	.220
Larry Doby	2B4, 1B1, SS1	L	23	29	32	3	5	1	0	0	2	1	11	0	.156	.188
Hank Ruszkowski	C16	R	21	23	27	5	7	2	0	3	4	2	6	0	.259	.667
1 Ted Sepkowski	OF1	L	23	10	8	0	1	1	0	0	0	1	1	0	.125	.250
Joe Frazier	OF5	L	24	9	14	1	1	1	0	0	0	1	1	0	.071	.143
Al Rosen	3B2, OF1	R	23	7	9	1	1	0	0	0	0	0	3	0	.111	.111
Heinz Becker		B	31	2	2	0	0	0	0	0	0	0	1	0	.000	.000
1 Felix Mackiewicz	OF2	R	29	2	5	0	0	0	0	0	0	0	2	0	.000	.000
Jimmy Wasdell		L	33	1	1	0	0	0	0	0	0	0	0	0	.000	.000

NAME	T	AGE	W	L	PCT	SV	G	GS	CG	IP	H	BB	SO	ShO	ERA
		30	80	74	.519	29	157	157	55	1402	1244	628	590	13	3.44
Bob Feller	R	28	20	11	.645	3	42	37	20	299	230	127	196	5	2.68
Al Gettel	R	29	11	10	.524	0	31	21	9	149	122	62	64	2	3.20
Bob Lemon	R	26	11	5	.688	3	37	15	6	167	150	97	65	1	3.45
Don Black	R	30	10	12	.455	0	30	28	8	191	177	85	72	3	3.91
Red Embree	R	29	8	10	.444	0	27	21	6	163	137	67	56	0	3.15
Mel Harder	R	37	6	4	.600	0	15	15	4	80	91	27	17	1	4.50
Eddie Klieman	R	29	5	4	.556	17	58	0	0	92	78	39	21	0	3.03
Bryan Stephens	R	26	5	10	.333	1	31	5	1	92	79	39	34	0	4.01
Steve Gromek	R	27	3	5	.375	4	29	7	0	84	77	36	39	0	3.75
Bob Kuzava	L	24	1	1	.500	0	4	4	1	22	22	9	9	0	4.09
Les Willis	L	38	0	2	.000	1	22	2	0	44	58	24	10	0	3.48
1 Roger Wolff	R	36	0	0	.000	0	7	2	0	16	15	10	5	0	3.94
Cal Dorsett	R	34	0	0	.000	0	2	0	0	1	3	3	1	0	36.00
Ernie Groth	R	25	0	0	.000	0	2	0	0	1	0	1	1	0	0.00
Gene Bearden	L	26	0	0	.000	0	1	0	0	.1	2	1	0	0	81.00
Lyman Linde	R	26	0	0	.000	0	1	0	0	1	3	1	0	0	18.00

PHILADELPHIA 5th 78-76 .506 19

CONNIE MACK

NAME	G by POS	B	AGE	G	AB	R	H	2B	3B	HR	RBI	BB	SO	SB	BA	SA
TOTALS			30	156	5198	633	1311	218	52	61	581	605	563	37	.252	.349
Ferris Fain	1B132	L	26	136	461	70	134	28	6	7	71	95	34	4	.291	.423
Pete Suder	2B140, SS3, 3B2	R	31	145	528	45	127	28	4	5	60	35	44	0	.241	.337
Eddie Joost	SS151	R	31	151	540	76	111	22	3	13	64	114	110	6	.206	.330
Hank Majeski	3B134, SS4, 2B1	R	30	141	497	54	134	26	5	8	72	53	31	1	.280	.405
Elmer Valo	OF104	L	26	112	370	60	111	12	6	5	36	64	21	11	.300	.405
Sam Chapman	OF146	R	31	149	551	84	139	18	5	14	83	65	70	3	.252	.379
Barney McCosky	OF136	L	29	137	546	77	179	22	7	1	52	57	29	1	.328	.399
Buddy Rosar	C102	R	32	102	359	40	93	20	2	1	33	40	13	1	.259	.334
George Binks	OF75, 1B13	L	32	104	333	33	86	19	4	2	34	23	36	8	.258	.357
Mike Guerra	C62	R	34	72	209	20	45	2	2	0	18	10	15	1	.215	.244
Dick Adams	1B24, OF3	R	27	37	89	9	18	2	3	2	11	2	18	0	.202	.360
Gene Handley (KJ)	2B17, 3B10, SS1	R	32	36	90	10	23	2	1	0	8	10	2	1	.256	.300
Austin Knickerbocker	OF14	R	28	21	48	8	12	3	2	0	2	3	4	0	.250	.396
Don Richmond	3B4, 2B1	L	27	19	21	2	4	1	1	0	4	3	3	0	.190	.333
Chet Laabs	OF7	R	35	15	32	5	7	1	0	1	5	4	4	0	.219	.344
Pat Cooper	1B1	R	29	13	16	0	4	2	0	0	3	0	5	0	.250	.375
Ray Poole		L	27	13	13	1	3	0	0	0	1	1	4	0	.231	.231
Mickey Rutner	3B11	R	27	12	48	4	12	1	0	1	4	3	2	0	.250	.333
Herman Franks	C4	R	33	8	15	2	3	0	1	0	1	4	4	0	.200	.333
Nellie Fox	2B1	L	19	7	3	2	0	0	0	0	0	1	0	0	.000	.000
Tom Kirk		L	19	1	1	0	0	0	0	0	0	0	0	0	.000	.000

Bobby Estalella (SM)36

NAME	T	AGE	W	L	PCT	SV	G	GS	CG	IP	H	BB	SO	ShO	ERA
		27	78	76	.506	15	156	156	70	1391	1291	597	493	12	3.51
Phil Marchildon	R	33	19	9	.679	0	35	35	21	277	228	141	128	2	3.22
Dick Fowler	R	26	12	11	.522	0	36	31	16	227	210	85	75	3	2.81
Bill McCahan	R	26	10	5	.667	0	29	19	10	165	160	62	47	1	3.33
Russ Christopher	R	29	10	7	.588	12	44	0	0	81	70	33	33	0	2.89
Bob Savage	R	25	8	10	.444	2	44	8	2	146	135	55	56	1	3.76
Joe Coleman	R	24	6	12	.333	1	32	21	9	160	171	62	65	2	4.33
Bill Dietrich	R	37	5	2	.714	0	11	9	2	61	48	40	18	1	3.10
Carl Scheib	R	20	4	6	.400	0	21	12	6	116	121	55	26	2	5.04
Jesse Flores	R	32	4	13	.235	0	28	20	4	151	139	59	41	0	3.40
Lou Brissie	L	23	0	1	.000	0	1	1	0	7	9	5	4	0	6.43

CHICAGO 6th 70-84 .455 27

TED LYONS

NAME	G by POS	B	AGE	G	AB	R	H	2B	3B	HR	RBI	BB	SO	SB	BA	SA
TOTALS			30	155	5274	553	1350	211	41	53	519	492	527	91	.256	.342
2 Rudy York	1B102	R	33	102	400	40	97	18	4	15	64	36	55	1	.243	.420
Don Kolloway	2B99, 1B11, 3B8	R	28	124	485	49	135	25	4	2	35	17	34	11	.278	.359
Luke Appling	SS129, 3B2	R	40	139	503	67	154	29	0	8	49	64	28	8	.306	.412
Floyd Baker	3B101, 2B1, SS1	L	30	105	371	61	98	12	3	0	22	66	28	9	.264	.313
Bob Kennedy	OF106, 3B1	R	26	115	428	47	112	19	3	6	48	18	38	3	.262	.362
Dave Philley	OF133, 3B4	B	27	143	551	55	142	25	11	2	45	35	39	21	.258	.354
Taffy Wright	OF100	L	35	124	401	48	130	13	0	4	54	48	17	8	.324	.387
Mike Tresh	C89	R	33	90	274	19	66	6	2	0	20	26	26	2	.241	.277
Cass Michaels	2B60, 3B44, SS2	R	21	110	355	31	97	15	4	3	34	39	28	10	.273	.363
Thurman Tucker	OF65	L	29	89	254	28	60	9	4	1	17	38	25	10	.236	.315
George Dickey	C80	B	31	83	211	15	47	6	0	1	27	34	25	4	.223	.265
Jack Wallaesa	SS27, OF22, 3B1	B	27	81	205	25	40	9	1	7	32	23	51	2	.195	.351
Ralph Hodgin (PB)	OF41	L	31	59	180	26	53	10	3	1	24	13	4	1	.294	.400
1 Jake Jones	1B43	R	26	45	171	15	41	7	1	3	20	13	25	1	.240	.345
Joe Stephenson	C13	R	26	16	35	3	5	0	0	0	3	1	7	0	.143	.143
Loyd Christopher	OF7	R	27	7	23	1	5	0	1	0	0	2	4	0	.217	.304
Joe Kuhel		L	41	4	4	0	0	0	0	0	0	0	3	0	.000	.000

NAME	T	AGE	W	L	PCT	SV	G	GS	CG	IP	H	BB	SO	ShO	ERA
		31	70	84	.455	27	155	155	47	1391	1384	603	522	11	3.64
Ed Lopat	L	29	16	13	.552	0	31	31	22	253	241	73	109	3	2.81
Joe Haynes	R	29	14	6	.700	0	29	22	7	182	174	61	50	2	2.42
Frank Papish	L	29	12	12	.500	3	38	26	6	199	185	98	79	1	3.26
Orval Grove	R	27	6	8	.429	0	25	19	6	136	158	70	33	1	4.43
Bob Gillespie	R	28	5	8	.385	0	25	17	1	118	133	53	36	0	4.73
Red Ruffing (KJ)	R	43	3	5	.375	0	9	9	1	53	63	16	11	0	6.11
Thornton Lee	L	40	3	7	.300	1	21	11	2	87	86	56	57	1	4.45
Earl Harrist	R	27	3	8	.273	5	33	4	0	94	85	49	55	0	3.54
Pete Gebrian	R	23	2	3	.400	5	27	4	0	66	61	33	17	0	4.50
Johnny Rigney	R	32	2	3	.400	0	11	7	2	51	42	15	19	0	1.94
Hi Bithorn	R	31	1	0	1.000	0	2	0	0	2	2	0	0	0	0.00
1 Eddie Smith	L	33	1	3	.250	0	15	5	0	33	40	24	12	0	7.36
Earl Caldwell	R	42	1	4	.200	8	40	0	0	54	53	30	22	0	3.67
Gordon Maltzberger	R	34	1	4	.200	5	33	0	0	64	61	25	22	0	3.38

WASHINGTON 7th 64-90 .416 33

OSSIE BLUEGE

NAME	G by POS	B	AGE	G	AB	R	H	2B	3B	HR	RBI	BB	SO	SB	BA	SA
TOTALS			30	154	5112	496	1234	186	48	42	458	525	534	53	.241	.321
Mickey Vernon	1B154	L	29	154	600	77	159	29	12	7	85	49	42	12	.265	.388
Jerry Priddy	2B146	R	27	147	505	42	108	20	3	3	49	62	79	7	.214	.283
Mark Christman	SS106, 2B1	R	33	110	374	27	83	15	2	1	33	33	16	4	.222	.281
Eddie Yost	3B114	R	20	115	428	52	102	17	3	0	14	45	57	3	.238	.292
Buddy Lewis	OF130	L	30	140	506	67	132	15	4	6	48	51	27	6	.261	.342
Stan Spence	OF142	L	32	147	506	62	141	22	6	16	73	81	41	2	.279	.441
Joe Grace	OF67	L	33	78	234	25	58	9	4	3	17	35	15	1	.248	.359
Al Evans	C94	R	30	99	319	17	77	8	3	2	23	28	25	2	.241	.304
Sherry Robertson	OF55, 3B10, 2B4	L	28	95	266	25	62	9	3	1	23	32	52	4	.233	.301
Cecil Travis	3B39, SS15	R	33	74	204	10	44	4	1	1	10	16	19	1	.216	.240
2 Tom McBride	OF51, 3B1	R	32	56	166	19	45	4	2	0	15	15	9	3	.271	.319
Early Wynn	P33	B	27	54	120	6	33	6	0	2	13	1	19	0	.275	.375
John Sullivan	SS40, 2B1	R	26	49	133	13	34	0	1	0	5	22	14	0	.256	.271
Frank Mancuso	C35	R	29	43	131	5	30	5	1	0	13	5	11	0	.229	.282
Rick Ferrell	C37	R	41	37	99	10	30	11	0	0	12	14	7	0	.303	.414
George Case	OF21	R	31	36	80	11	12	1	0	0	2	8	8	5	.150	.163
George Myatt	2B1	L	33	12	7	1	0	0	0	0	0	4	4	0	.000	.000
Gil Coan	OF11	L	25	11	42	5	21	3	2	0	3	5	6	2	.500	.667
Ed Lyons	2B7	R	24	7	26	2	4	0	0	0	0	2	2	0	.154	.154
Earl Wooten	OF6	R	23	6	24	0	2	0	0	0	1	0	4	1	.083	.083
2 Felix Mackiewicz	OF3	R	29	3	6	1	1	1	0	0	0	0	1	0	.167	.333

Cal Ermer 23 R 0-3, Roberto Ortiz (SM) 32

NAME	T	AGE	W	L	PCT	SV	G	GS	CG	IP	H	BB	SO	ShO	ERA
		29	64	90	.416	12	154	154	67	1362	1408	579	551	15	3.97
Early Wynn	R	27	17	15	.531	0	33	31	22	247	251	90	73	2	3.64
Walt Masterson	R	27	12	16	.429	1	35	31	14	253	215	97	135	4	3.13
Mickey Haefner	L	34	10	14	.417	1	31	28	14	193	195	85	77	4	3.64
Sid Hudson (HJ)	R	32	6	9	.400	0	20	17	5	106	113	58	37	1	5.60
Ray Scarborough	R	29	6	13	.316	0	33	18	8	161	165	67	63	2	3.41
1 Bobo Newsom	R	39	4	6	.400	0	14	13	1	84	99	37	40	0	4.07
Scott Cary	L	24	3	1	.750	0	23	3	1	55	73	20	25	0	5.89
Milo Candini	R	29	3	4	.429	1	38	2	0	87	96	35	31	0	5.17
Marino Pieretti	R	26	2	4	.333	0	23	10	2	83	97	47	32	1	4.23
Tom Ferrick	R	32	1	7	.125	9	31	0	0	60	57	20	23	0	3.15
Hal Toenes	R	29	0	1	.000	0	3	1	0	7	11	2	5	0	6.43
Lou Knerr	R	25	0	0	.000	0	6	0	0	9	17	8	5	0	11.00
Lum Harris	R	32	0	0	.000	0	3	0	0	6	7	7	2	0	3.00
Buzz Dozier	R	19	0	0	.000	0	2	0	0	5	2	1	2	0	0.00
Bill Kennedy	L	28	0	0	.000	0	2	0	0	7	10	5	1	0	7.71

Alex Carrasquell (SM) 34

ST. LOUIS 8th 59-95 .383 38

MUDDY RUEL

NAME	G by POS	B	AGE	G	AB	R	H	2B	3B	HR	RBI	BB	SO	SB	BA	SA
TOTALS			28	154	5145	564	1238	189	52	90	526	583	664	69	.241	.350
Walt Judnich	1B129, OF15	L	29	144	500	58	129	24	3	18	64	60	62	2	.258	.426
Johnny Berardino (JJ)	2B86	R	30	90	306	29	80	22	1	1	20	44	26	6	.261	.350
Vern Stephens	SS149	R	26	150	562	74	157	18	4	15	83	70	61	8	.279	.406
Bob Dillinger	3B137	R	28	137	571	70	168	23	6	3	37	56	38	34	.294	.371
Al Zarilla	OF110	L	28	127	380	34	85	15	6	3	38	40	45	3	.224	.318
Paul Lehner	OF127	L	27	135	483	59	120	25	9	7	48	28	29	5	.248	.381
Jeff Heath	OF140	L	32	141	491	81	123	20	7	27	85	88	87	2	.251	.485
Les Moss	C96	R	22	96	274	17	43	5	2	6	27	35	48	0	.157	.255
Ray Coleman	OF93	L	25	110	343	34	89	9	7	2	30	26	32	2	.259	.344
Jake Early	C85	L	30	87	214	25	48	9	3	3	19	54	34	0	.224	.336
Billy Hitchcock	2B46, 3B17, SS7, 1B5	R	30	80	275	25	61	2	2	1	28	21	34	3	.222	.255
Joe Schultz		L	28	43	38	3	7	0	0	1	1	4	5	0	.184	.263
Rusty Peters	2B13, SS2	R	32	39	47	10	16	4	0	0	2	6	8	0	.340	.426
Jerry Witte	1B27	R	31	34	99	4	14	2	1	2	12	11	22	0	.141	.242
Hank Thompson	2B19	L	21	27	78	10	20	1	1	0	5	10	7	2	.256	.295
Willard Brown	OF18	R	32	21	67	4	12	3	0	1	6	0	7	2	.179	.269
Perry Currin	SS1	L	18	3	2	0	0	0	0	0	0	1	0	0	.000	.000
Glenn McQuillen		R	32	1	1	0	0	0	0	0	0	0	0	0	.000	.000

NAME	T	AGE	W	L	PCT	SV	G	GS	CG	IP	H	BB	SO	ShO	ERA
		30	59	95	.383	13	154	154	50	1365	1426	604	552	7	4.33
Jack Kramer	R	29	11	16	.407	1	33	28	9	199	206	89	77	1	4.97
Sam Zoldak	L	28	9	10	.474	1	35	19	6	171	162	76	36	1	3.47
Bob Muncrief	R	31	8	14	.364	0	31	23	7	176	210	51	74	0	4.91
Ellis Kinder	R	32	8	15	.348	1	34	26	10	194	201	82	110	2	4.50
Fred Sanford	R	27	7	16	.304	4	34	23	9	187	186	76	62	0	3.71
Cliff Fannin	L	23	6	8	.429	1	26	18	6	146	134	77	77	2	3.58
Glen Moulder	R	29	4	2	.667	2	32	2	0	73	78	43	23	0	3.82
Nels Potter	R	35	4	10	.286	2	32	10	3	123	130	44	65	0	4.02
Walter Brown	R	32	1	0	1.000	0	19	0	0	46	50	28	10	0	4.89
1 Denny Galehouse	R	35	1	3	.250	1	9	4	0	32	42	16	11	0	6.19
1 Hooks Iott	L	27	0	1	.000	0	4	0	0	8	15	14	6	0	16.88
Bud Swartz	L	18	0	0	.000	0	5	0	0	5	9	7	1	0	7.20
Dizzy Dean	R	36	0	0	.000	0	1	1	0	4	3	1	0	0	0.00

BROOKLYN 1st 94-60 .610 — CLYDE SUKEFORTH 1-0 1.000, BURT SHOTTON 93-60 .608

NAME	G by POS	B	AGE	G	AB	R	H	2B	3B	HR	RBI	BB	SO	SB	BA	SA
TOTALS			28	155	5249	774	1428	241	50	83	719	732	561	88	.272	.384
Jackie Robinson	1B151	R	28	151	590	125	175	31	5	12	48	74	36	29	.297	.427
Eddie Stanky	2B146	R	30	146	559	97	141	24	5	3	53	103	39	3	.252	.329
Pee Wee Reese	SS142	R	28	142	476	81	135	24	4	12	73	104	67	7	.284	.426
Spider Jorgensen	3B128	L	27	129	441	57	121	29	8	5	67	58	45	4	.274	.410
Dixie Walker	OF147	L	36	148	529	77	162	31	3	9	94	97	26	6	.306	.427
Carl Furillo	OF121	R	25	124	437	61	129	24	7	8	88	34	24	7	.295	.437
Pete Reiser (CN)	OF108	L	28	110	388	68	120	23	2	5	46	68	41	14	.309	.418
Bruce Edwards	C128	R	23	130	471	53	139	15	8	9	80	49	55	2	.295	.418
Gene Hermanski	OF66	L	27	79	189	36	52	7	1	7	39	28	7	5	.275	.434
Arky Vaughan	OF22, 3B10	L	35	64	126	24	41	5	2	2	25	27	11	4	.325	.444
Eddie Miksis	2B13, OF11, 3B5, SS2	R	20	45	86	18	23	1	0	4	10	9	8	0	.267	.419
Cookie Lavagetto	3B18, 1B3	R	34	41	69	6	18	1	0	3	11	12	5	0	.261	.406
Duke Snider	OF25	L	20	40	83	6	20	3	1	0	5	3	24	2	.241	.301
2 Al Gionfriddo	OF17	L	25	37	62	10	11	2	1	0	6	16	11	2	.177	.242
Stan Rojek	SS17, 3B9, 2B7	R	28	32	80	7	21	0	1	0	7	7	3	1	.263	.288
Gil Hodges	C24	R	23	28	77	9	12	3	1	1	7	14	19	0	.156	.260
Bobby Bragan	C24	R	29	25	36	3	7	2	0	0	3	7	3	1	.194	.250
Marv Rackley	OF2	L	25	18	9	2	2	0	0	0	2	1	0	0	.222	.222
Tommy Brown (MS)	3B6, OF3, SS1	R	19	15	34	3	8	1	0	0	2	1	6	0	.235	.265
Don Lund	OF5	R	24	11	20	5	6	2	0	2	5	3	7	0	.300	.700
Ed Stevens	1B4	L	22	5	13	0	2	1	0	0	0	1	5	0	.154	.231
1 Tommy Tatum	OF3	R	27	4	6	0	0	0	0	0	0	0	1	0	.000	.000

Dick Whitman 26 L 4-10, 1 Howie Schultz 24 R 0-1, Leo Durocher (SL) 41, Luis Olmo (SM) 27, Mickey Owen (SM) 31

NAME	T	AGE	W	L	PCT	SV	G	GS	CG	IP	H	BB	SO	ShO	ERA
		26	94	60	.610	34	155	155	47	1375	1299	626	592	14	3.82
Ralph Branca	R	21	21	12	.636	1	43	36	15	280	251	98	148	4	2.67
Joe Hatten	L	30	17	8	.680	0	42	32	11	225	211	105	76	3	3.64
Vic Lombardi	L	24	12	11	.522	3	33	20	7	175	156	65	72	3	2.98
Hugh Casey	R	33	10	4	.714	18	46	0	0	77	75	29	40	0	3.97
Harry Taylor	R	28	10	5	.667	1	33	20	10	162	130	83	58	2	3.11
Clyde King	R	22	6	5	.545	0	29	9	2	88	85	29	31	0	2.76
Rex Barney	R	22	5	2	.714	0	28	9	0	78	66	59	36	0	4.96
13 Hank Behrman	R	26	5	3	.625	8	40	6	0	92	97	48	33	0	5.48
Hal Gregg	R	25	4	5	.444	1	37	16	2	104	115	55	59	1	5.88
1 Kirby Higbe	R	32	2	0	1.000	0	4	3	0	16	18	12*	10	0	5.06
Phil Haugstad	R	23	1	0	1.000	0	6	1	0	13	14	4	4	0	2.77
Willie Ramsdell	R	31	1	1	.500	0	2	0	0	3	4	3	3	0	6.00
Ed Chandler	R	25	0	1	.000	1	15	1	0	30	31	12	8	0	6.30
Rube Melton	R	30	0	1	.000	0	4	1	0	5	7	7	1	0	12.60
Jack Banta	R	22	0	1	.000	0	3	1	0	8	7	4	3	0	6.75
Erv Palica	R	19	0	1	.000	0	3	0	0	3	2	2	1	0	3.00
Dan Bankhead	R	27	0	0	.000	1	4	0	0	10	15	8	6	0	7.20
George Dockins	L	30	0	0	.000	0	4	0	0	5	10	2	1	0	12.60
Johnny Van Cuyk	L	25	0	0	.000	0	2	0	0	3	5	1	2	0	6.00

*Higbe, also with Pittsburgh, league leader in BB with 122

ST. LOUIS 2nd 89-65 .578 5 — EDDIE DYER

NAME	G by POS	B	AGE	G	AB	R	H	2B	3B	HR	RBI	BB	SO	SB	BA	SA
TOTALS			27	156	5422	780	1462	235	65	115	718	612	511	28	.270	.401
Stan Musial	1B149	L	26	149	587	113	183	30	13	19	95	80	24	4	.312	.504
Red Schoendienst	2B142, 3B5, OF1	B	24	151	659	91	167	25	9	3	48	48	27	6	.253	.332
Marty Marion	SS149	R	29	149	540	57	147	19	6	4	74	49	58	3	.272	.352
Whitey Kurowski	3B141	R	29	146	513	108	159	27	6	27	104	87	56	4	.310	.544
Erv Dusak	OF89, 3B7	R	26	111	328	56	93	7	3	6	28	50	34	1	.284	.378
Terry Moore	OF120	R	35	127	460	61	130	17	1	7	45	38	39	1	.283	.370
Enos Slaughter	OF142	L	31	147	551	100	162	31	13	10	86	59	27	4	.294	.452
Del Rice	C94	R	24	97	261	28	57	7	3	12	44	36	40	1	.218	.406
2 Ron Northey	OF94, 3B2	L	27	110	311	52	91	19	3	15	63	48	29	0	.293	.518
Chuck Diering	OF75	R	24	105	74	22	16	3	1	2	11	19	22	3	.216	.365
Joe Garagiola	C74	L	21	77	183	20	47	10	2	5	25	40	14	0	.257	.415
Joe Medwick	OF43	R	35	75	150	19	46	12	0	4	28	16	12	0	.307	.467
Del Wilber	C34	R	28	51	99	7	23	8	1	0	12	5	13	0	.232	.333
Jeff Cross	3B15,SS14,2B2	R	28	51	49	4	5	1	0	0	3	10	6	0	.102	.122
Dick Sisler	1B10, OF5	L	26	46	74	4	15	2	1	0	9	3	8	0	.203	.257
Nippy Jones	2B13, OF2	R	22	23	73	6	18	4	0	1	5	2	10	0	.247	.342
Bernie Creger	SS13	R	20	15	16	3	3	1	0	0	0	1	3	1	.188	.250
1 Harry Walker	OF9	L	30	10	25	2	5	1	0*	0	0	4	2	0	.200*	.240

Lou Klein (SM) 28

NAME	T	AGE	W	L	PCT	SV	G	GS	CG	IP	H	BB	SO	ShO	ERA
		28	89	65	.578	20	156	156	65	1399	1417	495	642	12	3.53
George Munger	R	28	16	5	.762	3	40	31	13	224	218	76	123	6	3.38
Harry Brecheen	L	32	16	11	.593	1	29	28	18	223	220	66	89	1	3.31
Al Brazle	L	33	14	8	.636	4	44	19	7	168	186	48	85	0	2.84
Murry Dickson	R	30	13	16	.448	3	47	25	11	232	211	88	111	4	3.06
Jim Hearn	R	26	12	7	.632	1	37	21	4	162	151	63	57	1	3.22
Howie Pollet	L	26	9	11	.450	2	37	24	9	176	195	87	73	0	4.35
Ted Wilks	R	31	4	0	1.000	5	37	0	0	50	57	11	28	0	5.04
Ken Burkhart	R	30	3	6	.333	1	34	6	1	95	108	23	44	0	5.21
Ken Johnson	L	24	1	0	1.000	0	2	1	1	10	2	5	8	0	0.00
Gerry Staley	R	26	1	0	1.000	0	18	1	1	29	33	8	14	0	2.79
Johnny Grodzicki	R	30	0	1	.000	0	16	0	0	23	21	19	8	0	5.48
1 Freddy Schmidt	R	31	0	0	.000	0	2	0	0	4	5	1	2	0	2.25

Max Lanier (SM) 31
Freddie Martin (SM) 32

*Walker, also with Philadelphia, league leader in 3B (16), BA (.363)

BOSTON 3rd 86-68 .558 8 — BILLY SOUTHWORTH

NAME	G by POS	B	AGE	G	AB	R	H	2B	3B	HR	RBI	BB	SO	SB	BA	SA
TOTALS			30	154	5253	701	1444	265	42	85	645	558	500	58	.275	.390
Earl Torgeson	1B117	L	23	128	399	73	112	20	6	16	78	82	59	11	.281	.481
Connie Ryan	2B150, SS1	R	27	150	544	60	144	33	5	5	69	71	60	5	.265	.371
Dick Culler	SS75	R	32	77	214	20	53	5	1	0	19	19	15	1	.248	.280
Bob Elliott	3B148	R	30	150	555	93	176	35	5	22	113	87	60	3	.317	.517
Tommy Holmes	OF147	L	30	150	618	90	191	33	3	9	53	44	16	3	.309	.416
Johnny Hopp	OF125	L	30	134	430	74	124	20	2	2	32	58	30	13	.288	.358
Bama Rowell	OF100, 2B7, 3B4	L	31	113	384	48	106	23	2	5	40	18	14	7	.276	.385
Phil Masi	C123	R	30	126	411	54	125	22	4	9	50	47	27	7	.304	.443
Mike McCormick	OF79	R	30	92	284	42	81	13	7	3	36	20	21	1	.285	.412
Danny Litwhiler	OF66	R	30	91	226	38	59	5	2	7	31	25	43	1	.261	.394
Nanny Fernandez	SS62, OF8, 3B6	R	28	83	209	16	43	4	0	2	21	22	20	2	.206	.254
2 Frank McCormick	1B48	R	36	81	212	24	75	18	2	2	43	11	8	2	.354	.486
Sibby Sisti	SS51, 2B1	R	26	56	153	22	43	8	0	2	15	20	17	2	.281	.373
Hank Camelli	C51	R	32	52	150	10	29	8	1	1	11	18	18	0	.193	.280
Johnny Sain	P38	R	29	40	107	13	37	7	0	0	18	3	1	0	.346	.411
Tommy Neill	OF2	L	27	7	10	1	2	0	1	0	0	1	2	0	.200	.400
Danny Murtaugh	2B2, 3B2	R	29	3	8	0	1	0	0	0	0	1	2	0	.125	.125

Bob Brady 24 L 0-1, Ray Sanders (BA) 30

NAME	T	AGE	W	L	PCT	SV	G	GS	CG	IP	H	BB	SO	ShO	ERA
		31	86	68	.558	13	154	154	74	1363	1352	453	494	14	3.62
Warren Spahn	L	26	21	10	.677	3	40	35	22	290	245	84	123	7	2.33
Johnny Sain	R	29	21	12	.636	1	38	35	22	266	265	79	132	3	3.52
Red Barrett	R	32	11	12	.478	1	36	30	12	211	200	53	53	3	3.54
2 Bill Voiselle	R	28	8	7	.533	0	22	20	7	131	146	51	59	0	4.33
Si Johnson	R	40	6	8	.429	2	36	10	3	113	124	34	27	0	4.22
2 Clyde Shoun	L	35	5	3	.625	1	26	3	1	74	73	21	23	1	4.38
Walt Lanfranconi	R	30	4	4	.500	1	36	4	1	64	65	27	18	0	2.95
Ed Wright	R	28	3	3	.500	0	23	6	1	65	80	35	14	0	6.37
Johnny Beazley (SA)	R	29	2	0	1.000	0	9	2	2	29	30	19	12	0	4.34
Andy Karl	R	33	2	3	.400	3	27	0	0	35	41	13	5	0	3.86
1 Mort Cooper	R	34	2	5	.286	0	10	7	2	47	48	13	15	0	4.02
Ray Martin	R	22	1	0	1.000	0	1	1	1	9	7	4	2	0	1.00
Glenn Elliott	L	27	0	1	.000	1	11	0	0	19	18	11	8	0	4.74
Johnny Lanning	R	36	0	0	.000	0	3	0	0	4	4	6	0	0	9.00
Max Macon	L	31	0	0	.000	0	1	0	0	2	1	1	1	0	0.00
Dick Mulligan	L	29	0	0	.000	0	1	0	0	2	4	1	1	0	9.00
Ernie White (SA)	L	30	0	0	.000	0	1	1	0	4	1	1	1	0	0.00

NEW YORK 4th 81-73 .526 13 — MEL OTT

NAME	G by POS	B	AGE	G	AB	R	H	2B	3B	HR	RBI	BB	SO	SB	BA	SA
TOTALS			27	155	5343	830	1446	220	48	221	790	494	568	29	.271	.454
Johnny Mize	1B154	L	32	154	586	137	177	26	2	51	138	74	42	2	.302	.614
Bill Rigney	2B72, 3B41, SS24	R	28	130	531	84	142	24	3	17	59	51	54	7	.267	.420
Buddy Kerr	SS138	R	24	138	547	73	157	23	5	7	49	36	49	2	.287	.386
Lucky Lohrke	3B111	R	23	112	329	44	79	12	4	11	35	46	29	3	.240	.401
Willard Marshall	OF155	L	26	155	587	102	171	19	6	36	107	67	30	3	.291	.528
Bobby Thomson	OF127, 2B9	R	23	138	545	105	154	26	5	29	85	40	78	1	.283	.508
Sid Gordon	OF124, 3B2	R	29	130	437	57	119	19	8	13	57	50	21	2	.272	.442
Walker Cooper	C132	R	32	140	515	79	157	24	8	35	122	24	43	2	.305	.586
Lloyd Gearhart	OF44	R	23	73	179	26	44	9	0	6	17	17	30	1	.246	.397
Joe Lafata	OF19, 1B2	L	25	62	95	13	21	1	0	2	18	15	18	1	.221	.295
Buddy Blattner	2B34, 3B11	R	27	55	153	28	40	9	2	0	13	21	19	4	.261	.346
Mickey Witek	2B40, 3B3	R	31	51	160	22	35	4	1	3	17	15	12	1	.219	.313
Ernie Lombardi	C24	R	39	48	110	8	31	5	0	4	21	7	9	0	.282	.436
Clint Hartung	P23, OF7	R	24	34	94	13	29	4	3	4	13	3	21	0	.309	.543
1 Babe Young		L	32	14	14	0	1	1	0	0	0	0	1	0	.071	.143
Bobby Rhawn	2B8, 3B5	R	28	13	45	7	14	3	0	1	3	8	1	0	.311	.444
Fuzz White	OF5	L	29	7	13	3	3	0	0	0	0	0	0	0	.231	.231
Wes Westrum	C2	R	24	6	12	1	5	1	0	0	2	0	2	0	.417	.500
2 Mickey Livingston	C2	R	32	5	6	0	1	0	0	0	0	1	2	0	.167	.167
Mel Ott		L	38	4	4	0	0	0	0	0	0	0	0	0	.000	.000

Bennie Warren 35 R 1-5, Whitey Lockman (BN) 20 L 1-2, Sal Yvars 23 R 1-5, Danny Gardella (SM) 27, George Hausmann (SM) 31, Nap Reyes (SM) 27, Ace Adams (SM) 35

NAME	T	AGE	W	L	PCT	SV	G	GS	CG	IP	H	BB	SO	ShO	ERA
		27	81	73	.526	14	155	155	58	1364	1418	590	553	6	4.44
Larry Jansen	R	26	21	5	.808	1	42	30	20	248	241	57	104	1	3.16
Dave Koslo	L	27	15	10	.600	0	39	31	10	217	223	82	86	3	4.40
Clint Hartung	R	24	9	7	.563	0	23	20	8	138	140	69	54	1	4.57
Monte Kennedy	L	25	9	12	.429	0	34	24	9	148	158	88	60	0	4.86
Ken Trinkle	R	27	8	4	.667	10	62	0	0	94	100	48	37	0	3.73
Junior Thompson	R	30	4	2	.667	0	15	0	0	36	36	27	13	0	4.25
Ray Poat	R	29	4	3	.571	0	7	7	5	60	53	13	25	0	2.55
2 Joe Beggs	R	36	3	3	.500	2	32	0	0	66	81	18	23	0	4.23
2 Hooks Iott	L	27	3	8	.273	0	20	9	2	71	67	52	46	1	5.96
Sheldon Jones	R	25	2	2	.500	0	15	6	0	56	51	29	24	0	3.86
1 Bill Voiselle	R	28	1	4	.200	0	11	5	1	43	44	22	20	0	4.60
Andy Hansen	R	22	1	5	.167	0	27	9	1	82	78	38	18	0	4.39
2 Mort Cooper	R	34	1	5	.167	0	8	8	2	37	51	13	12	0	7.05
Bill Ayers	R	28	0	3	.000	1	13	4	0	35	46	14	22	0	8.23
Hub Andrews	R	24	0	0	.000	0	7	0	0	9	14	4	2	0	6.00
Mike Budnick	R	27	0	0	.000	0	7	1	0	12	16	10	6	0	10.50
1 Bob Carpenter	R	29	0	0	.000	0	2	0	0	3	5	3	0	0	12.00
Mario Picone	R	20	0	0	.000	0	2	1	0	7	10	2	1	0	7.71
Woody Abernathy	L	32	0	0	.000	0	1	0	0	2	4	1	0	0	9.00

Sal Maglie (SM) 30, Adrian Zabala (SM) 30, Harry Feldman (SM) 27

CINCINNATI 5th 73-81 .474 21 — JOHNNY NEUN

NAME	G by POS	B	AGE	G	AB	R	H	2B	3B	HR	RBI	BB	SO	SB	BA	SA
TOTALS			29	154	5299	681	1372	242	43	95	637	539	530	46	.259	.375
2 Babe Young	1B93	L	32	95	364	55	103	21	3	14	79	35	26	0	.283	.473
Benny Zientara	2B100, 3B13	R	27	117	418	60	108	18	1	2	24	23	23	2	.258	.321
Eddie Miller	SS151	R	30	151	545	69	146	38	4	19	87	49	40	5	.268	.457
Grady Hatton	3B136	L	24	146	524	91	147	24	8	16	77	81	50	7	.281	.448
Frankie Baumholtz	OF150	L	28	151	643	96	182	32	9	5	45	56	53	6	.283	.384
Bert Haas	OF69, 1B53	R	33	135	482	58	138	17	7	3	67	42	27	9	.286	.369
Augie Galan	OF118	L	35	124	392	60	123	18	2	6	61	94	19	0	.314	.416
Ray Lammanno	C109	R	27	118	413	33	106	21	3	5	50	28	39	0	.257	.358
Eddie Lukon	OF55	L	26	86	200	26	41	6	1	11	33	28	36	0	.205	.410
Bobby Adams	2B69	R	25	81	217	39	59	11	2	4	20	25	23	9	.272	.396
Clyde Vollmer	OF66	R	25	78	155	19	34	10	0	1	13	9	18	0	.219	.303
Ray Mueller	C55	R	35	71	192	17	48	11	0	6	33	16	25	1	.250	.401
2 Tommy Tatum	OF49, 2B1	R	27	69	176	19	48	5	2	1	16	16	16	7	.273	.341
Kermit Wahl	3B20, SS9, 2B2	R	24	39	81	8	14	0	0	1	4	6	12	0	.173	.210
2 Hugh Poland	C3	L	34	16	18	1	6	1	0	0	2	1	4	0	.333	.389
Charlie Kress	1B8	L	25	11	27	4	4	0	0	0	0	6	4	0	.148	.148
Ted Kluszewski	1B2	L	22	9	10	1	1	0	0	0	2	1	2	0	.100	.100
Bob Usher	OF8	R	22	9	22	2	4	0	0	1	1	2	2	0	.182	.318
Virgil Stallcup	SS1	R	25	8	1	1	0	0	0	0	0	0	1	0	.000	.000
1 Al Lakeman		R	28	2	2	0	0	0	0	0	0	0	1	0	.000	.000

NAME	T	AGE	W	L	PCT	SV	G	GS	CG	IP	H	BB	SO	ShO	ERA
		28	73	81	.474	13	154	154	54	1365	1442	589	633	13	4.41
Ewell Blackwell	R	24	22	8	.733	0	33	33	23	273	227	95	193	6	2.47
Harry Gumbert	R	37	10	10	.500	10	46	0	0	90	88	47	43	0	3.90
Johnny Vander Meer	L	32	9	14	.391	0	30	29	9	186	186	87	79	3	4.40
Bucky Walters	R	38	8	8	.500	0	20	20	5	122	137	49	43	2	5.75
2 Ken Raffensberger	L	29	6	5	.545	1	19	15	7	107	132	29	38	0	4.12
Kent Peterson	L	21	6	13	.316	2	37	17	3	152	156	62	78	1	4.26
Bud Lively	R	22	4	7	.364	0	38	17	3	123	126	63	52	1	4.68
Eddie Erautt	R	22	4	9	.308	0	36	10	2	119	146	53	43	0	5.07
Johnny Hetki	R	25	3	4	.429	0	37	5	2	96	110	48	33	0	5.81
Elmer Riddle	R	32	1	0	1.000	0	16	3	0	30	42	31	8	0	8.40
1 Joe Beggs	R	36	0	3	.000	0	11	4	0	32	42	6	11	0	5.34
1 Clyde Shoun	L	35	0	0	.000	0	10	0	0	14	16	5	7	0	5.14
Clay Lambert	R	30	0	0	.000	0	3	0	0	6	12	6	1	0	15.00
Harry Perkowski	L	24	0	0	.000	0	3	1	0	7	12	3	2	0	3.86
Ken Polivka	L	26	0	0	.000	0	2	0	0	3	3	3	1	0	3.00
Bob Malloy	R	29	0	0	.000	0	1	0	0	1	3	0	1	0	18.00
Mike Schultz	L	26	0	0	.000	0	1	0	0	2	4	2	0	0	4.50
Herm Wehmeier	R	20	0	0	.000	0	1	0	0	1	0	0	0	0	0.00

CHICAGO 6th 69-85 .448 25 — **CHARLIE GRIMM**

NAME	G by POS	B	AGE	G	AB	R	H	2B	3B	HR	RBI	BB	SO	SB	BA	SA
TOTALS			30	155	5305	567	1373	231	48	71	540	471	578	22	.259	.361
Eddie Waitkus	1B126	L	27	130	514	60	150	28	6	2	35	32	17	3	.292	.381
Don Johnson	2B108, 3B6	R	35	120	402	33	104	17	2	3	26	24	45	2	.259	.333
Lennie Merullo	SS108	R	30	108	373	24	90	16	1	0	29	15	26	4	.241	.290
Peanuts Lowrey	3B91, OF25, 2B6	R	28	115	448	56	126	17	5	5	37	38	26	2	.281	.375
Bill Nicholson	OF140	L	32	148	487	69	119	28	1	26	75	87	83	1	.244	.466
Andy Pafko	OF127	R	26	129	513	68	155	25	7	13	66	31	39	4	.302	.454
Phil Cavarretta	OF100, 1B24	L	30	127	459	56	144	22	5	2	63	58	35	2	.314	.397
Bob Scheffing	C97	R	31	110	363	33	96	11	5	5	50	25	25	2	.264	.364
Bobby Sturgeon	SS46, 2B30, 3B5	R	27	87	232	16	59	10	5	0	21	7	12	0	.254	.341
Clyde McCullough	C64	R	30	86	234	25	59	12	4	3	30	20	20	1	.252	.376
Stan Hack	3B66	L	37	76	240	28	65	11	2	0	12	41	19	0	.271	.333
Marv Rickert	OF30, 1B7	L	26	71	137	7	20	0	0	2	15	15	17	0	.146	.190
Dom Dallessandro	OF28	L	33	66	115	18	33	7	1	1	14	21	11	0	.287	.391
Cliff Aberson	OF40	R	25	47	140	24	39	6	3	4	20	20	32	0	.279	.450
1 Lonny Frey	2B9	L	36	24	43	4	9	0	0	0	3	4	6	0	.209	.209
2 Ray Mack	2B21	R	30	21	78	9	17	6	0	2	12	5	15	0	.218	.372
1 Mickey Livingston	C7	R	32	19	33	2	7	2	0	0	3	1	5	0	.212	.273
Billy Jurges	SS14	R	39	14	40	5	8	2	0	1	2	9	9	0	.200	.325
Sal Madrid	SS8	R	27	8	24	0	3	1	0	0	1	1	6	0	.125	.167

Hank Schenz 28 R 1-14, Dewey Williams 31 R 0-2

NAME	T	AGE	W	L	PCT	SV	G	GS	CG	IP	H	BB	SO	ShO	ERA
		29	69	85	.448	15	155	155	46	1367	1449	618	571	8	4.10
Johnny Schmitz	L	26	13	18	.419	4	38	28	10	207	209	80	97	3	3.22
Doyle Lade	R	26	11	10	.524	0	34	25	7	187	202	79	62	1	3.95
Emil Kush	R	30	8	3	.727	5	47	1	1	91	80	53	44	0	3.36
Hank Borowy	R	31	8	12	.400	2	40	25	7	183	190	63	75	1	4.38
Bob Chipman	L	28	7	6	.538	0	32	17	5	135	135	66	51	1	3.67
Paul Erickson	R	31	7	12	.368	1	40	20	6	174	179	93	82	0	4.34
Hank Wyse	R	29	6	9	.400	1	37	19	5	142	158	64	53	1	4.31
Russ Meyer (NJ)	R	23	3	2	.600	0	23	2	1	45	43	14	22	0	3.40
Russ Meers	L	28	2	0	1.000	0	35	1	0	64	61	38	28	0	4.50
Claude Passeau	R	38	2	6	.250	2	19	6	1	63	97	24	26	1	6.29
Ox Miller	R	32	1	2	.333	0	4	4	1	16	31	5	7	0	10.13
Ralph Hamner	R	30	1	2	.333	0	3	3	2	25	24	16	14	0	2.52
2 Bob Carpenter	R	29	0	1	.000	0	4	1	0	7	10	4	1	0	5.14
Bill Lee	R	37	0	2	.000	0	14	2	0	24	26	14	9	0	4.50
3 Freddy Schmidt	R	31	0	0	.000	0	1	1	0	3	4	5	0	0	9.00

PHILADELPHIA 7th (Tie) 62-92 .403 32 — **BEN CHAPMAN**

NAME	G by POS	B	AGE	G	AB	R	H	2B	3B	HR	RBI	BB	SO	SB	BA	SA
TOTALS			29	155	5256	589	1354	210	52	60	544	464	594	60	.258	.352
2 Howie Schultz	1B114	R	24	114	403	30	90	19	1	6	35	21	70	0	.223	.320
Emil Verban	2B155	R	31	155	540	50	154	14	8	0	42	23	8	5	.285	.341
Skeeter Newsome	SS85, 2B6, 3B1	R	36	95	310	36	71	8	2	2	22	24	24	4	.229	.287
Lee Handley	3B83, 2B3, SS1	R	33	101	277	17	70	10	3	0	42	24	18	1	.253	.310
Johnny Wyrostek	OF126	L	27	128	454	68	124	24	7	5	51	61	45	7	.273	.390
2 Harry Walker	OF127, 1B4	L	30	130	488	79	181	28	16*	1	41	59	37	13	.371*	.500
Del Ennis	OF135	R	22	139	541	71	149	25	6	12	81	37	51	9	.275	.410
Andy Seminick	C109	R	26	111	337	48	85	16	2	13	50	58	69	4	.252	.427
Charlie Gilbert	OF37	L	27	83	152	20	36	5	2	2	10	13	14	1	.237	.336
Jim Tabor	3B67	R	33	75	251	27	59	14	0	4	31	20	21	2	.235	.339
Don Padgett	C39	L	35	75	158	14	50	8	1	0	24	16	5	0	.316	.380
Buster Adams	OF51	R	32	69	182	21	45	11	1	2	15	26	29	2	.247	.352
Ralph LaPointe	SS54	R	25	56	211	33	65	7	0	1	15	17	15	8	.308	.355
2 Al Lakeman	1B29, C23	R	28	55	182	11	29	3	0	6	19	5	39	0	.159	.275
Schoolboy Rowe	P31	R	37	43	79	9	22	2	0	2	11	13	18	0	.278	.380
Jack Albright (BL)	SS33	R	26	41	99	9	23	4	0	2	5	10	11	1	.232	.333
Willie Jones	3B17	R	21	18	62	5	14	0	1	0	10	7	0	2	.226	.258
1 Frank McCormick	1B12	R	36	15	40	7	9	2	0	1	8	3	2	0	.225	.350
Nick Etten	1B11	L	33	14	41	5	10	4	0	1	8	5	4	0	.244	.415
1 Ron Northey	OF13	L	27	13	47	7	12	3	0	0	3	6	3	1	.255	.319

Lou Finney 36 L 0-4, 1 Hugh Poland 34 L 0-8, Putsy Caballero 19 R 1-7, Granny Hamner 20 R 2-7, Rollie Hemsley 40 R 1-3, Jesse Levan 20 L 4-9

NAME	T	AGE	W	L	PCT	SV	G	GS	CG	IP	H	BB	SO	ShO	ERA
		32	62	92	.403	14	155	155	70	1362	1399	501	514	8	3.96
Dutch Leonard	R	38	17	12	.586	0	32	29	19	235	224	57	103	3	2.68
Schoolboy Rowe	R	37	14	10	.583	1	31	28	15	196	232	45	74	1	4.32
2 Ken Heintzelman	L	31	7	10	.412	1	24	19	8	136	144	46	55	0	4.04
2 Freddy Schmidt	R	31	5	8	.385	0	29	5	0	77	76	43	24	0	4.68
Blix Donnelly	R	33	4	6	.400	5	38	10	5	121	113	46	31	1	2.98
Tommy Hughes	R	27	4	11	.267	1	29	15	4	127	121	59	44	1	3.47
Oscar Judd	L	39	4	15	.211	0	32	19	8	147	155	69	54	1	4.69
Charley Schanz	R	28	2	4	.333	2	34	6	1	102	107	47	42	0	4.15
1 Ken Raffensberger	L	29	2	6	.250	0	10	7	3	41	50	8	16	1	5.49
Curt Simmons	L	18	1	0	1.000	0	1	1	1	9	5	6	9	0	1.00
Frank Hoerst	L	29	1	1	.500	0	4	1	0	11	19	3	0	0	8.18
Al Jurisich	R	25	1	7	.125	3	34	12	5	118	110	52	48	0	4.96
Dick Koecher	L	21	0	2	.000	0	3	2	1	17	20	10	4	0	4.76
Dick Mauney	R	27	0	0	.000	1	9	1	0	16	15	7	6	0	3.94
Homer Spragins	R	26	0	0	.000	0	4	0	0	5	3	3	3	0	7.20
Lou Possehl	R	21	0	0	.000	0	2	0	0	1	5	0	1	0	1.00

*Walker, also with St. Louis, league leader in 3B (16), BA (.363)

PITTSBURGH 7th (Tie) 62-92 .403 32 — **BILLY HERMAN** 61-92 .399 — **BILL BURWELL** 1-0 1.000

NAME	G by POS	B	AGE	G	AB	R	H	2B	3B	HR	RBI	BB	SO	SB	BA	SA
TOTALS			29	156	5307	744	1385	216	44	156	699	607	687	30	.261	.406
Hank Greenberg	1B119	R	36	125	402	71	100	13	2	25	74	104	73	0	.249	.478
Jimmy Bloodworth	2B87	R	29	88	316	27	79	9	0	7	48	16	39	1	.250	.345
Billy Cox	SS129	R	27	132	529	75	145	30	7	15	54	29	28	5	.274	.442
Frankie Gustine	3B156	R	27	156	616	102	183	30	6	9	67	63	65	5	.297	.409
Wally Westlake	OF109	R	26	112	407	59	111	17	4	17	69	27	63	5	.273	.459
Jim Russell	OF119	B	28	128	478	68	121	21	8	8	51	63	58	7	.253	.381
Ralph Kiner	OF152	R	24	152	565	118	177	23	4	51	127	98	81	1	.313	.639
Dixie Howell	C74	R	28	76	214	23	59	11	0	4	25	27	34	1	.276	.383
Culley Rikard	OF79	L	33	109	324	57	93	16	4	4	32	50	39	1	.287	.398
Clyde Kluttz	C69	R	29	73	232	26	70	9	2	6	42	17	18	1	.302	.435
Elbie Fletcher	1B50	L	31	69	157	22	38	9	1	1	22	29	24	2	.242	.331
Eddie Basinski	2B56	R	24	56	161	15	32	6	2	4	17	18	27	0	.199	.335
W. Wietelmann	SS22, 2B14, 3B6, 1B1	B	28	48	128	21	30	4	1	1	7	12	10	0	.234	.305
Bill Salkeld	C15	L	30	47	61	5	13	2	0	0	8	6	8	0	.213	.246
Billy Sullivan	C12	L	36	38	55	1	14	3	0	0	8	6	3	1	.255	.309
Gene Woodling	OF21	L	24	22	79	7	21	2	2	0	10	7	5	0	.266	.342
Roy Jarvis	C15	R	21	18	45	4	7	1	0	1	4	6	5	0	.156	.244
Gene Mauch	2B6, SS4	R	21	16	30	8	9	0	0	0	1	7	6	0	.300	.300
Billy Herman	2B10, 1B2	R	37	15	47	3	10	4	0	0	6	2	7	0	.213	.298

Pete Castiglione 26 R 14-50, 1 Al Gionfriddo 25 L 0-1

NAME	T	AGE	W	L	PCT	SV	G	GS	CG	IP	H	BB	SO	ShO	ERA
		33	62	92	.403	13	156	156	44	1374	1488	592	530	9	4.68
Fritz Ostermueller	L	39	12	10	.545	0	26	24	12	183	181	68	66	3	3.84
Ernie Bonham	R	33	11	8	.579	3	33	18	7	150	167	35	63	3	3.84
2 Kirby Higbe	R	32	11	17	.393	5	46	30	10	225	204	110*	99	1	3.72
Rip Sewell	R	40	6	4	.600	0	24	12	4	121	121	36	36	1	3.57
Jim Bagby	R	30	5	4	.556	0	37	6	2	116	143	37	23	0	4.66
Preacher Roe	L	32	4	15	.211	2	38	22	4	144	156	63	59	1	5.25
Ed Bahr	R	27	3	5	.375	0	19	11	1	82	82	43	25	0	4.61
2 Mel Queen	R	29	3	7	.300	0	14	12	2	74	70	51	34	0	4.01
Elmer Singleton	R	29	2	2	.500	1	36	3	0	67	70	39	24	0	6.31
2 Al Lyons	R	28	1	2	.333	0	13	0	0	28	36	12	16	0	7.39
Art Herring	R	40	1	3	.250	2	11	0	0	11	18	4	6	0	8.18
Steve Nagy	L	28	1	3	.250	0	6	1	0	14	18	9	4	0	5.79
2 Roger Wolff	R	36	1	4	.200	0	13	6	1	30	49	18	7	0	8.70
Nick Strincevich	R	32	1	6	.143	0	32	7	1	89	111	37	22	0	5.26
2 Hank Behrman	R	26	0	2	.000	0	10	2	0	25	33	17	11	0	9.00
1 Ken Heintzelman	L	31	0	0	.000	0	2	1	0	4	9	6	2	0	20.25
Lee Howard	L	23	0	0	.000	0	2	0	0	3	4	0	2	0	3.00
Hugh Mulcahy	R	33	0	0	.000	0	2	1	0	7	8	7	2	0	3.86
Ken Gables	R	28	0	0	.000	0	1	0	0	.1	3	0	0	0	54.00

Cal McLish 21 R 0-0, Lou Tost 36 L 0-0

*Higbe, also with Brooklyn, league leader in BB with 122

WORLD SERIES – NEW YORK (AL) 4 BROOKLYN (NL) 3

LINE SCORES

TEAM	1	2	3	4	5	6	7	8	9	10	11	12	R	H	E
Game 1 September 30 at New York															
BKN (NL)	1	0	0	0	0	1	1	0	0				3	6	0
NY (AL)	0	0	0	0	5	0	0	0	X				5	4	0
Game 2 October 1 at New York															
BKN	0	0	1	1	0	0	0	0	1				3	9	2
NY	1	0	1	1	2	1	4	0	X				10	15	1
Game 3 October 2 at Brooklyn															
NY	0	0	2	2	2	1	1	0	0				8	13	0
BKN	0	6	1	2	0	0	0	0	X				9	13	1
Game 4 October 3 at Brooklyn															
NY	1	0	0	1	0	0	0	0	0				2	8	1
BKN	0	0	0	0	1	0	0	0	2				3	1	3
Game 5 October 4 at Brooklyn															
NY	0	0	0	1	1	0	0	0	0				2	5	0
BKN	0	0	0	0	0	1	0	0	0				1	4	1
Game 6 October 5 at New York															
BKN	2	0	2	0	0	4	0	0	0				8	12	1
NY	0	0	4	1	0	0	0	0	1				6	15	2
Game 7 October 6 at New York															
BKN	0	2	0	0	0	0	0	0	0				2	7	0
NY	0	1	0	2	0	1	1	0	X				5	7	0

Game 1: **Branca**, Behrman (5), Casey (7) — **Shea**, Page (6)

Game 2: **Lombardi**, Gregg (5), Behrman (7), Barney (7) — **Reynolds**

Game 3: **Newsom**, Raschi (2), Drews (3), Chandler (4), Page (6) — Hatten, Branca (5), **Casey** (7)

Game 4: **Bevens** — Taylor, Gregg (1), Behrman (8), **Casey** (9)

Game 5: **Shea** — **Barney**, Hatten (5), Behrman (7), Casey (8)

Game 6: Lombardi, **Branca** (3), Hatten (6), Casey (9) — Reynolds, Drews (3), **Page** (5), Newsom (6), Raschi (7), Wensloff (8)

Game 7: **Gregg**, Behrman (4), Hatten (6), Barney (6), Casey (7) — Shea, Bevens (2), **Page** (5)

COMPOSITE BATTING

NAME	POS	G	AB	R	H	2B	3B	HR	RBI	BA
New York (AL) Totals		7	238	38	67	11	5	4	36	.282
Henrich	OF	7	31	2	10	2	0	1	5	.323
Stirnweiss	2B	7	27	3	7	0	1	0	3	.259
Rizzuto	SS	7	26	3	8	1	0	0	2	.308
Johnson	3B	7	26	8	7	0	3	0	2	.269
DiMaggio	OF	7	26	4	6	0	0	2	5	.231
McQuinn	1B	7	23	3	3	0	0	0	1	.130
Berra	C-OF	6	19	2	3	0	0	1	2	.158
Lindell	OF	6	18	3	9	3	1	0	7	.500
A. Robinson	C	3	10	2	2	0	0	0	1	.200
Shea	P	3	5	0	2	1	0	0	1	.400
Lollar	C	2	4	3	3	2	0	0	1	.750
Reynolds	P	2	4	2	2	0	0	0	1	.500
Page	P	4	4	0	0	0	0	0	0	.000
Bevens	P	2	4	0	0	0	0	0	0	.000
Brown	PH	4	3	2	3	2	0	0	3	1.000
Clark	OF	3	2	1	1	0	0	0	1	.500
Phillips	1B	2	2	0	0	0	0	0	0	.000
Drews	P	2	2	0	0	0	0	0	0	.000
Houk	PH	1	1	0	1	0	0	0	0	1.000
Frey	PH	1	1	0	0	0	0	0	1	.000

Newsom P 0-0, Raschi P 0-0, Chandler P 0-0, Wensloff P 0-0

NAME	POS	G	AB	R	H	2B	3B	HR	RBI	BA
Brooklyn (NL) Totals		7	226	29	52	13	1	1	26	.230
J. Robinson	1B	7	27	3	7	2	0	0	3	.259
Walker	OF	7	27	1	6	1	0	1	4	.222
Edwards	C	7	27	3	6	1	0	0	2	.222
Stanky	2B	7	25	4	6	1	0	0	2	.240
Reese	SS	7	23	5	7	1	0	0	4	.304
Jorgensen	3B	7	20	1	4	2	0	0	3	.200
Hermanski	OF	7	19	4	3	0	1	0	1	.158
Furillo	OF	6	17	2	6	2	0	0	3	.353
Reiser	OF	5	8	1	2	0	0	0	0	.250
Lavagetto	3B	5	7	0	1	1	0	0	3	.143
Miksis	2B-OF	5	4	1	1	0	0	0	0	.250
Branca	P	3	4	0	0	0	0	0	0	.000
Hatten	P	4	3	1	1	0	0	0	0	.333
Gionfriddo	OF	4	3	2	0	0	0	0	0	.000
Gregg	P	3	3	0	0	0	0	0	0	.000
Lombardi	P	3	3	0	0	0	0	0	0	.000
Vaughan	PH	3	2	0	1	1	0	0	0	.500
Bragan	PH	1	1	0	1	1	0	0	1	1.000

Hodges PH 0-1, Casey P 0-1, Barney P 0-1, Taylor P 0-0, Bankhead PR 0-0

COMPOSITE PITCHING

NAME	G	IP	H	BB	SO	W	L	SV	ERA
New York (AL) Totals	7	61.2	52	30	32	4	3	1	4.09
Shea	3	15.1	10	8	10	2	0	0	2.35
Page	4	13	12	2	7	1	1	1	4.15
Bevens	2	11.1	3	11	7	0	1	0	2.38
Reynolds	2	11.1	15	3	6	1	0	0	4.76
Drews	2	3	2	1	0	0	0	0	3.00
Newsom	2	2.1	6	2	0	0	1	0	19.29
Wensloff	1	2	0	0	0	0	0	0	0.00
Chandler	1	2	2	3	1	0	0	0	9.00
Raschi	2	1.1	2	0	1	0	0	0	6.75
Brooklyn (NL) Totals	7	60	67	38	37	3	4	1	5.55
Gregg	3	12.2	9	8	10	0	1	0	3.55
Casey	6	10.1	5	1	3	2	0	1	0.87
Hatten	4	9	12	7	5	0	0	0	7.00
Branca	3	8.1	12	5	8	1	1	0	8.64
Barney	3	6.2	4	10	3	0	1	0	2.70
Lombardi	2	6.2	14	1	5	0	1	0	12.16
Behrman	5	6.1	9	5	3	0	0	0	7.11
Taylor	1	0	2	1	0	0	0	0	0.00

1948 Nylons and Orchids

The Boston Red Sox and Cleveland Indians struggled through their 154-game schedule, only to find themselves having to play another game before the American League had a team to present to the World Series. What had happened for the first time in junior circuit history was a flat-footed tie for first place. Contributing to the excitement was the fact that the Yankees, led by Joe DiMaggio, stayed in the race until they were eliminated by the Red Sox on the next to last day of the season.

The winner-take-all playoff game was set in motion when Cleveland dropped their finale to Detroit, and Boston again got by New York. The climax was staged in Boston and was short-lived as Lou Boudreau poled two home runs, and rookie Gene Bearden allowed five hits in an 8-3 rout.

Despite producing the league batting champion in Ted Williams (.369), getting Joe McCarthy out of retirement, and making a great rush after a dismal 14-23 Memorial Day record, the Red Sox—in a sense—never stood a chance against the Cleveland spirit, promoted by Indian owner Bill Veeck. Included in Veeck's bag of surprises, which was vital and fresh enough to snap the turnstiles 2,260,627 times, (a then all-time high) were: giving away nylons to women fans, flying in thousands of orchids from Hawaii, opening a nursery under the stands of Memorial Stadium so mothers could attend games, honoring Mr. Average Fan—Joe Earley—with gifts at home plate, having a special night and raising $40,000 for pitcher Don Black, who days before had suffered a cerebral hemorrhage while at bat, and signing the 41-year-old legendary black pitcher from the Kansas City Monarchs, Leroy Satchel Paige.

Stunts and promotions alone did not bring Veeck a pennant. In addition to Boudreau, who finished second in batting with .355 and won the MVP, there was Bearden, tops with a 2.43 E.R.A., Bob Lemon, and Bob Feller, as well as ace reliever Russ Christopher and southpaw Sam Zoldak, whom Veeck picked up in trades.

Stan Musial dominated the National League statistics and narrowly missed the Triple Crown by one home run, while the Braves climaxed an upsurge under manager Billy Southworth to clinch their first flag since their miraculous predecessors turned the trick in 1914. The story for the Braves began with a phrase glorifying two of their pitchers that is certain to be echoed whenever the National League winner of 1948 is mentioned—"Spahn and Sain and two days of rain", attributed to Warren Spahn and Johnny Sain, who combined for 39 victories with Sain contributing a league high of 24.

Also responsible for the Braves' success was shortstop Al Dark, who hit .322 in his first full season and second baseman Eddie Stanky, who was acquired in a trade from Brooklyn during spring training and hit .320 before being sidelined in early July with a broken ankle.

In the Series opener, Feller allowed two hits and lost 1-0 to Sain on a run scored by Phil Masi after the Indians were sure that he had been picked off second base. The umpire disagreed and Tommy Holmes promptly singled Masi home. Lemon evened matters the next day with a 4-1 win over Spahn, and Bearden put the Indians in front to stay with a 2-0 win over the Braves in the third game. In the fourth game, Boston finally got Sain a run, but fell short as the Indians put two across for Steve Gromek. The Braves' last surge came in the next game as Bob Elliott hit two homers in leading an assault, before Lemon and Bearden combined with a 4-3 win to bring Cleveland their first Series win since 1920.

1948 AMERICAN LEAGUE

NAME	G by POS	B	AGE	G	AB	R	H	2B	3B	HR	RBI	BB	SO	SB	BA	SA
CLEVELAND 1st 97-58 .626		LOU BOUDREAU (Defeated Boston in a 1 game playoff)														
TOTALS			28	156	**5446**	840	**1534**	242	54	**155**	802	646	**575**	54	**.283**	.431
Eddie Robinson	1B131	L	27	134	493	53	125	18	5	16	83	36	42	1	.254	.408
Joe Gordon	2B144, SS2	R	33	144	550	96	154	21	4	32	124	77	68	5	.280	.507
Lou Boudreau	SS151, C1	R	30	152	560	116	199	34	6	18	106	98	9	3	.355	.534
Ken Keltner	3B153	R	31	153	558	91	166	24	4	31	119	89	52	2	.297	.522
Larry Doby	OF114	L	24	121	439	83	132	23	9	14	66	54	77	9	.301	.490
Thurman Tucker	OF66	L	30	83	242	52	63	13	2	1	19	31	17	11	.260	.343
Dale Mitchell	OF140	L	26	141	608	82	204	30	8	4	56	45	17	13	.336	.431
Jim Hegan	C142	R	27	144	472	60	117	21	6	14	61	48	74	6	.248	.407
Allie Clark	OF65, 3B5, 1B1	R	25	81	271	43	84	5	2	9	38	23	13	0	.310	.443
Walt Judnich	OF49, 1B20	L	30	79	218	36	56	13	3	2	29	56	23	2	.257	.372
J. Berardino	2B20, 1B18, SS12, 3B3	R	31	66	147	19	28	5	1	2	10	27	16	0	.190	.279
2 Bob Kennedy	OF50, 2B2, 1B1	R	27	66	73	10	22	3	2	0	5	4	6	0	.301	.397
Hank Edwards (SJ)	OF41	L	29	55	160	27	43	9	2	3	18	18	18	1	.269	.406
Bob Lemon	P43	L	27	52	119	20	34	9	0	5	21	8	23	0	.286	.487
Joe Tipton	C40	R	25	47	90	11	26	3	0	1	13	4	10	0	.289	.356
Hal Peck	OF9	L	31	45	63	12	18	3	0	0	8	4	8	1	.286	.333
1 Pat Seerey	OF7	R	25	10	23	7	6	0	0	1	6	7	**8***	0	.261	.391
Ray Boone	SS4	R	24	6	5	0	2	1	0	0	1	0	1	0	.400	.600
Al Rosen	3B2	R	24	5	5	0	1	0	0	0	0	0	2	0	.200	.200
Ray Murray		R	30	4	4	0	0	0	0	0	0	0	3	0	.000	.000
BOSTON 2nd 96-59 .619 1		JOE McCARTHY (Defeated by Cleveland in a 1 game playoff)														
TOTALS			30	155	5363	**907**	1471	**277**	40	121	**854**	**823**	552	38	.274	.409
Billy Goodman	1B117, 2B2, 3B2	L	22	127	445	65	138	27	2	1	66	74	44	5	.310	.387
Bobby Doerr	2B138	R	30	140	527	94	150	23	6	27	111	83	49	3	.285	.505
Vern Stephens	SS155	R	27	155	635	114	171	25	8	29	137	77	56	1	.269	.471
Johnny Pesky	3B141	L	28	143	565	124	159	26	6	3	55	99	32	3	.281	.365
Stan Spence	OF92, 1B14	L	33	114	391	71	92	17	4	12	61	82	33	0	.235	.391
Dom DiMaggio	OF155	R	31	155	**648**	127	185	40	4	9	87	101	58	10	.285	.401
Ted Williams	OF134	L	29	137	509	124	188	**44**	3	25	127	**126**	41	4	**.369**	**.615**
Birdie Tebbetts	C126	R	38	128	446	54	125	26	2	5	68	62	32	5	.280	.381
Wally Moses	OF45	L	37	78	189	26	49	12	1	2	29	21	19	5	.259	.365
Sam Mele	OF55	R	25	66	180	25	42	12	1	2	25	13	21	1	.233	.344
Billy Hitchcock	2B15, 3B15	R	31	49	124	15	37	3	2	1	20	7	9	0	.298	.379
Matt Batts	C41	R	26	46	118	13	37	12	0	1	24	15	9	0	.314	.441
Jake Jones	1B31	R	27	36	105	3	21	4	0	1	8	11	26	1	.200	.267
Babe Martin	C1	R	28	4	4	0	2	0	0	0	0	0	1	0	.500	.500
Lou Stringer	2B2	R	31	4	11	1	1	0	0	1	1	0	3	0	.091	.364
Tom Wright		L	24	3	2	1	1	0	1	0	0	0	0	0	.500	1.500
Neill Sheridan		R	26	2	1	0	0	0	0	0	0	0	1	0	.000	.000
John Ostrowski		R	30	1	1	0	0	0	0	0	0	0	1	0	.000	.000
NEW YORK 3rd 94-60 .610 2.5		BUCKY HARRIS														
TOTALS			30	154	5324	857	1480	251	**75**	139	806	623	478	24	.278	**.432**
George McQuinn	1B90	L	39	94	302	33	75	11	4	11	41	40	38	0	.248	.421
Snuffy Stirnweiss	2B141	R	29	141	515	90	130	20	7	3	32	86	62	5	.252	.336
Phil Rizzuto	SS128	R	30	128	464	65	117	13	2	6	50	60	24	6	.252	.328
Billy Johnson	3B118	R	29	127	446	59	131	20	6	12	64	41	30	0	.294	.446
Tommy Henrich	OF102, 1B46	L	35	146	588	**138**	181	42	**14**	25	100	76	42	2	.308	.554
Joe DiMaggio	OF152	R	33	153	594	110	190	26	11	**39**	**155**	67	30	1	.320	.598
Johnny Lindell	OF79	R	31	88	309	58	98	17	2	13	55	35	50	0	.317	.511
Gus Niarhos	C82	R	27	83	228	41	61	12	2	0	19	52	15	1	.268	.338
Yogi Berra	C71, OF50	L	23	125	469	70	143	24	10	14	98	25	24	3	.305	.488
Bobby Brown	3B41, SS26, 2B17, OF4	L	23	113	363	62	109	19	5	3	48	48	16	0	.300	.405
Charlie Keller (BH)	OF66	L	31	83	247	41	66	15	2	6	44	41	25	1	.267	.417
Cliff Mapes	OF21	L	26	53	88	19	22	11	1	1	12	6	13	1	.250	.432
Steve Souchock	1B32	R	29	44	118	11	24	3	1	3	11	7	13	3	.203	.322
Sherm Lollar	C10	R	23	22	38	0	8	0	0	0	4	1	6	0	.211	.211
Hank Bauer	OF14	R	25	19	50	6	9	1	1	1	9	6	13	1	.180	.300
Frankie Crosetti	2B6, SS5	R	37	17	14	4	4	0	1	0	0	2	0	0	.286	.429
Ralph Houk	C14	R	28	14	29	3	8	2	0	0	3	0	0	0	.276	.345
1 Bud Stewart		L	32	6	5	1	1	1	0	0	0	0	0	0	.200	.400
Joe Collins		L	25	5	5	0	1	1	0	0	2	0	1	0	.200	.400
Charlie Silvera	C4	R	23	4	14	1	8	0	1	0	1	0	1	0	.571	.714
1 Lonny Frey		L	37	1	0	1	0	0	0	0	0	0	0	0	.000	.000
Jack Phillips	1B1	R	26	1	2	0	0	0	0	0	0	0	1	0	.000	.000

NAME	T	AGE	W	L	PCT	SV	G	GS	CG	IP	H	BB	SO	ShO	ERA
		30	**97**	58	**.626**	**30**	156	156	66	**1409**	1246	628	595	**26**	**3.23**
Gene Bearden	L	27	20	7	.741	1	37	29	15	230	187	106	80	6	**2.43**
Bob Lemon	R	27	20	14	.588	2	43	37	**20**	**294**	231	129	147	**10**	2.82
Bob Feller	R	29	19	15	.559	3	44	**38**	18	280	**255**	116	**164**	2	3.57
Steve Gromek	R	28	9	3	.750	2	38	9	4	130	109	51	50	1	2.84
2 Sam Zoldak	L	29	9	6	.600	0	23	12	4	106	104	24	17	1	2.80
Satchel Paige	R	41	6	1	.857	1	21	7	3	73	61	25	45	2	2.47
Bob Muncrief	R	32	5	4	.556	0	21	9	1	72	76	31	24	1	4.00
Russ Christopher	R	30	3	2	.600	**17**	45	0	0	59	55	27	14	0	2.90
Eddie Klieman	R	30	3	2	.600	4	44	0	0	80	62	46	18	0	2.59
Don Black (OJ)	R	31	2	2	.500	0	18	10	1	52	57	40	16	0	5.37
1 Bill Kennedy	L	27	1	0	1.000	0	6	3	0	11	16	13	12	0	11.45
1 Al Gettel	R	30	0	1	.000	0	5	2	0	8	15	10	4	0	16.88
Butch Wensloff	R	32	0	1	.000	0	1	0	0	2	2	3	2	0	9.00
Lyman Linde	R	27	0	0	.000	0	3	0	0	10	9	4	0	0	5.40
Ernie Groth	R	26	0	0	.000	0	1	0	0	1	1	2	0	0	9.00
Mike Garcia	R	24	0	0	.000	0	1	0	0	2	3	0	1	0	0 00
Les Webber	R	33	0	0	.000	0	1	0	0	1	3	1	1	0	27.00

*Seerey, also with Chicago, league leader in SO with 102

NAME	T	AGE	W	L	PCT	SV	G	GS	CG	IP	H	BB	SO	ShO	ERA
		30	96	59	.619	13	155	155	70	1379	1445	592	513	111	4.26
Jack Kramer	R	30	18	5	**.783**	0	29	29	14	205	233	64	72	2	4.35
Joe Dobson	R	31	16	10	.615	2	38	32	16	245	237	92	116	5	3.56
Mel Parnell	L	26	15	8	.652	0	35	27	16	212	205	90	77	1	3.14
Earl Johnson	L	29	10	4	.714	5	35	3	1	91	98	42	45	0	4.55
Ellis Kinder	R	33	10	7	.588	0	28	22	10	178	183	63	53	1	3.74
Denny Galehouse	R	36	8	8	.500	3	27	15	6	137	152	46	38	1	4.01
Boo Ferriss	R	26	7	3	.700	3	31	9	1	115	127	61	30	0	5.24
Mickey Harris	L	31	7	10	.412	0	20	17	6	114	120	59	42	1	5.29
Tex Hughson (SA)	R	32	3	1	.750	0	15	0	0	19	21	7	6	0	5.21
Cot Deal	R	25	1	0	1.000	0	4	0	0	4	3	3	2	0	0.00
2 Earl Caldwell	R	43	1	1	.500	0	8	0	0	9	11	11	5	0	13.00
Harry Dorish	R	26	0	1	.000	0	9	0	0	14	18	6	5	0	5.79
Windy McCall	L	22	0	1	.000	0	1	1	0	1	6	1	0	0	27.00
Mickey McDermott	L	19	0	0	.000	0	7	0	0	23	16	35	17	0	6.26
Chuch Stobbs	L	18	0	0	.000	0	6	0	0	7	9	7	4	0	6.43
Mike Palm	R	23	0	0	.000	0	3	0	0	3	6	5	1	0	6.00

NAME	T	AGE	W	L	PCT	SV	G	GS	CG	IP	H	BB	SO	ShO	ERA
		29	94	60	.610	24	154	154	62	1366	1289	641	654	16	3.75
Vic Raschi	R	29	19	8	.704	1	36	31	18	223	208	74	124	6	3.83
Ed Lopat	L	30	17	11	.607	0	33	31	13	227	246	66	83	3	3.65
Allie Reynolds	R	33	16	7	.696	3	39	31	11	236	240	111	101	1	3.78
Spec Shea	R	27	9	10	.474	1	28	22	8	156	117	87	71	3	3.40
Tommy Byrne	L	28	8	5	.615	2	31	11	5	134	79	101	93	1	3.29
Joe Page	L	30	7	8	.467	16	**55**	1	0	108	116	66	77	0	4.25
Frank Hiller	R	27	5	2	.714	0	22	5	1	62	59	30	25	0	4.06
Red Embree	R	30	5	3	.625	0	20	8	4	77	77	30	25	0	3.74
Bob Porterfield	R	24	5	3	.625	0	16	12	2	78	85	34	30	1	4.50
1 Karl Drews	R	28	2	3	.400	1	19	2	0	38	35	31	11	0	3.79
1 Randy Gumpert	R	30	1	0	1.000	0	15	0	0	25	27	6	12	0	2.88
Cuddles Marshall	R	23	0	0	.000	0	1	0	0	1	0	3	0	0	0.00
Dick Starr	R	27	0	0	.000	0	1	0	0	2	0	2	2	0	4.50

PHILADELPHIA 4th 84-70 .545 12.5 — CONNIE MACK

NAME	G by POS	B	AGE	G	AB	R	H	2B	3B	HR	RBI	BB	SO	SB	BA	SA
TOTALS			30	154	5181	729	1345	231	47	68	685	726	523	40	.260	.362
Ferris Fain	1B145	L	27	145	520	81	146	27	6	7	88	113	37	10	.281	.396
Pete Suder	2B148	R	32	148	519	64	125	23	5	7	60	60	60	1	.241	.345
Eddie Joost	SS135	R	32	135	509	99	127	22	2	16	55	119	87	2	.250	.395
Hank Majeski	3B142, SS8	R	31	148	590	88	183	41	4	12	120	48	43	2	.310	.454
Elmer Valo	OF109	L	27	113	383	72	117	17	4	3	46	81	13	10	.305	.394
Sam Chapman	OF118	R	32	123	445	58	115	18	6	13	70	55	50	6	.258	.413
Barney McCoskey	OF134	L	30	135	515	95	168	21	5	0	46	68	22	1	.326	.386
Buddy Rosar	C90	R	33	90	302	30	77	13	0	4	41	39	12	0	.255	.338
Don White	OF54, 3B17	R	29	86	253	29	62	14	2	1	28	19	16	0	.245	.328
2 Ray Coleman	OF53	L	26	68	210	32	51	6	6	0	21	31	17	4	.243	.329
Mike Guerra	C47	R	35	53	142	18	30	4	2	1	23	18	13	2	.211	.289
Carl Scheib	P32, OF2	R	21	52	104	14	31	8	3	2	21	8	17	0	.298	.490
Herman Franks	C27	R	34	40	98	10	22	7	1	1	14	16	11	0	.224	.347
Rudy York	1B14	R	34	31	51	4	8	0	0	0	6	7	15	0	.157	.157
Skeeter Webb	2B9, SS8	R	38	23	54	5	8	2	0	0	3	0	9	0	.148	.185
Billy DeMars	SS9, 2B1, 3B1	R	22	18	29	3	5	0	0	0	1	5	3	0	.172	.172
1 George Binks	OF13	L	33	17	41	2	4	1	0	0	2	2	2	1	.098	.122
Bob Wellman	1B2, OF1	R	22	4	10	1	2	0	1	0	0	3	2	0	.200	.400

Nellie Fox 20 L 2-13, Earle Brucker 22 L 1-6, Bobby Estalella (SM) 37

NAME	T	AGE	W	L	PCT	SV	G	GS	CG	IP	H	BB	SO	ShO	ERA
		26	84	70	.545	18	154	154	74	1369	1456	638	486	7	4.42
Dick Fowler (AJ)	R	27	15	8	.652	2	29	26	16	205	221	76	50	2	3.78
Carl Scheib	R	21	14	8	.636	0	32	24	15	199	219	76	44	1	3.93
Lou Brissie	L	24	14	10	.583	5	39	25	11	194	202	95	127	0	4.13
Joe Coleman	R	25	14	13	.519	0	33	29	13	216	224	90	86	3	4.08
Phil Marchildon	R	34	9	15	.375	0	33	30	12	226	214	131	66	1	4.54
Bob Savage	R	26	5	1	.833	5	33	1	1	75	98	33	26	0	6.24
Charlie Harris	R	22	5	2	.714	5	45	0	0	94	89	35	32	0	4.12
Bill McCahan (SA)	R	27	4	7	.364	0	17	15	5	87	98	65	20	0	5.69
2 Nels Potter	R	36	2	2	.500	1	8	0	0	18	17	5	13	0	4.00
Walt Holborow	R	34	1	2	.333	0	5	1	1	17	32	7	3	0	5.82
Bill Dietrich	R	38	1	2	.333	0	4	2	0	15	21	9	5	0	6.00
Alex Kellner	L	23	0	0	.000	0	13	1	0	23	21	16	14	0	7.83

DETROIT 5th 78-76 .506 18.5 — STEVE O'NEILL

NAME	G by POS	B	AGE	G	AB	R	H	2B	3B	HR	RBI	BB	SO	SB	BA	SA
TOTALS			29	154	5235	700	1396	219	58	78	661	671	504	22	.267	.375
George Vico	1B142	L	24	144	521	50	139	23	9	8	58	39	39	2	.267	.392
Eddie Mayo	2B86, 3B10	L	38	106	370	35	92	20	1	2	42	30	19	1	.249	.324
Johnny Lipon	SS117, 2B1, 3B1	R	25	121	458	65	133	18	8	5	52	68	22	4	.290	.397
George Kell (BW-BJ)	3B92	R	25	92	368	47	112	24	3	2	44	33	15	2	.304	.402
Pat Mullin	OF131	L	30	138	496	91	143	16	11	23	80	77	57	1	.288	.504
Hoot Evers	OF138	R	27	139	538	81	169	33	6	10	103	51	31	3	.314	.454
Vic Wertz	OF98	L	23	119	391	49	97	19	9	7	67	48	70	0	.248	.396
Bob Swift	C112	R	33	113	292	23	65	6	0	4	33	51	29	1	.223	.284
Dick Wakefield	OF86	L	27	110	322	50	89	20	5	11	53	70	55	0	.276	.472
Neil Berry	SS41, 2B26	R	26	87	256	46	68	8	1	0	16	37	23	1	.266	.305
Fred Hutchinson	P33	R	28	76	112	11	23	1	0	1	12	23	9	3	.205	.241
Jimmy Outlaw	3B47, OF13	R	35	74	198	33	56	12	0	0	25	31	15	0	.283	.343
Eddie Lake (BG)	2B45, 3B17	R	32	64	198	51	52	6	0	2	18	57	20	3	.263	.323
Paul Campbell	1B27	L	30	59	83	15	22	1	1	1	11	1	10	0	.265	.337
1 Hal Wagner	C52	L	32	54	109	10	22	3	0	0	10	20	11	1	.202	.229
Hank Riebe	C24	R	26	25	62	0	12	0	0	0	5	0	3	0	.194	.194
Joe Ginsberg	C11	L	21	11	36	7	13	0	0	0	1	3	1	0	.361	.361
Johnny Groth	OF4	R	21	6	17	3	8	3	0	1	5	1	1	0	.471	.824
Johnny Bero	2B2	L	25	4	9	2	0	0	0	0	0	1	1	0	.000	.000
Doc Cramer	OF1	L	42	4	4	1	0	0	0	0	1	3	0	0	.000	.000
Ed Mierkowicz	OF1	R	24	3	5	0	1	0	0	0	1	2	2	0	.200	.200
John McHale		L	26	1	1	0	0	0	0	0	0	0	0	0	.000	.000

NAME	T	AGE	W	L	PCT	SV	G	GS	CG	IP	H	BB	SO	ShO	ERA
		28	78	76	.506	22	154	154	60	1377	1367	589	678	5	4.15
Hal Newhouser	L	27	21	12	.636	1	39	35	19	272	249	99	143	2	3.01
Virgil Trucks	R	29	14	13	.519	2	43	26	7	212	190	85	123	0	3.78
Fred Hutchinson	R	28	13	11	.542	0	33	28	15	221	223	48	92	0	4.32
Dizzy Trout	R	33	10	14	.417	2	32	23	11	184	193	73	91	2	3.42
Ted Gray	L	23	6	2	.750	0	26	11	3	85	73	72	60	1	4.24
Billy Pierce	L	21	3	0	1.000	0	22	5	0	55	47	51	36	0	6.38
Stubby Overmire	L	29	3	4	.429	3	37	4	0	66	89	31	14	0	6.00
Hal White	R	29	2	1	.667	1	27	0	0	43	46	26	17	0	6.07
Lou Kretlow	R	25	2	1	.667	0	5	2	1	23	21	11	9	0	4.70
Al Benton	R	37	2	2	.500	3	30	0	0	44	45	36	18	0	5.73
Art Houtteman	R	20	2	16	.111	10	43	20	4	164	186	52	74	0	4.66
Rufe Gentry	R	30	0	0	.000	0	4	0	0	7	5	5	1	0	2.57

ST. LOUIS 6th 59-94 .386 37 — ZACK TAYLOR

NAME	G by POS	B	AGE	G	AB	R	H	2B	3B	HR	RBI	BB	SO	SB	BA	SA
TOTALS			27	155	5303	671	1438	251	62	63	623	578	572	63	.271	.378
Chuck Stevens	1B85	B	29	85	288	34	75	12	4	1	26	41	26	2	.260	.340
Jerry Priddy	2B146	R	28	151	560	96	166	40	9	8	79	86	71	6	.296	.443
Eddie Pellagrini	SS98	R	30	105	290	31	69	8	3	2	27	34	40	1	.238	.307
Bob Dillinger	3B153	R	29	153	644	110	**207**	34	10	2	44	65	34	**28**	.321	.415
Al Zarilla	OF136	L	29	144	529	77	174	39	3	12	74	48	48	11	.329	.482
Paul Lehner	OF89, 1B2	L	28	103	333	23	92	15	4	2	46	30	19	0	.276	.363
Whitey Platt	OF114	R	27	123	454	57	123	22	10	7	82	39	51	1	.271	.410
Les Moss	C103	R	23	107	335	35	86	12	1	14	46	39	50	0	.257	.424
Sam Dente	SS76, 3B6	R	26	98	267	26	72	11	2	0	22	22	8	1	.270	.326
Roy Partee	C76	R	30	82	231	14	47	8	1	0	17	25	21	2	.203	.247
Dick Kokos	OF71	L	20	71	258	40	77	15	3	4	40	28	32	4	.298	.426
Hank Arft	1B69	L	26	69	248	25	59	10	3	5	38	45	43	1	.238	.363
2 Don Lund	OF45	R	25	63	161	21	40	7	4	3	25	10	17	0	.248	.398
Andy Anderson	2B21, SS10, 1B2	R	25	51	87	13	24	5	1	1	12	8	15	0	.276	.391
Joe Schultz		L	29	43	37	0	7	0	0	0	6	9	3	0	.189	.189
Pete Layden	OF30	R	28	41	104	11	26	2	1	0	4	6	10	4	.250	.288
1 Ray Coleman	OF5	L	26	17	29	2	5	0	1	0	2	2	5	1	.172	.241
2 George Binks	OF6, 1B4	L	33	15	23	2	5	0	0	0	1	2	1	0	.217	.217
Ken Wood	OF5	R	24	10	24	2	2	0	1	0	2	1	4	0	.083	.167
Jerry McCarthy	1B2	L	25	2	3	0	1	0	0	0	0	0	0	0	.333	.333
Tom Jordan		R	28	1	1	0	0	0	0	0	0	0	0	0	.000	.000

NAME	T	AGE	W	L	PCT	SV	G	GS	CG	IP	H	BB	SO	ShO	ERA
		27	59	94	.386	20	155	155	35	1373	**1513**	**737**	531	4	5.01
Fred Sanford	R	28	12	**21**	.364	2	42	33	9	227	250	91	79	1	4.64
Cliff Fannin	L	24	10	14	.417	1	34	29	10	214	198	104	102	3	4.16
2 Bill Kennedy	L	27	7	8	.467	0	26	20	3	132	132	104	77	0	4.70
Ned Garver	R	22	7	11	.389	5	38	24	7	198	200	95	75	0	3.41
Frank Biscan	L	28	6	7	.462	2	47	4	1	99	129	71	45	0	6.09
Joe Ostrowski	L	31	4	6	.400	3	26	9	3	78	108	17	20	0	6.00
2 Karl Drews	R	28	3	2	.600	2	20	2	0	38	43	38	11	0	8.05
Bryan Stephens	R	27	3	6	.333	3	43	12	2	123	141	67	35	0	6.00
1 Sam Zoldak	L	29	2	4	.333	0	11	9	0	54	64	19	13	0	4.67
Al Widmar	R	23	2	6	.250	1	49	0	0	83	88	48	34	0	4.45
Blackie Schwamb	R	21	1	1	.500	0	12	5	0	32	44	21	7	0	8.44
1 Nels Potter	R	36	1	1	.500	0	2	2	0	10	11	4	4	0	5.40
Ray Shore	R	27	1	2	.333	0	17	4	0	38	40	35	12	0	6.39
1 Clem Dreisewerd	L	32	0	2	.000	1	13	0	0	22	28	8	6	0	5.73
Al Gerheauser	L	31	0	3	.000	0	14	2	0	23	32	10	10	0	7.43
Jim Wilson	R	26	0	0	.000	0	4	0	0	3	5	5	1	0	12.00

WASHINGTON 7th 56-97 .366 40 — JOE KUHEL

NAME	G by POS	B	AGE	G	AB	R	H	2B	3B	HR	RBI	BB	SO	SB	BA	SA
TOTALS			29	154	5111	578	1245	203	**75**	31	538	568	572	**76**	.244	.331
Mickey Vernon	1B150	L	30	150	558	78	135	27	7	3	48	54	43	15	.242	.332
Al Kozar	2B149	R	25	150	577	61	144	25	8	1	58	66	52	4	.250	.326
Mark Christman	SS102, 3B9, 2B3	R	34	120	409	38	106	17	2	1	40	25	19	0	.259	.318
Eddie Yost	3B145	R	21	145	555	74	138	32	11	2	50	82	51	4	.249	.357
2 Bud Stewart	OF114	L	32	118	401	56	112	17	13	7	69	49	27	8	.279	.439
Carden Gillenwater	OF67	R	30	77	221	23	54	10	4	3	21	39	36	4	.244	.367
Gil Coan	OF131	L	26	138	513	56	119	13	9	7	60	41	78	23	.232	.333
Jake Early	C92	L	31	97	246	22	54	7	2	1	28	36	33	2	.220	.276
Al Evans	C85	R	31	93	228	19	59	6	3	2	28	38	20	1	.259	.338
Tom McBride	OF55	R	33	92	206	22	53	9	1	1	29	28	15	2	.257	.325
Earl Wooten	OF73, 1B6, P1	R	24	88	258	34	66	8	3	1	23	24	21	2	.256	.322
John Sullivan	SS57, 2B4	R	27	85	173	25	36	4	1	0	12	22	25	2	.208	.243
Early Wynn	P33	B	28	73	106	9	23	3	1	0	16	14	22	0	.217	.264
Sherry Robertson	OF51	R	29	71	187	19	46	11	3	2	22	24	26	8	.246	.369
Sammy Meeks	SS10, 2B1	R	25	24	33	4	4	1	0	0	2	1	12	0	.121	.152
Len Okrie	C17	R	24	19	42	1	10	0	1	0	1	1	7	0	.238	.286
Angel Fleitas	SS7	R	33	15	13	1	1	0	0	0	1	3	5	0	.077	.077
Leon Culberson	OF11	R	28	12	29	1	5	0	0	0	2	8	5	0	.172	.172
Jim Clark	SS1, 3B1	L	20	9	12	1	3	0	0	0	0	0	2	0	.250	.250
Larry Drake	OF2	L	27	4	7	0	2	0	0	0	1	1	3	0	.286	.286

Jay Difani R 24 0-2, 2 Clyde Vollmer R 26 2-5, Roberto Ortiz (SM) 33

NAME	T	AGE	W	L	PCT	SV	G	GS	CG	IP	H	BB	SO	ShO	ERA
		30	56	97	.366	22	154	154	42	1357	1439	734	446	4	4.66
Ray Scarborough	R	30	15	8	.652	1	31	26	9	185	166	72	76	0	2.82
Walt Masterson	R	28	8	15	.348	2	33	27	9	188	171	122	72	2	3.83
Early Wynn	R	28	8	19	.296	0	33	31	15	198	236	94	49	1	5.82
Forrest Thompson	L	30	6	10	.375	4	46	7	0	131	134	54	40	0	3.85
Mickey Haefner	L	35	5	13	.278	0	28	20	4	148	151	61	45	0	4.01
Sid Hudson	R	33	4	16	.200	1	39	29	4	182	217	107	53	0	5.88
2 Earl Harrist	R	28	3	3	.500	0	23	4	0	60	70	37	21	0	4.57
Dick Welteroth	R	20	2	1	.667	1	33	2	0	65	73	50	16	0	5.54
Milo Candini	R	30	2	3	.400	3	35	4	1	94	96	63	23	0	5.17
Tom Ferrick	R	33	2	5	.286	10	37	0	0	74	75	38	34	0	4.14
Dick Weik	R	20	1	2	.333	0	3	3	0	13	14	22	8	0	5.54
1 Marino Pieretti	R	27	0	2	.000	0	8	1	0	12	18	7	6	0	10.50
Ramon Garcia	R	24	0	0	.000	0	4	0	0	4	11	4	2	0	15.75
Earl Wooten	R	24	0	0	.000	0	1	0	0	2	2	2	1	0	9.00
Cal Cooper	R	25	0	0	.000	0	1	0	0	1	5	1	0	0	45.00

Alex Carrasquel (SM) 35

CHICAGO 8th 51-101 .336 44.5 — TED LYONS

NAME	G by POS	B	AGE	G	AB	R	H	2B	3B	HR	RBI	BB	SO	SB	BA	SA
TOTALS			30	154	5192	559	1303	172	39	55	532	695	528	46	.251	.321
Tony Lupien	1B154	L	31	154	617	69	152	19	3	6	54	74	38	11	.246	.316
Don Kolloway	2B83, 3B18	R	29	119	417	60	114	14	4	6	38	18	18	2	.273	.369
Cass Michaels	SS85, 2B55, OF1	R	22	145	484	47	120	12	6	5	56	69	42	8	.248	.329
Luke Appling	3B72, SS64	R	41	139	497	63	156	16	2	0	47	94	35	10	.314	.354
Taffy Wright	OF114	L	36	134	455	50	127	15	6	4	61	39	18	2	.279	.365
Dave Philley	OF128	B	28	137	488	51	140	28	3	5	42	50	33	8	.287	.387
2 Pat Seerey	OF93	R	25	95	340	44	78	11	0	18	64	83	**94***	0	.229	.421
Aaron Robinson	C92	L	33	98	326	47	82	14	2	8	39	46	30	0	.252	.380
Ralph Hodgin	OF79	L	32	114	331	28	88	11	5	1	34	21	11	0	.266	.338
Floyd Baker	3B71, 2B18, SS1	L	31	104	335	47	72	8	3	0	18	73	26	4	.215	.257
Ralph Weigel	C39, OF2	R	26	66	163	8	38	7	3	0	26	13	18	1	.233	.313
Mike Tresh	C34	R	34	39	108	10	27	1	0	1	11	9	9	0	.250	.287
Jack Wallaesa	SS5, OF1	B	28	33	48	2	9	0	0	1	3	1	12	0	.188	.250
1 Bob Kennedy	OF30	R	27	30	113	4	28	8	1	0	14	4	17	0	.248	.336
Jim Delsing	OF15	L	22	20	63	5	12	0	0	0	5	5	12	0	.190	.190
Herb Adams	OF4	L	20	5	11	1	3	1	0	0	0	1	1	0	.273	.364
Jerry Scala	OF2	L	21	3	6	1	0	0	0	0	0	0	3	0	.000	.000
Frank Whitman	SS1	R	23	3	6	0	0	0	0	0	0	0	3	0	.000	.000

NAME	T	AGE	W	L	PCT	SV	G	GS	CG	IP	H	BB	SO	ShO	ERA
		30	51	**101**	.336	23	154	154	35	1346	1454	673	403	2	4.89
Joe Haynes	R	30	9	10	.474	0	27	22	6	150	167	52	40	0	3.96
Bill Wight	L	26	9	20	.310	1	34	32	7	223	238	**135**	68	1	4.80
2 Al Gettel	R	30	8	10	.444	1	22	19	7	148	154	60	49	0	4.01
2 Marino Pieretti	R	27	8	10	.444	1	21	18	4	120	117	52	28	0	4.95
Howie Judson	R	22	4	5	.444	8	40	5	1	107	102	56	38	0	4.79
Glen Moulder	R	30	3	6	.333	2	33	9	0	86	108	54	26	0	6.38
Ike Pearson	R	31	2	3	.400	1	23	2	0	53	62	27	12	0	4.92
2 Randy Gumpert	R	30	2	6	.250	0	16	11	6	97	103	13	31	1	3.80
Frank Papish	L	30	2	8	.200	4	32	14	2	95	97	75	41	0	5.02
Orval Grove	R	28	2	10	.167	1	32	11	1	88	110	42	18	0	6.14
1 Earl Harrist	R	28	1	3	.250	0	11	1	0	23	23	13	14	0	5.87
1 Earl Caldwell	R	43	1	5	.167	3	25	1	0	39	53	22	10	0	5.31
Marv Rotblatt	L	20	0	1	.000	0	7	2	0	18	19	23	4	0	8.00
Bob Gillespie	R	29	0	4	.000	0	25	6	1	72	81	33	19	0	5.13
Fred Bradley	R	27	0	0	.000	0	8	0	0	16	11	4	2	0	4.50
Jim Goodwin	L	21	0	0	.000	1	8	1	0	10	9	12	3	0	9.00

*Seerey, also with Cleveland, league leader in SO with 102

BOSTON 1st 91-62 .595 — BILLY SOUTHWORTH

NAME	G by POS	B	AGE	G	AB	R	H	2B	3B	HR	RBI	BB	SO	SB	BA	SA
TOTALS			30	154	5297	739	**1458**	**272**	49	95	695	**671**	536	43	**.275**	.399
Earl Torgeson	1B129	L	24	134	438	70	111	23	5	10	67	81	54	19	.253	.397
Eddie Stanky (BN)	2B66	R	31	67	247	49	79	14	2	2	29	61	13	3	.320	.417
Al Dark	SS133	R	26	137	543	85	175	39	6	3	48	24	36	4	.322	.433
Bob Elliott	3B150	R	31	151	540	99	153	24	5	23	100	**131**	57	6	.283	.474
Tommy Holmes	OF137	L	31	139	585	85	190	35	7	6	61	46	20	1	.325	.439
Mike McCormick	OF100	R	31	115	343	45	104	22	7	1	39	32	34	1	.303	.417
Jeff Heath (BN)	OF106	L	33	115	364	64	116	26	5	20	76	51	46	2	.319	.582
Phil Masi	C109	R	31	113	376	43	95	19	0	5	44	35	26	2	.253	.343
Clint Conatser	OF76	R	26	90	224	30	62	9	3	3	23	32	27	0	.277	.384
Jim Russell (IL)	OF84	B	29	89	322	44	85	18	1	9	54	46	31	4	.264	.410
Sibby Sisti	2B44, SS26	R	27	83	221	30	54	6	2	0	21	31	34	0	.244	.290
Bill Salkeld	C59	L	31	78	198	26	48	8	1	8	28	42	37	1	.242	.414
Frank McCormick	1B50	R	37	75	180	14	45	9	2	4	34	10	9	0	.250	.389
Connie Ryan	2B40, 3B4	R	28	51	122	14	26	3	0	0	10	21	16	0	.213	.238
Bobby Sturgeon	2B18, SS4, 3B4	R	28	34	78	10	17	3	1	0	4	4	5	0	.218	.282
Al Lyons	P7, OF4	R	29	16	12	2	2	0	0	0	0	2	4	0	.167	.167
1 Danny Litwhiler	OF8	R	31	13	33	0	9	2	0	0	6	4	2	0	.273	.333
Ray Sanders		L	31	5	4	0	1	0	0	0	2	1	0	0	.250	.250

2 Marv Rickert 27 L 3-13, Paul Burris 24 R 2-4

NAME	T	AGE	W	L	PCT	SV	G	GS	CG	IP	H	BB	SO	ShO	ERA
		31	**91**	62	**.595**	17	154	154	**70**	1389	1354	430	579	10	**3.38**
Johnny Sain	R	30	**24**	15	.615	1	42	**39**	**28**	**315**	**297**	83	137	4	2.60
Warren Spahn	L	27	15	12	.556	1	36	35	16	257	237	77	114	3	3.71
Bill Voiselle	R	29	13	13	.500	2	37	30	9	216	226	90	89	2	3.63
Vern Bickford	R	27	11	5	.688	1	33	22	10	146	125	63	60	1	3.27
Bobby Hogue	R	27	8	2	.800	2	40	1	0	86	88	19	43	0	3.24
Red Barrett	R	33	7	8	.467	0	34	13	3	128	132	26	40	0	3.66
Clyde Shoun	L	36	5	1	.833	4	36	2	1	74	77	20	25	0	4.01
3 Nels Potter	R	36	5	2	.714	2	18	7	3	85	77	8	47	0	2.33
Al Lyons	R	29	1	0	1.000	0	7	0	0	13	17	8	5	0	7.62
Glenn Elliott	L	28	1	0	1.000	0	1	1	0	3	5	1	2	0	3.00
Jim Prendergast	L	30	1	1	.500	1	10	2	0	17	30	5	3	0	10.06
Johnny Beazley (SA)	R	30	0	1	.000	0	3	2	0	16	19	7	4	0	4.50
Ernie White	L	31	0	2	.000	2	15	0	0	23	13	17	8	0	1.96
Johnny Antonelli	L	18	0	0	.000	1	4	0	0	4	2	3	0	0	2.25
Ed Wright	R	29	0	0	.000	0	3	0	0	5	9	2	2	0	1.80
Ray Martin	R	23	0	0	.000	0	2	0	0	2	0	1	0	0	0.00

ST. LOUIS 2nd 85-69 .552 6.5 — EDDIE DYER

NAME	G by POS	B	AGE	G	AB	R	H	2B	3B	HR	RBI	BB	SO	SB	BA	SA
TOTALS			29	155	5302	742	1396	238	**58**	105	680	594	521	24	.263	.389
Nippy Jones	1B128	R	23	132	481	58	122	21	9	10	81	36	45	2	.254	.397
Red Schoendienst	2B96	B	25	119	408	64	111	21	4	4	36	28	16	1	.272	.373
Marty Marion	SS142	R	30	144	567	70	143	26	4	4	43	37	54	1	.252	.333
Don Lang	3B95, 2B2	R	33	117	323	30	87	14	1	4	31	47	38	2	.269	.356
Enos Slaughter	OF146	L	32	146	549	91	176	27	11	11	90	81	29	4	.321	.470
Terry Moore	OF71	R	36	91	207	30	48	11	0	4	18	27	12	0	.232	.343
Stan Musial	OF155, 1B2	L	27	155	611	**135**	**230**	**46**	**18**	39	**131**	79	34	7	**.376**	**.702**
Del Rice	C99	R	25	100	290	24	57	10	1	4	34	37	46	1	.197	.279
Erv Dusak	OF68, 2B29, 3B9, SS1, P1	R	27	114	311	60	65	9	2	6	19	49	55	3	.209	.309
Ron Northey	OF67	L	28	96	246	40	79	10	1	13	64	38	25	0	.321	.528
Ralph LaPointe	2B44, SS25, 3B1	R	26	87	222	27	50	3	0	0	15	18	19	1	.225	.239
Whitey Kurowski (AJ)	3B65	R	30	77	220	34	47	8	0	2	33	42	28	0	.214	.277
Bill Baker	C36	R	37	45	119	13	35	10	1	0	15	15	7	1	.294	.395
Murry Dickson	P42	R	31	43	96	7	27	2	0	0	11	1	1	0	.281	.302
2 Babe Young	1B35	L	33	41	111	14	27	5	2	1	13	16	6	0	.243	.351
Del Wilber	C26	R	29	27	58	5	11	2	0	0	10	4	9	0	.190	.224
Joe Garagiola	C23	L	22	24	56	9	6	1	0	2	7	12	9	0	.107	.232
Joe Medwick	OF1	R	36	20	19	0	4	0	0	0	2	1	2	0	.211	.211
Hal Rice	OF8	L	24	8	31	3	10	1	2	0	3	2	4	0	.323	.484
Chuck Diering	OF5	R	25	7	7	2	0	0	0	0	0	2	2	1	.000	.000
Eddie Kazak	3B6	R	27	6	22	1	6	3	0	0	2	0	2	0	.273	.409

Bobby Young 23 L 0-1, Johnny Bucha 23 R 0-1, 1 Jeff Cross 29 R 0-0, Larry Miggins 22 R 0-1, Lou Klein (SM) 29

NAME	T	AGE	W	L	PCT	SV	G	GS	CG	IP	H	BB	SO	ShO	ERA
		30	85	69	.552	18	155	155	60	1369	1392	476	635	13	3.91
Harry Brecheen	L	33	20	7	**.741**	1	33	30	21	233	193	49	**149**	**7**	**2.24**
Howie Pollet	L	27	13	8	.619	0	36	26	11	186	216	67	80	0	4.55
Murry Dickson	R	31	12	16	.429	1	42	29	11	252	257	85	113	1	4.14
Al Brazle	L	34	10	6	.625	1	42	23	6	156	171	50	55	3	3.81
George Munger	R	29	10	11	.476	0	39	25	7	166	179	74	72	2	4.50
Jim Hearn	R	27	8	6	.571	1	34	13	3	90	92	35	27	0	4.20
Ted Wilks	R	32	6	6	.500	13	57	2	1	131	113	39	71	0	2.61
Gerry Staley	R	27	4	4	.500	0	31	3	0	52	61	21	23	0	6.92
Ken Johnson	L	25	2	4	.333	0	13	4	0	45	43	30	20	0	4.80
Al Papai	R	29	0	1	.000	0	10	0	0	16	14	7	8	0	5.06
1 Ken Burkhart	R	31	0	0	.000	1	20	0	0	37	50	14	16	0	5.59
Clarence Beers	R	29	0	0	.000	0	1	0	0	1	3	1	0	0	27.00
Erv Dusak	R	27	0	0	.000	0	1	0	0	1	0	1	0	0	0.00
Ray Yochim	R	25	0	0	.000	0	1	0	0	1	0	3	1	0	0.00

Max Lanier (SM) 32
Freddie Martin (SM) 33

BROOKLYN 3rd 84-70 .545 7.5 — LEO DUROCHER 36-37 .493 BURT SHOTTON 48-33 .593

NAME	G by POS	B	AGE	G	AB	R	H	2B	3B	HR	RBI	BB	SO	SB	BA	SA
TOTALS			26	155	5328	744	1393	256	54	91	671	601	**684**	**114**	.261	.381
Gil Hodges	1B96, C38	R	24	134	481	48	120	18	5	11	70	43	61	7	.249	.376
Jackie Robinson	2B116, 1B30, 3B6	R	29	147	574	108	170	38	8	12	85	57	37	22	.296	.453
Pee Wee Reese	SS149	R	29	151	566	96	155	31	4	9	75	79	63	25	.274	.390
Billy Cox	3B70, SS6, 2B1	R	28	88	237	36	59	13	2	3	15	38	19	3	.249	.359
Gene Hermanski	OF119	L	28	133	400	63	116	22	7	15	60	64	46	15	.290	.493
Carl Furillo	OF104	R	26	108	364	55	108	20	4	4	44	43	32	6	.297	.407
Marv Rackley	OF74	L	26	88	281	55	92	13	5	0	15	19	25	8	.327	.409
Roy Campanella	C78	R	26	83	279	32	72	11	3	9	45	36	45	3	.258	.416
B. Edwards (SA)	C48, OF21, 3B14, 1B1	R	24	96	286	36	79	17	2	8	54	26	28	4	.276	.434
Eddie Miksis	2B54, 3B22, SS5	R	21	86	221	28	47	7	1	2	16	19	27	5	.213	.281
Arky Vaughan	OF26, 3B8	L	36	65	123	19	30	3	0	3	22	21	8	0	.244	.341
Pete Reiser (JJ)	OF30, 3B4	L	29	64	127	17	30	8	2	1	19	29	21	4	.236	.354
George Shuba	OF56	L	23	63	161	21	43	6	0	4	32	34	31	1	.267	.379
Dick Whitman	OF48	L	27	60	165	24	48	13	0	0	20	14	12	4	.291	.370
Tommy Brown	3B43, 1B1	R	20	54	145	18	35	4	0	2	20	7	17	1	.241	.310
Duke Snider	OF47	L	21	53	160	22	39	6	6	5	21	12	27	4	.244	.450
Preston Ward	1B38	L	20	42	146	9	38	9	2	1	21	15	23	0	.260	.370
Spider Jorgensen (AJ)	3B24	L	28	31	90	15	27	6	2	1	13	16	13	1	.300	.444
1 Don Lund	OF25	R	25	27	69	9	13	4	0	1	5	5	16	1	.188	.290
1 Gene Mauch	2B7, SS1	R	22	12	13	1	2	0	0	0	0	1	4	0	.154	.154
Bobby Bragan	C5	R	30	9	12	0	2	0	0	0	0	1	0	0	.167	.167

Bob Ramazotti 31 R 0-3, Luis Olmo (SM) 28, Mickey Owen (SM) 32

NAME	T	AGE	W	L	PCT	SV	G	GS	CG	IP	H	BB	SO	ShO	ERA
		27	84	70	.545	**22**	155	155	52	**1392**	1316	**633**	**670**	9	3.76
Rex Barney	R	23	15	13	.536	0	44	34	12	247	193	122	138	4	3.10
Ralph Branca	R	22	14	9	.609	1	36	28	11	216	189	80	122	1	3.50
Joe Hatten	L	31	13	10	.565	0	42	30	11	209	228	94	73	1	3.57
Preacher Roe	L	33	12	8	.600	2	34	22	8	178	156	33	86	2	2.63
Carl Erskine	R	21	6	3	.667	0	17	9	3	64	51	35	29	0	3.23
Erv Palica	R	20	6	6	.500	3	41	10	3	125	111	58	74	0	4.46
Hank Behrman	R	27	5	4	.556	7	34	4	2	91	95	42	42	1	4.05
Paul Minner	L	24	4	3	.571	1	28	2	0	63	61	26	23	0	2.43
Willie Ramsdell	R	32	4	4	.500	4	27	1	0	50	48	41	34	0	5.22
Hugh Casey (XJ)	R	34	3	0	1.000	4	22	0	0	36	59	17	7	0	8.00
Harry Taylor (IL)	R	29	2	7	.222	0	17	13	2	81	90	61	32	0	5.33
Clyde King	R	23	0	1	.000	0	9	0	0	12	14	6	5	0	8.25
Dwain Sloat	L	30	0	1	.000	0	4	1	0	7	7	8	1	0	6.43
Jack Banta	R	23	0	1	.000	0	2	1	0	3	5	5	1	0	9.00
Johnny Hall	R	24	0	0	.000	0	3	0	0	4	4	2	2	0	6.75
Johnny Van Cuyk	L	26	0	0	.000	0	3	0	0	5	4	1	1	0	3.60
Elmer Sexauer	R	22	0	0	.000	0	2	0	0	1	0	2	0	0	9.00
Phil Haugstad	R	24	0	0	.000	0	1	0	0	1	1	0	0	0	0.00

PITTSBURGH 4th 83-71 .539 8.5 — BILLY MEYER

NAME	G by POS	B	AGE	G	AB	R	H	2B	3B	HR	RBI	BB	SO	SB	BA	SA
TOTALS			28	156	5286	706	1388	191	54	108	650	580	578	68	.263	.380
Ed Stevens	1B117	L	23	128	429	47	109	19	6	10	69	35	53	4	.254	.396
Danny Murtaugh	2B146	R	30	146	514	56	149	21	5	1	71	60	40	10	.290	.356
Stan Rojek	SS156	R	29	156	**641**	85	186	27	5	4	51	61	41	24	.290	.367
Frankie Gustine	3B119	R	28	131	449	68	120	19	2	9	42	42	62	5	.267	.379
Dixie Walker	OF112	L	37	129	408	39	129	19	3	2	54	52	18	1	.316	.392
Wally Westlake	OF125	R	27	132	428	78	122	10	6	17	65	46	40	2	.285	.456
Ralph Kiner	OF154	R	25	156	555	104	147	19	5	**40**	123	112	61	1	.265	.533
Ed Fitzgerald	C96	R	24	102	262	31	70	9	3	1	35	32	37	3	.267	.336
Johnny Hopp	OF80, 1B25	L	31	120	392	64	109	15	12	1	31	40	25	5	.278	.385
Clyde Kluttz	C91	R	30	94	271	26	60	12	2	4	20	20	19	3	.221	.325
Max West	1B32, OF16	L	31	87	146	19	26	4	0	8	21	27	29	1	.178	.370
Eddie Bockman	3B51, 2B1	R	27	70	176	23	42	7	1	4	23	17	35	2	.239	.358
Monty Basgall	2B22	R	26	38	51	12	11	1	0	2	6	3	5	0	.216	.353
Ted Beard	OF22	L	27	25	81	15	16	1	3	0	7	12	18	5	.198	.284
Grady Wilson	SS7	R	25	12	10	1	1	1	0	0	1	0	3	0	.100	.200
Johnny Riddle	C10	R	42	10	15	1	3	0	0	0	0	1	2	0	.200	.200

Pete Castiglione 27 R 0-2, Don Gutteridge 36 R 0-2, Earl Turner 25 R 0-1

NAME	T	AGE	W	L	PCT	SV	G	GS	CG	IP	H	BB	SO	ShO	ERA
		31	83	71	.539	19	156	156	65	1371	1373	564	519	5	4.15
Bob Chesnes	B	27	14	6	.700	0	25	23	15	194	180	90	69	0	3.57
Rip Sewell	R	41	13	3	.813	0	21	17	7	122	126	37	36	0	3.47
Elmer Riddle	R	33	12	10	.545	1	28	27	12	191	184	81	63	3	3.49
Vic Lombardi	L	25	10	9	.526	4	38	17	9	163	156	67	54	0	3.70
Kirby Higbe	R	33	8	7	.533	10	56	8	3	158	140	83	86	0	3.36
Fritz Ostermueller	L	40	8	11	.421	0	23	22	10	134	143	41	43	2	4.43
Ernie Bonham	R	34	6	10	.375	0	22	20	7	136	145	23	42	0	4.30
Mel Queen	R	30	4	4	.500	1	25	8	0	66	82	40	34	0	6.68
Elmer Singleton	R	30	4	6	.400	2	38	5	1	92	90	40	53	0	4.99
Hal Gregg	R	26	2	4	.333	1	22	8	1	74	72	34	25	0	4.62
Junior Walsh	R	29	1	0	1.000	0	2	0	0	4	4	5	0	0	11.25
Woody Main	R	26	1	1	.500	0	17	0	0	27	35	19	12	0	8.33
1 Nick Strincevich	R	33	0	0	.000	0	3	0	0	4	8	2	1	0	9.00
Cal McLish	R	22	0	0	.000	0	2	1	0	5	8	2	1	0	9.00

NEW YORK 5th 78-76 .506 13.5 — MEL OTT 27-38 .415 LEO DUROCHER 51-38 .573

NAME	G by POS	B	AGE	G	AB	R	H	2B	3B	HR	RBI	BB	SO	SB	BA	SA
TOTALS			28	155	5277	**780**	1352	210	49	**164**	**733**	599	648	51	.256	**.408**
Johnny Mize	1B152	L	35	152	560	110	162	26	4	**40**	125	94	37	4	.289	.564
Bill Rigney	2B105, SS7	R	29	113	424	72	112	17	3	10	43	47	54	4	.264	.389
Buddy Kerr	SS143	R	25	144	496	41	119	16	4	0	46	56	36	9	.240	.288
Sid Gordon	3B115, OF23	R	30	142	521	100	156	26	4	30	107	74	39	8	.299	.537
Willard Marshall	OF142	L	27	143	537	72	146	21	8	14	86	64	34	2	.272	.419
Whitey Lockman	OF144	L	21	146	584	117	167	24	10	18	59	68	63	8	.286	.454
Bobby Thomson	OF125	R	24	138	471	75	117	20	2	16	63	30	77	2	.248	.401
Walker Cooper (KJ)	C79	R	33	91	290	40	77	12	0	16	54	28	29	1	.266	.472
Lucky Lohrke	3B50, 2B36	R	24	97	280	35	70	15	1	5	31	30	30	3	.250	.364
Wes Westrum	C63	R	25	66	125	14	20	3	1	4	16	20	30	3	.160	.296
Les Layton	OF20	R	26	63	91	14	21	4	4	2	12	6	21	1	.231	.429
Johnny McCarthy	1B6	L	38	56	57	6	15	0	1	2	12	3	2	0	.263	.404
Mickey Livingston	C42	R	33	45	99	9	21	4	1	2	12	21	11	1	.212	.333
Don Mueller	OF22	L	21	36	81	12	29	4	1	1	9	0	3	0	.358	.469
Bobby Rhawn	SS14, 3B7	R	29	36	44	11	12	2	1	1	8	8	6	3	.273	.432
2 Lonny Frey	2B13	L	37	29	51	6	13	1	0	1	6	4	6	0	.255	.333
Jack Conway	2B13, SS6, 3B3	R	28	24	49	8	12	2	1	1	3	5	10	0	.245	.388
Sal Yvars	C15	R	24	15	38	4	8	1	0	1	6	3	1	0	.211	.316
Pete Milne	OF9	L	23	12	27	0	6	1	0	1	2	1	6	0	.222	.296
Buddy Blattner	2B7	R	28	8	20	3	4	1	0	0	0	3	2	2	.200	.250

Hal Bamberger 23 L 1-12, Jack Harshman 20 L 2-8, Joe Lafata 26 L 0-1, Danny Gardella (SM) 28, George Hausmann (SM) 32, Nap Reyes (SM) 28, Ace Adams (SM) 36

NAME	T	AGE	W	L	PCT	SV	G	GS	CG	IP	H	BB	SO	ShO	ERA
		26	78	76	.506	21	155	155	54	1373	**1425**	551	527	**15**	3.93
Larry Jansen	R	27	18	12	.600	2	42	36	15	277	283	54	126	4	3.61
Sheldon Jones	R	26	16	8	.667	5	55	21	8	201	204	90	82	2	3.36
Ray Poat	R	30	11	10	.524	0	39	24	7	158	162	67	57	3	4.33
Clint Hartung	R	25	8	8	.500	1	36	19	6	153	146	72	42	2	4.76
Dave Koslo	L	28	8	10	.444	3	35	18	5	149	168	62	58	3	3.87
Andy Hansen	R	23	5	3	.625	1	36	9	3	100	96	36	27	0	2.97
Ken Trinkle	R	28	4	5	.444	7	53	0	0	71	66	41	20	0	3.17
Monte Kennedy	L	26	3	9	.250	0	25	16	7	114	118	57	63	1	4.03
Red Webb	R	23	2	1	.667	0	5	3	2	28	27	10	9	0	3.21
Alex Konikowski	R	20	2	3	.400	1	22	1	0	33	46	17	9	0	7.64
Thornton Lee	L	41	1	3	.250	0	11	4	1	33	41	12	17	0	4.36
Bobo Newsom	R	40	0	4	.000	0	11	4	0	26	35	13	9	0	4.15
2 Chem Dreisewerd	L	32	0	0	.000	1	4	0	0	13	17	5	2	0	5.54
Mickey McGowan	L	26	0	0	.000	0	3	0	0	4	3	4	2	0	6.75
3 Paul Erickson	R	32	0	0	.000	0	2	0	0	1	0	2	1	0	0.00
Jack Hallett	R	34	0	0	.000	0	2	0	0	4	3	4	3	0	4.50
Lou Lombardo	L	19	0	0	.000	0	2	0	0	5	5	5	0	0	7.20
Hub Andrews	R	25	0	0	.000	0	1	0	0	3	3	0	0	0	0.00
Joe Beggs	R	37	0	0	.000	0	1	0	0	.1	2	0	0	0	0.00

Sal Maglie (SM) 31, Adrian Zabala (SM) 31, Harry Feldman (SM) 28

PHILADELPHIA 6th 66-88 .429 25.5 — BEN CHAPMAN 37-42 .468 — DUSTY COOKE 6-5 .545 — EDDIE SAWYER 23-41 .359

NAME	G by POS	B	AGE	G	AB	R	H	2B	3B	HR	RBI	BB	SO	SB	BA	SA
TOTALS			27	155	5287	591	1367	227	39	91	548	440	598	68	.259	.368
Dick Sisler	1B120	L	27	121	446	60	122	21	3	11	56	47	46	1	.274	.408
Granny Hamner	2B87, SS37, 3B3	R	21	129	446	42	116	21	5	3	48	22	39	2	.260	.350
Eddie Miller	SS122	R	31	130	468	45	115	20	1	14	61	19	40	1	.246	.382
Putsy Caballero	3B79, 2B23	R	20	113	351	33	86	12	1	0	19	24	18	7	.245	.285
Del Ennis	OF151	R	23	152	589	86	171	40	4	30	95	47	58	2	.290	.525
Richie Ashburn (BG)	OF116	L	21	117	463	78	154	17	4	2	40	60	22	**32**	.333	.400
Johnny Blatnik	OF105	R	27	121	415	56	108	27	8	6	45	31	77	3	.260	.407
Andy Seminick	C124	R	27	125	391	49	88	11	3	13	44	58	68	4	.225	.368
Harry Walker	OF81, 1B4, 3B1	L	31	112	332	34	97	11	2	2	23	33	30	4	.292	.355
Bert Haas (CN)	3B54, 1B35	R	34	95	333	35	94	9	2	4	34	36	25	8	.282	.357
Bama Rowell	3B18, OF17, 2B12	L	32	77	196	15	47	16	2	1	22	8	14	2	.240	.357
1 Emil Verban	2B54	R	32	55	169	14	39	5	1	0	11	11	5	0	.231	.272
Don Padgett	C19	L	36	36	74	3	17	3	0	0	7	3	2	0	.230	.270
Al Lakeman	C22, P1	R	29	32	68	2	11	2	0	1	4	5	22	0	.162	.235
Willie Jones	3B17	R	22	17	60	9	20	2	0	2	9	3	5	0	.333	.467
Jackie Mayo	OF11	L	22	12	35	7	8	2	1	0	3	7	7	1	.229	.343
Stan Lopata	C4	R	22	6	15	2	2	1	0	0	2	0	4	0	.133	.200
1 Howie Schultz	1B3	R	25	6	13	0	1	0	0	0	1	1	2	0	.077	.077
2 Hal Wagner	C1	L	32	3	4	0	0	0	0	0	0	0	0	0	.000	.000

NAME	T	AGE	W	L	PCT	SV	G	GS	CG	IP	H	BB	SO	ShO	ERA
		30	66	88	.429	15	155	155	61	1362	1385	561	552	6	4.08
Dutch Leonard	R	39	12	**17**	.414	0	34	31	16	226	226	54	92	1	2.51
Schoolboy Rowe	R	38	10	10	.500	2	30	20	8	148	167	31	46	0	4.07
Monk Dubiel	R	29	8	10	.444	4	37	17	6	150	139	58	42	2	3.90
Robin Roberts	R	21	7	9	.438	0	20	20	9	147	148	61	84	0	3.18
Curt Simmons	L	19	7	13	.350	0	31	22	7	170	169	108	86	0	4.87
Ken Heintzelman	L	32	6	11	.353	2	27	16	5	130	117	45	57	2	4.29
Blix Donnelly	R	34	5	7	.417	2	26	19	8	132	125	49	46	1	3.68
Ed Heusser	R	39	3	2	.600	3	33	0	0	74	89	28	22	0	4.99
Sam Nahem	R	32	3	3	.500	0	28	1	0	59	68	45	30	0	7.02
2 Paul Erickson	R	**32**	2	0	1.000	0	4	2	0	17	19	17	5	0	5.29
Jim Konstanty	R	31	1	0	1.000	2	6	0	0	10	7	2	7	0	0.90
Jocko Thompson	L	28	1	0	1.000	0	2	2	1	13	10	9	7	0	2.77
Lou Possehl	R	22	1	1	.500	0	3	2	1	15	17	4	7	0	4.80
Charlie Bicknell	R	19	0	1	.000	0	17	1	0	26	29	17	5	0	5.88
2 Nick Strincevich	R	33	0	1	.000	0	6	1	0	17	26	10	4	0	9.00
Dick Koecher	L	22	0	1	.000	0	3	0	0	6	4	3	2	0	3.00
Oscar Judd	L	40	0	2	.000	0	4	1	0	14	19	11	7	0	7.07
Al Porto	L	22	0	0	.000	0	3	0	0	4	2	1	1	0	0.00
Lou Grasmick	R	23	0	0	.000	0	2	0	0	5	3	8	2	0	7.20
Al Lakeman	R	29	0	0	.000	0	1	0	0	1	1	0	0	0	9.00

CINCINNATI 7th 64-89 .418 27 — JOHNNY NEUN 44-56 .440 — BUCKY WALTERS 20-33 .377

NAME	G by POS	B	AGE	G	AB	R	H	2B	3B	HR	RBI	BB	SO	SB	BA	SA
TOTALS			28	153	5127	588	1266	221	37	104	548	478	586	42	.247	.365
Ted Kluszewski	1B98	L	23	113	379	49	104	23	4	12	57	18	32	1	.274	.451
Bobby Adams	2B64, 3B7	R	26	87	262	33	78	20	3	1	21	25	23	6	.298	.408
Virgil Stallcup	SS148	R	26	149	539	40	123	30	4	3	65	18	52	2	.228	.315
Grady Hatton	3B123, 2B3, SS2, OF1	L	25	133	458	58	110	17	2	9	44	72	50	7	.240	.345
Frankie Baumholtz	OF110	L	29	128	415	57	123	19	5	4	30	27	32	8	.296	.395
Johnny Wyrostek	OF130	L	28	136	512	74	140	24	9	17	76	52	63	7	.273	.455
Hank Sauer	OF132, 1B12	R	29	145	530	78	138	22	1	35	97	60	**85**	2	.260	.504
Ray Lammana	C125	R	28	127	385	31	93	12	0	0	27	48	32	2	.242	.273
2 Danny Litwhiler	OF83, 3B15	R	31	106	338	51	93	19	2	14	44	48	41	1	.275	.467
Claude Corbitt	2B52, 3B16, SS11	R	32	87	258	24	66	11	0	0	18	14	16	4	.256	.298
Benny Zientara	2B60, 3B3, SS2	R	28	74	187	17	35	1	2	0	7	12	11	0	.187	.214
Augie Galan	OF18	L	36	54	77	18	22	3	2	2	16	26	4	0	.286	.455
1 Babe Young	1B31, OF1	L	33	49	130	11	30	7	2	1	12	19	12	0	.231	.338
Dewey Williams	C47	R	32	48	95	9	16	2	0	1	5	10	18	0	.168	.221
2 Howie Schultz	1B26	R	25	36	72	9	12	0	0	2	9	4	7	2	.167	.250
Ray Mueller (BN)	C10	R	36	14	34	2	7	1	0	0	2	4	3	0	.206	.235
1 Marv Rickert		L	27	8	6	0	1	0	0	0	0	0	0	0	.167	.167
Steve Filipowicz	OF7	R	27	7	26	0	9	0	1	0	3	2	1	0	.346	.423
1 Clyde Vollmer	OF2	R	26	7	9	0	1	0	0	0	0	1	1	0	.111	.111
Hugh Poland		L	35	3	3	0	1	0	0	0	0	0	0	0	.333	.333

NAME	T	AGE	W	L	PCT	SV	G	GS	CG	IP	H	BB	SO	ShO	ERA
		28	64	89	.418	20	153	153	40	1343	1410	572	599	8	4.48
Johnny Vander Meer	L	33	17	14	.548	0	33	33	14	232	204	**124**	120	3	3.41
Herm Wehmeier	R	21	11	8	.579	0	33	24	6	147	179	75	56	0	5.88
Ken Raffensberger	L	30	11	12	.478	0	40	24	7	180	187	37	57	4	3.85
Harry Gumbert	R	38	10	8	.556	**17**	**61**	0	0	106	123	34	25	0	3.48
Ewell Blackwell (AJ)	R	25	7	9	.438	1	22	20	4	139	134	52	114	1	4.53
Howie Fox	R	27	6	9	.400	1	34	24	5	171	185	62	63	0	4.53
Kent Peterson	L	22	2	15	.118	1	43	17	2	137	146	59	64	0	4.60
Walker Cress	R	31	0	1	.000	0	30	2	1	60	60	42	33	0	4.50
Johnny Hetki	R	26	0	1	.000	0	3	0	0	7	8	3	3	0	9.00
Jim Blackburn	R	24	0	2	.000	0	16	0	0	32	38	14	10	0	4.22
2 Ken Burkhart	R	31	0	3	.000	0	16	0	0	42	42	16	14	0	6.86
Bucky Walters	R	39	0	3	.000	0	7	5	1	35	42	18	19	0	4.63
Tommy Hughes	R	28	0	4	.000	0	12	4	0	27	43	24	7	0	9.00
Bud Lively	R	23	0	0	.000	0	10	0	0	23	13	11	12	0	2.35
Eddie Erautt	R	23	0	0	.000	0	2	0	0	3	3	1	0	0	6.00
Ken Holcombe	R	29	0	0	.000	0	2	0	0	2	3	0	2	0	9.00

CHICAGO 8th 64-90 .416 27.5 — CHARLIE GRIMM

NAME	G by POS	B	AGE	G	AB	R	H	2B	3B	HR	RBI	BB	SO	SB	BA	SA
TOTALS			28	155	**5352**	597	1402	225	44	87	564	443	578	39	.262	.369
Eddie Waitkus	1B116, OF20	L	28	139	562	87	166	27	10	7	44	43	19	11	.295	.416
Hank Schenz	2B78, 3B5	R	29	96	337	43	88	17	1	1	14	18	15	3	.261	.326
Roy Smalley	SS124	R	22	124	361	25	78	11	4	4	36	23	76	0	.216	.302
Andy Pafko	3B139	R	27	142	548	82	171	30	2	26	101	50	50	3	.312	.516
Bill Nicholson	OF136	L	33	143	494	68	129	24	5	19	67	81	60	2	.261	.445
Hal Jeffcoat	OF119	R	23	134	473	53	132	16	4	4	42	24	68	8	.279	.355
Peanuts Lowrey	OF103, 3B9, 2B2, SS1	R	29	129	435	47	128	12	3	2	54	34	31	2	.294	.349
Bob Scheffing	C78	R	32	102	293	23	88	18	2	5	45	22	27	0	.300	.427
Phil Cavarretta	1B41, OF40	L	31	111	334	41	93	16	5	3	40	35	29	4	.278	.383
Clarence Maddern	OF55	R	26	80	214	16	54	12	1	4	27	10	25	0	.252	.374
Rube Walker	C44	L	22	79	171	17	47	8	0	5	26	24	17	0	.275	.409
Clyde McCullough	C51	R	31	69	172	10	36	4	2	1	7	15	25	0	.209	.273
2 Emil Verban	2B56	R	32	56	248	37	73	15	1	1	16	4	7	4	.294	.375
2 Gene Mauch	2B26, SS19	R	22	53	138	18	28	3	2	1	7	26	10	1	.203	.275
Dick Culler	SS43, 2B2	R	33	48	89	4	15	2	0	0	5	13	3	0	.169	.191
2 Jeff Cross	SS9, 2B1	R	29	16	20	1	2	0	0	0	0	0	4	0	.100	.100
Cliff Aberson	OF8	R	26	12	32	1	6	1	0	1	6	5	10	0	.188	.313
Dummy Lynch	2B1	R	21	7	7	3	2	0	0	1	1	1	1	0	.286	.714
Don Johnson	2B2, 3B2	R	36	6	12	0	3	0	0	0	0	0	1	1	.250	.250
Carmen Mauro	OF2	L	21	3	5	2	1	0	0	1	1	2	0	0	.200	.800
Carl Sawatski		L	20	2	2	0	0	0	0	0	0	0	0	0	.000	.000

NAME	T	AGE	W	L	PCT	SV	G	GS	CG	IP	H	BB	SO	ShO	ERA
		28	64	**90**	.416	10	155	155	51	1356	1355	609	636	7	4.00
Johnny Schmitz	L	27	18	13	.581	1	34	30	18	242	186	97	100	2	2.64
Russ Meyer	R	24	10	10	.500	0	29	26	8	165	157	77	89	3	3.65
Jess Dobernic	R	30	7	2	.778	1	54	0	0	86	67	40	48	0	3.14
Doyle Lade	R	27	5	6	.455	0	19	12	6	87	99	31	29	0	4.03
Ralph Hamner	R	31	5	9	.357	0	27	17	5	111	110	69	53	0	4.70
Hank Borowy	R	32	5	10	.333	1	39	17	2	127	156	49	50	1	4.89
Bob Rush	R	22	5	11	.313	0	36	16	4	133	153	37	72	0	3.92
Dutch McCall	L	27	4	13	.235	0	30	20	5	151	158	85	89	0	4.83
Bob Chipman	L	29	2	1	.667	4	34	3	0	60	73	24	16	0	3.60
Cliff Chambers	L	26	2	9	.182	0	29	12	3	104	100	48	51	1	4.41
Emil Kush	R	31	1	4	.200	3	34	1	0	72	70	37	31	0	4.38
Warren Hacker	R	23	0	1	.000	0	3	1	0	3	7	3	0	0	21.00
Ben Wade	R	25	0	1	.000	0	2	0	0	5	4	4	1	0	7.20
1 Paul Erickson	R	**32**	0	0	.000	0	3	0	0	6	7	6	4	0	6.00
Don Carlsen	R	21	0	0	.000	0	1	0	0	1	5	2	1	0	36.00
Tony Jacobs	R	22	0	0	.000	0	1	0	0	2	3	0	2	0	4.50
Hank Wyse (AJ) 30															

WORLD SERIES – CLEVELAND (AL) 4 BOSTON (NL) 2

LINE SCORES

TEAM	1	2	3	4	5	6	7	8	9	10	11	12	R	H	E
Game 1 October 6 at Boston															
CLE (AL)	0	0	0	0	0	0	0	0	0				0	4	0
BOS (NL)	0	0	0	0	0	0	0	1	X				1	2	2
Feller — **Sain**															
Game 2 October 7 at Boston															
CLE	0	0	0	2	1	0	0	0	1				4	8	1
BOS	1	0	0	0	0	0	0	0	0				1	8	3
Lemon — **Spahn**, Barrett (5), Potter (8)															
Game 3 October 8 at Cleveland															
BOS	0	0	0	0	0	0	0	0	0				0	5	1
CLE	0	0	1	1	0	0	0	0	X				2	5	0
Bickford, Voiselle (4), Barrett (8) — **Bearden**															
Game 4 October 9 at Cleveland															
BOS	0	0	0	0	0	0	1	0	0				1	7	0
CLE	1	0	1	0	0	0	0	0	X				2	5	0
Sain — **Gromek**															
Game 5 October 10 at Cleveland															
BOS	3	0	1	0	0	1	6	0	0				11	12	0
CLE	1	0	0	4	0	0	0	0	0				5	6	2
Potter, **Spahn** (4) — **Feller**, Klieman (7), Christopher (7), Paige (7), Muncrief (8)															
Game 6 October 11 at Boston															
CLE	0	0	1	0	0	2	0	1	0				4	10	0
BOS	0	0	0	1	0	0	0	2	0				3	9	0
Lemon, Bearden (8) — **Voiselle**, Spahn (8)															

COMPOSITE BATTING

NAME	POS	G	AB	R	H	2B	3B	HR	RBI	BA
Cleveland (AL)										
Totals		6	191	17	38	7	0	4	16	.199
Mitchell	OF	6	23	**4**	4	1	0	1	1	.174
Doby	OF	6	22	1	**7**	1	0	1	2	.318
Boudreau	SS	6	22	1	6	**4**	0	0	3	.273
Gordon	2B	6	22	3	4	0	0	1	2	.182
Keltner	3B	6	21	3	2	0	0	0	0	.095
Robinson	1B	6	20	0	6	0	0	0	1	.300
Hegan	C	6	19	2	4	0	0	1	**5**	.211
Judnich	OF	4	13	1	1	0	0	0	1	.077
Lemon	P	2	7	0	0	0	0	0	0	.000
Bearden	P	2	4	1	2	1	0	0	0	.500
Feller	P	2	4	0	0	0	0	0	0	.000
Tucker	OF	1	3	1	1	0	0	0	0	.333
Clark	OF	1	3	0	0	0	0	0	0	.000
Gromek	P	1	3	0	0	0	0	0	0	.000
Kennedy	OF	3	2	0	1	0	0	0	1	.500
Boone	PH	1	1	0	0	0	0	0	0	.000
Rosen	PH	1	1	0	0	0	0	0	0	.000
Tipton	PH	1	1	0	0	0	0	0	0	.000
Peck	OF	1	0	0	0	0	0	0	0	.000

Christopher P 0-0, Klieman P 0-0, Muncrief P 0-0, Paige P 0-0

NAME	POS	G	AB	R	H	2B	3B	HR	RBI	BA
Boston (NL)										
Totals		6	187	17	43	6	0	4	16	.230
Holmes	OF	6	**26**	3	5	0	0	0	1	.192
Dark	SS	6	24	2	4	1	0	0	0	.167
M. McCormick	OF	6	23	1	6	0	0	0	2	.261
Elliott	3B	6	21	**4**	**7**	0	0	**2**	**5**	.333
Rickert	OF	5	19	2	4	0	0	1	2	.211
Torgeson	1B	5	18	2	7	3	0	0	1	**.389**
Stanky	2B	6	14	0	4	1	0	0	1	.286
Salkeld	C	5	9	2	2	0	0	1	1	.222
Masi	C	5	8	1	1	1	0	0	1	.125
F. McCormick	1B	3	5	0	1	0	0	0	0	.200
Sain	P	2	5	0	1	0	0	0	0	.200
Conatser	OF	2	4	0	0	0	0	0	1	.000
Spahn	P	3	4	0	0	0	0	0	1	.000
Potter	P	2	2	0	1	0	0	0	0	.500
Voiselle	P	2	2	0	0	0	0	0	0	.000
Sisti	2B	2	1	0	0	0	0	0	0	.000
Ryan	PH	2	1	0	0	0	0	0	0	.000
Sanders	PH	1	1	0	0	0	0	0	0	.000
Barrett	P	2	0	0	0	0	0	0	0	.000
Bickford	P	1	0	0	0	0	0	0	0	.000

COMPOSITE PITCHING

NAME	G	IP	H	BB	SO	W	L	SV	ERA
Cleveland (AL)									
Totals	6	53	43	16	19	4	2	1	2.72
Lemon	2	16.1	**16**	7	6	**2**	0	0	1.65
Feller	2	14.1	10	5	7	0	**2**	0	5.02
Bearden	2	10.2	6	1	4	1	0	1	**0.00**
Gromek	1	9	7	1	2	1	0	0	1.00
Muncrief	1	2	1	0	0	0	0	0	0.00
Paige	1	.2	0	0	0	0	0	0	0.00
Klieman	1	0	1	2	0	0	0	0	∞
Christopher	1	0	2	0	0	0	0	0	∞
Boston (NL)									
Totals	6	52	38	12	26	2	4	0	2.60
Sain	2	**17**	9	0	9	1	1	0	1.06
Spahn	**3**	12	10	3	**12**	1	1	0	3.00
Voiselle	2	10.2	8	2	2	0	1	0	2.53
Potter	2	5.1	6	2	1	0	0	0	8.44
Barrett	2	3.2	1	0	1	0	0	0	0.00
Bickford	1	3.1	4	5	1	0	1	0	2.70

⊖ ⊖ 1949 The Arrival of Casey and His Magic Bag ⊖ ⊖

The Yankees' dynasty showed every sign of having crumbled before the start of the season. The Bombers had fallen to third place the past season, age was slowing up several key pinstripers, and both Cleveland and Boston seemed stronger on paper than their 1948 contending squads. Add the fact that Joe DiMaggio would miss the first half of the campaign with a heel injury, and almost no one could realistically forecast a Yankee pennant. But the prognosticators did not take into account that the Yankees had a magician who could change the picture in any crystal ball. Double-talking paragraphs and fashioning a language that reporters struggled to comprehend, Casey Stengel, the 1890-Kansas City, Missouri, product, had little to recommend him for the task. Although he had been a successful manager in the minors, he was better known as a clown in his two previous managerial trials in the majors. But Stengel showed no regard for his past and quickly proved the alchemist as he made moves which turned everything to gold for New York from the opening game.

No one laughed, but Yankee fans smiled as the pinstripers tore out to a quick lead under Stengel's deft direction. Injuries began to knock regulars out of the lineup for sizeable periods, but Casey kept coming up with the right sub at the right time. DiMaggio returned to the lineup in June and belted the ball at a .346 clip the rest of the way. Yogi Berra missed a month with a broken finger but still found time to drive 91 runs across the plate. Only star shortstop Phil Rizzuto escaped the injury hex the entire year. Although Vic Raschi chalked up 21 wins to lead the starters, Stengel relied most heavily on fast-balling reliever Joe Page of all his hurlers.

A strong rush by the Red Sox brought the heavy-hitting Beantowners within shouting distance of the top late in the season, and Stengel had apparently hit the bottom of his magic bag when Boston swept three games from New York on the next-to-last weekend to dump the Yankees into second place. The Sox still held a one-game lead as they came into Yankee Stadium for the final two games of the season. The Bombers knotted the race with an inspirational 5-4 triumph on Saturday, and the next day Stengel proved his magic by taking the pennant on a 5-3 victory. The one prize Stengel did not have in his bag was most valuable player honors. Despite DiMaggio's second-half performance, Boston's Ted Williams was awarded the MVP for leading the Red Sox late season surge.

A veteran St. Louis Cardinal squad, featuring the batting of Stan Musial and Enos Slaughter, the fielding of Marty Marion, and the pitching of Howie Pollet, battled all season long for the top spot in the National League with the youthful Brooklyn Dodgers. Brooklyn, boasting of a fine attack which carried a mediocre pitching staff, was expected to fold at any juncture, but the Cardinals instead reacted to the pressure by dropping four straight tilts in the final week to give Brooklyn a chance to climb in front. The Dodgers applied the coup de grace with a tenth-inning 9-7 win over the Phillies in the curtain-dropper to clinch the title with a narrow one-game edge over the crestfallen Cardinals. The Dodgers' return to the top was spearheaded by Jackie Robinson, who led the league in batting and won the MVP Award, and Gil Hodges and Carl Furillo, who were blossoming into power threats.

The young Brooklyn squad squared off with the veteran Bronx Bombers in Yankee Stadium in game one of the Series and for eight innings both Newcombe and Yankee starter Allie Reynolds kept all runners away from home. Leading off the bottom of the ninth, Old Reliable Tommy Henrich clouted a home run to beat Newcombe and presage the final outcome. Despite a shutout victory behind Preacher Roe the next day, the Dodgers went on to drop the fall classic in five games to prove that Stengel's magic was no laughing matter.

1949 AMERICAN LEAGUE

NAME	G by POS	B	AGE	G	AB	R	H	2B	3B	HR	RBI	BB	SO	SB	BA	SA
NEW YORK 1st 97-57 .630																
CASEY STENGEL																
TOTALS			28	155	5196	829	1396	215	60	115	759	731	539	58	.269	.400
Tommy Henrich	OF61, 1B52	L	36	115	411	90	118	20	3	24	85	86	34	2	.287	.526
Jerry Coleman	2B122, SS4	R	24	128	447	54	123	21	5	2	42	63	44	8	.275	.358
Phil Rizzuto	SS152	R	31	153	614	110	169	22	7	5	65	72	34	18	.275	.358
Bobby Brown	3B86, OF3	L	24	104	343	61	97	14	4	6	61	38	18	4	.283	.399
Hank Bauer	OF95	R	26	103	301	56	82	6	6	10	45	37	42	2	.272	.432
Cliff Mapes	OF108	L	27	111	304	56	75	13	3	7	38	58	50	6	.247	.378
Gene Woodling	OF98	L	26	112	296	60	80	13	7	5	44	52	21	2	.270	.412
Yogi Berra (BG)	C109	L	24	116	415	59	115	20	2	20	91	22	25	2	.277	.480
Billy Johnson	3B81, 1B21, 2B1	R	30	113	329	48	82	11	3	8	56	48	44	1	.249	.374
Johnny Lindell	OF65	R	32	78	211	33	51	10	0	6	27	35	27	3	.242	.374
Joe DiMaggio (FJ)	OF76	R	34	76	272	58	94	14	6	14	67	55	18	0	.346	.596
Snuffy Stirnweiss	2B51, 3B4	R	30	70	157	29	41	8	2	0	11	29	20	3	.261	.338
Charlie Keller	OF31	L	32	60	116	17	29	4	1	3	16	25	15	2	.250	.379
Charlie Silvera	C51	R	24	58	130	8	41	2	0	0	13	18	5	2	.315	.331
Dick Kryhoski	1B51	L	24	54	177	18	52	10	3	1	27	9	17	2	.294	.401
1 Jack Phillips	1B38	R	27	45	91	16	28	4	1	1	10	12	9	1	.308	.407
Gus Niarhos	C30	R	28	32	43	7	12	2	1	0	6	13	8	0	.279	.372
2 Johnny Mize	1B6	L	36	13	23	4	6	1	0	1	2	4	2	0	.261	.435
Fenton Mole	1B8	L	24	10	27	2	5	2	1	0	2	3	5	0	.185	.333
Jim Delsing	OF5	L	23	9	20	5	7	1	0	1	3	1	2	0	.350	.550
Joe Collins	1B5	L	26	7	10	2	1	0	0	0	4	6	2	0	.100	.100
Ralph Houk 29 R 4-7, Mickey Witek 33 R 1-1																
BOSTON 2nd 96-58 .623 1																
JOE McCARTHY																
TOTALS			30	155	**5320**	**896**	**1500**	**272**	36	**131**	**835**	**835**	510	43	**.282**	**.420**
Billy Goodman	1B117	L	23	122	443	54	132	23	3	0	56	58	21	2	.298	.363
Bobby Doerr	2B139	R	31	139	541	91	167	30	9	18	109	75	33	2	.309	.497
Vern Stephens	SS155	R	28	155	610	113	177	31	2	39	**159**	101	73	2	.290	.539
Johnny Pesky	3B148	L	29	148	604	111	185	27	7	2	69	100	19	8	.306	.384
2 Al Zarilla	OF122	L	30	124	474	68	133	32	4	9	71	48	51	4	.281	.422
Dom DiMaggio	OF144	R	32	145	605	126	186	34	5	8	60	96	55	9	.307	.420
Ted Williams	OF155	L	30	155	566	**150**	194	**39**	3	**43**	**159**	**162**	48	1	.343	**.650**
Birdie Tebbetts	C118	R	39	122	403	42	109	14	0	5	48	62	22	8	.270	.342
Matt Batts	C50	R	27	60	157	23	38	9	1	3	31	25	22	1	.242	.369
Billy Hitchcock	1B29, 2B8	R	32	55	147	22	30	6	1	0	9	17	11	2	.204	.259
Tommy O'Brien	OF32	R	30	49	125	24	28	5	0	3	10	21	12	1	.224	.336
Lou Stringer	2B9	R	32	35	41	10	11	4	0	1	6	5	10	0	.268	.439
1 Sam Mele	OF11	R	26	18	46	1	9	1	1	0	7	7	14	2	.196	.261
Merrill Combs	3B9, SS1	L	29	14	24	5	5	1	0	0	1	9	0	0	.208	.250
Walt Dropo	1B11	R	26	11	41	3	6	2	0	0	1	3	7	0	.146	.195
1 Stan Spence	OF5	L	34	7	20	3	3	1	0	0	1	6	1	0	.150	.200
Tom Wright		L	25	5	4	1	1	1	0	0	1	2	1	0	.250	.500
Babe Martin	C1	R	29	2	2	0	0	0	0	0	0	0	0	0	.000	.000
CLEVELAND 3rd 89-65 .578 8																
LOU BOUDREAU																
TOTALS			29	154	5221	675	1358	194	58	112	640	601	534	44	.260	.384
Mickey Vernon	1B153	L	31	153	584	72	170	27	4	18	83	58	51	9	.291	.443
Joe Gordon	2B145	R	34	148	541	74	136	18	3	20	84	83	33	5	.251	.407
Lou Boudreau	SS88, 3B38, 1B6, 2B1	R	31	134	475	53	135	20	3	4	60	70	10	0	.284	.364
Ken Keltner	3B69	R	32	80	246	35	57	9	2	8	30	38	26	0	.232	.382
Bob Kennedy	OF98, 3B21	R	28	121	424	49	117	23	5	9	57	37	40	5	.276	.417
Larry Doby	OF147	L	25	147	547	106	153	25	3	24	85	91	90	10	.280	.468
Dale Mitchell	OF147	L	27	149	**640**	81	**203**	16	**23**	3	56	43	11	10	.317	.428
Jim Hegan	C152	R	28	152	468	54	105	19	5	8	55	49	89	1	.224	.338
Ray Boone	SS76	R	25	86	258	39	65	4	4	4	26	38	17	0	.252	.345
Thurman Tucker	OF52	L	31	80	197	28	48	5	2	0	14	18	19	4	.244	.289
Johnny Berardino	3B25, 2B8, SS3	R	32	50	116	11	23	6	1	0	13	14	14	0	.198	.267
Bob Lemon	P37	L	28	46	108	17	29	6	2	7	19	10	20	0	.269	.556
Mike Tresh	C38	R	35	38	37	4	8	0	0	0	1	5	7	0	.216	.216
Allie Clark	OF17, 1B1	R	26	35	74	8	13	4	0	1	9	4	7	0	.176	.270
Hal Peck (KJ)	OF2	L	32	33	29	1	9	1	0	0	9	3	3	0	.310	.345
Bobby Avila	2B5	R	25	31	14	3	3	0	0	0	3	1	3	0	.214	.214
Al Rosen	3B10	R	25	23	44	3	7	2	0	0	5	7	4	0	.159	.205
Luke Easter	OF12	L	34	21	45	6	10	3	0	0	2	8	6	0	.222	.289
Minnie Minoso	OF7	R	26	9	16	2	3	0	0	1	1	2	2	0	.188	.375
1 Hank Edwards	OF5	L	30	5	15	3	4	0	0	1	1	1	2	0	.267	.467
Milt Nielsen 24 L 1-9, Freddie Marsh 25 R 0-0, 2 Herm Reich 31 R 1-2																

NAME	T	AGE	W	L	PCT	SV	G	GS	CG	IP	H	BB	SO	ShO	ERA
NEW YORK		30	**97**	57	**.630**	**36**	155	155	59	1371	1231	**812**	**671**	12	3.70
Vic Raschi	R	30	21	10	.677	0	38	**37**	21	275	247	138	124	3	3.34
Allie Reynolds	R	34	17	6	.739	1	35	31	4	214	200	123	105	2	4.00
Tommy Byrne	L	29	15	7	.682	0	32	30	12	196	125	**179**	129	3	3.72
Ed Lopat	L	31	15	10	.600	1	31	30	14	215	222	69	70	4	3.27
Joe Page	L	31	13	8	.619	**27**	**60**	0	0	135	103	75	99	0	2.60
Fred Sanford	R	29	7	3	.700	0	29	11	3	95	100	57	51	0	3.88
Cuddles Marshall	R	24	3	0	1.000	3	21	2	0	49	48	48	13	0	5.14
Duane Pillette	R	26	2	4	.333	0	12	3	2	37	43	19	9	0	4.38
Bob Porterfield (AJ)	R	25	2	5	.286	0	12	8	3	58	53	29	25	0	4.03
2 Hugh Casey	R	35	1	0	1.000	0	4	0	0	8	11	8	5	0	7.88
Spec Shea	R	28	1	1	.500	1	20	3	0	52	48	43	22	0	5.37
Ralph Buxton	R	38	0	1	.000	2	14	0	0	27	22	16	14	0	4.00
Frank Hiller	R	28	0	2	.000	1	4	0	0	8	9	7	3	0	5.63
Wally Hood	R	23	0	0	.000	0	2	0	0	2	0	1	2	0	0.00
BOSTON		29	96	58	.623	16	155	155	84	1377	1375	661	598	16	3.97
Mel Parnell	L	27	**25**	7	.781	2	39	33	**27**	**295**	258	134	122	4	**2.78**
Ellis Kinder	R	34	23	6	**.793**	4	43	30	19	252	251	99	138	**6**	3.36
Joe Dobson	R	32	14	12	.538	2	33	27	12	213	219	97	87	2	3.85
Chuck Stobbs	L	19	11	6	.647	0	26	19	10	152	145	75	70	0	4.03
Jack Kramer	R	31	6	8	.429	1	21	18	7	112	126	49	24	2	5.14
Mickey McDermott	L	20	5	4	.556	0	12	12	6	80	63	52	50	2	4.05
Tex Hughson	R	33	4	2	.667	3	29	2	0	78	82	41	35	0	5.31
2 Walt Masterson	R	29	3	4	.429	4	18	5	1	55	58	35	19	0	4.25
Earl Johnson	L	30	3	6	.333	0	19	3	0	49	65	29	20	0	7.53
1 Mickey Harris	L	32	2	3	.400	0	7	6	2	38	53	20	14	0s	4.97
Frank Quinn	R	21	0	0	.000	0	8	0	0	22	18	9	4	0	2.86
Harry Dorish	R	27	0	0	.000	0	5	0	0	8	7	1	5	0	2.25
Windy McCall	L	23	0	0	.000	0	5	0	0	9	13	10	8	0	12.00
Boo Ferriss (SA)	R	27	0	0	.000	0	4	0	0	7	7	4	1	0	3.88
Jack Robinson	R	28	0	0	.000	0	3	0	0	4	4	1	1	0	2.25
Denny Galehouse	R	37	0	0	.000	0	2	0	0	2	4	3	0	0	13.50
Johnnie Wittig	R	35	0	0	.000	0	1	0	0	2	2	2	0	0	9.00
CLEVELAND		31	89	65	.578	19	154	154	65	1384	1275	611	594	10	**3.36**
Bob Lemon	R	28	22	10	.688	1	37	33	22	280	211	137	138	2	2.99
Bob Feller	R	30	15	14	.517	0	36	28	15	211	198	84	108	0	3.75
Mike Garcia	R	25	14	5	.737	2	41	20	8	176	154	60	94	5	2.35
Early Wynn	R	29	11	7	.611	0	26	23	6	165	186	57	62	0	4.15
Al Benton	R	38	9	6	.600	10	40	11	4	136	116	51	41	2	2.12
Gene Bearden	L	28	8	8	.500	0	32	19	5	127	140	92	41	0	5.10
Steve Gromek	R	29	4	6	.400	0	27	12	3	92	86	40	22	0	3.33
Satchel Paige	R	42	4	7	.364	5	31	5	1	83	70	33	54	0	3.04
Frank Papish	L	31	1	0	1.000	1	25	3	1	62	54	39	23	0	3.19
Sam Zoldak	L	30	1	2	.333	0	27	0	0	53	60	18	11	0	4.25
Russ Christopher (IL) 31															

DETROIT 4th 87-67 .565 10 — **RED ROLFE**

NAME	G by POS	B	AGE	G	AB	R	H	2B	3B	HR	RBI	BB	SO	SB	BA	SA
TOTALS			29	155	5259	751	1405	215	51	88	709	751	502	39	.267	.378
Paul Campbell	1B74	L	31	87	255	38	71	15	4	3	30	24	32	3	.278	.404
Neil Berry	2B95, SS4	R	27	109	329	38	78	9	1	0	18	27	24	4	.237	.271
Johnny Lipon	SS120	R	26	127	439	57	110	14	6	3	59	75	24	2	.251	.330
George Kell	3B134	R	26	134	522	97	179	38	9	3	59	71	13	7	**.343**	.467
Vic Wertz	OF155	L	24	155	608	96	185	26	6	20	133	80	61	2	.304	.465
Johnny Groth	OF99	R	22	103	348	60	102	19	5	11	73	65	27	3	.293	.471
Hoot Evers	OF123	R	28	132	432	68	131	21	6	7	72	70	38	6	.303	.428
Aaron Robinson	C108	L	34	110	331	38	89	12	0	13	56	73	21	0	.269	.423
2 Don Kolloway	2B62, 1B57, 3B7	R	30	126	483	71	142	19	3	2	47	49	25	7	.294	.358
Pat Mullin	OF79	L	31	104	310	55	83	8	6	12	59	42	29	1	.268	.448
Eddie Lake	SS38, 2B19, 3B18	R	33	94	240	38	47	9	1	1	15	61	33	2	.196	.254
Bob Swift	C69	R	34	74	189	16	45	6	0	2	18	26	20	0	.238	.302
George Vico	1B53	L	25	67	142	15	27	5	2	4	18	21	17	0	.190	.338
Dick Wakefield	OF32	L	28	59	126	17	26	3	1	6	19	32	24	0	.206	.389
Hank Riebe	C11	R	27	17	33	1	6	2	0	0	2	0	5	1	.182	.242
Jimmy Outlaw		R	36	5	4	1	1	0	0	0	0	0	1	0	.250	.250
Don Lund		R	26	2	2	0	0	0	0	0	0	0	1	0	.000	.000
Bob Mavis		L	31	1	0	0	0	0	0	0	0	0	0	0	.000	.000
1 Earl Rapp		L	28	1	1	0	0	0	0	0	0	1	0	0	.000	.000

NAME	T	AGE	W	L	PCT	SV	G	GS	CG	IP	H	BB	SO	ShO	ERA
		28	87	67	.565	12	155	155	70	**1394**	1338	628	631	**19**	3.77
Virgil Trucks	R	30	19	11	.633	4	41	32	17	275	209	124	**153**	6	2.81
Hal Newhouser	L	28	18	11	.621	1	38	35	22	292	277	111	144	3	3.36
Fred Hutchinson	R	29	15	7	.682	1	33	21	9	189	167	52	54	4	2.95
Art Houtteman (FS)	R	21	15	10	.600	0	34	25	13	204	227	59	85	2	3.71
Ted Gray	L	24	10	10	.500	1	34	27	8	195	163	103	96	3	3.51
Lou Kretlow	R	26	3	2	.600	0	25	10	1	76	85	69	40	0	6.16
Dizzy Trout	R	34	3	6	.333	3	33	0	0	59	68	21	19	0	4.42
Marv Grissom	R	31	2	4	.333	0	27	2	0	39	56	34	17	0	6.46
Hal White	R	30	1	0	1.000	2	9	0	0	12	5	4	4	0	0.00
Stubby Overmire	L	30	1	3	.250	0	14	1	0	17	29	9	3	0	10.06
Saul Rogovin	R	26	0	1	.000	0	5	0	0	6	13	7	2	0	13.50
Marlin Stuart	R	30	0	2	.000	0	14	2	0	30	39	35	14	0	9.00

PHILADELPHIA 5th 81-73 .526 16 — **CONNIE MACK**

NAME	G by POS	B	AGE	G	AB	R	H	2B	3B	HR	RBI	BB	SO	SB	BA	SA
TOTALS			31	154	5123	726	1331	214	49	82	680	783	493	36	.260	.369
Ferris Fain	1B150	L	28	150	525	81	138	21	5	3	78	136	51	8	.263	.339
Pete Suder	2B89, 3B36, SS2	R	33	118	445	44	119	24	6	10	75	23	35	0	.267	.416
Eddie Joost	SS144	R	33	144	525	128	138	25	3	23	81	149	80	2	.263	.453
Hank Majeski	3B113	R	32	114	448	62	124	26	5	9	67	29	23	0	.277	.417
Wally Moses	OF92	L	38	110	308	49	85	19	3	1	25	51	19	1	.276	.367
Sam Chapman	OF154	R	33	154	589	89	164	24	4	24	108	80	68	3	.278	.455
Elmer Valo	OF150	L	28	150	547	86	155	27	12	5	85	119	32	14	.283	.404
Mike Guerra	C95	R	36	98	298	41	79	14	1	3	31	37	26	3	.265	.349
Nellie Fox	2B77	L	21	88	247	42	63	6	2	0	21	32	9	2	.255	.296
Taffy Wright	OF35	L	37	59	149	14	35	2	5	2	25	16	6	0	.235	.356
Don White	OF47, 3B4	R	30	57	169	12	36	6	0	0	10	14	12	2	.213	.249
Joe Astroth	C44	R	26	55	148	18	36	4	1	0	12	21	13	1	.243	.284
Buddy Rosar	C31	R	34	32	95	7	19	2	0	0	6	16	5	0	.200	.221
Tod Davis	SS14, 3B12, 2B1	R	24	31	75	7	20	0	1	1	6	9	16	0	.267	.333
Hank Biasatti	1B8	L	27	21	24	6	2	2	0	0	2	8	5	0	.083	.167
2 Augie Galan	OF9	L	37	12	26	4	8	2	0	0	0	9	2	0	.308	.385
Bobby Estalella (SM)	OF6	R	38	8	20	2	5	0	0	0	3	1	2	0	.250	.250

Barney McCoskey (XJ) 31

NAME	T	AGE	W	L	PCT	SV	G	GS	CG	IP	H	BB	SO	ShO	ERA
		24	81	73	.526	11	154	154	**85**	1365	1359	758	490	9	4.23
Alex Kellner	L	24	20	12	.625	1	38	27	19	245	243	129	94	0	3.75
Lou Brissie	L	25	16	11	.593	3	34	29	18	229	220	118	118	0	4.28
Dick Fowler	R	28	15	11	.577	1	31	28	15	214	210	115	43	4	3.74
Joe Coleman	R	26	13	14	.481	1	33	30	18	240	249	127	109	1	3.86
Carl Scheib	R	22	9	12	.429	0	38	23	11	183	191	118	43	2	5.11
Bobby Shantz	L	23	6	8	.429	2	33	7	4	127	100	74	58	1	3.40
Charlie Harris	R	23	1	1	.500	3	37	0	0	84	92	42	18	0	5.46
Bill McCahan	R	28	1	1	.500	0	7	4	0	21	23	9	3	0	2.57
Phil Marchildon (SA)	R	35	0	3	.000	0	7	6	0	16	24	19	2	0	11.81
Jim Wilson	R	27	0	0	.000	0	2	0	0	5	7	5	2	0	14.40
Clem Housmann	R	29	0	0	.000	0	1	0	0	1	0	2	0	0	9.00

CHICAGO 6th 63-91 .409 34 — **JACK ONSLOW**

NAME	G by POS	B	AGE	G	AB	R	H	2B	3B	HR	RBI	BB	SO	SB	BA	SA
TOTALS			28	154	5204	648	1340	207	**66**	43	591	702	596	**62**	.257	.347
2 Charlie Kress	1B95	L	27	97	353	45	98	17	6	1	44	39	44	6	.278	.368
Cass Michaels	2B154	R	23	154	561	73	173	27	9	6	83	101	50	5	.308	.421
Luke Appling	SS141	R	42	142	492	82	148	21	5	5	58	121	24	7	.301	.394
Floyd Baker	3B122, SS3, 2B1	L	32	125	388	38	101	15	4	1	40	84	32	3	.260	.327
Dave Philley	OF145	B	29	146	598	84	171	20	8	0	44	54	51	13	.286	.346
Catfish Metkovich	OF87	L	27	93	338	50	80	9	4	5	45	41	24	5	.237	.331
Herb Adams (BG)	OF48	L	21	56	208	26	61	5	3	0	16	9	16	1	.293	.346
Don Wheeler	C58	R	26	67	192	17	46	9	2	1	22	27	19	2	.240	.323
Steve Souchock	OF39, 1B30	R	30	84	252	29	59	13	5	7	37	25	38	5	.234	.409
Gus Zernial	OF46	R	26	73	198	29	63	17	2	5	38	15	26	0	.318	.500
Joe Tipton	C53	R	26	67	191	20	39	5	3	3	19	27	17	1	.204	.309
Eddie Malone	C51	R	29	55	170	17	46	7	2	1	16	29	19	2	.271	.353
John Ostrowski	OF41, 3B8	R	31	49	158	19	42	9	4	5	31	15	41	4	.266	.468
Gordon Goldsberry	1B38	L	21	39	145	25	36	3	2	1	13	18	9	2	.248	.317
Fred Hancock	SS27, 3B3, OF1	R	29	39	52	7	7	2	1	0	9	8	9	0	.135	.212
Jerry Scala	OF37	L	22	37	120	17	30	7	1	1	13	17	19	3	.250	.350
Billy Bowers	OF20	L	26	26	78	5	15	2	1	0	6	4	5	1	.192	.244
3 Bobby Rhawn	3B19, SS3	R	30	24	73	12	15	4	1	0	5	12	8	0	.205	.288
2 Earl Rapp	OF13	L	28	19	54	3	14	1	1	0	11	5	6	1	.259	.315
Rocky Krsnich	2B16	R	21	16	55	7	12	3	1	1	9	6	4	0	.218	.364
Dick Lane	OF11	R	22	12	42	4	5	0	0	0	4	5	3	0	.119	.119
George Yankowski	C6	R	26	12	18	0	3	1	0	0	2	0	2	0	.167	.222
Bill Higdon	OF6	L	24	11	23	3	7	3	0	0	1	6	3	1	.304	.435
Jim Baumer	SS7	R	18	8	10	2	4	1	1	0	2	2	1	0	.400	.700
1 Don Kolloway	3B2	R	30	4	4	0	0	0	0	0	0	0	1	0	.000	.000
Pat Seerey	OF2	R	26	4	4	1	0	0	0	0	0	3	1	0	.000	.000

NAME	T	AGE	W	L	PCT	SV	G	GS	CG	IP	H	BB	SO	ShO	ERA
		28	63	91	.409	17	154	154	57	1363	1362	693	502	10	4.30
Bill Wight	L	27	15	13	.536	1	35	33	14	245	254	96	78	3	3.31
Randy Gumpert	R	31	13	16	.448	1	34	32	18	234	223	83	78	3	3.81
Bob Kuzava	L	26	10	6	.625	0	29	18	9	157	139	91	83	1	4.01
Billy Pierce	L	22	7	15	.318	0	32	26	8	172	145	112	95	0	3.87
Marino Pieretti	R	28	4	6	.400	4	39	9	0	116	131	54	25	0	5.51
2 Mickey Haefner	L	36	4	6	.400	1	14	12	4	80	84	41	17	1	4.39
Max Surkont	R	27	3	5	.375	4	44	2	0	96	92	60	38	0	4.78
2 Eddie Klieman	R	31	2	0	1.000	3	18	0	0	33	33	15	9	0	3.00
1 Al Gettel	R	31	2	5	.286	1	19	7	1	63	69	26	22	1	6.43
2 Clyde Shoun	L	37	1	1	.500	0	19	0	0	23	37	13	8	0	5.87
Jack Bruner	L	25	1	2	.333	0	4	2	0	8	10	8	4	0	7.88
Howie Judson	R	23	1	14	.067	1	26	12	3	108	114	70	36	0	4.58
Bill Evans	R	30	0	1	.000	0	4	0	0	6	6	8	1	0	7.50
Ernie Groth	R	27	0	1	.000	0	3	0	0	5	2	3	1	0	5.40
Bob Cain	L	24	0	0	.000	1	6	0	0	11	7	5	5	0	2.45
Alex Carrasquel (SM)	R	36	0	0	.000	0	3	0	0	4	8	4	1	0	13.50
Fred Bradley	R	28	0	0	.000	0	1	1	0	2	4	3	0	0	13.50
Orval Grove	R	29	0	0	.000	0	1	0	0	1	4	1	1	0	36.00

ST. LOUIS 7th 53-101 .344 44 — **ZACK TAYLOR**

NAME	G by POS	B	AGE	G	AB	R	H	2B	3B	HR	RBI	BB	SO	SB	BA	SA
TOTALS			28	155	5112	667	1301	213	30	117	624	631	**700**	38	.254	.377
Jack Graham	1B136	L	32	137	500	71	119	22	1	24	79	61	62	0	.238	.430
Jerry Priddy	2B145	R	29	145	544	83	158	26	4	11	63	80	81	5	.290	.414
Eddie Pellagrini	SS76	R	31	79	235	26	56	8	1	2	15	14	24	2	.238	.306
Bob Dillinger	3B133	R	30	137	544	68	176	22	13	1	51	51	40	**20**	.324	.417
Dick Kokos	OF138	L	21	143	501	80	131	28	1	23	77	66	91	3	.261	.459
2 Stan Spence	OF85, 1B1	L	34	104	314	46	77	13	3	13	45	52	36	1	.245	.430
Roy Sievers	OF125, 3B7	R	22	140	471	84	144	28	1	16	91	70	75	1	.306	.471
Sherm Lollar	C93	R	24	109	284	28	74	9	1	8	49	32	22	0	.261	.384
John Sullivan	SS71, 3B23, 2B6	R	28	105	243	29	55	8	3	0	18	38	35	5	.226	.284
Paul Lehner	OF55, 1B18	L	29	104	297	25	68	13	0	3	37	16	20	0	.229	.303
Whitey Platt	OF59, 1B2	R	28	102	244	29	63	8	2	3	29	24	27	0	.258	.344
Les Moss	C83	R	24	97	278	28	81	11	0	10	39	49	32	0	.291	.439
Andy Anderson	SS44, 2B8, 3B8	R	26	71	136	10	17	3	0	1	5	14	21	0	.125	.169
George Elder	OF10	L	28	41	44	9	11	3	0	0	2	4	11	0	.250	.318
1 Al Zarilla	OF15	L	30	15	56	10	14	1	0	1	6	8	2	1	.250	.321
Ken Wood	OF3	R	25	7	6	0	0	0	0	0	0	1	2	0	.000	.000
Hank Arft		L	27	6	5	1	1	1	0	0	2	0	1	0	.200	.400
Owen Friend	2B2	R	22	2	8	1	3	0	0	0	1	0	0	0	.375	.375

Al Naples 21 R 1-7, Frankie Pack 21 L 0-1

NAME	T	AGE	W	L	PCT	SV	G	GS	CG	IP	H	BB	SO	ShO	ERA
		29	53	101	.344	16	155	155	43	1341	**1583**	685	432	3	5.21
Ned Garver	R	23	12	**17**	.414	3	41	32	16	224	245	102	70	1	3.98
Joe Ostrowski	L	32	8	8	.500	2	40	13	4	141	185	27	34	0	4.79
Cliff Fannin	R	25	8	14	.364	1	30	25	5	143	177	93	57	0	6.17
Tom Ferrick	R	34	6	4	.600	6	50	0	0	104	102	41	34	0	3.89
Bill Kennedy	L	28	4	11	.267	1	48	16	2	154	172	73	69	0	4.68
Al Papai	R	30	4	11	.267	2	42	15	6	142	175	81	31	0	5.07
Karl Drews	R	29	4	12	.250	0	31	23	3	140	180	66	35	1	6.62
Red Embree	R	31	3	13	.188	1	35	19	4	127	146	89	24	0	5.39
Ed Albrecht	R	20	1	0	1.000	0	1	1	1	5	1	4	1	0	5.40
Bob Malloy	R	31	1	1	.500	0	5	0	0	10	6	7	2	0	2.70
Ribs Raney	R	26	1	2	.333	0	3	3	1	16	23	12	5	0	7.88
Dick Starr (IL)	R	28	1	7	.125	0	30	8	1	83	96	48	44	1	4.34
Ray Shore	R	28	0	1	.000	0	13	0	0	23	27	31	13	0	10.96
Ralph Winegarner	R	39	0	0	.000	0	9	0	0	17	24	2	8	0	7.41
Bob Savage	R	27	0	0	.000	0	4	0	0	7	12	3	1	0	6.43
Irv Medlinger	L	22	0	0	.000	0	3	0	0	4	11	3	4	0	27.00
Jim Bilbrey	R	25	0	0	.000	0	1	0	0	1	1	3	0	0	18.00

WASHINGTON 8th 50-104 .325 47 — **JOE KUHEL**

NAME	G by POS	B	AGE	G	AB	R	H	2B	3B	HR	RBI	BB	SO	SB	BA	SA
TOTALS			28	154	5234	584	1330	207	41	81	546	593	495	46	.254	.356
Eddie Robinson	1B143	L	28	143	527	66	155	27	3	18	78	67	30	3	.294	.459
Al Kozar	2B102	R	26	105	350	46	94	15	2	4	31	25	23	2	.269	.357
Sam Dente	SS153	R	27	153	590	48	161	24	4	1	53	31	24	4	.273	.332
Eddie Yost	3B122	R	22	124	435	57	110	19	7	9	45	91	41	3	.253	.391
Bud Stewart	OF105	L	33	118	388	58	110	23	4	8	43	49	33	6	.284	.425
Clyde Vollmer	OF114	R	27	129	443	58	112	17	1	14	59	53	62	1	.253	.391
Gil Coan	OF97	L	27	111	358	36	78	7	8	3	25	29	58	9	.218	.307
Al Evans	C107	R	32	109	321	32	87	12	3	2	42	50	19	4	.271	.346
Sherry Robertson	2B71, 3B19, OF13	R	30	110	374	59	94	17	3	11	42	42	35	10	.251	.401
Buddy Lewis	OF67	L	32	95	257	25	63	14	4	3	28	41	12	2	.245	.366
2 Sam Mele	OF63, 1B11	R	26	78	264	21	64	12	2	3	25	17	34	2	.242	.337
John Simmons	OF26	R	24	62	93	12	20	0	0	0	5	11	6	0	.215	.215
Jake Early	C53	L	32	53	138	12	34	4	0	1	11	26	11	0	.246	.297
Mark Christman	3B23, 1B6, SS4, 2B1	R	35	49	112	8	24	2	0	3	18	8	7	0	.214	.313
Roberto Ortiz (SM)	OF32	R	34	40	129	12	36	3	0	1	11	9	12	0	.279	.326
Ralph Weigel	C21	R	27	34	60	4	14	2	0	0	4	8	6	0	.233	.267
Hal Keller		L	21	3	3	1	1	0	0	0	0	0	0	0	.333	.333
Jay Difani	2B1	R	25	2	1	0	1	1	0	0	0	0	0	0	1.000	2.000
1 Herm Reich		R	31	2	2	0	0	0	0	0	0	0	1	0	.000	.000

NAME	T	AGE	W	L	PCT	SV	G	GS	CG	IP	H	BB	SO	ShO	ERA
		29	50	**104**	.325	9	154	154	44	1346	1438	779	451	9	5.10
Ray Scarborough	R	31	13	11	.542	0	34	27	11	200	204	88	81	1	4.59
Sid Hudson	R	34	8	17	.320	1	40	27	11	209	234	91	54	2	4.22
Paul Calvert	R	31	6	**17**	.261	1	34	23	5	161	175	86	52	0	5.42
1 Mickey Haefner	L	36	5	5	.500	0	19	12	4	92	85	53	23	1	4.40
Lloyd Hittle	L	25	5	7	.417	0	36	9	3	109	123	57	32	2	4.21
1 Walt Masterson	R	29	3	2	.600	0	10	7	2	42	21	21	17	0	3.23
Dick Weik	R	21	3	12	.200	1	27	14	2	95	78	103	58	2	5.40
Dick Welteroth	R	21	2	5	.286	2	52	2	0	95	107	89	37	0	7.39
Joe Haynes	R	31	2	9	.182	2	37	10	0	96	106	55	19	0	6.28
2 Mickey Harris	L	32	2	12	.143	0	23	19	4	129	151	55	54	0	5.16
Forrest Thompson	L	31	1	3	.250	0	9	1	1	16	22	9	8	0	4.50
Jim Pearce	R	24	0	1	.000	0	2	1	0	5	9	5	1	0	9.00
Dizzy Sutherland	L	26	0	1	.000	0	1	1	0	1	2	6	0	0	45.00
2 Al Gettel	R	31	0	2	.000	1	16	1	0	35	43	24	7	0	5.40
Julio Gonzales	R	28	0	0	.000	0	13	0	0	34	33	27	5	0	4.76
Milo Candini	R	31	0	0	.000	1	3	0	0	6	4	1	1	0	4.50
Buzz Dozier	R	21	0	0	.000	0	2	0	0	6	12	6	1	0	12.00
1 Eddie Klieman	R	31	0	0	.000	0	2	0	0	3	8	3	1	0	18.00

BROOKLYN 1st 97-57 .630 — BURT SHOTTON

NAME	G by POS	B	AGE	G	AB	R	H	2B	3B	HR	RBI	BB	SO	SB	BA	SA
TOTALS			27	156	5400	**879**	1477	236	47	**152**	**816**	638	570	**117**	.274	**.419**
Gil Hodges	1B156	R	25	156	596	94	170	23	4	23	115	66	64	10	.285	.453
Jackie Robinson	2B156	R	30	156	593	122	203	38	12	16	124	86	27	**37**	**.342**	.528
Pee Wee Reese	SS155	R	30	155	617	**132**	172	27	3	16	73	116	59	26	.279	.410
Billy Cox	3B100	R	29	100	390	48	91	18	2	8	40	30	18	5	.233	.351
Carl Furillo	OF142	R	27	142	549	95	177	27	10	18	106	37	29	4	.322	.506
Duke Snider	OF145	L	22	146	552	100	161	28	7	23	92	56	**92**	12	.292	.493
Gene Hermanski	OF77	L	29	87	224	48	67	12	3	8	42	47	21	12	.299	.487
Roy Campanella	C127	R	27	130	436	65	125	22	2	22	82	67	36	3	.287	.498
Bruce Edwards	C41, OF4, 3B1	R	25	64	148	24	31	3	0	8	25	25	15	0	.209	.392
13 Marv Rackley	OF47	L	27	63	150	25	45	5	1	1	15	14	8	1	.300	.367
Mike McCormick	OF49	R	32	55	139	17	29	5	1	2	14	14	12	1	.209	.302
Spider Jorgensen	3B36	L	29	53	134	15	36	5	1	1	14	23	13	0	.269	.343
Eddie Miksis	3B29, SS4, 2B3, 1B1	R	22	50	113	17	25	5	0	1	6	7	8	3	.221	.292
Tommy Brown	OF27	R	21	41	89	14	27	2	0	3	18	6	8	0	.303	.427
Luis Olmo (SM)	OF34	R	29	38	105	15	32	4	1	1	14	5	11	2	.305	.390
Dick Whitman	OF11	L	28	23	49	8	9	2	0	0	2	4	4	0	.184	.224
Cal Abrams	OF7	L	25	8	24	6	2	1	0	0	0	7	6	1	.083	.125
2 Johnny Hopp	OF4, 1B2	L	32	8	14	0	0	0	0	0	0	0	3	0	.000	.000

1 Bob Ramazzotti 32 R 2-13, Chuck Connors 28 L 0-1, George Shuba 24 L 0-1

NAME	T	AGE	W	L	PCT	SV	G	GS	CG	IP	H	BB	SO	ShO	ERA
TOTALS		25	**97**	57	**.630**	17	156	156	62	**1409**	1306	582	**743**	**15**	3.80
Don Newcombe	R	23	17	8	.680	1	38	31	19	244	223	73	149	**5**	3.17
Preacher Roe	L	34	15	6	**.714**	1	30	27	13	213	201	44	109	3	2.79
Ralph Branca	R	23	13	5	.722	1	34	27	9	187	181	91	109	2	4.38
Joe Hatten	L	32	12	8	.600	2	37	29	11	187	194	69	58	2	4.19
Jack Banta	R	24	10	6	.625	3	48	12	2	152	125	68	97	1	3.38
Rex Barney	R	24	9	8	.529	1	38	20	6	141	108	89	80	2	4.40
Carl Erskine	R	22	8	1	.889	0	22	3	2	80	68	51	49	0	4.61
Erv Palica	R	21	8	9	.471	6	49	1	0	97	93	49	44	0	3.62
Paul Minner	L	25	3	1	.750	2	27	1	0	47	49	18	17	0	3.83
Pat McGlothin	R	28	1	1	.500	0	7	0	0	16	13	5	11	0	4.50
Morrie Martin	L	26	1	3	.250	0	10	4	0	31	39	15	15	0	6.97
Bud Podbielan	R	25	0	1	.000	0	7	1	0	12	9	9	5	0	3.75
Johnny Van Cuyk	L	27	0	0	.000	0	2	0	0	2	3	1	0	0	9.00

ST. LOUIS 2nd 96-58 .623 1 — EDDIE DYER

NAME	G by POS	B	AGE	G	AB	R	H	2B	3B	HR	RBI	BB	SO	SB	BA	SA
TOTALS			27	157	**5463**	766	**1513**	**281**	54	102	720	569	482	17	**.277**	.404
Nippy Jones	1B98	R	24	110	380	51	114	20	2	8	62	16	20	1	.300	.426
Red Schoendienst	2B138, SS14, 3B6, OF2	B	26	151	640	102	190	25	2	3	54	51	18	8	.297	.356
Marty Marion	SS134	R	31	134	515	61	140	31	2	5	70	37	42	0	.272	.369
Eddie Kazak (JJ)	3B80, 2B5	R	28	92	326	43	99	15	3	6	42	29	17	0	.304	.423
Stan Musial	OF156, 1B1	L	28	157	612	128	**207**	**41**	**13**	36	123	107	38	3	.338	.624
Chuck Diering	OF124	R	26	131	369	60	97	21	8	3	38	35	49	1	.263	.388
Enos Slaughter	OF150	L	33	151	568	92	191	34	**13**	13	96	79	37	3	.336	.511
Del Rice	C92	R	26	92	284	25	67	16	1	4	29	30	40	0	.236	.342
Ron Northey	OF73	L	29	90	265	28	69	18	2	7	50	31	15	0	.260	.423
Tommy Glaviano	3B73, 2B7	R	25	87	258	32	69	16	1	6	36	41	35	0	.267	.407
Rocky Nelson	1B70	L	24	82	244	28	54	8	4	4	32	11	12	1	.221	.337
Joe Garagiola	C80	L	23	81	241	25	63	14	0	3	26	31	19	0	.261	.357
Lou Klein (SM)	SS21, 2B9, 3B7	R	30	58	114	25	25	6	0	2	12	22	20	0	.219	.325
Hal Rice	OF10	L	25	40	46	3	9	2	1	1	9	3	7	0	.196	.348
1 Ed Sauer	OF10	R	29	24	45	5	10	2	1	0	1	3	8	0	.222	.311
Bill Baker	C10	R	38	20	30	2	4	1	0	0	4	2	2	0	.133	.167
Solly Hemus	2B16	L	26	20	33	8	11	1	0	0	2	7	3	0	.333	.364
Whitey Kurowski (EJ)	3B2	R	31	10	14	0	2	0	0	0	0	1	0	0	.143	.143
Bill Howerton	OF6	L	27	9	13	1	4	1	0	0	1	0	2	0	.308	.385

Steve Bilko 20 R 5-17, Russ Derry 32 L 0-2, Del Wilber 30 R 1-4, Erv Dusak 28 R 0-0

NAME	T	AGE	W	L	PCT	SV	G	GS	CG	IP	H	BB	SO	ShO	ERA
TOTALS		31	96	58	.623	**19**	157	157	64	1408	1356	506	606	13	**3.44**
Howie Pollet	L	28	20	9	.690	1	39	28	17	231	228	59	108	**5**	2.77
George Munger	R	30	15	8	.652	2	35	28	12	188	179	87	82	2	3.88
Al Brazle	L	35	14	8	.636	0	39	25	9	206	208	61	75	1	3.19
Harry Brecheen	L	34	14	11	.560	1	32	31	14	215	207	65	88	2	3.35
Ted Wilks	R	33	10	3	.769	**9**	**59**	0	0	118	103	[illegible]	71	0	[illegible]
Gerry Staley	R	28	10	10	.500	6	45	17	5	171	154	41	55	2	2.74
Freddie Martin (SM)	R	34	6	0	1.000	0	21	5	3	70	65	20	30	0	2.44
Max Lanier (SM)	L	33	5	4	.556	0	15	15	4	92	92	35	37	1	3.82
Bill Reeder	R	27	1	1	.500	0	21	1	0	34	33	30	21	0	5.03
Jim Hearn	R	28	1	3	.250	0	17	4	0	42	48	23	18	0	5.14
Ken Johnson	L	26	0	1	.000	0	14	2	0	34	29	35	18	0	6.35
Cloyd Boyer	R	21	0	0	.000	0	4	1	0	3	5	7	0	0	12.00
Ray Yochim	R	26	0	0	.000	0	3	0	0	2	3	4	3	0	18.00
Kurt Krieger	R	22	0	0	.000	0	1	0	0	1	0	1	0	0	0.00

PHILADELPHIA 3rd 81-73 .526 16 — EDDIE SAWYER

NAME	G by POS	B	AGE	G	AB	R	H	2B	3B	HR	RBI	BB	SO	SB	BA	SA
TOTALS			26	154	5307	662	1349	232	**55**	122	622	528	**670**	27	.254	.388
Dick Sisler	1B96	L	28	121	412	42	119	19	6	7	50	25	38	0	.289	.415
Eddie Miller	2B82, SS1	R	32	85	266	21	55	10	1	6	29	29	21	1	.207	.320
Granny Hamner	SS154	R	22	154	**662**	83	174	32	5	6	53	25	47	6	.263	.353
Willie Jones	3B145	R	23	149	532	71	130	35	1	19	77	65	66	3	.244	.421
Bill Nicholson	OF91	L	34	98	299	42	70	8	3	11	40	45	53	1	.234	.391
Richie Ashburn	OF154	L	22	154	**662**	84	188	18	11	1	37	58	38	9	.284	.349
Del Ennis	OF154	R	24	154	610	92	184	39	11	25	110	59	61	2	.302	.525
Andy Seminick	C98	R	28	109	334	52	81	11	2	24	68	69	74	0	.243	.503
Stan Lopata	C58	R	23	83	240	31	65	9	2	8	27	21	44	1	.271	.425
Stan Hollmig	OF66	R	23	81	251	28	64	11	6	2	26	20	43	1	.255	.371
Buddy Blattner	2B15, 3B12, SS7	R	29	64	97	15	24	6	0	5	21	19	17	0	.247	.464
Mike Goliat	2B50, 1B5	R	23	55	189	24	40	6	3	3	19	20	32	0	.212	.323
Eddie Waitkus (GW)	1B54	L	29	54	209	41	64	16	3	1	28	33	12	3	.306	.426
Jackie Mayo	OF25	L	23	45	39	3	5	0	0	0	2	4	5	0	.128	.128
Putsy Caballero	2B21, SS1	R	21	29	68	8	19	3	0	0	3	0	3	0	.279	.324
Bill Glynn	1B1	L	24	8	10	0	2	0	0	0	1	0	3	0	.200	.200
Ed Sanicki	OF6	R	24	7	13	4	3	0	0	3	7	1	4	0	.231	.923
Johnny Blatnik	OF2	R	28	6	8	3	1	0	0	0	0	4	1	0	.125	.125

Ken Silvestri 33 B 0-4, 1 Bert Haas 35 R 0-1, Hal Wagner 33 L 0-4

NAME	T	AGE	W	L	PCT	SV	G	GS	CG	IP	H	BB	SO	ShO	ERA
TOTALS		30	81	73*	.526	15	154	154	58	1392	1389	502	495	12	3.89
Russ Meyer	R	25	17	8	.680	1	37	28	14	213	199	70	78	2	3.08
Ken Heintzelman	L	33	17	10	.630	0	33	32	15	250	239	93	65	5	3.02
Robin Roberts	R	22	15	15	.500	4	43	31	11	227	229	75	95	3	3.69
Hank Borowy	R	33	12	12	.500	0	28	28	12	193	188	63	43	2	4.20
Jim Konstanty	R	32	9	5	.643	7	53	0	0	97	98	29	43	0	3.25
Curt Simmons	L	20	4	10	.286	1	38	14	2	131	133	55	83	0	4.60
Schoolboy Rowe	R	39	3	7	.300	0	23	6	2	65	68	17	22	0	4.85
Blix Donnelly	R	35	2	1	.667	0	23	10	1	78	84	40	36	0	5.08
Ken Trinkle	R	29	1	1	.500	2	42	0	0	74	79	30	14	0	4.04
Jocko Thompson	L	29	1	3	.250	0	8	5	1	31	38	11	12	0	6.97
Charlie Bicknell	R	20	0	0	.000	0	13	0	0	28	32	17	4	0	7.71
Bob Miller	R	23	0	0	.000	0	3	0	0	3	2	2	0	0	0.00

*1 loss by forfeit

BOSTON 4th 75-79 .487 22 — BILLY SOUTHWORTH

NAME	G by POS	B	AGE	G	AB	R	H	2B	3B	HR	RBI	BB	SO	SB	BA	SA
TOTALS			29	157	5336	706	1376	246	33	103	654	**684**	656	28	.258	.374
Elbie Fletcher	1B121	L	33	122	413	57	108	19	3	11	51	84	65	1	.262	.402
Eddie Stanky	2B135	R	32	138	506	90	144	24	5	1	42	113	41	3	.285	.358
Al Dark	SS125, 3B4	R	27	130	529	74	146	23	5	3	53	31	43	5	.276	.355
Bob Elliott	3B130	R	32	139	482	77	135	29	5	17	76	90	38	0	.280	.467
Tommy Holmes	OF103	L	32	117	380	47	101	20	4	8	59	39	6	1	.266	.403
Jim Russell	OF120	B	30	130	415	57	96	22	1	8	54	64	68	3	.231	.347
Marv Rickert	OF75, 1B12	L	28	100	277	44	81	18	3	6	49	23	38	1	.292	.444
Del Crandall	C63	R	19	67	228	21	60	10	1	4	34	9	18	2	.263	.368
Sibby Sisti	OF48, 2B21, SS18, 3B1	R	28	101	268	39	69	12	0	5	22	34	42	1	.257	.358
Connie Ryan	3B25, SS18, 2B16, 1B3	R	29	85	208	28	52	13	1	6	20	21	30	1	.250	.409
Pete Reiser	OF63, 3B4	L	30	84	221	32	60	8	3	8	40	33	42	3	.271	.443
2 Ed Sauer	OF71, 3B2	R	29	79	214	26	57	12	0	3	31	17	34	0	.266	.364
Bill Salkeld	C63	L	32	66	161	17	41	5	0	5	25	44	24	1	.255	.379
Clint Conatser		R	27	53	152	10	40	6	0	3	16	14	19	0	.263	.362
1 Phil Masi	C37	R	32	37	105	13	22	2	0	0	6	14	10	1	.210	.229
Jeff Heath (BN)	OF31	L	34	36	111	17	34	7	0	9	23	15	26	0	.306	.613
2 Mickey Livingston (BG)	C22	R	34	28	64	6	15	2	1	0	6	3	5	0	.234	.297
Earl Torgeson (SJ)	1B25	L	25	25	100	17	26	5	1	4	19	13	4	4	.260	.450
Ray Sanders (BW)	1B7	L	32	9	21	0	3	1	0	0	0	4	9	0	.143	.190
Don Thompson	OF2	L	25	7	11	0	2	0	0	0	0	0	2	0	.182	.182

Al Lakeman 30 R 1-6, Steve Kuczek 24 R 1-1

NAME	T	AGE	W	L	PCT	SV	G	GS	CG	IP	H	BB	SO	ShO	ERA
TOTALS		29	75	79	.487	11	157	157	**68**	1400	**1466**	520	591	12	3.99
Warren Spahn	L	28	**21**	14	.600	0	38	**38**	**25**	**302**	283	86	**151**	4	3.07
Vern Bickford	R	28	16	11	.593	0	37	36	15	231	246	106	101	2	4.25
Johnny Sain	R	31	10	17	.370	0	37	36	16	243	285	75	73	1	4.81
Bill Voiselle	R	30	7	8	.467	1	30	22	5	169	170	78	63	4	4.05
Bob Hall	R	25	6	4	.600	0	31	6	2	74	77	41	43	0	4.38
Nels Potter	R	37	6	11	.353	7	41	3	1	97	99	30	57	0	4.18
Glenn Elliott	L	29	3	4	.429	0	22	6	1	68	70	27	15	0	3.97
Johnny Antonelli	L	19	3	7	.300	0	22	10	3	96	99	42	48	1	3.56
Bobby Hogue	R	28	2	2	.500	3	33	0	0	72	78	25	23	0	3.13
Red Barrett	R	34	1	1	.500	0	23	0	0	44	58	10	17	0	5.73
Johnny Beazley	R	31	0	0	.000	0	1	0	0	2	0	0	0	0	0.00
1 Clyde Shoun	L	37	0	0	.000	0	1	0	0	1	1	0	0	0	0.00

NEW YORK 5th 73-81 .474 24 — LEO DUROCHER

NAME	G by POS	B	AGE	G	AB	R	H	2B	3B	HR	RBI	BB	SO	SB	BA	SA
TOTALS			28	156	5308	736	1383	203	52	147	690	613	523	43	.261	.401
1 Johnny Mize	1B101	L	36	106	388	59	102	15	0	18	62	50	19	1	.263	.441
Hank Thompson	2B69, 3B1	L	23	75	275	51	77	10	4	9	34	42	30	5	.280	.444
Buddy Kerr	SS89	R	26	90	220	16	46	4	0	0	19	21	23	0	.209	.227
Sid Gordon	3B123, OF15, 1B1	R	31	141	489	87	139	26	2	26	90	95	37	1	.284	.505
Willard Marshall	OF138	L	28	141	499	81	153	19	3	12	70	78	20	4	.307	.429
Bobby Thomson	OF156	R	25	156	641	99	198	35	9	27	109	44	45	10	.309	.518
Whitey Lockman	OF151	L	22	151	617	97	186	32	7	11	65	62	31	12	.301	.429
Wes Westrum	C62	R	26	64	169	23	41	4	1	7	28	37	39	1	.243	.402
Bill Rigney	SS81, 2B26, 3B14	R	30	122	389	53	108	19	6	6	47	47	38	3	.278	.404
Joe Lafata (IL)	1B47	L	27	64	140	18	33	2	2	3	16	9	23	1	.236	.343
2 Ray Mueller	C56	R	37	56	170	17	38	2	2	5	23	13	14	1	.224	.347
Lucky Lohrke	2B23, 3B19, SS15	R	25	55	180	32	48	11	4	5	22	16	12	3	.267	.456
2 Bert Haas	1B23, 3B11	R	35	54	104	12	27	2	3	1	10	5	8	0	.260	.365
Don Mueller	OF6	L	22	51	56	5	13	4	0	0	1	5	6	0	.232	.304
1 Walker Cooper	C40	R	34	42	147	14	31	4	2	4	21	7	8	0	.211	.347
Monte Irvin	OF10, 3B5, 1B5	R	30	36	76	7	17	3	2	0	7	17	11	0	.224	.316
Pete Milne	OF1	L	24	31	29	5	7	1	0	1	6	3	6	0	.241	.379
1 Augie Galan	1B3, OF1	L	37	22	17	0	1	1	0	0	2	5	3	0	.059	.118
Bobby Hofman	2B16	R	23	19	48	4	10	0	0	0	3	5	6	0	.208	.208
1 Mickey Livingston	C19	R	34	19	57	6	17	2	0	4	12	2	8	0	.298	.544

George Hausmann (SM) 33 R 6-47, 1 Bobby Rhawn 30 R 5-29, Davey Williams 21 R 12-50, Dick Culler 34 R 0-1, Rudy Rufer 22 R 1-15, Sal Yvars 25 R 0-8, Herman Franks 35 R 2-3, Danny Gardella (SM) 29, Nap Reyes (SM) 29

NAME	T	AGE	W	L	PCT	SV	G	GS	CG	IP	H	BB	SO	ShO	ERA
TOTALS		28	73*	81	.474	9	156	156	**68**	1375	1328	544	516	10	3.82
Sheldon Jones	R	27	15	12	.556	0	42	27	11	207	198	88	79	1	3.35
Larry Jansen	R	28	15	16	.484	0	37	35	17	260	271	62	113	3	3.84
Monte Kennedy	L	27	12	14	.462	1	38	32	14	223	208	100	95	4	3.43
Dave Koslo	L	29	11	14	.440	4	38	23	15	212	193	43	64	0	**2.50**
Clint Hartung	R	26	9	11	.450	0	33	25	8	155	156	86	48	0	4.99
Hank Behrman	R	28	3	3	.500	0	43	4	1	71	64	52	25	1	4.94
2 Kirby Higbe	R	34	2	0	1.000	2	37	2	0	81	72	41	38	0	3.44
Adrian Zabala (SM)	L	32	2	3	.400	1	15	4	2	41	44	10	13	1	5.27
Andy Hansen	R	24	2	6	.250	1	33	2	0	66	58	28	26	0	4.64
Red Webb	R	24	1	1	.500	0	20	0	0	45	41	21	9	0	4.00
Andy Tomasic	R	29	0	1	.000	0	2	0	0	5	9	5	2	0	18.00
Roger Bowman	L	21	0	0	.000	0	2	2	0	6	6	7	4	0	4.50
1 Ray Poat	R	31	0	0	.000	0	2	0	0	2	8	1	0	0	22.50

Sal Maglie (SM) 32, Ace Adams (SM) 37, Harry Feldman (SM) 29

*1 win by forfeit

PITTSBURGH 6th 71-83 .461 26 — BILLY MEYER

NAME	G by POS	B	AGE	G	AB	R	H	2B	3B	HR	RBI	BB	SO	SB	BA	SA
TOTALS			29	154	5214	681	1350	191	41	126	626	548	554	48	.259	.384
13 Johnny Hopp	1B77, OF16	L	32	105	371	55	118	14	5	5	39	37	29	9	.318	.423
Monty Basgall	2B98, 3B3	R	27	107	308	25	67	9	1	2	26	31	32	1	.218	.273
Stan Rojek	SS144	R	30	144	557	72	136	19	2	0	31	50	31	4	.244	.285
Pete Castiglione	3B98, SS17, OF2	R	28	118	448	57	120	20	2	6	43	20	43	2	.268	.362
Wally Westlake	OF143	R	28	147	525	77	148	24	8	23	104	45	69	6	.282	.490
Dino Restelli	OF61, 1B1	R	24	72	232	41	58	11	0	12	40	35	26	3	.250	.453
Ralph Kiner	OF152	R	26	152	549	116	170	19	5	**54**	**127**	**117**	61	6	.310	**.658**
Clyde McCullough	C90	R	32	91	241	30	57	9	3	4	21	24	30	1	.237	.349
Dixie Walker	OF39, 1B3	L	38	88	181	26	51	4	1	1	18	26	11	0	.282	.331
Eddie Bockman	3B68, 2B5	R	28	79	220	21	49	6	1	6	19	23	31	3	.223	.341
Danny Murtaugh	2B74	R	31	75	236	16	48	7	2	2	24	29	17	2	.203	.275
Ed Fitzgerald	C56	R	25	75	160	16	42	7	0	2	18	8	27	1	.263	.344
Tom Saffell	OF53	L	27	73	205	36	66	7	1	2	25	21	27	5	.322	.395
Ed Stevens	1B58	L	24	67	221	22	58	10	1	4	32	22	24	1	.262	.371
2 Phil Masi	C44, 1B2	R	32	48	135	16	37	6	1	2	13	17	16	1	.274	.378
Les Fleming	1B5	L	33	24	31	0	8	0	2	0	7	6	2	0	.258	.387
2 Jack Phillips	1B16, 3B1	R	27	18	56	6	13	3	1	0	3	4	6	1	.232	.321
Ted Beard	OF10	L	28	14	24	1	2	0	0	0	1	2	2	0	.083	.083

2 Marv Rackley 27 L 11-35, Walt Judnich 31 L 8-35, Jack Cassini 29 R 0-0, 2 Bobby Rhawn 30 R 1-7

NAME	T	AGE	W	L	PCT	SV	G	GS	CG	IP	H	BB	SO	ShO	ERA
		33	71	83	.461	15	154	154	53	1356	1452	535	556	9	4.57
Cliff Chambers	L	27	13	7	.650	0	34	21	10	177	186	58	93	1	3.97
Bill Werle	L	28	12	13	.480	0	35	29	10	221	243	51	106	2	4.24
Murry Dickson	R	32	12	14	.462	0	44	20	11	224	216	80	89	2	3.29
Ernie Bonham (DD)	R	35	7	4	.636	0	18	14	5	89	81	23	25	1	4.25
Bob Chesnes	R	28	7	13	.350	1	27	25	8	145	153	82	49	1	5.90
Rip Sewell	R	42	6	1	.857	1	28	6	2	76	82	32	26	1	3.91
Vic Lombardi	L	26	5	5	.500	1	34	12	4	134	149	68	64	0	4.57
1 Hugh Casey	R	35	4	1	.800	5	33	0	0	39	50	14	9	0	4.62
Hal Gregg	R	27	1	1	.500	0	8	1	0	19	20	8	9	0	3.32
2 Harry Gumbert	R	39	1	4	.200	3	16	0	0	28	30	18	5	0	5.79
Junio Walsh	R	30	1	4	.200	0	9	7	1	43	40	16	24	1	5.02
1 Bob Muncrief	R	33	1	5	.167	3	13	4	1	36	44	13	11	0	6.25
Elmer Riddle	R	34	1	8	.111	1	16	12	1	74	81	45	24	0	5.35
2 Ray Poat	R	31	0	1	.000	0	11	2	0	36	52	15	17	0	6.25
1 Kirby Higbe	R	34	0	2	.000	0	7	1	0	15	25	12	5	0	13.80

CINCINNATI 7th 62-92 .403 35 — BUCKY WALTERS 61-90 .404 LUKE SEWELL 1-2 .333

NAME	G by POS	B	AGE	G	AB	R	H	2B	3B	HR	RBI	BB	SO	SB	BA	SA
TOTALS			29	156	5469	627	1423	264	35	86	588	429	559	31	.260	.368
Ted Kluszewski	1B134	L	24	136	531	63	164	26	2	8	68	19	24	3	.309	.411
Jimmy Bloodworth	2B92, 1B23, 3B8	R	31	134	452	40	118	27	1	9	59	27	36	1	.261	.385
Virgil Stallcup	SS141	R	27	141	575	49	146	28	5	3	45	9	44	1	.254	.336
Grady Hatton	3B136	L	26	137	537	71	141	38	5	11	69	62	48	4	.263	.413
Johnny Wyrostek	OF129	L	29	134	474	54	118	20	4	9	46	58	63	7	.249	.365
Lloyd Merriman	OF86	L	24	103	287	35	66	12	5	4	26	21	36	2	.230	.348
2 Peanuts Lowrey	OF78	R	30	89	309	48	85	16	2	2	25	37	11	1	.275	.359
2 Walker Cooper	C77	R	34	82	307	34	86	9	2	16	62	21	24	0	.280	.479
Bobby Adams	2B63, 3B14	R	27	107	277	32	70	16	2	0	25	26	36	4	.253	.325
Danny Litwhiler	OF82, 3B3	R	32	102	292	35	85	18	1	11	48	44	42	0	.291	.473
2 Harry Walker	OF77, 1B1	L	32	86	314	53	100	15	2	1	23	34	17	4	.318	.389
Dixie Howell	C56	R	30	64	172	17	42	6	1	2	18	8	21	0	.244	.326
Claude Corbitt	SS18, 2B17, 3B1	R	33	44	94	10	17	1	0	0	3	9	1	1	.181	.191
1 Hank Sauer	OF39, 1B1	R	30	42	152	22	36	6	0	4	16	18	19	0	.237	.355
1 Ray Mueller	C31	R	37	32	106	7	29	4	0	1	13	5	13	1	.274	.340
1 Frankie Baumholtz	OF20	L	30	27	81	12	19	5	3	1	8	6	8	0	.235	.407
1 Charlie Kress	1B16	L	27	27	29	3	6	3	0	0	3	3	5	0	.207	.310
Johnny Pramesa	C13	R	23	17	25	2	6	1	0	1	2	3	5	0	.240	.400
Sammy Meeks	2B8, SS3	R	26	16	36	10	11	2	0	2	6	2	6	1	.306	.528
Wally Post	OF3	R	19	6	8	1	2	0	0	0	1	0	3	0	.250	.250

NAME	T	AGE	W	L	PCT	SV	G	GS	CG	IP	H	BB	SO	ShO	ERA
		28	62	92	.403	6	156	156	55	1401	1423	**640**	538	10	4.34
Ken Raffensberger	L	31	18	17	.514	0	41	**38**	20	284	**289**	80	103	**5**	3.39
Herm Wehmeier	R	22	11	12	.478	0	33	29	11	213	202	**117**	80	1	4.69
Howie Fox	R	28	6	**19**	.240	0	38	30	9	215	221	77	60	0	3.98
Ewell Blackwell	R	26	5	5	.500	1	30	4	0	77	80	34	55	0	4.21
Johnny Vander Meer	L	34	5	10	.333	0	28	24	7	160	172	85	76	3	4.89
1 Harry Gumbert	R	39	4	3	.571	2	29	0	0	41	58	8	12	0	5.49
Kent Peterson	L	23	4	5	.444	0	30	7	2	66	66	46	28	0	6.29
Bud Lively	R	24	4	6	.400	1	31	10	3	103	91	53	30	1	3.93
Eddie Erautt	R	24	4	11	.267	1	39	9	1	113	99	61	43	0	3.35
Harry Perkowski	L	26	1	1	.500	0	5	3	2	24	21	14	3	0	4.50
Dixie Howell	R	29	0	1	.000	0	5	1	0	13	21	8	7	0	8.31
Frank Fanovich	L	27	0	2	.000	0	29	1	0	43	44	28	27	0	5.44
2 Jess Dobernic	R	31	0	0	.000	0	14	0	0	19	28	16	6	0	9.95
Ken Burkhart	R	32	0	0	.000	1	11	0	0	28	29	10	8	0	3.21
Walker Cress	R	32	0	0	.000	0	3	0	0	2	2	3	0	0	0.00

CHICAGO 8th 61-93 .396 36 — CHARLIE GRIMM 19-31 .380 FRANKIE FRISCH 42-62 .404

NAME	G by POS	B	AGE	G	AB	R	H	2B	3B	HR	RBI	BB	SO	SB	BA	SA
TOTALS			29	154	5214	593	1336	212	53	97	539	396	573	53	.256	.373
3 Herm Reich	1B85, OF16	R	31	108	386	43	108	18	2	3	34	13	32	4	.280	.360
Emil Verban	2B88	R	33	98	343	38	99	11	1	0	22	8	2	3	.289	.327
Roy Smalley	SS132	R	23	135	477	57	117	21	10	8	35	36	77	2	.245	.382
Frankie Gustine	3B55, 2B16	R	29	76	261	29	59	13	4	4	27	18	22	3	.226	.352
Hal Jeffcoat	OF101	R	24	108	363	43	89	18	6	2	26	20	48	12	.245	.344
Andy Pafko	OF98, 3B49	R	28	144	519	79	146	29	2	18	69	63	33	4	.281	.449
2 Hank Sauer	OF96	R	30	96	357	59	104	17	1	27	83	37	47	0	.291	.571
Mickey Owen (SM)	C59	R	33	62	198	15	54	9	3	2	18	12	13	1	.273	.379
Phil Cavarretta	1B70, OF25	L	32	105	360	46	106	22	4	8	49	45	31	2	.294	.444
Gene Mauch	2B25, SS19, 3B7	R	23	72	150	15	37	6	2	1	7	21	15	3	.247	.333
2 Bob Ramazzotti	3B36, SS12, 2B4	R	32	65	190	14	34	3	1	0	6	5	33	9	.179	.205
2 Hank Edwards (SJ)	OF51	L	30	58	176	25	51	8	4	7	21	19	22	0	.290	.500
2 Frankie Baumholtz	OF43	L	30	58	164	15	37	4	2	1	15	9	21	2	.226	.293
Rube Walker	C43	L	23	56	172	11	42	4	1	3	22	9	18	0	.244	.331
Bob Scheffing (IL)	C40	R	33	55	149	12	40	6	1	3	19	9	9	0	.268	.383
Smokey Burgess	C8	L	22	46	56	4	15	0	0	1	12	4	4	0	.268	.321
1 Harry Walker	OF39	L	32	42	159	20	42	6	3	1	14	11	6	2	.264	.358
1 Peanuts Lowrey	OF31, 3B1	R	30	38	111	18	30	5	0	2	10	9	8	3	.270	.360
Wayne Terwilliger	2B34	R	24	36	112	11	25	2	1	2	10	16	22	0	.223	.313
Rube Novotney	C20	R	24	22	67	4	18	2	1	0	6	3	11	0	.269	.328

Bill Serena 24 R 8-37, Clarence Maddern 27 R 3-9, Hank Schenz 30 R 6-14, Cliff Aberson 27 R 0-7, Jim Kirby 26 R 1-2

NAME	T	AGE	W	L	PCT	SV	G	GS	CG	IP	H	BB	SO	ShO	ERA
		30	61	**93**	.396	17	154	154	44	1358	1463	564	532	8	4.50
Johnny Schmitz	L	28	11	13	.458	3	36	31	9	207	227	92	75	3	4.35
Bob Rush	R	23	10	18	.357	4	35	27	9	201	197	79	80	1	4.07
Bob Chipman	L	30	7	8	.467	1	38	11	3	113	110	63	46	1	3.98
Dutch Leonard	R	40	7	16	.304	0	33	28	10	180	198	43	83	1	4.15
Monk Dubiel	R	30	6	9	.400	4	32	20	3	148	142	54	52	1	4.14
2 Bob Muncrief	R	33	5	6	.455	2	34	3	1	75	80	31	36	0	4.56
Warren Hacker	R	24	5	8	.385	0	30	12	3	126	141	53	40	0	4.21
Doyle Lade	R	28	4	5	.444	1	36	13	5	130	141	58	43	1	4.98
Emil Kush	R	32	3	3	.500	2	26	0	0	48	51	24	22	0	3.75
Dewey Adkins	R	31	2	4	.333	0	30	5	1	82	98	39	43	0	5.71
Cal McLish	R	23	1	1	.500	0	8	2	0	23	31	12	6	0	5.87
Ralph Hamner	R	32	0	2	.000	0	6	1	0	12	22	8	3	0	9.00
Dwain Sloat	L	31	0	0	.000	0	5	1	0	9	14	3	3	0	7.00
1 Jess Dobernic	R	31	0	0	.000	0	4	0	0	4	9	4	0	0	20.25
Mort Cooper	R	36	0	0	.000	0	1	0	0	0	2	1	0	0	∞

WORLD SERIES – NEW YORK (AL) 4 BROOKLYN (NL) 1

LINE SCORES

TEAM	1	2	3	4	5	6	7	8	9	10	11	12	R	H	E
Game 1 October 5 at New York															
BKN (NL)	0	0	0	0	0	0	0	0	0				0	2	0
NY (AL)	0	0	0	0	0	0	0	0	1				1	5	1
Newcombe — **Reynolds**															
Game 2 October 6 at New York															
BKN	0	1	0	0	0	0	0	0	0				1	7	2
NY	0	0	0	0	0	0	0	0	0				0	6	1
Roe — Raschi, Page (9)															
Game 3 October 7 at Brooklyn															
NY	0	0	1	0	0	0	0	0	3				4	5	0
BKN	0	0	0	1	0	0	0	0	2				3	5	0
Byrne, **Page** (4) — **Branca**, Banta (9)															
Game 4 October 8 at Brooklyn															
NY	0	0	0	3	3	0	0	0	0				6	10	0
BKN	0	0	0	0	0	4	0	0	0				4	9	1
Lopat, Reynolds (6) — **Newcombe**, Hatten (4), Erskine (6), Banta (7)															
Game 5 October 9 at Brooklyn															
NY	2	0	3	1	1	3	0	0	0				10	11	1
BKN	0	0	1	0	0	1	4	0	0				6	11	2
Raschi, Page (7) — **Barney**, Banta (3), Erskine (6), Hatten (6), Palica (7), Minner (9)															

COMPOSITE BATTING

NAME	POS	G	AB	R	H	2B	3B	HR	RBI	BA
New York (AL) Totals		5	164	21	37	10	2	2	20	.226
Coleman	2B	5	20	0	5	**3**	0	0	4	.250
Henrich	1B	5	19	**4**	5	0	0	1	1	.263
Rizzuto	SS	5	18	2	3	0	0	0	1	.167
DiMaggio	OF	5	18	2	2	0	0	1	2	.111
Berra	C	4	16	2	1	0	0	0	1	.063
B. Brown	3B	4	12	**4**	**6**	1	**2**	0	**5**	**.500**
Woodling	OF	3	10	**4**	4	**3**	0	0	0	.400
Mapes	OF	4	10	3	1	1	0	0	2	.100
Johnson	3B	2	7	0	1	0	0	0	0	.143
Lindell	OF	2	7	0	1	0	0	0	0	.143
Bauer	OF	3	6	0	1	0	0	0	0	.167
Raschi	P	2	5	0	1	0	0	0	1	.200
Reynolds	P	2	4	0	2	1	0	0	0	.500
Page	P	3	4	0	0	0	0	0	0	.000
Lopat	P	1	3	0	1	1	0	0	1	.333
Mize	PH	2	2	0	2	0	0	0	2	1.000
Silvera	C	1	2	0	0	0	0	0	0	.000
Byrne	P	1	1	0	1	0	0	0	0	1.000

Stirnweiss PR 0-0, Niarhos C 0-0

NAME	POS	G	AB	R	H	2B	3B	HR	RBI	BA
Brooklyn (NL) Totals		5	162	14	34	7	1	4	14	.210
Snider	OF	5	**21**	2	3	1	0	0	0	.143
Reese	SS	5	19	2	**6**	1	0	1	2	.316
Hodges	1B	5	17	2	4	0	0	1	4	.235
Robinson	2B	5	16	2	3	1	0	0	2	.188
Campanella	C	5	15	2	4	1	0	1	2	.267
Hermanski	OF	4	13	1	4	0	1	0	2	.308
Olmo	OF	4	11	2	3	0	0	1	2	.273
Jorgensen	3B	4	11	1	2	2	0	0	0	.182
Furillo	OF	3	8	0	1	0	0	0	0	.125
Miksis	3B	3	7	0	2	1	0	0	0	.286
Rackley	OF	2	5	0	0	0	0	0	0	.000
Newcombe	P	2	4	0	0	0	0	0	0	.000
Cox	3B	2	3	0	1	0	0	0	0	.333
Branca	P	1	3	0	0	0	0	0	0	.000
Roe	P	1	3	0	0	0	0	0	0	.000
Edwards	PH	2	2	0	1	0	0	0	0	.500
T. Brown	PH	2	2	0	0	0	0	0	0	.000
Banta	P	3	1	0	0	0	0	0	0	.000
Whitman	PH	1	1	0	0	0	0	0	0	.000
Hatten	P	2	0	0	0	0	0	0	0	.000

Barney P 0-0, Erskine P 0-0, Minner P 0-0, Palica P 0-0, McCormick OF 0-0

COMPOSITE PITCHING

NAME	G	IP	H	BB	SO	W	L	SV	ERA
New York (AL) Totals	5	45	34	15	38	4	1	2	2.80
Raschi	2	**14.2**	**15**	5	11	1	1	0	4.30
Reynolds	2	12.1	2	4	**14**	1	0	1	**0.00**
Page	**3**	9	6	3	8	1	0	1	2.00
Lopat	1	5.2	9	1	4	1	0	0	6.35
Byrne	1	3.1	2	2	1	0	0	0	2.70
Brooklyn (NL) Totals	5	44	37	18	27	1	4	0	4.29
Newcombe	2	11.2	10	3	11	0	**2**	0	3.09
Roe	1	9	6	0	3	1	0	0	**0.00**
Branca	1	8.2	4	4	6	0	1	0	4.15
Banta	**3**	5.2	5	1	4	0	0	0	3.18
Barney	1	2.2	3	**6**	2	0	1	0	16.88
Palica	1	2	1	1	1	0	0	0	0.00
Erskine	2	1.2	3	1	0	0	0	0	16.20
Hatten	2	1.2	4	2	0	0	0	0	16.20
Minner	1	1	1	0	0	0	0	0	0.00

⊜ ⊜ 1950 Whiz, Sweep, and a Couple of Farewells ⊜ ⊜

The bandbox that was Ebbets Field pulsated as the 35,073 fans took their seats to watch their beloved Bums pull another pennant from the National League fires. It was Sunday, October 1. The schedule showed one remaining game for the Dodgers and Phillies. The standings told the tale: Philadelphia, 90-63; Brooklyn, 89-64. The prospects for Brooklyn looked excellent. The Phillies were skidding badly, having dissipated a seven-game lead in nine days. On Saturday, Erv Palica beat the Philadelphia Whiz Kids, 7-3. The Phils' manager Eddie Sawyer was forced to go with Robin Roberts, making his third start in the last five days, while Burt Shotton had his own iron man in Don Newcombe, who weeks before almost single-handedly beat the Phils in a doubleheader (a 2-0 shutout in the first game, and seven innings of the nightcap before departing for a pinch hitter).

To further boost Brooklyn's hopes, the Phillies' catcher Andy Seminick was playing with a painful ankle injury suffered four days before when the Giants' Monte Irvin crashed into Seminick at the plate in the last play of a twin bill. Sawyer's troops were also without the services of their lefty pitching ace Curt Simmons, who was called to active military duty on September 10. Aside from MVP Jim Konstanty, who had already appeared in a league high 74 games and had 22 saves to go along with his 16 wins, there was little else Sawyer could count on. His two promising rookie hurlers, Bubba Church and Bob Miller, were nursing their wounds. Miller had a bad arm, and Church was hit in the face by a line drive on September 15.

All of Brooklyn's dreams seemed assured when Pee Wee Reese wedged a freak homer between the scoreboard and the right field fence to tie the game at 1-1 in the sixth inning. The fact that the Dodgers threw away the game in the ninth when Richie Ashburn nailed Cal Abrams at the plate, and Roberts retired Carl Furillo and Gil Hodges with the bases loaded, did not completely destroy the rousing throng in the stands. Although the fans were feeling as empty as a Brooklyn heart could be, there was still the recent memory of 1949 when the Dodgers beat the Phils in ten innings, to win the pennant by one game over St. Louis. But 1950 was not 1949, and Dick Sisler climaxed a seven year rebuilding program with a tenth-inning, three-run homer that brought the Whiz Kids their first pennant since 1915.

By comparison, the American League finish was ho-hum. Casey Stengel, traipsing on the magic that was to guide him to the Hall of Fame, brought up a southpaw sensation in late June by the name of Whitey Ford. That move, coupled with Joe DiMaggio's late season comeback, and the clutch hitting of Big Jawn Mize, and Phil Rizzuto's MVP year at shortstop, was enough to edge Detroit, Boston, and Cleveland.

Stengel was also aided by a big trade with the St. Louis Browns, which brought him pitchers, Tom Ferrick and Joe Ostrowski, plus a cleverly manuevered waiver deal which landed him Johnny Hopp from Pittsburgh, the then No. 2 batter in the National League with a .340 average. Detroit missed the flag by three games and blamed their woes on losing their ace, Virgil Trucks, to arm trouble early in the season. Boston's pennant hopes faded when Ted Williams fractured his elbow in the annual All-Star Game and Cleveland, never really able to get going, was destroyed when the lowly Browns beat them four straight in September.

The World Series had its excitement, although the Yankees swept the Whiz Kids four straight. Perhaps more significant than New York's victory was Luke Appling's retirement, after toiling at shortstop for the White Sox since 1931, and Connie Mack's finally stepping down as manager of the Athletics after 50 years of service.

1950 AMERICAN LEAGUE

NAME	G by POS	B	AGE	G	AB	R	H	2B	3B	HR	RBI	BB	SO	SB	BA	SA
NEW YORK 1st 98-56 .636		CASEY STENGEL														
TOTALS			29	155	5361	914	1511	234	**70**	159	863	687	463	41	.282	.441
Johnny Mize	1B72	L	37	90	274	43	76	12	0	25	72	29	24	0	.277	.595
Jerry Coleman	2B152, SS6	R	25	153	522	69	150	19	6	6	69	67	38	3	.287	.381
Phil Rizzuto	SS155	R	32	155	617	125	200	36	7	7	66	91	38	12	.324	.439
Billy Johnson	3B100, 1B5	R	31	108	327	44	85	16	2	6	40	42	30	1	.260	.376
Hank Bauer	OF110	R	27	113	415	72	133	16	2	13	70	33	41	2	.320	.463
Joe DiMaggio	OF137, 1B1	R	35	139	525	114	158	33	10	32	122	80	33	0	.301	**.585**
Gene Woodling	OF118	L	27	122	449	81	127	20	10	6	60	69	31	5	.283	.412
Yogi Berra	C148	L	25	151	597	116	192	30	6	28	124	55	12	4	.322	.533
Cliff Mapes	OF102	L	28	108	356	60	88	14	6	12	61	47	61	1	.247	.421
Joe Collins	1B99, OF2	L	27	108	205	47	48	8	3	8	28	31	34	5	.234	.420
Bobby Brown	3B82	L	25	95	277	33	74	4	2	4	37	39	18	3	.267	.339
Tommy Henrich (KJ)	1B34	L	37	73	151	20	41	6	8	6	34	27	6	0	.272	.536
Jackie Jensen	OF23	R	23	45	70	13	12	2	2	1	5	7	8	4	.171	.300
Billy Martin	2B22, 3B1	R	22	34	36	10	9	1	0	1	8	3	3	0	.250	.361
2 Johnny Hopp	1B12, OF6	L	33	19	27	9	9	2	1	1	8	9	1	0	.333	.593
Charlie Silvera	C15	R	25	18	25	2	4	0	0	0	1	1	2	0	.160	.160
1 Jim Delsing		L	24	12	10	2	4	0	0	0	2	2	0	0	.400	.400
Ralph Houk	C9	R	30	10	9	0	1	1	0	0	1	0	2	0	.111	.222
1 Johnny Lindell	OF6	R	33	7	21	2	4	0	0	0	2	4	2	0	.190	.190
1 Snuffy Stirnweiss	2B4, 3B1	R	31	7	2	0	0	0	0	0	0	0	0	0	.000	.000
Dick Wakefield		L	29	3	2	0	1	0	0	0	1	1	1	0	.500	.500
Hank Workman	1B1	L	24	2	5	1	1	0	0	0	0	0	1	0	.200	.200
1 Gus Niarhos		R	29	1	0	0	0	0	0	0	0	0	0	0	.000	.000
DETROIT 2nd 95-59 .617 3		RED ROLFE														
TOTALS			28	157	5381	837	1518	285	50	114	787	**722**	480	23	.282	.417
Don Kolloway	1B118, 2B1	R	31	125	467	55	135	20	4	6	62	29	28	1	.289	.388
Jerry Priddy	2B157	R	30	157	618	104	171	26	6	13	75	95	95	2	.277	.401
Johnny Lipon	SS147	R	27	147	601	104	176	27	6	2	63	81	26	9	.293	.368
George Kell	3B157	R	27	157	**641**	114	**218**	**56**	6	8	101	66	18	3	.340	.484
Vic Wertz	OF145	L	25	149	559	99	172	37	4	27	123	91	55	0	.308	.533
Johnny Groth	OF157	R	23	157	566	95	173	30	8	12	85	95	27	1	.306	.451
Hoot Evers	OF139	R	29	143	526	100	170	35	**11**	21	103	71	40	5	.323	.551
Aaron Robinson	C103	L	35	107	283	37	64	7	0	9	37	75	35	0	.226	.346
Pat Mullin	OF32	L	32	69	142	16	31	5	0	6	23	20	23	1	.218	.380
Bob Swift	C66	R	35	67	132	14	30	4	0	2	9	25	6	0	.227	.303
Dick Kryhoski	1B47	L	25	53	169	20	37	10	0	4	19	8	11	0	.219	.349
Charlie Keller	OF6	L	33	50	51	7	16	1	3	2	16	13	6	0	.314	.569
Fred Hutchinson	P39	L	30	44	95	15	31	7	0	0	20	12	3	0	.326	.400
Neil Berry	SS11, 2B2, 3B1	R	28	38	39	9	10	1	0	0	7	6	11	0	.256	.282
Joe Ginsberg	C31	L	23	36	95	12	22	6	0	0	12	11	6	1	.232	.295
Eddie Lake	3B1, SS1	R	34	20	7	3	0	0	0	0	1	1	3	0	.000	.000
Frank House	C5	L	20	5	5	1	2	1	0	0	0	0	1	0	.400	.600
Paul Campbell		L	32	3	1	1	0	0	0	0	0	0	0	0	.000	.000
BOSTON 3rd 94-60 .610 4		JOE McCARTHY 32-30 .516 STEVE O'NEILL 62-30 .674														
TOTALS			30	154	**5516**	**1027**	**1665**	**287**	61	161	**974**	719	582	32	**.302**	**.464**
Walt Dropo	1B134	R	27	136	559	101	180	28	8	34	**144**	45	75	0	.322	.583
Bobby Doerr	2B149	R	32	149	586	103	172	29	**11**	27	120	67	42	3	.294	.519
Vern Stephens	SS146	R	29	149	628	125	185	34	6	30	**144**	65	43	1	.295	.511
Johnny Pesky	3B116, SS8	L	30	127	490	112	153	22	6	1	49	104	31	2	.312	.388
Al Zarilla	OF128	L	31	130	471	92	153	32	10	9	74	76	47	2	.325	.493
Dom DiMaggio	OF140	R	33	141	588	**131**	193	30	**11**	7	70	82	68	**15**	.328	.452
Ted Williams (BE)	OF86	L	31	89	334	82	106	24	1	28	97	82	21	3	.317	.647
Birdie Tebbetts	C74	R	40	79	268	33	83	10	1	8	45	29	26	1	.310	.444
B. Goodman	OF45, 3B27, 1B21, 2B5, SS1	L	24	110	424	91	150	25	3	4	68	52	25	2	**.354**	.455
Matt Batts	C73	R	28	75	238	27	65	15	3	4	34	18	19	0	.273	.412
2 Clyde Vollmer	OF39	R	28	57	169	35	48	10	0	7	37	21	35	1	.284	.467
Tom Wright	OF24	L	26	54	107	17	34	7	0	0	20	6	18	0	.318	.383
Buddy Rosar	C25	R	35	27	84	13	25	2	0	1	12	7	4	0	.298	.357
Lou Stringer	3B3, 2B1, SS1	R	33	24	17	7	5	1	0	0	2	0	4	1	.294	.353
Ken Keltner	3B8, 1B1	R	33	13	28	2	9	2	0	0	2	3	6	0	.321	.393
Fred Hatfield	3B3	L	25	10	12	3	3	0	0	0	2	3	1	0	.250	.250
1 Tommy O'Brien	OF9	R	31	9	31	0	4	1	0	0	3	3	5	0	.129	.161
Jimmy Piersall	OF2	R	20	6	7	4	2	0	0	0	0	4	0	0	.286	.286
Charlie Maxwell	OF2	L	23	3	8	1	0	0	0	0	0	1	3	0	.000	.000

1 Merrill Combs 30 L 0-0, Bob Scherbarth 24 R 0-0

NAME	T	AGE	W	L	PCT	SV	G	GS	CG	IP	H	BB	SO	ShO	ERA
NEW YORK		31	**98**	56	**.636**	**31**	155	155	66	1373	1322	708	**712**	**12**	4.15
Vic Raschi	R	31	21	8	**.724**	1	33	32	17	257	232	116	155	2	3.99
Ed Lopat	L	32	18	8	.692	1	35	32	15	236	244	65	72	3	3.47
Allie Reynolds	R	35	16	12	.571	2	35	29	14	241	215	138	160	2	3.73
Tommy Byrne	L	30	15	9	.625	0	31	31	10	203	188	**160**	118	2	4.74
Whitey Ford	L	21	9	1	.900	1	20	12	7	112	87	52	59	2	2.81
2 Tom Ferrick	R	35	8	4	.667	9	30	0	0	57	49	22	20	0	3.63
Fred Sanford	R	30	5	4	.556	0	26	12	2	113	103	79	54	0	4.54
Joe Page	L	32	3	7	.300	13	37	0	0	55	66	31	33	0	5.07
2 Joe Ostrowski	L	33	1	1	.500	3	21	4	1	44	50	15	15	0	5.11
Bob Porterfield (AJ-BJ)	R	26	1	1	.500	1	10	2	0	20	28	8	9	0	8.55
1 Don Johnson	R	23	1	0	1.000	0	8	0	0	18	35	12	9	0	10.00
1 Duane Pillette	R	27	0	0	.000	0	4	0	0	7	9	3	4	0	1.29
Ernie Nevel	R	30	0	1	.000	0	3	1	0	6	10	6	3	0	10.50
Lew Burdette	R	23	0	0	.000	0	2	0	0	1	3	0	0	0	9.00
Dave Madison	R	29	0	0	.000	0	1	0	0	3	3	1	1	0	6.00
DETROIT		29	95	59	.617	20	157	157	**72**	**1407**	1444	553	576	9	4.13
Art Houtteman	R	22	19	12	.613	4	41	34	21	275	257	99	88	**4**	3.53
Fred Hutchinson	R	30	17	8	.680	0	39	26	10	232	269	48	71	1	3.96
Hal Newhouser	L	29	15	13	.536	3	35	30	15	214	232	81	87	1	4.33
Dizzy Trout	R	35	13	5	.722	4	34	20	11	185	190	64	88	1	3.75
Ted Gray (IL)	L	25	10	7	.588	1	27	21	7	149	139	72	102	0	4.41
Hal White	R	31	9	6	.600	1	42	8	3	111	96	65	53	1	4.54
Marlin Stuart	R	31	3	1	.750	2	19	1	0	44	59	22	19	0	5.52
Virgil Trucks (SA)	R	31	3	1	.750	0	7	7	2	48	45	21	25	1	3.56
Paul Calvert	R	32	2	2	.500	4	32	0	0	51	71	25	14	0	6.35
Saul Rogovin	R	27	2	1	.667	0	11	5	1	40	39	26	11	0	4.50
3 Hank Borowy	R	34	1	1	.500	0	13	2	1	33	23	16	12	0	3.27
Ray Herbert	R	20	1	2	.333	1	8	3	1	22	20	12	5	0	3.68
2 Bill Connelly	R	25	0	0	.000	0	2	0	0	4	4	2	1	0	6.75
BOSTON		27	94	60	.610	28	154	154	66	1362	1413	**748**	630	6	4.88
Mel Parnell	L	28	18	10	.643	3	40	31	21	249	244	106	93	2	3.61
Joe Dobson	R	33	15	10	.600	4	39	27	12	207	217	81	81	1	4.17
Ellis Kinder	R	35	14	12	.538	9	48	23	11	207	212	78	95	1	4.26
Chuch Stobbs	L	20	12	7	.632	1	32	21	6	169	158	88	78	0	5.11
Walt Masterson	R	30	8	6	.571	1	33	15	6	129	145	82	60	0	5.65
Willard Nixon	R	22	8	6	.571	2	22	15	2	101	126	58	57	0	6.06
Mickey McDermott	L	21	7	3	.700	5	38	15	4	130	119	124	96	0	5.19
1 Al Papai	R	31	4	2	.667	2	16	3	2	51	61	28	19	0	6.71
Charley Schanz	R	31	3	2	.600	0	14	0	0	23	25	24	14	0	8.22
Dick Littlefield	L	24	2	2	.500	1	15	2	0	23	27	24	13	0	9.39
Harry Taylor	R	31	2	0	1.000	0	3	2	2	19	13	8	8	1	1.42
Jim McDonald	R	23	1	0	1.000	0	9	0	0	19	23	10	5	0	3.79
Earl Johnson	L	31	0	0	.000	0	11	0	0	14	18	8	6	0	7.07
Gordy Mueller	R	27	0	0	.000	0	8	0	0	7	11	13	1	0	10.29
Jim Suchecki	R	23	0	0	.000	0	4	0	0	4	3	4	3	0	4.50
Jim Atkins	R	29	0	0	.000	0	1	0	0	5	4	4	0	0	3.60
Boo Ferriss	R	28	0	0	.000	0	1	0	0	1	2	1	1	0	18.00
Bob Gillespie	R	31	0	0	.000	0	1	0	0	1	2	4	0	0	27.00
Phil Marchildon	R	36	0	0	.000	0	1	0	0	1	1	2	0	0	9.00
Frank Quinn	R	22	0	0	.000	0	1	0	0	2	2	1	0	0	9.00

CLEVELAND 4th 92-62 .597 6 — LOU BOUDREAU

NAME	G by POS	B	AGE	G	AB	R	H	2B	3B	HR	RBI	BB	SO	SB	BA	SA
TOTALS			29	155	5263	806	1417	222	46	**164**	758	693	624	40	.269	.422
Luke Easter	1B128, OF13	L	35	141	540	96	151	20	4	28	107	70	95	0	.280	.487
Joe Gordon	2B105	R	35	119	368	59	87	12	1	19	57	56	44	4	.236	.429
Ray Boone	SS102	R	26	109	365	53	110	14	6	7	58	56	27	4	.301	.430
Al Rosen	3B154	R	26	155	554	100	159	23	4	**37**	116	100	72	5	.287	.543
Bob Kennedy	OF144	R	29	146	540	79	157	27	5	9	54	53	31	3	.291	.409
Larry Doby	OF140	L	25	142	503	110	164	25	5	25	102	98	71	8	.326	.545
Dale Mitchell	OF127	L	28	130	506	81	156	27	5	3	49	67	21	3	.308	.399
Jim Hegan	C129	R	29	131	415	53	91	16	5	14	58	42	52	1	.219	.383
Lou Boudreau	SS61, 1B8, 2B2, 3B2	R	32	81	260	23	70	13	2	1	29	31	5	1	.269	.346
Bobby Avila	2B62, SS2	R	26	80	201	39	60	10	2	1	21	29	17	5	.299	.383
Bob Lemon	P44	L	29	72	136	21	37	9	1	6	26	13	25	0	.272	.485
Allie Clark	OF41	R	27	59	163	19	35	6	1	6	21	11	10	0	.215	.374
Thurman Tucker	OF34	L	32	57	101	13	18	2	0	1	7	14	14	1	.178	.228
Ray Murray	C45	R	32	55	139	16	38	8	2	1	13	12	13	1	.273	.381
1 Mickey Vernon	1B25	L	32	28	90	8	17	0	0	0	10	12	10	2	.189	.189
Jim Lemon	OF10	R	22	12	34	4	6	1	0	1	1	3	12	0	.176	.294
Herb Conyers	1B1	L	29	7	9	2	3	0	0	1	1	1	2	1	.333	.667
1 Johnny Berardino	2B1, 3B1	R	33	4	5	1	2	0	0	0	3	1	0	0	.400	.400

NAME	T	AGE	W	L	PCT	SV	G	GS	CG	IP	H	BB	SO	ShO	ERA
		31	92	62	.597	16	155	155	69	1379	1289	647	674	11	**3.75**
Bob Lemon	R	29	**23**	11	.676	3	44	**37**	**22**	**288**	**281**	146	**170**	3	3.84
Early Wynn	R	30	18	8	.692	0	32	28	14	214	166	101	143	2	**3.20**
Bob Feller	R	31	16	11	.593	0	35	34	16	247	230	103	119	3	3.43
Mike Garcia	R	26	11	11	.500	0	33	29	11	184	191	74	76	0	3.86
Steve Gromek	R	30	10	7	.588	0	31	13	4	113	94	36	43	1	3.66
Al Benton	R	39	4	2	.667	4	36	0	0	63	57	30	26	0	3.57
Sam Zoldak	L	31	4	2	.667	4	33	3	0	64	64	21	15	0	3.94
Jesse Flores	R	35	3	3	.500	4	28	2	1	53	53	25	27	1	3.74
1 Gene Bearden	L	29	1	3	.250	0	14	3	0	45	57	32	10	0	6.20
2 Dick Welk	R	22	1	3	.250	0	11	2	0	26	18	26	16	0	3.81
Al Aber	L	22	1	0	1.000	0	1	1	1	9	5	4	4	0	2.00
Marino Pieretti	R	29	0	1	.000	1	29	1	0	47	45	30	11	0	4.21
Dick Rozek	L	23	0	0	.000	0	12	2	0	25	28	19	14	0	5.04

WASHINGTON 5th 67-87 .435 31 — BUCKY HARRIS

NAME	G by POS	B	AGE	G	AB	R	H	2B	3B	HR	RBI	BB	SO	SB	BA	SA
TOTALS			28	155	5251	690	1365	190	53	76	659	671	606	**42**	.260	.360
2 Mickey Vernon	1B85	L	32	90	327	47	100	17	3	9	65	50	29	6	.306	.459
2 Cass Michaels	2B104	R	24	106	388	48	97	8	4	4	47	55	39	2	.250	.322
Sam Dente	SS128, 2B29	R	28	155	603	56	144	20	5	2	59	39	19	1	.239	.299
Eddie Yost	3B155	R	23	155	573	114	169	26	2	11	58	**141**	63	6	.295	.405
Bud Stewart	OF100	L	34	118	378	46	101	15	6	4	35	46	33	5	.267	.370
Irv Noren	OF121, 1B17	L	25	138	542	80	160	27	10	14	98	67	77	5	.295	.459
Gil Coan (FS)	OF98	L	28	104	366	58	111	17	4	7	50	28	46	10	.303	.429
Al Evans	C88	R	33	90	289	24	68	8	3	2	30	29	21	0	.235	.304
Sam Mele	OF99, 1B16	R	27	126	435	57	119	21	6	12	86	51	40	2	.274	.432
Mickey Grasso	C69	R	30	75	195	25	56	4	1	1	22	25	31	1	.287	.333
Sherry Robertson	OF14, 2B12, 3B1	R	31	71	123	19	32	3	3	2	16	22	18	1	.260	.382
2 John Ostrowski	OF45	R	32	55	141	16	32	2	1	4	23	20	31	2	.227	.340
1 Roberto Ortiz	OF19	R	35	39	75	4	17	2	1	0	8	7	12	0	.227	.280
2 Merrill Combs	SS30	L	30	37	102	19	25	1	0	0	6	22	16	0	.245	.255
1 Eddie Robinson	1B36	L	29	36	125	21	30	4	2	1	13	25	4	0	.240	.328
1 Al Kozar	2B15	R	27	20	55	7	11	1	0	0	3	5	8	0	.200	.218
Len Okrie	C17	R	26	17	27	1	6	0	0	0	2	6	7	0	.222	.222
Hal Keller	C8	L	22	11	28	1	6	3	0	1	5	2	2	0	.214	.429
Fred Taylor	1B3	L	25	6	16	1	2	0	0	0	0	1	2	0	.125	.125
1 Clyde Vollmer	OF3	R	28	6	14	4	4	0	0	0	1	2	3	1	.286	.286
2 Tommy O'Brien	OF3	R	31	3	9	1	1	0	0	0	1	1	0	0	.111	.111
George Genovese		L	28	3	1	1	0	0	0	0	0	1	0	0	.000	.000

NAME	T	AGE	W	L	PCT	SV	G	GS	CG	IP	H	BB	SO	ShO	ERA
		31	67	87	.435	18	155	155	59	1365	1479	648	486	7	4.65
Sid Hudson	R	35	14	14	.500	0	30	30	17	238	261	98	75	0	4.08
2 Bob Kuzava	L	27	8	7	.533	0	22	22	8	155	156	75	84	1	3.95
Joe Haynes	R	32	7	5	.583	0	27	10	1	102	124	46	15	1	5.82
Sandy Consuegra	R	29	7	8	.467	2	21	18	8	125	132	57	38	2	4.39
Connie Marrero	R	39	6	10	.375	1	27	19	8	152	159	55	63	1	4.50
Mickey Harris	L	33	5	9	.357	**15**	**53**	0	0	98	93	46	41	0	4.78
Al Sima	L	28	4	5	.444	0	17	9	1	77	89	26	23	0	4.79
2 Gene Bearden	L	29	3	5	.375	0	12	9	4	69	81	33	20	0	4.17
1 Ray Scarborough	R	32	3	5	.375	0	8	8	4	58	62	22	24	2	4.03
Jim Pearce	R	25	2	1	.667	0	20	3	1	57	58	37	18	0	6.00
Steve Nagy	L	31	2	5	.286	0	9	9	2	53	69	29	17	0	6.62
Lloyd Hittle	L	26	2	4	.333	0	11	4	1	43	60	17	9	0	5.02
Elmer Singleton	R	32	1	2	.333	0	21	1	0	36	39	17	19	0	5.25
1 Dick Weik	R	22	1	3	.250	0	14	5	1	44	38	47	26	0	4.30
Julio Moreno	R	29	1	1	.500	0	4	3	1	21	22	12	7	0	4.71
Carlos Pascual	R	20	1	1	.500	0	2	2	2	17	12	8	3	0	2.12
Bob Ross	L	21	0	1	.000	0	6	2	0	13	15	15	2	0	8.31
Dick Welteroth	R	22	0	0	.000	0	5	0	0	6	5	6	2	0	3.00
Rogelio Martinez	R	31	0	1	.000	0	2	1	0	1	4	2	0	0	36.00

CHICAGO 6th 60-94 .390 38 — JACK ONSLOW 8-22 .267 RED CORRIDEN 52-72 .419

NAME	G by POS	B	AGE	G	AB	R	H	2B	3B	HR	RBI	BB	SO	SB	BA	SA
TOTALS			29	156	5260	625	1368	172	47	93	592	551	566	19	.260	.364
2 Eddie Robinson	1B119	L	29	119	428	62	133	11	2	20	73	60	28	0	.311	.486
Nellie Fox	2B121	L	22	130	457	45	113	12	7	0	30	35	17	4	.247	.304
Chico Carrasquel	SS141	R	22	141	524	72	148	21	5	4	46	66	46	0	.282	.365
Hank Majeski	3B112	R	33	122	414	47	128	18	2	6	46	42	34	1	.309	.406
2 Marv Rickert	OF78, 1B1	L	29	84	278	38	66	9	2	4	27	21	42	0	.237	.327
Dave Philley	OF154	B	30	156	619	69	150	21	5	14	80	52	57	6	.242	.360
Gus Zernial	OF137	R	27	143	543	75	152	16	4	29	93	38	**110**	0	.280	.484
Phil Masi	C114	R	33	122	377	38	105	17	2	7	55	49	36	2	.279	.390
Floyd Baker	3B53, 2B3, OF2	L	33	83	186	26	59	7	0	0	11	32	10	1	.317	.355
Gordon Goldsberry	1B40, OF3	L	22	82	127	19	34	8	2	2	25	26	18	0	.268	.409
2 Mike McCormick	OF44	R	33	55	138	16	32	4	3	0	10	16	6	0	.232	.304
Luke Appling	SS20, 1B13, 2B1	R	43	50	128	11	30	3	4	0	13	12	8	2	.234	.320
2 Gus Niarhos	C36	R	29	41	105	17	34	4	0	0	16	14	6	0	.324	.362
Jerry Scala	OF23	L	23	40	67	8	13	2	1	0	6	10	10	0	.194	.254
1 Cass Michaels	2B35	R	24	36	138	21	43	6	3	4	19	13	8	0	.312	.486
Herb Adams	OF33	L	22	34	118	12	24	2	3	0	2	12	7	3	.203	.271
Eddie Malone	C21	R	30	31	71	2	16	2	0	0	10	10	8	0	.225	.254
1 John Ostrowski	OF15	R	32	22	49	10	12	2	1	2	2	9	9	0	.245	.449
Jim Busby	OF12	R	23	18	48	5	10	0	0	0	4	1	5	0	.208	.208
Joe Erautt	C5	R	28	16	18	0	4	0	0	0	1	1	3	0	.222	.222
2 Al Kozar	2B4, 3B1	R	27	10	10	4	3	0	0	1	2	0	3	0	.300	.600
Charlie Kress	1B2	L	28	3	8	0	0	0	0	0	0	0	2	0	.000	.000
Ed McGhee	OF1	R	25	3	6	0	1	0	1	0	0	0	1	0	.167	.500
Bill Wilson	OF2	R	21	3	6	0	0	0	0	0	0	2	2	0	.000	.000

Joe Kirrene 18 R 1-4, Bill Salkeld 33 L 0-3

NAME	T	AGE	W	L	PCT	SV	G	GS	CG	IP	H	BB	SO	ShO	ERA
		29	60	94	.390	9	156	156	62	1366	1370	734	566	7	4.41
Billy Pierce	L	23	12	16	.429	1	33	29	15	219	189	137	118	1	3.99
2 Ray Scarborough	R	32	10	13	.435	1	27	23	8	150	160	62	70	1	5.28
Bill Wight	L	28	10	16	.385	0	30	28	13	206	213	79	62	3	3.58
Bob Cain	L	25	9	12	.429	2	34	23	11	172	153	109	77	1	3.92
Luis Aloma	R	27	7	2	.778	4	42	0	0	88	77	53	49	0	3.78
Randy Gumpert	R	32	5	12	.294	0	40	17	6	155	165	58	48	1	4.76
Ken Holcombe	R	31	3	10	.231	1	24	15	5	96	122	45	37	0	4.59
Howie Judson	R	24	2	3	.400	0	46	3	1	112	105	63	34	0	3.94
1 Mickey Haefner	L	37	1	6	.143	0	24	9	2	71	83	45	17	0	5.70
1 Bob Kuzava	L	27	1	3	.250	0	10	7	1	44	43	27	21	0	4.34
2 Lou Kretlow	R	27	0	0	.000	0	11	1	0	22	17	27	14	0	3.68
1 Jack Bruner	L	26	0	0	.000	0	9	0	0	12	7	14	8	0	3.75
1 Bill Connelly	R	25	0	0	.000	0	2	0	0	2	5	1	0	0	13.50
Charlie Cuellar	R	32	0	0	.000	0	2	0	0	1	6	3	1	0	45.00
Marv Rotblatt	L	22	0	0	.000	0	2	0	0	9	11	5	6	0	6.00
Gus Keriazakos	R	18	0	1	.000	0	1	1	0	2	7	5	1	0	22.50
John Perkovich	R	26	0	0	.000	0	1	0	0	5	7	1	3	0	7.20

ST. LOUIS 7th 58-96 .377 40 — ZACK TAYLOR

NAME	G by POS	B	AGE	G	AB	R	H	2B	3B	HR	RBI	BB	SO	SB	BA	SA
TOTALS			25	154	5163	684	1269	235	43	106	642	690	**744**	39	.246	.370
Don Lenhardt	1B86, OF39, 3B10	R	27	139	480	75	131	22	6	22	81	90	94	3	.273	.481
Owen Friend	2B93, 3B24, SS3	R	23	119	372	48	88	15	2	8	50	40	68	2	.237	.352
Tom Upton	SS115, 2B2, 3B1	R	23	124	389	50	92	5	6	2	30	52	45	7	.237	.296
Bill Sommers	3B37, 2B21	R	26	65	137	24	35	5	1	0	14	25	14	0	.255	.307
Ken Wood	OF94	R	26	128	369	42	83	24	0	13	62	38	58	0	.225	.396
Ray Coleman	OF98	L	28	117	384	54	104	25	6	8	55	32	37	7	.271	.430
Dick Kokos	OF127	L	22	143	490	77	128	27	5	18	67	88	73	8	.261	.447
Sherm Lollar	C109	R	25	126	396	55	111	22	3	13	65	64	25	2	.280	.449
Roy Sievers	OF78, 3B21	R	23	113	370	46	88	20	4	10	57	34	42	1	.238	.395
Hank Arft	1B84	L	28	98	280	45	75	16	4	1	32	46	48	3	.268	.364
2 Snuffy Stirnweiss	2B62, 3B31, SS5	R	31	93	326	32	71	16	2	1	24	51	49	3	.218	.288
Les Moss	C60	R	25	84	222	24	59	6	0	8	34	26	32	0	.266	.401
2 Jim Delsing	OF53	L	24	69	209	25	55	5	2	0	15	20	23	1	.263	.306
Billy DeMars (NJ)	SS54, 3B5	R	24	61	178	25	44	5	1	0	13	22	13	0	.247	.287
Ned Garver	P37, OF1	R	24	51	91	13	26	4	0	1	10	8	9	0	.286	.363
Leo Thomas	3B35	R	25	35	121	19	24	6	0	1	9	20	14	0	.198	.273
Frankie Gustine	3B6	R	30	9	19	1	3	1	0	0	2	3	8	0	.158	.211

NAME	T	AGE	W	L	PCT	SV	G	GS	CG	IP	H	BB	SO	ShO	ERA
		27	58	96	.377	14	154	154	56	1365	**1629**	651	448	7	5.20
Ned Garver	R	24	13	18	.419	0	37	31	**22**	260	264	108	85	2	3.39
Stubby Overmire	L	31	9	12	.429	0	31	19	8	161	200	45	39	2	4.19
Al Widmar	R	25	7	15	.318	4	36	26	8	195	211	74	78	1	4.75
Dick Starr	R	29	7	5	.583	2	32	16	4	124	140	74	30	1	5.01
Cliff Fannin	L	26	5	9	.357	1	25	16	3	102	116	58	42	0	6.53
2 Don Johnson	R	23	5	6	.455	1	25	12	4	96	126	55	31	0	6.09
Harry Dorish	R	28	4	9	.308	0	29	13	4	109	162	36	36	0	6.44
2 Duane Pillette	R	27	3	5	.375	2	24	7	1	74	104	44	18	0	7.05
1 Joe Ostrowski	L	33	2	4	.333	0	9	7	2	57	57	7	15	0	2.53
Cuddles Marshall	R	25	1	3	.250	1	28	2	0	54	72	51	24	0	7.83
1 Tom Ferrick	R	35	1	3	.250	2	16	0	0	24	24	7	6	0	4.13
2 Jack Bruner	L	26	1	2	.333	1	13	1	0	35	36	23	16	0	4.63
Tommy Fine	R	35	0	1	.000	0	14	0	0	37	53	25	6	0	8.03
1 Lou Kretlow	R	27	0	2	.000	0	9	2	0	14	25	18	10	0	12.21
Sid Schacht	R	32	0	0	.000	0	8	1	0	11	24	14	7	0	15.54
Ed Albrecht	P	21	0	1	.000	0	2	1	0	7	6	7	1	0	5.14
Ribs Raney	R	27	0	1	.000	0	1	0	0	2	2	2	2	0	4.50

Russ Bauers 36 R 0-0, Bill Kennedy 29 L 0-0, Lou Sleater 23 L 0-0

PHILADELPHIA 8th 52-102 .338 46 — CONNIE MACK

NAME	G by POS	B	AGE	G	AB	R	H	2B	3B	HR	RBI	BB	SO	SB	BA	SA
TOTALS			32	154	5212	670	1361	204	53	100	627	685	493	**42**	.261	.378
Ferris Fain	1B151	L	29	151	522	83	147	25	4	10	83	132	26	8	.282	.402
Billy Hitchcock	2B107, SS1	R	33	115	399	35	109	22	5	1	54	44	32	3	.273	.361
Eddie Joost	SS131	R	34	131	476	79	111	12	3	18	58	101	68	5	.233	.384
1 Bob Dillinger	3B84	R	31	84	356	55	110	21	9	3	41	29	20	5	.309	.444
Elmer Valo	OF117	L	29	129	446	62	125	16	5	10	46	83	22	12	.280	.406
Sam Chapman	OF140	R	34	144	553	93	139	20	6	23	95	67	79	3	.251	.434
Paul Lehner	OF101	L	30	114	427	48	132	17	5	9	52	31	33	1	.309	.436
Mike Guerra	C78	R	37	87	252	25	71	10	4	2	26	16	12	1	.282	.377
Kermit Wahl	3B61, SS18, 2B2	R	27	89	280	26	72	12	3	2	27	30	30	1	.257	.343
Wally Moses	OF62	L	39	88	265	47	70	16	5	2	21	40	17	0	.264	.385
Pete Suder	2B47, 3B11, SS10, 1B4	R	34	77	248	34	61	10	0	8	35	23	31	2	.246	.383
Barney McCosky	OF42	L	32	66	179	19	43	10	1	0	11	22	12	0	.240	.307
Joe Tipton	C59	R	27	64	184	15	49	5	1	6	20	19	16	0	.266	.402
Joe Astroth	C38	R	27	39	110	11	36	3	1	1	18	18	3	0	.327	.400
Bob Wellman	OF2	R	24	11	15	1	5	0	0	1	1	0	3	0	.333	.533
2 Roberto Ortiz	OF3	R	35	6	14	1	1	0	0	0	3	0	3	0	.071	.071
Gene Markland	2B5	R	30	5	8	2	1	0	0	0	0	3	0	0	.125	.125
Ben Guintini	OF1	R	30	3	4	0	0	0	0	0	0	0	1	0	.000	.000
Bob Rinker	C1	R	29	3	3	0	1	0	0	0	0	0	0	0	.333	.333

NAME	T	AGE	W	L	PCT	SV	G	GS	CG	IP	H	BB	SO	ShO	ERA
		26	52	**102**	.338	18	154	154	50	1346	1528	729	466	3	5..49
Bob Hooper	R	28	15	10	.600	5	45	20	3	170	181	91	58	0	5.03
Hank Wyse	R	32	9	14	.391	0	41	23	4	171	192	87	33	0	5.84
Bobby Shantz	L	24	8	14	.364	0	36	23	6	215	251	85	93	1	4.60
Alex Kellner	L	25	8	**20**	.286	2	36	29	15	225	253	112	85	0	5.48
Lou Brissie	L	25	7	19	.269	8	46	31	15	246	237	117	101	2	4.02
Carl Scheib	R	23	3	10	.231	3	43	8	1	106	138	70	37	0	7.22
Dick Fowler (AJ)	R	29	1	5	.167	0	11	9	2	67	75	56	15	0	6.45
Johnny Kucab	R	30	1	1	.500	0	4	2	2	26	29	8	8	0	3.46
Joe Coleman	R	27	0	5	.000	0	15	6	2	54	74	50	12	0	8.50
Moe Burtschy (EJ)	R	28	0	1	.000	0	9	1	0	19	22	21	12	0	7.11
Joe Murray	L	29	0	3	.000	0	8	2	0	30	34	21	8	0	5.70
Harry Byrd	R	25	0	0	.000	0	6	0	0	11	25	9	2	0	16.36
Eddie Klieman	R	32	0	0	.000	0	5	0	0	6	10	2	0	0	9.00
Les McCrabb	R	35	0	0	.000	0	2	0	0	1	7	0	2	0	36.00

PHILADELPHIA 1st 91-63 .591 — EDDIE SAWYER

NAME	G by POS	B	AGE	G	AB	R	H	2B	3B	HR	RBI	BB	SO	SB	BA	SA
TOTALS			26	157	**5426**	722	1440	225	55	125	673	535	569	33	.265	.396
Eddie Waitkus	1B154	L	30	154	641	102	182	32	5	2	44	55	29	3	.284	.359
Mike Goliat	2B145	R	24	145	483	49	113	13	6	13	64	53	75	3	.234	.366
Granny Hamner	SS157	R	23	157	637	78	172	27	5	11	82	39	35	2	.270	.380
Willie Jones	3B157	R	24	157	610	100	163	28	6	25	88	61	40	5	.267	.456
Del Ennis	OF149	R	25	153	595	92	185	34	8	31	**126**	56	59	2	.311	.551
Richie Ashburn	OF147	L	23	151	594	84	180	25	**14**	2	41	63	32	14	.303	.402
Dick Sisler	OF137	L	29	141	523	79	155	29	4	13	83	64	50	1	.296	.442
Andy Seminick	C124	R	29	130	393	55	113	15	3	24	68	68	50	0	.288	.524
Dick Whitman	OF32	L	29	75	132	21	33	7	0	0	12	10	10	1	.250	.303
Stan Lopata	C51	R	24	58	129	10	27	2	2	1	11	22	25	1	.209	.279
2 Jimmy Bloodworth	2B27, 1B7, 3B2	R	32	54	96	6	22	2	0	0	13	6	12	0	.229	.250
Putsy Caballero	2B5, 3B4, SS2	R	22	46	24	12	4	0	0	0	0	2	2	1	.167	.167
Bill Nicholson	OF15	L	35	41	58	3	13	2	1	3	10	8	16	0	.224	.448
Jackie Mayo	OF15	L	24	18	36	1	8	3	0	0	3	2	5	0	.222	.306
Ken Silvestri	C9	B	34	11	20	2	5	0	1	0	4	4	3	0	.250	.350
Stan Hollmig	OF3	R	24	11	12	1	3	2	0	0	1	0	3	0	.250	.417
1 Johnny Blatnik	OF1	R	24	4	4	0	1	0	0	0	0	2	3	0	.250	.250

NAME	T	AGE	W	L	PCT	SV	G	GS	CG	IP	H	BB	SO	ShO	ERA
		27	**91**	63	**.591**	**27**	157	157	57	**1406**	1324	530	620	13	**3.50**
Robin Roberts	R	23	20	11	.645	1	40	**39**	21	304	282	77	146	**5**	3.02
Curt Simmons	L	21	17	8	.680	1	31	27	11	215	178	88	146	2	3.39
Jim Konstanty	R	33	16	7	.696	**22**	**74**	0	0	152	108	50	56	0	2.66
Bob Miller	R	24	11	6	.647	1	35	22	7	174	190	57	44	2	3.57
Russ Meyer	R	26	9	11	.450	1	32	25	3	160	193	67	74	0	5.29
Bubba Church	R	25	8	6	.571	1	31	18	8	142	113	56	50	2	2.73
2 Ken Johnson	L	27	4	1	.800	0	14	8	3	61	61	43	32	1	3.98
Ken Heintzelman	L	34	3	9	.250	0	23	17	4	125	122	54	39	1	4.10
Blix Donnelly	R	36	2	4	.333	0	14	1	0	21	30	10	10	0	4.29
Milo Candini	R	32	1	0	1.000	0	18	0	0	30	32	15	10	0	2.70
1 Hank Borowy	R	34	0	0	.000	0	3	0	0	6	5	4	3	0	6.00
John Brittin	R	26	0	0	.000	0	3	0	0	4	2	3	3	0	4.50
Paul Stuffel	R	23	0	0	.000	0	3	0	0	5	4	1	3	0	1.80
Jocko Thompson	L	30	0	0	.000	0	2	0	0	4	1	4	2	0	0.00
Steve Ridzik	R	31	0	0	.000	0	1	0	0	3	3	1	2	0	6.00

BROOKLYN 2nd 89-65 .578 2 — BURT SHOTTON

NAME	G by POS	B	AGE	G	AB	R	H	2B	3B	HR	RBI	BB	SO	SB	BA	SA
TOTALS			28	155	5364	**847**	**1461**	247	46	**194**	**774**	607	632	**77**	**.272**	**.444**
Gil Hodges	1B153	R	26	153	561	98	159	26	2	32	113	73	73	6	.283	.508
Jackie Robinson	2B144	R	31	144	518	99	170	39	4	14	81	80	24	12	.328	.500
Pee Wee Reese	SS134, 3B7	R	31	141	531	97	138	21	5	11	52	91	62	17	.260	.380
Billy Cox	3B107, 2B13, SS9	R	30	119	451	62	116	17	2	8	44	35	24	6	.257	.357
Carl Furillo	OF153	R	28	153	620	99	189	30	6	18	106	41	40	8	.305	.460
Duke Snider	OF151	L	23	152	620	109	**199**	31	10	31	107	58	79	16	.321	.553
Gene Hermanski	OF78	L	30	94	289	36	86	17	3	7	34	36	26	2	.298	.450
Roy Campanella	C123	R	28	126	437	70	123	19	3	31	89	55	51	1	.281	.551
Jim Russell	OF55	B	31	77	214	37	49	8	2	10	32	31	36	1	.229	.425
Bobby Morgan	3B52, SS10	R	24	67	199	38	45	10	3	7	21	32	43	0	.226	.412
Eddie Miksis	2B15, SS15, 3B7	R	23	51	76	13	19	2	1	2	10	5	10	3	.250	.382
Bruce Edwards	C38, 1B2	R	26	50	142	16	26	4	1	8	16	13	22	1	.183	.394
Tommy Brown	OF16	R	22	48	86	15	25	2	1	8	20	11	9	0	.291	.616
Cal Abrams	OF15	L	26	38	44	5	9	1	0	0	4	9	13	0	.205	.227
George Shuba	OF27	L	25	34	111	15	23	8	2	3	12	13	22	2	.207	.396
Wayne Belardi	1B1	L	19	10	10	0	0	0	0	0	0	0	4	0	.000	.000
Steve Lembo	C5	R	23	5	6	0	1	0	0	0	0	1	0	0	.167	.167
1 Spider Jorgensen	3B1	L	30	2	2	0	0	0	0	0	1	1	0	0	.000	.000

NAME	T	AGE	W	L	PCT	SV	G	GS	CG	IP	H	BB	SO	ShO	ERA
		27	89	65	.578	21	155	155	62	1389	1397	591	**772**	10	4.24
Don Newcombe	R	24	19	11	.633	3	40	35	20	267	258	75	130	4	3.71
Preacher Roe	L	35	19	11	.633	1	36	32	16	251	245	66	125	2	3.30
Erv Palica	R	22	13	8	.619	1	43	19	10	201	176	98	131	2	3.58
Dan Bankhead	R	30	9	4	.692	3	41	12	2	129	119	88	96	1	5.51
Ralph Branca	R	24	7	9	.438	7	43	15	5	142	152	55	100	0	4.69
Carl Erskine	R	23	7	6	.538	1	22	13	3	103	109	35	50	0	4.72
Bud Podbielan	R	26	5	4	.556	1	20	10	2	73	93	29	28	0	5.30
Jack Banta (SA)	R	25	4	4	.500	2	16	5	1	41	39	36	15	0	4.39
Joe Hatten	L	33	2	2	.500	0	23	8	2	69	82	31	29	1	4.57
Rex Barney	R	25	2	1	.667	0	20	1	0	34	25	48	23	0	6.35
Chris Van Cuyk	L	23	1	3	.250	0	12	4	1	33	33	12	21	0	4.91
1 Willie Ramsdell	R	34	1	2	.333	1	5	0	0	6	7	2	2	0	3.00
Billy Loes	R	20	0	0	.000	0	10	0	0	13	16	5	2	0	7.62
Joe Landrum	R	21	0	0	.000	1	7	0	0	7	12	1	5	0	7.71
Al Epperly	R	32	0	0	.000	0	5	0	0	9	14	5	3	0	5.00
Jim Romano	R	23	0	0	.000	0	3	1	0	6	8	2	8	0	6.00
Mal Mallette	L	28	0	0	.000	0	2	0	0	1	2	1	2	0	0.00
Clem Labine	R	23	0	0	.000	0	1	0	0	2	2	1	0	0	4.50
Pat McGlothin	R	24	0	0	.000	0	1	0	0	2	5	1	2	0	13.50

NEW YORK 3rd 86-68 .558 5 — LEO DUROCHER

NAME	G by POS	B	AGE	G	AB	R	H	2B	3B	HR	RBI	BB	SO	SB	BA	SA
TOTALS			26	154	5238	735	1352	204	50	133	684	**627**	629	42	.258	.392
Tookie Gilbert	1B111	L	21	113	322	40	71	12	2	4	32	43	36	3	.220	.307
Eddie Stanky	2B151	R	33	152	527	115	158	25	5	8	51	**144**	50	9	.300	.412
Al Dark	SS154	R	28	154	587	79	164	36	5	16	67	39	60	9	.279	.440
Hank Thompson	3B138, OF10	L	24	148	512	82	148	17	6	20	91	83	60	8	.289	.463
Don Mueller	OF125	L	23	132	525	60	153	15	6	7	84	10	26	1	.291	.383
Bobby Thomson	OF149	R	26	149	563	79	142	22	7	25	85	55	45	3	.252	.449
Whitey Lockman	OF128	L	23	129	532	72	157	28	5	6	52	42	29	1	.295	.400
Wes Westrum	C139	R	27	140	437	68	103	13	3	23	71	92	73	2	.236	.437
Monte Irvin	1B59, OF49, 3B1	R	31	110	374	61	112	19	5	15	66	52	41	3	.299	.497
Bill Rigney	2B23, 3B11	R	31	56	83	8	15	2	0	0	8	8	13	0	.181	.205
Roy Weatherly	OF15	L	35	52	69	10	18	3	3	0	11	13	10	0	.261	.391
Sammy Calderone	C33	R	24	34	67	9	20	1	0	1	12	2	5	0	.299	.358
Lucky Lohrke	3B16, 2B1	R	26	30	43	4	8	0	0	0	4	4	8	0	.186	.186
Jack Maguire	OF9, 1B2	R	25	29	40	3	7	2	0	0	3	3	13	0	.175	.225
2 Spider Jorgensen	3B5	L	30	24	37	5	5	0	0	0	4	5	2	0	.135	.135
Rudy Rufer	SS8	R	23	15	11	1	1	0	0	0	0	0	1	1	.091	.091
Jack Harshman	1B9	L	22	9	32	3	4	0	0	2	4	3	6	0	.125	.313
Sal Yvars	C9	R	26	9	14	0	2	0	0	0	0	1	2	0	.143	.143
Pete Milne		L	25	4	4	1	1	0	1	0	1	0	1	0	.250	.750
1 Ray Mueller	C4	R	38	4	11	0	1	1	0	0	0	0	2	0	.091	.182
1 Mike McCormick		R	33	4	4	0	0	0	0	0	0	0	2	0	.000	.000
Marv Blaylock		L	20	1	1	0	0	0	0	0	0	0	0	0	.000	.000
Nap Reyes	1B1	R	30	1	1	0	0	0	0	0	0	0	0	0	.000	.000

NAME	T	AGE	W	L	PCT	SV	G	GS	CG	IP	H	BB	SO	ShO	ERA
		29	86	68	.558	15	154	154	70	1375	1268	536	596	**19**	3.71
Larry Jansen	R	29	19	13	.594	3	40	35	21	275	238	55	161	**5**	3.01
Sal Maglie	R	33	18	4	**.818**	1	47	16	12	206	169	86	96	**5**	2.71
Sheldon Jones	R	28	13	16	.448	2	40	28	11	199	188	90	97	2	4.61
Dave Koslo	L	30	13	15	.464	3	40	22	7	187	190	68	56	2	3.90
2 Jim Hearn	R	29	11	3	.786	0	16	16	11	125	72	38	54	**5**	**1.94***
Monte Kennedy	L	28	5	4	.556	2	36	17	5	114	120	53	41	0	4.74
Jack Kramer	R	32	3	6	.333	1	35	9	1	87	91	39	27	0	3.52
Clint Hartung	R	27	3	3	.500	0	20	8	1	65	87	44	23	0	6.65
George Spencer	R	23	1	0	1.000	0	10	1	1	25	12	7	5	0	2.52
Andy Hansen	R	25	0	1	.000	3	31	1	0	57	64	26	19	0	5.53
Kirby Higbe	R	35	0	3	.000	0	18	1	0	35	37	30	17	0	4.89

*Hearn, also with St. Louis, league leader in ERA with 2.49

BOSTON 4th 83-71 .539 8 — BILLY SOUTHWORTH

NAME	G by POS	B	AGE	G	AB	R	H	2B	3B	HR	RBI	BB	SO	SB	BA	SA
TOTALS			29	156	5363	785	1411	246	36	148	726	615	616	71	.263	.405
Earl Torgeson	1B156	L	26	156	576	**120**	167	30	3	23	87	119	69	15	.290	.472
Roy Hartsfield	2B96	R	24	107	419	62	116	15	2	7	24	27	61	7	.277	.372
Buddy Kerr	SS155	R	27	155	507	45	115	24	6	2	46	50	50	0	.227	.310
Bob Elliott	3B137	R	33	142	531	94	162	28	5	24	107	68	67	2	.305	.512
Tommy Holmes	OF88	L	33	105	322	44	96	20	1	9	51	33	8	0	.298	.450
Sam Jethroe	OF141	B	28	141	582	100	159	28	8	18	58	52	93	**35**	.273	.442
Sid Gordon	OF123, 3B10	R	32	134	481	78	146	33	4	27	103	78	31	2	.304	.557
2 Walker Cooper	C88	R	35	102	337	52	111	19	3	14	60	30	26	1	.329	.528
Willard Marshall	OF85	L	29	105	298	38	70	10	2	5	40	36	5	1	.235	.332
Del Crandall	C75, 1B1	R	20	79	255	21	56	11	0	4	37	13	24	0	.220	.310
Luis Olmo	OF55, 3B1	R	30	69	154	23	35	7	1	5	22	18	23	3	.227	.383
Sibby Sisti	SS23, 2B19, 3B13, 1B1, OF1	R	29	69	105	21	18	3	1	2	11	16	19	1	.171	.276
Pete Reiser	OF24, 3B1	L	31	53	78	12	16	2	0	1	10	18	22	1	.205	.269
Gene Mauch	2B28, 3B7, SS5	R	24	48	121	17	28	5	0	1	15	14	9	1	.231	.298
1 Connie Ryan	2B20	R	30	20	72	12	14	2	0	3	6	12	9	0	.194	.347
Bob Addis	OF7	L	24	16	28	7	7	1	0	0	2	3	5	1	.250	.286
Paul Burris	C8	R	26	10	23	1	4	1	0	0	3	1	2	0	.174	.217
2 Emil Verban	2B2	R	34	4	5	1	0	0	0	0	0	0	0	0	.000	.000
Walt Linden	C3	R	26	3	5	0	2	1	0	0	0	1	0	0	.400	.600

NAME	T	AGE	W	L	PCT	SV	G	GS	CG	IP	H	BB	SO	ShO	ERA
		27	83	71	.539	10	156	156	**88**	1388	1411	554	615	7	4.13
Warren Spahn	L	29	**21**	17	.553	1	41	**39**	25	293	248	111	**191**	1	3.16
Johnny Sain	R	32	20	13	.606	0	37	37	25	278	**294**	70	96	3	3.95
Vern Bickford	R	29	19	14	.576	0	40	**39**	**27**	**312**	293	122	126	2	3.46
Bob Chipman	L	31	7	7	.500	1	27	12	4	124	127	37	40	0	4.43
Max Surkont	R	28	5	2	.714	0	9	6	2	56	63	20	21	0	3.21
Norm Roy	R	21	4	3	.571	1	19	6	2	60	72	39	25	0	5.10
Bobby Hogue	R	29	3	5	.375	7	36	1	0	63	69	31	15	0	5.00
Johnny Antonelli	L	20	2	3	.400	0	20	6	2	58	81	22	33	1	5.93
Ernie Johnson	R	26	2	0	1.000	0	16	1	0	21	37	13	15	0	6.86
Bob Hall	R	26	0	2	.000	0	21	4	0	50	58	33	22	0	7.02
Dick Donovan	R	22	0	2	.000	0	10	3	0	30	28	34	9	0	8.10
2 Mickey Haefner	L	37	0	2	.000	0	8	2	1	24	23	12	10	0	5.63
Dave Cole	R	19	0	1	.000	0	4	0	0	8	7	3	8	0	1.13
Dick Manville	R	23	0	0	.000	0	1	0	0	2	0	3	2	0	0.00
Murray Wall	R	23	0	0	.000	0	1	0	0	4	6	2	2	0	9.00
Bucky Walters	R	40	0	0	.000	0	1	0	0	4	5	2	0	0	4.50

ST. LOUIS 5th 78-75 .510 12.5 — EDDIE DYER

NAME	G by POS	B	AGE	G	AB	R	H	2B	3B	HR	RBI	BB	SO	SB	BA	SA
TOTALS			29	153	5215	693	1353	255	50	102	646	606	604	23	.259	.386
Stan Musial	OF77, 1B69	L	29	146	555	105	192	41	7	28	109	87	36	5	**.346**	**.596**
Red Schoendienst	2B143, SS10, 3B1	B	27	153	**642**	81	177	**43**	9	7	63	33	32	3	.276	.403
Marty Marion	SS101	R	32	106	372	36	92	10	2	4	40	44	55	1	.247	.317
Tommy Glaviano	3B106, 2B5, SS1	R	26	115	410	92	117	29	2	11	44	90	74	6	.285	.446
Enos Slaughter	OF145	L	34	148	556	82	161	26	7	10	101	66	33	3	.290	.415
Chuck Diering (BE)	OF81	R	27	89	204	34	51	12	0	3	18	35	38	1	.250	.353
Bill Howerton	OF94	L	28	110	313	50	88	20	8	10	59	47	60	0	.281	.492
Del Rice	C130	R	27	130	414	39	101	20	3	9	54	43	65	0	.244	.372
Eddie Kazak	3B48	L	29	93	207	21	53	2	2	5	23	18	19	0	.256	.357
Rocky Nelson	1B70	L	25	76	235	27	58	10	4	1	20	26	9	4	.247	.336
Eddie Miller	SS51, 2B1	R	33	64	172	17	39	8	0	3	22	19	21	0	.227	.326
Harry Walker	OF46, 1B2	L	33	60	150	17	31	5	0	0	7	18	12	0	.207	.240
Hal Rice	OF37	L	26	44	128	12	27	3	1	2	11	10	10	0	.211	.297
2 Johnny Lindell	OF33	R	33	36	113	16	21	5	2	5	16	15	24	0	.186	.398
Joe Garagiola (SJ)	C30	L	24	34	88	8	28	6	1	2	20	10	7	0	.318	.477
Johnny Bucha	C17	R	25	22	36	1	5	1	0	0	1	4	7	0	.139	.167
2 Peanuts Lowery	2B6, 3B5, OF4	R	31	17	56	10	15	0	0	1	4	6	1	0	.268	.321
Nippy Jones(XJ)	1B8	R	25	13	26	0	6	1	0	0	6	3	1	0	.231	.269
Solly Hemus	3B5	L	27	11	15	1	2	1	0	0	0	2	4	0	.133	.200
Steve Bilko	1B9	R	21	10	33	1	6	1	0	0	2	4	10	0	.182	.212
2 Johnny Blatnik	OF7	R	29	7	20	0	3	0	0	0	1	3	2	0	.150	.150
Ed Mickelson	1B4	R	23	5	10	1	1	0	0	0	0	2	3	0	.100	.100
Don Bollweg	1B4	L	29	4	11	1	2	0	0	0	1	1	1	0	.182	.182

Danny Gardella 30 L 0-1, Ed Mierkowicz 26 R 0-1

NAME	T	AGE	W	L	PCT	SV	G	GS	CG	IP	H	BB	SO	ShO	ERA
		32	78	75	.510	14	153	153	57	1355	1398	535	603	10	3.97
Howie Pollet	L	29	14	13	.519	2	37	30	14	232	228	68	117	2	3.30
Gerry Staley	R	29	13	13	.500	3	42	22	7	170	201	61	62	1	4.98
Al Brazle	L	36	11	9	.550	6	46	12	3	165	188	80	47	0	4.09
Max Lanier	L	34	11	9	.550	0	27	27	10	181	173	68	89	2	3.13
Harry Brecheen	L	35	8	11	.421	1	27	23	12	163	151	45	80	2	3.81
Cloyd Boyer	R	22	7	7	.500	1	36	14	6	120	105	49	82	2	3.53
George Munger	R	31	7	8	.467	0	32	20	5	155	158	70	61	1	3.89
Freddie Martin	R	35	4	2	.667	0	30	2	0	63	87	30	19	0	5.14
Ted Wilks	R	34	2	0	1.000	0	18	0	0	24	27	9	15	0	6.75
2 Al Papai	R	31	1	0	1.000	0	13	0	0	19	21	14	7	0	5.21
Erv Dusak	R	29	0	2	.000	1	14	2	0	36	27	27	16	0	3.75
1 Jim Hearn	R	29	0	1	.000	0	6	0	0	9	12	6	4	0	**10.00***
Tom Poholsky	R	20	0	0	.000	0	5	1	0	15	16	3	2	0	3.60
Cot Deal	R	27	0	0	.000	0	3	0	0	1	3	2	1	0	18.00
1 Ken Johnson	L	27	0	0	.000	0	2	0	0	2	1	3	1	0	0.00

*Hearn, also with New York, league leader in ERA with 2.49

CINCINNATI 6th 66-87 .431 24.5 — **LUKE SEWELL**

NAME	G by POS	B	AGE	G	AB	R	H	2B	3B	HR	RBI	BB	SO	SB	BA	SA
TOTALS			27	153	5253	654	1366	**257**	27	99	617	504	497	37	.260	.376
Ted Kluszewski	1B131	L	25	134	538	76	165	37	0	25	111	33	28	3	.307	.515
2 Connie Ryan	2B103	R	30	106	367	45	95	18	5	3	43	52	46	4	.259	.360
Virgil Stallcup	SS136	R	28	136	483	44	121	23	2	8	54	17	39	4	.251	.356
Grady Hatton	3B126, 2B1, SS1	L	27	130	438	67	114	17	1	11	54	70	39	6	.260	.379
Johnny Wyrostek	OF129, 1B4	L	30	131	509	70	145	34	5	8	76	52	38	1	.285	.418
Lloyd Merriman	OF84	L	25	92	298	44	77	15	3	2	31	30	23	6	.258	.349
Bob Usher	OF95	R	25	106	321	51	83	17	0	6	35	27	38	3	.259	.368
Dixie Howell	C81	R	31	82	224	30	50	9	1	2	22	32	31	0	.223	.299
Bobby Adams	2B53, 3B42	R	28	115	348	57	98	21	8	3	25	43	29	7	.282	.414
Joe Adcock	OF75, 1B24	R	22	102	372	46	109	16	1	8	55	24	24	2	.293	.406
1 Peanuts Lowery	OF72, 2B1	R	31	91	264	34	60	14	0	1	11	36	7	0	.227	.292
Johnny Pramesa	C73	R	24	74	228	14	70	10	1	5	30	19	15	0	.307	.425
Danny Litwhiler	OF29	R	33	54	112	15	29	4	0	6	12	20	21	0	.259	.455
Sammy Meeks	SS29, 3B2	R	27	39	95	7	27	5	0	1	8	6	14	1	.284	.368
1 Ron Northey	OF24	L	30	27	77	11	20	5	0	5	9	15	6	0	.260	.519
2 Bob Scheffing	C11	R	34	21	47	4	13	0	0	2	6	4	2	0	.277	.404
1 Walker Cooper	C13	R	35	15	47	3	9	3	0	0	4	0	5	0	.191	.255
1 Jimmy Bloodworth	2B4	R	32	4	14	1	3	1	0	0	1	2	0	0	.214	.286

Jim Bolger 18 R 0-1, Hobie Landrith 20 L 3-14, Marv Rackley 28 L 1-2, Ted Tappe 19 L 1-5

NAME	T	AGE	W	L	PCT	SV	G	GS	CG	IP	H	BB	SO	ShO	ERA
TOTALS		27	66	87	.431	13	153	153	67	1357	1363	582	686	7	4.31
Ewell Blackwell	R	27	17	15	.531	4	40	32	18	261	203	112	188	1	2.97
Ken Raffensberger	L	32	14	19	.424	0	38	35	18	239	271	40	87	4	4.26
Howie Fox	R	29	11	8	.579	1	34	22	10	187	196	85	64	1	4.33
Herm Wehmeier	R	23	10	18	.357	4	41	32	12	230	255	**135**	121	0	5.67
2 Willie Ramsdell	R	34	7	12	.368	0	27	22	8	157	151	75	83	1	3.73
Eddie Erautt	R	25	4	2	.667	1	33	2	1	65	82	22	35	0	5.68
Frank Smith	R	22	2	7	.222	3	38	4	0	91	73	39	55	0	3.86
Johnny Hetki	R	28	1	2	.333	0	22	1	0	53	53	27	21	0	5.09
Harry Perkowski	L	27	0	0	.000	0	22	0	0	34	36	23	19	0	5.29
Kent Peterson	L	24	0	3	.000	0	9	2	0	20	25	17	6	0	7.20
Bud Byerly	R	29	0	1	.000	0	4	1	0	15	12	4	5	0	2.40
Jim Avrea	R	29	0	0	.000	0	2	0	0	5	6	3	2	0	3.60

CHICAGO 7th 64-89 .418 26.5 — **FRANKIE FRISCH**

NAME	G by POS	B	AGE	G	AB	R	H	2B	3B	HR	RBI	BB	SO	SB	BA	SA
TOTALS			27	154	5230	643	1298	224	47	161	615	479	**767**	46	.248	.401
Preston Ward (NJ)	1B76	L	22	80	285	31	72	11	2	6	33	27	42	3	.253	.368
Wayne Terwilliger	2B126, 3B1, 1B1, OF1	R	25	133	480	63	116	22	3	10	32	43	63	13	.242	.363
Roy Smalley	SS154	R	24	154	557	58	128	21	9	21	85	49	**114**	2	.230	.413
Bill Serena	3B125	R	25	127	435	56	104	20	4	17	61	65	75	1	.239	.421
Bob Borkowski	OF65, 1B1	R	24	85	256	27	70	7	4	4	29	16	30	1	.273	.379
Andy Pafko	OF144	R	29	146	514	95	156	24	8	36	92	69	32	4	.304	.591
Hank Sauer	OF125, 1B18	R	31	145	540	85	148	32	2	32	103	60	67	1	.274	.519
Mickey Owen	C86	R	34	86	259	22	63	11	0	2	21	13	16	2	.243	.309
Phil Cavarretta (BA)	1B67, OF3	L	33	82	256	49	70	11	1	10	31	40	31	1	.273	.441
Rube Walker	C62	L	24	74	213	19	49	7	1	6	16	18	34	0	.230	.357
Hal Jeffcoat (BC)	OF53	R	25	66	179	21	42	13	1	2	18	6	23	7	.235	.352
Carmen Mauro	OF49	L	23	62	185	19	42	4	3	1	10	13	31	3	.227	.297
Bob Ramazzotti	2B31, 3B10, SS3	R	33	61	145	19	38	3	3	1	6	4	16	3	.262	.345
2 Ron Northey	OF27	L	30	53	114	11	32	9	0	4	20	10	9	0	.281	.465
1 Emil Verban	2B8, SS3, 3B1, OF1	R	34	45	37	7	4	1	0	0	1	3	5	0	.108	.135
Hank Edwards	OF29	L	31	41	110	13	40	11	1	2	21	10	13	0	.364	.536
Carl Sawatski	C32	L	22	38	103	4	18	1	0	1	7	11	10	0	.175	.211
Randy Jackson	3B27	R	24	34	111	13	25	4	3	3	6	7	25	4	.225	.396

Harry Chiti 17 R 2-6, 1 Bob Scheffing 34 R 3-16

NAME	T	AGE	W	L	PCT	SV	G	GS	CG	IP	H	BB	SO	ShO	ERA
TOTALS		30	64	89	.418	19	154	154	55	1372	1452	593	559	9	4.28
Bob Rush	R	24	13	**20**	.394	1	39	34	19	255	261	93	93	1	3.71
Frank Hiller	R	29	12	5	.706	1	38	17	9	153	153	32	55	2	3.53
Johnny Schmitz	L	29	10	16	.385	0	39	27	8	193	217	91	75	3	4.99
Paul Minner	L	26	8	13	.381	4	39	24	9	190	217	72	99	1	4.12
Monk Dubiel	R	31	6	10	.375	2	39	12	4	143	152	67	51	2	4.15
Dutch Leonard	R	41	5	1	.833	6	35	1	0	74	70	27	28	0	3.77
Doyle Lade	R	29	5	6	.455	2	34	12	2	118	126	50	36	0	4.73
Johnny Vander Meer	L	35	3	4	.429	1	32	6	0	74	60	59	41	0	3.77
Johnny Klippstein	R	22	2	9	.182	1	33	11	3	105	112	64	51	0	5.23
Bill Voiselle	R	31	0	4	.000	0	19	7	0	51	64	29	25	0	5.82
Warren Hacker	R	25	0	1	.000	1	5	3	1	15	20	8	5	0	5.40
Andy Varga	L	19	0	0	.000	0	1	0	0	1	0	1	0	0	0.00

PITTSBURGH 8th 57-96 .373 33.5 — **BILLY MEYER**

NAME	G by POS	B	AGE	G	AB	R	H	2B	3B	HR	RBI	BB	SO	SB	BA	SA
TOTALS			30	154	5327	681	1404	227	**59**	138	634	564	693	43	.264	.406
1 Johnny Hopp	1B70, OF7	L	33	106	318	51	108	24	5	8	47	43	17	7	.340	.522
Danny Murtaugh	2B108	R	32	118	367	34	108	20	5	2	37	47	42	2	.294	.392
Danny O'Connell	SS65, 3B12	R	23	79	315	39	92	16	1	8	32	24	33	7	.292	.425
2 Bob Dillinger	3B51	R	31	58	222	23	64	8	2	1	9	13	22	4	.288	.356
Gus Bell	OF104	L	21	111	422	62	119	22	11	8	53	28	46	4	.282	.443
Wally Westlake	OF123	R	29	139	477	69	136	15	6	24	95	48	78	1	.285	.493
Ralph Kiner	OF150	R	27	150	547	112	149	21	6	**47**	118	122	79	2	.272	.590
Clyde McCullough (BW)	C100	R	33	103	279	28	71	16	4	6	34	31	35	3	.254	.405
Pete Castiglione	3B35, SS29, 2B9, 1B3	R	29	94	263	29	67	10	3	3	22	23	23	1	.255	.350
Stan Rojek	SS68, 2B3	R	31	76	230	28	59	12	1	0	17	18	13	2	.257	.317
Jack Phillips	1B54, 3B3, P1	R	28	69	208	25	61	7	6	5	34	20	17	1	.293	.457
Tom Saffell	OF43	L	28	67	182	18	37	7	0	2	6	14	34	1	.203	.275
2 Ray Mueller	C63	R	38	67	156	17	42	7	0	6	24	11	14	2	.269	.429
Nanny Fernandez	3B52	R	31	65	198	23	51	11	0	6	27	19	17	2	.258	.404
Ted Beard (BH)	OF49	L	29	61	177	32	41	6	2	4	12	27	45	3	.232	.356
Hank Schenz	2B21, 3B12, SS4	R	31	58	101	17	23	4	2	1	5	6	7	0	.228	.337
Dale Coogan	1B32	L	19	53	129	19	31	6	1	1	13	17	24	0	.240	.326
2 Johnny Berardino	2B36, 3B3	R	33	40	131	12	27	3	1	1	12	19	11	0	.206	.267
Earl Turner	C34	R	27	40	74	10	18	0	0	3	5	4	13	1	.243	.365
Cliff Chambers	P37	L	28	37	00	10	20	1	1	2	9	4	18	0	.289	.389
George Strickland	SS19, 3B1	R	24	23	27	0	3	0	0	0	2	3	8	0	.111	.111
Ed Stevens	1B12	L	25	17	46	2	9	2	0	0	3	4	5	0	.196	.239

1 Marv Rickert 29 L 3-20, Ed Fitzgerald 26 R 1-15

NAME	T	AGE	W	L	PCT	SV	G	GS	CG	IP	H	BB	SO	ShO	ERA
TOTALS		28	57	**96**	.373	16	154	154	42	1368	**1472**	**616**	556	6	4.96
Cliff Chambers	L	28	12	15	.444	0	37	33	11	249	262	92	93	2	4.30
Murry Dickson	R	33	10	15	.400	3	51	22	8	225	227	83	76	0	3.80
Bill Werle	L	29	8	16	.333	8	48	22	6	215	249	65	78	0	4.60
Bill Macdonald	R	21	8	10	.444	1	32	20	6	153	138	88	60	2	4.29
Vern Law	R	20	7	9	.438	0	27	17	5	128	137	49	57	1	4.92
Mel Queen	R	32	5	14	.263	0	33	21	4	120	135	73	76	1	6.00
Bob Chesnes	R	29	3	3	.500	0	9	7	2	39	44	17	12	0	5.54
Junior Walsh	R	31	1	1	.500	2	38	2	0	62	56	34	33	0	5.08
Woody Main	R	28	1	0	1.000	1	12	0	0	20	21	11	12	0	4.95
2 Hank Borowy	R	34	1	3	.250	0	11	3	0	25	32	9	9	0	6.48
Frank Barrett	R	37	1	2	.333	0	5	0	0	4	5	1	0	0	4.50
Vic Lombardi	L	27	0	5	.000	1	39	2	0	76	93	48	26	0	6.63
Bill Pierro	R	24	0	2	.000	0	12	3	0	29	33	28	13	0	10.55
Hal Gregg	R	28	0	1	.000	0	5	1	0	5	10	7	3	0	14.40
Frank Papish	L	32	0	0	.000	0	4	1	0	2	8	4	1	0	31.50
Windy McCall	L	24	0	0	.000	0	2	0	0	7	12	4	5	0	9.00
Harry Gumbert	R	40	0	0	.000	0	1	0	0	2	3	2	0	0	4.50
Jack Phillips	R	28	0	0	.000	0	1	0	0	5	7	1	2	0	7.20

WORLD SERIES – NEW YORK (AL) 4 PHILADELPHIA (NL) 0

LINE SCORES

TEAM	1	2	3	4	5	6	7	8	9	10	11	12	R	H	E
Game 1 October 4 at Philadelphia															
NY (AL)	0	0	0	1	0	0	0	0	0				1	5	0
PHI (NL)	0	0	0	0	0	0	0	0	0				0	2	1
Raschi	**Konstanty**, Meyer (9)														
Game 2 October 5 at Philadelphia															
NY	0	1	0	0	0	0	0	0	0	1			2	10	0
PHI	0	0	0	0	1	0	0	0	0	0			1	7	0
Reynolds	**Roberts**														
Game 3 October 6 at New York															
PHI	0	0	0	0	0	1	1	0	0				2	10	2
NY	0	0	1	0	0	0	0	1	1				3	7	0
Heintzelman, Konstanty (8), **Meyer** (9)	Lopat, **Ferrick** (9)														
Game 4 October 7 at New York															
PHI	0	0	0	0	0	0	0	0	2				2	7	1
NY	2	0	0	0	0	3	0	0	X				5	8	2
Miller, Konstanty (1), Roberts (8),	**Ford**, Reynolds (9)														

COMPOSITE BATTING

NAME	POS	G	AB	R	H	2B	3B	HR	RBI	BA
New York (AL)										
Totals		4	135	11	30	3	1	2	10	.222
Berra	C	4	15	**2**	3	0	0	1	2	.200
Mize	1B	4	15	0	2	0	0	0	0	.133
Bauer	OF	4	15	0	2	0	0	0	1	.133
Woodling	OF	4	14	**2**	**6**	0	0	0	1	**.429**
Coleman	2B	4	14	**2**	4	1	0	0	**3**	.286
Rizzuto	SS	4	14	1	2	0	0	0	0	.143
DiMaggio	OF	4	13	**2**	4	1	0	1	2	.308
Brown	3B	4	12	**2**	4	1	1	0	1	.333
W. Johnson	3B	4	6	0	0	0	0	0	0	.000
Mapes	OF	1	4	0	0	0	0	0	0	.000
Raschi	P	1	3	0	1	0	0	0	0	.333
Reynolds	P	2	3	0	1	0	0	0	0	.333
Ford	P	1	3	0	0	0	0	0	0	.000
Lopat	P	1	2	0	1	0	0	0	0	.500
Hopp	1B	3	2	0	0	0	0	0	0	.000
Collins	1B	1	0	0	0	0	0	0	0	.000
Ferrick	P	1	0	0	0	0	0	0	0	.000
Jensen	PR	1	0	0	0	0	0	0	0	.000
Philadelphia (NL)										
Totals		4	128	5	26	6	1	0	3	.203
Ashburn	OF	4	**17**	0	3	1	0	0	1	.176
Sisler	OF	4	**17**	0	1	0	0	0	1	.059
Waitkus	1B	4	15	0	4	1	0	0	0	.267
Hamner	SS	4	14	1	**6**	**2**	1	0	0	**.429**
Jones	3B	4	14	1	4	1	0	0	0	.286
Goliat	2B	4	14	1	3	0	0	0	1	.214
Ennis	OF	4	14	1	2	1	0	0	0	.143
Seminick	C	4	11	0	2	0	0	0	0	.182
Konstanty	P	3	4	0	1	0	0	0	0	.250
Roberts	P	2	2	0	0	0	0	0	0	.000
Heintzelman	P	1	2	0	0	0	0	0	0	.000
Whitman	PH	3	2	0	0	0	0	0	0	.000
Lopata	C	2	1	0	0	0	0	0	0	.000
Caballero	PH	3	1	0	0	0	0	0	0	.000
K. Johnson	PR	1	0	1	0	0	0	0	0	.000
Silvestri	C	1	0	0	0	0	0	0	0	.000
Bloodworth	2B	1	0	0	0	0	0	0	0	.000
Mayo	OF	3	0	0	0	0	0	0	0	.000
Meyer	P	2	0	0	0	0	0	0	0	.000
Miller	P	1	0	0	0	0	0	0	0	.000

COMPOSITE PITCHING

NAME	G	IP	H	BB	SO	W	L	SV	ERA
New York (AL)									
Totals	4	37	26	7	24	4	0	1	0.72
Reynolds	2	10.1	7	4	7	1	0	1	0.87
Raschi	1	9	2	1	5	1	0	0	**0.00**
Ford	1	8.2	7	1	7	1	0	0	**0.00**
Lopat	1	8	9	0	5	0	0	0	2.25
Ferrick	1	1	1	1	0	1	0	0	0.00
Philadelphia (NL)									
Totals	4	35.2	30	13	12	0	4	0	2.27
Konstanty	**3**	**15**	9	4	3	0	1	0	2.40
Roberts	2	11	**11**	3	5	0	1	0	1.64
Heintzelman	1	7.2	4	**6**	3	0	0	0	1.17
Meyer	2	1.2	4	0	1	0	1	0	5.40
Miller	1	.1	2	0	0	0	1	0	27.00

1951: Ouch

The season began with Ford Frick succeeding Happy Chandler as Commissioner of Baseball. Midway through the campaign, Browns' owner Bill Veeck pulled the most famous stunt of his promotional career by unfurling, for one turn at bat, the smallest man ever to wear a major league uniform—3'7" Eddie Gaedel.

At the season's end, there was a broken heart for every foot of trolley track in the borough of Brooklyn. The story of the Dodgers and their misery, and the Giants and their joy, began in April with no indications as to the outcome which would astonish the baseball world in October.

The Giants and their hated rival, the Brooklyn Dodgers, were both strong enough to take the pennant. But while the Dodgers, led by MVP Roy Campanella, sprinted out to a comfortable lead, the Giants lost their first 11 games. By August 12, the Dodgers lead over the second place Giants was 13½ games.

Part two of the story began on that August date, as the Giants won again and again by running off 16 straight victories to climb up Brooklyn's back. Manager Leo Durocher masterfully guided the assault by whipping his charges into victory in 39 of the final 47 matches. Oddly enough, it was a 20-year-old rookie by the name of Willie Mays who proved the main spark of the team with his centerfield play and infectious enthusiasm. The second part of the story concluded as the Giants climbed into the top spot by winning their last seven contests, while the hapless Dodgers could only hang onto a tie by downing the Phils in 14 innings in the season's finale.

The feuding neighbors squared off in a three-game play-off for the flag to end the saddest story ever to be told in Brooklyn. A split of the first two tilts placed the issue directly on the line at the Polo Grounds on October 3. Those who now claim to have been present at the game number in the hundreds of thousands, but 34,320 ticket stubs were collected at the turnstiles on that overcast day in New York. Going into the bottom of the ninth, Giant fans were prepared to slink out into the street as quietly as possible, for Brooklyn was up 4-1 with big Don Newcombe needing only three more outs to wrap up the title. Alvin Dark opened up the fateful frame with an apparently harmless single, but Don Mueller raised some hopes by lashing another single to right. The tiring Newcombe managed to coax Monte Irvin into popping out, but Whitey Lockman bashed a double to left, plating Dark and sending Mueller sliding into third. An ankle injury forced Durocher to send in a pinch-runner for Mueller, and Dodger Skipper, Dressen, took advantage of the delay to wave big Ralph Branca to the mound to bail Newcombe out.

Branca, the proud bearer of uniform number 13, entered the fray to face slugger Bobby Thomson at the plate. Although first base stood empty, Dressen decided against an intentional pass to Thomson, which would have put the potential winning run on base with Mays at bat. Branca dauntlessly fired the first pitch down the middle for strike one, but his second serve needed no umpire's decision. On the next big pitch, Thomson swung and drilled a rising line drive into the left field stands to score the incredible winning runs. For a full second the crowd sat quietly stunned before spontaneously erupting into delirium at the realization that the Giants had pulled off the impossible. As Thomson circled the bases, Eddie Stanky hopped on manager Durocher's back in the third-base coaching box, typewriters clacked out headline stories, Mueller rejoiced from his stretcher in the dressing room, and the Dodgers could only wish quiet graves in their funeral march to the distant centerfield clubhouse.

With all the drama of the National League chase monopolizing the press coverage, the Yankees quietly retained the junior loop flag by outlasting threats from Cleveland and Boston—both of which died in the final two weeks. Phil Rizzuto and MVP Yogi Berra starred at bat and in the field, and Allie Reynolds hurled a pair of no-hitters in joining Vic Raschi and Eddie Lopat as Casey Stengel's mound aces. Only Joe DeMaggio's final year in pinstripes after a 13-season career, which netted him a .325 lifetime batting average, and the brief appearance of a green 19-year-old rookie outfielder named Mickey Mantle, gave Yankee fans any historical memory. The World Series, won by Stengel for the third time in as many tries, proved insignificant when compared to the miracle of Coogan's Bluff.

1951 AMERICAN LEAGUE

NAME	G by POS	B	AGE	G	AB	R	H	2B	3B	HR	RBI	BB	SO	SB	BA	SA
NEW YORK 1st 98-56 .636	CASEY STENGEL															
TOTALS			28	154	5194	798	1395	208	48	140	741	605	547	78	.269	.408
Johnny Mize	1B93	L	38	113	332	37	86	14	1	10	49	36	24	1	.259	.398
Jerry Coleman	2B102, SS18	R	26	121	362	48	90	11	2	3	43	31	36	6	.249	.315
Phil Rizzuto	SS144	R	33	144	540	87	148	21	6	2	43	58	27	18	.274	.346
Bobby Brown	3B90	L	26	103	313	44	84	15	2	6	51	47	18	1	.268	.387
Hank Bauer	OF107	R	28	118	348	53	103	19	3	10	54	42	39	5	.296	.454
Joe DiMaggio	OF113	R	36	116	415	72	109	22	4	12	71	61	36	0	.263	.422
Gene Woodling	OF116	L	28	120	420	65	118	15	8	15	71	62	37	0	.281	.462
Yogi Berra	C141	L	26	141	547	92	161	19	4	27	88	44	20	5	.294	.492
Gil McDougald	3B82, 2B55	R	23	131	402	72	123	23	4	14	63	56	54	14	.306	.488
Joe Collins	1B114, OF15	L	28	125	262	52	75	8	5	9	48	34	23	9	.286	.458
Mickey Mantle	OF86	B	19	96	341	61	91	11	5	13	65	43	74	8	.267	.443
Jackie Jensen	OF48	R	24	56	168	30	50	8	1	8	25	18	18	8	.298	.500
Billy Martin	2B23, SS6, 3B2, OF1	R	23	51	58	10	15	1	2	0	2	4	9	0	.259	.345
Johnny Hopp	1B25	L	34	46	63	10	13	1	0	2	4	9	11	2	.206	.317
1 Cliff Mapes	OF34	L	29	45	51	6	11	3	1	2	8	4	14	0	.216	.431
Charlie Silvera	C18	R	26	18	51	5	14	3	0	1	7	5	3	0	.275	.392
1 Billy Johnson	3B13	R	32	15	40	5	12	3	0	0	4	7	0	0	.300	.375
Bob Cerv	OF9	R	25	12	28	4	6	1	0	0	2	4	6	0	.214	.250
Jim Brideweser 24 R 3-8, Clint Courtney 24 L 0-2, Ralph Houk 31 R 1-5, Archie Wilson 27 R 0-4											Whitey Ford (MS) 22					
CLEVELAND 2nd 93-61 .604 5	AL LOPEZ															
TOTALS			29	155	5250	696	1346	208	35	140	658	606	632	52	.256	.389
Luke Easter	1B125	L	36	128	486	65	131	12	5	27	103	37	71	0	.270	.481
Bobby Avila	2B136	R	27	141	542	76	165	21	3	10	58	60	31	14	.304	.410
Ray Boone	SS151	R	27	151	544	65	127	14	1	12	51	48	36	5	.233	.329
Al Rosen	3B154	R	27	154	573	82	152	30	1	24	102	85	71	7	.265	.447
Bob Kennedy	OF106	R	30	108	321	30	79	15	4	7	29	34	33	4	.246	.383
Larry Doby	OF132	L	27	134	447	84	132	27	5	20	69	101	81	4	.295	.512
Dale Mitchell	OF124	L	29	134	510	83	148	21	7	11	62	53	16	7	.290	.424
Jim Hegan	C129	R	30	133	416	60	99	17	5	6	43	38	72	0	.238	.346
Harry Simpson	OF68, 1B50	L	25	122	332	51	76	7	0	7	24	45	48	6	.229	.313
2 Sam Chapman	OF84, 1B1	R	35	94	246	24	56	9	1	6	36	27	32	3	.228	.346
Birdie Tebbetts	C44	R	41	55	137	8	36	6	0	2	18	8	7	0	.263	.350
Snuffy Stirnweiss	2B25, 3B2	R	32	50	88	10	19	1	0	1	4	22	25	1	.216	.261
3 Berney McCosky	OF16	L	33	31	61	8	13	3	0	0	2	8	5	1	.213	.262
Merrill Combs	SS16	L	31	19	28	2	5	2	0	0	2	2	3	0	.179	.250
Milt Nielsen		L	26	16	6	1	0	0	0	0	0	1	1	0	.000	.000
4 Paul Lehner	OF1	L	31	12	13	2	3	0	0	0	1	1	2	0	.231	.231
Clarence Maddern	OF1	R	29	11	12	0	2	0	0	0	0	0	1	0	.167	.167
1 Minnie Minoso	1B7	R	28	8	14	3	6	2	0*	0	2	1	1	0*	.429	.571
1 Allie Clark 28 R 3-10, Doug Hansen 22 R 0-0, 1 Lou Klein 32 R 0-2, 1 Ray Murray 33 R 1-1, Hal Naragon 22 L 2-8, Thurman Tucker 33 L 0-1																
BOSTON 3rd 87-67 .565 11	STEVE O'NEILL															
TOTALS			30	154	5378	804	1428	233	32	127	757	756	594	20	.266	.392
Walt Dropo	1B93	R	28	99	360	37	86	14	0	11	57	38	52	0	.239	.369
Bobby Doerr (XJ)	2B106	R	33	106	402	60	116	21	2	13	73	57	33	2	.289	.448
Johnny Pesky	SS106, 3B11, 2B5	L	31	131	480	93	150	20	6	3	41	84	15	2	.313	.398
Vern Stephens (LJ)	3B89, SS2	R	30	109	377	62	113	21	2	17	78	38	33	1	.300	.501
Clyde Vollmer	OF106	R	29	115	386	66	97	9	2	22	85	55	66	0	.251	.456
Dom DiMaggio	OF146	R	34	146	639	113	189	34	4	12	72	73	53	4	.296	.418
Ted Williams	OF147	L	32	148	531	109	169	28	4	30	126	144	45	1	.318	.556
2 Les Moss	C69	R	26	71	202	18	40	6	0	3	26	25	34	0	.198	.272
Billy Goodman	1B62, 2B44, OF38, 3B1	L	25	141	546	92	162	34	4	0	50	79	37	7	.297	.374
Lou Boudreau	SS52, 3B15, 1B2	R	33	82	273	37	73	18	1	5	47	30	12	1	.267	.396
Fred Hatfield	3B49	L	26	80	163	23	28	4	2	2	14	22	27	1	.172	.258
Buddy Rosar	C56	R	36	58	170	11	39	7	0	1	13	19	14	0	.229	.288
Charlie Maxwell	OF13	L	24	49	80	8	15	1	0	3	12	9	18	0	.188	.313
Mel Parnell	P36	L	29	37	81	12	25	1	1	0	5	7	10	0	.309	.346
Tom Wright	OF18	L	27	28	63	8	14	1	1	1	9	11	8	0	.222	.317
2 Aaron Robinson	C25	L	36	26	74	9	15	1	1	2	7	17	10	0	.203	.324
Al Evans	C10	R	34	12	24	1	3	1	0	0	2	4	2	0	.125	.167
1 Matt Batts	C11	R	29	11	29	1	4	1	0	0	2	1	2	0	.138	.172
1 Mike Guerra	C10	R	38	10	32	1	5	0	0	0	2	6	5	1	.156	.156
Mel Hoderlein 28 B 5-14, Bob Di Pietro 23 R 1-11, Karl Olson 20 R 1-10, Al Richter 24 R 1-11, Sammy White R 22 2-11, Norm Zauchin 21 R 2-12																

NAME	T	AGE	W	L	PCT	SV	G	GS	CG	IP	H	BB	SO	ShO	ERA
		31	98	56	.636	22	154	154	66	1367	1290	562	664	24	3.56
Ed Lopat	L	33	21	9	.700	0	31	31	20	235	209	71	93	4	2.91
Vic Raschi	R	32	21	10	.677	0	35	34	15	258	233	103	164	4	3.28
Allie Reynolds	R	36	17	8	.680	7	40	26	16	221	171	100	126	7	3.05
Tom Morgan	R	21	9	3	.750	2	27	16	4	125	119	36	57	2	3.67
2 Bob Kuzava	L	28	8	4	.667	5	23	8	4	82	76	27	50	1	2.41
Joe Ostrowski	L	34	6	4	.600	5	34	3	2	95	103	18	30	0	3.51
Spec Shea	R	30	5	5	.500	0	25	11	2	96	112	50	38	2	4.31
Art Schallock	L	27	3	1	.750	0	11	6	1	46	50	20	19	0	3.91
1 Tommy Byrne	L	31	2	1	.667	0	9	3	0	21	16	36*	14	0	6.86
2 Johnny Sain	R	33	2	1	.667	1	7	4	1	37	41	8	21	0	4.14
3 Bobby Hogue	R	30	1	0	1.000	0	7	0	0	7	4	3	2	0	0.00
1 Tom Ferrick	R	36	1	1	.500	1	9	0	0	12	21	7	3	0	7.50
2 Stubby Overmire	L	32	1	1	.500	0	15	4	1	45	50	18	14	0	4.60
2 Jack Kramer	R	33	1	3	.250	0	19	3	0	41	46	21	15	0	4.61
Bob Muncrief	R	35	0	0	.000	0	2	0	0	3	5	4	2	0	9.00
Ernie Nevel	R	31	0	0	.000	1	1	0	0	4	1	1	1	0	0.00
1 Bob Porterfield	R	27	0	0	.000	0	2	0	0	3	5	3	2	0	15.00
Bob Wiesler (MS)	L	20	0	2	.000	0	4	3	0	9	13	11	3	0	14.00
1 Fred Sanford	R	31	0	3	.000	0	11	2	0	27	15	25	10	0	3.67
*Byrne, also with St. Louis, league leader in BB with 150															
		28	93	61	.604	19	155	155	76	1391	1287	577	642	10	3.38
Bob Feller	R	32	22	8	.733	0	33	32	16	250	239	95	111	4	3.49
Mike Garcia	R	27	20	13	.606	6	47	30	15	254	239	82	118	1	3.15
Early Wynn	R	31	20	13	.606	1	37	34	21	274	227	107	133	3	3.02
Bob Lemon	R	30	17	14	.548	2	42	34	17	263	244	124	132	1	3.52
Steve Gromek	R	31	7	4	.636	1	27	8	4	107	98	29	40	0	2.78
2 Lou Brissie	L	27	4	3	.571	9	54	4	1	112	90	61	50	0	3.21
Bob Chakales	R	23	3	4	.429	0	17	10	2	68	80	43	32	1	4.76
Sam Jones	R	25	0	1	.000	0	2	1	0	9	4	5	4	0	2.00
Johnny Vander Meer	L	36	0	1	.000	0	1	1	0	3	8	1	2	0	18.00
George Zuverink	R	26	0	0	.000	0	16	0	0	25	24	13	14	0	5.40
Dick Rozek	L	24	0	0	.000	0	7	1	0	15	18	11	5	0	3.00
Red Fahr	R	26	0	0	.000	0	5	0	0	6	11	2	0	0	4.50
2 Charlie Harris	R	25	0	0	.000	0	2	0	0	4	5	4	1	0	4.50
Al Aber (MS) 23															
Dick Weik (MS) 23															
*Minoso, also with Chicago, league leader in 3B(14) and SB(31)															
		28	87	67	.565	24	154	154	46	1399	1413	599	658	7	4.14
Mel Parnell	L	29	18	11	.621	2	36	29	11	221	229	77	77	3	3.26
Ray Scarborough	R	33	12	9	.571	0	37	22	8	184	201	61	71	0	5.09
Ellis Kinder	R	36	11	2	.846	14	63	2	1	127	108	46	84	0	2.55
Chuck Stobbs	L	21	10	9	.526	0	34	25	6	170	180	74	75	0	4.76
Mickey McDermott	L	22	8	8	.500	3	34	19	9	172	141	92	127	1	3.35
Willard Nixon	R	23	7	4	.636	1	33	14	2	125	136	56	70	1	4.90
Bill Wight	L	29	7	7	.500	0	34	17	4	118	128	63	38	2	5.11
Leo Kiely	L	21	7	7	.500	0	17	16	4	113	106	39	46	0	3.35
Harry Taylor	R	32	4	9	.308	2	31	8	1	81	100	42	22	0	5.78
Walt Masterson	R	31	3	0	1.000	2	30	1	0	59	53	32	39	0	3.36
Harley Hisner	R	24	0	1	.000	0	1	1	0	6	7	4	3	0	4.50
Bill Evans	R	32	0	0	.000	0	9	0	0	15	15	8	3	0	4.20
Paul Hinrichs	R	25	0	0	.000	0	4	0	0	3	7	4	1	0	24.00
Ben Flowers	R	24	0	0	.000	0	1	0	0	3	2	1	2	0	0.00

CHICAGO 4th 81-73 .526 17 — PAUL RICHARDS

NAME	G by POS	B	AGE	G	AB	R	H	2B	3B	HR	RBI	BB	SO	SB	BA	SA
TOTALS			29	155	**5378**	714	**1453**	229	**64**	86	668	596	524	**99**	**.270**	.385
Eddie Robinson	1B147	L	30	151	564	85	159	23	5	29	117	77	54	2	.282	.495
Nellie Fox	2B147	L	23	147	604	93	189	32	12	4	55	43	11	9	.313	.425
Chico Carrasquel	SS147	R	23	147	538	41	142	22	4	2	58	46	39	14	.264	.331
Bob Dillinger	3B70	R	32	89	299	39	90	6	4	0	20	15	17	5	.301	.348
Al Zarilla	OF117	L	32	120	382	56	98	21	2	10	60	60	57	2	.257	.401
Jim Busby	OF139	R	24	143	477	59	135	15	2	5	68	40	46	26	.283	.354
2 Minnie Minoso	OF82, 3B68, SS1	R	28	138	516	109	167	32	**14†**	10	74	71	41	**31†**	.324	.498
Phil Masi	C78	R	34	84	225	24	61	11	2	4	28	32	27	1	.271	.391
Bud Stewart	OF63	L	35	95	217	40	60	13	6	6	40	29	9	1	.276	.465
Floyd Baker	3B44, 2B5, SS3	L	34	82	133	24	35	6	1	0	14	25	12	0	.263	.323
Gus Niarhos (BW)	C59	R	30	66	168	27	43	6	0	1	10	47	9	4	.256	.310
2 Don Lenhardt	OF53, 1B2	R	28	64	199	23	53	9	1	10	45	24	25	1	.266	.472
Joe DeMaestri	SS27, 2B11, 3B8	R	22	56	74	8	15	0	2	1	3	5	11	0	.203	.297
2 Ray Coleman	OF51	L	29	51	181	21	50	8	7	3	21	15	14	2	.276	.448
Bud Sheely	C33	L	30	34	89	2	16	2	0	0	7	6	7	0	.180	.202
2 Paul Lehner	OF20	L	31	23	72	9	15	3	1	0	3	10	4	0	.208	.278
Bert Haas	1B7, OF4, 3B1	R	37	23	43	1	7	0	1	1	2	5	4	0	.163	.279
1 Gus Zernial	OF4	R	28	4	19	2	2	0	0	**0#**	**4#**	2	**2#**	0	.105	.105

Joe Erautt 29 R 4-25, 1 Hank Majeski 34 R 9-35, Bob Boyd 24 L 3-18, Gordon Goldsberry 23 L 1-11, 1 Dave Philley 31 B 6-25,
3 Rocky Nelson 26 L 0-5, Sam Hairston 31 R 2-5, Red Wilson 22 R 3-11, Herb Adams (MS) 23, Bill Wilson (MS) 22

NAME	T	AGE	W	L	PCT	SV	G	GS	CG	IP	H	BB	SO	ShO	ERA
		28	81	73	.526	14	155	155	74	**1418**	1353	549	572	11	3.50
Billy Pierce	L	24	15	**14**	.517	2	37	28	18	240	237	73	113	1	3.04
2 Saul Rogovin	R	28	11	7	.611	0	22	22	17	193	166	67	77	3	**2.47***
Ken Holcombe	R	32	11	12	.478	0	28	23	12	159	142	68	39	2	3.79
Randy Gumpert	R	33	9	8	.529	2	33	16	7	142	156	34	45	1	4.31
Joe Dobson	R	34	7	6	.538	3	28	21	6	147	136	51	67	0	3.61
Luis Aloma (AJ)	R	28	6	0	1.000	3	25	1	1	69	52	24	25	1	1.83
Lou Kretlow	R	28	6	9	.400	0	26	18	7	137	129	74	89	1	4.20
Harry Dorish	R	29	5	6	.455	0	32	4	2	97	101	31	29	1	3.53
Howie Judson	R	25	5	6	.455	1	27	14	3	122	124	55	43	0	3.76
Marv Rotblatt	L	23	4	2	.667	2	26	2	0	48	44	23	20	0	3.38
Dick Littlefield	L	25	1	1	.500	0	4	2	0	10	9	17	7	0	8.10
1 Bob Cain	L	26	1	2	.333	0	4	4	1	26	25	13	3	0	3.81
Ross Grimsley	L	29	0	0	.000	0	7	0	0	14	12	10	8	0	3.86
Hal Brown	R	26	0	0	.000	1	3	0	0	9	15	4	4	0	9.00
1 Bob Mahoney	R	23	0	0	.000	0	3	0	0	7	5	5	3	0	5.14

***Rogovin, also with Detroit, league leader in ERA with 2.78**
†Minoso, also with Cleveland, league leader in 3B (14), SB (31)
#Zernial, also with Philadelphia, league leader in HR (33), RBI (129), SO (101)

DETROIT 5th 73-81 .474 25 — RED ROLFE

NAME	G by POS	B	AGE	G	AB	R	H	2B	3B	HR	RBI	BB	SO	SB	BA	SA
TOTALS			29	154	5336	685	1413	231	35	104	636	568	525	37	.265	.380
Dick Kryhoski	1B112	L	26	119	421	58	121	19	4	12	57	28	29	1	.287	.437
Jerry Priddy	2B154, SS1	R	31	154	584	73	152	22	6	8	57	69	73	4	.260	.360
Johnny Lipon	SS125	R	28	129	487	56	129	15	1	0	38	49	27	7	.265	.300
George Kell	3B147	R	28	147	598	92	**191**	**36**	3	2	59	61	18	10	.319	.400
Vic Wertz	OF131	L	26	138	501	86	143	24	4	27	94	78	61	0	.285	.511
Johnny Groth	OF112	R	24	118	428	41	128	29	1	3	49	31	32	1	.299	.393
Hoot Evers	OF108	R	30	116	393	47	88	15	2	11	46	40	47	5	.224	.356
Joe Ginsberg	C95	L	24	102	304	44	79	10	2	8	37	43	21	0	.260	.385
Pat Mullin	OF83	L	33	110	295	41	83	11	6	12	51	40	38	2	.281	.481
Steve Souchock	OF59, 1B1, 2B1	R	32	91	188	33	46	10	3	11	28	18	27	0	.245	.505
Don Kolloway	1B59	R	32	78	212	28	54	7	0	1	17	15	12	2	.255	.302
Neil Berry	SS38, 2B10, 3B7	R	29	67	157	17	36	5	2	0	9	10	15	4	.229	.287
Charlie Keller	OF8	L	34	54	62	6	16	2	0	3	21	11	12	0	.258	.435
Bob Swift (IL)	C43	R	36	44	104	8	20	0	0	0	5	12	10	0	.192	.192
1 Aaron Robinson	C35	L	36	36	82	3	17	6	0	0	9	17	9	0	.207	.280
Frank House	C18	L	21	18	41	3	9	2	0	1	4	6	2	1	.220	.341

Doc Daugherty 23 R 0-1, Al Federoff 26 R 0-4, Russ Sullivan 28 L 5-26

NAME	T	AGE	W	L	PCT	SV	G	GS	CG	IP	H	BB	SO	ShO	ERA
		31	73	81	.474	17	154	154	51	1384	1385	602	597	8	4.29
Virgil Trucks	R	32	13	8	.619	1	37	18	6	154	153	75	89	1	4.32
2 Bob Cain	L	26	11	10	.524	2	35	22	6	149	135	82	58	1	4.71
Fred Hutchinson	R	31	10	10	.500	2	31	20	9	188	204	27	53	2	3.69
Dizzy Trout	R	36	9	**14**	.391	5	42	22	7	192	172	75	89	0	4.03
Ted Gray	L	26	7	**14**	.333	1	34	28	9	197	194	95	131	1	4.07
Hal Newhouser (SA)	L	30	6	6	.500	0	15	14	7	96	98	19	37	1	3.94
Ray Herbert (MS)	R	21	4	0	1.000	0	5	0	0	13	8	9	9	0	1.38
Marlin Stuart	R	32	4	6	.400	1	29	15	5	124	119	71	46	0	3.77
Hal White	R	32	3	4	.429	4	38	4	0	76	74	49	23	0	4.74
2 Gene Bearden	L	30	3	4	.429	0	37	4	2	106	112	58	38	1	4.33
Hank Borowy	R	35	2	2	.500	0	26	1	0	45	58	27	16	0	7.00
1 Saul Rogovin	R	28	1	1	.500	0	5	4	0	24	23	7	5	0	**5.25***
Wayne McLeland	R	26	0	1	.000	0	6	1	0	11	20	4	0	0	8.18
Dick Marlowe	R	22	0	1	.000	0	2	1	0	2	5	2	1	0	27.00
Earl Johnson	L	32	0	0	.000	1	6	0	0	6	9	2	2	0	6.00
Paul Calvert	R	33	0	0	.000	0	1	0	0	1	1	0	0	0	0.00

Art Houtteman (MS)23

***Rogovin, also with Chicago, league leader in ERA with 2.78**

PHILADELPHIA 6th 70-84 .455 28 — JIMMY DYKES

NAME	G by POS	B	AGE	G	AB	R	H	2B	3B	HR	RBI	BB	SO	SB	BA	SA
TOTALS			31	154	5277	736	1381	**262**	43	102	685	677	565	48	.262	.386
Ferris Fain (BF)	1B108, OF11	L	30	117	425	63	146	30	3	6	57	80	20	0	**.344**	.471
Pete Suder	2B103, SS18, 3B3	R	35	123	440	46	108	18	1	1	42	30	42	5	.245	.298
Eddie Joost	SS140	R	35	140	553	107	160	28	5	19	78	106	70	10	.289	.461
2 Hank Majeski	3B88	R	34	89	323	41	92	19	4	5	42	35	24	1	.285	.415
Elmer Valo	OF116	L	30	123	444	75	134	27	8	7	55	75	20	11	.302	.446
2 Dave Philley	OF120	B	31	125	468	71	123	18	7	7	59	63	38	9	.263	.376
2 Gus Zernial	OF138	R	28	139	552	90	151	30	5	**33***	**125***	61	**99***	2	.274	.525
Joe Tipton	C72	R	28	72	213	23	51	9	0	3	20	51	25	1	.239	.324
Lou Limmer	1B58	L	26	94	214	25	34	9	1	5	30	28	40	1	.159	.280
Billy Hitchcock	3B45, 2B23, 1B1	R	34	77	222	27	68	10	4	1	36	21	23	2	.306	.401
Wally Moses	OF27	L	40	70	136	17	26	6	0	0	9	21	9	2	.191	.235
Joe Astroth	C57	R	28	64	187	30	46	10	2	2	19	18	13	0	.246	.353
2 Allie Clark	OF32, 3B10	R	28	56	161	20	40	10	1	4	22	15	7	2	.248	.398
2 Lou Klein	2B42	R	32	49	144	22	33	7	0	5	17	10	12	0	.229	.382
Carl Scheib	P46	R	24	48	53	9	21	2	2	2	8	1	5	0	.396	.623
2 Ray Murray	C39	R	33	40	122	10	26	6	0	0	13	14	8	0	.213	.262
1 Kermit Wahl	3B18	R	28	20	59	4	11	2	0	0	6	9	5	0	.186	.220
1 Sam Chapman	OF17	R	35	18	65	7	11	1	0	0	5	12	12	0	.169	.185
1 Barney McCosky	OF7	L	33	12	27	4	8	2	0	1	1	3	4	0	.296	.481

Tod Davis 26 R 1-15, 1 Paul Lehner 31 L 4-28, Eddie Samcoff 26 R 0-11

NAME	T	AGE	W	L	PCT	SV	G	GS	CG	IP	H	BB	SO	ShO	ERA
		28	70	84	.455	22	154	154	52	1358	1421	569	437	7	4.47
Bobby Shantz	L	25	18	10	.643	0	32	25	13	205	213	70	77	3	3.95
Bob Hooper	R	29	12	10	.545	5	38	23	9	189	192	61	64	0	4.38
Morrie Martin	L	28	11	4	.733	0	35	13	3	138	139	63	35	1	3.78
Alex Kellner	L	26	11	**14**	.440	2	33	29	11	210	218	93	94	1	4.46
Sam Zoldak	L	32	6	10	.375	0	26	18	8	128	127	24	18	1	3.16
Dick Fowler	R	30	5	11	.313	0	22	22	4	125	141	72	29	0	5.62
Johnny Kucab	R	31	4	3	.571	4	30	1	0	75	76	23	23	0	4.20
1 Hank Wyse	R	33	1	2	.333	0	9	1	0	15	24	8	5	0	7.80
Joe Coleman	R	28	1	6	.143	1	28	9	1	96	117	59	34	0	6.00
Carl Scheib	R	24	1	12	.077	10	46	11	3	143	132	71	49	0	4.47
1 Lou Brissie	L	27	0	2	.000	0	2	2	0	13	20	8	3	0	6.92
Moe Burtschy (EJ)	R	29	0	0	.000	0	7	0	0	17	18	12	4	0	5.29
1 Charlie Harris	R	25	0	0	.000	0	3	0	0	4	4	5	2	0	9.00

***Zernial, also with Chicago, league leader in HR (33), RBI (129), SO (101)**

WASHINGTON 7th 62-92 .403 36 — BUCKY HARRIS

NAME	G by POS	B	AGE	G	AB	R	H	2B	3B	HR	RBI	BB	SO	SB	BA	SA
TOTALS			29	154	5329	672	1399	242	45	54	627	560	515	45	.263	.355
Mickey Vernon	1B137	L	33	141	546	69	160	30	7	9	87	53	45	7	.293	.423
Cass Michaels	2B128	R	25	138	485	59	125	20	4	4	45	61	41	1	.258	.340
Pete Runnels	SS73	L	23	78	273	31	76	12	2	0	25	31	24	0	.278	.337
Eddie Yost	3B152, OF3	R	24	154	568	109	161	**36**	4	12	65	126	55	6	.283	.424
Sam Mele	OF124, 1B15	R	28	143	558	58	153	**36**	7	5	94	32	31	2	.274	.391
Irv Noren	OF126	L	26	129	509	82	142	33	5	8	86	51	35	10	.279	.411
Gil Coan	OF132	L	29	135	538	85	163	25	7	9	62	39	62	8	.303	.426
2 Mike Guerra	C66	R	38	72	214	20	43	2	1	1	20	16	18	4	.201	.234
Sam Dente	SS65, 2B10, 3B5	R	29	88	273	21	65	8	1	0	29	25	10	3	.238	.275
Mike McCormick	OF62	R	34	81	243	31	70	9	3	1	23	29	20	1	.288	.362
Gene Verble	SS28, 2B19, 3B1	R	23	68	177	16	36	3	2	0	15	18	10	1	.203	.243
Sherry Robertson	OF22	R	32	62	111	14	21	2	1	1	10	9	22	2	.189	.252
2 Clyde Kluttz	C44	R	33	53	159	15	49	9	0	1	22	20	8	0	.308	.384
Mickey Grasso	C49	R	31	52	175	16	36	3	0	1	14	14	17	0	.206	.240
Dan Porter	OF3	L	19	13	19	2	4	0	0	0	0	2	4	0	.211	.211
Frank Campos	OF7	L	27	8	26	4	11	3	1	0	3	0	1	0	.423	.615
Willie Miranda	SS2, 1B1	B	25	7	9	2	4	0	0	0	0	0	0	0	.444	.444

Roy Hawes 24 L 1-6, Len Okrie 27 R 1-8, Frank Sacka 26 R 4-16, Fred Taylor 26 L 2-12

NAME	T	AGE	W	L	PCT	SV	G	GS	CG	IP	H	BB	SO	ShO	ERA
		32	62	92	.403	13	154	154	58	1366	1429	630	475	6	4.49
Connie Marrero	R	40	11	9	.550	0	25	25	16	187	198	71	66	2	3.90
2 Bob Porterfield	R	27	9	8	.529	0	19	19	10	133	109	54	53	3	3.25
Sandy Consuegra	R	30	7	8	.467	3	40	12	5	146	140	63	31	0	4.01
2 Don Johnson	R	24	7	11	.389	0	21	20	8	144	138	58	52	1	3.94
Mickey Harris	L	34	6	8	.429	4	41	0	0	87	87	43	47	0	3.83
Julio Moreno	R	30	5	11	.313	2	31	18	5	133	132	80	37	0	4.87
Sid Hudson	R	36	5	12	.294	0	23	19	8	139	168	52	43	0	5.12
1 Bob Kuzava	L	28	3	3	.500	0	8	8	3	52	57	28	22	0	5.54
Al Sima	L	29	3	7	.300	0	18	8	1	77	79	41	26	0	4.79
2 Tom Ferrick	R	36	2	0	1.000	2	22	0	0	42	36	7	17	0	2.36
2 Fred Sanford	R	31	2	3	.400	0	7	7	0	37	51	27	12	0	6.57
Joe Haynes	R	33	1	4	.200	2	26	3	1	73	85	37	18	0	4.56
2 Dick Starr	R	30	1	7	.125	0	11	11	1	61	76	24	17	0	5.61
Bob Ross	L	22	0	1	.000	0	11	1	0	32	36	21	23	0	6.47
Alton Brown	R	26	0	0	.000	0	7	0	0	12	14	12	7	0	9.00
2 Hank Wyse	R	33	0	0	.000	0	3	2	0	9	17	10	3	0	10.00
1 Gene Bearden	L	30	0	0	.000	0	1	1	0	3	6	2	1	0	15.00

ST. LOUIS 8th 52-102 .338 46 — ZACK TAYLOR

NAME	G by POS	B	AGE	G	AB	R	H	2B	3B	HR	RBI	BB	SO	SB	BA	SA
TOTALS			27	154	5219	611	1288	223	47	86	555	521	**693**	35	.247	.357
Hank Arft	1B97	L	29	112	345	44	90	16	5	7	42	41	34	4	.261	.397
Bobby Young	2B147	L	26	147	611	75	159	13	9	1	31	44	51	8	.260	.316
Bill Jennings	SS64	R	25	64	195	20	35	10	2	0	13	26	42	1	.179	.251
Freddie Marsh	3B117, SS3, 2B2	R	27	130	445	44	108	21	4	4	43	36	56	4	.243	.335
Ken Wood	OF100	R	27	109	333	40	79	19	0	15	44	27	49	1	.237	.429
Jim Delsing	OF124	L	25	131	449	59	112	20	2	8	45	56	39	2	.249	.356
1 Ray Coleman	OF87	L	29	91	341	41	96	16	5	5	55	24	32	3	.282	.402
Sherm Lollar	C85, 3B1	R	26	98	310	44	78	21	0	8	44	43	26	1	.252	.397
2 Matt Batts	C64	R	29	79	248	26	75	17	1	5	31	21	21	2	.302	.440
Johnny Bero	SS55, 2B1	L	28	61	160	24	34	5	0	5	17	26	30	1	.213	.338
2 Cliff Mapes	OF53	L	29	56	201	32	55	7	2	7	30	26	33	0	.274	.433
Tom Upton	SS47	R	24	52	131	9	26	4	3	0	12	12	22	1	.198	.275
Ned Garver	P33	R	25	49	95	8	29	6	1	1	9	9	9	0	.305	.421
3 Jack Maguire	OF26, 3B5, 2B2	R	26	41	127	15	31	2	1	1	14	12	21	1	.244	.299
Johnny Berardino	3B31, 2B2, 1B1, OF1	R	34	39	119	13	27	7	1	0	13	17	18	1	.227	.303
2 Dale Long	1B28, OF1	L	25	34	105	11	25	5	1	2	11	10	22	0	.238	.362
Roy Sievers (SJ)	OF25	R	24	31	89	10	20	2	1	1	11	9	21	0	.225	.303
1 Don Lenhardt	OF27, 1B1	R	28	31	103	9	27	3	0	5	18	6	13	1	.262	.437
Bennie Taylor	1B25	L	26	33	93	14	24	2	1	3	6	9	22	1	.258	.398
2 Earl Rapp	OF25	L	30	26	98	14	32	5	3	2	14	11	11	1	.327	.500
3 Paul Lehner	OF18	L	31	21	67	2	9	5	0	1	2	6	5	0	.134	.254
Frank Saucier	OF3	L	25	18	14	4	1	1	0	0	1	3	4	0	.071	.143
1 Les Moss	C12	R	26	16	47	5	8	2	0	1	7	6	8	0	.170	.277
Bob Nieman	OF11	R	24	12	43	6	16	3	1	2	8	3	5	0	.372	.628

Billy DeMars 25 R 1-4, Jim Dyck 29 R 1-15, Eddie Gaedel 26 R 0-0, 2 Mike Goliat 25 R 2-11, 1 Clyde Kluttz 33 R 2-4,
Joe Lutz 26 L 6-36, Bud Thomas 22 R 7-20, 2 Kermit Wahl 28 R 9-27, Owen Friend (MS) 24, Dick Kokos (MS) 23

NAME	T	AGE	W	L	PCT	SV	G	GS	CG	IP	H	BB	SO	ShO	ERA
		28	52	**102**	.338	9	154	154	56	1370	**1525**	**801**	550	5	5.17
Ned Garver	R	25	20	12	.625	0	33	30	**24**	246	237	96	84	1	3.73
Duane Pillette	R	28	6	**14**	.300	0	35	24	6	191	205	115	65	1	4.99
Jim McDonald	R	24	4	7	.364	1	16	11	5	84	84	46	28	0	4.07
Al Widmar	R	26	4	9	.308	0	26	16	4	108	157	52	28	0	6.50
2 Tommy Byrne	L	31	4	10	.286	0	19	17	7	123	104	***114**	57	2	3.80
Satchel Paige	R	44	3	4	.429	5	23	3	0	62	67	29	48	0	4.79
3 Fred Sanford	R	31	2	4	.333	0	9	7	1	27	37	23	7	0	10.33
2 Bob Mahoney	R	23	2	5	.286	0	30	4	0	81	86	41	30	0	4.44
1 Dick Starr	R	30	2	5	.286	0	15	9	0	62	66	42	26	0	7.40
2 Bobby Hogue	R	30	1	1	.500	1	18	0	0	30	31	23	11	0	5.10
Duke Markell	R	27	1	1	.500	0	5	2	1	21	25	20	10	0	6.43
Bill Kennedy	L	30	1	5	.167	0	19	5	1	56	76	37	29	0	5.79
1 Stubby Overmire	L	32	1	6	.143	0	8	7	3	53	61	21	13	0	3.57
Lou Sleater	L	24	1	9	.100	1	20	8	4	81	88	53	33	0	5.11
1 Don Johnson	R	24	0	1	.000	0	6	3	0	15	27	18	8	0	12.60
Bob Turley	R	20	0	1	.000	0	1	1	0	7	11	3	5	0	7.71
Cliff Fannin	L	27	0	2	.000	0	7	1	0	15	20	5	11	0	6.60
Irv Medlinger	L	24	0	0	.000	0	6	0	0	10	10	12	5	0	8.10
1 Sid Schacht	R	33	0	0	.000	1	6	0	0	6	14	5	4	0	21.00
Jim Suchecki	R	24	0	6	.000	0	29	6	0	90	113	42	47	0	5.40
Tito Herrera	R	24	0	0	.000	0	3	0	0	2	6	4	1	0	31.50

Dave Madison (MS)30

***Byrne, also with New York, league leader in BB with 150**

NEW YORK 1st 98-59 .624 — **LEO DUROCHER (Defeated Brooklyn in playoff 2 games to 1)**

NAME	G by POS	B	AGE	G	AB	R	H	2B	3B	HR	RBI	BB	SO	SB	BA	SA
TOTALS			27	157	5360	781	1396	201	53	179	734	671	624	55	.260	.418
Whitey Lockman	1B119, OF34	L	24	153	614	85	173	27	7	12	73	50	32	4	.282	.407
Eddie Stanky	2B140	R	34	145	515	88	127	17	2	14	43	127	63	8	.247	.369
Al Dark	SS156	R	29	156	646	114	196	41	7	14	69	42	39	12	.303	.454
Hank Thompson	3B71	L	25	87	264	37	62	8	4	8	33	43	23	1	.235	.386
Don Mueller	OF115	L	24	122	469	58	130	10	7	16	69	19	13	1	.277	.431
Willie Mays	OF121	R	20	121	464	59	127	22	5	20	68	56	60	7	.274	.472
Monte Irvin	OF112, 1B39	R	32	151	558	94	174	19	11	24	121	89	44	12	.312	.514
Wes Westrum	C122	R	28	124	361	59	79	12	0	20	70	104	93	1	.219	.418
Bobby Thomson	OF77, 3B69	R	27	148	518	89	152	27	8	32	101	73	57	5	.293	.562
Ray Noble	C41	R	29	55	141	16	33	6	0	5	26	6	26	0	.234	.383
Bill Rigney	3B12, 2B9	R	32	44	69	9	16	2	0	4	9	8	7	0	.232	.435
Davey Williams	2B22	R	23	30	64	17	17	1	0	2	8	5	8	1	.266	.375
Spider Jorgensen	OF11, 3B1	L	31	28	51	5	12	0	0	2	8	3	2	0	.235	.353
Sal Yvars	C23	R	27	25	41	9	13	2	0	2	3	5	7	0	.317	.512
Lucky Lohrke	3B17, SS1	R	27	23	40	3	8	0	0	1	3	10	2	0	.200	.275
Clint Hartung	OF12	R	28	21	44	4	9	1	0	0	2	1	9	0	.205	.227
Artie Wilson	2B3, SS3, 1B2	L	30	19	22	2	4	0	0	0	1	2	1	2	.182	.182
1 Jack Maguire	OF8	R	26	16	20	6	8	1	1	1	4	2	2	0	.400	.700
1 Earl Rapp		L	30	13	11	0	1	0	0	0	1	2	3	0	.091	.091

2 Hank Schenz 32 R 0-0, Sammy Calderone (MS) 25

NAME	T	AGE	W	L	PCT	SV	G	GS	CG	IP	H	BB	SO	ShO	ERA
		28	98	59	.624	18	157	157	64	1413	1334	482	625	9	3.48
Sal Maglie	R	34	23	6	.793	4	42	37	22	298	254	86	146	3	2.93
Larry Jansen	R	30	23	11	.676	0	39	34	18	279	254	56	145	3	3.03
Jim Hearn	R	30	17	9	.654	0	34	34	11	211	204	82	66	0	3.63
George Spencer	R	24	10	4	.714	6	57	4	2	132	125	56	36	0	3.75
Dave Koslo	L	31	10	9	.526	3	39	16	5	150	153	45	54	2	3.30
Sheldon Jones	R	29	6	11	.353	4	41	12	2	120	119	52	58	0	4.28
Al Corwin	R	24	5	1	.833	1	15	8	3	59	49	21	30	1	3.66
Roger Bowman	L	23	2	4	.333	0	9	5	0	26	35	22	24	0	6.23
Al Gettel	R	33	1	2	.333	0	30	1	0	57	52	25	36	0	4.89
Monte Kennedy	L	29	1	2	.333	0	29	5	1	68	68	31	22	0	2.25
1 Jack Kramer	R	33	0	0	.000	0	4	1	0	5	11	3	2	0	14.40
Alex Konikowski	R	23	0	0	.000	0	3	0	0	4	2	0	5	0	0.00
George Bamberger	R	25	0	0	.000	0	2	0	0	2	4	2	1	0	18.00
Red Hardy	R	28	0	0	.000	0	2	0	0	1	4	1	0	0	9.00

BROOKLYN 2nd 97-60 .618 1 — **CHUCK DRESSEN (Defeated by New York in playoff 2 games to 1)**

NAME	G by POS	B	AGE	G	AB	R	H	2B	3B	HR	RBI	BB	SO	SB	BA	SA
TOTALS			29	158	5492	855	1511	249	37	184	794	603	649	89	.275	.434
Gil Hodges	1B158	R	27	158	582	118	156	25	3	40	103	93	99	9	.268	.527
Jackie Robinson	2B150	R	32	153	548	106	185	33	7	19	88	79	27	25	.338	.527
Pee Wee Reese	SS154	R	32	154	616	94	176	20	8	10	84	81	57	20	.286	.393
Billy Cox	3B139, SS1	R	31	142	455	62	127	25	4	9	51	37	30	5	.279	.411
Carl Furillo	OF157	R	29	158	667	93	197	32	4	16	91	43	33	8	.295	.427
Duke Snider	OF150	L	24	150	606	96	168	26	6	29	101	62	97	14	.277	.483
2 Andy Pafko	OF78	R	30	84	277	42	69	11	0	18	58	35	27	1	.249	.484
Roy Campanella	C140	R	29	143	505	90	164	33	1	33	108	53	51	1	.325	.590
Don Thompson	OF61	L	27	80	118	25	27	3	0	0	6	12	12	2	.229	.254
Cal Abrams	OF34	L	27	67	150	27	42	8	0	3	19	36	26	3	.280	.393
Rocky Bridges	3B40, 2B10, SS9	R	23	63	134	13	34	7	0	1	15	10	10	0	.254	.328
2 Wayne Terwilliger	2B24, 3B1	R	26	37	50	11	14	1	0	0	4	8	7	1	.280	.300
2 Rube Walker	C23	L	25	36	74	6	18	4	0	2	9	6	14	0	.243	.378
1 Hank Edwards		L	32	35	31	1	7	3	0	0	3	4	9	0	.226	.323
1 Gene Hermanski	OF19	L	31	31	80	8	20	4	0	1	5	10	12	0	.250	.338
Dick Williams	OF15	R	22	23	60	5	12	3	1	1	5	4	10	0	.200	.333
1 Eddie Miksis	3B6, 2B1	R	24	19	10	6	2	1	0	0	0	1	2	0	.200	.300
1 Bruce Edwards	C14	R	27	17	36	6	9	2	0	1	8	1	3	0	.250	.389
Jim Russell	OF4	B	32	16	13	2	0	0	0	0	0	4	6	0	.000	.000
1 Tommy Brown	OF5	R	23	11	25	2	4	2	0	0	1	2	4	0	.160	.240

Wayne Belardi 20 L 1-3, Mickey Livingston 36 R 2-5

NAME	T	AGE	W	L	PCT	SV	G	GS	CG	IP	H	BB	SO	ShO	ERA
		27	97	60	.618	13	158	158	64	1423	1360	549	693	10	3.88
Preacher Roe	L	36	22	3	.880	0	34	33	19	258	247	64	113	2	3.03
Don Newcombe	R	25	20	9	.690	0	40	36	18	272	235	91	164	3	3.28
Carl Erskine	R	24	16	12	.571	4	46	19	7	190	208	78	95	0	4.46
Clyde King	R	26	14	7	.667	6	48	3	1	121	118	50	33	0	4.17
Ralph Branca	R	25	13	12	.520	3	42	27	13	204	180	85	118	3	3.26
Clem Labine	R	24	5	1	.833	0	14	6	5	65	52	20	39	2	2.22
Bud Podbielan	R	27	2	2	.500	0	27	5	1	80	67	36	26	0	3.49
Erv Palica	R	23	2	6	.250	0	19	8	0	53	55	20	15	0	4.75
1 Joe Hatten	L	34	1	0	1.000	0	11	6	0	49	55	21	22	0	4.59
Chris Van Cuyk	L	24	1	2	.333	0	9	6	0	29	33	11	16	0	5.59
1 Johnny Schmitz	L	30	1	4	.200	0	16	7	0	56	55	28	20	0	5.30
Phil Haugstad	R	27	0	1	.000	0	21	1	0	31	28	24	22	0	6.39
Dan Bankhead	R	31	0	1	.000	0	7	1	0	14	27	14	9	0	15.43
Earl Mossor	R	25	0	0	.000	0	3	0	0	2	2	7	1	0	27.00

Joe Landrum (VR) 22
Billy Loes (MS) 21

ST. LOUIS 3rd 81-73 .526 15.5 — **MARTY MARION (XJ)**

NAME	G by POS	B	AGE	G	AB	R	H	2B	3B	HR	RBI	BB	SO	SB	BA	SA
TOTALS			30	155	5317	683	1404	230	57	95	629	569	492	30	.264	.382
Nippy Jones	1B71	R	26	80	300	20	79	12	0	3	41	9	13	1	.263	.333
Red Schoendienst	2B124, SS9	B	28	135	553	88	160	32	7	6	54	35	23	0	.289	.405
Solly Hemus	SS105, 2B12	L	28	120	420	68	118	18	9	2	32	75	31	7	.281	.381
2 Billy Johnson	3B124	R	32	124	442	52	116	23	1	14	64	46	49	5	.262	.414
Enos Slaughter	OF106	L	35	123	409	48	115	17	8	4	64	67	25	7	.281	.391
Peanuts Lowery	OF85, 3B11, 2B3	R	32	114	370	52	112	19	5	5	40	35	12	0	.303	.422
Stan Musial	OF91, 1B60	L	30	152	578	124	205	30	12	32	108	98	40	4	.355	.614
Del Rice	C120	R	28	122	374	34	94	13	1	9	47	34	26	0	.251	.364
2 Wally Westlake	OF68	R	30	73	267	36	68	8	5	6	39	24	42	1	.255	.390
Hal Rice	OF63	L	27	69	236	20	60	12	1	4	38	24	22	0	.254	.364
Chuck Diering	OF44	R	28	64	85	9	22	5	1	0	8	6	15	0	.259	.341
Tommy Glaviano	OF35, 2B9	R	27	54	104	20	19	4	0	1	4	26	18	3	.183	.250
2 Stan Rojek	SS51	R	32	51	186	21	51	7	3	0	14	10	10	0	.274	.344
Bill Sarni	C35	R	23	36	86	7	15	1	0	0	2	9	13	1	.174	.186
1 Joe Garagiola	C23	L	25	27	72	9	14	3	2	2	9	9	7	0	.194	.375
1 Bill Howerton	OF17	L	29	24	65	10	17	4	1	1	4	10	12	0	.262	.400
Steve Bilko	1B19	R	22	21	72	5	16	4	0	2	12	9	10	0	.222	.361
1 Dick Cole	2B14	R	25	15	36	4	7	1	0	0	3	6	5	0	.194	.222
Vern Benson	3B9, OF4	L	26	13	46	8	12	3	1	1	7	6	8	0	.261	.435
Don Richmond	3B11	L	31	12	34	3	3	1	0	1	4	3	3	0	.088	.206
2 Bob Scheffing	C11	R	35	12	18	0	2	0	0	0	2	3	5	0	.111	.111
Eddie Kazak	3B10	R	30	11	33	2	6	2	0	0	4	5	5	0	.182	.242

Don Bollweg 30 L 1-9, Larry Ciaffone 26 R 0-5, 1 Rocky Nelson 26 L 4-18, Jay Van Noy 22 L 0-7, Harry Walker 34 L 8-26, 1 Erv Dusak 30 R 1-2

NAME	T	AGE	W	L	PCT	SV	G	GS	CG	IP	H	BB	SO	ShO	ERA
		29	81	73	.526	23	155	155	58	1388	1391	558	546	9	3.95
Gerry Staley	R	30	19	13	.594	3	42	30	10	227	244	74	67	4	3.81
2 Cliff Chambers	L	29	11	6	.647	0	21	16	9	129	120	56	45	1	3.84
Max Lanier	L	35	11	9	.550	1	31	23	9	160	149	50	59	2	3.26
Harry Brecheen	L	36	8	4	.667	2	24	16	5	139	134	54	57	0	3.24
Joe Presko	R	22	7	4	.636	2	15	12	5	89	86	20	38	0	3.44
Tom Poholsky	R	21	7	13	.350	1	38	26	10	195	204	68	70	1	4.43
Al Brazle	L	37	6	5	.545	7	56	8	5	154	139	60	66	0	3.10
George Munger	R	32	4	6	.400	0	23	11	3	95	106	46	44	0	5.31
Dick Bakelmann	R	24	3	3	.500	3	20	1	0	52	49	31	22	0	3.81
Jackie Collum	L	24	2	1	.667	0	3	2	1	17	11	10	5	1	1.59
Cloyd Boyer	R	23	2	5	.286	1	19	8	1	63	68	46	40	0	5.29
Jack Crimian	R	25	1	0	1.000	1	11	0	0	17	24	8	5	0	9.00
Dan Lewandowski	R	23	0	1	.000	0	2	0	0	1	3	1	1	0	9.00
1 Howie Pollet	L	30	0	3	.000	1	6	2	0	12	10	8	10	0	4.50
1 Ted Wilks	R	35	0	0	.000	1	17*	0	0	18	19	5	5	0	3.00
1 Erv Dusak	R	30	0	0	.000	0	5	0	0	10	14	7	8	0	7.20
Bob Habenicht	R	25	0	0	.000	0	3	0	0	5	5	9	1	0	7.20
Kurt Krieger	R	24	0	0	.000	0	2	0	0	4	6	5	3	0	15.75

*Wilks, also with Pittsburgh, league leader in G with 65.

BOSTON 4th 76-78 .494 20.5 — **BILLY SOUTHWORTH 28-31 .475 TOMMY HOLMES 48-47 .505**

NAME	G by POS	B	AGE	G	AB	R	H	2B	3B	HR	RBI	BB	SO	SB	BA	SA
TOTALS			29	155	5293	723	1385	234	37	130	683	565	617	80	.262	.394
Earl Torgeson	1B155	L	27	155	581	99	153	21	4	24	92	102	70	20	.263	.437
Roy Hartsfield	2B114	R	25	120	450	63	122	11	2	6	31	41	73	7	.271	.344
Buddy Kerr	SS63, 2B5	R	28	69	172	18	32	4	0	1	18	22	20	0	.186	.227
Bob Elliott	3B127	R	34	136	480	73	137	29	2	15	70	65	56	2	.285	.448
Willard Marshall	OF127	L	30	136	469	65	132	24	7	11	62	48	18	0	.281	.433
Sam Jethroe	OF140	B	29	148	572	101	160	29	10	18	65	57	88	35	.280	.460
Sid Gordon	OF122, 3B34	R	33	150	550	96	158	28	1	29	109	80	32	2	.287	.500
Walker Cooper	C90	R	36	109	342	42	107	14	1	18	59	28	18	1	.313	.518
Sibby Sisti	2B52, SS25, 3B6, OF1, 1B1	R	30	114	362	46	101	20	2	2	38	32	50	4	.279	.362
Bob Addis	OF46	L	25	85	199	23	55	7	0	1	24	9	10	3	.276	.327
Ebba St. Claire (BG)	C62	B	29	72	220	22	62	17	2	1	25	12	24	2	.282	.391
Luis Marquez	OF43	R	25	68	122	19	24	5	1	0	11	10	20	4	.197	.254
Johnny Logan	SS58	R	24	62	169	14	37	7	1	0	16	18	13	0	.219	.272
Ray Mueller	C23	R	39	28	70	8	11	2	0	1	9	7	11	0	.157	.229
Tommy Holmes	OF3	L	34	27	29	1	5	2	0	0	5	3	4	0	.172	.241
Luis Olmo	OF16	R	31	21	56	4	11	1	1	0	4	4	4	0	.196	.250
Gene Mauch	SS10, 3B3, 2B2	R	25	19	20	5	2	0	0	0	1	7	4	0	.100	.100

Bob Thorpe 24 R 1-2, Del Crandall (MS) 21

NAME	T	AGE	W	L	PCT	SV	G	GS	CG	IP	H	BB	SO	ShO	ERA
		27	76	78	.494	12	155	155	73	1389	1378	595	604	16	3.75
Warren Spahn	L	30	22	14	.611	0	39	36	26	311	278	109	164	7	2.98
Max Surkont	R	29	12	16	.429	1	37	33	11	237	230	89	110	2	3.99
Chet Nichols	L	20	11	8	.579	2	33	19	12	156	142	69	71	3	2.88
Vern Bickford (BG)	R	30	11	9	.550	0	25	20	12	165	146	76	76	3	3.11
Jim Wilson	R	29	7	7	.500	1	20	15	5	110	131	40	33	0	5.40
1 Johnny Sain	R	33	5	13	.278	1	26	22	6	160	195	45	63	1	4.22
Bob Chipman	L	32	4	3	.571	4	33	0	0	52	59	19	17	0	4.85
Phil Paine	R	21	2	0	1.000	0	21	0	0	35	36	20	17	0	3.09
Dave Cole	R	20	2	4	.333	0	23	7	1	68	64	64	33	0	4.24
Blix Donnelly	R	37	0	1	.000	0	6	0	0	7	8	6	3	0	7.71
George Estock	R	26	0	1	.000	3	37	1	0	60	56	37	11	0	4.35
2 Sid Schacht	R	33	0	2	.000	0	5	0	0	5	6	2	1	0	1.80
Dick Donovan	R	23	0	0	.000	0	8	2	0	14	17	11	4	0	5.14
1 Bobby Hogue	R	30	0	0	.000	0	3	0	0	5	4	3	0	0	5.40
Lew Burdette	R	24	0	0	.000	0	3	0	0	4	6	5	1	0	6.75

Johnny Antonelli (MS)21

PHILADELPHIA 5th 73-81 .474 23.5 — **EDDIE SAWYER**

NAME	G by POS	B	AGE	G	AB	R	H	2B	3B	HR	RBI	BB	SO	SB	BA	SA
TOTALS			28	154	5332	648	1384	199	47	108	609	505	525	63	.260	.375
Eddie Waitkus	1B144	L	31	145	610	65	157	27	4	1	46	53	22	0	.257	.320
Putsy Caballero	2B57, SS3, 3B3	R	23	84	161	15	30	3	2	1	11	12	7	1	.186	.248
Granny Hamner	SS150	R	24	150	589	61	150	23	7	9	72	29	32	10	.255	.363
Willie Jones	3B147	R	25	148	564	79	161	28	5	22	81	60	47	6	.285	.470
Del Ennis	OF144	R	26	144	532	76	142	20	5	15	73	68	42	4	.267	.408
Richie Ashburn	OF154	L	24	154	643	92	221	31	5	4	63	50	37	29	.344	.426
Dick Sisler	OF111	L	30	125	428	46	123	20	5	8	52	40	39	1	.287	.414
Andy Seminick	C91	R	30	101	291	42	66	8	1	11	37	63	67	1	.227	.375
Eddie Pellagrini	2B53, SS8, 3B6	R	33	86	197	31	46	4	5	5	30	23	25	5	.234	.381
Bill Nicholson	OF41	L	36	85	170	23	41	9	2	8	30	25	24	0	.241	.459
Del Wilbur	C73	R	32	84	245	30	68	7	3	8	34	17	26	0	.278	.429
2 Tommy Brown	OF32, 2B14, 1B12, 3B1	R	23	78	196	24	43	2	1	10	32	15	21	1	.219	.393
1 Mike Goliat	2B37, 3B2	R	25	41	138	14	31	2	1	4	15	9	18	0	.225	.341
Jimmy Bloodworth	2B8, 1B6	R	33	21	42	2	6	0	0	0	1	3	9	1	.143	.143
Dick Whitman	OF6	L	30	19	17	0	2	0	0	0	0	0	1	0	.118	.118
Dick Young	2B15	L	23	15	68	7	16	5	0	0	2	3	6	0	.235	.309
Ed Sanicki	OF10	R	26	13	4	1	2	1	0	0	1	1	1	1	.500	.750
Mel Clark	OF7	R	24	10	31	2	10	1	0	1	3	0	3	0	.323	.452

Stan Hollmig 25 R 0-2, Stan Lopata 25 R 0-5, Jackie Mayo 25 L 1-7, Ken Silvestri 35 B 2-9

NAME	T	AGE	W	L	PCT	SV	G	GS	CG	IP	H	BB	SO	ShO	ERA
		29	73	81	.474	15	154	154	57	1385	1373	496	570	19	3.81
Robin Roberts	R	24	21	15	.583	2	44	39	22	315	284	64	127	6	3.03
Bubba Church	R	26	15	11	.577	1	38	33	15	247	246	90	104	4	3.53
Russ Meyer	R	27	8	9	.471	0	28	24	7	168	172	55	65	2	3.48
Ken Heintzelman	L	35	6	12	.333	2	35	12	3	118	119	53	55	1	4.19
Ken Johnson	L	28	5	8	.385	0	20	18	4	106	103	68	58	3	4.58
Jocko Thompson	L	31	4	8	.333	1	29	14	3	119	102	59	60	2	3.86
Jim Konstanty	R	34	4	11	.267	9	58	1	0	116	127	31	27	0	4.03
Andy Hansen	R	26	3	1	.750	0	24	0	0	39	34	7	11	0	2.54
Bob Miller (SA)	R	25	2	1	.667	0	17	3	0	34	47	18	10	0	6.88
Niles Jordan	L	25	2	3	.400	0	5	5	2	37	35	8	11	1	3.16
Milo Candini	R	33	1	0	1.000	0	15	0	0	30	33	18	14	0	6.00
Karl Drews	R	31	1	0	1.000	0	5	3	1	23	29	7	13	0	6.26
Leo Cristante	R	24	1	1	.500	0	10	1	0	22	28	9	6	0	4.91
Lou Possehl	R	25	0	1	.000	0	2	1	0	6	9	3	6	0	6.00
John Brittin	R	27	0	0	.000	0	3	0	0	4	5	6	3	0	9.00

Curt Simmons (MS) 22

CINCINNATI 6th 68-86 .442 28.5 — LUKE SEWELL

NAME	G by POS	B	AGE	G	AB	R	H	2B	3B	HR	RBI	BB	SO	SB	BA	SA
TOTALS			27	155	5285	559	1309	215	33	88	528	415	577	44	.248	.351
Ted Kluszewski	1B154	L	26	154	607	74	157	35	2	13	77	35	33	6	.259	.387
Connie Ryan	2B121, 3B3, 1B2, OF1	R	31	136	473	75	112	17	4	16	53	79	72	11	.237	.391
Virgil Stallcup	SS117	R	29	121	428	33	103	17	2	8	49	6	40	2	.241	.346
Grady Hatton (BG)	3B87, OF2	L	28	96	331	41	84	9	3	4	37	33	32	4	.254	.335
Johnny Wyrostek	OF139	L	31	142	537	52	167	31	3	2	61	54	54	2	.311	.391
Lloyd Merriman	OF102	L	26	114	359	34	87	23	2	5	36	31	34	8	.242	.359
Joe Adcock	OF107	R	23	113	395	40	96	16	4	10	47	24	29	1	.243	.380
Dixie Howell	C73	R	32	77	207	22	52	6	1	2	18	15	34	0	.251	.319
Bobby Adams	3B60, 2B42, OF1	R	29	125	403	57	107	12	5	5	24	43	40	4	.266	.357
Bob Usher	OF90	R	26	114	303	27	63	12	2	5	25	19	36	4	.208	.310
Roy McMillan	SS54, 3B12, 2B1	R	20	85	199	21	42	4	0	1	8	17	26	0	.211	.246
Johnny Pramesa	C63	R	25	72	227	12	52	5	2	6	22	5	17	0	.229	.348
1 Bob Scheffing	C41	R	35	47	122	9	31	2	0	2	14	16	9	0	.254	.320
2 Hank Edwards (HJ)	OF34	L	32	41	127	14	40	9	1	3	20	13	17	0	.315	.472
Ewell Blackwell	P38	R	28	39	82	10	24	3	1	1	6	5	12	0	.293	.390
2 Barney McCosky	OF11	L	32	25	50	2	16	2	1	1	11	4	2	0	.320	.460

Jim Bolger 19 R 0-0, Hobie Landrith 21 L 5-13, Danny Litwhiler 34 R 8-29, Sammy Meeks 28 R 8-35, Wally Post 21 R 9-41, Ted Tappe 20 L 1-3

NAME	T	AGE	W	L	PCT	SV	G	GS	CG	IP	H	BB	SO	ShO	ERA
		29	68	86	.442	**23**	155	155	55	1391	1357	490	584	14	3.70
Ewell Blackwell	R	28	16	15	.516	2	38	32	11	233	204	97	120	2	3.44
Ken Raffensberger	L	33	16	**17**	.485	5	42	33	14	249	232	38	81	5	3.43
Howie Fox	R	39	9	14	.391	2	40	30	9	228	239	69	57	4	3.83
Willie Ramsdell	R	35	9	**17**	.346	0	31	31	10	196	204	70	88	1	4.04
Herm Wehmeier	R	24	7	10	.412	2	39	22	10	185	167	89	93	2	3.70
Frank Smith	R	23	5	5	.500	11	50	0	0	76	65	22	34	0	3.20
Harry Perkowski	L	28	3	6	.333	1	35	7	1	102	96	46	56	0	2.82
Bud Byerly	R	30	2	1	.667	0	40	0	0	66	69	25	28	0	3.27
Kent Peterson	L	25	1	1	.500	0	9	0	0	10	13	8	5	0	6.30
Eddie Erautt	R	26	0	0	.000	0	30	0	0	39	50	23	20	0	5.77
Ed Blake	R	25	0	0	.000	0	3	0	0	4	10	1	1	0	11.25
Jim Blackburn	R	27	0	0	.000	0	2	0	0	4	8	2	1	0	15.75

PITTSBURGH 7th 64-90 .416 32.5 — BILLY MEYER

NAME	G by POS	B	AGE	G	AB	R	H	2B	3B	HR	RBI	BB	SO	SB	BA	SA
TOTALS			28	155	5318	689	1372	218	56	137	648	557	615	29	.258	.397
Jack Phillips	1B53, 3B4	R	29	70	156	12	37	7	3	0	12	15	17	1	.237	.321
Danny Murtaugh	2B65, 3B3	R	33	77	151	9	30	7	0	1	11	16	19	0	.199	.265
George Strickland	SS125, 2B13	R	25	138	454	59	98	12	7	9	47	65	83	4	.216	.333
Pete Castiglione	3B99, SS28	R	30	132	482	62	126	19	4	7	42	34	28	2	.261	.361
Gus Bell	OF145	L	22	149	600	80	167	27	**12**	16	89	42	41	1	.278	.443
Catfish Metkovich	OF69, 1B37	L	29	120	423	51	124	21	3	3	40	28	23	3	.293	.378
Ralph Kiner	OF94, 1B58	R	28	151	531	**124**	164	31	6	**42**	109	**137**	57	2	.309	**.627**
Clyde McCullough	C86	R	34	92	259	26	77	9	2	8	39	27	31	2	.297	.440
2 Bill Howerton	OF53, 3B4	L	29	80	219	29	60	12	2	11	37	26	44	1	.274	.498
Pete Reiser	OF27, 3B5	L	32	74	140	22	38	9	3	2	13	27	20	4	.271	.421
2 Joe Garagiola	C61	L	25	72	212	24	54	8	2	9	35	32	20	4	.255	.439
2 Rocky Nelson	1B32, OF12	L	26	71	195	29	52	7	4	1	14	10	7	1	.267	.359
Monty Basgall	2B55	R	29	55	153	15	32	5	2	0	9	12	14	0	.209	.268
Ed FitzGerald	C38	R	27	55	97	8	22	6	0	0	13	7	10	1	.227	.289
1 Wally Westlake	3B34, OF11	R	30	50	181	28	51	4	0	16	45	9	26	0	.282	.569
Tom Saffell	OF17	L	29	49	65	11	13	0	0	1	5	5	18	1	.200	.246
2 Dick Cole	2B34, SS8	R	25	42	106	9	25	4	0	1	11	15	9	0	.236	.302
Frank Thomas	OF37	R	22	39	148	21	39	9	2	2	16	9	15	0	.264	.392
1 Hank Schenz	2B19, 3B2	R	32	25	61	5	13	1	0	0	3	0	2	0	.213	.230
Ted Beard	OF15	L	30	22	48	7	9	1	0	1	3	6	14	0	.188	.271
Dino Restelli	OF11	R	26	21	38	1	7	1	0	1	3	2	4	0	.184	.289
2 Erv Dusak	OF12, P3, 2B2, 3B2	R	30	21	39	6	12	3	0	1	7	3	11	0	.308	.462

1 Bob Dillinger 32 R 10-43, Harry Fisher 25 R 0-3, 1 Dale Long 25 L 2-12, 2 Jack Maguire 26 R 0-5, Jack Merson 29 R 18-50, 1 Stan Rojek 32 R 3-16, Dick Smith 23 R 8-46, Danny O'Connell (MS) 24

NAME	T	AGE	W	L	PCT	SV	G	GS	CG	IP	H	BB	SO	ShO	ERA
		29	64	90	.416	22	155	155	40	1380	**1479**	**627**	580	9	4.80
Murry Dickson	R	34	20	16	.556	2	45	35	19	289	**294**	101	112	3	4.02
Bill Werle	L	30	8	6	.571	6	59	9	2	150	181	51	57	0	5.64
Mel Queen	R	33	7	9	.438	0	39	21	4	168	149	99	123	1	4.45
Vern Law	R	21	6	9	.400	2	28	14	2	114	109	51	41	1	4.50
Bob Friend	R	20	6	10	.375	0	34	22	3	150	173	68	41	1	4.26
2 Howie Pollet	L	30	6	10	.375	0	21	21	4	129	149	51	47	1	5.02
2 Ted Wilks	R	35	3	5	.375	12	**48***	1	1	83	69	24	43	0	2.82
1 Cliff Chambers	L	29	3	6	.333	0	10	10	2	60	64	31	19	1	5.55
Don Carlsen	R	24	2	3	.400	0	7	6	2	43	50	14	20	0	4.19
Len Yochim	L	22	1	1	.500	0	2	2	0	9	10	11	5	0	8.00
Junior Walsh	R	32	1	4	.200	0	36	1	0	73	92	46	32	0	6.90
Paul LaPalme	L	27	1	5	.167	0	22	8	1	54	79	31	24	1	6.33
Bill Koski	R	19	0	1	.000	0	13	1	0	27	26	28	6	0	6.67
2 Erv Dusak	R	30	0	1	.000	0	3	1	0	7	10	9	2	0	11.57
Joe Muir	L	28	0	2	.000	0	9	1	0	16	11	7	5	0	2.81
Con Dempsey	R	27	0	2	.000	0	3	2	0	7	11	4	3	0	9.00
Paul Pettit	L	19	0	0	.000	0	2	0	0	3	2	1	0	0	3.00

Bill Macdonald (MS) 22

*Wilks, also with St. Louis, league leader in G with 65.

CHICAGO 8th 62-92 .403 34.5 — FRANKIE FRISCH 35-45 .412 — PHIL CAVARRETTA 27-47 .365

NAME	G by POS	B	AGE	G	AB	R	H	2B	3B	HR	RBI	BB	SO	SB	BA	SA
TOTALS			28	155	5307	614	1327	200	47	103	572	477	647	63	.250	.364
Chuck Connors	1B57	L	30	66	201	16	48	5	1	2	18	12	25	4	.239	.303
2 Eddie Miksis	2B102	R	24	102	421	48	112	13	3	4	35	33	36	11	.266	.340
Roy Smalley (BL)	SS74	R	25	79	238	24	55	7	4	8	31	25	53	0	.231	.395
Randy Jackson	3B143	R	25	145	557	78	153	24	6	16	76	47	44	14	.275	.425
Hal Jeffcoat	OF87	R	26	113	278	44	76	20	2	4	27	16	23	8	.273	.403
Frankie Baumholtz	OF140	L	32	146	560	62	159	28	10	2	50	49	36	5	.284	.380
Hank Sauer	OF132	R	32	141	525	77	138	19	4	30	89	45	77	2	.263	.486
Smoky Burgess	C64	L	24	94	219	21	55	4	2	2	20	21	12	2	.251	.315
Phil Cavarretta	1B53	L	34	89	206	24	64	7	1	6	28	27	28	0	.311	.442
2 Gene Hermanski	OF75	L	31	75	231	28	65	12	1	3	20	35	30	0	.281	.381
Bob Ramazzotti	SS51, 2B6, 3B1	R	34	73	158	13	39	5	2	1	15	10	23	0	.247	.323
Jack Cusick	SS56	R	23	65	164	16	29	3	2	2	16	17	29	2	.177	.256
Mickey Owen	C57	R	35	58	125	10	23	6	0	0	15	19	13	1	.184	.232
Bob Borkowski	OF25	R	25	58	89	9	14	1	0	0	10	3	16	0	.157	.169
2 Bruce Edwards	C28, 1B9	R	27	51	141	19	33	9	2	3	17	16	14	1	.234	.390
1 Wayne Terwilliger	2B49	R	26	50	192	26	41	6	0	0	10	29	21	3	.214	.245
1 Andy Pafko	OF48	R	30	49	178	26	47	5	3	12	35	17	10	1	.264	.528
Dee Fondy	1B44	L	26	49	170	23	46	7	2	3	20	11	20	5	.271	.388
1 Rube Walker	C31	L	25	37	107	9	25	4	0	2	5	12	13	0	.234	.327

Harry Chiti 18 R 11-31, Carmen Mauro 24 L 5-29, Fred Richards 23 L 8-27, Bill Serena (BW) 26 R 13-39, Carl Sawatski (MS) 23, Preston Ward (MS) 23

NAME	T	AGE	W	L	PCT	SV	G	GS	CG	IP	H	BB	SO	ShO	ERA
		29	62	**92**	.403	10	155	155	48	1386	1416	572	544	10	4.34
Bob Rush	R	25	11	12	.478	2	37	29	12	211	212	68	129	2	3.84
Dutch Leonard	R	42	10	6	.625	3	41	1	0	82	69	28	30	0	2.63
Bob Kelly	R	23	7	4	.636	0	35	11	4	124	130	55	48	0	4.65
Johnny Klippstein	R	23	6	6	.500	2	35	11	1	124	125	53	56	1	4.28
Frank Hiller	R	30	6	12	.333	1	24	21	6	141	147	31	50	2	4.85
Paul Minner	L	27	6	**17**	.261	1	33	28	14	202	219	64	68	3	3.79
Turk Lown	R	27	4	9	.308	0	31	18	3	127	125	90	39	1	5.46
Cal McLish	R	25	4	10	.286	0	30	17	5	146	159	52	46	1	4.44
Bob Schultz	L	27	3	6	.333	0	17	10	2	77	75	51	27	0	5.26
Monk Dubiel	R	32	2	2	.500	1	22	0	0	55	46	22	19	0	2.29
2 Joe Hatten	L	34	2	6	.250	0	23	6	1	75	82	37	23	0	5.16
1 Johnny Schmitz	L	30	1	2	.333	0	8	3	0	18	22	15	6	0	8.00
Warren Hacker	R	26	0	0	.000	0	2	0	0	1	3	0	2	0	18.00
Andy Varga	L	20	0	0	.000	0	2	0	0	3	2	6	1	0	3.00

WORLD SERIES – NEW YORK (AL) 4 NEW YORK (NL) 2

LINE SCORES

TEAM	1	2	3	4	5	6	7	8	9	10	11	12	R	H	E
Game 1 October 4 at Yankee Stadium															
NY (NL)	2	0	0	0	0	3	0	0	0				5	10	1
NY (AL)	0	1	0	0	0	0	0	0	0				1	7	1
Koslo — **Reynolds**, Hogue (7), Morgan (8)															
Game 2 October 5 at Yankee Stadium															
NY (NL)	0	0	0	0	0	0	1	0	0				1	5	1
NY (AL)	1	1	0	0	0	0	0	1	X				3	6	0
Jansen, Spencer (7) — **Lopat**															
Game 3 October 6 at Polo Grounds															
NY(AL)	0	0	0	0	0	0	0	1	1				2	5	2
NY (NL)	0	1	0	0	5	0	0	0	X				6	7	2
Raschi, Hogue (5), Ostrowski (7) — **Hearn**, Jones (8)															
Game 4 October 8 at Polo Grounds															
NY (AL)	0	1	0	1	2	0	2	0	0				6	12	0
NY (NL)	1	0	0	0	0	0	0	0	1				2	8	2
Reynolds — **Maglie**, Jones (6), Kennedy (9)															
Game 5 October 9 at Polo Grounds															
NY (AL)	0	0	5	2	0	2	4	0	0				13	12	1
NY (NL)	1	0	0	0	0	0	0	0	0				1	5	3
Lopat — **Jansen**, Kennedy (4), Spencer (6), Corwin (7), Konikowski (9)															
Game 6 October 10 at Yankee Stadium															
NY (NL)	0	0	0	0	1	0	0	0	2				3	11	1
NY (AL)	1	0	0	0	0	3	0	0	X				4	7	0
Koslo, Hearn (7), Jansen (8) — **Raschi**, Sain (7), Kuzava (9)															

COMPOSITE BATTING

NAME	POS	G	AB	R	H	2B	3B	HR	RBI	BA
New York (AL)										
Totals		6	199	29	49	7	2	5	25	.246
Rizzuto	SS	6	**25**	5	8	0	0	1	3	.320
DiMaggio	OF	6	23	3	6	2	0	1	5	.261
Berra	C	6	23	4	6	1	0	0	0	.261
McDougald	3B-2B	6	23	2	6	1	0	1	**7**	.261
Collins	1B-OF	6	18	2	4	0	0	1	3	.222
Bauer	OF	6	18	0	3	0	1	0	3	.167
Woodling	OF	6	18	**6**	3	1	1	1	1	.167
Brown	3B	5	14	1	5	1	0	0	0	.357
Coleman	2B	5	8	2	2	0	0	0	0	.250
Lopat	P	2	8	0	1	0	0	0	1	.125
Mize	1B	4	7	2	2	1	0	0	1	.286
Reynolds	P	2	6	0	2	0	0	0	1	.333
Mantle	OF	2	5	1	1	0	0	0	0	.200
Raschi	P	2	2	0	0	0	0	0	0	.000
Sain	P	1	1	0	0	0	0	0	0	.000
Martin	PR	1	0	1	0	0	0	0	0	.000
Hogue	P	2	0	0	0	0	0	0	0	.000
Hopp	PH	1	0	0	0	0	0	0	0	.000

Morgan P 0-0, Ostrowski P 0-0, Kuzava P 0-0

NAME	POS	G	AB	R	H	2B	3B	HR	RBI	BA
New York (NL)										
Totals		6	194	18	46	7	1	2	15	.237
Lockman	1B	6	**25**	1	6	2	0	1	4	.240
Irvin	OF	6	24	3	**11**	0	1	0	2	**.458**
Dark	SS	6	24	5	10	**3**	0	1	4	.417
Mays	OF	6	22	1	4	0	0	0	1	.182
Stanky	2B	6	22	3	3	0	0	0	1	.136
Thomson	3B	6	21	1	5	1	0	0	2	.238
Westrum	C	6	17	1	4	1	0	0	0	.235
Thompson	OF	5	14	3	2	0	0	0	0	.143
Koslo	P	2	5	0	0	0	0	0	0	.000
Rigney	PH	4	4	0	1	0	0	0	1	.250
Hartung	OF	2	4	0	0	0	0	0	0	.000
Hearn	P	2	3	0	0	0	0	0	0	.000
Noble	C	2	2	0	0	0	0	0	0	.000
Lohrke	PH	2	2	0	0	0	0	0	0	.000
Jansen	P	3	2	0	0	0	0	0	0	.000
Yvars	PH	1	1	0	0	0	0	0	0	.000
Williams	PH	2	1	0	0	0	0	0	0	.000
Maglie	P	1	1	0	0	0	0	0	0	.000
Schenz	PR	1	0	0	0	0	0	0	0	.000
Spencer	P	2	0	0	0	0	0	0	0	.000

Jones P 0-0, Kennedy P 0-0, Corwin P 0-0, Konikowski P 0-0

COMPOSITE PITCHING

NAME	G	IP	H	BB	SO	W	L	SV	ERA
New York (AL)									
Totals	6	53	46	25	22	4	2	1	1.87
Lopat	2	**18**	10	3	4	**2**	0	0	**0.50**
Reynolds	2	15	**16**	**11**	**8**	1	1	0	4.20
Raschi	2	10.1	12	8	4	1	1	0	0.87
Hogue	2	2.2	1	0	0	0	0	0	0.00
Morgan	1	2	2	1	3	0	0	0	0.00
Ostrowski	1	2	1	0	1	0	0	0	0.00
Sain	1	2	4	2	2	0	0	0	9.00
Kuzava	1	1	0	0	0	0	0	1	0.00
New York (NL)									
Totals	6	52	49	26	23	2	4	1	4.67
Koslo	2	15	12	7	6	1	1	0	3.00
Jansen	**3**	10	8	4	6	0	**2**	0	6.30
Hearn	2	8.2	5	8	1	1	0	0	1.04
Maglie	1	5	8	2	3	0	1	0	7.20
Jones	2	4.1	5	1	2	0	0	1	2.08
Spencer	2	3.1	6	3	0	0	0	0	18.90
Kennedy	2	3	3	1	4	0	0	0	6.00
Corwin	1	1.2	1	0	1	0	0	0	0.00
Konikowski	1	1	1	0	0	0	0	0	0.00

1952 A Lesson from the Old Professor

After winning three straight world championships, Casey Stengel was up against it as the season opened. Joe DiMaggio, after posting a lifetime .325 batting average, retired. Starting infielders, Bobby Brown and Jerry Coleman, were off to the service along with pitcher Tom Morgan. It was doubtful the Old Professor would achieve a fourth pennant. The experts didn't think so and neither did Cleveland, which was starting the campaign with the best pitching staff in the league.

Except for one demoralizing setback late in April, when St. Louis' Bob Cain bested the Indians' Bob Feller, 1-0, in a double one-hit game and unbelievably put the Browns in first place for a day, Cleveland got off to a fine start. By contrast, the Yankees were well off the pennant road, showing an 18-17 record at the end of May. To further complicate Stengel's life, Ed Lopat, his 1951 ace, hurt the shoulder of his pitching arm and could only post a mediocre 5-5 record when he was shelved at the All-Star break until mid-August.

But Stengel, who seemed to have a direct pipeline to the Gods, took Billy Martin off the bench and plugged up the vacancy Coleman left at second. Gil McDougald, who alternated between second and third in 1951, was made the regular at third and turned in a fine job. And a switch-hitting powerhouse by the name of Mickey Charles Mantle, out of Spavinaw, Oklahoma, took over DiMaggio's chores in center field and quickly blossomed in his second year in the majors, with 23 homers and a .311 batting average.

When Labor Day arrived, the Yankees found themselves 2½ games ahead of the pack but were faced with 18 of their last 21 games on the road compared to runner-up Cleveland, which had 20 of 22 to play at home. Both clubs met in a showdown in mid-September before 73,609 fans—the largest crowd of the season—and the Yankees stopped Mike Garcia, 7-1.

A few days later Bobby Shantz, the A's 5'6", 139-pound wonder southpaw, shook the Yankees, 2-0, to whittle their lead to 1½ games. But Allie Reynolds, who led the league with a 2.06 E.R.A. assured New York of at least a tie when he beat Boston, 3-2, before Lopat and Johnny Sain combined to send them over the top with a 5-2 victory at Philadelphia.

The failure for the Indians came when they could not get together with their long-time ace Bob Feller who, after pitching winning ball for 13 years, ran into a disappointing 9-13 season.

Over in the National League, the Dodgers made good after their humiliating loss in 1951. It was mostly because of Joe Black, a 28-year-old rookie who wasn't even on the roster at spring, and their feasting on the National League's tail—the Pirates, Braves, and Reds—for a combined 54-11 record.

Giant fans thought their team would have no trouble repeating as National League winners after they watched Leo Durocher manage his way to a 16-2 start. Such was not the case, especially when it was remembered that Monte Irvin, the 1951 RBI leader, broke an ankle in spring training and would not be with the team until late in the year. And Willie Mays, the Giants' super soph, would only remain until May when he had to depart for military service. If the Giants could have survived losing two key players, it was doubtful they could have done anything without their aces, Sal Maglie and Larry Jansen, who both suffered back trouble. The arrival of rookie knuckle-baller Hoyt Wilhelm, who posted the best E.R.A. in the league with 2.43, was enough for at least a second-place finish.

As far as the Series was concerned, it took Stengel and his Yankees the full seven games to prove the pre-season experts wrong.

1952 AMERICAN LEAGUE

NEW YORK 1st 95-59 .617 — **CASEY STENGEL**

NAME	G by POS	B	AGE	G	AB	R	H	2B	3B	HR	RBI	BB	SO	SB	BA	SA
TOTALS			27	154	5294	727	**1411**	221	**56**	129	672	566	652	52	**.267**	.403
Joe Collins	1B119	L	29	122	428	69	120	16	8	18	59	55	47	4	.280	.481
Billy Martin (BN)	2B107	R	24	109	363	32	97	13	3	3	33	22	31	3	.267	.344
Phil Rizzuto	SS152	R	34	152	578	89	147	24	10	2	43	67	42	17	.254	.341
Gil McDougald	3B117, 2B38	R	24	152	555	65	146	16	5	11	78	57	73	6	.263	.369
Hank Bauer	OF139	R	29	141	553	86	162	31	6	17	74	50	61	6	.293	.463
Mickey Mantle	OF141, 3B1	B	20	142	549	94	171	37	7	23	87	75	**111**	4	.311	.530
Gene Woodling	OF118	L	29	122	408	58	126	19	6	12	63	59	31	1	.309	.473
Yogi Berra	C140	L	27	142	534	97	146	17	1	30	98	66	24	2	.273	.478
2 Irv Noren	OF60, 1B19	L	27	93	272	36	64	13	2	5	21	26	34	4	.235	.353
Johnny Mize	1B27	L	39	78	137	9	36	9	0	4	29	11	15	0	.263	.416
Jim Brideweser	SS22, 2B4, 3B1	R	25	42	38	12	10	0	0	0	2	3	5	0	.263	.263
Bob Cerv	OF27	R	26	36	87	11	21	3	2	1	8	9	22	0	.241	.356
Bobby Brown (MS)	3B24	L	27	29	89	6	22	2	0	1	14	9	6	1	.247	.303
Charlie Silvera	C20	R	27	20	55	4	18	3	0	0	11	5	2	0	.327	.382
Andy Carey	3B14, SS1	R	20	16	40	6	6	0	0	0	1	3	10	0	.150	.150
1 Johnny Hopp	1B12	L	30	15	25	4	4	0	0	0	2	2	3	2	.160	.160
Jerry Coleman (MS)	2B11	R	27	11	42	6	17	2	1	0	4	5	4	0	.405	.500

Loren Babe 24 L 2-21, Ralph Houk 32 R 2-6, 1 Jackie Jenson 25 R 2-19, Charlie Keller 35 L 0-1, Kal Segrist 21 R 1-23, 1 Archie Wilson 28 R 1-2

NAME	T	AGE	W	L	PCT	SV	G	GS	CG	IP	H	BB	SO	ShO	ERA
		30	**95**	50	**.617**	27	154	154	72	1381	1240	581	666	**17**	**3.14**
Allie Reynolds	R	37	20	8	.714	6	35	29	24	244	194	97	**160**	**6**	**2.07**
Vic Raschi	R	33	16	6	.727	0	31	31	13	223	174	91	127	4	2.78
Johnny Sain	R	34	11	6	.647	7	35	16	8	148	149	38	57	0	3.47
Ed Lopat (SJ)	L	34	10	5	.667	0	20	19	10	149	127	53	56	2	2.54
Bob Kuzava	L	29	8	8	.500	3	28	12	6	133	115	63	67	1	3.45
Tom Gorman	R	27	6	2	.750	1	12	6	1	61	63	22	31	1	4.57
2 Ray Scarborough	R	34	5	1	,833	0	9	4	1	34	27	15	13	0	2.91
Tom Morgan (MS)	R	22	5	4	.556	2	16	12	2	94	86	33	35	1	3.06
Bill Miller	L	24	4	6	.400	0	21	13	5	88	78	49	45	2	3.48
Jim McDonald	R	25	3	4	.429	0	26	5	1	69	71	40	20	0	3.52
1 Bobby Hogue	R	31	3	5	.375	4	27	0	0	47	52	25	12	0	5.36
Joe Ostrowski	L	35	2	2	.500	2	20	1	0	40	56	14	17	0	5.63
2 Ewell Blackwell	R	29	1	0	1.000	1	5	2	0	16	12	12	7	0	0.56
2 Johnny Schmitz	L	31	1	1	.500	1	5	2	1	15	15	9	3	0	3.60
Harry Schaeffer	L	27	0	1	.000	0	5	2	0	17	18	18	15	0	5.29
Art Schallock	L	28	0	0	.000	0	2	0	0	2	3	2	1	0	9.00

Whitey Ford (MS) 23
Bob Wiesler (MS) 21

CLEVELAND 2nd 93-61 .604 2 — **AL LOPEZ**

NAME	G by POS	B	AGE	G	AB	R	H	2B	3B	HR	RBI	BB	SO	SB	BA	SA
TOTALS			29	155	5330	**763**	1399	211	49	**148**	**721**	626	**749**	46	.262	**.404**
Luke Easter	1B118	L	37	127	437	63	115	10	3	31	97	44	84	1	.263	.513
Bobby Avila	2B149	R	28	150	597	102	179	26	**11**	7	45	67	36	12	.300	.415
Ray Boone	SS96, 3B2, 2B1	R	28	103	316	57	83	8	2	7	45	53	33	0	.263	.367
Al Rosen	3B147, 1B4, SS3	R	28	148	567	101	171	32	5	28	**105**	75	54	8	.302	.524
Harry Simpson	OF127, 1B28	L	26	146	545	66	145	21	10	10	65	56	82	5	.266	.396
Larry Doby	OF136	L	28	140	519	**104**	143	26	8	**32**	104	90	**111**	5	.276	**.541**
Dale Mitchell	OF128	L	30	134	511	61	165	26	3	5	58	52	9	6	.323	.415
Jim Hegan	C107	R	31	112	333	39	75	17	2	4	41	29	47	0	.225	.324
Jim Fridley	OF54	R	27	62	175	23	44	2	0	4	16	14	40	3	.251	.331
Barney McCosky	OF19	L	34	54	80	14	17	4	1	1	6	8	5	1	.213	.325
Merrill Combs	SS49, 2B3	L	32	52	139	11	23	1	1	1	10	14	15	0	.165	.209
Bill Glynn	1B32	L	27	44	92	15	25	5	0	2	7	5	16	1	.272	.391
2 Joe Tipton	C35	R	29	43	105	15	26	2	0	6	22	21	21	1	.248	.438
Birdie Tebbetts	C37	R	42	42	101	4	25	4	0	1	8	12	9	0	.248	.317
2 Hank Majeski	3B11, 2B3	R	35	36	54	7	16	2	0	0	9	7	7	0	.296	.333
1 Johnny Berardino	2B8, SS8, 3B4, 1B2	R	35	35	32	5	3	0	0	0	2	10	8	0	.094	.094
Pete Reiser	OF10	B	33	34	44	7	6	1	0	3	7	4	16	1	.136	.364
2 George Strickland	SS30, 2B1	R	26	31	88	8	19	4	0	1	8	14	15	0	.216	.295
3 Wally Westlake	OF28	R	31	29	69	11	16	4	1	1	9	8	16	1	.232	.362
Bob Kennedy (MS)	OF13, 3B3	R	31	22	40	6	12	3	1	0	12	9	5	1	.300	.425
Dave Pope	OF10	L	27	12	34	9	10	1	1	1	4	1	7	0	.294	.471

Snuffy Stirnweiss 33 R 0-0, Quincy Troupe 39 B 1-10, Hal Naragon (MS) 23

NAME	T	AGE	W	L	PCT	SV	G	GS	CG	IP	H	BB	SO	ShO	ERA
		31	93	61	.604	18	155	155	**80**	1407	1278	556	671	**17**	3.32
Early Wynn	R	32	23	12	.657	3	42	33	19	286	239	**132**	153	4	2.90
Mike Garcia	R	28	22	11	.667	4	46	**36**	19	292	**284**	87	143	**6**	2.37
Bob Lemon	R	31	22	11	.667	4	42	**36**	**28**	**310**	236	105	131	5	2.50
Bob Feller	R	33	9	13	.409	0	30	30	11	192	219	83	81	0	4.73
Steve Gromek	R	32	7	7	.500	1	29	13	3	123	109	28	65	1	3.66
2 Mickey Harris	L	35	3	0	1.000	1	29	0	0	47	42	21	23	0	4.60
Lou Brissie	L	28	3	2	.600	2	42	1	0	83	68	34	28	0	3.47
Sam Jones	R	26	2	3	.400	1	14	4	0	36	38	37	28	0	7.25
Dick Rozek	L	25	1	0	1.000	0	10	1	0	13	11	13	5	0	4.85
Bob Chakales	R	24	1	2	.333	0	5	1	0	12	19	8	7	0	9.75
2 Ted Wilks	R	36	0	0	.000	1	7	0	0	12	8	7	6	0	3.75
Bill Abernathie	R	23	0	0	.000	1	1	0	0	2	4	1	0	0	13.50
George Zuverink	R	27	0	0	.000	0	1	0	0	1	1	0	1	0	0.00

Al Aber (MS) 24
Dick Weik (MS) 24

CHICAGO 3rd 81-73 .526 14 — **PAUL RICHARDS**

NAME	G by POS	B	AGE	G	AB	R	H	2B	3B	HR	RBI	BB	SO	SB	BA	SA
TOTALS			29	156	5316	610	1337	199	38	80	560	541	521	**61**	.252	.348
Eddie Robinson	1B155	L	31	155	594	79	176	33	1	22	104	70	49	2	.296	.466
Nellie Fox	2B151	L	24	152	**648**	76	**192**	25	10	0	39	34	14	5	.296	.366
Chico Carrasquel (BG)	SS99	R	24	100	359	36	89	7	4	1	42	33	27	2	.248	.298
Hector Rodriquez	3B113	R	32	124	407	55	108	14	0	1	40	47	22	7	.265	.307
2 Sam Mele	OF112, 1B3	R	29	123	423	46	105	18	2	14	59	48	40	1	.248	.400
2 Jim Rivera	OF53	L	29	53	201	27	50	7	3	3	18	21	27	13	.249	.358
Minnie Minoso	OF143, 3B9, SS1	R	29	147	569	96	160	24	9	13	61	71	46	**22**	.281	.424
Sherm Lollar	C120	R	27	132	375	35	90	15	0	13	50	54	34	1	.240	.384
Bud Stewart	OF60	L	36	92	225	23	60	10	0	5	30	28	17	3	.267	.378
1 Ray Coleman	OF73	L	30	85	195	19	42	7	1	2	14	13	17	0	.215	.292
13 Willie Miranda	SS54, 3B5, 2B1	B	26	70	150	14	33	4	1	0	7	13	14	1	.220	.260
Sam Dente	SS27, 3B18, 2B6, OF6, 1B2	R	30	62	145	12	32	0	1	0	11	5	8	0	.221	.234
2 Tom Wright	OF34	L	28	60	132	15	34	10	2	1	21	16	16	1	.258	.386
Rocky Krsnich	3B37	R	24	40	91	11	21	7	2	1	15	12	9	0	.231	.385
1 Al Zarilla	OF32	L	33	39	99	14	23	4	1	2	7	14	6	1	.232	.354
Bud Sheely	C31	L	31	36	75	1	18	2	0	0	3	12	7	0	.240	.267
Phil Masi	C25	R	35	30	63	9	16	1	1	0	7	10	10	0	.254	.302
2 Darrell Johnson	C21	R	23	22	37	3	4	0	0	0	1	5	9	1	.108	.108
2 Leo Thomas	3B9	R	27	19	24	1	4	0	0	0	6	6	4	0	.167	.167

1 Jim Busby 25 R 5-39, 2 Hank Edwards 33 L 6-18, Sammy Esposito (MS) 20 R 1-4, Ken Landenberger 23 L 1-5, Don Nicholas 21 L 0-2, 1 George Wilson 26 L 1-9, Red Wilson 23 R 0-3, Herb Adams (MS) 24, Joe Kirrene (MS) 20, Bill Wilson (MS) 23

NAME	T	AGE	W	L	PCT	SV	G	GS	CG	IP	H	BB	SO	ShO	ERA
		29	81	73	.526	**28**	156	156	53	1417	1251	578	**774**	13	3.25
Billy Pierce	L	25	15	12	.556	1	33	32	14	255	214	79	144	4	2.58
Saul Rogovin	R	29	14	9	.609	1	33	30	12	232	224	79	121	3	3.84
Joe Dobson	R	35	14	10	.583	1	29	25	11	201	164	60	101	3	2.51
Marv Grissom	R	34	12	10	.545	0	28	24	7	166	156	79	97	1	3.74
Harry Dorish	R	30	8	4	.667	**11**	39	1	1	91	66	42	47	0	2.47
Chuck Stobbs	L	22	7	12	.368	1	38	17	2	135	118	72	73	0	3.13
Lou Kretlow	R	29	4	4	.500	1	19	11	4	79	52	56	63	2	2.96
Luis Aloma (SA)	R	29	3	1	.750	6	25	0	0	40	42	11	18	0	4.28
Bill Kennedy	L	31	2	2	.500	5	**47**	1	0	71	54	38	46	0	2.79
Hal Brown	R	27	2	3	.400	0	24	8	1	72	82	21	31	0	4.25
Howie Judson	R	26	0	1	.000	1	21	0	0	34	30	22	15	0	4.24
1 Ken Holcombe	R	33	0	5	.000	0	7	7	1	35	38	18	12	0	6.17
2 Hal Hudson	L	25	0	0	.000	0	2	0	0	4	7	1	4	0	2.25
Al Widmar	R	27	0	0	.000	0	1	0	0	2	4	0	2	0	4.50

PHILADELPHIA 4th 79-75 .513 16 — JIMMY DYKES

NAME	G by POS	B	AGE	G	AB	R	H	2B	3B	HR	RBI	BB	SO	SB	BA	SA
TOTALS			31	155	5163	664	1305	212	35	89	634	683	561	52	.253	.359
Ferris Fain	1B144	L	31	145	538	82	176	43	3	2	59	105	26	3	.327	.429
Skeeter Kell	2B68	R	22	75	213	24	47	8	3	0	17	14	18	5	.221	.286
Eddie Joost	SS146	R	36	146	540	94	132	26	3	20	75	122	94	5	.244	.415
Billy Hitchcock	3B104, 1B13	R	35	119	407	45	100	8	4	1	56	39	45	1	.246	.292
Elmer Valo	OF121	L	31	129	388	69	109	26	4	5	47	101	16	12	.281	.407
Dave Philley	OF149, 3B2	B	32	151	586	80	154	25	4	7	71	59	35	11	.263	.355
Gus Zernial	OF141	R	29	145	549	76	144	15	1	29	100	70	87	5	.262	.452
Joe Astroth	C102	R	29	104	337	24	84	7	2	1	36	25	27	2	.249	.291
Kite Thomas	OF29	R	28	75	116	24	29	6	1	6	18	20	27	0	.250	.474
Pete Suder	2B43, SS17, 3B16	R	36	74	228	22	55	7	2	1	20	16	17	1	.241	.303
Allie Clark (BW)	OF48, 1B2	R	29	71	186	23	51	12	0	7	29	10	19	0	.274	.452
3 Cass Michaels	2B55	R	26	55	200	22	50	4	5	1	18	23	11	3	.250	.335
Ray Murray	C42	R	34	44	136	14	28	5	0	1	10	9	13	0	.206	.265
2 Sherry Robertson	2B8, OF7, 3B2	R	33	43	60	8	12	3	0	0	5	21	15	1	.200	.250
1 Hank Majeski	3B34	R	35	34	117	14	30	2	2	2	20	19	10	0	.256	.359
1 Joe Tipton	C23	R	29	23	68	6	13	4	0	3	8	15	10	0	.191	.382

2 Hal Bevan (BL) 21 R 6-17, Tom Hamilton 26 L 2-10, Jack Littrell 23 R 0-2

NAME	T	AGE	W	L	PCT	SV	G	GS	CG	IP	H	BB	SO	ShO	ERA
		29	79	75	.513	16	155	155	73	1384	1402	526	562	11	4.16
Bobby Shantz	L	26	24	7	.774	0	33	33	27	280	230	63	152	5	2.48
Harry Byrd	R	27	15	15	.500	2	37	28	15	228	244	98	116	3	3.32
Alex Kellner	L	27	12	14	.462	0	34	33	14	231	223	86	105	2	4.36
Bob Hooper	R	25	8	15	.348	6	43	14	4	144	158	68	40	0	5.19
Carl Scheib	R	30	11	7	.611	2	30	19	8	158	153	50	42	1	4.39
2 Bobo Newsom	R	44	3	3	.500	1	14	5	1	48	38	23	22	0	3.59
Ed Wright	R	33	2	1	.667	1	24	0	0	41	55	20	9	0	6.59
Charlie Bishop	R	28	2	2	.500	0	6	5	1	31	29	24	17	0	6.39
Marion Fricano	R	28	1	0	1.000	0	2	0	0	5	5	1	0	0	1.80
Dick Fowler	R	31	1	2	.333	0	18	3	1	59	71	28	14	0	6.41
Johnny Kucab	R	32	0	1	.000	2	25	0	0	51	64	20	17	0	5.29
Morrie Martin (BG)	L	29	0	2	.000	0	5	5	0	25	32	15	13	0	6.48
Sam Zoldak	L	33	0	6	.000	1	16	10	2	75	86	25	12	0	4.08
Tex Hoyle	R	30	0	0	.000	0	3	0	0	2	9	1	1	0	31.50
Walt Kellner	R	23	0	0	.000	1	1	0	0	4	4	3	2	0	6.75
Len Matarazzo	R	23	0	0	.000	0	1	0	0	1	1	1	0	0	0.00

WASHINGTON 5th 78-76 .506 17 — BUCKY HARRIS

NAME	G by POS	B	AGE	G	AB	R	H	2B	3B	HR	RBI	BB	SO	SB	BA	SA
TOTALS			29	157	5357	598	1282	225	44	50	555	580	607	48	.239	.326
Mickey Vernon	1B153	L	34	154	569	71	143	33	9	10	80	89	66	7	.251	.394
Floyd Baker	2B68, SS7, 3B1	L	35	79	263	27	69	8	0	0	33	30	17	1	.262	.293
Pete Runnels	SS147, 2B1	L	24	152	555	70	158	18	3	1	64	72	55	0	.285	.333
Eddie Yost	3B157	R	25	157	587	92	137	32	3	12	49	129	73	4	.233	.359
2 Jackie Jensen	OF143	R	25	144	570	80	163	29	5	10	80	63	40	17	.286	.407
2 Jim Busby	OF128	R	25	129	512	58	125	24	4	2	47	22	48	5	.244	.318
Gil Coan	OF86	L	30	107	332	50	68	11	6	5	20	32	35	9	.205	.319
Mickey Grasso	C114	R	32	115	361	22	78	9	0	0	27	29	36	1	.216	.241
Mel Hoderlein	2B58	B	29	72	208	16	56	8	2	0	17	18	22	2	.269	.327
2 Ken Wood	OF56	R	28	61	210	26	50	8	6	6	32	30	21	0	.238	.419
Clyde Kluttz	C52	R	34	58	144	7	33	5	0	1	11	12	11	0	.229	.285
Frank Campos	OF23	L	28	53	112	9	29	6	1	0	8	1	13	0	.259	.330
2 Earl Rapp	OF10	L	31	46	67	7	19	6	0	0	9	6	13	0	.284	.373
Jerry Snyder	2B19, SS4	R	22	36	57	5	9	2	0	0	2	5	8	1	.158	.193
2 Archie Wilson	OF24	R	28	26	96	8	20	2	3	0	14	5	11	0	.208	.292
1 Cass Michaels	2B22	R	25	22	86	10	20	4	1	1	7	7	15	0	.233	.337

George Bradshaw 27 R 5-23, Hal Keller 24 L 4-23, 2 Freddie Marsh 28 R 1-24, 1 Sam Mele 29 R 12-28, 1 Irv Noren 27 L 12-49,
1 Sherry Robertson 33 R 0-0, Fred Taylor 27 L 5-19, Tom Upton 25 R 0-5, Buck Varner 21 L 0-4, Don Porter (MS) 20, Bob Ross (MS) 23

NAME	T	AGE	W	L	PCT	SV	G	GS	CG	IP	H	BB	SO	ShO	ERA
		32	78	76	.506	15	157	157	75	1430	1405	577	574	10	3.37
Bob Porterfield	R	28	13	14	.481	0	31	29	15	231	222	85	80	3	2.73
Spec Shea	R	31	11	7	.611	0	22	21	12	169	144	92	65	2	2.93
Connie Marrero	R	41	11	8	.579	0	22	22	16	184	175	53	77	2	2.89
2 Walt Masterson	R	32	9	8	.529	2	24	21	11	161	153	72	89	0	3.69
Julio Moreno	R	31	9	9	.500	0	26	22	7	147	154	52	62	0	3.98
Sandy Consuegra	R	31	6	0	1.000	5	30	2	0	74	80	27	19	0	3.04
2 Lou Sleater	L	25	4	2	.667	0	14	9	3	57	56	30	22	1	3.63
Tom Ferrick	R	37	4	3	.571	1	27	0	0	51	53	11	28	0	3.00
2 Randy Gumpert	R	34	4	9	.308	0	20	12	2	104	112	30	29	0	4.24
1 Sid Hudson	R	37	3	4	.429	0	7	7	6	63	59	29	24	0	2.71
Mike Fornieles	R	20	2	2	.500	0	4	2	2	26	13	11	12	1	1.38
1 Bobo Newsom	R	44	1	1	.500	2	10	0	0	13	16	9	5	0	4.85
Raul Sanchez	R	21	1	1	.500	0	3	2	1	13	13	7	6	1	3.85
Joe Haynes	R	34	0	3	.000	3	22	2	0	66	70	35	18	0	4.50
Don Johnson	R	25	0	5	.000	2	29	6	0	69	80	33	37	0	4.43
1 Mickey Harris	L	35	0	0	.000	0	1	0	0	1	1	0	0	0	9.00
Harley Grossman	R	22	0	0	.000	0	1	0	0	1	2	0	0	0	18.00
Bunky Stewart	L	21	0	0	.000	0	1	0	0	1	2	1	1	0	18.00

BOSTON 6th 76-78 .494 19 — LOU BOUDREAU

NAME	G by POS	B	AGE	G	AB	R	H	2B	3B	HR	RBI	BB	SO	SB	BA	SA
TOTALS			27	154	5246	668	1338	233	34	113	628	542	739	59	.255	.377
Dick Gernert	1B99	R	23	102	367	58	89	20	2	19	67	35	83	4	.243	.463
Billy Goodman	2B103, 1B23, 3B5, OF4	L	26	138	513	79	157	27	3	4	56	48	23	8	.306	.394
2 Johnny Lipon	SS69, 3B7	R	29	79	234	25	48	8	1	0	18	32	20	1	.205	.248
2 George Kell	3B73	R	29	75	276	41	88	15	2	6	40	31	10	0	.319	.453
Faye Throneberry	OF86	L	21	98	310	38	80	11	3	5	23	33	67	16	.258	.361
Dom DiMaggio	OF123	R	35	128	486	81	143	20	1	6	33	57	61	6	.294	.377
2 Hoot Evers (BG)	OF105	R	31	106	401	53	105	17	4	14	59	29	55	5	.262	.429
Sammy White	C110	R	23	115	381	35	107	20	2	10	49	16	43	2	.281	.423
Vern Stephens (KJ)	SS53, 3B29	R	31	92	295	35	75	13	2	7	44	39	31	2	.254	.383
Clyde Vollmer	OF70	R	30	90	250	35	66	12	4	11	50	39	47	2	.264	.476
Ted Lepcio	2B57, 3B25, SS1	R	21	84	274	34	72	17	2	5	26	24	41	3	.263	.394
Jimmy Piersall (IL)	SS30, OF22, 3B1	R	22	56	161	28	43	8	0	1	16	28	26	3	.267	.335
2 Del Wilber	C39	R	33	47	135	7	36	10	1	3	23	7	20	1	.267	.422
2 George Schmees	OF29, 1B2, P2	L	27	42	64	8	13	3	0	0	3	10	11	0	.203	.250
1 Walt Dropo	1B35	R	29	37	132	13	35	7	1	6	27	11	22	0	.265	.470
1 Don Lenhardt	OF27	R	29	30	105	18	31	4	0	7	24	15	18	0	.295	.533
Gus Niarhos	C25	R	31	29	58	4	6	0	0	0	4	12	9	0	.103	.103
1 Johnny Pesky	3B19, SS2	L	32	25	67	10	10	2	0	0	2	15	5	0	.149	.179
Gene Stephens	OF13	L	19	21	53	10	12	5	0	0	5	3	8	4	.226	.321
3 Al Zarilla	OF19	L	33	21	60	9	11	0	1	2	8	7	8	2	.183	.317
1 Fred Hatfield	3B17	L	27	19	25	6	8	1	1	1	3	4	2	0	.320	.560

1 Hal Bevan 21 R 0-1, Milt Bolling 21 R 8-36, Lou Boudreau 34 R 0-2, Paul Lehner 32 L 2-3, Charlie Maxwell 25 L 1-15, Len Okrie 28 R 0-1,
Ted Williams (MS) 33 L 4-10, 3 Archie Wilson 28 R 10-30, 1 Ken Wood 28 R 2-20, Karl Olson (MS) 21, Norm Zauchin (MS) 22

NAME	T	AGE	W	L	PCT	SV	G	GS	CG	IP	H	BB	SO	ShO	ERA
		30	76	78	.494	24	154	154	53	1372	1332	623	624	7	3.80
Mel Parnell	L	30	12	12	.500	2	33	29	15	214	207	89	107	3	3.62
Mickey McDermott	L	23	10	9	.526	0	30	21	7	162	139	92	117	2	3.72
2 Dizzy Trout	R	37	9	8	.529	1	26	17	2	134	133	68	57	0	3.63
2 Sid Hudson	R	37	7	9	.438	0	21	18	7	134	145	36	50	0	3.63
Willard Nixon	R	24	5	4	.556	0	23	13	5	104	115	61	50	0	4.85
Bill Henry	L	24	5	4	.556	0	13	10	5	77	75	36	23	0	3.86
Dick Brodowski	R	19	5	5	.500	0	20	12	4	115	111	50	42	0	4.38
Ellis Kinder	R	37	5	6	.455	4	23	10	4	98	85	28	50	0	2.57
Al Benton	R	41	4	3	.571	6	24	0	0	38	37	17	20	0	2.37
Ike Delock	R	22	4	9	.308	5	39	7	1	95	88	50	46	1	4.26
Ralph Brickner	R	27	3	1	.750	1	14	1	0	33	32	11	9	0	2.18
1 Bill Wight	L	30	2	1	.667	0	10	2	0	24	14	14	5	0	3.00
1 Randy Gumpert	R	34	1	0	1.000	0	10	1	0	20	15	5	6	0	4.05
Hersh Freeman	R	24	1	0	1.000	0	4	1	1	14	13	5	5	0	3.21
Harry Taylor	R	33	1	0	1.000	0	2	1	1	10	6	6	1	0	1.80
1 Walt Masterson	R	32	1	1	.500	0	5	1	0	9	18	11	3	0	12.00
1 Ray Scarborough	R	34	1	5	.167	4	28	8	1	77	79	35	29	1	4.79
Jim Atkins	R	31	0	1	.000	0	3	1	0	10	11	7	2	0	3.60
2 George Schmees	L	27	0	0	.000	0	2	1	0	6	9	2	2	0	3.00
Leo Kiely (MS) 22															

ST. LOUIS 7th 64-90 .416 31 — ROGERS HORNSBY 22-28 .440 MARTY MARION 42-62 .404

NAME	G by POS	B	AGE	G	AB	R	H	2B	3B	HR	RBI	BB	SO	SB	BA	SA
TOTALS			27	155	5353	604	1340	225	46	82	574	540	720	30	.250	.356
Dick Kryhoski	1B86	L	27	111	342	38	83	13	1	11	42	23	42	2	.243	.383
Bobby Young	2B149	L	27	149	575	59	142	15	9	4	39	56	48	3	.247	.325
Joe DeMaestri	SS77, 3B1, 2B1	R	23	81	186	13	42	9	1	1	18	8	25	0	.226	.301
Jim Dyck	3B74, OF48	R	30	122	402	60	108	22	3	15	64	50	68	0	.269	.450
Bob Nieman	OF125	R	25	131	478	66	138	22	2	18	74	46	73	0	.289	.456
1 Jim Rivera	OF88	L	29	97	336	45	86	13	6	4	30	29	59	8	.256	.366
1 Jim Delsing	OF85	L	26	93	298	34	76	13	6	1	34	25	29	3	.255	.349
Clint Courtney	C113	L	25	119	413	38	118	24	3	5	50	39	26	0	.286	.395
13Freddie Marsh	SS60, 3B21, 2B9	R	28	87	247	28	69	9	1	2	27	27	33	3	.279	.348
Gordon Goldsberry	1B72, OF2	L	24	86	227	30	52	9	3	3	17	34	37	0	.229	.335
Marty Marion	SS63	R	34	67	186	16	46	11	0	2	19	19	17	0	.247	.339
2 Cass Michaels	3B42, 2B8	R	26	55	166	21	44	8	2	3	25	23	16	1	.265	.392
Les Moss	C39	R	27	52	118	11	29	3	0	3	12	15	13	0	.246	.347
2 Al Zarilla	OF35	L	33	48	130	20	31	6	0	1	9	27	15	1	.238	.308
1 Leo Thomas	3B37, SS3, 2B1	R	27	41	124	12	29	5	1	0	12	17	7	2	.234	.290
2 Vic Wertz	OF36	L	27	37	130	22	45	5	0	6	19	23	20	0	.346	.523
1 George Schmees	OF19, 1B2	L	27	34	61	9	8	1	1	0	3	2	18	0	.131	.180
Jay Porter	OF29, 3B2	R	19	33	104	12	26	4	1	0	7	10	10	4	.250	.308
1 Earl Rapp	OF7	L	31	30	49	3	7	4	0	0	4	0	8	0	.143	.224
1 Darrell Johnson	C22	R	23	29	78	9	22	2	1	0	9	11	4	0	.282	.333

Hank Arft (PB) 30 L 4-28, Rufus Crawford 24 R 2-11, Mike Goliat 26 R 0-4 Gene Bearden 31 L 23-65, 3 Don Lenhardt 29 R 13-48, 2 Ray Coleman 30 L 9-46, 2 Willie Miranda 26 B 1-11,
Stan Rojek 33 R 1-7, Roy Sievers (BC) 25 R 6-30, 1 Tom Wright 28 L 16-66, Owen Friend (MS) 25, Dick Kokos (MS) 24, Frank Saucier (MS) 26

NAME	T	AGE	W	L	PCT	SV	G	GS	CG	IP	H	BB	SO	ShO	ERA
		32	64	90	.416	18	155	155	48	1399	1388	598	581	6	4.12
Satchel Paige	R	45	12	10	.545	10	46	6	3	138	116	57	91	2	3.07
Bob Cain	L	27	12	10	.545	2	29	27	8	170	169	62	70	1	4.13
Duane Pillette	R	29	10	13	.435	0	30	30	9	205	222	55	62	1	3.60
Gene Bearden	L	31	7	8	.467	0	34	16	3	151	158	78	45	0	4.29
1 Ned Garver	R	26	7	10	.412	0	21	21	7	149	130	55	60	2	3.68
Tommy Byrne	L	32	7	14	.333	0	29	24	14	196	182	112	91	0	4.68
1 Dave Madison	R	31	4	2	.667	0	31	4	0	78	78	48	35	0	4.38
2 Dick Littlefield	L	26	2	3	.400	0	7	5	3	46	35	17	34	0	2.74
Earl Harrist	R	32	2	8	.200	5	36	9	1	117	119	47	49	0	4.00
2 Marlin Stuart	R	33	1	2	.333	1	12	2	0	26	26	9	13	0	4.15
2 Bobby Hogue	R	31	0	1	.000	0	8	1	0	16	10	13	2	0	2.76
1 Lou Sleater	L	25	0	1	.000	0	4	2	0	9	9	5	1	0	7.00
Johnny Hetki	R	30	0	1	.000	0	3	1	0	9	15	2	4	0	4.00
2 Ken Holcombe	R	33	0	2	.000	0	12	1	0	21	20	9	7	0	3.86
Cliff Fannin	L	28	0	2	.000	0	10	2	0	16	34	9	6	0	12.94
Stubby Overmire	L	33	0	3	.000	0	17	4	0	41	44	7	10	0	3.73
1 Hal Hudson	L	25	0	0	.000	0	3	0	0	6	9	6	0	0	12.00
Bob Mahoney	R	24	0	0	.000	0	3	0	0	3	8	4	1	0	18.00
Pete Taylor	R	24	0	0	.000	0	1	0	0	2	4	3	0	0	13.50
Bob Turley (MS) 21															

DETROIT 8th 50-104 .325 45 — RED ROLFE 23-49 .319 FRED HUTCHINSON 27-55 .329

NAME	G by POS	B	AGE	G	AB	R	H	2B	3B	HR	RBI	BB	SO	SB	BA	SA
TOTALS			30	156	5258	557	1278	190	37	103	529	553	605	27	.243	.352
2 Walt Dropo	1B115	R	29	115	459	56	128	17	3	23	70	26	63	2	.279	.479
Jerry Priddy (BL)	2B75	R	32	75	279	37	79	23	3	4	20	43	29	1	.283	.430
Neil Berry	SS66, 3B2	R	30	73	189	22	43	4	3	0	13	22	19	1	.228	.280
2 Fred Hatfield	3B107, SS9	L	27	112	441	42	104	12	2	2	25	35	51	2	.236	.286
1 Vic Wertz	OF79	L	27	85	285	46	70	15	3	17	51	46	44	1	.246	.498
Johnny Groth	OF139	R	25	141	524	56	149	22	2	4	51	51	39	2	.284	.357
Pat Mullin	OF65	L	34	97	255	29	64	13	5	7	35	31	30	4	.251	.424
Joe Ginsberg	C101	L	25	113	307	29	68	13	2	6	36	51	21	1	.221	.336
Steve Souchock	OF56, 3B13, 1B9	R	33	92	265	40	66	16	4	13	45	21	28	1	.249	.487
Cliff Mapes	OF62	L	30	86	193	26	38	7	0	9	23	27	42	0	.197	.373
Al Federoff	2B70, SS7	R	27	74	231	14	56	4	2	0	14	16	13	1	.242	.277
2 Johnny Pesky	SS41, 2B22, 3B3	L	32	69	177	26	45	4	0	1	9	41	11	1	.254	.294
Don Kolloway	1B32, 2B8	R	33	65	173	19	42	9	0	2	21	7	19	0	.243	.329
Matt Batts (IL)	C55	R	30	56	173	11	41	4	1	3	13	14	22	1	.237	.324
2 Don Lenhardt	OF43	R	29	45	144	18	27	2	1	3	13	28	18	0	.188	.278
2 Johnny Hopp	OF4, 1B1	L	35	42	46	5	10	1	0	0	3	6	7	0	.217	.239
1 George Kell	3B39	R	29	39	152	11	45	8	0	1	17	14	13	0	.296	.368
1 Johnny Lipon	SS39	R	29	39	136	17	30	4	2	0	12	16	6	3	.221	.279
2 Jim Delsing	OF32	L	26	33	113	14	31	2	1	3	11	15	8	1	.274	.389

1 Hoot Evers 31 R 1-1, Alex Garbowski 27 R 0-0, Harvey Kuenn 21 R 26-80, George Lerchen 29 B 5-32, Carl Linhart 22 L 0-2, Don Lund 29 R 7-23,
Russ Sullivan 29 L 17-52, Bob Swift 37 R 8-58, Bennie Taylor 27 L 3-18, Bill Tuttle 22 R 6-25, Frank House (MS) 22

NAME	T	AGE	W	L	PCT	SV	G	GS	CG	IP	H	BB	SO	ShO	ERA
		29	50	104	.325	14	156	156	51	1388	1394	591	702	10	4.25
Ted Gray	L	27	12	17	.414	0	35	32	13	224	212	101	138	2	4.14
Hal Newhouser	L	31	9	9	.500	0	25	19	8	154	148	47	57	0	3.74
Art Houtteman	R	24	8	20	.286	1	35	28	10	221	218	65	109	2	4.36
2 Bill Wight	L	30	5	9	.357	0	23	19	8	144	167	55	65	3	3.88
Virgil Trucks	R	33	5	19	.208	1	35	29	8	197	190	82	129	3	3.97
1 Marlin Stuart	R	33	3	2	.600	1	30	9	2	91	91	48	32	0	4.95
Fred Hutchinson	R	32	2	1	.667	0	12	1	0	37	40	9	12	0	3.41
Billy Hoeft	L	20	2	7	.222	4	34	10	1	125	123	63	67	0	4.32
2 Ned Garver	R	26	1	0	1.000	0	1	1	1	9	9	3	3	0	2.00
2 Dave Madison	R	31	1	1	.500	0	10	1	0	15	16	10	7	0	7.80
1 Dizzy Trout	R	37	1	5	.167	1	10	2	0	27	30	19	20	0	5.33
Hal White	R	33	1	8	.111	5	41	0	0	63	53	39	18	0	3.71
Bill Black	R	19	0	1	.000	0	2	2	0	8	14	5	0	0	10.13
Dick Marlowe	R	23	0	2	.000	0	4	1	0	11	21	3	3	0	7.36
1 Dick Littlefield	L	26	0	3	.000	1	28	1	0	48	46	25	32	0	4.31
Ken Johnson	L	29	0	0	.000	0	9	1	0	11	12	11	10	0	6.55
Wayne McLeland	R	27	0	0	.000	0	4	0	0	3	4	6	0	0	9.00
Ray Herbert (MS) 22															

BROOKLYN 1st 96-57 .627 — CHUCK DRESSEN

NAME	G by POS	B	AGE	G	AB	R	H	2B	3B	HR	RBI	BB	SO	SB	BA	SA
TOTALS			30	155	5266	775	1380	199	32	153	725	663	699	90	.262	.399
Gil Hodges	1B153	R	28	153	508	87	129	27	1	32	102	107	90	2	.254	.500
Jackie Robinson	2B146	R	33	149	510	104	157	17	3	19	75	106	40	24	.308	.465
Pee Wee Reese	SS145	R	33	149	559	94	152	18	8	6	58	86	59	30	.272	.365
Billy Cox (EJ)	3B100, SS10, 2B9	R	32	116	455	56	118	12	3	6	34	25	32	10	.259	.338
Carl Furillo	OF131	R	30	134	425	52	105	18	1	8	59	31	33	1	.247	.351
Duke Snider	OF141	L	25	144	534	80	162	25	7	21	92	55	77	7	.303	.494
Andy Pafko	OF139, 3B13	R	31	150	551	76	158	17	5	19	85	64	48	4	.287	.439
Roy Campanella	C122	R	30	128	468	73	126	18	1	22	97	57	59	8	.269	.453
George Shuba	OF67	L	27	94	256	40	78	12	1	9	40	38	29	1	.305	.465
Bobby Morgan	3B60, 2B5, SS4	R	26	67	191	36	45	8	0	7	16	46	35	2	.236	.387
Rocky Bridges	2B24, SS13, 3B6	R	24	51	56	9	11	3	0	0	2	7	9	0	.196	.250
Rube Walker	C40	L	26	46	139	9	36	8	0	1	19	8	17	0	.259	.338
Rocky Nelson	1B5	L	27	37	39	6	10	1	0	0	3	7	4	0	.256	.282
Dick Williams (JJ)	OF25, 1B1, 3B1	R	23	36	68	13	21	4	1	0	11	2	10	0	.309	.397
2 Tommy Holmes	OF6	L	35	31	36	2	4	1	0	0	1	4	4	0	.111	.139
Sandy Amoros	OF10	L	22	20	44	10	11	3	1	0	3	5	14	1	.250	.364
1 Cal Abrams	OF1	L	28	10	10	1	2	0	0	0	0	2	4	0	.200	.200
Steve Lembo	C2	R	25	2	5	0	1	0	0	0	1	0	1	0	.200	.200

NAME	T	AGE	W	L	PCT	SV	G	GS	CG	IP	H	BB	SO	ShO	ERA
		27	96	57	.627	24	155	155	45	1399	1295	544	773	11	3.53
Joe Black	R	28	15	4	.789	15	56	2	1	142	102	41	85	0	2.15
Carl Erskine	R	25	14	6	.700	2	33	26	10	207	167	71	131	4	2.70
Billy Loes	R	22	13	8	.619	1	39	21	8	187	154	71	115	4	2.70
Preacher Roe	L	37	11	2	.846	0	27	25	8	159	163	39	83	2	3.11
Ben Wade	R	29	11	9	.550	3	37	24	5	180	166	94	118	1	3.60
Clem Labine	R	25	8	4	.667	0	25	9	0	77	76	47	43	0	5.14
Johnny Rutherford	R	27	7	7	.500	2	22	11	4	97	97	29	29	0	4.27
Chris Van Cuyk	L	25	5	6	.455	1	23	16	4	98	104	40	66	0	5.14
Ralph Branca (SA)	R	26	4	2	.667	0	16	7	2	61	52	21	26	0	3.84
Clyde King	R	27	2	0	1.000	0	23	0	0	43	56	12	17	0	5.02
Jim Hughes	R	29	2	1	.667	0	6	0	0	19	16	11	8	0	1.42
1 Johnny Schmitz	L	31	1	1	.500	0	10	3	1	33	29	18	11	0	4.36
Ray Moore	R	26	1	2	.333	0	14	2	0	28	29	26	11	0	4.82
Ken Lehman	L	24	1	2	.333	0	4	3	0	15	19	6	7	0	5.40
Joe Landrum	R	23	1	3	.250	0	9	5	2	38	46	10	17	0	5.21
Ron Negray	R	22	0	0	.000	0	4	1	0	13	15	5	5	0	3.46
1 Bud Podbielan	R	28	0	0	.000	0	3	0	0	2	4	3	1	0	18.00

Don Newcombe (MS) 26
Erv Palica (MS) 24

NEW YORK 2nd 92-62 .597 4.5 — LEO DUROCHER

NAME	G by POS	B	AGE	G	AB	R	H	2B	3B	HR	RBI	BB	SO	SB	BA	SA
TOTALS			27	154	5229	722	1337	186	56	151	663	536	672	30	.256	.399
Whitey Lockman	1B154	L	25	154	606	99	176	17	4	13	58	67	52	2	.290	.396
Davey Williams	2B138	R	24	138	540	70	137	26	3	13	55	48	63	2	.254	.385
Al Dark	SS150	R	30	151	589	92	177	29	3	14	73	47	39	6	.301	.431
Bobby Thomson	[illegible]	[illegible]	[illegible]	[illegible]	608	89	164	29	14	24	108	52	74	5	.270	.482
Don Mueller	OF120	L	25	126	456	61	128	14	7	12	49	34	24	2	.281	.421
Hank Thompson	OF72, 3B46, 2B4	L	26	128	423	67	110	13	9	17	67	50	38	4	.260	.454
Bob Elliott	OF65, 3B13	R	35	98	272	33	62	6	2	10	35	36	20	1	.228	.375
Wes Westrum	C112	R	29	114	322	47	71	11	0	14	43	76	68	1	.220	.385
Dusty Rhodes	OF56	L	25	67	176	34	44	8	1	10	36	23	33	1	.250	.477
Sal Yvars	C59	R	28	66	151	15	37	3	0	4	18	10	16	0	.245	.344
2 George Wilson	OF21, 1B2	L	26	62	112	9	27	7	0	2	16	3	14	0	.241	.357
Bill Rigney	3B10, 2B9, SS4, 1B1	R	33	60	90	15	27	5	1	1	14	11	6	2	.300	.411
Monte Irvin (BN)	OF32	R	33	46	126	10	39	2	1	4	21	10	11	0	.310	.437
Chuck Diering	OF36	R	29	41	23	2	4	1	1	0	2	4	3	0	.174	.304
Willie Mays (MS)	OF34	R	21	34	127	17	30	2	4	4	23	16	17	4	.236	.409
Bobby Hofman	2B21, 3B2, 1B1	R	26	32	63	11	18	2	2	2	4	8	10	0	.286	.476
Clint Hartung	OF24	R	29	28	78	6	17	2	1	3	8	9	24	0	.218	.385
2 Bill Howerton	OF3	L	30	11	15	2	1	1	0	0	1	3	2	0	.067	.133
Ray Katt	C8	R	25	9	27	4	6	0	0	0	1	1	5	1	.222	.222
Daryl Spencer	SS3, 3B3	R	22	7	17	0	5	0	1	0	3	1	4	0	.294	.412
Ray Noble	C5	R	30	6	5	0	0	0	0	0	0	0	1	0	.000	.000

Dick Wakefield 31 L 0-2, Sammy Calderone (MS) 26

NAME	T	AGE	W	L	PCT	SV	G	GS	CG	IP	H	BB	SO	ShO	ERA
		30	92	62	.597	31	154	154	49	1371	1282	538	655	12	3.59
Sal Maglie	R	35	18	8	.692	1	35	31	12	216	199	75	112	5	2.92
Hoyt Wilhelm	R	28	15	3	.833	11	71	0	0	159	127	57	108	0	2.43
Jim Hearn	R	31	14	7	.667	1	37	34	11	224	208	97	89	1	3.78
Larry Jansen (XJ)	R	31	11	11	.500	2	34	27	8	167	183	47	74	1	4.10
Dave Koslo	L	[illegible]	10	7	[illegible]	[illegible]	41	17	8	166	154	47	67	2	3.20
Max Lanier	L	36	7	12	.368	5	37	16	6	137	124	65	47	1	3.94
Al Corwin	R	25	6	1	.857	2	21	7	1	68	58	36	36	0	2.65
Bill Connelly	R	27	5	0	1.000	0	11	4	0	32	22	25	22	0	4.50
Monte Kennedy	L	30	3	4	.429	0	31	6	2	83	73	31	48	1	3.04
George Spencer	R	25	3	5	.375	3	35	4	0	60	57	21	27	0	5.55
Hal Gregg	R	30	0	1	.000	1	16	4	1	36	42	17	13	0	4.75
Mario Picone	R	25	0	1	.000	0	2	1	0	9	11	5	3	0	7.00
Jack Harshman	L	24	0	2	.000	0	2	2	0	6	12	6	6	0	15.00
George Bamberger	R	26	0	0	.000	0	5	0	0	4	6	6	0	0	9.00
Roger Bowman	L	24	0	0	.000	0	2	1	0	3	6	3	3	0	12.00

Alex Konikowski (MS) 24

ST. LOUIS 3rd 88-66 .571 8.5 — EDDIE STANKY

NAME	G by POS	B	AGE	G	AB	R	H	2B	3B	HR	RBI	BB	SO	SB	BA	SA
TOTALS			31	154	5200	677	1386	247	54	97	643	537	479	33	.267	.391
2 Dick Sisler	1B114	L	31	119	418	48	109	14	5	13	60	29	35	3	.261	.411
Red Schoendienst	2B142, 3B11, SS3	B	29	152	620	91	188	40	7	7	67	42	30	9	.303	.424
Solly Hemus	SS148, 3B2	L	29	151	570	105	153	28	8	15	52	96	55	1	.268	.425
Billy Johnson	3B89	R	33	94	282	23	71	10	2	2	34	34	21	1	.252	.323
Enos Slaughter	OF137	L	36	140	510	73	153	17	12	11	101	70	25	6	.300	.445
Stan Musial	OF135, 1B25, P1	L	31	154	578	105	194	42	6	21	91	96	29	7	.336	.538
Peanuts Lowery	OF106, 3B6	R	33	132	374	48	107	18	2	1	48	34	13	3	.286	.353
Del Rice	C147	R	29	147	495	43	128	27	2	11	65	33	38	0	.259	.388
Hal Rice	OF81	L	28	98	295	37	85	14	5	7	45	16	26	1	.288	.441
Tommy Glaviano	3B52, 2B1	R	28	80	162	30	39	5	1	3	19	27	26	0	.241	.340
Eddie Stanky	2B20	R	35	53	83	13	19	4	0	0	7	19	9	0	.229	.277
Larry Miggins	OF25, 1B1	R	26	42	96	7	22	5	1	2	10	3	19	0	.229	.365
Les Fusselman	C32	R	31	32	63	5	10	3	0	1	3	0	9	0	.159	.254
2 Virgil Stallcup	SS12	R	30	29	31	4	4	1	0	0	1	1	5	0	.129	.161
1 Wally Westlake	OF20	R	31	21	74	7	16	3	0	0	10	8	11	1	.216	.257
Vern Benson (BL)	3B15	L	27	20	47	6	9	2	0	2	5	5	9	0	.191	.362
Steve Bilko (BA)	1B20	R	23	20	72	7	19	6	1	1	6	4	15	0	.264	.417
Gene Mauch	SS2	R	26	7	3	0	0	0	0	0	0	1	2	0	.000	.000
1 Eddie Kazak	3B1	R	31	3	2	1	0	0	0	0	0	0	0	0	.000	.000
Bill Sarni	C3	R	24	3	5	0	1	0	0	0	0	0	1	0	.200	.200

Neal Hertweck 20 L 0-6, Herb Gorman 27 L 0-1

NAME	T	AGE	W	L	PCT	SV	G	GS	CG	IP	H	BB	SO	ShO	ERA
		29	88	66	.571	27	154	154	49	1361	1274	501	712	12	3.66
Gerry Staley	R	31	17	14	.548	0	35	33	15	240	238	52	93	0	3.26
Eddie Yuhas	R	27	12	2	.857	6	54	2	0	99	90	35	39	0	2.73
Al Brazle	L	38	12	5	.706	16	46	6	3	109	75	42	55	2	2.72
Vinegar Bend Mizell	L	21	10	8	.556	0	30	30	7	190	171	103	146	2	3.65
Harry Brecheen	L	37	7	5	.583	2	25	13	4	100	82	28	54	1	3.33
Joe Presko	R	23	7	10	.412	0	28	18	5	147	140	57	63	1	4.04
Stu Miller	R	24	6	3	.667	0	12	11	6	88	63	26	64	2	2.05
Cloyd Boyer	R	24	6	6	.500	0	23	14	4	110	108	47	44	2	4.25
Cliff Chambers	L	30	4	4	.500	1	26	13	2	98	110	33	47	1	4.13
Mike Clark	R	30	2	0	1.000	0	12	4	0	25	32	14	10	0	6.12
Harvey Haddix	L	26	2	2	.500	0	7	6	3	42	31	10	31	0	2.79
Willard Schmidt	R	24	2	3	.400	1	18	3	0	35	36	18	30	0	5.14
2 Bill Werle	L	31	1	2	.333	1	19	0	0	39	40	15	23	0	4.85
Dick Bokelmann	R	25	0	1	.000	0	11	0	0	13	20	7	5	0	9.00
1 George Munger	R	33	0	1	.000	0	1	1	0	4	7	1	1	0	13.50
Bobby Tiefenauer	R	22	0	0	.000	0	6	0	0	8	12	7	3	0	7.88
Hack Crimian	R	26	0	0	.000	0	5	0	0	8	15	4	4	0	10.13
Jackie Collum	L	25	0	0	.000	0	2	0	0	3	2	1	0	0	0.00
Fred Hahn	L	23	0	0	.000	0	1	0	0	2	2	1	0	0	0.00
Stan Musial	L	31	0	0	.000	0	1	0	0	0	0	0	0	0	0.00

Tom Poholsky (MS)22

PHILADELPHIA 4th 87-67 .565 9.5 — EDDIE SAWYER 28-35 .444 STEVE O'NEILL 59-32 .648

NAME	G by POS	B	AGE	G	AB	R	H	2B	3B	HR	RBI	BB	SO	SB	BA	SA
TOTALS			28	154	5205	657	1353	237	45	93	606	540	534	60	.260	.376
Eddie Waitkus	1B143	L	32	146	499	51	144	29	4	2	49	64	23	2	.289	.375
Connie Ryan	2B154	R	32	154	577	81	139	24	6	12	49	69	72	13	.241	.366
Granny Hamner	SS151	R	25	151	596	74	164	30	5	17	87	27	51	7	.275	.428
Willie Jones	3B147	R	26	147	541	60	135	12	3	18	72	53	36	5	.250	.383
2 Johnny Wyrostek	OF88	L	32	98	321	45	88	16	3	1	37	44	26	1	.274	.352
Richie Ashburn	OF154	L	25	154	613	93	173	31	6	1	42	75	30	16	.282	.357
Del Ennis	OF149	R	27	151	592	90	171	30	10	20	107	47	65	6	.289	.475
Smoky Burgess	C104	L	25	110	371	49	110	27	2	6	56	49	21	3	.296	.429
Stan Lopata	C55	R	26	57	179	25	49	9	1	4	27	36	33	1	.274	.402
Bill Nicholson	OF19	L	37	55	88	17	24	3	0	6	19	14	26	0	.273	.511
Jackie Mayo	OF27, 1B6	L	26	50	119	13	29	5	0	1	4	12	17	1	.244	.311
Mel Clark	OF38, 3B1	R	25	47	155	20	52	6	4	1	15	6	13	2	.335	.445
Putsy Caballero	SS8, 2B7, 3B7	R	24	35	42	10	10	3	0	0	6	2	3	1	.238	.310
Lucky Lohrke	SS5, 3B3, 2B1	R	28	25	29	4	6	0	0	0	1	4	3	0	.207	.207
1 Tommy Brown	OF3, 1B3	R	24	18	25	2	4	1	0	1	2	4	3	0	.160	.320
Nippy Jones	1B8	R	27	8	30	3	5	0	0	1	5	0	4	0	.167	.267
Dick Young	2B2	B	24	5	9	3	2	1	0	0	0	1	3	1	.222	.333
1 Del Wilber		R	33	2	2	0	0	0	0	0	0	0	1	0	.000	.000

NAME	T	AGE	W	L	PCT	SV	G	GS	CG	IP	H	BB	SO	ShO	ERA
		29	87	67	.565	16	154	154	80	1387	1301	373	609	17	3.07
Robin Roberts	R	25	28	7	.800	2	39	37	30	330	292	45	148	3	2.59
Curt Simmons	L	23	14	8	.636	0	28	28	15	201	170	70	141	6	2.82
Karl Drews	R	32	14	15	.483	0	33	30	15	229	213	52	96	5	2.71
Russ Meyer	R	28	13	14	.481	1	37	32	14	232	235	65	92	1	3.14
Jim Konstanty	R	35	5	3	.625	6	42	2	2	80	87	21	16	1	3.94
Andy Hansen	R	27	5	6	.455	4	43	0	0	77	76	27	18	0	3.27
Steve Ridzik	R	23	4	2	.667	0	24	9	2	93	74	37	43	0	3.00
Howie Fox	R	31	2	7	.222	0	13	11	2	62	70	26	16	0	5.08
Paul Stuffel	R	25	1	0	1.000	0	2	1	0	6	5	7	3	0	3.00
Ken Heintzelman	L	36	1	3	.250	1	23	1	0	43	41	12	20	0	3.14
Lou Possehl	R	26	0	1	.000	0	4	1	0	13	12	7	4	0	4.85
Bob Miller	R	26	0	1	.000	0	3	1	0	9	13	1	2	0	6.00
Kent Peterson	L	26	0	0	.000	2	3	0	0	7	2	2	7	0	0.00
1 Bubba Church	R	27	0	0	.000	0	2	1	0	5	11	1	3	0	10.80

CHICAGO 5th 77-77 .500 19.5 — PHIL CAVARRETTA

NAME	G by POS	B	AGE	G	AB	R	H	2B	3B	HR	RBI	BB	SO	SB	BA	SA
TOTALS			28	155	5330	628	1408	223	45	107	595	422	712	50	.264	.383
Dee Fondy	1B143	L	27	145	554	69	166	21	9	10	67	28	60	13	.300	.424
Eddie Miksis	2B54, SS40	R	25	93	383	44	89	20	1	2	19	20	32	4	.232	.305
Roy Smalley	SS82	R	26	87	261	36	58	14	1	5	30	29	58	0	.222	.341
Randy Jackson	3B104, OF1	R	25	116	379	44	88	8	5	9	34	27	42	6	.232	.351
Frankie Baumholtz	OF101	L	33	103	409	59	133	17	4	4	35	27	27	5	.325	.416
Hal Jeffcoat	OF95	R	27	102	297	29	65	17	2	4	30	15	40	7	.219	.330
Hank Sauer	OF151	R	33	151	567	89	153	31	3	37	121	77	92	1	.270	.531
Toby Atwell	C101	L	28	107	362	36	105	16	3	2	31	40	22	2	.290	.367
Bill Serena	3B58, 2B49	R	27	122	390	49	107	21	5	15	61	39	83	1	.274	.469
Gene Hermanski	OF76	L	32	99	275	28	70	6	0	4	34	29	32	2	.255	.320
Bob Addis	OF76	L	26	93	292	38	86	13	2	1	20	23	30	4	.295	.363
2 Tommy Brown	SS39, 2B10, 1B5	R	24	61	200	24	64	11	0	3	24	12	24	1	.320	.420
Bob Ramazzotti (JJ)	2B50	R	35	50	183	26	52	5	3	1	12	14	14	3	.284	.361
Bruce Edwards (SA)	C22, 2B1	R	28	50	94	7	23	2	2	1	12	8	12	0	.245	.340
Phil Cavarretta	1B13	L	35	41	63	7	15	1	1	1	8	9	3	0	.238	.333
Bob Rush		R	26	34	96	5	28	5	1	0	15	1	35	0	.292	.365
Harry Chiti	C32	R	19	32	113	14	31	5	0	5	13	5	8	0	.274	.451
Johnny Pramesa	C17	R	26	22	46	1	13	1	0	1	5	4	4	0	.283	.370
Leon Brinkopf	SS6	R	25	9	22	1	4	0	0	0	2	4	5	0	.182	.182
Bud Hardin (JJ)	SS2, 2B1	R	30	3	7	1	1	0	0	0	0	0	0	0	.143	.143
Ron Northey		L	32	1	1	0	0	0	0	0	0	0	0	0	.000	.000

Bob Usher 27 R 0-0, Carl Sawatski (MS) 24, Preston Ward (MS) 24

NAME	T	AGE	W	L	PCT	SV	G	GS	CG	IP	H	BB	SO	ShO	ERA
		29	77	77	.500	15	155	155	59	1386	1265	534	661	15	3.58
Bob Rush	R	26	17	13	.567	0	34	32	17	250	205	81	157	4	2.70
Warren Hacker	R	27	15	9	.625	1	33	20	12	185	144	31	84	5	2.58
Paul Minner	L	28	14	9	.609	0	28	27	12	181	180	54	61	2	3.73
Johnny Klippstein	R	24	9	14	.391	3	41	25	7	203	208	89	110	2	4.43
Bob Schultz	L	28	6	3	.667	0	29	5	1	74	63	51	31	0	4.01
Joe Hatten	L	35	4	4	.500	0	13	8	2	50	65	25	15	0	6.12
Bob Kelly	R	24	4	9	.308	0	31	15	3	125	114	46	50	2	3.60
Turk Lown	R	28	4	11	.267	0	33	19	5	157	154	93	73	0	4.36
Dutch Leonard	R	43	2	2	.500	11	45	0	0	67	56	24	37	0	2.15
Willie Ramsdell	R	36	2	3	.400	0	19	4	0	67	41	24	30	0	2.42
Dick Manville	R	25	0	0	.000	0	11	0	0	17	25	12	6	0	7.94
Vern Fear	R	27	0	0	.000	0	4	0	0	8	9	3	4	0	7.88
Monk Dubiel	R	33	0	0	.000	0	1	0	0	1	1	0	1	0	0.00
Cal Howe	L	27	0	0	.000	0	1	0	0	2	0	1	2	0	0.00

CINCINNATI 6th 69-85 .448 27.5 — LUKE SEWELL 39-59 .398 EARLE BRUCKER 3-2 6.00 ROGERS HORNSBY 27-24 .529

NAME	G by POS	B	AGE	G	AB	R	H	2B	3B	HR	RBI	BB	SO	SB	BA	SA
TOTALS			28	154	5234	615	1303	212	45	104	562	480	709	32	.249	.366
Ted Kluszewski	1B133	L	27	135	497	62	159	24	11	16	86	47	28	3	.320	.509
Grady Hatton	2B120	L	29	128	433	48	92	14	1	9	57	66	60	5	.212	.312
Roy McMillan	SS154	R	21	154	540	60	132	32	2	7	57	45	81	4	.244	.350
Bobby Adams	3B154	R	30	154	**637**	85	180	25	4	6	48	49	67	11	.283	.363
2 Willard Marshall	OF105	L	31	107	397	52	106	23	1	8	46	37	21	0	.267	.390
Bob Borkowski	OF103, 1B5	R	26	126	377	42	95	11	4	4	24	26	53	1	.252	.334
Joe Adcock	OF85, 1B17	R	24	117	378	43	105	22	4	13	52	23	38	1	.278	.460
Andy Seminick	C99	R	31	108	336	38	86	16	1	14	50	35	65	1	.256	.435
1 Hank Edwards	OF51	R	33	74	184	24	52	7	6	6	28	19	22	0	.283	.484
2 Cal Abrams	OF46	L	28	71	158	23	44	9	2	2	13	19	25	1	.278	.399
2 Wally Westlake	OF56	R	31	59	183	29	37	4	0	3	14	31	29	0	.202	.273
Joe Rossi	C46	R	29	55	145	14	32	0	1	1	6	20	20	1	.221	.255
Eddie Pellagrini	2B22, 1B8, 3B1, SS1	R	34	46	100	15	17	2	0	1	3	8	18	1	.170	.220
1 Johnny Wyrostek	OF29, 1B1	L	32	30	106	12	25	1	3	1	10	18	7	1	.236	.330
Johnny Temple	2B22	R	23	30	97	8	19	3	0	1	5	5	1	2	.196	.258
Wally Post (IL)	OF16	R	22	19	58	5	9	1	0	2	7	4	20	0	.155	.276
Jim Greengrass	OF17	R	24	18	68	10	21	2	1	5	24	7	12	0	.309	.588
Dixie Howell	C12	R	33	17	37	4	7	1	1	2	4	3	9	0	.189	.432
Hobie Landrith	C14	L	22	15	50	1	13	4	0	0	4	0	4	0	.260	.340

2 Eddie Kazak 31 R 1-15, 1 Dick Sisler 31 L 5-27, 1 Virgil Stallcup 30 R 0-1, Lloyd Merriman (MS) 27

NAME	T	AGE	W	L	PCT	SV	G	GS	CG	IP	H	BB	SO	ShO	ERA
TOTALS		28	69	85	.448	12	154	154	56	1363	1377	517	579	11	4.00
Ken Raffensberger	L	34	17	13	.567	1	38	33	18	247	247	45	93	**6**	2.81
Harry Perkowski	L	29	12	10	.545	0	33	24	11	194	197	89	86	1	3.80
Frank Smith	R	24	12	11	.522	7	53	2	1	122	109	41	77	0	3.76
Herm Wehmeier	R	25	9	11	.450	0	33	26	6	190	197	**103**	83	1	5.16
Frank Hiller	R	31	5	8	.385	1	28	15	6	124	129	37	50	1	4.65
2 Bubba Church	R	27	5	9	.357	0	29	22	5	153	173	48	47	1	4.35
2 Bud Podbielan	R	28	4	5	.444	1	24	7	4	87	78	26	22	1	2.79
1 Ewell Blackwell	R	29	3	12	.200	0	23	17	3	102	107	60	48	0	5.30
3 Johnny Schmitz	L	31	1	0	1.000	0	3	0	0	5	3	3	3	0	0.00
Joe Nuxhall	L	23	1	4	.200	1	37	5	2	92	83	42	52	0	3.23
Bud Byerly	R	31	0	1	.000	1	12	2	0	25	29	7	14	0	5.04
Niles Jordan	L	26	0	1	.000	0	3	1	0	6	14	3	2	0	10.50
Phil Haugstad	R	28	0	0	.000	0	9	0	0	12	8	13	2	0	6.75
Ed Blake	R	26	0	0	.000	0	2	0	0	3	3	0	0	0	0.00

BOSTON 7th 64-89 .418 32 — 1 TOMMY HOLMES 13-22 .371 CHARLIE GRIMM 51-67 .432

NAME	G by POS	B	AGE	G	AB	R	H	2B	3B	HR	RBI	BB	SO	SB	BA	SA
TOTALS			28	155	5221	569	1214	187	31	110	530	483	711	58	.233	.343
Earl Torgeson	1B105, OF5	L	28	122	382	49	88	17	0	5	34	81	38	11	.230	.314
Jack Dittmer	2B90	L	24	93	326	26	63	7	2	7	41	26	26	1	.193	.291
Johnny Logan	SS117	R	25	117	456	56	129	21	3	4	42	31	33	1	.283	.368
Eddie Mathews	3B142	L	20	145	528	80	128	23	5	25	58	59	**115**	6	.242	.447
Bob Thorpe	OF72	R	25	81	292	20	76	8	2	3	26	5	42	3	.260	.332
Sam Jethroe	OF151	B	30	151	608	79	141	23	7	13	58	68	112	28	.232	.357
Sid Gordon	OF142, 3B2	R	34	144	522	69	151	22	2	25	75	77	49	0	.289	.483
Walker Cooper	C89	R	37	102	349	33	82	12	1	10	55	22	32	1	.235	.361
Jack Daniels	OF87	L	24	106	219	31	41	5	1	2	14	28	30	3	.187	.247
Sibby Sisti	2B33, OF23, SS18, 3B9	R	31	90	245	19	52	10	1	4	24	14	43	2	.212	.310
George Crowe	1B55	L	29	73	217	25	56	13	1	4	20	18	25	0	.258	.382
Paul Burris	C50	R	28	55	168	14	37	4	0	2	21	7	19	0	.220	.280
Jack Cusick	SS28, 3B3	R	24	49	78	5	13	1	0	0	6	6	9	0	.167	.179
Ebba St. Claire	C34	B	30	39	108	5	23	2	0	2	4	8	12	0	.213	.287
Roy Hartsfield	2B29	R	26	38	107	13	28	4	3	0	4	5	12	0	.262	.355
Pete Whisenant	OF14	R	22	24	52	3	10	2	0	0	7	4	13	1	.192	.231
1 Willard Marshall	OF16	L	31	21	66	5	15	4	1	2	11	4	4	0	.227	.409
Bill Reed	2B14	L	29	15	52	4	13	0	0	0	0	0	5	0	.250	.250

Bus Clarkson 34 R 5-25, Billy Klaus 23 L 0-4, Del Crandall (MS) 21

NAME	T	AGE	W	L	PCT	SV	G	GS	CG	IP	H	BB	SO	ShO	ERA
TOTALS		28	64	89	.418	13	155	155	63	1396	1388	525	687	11	3.78
Warren Spahn	L	31	14	19	.424	3	40	35	19	290	263	73	**183**	5	2.98
Max Surkont	R	30	12	13	.480	0	31	29	12	215	201	76	125	3	3.77
Jim Wilson	R	30	12	14	.462	0	33	33	14	234	234	90	104	0	4.23
Vern Bickford	R	31	7	12	.368	0	26	22	7	161	165	64	62	1	3.75
Ernie Johnson	R	28	6	3	.667	1	29	10	2	92	100	31	45	1	4.11
Lew Burdette	R	25	6	11	.353	7	45	9	5	137	138	47	47	0	3.61
Virgil Jester	R	24	3	5	.375	0	19	8	4	73	80	23	25	1	3.33
Bob Chipman	L	33	1	1	.500	0	29	0	0	42	28	20	16	0	2.79
Dave Cole	R	21	1	1	.500	0	22	3	0	45	38	42	22	0	4.00
Bert Thiel	R	26	1	1	.500	0	4	0	0	7	11	4	6	0	7.71
Sheldon Jones	R	30	1	4	.200	1	39	1	0	70	81	31	40	0	4.76
Dick Donovan	R	24	0	2	.000	1	7	2	0	13	18	12	6	0	5.54
Gene Conley	R	21	0	3	.000	0	4	3	0	13	23	9	6	0	7.62
Dick Hoover	L	26	0	0	.000	0	2	0	0	5	8	3	0	0	7.20

Johnny Antonelli (MS) 22
Chet Nichols (MS) 21
Phil Paine (MS) 23

PITTSBURGH 8th 42-112 .273 54.5 — BILLY MEYER

NAME	G by POS	B	AGE	G	AB	R	H	2B	3B	HR	RBI	BB	SO	SB	BA	SA
TOTALS			26	155	5193	515	1201	181	30	92	478	486	**724**	43	.231	.331
Tony Bartirome	1B118	L	20	124	355	32	78	10	3	0	16	26	37	3	.220	.265
Jack Merson	2B81, 3B27	R	30	111	398	41	98	20	2	5	38	22	38	1	.246	.344
Dick Groat	SS94	R	21	95	384	38	109	6	1	1	29	19	27	2	.284	.313
Pete Castiglione (BE)	3B57, 1B1, OF1	R	31	67	214	27	57	9	1	4	18	17	8	3	.266	.374
Gus Bell	OF123	L	23	131	468	53	117	21	5	16	59	36	72	1	.250	.419
Bobby Del Greco	OF93	R	19	99	341	34	74	14	2	1	20	38	70	6	.217	.279
Ralph Kiner	OF149	R	29	149	516	90	126	17	2	**37**	87	**110**	77	3	.244	.500
Joe Garagiola	C105	L	26	118	344	35	94	15	4	8	54	50	24	0	.273	.410
Catfish Metkovich	1B72, OF33	L	30	125	373	41	101	18	3	7	41	32	29	5	.271	.391
Clem Koshorek	SS33, 2B27, 3B26	R	26	98	322	27	84	17	0	0	15	26	39	4	.261	.314
1 G. Strickland	2B45, SS28, 3B1, 1B1	R	26	76	232	17	41	6	2	5	22	21	45	4	.177	.284
Clyde McCullough	C61, 1B1	R	35	66	172	10	40	5	1	1	15	10	18	0	.233	.291
Brandy Davis	OF29	R	23	55	95	14	17	1	1	0	1	11	28	9	.179	.211
Ed Fitzgerald	C18, 3B2	R	28	51	73	4	17	1	0	1	7	7	15	0	.233	.288
Lee Walls	OF19	R	19	32	80	6	15	0	1	2	5	8	22	0	.188	.288
Sonny Senerchia	3B28	R	21	29	100	5	22	5	0	3	11	4	21	0	.220	.360
Dick Smith	3B16, SS4, 2B4	R	24	29	66	8	7	1	0	0	5	9	3	0	.106	.121
Dick Hall	OF14, 3B5	R	21	26	80	6	11	1	0	0	2	2	17	0	.138	.150
Erv Dusak	OF11	R	31	20	27	1	6	0	0	1	3	2	8	0	.222	.333
2 Johnny Berardino	2B18	R	35	19	56	2	8	4	0	0	4	4	6	0	.143	.214

Tod Board 31 L 0-44, 1 Bill Howerton 30 L 8-26, Jim Mangan 22 R 2-13, Frank Thomas 23 R 2-21, Jack Phillips 30 R 0-1, Danny O'Connell (MS) 25

NAME	T	AGE	W	L	PCT	SV	G	GS	CG	IP	H	BB	SO	ShO	ERA
TOTALS		27	42	**112**	.273	8	155	155	43	1364	**1395**	**625**	564	5	4.65
Murry Dickson	R	35	14	**21**	.400	2	43	34	21	278	278	76	112	2	3.56
Howie Pollet	L	31	7	16	.304	0	31	30	9	214	217	71	90	1	4.12
Bob Friend	R	21	7	17	.292	0	35	23	6	185	186	84	75	1	4.18
1 Ted Wilks	R	36	5	5	.500	4	44	0	0	72	65	31	24	0	3.63
Joe Muir	L	29	2	3	.400	0	12	5	1	36	42	18	17	0	6.25
Woody Main	R	30	2	12	.143	2	48	11	2	153	149	52	79	0	4.47
Paul LaPalme	L	28	1	2	.333	0	31	2	0	60	56	37	25	0	3.90
Harry Fisher	R	26	1	2	.333	0	8	3	0	18	17	13	5	0	7.00
Jim Waugh	R	18	1	6	.143	0	17	7	1	52	61	32	18	0	6.40
Ron Necciai	R	20	1	6	.143	0	12	9	0	55	63	32	31	0	7.04
Cal Hogue	R	24	1	8	.111	0	19	12	3	84	79	68	34	0	4.82
Don Carlsen	R	25	0	1	.000	0	5	1	0	10	20	5	2	0	10.80
Bill Bell	R	18	0	1	.000	0	4	1	0	16	16	13	4	0	4.50
Mel Queen	R	34	0	2	.000	0	2	2	0	3	8	4	3	0	33.00
2 George Munger	R	34	0	3	.000	0	5	4	0	26	30	10	8	0	7.27
Ron Kline	R	20	0	7	.000	0	27	11	0	79	74	66	27	0	5.47
1 Bill Werle	L	31	0	0	.000	0	5	0	0	4	9	1	1	0	9.00
Jim Suchecki	R	25	0	0	.000	0	5	0	0	10	14	4	6	0	5.40
Jim Dunn	R	21	0	0	.000	0	3	0	0	6	4	3	2	0	3.60
Ed Wolfe	R	23	0	0	.000	0	3	0	0	4	7	5	1	0	6.75

Bill Koski (MS) 20, Vern Law (MS) 22, Bill Macdonald (MS) 23

WORLD SERIES – NEW YORK (AL) 4 BROOKLYN (NL) 3

LINE SCORES

TEAM	1	2	3	4	5	6	7	8	9	10	11	12	R	H	E
Game 1 October 1 at Brooklyn															
NY (AL)	0	0	1	0	0	0	0	1	0				2	6	2
BKN (NL)	0	1	0	0	0	2	0	1	X				4	6	0
Reynolds, Scarborough (8) — **Black**															
Game 2 October 2 at Brooklyn															
NY	0	0	0	1	1	5	0	0	0				7	10	0
BKN	0	0	1	0	0	0	0	0	0				1	3	1
Raschi — **Erskine**, Loes (6), Lehman (8)															
Game 3 October 3 at New York															
BKN	0	0	1	0	1	0	0	1	2				5	11	0
NY	0	1	0	0	0	0	0	1	1				3	6	2
Roe — **Lopat**, Gorman (9)															
Game 4 October 4 at New York															
BKN	0	0	0	0	0	0	0	0	0				0	4	1
NY	0	0	0	1	0	0	0	1	X				2	4	1
Black, Rutherford (8) — **Reynolds**															
Game 5 October 5 at New York															
BKN	0	1	0	0	3	0	1	0	0	0	1		6	10	0
NY	0	0	0	0	5	0	0	0	0	0	0		5	5	1
Erskine — **Blackwell, Sain** (6)															
Game 6 October 6 at Brooklyn															
NY	0	0	0	0	0	0	2	1	0				3	9	0
BKN	0	0	0	0	0	1	0	1	0				2	8	1
Raschi, Reynolds (8) — **Loes**, Roe (9)															
Game 7 October 7 at Brooklyn															
NY	0	0	0	1	1	1	1	0	0				4	10	4
BKN	0	0	0	1	1	0	0	0	0				2	8	1
Lopat, **Reynolds** (4), Raschi (7), Kuzava (7) — **Black**, Roe (6), Erskine (8)															

COMPOSITE BATTING

NAME	POS	G	AB	R	H	2B	3B	HR	RBI	BA
New York (AL)										
Totals		7	232	26	50	5	2	10	24	.216
Mantle	OF	7	**29**	**5**	**10**	1	1	2	3	.345
Berra	C	7	28	2	6	1	0	2	3	.214
Rizzuto	SS	7	27	2	4	1	0	0	0	.148
McDougald	3B	7	25	**5**	5	0	0	1	3	.200
Woodling	OF	7	23	4	8	1	1	1	1	.348
Martin	2B	7	23	2	5	0	0	1	4	.217
Bauer	OF	7	18	2	1	0	0	0	1	.056
Mize	1B	5	15	3	6	1	0	3	6	**.400**
Collins	1B	6	12	1	0	0	0	0	0	.000
Noren	OF	4	10	0	3	0	0	0	1	.300
Reynolds	P	4	7	0	0	0	0	0	0	.000
Raschi	P	3	6	0	1	0	0	0	1	.167
Lopat	P	2	3	0	1	0	0	0	1	.333
Sain	P	2	3	0	0	0	0	0	0	.000
Houk	PH	1	1	0	0	0	0	0	0	.000
Blackwell	P	1	1	0	0	0	0	0	0	.000
Kuzava	P	1	1	0	0	0	0	0	0	.000
Scarborough	P	1	0	0	0	0	0	0	0	.000
Gorman	P	1	0	0	0	0	0	0	0	.000
Brooklyn (NL)										
Totals		7	233	20	50	7	0	6	18	.215
Snider	OF	7	**29**	**5**	**10**	**2**	0	**4**	**8**	.345
Reese	SS	7	**29**	4	**10**	0	0	1	4	.345
Campanella	C	7	28	0	6	0	0	0	1	.214
Cox	3B	7	27	4	8	**2**	0	0	0	.296
Robinson	2B	7	23	4	4	0	0	1	2	.174
Furillo	OF	7	23	1	4	**2**	0	0	0	.174
Pafko	OF	7	21	0	4	0	0	0	2	.190
Hodges	1B	7	21	1	0	0	0	0	1	.000
Shuba	OF	4	10	0	3	1	0	0	0	.300
Black	P	3	6	0	0	0	0	0	0	.000
Erskine	P	3	6	1	0	0	0	0	0	.000
Loes	P	2	3	0	1	0	0	0	0	.333
Nelson	PH	4	3	0	0	0	0	0	0	.000
Roe	P	3	2	0	0	0	0	0	0	.000
Holmes	OF	3	1	0	0	0	0	0	0	.000
Morgan	3B	2	1	0	0	0	0	0	0	.000
Lehman	P	1	0	0	0	0	0	0	0	.000
Rutherford	P	1	0	0	0	0	0	0	0	.000
Amoros	PR	1	0	0	0	0	0	0	0	.000

COMPOSITE PITCHING

NAME	G	IP	H	BB	SO	W	L	SV	ERA
New York (AL)									
Totals	7	64	50	24	49	4	3	2	2.81
Reynolds	**4**	20.1	12	6	**18**	**2**	1	1	1.77
Raschi	3	17	12	8	**18**	**2**	0	0	**1.59**
Lopat	2	11.1	14	4	3	0	1	0	4.76
Sain	1	6	6	3	3	0	1	0	3.00
Blackwell	1	5	4	3	4	0	0	0	7.20
Kuzava	1	2.2	0	0	2	0	0	1	0.00
Scarborough	1	1	1	0	1	0	0	0	9.00
Gorman	1	.2	1	0	0	0	0	0	0.00
Brooklyn (NL)									
Totals	7	64	50	31	32	3	4	0	3.52
Black	3	**21.1**	**15**	8	9	1	**2**	0	2.53
Erskine	3	18	12	**10**	10	1	1	0	4.50
Roe	3	11.1	9	6	7	1	0	0	3.18
Loes	2	10.1	11	5	5	0	1	0	4.35
Lehman	1	2	2	1	0	0	0	0	0.00
Rutherford	1	1	1	1	1	0	0	0	9.00

1953 One More Time

Casey Stengel wasn't waiting for anyone. Part of the reason may have been the scare of 1952 when the Yankees almost lost the pennant. But, more than proximity itself, Stengel realized he had one foot on the doorstep of history—where only a few men had stood before. He did not want to lose his footing nor the chance to become the first man to manage five straight pennant winners. After bowing in the opener, the Yankees went on to win nine out of ten, giving them a lead they never relinquished. Any thought that the runner-up Indians had a chance was dispelled in late May when the Yankees went on an 18-game winning streak, falling one short of the American League record established by the 1906 White Sox, but enough of a surge to assure Stengel his well-deserved place in the record books.

The Yankees' victory was attributed to a veteran pitching staff and the left arm of a 24-year-old youngster by the name of Whitey Ford, who rejoined the team after a two-year military absence. Ford led the staff with 18 victories, while Eddie Lopat led the league with a 2.42 E.R.A. Allie Reynolds, at 38, Vic Raschi, at 34, and Johnny Sain, at 35, were the other pitching mainstays. These five men combined for an impressive 74-30 record. Catcher Yogi Berra led the offense with 27 home runs and 108 runs batted in, while Mickey Mantle, in his second year, hit 21 home runs, one of which astounded the baseball word in mid-April, a prodigious 565-foot shot off Chuck Stobbs in Washington.

Yet, while the Yankees collected team honors, individual laurels were taken by Al Rosen of Cleveland who was named the MVP with a near Triple Crown performance, losing out only to Mickey Vernon of Washington, who won the batting title by one point. But the Browns' Bobo Holloman suffered a greater disappointment than Rosen. Holloman started his first major league game on May 6, and threw a no-hitter against Philadelphia. Then, in July, with a 3-7 record he found himself optioned to Toronto, never again to return to the majors.

The National League headlines also belonged to New York. Not the Giants, but the Dodgers, who became the first team to repeat as pennant winners since the 1944 Cardinals. Led by MVP catcher Roy Campanella, the Brooklynites cracked the race open after the All-Star break and finished a strong 13 games in front of the surprising Braves. In their victory route, the Dodgers paced the league in runs, home runs, and batting average. Their 105 victories set an all-time high for the team, and Duke Snider's 42 home runs, coupled with Campanella's 41, marked the first time in the National League that two men on the same club went over the 40 home run mark. Carl Furillo won a lame duck batting title by hitting .344 and spending the last three weeks of the season on the sidelines after breaking his hand in a free-for-all with the Giants—a rhubarb which started after Furillo was hit by a pitch which he claimed Giants' manager Leo Durocher had ordered.

The underlying story of the year came from Milwaukee, where owner Lou Perini had shifted his Braves from Boston, marking the first major league franchise transplant since 1903. The Braves, infused by new blood as the result of trades which brought Andy Pafko from the Dodgers and Joe Adcock from Cincinnati, and the blossoming of sophomore third baseman Eddie Matthews, who broke Ralph Kiner's seven year hold on the home run title, produced a National League attendance mark of 1,826,397. It was a figure which was also greatly credited to the franchise shift and one which would start the machinery in many owners' heads whizzing for some time to come.

The Dodgers entered the fall classic with a regular lineup boasting of five .300 plus batters and seemed destined to win their first World Series. Such was not the case. Stengel had a lock on destiny and took the Series in six games to make it five world championships in five years. There seemed little remaining that the Old Professor had to prove.

1953 AMERICAN LEAGUE

NAME	G by POS	B	AGE	G	AB	R	H	2B	3B	HR	RBI	BB	SO	SB	BA	SA
NEW YORK 1st 99-52 .656		CASEY STENGEL														
TOTALS			29	151	5194	**801**	1420	226	52	139	**762**	**656**	644	34	**.273**	**.417**
Joe Collins	1B113, OF4	L	30	127	387	72	104	11	2	17	44	59	36	2	.269	.439
Billy Martin	2B146, SS18	R	25	149	587	72	151	24	6	15	75	43	56	6	.257	.395
Phil Rizzuto	SS133	R	35	134	413	54	112	21	3	2	54	71	39	4	.271	.351
Gil McDougald	3B136, 2B26	R	25	141	541	82	154	27	7	10	83	60	65	3	.285	.416
Hank Bauer	OF126	R	30	133	437	77	133	20	6	10	57	59	45	2	.304	.446
Mickey Mantle	OF121, SS1	B	21	127	461	105	136	24	3	21	92	79	90	8	.295	.497
Gene Woodling	OF119	L	30	125	395	64	121	26	4	10	58	82	29	2	.306	.468
Yogi Berra	C133	L	28	137	503	80	149	23	5	27	108	50	32	0	.296	.523
Irv Noren	OF96	L	28	109	345	55	92	12	6	6	46	42	39	3	.267	.388
Johnny Mize	1B15	L	40	81	104	6	26	3	0	4	27	12	17	0	.250	.394
Don Bollweg	1B43	L	32	70	155	24	46	6	4	6	24	21	31	1	.297	.503
Bill Renna	OF40	R	28	61	121	19	38	6	3	2	13	13	31	0	.314	.463
Andy Carey	3B40, SS2, 2B1	R	21	51	81	14	26	5	0	4	8	9	12	2	.321	.531
2 Willie Miranda	SS45	B	27	48	58	12	13	0	0	1	5	5	10	1	.224	.276
Charlie Silvera	C39, 3B1	R	28	42	82	11	23	3	1	0	12	9	5	0	.280	.341
Gus Triandos	1B12, C5	R	22	18	51	5	8	2	0	1	6	3	9	0	.157	.255
Ralph Houk	C8	R	33	8	9	2	2	0	0	0	1	0	1	0	.222	.222
Jerry Coleman (MS)	2B7, SS1	R	28	8	10	1	2	0	0	0	0	0	2	0	.200	.200
Bob Cerv 27 R 0-6, Art Schult 25 R 0-0, 1 Loren Babe 25 L 6-18, Jim Brideweser 26 R 3-3, Frank Verdi 27 R 0-0, Bobby Brown (MS) 27																
CLEVELAND 2nd 92-62 .597 8.5		AL LOPEZ														
TOTALS			30	155	5285	770	1426	201	29	**160**	729	609	**683**	33	.270	.410
Bill Glynn	1B135, OF2	L	28	147	411	60	100	14	2	3	30	44	65	1	.243	.309
Bobby Avila	2B140	R	29	141	559	85	160	22	3	8	55	58	27	10	.286	.379
George Strickland	SS122, 1B1	R	27	123	419	43	119	17	4	5	47	51	52	0	.284	.379
Al Rosen	3B154, 1B1, SS1	R	29	155	599	**115**	201	27	5	**43**	**145**	85	48	8	.336	**.613**
Wally Westlake	OF72	R	32	82	218	42	72	7	1	9	46	35	29	2	.330	.495
Larry Doby	OF146	L	29	149	513	92	135	18	5	29	102	96	**121**	3	.263	.487
Dale Mitchell	OF125	L	31	134	500	76	150	26	4	13	60	42	20	3	.300	.446
Jim Hegan	C106	R	32	112	299	37	65	10	1	9	37	25	41	1	.217	.348
Bob Kennedy	OF89	R	32	100	161	22	38	5	0	3	22	19	11	0	.236	.323
Harry Simpson	OF69, 1B2	L	27	82	242	25	55	3	1	7	22	18	27	0	.227	.335
Luke Easter (BF)	1B56	L	38	68	211	26	64	9	0	7	31	15	35	0	.303	.445
Hank Majeski	2B10, 3B7, OF1	R	36	50	50	6	15	1	0	2	12	3	8	0	.300	.440
Al Smith	OF39, 3B2	R	25	47	150	28	36	9	0	3	14	20	25	2	.240	.360
Joe Tipton	C46	R	30	47	109	17	25	2	0	6	13	19	13	0	.229	.413
2 Joe Ginsberg	C39	L	26	46	109	10	31	4	0	0	10	14	4	0	.284	.321
Early Wynn	P36	B	33	37	91	11	25	2	0	3	10	7	17	0	.275	.396
1 Ray Boone	SS31	R	29	34	112	21	27	1	2	4	21	24	21	1	.241	.393
2 Owen Friend	2B19, SS8, 3B1	R	26	34	68	7	16	2	0	2	13	5	16	0	.235	.353
Barney McCosky		L	35	22	21	3	4	3	0	0	3	1	4	0	.190	.333
Jim Lemon	OF11, 1B2	R	25	16	46	5	8	1	0	1	5	3	15	0	.174	.261
2 Hank Foiles	C7	R	24	7	7	2	1	0	0	0	0	1	1	0	.143	.143
Dick Aylward 28 R 0-3, 1Dick Weik 25 R 0-0, Hal Naragon (MS) 24																
CHICAGO 3rd 89-65 .578 11.5		PAUL RICHARDS														
TOTALS			29	156	5212	716	1345	226	**53**	74	676	601	530	**73**	.258	.364
Ferris Fain	1B127	L	32	128	446	73	114	18	2	6	52	108	28	3	.256	.345
Nellie Fox	2B154	L	25	154	624	92	178	31	8	3	72	49	18	4	.285	.375
Chico Carrasquel	SS149	R	25	149	552	72	154	30	4	2	47	38	47	5	.279	.359
2 Bob Elliott	3B58, OF2	R	36	67	208	24	54	11	1	4	32	31	21	1	.260	.380
Sam Mele	OF138, 1B2	R	30	140	481	64	132	26	8	12	82	58	47	3	.274	.437
Jim Rivera	OF156	L	30	156	567	79	147	26	**16**	11	78	53	70	22	.259	.420
Minnie Minoso	OF147, 3B10	R	30	151	556	104	174	24	8	15	104	74	43	**25**	.313	.466
Sherm Lollar	C107, 1B1	R	28	113	334	46	96	19	0	8	54	47	29	1	.287	.416
Tom Wright	OF33	L	29	77	132	14	33	5	3	2	25	12	21	0	.250	.379
Red Wilson	C63	R	24	71	164	21	41	6	1	0	10	26	12	2	.250	.299
Freddie Marsh	3B32, SS17, 1B5, 2B2	R	29	67	95	22	19	1	0	2	2	13	26	0	.200	.274
Rocky Krsnich	3B57	R	25	64	129	9	26	8	0	1	14	12	11	0	.202	.287
Bob Boyd	1B29, OF16	L	26	55	165	20	49	6	2	3	23	13	11	1	.297	.412
Bud Stewart (IL)	OF16	L	37	53	59	16	16	2	0	2	13	14	3	1	.271	.407
1 Vern Stephens	3B38, SS3	R	32	44	129	14	24	6	0	1	14	13	18	2	.186	.256
Bud Sheely	C17	L	32	31	46	4	10	1	0	0	2	9	8	0	.217	.239
1 Tommy Byrne	P6	L	33	18	18	2	3	0	0	1	5	2	6	0	.167	.333
2 Connie Ryan	3B16	R	33	17	54	6	12	1	0	0	6	9	12	2	.222	.241
2 Allie Clark	OF1, 1B1	R	30	9	15	0	1	0	0	0	0	0	5	0	.067	.067
Bill Wilson 24 R 1-17, 2 Neil Berry 31 R 1-8, Sam Dente 31 R 0-0, Sammy Esposito (MS) 21, Joe Kirrene (MS) 20																

NAME	T	AGE	W	L	PCT	SV	G	GS	CG	IP	H	BB	SO	ShO	ERA
		32	99	52	.656	**39**	151	151	50	1358	1286	500	604	**16**	**3.20**
Whitey Ford	L	24	18	6	.750	0	32	30	11	207	187	110	110	3	3.00
Ed Lopat	L	35	16	4	**.800**	0	25	24	9	178	169	32	50	3	**2.43**
Johnny Sain	R	35	14	7	.667	9	40	19	10	189	189	45	84	1	3.00
Vic Raschi	R	34	13	6	.684	1	28	26	7	181	150	55	76	4	3.33
Allie Reynolds	R	38	13	7	.650	13	41	15	5	145	140	61	86	1	3.41
Jim McDonald	R	26	9	7	.563	0	27	18	6	130	128	39	43	2	3.81
Bob Kuzava	L	30	6	5	.545	4	33	6	2	92	92	34	48	2	3.33
Tom Gorman	R	28	4	5	.444	6	40	1	0	77	65	32	38	0	3.39
Ewell Blackwell (SA)	R	30	2	0	1.000	1	8	4	0	20	17	13	11	0	3.60
Bill Miller	L	25	2	1	.667	1	13	3	0	34	46	19	17	0	4.76
1 Ray Scarborough	R	35	2	2	.500	2	25	1	0	55	52	26	20	0	3.27
Steve Kraly	L	24	0	2	.000	1	5	3	0	25	19	16	8	0	3.24
Art Schallock	L	29	0	0	.000	1	7	1	0	21	30	15	13	0	3.00
1 Johnny Schmitz	L	32	0	0	.000	0	3	0	0	4	2	3	0	0	2.25
Tom Morgan (MS) 23															
		30	92	62	.597	15	155	155	**81**	1373	1311	519	586	11	3.64
Bob Lemon	R	32	21	15	.583	1	41	**36**	23	**287**	**283**	110	98	5	3.36
Mike Garcia	R	29	18	9	.667	0	38	35	21	272	260	81	134	3	3.24
Early Wynn	R	33	17	12	.586	0	36	34	16	252	234	107	138	1	3.93
Bob Feller	R	34	10	7	.588	0	25	25	10	176	163	60	60	1	3.58
Dave Hoskins	R	27	9	3	.750	1	26	7	3	113	102	38	55	0	3.98
2 Art Houtteman	R	25	7	7	.500	3	22	13	6	109	113	25	40	1	3.80
Bob Hooper	R	31	5	4	.556	7	43	0	0	69	50	38	16	0	4.04
2 Bill Wight	L	31	2	1	.667	1	20	0	0	27	29	16	14	0	3.67
Dick Tomanek	L	22	1	0	1.000	0	1	1	1	9	6	6	6	0	2.00
1 Al Aber	L	25	1	1	.500	0	6	0	0	6	6	9	4	0	7.50
1 Steve Gromek	R	33	1	1	.500	0	5	1	0	11	11	3	8	0	3.27
Bob Chakales	R	25	0	2	.000	0	7	3	1	27	28	10	6	0	2.67
Lou Brissie	L	29	0	0	.000	2	16	0	0	13	21	13	5	0	7.62
Ted Wilks	R	37	0	0	.000	0	4	0	0	4	5	3	2	0	6.75
		30	89	65	.578	33	156	156	57	1404	1299	583	**714**	**16**	3.41
Billy Pierce	L	26	18	12	.600	3	40	33	19	271	216	102	**186**	7	2.72
2 Virgil Trucks	R	34	15	6	.714	1	24	21	13	176	151	67	102	3	2.86
Harry Dorish	R	31	10	6	.625	18	55	6	2	146	140	52	69	0	3.39
Mike Fornieles	R	21	8	7	.533	3	39	16	5	153	160	61	72	0	3.59
2 Sandy Consuegra	R	32	7	5	.583	3	29	13	5	124	122	28	30	1	2.54
Bob Keegan (SA)	R	32	7	5	.583	1	22	11	4	99	80	33	32	2	2.73
Saul Rogovin (EJ)	R	30	7	12	.368	1	22	19	4	131	151	48	62	1	5.22
Joe Dobson	R	36	5	5	.500	1	23	15	3	101	96	37	50	1	3.65
Connie Johnson	R	30	4	4	.500	0	14	10	2	61	55	38	44	1	3.54
Gene Bearden	L	32	3	3	.500	0	25	3	0	58	48	33	24	0	2.95
Luis Aloma	R	30	2	0	1.000	2	24	0	0	38	41	23	23	0	4.74
1 Tommy Byrne	L	33	2	0	1.000	0	6	6	0	16	18	26	4	0	10.13
1 Earl Harrist	R	33	1	0	1.000	0	7	0	0	8	9	5	1	0	7.88
1 Lou Kretlow	R	30	0	0	.000	0	9	3	0	21	12	30	15	0	3.43
Hal Hudson	L	26	0	0	.000	0	1	0	0	1	0	0	0	0	0.00

BOSTON 4th 84-69 .549 16 — LOU BOUDREAU

NAME	G by POS	B	AGE	G	AB	R	H	2B	3B	HR	RBI	BB	SO	SB	BA	SA
TOTALS			26	153	5246	656	1385	255	37	101	614	496	601	33	.264	.384
Dick Gernert	1B136	R	24	139	494	73	125	15	1	21	71	88	82	0	.253	.415
Billy Goodman	2B112, 1B20	L	27	128	514	73	161	33	5	2	41	57	11	1	.313	.409
Milt Bolling	SS109	R	22	109	323	30	85	12	1	5	28	24	41	1	.263	.353
George Kell	3B124, OF7	R	30	134	460	68	141	41	2	12	73	52	22	5	.307	.483
Jimmy Piersall	OF151	R	23	151	585	76	159	21	9	3	52	41	52	11	.272	.354
Tommy Umphlett	OF136	R	23	137	495	53	140	27	5	3	59	34	30	4	.283	.376
Hoot Evers	OF93	R	32	99	300	39	72	10	1	11	31	23	41	2	.240	.390
Sammy White	C131	R	24	136	476	59	130	34	2	13	64	29	48	3	.273	.435
2 Floyd Baker	3B37, 2B16	L	36	81	172	22	47	4	2	0	24	24	10	0	.273	.320
Gene Stephens	OF72	L	20	78	221	30	45	6	2	3	18	29	56	3	.204	.290
Ted Lepcio	2B34, SS20, 3B11	R	22	66	161	17	38	4	2	4	11	17	24	0	.236	.360
1 Johnny Lipon	SS58	R	30	60	145	18	31	7	0	0	13	14	16	1	.214	.262
Del Wilber	C28, 1B2	R	34	58	112	16	27	6	1	7	29	6	21	0	.241	.500
Al Zarilla	OF18	L	34	57	67	11	13	2	0	0	4	14	13	0	.194	.224
Billy Consolo	3B16, 2B11	R	18	47	65	9	14	2	1	1	6	2	23	1	.215	.323
Mickey McDermott	P32	L	24	45	93	9	28	8	0	1	13	2	13	0	.301	.419
Ted Williams (MS)	OF26	L	34	37	91	17	37	6	0	13	34	19	10	0	.407	.901
Karl Olson(MS)	OF24	R	22	25	57	5	7	2	0	1	6	1	9	0	.123	.211
Gus Niarhos	C16	R	32	16	35	6	7	1	1	0	2	4	4	0	.200	.286

Dom DiMaggio 36 R 1-3, Jack Merson 31 R 0-4, Al Richter 26 R 0-0, 1 Clyde Vollmer 31 R 0-0, Faye Throneberry (MS) 22, Norm Zauchin (MS) 23

NAME	T	AGE	W	L	PCT	SV	G	GS	CG	IP	H	BB	SO	ShO	ERA
TOTALS		30	84	69	.549	37	153	153	41	1373	1333	584	642	14	3.58
Mel Parnell	L	31	21	8	.724	0	38	34	12	241	217	116	136	5	3.06
Mickey McDermott	L	34	18	10	.643	0	32	30	8	206	169	109	92	4	3.01
Hal Brown	R	28	11	6	.647	0	30	25	6	166	177	57	62	1	4.66
Ellis Kinder	R	38	10	6	.625	27	69	0	0	107	84	38	39	0	1.85
Sid Hudson	R	38	6	9	.400	2	30	17	4	156	164	49	60	0	3.52
Bill Henry	L	25	5	5	.500	1	21	12	4	86	86	33	56	1	3.24
Willard Nixon	R	25	4	8	.333	0	23	15	5	117	114	59	57	1	3.92
Ike Delock	R	23	3	1	.750	1	23	1	0	49	60	20	22	0	4.41
1 Marv Grissom	R	35	2	6	.250	0	13	11	1	59	61	30	31	1	4.73
Ken Holcombe	R	34	1	0	1.000	1	3	0	0	6	9	3	1	0	6.00
Frank Sullivan	R	23	1	1	.500	0	14	0	0	26	24	11	17	0	5.54
Ben Flowers	R	26	1	4	.200	3	32	6	1	79	87	24	36	1	3.87
Hersh Freeman	R	25	1	4	.200	0	18	2	0	39	50	17	15	0	5.54
Bill Werle	L	32	0	1	.000	0	5	0	0	12	7	1	4	0	1.50
Bill Kennedy	L	32	0	0	.000	2	16	0	0	24	24	17	14	0	3.75

Dick Brodowski (MS) 20
Leo Kiely (MS) 22

WASHINGTON 5th 76-76 .500 23.5 — BUCKY HARRIS

NAME	G by POS	B	AGE	G	AB	R	H	2B	3B	HR	RBI	BB	SO	SB	BA	SA
TOTALS			29	152	5149	687	1354	230	53	69	647	596	604	65	.263	.368
Mickey Vernon	1B152	L	35	152	608	101	205	43	11	15	115	63	57	4	.337	.518
Wayne Terwilliger	2B133	R	28	134	464	62	117	24	4	4	46	64	65	7	.252	.347
Pete Runnels	SS121, 2B11	L	25	137	486	64	125	15	5	2	50	64	36	3	.257	.321
Eddie Yost	3B152	R	26	152	577	107	157	30	7	9	45	123	59	7	.272	.395
Jackie Jensen	OF146	R	26	147	552	87	147	32	8	10	84	73	51	18	.266	.408
Jim Busby	OF150	R	26	150	586	68	183	28	7	6	82	38	45	13	.312	.415
2 Clyde Vollmer	OF106	R	31	118	408	54	106	15	3	11	74	48	59	0	.260	.392
2 Ed Fitzgerald	C85	R	29	88	288	23	72	13	0	3	39	19	34	2	.250	.326
Gil Coan	OF46	L	31	68	168	28	33	1	4	2	17	22	23	7	.196	.286
Mickey Grasso	C59	R	33	61	196	13	41	7	0	2	22	9	20	0	.209	.276
2 Kite Thomas	OF8, C1	R	29	38	58	10	17	3	2	1	12	11	7	0	.293	.466
Jerry Snyder	SS17, 2B4	R	23	29	62	10	21	4	0	0	4	5	8	1	.339	.403
Mel Hoderlein	2B11, SS2	B	30	23	47	5	9	0	0	0	5	6	9	0	.191	.191
Yo-Yo Davalillo	SS17	R	22	19	58	10	17	1	0	0	2	1	7	1	.293	.310
2 Carmen Mauro	OF6	L	26	17	23	1	4	0	1	0	2	1	3	0	.174	.261
2 Tommy Byrne	P6	L	33	14	17	0	1	0	0	0	0	3	7	0	.059	.059
Gene Verble	SS8	R	25	13	21	4	4	0	0	0	2	2	1	0	.190	.190
Ken Wood	OF7	R	29	12	33	0	7	1	0	0	3	2	3	0	.212	.242
Frank Campos		L	29	10	9	0	1	0	0	0	2	1	0	0	.111	.111
Les Peden	C8	R	29	9	28	4	7	1	0	1	1	4	3	0	.250	.393

1 Floyd Baker 36 L 0-7, Bob Oldis 25 R 4-16, Frank Sacka 28 R 5-18, Bruce Barmes 23 L 1-5, Tony Roig 24 R 1-8, Dan Porter (MS) 21

NAME	T	AGE	W	L	PCT	SV	G	GS	CG	IP	H	BB	SO	ShO	ERA
TOTALS		31	76	76	.500	10	152	152	76	1345	1313	478	515	16	3.66
Bob Porterfield	R	29	22	10	.688	0	34	32	24	255	243	73	77	9	3.35
Spec Shea	R	32	12	7	.632	0	23	23	11	165	151	75	38	1	3.93
Chuck Stobbs	L	23	11	8	.579	0	27	20	8	153	146	44	67	0	3.29
Walt Masterson	R	33	10	12	.455	0	29	20	10	166	145	62	95	4	3.63
Connie Marrero	R	42	8	7	.533	2	22	20	10	146	130	48	65	2	3.02
Sonny Dixon	R	28	5	8	.385	3	43	6	3	120	123	31	40	0	3.75
Julio Moreno	R	32	3	1	.750	0	12	2	1	35	41	13	13	0	2.83
Al Sima	L	31	2	3	.400	1	31	5	1	68	63	31	25	0	3.44
2 Johnny Schmitz	L	32	2	7	.222	4	24	13	5	108	118	37	39	0	3.67
Jerry Lane	R	27	1	4	.200	0	20	2	0	57	64	16	26	0	4.89
Jim Pearce	R	28	0	1	.000	0	4	1	0	9	15	6	0	0	8.00
Dean Stone	L	22	0	1	.000	0	3	1	0	9	13	5	5	0	8.00
Bunky Stewart	L	22	0	2	.000	0	2	2	1	15	17	11	3	0	4.80
2 Tommy Byrne	L	33	0	5	.000	0	6	5	2	34	35	22	22	0	4.24
1 Sandy Consuegra	R	32	0	0	.000	0	4	0	0	5	9	4	0	0	10.80

Bob Ross (MS) 24

DETROIT 6th 60-94 .390 40.5 — FRED HUTCHINSON

NAME	G by POS	B	AGE	G	AB	R	H	2B	3B	HR	RBI	BB	SO	SB	BA	SA
TOTALS			29	158	5553	695	1479	259	44	108	660	506	603	30	.266	.387
Walt Dropo	1B150	R	30	152	606	61	150	30	3	13	96	29	69	2	.248	.371
Johnny Pesky	2B73	L	33	103	308	43	90	22	1	2	24	27	10	3	.292	.390
Harvey Kuenn	SS155	R	22	155	679	94	209	33	7	2	48	50	31	6	.308	.386
2 Ray Boone	3B97, SS3	R	29	101	385	73	120	16	6	22	93	48	47	2	.312	.556
Don Lund	OF123	R	30	131	421	51	108	21	4	9	47	39	65	3	.257	.390
Jim Delsing	OF133	L	27	138	479	77	138	26	6	11	62	66	39	1	.288	.436
Bob Nieman	OF135	R	26	142	508	72	143	32	5	15	69	57	57	0	.281	.453
Matt Batts	C103	R	31	116	374	38	104	24	3	6	42	24	36	2	.278	.406
Fred Hatfield	3B54, 2B28, SS1	L	28	109	311	41	79	11	1	3	19	40	34	3	.254	.325
Steve Souchock	OF80, 1B1	R	34	89	278	29	84	13	3	11	46	8	35	5	.302	.489
Pat Mullin	OF14	L	35	79	97	11	26	1	0	4	17	14	15	0	.268	.402
Jerry Priddy	2B45, 1B11, 3B2	R	33	65	196	14	46	6	2	1	24	17	19	1	.235	.301
Johnny Bucha	C56	R	28	60	158	17	35	9	0	1	14	20	14	1	.222	.297
1 Owen Friend	2B26	R	26	31	96	10	17	4	0	3	10	6	9	0	.177	.313
Al Kaline	OF20	R	18	30	28	9	7	0	0	1	2	1	5	1	.250	.357
Russ Sullivan	OF20	L	30	23	72	7	18	5	1	1	6	13	5	0	.250	.389
Billy Hitchcock	3B12, 2B1, SS1	R	36	22	38	8	8	0	0	0	0	3	3	0	.211	.211
1 Joe Ginsberg	C15	L	26	18	53	6	16	2	0	0	3	10	1	0	.302	.340
Frank Carswell	OF3	R	33	16	15	2	4	0	0	0	2	3	1	0	.267	.267
John Baumgartner	3B7	R	22	7	27	3	5	0	0	0	2	0	5	0	.185	.185

Bob Swift 38 R 1-3, Reno Bertoia 18 R 0-1, George Freese 26 R 0-1, Frank House (MS) 23

NAME	T	AGE	W	L	PCT	SV	G	GS	CG	IP	H	BB	SO	ShO	ERA
TOTALS		27	60	94	.390	16	158	158	50	1415	1633	585	645	2	5.25
Ned Garver	R	27	11	11	.500	1	30	26	13	198	228	66	69	0	4.45
Ted Gray	L	28	10	15	.400	0	30	28	8	176	166	76	115	0	4.60
Billy Hoeft	L	21	9	14	.391	2	29	27	9	198	223	58	90	0	4.82
Dick Marlowe	R	24	6	7	.462	0	42	11	2	120	152	42	52	0	5.25
2 Steve Gromek	R	33	6	8	.429	1	19	17	6	126	138	36	59	1	4.50
2 Al Aber	L	25	4	3	.571	0	17	10	2	67	63	41	34	0	4.43
Ray Herbert	R	23	4	6	.400	6	43	3	0	88	109	46	37	0	5.22
2 Ralph Branca	R	27	4	7	.364	1	17	14	7	102	98	31	50	0	4.15
Dave Madison	R	32	3	4	.429	0	32	1	0	62	76	44	27	0	6.82
1 Art Houtteman	R	25	2	6	.250	1	16	9	3	69	87	29	28	1	5.87
Bob Miller	L	17	1	2	.333	0	13	1	0	36	43	21	9	0	6.00
Hal Erickson	R	33	0	1	.000	1	18	0	0	32	43	10	19	0	4.78
2 Dick Weik	R	25	0	1	.000	0	12	1	0	19	32	23	6	0	14.21
Milt Jordan	R	26	0	1	.000	0	8	1	0	17	26	5	4	0	5.82
Hal Newhouser (SA)	L	32	0	1	.000	1	7	4	0	22	31	8	6	0	6.95
2 Ray Scarborough	R	35	0	2	.000	2	13	0	0	21	34	11	12	0	8.14
2 Earl Harrist	R	33	0	2	.000	0	8	1	0	19	25	15	7	0	8.53
1 Bill Wight	L	31	0	3	.000	0	13	4	0	25	35	14	10	0	9.00
Paul Foytack	R	22	0	0	.000	0	6	0	0	10	15	9	7	0	10.80
Fred Hutchinson	R	33	0	0	.000	0	3	0	0	10	9	0	4	0	2.70

Bill Black (MS) 20

PHILADELPHIA 7th 59-95 .383 41.5 — JIMMY DYKES

NAME	G by POS	B	AGE	G	AB	R	H	2B	3B	HR	RBI	BB	SO	SB	BA	SA
TOTALS			30	157	5455	632	1398	205	38	116	588	498	602	41	.256	.372
Eddie Robinson	1B155	L	32	156	615	64	152	28	4	22	102	63	56	1	.247	.413
Cass Michaels	2B110	R	27	117	411	53	103	10	0	12	42	51	56	7	.251	.363
Joe DeMaestri	SS108	R	24	111	420	53	107	17	3	6	35	24	39	0	.255	.352
2 Loren Babe	3B93, SS1	L	25	103	343	34	77	16	2	0	20	35	20	0	.224	.283
Dave Philley	OF157, 3B1	B	33	157	620	80	188	30	9	9	59	51	35	13	.303	.424
Ed McGhee	OF99	R	28	104	358	36	94	11	4	1	29	32	43	4	.263	.324
Gus Zernial	OF141	R	30	147	556	85	158	21	3	42	108	57	79	4	.284	.559
Joe Astroth	C79	R	30	82	260	28	77	15	2	3	24	27	12	1	.296	.404
Pete Suder	3B72, 2B38, SS7	R	37	115	454	44	130	11	3	4	35	17	35	3	.286	.350
Ray Murray	C78	R	35	84	268	25	76	14	3	6	41	18	25	0	.284	.425
3 Carmen Mauro	OF49, 3B1	L	26	64	165	14	44	4	4	0	17	19	21	3	.267	.339
Tom Hamilton	1B7, OF2	L	27	58	56	8	11	2	0	0	5	7	11	0	.196	.232
Eddie Joost	SS51	R	37	51	177	39	44	6	0	6	15	45	24	3	.249	.384
Elmer Valo (BG)	OF25	L	32	50	85	15	19	3	0	0	9	22	7	0	.224	.259
1 Kite Thomas	OF15	R	29	24	49	1	6	0	0	0	2	3	6	0	.122	.122
Neal Watlington	C9	L	30	21	44	4	7	1	0	0	3	3	8	0	.159	.182
1 Allie Clark	OF19	R	30	20	74	6	15	4	0	3	13	3	5	0	.203	.378
Tommy Giordano	2B11	R	27	11	40	6	7	2	0	2	5	5	6	0	.175	.375

Spider Wilhelm 24 R 2-7, Don Kolloway 34 R 0-1

NAME	T	AGE	W	L	PCT	SV	G	GS	CG	IP	H	BB	SO	ShO	ERA
TOTALS		30	59	95	.383	11	157	157	51	1409	1475	594	566	6	4.67
Alex Kellner	L	28	11	12	.478	0	25	25	14	202	210	51	81	2	3.92
Harry Byrd	R	28	11	20	.355	0	40	37	11	237	279	115	122	2	5.51
Morrie Martin	L	30	10	12	.455	7	58	11	2	156	158	59	64	0	4.44
Marion Fricano	R	29	9	12	.429	0	39	23	10	211	206	90	67	0	3.88
Bobby Shantz (SA)	L	27	5	9	.357	0	16	16	6	106	107	26	58	0	4.08
Joe Coleman (IL)	R	30	3	4	.429	0	21	9	2	90	85	49	18	1	4.00
Carl Scheib	R	26	3	7	.300	2	28	8	3	96	99	29	25	0	4.88
Charlie Bishop	R	29	3	14	.176	2	39	20	1	161	174	86	66	1	5.65
Bobo Newsom	R	45	2	1	.667	0	17	2	1	39	44	24	16	0	4.85
Bob Trice	R	24	2	1	.667	0	3	3	1	23	25	6	4	0	5.48
Frank Fanovich	L	31	0	3	.000	0	26	3	0	62	62	37	37	0	5.52
Rinty Monahan	R	25	0	0	.000	0	4	0	0	11	11	7	2	0	3.64
Walt Kellner	R	24	0	0	.000	0	2	0	0	3	1	4	4	0	6.00
Dick Rozek	L	26	0	0	.000	0	2	0	0	11	8	9	2	0	4.91
Bill Harrington (MS)	R	25	0	0	.000	0	1	0	0	2	5	0	0	0	13.50
Johnny Mackinson	R	29	0	0	.000	0	1	0	0	1	1	2	0	0	0.00

ST. LOUIS 8th 54-100 .351 46.5 — MARTY MARION

NAME	G by POS	B	AGE	G	AB	R	H	2B	3B	HR	RBI	BB	SO	SB	BA	SA
TOTALS			28	154	5264	555	1310	215	25	112	522	507	644	17	.249	.363
Dick Kryhoski	1B88	L	28	104	338	35	94	18	4	16	50	26	33	0	.278	.497
Bobby Young	2B148	L	28	148	537	48	137	22	2	4	25	41	40	2	.255	.326
Billy Hunter	SS152	R	25	154	567	50	124	18	1	1	37	24	45	3	.219	.259
Jim Dyck	OF55, 3B51	R	31	112	334	38	71	15	1	9	27	38	40	3	.213	.344
Vic Wertz	OF121	L	28	128	440	61	118	18	6	19	70	72	44	1	.268	.466
Johnny Groth	OF141	R	26	141	557	65	141	27	4	10	57	42	53	5	.253	.370
Dick Kokos	OF83	L	25	107	299	41	72	12	0	13	38	56	53	0	.241	.411
Clint Courtney	C103	L	26	106	355	28	89	12	2	4	19	25	20	0	.251	.330
Don Lenhardt	OF77, 3B6	R	30	97	303	37	96	15	0	10	35	41	41	1	.317	.465
Roy Sievers	1B76	R	26	92	285	37	77	15	0	8	35	32	47	0	.270	.407
Les Moss	C71	R	28	78	239	21	66	14	1	2	28	18	31	0	.276	.368
Hank Edwards	OF21	L	34	65	106	6	21	3	0	0	9	13	10	0	.198	.226
1 Neil Berry	3B18, 2B15, SS6	R	31	57	99	14	28	1	2	0	11	9	10	1	.283	.333
Don Larsen	P38, OF1	R	23	50	81	11	23	3	1	3	10	4	14	0	.284	.457
1 Bob Elliott	3B45	R	36	48	160	19	40	8	1	5	29	30	18	0	.250	.406
2 Vern Stephens	3B46	R	32	46	165	16	53	8	0	4	17	18	24	0	.321	.442
1 Willie Miranda	SS8, 3B6	B	27	17	6	2	1	0	0	0	0	1	1	1	.167	.167
Dixie Upright		L	27	9	8	3	2	0	0	1	1	1	3	0	.250	.625
2 Johnny Lipon	3B6, 2B1	R	30	7	9	0	2	0	0	0	1	0	1	0	.222	.222

Ed Mickelson 26 R 2-15, Babe Martin 33 R 0-2, Jim Pisoni 23 R 1-12, Marty Marion 35 R 0-7, Frank Kellert 28 R 0-4, Jay Porter (MS) 20, Frank Saucier (MS) 27

NAME	T	AGE	W	L	PCT	SV	G	GS	CG	IP	H	BB	SO	ShO	ERA
TOTALS		31	54	100	.351	24	154	154	28	1384	1467	626	639	7	4.47
Marlin Stuart	R	34	8	2	.800	7	60	2	0	114	136	44	46	0	3.95
Don Larsen	R	23	7	12	.368	2	38	22	7	193	201	64	96	2	4.15
Dick Littlefield	L	27	7	12	.368	0	36	22	2	152	153	84	104	0	5.09
Duane Pillette	R	30	7	13	.350	0	31	25	5	167	181	62	58	1	4.47
1 Virgil Trucks	R	34	5	4	.556	2	16	12	4	88	83	32	47	2	3.07
Harry Brecheen	L	38	5	13	.278	1	26	16	3	117	122	31	44	0	3.08
Bob Cain	L	28	4	10	.286	1	32	13	1	100	129	45	36	0	6.21
Bobo Holloman	R	28	3	7	.300	0	22	10	1	65	69	50	25	1	5.26
Satchel Paige	R	46	3	9	.250	11	57	4	0	117	114	39	51	0	3.54
Mike Blyzka	R	24	2	6	.250	0	33	9	2	94	110	56	23	0	6.41
Bob Turley (MS)	R	22	2	6	.250	0	10	7	3	60	39	44	61	1	3.30
2 Lou Kretlow	R	30	1	5	.167	0	22	11	0	81	93	52	37	0	5.11
2 Max Lanier	L	37	0	1	.000	0	10	1	0	22	28	19	8	0	7.36
1 Hal White	R	34	0	0	.000	0	10	0	0	10	8	3	2	0	2.70
Bob Habenicht	R	27	0	0	.000	0	1	0	0	2	1	1	1	0	4.50

BROOKLYN 1st 105-49 .682 — **CHUCK DRESSEN**

NAME	G by POS	B	AGE	G	AB	R	H	2B	3B	HR	RBI	BB	SO	SB	BA	SA
TOTALS			29	155	5373	955	1529	274	59	208	887	655	686	90	.285	.474
Gil Hodges	1B127, OF24	R	29	141	520	101	157	22	7	31	122	75	84	1	.302	.550
Jim Gilliam	2B149	B	24	151	605	125	168	31	17	6	63	100	38	21	.278	.415
Pee Wee Reese	SS135	R	34	140	524	108	142	25	7	13	61	82	61	22	.271	.420
Billy Cox	3B89, SS6, 2B1	R	33	100	327	44	95	18	1	10	44	37	21	2	.291	.443
Carl Furillo	OF131	R	31	132	479	82	165	38	6	21	92	34	32	1	.344	.580
Duke Snider	OF151	L	26	153	590	132	198	38	4	42	126	82	90	16	.336	.627
J. Robinson	OF76, 3B44, 2B9, 1B6, SS1	R	34	136	484	109	159	34	7	12	95	74	30	17	.329	.502
Roy Campanella	C140	R	31	144	519	103	162	26	3	41	142	67	58	4	.312	.611
Don Thompson	OF81	L	29	96	153	25	37	5	0	1	12	14	13	2	.242	.294
George Shuba	OF44	L	28	74	169	19	43	12	1	5	23	17	20	1	.254	.426
Bobby Morgan	3B36, SS21	R	27	69	196	35	51	6	2	7	33	33	47	2	.260	.418
Wayne Belardi (AJ)	1B38	L	22	69	163	19	39	3	2	11	34	16	40	0	.239	.485
Rube Walker	C28	L	27	43	95	5	23	6	0	3	9	7	11	0	.242	.400
Bill Antonello	OF25	R	26	40	43	9	7	1	1	1	4	2	11	0	.163	.302
Dick Williams	OF24	R	24	30	55	4	12	2	0	2	5	3	10	0	.218	.364
1 Carmen Mauro	OF1	L	26	8	9	1	0	0	0	0	0	0	4	0	.000	.000
Dixie Howl		R	34	1	1	0	0	0	0	0	0	0	1	0	.000	.000
Dick Teed		B	27	1	1	0	0	0	0	0	0	0	1	0	.000	.000

NAME	T	AGE	W	L	PCT	SV	G	GS	CG	IP	H	BB	SO	ShO	ERA
		28	105	49	.682	29	155	155	51	1381	1337	509	817	11	4.10
Carl Erskine	R	26	20	6	.769	3	39	33	16	247	213	95	187	4	3.53
Russ Meyer	R	29	15	5	.750	0	34	32	10	191	201	63	106	2	4.57
Billy Loes	R	23	14	8	.636	0	32	25	9	163	165	53	75	1	4.53
Preacher Roe	L	38	11	3	.786	0	25	24	9	157	171	40	85	1	4.36
Clem Labine	R	26	11	6	.647	7	37	7	0	110	92	30	44	0	2.78
Johnny Podres	L	20	9	4	.692	0	33	18	3	115	126	64	82	1	4.23
Bob Milliken	R	26	8	4	.667	2	37	10	3	118	94	42	65	0	3.36
Ben Wade	R	30	7	5	.583	3	32	0	0	90	79	33	65	0	3.80
Joe Black	R	29	6	3	.667	5	34	3	0	73	74	27	42	0	5.30
Jim Hughes	R	30	4	3	.571	9	48	0	0	86	80	41	49	0	3.45
Glenn Mickens	R	22	0	1	.000	0	4	2	0	6	11	4	5	0	12.00
Ray Moore	R	27	0	1	.000	0	1	1	1	8	6	4	4	0	3.38
1 Ralph Branca	R	27	0	0	.000	0	7	0	0	11	15	5	5	0	9.82
Erv Palica (MS)	R	25	0	0	.000	0	4	0	0	6	10	8	3	0	12.00
Don Newcombe (MS) 27															

MILWAUKEE 2nd 92-62 .597 13 — **CHARLIE GRIMM**

NAME	G by POS	B	AGE	G	AB	R	H	2B	3B	HR	RBI	BB	SO	SB	BA	SA
TOTALS			27	157	5349	738	1422	227	52	156	691	439	637	46	.266	.415
Joe Adcock	1B157	R	25	157	590	71	168	33	6	18	80	42	82	3	.285	.453
Jack Dittmer	2B138	L	25	138	504	54	134	22	1	9	63	18	35	1	.266	.367
Johnny Logan	SS150	R	26	150	611	100	167	27	8	11	73	41	33	2	.273	.398
Eddie Mathews	3B157	L	21	157	579	110	175	31	8	47	135	99	83	1	.302	.627
Andy Pafko	OF139	R	32	140	516	70	153	23	4	17	72	37	33	2	.297	.455
Bill Bruton	OF150	L	27	151	613	82	153	18	14	1	41	44	100	26	.250	.330
Sid Gordon	OF137	R	35	140	464	67	127	22	4	19	75	71	40	1	.274	.461
Del Crandall	C108	R	23	116	382	55	104	13	1	15	51	33	47	2	.272	.429
Jim Pendleton	OF105, SS7	R	29	120	251	48	75	12	4	7	27	7	36	6	.299	.462
Walker Cooper	C35	R	38	53	137	12	30	6	0	3	16	12	15	1	.219	.328
Harry Hanebrink	2B21, 3B1	L	25	51	80	8	19	1	1	1	8	6	8	1	.238	.313
George Crowe	1B9	L	30	47	42	6	12	2	0	2	6	2	7	0	.286	.476
Sibby Sisti	2B13, SS6, 3B4	R	32	38	23	8	5	1	0	0	4	5	2	0	.217	.261
Ebba St. Claire	C27	B	31	33	80	7	16	3	0	2	5	3	9	0	.200	.313
Bob Thorpe	OF18	R	26	27	37	1	6	1	0	0	5	1	6	0	.162	.189
Mel Roach	2B1	R	20	5	2	1	0	0	0	0	0	0	1	0	.000	.000
Paul Burris	C2	R	29	2	1	0	0	0	0	0	0	0	0	0	.000	.000
Billy Klaus		L	24	2	2	1	0	0	0	0	1	0	0	0	.000	.000

NAME	T	AGE	W	L	PCT	SV	G	GS	CG	IP	H	BB	SO	ShO	ERA
		28	92	62	.597	15	157	157	72	1387	1282	539	738	14	3.30
Warren Spahn	L	32	23	7	.767	3	35	32	24	266	211	70	148	5	2.10
Lew Burdette	R	26	15	5	.750	8	46	13	6	175	177	56	58	1	3.24
Bob Buhl	R	24	13	8	.619	0	30	18	8	154	133	73	83	3	2.98
Johnny Antonelli	L	23	12	12	.500	1	31	26	11	175	167	71	131	2	3.18
Max Surkont	R	31	11	5	.688	0	28	24	11	170	168	64	83	2	4.18
Don Liddle	L	28	7	6	.538	2	31	15	4	129	119	55	63	0	3.07
Ernie Johnson	R	29	4	3	.571	0	36	1	0	81	79	22	36	0	2.67
Jim Wilson	R	31	4	9	.308	0	20	18	5	114	107	43	71	0	4.34
Vern Bickford	R	32	2	5	.286	1	20	9	2	58	60	35	25	0	5.28
Joey Jay	R	17	1	0	1.000	0	3	1	1	10	6	5	4	1	0.00
Dave Jolly	R	28	0	1	.000	0	24	0	0	38	34	27	23	0	3.55
Dave Cole	R	22	0	1	.000	0	10	0	0	15	17	14	13	0	8.40
Virgil Jester	R	25	0	0	.000	0	2	0	0	2	4	4	0	0	22.50
Chet Nichols (MS) 22															
Phil Paine (MS) 23															

PHILADELPHIA 3rd (Tie) 83-71 .539 22 — **STEVE O'NEILL**

NAME	G by POS	B	AGE	G	AB	R	H	2B	3B	HR	RBI	BB	SO	SB	BA	SA
TOTALS			28	156	5290	716	1400	228	62	115	657	530	597	42	.265	.396
Earl Torgeson	1B105	L	33	111	379	58	104	25	8	11	64	53	57	7	.274	.470
Granny Hamner	2B93, SS71	R	26	154	609	90	168	30	8	21	92	32	28	2	.276	.455
Ted Kazanski	SS95	R	19	95	360	39	78	17	5	2	27	26	53	1	.217	.308
Willie Jones	3B147	R	27	149	481	61	108	16	2	19	70	85	45	1	.225	.385
Johnny Wyrostek	OF110	L	33	125	409	42	111	14	2	6	47	38	43	0	.271	.359
Richie Ashburn	OF156	L	26	156	622	110	205	25	9	2	57	61	35	14	.330	.408
Del Ennis	OF150	R	28	152	578	79	165	22	3	29	125	57	53	1	.285	.484
Smoky Burgess	C95	L	26	102	312	31	91	17	5	4	36	37	17	3	.292	.417
1 Connie Ryan	2B65, 1B2	R	33	90	247	47	73	14	6	5	26	30	35	5	.296	.462
Eddie Waitkus	1B59	L	33	81	247	24	72	9	2	1	16	13	23	1	.291	.356
Stan Lopata	C80	R	27	81	234	34	56	12	3	8	31	28	39	3	.239	.419
Mel Clark (KJ)	OF51	R	26	60	198	31	59	10	4	0	19	11	17	1	.298	.389
Tommy Glaviano	3B14, 2B12, SS1	R	29	53	74	17	15	1	2	3	5	24	20	2	.203	.392
Bill Nicholson	OF12	L	38	38	62	12	13	5	1	2	16	12	20	0	.210	.419
Lucky Lohrke	SS2, 2B2, 3B1	R	29	12	13	3	2	0	0	0	0	1	2	0	.154	.154
2 Johnny Lindell	P5, OF2	R	36	11	18	3	7	1	0	0	2	6	2	0	.389	.444
Jackie Mayo	OF1	L	27	5	4	0	0	0	0	0	0	0	1	0	.000	.000
Stan Palys	OF1	R	23	2	2	0	0	0	0	0	0	1	0	0	.000	.000

NAME	T	AGE	W	L	PCT	SV	G	GS	CG	IP	H	BB	SO	ShO	ERA
		28	83	71	.539	15	156	156	76	1369	1410	410	637	13	3.80
Robin Roberts	R	26	23	16	.590	2	44	41	33	347	324	61	198	5	2.75
Curt Simmons (FJ)	L	24	16	13	.552	0	32	30	19	238	211	82	138	4	3.21
Jim Konstanty	R	36	14	10	.583	5	48	19	7	171	198	42	45	0	4.42
Steve Ridzik	R	24	9	6	.600	0	42	12	1	124	119	48	53	0	3.77
Karl Drews	R	33	9	10	.474	3	47	27	6	185	218	50	72	0	4.52
Bob Miller	R	27	8	9	.471	2	35	20	8	157	169	42	63	3	4.01
Thornton Kipper	R	24	3	3	.500	0	20	3	0	46	59	12	15	0	4.70
2 Johnny Lindell	R	36	1	1	.500	0	5	3	2	23	22	23*	16	0	4.30
Kent Peterson	L	27	0	1	.000	0	15	0	0	27	26	21	20	0	6.67
Andy Hansen	R	28	0	2	.000	3	30	1	0	51	60	24	17	0	4.06
Paul Stuffel	R	26	0	0	.000	0	2	0	0	0	0	4	0	0	∞
Tom Qualters	L	18	0	0	.000	0	1	0	0	.1	4	1	0	0	162.00

*Lindell, also with Pittsburgh, league leader in BB with 139.

ST. LOUIS 3rd (Tie) 83-71 .539 22 — **EDDIE STANKY**

NAME	G by POS	B	AGE	G	AB	R	H	2B	3B	HR	RBI	BB	SO	SB	BA	SA
TOTALS			30	157	5397	768	1474	281	56	140	722	574	617	18	.273	.424
Steve Bilko	1B154	R	24	154	570	72	143	23	3	21	84	70	125	0	.251	.412
Red Schoendienst	2B140	B	30	146	564	107	193	35	5	15	79	60	23	3	.342	.502
Solly Hemus	SS150, 2B3	L	30	154	585	110	163	32	11	14	61	86	40	2	.279	.443
Ray Jablonski	3B157	R	26	157	604	64	162	23	5	21	112	34	61	2	.268	.427
Enos Slaughter	OF137	L	37	143	492	64	143	34	9	6	89	80	28	4	.291	.433
Rip Repulski	OF153	R	25	153	567	75	156	25	4	15	66	33	71	3	.275	.413
Stan Musial	OF157	L	32	157	593	127	200	53	9	30	113	105	32	3	.337	.609
Del Rice	C135	R	30	135	419	32	99	22	1	6	37	48	49	0	.236	.337
Peanuts Lowery	OF38, 2B10, 3B1	R	34	104	182	26	49	9	2	5	27	15	21	1	.269	.423
2 Pete Castiglione	3B51, 2B9, SS3	R	32	67	52	9	9	2	0	0	3	2	5	0	.173	.212
Harvey Haddix	P36	L	27	48	97	21	28	3	3	1	11	5	19	0	.289	.412
Dick Schofield	SS15	B	18	33	39	9	7	0	0	2	4	2	11	0	.179	.333
Dick Sisler	1B10	L	32	32	43	3	11	1	1	0	4	1	4	0	.256	.326
2 Sal Yvars	C26	R	29	30	57	4	14	2	0	1	6	4	6	0	.246	.333
Harry Elliott	OF17	R	27	24	59	6	15	6	1	1	6	3	8	0	.254	.441
Ferrell Anderson	C12	R	35	18	35	1	10	2	0	0	1	0	4	0	.286	.343
Eddie Stanky	2B8	R	36	17	30	5	8	0	0	0	1	6	4	0	.267	.267
Grant Dunlap	OF1	R	29	16	17	2	6	0	1	1	3	0	2	0	.353	.647
Vern Benson		L	28	13	4	2	0	0	0	0	0	1	2	0	.000	.000
Billy Johnson	3B11	R	34	11	5	0	1	1	0	0	1	1	1	0	.200	.400
Les Fusselman	C11	R	32	11	8	1	2	1	0	0	0	0	0	0	.250	.375
Dick Rand	C9	R	22	9	31	3	9	1	0	0	1	2	6	0	.290	.323
Ed Phillips		B	21	9	0	4	0	0	0	0	0	0	0	0	.000	.000
1 Hal Rice		L	29	8	8	0	2	0	0	0	0	0	3	0	.250	.250
Virgil Stallcup		R	31	1	1	0	0	0	0	0	0	0	0	0	.000	.000
Fred Marolewski	1B1	R	24	1	1	0	0	0	0	0	0	0	0	0	.000	.000
Herb Gorman (DD) 28																

NAME	T	AGE	W	L	PCT	SV	G	GS	CG	IP	H	BB	SO	ShO	ERA
		29	83	71	.539	36	157	157	51	1387	1406	533	732	11	4.22
Harvey Haddix	L	27	20	9	.690	1	36	33	19	253	220	69	163	6	3.06
Gerry Staley	R	32	18	9	.667	4	40	32	10	230	243	54	88	1	3.99
Vinegar Bend Mizell	L	22	13	11	.542	0	33	33	10	224	193	114	173	1	3.50
Stu Miller	R	25	7	8	.467	4	40	18	8	138	161	47	79	2	5.54
2 Hal White	R	34	6	5	.545	7	49	0	0	85	84	39	32	0	2.96
Al Brazle	L	39	6	7	.462	18	60	0	0	92	101	43	57	0	4.21
Joe Presko	R	24	6	13	.316	1	34	25	4	162	165	65	56	0	5.00
2 Eddie Erautt	R	28	3	1	.750	0	20	1	0	36	43	16	15	0	6.25
Cliff Chambers	L	31	3	6	.333	0	32	8	0	80	82	43	26	0	4.84
Mike Clark	R	31	1	0	1.000	1	23	2	0	36	46	21	17	0	4.75
Willard Schmidt	R	25	0	2	.000	0	6	2	0	18	21	13	11	0	9.00
1 Jackie Collum	L	26	0	0	.000	0	7	0	0	11	15	4	5	0	6.55
Jack Faszholz	R	26	0	0	.000	0	4	1	0	12	16	1	7	0	6.75
Dick Bokelmann	R	26	0	0	.000	0	3	0	0	3	4	0	0	0	6.00
John Romonosky	R	23	0	0	.000	0	2	2	0	8	9	4	3	0	4.50
Eddie Yuhas (SA)	R	28	0	0	.000	0	2	0	0	1	3	0	0	0	18.00
Tom Poholsky (MS) 23															

NEW YORK 5th 70-84 .455 35 — **LEO DUROCHER**

NAME	G by POS	B	AGE	G	AB	R	H	2B	3B	HR	RBI	BB	SO	SB	BA	SA
TOTALS			28	155	5362	768	1452	195	45	176	739	499	608	31	.271	.422
Whitey Lockman	1B120, OF30	L	26	150	607	85	179	22	4	9	61	52	36	3	.295	.389
Davey Williams	2B95	R	25	112	340	51	101	11	2	3	34	44	19	2	.297	.368
Al Dark	SS110, 2B26, OF17, 3B8, P1	R	31	155	647	126	194	41	6	23	88	28	34	7	.300	.488
Hank Thompson	3B101, OF9, 2B1	L	27	114	388	80	117	15	8	24	74	60	39	6	.302	.567
Don Mueller	OF122	L	26	131	480	56	160	12	2	6	60	19	13	2	.333	.404
Bobby Thomson	OF154	R	29	154	608	80	175	22	6	26	106	43	57	4	.288	.472
Monte Irvin	OF113	R	34	124	444	72	146	21	5	21	97	55	34	2	.329	.541
Wes Westrum	C106, 3B1	R	30	107	290	40	65	5	0	12	30	56	73	2	.224	.366
Daryl Spencer	SS53, 3B36, 2B32	R	26	118	408	55	85	18	5	20	56	42	74	0	.208	.424
Dusty Rhodes	OF47	L	26	76	163	18	38	7	0	11	30	10	28	0	.233	.479
Bobby Hofman	3B23, 2B17	R	27	74	169	21	45	7	2	12	34	12	23	1	.266	.544
Tookie Gilbert	1B44	L	24	70	160	12	27	3	0	3	16	22	21	1	.169	.244
Ray Noble	C41	R	31	46	97	15	20	0	1	4	14	19	14	1	.206	.351
Sammy Calderone	C31	R	27	35	45	4	10	2	0	0	8	1	4	0	.222	.267
1 Sal Yvars	C20	R	29	23	47	1	13	0	0	0	1	7	1	0	.277	.277
Bill Rigney	3B2, 2B1	R	34	19	20	2	5	0	0	0	1	0	5	0	.250	.250
George Wilson		L	27	11	8	0	1	0	0	0	0	2	2	0	.125	.125
Ray Katt	C8	R	26	8	29	2	5	1	0	0	1	1	3	0	.172	.207
Willie Mays (MS) 22																

NAME	T	AGE	W	L	PCT	SV	G	GS	CG	IP	H	BB	SO	ShO	ERA
		30	70	84	.455	20	155	155	46	1366	1403	610	647	10	4.25
Ruben Gomez	R	25	13	11	.542	0	29	26	13	204	166	101	113	3	3.40
Larry Jansen	R	32	11	16	.407	1	36	26	6	185	185	55	88	0	4.14
Jim Hearn	R	32	9	12	.429	0	36	32	6	197	206	84	77	0	4.52
Sal Maglie	R	36	8	9	.471	0	27	24	9	145	158	47	80	3	4.16
Hoyt Wilhelm	R	29	7	8	.467	15	68	0	0	145	127	77	71	0	3.04
Al Corwin	R	26	6	4	.600	2	48	7	2	107	122	68	49	1	4.96
Dave Koslo	L	33	6	12	.333	2	37	12	2	112	135	36	36	0	4.74
2 Marv Grissom	R	35	4	2	.667	0	21	7	3	84	83	31	46	0	3.96
Al Worthington	R	24	4	8	.333	0	20	17	5	102	103	54	52	2	3.44
Frank Hiller	R	32	2	1	.667	0	19	1	0	34	43	15	10	0	6.09
Bill Connelly	R	28	0	1	.000	0	8	2	0	20	33	17	11	0	11.25
Monte Kennedy	L	31	0	0	.000	0	18	0	0	23	30	19	11	0	7.04
1 Max Lanier	L	37	0	0	.000	0	3	0	0	5	8	3	2	0	7.20
George Spencer	R	26	0	0	.000	0	1	0	0	2	3	2	1	0	9.00
Al Dark	R	31	0	0	.000	0	1	1	0	1	1	1	0	0	18.00
Alex Konikowski (MS) 25															

CINCINNATI 6th 68-86 .442 37 — ROGERS HORNSBY 64-82 .438 BUSTER MILLS 4-4 .500

NAME	G by POS	B	AGE	G	AB	R	H	2B	3B	HR	RBI	BB	SO	SB	BA	SA
TOTALS			27	155	5343	714	1396	190	34	166	669	485	701	25	.261	.403
Ted Kluszewski	1B147	L	28	149	570	97	180	25	0	40	108	55	34	2	.316	.570
Rocky Bridges	2B115, SS6, 3B3	R	25	122	432	52	98	13	2	1	21	37	42	6	.227	.273
Roy McMillan	SS155	R	22	155	557	51	130	15	4	5	43	43	52	2	.233	.302
Bobby Adams	3B150	R	31	150	607	99	167	14	6	8	49	58	67	3	.275	.357
Willard Marshall	OF95	L	32	122	357	51	95	14	6	17	62	41	28	0	.266	.482
Gus Bell	OF151	L	24	151	610	102	183	37	5	30	105	48	72	0	.300	.525
Jim Greengrass	OF153	R	25	154	606	86	173	22	7	20	100	47	83	6	.285	.444
Andy Seminick	C112	R	32	119	387	46	91	12	0	19	64	49	82	2	.235	.413
Bob Borkowski	OF67, 1B2	R	27	94	249	32	67	11	1	7	29	21	41	0	.269	.406
Grady Hatton	2B35, 1B10, 3B5	L	30	83	159	22	37	3	1	7	22	29	24	0	.233	.396
Johnny Temple	2B44	R	24	63	110	14	29	4	0	1	9	7	12	1	.264	.327
Hobie Landrith	C47	L	23	52	154	15	37	3	1	3	16	12	8	2	.240	.331
Bob Marquis	OF10	L	28	40	44	9	12	1	1	2	3	4	11	0	.273	.477
George Lerchen	OF1	L	30	22	17	2	5	1	0	0	2	5	6	0	.294	.353
Frank Baldwin	C6	R	24	16	20	0	2	0	0	0	0	1	9	0	.100	.100

Wally Post 23 R 8-33, 1 Hank Foiles 24 R 2-13, Joe Szekely 28 R 1-13, Ed Bailey 22 L 3-8, Lloyd Merriman (MS) 28

NAME	T	AGE	W	L	PCT	SV	G	GS	CG	IP	H	BB	SO	ShO	ERA
		28	68	86	.442	15	155	155	47	1365	1484	488	506	7	4.64
Harry Perkowski	L	30	12	11	.522	2	33	25	7	193	204	62	70	2	4.52
2 Fred Baczewski	L	27	11	4	.733	1	24	18	10	138	125	52	58	1	3.46
Joe Nuxhall	L	24	9	11	.450	2	30	17	5	142	136	69	52	1	4.31
Frank Smith	R	25	8	1	.889	2	50	1	0	84	89	25	42	0	5.46
2 Jackie Collum	L	26	7	11	.389	3	30	12	4	125	123	39	51	1	3.74
Ken Raffensberger	L	35	7	14	.333	0	26	26	9	174	200	33	47	1	3.93
Bud Podbielan	R	29	6	16	.273	1	36	24	8	186	214	67	74	1	4.74
1 Bubba Church	R	28	3	3	.500	0	11	7	2	44	55	19	12	0	5.93
Clyde King	R	28	3	6	.333	2	35	4	0	76	78	32	21	0	5.21
2 Bob Kelly	R	25	1	2	.333	2	28	5	0	66	71	26	29	0	4.36
Herm Wehmeier	R	26	1	6	.143	0	28	10	2	82	100	47	32	0	7.13
Howie Judson	R	27	0	1	.000	0	10	6	0	39	58	11	11	0	5.54
Ernie Nevel	R	33	0	0	.000	0	10	0	0	10	16	1	5	0	6.30
1 Eddie Erautt	R	28	0	0	.000	0	4	0	0	5	11	3	1	0	5.40
Ed Blake	R	27	0	0	.000	0	1	0	0	0	1	1	0	0	∞
Barney Martin	R	30	0	0	.000	0	1	0	0	2	3	1	1	0	9.00

CHICAGO 7th 65-89 .422 40 — PHIL CAVARRETTA

NAME	G by POS	B	AGE	G	AB	R	H	2B	3B	HR	RBI	BB	SO	SB	BA	SA
TOTALS			30	155	5272	633	1372	204	57	137	588	514	**746**	49	.260	.399
Dee Fondy	1B149	L	28	150	595	79	184	24	11	18	78	44	106	10	.309	.477
Eddie Miksis	2B92, SS53	R	26	142	577	61	145	17	6	8	39	33	59	13	.251	.343
Roy Smalley	SS77	R	27	82	253	20	63	9	0	6	25	28	57	0	.249	.356
Randy Jackson	3B133	R	27	139	498	61	142	22	8	19	66	42	61	8	.285	.476
Hank Sauer (BG)	OF105	R	34	108	395	61	104	16	5	19	60	50	56	0	.263	.473
Frankie Baumholtz	OF130	L	34	133	520	75	159	36	7	3	25	42	36	3	.306	.419
2 Ralph Kiner	OF116	R	30	117	414	73	117	14	2	28	87	75	67	1	.283	.529
Clyde McCullough	C73	R	36	77	229	21	59	3	2	6	23	15	23	0	.258	.367
Hal Jeffcoat	OF100	R	28	106	183	22	43	3	1	4	22	21	26	5	.235	.328
Bill Serena	2B49, 3B28	R	28	93	275	30	69	10	5	10	52	41	46	0	.251	.433
2 Joe Garagiola	C68	L	27	74	228	21	62	9	4	1	21	21	23	0	.272	.360
Tommy Brown	SS25, OF6	R	25	65	138	19	27	7	1	2	13	13	17	1	.196	.304
2 Catfish Metkovich	OF38, 1B7	L	31	61	124	19	29	9	0	2	12	16	10	2	.234	.355
Carl Sawatski	C15	L	25	43	59	5	13	3	0	1	5	7	7	0	.220	.322
1 Preston Ward	OF27, 1B7	L	25	33	100	10	23	5	0	4	12	18	21	3	.230	.400
Phil Cavaretta		L	36	27	21	3	6	3	0	0	3	6	3	0	.286	.429
Bob Ramazotti (HJ)	2B18	R	36	26	39	3	6	2	0	0	4	3	4	0	.154	.205
1 Toby Atwell	C24	L	29	24	74	10	17	2	0	1	8	13	7	0	.230	.297
1 Gene Hermanski	OF13	L	33	18	40	1	6	1	0	0	1	4	7	1	.150	.175

Ernie Banks 22 R 11-35, 1 Bob Addis 27 L 2-12, Dale Talbot 26 R 10-30, Gene Baker 28 R 5-22, Paul Schramke 25 L 0-0, Harry Chiti (MS) 20

NAME	T	AGE	W	L	PCT	SV	G	GS	CG	IP	H	BB	SO	ShO	ERA
		30	65	89	.422	22	155	155	38	1360	1491	554	623	3	4.79
Paul Minner	L	29	12	15	.444	1	31	27	9	201	227	40	64	2	4.21
Warren Hacker	R	28	12	**19**	.387	2	39	32	9	222	225	54	106	0	4.38
Johnny Klippstein	R	25	10	11	.476	6	48	20	5	168	169	107	113	0	4.82
Bob Rush	R	27	9	14	.391	0	29	28	8	167	177	66	84	1	4.53
Turk Lown	R	29	8	7	.533	3	49	12	2	148	166	84	76	0	5.17
2 Howie Pollet	L	32	5	6	.455	1	25	16	2	111	120	44	45	0	4.13
2 Bubba Church	R	28	4	5	.444	1	27	11	1	104	115	49	47	0	5.02
Jim Willis	R	26	2	1	.667	0	13	3	2	43	37	17	15	0	3.14
Dutch Leonard	R	44	2	3	.400	8	45	0	0	63	72	24	27	0	4.57
Duke Simpson	R	25	1	2	.333	0	30	1	0	45	60	25	21	0	8.00
1 Bob Kelly	R	25	0	1	.000	0	14	0	0	17	27	9	6	0	9.53
Don Elston	R	24	0	1	.000	0	2	1	0	5	11	0	2	0	14.40
Sheldon Jones	R	31	0	2	.000	0	22	2	0	38	47	16	9	0	5.45
1 Bob Schultz	L	29	0	2	.000	0	7	2	0	12	13	11	4	0	5.25
1 Fred Baczewski	L	27	0	0	.000	0	9	0	0	10	20	6	3	0	6.30
Bill Moisan	R	27	0	0	.000	0	3	0	0	5	5	2	1	0	5.40

PITTSBURGH 8th 50-104 .325 55 — FRED HANEY

NAME	G by POS	B	AGE	G	AB	R	H	2B	3B	HR	RBI	BB	SO	SB	BA	SA
TOTALS			27	154	5253	622	1297	178	49	99	571	524	715	41	.247	.356
2 Preston Ward	1B78	L	25	88	281	35	59	7	1	8	27	44	39	1	.210	.327
Johnny O'Brien	2B77, SS1	R	22	89	279	28	69	13	2	2	22	21	36	1	.247	.330
Eddie O'Brien	SS81	R	22	89	261	21	62	5	3	0	14	17	30	6	.238	.280
Danny O'Connell	3B104, 2B47	R	26	149	588	88	173	26	8	7	55	57	42	3	.294	.401
Cal Abrams	OF112	L	29	119	448	66	128	10	6	15	43	58	70	4	.286	.435
Carlos Bernier	OF87	R	24	105	310	48	66	7	8	3	31	51	53	15	.213	.316
Frank Thomas	OF118	R	24	128	455	68	116	22	1	30	102	50	93	1	.255	.505
Mike Sandlock	C64	B	37	64	186	10	43	5	0	0	12	12	19	0	.231	.258
Paul Smith	1B74, OF19	L	22	118	389	41	110	12	7	4	44	24	23	3	.283	.380
Dick Cole	SS77, 2B7, 1B1	R	27	97	235	29	64	13	1	0	23	38	26	2	.272	.336
2 Hal Rice	OF70	L	29	78	286	39	89	16	1	4	42	17	22	0	.311	.416
Eddie Pellagrini	2B31, 3B12, SS3	R	35	78	174	16	44	3	2	4	19	14	20	1	.253	.362
1 Johnny Lindell	P27, 1B2	R	36	58	91	11	26	6	1	4	15	16	15	0	.286	.505
2 Toby Atwell	C44	L	29	53	139	11	34	6	0	0	17	20	12	0	.245	.288
1 Pete Castiglione	3B43	R	32	45	159	14	33	2	1	4	21	5	14	1	.208	.308
Vic Janowicz	C35	R	23	42	123	10	31	3	1	2	8	5	31	0	.252	.341
1 Ralph Kiner	OF41	R	30	41	148	27	40	6	1	7	29	25	21	1	.270	.466
2 Gene Hermanski	OF13	L	33	41	62	7	11	0	0	1	4	8	14	0	.177	.226
Felipe Montemayor	OF12	L	23	28	55	5	6	4	0	0	2	4	13	0	.109	.182
1 Joe Garagiola	C22	L	27	27	73	9	17	5	0	2	14	10	11	1	.233	.384
1 Catfish Metkovich	1B5, OF4	L	31	26	41	5	6	0	1	1	7	6	3	0	.146	.268
Dick Smith	SS13	R	26	13	43	4	7	0	1	0	2	6	6	0	.163	.209

Brandy Davis 24 R 8-39, Dick Hall 22 R 4-24, Nick Koback 17 R 2-16, Pete Naton (MS) 21 R 2-12, 1 Ed Fitz Gerald 29 R 2-17, 2 Bob Addis 27 L 0-3, Jack Shepard 21 R 1-4, Clem Koshorek 27 R 0-1, Tony Bartirome (MS) 21, Dick Groat (MS) 22, Jim Mangan (MS) 23

NAME	T	AGE	W	L	PCT	SV	G	GS	CG	IP	H	BB	SO	ShO	ERA
		28	50	**104**	.325	10	154	154	49	1358	**1529**	577	607	4	5.22
Murry Dickson	R	36	10	**19**	.345	4	45	26	10	201	240	58	88	1	4.52
Bob Friend	R	22	8	11	.421	0	32	24	8	171	193	57	66	0	4.89
Paul LaPalme	L	29	8	16	.333	2	35	24	7	176	191	64	86	1	4.60
Roy Face	R	25	6	8	.429	0	41	13	2	119	145	30	56	0	6.58
1 Johnny Lindell	R	36	5	16	.238	0	27	23	13	176	173	**116***	102	1	4.70
Jim Waugh	R	19	4	5	.444	0	29	11	1	90	108	56	23	0	6.50
Johnny Hetki	R	31	3	6	.333	3	54	2	0	118	120	33	37	0	3.97
Bob Hall	R	29	3	12	.200	1	37	17	6	152	172	72	68	1	5.39
1 Howie Pollet	L	32	1	1	.500	0	5	2	0	13	27	6	8	0	10.38
Cal Hogue	R	25	1	1	.500	0	3	2	2	19	19	16	10	0	5.21
Paul Pettit	L	21	1	2	.333	0	10	5	0	28	33	20	14	0	7.71
Bill Macdonald	R	24	0	1	.000	0	4	1	0	7	12	8	4	0	12.86
2 Bob Schultz	L	29	0	2	.000	0	11	2	0	19	26	10	5	0	8.05
Roger Bowman	L	25	0	4	.000	0	30	2	0	65	65	29	36	0	4.85
Woody Main	R	31	0	0	.000	0	2	0	0	4	5	2	4	0	11.25
Bill Bell (MS) 19															
Ron Kline (MS) 21															
Bill Koski (MS) 21															
Vern Law (MS) 23															
Ron Necciai (MS) 21															

*Lindell, also with Philadelphia, league leader in BB with 139.

WORLD SERIES – NEW YORK (AL) 4 BROOKLYN (NL) 3

LINE SCORES

Game 1 September 30 at New York

TEAM	1	2	3	4	5	6	7	8	9	10	11	12	R	H	E
BKN (NL)	0	0	0	0	1	3	1	0	0				5	12	2
NY (AL)	4	0	0	0	1	0	1	3	X				9	12	0

Erskine, Hughes (2), Labine (6), Wade (7) — Reynolds, **Sain** (6)

Game 2 October 1 at New York

TEAM	1	2	3	4	5	6	7	8	9	10	11	12	R	H	E
BKN	0	0	0	2	0	0	0	0	0				2	9	1
NY	1	0	0	0	0	0	1	2	X				4	5	0

Roe — **Lopat**

Game 3 October 2 at Brooklyn

TEAM	1	2	3	4	5	6	7	8	9	10	11	12	R	H	E
NY	0	0	0	0	1	0	0	1	0				2	6	0
BKN	0	0	0	0	1	1	0	1	X				3	9	0

Raschi — **Erskine**

Game 4 October 3 at Brooklyn

TEAM	1	2	3	4	5	6	7	8	9	10	11	12	R	H	E
NY	0	0	0	0	2	0	0	0	1				3	9	0
BKN	3	0	0	1	0	2	1	0	X				7	12	0

Ford, Gorman (2), Sain (5), Schallock (7) — **Loes**, Labine (9)

Game 5 October 4 at Brooklyn

TEAM	1	2	3	4	5	6	7	8	9	10	11	12	R	H	E
NY	1	0	5	0	0	0	3	1	1				11	11	1
BKN	0	1	0	0	1	0	0	4	1				7	14	1

McDonald, Kuzava (8), Reynolds (9) — Podres, Meyer (3), Wade (8), Black (9)

Game 6 October 5 at New York

TEAM	1	2	3	4	5	6	7	8	9	10	11	12	R	H	E
BKN	0	0	0	0	0	1	0	0	2				3	8	3
NY	2	1	0	0	0	0	0	0	1				4	13	0

Erskine, Milliken (5), Labine (7) — Ford, **Reynolds** (8)

COMPOSITE BATTING

NAME	POS	G	AB	R	H	2B	3B	HR	RBI	BA
New York (AL) Totals		6	201	33	56	6	4	9	32	.279
Martin	2B	6	24	5	**12**	1	**2**	**2**	**8**	**.500**
Mantle	OF	6	24	3	5	0	0	**2**	7	.208
McDougald	3B	6	24	2	4	0	1	**2**	4	.167
Collins	1B	6	24	4	4	1	0	1	2	.167
Bauer	OF	6	23	**6**	6	0	1	0	1	.261
Berra	C	6	21	3	9	1	0	1	4	.429
Woodling	OF	6	20	5	6	0	0	1	3	.300
Rizzuto	SS	6	19	4	6	1	0	0	0	.316
Ford	P	2	3	0	1	0	0	0	0	.333
Lopat	P	1	3	0	0	0	0	0	0	.000
Mize	PH	3	3	0	0	0	0	0	0	.000
McDonald	P	1	2	0	1	1	0	0	0	.500
Reynolds	P	3	2	0	1	0	0	0	0	.500
Sain	P	2	2	1	1	1	0	0	2	.500
Bollweg	1B	3	2	0	0	0	0	0	0	.000
Raschi	P	1	2	0	0	0	0	0	0	.000
Noren	PH	2	1	0	0	0	0	0	0	.000

Gorman P 0-1, Kuzava P 0-1, Schallock P 0-0

NAME	POS	G	AB	R	H	2B	3B	HR	RBI	BA
Brooklyn (NL) Totals		6	213	27	64	13	1	8	26	.300
Gilliam	2B	6	**27**	4	8	**3**	0	**2**	4	.296
Snider	OF	6	25	3	8	**3**	0	1	5	.320
Robinson	OF	6	25	3	8	2	0	0	2	.320
Furillo	OF	6	24	4	8	2	0	1	4	.333
Reese	SS	6	24	0	5	0	1	0	0	.208
Cox	3B	6	23	3	7	**3**	0	1	6	.304
Hodges	1B	6	22	3	8	0	0	1	1	.364
Campanella	C	6	22	**6**	6	0	0	1	2	.273
Erskine	P	3	4	0	1	0	0	0	0	.250
Loes	P	1	3	0	2	0	0	0	0	.667
Roe	P	1	3	0	0	0	0	0	0	.000
Williams	PH	3	2	0	1	0	0	0	0	.500
Labine	P	3	2	0	0	0	0	0	0	.000
Belardi	PH	2	2	0	0	0	0	0	0	.000
Shuba	PH	2	1	1	1	0	0	1	2	1.000
Podres	P	1	1	0	1	0	0	0	0	1.000
Hughes	P	1	1	0	0	0	0	0	0	.000
Meyer	P	1	1	0	0	0	0	0	0	.000
Morgan	PH	1	1	0	0	0	0	0	0	.000
Thompson	OF	2	0	0	0	0	0	0	0	.000
Wade	P	2	0	0	0	0	0	0	0	.000

Black P 0-0, Milliken P 0-0

COMPOSITE PITCHING

NAME	G	IP	H	BB	SO	W	L	SV	ERA
New York (AL) Totals	6	52	64	15	30	4	2	1	4.50
Lopat	1	9	9	4	3	1	0	0	**2.00**
Raschi	1	8	9	3	4	0	1	0	3.38
Ford	2	8	9	2	7	0	1	0	4.50
Reynolds	3	8	9	4	9	1	0	1	6.75
McDonald	1	7.2	12	1	0	1	0	0	5.63
Sain	2	5.2	8	1	1	1	0	0	4.50
Gorman	1	3	4	0	1	0	0	0	3.00
Schallock	1	2	2	1	1	0	0	0	4.50
Kuzava	1	.2	2	0	1	0	0	0	13.50
Brooklyn (NL) Totals	6	51.1	56	25	43	2	4	1	4.91
Erskine	3	**14**	**14**	**9**	**16**	1	0	0	5.79
Loes	1	8	8	2	8	1	0	0	3.38
Roe	1	8	5	4	4	0	1	0	4.50
Labine	3	5	10	1	3	0	2	1	3.60
Meyer	1	4.1	8	4	5	0	0	0	6.23
Hughes	1	4	3	1	3	0	0	0	2.25
Podres	1	2.2	1	2	0	0	1	0	3.38
Wade	2	2.1	4	1	2	0	0	0	15.43
Milliken	1	2	2	1	0	0	0	0	0.00
Black	1	1	1	0	2	0	0	0	9.00

1954 The Year the Indians Almost Took It All Apart

There were two notable absences as the season opened. Chuck Dressen, after leading the Dodgers to two straight pennants, demanded a three-year contract from owner Walter O'Malley and was promptly fired. In his place came Walter Alston, an unassuming man with one major league at-bat to his credit. The other vacancy was in St. Louis. After the 1953 season, financially-plagued Bill Veeck sold the team to a syndicate which moved the club to Baltimore—a town that hadn't been in the majors since 1902, when the franchise had been moved to New York.

Beyond the franchise shifts, which were beginning to unsettle baseball's grinning complacency, there was a more immediate problem to handle. Could anyone loosen the Yankees' grip on the pennant? After five years of dominance, people were beginning to wonder if Casey Stengel had a contract with some higher authority than the Yankee owners. As it turned out, Casey proved mortal, even though the Yankees registered 103 victories—more than any of his previous five pennant winners could claim. But the Cleveland Indians, with Bobby Avila, Larry Doby, and Al Rosen, plus pitchers, Early Wynn, Bob Lemon, Mike Garcia, and Bob Feller, set a torrid pace and won 111 games to set a new American League record.

Part of the story of Cleveland's victory was pitching. While some of the Yankee's hurlers were beginning to show signs of age, Cleveland came up with rookies, Don Mossi and Ron Narleski, who accounted for nine wins and 20 saves, and Hal Newhouser, who decided not to retire and chalked up a 7-2 record with seven saves. Also, getting Vic Wertz from Baltimore and putting him on first base did no harm. The Yankees had to be content with an MVP performance from catcher Yogi Berra and 20 wins from rookie Bob Grim.

In the National League, the Dodgers were expected to repeat. Instead, the 1953 fifth-place Giants surprised everyone by winning the flag by five games over Brooklyn. The return of Willie Mays—after two years in the army—and the trade to the Braves of outfielder Bobby Thomson for pitcher Johnny Antonelli made the difference. While Mays got red hot after the All-Star break and hit 31 home runs to win MVP honors, Antonelli came through with 21 wins and a league low 2.29 E.R.A. Ruben Gomez and Sal Maglie also proved reliable starters, but the main thrust came from the bullpen, where Marv Grissom and Hoyt Wilhelm combined to win 22 games and save 26 more. Brooklyn's near miss could be traced to their pitching, especially Don Newcombe, who returned from the service and won only nine, and a hand injury to catcher Roy Campanella, which dropped his average by 105 points.

One departure and several new arrivals also added to the story of 1954. Arnold Johnson bought out the interests of Connie Mack and his family and transplanted the Philadelphia Athletics to Kansas City for the start of the 1955 season. In Milwaukee, Bobby Thomson broke an ankle and forced the Braves to try a young infielder by the name of Hank Aaron in left field. Wally Moon hit well enough for the Cardinals to cause them to trade Enos Slaughter to the Yankees, while Ernie Banks took over as shortstop for the Cubs and Al Kaline right field for the Tigers.

The World Series only lasted for four games, mostly because of the Giants' Mays and their ace pinch hitter Dusty Rhodes. In the first game, with the score knotted at 2-2 and two men on, Wertz of the Indians hit a booming fly ball to the deepest caverns of the Polo Grounds. Mays tore full speed with his back to the plate and caught the drive over his shoulder some 460 feet from home plate. After the miraculous catch, he pivoted and made a great throw to prevent the runners from advancing. Rhodes capped the game in the tenth inning with a three-run pinch-hit homer. In the second game, Rhodes again provided the heroics with a pinch-hit single that tied the game before delivering an insurance homer in the seventh. The third game was again Rhodes', as he came in with the bases loaded and singled to score two runs to give the Giants a 3-0 lead in a 6-2 finale. The last game was all the Giants'. They jumped on the Indians for seven runs to capture the first championship for the National League since 1946.

1954 AMERICAN LEAGUE

CLEVELAND 1st 111-43 .721 — AL LOPEZ

NAME	G by POS	B	AGE	G	AB	R	H	2B	3B	HR	RBI	BB	SO	SB	BA	SA
TOTALS			30	156	5222	746	1368	188	39	**156**	714	637	668	30	.262	.403
2 Vic Wertz	1B83, OF5	L	29	94	295	33	81	14	2	14	48	34	40	0	.275	.478
Bobby Avila	2B141, SS7	R	30	143	555	112	189	27	2	15	67	59	31	9	**.341**	.477
George Strickland (BJ)	SS112	R	28	112	361	42	77	12	3	6	37	55	62	2	.213	.313
Al Rosen	3B87, 1B46, 2B1, SS1	R	30	137	466	76	140	20	2	24	102	85	43	6	.300	.506
Dave Philley	OF129	B	34	133	452	48	102	13	3	12	60	57	48	2	.226	.347
Larry Doby	OF153	L	30	153	577	94	157	18	4	**32**	**126**	85	94	3	.272	.484
Al Smith	OF109, 3B21, SS4	R	26	131	481	101	135	29	6	11	50	88	65	2	.281	.435
Jim Hegan	C137	R	33	139	423	56	99	12	7	11	40	34	48	0	.234	.374
Billy Glynn	1B96, OF1	L	29	111	171	19	43	3	2	5	18	12	21	3	.251	.380
Wally Westlake	OF70	R	33	85	240	36	63	9	2	11	42	26	37	0	.263	.454
Sam Dente	SS60, 2B7	R	32	68	169	18	45	7	1	1	19	14	4	0	.266	.337
Rudy Regalado	3B50, 2B2	R	24	65	180	21	45	5	0	2	24	19	16	0	.250	.311
Dave Pope	OF29	L	29	60	102	21	30	2	1	4	13	10	22	2	.294	.451
Hank Majeski	2B25, 3B10	R	37	57	121	10	34	4	0	3	17	7	14	0	.281	.388
Dale Mitchell	OF6, 1B1	L	32	53	60	6	17	1	0	1	6	9	1	0	.283	.350
Hal Naragon	C45	L	25	46	101	10	24	2	2	0	12	9	12	0	.238	.297

Mickey Grasso 34 R 2-6, Luke Easter 39 L 1-6, Rocky Nelson 24 L 0-4, Joe Ginsberg 27 L 1-2, Jim Dyck 32 R 1-1, 1 Bob Kennedy 33 R 0-0

NAME	T	AGE	W	L	PCT	SV	G	GS	CG	IP	H	BB	SO	ShO	ERA
		30	**111**	43	**.721**	36	156	156	**77**	**1419**	1220	486	678	12	**2.78**
Bob Lemon	R	33	**23**	7	.767	0	36	33	**21**	258	228	92	110	2	2.72
Early Wynn	R	34	**23**	11	.676	2	40	**36**	20	**271**	225	83	155	3	2.72
Mike Garcia	R	30	19	8	.704	5	45	34	13	259	220	71	129	**5**	**2.64**
Art Houtteman	R	26	15	7	.682	0	32	25	11	188	198	59	68	1	3.35
Bob Feller	R	35	13	3	.813	0	19	19	9	140	127	39	59	1	3.09
Hal Newhouser	L	33	7	2	.778	7	26	1	0	47	34	18	25	0	2.49
Don Mossi	L	25	6	1	.857	7	40	5	2	93	56	39	55	0	1.94
Ray Narleski	R	25	3	3	.500	13	42	2	1	89	59	44	52	0	2.22
1 Bob Chakales	R	26	2	0	1.000	0	3	0	0	10	4	12	3	0	0.90
Dave Hoskins	R	28	0	1	.000	0	14	1	0	27	29	10	9	0	3.00
Bob Hooper	R	32	0	0	.000	2	17	0	0	35	39	16	12	0	4.89
Jose Santiago	R	25	0	0	.000	0	1	0	0	2	0	2	1	0	0.00
Dick Tomanek	L	23	0	0	.000	0	1	0	0	2	1	1	0	0	4.50

NEW YORK 2nd 103-51 .669 8 — CASEY STENGEL

NAME	G by POS	B	AGE	G	AB	R	H	2B	3B	HR	RBI	BB	SO	SB	BA	SA
TOTALS			28	155	5226	**805**	1400	215	59	133	**747**	650	632	34	**.268**	**.408**
Joe Collins	1B117	L	31	130	343	67	93	20	2	12	46	51	37	2	.271	.446
Gil McDougald	2B92, 3B35	R	26	126	394	66	102	22	2	12	48	62	64	3	.259	.416
Phil Rizzuto	SS126, 2B1	R	36	127	307	47	60	11	0	2	15	41	23	3	.195	.251
Andy Carey	3B120	R	22	122	411	60	124	14	6	8	65	43	38	5	.302	.423
Hank Bauer	OF108	R	31	114	377	73	111	16	5	12	54	40	42	4	.294	.459
Mickey Mantle	OF144, SS4, 2B1	B	22	146	543	**129**	163	17	12	27	102	102	**107**	5	.300	.525
Irv Noren	OF116, 1B1	L	29	125	426	70	136	21	6	12	66	43	38	4	.319	.481
Yogi Berra	C149, 3B1	L	29	151	584	88	179	28	6	22	125	56	29	0	.307	.488
Jerry Coleman	2B79, SS30, 3B1	R	29	107	300	39	65	7	1	3	21	26	29	3	.217	.277
Gene Woodling (HJ)	OF89	L	31	97	304	33	76	12	5	3	40	53	35	3	.250	.352
Willie Miranda	SS88, 2B4, 3B1	B	28	92	116	12	29	4	2	1	12	10	10	0	.250	.345
Bill Skowron	1B61, 3B5, 2B2	R	23	87	215	37	73	12	9	7	41	19	18	2	.340	.577
Eddie Robinson	1B29	L	33	85	142	11	37	9	0	3	27	19	21	0	.261	.387
Enos Slaughter (BW)	OF30	L	38	69	125	19	31	4	2	1	19	28	8	0	.248	.336
Bob Cerv	OF24	R	28	56	100	14	26	6	0	5	13	11	17	0	.260	.470
Bobby Brown (MS)	3B17	L	29	28	60	5	13	1	0	1	7	8	3	0	.217	.283
Charlie Silvera	C18	R	29	20	37	1	10	1	0	0	4	3	2	0	.270	.297
Frank Leja	1B6	L	18	12	5	2	1	0	0	0	0	0	1	0	.200	.200

Lou Berberet 24 L 2-5, Woodie Held 22 R 0-3, Gus Triandos 23 R 0-1, Ralph Houk 34 R 0-1, Billy Martin (MS) 26

NAME	T	AGE	W	L	PCT	SV	G	GS	CG	IP	H	BB	SO	ShO	ERA
		30	103	51	.669	**37**	155	155	51	1379	1284	552	655	16	3.26
Bob Grim	R	24	20	6	.769	0	37	20	8	199	175	85	108	1	3.26
Whitey Ford	L	25	16	8	.667	1	34	28	11	211	170	101	125	3	2.82
Allie Reynolds	R	39	13	4	.765	7	36	18	5	157	133	66	100	4	3.32
Ed Lopat	L	36	12	4	.750	0	26	23	7	170	189	33	54	0	3.55
Tom Morgan	R	24	11	5	.688	1	32	17	7	143	149	40	34	4	3.34
Harry Byrd	R	29	9	7	.563	0	25	21	5	132	131	43	52	1	3.00
Johnny Sain	R	36	6	6	.500	**22**	45	0	0	77	66	15	33	0	3.16
Jim McDonald (GJ)	R	27	4	1	.800	0	16	10	3	71	54	45	20	1	3.17
2 Marlin Stuart	R	35	3	0	1.000	1	10	0	0	18	28	12	2	0	5.50
Bob Wiesler	L	23	3	2	.600	0	6	5	0	30	28	30	25	0	4.20
Tommy Byrne	L	34	3	2	.600	0	5	5	4	40	36	19	24	1	2.70
2 Ralph Branca	R	28	1	0	1.000	0	5	3	0	13	9	13	7	0	2.77
2 Jim Konstanty	R	37	1	1	.500	2	9	0	0	18	11	6	3	0	1.00
1 Bob Kuzava	L	31	1	3	.250	1	20	3	0	40	46	18	22	0	5.40
Art Schallock	L	30	0	1	.000	0	6	1	1	17	20	11	9	0	4.24
Bill Miller	L	26	0	1	.000	0	2	1	0	6	9	1	6	0	6.00
Tom Gorman	R	29	0	0	.000	2	23	0	0	37	30	14	31	0	2.19

CHICAGO 3rd 94-60 .610 17 — PAUL RICHARDS 91-54 .628 — MARTY MARION 3-6 .333

NAME	G by POS	B	AGE	G	AB	R	H	2B	3B	HR	RBI	BB	SO	SB	BA	SA
TOTALS			30	155	5168	711	1382	203	47	94	655	604	536	**98**	.267	.379
Ferris Fain (KJ)	1B64	L	33	65	235	30	71	10	1	5	51	40	14	5	.302	.417
Nellie Fox	2B155	L	26	155	631	111	**201**	24	8	2	47	51	12	16	.319	.391
Chico Carrasquel	SS155	R	26	155	620	106	158	28	3	12	62	85	67	7	.255	.368
Cass Michaels (FS)	3B91, 2B2	R	28	101	282	35	74	13	2	7	44	56	31	10	.262	.397
Jim Rivera	OF143	L	31	145	490	62	140	16	8	13	61	49	68	18	.286	.431
Johnny Groth	OF125	R	27	125	422	41	116	20	0	7	60	42	37	3	.275	.372
Minnie Minoso	OF146, 3B9	R	31	153	568	119	182	29	**18**	19	116	77	46	18	.320	.535
Sherm Lollar	C93	R	29	107	316	31	77	13	0	7	34	37	28	0	.244	.351
2 George Kell (KJ)	1B32, 3B31, OF2	R	31	71	233	25	66	10	0	5	48	18	12	1	.283	.391
Phil Cavaretta	1B44, OF9	L	37	71	158	21	50	6	0	3	24	26	12	4	.316	.411
Freddie Marsh	3B36, SS3, 1B2, OF1	R	30	62	98	21	30	5	2	0	4	9	16	4	.306	.398
2 Matt Batts	C42	R	32	55	158	16	36	7	1	3	19	17	15	0	.228	.342
Willard Marshall	OF29	L	33	47	71	7	18	2	0	1	7	11	9	0	.254	.324
Carl Sawatski	C33	L	26	43	109	6	20	3	3	1	12	15	20	0	.183	.294
2 Ed McGlee	OF34	R	29	42	75	12	17	1	0	0	5	12	8	5	.227	.240
Ron Jackson	1B35	R	20	40	93	10	26	4	0	4	10	6	20	2	.280	.452
Bob Boyd	OF13, 1B12	L	27	29	56	10	10	3	0	0	5	4	3	2	.179	.232
1 Bill Wilson	OF19	R	25	20	35	4	6	1	0	2	5	7	5	0	.171	.371
Bud Stewart	OF2	L	38	18	13	0	1	0	0	0	0	3	2	0	.077	.077
2 Grady Hatton	3B10, 1B3	L	31	13	30	3	5	1	0	0	3	5	3	1	.167	.200
Joe Kirrene	3B9	R	22	9	23	4	7	1	0	0	4	5	2	1	.304	.348

1 Red Wilson 25 R 4-20, Don Nicholas 23 L 0-0, 2 Stan Jok 28 R 2-12, Bob Cain 29 L 0-0, Sammy Esposito (MS) 22

NAME	T	AGE	W	L	PCT	SV	G	GS	CG	IP	H	BB	SO	ShO	ERA
		30	94	60	.610	33	155	155	60	1383	1255	517	701	**23**	3.05
Virgil Trucks	R	35	19	12	.613	3	40	33	16	265	224	95	152	5	2.78
Sandy Consuegra	R	33	16	3	**.842**	3	39	17	3	154	142	35	31	2	2.69
Bob Keegan	R	33	16	9	.640	2	31	27	14	210	211	82	61	2	3.09
Jack Harshman	L	26	14	8	.636	1	35	21	9	177	157	96	134	4	2.95
Billy Pierce	L	27	9	10	.474	3	36	26	12	189	179	86	148	4	3.48
Don Johnson	R	27	8	7	.533	7	46	16	3	144	129	43	68	3	3.13
Harry Dorish	R	32	6	4	.600	6	37	6	2	109	88	29	48	1	2.72
2 Morrie Martin	L	31	5	4	.556	5	35	2	1	70	52	24	31	0	2.06
Mike Fornieles	R	22	1	2	.333	1	15	6	0	42	41	14	18	0	4.29
1 Al Sima	L	32	0	1	.000	1	5	1	0	7	11	2	1	0	5.14
Dick Strahs	R	29	0	0	.000	1	9	0	0	14	16	8	8	0	5.79
Tom Flanigan	L	19	0	0	.000	0	2	0	0	2	1	1	0	0	0.00
Vito Valentinetti	R	25	0	0	.000	0	1	0	0	1	4	2	1	0	54.00

BOSTON 4th 69-85 .448 42 — LOU BOUDREAU

NAME	G by POS	B	AGE	G	AB	R	H	2B	3B	HR	RBI	BB	SO	SB	BA	SA
TOTALS			26	156	5399	700	1436	244	41	123	657	654	660	51	.266	.395
Harry Agganis	1B119	L	24	132	434	54	109	13	8	11	57	47	57	6	.251	.394
Ted Lepcio	2B80, 3B24, SS14	R	23	116	398	42	102	19	4	8	45	42	62	3	.256	.384
Milt Bolling	SS107, 3B5	R	23	113	370	42	92	20	3	6	36	47	55	2	.249	.368
3 Grady Hatton	3B93, SS1, 1B1	L	31	99	302	40	85	12	3	5	33	58	25	1	.281	.391
Jimmy Piersall	OF126	R	24	133	474	77	135	24	2	8	38	36	42	5	.285	.395
Jackie Jensen	OF151	R	27	152	580	92	160	25	7	25	117	79	52	22	.276	.472
Ted Williams (BS)	OF115	L	35	117	386	93	133	23	1	29	89	136	32	0	.345	.635
Sammy White	C133	R	25	137	493	46	139	25	2	14	75	21	50	1	.282	.426
Billy Goodman	2B72, 1B27, OF13, 3B12	L	28	127	489	71	148	25	4	1	36	51	15	3	.303	.376
Karl Olson (MS)	OF78	R	23	101	227	25	59	12	2	1	20	12	23	2	.260	.344
Billy Consolo	SS50, 3B18, 2B12	R	19	91	242	23	55	7	1	1	11	33	69	2	.227	.277
Charlie Maxwell	OF27	L	27	74	104	9	26	4	1	0	5	12	21	3	.250	.308
2 Don Lenhardt	OF13, 3B1	R	31	44	66	5	18	4	0	3	17	3	9	0	.273	.470
2 Sam Mele	1B22, OF13	R	31	42	132	22	42	6	0	7	23	12	12	0	.318	.523
Mickey Owen	C30	R	38	32	68	6	16	3	0	1	11	9	6	0	.235	.324
1 George Kell	3B25	R	31	26	93	15	24	3	0	0	10	15	3	0	.258	.290
Del Wilber	C18	R	35	24	61	2	8	2	1	1	7	4	6	0	.131	.246
1 Floyd Baker	3B7, 2B1	L	37	21	20	1	4	2	0	0	3	0	1	0	.200	.300
Dick Gernert	1B6	R	25	14	23	2	6	2	0	0	1	6	4	0	.261	.348

1 Hoot Evers 33 R 0-8, Guy Morton 23 R 0-1, Faye Throneberry (MS) 23

NAME	T	AGE	W	L	PCT	SV	G	GS	CG	IP	H	BB	SO	ShO	ERA
TOTALS		28	69	85	.448	22	156	156	41	1412	1434	612	707	10	4.02
Frank Sullivan	R	24	15	12	.556	1	36	26	11	206	185	66	124	3	3.15
Willard Nixon	R	26	11	12	.478	0	31	30	8	200	182	87	102	2	4.05
Tom Brewer	R	22	10	9	.526	0	33	23	7	163	152	95	69	0	4.64
Ellis Kinder	R	39	8	8	.500	15	48	2	0	107	106	36	67	0	3.62
Russ Kemmerer	R	22	5	3	.625	0	19	9	2	75	71	41	37	1	3.84
Leo Kiely	L	24	5	8	.385	0	28	19	4	131	153	58	59	1	3.50
Sid Hudson	R	39	3	4	.429	5	33	5	0	71	83	30	27	0	4.44
Bill Henry	L	26	3	7	.300	0	24	13	3	96	104	49	38	1	4.50
Mel Parnell (BA)	L	32	3	7	.300	0	19	15	4	92	104	35	38	1	3.72
Tom Hurd	R	30	2	0	1.000	1	16	0	0	30	21	12	14	0	3.00
Tex Clevenger	R	21	2	4	.333	0	23	8	1	68	67	29	43	0	4.76
Tom Herrin	R	24	1	2	.333	0	14	1	0	28	34	22	8	0	7.39
Hal Brown	R	29	1	8	.111	0	40	5	1	118	126	41	66	0	4.12
Bill Werle	L	33	0	1	.000	0	14	0	0	25	41	10	14	0	4.32
Joe Dobson	R	37	0	0	.000	0	2	0	0	3	5	1	1	0	6.00

Dick Brodowski (MS) 21

DETROIT 5th 68-86 .442 43 — FRED HUTCHINSON

NAME	G by POS	B	AGE	G	AB	R	H	2B	3B	HR	RBI	BB	SO	SB	BA	SA
TOTALS			25	155	5233	584	1351	215	41	90	552	492	603	48	.258	.367
Walt Dropo	1B95	R	31	107	320	27	90	14	2	4	44	24	41	0	.281	.375
Frank Bolling	2B113	R	22	117	368	46	87	15	2	6	38	36	51	3	.236	.337
Harvey Kuenn	SS155	R	23	155	656	81	201	28	6	5	48	29	13	9	.306	.390
Ray Boone	3B148, SS1	R	30	148	543	76	160	19	7	20	85	71	53	4	.295	.466
Al Kaline	OF135	R	19	138	504	42	139	18	3	4	43	22	45	9	.276	.347
Bill Tuttle	OF145	R	24	147	530	64	141	20	11	7	58	62	60	5	.266	.385
Jim Delsing	OF108	L	28	122	371	39	92	24	2	6	38	49	38	4	.248	.372
Frank House	C107	L	24	114	352	35	88	12	1	9	38	31	34	2	.250	.366
Bob Nieman	OF62	R	27	91	251	24	66	14	1	8	35	22	32	0	.263	.422
2 Wayne Belardi	1B79	L	23	88	250	27	58	7	1	11	24	33	34	1	.232	.400
Fred Hatfield	2B54, 3B15	L	29	81	218	31	64	12	0	2	25	28	24	4	.294	.376
2 Red Wilson	C53	R	25	54	170	22	48	11	1	2	22	27	12	3	.282	.394
Reno Bertoia	2B15, 3B8, SS3	R	19	54	37	13	6	2	0	1	2	5	9	1	.162	.297
Don Lund	OF31	R	31	35	54	4	7	2	0	0	3	4	3	1	.130	.167
3 Hoot Evers	OF24	R	33	30	60	5	11	4	0	0	5	5	8	1	.183	.250
Steve Souchock (BW)	OF9, 3B2	R	35	25	39	6	7	0	1	3	8	2	10	1	.179	.462
1 Charlie Kress	1B7, OF1	L	32	24	37	4	7	0	1	0	3	1	4	0	.189	.243
1 Johnny Pesky		L	34	20	17	5	3	0	0	1	1	3	1	0	.176	.353
1 Matt Batts	C8	R	32	12	21	1	6	1	0	0	5	2	4	0	.286	.333
Charlie King	OF7	R	23	11	28	4	6	0	1	0	3	3	8	0	.214	.286

Al Lakeman 35 R 0-6, George Bullard 25 R 0-1, Walt Streuli 18 R 0-0,

NAME	T	AGE	W	L	PCT	SV	G	GS	CG	IP	H	BB	SO	ShO	ERA
TOTALS		26	68	86	.442	13	155	155	58	1383	1375	506	603	12	3.81
Steve Gromek	R	34	18	16	.529	1	36	32	17	253	236	57	102	4	2.74
Ned Garver	R	28	14	11	.560	1	35	32	16	246	216	62	93	3	2.82
2 George Zuverink	R	29	9	13	.409	4	35	25	9	203	201	62	70	2	3.59
Billy Hoeft	L	22	7	15	.318	1	34	25	10	175	180	59	114	4	4.58
Dick Marlowe	R	25	5	4	.556	2	38	2	0	84	76	40	39	0	4.18
Al Aber	L	26	5	11	.313	3	32	18	4	125	121	40	54	0	3.96
1 Ralph Branca	R	28	3	3	.500	0	17	5	0	45	63	30	15	0	5.80
Ted Gray (AJ)	L	29	3	5	.375	0	19	10	2	72	70	56	29	0	5.38
Ray Herbert	R	24	3	6	.333	0	42	4	0	84	114	50	44	0	5.89
Bob Miller	L	18	1	1	.500	1	32	1	0	70	62	26	27	0	2.44
Dick Weik	R	26	0	1	.000	0	9	1	0	16	23	16	9	0	7.31
Frank Lary	R	24	0	0	.000	0	3	0	0	4	4	3	5	0	2.25
Dick Donovan	R	26	0	0	.000	0	2	0	0	6	9	5	2	0	10.50

Bill Black (MS) 21

WASHINGTON 6th 66-88 .429 45 — BUCKY HARRIS

NAME	G by POS	B	AGE	G	AB	R	H	2B	3B	HR	RBI	BB	SO	SB	BA	SA
TOTALS			29	155	5249	632	1292	188	69	81	592	610	719	37	.246	.355
Mickey Vernon	1B148	L	36	151	597	90	173	33	14	20	97	61	61	1	.290	.492
Wayne Terwilliger	2B90, 3B10, SS3	R	29	106	337	42	70	10	1	3	24	32	40	3	.208	.270
Pete Runnels	SS107, 2B27, OF1	L	26	139	488	75	131	17	15	3	56	78	60	2	.268	.383
Eddie Yost	3B155	R	27	155	539	101	138	26	4	11	47	131	71	7	.256	.380
Tommy Umphlett	OF101	R	24	114	342	21	75	8	3	1	33	17	42	1	.219	.269
Jim Busby	OF155	R	27	155	628	83	187	22	7	7	80	43	56	17	.298	.389
Roy Sievers	OF133, 1B8	R	27	145	514	75	119	26	6	24	102	80	77	2	.232	.446
Ed Fitz Gerald	C107	R	30	115	360	33	104	13	5	4	40	33	22	0	.289	.386
Tom Wright	OF43	L	30	76	171	13	42	4	4	1	17	18	38	0	.246	.333
Jerry Snyder	SS48, 2B3	R	24	64	154	17	36	3	1	0	17	15	18	3	.234	.266
Clyde Vollmer	OF26	R	32	62	117	8	30	4	0	2	15	12	28	0	.256	.342
Joe Tipton	C52	R	31	54	157	9	35	6	1	1	10	30	30	0	.223	.293
Mickey McDermott	P30	L	25	54	95	7	19	3	0	0	4	7	12	0	.200	.232
2 Johnny Pesky	2B37, SS1	L	34	49	158	17	40	4	3	0	9	10	7	1	.253	.316
Jim Lemon	OF33	R	26	37	128	12	30	2	3	2	13	9	34	0	.234	.344
Mel Hoderlein	[illegible], 2B5	B	31	14	25	0	4	1	0	0	1	1	4	0	.160	.200
Bob Oldis	C8, 3B2	R	26	11	24	1	8	1	0	0	0	1	3	0	.333	.375
Harmon Killebrew	2B3	R	18	9	13	1	4	1	0	0	3	2	3	0	.308	.385
Roy Dietzel	2B7, 3B2	R	23	9	21	1	5	0	0	0	1	5	4	0	.238	.238

Carlos Paula 25 R 4-24, Jesse Levan 27 L 3-10, Steve Korcheck 21 R 1-7

NAME	T	AGE	W	L	PCT	SV	G	GS	CG	IP	H	BB	SO	ShO	ERA
TOTALS		28	66	88	.429	7	155	155	69	1383	1396	573	562	10	3.84
Bob Porterfield	R	30	13	15	.464	0	32	31	21	244	249	77	82	2	3.32
Dean Stone	L	23	12	10	.545	0	31	23	10	179	161	69	87	2	3.22
Johnny Schmitz	L	33	11	8	.579	1	29	23	12	185	176	64	56	2	2.92
Chuck Stobbs	L	24	11	11	.500	0	31	24	10	182	189	67	67	3	4.10
Mickey McDermott	L	25	7	15	.318	1	30	26	11	196	172	110	95	1	3.44
Camilo Pascual	R	20	4	7	.364	3	48	4	1	119	126	61	60	0	4.24
Connie Marrero	R	43	3	6	.333	0	22	8	1	66	74	22	26	0	4.77
Gus Keriazakos	R	22	2	3	.400	0	22	3	2	60	59	30	33	0	3.75
Spec Shea	R	33	2	9	.182	0	23	11	1	71	97	34	22	0	6.21
1 Sonny Dixon	R	29	1	2	.333	1	16*	0	0	30	26	12	7	0	3.00
Bunky Stewart	L	23	0	2	.000	1	29	2	0	51	67	27	27	0	7.59

*Dixon, also with Philadelphia, league leader in G with 54.

BALTIMORE 7th 54-100 .351 57 — JIMMY DYKES

NAME	G by POS	B	AGE	G	AB	R	H	2B	3B	HR	RBI	BB	SO	SB	BA	SA
TOTALS			30	154	5206	483	1309	195	49	52	451	468	634	30	.251	.338
Eddie Waitkus	1B78	L	34	95	311	35	88	17	4	2	33	28	25	0	.283	.383
Bobby Young	2B127	L	29	130	432	43	106	13	6	4	24	54	42	4	.245	.331
Billy Hunter	SS124	R	26	125	411	28	100	9	5	2	27	21	38	5	.243	.304
Vern Stephens	3B96	R	33	101	365	31	104	17	1	8	46	17	36	0	.285	.403
2 Cal Abrams	OF115	L	30	115	423	67	124	22	7	6	25	72	67	1	.293	.421
Chuck Diering	OF119	R	31	128	418	35	108	14	1	2	29	56	57	3	.258	.311
Gil Coan	OF67	L	32	94	265	29	74	11	1	2	20	16	17	9	.279	.351
Clint Courtney	C111	L	27	122	397	25	107	18	3	4	37	30	7	2	.270	.360
2 Bob Kennedy	3B71, OF21	R	33	106	323	37	81	13	2	6	45	28	43	2	.251	.359
Dick Kryhoski	1B69	L	29	100	300	32	78	13	2	1	34	19	24	0	.260	.327
Jim Fridley	OF67	R	29	85	240	25	59	8	5	4	36	21	41	0	.246	.371
Jim Brideweser	SS48, 2B19	R	27	73	204	18	54	7	2	0	12	15	27	1	.265	.319
1 Sam Mele	OF62	R	31	72	230	17	55	9	4	5	32	18	26	1	.239	.378
Les Moss	C38	R	29	50	126	7	31	3	0	0	5	14	16	0	.246	.270
Chico Garcia	2B24	R	29	39	62	6	7	0	2	0	5	8	3	0	.113	.177
1 Vic Wertz	OF27	L	29	29	94	5	19	1	0	1	13	11	17	0	.202	.245
Ray Murray	C21	R	36	22	61	4	15	4	1	0	2	2	5	0	.246	.344
1 Don Lenhardt	OF7, 1B2	R	31	13	33	2	5	1	0	0	1	3	9	0	.152	.182
Dick Kokos	OF1	L	26	11	10	1	2	0	0	1	1	4	3	0	.200	.500
Joe Durham	OF10	R	22	10	40	4	9	0	0	1	3	4	7	0	.225	.300
Frank Kellert	1B9	R	29	10	34	3	7	2	0	0	1	5	4	0	.206	.265

Neil Berry 32 R 1-9, Jay Porter (MS) 21, Frank Saucier (MS) 28

NAME	T	AGE	W	L	PCT	SV	G	GS	CG	IP	H	BB	SO	ShO	ERA
TOTALS		29	54	100	.351	8	154	154	58	1373	1279	688	668	6	3.88
Bob Turley	R	23	14	15	.483	0	35	35	14	247	178	181	185	0	3.46
Joe Coleman	R	31	13	17	.433	0	33	32	15	221	184	96	103	4	3.50
Duane Pillette	R	31	10	14	.417	0	25	25	11	179	158	67	66	1	3.12
Lou Kretlow	R	31	6	11	.353	0	32	20	5	167	169	82	82	0	4.37
2 Bob Chakales	R	26	3	7	.300	3	38	6	0	89	81	43	44	0	3.74
Don Larsen	R	24	3	21	.125	0	29	28	12	202	213	89	80	1	4.37
Billy O'Dell	L	21	1	1	.500	0	7	2	1	16	15	5	6	0	2.81
Howie Fox	R	33	1	2	.333	2	38	0	0	74	80	34	27	0	3.65
1 Marlin Stuart	R	35	1	2	.333	2	22	0	0	38	46	15	13	0	4.50
2 Bob Kuzava	L	31	1	3	.250	0	4	4	0	24	30	11	15	0	4.13
Mike Blyzka	R	25	1	5	.167	1	37	0	0	86	83	51	35	0	4.71
1 Dave Koslo	L	34	0	1	.000	0	3	1	0	14	20	3	3	0	3.21
Vern Bickford	R	33	0	1	.000	0	1	1	0	4	5	1	0	0	9.00
1 Dick Littlefield	L	28	0	0	.000	0	3	0	0	6	8	6	5	0	10.50
Jay Heard	R	29	0	0	.000	0	2	0	0	3	6	3	2	0	15.00
Ryne Duren	R	25	0	0	.000	0	1	0	0	2	3	1	2	0	9.00

PHILADELPHIA 8th 51-103 .331 60 — EDDIE JOOST

NAME	G by POS	B	AGE	G	AB	R	H	2B	3B	HR	RBI	BB	SO	SB	BA	SA
TOTALS			29	156	5206	542	1228	191	41	94	503	504	677	30	.236	.342
Lou Limmer	1B79	L	29	115	316	41	73	10	3	14	32	35	37	2	.231	.415
Spook Jacobs	2B131	R	28	132	508	63	131	11	1	0	26	60	22	17	.258	.283
Joe DeMaestri	SS142, 3B1, 2B1	R	25	146	539	49	124	16	3	8	40	20	63	1	.230	.315
Jim Finigan	3B136	R	25	136	487	57	147	25	6	7	51	64	66	2	.302	.421
Bill Renna	OF115	R	29	123	422	52	98	15	4	13	53	41	60	1	.232	.379
2 Bill Wilson	OF91	R	25	94	323	43	77	10	1	15	33	39	59	1	.238	.415
Vic Power	OF101, 1B21, 3B1, SS1	R	22	127	462	36	118	17	5	8	38	19	19	2	.255	.366
Joe Astroth	C71	R	31	77	226	22	50	8	1	1	23	21	19	0	.221	.279
Don Bollweg	1B71	L	33	103	268	35	60	15	3	5	24	35	33	1	.224	.358
Gus Zernial (BC)	OF90, 1B2	R	31	97	336	42	84	8	2	14	62	30	60	0	.250	.411
Elmer Valo	OF62	L	33	95	224	28	48	11	6	1	33	51	18	2	.214	.330
Pete Suder	2B35, 3B20, SS2	R	38	69	205	8	41	11	1	0	16	7	16	0	.200	.263
Jim Robertson	C50	R	26	63	147	9	27	8	0	0	8	23	25	0	.184	.238
Billy Shantz	C51	R	26	51	164	13	42	9	3	1	17	17	23	0	.256	.366
1 Ed McGhee	OF13	R	29	21	53	5	11	2	0	2	9	4	8	0	.208	.358
Eddie Joost	SS9, 3B5, 2B1	R	38	19	47	7	17	3	0	1	9	10	10	0	.362	.489
Joe Taylor	OF16	L	28	18	58	5	13	1	1	1	8	2	9	0	.224	.328
Jack Littrell	SS9	R	25	9	30	7	9	2	0	1	3	6	3	1	.300	.467

NAME	T	AGE	W	L	PCT	SV	G	GS	CG	IP	H	BB	SO	ShO	ERA
TOTALS		28	51	103	.331	13	156	156	49	1371	1523	685	665	3	5.18
Arnie Portocarrero	R	22	9	18	.333	0	34	33	16	248	233	114	132	1	4.06
Bob Trice	R	25	7	8	.467	0	19	18	8	119	146	48	22	1	5.60
Alex Kellner	L	29	6	17	.261	0	27	27	8	174	204	88	69	1	5.38
Moe Burtschy	R	32	5	4	.556	4	46	0	0	95	80	53	54	0	3.79
2 Sonny Dixon	R	29	5	7	.417	4	38*	6	1	107	136	27	42	0	4.88
Marion Fricano	R	30	5	11	.313	1	37	20	4	152	163	64	43	0	5.15
Charlie Bishop	R	30	4	6	.400	1	20	12	4	96	98	50	34	0	4.41
John Gray	R	26	3	12	.200	0	18	16	5	105	111	91	51	0	6.51
1 Morrie Martin	L	31	2	4	.333	0	13	6	2	53	57	19	24	0	5.43
2 Al Sima	L	32	2	5	.286	2	29	7	1	79	101	32	36	0	5.24
Bobby Shantz (SA)	L	28	1	0	1.000	0	2	1	0	8	12	3	3	0	7.88
Dutch Romberger	R	27	1	1	.500	0	10	0	0	16	28	12	6	0	11.25
Art Ditmar	R	25	1	4	.200	0	14	5	0	39	50	36	14	0	6.46
Bill Oster	L	21	0	1	.000	0	8	1	0	16	19	12	5	0	6.19
1 Carl Scheib	R	27	0	1	.000	0	1	1	0	2	5	1	1	0	22.50
Ozzie Van Brabant	R	27	0	2	.000	0	9	2	0	27	35	18	10	0	7.00
Lee Wheat	R	24	0	2	.000	0	8	1	0	28	38	9	7	0	5.79
Bill Upton	R	25	0	0	.000	1	2	0	0	5	6	1	2	0	1.80

Dick Rozek 27 L 0-0, Hal Raether 21 R 0-0, Bill Harrington (MS) 26

*Dixon (See Washington)

NEW YORK 1st 97-57 .630 — LEO DUROCHER

NAME	G by POS	B	AGE	G	AB	R	H	2B	3B	HR	RBI	BB	SO	SB	BA	SA
TOTALS			28	154	5245	732	1386	194	42	**186**	701	522	561	30	.264	.424
Whitey Lockman	1B145, OF2	L	27	148	570	73	143	17	3	16	60	59	31	2	.251	.375
Davey Williams	2B142	R	26	142	544	65	121	18	3	9	46	43	33	1	.222	.316
Al Dark	SS154	R	32	154	**644**	98	189	26	6	20	70	27	40	5	.293	.446
Hank Thompson	3B130, 2B2, OF1	L	28	136	448	76	118	18	1	26	86	90	58	3	.263	.482
Don Mueller	OF153	L	27	153	619	90	**212**	35	8	4	71	22	17	2	.342	.444
Willie Mays	OF151	R	23	151	565	119	195	33	**13**	41	110	66	57	8	**.345**	**.667**
Monte Irvin	OF128, 3B1, 1B1	R	35	135	432	62	113	13	3	19	64	70	23	7	.262	.438
Wes Westrum	C98	R	31	98	246	25	46	3	1	8	27	45	60	0	.187	.305
Ray Katt	C82	R	27	86	200	26	51	7	1	9	33	19	29	1	.255	.435
Dusty Rhodes	OF37	L	27	82	164	31	56	7	3	15	50	18	25	1	.341	.695
Bobby Hofman	1B21, 2B10, 3B8	R	28	71	125	12	28	5	0	8	30	17	15	0	.224	.456
Billy Gardner	3B30, 2B13, SS5	R	26	62	108	10	23	5	0	1	7	6	19	0	.213	.287
Bill Taylor	OF9	L	24	55	65	4	12	1	0	2	10	3	15	0	.185	.292
Ebba St. Claire	C16	B	32	20	42	5	11	1	0	2	6	12	7	0	.262	.429
Foster Castleman	2B2	R	23	13	12	0	3	0	0	0	1	0	3	0	.250	.250
2 Hoot Evers	OF4	R	33	12	11	1	1	0	0	1	3	0	6	0	.091	.364
Ron Samford	2B3	R	24	12	5	2	0	0	0	0	0	0	1	0	.000	.000
Joey Amalfitano	3B4, 2B1	R	20	9	5	2	0	0	0	0	0	0	4	0	.000	.000
2 Joe Garagiola	C3	L	28	5	11	1	3	2	0	0	1	1	2	0	.273	.455
Eric Rodin	OF3	R	24	5	6	0	0	0	0	0	0	0	2	0	.000	.000
Harvey Gentry		L	28	5	4	0	1	0	0	0	1	1	0	0	.250	.250
Bob Lennon		L	25	3	3	0	0	0	0	0	0	0	0	0	.000	.000
Daryl Spencer (MS) 24																

NAME	T	AGE	W	L	PCT	SV	G	GS	CG	IP	H	BB	SO	ShO	ERA
TOTALS		30	**97**	57	**.630**	33	154	154	45	1390	1258	613	692	**19**	**3.09**
Johnny Antonelli	L	24	21	7	**.750**	2	39	37	18	259	209	94	152	**6**	**2.29**
Ruben Gomez	R	26	17	9	.654	0	37	32	10	222	202	**109**	106	4	2.88
Sal Maglie	R	37	14	6	.700	2	34	32	9	218	222	70	117	1	3.26
Hoyt Wilhelm	R	30	12	4	.750	7	57	0	0	111	77	52	64	0	2.11
Marv Grissom	R	36	10	7	.588	19	56	3	1	122	100	50	64	1	2.36
Don Liddle	L	29	9	4	.692	0	28	19	4	127	100	55	44	3	3.05
Jim Hearn	R	33	8	8	.500	1	29	18	3	130	137	66	45	2	4.15
Larry Jansen	R	33	2	2	.500	0	13	7	0	41	57	15	15	0	5.93
Windy McCall	L	28	2	5	.286	2	33	4	0	61	50	29	38	0	3.25
George Spencer	R	27	1	0	1.000	0	6	0	0	12	9	8	4	0	3.75
Al Corwin	R	27	1	3	.250	0	20	0	0	31	35	14	14	0	4.06
Al Worthington	R	25	0	2	.000	0	10	1	0	18	21	15	8	0	3.50
Alex Konikowski	R	26	0	0	.000	0	10	0	0	12	10	12	6	0	7.50
Paul Giel	R	21	0	0	.000	0	6	0	0	4	8	2	4	0	9.00
Ray Monzant	R	21	0	0	.000	0	6	1	0	8	8	11	5	0	4.50
1 Mario Picone	R	27	0	0	.000	0	5	0	0	14	13	11	6	0	5.14

BROOKLYN 3rd 92-62 .597 5 — WALT ALSTON

NAME	G by POS	B	AGE	G	AB	R	H	2B	3B	HR	RBI	BB	SO	SB	BA	SA
TOTALS			30	154	5251	778	1418	246	56	**186**	741	**634**	625	46	.270	**.444**
Gil Hodges	1B154	R	30	154	579	106	176	23	5	42	130	74	84	3	.304	.579
Jim Gilliam	2B143, OF5	B	25	146	607	107	171	28	8	13	52	76	30	8	.282	.418
Pee Wee Reese	SS140	R	35	141	554	98	171	35	8	10	69	90	62	8	.309	.455
Don Hoak	3B75	R	26	88	261	41	64	9	5	7	26	25	39	8	.245	.398
Carl Furillo	OF149	R	32	150	547	56	161	23	1	19	96	49	35	2	.294	.444
Duke Snider	OF148	L	27	149	584	**120**	199	39	10	40	130	84	**96**	6	.341	.647
Jackie Robinson	OF64, 3B50, 2B4	R	35	124	386	62	120	22	4	15	59	63	20	7	.311	.505
Roy Campanella (HJ)	C111	R	32	111	397	43	82	14	3	19	51	42	49	1	.207	.401
Sandy Amoros	OF70	L	24	79	263	44	72	18	6	9	34	31	24	1	.274	.490
Billy Cox	3B58, 2B11, SS8	R	34	77	226	26	53	9	2	2	17	21	13	0	.235	.319
Rube Walker	C47	L	28	50	155	12	28	7	0	5	23	24	17	0	.181	.323
Walt Moryn	OF21	L	28	48	91	16	25	4	2	2	14	7	11	0	.275	.429
George Shuba	OF13	L	29	45	65	3	10	5	0	2	10	7	10	0	.154	.323
Don Thompson	OF29	L	30	34	25	2	1	0	0	0	1	5	5	0	.040	.040
Don Zimmer	SS13	R	23	24	33	3	6	0	1	0	0	3	8	2	.182	.242
Dick Williams	OF14	R	25	16	34	5	5	0	0	1	2	2	7	0	.147	.235
2 Charlie Kress	1B1	L	32	13	12	1	1	0	0	0	2	0	0	0	.083	.083
1 Wayne Belardi		L	23	11	9	0	2	0	0	0	1	2	3	0	.222	.222
Tim Thompson	C2, OF1	L	30	10	13	2	2	1	0	0	1	1	1	0	.154	.231

NAME	T	AGE	W	L	PCT	SV	G	GS	CG	IP	H	BB	SO	ShO	ERA
TOTALS		28	92	62	.597	**36**	154	154	39	1394	1399	533	**762**	8	4.31
Carl Erskine	R	27	18	15	.545	1	38	37	12	260	239	92	166	2	4.15
Billy Loes	R	24	13	5	.722	0	28	21	6	148	154	60	97	0	4.14
Russ Meyer	R	30	11	6	.647	0	36	28	6	180	193	49	70	2	4.00
Johnny Podres (IL)	L	21	11	7	.611	0	29	21	6	152	147	53	79	2	4.26
Don Newcombe	R	28	9	8	.529	0	29	25	6	144	158	49	82	0	4.56
Jim Hughes	R	31	8	4	.667	**24**	**60**	0	0	87	76	44	58	0	3.21
Clem Labine	R	27	7	6	.538	5	47	2	0	108	101	56	43	0	4.17
Bob Milliken	R	27	5	2	.714	2	24	3	0	63	58	18	25	0	4.00
Erv Palica	R	26	3	3	.500	0	25	3	0	68	77	31	25	0	5.29
Preacher Roe	L	39	3	4	.429	0	15	10	1	63	69	23	31	0	5.00
Karl Spooner	L	23	2	0	1.000	0	2	2	2	18	7	6	27	2	0.00
1 Ben Wade	R	31	1	1	.500	3	23	0	0	45	62	21	25	0	8.20
Pete Wojey	R	34	1	1	.500	1	14	1	0	28	24	14	21	0	3.21
Bob Darnell	R	23	0	0	.000	0	6	1	0	14	15	7	5	0	3.21
Joe Black (SA)	R	30	0	0	.000	0	5	0	0	7	11	5	3	0	11.57
Tom Lasorda	L	26	0	0	.000	0	4	0	0	9	8	5	5	0	5.00

MILWAUKEE 3rd 89-65 .578 8 — CHARLIE GRIMM

NAME	G by POS	B	AGE	G	AB	R	H	2B	3B	HR	RBI	BB	SO	SB	BA	SA
TOTALS			26	154	5261	670	1395	217	41	139	636	471	619	54	.265	.401
Joe Adcock	1B133	R	26	133	500	73	154	27	5	23	87	44	58	1	.308	.520
Danny O'Connell	2B103, 3B35, 1B8, SS1	R	27	146	541	61	151	28	4	2	37	38	46	2	.279	.357
Johnny Logan	SS154	R	27	154	560	66	154	17	7	8	66	51	51	2	.275	.373
Eddie Mathews	3B127, OF10	L	22	138	476	96	138	21	4	40	103	113	61	10	.290	.603
Andy Pafko	OF138	R	33	138	510	61	146	22	4	14	69	37	36	1	.286	.427
Bill Bruton	OF141	L	28	142	567	89	161	20	7	4	30	40	78	**34**	.284	.365
Hank Aaron (BN)	OF116	R	20	122	468	58	131	27	6	13	69	28	39	2	.280	.447
Del Crandall	C136	R	24	138	463	60	112	18	2	21	64	40	56	0	.242	.425
Jim Pendleton	OF50	R	30	71	173	20	38	3	1	1	16	4	21	2	.220	.266
Catfish Metkovich	1B18, OF13	L	32	68	123	7	34	5	1	1	15	15	15	0	.276	.358
Jack Dittmer	2B55	L	26	66	192	22	47	8	0	6	20	19	17	0	.245	.380
Charlie White	C28	L	25	50	93	14	22	4	0	1	8	9	8	0	.237	.312
Bobby Thomson (BN)	OF26	R	30	43	99	7	23	3	0	2	15	12	29	0	.232	.323
Roy Smalley	SS9, 2B7, 1B2	R	28	25	36	5	8	0	0	1	7	4	9	0	.222	.306
Sammy Calderone	C16	R	28	22	29	3	11	2	0	0	5	4	4	0	.379	.448
Sibby Sisti		R	33	9	0	2	0	0	0	0	0	0	0	0	.000	.000
Mel Roach	1B1	R	21	3	4	0	0	0	0	0	0	0	1	0	.000	.000
Billy Queen	OF1	R	25	3	2	0	0	0	0	0	0	0	2	0	.000	.000

NAME	T	AGE	W	L	PCT	SV	G	GS	CG	IP	H	BB	SO	ShO	ERA
TOTALS		26	89	65	.578	21	154	154	63	**1395**	1296	553	698	13	3.19
Warren Spahn	L	33	21	12	.636	3	39	34	23	283	262	86	136	1	3.15
Lew Burdette	R	27	15	14	.517	0	38	32	13	238	224	62	79	4	2.76
Gene Conley	R	23	14	9	.609	0	28	27	12	194	171	79	113	2	2.97
Dave Jolly	R	29	11	6	.647	10	47	1	0	111	87	64	62	0	2.43
Chet Nichols	L	23	9	11	.450	1	35	20	5	122	132	65	55	1	4.43
Jim Wilson	R	32	8	2	.800	0	27	19	6	128	129	36	52	4	3.52
Ernie Johnson	R	30	5	2	.714	2	40	4	1	99	77	34	68	0	2.82
Bob Buhl	R	25	2	7	.222	3	31	14	2	110	117	65	57	1	4.01
Ray Crone	R	22	1	0	1.000	1	19	2	1	49	44	19	33	0	2.02
Joey Jay	R	18	1	0	1.000	0	15	1	0	18	21	16	13	0	6.50
Phil Paine	R	24	1	0	1.000	0	11	0	0	14	14	12	11	0	3.86
2 Dave Koslo	L	34	1	1	.500	1	12	0	0	17	13	9	7	0	3.18
Charlie Gorin	L	26	0	1	.000	0	5	0	0	10	5	6	12	0	1.80

PHILADELPHIA 4th 75-79 .487 22 — STEVE O'NEILL 40-37 .519 TERRY MOORE 35-42 .455

NAME	G by POS	B	AGE	G	AB	R	H	2B	3B	HR	RBI	BB	SO	SB	BA	SA
TOTALS			28	154	5184	659	1384	243	**58**	102	620	604	620	30	.267	.395
Earl Torgeson	1B133	L	30	135	490	63	133	22	6	5	54	75	52	7	.271	.371
Granny Hamner	2B152, SS1	R	27	152	596	83	178	39	11	13	89	53	44	1	.299	.466
Bobby Morgan	SS129, 3B8, 2B5	R	28	135	455	58	119	25	2	14	50	70	68	3	.262	.418
Willie Jones	3B141	R	28	142	535	64	145	28	3	12	56	61	54	4	.271	.402
Danny Schell	OF69	R	26	92	272	25	77	14	3	7	33	17	31	0	.283	.434
Richie Ashburn	OF153	L	27	153	559	111	175	16	8	1	41	**125**	46	11	.313	.376
Del Ennis	OF142, 1B1	R	29	145	556	73	145	23	2	25	119	50	60	2	.261	.444
Smoky Burgess	C91	L	27	108	345	41	127	27	5	4	46	42	11	1	.368	.510
Johnny Wyrostek	OF55, 1B22	L	34	92	259	28	62	12	4	3	28	29	39	0	.239	.351
Stan Lopata	C75, 1B1	R	28	86	259	42	75	14	5	14	42	33	37	1	.290	.544
Mel Clark	OF63	R	27	83	233	26	56	9	7	1	24	17	21	0	.240	.352
Ted Kazanski	SS38	R	20	39	104	7	14	2	0	1	8	4	14	0	.135	.183
2 Floyd Baker	3B7, 2B2	L	37	23	22	0	5	0	0	0	0	5	4	0	.227	.227
Bob Micelotta	SS1	R	25	13	3	2	0	0	0	0	0	1	1	0	.000	.000
Jim Command	3B6	L	25	9	18	1	4	1	0	1	6	2	4	0	.222	.444
Johnny Lindell		R	37	7	5	0	1	0	0	0	2	2	3	0	.200	.200
Gus Niarhos	C3	R	33	3	5	0	1	0	0	0	0	0	1	0	.200	.200
1 Stan Jok		R	28	3	3	0	0	0	0	0	0	0	2	0	.000	.000
Stan Palys	OF1	R	24	2	4	0	1	0	0	0	0	1	1	0	.250	.250

NAME	T	AGE	W	L	PCT	SV	G	GS	CG	IP	H	BB	SO	ShO	ERA
TOTALS		29	75*	79	.487	12	154	153	**78**	1365	1329	450	570	14	3.59
Robin Roberts	R	27	**23**	15	.605	4	45	**38**	**29**	**337**	**289**	56	**185**	4	2.96
Curt Simmons	L	25	14	15	.483	1	34	33	21	253	226	98	125	3	2.81
2 Herm Wehmeier	R	27	10	8	.556	0	25	17	10	138	117	51	49	2	3.85
Murry Dickson	R	37	10	**20**	.333	3	40	31	12	226	256	73	64	4	3.78
Bob Miller	R	28	7	9	.438	0	30	16	5	150	176	39	42	0	4.56
Steve Ridzik	R	25	4	5	.444	0	35	6	0	81	72	44	45	0	4.11
1 Jim Konstanty	R	37	2	3	.400	3	33	1	0	50	62	12	11	0	3.78
1 Karl Drews	R	34	1	0	1.000	0	8	0	0	16	18	8	6	0	5.63
Ron Mrozinski	L	23	1	1	.500	0	15	4	1	48	49	25	26	0	4.50
Paul Penson	R	22	1	1	.500	0	5	3	0	16	14	14	3	0	4.50
Bob Greenwood (JJ)	R	26	1	2	.333	0	11	4	0	37	28	18	9	0	3.16
Thornton Kipper	R	25	0	0	.000	1	11	0	0	14	22	12	5	0	7.71
Tom Qualters (DP) 19															

*1 win by forfeit

CINCINNATI 5th 74-80 .481 23 — BIRDIE TEBBETTS

NAME	G by POS	B	AGE	G	AB	R	H	2B	3B	HR	RBI	BB	SO	SB	BA	SA
TOTALS			27	154	5234	729	1369	221	46	147	685	557	645	47	.262	.406
Ted Kluszewski	1B149	L	29	149	573	104	187	28	3	**49**	**141**	78	35	0	.326	.642
Johnny Temple	2B144	R	25	146	505	60	155	14	8	0	44	62	24	21	.307	.366
Roy McMillan	SS154	R	23	154	588	86	147	21	2	4	42	47	54	4	.250	.313
Bobby Adams	3B93, 2B2	R	32	110	390	69	105	25	6	3	23	55	46	2	.269	.387
Wally Post	OF116	R	24	130	451	46	115	21	3	18	83	26	70	2	.255	.435
Gus Bell	OF153	L	25	153	619	104	185	38	7	17	101	48	58	5	.299	.465
Jim Greengrass	OF137	R	26	139	542	79	152	27	4	27	95	41	81	0	.280	.494
Andy Seminick	C82	R	33	86	247	25	58	9	4	7	30	48	39	0	.235	.389
Chuck Harmon	3B67, 1B3	R	28	94	286	39	68	7	3	2	25	17	27	7	.238	.304
Ed Bailey	C61	L	23	73	183	21	36	2	3	9	20	35	34	1	.197	.388
Bob Borkowski	OF36, 1B3	R	28	73	162	13	43	12	1	1	19	8	18	0	.265	.370
Lloyd Merriman	OF25	L	29	73	112	12	30	8	1	0	16	23	10	3	.268	.357
Nino Escalera	OF14, 1B8, SS1	L	24	73	69	15	11	1	1	0	3	7	11	1	.159	.203
Rocky Bridges	SS20, 2B19, 3B13	R	26	53	52	4	12	1	0	0	2	7	7	0	.231	.250
Hobie Landrith	C42	L	24	48	81	12	16	0	0	5	14	18	9	1	.198	.383
Dick Murphy		L	22	6	1	1	0	0	0	0	0	0	1	0	.000	.000
Jim Bolger	OF2	R	22	5	3	1	1	0	0	0	0	0	1	0	.333	.333
1 Grady Hatton		L	31	1	1	0	0	0	0	0	0	0	0	0	.000	.000
Johnny Lipon		R	31	1	1	0	0	0	0	0	0	0	0	0	.000	.000
Connie Ryan		R	34	1	0	0	0	0	0	0	0	1	0	0	.000	.000

NAME	T	AGE	W	L	PCT	SV	G	GS	CG	IP	H	BB	SO	ShO	ERA
TOTALS		28	74	80	.481	27	154	154	34	1368	1491	547	537	8	4.50
Joe Nuxhall	L	25	12	5	.706	0	35	14	5	167	188	59	85	1	3.88
Art Fowler	R	31	12	10	.545	0	40	29	8	228	256	85	93	1	3.83
Corky Valentine	R	25	12	11	.522	1	36	28	7	194	211	60	73	3	4.45
Jackie Collum	L	27	7	3	.700	0	36	2	1	79	86	32	28	0	3.76
Bud Podbielan	R	30	7	10	.412	0	27	24	4	131	157	58	42	0	5.36
Fred Baczewski	L	28	6	6	.500	0	29	22	4	130	159	53	43	1	5.26
Howie Judson	R	28	5	7	.417	3	37	8	0	93	86	42	27	0	3.97
Frank Smith	R	26	5	8	.385	20	50	0	0	81	60	29	51	0	2.67
2 Karl Drews	R	34	4	4	.500	0	22	9	1	60	79	19	29	1	6.00
Harry Perkowski	L	31	2	8	.200	0	28	12	3	96	100	62	32	1	6.09
Jerry Lane	R	28	1	0	1.000	0	3	0	0	11	9	3	2	0	1.64
Jim Pearce	R	29	1	0	1.000	0	2	1	1	11	7	5	3	0	0.00
2 Mario Picone	R	27	0	1	.000	0	4	1	0	10	9	7	1	0	6.30
Moe Savransky	L	25	0	2	.000	0	16	0	0	24	23	8	7	0	4.88
Ken Raffensberger	L	36	0	2	.000	0	6	1	0	10	15	3	5	0	8.10
1 Herm Wehmeier	R	27	0	3	.000	2	12	3	0	34	36	21	13	0	6.62
Cliff Ross	L	25	0	0	.000	1	4	0	0	3	0	0	1	0	0.00
1 George Zuverink	R	29	0	0	.000	0	2	0	0	6	10	1	2	0	9.00

ST. LOUIS 6th 72-82 .468 25 — EDDIE STANKY

NAME	G by POS	B	AGE	G	AB	R	H	2B	3B	HR	RBI	BB	SO	SB	BA	SA
TOTALS			27	154	5405	799	1518	285	58	119	748	582	586	63	.281	.421
Joe Cunningham	1B85	L	22	85	310	40	88	11	3	11	50	43	40	1	.284	.445
Red Schoendienst	2B144	B	31	148	610	98	192	38	8	5	79	54	22	4	.315	.428
Alex Grammas	SS142, 3B1	R	27	142	401	57	106	17	4	2	29	40	29	6	.264	.342
Ray Jablonski	3B149, 1B1	R	27	152	611	80	181	33	3	12	104	49	42	9	.296	.419
Stan Musial	OF152, 1B10	L	33	153	591	120	195	41	9	35	126	103	39	1	.330	.607
Wally Moon	OF148	L	24	151	635	106	193	29	9	12	76	71	73	18	.304	.435
Rip Repulski	OF152	R	26	152	619	99	175	39	5	19	79	43	75	8	.283	.454
Bill Sarni	C118	R	26	123	380	40	114	18	4	9	70	25	42	3	.300	.439
Solly Hemus	SS66, 3B27, 2B12	L	31	124	214	43	65	15	3	2	27	55	27	5	.304	.430
Joe Frazier	OF11, 1B1	L	31	81	88	8	26	5	2	3	18	13	17	0	.295	.500
Peanuts Lowery	OF12	R	35	74	61	6	7	1	2	0	5	9	9	0	.115	.197
Tom Alston	1B65	L	23	66	244	28	60	14	2	4	34	24	41	3	.246	.369
Del Rice	C52	R	31	56	147	13	37	10	1	2	16	16	21	0	.252	.374
Dick Schofield	SS11	B	19	43	7	17	1	0	1	0	1	0	3	1	.143	.429
Sal Yvars	C21	R	30	38	57	8	14	4	0	2	8	6	5	1	.246	.421
Tom Burgess	OF4	L	26	17	21	2	1	1	0	0	1	3	9	0	.048	.095

1 Steve Bilko 25 R 2-14, Pete Castiglione 33 R 0-0, Vinegar Bend Mizell (MS) 23

NAME	T	AGE	W	L	PCT	SV	G	GS	CG	IP	H	BB	SO	ShO	ERA
		30	72	82*	.468	18	154	153	40	1390	1484	535	680	11	4.50
Harvey Haddix	L	28	18	13	.581	4	43	35	13	260	247	77	184	3	3.57
Brooks Lawrence	R	29	15	6	.714	1	35	18	8	159	141	72	72	0	3.74
Vic Raschi	R	35	8	9	.471	0	30	29	6	179	182	71	73	2	4.73
Gerry Staley	R	33	7	13	.350	2	48	20	3	156	198	47	50	1	5.25
Al Brazle	L	40	5	4	.556	8	58	0	0	84	93	24	30	0	4.18
Tom Poholsky	R	24	5	7	.417	0	25	13	4	106	101	20	55	0	3.06
Gordon Jones	R	24	4	4	.500	0	11	10	4	81	78	19	48	2	2.00
Joe Presko	R	25	4	9	.308	0	37	6	1	72	97	41	36	1	6.88
Cot Deal	R	31	2	3	.400	1	33	0	0	72	85	36	25	0	6.25
Royce Lint	L	33	2	3	.400	0	30	4	1	70	75	30	36	1	4.89
Stu Miller	R	26	2	3	.400	2	19	4	0	47	55	29	22	0	5.74
2 Carl Scheib	R	27	0	1	.000	0	3	1	0	5	6	5	5	0	10.80
Willie Greason	R	29	0	1	.000	0	3	2	0	4	8	4	2	0	13.50
Memo Luna	L	24	0	1	.000	0	1	1	0	1	2	2	0	0	18.00
Ralph Beard	R	25	0	4	.000	0	13	10	0	58	62	28	17	0	3.72
2 Ben Wade	R	31	0	0	.000	0	13	0	0	23	27	15	19	0	5.48
Mel Wright	R	26	0	0	.000	0	9	0	0	10	16	11	4	0	10.80
Hal White	R	35	0	0	.000	0	4	0	0	5	11	4	2	0	19.80

*1 loss by forfeit

CHICAGO 7th 64-90 .416 33 — STAN HACK

NAME	G by POS	B	AGE	G	AB	R	H	2B	3B	HR	RBI	BB	SO	SB	BA	SA
TOTALS			28	154	5359	700	1412	229	45	159	640	478	693	46	.263	.412
Dee Fondy	1B138	L	29	141	568	77	162	30	4	9	49	35	84	20	.285	.400
Gene Baker	2B134	R	29	135	541	68	149	32	5	13	61	47	55	4	.275	.425
Ernie Banks	SS154	R	23	154	593	70	163	19	7	19	79	40	50	6	.275	.427
Randy Jackson	3B124	R	28	126	484	77	132	17	6	19	67	44	55	2	.273	.450
Hank Sauer	OF141	R	35	142	520	98	150	18	1	41	103	70	68	2	.288	.563
Dale Talbot	OF110	R	27	114	403	45	97	15	4	1	19	16	25	3	.241	.305
Ralph Kiner	OF147	R	31	147	557	88	159	36	5	22	73	76	90	2	.285	.487
1 Joe Garagiola	C55	L	28	63	153	16	43	5	0	5	21	28	12	0	.281	.412
Frankie Baumholtz	OF71	L	35	90	303	38	90	12	6	4	28	20	15	1	.297	.416
2 Walker Cooper	C48	R	39	57	158	21	49	10	2	7	32	21	23	0	.310	.532
2 Hal Rice	OF24	L	30	51	72	5	11	0	0	0	5	8	15	0	.153	.153
2 Steve Bilko	1B22	R	25	47	92	11	22	8	1	4	12	11	24	0	.239	.478
El Tappe	C46	R	27	46	119	5	22	3	0	0	4	10	9	0	.185	.210
Bill Serena	3B12, 2B2	R	29	41	63	8	10	0	1	4	13	14	18	0	.159	.381
Eddie Miksis	2B21, 3B2, OF1	R	27	38	99	9	20	3	0	2	3	3	9	1	.202	.293
Bob Rush	P33	R	28	33	83	6	23	4	1	2	9	3	23	0	.277	.422
Clyde McCullough (SA)	C26, 3B3	R	37	31	81	9	21	7	0	3	17	5	5	0	.259	.457
Vern Morgan	3B15	L	25	24	64	3	15	2	0	0	2	1	10	0	.234	.266
1 Luis Marquez	OF14	R	28	17	12	2	1	0	0	0	0	2	4	3	.083	.083
Don Robertson	OF6	L	23	14	6	2	0	0	0	0	0	0	2	0	.000	.000
Jim Fanning	C11	R	26	11	38	2	7	0	0	0	1	1	7	0	.184	.184

Bruce Edwards 30 R 0-3, Chris Kitsos 26 B 0-0, Harry Chiti (MS) 21

NAME	T	AGE	W	L	PCT	SV	G	GS	CG	IP	H	BB	SO	ShO	ERA
		28	64	90	.416	19	154	154	41	1374	1375	619	622	6	4.51
Bob Rush	R	28	13	15	.464	0	33	32	11	236	213	103	124	0	3.78
Jim Davis	L	29	11	7	.611	4	46	12	2	128	114	51	58	0	3.52
Paul Minner	L	30	11	11	.500	1	32	29	12	218	236	50	79	0	3.96
Howie Pollet	L	33	8	10	.444	0	20	20	4	128	131	54	58	2	3.59
Warren Hacker	R	29	6	13	.316	2	39	18	4	159	157	37	80	1	4.25
Hal Jeffcoat	R	29	5	6	.455	7	43	3	1	104	110	58	35	0	5.19
Johnny Klippstein	R	26	4	11	.267	1	36	21	4	148	155	96	69	0	5.29
Dave Cole (SA)	R	23	3	8	.273	0	18	14	2	84	74	62	37	1	5.36
Jim Brosnan	R	24	1	0	1.000	0	18	0	0	33	44	18	17	0	9.55
Bill Tremel	R	24	1	2	.333	4	33	0	0	51	45	28	21	0	4.24
Bubba Church	R	29	1	3	.250	0	7	3	1	15	21	13	8	0	9.60
Jim Willis	R	27	0	1	.000	0	14	1	0	23	22	18	5	0	3.91
John Pyecha	R	22	0	1	.000	0	1	0	0	3	4	2	2	0	9.00
Turk Lown	R	30	0	2	.000	0	15	0	0	22	23	15	16	0	6.14
Bob Zick	R	27	0	0	.000	0	8	0	0	16	23	7	9	0	8.44
Al Lary	R	24	0	0	.000	0	1	1	0	6	3	7	4	0	3.00

PITTSBURGH 8th 53-101 .344 44 — FRED HANEY

NAME	G by POS	B	AGE	G	AB	R	H	2B	3B	HR	RBI	BB	SO	SB	BA	SA
TOTALS			25	154	5088	557	1260	181	57	76	526	566	737	21	.248	.350
Bob Skinner	1B118, OF2	L	22	132	470	67	117	15	9	8	46	47	59	4	.249	.370
Curt Roberts	2B131	R	24	134	496	47	115	18	7	1	36	55	49	6	.232	.302
Gair Allie	SS95, 3B19	R	22	121	418	38	83	8	6	3	30	56	84	1	.199	.268
Dick Cole	SS66, 3B55, 2B17	R	28	138	486	40	131	22	5	1	40	41	48	0	.270	.342
Sid Gordon	OF73, 3B40	R	26	131	363	38	111	12	0	12	49	67	24	0	.306	.438
Dick Hall	OF102	R	23	112	310	38	74	8	4	2	27	33	46	3	.239	.310
Frank Thomas	OF153	R	25	153	577	81	172	32	7	23	94	51	74	3	.298	.497
Toby Atwell	C88	L	30	96	287	36	83	8	4	3	26	43	21	2	.289	.376
Preston Ward	1B48, OF42, 3B11	L	26	117	360	37	97	16	2	7	48	39	61	0	.269	.383
Jerry Lynch	OF83	L	23	98	284	27	68	4	5	8	36	20	43	2	.239	.373
Jack Shepard	C67	R	22	82	227	24	69	8	2	3	22	26	33	0	.304	.396
Eddie Pellagrini	3B31, 2B7, SS1	R	36	73	125	12	27	6	0	0	16	9	21	0	.216	.264
Vic Janowicz	3B18, OF1	R	24	41	73	10	11	3	0	0	2	7	23	0	.151	.192
1 Hal Rice	OF24	L	30	28	81	10	14	4	1	1	9	14	24	0	.173	.284
1 Cal Abrams	OF13	L	30	17	42	6	6	1	1	0	2	10	9	0	.143	.214
Gail Henley	OF9	L	25	14	30	7	9	1	0	1	2	4	4	0	.300	.433
Jim Mangan (MS)	C7	R	24	14	26	2	5	0	0	0	2	4	9	0	.192	.192
2 Luis Marquez	OF4	R	28	14	9	3	1	0	0	0	0	4	0	0	.111	.111
1 Walker Cooper	C2	R	39	14	15	0	3	2	0	0	1	2	1	0	.200	.333
Dick Smith	3B9	R	26	12	31	2	3	1	1	0	0	6	5	0	.097	.194

Bill Hall 25 L 0-7, Nick Koback 18 R 0-10, Sam Jethroe 32 B 0-1, Tony Bartirome (MS) 22, Dick Groat (MS) 23, Pete Naton (MS) 22, Eddie O'Brien (MS) 23, Johnny O'Brien (MS) 23

NAME	T	AGE	W	L	PCT	SV	G	GS	CG	IP	H	BB	SO	ShO	ERA
		27	53	101	.344	15	154	154	37	1346	1510	564	525	4	4.92
2 Dick Littlefield	L	28	10	11	.476	0	23	21	7	155	140	85	92	1	3.60
Vern Law	R	24	9	13	.409	3	39	18	7	162	201	56	57	0	5.50
Max Surkont	R	32	9	18	.333	0	33	29	11	208	216	78	78	0	4.41
Bob Friend	R	23	7	12	.368	2	35	20	4	170	204	58	73	2	5.08
Johnny Hetki	R	32	4	4	.500	9	58	1	0	83	102	30	27	0	4.99
Paul LaPalme	L	30	4	10	.286	0	33	15	2	121	147	54	57	0	5.50
Bob Purkey	R	24	3	8	.273	0	36	11	0	131	145	62	38	0	5.08
Jake Theis	R	28	3	9	.250	0	33	18	3	130	120	49	57	1	3.88
George O'Donnell	R	25	3	9	.250	1	21	10	3	87	105	21	8	0	4.55
Laurin Pepper	R	23	1	5	.167	0	14	8	0	51	63	43	17	0	7.94
Len Yochim	L	25	0	1	.000	0	10	1	0	20	30	8	7	0	7.20
Cal Hogue	R	26	0	1	.000	0	3	2	0	11	11	12	7	0	4.91
Joe Page	L	36	0	0	.000	0	7	0	0	10	16	7	4	0	10.80
Nellie King	R	26	0	0	.000	0	4	0	0	7	10	1	3	0	5.14

Bill Bell (MS) 20
Ron Kline (MS) 22
Bill Koski (MS) 22

WORLD SERIES – NEW YORK (NL) 4 CLEVELAND (AL) 0

LINE SCORES

TEAM	1	2	3	4	5	6	7	8	9	10	11	12	R	H	E
Game 1 September 29 at New York															
CLE (AL)	2	0	0	0	0	0	0	0	0	0			2	8	0
NY (NL)	0	0	2	0	0	0	0	0	0	3			5	9	3
Game 2 September 30 at New York															
CLE	1	0	0	0	0	0	0	0	0				1	8	0
NY	0	0	0	0	2	0	1	0	X				3	4	0
Game 3 October 1 at Cleveland															
NY	1	0	3	0	1	1	0	0	0				6	10	1
CLE	0	0	0	0	0	0	1	1	0				2	4	2
Game 4 October 2 at Cleveland															
NY	0	2	1	0	4	0	0	0	0				7	10	3
CLE	0	0	0	0	3	0	1	0	0				4	6	2

Game 1 pitchers: **Lemon**; Maglie, Liddle (8), **Grissom** (8)

Game 2 pitchers: **Wynn**, Mossi (8); **Antonelli**

Game 3 pitchers: **Gomez**, Wilhelm (8); **Garcia**, Houtteman (4), Narleski (6), Mossi (9)

Game 4 pitchers: **Liddle**, Wilhelm (7), Antonelli (8); **Lemon**, Newhouser (5), Narleski (5), Mossi (6), Garcia (8)

COMPOSITE BATTING

NAME	POS	G	AB	R	H	2B	3B	HR	RBI	BA
New York (NL) Totals		4	130	21	33	3	0	2	20	.254
Mueller	OF	4	18	4	7	0	0	0	1	.389
Lockman	1B	4	18	2	2	0	0	0	0	.111
Dark	SS	4	17	2	7	0	0	0	0	.412
Mays	OF	4	14	4	4	1	0	0	3	.286
Thompson	3B	4	11	6	4	1	0	0	2	.364
Westrum	C	4	11	0	3	0	0	0	3	.273
Williams	2B	4	11	0	0	0	0	0	1	.000
Irvin	OF	4	9	1	2	1	0	0	2	.222
Rhodes	OF	4	6	2	4	0	0	2	7	.667
Gomez	P	1	4	0	0	0	0	0	0	.000
Maglie	P	1	3	0	0	0	0	0	0	.000
Liddle	P	2	3	0	0	0	0	0	0	.000
Antonelli	P	2	3	0	0	0	0	0	1	.000
Wilhelm	P	2	1	0	0	0	0	0	0	.000
Grissom	P	1	1	0	0	0	0	0	0	.000
Cleveland (AL) Totals		4	137	9	26	5	1	3	9	.190
Wertz	1B	4	16	2	8	2	1	1	3	.500
Doby	OF	4	16	0	2	0	0	0	0	.125
Avila	2B	4	15	1	2	0	0	0	0	.133
Smith	OF	4	14	2	3	0	0	1	2	.214
Hegan	C	4	13	1	2	1	0	0	0	.154
Rosen	3B	3	12	0	3	0	0	0	0	.250
Strickland	SS	3	9	0	0	0	0	0	0	.000
Philley	OF	4	8	0	1	0	0	0	0	.125
Westlake	OF	2	7	0	1	0	0	0	0	.143
Majeski	3B	4	6	1	1	0	0	1	3	.167
Lemon	P	3	6	0	0	0	0	0	0	.000
Regalado	3B	4	3	0	1	0	0	0	1	.333
Dente	SS	3	3	1	0	0	0	0	0	.000
Pope	OF	3	3	0	0	0	0	0	0	.000
Wynn	P	1	2	0	1	1	0	0	0	.500
Glynn	1B	2	2	1	1	0	0	0	0	.500
Mitchell	PH	2	2	0	0	0	0	0	0	.000
Grasso	C	1	0	0	0	0	0	0	0	.000
Naragon	C	1	0	0	0	0	0	0	0	.000
Mossi	P	3	0	0	0	0	0	0	0	.000
Garcia	P	2	0	0	0	0	0	0	0	.000
Narleski	P	2	0	0	0	0	0	0	0	.000
Houtteman	P	1	0	0	0	0	0	0	0	.000
Newhouser	P	1	0	0	0	0	0	0	0	.000

COMPOSITE PITCHING

NAME	G	IP	H	BB	SO	W	L	SV	ERA
New York (NL) Totals	4	37	26	16	23	4	0	2	1.46
Antonelli	2	10.2	8	7	12	1	0	1	0.84
Gomez	1	7.1	4	3	2	1	0	0	2.45
Liddle	2	7	5	1	2	1	0	0	1.29
Maglie	1	7	7	2	2	0	0	0	2.57
Grissom	1	2.2	1	3	2	1	0	0	0.00
Wilhelm	2	2.1	1	0	3	0	0	1	0.00
Cleveland (AL) Totals	4	35.1	33	17	24	0	4	0	4.84
Lemon	2	13.1	16	8	11	0	2	0	6.75
Wynn	1	7	4	2	5	0	1	0	3.86
Garcia	2	5	6	4	4	0	1	0	5.40
Mossi	3	4	3	0	1	0	0	0	0.00
Narleski	2	4	1	1	2	0	0	0	2.25
Houtteman	1	2	2	1	1	0	0	0	4.50
Newhouser	1	0	1	1	0	0	0	0	∞

1955 Forget about Next Year

After winning five championships in a row with teams that never topped 100 victories, Casey Stengel broke the barrier in 1954 only to finish a good second. In 1955, Stengel and the Yankees returned to their old ways and won less than 100 games—a feat which was good enough for a sixth pennant in seven years under the helm of the Old Professor. But Stengel, to his regret, was not the *big story* of the year. Baseball's dynamite, for once, belonged to Brooklyn. While the Yankees topped the American League with 175 home runs, the Dodgers outdid them by proving the powerhouse of the majors with 201 clouts.

The Dodgers, in fact, were devastating. They opened their campaign by reeling off ten wins in a row and taking 22 of their first 24 games to find themselves 12½ over the pack by July 4. Even an August slump couldn't harm them as they finished a strong 13½ games in front of Milwaukee, the pre-season favorites.

Roy Campanella recovered sufficiently from a 1954 hand injury and proved the anchor in his performance behind the plate, as well as behind the bat, as he hit .318, collected 32 home runs, and was voted league MVP. Duke Snider led the league with 136 RBI's while batting .309 and hitting 42 home runs, while Don Newcombe returned to form and posted a 20-5 season. Clem Labine led the relief corps with 13 victories and 11 saves to round out the most balanced Dodgers' attack in years. Milwaukee finished second mostly due to sophomore Hank Aaron's maturing year and Eddie Mathews' 41 home runs. Willie Mays again gave the Giants a good year with a league-leading 51 homers and a .319 average, but could not make up for the reversal of form by Johnny Antonelli and Rubin Gomez, who could only combine for 23 wins instead of the 38 they bunched in 1954.

While Campanella was leading the Dodgers to victory, Yogi Berra was doing the same for the Yankees. Although his batting stats did not compare with those of his Dodger rival, his performance was also good enough to earn him MVP honors. The Yankees edged out Cleveland by three games, mostly due to a shake-up in the pitching department and Stengel's being able to compensate for off years and injuries—something Cleveland manager Al Lopez was unable to do. With Allie Reynolds retired, Bob Grim suffering from arm trouble, and Vic Raschi, Johnny Sain, and Eddie Lopat sold, Stengel brought Tommy Byrne back from the minors and got good mileage out of Bob Turley and Don Larsen, obtained during the winter from Baltimore as part of an 18-man trade. Stengel's big problem at shortstop, where Phil Rizzuto became a part-timer, was solved by using Billy Hunter until Jerry Coleman was able to recover from a broken collarbone.

Cleveland's one compensation for their regulars' off-year, and the polio which sidelined Vic Wertz in late August, was the debut of Herb Score, who created much excitement with his 16 victories and 245 strikeouts. Detroit produced a batting champion in 20-year-old sophomore Al Kaline—a feat which tied him with Ty Cobb as the youngest batting champion ever.

As the Series got underway, and the Yankees won the first two games, it seemed as if, indeed, the Dodgers would have to "wait till next year". But the Dodgers came home to Ebbets Field and won the next three games. Back at Yankee Stadium, Whitey Ford cooled off Brooklyn, 5-1, and the old rivals entered the final game. With Johnny Podres throwing shutout ball and the Dodgers up two runs on Gil Hodges' hitting, Billy Martin started off the sixth inning with a walk, followed by Gil McDougald's infield single. Berra then came up and hit a high fly ball into the leftfield corner. Sandy Amoros, playing in left center, started running toward the ball in desperation. At the last second, he made a lunge and speared the ball just inside the foul line. Amoros recovered in time to throw to Reese who, in turn, relayed the ball to Hodges to double McDougald off first base. Podres hung on to shut out the Yankees and to evoke the cry, "this is next year."

1955 AMERICAN LEAGUE

NEW YORK 1st 96-58 .623 — CASEY STENGEL

NAME	G by POS	B	AGE	G	AB	R	H	2B	3B	HR	RBI	BB	SO	SB	BA	SA
TOTALS			28	154	5161	762	1342	179	55	175	722	609	658	55	.260	.418
Bill Skowron	1B74, 3B3	R	24	108	288	46	92	17	3	12	61	21	32	1	.319	.524
Gil McDougald	2B126, 3B17	R	27	141	533	79	152	10	8	13	53	65	77	6	.285	.407
Billy Hunter	SS98	R	27	98	255	14	58	7	1	3	20	15	18	9	.227	.298
Andy Carey	3B135	R	23	135	510	73	131	19	11	7	47	44	51	3	.257	.378
Hank Bauer	OF133, C1	R	32	139	492	97	137	20	5	20	53	56	65	8	.278	.461
Mickey Mantle	OF145, SS2	B	23	147	517	121	158	25	11	37	99	113	97	8	.306	.611
Irv Noren	OF126	L	30	132	371	49	94	19	1	8	59	43	33	5	.253	.375
Yogi Berra	C145	L	30	147	541	84	147	20	3	27	108	60	20	1	.272	.470
Joe Collins	1B73, OF27	L	32	105	278	40	65	9	1	13	45	44	32	0	.234	.414
Elston Howard	OF75, C9	R	26	97	279	33	81	8	7	10	43	20	36	0	.290	.477
Eddie Robinson	1B46	L	34	88	173	25	36	1	0	16	42	36	26	0	.208	.491
Phil Rizzuto	SS79, 2B1	R	37	81	143	19	37	4	1	1	9	22	18	7	.259	.322
Bob Cerv	OF20	R	29	55	85	17	29	4	2	3	22	7	16	4	.341	.541
Jerry Coleman (BC)	SS29, 2B13, 3B1	R	30	43	96	12	22	5	0	0	8	11	11	0	.229	.281
Billy Martin (MS)	2B17, SS3	R	27	20	70	8	21	2	0	1	9	7	9	1	.300	.371
Tommy Carroll	SS4	R	18	14	6	3	2	0	0	0	0	0	2	0	.333	.333

Charlie Silvera 30 R 5-26, Bobby Richardson 19 R 4-26, 1 Enos Slaughter 39 L 1-9, Frank Leja 19 L 0-2, Lou Berberet 25 L 2-5, Dick Tettelbach 26 R 0-5, Marv Throneberry 21 L 2-2, Johnny Blanchard 22 L 0-3

NAME	T	AGE	W	L	PCT	SV	G	GS	CG	IP	H	BB	SO	ShO	ERA
		28	96	58	.623	33	154	154	52	1372	1163	688	732	19	3.23
Whitey Ford	L	26	18	7	.720	2	39	33	18	254	188	113	137	5	2.62
Bob Turley	R	24	17	13	.567	1	36	34	13	247	168	177	210	6	3.06
Tommy Byrne	L	35	16	5	.762	2	27	22	9	160	137	87	76	3	3.15
Don Larsen	R	25	9	2	.818	2	19	13	5	97	81	51	44	1	3.06
Johnny Kucks	R	21	8	7	.533	0	29	13	3	127	122	44	49	1	3.40
Jim Konstanty	R	38	7	2	.778	11	45	0	0	74	68	24	19	0	2.31
Tom Morgan	R	25	7	3	.700	10	40	1	0	72	72	24	17	0	3.25
Bob Grim (SA)	R	25	7	5	.583	4	26	11	1	92	81	42	63	1	4.21
1 Ed Lopat	L	37	4	8	.333	0	16	12	3	87	101	16	24	1	3.72
Rip Coleman	L	23	2	1	.667	1	10	6	0	29	40	16	15	0	5.28
Tom Sturdivant	R	25	1	3	.250	0	33	1	0	68	48	42	48	0	3.18
Bob Wiesler	L	24	0	2	.000	0	16	7	0	53	39	49	22	0	3.91
1 Johnny Sain	R	37	0	0	.000	0	3	0	0	5	6	1	5	0	7.20
1 Art Schallock	L	31	0	0	.000	0	2	0	0	3	4	1	2	0	6.00
2 Gerry Staley	R	34	0	0	.000	0	2	0	0	2	5	1	0	0	13.50
3 Ted Gray	L	30	0	0	.000	0	1	1	0	3	3	0	1	0	3.00

CLEVELAND 2nd 93-61 .604 3 — AL LOPEZ

NAME	G by POS	B	AGE	G	AB	R	H	2B	3B	HR	RBI	BB	SO	SB	BA	SA
TOTALS			31	154	5146	698	1325	195	31	148	657	723	715	28	.257	.394
Vic Wertz (IL)	1B63, OF9	L	30	74	257	30	65	11	2	14	55	32	33	1	.253	.475
Bobby Avila	2B141	R	31	141	537	83	146	22	4	13	61	82	47	1	.272	.400
George Strickland	SS128	R	29	130	388	34	81	9	5	2	34	49	60	1	.209	.273
Al Rosen	3B106, 1B41	R	31	139	492	61	120	13	1	21	81	92	44	4	.244	.402
Al Smith	OF120, 3B45, SS5, 2B1	R	27	154	607	123	186	27	4	22	77	93	77	11	.306	.473
Larry Doby	OF129	L	31	131	491	91	143	17	5	26	75	61	100	2	.291	.505
Ralph Kiner	OF87	R	32	113	321	56	78	13	0	18	54	65	46	0	.243	.452
Jim Hegan	C111	R	34	116	304	30	67	5	2	9	40	34	33	0	.220	.339
2 Gene Woodling	OF70	L	32	79	259	33	72	15	1	5	35	36	15	2	.278	.402
Sam Dente	SS53, 3B13, 2B4	R	33	73	105	10	27	4	0	0	10	12	8	0	.257	.295
Hank Foiles	C41	R	26	62	111	13	29	9	0	1	7	17	18	0	.261	.369
Dale Mitchell	1B8, OF3	L	33	61	58	4	15	2	1	0	10	4	3	0	.259	.328
Hal Naragon	C52	L	26	57	127	12	41	9	2	1	14	15	8	1	.323	.449
2 Ferris Fain	1B51	L	34	56	118	9	30	3	0	0	8	42	13	3	.254	.280
1 Dave Philley	OF34	B	35	43	104	15	31	4	2	2	9	12	10	0	.298	.433
Joe Altobelli	1B40	L	23	42	75	8	15	3	0	2	5	5	14	0	.200	.320
2 Hoot Evers	OF25	R	34	39	66	10	19	7	1	2	9	3	12	0	.288	.515
1 Hank Majeski	3B9, 2B4	R	38	36	48	3	9	2	0	2	6	8	3	0	.188	.354
1 Dave Pope	OF31	L	30	35	104	17	31	5	0	6	22	12	31	0	.298	.519

2 Bobby Young 30 L 14-45, 1 Wally Westlake 34 R 5-20, Stu Locklin 26 L 3-18, Billy Harrell 26 R 8-19, Rudy Regalado 25 R 7-26, Rocky Colavito 21 R 4-9, Kenny Kuhn 18 L 2-6, 1 Harry Simpson 29 L 0-1, Stan Pawloski 23 R 1-8

NAME	T	AGE	W	L	PCT	SV	G	GS	CG	IP	H	BB	SO	ShO	ERA
		30	93	61	.604	36	154	154	45	1386	1285	558	877	15	3.39
Bob Lemon	R	34	18	10	.643	2	35	31	5	211	218	74	100	0	3.88
Early Wynn	R	35	17	11	.607	0	32	31	16	230	207	80	122	6	2.82
Herb Score	L	22	16	10	.615	0	33	32	11	227	158	154	245	2	2.85
Mike Garcia	R	31	11	13	.458	3	38	31	6	211	230	56	120	2	4.01
Art Houtteman	R	27	10	6	.625	0	35	12	3	124	126	44	53	1	3.99
Ray Narleski	R	26	9	1	.900	19	60	1	1	112	91	52	94	0	3.70
Don Mossi	L	26	4	3	.571	9	57	1	0	82	81	18	69	0	2.41
Bob Feller	R	36	4	4	.500	0	25	11	2	83	71	31	25	1	3.47
Jose Santiago	R	26	2	0	1.000	0	17	0	0	33	31	14	19	0	2.45
Hank Aquirre	L	23	2	0	1.000	0	4	1	1	13	6	12	6	1	1.38
Bud Daley	L	22	0	1	.000	0	2	1	0	7	10	1	2	0	6.43
2 Sal Maglie	R	38	0	2	.000	2	10	2	0	26	26	7	11	0	3.81
1 Bill Wight	L	33	0	0	.000	1	17	0	0	24	24	9	9	0	2.63
2 Ted Gray	L	30	0	0	.000	0	2	0	0	2	5	2	1	0	18.00
Hal Newhouser	L	34	0	0	.000	0	2	0	0	2	1	4	1	0	0.00

CHICAGO 3rd 91-63 .591 5 — MARTY MARION

NAME	G by POS	B	AGE	G	AB	R	H	2B	3B	HR	RBI	BB	SO	SB	BA	SA
TOTALS			30	155	5220	725	1401	204	36	116	678	567	595	69	.268	.388
Walt Dropo	1B140	R	32	141	453	55	127	15	2	19	79	42	71	0	.280	.448
Nellie Fox	2B154	L	27	154	636	100	198	28	7	6	59	38	15	7	.311	.406
Chico Carrasquel	SS144	R	27	145	523	83	134	11	2	11	52	61	59	1	.256	.348
George Kell	3B105, 1B24, OF1	R	32	128	429	44	134	24	1	8	81	51	36	2	.312	.429
Jim Rivera	OF143	L	32	147	454	71	120	24	4	10	52	62	59	25	.264	.401
2 Jim Busby	OF99	R	28	99	337	38	82	13	4	1	27	25	37	7	.243	.315
Minnie Minoso	OF138, 3B2	R	32	139	517	79	149	26	7	10	70	76	43	19	.288	.424
Sherm Lollar	C136	R	30	138	426	67	111	13	1	16	61	68	34	2	.261	.408
Bob Nieman	OF78	R	28	99	272	36	77	11	2	11	53	36	37	1	.283	.460
2 Bob Kennedy	3B55, OF20, 1B3	R	34	83	214	28	65	10	2	9	43	16	16	0	.304	.495
Ron Jackson	1B29	R	21	40	74	10	15	1	1	2	7	8	22	1	.203	.324
Jim Brideweser	SS26, 3B3, 2B2	R	28	34	58	6	12	3	2	0	4	3	7	0	.207	.328
1 Johnny Groth	OF26	R	28	32	77	13	26	7	0	2	11	6	13	1	.338	.506
2 Les Moss	C32	R	30	32	59	5	15	2	0	2	7	6	10	0	.254	.390
2 Bobby Adams	3B9, 2B1	R	33	28	21	8	2	0	1	0	3	4	4	0	.095	.190
Ed McGhee	OF17	R	30	26	13	6	1	0	0	0	0	6	1	2	.077	.077
2 Vern Stephens	3B18	R	34	22	56	10	14	3	0	3	7	7	11	0	.250	.464
Willard Marshall	OF12	L	34	22	41	6	7	0	0	0	6	13	1	0	.171	.171
1 Clint Courtney	C17	L	28	19	37	7	14	3	0	1	10	7	0	0	.378	.541
2 Gil Coan	OF3	L	33	17	17	0	3	0	0	0	1	0	5	0	.176	.176

Ron Northey 35 L 5-14, Buddy Peterson 30 R 6-21, Stan Jok 29 R 1-4, Phil Cavaretta 38 L 0-4, Earl Battey 20 R 2-7, Sammy Esposito (MS) 23 R 0-4, Ed White 29 R 2-4, 1 Lloyd Merriman 30 L 0-1, Bob Powell 21 R 0-0

NAME	T	AGE	W	L	PCT	SV	G	GS	CG	IP	H	BB	SO	ShO	ERA
		31	91	63	.591	23	155	155	55	1378	1301	497	720	20	3.37
Dick Donovan	R	27	15	9	.625	0	29	24	11	187	186	48	88	5	3.32
Billy Pierce	L	28	15	10	.600	1	33	26	16	206	162	64	157	6	1.97
Virgil Trucks	R	36	13	8	.619	0	32	26	7	175	176	61	91	3	3.96
Jack Harshman	L	27	11	7	.611	0	32	23	9	179	144	97	116	0	3.37
Dixie Howell	R	35	8	3	.727	9	35	0	0	74	70	25	25	0	2.92
Connie Johnson	R	32	7	4	.636	0	17	16	5	99	95	52	72	2	3.45
Mike Fornieles	R	23	6	3	.667	2	26	9	2	86	84	29	23	0	3.87
Sandy Consuegra	R	34	6	5	.545	7	44	7	3	126	120	18	35	0	2.64
2 Harry Byrd	R	30	4	6	.400	1	25	12	1	91	85	30	44	1	4.65
1 Harry Dorish	R	33	2	0	1.000	1	13	0	0	17	16	9	6	0	1.59
Morrie Martin	L	32	2	3	.400	2	37	0	0	52	50	20	22	0	3.63
Bob Keegan (KJ)	R	34	2	5	.286	0	18	11	1	59	83	28	29	0	5.80
1 Bob Chakales	R	27	0	0	.000	0	7	0	0	12	11	6	6	0	1.50
Al Papai	R	36	0	0	.000	0	7	0	0	12	10	8	5	0	3.75
1 Ted Gray	L	30	0	0	.000	0	2	1	0	3	9	2	1	0	18.00

BOSTON 4th 84-70 .545 12

PINKY HIGGINS

NAME	G by POS	B	AGE	G	AB	R	H	2B	3B	HR	RBI	BB	SO	SB	BA	SA
TOTALS			28	154	5273	755	1392	**241**	39	137	710	707	733	43	.264	.402
Norm Zauchin	1B126	R	25	130	477	65	114	10	0	27	93	69	**105**	3	.239	.430
Billy Goodman	2B143, 1B5, OF1	L	29	149	599	100	176	31	2	0	52	99	44	5	.294	.352
Billy Klaus	SS126, 3B8	L	26	135	541	83	153	26	2	7	60	60	44	6	.283	.377
Grady Hatton	3B111, 2B1	L	32	126	380	48	93	11	4	4	49	76	28	0	.245	.326
Jackie Jensen	OF150	R	28	152	574	95	158	27	6	26	**116**	89	63	16	.275	.479
Jimmy Piersall	OF147	R	25	149	515	68	146	25	5	13	62	67	52	6	.283	.427
Ted Williams(RP)	OF93	L	36	98	320	77	114	21	3	28	83	91	24	2	.356	.703
Sammy White	C143	R	26	143	544	65	142	30	4	11	64	44	58	1	.261	.392
Gene Stephens	OF75	L	22	109	157	25	46	9	4	3	18	20	34	0	.293	.459
Faye Throneberry	OF34	L	24	60	144	20	37	7	3	6	27	14	31	0	.257	.472
Eddie Joost	SS20, 2B17, 3B2	R	39	55	119	15	23	2	0	5	17	17	21	0	.193	.336
Ted Lepcio	3B45	R	24	51	134	19	31	9	0	6	15	13	36	1	.231	.433
Karl Olson	OF21	R	24	26	48	7	12	1	2	0	1	1	10	0	.250	.354
Harry Agganis (DD)	1B20	L	25	25	83	11	26	10	1	0	10	10	10	2	.313	.458
Pete Daley	C14	R	25	17	50	4	11	2	1	0	5	3	6	0	.220	.300
1 Owen Friend	SS14, 2B1	R	28	14	42	3	11	3	0	0	2	4	11	0	.262	.333
1 Sam Mele	OF7	R	32	14	31	1	4	2	0	0	1	0	7	1	.129	.194

Billy Consolo 20 R 4-18, Dick Gernert 26 R 4-10, Frank Malzone 25 R 7-20, Milt Bolling (BE) 24 R 1-5, Haywood Sullivan 24 R 0-6, Jim Pagliaroni 17 R 0-0

NAME	T	AGE	W	L	PCT	SV	G	GS	CG	IP	H	BB	SO	ShO	ERA
		27	84	70	.545	34	154	154	44	1384	1333	582	674	9	3.72
Frank Sullivan	R	25	**18**	13	.581	0	35	**35**	16	**260**	235	100	129	3	2.91
Willard Nixon	R	27	12	10	.545	0	31	31	7	208	207	85	95	3	4.07
Tom Brewer	R	23	11	10	.524	0	31	28	9	193	198	87	91	2	4.20
Ike Delock	R	25	9	7	.563	3	29	18	6	144	136	61	88	0	3.75
George Susce	R	23	9	7	.563	1	29	15	6	144	123	49	60	1	3.06
Tom Hurd	R	31	8	6	.571	5	43	0	0	81	72	38	48	0	3.00
Ellis Kinder	R	40	5	5	.500	18	43	0	0	67	57	15	31	0	2.82
Leo Kiely	L	25	3	3	.500	6	33	4	0	90	91	37	36	0	2.80
Frank Baumann	L	22	2	1	.667	0	7	5	0	34	38	17	27	0	5.82
Mel Parnell	L	33	2	3	.400	1	13	9	0	46	62	25	18	0	7.83
Bill Henry	L	27	2	4	.333	0	17	7	0	60	56	21	23	0	3.30
Dick Brodowski	R	22	1	0	1.000	0	16	0	0	32	36	25	10	0	5.63
1 Hal Brown	R	30	1	0	1.000	0	2	0	0	4	2	2	2	0	2.25
Russ Kemmerer	R	23	1	1	.500	0	7	2	0	17	18	15	13	0	7.41
1 Hersh Freeman	R	27	0	0	.000	0	2	0	0	2	1	1	1	0	0.00
Joe Trimble	R	24	0	0	.000	0	2	0	0	2	0	3	1	0	0.00
Bob Smith	L	24	0	0	.000	0	1	0	0	2	1	1	1	0	0.00

DETROIT 5th 79-75 .513 17

BUCKY HARRIS

NAME	G by POS	B	AGE	G	AB	R	H	2B	3B	HR	RBI	BB	SO	SB	BA	SA
TOTALS			27	154	5283	**775**	**1407**	211	38	130	**724**	641	583	41	.266	.394
2 Earl Torgeson	1B83	L	31	89	300	58	85	10	1	9	50	61	29	9	.283	.413
Fred Hatfield	2B92, 3B16, SS14	L	30	122	413	51	96	15	3	8	33	61	49	3	.232	.341
Harvey Kuenn	SS141	R	24	145	620	101	190	**38**	5	8	62	40	27	8	.306	.423
Ray Boone	3B126	R	31	135	500	61	142	22	7	20	**116**	50	49	1	.284	.476
Al Kaline	OF152	R	20	152	588	121	**200**	24	8	27	102	82	57	6	**.340**	.546
Bill Tuttle	OF154	R	25	154	603	102	168	23	4	14	78	76	54	6	.279	.400
Jim Delsing	OF101	L	29	114	356	49	85	14	2	10	60	48	40	2	.239	.374
Frank House	C93	L	25	102	328	37	85	11	1	15	53	22	25	0	.259	.436
Bubba Phillips	OF65, 3B4	R	25	95	184	18	43	4	0	3	23	14	20	2	.234	.304
Red Wilson	C72	R	26	78	241	26	53	9	0	2	17	26	23	1	.220	.282
Harry Malmberg	2B65	R	28	67	208	25	45	5	2	0	19	29	19	0	.216	.260
1 Ferris Fain	1B44	L	34	58	140	23	37	8	0	2	23	52	12	2	.264	.364
Jack Phillips	1B35, 3B3	R	33	55	117	15	37	8	2	1	20	10	12	0	.316	.444
2 Charlie Maxwell	OF26, 1B2	L	28	55	109	19	29	7	1	7	18	8	20	0	.266	.541
Reno Bertoia	3B14, 2B6, SS5	R	20	38	68	13	14	2	1	1	10	5	11	0	.206	.309
Jay Porter	1B6, C4, OF4	R	22	24	55	6	13	2	0	0	3	8	15	0	.236	.273

Jim Small 18 L 0-4, Charlie King 24 R 5-21, Wayne Belardi 24 L 0-3, Walt Strevli 19 R 1-4, Ron Samford 25 R 0-1, Steve Souchock 36 R 1-1, Frank Bolling (MS) 23

NAME	T	AGE	W	L	PCT	SV	G	GS	CG	IP	H	BB	SO	ShO	ERA
		27	79	75	.513	12	154	154	**66**	1381	1381	517	629	16	3.79
Billy Hoeft	L	23	16	7	.696	0	32	29	17	220	187	75	133	7	2.99
Frank Lary	R	25	14	15	.483	1	36	31	16	235	232	89	98	2	3.10
Steve Gromek	R	35	13	10	.565	0	28	25	8	181	183	37	73	2	3.98
Ned Garver	R	29	12	16	.429	0	33	32	16	231	**251**	67	83	1	3.97
Al Aber	L	27	6	3	.667	3	39	1	0	80	86	28	37	0	3.38
Duke Maas	R	26	5	6	.455	0	18	16	5	87	91	50	42	2	4.86
Babe Birrer	R	26	4	3	.571	3	36	3	1	80	77	29	28	0	4.16
Jim Bunning	R	23	3	5	.375	1	15	8	0	51	59	32	37	0	6.35
2 Joe Coleman (SA)	R	32	2	1	.667	3	17	0	0	25	22	14	5	0	3.24
Bob Miller	L	19	2	1	.667	0	7	3	1	25	26	12	11	0	2.52
Dick Marlowe	R	26	1	0	1.000	1	4	1	1	15	12	4	9	0	1.80
Bill Black	R	22	1	1	.500	0	3	2	1	14	12	8	7	1	1.29
Paul Foytack	R	24	0	1	.000	0	22	1	0	50	48	36	38	0	5.22
Leo Cristante	R	28	0	1	.000	0	20	1	0	37	37	14	9	0	3.16
1 George Zuverink	R	30	0	5	.000	0	14	1	0	28	38	14	13	0	7.07

Van Fletcher 30 R 0-0, 1 Ben Flowers 28 R 0-0, Bill Froats 24 L 0-0, Bob Schultz 31 L 0-0

KANSAS CITY 6th 63-91 .409 33

LOU BOUDREAU

NAME	G by POS	B	AGE	G	AB	R	H	2B	3B	HR	RBI	BB	SO	SB	BA	SA
TOTALS			28	155	**5335**	638	1395	189	46	121	593	463	725	22	.261	.382
Vic Power	1B144	R	23	147	596	91	190	34	10	19	76	35	27	0	.319	.505
Jim Finigan	2B90, 3B59	R	26	150	545	72	139	30	7	9	68	61	49	1	.255	.385
Joe DeMaestri	SS122	R	26	123	457	42	114	14	1	6	37	20	47	3	.249	.324
Hector Lopez	3B93, 2B36	R	22	128	483	50	140	15	2	15	68	33	58	1	.290	.422
Bill Wilson	OF82, P1	R	26	98	273	39	61	12	0	15	38	24	63	1	.223	.432
2 Harry Simpson	OF100, 1B3	L	29	112	396	42	119	16	7	5	52	34	61	3	.301	.414
Gus Zernial	OF103	R	32	120	413	62	105	9	3	30	84	30	90	1	.254	.508
Joe Astroth	C100	R	32	101	274	29	69	4	1	5	23	47	33	2	.252	.328
Elmer Valo	OF72	L	34	112	283	50	103	17	4	3	37	52	18	5	.364	.484
2 Enos Slaughter	OF77	L	39	108	267	49	86	12	4	5	34	40	17	2	.322	.453
Bill Renna	OF79	R	30	100	249	33	53	7	3	7	28	31	42	0	.213	.349
Billy Shantz	C78	R	27	79	217	18	56	4	1	1	12	11	14	0	.258	.300
Clete Boyer	SS12, 3B11, 2B10	R	18	47	79	3	19	1	0	0	6	3	17	0	.241	.253
Jack Littrell (NJ)	SS22, 1B6, 2B4	R	26	37	70	7	14	0	1	0	1	4	12	0	.200	.229
Dick Kryhoski	1B14	L	30	28	47	2	10	2	0	0	2	6	7	0	.213	.255
Pete Suder	2B24	R	39	26	81	3	17	4	1	0	1	2	13	0	.210	.284
Jerry Schypinski	SS21, 2B2	L	23	22	69	7	15	2	0	0	5	1	6	0	.217	.246
Spook Jacobs	2B7	R	29	13	23	7	6	0	0	0	1	3	0	1	.261	.261

Don Bollweg 34 L 1-9, Bill Stewart 27 R 2-18, 2 Tom Saffell 33 L 8-37, Don Plarski 25 R 1-11,
Jim Robertson 27 R 2-8, Alex George 26 L 1-10, Hal Bevan 24 R 0-3, Eric MacKenzie 22 L 0-1

NAME	T	AGE	W	L	PCT	SV	G	GS	CG	IP	H	BB	SO	ShO	ERA
		29	63	91	.409	23	155	155	29	1382	**1486**	**707**	573	9	5.35
Art Ditmar	R	26	12	12	.500	1	35	22	7	175	180	86	79	1	5.04
Alex Kellner	L	30	11	8	.579	0	30	24	6	163	164	60	75	3	4.20
Tom Gorman	R	30	7	6	.538	18	57	0	0	109	98	36	46	0	3.55
Cloyd Boyer	R	27	5	5	.500	0	30	11	2	98	107	69	32	0	6.24
A. Portocarrero (SJ)	R	23	5	9	.357	0	24	20	4	111	109	67	34	1	4.78
Bobby Shantz	L	29	5	10	.333	0	23	17	4	125	124	66	58	1	4.54
2 Vic Raschi	R	36	4	6	.400	0	20	18	1	101	132	35	38	0	5.44
Art Ceccarelli	L	25	4	7	.364	0	31	16	3	124	123	71	68	1	5.30
Bill Harrington (MS)	R	27	3	3	.500	2	34	1	0	77	69	41	26	0	4.09
Moe Burtschy	R	33	2	0	1.000	0	7	0	0	11	17	10	9	0	10.64
2 Johnny Sain	R	37	2	5	.286	1	25	0	0	45	54	10	12	0	5.40
Charlie Bishop	R	31	1	0	1.000	0	4	0	0	7	6	8	4	0	7.71
Lou Sleater	L	28	1	1	.500	0	16	1	0	26	33	21	11	0	7.62
Ray Herbert	R	25	1	8	.111	0	23	11	2	88	99	40	30	0	6.24
Gus Keriazakos	R	23	0	1	.000	0	5	1	0	12	15	7	8	0	12.00
John Kume	R	29	0	2	.000	0	6	4	0	24	35	15	7	0	7.88
Walt Craddock	L	23	0	2	.000	0	4	2	0	15	18	10	9	0	7.80
Glen Cox	R	24	0	2	.000	0	2	2	0	2	11	1	2	0	36.00
John Gray	R	27	0	3	.000	0	8	5	0	27	28	24	11	0	6.33

E. Blackwell 32 R 0-1, Marion Fricano 31 R 0-0, Bob Trice 26 R 0-0, Lee Wheat 25 R 0-0,
S. Dixon 30 R 0-0, Bob Spicer 30 R 0-0, Ozzie Van Brabant 28 R 0-0, Bill Wilson 26 R 0-0

BALTIMORE 7th 57-97 .370 39

PAUL RICHARDS

NAME	G by POS	B	AGE	G	AB	R	H	2B	3B	HR	RBI	BB	SO	SB	BA	SA
TOTALS			29	156	5257	540	1263	177	39	54	503	560	**742**	34	.240	.320
Gus Triandos	1B103, C36, 3B1	R	24	140	481	47	133	17	3	12	65	40	55	0	.277	.399
Freddie Marsh (BE-LJ)	2B76, 3B18, SS16	R	31	89	303	30	66	7	1	2	19	35	33	1	.218	.267
Willie Miranda	SS153, 2B1	B	29	153	487	42	124	12	6	1	38	42	58	4	.255	.310
Wayne Causey	3B55, 2B7, SS1	L	18	68	175	14	34	2	1	1	9	17	25	0	.194	.234
Cal Abrams	OF96, 1B4	L	31	118	309	56	75	12	3	6	32	89	69	2	.243	.359
Chuck Diering	OF107, 3B34, SS12	R	32	137	371	38	95	16	2	3	31	57	45	5	.256	.334
2 Dave Philley	OF82, 3B2	B	35	83	311	50	93	13	3	6	41	34	38	1	.299	.418
Hal Smith	C125	R	24	135	424	41	115	23	4	4	52	30	21	1	.271	.373
2 Dave Pope	OF73	L	30	86	222	21	55	8	4	1	30	16	34	5	.248	.333
Bob Hale	1B44	L	21	67	182	13	65	7	1	0	29	5	19	0	.357	.407
Jim Dyck	OF45, 3B17	R	33	61	197	32	55	13	1	2	22	28	21	1	.279	.386
1 Gil Coan	OF42	L	33	61	130	18	31	7	1	1	11	13	15	4	.238	.331
1 Hoot Evers	OF55	R	34	60	185	21	44	10	1	6	30	19	28	2	.238	.400
1 Bobby Young	2B58	L	30	59	186	5	37	3	0	1	8	11	23	1	.199	.231
Billy Cox	3B37, 2B18, SS6	R	35	53	194	25	41	7	2	3	14	17	16	1	.211	.314
1 Gene Woodling	OF47	L	32	47	145	22	32	6	2	3	18	24	18	1	.221	.352
Don Leppert	2B35	L	24	40	70	6	8	0	1	0	2	9	10	1	.114	.143
Jim Pyburn (XJ)	3B33, OF1	R	22	39	98	5	20	2	2	0	7	8	24	1	.204	.265
1 Eddie Waitkus	1B26	L	35	38	85	2	22	1	1	0	9	11	10	2	.259	.294
1 Les Moss	C17	R	30	29	56	5	19	1	0	2	6	7	4	0	.339	.464
1 Bob Kennedy	OF14, 1B6, 3B1	R	34	26	70	10	10	1	0	0	5	10	10	0	.143	.157
Bob Nelson	OF6, 1B2	L	18	25	31	4	6	0	0	0	1	7	13	0	.194	.194
Tommy Gastall	C15	R	23	20	27	4	4	1	0	0	0	3	5	0	.148	.185

2 Hank Majeski 38 R 7-41, 2 Wally Westlake 34 R 3-24, Angie Dagres 20 L 4-15, Kal Segrist 24 R 3-9, Brooks Robinson 18 R 2-22, 1 Charlie Maxwell 28 L 0-4,
1 Vern Stephens 34 R 1-6, Roger Marquis 18 L 0-1, Joe Durham (MS) 23

NAME	T	AGE	W	L	PCT	SV	G	GS	CG	IP	H	BB	SO	ShO	ERA
		30	57	97	.370	22	156	156	35	**1389**	1403	625	594	10	4.21
Jim Wilson	R	34	12	**18**	.400	0	34	31	14	235	200	87	96	4	3.45
Ray Moore	R	29	10	10	.500	6	46	14	3	152	128	80	80	1	3.91
2 Bill Wight	L	33	6	8	.429	2	19	14	8	117	111	39	54	2	2.46
Erv Palica	R	27	5	11	.313	2	33	25	5	170	165	83	68	1	4.13
2 George Zuverink	R	30	4	3	.571	4	28	5	0	86	80	17	31	0	2.20
1 Harry Byrd	R	30	3	2	.600	1	14	8	1	65	64	28	25	1	4.57
2 Harry Dorish	R	33	3	3	.500	6	35	1	0	66	58	28	22	0	3.14
2 Ed Lopat	L	37	3	4	.429	0	10	7	1	49	57	9	10	0	4.22
2 Art Schallock	L	31	3	5	.375	0	30	6	1	80	92	42	33	0	4.16
Jim McDonald	R	28	3	5	.375	0	21	8	0	52	76	30	20	0	7.10
Don Johnson	R	28	2	4	.333	1	31	5	0	68	89	35	27	0	5.82
Bob Alexander	R	32	1	0	1.000	0	4	0	0	4	8	2	1	0	13.50
4 Ted Gray	L	30	1	2	.333	0	9	1	0	15	21	11	8	0	8.40
1 Saul Rogovin	R	32	1	8	.111	0	14	12	1	71	79	27	35	0	4.56
1 Joe Coleman	R	32	0	1	.000	0	6	2	0	12	19	10	4	0	10.50
1 Bob Kuzava	L	32	0	1	.000	0	6	1	0	12	10	4	5	0	3.75
Bill Miller	L	27	0	1	.000	0	5	1	0	4	3	10	4	0	13.50
Duane Pillette	R	32	0	3	.000	0	7	5	0	21	31	14	13	0	6.43
2 Hal Brown	R	30	0	4	.000	0	15	5	1	57	51	26	26	0	4.11
Lou Kretlow	R	32	0	4	.000	0	15	5	0	38	50	27	26	0	8.29
Don Ferrarese	L	26	0	0	.000	0	6	0	0	9	8	11	5	0	3.00
Charlie Locke	R	23	0	0	.000	0	2	0	0	3	0	1	1	0	0.00
Bob Harrison	R	24	0	0	.000	0	1	0	0	2	3	4	0	0	9.00

Billy O'Dell (MS) 22

WASHINGTON 8th 53-101 .344 43

CHUCK DRESSEN

NAME	G by POS	B	AGE	G	AB	R	H	2B	3B	HR	RBI	BB	SO	SB	BA	SA
TOTALS			28	154	5142	598	1277	178	54	80	556	538	654	25	.248	.351
Mickey Vernon	1B144	L	37	150	538	74	162	23	8	14	85	74	50	0	.301	.452
Pete Runnels	2B132, SS2	L	27	134	503	66	143	16	4	2	49	55	51	3	.284	.346
Jose Valdivielso	SS94	R	21	94	294	32	65	12	5	2	28	21	38	1	.221	.316
Eddie Yost	3B107	R	28	122	375	64	91	17	5	7	48	95	54	4	.243	.371
Carlos Paula	OF85	R	26	115	351	34	105	20	7	6	45	17	43	2	.299	.447
Tommy Umphlett	OF103	R	25	110	323	34	70	10	0	2	19	24	35	2	.217	.266
Roy Sievers	OF129, 1B17, 3B2	R	28	144	509	74	138	20	8	25	106	73	66	1	.271	.489
Ed Fitz Gerald	C72	R	31	74	236	28	56	3	1	4	19	25	23	0	.237	.309
Ernie Oravetz	OF57	B	23	100	263	24	71	5	1	0	25	26	19	1	.270	.297
Bobby Kline	SS69, 2B4, 3B3, P1	R	26	77	140	12	31	5	0	0	9	11	27	0	.221	.257
2 Clint Courtney	C67	L	28	75	238	26	71	8	4	2	30	19	9	0	.298	.395
Mickey McDermott	P31	L	26	70	95	10	25	4	0	1	10	6	16	1	.263	.337
2 Johnny Groth	OF48	R	28	63	183	22	40	4	5	2	17	18	18	2	.219	.328
Juan Delis	3B24, OF8, 2B1	R	27	54	132	12	25	3	1	0	11	3	15	1	.189	.227
1 Jim Busby	OF47	R	28	47	191	23	44	6	2	6	14	13	22	5	.230	.377
Jerry Snyder	2B22, SS20	R	25	46	107	7	24	5	0	0	5	6	6	1	.224	.271
Harmon Killebrew	3B23, 2B3	R	19	38	80	12	16	1	0	4	7	9	31	0	.200	.363
Bruce Edwards	C22, 3B5	R	31	30	57	5	10	2	0	0	3	16	6	0	.175	.211
Tony Roig	SS21, 3B8, 2B1	R	26	29	57	3	13	1	1	0	4	2	15	0	.228	.281
Jerry Schoonmaker	OF15	R	21	20	46	5	7	0	1	1	4	5	11	1	.152	.261

Jesse Levan 28 L 3-16, Steve Korcheck 22 R 10-36, Jim Lemon 27 R 5-25, Julio Becquer 23 L 3-14, Tom Wright 31 L 0-7, Bob Oldis 27 R 0-6

NAME	T	AGE	W	L	PCT	SV	G	GS	CG	IP	H	BB	SO	ShO	ERA
		26	53	**101**	.344	16	154	154	37	1355	1450	634	607	10	4.62
Mickey McDermott	L	26	10	10	.500	1	31	20	8	156	140	100	78	1	3.74
Bob Porterfield	R	31	10	17	.370	0	30	27	8	178	197	54	74	2	4.45
Johnny Schmitz	L	34	7	10	.412	1	32	21	6	165	187	54	49	1	3.71
Dean Stone	L	24	6	13	.316	1	43	24	5	180	180	114	84	1	4.15
Ted Abernathy	R	22	5	9	.357	0	40	14	3	119	136	67	79	2	5.97
Pedro Ramos	R	20	5	11	.313	5	45	9	3	130	121	39	34	1	3.88
Chuck Stobbs	L	25	4	14	.222	3	41	16	2	140	169	57	60	0	5.01
Spec Chea	R	34	2	2	.500	2	27	4	1	56	53	27	16	1	4.02
2 Bob Chakales	R	27	2	3	.400	0	29	0	0	55	55	25	28	0	5.24
Camilo Pascual	R	21	2	12	.143	3	43	16	1	129	158	70	82	0	6.14
Bunky Stewart	L	24	0	0	.000	0	7	1	0	15	18	6	10	0	4.20
Webbo Clarke	L	27	0	0	.000	0	7	2	0	21	17	14	9	0	4.71
Bill Currie	R	26	0	0	.000	0	3	0	0	4	7	2	2	0	13.50
Dick Hyde	R	26	0	0	.000	0	3	0	0	2	2	1	1	0	4.50
Vince Gonzales	L	29	0	0	.000	0	1	0	0	2	6	3	1	0	27.00
Bobby Kline	R	26	0	0	.000	0	1	0	0	1	4	1	0	0	27.00

BROOKLYN 1st 98-55 .641 — WALT ALSTON

NAME	G by POS	B	AGE	G	AB	R	H	2B	3B	HR	RBI	BB	SO	SB	BA	SA
TOTALS			30	154	5193	**857**	1406	**230**	44	**201**	**800**	**674**	718	**79**	**.271**	**.448**
Gil Hodges	1B139, OF16	R	31	150	546	75	158	24	5	27	102	80	91	2	.289	.500
Jim Gilliam	2B99, OF46	B	26	147	538	110	134	20	8	7	40	70	37	15	.249	.355
Pee Wee Reese	SS142	R	36	145	553	99	156	29	4	10	61	78	60	8	.282	.403
Jackie Robinson	3B84, OF10, 2B1, 1B1	R	36	105	317	51	81	6	2	8	36	61	18	12	.256	.363
Carl Furillo	OF140	R	33	140	523	83	164	24	3	26	95	43	43	4	.314	.520
Duke Snider	OF146	L	28	148	538	**126**	166	34	6	42	**136**	104	87	9	.309	.628
Sandy Amoros	OF109	L	25	119	388	59	96	16	7	10	51	55	45	10	.247	.402
Roy Campanella	C121	R	33	123	446	81	142	20	1	32	107	56	41	2	.318	.583
Don Hoak	3B78	R	27	94	279	50	67	13	3	5	19	46	50	9	.240	.362
Don Zimmer	2B62, SS21, 3B8	R	24	88	280	38	67	10	1	15	50	19	66	5	.239	.443
Don Newcombe	P34	L	29	57	117	18	42	9	1	7	23	6	18	1	.359	.632
Rube Walker	C35	L	29	48	103	6	26	5	0	2	13	15	11	1	.252	.359
George Shuba	OF9	L	30	44	51	8	14	2	0	1	8	11	10	0	.275	.373
Frank Kellert	1B22	R	30	39	80	12	26	4	2	4	19	9	10	0	.325	.575
Dixie Howell	C13	R	36	16	42	2	11	4	0	0	5	1	7	0	.262	.357
Walt Moryn	OF7	L	29	11	19	3	5	1	0	1	3	5	4	0	.263	.474
2 Bob Borkowski	OF9	R	29	9	19	2	2	0	0	0	0	1	6	0	.105	.105
Bert Hamric		L	27	2	1	0	0	0	0	0	0	0	1	0	.000	.000

NAME	T	AGE	W	L	PCT	SV	G	GS	CG	IP	H	BB	SO	ShO	ERA
		26	**98**	55	**.641**	**37**	154	154	46	1378	1296	483	**773**	11	**3.68**
Don Newcombe	R	29	20	5	**.800**	0	34	31	17	234	222	38	143	1	3.19
Clem Labine	R	28	13	5	.722	11	**60**	8	1	144	121	55	67	0	3.25
Carl Erskine	R	28	11	8	.579	1	31	29	7	195	185	64	84	2	3.78
Billy Loes	R	25	10	4	.714	0	22	19	6	128	116	46	85	0	3.59
Johnny Podres	L	22	9	10	.474	0	27	24	5	159	160	57	114	2	3.96
Don Bessent	R	24	8	1	.889	3	24	2	1	63	51	21	29	0	2.71
Karl Spooner (SA)	L	24	8	6	.571	2	29	14	2	99	79	41	78	1	3.64
Russ Meyer (XJ)	R	31	6	2	.750	0	18	11	2	73	86	31	26	1	5.42
Roger Craig	R	24	5	3	.625	2	21	10	3	91	81	43	48	0	2.77
Ed Roebuck	R	23	5	6	.455	12	47	0	0	84	96	24	33	0	4.71
Sandy Koufax (NJ)	L	19	2	2	.500	0	12	5	2	42	33	28	30	2	3.00
1 Joe Black	R	31	1	0	1.000	0	6	0	0	15	15	5	9	0	3.00
Chuck Templeton	L	23	0	1	.000	0	4	0	0	5	5	5	3	0	10.80
Jim Hughes	R	32	0	2	.000	6	24	0	0	43	41	19	20	0	4.19
Tom Lasorda	L	27	0	0	.000	0	4	1	0	4	5	6	4	0	13.50

MILWAUKEE 2nd 85-69 .552 13.5 — CHARLIE GRIMM

NAME	G by POS	B	AGE	G	AB	R	H	2B	3B	HR	RBI	BB	SO	SB	BA	SA
TOTALS			28	154	5277	743	1377	219	55	182	699	504	735	42	.261	.427
George Crowe	1B79	L	32	104	303	41	85	12	4	15	55	45	44	1	.281	.495
Danny O'Connell	2B114, 3B7, SS1	R	28	124	453	47	102	15	4	6	40	28	43	2	.225	.316
Johnny Logan	SS154	R	28	154	595	95	177	**37**	5	13	83	58	58	3	.297	.442
Eddie Mathews	3B137	L	23	141	499	108	144	23	5	41	101	**109**	98	3	.289	.601
Hank Aaron	OF126, 2B27	R	21	153	602	105	189	**37**	9	27	106	49	61	3	.314	.540
Bill Bruton	OF149	L	29	149	**636**	106	175	30	12	9	47	43	72	**25**	.275	.403
Bobby Thomson	OF91	R	31	101	343	40	88	12	3	12	56	34	52	2	.257	.414
Del Crandall	C131	R	25	133	440	61	104	15	2	26	62	40	56	2	.236	.457
Chuck Tanner	OF62	L	25	97	243	27	60	9	3	6	27	27	32	0	.247	.383
Andy Pafko	OF58, 3B12	R	34	86	252	29	67	3	5	5	34	7	23	1	.266	.377
Joe Adcock (BA)	1B78	R	27	84	288	40	76	14	0	15	45	31	44	0	.264	.469
Warren Spahn	P39	L	34	40	81	7	17	1	1	4	14	4	20	0	.210	.395
Jack Dittmer	2B28	L	27	38	72	4	9	1	1	1	4	4	15	0	.125	.208
2 Del Rice	C22	R	32	27	71	5	14	0	1	2	7	6	12	0	.197	.310
Charlie White	C10	L	26	12	30	3	7	1	0	0	4	5	7	0	.233	.267
Bennie Taylor	1B1	L	30	12	10	2	1	0	0	0	0	2	4	0	.100	.100

Jim Pendleton 31 R 0-10, Bob Roselli 23 R 2-9, Mel Roach (MS) 22

NAME	T	AGE	W	L	PCT	SV	G	GS	CG	IP	H	BB	SO	ShO	ERA
		27	85	69	.552	12	154	154	**61**	1383	1339	591	654	5	3.85
Warren Spahn	L	34	17	14	.548	1	39	32	16	246	249	65	110	1	3.26
Lew Burdette	R	28	13	8	.619	0	42	33	11	230	253	73	70	2	4.03
Bob Buhl	R	26	13	11	.542	1	38	27	11	202	168	109	117	1	3.21
Gene Conley	R	24	11	7	.611	0	22	21	10	158	152	52	107	0	4.16
Ray Crone	R	23	10	9	.526	0	33	15	6	140	117	42	76	1	3.47
Chet Nichols	L	24	9	8	.529	1	34	21	6	144	139	67	44	0	4.00
Ernie Johnson	R	31	5	7	.417	4	40	2	0	92	81	55	43	0	3.42
Humberto Robinson	R	25	3	1	.750	2	13	2	1	38	31	25	19	0	3.08
Phil Paine	R	25	2	0	1.000	0	15	0	0	25	20	14	26	0	2.52
Dave Jolly	R	30	2	3	.400	1	36	0	0	58	58	51	23	0	5.74
Dave Koslo	L	35	0	1	.000	0	1	0	0	0	1	0	0	0	∞
Roberto Vargas	L	26	0	0	.000	2	25	0	0	25	39	14	13	0	8.64
Joey Jay	R	19	0	0	.000	0	12	1	0	19	23	13	3	0	4.74
John Edelman	R	19	0	0	.000	0	5	0	0	6	7	8	3	0	10.50
Charlie Gorin	L	27	0	0	.000	0	2	0	0	0	1	3	0	0	∞

NEW YORK 3rd 80-74 .519 18.5 — LEO DUROCHER

NAME	G by POS	B	AGE	G	AB	R	H	2B	3B	HR	RBI	BB	SO	SB	BA	SA
TOTALS			28	154	**5288**	702	1377	173	34	169	643	497	581	38	.260	.402
Gail Harris	1B75	L	23	79	263	27	61	9	0	12	36	20	46	0	.232	.403
Wayne Terwilliger	2B78, SS1, 3B1	R	30	80	257	29	66	16	1	1	18	36	42	2	.257	.339
Al Dark (SJ)	SS115	R	33	115	475	77	134	20	3	9	45	22	32	2	.282	.394
Hank Thompson	3B124, 2B7, SS1	L	29	135	432	65	106	13	1	17	63	84	56	2	.245	.398
Don Mueller	OF146	L	28	147	605	67	185	21	4	8	83	19	12	1	.306	.393
Willie Mays	OF152	R	24	152	580	123	185	18	**13**	**51**	127	79	60	24	.319	**.659**
Whitey Lockman	OF81, 1B68	L	28	147	576	76	157	19	0	15	49	39	34	3	.273	.384
Ray Katt	C122	R	28	124	326	27	70	7	2	7	28	22	38	0	.215	.313
Bobby Hofman	1B24, 2B19, C19, 3B5	R	29	96	207	32	55	7	2	10	28	22	31	0	.266	.464
Dusty Rhodes	OF45	L	28	94	187	22	57	5	2	6	32	27	26	1	.305	.449
Davey Williams (JJ)	2B71	R	27	82	247	25	62	4	1	4	15	17	17	0	.251	.324
Wes Westrum	C68	R	32	69	137	11	29	1	0	4	18	24	18	0	.212	.307
2 Sid Gordon	3B31, OF17	R	37	66	144	19	35	6	1	7	25	25	15	0	.243	.444
Bill Taylor	OF2	L	25	65	64	9	17	4	0	4	12	1	16	0	.266	.516
Billy Gardner	SS38, 3B10, 2B4	R	27	59	187	26	38	10	1	3	17	13	19	0	.203	.316
Monte Irvin	OF45	R	36	51	150	16	38	7	1	1	17	17	15	3	.253	.333
Jim Hearn	P39	R	34	41	77	11	12	0	0	4	6	4	26	0	.156	.312
Johnny Antonelli	P38	L	25	38	82	8	17	1	0	4	15	3	18	0	.207	.366
Joey Amalfitano	SS5, 3B2	R	21	36	22	8	5	1	1	0	1	2	2	0	.227	.364
Foster Castleman	2B6, 3B1	R	24	15	28	3	6	1	0	2	4	2	4	0	.214	.464

3 Gil Coan 33 L 2-13, Mickey Grasso 35 R 0-2, Daryl Spencer (MS) 25

NAME	T	AGE	W	L	PCT	SV	G	GS	CG	IP	H	BB	SO	ShO	ERA
		30	80	74	.519	14	154	154	52	**1387**	1347	560	721	6	3.77
Jim Hearn	R	34	14	16	.467	0	39	33	11	227	225	66	86	1	3.73
Johnny Antonelli	L	25	14	16	.467	1	38	34	14	235	206	82	143	2	3.33
Don Liddle	L	30	10	4	.714	1	33	13	4	106	97	61	56	0	4.25
1 Sal Maglie	R	38	9	5	.643	0	23	21	6	130	142	48	71	0	3.74
Ruben Gomez	R	27	9	10	.474	1	33	31	9	185	207	63	79	3	4.57
Windy McCall	L	29	6	5	.545	3	42	6	4	95	86	37	50	0	3.69
Marv Grissom	R	37	5	4	.556	8	55	0	0	89	76	41	49	0	2.93
Hoyt Wilhelm	R	31	4	1	.800	0	59	0	0	103	104	40	71	0	3.93
Paul Giel	R	22	4	4	.500	0	34	2	0	82	70	50	47	0	3.40
Ray Monzant	R	22	4	8	.333	0	28	12	3	95	98	43	54	0	3.98
Pete Burnside	L	24	1	0	1.000	0	2	2	1	13	10	9	2	0	2.77
Al Corwin	R	28	0	1	.000	0	13	0	0	25	25	17	13	0	3.96
George Spencer	R	28	0	0	.000	0	1	0	0	2	1	3	0	0	4.50

PHILADELPHIA 4th 77-77 .500 21.5 — MAYO SMITH

NAME	G by POS	B	AGE	G	AB	R	H	2B	3B	HR	RBI	BB	SO	SB	BA	SA
TOTALS			28	154	5092	675	1300	214	50	132	631	652	673	44	.255	.395
Marv Blaylock	1B77, OF6	L	25	113	259	30	54	7	7	3	24	31	43	6	.208	.324
Bobby Morgan	2B88, SS41, 3B6, 1B1	R	29	136	483	61	112	20	2	10	49	73	72	6	.232	.344
Roy Smalley	SS87, 3B1, 2B1	R	29	92	260	33	51	11	1	7	39	39	58	0	.196	.327
Willie Jones	3B146	R	29	146	516	65	133	20	3	16	81	77	51	6	.258	.401
2 Jim Greengrass	OF83, 3B2	R	27	94	323	43	88	20	2	12	37	33	43	0	.272	.458
Richie Ashburn	OF140	L	28	140	533	91	180	32	9	3	42	105	36	12	**.338**	.448
Del Ennis	OF145	R	30	146	564	82	167	24	7	29	120	46	46	4	.296	.518
2 Andy Seminick	C88	R	34	93	289	32	71	12	1	11	34	32	59	1	.246	.408
Granny Hamner	2B82, SS32	R	28	104	405	57	104	12	4	5	43	41	30	0	.257	.343
Stan Lopata	C66, 1B24	R	29	99	303	49	82	9	3	22	58	58	62	4	.271	.538
2 Glen Gorbous	OF57	L	24	91	224	25	53	9	1	4	23	21	17	0	.237	.339
Peanuts Lowery	OF28, 2B2, 1B1	R	36	54	106	9	20	4	0	0	8	7	10	2	.189	.226
1 Earl Torgeson	1B43	L	31	47	150	29	40	5	3	1	17	32	20	2	.267	.360
Herm Wehmeier	P31	R	28	34	72	10	20	1	1	0	7	2	26	0	.278	.319
2 Eddie Waitkus	1B31	L	35	33	107	10	30	5	0	2	14	17	7	0	.280	.383
1 Stan Palys	OF15	R	25	15	52	8	15	3	0	1	8	6	5	1	.288	.404
Mel Clark	OF8	R	28	10	32	3	5	3	0	0	1	3	4	0	.156	.250
Ted Kazanski	SS4, 3B4	R	21	9	12	1	1	0	0	1	1	1	1	0	.083	.333
Gus Niarhos	C7	R	34	7	9	1	1	0	0	0	0	0	2	0	.111	.111
1 Smoky Burgess	C6	L	28	7	21	4	4	2	0	1	1	3	1	0	.190	.429

Floyd Baker 38 L 0-8, Jim Command 26 L 0-5, Bob Micelotta 26 R 0-4, Bob Bowman 24 R 0-3, Danny Schell 27 R 0-2, John Easton 22 R 0-0, Fred Van Dusen 17 L 0-0, Jim Westlake 24 L 0-1

NAME	T	AGE	W	L	PCT	SV	G	GS	CG	IP	H	BB	SO	ShO	ERA
		28	77	77	.500	21	154	154	58	1357	1291	477	657	11	3.93
Robin Roberts	R	28	**23**	14	.622	3	41	**38**	**26**	**305**	**292**	53	160	1	3.28
Murry Dickson	R	38	12	11	.522	0	36	28	12	216	190	82	92	4	3.50
Herm Wehmeier	R	28	10	12	.455	0	31	29	10	194	176	67	85	1	4.41
Bob Miller	R	29	8	4	.667	1	40	0	0	90	80	28	28	0	2.40
Curt Simmons	L	26	8	8	.500	0	25	22	3	130	148	50	58	0	4.92
Jack Meyer	R	23	6	11	.353	**16**	50	5	0	110	75	66	97	0	3.44
2 Saul Rogovin	R	32	5	3	.625	0	12	11	5	73	60	17	27	2	3.08
Ron Negray	R	25	4	3	.571	0	19	10	2	72	71	21	30	0	3.50
2 Bob Kuzava	L	32	1	0	1.000	0	17	4	0	32	47	12	13	0	7.31
Thornton Kipper	R	26	0	1	.000	0	24	0	0	40	47	22	15	0	4.95
Lynn Lovenguth	R	32	0	1	.000	0	14	0	0	18	17	10	14	0	4.50
1 Steve Ridzik	R	26	0	1	.000	0	3	1	0	11	7	8	6	0	2.45
Jack Spring	L	22	0	1	.000	0	2	0	0	3	2	1	2	0	6.00
Ron Mrozinski	L	24	0	2	.000	1	22	1	0	34	38	19	18	0	6.62
Jim Owens	R	21	0	2	.000	0	3	2	0	9	13	7	6	0	8.00
Dave Cole	R	24	0	3	.000	0	7	3	0	18	21	14	6	0	6.50
Bob Greenwood	R	27	0	0	.000	0	1	0	0	2	7	0	0	0	18.00

CINCINNATI 5th 75-79 .487 23.5 — BIRDIE TEBBETTS

NAME	G by POS	B	AGE	G	AB	R	H	2B	3B	HR	RBI	BB	SO	SB	BA	SA
TOTALS			27	154	5270	761	**1424**	216	28	181	726	556	657	51	.270	.425
Ted Kluszewski	1B153	L	30	153	612	116	**192**	25	0	47	113	66	40	1	.314	.585
Johnny Temple	2B149, SS1	R	26	150	588	94	165	20	3	0	50	80	32	19	.281	.325
Roy McMillan	SS150	R	24	151	470	50	126	21	2	1	37	66	33	4	.268	.328
Rocky Bridges	3B59, SS26, 2B9	R	27	95	168	20	48	4	0	1	18	15	19	1	.286	.327
Wally Post	OF154	R	25	154	601	116	186	33	3	40	109	60	**102**	7	.309	.574
Gus Bell	OF154	L	26	154	610	88	188	30	6	27	104	54	57	4	.308	.510
2 Stan Palys	OF55, 1B1	R	25	79	222	29	51	14	0	7	30	12	35	1	.230	.387
2 Smoky Burgess	C107	L	28	116	421	67	129	15	3	20	77	47	35	1	.306	.499
Chuck Harmon	3B39, OF32, 1B4	R	29	96	198	31	50	6	3	5	28	26	24	9	.253	.389
Bob Thurman	OF36	L	34	82	152	19	33	2	3	7	22	17	26	0	.217	.408
Ray Jablonski	3B28, OF28	R	28	74	221	28	53	9	0	9	28	13	35	0	.240	.403
1 Bobby Adams	3B42, 2B5	R	33	64	150	23	41	11	2	2	20	20	21	2	.273	.413
Hobie Landrith (BC)	C27	L	25	43	87	9	22	3	0	4	7	10	14	0	.253	.425
Milt Smith	3B28, 2B5	R	26	36	102	15	20	3	1	3	8	13	24	2	.196	.333
2 Sam Mele	OF13, 1B1	R	32	35	62	4	13	1	0	2	7	5	13	0	.210	.323
Matt Batts	C21	R	33	26	71	4	18	4	1	0	13	4	11	0	.254	.338
1 Bob Borkowski	OF11, 1B1	R	29	25	18	1	3	1	0	0	1	1	2	0	.167	.222
Ed Bailey	C11	L	24	21	39	3	8	1	1	1	4	4	10	0	.205	.359
Joe Brovia		L	33	21	18	0	2	0	0	0	4	1	6	0	.111	.111
1 Jim Greengrass	OF111	R	27	13	39	1	4	2	0	0	1	9	9	0	.103	.154
Al Silvera	OF1	R	19	13	7	3	1	0	0	0	2	0	1	0	.143	.143
1 Glen Gorbous	OF5	L	24	8	18	2	6	3	0	0	4	3	1	0	.333	.500

1 Andy Seminick 34 R 2-15, Bob Hazle 24 L 3-13

NAME	T	AGE	W	L	PCT	SV	G	GS	CG	IP	H	BB	SO	ShO	ERA
		29	75	79	.487	22	154	154	38	1363	1373	443	576	**12**	3.95
Joe Nuxhall	L	26	17	12	.586	3	50	33	14	257	240	78	98	5	3.47
Art Fowler	R	32	11	10	.524	2	46	28	8	208	198	63	94	3	3.89
Jackie Collum	L	28	9	8	.529	1	32	17	5	134	128	37	49	0	3.63
Johnny Klippstein	R	27	9	10	.474	0	39	14	3	138	120	60	68	2	3.39
2 Hersh Freeman	R	27	7	4	.636	11	52	0	0	92	94	30	37	0	2.15
2 Joe Black	R	31	5	2	.714	3	32	11	1	102	106	25	54	0	4.24
1 Gerry Staley	R	34	5	8	.383	0	30	18	2	120	146	28	40	0	4.65
Rudy Minarcin	R	25	5	9	.357	1	41	12	3	116	116	51	45	1	4.89
Don Gross	L	24	4	5	.444	0	17	11	2	67	79	16	33	1	4.16
Corky Valentine	R	26	2	1	.667	0	10	5	0	27	29	16	14	0	7.33
Bud Podbielan (JJ)	R	31	1	2	.333	0	17	2	0	42	36	11	26	0	3.21
Jim Pearce	R	30	0	1	.000	0	2	1	0	3	8	0	0	0	12.00
Jerry Lane	R	29	0	2	.000	1	8	0	0	11	11	6	5	0	4.91
Bob Hooper	R	33	0	2	.000	0	8	0	0	13	20	6	6	0	7.62
2 Steve Ridzik	R	26	0	3	.000	0	13	2	0	30	35	14	6	0	4.50
Fred Baczewski	L	29	0	0	.000	0	1	0	0	1	2	0	0	0	18.00
Maury Fisher	R	24	0	0	.000	0	1	0	0	3	5	2	1	0	6.00

CHICAGO 6th 72-81 .471 26 — STAN HACK

NAME	G by POS	B	AGE	G	AB	R	H	2B	3B	HR	RBI	BB	SO	SB	BA	SA
TOTALS			28	154	5214	626	1287	187	55	164	597	428	**806**	37	.247	.398
Dee Fondy	1B147	L	30	150	574	69	152	23	8	17	65	35	87	8	.265	.422
Gene Baker	2B154	R	30	154	609	82	163	29	7	11	52	49	57	9	.268	.392
Ernie Banks	SS154	R	24	154	596	98	176	29	9	44	117	45	72	9	.295	.596
Randy Jackson	3B134	R	29	138	499	73	132	13	7	21	70	58	58	0	.265	.445
Jim King	OF93	L	22	113	301	43	77	12	3	11	45	24	39	2	.256	.425
Eddie Miksis	OF111, 3B18	R	28	131	481	52	113	14	2	9	41	32	55	3	.235	.328
Hank Sauer	OF68	R	36	79	261	29	55	8	1	12	28	26	47	0	.211	.387
Harry Chiti	C113	R	22	113	338	24	78	6	1	11	41	25	68	0	.231	.352
Frankie Baumholtz	OF63	L	36	105	280	23	81	12	5	1	27	16	24	0	.289	.379
Bob Speake	OF55, 1B8	L	24	95	261	36	57	9	5	12	43	28	71	3	.218	.429
2 Lloyd Merriman	OF49	L	30	72	145	15	31	6	1	1	8	21	21	1	.214	.290
Jim Bolger	OF51	R	23	64	160	19	33	5	4	0	7	9	17	2	.206	.288
Walker Cooper	C31	R	40	54	111	11	31	8	1	7	15	6	19	0	.279	.559
Clyde McCullough	C37	R	38	44	81	7	16	0	0	0	10	8	15	0	.198	.198
Ted Tappe (FJ)	OF15	L	24	23	50	12	13	2	0	4	10	11	11	0	.260	.540
Gale Wade	OF9	L	26	9	33	5	6	1	0	1	1	4	3	0	.182	.303
Vern Morgan	3B2	L	26	7	7	1	1	0	0	0	1	3	4	0	.143	.143

2 Owen Friend 28 R 1-10, Jim Fanning 27 R 0-10, Al Lary 25 R 0-0, El Tappe 28 R 0-0

NAME	T	AGE	W	L	PCT	SV	G	GS	CG	IP	H	BB	SO	ShO	ERA
TOTALS		30	72	81	.471	23	154	154	47	1378	1306	**601**	686	10	4.17
Sam Jones	R	29	14	**20**	.412	0	36	34	12	242	175	**185**	**198**	4	4.09
Bob Rush	R	29	13	11	.542	0	33	33	14	234	204	73	130	3	3.50
Warren Hacker	R	30	11	15	.423	3	35	30	13	213	202	43	80	0	4.27
Paul Minner	L	31	9	9	.500	0	22•	22	7	158	173	47	53	1	3.47
Hal Jeffcoat	R	30	8	6	.571	6	50	1	0	101	107	53	32	0	2.94
Jim Davis	L	30	7	11	.389	3	42	16	0	134	122	58	62	0	4.43
Howie Pollet	L	34	4	3	.571	5	24	7	1	61	62	27	27	1	5.61
Bill Tremel	R	25	3	0	1.000	2	23	0	0	39	33	18	13	0	3.69
Harry Perkowski	L	32	3	4	.429	2	25	4	0	48	53	25	28	0	5.26
John Andre	R	32	0	1	.000	1	22	3	0	45	45	28	19	0	5.80
Vicente Amor	R	22	0	1	.000	0	4	0	0	6	11	3	3	0	4.50
Dave Hillman	R	27	0	0	.000	0	25	3	0	58	63	25	23	0	5.28
Don Kaiser	R	20	0	0	.000	0	11	0	0	18	20	5	11	0	5.50
Hy Cohen	R	24	0	0	.000	0	7	1	0	17	28	10	4	0	7.94
Bubba Church	R	30	0	0	.000	1	2	0	0	3	4	1	3	0	6.00
Bob Thorpe	R	20	0	0	.000	0	2	0	0	3	4	0	0	0	3.00

ST. LOUIS 7th 68-86 .442 30.5 — EDDIE STANKY 17-19 .472 HARRY WALKER 51-67 .432

NAME	G by POS	B	AGE	G	AB	R	H	2B	3B	HR	RBI	BB	SO	SB	BA	SA
TOTALS			29	154	5266	654	1375	228	36	143	608	458	597	64	.261	.400
Stan Musial	1B110, OF51	L	34	154	562	97	179	30	5	33	108	80	39	5	.319	.566
Red Schoendienst	2B142	B	32	145	553	68	148	21	3	11	51	54	28	7	.268	.376
Alex Grammas	SS126	R	28	128	366	32	88	19	2	3	25	33	36	4	.240	.328
Ken Boyer	3B139, SS18	R	24	147	530	78	140	27	2	18	62	37	67	22	.264	.425
Wally Moon	OF100, 1B51	L	25	152	593	86	175	24	8	19	76	47	65	11	.295	.459
Bill Virdon	OF142	L	24	144	534	58	150	18	6	17	68	36	64	2	.281	.433
Rip Repulski	OF141	R	27	147	512	64	138	28	2	23	73	49	66	5	.270	.467
Bill Sarni	C99	R	27	107	325	32	83	15	2	3	34	27	33	1	.255	.342
Solly Hemus	3B43, 2B40, SS2	L	32	96	206	36	50	10	2	5	21	27	22	1	.243	.383
Harry Elliott	OF28	R	29	68	117	9	30	4	0	1	12	11	9	0	.256	.316
Bobby Stephenson	SS48, 2B7, 3B1	R	26	67	111	19	27	3	0	0	6	5	18	2	.243	.270
Nels Burbrink	C55	R	33	58	170	11	47	8	1	0	15	14	13	1	.276	.335
Pete Whisenant	OF40	R	25	58	115	10	22	5	1	2	9	5	29	2	.191	.304
Joe Frazier	OF14	L	32	58	70	12	14	1	0	4	9	6	12	0	.200	.386
1 Del Rice	C18	R	32	20	59	6	12	3	0	1	7	7	6	0	.203	.305
Tom Alston	1B7	L	24	13	8	0	1	0	0	0	0	0	0	0	.125	.125
Dick Schofield	SS3	B	20	12	4	3	0	0	0	0	0	0	1	0	.000	.000
Harry Walker	OF1	L	38	11	14	2	5	2	0	0	1	1	0	0	.357	.500
Don Blasingame	2B3, SS2	L	23	5	16	4	6	1	0	0	0	6	0	1	.375	.438
Dick Rand	C3	R	24	3	10	1	3	0	0	1	3	1	1	0	.300	.600

NAME	T	AGE	W	L	PCT	SV	G	GS	CG	IP	H	BB	SO	ShO	ERA
TOTALS		27	68	86	.442	15	154	154	42	1377	1376	549	730	10	4.56
Harvey Haddix	L	29	12	16	.429	1	37	30	9	208	216	62	150	2	4.46
Luis Arroyo	L	28	11	8	.579	0	35	24	9	159	162	63	68	1	4.19
Tom Poholsky	R	25	9	11	.450	0	30	24	8	151	143	35	66	2	3.81
Larry Jackson	R	24	9	14	.391	2	37	25	4	177	189	72	88	1	4.32
Willard Schmidt	R	27	7	6	.538	0	20	15	8	130	89	57	86	1	2.77
Paul LaPalme	L	31	4	3	.571	3	56	0	0	92	76	34	39	0	2.74
Frank Smith (AJ)	R	27	3	1	.750	1	28	0	0	39	27	23	17	0	3.23
Brooks Lawrence	R	30	3	8	.273	1	46	10	2	96	102	58	52	1	6.56
Mel Wright	R	27	2	2	.500	1	29	0	0	36	44	9	18	0	6.25
Floyd Wooldridge	R	26	2	4	.333	0	18	8	2	58	64	27	14	0	4.81
Al Gettel	R	37	1	0	1.000	0	8	0	0	17	26	10	7	0	9.00
2 Ben Flowers	R	28	1	0	1.000	0	4	4	0	27	27	12	19	0	3.67
Herb Moford	R	26	1	1	.500	2	14	1	0	24	29	15	8	0	7.88
Barney Schultz	R	28	1	2	.333	4	19	0	0	30	28	15	19	0	7.80
Bobby Tiefenauer	R	25	1	4	.200	0	18	0	0	33	31	10	16	0	4.36
Gordon Jones	R	25	1	4	.200	0	15	9	0	57	66	28	46	0	5.84
Johnny Mackinson	R	31	0	1	.000	0	8	1	0	21	24	10	8	0	7.71
1 Vic Raschi	R	36	0	1	.000	0	1	1	0	2	5	1	1	0	18.00
Lindy McDaniel	R	19	0	0	.000	0	4	2	0	19	22	7	7	0	4.74
Tony Jacobs	R	29	0	0	.000	0	1	0	0	2	6	1	1	0	18.00

Vinegar Bend Mizell (MS) 24

PITTSBURGH 8th 60-94 .390 38.5 — FRED HANEY

NAME	G by POS	B	AGE	G	AB	R	H	2B	3B	HR	RBI	BB	SO	SB	BA	SA
TOTALS			25	154	5173	560	1262	210	**60**	91	532	471	652	22	.244	.361
Dale Long	1B119	L	29	131	419	59	122	19	**13**	16	79	48	72	0	.291	.513
Johnny O'Brien (MS-JJ)	2B78	R	24	84	278	22	83	15	2	1	25	20	19	1	.299	.378
Dick Groat	SS149	R	24	151	521	45	139	28	2	4	51	38	26	0	.267	.351
Gene Freese	3B65, 2B57	R	21	134	455	69	115	21	8	14	44	34	57	5	.253	.426
Roberto Clemente	OF118	R	20	124	474	48	121	23	11	5	47	18	60	2	.255	.382
Eddie O'Brien (MS)	OF56, 3B7, SS4	R	24	75	236	26	55	3	1	0	8	18	13	4	.233	.254
Frank Thomas	OF139	R	26	142	510	72	125	16	2	25	72	60	76	2	.245	.431
Jack Shepard	C77	R	23	94	264	24	63	10	2	2	23	33	25	1	.239	.314
Jerry Lynch	OF71, C2	L	24	88	282	43	80	18	6	5	28	22	33	2	.284	.443
Preston Ward	1B48, OF1	L	27	84	179	16	38	7	4	5	25	22	28	0	.212	.380
Dick Cole	3B33, 2B24, SS12	R	29	77	239	16	54	8	3	0	21	18	22	0	.226	.285
1 Tom Saffell	OF47	L	33	73	113	21	19	1	0	1	3	15	22	1	.168	.204
Toby Atwell	C67	L	31	71	207	21	44	8	0	1	18	40	16	0	.213	.266
Roman Mejias	OF43	R	24	71	167	14	36	8	1	3	21	9	13	1	.216	.329
George Freese	3B50	R	28	51	179	17	46	8	2	3	22	17	18	1	.257	.374
Felipe Montemayor	OF28	L	25	36	95	10	20	1	3	2	8	18	24	1	.211	.347
Hardy Peterson	C31	R	25	32	81	7	20	6	0	1	10	7	7	0	.247	.358
1 Sid Gordon	3B8, OF4	R	37	16	47	2	8	1	0	0	1	2	6	0	.170	.191
Curt Roberts	2B6	R	26	6	17	1	2	1	0	0	0	2	1	0	.118	.176
Earl Smith	OF5	R	27	5	16	1	1	0	0	0	0	4	2	0	.063	.063
Nick Koback	C2	R	19	5	7	0	2	0	0	0	0	0	1	0	.286	.286

Dick Smith 27 R 0-0, Johnny Powers 25 L 1-4, Paul Smith (MS) 24

NAME	T	AGE	W	L	PCT	SV	G	GS	CG	IP	H	BB	SO	ShO	ERA
TOTALS		27	60	**94**	.390	16	154	154	41	1362	**1480**	536	622	5	4.39
Bob Friend	R	24	14	9	.609	2	44	20	9	200	178	52	98	2	**2.84**
Vern Law	R	25	10	10	.500	1	43	24	8	201	221	61	82	1	3.81
Max Surkont	R	33	7	14	.333	2	35	22	5	166	194	78	84	0	5.58
Dick Hall	R	24	6	6	.500	1	15	13	4	94	92	28	46	0	3.93
Ron Kline	R	23	6	13	.316	2	36	19	2	137	161	53	48	1	4.14
Roy Face	R	27	5	7	.417	5	42	10	4	126	128	40	84	0	3.57
Dick Littlefield	L	29	5	12	.294	0	35	17	4	130	148	68	70	1	5.12
Lino Donoso	L	32	4	6	.400	1	25	9	3	95	106	35	38	0	5.31
Bob Purkey	R	25	2	7	.222	1	14	10	2	68	77	25	24	0	5.29
Nellie King	R	27	1	3	.250	0	17	4	0	54	60	14	21	0	3.00
Laurin Pepper	R	24	0	1	.000	0	14	1	0	20	30	25	7	0	10.35
Ben Wade	R	32	0	1	.000	1	11	1	0	28	26	14	7	0	3.21
Paul Martin	R	23	0	1	.000	0	7	1	0	7	13	17	3	0	14.14
Jake Theis	R	29	0	1	.000	0	1	1	0	4	5	3	0	0	4.50
Roger Bowman	L	27	0	3	.000	0	7	2	0	17	25	10	8	0	8.47
Al Grunwald	L	25	0	0	.000	0	3	0	0	8	7	7	2	0	4.50
Fred Waters	L	28	0	0	.000	0	2	0	0	5	7	2	0	0	3.60
Bill Bell	R	21	0	0	.000	0	1	0	0	1	0	1	0	0	0.00
Red Swanson	R	18	0	0	.000	0	1	0	0	2	2	3	0	0	18.00

WORLD SERIES – BROOKLYN (NL) 4 NEW YORK (AL) 3

LINE SCORES

TEAM	1	2	3	4	5	6	7	8	9	10	11	12	R	H	E
Game 1 September 28 at New York															
BKN (NL)	0	2	1	0	0	0	0	2	0				5	10	0
NY (AL)	0	2	1	1	0	2	0	0	X				6	9	1
Newcombe, Bessent (6), Labine (8) — **Ford**, Grim (9)															
Game 2 September 29 at New York															
BKN	0	0	0	1	1	0	0	0	0				2	5	2
NY	0	0	0	4	0	0	0	0	X				4	8	0
Loes, Bessent (4), Spooner (5), Labine (8) — **Byrne**															
Game 3 September 30 at Brooklyn															
NY	0	2	0	0	0	0	1	0	0				3	7	0
BKN	2	2	0	2	0	0	2	0	X				8	11	1
Turley, Morgan (2), Kucks (5), Sturdivant (7) — **Podres**															
Game 4 October 1 at Brooklyn															
NY	1	1	0	1	0	2	0	0	0				5	9	0
BKN	0	0	1	3	3	0	1	0	X				8	14	0
Larsen, Kucks (5), R. Coleman (6), Morgan (7), Sturdivant (8) — Erskine, Bessent (3), **Labine** (5)															
Game 5 October 2 at Brooklyn															
NY	0	0	0	1	0	0	1	1	0				3	6	0
BKN	0	2	1	0	1	0	0	1	X				5	9	2
Grim, Turley (7) — **Craig**, Labine (7)															
Game 6 October 3 at New York															
BKN	0	0	0	1	0	0	0	0	0				1	4	1
NY	5	0	0	0	0	0	0	0	X				5	8	0
Spooner, Meyer (1), Roebuck (7) — **Ford**															
Game 7 October 4 at New York															
BKN	0	0	0	1	0	1	0	0	0				2	5	0
NY	0	0	0	0	0	0	0	0	0				0	8	1
Podres — **Byrne**, Grim (6), Turley (8)															

COMPOSITE BATTING

NAME	POS	G	AB	R	H	2B	3B	HR	RBI	BA
Brooklyn (NL)										
Totals		7	223	31	58	8	1	9	30	.260
Reese	SS	7	**27**	5	8	1	0	0	2	.296
Furillo	OF	7	**27**	4	8	1	0	1	3	.296
Campanella	C	7	**27**	4	7	**3**	0	2	4	.259
Snider	OF	7	25	5	8	1	0	**4**	**7**	.320
Gilliam	OF-2B	7	24	2	7	1	0	0	3	.292
Hodges	1B	7	24	2	7	0	0	1	5	.292
J. Robinson	3B	6	22	5	4	1	1	0	1	.182
Amoros	OF	5	12	3	4	0	0	1	3	.333
Zimmer	2B	4	9	0	2	0	0	0	2	.222
Podres	P	2	7	1	1	0	0	0	0	.143
Labine	P	4	4	0	0	0	0	0	0	.000
Kellert	PH	3	3	0	1	0	0	0	0	.333
Hoak	3B	3	3	0	1	0	0	0	0	.333
Newcombe	P	1	3	0	0	0	0	0	0	.000
Meyer	P	1	2	0	0	0	0	0	0	.000
Shuba	PH	1	1	0	0	0	0	0	0	.000
Bessent	P	3	1	0	0	0	0	0	0	.000
Loes	P	1	1	0	0	0	0	0	0	.000
Erskine	P	1	1	0	0	0	0	0	0	.000

Spooner P 0-0, Craig P 0-0, Roebuck P 0-0

NAME	POS	G	AB	R	H	2B	3B	HR	RBI	BA
New York (AL)										
Totals		7	222	26	55	4	2	8	25	.248
McDougald	3B	7	**27**	2	7	0	0	1	1	.259
Howard	OF	7	26	3	5	0	0	1	3	.192
Martin	2B	7	25	2	8	1	1	0	4	.320
Berra	C	7	24	5	**10**	1	0	1	2	.417
Cerv	OF	5	16	1	2	0	0	1	1	.125
Noren	OF	5	16	0	1	0	0	0	1	.063
Rizzuto	SS	7	15	2	4	0	0	0	1	.267
Bauer	OF	6	14	1	6	0	0	0	1	**.429**
Skowron	1B	5	12	2	4	2	0	1	3	.333
Collins	1B-OF	5	12	**6**	2	0	0	2	3	.167
Mantle	OF	3	10	1	2	0	0	1	1	.200
Byrne	P	3	6	0	1	0	0	0	2	.167
Ford	P	2	6	1	0	0	0	0	0	.000
E. Robinson	1B	4	3	0	2	0	0	0	1	.667
Carey	PH	2	2	0	1	0	1	0	1	.500
J. Coleman	SS	3	3	0	0	0	0	0	0	.000
Grim	P	3	2	0	0	0	0	0	0	.000
Turley	P	3	1	0	0	0	0	0	0	.000

Larsen P 0-2, Morgan P 0-0, Kucks P 0-0, Sturdivant P 0-0, R. Coleman P 0-0, Carroll PR 0-0

COMPOSITE PITCHING

NAME	G	IP	H	BB	SO	W	L	SV	ERA
Brooklyn (NL)									
Totals	7	60	55	22	39	4	3	1	3.75
Podres	2	**18**	**15**	4	**10**	**2**	0	0	**1.00**
Labine	**4**	9.1	6	2	2	1	0	1	2.89
Craig	1	6	4	5	4	1	0	0	3.00
Meyer	1	5.2	4	2	4	0	0	0	0.00
Newcombe	1	5.2	8	2	4	0	1	0	9.53
Loes	1	3.2	7	1	5	0	1	0	9.82
Bessent	3	3.1	3	1	1	0	0	0	0.00
Spooner	2	3.1	4	3	6	0	1	0	13.50
Erskine	1	3	3	2	3	0	0	0	9.00
Roebuck	1	2	1	0	0	0	0	0	0.00
New York (AL)									
Totals	7	60	58	33	38	3	4	1	4.20
Ford	2	17	13	**8**	**10**	**2**	0	0	2.12
Byrne	2	14.1	8	**8**	8	1	1	0	1.88
Grim	3	8.2	8	5	8	0	1	1	4.15
Turley	3	5.1	7	4	7	0	1	0	8.44
Larsen	1	4	5	2	2	0	1	0	11.25
Morgan	2	3.2	3	3	1	0	0	0	4.91
Kucks	2	3	4	1	1	0	0	0	6.00
Sturdivant	2	3	5	2	0	0	0	0	6.00
R. Coleman	1	1	5	0	1	0	0	0	9.00

1956 October's Revenge

Casey Stengel was not a man to hold a grudge. But as the season started, his Yankees were only the second best in the world to the Brooklyn Dodgers. Stengel had spent too many years getting used to being first, and began the season with that goal in mind. The Yankees roared to seven victories in their first eight matches, hovering near the top until permanently staking their claim to the lead on May 16, and waltzing home to their seventh pennant in the Old Professor's eight year reign.

A successor to Ruth, Gehrig, and DiMaggio finally came to fruition in the person of Mickey Mantle. The 24-year-old Oklahoman hit 52 home runs en route to his Triple Crown and was voted the MVP. While Mantle provided the heavy artillery, Stengel had other key performers at his beck and call. Yogi Berra hit .298 with 30 homers and 105 RBI's, Hank Bauer belted 26 homers, and both Bill Skowron and Gil McDougald were .300 batters. The pitching did not come as easy, causing Stengel to again provide some magic. He patched up his pitching by coming up with two trump cards in the form of Tom Sturdivant and Johnny Kucks. With Don Larsen, Bob Turley, Tommy Byrne, and Bob Grim all disappointing, Sturdivant, a 26-year-old ex-minor league infielder, and Kucks, a 22-year-old-baby-faced sophomore, both came out of the bullpen to win 16 and 18 games respectively in the starting rotation. Whitey Ford provided continuity to the staff by winning 19 games, missing the 20th only by losing on the final day of the season. Runner-up Cleveland boasted superior pitching by flashing three 20-game winners in Bob Lemon, Early Wynn, and strikeout phenom Herb Score, but could not keep pace with New York's offense.

In the National League, the Dodgers almost failed to accommodate Stengel for another showdown, winning the pennant only on the final day of the season by one game over the Milwaukee Braves and two over the Cincinnati Reds. All three teams battled for the top spot all season—Brooklyn's aging championship squad, Milwaukee's maturing young team, and Cincinnati's surprising Reds, who made a strong run on overwhelming home run power and not much else. Don Newcombe chalked up 27 wins for Brooklyn in carrying them most of the way; his crackling fastball won him the MVP and the first Cy Young Award. Down the stretch, though, Sal Maglie booted the Dodgers home. Obtained on waivers from Cleveland in May, Sal the Barber won 13 games, threw a no-hitter against the Phils on September 25, in the peak of the flag fight, and won key games whenever they were there to win.

The Braves' attack centered around young Hank Aaron, whose .328 batting average led the league and whose 26 homers and 92 RBI's provided much firewater for the Braves' attack. Warren Spahn won 20 games for the Tribe but late season slumps by Bob Buhl, Lew Burdette, Eddie Mathews, and Joe Adcock took the edge off their fine season. The Reds' 221 homers, tying the 1947 Giants for the most ever by a team in one season, kept them in the race until the end. The final weekend of the season saw Milwaukee in front of Brooklyn by one game with three left to play. But, while the Dodgers, behind Clem Labine, Maglie, and Newcombe, were taking three straight from the Pirates, the Braves dropped two of three to St. Louis.

Finally, Stengel had his chance. But after the second World Series game was over, Stengel found himself on the bottom of a 13-8 score and a two game deficit. As the experts pondered whether the Yankees would suddenly start chanting Brooklyn's cry of "wait till next year", Whitey Ford returned with the help of a three-run homer from Enos Slaughter to give the Yankees a 5-3 win. The muscle of Mantle and Bauer combined with Sturdivant's pitching to give the Yankees a 6-2 Series. Game No. 5 made history. Don Larsen made his second Series start after being shelled in the second inning of the second game and threw an unprecedented perfect game. Although Labine restored Brooklyn's hopes in the sixth game with a brilliant 1-0 pitching triumph in ten innings over Bob Turley, who was the victim of a misjudged fly ball by Slaughter, the final game proved anticlimatic. Newcombe made his second start and again failed to go beyond the third inning. as the Yankees won in a 9-0 rout; which, of many things, gave proof through the night that Stengel and the Yankees were again supreme.

1956 AMERICAN LEAGUE

NEW YORK 1st 97-57 .630 — CASEY STENGEL

NAME	G by POS	B	AGE	G	AB	R	H	2B	3B	HR	RBI	BB	SO	SB	BA	SA
TOTALS			28	154	5312	857	1433	193	55	190	788	615	755	51	.270	.434
Bill Skowron	1B120, 3B2	R	25	134	464	78	143	21	6	23	90	50	60	4	.308	.528
Billy Martin	2B105, 3B16	R	28	121	458	76	121	24	5	9	49	30	56	7	.264	.397
Gil McDougald	SS92, 2B31, 3B5	R	28	120	438	79	136	13	3	13	56	68	59	3	.311	.443
Andy Carey	3B131	R	24	132	422	54	100	18	2	7	50	45	53	9	.237	.339
Hank Bauer	OF146	R	33	147	539	96	130	18	7	26	84	59	72	4	.241	.445
Mickey Mantle	OF144	B	24	150	533	132	188	22	5	52	130	112	99	10	.353	.705
Elston Howard	OF65, C26	R	27	98	290	35	76	8	3	5	34	21	30	0	.262	.362
Yogi Berra	C135, OF1	L	31	140	521	93	155	29	2	30	105	65	29	3	.298	.534
Joe Collins	OF51, 1B43	L	33	100	262	38	59	5	3	7	43	34	33	3	.225	.347
Jerry Coleman	2B41, SS24, 3B18	R	31	80	183	15	47	5	1	0	18	12	33	1	.257	.295
Norm Siebern (KJ)	OF51	L	22	54	162	27	33	1	4	4	21	19	38	1	.204	.333
Bob Cerv (JJ)	OF44	R	30	54	115	16	35	5	6	3	25	18	13	0	.304	.530
Mickey McDermott	P23	L	27	46	52	4	11	0	0	1	4	8	13	0	.212	.269
Billy Hunter (NJ)	SS32, 3B4	R	28	39	75	8	21	3	4	0	11	2	4	0	.280	.427
Tommy Carroll	3B11, SS1	R	19	36	17	11	6	0	0	0	0	1	3	1	.353	.353
Tom Sturdivant	P32	L	26	32	64	5	20	1	1	0	5	0	7	0	.313	.359
Phil Rizzuto	SS30	R	38	31	52	6	12	0	0	0	6	6	6	3	.231	.231
Irv Noren (KJ)	OF10, 1B1	L	31	29	37	4	8	1	0	0	6	12	7	0	.216	.243
1 Eddie Robinson	1B14	L	35	26	54	7	12	1	0	5	11	5	3	0	.222	.519
2 Enos Slaughter	OF20	L	40	24	83	15	24	4	2	0	4	5	6	1	.289	.386

Jerry Lumpe 23 L 16-62, 2 George Wilson 30 L 2-12, Charlie Silvera 31 R 2-9, 1 Lou Skizas 24 R 1-6, Bobby Richardson 20 R 1-7

NAME	T	AGE	W	L	PCT	SV	G	GS	CG	IP	H	BB	SO	ShO	ERA
		27	97	57	.630	35	154	154	50	1382	1285	652	732	10	3.63
Whitey Ford	L	27	19	6	.760	1	31	30	18	226	187	84	141	2	2.47
Johnny Kucks	R	22	18	9	.667	0	34	31	12	224	223	72	67	3	3.86
Tom Sturdivant	R	26	16	8	.667	5	32	17	6	158	134	52	110	2	3.30
Don Larsen	R	26	11	5	.688	1	38	20	6	180	133	96	107	1	3.25
Bob Turley	R	25	8	4	.667	1	27	21	5	132	138	103	91	1	5.05
Tommy Byrne	L	36	7	3	.700	6	37	8	1	110	108	72	52	0	3.35
Bob Grim	R	26	6	1	.857	5	26	6	1	75	64	31	48	0	2.76
Tom Morgan	R	26	6	7	.462	11	41	0	0	71	74	27	20	0	4.18
Rip Coleman	L	24	3	5	.375	2	29	9	0	88	97	42	42	0	3.68
Mickey McDermott	L	27	2	6	.250	0	23	9	1	87	85	47	38	0	4.24
Ralph Terry	R	20	1	2	.333	0	3	3	0	13	17	11	8	0	9.69
Sonny Dixon	R	31	0	1	.000	1	3	0	0	4	5	5	1	0	2.08
1 Jim Konstanty	R	39	0	0	.000	2	8	0	0	11	15	6	6	0	4.91
1 Gerry Staley	R	35	0	0	.000	0	.1	0	0	.1	4	0	1	0	108.00
Jim Coates	R	23	0	0	.000	0	2	0	0	2	1	4	0	0	13.50

CLEVELAND 2nd 88-66 .571 9 — AL LOPEZ

NAME	G by POS	B	AGE	G	AB	R	H	2B	3B	HR	RBI	BB	SO	SB	BA	SA
TOTALS			30	155	5148	712	1256	199	23	153	675	681	764	40	.244	.381
Vic Wertz	1B133	L	31	136	481	65	127	22	0	32	106	75	87	0	.264	.509
Bobby Avila	2B135	R	32	138	513	74	115	14	2	10	54	70	68	17	.224	.318
Chico Carrasquel	SS141, 3B1	R	28	141	474	60	115	15	1	7	48	52	61	0	.243	.323
Al Rosen	3B116	R	32	121	416	64	111	18	2	15	61	58	44	1	.267	.428
Rocky Colavito	OF98	R	22	101	322	55	89	11	4	21	65	49	46	0	.276	.531
Jim Busby	OF133	R	29	135	494	72	116	17	3	12	50	43	47	8	.235	.354
Al Smith	OF122, 3B28, 2B1	R	28	141	526	87	144	26	5	16	71	84	72	6	.274	.433
Jim Hegan	C118	R	35	122	315	42	70	15	2	6	34	49	54	1	.222	.340
Gene Woodling (IL)	OF85	L	33	100	317	56	83	17	0	8	38	69	29	2	.262	.391
2 Preston Ward	1B60, OF17	L	28	87	150	18	38	10	0	6	21	16	20	0	.253	.440
George Strickland	SS28, 2B28, 3B26	R	30	85	171	22	36	1	2	3	17	22	27	0	.211	.292
Sam Mele	OF20, 1B8	R	33	57	114	17	29	7	0	4	20	12	20	0	.254	.421
Hal Naragon	C48	L	27	53	122	11	35	3	1	3	18	13	9	0	.287	.402
Bob Lemon	P39	L	35	43	93	8	18	0	0	5	12	9	21	0	.194	.355
Earl Averill	C34	R	24	42	93	12	22	6	0	3	14	14	25	0	.237	.398
1 Dale Mitchell	OF1	L	34	38	30	2	4	0	0	0	6	7	2	0	.133	.133
2 Dave Pope	OF18	L	31	25	70	6	17	3	1	0	3	1	12	0	.243	.314

Kenny Kuhn 19 L 6-22, Rudy Regalado 26 R 11-47, Joe Caffie 25 L 13-38, Stu Locklin 27 L 1-6, 1 Hoot Evers 35 R 0-0, 1 Hank Foiles 27 R 0-0, Bobby Young 31 L 0-0

NAME	T	AGE	W	L	PCT	SV	G	GS	CG	IP	H	BB	SO	ShO	ERA
		30	88	66	.571	24	155	155	67	1384	1233	564	845	17	3.32
Early Wynn	R	36	20	9	.690	2	38	35	18	278	233	91	158	4	2.72
Herb Score	L	23	20	9	.690	0	35	33	16	249	162	129	263	5	2.53
Bob Lemon	R	35	20	14	.588	3	39	35	21	255	230	89	94	2	3.04
Mike Garcia	R	32	11	12	.478	0	35	30	8	198	213	74	119	4	3.77
Don Mossi	L	27	6	5	.545	11	48	3	0	88	79	33	59	0	3.58
Ray Narleski (EJ)	R	27	3	2	.600	4	32	0	0	59	36	19	42	0	1.53
Hank Aguirre	L	24	3	5	.375	1	16	9	2	65	63	27	31	1	3.74
Art Houtteman	R	28	2	2	.500	1	22	4	0	47	60	31	19	0	6.51
Cal McLish	R	30	2	4	.333	1	37	2	0	62	67	32	27	0	4.94
Bud Daley	L	23	1	0	1.000	0	14	0	0	20	21	14	13	0	6.30
Bob Feller	R	37	0	4	.000	1	19	4	2	58	63	23	18	0	4.97
1 Sal Maglie	R	39	0	0	.000	0	2	0	0	5	6	2	2	0	3.60

CHICAGO 3rd 85-69 .552 12 — MARTY MARION

NAME	G by POS	B	AGE	G	AB	R	H	2B	3B	HR	RBI	BB	SO	SB	BA	SA
TOTALS		·	30	154	5286	776	1412	218	43	128	729	619	660	70	.267	.397
Walt Dropo	1B117	R	33	125	361	42	96	13	1	8	52	37	51	1	.266	.374
Nellie Fox	2B154	L	28	154	649	109	192	20	10	4	52	44	14	8	.296	.376
Luis Aparicio	SS152	R	22	152	533	69	142	19	6	3	56	34	63	21	.266	.341
2 Fred Hatfield	3B100, SS3	L	31	106	321	46	84	9	1	7	33	37	36	1	.262	.361
Jim Rivera	OF134	L	33	139	491	76	125	23	5	12	66	49	75	20	.255	.395
Larry Doby	OF137	L	32	140	504	89	135	22	3	24	102	102	105	0	.268	.466
Minnie Minoso	OF148, 3B8, 1B1	R	33	151	545	106	172	29	11	21	88	86	40	12	.316	.525
Sherm Lollar	C132	R	31	136	450	55	132	28	2	11	75	53	34	2	.293	.438
2 Dave Philley	1B51, OF30	B	36	86	279	44	74	14	2	4	47	28	27	1	.265	.373
Sammy Esposito	3B61, SS19, 2B3	R	24	81	184	30	42	8	2	3	25	41	19	1	.228	.342
Bubba Phillips	OF35, 3B2	R	26	67	99	16	27	6	0	2	11	6	12	1	.273	.394
Les Moss	C49	R	31	56	127	20	31	4	0	10	22	18	15	0	.244	.512
2 Jim Delsing	OF29	L	30	55	41	11	5	3	0	0	2	10	13	1	.122	.195
Ron Northey	OF4	L	36	53	48	4	17	2	0	3	23	8	1	0	.354	.583
Jack Harshman	P34	L	28	36	71	8	12	1	0	6	19	11	21	0	.169	.437
Ron Jackson	1B19	R	22	22	56	7	12	3	0	1	4	10	13	1	.214	.321
1 George Kell	3B18, 1B4	R	33	21	80	7	25	5	0	1	11	8	6	0	.313	.413

1 Bob Nieman 29 R 12-40, 1 Jim Brideweser 29 R 2-11, 1 Bob Kennedy 35 R 1-13, Earl Battey 21 R 1-4, Cal Abrams 32 L 1-3, Bob Powell (MS) 22

NAME	T	AGE	W	L	PCT	SV	G	GS	CG	IP	H	BB	SO	ShO	ERA
		33	85	69	.552	13	154	154	65	1389	1351	524	722	11	3.73
Billy Pierce	L	29	20	9	.690	1	35	33	21	276	261	100	192	1	3.33
Jack Harshman	L	28	15	11	.577	0	34	30	15	227	183	102	143	4	3.09
Dick Donovan	R	28	12	10	.545	0	34	31	14	235	212	59	120	3	3.64
2 Jim Wilson	R	35	9	12	.429	0	28	21	6	160	149	70	82	3	4.05
2 Gerry Staley	R	35	8	3	.727	0	26	10	5	102	98	20	25	0	2.91
Dixie Howell	R	36	5	6	.455	4	34	1	0	64	79	36	28	0	4.64
Bob Keegan	R	35	5	7	.417	0	20	16	4	105	119	35	32	0	3.94
2 Ellis Kinder	R	41	3	1	.750	3	29	0	0	30	33	8	19	0	2.70
3 Paul LaPalme	L	32	3	1	.750	2	29	0	0	46	31	27	23	0	2.35
1 Howie Pollet	L	35	3	1	.750	0	11	4	0	26	27	11	14	0	4.15
1 Morrie Martin	L	33	1	0	1.000	0	10	0	0	18	21	7	9	0	5.00
1 Sandy Consuegra	R	35	1	2	.333	3	28	1	0	38	45	11	7	0	5.21
1 Mike Fornieles	R	24	0	1	.000	0	6	0	0	16	22	6	6	0	4.50
1 Connie Johnson	R	33	0	1	.000	0	5	2	0	12	11	7	6	0	3.75
Harry Byrd	R	31	0	1	.000	0	3	1	0	4	9	4	0	0	11.25
Jim McDonald	R	29	0	2	.000	0	8	3	0	19	29	7	10	0	8.53
Jim Derrington	L	16	0	1	.000	0	1	1	0	6	9	6	3	0	7.50

Jerry Dahlke 26 R 0-0, Bill Fischer 25 R 0-0, 2 Dick Marlowe 27 R 0-0

BOSTON 4th 84-70 .545 13 — **PINKY HIGGINS**

NAME	G by POS	B	AGE	G	AB	R	H	2B	3B	HR	RBI	BB	SO	SB	BA	SA
TOTALS			29	155	5349	780	1473	**261**	45	139	752	**727**	687	28	.275	.419
Mickey Vernon	1B108	L	38	119	403	67	125	28	4	15	84	57	40	1	.310	.511
Billy Goodman	2B95	L	30	105	399	61	117	22	8	2	38	40	22	0	.293	.404
Don Buddin	SS113	R	22	114	377	49	90	24	0	5	37	65	62	2	.239	.342
Billy Klaus	3B106, SS26	L	27	135	520	91	141	29	5	7	59	90	43	1	.271	.387
Jackie Jensen	OF151	R	29	151	578	80	182	23	**11**	20	97	89	43	11	.315	.497
Jimmy Piersall	OF155	R	26	155	601	91	176	**40**	6	14	87	58	48	7	.293	.449
Ted Williams	OF110	L	37	136	400	71	138	28	2	24	82	102	39	0	.345	.605
Sammy White	C114	R	27	114	392	28	96	15	2	5	44	35	40	2	.245	.332
Dick Gernert	OF50, 1B37	R	27	106	306	53	89	11	0	16	68	56	57	1	.291	.484
Gene Stephens	OF71	L	23	104	63	22	17	2	0	1	7	12	12	0	.270	.349
Ted Lepcio	2B57, 3B22	R	25	83	284	34	74	10	0	15	51	30	77	1	.261	.454
Pete Daley	C57	R	26	59	187	22	50	11	3	5	29	18	30	1	.267	.439
Billy Consolo	2B25	R	21	48	11	13	2	0	0	0	1	3	5	0	.182	.182
Milt Bolling	SS26, 3B11, 2B1	R	25	45	118	19	25	3	2	3	8	18	20	0	.212	.347
Norm Zauchin	1B31	R	26	44	84	12	18	2	0	2	11	14	22	0	.214	.310
Tom Brewer	P32	R	24	38	94	14	28	0	1	1	13	5	19	0	.298	.351
Frank Malzone	3B26	R	26	27	103	15	17	3	1	2	11	9	8	1	.165	.272
Faye Throneberry (IL)	OF13	L	25	24	50	6	11	2	0	1	3	3	16	0	.220	.320

Gene Mauch 30 R 8-25, 1 Grady Hatton 33 L 2-5, Marty Keough 21 L 0-2, Jim Pagliaroni (MS) 18

NAME	T	AGE	W	L	PCT	SV	G	GS	CG	IP	H	BB	SO	ShO	ERA
		28	84	70	.545	20	155	155	50	**1398**	1354	668	712	8	4.17
Tom Brewer	R	24	19	9	.679	0	32	32	15	244	200	112	127	4	3.50
Frank Sullivan	R	26	14	7	.667	0	34	33	12	242	253	82	116	1	3.42
Ike Delock	R	26	13	7	.650	9	48	8	1	128	122	80	105	0	4.22
Dave Sisler	R	24	9	8	.529	3	39	14	3	142	120	72	93	0	4.63
Willard Nixon	R	28	9	8	.529	0	23	22	9	145	142	57	74	1	4.22
Mel Parnell (NJ)	L	34	7	6	.538	0	21	20	6	131	129	59	41	1	3.78
Tom Hurd	R	32	3	4	.429	5	40	0	0	76	84	47	34	0	5.33
Bob Porterfield	R	32	3	12	.200	0	25	18	4	126	127	64	53	1	5.14
Frank Baumann	L	23	2	1	.667	0	7	1	0	25	22	14	18	0	3.24
Leo Kiely	L	26	2	2	.500	3	23	0	0	31	47	14	9	0	5.23
George Susce (IL)	R	24	2	4	.333	0	21	6	0	70	71	44	26	0	6.17
Rudy Minarcin	R	26	1	0	1.000	0	3	1	0	10	9	8	5	0	2.70
2 Harry Dorish	R	34	0	2	.000	0	15	0	0	23	23	10	11	0	3.52
1 Johnny Schmitz	L	35	0	0	.000	0	2	0	0	4	5	4	0	0	0.00

DETROIT 5th 82-72 .532 15 — **BUCKY HARRIS**

NAME	G by POS	B	AGE	G	AB	R	H	2B	3B	HR	RBI	BB	SO	SB	BA	SA
TOTALS			28	155	**5364**	789	**1494**	209	50	150	745	644	618	43	**.279**	.420
Earl Torgeson	1B83	L	32	117	318	61	84	9	3	12	42	78	47	6	.264	.425
Frank Bolling	2B102	R	24	102	366	53	103	21	7	7	45	42	51	6	.281	.434
Harvey Kuenn	SS141, OF1	R	25	146	591	96	**196**	32	7	12	88	55	34	9	.332	.470
Ray Boone	3B130	R	32	131	481	77	148	14	6	25	81	77	46	0	.308	.518
Al Kaline	OF153	R	21	153	617	96	194	32	10	27	128	70	55	7	.314	.530
Bill Tuttle	OF137	R	26	140	546	61	138	22	4	9	65	38	48	5	.253	.357
Charlie Maxwell	OF136	L	29	141	500	96	163	14	3	28	87	79	74	1	.326	.534
Frank House	C88	L	26	94	321	44	77	6	2	10	44	21	19	1	.240	.364
Wayne Belardi	1B31, OF2	L	25	79	154	24	43	3	1	6	15	15	13	0	.279	.429
Red Wilson	C78	R	27	78	228	32	66	12	2	7	38	42	18	2	.289	.452
2 Jim Brideweser	SS32, 2B31, 3B4	R	29	70	156	23	34	4	0	0	10	20	19	3	.218	.244
2 Bob Kennedy	OF29, 3B27	R	35	69	177	17	41	5	0	4	22	24	19	2	.232	.328
Jack Phillips	1B56, OF1, 2B1	R	34	67	224	31	66	13	2	1	20	21	19	1	.295	.384
Jim Small	OF26	L	19	58	91	13	29	4	2	0	10	6	10	0	.319	.407
Buddy Hicks	SS16, 2B6, 3B1	B	29	26	47	5	10	2	0	0	5	3	2	0	.213	.255
Reno Bertoia	2B18, 3B2	R	21	22	66	7	12	2	0	1	5	6	12	0	.182	.258
Jay Porter	C2, OF2	R	23	14	21	0	2	0	0	0	3	0	8	0	.095	.095
1 Jim Delsing	OF3	L	30	10	12	0	0	0	0	0	0	3	3	0	.000	.000

1 Fred Hatfield 31 L 3-12, Charlie King 25 R 2-9, Charlie Lau 23 L 2-9, Walt Strevli 20 R 2-8

NAME	T	AGE	W	L	PCT	SV	G	GS	CG	IP	H	BB	SO	ShO	ERA
		29	82	72	.532	15	155	155	62	1379	1389	655	788	10	4.06
Frank Lary	R	26	**21**	13	.618	1	41	**38**	20	**294**	**289**	116	165	3	3.15
Billy Hoeft	L	24	20	14	.588	0	38	34	18	248	276	104	172	4	4.06
Paul Foytack	R	25	15	13	.536	1	43	33	16	256	211	**142**	184	1	3.59
Steve Gromek	R	36	8	6	.571	4	40	13	4	141	142	47	64	0	4.28
Virgil Trucks	R	37	6	5	.545	1	22	16	3	120	104	63	43	1	3.83
Jim Dunning	R	24	5	1	.833	1	15	3	0	53	55	28	34	0	3.74
Al Aber	L	28	4	4	.500	7	42	0	0	63	65	25	21	0	3.43
Walt Masterson	R	36	1	1	.500	0	35	0	0	50	54	32	28	0	4.14
1 Dick Marlowe	R	27	1	1	.500	0	7	1	0	11	12	9	4	0	5.73
Bill Black	R	23	1	1	.500	0	5	1	0	10	10	5	7	0	3.60
Bob Miller	L	20	0	2	.000	0	11	3	0	32	37	22	16	0	5.63
Ned Garver (SA)	R	30	0	2	.000	0	6	3	1	18	15	13	6	0	4.00
Hal Woodeshick	L	23	0	2	.000	0	2	2	0	5	12	3	1	0	14.40
Duke Maas	R	27	0	7	.000	0	26	7	0	63	81	32	34	0	6.57
Jim Brady	L	20	0	0	.000	0	6	0	0	6	15	11	3	0	30.00
Pete Wojey	R	36	0	0	.000	0	2	0	0	4	2	1	1	0	2.25
Gene Host	L	23	0	0	.000	0	1	1	0	5	9	2	5	0	7.20

BALTIMORE 6th 69-85 .448 28 — **PAUL RICHARDS**

NAME	G by POS	B	AGE	G	AB	R	H	2B	3B	HR	RBI	BB	SO	SB	BA	SA
TOTALS			27	154	5090	571	1242	198	34	91	515	563	725	39	.244	.350
Bob Boyd (BE)	1B60, OF8	L	29	70	225	28	70	8	3	2	11	30	14	0	.311	.400
Billy Gardner	2B132, SS25, 3B6	R	28	144	515	53	119	16	2	11	50	29	53	5	.231	.334
Willie Miranda	SS147	B	30	148	461	38	100	16	4	2	34	46	73	3	.217	.282
2 George Kell	3B97, 1B2, 2B1	R	33	102	345	45	90	17	2	8	37	25	31	0	.261	.391
Tito Francona	OF122, 1B21	L	22	139	445	62	115	16	4	9	57	51	60	11	.258	.373
2 Dick Williams	OF81, 1B10, 2B10, 3B4	R	27	87	353	45	101	18	4	11	37	30	40	5	.286	.453
2 Bob Nieman	OF114	R	29	114	388	60	125	20	6	12	64	86	59	1	.322	.497
Gus Triandos	C89, 1B52	R	25	131	452	47	126	18	1	21	88	48	73	0	.279	.462
Bob Hale	1B51	L	22	85	207	18	49	10	1	1	24	11	10	0	.237	.309
Jim Pyburn	OF77	R	23	84	156	23	27	3	3	2	11	17	26	4	.173	.269
1 Hal Smith	C71	R	25	78	229	16	60	14	0	3	18	17	22	1	.262	.362
Wayne Causey	3B30, 2B7	L	19	53	88	7	15	0	1	1	4	8	23	0	.170	.227
Chuck Diering	OF40, 3B2	R	33	50	97	15	18	4	0	1	4	23	19	2	.186	.258
2 Hoot Evers	OF36	R	35	48	112	20	27	3	0	1	4	24	18	1	.241	.295
3 Joe Frazier	OF19	L	33	45	74	7	19	6	0	1	12	11	6	0	.257	.378
Bobby Adams	3B24, 2B18	R	34	41	111	19	25	6	1	0	7	25	15	1	.225	.297
Bob Nelson	OF24	L	19	39	68	5	14	2	0	0	5	7	22	0	.206	.235
1 Dave Philley	OF31, 3B5	B	36	32	117	13	24	4	2	1	17	18	13	3	.205	.299
Tommy Gastall (DD)	C20	R	24	32	56	3	11	2	0	0	4	3	8	0	.196	.232
3 Grady Hatton	2B15, 3B12	L	33	27	61	4	9	1	0	1	3	13	6	0	.148	.213
Freddie Marsh	3B8, SS8, 2B5	R	32	20	24	2	3	0	0	0	0	4	3	1	.125	.125
Brooks Robinson	3B14, 2B1	R	19	15	44	5	10	4	0	1	1	1	5	0	.227	.386
2 Joe Ginsberg	C8	L	29	15	28	0	2	0	0	0	2	2	4	0	.071	.071

1 Jim Dyck 34 R 5-23, 1 Dave Pope 31 L 3-19, Joe Durham (MS) 24

NAME	T	AGE	W	L	PCT	SV	G	GS	CG	IP	H	BB	SO	ShO	ERA
		30	69	85	.448	24	154	154	38	1361	1362	547	715	10	4.20
Ray Moore	R	30	12	7	.632	0	32	27	9	185	161	99	105	1	4.18
Hal Brown	R	31	9	7	.563	2	35	14	4	152	142	37	57	1	4.03
2 Connie Johnson	R	33	9	10	.474	0	26	25	9	184	165	62	130	2	3.42
Bill Wight	L	34	9	12	.429	0	35	26	7	175	198	72	84	1	4.01
George Zuverink	R	31	7	6	.538	**16**	**62**	0	0	97	112	34	33	0	4.18
1 Jim Wilson	R	35	4	2	.667	0	7	7	1	48	49	16	31	0	5.06
2 Mike Fornieles	R	24	4	7	.364	1	30	11	1	111	109	25	53	1	3.97
Don Ferrarese	L	27	4	10	.286	2	36	14	3	102	86	64	81	1	5.03
Erv Palica	R	28	4	11	.267	0	29	14	2	116	117	50	62	0	4.50
Charlie Beamon	R	21	2	0	1.000	0	2	1	1	13	9	8	14	1	1.38
2 Billy Loes	R	26	2	7	.222	3	21	6	1	57	65	23	22	0	4.74
Fred Besana	L	25	1	0	1.000	0	7	2	0	18	22	14	7	0	5.50
2 Morrie Martin	L	33	1	1	.500	0	9	0	0	5	10	2	3	0	10.80
2 Sandy Consuegra	R	35	1	1	.500	0	4	1	0	9	10	2	1	0	4.00
Ron Moeller	L	17	0	1	.000	0	4	1	0	9	10	3	2	0	4.00
2 Johnny Schmitz	L	35	0	3	.000	0	18	3	0	38	49	14	15	0	4.03
1 Harry Dorish	R	34	0	0	.000	0	13	0	0	20	22	3	4	0	4.05
Babe Birrer	R	27	0	0	.000	0	4	0	0	5	9	1	1	0	7.20
Mel Held	R	27	0	0	.000	0	4	0	0	7	7	3	4	0	5.14
Billy O'Dell (MS)	L	23	0	0	.000	0	4	1	0	8	6	6	6	0	1.13
Bob Harrison	R	25	0	0	.000	0	1	1	0	2	3	5	0	0	13.50
Gordie Sundin	R	18	0	0	.000	0	1	0	0	0	0	2	0	0	∞
George Werley	R	17	0	0	.000	0	1	0	0	1	1	2	0	0	9.00

WASHINGTON 7th 59-95 .383 38 — **CHUCK DRESSEN**

NAME	G by POS	B	AGE	G	AB	R	H	2B	3B	HR	RBI	BB	SO	SB	BA	SA
TOTALS			27	155	5202	652	1302	198	**62**	112	613	690	**877**	37	.250	.377
Pete Runnels	1B81, 2B69, SS3	L	28	147	578	72	179	29	9	8	76	58	64	5	.310	.433
Herb Plews	2B66, SS5, 3B2	L	28	91	256	24	69	10	7	1	25	26	40	1	.270	.375
Jose Valdivielso	SS90	R	22	90	246	18	58	8	2	4	29	29	36	3	.236	.333
Eddie Yost	3B135, OF8	R	29	152	515	94	119	17	2	11	53	**151**	82	8	.231	.336
Jim Lemon	OF141	R	28	146	538	77	146	21	**11**	27	96	65	**138**	2	.271	.502
Karl Olson	OF101	R	25	106	313	34	77	10	2	4	22	28	41	1	.246	.329
Whitey Herzog	OF103, 1B5	L	24	117	421	49	103	13	7	4	35	35	74	8	.245	.337
Clint Courtney	C76	L	29	101	283	31	85	20	3	5	44	20	10	0	.300	.445
Roy Sievers	OF78, 1B76	R	29	152	550	92	139	27	2	29	95	100	88	0	.253	.467
Lou Berberet	C59	L	26	95	207	25	54	6	3	4	27	46	33	0	.261	.377
Ernie Oravetz	OF31	B	24	88	137	20	34	3	2	0	11	27	20	1	.248	.299
Ed Fitz Gerald	C50	R	32	64	148	15	45	8	0	2	12	20	16	0	.304	.399
Tony Roig	2B27, SS19	R	27	44	119	11	25	5	2	0	7	20	29	0	.210	.286
Harmon Killebrew	3B20, 2B4	R	20	44	99	10	22	2	0	5	13	10	39	0	.222	.394
Jerry Snyder (BW)	SS35, 2B7	R	26	43	148	14	40	3	1	2	14	10	9	1	.270	.345
Lyle Luttrell	SS37	R	26	38	122	17	23	5	3	2	9	8	19	5	.189	.328
Carlos Paula	OF20	R	27	33	82	8	15	2	1	3	13	8	15	0	.183	.341
Dick Tettelbach	OF18	R	27	18	64	10	10	1	2	1	9	14	15	0	.156	.281

Tom Wright 32 L 0-1, Steve Korcheck (MS) 23, Jerry Schoonmaker (MS) 22

NAME	T	AGE	W	L	PCT	SV	G	GS	CG	IP	H	BB	SO	ShO	ERA
		25	59	95	.383	18	155	155	36	1369	**1539**	**730**	663	1	5.33
Chuck Stobbs	L	26	15	15	.500	1	37	33	15	240	264	54	97	1	3.60
Pedro Ramos	R	21	12	10	.545	0	37	18	4	152	178	76	54	0	5.27
Camilo Pascual	R	22	6	18	.250	2	39	27	6	189	194	89	162	0	5.86
Dean Stone	L	25	5	7	.417	3	41	21	2	132	148	93	86	0	6.27
Bunky Stewart	L	25	5	7	.417	2	33	9	1	105	111	82	36	0	5.57
Bob Chakales	R	28	4	4	.500	4	43	1	0	96	94	57	33	0	4.03
Connie Grob	R	23	4	5	.444	1	37	1	0	79	121	26	27	0	7.86
Bob Wiesler	L	25	3	12	.200	0	37	21	3	123	141	112	49	0	6.44
Bud Byerly	R	35	2	4	.333	4	25	0	0	52	45	14	19	0	2.94
Evelio Hernandez	R	25	1	1	.500	0	4	4	1	23	24	8	9	0	4.70
Ted Abernathy (SA)	R	23	1	3	.250	0	5	4	2	30	35	10	18	0	4.20
Hal Griggs	R	27	1	6	.143	1	34	12	1	99	120	76	48	0	6.00
Dick Brodowski	R	23	0	3	.000	0	7	3	1	18	31	12	8	0	9.00
Tex Clevenger	R	23	0	0	.000	0	20	1	0	32	33	21	17	0	5.34

KANSAS CITY 8th 52-102 .338 45 — **LOU BOUDREAU**

NAME	G by POS	B	AGE	G	AB	R	H	2B	3B	HR	RBI	BB	SO	SB	BA	SA
TOTALS			29	154	5256	619	1325	204	41	112	581	480	727	40	.252	.370
Vic Power	1B76, 2B47, OF7	R	24	127	530	77	164	21	5	14	63	24	16	2	.309	.447
Jim Finigan	2B52, 3B32	R	27	91	250	29	54	7	2	2	21	30	28	3	.216	.284
Joe DeMaestri	SS132, 2B2	R	27	133	434	41	101	16	1	6	39	25	73	3	.233	.316
Hector Lopez	3B121, OF20, 2B8, SS4	R	23	151	561	91	153	27	3	18	69	63	73	4	.273	.428
Harry Simpson	OF111, 1B32	L	30	141	543	76	159	22	**11**	21	105	47	82	2	.293	.490
Johnny Groth	OF84	R	29	95	244	22	63	13	3	5	37	30	31	1	.258	.398
2 Lou Skizas	OF74	R	24	83	297	39	94	11	3	11	39	15	17	3	.316	.485
Tim Thompson	C68	L	32	92	268	21	73	13	2	1	27	17	23	2	.272	.347
Gus Zernial	OF69	R	33	109	272	36	61	12	0	16	44	33	66	2	.224	.445
1 Enos Slaughter	OF56	L	40	91	223	37	62	14	3	2	23	29	20	1	.278	.395
2 Eddie Robinson	1B47	L	35	75	172	13	34	5	1	2	12	26	20	0	.198	.273
Mike Baxes	SS62, 2B1	R	25	73	106	9	24	3	1	1	5	18	15	0	.226	.302
1 Joe Ginsberg	C57	L	29	71	195	15	48	8	1	1	12	23	17	1	.246	.313
Al Pilarcik	OF67	L	25	69	239	28	60	10	1	4	22	30	32	9	.251	.351
Clete Boyer	2B51, 3B7	R	19	67	129	15	28	3	1	1	4	11	24	1	.217	.279
Rance Pless	1B15, 3B5	R	30	48	85	4	23	3	1	0	9	10	13	0	.271	.329
2 Hal Smith	C36	R	25	36	142	15	39	9	2	2	24	3	12	1	.275	.408
Bill Renna	OF25	R	31	33	48	12	13	3	0	2	5	3	10	1	.271	.458
1 Spook Jacobs	2B31	R	30	32	97	13	21	3	0	0	5	15	5	4	.216	.247

Jim Pisoni 26 R 8-30, 1 Elmer Valo 35 L 2-9, Joe Astroth 33 R 1-13, Dave Melton 27 R 1-3

NAME	T	AGE	W	L	PCT	SV	G	GS	CG	IP	H	BB	SO	ShO	ERA
		29	52	**102**	.338	18	154	154	30	1370	1424	679	636	3	4.86
Art Ditmar	R	27	12	**22**	.353	1	44	34	14	254	254	108	126	2	4.43
Tom Gorman	R	31	9	10	.474	3	52	13	1	171	168	68	56	0	3.84
Alex Kellner	L	31	7	4	.636	0	20	17	5	92	103	33	44	0	4.30
Wally Burnette	R	27	6	8	.429	0	18	14	4	121	115	39	54	1	2.90
Jack Crimian	R	30	4	8	.333	3	54	7	0	129	129	49	59	0	5.51
Lou Kretlow	R	33	4	9	.308	0	25	20	3	119	121	74	61	0	5.29
Moe Burtschy	R	34	3	1	.750	0	21	0	0	43	41	30	18	0	3.98
Bill Harrington	R	28	2	2	.500	1	23	1	0	38	40	26	14	0	6.39
Bobby Shantz (XJ)	L	30	2	7	.222	9	45	2	1	101	95	37	67	0	4.37
Carl Duser	L	23	1	1	.500	0	2	2	0	6	14	2	5	0	9.00
Jose Santiago	R	27	1	2	.333	0	9	5	0	22	36	17	9	0	8.18
Troy Herriage	R	25	1	13	.071	0	31	16	1	103	135	64	59	0	6.64
Art Ceccarelli	L	26	0	1	.000	0	3	2	0	10	13	4	2	0	7.20
Arnie Portocarrero	R	24	0	1	.000	0	3	1	0	8	9	7	2	0	10.13
Glenn Cox	R	25	0	2	.000	0	3	3	1	23	15	22	6	0	4.30
Walt Craddock	L	24	0	2	.000	0	2	2	0	9	9	10	8	0	7.00
Tom Lasorda	L	28	0	4	.000	1	18	5	0	45	40	45	28	0	6.20
2 Jack McMahan	L	23	0	5	.000	0	23	9	0	62	69	31	13	0	4.79
George Brunet	L	21	0	0	.000	0	6	1	0	9	10	11	5	0	7.00
Bob Spicer	R	31	0	0	.000	0	2	0	0	2	6	1	0	0	22.50
Bill Bradford	R	34	0	0	.000	0	1	0	0	2	2	1	0	0	9.00

BROOKLYN 1st 93-61 .604 — **WALT ALSTON**

NAME	G by POS	B	AGE	G	AB	R	H	2B	3B	HR	RBI	BB	SO	SB	BA	SA
TOTALS			32	154	5098	720	1315	212	36	179	680	**649**	738	65	.258	.419
Gil Hodges	1B138, OF30, C1	R	32	153	550	86	146	29	4	32	87	76	91	3	.265	.507
Jim Gilliam	2B102, OF56	B	27	153	594	102	178	23	8	6	43	95	39	21	.300	.396
Pee Wee Reese	SS136, 3B12	R	37	147	572	85	147	19	2	9	46	56	69	13	.257	.344
Randy Jackson	3B80	R	30	101	307	37	84	15	7	8	53	28	38	2	.274	.446
Carl Furillo	OF146	R	34	149	523	66	151	30	0	21	83	57	41	1	.289	.467
Duke Snider	OF150	L	29	151	542	112	158	33	2	**43**	101	**99**	101	3	.292	**.598**
Sandy Amoros	OF86	L	26	114	292	53	76	11	8	16	58	59	51	3	.260	.517
Roy Campanella	C121	R	34	124	388	39	85	6	1	20	73	66	61	1	.219	.394
Jackie Robinson	3B72, 2B22, 1B9, OF2	R	37	117	357	61	98	15	2	10	43	60	32	12	.275	.412
Gino Cimoli	OF62	R	26	73	36	3	4	1	0	0	4	1	8	1	.111	.139
Charlie Neal	2B51, SS1	R	25	62	136	22	39	5	1	2	14	14	19	2	.287	.382
Rube Walker	C43	L	30	54	146	5	31	6	1	3	20	7	18	0	.212	.329
Chico Fernandez	SS25	R	24	34	66	11	15	2	0	1	9	3	10	2	.227	.303
1 Rocky Nelson	1B25	L	31	31	96	7	20	2	0	4	15	4	10	0	.208	.354
2 Dale Mitchell	OF2	L	34	19	24	3	7	1	0	0	1	0	3	0	.292	.333
Don Zimmer (BY)	SS8, 3B3, 2B1	R	25	17	20	4	6	1	0	0	2	0	7	0	.300	.350
Dixie Howell	C6	R	37	7	13	0	3	2	0	0	1	1	3	0	.231	.385

1 Dick Williams 27 R 2-7, Don Demeter 21 R 1-3, Bob Aspromonte 18 R 0-1

NAME	T	AGE	W	L	PCT	SV	G	GS	CG	IP	H	BB	SO	ShO	ERA
		27	**93**	61	**.604**	**30**	154	154	46	1369	1251	441	**772**	**12**	3.57
Don Newcombe	R	30	**27**	7	**.794**	0	38	36	18	268	219	46	139	5	3.06
2 Sal Maglie	R	39	13	5	.722	0	28	26	9	191	154	52	108	3	2.87
Carl Erskine	R	29	13	11	.542	0	31	28	8	186	189	57	95	1	4.26
Roger Craig	R	25	12	11	.522	1	35	32	8	199	169	87	109	2	3.71
Clem Labine	R	29	10	6	.625	**19**	62	3	1	116	111	39	75	0	3.34
Ed Roebuck	R	24	5	4	.556	1	43	0	0	89	83	29	60	0	3.94
Don Drysdale	R	19	5	5	.500	0	25	12	2	99	95	31	55	0	2.64
Don Bessent	R	25	4	3	.571	9	38	0	0	79	63	31	52	0	2.51
Ken Lehman	L	28	2	3	.400	0	25	4	0	49	65	23	29	0	5.69
Sandy Koufax	L	20	2	4	.333	0	16	10	0	59	66	29	30	0	4.88
Chuck Templeton	L	24	0	1	.000	0	6	2	0	16	20	10	8	0	6.75
1 Billy Loes	R	26	0	1	.000	0	1	1	0	1	5	1	2	0	54.00
1 Jim Hughes	R	33	0	0	.000	0	5	0	0	12	10	4	8	0	5.25
Ralph Branca	R	30	0	0	.000	0	1	0	0	2	1	2	2	0	0.00
Bob Darnell	R	25	0	0	.000	0	1	0	0	1	1	0	0	0	0.00

Johnny Podres (MS) 23

MILWAUKEE 2nd 92-62 .597 1 — **CHARLIE GRIMM 24-22 .522** — **FRED HANEY 68-40 .630**

NAME	G by POS	B	AGE	G	AB	R	H	2B	3B	HR	RBI	BB	SO	SB	BA	SA
TOTALS			28	155	5207	709	1350	212	54	177	667	486	714	29	.259	.423
Joe Adcock	1B129	R	28	137	454	76	132	23	1	38	103	32	86	1	.291	.597
Danny O'Connell	2B138, 3B4, SS1	R	29	139	498	71	119	17	9	2	42	76	42	3	.239	.321
Johnny Logan	SS148	R	29	148	545	69	153	27	5	15	46	46	49	3	.281	.431
Eddie Mathews	3B150	L	24	151	552	103	150	21	2	37	95	91	86	6	.272	.518
Hank Aaron	OF152	R	22	153	609	106	**200**	**34**	14	26	92	37	54	2	**.328**	.558
Bill Bruton	OF145	L	30	147	525	73	143	23	**15**	8	56	26	63	8	.272	.419
Bobby Thomson	OF136, 3B3	R	32	142	451	59	106	10	4	20	74	43	75	2	.235	.408
Del Crandall	C109	R	26	112	311	37	74	14	2	16	48	35	30	1	.238	.450
Frank Torre	1B89	L	24	111	159	17	41	6	0	0	16	11	4	1	.258	.296
Wes Covington	OF35	L	24	75	138	17	39	4	0	2	16	16	20	1	.283	.355
Del Rice	C65	R	33	71	188	15	40	9	1	3	17	18	34	0	.213	.319
Chuck Tanner	OF8	L	26	60	63	6	15	2	0	1	4	10	10	0	.238	.317
Andy Pafko	OF37	R	35	45	93	15	24	5	0	2	9	10	13	0	.258	.376
Jack Dittmer	2B42	L	28	44	102	8	25	4	0	1	6	8	8	0	.245	.314
Felix Mantilla	SS15, 3B3	R	21	35	53	9	15	1	1	0	3	1	8	0	.283	.340
2 Toby Atwell	C10	L	32	15	30	2	5	1	0	2	7	4	1	0	.167	.400
Jim Pendleton	SS3, 3B2, 2B1, 1B1	R	32	14	11	0	0	0	0	0	0	1	3	0	.000	.000

Earl Hersh 24 L 3-13, Bob Roselli 24 R 1-2, Mel Roach (MS) 23

NAME	T	AGE	W	L	PCT	SV	G	GS	CG	IP	H	BB	SO	ShO	ERA
		28	92	62	.597	27	155	155	**64**	**1393**	1295	467	639	**12**	**3.11**
Warren Spahn	L	35	20	11	.645	3	39	35	20	281	249	52	128	3	2.79
Lew Burdette	R	29	19	10	.655	1	39	35	16	256	234	52	110	**6**	**2.71**
Bob Buhl	R	27	18	8	.692	0	38	33	13	217	190	105	86	2	3.32
Ray Crone	R	24	11	10	.524	2	35	21	6	170	173	44	73	0	3.86
Gene Conley	R	25	8	9	.471	3	31	19	5	158	169	52	68	1	3.13
Taylor Phillips	L	23	5	3	.625	2	23	6	3	88	69	33	36	0	2.25
Ernie Johnson	R	32	4	3	.571	6	36	0	0	51	54	21	26	0	3.71
Bob Trowbridge	R	26	3	2	.600	0	19	4	1	51	38	34	40	0	2.65
Lou Sleater	L	29	2	2	.500	2	25	1	0	46	42	27	32	0	3.13
Dave Jolly	R	31	2	3	.400	7	29	0	0	46	39	35	20	0	3.72
Chet Nichols	L	25	0	1	.000	0	2	0	0	4	9	3	2	0	6.75
Red Murff (XJ)	R	35	0	0	.000	1	14	1	0	24	25	7	18	0	4.50
Phil Paine	R	26	0	0	.000	0	1	0	0	0	3	0	0	0	∞
Humberto Robinson	R	26	0	0	.000	0	1	0	0	2	1	2	0	0	0.00

CINCINNATI 3rd 91-63 .591 2 — **BIRDIE TEBBETTS**

NAME	G by POS	B	AGE	G	AB	R	H	2B	3B	HR	RBI	BB	SO	SB	BA	SA
TOTALS			27	155	5291	**775**	1406	201	32	**221**	**734**	528	760	45	.266	**.441**
Ted Kluszewski	1B131	L	31	138	517	91	156	14	1	35	102	49	31	1	.302	.536
Johnny Temple	2B154, OF1	R	27	154	**632**	88	180	18	3	2	41	58	40	14	.285	.332
Roy McMillan	SS150	R	25	150	479	51	126	16	7	3	62	76	54	4	.263	.344
Ray Jablonski	3B127, 2B1	R	29	130	407	42	104	25	1	15	66	37	57	2	.256	.432
Wally Post	OF136	R	26	143	539	94	134	25	3	36	83	37	**124**	6	.249	.506
Gus Bell	OF149	L	27	150	603	82	176	31	4	29	84	50	66	6	.292	.501
Frank Robinson	OF152	R	20	152	572	**122**	166	27	6	38	83	64	95	8	.290	.558
Ed Bailey	C106	L	25	118	383	59	115	8	2	28	75	52	50	2	.300	.551
Smoky Burgess	C55	L	29	90	229	28	63	10	0	12	39	26	18	0	.275	.476
Bob Thurman	OF29	L	35	80	139	25	41	5	2	8	22	10	14	0	.295	.532
2 Alex Grammas	3B58, SS12, 2B5	R	29	77	140	17	34	11	0	0	16	16	18	0	.243	.321
George Crowe	1B32	L	33	77	144	22	36	2	1	10	23	11	28	0	.250	.486
Rocky Bridges	3B51, 2B8, SS7, OF1	R	28	71	19	9	4	0	0	0	1	4	3	1	.211	.211
Stan Palys	OF10	R	26	40	53	5	12	0	0	2	5	6	13	0	.226	.340
2 Jim Dyck	3B1, 1B1	R	34	18	11	5	1	0	0	0	0	3	5	0	.091	.091
1 Chuck Harmon	OF6, 1B2	R	30	13	4	2	0	0	0	0	0	0	0	1	.000	.000
2 Joe Frazier	OF4	L	33	10	17	2	4	0	0	1	2	1	7	0	.235	.412
Bruce Edwards	C2, 3B1, 2B1	R	32	7	5	0	1	0	0	0	0	0	2	0	.200	.200
Bobby Balcena	OF2	R	27	7	2	2	0	0	0	0	0	0	1	0	.000	.000

Art Schult 28 R 3-7, Curt Flood 18 R 0-1, Matt Batts 34 R 0-2, John Oldham 23 R 0-0, Al Silvera 20 R 0-0, Dick Murphy (MS) 24

NAME	T	AGE	W	L	PCT	SV	G	GS	CG	IP	H	BB	SO	ShO	ERA
		29	91	63	.591	29	155	155	47	1389	1406	458	653	4	3.85
Brooks Lawrence	R	31	19	10	.655	0	49	30	11	219	210	71	96	1	3.99
Hersh Freeman	R	28	14	5	.737	18	64	0	0	109	112	34	50	0	3.39
Joe Nuxhall	L	27	13	11	.542	3	44	32	10	201	196	87	120	2	3.72
Johnny Klippstein	R	28	12	11	.522	1	37	29	11	211	219	82	86	0	4.09
Art Fowler	R	33	11	11	.500	1	45	23	8	178	191	35	86	0	4.04
Hal Jeffcoat	R	31	8	2	.800	2	38	16	2	171	189	55	55	0	3.84
Tom Acker	R	26	4	3	.571	1	29	7	1	84	60	29	54	1	2.36
Don Gross	L	25	3	0	1.000	0	19	7	2	69	69	20	47	0	1.96
Joe Black	R	32	3	2	.600	2	32	0	0	62	61	25	27	0	4.50
Larry Jansen	R	35	2	3	.400	1	8	7	2	35	39	9	16	0	5.14
2 Paul LaPalme	L	32	2	4	.333	0	11	2	0	27	26	4	4	0	4.67
Pat Scantlebury	L	30	0	1	.000	0	6	2	0	19	24	5	10	0	6.63
Frank Smith	R	28	0	0	.000	0	2	0	0	3	3	2	1	0	12.00
2 Russ Meyer	R	32	0	0	.000	0	1	0	0	1	1	0	1	0	0.00
Bill Kennedy	L	35	0	0	.000	0	1	0	0	2	6	0	0	0	18.00

ST. LOUIS 4th 76-78 .494 17 — **FRED HUTCHINSON**

NAME	G by POS	B	AGE	G	AB	R	H	2B	3B	HR	RBI	BB	SO	SB	BA	SA
TOTALS			28	156	**5378**	678	**1443**	**234**	49	124	628	503	622	41	**.268**	.399
Stan Musial	1B103, OF53	L	35	156	594	87	184	33	6	27	**109**	75	39	2	.310	.522
Don Blasingame	2B98, SS49, 3B12	L	24	150	587	94	153	22	7	0	27	72	52	8	.261	.322
2 Al Dark	SS99	R	34	100	413	54	118	14	7	4	37	21	33	3	.286	.383
Ken Boyer	3B149	R	25	150	595	91	182	30	2	26	98	38	65	8	.306	.494
Wally Moon	OF97, 1B52	L	26	149	540	86	161	22	11	16	68	80	50	12	.298	.469
2 Bobby Del Greco	OF99	R	23	102	270	29	58	16	2	5	18	32	50	1	.215	.344
Rip Repulski	OF100	R	28	112	376	44	104	18	3	11	55	24	46	2	.277	.428
Hal Smith	C66	R	25	75	227	27	64	12	0	5	23	15	22	1	.282	.401
Hank Sauer	OF37	R	37	75	151	11	45	4	0	5	24	25	31	0	.298	.424
2 Whitey Lockman	OF57, 1B2	L	29	70	193	14	48	0	2	0	10	18	8	2	.249	.269
2 Bobby Morgan	2B13, 3B11, SS6	R	30	61	113	14	22	7	0	3	20	15	24	0	.195	.336
2 Ray Katt	C47	R	29	47	158	11	41	4	0	6	20	6	24	0	.259	.399
2 Grady Hatton	2B13, 3B1	L	33	44	73	10	18	1	2	0	7	13	7	1	.247	.315
1 Bill Sarni	C41	R	28	43	148	12	43	7	2	5	22	8	15	1	.291	.466
1 Red Schoendienst	2B36	B	33	40	153	22	48	9	0	0	15	13	5	0	.314	.373
Walker Cooper	C16	R	41	40	68	5	18	5	1	2	14	3	8	0	.265	.456
2 Rocky Nelson	1B14, OF8	L	31	38	56	6	13	5	0	3	8	6	6	0	.232	.482
1 Jackie Brandt	OF26	R	22	27	42	9	12	3	0	1	3	4	5	0	.286	.429
1 Bill Virdon	OF24	L	25	24	71	10	15	2	0	2	9	5	8	0	.211	.324
Charlie Peete	OF21	L	25	23	52	3	10	2	2	0	6	6	10	0	.192	.308
2 Chuck Harmon	OF11, 1B2, 3B1	R	30	20	15	2	0	0	0	0	0	2	2	0	.000	.000
Dick Schofield	SS9	B	21	16	30	3	3	2	0	0	1	0	6	0	.100	.167
1 Joe Frazier	OF3	L	33	14	19	1	4	2	0	1	4	3	3	0	.211	.474
1 Alex Grammas	SS5	R	29	6	12	1	3	0	0	0	1	1	2	0	.250	.250

1 Solly Hemus 33 L 1-5, Joe Cunningham 24 L 0-3, Tom Alston 25 L 0-2

NAME	T	AGE	W	L	PCT	SV	G	GS	CG	IP	H	BB	SO	ShO	ERA
		30	76	78	.494	**30**	156	156	41	1389	1339	546	709	**12**	3.97
Vinegar Bend Mizell	L	25	14	14	.500	0	33	33	11	209	172	92	153	3	3.62
2 Murry Dickson	R	39	13	8	.619	0	28	27	12	196	175	57	109	3	3.08
2 Herm Wehmeier	R	29	12	9	.571	1	34	19	7	171	150	71	68	2	3.68
Tom Poholsky	R	26	9	14	.391	0	33	29	7	203	210	44	95	2	3.59
Willard Schmidt	R	28	6	8	.429	1	33	21	2	148	131	78	52	0	3.83
Lindy McDaniel	R	20	7	6	.538	0	39	7	1	116	121	42	59	0	3.41
Jackie Collum	L	29	6	2	.750	7	38	1	0	60	63	27	17	0	4.20
1 Ellis Kinder	R	41	2	0	1.000	6	22	0	0	26	23	9	4	0	3.46
Larry Jackson	R	25	2	2	.500	9	51	1	0	85	75	45	50	0	4.13
1 Harvey Haddix	L	30	1	0	1.000	0	4	4	1	24	28	10	16	1	5.25
2 Jim Konstanty	R	39	1	1	.500	5	27	0	0	39	46	6	7	0	4.62
1 Ben Flowers	R	29	1	1	.500	0	3	3	0	12	15	5	5	0	6.75
2 Don Liddle	L	31	1	2	.333	0	14	2	0	25	36	18	14	0	8.28
Bob Blaylock	R	21	1	6	.143	0	14	6	0	41	45	24	39	0	6.37
1 Stu Miller	R	28	0	1	.000	1	3	0	0	7	12	5	5	0	5.14
2 Dick Littlefield	L	30	0	2	.000	0	3	2	0	10	9	4	5	0	7.20
Gordon Jones	R	26	0	2	.000	0	5	1	0	11	14	5	6	0	5.73
2 Max Surkont	R	34	0	0	.000	0	5	0	0	6	10	2	5	0	9.00
1 Paul LaPalme	L	32	0	0	.000	0	1	0	0	1	4	2	0	0	54.00

PHILADELPHIA 5th 71-83 .461 22 — **MAYO SMITH**

NAME	G by POS	B	AGE	G	AB	R	H	2B	3B	HR	RBI	BB	SO	SB	BA	SA
TOTALS			30	154	5204	668	1313	207	49	121	616	585	673	45	.252	.381
Marv Blaylock	1B124, OF1	L	26	136	460	61	117	14	8	10	50	50	86	5	.254	.385
Ted Kazanski	2B116, SS1	R	22	117	379	35	80	11	1	4	34	20	41	0	.211	.277
Granny Hamner	SS110, 2B11, P3	R	29	122	401	42	90	24	3	4	42	30	42	2	.224	.329
Willie Jones	3B149	R	30	149	520	88	144	20	4	17	78	92	49	5	.277	.429
2 Elmer Valo	OF87	L	35	98	291	40	84	13	3	5	37	48	21	7	.289	.405
Richie Ashburn	OF154	L	29	154	628	94	190	26	8	3	50	79	45	10	.303	.384
Del Ennis	OF153	R	31	153	630	80	164	23	3	26	95	33	62	7	.260	.430
Stan Lopata	C102, 1B39	R	30	146	535	96	143	33	7	32	95	75	93	5	.267	.535
Jim Greengrass	OF62	R	28	86	215	24	44	9	2	5	25	28	43	0	.205	.335
2 Solly Hemus	2B49, 3B1	L	33	78	187	24	54	10	4	5	24	28	21	1	.289	.465
Frank Baumholtz	OF15	L	37	76	100	13	27	0	0	0	9	6	6	0	.270	.270
Roy Smalley	SS60	R	30	65	168	14	38	9	3	0	16	23	29	0	.226	.315
Andy Seminick	C54	R	35	60	161	16	32	3	1	7	23	31	38	3	.199	.360
Joé Lonnett	C7	R	29	16	22	2	4	0	0	0	0	2	7	0	.182	.182
Glen Gorbous	OF8	L	25	15	33	1	6	0	0	0	1	0	1	0	.182	.182
Mack Burk	C1	R	21	15	1	3	1	0	0	0	0	0	0	0	1.000	1.000
Ed Bouchee	1B6	L	23	9	22	0	6	2	0	0	1	5	6	0	.273	.364
1 Bobby Morgan	3B5, 2B3	R	30	8	25	1	5	0	0	0	1	6	4	0	.200	.200
Bob Bowman	OF5	R	25	6	16	2	3	0	1	1	2	0	6	0	.188	.500
2 Wally Westlake		R	35	5	4	0	0	0	0	0	0	1	3	0	.000	.000

NAME	T	AGE	W	L	PCT	SV	G	GS	CG	IP	H	BB	SO	ShO	ERA
		29	71	83	.461	15	154	154	57	1377	**1407**	437	750	4	4.20
Robin Roberts	R	29	19	**18**	.514	3	43	37	**22**	297	**328**	40	157	1	4.45
Curt Simmons	L	27	15	10	.600	0	33	27	14	198	186	65	88	0	3.36
2 Harvey Haddix	L	30	12	8	.600	2	31	26	11	207	196	55	154	2	3.48
Saul Rogovin	R	33	7	6	.538	0	22	18	3	107	122	27	48	0	4.96
Jack Meyer	R	24	7	11	.389	2	41	7	2	96	86	51	66	0	4.41
2 Stu Miller	R	28	5	8	.385	0	24	15	2	107	109	51	65	0	4.46
Bob Miller	R	30	3	6	.333	5	49	6	3	122	115	34	53	1	3.25
Ron Negray	R	26	2	3	.400	3	39	4	0	67	72	24	44	0	4.16
Jack Sanford	R	27	1	0	1.000	0	3	1	0	13	7	13	6	0	1.38
Granny Hamner	R	29	0	1	.000	0	3	1	0	8	10	2	4	0	4.50
Dick Farrell	R	22	0	1	.000	0	1	1	0	4	6	3	0	0	13.50
2 Ben Flowers	R	29	0	2	.000	0	32	0	0	41	54	10	22	0	5.71
1 Herm Wehmeier	R	29	0	2	.000	0	3	3	0	20	18	11	8	0	4.05
1 Murry Dickson	R	39	0	3	.000	0	3	3	0	23	20	12	1	0	5.09
Jim Owens	R	22	0	4	.000	0	10	5	0	30	35	22	22	0	7.20
Duane Pillette	R	33	0	0	.000	0	20	0	0	23	32	12	10	0	6.65
Angelo LiPetri	R	25	0	0	.000	0	6	0	0	11	7	3	8	0	3.27
Bob Ross	L	27	0	0	.000	0	3	0	0	3	4	2	4	0	9.00

NEW YORK 6th 67-87 .435 26 — BILL RIGNEY

NAME	G by POS	B	AGE	G	AB	R	H	2B	3B	HR	RBI	BB	SO	SB	BA	SA
TOTALS			29	154	5190	540	1268	192	45	145	497	402	659	67	.244	.382
Bill White	1B138, OF2	L	22	138	508	63	130	23	7	22	59	47	72	15	.256	.459
2 Red Schoendienst	2B85	B	33	92	334	39	99	12	3	2	14	28	10	1	.296	.368
Daryl Spencer	2B70, SS66, 3B12	R	26	146	489	46	108	13	2	14	42	35	65	1	.221	.342
Foster Castleman	3B107, SS2, 2B1	R	25	124	385	33	87	16	3	14	45	15	50	2	.226	.392
Don Mueller	OF117	L	29	138	453	38	122	12	1	5	41	15	7	0	.269	.333
Willie Mays	OF152	R	25	152	578	101	171	27	8	36	84	68	65	40	.296	.557
2 Jackie Brandt	OF96	R	22	98	351	45	105	16	8	11	47	17	31	3	.299	.484
2 Bill Sarni (IL)	C75	R	28	78	238	16	55	9	3	5	23	20	31	0	.231	.357
Dusty Rhodes	OF68	L	29	111	244	20	53	10	3	8	33	30	41	0	.217	.381
Hank Thompson	3B44, OF10, SS1	L	30	83	183	24	43	9	0	8	29	31	26	2	.235	.415
Wes Westrum	C67	R	33	68	132	10	29	5	2	3	8	25	28	0	.220	.356
1 George Wilson	OF8	L	30	53	68	5	9	1	0	1	2	5	14	0	.132	.191
Ed Bressoud	SS48	R	24	49	163	15	37	4	2	0	9	12	20	1	.227	.276
1 Al Dark	SS48	R	34	48	206	19	52	12	0	2	17	8	13	0	.252	.340
1 Whitey Lockman	OF39, 1B7	L	29	48	169	13	46	7	1	1	10	16	17	0	.272	.343
Bobby Hofman	3B7, C7, 1B3, 2B2	R	30	47	56	1	10	1	0	0	2	6	8	0	.179	.196
1 Ray Katt	C37	R	29	37	101	10	23	4	0	7	14	6	16	0	.228	.475
Bob Lennon	OF21	L	27	26	55	3	10	1	0	0	1	4	17	0	.182	.200
Jim Mangan	C15	R	26	20	20	2	2	0	0	0	1	4	6	0	.100	.100
Wayne Terwilliger	2B6	R	31	14	18	0	4	1	0	0	0	0	5	0	.222	.278
Gail Harris	1B11	L	24	12	38	2	5	0	1	1	1	3	10	0	.132	.263

Gil Coan 34 L 0-1, Ozzie Virgil 23 R 5-12, Bill Taylor 26 L 1-4

NAME	T	AGE	W	L	PCT	SV	G	GS	CG	IP	H	BB	SO	ShO	ERA
		30	67	87	.435	28	154	154	31	1378	1287	551	765	9	3.78
John Antonelli	L	26	20	13	.606	1	41	36	15	258	225	75	145	5	2.86
Al Worthington (XJ)	R	27	7	14	.333	0	28	24	4	166	158	74	95	0	3.96
Ruben Gomez	R	28	7	17	.292	0	40	31	4	196	191	77	76	2	4.59
Steve Ridzik	R	27	6	2	.750	0	41	5	1	92	80	65	53	1	3.82
Joe Margoneri	L	26	6	6	.500	0	23	13	2	92	88	49	49	0	3.91
Jim Hearn	R	35	5	11	.313	1	30	19	2	129	124	44	66	0	3.98
2 Dick Littlefield	L	30	4	4	.500	2	31	7	0	97	78	39	65	0	4.08
Hoyt Wilhelm	R	32	4	9	.308	8	64	0	0	89	97	43	71	0	3.84
Windy McCall	L	30	3	4	.429	7	46	4	0	77	74	20	41	0	3.62
3 Max Surkont	R	34	2	2	.500	1	8	4	1	32	24	9	18	0	4.78
Ray Monzant	R	23	1	0	1.000	0	4	1	1	13	8	7	11	0	4.15
Marv Grissom	R	38	1	1	.500	7	43	2	0	81	71	16	49	0	1.56
1 Don Liddle	L	31	1	2	.333	1	11	5	1	41	45	14	21	0	3.95
Mike McCormick	L	17	0	1	.000	0	3	2	0	7	7	10	4	0	9.00
Roy Wright	R	22	0	1	.000	0	1	1	0	3	8	2	0	0	15.00
Jim Constable	L	23	0	0	.000	0	3	0	0	4	9	7	1	0	15.75

Paul Giel (MS) 23

PITTSBURGH 7th 66-88 .429 27 — BOBBY BRAGAN

NAME	G by POS	B	AGE	G	AB	R	H	2B	3B	HR	RBI	BB	SO	SB	BA	SA
TOTALS			24	157	5221	588	1340	199	57	110	546	383	752	24	.257	.380
Dale Long	1B138	L	30	148	517	64	136	20	7	27	91	54	85	1	.263	.485
Bill Mazeroski	2B81	R	19	81	255	30	62	8	1	3	14	18	24	0	.243	.318
Dick Groat	SS141, 3B2	R	25	142	520	40	142	19	3	0	37	35	25	0	.273	.321
Frank Thomas	3B111, OF56, 2B4	R	27	157	588	69	166	24	3	25	80	36	61	0	.282	.461
Roberto Clemente	OF139, 2B2, 3B1	R	21	147	543	66	169	30	7	7	60	13	58	6	.311	.431
2 Bill Virdon	OF130	L	25	133	509	67	170	21	10	8	37	33	63	6	.334	.462
Lee Walls	OF133, 3B1	R	23	143	474	72	130	20	11	11	54	50	83	3	.274	.432
Jack Shepard	C86, 1B2	R	24	100	256	24	62	11	2	7	30	25	37	1	.242	.383
Bob Skinner	OF36, 1B24, 3B1	L	24	113	233	29	47	8	3	5	29	26	50	1	.202	.326
2 Hank Foiles	C73	R	27	79	222	24	47	10	2	7	25	17	56	0	.212	.369
Johnny O'Brien	2B53, P8, SS1	R	25	73	104	13	18	1	0	0	3	5	7	0	.173	.183
Dick Cole	3B18, 2B12, SS6	R	30	72	99	7	21	2	1	0	9	11	9	0	.212	.253
Gene Freese	3B47, 2B26	R	22	65	207	17	43	9	0	3	14	16	45	2	.208	.295
Eddie O'Brien	SS23, OF6, 3B4, 2B2, P1	R	25	63	53	17	14	2	0	0	3	2	2	1	.264	.302
Danny Kravitz	C26, 3B2	L	25	32	68	6	18	2	2	2	10	5	9	1	.265	.441
Curt Roberts	2B27	R	26	31	62	6	11	5	2	0	4	5	12	1	.177	.323
Jerry Lynch (IL)	OF1	L	25	19	19	1	3	0	1	0	0	1	4	0	.158	.263
1 Preston Ward	OF5, 3B5	L	28	16	30	3	10	0	1	1	11	6	4	0	.333	.500
1 Bobby Del Greco	OF8, 3B3	R	23	14	20	4	4	0	0	2	3	3	3	0	.200	.500
1 Toby Atwell	C9	L	32	12	18	0	2	0	0	0	3	1	5	0	.111	.111
2 Spook Jacobs	2B11	R	30	11	37	4	6	2	0	0	1	2	5	0	.162	.216

Johnny Powers 26 L 1-21, Bill Hall 27 L 0-3, Paul Smith (MS) 25

NAME	T	AGE	W	L	PCT	SV	G	GS	CG	IP	H	BB	SO	ShO	ERA
		28	66	88	.429	24	157	157	37	1376	1406	469	662	8	3.74
Bob Friend	R	25	17	17	.500	3	49	42	19	314	310	85	166	4	3.47
Ron Kline	R	24	14	18	.438	2	44	39	9	264	263	81	125	2	3.38
Roy Face	R	28	12	13	.480	6	68	3	0	135	131	42	96	0	3.53
Vern Law	R	26	8	16	.333	2	39	32	6	196	218	49	60	0	4.32
Nellie King	R	28	4	1	.800	5	38	0	0	60	54	19	25	0	3.15
Luis Arroyo	L	29	3	3	.500	0	18	2	1	29	36	12	17	0	4.66
George Munger	R	37	3	4	.429	2	35	13	0	107	126	41	45	0	4.04
Fred Waters	L	29	2	2	.500	0	23	5	1	51	48	30	14	0	2.82
Johnny O'Brien	R	25	1	0	1.000	0	8	0	0	19	8	9	9	0	2.84
Laurin Pepper	R	25	1	1	.500	0	11	7	0	30	30	25	12	0	3.00
Cholly Naranjo	R	21	1	2	.333	0	17	3	0	34	37	17	26	0	4.50
2 Howie Pollet	L	35	0	4	.000	3	19	0	0	23	18	8	10	0	3.13
Dick Hall (FJ)	R	25	0	7	.000	1	19	9	1	62	64	21	27	0	4.79
1 Jack McMahan	L	23	0	0	.000	0	11	0	0	13	18	9	9	0	6.23
Red Swanson	R	19	0	0	.000	0	9	0	0	12	21	8	5	0	9.75
1 Dick Littlefield	L	30	0	0	.000	0	6	2	0	13	14	6	10	0	4.15
Lino Donoso	L	33	0	0	.000	0	3	0	0	2	2	1	1	0	0.00
Bob Garber	R	27	0	0	.000	0	2	0	0	4	3	3	3	0	2.25
Bob Purkey	R	26	0	0	.000	0	2	0	0	4	2	0	1	0	2.25
1 Max Surkont	R	34	0	0	.000	0	1	0	0	2	2	3	1	0	4.50
Eddie O'Brien	R	25	0	0	.000	0	1	0	0	2	1	0	0	0	0.00

CHICAGO 8th 60-94 .390 33 — STAN HACK

NAME	G by POS	B	AGE	G	AB	R	H	2B	3B	HR	RBI	BB	SO	SB	BA	SA
TOTALS			28	157	5260	597	1281	202	50	142	563	446	776	55	.244	.382
Dee Fondy	1B133	L	31	137	543	52	146	22	9	9	46	20	74	9	.269	.392
Gene Baker	2B140	R	31	140	546	65	141	23	3	12	57	39	54	4	.258	.377
Ernie Banks	SS139	R	25	139	538	82	160	25	8	28	85	52	62	6	.297	.530
Don Hoak	3B110	R	28	121	424	51	91	18	4	5	37	41	46	8	.215	.311
Walt Moryn	OF141	L	30	147	529	69	151	27	3	23	67	50	67	4	.285	.478
Pete Whisenant	OF93	R	26	103	314	37	75	16	3	11	46	24	53	8	.239	.414
Monte Irvin	OF96	R	37	111	339	44	92	13	3	15	50	41	41	1	.271	.460
Hobie Landrith	C99	L	26	111	312	22	69	10	3	4	32	39	38	0	.221	.311
Jim King	OF82	L	23	118	317	32	79	13	2	15	54	30	40	1	.249	.445
Eddie Miksis	3B48, OF33, 2B19, SS2	R	29	114	356	54	85	10	3	9	27	32	40	4	.239	.360
Harry Chiti	C67	R	23	72	203	17	43	6	4	4	18	19	35	0	.212	.340
Frank Kellert	1B27	R	31	71	129	10	24	3	1	4	17	12	22	0	.186	.318
Solly Drake	OF53	B	25	65	215	29	55	9	1	2	15	23	35	9	.256	.335
Jerry Kindall	SS18	R	21	32	55	7	9	1	1	0	0	6	17	1	.164	.218
Ed Winceniak	3B4, 2B1	R	27	15	17	1	2	0	0	0	0	1	3	0	.118	.118
Clyde McCullough	C7	R	39	14	19	0	4	1	0	0	1	0	5	0	.211	.263

Gale Wade 27 L 0-12, Richie Myers 26 R 0-1, El Tappe 29 R 0-1, Owen Friend 29 R 0-2, Jim Fanning 28 R 1-4, Ted Tappe (IL) 25

NAME	T	AGE	W	L	PCT	SV	G	GS	CG	IP	H	BB	SO	ShO	ERA
		29	60	94	.390	17	157	157	37	1392	1325	613	744	6	3.96
Bob Rush	R	30	13	10	.565	0	32	32	13	240	210	59	104	1	3.19
Turk Lown	R	32	9	8	.529	13	61	0	0	111	95	78	74	0	3.57
Sam Jones	R	30	9	14	.391	0	33	28	8	189	155	115	176	2	3.90
Vito Valentinetti	R	27	6	4	.600	1	42	2	0	95	84	36	26	0	3.79
Jim Davis	L	31	5	7	.417	2	46	11	2	120	116	59	66	1	3.68
Jim Brosnan	R	26	5	9	.357	1	30	10	1	95	95	45	51	1	3.79
Don Kaiser	R	21	4	9	.308	0	27	22	5	150	144	52	74	1	3.60
Warren Hacker	R	31	3	13	.188	0	34	24	4	168	190	44	65	0	4.66
Moe Drabowski	R	20	2	4	.333	0	9	7	3	51	37	39	36	0	2.47
Paul Minner (YJ)	L	32	2	5	.286	0	10	9	1	47	60	19	14	0	6.89
2 Jim Hughes	R	33	1	3	.250	0	25	1	0	45	43	30	20	0	5.20
1 Russ Meyer (SJ)	R	32	1	6	.143	0	20	9	0	57	71	26	28	0	6.32
Dave Hillman	R	28	0	2	.000	0	2	2	0	12	11	5	6	0	2.25
Johnny Briggs	R	22	0	0	.000	0	3	0	0	5	5	4	1	0	1.80
George Piktuzis	L	24	0	0	.000	0	2	0	0	5	6	2	3	0	7.20
Bill Tremel	R	26	0	0	.000	0	1	0	0	1	3	0	0	0	9.00

WORLD SERIES — NEW YORK (AL) 4 BROOKLYN (NL) 3

LINE SCORES

TEAM	1	2	3	4	5	6	7	8	9	10	11	12	R	H	E
Game 1 October 3 at Brooklyn															
NY (AL)	2	0	0	1	0	0	0	0	0				3	9	1
BKN (NL)	0	2	3	1	0	0	0	0	X				6	9	0
Game 2 October 5 at Brooklyn															
NY	1	5	0	1	0	0	0	0	1				8	12	2
BKN	0	6	1	2	2	0	0	2	X				13	12	0
Game 3 October 6 at New York															
BKN	0	1	0	0	0	1	1	0	0				3	8	1
NY	0	1	0	0	0	3	0	1	X				5	8	1
Game 4 October 7 at New York															
BKN	0	0	0	1	0	0	0	0	1				2	6	0
NY	1	0	0	2	0	1	2	0	X				6	7	2
Game 5 October 8 at New York															
BKN	0	0	0	0	0	0	0	0	0				0	0	0
NY	0	0	0	1	0	1	0	0	X				2	5	0
Game 6 October 9 at Brooklyn															
NY	0	0	0	0	0	0	0	0	0	0			0	7	0
BKN	0	0	0	0	0	0	0	0	0	1			1	4	0
Game 7 October 10 at Brooklyn															
NY	2	0	2	1	0	0	4	0	0				9	10	0
BKN	0	0	0	0	0	0	0	0	0				0	3	1

Game 1: **Ford, Kucks (4), Morgan (6), Turley (8)** — **Maglie**

Game 2: Larsen, Kucks (2), Byrne (2), Sturdivant (3), **Morgan (3)**, Turley (5), McDermott (6) — Newcombe, Roebuck (2), **Bessent (3)**

Game 3: **Craig**, Labine (7) — **Ford**

Game 4: **Erskine**, Roebuck (5), Drysdale (7) — **Sturdivant**

Game 5: **Maglie** — **Larsen**

Game 6: **Turley** — **Labine**

Game 7: **Kucks** — **Newcombe**, Bessent (4), Craig (7), Roebuck (7), Erskine (9)

COMPOSITE BATTING

NAME	POS	G	AB	R	H	2B	3B	HR	RBI	BA
New York (AL) Totals		7	229	33	58	6	0	12	33	.253
Bauer	OF	7	32	3	9	0	0	1	3	.281
Martin	2B-3B	7	27	5	8	0	0	2	3	.296
Berra	C	7	25	5	9	2	0	3	10	.360
Mantle	OF	7	24	6	6	1	0	3	4	.250
Collins	1B	6	21	2	5	2	0	0	2	.238
McDougald	SS	7	21	0	3	0	0	0	1	.143
Slaughter	OF	6	20	6	7	0	0	1	4	.350
Carey	3B	7	19	2	3	0	0	0	0	.158
Skowron	1B	3	10	1	1	0	0	1	4	.100
Howard	OF	1	5	1	2	1	0	1	1	.400
Larsen	P	2	3	1	1	0	0	0	1	.333
Sturdivant	P	2	3	0	1	0	0	0	0	.333
Coleman	2B	2	2	0	0	0	0	0	0	.000
Turley	P	3	4	0	0	0	0	0	0	.000
Cerv	PH	1	1	0	1	0	0	0	0	1.000
McDermott	P	1	1	0	1	0	0	0	0	1.000
Morgan	P	2	1	1	1	0	0	0	0	1.000
Siebern	PH	1	1	0	0	0	0	0	0	.000
Wilson	PH	1	1	0	0	0	0	0	0	.000

Ford P 0-4, Kucks P 0-3, Byrne P 0-1

NAME	POS	G	AB	R	H	2B	3B	HR	RBI	BA
Brooklyn (NL) Totals		7	215	25	42	8	1	3	24	.195
Reese	SS	7	27	3	6	0	1	0	2	.222
Furillo	OF	7	25	2	6	2	0	0	1	.240
Robinson	3B	7	24	5	6	1	0	1	2	.250
Gilliam	2B-OF	7	24	2	2	0	0	0	2	.083
Snider	OF	7	23	5	7	1	0	1	4	.304
Hodges	1B	7	23	5	7	2	0	1	8	.304
Campanella	C	7	22	2	4	1	0	0	3	.182
Amoros	OF	6	19	1	1	0	0	0	1	.053
Maglie	P	2	5	0	0	0	0	0	0	.000
Labine	P	2	4	0	1	1	0	0	0	.250
Neal	2B	1	4	0	0	0	0	0	0	.000
Mitchell	PH	4	4	0	0	0	0	0	0	.000
Jackson	PH	3	3	0	0	0	0	0	0	.000
Bessent	P	2	2	0	1	0	0	0	0	.500
Craig	P	2	2	0	1	0	0	0	0	.500
Walker	PH	2	2	0	0	0	0	0	0	.000
Newcombe	P	2	1	0	0	0	0	0	0	.000
Erskine	P	2	1	0	0	0	0	0	0	.000
Cimoli	OF	1	0	0	0	0	0	0	0	.000

Roebuck P 0-0, Drysdale P 0-0

COMPOSITE PITCHING

NAME	G	IP	H	BB	SO	W	L	SV	ERA
New York (AL) Totals	7	61.2	42	32	47	4	3	0	2.48
Ford	2	12	14	2	8	1	1	0	5.25
Turley	3	11	4	8	14	0	1	0	0.82
Kucks	3	11	6	3	2	1	0	0	0.82
Larsen	2	10.2	1	4	7	1	0	0	0.00
Sturdivant	2	9.2	8	8	9	1	0	0	2.79
Morgan	2	4	6	4	3	0	1	0	9.00
McDermott	1	3	2	3	3	0	0	0	3.00
Byrne	1	.1	1	0	1	0	0	0	0.00
Brooklyn (NL) Totals	7	61	58	21	43	3	4	0	4.72
Maglie	2	17	14	6	15	1	1	0	2.65
Labine	2	12	8	3	7	1	0	0	0.00
Bessent	2	10	8	3	5	1	0	0	1.80
Craig	2	6	10	3	4	0	1	0	12.00
Erskine	2	5	4	2	2	0	1	0	5.40
Newcombe	2	4.2	11	3	4	0	1	0	21.21
Roebuck	3	4.1	1	0	5	0	0	0	2.08
Drysdale	1	2	2	1	1	0	0	0	9.00

1957 Glory for the Older Gentry and a Championship to the Young

Part of the scenery was gone. The Dodgers had wanted to trade Jackie Robinson to the Giants, but he retired instead. Along with baseball's first black performer went Bob Feller, Phil Rizzuto, and Al Rosen. All had left a heavy enough impression upon the game to give the feeling that the times were changing. For Fred Haney, things had changed for the better.

In 1955, Haney had little thought that he would manage a World Series winner two years later. From 1953 through 1955, Haney managed the Pirates to three straight last place finishes. Yet, when the Milwaukee Braves got off to a slow start in 1956, they gave him the nod to succeed Charlie Grimm as manager—and suddenly Haney found himself with a contending club to work with for the first time in his managerial career. After coming alive in mid-1956 but fading at the end to finish only one game behind Brooklyn, the 1957 Braves outlasted mid-summer challenges from St. Louis and Cincinnati to win the National League flag by a margin of eight games.

Brooklyn was plagued by age's toll on Pee Wee Reese, Don Newcombe, Carl Erskine, and Roy Campanella, and never made a serious run at the top. While the Braves were paced by sluggers, Hank Aaron and Eddie Mathews, and a Big Three pitching staff of Warren Spahn, Lew Burdette, and Bob Buhl, Haney kept pulling rabbits out of his hat to stock the supporting cast. He sent three players to the Giants in June in exchange for Red Schoendienst, who proceeded to hit .310 and make all the plays at second base. Billy Bruton and Joe Adcock were put out of action in mid-season by injuries, only to see Wes Covington and Bob "Hurricane" Hazle recalled from Wichita. Covington knocked 21 homers and Hazle batted a torrid .403. When a relief pitcher was needed, Haney was able to come up with Don McMahon from Wichita. Aaron took the MVP Award, leading the senior circuit in homers and RBI's, losing only the batting crown to 36-year-old Stan Musial.

In the American League, there was almost a final surprise, as the White Sox came out of the gate fast. But the Chicago attack, devoid of power and long on singles and stolen bases, could only support their strong pitching well enough to remain on top through June. They proved no match for the Yankees, who took 14 of 22 contests from Al Lopez's squad to win their eighth pennant in nine years. The Chicago guerrilla attack of Luis Aparicio, Nellie Fox, and Minnie Minoso turned out to be no match for the big guns of Mickey Mantle, Yogi Berra, and Bill Skowron. Mantle won a second consecutive MVP Award with a .365 batting average and logs of 34 homers and 94 RBI's. Berra's 24 homers, Skowron's .304 batting, and a .297 rookie season by Tony Kubek fleshed out the Yankee offense, while Stengel again had to patch together a pitching staff. Whitey Ford was troubled by a bad shoulder and won only 11 games, but Tom Sturdivant continued his good work of 1956, Bob Turley made a comeback from an off-season, and Bobby Shantz, the diminutive left-hander obtained from Kansas City during the winter, recovered from arm ills to lead the American League in E.R.A. with 2.45.

The rest of the league saw several key events. Boston's 38-year-old Ted Williams took the batting crown with a .388 mark, becoming the oldest batting champ ever. Washington's Roy Sievers won the home run and RBI titles, but the Senators still finished eighth. Cleveland lost baseball's most promising young pitcher when lefty Herb Score was struck on the eye by a line drive hit by the Yankees' Gil McDougald on May 7.

The Series saw the world championship flag fly west of the Hudson River for the first time since 1948, as the Braves knocked off the Yanks in seven games. Aaron hit a rousing .393, but the big story was Lew Burdette. In throwing three complete game victories, Burdette became the first to perform that feat since Stan Coveleski in 1920.

Beyond Stengel's having to again settle for second-best, the most far-reaching story of the year was the decision of the Brooklyn Dodgers and the New York Giants to abandon their traditional turf for new California sod. Unlike previous franchise shifts, both teams were still fairly good gate draws, but each cited outmoded ball parks and inadequate parking facilities and wanted the unlimited potential which Los Angeles and San Francisco offered.

1957 AMERICAN LEAGUE

NAME	G by POS	B	AGE	G	AB	R	H	2B	3B	HR	RBI	BB	SO	SB	BA	SA
NEW YORK 1st 98-56 .636		CASEY STENGEL														
TOTALS			29	154	5271	**723**	**1412**	200	**54**	145	682	562	709	49	**.268**	**.409**
Bill Skowron	1B115	R	26	122	457	54	139	15	5	17	88	31	60	3	.304	.470
Bobby Richardson	2B93	R	21	97	305	36	78	11	1	0	19	9	26	1	.256	.298
Gil McDougald	SS121, 2B21, 3B7	R	29	141	539	87	156	25	**9**	13	62	59	71	2	.289	.442
Andy Carey	3B81	R	25	85	247	30	63	6	5	6	33	15	42	2	.255	.393
Hank Bauer	OF135	R	34	137	479	70	124	22	**9**	18	65	42	64	7	.259	.455
Mickey Mantle	OF139	B	25	144	474	**121**	173	28	6	34	94	**146**	75	16	.365	.665
Enos Slaughter	OF64	L	41	96	209	24	53	7	1	5	34	40	19	0	.254	.368
Yogi Berra	C121, OF6	L	32	134	482	74	121	14	2	24	82	57	24	1	.251	.438
Tony Kubek	OF50, SS41, 3B38, 2B1	L	20	127	431	56	128	21	3	3	39	24	48	6	.297	.381
Elston Howard	OF71, C32, 1B2	R	28	110	356	33	90	13	4	8	44	16	43	2	.253	.379
Joe Collins	1B32, OF15	L	34	79	149	17	30	1	0	2	10	24	18	2	.201	.248
2 Harry Simpson	OF42, 1B21	L	31	75	224	27	56	7	3*	7	39	19	36	1	.250	.402
Jerry Coleman	2B45, 3B21, SS4	R	32	72	157	23	42	7	2	2	12	20	21	1	.268	.376
1 Billy Martin	2B27, 3B13	R	29	43	145	12	35	5	2	1	12	3	14	2	.241	.324
Jerry Lumpe	3B30, SS6	L	24	40	103	15	35	6	2	0	11	9	13	2	.340	.437
Darrell Johnson	C20	R	28	21	46	4	10	1	0	1	8	3	10	0	.217	.304
2 Bobby Del Greco	OF6	R	24	8	7	3	3	0	0	0	0	2	2	1	.429	.429
Zeke Bella	OF4	R	26	5	10	0	1	0	0	0	0	1	2	0	.100	.100
1 Woodie Held		R	25	1	1	0	0	0	0	0	0	0	0	0	.000	.000

NAME	T	AGE	W	L	PCT	SV	G	GS	CG	IP	H	BB	SO	ShO	ERA
		28	**98**	56	**.636**	**42**	154	154	41	1395	1198	580	**810**	13	**3.00**
Tom Sturdivant	R	27	16	6	.727	0	28	28	7	202	170	80	118	2	2.54
Bob Turley	R	26	13	6	.684	3	32	23	9	176	120	85	152	4	2.71
Bob Grim	R	27	12	8	.600	**19**	46	0	0	72	60	36	52	0	2.53
Bobby Shantz	L	31	11	5	.688	5	30	21	9	173	157	40	72	1	**2.45**
Whitey Ford (SJ)	L	28	11	5	.688	0	24	17	5	129	114	53	84	0	2.58
Don Larsen	R	27	10	4	.714	0	27	20	4	140	113	87	81	1	3.73
Art Ditmar	R	28	8	3	.727	6	46	11	0	127	128	35	64	0	3.26
Johnny Kucks	R	23	8	10	.444	2	37	23	4	179	169	59	78	1	3.57
Tommy Byrne	L	37	4	6	.400	2	30	4	1	85	70	60	57	0	4.34
2 Sal Maglie	R	40	2	0	1.000	3	6	3	1	26	22	7	9	1	1.73
Al Cicotte	R	27	2	2	.500	2	20	2	0	65	57	30	36	0	3.05
1 Ralph Terry	R	21	1	1	.500	0	7	2	1	21	18	8	7	1	3.00

*Simpson also with Kansas City, tied for league lead in 3B with 9

NAME	G by POS	B	AGE	G	AB	R	H	2B	3B	HR	RBI	BB	SO	SB	BA	SA
CHICAGO 2nd 90-64 .584 8		AL LOPEZ														
TOTALS			30	155	5265	707	1369	208	41	106	671	**633**	745	**109**	.260	.375
2 Earl Torgeson	1B70, OF1	L	33	86	251	53	74	11	2	7	46	49	44	7	.295	.295
Nellie Fox	2B155	L	29	155	619	110	**196**	27	8	6	61	75	13	5	.317	.415
Luis Aparicio	SS142	R	23	143	575	82	148	22	6	3	41	52	55	**28**	.257	.332
Bubba Phillips	3B97, OF20	R	27	121	393	38	106	13	3	7	42	28	32	5	.270	.372
Jim Rivera	OF82, 1B31	L	34	125	402	51	103	21	6	14	52	40	80	18	.256	.443
Larry Doby	OF110	L	33	119	416	57	120	27	2	14	79	56	79	2	.288	.464
Minnie Minoso	OF152, 3B1	R	34	153	568	96	176	**36**	5	12	103	79	54	18	.310	.454
Sherm Lollar (BW)	C96	R	32	101	351	33	90	11	2	11	70	35	24	2	.256	.393
Jim Landis	OF90	R	23	96	274	38	58	11	3	2	16	45	61	14	.212	.296
Sammy Esposito	3B53, SS22, 2B4, OF1	R	25	94	176	26	36	3	0	2	15	38	27	5	.205	.256
Walt Dropo	1B69	R	34	93	223	24	57	2	0	13	49	16	40	0	.256	.439
Fred Hatfield	3B44	L	32	69	114	14	23	3	0	0	8	15	20	1	.202	.228
Earl Battey	C43	R	22	48	115	12	20	2	3	3	6	11	38	0	.174	.322
Les Moss	C39	R	32	42	115	10	31	3	0	2	12	20	18	0	.270	.348
1 Ron Northey		L	37	40	27	0	5	1	0	0	7	11	5	0	.185	.222
Ted Beard	OF28	L	36	38	78	15	16	1	0	0	7	18	14	3	.205	.218
1 Dave Philley	OF17, 1B2	B	37	22	71	9	23	4	0	0	9	4	10	1	.324	.380
Ron Jackson	1B13	R	23	13	60	4	19	3	0	2	8	1	12	0	.317	.467
1 Bob Kennedy		R	36	4	2	0	0	0	0	0	0	0	1	0	.000	.000
Bob Powell		R	23	1	0	1	0	0	0	0	0	0	0	0	.000	.000

NAME	T	AGE	W	L	PCT	SV	G	GS	CG	IP	H	BB	SO	ShO	ERA
		31	90	64	.584	27	155	155	**59**	1402	1305	470	665	**16**	3.35
Billy Pierce	L	30	**20**	12	.625	2	37	34	**16**	257	228	71	171	4	3.76
Dick Donovan	R	29	16	6	.727	0	28	28	**16**	221	203	45	88	2	2.77
Jim Wilson	R	36	15	8	.652	0	30	29	12	202	189	65	100	**5**	3.48
Bob Keegan	R	36	10	8	.556	2	30	20	6	143	131	37	36	2	3.52
Jack Harshman	L	29	8	8	.500	1	30	26	6	151	142	82	83	0	4.11
Bill Fischer	R	26	7	8	.467	1	33	11	3	124	139	35	48	1	3.48
Dixie Howell	R	37	6	5	.545	6	37	0	0	68	64	30	37	0	3.31
Gerry Staley	R	36	5	1	.833	7	47	0	0	105	95	27	44	0	2.06
Don Rudolph	L	25	1	0	1.000	0	5	0	0	12	6	2	2	0	2.25
Barry Latman	R	21	1	2	.333	1	7	2	0	12	12	13	9	0	8.25
Paul LaPalme	L	33	1	4	.200	7	35	0	0	40	35	19	19	0	3.38
Jim Derrington	L	17	0	1	.000	0	20	5	0	37	29	29	14	0	4.86
Jim McDonald	R	30	0	1	.000	0	10	0	0	22	18	10	12	0	2.05
Jim Hughes	R	34	0	0	.000	0	4	0	0	5	12	3	2	0	10.80
Ellis Kinder	R	42	0	0	.000	0	1	0	0	1	0	1	0	0	0.00
Stover McIlwain	R	17	0	0	.000	0	1	0	0	1	2	1	0	0	0.00

NAME	G by POS	B	AGE	G	AB	R	H	2B	3B	HR	RBI	BB	SO	SB	BA	SA
BOSTON 3rd 82-72 .532 16		PINKY HIGGINS														
TOTALS			29	154	5267	721	1380	**231**	32	153	**695**	624	739	29	.262	.405
Dick Gernert	1B71, OF16	R	28	99	316	45	75	13	3	14	58	39	62	1	.237	.430
Ted Lepcio	2B68	R	26	79	232	24	56	10	2	9	37	29	61	0	.241	.418
Billy Klaus	SS118	L	28	127	477	76	120	18	4	10	42	55	53	2	.252	.369
Frank Malzone	3B153	R	27	153	634	82	185	31	5	15	103	31	41	2	.292	.427
Jackie Jensen	OF144	R	30	145	544	82	153	29	2	23	103	75	66	8	.281	.469
Jimmy Piersall	OF151	R	27	151	609	103	159	27	5	19	63	62	54	14	.261	.415
Ted Williams	OF125	L	38	132	420	96	163	28	1	38	87	119	43	0	**.388**	**.731**
Sammy White	C111	R	28	111	340	24	73	10	1	3	31	25	38	0	.215	.276
Gene Stephens	OF90	L	24	120	173	25	46	6	4	3	26	26	20	0	.265	.399
Mickey Vernon	1B70	L	39	102	270	36	65	18	1	7	38	41	35	0	.241	.393
Pete Daley	C77	R	27	78	191	17	43	10	0	3	25	16	31	0	.225	.325
Billy Consolo	SS42, 2B16, 3B2	R	22	68	196	26	53	6	1	4	19	23	48	1	.270	.372
Gene Mauch (VJ)	2B58	R	31	65	222	23	60	10	3	2	28	22	26	1	.270	.369
Norm Zauchin (BW)	1B36	R	27	52	91	11	24	3	0	3	14	9	13	0	.264	.396
Willard Nixon	P29	L	29	32	75	7	22	1	0	0	4	6	16	0	.293	.307
Ken Aspromonte	2B24	R	25	24	78	9	21	5	0	0	4	17	10	0	.269	.333
1 Billy Goodman		L	31	18	16	1	1	1	0	0	0	2	1	0	.063	.125
Marty Keough	OF7	L	22	9	17	1	1	0	0	0	0	4	3	0	.059	.059
Haywood Sullivan	C1	R	26	2	1	0	0	0	0	0	0	0	0	0	.000	.000
1 Milt Bolling		R	26	1	1	0	0	0	0	0	0	0	0	0	.000	.000

1 Faye Throneberry 26 L 0-1, Jim Pagliaron: (MS)19

NAME	T	AGE	W	L	PCT	SV	G	GS	CG	IP	H	BB	SO	ShO	ERA
		27	82	72	.532	23	154	154	55	1377	1391	498	692	9	3.88
Tom Brewer	R	25	16	13	.552	0	32	32	15	238	225	93	128	2	3.86
Frank Sullivan	R	27	14	11	.560	0	31	30	14	241	206	48	127	3	2.73
Willard Nixon	R	29	12	13	.480	0	29	29	11	191	207	56	96	1	3.68
Ike Delock	R	27	9	8	.529	11	49	2	0	94	80	45	62	0	3.83
2 Mike Fornieles	R	25	8	7	.125	2	25	18	7	125	136	38	64	1	3.53
George Susce	R	25	7	3	.700	1	29	5	0	88	93	41	40	0	4.30
Dave Sisler	R	25	7	8	.467	1	22	19	5	122	135	61	55	0	4.72
Bob Porterfield	R	33	4	4	.500	1	28	9	3	102	107	30	28	1	4.06
Murray Wall	R	30	3	0	1.000	1	11	0	0	24	21	2	13	0	3.38
Frank Baumann	L	24	1	0	1.000	0	4	1	0	12	13	3	7	0	3.75
2 Dean Stone	L	26	1	3	.250	1	17	8	0	51	56	35	32	0	5.12
2 Bob Chakales	R	29	0	2	.000	3	18	0	0	32	53	11	16	0	8.16
Rudy Minarcin	R	27	0	0	.000	2	26	0	0	45	44	30	20	0	4.40
Russ Meyer	R	33	0	0	.000	0	2	1	0	5	10	3	1	0	5.40
1 Russ Kemmerer	R	25	0	0	.000	0	1	0	0	4	5	2	1	0	4.50
Jack Spring	L	24	0	0	.000	0	1	0	0	1	0	0	2	0	0.00

DETROIT 4th 78-76 .506 20 — JACK TIGHE

NAME	G by POS	B	AGE	G	AB	R	H	2B	3B	HR	RBI	BB	SO	SB	BA	SA
TOTALS			28	154	5348	614	1376	224	37	116	574	504	643	36	.257	.378
Ray Boone	1B117, 3B4	R	33	129	462	48	126	25	3	12	65	57	47	1	.273	.418
Frank Bolling	2B146	R	25	146	576	72	149	27	6	15	40	57	64	4	.259	.405
Harvey Kuenn	SS136, 3B17, 1B1	R	26	151	624	74	173	30	6	9	44	47	28	5	.277	.388
Reno Bertoia	3B83, SS7, 2B2	R	22	97	295	28	81	16	2	4	28	19	43	2	.275	.383
Al Kaline	OF145	R	22	149	577	83	170	29	4	23	90	43	38	11	.295	.478
Bill Tuttle	OF128	R	27	133	451	49	113	12	4	5	47	44	41	2	.251	.328
Charlie Maxwell	OF137	L	30	138	492	75	136	23	3	24	82	76	84	3	.276	.482
Frank House	C97	L	27	106	348	31	90	9	0	7	36	35	26	1	.259	.345
2 Dave Philley	1B27, OF12, 3B1	B	37	65	173	15	49	8	1	2	16	7	16	3	.283	.376
Jim Finigan	3B59, 2B3	R	28	64	174	20	47	4	2	0	17	23	18	1	.270	.316
Red Wilson	C59	R	28	59	178	21	43	8	1	3	13	24	19	2	.242	.348
Jay Porter	OF27, C12, 1B3	R	24	58	140	14	35	8	0	2	18	14	20	0	.250	.350
Ron Samford	SS35, 2B11, 3B4	R	27	54	91	6	20	1	2	0	5	6	15	1	.220	.275
2 Johnny Groth	OF36	R	30	38	103	11	30	10	0	0	16	6	7	0	.291	.388
Jim Small	OF14	L	20	36	42	7	9	2	0	0	0	2	11	0	.214	.262
1 Earl Torgeson	1B17	L	33	30	50	5	12	2	1	1	5	12	10	0	.240	.380
Steve Boros	3B9, SS5	R	20	24	41	4	6	1	0	0	2	1	8	0	.146	.171
Jack Dittmer	3B3, 2B1	L	29	16	22	3	5	1	0	0	2	2	1	0	.227	.273
1 Eddie Robinson	1B1	L	36	13	9	0	0	0	0	0	0	3	0	0	.000	.000

Bobo Osborne 21 L 4-27, 2 Bill Taylor 27 L 8-23, 2 Karl Olson 26 R 2-14, Mel Clark 30 R 0-7, Jack Phillips 35 R 0-1, George Thomas 19 R 0-1, Tom Yewcic 25 R 0-1

NAME	T	AGE	W	L	PCT	SV	G	GS	CG	IP	H	BB	SO	ShO	ERA
TOTALS		29	78	76	.506	21	154	154	52	1417	1330	505	756	9	3.56
Jim Bunning	R	25	20	8	.714	1	45	30	14	267	214	72	182	1	2.70
Paul Foytack	R	26	14	11	.560	1	38	27	8	212	175	104	118	1	3.14
Frank Lary	R	27	11	16	.407	3	40	35	12	238	250	72	107	2	3.97
Duke Maas	R	28	10	14	.417	6	45	26	8	219	210	65	116	2	3.29
Billy Hoeft	L	25	9	11	.450	1	34	28	10	207	188	69	111	1	3.48
Harry Byrd	R	32	4	3	.571	5	37	1	0	59	53	28	20	0	3.36
Lou Sleator	L	30	3	3	.500	2	41	0	0	69	61	28	43	0	3.78
2 Al Aber	L	29	3	3	.500	1	28	0	0	37	46	11	15	0	6.81
John Tsitouris	R	21	1	0	1.000	0	2	0	0	3	8	2	2	0	9.00
Jim Stump	R	25	1	0	1.000	0	6	0	0	13	11	8	2	0	2.08
Joe Presko	R	28	1	1	.500	0	7	0	0	11	10	4	3	0	1.64
Don Lee	R	23	1	3	.250	0	11	6	0	39	48	18	19	0	4.62
Steve Gromek	R	37	0	1	.000	1	15	1	0	24	32	13	11	0	6.00
Bob Shaw	R	24	0	1	.000	0	7	0	0	10	11	7	4	0	7.20
Jack Crimian	R	31	0	1	.000	0	4	0	0	6	9	4	1	0	12.00
Pete Wojey	R	37	0	0	.000	0	2	0	0	1	1	0	0	0	0.00
Chuck Daniel	R	23	0	0	.000	0	1	0	0	2	3	0	2	0	9.00

BALTIMORE 5th 76-76 .500 21 — PAUL RICHARDS

NAME	G by POS	B	AGE	G	AB	R	H	2B	3B	HR	RBI	BB	SO	SB	BA	SA
TOTALS			29	154	5264	597	1326	191	39	87	554	504	699	57	.252	.353
Bob Boyd	1B132, OF1	L	30	141	485	73	154	16	8	4	34	55	31	2	.318	.408
Billy Gardner	2B148, SS9	R	29	154	644	79	169	36	3	6	55	53	67	10	.262	.356
Willie Miranda	SS115	B	31	115	314	29	61	3	0	0	20	24	42	2	.194	.204
George Kell	3B80, 1B22	R	34	99	310	28	92	9	0	9	44	25	16	2	.297	.413
Al Pilarcik	OF126	L	26	142	407	52	113	16	3	9	49	53	28	14	.278	.398
2 Jim Busby	OF85	R	30	86	288	31	72	10	1	3	19	23	36	6	.250	.323
Bob Nieman	OF120	R	30	129	445	61	123	17	6	13	70	63	86	4	.276	.429
Gus Triandos	C120	R	26	129	418	44	106	21	1	19	72	38	73	0	.254	.445
Tito Francona	OF73, 1B4	L	23	97	279	35	65	8	3	7	38	29	48	7	.233	.358
Jim Brideweser	SS74, 3B3, 2B1	R	30	91	142	16	38	6	1	1	18	21	16	2	.268	.345
Joe Ginsberg	C66	L	30	85	175	15	48	8	2	1	18	18	19	2	.274	.360
Joe Durham	OF59	R	25	77	157	19	29	2	0	4	17	16	42	1	.185	.274
2 Billy Goodman	3B54, OF9, 1B8, 2B5, SS5	L	31	73	263	36	81	10	3	3	33	21	18	0	.308	.403
Brooks Robinson (KJ)	3B47	R	20	50	117	13	28	6	1	2	14	7	10	1	.239	.359
1 Dick Williams	OF26, 3B15, 1B12	R	28	47	167	16	39	10	2	1	17	14	21	0	.234	.335
Bob Hale	1B5	L	23	42	44	2	11	0	0	0	7	2	2	0	.250	.250
Jim Pyburn	OF28, C1	R	24	35	40	8	9	0	0	1	2	9	6	1	.225	.300
Lenny Green	OF15	L	23	19	33	2	6	1	1	1	5	1	4	0	.182	.364
Carl Powis	OF13	R	29	15	41	4	8	3	1	0	2	7	9	2	.195	.317
Bob Nelson	OF8	L	20	15	23	2	5	0	2	0	5	1	5	0	.217	.391

Wayne Causey 20 L 2-10, Frank Zupo 17 L 1-12, Buddy Peterson 32 R 3-17, 3 Eddie Robinson 36 L 0-3, 2 Eddie Miksis 30 R 0-1, Tom Patton 21 R 0-2

NAME	T	AGE	W	L	PCT	SV	G	GS	CG	IP	H	BB	SO	ShO	ERA
TOTALS		30	76	76	.500	25	154	154	44	1408	1272	493	767	13	3.46
Connie Johnson	R	34	14	11	.560	0	35	30	14	242	212	66	177	3	3.70
Billy Loes	R	27	12	7	.632	4	31	18	8	155	142	37	86	3	3.25
Ray Moore	R	31	11	13	.458	0	34	32	7	227	196	112	117	1	3.73
George Zuverink	R	32	10	6	.625	9	56	0	0	113	105	39	36	0	2.47
2 Ken Lehman	L	29	8	3	.727	6	30	3	1	68	57	22	32	0	2.78
Hal Brown	R	32	7	8	.467	1	25	20	7	150	132	37	62	2	3.90
Bill Wight	L	35	6	6	.500	0	27	17	2	121	122	54	50	0	3.64
Billy O'Dell	L	24	4	10	.286	4	35	15	2	140	107	39	97	1	2.70
1 Mike Fornieles	R	25	2	6	.250	0	15	4	1	57	57	17	43	1	4.26
Jerry Walker	R	18	1	0	1.000	1	13	3	1	28	24	14	13	1	2.89
Don Ferrarese	L	28	1	1	.500	0	8	2	0	19	14	12	13	0	4.74
Art Ceccarelli	L	27	0	5	.000	0	20	8	1	58	62	31	30	0	4.50
2 Art Houtteman	R	29	0	0	.000	0	5	1	0	7	20	3	3	0	16.71
1 Sandy Consuegra	R	36	0	0	.000	0	5	0	0	5	4	0	0	0	1.80
Charlie Beamon	R	22	0	0	.000	0	4	1	0	9	8	7	5	0	5.00
Milt Pappas	R	18	0	0	.000	0	4	0	0	9	6	3	3	0	1.00
Dizzy Trout	R	42	0	0	.000	0	2	0	0	.1	4	0	0	0	81.00

CLEVELAND 6th 76-77 .497 21.5 — KERBY FARRELL

NAME	G by POS	B	AGE	G	AB	R	H	2B	3B	HR	RBI	BB	SO	SB	BA	SA
TOTALS			28	153	5171	682	1304	199	26	140	649	591	786	40	.252	.382
Vic Wertz	1B139	L	32	144	515	84	145	21	0	28	105	78	88	2	.282	.485
Bobby Avila	2B107, 3B16	R	33	129	463	60	124	19	3	5	48	46	47	2	.268	.354
Chico Carrasquel	SS122	R	29	125	392	37	108	14	1	8	57	41	53	0	.276	.378
Al Smith	3B84, OF50	R	29	135	507	78	125	23	5	11	49	79	70	12	.247	.377
Rocky Colavito	OF130	R	23	134	461	66	116	26	0	25	84	71	80	1	.252	.471
Roger Maris	OF112	L	22	116	358	61	84	9	5	14	51	60	79	8	.235	.405
Gene Woodling	OF113	L	34	133	430	74	138	25	2	19	78	64	35	0	.321	.521
Jim Hegan	C58	R	36	58	148	14	32	7	0	4	15	16	23	0	.216	.345
Larry Raines	3B27, SS25, 2B10, OF8	R	27	96	244	39	64	14	0	2	16	19	40	5	.262	.344
George Strickland	2B48, SS23, 3B19	R	31	89	201	21	47	8	2	1	19	26	29	0	.234	.308
Joe Altobelli	1B56, OF7	L	25	83	87	9	18	3	2	0	9	5	14	3	.207	.287
2 Dick Williams	OF37, 3B19	R	28	67	205	33	58	7	0	6	17	12	19	3	.283	.405
Russ Nixon	C57	L	22	65	185	15	52	7	1	2	18	12	12	0	.281	.362
Hal Naragon	C39	L	28	57	121	12	31	1	1	0	8	12	9	0	.256	.281
Kenny Kuhn	2B14, 3B2, SS1	L	20	40	53	5	9	0	0	0	5	4	9	0	.170	.170
Dick Brown	C33	R	22	34	114	10	30	4	0	4	22	4	23	1	.263	.404
Joe Caffie	OF19	L	26	32	89	14	24	2	1	3	10	4	11	0	.270	.416
1 Jim Busby	OF26	R	30	30	74	9	14	2	1	2	4	1	8	0	.189	.324
Billy Harrell	SS14, 3B6, 2B1	R	28	22	57	6	15	1	1	1	5	4	7	3	.263	.368
2 Eddie Robinson	1B7	L	36	19	27	1	6	1	0	1	3	0	3	0	.222	.370

1 Bob Usher 32 R 1-8, Preston Ward 29 L 2-11

NAME	T	AGE	W	L	PCT	SV	G	GS	CG	IP	H	BB	SO	ShO	ERA
TOTALS		30	76	77	.497	23	153	153	46	1381	1381	618	807	7	4.06
Early Wynn	R	37	14	17	.452	1	40	37	13	263	270	140	184	1	4.31
Mike Garcia	R	33	12	8	.600	0	38	27	9	211	221	73	110	1	3.75
Ray Narleski	R	28	11	5	.688	16	46	15	7	154	136	70	93	1	3.10
Don Mossi	L	28	11	10	.524	2	36	22	6	159	165	57	97	1	4.13
Cal McLish	R	31	9	7	.563	1	42	7	2	144	118	67	88	0	2.75
Bob Lemon	R	36	6	11	.353	0	21	17	2	117	129	64	45	0	4.62
Dick Tomanek	L	26	2	1	.667	0	34	2	0	70	67	37	55	0	5.66
Herb Score (IJ)	L	24	2	1	.667	0	5	5	3	36	18	26	39	1	2.00
Stan Pitula (AJ)	R	26	2	2	.500	0	23	5	1	60	67	32	17	0	4.95
2 Vito Valentinetti	R	28	2	2	.500	0	11	2	1	24	26	13	9	0	4.87
Bud Daley	L	24	2	8	.200	2	34	10	1	87	99	40	54	0	4.45
2 Hoyt Wilhelm	R	33	1	0	1.000	1	2	0	0	4	2	1	0	0	2.25
Hank Aguirre	L	25	1	1	.500	0	10	1	0	20	26	13	9	0	5.85
John Gray	R	29	1	3	.250	0	7	3	1	20	21	13	3	1	5.85
Bob Alexander	R	34	0	1	.000	0	5	0	0	7	10	5	1	0	9.00
1 Art Houtteman	R	29	0	0	.000	0	3	0	0	4	6	3	3	0	6.75

KANSAS CITY 7th 59-94 .386 38.5 — LOU BOUDREAU 36-67 .340 HARRY CRAFT 23-27 .460

NAME	G by POS	B	AGE	G	AB	R	H	2B	3B	HR	RBI	BB	SO	SB	BA	SA
TOTALS			28	154	5170	563	1262	195	40	166	535	364	760	35	.244	.394
Vic Power	1B113, OF6, 2B4	R	25	129	467	48	121	15	1	14	42	19	21	3	.259	.385
Billy Hunter	2B64, SS35, 3B17	R	29	116	319	39	61	10	4	8	29	27	43	1	.191	.323
Joe DeMaestri	SS134	R	28	135	461	44	113	14	6	9	33	22	82	6	.245	.360
Hector Lopez	3B111, 2B4, OF3	R	24	121	391	51	115	19	4	11	35	41	66	1	.294	.448
Bob Cerv	OF89	R	31	124	345	35	94	14	2	11	44	20	57	1	.272	.420
2 Woodie Held	OF92	R	25	92	326	48	78	14	3	20	50	37	81	4	.239	.485
Gus Zernial	OF113, 1B1	R	34	131	437	56	103	20	1	27	69	34	84	1	.236	.471
Hal Smith	C103	R	26	107	360	41	109	26	0	13	41	14	44	2	.303	.483
Lou Skizas	OF76, 3B32	R	25	119	376	34	92	14	1	18	44	27	15	5	.245	.431
Tim Thompson	C62	L	33	81	230	25	47	10	0	7	19	18	26	0	.204	.339
1 Irv Noren	1B25, OF6	L	32	81	160	8	34	8	0	2	16	11	19	0	.213	.300
2 Billy Martin	2B51, 3B20, SS2	R	29	73	265	33	68	9	3	9	27	12	20	7	.257	.415
Bob Martyn	OF49	L	26	58	131	10	35	2	4	1	12	11	20	1	.267	.366
Mickey McDermott	P29, 1B2	L	28	58	49	6	12	1	0	4	7	9	16	0	.245	.510
Milt Graff	2B53	L	26	56	155	16	28	4	3	0	10	15	10	2	.181	.245
1 Johnny Groth	OF50	R	30	55	59	10	15	0	0	0	2	7	6	0	.254	.254
1 Harry Simpson	1B27, OF21	L	31	50	179	24	53	9	6*	6	24	12	28	0	.296	.514
Jim Pisoni	OF44	R	27	44	97	14	23	2	2	3	12	10	17	0	.237	.392
Clete Boyer	3B1, 2B1	R	20	10	0	0	0	0	0	0	0	0	0	0	.000	.000

NAME	T	AGE	W	L	PCT	SV	G	GS	CG	IP	H	BB	SO	ShO	ERA
TOTALS		29	59	94	.386	19	154	154	26	1370	1344	565	626	6	4.19
Virgil Trucks	R	38	9	7	.563	7	48	7	0	116	106	62	55	0	3.03
Tom Morgan	R	27	9	7	.563	7	46	13	5	144	160	61	32	0	4.63
Jack Urban	R	28	7	4	.636	0	31	13	3	129	111	45	55	0	3.35
Wally Burnette	R	28	7	12	.368	1	38	9	1	113	115	44	57	0	4.30
Alex Kellner	L	32	6	5	.545	0	28	21	3	133	141	41	72	0	4.26
Ned Garver	R	31	6	13	.316	0	24	23	6	145	120	55	61	1	3.85
Tom Gorman	R	32	5	9	.357	3	38	12	3	125	125	33	66	1	3.82
Arnie Portocarrero	R	25	4	9	.308	0	33	17	1	115	103	34	42	0	3.91
2 Ralph Terry	R	21	4	11	.267	0	21	19	3	131	119	47	80	1	3.37
Glenn Cox	R	26	1	0	1.000	0	10	0	0	14	18	9	8	0	5.14
Mickey McDermott	L	28	1	4	.200	0	29	4	0	69	68	50	29	0	5.48
George Brunet	L	22	0	1	.000	0	4	2	0	11	13	4	3	0	5.73
Gene Host	L	24	0	2	.000	0	11	2	0	24	29	14	9	0	7.12
Ryne Duren	R	28	0	3	.000	1	14	6	1	43	37	30	37	0	5.23
Rip Coleman	L	25	0	7	.000	0	19	6	1	41	53	25	15	1,	5.93
2 Al Aber	L	29	0	0	.000	0	3	0	0	3	6	2	0	0	12.00
Ed Blake	R	31	0	0	.000	0	2	0	0	2	1	2	0	0	4.50
Harry Taylor	R	21	0	0	.000	0	2	0	0	9	11	4	4	0	3.00
Dave Hill	L	19	0	0	.000	0	2	0	0	2	6	3	1	0	31.50
Hal Raether	R	24	0	0	.000	0	1	0	0	2	2	0	0	0	9.00

*Simpson, also with New York, tied for league lead in 3B with 9

WASHINGTON 8th 55-99 .357 43 — CHUCK DRESSEN 5-16 .238 COOKIE LAVAGETTO 50-83 .376

NAME	G by POS	B	AGE	G	AB	R	H	2B	3B	HR	RBI	BB	SO	SB	BA	SA
TOTALS			29	154	5231	603	1274	215	38	111	576	527	733	13	.244	.363
Pete Runnels	1B72, 3B32, 2B23	L	29	134	473	53	109	18	4	2	35	55	51	2	.230	.298
Herb Plews	2B79, 3B11, SS4	L	29	104	329	51	89	19	4	1	26	28	39	0	.271	.362
2 Rocky Bridges	SS108, 2B14, 3B1	R	29	120	391	40	89	17	2	3	47	40	32	0	.228	.304
Eddie Yost (GJ)	3B107	R	30	110	414	47	104	13	5	9	38	73	49	1	.251	.372
Jim Lemon	OF131, 1B3	R	29	137	518	58	147	22	6	17	64	49	94	1	.284	.448
2 Bob Usher	OF95	R	32	96	295	36	77	7	1	5	27	27	30	0	.261	.342
Roy Sievers	OF130, 1B21	R	30	152	572	99	172	23	5	42	114	76	55	1	.301	.579
Lou Berberet	C77	L	27	99	264	24	69	11	2	7	36	41	38	0	.261	.398
Julio Becquer	1B43	L	25	105	186	14	42	6	2	2	22	10	29	3	.226	.312
2 Milt Bolling	2B53, SS35, 3B1	R	26	91	277	29	63	12	1	4	19	18	59	2	.227	.321
Clint Courtney	C59	L	30	91	232	23	62	14	1	6	27	16	11	0	.267	.414
2 Art Schult	1B35, OF31	R	29	77	247	30	65	14	0	4	35	14	30	0	.263	.368
2 Faye Throneberry	OF58	L	26	68	195	21	36	8	2	2	12	17	37	0	.185	.277
Ed Fitz Gerald	C37	R	33	45	125	14	34	8	0	1	13	10	9	2	.272	.360
Jerry Snyder	SS15, 2B13, 3B1	R	27	42	93	6	14	1	0	1	4	4	9	0	.151	.194
Whitey Herzog	OF28	L	25	36	78	7	13	3	0	0	4	13	12	1	.167	.205
Jerry Schoonmaker	OF13	R	23	30	23	5	2	1	0	0	0	2	11	0	.087	.130
Neil Chrisley	OF11	L	25	26	51	6	8	2	1	0	3	7	7	0	.157	.235
Lyle Luttrell	SS17	R	27	19	45	4	9	4	0	0	5	3	8	0	.200	.289

Harmon Killebrew 21 R 9-31, Dick Tettelbach 28 R 2-11, 1 Karl Olson 26 R 2-12, Steve Korcheck (MS) 24

NAME	T	AGE	W	L	PCT	SV	G	GS	CG	IP	H	BB	SO	ShO	ERA
TOTALS		26	55	99	.357	16	154	154	31	1377	1482	580	691	5	4.85
Pedro Ramos	R	22	12	16	.429	0	43	30	7	231	251	69	91	1	4.79
Camilo Pascual	R	23	8	17	.320	0	29	26	8	176	168	76	113	2	4.09
Chuck Stobbs	L	27	8	20	.286	1	42	31	5	212	235	80	114	2	5.36
Tex Clevenger	R	24	7	6	.538	8	52	9	2	140	139	47	75	0	4.18
2 Russ Kemmerer	R	25	7	11	.389	0	39	26	6	172	214	71	81	0	4.97
Bud Byerly	R	36	6	6	.500	6	47	0	0	95	94	22	39	0	3.13
Dick Hyde	R	28	4	3	.571	1	52	2	0	109	104	56	46	0	4.13
Ted Abernathy	R	24	2	10	.167	0	26	16	2	85	100	65	50	0	6.78
Bob Wiesler	L	26	1	1	.500	0	3	2	1	16	15	11	9	0	4.50
Joe Black	R	33	0	1	.000	0	7	0	0	13	22	1	2	0	6.92
Dick Brodowski	R	24	0	1	.000	0	6	0	0	11	12	10	4	0	11.46
1 Bob Chakales	R	29	0	1	.000	0	4	2	0	18	20	10	12	0	5.50
Ralph Lumenti	L	20	0	1	.000	0	3	2	0	9	9	5	8	0	7.00
Hal Griggs	R	28	0	1	.000	0	2	2	0	14	11	7	12	0	3.21
Don Minnick	R	26	0	1	.000	0	2	1	0	9	14	2	7	0	5.00
Jim Heise	R	24	0	3	.000	0	8	2	0	19	25	16	8	0	8.05
Evelio Hernandez	R	26	0	0	.000	0	14	2	0	36	38	20	15	0	4.25
Garland Shifflett	R	22	0	0	.000	0	6	1	0	8	6	10	2	0	10.13
1 Dean Stone	L	26	0	0	.000	0	3	0	0	3	5	2	3	0	9.00

MILWAUKEE 1st 95-59 .617 — FRED HANEY

NAME	G by POS	B	AGE	G	AB	R	H	2B	3B	HR	RBI	BB	SO	SB	BA	SA
TOTALS			28	155	5458	772	1469	221	62	199	722	461	729	35	.269	.442
Frank Torre	1B117	L	25	129	364	46	99	19	5	5	40	29	19	0	.272	.393
2 Red Schoendienst	2B92, OF2	B	34	93	394	56	122*	23	4	6	32	23	7	2	.310	.434
Johnny Logan	SS129	R	30	129	494	59	135	19	7	10	49	31	49	5	.273	.401
Eddie Mathews	3B147	L	25	148	572	109	167	28	9	32	94	90	79	3	.292	.540
Hank Aaron	OF150	R	23	151	615	118	198	27	6	44	132	57	58	1	.322	.600
Bill Bruton (KJ)	OF79	L	31	79	306	41	85	16	9	5	30	19	35	11	.278	.438
Wes Covington	OF89	L	25	96	328	51	93	4	8	21	65	29	44	4	.284	.537
Del Crandall	C102, OF9, 1B1	R	27	118	383	45	97	11	2	15	46	30	38	1	.253	.410
Andy Pafko	OF69	R	36	83	220	31	61	6	1	8	27	10	22	1	.277	.423
Felix Mantilla	SS35, 2B13, 3B7, OF1	R	22	71	182	28	43	9	1	4	21	14	34	2	.236	.363
Joe Adcock (BL)	1B56	R	29	65	209	31	60	13	2	12	38	20	51	0	.287	.541
Carl Sawatski	C28	L	29	58	105	13	25	4	0	6	17	10	15	0	.238	.448
Del Rice (BG)	C48	R	34	54	144	15	33	1	1	9	20	17	37	0	.229	.438
1 Danny O'Connell	2B48	R	30	48	183	29	43	9	1	1	8	19	20	1	.235	.311
Bob Hazle	OF40	L	26	41	134	26	54	12	0	7	27	18	15	1	.403	.649
1 Bobby Thomson	OF38	R	33	41	148	15	35	5	3	4	23	8	27	2	.236	.392
John DeMerit	OF13	R	21	33	34	8	5	0	0	0	1	0	8	1	.147	.147
Nippy Jones	1B20, OF1	R	32	30	79	5	21	2	1	2	8	3	7	0	.266	.392
1 Chuck Tanner	OF18	L	27	22	69	5	17	3	0	2	6	5	4	0	.246	.377
Dick Cole	2B10, 3B1, 1B1	R	31	15	14	1	1	0	0	0	0	3	5	0	.071	.071
Bobby Malkmus	2B7	R	25	13	22	6	2	0	1	0	0	3	3	0	.091	.182
Mel Roach	2B5	R	24	7	6	1	1	0	0	0	0	0	3	0	.167	.167
Hawk Taylor	C1	R	18	7	1	2	0	0	0	0	0	0	0	0	.000	.000
Harry Hanebrink	3B2	L	29	6	7	0	2	0	0	0	0	1	2	0	.286	.286
Ray Shearer	OF1	R	27	2	2	1	1	0	0	0	0	1	1	0	.500	.500

NAME	T	AGE	W	L	PCT	SV	G	GS	CG	IP	H	BB	SO	ShO	ERA
TOTALS		28	95	59	.617	24	155	155	60	1411	1347	570	693	9	3.47
Warren Spahn	L	36	21	11	.656	3	39	35	18	271	241	78	111	4	2.69
Bob Buhl	R	28	18	7	.720	0	34	31	14	217	191	121	117	2	2.74
Lew Burdette	R	30	17	9	.654	0	37	33	14	257	260	59	78	1	3.71
Gene Conley	R	26	9	9	.500	1	35	18	6	148	133	64	61	1	3.16
Ernie Johnson	R	33	7	3	.700	4	30	0	0	65	67	26	44	0	3.88
Bob Trowbridge	R	27	7	5	.583	1	32	16	3	126	118	52	75	1	3.64
Juan Pizarro	L	20	5	6	.455	0	24	10	3	99	99	51	68	0	4.64
1 Ray Crone	R	25	3	1	.750	0	11	5	2	42	54	15	15	0	4.50
Taylor Phillips	L	24	3	2	.600	2	27	6	0	73	82	40	36	0	5.55
Red Murff	R	36	2	2	.500	2	12	1	0	26	31	11	13	0	4.85
Don McMahon	R	27	2	3	.400	9	32	0	0	47	33	29	46	0	1.53
Dave Jolly	R	32	1	1	.500	1	23	0	0	38	37	21	27	0	4.97
Joey Jay	R	21	0	0	.000	1	1	0	0	1	0	0	0	0	0.00
Phil Paine	R	27	0	0	.000	0	1	0	0	2	1	3	2	0	0.00

*Schoendienst, also with New York, league leader in H with 200

ST. LOUIS 2nd 87-67 .565 8 — FRED HUTCHINSON

NAME	G by POS	B	AGE	G	AB	R	H	2B	3B	HR	RBI	BB	SO	SB	BA	SA
TOTALS			28	154	5472	737	1497	235	43	132	685	493	672	58	.274	.405
Stan Musial	1B130	L	36	134	502	82	176	38	3	29	102	66	34	1	.351	.612
Don Blasingame	2B154	L	25	154	650	108	176	25	7	8	58	71	49	21	.271	.368
Al Dark	SS139, 3B1	R	35	140	583	80	169	25	8	4	64	29	56	3	.290	.381
Eddie Kasko	3B120, SS13, 2B1	R	25	134	479	59	131	16	5	1	35	33	53	6	.273	.334
Del Ennis	OF127	R	32	136	490	61	140	24	3	24	105	37	50	1	.286	.494
Ken Boyer	OF105, 3B41	R	26	142	544	79	144	18	3	19	62	44	77	12	.265	.414
Wally Moon	OF133	L	27	142	516	86	152	28	5	24	73	62	57	5	.295	.508
Hal Smith	C97	R	26	100	333	25	93	12	3	2	37	18	18	2	.279	.351
Joe Cunningham	1B57, OF46	L	25	122	261	50	83	15	0	9	52	56	29	3	.318	.479
Bobby Gene Smith	OF79	R	23	93	185	24	39	7	1	3	18	13	35	1	.211	.308
Hobie Landrith	C67	L	27	75	214	18	52	6	0	3	26	25	27	1	.243	.313
Dick Schofield	SS23	B	22	65	56	10	9	0	0	0	1	7	13	1	.161	.161
1 Eddie Miksis	OF31	R	30	49	38	3	8	0	0	1	2	7	7	0	.211	.289
Walker Cooper	C13	R	42	48	78	7	21	5	1	3	10	5	10	0	.269	.474
Jim King	OF8	L	24	22	35	1	11	0	0	0	2	4	2	0	.314	.314
2 Irv Noren	OF8	L	32	17	30	3	11	4	1	1	10	4	6	0	.367	.667
1 Chuck Harmon	OF8	R	31	9	3	2	1	0	1	0	1	0	0	1	.333	1.000
Tom Alston (IL)	1B6	L	26	9	17	2	5	1	0	0	2	1	5	0	.294	.353
Gene Green	OF3	R	24	6	15	0	3	1	0	0	2	0	3	0	.200	.267
Don Lassetter	OF3	R	24	4	13	2	2	0	1	0	0	1	3	0	.154	.308

Charlie Peete (DD)25

NAME	T	AGE	W	L	PCT	SV	G	GS	CG	IP	H	BB	SO	ShO	ERA
TOTALS		26	87	67	.565	29	154	154	46	1413	1385	506	778	11	3.78
Larry Jackson	R	26	15	9	.625	1	41	22	6	210	196	57	96	2	3.47
Lindy McDaniel	R	21	15	9	.625	0	30	26	10	191	196	53	75	1	3.49
Sam Jones	R	31	12	9	.571	0	28	27	10	183	164	71	154	2	3.59
Willard Schmidt	R	29	10	3	.769	0	40	8	1	117	146	49	63	0	4.77
Herm Wehmeier	R	30	10	7	.588	0	36	18	5	165	165	54	91	0	4.31
Vinegar Bend Mizell	L	26	8	10	.444	0	33	21	7	149	136	51	87	2	3.74
Von McDaniel	R	18	7	5	.583	0	17	13	4	87	71	31	45	2	3.21
Murry Dickson	R	40	5	3	.625	0	14	13	3	74	87	25	29	1	4.14
Billy Muffett	R	26	3	2	.600	8	23	0	0	44	35	13	21	0	2.25
Lloyd Merritt	R	24	1	2	.333	7	44	0	0	65	60	28	35	0	3.32
1 Hoyt Wilhelm	R	33	1	4	.200	11	40	0	0	55	52	21	29	0	4.25
1 Jim Davis	L	32	0	1	.000	1	10	0	0	14	18	6	5	0	5.15
Tom Cheney	R	22	0	1	.000	0	4	3	0	9	6	15	10	0	5.00
Frank Barnes	R	28	0	1	.000	0	3	1	0	10	13	9	5	0	4.50
Lynn Lovenguth	R	34	0	1	.000	0	2	1	0	9	6	6	6	0	2.00
Bob Miller	R	18	0	0	.000	0	5	0	0	9	13	5	7	0	7.00
1 Bob Smith	L	26	0	0	.000	1	6	0	0	10	12	6	11	0	4.50
Morrie Martin	L	34	0	0	.000	0	4	1	0	11	5	4	7	0	2.45
2 Bob Kuzava	L	34	0	0	.000	0	3	0	0	2	4	2	2	0	4.50

BROOKLYN 3rd 84-70 .545 11 — WALT ALSTON

NAME	G by POS	B	AGE	G	AB	R	H	2B	3B	HR	RBI	BB	SO	SB	BA	SA
TOTALS			31	154	5242	690	1325	188	38	147	648	550	848	60	.253	.387
Gil Hodges	1B150, 3B2, 2B1	R	33	150	579	94	173	28	7	27	98	63	91	5	.299	.511
Jim Gilliam	2B148, OF2	B	28	149	617	89	154	26	4	2	37	64	31	26	.250	.314
Charlie Neal	SS100, 3B23, 2B3	R	26	128	448	62	121	13	7	12	62	53	83	11	.270	.411
Pee Wee Reese	3B75, SS23	R	38	103	330	33	74	3	1	1	29	39	32	5	.224	.248
Carl Furillo	OF107	R	35	119	395	61	121	17	4	12	66	29	33	0	.306	.461
Duke Snider	OF136	L	30	139	508	91	139	25	7	40	92	77	104	3	.274	.587
Gino Cimoli	OF138	R	27	142	532	88	156	22	5	10	57	39	86	3	.293	.410
Roy Campanella	C100	R	35	103	330	31	80	9	0	13	62	34	50	1	.242	.388
Sandy Amoros	OF66	L	27	106	238	40	66	7	1	7	26	46	42	3	.277	.403
Don Zimmer	3B39, SS37, 2B5	R	26	84	269	23	59	9	1	6	19	16	63	1	.219	.327
Elmer Valo	OF36	L	36	81	161	14	44	10	1	4	26	25	16	0	.273	.422
Rube Walker	C50	L	31	60	166	12	30	8	0	2	23	15	33	2	.181	.265
Randy Jackson(KJ)	3B34	R	31	48	131	7	26	1	0	2	16	9	20	0	.198	.252
Johnny Roseboro	C19, 1B5	L	24	35	69	6	10	2	0	2	6	10	20	0	.145	.261
2 Bob Kennedy	OF9, 3B3	R	36	19	31	5	4	1	0	1	4	1	5	0	.129	.258
Joe Pignatano	C6	R	27	8	14	0	3	1	0	0	1	0	5	0	.214	.286
Jim Gentile	1B2	L	23	4	6	1	1	0	0	1	1	1	1	0	.167	.667
Rod Miller		L	17	1	1	0	0	0	0	0	0	0	1	0	.000	.000

NAME	T	AGE	W	L	PCT	SV	G	GS	CG	IP	H	BB	SO	ShO	ERA
TOTALS		27	84	70	.545	29	154	154	44	1399	1285	456	891	18	3.35
Don Drysdale	R	20	17	9	.654	0	34	29	9	221	197	61	148	4	2.69
Johnny Podres	L	24	12	9	.571	3	31	27	10	196	168	44	109	6	2.66
Don Newcombe	R	31	11	12	.478	0	28	28	12	199	199	33	90	4	3.48
Ed Roebuck	R	25	8	2	.800	8	44	1	0	96	70	46	73	0	2.72
Danny McDevitt	L	24	7	4	.636	0	22	17	5	119	105	72	90	2	3.25
1 Sal Maglie	R	40	6	6	.500	1	19	17	4	101	94	26	50	1	2.94
Roger Craig	R	26	6	9	.400	0	32	13	1	111	102	47	69	0	4.62
Carl Erskine (SA)	R	30	5	3	.625	0	15	7	1	66	62	20	26	0	3.55
Sandy Koufax	L	21	5	4	.556	0	34	13	2	104	83	51	122	0	3.89
Clem Labine	R	30	5	7	.417	17	58	0	0	105	104	27	67	0	3.43
Rene Valdes	R	28	1	1	.500	0	5	1	0	13	13	7	10	0	5.54
Don Bessent	R	26	1	3	.250	0	27	0	0	44	58	19	24	0	5.73
Bill Harris	R	25	0	1	.000	0	1	1	0	7	9	1	3	0	3.86
2 Jackie Collum	L	30	0	0	.000	0	3	0	0	4	7	1	3	0	9.00
1 Ken Lehman	L	29	0	0	.000	0	3	0	0	7	7	1	3	0	0.00
1 Don Elston	R	28	0	0	.000	0	1	0	0	1	1	0	1	0	0.00
Fred Kipp	L	25	0	0	.000	0	1	0	0	4	6	0	3	0	9.00

CINCINNATI 4th 80-74 .519 15 — BIRDIE TEBBETTS

NAME	G by POS	B	AGE	G	AB	R	H	2B	3B	HR	RBI	BB	SO	SB	BA	SA
TOTALS			29	154	5389	747	1452	251	33	187	713	546	752	51	.269	.432
George Crowe	1B120	L	34	133	494	71	134	20	1	31	92	32	62	1	.271	.504
Johnny Temple	2B145	R	28	145	557	85	158	24	4	0	37	94	34	19	.284	.341
Roy McMillan	SS151	R	26	151	448	50	122	25	5	1	55	66	44	5	.272	.357
Don Hoak	3B149, 2B1	R	29	149	529	78	155	39	2	19	89	74	54	8	.293	.482
Wally Post	OF124	R	27	134	467	68	114	26	2	20	74	33	84	2	.244	.437
Gus Bell	OF121	L	28	121	510	65	149	20	3	13	61	30	54	0	.292	.420
Frank Robinson	OF136, 1B24	R	21	150	611	97	197	29	5	29	75	44	92	10	.322	.529
Ed Bailey	C115	L	26	122	391	54	102	15	2	20	48	73	69	5	.261	.463
Smoky Burgess	C45	L	30	90	205	29	58	14	1	14	39	24	16	0	.283	.566
Bob Thurman	OF44	L	36	74	190	38	47	4	2	16	40	15	33	0	.247	.542
Alex Grammas	SS42, 2B20, 3B9	R	30	73	99	14	30	4	0	0	8	10	6	1	.303	.343
Ted Kluszewski (XJ)	1B23	L	32	69	127	12	34	7	0	6	21	5	5	0	.268	.465
Jerry Lynch	OF24, C2	L	26	67	124	11	32	4	1	4	13	6	18	0	.258	.403
Pete Whisenant	OF43	R	27	67	90	18	19	3	2	5	11	5	24	0	.211	.456
Joe Taylor	OF27	L	31	33	107	14	28	7	0	4	9	6	24	0	.262	.439
Bobby Henrich	SS7, OF6, 3B2, 2B1	R	18	29	10	8	2	0	0	0	1	1	4	0	.200	.200
1 Art Schult	OF5	R	29	21	34	4	9	2	0	0	4	0	2	0	.265	.324

1 Rocky Bridges 29 R 0-1, Dutch Dotterer 25 R 1-12, Curt Flood 19 R 1-3, Bobby Durnbaugh 24 R 0-1, Don Pavletich (MS) 18 R 0-1, Dick Murphy (MS) 25

NAME	T	AGE	W	L	PCT	SV	G	GS	CG	IP	H	BB	SO	ShO	ERA
TOTALS		30	80	74	.519	29	154	154	40	1396	1486	429	707	5	4.62
Brooks Lawrence	R	32	16	13	.552	4	49	32	12	250	234	76	121	1	3.53
Hal Jeffcoat	R	32	12	13	.480	0	37	31	10	207	236	46	63	1	4.52
Tom Acker	R	27	10	5	.667	4	49	6	1	109	122	41	67	0	4.95
Joe Nuxhall	L	28	10	10	.500	1	39	28	6	174	192	53	99	2	4.76
Johnny Klippstein	R	29	8	11	.421	3	46	18	3	146	146	68	99	1	5.05
Hersh Freeman	R	29	7	2	.778	8	52	0	0	84	90	14	36	0	4.50
Don Gross	L	26	7	9	.438	1	43	16	5	148	152	33	73	0	4.32
Art Fowler	R	34	3	0	1.000	0	33	7	1	88	111	24	45	0	6.44
Raul Sanchez	R	26	3	2	.600	5	38	0	0	62	61	25	37	0	4.79
1 Warren Hacker	R	32	3	2	.600	0	15	6	0	43	50	13	18	0	5.23
Vicente Amor	R	24	1	2	.333	0	9	4	1	27	39	10	9	0	6.00
Bud Podbielan	R	33	0	1	.000	0	5	3	1	16	18	4	13	0	6.19
Jay Hook	R	20	0	1	.000	0	3	2	0	10	6	8	6	0	4.50
Charlie Rabe	L	25	0	1	.000	0	2	1	0	8	5	0	6	0	2.25
Bill Kennedy	L	36	0	2	.000	3	8	0	0	13	16	5	8	0	6.23
Claude Osteen	L	17	0	0	.000	0	3	0	0	4	4	3	3	0	2.25
Dave Skaugstad	L	17	0	0	.000	0	2	0	0	6	4	6	4	0	1.50

PHILADELPHIA 5th 77-77 .500 18 — MAYO SMITH

NAME	G by POS	B	AGE	G	AB	R	H	2B	3B	HR	RBI	BB	SO	SB	BA	SA
TOTALS			28	156	5241	623	1311	213	44	117	569	534	758	57	.250	.375
Ed Bouchee	1B154	L	24	154	574	78	168	35	8	17	76	84	91	1	.293	.470
Granny Hamner	2B125, SS5, P1	R	30	133	502	59	114	19	5	10	62	34	42	3	.227	.345
Chico Fernandez	SS149	R	25	149	500	42	131	14	4	5	51	31	64	18	.262	.336
Willie Jones	3B126	R	31	133	440	58	96	19	2	9	47	61	41	1	.218	.332
Rip Repulski	OF130	R	29	134	516	65	134	23	4	20	68	19	74	7	.260	.436
Richie Ashburn	OF156	L	30	156	626	93	186	26	8	0	33	94	44	13	.297	.364
Harry Anderson	OF109	L	25	118	400	53	107	15	4	17	61	36	61	2	.268	.453
Stan Lopata	C108	R	31	116	388	50	92	18	2	18	67	56	81	2	.237	.433
Bob Bowman	OF81	R	26	99	237	31	63	8	2	6	23	27	50	0	.266	.392
Solly Hemus	2B24	L	34	70	108	8	20	6	1	0	5	20	8	1	.185	.259
Joe Lonnett	C65	R	30	67	160	12	275	5	0	5	15	22	39	0	.169	.294
Ted Kazanski	3B36, 2B22, SS3	R	23	62	185	15	49	7	1	3	11	17	20	1	.265	.362
2 Chuck Harmon	OF25, 3B5, 1B2	R	31	57	86	14	22	2	1	0	5	1	4	7	.256	.302
Harvey Haddix	P27	L	31	41	68	6	21	3	1	0	6	3	12	1	.309	.382
Marv Blaylock	1B12, OF1	L	27	37	26	5	4	0	0	2	4	3	8	0	.154	.385
2 Ron Northey		L	37	33	26	1	7	0	0	1	5	6	6	0	.269	.385
Roy Smalley	SS20	R	31	28	31	5	5	0	1	1	1	1	9	0	.161	.323
Andy Seminick	C8	R	36	8	11	0	1	0	0	0	0	1	3	0	.091	.091

John Kennedy 22 R 0-2, Glen Garbous 26 L 1-2, 1 Bobby Morgan 31 R 0-0, Don Landrum 21 L 1-7, Frankie Baumholtz 38 L 0-2

NAME	T	AGE	W	L	PCT	SV	G	GS	CG	IP	H	BB	SO	ShO	ERA
TOTALS		28	77	77	.500	23	156	156	54	1401	1363	412	858	9	3.80
Jack Sanford	R	28	19	8	.704	0	33	33	15	237	194	94	188	3	3.08
Curt Simmons	L	28	12	11	.522	0	32	29	9	212	214	50	92	2	3.44
Dick Farrell	R	23	10	2	.833	10	52	0	0	83	74	36	54	0	2.39
Harvey Haddix	L	31	10	13	.435	0	27	25	8	171	176	39	136	1	4.05
Robin Roberts	R	30	10	22	.313	2	39	32	14	250	246	43	128	2	4.07
Jim Hearn	R	36	5	1	.833	3	36	4	1	74	79	18	46	0	3.65
2 Warren Hacker	R	32	4	4	.500	0	20	10	1	74	72	18	33	0	4.50
Don Cardwell	R	21	4	8	.333	1	30	19	5	128	122	42	92	1	4.92
Bob Miller	R	31	2	5	.286	6	32	1	0	60	61	17	12	0	2.70
Seth Morehead	L	22	1	1	.500	1	34	1	1	59	57	20	36	0	3.66
Jack Meyer	R	25	0	2	.000	0	19	2	0	38	44	28	34	0	5.68
Tom Qualters	L	22	0	0	.000	0	6	0	0	7	12	4	6	0	7.71
Saul Rogovin	R	34	0	0	.000	0	4	0	0	8	11	3	0	0	9.00
Granny Hamner	R	30	0	0	.000	0	1	0	0	1	1	0	1	0	0.00

Jim Owens (MS) 23

NEW YORK 6th 69-85 .448 26 — BILL RIGNEY

NAME	G by POS	B	AGE	G	AB	R	H	2B	3B	HR	RBI	BB	SO	SB	BA	SA
TOTALS			30	154	5346	643	1349	171	54	157	612	447	669	**64**	.252	.393
Whitey Lockman	1B102, OF27	L	30	133	456	51	113	9	4	7	30	39	19	5	.248	.331
2 Danny O'Connell	2B68, 3B30	R	30	95	364	57	97	18	3	7	28	33	30	8	.266	.390
Daryl Spencer	SS110, 2B36, 3B6	R	27	148	534	65	133	31	2	11	50	50	50	3	.249	.376
Ray Jablonski	3B70, 1B6, OF1	R	30	107	305	37	88	15	1	9	57	31	47	0	.289	.433
Don Mueller	OF115	L	30	135	450	45	116	7	1	6	37	13	16	2	.258	.318
Willie Mays	OF150	R	26	152	585	112	195	26	**20**	35	97	76	62	**38**	.333	**.626**
Hank Sauer	OF98	R	38	127	378	46	98	14	1	26	76	49	59	1	.259	.508
Valmy Thomas	C88	R	28	88	241	30	60	10	3	6	31	16	29	0	.249	.390
Ozzie Virgil	3B62, OF24, SS1	R	24	96	226	26	53	0	2	4	24	14	27	2	.235	.305
Dusty Rhodes	OF44	L	30	92	190	20	39	5	1	4	19	18	34	0	.205	.305
Gail Harris	1B61	L	25	90	225	28	54	7	3	9	31	16	28	1	.240	.418
2 Bobby Thomson	OF71, 3B1	R	33	81	215	24	52	7	4	8	38	19	39	1	.242	.423
Ray Katt	C68	R	30	72	165	11	38	3	1	2	17	15	35	1	.230	.297
Wes Westrum	C63	R	34	63	91	4	15	1	0	1	2	10	24	0	.165	.209
1 Red Schoendienst	2B57	B	34	57	254	35	**78***	8	4	9	33	10	8	2	.307	.476
Ed Bressoud	SS33, 3B12	R	25	49	127	11	34	2	2	5	10	4	19	0	.268	.433
Andre Rodgers	SS20, 3B8	R	22	32	86	8	21	2	1	3	9	9	21	0	.244	.395
Foster Castleman	3B7, SS1, 2B1	R	26	18	37	7	6	2	0	1	1	2	8	0	.162	.297

1 Bill Taylor 27 L 0-9, Bobby Hofman 31 R 0-2, Jackie Brandt (MS) 23, Bill White (MS) 23, Paul Giel (MS) 24

NAME	T	AGE	W	L	PCT	SV	G	GS	CG	IP	H	BB	SO	ShO	ERA
		27	69	85	.448	20	154	154	35	1399	1436	471	701	9	4.01
Ruben Gomez	R	29	15	13	.536	0	38	36	16	238	233	71	92	1	3.78
Johnny Antonelli	L	27	12	18	.400	0	40	30	8	212	228	67	114	3	3.78
Curt Barclay	R	25	9	9	.500	0	37	28	5	183	196	48	67	2	3.44
Al Worthington	R	28	8	11	.421	4	55	12	1	158	140	56	90	1	4.22
Stu Miller	R	29	7	9	.438	1	38	13	0	124	110	45	60	0	3.63
Marv Grissom	R	39	4	4	.500	14	55	0	0	83	74	23	51	0	2.60
2 Ray Crone	R	25	4	8	.333	1	25	17	2	121	131	40	56	0	4.31
Mike McCormick	L	18	3	1	.750	0	24	5	1	75	79	32	50	0	4.08
Ray Monzant	R	24	3	2	.600	0	24	2	0	50	55	16	37	0	3.96
2 Jim Davis	L	32	1	0	1.000	0	10	0	0	11	13	5	6	0	6.55
Jim Constable	L	24	1	1	.500	0	16	0	0	28	27	7	13	0	2.89
Joe Margoneri	L	27	1	1	.500	0	13	2	1	34	44	21	18	0	5.29
Pete Burnside	L	26	1	4	.200	0	10	9	1	31	47	13	18	1	8.71
Gordon Jones	R	27	0	1	.000	0	10	0	0	12	16	3	5	0	6.00
Max Surkont	R	35	0	1	.000	0	5	0	0	6	9	2	8	0	10.50
Steve Ridzik	R	28	0	2	.000	0	15	0	0	27	19	19	13	0	4.67
Windy McCall	L	31	0	0	.000	0	5	0	0	3	8	2	2	0	15.00
2 Sandy Consuegra	R	36	0	0	.000	0	4	0	0	4	7	1	1	0	2.25

***Schoendienst, also with St. Louis, league leader in H with 200**

CHICAGO 7th (Tie) 62-92 .403 33 — BOB SCHEFFING

NAME	G by POS	B	AGE	G	AB	R	H	2B	3B	HR	RBI	BB	SO	SB	BA	SA
TOTALS			28	156	5369	628	1312	223	31	147	590	461	**989**	28	.244	.380
2 Dale Long	1B104	L	31	123	397	55	121	19	0	21	62	52	63	1	.305	.511
2 Bobby Morgan	2B116, 3B12	R	31	125	425	43	88	20	2	5	27	52	87	5	.207	.299
Ernie Banks	SS100, 3B58	R	26	156	594	113	169	34	6	43	102	70	85	8	.285	.579
Bobby Adams	3B47, 2B1	R	35	60	187	21	47	10	2	1	10	17	28	0	.251	.342
Walt Moryn	OF147	L	31	149	568	76	164	33	0	19	88	50	90	0	.289	.447
2 Chuck Tanner	OF82	L	27	95	318	42	91	16	2	7	42	23	20	0	.286	.415
2 Lee Walls	OF94, 3B1	R	24	117	366	42	88	10	5	6	33	27	67	5	.240	.344
Cal Neeman	C118	R	28	122	415	37	107	17	1	10	39	22	87	0	.258	.376
Bob Speake	OF60, 1B39	L	26	129	418	65	97	14	5	16	50	38	68	5	.232	.404
Jim Bolger	OF63, 3B3	R	25	112	273	28	75	4	1	5	29	10	36	0	.275	.352
Jerry Kindall	2B28, 3B19, SS9	R	22	72	181	18	29	3	0	6	12	8	48	1	.160	.276
Bob Will	OF30	L	25	70	112	13	25	3	0	1	10	5	21	1	.223	.277
Jack Littrell	SS47, 2B6, 3B5	R	28	61	153	8	29	4	2	1	13	9	43	0	.190	.261
Jim Fanning	C35	R	29	47	89	3	16	2	0	0	4	4	17	0	.180	.202
Casey Wise	2B31, SS5	B	24	43	106	12	19	3	1	0	7	11	14	0	.179	.226
Charlie Silvera	C26	R	32	26	53	1	11	3	0	0	2	4	5	0	.208	.264
1 Bobby Del Greco	OF16	R	24	20	40	2	8	2	0	0	3	10	17	1	.200	.250
Frank Ernaga	OF10	R	26	20	35	9	11	3	2	2	7	9	14	0	.314	.686
Ed Winceniak	SS5, 3B4, 2B3	R	28	17	50	5	12	3	0	1	8	2	9	0	.240	.360
1 Gene Baker	3B12	R	32	12	44	4	11	3	1	1	10	6	3	0	.250	.432
1 Dee Fondy	1B11	L	32	11	51	3	16	3	1	0	2	0	9	1	.314	.412

Eddie Haas 22 L 5-24, Johnny Goryl 23 R 8-38, Bob Lennon 28 L 3-21, Gordon Massa 21 L 7-15, Ed Mickelson 30 R 0-12, Jim Woods 17 R 0-0

NAME	T	AGE	W	L	PCT	SV	G	GS	CG	IP	H	BB	SO	ShO	ERA
		27	62	**92**	.403	26	156	156	30	1403	1397	**601**	859	5	4.13
Dick Drott	R	21	15	11	.577	0	38	32	7	229	200	**129**	170	3	3.58
Moe Drabowsky	R	21	13	15	.464	0	36	33	12	240	214	94	170	2	3.53
2 Don Elston	R	28	6	7	.462	8	39	14	2	144	139	55	102	0	3.56
Dave Hillman	R	29	6	11	.353	1	32	14	1	103	115	37	53	0	4.37
Bob Rush	R	31	6	16	.273	0	31	29	5	205	211	66	103	0	4.39
Jim Brosnan	R	27	5	5	.500	0	41	5	1	99	79	46	73	0	3.36
Turk Lown	R	33	5	7	.417	12	**67**	0	0	93	74	51	51	0	3.77
Dick Littlefield	L	31	2	3	.400	4	48	2	0	66	76	37	51	0	5.32
Don Kaiser	R	22	2	6	.250	0	20	13	1	72	91	28	23	0	5.00
1 Jackie Collum	L	30	1	1	.500	1	9	0	0	11	8	9	7	0	6.55
Tom Poholsky	R	27	1	7	.125	0	28	11	1	84	117	22	28	0	4.93
Bob Anderson	R	21	0	1	.000	0	8	0	0	16	20	8	7	0	7.88
Elmer Singleton (EJ)	R	39	0	1	.000	0	5	2	0	13	20	2	6	0	6.92
Johnny Briggs	R	23	0	1	.000	0	3	0	0	4	7	3	1	0	13.50
1 Vito Valentinetti	R	28	0	0	.000	0	9	0	0	12	12	7	8	0	2.25
Ed Mayer	L	25	0	0	.000	0	3	1	0	8	8	2	3	0	5.63
Glen Hobbie	R	21	0	0	.000	0	2	0	0	4	6	5	3	0	11.25

PITTSBURGH 7th (Tie) 62-92 .403 33 — BOBBY BRAGAN 36-67 .350 DANNY MURTAUGH 26-25 .510

NAME	G by POS	B	AGE	G	AB	R	H	2B	3B	HR	RBI	BB	SO	SB	BA	SA
TOTALS			26	155	5402	586	1447	231	60	92	551	374	733	46	.268	.384
2 Dee Fondy	1B73	L	32	95	323	42	101	13	2	2	35	25	59	11	.313	.384
Bill Mazeroski	2B144	R	20	148	526	59	149	27	7	8	54	27	49	3	.283	.407
Dick Groat	SS123, 3B2	R	26	125	501	58	158	30	5	7	54	27	28	0	.315	.437
Gene Freese	3B74, 2B10, OF10	R	23	114	346	44	98	18	2	6	31	17	42	9	.283	.399
Roberto Clemente	OF109	R	22	111	451	42	114	17	7	4	30	23	45	0	.253	.348
Bill Virdon	OF141	L	26	144	561	59	141	28	11	8	50	33	69	3	.251	.383
Bob Skinner	OF93, 1B9, 3B1	L	25	126	387	58	118	12	6	13	45	38	50	10	.305	.468
Hank Foiles	C109	R	28	109	281	32	76	10	4	9	36	37	53	1	.270	.431
Frank Thomas	1B71, OF59, 3B31	R	28	151	594	72	172	30	1	23	89	44	66	3	.290	.460
2 Gene Baker	3B60, SS28, 2B13	R	32	111	365	36	97	19	4	2	36	29	29	3	.266	.356
Paul Smith	OF33, 1B1	L	26	81	150	12	38	4	0	3	11	12	17	0	.253	.340
Dick Rand	C57	R	26	60	105	7	23	2	1	1	9	11	24	0	.219	.286
Roman Mejias (VJ)	OF42	R	26	58	142	12	39	7	4	2	15	6	13	2	.275	.423
Jim Pendleton	OF9, 3B2, SS1	R	33	46	59	9	18	1	1	0	9	9	14	0	.305	.356
Johnny O'Brien	P16, SS8, 2B2	R	26	34	35	7	11	2	1	0	1	1	4	0	.314	.429
Hardy Peterson	C30	R	27	30	73	10	22	2	1	2	11	9	10	0	.301	.438
Johnny Powers	OF8, 2B1	L	27	20	35	7	10	3	0	2	8	5	9	0	.286	.543
Danny Kravitz	C15	L	26	19	41	2	6	1	0	0	4	2	10	0	.146	.171

Buddy Pritchard 21 R 1-11, 1 Lee Walls 24 R 4-22, 1 Dale Long 31 L 4-22, Ken Hamlin 22 R 0-1

NAME	T	AGE	W	L	PCT	SV	G	GS	CG	IP	H	BB	SO	ShO	ERA
		27	62	**92**	.403	15	155	155	47	1395	1463	421	663	9	3.88
Bob Friend	R	26	14	18	.438	0	40	**38**	17	**277**	**273**	68	143	3	3.38
Bob Purkey	R	27	11	14	.440	2	48	21	6	180	194	38	51	1	3.85
Vern Law	R	27	10	8	.556	1	31	25	9	173	172	32	55	3	2.86
Ron Kline	R	25	9	16	.360	0	40	31	11	205	214	61	88	2	4.04
Roy Face	R	29	4	6	.400	10	59	1	0	94	97	24	53	0	3.06
Red Swanson	R	20	3	3	.500	0	32	8	1	73	68	31	29	0	3.70
Whammy Douglas	R	22	3	3	.500	0	11	8	0	47	48	30	28	0	3.26
Luis Arroyo	L	30	3	11	.214	1	54	10	0	131	151	31	101	0	4.67
Nellie King	R	29	2	1	.667	1	36	0	0	52	69	16	23	0	4.50
2 Bob Smith (EJ)	L	26	2	4	.333	0	20	4	2	55	48	25	35	0	3.11
Eddie O'Brien	R	26	1	0	1.000	0	3	1	1	12	11	3	10	0	2.25
Laurin Pepper	R	26	0	1	.000	0	5	1	0	9	11	5	4	0	8.00
Bennie Daniels	R	25	0	1	.000	0	1	1	0	7	5	3	2	0	1.29
George Witt	R	23	0	1	.000	0	1	1	0	1	4	5	1	0	54.00
Joe Trimble	R	26	0	2	.000	0	5	4	0	20	23	13	9	0	8.10
Johnny O'Brien	R	26	0	3	.000	0	16	1	0	40	46	24	19	0	6.08
Dick Hall (AJ)	R	26	0	0	.000	0	8	0	0	10	17	5	7	0	10.80
Chuck Churn	R	27	0	0	.000	0	5	0	0	8	9	4	4	0	4.50
1 Bob Kuzava	L	34	0	0	.000	0	4	0	0	2	3	3	1	0	9.00

WORLD SERIES – MILWAUKEE (NL) 4 NEW YORK (AL) 3

LINE SCORES

TEAM	1	2	3	4	5	6	7	8	9	10	11	12	R	H	E
Game 1 October 2 at New York															
MIL (NL)	0	0	0	0	0	0	1	0	0				1	5	0
NY (AL)	0	0	0	0	1	2	0	0	X				3	9	1
Spahn, Johnson (6), McMahon (7) — **Ford**															
Game 2 October 3 at New York															
MIL	0	1	1	2	0	0	0	0	0				4	8	0
NY	0	1	1	0	0	0	0	0	0				2	7	2
Burdette — **Shantz**, Ditmar (4), Grim (8)															
Game 3 October 5 at Milwaukee															
NY	3	0	2	2	0	0	5	0	0				12	9	0
MIL	0	1	0	0	2	0	0	0	0				3	8	1
Turley, **Larsen** (2) — **Buhl**, Pizarro (1), Conley (3), Johnson (5), Trowbridge (7), McMahon (8)															
Game 4 October 6 at Milwaukee															
NY	1	0	0	0	0	0	0	0	3	1			5	11	0
MIL	0	0	0	4	0	0	0	0	0	3			7	7	0
Sturdivant, Shantz (5), Kucks (8), Byrne (8), **Grim** (10) — **Spahn**															
Game 5 October 7 at Milwaukee															
NY	0	0	0	0	0	0	0	0	0				0	7	0
MIL	0	0	0	0	0	1	0	0	X				1	6	1
Ford, Turley (8) — **Burdette**															
Game 6 October 9 at New York															
MIL	0	0	0	0	1	0	1	0	0				2	4	0
NY	0	0	2	0	0	0	1	0	X				3	7	0
Buhl, **Johnson** (3), McMahon (8) — **Turley**															
Game 7 October 10 at New York															
MIL	0	0	4	0	0	0	0	1	0				5	9	1
NY	0	0	0	0	0	0	0	0	0				0	7	3
Burdette — **Larsen**, Shantz (3), Ditmar (4), Sturdivant (6), Byrne (8)															

COMPOSITE BATTING

NAME	POS	G	AB	R	H	2B	3B	HR	RBI	BA
Milwaukee (NL)										
Totals		7	225	23	47	6	1	8	22	.209
Aaron	OF	7	28	**5**	**11**	0	1	**3**	**7**	**.393**
Logan	SS	7	27	**5**	5	1	0	1	2	.185
Covington	OF	7	24	1	5	1	0	0	1	.208
Mathews	3B	7	22	4	5	**3**	0	1	4	.227
Crandall	C	6	19	1	4	0	0	1	1	.211
Schoendienst	2B	5	18	0	5	1	0	0	2	.278
Adcock	1B	5	15	1	3	0	0	0	2	.200
Pafko	OF	6	14	1	3	0	0	0	0	.214
Hazle	OF	4	13	2	2	0	0	0	0	.154
Torre	1B	7	10	2	3	0	0	2	3	.300
Mantilla	2B	4	10	1	0	0	0	0	0	.000
Burdette	P	3	8	0	0	0	0	0	0	.000
Rice	C	2	6	0	1	0	0	0	0	.167
Spahn	P	2	4	0	0	0	0	0	0	.000
Jones	PH	3	2	0	0	0	0	0	0	.000
Sawatski	PH	2	2	0	0	0	0	0	0	.000
Johnson	P	3	1	0	0	0	0	0	0	.000
Buhl	P	2	1	0	0	0	0	0	0	.000
Pizarro	P	1	1	0	0	0	0	0	0	.000

Trowbridge P 0-0, McMahon P 0-0, Conley P 0-0, DeMerit PR 0-0

NAME	POS	G	AB	R	H	2B	3B	HR	RBI	BA
New York (AL)										
Totals		7	230	25	57	7	1	7	25	.248
Bauer	OF	7	**31**	3	8	2	1	2	6	.258
Kubek	3B-OF	7	28	4	8	0	0	2	4	.286
Berra	C	7	25	5	8	1	0	1	2	.320
McDougald	SS	7	24	3	6	0	0	0	2	.250
Coleman	2B	7	22	2	8	2	0	0	2	.364
Mantle	OF	6	19	3	5	0	0	1	2	.263
Lumpe	3B	6	14	0	4	0	0	0	2	.286
Slaughter	OF	5	12	2	3	1	0	0	0	.250
Simpson	1B	5	12	0	1	0	0	0	1	.083
Howard	1B	6	11	2	3	0	0	1	3	.273
Carey	3B	2	7	0	2	1	0	0	1	.286
Collins	1B	6	5	0	0	0	0	0	0	.000
Ford	P	2	5	0	0	0	0	0	0	.000
Skowron	1B	2	4	0	0	0	0	0	0	.000
Turley	P	3	4	0	0	0	0	0	0	.000
Byrne	P	2	2	0	1	0	0	0	0	.500
Larsen	P	2	2	1	0	0	0	0	0	.000
Richardson	2B	2	0	0	0	0	0	0	0	.000
Sturdivant	P	2	1	0	0	0	0	0	0	.000

Shantz P 0-1, Ditmar P 0-1, Grim P 0-0, Kucks P 0-0

COMPOSITE PITCHING

NAME	G	IP	H	BB	SO	W	L	SV	ERA
Milwaukee (NL)									
Totals	7	62	57	22	34	4	3	0	3.48
Burdette	**3**	**27**	**21**	4	**13**	**3**	0	0	**0.67**
Spahn	2	15.1	18	2	2	1	1	0	4.70
Johnson	**3**	7	2	1	8	0	1	0	1.29
McMahon	**3**	5	3	3	5	0	0	0	0.00
Buhl	2	3.1	6	**6**	4	0	1	0	10.80
Pizarro	1	1.2	3	2	1	0	0	0	10.80
Conley	1	1.2	2	1	0	0	0	0	10.80
Trowbridge	1	1	2	3	1	0	0	0	45.00
New York (AL)									
Totals	7	62.1	47	22	40	3	4	0	2.89
Ford	2	16	11	5	7	1	1	0	1.13
Turley	**3**	11.2	7	**6**	12	1	0	0	2.31
Larsen	2	9.2	8	5	6	1	1	0	3.72
Shantz	**3**	6.2	8	2	7	0	1	0	4.05
Ditmar	2	6	2	0	2	0	0	0	0.00
Sturdivant	2	6	6	1	2	0	0	0	6.00
Byrne	2	3.1	1	2	1	0	0	0	5.40
Grim	2	2.1	3	0	2	0	1	0	7.71
Kucks	1	.2	1	1	1	0	0	0	0.00

1958 O'Malley's Rambling Meadows

Ebbets Field felt the wrecker's steel ball, the Polo Grounds played only to yesterday's ghosts, and the West coast had its first taste of major league baseball. Walter O'Malley's Dodgers set up shop in the Los Angeles Memorial Coliseum, which proved to be as colorful a home as Ebbets Field had been. The huge football stadium had a monstrously vast right field, ranging to 440 feet in the power lane, and a short 251-foot left field target, which was crowned by a 40-foot high screen extending 140 feet into left center, a concoction designed to prevent a feared flood of cheap home runs.

Opening day on Friday, April 18, saw the largest curtain-raising crowd in history; 78,672 turned out to see the Giants knock off the Dodgers in the first renewal of the newly transplanted geographical rivalry. The opening three-game series between the two teams additionally set an attendance record for a three-game series, 167,204. The 94,000 capacity coliseum counted 1,845,556 clicks of the turnstile during the season, surpassing the 1947 Brooklyn record of 1,807,526.

The Giants' new home was San Francisco's Seals Stadium, which seated only 22,900. Nevertheless, 1,272,625 fans viewed the team, only 300,000 short of the Giants' 1947 record attendance, and almost double the 1957 Polo Grounds' count.

Both teams planned new stadiums. A municipally-built and owned Candlestick Park received quick approval in San Francisco, and mid-1959 was a hoped-for time of occupancy. The Dodgers, of course, showed much more flair. An agreement was reached with the Los Angeles city fathers, in which the valuable Chavez Ravine land tract would be turned over to the Dodgers where they were to build themselves a $12 million stadium. Opponents to the project put the agreement onto a highly-contested referendum, which was approved and then brought into court, where it remained until the California Supreme Court passed the final decision approving the agreement in January, 1959.

On the field, the Dodgers and Giants passed each other in opposite directions. The Dodgers were expected to continue as strong contenders but got off to a slow start, spent most of the year in the basement, and limped home in seventh place. The Dodgers had lost their field leader during the winter, when catcher Roy Campanella was tragically paralyzed in an early-morning car accident in New York. Pee Wee Reese and Carl Erskine became part-time players and were obviously playing out the string. Don Newcombe started slowly and was traded to Cincinnati in June with an 0-6 record. Duke Snider had his bat taken out of his hands by the vast right field playing area in Los Angeles. Without the cozy Ebbets Field right field screen, and plagued by a bad knee, Snider fell from 40 homers in 1957 to a mere 15. Charging up from a sixth-place finish in New York, the Giants flashed a hand of six rookie aces, the most promising being Orlando Cepeda to finish a strong third.

Yet, while the Dodgers and Giants were moving, the National League pennant wasn't; it stayed put in Milwaukee. Overcoming injuries to Bob Buhl and Billy Bruton, and Red Schoendienst being disabled by tuberculosis, the Braves again won by eight games, spearheaded by Hank Aaron and Ed Mathews at bat, and Warren Spahn and Lew Burdette on the hill. A trio of young pitchers, Carl Willey, Joey Jay, and Juan Pizarro, took up the slack left by the injury to Buhl and the off season of Gene Conley. The Pirates finished in the first division for the first time since 1948, by closing fast and winding up in second place. Bob Friend won 22 games for the Bucs, and several young hitters—such as Roberto Clemente, Dick Groat, and Bill Mazeroski—matured into stardom. The second division boasted stars in the Cubs' Ernie Banks, the homer and RBI champ and MVP, and Richie Ashburn of the Phils, the batting champ.

The Yankees, as usual, took the American League pennant, this time by ten games over Chicago. Mickey Mantle and Bob Turley were the stars of this season's production, though Boston again boasted of the batting champ in Ted Williams, and the MVP—Jackie Jensen.

In the Series, the Yanks dropped three of four to the Braves, then became the first team since 1925 to win the championship after being down 3 games to 1, to give Stengel his seventh world's title in nine years—making it, perhaps, the sweetest victory the Old Professor ever enjoyed.

1958 AMERICAN LEAGUE

NAME	G by POS	B	AGE	G	AB	R	H	2B	3B	HR	RBI	BB	SO	SB	BA	SA
NEW YORK 1st 92-62 .597		CASEY STENGEL														
TOTALS			27	155	**5294**	**759**	**1418**	212	39	**164**	**715**	537	**822**	48	**.268**	**.416**
Bill Skowron	1B118, 3B2	R	27	126	465	61	127	22	3	14	73	28	69	1	.273	.424
Gil McDougald	2B115, SS19	R	30	138	503	69	126	19	1	14	65	59	75	6	.250	.376
Tony Kubek	SS134, OF3, 2B1, 1B1	L	21	138	559	66	148	21	1	2	48	25	57	5	.265	.317
Andy Carey	3B99	R	26	102	315	39	90	19	4	12	45	34	43	1	.286	.486
Hank Baver	OF123	R	35	128	452	62	121	22	6	12	50	32	56	3	.268	.423
Mickey Mantle	OF150	B	26	150	519	**127**	158	21	1	**42**	97	**129**	**120**	18	.304	.592
Norm Siebern	OF133	L	24	134	460	79	138	19	5	14	55	66	87	5	.300	.454
Yogi Berra	C88, OF21, 1B2	L	33	122	433	60	115	17	3	22	90	35	35	3	.266	.471
Elston Howard	C67, OF24, 1B5	R	29	103	376	45	118	19	5	11	66	22	60	1	.314	.479
Jerry Lumpe	3B65, SS5	L	25	81	232	34	59	8	4	3	32	23	21	1	.254	.362
Enos Slaughter	OF35	L	42	77	138	21	42	4	1	4	19	21	16	2	.304	.435
Bobby Richardson	2B51, 3B13, SS2	R	22	73	182	18	45	6	2	0	14	8	5	1	.247	.302
Marv Throneberry	1B40, OF5	L	24	60	150	30	34	5	2	7	19	19	40	1	.227	.427
Don Larsen (EJ)	P19	R	28	28	49	9	15	1	0	4	13	5	9	0	.306	.571
1 Harry Simpson	OF15	L	32	24	51	1	11	2	1	0	6	6	12	0	.216	.294
Bobby Del Greco	OF12	R	25	12	5	1	1	0	0	0	0	1	1	0	.200	.200

Darrell Johnson 29 R 4-16, Fritzie Brickell 23 R 0-0, Tommy Carroll (MS) 21

NAME	T	AGE	W	L	PCT	SV	G	GS	CG	IP	H	BB	SO	ShO	ERA
		29	**92**	62	**.597**	**33**	155	155	53	1379	1201	557	796	**21**	**3.22**
Bob Turley	R	27	**21**	7	**.750**	1	33	31	**19**	245	178	**128**	168	6	2.98
Whitey Ford	L	29	14	7	.667	1	30	29	15	219	174	62	145	**7**	**2.01**
Don Larsen (EJ)	R	28	9	6	.600	0	19	19	5	114	100	52	55	3	3.08
Art Ditmar	R	29	9	8	.529	4	38	13	4	140	124	38	52	0	3.41
Johnny Kucks	R	24	8	8	.500	4	34	15	4	126	132	39	46	1	3.93
2 Duke Maas	R	29	7	3	.700	0	22	13	2	101	93	36	50	1	3.83
Bobby Shantz	L	32	7	6	.538	0	33	13	3	126	127	35	80	0	3.36
Ryne Duren	R	29	6	4	.600	**20**	44	1	0	76	40	43	87	0	2.01
Zack Monroe	R	26	4	2	.667	1	21	6	1	58	57	27	18	0	3.26
Tom Sturdivant (SA)	R	28	3	6	.333	0	15	10	0	71	77	38	41	0	4.18
2 Virgil Trucks	R	39	2	1	.667	1	25	0	0	40	40	24	26	0	4.50
1 Sal Maglie	R	41	1	1	.500	0	7	3	0	23	27	9	7	0	4.70
2 Murry Dickson	R	41	1	2	.333	1	6	2	0	20	18	12	9	0	5.85
1 Bob Grim	R	28	0	1	.000	0	11	0	0	16	12	10	11	0	5.63
Johnny James	R	24	0	0	.000	0	1	0	0	3	2	4	1	0	0.00

NAME	G by POS	B	AGE	G	AB	R	H	2B	3B	HR	RBI	BB	SO	SB	BA	SA
CHICAGO 2nd 82-72 .532 10		AL LOPEZ														
TOTALS			30	155	5249	634	1348	191	42	101	600	518	669	**101**	.257	.367
2 Ray Boone	1B63	R	34	77	246	25	60	12	1	7	41	18	33	1	.244	.386
Nellie Fox	2B155	L	30	155	623	82	**187**	21	6	0	49	47	11	5	.300	.353
Luis Aparicio	SS145	R	24	145	557	76	148	20	9	2	40	35	38	**29**	.266	.345
Billy Goodman	3B111, 1B3, 2B1, SS1	L	32	116	425	41	127	15	5	0	40	37	21	1	.299	.358
Jim Rivera	OF99	L	35	116	276	37	62	8	4	9	35	24	49	21	.225	.380
Jim Landis	OF142	R	24	142	523	72	145	23	7	15	64	52	80	19	.277	.434
Al Smith	OF138, 3B1	R	30	139	480	61	121	23	5	12	58	48	77	3	.252	.396
Sherm Lollar	C116	R	33	127	421	53	115	16	0	20	84	57	37	2	.273	.454
Sammy Esposito	3B63, SS22, 2B2, OF1	R	26	98	81	16	20	3	0	0	3	12	6	1	.247	.284
Earl Torgeson	1B73	L	34	96	188	37	50	8	0	10	30	48	29	7	.266	.468
Bubba Phillips (BF)	3B47, OF37	R	28	84	260	26	71	10	0	5	30	15	14	3	.273	.369
Don Mueller	OF43	L	31	70	166	7	42	5	0	0	16	11	9	0	.253	.283
Earl Battey	C49	R	23	68	168	24	38	8	0	8	26	24	34	1	.226	.417
Ron Jackson	1B38	R	24	61	146	19	34	4	0	7	21	18	46	2	.233	.404
1 Tito Francona	OF35	L	24	41	128	10	33	3	2	1	10	14	24	2	.258	.336
1 Walt Dropo	1B16	R	35	28	52	3	10	1	0	2	8	5	11	0	.192	.327
Ted Beard	OF15	L	37	19	22	5	2	0	0	1	2	6	5	3	.091	.227
Johnny Callison	OF18	L	19	18	64	10	19	4	2	1	12	6	14	1	.297	.469
Norm Cash	OF4	L	23	13	8	2	2	0	0	0	0	0	1	0	.250	.250
Jim McAnany	OF3	R	21	5	13	0	0	0	0	0	0	0	5	0	.000	.000

Johnny Romano 23 R 2-7, Les Moss 33 R 0-1, Chuck Lindstrom 21 R 1-1

NAME	T	AGE	W	L	PCT	SV	G	GS	CG	IP	H	BB	SO	ShO	ERA
		31	82	72	.532	25	155	155	55	1390	1296	515	751	15	3.61
Billy Pierce	L	31	17	11	.607	2	35	32	19	245	204	66	144	3	2.68
Dick Donovan	R	30	15	14	.517	0	34	34	16	248	240	53	127	4	3.01
Early Wynn	R	38	14	16	.467	2	40	34	11	240	214	104	**179**	4	4.13
Ray Moore	R	32	9	7	.563	2	32	20	4	137	107	70	73	2	3.81
Jim Wilson	R	37	9	9	.500	1	28	23	4	156	156	63	70	1	4.10
2 Bob Shaw	R	25	4	2	.667	1	29	3	0	64	67	28	18	0	4.64
Gerry Staley	R	37	4	5	.444	8	50	0	0	85	81	24	27	0	3.18
Barry Latman	R	22	3	0	1.000	0	13	3	1	48	27	17	28	1	0.75
3 Turk Lown	R	34	3	3	.500	8	27	0	0	41	49	28	40	0	3.95
1 Bill Fischer	R	27	2	3	.400	0	17	3	0	36	43	13	16	0	6.75
Don Rudolph	L	26	1	0	1.000	1	7	0	0	7	4	5	2	0	2.57
Hal Trosky	R	21	1	0	1.000	0	2	0	0	3	5	2	1	0	6.00
Bob Keegan	R	37	0	2	.000	0	14	2	0	30	44	18	8	0	6.00
2 Tom Qualters	R	23	0	0	.000	0	26	0	0	43	45	20	14	0	4.19
Jim McDonald	R	31	0	0	.000	0	3	0	0	2	6	4	0	0	22.50
Dixie Howell	R	38	0	0	.000	0	1	0	0	2	0	0	0	0	0.00
Stover McIlwain	R	18	0	0	.000	0	1	1	0	4	4	0	4	0	2.25

NAME	G by POS	B	AGE	G	AB	R	H	2B	3B	HR	RBI	BB	SO	SB	BA	SA
BOSTON 3rd 79-75 .513 13		PINKY HIGGINS														
TOTALS			29	155	5218	697	1335	**229**	30	155	665	**638**	820	29	.256	.400
Dick Gernert	1B114	R	29	122	431	59	102	19	1	20	69	59	78	2	.237	.425
Pete Runnels	2B106, 1B42	L	30	147	568	103	183	32	5	8	59	87	49	1	.322	.438
Don Buddin	SS136	R	24	136	497	74	118	25	2	12	43	82	106	0	.237	.368
Frank Malzone	3B155	R	28	155	**627**	76	185	30	2	15	87	33	53	1	.295	.421
Jackie Jensen	OF153	R	31	154	548	83	157	31	0	35	**122**	99	65	9	.286	.535
Jimmy Piersall	OF125	R	28	130	417	55	99	13	5	8	48	42	43	12	.237	.350
Ted Williams	OF114	L	39	129	411	81	135	23	2	26	85	98	49	1	**.328**	.584
Sammy White	C102	R	29	102	328	25	85	15	3	6	35	21	37	1	.259	.378
Gene Stephens	OF110	L	25	134	270	38	59	10	1	9	25	22	46	1	.219	.363
Marty Keough	OF25, 1B2	L	23	68	118	21	26	3	3	1	9	7	29	1	.220	.322
Billy Klaus	SS27	L	29	61	88	5	14	4	0	1	7	5	16	0	.159	.239
2 Lou Berberet	C49	L	28	57	167	11	35	5	3	2	18	31	32	0	.210	.311
Ted Lepcio	2B40	R	27	50	136	10	27	3	0	6	14	12	47	0	.199	.353
Billy Consolo	2B13, SS11, 3B1	R	23	46	72	13	9	2	1	0	5	6	14	0	.125	.181
Bill Renna	OF11	R	33	39	56	5	15	5	0	4	18	6	14	0	.268	.571
Pete Daley	C27	R	28	27	56	10	18	2	1	2	8	7	11	0	.321	.500
1 Ken Aspromonte	2B6	R	26	6	16	0	2	0	0	0	0	3	1	0	.125	.125

Haywood Sullivan (JJ) 27

NAME	T	AGE	W	L	PCT	SV	G	GS	CG	IP	H	BB	SO	ShO	ERA
		28	79	75	.513	28	155	155	44	1380	1396	521	695	5	3.92
Ike Delock	R	28	14	8	.636	2	31	19	9	160	155	56	82	1	3.38
Frank Sullivan	R	28	13	9	.591	3	32	29	10	199	216	49	103	2	3.57
Tom Brewer	R	26	12	12	.500	0	33	32	10	227	227	93	124	1	3.73
Murray Wall	R	31	8	9	.471	10	52	1	0	114	109	33	53	0	3.63
Dave Sisler	R	26	8	9	.471	0	30	25	4	149	157	79	71	1	4.95
Leo Kiely	L	28	5	2	.714	12	47	0	0	81	77	18	26	0	3.00
Ted Bowsfield	L	22	4	2	.667	0	16	10	2	66	58	36	38	0	3.82
Riverboat Smith	R	30	4	3	.571	0	17	7	1	67	61	45	43	0	3.76
Mike Fornieles	R	26	4	6	.400	1	37	7	1	111	123	33	49	0	4.95
Bill Monbouquette	R	21	3	4	.429	0	10	8	3	54	52	20	30	0	3.33
Frank Baumann	L	25	2	2	.500	0	10	7	2	52	56	27	31	0	4.50
2 Bud Byerly	R	37	1	2	.333	0	18	0	0	30	31	7	16	0	1.80
Willard Nixon (JJ)	R	30	1	7	.125	0	10	8	2	43	48	11	15	0	6.07
Al Schroll	R	26	0	0	.000	0	5	0	0	10	6	4	7	0	4.50
Jerry Casale	R	24	0	0	.000	0	2	0	0	3	1	2	3	0	0.00
1 Bob Porterfield	R	34	0	0	.000	0	2	0	0	4	3	0	1	0	4.50
1 George Susce	R	26	0	0	.000	0	2	0	0	2	6	1	0	0	18.00
Duane Wilson	L	24	0	0	.000	0	2	2	0	6	10	7	3	0	6.00

CLEVELAND 4th 77-76 .503 14.5 — BOBBY BRAGAN 31-36 .463 JOE GORDON 46-40 .535

NAME	G by POS	B	AGE	G	AB	R	H	2B	3B	HR	RBI	BB	SO	SB	BA	SA
TOTALS			28	153	5201	694	1340	210	31	161	653	494	819	50	.258	.403
Mickey Vernon	1B96	L	40	119	355	49	104	22	3	8	55	44	56	0	.293	.439
Bobby Avila	2B82, 3B33	R	34	113	375	54	95	21	3	5	30	56	45	5	.253	.365
2 Billy Hunter	SS75, 3B2	R	30	76	190	21	37	10	2	0	9	17	37	4	.195	.268
Billy Harrell	3B46, SS45, 2B7, OF1	R	29	101	229	36	50	4	0	7	19	15	36	12	.218	.328
Rocky Colavito	OF129, 1B11, P1	R	24	143	489	80	148	26	3	41	113	84	89	0	.303	**.620**
Larry Doby	OF68	L	34	89	247	41	70	10	1	13	45	26	49	0	.283	.490
Minnie Minoso	OF147, 3B1	R	35	149	556	94	168	25	2	24	80	59	53	14	.302	.484
Russ Nixon	C101	L	23	113	376	42	113	17	4	9	46	13	38	0	.301	.439
Billy Moran	2B74, SS38	R	24	115	257	26	58	11	0	1	18	13	23	3	.226	.280
2 Vic Power	3B42, 1B40, 2B27, SS2, OF1	R	26	93	385	63	122	24	**6***	12	53	13	11	2	.317	.504
Gary Geiger	OF53, 3B2, P1	L	21	91	195	28	45	3	1	1	6	27	43	2	.231	.272
Dick Brown	C62	R	23	68	173	20	41	5	0	7	20	12	27	1	.237	.387
2 Woodie Held	OF43, SS14, 3B4	R	26	67	144	12	28	4	1	3	17	15	36	1	.194	.299
1 Roger Maris	OF48	L	23	51	182	26	41	5	1	9	27	17	33	4	.225	.412
1 Chico Carrasquel	SS32, 3B14	R	30	49	156	14	40	6	0	2	21	14	12	0	.256	.333
1 Preston Ward	3B24, 1B21	L	30	48	148	22	50	3	1	4	21	10	27	0	.338	.453
Jay Porter	C20, 1B4, 3B1	R	25	40	85	13	17	1	0	4	19	9	23	0	.200	.353
2 Randy Jackson	3B24	R	32	29	91	7	22	3	1	4	13	3	18	0	.242	.429
Carroll Hardy	OF17	R	25	27	49	10	10	3	0	1	6	6	14	1	.204	.327
Vic Wertz (BN)	1B8	L	33	25	43	5	12	1	0	3	12	5	7	0	.279	.512
Earl Averill	3B17	R	26	17	55	2	10	1	0	2	7	4	7	1	.182	.309

Hal Naragon 29 L 3-9, Larry Raines 28 R 0-9, Rod Graber 27 L 1-8, 1Fred Hatfield 33 L 1-8, George Strickland (VR)32

NAME	T	AGE	W	L	PCT	SV	G	GS	CG	IP	H	BB	SO	ShO	ERA
TOTALS		28	77	76	.503	20	153	153	51	1373	1283	**604**	766	2	3.73
Cal McLish	R	32	16	8	.667	1	39	30	13	226	214	70	97	0	2.99
Ray Narleski	R	29	13	10	.565	1	44	24	7	183	179	91	102	0	4.08
Gary Bell	R	21	12	10	.545	1	33	23	10	182	141	73	110	0	3.31
Mudcat Grant	R	22	10	11	.476	4	44	28	11	204	173	104	111	1	3.84
Don Mossi	L	29	7	8	.467	3	43	5	0	102	106	30	55	0	3.88
Hal Woodeshick	L	25	6	6	.500	0	14	9	3	72	71	25	27	0	3.63
Don Ferrarese	L	29	3	4	.429	1	28	10	2	95	91	46	62	0	3.69
2 Morrie Martin	L	35	2	0	1.000	1	14	0	0	19	20	8	5	0	2.37
1 Dick Tomanek	L	27	2	3	.400	0	18	6	2	58	61	28	42	0	5.62
Herb Score (IJ)	L	25	2	3	.400	3	12	5	2	41	29	34	48	1	3.95
1 Hoyt Wilhelm	R	34	2	7	.222	5	30	6	1	90	70	35	57	0	2.50
Mike Garcia (SA)	R	34	1	0	1.000	0	6	1	0	8	15	7	2	0	9.00
Dick Brodowski	R	25	1	0	1.000	0	5	0	0	10	3	6	12	0	0.00
Bob Lemon	R	37	0	1	.000	0	11	1	0	25	41	16	8	0	5.40
2 Jim Constable	L	25	0	1	.000	0	6	2	0	9	17	4	3	0	12.00
2 Bob Kelly	R	30	0	2	.000	0	13	3	0	28	29	13	12	0	5.14
Steve Ridzik	R	29	0	2	.000	0	6	0	0	9	9	5	6	0	2.00
Chuck Churn	R	28	0	0	.000	0	6	0	0	9	12	5	4	0	6.00
Rocky Colavito	R	24	0	0	.000	0	1	0	0	3	0	3	1	0	0.00
Gary Geiger	R	21	0	0	.000	0	1	0	0	2	2	1	2	0	9.00

*Power, also with Kansas City, league leader in 3B with 10

DETROIT 5th 77-77 .500 15 — JACK TIGHE 21-28 .429 BILL NORMAN 56-49 .533

NAME	G by POS	B	AGE	G	AB	R	H	2B	3B	HR	RBI	BB	SO	SB	BA	SA
TOTALS			27	154	5194	659	1384	**229**	41	109	612	463	678	48	.266	.389
Gail Harris	1B122	L	26	134	451	63	123	18	8	20	83	36	60	1	.273	.481
Frank Bolling	2B154	R	26	154	610	91	164	25	4	14	75	54	54	6	.269	.392
Billy Martin	SS88, 3B41	R	30	131	498	56	127	19	1	7	42	16	62	5	.255	.339
Reno Bertoia	3B68, SS5, OF1	R	23	86	240	28	56	6	0	6	27	20	35	5	.233	.333
Al Kaline	OF145	R	23	146	543	84	170	34	7	16	85	54	47	7	.313	.490
Harvey Kuenn	OF138	R	27	139	561	73	179	**39**	3	8	54	51	34	5	.319	.442
Charlie Maxwell	OF114, 1B14	L	31	131	397	56	108	14	4	13	65	64	54	6	.272	.426
Red Wilson	C101	R	29	103	298	31	89	13	1	3	29	35	30	10	.299	.379
Johnny Groth	OF80	R	31	88	146	24	41	5	2	2	11	13	19	0	.281	.384
Gus Zernial	OF24	R	35	66	124	8	40	7	1	5	23	6	25	0	.323	.516
Coot Veal	SS58	R	25	58	207	29	53	10	2	0	16	14	21	1	.256	.324
Ozzie Virgil	3B49	R	25	49	193	19	47	10	2	3	19	8	20	1	.244	.363
1 Jim Hegan	C45	R	37	45	130	14	25	6	0	1	7	10	32	0	.192	.262
2 Tito Francona	OF18, 1B1	L	24	45	69	11	17	5	0	0	10	15	16	0	.246	.319
2 Bob Hazle	OF12	L	27	43	58	5	14	2	0	2	5	5	13	0	.241	.379
1 Ray Boone	1B32	R	34	39	114	16	27	4	1	6	20	14	13	0	.237	.447
Charlie Lau	C27	L	25	30	68	8	10	1	2	0	6	12	15	0	.147	.221
Milt Bolling	SS13, 2B1, 3B1	R	27	24	31	3	6	2	0	0	0	5	7	0	.194	.258
Lou Skizas	OF5, 3B4	R	26	23	33	4	8	2	0	1	2	5	1	0	.242	.394
Bill Taylor	OF1	L	28	8	8	0	3	0	0	0	1	0	2	0	.375	.375

Steve Boros 21 R 0-2, Tim Thompson 34 L 1-6, George Alusik 23 R 0-2, Bobo Osborne 22 L 0-2, Jack Feller 21 R 0-0, George Thomas 20 R 0-0

NAME	T	AGE	W	L	PCT	SV	G	GS	CG	IP	H	BB	SO	ShO	ERA
TOTALS		27	77	77	.500	19	154	154	**59**	1357	1294	437	**797**	8	3.59
Frank Lary	R	28	16	15	.516	1	39	34	**19**	**260**	249	68	131	3	2.91
Paul Foytack	R	27	15	13	.536	1	39	33	16	230	198	77	135	2	3.44
Jim Bunning	R	26	14	12	.538	0	35	34	10	220	188	79	177	3	3.52
Billy Hoeft	L	26	10	9	.526	3	36	21	6	143	148	49	94	0	4.15
2 George Susce	R	26	4	3	.571	1	27	10	2	91	90	26	42	0	3.66
Herb Moford	R	29	4	8	.308	1	25	11	6	110	83	42	58	0	3.60
2 Al Cicotte	R	28	3	1	.750	0	14	2	0	43	50	15	21	0	3.56
Hank Aguirre	L	26	3	4	.429	5	44	3	0	70	67	27	38	0	3.73
2 Bill Fischer	R	27	2	4	.333	2	22	0	0	31	46	13	16	0	7.55
Tom Morgan	R	28	2	5	.286	1	39	1	0	63	70	4	32	0	3.14
1 Vito Valentinetti	R	29	1	0	1.000	2	15	0	0	19	18	5	10	0	3.38
George Spencer	R	31	1	0	1.000	0	7	0	0	10	11	4	5	0	2.70
2 Herm Wehmeier	R	31	1	0	1.000	0	7	3	0	23	21	5	11	0	2.35
1 Bob Shaw	R	25	1	2	.333	0	11	2	0	27	32	13	17	0	5.00
Joe Presko	R	29	0	0	.000	2	7	0	0	11	13	1	6	0	3.27
1 Lou Sleater	L	31	0	0	.000	0	4	0	0	5	3	6	4	0	7.20
Mickey McDermott	L	29	0	0	.000	0	2	0	0	2	6	2	0	0	9.00
Don Lee	R	24	0	0	.000	0	1	0	0	2	1	1	0	0	9.00

BALTIMORE 6th 74-79 .484 17.5 — PAUL RICHARDS

NAME	G by POS	B	AGE	G	AB	R	H	2B	3B	HR	RBI	BB	SO	SB	BA	SA
TOTALS			29	154	5111	521	1233	195	19	108	493	483	731	33	.241	.350
Bob Boyd	1B99	L	31	125	401	58	124	21	5	7	36	25	24	1	.309	.439
Billy Gardner	2B151, SS13	R	30	151	560	32	126	28	2	3	33	34	53	2	.225	.298
Willie Miranda	SS102	B	32	102	214	15	43	6	0	1	8	14	25	1	.201	.243
Brooks Robinson	3B140, 2B16	R	21	145	463	31	110	16	3	3	32	31	51	1	.238	.305
Al Pilarcik	OF118	L	27	141	379	40	92	21	0	1	24	42	37	7	.243	.306
Jim Busby	OF103, 3B1	R	31	113	215	32	51	7	2	3	19	24	37	6	.237	.330
Gene Woodling	OF116	L	35	133	413	57	114	16	1	15	65	66	49	4	.276	.429
Gus Triandos	C132	R	27	137	474	59	116	10	0	30	79	60	65	1	.245	.456
Dick Williams	OF70, 3B45, 1B26, 2B7	R	29	128	409	36	113	17	0	4	32	37	47	0	.276	.347
Bob Nieman (HJ)	OF100	R	31	105	366	56	119	20	2	16	60	44	57	2	.325	.522
Foster Castleman	SS91, 2B4, 3B4, OF1	R	27	98	200	15	34	5	0	3	14	16	34	2	.170	.240
1 Jim Marshall	1B52, OF8	L	26	85	191	17	41	4	3	5	19	18	30	3	.215	.346
Lenny Green	OF53	L	24	69	91	10	21	4	0	0	4	9	10	0	.231	.275
Joe Ginsberg	C39	L	31	61	109	4	23	1	0	3	16	13	14	0	.211	.303
Jack Harshman	P34, OF1	L	30	47	82	11	16	1	0	6	14	17	22	0	.195	.427
2 Joe Taylor	OF21	L	32	36	77	11	21	4	0	2	9	7	19	0	.273	.403
Bob Hale	1B2	L	24	19	20	2	7	2	0	0	3	2	1	0	.350	.450
Willie Tasby	OF16	R	25	18	50	6	10	3	0	1	1	7	15	1	.200	.320
Chuck Oertel	OF2	L	27	14	12	4	2	0	0	1	1	1	1	0	.167	.417
Jerry Adair	SS10, 2B1	R	21	11	19	1	2	0	0	0	0	1	7	0	.105	.105

Ron Hansen 20 R 0-19, Bert Hamric 30 L 1-8, Leo Burke 24 R 5-11, 1Eddie Mikisis 31 R 0-2, Frank Zupo 18 L 0-2

NAME	T	AGE	W	L	PCT	SV	G	GS	CG	IP	H	BB	SO	ShO	ERA
TOTALS		28	74	79	.484	28	154	154	55	1370	1277	403	749	15	3.40
Arnie Portocarrero	R	26	15	11	.577	2	32	27	10	205	173	57	90	3	3.25
Billy O'Dell	L	25	14	11	.560	8	41	25	12	221	201	51	137	3	2.97
Jack Harshman	L	30	12	15	.444	4	34	29	17	236	204	75	161	3	2.90
Milt Pappas	R	19	10	10	.500	0	31	21	3	135	135	48	72	0	4.07
Hal Brown (JJ)	R	33	7	5	.583	1	19	17	4	97	96	20	44	2	3.06
Connie Johnson	R	35	6	9	.400	1	26	17	4	118	116	32	68	0	3.89
Billy Loes	R	28	3	9	.250	5	32	10	1	114	106	44	44	0	3.63
Ken Lehman	L	30	2	1	.667	0	31	1	1	62	64	18	36	0	3.48
George Zuverink	R	33	2	2	.500	7	45	0	0	69	74	17	22	0	3.39
2 Lou Sleater	L	31	1	0	1.000	0	6	0	0	7	14	2	5	0	12.86
Charlie Beamon	R	23	1	3	.250	0	21	3	0	50	47	21	26	0	4.32
2 Hoyt Wilhelm	R	34	1	3	.250	0	9	4	3	41	25	10	35	1	1.98
Jerry Walker	R	19	0	0	.000	0	6	0	0	10	16	5	6	0	7.20
Ron Moeller	L	19	0	0	.000	0	4	0	0	4	6	3	3	0	4.50

KANSAS CITY 7th 73-81 .474 19 — HARRY CRAFT

NAME	G by POS	B	AGE	G	AB	R	H	2B	3B	HR	RBI	BB	SO	SB	BA	SA
TOTALS			28	156	5261	642	1297	196	**50**	138	605	452	747	22	.247	.381
1 Vic Power	1B51, 2B1	R	26	52	205	35	62	13	**4***	4	27	7	3	1	.302	.463
Hector Lopez	2B96, 3B55, SS1, OF1	R	25	151	564	84	147	28	4	17	73	49	61	2	.261	.415
Joe DeMaestri	SS137	R	29	139	442	32	97	11	1	6	38	16	84	1	.219	.290
Hal Smith	3B43, C31, 1B14	R	27	99	315	32	86	19	2	5	46	25	47	0	.273	.394
2 Roger Maris	OF98	L	23	99	401	61	99	14	3	19	53	28	52	0	.247	.439
Bill Tuttle	OF145	R	28	148	511	77	118	14	9	11	51	74	58	7	.231	.358
Bob Cerv	OF136	R	32	141	515	93	157	20	7	38	104	50	82	3	.305	.592
Harry Chiti	C83	R	25	103	295	32	79	11	3	9	44	18	48	3	.268	.417
Bob Martyn	OF63	L	27	95	226	25	59	10	7	2	23	26	36	1	.261	.394
2 Whitey Herzog	OF37, 1B22	L	26	88	96	11	23	1	2	0	9	16	21	0	.240	.292
2 Preston Ward	1B39, 3B34, OF2	L	30	81	268	28	68	10	1	6	24	27	36	0	.254	.366
2 Harry Simpson	1B43, OF11	L	32	78	212	21	56	7	1	7	27	26	33	0	.264	.406
Frank House	C55	L	28	76	202	16	51	6	3	4	24	12	13	1	.252	.371
Mike Baxes	2B61, SS4	R	27	73	231	31	49	10	1	0	8	21	24	1	.212	.264
2 Chico Carrasquel	3B32, SS22	R	30	59	160	19	34	5	1	2	13	21	15	0	.213	.294
1 Woodie Held	OF41, 3B4, SS1	R	26	47	131	13	28	2	0	4	16	10	28	0	.214	.321
1 Billy Hunter	SS12, 2B8, 3B1	R	30	22	58	6	9	1	1	2	11	5	7	1	.155	.310

Dave Melton 29 R 0-6, Milt Graff 27 L 0-1, Kent Hadley 23 L 2-11, Lou Klimchock 18 L 2-10, Jim Small 21 L 0-4

NAME	T	AGE	W	L	PCT	SV	G	GS	CG	IP	H	BB	SO	ShO	ERA
TOTALS		30	73	81	.474	25	156	156	42	**1398**	1405	467	721	9	4.15
Ned Garver	R	32	12	11	.522	1	31	28	10	201	192	66	72	3	4.03
Ralph Terry	R	22	11	13	.458	2	40	33	8	217	217	61	134	3	4.23
1 Murry Dickson	R	41	9	5	.643	1	27	9	3	99	99	31	46	0	3.27
Ray Herbert	R	28	8	8	.500	3	42	16	5	175	161	55	108	0	3.50
Jack Urban	R	29	8	11	.421	1	30	24	5	132	150	51	54	1	5.93
2 Bob Grim	R	28	7	6	.538	0	26	14	5	114	118	41	54	1	3.55
2 Dick Tomanek	L	27	5	5	.500	5	36	2	1	72	69	28	50	0	3.63
Tom Gorman	R	33	4	4	.500	8	50	1	0	90	86	20	44	0	3.50
1 Duke Maas	R	29	4	5	.444	1	10	7	3	55	49	13	19	1	3.93
Bud Daley	L	25	3	2	.600	0	26	5	1	71	67	19	39	0	3.30
Howie Reed	R	21	1	0	1.000	0	3	1	1	10	5	4	5	0	0.90
Wally Burnette	R	29	1	1	.500	0	12	4	0	28	29	14	11	0	3.54
1 Virgil Trucks	R	39	0	1	.000	3	16	0	0	22	18	15	15	0	2.05
1 Alex Kellner	L	33	0	2	.000	0	7	6	0	34	40	8	22	0	5.82
Walt Craddock	L	26	0	3	.000	0	23	1	0	37	41	20	22	0	5.84
Bob Davis	R	24	0	4	.000	0	8	4	0	31	45	12	22	0	7.84
Glenn Cox	R	27	0	0	.000	0	2	0	0	4	6	3	1	0	9.00
Ken Johnson	R	25	0	0	.000	0	2	0	0	2	6	3	1	0	31.50

Carl Duser 25 L 0-0, John Tsitouris 22 R 0-0 *Power-See Cleveland

WASHINGTON 8th 61-93 .396 31 — COOKIE LAVAGETTO

NAME	G by POS	B	AGE	G	AB	R	H	2B	3B	HR	RBI	BB	SO	SB	BA	SA
TOTALS			28	156	5156	553	1240	161	38	121	526	477	751	22	.240	.357
Norm Zauchin	1B91	R	28	96	303	35	69	8	2	15	37	38	68	0	.228	.416
2 Ken Aspromonte	2B72, 3B11, SS1	R	26	92	253	15	57	9	1	5	27	25	28	1	.225	.328
Rocky Bridges	SS112, 2B3, 3B3	R	30	116	377	38	99	14	3	5	28	27	32	0	.263	.355
Eddie Yost	3B114, OF4, 1B2	R	31	134	406	55	91	16	0	8	37	81	43	3	.224	.323
Jim Lemon	OF137	R	30	142	501	65	123	15	9	26	75	50	**120**	2	.246	.467
Albie Pearson	OF141	L	23	146	530	63	146	25	5	3	33	64	31	7	.275	.358
Roy Sievers	OF114, 1B33	R	31	148	550	85	162	18	1	39	108	53	63	3	.295	.544
Clint Courtney	C128	L	31	134	450	46	113	18	0	8	62	48	23	1	.251	.344
Herb Plews	2B64, 3B36	L	30	111	380	46	98	12	6	2	29	17	45	2	.258	.337
Neil Chrisley	OF69, 3B1	L	26	105	233	19	50	7	4	5	26	16	18	1	.215	.343
Ossie Alvarez	SS64, 2B14, 3B3	R	24	87	196	20	41	3	0	0	5	16	26	1	.209	.224
Julio Becquer	1B42, OF1	L	26	86	164	10	39	3	0	0	12	8	21	1	.238	.256
Ed Fitz Gerald	C21, 1B5	R	34	58	114	7	30	3	0	0	11	8	15	0	.263	.289
Faye Throneberry	OF26	L	27	44	87	12	16	1	1	4	7	4	28	0	.184	.356
Bobby Malkmus	2B26, 3B2, SS1	R	26	41	70	5	13	2	1	0	3	4	15	0	.186	.243
Steve Korcheck	C20	R	25	21	51	6	4	2	1	0	1	1	16	0	.078	.157
Harmon Killebrew	3B9	R	22	13	31	2	6	0	0	0	2	0	12	0	.194	.194
Bob Allison	OF11	R	23	11	35	1	7	1	0	0	0	2	5	0	.200	.229

1 Whitey Herzog 26 L 0-5, Johnny Schaive 24 R 6-24, Jerry Snyder 28 R 1-9, 1 Lou Berberet 28 L 1-6

NAME	T	AGE	W	L	PCT	SV	G	GS	CG	IP	H	BB	SO	ShO	ERA
TOTALS		28	61	**93**	.396	28	156	156	28	1377	**1443**	558	762	6	4.53
Pedro Ramos	R	23	14	**18**	.438	3	43	**37**	10	259	**277**	77	132	4	4.24
Dick Hyde	R	29	10	3	.769	18	53	0	0	103	82	35	49	0	1.75
Tex Clevenger	R	25	9	9	.500	6	**55**	4	0	124	119	50	70	0	4.35
Camilo Pascual	R	24	8	12	.400	0	31	27	6	177	166	60	146	2	3.15
Russ Kemmerer	R	26	6	15	.286	0	40	30	6	224	234	74	111	0	4.62
2 Vito Valentinetti	R	29	4	6	.400	0	23	10	2	96	106	49	33	0	5.06
Hal Griggs	R	29	3	11	.214	0	32	21	3	137	138	74	69	0	5.52
1 Bud Byerly	R	37	2	0	1.000	1	17	0	0	24	34	11	13	0	6.75
John Romonosky	R	28	2	4	.333	0	18	5	1	55	52	28	38	0	6.55
1 Chuck Stobbs	L	28	2	6	.250	0	19	8	0	57	87	16	23	0	6.00
Ralph Lumenti	L	21	1	2	.333	0	8	4	0	21	21	36	20	0	8.57
3 Jim Constable	L	25	0	1	.000	0	15	2	0	28	29	15	25	0	4.82
1 Al Cicotte	R	28	0	3	.000	0	8	4	0	28	36	14	14	0	4.82
3 Bill Fischer	R	27	0	3	.000	0	3	3	0	21	24	5	10	0	3.86
Joe Albanese	R	25	0	0	.000	0	6	0	0	6	8	2	3	0	4.50
Bob Wiesler	L	27	0	0	.000	0	4	0	0	9	14	5	5	0	7.00
Jack Spring	L	25	0	0	.000	0	3	1	0	7	16	7	1	0	14.14

MILWAUKEE 1st 92-62 .597 — **FRED HANEY**

NAME	G by POS	B	AGE	G	AB	R	H	2B	3B	HR	RBI	BB	SO	SB	BA	SA
TOTALS			29	154	5225	675	1388	221	21	167	641	478	646	26	**.266**	.412
Frank Torre	1B122	L	26	138	372	41	115	22	5	6	55	42	14	2	.309	.444
Red Schoendienst (IL)	2B105	B	35	106	427	47	112	23	1	1	24	31	21	3	.262	.328
Johnny Logan	SS144	R	31	145	530	54	120	20	0	11	53	40	57	1	.226	.326
Eddie Mathews	3B149	L	26	149	546	97	137	18	1	31	77	85	85	5	.251	.458
Hank Aaron	OF153	R	24	153	601	109	196	34	4	30	95	59	49	4	.326	.546
Bill Bruton (KJ)	OF96	L	32	100	325	47	91	11	3	3	28	27	37	4	.280	.360
Wes Covington	OF82	L	26	90	294	43	97	12	1	24	74	20	35	0	.330	.622
Del Crandall	C124	R	28	131	427	50	116	23	1	18	63	48	38	4	.272	.457
Joe Adcock	1B71, OF22	R	30	105	320	40	88	15	1	19	54	21	63	0	.275	.506
Andy Pafko	OF93	R	37	95	164	17	39	7	1	3	23	15	17	0	.238	.348
Felix Mantilla	OF43, 2B21, SS5, 3B2	R	23	85	226	37	50	5	1	7	19	20	20	2	.221	.345
Harry Hanebrink	OF33, 3B7	L	30	63	133	14	25	3	0	4	10	13	9	0	.188	.301
Mel Roach (KJ)	2B27, OF7, 1B1	R	25	44	136	14	42	7	0	3	10	6	15	0	.309	.426
Del Rice	C38	R	35	43	121	10	27	7	0	1	8	8	30	0	.223	.306
Warren Spahn	P38	L	37	41	108	10	36	6	1	2	15	7	24	0	.333	.463
Casey Wise	2B10, SS7, 3B1	B	25	31	71	8	14	1	0	0	0	4	8	1	.197	.211
1 Bob Hazle	OF20	L	27	20	56	6	10	0	0	0	5	9	4	0	.179	.179
Joe Koppe	SS3	R	27	16	9	3	4	0	0	0	0	1	1	0	.444	.444

1 Carl Sawatski 30 L 1-10, Eddie Haas 23 L 5-14, Hawk Taylor 19 R 1-8, John DeMerit 22 R 2-3, Bob Roselli 26 R 0-1

NAME	T	AGE	W	L	PCT	SV	G	GS	CG	IP	H	BB	SO	ShO	ERA
		29	**92**	62	**.597**	17	154	154	**72**	1376	1261	426	773	**16**	**3.21**
Warren Spahn	L	37	**22**	11	**.667**	1	38	36	**23**	**290**	257	76	150	2	3.07
Lew Burdette	R	31	20	10	**.667**	0	40	36	19	275	279	50	113	3	2.91
Bob Rush	R	32	10	6	.625	0	28	20	5	147	142	31	84	2	3.43
Carl Willey	R	27	9	7	.563	0	23	19	9	140	110	53	74	**4**	2.70
Don McMahon	R	28	7	2	.778	8	38	0	0	59	50	29	37	0	3.66
Joey Jay	R	22	7	5	.583	0	18	12	6	97	60	43	74	3	2.13
Juan Pizarro	L	21	6	4	.600	1	16	10	7	97	75	47	84	1	2.69
Bob Buhl (SA)	R	29	5	2	.714	1	11	10	3	73	74	30	27	0	3.45
Ernie Johnson	R	34	3	1	.750	1	15	0	0	23	35	10	13	0	8.22
Humberto Robinson	R	28	2	4	.333	1	19	0	0	42	30	13	26	0	3.00
Bob Trowbridge	R	28	1	3	.333	1	27	4	0	55	53	26	31	0	3.93
Dick Littlefield	L	32	0	1	.000	1	4	0	0	6	7	1	7	0	4.50
Gene Conley (AJ)	R	27	0	6	.000	2	26	7	0	72	89	17	53	0	4.88

PITTSBURGH 2nd 84-70 .545 8 — **DANNY MURTAUGH**

NAME	G by POS	B	AGE	G	AB	R	H	2B	3B	HR	RBI	BB	SO	SB	BA	SA
TOTALS			27	154	5247	662	1386	229	**68**	134	625	396	753	30	.264	.410
Ted Kluszewski	1B72	L	33	100	301	29	88	13	4	4	37	26	16	0	.292	.402
Bill Mazeroski	2B152	R	21	152	567	69	156	24	6	19	68	25	71	1	.275	.439
Dick Groat	SS149	R	27	151	584	67	175	36	9	3	66	23	32	2	.300	.408
Frank Thomas	3B139, OF8, 1B2	R	29	149	562	89	158	26	4	35	109	42	79	0	.281	.528
Roberto Clemente	OF135	R	23	140	519	69	150	24	10	6	50	31	41	8	.289	.408
Bill Virdon	OF143	L	27	144	604	75	161	24	11	9	46	52	70	5	.267	.387
Bob Skinner	OF141	L	26	144	529	93	170	33	9	13	70	58	55	12	.321	.491
Hank Foiles	C103	R	29	104	264	31	54	10	2	8	30	45	53	0	.205	.348
Roman Mejias	OF57	R	27	76	157	17	42	3	2	5	19	2	27	2	.268	.408
Dick Stuart	1B64	R	25	67	254	38	68	12	5	16	48	11	75	0	.268	.543
R C Stevens	1B52	R	23	59	90	16	24	3	1	7	18	5	25	0	.267	.556
Johnny Powers	OF14	L	28	57	82	6	15	1	0	2	2	8	19	0	.183	.268
Bill Hall	C51	L	29	51	116	15	33	6	0	1	15	15	13	0	.284	.362
Danny Kravitz	C37	L	27	45	100	9	24	3	2	1	5	11	10	0	.240	.340
Gene Baker (KJ)	3B11, 2B3	R	33	29	56	3	14	2	1	0	7	8	6	0	.250	.321
2 Dick Schofield	SS5, 3B2	B	23	26	27	4	4	0	1	0	2	3	6	0	.148	.222
1 Gene Freese	3B1	R	24	17	18	1	3	0	0	1	2	1	2	0	.167	.333
Harry Bright	3B7	R	28	15	24	4	6	1	0	1	3	1	6	0	.250	.417

1 Paul Smith 27 L 1-3, 1 Johnny O'Brien 27 R 0-1, Jim Pendleton 34 R 1-3, Hardy Peterson 28 R 2-6

NAME	T	AGE	W	L	PCT	SV	G	GS	CG	IP	H	BB	SO	ShO	ERA
		27	84	70	.545	41	154	154	43	1367	1344	470	679	10	3.56
Bob Friend	R	27	**22**	14	.611	0	38	**38**	16	274	**299**	61	135	1	3.68
Vern Law	R	28	14	12	.538	3	35	29	6	202	235	39	56	1	3.97
Ron Kline	R	26	13	**16**	.448	0	32	32	11	237	220	92	109	2	3.53
George Witt	R	24	9	2	.818	0	18	15	5	106	78	59	81	3	1.61
Curt Raydon	R	24	8	4	.667	1	32	20	2	134	118	61	85	1	3.62
Roy Face	R	30	5	2	.714	**20**	57	0	0	84	77	22	47	0	2.89
Don Gross	L	27	5	7	.417	7	40	3	0	75	67	38	59	0	3.96
2 Bob Porterfield	R	34	4	6	.400	5	37	6	2	88	78	19	39	1	3.27
Ron Blackburn	R	23	2	1	.667	3	38	2	0	64	61	27	31	0	3.38
Bob Smith	L	27	2	2	.500	1	35	4	0	61	61	31	24	0	4.43
George Perez	R	20	0	1	.000	1	4	0	0	8	9	4	2	0	5.63
Bennie Daniels	R	26	0	3	.000	0	8	5	1	28	31	15	7	0	5.46
Don Williams	R	26	0	0	.000	0	2	0	0	4	6	1	3	0	6.75
Eddie O'Brien	R	27	0	0	.000	0	1	0	0	2	4	1	1	0	13.50

Dick Hall (VR) 27

SAN FRANCISCO 3rd 80-74 .519 12 — **BILL RIGNEY**

NAME	G by POS	B	AGE	G	AB	R	H	2B	3B	HR	RBI	BB	SO	SB	BA	SA
TOTALS			27	154	5318	**727**	1399	**250**	42	170	**682**	531	817	64	.263	.422
Orlando Cepeda	1B147	R	20	148	603	88	188	**38**	4	25	96	29	84	15	.312	.512
Danny O'Connell	2B104, 3B3	R	31	107	306	44	71	12	2	3	23	51	35	2	.232	.314
Daryl Spencer	SS134, 2B17	R	28	148	539	71	138	20	5	17	74	73	60	1	.256	.406
Jim Davenport	3B130, SS5	R	24	134	434	70	111	22	3	12	41	33	64	1	.256	.403
Willie Kirkland	OF115	L	24	122	418	48	108	25	6	14	56	43	69	3	.258	.447
Willie Mays	OF151	R	27	152	600	**121**	208	33	11	29	96	78	56	**31**	.347	.583
Felipe Alou	OF70	R	23	75	182	21	46	9	2	4	16	19	34	4	.253	.390
Bob Schmidt	C123	R	25	127	393	46	96	20	2	14	54	33	59	0	.244	.412
Whitey Lockman	OF25, 2B15, 1B7	L	31	92	122	15	29	5	0	2	7	13	8	0	.238	.328
Hank Sauer	OF67	R	39	88	236	27	59	8	0	12	46	35	37	0	.250	.436
Ray Jablonski	3B57	R	31	86	230	28	53	15	1	12	46	17	50	2	.230	.461
Leon Wagner	OF57	L	24	74	221	31	70	9	0	13	35	18	34	1	.317	.534
Ed Bressoud	2B57, 3B6, SS4	R	26	66	137	19	36	5	3	0	8	14	22	0	.263	.343
Bob Speake	OF10	L	27	66	71	9	15	3	0	3	10	13	15	0	.211	.380
Valmy Thomas	C61	R	29	63	143	14	37	5	0	3	16	13	24	1	.259	.357
Don Taussig	OF36	R	26	39	50	10	10	0	0	1	4	3	8	0	.200	.260
Jim King	OF15	L	25	34	56	8	12	2	1	2	8	10	8	0	.214	.393
Bill White (MS)	1B3, OF2	L	24	26	29	5	7	1	0	1	4	7	5	1	.241	.379
Jim Finigan	2B8, 3B4	R	29	23	25	3	5	2	0	0	1	3	5	0	.200	.280
Andre Rodgers	SS18	R	23	22	63	7	13	3	1	2	11	4	14	0	.206	.381
Jackie Brandt (MS)	OF14	R	24	18	52	7	13	1	0	0	3	6	5	1	.250	.269
Nick Testa	C1	R	30	1	0	0	0	0	0	0	0	0	0	0	.000	.000

NAME	T	AGE	W	L	PCT	SV	G	GS	CG	IP	H	BB	SO	ShO	ERA
		29	80	74	.519	25	154	154	38	1389	1400	512	775	7	3.98
Johnny Antonelli	L	28	16	13	.552	3	41	34	13	242	216	87	143	0	3.27
Al Worthington	R	29	11	7	.611	6	54	12	1	151	152	57	76	0	3.64
Mike McCormick	L	19	11	8	.579	1	42	28	8	178	192	60	82	2	4.60
Ruben Gomez	R	30	10	12	.455	1	42	30	8	208	204	77	112	1	4.37
Ray Monzant	R	25	8	11	.421	1	43	16	4	151	160	57	93	1	4.71
Marv Grissom	R	40	7	5	.583	10	51	0	0	65	71	26	46	0	4.02
Stu Miller	R	30	6	9	.400	0	41	20	4	182	160	49	119	1	**2.47**
Paul Giel	R	25	4	5	.444	0	29	9	0	92	89	55	55	0	4.70
Gordon Jones	R	28	3	1	.750	1	11	1	0	30	33	5	8	0	2.40
1 Jim Constable	L	25	1	0	1.000	1	9	0	0	8	10	3	4	0	5.63
Curt Barclay	R	26	1	0	1.000	0	6	1	0	16	16	5	6	0	2.81
Dom Zanni	R	26	1	0	1.000	0	1	0	0	4	7	1	3	0	2.25
Ray Crone	R	26	1	2	.333	0	14	1	0	24	35	13	7	0	6.75
Don Johnson	R	31	0	1	.000	1	17	0	0	23	31	8	14	0	6.26
Pete Burnside	L	27	0	0	.000	0	6	1	0	11	20	5	4	0	6.55
John Fitzgerald	L	24	0	0	.000	0	1	1	0	3	1	1	3	0	3.00
Joe Shipley	R	23	0	0	.000	0	1	0	0	1	3	3	0	0	45.00

CINCINNATI 4th 76-78 .494 16 — **BIRDIE TEBBETTS 52-61 .460 JIMMY DYKES 24-17 .585**

NAME	G by POS	B	AGE	G	AB	R	H	2B	3B	HR	RBI	BB	SO	SB	BA	SA
TOTALS			30	154	5273	695	1359	242	40	123	649	572	765	61	.258	.389
George Crowe	1B93, 2B1	L	35	111	345	31	95	12	5	7	61	41	51	1	.275	.400
Johnny Temple	2B141, 1B1	R	29	141	542	82	166	31	6	3	47	91	41	15	.306	.402
Roy McMillan	SS145	R	27	145	393	48	90	18	3	1	25	47	33	5	.229	.298
Don Hoak	3B112, SS1	R	30	114	417	51	109	30	0	6	50	43	36	6	.261	.376
Jerry Lynch	OF101	L	27	122	420	58	131	20	5	16	68	18	54	1	.312	.498
Gus Bell	OF107	L	29	112	385	42	97	16	2	10	46	36	40	2	.252	.382
Frank Robinson	OF138, 3B11	R	22	148	554	90	149	25	6	31	83	62	80	10	.269	.504
Ed Bailey	C99	L	27	112	360	39	90	23	1	11	59	47	61	2	.250	.411
Alex Grammas	SS61, 3B38, 2B14	R	31	105	216	25	47	8	0	0	12	34	24	2	.218	.255
Smoky Burgess	C58	L	31	99	251	28	71	12	1	6	31	22	20	0	.283	.410
Bob Thurman	OF41	L	37	94	178	23	41	7	4	4	20	20	38	1	.230	.382
Dee Fondy	1B36, OF22	L	33	89	124	23	27	1	1	1	11	5	27	7	.218	.266
Pete Whisenant	OF66, 2B1	R	28	85	203	33	48	9	2	11	40	18	37	3	.236	.463
2 Eddie Miksis	OF32, 3B14, 2B7, SS5, 1B1	R	31	69	50	15	7	0	0	0	4	5	5	1	.140	.140
2 Walt Dropo	1B43	R	35	63	162	18	47	7	2	7	31	12	31	0	.290	.488
2 Don Newcombe	P20	L	32	39	60	9	21	1	0	1	9	8	10	0	.350	.417
1 Steve Bilko	1B21	R	29	31	87	12	23	4	2	4	17	10	20	0	.264	.494
Vada Pinson	OF27	L	19	27	96	20	26	7	0	1	8	11	18	2	.271	.375
Dutch Dotterer	C8	R	26	11	28	1	7	1	0	1	2	2	4	0	.250	.393

Dan Morejon 27 R 5-26, Chuck Coles 27 L 2-11, Bobby Henrich 19 R 0-3, Jim Fridley 33 R 2-9, 2Fred Hatfield 33 L 0-1, Don Pavletich (MS) 19

NAME	T	AGE	W	L	PCT	SV	G	GS	CG	IP	H	BB	SO	ShO	ERA
		31	76	78	.494	20	154	154	50	1385	1422	419	705	7	3.73
Bob Purkey	R	28	17	11	.607	0	37	34	17	250	259	49	70	3	3.60
Joe Nuxhall	L	29	12	11	.522	0	36	26	5	176	169	63	111	0	3.78
Harvey Haddix	L	32	8	7	.533	0	29	26	8	184	191	43	110	1	3.52
Brooks Lawrence	R	33	8	13	.381	5	46	23	6	181	194	55	74	2	4.13
2 Alex Kellner	L	33	7	3	.700	0	18	7	4	82	74	20	42	0	2.30
2 Don Newcombe	R	32	7	7	.500	1	20	18	7	133	159	28	53	0	3.86
Hal Jeffcoat	R	33	6	8	.429	9	49	0	0	75	76	26	35	0	3.72
Tom Acker	R	28	4	3	.571	1	38	10	3	125	126	43	90	0	4.54
1 Johnny Klippstein	R	30	3	2	.600	1	12	4	0	33	37	14	22	0	4.91
Willard Schmidt	R	30	3	5	.375	0	41	2	0	69	60	33	41	0	2.87
Orlando Pena	R	24	1	0	1.000	3	9	0	0	15	10	4	11	0	0.60
1 Bill Wight	L	36	0	1	.000	0	7	0	0	7	7	4	5	0	3.86
Jay Hook	R	21	0	1	.000	0	1	1	0	3	3	2	5	0	12.00
Jim O'Toole	L	21	0	1	.000	0	1	1	0	7	4	5	4	0	1.29
2 Turk Lown	R	34	0	2	.000	0	11	0	0	12	12	12	9	0	5.25
Charlie Rabe	L	26	0	3	.000	0	9	1	0	19	25	9	10	0	4.26
1 Hersh Freeman	R	30	0	0	.000	0	3	0	0	8	4	5	7	0	3.38
Gene Hayden	L	23	0	0	.000	0	3	0	0	4	5	1	3	0	4.50
1 Bob Kelly	R	30	0	0	.000	0	2	1	0	2	3	3	1	0	4.50
Ted Wieand	R	25	0	0	.000	0	1	0	0	2	4	0	2	0	9.00

CHICAGO 5th (Tie) 72-82 .468 20 — **BOB SCHEFFING**

NAME	G by POS	B	AGE	G	AB	R	H	2B	3B	HR	RBI	BB	SO	SB	BA	SA
TOTALS			29	154	5289	709	1402	207	49	**182**	666	487	853	39	.265	**.426**
Dale Long	1B137, C2	L	32	142	480	68	130	26	4	20	75	66	64	2	.271	.467
Tony Taylor	2B137, 3B1	R	22	140	497	63	117	15	3	6	27	40	93	21	.235	.314
Ernie Banks	SS154	R	27	154	**617**	119	193	23	11	**47**	**129**	52	87	4	.313	**.614**
2 Al Dark	3B111	R	36	114	464	54	137	16	4	3	43	29	23	1	.295	.366
Lee Walls	OF132	R	25	136	513	80	156	19	3	24	72	47	62	4	.304	.493
Bobby Thomson	OF148, 3B4	R	34	152	547	67	155	27	5	21	82	56	76	0	.283	.466
Walt Moryn	OF141	L	32	143	512	77	135	26	7	26	77	62	83	1	.264	.494
Sammy Taylor	C87	L	25	96	301	30	78	12	2	6	36	27	46	2	.259	.372
Jim Bolger	OF37	R	26	84	120	15	27	4	1	1	11	9	20	0	.225	.300
Johnny Goryl	3B44, 2B35	R	24	83	219	27	53	9	3	4	14	27	34	0	.242	.365
Cal Neeman	C71	R	29	76	201	30	52	7	0	12	29	21	41	0	.259	.473
Chuck Tanner	OF15	L	28	73	103	10	27	6	0	4	17	9	10	1	.262	.437
Bobby Adams	1B11, 3B9, 2B7	R	36	62	96	14	27	4	4	0	4	6	15	2	.281	.406
2 Jim Marshall	1B15, OF11	L	26	26	81	12	22	2	0	5	11	12	13	1	.272	.481
Lou Jackson	OF12	L	22	24	35	5	6	2	1	1	6	1	9	0	.171	.371
2 Paul Smith	1B4	L	27	18	20	1	3	0	0	0	1	3	4	0	.150	.150
El Tappe	C16	R	31	17	28	2	6	0	0	0	4	3	1	0	.214	.214
Moe Thacker	C9	R	24	11	24	4	6	1	0	2	3	1	7	0	.250	.542
Frank Ernaga		R	27	9	8	0	1	0	0	0	0	0	2	0	.125	.125
Charlie King	OF7	R	27	8	8	1	2	0	0	0	1	3	1	0	.250	.250

Dick Johnson 26 L 0-5, Bob Will 26 L 1-4, Jerry Kindall 23 R 1-6, Bill Gabler 27 L 0-3. Gordon Massa 22 L 0-2, Bobby Morgan 32 R 0-1

NAME	T	AGE	W	L	PCT	SV	G	GS	CG	IP	H	BB	SO	ShO	ERA
		26	72	82	.468	24	154	154	27	1361	1322	**619**	805	5	4.22
Glen Hobbie	R	22	10	6	.625	2	55	16	2	168	163	93	91	1	3.75
Don Elston	R	29	9	8	.529	10	**69**	0	0	97	75	39	84	0	2.88
Moe Drabowsky	R	22	9	11	.450	0	22	20	4	126	118	73	77	1	4.50
Taylor Phillips	L	25	7	10	.412	1	39	27	5	170	178	79	102	1	4.76
Dick Drott	R	22	7	11	.389	0	39	31	4	167	156	99	127	0	5.44
Bill Henry	L	30	5	4	.556	6	44	0	0	81	63	17	58	0	2.89
Johnny Briggs	R	24	5	5	.500	0	20	17	3	96	99	45	46	1	4.50
Dave Hillman	R	30	4	8	.333	1	31	16	3	126	132	31	65	0	3.14
John Buzhardt	R	21	3	0	1.000	0	6	2	1	24	16	7	9	0	1.88
Bob Anderson	R	22	3	3	.500	0	17	8	2	66	61	29	51	0	3.95
Marcelino Solis	L	27	3	3	.500	0	15	4	0	52	74	20	15	0	6.06
1 Jim Brosnan	R	28	3	4	.429	0	8	8	2	52	41	29	24	0	3.12
Ed Mayer	R	26	2	2	.500	1	19	0	0	24	15	16	14	0	3.75
Elmer Singleton	R	40	1	0	1.000	0	2	0	0	5	1	1	2	0	0.00
Gene Fodge	R	26	1	1	.500	0	16	4	1	40	47	11	15	0	4.73
2 Hersh Freeman	R	30	0	1	.000	0	9	0	0	13	23	3	7	0	8.31
Dick Ellsworth	L	18	0	1	.000	0	1	1	0	2	4	3	0	0	18.00
Dolan Nichols	R	28	0	4	.000	1	24	0	0	41	46	16	9	0	5.05
1 Turk Lown	R	34	0	0	.000	0	4	0	0	4	2	3	4	0	4.50
Freddy Rodriguez	R	30	0	0	.000	2	7	0	0	7	8	5	5	0	7.71

ST. LOUIS 5th (Tie) 72-82 .468 20 — FRED HUTCHINSON 69-75 .479 — STAN HACK 3-7 .300

NAME	G by POS	B	AGE	G	AB	R	H	2B	3B	HR	RBI	BB	SO	SB	BA	SA
TOTALS			28	154	5255	619	1371	216	39	111	570	533	637	44	.261	.380
Stan Musial	1B124	L	37	135	472	64	159	35	2	17	62	72	26	0	.337	.528
Don Blasingame	2B137	L	26	143	547	71	150	19	10	2	36	57	47	20	.274	.356
Eddie Kasko	SS77, 2B12, 3B1	R	26	104	259	20	57	8	1	2	22	21	25	1	.220	.282
Ken Boyer	3B144, OF6, SS1	R	27	150	570	101	175	21	9	23	90	49	53	11	.307	.496
Wally Moon	OF82	L	28	108	290	36	69	10	3	7	38	47	30	2	.238	.366
Curt Flood	OF120, 3B1	R	20	121	422	50	110	17	2	10	41	31	56	2	.261	.382
Del Ennis	OF84	R	33	106	329	22	86	18	1	3	47	15	35	0	.261	.350
Hal Smith	C71	R	27	77	220	13	50	4	1	1	24	14	14	0	.227	.268
Gene Green	OF75, C48	R	25	137	442	47	124	18	3	13	55	37	48	2	.281	.423
Joe Cunningham	1B67, OF66	L	26	131	337	61	105	20	3	12	57	82	23	4	.312	.496
Irv Noren	OF77	L	33	117	178	24	47	9	1	4	22	13	21	0	.264	.393
Hobie Landrith	C45	L	28	70	144	9	31	4	0	3	13	26	21	0	.215	.306
2 Gene Freese	SS28, 2B14, 3B3	R	24	62	191	28	49	11	1	6	16	10	32	1	.257	.419
Ruben Amaro	SS36, 2B1	R	22	40	76	8	17	2	1	0	0	5	8	0	.224	.276
1 Dick Schofield	SS27	B	23	39	108	16	23	4	0	1	8	23	15	0	.213	.278
Bobby Gene Smith	OF27	R	24	28	88	8	25	3	0	2	5	2	18	1	.284	.386
Ray Katt	C14	R	31	19	41	1	7	1	0	1	4	4	6	0	.171	.268
1 Al Dark	SS8, 3B8	R	36	18	64	7	19	0	0	1	5	2	6	0	.297	.344
1 Joe Taylor	OF5	L	32	18	23	2	7	3	0	1	3	2	4	0	.304	.565

2 Johnny O'Brien 27 R 0-2, Lee Tate 26 R 7-35, Benny Valenzuela 25 R 3-14, Ellis Burton 21 B 7-30

NAME	T	AGE	W	L	PCT	SV	G	GS	CG	IP	H	BB	SO	ShO	ERA
		29	72	82	.468	25	154	154	45	1382	1398	567	822	6	4.12
Sam Jones	R	32	14	13	.519	0	35	35	14	250	204	107	225	2	2.88
Larry Jackson	R	27	13	13	.500	8	49	23	11	198	211	51	124	1	3.68
Vinegar Bend Mizell	L	27	10	14	.417	0	30	29	8	190	178	91	80	2	3.41
2 Jim Brosnan	R	28	8	4	.667	7	33	12	2	115	107	50	65	0	3.44
Phil Paine	R	28	5	1	.833	1	46	0	0	73	70	31	45	0	3.58
Lindy McDaniel	R	22	5	7	.417	0	26	17	2	109	139	31	47	1	5.78
Billy Muffet	R	27	4	6	.400	5	35	6	1	84	107	42	41	0	4.93
2 Bill Wight	L	36	3	0	1.000	2	28	1	1	57	64	32	10	0	5.05
1 Morrie Martin	L	35	3	1	.750	0	17	0	0	25	19	12	16	0	4.68
Bob Mabe	R	28	3	9	.250	0	31	13	4	112	113	41	74	0	4.50
2 Sal Maglie	R	41	2	6	.250	0	10	10	2	53	46	25	21	0	4.75
Frank Barnes	R	29	1	1	.500	0	8	1	0	19	19	16	17	0	7.58
2 Chuck Stobbs	L	28	1	3	.250	1	17	0	0	40	40	14	25	0	3.60
Nels Chittum	R	25	0	1	.000	0	13	2	0	29	31	7	13	0	6.52
Phil Clark	R	25	0	1	.000	1	7	0	0	8	11	3	1	0	3.38
1 Herm Wehmeier	R	31	0	1	.000	0	3	3	0	6	13	2	4	0	13.50
Bill Smith	L	24	0	1	.000	0	2	1	0	10	12	4	4	0	6.30
Von McDaniel (SA)	R	19	0	0	.000	0	2	1	0	2	5	5	0	0	13.50
2 Johnny O'Brien	R	27	0	0	.000	0	1	0	0	2	7	2	2	0	22.50
Tom Flanigan	L	23	0	0	.000	0	1	0	0	1	2	1	0	0	9.00
Tom Cheney (MS) 23															

LOS ANGELES 7th 71-83 .461 21 — WALT ALSTON

NAME	G by POS	B	AGE	G	AB	R	H	2B	3B	HR	RBI	BB	SO	SB	BA	SA
TOTALS			29	154	5173	668	1297	166	50	172	627	495	850	73	.251	.402
Gil Hodges	1B122, 3B15, OF9, C1	R	34	141	475	68	123	15	1	22	64	52	87	8	.259	.434
Charlie Neal	2B132, 3B9	R	27	140	473	87	120	9	6	22	65	61	91	7	.254	.438
Don Zimmer	SS114, 3B12, 2B1	R	27	127	455	52	119	15	2	17	60	28	92	14	.262	.415
Dick Gray	3B55	R	26	58	197	25	49	5	6	9	30	19	30	1	.249	.472
Carl Furillo	OF119	R	36	122	411	54	119	19	3	18	83	35	28	0	.290	.482
Duke Snider	OF92	L	31	106	327	45	102	12	3	15	58	32	49	2	.312	.505
Gino Cimoli	OF104	R	28	109	325	35	80	6	3	9	27	18	49	3	.246	.366
Johnny Roseboro	C104, OF5	L	25	114	384	52	104	11	9	14	43	36	56	11	.271	.456
Jim Gilliam	OF75, 3B44, 2B32	B	29	147	555	81	145	25	5	2	43	78	22	18	.261	.335
Norm Larker	OF43, 1B25	L	27	99	253	32	70	16	5	4	29	29	21	1	.277	.427
Elmer Valo	OF26	L	37	65	101	9	25	2	1	1	14	12	11	0	.248	.317
Joe Pignatano	C57	R	28	63	142	18	31	4	0	9	17	16	26	4	.218	.437
Pee Wee Reese	SS22, 3B21	R	39	59	147	21	33	7	2	4	17	26	15	1	.224	.381
2 Steve Bilko	1B25	R	29	47	101	13	21	1	2	7	18	8	37	0	.208	.465
Don Drysdale	P44	R	21	47	66	9	15	1	1	7	12	3	25	0	.227	.591
Don Demeter	OF39	R	23	43	106	11	20	2	0	5	8	5	32	2	.189	.349
1 Randy Jackson	3B17	R	32	35	65	8	12	3	0	1	4	5	10	0	.185	.277
Rube Walker	C20	L	32	25	44	3	5	2	0	1	7	5	10	0	.114	.227
Bob Lillis	SS19	R	28	20	69	10	27	3	1	1	5	4	2	1	.391	.507
Ron Fairly	OF15	L	19	15	53	6	15	1	0	2	8	6	7	0	.283	.415

Jim Gentile 24 L 4-30, 1Don Newcombe 32 L 5-12, Frank Howard 21 R 7-29, Don Miles 22 L 4-22, Earl Robinson 21 R 3-15, Bob Wilson 30 R 1-5, Roy Campanella (BX) 36

NAME	T	AGE	W	L	PCT	SV	G	GS	CG	IP	H	BB	SO	ShO	ERA
		26	71	83	.461	31	154	154	30	1368	1399	606	855	7	4.47
Johnny Podres	L	25	13	15	.464	1	39	31	10	210	208	78	143	2	3.73
Don Drysdale	R	21	12	13	.480	0	44	29	6	212	214	72	131	1	4.16
Sandy Koufax	L	22	11	11	.500	1	40	26	5	159	132	105	131	0	4.47
Stan Williams	R	21	9	7	.563	0	27	21	3	119	99	65	80	2	4.01
Clem Labine	R	31	6	6	.500	14	52	2	0	104	112	33	43	0	4.15
Fred Kipp	L	26	6	6	.500	0	40	9	0	102	107	45	58	0	5.03
Carl Erskine	R	31	4	4	.500	0	31	9	2	98	115	35	54	1	5.14
2 Johnny Klippstein	R	30	3	5	.375	9	45	0	0	90	81	44	73	0	3.80
Roger Craig	R	27	2	1	.667	0	9	2	1	32	30	12	16	0	4.50
Danny McDevitt	L	25	2	6	.250	0	13	10	2	48	71	31	26	0	7.50
Don Bessent (SA)	R	27	1	0	1.000	0	19	0	0	24	24	17	13	0	3.38
Bob Giallombardo	L	21	1	1	.500	0	6	5	0	26	29	15	14	0	3.81
Ralph Mauriello	R	23	1	1	.500	0	3	2	0	12	10	8	11	0	4.50
Ed Roebuck	R	26	0	1	.000	5	32	0	0	44	45	15	26	0	3.48
1 Don Newcombe	R	32	0	6	.000	0	11	8	1	34	53	8	16	0	7.94
Babe Birrer	R	29	0	0	.000	1	16	0	0	34	43	7	16	0	4.50
Larry Sherry	R	22	0	0	.000	0	5	0	0	4	10	7	2	0	13.50
Ron Negray	R	28	0	0	.000	0	4	0	0	11	12	7	2	0	7.36
Jackie Collum	L	31	0	0	.000	0	2	0	0	3	4	2	0	0	9.00

PHILADELPHIA 8th 69-85 .448 23 — MAYO SMITH 39-44 .470 — EDDIE SAYWER 30-41 .423

NAME	G by POS	B	AGE	G	AB	R	H	2B	3B	HR	RBI	BB	SO	SB	BA	SA
TOTALS			30	154	5363	664	1424	238	56	124	630	573	871	51	.266	.400
Ed Bouchee (IL)	1B89	L	25	89	334	55	86	19	5	9	39	51	74	1	.257	.425
Solly Hemus	2B84, 3B1	L	35	105	334	53	95	14	3	8	36	51	34	3	.284	.416
Chico Fernandez	SS148	R	26	148	522	38	120	18	5	6	51	37	48	12	.230	.318
Willie Jones	3B110, 1B1	R	32	118	398	52	108	15	1	14	60	49	45	1	.271	.420
Wally Post	OF91	R	28	110	379	51	107	21	3	12	62	32	74	0	.282	.449
Richie Ashburn	OF152	L	31	152	615	98	215	24	13	2	33	97	48	30	.350	.441
Harry Anderson	OF87, 1B49	L	26	140	515	80	155	34	6	23	97	59	95	0	.301	.524
Stan Lopata	C80	R	32	86	258	36	64	9	0	9	33	60	63	0	.248	.388
Ted Kazanski	2B59, SS22, 3B16	R	24	95	289	21	66	12	2	3	35	22	34	2	.228	.315
Dave Philley	OF24, 1B18	B	38	91	207	30	64	11	4	3	31	15	20	1	.309	.444
Bob Bowman	OF57	R	27	91	184	31	53	11	2	8	24	16	30	0	.288	.500
Rip Repulski	OF56	R	30	85	238	33	58	9	4	13	40	15	47	0	.244	.479
2 Carl Sawatski	C53	L	30	60	183	12	42	4	1	5	12	16	42	0	.230	.344
Chuck Essegian	OF30	R	26	39	114	15	28	5	2	5	16	12	34	0	.246	.456
Granny Hamner (KJ)	3B22, 2B11, SS3	R	31	35	133	18	40	7	3	2	18	8	16	0	.301	.444
Bobby Young	2B21	L	33	32	60	7	14	1	1	1	4	1	5	0	.233	.333
Pancho Herrera	3B16, 1B11	R	24	29	63	5	17	3	0	1	6	7	15	1	.270	.365
2 Jim Hegan	C25	R	37	25	59	5	13	6	0	0	6	4	16	0	.220	.322

Joe Lonnett 31 R 7-50, Jimmie Coker 22 R 1-6, Roy Smalley 32 R 0-2, Mack Burk (MS) 23 0-1

NAME	T	AGE	W	L	PCT	SV	G	GS	CG	IP	H	BB	SO	ShO	ERA
		28	69	85	.448	15	154	154	51	1397	1480	446	778	6	4.32
Robin Roberts	R	31	17	14	.548	0	35	34	21	270	270	51	130	1	3.23
Ray Semproch	R	27	13	11	.542	0	36	30	12	204	211	58	92	2	3.93
Jack Sanford	R	29	10	13	.435	0	38	27	7	186	197	81	106	2	4.45
Dick Farrell	R	24	8	9	.471	11	54	0	0	94	84	40	73	0	3.35
Curt Simmons	L	29	7	14	.333	1	29	27	7	168	196	40	78	1	4.39
Jim Hearn	R	37	5	3	.625	0	39	1	0	73	88	27	33	0	4.19
Jack Meyer	R	26	3	6	.333	2	37	5	1	90	77	33	87	0	3.60
Don Cardwell	R	22	3	6	.333	0	16	14	3	108	99	37	77	0	4.50
Jim Owens (MS)	R	24	1	0	1.000	0	1	1	0	7	4	5	3	0	2.57
Bob Miller	R	32	1	1	.500	0	17	0	0	22	36	9	9	0	11.86
Seth Morehead	L	23	1	6	.143	0	27	11	0	92	121	26	54	0	5.87
Warren Hacker	R	33	0	1	.000	0	9	1	0	17	24	8	4	0	7.41
Don Erickson	R	26	0	1	.000	1	9	0	0	12	11	9	9	0	4.50
John Gray	R	30	0	0	.000	0	15	0	0	17	12	14	10	0	4.24
John Anderson	R	25	0	0	.000	0	5	1	0	16	26	4	9	0	7.88
Angelo LiPetri	R	27	0	0	.000	0	4	0	0	4	6	0	1	0	11.25
Bob Conley	R	24	0	0	.000	0	2	2	0	8	9	1	0	0	7.88
1 Tom Qualters	R	23	0	0	.000	0	1	0	0	2	2	1	0	0	4.50
Hank Mason	R	27	0	0	.000	0	1	0	0	5	7	2	3	0	10.80

WORLD SERIES – NEW YORK (AL) 4 MILWAUKEE (NL) 3

LINE SCORES

TEAM	1	2	3	4	5	6	7	8	9	10	11	12	R	H	E
Game 1 October 1 at Milwaukee															
NY (AL)	0	0	0	1	2	0	0	0	0	0			3	8	1
MIL (NL)	0	0	0	2	0	0	0	1	0	1			4	10	0
Ford, Duren (8) — Spahn															
Game 2 October 2 at Milwaukee															
NY	1	0	0	1	0	0	0	0	3				5	7	0
MIL	7	1	0	0	0	0	2	3	X				13	15	1
Turley, Maas (1), Kucks (1), Dickson (5), Monroe (8) — Burdette															
Game 3 October 4 at New York															
MIL	0	0	0	0	0	0	0	0	0				0	6	0
NY	0	0	0	0	2	0	2	0	X				4	4	0
Rush, McMahon (8) — Larsen, Duren (8)															
Game 4 October 5 at New York															
MIL	0	0	0	0	0	1	1	1	0				3	9	0
NY	0	0	0	0	0	0	0	0	0				0	2	1
Spahn — Ford, Kucks (8), Dickson (9)															
Game 5 October 6 at New York															
MIL	0	0	0	0	0	0	0	0	0				0	5	0
NY	0	0	1	0	0	6	0	0	X				7	10	0
Burdette, Pizarro (6), Willey (8) — Turley															
Game 6 October 8 at Milwaukee															
NY	1	0	0	0	0	1	0	0	0	2			4	10	1
MIL	1	1	0	0	0	0	0	0	0	1			3	10	4
Ford, Ditmar (2), Duren (6), Turley (10) — Spahn, McMahon (10)															
Game 7 October 9 at Milwaukee															
NY	0	2	0	0	0	0	0	4	0				6	8	0
MIL	1	0	0	0	0	1	0	0	0				2	5	2
Larsen, Turley (3) — Burdette, McMahon (9)															

COMPOSITE BATTING

NAME	POS	G	AB	R	H	2B	3B	HR	RBI	BA
New York (AL) Totals		7	233	29	49	5	1	10	29	.210
Bauer	OF	7	31	6	10	0	0	4	8	.323
McDougald	2B	7	28	5	9	2	0	2	4	.321
Skowron	1B	7	28	3	7	0	0	2	7	.259
Berra	C	7	27	3	6	3	0	0	2	.222
Mantle	OF	7	24	4	6	0	1	2	3	.250
Kubek	SS	7	21	0	1	0	0	0	1	.048
Howard	OF	6	18	4	4	0	0	0	2	.222
Lumpe	3B-SS	6	12	0	2	0	0	0	0	.167
Carey	3B	5	12	1	1	0	0	0	0	.083
Siebern	OF	3	8	1	1	0	0	0	0	.125
Turley	P	4	5	0	1	0	0	0	2	.200
Richardson	3B	4	5	0	0	0	0	0	0	.000
Ford	P	3	4	1	0	0	0	0	0	.000
Duren	P	3	3	0	0	0	0	0	0	.000
Slaughter	PH	4	3	1	0	0	0	0	0	.000
Larsen	P	2	2	0	0	0	0	0	0	.000
Kucks	P	2	1	0	1	0	0	0	0	1.000
Throneberry	PH	1	1	0	0	0	0	0	0	.000
Ditmar	P	1	1	0	0	0	0	0	0	.000
Dickson	P	2	0	0	0	0	0	0	0	.000
Maas	P	1	0	0	0	0	0	0	0	.000
Monroe	P	1	0	0	0	0	0	0	0	.000
Milwaukee (NL) Totals		7	240	25	60	10	1	3	24	.250
Schoendienst	2B	7	30	5	9	3	1	0	0	.300
Aaron	OF	7	27	3	9	2	0	0	2	.333
Covington	OF	7	26	2	7	0	0	0	4	.269
Mathews	3B	7	25	3	4	2	0	0	3	.160
Logan	SS	7	25	3	3	2	0	0	2	.120
Crandall	C	7	25	4	6	0	0	1	3	.240
Bruton	OF	7	17	2	7	0	0	1	2	.412
Torre	1B	7	17	0	3	0	0	0	0	.176
Adcock	1B	4	13	1	4	0	0	0	0	.308
Spahn	P	3	12	0	4	0	0	0	3	.333
Pafko	OF	4	9	0	3	1	0	0	1	.333
Burdette	P	3	9	1	1	0	0	1	3	.111
Hanebrink	PH	2	2	0	0	0	0	0	0	.000
Rush	P	1	2	0	0	0	0	0	0	.000
Wise	PH	2	1	0	0	0	0	0	0	.000
Mantilla	SS	4	0	1	0	0	0	0	0	.000
McMahon	P	3	0	0	0	0	0	0	0	.000
Pizarro	P	1	0	0	0	0	0	0	0	.000

COMPOSITE PITCHING

NAME	G	IP	H	BB	SO	W	L	SV	ERA
New York (AL) Totals	7	63.2	60	27	56	4	3	2	3.39
Turley	4	16.1	10	7	13	2	1	1	2.76
Ford	3	15.1	19	5	16	0	1	0	4.11
Larsen	2	9.1	9	6	9	1	0	0	0.96
Duren	3	9.1	7	6	14	1	1	1	1.93
Kucks	2	4.1	4	1	0	0	0	0	2.08
Dickson	2	4	4	0	1	0	0	0	4.50
Ditmar	1	3.2	2	0	2	0	0	0	0.00
Monroe	1	1	3	1	1	0	0	0	27.00
Maas	1	.1	2	1	0	0	0	0	81.00
Milwaukee (NL) Totals	7	63	49	21	42	3	4	0	3.71
Spahn	3	28.2	19	8	18	2	1	0	2.20
Burdette	3	22.1	22	4	12	1	2	0	5.64
Rush	1	6	3	5	2	0	1	0	3.00
McMahon	3	3.1	3	3	5	0	0	0	5.40
Pizarro	1	1.2	2	1	3	0	0	0	5.40
Willey	1	1	0	0	2	0	0	0	0.00

1959 Don't Count Your Pennants until They Hatch

Late in the season, San Francisco Giant officials were considering whether to play the World Series in Seals Stadium or to open the still-unfinished Candlestick Park. With eight games remaining on the schedule, the Giants led the Braves and Dodgers by two games. A decision would have to be made soon. It was, but not in the Giants' front office. The Dodgers came into Seals Stadium on the weekend of September 19-20, and bumped off the Jints three straight times, sending them reeling into third place. Milwaukee kept pace with the Dodgers the final week, each team winning and losing on alternate days, while the Giants were dropping four out of five to the Cubs and Cards, making it seven losses in their final eight games. On Sunday, Roger Craig and Bob Buhl hurled victories to end the National League race in a tie for the third time. The three-game play-off only went two games, as the Dodgers beat the Braves two straight to take the pennant and break their post-season jinx, after having been the victims in 1946 and 1951.

Shooting from seventh to the top in one year, the heart of the team consisted of two old Brooklyn veterans, one young veteran, one newly acquired veteran, and three mid-season recalls from Spokane. Duke Snider and Gil Hodges provided power, Don Drysdale won 17 games, and ex-Cardinal Wally Moon hit .302 with 74 RBI's. Roger Craig fit into the starting rotation, Larry Sherry was a strong reliever, and Maury Wills plugged a gapping hole in the infield at shortstop. A blend of old and new, the Dodgers had no standout stars, unlike their rivals. Hank Aaron and Eddie Mathews *were* the Brave offense; Spahn, Burdette, and Buhl *were* the hill staff. Willie Mays and Orlando Cepeda carried the Giant attack, joined in August by a young powerhouse named Willie McCovey. The Giants' five-man pitching staff of Johnny Antonelli, Sam Jones, Jack Sanford, Mike McCormick, and Stu Miller collapsed in the stretch due to overuse by manager Bill Rigney. The trailing teams boasted of a second straight MVP in Ernie Banks of Chicago—and the Pirates had an 18-1 relief pitcher in Elroy Face and a superb performance from Harvey Haddix, who threw 12 perfect innings only to be defeated in the 13th.

For once, all was not ho-hum in the American League. The fact that it was not become clear on May 20, when the New York Yankees shocked the world by falling into last place. While Cleveland and Chicago were fighting over first, the heavily-favored Yankees trailed the lowly Senators. New York was able to climb back into contention but never could forge ahead of the White Sox or Indians. The Go-Go Sox, with a high-octane running team, took over first for keeps on July 28, but could shake the Indians only by sweeping a four-game series from them August 28-30. MVP Nellie Fox, and Luis Aparicio ran the guerrilla attack and provided an air-tight defense. Jim Landis and Sherm Lollar also starred, while 39-year-old Early Wynn won 22 games, Bob Shaw won 18 games and a starter's job, and oldsters, Gerry Staley and Turk Lown, provided solid relief work. Ted Kluszewski came over from the National League on waivers August 25, and provided punch in the stretch. Although Cleveland paced the loop in homers and batting, their pitching was no match for Chicago; Rocky Colavito belted 42 home runs for the Tribe, while Tito Francona hit .363 after coming off the bench.

The White Sox expected to run on the Dodgers in the World Series, but catcher John Roseboro's arm put an end to Al Lopez's ideas. After Ted Kluszewski led Chicago to an 11-0 first-game victory, the Dodgers took four of the next five games behind Larry Sherry's two wins and two saves, to give California a championship in its second year in the majors.

The year also saw old-timers, Stan Musial and Ted Williams, experience the first off-seasons in their long careers, as both became part-time players. Another old-timer, former Brooklyn general manager Branch Rickey, attempted a comeback as president of the proposed Continental League. The threat of a new major league painfully forced big league owners to consider expansion—a move which baseball had avoided for 58 years.

1959 AMERICAN LEAGUE

NAME	G by POS	B	AGE	G	AB	R	H	2B	3B	HR	RBI	BB	SO	SB	BA	SA
CHICAGO 1st 94-60 .610	AL LOPEZ															
TOTALS			30	156	5297	669	1325	220	46	97	620	580	634	113	.250	.364
Earl Torgeson	1B103	L	35	127	277	40	61	5	3	9	45	62	55	7	.220	.357
Nellie Fox	2B156	L	31	156	**624**	84	191	34	6	2	70	71	13	5	.306	.389
Luis Aparicio	SS152	R	25	152	612	98	157	18	5	6	51	52	40	**56**	.257	.332
Bubba Phillips	3B100, OF23	R	29	117	379	43	100	27	1	5	40	27	28	1	.264	.380
Jim McAnany	OF67	R	22	67	210	22	58	9	3	0	27	19	26	2	.276	.348
Jim Landis	OF148	R	25	149	515	78	140	26	7	5	60	78	68	20	.272	.379
Al Smith	OF128, 3B1	R	31	129	472	65	112	16	4	17	55	46	74	7	.237	.396
Sherm Lollar	C122, 1B24	R	34	140	505	63	134	22	3	22	84	55	49	4	.265	.451
Billy Goodman	3B74, 2B3	L	33	104	268	21	67	14	1	1	28	19	20	3	.250	.321
Jim Rivera	OF69	L	36	80	177	18	39	9	4	4	19	11	19	5	.220	.384
Sammy Esposito	3B45, SS14, 2B2	R	27	69	66	12	11	1	0	1	5	11	16	0	.167	.227
Norm Cash	1B31	L	24	58	104	16	25	0	1	4	16	18	9	1	.240	.375
Johnny Romano	C38	R	24	53	126	20	37	5	1	5	25	23	18	0	.294	.468
Johnny Callison	OF41	L	20	49	104	12	18	3	0	3	12	13	20	0	.173	.288
2 Harry Simpson	OF12, 1B1	L	33	38	75	5	14	5	1	2	13	4	14	0	.187	.360
2 Ted Kluszewski	1B29	L	34	31	101	11	30	2	1	2	10	9	10	0	.297	.396
2 Del Ennis	OF25	R	34	26	96	10	21	6	0	2	7	4	10	0	.219	.344
Earl Battey	C20	R	24	26	64	9	14	1	2	2	7	8	13	0	.219	.391
2 Larry Doby (BN)	OF12, 1B2	L	35	21	58	1	14	1	1	0	9	2	13	1	.241	.293
Ron Jackson	1B5	R	25	10	14	3	3	1	0	1	2	1	0	0	.214	.500

1 Ray Boone 35 R 5-21, Lou Skizas 27 R 1-13, Joe Hicks 26 L 3-7, Don Mueller 32 L 2-4, J. C. Martin 22 L 1-4, Cam Carreon 21 R 0-1

NAME	T	AGE	W	L	PCT	SV	G	GS	CG	IP	H	BB	SO	ShO	ERA
		32	**94**	60	**.610**	**36**	156	156	44	**1425**	1297	525	761	13	**3.29**
Early Wynn	R	39	**22**	10	.688	0	37	**37**	14	**256**	202	**119**	179	5	3.16
Bob Shaw	R	26	18	6	**.750**	3	47	26	8	231	217	54	89	3	2.69
Billy Pierce	L	32	14	15	.483	0	34	33	12	224	217	62	114	2	3.62
Turk Lown	R	35	9	2	.818	**15**	60	0	0	93	73	42	63	0	2.90
Dick Donovan	R	31	9	10	.474	0	31	29	5	180	171	58	71	1	3.65
Gerry Staley	R	38	8	5	.615	14	**67**	0	0	116	111	25	54	0	2.25
Barry Latman	R	23	8	5	.615	0	37	21	5	156	138	72	97	2	3.75
Ray Moore	R	33	3	6	.333	0	29	8	0	90	86	46	49	0	4.10
Rudy Arias	L	28	2	0	1.000	2	34	0	0	44	49	20	28	0	4.09
Joe Stanka	R	27	1	0	1.000	0	2	0	0	5	2	4	3	0	3.60
Ken McBride	R	23	0	1	.000	1	11	2	0	23	20	17	12	0	3.13
1 Don Rudolph	L	27	0	0	.000	1	4	0	0	3	4	2	0	0	0.00
Claude Raymond	R	22	0	0	.000	0	3	0	0	4	5	2	1	0	9.00
Gary Peters	L	22	0	0	.000	0	2	0	0	1	2	2	1	0	0.00

NAME	G by POS	B	AGE	G	AB	R	H	2B	3B	HR	RBI	BB	SO	SB	BA	SA
CLEVELAND 2nd 89-65 .578 5	JOE GORDON															
TOTALS			29	154	5288	**745**	1390	216	25	**167**	**682**	433	721	33	**.263**	**.408**
Vic Power	1B121, 2B21, 3B7	R	27	145	595	102	172	31	6	10	60	40	22	9	.289	.412
Billy Martin (SJ-BY)	2B67, 3B4	R	31	73	242	37	63	7	0	9	24	7	18	0	.260	.401
Woodie Held	SS103, 3B40, OF6, 2B3	R	27	143	525	82	132	19	3	29	71	47	118	1	.251	.465
George Strickland	3B80, SS50, 2B4	R	33	132	441	55	105	15	2	3	48	52	64	1	.238	.302
Rocky Colavito	OF154	R	25	154	588	90	151	24	0	**42**	111	71	86	3	.257	.512
Jimmy Piersall	OF91, 3B1	R	29	100	317	42	78	13	2	4	30	24	31	6	.246	.338
Minnie Minoso	OF148	R	36	148	570	92	172	32	0	21	92	54	46	8	.302	.468
Russ Nixon	C74	L	24	82	258	23	62	10	3	1	29	15	28	0	.240	.314
Tito Francona	OF64, 1B35	L	25	122	399	68	145	17	2	20	79	35	42	2	.363	.566
2 Jim Baxes	2B48, 3B22	R	30	77	247	35	59	11	0	15	34	21	47	0	.239	.466
2 Ed Fitz Gerald (BG)	C45	R	35	49	129	12	35	6	1	1	4	12	14	0	.271	.357
Dick Brown	C48	R	24	48	141	15	31	7	0	5	16	11	39	0	.220	.376
Ray Webster	2B24, 3B4	R	21	40	74	10	15	2	1	2	10	5	7	1	.203	.338
Elmer Valo	OF2	L	38	34	24	3	7	0	0	0	5	7	0	0	.292	.292
Carroll Hardy	OF15	R	26	32	53	12	11	1	0	0	2	3	7	1	.208	.226
2 Granny Hamner	SS10, 2B7, 3B5	R	32	27	67	4	11	1	1	1	3	1	8	0	.164	.254
1 Hal Naragon	C10	L	30	14	36	6	10	4	1	0	5	3	2	0	.278	.444
Chuck Tanner	OF10	L	29	14	48	6	12	2	0	1	5	2	9	0	.250	.354
Gene Leek	3B13, SS1	R	22	13	36	7	8	3	0	1	5	2	7	0	.222	.389

2 Willie Jones 33 R 4-18, Don Dillard 22 L 4-10, Billy Moran 25 R 5-17, 1 Jim Bolger 27 R 0-7, Gordy Coleman 24 L 8-15, 1 Randy Jackson 33 R 1-7

NAME	T	AGE	W	L	PCT	SV	G	GS	CG	IP	H	BB	SO	ShO	ERA
		27	89	65	.578	23	154	154	**58**	1384	1230	**635**	799	7	3.75
Cal McLish	R	33	19	8	.704	1	35	32	13	235	**253**	72	113	0	3.64
Gary Bell	R	22	16	11	.593	5	44	28	12	234	208	105	136	1	4.04
Jim Perry	R	23	12	10	.545	4	44	13	8	153	122	55	79	2	2.65
Mudcat Grant	R	23	10	7	.588	3	38	19	6	165	140	81	85	1	4.15
Herb Score	L	26	9	11	.450	0	30	25	9	161	123	115	147	1	4.70
3 Jack Harshman	L	31	5	1	.833	1	13	6	5	66	46	13	35	1	2.59
Don Ferrarese	L	30	5	3	.625	0	15	10	4	76	58	51	45	0	3.20
Al Cicotte	R	29	3	1	.750	1	26	1	0	44	46	25	23	0	5.32
Bobby Locke	R	25	3	2	.600	2	24	7	0	78	66	41	40	0	3.12
Mike Garcia	R	35	3	6	.333	1	29	8	1	72	72	31	49	0	4.00
Dick Brodowski	R	26	2	2	.500	5	18	0	0	30	19	21	9	0	1.80
1 Humberto Robinson	R	29	1	0	1.000	0	5	0	0	9	9	4	6	0	4.00
Jake Striker	L	25	1	0	1.000	0	1	1	0	7	8	4	5	0	2.57
2 Riverboat Smith	L	31	0	1	.000	0	12	3	0	29	31	12	17	0	5.28
Bud Podbielan	R	35	0	1	.000	0	6	0	0	12	17	2	5	0	6.00
Johnny Briggs	R	25	0	1	.000	0	4	1	0	13	12	3	5	0	2.08

NAME	G by POS	B	AGE	G	AB	R	H	2B	3B	HR	RBI	BB	SO	SB	BA	SA
NEW YORK 3rd 79-75 .513 15	CASEY STENGEL															
TOTALS			28	155	**5379**	687	**1397**	224	40	153	651	457	828	45	.260	.402
Bill Skowron (XJ)	1B72	R	28	74	282	39	84	13	5	15	59	20	47	1	.298	.539
Bobby Richardson	2B109, SS14, 3B12	R	23	134	469	53	141	18	6	2	33	26	20	5	.301	.377
Tony Kubek	SS67, OF53, 3B17, 2B1	L	22	132	512	67	143	25	7	6	51	24	46	3	.279	.391
2 Hector Lopez	3B76, OF35	R	26	112	406	60	115	16	2	16	69	28	54	3	.283	.451
Hank Bauer	OF111	R	36	114	341	44	81	20	0	9	39	33	54	4	.238	.375
Mickey Mantle	OF143	B	27	144	541	104	154	23	4	31	75	94	**126**	21	.285	.514
Norm Siebern	OF93, 1B2	L	25	120	380	52	103	17	0	11	53	41	71	3	.271	.403
Yogi Berra	C116, OF7	L	34	131	472	64	134	25	1	19	69	43	38	1	.284	.462
Gil McDougald	2B53, SS52, 3B25	R	31	127	434	44	109	16	8	4	34	35	40	0	.251	.353
Elston Howard	1B50, C43, OF28	R	30	125	443	59	121	24	6	18	73	20	57	0	.273	.476
Marv Throneberry	1B54, OF13	L	25	80	192	27	46	5	0	8	22	18	51	0	.240	.391
1 Enos Slaughter	OF26	L	43	74	99	10	17	2	0	6	21	13	19	1	.172	.374
Johnny Blanchard	C12, OF8, 1B1	L	26	49	59	6	10	1	0	2	4	7	12	0	.169	.288
Clete Boyer	SS26, 3B16	R	22	47	114	4	20	2	0	0	3	6	23	1	.175	.193
Andy Carey (IL)	3B34	R	27	41	101	11	26	1	0	3	9	7	17	1	.257	.356
Fritzie Brickell	SS15, 2B3	R	24	18	39	4	10	1	0	1	4	1	10	0	.256	.359
1 Jerry Lumpe	3B12, SS4, 2B1	L	26	18	45	2	10	0	0	0	2	6	7	0	.222	.222
2 Jim Pisoni	OF15	R	29	17	17	2	3	0	1	0	1	1	9	0	.176	.294

Gordon Windhorn 25 R 0-11, Ken Hunt 24 R 4-12

NAME	T	AGE	W	L	PCT	SV	G	GS	CG	IP	H	BB	SO	ShO	ERA
		28	79	75	.513	28	155	155	38	1399	1281	594	**836**	**15**	3.60
Whitey Ford	L	30	16	10	.615	1	35	29	9	204	194	89	114	2	3.04
Duke Maas	R	30	14	8	.636	4	38	21	3	138	149	53	67	1	4.43
Art Ditmar	R	30	13	9	.591	1	38	25	7	202	156	52	96	1	2.90
Bob Turley	R	28	8	11	.421	0	33	22	7	154	141	83	111	3	4.32
Bobby Shantz	L	33	7	3	.700	3	33	4	2	95	64	33	66	2	2.37
Jim Coates	R	26	6	1	.857	3	37	4	2	100	89	36	64	0	2.88
Don Larsen	R	29	6	7	.462	0	25	18	3	125	122	76	69	1	4.32
Ryne Duren	R	30	3	6	.333	14	41	0	0	77	49	43	96	0	1.87
2 Ralph Terry	R	23	3	7	.300	0	24	16	5	127	130	30	55	1	3.40
Eli Grba	R	24	2	5	.286	0	19	6	0	50	52	39	23	0	6.48
John Gabler	R	28	1	1	.500	0	3	1	0	19	21	10	11	0	2.84
2 Gary Blaylock	R	27	0	1	.000	0	15	1	0	26	30	15	20	0	3.46
1 Johnny Kucks	R	25	0	1	.000	0	9	1	0	17	21	9	9	0	8.47
1 Tom Sturdivant	R	29	0	2	.000	0	7	3	0	25	20	9	16	0	5.04
Jim Bronstad	R	23	0	3	.000	2	16	3	0	29	34	13	14	0	5.28
Zack Monroe	R	27	0	0	.000	0	3	0	0	3	3	2	1	0	6.00
1 Mark Freeman	R	28	0	0	.000	0	1	1	0	7	6	2	4	0	2.57

DETROIT 4th 76-78 .494 18 — BILL NORMAN 2-15 .118 JIMMY DYKES 74-63 .540

NAME	G by POS	B	AGE	G	AB	R	H	2B	3B	HR	RBI	BB	SO	SB	BA	SA
TOTALS			28	154	5211	713	1346	196	30	160	667	580	737	34	.258	.400
Gail Harris	1B93	L	27	114	349	39	77	4	3	9	39	29	49	0	.221	.327
Frank Bolling	2B126	R	27	127	459	56	122	18	3	13	55	45	37	2	.266	.403
Rocky Bridges	SS110, 2B5	R	31	116	381	38	102	16	3	3	35	30	35	1	.268	.349
Eddie Yost	3B146, 2B1	R	32	148	521	**115**	145	19	0	21	61	**135**	77	9	.278	.436
Harvey Kuenn	OF137	R	28	139	561	99	**198**	**42**	7	9	71	48	37	7	**.353**	.501
Al Kaline	OF136	R	24	136	511	86	167	19	2	27	94	72	42	10	.327	**.530**
Charlie Maxwell	OF136	L	32	145	518	81	130	12	2	31	95	81	91	0	.251	.461
Lou Berberet	C95	L	29	100	338	38	73	8	2	13	44	35	59	0	.216	.367
Bobo Osborne	1B56, OF1	L	23	86	209	27	40	7	1	3	21	16	41	1	.191	.278
Coot Veal	SS72	R	26	77	89	12	18	1	0	1	15	8	7	0	.202	.247
2 Ted Lepcio	SS35, 2B24, 3B11	R	28	76	215	25	60	8	0	7	24	17	49	2	.279	.414
Red Wilson	C64	R	30	67	228	28	60	17	2	4	35	10	23	2	.263	.408
Neil Chrisley	OF21	L	27	65	106	7	14	3	0	6	11	12	10	0	.132	.330
Gus Zernial	1B32, OF1	R	36	60	132	11	30	4	0	7	26	7	27	0	.227	.417
Johnny Groth	OF41	R	32	55	102	12	24	7	1	1	10	7	14	0	.235	.353
1 Larry Doby	OF16	L	35	18	55	5	12	3	1	0	3	8	9	0	.218	.309

Steve Demeter 24 R 2-18, Ossie Alvarez 25 R 1-2, Ron Shoop 27 R 1-7, Charlie Lau 26 L 1-6

NAME	T	AGE	W	L	PCT	SV	G	GS	CG	IP	H	BB	SO	ShO	ERA
TOTALS		29	76	78	.494	24	154	154	53	1360	1327	432	829	9	4.20
Don Mossi	L	30	17	9	.654	0	34	30	15	228	210	49	125	3	3.36
Frank Lary	R	29	17	10	.630	0	32	32	11	223	225	46	137	3	3.55
Jim Bunning	R	27	17	13	.567	1	40	35	14	250	220	75	**201**	1	3.89
Paul Foytack	R	28	14	14	.500	1	39	**37**	11	240	239	64	110	2	4.65
Ray Narleski	R	30	4	12	.250	5	42	10	1	104	105	59	71	0	5.80
Jerry Davie	R	26	2	2	.500	0	11	5	1	37	40	17	20	0	4.14
1 Billy Hoeft	L	27	1	1	.500	0	2	2	0	9	6	4	2	0	5.00
Barney Schultz	R	32	1	2	.333	0	13	0	0	18	17	14	17	0	4.50
2 Dave Sisler	R	27	1	3	.250	7	32	0	0	52	46	36	29	0	3.98
Pete Burnside	L	28	1	3	.250	1	30	0	0	62	55	25	49	0	3.77
Tom Morgan	R	29	1	4	.200	9	46	1	0	93	94	18	39	0	3.97
Bob Bruce	R	26	0	1	.000	0	2	1	0	2	2	3	1	0	9.00
Jim Proctor	R	23	0	1	.000	0	2	1	0	3	8	3	0	0	15.00
2 Bob Smith	L	28	0	3	.000	0	9	0	0	11	20	3	10	0	8.18
George Susce	R	27	0	0	.000	0	9	0	0	15	24	9	9	0	12.60
Jim Stump	R	27	0	0	.000	0	5	0	0	11	12	4	6	0	2.45
Hank Aguirre	L	27	0	0	.000	0	3	0	0	3	4	3	3	0	3.00

BOSTON 5th 75-79 .487 19 — PINKY HIGGINS 31-41 .425 RUDY YORK 0-1 .000 BILLY JURGES 44-36 .550

NAME	G by POS	B	AGE	G	AB	R	H	2B	3B	HR	RBI	BB	SO	SB	BA	SA
TOTALS			29	154	5225	726	1335	**248**	28	125	671	**626**	810	68	.256	.385
Dick Gernert	1B75, OF25	R	30	117	298	41	78	14	1	11	42	52	49	1	.262	.426
Pete Runnels	2B101, 1B44, SS9	L	31	147	560	95	176	33	6	6	57	95	48	6	.314	.427
Don Buddin	SS150	R	25	151	485	75	117	24	1	10	53	92	99	6	.241	.357
Frank Malzone	3B154	R	29	154	604	90	169	34	2	19	92	42	58	6	.280	.437
Jackie Jensen	OF146	R	32	148	535	101	148	31	0	28	**112**	88	67	20	.277	.492
Gary Geiger	OF95	L	22	120	335	45	82	10	4	11	48	21	55	9	.245	.397
Ted Williams	OF76	L	40	103	272	32	69	15	0	10	43	52	27	0	.254	.419
Sammy White	C119	R	30	119	377	34	107	13	4	1	42	23	39	4	.284	.347
Marty Keough	OF69, 1B3	L	24	96	251	40	61	13	5	7	27	26	40	3	.243	.418
Vic Wertz	1B64	L	34	94	247	38	68	13	0	7	49	22	32	0	.275	.413
Gene Stephens (BA)	OF85	L	26	92	270	34	75	13	1	3	39	29	33	5	.278	.367
Pete Daley	C58	R	29	65	169	9	38	7	0	1	11	13	31	1	.225	.284
Jim Busby	OF34	R	32	61	102	16	23	8	0	1	5	5	18	0	.225	.333
Pumpsie Green	2B45, SS1	B	25	50	172	30	40	6	3	1	10	29	22	4	.233	.320
Jim Mahoney	SS30	R	25	31	23	10	3	0	0	1	4	3	7	0	.130	.261
2 Bobby Avila	2B11	R	35	22	45	7	11	0	0	3	6	6	11	0	.244	.444
Bill Renna	OF7	R	34	14	22	2	2	0	0	0	2	5	9	0	.091	.091

1 Billy Consolo 24 R 3-14, Jerry Mallett 23 R 4-15, Haywood Sullivan 28 R 0-2, 1 Ted Lepcio 28 R 1-3, Don Gile 24 R 2-10, 2 Herb Plews 31 L 1-12

NAME	T	AGE	W	L	PCT	SV	G	GS	CG	IP	H	BB	SO	ShO	ERA
TOTALS		27	75	79	.487	25	154	154	38	1364	1386	589	724	9	4.17
Jerry Casale	R	25	13	8	.619	0	31	26	9	180	162	89	93	3	4.30
Ike Delock	R	29	11	6	.647	0	28	17	4	134	120	62	55	0	2.96
Tom Brewer	R	27	10	12	.455	2	36	32	11	215	219	88	121	3	3.77
Frank Sullivan	R	29	9	11	.450	1	30	26	5	178	172	67	107	2	3.94
Bill Monbouquette	R	22	7	7	.500	0	34	17	4	152	165	33	87	0	4.14
Frank Baumann	L	26	6	4	.600	1	26	10	2	96	96	55	48	0	4.03
Mike Fornieles	R	27	5	3	.625	11	46	0	0	82	77	29	54	0	3.07
Nels Chittum	R	26	3	0	1.000	0	21	0	0	30	29	11	12	0	1.20
Leo Kiely	L	29	3	3	.500	7	41	0	0	56	67	18	30	0	4.18
2 Jack Harshman	L	31	2	3	.400	0	8	2	0	25	29	10	14	0	6.48
13Murray Wall	R	32	2	5	.286	3	26	0	0	49	57	26	14	0	5.51
Ted Wills	L	25	2	6	.250	0	9	8	2	56	68	24	24	0	5.30
Earl Wilson	R	24	1	1	.500	0	9	4	0	24	21	31	17	0	6.00
1 Al Schroll	R	27	1	4	.200	0	14	5	1	46	47	22	26	0	4.70
Ted Bowsfield	L	23	0	1	.000	0	5	2	0	9	16	9	4	0	15.00
Herb Moford	R	30	0	2	.000	0	4	2	0	9	10	6	7	0	11.00
2 Billy Hoeft	L	27	0	3	.000	0	5	3	0	18	22	8	8	0	5.50
1 Dave Sisler	R	27	0	0	.000	0	3	0	0	7	9	1	3	0	6.43

BALTIMORE 6th 74-80 .481 20 — PAUL RICHARDS

NAME	G by POS	B	AGE	G	AB	R	H	2B	3B	HR	RBI	BB	SO	SB	BA	SA
TOTALS			30	155	5208	551	1240	182	23	109	514	536	690	36	.238	.345
Bob Boyd	1B109	L	32	128	415	42	110	20	2	3	41	29	14	3	.265	.345
Billy Gardner	2B139, 3B1, SS12	R	31	140	401	34	87	13	2	6	27	38	61	2	.217	.304
Chico Carrasquel	SS89, 2B22, 3B2, 1B1	R	30	114	346	28	77	13	0	4	28	34	41	2	.223	.295
Brooks Robinson	3B87, 2B1	R	22	88	313	29	89	15	2	4	24	17	37	2	.284	.383
Gene Woodling	OF124	L	36	140	440	63	132	22	2	14	77	78	35	1	.300	.455
Willie Tasby	OF137	R	26	142	505	69	126	16	5	13	48	34	80	3	.250	.378
Bob Nieman	OF97	R	32	118	360	49	105	18	2	21	60	42	55	1	.292	.528
Gus Triandos	C125	R	28	126	393	43	85	7	1	25	73	65	56	0	.216	.430
Al Pilarcik	OF106	L	28	130	273	37	77	12	1	3	16	30	25	9	.282	.366
Billy Klaus	SS59, 3B49, 2B1	L	30	104	321	33	80	11	0	3	25	51	38	2	.249	.312
2 Albie Pearson	OF49	L	24	80	138	22	32	4	2	0	6	13	5	4	.232	.290
Joe Ginsberg	C62	L	32	65	166	14	30	2	0	1	14	21	13	1	.181	.211
Willie Miranda	SS47, 3B11, 2B5	B	33	65	88	8	14	5	0	0	7	7	16	0	.159	.216
2 Walt Dropo	1B54, 3B2	R	36	62	151	17	42	9	0	6	21	12	20	0	.278	.457
Jim Finigan	3B42, 2B6, SS2	R	30	48	119	14	30	6	0	1	10	9	10	1	.252	.328
Bob Hale	1B8	L	25	40	54	2	10	3	0	0	7	2	6	0	.185	.241
1 Whitey Lockman	1B22, 2B5, OF1	L	32	38	69	7	15	1	1	0	2	8	4	0	.217	.261
Barry Shetrone	OF23	L	20	33	79	8	16	1	1	0	5	5	9	3	.203	.241
1 Lenny Green	OF23	L	25	27	24	3	7	0	0	1	2	1	3	0	.292	.417
1 Bobby Avila	OF10, 2B8, 3B1	R	35	20	47	1	8	0	0	0	0	4	5	0	.170	.170

Joe Taylor 33 L 5-32, Jerry Adair 22 R 11-35, Fred Valentine 24 B 6-19, Leo Burke 25 R 2-10, Ron Hansen 21 R 0-4, Bob Saverine 18 B 0-0

NAME	T	AGE	W	L	PCT	SV	G	GS	CG	IP	H	BB	SO	ShO	ERA
TOTALS		27	74	80	.481	30	155	155	45	1400	1290	476	735	**15**	3.56
Milt Pappas	R	20	15	9	.625	3	33	27	15	209	175	75	120	4	3.27
Hoyt Wilhelm	R	35	15	11	.577	0	32	27	13	226	178	77	139	3	**2.19**
Hal Brown	R	34	11	9	.550	3	31	21	2	164	158	32	81	0	3.79
Jerry Walker	R	20	11	10	.524	4	30	22	7	182	160	52	100	2	2.92
Billy O'Dell	L	26	10	12	.455	1	38	24	6	199	163	67	88	2	2.94
Ernie Johnson	R	35	4	1	.800	1	31	1	0	50	57	19	29	0	4.14
Billy Loes	R	29	4	7	.364	14	37	0	0	64	58	25	34	0	4.08
Arnie Portocarrero	R	27	2	7	.222	0	27	14	1	90	107	32	23	0	6.80
3 Billy Hoeft	L	27	1	1	.500	0	16	3	0	41	50	19	30	0	5.71
Jack Fisher	R	20	1	6	.143	2	27	7	1	89	76	38	52	1	3.03
George Zuverink (SJ)	R	34	0	1	.000	0	6	0	0	13	15	6	1	0	4.15
1 Jack Harshman	L	31	0	6	.000	0	14	8	0	47	58	28	24	0	6.89
Wes Stock	R	25	0	0	.000	1	7	0	0	13	16	2	8	0	3.46
2 Rip Coleman	L	27	0	0	.000	0	3	0	0	4	4	2	4	0	0.00
George Bamberger	R	33	0	0	.000	1	3	1	0	8	15	2	2	0	7.88

KANSAS CITY 7th 66-88 .429 28 — HARRY CRAFT

NAME	G by POS	B	AGE	G	AB	R	H	2B	3B	HR	RBI	BB	SO	SB	BA	SA
TOTALS			28	154	5264	681	1383	231	43	117	638	481	780	34	**.263**	.390
Kent Hadley	1B95	L	24	113	288	40	73	11	1	10	39	24	74	1	.253	.403
Wayne Terwilliger	2B63, SS2, 3B1	R	34	74	180	27	48	11	0	2	18	19	31	2	.267	.361
Joe DeMaestri	SS115	R	30	118	352	31	86	16	5	6	34	28	65	1	.244	.369
Dick Williams	3B80, 1B32, OF23, 2B3	R	30	130	488	72	130	33	1	16	75	28	60	4	.266	.436
Roger Maris (IL)	OF117	L	24	122	433	69	118	21	7	16	72	58	53	2	.273	.464
Bill Tuttle	OF121	R	29	126	463	74	139	19	6	7	43	48	38	10	.300	.413
Bob Cerv	OF119	R	33	125	463	61	132	22	4	20	87	35	87	3	.285	.479
Frank House	C95	L	29	98	347	32	82	14	3	1	30	20	23	0	.236	.303
2 Jerry Lumpe	2B61, SS56, 3B4	L	26	108	403	47	98	11	5	3	28	41	32	2	.243	.318
Hal Smith	3B77, C22	R	28	108	292	36	84	12	0	5	31	34	39	0	.288	.380
Russ Snyder	OF64	L	25	73	243	41	76	13	2	3	21	19	29	6	.313	.420
2 Ray Boone	1B38, 3B3	R	35	61	132	19	36	6	0	2	12	27	17	1	.273	.364
Preston Ward	1B22, OF1	L	31	58	109	8	27	4	1	2	19	7	12	0	.248	.358
Harry Chiti	C47	R	26	55	162	20	44	11	1	5	25	17	26	0	.272	.444
Zeke Bella	OF25, 1B1	R	28	47	82	10	17	2	1	1	9	9	14	0	.207	.293
Bud Daley	P39	L	26	39	78	5	23	1	0	0	13	2	11	0	.295	.308
Whitey Herzog (IL)	OF34, 1B1	L	27	38	123	25	36	7	1	1	9	34	23	1	.293	.390
1 Hector Lopez	2B33	R	26	35	135	22	38	10	3	6	24	8	23	1	.281	.533
Ned Garver	P32	R	33	32	71	9	20	2	1	2	9	4	7	0	.282	.423
2 Ray Jablonski	3B17	R	32	25	65	4	17	1	0	2	8	3	11	0	.262	.369
2 Joe Morgan	3B2	L	28	20	21	2	4	0	1	0	3	3	7	0	.190	.286
Lou Klimchock	2B16	L	19	17	66	10	18	1	0	4	13	1	6	0	.273	.470

Tommy Carroll 22 R 1-7, 1 Harry Simpson 33 L 4-14, Bob Martyn 28 L 0-0

NAME	T	AGE	W	L	PCT	SV	G	GS	CG	IP	H	BB	SO	ShO	ERA
TOTALS		30	66	88	.429	21	154	154	44	1361	**1452**	492	703	8	4.35
Bud Daley	L	26	16	13	.552	1	39	29	12	216	212	62	125	2	3.17
Ray Herbert	R	29	11	11	.500	1	37	26	10	184	196	62	99	2	4.84
Ned Garver	R	33	10	13	.435	1	32	30	9	201	214	42	61	2	3.72
2 Johnny Kucks	R	25	8	11	.421	1	33	23	6	151	163	42	51	1	3.87
Bob Grim	R	29	6	10	.375	4	40	9	3	125	124	57	65	1	4.10
John Tsitouris	R	23	4	3	.571	0	24	10	0	83	90	35	50	0	4.99
Murry Dickson	R	42	2	1	.667	0	38	0	0	71	85	27	36	0	4.94
1 Ralph Terry	R	23	2	4	.333	0	9	7	2	46	56	19	35	0	5.28
2 Tom Sturdivant	R	29	2	6	.250	5	36	3	0	72	70	34	57	0	4.63
1 Rip Coleman	L	27	2	10	.167	2	29	11	2	81	85	34	54	0	4.56
Russ Meyer	R	35	1	0	1.000	1	18	0	0	24	24	11	10	0	4.50
Tom Gorman	R	34	1	0	1.000	1	17	0	0	20	24	14	9	0	7.20
Ken Johnson	R	26	1	1	.500	0	2	2	0	11	11	5	8	0	4.09
Dick Tomanek	L	28	0	1	.000	2	16	0	0	21	27	12	13	0	6.43
Al Grunwald	L	29	0	1	.000	1	6	1	0	11	18	11	9	0	8.18
Howie Reed	R	22	0	3	.000	0	6	3	0	21	26	10	11	0	7.29
Evans Killeen	R	23	0	0	.000	0	4	0	0	6	4	4	1	0	4.50
Marty Kutyna	R	26	0	0	.000	1	4	0	0	7	7	1	1	0	0.00
2 Mark Freeman	R	28	0	0	.000	0	3	0	0	4	6	3	1	0	9.00
George Brunet	L	24	0	0	.000	0	2	0	0	5	10	7	7	0	10.80

WASHINGTON 8th 63-91 .409 31 — COOKIE LAVAGETTO

NAME	G by POS	B	AGE	G	AB	R	H	2B	3B	HR	RBI	BB	SO	SB	BA	SA
TOTALS			27	154	5092	619	1205	173	32	163	579	517	**881**	51	.237	.379
Roy Sievers	1B93, OF13	R	32	115	385	55	93	19	0	21	49	53	62	1	.242	.455
Reno Bertoia	2B71, 3B5, SS1	R	24	90	308	33	73	10	0	8	29	29	48	2	.237	.347
2 Billy Consolo	SS75, 2B4	R	24	79	202	25	43	5	3	0	10	36	54	1	.213	.267
Harmon Killebrew	3B150, OF4	R	23	153	546	98	132	20	2	**42**	105	90	116	3	.242	.516
Faye Throneberry	OF86	L	28	117	327	36	82	11	2	10	42	33	61	6	.251	.388
Bob Allison	OF149	R	24	150	570	83	149	18	**9**	30	85	60	92	13	.261	.482
Jim Lemon	OF142	R	31	147	531	73	148	18	3	33	100	46	99	5	.279	.510
2 Hal Naragon	C54	L	30	71	195	12	47	3	2	0	11	8	9	0	.241	.277
Julio Becquer	1B53	L	27	108	220	20	59	12	5	1	26	8	17	3	.268	.382
Ron Samford	SS64, 2B23	R	29	91	237	23	53	13	0	5	22	11	29	1	.224	.342
2 Lenny Green	OF58	L	25	88	190	29	46	6	1	2	15	20	15	9	.242	.316
Clint Courtney (IL)	C53	L	32	72	189	19	44	4	1	2	18	20	19	0	.233	.296
Ken Aspromonte	2B52, SS12, 1B1, OF1	R	27	70	225	31	55	12	0	2	14	26	39	2	.244	.324
1 Jay Porter	C34, 1B2	R	26	37	106	8	24	4	0	1	10	11	16	0	.226	.292
Camilo Pascual	P32	R	25	32	86	10	26	2	0	0	3	5	11	0	.302	.326
Zoilo Versalles	SS29	R	19	29	59	4	9	0	0	1	1	4	15	1	.153	.203
1 Herb Plews	2B6	L	31	27	40	4	9	0	0	0	2	3	5	0	.225	.225
1 Albie Pearson	OF22	L	24	25	80	9	15	1	0	0	2	14	3	1	.188	.200
Josie Valdivielso	SS21	R	25	24	14	1	4	0	0	0	0	1	3	0	.286	.286
1 Ed Fitz Gerald	C16	R	35	19	62	5	12	3	0	0	5	4	8	0	.194	.242
Norm Zauchin	1B19	R	29	19	71	11	15	4	0	3	4	7	14	2	.211	.394

Steve Korcheck 26 R 8-51, Dan Dobbek 24 L 15-60, Johnny Schaive 25 R 9-59, Bobby Malkmus 27 R 0-0

NAME	T	AGE	W	L	PCT	SV	G	GS	CG	IP	H	BB	SO	ShO	ERA
TOTALS		27	63	**91**	.409	21	154	154	46	1360	1358	467	694	10	4.01
Camilo Pascual	R	25	17	10	.630	0	32	30	**17**	239	202	69	185	**6**	2.64
Pedro Ramos	R	24	13	**19**	.406	0	37	35	11	234	233	52	95	0	4.15
Bill Fischer	R	28	9	11	.450	0	34	29	6	187	211	43	62	1	4.28
Tex Clevenger	R	26	8	5	.615	8	50	7	2	117	114	51	71	2	3.92
Russ Kemmerer	R	27	8	17	.320	0	37	28	8	206	221	71	89	0	4.50
Hal Woodeschick	L	26	2	4	.333	0	31	3	0	61	58	36	30	0	3.69
Dick Hyde (SA)	R	30	2	5	.286	4	37	0	0	54	56	27	29	0	5.00
Hal Griggs	R	30	2	8	.200	2	37	10	2	98	103	52	43	1	5.23
John Romonosky	R	29	1	0	1.000	0	12	2	0	38	36	19	22	0	3.32
Chuck Stobbs	L	29	1	8	.111	7	41	7	0	91	82	24	50	0	2.97
Vito Valentinetti	R	30	0	2	.000	0	7	1	0	11	16	10	7	0	10.92
Jim Kaat	L	20	0	2	.000	0	3	2	0	5	7	4	2	0	12.60
Jack Kralick	L	24	0	0	.000	0	6	0	0	12	13	8	7	0	7.75
Ralph Lumenti	L	22	0	0	.000	0	2	0	0	3	2	1	2	0	0.00
2 Murray Wall	R	33	0	0	.000	0	1	0	0	1	3	0	0	0	9.00
Tom McAvoy	L	22	0	0	.000	0	1	0	0	3	1	2	0	0	0.00

LOS ANGELES 1st 88-68 .564 — WALT ALSTON (Defeated Milwaukee in playoff 2 games to 0)

NAME	G by POS	B	AGE	G	AB	R	H	2B	3B	HR	RBI	BB	SO	SB	BA	SA
TOTALS			28	156	5282	705	1360	196	46	148	667	**591**	891	**84**	.257	.396
Gil Hodges	1B113, 3B4	R	35	124	413	57	114	19	2	25	80	58	92	3	.276	.513
Charlie Neal	2B151, SS1	R	28	151	616	103	177	30	**11**	19	83	43	86	17	.287	.464
Don Zimmer	SS88, 3B5, 2B1	R	28	97	249	21	41	7	1	4	28	37	56	3	.165	.249
Jim Gilliam	3B132, 2B8, OF4	B	30	145	553	91	156	18	4	3	34	**96**	25	23	.282	.345
Duke Snider	OF107	L	32	126	370	59	114	11	2	23	88	58	71	1	.308	.535
Don Demeter	OF124	R	24	139	371	55	95	11	1	18	70	16	87	5	.256	.437
Wally Moon	OF143, 1B1	L	29	145	543	93	164	26	**11**	19	74	81	64	15	.302	.495
Johnny Roseboro	C117	L	26	118	397	39	92	14	7	10	38	52	69	7	.232	.378
Ron Fairly	OF88	L	20	118	244	27	58	12	1	4	23	31	29	0	.238	.344
Norm Larker	1B55, OF30	L	28	108	311	37	90	14	1	8	49	26	25	0	.289	.418
Maury Wills	SS82	B	26	83	242	27	63	5	2	0	7	13	27	7	.260	.298
Rip Repulski	OF31	R	31	53	94	11	24	4	0	2	14	13	23	0	.255	.362
Joe Pignatano	C49	R	29	52	139	17	33	4	1	1	11	21	15	1	.237	.302
Carl Furillo	OF25	R	37	50	93	8	27	4	0	0	13	7	11	0	.290	.333
Don Drysdale	P44	R	22	46	91	9	15	1	1	4	12	4	31	0	.165	.330
Bob Lillis	SS20	R	29	30	48	7	11	2	0	0	2	3	4	0	.229	.271
2 Chuck Essegian	OF10	R	27	24	46	6	14	6	0	1	5	4	11	0	.304	.500
1 Dick Gray	3B11	R	27	21	52	8	8	1	0	2	4	6	12	0	.154	.288
1 Jim Baxes	3B10	R	30	11	33	4	10	1	0	2	5	4	7	1	.303	.515
Frank Howard	OF6	R	22	9	21	2	3	0	1	1	6	2	9	0	.143	.381
1 Solly Drake	OF4	B	28	9	8	2	2	0	0	0	0	1	3	1	.250	.250

Sandy Amoros 29 L 1-5, Norm Sherry 27 R 1-3, Tommy Davis 20 R 0-1

NAME	T	AGE	W	L	PCT	SV	G	GS	CG	IP	H	BB	SO	ShO	ERA
		27	**88**	68	**.564**	**26**	156	156	43	**1412**	1317	**614**	**1077**	14	3.79
Don Drysdale	R	22	17	13	.567	2	44	36	15	271	237	93	**242**	**4**	3.45
Johnny Podres	L	26	14	9	.609	0	34	29	6	195	192	74	145	2	4.11
Roger Craig	R	28	11	5	.688	0	29	17	7	153	122	45	76	**4**	2.06
Danny McDevitt	L	26	10	8	.556	4	39	22	6	145	149	51	106	2	3.97
Sandy Koufax	L	23	8	6	.571	2	35	23	6	153	136	92	173	1	4.06
Larry Sherry	R	23	7	2	.778	3	23	9	1	94	75	43	72	1	2.20
Stan Williams	R	22	5	5	.500	0	35	15	2	125	102	86	89	0	3.96
Clem Labine	R	32	5	10	.333	9	56	0	0	85	91	25	37	0	3.92
Johnny Klippstein	R	31	4	0	1.000	2	28	0	0	46	48	33	30	0	5.87
Chuck Churn	R	29	3	2	.600	1	14	0	0	31	28	10	24	0	4.94
Art Fowler	R	36	3	4	.429	2	36	0	0	61	70	23	47	0	5.31
Gene Snyder	L	28	1	1	.500	0	11	2	0	26	32	20	20	0	5.54
Carl Erskine	R	32	0	3	.000	1	10	3	0	23	33	13	15	0	7.83
Fred Kipp	L	27	0	0	.000	0	2	0	0	3	2	3	1	0	0.00
Bill Harris	R	27	0	0	.000	0	1	0	0	2	0	3	0	0	0.00

MILWAUKEE 2nd 86-70 .551 2 — FRED HANEY (Defeated by Los Angeles in playoff 2 games to 0)

NAME	G by POS	B	AGE	G	AB	R	H	2B	3B	HR	RBI	BB	SO	SB	BA	SA
TOTALS			30	157	5388	724	1426	216	36	**177**	683	488	765	41	.265	.417
Joe Adcock	1B89, OF21	R	31	115	404	53	118	19	2	25	76	32	77	0	.292	.535
Felix Mantilla	2B60, SS23, 3B9, OF7	R	24	103	251	26	54	5	0	3	19	16	31	6	.215	.271
Johnny Logan	SS138	R	32	138	470	59	137	17	0	13	50	57	45	1	.291	.411
Eddie Mathews	3B148	L	27	148	594	118	182	16	8	**46**	114	80	71	2	.306	.593
Hank Aaron	OF152, 3B5	R	25	154	629	116	**223**	46	7	39	123	51	54	8	**.355**	**.636**
Bill Bruton	OF133	L	33	133	478	72	138	22	6	6	41	35	54	13	.289	.397
Wes Covington (KJ)	OF94	L	27	103	373	38	104	17	3	7	45	26	41	0	.279	.397
Del Crandall	C146	R	29	150	518	65	133	19	2	21	72	46	48	5	.257	.423
Frank Torre	1B87	L	27	115	263	23	60	15	1	1	33	35	12	0	.228	.304
Mickey Vernon	1B10, OF4	L	41	74	91	8	20	4	0	3	14	7	20	0	.220	.363
Andy Pafko	OF64	R	38	71	142	17	31	8	2	1	15	14	15	0	.218	.324
3 Bobby Avila	2B51	R	35	51	172	29	41	3	2	3	19	24	31	3	.238	.331
Lee Maye	OF44	L	24	51	140	17	42	5	1	4	16	7	26	2	.300	.436
Johnny O'Brien	2B37	R	28	44	116	16	23	4	0	1	8	11	15	0	.198	.259
Stan Lopata	C11, 1B2	R	33	25	48	0	5	0	0	0	4	3	13	0	.104	.104
Casey Wise	2B20, SS5	B	26	22	76	11	13	2	0	1	5	10	5	0	.171	.237
Mel Roach (KJ)	2B8, OF4, 3B1	R	26	19	31	1	3	0	0	0	0	2	4	0	.097	.097
Del Rice (BL)	C9	R	36	13	29	3	6	0	0	0	1	2	3	0	.207	.207
1 Joe Morgan	2B7	L	28	13	23	2	5	1	0	0	1	2	4	0	.217	.261
3 Ray Boone	1B3	R	35	13	15	3	3	0	0	1	2	4	2	0	.200	.400
2 Enos Slaughter	OF6	L	43	11	18	0	3	0	0	0	1	3	3	0	.167	.167
Chuck Cottier	2B10	R	23	10	24	1	3	1	0	0	1	3	7	0	.125	.167
1 Jim Pisoni	OF9	R	29	9	24	4	4	1	0	0	0	2	6	0	.167	.208
Al Spangler	OF4	L	25	6	12	3	5	0	1	0	0	1	1	1	.417	.583

John DeMerit 23 R 1-5, Red Schoendienst (IL) 36 B 0-3

NAME	T	AGE	W	L	PCT	SV	G	GS	CG	IP	H	BB	SO	ShO	ERA
		29	86	70	.551	18	157	157	**69**	1401	1406	429	775	**18**	3.51
Lew Burdette	R	32	**21**	15	.583	1	41	**39**	20	290	**312**	38	105	**4**	4.07
Warren Spahn	L	38	**21**	15	.583	0	40	36	**21**	**292**	282	70	143	**4**	2.96
Bob Buhl (SA)	R	30	15	9	.625	0	31	25	12	198	181	74	105	**4**	2.86
Juan Pizarro	L	22	6	2	.750	0	29	14	6	134	117	70	126	2	3.76
Joey Jay	R	23	6	11	.353	0	34	19	4	136	130	64	88	1	4.10
Don McMahon	R	29	5	3	.625	**15**	60	0	0	81	81	37	55	0	2.56
Bob Rush	R	33	5	6	.455	0	31	9	1	101	102	23	64	1	2.41
Carl Willey	R	28	5	9	.357	0	26	15	5	117	126	31	51	2	4.15
Bob Trowbridge	R	29	1	0	1.000	1	16	0	0	30	45	10	22	0	6.00
Bob Giggie	R	25	1	0	1.000	1	13	0	0	20	24	10	15	0	4.05
Bob Hartman	L	21	0	0	.000	0	3	0	0	2	6	2	1	0	22.50

SAN FRANCISCO 3rd 83-71 .539 4 — BILL RIGNEY

NAME	G by POS	B	AGE	G	AB	R	H	2B	3B	HR	RBI	BB	SO	SB	BA	SA
TOTALS			25	154	5281	705	1377	239	35	167	660	473	875	81	.261	.414
Orlando Cepeda	1B122, OF44, 3B4	R	21	151	605	92	192	35	4	27	105	33	100	23	.317	.522
Daryl Spencer	2B151, SS4	R	29	152	555	59	147	20	1	12	62	58	67	5	.265	.369
Ed Bressoud	SS92, 1B1, 2B1, 3B1	R	27	104	315	36	79	17	2	9	26	28	55	0	.251	.403
Jim Davenport	3B121, SS1	R	25	123	469	65	121	16	3	6	38	28	65	0	.258	.343
Willie Kirkland	OF117	L	25	126	463	64	126	22	3	22	68	42	84	5	.272	.475
Willie Mays	OF147	R	28	151	575	125	180	43	5	34	104	65	58	**27**	.313	.583
Jackie Brandt	OF116, 3B18, 1B3, 2B1	R	25	137	429	63	116	16	5	12	57	35	69	11	.270	.415
Hobie Landrith	C109	L	29	109	283	30	71	14	0	3	29	43	23	0	.251	.332
Felipe Alou	OF69	R	24	95	247	38	68	13	2	10	33	17	38	5	.275	.466
Leon Wagner	OF28	L	25	87	129	20	29	4	3	5	22	25	24	0	.225	.419
Andre Rodgers	SS66	R	24	71	228	32	57	12	1	6	24	32	50	2	.250	.390
Bob Schmidt	C70	R	26	71	181	17	44	7	1	5	20	13	24	0	.243	.376
Dusty Rhodes		L	32	54	48	1	9	2	0	0	7	5	9	0	.188	.229
Willie McCovey	1B51	L	21	52	192	32	68	9	5	13	38	22	35	2	.354	.656
Danny O'Connell	3B26, 2B8	R	32	34	58	6	11	3	0	0	0	5	15	0	.190	.241
Jose Pagan	3B18, SS5, 2B3	R	24	31	46	7	8	1	0	0	1	2	8	1	.174	.196
2 Jim Hegan	C21	R	38	21	30	0	4	1	0	0	0	1	10	0	.133	.167

Bob Speake 28 L 1-11, Hank Sauer 40 R 1-15, Roger McCardell 26 R 0-4

NAME	T	AGE	W	L	PCT	SV	G	GS	CG	IP	H	BB	SO	ShO	ERA
		28	83	71	.539	23	154	154	52	1376	1279	500	873	12	**3.47**
Sam Jones	R	33	**21**	15	.583	4	50	35	16	271	232	**109**	209	**4**	**2.82**
Johnny Antonelli	L	29	19	10	.655	1	40	38	17	282	247	76	165	**4**	3.10
Jack Sanford	R	30	15	12	.556	1	36	31	10	222	198	70	132	0	3.16
Mike McCormick	L	20	12	16	.429	4	47	31	7	226	213	86	151	3	3.98
Stu Miller	R	31	8	7	.533	8	59	9	2	168	164	57	95	0	2.84
Gordon Jones	R	29	3	2	.600	2	31	0	0	44	45	19	29	0	4.30
Al Worthington	R	30	2	3	.400	2	42	3	0	73	68	37	45	0	3.70
Eddie Fisher	R	22	2	6	.250	1	17	5	0	40	57	8	15	0	7.88
Bud Byerly	R	38	1	0	1.000	0	11	0	0	13	11	5	4	0	1.38
Joe Shipley	R	24	0	0	.000	0	10	1	0	18	16	17	11	0	4.50
Dom Zanni	R	27	0	0	.000	0	9	0	0	11	12	8	11	0	6.55
Billy Muffett	R	28	0	0	.000	0	5	0	0	7	11	3	3	0	5.14
Curt Barclay	R	27	0	0	.000	0	1	0	0	0	2	2	0	0	∞
Marshall Renfroe	L	23	0	0	.000	0	1	1	0	2	3	3	3	0	27.00

Ray Monzant (VR) 26

PITTSBURGH 4th 78-76 .506 9 — DANNY MURTAUGH

NAME	G by POS	B	AGE	G	AB	R	H	2B	3B	HR	RBI	BB	SO	SB	BA	SA
TOTALS			28	155	5369	651	1414	230	42	112	617	442	715	32	.263	.384
Dick Stuart	1B105, OF1	R	26	118	397	64	118	15	2	27	78	42	86	1	.297	.549
Bill Mazeroski	2B133	R	22	135	493	50	119	15	6	7	59	29	54	1	.241	.339
Dick Groat	SS145	R	28	147	593	74	163	22	7	5	51	32	35	0	.275	.361
Don Hoak	3B155	R	31	155	564	60	166	29	3	8	65	71	75	9	.294	.399
Roberto Clemente (EJ)	OF104	R	24	105	432	60	128	17	7	4	50	15	51	2	.296	.396
Bill Virdon	OF144	L	28	144	519	67	132	24	2	8	41	55	65	7	.254	.355
Bob Skinner	OF142, 1B1	L	27	143	547	78	153	18	4	13	61	67	65	10	.280	.399
Smoky Burgess	C101	L	32	114	377	41	112	28	5	11	59	31	16	0	.297	.485
Rocky Nelson	1B56, OF2	L	34	98	175	31	51	11	0	6	32	23	19	0	.291	.457
Roman Mejias	OF85	R	28	96	276	28	65	6	1	7	28	21	48	1	.236	.341
Dick Schofield	2B28, SS8, OF3	B	24	81	145	21	34	10	1	1	9	16	22	1	.234	.338
1 Ted Kluszewski	1B20	L	34	60	122	11	32	10	1	2	17	5	14	0	.262	.410
Hank Foiles (KJ)	C51	R	30	53	80	10	18	3	0	3	4	7	16	0	.225	.375
Danny Kravitz	C45	L	28	52	162	18	41	9	1	3	21	5	14	0	.253	.377
Harry Bright	OF4, 3B3, 2B1	R	29	40	48	4	12	1	0	3	8	5	10	0	.250	.458

3 Harry Simpson 33 L 4-15, Joe Christopher 23 R 0-12, Ken Hamlin 24 R 1-8, R C Stevens 24 R 2-7,
Hardy Peterson 29 R 0-1, Gene Baker (KJ) 34

NAME	T	AGE	W	L	PCT	SV	G	GS	CG	IP	H	BB	SO	ShO	ERA
		28	78	76	.506	17	155	155	48	1393	1432	418	730	7	3.90
Roy Face	R	31	18	1	**.947**	10	57	0	0	93	91	25	69	0	2.71
Vern Law	R	29	18	9	.667	1	34	33	20	266	245	53	110	2	2.98
Harvey Haddix	L	33	12	12	.500	0	31	29	14	224	189	49	149	2	3.13
Ron Kline	R	27	11	13	.458	0	33	29	7	186	186	70	91	0	4.26
Bob Friend	R	28	8	**19**	.296	0	35	35	7	235	267	52	104	2	4.02
Bennie Daniels	R	27	7	9	.438	1	34	12	0	101	115	39	67	0	5.44
Ron Blackburn (MS)	R	24	1	1	.500	1	26	0	0	44	50	15	19	0	3.68
Don Gross	L	28	1	1	.500	2	21	0	0	33	28	10	15	0	3.55
13Bob Porterfield	R	35	1	2	.333	1	36	0	0	41	51	19	19	0	4.39
Freddie Green	L	25	1	2	.333	1	17	1	0	37	37	15	20	0	3.16
George Witt (SA)	R	25	0	7	.000	0	15	11	0	51	58	32	30	0	6.88
1 Bob Smith	L	28	0	0	.000	0	20	0	0	28	32	17	12	0	3.54
Al Jackson	L	23	0	0	.000	0	8	3	0	18	30	8	13	0	6.50
Don Williams	R	27	0	0	.000	0	6	0	0	12	17	3	3	0	6.75
Paul Giel	R	26	0	0	.000	0	4	0	0	8	17	6	3	0	13.50
Dick Hall	R	28	0	0	.000	0	2	1	0	9	12	1	3	0	3.00
Jim Umbricht	R	28	0	0	.000	0	1	1	0	7	7	4	3	0	6.43

CHICAGO 5th (Tie) 74-80 .481 13 — BOB SCHEFFING

NAME	G by POS	B	AGE	G	AB	R	H	2B	3B	HR	RBI	BB	SO	SB	BA	SA
TOTALS			30	155	5296	673	1321	209	44	163	635	498	**911**	32	.249	.398
Dale Long	1B85	L	33	110	296	34	70	10	3	14	37	31	53	0	.236	.432
Tony Taylor	2B149, SS2	R	23	150	624	96	175	30	8	8	38	45	86	23	.280	.393
Ernie Banks	SS154	R	28	155	589	97	179	25	6	45	**143**	64	72	2	.304	.596
Al Dark	3B131, 1B4, SS1	R	37	136	477	60	126	22	9	6	45	55	50	1	.264	.386
Lee Walls	OF119	R	26	120	354	43	91	18	3	8	33	42	73	0	.257	.393
George Altman	OF121	L	26	135	420	54	103	14	4	12	47	34	80	1	.245	.383
Bobby Thomson	OF116	R	35	122	374	55	97	15	2	11	52	35	50	1	.259	.398
Sammy Taylor	C109	L	26	110	353	41	95	13	2	13	43	35	47	1	.269	.428
Walt Moryn	OF104	L	33	117	381	41	89	14	1	14	48	44	66	0	.234	.386
Jim Marshall	1B72, OF8	L	27	108	294	39	74	10	1	11	40	33	39	0	.252	.405
Earl Averill	C32, 3B13, OF5, 2B2	R	27	74	186	22	44	10	0	10	34	15	39	0	.237	.452
2 Irv Noren	OF40, 1B1	L	34	65	156	27	50	6	2	4	19	13	24	2	.321	.462
Cal Neeman	C38	R	30	44	105	7	17	2	0	3	9	11	23	0	.162	.267
Art Schult	1B23, OF15	R	31	42	118	17	32	7	0	2	14	7	14	0	.271	.381
2 Randy Jackson	3B22, OF1	R	33	41	74	7	18	5	1	1	10	11	10	0	.243	.378
Johnny Goryl	2B11, 3B4	R	25	25	48	1	9	3	1	1	6	5	3	1	.188	.354
Billy Williams	OF10	L	21	18	33	0	5	0	1	0	2	1	7	0	.152	.212
Lou Jackson		L	23	6	4	2	1	0	0	0	1	0	2	0	.250	.250

Don Eaddy 25 R 0-1, 1 Charlie King 28 R 0-3, Bobby Adams 37 R 0-2, Gordon Massa (MS) 23

NAME	T	AGE	W	L	PCT	SV	G	GS	CG	IP	H	BB	SO	ShO	ERA
		28	74	80	.481	25	155	155	30	1391	1337	519	765	11	4.01
Glen Hobbie	R	23	16	13	.552	0	46	33	10	234	204	106	138	3	3.69
Bob Anderson	R	23	12	13	.480	0	37	36	7	235	245	77	113	1	4.14
Don Elston	R	30	10	8	.556	13	**65**	0	0	98	77	46	82	0	3.31
Bill Henry	L	31	9	8	.529	12	**65**	0	0	134	111	26	115	0	2.69
Dave Hillman	R	31	8	11	.421	0	39	24	4	191	178	43	88	1	3.53
Art Ceccarelli	L	29	5	5	.500	0	18	15	4	102	95	37	56	2	4.76
Moe Drabowsky	R	23	5	10	.333	0	31	23	3	142	138	75	70	1	4.12
John Buzhardt	R	22	4	5	.444	0	31	10	1	101	107	29	33	1	4.99
Elmer Singleton	R	41	2	1	.667	0	21	1	0	43	40	12	25	0	2.72
Joe Schaffernoth (EJ)	R	21	1	0	1.000	0	5	1	0	8	11	4	3	0	7.88
Ed Donnelly	R	24	1	1	.500	0	9	0	0	14	18	9	6	0	3.21
Dick Drott (BA)	R	23	1	2	.333	0	8	6	1	27	25	26	15	1	6.00
2 Seth Morehead	L	24	0	1	.000	0	11	2	0	19	25	8	9	0	4.74
1 Taylor Phillips	L	26	0	2	.000	0	7	2	0	17	22	11	5	0	7.41
Ben Johnson	R	28	0	0	.000	0	4	2	0	17	17	4	6	0	2.12
2 Bob Porterfield	R	35	0	0	.000	0	4	0	0	6	14	3	0	0	12.00
Morrie Martin	L	36	0	0	.000	0	3	0	0	2	5	1	1	0	22.50
1 Riverboat Smith	L	31	0	0	.000	0	1	0	0	1	5	2	0	0	54.00

CINCINNATI 5th (Tie) 74-80 .481 13 — MAYO SMITH 35-45 .438 — FRED HUTCHINSON 39-35 .527

NAME	G by POS	B	AGE	G	AB	R	H	2B	3B	HR	RBI	BB	SO	SB	BA	SA
TOTALS			28	154	5288	**764**	**1448**	**258**	34	161	**721**	499	763	65	**.274**	**.427**
Frank Robinson	1B125, OF40	R	23	146	540	106	168	31	4	36	125	69	93	18	.311	.583
Johnny Temple	2B149	R	30	149	598	102	186	35	6	8	67	72	40	14	.311	.430
Eddie Kasko	SS84, 3B31, 2B2	R	27	118	329	39	93	14	1	2	31	14	38	2	.283	.350
3 Willie Jones	3B68	R	33	72	233	33	58	12	1	7	31	28	26	0	.249	.399
Gus Bell	OF145	L	30	148	580	59	170	27	2	19	115	29	44	2	.293	.445
Vada Pinson	OF154	L	20	154	**648**	**131**	205	**47**	9	20	84	55	98	21	.316	.509
Jerry Lynch	OF98	L	28	117	379	49	102	16	3	17	58	29	50	2	.269	.462
Ed Bailey	C117	L	28	121	379	43	100	13	0	12	40	62	53	2	.264	.393
Frank Thomas	3B64, OF33, 1B14	R	30	108	374	41	84	18	2	12	47	27	56	0	.225	.380
Roy McMillan (BC)	SS73	R	28	79	246	38	65	14	2	9	24	27	27	0	.264	.447
Jim Pendleton	OF24, 3B16, SS3	R	35	65	113	13	29	2	0	3	9	8	18	3	.257	.354
Don Newcombe	P30	L	33	61	105	10	32	2	0	3	21	17	23	0	.305	.410
Dutch Dotterer	C51	R	27	52	161	21	43	7	0	2	17	16	23	0	.267	.348
2 Whitey Lockman	1B20, 2B6, OF1, 3B1	L	32	52	84	10	22	5	1	0	7	4	6	0	.262	.345
Johnny Powers	OF5	L	29	43	43	8	11	2	1	2	4	3	13	0	.256	.488
Pete Whisenant	OF21	R	29	36	71	13	17	2	0	5	11	8	18	0	.239	.479
1 Walt Dropo	1B23	R	36	26	39	4	4	1	0	1	2	4	7	0	.103	.205
Cliff Cook	3B9	R	22	9	21	3	8	2	1	0	5	2	8	1	.381	.571

Bobby Henrich 20 R 0-3, Buddy Gilbert 23 L 3-20, 1 Del Ennis 34 R 4-12, Bob Thurman 38 L 1-4, Don Pavletich 20 R 0-0

NAME	T	AGE	W	L	PCT	SV	G	GS	CG	IP	H	BB	SO	ShO	ERA
		29	74	80	.481	**26**	154	154	44	1357	**1460**	456	690	7	4.31
Don Newcombe	R	33	13	8	.619	1	30	29	17	222	216	27	100	2	3.16
Bob Purkey	R	29	13	18	.419	1	38	33	9	218	241	43	78	1	4.25
Joe Nuxhall	L	30	9	9	.500	1	28	21	6	132	155	35	75	1	4.23
2 Jim Brosnan	R	29	8	3	.727	2	26	9	1	83	79	26	56	1	3.36
Brooks Lawrence	R	34	7	12	.368	10	43	14	3	128	144	45	64	0	4.78
Jay Hook	R	22	5	5	.500	0	17	15	4	79	79	39	37	0	5.13
Jim O'Toole	L	22	5	8	.385	0	28	19	3	129	144	73	68	1	5.16
Orlando Pena	R	25	5	9	.357	5	46	8	1	136	150	39	76	0	4.76
Bob Mabe	R	29	4	2	.667	3	18	1	0	30	29	19	8	0	5.40
Willard Schmidt	R	31	3	2	.600	0	36	4	0	71	80	30	40	0	3.93
Luis Arroyo	L	32	1	0	1.000	0	10	0	0	14	17	11	8	0	3.86
Tom Acker	R	29	1	2	.333	2	37	0	0	63	57	37	45	0	4.14
1 Hal Jeffcoat	R	34	0	1	.000	1	17	0	0	22	21	10	12	0	3.27
Jim Bailey	L	24	0	1	.000	0	3	1	0	12	17	6	7	0	6.00
2 Don Rudolph	L	27	0	0	.000	0	5	0	0	7	13	3	8	0	5.14
Mike Cuellar	L	22	0	0	.000	0	2	0	0	4	7	4	5	0	15.75
Claude Osteen	L	19	0	0	.000	0	2	0	0	8	11	9	3	0	6.75

ST. LOUIS 7th 71-83 .461 16 — SOLLY HEMUS

NAME	G by POS	B	AGE	G	AB	R	H	2B	3B	HR	RBI	BB	SO	SB	BA	SA
TOTALS			28	154	5317	641	1432	244	**49**	118	605	485	747	65	.269	.400
Stan Musial	1B90, OF3	L	38	115	341	37	87	13	2	14	44	60	25	0	.255	.428
Don Blasingame	2B150	L	27	150	615	90	178	26	7	1	24	67	42	15	.289	.359
Alex Grammas	SS130	R	32	131	368	43	99	14	2	3	30	38	26	3	.269	.342
Ken Boyer	3B143, SS12	R	28	149	563	86	174	18	5	28	94	67	77	12	.309	.508
Joe Cunningham	OF121, 1B35	L	27	144	458	65	158	28	6	7	60	88	47	2	.345	.478
Gino Cimoli	OF141	R	29	143	519	61	145	40	7	8	72	37	83	7	.279	.430
Bill White	OF92, 1B71	L	25	138	517	77	156	33	9	12	72	34	61	15	.302	.470
Hal Smith	C141	R	28	142	452	35	122	15	3	13	60	15	20	2	.270	.403
Curt Flood	OF106, 2B1	R	21	121	208	24	53	7	3	7	26	16	35	2	.255	.418
George Crowe	1B14	L	36	77	103	14	31	6	0	8	29	5	12	0	.301	.592
Gene Oliver	OF42, C9, 1B5	R	23	68	172	14	42	9	0	6	28	7	41	3	.244	.401
1 Ray Jablonski	3B19, SS1	R	32	60	87	11	22	4	0	3	14	8	19	1	.253	.402
Wally Shannon	SS21, 2B10	L	25	47	95	5	27	5	0	0	5	0	12	0	.284	.337
Bobby Gene Smith	OF32	R	25	43	60	11	13	1	1	1	7	1	9	0	.217	.317
Lee Tate	SS39, 2B2, 3B2	R	27	41	50	5	7	1	1	1	4	5	7	0	.140	.260
2 Dick Gray	SS13, 3B6, 2B2, OF1	R	27	36	51	9	16	1	0	1	6	6	8	3	.314	.392
Gene Green	OF19, C11	R	26	30	74	8	14	6	0	1	3	5	18	0	.189	.311
Solly Hemus	2B1, 3B1	L	36	24	17	2	4	2	0	0	1	8	2	0	.235	.353
2 Jay Porter	C19, 1B1	R	26	23	33	5	7	3	0	1	2	1	4	0	.212	.394
1 Chuck Essegian	OF9	R	27	17	39	2	7	2	1	0	5	1	13	0	.179	.282
Ray Katt	C14	R	31	15	24	0	7	2	0	0	2	0	8	0	.292	.375

Duke Carmel 22 L 3-23, Tim McCarver 17 L 4-24, 1 Irv Noren 34 L 1-8, Joe Durham 27 R 0-5, 2 Charlie King 28 R 3-7, Charlie O'Rourke 22 R 0-2

NAME	T	AGE	W	L	PCT	SV	G	GS	CG	IP	H	BB	SO	ShO	ERA
		26	71	83	.461	21	154	154	36	1363	1427	564	846	8	4.34
Lindy McDaniel	R	23	14	12	.538	**15**	62	7	1	132	144	41	86	0	3.82
Larry Jackson	R	28	14	13	.519	0	40	37	12	256	271	64	145	3	3.30
Vinegar Bend Mizell	L	28	13	10	.565	0	31	30	8	201	196	89	108	1	4.21
Ernie Broglio	R	23	7	12	.368	0	35	25	6	181	174	89	133	3	4.72
Marshall Bridges	L	28	6	3	.667	1	27	4	1	76	67	37	76	0	4.26
Bob Miller	R	20	4	3	.571	0	11	10	3	71	66	21	43	0	3.30
1 Gary Blaylock	R	27	4	5	.444	0	26	12	3	100	117	43	61	0	5.13
Bob Gibson	R	23	3	5	.375	0	13	9	2	76	77	39	48	1	3.32
Alex Kellner (EJ)	L	34	2	1	.667	0	12	4	0	37	31	10	19	0	3.16
Howie Nunn	R	23	2	2	.500	0	16	0	0	21	23	15	20	0	7.71
1 Jim Brosnan	R	29	1	3	.250	2	20	1	0	33	34	15	18	0	4.91
Dick Ricketts	R	25	1	6	.143	0	12	9	0	56	68	30	25	0	5.79
Dean Stone	L	28	0	1	.000	1	18	1	0	30	30	16	17	0	4.20
2 Hal Jeffcoat	R	34	0	1	.000	0	11	0	0	18	33	9	7	0	9.00
Tom Cheney	R	24	0	1	.000	0	11	2	0	12	17	11	8	0	6.75
Bob Duliba	R	24	0	1	.000	1	11	0	0	23	19	12	14	0	2.74
Phil Clark	R	26	0	1	.000	0	7	0	0	7	8	8	5	0	12.86
Bob Blaylock	R	24	0	1	.000	0	3	1	0	9	8	3	3	0	4.00
Tom Hughes	R	24	0	2	.000	0	2	2	0	4	9	2	2	0	15.75
Jack Urban	R	30	0	0	.000	0	8	0	0	11	18	7	4	0	9.00
Bill Smith	L	25	0	0	.000	1	6	0	0	8	11	3	4	0	1.13
Marv Grissom	R	41	0	0	.000	0	3	0	0	2	6	0	0	0	22.50

PHILADELPHIA 8th 64-90 .416 23 — EDDIE SAWYER

NAME	G by POS	B	AGE	G	AB	R	H	2B	3B	HR	RBI	BB	SO	SB	BA	SA
TOTALS			30	155	5109	599	1237	196	38	113	560	498	858	39	.242	.362
Ed Bouchee	1B134	L	26	136	499	75	142	29	4	15	74	70	74	0	.285	.449
Sparky Anderson	2B152	R	25	152	477	42	104	9	3	0	34	42	53	6	.218	.249
Joe Koppe	SS113, 2B11	R	28	126	422	68	110	18	7	7	28	41	80	7	.261	.386
Gene Freese	3B109, 2B6	R	25	132	400	60	107	14	5	23	70	43	61	8	.268	.500
Wally Post	OF120	R	29	132	468	62	119	17	6	22	94	36	**101**	0	.254	.457
Richie Ashburn	OF149	L	32	153	564	86	150	16	2	1	20	79	42	9	.266	.307
Harry Anderson	OF137	L	27	142	508	50	122	28	6	14	63	43	95	1	.240	.402
Carl Sawatski	C69	L	31	74	198	15	58	10	0	9	43	32	36	0	.293	.480
Dave Philley	OF34, 1B24	B	39	99	254	32	74	18	2	7	37	18	27	0	.291	.461
2 Solly Drake	OF37	B	28	67	62	10	9	1	0	0	3	8	15	5	.145	.161
Valmy Thomas	C65, 3B1	R	30	66	140	5	28	2	0	1	7	9	19	1	.200	.236
Harry Hanebrink	2B15, 3B9, OF1	L	31	57	97	10	25	3	1	1	7	2	12	0	.258	.340
Bob Bowman	OF20, P5	R	28	57	79	7	10	0	0	2	5	5	23	0	.127	.203
1 Willie Jones	3B46	R	33	47	160	23	43	9	1	7	24	19	14	0	.269	.469
Chico Fernandez	SS40, 2B2	R	27	45	123	15	26	5	1	0	3	10	11	2	.211	.268
Joe Lonnett	C43	R	32	43	93	8	16	1	0	1	10	14	17	0	.172	.215
1 Jim Hegan	C25	R	38	25	51	1	10	1	0	0	8	3	10	0	.196	.216
1 Granny Hamner	SS15, 3B1	R	32	21	64	10	19	4	0	2	6	5	5	0	.297	.453

2 Jim Bolger 27 R 4-48, John Easton 26 R 0-3

NAME	T	AGE	W	L	PCT	SV	G	GS	CG	IP	H	BB	SO	ShO	ERA
		29	64	**90**	.416	15	155	155	54	1354	1357	474	769	8	4.27
Robin Roberts	R	32	15	17	.469	0	35	35	19	257	267	35	137	2	4.27
Gene Conley (BH)	R	28	12	7	.632	1	25	22	12	180	159	42	102	3	3.00
Jim Owens	R	25	12	12	.500	1	31	30	11	221	203	73	135	1	3.22
Don Cardwell	R	23	9	10	.474	0	25	22	5	153	135	65	106	1	4.06
Jack Meyer	R	27	5	3	.625	1	47	1	1	94	76	53	71	0	3.35
Ruben Gomez	R	31	3	8	.273	1	20	12	2	72	90	24	37	1	6.13
Ray Semproch	R	28	3	10	.231	3	30	18	2	112	119	59	54	0	5.38
2 Humberto Robinson	R	29	2	4	.333	1	31	4	1	73	70	24	32	0	3.33
2 Al Schroll	R	27	1	1	.500	0	3	0	0	9	12	6	4	0	9.00
2 Taylor Phillips	L	26	1	4	.200	1	32	3	1	63	72	31	35	0	5.00
Dick Farrell	R	25	1	6	.143	6	38	0	0	57	61	25	31	0	4.74
Bob Bowman	R	28	0	1	.000	0	5	0	0	6	5	5	0	0	6.00
Jim Hearn	R	38	0	2	.000	0	6	0	0	11	15	6	1	0	5.73
1 Seth Morehead	L	24	0	2	.000	0	3	3	0	10	15	3	8	0	9.90
Ed Keegan	R	19	0	3	.000	0	3	3	0	9	19	13	3	0	18.00
Curt Simmons (SA)	L	30	0	0	.000	0	7	0	0	10	16	0	4	0	4.50
Chris Short	L	21	0	0	.000	0	3	2	0	14	19	10	8	0	8.36
Freddy Rodriguez	R	31	0	0	.000	0	1	0	0	2	4	0	1	0	13.50

WORLD SERIES – LOS ANGELES (NL) 4 CHICAGO (AL) 2

LINE SCORES

TEAM	1	2	3	4	5	6	7	8	9	10	11	12	R	H	E
Game 1 October 1 at Chicago															
LA (NL)	0	0	0	0	0	0	0	0	0				0	8	3
CHI (AL)	2	0	7	2	0	0	0	0	X				11	11	0

Craig, Churn (3), Labine (4), Koufax (5), Klippstein (7) — **Wynn**, Staley (8)

TEAM	1	2	3	4	5	6	7	8	9	10	11	12	R	H	E
Game 2 October 2 at Chicago															
LA	0	0	0	0	1	0	3	0	0				4	9	1
CHI	2	0	0	0	0	0	0	1	0				3	8	0

Podres, Sherry (3) — **Shaw**, Lown (7)

TEAM	1	2	3	4	5	6	7	8	9	10	11	12	R	H	E
Game 3 October 4 at Los Angeles															
CHI	0	0	0	0	0	0	0	1	0				1	12	0
LA	0	0	0	0	0	0	2	1	X				3	5	0

Donovan, Staley (7) — **Drysdale**, Sherry (8)

TEAM	1	2	3	4	5	6	7	8	9	10	11	12	R	H	E
Game 4 October 5 at Los Angeles															
CHI	0	0	0	0	0	0	4	0	0				4	10	3
LA	0	0	4	0	0	0	0	1	X				5	9	0

Wynn, Lown (3), Pierce (4), **Staley** (7) — Craig, **Sherry** (8)

TEAM	1	2	3	4	5	6	7	8	9	10	11	12	R	H	E
Game 5 October 6 at Los Angeles															
CHI	0	0	0	1	0	0	0	0	0				1	5	0
LA	0	0	0	0	0	0	0	0	0				0	9	0

Shaw, Pierce (8), Donovan (8) — **Koufax**, Williams (8)

TEAM	1	2	3	4	5	6	7	8	9	10	11	12	R	H	E
Game 6 October 8 at Chicago															
LA	0	0	2	6	0	0	0	0	1				9	13	0
CHI	0	0	0	3	0	0	0	0	0				3	6	1

Podres, **Sherry** (4) — **Wynn**, Donovan (4), Lown (4), Staley (5), Pierce (8), Moore (9)

COMPOSITE BATTING

NAME	POS	G	AB	R	H	2B	3B	HR	RBI	BA
Los Angeles (NL)										
Totals		6	203	21	53	3	1	7	19	.261
Neal	2B	6	**27**	4	**10**	2	0	2	6	.370
Gilliam	3B	6	25	2	6	0	0	0	0	.240
Hodges	1B	6	23	2	9	0	1	1	2	**.391**
Moon	OF	6	23	3	6	0	0	1	2	.261
Roseboro	C	6	21	0	2	0	0	0	1	.095
Wills	SS	6	20	2	5	0	0	0	1	.250
Larker	OF	6	16	2	3	0	0	0	0	.188
Demeter	OF	6	12	2	3	0	0	0	0	.250
Snider	OF	4	10	1	2	0	0	1	2	.200
Sherry	P	5	4	0	2	0	0	0	0	.500
Podres	P	3	4	1	2	1	0	0	1	.500
Furillo	OF	4	4	0	1	0	0	0	2	.250
Essegian	PH	4	3	2	2	0	0	2	2	.667
Fairly	OF	6	3	0	0	0	0	0	0	.000
Craig	P	2	3	0	0	0	0	0	0	.000
Koufax	P	2	2	0	0	0	0	0	0	.000
Drysdale	P	1	2	0	0	0	0	0	0	.000
Zimmer	SS	1	1	0	0	0	0	0	0	.000
Pignatano	C	1	0	0	0	0	0	0	0	.000
Repulski	PH	1	0	0	0	0	0	0	0	.000

Churn P 0-0, Labine P 0-0, Klippstein P 0-0, Williams P 0-0

NAME	POS	G	AB	R	H	2B	3B	HR	RBI	BA
Chicago (AL)										
Totals		6	199	23	52	10	0	4	19	.261
Aparicio	SS	6	26	1	8	1	0	0	0	.308
Fox	2B	6	24	4	9	**3**	0	0	0	.375
Landis	OF	6	24	**6**	7	0	0	0	1	.292
Kluszewski	1B	6	23	5	9	1	0	**3**	**10**	**.391**
Lollar	C	6	22	3	5	0	0	1	5	.227
Smith	OF	6	20	1	5	**3**	0	0	1	.250
Goodman	3B	5	13	1	3	0	0	0	1	.231
Rivera	OF	5	11	1	0	0	0	0	0	.000
Phillips	3B-OF	3	10	0	3	1	0	0	0	.300
Wynn	P	3	5	0	1	1	0	0	1	.200
McAnany	OF	3	5	0	0	0	0	0	0	.000
Shaw	P	2	4	0	1	0	0	0	0	.250
Cash	PH	4	4	0	0	0	0	0	0	.000
Donovan	P	3	3	0	1	0	0	0	0	.333
Esposito	3B	2	2	0	0	0	0	0	0	.000
Torgeson	1B	3	1	1	0	0	0	0	0	.000
Romano	PH	2	1	0	0	0	0	0	0	.000
Staley	P	4	1	0	0	0	0	0	0	.000

Lown P 0-0, Pierce P 0-0, Moore P 0-0

COMPOSITE PITCHING

NAME	G	IP	H	BB	SO	W	L	SV	ERA
Los Angeles (NL)									
Totals	6	53	52	20	33	4	2	2	3.23
Sherry	**4**	12.2	8	2	5	**2**	0	**2**	**0.71**
Podres	2	9.1	7	**6**	4	1	0	0	4.82
Craig	2	9.1	15	5	8	0	1	0	8.68
Koufax	2	9	5	1	7	0	1	0	1.00
Drysdale	1	7	11	4	5	1	0	0	1.29
Williams	1	2	0	2	1	0	0	0	0.00
Klippstein	1	2	1	0	2	0	0	0	0.00
Labine	1	1	0	0	1	0	0	0	0.00
Churn	1	.2	5	0	0	0	0	0	27.00
Chicago (AL)									
Totals	6	52	53	12	27	2	4	2	3.46
Shaw	2	**14**	17	2	2	1	1	0	2.57
Wynn	3	13	**19**	4	**10**	1	1	0	5.54
Staley	**4**	8.1	8	0	3	0	1	1	2.16
Donovan	3	8.1	4	3	5	0	1	1	5.40
Pierce	3	4	2	2	3	0	0	0	0.00
Lown	3	3.1	2	1	3	0	0	0	0.00
Moore	1	1	1	0	1	0	0	0	9.00

1960 Stengel's Last Hurrah

On the eve of the Series opener, the Pirates had to be thirsting for revenge. Pittsburgh had last taken the National League flag in 1927, only to run up against the Yankees of Babe Ruth and Lou Gehrig and be blown out of the park in four games. And if the Pirates weren't giving much thought to the holocaust which had erupted 33 years before, the press was—if for no other reason than the fact that the 1960 rendition of the Yankees featured Mickey Mantle and Roger Maris.

The Pirates' seven-game margin over runner-up Milwaukee gave little evidence that they were a team of destiny. They had earned the chance to vindicate their image by leading the National League race practically the entire way and beating back challenges by Milwaukee and St. Louis. Pittsburgh had Roberto Clemente and Bill Mazeroski, league All-Stars, at right field and second base, a fiery inspirational leader in ex-Marine Don Hoak at third base, and the league batting champ in Dick Groat, who spent September on the bench with a fractured wrist while watching a .403 performance from his substitute, Dick Schofield. The final balance of Danny Murtaugh's club was provided by pitching aces, Vern Law, Bob Friend, and Roy Face, plus the healthy addition of left-hander Vinegar Bend Mizell, who came from the Cardinals in a May trade.

The Yankees began the season unlike a pennant contender, and it seemed as if Casey Stengel's magic was finally gone. After stumbling through May as the White Sox and Orioles led the pack, a repeat of 1959 looked imminent. But the weather warmed, and Stengel got his juggernaut going to make it a three-team race by the time August rolled around. Then, in typical Yankee fashion, they broke the race wide open by winning their last 15 in a row, a pace too rich for the rookie-laden Orioles and the newly-powerful White Sox.

Stengel's magic, which could be traced to his genius for knowing when to say "goodbye" and when to say "hello" to his players, cemented the Yankee cause by trading a few young players over the winter to Kansas City in return for Roger Maris. There was no doubt that the young lefty slugger was a perfect fit for a Yankee uniform and the short right field Yankee Stadium fence 301 feet away. While Maris endorsed Stengel's wizardry by hitting 39 homers and driving in a league-leading 112 runs to be named MVP, Mantle once again provided the supercharge with his league-leading 40 home runs. It was a good thing for Yankee power, because Yankee pitching was not the name of the game. Art Ditmar led the starters with 15 wins and Bobby Shantz the relievers with 11 saves, but the offense led the American League record books with 193 round trippers.

The World Series opened at Pittsburgh, and the Pirates wasted no time in refurbishing their image with a 6-4 win. But reality and shades of 1927 occurred in games two and three, as the Yankees blasted the Bucs by embarrassing scores of 16-3 and 10-0. In the next game, the Pirates shook off the Yankees' savage attack and recovered for a 3-2 win to knot the Series. In the fifth game, Haddix and Face combined to give the Pirates a 5-2 victory, only to watch the Yankees rise up in arms in the next game for a 12-0 rout and the third Series tie. That left it all up to the seventh game.

Pittsburgh scored two runs in the first and second and were coasting on a 4-0 lead until the sixth, when Bill Skowron and Yogi Berra homered to give New York a 5-4 lead. The Yankees added two more in their half of the eighth to bring a curtain of gloom over the Forbes Field crowd. But destiny was not be be denied. An apparent double play ground ball took a bad hop and hit shortstop Tony Kubek in the neck, opening the gates for five runs and a Pittsburgh 9-7 lead. Three more outs and the Pirates would be renewed, but the script was more involved as Friend, the old reliable, failed and allowed the Yankees to tie the score. Throats in Forbes Field were sore, and expectations confused, as Bill Mazerowski stepped in to start the Pirates' last turn at bat in regulation play. Ralph Terry, who had finally put out the Pirates' fire in the eighth, was on the mound. He sadly watched his pitch sail over the left field wall, to end the gruelling slugfest at 10-9.

Terry apologized to Stengel for failing the old master, but it mattered little at the Yankee front office as—after 12 years, ten pennants, and seven World Series victories—the services of Charles Dillon Stengel were no longer needed. The Yankees gave the reason as age, but most fans felt they knew better.

1960 AMERICAN LEAGUE

NAME	G by POS	B	AGE	G	AB	R	H	2B	3B	HR	RBI	BB	SO	SB	BA	SA
NEW YORK 1st 97-57 .630			CASEY STENGEL													
TOTALS			28	155	5290	**746**	1377	215	40	**193**	**699**	537	818	37	.260	**.426**
Bill Skowron	1B142	R	29	146	538	63	166	34	3	26	91	38	95	2	.309	.528
Bobby Richardson	2B141, 3B11	R	24	150	460	45	116	12	3	1	26	35	19	6	.252	.298
Tony Kubek	SS136, OF29	L	23	147	568	77	155	25	3	14	62	31	42	3	.273	.401
Clete Boyer	3B99, SS33	R	23	124	393	54	95	20	1	14	46	23	85	2	.242	.405
Roger Maris	OF131	L	25	136	499	98	141	18	7	39	**112**	70	65	2	.283	**.581**
Mickey Mantle	OF150	B	28	153	527	**119**	145	17	6	**40**	94	111	**125**	14	.275	.558
Hector Lopez	OF106, 2B5, 3B1	R	27	131	408	66	116	14	6	9	42	46	64	1	.284	.414
Elston Howard	C91, OF1	R	31	107	323	29	79	11	3	6	39	28	43	3	.245	.353
Yogi Berra	C63, OF36	L	35	120	359	46	99	14	1	15	62	38	23	2	.276	.446
Gil McDougald	3B84, 2B42	R	32	119	337	54	87	16	4	8	34	38	45	2	.258	.401
2 Bob Cerv	OF51, 1B3	R	34	87	216	32	54	11	1	8	28	30	36	0	.250	.421
Kent Hadley	1B24	L	25	55	64	8	13	2	0	4	11	6	19	0	.203	.422
Johnny Blanchard (IL)	C28	L	27	53	99	8	24	3	1	4	14	6	17	0	.242	.414
Joe DeMaestri	2B19, SS17	R	31	49	35	8	8	1	0	0	2	0	9	0	.229	.257
2 Dale Long	1B11	L	34	26	41	6	15	3	1	3	10	5	6	0	.366	.707
Ken Hunt	OF24	R	25	25	22	4	6	2	0	0	1	4	4	0	.273	.364
Jim Pisoni	OF18	R	30	20	9	1	1	0	0	0	1	1	2	0	.111	.111

Deron Johnson 21 R 2-4, 1 Elmer Valo 39 L 0-5, Jesse Gonder 24 L 2-7, 1 Andy Carey 28 R 1-3, Billy Shantz 32 R 0-0

NAME	T	AGE	W	L	PCT	SV	G	GS	CG	IP	H	BB	SO	ShO	ERA
NEW YORK (totals)		29	97	57	.630	42	155	155	38	1398	1225	609	712	16	3.52
Art Ditmar	R	31	15	9	.625	0	34	28	8	200	195	56	65	1	3.06
Jim Coates	R	27	13	3	.813	1	35	18	6	149	139	66	73	2	4.29
Whitey Ford	L	31	12	9	.571	0	33	29	8	193	168	65	85	**4**	3.08
Ralph Terry	R	24	10	8	.556	1	35	23	7	167	149	52	92	3	3.40
Bob Turley	R	29	9	3	.750	5	34	24	4	173	138	87	87	1	3.28
Eli Grba	R	25	6	4	.600	1	24	9	1	81	65	46	32	0	3.67
Duke Maas	R	31	5	1	.833	4	35	1	0	70	70	35	28	0	4.11
Luis Arroyo	L	33	5	1	.833	7	29	0	0	41	30	22	29	0	2.85
Johnny James	R	26	5	1	.833	2	28	0	0	43	38	26	29	0	4.40
Bobby Shantz	L	34	5	4	.556	11	42	0	0	68	57	24	54	0	2.78
Bill Stafford	R	20	3	1	.750	0	11	8	2	60	50	18	36	1	2.25
John Gabler	R	29	3	3	.500	1	21	4	0	52	46	32	19	0	4.15
Ryne Duren	R	31	3	4	.429	9	42	1	0	49	27	49	67	0	4.96
Bill Short	L	22	3	5	.375	0	10	10	2	47	49	30	14	0	4.79
Fred Kipp	L	28	0	1	.000	0	4	0	0	4	4	0	2	0	6.75
Hal Stowe	L	22	0	0	.000	0	1	0	0	1	0	1	0	0	9.00

NAME	G by POS	B	AGE	G	AB	R	H	2B	3B	HR	RBI	BB	SO	SB	BA	SA
BALTIMORE 2nd 89-65 .578 8			PAUL RICHARDS													
TOTALS			29	154	5170	682	1307	206	33	123	640	596	801	37	.253	.377
Jim Gentile	1B124	L	26	138	384	67	112	17	0	21	98	68	72	0	.292	.500
Marv Breeding	2B152	R	26	152	551	69	147	25	2	3	43	35	80	10	.267	.336
Ron Hansen	SS153	R	22	153	530	72	135	22	5	22	86	69	94	3	.255	.440
Brooks Robinson	3B152, 2B3	R	23	152	595	74	175	27	9	14	88	35	49	2	.294	.440
2 Gene Stephens	OF77	L	27	84	193	38	46	11	0	5	11	25	25	4	.238	.373
Jackie Brandt	OF142, 3B2, 1B1	R	26	145	511	73	130	24	6	15	65	47	69	5	.254	.413
Gene Woodling	OF124	L	37	140	435	68	123	18	3	11	62	84	40	3	.283	.414
Gus Triandos (HJ)	C105	R	29	109	364	36	98	18	0	12	54	41	62	0	.269	.418
Al Pilarcik	OF75	L	29	104	194	30	48	5	1	4	17	15	16	0	.247	.345
Clint Courtney	C58	L	33	83	154	14	35	3	0	1	12	30	14	0	.227	.266
Walt Dropo	1B67, 3B1	R	37	79	179	16	48	8	0	4	21	20	19	0	.268	.380
2 Jim Busby	OF71	R	33	79	159	25	41	7	1	0	12	20	14	2	.258	.314
Bob Boyd	1B17	L	33	71	82	9	26	5	2	0	9	6	5	0	.317	.427
Dave Nicholson	OF44	R	20	54	113	17	21	1	1	5	11	20	55	0	.186	.345
Albie Pearson	OF32	L	25	48	82	17	20	2	0	1	6	17	3	4	.244	.305
Billy Klaus	2B30, SS12, 3B2	L	31	46	43	8	9	2	0	1	6	9	9	0	.209	.326
1 Willie Tasby	OF36	R	27	39	85	9	18	2	1	0	3	9	12	1	.212	.259

1 Joe Ginsberg 33 L 8-30, 3 Dave Philley 40 B 9-34, 1 Johnny Powers 30 L 2-18, Valmy Thomas 31 R 1-16, Ray Barker 24 L 0-6, Jerry Adair 23 R 1-5,
2 Bobby Thomson 36 R 0-6, Gene Green 27 R 1-4, 3 Del Rice 37 R 0-1, Barry Shetrone 21 L 0-0

NAME	T	AGE	W	L	PCT	SV	G	GS	CG	IP	H	BB	SO	ShO	ERA
BALTIMORE (totals)		26	89	65	.578	22	154	154	**48**	1376	1222	552	785	11	**3.52**
Chuck Estrada	R	22	**18**	11	.621	2	36	25	12	209	162	101	144	1	3.57
Milt Pappas	R	21	15	11	.577	0	30	27	11	206	184	83	126	3	3.36
Hal Brown	R	35	12	5	.706	0	30	20	6	159	155	22	66	1	3.06
Jack Fisher	R	21	12	11	.522	2	40	20	8	198	174	78	99	3	3.41
Hoyt Wilhelm	R	36	11	8	.579	7	41	11	3	147	125	39	107	1	3.31
Steve Barber	L	21	10	7	.588	2	36	27	6	182	148	**113**	112	1	3.21
Arnie Portocarrero	R	28	3	2	.600	0	13	5	1	41	44	9	15	0	4.39
Jerry Walker	R	21	3	4	.429	5	29	18	1	118	107	56	48	0	3.74
Billy Hoeft	L	28	2	1	.667	0	19	0	0	19	18	14	14	0	4.26
Wes Stock	R	26	2	2	.500	2	17	0	0	34	26	14	23	0	2.91
Gordon Jones	R	30	1	1	.500	2	29	0	0	55	59	13	30	0	4.42
Rip Coleman	L	27	0	2	.000	0	5	1	0	4	8	5	0	0	11.25
John Anderson	R	27	0	0	.000	0	4	0	0	5	8	4	1	0	12.60
Bob Mabe	R	30	0	0	.000	0	2	0	0	1	4	1	0	0	18.00

NAME	G by POS	B	AGE	G	AB	R	H	2B	3B	HR	RBI	BB	SO	SB	BA	SA
CHICAGO 3rd 87-67 .565 10			AL LOPEZ													
TOTALS			31	154	5191	741	1402	**242**	38	112	684	567	648	**122**	**.270**	.396
Roy Sievers	1B114, OF6	R	33	127	444	87	131	22	0	28	93	74	69	1	.295	.534
Nellie Fox	2B149	L	32	150	**605**	85	175	24	**10**	2	59	50	13	2	.289	.372
Luis Aparicio	SS153	R	26	153	600	86	166	20	7	2	61	43	39	**51**	.277	.343
Gene Freese	3B122	R	26	127	455	60	124	32	6	17	79	29	65	10	.273	.481
Al Smith	OF141	R	32	142	536	80	169	31	3	12	72	50	65	8	.315	.451
Jim Landis	OF147	R	26	148	494	89	125	25	6	10	49	80	84	23	.253	.389
Minnie Minoso	OF154	R	37	154	591	89	**184**	32	4	20	105	52	63	17	.311	.481
Sherm Lollar	C123	R	35	129	421	43	106	23	0	7	46	42	39	2	.252	.356
Ted Kluszewski	1B39	L	35	81	181	20	53	9	0	5	39	22	10	0	.293	.425
Earl Torgeson	1B10	L	36	68	57	12	15	2	0	2	9	21	8	1	.263	.404
Sammy Esposito	3B37, SS11, 2B5	R	28	57	77	14	14	5	0	1	11	10	20	0	.182	.286
Jim Rivera	OF24	L	37	48	17	17	5	0	0	1	1	3	3	4	.294	.471
Joe Hicks	OF14	L	27	36	47	3	9	1	0	0	2	6	3	0	.191	.213
Billy Goodman	3B20, 2B7	L	34	30	77	5	18	4	0	0	6	12	8	0	.234	.286
2 Joe Ginsberg	C25	L	33	28	75	8	19	4	0	0	9	10	8	1	.253	.307
Floyd Robinson	OF17	L	24	22	46	7	13	0	0	0	1	11	8	2	.283	.283

Dick Brown 25 R 7-43, Earl Averill 28 R 3-14, Cam Carreon 22 R 4-17, J. C. Martin 23 L 2-20, Stan Johnson 23 L 1-6, Jim McAnany 23 R 0-2

NAME	T	AGE	W	L	PCT	SV	G	GS	CG	IP	H	BB	SO	ShO	ERA
CHICAGO (totals)		33	87	67	.565	26	154	154	42	1381	1338	533	695	11	3.60
Billy Pierce	L	33	14	7	.667	0	32	30	8	196	201	46	108	1	3.63
Frank Baumann	L	27	13	6	.684	3	47	20	7	185	169	53	71	2	**2.68**
Gerry Staley	R	39	13	8	.619	10	64	0	0	115	94	25	52	0	2.43
Early Wynn	R	40	13	12	.520	1	36	35	13	237	220	112	158	**4**	3.49
Bob Shaw	R	27	13	13	.500	0	36	32	7	193	221	62	46	1	4.06
Dick Donovan	R	32	6	1	.857	3	33	8	0	79	87	25	30	0	5.35
2 Russ Kemmerer	R	28	6	3	.667	2	36	7	2	121	111	45	76	1	2.98
Herb Score	L	27	5	10	.333	0	23	22	5	114	91	87	78	1	3.71
Turk Lown	R	36	2	3	.400	5	45	0	0	67	60	34	39	0	3.90
1 Ray Moore	R	34	1	1	.500	0	14	0	0	21	19	11	3	0	5.57
2 Al Worthington	R	31	1	1	.500	0	4	0	0	5	3	4	1	0	3.60
Don Ferrarese	L	31	0	1	.000	0	5	0	0	4	8	9	4	0	18.00
Ken McBride	R	24	0	1	.000	0	5	0	0	5	6	3	4	0	3.60
Mike Garcia	R	36	0	0	.000	2	15	0	0	18	23	10	8	0	4.50
2 Bob Rush	R	34	0	0	.000	0	9	0	0	14	16	5	12	0	5.79
Gary Peters	L	23	0	0	.000	0	2	0	0	3	4	1	4	0	3.00
Jake Striker	L	26	0	0	.000	0	2	0	0	4	5	1	1	0	4.50

CLEVELAND 4th 76-78 .494 21 — **JOE GORDON** 49-46 .516 **JO-JO WHITE** 1-0 1.000 **JIMMY DYKES** 26-32 .448

NAME	G by POS	B	AGE	G	AB	R	H	2B	3B	HR	RBI	BB	SO	SB	BA	SA
TOTALS			28	154	5296	667	1415	218	20	127	632	444	573	58	.267	.388
Vic Power	1B147, SS5, 3B4	R	28	147	580	69	167	26	3	10	84	24	20	9	.288	.395
2 Ken Aspromonte	2B80, 3B36	R	28	117	459	65	133	20	1	10	48	53	32	4	.290	.403
Woodie Held (BC)	SS109	R	28	109	376	45	97	15	1	21	67	44	73	0	.258	.471
Bubba Phillips	3B85, OF25, SS1	R	30	113	304	34	63	14	1	4	33	14	37	1	.207	.299
Harvey Kuenn	OF119, 3B5	R	29	126	474	65	146	24	0	9	54	55	25	3	.308	.416
Jimmy Piersall	OF134	R	30	138	486	70	137	12	4	18	66	24	38	18	.282	.434
Tito Francona	OF138, 1B13	L	26	147	544	84	159	36	2	17	79	67	67	4	.292	.460
Johnny Romano	C99	R	25	108	316	40	86	12	2	16	52	37	50	0	.272	.475
Johnny Temple	2B77, 3B17	R	31	98	381	50	102	13	1	2	19	32	20	11	.268	.323
Bob Hale	1B5	L	26	70	70	2	21	7	0	0	12	3	6	0	.300	.400
2 Marty Keough	OF42	L	25	65	149	19	37	5	0	3	11	9	23	2	.248	.342
Mike de la Hoz	SS38, 3B8	R	20	49	160	20	41	6	2	6	23	9	12	0	.256	.431
Walt Bond	OF36	L	22	40	131	19	29	2	1	5	18	13	14	4	.221	.366
2 Red Wilson	C30	R	31	32	88	5	19	3	0	1	10	6	7	0	.216	.284
George Strickland	SS14, 3B12, 2B2	R	34	32	42	4	7	0	0	1	3	4	8	0	.167	.238
1 Russ Nixon	C25	L	25	25	82	6	20	5	0	1	6	6	6	0	.244	.341
2 Hank Foiles	C22	R	31	24	68	9	19	1	0	1	6	7	5	0	.279	.338
2 Joe Morgan	3B12, OF2	L	29	22	47	6	14	2	0	2	4	6	4	0	.298	.468
Chuck Tanner	OF4	L	30	21	25	2	7	1	0	0	4	4	6	1	.280	.320
2 Rocky Bridges	SS7, 3B3	R	32	10	27	1	9	0	0	0	3	1	2	0	.333	.333
Ty Cline	OF6	L	21	7	26	2	8	1	1	0	2	0	4	0	.308	.423

1 Carroll Hardy 27 R 2-18, 2 Johnny Powers 30 L 2-12, 2 Pete Whisenant 30 R 1-6, Don Dillard 23 L 1-7, Steve Demeter 25 R 0-5

NAME	T	AGE	W	L	PCT	SV	G	GS	CG	IP	H	BB	SO	ShO	ERA
		27	76	78	.494	30	154	154	32	1382	1308	636	771	10	3.95
Jim Perry	R	24	18	10	.643	1	41	36	10	261	257	91	120	4	3.62
Mudcat Grant	R	24	9	8	.529	0	33	19	5	160	147	78	75	0	4.39
Gary Bell	R	23	9	10	.474	1	28	23	6	155	139	82	109	2	4.12
Barry Latman	R	24	7	7	.500	0	31	20	4	147	146	72	94	0	4.04
Johnny Klippstein	R	32	5	5	.500	14	49	0	0	74	53	35	46	0	2.92
Dick Stigman	L	24	5	11	.313	9	41	18	3	134	118	87	104	0	4.50
1 Johnny Briggs	R	26	4	2	.667	1	21	2	0	36	32	15	19	0	4.50
Frank Funk	R	24	4	2	.667	1	9	0	0	32	27	9	18	0	1.97
Wynn Hawkins	R	24	4	4	.500	0	15	9	1	66	68	39	39	0	4.23
2 Ted Bowsfield	L	24	3	4	.429	0	11	6	1	41	47	20	14	1	5.05
Bobby Locke	R	26	3	5	.375	2	32	11	2	123	121	37	53	2	3.37
2 Don Newcombe	R	34	2	3	.400	1	20	2	0	54	61	8	27	0	4.33
Jack Harshman	L	32	2	4	.333	0	15	8	0	54	50	30	25	0	4.00
Carl Thomas	R	28	1	0	1.000	0	4	0	0	10	8	10	5	0	7.20
Carl Mathias	L	24	0	1	.000	0	7	0	0	15	14	8	13	0	3.60
Bobby Tiefenauer	R	30	0	1	.000	0	6	0	0	9	8	3	2	0	2.00
1 Bob Grim	R	30	0	1	.000	0	3	0	0	2	6	1	2	0	13.50
Mike Lee	L	19	0	0	.000	0	7	0	0	9	6	11	6	0	2.00

WASHINGTON 5th 73-81 .474 24 — **COOKIE LAVAGETTO**

NAME	G by POS	B	AGE	G	AB	R	H	2B	3B	HR	RBI	BB	SO	SB	BA	SA
TOTALS			28	154	5248	672	1283	205	43	147	626	584	883	52	.244	.384
Julio Becquer	1B77, P1	L	28	110	298	41	75	15	7	4	35	12	35	1	.252	.389
Billy Gardner	2B145, SS13	R	32	145	592	71	152	26	5	9	56	43	76	0	.257	.363
Jose Valdivielso	SS115, 3B1	R	26	117	268	23	57	1	1	2	19	20	36	1	.213	.246
Reno Bertoia	3B112, 2B21	R	25	121	460	44	122	17	7	4	45	26	58	3	.265	.359
Bob Allison	OF140, 1B4	R	25	144	501	79	126	30	3	15	69	92	94	11	.251	.413
Lenny Green	OF100	L	26	127	330	62	97	16	7	5	33	43	25	21	.294	.430
Jim Lemon	OF145	R	32	148	528	81	142	10	1	38	100	67	114	2	.269	.508
Earl Battey	C136	R	35	137	466	49	126	24	2	15	60	48	68	4	.270	.427
Harmon Killebrew	1B71, 3B65	R	24	124	442	84	122	19	1	31	80	71	106	1	.276	.534
Dan Dobbek	OF78	L	25	110	248	32	54	8	2	10	30	35	41	4	.218	.387
Billy Consolo	SS82, 2B12, 3B2	R	25	100	174	23	36	4	2	3	15	25	29	1	.207	.305
Faye Throneberry	OF34	L	29	85	157	18	39	7	1	1	23	18	33	1	.248	.325
2 Elmer Valo	OF6	L	39	76	64	6	18	3	0	0	16	17	4	0	.281	.328
3 Pete Whisenant	OF47	R	30	58	115	19	26	9	0	3	9	19	14	2	.226	.383
Hal Naragon	C29	L	31	33	92	7	19	2	0	0	5	8	4	0	.207	.228
Don Mincher	1B20	L	22	27	79	10	19	4	1	2	5	11	11	0	.241	.392
Zoilo Versalles	SS15	R	20	15	45	2	6	2	2	0	4	2	5	0	.133	.267

Johnny Schaive 26 R 3-12, Lamar Jacobs 23 R 0-2, 1 Ken Aspromonte 28 R 0-3

NAME	T	AGE	W	L	PCT	SV	G	GS	CG	IP	H	BB	SO	ShO	ERA
		28	73	81	.474	35	154	154	34	1405	1392	538	775	10	3.77
Chuck Stobbs	L	30	12	7	.632	2	40	13	1	119	115	38	72	1	3.33
Camilo Pascual	R	26	12	8	.600	2	26	22	8	152	139	53	143	3	3.02
Pedro Ramos	R	25	11	18	.379	2	43	36	14	274	254	99	160	1	3.45
Jack Kralick	L	25	8	6	.571	1	35	18	7	151	139	46	71	2	3.04
Don Lee	R	26	8	7	.533	3	44	20	1	165	160	64	88	0	3.44
Tex Clevenger	R	27	5	11	.313	7	53	11	1	129	150	49	49	0	4.19
Rudy Hernandez	R	28	4	1	.800	0	21	0	0	35	34	21	22	0	4.37
Hal Woodeshick	L	27	4	5	.444	4	41	14	1	115	131	60	46	0	4.70
2 Ray Moore	R	34	3	2	.600	13	37	0	0	66	49	27	29	0	2.86
1 Bill Fischer	R	29	3	5	.375	0	20	7	1	77	85	17	31	0	4.91
Ted Sadowski	R	24	1	0	1.000	1	9	1	0	17	17	9	12	0	5.29
2 Tom Morgan	R	30	1	3	.250	0	14	0	0	24	36	5	11	0	3.75
Jim Kaat	L	21	1	5	.167	0	13	9	0	50	48	31	25	0	5.58
Dick Hyde	R	31	0	1	.000	0	9	0	0	9	11	5	4	0	4.00
1 Russ Kemmerer	R	28	0	2	.000	0	3	3	0	17	18	10	10	0	7.94
Ted Abernathy	R	27	0	0	.000	0	2	0	0	3	4	4	1	0	12.00
Hector Maestri	R	25	0	0	.000	0	1	0	0	2	1	1	1	0	0.00
Julio Becquer	L	28	0	0	.000	0	1	0	0	1	1	0	0	0	9.00

DETROIT 6th 71-83 .461 26 — **JIMMY DYKES** 44-52 .458 **BILLY HITCHCOCK** 1-0 1.000 **JOE GORDON** 26-31 .456

NAME	G by POS	B	AGE	G	AB	R	H	2B	3B	HR	RBI	BB	SO	SB	BA	SA
TOTALS			29	154	5202	633	1243	188	34	150	601	636	728	66	.239	.375
Norm Cash	1B99, OF4	L	25	121	353	64	101	16	3	18	63	65	58	4	.286	.501
Frank Bolling	2B138	R	28	139	536	64	136	20	4	9	59	40	48	7	.254	.356
Chico Fernandez	SS130	R	28	133	435	44	105	13	3	4	35	39	50	13	.241	.313
Eddie Yost	3B142	R	33	143	497	78	129	23	5	14	47	125	69	5	.260	.398
Rocky Colavito	OF144	R	26	145	555	67	138	18	1	35	87	53	80	3	.249	.474
Al Kaline	OF142	R	25	147	551	77	153	29	4	15	68	65	47	19	.278	.426
Charlie Maxwell	OF120	L	33	134	482	70	114	16	2	24	81	58	75	5	.237	.440
Lou Berberet	C81	L	30	85	232	18	45	4	0	5	23	41	31	2	.194	.276
Neil Chrisley	OF47, 1B2	L	28	96	220	27	56	10	3	5	24	19	26	2	.255	.395
Steve Bilko	1B62	R	31	78	222	20	46	11	2	9	25	27	31	0	.207	.396
2 Sandy Amoros	OF10	L	30	65	67	7	10	0	0	1	7	12	10	0	.149	.194
Ozzie Virgil	3B42, 2B8, SS5, C1	R	27	62	132	16	30	4	2	3	13	4	14	1	.227	.356
1 Red Wilson	C45	R	31	45	134	17	29	4	0	1	14	16	14	3	.216	.269
2 Harry Chiti	C36	R	27	37	104	9	17	0	0	2	5	10	12	0	.163	.221
Casey Wise	2B17, SS10, 3B1	B	27	30	68	6	10	0	2	2	5	4	9	1	.147	.294
Coot Veal	SS22, 3B3, 2B1	R	27	27	64	8	19	5	1	0	8	11	7	0	.297	.406
3 Hank Foiles	C22	R	31	26	56	5	14	3	0	0	3	1	8	1	.250	.304
Johnny Groth	OF8	R	33	25	19	3	7	1	0	0	2	3	1	0	.368	.421
2 Dick Gernert	1B13, OF6	R	31	21	50	6	15	4	0	1	5	4	5	0	.300	.440

1 Rocky Bridges 32 R 1-5, Dick McAuliffe 20 L 7-27, Gail Harris 28 L 0-5, Em Lindbeck 24 L 0-1

NAME	T	AGE	W	L	PCT	SV	G	GS	CG	IP	H	BB	SO	ShO	ERA
		28	71	83	.461	25	154	154	40	1406	1336	474	824	7	3.64
Frank Lary	R	30	15	15	.500	1	38	36	15	274	262	62	149	2	3.51
Jim Bunning	R	28	11	14	.440	0	36	34	10	252	217	64	201	3	2.79
Don Mossi	L	31	9	8	.529	0	23	22	9	158	158	32	69	2	3.47
Dave Sisler	R	28	7	5	.583	6	41	0	0	80	56	45	47	0	2.48
Pete Burnside	L	29	7	7	.500	2	31	15	2	114	122	50	71	0	4.26
Hank Aguirre	L	28	5	3	.625	10	37	6	1	95	75	30	80	0	2.84
2 Bill Fischer	R	29	5	3	.625	0	20	6	1	55	50	18	24	0	3.44
Bob Bruce	R	27	4	7	.364	0	34	15	1	130	127	56	76	0	3.74
Ray Semproch	R	29	3	0	1.000	0	17	0	0	27	29	16	9	0	4.00
1 Tom Morgan	R	30	3	2	.600	1	22	0	0	29	33	10	12	0	4.66
Paul Foytack	R	29	2	11	.154	2	28	13	1	97	108	49	38	0	6.12
George Spencer	R	33	0	1	.000	0	5	0	0	8	10	5	4	0	3.38
2 Clem Labine	R	33	0	3	.000	2	14	0	0	19	19	12	6	0	5.21
Phil Regan	R	23	0	4	.000	1	17	7	0	68	70	25	38	0	4.50

BOSTON 7th 65-89 .422 32 — **BILLY JURGES** 34-47 .420 **PINKY HIGGINS** 31-42 .425

NAME	G by POS	B	AGE	G	AB	R	H	2B	3B	HR	RBI	BB	SO	SB	BA	SA
TOTALS			29	154	5215	658	1359	234	32	124	623	570	798	34	.261	.389
Vic Wertz	1B117	L	35	131	443	45	125	22	0	19	103	37	54	0	.282	.460
Pete Runnels	2B129, 1B57, 3B3	L	32	143	528	80	169	29	2	2	35	71	51	5	.320	.394
Don Buddin	SS124	R	26	124	428	62	105	21	5	6	36	62	59	4	.245	.360
Frank Malzone	3B151	R	30	152	595	60	161	30	2	14	79	36	42	2	.271	.398
Lu Clinton	OF89	R	22	96	298	37	68	17	5	6	37	20	66	4	.228	.379
2 Willie Tasby	OF102	R	27	105	385	68	108	17	1	7	37	51	54	3	.281	.384
Ted Williams	OF87	L	41	113	310	56	98	15	0	29	72	75	41	1	.316	.645
2 Russ Nixon	C74	L	25	80	272	24	81	17	3	5	33	13	23	0	.298	.438
Pumpsie Green	2B69, SS41	B	26	133	260	36	63	10	3	3	21	44	47	3	.242	.338
Gary Geiger (IL)	OF66	L	23	77	245	32	74	13	3	9	33	23	38	2	.302	.490
2 Carroll Hardy	OF59	R	27	73	145	26	34	5	2	2	15	17	40	3	.234	.338
2 Rip Repulski	OF33	R	32	73	136	14	33	6	1	3	20	10	25	0	.243	.368
Haywood Sullivan	C50	R	29	52	124	9	20	1	0	3	10	16	24	0	.161	.242
1 Bobby Thomson	OF27, 1B1	R	36	40	114	12	30	3	1	5	20	11	15	0	.263	.439
1 Marty Keough	OF29	L	25	38	105	15	26	6	1	1	9	8	8	2	.248	.352
Eddie Sadowski (BG)	C36	R	28	38	93	10	20	2	0	3	8	8	13	0	.215	.333
1 Gene Stephens	OF31	L	27	35	109	9	25	4	0	2	11	14	22	5	.229	.321
2 Ray Boone	1B22	R	36	34	78	6	16	1	0	1	11	11	15	0	.205	.256
Don Gile	C15, 1B11	R	25	29	51	6	9	1	1	1	4	1	13	0	.176	.294
Jim Pagliaroni	C18	R	22	28	62	7	19	5	2	2	9	13	11	0	.306	.548
Ron Jackson	1B9	R	26	10	31	1	7	2	0	0	0	1	6	0	.226	.290

Marlan Coughtry 25 L 3-19, Ray Webster 22 R 0-3, 1 Jim Busby 33 R 0-0, Jack Jensen (VR) 33, Sammy White (VR) 31

NAME	T	AGE	W	L	PCT	SV	G	GS	CG	IP	H	BB	SO	ShO	ERA
		28	65	89	.422	23	154	154	34	1361	1440	580	767	6	4.62
Bill Monbouquette	R	23	14	11	.560	0	35	30	12	215	217	68	134	3	3.64
Mike Fornieles	R	28	10	5	.667	14	70	0	0	109	86	49	64	0	2.64
Tom Brewer	R	28	10	15	.400	1	34	29	8	187	220	72	60	1	4.81
Ike Delock	R	30	9	10	.474	0	24	23	3	129	145	52	49	1	4.74
Billy Muffet	R	29	6	4	.600	0	23	14	4	125	116	36	75	1	3.24
Frank Sullivan	R	30	6	16	.273	1	40	22	4	154	164	52	98	0	5.08
Earl Wilson	R	25	3	2	.600	0	13	9	2	65	61	48	40	0	4.71
Tom Sturdivant	R	30	3	3	.500	1	40	3	0	101	106	45	67	0	4.99
Jerry Casale	R	26	2	9	.182	0	29	14	1	96	113	67	54	0	6.19
Ted Wills	L	26	1	1	.500	1	15	0	0	30	38	16	28	0	7.50
1 Ted Bowsfield	L	24	1	2	.333	2	17	2	0	21	20	13	18	0	5.14
1 Al Worthington	R	31	0	1	.000	0	6	0	0	12	17	11	7	0	7.50
Arnie Earley	L	27	0	1	.000	0	2	0	0	4	9	4	5	0	15.75
Chet Nichols	L	29	0	2	.000	0	6	1	0	13	12	4	11	0	4.15
Dave Hillman (RJ)	R	32	0	3	.000	0	16	3	0	37	41	12	14	0	5.59
Tom Borland	L	27	0	4	.000	3	26	4	0	51	67	23	32	0	6.53
Nels Chittum	R	27	0	0	.000	0	6	0	0	8	8	6	5	0	4.50
Tracy Stallard	R	22	0	0	.000	0	4	0	0	4	0	2	6	0	0.00

KANSAS CITY 8th 58-96 .377 39 — **BOB ELLIOTT**

NAME	G by POS	B	AGE	G	AB	R	H	2B	3B	HR	RBI	BB	SO	SB	BA	SA
TOTALS			28	155	5226	615	1303	212	34	110	566	513	744	16	.249	.366
Marv Throneberry	1B71	L	26	104	236	29	59	9	2	11	41	23	60	0	.250	.445
Jerry Lumpe	2B134, SS15	L	27	146	574	69	156	19	3	8	53	48	49	1	.272	.367
Ken Hamlin	SS139	R	25	140	428	51	96	10	2	2	24	44	48	1	.224	.271
2 Andy Carey	3B91	R	28	102	343	30	80	14	4	12	53	26	52	0	.233	.402
Russ Snyder	OF91	L	26	125	304	45	79	10	5	4	26	20	28	7	.260	.365
Bill Tuttle	OF148	R	30	151	559	75	143	21	3	8	40	66	52	1	.256	.347
Norm Siebern	OF75, 1B69	L	26	144	520	69	145	31	6	19	69	72	68	0	.279	.471
Pete Daley	C61, OF1	R	30	73	228	19	60	10	2	5	25	16	41	0	.263	.390
Dick Williams	3B57, 1B34, OF25	R	31	127	420	47	121	31	0	12	65	39	68	0	.288	.448
Hank Bauer	OF67	R	37	95	255	30	70	15	0	3	31	21	36	1	.275	.369
Whitey Herzog (IL)	OF69, 1B2	L	28	83	252	43	67	10	2	8	38	40	32	0	.266	.417
Bob Johnson	SS30, 2B27, 3B11	R	24	76	146	12	30	4	0	1	9	19	23	2	.205	.253
2 Danny Kravitz	C47	L	29	59	175	17	41	7	2	4	14	11	19	0	.234	.366
1 Harry Chiti	C52	R	27	58	190	16	42	7	0	5	28	17	33	1	.221	.337
1 Bob Cerv	OF21	R	34	23	78	14	20	1	1	6	12	10	17	0	.256	.526
Ray Jablonski	3B6	R	33	21	32	3	7	1	0	0	3	4	8	0	.219	.250
Jim Delsing	OF10	L	34	16	40	2	10	3	0	0	5	3	5	0	.250	.325
Leo Posada	OF9	R	24	10	36	8	13	0	2	1	2	3	7	1	.361	.556

Lou Klimchock 20 L 3-10, 1 Hank Foiles 31 R 4-7, Chet Boak 25 R 2-13, Jim McManus 23 L 4-13, Wayne Terwilliger 35 R 0-1

NAME	T	AGE	W	L	PCT	SV	G	GS	CG	IP	H	BB	SO	ShO	ERA
		29	58	96	.377	14	155	155	44	1374	1428	525	664	4	4.38
Bud Daley	L	27	16	16	.500	0	37	35	13	231	234	96	126	1	4.56
Ray Herbert	R	30	14	15	.483	1	37	33	14	253	256	72	122	0	3.27
Dick Hall	R	29	8	13	.381	0	29	28	9	182	183	38	79	1	4.05
Ken Johnson	R	27	5	10	.333	3	42	6	2	120	120	45	83	0	4.28
Ned Garver	R	34	4	9	.308	0	28	15	5	122	110	35	50	2	3.84
Johnny Kucks	R	26	4	10	.286	0	31	17	1	114	140	43	38	0	6.00
Marty Kutyna	R	27	3	2	.600	4	51	0	0	62	64	32	20	0	3.92
2 Bob Giggie	R	26	1	0	1.000	0	10	0	0	19	24	15	8	0	5.68
Leo Kiely	L	30	1	2	.333	1	20	0	0	21	21	5	6	0	1.75
Bob Trowbridge	R	30	1	3	.250	2	22	1	0	68	70	34	33	0	4.63
Don Larsen	R	30	1	10	.091	0	22	15	0	84	97	42	43	0	5.36
John Tsitouris (BJ)	R	24	0	2	.000	0	14	2	0	33	38	21	12	0	6.55
2 Johnny Briggs	R	26	0	2	.000	0	8	1	0	11	19	12	8	0	13.05
1 George Brunet	L	25	0	2	.000	0	3	2	0	10	12	10	4	0	4.50
Bob Davis	R	26	0	0	.000	1	21	0	0	32	31	22	28	0	3.66
Dave Wickersham	R	24	0	0	.000	2	5	0	0	8	4	1	3	0	1.13
Ray Blemker	L	22	0	0	.000	0	1	0	0	2	3	2	0	0	22.50
Howie Reed	R	23	0	0	.000	0	1	0	0	2	2	0	1	0	0.00

PITTSBURGH 1st 95-59 .617 — **DANNY MURTAUGH**

NAME	G by POS	B	AGE	G	AB	R	H	2B	3B	HR	RBI	BB	SO	SB	BA	SA
TOTALS			29	155	5406	734	1493	236	56	120	689	486	747	34	.276	.407
Dick Stuart	1B108	R	27	122	438	48	114	17	5	23	83	39	107	0	.260	.479
Bill Mazeroski	2B151	R	23	151	538	58	147	21	5	11	64	40	50	4	.273	.392
Dick Groat	SS136	R	29	138	573	85	186	26	4	2	50	39	35	0	.325	.394
Don Hoak	3B155	R	32	155	553	97	156	24	9	16	79	74	74	3	.282	.445
Roberto Clemente	OF142	R	25	144	570	89	179	22	6	16	94	39	72	4	.314	.458
Bill Virdon	OF109	L	29	120	409	60	108	16	9	8	40	40	44	8	.264	.406
Bob Skinner	OF141	L	28	145	571	83	156	33	6	15	86	59	86	11	.273	.431
Smoky Burgess	C89	L	33	110	337	33	99	15	2	7	39	35	13	0	.294	.412
Gino Cimoli	OF91	R	30	101	307	36	82	14	4	0	28	32	43	1	.267	.339
Rocky Nelson	1B73	L	35	93	200	34	60	11	1	7	35	24	15	1	.300	.470
Hal Smith	C71	R	29	77	258	37	76	18	2	11	45	22	48	1	.295	.508
Dick Schofield	SS23, 2B10, 3B1	B	25	65	102	9	34	4	1	0	10	16	20	0	.333	.392
Joe Christopher	OF17	R	24	50	56	21	13	2	0	1	3	5	8	1	.232	.321
Gene Baker	3B7, 2B1	R	35	33	37	5	9	0	0	0	4	2	9	0	.243	.243
Bob Oldis	C22	R	32	22	20	1	4	1	0	0	1	1	2	0	.200	.250

R C Stevens 25 R 0-3, Mickey Vernon 42 L 1-8, 1 Danny Kravitz 29 L 0-6, Harry Bright 30 R 0-4, Dick Barone 27 R 0-6, Roman Mejias 29 0-1

NAME	T	AGE	W	L	PCT	SV	G	GS	CG	IP	H	BB	SO	ShO	ERA
		29	95	59	.617	33	155	155	47	1400	1363	386	811	11	3.49
Vern Law	R	30	20	9	.690	0	35	35	18	272	266	40	120	3	3.08
Bob Friend	R	29	18	12	.600	1	38	37	16	276	266	45	183	4	3.00
2 Vinegar Bend Mizell	L	29	13	5	.722	0	23	23	8	156	141	46	71	3	3.12
Harvey Haddix	L	34	11	10	.524	1	29	28	4	172	189	38	101	0	3.98
Roy Face	R	32	10	8	.556	24	68	0	0	115	93	29	72	0	2.90
Freddie Green	L	26	8	4	.667	3	45	0	0	70	61	33	49	0	3.21
Joe Gibbon	L	25	4	2	.667	0	27	9	0	80	87	31	60	0	4.05
3 Clem Labine	R	33	3	0	1.000	3	15	0	0	30	29	11	21	0	1.50
Paul Giel	R	27	2	0	1.000	0	16	0	0	33	35	15	21	0	5.73
Tom Cheney	R	25	2	2	.500	0	11	8	1	52	44	33	35	1	3.98
Earl Francis	R	23	1	0	1.000	0	7	0	0	18	14	4	8	0	2.00
Jim Umbricht	R	29	1	2	.333	1	17	3	0	41	40	27	26	0	5.05
George Witt	R	26	1	2	.333	0	10	6	0	30	33	12	15	0	4.20
Bennie Daniels	R	28	1	3	.250	0	10	6	0	40	52	17	16	0	7.88
Don Gross	L	29	0	0	.000	0	5	0	0	5	5	0	3	0	3.60
Diomedes Olivo	L	41	0	0	.000	0	4	0	0	10	8	5	10	0	2.70

MILWAUKEE 2nd 88-66 .571 7 — **CHUCK DRESSEN**

NAME	G by POS	B	AGE	G	AB	R	H	2B	3B	HR	RBI	BB	SO	SB	BA	SA
TOTALS			30	154	5263	724	1393	198	48	170	681	463	793	69	.265	.417
Joe Adcock	1B136	R	32	138	514	55	153	21	4	25	91	46	86	2	.298	.500
Chuck Cottier	2B92	R	24	95	229	29	52	8	0	3	19	14	21	1	.227	.301
Johnny Logan	SS136	R	33	136	482	52	118	14	4	7	42	43	40	1	.245	.334
Eddie Mathews	3B153	L	28	153	548	108	152	19	7	39	124	111	113	7	.277	.551
Hank Aaron	OF153, 2B2	R	26	153	590	102	172	20	11	40	126	60	63	16	.292	.566
Bill Bruton	OF149	L	34	151	629	112	180	27	13	12	54	41	97	22	.286	.428
Wes Covington	OF72	L	28	95	281	25	70	16	1	10	35	15	37	1	.249	.420
Del Crandall	C141	R	30	142	537	81	158	14	1	19	77	34	36	4	.294	.430
Al Spangler	OF92	L	26	101	105	26	28	5	2	0	6	14	17	6	.267	.352
Red Schoendienst	2B62	B	37	68	226	21	58	9	1	1	19	17	13	1	.257	.319
Felix Mantilla	2B26, SS25, OF8	R	25	63	148	21	38	7	0	3	11	7	16	3	.257	.365
2 Al Dark	OF25, 1B10, 3B4, 2B3	R	38	50	141	16	42	6	2	1	18	7	13	0	.298	.390
Mel Roach	OF21, 2B20, 3B1, 1B1	R	27	48	140	12	42	12	0	3	18	6	19	0	.300	.450
Lee Maye	OF19	L	25	41	83	14	25	6	0	0	2	7	21	5	.301	.373
Eddie Haas	OF2	L	25	32	32	4	7	2	0	0	5	5	14	0	.219	.275
Frank Torre	1B17	L	28	21	44	2	9	1	0	0	5	3	2	0	.205	.227
Charlie Lau	C16	L	27	21	53	4	10	2	0	0	2	6	10	0	.189	.226
1 Ray Boone	1B4	R	36	7	12	3	3	1	0	0	4	5	1	0	.250	.333

Stan Lopata 34 R 1-8, Mike Krsnich 28 R 3-9, Len Gabrielson 20 L 0-3, Joe Torre 19 R 1-2

NAME	T	AGE	W	L	PCT	SV	G	GS	CG	IP	H	BB	SO	ShO	ERA
		29	88	66	.571	28	154	154	55	1387	1327	518	807	13	3.76
Warren Spahn	L	39	21	10	.677	2	40	33	18	268	254	74	154	4	3.49
Lew Burdette	R	33	19	13	.594	4	45	32	18	276	277	35	83	4	3.36
Bob Buhl	R	31	16	9	.640	0	36	33	11	239	202	103	121	2	3.09
Joey Jay	R	24	9	8	.529	1	32	11	3	133	128	59	90	0	3.25
Carl Willey	R	29	6	7	.462	0	28	21	2	145	136	65	109	1	4.34
Juan Pizarro	L	23	6	7	.462	0	21	17	3	115	105	72	88	0	4.54
Ron Piche	R	25	3	5	.375	9	37	0	0	48	48	23	38	0	3.56
Don McMahon	R	30	3	6	.333	10	48	0	0	64	66	32	50	0	5.91
2 George Brunet	L	25	2	0	1.000	0	17	6	0	50	53	22	39	0	5.04
1 Bob Rush	R	34	2	0	1.000	1	10	0	0	15	24	5	8	0	4.20
Don Nottebart	R	24	1	0	1.000	1	5	1	0	15	14	15	8	0	4.20
Ken MacKenzie	L	26	0	1	.000	0	9	0	0	8	9	3	9	0	6.75
Terry Fox	R	24	0	0	.000	0	5	0	0	8	6	6	5	0	4.50
1 Bob Giggie	R	26	0	0	.000	0	3	0	0	4	5	4	5	0	4.50

ST. LOUIS 3rd 86-68 .558 9 — **SOLLY HEMUS**

NAME	G by POS	B	AGE	G	AB	R	H	2B	3B	HR	RBI	BB	SO	SB	BA	SA
TOTALS			30	155	5187	639	1317	213	48	138	592	501	792	48	.254	.393
Bill White	1B123, OF29	L	26	144	554	81	157	27	10	16	79	42	83	12	.283	.455
Julian Javier	2B119	R	23	119	451	55	107	19	8	4	21	21	72	19	.237	.341
Daryl Spencer	SS138, 2B16	R	30	148	507	70	131	20	3	16	58	81	74	1	.258	.404
Ken Boyer	3B146	R	29	151	552	95	168	26	10	32	97	56	77	8	.304	.562
Joe Cunningham	OF116, 1B15	L	28	139	492	68	138	28	3	6	39	59	59	1	.280	.386
Curt Flood	OF134, 3B1	R	22	140	396	37	94	20	1	8	38	35	54	0	.237	.354
Stan Musial	OF59, 1B29	L	39	116	331	49	91	17	1	17	63	41	34	1	.275	.486
Hal Smith	C124	R	29	127	337	20	77	16	0	2	28	29	33	1	.228	.294
Alex Grammas	SS40, 2B38, 3B13	R	33	102	196	20	48	4	1	4	17	12	15	0	.245	.337
Bob Nieman	OF55	R	33	81	188	19	54	13	5	4	31	24	31	0	.287	.473
Carl Sawatski	C67	L	32	78	179	16	41	4	0	6	27	22	24	0	.229	.352
2 Walt Moryn	OF62	L	34	75	200	24	49	4	3	11	35	17	38	0	.245	.460
George Crowe	1B5	L	37	73	72	5	17	3	0	4	13	5	16	0	.236	.444
Charlie James	OF37	R	22	43	50	5	9	1	0	2	5	1	12	0	.180	.320
Leon Wagner	OF32	L	26	39	98	12	21	2	0	4	11	17	17	0	.214	.357
John Glenn	OF28	R	31	32	31	4	8	0	1	0	5	0	9	0	.258	.323
Ellis Burton	OF23	B	23	29	28	5	6	1	0	0	2	4	14	0	.214	.250
Wally Shannon	2B15, SS1	L	26	18	23	2	4	0	0	0	1	3	6	0	.174	.174
Don Landrum	OF13	L	24	13	49	7	12	0	1	2	3	4	6	3	.245	.408
Tim McCarver	C5	L	18	10	10	3	2	0	0	0	0	0	2	0	.200	.200
Dick Gray	2B4, 3B1	R	28	9	5	1	0	0	0	0	1	2	2	0	.000	.000
Gary Kolb	OF2	L	20	9	3	1	0	0	0	0	0	0	0	0	.000	.000
Chris Cannizzaro	C6	R	22	7	9	0	2	0	0	0	1	1	3	0	.222	.222
Julio Gotay	SS2, 3B1	R	21	3	8	1	3	0	0	0	0	0	2	1	.375	.375
Ed Olivares	2B1	R	21	3	5	0	0	0	0	0	0	0	3	0	.000	.000

Darrell Johnson 31 R 0-2, Duke Carmel 23 L 0-3, 3 Rocky Bridges 32 R 0-0, 2 Del Rice 37 R 0-2, Bob Sadowski 23 L 0-1, Doug Clemens 21 L 0-0

NAME	T	AGE	W	L	PCT	SV	G	GS	CG	IP	H	BB	SO	ShO	ERA
		26	86	68	.558	30	155	155	37	1371	1316	511	906	11	3.64
Ernie Broglio	R	24	21	9	.700	0	52	24	9	226	172	100	188	3	2.75
Larry Jackson	R	29	18	13	.581	0	43	38	14	282	277	70	171	3	3.48
Lindy McDaniel	R	24	12	4	.750	26	65	2	1	116	85	24	105	0	2.09
Ray Sadecki	L	19	9	9	.500	0	26	26	7	157	148	86	95	1	3.78
2 Curt Simmons	L	31	7	4	.636	0	23	17	3	152	149	31	63	1	2.66
Bob Miller	R	21	4	3	.571	0	15	7	0	53	[illegible]	17	33	0	3.40
Bob Duliba (JJ)	R	25	4	4	.500	0	27	0	0	41	49	16	23	0	4.17
Ron Kline	R	28	4	9	.308	1	34	17	1	118	133	43	54	0	6.03
Bob Gibson	R	24	3	6	.333	0	27	12	2	87	97	48	69	0	5.59
1 Marshall Bridges	L	29	2	2	.500	1	20	1	0	31	33	16	27	0	3.48
3 Bob Grim	R	30	1	0	1.000	0	15	0	0	21	22	9	15	0	3.00
1 Vinegar Bend Mizell	L	29	1	3	.250	0	9	9	0	55	64	28	42	0	4.58
Frank Barnes	R	31	0	1	.000	1	4	1	0	8	8	9	8	0	3.38
Mel Nelson	L	24	0	1	.000	0	2	1	0	8	7	2	7	0	3.38
Ed Bauta	R	25	0	0	.000	1	9	0	0	16	14	11	6	0	6.19
Cal Browning	L	22	0	0	.000	0	1	0	0	1	5	1	0	0	27.00

LOS ANGELES 4th 82-72 .532 13 — **WALT ALSTON**

NAME	G by POS	B	AGE	G	AB	R	H	2B	3B	HR	RBI	BB	SO	SB	BA	SA
TOTALS			28	154	5227	662	1333	216	38	126	606	529	837	95	.255	.383
Norm Larker	1B119, OF2	L	29	133	440	56	142	26	3	5	78	36	24	1	.323	.430
Charlie Neal	2B136, SS3	R	29	139	477	60	122	23	2	8	40	48	75	5	.256	.363
Maury Wills	SS145	B	27	148	516	75	152	15	2	0	27	35	47	50	.295	.331
Jim Gilliam	3B130, 2B30	B	31	151	557	96	138	20	2	5	40	96	28	12	.248	.318
Frank Howard	OF115, 1B4	R	23	117	448	54	120	15	2	23	77	32	108	0	.268	.464
Tommy Davis	OF87, 3B5	R	21	110	352	43	97	18	1	11	44	13	35	6	.276	.426
Wally Moon	OF127	L	30	138	469	74	140	21	6	13	69	67	53	6	.299	.452
Johnny Roseboro	C87, 1B1, 3B1	L	27	103	287	22	61	15	3	8	42	44	53	7	.213	.369
Duke Snider	OF75	L	33	101	235	38	57	13	5	14	36	46	54	1	.243	.519
Gil Hodges	1B92, 3B10	R	36	101	197	22	39	8	1	8	30	26	37	0	.198	.371
Don Demeter	OF62	R	25	64	168	23	46	7	1	9	29	8	34	0	.274	.488
Joe Pignatano	C40	R	30	58	90	11	21	4	0	2	9	15	17	1	.233	.344
Chuck Essegian	OF18	R	28	52	79	8	17	3	0	3	11	8	24	0	.215	.367
Bob Lillis	SS23, 3B14, 2B1	R	30	48	60	6	16	4	0	0	6	2	6	2	.267	.333
Norm Sherry	C44	R	28	47	138	22	39	4	1	8	19	12	29	0	.283	.500
2 Irv Noren		L	35	26	25	1	5	0	0	1	1	1	8	0	.200	.320
Willie Davis	OF22	L	20	22	88	12	28	6	1	2	10	4	12	3	.318	.477
Bob Aspromonte	SS15, 3B4	R	22	21	55	1	10	1	0	1	6	0	6	1	.182	.255
Charley Smith	3B18	R	22	18	60	2	10	1	1	0	5	1	15	0	.167	.217
Ron Fairly	OF13	L	21	14	37	6	4	0	3	1	3	7	12	0	.108	.351
Doug Camilli	C6	R	23	6	24	4	8	2	0	1	3	1	4	0	.333	.542

1 Sandy Amoros 30 L 2-14, Carl Furillo 38 R 2-10, 1 Rip Repulski 32 R 1-5

NAME	T	AGE	W	L	PCT	SV	G	GS	CG	IP	H	BB	SO	ShO	ERA
		26	82	72	.532	20	154	154	46	1398	1218	564	1122	13	3.40
Don Drysdale	R	23	15	14	.517	2	41	36	15	269	214	72	246	5	2.84
Larry Sherry	R	24	14	10	.583	7	57	3	1	142	125	82	114	0	3.80
Stan Williams	R	23	14	10	.583	1	38	30	9	207	162	72	175	2	3.00
Johnny Podres	L	27	14	12	.538	0	34	33	8	228	217	71	159	1	3.08
Ed Roebuck	R	28	8	3	.727	8	58	0	0	117	109	38	77	0	2.77
Roger Craig (BS)	R	29	8	3	.727	0	21	15	6	116	99	43	69	1	3.26
Sandy Koufax	L	24	8	13	.381	1	37	26	7	175	133	100	197	2	3.91
Jim Golden	R	24	1	0	1.000	0	1	1	0	7	6	4	4	0	6.43
Ed Palmquist	R	27	0	1	.000	0	22	0	0	39	34	16	23	0	2.54
1 Clem Labine	R	33	0	1	.000	1	13	0	0	17	26	8	15	0	5.82
Ed Rakow	R	24	0	1	.000	0	9	2	0	22	30	11	9	0	7.36
Danny McDevitt	L	27	0	4	.000	0	24	7	0	53	51	42	30	0	4.25
Phil Ortega	R	20	0	0	.000	0	3	1	0	6	12	5	4	0	18.00

SAN FRANCISCO 5th 79-75 .513 16 — **BILL RIGNEY 33-25 .569 TOM SHEEHAN 46-50 .479**

NAME	G by POS	B	AGE	G	AB	R	H	2B	3B	HR	RBI	BB	SO	SB	BA	SA
TOTALS			26	156	5324	671	1357	220	62	130	622	467	846	86	.255	.393
Willie McCovey	1B71	L	22	101	260	37	62	15	3	13	51	45	53	1	.238	.469
Don Blasingame	2B133	L	28	136	523	72	123	12	8	2	31	49	53	14	.235	.300
Ed Bressoud	SS115	R	28	116	386	37	87	19	6	9	43	35	72	1	.225	.376
Jim Davenport	3B103, SS7	R	26	112	363	43	91	15	3	6	38	26	58	0	.251	.358
Willie Kirkland	OF143	L	26	146	515	59	130	21	10	21	65	44	86	12	.252	.454
Willie Mays	OF152	R	29	153	595	107	190	29	12	29	103	61	70	25	.319	.555
Orlando Cepeda	OF91, 1B63	R	22	151	569	81	169	36	3	24	96	34	91	15	.297	.497
Bob Schmidt	C108	R	27	110	344	31	92	12	1	8	37	26	51	0	.267	.378
Joey Amalfitano	3B63, 2B33, SS3, OF1	R	26	106	328	47	91	15	3	1	27	26	31	2	.277	.351
Felipe Alou	OF95	R	25	106	322	48	85	17	3	8	44	16	42	10	.264	.410
Andre Rodgers	SS41, 3B21, 1B6, OF2	R	25	81	217	22	53	8	5	2	22	24	44	1	.244	.355
Jim Marshall	OF6	L	28	75	118	19	28	2	2	2	13	17	24	0	.237	.339
Hobie Landrith	C70	L	30	71	190	18	46	10	0	1	20	23	11	1	.242	.311
2 Dave Philley	OF10, 3B3	B	40	39	61	5	10	0	0	1	7	6	14	0	.164	.213
1 Dale Long	1B10	L	34	37	54	4	9	0	0	3	6	7	7	0	.167	.333
Jose Pagan	SS11, 3B1	R	25	18	49	8	14	2	2	0	2	1	6	2	.286	.408

Neil Wilson 25 L 0-10, Matty Alou 21 L 1-3

NAME	T	AGE	W	L	PCT	SV	G	GS	CG	IP	H	BB	SO	ShO	ERA
		29	79	75	.513	26	156	156	55	1396	1288	512	897	16	3.44
Sam Jones	R	34	18	14	.563	0	39	35	13	234	200	91	190	3	3.19
Mike McCormick	L	21	15	12	.556	3	40	34	15	253	228	65	154	4	2.70
Jack Sanford	R	31	12	14	.462	0	37	34	11	219	199	99	125	6	3.82
Billy O'Dell	L	27	8	13	.381	2	43	24	6	203	198	72	145	1	3.19
Stu Miller	R	32	7	6	.538	2	47	3	2	102	100	31	65	0	3.88
Juan Marichal	R	22	6	2	.750	0	11	11	6	81	59	28	58	1	2.67
Johnny Antonelli	L	30	6	7	.462	11	41	10	1	112	106	47	57	1	3.78
Billy Loes	R	30	3	2	.600	5	37	0	0	46	40	17	28	0	4.89
Bud Byerly	R	39	1	0	1.000	2	19	0	0	22	32	6	13	0	5.32
Eddie Fisher	R	23	1	0	1.000	0	3	1	1	13	11	2	7	0	3.46
Sherman Jones	R	25	1	1	.500	1	16	0	0	32	37	11	10	0	3.09
Georges Maranda	R	28	1	4	.200	0	17	4	0	51	50	30	28	0	4.59
Joe Shipley	R	25	0	0	.000	0	15	0	0	20	20	9	9	0	5.40
Don Choate	R	21	0	0	.000	0	4	0	0	8	7	4	7	0	2.25
Ray Monzant	R	27	0	0	.000	0	1	0	0	1	1	0	1	0	9.00

CINCINNATI 6th 67-87 .435 28 — FRED HUTCHINSON

NAME	G by POS	B	AGE	G	AB	R	H	2B	3B	HR	RBI	BB	SO	SB	BA	SA
TOTALS			28	154	5289	640	1324	230	40	140	604	512	858	73	.250	.388
Frank Robinson	1B78, OF51, 3B1	R	24	139	464	86	138	33	6	31	83	82	67	13	.297	**.595**
Billy Martin	2B97	R	32	103	317	34	78	17	1	3	16	27	34	0	.246	.334
Roy McMillan	SS116, 2B10	R	29	124	399	42	94	12	2	10	42	35	40	2	.236	.351
Eddie Kasko	3B86, 2B33, SS15	R	28	126	479	56	140	21	1	6	51	46	37	9	.292	.378
Gus Bell	OF131	L	31	143	515	65	135	19	5	12	62	29	40	4	.262	.388
Vada Pinson	OF154	L	21	154	**652**	107	187	**37**	12	20	61	47	96	32	.287	.472
2 Wally Post	OF67	R	30	77	249	36	70	14	0	17	38	28	51	0	.281	.542
Ed Bailey	C129	L	29	133	441	52	115	19	3	13	67	59	70	1	.261	.406
Jerry Lynch	OF32	L	29	102	159	23	46	8	2	6	27	16	25	0	.289	.478
Willie Jones	3B46, 2B1	R	34	79	149	16	40	7	0	3	27	31	16	1	.268	.376
Gordy Coleman	1B66	L	25	66	251	26	68	10	1	6	32	12	32	1	.271	.390
Cliff Cook	3B47, OF4	R	23	54	149	9	31	7	0	3	13	8	51	0	.208	.315
Elio Chacon	2B43, OF2	R	23	49	116	14	21	1	0	0	7	14	23	7	.181	.190
Leo Cardenas	SS47	R	21	48	142	13	33	2	4	1	12	6	32	0	.232	.324
1 Tony Gonzalez	OF31	L	23	39	99	10	21	5	1	3	14	4	27	1	.212	.374
Dutch Dotterer	C31	R	28	33	79	4	18	5	0	2	11	13	10	0	.228	.367
1 Lee Walls	OF24, 1B2	R	27	29	84	12	23	3	2	1	7	17	20	2	.274	.393

2 Harry Anderson 28 L 11-66, Frank House 30 L 5-28, Whitey Lockman 33 L 2-10, Joe Azcue 20 R 3-31, Joe Gaines 23 R 3-15, Rogelio Alvarez 22 R 1-9, Pete Whisenant 30 R 0-1

NAME	T	AGE	W	L	PCT	SV	G	GS	CG	IP	H	BB	SO	ShO	ERA
		29	67	87	.435	**35**	154	154	33	1390	1417	442	740	8	4.00
Bob Purkey	R	30	17	11	.607	0	41	33	11	253	259	59	97	1	3.59
Jim O'Toole	L	23	12	12	.500	1	34	31	7	196	198	66	124	2	3.81
Jay Hook	R	23	11	18	.379	0	36	33	10	222	222	73	103	2	4.50
Jim Brosnan	R	30	7	2	.778	12	57	2	0	99	79	22	62	0	2.36
2 Marshall Bridges	L	29	4	0	1.000	2	14	0	0	25	14	7	26	0	1.08
1 Don Newcombe	R	34	4	6	.400	0	16	15	1	83	99	14	36	0	4.55
Cal McLish	R	34	4	14	.222	0	37	21	2	151	170	48	56	1	4.17
2 Bob Grim	R	30	2	2	.500	2	26	0	0	30	32	10	22	0	4.50
Jim Maloney	R	20	2	6	.250	0	11	10	2	64	61	37	48	1	4.64
Raul Sanchez	R	29	1	0	1.000	0	8	0	0	15	12	11	5	0	4.80
Brooks Lawrence	R	35	1	0	1.000	1	7	0	0	8	9	8	2	0	10.13
Bill Henry	L	32	1	5	.167	17	51	0	0	68	62	20	58	0	3.18
Joe Nuxhall	L	31	1	8	.111	0	38	6	0	112	130	27	72	0	4.42
Claude Osteen	L	20	0	1	.000	0	20	3	0	48	53	30	15	0	5.06
Ted Wieand	R	27	0	1	.000	0	5	0	0	4	4	5	3	0	11.25
Orlando Pena	R	26	0	1	.000	0	4	0	0	9	8	3	9	0	3.00
Duane Richards	R	23	0	0	.000	0	2	0	0	3	5	2	2	0	9.00

CHICAGO 7th 60-94 .390 35 — CHARLIE GRIMM 6-11 .353 LOU BOUDREAU 54-83 .394

NAME	G by POS	B	AGE	G	AB	R	H	2B	3B	HR	RBI	BB	SO	SB	BA	SA
TOTALS			28	156	5311	634	1293	213	48	119	600	**531**	897	51	.243	.369
2 Ed Bouchee	1B80	L	27	98	299	33	71	11	1	5	44	45	51	2	.237	.331
Jerry Kindall	2B82, SS2	R	25	89	246	17	59	16	2	2	23	5	52	4	.240	.346
Ernie Banks	SS156	R	29	156	597	94	162	32	7	**41**	117	71	69	1	.271	.554
Ron Santo	3B94	R	20	95	347	44	87	24	2	9	44	31	44	0	.251	.409
Bob Will	OF121	L	28	138	475	58	121	20	9	6	53	47	54	1	.255	.373
Richie Ashburn	OF146	L	33	151	547	99	159	16	5	0	40	**116**	50	16	.291	.338
George Altman	OF79, 1B21	L	27	119	334	50	89	16	4	13	51	32	67	4	.266	.455
El Tappe	C49	R	33	51	103	11	24	7	0	0	3	11	12	0	.233	.301
Frank Thomas	1B50, OF49, 3B33	R	31	135	479	54	114	12	1	21	64	28	74	1	.238	.399
Don Zimmer	2B75, 3B45, SS5, OF2	R	29	132	368	37	95	16	7	6	35	27	56	8	.258	.389
Sammy Taylor (AJ)	C43	L	27	74	150	14	31	9	0	3	17	6	18	0	.207	.327
Moe Thacker	C50	R	26	54	90	5	14	1	0	0	6	14	20	1	.156	.167
1 Earl Averill	C34, 3B1, OF1	R	28	52	102	14	24	4	0	1	13	11	16	1	.235	.304
1 Dick Gernert	1B18, OF5	R	31	52	96	8	24	3	0	0	11	10	19	1	.250	.281
Al Heist	OF33	R	32	41	102	11	28	5	3	1	6	10	12	3	.275	.412
1 Walt Moryn	OF30	L	34	38	109	12	32	4	0	2	11	13	19	2	.294	.385
Lou Johnson	OF25	R	25	34	68	6	14	2	1	0	1	5	19	3	.206	.265
2 Don Cardwell	P31	R	24	33	69	9	14	1	0	3	6	0	30	1	.203	.348
Danny Murphy	OF21	L	17	31	75	7	9	2	0	1	6	4	13	0	.120	.187
1 Tony Taylor	2B19	R	24	19	76	14	20	3	3	1	9	8	12	2	.263	.421

Grady Hatton 37 L 13-38, Jim Hegan 39 R 9-43, 1 Del Rice 37 R 12-52, Sammy Drake 25 B 1-15, Billy Williams 22 L 13-47, Art Schult 32 R 2-15,
1 Irv Noren 35 L 1-11, 1 Cal Neeman 31 R 2-13, Dick Bertell 24 R 2-15, Nelson Mathews 18 R 2-8, Jim McKnight 24 R 2-6

NAME	T	AGE	W	L	PCT	SV	G	GS	CG	IP	H	BB	SO	ShO	ERA
		25	60	94	.390	25	156	156	36	**1403**	1393	**565**	805	6	4.35
Glen Hobbie	R	24	16	**20**	.444	1	46	36	16	259	253	101	134	4	3.96
Bob Anderson	R	24	9	11	.450	1	38	30	5	204	201	68	115	0	4.10
Don Elston	R	31	8	9	.471	11	60	0	0	127	109	55	85	0	3.40
2 Don Cardwell	R	24	8	14	.364	0	31	26	6	177	166	68	129	1	4.37
Dick Ellsworth	L	20	7	13	.350	0	31	27	6	177	170	72	94	0	3.71
Moe Drabowsky	R	24	3	1	.750	1	32	7	0	50	71	23	26	0	6.48
Mark Freeman	R	29	3	3	.500	1	30	8	1	77	70	33	50	0	5.61
Ben Johnson	R	29	2	1	.667	1	17	0	0	29	39	11	9	0	4.97
Joe Schaffernoth	R	22	2	3	.400	3	33	0	0	55	46	17	33	0	2.78
Seth Morehead	L	25	2	9	.182	4	45	7	2	123	123	46	64	0	3.95
Mel Wright	R	32	0	1	.000	2	9	0	0	16	17	3	8	0	5.06
Jim Brewer (BJ)	L	22	0	3	.000	0	5	4	0	22	25	6	7	0	5.73
Dick Drott	R	24	0	6	.000	0	23	9	0	55	63	42	32	0	7.20
Art Ceccarelli	L	30	0	0	.000	0	7	1	0	13	16	4	10	0	5.54
John Goetz	R	22	0	0	.000	0	4	0	0	6	10	4	6	0	13.50
Dick Burwell	R	20	0	0	.000	0	3	1	0	10	11	7	1	0	5.40
Al Schroll	R	28	0	0	.000	0	2	0	0	3	3	5	2	0	9.00

PHILADELPHIA 8th 59-95 .383 36 — EDDIE SAWYER 1-0 1.000 ANDY COHEN 0-1 .000 GENE MAUCH 58-94 .382

NAME	G by POS	B	AGE	G	AB	R	H	2B	3B	HR	RBI	BB	SO	SB	BA	SA
TOTALS			26	154	5169	546	1235	196	44	99	503	448	**1054**	45	.239	.351
Pancho Herrera	1B134, 2B17	R	26	145	512	61	144	26	6	17	71	51	**136**	2	.281	.455
2 Tony Taylor	2B123, 3B4	R	24	127	505	66	145	22	4	4	35	33	86	24	.287	.370
Ruben Amaro	SS92	R	24	92	264	25	61	9	1	0	16	21	32	0	.231	.273
1 Al Dark	3B53, 1B1	R	38	55	198	29	48	5	1	3	14	19	14	1	.242	.323
Ken Walters	OF119	R	26	124	426	42	102	10	0	8	37	16	50	4	.239	.319
Bobby Del Greco	OF89	R	27	100	300	48	71	16	4	10	26	54	64	1	.237	.417
Johnny Callison (KJ)	OF86	L	21	99	288	36	75	11	5	9	30	45	70	0	.260	.427
Jimmie Coker	C76	R	24	81	252	18	54	5	3	6	34	23	45	0	.214	.329
Bobby Gene Smith	OF70, 3B1	R	26	98	217	24	62	5	2	4	27	10	28	2	.286	.382
Tony Curry	OF64	L	21	95	245	26	64	14	2	6	34	16	53	0	.261	.408
Clay Dalrymple	C48	L	23	82	158	11	43	6	2	4	21	15	21	0	.272	.411
Bobby Malkmus	SS29, 2B23, 3B12	R	28	79	133	16	28	4	1	1	12	11	28	2	.211	.278
2 Tony Gonzalez	OF67	L	23	78	241	27	72	17	5	6	33	11	47	2	.299	.485
Ted Lepcio	3B50, SS14, 2B5	R	29	69	141	16	32	7	0	2	8	17	41	0	.227	.319
2 Lee Walls	3B34, OF13, 1B7	R	27	65	181	19	36	6	1	3	19	14	32	3	.199	.293
2 Cal Neeman	C52	R	31	59	160	13	29	6	2	4	13	16	42	0	.181	.319
Joe Koppe (WJ)	SS55, 3B2	R	29	58	170	13	29	6	1	1	13	23	47	3	.171	.235
1 Harry Anderson	OF16, 1B12	L	28	38	93	10	23	2	0	5	12	10	19	0	.247	.430
1 Wally Post	OF22	R	30	34	84	11	24	8	1	2	12	9	24	0	.286	.452

1 Joe Morgan 29 L 11-83, 1 Ed Bouchee 27 L 17-65, 1 Dave Philley 40 B 5-15, Jim Woods 20 R 6-34, 1 Don Cardwell 24 R 2-8, Bobby Wine 21 R 2-14

NAME	T	AGE	W	L	PCT	SV	G	GS	CG	IP	H	BB	SO	ShO	ERA
		27	59	**95**	.383	16	154	154	45	1375	**1423**	439	736	6	4.01
Robin Roberts	R	33	12	16	.429	1	35	33	13	237	256	34	122	2	4.03
Dick Farrell	R	26	10	6	.625	11	59	0	0	103	88	29	70	0	2.71
Gene Conley	R	29	8	14	.364	0	29	25	9	183	192	42	117	2	3.69
Art Mahaffey	R	22	7	3	.700	0	14	12	5	93	78	34	56	1	2.32
Chris Short	L	22	6	9	.400	3	42	10	2	107	101	52	54	0	3.95
John Buzhardt	R	23	5	16	.238	0	30	29	5	200	198	68	73	0	3.87
Jim Owens	R	26	4	14	.222	0	31	22	6	150	182	64	83	0	5.04
Jack Meyer (XJ)	R	28	3	1	.750	0	7	4	0	25	25	11	18	0	4.32
Dallas Green	R	25	3	6	.333	0	23	10	5	109	100	44	51	1	4.05
1 Don Cardwell	R	24	1	2	.333	0	5	4	0	28	28	11	21	0	4.50
Taylor Phillips	L	27	0	1	.000	0	10	1	0	14	21	4	6	0	8.36
Ruben Gomez	R	32	0	3	.000	1	22	1	0	52	68	9	24	0	5.37
Humberto Robinson	R	30	0	4	.000	0	33	1	0	50	48	22	31	0	3.42
Al Neiger	L	21	0	0	.000	0	6	0	0	13	16	4	3	0	5.54
Curt Simmons	L	31	0	0	.000	0	4	2	0	4	13	6	4	0	18.00
Hank Mason	R	29	0	0	.000	0	3	0	0	6	9	5	3	0	9.00

WORLD SERIES – PITTSBURGH (NL) 4 NEW YORK (AL) 3

LINE SCORES

TEAM	1	2	3	4	5	6	7	8	9	10	11	12	R	H	E
Game 1 October 5 at Pittsburgh															
NY (AL)	1	0	0	1	0	0	0	0	2				4	13	2
PIT (NL)	3	0	0	2	0	1	0	0	X				6	8	0
Game 2 October 6 at Pittsburgh															
NY	0	0	2	1	2	7	3	0	1				16	19	1
PIT	0	0	0	1	0	0	0	0	2				3	13	1
Game 3 October 8 at New York															
PIT	0	0	0	0	0	0	0	0	0				0	4	0
NY	6	0	0	4	0	0	0	0	X				10	16	1
Game 4 October 9 at New York															
PIT	0	0	0	0	3	0	0	0	0				3	7	0
NY	0	0	0	1	0	0	1	0	0				2	8	0
Game 5 October 10 at New York															
PIT	0	3	1	0	0	0	0	0	1				5	10	2
NY	0	1	1	0	0	0	0	0	0				2	5	2
Game 6 October 12 at Pittsburgh															
NY	0	1	5	0	0	2	2	2	0				12	17	1
PIT	0	0	0	0	0	0	0	0	0				0	7	1
Game 7 October 13 at Pittsburgh															
NY	0	0	0	0	1	4	0	2	2				9	13	1
PIT	2	2	0	0	0	0	0	5	1				10	11	0

Game 1: **Ditmar**, Coates (1), Maas (5), Duren (7) — **Law**, Face (8)

Game 2: **Turley**, Shantz (9) — **Friend**, Green (5), Labine (6), Witt (6), Gibbon (7), Cheney (9)

Game 3: **Mizell**, Labine (1), Green (1), Witt (4), Cheney (6), Gibbon (8) — **Ford**

Game 4: **Law**, Face (7) — **Terry**, Shantz (7), Coates (8)

Game 5: **Haddix**, Face (7) — **Ditmar**, Arroyo (2), Stafford (5), Duren (8)

Game 6: **Ford** — **Friend**, Cheney (3), Mizell (4), Green (6), Labine (6), Witt (9)

Game 7: Turley, Stafford (2), Shantz (3), Coates (8), **Terry** (8) — Law, Face (6), Friend (9), **Haddix** (9)

COMPOSITE BATTING

NAME	POS	G	AB	R	H	2B	3B	HR	RBI	BA
Pittsburgh (NL)										
Totals		7	234	27	60	11	0	4	26	.256
Clemente	OF	7	29	1	9	0	0	0	3	.310
Virdon	OF	7	29	2	7	**3**	0	0	5	.241
Groat	SS	7	28	3	6	2	0	0	2	.214
Mazeroski	2B	7	25	4	8	2	0	2	5	.320
Hoak	3B	7	23	3	5	2	0	0	3	.217
Cimoli	OF	7	20	4	5	0	0	0	1	.250
Stuart	1B	5	20	0	3	0	0	0	0	.150
Burgess	C	5	18	2	6	1	0	0	0	.333
Nelson	1B	4	9	2	3	0	0	1	2	.333
Smith	C	3	8	1	3	0	0	1	3	.375
Law	P	3	6	1	2	1	0	0	1	.333
Skinner	OF	2	5	2	1	0	0	0	1	.200
Schofield	SS	3	3	0	1	0	0	0	0	.333
Haddix	P	2	3	0	1	0	0	0	0	.333
Face	P	4	3	0	0	0	0	0	0	.000
Baker	PH	3	3	0	0	0	0	0	0	.000
Christopher	PR	3	0	2	0	0	0	0	0	.000
Oldis	C	2	0	0	0	0	0	0	0	.000

Friend P 0-1, Green P 0-1, Cheney P 0-0, Labine P 0-0, Witt P 0-0, Gibbon P 0-0, Mizell P 0-0

NAME	POS	G	AB	R	H	2B	3B	HR	RBI	BA
New York (AL)										
Totals		7	269	55	91	13	4	10	54	.338
Skowron	1B	7	**32**	7	**12**	2	0	2	6	.375
Richardson	2B	7	30	**8**	11	2	**2**	1	**12**	.367
Kubek	SS-OF	7	30	6	10	1	0	0	3	.333
Maris	OF	7	30	6	8	1	0	2	2	.267
Mantle	OF	7	25	**8**	10	1	0	**3**	11	.400
Berra	C-OF	7	22	6	7	0	0	1	8	.218
McDougald	3B	6	18	4	5	1	0	0	2	.278
Cerv	OF	4	14	1	5	0	0	0	0	.357
Howard	C	5	13	4	6	1	1	1	4	**.462**
Boyer	3B-SS	4	12	1	3	2	1	0	1	.250
Blanchard	C	5	11	2	5	2	0	0	2	.455
Ford	P	2	8	1	2	0	0	0	2	.250
Lopez	OF	3	7	0	3	0	0	0	0	.429
Turley	P	2	4	0	1	0	0	0	1	.250
Long	PH	3	3	0	1	0	0	0	0	.333
Shantz	P	3	3	0	1	0	0	0	0	.333
DeMaestri	SS	4	2	1	1	0	0	0	0	.500
Terry	P	2	2	0	0	0	0	0	0	.000

Coates P 0-1, Stafford P 0-1, Arroyo P 0-1, Ditmar P 0-0, Duren P 0-0, Maas P 0-0, Grba PR 0-0

COMPOSITE PITCHING

NAME	G	IP	H	BB	SO	W	L	SV	ERA
Pittsburgh (NL)									
Totals	7	62	91	18	40	4	3	3	7.11
Law	3	**18.1**	**22**	3	**8**	2	0	0	3.44
Face	**4**	10.1	9	2	4	0	0	**3**	5.23
Haddix	2	7.1	6	2	6	2	0	0	2.45
Friend	3	6	13	3	7	0	2	0	13.50
Cheney	3	4	4	1	6	0	0	0	4.50
Labine	3	4	13	1	2	0	0	0	13.50
Green	3	4	11	1	3	0	0	0	22.50
Gibbon	2	3	4	1	2	0	0	0	9.00
Witt	3	2.2	5	2	1	0	0	0	0.00
Mizell	2	2.1	4	2	1	0	1	0	15.43
New York (AL)									
Totals	7	61	60	12	26	3	4	1	3.54
Ford	2	18	11	2	**8**	2	0	0	**0.00**
Turley	2	9.1	15	**4**	0	1	0	0	4.82
Terry	2	6.2	7	1	5	0	2	0	5.40
Shantz	3	6.1	4	1	1	0	0	1	4.26
Coates	3	6.1	6	1	3	0	0	0	5.68
Stafford	2	6	5	1	2	0	0	0	1.50
Duren	2	4	2	1	5	0	0	0	2.25
Maas	1	2	2	0	1	0	0	0	4.50
Ditmar	2	1.2	6	1	0	0	2	0	21.60
Arroyo	1	.2	2	0	1	0	0	0	13.50

USE NAME – GIVEN NAMES (NICKNAMES)	TEAM BY YEAR	BIRTH DATE	BIRTH PLACE	DEATH DATE	B	T	HGT	WGT	G	AB	R	H	2B	3B	HR	RBI	BB	SO	SB	BA	SA
					LIFETIME BATTING TOTALS																
Aberson, Cliff-Clifford Alexander 46 played in N.F.L.	47-49ChiN	8-28-21	Chicago, Ill.	6-23-73	R	R	6'	200	63	179	25	45	7	3	5	26	25	44	0	.251	.408
Abrams, Cal-Calvin Ross	49-51BknN 52CinN 53-54PitN 54-55BalA 56ChiA	3- 2-24	Philadelphia, Pa.		L	L	5'11	195	567	1611	257	433	64	19	32	138	304	290	12	.269	.392
Adams, Bobby-Robert Henry	46-55CinN 55ChiA 56BalA 57-59ChiN	12-14-21	Tuolumne, Cal.		R	R	5'10	170	1281	4019	591	1082	188	49	37	303	414	447	67	.269	.368
Adams, Dick-Richard Leroy	47PhiA	4- 8-20	Tuolumne, Cal.		R	L	6'	185	37	89	9	18	2	3	2	11	2	18	0	.202	.360
Adams, Herb-Herbert Loren	48-50ChiA 51-52MS	4-14-28	Hollywood, Cal.		L	L	5'9	160	95	337	39	88	8	6	0	18	22	24	4	.261	.320
Adcock, Joe-Joseph Wilbur	50-52CinN 53-62MilN 63CleA 64LAA 65-66CalA M67CleA	10-30-27	Coushatta, La.		R	R	6'4	220	1959	6606	823	1832	295	35	336	1122	594	1059	20	.277	.485
Addis, Bob-Robert Gordon	50-51BosN 52-53ChiN 53PitN	11- 6-25	Mineral, Ohio		L	R	6'	180	208	534	70	150	22	2	2	47	37	47	8	.281	.341
Agganis, Harry-Harry (The Golden Greek)	54-55BosA	4-20-30	Lynn, Mass.	6-27-55	L	L	6'2	200	157	517	65	135	23	9	11	67	57	67	8	.261	.404
Albright, Jack-Harold John	47PhiN	6-30-21	St. Petersburg, Fla.		R	R	5'9	175	41	99	9	23	4	0	2	5	10	11	1	.232	.333
Allie, Gair-Gair Roosevelt	54PitN	10-29-31	Statesville, N.C.		R	R	6'1	190	121	418	38	83	8	6	3	30	56	84	1	.199	.268
Alston, Tom-Thomas Edison	54-57StLN	1-31-31	Greensboro, N.C.		L	R	6'5	210	91	271	30	66	15	2	4	36	25	46	3	.244	.358
Altobelli, Joe-Joseph Salvatore	55,57CleA 61MinA	5-26-32	Detroit, Mich.		L	L	6'	185	166	257	27	54	8	3	5	28	23	42	3	.210	.323
Alvarez, Ossie-Oswaldo [Gonzalez]	58WasA 59DetA	10-19-33	Matanzas, Cuba		R	R	5'10	165	95	198	20	42	3	0	0	5	16	27	1	.212	.227
Amoros, Sandy-Edmundo Isasi	52,54-57BknN 59-60LAN 60DetA	1-30-30	Havana, Cuba		L	L	5'7	170	517	1311	215	334	55	23	43	180	211	189	18	.255	.430
Anderson, Andy-Andy Holm	48-49StLA	11-13-22	Bremerton, Wash.		R	R	5'11	172	122	223	23	41	8	1	2	17	22	36	0	.184	.256
Anderson, Ferrell-Ferrell Jack	46BknN 53StLN	1- 9-18	Maple City, Kans.		R	R	6'1	200	97	234	20	61	12	0	2	15	18	25	1	.261	.338
Anderson, Harry-Harry Walter	57-60PhiN 60-61CinN	9-10-31	North East, Md.		L	R	6'3	205	484	1586	199	419	82	16	60	242	159	291	3	.264	.450
Anderson, Sparky-George Lee	59PhiN M70-75CinN	2-22-34	Bridgewater, S.D.		R	R	5'9	170	152	477	42	104	9	3	0	34	42	53	6	.218	.249
Andres, Ernie-Ernest Henry (Junie) 39-40,45-48 played in N.B.L.	46BosA	1-11-18	Jeffersonville, Ind.		R	R	6'1	200	15	41	0	4	2	0	0	1	3	5	0	.098	.146
Antonello, Bill-William James	53BknN	5-19-27	Brooklyn, N.Y.		R	R	5'11	185	40	43	9	7	1	1	1	4	2	11	0	.163	.302
Arft, Hank-Henry Irven (Bow Bow)	48-52StLA	1-28-22	Manchester, Mo.		L	L	5'11	190	300	906	116	229	46	13	13	118	137	133	8	.253	.375
Armstrong, George-George Noble (Dodo)	46PhiA	6- 3-24	Orange, N.J.		R	R	5'10	190	8	6	0	1	1	0	0	0	1	1	0	.167	.333
Ashburn, Richie-Don Richie (Whitey)	48-59PhiN 60-61ChiN 62NYN	3-19-27	Tilden, Neb.		L	R	5'10	170	2189	8365	1322	2574	317	109	29	586	1198	571	234	.308	.382
Aspromonte, Ken-Kenneth Joseph	57-58BosA 58-60WasA 60CleA 61LAA 61-62CleA 62MilN 63ChiN M72-74CleA	9-22-31	Brooklyn, N.Y.		R	R	6'	180	475	1483	171	369	69	3	19	124	179	149	7	.249	.338
Astroth, Joe-Joseph Henry	45-46,49-54PhiA 55-56KCA	9- 1-22	East Alton, Ill.		R	R	5'9	187	544	1579	163	401	51	10	13	156	177	124	6	.254	.324
Atwell, Toby-Maurice Dailey	52-53ChiN 53-56PitN 56MilN	3- 8-24	Leesburg, Va.		L	R	5'9	185	378	1117	116	290	41	7	9	110	161	84	4	.260	.333
Aulds, Doyle-Leycester Doyle (Tex)	47BosA	12-28-20	Farmerville, La.		R	R	6'2	185	3	4	0	1	0	0	0	0	0	1	0	.250	.250
Avila, Bobby-Roberto Francisco [Gonzalez] (Beto)	49-58CleA 59BalA 59BosA 59MilN	4- 2-24	Veracruz, Mexico		R	R	5'10	175	1300	4620	725	1296	185	35	80	467	562	399	78	.281	.388
Aylward, Dick-Richard John	53CleA	6- 4-25	Baltimore, Md.		R	R	6'	190	4	3	0	0	0	0	0	0	0	1	0	.000	.000
Babe, Loren-Loren Rolland (Bee Bee)	52-53NYA 53PhiA	1-11-28	Pisgah, Iowa		L	R	5'10	180	120	382	37	85	18	2	2	26	39	26	1	.223	.296
Bailey, Ed-Lonas Edgar	53-61CinN 61-63SFN 64MilN 65SFN 65ChiN 66CalA	4-15-31	Strawberry Pl., Tenn.		L	R	6'2	205	1212	3583	432	915	128	15	155	540	545	577	17	.256	.429
Baker, Floyd-Floyd Wilson	43-44StLA 45-51ChiA 52-53WasA 53-54BosA 54-55PhiN	10-10-16	Luray, Va.		L	R	5'9	160	874	2280	285	573	76	13	1	196	382	165	23	.251	.297
Baker, Gene-Eugene Walter	53-57ChiN 57-58,60-61PitN	6-15-25	Davenport, Iowa		R	R	6'1	175	630	2230	265	590	109	21	39	227	184	219	21	.265	.385
Balcena, Bobby-Robert Rudolph	56CinN	8- 1-28	San Pedro, Cal.		R	L	5'7	160	7	2	2	0	0	0	0	0	0	1	0	.000	.000
Baldwin, Frank-Frank DeWitt	53CinN	12-25-28	High Bridge, N.J.		R	R	5'11	195	16	20	0	2	0	0	0	0	1	9	0	.100	.100
Bamberger, Hal-Harold Earl (Dutch)	48NYN	10-29-24	Lebanon, Pa.		L	R	6'	173	7	12	0	1	0	0	0	0	1	2	0	.083	.083
Barmes, Bruce-Bruce Raymond (Squeaky)	53WasA	10-23-29	Vincennes, Ind.		L	R	5'8	165	5	5	1	1	0	0	0	0	0	0	0	.200	.200
Barone, Dick-Richard Anthony	60PitN	10-13-32	San Jose, Cal.		R	R	5'9	165	3	6	0	0	0	0	0	0	0	1	0	.000	.000
Bartirome, Tony-Anthony Joseph	52PitN 53-54MS	5- 9-32	Pittsburgh, Pa.		L	L	5'10	155	124	355	32	78	10	3	0	16	26	37	3	.220	.265
Basgall, Monty-Romanus	48-49,51PitN	2- 8-22	Pfeifer, Kans.		R	R	5'10	175	200	512	52	110	15	3	4	41	46	51	1	.215	.279
Batts, Matt-Matthew Daniel	47-51BosA 51StLA 52-54DetA 54ChiA 55-56CinN	10-16-21	San Antonio, Tex.		R	R	5'11	200	546	1605	163	432	95	11	26	219	143	163	6	.269	.391
Bauer, Hank-Henry Albert	48-59NYA 60-61,M61-62KCA M64-68BalA M69OakA	7-31-22	East St. Louis, Ill.		R	R	6'	192	1544	5145	833	1424	229	57	164	703	519	638	50	.277	.439
Baumgartner, John-John Edward	53DetA	5-29-31	Birmingham, Ala.		R	R	6'1	190	7	27	3	5	0	0	0	2	0	5	0	.185	.185
Baumholtz, Frankie-Frank Conrad 45-46 played in N.B.L., 46-47 played in B.A.A.	47-49CinN 49,51-55ChiN 56-57PhiN	10- 7-18	Midvale, Ohio		L	L	5'10	175	1019	3477	450	1010	165	51	25	272	258	258	30	.290	.389
Baxes, Jim-Dimitrios S.	59LAN 59CleA	7- 5-28	San Francisco, Cal.		R	R	6'1	190	88	280	39	69	12	0	17	39	25	54	1	.246	.471
Baxes, Mike-Michael	56,58KCA	12-18-30	San Francisco, Cal.		R	R	5'10	175	146	337	40	73	13	2	1	13	39	39	1	.217	.276
Beard, Ted-Cramer Theodore	48-52PitN 57-58ChiA	1- 7-21	Woodsboro, Md.		L	L	5'8	165	194	474	80	94	11	6	6	35	78	107	16	.198	.285
Becquer, Julio-Julio [Villegas]	55,57-60WasA 61LAA 61,63MinA	12-20-31	Havana, Cuba		L	L	5'11	178	488	974	100	238	37	16	12	114	41	120	8	.244	.352
Belardi, Wayne-Carroll Wayne (Footsie)	50-51,53-54BknN 54-56DetA	9- 5-30	Calistoga, Cal.		L	L	6'1	185	263	592	71	143	13	5	28	74	66	97	1	.242	.422
Bell, Gus-David Russell	50-52PitN 53-61CinN 62NYN 62-64MilN	11-15-28	Louisville, Ky.		L	R	6'1	196	1741	6478	865	1823	311	66	206	942	470	636	30	.281	.445
Bella, Zeke-John	57NYA 59KCA	8-23-30	Greenwich, Conn.		R	L	5'11	185	52	98	10	18	2	1	1	9	10	16	0	.196	.272
Benson, Vern-Vernon Adair	43PhiA 44-45MS 46PhiA 51-53StLN	9-19-24	Granite Quarry, N.C.		L	R	5'11	185	55	104	17	21	5	1	3	12	13	22	0	.202	.356
Berardino, Johnny-John	39-42StLA 43-45MS 46-47StLA 48-50CleA 50PitN 51StLA 52CleA 52PitN	5- 1-17	Los Angeles, Cal.		R	R	5'11	175	912	3028	334	755	167	23	36	387	284	268	27	.249	.355
Berberet, Lou-Louis Joseph	54-55NYA 56-58WasA 58BosA 59-60DetA	11-20-29	Long Beach, Cal.		L	R	5'11	200	448	1224	118	281	34	10	31	153	200	195	2	.230	.350
Bernier, Carlos-Carlos [Rodriguez]	53PitN	1-28-29	Juana Diaz, P.R.		R	R	5'9	180	105	310	48	66	7	8	3	31	51	53	15	.213	.316
Bero, Johnny-John George	48DetA 51StLA	12-22-22	Gary, W.Va.		L	R	6'	170	65	169	26	34	5	0	5	17	27	31	1	.201	.320
Berra, Yogi-Lawrence Peter	46-63,M64NYA 65,M72-75NYN	5-12-25	St. Louis, Mo.		L	R	5'8	195	2120	7555	1175	2150	321	49	358	1430	704	414	30	.285	.482
Berry, Neil-Cornelius John	48-52DetA 53StLA 53ChiA 54BalA	1-11-22	Kalamazoo, Mich.		R	R	5'10	168	441	1086	148	265	28	9	0	74	113	105	11	.244	.286
Bertoia, Reno-Reno Peter	53-58DetA 59-60WasA 61MinA 61KCA 61-62DetA	1- 8-35	St. Vito Udine, Italy		R	R	5'11	185	612	1745	204	425	60	10	27	171	142	252	16	.244	.336
Bevan, Hal-Harold Joseph	52BosA 52PhiA 55KCA 61CinN	11-15-30	New Orleans, La.	10- 5-68	R	R	6'2	198	15	24	2	7	0	0	1	5	0	3	2	.292	.417
Biasatti, Hank-Henry Arcado 46-47 played in B.A.A.	49PhiA	1-14-22	Beano, Italy		L	L	5'11	175	21	24	6	2	2	0	0	2	8	5	0	.083	.167
Bilko, Steve-Stephen Thomas	49-54StLN 54ChiN 58CinN 58LAN 60DetA 61-62LAA	11-13-28	Nanticoke, Pa.		R	R	6'1	230	600	1738	220	432	85	13	76	276	234	395	2	.249	.444
Binks (Binkowski), George-George Alvin (Bingo)	44-46WasA 47-48PhiA 48StLA	7-11-14	Chicago, Ill.		L	L	6'	175	351	1093	112	277	55	10	8	130	67	108	21	.253	.344
Blasingame, Don-Don Lee (Blazer)	55-59StLN 60-61SFN 61-63CinN 63-66WasA 66KCA	3-16-32	Corinth, Miss.		L	R	5'10	160	1444	5296	731	1366	178	62	21	308	552	462	105	.258	.327
Blatnik, Johnny-John Louis (Chief)	48-50PhiN 50StLN	3-10-21	Bridgeport, Ohio		R	R	6'	195	138	447	59	113	27	8	6	46	40	83	3	.253	.389
Blattner, Buddy-Robert Garnett	42StLN 43-45MS 46-48NYN 49PhiN	2- 2-20	St. Louis, Mo.		R	R	6'	180	272	713	112	176	34	8	16	84	102	96	18	.247	.384
Blaylock, Marv-Marvin Edward	50NYN 55-57PhiN	9-30-29	Fort Smith, Ark.		L	L	6'1	175	287	746	96	175	21	15	15	78	84	137	11	.235	.363
Boak, Chet-Chester Robert	60KCA 61WasA	6-19-35	New Castle, Pa.		R	R	6'	180	10	20	1	2	0	0	0	1	1	3	1	.100	.100
Bockman, Eddie-Joseph Edward	46NYA 47CleA 48-49PitN	7-26-20	Santa Ana, Cal.		R	R	5'9	175	199	474	54	109	16	4	11	56	46	87	5	.230	.350
Bolger, Jim-James Cyril (Dutch)	50-51,54CinN 55,57-58ChiN 59CleA 59PhiN	2-23-32	Cincinnati, Ohio		R	R	6'2	180	312	612	65	140	14	6	6	48	32	83	3	.229	.301
Bolling, Frank-Frank Elmore	54DetA 55MS 56-60DetA 61-65MilN 66AtlN	11-16-31	Mobile, Ala.		R	R	6'1	175	1540	5562	692	1415	221	40	106	556	462	558	40	.254	.366
Bolling, Milt-Milton Joseph	52-57BosA 57WasA 58DetA	8- 9-30	Mississippi C., Miss.		R	R	6'1	177	400	1161	127	280	50	7	19	94	115	188	5	.241	.345
Bollweg, Don-Donald Raymond	50-51StLN 53NYA 54PhiA 55KCA	2-12-21	Wheaton, Ill.		L	L	6'1	190	195	452	62	110	22	7	11	53	60	68	2	.243	.396
Boone, Ray-Raymond Otis (Ike)	48-53CleA 53-58DetA 58-59ChiA 59KCA 59-60MilN 60BosA	7-27-23	San Diego, Cal.		R	R	6'	180	1373	4589	645	1260	162	46	151	737	608	463	21	.275	.429
Borkowski, Bob-Robert Vilarian (Bush)	50-51ChiN 52-55CinN 55BknN	1-27-26	Dayton, Ohio		R	R	6'2	182	470	1170	126	294	43	10	16	112	76	166	2	.251	.346
Bouchee, Ed-Edward Francis	56-60PhiN 60-61ChiN 62NYN	3- 7-33	Livingston, Mont.		L	L	6'	210	670	2199	298	583	114	21	61	290	340	401	5	.265	.419
Bowers, Billy-Grover Bill	49ChiA	3-25-23	Parkin, Ark.		L	R	5'9	176	26	78	5	15	2	1	0	6	4	5	1	.192	.244
Bowman, Bob-Robert Leroy	55-59PhiN	5-10-31	Laytonville, Cal.		R	R	6'1	195	256	519	71	129	19	5	17	54	48	109	0	.249	.403
Boyd, Bob-Robert Richard (The Rope)	51,53-54ChiA 56-60BalA 61KCA 61MilN	10- 1-26	Potts Camp, Miss.		L	L	5'10	170	693	1936	253	567	81	23	19	175	167	114	9	.293	.388
Bradley, George-George Washington	46StLA	4- 1-14	Greenwood, Ark.		R	R	6'1	185	4	12	2	2	1	0	0	3	0	1	0	.167	.250
Bradshaw, George-George Thomas	52WasA	9-12-24	Salisbury, N.C.		R	R	6'2	185	10	23	3	5	2	0	0	6	1	2	0	.217	.304
Brady, Bob-Robert Jay	46-47BosN	11- 8-22	Lewistown, Pa.		L	R	6'1	175	4	6	0	1	0	0	0	0	1	1	0	.167	.167
Brideweser, Jim-James Ehrenfeld	51-53NYA 54BalA 55-56ChiA 56DetA 57BalA	2-13-27	Lancaster, Ohio		R	R	6'	165	329	620	79	156	21	6	1	50	63	78	6	.252	.310
Bridges, Rocky-Everett Lamar	51-52BknN 53-57CinN 57-58WasA 59-60DetA 60CleA 60StLN 61LAA	8- 7-27	Refugio, Tex.		R	R	5'8	176	919	2272	245	562	80	11	16	187	205	229	10	.247	.313
Brinkopf, Leon-Leon Clarence	52ChiN	10-20-26	Cape Girardeau, Mo.		R	R	5'11	185	9	22	1	4	0	0	0	2	4	5	0	.182	.182
Brovia, Joe-Joseph John (Ox)	55CinN	2-18-22	Davenport, Cal.		L	R	6'3	195	21	18	0	2	0	0	0	4	1	6	0	.111	.111
Brown, Bobby-Robert William (Doc)	46-52NYA 53MS 54NYA	10-25-24	Seattle, Wash.		L	R	6'1	180	548	1619	233	452	62	14	22	237	214	88	9	.279	.376
Brown, Tommy-Thomas Michael (Buckshot)	44-45BknN 46MS 47-51BknN 51-52PhiN 52-53ChiN	12- 6-27	Brooklyn, N.Y.		R	R	6'1	170	494	1280	151	309	39	7	31	159	85	142	7	.241	.355
Brown, Willard-Willard Jessie	47StLA	6-26-15	Shreveport, La.		R	R	5'11	200	21	67	4	12	3	0	1	6	0	7	2	.179	.269
Brucker, Earle-Earle Francis	48PhiA	8-29-25	Los Angeles, Cal.		L	R	6'2	210	2	6	0	1	1	0	0	0	1	1	0	.167	.333
Bruton, Bill-William Haron	53-60MilN 61-64DetA	12-22-25	Panola, Ala.		L	R	6'	169	1610	6056	937	1651	241	102	94	545	482	793	207	.273	.393
Bucha, Johnny-John George	48,50StLN 53DetA	1-22-25	Allentown, Pa.		R	R	5'11	190	84	195	18	40	10	0	1	15	25	21	1	.205	.272
Buddin, Don-Donald Thomas	56,58-61BosA 62HouN 62DetA	5- 5-34	Turbeville, S.C.		R	R	5'11	178	711	2289	342	551	123	12	41	225	410	404	15	.241	.359

USE NAME – GIVEN NAMES (NICKNAMES)	TEAM BY YEAR	BIRTH DATE	BIRTH PLACE	DEATH DATE	B	T	HGT	WGT	G	AB	R	H	2B	3B	HR	RBI	BB	SO	SB	BA	SA
					LIFETIME BATTING TOTALS																
Bullard, George-George Donald	54DetA	10-24-28	Lynn, Mass.		R	R	5'9	165	4	1	0	0	0	0	0	0	0	0	0	.000	.000
Burbrink, Nels-Nelson Edward	55StLN	12-28-21	Cincinnati, Ohio		R	R	5'10	195	58	170	11	47	8	1	0	15	14	13	1	.276	.335
Burgess, Smoky-Forrest Harrill	49,51ChiN 52-55PhiN 55-58CinN 59-64PitN 64-67ChiA	2- 6-27	Caroleen, N.C.		L	R	5'8	190	1691	4471	485	1318	230	33	126	673	477	270	13	.295	.446
Burk, Mack-Mack Edwin	56PhiN 57MS 58PhiN	4-21-35	Nacogdoches, Tex.		R	R	6'4	190	16	2	3	1	0	0	0	0	0	1	0	.500	.500
Burris, Paul-Paul Robert	48,50,52BosN 53MilN	7-21-23	Hickory, N.C.		R	R	6'	190	69	196	15	43	5	0	2	24	8	21	0	.219	.276
Busby, Jim-James Franklin	50-52ChiA 52-55WasA 55ChiA 56-57CleA 57-58BalA	1- 8-27	Kenedy, Tex.		R	R	6'1	175	1352	4250	541	1113	162	35	48	438	310	439	97	.262	.350
	59-60BosA 60-61BalA 62HouN																				
Caballero, Putsy-Ralph Joseph	44-45,47-52PhiN	11- 5-27	New Orleans, La.		R	R	5'10	170	322	658	81	150	21	3	1	40	41	34	10	.228	.274
Caffie, Joe-Joseph Clifford (Rabbit)	56-57CleA	2-14-31	Ramer, Ala.		L	R	5'10	180	44	127	21	37	2	1	3	11	8	19	3	.291	.394
Calderone, Sammy-Samuel Francis	50NYN 51-52MS 53NYN 54MilN	2- 6-26	Beverly, N.J.		R	R	5'10	185	91	141	16	41	5	0	1	25	7	13	0	.291	.348
Camelli, Hank-Henry Richard	43-46PitN 47BosN	12- 9-14	Gloucester, Mass.		R	R	5'11	190	159	376	33	86	15	4	2	26	46	39	0	.229	.306
Campanella, Roy-Roy	48-57BknN 58BX	11-19-21	Philadelphia, Pa.		R	R	5'9	205	1215	4205	627	1161	178	18	242	856	533	501	25	.276	.500
Campbell, Paul-Paul McLaughlin	41-42BosA 43-45MS 46BosA 48-50DetA	9- 1-17	Paw Creek, N.C.		L	L	5'10	185	204	380	61	97	17	5	4	41	28	54	4	.255	.358
Campos, Frank-Francisco Jose [Lopez]	51-53WasA	5-11-24	Havana, Cuba		L	L	5'10	170	71	147	13	41	9	2	0	13	2	14	0	.279	.367
Carey (Nordstrom), Andy-Andrew Arthur	52-60NYA 60-61KCA 61ChiA 62LAN	10-18-31	Oakland, Cal.		R	R	6'1	190	938	2850	371	741	119	38	64	350	268	389	23	.260	.396
Carrasquel, Chico-Alfonso [Colon]	50-55ChiA 56-58CleA 58KCA 59BalA	1-23-28	Caracas, Venezuela		R	R	6'	170	1325	4644	568	1199	172	25	55	474	491	467	31	.258	.342
Carroll, Tommy-Thomas Edward	55-56NYA 58MS 59KCA	9-17-36	Queens, N.Y.		R	R	6'3	186	64	30	15	9	0	0	0	1	1	6	1	.300	.300
Carswell, Frank-Frank Willis (Wheels, Tex)	53DetA	11- 6-19	Palestine, Tex.		R	R	6'	195	16	15	2	4	0	0	0	2	3	1	0	.267	.267
Cassini, Jack-Jack Dempsey (Scat)	49PitN	10-26-19	Dearborn, Mich.		R	R	5'10	175	8	0	3	0	0	0	0	0	0	0	0	–	–
Castiglione, Pete-Peter Paul	47-53PitN 53-54StLN	2-13-21	Greenwich, Conn.		R	R	5'11	175	545	1670	205	426	62	11	24	150	103	126	10	.255	.349
Castleman, Foster Ephraim	54-57NYN 58BalA	1- 1-31	Nashville, Tenn.		R	R	6'	175	268	662	58	136	24	3	20	65	35	99	4	.205	.341
Caulfield, John-John Joseph (Jake)	46PhiA	11-23-18	Los Angeles, Cal.		R	R	5'11	170	44	94	13	26	8	0	0	10	4	11	0	.277	.362
Cerv, Bob-Robert Henry	51-56NYA 57-60KCA 60NYA 61LAA 61-62NYA 62HouN	5- 5-26	Weston, Neb.		R	R	6'	210	829	2261	320	624	96	26	105	374	212	392	12	.276	.481
Chapman, Sam-Samuel Blake	38-41PhiA 42-44MS 45-51PhiA 51CleA	4-11-16	Tiburon, Cal.		R	R	6'	180	1368	4988	754	1329	210	52	180	773	561	682	41	.266	.438
Chiti, Harry-Harry	50-52ChiN 53-54MS 55-56ChiN 58-60KCA 60-61DetA 62NYN	11-16-32	Kincaid, Ill.		R	R	6'2	221	502	1495	135	356	49	9	41	179	115	242	4	.238	.365
Chrisley, Neil-Barbara O'Neil	57-58WasA 59-60DetA 61MilN	12-16-31	Calhoun Falls, S.C.		L	R	6'3	187	302	619	60	130	22	8	16	64	55	62	3	.210	.349
Christopher, Loyd-Loyd Eugene	45BosA 45ChiN 47ChiA	12-31-19	Richmond, Cal.		R	R	6'2	190	16	37	5	9	0	1	0	4	5	6	0	.243	.297
Ciaffone, Larry-Lawrence Thomas (Symphony)	51StLN	8-17-24	Brooklyn, N.Y.		R	R	5'10	185	5	5	0	0	0	0	0	0	1	2	0	.000	.000
Cimoli, Gino-Gino Nicholas	56-57BknN 58LAN 59StLN 60-61PitN 61MilN 62-64KCA	12-18-29	San Francisco, Cal.		R	R	6'1	195	969	3054	370	808	133	48	44	321	221	474	21	.265	.383
	64BalA 65CalA																				
Clark, Allie-Alfred Aloysius	47NYA 48-51CleA 51-53PhiA 53ChiA	6-16-23	South Amboy, N.J.		R	R	6'	195	358	1021	131	267	48	4	32	149	72	70	2	.262	.410
Clark (Petrosky), Jim-James	48WasA	9- 1-27	Bagley, Pa.		L	R	5'10	162	9	12	1	3	0	0	0	0	0	2	0	.250	.250
Clark, Mel-Melvin Earl	51-55PhiN 57DetA	7- 7-26	Letart, W.Va.		R	R	6'	[illegible]	215	656	82	183	29	15	3	63	37	61	3	.277	.381
Clarkson, Bus-James Buster	52BosN	3-13-18	Hopkins, S.C.		R	R	5'11	195	14	25	3	5	0	0	0	1	3	3	0	.200	.200
Coan, Gil-Gilbert Fitzgerald (Citation)	46-53WasA 54-55BalA 55ChiA 55-56NYN	5-18-22	Monroe, N.C.		L	R	6'	180	918	2877	384	731	98	44	39	278	232	384	83	.254	.359
Cole, Dick-Richard Roy	51StLN 51,53-56PitN 57MilN	5- 6-26	Long Beach, Cal.		R	R	6'2	180	456	1215	106	303	50	10	2	107	132	124	2	.249	.312
Coleman, Jerry-Gerald Francis	49-57NYA	9-14-24	San Jose, Cal.		R	R	6'	165	723	2119	267	558	77	18	16	217	235	218	22	.263	.339
Coleman, Ray-Raymond Leroy	47-48StLA 48PhiA 50-51StLA 51-52ChiA 52StLA	6- 4-22	Dunsmuir, Cal.		L	R	6'	185	559	1729	208	446	74	33	20	199	148	158	19	.258	.374
Coles, Chuck-Charles Edward	58CinN	6-27-31	Fredericktown, Pa.		L	L	5'9	180	5	11	0	2	1	0	0	2	2	6	0	.182	.273
Collins (Kollonige), Joe-Joseph Edward	48-57NYA	12- 3-22	Scranton, Pa.		L	L	6'	195	908	2329	404	596	79	24	86	329	338	263	27	.256	.421
Combs, Merrill-Merrill Russell	47,49-50BosA 50WasA 51-52CleA	12-11-19	Los Angeles, Cal.		R	R	6'	172	140	361	45	73	6	1	2	25	57	43	0	.202	.241
Command, Jim-James Dalton (Igor)	54-55PhiN	10-15-28	Grand Rapids, Mich.		L	R	6'2	200	14	23	1	4	1	0	1	6	2	4	0	.174	.348
Conatser, Clint-Clinton Astor (Connie)	48-49BosN	7-24-21	Los Angeles, Cal.		R	R	5'11	182	143	376	40	102	15	3	6	39	46	46	0	.271	.375
Connors, Chuck-Kevin Joseph 45-46 played in N.B.L.	49BknN 51ChiN	4-10-21	Brooklyn, N.Y.		L	L	6'5	190	67	202	16	48	5	1	2	18	12	25	4	.238	.302
46-48 played in B.A.A.																					
Consolo, Billy-William Angelo	53-59BosA 59-60WasA 61MinA 62PhiN 62LAA 62KCA	8-18-34	Cleveland, Ohio		R	R	5'11	180	603	1178	158	260	31	11	9	83	161	297	9	.221	.289
Conway, Jack-Jack Clements	41CleA 42-45MS 46-47CleA 48NYN	7-30-19	Bryan, Tex.		R	R	5'11	175	128	359	35	80	10	3	1	27	28	54	2	.223	.276
Conyers, Herb-Herbert Leroy	50CleA	1- 8-21	Cogwill, Mo.	9-16-64	L	R	6'5	210	7	9	2	3	0	0	1	1	1	2	1	.333	.667
Coogan, Dale-Dale Roger	50PitN	8-14-30	Los Angeles, Cal.		L	L	6'1	190	53	129	19	31	6	1	1	13	17	24	0	.240	.326
Cooper, Pat-Orge Patterson (See P46-60)	46-47PhiA	11-26-17	Albermarle, N.C.		R	R	6'3	180	14	16	0	4	2	0	0	3	0	5	0	.250	.375
Cooper, Walker-William Walker	40-45StLN 46-49NYN 49-50CinN 50-52BosN	1- 8-15	Atherton, Mo.		R	R	6'3	210	1473	4702	573	1341	240	40	173	812	309	357	18	.285	.464
	53MilN 54PitN 54-55ChiN 56-57StLN																				
Corbitt, Claude-Claude Elliott	45BknN 46,48-49CinN	7-21-15	Sunbury, N.C.		R	R	5'10	170	215	630	60	153	22	1	1	37	47	30	8	.243	.286
Corriden, John-John Michael Jr.	46BknN	10- 6-18	Logansport, Ind.		B	R	5'6	160	1	0	1	0	0	0	0	0	0	0	0	–	–
Courtney, Clint-Clinton Dawson (Scrap Iron)	51NYA 52-53StLA 54BalA 55ChiA	3-16-27	Hall Summit, La.	6-16-75	L	R	5'8	180	946	2796	260	750	126	17	38	313	265	143	3	.268	.366
	55-59WasA 60BalA 61KCA 61BalA																				
Cox, Billy-William Richard	41PitN 42-45MS 46-47PitN 48-54BknN 55BalA	8-29-19	Newport, Pa.		R	R	5'10	150	1058	3712	470	974	174	32	66	351	298	218	42	.262	.380
Crandall, Del-Delmar Wesley	49-50BosN 51-52MS 53-63MilN 64SFN 65PitN	3- 5-30	Ontario, Cal.		R	R	6'1	200	1573	5026	585	1276	179	18	179	657	424	477	26	.254	.404
	66CleA M72-75MilA																				
Crawford, Rufus-Rufus (Jake)	52StLA	3-20-28	Campbell, Mo.		R	R	6'1	185	7	11	1	2	1	0	0	0	1	5	1	.182	.273
Cregor, Bernie-Bernard Udell	47StLN	2-21-27	Wytheville, Va		R	R	6'	175	15	16	3	3	1	0	0	0	1	3	1	.188	.250
Cross, Jeff-Joffre James	42StLN 43-45MS 46-48StLN 48ChiN	8-28-18	Tulsa, Okla.		R	R	5'11	160	119	142	22	23	4	0	0	10	20	18	4	.162	.190
Crowe, George-George Daniel	52BosN 53,55MilN 56-58CinN 59-61StLN	3-22-23	Whiteland, Ind.		L	L	6'2	210	702	1727	215	467	70	12	81	299	159	246	3	.270	.466
48-49 played in N.B.L.																					
Culler, Dick-Richard Broadus	36PhiA 43ChiA 44-47BosN 48ChiN 49NYN	1-25-15	High Point, N.C.	6-16-64	R	R	5'9	155	472	1527	195	372	39	6	2	99	166	87	19	.244	.281
Cunningham, Joe-Joseph Robert	54,56-61StLN 62-64ChiA 64-66WasA	8-27-31	Paterson, N.J.		L	L	6'	188	1141	3362	525	980	177	26	64	436	599	368	16	.291	.417
Currin, Perry-Perry Gilmore	47StLA	9-27-28	Washington, D.C.		L	R	6'	175	3	2	0	0	0	0	0	0	1	0	0	.000	.000
Curry, Tony-George Anthony	60-61PhiN 66CleA	12-22-38	Nassau, Bahamas		L	L	5'11	185	129	297	33	73	16	2	6	40	20	69	0	.246	.374
Cusick, Jack-John Peter	51ChiN 52BosN	6-12-28	Weehawken, N.J.		R	R	6'	170	114	242	21	42	4	2	2	22	23	38	2	.174	.231
Dagres, Angie-Angelo George (Junior)	55BalA	8-22-34	Newburyport, Mass.		L	L	5'11	175	8	15	5	4	0	0	0	3	1	2	0	.267	.267
Daley, Pete-Peter Harvey	55-59BosA 60KCA 61WasA	1-14-30	Grass Valley, Cal.		R	R	6'	195	391	1084	93	259	49	8	18	120	87	187	2	.239	.349
Daniels, Jack-Harold Jack (Sour Mash)	52BosN	12-21-27	Chester, Pa.		L	L	5'10	165	106	219	31	41	5	1	2	14	28	30	3	.187	.247
Dark, Al-Alvin Ralph (Blackie)	46,48-49BosN 50-56NYN 56-58StLN 58-59ChiN	1- 7-22	Comanche, Okla.		R	R	5'11	185	1828	7219	1064	2089	358	72	126	757	430	534	59	.289	.411
	60PhiN 60MilN M61-64SFN M66-67KCA M68-71CleA M74-75OakA																				
Daugherty, Doc-Harold Ray	51DetA	10-12-27	Paris, Pa.		R	R	6'	180	1	1	0	0	0	0	0	0	0	1	0	.000	.000
Davalillo, Yo-Yo-Pompeyo Antonio [Rodriguez]	53WasA	6-30-31	Caracas, Venezuela		R	R	5'3	140	19	58	10	17	1	0	0	2	1	7	1	.293	.310
Davis, Brandy-Robert Brandon	52-53PitN	9-10-28	Newark, Del.		R	R	6'	170	67	134	19	25	3	1	0	3	11	31	9	.187	.224
Davis, Otis-Otis Allen (Scat)	46BknN	9-24-20	Charleston, Ark.		L	R	6'	160	1	0	1	0	0	0	0	0	0	0	0	–	–
Davis, Tod-Thomas Oscar	49,51PhiA	7-24-24	Los Angeles, Cal.		R	R	6'2	190	42	90	7	21	0	1	1	6	10	19	0	.233	.289
Delis, Juan-Juan Francisco	55WasA	2-27-28	Santiago de Cuba, Cuba		R	R	5'11	170	54	132	12	25	3	1	0	11	3	15	1	.189	.227
Delsing, Jim-James Henry	48ChiA 49-50NYA 50-52StLA 52-56DetA 56ChiA 60KCA	11-13-25	Rudolph, Wis.		L	R	5'10	175	822	2461	322	627	111	21	40	286	299	251	15	.255	.366
DeMaestri, Joe-Joseph Paul (Oats)	51ChiA 52StLA 53-54PhiA 55-59KCA 60-61NYA	12- 9-28	San Francisco, Cal.		R	R	6'	180	1121	3441	322	813	114	23	49	281	168	511	15	.236	.325
DeMars, Billy-William Lester (Kid)	48PhiA 50-51StLA	8-26-25	Brooklyn, N.Y.		R	R	5'10	160	80	211	29	50	5	1	0	14	28	16	0	.237	.270
Demeter, Steve-Stephen	59DetA 60CleA	1-27-35	Homer City, Pa.		R	R	5'10	185	15	23	1	2	1	0	0	1	0	2	0	.087	.130
Dente, Sam-Samuel Joseph (Blackie)	47BosA 48StLA 49-51WasA 52-53ChiA 54-55CleA	4-26-22	Harrison, N.J.		R	R	5'11	175	745	2320	205	585	78	16	4	214	167	96	9	.252	.305
Dickey, George-George Willard (Skeets)	35-36BosA 41-42,46-47ChiA 43-45MS	7-10-15	Kensett, Ark.		B	R	6'2	180	226	494	36	101	12	0	4	54	63	62	4	.204	.253
Diering, Chuck-Charles Edward Allen	47-51StLN 52NYN 54-56BalA	2- 5-23	St. Louis, Mo.		R	R	5'10	165	752	1648	217	411	76	14	14	141	237	250	16	.249	.338
Dietzel, Roy-Leroy Louis	54WasA	1- 9-31	Baltimore, Md.		R	R	6'	190	9	21	1	5	0	0	0	1	5	4	0	.238	.238
Difani, Jay-Clarence Joseph	48-49WasA	12-21-23	Crystal City, Mo.		R	R	6'	170	4	3	0	1	1	0	0	0	0	2	0	.333	.667
Dillinger, Bob-Robert Bernard	46-49StLA 50PhiA 50-51PitN 51ChiA	9-17-18	Glendale, Cal.		R	R	5'11	170	753	2904	401	888	123	47	10	213	249	203	106	.306	.391
DiMaggio, Dom-Dominic Paul (The Little Professor)	40-42BosA 43-45MS 46-53BosA	2-12-17	San Francisco, Cal.		R	R	5'9	168	1399	5640	1046	1680	308	57	87	618	750	571	100	.298	.419
DiPiefro, Bob-Robert Louis Paul	51BosA	9- 1-27	San Francisco, Cal.		R	R	5'11	185	4	11	0	1	0	0	0	0	1	1	0	.091	.091
Dittmer, Jack-John Douglas	52BosN 53-56MilN 57DetA	1-10-28	Elkader, Iowa		L	R	6'1	175	395	1218	117	283	43	4	24	136	77	102	2	.232	.333
Dobbek, Dan-Daniel John	59-60WasA 61MinA	12- 6-34	Ontonagon, Mich.		L	R	6'	195	198	433	52	90	12	5	15	49	53	72	5	.208	.363
Doby, Larry-Lawrence Eugene	47-55CleA 56-57ChiA 58CleA 59DetA 59ChiA	12-13-23	Camden, S.C.		L	R	6'1	180	1533	5348	960	1515	243	52	253	969	871	1011	47	.283	.490
Dotterer, Dutch-Henry John	57-60CinN 61WasA	11-11-31	Syracuse, N.Y.		R	R	6'	209	107	299	27	74	15	0	5	33	35	44	0	.247	.348
Drake, Larry-Larry Francis	45PhiA 48WasA	5- 4-21	McKinney, Tex.		L	R	6'1	195	5	9	0	2	0	0	0	1	1	5	0	.222	.222
Drake, Solly-Solomon Louis	56ChiN 59LAN 59PhiN	10-23-30	Little Rock, Ark.		B	R	6'	170	141	285	41	66	10	1	2	18	32	53	15	.232	.295
Dropo, Walt-Walter (Moose)	49-52BosA 52-54DetA 55-58ChiA 58-59CinN	1-30-23	Moosup, Conn.		R	R	6'5	220	1288	4124	478	1113	168	22	152	704	328	582	5	.270	.432
	59-61BalA																				
Dunlap, Grant-Grant Lester (Snap)	53StLN	12-20-23	Stockton, Cal.		R	R	6'2	180	16	17	2	6	0	1	1	3	0	2	0	.353	.647

USE NAME – GIVEN NAMES (NICKNAMES)	TEAM BY YEAR	BIRTH DATE	BIRTH PLACE	DEATH DATE	LIFETIME BATTING TOTALS																
					B	T	HGT	WGT	G	AB	R	H	2B	3B	HR	RBI	BB	SO	SB	BA	SA
Durham, Joe-Joseph Vann (Pop)	54BalA 55-56MS 57BalA 59StLN	7-31-31	Newport News, Va.		R	R	6'1	186	93	202	25	38	2	0	5	20	20	50	1	.188	.272
Durnbaugh, Bobby-Robert Eugene (Scroggy)	57CinN	1-15-33	Dayton, Ohio		R	R	5'8	170	2	1	0	0	0	0	0	0	0	0	0	.000	.000
Dusak, Erv-Ervin Frank (Four Sack) See P46-60)	41-42StLN 43-45MS 46-51StLN 51-52PitN	7-29-20	Chicago, Ill.		R	R	6'2	185	413	1035	168	251	32	6	24	106	142	188	12	.243	.355
Dyck, Jim-James Robert	51-53StLA 54CleA 55-56BalA 56CinN	2- 3-22	Omaha, Neb.		R	R	6'2	200	330	983	139	242	52	5	26	114	131	140	4	.246	.389
Eaddy, Don-Donald Johnson	59ChiN	2-16-34	Grand Rapids, Mich.		R	R	5'11	165	15	1	3	0	0	0	0	0	0	1	0	.000	.000
Easter, Luke-Lusious Luke	49-54CleA	8- 4-14	St. Louis, Mo.		L	R	6'4	240	491	1725	256	472	54	12	93	340	174	293	1	.274	.481
Easton, John-John David (Goose)	55,59PhiN	3- 4-33	Trenton, N.J.		R	R	6'2	185	4	3	0	0	0	0	0	0	0	3	0	.000	.000
Edwards, Bruce-Charles Bruce (Bull)	46-51BknN 51-52,54ChiN 55WasA 56CinN	7-15-23	Quincy, Ill.	4-25-75	R	R	5'8	180	591	1675	191	429	67	20	39	241	190	179	9	.256	.390
Edwards, Hank-Henry Albert	41-43CleA 44-45MS 46-49CleA 49-50ChiN 51BknN 51-52CinN 52ChiA 53StLA	1-29-19	Elmwood Place, Ohio		L	L	6'	190	735	2191	285	613	116	41	51	276	208	264	9	.280	.440
Elder, George-George Rezin	49StLA	3-10-21	Lebanon, Ky.		L	R	5'11	180	41	44	9	11	3	0	0	2	4	11	0	.250	.318
Elliott, Bob-Robert Irving	39-46PitN 47-51BosN 52NYN 53StLA 53ChiA M60KCA	11-26-16	San Francisco, Cal.	5- 4-66	R	R	6'	185	1978	7141	1064	2061	383	94	170	1195	967	604	60	.289	.440
Elliott, Harry-Harry Lewis	53,55StLN	12-30-25	San Francisco, Cal.		R	R	5'10	175	92	176	15	45	10	1	2	18	14	17	0	.256	.358
Endicott, Bill-William Franklin	46StLN	9-14-18	Acorn, Mo.		L	L	5'11	175	20	20	2	4	3	0	0	3	4	4	0	.200	.350
Ennis, Del-Delmer	46-56PhiN 57-58StLN 59CinN 59ChiA	6- 8-25	Philadelphia, Pa.		R	R	6'	195	1903	7254	985	2063	358	69	288	1284	597	719	45	.284	.472
Erautt, Joe-Joseph Michael (Stubby)	50-51ChiA	9- 1-21	Vibank, Canada		R	R	5'9	175	32	43	3	8	1	0	0	1	4	5	0	.186	.209
Ermer, Cal-Calvin Collidge	47WASA M67-68MinA	11-10-23	Baltimore, Md.		R	R	6'	175	1	3	0	0	0	0	0	0	0	0	0	.000	.000
Ernaga, Frank-Frank John	57-58ChiN	8-22-30	Susanville, Cal.		R	R	6'1	195	29	43	9	12	3	2	2	7	9	16	0	.279	.581
Escalera, Nino-Saturnino Cuadrado	54CinN	12- 1-29	Santurce, P.R.		L	R	5'10	165	73	69	15	11	1	1	0	3	7	11	1	.159	.203
Esposito, Sammy-Samuel	52ChiA 53-54MS 55-63ChiA 63KCA	12-15-31	Chicago, Ill.		R	R	5'9	170	560	792	130	164	27	2	8	73	145	127	7	.207	.277
Evans, Al-Alfred Hubert	39-42WasA 43MS 44-50WasA 51BosA	9-28-16	Kenly, N.C.		R	R	5'11	190	704	2053	188	514	70	23	13	211	243	206	11	.250	.320
Evers, Hoot-Walter Arthur	41DetA 43-45MS 46-52DetA 52-54BosA 54NYN 54DetA 55BalA 55-56CleA 56BalA	2- 8-21	St. Louis, Mo.		R	R	6'2	180	1142	3801	556	1055	187	41	98	565	415	420	45	.278	.426
Fain, Ferris-Ferris Roy (Burrhead)	47-52PhiA 53-54ChiA 55DetA 55CleA	3-29-21	San Antonio, Tex.		L	L	5'11	180	1151	3930	595	1139	213	30	48	570	903	261	46	.290	.396
Fanning, Jim-William James	54-57ChiN	9-14-27	Chicago, Ill.		R	R	5'11	180	64	141	5	24	2	0	0	5	6	26	0	.170	.184
Federoff, Al-Alfred (Whitey)	51-52DetA	7-11-24	Bairford, Pa.		R	R	5'10	165	76	235	14	56	4	2	0	14	16	13	1	.238	.272
Feller, Jack-Jack Leland	58DetA	12-10-36	Adrian, Mich.		R	R	5'10	185	1	0	0	0	0	0	0	0	0	0	0	–	–
Fernandez, Chico-Humberto [Perez]	56BknN 57-59PhiN 60-63DetA 63NYN	3- 2-32	Havana, Cuba		R	R	6'	170	856	2778	270	666	91	19	40	259	213	338	68	.240	.329
Fernandez, Nanny-Frailan	42BosN 43-45MS 46-47BosN 50PitN	10-25-18	Wilmington, Cal.		R	R	5'9	170	408	1356	139	336	59	5	16	145	109	142	20	.248	.334
Finigan, Jim-James Leroy	54PhiA 55-56KCA 57DetA 58SFN 59BalA	8-19-28	Quincy, Ill.		R	R	5'11	175	512	1600	195	422	74	17	19	168	190	176	8	.264	.367
Fisher, Harry-Harry Devereux (See P46-60)	51-52PitN	1- 3-26	Newbury, Canada		L	R	6'	180	18	18	0	5	1	0	0	1	0	3	0	.278	.333
Fitz Gerald, Ed-Edward Raymond	48-53PitN 53-59WasA 59CleA	5-21-24	Santa Ynez, Cal.		R	R	6'	170	807	2086	199	542	82	10	19	217	185	235	9	.260	.336
Fleitas, Angel-Angel Felix Husta	48WasA	11-10-14	Cienfuegos, Cuba		R	R	5'9	160	15	13	1	1	0	0	0	1	3	5	0	.077	.077
Fleming, Les-Leslie Harvey (Moe)	39DetA 41-42CleA 43-44VR 45-47CleA 49PitN	8- 7-15	Singleton, Tex.		L	L	5'10	185	434	1330	168	369	69	15	29	199	226	152	7	.277	.417
Foiles, Hank-Henry Lee	53CinN 53,55-56CleA 56-59PitN 60KCA 60CleA 60DetA 61BalA 62-63CinN 63-64LAA	6-10-29	Richmond, Va.		R	R	6'	200	608	1455	171	353	59	10	46	166	170	295	3	.243	.392
Fondy, Dee-Dee Virgil	51-57ChiN 57PitN 58CinN	10-31-24	Slaton, Tex.		L	L	6'3	195	967	3502	437	1000	144	47	69	373	203	526	84	.286	.413
Fox, Nellie-Jacob Nelson	47-49PhiA 50-63ChiA 64-65HouN	12-25-27	St. Thomas, Pa.		L	R	5'10	160	2367	9232	1279	2663	355	112	35	790	719	216	76	.288	.363
Frazier, Joe-Joseph Filmore (Cobra Joe)	47CleA 54-56StLN 56CinN 56BalA	10- 6-22	Liberty, N.C.		L	R	6'	180	217	282	31	68	15	2	10	45	35	46	0	.241	.415
Freese, Gene-Eugene Lewis	55-58PitN 58StLN 59PhiN 60ChiA 61-63CinN 64-65PitN 65-66ChiA 66HouN	1- 8-34	Wheeling, W.Va.		R	R	5'11	185	1115	3446	429	877	161	28	115	432	243	535	51	.254	.418
Freese, George-George Walter (Bud)	53DetA 55PitN 61ChiN	9-12-26	Wheeling, W.Va.		R	R	6'	197	61	187	17	48	8	2	3	23	18	22	1	.257	.369
Fridley, Jim-James Riley (Big Jim)	52CleA 54BalA 58CinN	9- 6-24	Phillippi, W.Va.		R	R	6'2	205	154	424	50	105	12	5	8	53	35	83	3	.248	.356
Friend, Owen-Owen Lacey (Red)	49-50StLA 51-52MS 53DetA 53CleA 55BosA 55-56ChiN	3-21-27	Granite City, Ill.		R	R	6'1	180	208	598	69	136	24	2	13	76	55	109	2	.227	.339
Furillo, Carl-Carl Anthony (Skoonj, The Reading Rifle)	46-57BknN 58-60LAN	3- 8-22	Stony Creek Mills, Pa.		R	R	6'	190	1806	6378	895	1910	324	56	192	1058	514	436	48	.299	.458
Fusselman, Les-Lester LeRoy	52-53StLN	3- 7-21	Pryor, Okla.	5-21-70	R	R	6'1	195	43	71	6	12	4	0	1	3	0	9	0	.169	.268
Gabler, Bill-William Louis (Gabe)	58ChiN	8- 4-30	St. Louis, Mo.		L	L	6'1	190	3	3	0	0	0	0	0	0	0	3	0	.000	.000
Gaedel, Eddie-Edward Carl	51StLA	6- 8-25	Chicago, Ill.	6-18-61	R	L	3'7	65	1	0	0	0	0	0	0	0	1	0	0	–	–
Garagiola, Joe-Joseph Henry	46-51StLN 51-53PitN 53-54ChiN 54NYN	2-12-26	St. Louis, Mo.		L	R	6'	190	676	1872	198	481	82	16	42	255	267	173	5	.257	.385
Garbowski, Alex-Alexander	52DetA	6-25-25	Yonkers, N.Y.		R	R	6'1	185	2	0	0	0	0	0	0	0	0	0	0	–	–
Garcia, Chico-Vinicio Uzcanga	54BalA	12-24-24	Veracruz, Mexico		R	R	5'8	170	39	62	6	7	0	2	0	5	8	3	0	.113	.177
Gardner, Billy-William Frederick (Shotgun)	54-55NYN 56-59BalA 60WasA 61MinA 61-62NYA 62-63BosA	7-19-27	Waterford, Conn.		R	R	6'	180	1034	3544	356	841	159	18	41	271	246	439	19	.237	.327
Garriott, Rabbit-Virgil Cecil	46ChiN	8-15-16	Harristown, Ill.		L	R	5'8	165	6	5	1	0	0	0	0	0	0	2	0	.000	.000
Gastall, Tommy-Thomas Everett	55-56BalA	6-13-32	Fall River, Mass.	9-20-56	R	R	6'2	187	52	83	7	15	3	0	0	4	6	13	0	.181	.217
Gearhart, Lloyd-Lloyd William (Gary)	47NYN	8-10-23	New Lebanon, Ohio		R	L	5'11	180	73	179	26	44	9	0	6	17	17	30	1	.246	.397
Genovese, George-George Michael	50WasA	2-22-22	Staten Island, N.Y.		L	R	5'6	160	3	1	1	0	0	0	0	0	1	0	0	.000	.000
Gentry, Harvey-Harvey William	54NYN	5-27-26	Winston-Salem, N.C.		L	R	6'	170	5	4	0	1	0	0	0	1	1	0	0	.250	.250
George, Alex-Alex Thomas M.	55KCA	9-27-38	Kansas City, Mo.		L	R	5'11	170	5	10	0	1	0	0	0	0	1	7	0	.100	.100
Gernert, Dick-Richard Edward	52-59BosA 60ChiN 60-61DetA 61CinN 62HouN	9-28-28	Reading, Pa.		R	R	6'3	209	835	2493	357	632	104	8	103	402	363	462	10	.254	.426
Gilbert, Buddy-Drew Edward	59CinN	7-26-35	Knoxville, Tenn.		L	R	6'3	195	7	20	4	3	0	0	2	2	3	4	0	.150	.450
Gilbert, Tookie-Harold Joseph	50,53NYN	4- 4-29	New Orleans, La.	6-23-67	L	R	6'2	185	183	482	52	98	15	2	7	48	65	57	4	.203	.286
Gile, Don-Donald Loren (Bear)	59-62BosA	4-19-35	Modesto, Cal.		R	R	6'6	220	58	120	12	18	2	1	3	9	5	35	0	.150	.258
Gilliam, Jim-James William (Junior)	53-57BknN 58-66LAN	10-17-28	Nashville, Tenn.		B	R	5'11	180	1956	7119	1163	1889	304	71	65	558	1036	416	203	.265	.355
Ginsberg, Joe-Myron Nathan	48,50-53DetA 53-54CleA 56KCA 56-60BalA 60-61ChiA 61BosA 62NYN	10-11-26	New York, N.Y.		L	R	5'11	180	695	1716	168	414	59	8	20	182	226	135	7	.241	.320
Giordano, Tommy-Thomas Arthur (T-Bone)	53PhiA	10- 9-25	Newark, N.J.		R	R	6'	175	11	40	6	7	2	0	2	5	5	6	0	.175	.375
Gladd, Jim-James Walter	46NYN	10- 2-22	Fort Gibson, Okla.		R	R	6'2	190	4	11	0	1	0	0	0	0	1	4	0	.091	.091
Glaviano, Tommy-Thomas Giatano (Rabbit)	49-52StLN 53PhiN	10-26-23	Sacramento, Cal.		R	R	5'9	175	389	1008	191	259	55	6	24	108	208	173	11	.257	.395
Glenn, John-John	60StLN	7-10-28	Moultrie, Ga.		R	R	6'3	180	32	31	4	8	0	1	0	5	0	9	0	.258	.323
Glynn, Bill-William Vincent	49PhiN 52-54CleA	1-30-25	Sussex, N.J.		L	L	6'	190	310	684	94	170	22	4	10	56	61	105	5	.249	.336
Goldsberry, Gordon-Gordon Frederick	49-51ChiA 52StLA	8-30-27	Sacramento, Cal.		L	L	6'	170	217	510	78	123	20	7	6	56	80	66	2	.241	.343
Goliat, Mike-Mike Mitchel	49-51PhiN 51-52StLA	11- 5-25	Yatesboro, Pa.		R	R	6'	180	249	825	87	186	21	10	20	99	83	127	3	.225	.348
Goodman, Billy-William Dale	47-57BosA 57BalA 58-61ChiA 62HouN	3-22-26	Concord, N.C.		L	R	5'11	165	1623	5644	807	1691	299	44	19	591	669	329	37	.300	.378
Goolsby, Ray-Raymond Daniel (Ox)	46WasA	9- 5-19	Florala, Ala.		R	R	6'1	185	3	4	0	0	0	0	0	0	1	1	0	.000	.000
Gorbous, Glen-Glen Edward	55CinN 55-57PhiN	7- 8-30	Drumheller, Canada		L	R	6'2	175	117	277	29	66	13	1	4	29	25	19	0	.238	.336
Gordon, Sid-Sidney	41-43,46-49,55NYN 44-45MS 50-52BosN 53MilN 54-55PitN	8-13-17	Brooklyn, N.Y.	6-17-75	R	R	5'10	185	1475	4992	735	1415	220	43	202	805	731	356	19	.283	.466
Gorman, Herb-Herbert Allan	52StLN	12-22-24	San Francisco, Cal.	4- 5-53	L	L	5'11	180	1	1	0	0	0	0	0	0	0	0	0	.000	.000
Graber, Rod-Rodney Blaine	58CleA	6-20-31	Marshallville, Ohio		L	L	5'11	175	4	8	0	1	0	0	0	0	1	2	0	.125	.125
Graff, Milt-Milton Edward	57-58KCA	12-30-30	Jefferson Center, Pa.		L	R	5'7	158	61	156	16	28	4	3	0	10	15	10	2	.179	.244
Graham, Jack-Jack Bernard	46BknN 46NYN 49StLA	12-24-16	Minneapolis, Minn.		L	L	6'2	200	239	775	105	179	28	5	38	126	84	99	1	.231	.427
Grammas, Alex-Alexander Peter	54-56StLN 56-58CinN 59-62StLN 62-63ChiN M69PitN	4- 3-27	Birmingham, Ala.		R	R	6'	175	913	2073	236	512	90	10	12	163	206	193	17	.247	.317
Grasso, Mickey-Newton Michael	46NYN 50-53WasA 54CleA 55NYN	5-10-20	Newark, N.J.		R	R	6'	195	322	957	78	216	23	1	5	87	81	108	2	.226	.268
Gray, Dick-Richard Benjamin	58-59LAN 59-60StLN	7-11-31	Jefferson, Pa.		R	R	5'11	165	124	305	43	73	7	6	12	41	33	52	4	.239	.420
Green, Pumpsie-Elijah Jerry	59-62BosA 63NYN	10 27 33	Oakland, Cal.		B	R	6'	175	344	796	119	196	31	12	13	74	138	132	12	.246	.364
Greengrass, Jim-James Raymond	52-55CinN 55-56PhiN	10-24-27	Addison, N.Y.		R	R	6'1	200	504	1793	243	482	82	16	69	282	165	271	6	.269	.448
Groth, Johnny-John Thomas	46-52DetA 53StLA 54-55ChiA 55WasA 56-57KCA 57-60DetA	7-23-26	Chicago, Ill.		R	R	6'	182	1248	3808	480	1064	197	31	60	486	419	329	19	.279	.395
Guerra, Mike-Fermin Romero	37,44-46WasA 47-50PhiA 51BosA 51WasA	10-11-12	Havana, Cuba		R	R	5'9	150	565	1581	168	382	42	14	9	168	131	123	24	.242	.303
Guintini, Ben-Benjamin John	46PitN 50PhiA	1-13-20	Los Banos, Cal.		R	R	6'1	190	5	7	0	0	0	0	0	0	0	1	0	.000	.000
Haas, Bert-Berthold John	37-38BknN 42-43CinN 44-45MS 46-47CinN 48-49PhiN 49NYN 51ChiA	2- 8-14	Naperville, Ill.		R	R	5'11	178	721	2440	263	644	93	32	22	263	204	188	51	.264	.355
Haas, Eddie-George Edwin	57ChiN 58,60MilN	5-26-35	Paducah, Ky.		L	R	5'11	178	55	70	7	17	3	0	1	10	8	20	0	.243	.329
Hadley, Kent-Kent William	58-59KCA 60NYA	12-17-34	Pocatello, Idaho		L	L	6'3	190	171	363	49	88	13	1	14	50	30	97	1	.242	.399
Hairston, Sam-Samuel	51ChiA	1-28-20	Crawford, Miss.		R	R	5'10	187	4	5	1	2	1	0	0	1	2	0	0	.400	.600
Hale, Bob-Robert Houston	55-59BalA 60-61CleA 61NYA	11- 7-33	Sarasota, Fla.		L	L	5'10	195	376	626	41	171	29	2	2	89	26	51	0	.273	.335
Hall, Bill-William Lemuel	54,56,58PitN	7-30-28	Moultrie, Ga.		L	R	5'11	165	57	126	15	33	6	0	1	15	15	14	0	.262	.333
Hall, Dick-Richard Wallace (Turkey Neck) (See P61-73)	52-57PitN 58VR 59PitN 60KCA 61-66BalA 67-68PhiN 69-71BalA	9-27-30	St. Louis, Mo.		R	R	6'6	205	669	714	79	150	15	4	4	56	61	147	6	.210	.259

USE NAME – GIVEN NAMES (NICKNAMES)	TEAM BY YEAR	BIRTH DATE	BIRTH PLACE	DEATH DATE	B	T	HGT	WGT	G	AB	R	H	2B	3B	HR	RBI	BB	SO	SB	BA	SA
					LIFETIME BATTING TOTALS																
Hamilton, Tom-Thomas Ball (Ham)	52-53PhiA	9-29-25	Altoona, Kans.		L	R	6'4	213	67	66	9	13	3	0	0	6	8	12	0	.197	.242
Hamner, Granny-Granville Wilbur (See P46-60)	44-59PhiN 59CleA 62KCA	4-26-27	Richmond, Va.		R	R	5'10	163	1531	5839	711	1529	272	62	104	708	351	432	35	.262	.383
Hamric, Bert-Odbert Herman	55BknN 58BalA	3- 1-28	Clarksburg, W.Va.		L	R	6'	165	10	9	0	1	0	0	0	0	0	7	0	.111	.111
Hancock, Fred-Fred James	49ChiA	3-28-20	Allenport, Pa.		R	R	5'8	170	39	52	7	7	2	1	0	9	8	9	0	.135	.212
Handley, Gene-Eugene Louis	46-47PhiA	11-25-14	Kennett, Mo.		R	R	5'10	165	125	341	41	86	10	6	0	29	32	27	9	.252	.317
Hanebrink, Harry-Harry Aloysius	53,57-58MilN 59PhiN	11-12-27	St. Louis, Mo.		L	R	6'	185	177	317	32	71	7	2	6	25	22	31	1	.224	.315
Hansen, Doug-Douglas William	51CleA	12-16-28	Los Angeles, Cal.		R	R	6'	180	3	0	2	0	0	0	0	0	0	0	0	–	–
Hardin, Bud-William Edgar	52ChiN	6-14-22	Shelby, N.C.		R	R	5'10	165	3	7	1	1	0	0	0	0	0	0	0	.143	.143
Harmon, Chuck-Charles Byron	54-56CinN 56-57StLN 57PhiN	4-23-26	Washington, Ind.		R	R	6'2	175	289	592	90	141	15	8	7	59	46	57	25	.238	.326
Harrell, Billy-William	55,57-58CleA 61BosA	7-18-28	Norristown, Pa.		R	R	6'1	180	173	342	54	79	7	1	8	26	23	54	17	.231	.327
Harris, Gail-Boyd Gail	55-57NYN 58-60DetA	10-15-31	Abingdon, Va.		L	L	6'	200	437	1331	159	320	38	15	51	190	106	194	2	.240	.406
Harshman, Jack-John Elvin (See P46-60)	48,50,52NYN 54-57ChiA 58-59BalA 59BosA 59-60CleA	7-12-27	San Diego, Cal.		L	L	6'2	189	258	424	46	76	8	0	21	65	72	119	0	.179	.347
Hartsfield, Roy-Roy Thomas	50-52BosN	10-25-25	Chattahoochee, Ga.		R	R	5'9	165	265	976	138	266	30	7	13	59	73	146	14	.273	.358
Hartung, Clint-Clinton Clarence (The Hondo Hurricane, Floppy) (See P46-60)	47-52NYN	8-10-22	Hondo, Tex.		R	R	6'5	210	196	378	42	90	10	6	14	43	25	112	0	.238	.407
Hatfield, Fred-Fred James	50-52BosA 52-56DetA 56-57ChiA 58CleA 58CinN	3-18-25	Lanett, Ala.		L	R	6'1	171	722	2039	259	493	67	10	25	165	248	247	15	.242	.321
Hatton, Grady-Grady Edgebert	46-54CinN 54ChiA 54-56BosA 56StLN 56BalA 60ChiN M66-68HouN	10- 7-22	Beaumont, Tex.		L	R	5'8	170	1312	4206	562	1068	166	33	91	533	646	430	42	.254	.374
Hawes, Roy-Roy Lee	51WasA	7- 5-26	Shiloh, Ill.		L	L	6'2	190	3	6	0	1	0	0	0	0	0	1	0	.167	.167
Hazle, Bob-Robert Sidney (Hurricane)	55CinN 57-58MilN 58DetA	12- 9-30	Laurens, S.C.		L	R	6'	190	110	261	37	81	14	0	9	37	32	35	1	.310	.467
Hegan, Jim-James Edward	41-42CleA 43-45MS 46-57CleA 58DetA 58-59PhiN 59SFN 60ChiN	8- 3-20	Lynn, Mass.		R	R	6'2	195	1666	4772	550	1087	187	46	92	525	456	742	15	.228	.344
Helf, Hank-Henry Hartz	38,40CleA 44-45MS 46StLA	8-26-13	Austin, Tex.		R	R	6'1	196	78	196	18	36	11	0	6	22	10	41	0	.184	.332
Hemus, Solly-Solomon Joseph	49-56StLN 56-58PhiN 59,M59-61StLN	4-17-23	Phoenix, Ariz.		L	R	5'9	175	961	2694	459	736	137	41	51	263	456	247	21	.273	.411
Henley, Gail-Gail Curtice	54PitN	10-15-28	Wichita, Kans.		L	R	5'9	180	14	30	7	9	1	0	1	2	4	4	0	.300	.433
Henrich, Bobby-Robert Edward	57-59CinN	12-24-38	Lawrence, Kans.		R	R	6'1	185	48	16	13	2	0	0	0	1	1	7	0	.125	.125
Hermanski, Gene-Eugene Victor	43BknN 44-45MS 46-51BknN 51-53ChiN 53PitN	5-11-20	Pittsfield, Mass.		L	R	5'11	185	739	1960	276	533	85	18	46	259	289	212	43	.272	.404
Herrera, Pancho-Juan Francisco	58,50-61PhiN	6-16-34	Santiago de Cuba, Cuba		R	R	6'3	220	300	975	122	264	46	8	31	128	113	271	8	.271	.430
Hersh, Earl-Earl Walter	56MilN	5-21-32	Ebbvale, Md.		L	L	6'	205	7	13	0	3	3	0	0	0	0	5	0	.231	.462
Hertweck, Neal-Neal Charles	52StLN	11-22-31	St. Louis, Mo.		L	L	6'1	175	2	6	0	0	0	0	0	0	1	1	0	.000	.000
Herzog, Whitey-Dorrel Norman Elvert	56-58WasA 58-60KCA 61-62BalA 63DetA M73TexA M74CalA M75KCA	11- 9-31	New Athens, Ill.		L	L	5'11	187	634	1614	213	414	60	20	25	172	241	261	13	.257	.365
Hicks, Buddy-Clarence Walter	56DetA	2-15-27	Belvedere, Cal.		B	R	5'10	170	26	47	5	10	2	0	0	5	3	2	0	.213	.255
Higdon, Bill-William Travis	49ChiA	4-27-25	Camp Hill, Ala.		L	R	6'1	193	11	23	3	7	3	0	0	1	6	3	1	.304	.435
Hitchcock, Billy-William Clyde	42DetA 43-45MS 46DetA 46WasA 47StLA 48-49BosA 50-52PhiA 53,M60DetA M62-63BalA M66-67AtlN	7-31-16	Inverness, Ala.		R	R	6'1	185	703	2249	231	547	67	22	5	257	205	230	15	.243	.299
Hoak, Don-Donald Albert (Tiger)	54-55BknN 56ChiN 57-58CinN 59-62PitN 63-64PhiN	2- 5-28	Roulette, Pa.	10- 9-69	R	R	6'1	180	1263	4322	598	1144	214	44	89	498	523	530	64	.265	.396
Hoderlein, Mel-Melvin Anthony	51BosA 52-54WasA	6-24-23	Mt. Carmel, Ohio		B	R	5'10	185	118	294	22	74	10	3	0	24	31	37	2	.252	.306
Hodges, Gil-Gilbert Raymond	43BknN 44-45MS 47-57BknN 58-61LAN 62-63NYN M63-67WasA M68-71NYN	4- 4-24	Princeton, Ind.	4- 2-72	R	R	6'2	200	2071	7030	1105	1921	295	48	370	1274	943	1137	63	.273	.487
Hofman, Bobby-Robert George	49,52-57NYN	10- 5-25	St. Louis, Mo.		R	R	5'10	178	341	670	81	166	22	6	32	101	70	94	1	.248	.442
Hollmig, Stan-Stanley Ernest (Hondo)	49-51PhiN	1- 2-26	Fredericksburg, Tex.		R	R	6'2	190	94	265	29	67	13	6	2	27	20	46	1	.253	.370
Holmes, Tommy-Thomas Francis (Kelly)	42-51,M51-52BosN 52BknN	3-29-17	Brooklyn, N.Y.		L	L	5'10	180	1320	4992	698	1507	292	47	88	581	480	122	40	.302	.432
Hopp, Johnny-John Leonard (Hippity)	39-45StLN 46-47BosN 48-49PitN 49BknN 49-50PitN 50-52NYA 52DetA	7-18-16	Hastings, Neb.		L	L	5'10	170	1393	4260	698	1262	216	74	47	458	465	378	128	.296	.414
Houk, Ralph-Ralph George (Major)	47-54,M61-63,66-73NYA M74-75DetA	8- 9-19	Lawrence, Kans.		R	R	5'11	193	91	158	12	43	6	1	0	20	12	10	0	.272	.323
House, Frank-Henry Franklin (Pig)	50-51DetA 52-53MS 54-57DetA 58-59KCA 60CinN 61DetA	2-18-30	Bessemer, Ala.		L	R	6'1	190	653	1994	202	494	64	11	47	235	151	147	6	.248	.362
Howell, Dixie-Homer Elliott	47PitN 49-52CinN 53,55-56BknN	4-24-19	Louisville, Ky.		R	R	5'11	190	340	910	98	224	39	4	12	93	87	140	1	.246	.337
Howerton, Bill-William Ray (Hopalong)	49-51StLN 51-52PitN 52NYN	12-12-21	Lompoc, Cal.		L	R	5'11	185	247	650	95	178	39	12	22	106	92	125	1	.274	.472
Hunter, Billy-Gordon William	53StLA 54BalA 55-56NYA 57-58KCA 58CleA	6- 4-28	Punxsutawney, Pa.		R	R	6'	180	630	1875	166	410	58	18	16	144	111	192	23	.219	.294
Hutchinson, Fred-Frederick Charles (Big Bear) (See P46-60)	39-41DetA 42-45MS 46-53,M52-54DetA M56-58StLN M59-64CinN	8-12-19	Seattle, Wash.	11-12-64	L	R	6'2	190	354	650	71	171	23	3	4	83	67	30	6	.263	.326
Irvin, Monte-Monford	49-55NYN 56ChiN	2-25-19	Columbia, Ala.		R	R	6'1	195	764	2499	366	731	97	31	99	443	351	220	28	.293	.475
Jablonski, Ray-Raymond Leo (Jabbo)	53-54StLN 55-56CinN 57NYN 58SFN 59StLN 59-60KCA	12-17-26	Chicago, Ill.		R	R	5'10	180	812	2562	297	687	126	11	83	438	196	330	16	.268	.423
Jackson, Lou-Louis Clarence	58-59ChiN 64BalA	7-26-35	Riverton, La.	5-27-69	L	R	5'10	168	34	47	7	10	2	1	1	7	1	13	0	.213	.362
Jackson, Randy-Ransom Joseph (Handsome Ransom)	50-55ChiN 56-57BknN 58LAN 58-59CleA 59ChiN	2-10-26	Little Rock, Ark.		R	R	6'1	185	955	3203	412	835	115	44	103	415	281	382	36	.261	.421
Jackson, Ron-Ronald Harris	54-59ChiA 60BosA	10-22-33	Kalamazoo, Mich.		R	R	6'7	235	196	474	54	116	18	1	17	52	45	119	6	.245	.395
Jacobs, Spook-Forrest Vandergrift	54PhiA 55-56KCA 56PitN	11- 4-25	Cheswold, Del.		R	R	5'8	155	188	665	87	164	16	1	0	33	80	32	22	.247	.274
Janowicz, Vic-Victor Felix 54-55 played in N.F.L.	53-54PitN	2-26-30	Elyria, Ohio		R	R	5'9	185	83	196	20	42	6	1	2	10	12	54	0	.214	.286
Jarvis, Roy-LeRoy Gilbert	44BknN 45MS 46-47PitN	6- 7-26	Shawnee, Okla.		R	R	5'9	160	21	50	4	8	1	0	1	4	7	7	0	.160	.240
Jeffcoat, Hal-Harold Bentley (See P46-60)	48-55ChiN 56-59CinN 59StLN	9- 6-24	West Columbia, S.C.		R	R	5'10	185	918	1963	249	487	95	18	26	188	114	289	49	.248	.355
Jennings, Bill-William Lee	51StLA	9-28-25	St. Louis, Mo.		R	R	6'2	175	64	195	20	35	10	2	0	13	26	42	1	.179	.251
Jensen, Jackie-Jack Eugene	50-52NYA 52-53WasA 54-59BosA 60VR 61BosA	3- 9-27	San Francisco, Cal.		R	R	5'11	190	1438	5236	810	1463	259	45	199	929	750	546	143	.279	.460
Jethroe, Sam-Samuel (Jet)	50-52BosN 54PitN	1-20-22	East St. Louis, Ill.		B	R	6'1	178	442	1763	280	460	80	25	49	181	177	293	98	.261	.418
Johnson, Billy-William Russell (Bull)	43NYA 44-45MS 46-51NYA 51-53StLN	8-30-18	Montclair, N.J.		R	R	5'9	180	964	3253	419	882	141	33	61	487	347	290	13	.271	.391
Johnson, Darrell-Darrell Dean	52StLA 52ChiA 57-58NYA 60StLN 61PhiN 61-62CinN 62BalA M74-75BosA	8-25-28	Horace, Neb.		R	R	6'1	180	134	320	24	75	6	1	2	28	26	39	1	.234	.278
Johnson, Dick-Richard Allan (Footer, Treads)	58ChiN	2-15-32	Dayton, Ohio		L	L	5'11	175	8	5	1	0	0	0	0	0	0	1	0	.000	.000
Johnson, Stan-Stanley Lucius	60ChiA 61KCA	2-12-37	Dallas, Tex.		L	L	5'10	180	8	9	2	1	0	0	1	1	2	2	0	.111	.444
Jok, Stan-Stanley Edward (Tucker)	54PhiN 54-55ChiA	5- 3-26	Buffalo, N.Y.	3- 6-72	R	R	6'	190	12	19	4	3	0	0	1	4	2	5	0	.158	.316
Jones, Jake-James Murrell	41-42ChiA 43-45MS 46-47ChiA 47-48BosA	11-23-20	Epps, La.		R	R	6'3	197	224	790	80	181	31	5	23	117	69	130	8	.229	.368
Jones, Nippy-Vernal Leroy	46-51StLN 52PhiN 57MilN	6-29-25	Los Angeles, Cal.		R	R	6'1	185	412	1381	146	369	60	12	25	209	71	102	4	.267	.382
Jones, Willie-Willie Edward (Puddin' Head)	47-59PhiN 59CleA 59-61CinN	8-16-25	Dillon, S.C.		R	R	6'2	205	1691	5826	786	1502	252	33	190	812	755	541	40	.258	.410
Joost, Eddie-Edwin David	36-37,39-42CinN,43BosN 44VR 45BosN 47-54,M54PhiA 55BosA	6- 5-16	San Francisco, Cal.		R	R	6'	175	1574	5606	874	1339	238	35	134	601	1041	827	61	.239	.366
Jordan, Tom-Thomas Jefferson	44,46ChiA 46CleA 48StLA	9- 5-19	Lawton, Okla.		R	R	6'1	195	39	96	5	23	4	2	1	6	4	2	1	.240	.354
Jorgensen, Spider-John Donald	47-50BknN 50-51NYN	11- 3-19	Folsom, Cal.		L	R	5'9	155	267	755	97	201	40	11	9	107	106	75	5	.266	.384
Katt, Ray-Raymond Frederick	52-56NYN 56StLN 57NYN 58-59StLN	5- 9-27	New Braunfels, Tex.		R	R	6'2	200	417	1071	92	248	29	4	32	120	74	164	2	.232	.356
Kazak (Tkaczuk), Eddie-Edward Terrance	48-52StLN 52CinN	7-18-20	Steubenville, Ohio		R	R	6'	175	218	605	69	165	22	6	11	71	52	45	0	.273	.383
Kazanski, Ted-Theodore Stanley	53-58PhiN	1-25-34	Hamtramck, Mich.		R	R	6'1	180	417	1329	118	288	49	9	14	116	90	163	4	.217	.299
Kell, George-George Clyde	43-46PhiA 46-52DetA 52-54BosA 54-56ChiA 56-57BalA	8-23-22	Swifton, Ark.		R	R	5'9	175	1795	6702	881	2054	385	50	78	870	620	287	51	.306	.414
Kell, Skeeter-Everett Lee	52PhiA	10-11-29	Swifton, Ark.		R	R	5'9	160	75	213	24	47	8	3	0	17	14	18	5	.221	.286
Keller, Hal-Harold Kefauver	49-50,52WasA	7- 7-27	Middletown, Md.		L	R	6'1	200	25	54	4	11	5	0	1	5	3	3	0	.204	.352
Kellert, Frank-Frank William	53StLA 54BalA 55BknN 56ChiN	7- 6-24	Oklahoma City, Okla.		R	R	6'2	185	122	247	25	57	9	3	8	37	26	36	0	.231	.389
Kennedy, Bob-Robert Daniel	39-42ChiA 43-45MS 46-48ChiA 48-54CleA 54-55BalA 55-56ChiA 56DetA 57ChiA 57BknN M63-65ChiN M68OakA	8-18-20	Chicago, Ill.		R	R	6'2	193	1483	4624	514	1176	196	41	63	514	364	443	45	.254	.355
Kennedy, John-John Irvin	57PhiN	11-23-34	Sumter, S.C.		R	R	5'10	175	5	2	1	0	0	0	0	0	0	1	0	.000	.000
Kerr, Buddy-John Joseph	43-49NYN 50-51BosN	11- 6-22	Queens, N.Y.		R	R	6'2	175	1067	3631	378	903	145	25	31	333	324	280	38	.249	.328
Kiner, Ralph-Ralph McPherran	46-53PitN 53-54ChiN 55CleA	10-27-22	Santa Rita, N.M.		R	R	6'2	195	1472	5205	971	1451	216	39	369	1015	1011	749	22	.279	.548
King, Charlie-Charles Gilbert (Chick)	54-56DetA 58-59ChiN 59StLN	11-10-30	Paris, Tenn.		R	R	6'2	190	45	76	11	18	0	1	0	5	8	18	0	.237	.263
Kirby, Jim-James Herschel	49ChiN	5- 5-23	Nashville, Tenn.		R	R	5'11	175	3	2	0	1	0	0	0	0	0	0	0	.500	.500
Kirk, Tom-Thomas Daniel	47PhiA	9-27-27	Philadelphia, Pa.		L	L	5'10	182	1	1	0	0	0	0	0	0	0	0	0	.000	.000
Kirrene, Joe-Joseph John	50ChiA 52-53MS 54ChiA	10- 4-31	San Francisco, Cal.		R	R	6'2	195	10	27	4	8	1	0	0	4	5	3	1	.296	.333
Kitsos, Chris-Christopher Anestos	54ChiN	2-11-28	New York, N.Y.		B	R	5'9	165	1	0	0	0	0	0	0	0	0	0	0	–	–
Klaus, Billy-William Joseph	52BosN 53MilN 55-58BosA 59-60BalA 61WasA 62-63PhiN	12- 9-28	Fox Lake, Ill.		L	R	5'9	165	821	2513	357	626	106	15	40	250	331	285	14	.249	.351
Kline, Bobby-John Robert	55WasA	1-27-29	St. Petersburg, Fla.		R	R	6'	179	77	140	12	31	5	0	0	9	11	27	0	.221	.257
Kluszewski, Ted-Theodore Bernard (Klu)	47-57CinN 58-59PitN 59-60ChiA 61LAA	9-10-24	Argo, Ill.		L	L	6'2	235	1718	5929	848	1766	290	29	279	1028	492	365	20	.298	.498
Kluttz, Clyde-Clyde Franklin	42-45BosN 45-46NYN 46StLN 47-48PitN 51StLA 51-52WasA	12-12-17	Rockwell, N.C.		R	R	6'	193	656	1903	172	510	90	8	19	212	132	119	5	.268	.354
Knickerbocker, Austin-Austin Jay	47PhiA	10-15-18	Bangall, N.Y.		R	R	5'11	185	21	48	8	12	3	2	0	2	3	4	0	.250	.396

USE NAME – GIVEN NAMES (NICKNAMES)	TEAM BY YEAR	BIRTH DATE	BIRTH PLACE	DEATH DATE	B	T	HGT	WGT	G	AB	R	H	2B	3B	HR	RBI	BB	SO	SB	BA	SA
Koback, Hick-Nicholas Nicholie	53-55PitN	7-19-35	Hartford, Conn.		R	R	6'	187	16	33	1	4	0	1	0	0	1	13	0	.121	.182
Kokos (Kokoszka), Dick-Richard Jerome	48-50StLA 51-52MS 53StLA 54BalA	2-28-28	Chicago, Ill.		L	L	5'8	170	475	1558	239	410	82	9	59	223	242	252	15	.263	.441
Kolloway, Don-Donald Martin (Butch, Cab)	40-43ChiA 44-45MS 46-49ChiA 49-52DetA 53PhiA	8- 4-18	Posen, Ill.		R	R	6'3	200	1079	3993	466	1081	180	30	29	393	189	251	76	.271	.353
Konopka, Bruce-Bruno Bruce	42-43PhiA 44-45MS 46PhiA	9-16-19	Hammond, Ind.		L	L	6'2	190	45	105	9	25	4	1	0	10	5	9	0	.238	.295
Korcheck, Steve-Stephen Joseph (HossP	54-55WasA 56-57MS 58-59WasA	8-11-32	McClellandtown, Pa.		R	R	6'1	205	58	145	12	23	6	1	0	7	6	36	0	.159	.214
Koshorek, Clem-Clement John (Scooter)	52-53PitN	6-20-26	Royal Oak, Mich.		R	R	5'6	165	99	323	27	84	17	0	0	15	26	40	4	.260	.313
Kozar, Al-Albert Kenneth	48-50WasA 50ChiA	7- 5-22	McKees Rocks, Pa.		R	R	5'9	173	285	992	118	252	41	10	6	94	96	86	6	.254	.334
Kravitz, Danny-Daniel (Beak, Dusty)	56-60PitN 60KCA	12-21-30	Lopez, Pa.		L	R	5'11	200	215	552	52	130	22	7	10	54	35	64	1	.236	.355
Kress, Charlie-Charles Steven (Chuck)	47,49CinN 49-50ChiA 54DetA 54BknN	12- 9-21	Philadelphia, Pa.		L	L	6'	190	175	466	57	116	20	7	1	52	49	59	6	.249	.328
Krsnich, Rocky-Rocco Peter	49,52-53ChiA	8- 5-27	West Allis, Wis.		R	R	6'	180	120	275	27	59	18	3	3	38	30	24	0	.215	.335
Kryhoski, Dick-Richard David	49NYA 50-51DetA 52-53StLA 54BalA 55KCA	3-24-25	Leonia, N.J.		L	L	6'2	205	569	1794	203	475	85	14	45	231	119	163	5	.265	.403
Kuczek, Steve-Stanislaw Leo	49BosN	12-28-24	Amsterdam, N.Y.		R	R	6'	160	1	1	0	1	1	0	0	0	0	0	0	1.000	2.000
Kuenn, Harvey-Harvey Edward	52-59DetA 60CleA 61-65SFN 65-66ChiN 66PhiN	12- 4-30	West Allis, Wis.		R	R	6'2	192	1833	6913	951	2092	356	56	87	671	594	404	68	.303	.408
Kuhn, Kenny-Kenneth Harold	55-57CleA	3-20-37	Louisville, Ky.		L	R	5'10	175	71	81	12	17	1	0	0	7	5	13	1	.210	.222
Kwietniewski, Cass (See Cass Michaels)																					
Lafata, Joe-Joseph Joseph	47-49NYN	8- 3-21	Detroit, Mich.		L	L	6'	163	127	236	31	54	3	2	5	34	24	42	2	.229	.322
Lajeskie, Dick-Richard Edward	46NYN	1- 8-26	Passaic, N.J.		R	R	5'11	175	6	10	3	2	0	0	0	0	3	2	0	.200	.200
Lake, Eddie-Edward Erving	39-41StLN 43-45BosA 46-50DetA	3-18-16	Antioch, Cal.		R	R	5'7	159	835	2595	442	599	105	9	39	193	546	312	52	.231	.323
Lamanno, Ray-Raymond Simond	41-42CinN 43-45MS 46-48CinN	11-17-19	Oakland, Cal.		R	R	6'	185	442	1408	122	355	57	5	18	150	118	151	2	.252	.338
Landenberger, Ken-Kenneth Henry (Red)	52ChiA	7-29-28	Lyndhurst, Ohio	7-28-60	L	L	6'3	200	2	5	0	1	0	0	0	0	0	2	0	.200	.200
Landrith, Hobie-Hobart Neal	50-55CinN 56ChiN 57-58StLN 59-61SFN 62NYN 62-63BalA 63WasA	3-16-30	Decatur, Ill.		L	R	5'10	170	772	1929	179	450	69	5	34	203	253	188	5	.233	.327
Lane, Dick-Richard Harrison	49ChiA	6-28-27	Highland Park, Mich.		R	R	5'11	178	12	42	4	5	0	0	0	4	5	3	0	.119	.119
Lang, Don-Donald Charles	38CinN 48StLN	3-15-15	Selma, Cal.		R	R	6'	175	138	373	35	100	17	2	5	42	49	45	2	.268	.365
LaPointe, Ralph-Ralph Robert	47PhiN 48StLN	1- 8-22	Winooski, Vt.	9-13-67	R	R	5'11	185	143	433	60	115	10	0	1	30	35	34	9	.266	.296
Larker, Norm-Norman Howard John	58-61LAN 62HouN 63MilN 63SFN	12-27-30	Beaver Meadows, Pa.		L	L	6'	185	667	1953	227	538	97	15	32	271	211	165	3	.275	.390
Lassetter, Don-Donald O'Neal	57StLN	3-27-33	Newnan, Ga.		R	R	6'3	200	4	13	2	2	0	1	0	0	1	3	0	.154	.308
Lawing, Garland	46CinN 46NYN	8-26-19	Gastonia, N.C.		R	R	6'1	180	10	15	2	2	0	0	0	0	0	5	0	.133	.133
Layden, Pete-Peter John 48-49 played in A.A.F.C. 50 played in N.F.L.	48StLA	12-30-19	Dallas, Tex.		R	R	5'11	185	41	104	11	26	2	1	0	4	6	10	4	.250	.288
Layton, Les-Lester Lee	48NYN	11-1821	Nardin, Okla.		R	R	6'	165	63	91	14	21	4	4	2	12	6	21	1	.231	.429
Lehner, Paul-Paul Eugene	46-49StLA 50-51PhiA 51ChiA 51StLA 51CleA 52BosA	7- 1-20	Dolomite, Ala.	12-27-67	L	L	5'9	160	540	1768	175	455	80	21	22	197	126	118	6	.257	.364
Leja, Frank-Frank John	54-55NYA 62LAA	2- 7-36	Holyoke, Mass.		L	L	6'4	215	26	23	3	1	0	0	0	0	1	8	0	.043	.043
Lembo, Steve-Stephen Neal	50,52BknN	11-13-26	Brooklyn, N.Y.		R	R	6'1	185	7	11	0	2	0	0	0	1	1	1	0	.182	.182
Lemon, Bob-Robert Granville (See P46-60)	41-42,46-58CleA 43-45MS M70-72KCA	9-22-20	San Bernardino, Cal.		L	R	6'	180	615	1183	148	274	54	9	37	147	93	241	2	.232	.386
Lemon, Jim-James Robert	50,53CleA 54-60WasA 61-63MinA 63PhiN 63ChiA M68WasA	3-23-28	Covington, Va.		R	R	6'4	205	1010	3445	446	901	120	35	164	529	363	787	13	.262	.460
Lenhardt, Don-Donald Eugene (Footsie)	50-51StLA 51ChiA 52BosA 52DetA 52-53StLA 54BalA 54BosA	10- 4-22	Alton, Ill.		R	R	6'3	190	481	1481	192	401	64	9	61	239	214	235	6	.271	.450
Lennon, Bob-Robert Albert (Arch)	54,56NYN 57ChiN	9-15-28	Brooklyn, N.Y.		L	L	6'	200	38	79	5	13	2	0	1	4	5	26	0	.165	.228
Lepcio, Ted-Thaddeus Stanley	52-59BosA 59DetA 60PhiN 61ChiA 61MinA	7-28-30	Utica, N.Y.		R	R	5'10	177	729	2092	233	512	91	11	69	251	210	471	11	.245	.398
Leppert, Don-Don Eugene (Tiger)	55BalA	11-20-30	Memphia, Tenn.		L	R	5'8	175	40	70	6	8	0	1	0	2	9	10	1	.114	.143
Lerchen, George-George Edward	52DetA 53CinN	12- 1-22	Detroit, Mich.		B	R	5'11	175	36	49	3	10	2	0	1	5	12	16	1	.204	.306
Levan, Jesse-Jesse Roy	47PhiN 54-55WasA	7-15-26	Reading, Pa.		Bats Left 53 L	R	6'	205	25	35	5	10	0	0	1	5	0	2	0	.286	.371
Limmer, Lou-Louis	51,54PhiA	3-10-25	New York, N.Y.		L	L	6'2	190	209	530	66	107	19	4	19	62	63	77	3	.202	.360
Lindbeck, Em-Emerit Desmond	60DetA	8-27-35	Kewanee, Ill.		L	R	6'	185	2	1	0	0	0	0	0	0	1	0	0	.000	.000
Lindell, Johnny-John Harlan (See P46-60)	41-50NYA 50StLN 53PitN 53-54PhiN	8-30-16	Greeley, Colo.		R	R	6'4	217	854	2795	401	762	124	48	72	404	289	366	17	.273	.429
Linden, Walt-Walter Charles	50BosN	3-27-24	Chicago, Ill.		R	R	6'1	190	3	5	0	2	1	0	0	0	1	0	0	.400	.600
Lindstrom, Chuck-Charles William	58ChiA	9- 7-36	Chicago, Ill.		R	R	5'11	175	1	1	1	1	0	1	0	1	1	0	0	1.000	3.000
Linhart, Carl-Carl James	52DetA	12-14-29	Zborov, Czechoslovakia		L	R	5'11	184	3	2	0	0	0	0	0	0	0	0	0	.000	.000
Lipon, Johnny-John Joseph (Skids)	42DetA 43-45MS 46,48-52DetA 52-53BosA 53StLA 54CinN M71CleA	11-10-22	Martins Ferry, Ohio		R	R	6'	175	758	2661	351	690	95	24	10	266	347	152	28	.259	.324
Littrell, Jack-Jack Napier	52,54PhiA 55KCA 57ChiN	1-22-29	Louisville, Ky.		R	R	6'	185	111	255	22	52	6	3	2	17	20	60	1	.204	.275
Locklin, Stu-Stuart Carlton	55-56CleA	7-22-28	Appleton, Wis.		L	L	6'1	190	25	24	4	4	1	0	0	0	3	5	0	.167	.208
Lockman, Whitey-Carroll Walter	45NYN 46MS 47-56NYN 56StLN 57NYN 58SFN 59BalA 59-60CinN M72-74ChiN	7-25-26	Lowell, N.C.		L	R	6'1	180	1666	5940	836	1658	222	49	114	563	552	383	43	.279	.391
Logan, Johnny-John (Yatcha)	51-52BosN 53-61MilN 61-63PitN	3-23-27	Endicott, N.Y.		R	R	5'11	175	1503	5244	651	1407	216	41	93	547	451	472	19	.268	.378
Lohrke, Lucky-Jack Wayne	47-51NYN 52-53PhiN	2-25-24	Los Angeles, Cal.		R	R	6'	180	354	914	125	221	38	9	22	96	111	86	9	.242	.375
Lollar, Sherm-John Sherman	46CleA 47-48NYA 49-51StLA 52-63ChiA	8-23-24	Durham, Ark.		R	R	6'	195	1752	5351	623	1415	244	14	155	808	671	453	20	.264	.402
Long, Dale-Richard Dale	51PitN 51StLA 55-57PitN 57-59ChiN 60SFN 60NYA 61-62WasA 62-63NYA	2- 6-26	Springfield, Mo.		L	L	6'4	212	1013	3020	384	805	135	33	132	467	353	460	10	.267	.464
Lonnett, Joe-Joseph Paul	56-59PhiN	2- 7-27	Beaver Falls, Pa.		R	R	5'10	185	143	325	22	54	8	0	6	27	40	74	0	.166	.246
Lopata, Stan-Stanley Edward	48-58PhiN 59-60MilN	9-12-25	Delray, Mich.		R	R	6'2	210	853	2601	375	661	116	25	116	397	393	497	18	.254	.452
Lopez, Hector-Hector Headley	55-59KCA 59-66NYA	7- 8-32	Colon, Panama		R	R	5'11	174	1450	4644	623	1251	193	37	136	591	418	696	16	.269	.415
Lowrey, Peanuts-Harry Lee	42-43,45-49ChiN 44MS 49-50CinN 50-54StLN 55PhiN	8-27-18	Culver City, Cal.		R	R	5'8	170	1401	4317	564	1177	186	45	37	479	403	226	48	.273	.362
Lukon, Eddie-Edward Paul (Mongoose)	41CinN 43-44MS 45-47CinN	8- 5-20	Burgettstown, Pa.		L	L	5'10	168	213	606	64	143	17	9	23	70	60	72	4	.236	.408
Lund, Don-Donald Andrew	45,47-48BknN 48StLA 49,52-54DetA	5-18-23	Detroit, Mich.		R	R	6'	200	281	753	91	181	36	8	15	86	65	113	5	.240	.369
Luttrell, Lyle-Lyle Kenneth	56-57WasA	2-22-30	Bloomington, Ill.		R	R	6'	180	57	167	21	32	9	3	2	14	11	27	5	.192	.317
Lutz, Joe-Rollin Joseph	51StLA	2-18-25	Keokuk, Iowa		L	L	6'	195	14	36	7	6	0	1	0	2	6	9	0	.167	.222
Lynch, Dummy-Matthew Daniel	48ChiN	2- 7-27	Dallas, Tex.		R	R	5'11	174	7	7	3	2	0	0	1	1	1	1	0	.286	.714
Lynch, Jerry-Gerald Thomas	54-56PitN 57-63CinN 63-66PitN	7-17-30	Bay City, Mich.		L	R	6'1	190	1184	2879	364	798	123	34	115	470	224	416	12	.277	.463
Lyons, Ed-Edward Hoyte (Mouse)	47WasA	5-12-23	Winston-Salem, N.C.		R	R	5'9	165	7	26	2	4	0	0	0	0	2	2	0	.154	.154
MacKenzie, Eric-Eric Hugh	55KCA	8-29-32	Glendon, Canada		L	R	6'	185	1	1	0	0	0	0	0	0	0	0	0	.000	.000
Maddern, Clarence-Clarence James	46,48-49ChiN 51CleA	9-26-21	Bisbee, Ariz.		R	R	6'1	185	104	238	17	59	12	1	5	29	12	26	0	.248	.370
Madrid, Sal-Salvador	47ChiN	6-19-20	El Paso, Tex.		R	R	5'9	165	8	24	0	3	1	0	0	1	1	6	0	.125	.167
Maguire, Jack-Jack	50-51NYN 51PitN 51StLA	2- 5-25	St. Louis, Mo.		R	R	5'11	165	94	192	25	46	5	2	2	21	18	36	1	.240	.318
Majeski, Hank-Henry (Heinie)	39-41BosN 43-45MS 46NYA 46-49PhiA 50-51ChiA 51-52PhiA 52-55CleA 55BalA	12-13-16	Staten Island, N.Y.		R	R	5'9	185	1069	3241	404	956	181	27	57	501	299	260	10	.279	.398
Mallett, Jerry-Gerald Gordon	59BosA	9-18-35	Bonne Terre, Mo.		R	R	6'5	208	4	15	1	4	0	0	0	1	1	3	0	.267	.267
Malmberg, Harry-Harry William (Swede)	55DetA	7-31-26	Fairfield, Ala.		R	R	6'1	170	67	208	25	45	5	2	0	19	29	19	0	.216	.260
Malone, Eddie-Edward Russell	49-50ChiA	6-16-20	Chicago, Ill.		R	R	5'10	175	86	241	19	62	9	2	1	26	39	27	2	.257	.324
Mangan, Jim-James Daniel	52PitN 53MS 54PitN 56NYN	9-24-29	San Francisco, Cal.		R	R	5'10	190	45	59	5	9	0	0	0	5	9	18	0	.153	.153
Mantle, Mickey-Mickey Charles (The Commerce Comet)	51-68NYA	10-20-31	Spavinaw, Okla.		B	R	5'11	195	2401	8102	1677	2415	344	72	536	1509	1734	1710	153	.298	.557
Mapes, Cliff-Cliff Franklin (Tiger)	48-51NYA 51StLA 52DetA	3-13-22	Sutherland, Neb.		L	R	6'3	205	459	1193	199	289	55	13	38	172	168	213	8	.242	.406
Markland, Gene-Cleneth Eugene (Mousy)	50PhiA	12-26-19	Detroit, Mich.		R	R	5'10	160	5	8	2	1	0	0	0	0	3	0	0	.125	.125
Marolewski, Fred-Fred Daniel (Fritz)	53StLN	10- 6-28	Chicago, Ill.		R	R	6'2	205	1	0	0	0	0	0	0	0	0	0	0	–	–
Marquez, Luis-Luis Angel (Canena)	51BosN 54ChiN 54PitN	10-28-25	Aguadilla, P.R.		R	R	5'10	174	99	143	24	26	5	1	0	11	16	24	7	.182	.231
Marquis, Bob-Robert Rudolph	53CinN	12-23-24	Oklahoma City, Okla.		L	L	6'1	170	40	44	9	12	1	1	2	3	4	11	0	.273	.477
Marquis, Roger-Roger Julian (Noonie)	55BalA	4- 5-37	Holyoke, Mass.		L	L	6'	190	1	1	0	0	0	0	0	0	0	0	0	.000	.000
Marsh, Freddie-Fred Francis	49CleA 51-52StLA 52WasA 52StLA 53-54ChiA 55-56BalA	1- 5-24	Valley Falls, Kans.		R	R	5'10	180	465	1236	148	296	43	8	10	96	125	171	13	.239	.311
Marshall, Jim-Rufus James	58BalA 58-59ChiN 60-61SFN 62NYN 62PitN M74-75ChiN	5-25-32	Danville, Ill.		L	L	6'1	195	410	852	111	206	24	7	29	106	101	139	5	.242	.388
Marshall, Willard-Willard Warren	42NYN 43-45MS 46-49NYN 50-52BosN 52-53CinN 54-55ChiA	2- 8-21	Richmond, Va.		L	R	6'1	205	1246	4233	583	1160	163	39	130	604	458	219	14	.274	.423
Martin, Billy-Alfred Manuel	50-53NYA 54MS 55-57NYA 57KCA 58DetA 59CleA 60CinN 61MilN 61,M69MinA M71-73DetA M73-75TexA M75NYA	5-16-28	Berkeley, Cal.		R	R	5'11	165	1021	3419	425	877	137	28	64	333	187	355	34	.257	.369
Martyn, Bob-Robert Gordon	57-59KCA	8-15-30	Weiser, Idaho		L	R	6'	176	154	357	35	94	12	11	3	35	37	56	2	.263	.384
Masi, Phil-Philip Samuel	39-49BosN 49PitN 50-52ChiA	1- 6-17	Chicago, Ill.		R	R	5'10	185	1229	3468	420	917	164	31	47	417	410	311	45	.264	.370
Massa, Gordon-Gordon Richard (Moose, Duke)	57-58ChiN 59MS	9- 2-35	Cincinnati, Ohio		L	R	6'3	210	8	17	2	7	1	0	0	3	4	5	0	.412	.471
Mathews, Eddie-Edwin Lee	52BosN 53-65MilN 66AtlN 67HouN 67-68DetA M72-74AtlN	10-13-31	Texarkana, Tex.		L	R	6'1	200	2391	8537	1509	2315	354	72	512	1453	1444	1487	68	.271	.509

USE NAME – GIVEN NAMES (NICKNAMES)	TEAM BY YEAR	BIRTH DATE	BIRTH PLACE	DEATH DATE	B	T	HGT	WGT	G	AB	R	H	2B	3B	HR	RBI	BB	SO	SB	BA	SA
					LIFETIME BATTING TOTALS																
Mauch, Gene-Gene William (Skip)	44BknN 45MS 47PitN 48BknN 48-49ChiN	11-18-25	Salina, Kans.		R	R	5'10	165	304	737	93	176	25	7	5	62	104	82	6	.239	.312
	50-51BosN 52StLN 56-57BosA M60-68PhiN M69-75MonN																				
Mauro, Carmen-Carmen Louis	48,50-51ChiN 53BknN 53WasA 53PhiA	11-10-26	St. Paul, Minn.		L	R	6'	167	167	416	40	96	9	8	2	33	37	65	6	.231	.305
Mavis, Bob-Robert Henry	49DetA	4- 8-18	Milwaukee, Wis.		L	R	5'7	160	1	0	0	0	0	0	0	0	0	0	0	–	–
Maxwell, Charlie-Charles Richard	50-52,54BosA 55BalA 55-62DetA 62-64ChiA	4-28-27	Lawton, Mich.		L	L	5'11	190	1133	3245	478	856	110	26	148	532	484	545	18	.264	.451
Mayo, Jackie-John Lewis	48-53PhiN	7-26-25	Litchfield, Ill.		L	R	6'1	190	139	240	25	51	10	1	1	12	25	35	2	.213	.275
McAnany, Jim-James	58-60ChiA 61-62ChiN	9- 4-36	Los Angeles, Cal.		R	R	5'10	196	93	241	23	61	10	3	0	27	21	38	2	.253	.320
McCardell, Roger-Roger Morton	59SFN	8-29-32	Gorsuch Mills, Md.		R	R	6'	200	4	4	0	0	0	0	0	0	0	0	0	.000	.000
McCarthy, Jerry-Jerome Francis	48StLA	5-23-23	Brooklyn, N.Y.	10- 3-65	L	L	6'1	205	2	3	0	1	0	0	0	0	0	0	0	.333	.333
McCormick, Mike-Myron Winthrop	40-43CinN 44-45MS 46CinN 46-48BosN 49BknN	5- 6-17	Angels Camp, Cal.		R	R	6'	195	748	2325	302	640	100	29	14	215	188	174	16	.275	.361
	50NYN 50ChiA 51WasA																				
McCosky, Barney-William Barney	39-42DetA 43-45MS 46DetA 46-51PhiA 51CinN	4-11-18	Coal Run, Pa.		L	R	6'1	184	1170	4172	664	1301	214	71	24	397	497	261	58	.312	.414
	51-53CleA																				
McCullough, Clyde-Clyde Edward	40-43ChiN 44-45MS 46-48ChiN 49-52PitN	3- 4-17	Nashville, Tenn.		R	R	5'11	190	1098	3121	308	785	121	28	52	339	265	398	27	.252	.358
(1945-played in World Series game-Chi N)	53-56ChiN																				
McDermott, Mickey-Maurice Joseph (See P46-60)	48-53BosA 54-55WasA 56NYA	8-19-28	Poughkeepsie, N.Y.		L	L	6'2	185	443	619	71	156	29	2	9	74	52	112	1	.252	.349
	57KCA 58DetA 61StLN 61KCA																				
McDougald, Gil-Gilbert James	51-60NYA	5-19-28	San Francisco, Cal.		R	R	6'	180	1336	4676	697	1291	187	51	112	576	559	623	45	.276	.410
McGah, Ed-Edward Joseph	46-47BosA	9-30-21	Oakland, Cal.		R	R	6'	183	24	51	3	8	1	1	0	3	10	7	0	.157	.216
McGhee, Ed-Warren Edward	50ChiA 53-54PhiA 54-55ChiA	9-29-24	Perry, Cal.		R	R	5'11	182	196	505	59	124	14	5	3	43	54	61	11	.246	.311
McHale, John-John Joseph	43-45,47-48DetA	9-21-21	Detroit, Mich.		L	R	6'	200	64	114	10	22	1	0	3	12	9	29	1	.193	.281
McManus, Jim-James Michael	60KCA	7-20-36	Brookline, Mass.		L	L	6'4	215	5	13	3	4	0	0	1	2	1	2	0	.308	.538
McMillan, Roy-Roy David	51-60CinN 61-64MilN 64-66NYN M72MilA M75NYN	7-17-30	Bonham, Tex.		R	R	5'11	170	2093	6752	739	1639	253	35	68	594	665	711	41	.243	.321
Meeks, Sammy-Samuel Mack	48WasA 49-51CinN	4-23-23	Anderson, S.C.		R	R	5'9	160	102	199	25	50	8	0	3	18	9	36	3	.251	.337
Mele, Sam-Sabath Anthony	47-49BosA 49-52WasA 52-53ChiA 54BalA 54-55BosA	1-21-23	Queens, N.Y.		R	R	6'1	183	1046	3437	406	916	168	39	80	544	311	342	15	.267	.408
	55CinN 56CleA M61-67MinA																				
Melton, Dave-David Olin	56,58KCA	10- 3-28	Pampa, Tex.		R	R	6'	185	12	9	0	1	0	0	0	0	0	5	0	.111	.111
Merriman, Lloyd-Lloyd Archer (Citation)	49-51,54CinN 52-53MS 54ChiA 55ChiN	8- 2-24	Clovis, Cal.		L	L	6'	190	455	1202	140	291	64	12	12	117	126	124	20	.242	.345
Merson, Jack-John Warren	51-52PitN 53BosA	1-17-22	Elk Ridge, Md.		R	R	5'11	175	125	452	47	116	22	4	6	52	23	45	1	.257	.363
Metkovich, Catfish-George Michael	43-46BosA 47CleA 49ChiA 51-53PitN	10- 8-21	Angel's Camp, Cal.		L	L	6'1	185	1055	3585	476	934	167	36	47	373	307	359	61	.261	.367
	53ChiN 54MilN																				
Micelotta, Bob-Robert Peter (Mickey)	54-55PhiN	10-20-28	Queens, N.Y.		R	R	5'11	185	17	7	2	0	0	0	0	0	1	1	0	.000	.000
Michaels (Kwietniewski), Cass-Casimir Eugene	43-50ChiA 50-52WasA 52StLA	3- 4-26	Detroit, Mich.		R	R	5'11	175	1288	4367	508	1142	147	46	53	501	566	406	64	.262	.353
(Played as Cass Kwietniewski 43)	52-53PhiA 54ChiA																				
Mickelson, Ed-Edward Allen	50StLN 53StLA 57ChiN	9- 9-26	Ottawa, Ill.		R	R	6'3	205	18	37	2	3	1	0	0	3	4	13	0	.081	.108
Mierkowicz, Ed-Edward Frank (Butch)	45,47-48DetA 50StLN	3- 6-24	Wyandotte, Mich.		R	R	6'4	205	35	63	6	11	3	0	1	4	4	18	1	.175	.270
Miggins, Larry-Lawrence Edward (Irish)	48,52StLN	8-20-25	Bronx, N.Y.		R	R	6'4	198	43	97	8	22	5	1	2	10	3	19	0	.227	.361
Miksis, Eddie-Edward Thomas	44BknN 45MS 46-51BknN 51-56ChiN 57StLN	9-11-26	Burlington, N.J.		R	R	6'	185	1042	3053	383	722	95	17	44	228	215	313	52	.236	.322
	57-58BalA 58CinN																				
Miles, Don-Donald Ray	58LAN	3-13-36	Indianapolis, Ind.		L	L	6'1	210	8	22	2	4	0	0	0	0	0	6	0	.182	.182
Miller, Rod-Rodney Carter	57BknN	1-16-40	Portland, Ore.		L	R	5'9	150	1	1	0	0	0	0	0	0	0	1	0	.000	.000
Milne, Pete-William James	48-50NYN	4-10-25	Mobile, Ala.		L	L	6'1	180	47	60	6	14	1	2	1	9	4	13	0	.233	.367
Minoso, Minnie-Saturnino Orestes Armas [Arrieta]	49,51CleA 51-57ChiA	11-29-22	Havana, Cuba		R	R	5'10	175	1830	6569	1136	1962	336	83	186	1023	814	582	205	.299	.460
	58-59CleA 60-61ChiA 62StLN 63WasA 64ChiA																				
Miranda, Willie-Guillermo [Perez]	51WasA 52ChiA 52StLA 52ChiA 53StLA	5-24-26	Velasco, Cuba		B	R	5'9	150	824	1914	176	423	50	14	6	132	165	250	13	.221	.271
	53-54NYA 55-59BalA																				
Mitchell, Dale-Loren Dale	46-56CleA 56BknN	8-23-21	Colony, Okla.		L	L	6'1	195	1127	3984	555	1244	169	61	41	403	346	119	45	.312	.416
Mole, Fenton-Fenton LeRoy (Muscles)	49NYA	6-14-25	San Leandro, Cal.		L	L	6'1	200	10	27	2	5	2	1	0	2	3	5	0	.185	.333
Montemayor, Felipe-Felipe Angel (Monty)	53,55PitN	2- 7-30	Monterrey, Mexico		L	L	6'2	185	64	150	15	26	5	3	2	10	22	37	1	.173	.287
Moon, Wally-Wallace Wade	54-58StLN 59-65LAN	4- 3-30	Bay, Ark.		L	R	6'	175	1457	4843	737	1399	212	60	142	661	644	591	89	.289	.445
Moore, Anse-Anselm Winn	46DetA	9-22-17	Delhi, La.		L	R	6'1	190	51	134	16	28	4	0	1	8	12	9	1	.209	.261
Morejon, Dan-Daniel [Torres]	58CinN	7-21-30	Havana, Cuba		R	R	6'1	175	12	26	4	5	0	0	0	1	9	2	1	.192	.192
Morgan, Bobby-Robert Morris	50,52-53BknN 54-56PhiN 56StLN 57PhiN 57-58ChiN	6-29-26	Oklahoma City, Okla.		R	R	5'10	180	671	2088	286	487	96	11	53	217	327	381	18	.233	.366
Morgan, Joe-Joseph Michael	59MilN 59KCA 60PhiN 60-61CleA 64StLN	11-19-30	Walpole, Mass.		L	R	5'10	170	88	187	15	36	5	3	2	10	18	31	0	.193	.283
Morgan, Vern-Vernon Thomas	54-55ChiN	8- 8-28	Emporia, Va.		L	R	6'1	190	31	71	4	16	2	0	0	3	4	14	0	.225	.254
Morton, Guy-Guy Jr. (Moose)	54BosA	11- 4-30	Tuscaloosa, Ala.		R	R	6'2	200	1	1	0	0	0	0	0	0	0	1	0	.000	.000
Moryn, Walt-Walter Joseph (Moose)	54-55BknN 56-60ChiN 60-61StLN 61PitN	4-12-26	St. Paul, Minn.		L	R	6'2	210	785	2506	324	667	116	16	101	354	251	393	7	.266	.446
Moss, Howie-Howard Glenn	42NYN 43-45MS 46CinN 46CleA	10-17-19	Gastonia, N.C.		R	R	5'11	195	22	72	3	7	0	0	0	1	3	17	0	.097	.097
Moss, Les-John Lester	46-51StLA 51BosA 52-53StLA 54-55BalA 55-58,M68ChiA	5-14-25	Tulsa, Okla.		R	R	5'11	205	824	2234	210	552	75	4	63	276	282	316	2	.247	.369
Mueller, Don-Donald Frederick (Mandrake the Magician)	48-57NYN 58-59ChiA	4-14-27	St. Louis, Mo.		L	R	6'	185	1245	4364	499	1292	139	37	65	520	167	146	11	.296	.390
Mullin, Pat-Patrick Joseph	40-41DetA 42-45MS 46-53DetA	11- 1-17	Trotter, Pa.		L	R	6'2	190	864	2493	381	676	106	43	87	385	330	312	20	.271	.453
Murphy, Dick-Richard Lee	54CinN 55-57MS	10-25-31	Cincinnati, Ohio		L	L	5'11	170	6	1	1	0	0	0	0	0	0	1	0	.000	.000
Murray, Ray-Raymond Lee (Deacon)	48,50-51CleA 51-53PhiA 54BalA	10-12-17	Spring Hope, N.C.		R	R	6'3	204	250	731	69	184	37	6	8	80	55	67	1	.252	.362
Murtaugh, Danny-Daniel Edward	41-43PhiN 44-45MS 46PhiN 47BosN	10- 8-17	Chester, Pa.		R	R	5'9	165	767	2599	263	661	97	21	8	219	287	216	49	.254	.317
	48-51,M57-64,67,70-71,73-75PitN																				
Musial, Stan-Stanley Frank (Stan the Man)	41-44StLN 45MS 46-63StLN	11-21-20	Donora, Pa.		L	L	6'	175	3026	10972	1949	3630	725	177	475	1951	1599	696	78	.331	.559
Myers, Richie-Richard	56ChiN	4- 7-30	Sacramento, Cal.		R	R	5'6	150	4	1	1	0	0	0	0	0	0	0	0	.000	.000
Naples, Al-Aloysius Francis	49StLA	8-29-27	Staten Island, N.Y.		R	R	5'9	168	2	7	0	1	1	0	0	0	0	1	0	.143	.286
Naragon, Hal-Harold Richard	51CleA 52-53MS 54-59CleA 59-60WasA 61-62MinA	10- 1-28	Zanesville, Ohio		L	R	6'	180	424	985	83	262	27	11	6	87	76	62	1	.266	.334
Naton, Pete-Peter Alphonsus	53PitN 54MS	9- 9-31	Queens, N.Y.		R	R	6'1	200	6	12	2	2	0	0	0	1	2	1	0	.167	.167
Neal, Charlie-Charles Lenard	56-57BknN 58-61LAN 62-63NYN 63CinN	1-30-31	Longview, Tex.		R	R	5'10	165	970	3316	461	858	113	38	87	391	337	557	48	.259	.394
Neeman, Cal-Calvin Amandus	57-60ChiN 60-61PhiN 62PitN 63CleA 63WasA	2-18-29	Valmeyer, Ill.		R	R	6'1	192	376	1002	93	224	35	4	30	97	79	221	1	.224	.356
Neill, Tommy-Thomas White	46-47BosN	11- 7-19	Hartselle, Ala.		L	R	6'2	200	20	55	9	14	2	1	0	7	3	3	0	.255	.327
Nelson, Bob-Robert Sidney (Tex, Babe)	55-57BalA	8- 7-36	Dallas, Tex.		L	L	6'3	205	79	122	11	25	2	2	0	11	15	40	0	.205	.254
Nelson, Rocky-Glenn Richard	49-51StLN 51PitN 51ChiA 52BknN 54CleA 56BknN	11-18-24	Portsmouth, Ohio		L	L	5'10	175	620	1394	186	347	61	14	31	173	130	94	7	.249	.379
	56StLN 59-61PitN																				
Niarhos, Gus-Constantine Gregory	46,48-50NYA 50-51ChiA 52-53BosA 54-55PhiN	12- 6-20	Birmingham, Ala.		R	R	6'	160	315	691	114	174	26	5	1	59	153	56	6	.252	.308
Nicholas, Don-Donald Leigh	52,54ChiA	10-30-30	Phoenix, Ariz.		L	R	5'7	150	10	2	3	0	0	0	0	0	1	0	0	.000	.000
Nielsen, Milt-Milton Robert	49,51CleA	2- 8-25	Tyler, Minn.		L	L	5'11	190	19	15	2	1	0	0	0	0	3	5	0	.067	.067
Nieman, Bob-Robert Charles	51-52StLA 53-54DetA 55-56ChiA 56-59BalA	1-26-27	Cincinnati, Ohio		R	R	5'11	195	1113	3452	455	1018	180	32	125	544	435	512	10	.295	.474
	60-61StLN 61-62CleA 62SFN																				
Noble, Ray-Rafael Miguel	51-53NYN	3-15-22	Central Hatillo, Cuba		R	R	5'11	200	107	243	31	53	6	1	9	40	25	41	1	.218	.362
Noren, Irv-Irving Arnold	50-52WasA 52-56NYA 57KCA 57-59StLN 59-60ChiN	11-29-24	Jamestown, N.Y.		L	L	6'	190	1093	3119	443	857	157	35	65	453	335	350	34	.275	.410
46-47 played in N.B.L.	60LAN																				
Northey, Ron-Ronald James (The Round Man)	42-44PhiN 45MS 46-47PhiN	4-26-20	Mahanoy City, Pa.	4-16-71	L	R	5'10	195	1084	3172	385	874	172	28	108	513	361	297	7	.276	.450
	47-49StLN 50CinN 50,52ChiN 55-57ChiA 57PhiN																				
Novotney, Rube-Ralph Joseph	49ChiN	8- 5-24	Streator, Ill.		R	R	6'	187	22	67	4	18	2	1	0	6	3	11	0	.269	.328
O'Brien, Eddie-Edward Joseph (See P46-60)	53PitN 54MS 55-58PitN	12-11-30	South Amboy, N.J.		R	R	5'9	165	231	554	64	131	10	4	0	25	37	45	11	.236	.269
O'Brien, Johnny-John Thomas (See P46-60)	53,55-58PitN 54MS 58StLN 59MilN	12-11-30	South Amboy, N.J.		R	R	5'9	170	339	815	90	204	35	5	4	59	59	82	2	.250	.320
O'Connell, Danny-Daniel Francis	50PitN 51-52MS 53PitN 54-57MilN	1-21-27	Paterson, N.J.	10- 2-69	R	R	5'11	180	1143	4035	527	1049	181	35	39	320	431	396	48	.260	.351
	57NYN 58-59SFN 61-62WasA																				
Oertel, Chuck-Charles Frank (Snuffy, Ducky)	58BalA	3-12-31	Coffeyville, Kans.		L	R	5'8	165	14	12	4	2	0	0	1	1	1	1	0	.167	.417
Okrie, Len-Leonard Joseph	48,50-51DetA 52BosA	7-16-23	Detroit, Mich.		R	R	6'1	185	42	78	3	17	1	1	0	3	9	16	0	.218	.256
Oldham, John-John Hardin	56CinN	11- 6-32	Salinas, Cal.		R	L	6'3	198	1	0	0	0	0	0	0	0	0	0	0	–	–
Olson, Karl-Karl Arthur (Ole)	51BosA 52MS 53-55BosA 56-57WasA 57DetA	7- 6-30	Ross, Cal.		R	R	6'3	210	279	681	74	160	25	6	6	50	43	94	3	.235	.316
O'Neil, John-John Francis	46PhiN	4-19-20	Shelbiana, Ky.		R	R	5'9	155	46	94	12	25	3	0	0	9	5	12	0	.266	.298
Oravetz, Ernie-Ernest Eugene	55-56WasA	1-24-32	Johnstown, Pa.		B	L	5'4	145	188	400	44	105	8	3	0	36	53	39	2	.263	.298
O'Rourke, Charlie-James Patrick	59StLN	6-22-37	Walla Walla, Wash.		R	R	6'2	195	2	2	0	0	0	0	0	0	0	0	0	.000	.000
Ostrowski, John-John Thaddeus	43-46ChiN 48BosA 49-50ChiA 50WasA 50ChiA	10-17-17	Chicago, Ill.		R	R	5'10	170	216	561	73	131	20	9	14	74	68	125	7	.234	.376
Pack, Frankie-Frank	49StLA	4-10-28	Morristown, Tenn.		L	R	6'	190	1	1	0	0	0	0	0	0	0	1	0	.000	.000
Pafko, Andy-Andrew (Handy Andy, Pruschka)	43-51ChiN 51-52BknN 53-59MilN	2-25-21	Boyceville, Wis.		R	R	6'	190	1852	6292	844	1796	264	62	213	976	561	477	38	.285	.449
Palys, Stan-Stanley Francis	53-55PhiN 55-56CinN	5- 1-30	Blakely, Pa.		R	R	6'2	190	138	333	42	79	17	0	10	43	26	54	2	.237	.378
Patton, Tom-Thomas Allen	57BalA	9- 5-35	Honey Brook, Pa.		R	R	5'9	185	1	2	0	0	0	0	0	0	0	2	0	.000	.000
Paula, Carlos-Carlos Conill	54-56WasA	11- 4-28	Havana, Cuba		R	R	6'3	195	157	457	44	124	23	8	9	60	27	62	2	.271	.416
Pawelek, Ted-Theodore John (Porky)	46ChiN	8-15-19	Chicago Heights, Ill.	2-12-64	L	R	5'11	202	4	4	0	1	1	0	0	0	0	0	0	.250	.500
Pawloski, Stan-Stanley Walter	55CleA	9- 6-31	Wanamie, Pa.		R	R	6'1	175	2	8	0	1	0	0	0	0	0	2	0	.125	.125

USE NAME – GIVEN NAMES (NICKNAMES)	TEAM BY YEAR	BIRTH DATE	BIRTH PLACE	DEATH DATE	LIFETIME BATTING TOTALS																
					B	T	HGT	WGT	G	AB	R	H	2B	3B	HR	RBI	BB	SO	SB	BA	SA
Peck, Hal-Harold Arthur	43BknN 44-46PhiA 47-49CleA	4-20-17	Big Bend, Wis.		L	L	5'11	175	355	1092	136	305	52	13	15	112	87	86	10	.279	.392
Peden, Les-Leslie Earl	53WasA	9-17-23	Azle, Tex.		R	R	6'1	212	9	28	4	7	1	0	1	1	4	3	0	.250	.393
Peete, Charlie-Charles (Mule)	56StLN	2-22-31	Franklin, Va.	11-27-56	L	R	5'10	190	23	52	3	10	2	2	0	6	6	10	0	.192	.308
Pellagrini, Eddie-Edward Charles	46-47BosA 48-49StLA 51PhiN 52CinN 53-54PitN	3-13-18	Boston, Mass.		R	R	5'9	160	563	1423	167	321	42	13	20	133	128	201	13	.226	.316
Pendleton, Jim-James Edward	53-56MilN 57-58PitN 59CinN 62HouN	1- 7-24	St. Charles, Mo.		R	R	6'	185	444	941	120	240	30	8	19	97	43	151	11	.255	.365
Pesky (Paveskovich), Johnny-John Michael	42BosA 43-45MS 46-52BosA 52-54DetA 54WasA M63-64BosA	9-27-19	Portland, Ore.		L	R	5'9	168	1270	4745	867	1455	226	50	17	404	663	218	53	.307	.386
Peterson, Buddy-Carl Francis	55ChiA 57BalA	4-23-25	Portland, Ore.		R	R	5'9	170	13	38	8	9	3	0	0	2	5	4	0	.237	.316
Peterson, Hardy-Harding William	55,57-59PitN	10-17-29	Perth Amboy, N.J.		R	R	6'	205	66	161	17	44	8	1	3	21	17	17	0	.273	.391
Philley, Dave-David Earl	41ChiA 43-45MS 46-51ChiA 51-53PhiA 54-55CleA 55-56BalA 56-57ChiA 57DetA 58-60PhiN 60SFN 60-61BalA 62BosA	5-16-20	Paris, Tex.		B	R	6'	188	1904	6296	789	1700	276	72	84	729	594	551	102	.270	.377
Phillips, Bubba-John Melvin	55DetA 56-59ChiA 60-62CleA 63-64DetA	2-24-30	West Point, Miss.		R	R	5'9	180	1062	3278	348	835	135	8	62	356	182	314	25	.255	.358
Phillips, Ed-Howard Edward	53StLN	7- 8-31	St. Louis, Mo.		B	R	6'1	180	9	0	4	0	0	0	0	0	0	0	0	–	–
Phillips, Jack-Jack Dorn (Stretch)	47-49NYA 49-52PitN 55-57DetA	9- 6-21	Clarence, N.Y.		R	R	6'4	193	343	892	111	252	42	16	9	101	85	86	5	.283	.396
Piersall, Jimmy-James Anthony	50,52-58BosA 59-61CleA 62-63WasA 63NYN 63-64LAA 65-67CalA	11-14-29	Waterbury, Conn.		R	R	6'	190	1734	5890	811	1604	256	52	104	591	523	583	115	.272	.386
Pignatano, Joe-Joseph Benjamin	57BknN 58-60LAN 61KCA 62SFN 62NYN	8- 4-29	Brooklyn, N.Y.		R	R	5'10	180	307	689	81	161	25	4	16	62	94	116	8	.234	.351
Pike, Jess-Jess Willard	46NYN	7-31-16	Dustin, Okla.		L	R	6'2	180	16	41	4	7	1	1	1	6	6	9	0	.171	.317
Pilarcik, Al-Alfred James	56KCA 57-60BalA 61KCA 61ChiA	7- 3-30	Whiting, Ind.		L	L	5'10	180	668	1614	205	413	66	7	22	143	185	150	41	.256	.346
Pisoni, Jim-James Pete	53StLA 56-57KCA 59MilN 59-60NYA	8-14-29	St. Louis, Mo.		R	R	5'10	169	103	189	26	40	3	3	6	20	16	47	0	.212	.354
Plarski, Don-Donald Joseph	55KCA	11- 9-29	Chicago, Ill.		R	R	5'6	160	8	11	0	1	0	0	0	0	0	2	1	.091	.091
Platt, Whitey-Mizell George	42-43ChiN 44-45MS 46ChiA 48-49StLA	8-21-20	W. Palm Beach, Fla.	7-27-70	R	R	6'2	215	333	1002	117	256	41	17	13	147	81	122	2	.255	.369
Pless, Rance-Rance	56KCA	12- 6-25	Greeneville, Tenn.		R	R	6'	195	48	85	4	23	3	1	0	9	10	13	0	.271	.329
Plews, Herb-Herbert Eugene	[illegible]WasA [illegible]BosA	[illegible]	Helena, Mont.		[illegible]	R	5'11	165	346	1017	125	266	42	17	4	82	74	133	3	.262	.348
Poole, Ray-Raymond Herman	41PhiA 42-45MS 47PhiA	1-16-20	Salisbury, N.C.		L	R	6'	180	15	15	1	3	0	0	0	1	1	5	0	.200	.200
Pope, Dave-David	52,54-55CleA 55-56BalA 56CleA	6-17-25	Talladega, Ala.		L	R	5'10	170	230	551	75	146	19	7	12	73	40	113	7	.265	.390
Porter, Dan-Daniel Edward	51WasA 52-53MS	10-17-31	Decatur, Ill.		L	L	6'	164	13	19	2	4	0	0	0	0	2	4	0	.211	.211
Porter, Jay-J W	52StLA 53-54MS 55-57DetA 58CleA 59WasA 59StLN	1-17-33	Shawnee, Okla.		R	R	6'2	180	229	544	58	124	22	1	8	62	53	96	4	.228	.316
Post, Wally-Walter Charles	49,51-57CinN 58-60PhiN 60-63CinN 63MinA 64CleA	7- 9-29	St. Wendelin, Ohio		R	R	6'1	203	1204	4007	594	1064	194	28	210	699	331	813	19	.266	.485
Powell, Bob-Robert Leroy	55ChiA 56MS 57ChiA	10-17-33	Flint, Mich.		R	R	6'1	190	2	0	1	0	0	0	0	0	0	0	0	–	–
Power, Vic-Victor Pellot	54PhiA 55-58KCA 58-61CleA 62-64MinA 64PhiN 64LAA 65CalA	11- 1-31	Arecibo, P.R.		R	R	6'	195	1627	6046	765	1716	290	49	126	658	279	247	45	.284	.411
Powers, Johnny, John Calvin	55-58PitN 59CinN 60BalA 60CleA	7- 8-29	Birmingham, Ala.		L	R	6'1	197	151	215	26	42	7	2	6	14	22	48	0	.195	.330
Powis, Carl-Carl Edgar (Jug)	57BalA	1-11-28	Philadelphia, Pa.		R	R	6'	185	15	41	4	8	3	1	0	2	7	9	2	.195	.317
Pramesa, Johnny-John Steven	49-51CinN 52ChiN	8-28-25	Barton, Ohio		R	R	6'2	210	185	526	29	141	17	3	13	59	31	41	0	.268	.386
Price, Johnny-John Thomas Reid (Jackie)	46CleA	11-13-12	Winborn, Miss.	10- 2-67	L	R	5'10	150	7	13	1	3	0	0	0	0	0	0	0	.231	.231
Priddy, Jerry-Gerald Edward	41-42NYA 43WasA 44-45MS 46-47WasA 48-49StLA 50-53DetA	11- 9-19	Los Angeles, Cal.		R	R	5'11	180	1296	4720	612	1252	232	46	61	541	624	639	44	.265	.373
Pritchard, Buddy-Harold William	57PitN	1-25-36	South Gate, Cal.		R	R	6'	165	23	11	1	1	0	0	0	0	0	4	0	.091	.091
Pyburn, Jim-James Edward	55-57BalA	11- 1-32	Fairfield, Ala.		R	R	6'	190	158	294	36	56	5	5	3	20	34	56	6	.190	.272
Queen, Billy-Billy Eddleman (Doc)	54MilN	11-28-28	Gastonia, N.C.		R	R	6'1	185	3	2	0	0	0	0	0	0	0	2	0	.000	.000
Rackley, Marv-Marvin Eugene	47-49BknN 49PitN 49BknN 50CinN	7-25-21	Seneca, S.C.		L	L	5'10	170	185	477	87	151	20	6	1	35	36	36	10	.317	.390
Raines, Larry-Lawrence Glenn Hope	57-58CleA	3- 9-30	St. Albans, W.Va.		R	R	5'10	165	103	253	39	64	14	0	2	16	19	45	5	.253	.332
Ramazzotti, Bob-Robert Louis	46,48-49BknN 49-53ChiN	1-16-17	Elanora, Pa.		R	R	5'9	175	346	851	86	196	22	9	4	53	45	107	15	.230	.291
Rand, Dick-Richard Hilton	53,55StLN 57PitN	3- 7-31	South Gate, Cal.		R	R	6'2	185	72	146	11	35	3	1	2	13	14	31	0	.240	.315
Rapp, Earl-Earl Wellington	49DetA 49ChiA 51NYN 51-52StLA 52WasA	5-20-21	Corunna, Mich.		L	R	6'2	185	135	279	27	73	16	4	2	39	25	41	2	.262	.369
Reed, Bill-William Joseph	52BosN	11-12-22	Shawano, Wis.		L	R	5'10	185	15	52	4	13	0	0	0	0	0	5	0	.250	.250
Reese, Pee Wee-Harold Henry (The Little Colonel)	40-42BknN 43-45MS 46-57BknN 58LAN	7-23-18	Ekron, Ky.		R	R	5'10	175	2166	8058	1338	2170	330	80	126	885	1210	890	232	.269	.377
Regalado, Rudy-Rudolph Valentino	54-56CleA	5-21-30	Los Angeles, Cal.		R	R	6'1	185	91	253	27	63	8	0	2	31	25	21	0	.249	.304
Reich, Herm-Herman Charles	49WasA 49CleA 49ChiN	11-23-17	Bell, Cal.		R	L	6'2	200	111	390	43	109	18	2	3	34	14	33	4	.279	.359
Reiser, Pete-Harold Patrick (Pistol Pete)	40-42BknN 43-45MS 46-48BknN 49-50BosN 51PitN 52CleA	3-17-19	St. Louis, Mo.		L	R	5'11	185	861	2662	473	786	155	41	58	368	343	369	87	.295	.450
Renna, Bill-William Beneditto (Big Bill)	53NYA 54PhiA 55-56KCA 58-59BosA	10-14-24	Hanford, Cal.		R	R	6'3	218	370	918	123	219	36	10	28	119	99	166	2	.239	.391
Repulski, Rip-Eldon John	53-56StLN 57-58PhiN 59-60LAN 60-61BosA	10- 4-27	Sauk Rapids, Minn.		R	R	6'	195	928	3088	407	830	153	23	106	416	207	433	25	.269	.436
Restelli, Dino-Dino Paul (Dingo)	49,51PitN	9-23-24	St. Louis, Mo.		R	R	6'1	191	93	270	42	65	12	0	13	43	37	30	3	.241	.430
Rhawn, Bobby-Robert John (Rocky)	47-49NYN 49PitN 49ChiA	2-13-19	Catawissa, Pa.		R	R	5'8	180	90	198	38	47	9	2	2	18	35	17	4	.237	.333
Rhodes, Dusty-James Lamar	52-57NYN 59SFN	5-13-27	Mathews, Ala.		L	R	6'	178	576	1172	146	296	44	10	54	207	131	196	3	.253	.445
Rice, Del-Delbert W 45-46 played in N.B.L.	45-55StLN 55-59MilN 60ChiN 60StLN 60BalA 61LAA M72CalA	10-27-22	Portsmouth, Ohio		R	R	6'2	190	1309	3826	342	908	177	20	79	441	382	522	2	.237	.356
Rice, Hal-Harold Housten (Hoot)	48-53StLN 53-54PitN 54ChiN	2-11-24	Morganette, W.Va.		L	R	6'1	195	424	1183	129	307	52	12	19	162	94	133	1	.260	.372
Richards, Fred-Fred Charles (Fuzzy)	51ChiN	11- 3-27	Warren, Ohio		L	L	6'1	185	10	27	1	8	2	0	0	4	2	3	0	.296	.370
Richardson, Ken-Kenneth Franklin	42PhiA 46PhiN	5- 2-15	Orleans, Ind.		R	R	5'11	187	12	35	2	4	1	0	0	2	2	2	0	.114	.143
Richmond, Don-Donald Lester	41PhiA 42-45MS 46-47PhiA 51StLN	10-27-19	Gillett, Pa.		L	R	6'1	175	56	152	11	32	6	2	2	22	6	17	1	.211	.316
Richter, Al-Allen Gordon	51,53BosA	2- 7-27	Norfolk, Va.		R	R	6'	175	6	11	1	1	0	0	0	0	3	0	0	.091	.091
Rickert, Marv-Marvin August (Twitch)	42ChiN 43-45MS 46-47ChiN 48CinN 48-49BosN 50PitN 50ChiA	1- 8-21	Long Branch, Wash.		L	R	6'2	195	402	1149	139	284	45	9	19	145	88	161	4	.247	.352
Riebe, Hank-Harvey Donald	42DetA 43-45MS 47-49DetA	10-10-21	Cleveland, Ohio		R	R	5'9	175	61	137	2	29	4	0	0	11	3	18	1	.212	.241
Rigney, Bill-William Joseph (Specs, Cricket)	46-53,M56-57NYN M58-60SFN M61-64LAA M65-69CalA M70-72MinA	1-29-19	Alameda, Cal.		R	R	6'1	178	654	1966	281	510	78	14	41	212	208	206	25	.259	.376
Rikard, Culley-Culley	41-42PitN 43-45MS 47PitN	5- 9-14	Oxford, Miss.		L	R	6'	183	153	396	64	107	19	5	4	37	58	48	1	.270	.374
Rinker, Bob-Robert John	50PhiA	4-21-21	Audenried, Pa.		R	R	6'	190	3	3	0	1	0	0	0	0	0	0	0	.333	.333
Rivera, Jim-Manuel Joseph (Jungle Jim)	52StLA 52-61ChiA 61KCA	7-22-22	Bronx, N.Y.		L	L	6'	196	1171	3552	503	911	155	56	83	422	365	523	160	.256	.402
Rizzuto, Phil-Philip Francis (Scooter)	41-42NYA 43-45MS 46-56NYA	9-25-17	Brooklyn, N.Y.		R	R	5'6	150	1661	5816	877	1588	239	62	38	563	650	397	149	.273	.355
Roach, Mel-Melvin Earl	53-54MilN 55-56MS 57-61MilN 61ChiN 62PhiN	1-25-33	Richmond, Va.		R	R	6'1	190	227	499	42	119	25	0	7	43	24	75	1	.238	.331
Roberts, Curt-Curtis Benjamin	54-56PitN	8-16-29	Pineland, Tex.		R	R	5'8	165	171	575	54	128	24	9	1	40	62	62	7	.223	.301
Robertson, Don-Donald Alexander	54ChiN	10-15-30	Harvey, Ill.		L	L	5'10	180	14	6	2	0	0	0	0	0	0	2	0	.000	.000
Robertson, Jim-Alfred James	54PhiA 55KCA	1-29-28	Chicago, Ill.		R	R	5'9	183	69	155	10	29	8	0	0	8	24	27	0	.187	.239
Robertson, Sherry-Sherrard Alexander	40-41,43WasA 44-45MS 46-52WasA 52PhiA	1- 1-19	Montreal, Canada	10-23-70	L	R	6'	180	597	1507	200	346	55	18	26	151	202	238	32	.230	.342
Robinson, Aaron-Aaron Andrew	43NYA 44MS 45-47NYA 48ChiA 49-51DetA 51BosA	6-23-15	Lancaster, S.C.	3- 9-66	L	R	6'2	205	610	1839	208	478	74	11	61	272	337	194	0	.260	.412
Robinson, Eddie-William Edward	42CleA 43-45MS 46-48CleA 49-50WasA 50-52ChiA 53PhiA 54-56NYA 56KCA 57DetA 57CleA 57BalA	12-15-20	Paris, Tex.		L	R	6'2	210	1314	4279	545	1145	171	24	172	723	520	359	10	.268	.439
Robinson, Jackie-Jack Roosevelt	47-56BknN	1-31-19	Cairo, Ga.	10-24-72	R	R	5'11	195	1382	4877	947	1518	273	54	137	734	740	291	197	.311	.474
Rodin, Eric-Eric Chapman	54NYN	2- 5-30	Orange, N.J.		R	R	6'2	215	5	6	0	0	0	0	0	0	0	2	0	.000	.000
Rodriguez, Hector-Antonio [Ordenana]	52ChiA	6-13-20	Alquizar, Cuba		R	R	5'8	165	124	407	55	108	14	0	1	40	47	22	7	.265	.307
Roig, Tony-Anton Ambrose	53,55-56WasA	12-23-28	New Orleans, La.		R	R	6'2	188	76	184	14	39	7	3	0	11	22	45	2	.212	.283
Rojek, Stan-Stanley Andrew	42,46-47BknN 43-45MS 48-51PitN 51StLN 52StLA	4-21-19	N. Tonawanda, N.Y.		R	R	5'10	170	522	1764	225	470	67	13	4	122	152	100	32	.266	.326
Rosen, Al-Albert Leonard (Flip)	47-56CleA	2-29-24	Spartanburg, S.C.		R	R	5'10	180	1044	3725	603	1063	165	20	192	717	587	385	39	.285	.495
Rossi, Joe-Joseph Anthony	52CinN	3-13-23	Oakland, Cal.		R	R	6'1	205	55	145	14	32	0	1	1	6	20	20	1	.221	.255
Rufer, Rudy-Rudolph Joseph	49-50NYN	10-28-26	Queens, N.Y.		R	R	6'	165	22	26	2	2	0	0	0	2	2	1	1	.077	.077
Runnels (Runnells), Pete-James Edward	51-57WasA 58-62BosA 63-64HouN M66BosA	1-28-28	Lufkin, Tex.		L	R	6'	170	1799	6373	876	1854	282	64	49	630	844	627	37	.291	.378
Russell, Jim-James William	42-47PitN 48-49BosN 50-51BknN	10- 1-18	Fayette City, Pa.		B	R	6'1	181	1033	3595	554	959	171	51	67	428	503	427	59	.267	.400
Rutner, Mickey-Milton	47PhiA	3-18-20	Hempstead, N.Y.		R	R	5'11	185	12	48	4	12	1	0	1	4	3	2	0	.250	.333
Ryan, Connie-Cornelius Joseph	42NYN 43-44BosN 45MS 46-50BosN 50-51CinN 52-53PhiN 53ChiA 54CinN M75AtlN	2-27-20	New Orleans, La.		R	R	5'11	175	1184	3982	535	988	181	42	56	381	518	514	69	.248	.357
Sacka, Frank-Frank	51,53WasA	8-30-24	Romulus, Mich.		R	R	6'	195	14	34	3	9	0	0	0	6	3	6	0	.265	.265
Saffell, Tom-Thomas Judson	49-51,55PitN 55KCA	7-26-21	Etowah, Tenn.		L	R	5'11	170	271	602	91	143	15	1	6	40	59	108	9	.238	.296
St. Claire, Ebba-Edward Joseph	51-52BosN 53MilN 54NYN	8- 5-21	Whitehall, N.Y.		B	R	6'1	219	164	450	39	112	23	2	7	40	35	52	0	.249	.356
Salkeld, Bill-William Franklin	45-47PitN 48-49BosN 50ChiA	3-18-17	Pocatello, Idaho	4-22-67	L	R	5'10	190	356	850	111	232	39	2	31	132	182	101	6	.273	.433
Samcoff, Eddie-Edward William	51PhiA	9- 1-24	Sacramento, Cal.		R	R	5'10	165	4	11	0	0	0	0	0	0	1	2	0	.000	.000
Samford, Ron-Ronald Edward	54NYN 55,57DetA 59WasA	2-28-30	Dallas, Tex.		R	R	5'11	156	158	334	31	73	14	2	5	27	17	46	2	.219	.317
Sanicki, Ed-Edward Robert (Butch)	49,51PhiN	7- 7-24	Wallington, N.J.		R	R	5'9	175	20	17	5	5	1	0	3	8	2	5	1	.294	.882
Sarni, Bill-William F.	51-52,54-56StLN 56NYN 56IL	9-19-27	Los Angeles, Cal.		R	R	5'11	185	390	1182	107	311	50	11	22	151	89	135	6	.263	.380
Saucier, Frank-Francis Field	51StLA 52-54MS	5-28-26	Leslie, Mo.		L	R	6'1	180	18	14	4	1	1	0	0	1	3	4	0	.071	.143

USE NAME – GIVEN NAMES (NICKNAMES)	TEAM BY YEAR	BIRTH DATE	BIRTH PLACE	DEATH DATE	B	T	HGT	WGT	G	AB	R	H	2B	3B	HR	RBI	BB	SO	SB	BA	SA
									LIFETIME BATTING TOTALS												
Sauer, Ed-Edward (Horn)	43-45ChiN 49StLN 49BosN	1- 3-20	Pittsburgh, Pa.		R	R	6'1	188	189	457	45	117	25	2	5	57	33	77	3	.256	.352
Sauer, Hank-Henry John	41-42CinN 44MS 45,48-49CinN 49-55ChiN 56StLN 57NYN 58-59SFN	3-17-19	Pittsburgh, Pa.		R	R	6'2	198	1399	4796	709	1278	200	19	288	876	561	714	11	.266	.496
Sawatski, Carl-Carl Ernest (Swats)	48,50ChiN 51-52MS 53ChiN 54ChiA 57-58MilN 58-59PhiN 60-63StLN	11- 4-27	Shickshinny, Pa.		L	R	5'10	220	633	1449	133	351	46	5	58	213	191	251	2	.242	.401
Scala, Jerry-Gerard Michael	48-50ChiA	9-27-26	Bayonne, N.J.		L	R	5'11	178	80	193	26	43	9	2	1	19	27	32	3	.223	.306
Scheffing, Bob-Robert Boden	41-42ChiN 43-45MS 46-50ChiN 50-51CinN 51StLN M57-59ChiN M61-63DetA	8-11-15	Overland, Mo.		R	R	6'2	180	517	1357	105	357	53	9	20	187	103	127	6	.263	.360
Schell, Danny-Clyde Daniel	54-55PhiN	12-26-27	Fostoria, Mich.	5-11-72	R	R	6'1	195	94	274	25	77	14	3	7	33	17	32	0	.281	.431
Schenz, Hank-Henry Leonard	46-49ChiN 50-51PitN 51NYN	4-11-19	New Richmond, Ohio		R	R	5'9	175	207	538	70	133	22	3	2	24	27	25	8	.247	.310
Scherbarth, Bob-Robert Elmer	50BosA	1-18-26	Milwaukee, Wis.		R	R	6'	180	1	0	0	0	0	0	0	0	0	0	0		
Schmees, George-George Edward (Rocky)	52StLA 52BosA	9- 6-24	Cincinnati, Ohio		L	L	6'	190	76	125	17	21	4	1	0	6	12	29	0	.168	.216
Schmidt, Bob-Robert Benjamin	58-61SFN 61CinN 62-63WasA 65NYA	4-22-33	St. Louis, Mo.		R	R	6'2	205	454	1305	133	317	55	4	39	150	100	199	0	.243	.381
Schoendienst, Red-Albert Frederick	45-56StLN 56-57NYN 57-60MilN 61-63,M65-75StLN	2- 2-23	Germantown, Ill.		B	R	6'	170	2216	8479	1223	2449	427	78	84	773	606	346	89	.289	.387
Schoonmaker, Jerry-Jerald Lee	55WasA 56MS 57WasA	12-14-33	Seymour, Mo.		R	R	5'11	190	50	69	10	9	1	1	1	4	7	22	1	.130	.217
Schramka, Paul-Paul Edward	53ChiN	3-22-28	Milwaukee, Wis.		L	L	6'	185	2	0	0	0	0	0	0	0	0	0	0	–	–
Schult, Art-Arthur William (Dutch)	53NYA 56-57CinN 57WasA 59-60ChiN	6-20-28	Brooklyn, N.Y.		R	R	6'3	210	164	421	58	111	24	0	6	56	23	50	0	.264	.363
Schypinski, Jerry-Gerald Albert	55KCA	9-16-31	Detroit, Mich.		L	R	5'10	170	22	69	7	15	2	0	0	5	1	6	0	.217	.246
Seerey, Pat-James Patrick	43-48CleA 48-49ChiA	3-17-23	Wilburton, Okla.		R	R	5'10	200	561	1815	236	406	73	5	86	261	281	485	3	.224	.412
Segrist, Kal-Kal Hill	52NYA 55BalA	4- 4-31	Greenville, Tex.		R	R	6'	180	20	32	4	4	0	0	0	1	5	1	0	.125	.125
Seminick, Andy-Andrew Wasil	43-51PhiN 52-55CinN 55-57PhiN	9-12-20	Pierce, W.Va.		R	R	5'11	187	1304	3921	495	953	139	26	164	556	582	780	23	.243	.417
Senerchia, Sonny-Emanuel Robert	52PitN	4- 6-31	Newark, N.J.		R	R	6'1	195	29	100	5	22	5	0	3	11	4	21	0	.220	.360
Sepkowski (Szczepkowski), Ted-Theodore Walter	42CleA 44-45MS 46-47CleA 47NYA	11- 9-23	Baltimore, Md.		L	R	5'11	190	19	26	3	6	2	0	0	1	1	4	0	.231	.308
Serena, Bill-William Robert	49-54ChiN	10- 2-24	Alameda, Cal.		R	R	5'9	180	408	1239	154	311	57	16	48	198	177	235	2	.251	.439
Sessi, Walter-Walter Anthony (Watsie)	41StLN 42-45MS 46StLN	7-23-18	Finleyville, Pa.		L	L	6'3	225	20	27	4	2	0	0	1	2	2	6	0	.074	.185
Shannon, Wally-Walter Charles	59-60StLN	1-23-34	Cleveland, Ohio		L	R	6'	178	65	118	7	31	5	0	0	6	3	18	0	.263	.305
Shantz, Billy-Wilmer Ebert	54PhiA 55KCA 60NYA	7-31-27	Pottstown, Pa.		R	R	6'1	160	131	381	31	98	13	4	2	29	28	37	0	.257	.328
Shearer, Ray-Ray Solomon	57MilN	9-19-29	Jacobus, Pa.		R	R	6'	200	2	2	1	1	0	0	0	0	1	1	0	.500	.500
Sheely, Bud-Hollis Kimball	51-53ChiA	11-26-20	Spokane, Wash.		L	R	6'1	200	101	210	7	44	5	0	0	12	27	22	0	.210	.233
Shepard, Jack-Jack Leroy	53-56PitN	5-13-32	Clovis, Cal.		R	R	6'2	195	278	751	72	195	29	6	12	75	84	97	2	.260	.362
Sheridan, Neill-Neill Rawlins (Wild Horse)	48BosA	11-20-21	Sacramento, Cal.		R	R	6'1	195	2	1	0	0	0	0	0	0	0	1	0	.000	.000
Shetrone, Barry-Barry Stevan	59-62BalA 63WasA	7- 6-38	Baltimore, Md.		L	R	6'2	190	60	112	12	23	2	1	1	7	5	16	3	.205	.268
Shofner, Strick-Frank Strickland	47BosA	7-23-19	Crawford, Tex.		L	R	5'11	172	5	13	1	2	0	1	0	0	0	3	0	.154	.308
Shokes, Eddie-Edward Christopher	41CinN 43-45MS 46CinN	1-27-20	Charleston, S.C.		L	L	6'	170	32	84	3	10	1	0	0	5	18	22	1	.119	.131
Shoop, Ron-Ronald Lee	59DetA	9-19-31	Rural Valley, Pa.		R	R	5'11	180	3	7	1	1	0	0	0	1	0	1	0	.143	.143
Shuba, George-George Thomas (Shotgun)	48-50,52-55BknN	12-13-24	Youngstown, Ohio		L	R	5'11	180	355	814	106	211	45	4	24	125	120	122	5	.259	.413
Sievers, Roy-Roy Edward (Squirrel)	49-53StLA 54-59WasA 60-61ChiA 62-64PhiN 64-65WasA	11-18-26	St. Louis, Mo.		R	R	6'1	204	1887	6387	945	1703	292	42	318	1147	841	920	14	.267	.475
Silvera, Al-Aaron Albert	55-56CinN	8-26-35	San Diego, Cal.		R	R	6'	180	14	7	3	1	0	0	0	2	0	1	0	.143	.143
Silvera, Charlie-Charles Anthony Ryan (Swede)	48-56NYA 57ChiN	10-13-24	San Francisco, Cal.		R	R	5'10	175	227	482	34	136	15	2	1	52	53	32	2	.282	.328
Simmons, John-John Earl	49WasA	7- 7-24	Birmingham, Ala.		R	R	6'1	192	62	93	12	20	0	0	0	5	11	6	0	.215	.215
Simpson, Harry-Harry Leon (Suitcase)	51-53,55CleA 55-57KCA 57-58NYA 58-59KCA 59ChiA 59PitN	12- 3-25	Atlanta, Ga.		L	R	6'1	180	888	2829	343	752	101	41	73	381	271	429	17	.266	.408
Sisler, Dick-Richard Allan	46-47StLN 48-51PhiN 52CinN 52-53StLN M64-65CinN	11- 2-20	St. Louis, Mo.		L	R	6'2	205	799	2606	302	720	118	28	55	360	226	253	6	.276	.406
Sisti, Sibby-Sebastian Daniel	39-42BosN 43-45MS 46-52BosN 53-54MilN	7-26-20	Buffalo, N.Y.		R	R	5'11	185	1016	2999	401	732	121	19	27	260	283	440	30	.244	.324
Skinner, Bob-Robert Ralph	54,56-63PitN 63-64CinN 64-66StLN M68-69PhiN	10- 3-31	La Jolla, Cal.		L	R	6'4	190	1381	4318	642	1198	197	58	103	531	485	646	67	.277	.421
Skizas, Lou-Louis Peter (The Nervous Greek)	56NYA 56-57KCA 58DetA 59ChiA	6- 2-32	Chicago, Ill.		R	R	5'11	175	239	725	80	196	27	4	30	86	50	37	8	.270	.443
Slaughter, Enos-Enos Bradsher (Country)	38-42StLN 43-45MS 46-53StLN 54-55NYA 55-56KCA 56-59NYA 59MilN	4-27-16	Roxboro, N.C.		L	R	5'9	190	2380	7946	1247	2383	413	148	169	1304	1018	538	71	.300	.453
Small, Jim-James Arthur	55-57DetA 58KCA	3- 8-37	Portland, Ore.		L	L	6'	180	108	141	22	38	6	2	0	10	10	22	0	.270	.340
Smalley, Roy-Roy Frederick Jr.	48-53ChiN 54MilN 55-58PhiN	6- 9-26	Springfield, Mo.		R	R	6'3	190	872	2644	277	601	103	33	61	305	257	541	4	.227	.360
Smaza, Joe-Joseph Paul	46ChiA	7- 7-23	Detroit, Mich.		L	L	5'11	175	2	5	2	1	0	0	0	0	0	0	0	.200	.200
Smith, Al-Alphonse Eugene (Fuzzy)	53-57CleA 58-62ChiA 63BalA 64CleA 64BosA	2- 7-28	Kirkwood, Mo.		R	R	6'	196	1517	5357	843	1458	258	46	164	676	674	768	67	.272	.429
Smith, Bobby Gene-Bobby Gene	57-59StLN 60-61PhiN 62NYN 62ChiN 62StLN 65CalA	5-28-34	Hood River, Ore.		R	R	5'11	190	476	962	101	234	35	5	13	96	55	154	5	.243	.331
Smith, Dick-Richard Harrison	51-55PitN	7-21-27	Blandsburg, Pa.		R	R	5'8	160	70	186	17	25	2	2	0	11	30	22	0	.134	.167
Smith, Earl-Earl Calvin	55PitN	3-14-28	Sunnyside, Wash.		R	R	6'	185	5	16	1	1	0	0	0	0	4	2	0	.063	.063
Smith, Hal-Harold Raymond (Cura)	56-61StLN 62-64IL 65PitN	6- 1-31	Barling, Ark.		R	R	5'10	186	570	1697	126	437	63	8	23	172	102	128	6	.258	.345
Smith, Hal-Harold Wayne	55-56BalA 56-59KCA 60-61PitN 62-63HouN 64CinN	12- 7-30	West Frankfort, Ill.		R	R	6'	195	879	2682	269	715	148	10	58	323	196	361	7	.267	.394
Smith, Milt-Milton	55CinN	3-27-29	Columbus, Ga.		R	R	5'10	165	36	102	15	20	3	1	3	8	13	24	2	.196	.333
Smith, Paul-Paul Leslie	53PitN 55-56MS 57-58PitN 58ChiN	3-19-31	New Castle, Pa.		L	L	5'8	165	223	562	54	152	16	7	7	56	42	44	3	.270	.361
Snider, Duke-Edwin Donald (The Silver Fox)	47-57BknN 58-62LAN 63NYN 64SFN	9-19-26	Los Angeles, Cal.		L	R	6'	195	2143	7161	1259	2116	358	85	407	1333	971	1237	99	.295	.540
Snyder, Jerry-Gerald George	52-58WasA	7-21-29	Jenks, Okla.		R	R	6'	170	266	630	60	145	18	2	3	47	46	59	7	.230	.279
Sommers, Bill-William Dunn	50StLA	2-17-24	Brooklyn, N.Y.		R	R	6'	180	65	137	24	35	5	1	0	14	25	14	0	.255	.307
Souchock, Steve-Stephen (Bud)	46,48NYA 49ChiA 51-55DetA	3-13-19	Yatesboro, Pa.		R	R	6'2	203	473	1227	163	313	58	20	50	186	88	164	15	.255	.457
Speake, Bob-Robert Charles (Spook)	55,57ChiN 58-59SFN	8-22-30	Springfield, Mo.		L	L	6'1	178	305	761	110	170	26	10	31	104	80	158	8	.223	.406
Spencer, Daryl-Daryl Dean (Big Dee)	52-53NYN 54-55MS 56-57NYN 58-59SFN 60-61StLN 61-63LAN 63CinN	7-13-29	Wichita, Kans.		R	R	6'2	195	1098	3689	457	901	145	20	105	428	449	516	13	.244	.380
Stallcup, Virgil-Thomas Virgil (Red)	47-52CinN 52-53StLN	1- 3-22	Ravensford, N.C.		R	R	6'3	185	587	2059	171	497	99	13	22	214	51	181	9	.241	.334
Stanky, Eddie-Edward Raymond (The Brat, Muggsy)	43-44ChiN 44-47BknN 48-49BosN 50-51NYN 52-53,M52-55StLN M66-68ChiA	9- 3-16	Philadelphia, Pa.		R	R	5'8	170	1259	4301	811	1154	185	35	29	364	996	374	48	.268	.348
Stephens, Gene-Glen Eugene	52-53,55-60BosA 60-61BalA 61-62KCA 63-64ChiA	1-20-33	Gravette, Ark.		L	R	6'3	185	964	1913	283	460	78	15	37	207	233	322	27	.240	.355
Stephens, Vern-Vernon Decatur (Buster, Junior)	41-47StLA 48-52BosA 53ChiA 53StLA 54-55BalA 55ChiA	10-23-20	McAlister, N.M.	11- 3-68	R	R	5'10	185	1720	6497	1001	1859	307	42	247	1174	692	685	25	.286	.460
Stephenson, Bobby-Robert Lloyd	55StLN	8-11-28	Blair, Okla.		R	R	6'	165	67	111	19	27	3	0	0	6	5	18	2	.243	.270
Stephenson, Joe-Joseph Chester	43NYN 44ChiN 45MS 47ChiA	6-30-21	Detroit, Mich.		R	R	6'2	185	29	67	8	12	1	0	0	4	2	15	1	.179	.194
Stevens, Chuck-Charles Augustus	41StLA 43-45MS 46,48StLA	7-10-18	Van Houten, N.M.		B	L	6'1	180	211	733	89	184	29	8	4	55	88	89	6	.251	.329
Stevens, Ed-Edward Lee (Big Ed)	45-47BknN 48-50PitN	1-12-25	Galveston, Tex.		L	L	6'1	190	375	1220	134	308	59	17	28	193	121	151	7	.252	.398
Stevens, R C-R C	58-60PitN 61WasA	7-22-34	Moultrie, Ga.		R	L	6'5	219	104	162	21	34	4	1	8	21	12	41	1	.210	.395
Stewart, Bill-William Wayne	55KCA	4-11-28	Bay City, Mich.		R	R	5'11	200	11	18	2	2	1	0	0	0	1	6	0	.111	.167
Stewart, Bud-Edward Perry	41-42PitN 43-44VR 44-45MS 48NYA 48-50WasA 51-54ChiA	6-15-16	Sacramento, Cal.		L	R	5'11	160	773	2041	288	547	96	32	32	260	252	157	29	.268	.393
Stirnweiss, Snuffy-George Henry	43-50NYA 50StLA 51-52CleA	10-26-18	New York, N.Y.	9-15-58	R	R	5'8	175	1028	3695	604	989	157	68	29	281	541	447	134	.268	.371
Streuli, Walt-Walter Herbert	54-56DetA	9-26-35	Memphis, Tenn.		R	R	6'2	195	6	12	1	3	2	0	0	2	2	2	0	.250	.417
Strickland, George-George Bevan (Bo)	50-52PitN 52-57CleA 58VR 59-60,M66CleA	1-10-26	New Orleans, La.		R	R	6'1	175	971	2824	305	633	84	27	36	284	362	453	12	.224	.311
Suder, Pete-Peter (Pecky)	41-43PhiA 44-45MS 46-54PhiA 55KCA	4-16-16	Aliquippa, Pa.		R	R	6'	175	1421	5085	469	1268	210	44	49	541	288	456	19	.249	.337
Sullivan, Russ-Russell Guy	51-53DetA	2-19-23	Fredricksburg, Va.		L	R	6'	196	45	150	16	40	8	2	5	12	18	11	1	.267	.447
Szekely, Joe-Joseph	53CinN	2- 2-25	Cleveland, Ohio		R	R	5'11	180	5	13	1	1	0	0	0	0	0	1	0	.077	.077
Talbot, Dale-Robert Dale	53-54ChiN	6- 6-27	Visalia, Cal.		R	R	6'	170	122	433	50	107	15	5	1	19	16	29	4	.247	.312
Tanner, Chuck-Charles William	55-57MilN 57-58ChiN 59-60CleA 61-62LAA M70-75ChiA	7- 4-29	New Castle, Pa.		L	L	6'	185	396	885	98	231	39	5	21	105	82	93	2	.261	.388
Tappe, El-Elvin Walter	54-56,58,60,62,M61-62ChiN	5-21-27	Quincy, Ill.		R	R	5'11	180	145	304	21	63	10	0	0	17	29	25	0	.207	.240
Tappe, Ted-Theodore Nash	50-51CinN 55ChiN 56IL	2- 2-31	Seattle, Wash.		L	R	6'3	185	34	58	13	15	2	0	5	11	12	12	0	.259	.552
Tasby, Willie-Willie	58-60BalA 60BosA 61-62WasA 62-63CleA	1- 8-33	Shreveport, La.		R	R	5'11	180	583	1868	246	467	61	10	46	174	201	327	12	.250	.367
Tate, Lee-Lee Willie (Skeeter)	58-59StLN	3-18-32	Black Rock, Ark.		R	R	5'10	165	51	85	9	14	3	1	1	5	9	10	0	.165	.259
Tatum, Tommy-Tommy	41BknN 42-45MS 47BknN 47CinN	7-16-19	Boyd, Tex.		R	R	6'	185	81	194	20	50	6	2	1	17	17	20	7	.258	.325
Taylor, Bennie-Benjamin Eugene	51StLA 52DetA 55MilN	9-30-24	Metropolis, Ill.		L	L	6'	195	52	121	16	28	2	1	3	6	11	31	1	.231	.339
Taylor, Bill-William Michael (Moose)	54-57NYN 57-58DetA	12-30-29	Alhambra, Cal.		L	R	6'4	212	149	173	17	41	8	0	7	26	5	39	0	.237	.405
Taylor, Fred-Frederick Rankin	50-52WasA	12- 3-24	Zanesville, Ohio		L	R	6'3	201	22	47	5	9	2	0	0	4	4	8	0	.191	.234
Taylor, Joe-Joe Cephus (Cash)	54PhiA 57CinN 58StLN 58-59BalA	3- 2-26	Chapman, Ala.		L	L	6'1	185	119	297	34	74	16	1	9	31	28	61	0	.249	.401
Taylor, Sammy-Samuel Douglas	58-62ChiN 62-63NYN 63CinN 63CleA	2-27-33	Woodruff, S.C.		L	R	6'2	185	473	1263	127	309	47	9	33	147	122	181	3	.245	.275
Tebbetts, Birdie-George Robert	36-42DetA 43-45MS 46-47DetA 47-50BosA 51-52CleA M54-58CinN M61-62MilN M63-66CleA	11-10-09	Burlington, Vt.		R	R	5'11	190	1162	3704	357	1000	169	22	38	469	389	261	29	.270	.358

USE NAME – GIVEN NAMES (NICKNAMES)	TEAM BY YEAR	BIRTH DATE	BIRTH PLACE	DEATH DATE	B	T	HGT	WGT	G	AB	R	H	2B	3B	HR	RBI	BB	SO	SB	BA	SA
					LIFETIME BATTING TOTALS																
Teed, Dick-Richard Leroy	53BknN	3- 8-26	Springfield, Mass.		B	R	5'11	180	1	1	0	0	0	0	0	0	0	1	0	.000	.000
Temple, Johnny-John Ellis	52-59CinN 60-61CleA 62BalA 62-63HouN 64CinN	8- 8-28	Lexington, N.C.		R	R	5'11	165	1420	5218	720	1484	208	36	22	395	648	338	140	.284	.351
Tepsic, Joe-Joseph John	46BknN	9-18-23	Slovan, Pa.		R	R	5'9	170	15	5	2	0	0	0	0	0	1	1	0	.000	.000
Terwilliger, Wayne-Willard Wayne (Twig)	49-51ChiN 51BknN 53-54WasA 55-56NYN 59-60KCA	6-27-25	Clare, Mich.		R	R	5'11	165	666	2091	271	501	93	10	22	162	247	296	31	.240	.325
Testa, Nick-Nicholas	58SFN	6-29-28	New York, N.Y.		R	R	5'8	180	1	0	0	0	0	0	0	0	0	0	0	–	–
Tettlebach, Dick-Richard Morley (Tut)	55NYA 56-57WasA	6-26-29	New Haven, Conn.		R	R	6'	195	29	80	12	12	1	2	1	10	18	17	0	.150	.250
Thomas, Bud-John Tillman	51StLA	3-10-29	Sedalia, Mo.		R	R	6'	160	14	20	3	7	0	0	1	1	0	3	2	.350	.500
Thomas, Frank-Frank Joseph	51-58PitN 59CinN 60-61ChiN 61MilN 62-64NYN 64-65PhiN 65HouN 65MilN 66ChiN	6-11-29	Pittsburgh, Pa.		R	R	6'3	205	1766	6285	792	1671	262	31	286	962	484	894	15	.266	.454
Thomas, Kite-Keith Marshall	52-53PhiA 53WasA	4-27-24	Kansas City, Kans.		R	R	6'1	195	137	223	35	52	9	3	7	32	34	40	0	.233	.395
Thomas, Leo-Leo Raymond (Tommy)	50,52StLA 52ChiA	7-26-24	Turlock, Cal.		R	R	5'11	178	95	269	32	57	11	1	1	27	43	25	2	.212	.271
Thomas, Valmy-Valmy	57NYN 58SFN 59PhiN 60BalA 61CleA	10-21-28	Santurce, P.R.		R	R	5'9	160	252	626	56	144	20	3	12	60	45	79	2	.230	.329
Thompson, Don-Donald Newlin	49BosN 51,53-54BknN	12-28-23	Swepsonville, N.C.		L	L	6'	185	217	307	52	67	8	0	1	19	31	32	4	.218	.254
Thompson, Hank-Henry Curtis	47StLA 49-56NYN	12- 8-25	Oklahoma City, Okla.	9-30-69	L	R	5'9	174	933	3003	492	801	104	34	129	482	493	337	33	.267	.453
Thompson, Tim-Charles Lemoine	54BknN 56-57KCA 58DetA	3- 1-24	Coalport, Pa.		L	R	5'11	190	187	517	49	123	24	2	8	47	39	52	2	.238	.338
Thomson, Bobby-Robert Brown (The Staten Island Scot)	46-53NYN 54-57MilN 57NYN 58-59ChiN 60BosA 60BalA	10-25-23	Glasgow, Scotland		R	R	6'2	185	1779	6305	903	1705	267	74	264	1026	559	804	38	.270	.462
Thorpe, Bob-Benjamin Robert	51-52BosN 53MilN	11-19-26	Caryville, Fla.		R	R	6'1	190	110	331	22	83	9	3	3	32	6	48	3	.251	.323
Throneberry, Faye-Maynard Faye	52BosA 53-54MS 55-57BosA 57-60WasA 61LAA	6-22-31	Memphis, Tenn.		L	R	5'11	185	521	1302	152	307	48	12	29	137	127	284	23	.236	.358
Throneberry, Marv-Marvin Eugene (Marvelous Marv)	55,58-59NYA 60-61KCA 61-62BalA 62-63NYN	9- 2-33	Collierville, Tenn.		L	L	6'1	195	480	1186	143	281	37	8	53	170	130	295	3	.237	.416
Thurman, Bob-Roberts Burns	55-59CinN	5-14-21	Wichita, Kans.		L	L	6'1	205	334	663	106	163	18	11	35	106	62	112	1	.246	.465
Tipton, Joe-Joe Hicks	48CleA 49ChiA 50-52PhiA 52-53CleA 54WasA	2-18-23	McCaysville, Ga.		R	R	5'11	185	417	1117	116	264	36	5	29	125	186	142	3	.236	.355
Torgeson, Earl-Clifford Earl (The Earl of Snohomish)	47-52BosN 53-55PhiN 55-57DetA 57-61ChiA 61NYA	1- 1-24	Snohomish, Wash.		L	L	6'3	190	1668	4969	848	1318	215	46	149	740	980	653	133	.265	.417
Torre, Frank-Frank Joseph	56-60MilN 62-63PhiN	12-30-31	Brooklyn, N.Y.		L	L	6'4	205	714	1482	150	404	70	15	10	170	155	01	1	.270	.372
Triandos, Gus-Gus	53-54NYA 55-62BalA 63DetA 64-65PhiN 65HouN	7-30-30	San Francisco, Cal.		R	R	6'3	215	1206	3907	389	954	147	6	167	608	440	636	1	.244	.413
Troupe, Quincy-Quincy Thomas	52CleA	12-25-12	Dublin, Ga.		B	R	6'2	225	6	10	1	1	0	0	0	0	1	3	0	.100	.100
Tucker, Thurman-Thurman Lowell (Joe E.)	42-44ChiA 45MS 46-47ChiA 48-51CleA	9-26-17	Gordon, Tex.		L	R	5'10	165	701	2231	325	570	79	24	9	179	291	237	77	.255	.325
Turner, Earl-Earl Edwin	48,50PitN	5- 6-23	Pittsfield, Mass.		R	R	5'9	170	42	75	10	18	0	0	3	5	4	13	1	.240	.360
Tuttle, Bill-William Robert	52,54-57DetA 58-61KCA 61-63MinA	7- 4-29	Elwood, Ill.		R	R	6'	190	1270	4268	578	1105	149	47	67	443	480	416	38	.259	.363
Umphlett, Tommy-Thomas Mullen	53BosA 54-55WasA	5-12-30	Scotland Neck, N.C.		R	R	6'2	180	361	1160	108	285	45	8	6	111	75	107	7	.246	.314
Upright, Dixie-Roy T.	53StLA	5-30-26	Kannapolis, N.C.		L	L	6'	175	9	8	3	2	0	0	1	1	1	3	0	.250	.625
Upton, Tom-Thomas Herbert (Muscles)	50-51StLA 52WasA	12-29-26	Esther, Mo.		R	R	6'	160	181	525	60	118	9	9	2	42	65	67	8	.225	.288
Usher, Bob-Robert Royce	46-47,50-51CinN 52ChiN 57CleA 57WasA	3- 1-25	San Diego, Cal.		R	R	6'1	180	428	1101	133	259	41	4	18	102	90	136	9	.235	.329
Valdivielso, Jose-Jose [Lopez]	55-56,59-60WasA 61MinA	5-22-34	Matanzas, Cuba		R	R	6'1	175	401	971	89	213	26	8	9	85	79	132	6	.219	.290
Valenzuela, Benny-Benjamin Beltran (Papalero)	58StLN	6- 2-33	Los Mochis, Mexico		R	R	5'10	175	10	14	0	3	1	0	0	0	1	0	0	.214	.286
Valo, Elmer-Elmer William	40-43PhiA 44-45MS 46-54PhiA 55-56KCA 56PhiN 57BknN 58LAN 59CleA 60NYA 60WasA 61MinA 61PhiN	3- 5-21	Ribnik, Czechoslov.		L	R	5'11	190	1806	5029	768	1420	228	73	58	601	943	284	110	.282	.391
Van Dusen, Fred-Frederick William	55PhiN	7-31-37	Queens, N.Y.		L	L	6'3	180	1	0	0	0	0	0	0	0	0	0	0	–	–
Van Noy, Jay-Jay Lowell	51StLN	11- 4-28	Garland, Utah		L	R	6'1	200	6	7	1	0	0	0	0	0	1	6	0	.000	.000
Varner, Buck-Glen Gann	52WasA	8-17-30	Hixson, Tenn.		L	R	5'10	170	2	4	0	0	0	0	0	0	1	1	0	.000	.000
Veal, Coot-Orville Inman	58-60DetA 61WasA 62PitN 63DetA	7- 9-32	Sandersville, Ga.		R	R	6'1	165	247	611	75	141	26	3	1	51	56	69	2	.231	.288
Verban, Emil-Emil Matthew (Dutch, The Antelope)	44-46StLN 46-48PhiN 48-50ChiN 50BosN	8-27-15	Lincoln, Ill.		R	R	5'11	165	853	2911	301	793	99	26	1	241	108	74	21	.272	.325
Verble, Gene-Gene Kermit (Satchel)	51,53WasA	6-29-28	Concord, N.C.		R	R	5'10	163	81	198	20	40	3	2	0	17	20	11	1	.202	.237
Verdi, Frank-Frank Michael	53NYA	6- 2-26	Brooklyn, N.Y.		R	R	5'10	170	1	0	0	0	0	0	0	0	0	0	0	–	–
Vernon, Mickey-James Barton	39-43WasA 44-45MS 46-48WasA 49-50CleA 50-55WasA 56-57BosA 58CleA 59MilN 60PitN M61-63WasA	4-22-18	Marcus Hook, Pa.		L	L	6'2	184	2409	8731	1196	2495	490	120	172	1311	934	869	137	.286	.428
Vico, George-George Steve (Sam)	48-49DetA	8- 9-23	San Fernando, Cal.		L	R	6'4	200	211	663	65	166	28	11	12	76	60	56	2	.250	.380
Virdon, Bill-William Charles (Quail)	55-56StLN 56-65,68,M72-73PitN M74-75NYA M75HouN	6- 9-31	Hazel Park, Mich.		L	R	6'	185	1583	5980	735	1596	237	81	91	502	442	647	47	.267	.379
Virgil, Ozzie-Osvaldo Jose	56-57NYN 58,60-61DetA 61KCA 62BalA 65PitN 66,69SFN	5-17-33	Montecristi, Dom. Rep.		R	R	6'1	174	324	753	75	174	19	7	14	73	34	91	6	.231	.331
Vollmer, Clyde-Clyde Frederick	42CinN 43-45MS 46-48CinN 48-50WasA 50-53BosA 53-54WasA	9-24-21	Cincinnati, Ohio		R	R	6'1	190	685	2021	283	508	77	10	69	339	243	328	7	.251	.402
Wade, Gale-Galeard Lee	55-56ChiN	1-20-29	Hollister, Mo.		L	R	6'1	185	19	45	5	6	1	0	1	1	5	3	0	.133	.222
Wahl, Kermit-Kermit Emerson	44-45,47CinN 50-51PhiA 51StLA	11-18-22	Columbia, S.D.		R	R	5'11	170	231	642	58	145	23	6	3	50	68	72	3	.226	.294
Waitkus, Eddie-Edward Stephen	41ChiN 42-45MS 46-48ChiN 49-53PhiN 54-55BalA 55PhiN	9- 4-19	Cambridge, Mass.	9-15-72	L	L	6'	180	1140	4254	528	1214	215	44	24	373	372	204	28	.285	.374
Wakefield, Dick-Richard Cummings	41,43-44DetA 45MS 46-49DetA 50NYA 52NYN	5- 6-21	Chicago, Ill.		L	R	6'4	210	638	2132	334	625	102	29	56	315	360	270	10	.293	.447
Walker, Harry-Harry William (The Hat)	40-43StLN 44-45MS 46-47StLN 47-48PhiN 49ChiN 49CinN 50-51,55,M55StLN M65-67PitN M68-72HouN	10-22-16	Pascagoula, Miss.		L	R	6'2	175	807	2651	385	786	126	37	10	214	245	175	42	.296	.383
Walker, Rube-Albert Bluford	48-51ChiN 51-57BknN 58LAN	5-16-26	Lenoir, N.C.		L	R	6'	185	608	1585	114	360	69	3	35	192	150	213	3	.227	.341
Wallaesa, Jack-John	40,42PhiA 43-45MS 46PhiA 47-48ChiA	8-31-19	Easton, Pa.		B Bats Right 40	R	6'3	191	219	584	56	120	17	4	15	61	39	138	3	.205	.325
Walls, Lee-Ray Lee	52,56-57PitN 57-59ChiN 60CinN 60-61PhiN 62-64LAN	1- 6-33	San Diego, Cal.		R	R	6'3	205	902	2558	331	670	88	31	66	284	245	470	21	.262	.398
Walters, Ken-Kenneth Rogers	60-61PhiN 63CinN	11-11-33	Fresno, Cal.		R	R	6'1	180	259	681	71	157	20	2	11	58	25	89	6	.231	.314
Ward, Preston-Preston Meyer	48BknN 50ChiN 51-52MS 53ChiN 53-56PitN 56-58CleA 58-59KCA	7-24-27	Columbia, Mo.		L	R	6'4	190	744	2067	219	522	83	15	50	262	231	315	7	.253	.380
Watlington, Neal-Julius Neal	53PhiA	12-25-22	Yanceyville, N.C.		L	R	6'	195	21	44	4	7	1	0	0	3	3	8	0	.159	.182
Webster, Ray-Raymond George	59CleA 60BosA	11-15-37	Grass Valley, Cal.		R	R	6'	175	47	77	11	15	2	1	2	11	6	7	1	.195	.325
Weigel, Ralph-Ralph Richard (Wig)	46CleA 48ChiA 49WasA	10- 2-21	Coldwater, Ohio		R	R	6'1	180	106	235	12	54	9	3	0	30	21	26	2	.230	.294
Wellman, Bob-Robert Joseph	48,50PhiA	7-15-25	Cincinnati, Ohio		R	R	6'4	210	15	25	2	7	0	1	1	1	3	5	0	.280	.480
Wells, Leo-Leo Donald	42ChiA 43-45MS 46ChiA	7-18-17	Kansas City, Kans.		R	R	5'9	170	80	189	19	36	6	1	2	15	16	39	4	.190	.265
Wertz, Vic-Victor Woodrow	47-52DetA 52-53StLA 54BalA 54-58CleA 59-61BosA 61-63DetA 63MinA	2- 9-25	York, Pa.		L	R	6'	195	1862	6099	867	1692	289	42	266	1178	828	842	9	.277	.469
Westlake, Jim-James Patrick	55PhiN	7- 3-30	Sacramento, Cal.		L	L	6'1	190	1	1	0	0	0	0	0	0	0	1	0	.000	.000
Westlake, Wally-Waldon Thomas	47-51PitN 51-52StLN 52CinN 52-55CleA 55BalA 56PhiN	11- 8-20	Gridley, Cal.		R	R	6'	195	958	3117	474	848	107	33	127	539	317	453	19	.272	.450
Westrum, Wes-Wesley Noreen	47-57NYN M65-67NYN M74-75SFN	11-28-22	Clearbrook, Minn.		R	R	5'11	190	919	2322	302	503	59	8	96	315	489	508	10	.217	.373
Wheeler, Don-Donald Wesley (Scotty)	49ChiA	9-29-22	Minneapolis, Minn.		R	R	5'10	175	67	192	17	46	9	2	1	22	27	19	2	.240	.323
Whisenant, Pete-Thomas Peter	52BosN 55StLN 56ChiN 57-60CinN 60CleA 60WasA	12-14-29	Asheville, N.C.		R	R	6'2	200	475	988	140	221	46	8	37	134	86	196	17	.224	.399
White, Charlie-Charles	54-55MilN	8-12-28	Kingston, N.C.		L	R	5'11	192	62	123	17	29	5	0	1	12	14	15	0	.236	.301
White, Don-Donald William	48-49PhiA	1- 8-19	Everett, Wash.		R	R	6'1	195	143	422	41	98	20	2	1	38	33	28	2	.232	.296
White, Ed-Edward Perry	55ChiA	4- 6-26	Anniston, Ala.		R	R	6'2	200	3	4	0	2	0	0	0	0	1	1	0	.500	.500
White, Fuzz-Albert Eugene	40StLA 47NYN	6-27-18	Springfield, Mo.		L	R	6'	175	9	15	3	3	0	0	0	0	0	0	0	.200	.200
White, Sammy-Samuel Charles	51-59BosA 60VR 61MilN 62PhiN	7- 7-28	Wenatchee, Wash.		R	R	6'3	195	1043	3502	324	916	167	20	66	421	218	381	14	.262	.377
Whitman, Dick-Dick Corwin	46-49BknN 50-51PhiN	11- 9-20	Woodburn, Ore.		L	R	5'11	170	285	638	93	165	37	3	2	67	51	46	10	.259	.335
Whitman, Frank-Walter Franklin (Hooker)	46,48ChiA	8-15-24	Marengo, Ind.		R	R	6'2	175	20	22	7	1	0	0	0	1	2	9	0	.045	.045
Wilbur, Del-Delbert Quentin (Babe)	46-49StLN 51-52PhiN 52-54BosA M73TexA	2-24-19	Lincoln Park, Mich.		R	R	6'3	200	299	720	67	174	35	7	19	115	44	96	1	.242	.389
Wilhelm, Spider-Charles Ernest	53PhiA	5-23-29	Baltimore, Md.		R	R	5'9	170	7	7	1	2	1	0	0	0	0	3	0	.286	.429
Will, Bob-Robert Lee (Butch)	57-58,60-63ChiN	7-15-31	Irwin, Ill.		L	L	5'10	175	410	819	87	202	35	9	9	87	83	119	2	.247	.344
Williams, Davey-David Carlous	49,51-55NYN	11- 2-27	Dallas, Tex.		R	R	5'10	160	517	1785	235	450	61	10	32	163	164	144	6	.252	.351
Williams, Dick-Richard Hirschfeld	51-54,56BknN 56-57BalA 57CleA 58BalA 59-60KCA 61-62BalA 63-64,M67-69BosA M71-73OakA M74-75CalA	5- 7-29	St. Louis, Mo.		R	R	6'	190	475	1574	198	421	74	12	29	201	133	140	7	.267	.385
Williams, Ted-Theodore Samuel (Thumper, The Splendid Splinter)	39-42BosA 43-45MS 46-60BosA M69-71WasA M72TexA	8-30-18	San Diego, Cal.		L	R	6'3	200	2292	7706	1798	2654	525	71	521	1839	2019	709	24	.344	.634
Wilson, Archie-Archie Clifton	51-52NYA 52WasA 52BosA	11-25-23	Los Angeles, Cal.		R	R	5'11	175	51	140	9	31	5	3	0	17	7	14	0	.221	.300
Wilson, Artie-Arthur Lee	51NYN	10-28-20	Springfield, Ala.		L	R	5'11	168	19	22	2	4	0	0	0	1	2	1	2	.182	.182
Wilson, Bill-William Donald	50ChiA 51-52MS 53-54ChiA 54PhiA 55KCA	11- 6-28	Central City, Neb.		R	R	6'2	200	224	654	87	145	23	1	32	77	72	136	2	.222	.407
Wilson, Bob-Robert	58LAN	2-22-28	Dallas, Tex.		R	R	5'11	197	3	5	0	1	0	0	0	0	0	1	0	.200	.200
Wilson, George-George Washington (Teddy)	52ChiA 52-53,56NYN 56NYA	8-30-25	Cherryville, N.C.	10-29-74	L	R	6'1	185	145	209	15	40	8	0	3	19	14	32	0	.191	.273
Wilson, Grady-Grady Herbert	48PitN	11-23-22	Columbus, Ga.		R	R	6'	170	12	10	1	1	1	0	0	1	0	3	0	.100	.200
Wilson, Neil-Sammy O'Neil	60SFN	6-14-35	Lexington, Tenn.		L	R	6'1	175	6	10	0	0	0	0	0	0	1	2	0	.000	.000
Wilson, Red-Robert James	51-54ChiA 54-60DetA 60CleA	3- 7-29	Milwaukee, Wis.		R	R	6'	198	601	1763	206	455	84	8	24	189	214	163	25	.258	.356
Winceniak, Ed-Edward Joseph	56-57ChiN	4-16-29	Chicago, Ill.		R	R	5'9	165	32	67	6	14	3	0	1	8	3	12	0	.209	.299
Wise, Casey-Kendall Cole	57ChiN 58-59MilN 60DetA	9- 8-32	Lafayette, Ind.		B	R	6'	170	126	321	37	56	6	3	3	17	29	36	2	.174	.240

USE NAME – GIVEN NAMES (NICKNAMES)	TEAM BY YEAR	BIRTH DATE	BIRTH PLACE	DEATH DATE	B	T	HGT	WGT	G	AB	R	H	2B	3B	HR	RBI	BB	SO	SB	BA	SA
					LIFETIME BATTING TOTALS																
Witte, Jerry-Jerome Charles	46-47StLA	7-30-15	St. Louis, Mo.		R	R	6'1	190	52	172	11	28	4	1	4	16	11	40	0	.163	.267
Wood, Ken-Kenneth Lanier	48-51StLA 52BosA 52-53WasA	7- 1-24	Lincolnton, N.C.		R	R	6'	200	342	995	110	223	52	7	34	143	102	141	1	.224	.393
Woodling, Gene-Eugene Richard	43CleA 44-45MS 46CleA 47PitN 49-54NYA 55BalA 55-57CleA 58-60BalA 61-62WasA 62NYN	8-16-22	Akron, Ohio		L	R	5'10	195	1796	5587	830	1585	257	63	147	830	920	477	29	.284	.431
Wooten, Earl-Earl Hazwell (Junior)	47-48WasA	1-16-24	Pelzer, S.C.		R	L	5'11	160	94	282	34	68	8	3	1	24	24	25	3	.241	.301
Workman, Hank-Henry Kilgariff	50NYA	2- 5-26	Los Algeles, Cal.		L	R	6'1	185	2	5	1	1	0	0	0	0	0	1	0	.200	.200
Wright, Tom-Thomas Everette	48-51BosA 52StLA 52-53ChiA 54-56WasA	9-22-23	Shelby, N.C.		L	R	5'11	185	341	685	75	175	28	11	6	99	77	123	2	.255	.355
Wyrostek, Johnny-John Barney	42-43PitN 44-45MS 46-47PhiN 48-52CinN 52-54PhiN	7-12-19	Fairmont City, Ill.		L	R	6'2	180	1221	4240	525	1149	209	45	58	481	482	437	33	.271	.383
Yankowski, George-George Edward	42PhiA 43-46MS 49ChiA	11-19-22	Cambridge, Mass.		R	R	6'	180	10	31	0	5	2	0	0	4	0	4	0	.161	.226
Yewcic, Tom-Thomas J. (Kibby) 61-66 played in A.F.L.	57DetA	5- 9-32	Conemaugh, Pa.		R	R	5'11	180	1	1	0	0	0	0	0	0	0	0	0	.000	.000
Yost, Eddie-Edward Frederick Joseph (The Walking Man)	44WasA 45MS 46-58WasA 59-60DetA 61-62LAA	10-13-26	Brooklyn, N.Y.		R	R	5'10	180	2109	7346	1215	1863	337	56	139	683	1614	920	72	.254	.371
Young, Bobby-Robert George	48StLN 51-53StLA 54-55BalA 55-56CleA 58PhiN	11-22-25	Granite, Md.		L	R	6'1	175	687	2447	244	609	68	28	15	137	208	212	18	.249	.318
Young, Dick-Richard Ennis	51-52PhiN	6- 3-28	Seattle, Wash.		L	R	5'11	175	20	77	10	18	6	0	0	2	4	9	1	.234	.312
					Bats Both 52																
Yvars, Sal-Salvador Anthony	47-53NYN 53-54StLN	2-20-24	New York, N.Y.		R	R	5'10	193	210	418	41	102	12	0	10	42	37	41	1	.244	.344
Zarilla, Al-Allen Lee (Zeke)	43-44StLA 45MS 46-49STLA 49-50BosA 51-52ChiA 52StLA 52-53BosA	5- 1-19	Los Angeles, Cal.		L	R	5'11	185	1120	3535	507	975	186	43	61	456	415	382	33	.276	.405
Zauchin, Norm-Norbert Henry	51BosA 52-53MS 55-57BosA 58-59WasA	11-17-29	Royal Oak, Mich.		R	R	6'5	220	346	1038	134	242	28	2	50	159	137	226	5	.233	.408
Zernial, Gus-Gus Edward (Ozark Ike)	49-51ChiA 51-54PhiA 55-57KCA 58-59DetA	6-27-23	Beaumont, Tex.		R	R	6'2	210	1234	4131	572	1093	159	22	237	776	383	755	15	.265	.486
Zientara, Benny-Benedict Joseph	41CinN 42-45MS 46-48CinN	2-14-20	Chicago, Ill.		R	R	5'8	150	278	906	106	230	29	5	2	49	50	48	5	.254	.304
Zimmer, Don-Donald William	54-57BknN 58-59LAN 60-61ChiN 62NYN 62CinN 63LAN 63-65WasA M72-73SDN	1-17-31	Cincinnati, Ohio		R	R	5'9	175	1095	3283	353	773	130	22	91	352	246	678	45	.235	.372
Zupo, Frank-Frank Joseph (Noodles)	57-58,61BalA	8-29-39	San Francisco, Cal.		L	R	5'11	182	16	18	3	3	1	0	0	0	2	6	0	.167	.222

USE NAME – GIVEN NAMES (NICKNAMES)	TEAM BY YEAR	BIRTH DATE	BIRTH PLACE	DEATH DATE	LIFETIME PITCHING TOTALS																	BATTING TOTALS			
					B	T	HGT	WGT	W	L	PCT	SV	G	GS	CG	IP	H	BB	SO	ShO	ERA	AB	H	HR	BA
Aber, Al-Albert Julius	50CleA 51-52MS 53-CleA 53-57DetA 57KCA	7-31-27	Cleveland, Ohio		L	L	6'2	200	24	25	.490	14	168	30	7	390	398	160	169	0	4.18	100	14	0	.140
Abernathie, Bill-William Edward	52CleA	1-30-29	Torrance, Cal.		R	R	5'10	190	0	0	–	0	1	0	0	2	4	1	0	0	13.50	1	0	0	.000
Abernathy, Woody-Virgil Woodrow	46-47NYN	2- 1-15	Forest City, N.C.		L	L	6'	170	1	1	.500	1	16	1	0	42	36	11	6	0	3.64	8	0	0	.000
Acker, Tom-Thomas James (Shoulders)	56-59CinN	3- 7-30	Paterson, N.J.		R	R	6'4	220	19	13	.594	8	153	23	5	381	365	150	256	1	4.13	77	5	0	.065
Adams, Red-Charles Dwight	46ChiN	10- 7-21	Parlier, Cal.		R	R	6'2	200	0	1	.000	0	8	0	0	12	18	7	8	0	8.25	1	0	0	.000
Adkins, Dewey-John Dewey	42-43WasA 49ChiN	5-11-18	Norcatur, Kans.		R	R	6'2	195	2	4	.333	0	38	6	1	98	114	50	47	0	5.69	22	5	1	.227
Albanese, Joe-Joseph Peter	58WasA	6-26-33	New York, N.Y.		R	R	6'3	215	0	0	–	0	6	0	0	6	8	2	3	0	4.50	0	0	0	–
Albosta, Ed-Edward John (Rube)	41BknN 43-45MS 46PitN	10-27-18	Saginaw, Mich.		R	R	6'1	175	0	8	.000	0	19	8	0	53	52	43	24	0	6.11	12	1	0	.083
Albrecht, Ed-Edward Arthur	49-50StLA	2-28-29	St. Louis Co., Mo.		R	R	5'10	165	1	1	.500	0	3	2	1	12	7	11	2	0	5.25	3	0	0	.000
Alexander, Bob-Robert Somerville	55BalA CleA	8- 7-22	Vancouver, Canada		R	R	6'2	205	1	1	.500	0	9	0	0	11	18	7	2	0	10.64	1	0	0	.000
Aloma, Luis-Luis [Barba] (Witto)	50-53ChiA	6-19-23	Havana, Cuba		R	R	6'2	195	18	3	.857	15	116	1	1	235	212	111	115	1	3.45	48	8	0	.167
Amor, Vicente-Vicente [Alvarez]	55ChiN 57CinN	8- 8-32	Havana, Cuba		R	R	6'3	182	1	3	.250	0	13	4	1	33	50	13	12	0	5.73	6	1	0	.167
Anderson, Bob-Robert Carl	57-62ChiN 63DetA	9-29-35	East Chicago, Ind.		R	R	6'4	210	36	46	.439	13	246	93	15	841	858	319	502	1	4.26	246	33	2	.134
Andre, John-John Edward (Long John)	55ChiN	1- 3-23	Brockton, Mass.		L	R	6'4	200	0	1	.000	1	22	3	0	45	45	28	19	0	5.80	9	1	0	.111
Andrews, Hub-Hubert Carl	47-48NYN	8-31-22	Burbank, Okla.		R	R	6'	170	0	0	–	0	8	0	0	12	17	4	2	0	4.50	0	0	0	–
Antonelli, Johnny-John August	48-50BosN 51-52MS 53MilN 54-57NYN	4-12-30	Rochester, N.Y.		L	L	6'1	185	126	110	.534	21	377	268	102	1992	1870	687	1162	25	3.34	679	121	15	.178
	58-60SFN 61CleA 61MilN																								
Ardizoia, Rugger-Rinaldo Joseph	47NYA	11-20-19	Oleggio, Italy		R	R	5'11	180	0	0	–	0	1	0	0	2	4	1	0	0	9.00	0	0	0	–
Arias, Rudy-Rodolfo [Martinez]	59ChiA	6- 6-31	Mordoza, Cuba		L	L	5'10	165	2	0	1.00	2	34	0	0	44	49	20	28	0	4.09	4	0	0	.000
Arroyo, Luis-Luis Enrique (Yo-Yo)	55StLN 56-57PitN 59CinN 60-63NYA	2-18-27	Penuelas, P.R.		L	L	5'8	178	40	32	.556	44	244	36	10	533	524	208	336	1	3.92	128	29	1	.227
Atkins, Jim-James Curtis (Buddy)	50,52BosA	3-10-21	Birmingham, Ala.		L	R	6'3	205	0	1	.000	0	4	1	0	15	15	11	2	0	3.60	5	2	0	.400
Avrea, Jim-James Epherium (Jay)	50CinN	7- 6-20	Cleburne, Tex.		R	R	6'1	175	0	0	–	0	2	0	0	5	6	3	2	0	3.60	2	0	0	.000
Ayers, Bill-William Oscar	47NYN	8-27-18	Newnan, Ga.		R	R	6'3	185	0	3	.000	1	13	4	0	35	46	14	22	0	8.23	8	2	0	.250
Baczewski, Fred-Frederic John (Lefty)	53ChiN 53-55CinN	5-15-26	St. Paul, Minn.		L	L	6'2	185	17	10	.630	1	63	40	14	279	306	111	104	2	4.45	89	12	1	.135
Bahr, Ed-Edson Garfield	46-47PitN	10-16-19	Rouleau, Canada		R	R	6'1	172	11	11	.500	0	46	25	8	219	210	95	69	0	3.37	68	10	0	.147
Bailey, Jim-James Hopkins	59CinN	12-16-34	Strawberry Pl., Tenn.		B	L	6'2	210	0	1	.000	0	3	1	0	12	17	6	7	0	6.00	3	0	0	.000
Bamberger, George-George Irvin	51-52NYN 59BalA	8- 1-25	Staten Island, N.Y.		R	R	6'	175	0	0	–	1	10	1	0	14	25	10	3	0	9.64	2	0	0	.000
Bankhead, Dan-Daniel Robert	47,50-51BknN	5- 3-20	Empire, Ala.		R	R	6'1	184	9	5	.643	4	53	13	2	153	161	110	111	1	6.53	45	10	1	.222
Banta, Jack-John Kay	45-50BknN	6-24-25	Hutchinson, Kans.		L	R	6'2	175	14	12	.538	5	69	19	3	204	176	113	116	1	3.79	61	7	0	.115
Barclay, Curt-Curtis Cordell	57NYN 58-59SFN	8-22-31	Chicago, Ill.		R	R	6'3	210	10	9	.526	0	44	29	5	199	214	55	73	2	3.48	64	15	0	.234
Barnes, Frank-Frank	57-58,60StLN	8-26-28	Longwood, Miss.		R	R	6'	185	0	2	.000	1	6	3	0	17	23	16	2	0	7.94	10	1	0	.100
Barney, Rex-Rex Edward	43BknN 44-45MS 46-50BknN	12-19-24	Omaha, Neb.		R	R	6'3	185	35	31	.530	1	155	81	20	599	474	410	336	6	4.33	201	33	0	.164
Baumann, Frank-Frank Matt (The Beau)	55-59BosA 60-64ChiA 65ChiN	7- 1-33	St. Louis, Mo.		L	L	6'	205	45	38	.542	13	244	78	19	798	856	300	384	4	4.11	225	49	2	.218
Beamon, Charlie-Charles Alonzo	56-58BalA	12-25-34	Oakland, Cal.		R	R	5'11	195	3	3	.500	0	27	5	1	72	64	36	45	1	3.88	17	0	0	.000
Beard, Ralph-Ralph William	54StLN	2-11-29	Cincinnati, Ohio		R	R	6'5	200	0	4	.000	0	13	10	0	58	62	28	17	0	3.72	17	1	0	.059
Bearden, Gene-Henry Eugene	47-50CleA 50-51WasA 51DetA 52StLA 53ChiA	9- 5-20	Lexa, Ark.		L	L	6'4	198	45	38	.542	1	193	84	29	789	791	435	259	7	3.96	288	68	4	.236
Beers, Clarence-Clarence Scott	48StLN	12- 9-18	El Dorado, Kans.		R	R	6'	175	0	0	–	0	1	0	0	1	3	1	0	0	9.00	0	0	0	–
Behrman, Hank-Henry Bernard	46-47BknN 47PitN 47-48BknN 49NYN	6-27-21	Brooklyn, N.Y.		R	R	5'11	174	24	17	.585	19	174	27	5	430	427	228	189	2	4.40	115	14	0	.122
Bell, Bill-William Samuel (Ding Dong)	52PitN 53-54MS 55PitN	10-24-33	Goldsboro, N.C.	10-11-62	R	R	6'3	200	0	1	.000	0	5	1	0	17	16	14	4	0	4.24	4	0	0	.000
Besana, Fred-Frederick Cyril	56BalA	4- 5-31	Lincoln, Cal.		R	L	6'3	200	1	0	1.000	0	7	2	0	18	22	14	7	0	5.50	4	0	0	.000
Bessent, Don-Fred Donald (The Weasel)	55-57BknN 58LAN	3-13-31	Jacksonville, Fla.		R	R	6'	175	14	7	.667	12	108	2	1	210	196	88	118	0	3.34	44	5	0	.114
Bevens, Bill-Floyd Clifford	44-47NYA	10-21-16	Hubbard, Ore.		R	R	6'3	210	40	36	.526	0	96	84	46	643	598	236	289	6	3.08	221	22	3	.100
Bickford, Vern-Vernon Edgell	48-52BosN 53MilN 54BalA	8-27-20	Hellier, Ky.	5- 6-60	R	R	6'	180	66	57	.537	2	182	149	73	1077	1040	467	540	9	3.71	365	57	0	.156
Bicknell, Charlie-Charles Stephen (Bud)	48-49PhiN	7-27-28	Plainfield, N.J.		R	R	5'11	170	0	1	.000	0	30	1	0	54	61	34	9	0	6.83	6	0	0	.000
Bilbrey, Jim-James Melvin	49StLA	4-20-24	Rickman, Tenn.		R	R	6'2	205	0	0	–	0	1	0	0	1	1	3	0	0	18.00	0	0	0	–
Birrer, Babe-Werner Joseph	55DetA 56BalA 58LAN	7- 4-28	Buffalo, N.Y.		R	R	6'	195	4	3	.571	4	56	3	1	119	129	37	45	0	4.39	27	7	2	.259
Biscan, Frank-Frank Stephen (Porky)	42StLA 43-45MS 46,48StLA	3-13-20	Mt. Olive, Ill.	5-22-59	L	L	5'11	190	7	9	.438	4	74	4	1	149	170	104	64	0	5.26	35	5	0	.143
Bishop, Charlie-Charles Tuller	52-54PhiA 55KCA	1- 1-24	Atlanta, Ga.		R	R	6'2	195	10	22	.313	3	69	37	6	295	307	168	121	1	5.31	100	11	0	.110
Black, Bill-William Carroll (Bud)	52DetA 53-54MS 55-56DetA	7- 9-32	St. Louis, Mo.		R	R	6'3	197	2	3	.400	0	10	5	1	32	36	18	14	1	4.22	9	1	0	.111
Black, Joe-Joseph	52-55BknN 55-56CinN 57WasA	2- 8-24	Plainfield, N.J.		R	R	6'2	220	30	12	.714	25	172	16	2	415	391	129	222	0	3.90	96	13	0	.135
Blackburn, Jim-James Ray (Bones)	48,51CinN	6-19-24	Warsaw, Ky.	10-26-69	R	R	6'4	175	0	2	.000	0	18	0	0	36	46	16	11	0	5.50	6	0	0	.000
Blackburn, Ron-Ronald Hamilton	58-59PitN	4-23-35	Mt. Airy, N.C.		R	R	6'	160	3	2	.600	4	64	2	0	108	111	42	50	0	3.50	12	3	1	.250
Blackwell, Ewell-Ewell (The Whip)	42CinN 43-45MS 46-52CinN	10-23-22	Fresno, Cal.		R	R	6'6	195	82	78	.513	11	236	169	69	1322	1150	562	839	16	3.30	443	77	1	.174
	52-53NYA 55KCA																								
Blake, Ed-Edward James	51-53CinN 57KCA	2-23-25	E. St. Louis, Ill.		R	R	5'11	175	0	0	–	0	8	0	0	9	15	4	1	0	8.00	0	0	0	–
Blaylock, Bob-Robert Edward	56,59StLN	6-28-35	Chattanooga, Okla.		R	R	6'1	185	1	7	.125	0	17	7	0	50	53	27	42	0	5.94	12	1	0	.083
Blaylock, Gary-Gary Nelson	59StLN 59NYA	10-11-31	Clarkton, Mo.		R	R	6'	196	4	6	.400	0	41	13	3	126	147	58	81	0	4.79	36	5	2	.139
Blemker, Ray-Ray (Buddy)	60KCA	8- 9-37	Huntingberg, Ind.		R	L	5'11	190	0	0	–	0	1	0	0	2	3	2	0	0	22.50	0	0	0	–
Blyzka, Mike-Michael John	53StLA 54BalA	12-25-28	Hamtramck, Mich.		R	R	6'	205	3	11	.214	1	70	9	2	180	193	107	58	0	5.60	38	2	0	.053
Bokelmann, Dick-Richard Werner	51-53StLN	10-26-26	Arlington Hts., Ill.		R	R	6'	185	3	4	.429	3	34	1	0	68	73	38	27	0	4.90	14	0	0	.000
Borland, Tom-Thomas Bruce (Spike)	60-61BosA	2-14-33	El Dorado, Kans.		L	L	6'3	172	0	4	.000	3	27	4	0	52	70	23	32	0	6.75	13	0	0	.000
Bowman, Roger-Roger Clinton	49,51-52NYN 53,55PitN	8-18-27	Amsterdam, N.Y.		R	L	6'	175	2	11	.154	0	50	12	0	117	137	71	75	0	5.85	18	3	0	.167
Boyer, Cloyd-Cloyd Victor (Junior)	49-52StLN 55KCA	9- 1-27	Alba, Mo.		R	R	6'1	188	20	23	.465	2	112	48	13	394	393	218	198	4	4.75	120	20	0	.167
Bradford, Bill-William D	56KCA	8-28-21	Choctaw, Ark.		R	R	6'2	180	0	0	–	0	1	0	0	2	2	1	0	0	9.00	0	0	0	–
Bradley, Fred-Fred Langdon	48-49ChiA	7-31-20	Parsons, Kans.		R	R	6'1	180	0	0	–	0	9	1	0	18	15	7	2	0	5.50	2	0	0	.000
Brady, Jim-James Joseph (Diamond Jim)	56DetA	3- 2-36	Jersey City, N.J.		L	L	6'2	185	0	0	–	0	6	0	0	6	15	11	3	0	30.00	0	0	0	–
Branca, Ralph-Ralph Theodore Joseph (Hawk)	44-53BknN 53-54DetA	1- 6-26	Mt. Vernon, N.Y.		R	R	6'3	220	88	68	.564	19	322	188	71	1485	1372	663	829	12	3.79	464	66	2	.142
	54NYA 56BknN																								
Brazle, Al-Alpha Eugene (Cotton)	43StLN 44-45MS 46-54StLN	10-19-13	Loyal, Okla.	10-24-73	L	L	6'2	185	97	64	.602	60	441	117	41	1375	1387	492	554	9	3.31	453	80	0	.177
Brecheen, Harry-Harry David (The Cat)	40,43-52StLN 53StLA	10-14-14	Broken Bow, Okla.		L	L	5'10	165	133	92	.591	18	318	240	125	1905	1731	536	901	25	2.92	673	129	2	.192
Brewer, Tom-Thomas Austin	54-61BosA	9- 3-31	Wadesboro, N,C.		R	R	6'1	180	91	82	.526	3	241	217	75	1509	1478	669	733	13	4.00	551	114	3	.207
Brickner, Ralph-Ralph Harold (Brick)	52BosA	5- 2-25	Cincinnati, Ohio		R	R	6'3	215	3	1	.750	1	14	1	0	33	32	11	9	0	2.18	8	2	0	.250
Briggs, Johnny-Jonathan Tift	56-58ChiN 59-60CleA 60KCA	1-24-34	Natoma, Cal.		R	R	5'10	175	9	11	.450	1	59	21	3	166	174	82	80	1	4.99	48	10	0	.208
Brissie, Lou-Leland Victor	47-51PhiA 51-53CleA	6- 5-24	Anderson, S.C.		L	L	6'4	210	44	48	.478	29	234	93	45	898	867	451	436	2	4.07	295	67	0	.227
Brittin, John-John Albert	50-51PhiN	3- 4-24	Athens, Ill.		R	R	5'11	175	0	0	–	0	6	0	0	8	7	9	6	0	6.75	0	0	0	–
Brodowski, Dick-Richard Stanley	52BosA 53-54MS 55-BosA 56-57WasA	7-26-32	Bayonne, N.J.		R	R	6'1	182	9	11	.450	5	72	15	5	216	212	124	85	0	4.75	62	15	2	.242
	58-59CleA																								
Brosnan, Jim-James Patrick (Professor)	54,56-58ChiN 58-59StLN	10-24-29	Cincinnati, Ohio		R	R	6'4	210	55	47	.539	67	385	47	7	832	790	312	507	2	3.54	177	27	1	.153
	59-63CinN 63ChiA																								
Brown, Alton-Alton Leo (Deacon)	51WasA	4-16-25	Norfolk, Va.		R	R	6'2	195	0	0	–	0	7	0	0	12	14	12	7	0	9.00	1	0	0	.000
Brown, Hal-Hector Harold (Skinny)	51-52ChiA 53-55BosA 55-62BalA	12-11-24	Greensboro, N.C.		R	R	6'2	185	85	92	.480	11	358	211	47	1680	1677	389	710	13	3.81	484	82	2	.169
	62NYA 63-64HouN																								
Brown, Norm-Norman	43PhiA 44-45MS 46PhiA	2- 1-19	Evergreen, N.C.		B	R	6'3	180	0	1	.000	0	5	1	0	14	13	6	4	0	3.21	3	0	0	.000
Brown, Walter-Walter Irving	47StLA	4-23-15	Jamestown, N.Y.		R	R	5'11	175	1	0	1.000	0	19	0	0	46	50	28	10	0	4.89	11	0	0	.000
Browning, Cal-Calvin Duane	60StLN	3-16-38	Burns Flat, Okla.		L	L	5'11	190	0	0	–	0	1	0	0	1	5	1	0	0	27.00	0	0	0	–
Bruner, Jack-Jack Raymond (Pappy)	49-50ChiA 50StLA	7- 1-24	Waterloo, Iowa		L	L	6'1	185	2	4	.333	1	26	3	0	55	53	45	28	0	4.91	11	0	0	.000
Budnick, Mike-Michael Joe	46-47NYN	9-15-19	Astoria, Ore.		R	R	6'1	200	2	3	.400	3	42	8	1	100	95	58	42	1	4.05	24	7	1	.292
Buhl, Bob-Robert Ray	52-63MilN 62-66ChiN 66-67PhiN	8-12-28	Saginaw, Mich.		R	R	6'2	185	166	132	.557	6	457	369	111	2587	2446	1105	1268	20	3.55	857	76	0	.089
					Bats Both 52,58-60,66																				
Burdette, Lew-Selva Lewis	50NYA 51-52BosN 53-63MilN 63-64StLN	11-22-26	Nitro, W. Va.		R	R	6'2	190	203	144	.585	31	626	373	158	3068	3186	628	1074	33	3.66	1011	185	12	.183
	64-65ChiN 65PhiN 66-67CalA																								
Burkhart (Burkhardt), Ken-Kenneth William	45-48StLN 48-49CinN	11-18-16	Knoxville, Tenn.		R	R	6'1	190	27	20	.574	7	148	41	18	519	546	165	181	6	3.85	150	27	1	.180
Burnette, Wally-Wallace Harper	56-58KCA	6-20-29	Blairs, Va.		R	R	6'	178	14	21	.400	1	68	27	5	262	259	97	122	1	3.57	77	11	0	.143
Burpo, George-George Harvie	46CinN	6-19-22	Jenkins, Ky.		R	L	6'	195	0	0	–	0	2	0	0	2	4	5	1	0	18.00	0	0	0	–
Burtschy, Moe-Edward Frank	50-51,54PhiA 55-56KCA	4-18-22	Cincinnati, Ohio		R	R	6'3	208	10	6	.625	4	90	1	0	185	178	126	97	0	4.72	36	5	0	.139
Burwell, Dick-Richard Matthew	60-61ChiN	1-23-40	Alton, Ill.		R	R	6'1	190	0	0	–	0	5	1	0	14	17	11	1	0	6.43	4	1	0	.250
Buxton, Ralph-Ralph Stanley (Buck)	38PhiA 49NYA	6- 7-11	Weyburn, Canada		R	R	5'11	163	0	2	.000	2	19	0	0	36	34	21	23	0	4.25	4	0	0	.000
Byerly, Bud-Eldred William	43-45StLN 50-52CinN 56-58WasA 58BosA	10-26-20	Webster Groves, Mo.		R	R	6'2	185	22	22	.500	14	237	17	4	492	519	167	209	0	3.70	85	10	0	.118
	59-60SFN																								
Byrd, Harry-Harry Gladwin	50,52-53PhiA 54NYA 55BalA 55-56ChiA 57DetA	2- 3-25	Darlington, S.C.		R	R	6'1	215	46	54	.460	9	187	108	33	827	890	355	381	8	4.35	262	42	0	.160
					Bats Both 55																				

USE NAME – GIVEN NAMES (NICKNAMES)	TEAM BY YEAR	BIRTH DATE	BIRTH PLACE	DEATH DATE	B	T	HGT	WGT	W	L	PCT	SV	G	GS	CG	IP	H	BB	SO	ShO	ERA	AB	H	HR	BA
					LIFETIME PITCHING TOTALS																	BATTING TOTALS			
Byrne, Tommy-Thomas Joseph	43NYA 44-45MS 46-51NYA 51-52StLA 53ChiA 53WasA 54-57NYA	12-31-19	Baltimore, Md.		L	L	6'1	182	85	69	.552	12	281	170	65	1363	1138	1037	766	12	4.11	601	143	14	.238
Cain, Bob-Robert Max (Sugar)	49-51ChiA 51DetA 52-53StLA 54ChiA	10-16-24	Longford, Kans.		L	L	6'	165	37	44	.457	8	140	89	27	629	618	316	249	3	4.49	214	42	0	.196
Calvert, Paul-Paul Leo Emile	42-45CleA 49WasA 50-51DetA	10- 6-17	Montreal, Canada		R	R	6'	175	9	22	.290	5	109	27	5	301	345	158	102	0	5.32	74	11	0	.149
Candini, Milo-Mario Cain	43-44WasA 45MS 46-49WasA 50-51PhiN	8- 3-17	Manteca, Cal.		R	R	6'	187	26	21	.553	8	174	37	13	538	530	250	183	5	3.91	144	35	1	.243
Carden, John-John Bruton	46NYN	5-19-21	Killeen, Tex.	2- 8-49	R	R	6'5	210	0	0	–	0	1	0	0	2	4	4	1	0	22.50	0	0	0	–
Carlsen, Don-Donald Herbert	48ChiN 51-52PitN	10-15-26	Chicago, Ill.		R	R	6'1	180	2	4	.333	0	13	7	2	54	75	21	23	0	6.00	19	5	0	.263
Cary, Scott-Scott Russell (Red)	47WasA	4-11-23	Kendallville, Ind.		L	L	5'11	168	3	1	.750	0	23	3	1	55	73	20	25	0	5.89	13	1	0	.077
Casale, Jerry-Jerry Joseph	58-60BosA 61LAA 61-62DetA	9-27-33	Brooklyn, N.Y.		R	R	6'2	205	17	24	.415	1	96	49	10	371	376	204	207	3	5.07	116	25	4	.216
Ceccarelli, Art-Arthur Edward (Chic)	55-56KCA 57BalA 59-60ChiN	4- 2-30	New Haven, Conn.		R	L	6'	190	9	18	.333	0	79	42	8	307	309	147	166	3	5.04	88	6	0	.068
					Bats Both 57																				
Chakales, Bob-Robert Edward (Chick)	51-54CleA 54BalA 55ChiA 55-57WasA 57BosA	8-10-27	Asheville, N.C.		R	R	6'1	190	15	25	.375	10	171	23	3	420	445	225	187	1	4.54	96	26	1	.271
Chambers, Cliff-Clifford Day (Lefty)	48ChiN 49-51PitN 51-53StLN	1-10-22	Portland, Ore.		L	L	6'3	208	48	53	.475	1	189	113	37	897	924	361	374	6	4.29	294	69	3	.235
Chandler, Ed-Edward Oliver	47BknN	2-17-22	Pinson, Ala		R	R	6'2	190	0	1	.000	1	15	1	0	30	31	12	8	0	6.30	2	0	0	.000
Chesnes, Bob-Robert Vincent	48-50PitN	5- 6-21	Oakland, Cal.		B	R	6'	180	24	22	.522	1	61	55	25	378	377	189	130	1	4.67	172	44	2	.256
Chipman, Robert Howard (Mr. Chips)	41-44BknN 44-49ChiN 50-52BosN	10-11-18	Brooklyn, N.Y.	11- 8-73	L	L	6'2	190	51	46	.526	14	293	87	29	880	889	386	322	7	3.72	250	32	0	.128
Chittum, Nels-Nelson Boyd	58StLN 59-60BosA	3-25-33	Harrisonburg, Va.		R	R	6'1	180	3	1	.750	0	40	2	0	67	68	24	30	0	3.90	10	2	0	.200
Choate, Don-Donald Leon	60SFN	7- 2-38	Potosi, Mo.		R	R	6'	185	0	0	–	0	4	0	0	8	7	4	7	0	2.25	0	0	0	–
Church, Bubba-Emory Nicholas	50-52PhiN 52-53CinN 53-55ChiN	9-12-24	Birmingham, Ala.		R	R	6'	180	36	37	.493	4	147	95	32	713	738	277	274	7	4.10	235	53	3	.226
Churn, Chuck-Clarence Nottingham	57PitN 58CleA 59LAN	2- 1-30	Bridgetown, Va.		R	R	6'3	205	3	2	.600	1	25	0	0	48	49	19	32	0	5.06	7	1	0	.143
Cicotte, Al-Alva Warren (Bozo)	57NYA 58WasA 58DetA 59CleA 61StLN 62HouN	12-23-29	Melvindale, Mich.		R	R	6'3	190	10	13	.435	4	102	16	0	260	280	119	149	0	4.36	71	15	0	.211
Clark, Mike-Michael John	52-53StLN	2-12-22	Camden, N.J.		R	R	6'4	190	3	0	1.000	1	35	6	0	61	78	35	27	0	5.31	11	0	0	.000
Clark, Phil-Philip James	58-59StLN	10- 3-32	Albany, Ga.		R	R	6'3	210	0	2	.000	1	14	0	0	15	19	11	6	0	7.80	1	0	0	.000
Clarke, Webbo-Vibert Ernesto	55WasA	6- 8-28	Colon, Panama	6-14-70	L	L	6'	165	0	0	–	0	7	2	0	21	17	14	9	0	4.71	6	1	0	.167
Clevenger, Tex-Truman Eugene	54BosA 56-60WasA 61LAA 61-62NYA	7- 9-32	Visalia, Cal.		R	R	6'1	185	36	37	.493	30	307	40	6	696	706	298	361	2	4.18	127	20	0	.157
Cohen, Hy-Hyman	55ChiN	1-29-31	Brooklyn, N.Y.		R	R	6'5	215	0	0	–	0	7	1	0	17	28	10	4	0	7.94	3	0	0	.000
Cole, Dave-David Bruce	51-52BosN 53MilN 54ChiN 55PhiN	8-29-30	Williamsport, Md.		R	R	6'2	180	6	18	.250	0	84	27	3	238	221	199	119	1	4.92	61	14	3	.230
Coleman, Joe-Joseph Patrick	42PhiA 43-45MS 46-51,53PhiA 54-55BalA 55DetA	7-30-22	Medford, Mass.		R	R	6'2	200	52	76	.406	6	223	140	60	1133	1172	566	444	11	4.38	363	66	4	.182
Coleman, Rip-Walter Gary	55-56NYA 57,59KCA 59-60BalA	7-31-31	Troy, N.Y.		L	L	6'2	185	7	25	.219	5	95	33	3	247	287	124	130	1	4.59	69	5	0	.072
Collum, Jackie-Jack Dean	51-53StLN 53-55CinN 56StLN 57ChiN 57BknN 58LAN 62MinA 62CleA	6-21-27	Victor, Iowa		L	L	5'7	160	32	28	.533	12	171	37	11	464	480	173	171	2	4.15	118	29	1	.246
Conley, Bob-Robert Burns	58PhiN	2- 1-34	Knott Cy., Ky.		R	R	6'1	188	0	0	–	0	2	2	0	8	9	1	0	0	7.88	1	0	0	.000
Conley, Gene-Donald Eugene	52BosN 54-58MilN 59-60PhiN 61-63BosA	11-10-30	Muskogee, Okla.		R	R	6'8	225	91	96	.487	9	276	214	69	1589	1606	511	888	13	3.82	548	105	5	.192
52-53,58-61,62-64 played in N.B.A.																									
Connelly, Bill-William Wirt (Wild Bill)	45PhiA 50ChiA 50DetA 52-53NYN	6-29-25	Alberta, Va.		L	R	6'	175	6	2	.750	0	25	7	0	66	71	53	34	0	6.95	19	4	0	.211
Constable, Jim-Jimmy Lee (Sheriff)	56-57NYN 58SFN 58CleA 58WasA 62MilN 63SFN	6-14-33	Jonesboro, Tenn.		B	L	6'1	185	3	4	.429	2	56	6	1	97	109	41	59	1	4.92	17	4	0	.235
Consuegra, Sandy-Sandalio Simeon [Castellon]	50-53WasA 53-56ChiA 56-57BalA 57NYN	9- 3-20	Potrerillo, Cuba		R	R	5'11	165	51	32	.614	26	248	71	24	810	811	246	193	5	3.37	218	37	0	.170
Cooper, Cal-Calvin Asa	48WasA	8-11-22	Great Falls, S.C.		R	R	6'2	180	0	0	–	0	1	0	0	1	5	1	0	0	45.00	0	0	0	–
Cooper, Pat-Orge Patterson	46PhiA	11-26-17	Albemarle, N.C.		R	R	6'3	180	0	0	–	0	1	0	0	1	1	1	0	0	0.00	(See B46-60)			
Corwin, Al-Elmer Nathan	51-55NYN	12- 3-26	Newburgh, N.Y.		R	R	6'1	170	18	10	.643	5	117	22	6	290	289	156	142	2	3.97	79	12	2	.152
Cox, Glenn-Glenn Melvin (Jingles)	55-58KCA	2- 3-31	Montebello, Cal.		R	R	6'2	210	1	4	.200	0	17	5	1	43	50	35	17	0	6.49	10	0	0	.000
Craddock, Walt-Walter Anderson	55-56,58KCA	3-25-32	Pax, W.Va.		R	L	6'	176	0	7	.000	0	29	5	0	61	68	40	39	0	6.49	9	0	0	.000
Cress, Walker-Walker James (Foots)	48-49CinN	3- 6-17	Ben Hur, Va.		R	R	6'5	205	0	1	.000	0	33	2	1	62	62	45	33	0	4.35	8	4	0	.500
Crimian, Jack-John Melvin	51-52StLN 56KCA 57DetA	2-17-26	Philadelphia, Pa.		R	R	5'10	180	5	9	.357	4	74	7	0	160	177	65	69	0	6.35	26	6	0	.231
Cristante, Leo-Leo Dante	51PhiN 55DetA	12-10-26	Detroit, Mich.		R	R	6'1	205	1	2	.333	0	30	2	0	59	65	23	15	0	3.81	13	1	0	.077
Crone, Ray-Raymond Hayes	54-57MilN 57NYN 58SFN	8- 7-31	Memphis, Tenn.		R	R	6'2	185	30	30	.500	4	137	61	17	546	554	173	260	1	3.87	156	18	0	.115
Cuellar, Charlie-Jesus Patracis	50ChiA	9-24-17	Ybor City, Fla.		R	R	5'11	183	0	0	–	0	2	0	0	1	6	3	1	0	36.00	0	0	0	–
Currie, Bill-William Cleveland	55WasA	11-29-28	Leary, Ga.		R	R	6'	175	0	0	–	0	3	0	0	4	7	2	2	0	13.50	0	0	0	–
Dahlke, Jerry-Jerome Alex (Joe)	56ChiA	6- 8-30	Marathon, Wis.		R	R	6'	180	0	0	–	0	5	0	0	2	5	6	1	0	22.50	0	0	0	–
Daley, Buddy-Leavitt Leo	55-57CleA 58-61KCA 61-64NYA	10- 7-32	Orange, Cal.		L	L	6'1	185	60	64	.484	10	248	116	36	966	998	351	549	3	4.03	291	56	0	.192
Daniel, Chuck-Charles Edward	57DetA	9-17-33	Bluffton, Ark.		R	R	6'2	195	0	0	–	0	1	0	0	2	3	0	2	0	9.00	0	0	0	–
Darnell, Bob-Robert Jack	54,56BknN	11- 6-30	Wewoka, Okla.		R	R	5'10	175	0	0	–	0	7	1	0	15	16	7	5	0	3.00	2	0	0	.000
Davie, Jerry-Gerald Lee	59DetA	2-10-33	Detroit, Mich.		R	R	6'	180	2	2	.500	0	11	5	1	37	40	17	20	0	4.14	10	4	0	.400
Davis, Bob-Robert Edward	58,60KCA	9-11-33	New York, N.Y.		R	R	6'	170	0	4	.000	1	29	4	0	63	76	34	50	0	5.71	10	2	0	.200
Davis, Jim-James Bennett	54-56ChiN 57StLN 57NYN	9-15-24	Red Bluff, Cal.		B	L	6'	180	24	26	.480	10	154	39	4	407	383	179	197	1	4.00	99	9	0	.091
Deal, Cot-Ellis Fergason	47-48BosA 50,54StLN	1-23-23	Arapaho, Okla.		B	R	5'10	185	3	4	.429	1	45	2	0	90	111	48	34	0	6.50	24	4	1	.167
					Bats Left 47-48																				
Delock, Ike-Ivan Martin	52-53,55-63BosA 63BalA	11-11-29	Highland Pk., Mich.		R	R	5'11	175	84	75	.528	31	320	147	32	1237	1238	530	672	6	4.04	361	31	1	.086
Dempsey, Con-Cornelius Francis	51PitN	9-16-23	San Francisco, Cal.		R	R	6'4	190	0	2	.000	0	3	2	0	7	11	4	3	0	9.00	1	0	0	.000
Derrington, Jim-Charles James (Blackie)	56-57ChiA	11-29-39	Compton, Cal.		L	L	6'3	190	0	2	.000	0	21	6	0	43	38	35	17	0	5.23	6	1	0	.167
Deutsch, Mel-Melvin Elliott	46BosA	7-26-15	Caldwell, Tex.		R	R	6'4	215	0	0	–	0	3	0	0	6	7	3	2	0	6.00	2	0	0	.000
Dickson, Murry-Murry Monroe	39-40,42-43StLN 44-45MS 46-48StLN 49-53PitN 54-56PhiN 56-57StLN 58KCA 58NYA 59KCA	8-21-16	Tracy, Mo.		R	R	5'10	170	172	181	.487	23	625	338	149	3053	3024	1058	1281	27	3.66	1095	253	3	.231
Ditmar, Art-Arthur John	54PhiA 55-56KCA 57-61NYA 61-62KCA	4- 3-29	Winthrop, Mass.		R	R	6'2	195	72	77	.483	14	287	156	41	1267	1237	461	552	5	3.99	422	75	2	.178
Dixon, Sonny-John Craig	53-54WasA 54PhiA 55KCA 56NYA	11- 5-24	Charlotte, N.C.		B	R	6'2	205	11	18	.379	9	102	12	4	263	296	75	90	0	4.17	61	11	0	.180
Dobernic, Jess-Andrew Joseph	39ChiA 48-49ChiN 49CinN	11-20-17	Mt. Olive, Ill.		R	R	5'10	170	7	3	.700	1	76	0	0	112	107	66	55	0	5.22	13	2	0	.154
Dobson, Joe-Joseph Gordon (Burrhead)	39-40CleA 41-43BosA 44-45MS 46-50BosA 51-53ChiA 54BosA	1-20-17	Durant, Okla.		R	R	6'2	197	137	103	.571	18	414	273	112	2172	2048	851	992	22	3.62	697	106	2	.152
Donnelly, Blix-Sylvester Urban	44-46StLN 46-50PhiN 51BosN	1-21-14	Olivia, Minn.		R	R	5'10	166	27	36	.429	12	190	75	27	691	659	306	296	7	3.49	201	32	0	.159
Donnelly, Ed-Edward Vincent	59ChiN	12-10-34	Allen, Mich.		R	R	6'	175	8	12	.400	0	42	22	14	221	258	81	83	1	4.03	0	0	0	–
Donoso, Lino-Lino Galata	55-56PitN	9-23-22	Havana, Cuba		L	L	5'11	160	4	6	.400	1	28	9	3	97	108	36	39	0	5.20	27	5	0	.185
Donovan, Dick-Richard Edward	50-52BosN 54DetA 55-60ChiA 61WasA 62-65CleA	12- 7-27	Boston, Mass.		L	R	6'3	205	122	99	.552	5	345	273	101	2020	1988	495	880	25	3.66	694	113	15	.163
Dorish, Harry-Harry (Fritz)	47-49BosA 50StLA 51-55ChiA 55-56BalA 56BosA	7-13-21	Swoyersville, Pa.		R	R	5'11	204	45	43	.511	44	323	40	13	835	850	301	332	2	3.83	204	32	0	.157
Douglas, Whammy-Charles William	57PitN	2-17-35	Carrboro, N.C.		R	R	6'2	185	3	3	.500	0	11	8	0	47	48	30	28	0	3.26	16	1	0	.063
Dozier, Buzz-William Joseph	47,49WasA	8-31-27	Waco, Tex.		R	R	6'3	185	0	0	–	0	4	0	0	11	14	7	3	0	6.55	3	0	0	.000
Dreisewerd, Clem-Clement John (Steamboat)	44-46BosA 48StLA 48NYN	1-24-16	Old Monroe, Mo.		L	L	6'1	195	6	8	.429	2	46	10	3	141	160	39	39	0	4.53	38	4	0	.105
Drews, Karl-Karl August	46-48NYA 48-49StLA 51-54PhiN 54CinN	2-22-20	Staten Island, N.Y.	8-13-63	R	R	6'4	192	44	53	.454	7	218	107	26	827	913	332	322	7	4.76	254	21	0	.083
Drott, Dick-Richard Fred (Hummer)	57-61ChiN 62-63HouN	7- 1-36	Cincinnati, Ohio		R	R	6'	190	27	46	.370	0	176	101	14	687	626	405	460	5	4.78	202	34	0	.168
Dubiel, Monk-Walter John	44-45NYA 48PhiN 49-52ChiN	2-12-19	Hartford, Conn.	10-23-69	R	R	6'	190	45	53	.459	11	187	97	41	880	854	349	289	9	3.87	275	57	1	.207
Dunn, Jim-James William (Bill)	52PitN	2-25-31	Valdosta, Ga.		R	R	6'	185	0	0	–	0	3	0	0	5	4	3	2	0	3.60	1	0	0	.000
Dusak, Erv-Ervin Frank (Four Sack)	48,50-51StLN 51PitN	7-29-20	Chicago, Ill.		R	R	6'2	185	0	3	.000	1	23	3	0	54	51	44	26	0	5.33	(See B46-60)			
Duser, Carl-Carl Robert	56,58KCA	7-22-32	Hazleton, Pa.		L	L	6'1	175	1	1	.500	0	3	2	0	8	19	3	5	0	7.88	3	0	0	.000
Edelman, John-John Rogers	55MilN	7-27-35	Philadelphia, Pa.		R	R	6'3	185	0	0	–	0	5	0	0	6	7	8	3	0	10.50	0	0	0	–
Elliott, Glenn-Herbert Glenn (Lefty)	47-49BosN	11-11-19	Sapulpa, Okla.	7-27-69	L	L	5'10	170	11	24	.314	4	120	30	4	322	453	174	90	0	6.96	21	2	0	.095
Elston, Don-Donald Ray	53ChiN 57BknN 57-64ChiN	4-26-29	Campbellstown, O.		R	R	6'	170	49	54	.476	63	450	15	2	755	702	327	519	0	3.70	124	19	0	.153
Embree, Red-Charles Willard	41-42CleA 43VR 44-47CleA 48NYA 49StLA	8-30-17	El Monte, Cal.		R	R	6'	165	31	48	.392	1	141	90	29	707	653	330	286	1	3.72	223	37	0	.166
Erautt, Eddie-Edward Lorenz Sebastian	47-51,53CinN 53StLN	9-26-24	Portland, Ore.		R	R	5'11	185	15	23	.395	2	164	22	4	379	434	179	157	0	4.87	75	9	0	.120
Erickson, Don-Don Lee	58PhiN	12-13-31	Springfield, Ill.		R	R	6'	175	0	1	.000	1	9	0	0	12	11	9	9	0	4.50	1	0	0	.000
Erickson, Hal-Harold James	53DetA	7-17-19	Portland, Ore.		R	R	6'5	230	0	1	.000	1	18	0	0	32	43	10	19	0	4.78	4	0	0	.000
Erskine, Carl-Carl Daniel (Oisk)	48-57BknN 58-59LAN	12-13-26	Anderson, Ind.		R	R	5'10	165	122	78	.610	13	335	216	71	1719	1637	646	981	14	4.00	588	92	1	.156
Estock, George-George John	51BosN	11- 2-24	Stirling, N.J.		R	R	6'	185	0	1	.000	3	37	1	0	60	56	37	11	0	4.35	7	2	0	.288
Evans, Bill-William Lawrence	49ChiA 51BosA	3-26-19	Childress, Tex.		R	R	6'2	180	0	1	.000	0	13	0	0	21	21	16	4	0	5.14	5	0	0	.000
Fagan, Everett-Everett Joseph	43PhiA 44-45MS 46PhiA	1-13-18	Pottersville, N.J.		R	R	6'	195	2	7	.222	3	38	2	0	82	88	38	21	0	5.49	21	4	0	.190
Fahr, Red-Gerald Warren	51CleA	12- 9-24	Marmaduke, Ark.		R	R	6'5	185	0	0	–	0	5	0	0	6	11	2	0	0	4.50	0	0	0	–
Fannin, Cliff-Clifford Bryson (Mule)	45-52StLA	5-13-24	Louisa, Ky.	12-11-66	L	R	6'	170	34	51	.400	6	164	98	28	733	763	393	352	6	4.85	237	41	0	.173
Fanovich, Frank-Frank Joseph (Lefty)	49CinN 53PhiA	1-11-22	New York, N.Y.		L	L	5'11	180	0	5	.000	0	55	4	0	105	106	65	64	0	5.49	15	2	0	.133

									LIFETIME PITCHING TOTALS													BATTING TOTALS			
USE NAME – GIVEN NAMES (NICKNAMES)	TEAM BY YEAR	BIRTH DATE	BIRTH PLACE	DEATH DATE	B	T	HGT	WGT	W	L	PCT	SV	G	GS	CG	IP	H	BB	SO	ShO	ERA	AB	H	HR	BA
Faszholz, Jack-John Edward (Preacher)	53StLN	4-11-27	St. Louis, Mo.		R	R	6'3	205	0	0	–	0	4	1	0	12	16	1	7	0	6.75	3	0	0	.000
Fear, Vern-Luvern Carl	52ChiN	8-21-24	Everly, Iowa		B	R	6'	170	0	0	–	0	4	0	0	8	9	3	4	0	7.88	1	0	0	.000
Feller, Bob-Robert William Andrew (Rapid Robert)	36-41CleA 42-44MS 45-56CleA	11- 3-18	Van Meter, Iowa		R	R	6'	185	266	162	.621	21	570	484	279	3828	3271	1764	2581	44	3.25	1282	193	8	.151
Ferens, Stan-Stanley (Lefty)	42,46StLA	3- 5-15	Wendell, Pa.		B	L	5'11	170	5	13	.278	0	53	9	2	157	176	59	51	0	4.18	45	7	0	.156
Ferrarese, Don-Donald Hugh (Midget)	55-57BalA 58-59CleA 60ChiA 61-62PhiN 62StLN	6-19-29	Oakland, Cal.		R	L	5'9	170	19	36	.345	5	183	50	12	507	449	295	350	2	3.99	128	20	1	.156
Ferrick, Tom-Thomas Jerome	41PhiA 42CleA 43-45MS 46CleA 46StLA 47-48WasA 49-50StLA 50-51NYA 51-52WasA	1- 6-15	New York, N.Y.		R	R	6'2	220	40	40	.500	56	323	7	4	674	654	227	245	1	3.47	147	27	0	.184
Ferriss, Boo-David Meadow	45-50BosA	12- 5-21	Shaw, Miss.		L	R	6'2	208	65	30	.684	8	144	103	67	880	914	314	296	12	3.64	372	93	1	.250
Fine, Tommy-Thomas Morgan	47BosA 50StLA	10-10-14	Cleburne, Tex.		B	R	6'	180	1	3	.250	0	23	7	1	73	94	44	16	0	6.78	21	7	0	.333
Fischer, Bill-William Charles	56-58ChiA 58DetA 58-60WasA 60-61DetA 61-63KCA 64MinA	10-11-30	Wausau, Wis.		R	R	6'	195	45	58	.437	13	281	78	16	832	936	210	313	2	4.34	199	27	1	.136
Fisher, Harry-Harry Devereux	52PitN	1- 3-26	Newbury, Canada		L	R	6'	180	1	2	.333	0	8	3	0	18	17	13	5	0	7.00	(See B46-60)			
Fisher, Maury-Maurice Wayne	55CinN	2-16-31	Uniondale, Ind.		R	R	6'5	210	0	0	–	0	1	0	0	3	5	2	1	0	6.00	1	0	0	.000
Fitzgerald, John-John Francis	58SFN	9-15-33	Brooklyn, N.Y.		L	L	6'3	190	0	0	–	0	1	1	0	3	1	1	3	0	3.00	1	0	0	.000
Flanigan, Ray-Raymond Arthur	46CleA	1- 8-23	Morgantown, W.Va.		R	R	6'	190	0	1	.000	0	3	1	0	9	11	8	2	0	11.00	2	1	0	.500
Flanigan, Tom-Thomas Anthony	54ChiA 58StLN	9- 6-34	Cincinnati, Ohio		R	L	6'3	175	0	0	–	0	3	0	0	3	3	2	0	0	3.00	0	0	0	–
Fletcher, Van-Alfred Vanoide	55DetA	8- 6-24	East Bend, N.C.		R	R	6'2	185	0	0	–	0	9	0	0	12	13	2	4	0	3.00	0	0	0	–
Flowers, Ben-Bennett	51,53BosA 55DetA 55-56StLN 56PhiN	6-15-27	Wilson, N.C.		R	R	6'4	200	3	7	.300	3	76	13	1	168	190	54	86	1	4.50	36	4	0	.111
Fodge, Gene-Eugene Arlan (Suds)	58ChiN	7- 9-31	South Bend, Ind.		R	R	6'	175	1	1	.500	0	16	4	1	40	47	11	15	0	4.73	7	0	0	.000
Ford, Whitey-Edward Charles (The Chairman of the Board)	50NYA 51-52MS 53-67NYA	10-21-28	New York, N.Y.		L	L	5'10	178	236	106	.690	10	498	438	156	3171	2766	1086	1956	45	2.74	1023	177	3	.173
Fornieles, Mike-Jose Miguel [Torres]	52WasA 53-56ChiA 56-57BalA 57-63BosA 63MinA	1-18-32	Havana, Cuba		R	R	5'11	158	63	64	.496	55	432	76	20	1156	1165	421	576	4	3.96	308	52	1	.169
Fowler, Art-John Arthur	54-57CinN 59LAN 61-64LAA	7- 3-22	Converse, S.C.		R	R	5'11	180	54	51	.514	32	362	90	25	1025	1039	308	539	4	4.02	231	35	0	.152
Fowler, Dick-Richard John	41-42PhiA 43-44MS 45-52PhiA	3-30-21	Toronto, Canada	5-22-72	R	R	6'4	215	66	79	.455	4	221	170	79	1304	1307	578	382	11	4.11	477	88	1	.186
Fox, Howie-Howard Francis	44-46,48-51CinN 52PhiN 54BalA	3- 1-21	Coburg, Ore.	10- 9-55	R	R	6'3	210	43	72	.374	6	248	132	42	1108	1174	435	342	5	4.33	349	66	2	.189
Foytack, Paul-Paul Eugene	53,55-63DetA 63-64LAA	11-16-30	Scranton, Pa.		R	R	5'11	180	86	87	.497	7	312	193	63	1499	1381	662	827	7	4.14	461	82	1	.178
Freeman, Hersh-Hershell Baskin (Buster)	52-53,55BosA 55-58CinN 58ChiN	7- 1-28	Gadsden, Ala.		R	R	6'3	220	30	16	.652	37	204	3	1	360	387	109	158	0	3.73	63	9	1	.143
Freeman, Mark-Mark Price	59NYA 59KCA 60ChiN	12- 7-30	Memphis, Tenn.		R	R	6'4	220	3	3	.500	1	34	9	1	88	82	38	55	0	5.52	22	3	0	.136
Fricano, Marion-Marion John	52-54PhiA 55KCA	7-15-23	Brant, N.Y.		R	R	6'	170	15	23	.395	1	88	43	14	388	393	164	115	0	4.31	113	16	0	.142
Friend, Bob-Robert Bartmess (Warrior)	51-65PitN 66NYA 66NYN	11-24-30	Lafayette, Ind.		R	R	6'	195	197	230	.461	11	602	497	163	3612	3772	894	1734	36	3.58	1137	138	2	.121
Froats, Bill-William John	55DetA	10-20-30	New York, N.Y.		L	L	6'	180	0	0	–	0	1	0	0	2	0	2	0	0	0.00	0	0	0	–
Garber, Bob-Robert Mitchell	56PitN	9-10-28	Hunker, Pa.		R	R	6'1	190	0	0	–	0	2	0	0	4	3	3	3	0	2.25	0	0	0	–
Garcia, Mike-Edward Miguel (The Big Bear)	48-59CleA 60ChiA 61WasA	11-17-23	San Gabriel, Cal.		R	R	6'1	205	142	97	.594	23	428	281	111	2176	2148	719	1117	27	3.26	696	127	2	.182
Garcia, Ramon-Ramon [Garcia]	48WasA	3- 5-24	LaEsperanza, Cuba		R	R	5'10	170	0	0	–	0	4	0	0	4	11	4	2	0	15.75	1	1	0	1.000
Garver, Ned-Ned Franklin	48-52StLA 52-56DetA 57-60KCA 61LAA	12-25-25	Ney, Ohio		R	R	5'10	185	129	157	.451	12	402	330	153	2477	2471	881	881	18	3.73	827	180	7	.218
Gebrian, Pete-Peter (Gabe)	47ChiA	8-10-23	Bayonne, N.J.		R	R	6'	170	2	3	.400	5	27	4	0	66	61	33	17	0	4.50	13	0	0	.000
Gettel, Al-Allen Jones	45-46NYA 47-48CleA 48-49ChiA 49WasA 51NYN 55StLN	9-17-17	Norfolk, Va.		R	R	6'3	200	38	45	.458	6	184	79	31	735	711	310	310	5	4.27	241	55	0	.228
Giallombardo, Bob-Robert Paul	58LAN	5-20-37	Brooklyn, N.Y.		L	L	6'	175	1	1	.500	0	6	5	0	26	29	15	14	0	3.81	6	1	0	.167
Giel, Paul-Paul Robert	54-55NYN 56-57MS 58SFN 59-60PitN 61MinA 61KCA	9-29-32	Winona, Minn.		R	R	5'11	185	11	9	.550	0	102	11	0	240	249	148	145	0	5.40	55	4	0	.073
Giggie, Bob-Robert Thomas	59-60MilN 60,62KCA	8-13-33	Dorchester, Mass.		R	R	6'1	200	3	1	.750	1	30	2	0	57	70	32	32	0	5.21	7	0	0	.000
Gillespie, Bob-Robert William (Bunch)	44DetA 47-48ChiA 50BosA	10- 8-18	Columbus, Ohio		R	R	6'4	187	5	13	.278	0	58	23	2	202	223	102	59	0	5.08	51	2	0	.039
Goetz, John-John Hardy	60ChiN	10-24-37	Goetzville, Mich.		R	R	6'	185	0	0	–	0	4	0	0	6	10	4	6	0	13.50	1	0	0	.000
Gomez, Ruben-Ruben [Colon]	53-57NYN 58SFN 59-60PhiN 62CleA 62MinA 67PhiN	7-13-27	Arroyo, P.R.		R	R	6'	170	76	86	.469	5	289	205	63	1453	1436	574	677	15	4.09	477	95	3	.199
Gonzales, Julio-Julio Enrique	49WasA	12-20-20	Havana, Cuba		R	R	5'11	150	0	0	–	0	13	0	0	34	33	27	5	0	4.76	5	1	0	.200
Gonzales, Vince-Wenceslao [O'Reilly]	55WasA	9-28-25	Quivican, Cuba		L	L	6'1	165	0	0	–	0	1	0	0	2	6	3	1	0	27.00	0	0	0	–
Goodwin, Jim-James Patrick	48ChiA	8-15-26	St. Louis, Mo.		L	L	6'1	170	0	0	–	1	8	1	0	10	9	12	3	0	9.00	2	1	0	.500
Gorin, Charlie-Charles Perry	54-55MilN	2- 6-28	Waco, Tex.		L	L	5'10	165	0	1	.000	0	7	0	0	10	6	9	12	0	3.60	3	0	0	.000
Gorman, Tom-Thomas Aloysius	52-54NYA 55-59KCA	1- 4-25	New York, N.Y.		R	R	6'1	195	36	36	.500	42	289	33	5	690	659	239	321	2	3.77	155	14	0	.090
Grasmick, Lou-Louis Junior	48PhiN	9-11-24	Baltimore, Md.		R	R	6'	195	0	0	–	0	2	0	0	5	3	8	2	0	7.20	1	1	0	1.000
Gray, John-John Leonard	54PhiA 55KCA 57CleA 58PhiN	12-11-27	W. Palm Beach, Fla.		R	R	6'4	226	4	18	.182	0	48	24	6	169	172	142	75	1	6.18	47	2	0	.043
Gray, Ted-Ted Glenn	46,48-54DetA 55ChiA 55CleA 55NYA 55BalA	12-31-24	Detroit, Mich.		B Bats Right 46	L	5'11	175	59	74	.444	4	222	162	50	1133	1072	595	687	7	4.37	370	59	0	.159
Greason, Willie-William Henry (Booster)	54StLN	9- 3-24	Atlanta, Ga.		R	R	5'10	170	0	1	.000	0	3	2	0	4	8	4	2	0	13.50	1	0	0	.000
Green, Freddie-Fred Allen	59-61PitN 62WasA 64Pitn	9-14-33	Titusville, N.J.		R	L	6'4	190	9	7	.563	4	88	1	0	142	142	63	77	0	3.49	17	3	2	.176
Greenwood, Bob-Robert Chandler (Greenie)	54-55PhiN	3-13-28	Cananea, Mexico		R	R	6'4	205	1	2	.333	0	12	4	0	39	35	18	9	0	3.92	10	0	0	.000
Griffeth, Lee-Leon Clifford	46PhiA	5-20-25	Carmel, N.Y.		B	L	5'11	180	0	0	–	0	10	0	0	15	13	6	4	0	3.00	1	0	0	.000
Griggs, Hal-Harold Lloyd	56-59WasA	8-24-28	Shannon, Ga.		R	R	6'	170	6	26	.188	3	105	45	6	348	372	209	172	1	5.48	79	7	0	.089
Grim, Bob-Robert Anton	54-58NYA 58-59KCA 60CleA 60CinN 60StLN 62KCA	3- 8-30	New York, N.Y.		R	R	6'1	175	61	41	.598	37	268	60	18	759	708	330	443	4	3.62	189	24	3	.127
Grimsley, Ross-Ross Albert Sr. (Lefty)	51ChiA	6- 4-22	Americus, Kans.		L	L	6'	175	0	0	–	0	7	0	0	14	12	10	8	0	3.86	2	0	0	.000
Grissom, Marv-Marvin Edward	46NYN 49DetA 52ChiA 53BosA 53-57NYN 58SFN 59StLN	3-31-18	Los Molinos, Cal.		R	R	6'3	205	47	45	.511	58	356	52	12	810	771	343	459	3	3.41	189	23	0	.122
Grob, Connie-Conrad George	56WasA	11- 9-32	Cross Plains, Wis.		L	R	6'	180	4	5	.444	1	37	1	0	79	121	26	27	0	7.86	18	6	0	.333
Grodzicki, Johnny-John	41StLN 42-45MS 46-47StLN	2-26-17	Nanticoke, Pa.		R	R	6'1	200	2	2	.500	0	24	1	0	40	31	34	20	0	4.50	3	0	0	.000
Gromek, Steve-Stephen Joseph	41-53CleA 53-57DetA	1-15-20	Hamtramck, Mich.		B	R	6'2	195	123	108	.532	23	447	225	92	2065	1940	630	904	15	3.41	630	124	0	.197
Gross, Don-Donald John	55-57CinN 58-60PitN	6-30-31	Weidman, Mich.		L	L	5'11	186	20	22	.476	10	145	37	9	397	400	117	230	1	3.74	104	11	0	.106
Grossman, Harley-Harley Joseph	52WasA	5- 5-30	Evansville, Ind.		R	R	6'	170	0	0	–	0	1	0	0	.1	2	0	0	0	54.00	0	0	0	–
Groth, Ernie-Ernest William	47-48CleA 49ChiA	5- 3-22	Beaver Falls, Pa.		R	R	5'9	185	0	1	.000	0	6	0	0	7	3	6	2	0	5.14	0	0	0	–
Grunwald, Al-Alfred Henry (Stretch)	55PitN 59KCA	2-13-30	Los Angeles, Cal.		L	L	6'4	210	0	1	.000	1	9	1	0	19	25	18	11	0	6.63	8	2	0	.250
Gumpert, Randy-Randall Pennington	36-38PhiA 43-45MS 46-48NYA 48-51ChiA 52BosA 52WasA	1-23-18	Monocacy, Pa.		R	R	6'3	200	51	59	.464	7	261	113	47	1052	1099	346	352	6	4.17	329	60	0	.182
Habenicht, Bob-Robert Julius (Hobby)	51StLN 53StLA	2-13-26	St. Louis, Mo.		R	R	6'2	185	0	0	–	0	4	0	0	7	6	10	2	0	6.43	1	0	0	.000
Hacker, Warren-Warren Louis	48-56ChiN 57CinN 57-58PhiN 61ChiA	11-21-24	Marissa, Ill.		R	R	6'1	185	62	89	.411	17	306	157	47	1283	1297	320	557	6	4.21	401	78	0	.195
Haddix, Harvey-Harvey (The Kitten)	52-56StLN 56-57PhiN 58CinN 59-63PitN 64-65BalA	9-18-25	Medway, Ohio		L	L	5'9	170	136	113	.546	21	453	285	99	2235	2154	601	1575	20	3.63	798	169	4	.212
Haefner, Mickey-Milton Arnold	43-49WasA 49-50ChiA 50BosN	10- 9-12	Lenzburg, Ill.		L	L	5'8	160	78	91	.462	13	261	179	91	1467	1414	577	508	13	3.50	448	84	0	.188
Hahn, Fred-Frederick Aloys	52StLN	2-16-29	Nyack, N.Y.		R	L	6'3	174	0	0	–	0	1	0	0	2	2	1	0	0	0.00	0	0	0	–
Hall, Bob-Robert Lewis	49-50BosN 53PitN	12-22-23	Swissvale, Pa.		R	R	6'2	195	9	18	.333	1	89	27	8	276	307	146	133	1	5.41	72	15	1	.208
Hall, Johnny-John Sylvester	48BknN	1- 9-24	Muskogee, Okla.		R	R	6'2	170	0	0	–	0	3	0	0	4	4	2	2	0	6.75	0	0	0	–
Hamner, Granny-Granville Wilbur	56-57PhiN 62KCA	4-26-27	Richmond, Va.		R	R	5'10	163	0	2	.000	0	7	1	0	13	21	8	5	0	5.54	(See B46-60)			
Hamner, Ralph-Ralph Conant (Bruz)	46ChiA 47-49ChiN	9-12-16	Gibsland, La.		R	R	6'3	165	8	20	.286	1	61	28	8	219	236	132	99	0	4.60	61	10	1	.164
Hansen, Andy-Andrew Viggo (Swede)	44-45NYN 46MS 47-50NYN 51-53PhiN	11-12-24	Lake Worth, Fla.		R	R	6'3	185	23	30	.434	16	270	39	8	618	627	246	188	0	4.22	118	12	0	.102
Hardy, Red-Francis Joseph	51NYN	1- 6-23	Marmarth, N.D.		R	R	5'11	175	0	0	–	0	2	0	0	1	4	1	0	0	9.00	0	0	0	–
Harrington, Bill-Billy Womble	53PhiA 54MS 55-56KCA	10- 3-27	Sanford, N.C.		R	R	5'11	160	5	5	.500	3	58	2	0	117	114	67	40	0	5.00	24	2	0	.083
Harris, Bill-William Thomas (Billy)	57BknN 59LAN	12- 3-31	Dugayville, Canada		L	R	5'8	187	0	1	.000	0	2	1	0	9	9	4	3	0	3.00	2	1	0	.500
Harris, Charlie-Charles (Bubba)	48-49,51PhiA 51CleA	2-15-26	Sulligent, Ala.		R	R	6'4	204	6	3	.667	8	87	0	0	186	190	86	53	0	4.84	48	6	0	.125
Harris, Mickey-Maurice Charles	40-41BosA 42-45MS 46-49BosA 49-52WasA 52CleA	1-30-17	New York, N.Y.	4-15-71	L	L	6'	195	59	71	.454	21	271	109	42	1051	1097	455	534	2	4.18	288	54	0	.188
Harrison, Bob-Robert Lee	55-56BalA	9-22-30	St. Louis, Mo.		L	R	5'11	178	0	0	–	0	2	1	0	4	6	9	0	0	11.25	0	0	0	–
Harrist, Earl-Earl (Irish)	45CinN 47-48ChiA 48WasA 52StLA 53ChiA 53DetA	8-20-19	Dubach, La.		R	R	6'	175	12	28	.300	10	132	24	2	383	391	193	162	0	4.34	96	11	0	.115
Harshman, Jack-John Elvin	52NYN 54-57ChiA 58-59BalA 59BosA 59-60CleA	7-12-27	San Diego, Cal.		L	L	6'2	189	69	65	.515	7	217	155	61	1168	1025	539	741	12	3.51	(See B46-60)			
Hartung, Clint-Clinton Clarence (The Hondo Hurricane, Floppy)	47-50NYN	8-10-22	Hondo, Tex.		R	R	6'1	210	29	29	.500	1	112	72	23	511	529	271	167	3	5.02	(See B46-60)			
Hatten, Joe-Joseph Hilarian	46-51BknN 51-52ChiN	11- 7-16	Bancroft, Iowa		R	L	6'	176	65	49	.570	4	233	149	51	1087	1124	492	381	7	3.87	357	57	0	.160
Haugstad, Phil-Philip Donald	47-48,51BknN 52CinN	2-23-24	Black R. Falls, Wis.		R	R	6'2	165	1	1	.500	0	37	2	0	57	51	41	28	0	5.53	4	0	0	.000
Hayden, Gene-Eugene Franklin (Lefty)	58CinN	4-14-35	San Francisco, Cal.		L	L	6'2	175	0	0	–	0	3	0	0	4	5	1	3	0	4.50	0	0	0	–
Haynes, Joe-Joseph Walton	39-40WasA 41-48ChiA 49-52WasA	9-21-17	Lincolnton, Ga.	1- 7-67	R	R	6'2	190	76	82	.481	21	379	147	53	1580	1672	620	475	5	4.01	521	111	1	.213
Heard, Jay-Jehosie	54BalA	1-17-25	Atlanta, Ga.		L	L	5'7	147	0	0	–	0	2	0	0	3	6	3	2	0	15.00	0	0	0	–
Hearn, Jim-James Tolbert	47-50StLN 50-56NYN 57-59PhiN	4-11-21	Atlanta, Ga.		R	R	6'3	205	109	89	.551	8	396	229	63	1704	1661	655	669	10	3.81	548	77	9	.141

USE NAME – GIVEN NAMES (NICKNAMES)	TEAM BY YEAR	BIRTH DATE	BIRTH PLACE	DEATH DATE					LIFETIME PITCHING TOTALS													BATTING TOTALS			
					B	T	HGT	WGT	W	L	PCT	SV	G	GS	CG	IP	H	BB	SO	ShO	ERA	AB	H	HR	BA
Heintzelman, Ken-Kenneth Alphonse	37-42PitN 43-45MS 46-47PitN 47-52PhiN	10-14-15	Peruque, Mo.		R	L	5'11	185	77	98	.440	10	319	183	66	1502	1540	630	564	19	3.93	440	56	0	.127
Heise, Jim-James Edward	57WasA	10- 2-32	Scottsdale, Pa.		R	R	6'1	185	0	3	.000	0	8	2	0	19	25	16	8	0	8.05	4	0	0	.000
Held, Mel-Melvin Nicholas (Country)	56BalA	4-12-29	Edon, Ohio		R	R	6'1	178	0	0	–	0	4	0	0	7	7	3	4	0	5.14	0	0	0	–
Herbert, Ray-Raymond Ernest	50-51DetA 52MS 53-54DetA 55,58-61KCA 61-64ChiA 65-66PhiN	12-15-29	Detroit, Mich.		R	R	5'11	185	104	107	.493	15	407	236	68	1883	2000	571	864	13	4.01	569	109	7	.192
Hernandez, Evelio-Evelio Gregorio [Lopez]	56-57WasA	12-24-30	Guanabacoa, Cuba		R	R	6'1	180	1	1	.500	0	18	6	1	59	62	28	24	0	4.42	17	2	0	.118
Hernandez, Rudy-Rudolph Albert	60WasA 61WasA	12-10-31	Santiago, Dom. R.		R	R	6'3	185	4	2	.667	0	28	0	0	44	42	24	26	0	4.09	6	1	0	.167
Herrera, Tito-Procopio [Rodriguez] (Bobby)	51StLA	7-26-26	Nuevo Laredo, Mex.		R	R	6'	184	0	0	–	0	3	0	0	2	6	4	1	0	31.50	0	0	0	–
Herriage, Troy-William Troy (Dutch)	56KCA	12-20-30	Tipton, Okla.		R	R	6'1	170	1	13	.071	0	31	16	1	103	135	64	59	0	6.64	25	3	0	.120
Herrin, Tom-Thomas Edward	54BosA	9-12-29	Shreveport, La.		R	R	6'3	190	1	2	.333	0	14	1	0	28	34	22	8	0	7.39	8	1	0	.125
Hetki, Johnny-John Edward	45-48,50CinN 52StLA 53-54PitN	5-12-22	Leavenworth, Kans.		R	R	6'1	202	18	26	.409	13	214	23	8	525	557	185	175	0	4.39	115	27	0	.235
Hill, Dave-David Burnham	57KCA	11-11-37	New Orleans, La.		R	L	6'2	170	0	0	–	0	2	0	0	2	6	3	1	0	31.50	0	0	0	–
Hiller, Frank-Frank Walter (Dutch)	46,48-49NYA 50-51ChiN 52CinN 53NYN	7-13-20	Newark, N.Y.		R	R	6'	200	30	32	.484	4	138	60	22	533	553	158	197	5	4.42	148	26	0	.176
Hillman, Dave-Darius Dutton	55-59ChiN 60-61BosA 62CinN 62NYN	9-14-27	Dungannon, Va.		R	R	5'11	168	21	37	.362	3	188	64	8	624	639	185	296	1	3.87	163	16	0	.098
Hinrichs, Paul-Paul Edwin (Herky)	51BosA	8-31-25	Marengo, Iowa		R	R	6'	180	0	0	–	0	4	0	0	3	7	4	1	0	24.00	0	0	0	–
Hisner, Harley-Harley Parnell	51BosA	11- 6-26	Naples, Ind.		R	R	6'1	185	0	1	.000	0	1	1	0	6	7	4	3	0	4.50	2	1	0	.500
Hittle, Lloyd-Lloyd Eldon (Red)	49-50WasA	2-21-24	Lodi, Cal.		R	L	5'10	164	7	11	.389	0	47	13	4	152	183	74	41	2	4.44	41	5	0	.122
Hobbie, Glen-Glen Frederick	57-64ChiN 64StLN	4-24-36	Witt, Ill.		R	R	6'2	195	62	81	.434	6	284	170	45	1263	1283	495	682	11	4.20	398	52	4	.131
Hodkey, Eli-Aloysius Joseph	46PhiN	11- 3-17	Lorain, Ohio		L	L	6'4	185	0	1	.000	0	2	1	0	4	9	5	0	0	13.50	2	0	0	.000
Hoeft, Billy-William Frederick	52-59DetA 59BosA 59-61BalA 63SFN 64MilN 65-66ChiN 66SFN	5-17-32	Oshkosh, Wis.		L	L	6'3	195	97	101	.490	33	505	200	75	1848	1820	685	1140	17	3.94	531	107	3	.202
Hogue, Bobby-Robert Clinton	48-51BosN 51StLA 51-52NYA 52StLA	4- 5-21	Miami, Fla.		R	R	5'10	195	18	16	.529	17	172	3	0	327	336	142	108	0	3.96	73	17	0	.233
Hogue, Cal-Calvin Grey	52-54PitN	10-24-27	Dayton, Ohio		R	R	6'	185	2	10	.167	0	25	16	5	114	109	96	51	0	4.89	32	6	0	.188
Holcombe, Ken-Kenneth Edward	45NYA 48CinN 50-52ChiA 52StLA 53BosA	8-23-18	Burnsville, N.C.		R	R	5'11	185	18	32	.360	2	99	48	18	374	377	170	118	2	3.99	106	19	0	.179
Holloman, Bobo-Alva Lee	53StLA	3- 7-25	Thomaston, Ga.		R	R	6'2	207	3	7	.300	0	22	10	1	65	69	50	25	1	5.26	19	2	0	.105
Hood, Wally-Wallace James Jr.	49NYA	9-24-25	Los Angeles, Cal.		R	R	6'1	190	0	0	–	0	2	0	0	2	0	1	2	0	0.00	0	0	0	–
Hooper, Bob-Robert Nelson	50-52PhiA 53-54CleA 55CinN	5-30-22	Leamington, Canada		R	R	5'11	200	40	41	.494	25	194	57	16	620	640	280	196	0	4.80	187	31	4	.166
Hoover, Dick-Richard Lloyd	52BosN	12-11-25	Columbus, Ohio		L	L	6'	170	0	0	–	0	2	0	0	5	8	3	0	0	7.20	0	0	0	–
Hopper, Jim-James McDaniel	46PitN	9- 1-19	Charlotte, N.C.		R	R	6'1	170	0	1	.000	0	2	1	0	4	6	3	1	0	11.25	0	0	0	–
Hoskins, Dave-David Taylor	53-54CleA	8- 3-25	Greenwood, Miss.	4- 2-70	L	R	6'1	180	9	4	.692	1	40	8	3	140	131	48	64	0	3.79	66	15	1	.227
Host, Gene-Eugene Earl (Twinkles, Slick)	56DetA 57KCA	1- 1-33	Leeper, Pa.		B	L	5'11	190	0	2	.000	0	12	3	0	29	38	16	14	0	7.14	7	0	0	.000
Houtteman, Art-Arthur Joseph	45-50,52DetA 51MS 53-57CleA 57BalA	8- 7-27	Detroit, Mich.		R	R	6'2	188	87	91	.489	20	325	181	78	1556	1646	516	639	14	4.14	513	99	2	.193
Howard, Lee-Lee Vincent	46-47PitN	11-11-23	Staten Island, N.Y.		L	L	6'2	175	0	1	.000	0	5	2	1	16	18	9	8	0	2.25	5	0	0	.000
Howe, Cal-Calvin Earl	52ChiN	11-27-24	Rock Falls, Ill.		L	L	6'3	205	0	0	–	0	1	0	0	2	0	1	2	0	0.00	0	0	0	–
Howell, Dixie-Millard	40CleA 49CinN 55-58ChiA	1- 7-20	Bowman, Ky.	3-18-60	L	R	6'2	210	19	15	.559	19	115	2	0	226	236	103	99	0	3.78	74	18	5	.243
Hoyle, Tex-Roland Edison	52PhiA	7-17-21	Carbondale, Pa.		R	R	6'4	170	0	0	–	0	3	0	0	2	9	1	1	0	31.50	0	0	0	–
Hudson, Hal-Hal Campbell (Lefty)	52StLA 52-53ChiA	5- 4-27	Grosse Pt., Mich.		L	L	5'10	175	0	0	–	0	6	0	0	11	16	7	4	0	7.36	1	0	0	.000
Hudson, Sid-Sidney Charles	40-42WasA 43-45MS 46-52WasA 52-54BosA	1- 3-15	Coalfield, Tenn.		R	R	6'4	180	104	152	.406	13	380	279	123	2181	2384	835	734	11	4.28	746	164	0	.220
Hughes, Jim-James Robert	52-56BknN 56ChiN 57ChiA	3-21-23	Chicago, Ill.		R	R	6'1	200	15	13	.536	39	172	1	0	297	278	152	165	0	3.82	53	9	0	.170
Hughes, Tom-Thomas Edward	59StLN	9-13-34	Ancon, Canal Zone		L	R	6'2	180	0	2	.000	0	2	2	0	4	9	2	2	0	15.75	1	0	0	.000
Hughes, Tommy-Thomas Owen	41-42PhiN 43-45MS 46-47PhiN 48CinN	10- 7-19	Wilkes-Barre, Pa.		R	R	6'1	190	31	56	.356	3	144	87	31	688	698	308	221	5	3.92	213	25	0	.117
Hurd, Tom-Thomas Carr (Whitey)	54-56BosA	5-27-24	Danville, Va.		R	R	5'9	155	13	10	.565	11	99	0	0	187	177	97	96	0	3.95	29	8	0	.276
Hutchinson, Fred-Frederick Charles (Big Bear)	39-41DetA 42-45MS 46-53,M52-54DetA 56-58StLN M59-64CinN	8-12-19	Seattle, Wash.	11-12-64	L	R	6'2	190	95	71	.572	7	242	169	81	1465	1487	388	591	13	3.72	(See B46-60)			
Hyde, Dick-Richard Elde	55,57-60WasA 61BalA	8- 3-28	Hindsboro, Ill.		R	R	5'11	170	17	14	.548	23	169	2	0	298	273	137	144	0	3.56	43	4	0	.093
Iott, Hooks-Clarence Eugene	41StLA 43-45MS 47StLA 47NYN	12- 3-19	Mountain Grove, Mo.		B	L	6'2	200	3	9	.250	0	26	9	2	82	84	67	53	1	7.02	23	3	0	.130
Jacobs, Tony-Anthony Robert	48ChiN 55StLN	8- 5-25	Dixmoor, Ill.		B	R	5'9	150	0	0	–	0	2	0	0	4	9	1	3	0	11.25	1	0	0	.000
Jansen, Larry-Lawrence Joseph	47-54NYN 56CinN	7-16-20	Verboort, Ore.		R	R	6'2	190	122	89	.578	10	291	237	107	1767	1751	410	842	17	3.58	600	90	1	.150
Jeffcoat, Hal-Harold Bentley	54-55ChiN 56-59CinN 59StLN	9- 6-24	W. Columbia, S.C.		R	R	5'10	185	39	37	.513	26	246	51	13	697	772	267	239	1	4.22	(See B46-60)			
Jester, Virgil-Virgil Milton	52BosN 53MilN	7-23-27	Denver, Colo.		R	R	5'11	188	3	5	.375	0	21	8	4	75	84	27	25	1	3.84	19	4	0	.211
Johnson, Ben-Benjamin Franklin	59-60ChiN	5-16-31	Greenwood, S.C.		R	R	6'2	190	2	1	.667	1	21	2	0	46	56	15	15	0	3.91	6	0	0	.000
Johnson, Chet-Chester Lillis (Chesty Chet)	46StLA	8- 1-17	Redmond, Wash.		L	L	6'	175	0	0	–	0	5	3	0	18	20	13	8	0	5.00	6	0	0	.000
Johnson, Connie-Clifford	53,55-56ChiA 56-58BalA	12-27-22	Stone Mountain, Ga.		R	R	6'4	200	40	39	.506	1	123	100	34	716	654	257	497	8	3.44	237	40	0	.169
Johnson, Don-Donald Roy	47,50NYA 50-51StLA 51-52WasA 54ChiA 55BalA 58SFN	11-12-26	Portland, Ore.		R	R	6'3	200	27	38	.415	12	198	70	17	631	712	285	262	4	4.78	155	9	0	.058
Johnson, Earl-Earl Douglas (Lefty)	40-51,46-50BosA 42-45MS 51DetA	4- 2-19	Redmond, Wash.		L	L	6'3	190	40	32	.556	17	179	50	13	546	556	272	250	3	4.31	171	32	0	.187
Johnson, Ernie-Ernest Thorwald	50,52BosN 53-58MilN 59BalA	6-16-24	Brattleboro, Vt.		R	R	6'3	195	40	23	.635	19	273	19	3	574	587	231	319	1	3.78	100	18	1	.180
Johnson, Ken-Kenneth Wandersee (Hooks)	47-50StLN 50-51PhiN 52DetA	1-14-23	Topeka, Kans.		L	L	6'1	185	12	14	.462	0	74	34	8	269	251	195	147	4	4.58	89	19	0	.213
Jolly, Dave-David (Gabby)	53-57MilN	10-14-24	Stony Point, N.C.	5-27-63	R	R	6'	165	16	14	.533	19	159	1	0	291	255	198	155	0	3.77	48	14	1	.292
Jones, Gordon-Gordon Bassett	54-56StLN 57NYN 58-59SFN 60-61BalA 62KCA 64-65HouN	4- 2-30	Portland, Ore.		R	R	6'	185	15	18	.455	12	171	21	4	379	405	120	232	2	4.16	67	8	0	.119
Jones, Sam-Samuel (Toothpick, Sad Sam)	51-52CleA 55-56ChiN 57-58StLN 59-61SFN 62DetA 63StLN 64BalA	12-14-25	Stewartsville, O.	11- 5-71	R	R	6'4	205	102	101	.502	9	322	222	76	1644	1403	822	1376	17	3.59	522	78	1	.149
Jones, Sheldon-Sheldon Leslie (Available)	46-51NYN 52BosN 53ChiN	2- 2-22	Tecumseh, Neb.		R	R	6'	180	54	57	.486	12	260	101	33	919	909	413	413	5	3.97	257	35	0	.136
Jordan, Milt-Milton Mignot	53DetA	5-24-27	Mineral Sprs., Pa.		R	R	6'2	207	0	1	.000	0	8	1	0	17	26	5	4	0	5.82	2	1	0	.500
Jordan, Niles-Niles Chapman	51PhiN 52CinN	12- 1-25	Lyman, Wash.		L	L	5'11	180	2	4	.333	0	8	6	2	43	49	11	13	1	4.19	14	1	0	.071
Judson, Howie-Howard Kolls	48-52ChiA 53-54CinN	2-16-26	Hebron, Ill.		R	R	6'1	195	17	37	.315	14	207	48	8	615	619	319	204	0	4.29	154	14	0	.093
Kaiser, Don-Clyde Donald (Tiger)	55-57ChiN	2- 3-35	Byng, Okla.		R	R	6'5	195	6	15	.286	0	58	35	6	240	255	85	108	1	4.16	68	4	0	.059
Karpel, Herb-Herbert (Lefty)	46NYA	12-27-17	Brooklyn, N.Y.		L	L	5'9	180	0	0	–	0	2	0	0	2	4	0	0	0	9.00	0	0	0	–
Keegan, Bob-Robert Charles (Smiley)	53-58ChiA	8- 4-20	Rochester, N.Y.		R	R	6'2	207	40	36	.526	5	135	87	29	646	668	233	198	6	3.65	196	32	0	.163
Kellner, Alex-Alexander Raymond	48-54PhiA 55-58KCA 58CinN 59StLN	8-26-24	Tucson, Ariz.		R	L	6'	200	101	112	.474	5	321	250	99	1851	1925	747	816	9	4.41	643	138	4	.215
Kellner, Walt-Walter Joseph	52-53PhiA	4-26-29	Tucson, Ariz.		R	R	6'	200	0	0	–	1	3	0	0	7	5	7	6	0	6.43	1	0	0	.000
Kelly, Bob-Robert Edward	51-53ChiN 53,58CinN 58CleA	10- 4-27	Cleveland, Ohio		R	R	6'	180	12	18	.400	2	123	35	7	362	374	152	146	2	4.50	90	16	0	.178
Kemmerer, Russ-Russell Paul (Rusty, Dutch)	54-55,57BosA 57-60WasA 60-62ChiA 62-63HouN	11- 1-31	Pittsburgh, Pa.		R	R	6'2	198	43	59	.422	8	302	109	24	1066	1144	389	505	2	4.47	265	34	2	.128
Kennedy, Bill-William Aulton (Lefty)	48CleA 48-51StLA 52ChiA 53BosA 56-57CinN	3-14-21	Carnesville, Ga.		L	L	6'2	200	15	28	.349	11	172	45	6	465	497	289	256	0	4.70	120	25	0	.208
Kennedy, Bill-William Gorman	42WasA 43-45MS 46-47WasA	12-22-18	Alexandria, Va.		L	L	6'1	175	1	3	.250	5	31	4	1	64	71	44	23	0	6.75	14	1	0	.071
Kennedy, Monte-Montia Calvin (Lefty)	46-53NYN	5-11-22	Amelia, Va.		R	L	6'2	185	42	55	.433	4	249	127	48	960	928	495	411	7	3.84	301	46	1	.153
Keriazakos, Gus-Constantine Nicholas	50ChiA 54WasA 55KCA	7-28-31	West Orange, N.J.		R	R	6'3	187	2	5	.286	0	28	5	2	74	81	42	42	0	5.59	19	2	0	.105
Kiely, Leo-Leo Patrick	51BosA 52-53MS 54-56,58-59BosA 60KCA	11-30-29	Hoboken, N.J.		L	L	6'2	180	26	27	.491	29	209	39	8	523	562	189	212	1	3.37	139	20	1	.144
Killeen, Evans-Evans Henry	59KCA	2-27-36	Brooklyn, N.Y.		R	R	6'	190	0	0	–	0	4	0	0	6	4	4	1	0	4.50	0	0	0	–
Kinder, Ellis-Ellis Raymond (Old Folks)	46-47StLA 48-55BosA 56StLN 56-57ChiA	7-26-14	Atkins, Ark.	10-16-68	R	R	6'3	215	102	71	.590	102	484	122	56	1480	1421	539	749	10	3.43	444	63	1	.142
King, Clyde-Clyde Edward	44-45,47-48,51-52BknN 53CinN M69-70SFN M74-75AtlN	5-23-25	Goldsboro, N.C.		B	R	6'1	183	32	25	.561	11	200	21	4	496	524	189	150	0	4.14	114	13	0	.114
King, Nellie-Nelson Joseph	54-57PitN	3-15-28	Shenandoah, Pa.		R	R	6'6	185	7	5	.583	6	95	4	0	173	193	50	72	0	3.59	23	0	0	.000
Kipp, Fred-Fred Leo	57BknN 58-59LAN 60NYA	10- 1-31	Piqua, Kans.		L	L	6'4	200	6	7	.462	0	47	9	0	113	119	48	64	0	5.10	37	9	0	.243
Kipper, Thornton-Thornton John	53-55PhiN	9-27-28	Bagley, Wis.		R	R	6'3	195	3	4	.429	1	55	3	0	100	128	46	35	0	5.22	16	2	0	.125
Klieman, Eddie-Edward Frederick (Babe)	43-48CleA 49WasA 49ChiA 50PhiA	3-21-18	Norwood, Ohio		R	R	6'1	190	26	28	.481	33	222	32	10	542	525	239	130	2	3.49	144	21	1	.146
Klippstein, Johnny-John Calvin	50-54ChiN 55-58CinN 58-59LAN 60CleA 61WasA 62CinN 63-64PhiN 64-66MinA 67DetA	10-17-27	Washington, D.C.		R	R	6'1	185	101	118	.461	66	711	162	37	1970	1915	978	1158	6	4.24	502	63	5	.125
Knerr, Lou-Wallace Luther	45-46PhiA 47WasA	8-21-21	Denver, Pa.		R	R	6'1	210	8	27	.229	0	63	39	11	287	330	149	104	0	5.05	98	19	0	.194
Koecher, Dick-Richard Finlay (Highpockets)	46-48PhiN	3-30-26	Philadelphia, Pa.		L	L	6'5	196	0	4	.000	0	7	3	1	26	31	14	8	0	4.85	5	0	0	.000
Konikowski, Alex-Alexander James (Whitey)	48,51NYN 52-53MS 54NYN	6- 8-28	Throop, Pa.		R	R	6'1	187	2	3	.400	1	35	1	0	49	58	29	20	0	6.98	3	0	0	.000
Konstanty, Jim-Casimir James	44CinN 46BosN 48-54PhiN 54-56NYA 56StLN	3- 2-17	Strykersville, N.Y.		R	R	6'1	202	66	48	.579	74	433	36	14	947	957	269	268	2	3.46	202	33	0	.163
Koski, Bill-William John (T-Bone)	51PitN 52-54MS	2- 6-32	Madera, Cal.		R	R	6'4	185	0	1	.000	0	13	1	0	27	26	28	6	0	6.67	4	0	0	.000
Koslo (Koslowski), Dave-George Bernard	41-42NYN 43-45MS 46-53NYN 54BalA 54-55MilN	3-31-20	Menasha, Wis.		L	L	5'11	185	92	107	.462	22	348	189	74	1592	1597	538	606	16	3.68	516	56	3	.109
Kraly, Steve-Steve Charles (Lefty)	53NYA	4-18-29	Whiting, Ind.		L	L	5'10	152	0	2	.000	1	5	3	0	25	19	16	8	0	3.24	7	0	0	.000
Kramer, Jack-John Henry	39-41StLA 42WW 43-47StLA 48-49BosA 50-51NYN 51NYA	1- 5-18	New Orleans, La.		R	R	6'2	190	95	103	.480	7	322	215	88	1638	1761	682	613	14	4.24	501	72	5	.144

					LIFETIME PITCHING TOTALS																	BATTING TOTALS			
USE NAME – GIVEN NAMES (NICKNAMES)	TEAM BY YEAR	BIRTH DATE	BIRTH PLACE	DEATH DATE	B	T	HGT	WGT	W	L	PCT	SV	G	GS	CG	IP	H	BB	SO	ShO	ERA	AB	H	HR	BA
Kretlow, Lou-Louis Henry	46,48-49DetA 50StLA 50-53ChiA 53StLA	6-27-23	Apache, Okla.		R	R	6'2	195	27	47	.365	1	199	104	22	786	781	522	450	3	4.87	237	27	0	.114
	54-55BalA 56KCA																								
Krieger, Kurt-Kurt Ferdinand (Dutch)	49,51StLN	9-16-26	Traisen, Austria	8-16-70	R	R	6'3	212	0	0	–	0	3	0	0	5	6	6	3	0	12.60	0	0	0	–
Kucab, Johnny-John Albert	50-52PhiA	12-17-19	Olyphant, Pa.		R	R	6'2	185	5	5	.500	6	59	3	2	152	169	51	48	0	4.44	35	3	0	.086
Kucks, Johnny-John Charles	55-59NYA 59-60KCA	7-27-33	Hoboken, N.J.		R	R	6'3	190	54	56	.491	7	207	123	30	938	970	308	338	7	4.10	291	32	0	.110
Kume, John-John Mike	55KCA	5-19-26	Premier, W.Va.		R	R	6'1	195	0	2	.000	0	6	4	0	24	35	15	7	0	7.88	8	1	0	.125
Kush, Emil-Emil Benedict	41-42ChiN 43-45MS 46-49ChiN	11- 4-16	Chicago, Ill.		R	R	6'1	185	21	12	.636	12	150	8	2	347	324	158	150	1	3.48	82	18	0	.220
Kuzava, Bob-Robert LeRoy (Sarge)	46-47CleA 49-50ChiA 50-51WasA	5-28-23	Wyandotte, Mich.		B	L	6'2	202	49	44	.527	13	213	99	34	862	849	415	446	6	4.05	256	22	1	.086
	51-54NYA 54-55BalA 55PhiN 57PitN 57StLN																								
Labine, Clem-Clement Walter	50-57BknN 58-60LAN 60DetA 60-61PitN 62NYN	8- 6-26	Lincoln, R.I.		R	R	6'	190	77	56	.579	96	513	38	7	1080	1043	396	551	2	3.63	227	17	3	.075
Lade, Doyle-Doyle Marion (Porky)	46-50ChiN	2-17-21	Fairbury, Neb.		R	R	5'10	183	25	29	.463	3	126	64	20	537	583	221	178	2	4.39	164	36	0	.220
					Bats Both 46-47																				
LaMacchia, Al-Alfred Anthony	43,45-46StLA 46WasA	7-22-21	St. Louis, Mo.		R	R	5'10	190	2	2	.500	0	16	1	0	31	38	14	7	0	6.39	6	0	0	.000
Lambert, Clay-Clayton Patrick	46-47CinN	3-26-17	Summit, Ill.		R	R	6'2	185	2	2	.500	1	26	4	2	59	60	26	21	0	5.34	14	2	0	.143
Landrum, Joe-Joseph Butler	50BknN 51VR 52BknN	12-13-28	Columbia, S.C.		R	R	5'11	180	1	3	.250	1	16	5	2	45	58	11	22	0	5.60	8	1	0	.125
Lane, Jerry-Jerald Hal	53WasA 54-55CinN	2- 7-26	Ashland, N.Y.		R	R	6'	205	2	6	.250	1	31	2	0	79	84	25	33	0	4.44	13	1	0	.077
Lanfranconi, Walt-Walter Oswald	41ChiN 42-45MS 47BosN	11- 9-16	Barre, Vt.		R	R	5'7	155	4	5	.444	1	38	5	1	70	72	29	19	0	2.96	11	0	0	.000
LaPalme, Paul-Paul Edmore	51-54PitN 55-56StLN 56CinN 56-57ChiA	12-14-23	Springfield, Mass.		L	L	5'10	185	24	45	.348	14	253	51	10	616	645	272	277	2	4.42	147	20	0	.136
Larsen, Don-Donald James	53StLA 54BalA 55-59NYA 60-61KCA 61ChiA	8- 7-29	Michigan City, Ind.		R	R	6'4	225	81	91	.471	23	412	171	44	1549	1442	725	849	11	3.78	596	144	14	.242
	62-64SFN 64-65HouN 65BalA 67ChiN																								
Lary, Frank-Frank Strong (Mule, The Yankee Killer)	54-64DetA	4-10-30	Northport, Ala.		R	R	5'11	185	128	116	.525	11	350	292	126	2162	2123	616	1099	21	3.49	734	130	6	.177
	64NYN 64MilN 65NYN 65ChiA																								
Lasorda, Tom-Thomas Charles	54-55BknN 56KCA	9-22-27	Norristown, Pa.		L	L	5'10	175	0	4	.000	1	26	6	0	58	53	56	37	0	6.52	14	1	0	.071
Law, Vern-Vernon Sanders (Deacon)	50-51PitN 52-53MS 54-67PitN	3-12-30	Meridian, Idaho		R	R	6'2	200	162	147	.524	13	483	364	119	2673	2833	597	1092	28	3.76	883	191	11	.216
Lawrence, Brooks-Brooks Ulysses (Bull)	54-55StLN 56-60CinN	1-30-25	Springfield, Ohio		R	R	6'	205	69	62	.527	22	275	127	42	1041	1034	385	481	5	4.25	319	49	0	.154
Lehman, Ken-Kenneth Karl	52,56-57BknN 57-58BalA 61PhiN	6-10-28	Seattle, Wash.		L	L	6'	180	14	10	.583	7	134	13	2	204	270	[illegible]	101	0	3.02	66	0	0	.161
Lemon, Bob-Robert Granville	46-58CleA M70-72KCA	9-22-20	San Bernandino, Cal.		L	R	6'	180	207	128	.618	22	460	350	188	2849	2559	1251	1277	31	3.23	(See B46-60)			
Lewandowski, Dan-Daniel William	51StLN	1- 6-28	Buffalo, N.Y.		R	R	6'	180	0	1	.000	0	2	0	0	1	3	1	1	0	9.00	0	0	0	–
Liddle, Don-Donald Eugene	53MilN 54-56NYN 56StLN	5-25-25	Mt. Carmel, Ill.		L	L	5'10	165	28	18	.609	4	117	54	13	428	397	203	198	3	3.74	112	17	0	.152
Linde, Lyman-Lyman Gilbert	47-48CleA	9-20-20	Beaver Dam, Wis.		R	R	5'11	185	0	0	–	0	4	0	0	11	12	5	0	0	6.55	2	0	0	.000
Lindell, Johnny-John Harlan	42NYA 45MS 53PitN 53PhiN	8-30-16	Greeley, Colo.		R	R	6'4	217	8	18	.308	1	55	28	15	252	247	161	146	1	4.46	(See B46-60)			
Lint, Royce-Royce James	54StLN	1- 1-21	Birmingham, Ala.		L	L	6'1	165	2	3	.400	0	30	4	1	70	75	30	36	1	4.89	10	1	0	.100
LiPetri, Angelo-Michael Angelo	56,58PhiN	7- 6-30	Brooklyn, N.Y.		R	R	6'1	180	0	0	–	0	10	0	0	15	13	3	9	0	5.40	1	0	0	.000
Littlefield, Dick-Richard Bernard	50BosA 51ChiA 52DetA 52-53StLA	3-18-26	Detroit, Mich.		L	L	6'	180	33	54	.379	9	243	83	16	761	750	413	495	2	4.72	193	28	0	.145
	54BalA 54-56PitN 56StLN 56NYN 57ChiN 58MilN																								
Lively, Bud-Everett Adrian (Red)	47-49CinN	2-14-25	Birmingham, Ala.		R	R	6'	200	8	13	.381	1	79	27	6	249	230	127	94	2	4.16	60	10	0	.167
Locke, Charlie-Charles Edward (Chuck)	55BalA	5- 5-32	Malden, Mo.		R	R	5'11	185	0	0	–	0	2	0	0	3	0	1	1	0	0.00	0	0	0	–
Loes, Billy-William	50BknN 51MS 52-56BknN 56-59BalA 60-61SFN	12-13-29	Queens, N.Y.		R	R	6'1	180	80	63	.559	32	316	139	42	1191	1135	421	645	9	3.88	347	38	0	.110
Lombardi, Vic-Victor Alvin	45-47BknN 48-50PitN	9-20-22	Reedley, Cal.		L	L	5'7	158	50	51	.495	16	223	100	42	945	919	418	340	5	3.68	311	74	0	.238
Lombardo, Lou-Louis	48NYN	11-18-28	Carlstadt, N.J.		L	L	6'2	210	0	0	–	0	2	0	0	5	5	5	0	0	7.20	2	0	0	.000
Lopat (Lopatynski), Ed-Edmund Walter (Steady Eddie)	44-47ChiA 48-55NYA	6-21-18	New York, N.Y.		L	L	5'10	185	166	112	.597	3	340	318	164	2439	2464	650	859	27	3.21	887	187	5	.211
	55BalA M63-64KCA																								
Lovenguth, Lynn-Lynn Richard	55PhiN 57StLN	11-29-22	Camden, N.Y.		L	R	5'10	170	0	2	.000	0	16	1	0	27	23	16	20	0	3.67	4	0	0	.000
Lown, Turk-Omar Joseph	51-54,56-58ChiN 58CinN 58-62ChiA	5-30-24	Brooklyn, N.Y.		R	R	6'	185	55	61	.474	73	504	49	10	1031	978	590	574	1	4.12	214	35	1	.164
Lumenti, Ralph-Ralph Anthony (Commuter)	57-59WasA	12-21-36	Milford, Mass.		L	L	6'3	185	1	3	.250	0	13	6	0	33	32	42	30	0	7.36	10	2	0	.200
Luna, Memo-Guillermo Romero	54StLN	6-25-30	Tacubaya, Mexico		L	L	6'	168	0	1	.000	0	1	1	0	1	2	2	0	0	18.00	0	0	0	–
Lyons, Al-Albert Harold	44NYA 45MS 46-47NYA 47PitN 48BosN	7-18-18	St. Joseph, Mo.	12-20-65	R	R	6'2	195	3	3	.500	0	39	1	0	100	125	59	46	0	6.30	58	17	1	.293
Maas, Duke-Duane Fredrick	55-57DetA 58KCA 58-61NYA	1-31-29	Utica, Mich.		R	R	5'10	170	45	44	.506	15	195	91	21	734	745	284	356	7	4.19	214	25	1	.117
Mabe, Bob-Robert Lee	58StLN 59CinN 60BalA	10- 8-29	Danville, Va.		R	R	5'11	165	7	11	.389	3	51	14	4	143	146	61	82	0	4.78	31	1	0	.032
Macdonald, Bill-William Paul	50PitN 51-52MS 53PitN	3-28-29	Alameda, Cal.		R	R	5'11	175	8	11	.421	1	36	21	6	160	150	96	64	2	4.67	49	6	0	.122
Mackinson, Johnny-John Joseph	53PhiA 55StLN	10-29-23	Orange, N.J.		R	R	5'10	160	0	1	.000	0	9	1	0	22	25	12	8	0	7.36	4	0	0	.000
Madison, Dave-David Pledger	50NYA 51MS 52StLA 52-53DetA	2- 1-21	Brooksville, Miss.		R	R	6'3	190	8	7	.533	0	74	6	0	158	173	103	70	0	5.70	30	3	0	.100
Maglie, Sal-Salvatore Anthony (The Barber)	45NYN 46-49SM 50-55NYN	4-26-17	Niagara Falls, N.Y.		R	R	6'2	185	119	62	.657	14	303	232	93	1721	1591	652	862	25	3.15	563	76	2	.135
	55-56CleA 56-57BknN 57-58NYA 58StLN																								
Mahoney, Bob-Robert Paul	51ChiA 51-52StLA	6-20-28	LeRoy, Minn.		R	R	6'1	185	2	5	.286	0	36	4	0	91	99	50	34	0	4.95	18	4	0	.222
Main, Woody-Forrest Harry	48,50,52-53PitN	2-12-22	Delano, Cal.		R	R	6'3	195	4	13	.235	3	79	11	2	204	210	84	107	0	5.16	44	4	0	.091
Mallette, Mal-Malcolm Francis	50BknN	1-30-22	Syracuse, N.Y.		L	L	6'2	200	0	0	–	0	2	0	0	1	2	1	2	0	0.00	0	0	0	–
Malloy, Bob-Robert Paul	43-44CinN 45MS 46-47CinN 49StLA	5-28-18	Canonsburg, Pa.		R	R	5'11	185	4	7	.364	2	48	3	1	116	116	52	35	0	3.26	31	7	0	.226
Manville, Dick-Richard Wesley	50BosN 52ChiN	12-25-26	Des Moines, Iowa		R	R	6'5	200	0	0	–	0	12	0	0	19	25	15	8	0	7.11	2	1	0	.500
Marchildon, Phil-Philip Edward	40-42,45-49PhiA 43-44MS 50BosA	10-25-13	Penetanguishene, Cda.		R	R	5'10	175	68	75	.476	2	185	162	82	1214	1084	684	481	6	3.93	405	58	1	.143
Margoneri, Joe-Joseph Emanuel	56-57NYN	1-13-30	Somerset, Pa.		L	L	6'	185	7	7	.500	0	36	15	3	126	132	70	67	0	4.29	37	3	1	.081
Markell (Makowsky), Duke-Harry Duquesne	51StLA	8-17-23	Paris, France		R	R	6'1	209	1	1	.500	0	5	2	1	21	25	20	10	0	6.43	6	1	0	.167
Marlowe, Dick-Richard Burton	51-56DetA 56ChiA	6-27-29	Hickory, N.C.	12-30-68	R	R	6'2	165	13	15	.464	3	98	17	3	244	280	101	108	0	4.70	57	10	0	.175
Marrero, Connie-Conrado Eugenio [Ramos]	50-54WasA	4-25-11	Sagua, Cuba		R	R	5'7	165	39	40	.494	3	118	94	51	735	736	249	297	7	3.67	236	27	0	.114
Marshall, Cuddles-Clarence Westly	46,48-49NYA 50StLA	4-28-25	Bellingham, Wash.		R	R	6'3	200	7	7	.500	4	73	15	1	185	216	158	69	0	5.98	49	9	0	.184
Martin, Barney-Barnes Robertson	53CinN	3- 3-23	Columbia, S.C.		R	R	5'11	170	0	0	–	0	1	0	0	2	3	1	1	0	9.00	0	0	0	–
Martin, Freddie-Fred Turner	46StLN 47-48SM 49-50StLN	6-27-15	Williams, Okla.		R	R	6'1	185	12	3	.800	0	57	10	5	162	181	58	68	0	3.78	46	13	0	.283
Martin, Morrie-Morris Webster	49BknN 51-54PhiA 54-56ChiA 56BalA	9- 3-22	Dixon, Mo.		L	L	6'	180	38	34	.528	15	250	42	8	604	607	251	245	1	4.29	165	28	0	.170
	57-58StLN 58CleA 59ChiN																								
Martin, Paul-Paul Charles	55PitN	3-10-32	Brownstone, Pa.		R	R	6'6	235	0	1	.000	0	7	1	0	7	13	17	3	0	14.14	0	0	0	–
Martin, Ray-Raymond Joseph	43BosN 44-46MS 47-48BosN	3-13-25	Norwood, Mass.		R	R	6'2	177	1	0	1.000	0	5	1	1	14	10	6	3	0	2.57	4	0	0	.000
Martinez, Rogelio-Rogelio [Ulloa] (Limonar)	50WasA	11- 5-18	Matanzas, Cuba		R	R	6'	180	0	1	.000	0	2	1	0	1	4	2	0	0	36.00	0	0	0	–
Mason, Hank-Henry	58,60PhiN	6-19-31	Marshall, Mo.		R	R	6'	185	0	0	–	0	4	0	0	11	16	7	6	0	9.82	3	0	0	.000
Masterson, Walt-Walter Edward	39-42WasA 43-44MS 45-49WasA	6-22-20	Philadelphia, Pa.		R	R	6'2	189	78	100	.438	20	399	184	70	1648	1613	886	815	15	4.15	486	68	0	.140
	49-52BosA 52-53WasA 56DetA																								
Matarazzo, Len-Leonard	52PhiA	9-12-28	New Castle, Pa.		R	R	6'4	195	0	0	–	0	1	0	0	1	1	1	0	0	0.00	0	0	0	–
Mathias, Carl-Carl Lynwood (Stubby)	60CleA 61WasA	6-13-36	Bechtelsville, Pa.		B	L	5'11	195	0	2	.000	0	11	3	0	29	36	12	20	0	7.14	6	1	0	.167
Mauriello, Ralph-Ralph (Tami)	58LAN	8-25-34	Brooklyn, N.Y.		R	R	6'3	195	1	1	.500	0	3	2	0	12	10	8	11	0	4.50	4	0	0	.000
Mayer, Ed-Edwin David	57-58ChiN	11-30-31	San Francisco, Cal.		L	L	6'2	185	2	2	.500	1	22	1	0	32	23	18	17	0	4.22	7	2	0	.286
McAvoy, Tom-Thomas John	59WasA	8-12-36	Brooklyn, N.Y.		L	L	6'3	200	0	0	–	0	1	0	0	3	1	2	0	0	0.00	1	0	0	.000
McCabe, Ralph-Ralph Herbert	46CleA	10-21-18	Napanee, Canada		R	R	6'4	195	0	1	.000	0	1	1	0	4	5	2	3	0	11.25	1	0	0	.000
McCahan, Bill-William Glenn	46-47 played in N.B.L. 46-49PhiA	6- 7-21	Philadelphia, Pa.		R	R	5'11	200	16	14	.533	0	57	40	17	291	297	145	76	2	3.84	96	20	0	.208
McCall, Dutch-Robert Leonard	48ChiN	12-15-20	Columbia, Tenn.		L	L	6'1	184	4	13	.235	0	30	20	5	151	158	85	89	0	4.83	53	9	0	.170
McCall, Windy-John William	48-49BosA 50PitN 54-57NYN	7-18-25	San Francisco, Cal.		L	L	6'	180	11	15	.423	12	134	15	4	253	249	103	144	0	4.23	48	7	0	.146
McDaniel, Von-Max Von	57-58StLN	4-18-39	Hollis, Okla.		R	R	6'2	180	7	5	.583	0	19	14	4	89	76	36	45	2	3.44	26	0	0	.000
McDermott, Mickey, Maurice Joseph	48-53BosA 54-55WasA 56NYA	8-29-28	Poughkeepsie, N.Y.		L	L	6'2	185	69	69	.500	14	291	156	54	1316	1161	838	757	11	3.91	(See B46-60)			
	57KCA 58DetA 61StLN 61KCA																								
McDevitt, Danny-Daniel Eugene	57BknN 58-60LAN 61NYA 61MinA 62KCA	11-18-32	New York, N.Y.		L	L	5'10	175	21	27	.438	7	155	60	13	456	461	264	303	4	4.40	123	17	0	.138
McDonald, Jim-James LeRoy (Hot Rod)	50BosA 51StLA 52-54NYA 55BalA	5-17-27	Grants Pass, Ore.		R	R	5'10	192	24	27	.471	1	136	55	15	468	489	231	158	3	4.27	128	23	0	.180
	56-58ChiA				Bats Both 50-51																				
McGlothin, Pat-Ezra Mac	49-50BknN	10-20-20	Coalfield, Tenn.		L	R	6'3	180	1	1	.500	0	8	0	0	18	18	6	13	0	5.50	3	0	0	.000
McGowan, Mickey-Tullis Earl	48NYN	11-26-21	Dothan, Ala.		L	L	6'2	200	0	0	–	0	3	0	0	4	3	4	2	0	6.75	1	0	0	.000
McIlwain, Stover-William Stover (Smokey)	57-58ChiA	9-22-39	Savannah, Ga.	1-15-66	R	R	6'2	195	0	0	–	0	2	1	0	5	6	1	4	0	1.80	1	0	0	.000
McLeland, Wayne-Wayne Gaffney (Nubbin)	51-52DetA	8-29-24	Milton, Iowa		R	R	6'	185	0	1	.000	0	10	1	0	14	24	10	0	0	8.36	1	0	0	.000
McLish, Cal-Calvin Coolidge Julius Caesar Tuskahoma	44BknN 45MS 46BknN	12- 1-25	Anadarko, Okla.		B	R	6'1	200	92	92	.500	6	352	209	57	1609	1685	552	713	5	4.01	490	73	3	.149
	47-48PitN 49,51ChiN 56-59CleA 60CinN 61ChiA 62-64PhiN																								
McMahan, Jack-Jack Wally	56PitN 56KCA	7-22-32	Hot Springs, Ark.		R	L	6'	175	0	5	.000	0	34	9	0	75	87	40	22	0	5.04	15	0	0	.000
Medlinger, Irv-Irving John	49,51StLA	6-18-27	Chicago, Ill.		L	L	5'11	185	0	0	–	0	9	0	0	14	21	15	9	0	13.50	0	0	0	–
Meers, Russ-Russell Harlan (Babe)	41ChiN 42-45MS 46-47ChiN	11-28-18	Tilton, Ill.		L	L	5'10	170	3	3	.500	0	43	4	0	83	76	48	35	0	4.01	17	3	0	.176
Merritt, Lloyd-Lloyd Wesley	57StLN	4- 8-33	St. Louis, Mo.		R	R	6'	189	1	2	.333	7	44	0	0	65	60	28	35	0	3.32	7	0	0	.000
Meyer, Jack-John Robert	55-61PhiN	3-23-32	Philadelphia, Pa.	3- 9-67	R	R	6'1	175	24	34	.414	21	202	24	4	455	385	244	375	0	3.92	86	14	1	.163
Meyer, Russ-Russell Charles (The Mad Monk)	46-48ChiN 49-52PhiN	10-25-23	Peru, Ill.		B	R	6'1	175	94	73	.563	5	319	219	65	1531	1606	541	672	13	3.99	484	55	1	.114
	53-55BknN 56ChiN 56CinN 57BosA 59KCA																								
Mickens, Glenn-Glenn Roger	53BknN	7-26-30	Wilmar, Cal.		R	R	6'	175	0	1	.000	0	4	2	0	6	11	4	5	0	12.00	2	0	0	.000

USE NAME – GIVEN NAMES (NICKNAMES)	TEAM BY YEAR	BIRTH DATE	BIRTH PLACE	DEATH DATE	LIFETIME PITCHING TOTALS B	T	HGT	WGT	W	L	PCT	SV	G	GS	CG	IP	H	BB	SO	ShO	ERA	BATTING TOTALS AB	H	HR	BA
Miller, Bill-William Paul (Hooks)	52-54NYA 55BalA	7-26-27	Minersville, Pa.		L	L	5'11	180	6	9	.400	1	41	18	5	132	136	79	72	2	4.23	40	9	0	.225
Miller, Bob-Robert Gerald	53-56DetA 62CinN 62NYN	7-15-35	Berwyn, Ill.		R	L	6'1	185	6	8	.429	1	86	8	1	189	206	92	75	0	4.71	41	6	0	.146
Miller, Bob-Robert John	49-58PhiN	6-16-26	Detroit, Mich.		R	R	6'3	190	42	42	.500	15	261	69	23	821	889	247	263	6	3.97	223	41	2	.184
Miller, Ox-John Anthony	43WasA 43,45-46StLA 47ChiN	5- 4-15	Gause, Tex.		R	R	6'1	190	4	6	.400	1	24	10	4	91	123	33	27	0	6.43	27	7	1	.259
Milliken, Bob-Robert Fogle (Bobo)	53-54BknN	8-25-26	Majorsville, W.Va.		R	R	6'	195	13	6	.684	4	61	13	3	181	152	60	90	0	3.58	51	7	0	.137
Minarcin, Rudy-Rudy Anthony (Buster)	55CinN 56-57BosA	3-25-30	N. Vandergrift, Pa.		R	R	6'	195	6	9	.400	3	70	13	3	171	169	89	70	1	4.63	32	6	0	.188
Minner, Paul-Paul Edison (Lefty)	46,48-49BknN 50-56ChiN	7-30-23	New Wilmington, Pa.		L	L	6'5	200	69	84	.451	10	253	169	64	1311	1428	393	481	9	3.94	447	98	6	.219
Minnick, Don-Donald Athey	57WasA	4-14-31	Lynchburg, Va.		R	R	6'3	195	0	1	.000	0	2	1	0	9	14	2	7	0	5.00	2	0	0	.000
Mizell, Vinegar Bend-Wilmer David	52-53StLN 54-55MS 56-60StLN	8-13-30	Leakesville, Miss.		R	L	6'3	205	90	88	.506	0	268	230	61	1528	1434	680	918	15	3.85	513	57	1	.111
	60-62PitN 62NYN																								
Moford, Herb-Herbert	55StLN 58DetA 59BosA 62NYN	8- 6-28	Brooksville, Ky.		R	R	6'1	175	5	13	.278	3	50	14	6	158	143	64	78	0	5.01	44	2	0	.045
Moisan, Bill-William Joseph	53ChiN	7-30-25	Bradford, Mass.		L	R	6'1	170	0	0	–	0	3	0	0	5	5	2	1	0	5.40	0	0	0	–
Monahan, Rinty-Edward Francis	53PhiA	4-28-28	Brooklyn, N.Y.		R	R	6'1	195	0	0	–	0	4	0	0	11	11	7	2	0	4.09	2	0	0	.000
Monroe, Zack-Zachary Charles	58-59NYA	7- 8-31	Peoria, Ill.		R	R	6'	198	4	2	.667	1	24	6	1	61	60	29	19	0	3.39	17	2	0	.118
Monzant, Ray-Ramon [Segundo]	54-57NYN 58SFN 59VR 60SFN	1- 4-33	Maracaibo, Venez.		R	R	6'	160	16	21	.432	1	106	32	8	318	330	134	201	1	4.36	89	14	0	.157
Moore, Ray-Raymond Leroy (Farmer)	52-53BknN 55-57BalA 58-60ChiA	6- 1-26	Meadows, Md.		R	R	6'	200	63	59	.516	46	365	105	24	1073	935	560	612	5	4.06	299	56	6	.187
	60WasA 61-63MinA																								
Morehead, Seth-Seth Marvin (Moe)	57-59PhiN 59-60ChiN 61MilN	8-15-34	Houston, Tex.		L	L	6'	195	5	19	.208	5	132	24	3	318	357	110	184	0	4.81	62	9	0	.145
Moreno, Julio-Julio [Gonzalez]	50-53WasA	1-28-21	Guines, Cuba		R	R	5'8	160	18	22	.450	2	73	45	14	336	349	157	119	0	4.26	106	14	0	.132
Morgan, Tom-Tom Stephen (Plowboy)	51-52NYA 53MS 54-56NYA 57KCA	5-20-30	El Monte, Cal.		R	R	6'1	200	67	47	.588	64	443	61	18	1025	1040	300	364	7	3.60	247	46	5	.186
	58-60DetA 60WasA 61-63LAA																								
Mossi, Don-Donald Louis (The Spinx)	54-58CleA 59-63DetA 64ChiA 65KCA	1-11-29	St. Helena, Cal.		L	L	6'1	195	101	80	.558	50	460	165	55	1548	1493	385	932	8	3.43	436	71	2	.163
Mossor, Earl-Earl Dalton	51BknN	7-21-25	Forbes, Tenn.		L	R	6'1	175	0	0	–	0	3	0	0	2	2	7	1	0	27.00	1	1	0	1.000
Moulder, Glen-Glen Hubert	46BknN 47StLA 48ChiA	9-28-17	Cleveland, Okla.		R	R	6'1	180	7	8	.467	4	66	11	0	161	188	98	50	0	5.20	37	10	0	.270
Mrozinski, Ron-Ronald Frank	54-55PhiN	9-16-30	White Haven, Pa.		R	L	5'11	160	1	3	.250	1	37	5	1	82	87	44	44	0	5.38	16	1	0	.063
Mueller, Gordy-Joseph Gordon	50BosA	12-10-22	Baltimore, Md.		R	R	6'4	200	0	0	–	0	8	0	0	7	11	13	1	0	10.29	1	0	0	.000
Muffett, Billy-Billy Arnold (Muff)	57-58StLN 59SFN 60-62BosA	9-21-30	Hammond, Ind.		R	R	6'1	198	16	23	.410	15	125	32	7	377	407	132	188	1	4.32	92	20	1	.217
Muir, Joe-Joseph Allen	51-52PitN	11-26-22	Oriole, Md.		L	L	6'1	188	2	5	.286	0	21	6	1	52	53	25	22	0	5.19	10	1	0	.100
Mulligan, Dick-Richard Charles	41WasA 42-45MS 46PhiN 46-47BosN	3-18-18	Wilkes-Barre, Pa.		L	L	6'	167	3	3	.500	1	25	6	2	81	82	39	23	0	4.44	18	0	0	.000
Munger, George-George David (Red)	43-44,46-52StLN 45MS 52,56PitN	10- 4-18	Houston, Tex.		R	R	6'2	200	77	56	.579	12	273	161	54	1229	1243	500	564	13	3.83	402	70	1	.174
Murff, Red-John Robert	56-57MilN	4- 1-21	Burlington, Tex.		R	R	6'3	195	2	2	.500	3	26	2	0	50	56	18	31	0	4.68	11	1	0	.091
Murray, Joe-Joseph Ambrose	50PhiA	11-11-20	Wilkes-Barre, Pa.		L	L	6'	165	0	3	.000	0	8	2	0	30	34	21	8	0	5.70	11	0	0	.000
Nagy, Steve-Stephen	47PitN 50WasA	5-28-19	Franklin, N.J.		L	L	5'9	174	3	8	.273	0	15	10	2	67	87	38	21	0	6.45	26	6	1	.231
Naranjo, Cholly-Lazaro Ramon Gonzalo Couto	56PitN	11-25-34	Havana, Cuba		L	R	5'11	165	1	2	.333	0	17	3	0	34	37	17	26	0	4.50	7	1	0	.143
Narleski, Ray-Raymond Edmond	54-58CleA 59DetA	11-25-28	Camden, N.J.		R	R	6'1	195	43	33	.566	58	266	52	17	701	606	335	454	1	3.61	166	26	1	.157
Necciai, Ron-Ronald Andrew	52PitN 53MS	6-18-32	Manown, Pa.		R	R	6'5	185	1	6	.143	0	12	9	0	55	63	32	31	0	7.04	17	1	0	.059
Negray, Ron-Ronald Alvin	52BknN 55-56PhiN 58LAN	2-26-30	Akron, Ohio		R	R	6'1	185	6	6	.500	3	66	15	2	163	170	57	81	0	4.03	35	3	0	.086
Neiger, Al-Alvin Edward	60PhiN	3-26-39	Wilmington, Del.		L	L	6'	195	0	0	–	0	6	0	0	13	16	4	3	0	5.54	2	1	0	.500
Nevel, Ernie-Ernie Wyre	50-51NYA 53CinN	8-17-19	Charleston, Mo.		R	R	5'11	190	0	1	.000	1	14	1	0	20	27	8	9	0	6.30	2	0	0	.000
Newcombe, Don-Donald (Newk)	49-51BknN 52-53MS 54-57BknN 58LAN	6-14-26	Madison, N.J.		L	R	6'4	230	149	90	.623	7	344	294	136	2155	2102	490	1129	24	3.56	878	238	15	.271
Newhouser, Hal-Harold (Prince Hal)	39-53DetA 54-55CleA	5-20-21	Detroit, Mich.		L	L	6'2	180	207	150	.580	26	488	374	212	2993	2674	1249	1796	33	3.05	999	201	2	.201
Nichols, Chet-Chester Raymond Jr.	51BosN 52-53MS 54-56MilN	2-22-31	Providence, R.I.		B	L	6'1	180	34	36	.486	10	189	71	23	604	600	280	266	4	3.64	173	22	0	.127
	60-63BosA 64CinN																								
Nichols, Dolan-Dolan Levon (Nick)	58ChiN	2-28-30	Tishomingo, Miss.		R	R	6'	195	0	4	.000	1	24	0	0	41	46	16	9	0	5.05	5	0	0	.000
Nixon, Willard-Willard Lee	50-58BosA	6-17-28	Taylorsville, Ga.		L	R	6'2	195	69	72	.489	3	225	177	51	1234	1277	530	616	9	4.39	459	111	2	.242
Nuxhall, Joe-Joseph Henry	44,52-60CinN 61KCA 62LAA 62-66CinN	7-30-28	Hamilton, Ohio		L	L	6'3	215	135	117	.536	19	526	287	83	2304	2310	776	1372	20	3.90	766	152	15	.198
O'Brien, Eddie-Edward Joseph	56-58PitN	12-11-30	South Amboy, N.J.		R	R	5'9	165	1	0	1.000	0	5	1	1	16	16	4	11	0	3.38	(See B46-60)			
O'Brien, Johnny-John Thomas	56-58PitN	12-11-30	South Amboy, N.J.		R	R	5'9	170	1	3	.250	0	25	1	0	61	61	35	30	0	5.61	(See B46-60)			
O'Donnell, George-George Dana	54PitN	5-27-29	Winchester, Ill.		R	R	6'3	175	3	9	.250	1	21	10	3	87	105	21	8	0	4.55	23	2	1	.087
Oster, Bill-William Peter	54PhiA	1- 2-33	New York, N.Y.		L	L	6'3	198	0	1	.000	0	8	1	0	16	19	12	5	0	6.19	3	1	0	.333
Ostrowski, Joe-Joseph Paul (Professor)	48-50StLA 50-52NYA	11-15-16	West Wyoming, Pa.		L	L	6'	180	23	25	.479	15	150	37	12	455	559	98	131	0	4.55	118	19	0	.161
Overmire, Stubby-Frank	43-49DetA 50-51StLA 51NYA 52StLA	5-16-19	Moline, Mich.		R	L	5'7	170	58	67	.464	10	266	137	50	1130	1259	325	301	11	3.97	335	54	0	.161
Page, Joe-Joseph Francis (Fireman)	44-50NYA 54PitN	10-28-17	Cherry Valley, Pa.		L	L	6'3	200	57	49	.538	76	285	45	14	790	727	421	519	1	3.53	229	47	2	.205
Paige, Satchel-Leroy Robert (Satch)	48-49CleA 51-53StLA 65KCA	7- 7-06	Mobile, Ala.		R	R	6'3	185	28	31	.475	32	179	26	7	476	429	183	290	4	3.29	124	12	0	.097
Paine, Phil-Phillips Steere	51BosN 52-53MS 54-57MilN 58StLN	6- 8-30	Chepachet, R.I.		R	R	6'2	185	10	1	.909	1	95	0	0	149	144	80	101	0	3.38	14	3	0	.214
Palica (Pavliecivich), Erv-Ervin Martin	45,47-51BknN 52MS	2- 9-28	Lomita, Cal.		R	R	6'1	190	41	55	.427	12	246	80	20	839	806	399	423	3	4.23	243	48	1	.198
	53-54BknN 55-56BalA																								
Palm, Mike-Richard Paul	48BosA	2-13-25	Boston, Mass.		R	R	6'3	190	0	0	–	0	3	0	0	3	6	5	1	0	6.00	3	0	0	.000
Palmquist, Ed-Edwin Lee	60-61LAN 61MinA	6-10-33	Los Angeles, Cal.		R	R	6'3	195	1	3	.250	1	36	2	0	69	77	36	41	0	5.09	10	0	0	.000
Papai, Al-Alfred Thomas	48StLN 49StLA 50BosA 50StLN 55ChiA	5- 7-19	Divernon, Ill.		R	R	6'3	185	9	14	.391	4	88	18	8	240	281	138	70	0	5.36	62	6	0	.097
Papish, Frank-Frank Richard (Pap)	45-48ChiA 49CleA 50PitN	10-21-17	Pueblo, Colo.	8-30-65	R	L	6'2	192	26	29	.473	9	149	64	18	580	541	310	255	3	3.50	162	25	0	.154
Parnell, Mel-Melvin Lloyd (Dusty)	47-56BosA	6-13-22	New Orleans, La.		L	L	6'	180	123	75	.621	10	289	232	113	1752	1715	758	732	20	3.50	668	132	1	.198
Pascual, Carlos-Carlos Luis [Lus]	50WasA	3-13-30	Havana, Cuba		R	R	5'7	172	1	1	.500	0	2	2	2	17	12	8	3	0	2.12	4	1	0	.250
Pearce, Jim-James Madison	49-50,53WasA 54-55CinN	6- 9-25	Zebulon, N.C.		R	R	6'6	190	3	4	.429	0	30	7	2	85	97	53	22	0	5.82	19	2	0	.105
Penson, Paul-Paul Eugene	54PhiN	7-12-31	Kansas City, Kans.		R	R	6'1	185	1	1	.500	0	5	3	0	16	14	14	3	0	4.50	7	0	0	.000
Pepper, Laurin-Hugh McLaurin	54-57PitN	1-18-31	Vaughan, Miss.		R	R	5'11	190	2	8	.200	0	44	17	0	110	134	98	40	0	7.04	25	4	0	.160
Perez, George-George Thomas	58PitN	12-29-37	San Fernando, Cal.		R	R	6'2	200	0	1	.000	1	4	0	0	8	9	4	2	0	5.63	2	0	0	.000
Perkovich, John-John Joseph	50ChiA	3-10-24	Chicago, Ill.		R	R	5'11	175	0	0	–	0	1	0	0	5	7	1	3	0	7.20	1	0	0	.000
Perkowski, Harry-Harry Walter	47,49-54CinN 55ChiN	9- 6-22	Dante, Va.		L	L	6'2	196	33	40	.452	5	184	76	24	698	719	324	296	4	4.37	239	43	1	.180
Peterson, Kent-Kent Franklin	44CinN 45-46MS 47-51CinN 52-53PhiN	12-21-25	Goshen, Utah		R	L	5'10	170	13	38	.255	5	147	43	7	420	434	215	208	1	4.95	110	10	0	.091
Pettit, Paul-George William Paul (Lefty)	51,53PitN	11-29-31	Los Angeles, Cal.		L	L	6'2	195	1	2	.333	0	12	5	0	31	35	21	14	0	7.26	9	2	0	.222
Phillips, Taylor-William Taylor (Tay)	56-57MilN 58-59ChiN 59-60PhiN 63ChiA	6-18-33	Atlanta, Ga.		L	L	5'11	185	16	22	.421	6	147	45	9	439	460	211	233	1	4.82	113	6	0	.053
Picone, Mario-Mario Peter (Babe)	47,52,54NYN 54CinN	7- 5-26	Brooklyn, N.Y.		R	R	5'11	180	0	2	.000	0	13	3	0	40	43	25	11	0	6.30	6	1	0	.167
Pierce, Billy-Walter William	45,48DetA 49-61ChiA 62-64SFN	4- 2-27	Detroit, Mich.		L	L	5'10	170	211	169	.555	32	585	432	193	3305	2989	1178	1999	38	3.27	1102	203	0	.184
Pieretti, Marino-Marino Paul (Chick)	45-48WasA 48-49ChiA 50CleA	9-23-20	Lucca, Italy		R	R	5'7	153	30	38	.441	8	194	68	21	673	713	321	188	4	4.53	207	45	0	.217
Pierro, Bill-William Leonard (Wild Bill)	50PitN	4-15-26	Brooklyn, N.Y.		R	R	6'1	155	0	2	.000	0	12	3	0	29	33	28	13	0	10.55	9	2	0	.222
Piktuzis, George-George Richard	56ChiN	1- 3-32	Chicago, Ill.		R	L	6'2	200	0	0	–	0	2	0	0	5	6	2	3	0	7.20	0	0	0	–
Pillette, Duane-Duane Xavier (Dee)	49-50NYA 50-53StLA 54-55BalA 56PhiN	7-24-22	Detroit, Mich.		R	R	6'3	195	38	66	.365	2	188	119	34	904	985	391	305	4	4.40	271	38	1	.140
Pitula, Stan-Stanley	57CleA	3-23-31	Hackensack, N.J.	8-15-65	R	R	5'10	170	2	2	.500	0	23	5	1	60	67	32	17	0	4.95	15	3	0	.200
Poat, Ray-Raymond Willis	42-44CleA 45VR 47-49NYN 49PitN	12-19-17	Chicago, Ill.		R	R	6'2	200	22	30	.423	1	116	47	15	400	425	162	178	4	4.55	122	14	1	.115
Podbielan, Bud-Clarence Anthony	49-52BknN 52-55,57CinN 59CleA	3-26-24	Curlew, Wash.		R	R	6'1	180	25	42	.373	3	172	76	20	641	693	245	242	2	4.49	188	29	0	.154
Podres, Johnny-John Joseph	53-55BknN 56MS 57BknN 58-66LAN	9-30-32	Witherbee, N.Y.		L	L	5'11	180	148	116	.561	11	440	340	77	2265	2238	743	1435	24	3.67	762	145	2	.190
	66-67DetA 69SDN																								
Poholsky, Tom-Thomas George	50-51StLN 52-53MS 54-56StLN 57ChiN	8-26-29	Detroit, Mich.		R	R	6'3	205	31	52	.373	1	159	104	30	754	791	192	316	5	3.93	228	39	0	.171
Polivka, Ken-Kenneth Lyle	47CinN	1-21-21	Chicago, Ill.		L	L	5'10	175	0	0	–	0	2	0	0	3	3	3	1	0	3.00	0	0	0	–
Pollet, Howie-Howard Joseph	41-43StLN 44-45MS 46-51StLN	6-26-21	New Orleans, La.	8- 8-74	L	L	6'1	175	131	116	.530	20	403	277	116	2106	2096	745	934	25	3.51	698	129	0	.185
	51-53PitN 53-55ChiN 56ChiA 56PitN																								
Porterfield, Bob-Erwin Coolidge	48-51NYA 51-55WasA 56-58BosA	8-10-23	Newport, Va.		R	R	6'	190	87	97	.473	8	318	193	92	1568	1571	552	572	23	3.79	516	95	6	.184
	58-59PitN 59ChiN 59PitN																								
Porto, Al-Alfred (Lefty)	48PhiN	6-27-26	Heilwood, Pa.		L	L	5'11	176	0	0	–	0	3	0	0	4	2	1	1	0	0.00	0	0	0	–
Portocarrero, Arnie-Arnold Mario	54PhiA 55-57KCA 58-60BalA	7- 5-31	New York, N.Y.		R	R	6'3	200	38	57	.400	2	166	117	33	818	778	320	338	5	4.31	240	26	3	.108
Possehl, Lou-Louis Thomas	46-48,51-52PhiN	4-12-26	Chicago, Ill.		R	R	6'2	185	2	5	.286	0	15	8	1	52	62	24	22	0	5.19	10	1	0	.100
Prendergast, Jim-James Bartholomew	48BosN	8-23-17	Brooklyn, N.Y.		L	L	6'1	208	1	1	.500	1	10	2	0	17	30	5	3	0	10.06	5	0	0	.000
Presko, Joe-Joseph Edward (Little Joe)	51-54StLN 57-58DetA	10- 7-28	Kansas City, Mo.		R	R	5'9	165	25	37	.403	5	128	61	15	492	511	188	202	2	4.59	156	27	0	.173
Proctor, Jim-James Arthur	59DetA	9- 9-35	Brandywine, Md.		R	R	6'	165	0	1	.000	0	2	1	0	3	8	3	0	0	15.00	0	0	0	–
Purkey, Bob-Robert Thomas	54-57PitN 58-64CinN 65StLN 66PitN	7-14-29	Pittsburgh, Pa.		R	R	6'2	190	129	115	.529	9	386	276	92	2115	2170	510	793	13	3.79	645	71	6	.110
Pyecha, John-John Nicholas	54ChiN	11-25-31	Aliquippa, Pa.		R	R	6'5	200	0	1	.000	0	1	0	0	3	4	2	2	0	9.00	1	0	0	.000
Qualters, Tom-Thomas Francis (Money Bags)	53PhiN 54DP 57-58PhiN	4- 1-35	McKeesport, Pa.		R	R	6'	190	0	0	–	0	34	0	0	52	63	26	20	0	5.71	2	0	0	.000
	58ChiA																								
Queen, Mel-Melvin Joseph	42,44NYA 45MS 46-47NYA 47-52PitN	3- 4-18	Maxwell, Pa.		R	R	6'	204	27	40	.403	1	146	77	15	556	567	329	328	3	5.10	164	17	0	.104

									LIFETIME PITCHING TOTALS													BATTING TOTALS			
USE NAME – GIVEN NAMES (NICKNAMES)	TEAM BY YEAR	BIRTH DATE	BIRTH PLACE	DEATH DATE	B	T	HGT	WGT	W	L	PCT	SV	G	GS	CG	IP	H	BB	SO	ShO	ERA	AB	H	HR	BA
Quinn, Frank-Frank William	49-50BosA	11-27-27	Springfield, Mass.		R	R	6'2	180	0	0	–	0	9	0	0	24	20	10	4	0	3.38	6	1	0	.167
Rabe, Charlie-Charles Henry	57-58CinN	5- 6-32	Boyce, Tex.		L	L	6'1	180	0	4	.000	0	11	2	0	27	30	9	16	0	3.67	6	0	0	.000
Raether, Hal-Harold Herman (Bud)	54PhiA 57KCA	10-10-32	Lake Mills, Wis.		R	R	6'1	185	0	0	–	0	2	0	0	4	3	4	0	0	6.75	0	0	0	–
Raffensberger, Ken-Kenneth David	39StLN 40-41ChiN 43-47PhiN 47-54CinN	8- 8-17	York, Pa.		R	L	6'2	195	119	154	.436	16	396	282	133	2152	2257	449	806	31	3.60	688	97	4	.141
Ramsdell, Willie-James Willard (Willie the Knuck)	47-48,50BknN 50-51CinN 52ChiN	4- 4-16	Williamsburg, Kans.	10- 8-69	R	R	5'11	165	24	39	.381	5	111	58	18	480	455	215	240	2	3.83	141	22	0	.156
Raney (Raniszewski), Ribs-Frank Robert Donald	49-50StLA	2-26-23	Detroit, Mich.		R	R	6'4	190	1	3	.250	0	4	3	1	18	25	14	7	0	7.50	7	0	0	.000
Raschi, Vic-Victor John Angelo (The Springfield Rifle)	46-53NYA 54-55StLN 55KCA	3-28-19	W. Springfield, Mass.		R	R	6'1	205	132	66	.667	3	269	255	106	1820	1666	727	944	26	3.72	608	112	1	.184
Raydon, Curt-Curtis Lowell	58PitN	11-18-33	Bloomington, Ill.		R	R	6'4	190	8	4	.667	1	32	20	2	134	118	61	85	1	3.63	38	1	0	.026
Reeder, Bill-William Edgar	49StLN	2-20-22	Dike, Tex.		R	R	6'5	205	1	1	.500	0	21	1	0	34	33	30	21	0	5.03	3	0	0	.000
Reid, Earl-Earl Percy	46BosN	6- 8-13	Bangor, Ala.		L	R	6'3	190	1	0	1.000	0	2	0	0	3	4	3	2	0	3.00	0	0	0	–
Renfroe, Marshall-Marshall Daniel	59SFN	5-25-36	Century, Fla.	12-10-70	L	L	6'	185	0	0	–	0	1	1	0	2	3	3	3	0	27.00	1	0	0	.000
Reynolds, Allie-Allie Pierce (Superchief)	42-46CleA 47-54NYA	2-10-15	Bethany, Okla.		R	R	6'	195	182	107	.630	49	434	309	137	2492	2193	1261	1423	33	3.30	857	140	1	.163
Richards, Duane-Duane Lee	60CinN	12-16-36	Spartanburg, Ind.		R	R	6'3	200	0	0	–	0	2	0	0	3	5	2	2	0	9.00	0	0	0	–
Ricketts, Dick-Richard James 55-58 played in N.B.A.	59StLN	12- 4-33	Pottstown, Pa.		L	R	6'7	215	1	6	.143	0	12	9	0	56	68	30	25	0	5.79	18	1	0	.056
Ridzik, Steve-Stephen George	50,52-55PhiN 55CinN 56-57NYN 58CleA 63-65WasA 66PhiN	4-29-29	Yonkers, N.Y.		R	R	5'11	170	39	38	.506	11	314	48	4	784	709	351	406	1	3.79	198	38	1	.192
Roberts, Robin-Robin Evan	48-61PhiN 62-65BalA 65-66HouN 66ChiN	9-30-26	Springfield, Ill.		B	R	6'	190	286	245	.539	25	676	609	305	4689	4582	902	2357	45	3.40	1525	255	5	.167
					Bats Left 48-52																				
Robinson, Humberto-Humberto Valentino	55-56,58MilN 59CleA 59-60PhiN	6-25-30	Colon, Panama		R	R	6'1	155	8	13	.381	4	102	7	2	214	189	90	114	0	3.24	38	6	0	.158
Robinson, Jack-John Edward	49BosA	2-20-21	Orange, N.J.		R	R	6'	175	0	0	–	0	3	0	0	4	4	1	1	0	2.25	0	0	0	–
Rodriguez, Freddy-Fernando Pedro	58ChiN 59PhiN	4-29-28	Havana, Cuba		R	R	6'	180	0	0	–	2	8	0	0	9	12	5	6	0	9.00	1	0	0	.000
Roe, Preacher-Elwin Charles	38StLN 44-47PitN 48-54BknN	2-26-15	Ashflat, Ark.		R	L	6'2	170	127	84	.602	10	333	261	101	1916	1907	504	956	17	3.43	620	68	1	.110
Roebuck, Ed-Edward Jack	55-57BknN 58,60-63LAN 63-64WasA 64-66PhiN	7- 3-31	E. Millsboro, Pa.		R	R	6'2	185	52	31	.627	62	460	1	0	790	753	302	477	0	3.35	137	28	2	.204
Rogovin, Saul-Saul Walter	49-51DetA 51-53ChiA 55BalA 55-57PhiN	10-10-22	Brooklyn, N.Y.		R	R	6'2	205	48	48	.500	2	150	121	43	885	888	308	388	9	4.06	300	54	3	.180
Romano, Jim-James King	50BknN	4- 6-27	Brooklyn, N.Y.		R	R	6'4	190	0	0	–	0	3	1	0	6	8	2	8	0	6.00	1	0	0	.000
Romberger, Dutch-Allen Isaiah	54PhiA	5-26-27	Klingerstown, Pa.		R	R	6'	185	1	1	.500	0	10	0	0	16	28	12	6	0	11.25	2	0	0	.000
Romonosky, John-John	53StLN 58-59WasA	7- 7-29	Harrisburg, Ill.		R	R	6'2	195	3	4	.429	0	32	9	1	101	97	51	63	0	5.17	26	6	1	.231
Ross, Bob-Floyd Robert	50-51WasA 52-53MS 56PhiN	11- 2-28	Fullerton, Cal.		R	L	6'	165	0	2	.000	0	20	3	0	48	55	38	29	0	7.13	12	1	0	.083
Ross, Cliff-Clifford Davis	54CinN	8- 3-28	Philadelphia, Pa.		L	L	6'4	195	0	0	–	1	4	0	0	3	0	0	1	0	0.00	0	0	0	–
Rotblatt, Marv-Marvin Joseph	48,50-51ChiA	10-18-27	Chicago, Ill.		B	L	5'8	165	4	3	.571	2	35	4	0	75	74	51	30	0	4.80	15	0	0	.000
Roy, Jean Pierre-Jean Pierre	46BknN	6-26-20	Montreal, Canada		B	R	5'10	160	0	0	–	0	3	1	0	6	5	5	6	0	10.50	2	0	0	.000
Roy, Norm-Norman Brooks (Jumbo)	50BosN	11-15-28	Newton, Mass.		R	R	6'	200	4	3	.571	1	19	6	2	60	72	39	25	0	5.10	18	3	0	.167
Rozek, Dick-Richard Louis	50-52CleA 53-54PhiA	3-27-27	Clear Rapids, Iowa		L	L	6'	190	1	0	1.000	0	33	4	0	65	65	55	26	0	4.57	12	1	0	.083
Rush, Bob-Robert Ransom	48-57ChiN 58-60MilN 60ChiA	12-21-25	Battle Creek, Mich.		R	R	6'4	205	127	152	.455	8	417	321	118	2409	2327	789	1244	16	3.65	807	140	4	.173
Rutherford, Johnny-John William (Doc)	52BknN	5- 5-25	Belleville, Canada		L	R	5'10	170	7	7	.500	2	22	11	4	97	97	29	29	0	4.27	31	9	0	.290
Sain, Johnny-John Franklin	42,46-51BosN 43-45MS 51-55NYA 55KCA	9-25-17	Havana, Ark.		R	R	6'2	190	139	116	.545	51	412	245	140	2125	2145	619	910	16	3.49	774	190	3	.245
Sanchez, Raul-Raul Guadalupe [Rodriguez]	52WasA 57,60CinN	12-20-30	Marianao, Cuba		R	R	6'	150	5	3	.625	5	49	2	1	90	86	43	48	1	4.60	14	3	0	.214
Sanford, Fred-John Frederick	43StLA 44-45MS 46-48StLA 49-51NYA 51WasA 51StLA	8- 9-19	Garfield, Utah		B	R	6'1	200	37	55	.402	6	164	98	26	744	768	391	285	3	4.45	229	39	1	.170
					Bats Right 48																				
Santiago, Jose-Jose Guillermo (Pants)	54-55CleA 56KCA	9- 4-28	Coamo, P.R.		R	R	5'10	175	3	2	.600	0	27	5	0	57	67	33	29	0	4.58	9	4	0	.444
Savage, Bob-John Robert	42PhiA 43-45MS 46-48PhiA 49StLA	12- 1-21	Manchester, N.H.		R	R	6'2	180	16	27	.372	9	129	31	10	423	433	215	171	2	4.32	104	9	0	.087
Savransky, Moe-Morris	54CinN	1-13-29	Cleveland, Ohio		L	L	5'11	175	0	2	.000	0	16	0	0	24	23	8	7	0	4.88	2	1	0	.500
Scantlebury, Pat-Patricio Athelstan	56CinN	11-11-25	Gatun, Canal Zone		L	L	6'1	180	0	1	.000	0	6	2	0	19	24	5	10	0	6.63	3	0	0	.000
Scarborough, Ray-Ray Wilson	42-43WasA 44-45MS 46-50WasA 50ChiA 51-52BosA 52-53NYA 53DetA	7-23-17	Mt. Gilead, N.C.		R	R	6'	185	80	85	.485	14	318	168	59	1429	1487	611	564	9	4.13	456	85	1	.186
Schacht, Sid-Sidney	50-51StLA 51BosN	2- 3-18	Bogota, N.J.		R	R	5'11	170	0	2	.000	1	19	1	0	22	44	21	12	0	13.91	2	0	0	.000
Schaeffer, Harry-Harry Edward (Lefty)	52NYA	6-23-24	Reading, Pa.		L	L	6'2	175	0	1	.000	0	5	2	0	17	18	18	15	0	5.29	3	0	0	.000
Schaffernorth, Joe-Joseph Arthur	59-61ChiN 61CleA	8- 6-37	Trenton, N.J.		R	R	6'4	195	3	8	.273	3	74	1	0	118	116	53	68	0	4.58	16	2	0	.125
Schallock, Art-Arthur Lawrence	51-55NYA 55BalA	4-25-24	Mill Valley, Cal.		L	L	5'9	160	6	7	.462	1	58	14	3	169	199	91	77	0	4.05	45	9	0	.200
Scheib, Carl-Carl Alvin	43-45PhiA 46MS 47-54PhiA 54StLN	1- 1-27	Gratz, Pa.		R	R	6'1	204	45	65	.409	17	267	107	47	1072	1130	493	290	6	4.88	468	117	5	.250
Schmidt, Willard-Willard Raymond	52-53,55-57StLN 58-59CinN	5-29-28	Hays, Kans.		R	R	6'1	187	31	29	.517	2	194	55	11	588	563	278	323	1	3.92	153	25	0	.163
Schmitz, Johnny-John Albert (Bear Tracks)	41-42ChiN 43-45MS 46-51ChiN 51-52BknN 52NYA 52CinN 53NYA 53-55WasA 56BosA 56BalA	11-27-20	Wausau, Wis.		R	L	6'	170	93	114	.449	19	366	235	86	1813	1766	757	746	16	3.54	587	83	2	.141
Schroll, Al-Albert Bringhurst	58-59BosA 59PhiN 60ChiN 61MinA	3-22-33	New Orleans, La.		R	R	6'2	210	6	9	.400	0	35	13	3	118	121	64	63	0	5.34	33	9	1	.273
Schultz, Bob-Robert Duffy	51-53ChiN 53PitN 55DetA	11-27-23	Louisville, Ky.		R	L	6'3	205	9	13	.409	0	65	19	3	182	179	125	67	0	5.19	52	8	0	.154
Schultz, Mike-William Michael	47CinN	12-17-20	Syracuse, N.Y.		L	L	6'1	175	0	0	–	0	1	0	0	2	4	2	0	0	4.50	0	0	0	–
Schwamb, Blackie-Ralph Richard	48StLA	8- 6-26	Los Angeles, Cal.		R	R	6'5	198	1	1	.500	0	12	5	0	32	44	21	7	0	8.44	10	3	0	.300
Score, Herb-Herbert Jude	55-59CleA 60-62ChiA	6- 7-33	Rosedale, N.Y.		L	L	6'2	185	55	46	.545	3	150	127	47	858	609	573	837	11	3.36	281	36	1	.128
Semproch, Ray-Roman Anthony (Baby)	58-59PhiN 60DetA 61LAA	1- 7-31	Cleveland, Ohio		R	R	5'11	180	19	21	.475	3	85	48	14	344	360	136	156	2	4.42	112	13	0	.116
Sexauer, Elmer-Elmer George	48BknN	5-21-26	St. Louis Cy., Mo.		R	R	6'4	220	0	0	–	0	2	0	0	1	0	2	0	0	9.00	0	0	0	–
Shantz, Bobby-Robert Clayton	49-54PhiA 55-56KCA 57-60NYA 61PitN 62HouN 62-64StLN 64ChiN 64PhiN	9-26-25	Pottstown, Pa.		R	L	5'6	139	119	99	.546	48	537	171	78	1936	1795	643	1072	15	3.38	548	107	1	.195
Shea (O'Shea), Spec-Frank Joseph (The Naugatuck Nugget)	47-49,51NYA 52-55WasA	10- 2-20	Naugatuck, Conn.		R	R	6'	200	56	46	.549	5	195	118	48	944	849	497	361	12	3.79	298	58	1	.195
Shipley, Joe-Joseph Clark (Moses)	58-60SFN 63ChiA	5- 9-35	Morristown, Tenn.		R	R	6'4	210	0	1	.000	0	29	1	0	44	48	35	23	0	5.93	5	0	0	.000
Shore, Ray-Raymond Everett	46,48-49StLA	6- 9-21	Cincinnati, Ohio		R	R	6'3	210	1	3	.250	0	31	4	0	62	70	67	26	0	8.27	14	0	0	.000
Sima, Al-Albert	50-51,53WasA 54ChiA 54PhiA	10- 7-21	Mahwah, N.J.		L	L	6'	190	11	21	.344	4	100	30	4	308	343	132	111	0	4.62	82	9	1	.110
Simmons, Curt-Curtis Thomas	47-50PhiN 51MS 52-60PhiN 60-66StLN 66-67ChiN 67CalA	5-19-29	Egypt, Pa.		L	L	5'11	190	193	183	.513	5	569	461	163	3349	3313	1063	1697	36	3.54	1135	194	1	.171
Simpson, Duke-Thomas Leo	53ChiN	9-15-27	Columbus, Ohio		R	R	6'1	190	1	2	.333	0	30	1	0	45	60	25	21	0	8.00	8	2	0	.250
Singleton, Elmer-Bert Elmer (Smoky)	45-46BosN 47-48PitN 50WasA 57-59ChiN	6-26-18	Ogden, Utah		R	R	6'2	174	11	17	.393	4	145	19	2	327	322	146	160	0	4.84	68	9	0	.132
					Bats Both 57-58																				
Sisler, Dave-David Michael	56-59BosA 59-60DetA 61WasA 62CinN	10-16-31	St. Louis, Mo.		R	R	6'4	200	38	44	.463	29	247	59	12	655	622	368	355	1	4.34	159	25	0	.157
Skaugstad, Dave-David Wendell	57CinN	1-10-40	Algona, Iowa		L	L	6'1	180	0	0	–	0	2	0	0	6	4	6	4	0	1.50	1	0	0	.000
Sleater, Lou-Louis Mortimer	50-52StLA 52WasA 55KCA 56MilN 57-58DetA 58BalA	9- 8-26	St. Louis, Mo.		L	L	5'10	185	12	18	.400	5	131	21	7	301	306	172	152	1	4.69	103	21	4	.204
Sloat, Dwain-Dwain Clifford (Lefty)	48BknN 49ChiN	12- 1-18	Nokomis, Ill.		R	L	6'	168	0	1	.000	0	9	2	0	16	21	11	4	0	6.75	1	0	0	.000
Smith, Bob-Robert Gilchrist	55BosA 57StLN 57-59PitN 59DetA	2- 1-31	Woodsville, N.H.		R	L	6'1	190	4	9	.308	2	91	8	2	167	174	83	93	0	4.04	29	2	0	.069
Smith, Frank-Frank Thomas	50-54CinN 55StLN 56CinN	4- 4-28	Pierrepont Mr., N.Y.		R	R	6'3	200	35	33	.515	44	271	7	1	496	426	181	277	0	3.81	87	10	0	.115
Smith, Riverboat-Robert Walkup	58BosA 59ChiN 59CleA	5-13-28	Clarence, Mo.		L	L	6'	185	4	4	.500	0	30	10	1	97	97	59	60	0	4.73	25	2	0	.080
					Bats Both 59																				
Snyder, Gene-Gene Walter	59LAN	3-31-31	York, Pa.		R	L	5'11	175	1	1	.500	0	11	2	0	26	32	20	20	0	5.54	6	0	0	.000
Solis, Marcelino-Marcelino	58ChiN	7-19-30	San L. Potosi, Mex.		L	L	6'1	185	3	3	.500	0	15	4	0	52	74	20	15	0	6.06	20	5	0	.250
Spahn, Warren-Warren Edward	42BosN 43-45MS 46-52BosN 53-64MilN 65NYN 65SFN	4-23-21	Buffalo, N.Y.		L	L	6'	175	363	245	.597	29	750	665	382	5246	4830	1434	2583	63	3.08	1872	363	35	.194
Spencer, George-George Elwell	50-55NYN 58,60DetA	7- 7-26	Columbus, Ohio		R	R	6'1	215	16	10	.615	9	122	9	3	251	228	106	82	0	4.05	50	6	0	.120
Spicer, Bob-Robert Oberton	55-56KCA	4-11-25	Richmond, Va.		L	R	5'10	173	0	0	–	0	4	0	0	5	15	5	2	0	27.00	1	0	0	.000
Spooner, Karl-Karl Benjamin	54-55BknN	6-23-31	Oriskany Falls, N.Y.		R	L	6'	185	10	6	.625	2	31	16	4	117	86	47	105	3	3.08	34	9	0	.265
Spragins, Homer-Homer Franklin	47PhiN	11- 9-20	Grenada, Miss.		R	R	6'1	190	0	0	–	0	4	0	0	5	3	3	3	0	7.20	0	0	0	–
Staley, Gerry-Gerald Lee	47-54StLN 55CinN 55-56NYA 56-61ChiA 61KCA 61DetA	8-21-20	Brush Prairie, Wash.		R	R	6'	195	134	111	.547	61	640	186	58	1981	2070	529	727	9	3.70	525	66	1	.126
Stanceau, Charley-Charles	41NYA 42-45MS 46NYA 46PhiN	1- 9-16	Canton, Ohio	4- 3-69	R	R	6'2	190	5	7	.417	0	39	13	1	122	135	79	47	0	4.94	31	0	0	.000
Stanka, Joe-Joe Donald	59ChiA	7-23-31	Hammon, Okla.		R	R	6'5	201	1	0	1.000	0	2	0	0	5	2	4	3	0	3.60	3	1	0	.333
Starr, Dick-Richard Eugene	47-48NYA 49-51StLA 51WasA	3- 2-21	Kittanning, Pa.		R	R	6'3	190	12	24	.333	2	93	45	7	344	390	198	120	2	5.26	97	15	0	.155
Stephens, Bryan-Bryan Maris	47CleA 48StLA	7-14-20	Fayetteville, Ark.		R	R	6'4	175	8	16	.333	4	74	17	3	215	220	106	69	0	5.15	59	7	0	.119
Stewart, Bunky-Veston Goff	52-56WasA	1- 7-31	Jasper, N.C.		L	L	6'	154	5	11	.313	3	72	14	2	187	215	127	77	0	6.02	38	8	0	.211
Stobbs, Chuck-Charles Klein	47-51BosA 52ChiA 53-58WasA 58StLN 59-60WasA 61MinA	7- 2-29	Wheeling, W.Va.		L	L	6'1	192	107	130	.451	19	459	238	65	1920	2003	735	897	7	4.29	578	102	0	.176
Stone, Dean-Darrah Dean	53-57WasA 57BosA 59StLN 62HouN 62ChiA 63BalA	9- 1-30	Moline, Ill.		L	L	6'4	205	29	39	.426	12	215	85	19	687	705	373	380	5	4.47	170	15	1	.088
Stowe, Hal-Harold Rudolph (Rudy)	60NYA	3-29-37	Gastonia, N.C.		L	L	6'	170	0	0	–	0	1	0	0	1	0	1	0	0	9.00	0	0	0	–
Strahs, Dick-Richard Bernard	54ChiA	12- 4-24	Evanston, Ill.		L	R	6'	192	0	0	–	1	9	0	0	14	16	8	8	0	5.79	1	0	0	.000
Striker, Jake-Wilbur Scott	59CleA 60ChiA	10-23-33	New Washington, Ohio		L	L	6'2	200	1	0	1.000	0	3	1	0	11	13	5	6	0	3.27	1	0	0	.000

USE NAME – GIVEN NAMES (NICKNAMES)	TEAM BY YEAR	BIRTH DATE	BIRTH PLACE	DEATH DATE	B	T	HGT	WGT	W	L	PCT	SV	G	GS	CG	IP	H	BB	SO	ShO	ERA	AB	H	HR	BA
					LIFETIME PITCHING TOTALS																	BATTING TOTALS			
Stuart, Marlin-Marlin Henry	49-52DetA 52-53StLA 54BalA 54NYA	8- 8-18	Paragould, Ark.		L	R	6'2	185	23	17	.575	15	196	31	7	486	544	256	185	0	4.65	125	22	1	.176
Stuffel, Paul-Paul Harrington (Stu)	50,52-53PhiN	3-22-27	Canton, Ohio		R	R	6'2	185	1	0	1.000	0	7	1	0	11	9	12	6	0	5.73	2	0	0	.000
Stump, Jim-James Gilbert	57,59DetA	2-10-32	Lansing, Mich.		R	R	6'	188	1	0	1.000	0	11	0	0	24	23	12	8	0	2.25	3	2	0	.667
Sturdivant, Tom-Thomas Virgil (Snake)	55-59NYA 59KCA 60BosA	4-28-30	Gordon, Kans.		L	R	6'	180	59	51	.536	17	335	101	22	1136	1029	449	704	7	3.75	328	60	0	.183
	61WasA 61-63PitN 63DetA 63-64KCA 64NYN																								
Suchecki, Jim-James Joseph	50BosA 51StLA 52PitN	8-25-26	Chicago, Ill.		R	R	6'	185	0	6	.000	0	38	6	0	104	130	50	56	0	5.37	22	2	0	.091
Sullivan, Frank-Franklin Leal	53-60BosA 61-62PhiN 62-63MinA	1-23-30	Hollywood, Cal.		R	R	6'7	225	97	100	.492	18	351	219	73	1732	1702	559	959	15	3.60	529	76	0	.144
Sundin, Gordie-Gordon Vincent	56BalA	10-10-37	Minneapolis, Minn.		R	R	6'4	215	0	0	–	0	1	0	0	0	0	2	0	0	∞	0	0	0	–
Surkont, Max-Matthew Constantine	49ChiA 50-52BosN 53MilN	6-16-22	Central Falls, R.I.		R	R	6'1	210	61	76	.445	8	236	149	53	1194	1209	481	571	7	4.38	357	63	1	.176
	54-56PitN 56StLN 56-57NYN																								
Susce, George-George Daniel	55-58BosA 58-59DetA	9-13-31	Pittsburgh, Pa.		R	R	6'1	180	22	17	.564	3	117	36	8	410	407	170	177	1	4.41	117	17	0	.145
Sutherland, Dizzy-Howard Alvin	49WasA	4- 9-23	Washington, D.C.		L	L	6'	200	0	1	.000	0	1	1	0	1	2	6	0	0	45.00	0	0	0	–
Swanson, Red-Arthur Leonard	55-57PitN	10-15-36	Baton Rouge, La.		R	R	6'1	175	3	3	.500	0	42	8	1	87	91	42	34	0	4.86	13	0	0	.000
Swartz, Bud-Sherwin Merle	47StLA	6-13-29	Tulsa, Okla.		L	L	6'2	180	0	0	–	0	5	0	0	5	9	7	1	0	7.20	1	1	0	1.000
Tate, Al-Walter Alvin	46PitN	7- 1-18	Coleman, Okla.		R	R	6'	180	0	1	.000	0	2	1	1	9	8	7	2	0	5.00	3	1	0	.333
Taylor, Harry-Harry Evans	57KCA	12- 2-35	San Angelo, Tex.		R	R	6'	185	0	0	–	0	2	0	0	9	11	4	4	0	3.00	4	1	0	.250
Taylor, Harry-James Harry	46-48BknN 50-52BosA	5-20-19	East Glenn, Ind.		R	R	6'1	190	19	21	.475	4	90	44	16	358	344	201	127	3	4.10	124	20	0	.161
Taylor, Pete-Vernon Charles	52StLA	11-26-27	Severn, Md.		R	R	6'1	170	0	0	–	0	1	0	0	2	4	3	0	0	13.50	0	0	0	–
Templeton, Chuck-Charles Sherman	55-56BknN	6- 1-32	Detroit, Mich.		R	L	6'3	210	0	2	.000	0	10	2	0	21	25	15	11	0	7.71	3	0	0	.000
Thiel, Bert-Maynard Bert	52BosN	5- 4-26	Marion, Wis.		R	R	5'10	185	1	1	.500	0	4	0	0	7	11	4	6	0	7.71	0	0	0	–
Thies, Jake-Vernon Arthur	54-55PitN	4- 1-26	St. Louis, Mo.		R	R	5'11	170	3	10	.231	0	34	19	3	134	125	52	57	1	3.90	33	1	0	.030
Thomas, Carl-Carl Leslie	60CleA	5-28-32	Minneapolis, Minn.		R	R	6'5	245	1	0	1.000	0	4	0	0	10	8	10	5	0	7.20	3	1	0	.333
Thompson, Forrest-Forrest David	48-49WasA	3- 3-18	Morresville, N.C.		L	L	5'11	195	7	13	.350	4	55	8	1	147	156	63	48	0	3.92	40	13	0	.325
Thompson, Jocko-John Samuel	48-51PhiN	1-17-20	Beverly, Mass.		L	L	6'	185	6	11	.353	1	41	21	5	167	151	83	81	2	4.26	53	6	0	.113
Thorpe, Bob-Robert Joseph	55ChiN	1-12-35	San Diego, Cal.	3-17-60	R	R	6'1	170	0	0	–	0	2	0	0	3	4	0	0	0	3.00	0	0	0	–
Toenes, Hal-William Harrel	47WasA	10- 8-17	Mobile, Ala.		R	R	5'11	175	0	1	.000	0	3	1	0	7	11	2	5	0	6.43	1	0	0	.000
Tomanek, Dick-Richard Carl (Bones)	53-54,57-58CleA 58-59KCA	1- 6-31	Avon Lake, Ohio		L	L	6'1	175	10	10	.500	7	106	11	4	232	231	112	166	0	4.93	50	9	1	.180
Tomasic, Andy-Andrew John 42,46 played in N.F.L.	49NYN	12-10-19	Hokendauqua, Pa.		R	R	6'	175	0	1	.000	0	2	0	0	5	9	5	2	0	18.00	1	0	0	.000
Tremel, Bill-William Leonard (Mumbles)	54-56ChiN	7- 4-29	Lilly, Pa.		R	R	5'11	180	4	2	.667	6	57	0	0	91	81	46	34	0	4.05	15	4	0	.267
Trice, Bob-Robert Lee	53-54PhiA 55KCA	8-28-28	Newton, Ga.		R	R	6'2	190	9	9	.500	0	26	21	9	152	185	60	28	1	5.80	52	15	1	.288
Trimble, Joe-Joseph Gerard	55BosA 57PitN	10-12-30	Providence, R.I.		R	R	6'1	190	0	2	.000	0	7	4	0	22	23	16	10	0	7.36	7	1	0	.143
Trinkle, Ken-Kenneth Wayne	43NYN 44-45MS 46-48NYN 49PhiN	12-15-19	Paoli, Ind.		R	R	6'1	175	21	29	.420	21	216	19	3	436	442	208	130	0	3.74	80	11	0	.138
Trosky (Troyavesky), Hal-Harold Arthur Jr. (Hoot)	58ChiA	9-29-36	Cleveland, Ohio		R	R	6'3	205	1	0	1.000	0	2	0	0	3	5	2	1	0	6.00	0	0	0	–
Trowbridge, Bob-Robert	56-59MilN 60KCA	6-27-30	Hudson, N.Y.		R	R	6'1	195	13	13	.500	5	116	25	4	330	324	156	201	1	3.95	77	6	0	.078
Trucks, Virgil-Virgil Oliver (Fire)	41-43DetA 44MS 45-52DetA	4-26-19	Birmingham, Ala.		R	R	5'11	205	177	135	.567	30	517	328	124	2684	2416	1088	1534	33	3.38	949	171	2	.180
	53StLA 53-55ChiA 56DetA 57-58KCA 58NYA																								
Turley, Bob-Robert Lee (Bullet Bob)	51,53StLA 54BalA 55-62NYA	9-19-30	Troy, Ill.		R	R	6'2	215	101	85	.543	12	310	237	78	1711	1366	1068	1265	24	3.65	547	69	4	.126
	63LAA 63BosA																								
Upton, Bill-William Ray	54PhiA	6-18-29	Esther, Mo.		R	R	6'	167	0	0	–	0	2	0	0	5	6	1	2	0	1.80	0	0	0	–
Urban, Jack-Jack Elmer	57-58KCA 59StLN	12- 5-28	Omaha, Neb.		R	R	5'8	155	15	15	.500	1	69	37	8	272	279	103	113	1	4.83	86	18	0	.209
Valdes, Rene-Rene [Gutierrez] (El Latigo)	57BknN	6- 2-29	Guanabacoa, Cuba		R	R	6'3	175	1	1	.500	0	5	1	0	13	13	7	10	0	5.54	3	0	0	.000
Valentine, Corky-Harold Lewis	54-55CinN	1- 4-29	Troy, Ohio		R	R	6'1	203	14	12	.538	1	46	33	7	221	240	76	87	3	4.81	72	9	0	.125
Valentinetti, Vito-Vito John	54ChiA 56-57ChiN 57CleA 58DetA	9-16-28	W. New York, N.J.		R	R	6'	200	13	14	.481	3	108	15	3	257	266	122	94	0	4.73	55	12	0	.218
	58-59WasA																								
Van Brabant, Ozzie-Camille Oscar	54PhiA 55KCA	9-28-26	Kingsville, Canada		R	R	6'1	165	0	2	.000	0	11	2	0	29	39	20	11	0	7.76	5	1	0	.200
Van Cuyk, Chris-Christian Gerald	50-52BknN	3- 1-27	Kimberly, Wis.		L	L	6'6	220	7	11	.389	1	44	26	5	160	170	63	103	0	5.18	51	11	0	.216
Van Cuyk, Johnny-John Henry	47-49BknN	7- 7-21	Little Chute, Wis.		L	L	6'1	190	0	0	–	0	7	0	0	10	12	3	3	0	5.40	0	0	0	–
Varga, Andy-Andrew William	50-51ChiN	12-11-30	Chicago, Ill.		R	L	6'4	187	0	0	–	0	3	0	0	4	2	7	1	0	2.25	0	0	0	–
Vargas, Roberto-Roberto Enrique	55MilN	5-29-29	Santurce, P.R.		L	L	5'11	170	0	0	–	2	25	0	0	25	39	14	13	0	8.64	2	1	0	.500
Voiselle, Bill-William Symmes (Big Bill, 96)	42-47NYN 47-49BosN	1-29-19	Greenwood, S.C.		R	R	6'4	200	74	84	.468	3	245	190	74	1373	1370	588	645	13	3.83	464	68	0	.147
	50ChiN																								
Wade, Ben-Benjamin Styron	48ChiN 52-54BknN 54StLN 55PitN	11-26-22	Morehead C., N.C.		R	R	6'3	195	19	17	.528	10	118	25	5	371	364	181	235	1	4.34	98	11	4	.112
Wall, Murray-Murray Wesley (Tex)	50BosN 57-59BosA 59WasA 59BosA	9-19-26	Dallas, Tex.	10- 8-71	R	R	6'3	190	13	14	.481	14	91	1	0	192	196	63	82	0	4.22	46	5	0	.109
Walsh, Junior-James Gerald	46,48-51PitN	3- 7-19	Newark, N.J.		R	R	5'11	190	4	10	.286	2	89	12	1	192	201	111	91	1	5.91	31	2	0	.065
Waters, Fred-Fred Warren	55-56PitN	2- 2-27	Benton, Miss.		L	L	5'11	185	2	2	.500	0	25	5	1	56	55	32	14	0	2.89	21	1	0	.048
Waugh, Jim-James Elden	52-53PitN	11-25-33	Lancaster, Ohio		R	R	6'3	185	5	11	.313	0	46	18	2	142	169	88	41	0	6.46	32	6	0	.188
Webb, Red-Samuel Henry	48-49NYN	9-25-24	Washington, D.C.		L	R	6'	175	3	2	.600	0	25	3	2	73	68	31	18	0	3.70	19	6	0	.316
Wehmeier, Herm-Herman Ralph	45,47-54CinN 54-56PhiN 56-58StLN 58DetA	2-18-27	Cincinnati, Ohio	5-21-73	R	R	6'2	200	92	108	.460	9	361	240	79	1804	1806	852	794	9	4.79	633	124	3	.196
Weik, Dick-Richard Henry (Legs)	48-50WasA 50CleA 51-52MS 53CLeA	11-17-27	Waterloo, Iowa		R	R	6'3	184	6	22	.214	1	76	26	3	213	203	237	123	2	5.92	53	12	0	.226
	53-54DetA																								
Welteroth, Dick-Richard John	48-50WasA	8- 3-27	Williamsport, Pa.		R	R	5'11	165	4	6	.400	3	90	4	0	166	185	145	55	0	6.51	27	2	0	.074
Werle, Bill-William George (Bugs)	49-52PitN 52StLN 53-54BosA	12-21-20	Oakland, Cal.		L	L	6'2	192	29	39	.426	15	185	60	18	666	770	194	283	2	4.69	199	35	0	.176
Werley, George-George William	56BalA	9- 8-38	St. Louis, Mo.		R	R	6'2	196	0	0	–	0	1	0	0	1	1	2	0	0	9.00	0	0	0	–
Wheat, Lee-Leroy William	54PhiA 55KCA	9-15-29	Edwardsville, Ill.		R	R	6'4	200	0	2	.000	0	11	1	0	30	46	12	8	0	6.90	8	1	0	.125
White, Hal-Harold George	41-43DetA 44-45MS 46-52DetA 53StLA 53-54StLN	3-18-19	Utica, N.Y.		L	R	5'10	165	46	54	.460	25	336	67	23	921	875	460	349	7	3.78	255	37	0	.145
Widmar, Al-Albert Joseph	47BosA 48,50-51StLA 52ChiA	3-20-25	Cleveland, Ohio		R	R	6'3	185	13	30	.302	5	114	42	12	389	461	176	143	1	5.21	107	18	0	.168
Wieand, Ted-Franklin Delano Roosevelt	58,60CinN	4- 4-33	Walnutport, Pa.		R	R	6'2	195	0	1	.000	0	6	0	0	6	8	5	5	0	10.50	0	0	0	–
Wiesler, Bob-Robert George	51NYA 52MS 54-55NYA 56-58WasA	8-13-30	St. Louis, Mo.		B	L	6'3	195	7	19	.269	0	70	38	4	240	250	218	113	0	5.78	69	9	0	.130
Wight, Bill-William Robert (Lefty)	46-47NYA 48-50ChiA 51-52BosA	4-12-22	Rio Vista, Cal.		L	L	6'1	190	77	99	.438	8	347	198	66	1562	1656	714	574	15	3.95	480	55	0	.115
	52-53DetA 53,55CleA 55-57BalA 58CinN 58StLN																								
Wilks, Ted-Teddy (Cork)	44-51StLN 51-52PitN 52-53CleA	11-13-15	Fulton, N.Y.		R	R	5'9	195	59	30	.663	46	385	44	22	913	832	283	403	5	3.26	206	27	0	.131
Williams, Don-Donald Fred	58-59PitN 62KCA	9-14-31	Floyd, Va.		R	R	6'2	180	0	0	–	0	11	0	0	20	29	4	7	0	7.20	4	1	0	.250
Willis, Jim-James Gladden	53-54ChiN	3-20-27	Doyline, La.		L	R	6'3	175	2	2	.500	1	27	4	2	66	59	35	20	0	3.41	14	0	0	.000
Willis, Les-Lester Evans (Wimpy, Lefty)	47CleA	1-17-08	Nacogdoches, Tex.		L	L	5'9	195	0	2	.000	1	22	2	0	44	58	24	10	0	3.48	11	1	0	.091
Wilson, Duane-Duane Lewis	58BosA	6-29-34	Wichita, Kans.		L	L	6'1	185	0	0	–	0	2	2	0	6	10	7	3	0	6.00	1	0	0	.000
Wilson, Jim-James Alger	45-46BosA 48StLA 49PhiA 51-52BosN	2-20-22	San Diego, Cal.		R	R	6'1	200	86	89	.491	2	257	217	75	1540	1479	608	692	19	4.01	546	99	2	.181
	53-54MilN 55-56BalA 56-58ChiA																								
Wilson, Maxie-Charles Max	40PhiN 42-45MS 46WasA	6- 3-16	Haw River, N.C.		L	L	5'7	160	0	1	.000	0	12	0	0	20	32	11	11	0	9.00	4	0	0	.000
Witt, George-George Adrian (Red)	57-61PitN 62LAA 62HouN	11- 9-33	Long Beach, Cal.		R	R	6'3	200	11	16	.407	0	66	38	5	229	225	127	156	3	4.32	69	9	0	.130
Wojey, Pete-Peter Paul	54BknN 56-57DetA	12- 1-19	Stowe, Pa.		R	R	5'11	185	1	1	.500	1	18	1	0	33	27	15	22	0	3.00	3	0	0	.000
Wolfe, Ed-Edward Anthony	52PitN	1- 2-29	Los Angeles, Cal.		R	R	6'3	185	0	0	–	0	3	0	0	4	7	5	1	0	6.75	0	0	0	–
Wooldridge, Floyd-Floyd Lewis	55StLN	8-25-28	Jerico Springs, Mo.		R	R	6'1	185	2	4	.333	0	18	8	2	58	64	27	14	0	4.81	18	4	0	.222
Wright, Ed-Henderson Edward	45-48BosN 52PhiA	5-15-19	Dyersburg, Tenn.		R	R	6'1	180	25	16	.610	1	101	39	17	398	412	161	93	3	4.00	128	27	0	.211
Wright, Mel-Melvin James	54-55StLN 60-61ChiN	5-11-28	Manila, Ark.		R	R	6'3	210	2	4	.333	3	58	0	0	83	119	27	36	0	7.70	11	0	0	.000
Wright, Roy-Roy Earl	56NYN	9-26-33	Buchtel, Ohio		R	R	6'2	170	0	1	.000	0	1	1	0	3	8	2	0	0	15.00	1	0	0	.000
Wynn, Early-Early (Gus)	39,41-44WasA 45MS 46-48WasA 49-57CleA	1- 6-20	Hartford, Ala.		B	R	6'	200	300	244	.551	15	691	612	290	4566	4291	1775	2334	49	3.54	1704	365	17	.214
	58-62ChiA 63CleA				Bats Right 41-44																				
Yochim, Len-Leonard Joseph	51,54PitN	10-16-28	New Orleans, La.		L	L	6'2	200	1	2	.333	0	12	3	0	29	40	19	12	0	7.45	5	1	0	.200
Yochim, Ray-Raymond Austin Aloysius	48-49StLN	7-19-22	New Orleans, La.		R	R	6'1	170	0	0	–	0	4	0	0	3	3	7	4	0	12.00	0	0	0	–
Yuhas, Eddie-John Edward	52-53StLN	8- 5-24	Youngstown, Ohio		R	R	6'1	180	12	2	.857	6	56	2	0	100	93	35	39	0	2.88	21	4	0	.190
Zick, Bob-Robert George	54ChiN	4-26-27	Chicago, Ill.		L	R	6'	168	0	0	–	0	8	0	0	16	23	7	9	0	8.44	4	1	0	.250
Zoldak, Sam-Samuel Walter (Sad Sam)	44-48StLA 48-50CleA 51-52PhiA	12- 8-18	Brooklyn, N.Y.	8-25-66	L	L	5'11	185	43	53	.448	8	250	93	30	930	956	301	207	5	3.54	286	50	0	.175
Zuverink, George-George	51-52CleA 54CinN 54-55DetA 55-59BalA	8-20-24	Holland, Mich.		R	R	6'4	205	32	36	.471	40	265	31	9	642	660	203	223	2	3.54	142	21	0	.148

1961-1975
Unlocking the Floodgates

Until 1960, baseball had managed to preserve its limited franchise sanctuary of 16 teams since 1901, the year the American League first came into existence. Except for the slight intrusion of the Federal League in 1914-1915, the hallowed structure remained undisturbed through the season of 1960. But it could not survive Branch Rickey's plans for a third major circuit—the Continental League—the increasing reach of television, and jet travel shrinking the country, all of which led to the American League's expanding to ten teams in 1961. While the Washington Senators took advantage of the expansion by abandoning the attendance-starved capital city for the Minneapolis-St. Paul area and becoming the Minnesota Twins, a new team took residence in Washington, D.C. The League's other entrant seeded their destinies in the increasingly popular west as the Los Angeles Angels. The two new teams also meant an increase in the regular season schedule to 162 games—a feat partly responsible for the New York Yankees' Roger Maris hitting a record 61 home runs—one more than his legendary teammate Babe Ruth poled in 1927.

The National League followed suit a year later by adding a team in Houston, Texas, and one in the city of New York, which had been jilted in 1958 by the exodus of the Giants and Dodgers. The Texas team began its career as the Houston Colts before changing its nickname to the Astros in 1965—mostly to take advantage of the huge space complex, also located in Houston. New York's entry relied upon a newspaper contest for their nickname and simply called themselves the Mets—a name that later became synonomous with miracles, magic, and mayhem.

Although there was no further expansion until 1969, franchise movement continued to be popular as attendance figures became more important than the loyalty of one city. In 1966, the Milwaukee Braves moved to Atlanta after spending only 13 years in that mid-western city. Not unlike the Braves, the Athletics were also in search of a loyal following, and pulled up their stakes in Kansas City after a similar 13-year period to begin life anew in Oakland in time for the start of the 1968 season.

Then, in 1969, with the demand for major league representation still on the rise, both leagues expanded their circuits to 12 teams. The National League used great imagination by placing one of their tenants across the border in Montreal and the other in San Diego. The American League placed one team in abandoned Kansas City and one in Seattle, with the latter being able to survive only one year before declaring bankruptcy and having to change owners and move to Milwaukee for the 1970 season. Two years later, the age-old cry of "first in the heart of America and last in the American League" became a phrase for history as the Washington Senators not only left the capital city to the politicians but their familiar nicknames as well when they journeyed to the Dallas suburb of Arlington to take up residence as the Texas Rangers.

Along with the expansion came a major innovation. Because of the great number of teams and the fact that a 12th place club could only have a negative effect on attendance, both leagues initiated divisional play splitting their circuits into a six-team Western Division and a six-team Eastern Division. Although the same 162-game schedule remained intact, teams in the same league no longer played an equal number of games with each other team. The schedule now called for 18 games to be played with teams in the same division and 12 games with teams in the other division. Also, for the first time, a championship play-off series was established, with each divisional winner playing a best three-of-five games to decide the pennant winner.

Baseball's new look was also accompanied by a new generation of stadiums. In the National League, most clubs, with the exception of Montreal and Chicago, were playing in modern facilities which accomodated large crowds and ample parking. But while Montreal made plans for a new stadium, and San Diego waited to see if their future fortunes would find them still on the west coast, Chicago remained in Wrigley Field—a home the Cubs had enjoyed since 1916. In addition to retaining their sanctuary, which included an ivy-covered outfield and a greater intimacy between the fans and the players, the Cubs also remained the only club in the major leagues with no lights and consequently no night baseball.

By contrast, the American League did not keep up with the architectural pace. The only teams to build new stadiums were the California Angels, Kansas City Royals, Oakland Athletics, and Minnesota Twins. And New York, after being threatened with the loss of the Yankees due to an aging structure and inadequate parking, closed the stadium after the 1973 season, and the Yankees moved to share Shea Stadium with the Mets while major renovations were underway.

The new stadiums—the most famous of which was the enclosed, air-conditioned Astrodome in Houston—also brought with them synthetic grass and increased home run distances. But batting averages did not rise as home runs went down. The overriding reason for this was the pitcher, who began to take advantage of batter's swinging for the fences on every pitch. The pitcher was able to reestablish himself with better control and training and mastery of a whole array of pitches, including the slider, knuckle ball, palm ball, and fork ball. The pitcher's reemergence could also be traced to the minor leagues, which not only helped the hurler sharpen his talents at an earlier age, but also allowed some to begin concentrating on relief pitching as a specialty unto itself. One result of better pitching was a lowering of the pitching mound by six inches in 1969 to give the hitter a better opportunity. Yet, even with this alteration, the pitcher remained dominant and plummeting batting averages were accompanied by an increase in strikeouts and shutouts. It was this lack of offense, plus disappointing American League attendance, which caused the junior circuit to experimentally initiate the "designated hitter" rule in 1973. This rule allowed one player to bat for the pitcher the entire game without having to play the field—a move which increased scoring but also produced a record 12 20-game winners since good starting pitchers were not removed for pinch-hitters.

Beyond the expansion, franchise shifts, and new role of the pitcher, was the establishment of black and Latin players who not only provided a return of daring on the basepaths—highlighted by Maury Wills' and Lou Brock's record-breaking feats—but also contributed to most of the long ball artistry of the period. In the 26 years since the black athlete was allowed entry into the major leagues, three of the top four men attaining lifetime home run honors were Hank Aaron, Willie Mays, and Frank Robinson.

Whatever baseball's future may include, whether it be expansion across the Pacific, franchise shifts, rulings such as the designated hitter, or a rise in one playing statistic or another, it is certain that it will continue to provide the same color and thrills as it has since the first major league season of 1876.

1961-1975 SINGLE SINGLE LEADERS

BATTING

Batting Average

1	Rico Carty	1970	Atl	N	.366
2	Rod Carew	1974	Min	A	.364
3	Joe Torre	1971	StL	N	.363
4	Norm Cash	1961	Det	A	.361
5	Rod Carew	1975	Min	A	.359
6	Roberto Clemente	1967	Pit	N	.357
7	Bill Madlock	1975	Chi	N	.354
8	Ralph Garr	1974	Atl	N	.353
9	Roberto Clemente	1970	Pit	N	.352
10	Roberto Clemente	1961	Pit	N	.351
11	Rod Carew	1973	Min	A	.350

Slugging Average

1	Mickey Mantle	1961	NY	A	.687
2	Hank Aaron	1971	Atl	N	.669
3	Norm Cash	1961	Det	A	.662
4	Willie McCovey	1969	SF	N	.656
5	Willie Stargell	1973	Pit	N	.646
6	Jim Gentile	1961	Bal	A	.646
7	Willie Mays	1965	SF	N	.645
8	Frank Robinson	1966	Bal	A	.637
9	Dick Allen	1966	Phi	N	.632
10	Willie Stargell	1971	Pit	N	.628

Runs Batted In

1	Tommy Davis	1961	LA	N	153
2	Johnny Bench	1970	Cin	N	148
3	Orlando Cepeda	1961	SF	N	142
	Roger Maris	1961	NY	A	142
5	Jim Gentile	1961	Bal	A	141
	Willie Mays	1962	SF	N	141
7	Rocky Colavito	1961	Det	A	140
	Harmon Killebrew	1969	Min	A	140
9	Joe Torre	1971	StL	N	137
10	Frank Robinson	1961	Cin	N	136

Runs

1	Billy Williams	1970	Chi	N	137
2	Frank Robinson	1962	Cin	N	134
	Bobby Bonds	1970	SF	N	134
4	Mickey Mantle	1961	NY	A	132
	Roger Maris	1961	NY	A	132
6	Bobby Bonds	1973	SF	N	131
7	Willie Mays	1962	SF	N	130
	Maury Wills	1962	LA	N	130
9	Rocky Colavito	1961	Det	A	129
	Willie Mays	1961	SF	N	129

Bases on Balls

1	Jim Wynn	1969	Hou	N	148
2	Harmon Killebrew	1969	Min	A	145
3	Willie McCovey	1970	SF	N	137
4	Frank Howard	1970	Was	A	132
	Joe Morgan	1975	Cin	N	132
6	Harmon Killebrew	1967	Min	A	131
7	Harmon Killebrew	1970	Min	A	128
	Carl Yastrzemski	1970	Bos	A	128
9	Mickey Mantle	1961	NY	A	126
	Darrell Evans	1974	Atl	N	126

Strikeouts

1	Bobby Bonds	1969	SF	N	189
2	Bobby Bonds	1970	SF	N	187
3	Mike Schmidt	1975	Phi	N	180
4	Dave Nicholson	1963	Chi	A	175
5	Reggie Jackson	1968	Oak	A	171
6	Donn Clendenon	1968	Pit	N	163
7	Reggie Jackson	1971	Oak	A	161
8	Tommie Agee	1970	NY	N	156
9	Frank Howard	1967	Was	A	155
	Jeff Burroughs	1975	Tex	A	155

Hits

1	Matty Alou	1969	Pit	N	231
2	Tommy Davis	1962	LA	N	230
	Joe Torre	1971	StL	N	230
	Pete Rose	1973	Cin	N	230
5	Ralph Garr	1971	Atl	N	219
6	Felipe Alou	1966	Atl	N	218
	Pete Rose	1969	Cin	N	218
	Rod Carew	1974	Min	A	218
9	Tony Oliva	1964	Min	A	217
10	Ralph Garr	1974	Atl	N	214

Doubles

1	Frank Robinson	1962	Cin	N	52
2	Wes Parker	1970	LA	N	47
	Fred Lynn	1975	Bos	A	47
	Pete Rose	1975	Cin	N	47
5	Lou Brock	1968	StL	N	46
6	Floyd Robinson	1962	Chi	A	45
	Zoilo Versalles	1965	Min	A	45
	Carl Yastrzemski	1965	Bos	A	45
	Pete Rose	1974	Cin	N	45
10	Lee Maye	1964	Mil	N	44
	Rusty Staub	1967	Hou	N	44

Triples

1	Ralph Garr	1974	Atl	N	17
2	Johnny Callison	1965	Phi	N	16
	Willie Davis	1970	LA	N	16
4	Gino Cimoli	1962	KC	A	15
5	Jake Wood	1961	Det	A	14
	Vada Pinson	1963	Cin	N	14
	Dick Allen	1965	Phi	N	14
	Roberto Clemente	1965	Pit	N	14
	Donn Clendenon	1965	Pit	N	14
	Lou Brock	1968	StL	N	14
	Don Kessinger	1970	Chi	N	14
	Ralph Metzger	1973	Hou	N	14

Home Runs

1	Roger Maris	1961	NY	A	61
2	Mickey Mantle	1961	NY	A	54
3	Willie Mays	1965	SF	N	52
4	Willie Mays	1962	SF	N	49
	Harmon Killebrew	1964	Min	A	49
	Frank Robinson	1966	Bal	A	49
	Harmon Killebrew	1969	Min	A	49
8	Harmon Killebrew	1962	Min	A	48
	Frank Howard	1969	Was	A	48
	Willie Stargell	1971	Pit	N	48

Stolen Bases

1	Lou Brock	1974	StL	N	118
2	Maury Wills	1962	LA	N	104
3	Maury Wills	1965	LA	N	94
4	Dave Lopes	1975	LA	N	77
5	Lou Brock	1966	StL	N	74
6	Tommy Harper	1969	Sea	A	73
7	Lou Brock	1973	StL	N	70
	Mickey Rivers	1975	Cal	A	70
9	Joe Morgan	1973	Cin	N	67
	Joe Morgan	1975	Cin	N	67

At Bats

1	Dave Cash	1975	Phi	N	699
2	Matty Alou	1969	Pit	N	698
3	Maury Wills	1962	LA	N	695
4	Bobby Richardson	1962	NY	A	692
5	Lou Brock	1967	StL	N	689
	Sandy Alomar	1971	Cal	A	689
7	Dave Cash	1974	Phi	N	687
8	Horace Clarke	1970	NY	A	686
9	Pete Rose	1973	Cin	N	680
10	Curt Flood	1964	StL	N	679
	Bobby Richardson	1964	NY	A	679

PITCHING

Wins

1	Denny Mc Lain	1968	Det	A	31
2	Sandy Koufax	1966	LA	N	27
	Steve Carlton	1972	Phi	N	27
4	Sandy Koufax	1965	LA	N	26
	Juan Marichal	1968	SF	N	26
6	Whitey Ford	1961	NY	A	25
	Don Drysdale	1962	LA	N	25
	Sandy Koufax	1963	LA	N	25
	Juan Marichal	1963	SF	N	25
	Jim Kaat	1966	Min	A	25
	Juan Marichal	1966	SF	N	25
	Tom Seaver	1969	NY	N	25
	Mickey Lolich	1971	Det	A	25
	Catfish Hunter	1974	Oak	A	25
	Ferguson Jenkins	1974	Tex	A	25

Losses

1	Roger Craig	1962	NY	N	24
	Jack Fisher	1965	NY	N	24
3	Roger Craig	1963	NY	N	22
	Dick Ellsworth	1966	Chi	N	22
	Denny McLain	1971	Was	A	22
	Bill Bonham	1974	Chi	N	22
	Randy Jones	1974	SD	N	22
8	Steve Arlin	1972	SD	N	21
	Stan Bahnsen	1973	Chi	A	21
	Mickey Lolich	1974	Det	A	21

Saves

1	John Hiller	1973	Det	A	38
2	Clay Carroll	1972	Cin	N	37
3	Wayne Granger	1970	Cin	N	35
	Sparky Lyle	1972	NY	A	35
5	Ron Perranoski	1970	Min	A	34
6	Jack Aker	1966	KC	A	32
7	Ted Abernathy	1965	Chi	N	31
	Ron Perranoski	1969	Min	A	31
	Ken Sanders	1971	Mil	A	31
	Mike Marshall	1973	Mon	N	31

Games Pitched

1	Mike Marshall	1974	LA	N	106
2	Mike Marshall	1973	Mon	N	92
3	Wilbur Wood	1968	Chi	A	88
4	Ted Abernathy	1965	Chi	N	84
5	Ken Sanders	1971	Mil	A	83
6	Eddie Fisher	1965	Chi	A	82
7	John Wyatt	1964	KC	A	81
8	Mudcat Grant	1970	Oak-Pit	A-N	80
	Pedro Borbon	1973	Cin	N	80
10	Dick Radatz	1964	Bos	A	79

Games Started

1	Wilbur Wood	1972	Chi	A	49
2	Wilbur Wood	1973	Chi	A	48
3	Mickey Lolich	1971	Det	A	45
4	Wilbur Wood	1975	Chi	A	43
5	Don Drysdale	1963	LA	N	42
	Jack Sanford	1963	SF	N	42
	Don Drysdale	1965	LA	N	42
	Jim Kaat	1965	Min	A	42
	Ferguson Jenkins	1969	Chi	N	42
	Wilbur Wood	1971	Chi	A	42
	Stan Bahnsen	1973	Chi	A	42
	Mickey Lolich	1973	Det	A	42
	Wilbur Wood	1974	Chi	A	42

Complete Games

1	Juan Marichal	1968	SF	N	30
	Ferguson Jenkins	1971	Chi	N	30
	Steve Carlton	1972	Phi	N	30
	Catfish Hunter	1975	NY	A	30
5	Mickey Lolich	1971	Det	A	29
	Gaylord Perry	1972	Cle	A	29
	Gaylord Perry	1973	Cle	A	29
	Ferguson Jenkins	1974	Tex	A	29
9	Bob Gibson	1968	StL	N	28
	Denny McLain	1968	Det	A	28
	Bob Gibson	1969	StL	N	28
	Gaylord Perry	1974	Cle	A	28

Winning Percentage

1	Whitey Ford	1961	NY	A	.862
2	Ralph Terry	1961	NY	A	.842
	Ron Perranoski	1963	LA	N	.842
4	Denny McLain	1968	Det	A	.838
5	Sandy Koufax	1963	LA	N	.833
6	Roger Moret	1975	Bos	A	.824
7	Bob Purkey	1962	Cin	N	.821
8	Tommy John	1974	LA	N	.813
	Al Hrabosky	1975	StL	N	.813
10	Dave McNally	1971	Bal	A	.808
	Catfish Hunter	1973	Oak	A	.808

Earned Run Average

1	Bob Gibson	1968	StL	N	1.12
2	Luis Tiant	1968	Cle	A	1.60
3	Dean Chance	1964	LA	A	1.65
4	Sandy Koufax	1964	LA	N	1.73
5	Sandy Koufax	1966	LA	N	1.74
6	Tom Seaver	1971	NY	N	1.76
7	Sam McDowell	1968	Cle	A	1.81
8	Vida Blue	1971	Oak	A	1.82
9	Phil Niekro	1967	Atl	N	1.87
10	Sandy Koufax	1963	LA	N	1.88

Bases on Balls

1	Nolan Ryan	1974	Cal	A	202
2	Nolan Ryan	1973	Cal	A	162
3	Joe Coleman	1974	Det	A	158
4	Nolan Ryan	1972	Cal	A	157
5	Sam McDowell	1971	Cle	A	153
6	Bill Stoneman	1971	Mon	N	146
7	J.R. Richard	1975	Hou	N	138
8	Steve Carlton	1974	Phi	N	136
9	Steve Renko	1971	Mon	N	135
10	Mike Torrez	1975	Bal	A	133

Strikeouts

1	Nolan Ryan	1973	Cal	A	383
2	Sandy Koufax	1965	LA	N	382
3	Nolan Ryan	1974	Cal	A	367
4	Nolan Ryan	1972	Cal	A	329
5	Sam McDowell	1965	Cle	A	325
6	Sandy Koufax	1966	LA	N	317
7	Steve Carlton	1972	Phi	N	310
8	Mickey Lolich	1971	Det	A	308
9	Sandy Koufax	1963	LA	N	306
10	Sam McDowell	1970	Cle	A	304
11	Vida Blue	1971	Oak	A	301

Shutouts

1	Bob Gibson	1968	StL	N	13
2	Sandy Koufax	1963	LA	N	11
	Dean Chance	1964	LA	A	11
4	Juan Marichal	1965	SF	N	10
	Jim Palmer	1975	Bal	A	10
6	Luis Tiant	1968	Cle	A	9
	Denny McLain	1969	Det	A	9
	Nolan Ryan	1972	Cal	A	9
	Don Sutton	1972	LA	N	9
	Bert Blyleven	1973	Min	A	9

Innings Pitched

1	Wilbur Wood	1972	Chi	A	377
2	Mickey Lolich	1971	Det	A	376
3	Wilbur Wood	1973	Chi	A	359
4	Steve Carlton	1972	Pit	N	346
5	Gaylord Perry	1973	Cle	A	344
6	Gaylord Perry	1972	Cle	A	343
7	Sandy Koufax	1965	LA	N	336
	Denny McLain	1968	Det	A	336
9	Wilbur Wood	1971	Chi	A	334
10	Nolan Ryan	1974	Cal	A	333

1961-1975 PERIOD LEADERS

BATTING

Batting Average
(Minimum 1000 Games or 4000 At Bats)

1	Roberto Clemente	1961-72	.331
2	Rod Carew	*1967-	.328
3	Pete Rose	*1963-	.310
4	Rico Carty	*1963-	.308
5	Matty Alou	1961-74	.307
6	Tony Oliva	*1962-	.306
7	Manny Mota	*1962-	.303
8	Curt Flood	1961-71	.301
9	Hank Aaron	1961-	.301
10	Joe Torre	1961-	.298

Hits

1	Billy Williams	1961-	2619
2	Lou Brock	*1961-	2551
3	Pete Rose	*1963-	2547
4	Carl Yastrzemski	*1961-	2413
5	Hank Aaron	1961-	2400
6	Willie Davis	1961-	2387
7	Brooks Robinson	1961-	2381
8	Vada Pinson	1961-	2339
9	Joe Torre	1961-	2237
10	Ron Santo	1961-74	2167

Slugging Average
(Minimum 1000 Games or 4000 At Bats)

1	Hank Aaron	1961-	.558
2	Dick Allen	*1963-	.542
3	Willie McCovey	1961-	.537
4	Willie Mays	1961-73	.537
5	Willie Stargell	*1962-	.535
6	Frank Robinson	1961-	.533
7	Harmon Killebrew	1961-75	.511
8	Roberto Clemente	1961-72	.507
9	Reggie Jackson	*1967-	.503
10	Frank Howard	1961-73	.502

Home Runs

1	Hank Aaron	1961-	526
2	Harmon Killebrew	1962-75	489
3	Willie McCovey	1961-	432
4	Frank Robinson	1961-	418
5	Billy Williams	1961-	413
6	Willie Mays	1961-73	381
7	Willie Stargell	*1962-	368
8	Frank Howard	1961-73	357
9	Norm Cash	1961-74	355
10	Ron Santo	1961-74	333

Runs Batted In

1	Hank Aaron	1961-	1519
2	Billy Williams	1961-	1425
3	Harmon Killebrew	1961-75	1369
4	Frank Robinson	1961-	1353
5	Ron Santo	1961-74	1287
6	Carl Yastrzemski	*1961-	1261
7	Willie McCovey	1961-	1207
8	Willie Stargell	*1962-	1197
9	Brooks Robinson	1961-	1182
10	Boog Powell	*1961-	1149

Triples

1	Lou Brock	*1961-	126
2	Willie Davis	1961-	126
3	Roberto Clemente	1961-72	118
4	Vada Pinson	1961-	106
5	Pete Rose	*1963-	95
6	Billy Williams	1961-	85
7	Johnny Callison	1961-73	82
8	Dick Allen	*1963-	78
9	Jim Fregosi	*1961-	77
10	Joe Morgan	*1963-	73

Runs

1	Hank Aaron	1961-	1438
2	Lou Brock	*1961-	1381
3	Billy Williams	1961-	1370
4	Pete Rose	*1963-	1339
5	Carl Yastrzemski	*1961-	1331
6	Frank Robinson	1961-	1323
7	Willie Mays	1961-73	1178
8	Willie Davis	1961-	1135
9	Vada Pinson	1961-	1108
10	Ron Santo	1961-74	1094

Doubles

1	Carl Yastrzemski	*1961-	466
2	Pete Rose	*1963-	441
3	Billy Williams	1961-	422
4	Lou Brock	*1961-	416
5	Brooks Robinson	1961-	404
6	Vada Pinson	1961-	394
7	Hank Aaron	1961-	391
8	Frank Robinson	1961-	383
9	Willie Davis	1961-	369
10	Willie Stargell	*1962-	344

Bases on Balls

1	Harmon Killebrew	1961-75	1375
2	Carl Yastrzemski	*1961-	1348
3	Willie McCovey	1961-	1102
4	Frank Robinson	1961-	1088
5	Ron Santo	1961-74	1077
6	Jim Wynn	*1963-	1065
7	Joe Morgan	*1963-	1063
8	Hank Aaron	1961-	1026
9	Billy Williams	1961-	981
10	Norm Cash	1961-74	960

Stolen Bases

1	Lou Brock	*1961-	809
2	Maury Wills	1961-72	529
3	Bert Campaneris	*1964-	512
4	Joe Morgan	*1963-	445
5	Tommy Harper	*1962-	404
6	Willie Davis	1961-	380
7	Luis Aparicio	1961-73	321
8	Jose Cardenal	*1963-	297
9	Bobby Bonds	*1968-	295
10	Cesar Cedeno	*1970-	255

Strikeouts

1	Lou Brock	*1961-	1509
2	Willie Stargell	*1962-	1497
3	Dick Allen	*1963-	1457
4	Harmon Killebrew	1961-75	1384
5	Frank Howard	1961-73	1332
6	Deron Johnson	1961-	1307
7	Ron Santo	1961-74	1299
8	Jim Wynn	*1963-	1269
9	Boog Powell	*1961-	1174
10	Willie McCovey	1961-	1163

PITCHING

Wins

1	Bob Gibson	1961-75	245
2	Juan Marichal	1961-75	237
3	Jim Kaat	1961-	234
4	Gaylord Perry	*1962-	216
5	Mickey Lolich	*1963-	207
6	Claude Osteen	1961-	196
7	Ferguson Jenkins	*1965-	191
8	Mike Cuellar	1964-	189
9	Jim Perry	1961-75	185
10	Catfish Hunter	*1965-	184
	Dave McNally	*1962-75	184

Winning Percentage
(Minimum 100 Wins)

1	Sandy Koufax	1961-66	.733
2	Jim Palmer	*1965-	.655
3	Tom Seaver	*1967-	.636
4	Juan Marichal	1961-75	.629
5	Jim Maloney	1961-71	.629
6	Mike Cuellar	1964-	.609
7	Dave McNally	*1962-1975	.607
8	Bob Gibson	1961-75	.592
9	Catfish Hunter	*1965-	.592
10	Denny McLain	*1963-72	.590

Losses

1	Claude Osteen	1961-	194
2	Jim Kaat	1961-	180
3	Mickey Lolich	*1963-	175
4	Gaylord Perry	*1962-	174
5	Bob Gibson	1961-75	163
6	Jim Perry	1961-75	154
7	Juan Marichal	1961-75	140
8	Ferguson Jenkins	*1965-	139
	Mel Stottlemyre	*1964-74	139
10	Wilbur Wood	*1961-	135

Earned Run Average
(Minimum 1500 Innings Pitched or 100 Wins)

1	Sandy Koufax	1961-66	2.19
2	Tom Seaver	*1967-	2.46
3	Jim Palmer	*1965-	2.63
4	Andy Messersmith	*1968-	2.65
5	Bert Blyleven	*1970-	2.78
6	Don Drysdale	1961-69	2.83
7	Bob Gibson	1961-75	2.84
8	Phil Niekro	*1964-	2.87
9	Gaylord Perry	*1962-	2.88
10	Juan Marichal	1961-75	2.90

Saves

1	Ron Perranoski	*1961-73	179
2	Hoyt Wilhelm	1961-72	162
3	Sparky Lyle	*1967	152
4	Ted Abernathy	1961-72	148
5	Stu Miller	1961-68	136
6	Clay Carroll	*1964-	132
	Dave Giusti	*1962-	132
8	Lindy McDaniel	1961-75	131
9	Jim Brewer	1961-	130
10	Jim Aker	*1964-74	123

Strikeouts

1	Bob Gibson	1961-75	3000
2	Mickey Lolich	*1963-	2679
3	Gaylord Perry	*1962-	2527
4	Sam McDowell	*1961-75	2453
5	Juan Marichal	1961-75	2245
6	Ferguson Jenkins	*1965-	2202
7	Jim Kaat	1961-	2124
8	Tom Seaver	*1967-	2099
9	Jim Bunning	1961-71	2023
10	Steve Carlton	*1965-	1916

Games Pitched

1	Lindy McDaniel	1961-75	761
2	Ron Perranoski	*1961-73	737
3	Don McMahon	1961-74	696
4	Eddie Fisher	*1962-73	690
5	Bob Miller	1961-74	663
6	Clay Carroll	*1964-	641
7	Ted Abernathy	1961-72	608
8	Diego Segui	*1962-	597
	Hoyt Wilhelm	1961-72	597
10	Wilbur Wood	*1961-	592

Shutouts

1	Bob Gibson	1961-75	55
2	Juan Marichal	1961-75	51
3	Gaylord Perry	*1962-	42
4	Don Sutton	*1966-	40
	Claude Osteen	1961-	40
	Mel Stottlemyre	*1964-74	40
7	Mickey Lolich	*1963-	39
8	Catfish Hunter	*1965-	38
9	Ferguson Jenkins	*1965-	37
	Luis Tiant	*1964-	37

Games Started

1	Jim Kaat	1961-	509
2	Claude Osteen	1961-	485
3	Bob Gibson	1961-75	461
4	Mickey Lolich	*1963-	459
5	Juan Marichal	1961-75	446
6	Gaylord Perry	*1962-	438
7	Jim Perry	1961-75	398
8	Dave McNally	*1962-75	396
9	Milt Pappas	1961-73	390
10	Catfish Hunter	*1965-	379

Innings Pitched

1	Bob Gibson	1961-75	3722
2	Gaylord Perry	*1962-	3610
3	Jim Kaat	1961-	3581
4	Juan Marichal	1961-75	3425
5	Claude Osteen	1961-	3404
6	Mickey Lolich	*1963-	3363
7	Ferguson Jenkins	*1965-	2900
8	Jim Perry	1961-75	2873
9	Catfish Hunter	*1965-	2784
10	Dave McNally	*1962-75	2730

Complete Games

1	Bob Gibson	1971-75	251
2	Juan Marichal	1971-75	238
3	Gaylord Perry	*1962-	236
4	Ferguson Jenkins	*1965-	190
	Mickey Lolich	*1963-	190
6	Mike Cuellar	1964-	170
7	Jim Kaat	1961-	163
8	Mel Stottlemyre	*1964-74	152
9	Tom Seaver	*1967-	148
10	Catfish Hunter	*1965-	146

Complete Game Percentage
(Complete Games as a Percentage of Games Started — minimum 175 Games Started)

1	Sandy Koufax	1961-66	54.5
2	Bob Gibson	1961-75	54.4
3	Gaylord Perry	*1962-	53.9
4	Juan Marichal	1961-75	53.4
5	Ferguson Jenkins	*1965-	51.9
6	Mike Cuellar	1964-	47.4
7	Tom Seaver	*1967-	47.1
8	Luis Tiant	*1964-	45.9
9	Bert Blyleven	*1970-	45.5
10	Steve Carlton	*1965-	44.1

* — Entire major league career

1961 Preserving History with an Asterisk

In 1892, as a result of the collapse of the American Association, the National League reluctantly expanded its membership to 12 teams. The union lasted through 1899, the year Baltimore, Louisville, Cleveland, and Washington were sliced from the circuit. In 1900, the National League enjoyed the status quo of former times when it had confined baseball to the major eastern cities. The senior circuit had survived the rebellious antics of the Union Association in 1884, the Players League in 1890, and the American Association from 1882 to 1891. But, in 1901, when the fledgling American League was born, it brought an end to the monopolistic harmony of eight teams. The American League arrived with money, determination, and enough National League talent to field another eight major league teams. After much feuding, franchise shake-ups and the like, both circuits settled down to ward off the intrusion of the Federal League, 1914-15, and two major World Wars.

But as television replaced radio, and jet travel made the going faster than trains or conventional prop airplanes, westward expansion was inevitable. The move of the Giants and Dodgers in 1958 to California did not lessen the necessity for growth, but rather increased it—with the result that, by the time the 1961 season got underway, the American League found itself with ten teams and a 162-game schedule. The new teams included the Los Angeles Angels and the Washington Senators, the last of which replaced the old Senators who were transplanted to the St. Paul-Minnesota area under the name, Minnesota Twins. It was this expansion and the new 162-game schedule which provided baseball with the most exciting and controversial season in years, as the assault on the game's most precious single season's record was finally achieved.

On April 26, at Tiger Stadium, Paul Foytack's fastball got up too high, and Roger Maris launched his first circuit clout of the year into the right field stands. The next six months would see Maris chasing Babe Ruth's mark of 60 home runs in one season, clashing with a persistent press, and asterisks added to the record book by Commissioner Ford Frick. Along with Maris, teammate Mickey Mantle also got away to a fast start. Through May, Mantle had 14 home runs and Maris 12. By the end of July, Mantle had 39, Maris 40, and a buzz was universal in the baseball world. Mantle had been a star for years, and quote-hungry reporters did not bother him. For Maris, though, superstardom was new; the pressure of chasing Ruth's record and the unending pursuit of the press took a great toll on the right fielder, turning him surly and uncommunicative.

After Detroit had led the American League for the first half, the Yankees took charge after the All-Star break, and all interest turned from the pennant race to the M&M boys. The excitement was fueled by the first-time departure from the traditional 154-game schedule, with some writers and fans claiming that the extra eight games gave Maris an unfair advantage on the record. Commissioner Frick ended all doubt but not the clamour as he ruled, in July, that Ruth's record would fall only if broken in the first 154 games and, that if a new record was set in the final eight games, it would be entered in the record book with an asterisk alongside Ruth's treasured single-season mark.

With half the fans rooting for him, and the other half rooting against his reaching the "sacred" mark of the Babe, and with the press making copy out of his every action, Maris suffered from the pressure but continued to belt home runs. By September 1, Maris had 51 home runs and Mantle had 48, but Mantle was starting to be hounded by little injuries and an infection, which put him out of action for part of September, ending his chance of surpassing Ruth. In the final game which matched Ruth's schedule, Maris hit #59 but could not get #60, thus assuring that the Babe's mark would stand. On September 26, Jack Fisher of Baltimore served up Maris' 60th in the 159th game of the season. In the season's finale, a Tracy Stallard pitch landed in Yankee Stadium's right field stands to give Maris a season's mark of 61 homers and a new record, or at least part of a new record. Mantle wound up with 54 clouts to bring the duo's total to 115, eclipsing the two-man mark of 107 set by Ruth and Lou Gehrig in 1927.

With Maris and Mantle constant front page news, the Yankees' pennant drive took on a secondary aura. Finishing eight games ahead of the Tigers, new manager Ralph Houk used the long ball as his big weapon. In addition to Maris and Mantle, Moose Skowron, Yogi Berra, Elston Howard, and Johnny Blanchard all knocked over 20 home runs to set a new season's mark of 240 round trippers. Tony Kubek, Bobby Richardson, and Clete Boyer gave the infield an airtight look, and Houk made key changes by abandoning Casey Stengel's platooning policy. He moved aging Yogi Berra to left field and installed Johnny Blanchard as Elston Howard's relief behind the plate. Whitey Ford got a chance to start every fourth day and thrived on the additional work, as he logged a 25-4 mark. Ralph Terry ended at 16-3, and Bill Stafford at 14-9, to round out the big three of the starting staff. Luis Arroyo in using his screwball to chalk up a spectacular season in relief, posted a league-leading 29 saves. The fireman's performance was such that it became routine to see Ford start and pitch seven innings and then watch Arroyo mop up the final six outs. The assault of the pitching and the tremendous hitting moved observers to place the 1961 squad in a class with the 1927 Yankees as the greatest clubs of all time.

Detroit's early season run on first place was sparked by the heavy hitting of Norm Cash, Al Kaline, and Rocky Colavito. Cash reached stardom by hitting a league-leading .361 with 41 home runs and 132 RBI's. Kaline remained consistent with a .324 mark, as Colavito hit 45 homers and drove in 140 Tigers. Frank Lary notched 23 victories to take second-place league runner-up honors behind Ford, although his complete games far outdistanced the classy southpaw by a 22-11 margin.

Unlike the American League, the National still had eight teams and still played a 154-game schedule. And, unlike the power-bludgeoned junior circuit, the more subdued senior league produced an upset pennant winner in the Cincinnati Reds. The Reds were generally figured as a second division club but led almost all the way under the direction of tough manager Fred Hutchinson. Rookie manager Al Dark kept his San Francisco Giants out front through May, but from June 15, to July 10, the Reds won 21 of 28 to create a five-game bulge over Willie Mays and Co. The Dodgers, hot in July, fought for the top spot until stumbling into a ten-game losing streak in mid-August.

The heart of the Reds' attack came from Frank Robinson, who hit .323, hitting 37 home runs and driving in 124 runs. Vada Pinson hit .343 and Gordy Coleman, who became a full-time player, and Gene Freese, who was obtained from the White Sox, added fuel to the Rhinelander's fire by each belting 26 home runs. Oddly enough, Cincinnati bucked tradition by winning the pennant without a regular middle defense, as Don Blasingame and Elio Chacon shared second base, Eddie Kasko and Leo Cardenas split shortstop, and Jerry Zimmerman, Darrell Johnson, and Johnny Edwards combined to cover the catching duties. On the mound, Bob Purkey, Jim O'Toole, and winter-acquisition Joey Jay were ace starters, while Jim Brosnan and Bill Henry supplied top firefighting in their combined 32 saves.

Despite boasting of the league batting champion in Roberto Clemente, the Pirates fell off to sixth due to the sore arm of Vern Law, the off-season of Bob Friend, and the drop of 50 points in the batting average of Dick Groat, the 1960 league leader. Roy Face, although managing 17 saves to lead the league, lost twice as many as he won and posted a high 3.82 E.R.A.

In the Series it was no contest as the Yankees won the championship in five games. A Ford two-hitter gave New York game one, and home run power overwhelmed the Reds in games three, four, and five after a Joey Jay victory in game two. Even with Mantle hurt and Maris hitting .105, the Yankees outscored the Reds 27-13, due mostly to good hitting from Houk's reserves. In addition to Ruth suffering the eclipse of his home run record, a mark that was even more precious to the Babe also went. Ford, in winding up the Series with 32 scoreless innings, washed away the 29 2/3 consecutive zero frames once tossed by Ruth. The footnotes to baseball's explosive year included Willie Mays' four home runs in one game, Jim Gentile's record tying five grand-slams in one season, 18-year-old Lew Krausse's signing with the Athletics after his high school graduation and shutting out the Los Angeles Angels on three hits in his pro debut, and Leo Durocher's returning to uniform as a coach with the Dodgers to set off recurring rumors that he would replace stalwart Walter Alston as Dodger manager. There was also the arrival of Charley Finley who, in his first year as owner of the Athletics, fired his first manager and general manager, and the Chicago Cubs who went through the year with no manager but, rather, a rotating staff of head coaches. And while the All-Star Game played to its first tie, the Philadelphia Phillies set a record with 23 losses in a row. Finally, as the National League planned expansion in 1962 with a franchise in Houston and one in New York, 71-year-old Casey Stengel agreed to return to baseball after a year's retirement to pilot the New York entry.

NEW YORK 1st 109-53 .673 — RALPH HOUK

NAME	G by POS	B	AGE	G	AB	R	H	2B	3B	HR	RBI	BB	SO	SB	BA	SA
TOTALS			28	163	5559	827	1461	194	40	240	782	543	785	28	.263	.441
Bill Skowron	1B149	R	30	150	561	76	150	23	4	28	89	35	108	0	.267	.472
Bobby Richardson	2B161	R	25	162	662	80	173	17	5	3	49	30	23	9	.261	.316
Tony Kubek	SS145	L	24	153	617	84	170	38	6	8	46	27	60	1	.276	.395
Clete Boyer	3B141, SS12, OF1	R	24	148	504	61	113	19	5	11	55	63	83	1	.224	.347
Roger Maris	OF160	L	26	161	590	132	159	16	4	61	142	94	67	0	.269	.620
Mickey Mantle	OF150	B	29	153	514	132	163	16	6	54	128	126	112	12	.317	.687
Yogi Berra	OF87, C15	L	36	119	395	62	107	11	0	22	61	35	28	2	.271	.466
Elston Howard	C111, 1B9	R	32	129	446	64	155	17	5	21	77	28	65	0	.348	.549
Hector Lopez	OF72	R	28	93	243	27	64	7	2	3	22	24	38	1	.222	.305
Johnny Blanchard	C48, OF15	L	28	93	243	38	74	10	1	21	54	27	28	1	.305	.613
2 Bob Cerv	OF30, 1B3	R	35	57	118	17	32	5	1	6	20	12	17	1	.271	.483
2 Billy Gardner	3B33, 2B6	R	33	41	99	11	21	5	0	1	2	6	18	0	.212	.293
Joe DeMaestri	SS18, 2B5, 3B4	R	32	30	41	1	6	0	0	0	2	0	13	0	.146	.146
Jack Reed	OF27	R	28	28	13	4	2	0	0	0	1	1	1	0	.154	.154
2 Earl Torgeson	1B8	L	37	22	18	3	2	0	0	0	0	8	3	0	.111	.111
Jesse Gonder		L	25	15	12	2	4	1	0	0	3	3	1	0	.333	.417
1 Deron Johnson	3B8	R	22	13	19	1	2	0	0	0	2	2	5	0	.105	.105
2 Bob Hale	1B5	L	27	11	13	2	2	0	0	1	1	0	0	0	.154	.385

Tom Tresh 23 B 2-8, 1 Lee Thomas 25 L 1-2

NAME	T	AGE	W	L	PCT	SV	G	GS	CG	IP	H	BB	SO	ShO	ERA
		27	109	53	.673	39	163	163	47	1451	1288	542	866	14	3.46
Whitey Ford	L	32	25	4	.862	0	39	39	11	283	242	92	209	3	3.21
Ralph Terry	R	25	16	3	.842	0	31	27	9	188	162	42	86	2	3.16
Luis Arroyd	L	34	15	5	.750	29	65	0	0	119	83	49	87	0	2.19
Bill Stafford	R	21	14	9	.609	2	36	25	8	195	168	59	101	3	2.68
Jim Coates	R	28	11	5	.688	5	43	11	4	141	128	53	80	1	3.45
Rollie Sheldon	R	24	11	5	.688	0	35	21	6	163	149	55	84	2	3.59
2 Bud Daley	L	28	8	9	.471	0	23	17	7	130	127	51	83	0	3.95
Bob Turley (SA)	R	30	3	5	.375	0	15	12	1	72	74	51	48	0	5.75
Hal Reniff	R	22	2	0	1.000	2	25	0	0	45	31	31	21	0	2.60
1 Art Ditmar	R	32	2	3	.400	0	12	8	1	54	59	14	24	0	4.67
2 Tex Clevenger	R	28	1	1	.500	0	21	0	0	32	35	21	14	0	4.78
1 Danny McDevitt	L	28	1	2	.333	1	8	2	0	13	18	8	8	0	7.62
Al Downing	L	20	0	1	.000	0	5	1	0	9	7	12	12	0	8.00
1 Ryne Duren	R	32	0	1	.000	0	4	0	0	5	2	4	7	0	5.40
1 Johnny James	R	27	0	0	.000	0	1	0	0	1	1	0	2	0	0.00
Duke Maas	R	32	0	0	.00	0	1	0	0	0	2	0	0	0	∞

DETROIT 2nd 101-61 .623 8 — BOB SCHEFFING

NAME	G by POS	B	AGE	G	AB	R	H	2B	3B	HR	RBI	BB	SO	SB	BA	SA
TOTALS			27	163	5561	841	1481	215	53	180	779	673	867	98	.266	.421
Norm Cash	1B157	L	26	159	535	119	193	22	8	41	132	124	85	11	.361	.662
Jake Wood	2B162	R	24	162	663	96	171	17	14	11	69	58	141	30	.258	.376
Chico Fernandez	SS121, 3B8	R	29	133	435	41	108	15	4	3	40	36	45	8	.248	.322
Steve Boros (BC)	3B116	R	24	116	396	51	107	18	2	5	62	68	42	4	.270	.364
Al Kaline	OF147, 3B1	R	26	153	586	116	190	41	7	19	82	66	42	14	.324	.515
Bill Bruton	OF155	L	35	160	596	99	153	15	5	17	63	61	66	22	.257	.384
Rocky Colavito	OF161	R	27	163	583	129	169	30	2	45	140	113	75	1	.290	.580
Dick Brown (JJ)	C91	R	26	93	308	32	82	12	2	16	45	22	57	0	.266	.474
Mike Roarke	C85	R	30	86	229	21	51	6	1	2	22	20	31	0	.223	.284
Dick McAuliffe	SS55, 3B22	L	21	80	285	36	73	12	4	6	33	24	39	2	.256	.389
Charlie Maxwell	OF25	L	34	79	131	11	30	4	2	5	18	20	24	0	.229	.405
Bubba Morton	OF30	R	29	77	108	26	31	5	1	2	19	9	25	3	.287	.407
Bobo Osborne	1B11, 3B8	L	25	71	93	8	20	7	0	2	13	20	15	1	.215	.355
3 Reno Bertoia	3B13, 2B7, SS1	R	26	24	46	6	10	1	0	1	4	3	8	2	.217	.304
1 Ozzie Virgil	3B9, C3, 2B1, SS1	R	28	20	30	1	4	0	0	1	1	1	5	0	.133	.233
Frank House	C14	L	31	17	22	3	5	1	1	0	3	4	2	0	.227	.364
1 George Thomas	OF2, SS1	R	23	17	6	2	0	0	0	0	0	0	4	0	.000	.000
1 Chuck Cottier	SS8, 2B2	R	25	10	7	2	2	0	0	0	1	1	1	0	.286	.286

George Alusik 26 R 2-14, 2 Vic Wertz 36 L 1-6, 1 Dick Gernert 32 R 1-5, Harry Chiti 28 R 1-12, Bill Freehan 19 R 4-10

NAME	T	AGE	W	L	PCT	SV	G	GS	CG	IP	H	BB	SO	ShO	ERA
		29	101	61	.623	30	163	163	62	1459	1404	469	836	12	3.55
Frank Lary	R	31	23	9	.719	0	36	36	22	275	252	66	146	4	3.24
Jim Bunning	R	29	17	11	.607	1	38	37	12	268	232	71	194	4	3.19
Don Mossi	L	32	15	7	.682	1	35	34	12	240	237	47	137	1	2.96
Paul Foytack	R	30	11	10	.524	0	32	20	6	170	152	56	89	0	3.92
Phil Regan	R	24	10	7	.588	2	32	16	6	120	134	41	46	0	5.25
Terry Fox	R	25	5	2	.714	12	39	0	0	57	42	16	32	0	1.42
2 Ron Kline	R	29	5	3	.625	0	10	8	3	56	53	17	27	1	2.73
Hank Aguirre	L	29	4	4	.500	8	45	0	0	55	44	38	32	0	3.27
1 Bill Fischer	R	30	3	2	.600	3	26	1	0	47	54	17	18	0	4.98
Howie Koplitz	R	23	2	0	1.000	0	4	1	1	12	16	8	9	0	2.25
Fred Gladding	R	25	1	0	1.000	0	8	0	0	16	18	11	11	0	3.38
Joe Grzenda	L	24	1	0	1.000	0	4	0	0	6	9	2	0	0	7.50
1 Jim Donohue	R	22	1	1	.500	1	14	0	0	20	23	15	20	0	3.60
3 Gerry Staley	R	40	1	1	.500	2	13	0	0	13	15	6	8	0	3.46
2 Hal Woodeshick	L	28	1	1	.500	0	12	2	0	18	25	17	13	0	8.00
Bob Bruce (IJ)	R	28	1	2	.333	0	14	6	0	45	57	24	25	0	4.40
Ron Nischwitz	L	24	0	1	.000	0	6	1	0	11	13	8	8	0	5.73
2 Jerry Casale	R	27	0	0	.000	0	3	1	0	12	15	3	6	0	5.25
Manny Montejo	R	24	0	0	.000	0	12	0	0	16	13	6	15	0	3.94

BALTIMORE 3rd 95-67 .586 14 — PAUL RICHARDS 84-47 .641 LUM HARRIS 11-20 .355

NAME	G by POS	B	AGE	G	AB	R	H	2B	3B	HR	RBI	BB	SO	SB	BA	SA
TOTALS			27	163	5481	691	1393	227	36	149	638	581	902	39	.254	.390
Jim Gentile	1B144	L	27	148	486	96	147	25	2	46	141	96	106	1	.302	.646
Jerry Adair	2B107, SS27, 3B2	R	24	133	386	41	102	21	1	9	37	35	51	5	.264	.394
Ron Hansen	SS149, 2B7	R	23	155	533	51	132	13	2	12	51	66	96	1	.248	.347
Brooks Robinson	3B163, 2B2, SS1	R	24	163	668	89	192	38	7	7	61	47	57	1	.287	.397
Whitey Herzog	OF98	L	29	113	323	39	94	11	6	5	35	50	41	1	.291	.409
Jackie Brandt	OF136, 3B1	R	27	139	516	93	153	18	5	16	72	62	51	10	.297	.444
Russ Snyder	OF108	L	27	115	312	46	91	13	5	1	13	20	32	5	.292	.375
Gus Triandos	C114	R	30	115	397	35	97	21	0	17	63	44	60	0	.244	.426
Dick Williams	OF75, 1B20, 3B2	R	32	103	310	37	64	15	2	8	24	20	38	0	.206	.345
Dave Philley	OF25, 1B1	B	41	99	144	13	36	9	2	1	23	10	20	2	.250	.361
Earl Robinson	OF82	R	24	96	222	37	59	12	3	8	30	31	54	4	.266	.455
Marv Breeding	2B80	R	27	90	244	32	51	8	0	1	16	14	33	5	.209	.254
Jim Busby	OF71	R	34	75	89	15	23	3	1	0	6	8	10	2	.258	.315
2 Marv Throneberry	OF15, 1B11	L	27	56	96	9	20	3	0	5	11	12	20	0	.208	.396
Hank Foiles (RJ)	C38	R	32	43	124	18	34	6	0	6	19	12	27	0	.274	.468
1 Gene Stephens	OF30	L	28	32	58	4	11	2	0	0	2	14	7	1	.190	.224
2 Clint Courtney	C16	L	34	22	45	3	12	2	0	0	4	10	3	0	.267	.311
2 Charlie Lau	C17	L	28	17	47	3	8	0	0	1	4	1	3	0	.170	.234
Walt Dropo	1B12	R	38	14	27	1	7	0	0	1	2	4	3	0	.259	.370
Frank Zupo	C4	L	21	5	4	1	2	1	0	0	0	1	1	0	.500	.750
Barry Shetrone	OF2	L	22	3	7	0	1	0	0	0	1	0	2	0	.143	.143

Boog Powell 19 L 1-13, 1 Chuck Essegian 29 R 0-1

NAME	T	AGE	W	L	PCT	SV	G	GS	CG	IP	H	BB	SO	ShO	ERA
		28	95	67	.586	33	163	163	54	1471	1226	617	926	21	3.22
Steve Barber	L	22	18	12	.600	1	37	34	14	248	194	130	150	8	3.34
Chuck Estrada	R	23	15	9	.625	0	33	31	6	212	159	132	160	1	3.69
Milt Pappas (AJ)	R	22	13	9	.591	1	26	23	11	178	134	78	89	4	3.03
Hal Brown	R	36	10	6	.625	1	27	23	6	167	153	33	61	3	3.18
Jack Fisher	R	22	10	13	.435	1	36	25	10	196	205	75	118	1	3.90
Hoyt Wilhelm	R	37	9	7	.563	18	51	1	0	110	89	41	87	0	2.29
Billy Hoeft	L	29	7	4	.636	3	35	12	3	138	106	55	100	1	2.02
Dick Hall	R	30	7	5	.583	4	29	13	4	122	102	30	92	2	3.10
Wes Stock	R	27	5	0	1.000	3	35	1	0	72	58	27	47	0	3.00
Dick Hyde	R	32	1	2	.333	0	15	0	0	21	18	13	15	0	5.57
Gordon Jones	R	31	0	0	.000	1	3	0	0	5	5	0	4	0	5.40
Jim Lehew	R	23	0	0	.000	0	2	0	0	2	1	0	0	0	0.00
John Papa	R	20	0	0	.000	0	2	0	0	1	2	3	3	0	18.00

CHICAGO 4th 86-76 .531 23 — AL LOPEZ

NAME	G by POS	B	AGE	G	AB	R	H	2B	3B	HR	RBI	BB	SO	SB	BA	SA
TOTALS			30	163	5556	765	1475	216	46	138	704	550	612	100	.265	.395
Roy Sievers	1B132	R	34	141	492	76	145	26	6	27	92	61	62	1	.295	.537
Nellie Fox	2B159	L	33	159	606	67	152	11	5	2	51	59	12	2	.251	.295
Luis Aparicio	SS156	R	27	156	625	90	170	24	4	6	45	38	33	53	.272	.352
Al Smith	3B80, OF71	R	33	147	532	88	148	29	4	28	93	56	67	4	.278	.506
Floyd Robinson	OF106	L	25	132	432	69	134	20	7	11	59	52	32	7	.310	.465
Jim Landis	OF139	R	27	140	534	87	151	18	8	22	85	65	71	19	.283	.470
Minnie Minoso	OF147	R	38	152	540	91	151	28	3	14	82	67	46	9	.280	.420
Sherm Lollar	C107	R	36	116	337	38	95	10	1	7	41	37	22	0	.282	.380
J. C. Martin	1B60, 3B36	L	24	110	274	26	63	8	3	5	32	21	31	1	.230	.336
Cam Carreon	C71	R	23	78	229	32	62	5	1	4	27	21	24	0	.271	.354
Sammy Esposito	3B28, SS20, 2B11	R	29	63	94	12	16	5	0	1	8	12	21	0	.170	.255
2 Andy Carey	3B54	R	29	56	143	21	38	12	3	0	14	11	24	0	.266	.392
2 Al Pilarcik	OF17	L	30	47	62	9	11	1	0	1	6	9	5	1	.177	.242
Billy Goodman	3B7, 1B2, 2B1	L	35	41	51	4	13	4	0	1	10	7	6	0	.255	.392
2 Wes Covington	OF14	L	29	22	59	5	17	1	0	4	15	4	5	0	.288	.508
Bob Roselli	C10	R	29	22	38	2	10	3	0	0	4	0	11	0	.263	.342
1 Earl Torgeson	1B1	L	37	20	15	1	1	0	0	0	1	3	5	0	.067	.067
Mike Hershberger	OF13	R	21	15	55	9	17	3	0	0	5	2	2	1	.309	.364
1 Joe Ginsberg	C2	L	34	6	3	0	0	0	0	0	0	1	2	0	.000	.000

1 Ted Lepcio 30 R 0-2, Dean Look 23 R 0-6, 1 Jim Rivera 38 L 0-0

NAME	T	AGE	W	L	PCT	SV	G	GS	CG	IP	H	BB	SO	ShO	ERA
		33	86	76	.531	33	163	163	39	1449	1491	498	814	3	4.06
Juan Pizarro	L	24	14	7	.667	2	39	25	12	195	164	89	188	1	3.05
Billy Pierce	L	34	10	9	.526	3	39	28	5	180	190	54	106	1	3.80
Frank Baumann	L	28	10	13	.435	3	53	23	5	188	249	59	75	1	5.60
Cal McLish	R	35	10	13	.435	1	31	27	4	162	178	47	80	0	4.39
2 Ray Herbert	R	31	9	6	.600	0	21	20	4	138	142	36	50	0	4.04
Early Wynn (IL)	R	41	8	2	.800	0	17	16	5	110	88	47	64	0	3.52
2 Don Larsen	R	31	7	2	.778	2	25	3	0	74	64	29	53	0	4.14
Turk Lown	R	37	7	5	.583	11	59	0	0	101	87	35	50	0	2.76
Russ Kemmerer	R	29	3	3	.500	2	47	2	0	97	102	26	35	0	4.36
Warren Hacker	R	36	3	3	.500	8	42	0	0	57	62	8	40	0	3.79
1 Bob Shaw	R	28	3	4	.429	0	14	10	3	71	85	20	31	0	3.80
Herb Score	L	28	1	2	.333	0	8	5	1	24	22	24	14	0	6.75
Joe Horlen	R	23	1	3	.250	0	5	4	1	18	25	13	11	0	6.50
Alan Brice	R	23	0	1	.000	0	3	0	0	3	4	3	3	0	0.00
1 Gerry Staley	R	40	0	3	.000	0	16	0	0	18	17	5	8	0	5.00
Gary Peters	L	24	0	0	.000	1	3	0	0	10	10	2	6	0	1.80
Mike Degerick	R	18	0	0	.000	0	1	0	0	2	2	1	0	0	4.50

CLEVELAND 5th 78-83 .484 30.5 — JIMMY DYKES 78-82 .488 MEL HARDER 0-1 .000

NAME	G by POS	B	AGE	G	AB	R	H	2B	3B	HR	RBI	BB	SO	SB	BA	SA
TOTALS			28	161	5609	737	1493	257	39	150	682	492	720	34	.266	.406
Vic Power	1B141, 2B7	R	29	147	563	64	151	34	4	5	63	38	16	4	.268	.369
Johnny Temple	2B129	R	32	129	518	73	143	22	3	3	30	61	36	9	.276	.347
Woodie Held	SS144	R	29	146	509	67	136	23	5	23	78	69	111	0	.267	.468
Bubba Phillips	3B143	R	31	143	546	64	144	23	1	18	72	29	61	1	.264	.408
Willie Kirkland	OF138	L	27	146	525	84	136	22	5	27	95	48	77	7	.259	.474
Jimmy Piersall	OF120	R	31	121	484	81	156	26	7	6	40	43	46	8	.322	.442
Tito Francona	OF138, 1B14	L	27	155	592	87	178	30	8	16	85	56	52	2	.301	.459
Johnny Romano	C141	R	26	142	509	76	152	29	1	21	80	61	60	0	.299	.483
Don Dillard	OF39	L	24	74	147	27	40	5	0	7	17	15	28	0	.272	.449
Mike de la Hoz	2B17, SS17, 3B18	R	21	61	173	20	45	10	0	3	23	7	10	0	.260	.370
3 Chuck Essegian	OF49	R	29	60	166	25	48	7	1	12	35	10	33	0	.289	.560
1 Bob Hale		L	27	42	36	0	6	0	0	0	6	1	7	0	.167	.167
2 Bob Nieman	OF12	R	34	39	65	2	23	6	0	2	10	7	4	1	.354	.538
Walt Bond	OF12	L	23	38	52	7	9	1	1	2	7	6	10	1	.173	.346
Valmy Thomas	C27	R	32	27	86	7	18	3	0	2	6	6	7	0	.209	.314
Jack Kubiszyn	3B8, SS7, 2B2	R	24	25	42	4	9	0	0	0	0	2	5	0	.214	.214
2 Ken Aspromonte	2B21	R	29	22	70	5	16	6	1	0	5	6	3	0	.229	.343
Ty Cline	OF12	L	22	12	43	9	9	2	1	0	1	6	1	0	.209	.302
Hal Jones	1B10	R	25	12	35	2	6	0	0	2	4	2	12	0	.171	.343
Al Luplow	OF5	L	22	5	18	0	1	0	0	0	0	2	6	0	.056	.056
Joe Morgan	OF2	L	30	4	10	0	2	0	0	0	0	1	3	0	.200	.200

NAME	T	AGE	W	L	PCT	SV	G	GS	CG	IP	H	BB	SO	ShO	ERA
		25	78	83	.484	23	161	161	35	1444	1426	599	801	12	4.15
Mudcat Grant	R	25	15	9	.625	0	35	35	11	245	207	109	146	3	3.86
Barry Latman	R	25	13	5	.722	5	45	18	4	177	163	54	108	2	4.02
Gary Bell	R	24	12	16	.429	0	34	34	11	228	214	100	163	2	4.11
Frank Funk	R	25	11	11	.500	11	56	0	0	92	79	31	64	0	3.33
Jim Perry	R	25	10	17	.370	0	35	35	6	224	238	87	90	1	4.70
Wynn Hawkins	R	25	7	9	.438	1	30	21	3	133	139	59	51	1	4.06
Bobby Locke	R	27	4	4	.500	2	37	4	0	95	112	40	37	0	4.55
Bob Allen	L	23	3	2	.600	3	48	0	0	82	96	40	42	0	3.73
Dick Stigman (EJ)	L	25	2	5	.286	0	22	6	0	64	65	25	48	0	4.64
Bill Dailey	R	26	1	0	1.000	0	12	0	0	19	16	6	7	0	0.95
2 Joe Schaffernoth	R	23	0	1	.000	0	15	0	0	17	16	14	9	0	4.76
1 Johnny Antonelli	L	31	0	4	.000	0	11	7	0	48	68	18	23	0	6.56
1 Russ Heman	R	28	0	0	.000	1	6	0	0	10	8	8	4	0	3.60
Steve Hamilton	L	27	0	0	.000	0	2	0	0	3	2	3	4	0	3.00
Sam McDowell	L	18	0	0	.000	0	1	1	0	6	3	5	5	0	0.00

BOSTON 6th 76-86 .469 33 — PINKY HIGGINS

NAME	G by POS	B	AGE	G	AB	R	H	2B	3B	HR	RBI	BB	SO	SB	BA	SA
TOTALS			28	163	5508	729	1401	251	37	112	682	647	847	56	.254	.374
Pete Runnels	1B113, 3B11, 2B7, SS1	L	33	143	360	49	114	20	3	3	38	46	32	5	.317	.414
Chuck Schilling	2B158	R	23	158	646	87	167	25	2	5	62	78	77	7	.259	.327
Don Buddin	SS109	R	27	115	339	58	89	22	3	6	42	72	45	2	.263	.398
Frank Malzone	3B149	R	31	151	590	74	157	21	4	14	87	44	49	1	.266	.386
Jackie Jensen	OF131	R	34	137	498	64	131	21	2	13	66	66	69	9	.263	.392
Gary Geiger	OF137	L	24	140	499	82	116	21	6	18	64	87	91	16	.232	.407
Carl Yastrzemski	OF147	L	21	148	583	71	155	31	6	11	80	50	96	6	.266	.396
Jim Pagliaroni	C108	R	23	120	376	50	91	17	0	16	58	55	74	1	.242	.415
1 Vic Wertz	1B86	L	36	99	317	33	83	16	2	11	60	38	43	0	.262	.429
Pumpsie Green (IL)	SS57, 2B7	B	27	88	219	33	57	12	3	6	27	42	32	4	.260	.425
Russ Nixon	C66	L	26	87	242	24	70	12	2	1	19	13	19	0	.289	.368
Carroll Hardy	OF76	R	28	85	281	46	74	20	2	3	36	26	53	4	.263	.381
Billy Harrell	3B10, SS7, 1B2	R	32	37	37	10	6	2	0	0	1	1	8	1	.162	.216
2 Joe Ginsberg	C6	L	34	19	24	1	6	0	0	0	5	0	2	0	.250	.250
Lu Clinton	OF13	R	23	17	51	4	13	2	1	0	3	2	10	0	.255	.333
Rip Repulski	OF4	R	33	15	25	2	7	1	0	0	1	1	5	0	.280	.320
Don Gile	1B6, C1	R	26	8	18	2	5	0	0	1	1	1	5	0	.278	.444

NAME	T	AGE	W	L	PCT	SV	G	GS	CG	IP	H	BB	SO	ShO	ERA
		28	76	86	.469	30	163	163	35	1443	1472	679	831	6	4.29
Don Schwall	R	25	15	7	.682	0	25	25	10	179	167	110	91	2	3.22
Bill Monbouquette	R	24	14	14	.500	0	32	32	12	236	233	100	161	1	3.39
Gene Conley	R	30	11	14	.440	1	33	30	6	200	229	65	113	2	4.91
Mike Fornieles	R	29	9	8	.529	15	57	2	1	119	121	54	70	0	4.69
Ike Delock	R	31	6	9	.400	0	28	28	3	156	185	52	80	1	4.90
Dave Hillman	R	33	3	2	.600	0	28	1	0	78	70	23	39	0	2.77
Chet Nichols (BH)	L	30	3	2	.600	3	26	2	0	52	40	26	20	0	2.08
Ted Wills	L	27	3	2	.600	0	17	0	0	20	24	19	11	0	5.85
Tom Brewer	R	29	3	2	.600	0	10	9	0	42	37	29	13	0	3.43
Billy Muffet	R	30	3	11	.214	2	38	11	2	113	130	36	47	0	5.65
Arnie Earley	L	28	2	4	.333	7	33	0	0	50	42	34	44	0	3.96
Galen Cisco	R	25	2	4	.333	0	17	8	0	52	67	28	26	0	6.75
Tracy Stallard	R	23	2	7	.222	2	43	14	1	133	110	96	109	0	4.87
Wilbur Wood	L	19	0	0	.000	0	6	1	0	13	14	7	7	0	5.54
Tom Borland	L	28	0	0	.000	0	1	0	0	1	3	0	0	0	18.00

MINNESOTA 7th 70-90 .438 38 — COOKIE LAVAGETTO 29-45 .392 — SAM MELE 41-45 .477

NAME	G by POS	B	AGE	G	AB	R	H	2B	3B	HR	RBI	BB	SO	SB	BA	SA
TOTALS			28	161	5417	707	1353	215	40	167	665	597	840	47	.250	.397
Harmon Killebrew	1B119, 3B45, OF2	R	25	150	541	94	156	20	7	46	122	107	109	1	.288	.606
2 Billy Martin	2B105, SS1	R	33	108	374	44	92	15	5	6	36	13	42	3	.246	.361
Zoilo Versalles	SS129	R	21	129	510	65	143	25	5	7	53	25	61	16	.280	.390
2 Bill Tuttle	3B85, OF64, 2B2	R	31	113	370	38	91	12	3	5	38	43	41	1	.246	.335
Bob Allison	OF150, 1B18	R	26	159	556	83	136	21	3	29	105	103	100	2	.245	.450
Lenny Green	OF153	L	27	156	600	92	171	28	7	9	50	81	50	17	.285	.400
Jim Lemon	OF120	R	33	129	423	57	109	26	1	14	52	44	98	1	.258	.423
Earl Battey	C131	R	26	133	460	70	139	24	1	17	55	53	66	3	.302	.470
Jose Valdivielso	SS43, 2B15, 3B14	R	27	76	149	15	29	5	0	1	9	8	19	1	.195	.248
Dan Dobbek	OF48	L	26	72	125	12	21	3	1	4	14	13	18	1	.168	.304
Hal Naragon	C36	L	32	57	139	10	42	2	1	2	11	4	8	0	.302	.374
2 Julio Becquer	1B18, OF5, P1	L	29	57	84	13	20	1	2	5	18	2	12	0	.238	.476
2 Ted Lepcio	3B35, 2B22, SS6	R	30	47	112	11	19	3	1	7	19	8	31	1	.170	.402
1 Billy Gardner	2B41, 3B2	R	33	45	154	13	36	9	0	1	11	10	14	0	.234	.312
Joe Altobelli	OF25, 1B21	L	29	41	95	10	21	2	1	3	14	13	14	0	.221	.358
1 Reno Bertoia	3B32	R	26	35	104	17	22	2	0	1	8	20	12	0	.212	.260
Don Mincher	1B29	L	23	35	101	18	19	5	1	5	11	22	11	0	.188	.406
1 Elmer Valo	OF1	L	40	33	32	0	5	2	0	0	4	3	3	0	.156	.219

Ron Henry 24 R 4-28, Rich Rollins 23 R 5-17, Billy Consolo 26 R 0-5, 1 Pete Whisennant 31 R 0-6, Lamar Jacobs 24 R 2-8, Jim Snyder 28 R 0-5

NAME	T	AGE	W	L	PCT	SV	G	GS	CG	IP	H	BB	SO	ShO	ERA
		27	70	90	.438	23	161	161	49	1432	1415	570	914	14	4.28
Camilo Pascual	R	27	15	16	.484	0	35	33	15	252	205	100	**221**	**8**	3.46
Jack Kralick	L	26	13	11	.542	0	33	33	11	242	257	64	137	2	3.61
Pedro Ramos	R	26	11	**20**	.355	2	42	34	9	264	**265**	79	174	3	3.95
Jim Kaat	L	22	9	17	.346	0	36	29	8	201	188	82	122	1	3.90
Bill Pleis	L	23	4	2	.667	2	37	0	0	56	59	34	32	0	4.98
Ray Moore	R	35	4	4	.500	14	46	0	0	56	49	38	45	0	3.70
Al Schroll	R	29	4	4	.500	0	11	8	2	50	53	27	24	0	5.22
Don Lee	R	27	3	6	.333	3	37	10	4	115	93	35	65	0	3.52
Chuck Stobbs	L	31	2	3	.400	2	24	3	0	45	56	15	17	0	7.40
2 Danny McDevitt	L	28	1	0	1.000	0	16	1	0	27	20	19	15	0	2.33
1 Paul Giel	R	28	1	0	1.000	0	12	0	0	19	24	17	14	0	9.95
Lee Stange	R	24	1	0	1.000	0	7	0	0	12	15	10	10	0	3.00
2 Ed Palmquist	R	28	1	1	.500	0	9	2	0	21	33	13	13	0	9.43
Berto Cueto	R	23	1	3	.250	0	7	5	0	21	27	10	5	0	7.29
Jerry Arrigo	L	20	0	1	.000	0	7	2	0	10	9	10	6	0	9.90
Ted Sadowski	R	25	0	2	.000	0	15	1	0	33	49	11	12	0	6.82
Gary Dotter	L	18	0	0	.000	0	2	0	0	6	6	4	2	0	9.00
Fred Bruckbauer	R	23	0	0	.000	0	1	0	0	0	3	1	0	0	∞
2 Julio Becquer	L	29	0	0	.000	0	1	0	0	1	4	1	0	0	27.00

LOS ANGELES 8th 70-91 .435 38.5 — BILL RIGNEY

NAME	G by POS	B	AGE	G	AB	R	H	2B	3B	HR	RBI	BB	SO	SB	BA	SA
TOTALS			29	162	5424	744	1331	218	22	189	700	**681**	**1068**	37	.245	.398
Steve Bilko	1B86, OF3	R	32	114	294	49	82	16	1	20	59	58	81	1	.279	.544
1 Ken Aspromonte	2B62	R	29	66	238	29	53	10	0	2	14	33	21	0	.223	.290
2 Joe Koppe	SS88, 2B3, 3B1	R	30	91	338	46	85	12	2	5	40	45	77	3	.251	.343
Eddie Yost (BH)	3B67	R	34	76	213	29	43	4	0	3	15	50	48	0	.202	.263
Albie Pearson	OF113	L	26	144	427	92	123	21	3	7	41	96	40	11	.288	.400
Ken Hunt	OF134, 2B1	R	26	149	479	70	122	29	3	25	84	49	120	8	.255	.484
Leon Wagner	OF116	L	27	133	453	74	127	19	2	28	79	48	65	5	.280	.517
Earl Averill	C88, OF9, 2B1	R	29	115	323	56	86	9	0	21	59	62	70	1	.266	.489
2 Lee Thomas	OF86, 1B34	L	25	130	450	77	128	11	5	24	70	47	74	0	.284	.491
Ted Kluszewski	1B66	L	36	107	263	32	64	12	0	15	39	24	23	0	.243	.460
Rocky Bridges	2B58, SS25, 3B4	R	33	84	229	20	55	5	1	2	15	26	37	1	.240	.297
2 George Thomas	OF45, 3B38	R	23	79	282	39	79	12	1	13	59	21	66	3	.280	.468
Eddie Sadowski	C56	R	29	69	164	16	38	13	0	4	12	11	33	2	.232	.384
Gene Leek	3B49, SS7, OF1	R	24	57	199	16	45	9	1	5	20	7	54	0	.226	.357
Billy Moran	2B51, SS2	R	27	54	173	17	45	7	1	2	22	17	16	0	.260	.347
Del Rice	C30	R	38	44	83	11	20	4	0	4	11	20	19	0	.241	.434
Ken Hamlin	SS39	R	26	42	91	4	19	3	0	1	5	11	9	0	.209	.275
Tom Satriano	3B23, 2B10, SS1	L	20	35	96	15	19	5	1	1	8	12	16	2	.198	.302
Fritzie Brickell	SS17	R	26	21	49	3	6	0	0	0	3	6	9	0	.122	.122
1 Bob Cerv	OF15	R	35	18	57	3	9	3	0	2	6	1	8	0	.158	.316
Bob Rodgers	C14	B	22	16	56	8	18	2	0	2	13	1	6	0	.321	.464

Faye Thornberry 30 L 6-31, Jim Fregosi 19 R 6-27, 1 Julio Becquer 29 L 0-8, Chuch Tanner 31 L 1-8, Danny Ardell 20 L 1-4, Leo Burke 27 R 0-5, Lou Johnson 26 R 0-0

NAME	T	AGE	W	L	PCT	SV	G	GS	CG	IP	H	BB	SO	ShO	ERA
		28	70	91	.435	34	162	162	25	1438	1391	**713**	**973**	5	4.31
Ken McBride	R	25	12	15	.444	1	38	36	11	242	229	102	180	1	3.64
Ted Bowsfield	L	25	11	8	.579	0	41	21	4	157	154	63	88	1	3.73
Eli Grba	R	26	11	13	.458	2	40	30	8	212	197	114	105	0	4.25
Tom Morgan	R	31	8	2	.800	10	59	0	0	92	74	17	39	0	2.35
2 Ryne Duren	R	32	6	12	.333	2	40	14	1	99	87	75	108	1	5.18
Art Fowler	R	38	5	8	.385	11	53	3	0	89	68	29	78	0	3.64
2 Jim Donohue	R	22	4	6	.400	5	38	7	0	100	93	50	79	0	4.32
Ron Moeller	L	22	4	8	.333	0	33	18	1	113	122	83	87	1	5.81
Jack Spring	L	28	3	0	1.000	0	18	4	0	38	35	15	27	0	4.26
1 Ron Kline	R	29	3	6	.333	1	26	12	0	105	119	44	70	0	4.89
1 Tex Clevenger	R	28	2	1	.667	1	12	0	0	16	13	13	11	0	1.69
1 Jerry Casale	R	27	1	5	.167	1	13	7	0	43	52	25	35	0	6.49
2 Johnny James	R	27	0	2	.000	0	36	3	0	71	66	54	41	0	5.32
Dean Chance	R	20	0	2	.000	0	5	4	0	18	33	5	11	0	7.00
Ned Garver	R	35	0	3	.000	0	12	2	0	29	40	16	9	0	5.59
2 Russ Heman	R	28	0	0	.000	0	6	0	0	10	4	2	2	0	1.80
Ray Semproch	R	30	0	0	.000	0	2	0	0	1	1	3	1	0	9.00
Bob Sprout	L	19	0	0	.000	0	1	1	0	4	4	3	2	0	4.50

KANSAS CITY 9th (Tie) 61-100 .379 47.5 — JOE GORDON 26-43 .377 — HANK BAUER 35-57 .380

NAME	G by POS	B	AGE	G	AB	R	H	2B	3B	HR	RBI	BB	SO	SB	BA	SA
TOTALS			27	162	5423	683	1342	216	47	90	632	580	772	58	.247	.354
Norm Siebern	1B109, OF47	L	27	153	560	68	166	36	5	18	98	82	91	2	.296	.475
Jerry Lumpe	2B147	L	28	148	569	81	167	29	9	3	54	48	39	1	.293	.392
Dick Howser	SS157	R	24	158	611	108	171	29	6	3	45	92	38	37	.280	.362
Wayne Causey	3B88, SS11, 2B9	L	24	104	312	37	86	14	1	8	49	37	28	0	.276	.404
2 Deron Johnson	OF59, 3B19, 1B3	R	22	83	283	31	61	11	3	8	42	14	44	0	.216	.360
2 Bobby Del Greco	OF73	R	28	74	239	34	55	14	1	5	21	30	31	1	.230	.360
Leo Posada	OF102	R	25	116	344	37	87	10	4	7	53	36	84	0	.253	.366
Haywood Sullivan	C88, 1B16, OF5	R	30	117	331	42	80	16	2	6	40	46	45	1	.242	.356
Joe Pignatano	C83, 3B2	R	31	92	243	31	59	10	3	4	22	36	42	2	.243	.358
Jay Hankins	OF65	L	25	76	173	23	32	0	3	3	6	8	17	2	.185	.272
2 Jim Rivera	OF43	L	38	64	141	20	34	8	0	2	10	24	14	6	.241	.340
2 Gene Stephens	OF54	L	28	62	183	22	38	6	1	4	26	16	27	3	.208	.317
Lou Klimchock	1B11, OF7, 3B6, 2B1	L	21	57	121	8	26	4	1	1	16	5	13	0	.215	.289
Hank Bauer	OF35	R	38	43	106	11	28	3	1	3	18	9	8	1	.264	.396
1 Marv Throneberry	1B30, OF10	L	27	40	130	17	31	2	1	6	24	19	30	0	.238	.408
1 Andy Carey	3B39	R	29	39	123	20	30	6	2	3	11	15	23	0	.244	.398
2 Reno Bertoia	3B29, 2B6	R	26	39	120	12	29	2	0	0	13	9	15	1	.242	.258
1 Al Pilarcik	OF21	L	30	35	60	9	12	1	1	0	9	6	7	1	.200	.250
1 Bob Boyd	1B8	L	34	26	48	7	11	2	0	0	9	1	2	0	.229	.271
1 Bill Tuttle	OF25	R	31	25	84	15	22	2	2	0	8	9	9	0	.262	.333
3 Wes Covington	OF12	L	29	17	44	3	7	0	0	1	6	4	7	0	.159	.227
Frank Cipriani	OF11	R	20	13	36	2	9	0	0	0	2	2	4	0	.250	.250
Charlie Shoemaker	2B6	L	21	7	26	5	10	2	0	0	1	2	2	0	.385	.462

Gordon MacKenzie 23 R 3-24, 2 Ozzie Virgil 28 R 3-21, Bobby Prescott 30 R 1-12, Billy Bryan 22 L 3-19, 2 Chuck Essegian 29 R 2-6, Stan Johnson 24 L 0-3, 1 Clint Courtney 34 L 0-1

NAME	T	AGE	W	L	PCT	SV	G	GS	CG	IP	H	BB	SO	ShO	ERA
		28	61	**100**	.379	23	162	162	32	1415	**1519**	629	703	5	4.74
Norm Bass	R	22	11	11	.500	0	40	23	6	171	164	82	74	2	4.68
2 Bob Shaw	R	28	9	10	.474	0	26	24	6	151	165	58	60	0	4.32
Jim Archer	L	29	9	15	.375	5	39	27	9	205	204	60	110	2	3.20
Jerry Walker	R	22	8	14	.364	2	36	24	4	168	161	96	56	0	4.82
Joe Nuxhall	L	32	5	8	.385	1	37	13	1	128	135	65	81	0	5.34
1 Bud Daley	L	28	4	8	.333	1	16	10	2	64	84	22	36	0	4.92
Bill Kunkel	R	24	3	4	.429	4	58	2	0	89	103	32	46	0	5.16
1 Ray Herbert	R	31	3	6	.333	0	13	12	1	84	103	30	34	0	5.36
Dave Wickersham (XJ)	R	25	2	1	.667	2	17	0	0	21	25	5	10	0	5.14
Lew Krausse	R	18	2	5	.286	0	12	8	2	56	49	46	32	1	4.82
Ed Rakow	R	25	2	8	.200	1	45	11	1	125	131	49	81	0	4.75
1 Don Larsen	R	31	1	0	1.000	0	8	1	0	15	21	11	13	0	4.20
2 Bill Fischer	R	30	1	0	1.000	2	15	0	0	21	26	6	12	0	3.86
2 Gerry Staley	R	40	1	1	.500	2	23	0	0	30	32	10	16	0	3.60
1 Ken Johnson	R	28	0	4	.000	0	6	1	0	9	11	7	4	0	11.00
2 Art Ditmar	R	32	0	5	.000	1	20	5	0	54	60	23	19	0	5.67
2 Mickey McDermott	L	32	0	0	.000	0	4	0	0	6	14	10	3	0	13.50
Ed Keegan	R	21	0	0	.000	1	6	0	0	6	6	5	3	0	4.50
John Wyatt	R	26	0	0	.000	1	5	0	0	7	8	4	6	0	2.57
Dan Pfister	R	24	0	0	.000	0	2	0	0	2	5	4	3	0	18.00
2 Paul Giel	R	28	0	0	.000	0	1	0	0	2	6	3	1	0	31.50
Bill Kirk	L	25	0	0	.000	0	1	1	0	3	6	1	3	0	12.00

WASHINGTON 9th (Tie) 61-100 .379 47.5 — MICKEY VERNON

NAME	G by POS	B	AGE	G	AB	R	H	2B	3B	HR	RBI	BB	SO	SB	BA	SA
TOTALS			29	161	5366	618	1307	217	44	119	578	558	917	81	.244	.367
Dale Long	1B95	L	35	123	377	52	94	20	4	17	49	39	41	0	.249	.459
2 Chuck Cottier	2B100	R	25	101	337	37	79	14	4	2	34	30	51	9	.234	.318
Coot Veal	SS63	R	28	69	218	21	44	10	0	0	8	19	29	1	.202	.248
Danny O'Connell	3B73, 2B61	R	34	138	493	61	128	30	1	1	37	77	62	15	.260	.331
Marty Keough	OF100, 1B10	L	26	135	390	57	97	18	9	9	34	32	60	12	.249	.410
Willie Tasby	OF139	R	28	141	494	54	124	13	2	17	63	58	94	4	.251	.389
Chuck Hinton	OF92	R	27	106	339	51	88	13	5	6	34	40	81	22	.260	.381
Gene Green	C79, OF21	R	28	110	364	52	102	16	3	18	62	35	65	0	.280	.489
Gene Woodling	OF90	L	38	110	342	39	107	16	4	10	57	50	24	1	.313	.471
Jim King	OF91, C1	L	28	110	263	43	71	12	1	11	46	38	45	4	.270	.449
Billy Klaus	3B51, SS18, 2B1, OF1	L	32	91	251	26	57	8	2	7	30	30	34	2	.227	.359
Pete Daley	C72	R	31	72	203	12	39	7	1	2	17	14	37	0	.192	.266
Harry Bright	3B40, C8, 2B1	R	31	72	183	20	44	6	0	4	21	19	23	0	.240	.339
Bob Johnson	SS57, 2B2, 3B2	R	25	61	224	27	66	13	1	6	28	19	26	4	.295	.442
Bud Zipfel	1B44	L	22	50	170	17	34	7	5	4	18	15	49	1	.200	.371
Jim Mahoney	SS31, 2B2	R	27	43	108	10	26	0	1	0	6	5	23	1	.241	.259
R C Stevens	1B25	R	26	33	62	2	8	1	0	0	7	2	15	1	.129	.145
Ken Retzer	C16	L	27	16	53	7	18	4	0	1	3	4	5	1	.340	.472

Joe Hicks 28 L 5-29, Ron Stillwell 21 R 2-16, Dutch Dotterer 29 R 5-19, Chet Boak 26 R 0-7, Eddie Brinkman 19 R 1-11

NAME	T	AGE	W	L	PCT	SV	G	GS	CG	IP	H	BB	SO	ShO	ERA
		30	61	**100**	.379	21	161	161	39	1425	1405	586	666	8	4.23
Bennie Daniels	R	29	12	11	.522	0	32	28	12	212	184	80	110	1	3.44
Dick Donovan	R	33	10	10	.500	0	23	22	11	169	138	35	62	2	**2.40**
Joe McClain	R	28	8	18	.308	1	33	29	7	212	221	48	76	2	3.86
Ed Hobaugh	R	27	7	9	.438	0	26	18	3	126	142	64	67	0	4.43
Marty Kutyna	R	28	6	8	.429	3	50	6	0	143	147	48	64	0	3.97
Pete Burnside	L	30	4	9	.308	2	33	16	4	113	106	51	56	2	4.54
1 Hal Woodeshick	L	28	3	2	.600	0	7	6	1	40	38	24	24	0	4.05
John Gabler	R	30	3	8	.273	4	29	9	0	93	104	37	33	0	4.84
Johnny Klippstein	R	33	2	2	.500	0	42	1	0	72	83	43	41	0	6.75
1 Tom Sturdivant	R	31	2	6	.250	0	15	10	1	80	67	40	39	1	4.61
Dave Sisler	R	29	2	8	.200	11	45	1	0	60	55	48	30	0	4.00
2 Claude Osteen	L	21	1	1	.500	0	3	3	0	18	14	9	14	0	5.00
2 Tom Cheney (SA)	R	26	1	3	.250	0	10	7	0	30	32	26	20	0	8.70
Mike Garcia	R	37	0	1	.000	0	16	0	0	19	23	13	14	0	4.74
Rudy Hernandez	R	29	0	1	.000	0	7	0	0	9	8	3	4	0	3.00
Carl Mathias	L	25	0	1	.000	0	4	3	0	14	22	4	7	0	10.93
Carl Bouldin	R	21	0	1	.000	0	2	1	0	3	9	2	2	0	18.00
Hector Maestri	R	26	0	1	.000	0	1	1	0	6	6	2	2	0	1.50
Roy Heiser	R	19	0	0	.000	0	3	0	0	6	6	9	1	0	6.00

CINCINNATI 1st 93-61 .604 — **FRED HUTCHINSON**

NAME	G by POS	B	AGE	G	AB	R	H	2B	3B	HR	RBI	BB	SO	SB	BA	SA
TOTALS			27	154	5243	710	1414	247	35	158	675	423	761	70	.270	.421
Gordy Coleman	1B150	L	26	150	520	63	149	27	4	26	87	45	67	1	.287	.504
2 Don Blasingame	2B116	L	29	123	450	59	100	18	4	1	21	39	38	4	.222	.287
Eddie Kasko	SS112, 3B12, 2B6	R	29	126	469	64	127	22	1	2	27	32	36	4	.271	.335
Gene Freese	3B151, 2B1	R	27	152	575	78	159	27	2	26	87	27	78	8	.277	.466
Frank Robinson	OF150, 3B1	R	25	153	545	117	176	32	7	37	124	71	64	22	.323	.611
Vada Pinson	OF153	L	22	154	607	101	208	34	8	16	87	39	63	23	.343	.504
Wally Post	OF81	R	31	99	282	44	83	16	3	20	57	22	61	0	.294	.585
Jerry Zimmerman	C76	R	26	76	204	8	42	5	0	0	10	11	21	1	.206	.230
Gus Bell	OF75	L	32	103	235	27	60	10	1	3	33	18	21	1	.255	.345
Jerry Lynch	OF44	L	30	96	181	33	57	13	2	13	50	27	25	2	.315	.624
Leo Cardenas	SS63	R	22	74	198	23	61	18	1	5	24	15	39	1	.308	.485
Elio Chacon	2B42, OF8	R	24	61	132	26	35	4	2	2	5	21	22	1	.265	.371
Johnny Edwards	C52	L	23	52	145	14	27	5	0	2	14	18	28	1	.186	.262
2 Dick Gernert	1B21	R	32	40	63	4	19	1	0	0	7	7	9	0	.302	.317
2 Bob Schmidt	C27	R	28	27	70	4	9	0	0	1	4	8	14	0	.129	.171
2 Pete Whisenant	OF12, 3B1, C1	R	31	26	15	6	3	0	0	0	1	2	4	1	.200	.200
2 Darrell Johnson	C20	R	32	20	54	3	17	2	0	1	6	1	2	0	.315	.407
1 Ed Bailey	C12	L	30	12	43	4	13	4	0	0	2	3	5	0	.302	.395

Jim Baumer 30 R 3-24, Willie Jones 35 R 0-7, Joe Gaines 24 R 0-3, Cliff Cook 24 R 0-5, Harry Anderson 29 L 1-4, Hal Bevan 29 R 1-3

NAME	T	AGE	W	L	PCT	SV	G	GS	CG	IP	H	BB	SO	ShO	ERA
		26	93	61	.604	40	154	154	46	1370	1300	500	829	12	3.78
Joey Jay	R	25	21	10	.677	0	34	34	14	247	217	92	157	4	3.53
Jim O'Toole	L	24	19	9	.679	2	39	35	11	253	229	93	178	3	3.09
Bob Purkey	R	31	16	12	.571	1	36	34	13	246	245	51	116	1	3.73
Jim Brosnan	R	31	10	4	.714	16	53	0	0	80	77	18	40	0	3.04
Ken Hunt	R	22	9	10	.474	0	29	22	4	136	130	66	75	0	3.97
2 Ken Johnson	R	28	6	2	.750	1	15	11	3	83	71	22	42	1	3.25
Jim Maloney	R	21	6	7	.462	2	27	11	1	95	86	59	57	0	4.36
Bill Henry	L	33	2	1	.667	16	47	0	0	53	50	15	53	0	2.21
Howie Nunn (EJ)	R	25	2	1	.667	0	24	0	0	38	36	24	26	0	3.55
Sherman Jones	R	26	1	1	.500	2	24	2	0	55	51	27	32	0	4.42
Jay Hook	R	24	1	3	.250	0	22	5	0	63	83	22	36	0	7.71
Marshall Bridges	L	30	0	1	.000	0	13	0	0	21	26	11	17	0	7.71
1 Claude Osteen	L	21	0	0	.000	0	1	0	0	.1	0	0	0	0	0.00

LOS ANGELES 2nd 89-65 .578 4 — **WALT ALSTON**

NAME	G by POS	B	AGE	G	AB	R	H	2B	3B	HR	RBI	BB	SO	SB	BA	SA
TOTALS			28	154	5189	735	1358	193	40	157	673	596	796	86	.262	.405
Norm Larker	1B86, OF1	L	30	97	282	29	76	16	1	5	38	24	22	0	.270	.387
Charlie Neal	2B104	R	30	108	341	40	80	6	1	10	48	30	49	3	.235	.346
Maury Wills	SS148	B	28	148	613	105	173	12	10	1	31	59	50	35	.282	.339
Jim Gilliam	3B74, 2B71, OF11	B	32	144	439	74	107	26	3	4	32	79	34	8	.244	.344
Tommy Davis	OF86, 3B59	R	22	132	460	60	128	13	2	15	58	32	53	10	.278	.413
Willie Davis	OF114	L	21	128	339	56	86	19	6	12	45	27	46	12	.254	.451
Wally Moon	OF133	L	31	134	463	79	152	25	3	17	88	89	79	7	.328	.505
Johnny Roseboro	C125	L	28	128	394	59	99	16	6	18	59	56	62	6	.251	.459
Ron Fairly	OF71, 1B23	L	22	111	245	42	79	15	2	10	48	48	22	0	.322	.522
Gil Hodges	1B100	R	37	109	215	25	52	4	0	8	31	24	43	3	.242	.372
Frank Howard	OF65, 1B7	R	24	92	267	36	79	10	2	15	45	21	50	0	.296	.517
Duke Snider (BE)	OF66	L	34	85	233	35	69	8	3	16	56	29	43	1	.296	.562
2 Daryl Spencer	3B57, SS3	R	31	60	189	27	46	7	0	8	27	20	35	0	.243	.407
Norm Sherry	C45	R	29	47	121	10	31	2	0	5	21	9	30	0	.256	.397
Bob Aspromonte	3B9, SS4, 2B2	R	23	47	58	7	14	3	0	0	2	4	12	0	.241	.293
Don Drysdale	P40	R	24	40	83	9	16	1	0	5	12	6	24	0	.193	.386
Gordie Windhorn	OF17	R	27	34	33	10	8	2	1	2	6	4	3	0	.242	.545
1 Carl Warwick	OF12	R	24	19	11	2	1	0	0	0	1	2	3	0	.091	.091
1 Don Demeter	OF14	R	26	15	29	3	5	0	0	1	2	3	6	0	.172	.276
Doug Camilli	C12	R	24	13	30	3	4	0	0	3	4	1	9	0	.133	.433

1 Bob Lillis 31 R 1-9, 1 Charley Smith 23 R 6-24, Tim Harkness 23 L 4-8

NAME	T	AGE	W	L	PCT	SV	G	GS	CG	IP	H	BB	SO	ShO	ERA
		26	89	65	.578	35	154	154	40	1378	1346	544	1105	10	4.04
Johnny Podres	L	28	18	5	.783	0	32	29	6	183	192	51	124	1	3.74
Sandy Koufax	L	25	18	13	.581	1	42	35	15	256	212	96	269	2	3.52
Stan Williams	R	24	15	12	.556	0	41	35	6	235	213	108	205	2	3.91
Don Drysdale	R	24	13	10	.565	0	40	37	10	244	236	83	182	3	3.69
Ron Perranoski	L	25	7	5	.583	6	53	1	0	92	82	41	56	0	2.64
2 Dick Farrell	R	27	6	6	.500	10	50	0	0	89	107	43	80	0	5.06
Roger Craig	R	30	5	6	.455	2	40	14	2	113	130	52	63	0	6.13
Larry Sherry	R	25	4	4	.500	15	53	1	0	95	90	39	79	0	3.88
Ed Roebuck (SJ)	R	29	2	0	1.000	0	5	0	0	9	12	2	9	0	5.00
Jim Golden	R	25	1	1	.500	0	28	0	0	42	52	20	18	0	5.79
1 Ed Palmquist	R	28	0	1	.000	1	5	0	0	9	10	7	5	0	6.00
Phil Ortega	R	21	0	2	.000	0	4	2	1	13	10	2	15	0	5.54

SAN FRANCISCO 3rd 85-69 .552 8 — **AL DARK**

NAME	G by POS	B	AGE	G	AB	R	H	2B	3B	HR	RBI	BB	SO	SB	BA	SA
TOTALS			26	155	5233	773	1379	219	32	183	709	506	764	79	.264	.423
Willie McCovey	1B84	L	23	106	328	59	89	12	3	18	50	37	60	1	.271	.491
Joey Amalfitano	2B95, 3B6	R	27	109	384	64	98	11	4	2	23	44	59	7	.255	.320
Jose Pagan	SS132, OF4	R	26	134	434	38	110	15	2	5	46	31	45	8	.253	.332
Jim Davenport	3B132	R	27	137	436	64	121	28	4	12	65	45	65	4	.278	.443
Felipe Alou	OF122	R	26	132	415	59	120	19	0	18	52	26	41	11	.289	.465
Willie Mays	OF153	R	30	154	572	129	176	32	3	40	123	81	77	18	.308	.584
Harvey Kuenn	OF93, 3B32, SS1	R	30	131	471	60	125	22	4	5	46	47	34	5	.265	.361
2 Ed Bailey	C103, OF1	L	30	107	340	39	81	9	1	13	51	42	41	1	.238	.385
Orlando Cepeda	1B81, OF80	R	23	152	585	105	182	28	4	46	142	39	91	12	.311	.609
Matty Alou	OF58	L	22	81	200	38	62	7	2	6	24	15	18	3	.310	.455
Chuck Hiller	2B67	L	26	70	240	38	57	12	1	2	12	32	30	4	.238	.321
Ed Bressoud	SS34, 3B3, 2B1	R	29	59	114	14	24	6	0	3	11	11	23	1	.211	.342
Hobie Landrith	C30	L	31	43	71	11	17	4	0	2	10	12	7	0	.239	.380
Ernie Bowman	2B13, SS12, 3B7	R	23	38	38	10	8	0	2	0	2	1	8	2	.211	.316
Tom Haller	C25	L	24	30	62	5	9	1	0	2	8	9	23	0	.145	.258
John Orsino	C25	R	23	25	83	5	23	3	2	4	12	3	13	0	.277	.506

Jim Marshall 29 L 8-36, Bob Farley 23 L 2-20, 1 Don Blasingame 29 L 0-1, 1 Bob Schmidt 28 R 1-6

NAME	T	AGE	W	L	PCT	SV	G	GS	CG	IP	H	BB	SO	ShO	ERA
		27	85	69	.552	30	155	155	39	1388	1306	502	924	9	3.77
Stu Miller	R	33	14	5	.737	17	63	0	0	122	95	37	89	0	2.66
Jack Sanford	R	32	13	9	.591	0	38	33	6	217	203	87	112	0	4.23
Juan Marichal	R	23	13	10	.565	0	29	27	9	185	183	48	124	3	3.89
Mike McCormick	L	22	13	16	.448	0	40	35	13	250	235	75	163	3	3.20
Sam Jones	R	35	8	8	.500	1	37	17	2	128	134	57	105	0	4.50
Billy O'Dell	L	28	7	5	.583	2	46	14	4	130	132	33	110	1	3.60
Billy Loes	R	31	6	5	.545	0	26	18	3	115	114	39	55	1	4.23
Jim Duffalo	R	25	5	1	.833	1	24	4	1	62	59	32	37	0	4.21
Dick LeMay	L	22	3	6	.333	3	27	5	1	83	65	36	54	0	3.58
Bobby Bolin	R	22	2	2	.500	5	37	1	0	48	37	37	48	0	3.19
Dom Zanni	R	29	1	0	1.000	0	8	0	0	14	13	12	11	0	3.86
Eddie Fisher	R	24	0	2	.000	1	15	1	0	34	36	9	16	0	5.29

MILWAUKEE 4th 83-71 .539 10 — **CHUCK DRESSEN 71-58 .550 BIRDIE TEBBETTS 12-13 .480**

NAME	G by POS	B	AGE	G	AB	R	H	2B	3B	HR	RBI	BB	SO	SB	BA	SA
TOTALS			28	155	5288	712	1365	199	34	188	662	534	000	70	.258	.415
Joe Adcock	1B140	R	33	152	562	77	160	20	0	35	108	59	94	2	.285	.507
Frank Bolling	2B148	R	29	148	585	86	153	16	4	15	56	57	62	7	.262	.379
Roy McMillan	SS154	R	30	154	505	42	111	16	0	7	48	61	86	2	.220	.293
Eddie Mathews	3B151	L	29	152	572	103	175	23	6	32	91	93	95	12	.306	.535
Lee Maye	OF96	L	26	110	373	68	101	11	5	14	41	36	50	10	.271	.440
Hank Aaron	OF154, 3B2	R	27	155	603	115	197	39	10	34	120	56	64	21	.327	.594
2 Frank Thomas	OF109, 1B11	R	32	124	423	58	120	13	3	25	67	29	70	2	.284	.506
Joe Torre	C112	R	20	113	406	40	113	21	4	10	42	28	60	3	.278	.424
Al Spangler	OF44	L	27	68	97	23	26	2	0	0	6	28	9	4	.268	.289
Felix Mantilla	SS19, 2B10, OF10, 3B6	R	26	45	93	13	20	3	0	1	5	10	16	1	.215	.280
Warren Spahn	P38	L	40	39	94	13	21	7	0	4	15	7	33	0	.223	.426
2 Gino Cimoli	OF31	R	31	37	117	12	23	5	0	3	4	11	15	1	.197	.316
2 Bob Boyd	1B3	L	34	36	41	3	10	0	0	0	3	1	7	0	.244	.244
John DeMerit	OF21	R	25	32	74	5	12	3	0	2	5	5	19	0	.162	.284
Mack Jones	OF26	L	22	28	104	13	24	3	2	0	12	12	28	4	.231	.298
1 Charlie Lau	C25	L	28	28	82	3	17	5	0	0	5	14	11	1	.207	.268
Sammy White	C20	R	32	21	63	1	14	1	0	1	5	2	9	0	.222	.206
Hawk Taylor	OF5, C1	R	22	20	26	1	5	0	0	1	1	3	11	0	.192	.308
1 Mel Roach	OF9, 1B2	R	28	13	36	3	6	0	0	1	6	2	4	0	.167	.250

1 Johnny Logan 34 R 2-19, Del Crandell 31 R (SA) 6-30, Neil Chrisley 29 L 2-9, 1Wes Covington 29 L 4-21, 1Billy Martin 33 R 0-6, Phil Roof 20 R 0-0

NAME	T	AGE	W	L	PCT	SV	G	GS	CG	IP	H	BB	SO	ShO	ERA
		29	83	71	.539	16	155	155	57	1391	1367	493	652	8	3.90
Warren Spahn	L	40	21	13	.618	0	38	34	21	263	236	64	115	4	3.01
Lew Burdette	R	34	18	11	.621	0	40	36	14	272	295	33	92	3	4.00
Bob Buhl	R	32	9	10	.474	0	32	28	9	188	180	98	77	1	4.12
Tony Cloninger	R	20	7	2	.778	0	19	10	3	84	84	33	51	0	5.25
Don McMahon	R	31	6	4	.600	8	53	0	0	92	84	51	55	0	2.84
Don Nottebart	R	25	6	7	.462	3	38	11	2	126	117	48	66	0	4.07
Carl Willey	R	30	6	12	.333	0	35	22	4	160	147	65	91	0	3.83
Bob Hendley	L	22	5	7	.417	0	19	13	3	97	96	39	44	0	3.90
Ron Piche	R	26	2	2	.500	1	12	1	1	23	20	16	16	0	3.52
Claude Raymond	R	24	1	0	1.000	2	13	0	0	20	22	9	13	0	4.05
Seth Morehead	L	26	1	0	1.000	0	12	0	0	15	16	7	13	0	6.60
2 Johnny Antonelli	L	31	1	0	1.000	0	9	0	0	11	16	3	8	0	7.36
Ken MacKenzie	L	27	0	1	.000	0	5	0	0	7	8	2	5	0	5.14
Moe Drabowsky	R	25	0	2	.000	2	16	0	0	25	26	18	5	0	4.68
George Brunet (IL)	L	26	0	0	.000	0	5	0	0	5	7	2	0	0	5.40
Chi Chi Olivo	R	23	0	0	.000	0	3	0	0	2	3	5	1	0	18.00

ST. LOUIS 5th 80-74 .519 13 — **SOLLY HEMUS 33-41 .446 JOHNNY KEANE 47-33 .588**

NAME	G by POS	B	AGE	G	AB	R	H	2B	3B	HR	RBI	BB	SO	SB	BA	SA
TOTALS			29	155	5307	703	1436	236	51	103	657	494	745	46	.271	.393
Bill White	1B151	L	27	153	591	89	169	28	11	20	90	64	84	8	.286	.472
Julian Javier (LJ)	2B113	R	24	113	445	58	124	14	3	2	41	30	51	11	.279	.337
Alex Grammas	SS65, 2B18, 3B3	R	34	89	170	23	36	10	1	0	21	19	21	0	.212	.282
Ken Boyer	3B153	R	30	153	589	109	194	26	11	24	95	68	91	6	.329	.533
Charlie James	OF90	R	23	108	349	43	89	19	2	4	44	15	59	2	.255	.355
Curt Flood	OF119	R	23	132	335	53	108	15	5	2	21	35	33	6	.322	.415
Stan Musial	OF103	L	40	123	372	46	107	22	4	15	70	52	35	0	.288	.489
Jimmie Schaffer	C68	R	25	68	153	15	39	7	0	1	16	9	29	0	.255	.320
Joe Cunningham	OF86, 1B10	L	29	113	322	60	92	11	2	7	40	53	32	1	.286	.398
Don Taussig	OF87	R	29	98	188	27	54	14	5	2	25	16	34	2	.287	.447
2 Bob Lillis	SS56, 2B24	R	31	86	230	24	50	4	0	0	21	7	13	3	.217	.235
Carl Sawatski	C60, OF1	L	33	86	174	23	52	8	0	10	33	25	17	0	.299	.517
Red Schoendienst	2B32	B	38	72	120	9	36	9	0	1	12	12	6	1	.300	.400
2 Carl Warwick	OF48	R	24	55	152	27	38	6	2	4	16	18	33	3	.250	.395
Hal Smith (IL)	C45	R	30	45	125	6	31	4	1	0	10	11	12	0	.248	.296
1 Daryl Spencer	SS37	R	31	37	130	19	33	4	0	4	21	23	17	1	.254	.377
Curt Simmons	P30	L	32	32	66	9	20	3	0	0	6	8	22	0	.303	.348
Jerry Buchek	SS31	R	19	31	90	6	12	2	0	0	9	0	28	0	.133	.156
Don Landrum	OF25, 2B1	L	25	28	66	5	11	2	0	1	3	5	14	1	.167	.242
Gene Oliver	C15, OF1	R	25	22	52	8	14	2	0	4	9	6	10	0	.269	.538
Tim McCarver	C20	L	19	22	67	5	16	2	1	1	6	0	5	0	.239	.343
1 Walt Moryn	OF7	L	35	17	32	0	4	2	0	0	2	1	5	0	.125	.188
Julio Gotay	SS10	R	22	10	45	5	11	4	0	0	5	3	5	0	.244	.333

Ed Olivares 22 R 5-30, George Crowe 38 L 1-7, Chris Cannizzaro 23 R 1-2, 1 Bob Nieman 34 R 8-17, Doug Clemens 22 L 2-12

NAME	T	AGE	W	L	PCT	SV	G	GS	CG	IP	H	BB	SO	ShO	ERA
		27	80	74	.519	24	155	155	49	1369	1334	570	823	10	3.74
Ray Sadecki	L	20	14	10	.583	0	31	31	13	223	196	102	114	0	3.71
Larry Jackson (BJ)	R	30	14	11	.560	0	33	28	12	211	203	56	113	3	3.75
Bob Gibson	R	25	13	12	.520	1	35	27	10	211	186	119	166	2	3.24
Lindy McDaniel	R	25	10	6	.625	9	55	0	0	94	117	31	65	0	4.88
Curt Simmons	L	32	9	10	.474	0	30	29	6	196	203	64	99	2	3.12
Ernie Broglio	R	25	9	12	.429	0	29	26	7	175	166	75	113	2	4.11
Craig Anderson	R	23	4	3	.571	1	25	0	0	39	38	12	21	0	3.23
Ed Bauta	R	26	2	0	1.000	5	13	0	0	19	12	5	12	0	1.42
Al Cicotte	R	31	2	6	.250	1	29	7	0	75	83	34	51	0	5.28
1 Mickey McDermott	L	32	1	0	1.000	4	19	0	0	27	29	15	15	0	3.67
Ray Washburn	R	23	1	1	.500	0	3	2	1	20	10	7	12	0	1.80
Bob Miller	R	22	1	3	.250	3	34	5	0	74	82	46	39	0	4.26
Bobby Tiefenauer	R	31	0	0	.000	0	3	0	0	4	9	4	3	0	6.75

PITTSBURGH 6th 75-79 .487 18 — DANNY MURTAUGH

NAME	G by POS	B	AGE	G	AB	R	H	2B	3B	HR	RBI	BB	SO	SB	BA	SA
TOTALS			29	154	5311	694	**1448**	232	**57**	128	646	428	721	26	**.273**	.410
Dick Stuart	1B132, OF1	R	28	138	532	83	160	28	8	35	117	34	**121**	0	.301	.581
Bill Mazeroski	2B152	R	24	152	558	71	148	21	2	13	59	26	55	2	.265	.380
Dick Groat	SS144, 3B1	R	30	148	596	71	164	25	6	6	55	40	44	0	.275	.367
Don Hoak	3B143	R	33	145	503	72	150	27	7	12	61	73	53	4	.298	.451
Roberto Clemente	OF144	R	26	146	572	100	201	30	10	23	89	35	59	4	**.351**	.559
Bill Virdon	OF145	L	30	146	599	81	156	22	8	9	58	49	45	5	.260	.369
Bob Skinner	OF97	L	29	119	381	61	102	20	3	3	42	51	49	3	.268	.360
Smoky Burgess	C92	L	34	100	323	37	98	17	3	12	52	30	16	1	.303	.486
Joe Christopher	OF55	R	25	76	186	25	49	7	3	0	14	18	24	6	.263	.333
Rocky Nelson	1B35	L	36	75	127	15	25	5	1	5	13	17	11	0	.197	.370
Hal Smith	C65	R	30	67	193	12	43	10	0	3	26	11	38	0	.223	.321
Dick Schofield	3B11, SS9, 2B5, OF3	B	26	60	78	16	15	2	1	0	2	10	19	0	.192	.244
2 Walt Moryn	OF11	L	35	40	65	6	13	1	0	3	9	2	10	0	.200	.354
2 Johnny Logan	3B7, SS6	R	34	27	52	5	12	4	0	0	5	4	8	0	.231	.308
Don Leppert	C21	L	29	22	60	6	16	2	1	3	5	1	11	0	.267	.483
1 Gino Cimoli	OF19	R	31	21	67	4	20	3	1	0	6	2	13	0	.299	.373

Donn Clendenon 25 R 11-35, Gene Baker 36 R 1-10, Bob Oldis 33 R 0-5, Roman Mejias 30 R 0-1

NAME	T	AGE	W	L	PCT	SV	G	GS	CG	IP	H	BB	SO	ShO	ERA
		30	75	79	.487	29	154	154	34	1362	1442	400	759	9	3.92
Bob Friend	R	30	14	**19**	.424	1	41	35	10	236	271	45	108	1	3.85
Joe Gibbon	L	26	13	10	.565	0	30	29	7	195	185	57	145	3	3.32
Harvey Haddix	L	35	10	6	.625	0	29	22	5	156	159	41	99	2	4.10
Vinegar Bend Mizell	L	30	7	10	.412	0	25	17	2	100	120	31	37	1	5.04
Bobby Shantz	L	35	6	3	.667	2	43	6	2	89	91	26	61	1	3.34
Roy Face	R	33	6	12	.333	**17**	62	0	0	92	94	10	55	0	3.82
2 Tom Sturdivant	R	31	5	2	.714	1	13	11	6	86	81	17	45	1	2.83
Clem Labine	R	34	4	1	.800	8	56	1	0	93	102	31	49	0	3.68
Al McBean	R	23	3	2	.600	0	27	2	0	74	72	42	49	0	3.77
Vern Law (SA)	R	31	3	4	.429	0	11	10	1	59	72	18	20	0	4.73
Earl Francis	R	24	2	8	.200	0	23	15	0	103	110	47	53	0	4.19
Al Jackson	L	25	1	0	1.000	0	3	2	1	24	20	4	15	0	3.38
Larry Foss	R	25	1	1	.500	0	3	3	0	15	15	11	9	0	6.00
George Witt (SA)	R	27	0	1	.000	0	9	1	0	16	17	5	9	0	6.19
Freddie Green	L	27	0	0	.000	0	13	0	0	21	27	9	4	0	4.71
1 Tom Cheney	R	26	0	0	.000	0	1	0	0	0	1	4	0	0	∞
Jim Umbricht	R	30	0	0	.000	0	1	0	0	3	5	2	1	0	3.00

CHICAGO 7th 64-90 .416 29 — VEDIE HIMSL 10-21 .323 HARRY CRAFT 7-9 .438 EL TAPPE 42-53 .442 LOU KLEIN 5-7 .417

NAME	G by POS	B	AGE	G	AB	R	H	2B	3B	HR	RBI	BB	SO	SB	BA	SA
TOTALS			28	156	**5344**	689	1364	238	51	176	650	539	**1027**	35	.255	.418
Ed Bouchee	1B107	L	28	112	319	49	79	12	3	12	38	58	77	1	.248	.417
Don Zimmer	2B116, 3B5, OF1	R	30	128	477	57	120	25	4	13	40	25	70	5	.252	.403
Ernie Banks	SS104, OF23, 1B7	R	30	138	511	75	142	22	4	29	80	54	75	1	.278	.507
Ron Santo	3B153	R	21	154	578	84	164	32	6	23	83	73	77	2	.284	.479
George Altman	OF130, 1B3	L	28	138	518	77	157	28	**12**	27	96	40	92	6	.303	.560
Al Heist	OF99	R	33	109	321	48	82	14	3	7	37	33	51	0	.255	.383
Billy Willians	OF135	L	23	146	529	75	147	20	7	25	86	45	70	6	.278	.484
Dick Bertell	C90	R	25	92	267	20	73	7	1	2	33	15	33	0	.273	.330
Richie Ashburn	OF76	L	34	109	307	49	79	7	4	0	19	55	27	7	.257	.306
Jerry Kindall	2B50, SS47	R	26	96	310	37	75	22	3	9	44	18	89	2	.242	.419
Sammy Taylor	C75	L	28	89	235	26	56	8	2	8	23	23	39	0	.238	.391
Bob Will	OF30, 1B1	L	29	86	113	9	29	9	0	0	8	15	19	0	.257	.336
Andre Rodgers	1B42, SS24, OF2, 2B1	R	26	73	214	27	57	17	0	6	23	25	54	1	.266	.430
Moe Thacker	C25	R	27	25	35	3	6	0	0	0	2	11	11	0	.171	.171
2 Mel Roach	1B7, 2B7	R	28	23	39	1	5	2	0	0	1	3	9	1	.128	.179
1 Frank Thomas	OF10, 1B6	R	32	15	50	7	13	2	0	2	6	2	8	0	.260	.420
Jim McAnany	OF1	R	24	11	10	1	3	1	0	0	0	1	3	0	.300	.400
Cuno Barragan (BN)	C10	R	29	10	28	3	6	0	0	1	2	2	7	0	.214	.321
Ken Hubbs	2B8	R	19	10	28	4	5	1	1	1	2	0	8	0	.179	.393
Moe Morhardt	1B7	L	24	7	18	3	5	0	0	0	1	3	5	0	.278	.278

Sammy Drake 26 B 0-5, George Freese 34 R 2-7, Danny Murphy 18 L 5-13, Lou Brock 22 L 1-11, Nelson Mathews 19 R 1-9

NAME	T	AGE	W	L	PCT	SV	G	GS	CG	IP	H	BB	SO	ShO	ERA
		26	64	90	.416	25	156	156	34	1385	**1492**	465	755	6	4.48
Don Cardwell	R	25	15	14	.517	0	39	38	13	259	243	88	156	3	3.82
Dick Ellsworth	L	21	10	11	.476	0	37	31	7	187	213	48	91	1	3.85
Jack Curtis	L	24	10	13	.435	0	31	27	6	180	220	51	57	0	4.90
Barney Schultz	R	34	7	6	.538	7	41	0	0	67	57	25	59	0	2.69
Bob Anderson	R	25	7	10	.412	8	57	12	1	152	162	56	96	0	4.26
Glen Hobbie	R	25	7	13	.350	2	36	29	7	199	207	54	103	2	4.25
Don Elston	R	32	6	7	.462	8	58	0	0	93	108	45	59	0	5.61
Dick Drott	R	25	1	4	.200	0	35	8	0	98	75	51	48	0	4.22
Jim Brewer	L	23	1	7	.125	0	36	11	0	87	116	21	57	0	5.79
Mel Wright	R	33	0	1	.000	0	11	0	0	21	42	4	6	0	10.71
1 Joe Schaffernoth	R	23	0	4	.000	0	21	0	0	38	43	18	23	0	6.39
Dick Burwell (MS)	R	21	0	0	.000	0	2	0	0	4	6	4	0	0	9.00

PHILADELPHIA 8th 47-107 .305 46 — GENE MAUCH

NAME	G by POS	B	AGE	G	AB	R	H	2B	3B	HR	RBI	BB	SO	SB	BA	SA
TOTALS			26	155	5213	584	1265	185	50	103	549	475	928	56	.243	.357
Pancho Herrera	1B115	R	27	126	400	56	103	17	2	13	51	55	120	5	.258	.408
Tony Taylor (RJ)	2B91, 3B3	R	25	106	400	47	100	17	3	2	26	29	59	11	.250	.323
Ruben Amaro	SS132, 1B3, 2B1	R	25	135	381	34	98	14	9	1	32	53	59	1	.257	.349
2 Charley Smith	3B94, SS14	R	23	112	411	43	102	13	4	9	47	23	76	3	.248	.365
2 Don Demeter	OF79, 1B22	R	26	106	382	54	98	18	4	20	68	19	74	2	.257	.482
Tony Gonzalez	OF118	L	24	126	426	58	118	16	8	12	58	49	66	15	.277	.437
Johnny Callison	OF124	L	22	138	455	74	121	20	11	9	47	69	76	10	.266	.418
Clay Dalrymple	C122	L	24	129	378	23	83	11	1	5	42	30	30	0	.220	.294
Bobby Malkmus	2B58, SS34, 3B25	R	29	121	342	39	79	8	2	7	31	20	43	1	.231	.327
Lee Walls	1B28, 3B26, OF18	R	28	91	261	32	73	6	4	8	30	19	48	2	.280	.425
Ken Walters	OF56, 1B5, 3B1	R	27	86	180	23	41	8	2	2	14	5	25	2	.228	.328
Bobby Gene Smith	OF47	R	27	79	174	16	44	7	0	2	18	15	32	0	.253	.328
4 Wes Covington	OF45	L	29	57	165	23	50	9	0	7	26	15	17	0	.303	.485
2 Elmer Valo	OF1	L	40	50	43	4	8	2	0	1	8	8	6	0	.186	.302
1 Bobby Del Greco	OF32, 2B1, 3B1	R	28	41	112	14	29	5	0	2	11	12	17	0	.259	.357
Choo Choo Coleman	C14	L	23	34	47	3	6	1	0	0	4	2	8	0	.128	.149
Jim Woods	3B15	R	21	23	48	6	11	3	0	2	9	4	15	0	.229	.417
1 Darrell Johnson	C21	R	32	21	61	4	14	1	0	0	3	3	8	0	.230	.246
George Williams	2B15	R	21	17	36	4	9	0	0	0	1	4	4	0	.250	.250
Bob Sadowski	3B14	L	24	16	54	4	7	0	0	0	0	4	7	1	.130	.130
Jimmie Coker	C11	R	25	11	25	3	10	1	0	1	4	7	4	1	.400	.560

Cal Neeman 32 R 7-31, Tony Curry 22 L 7-36, Al Kenders 24 R 4-23, 1 Joe Koppe 30 R 0-3

NAME	T	AGE	W	L	PCT	SV	G	GS	CG	IP	H	BB	SO	ShO	ERA
		28	47	**107**	.305	13	155	155	29	1383	1452	521	775	9	4.61
Art Mahaffey	R	23	11	**19**	.367	0	36	32	12	219	205	70	158	3	4.11
Chris Short	L	23	6	12	.333	1	39	16	1	127	157	71	80	0	5.95
John Buzhardt	R	24	6	18	.250	0	41	27	6	202	200	65	92	1	4.50
Jack Baldschun	R	24	5	3	.625	3	**65**	0	0	100	90	49	59	0	3.87
Jim Owens	R	27	5	10	.333	0	20	17	3	107	119	32	38	0	4.46
Don Ferrarese	L	32	5	12	.294	1	42	14	3	139	120	68	89	1	3.76
Frank Sullivan	R	31	3	16	.158	6	49	18	1	159	161	55	114	1	4.30
1 Dick Farrell	R	27	2	1	.667	0	5	0	0	10	10	6	10	0	6.30
Dallas Green	R	26	2	4	.333	1	42	10	1	128	160	47	51	1	4.85
Ken Lehman	L	33	1	1	.500	1	41	2	0	63	61	25	27	0	4.29
Robin Roberts (KJ)	R	34	1	10	.091	0	26	18	2	117	154	23	54	0	5.85
Paul Brown	R	20	0	1	.000	0	5	1	0	10	13	8	1	0	8.10
Jack Meyer	R	29	0	0	.000	0	1	0	0	2	2	2	2	0	9.00

WORLD SERIES – NEW YORK (AL) 4 CINCINNATI (NL) 1

LINE SCORES

TEAM	1	2	3	4	5	6	7	8	9	10	11	12	R	H	E
Game 1 October 4 at New York															
CIN (NL)	0	0	0	0	0	0	0	0	0				0	2	0
NY (AL)	0	0	0	1	0	1	0	0	X				2	6	0
O'Toole, Brosnan (8) — **Ford**															
Game 2 October 5 at New York															
CIN	0	0	0	2	1	1	0	2	0				6	9	0
NY	0	0	0	2	0	0	0	0	0				2	4	3
Jay — **Terry**, Arroyo (8)															
Game 3 October 7 at Cincinnati															
NY	0	0	0	0	0	0	1	1	1				3	6	1
CIN	0	0	1	0	0	0	1	0	0				2	8	0
Stafford, Daley (7), **Arroyo** (8) — **Purkey**															
Game 4 October 8 at Cincinnati															
NY	0	0	0	1	1	2	3	0	0				7	11	0
CIN	0	0	0	0	0	0	0	0	0				0	5	1
Ford, Coates (6) — **O'Toole**, Brosnan (6), Henry (9)															
Game 5 October 9 at Cincinnati															
NY	5	1	0	5	0	2	0	0	0				13	15	1
CIN	0	0	3	0	2	0	0	0	0				5	11	3
Terry, **Daley** (3) — **Jay**, Maloney (1), K. Johnson (2), Henry (3), Jones (4), Purkey (5), Brosnan (7), Hunt (9)															

COMPOSITE BATTING

NAME	POS	G	AB	R	H	2B	3B	HR	RBI	BA
New York (AL)										
Totals		5	165	27	42	8	1	7	26	.255
Richardson	2B	5	**23**	2	**9**	1	0	0	0	.391
Kubek	SS	5	22	3	5	0	0	0	1	.227
Howard	C	5	20	**5**	5	**3**	0	1	1	.250
Maris	OF	5	19	4	2	1	0	1	2	.105
Skowron	1B	5	17	3	6	0	0	1	5	.353
Boyer	3B	5	15	0	4	2	0	0	3	.267
Berra	OF	4	11	2	3	0	0	1	3	.273
Blanchard	OF	4	10	4	4	1	0	**2**	3	**.400**
Lopez	OF	3	9	3	3	0	1	1	**7**	.333
Mantle	OF	2	6	0	1	0	0	0	0	.167
Ford	P	2	5	1	0	0	0	0	0	.000
Terry	P	2	3	0	0	0	0	0	0	.000
Stafford	P	1	2	0	0	0	0	0	0	.000
Daley	P	2	1	0	0	0	0	0	1	.000
Gardner	PH	1	1	0	0	0	0	0	0	.000
Coates	P	1	1	0	0	0	0	0	0	.000
Reed	OF	3	0	0	0	0	0	0	0	.000
Arroyo	P	2	0	0	0	0	0	0	0	.000
Cincinnati (NL)										
Totals		5	170	13	35	8	0	3	11	.206
Kasko	SS	5	22	1	7	0	0	0	1	.318
Pinson	OF	5	22	0	2	1	0	0	0	.091
Coleman	1B	5	20	2	5	0	0	1	2	.250
Post	OF	5	18	3	6	1	0	1	2	.333
Freese	3B	5	16	0	1	1	0	0	0	.063
Robinson	OF	5	15	3	3	2	0	1	4	.200
Chacon	2B	4	12	2	3	0	0	0	0	.250
Edwards	C	3	11	1	4	2	0	0	2	.364
Blasingame	2B	3	7	1	1	0	0	0	0	.143
D. Johnson	C	2	4	0	2	0	0	0	0	.500
Gernert	PH	4	4	0	0	0	0	0	0	.000
Jay	P	2	4	0	0	0	0	0	0	.000
Cardenas	PH	3	3	0	1	1	0	0	0	.333
Lynch	PH	4	3	0	0	0	0	0	0	.000
O'Toole	P	2	3	0	0	0	0	0	0	.000
Purkey	P	2	3	0	0	0	0	0	0	.000
Bell	PH	3	3	0	0	0	0	0	0	.000
Zimmerman	PH	2	0	0	0	0	0	0	0	.000
Brosnan	P	3	0	0	0	0	0	0	0	.000
Henry	P	2	0	0	0	0	0	0	0	.000
K. Johnson	P	1	0	0	0	0	0	0	0	.000

Hunt P 0-0, Jones P 0-0, Maloney P 0-0

COMPOSITE PITCHING

NAME	G	IP	H	BB	SO	W	L	SV	ERA
New York (AL)									
Totals	5	45	35	8	27	4	1	1	1.60
Ford	2	**14**	6	1	7	**2**	0	0	**0.00**
Terry	2	9.1	**12**	2	7	0	1	0	4.82
Daley	2	7	5	0	2	1	0	0	0.00
Stafford	1	6.2	7	2	5	0	0	0	2.70
Arroyo	2	4	4	2	3	1	0	0	2.25
Coates	1	4	1	1	2	0	0	1	0.00
Cincinnati (NL)									
Totals	5	44	42	24	25	1	4	0	4.91
O'Toole	2	12	11	7	4	0	2	0	3.00
Purkey	2	11	6	3	5	0	1	0	1.64
Jay	2	9.2	8	6	6	1	1	0	5.59
Brosnan	3	6	9	4	5	0	0	0	7.50
Henry	2	2.1	4	2	3	0	0	0	19.29
Hunt	1	2	0	1	1	0	0	0	0.00
K. Johnson	1	-.2	0	0	0	0	0	0	0.00
Jones	1	.2	0	0	0	0	0	0	0.00
Maloney	1	.2	4	1	1	0	0	0	27.00

1962 Circulating into Second Place

After much struggle with the city fathers of Los Angeles, Walter O'Malley finally opened his baseball emporium, Dodger Stadium, for the start of the 1962 season. O'Malley's highly regarded team drew a record 2,755,184 fans into the park, while pacing the National League all summer behind the star performances of Maury Wills, Tommy Davis, and Don Drysdale. Of the trio, Wills proved the most exciting while en route to the league's MVP Award by committing the grandest theft act ever witnessed on major league turf—104 steals to break the 1915 mark of the legendary Ty Cobb. Davis, by hitting .346 and knocking in 153 runs, captured two of the major batting categories while Drysdale won the coveted Cy Young Award on the strength of his 25 victories.

But all the individual glory could not make up for an unfortunate incident which took place on July 17, when ace southpaw Sandy Koufax was lost for the season with a circulatory ailment in his fingers. In the final 13 contests, the Dodgers could only win three, while the rival San Francisco Giants won seven to tie Los Angeles on the final day of the season.

In the first game of the play-offs, the Giants won easily behind Billy Pierce's 3-hit, 8-0 performance. The Dodgers came from behind to take the second game, 8-7, thus setting the stage for the showdown and evoking the memories of the 1951 play-offs. After eight innings, the Dodgers led 4-2. But the Giants crossed the plate four times in the ninth, with the winning run being walked across by Stan Williams.

The Giants stayed in contention all year with an attack centered on home run leader Willie Mays, and the slugging of Orlando Cepeda and Felipe Alou. Jack Sanford, by winning 16 games in a row and winding up with 24, led all the hurlers, which included Billy O'Dell's 19, Juan Marichal's 18, and 16 from the arm of the 35-year-old Pierce.

The Giant-Dodger pennant struggle partly overshadowed the league's expansion to ten teams, which brought Houston into the fold for the first time and a return of a National League team to New York in the unlikely name of the Mets. Led by Casey Stengel, also returning after his ouster by the Yankees, the Mets lost 120 games to set a modern record for futility.

In the American League, the fanfare took place before the final curtain. Cleveland, leading until the All-Star break, lost 19 of their next 24 games to drop into second division. While the Indians were faltering, the Los Angeles Angels and Minnesota Twins, the league's newest entries, were charging into contention. Although the joint efforts were commendable, both fell short. The Twins finished second on the strength of a strong batting attack, and the Angels third on the arms of their two colorful rookies, Dean Chance and Bo Belinsky.

As usual, the Yankees were on top when the season closed. Even in an off-year, New York mustered enough offense to win the pennant by five games. Mickey Mantle, although missing 39 games with injuries, also mustered enough of an attack, with his .321 batting and 30 home runs to win the league's MVP Award. Roger Maris cooled off greatly from his record 1961 cloudburst and polled 33 homers, while Bobby Richardson turned in his best year with a .302 average. Rookie Tom Tresh filled in admirably at shortstop until Tony Kubek returned from the army in August, and Ralph Terry led all the Yankees and the league with his 23 victories.

On October 4, when the World Series got underway at Candlestick Park in San Francisco, the Giants and Yankees were meeting in the fall classic for the seventh time. The rivalry, which first began in 1921, saw the Giants take a commanding 2-0 lead before the Yankees came back to take the next four Series. Both clubs had not met since the Giants' memorable year of 1951, and events had changed sufficiently enough so that the once-prized championship, as well as the love of New York City itself, was no longer up for grabs.

In the opener, Whitey Ford faced Billy O'Dell, and a homer by Clete Boyer in the seventh broke a 2-2 tie to give New York a final 6-2 victory and Ford his tenth win in Series play. Jack Sanford and Ralph Terry matched up the next day and the Giants, behind Chuck Hiller's double and Willie McCovey's home run, evened matters, 2-0, as Sanford held the Yankees to three hits. Both clubs travelled to New York for the third game which featured Billy Pierce and Bill Stafford. Much like the opener, the game remained tied until the seventh. This time for New York, Roger Maris came to the rescue with a single which scored two of the three runs collected in the inning in what turned out to be a 3-2 affair. Game four once again saw both clubs entering the seventh with identical scores, but the day belonged to the Giants in this go-around, or to be more precise, it was the possession of Chuck Hiller, who hit the first National League grand slam in Series play to once again even the contest.

Terry, who lost the second game to Sanford, returned to outpitch the Giants' ace right-hander, 5-3, behind a three-run homer by Tommy Tresh. With the Yankees up, 3-2, both clubs returned West, however, a rain delay of three days made the final result nearly anticlimactic. When play resumed on October 15,—five days since the last game—Pierce limited the Yankees to three hits in prolonging the seesaw battle another day. Finally, with Terry and Sanford hooking up for the third time, the Yankees won, 1-0, on a catch by Bobby Richardson of McCovey's line drive with two outs and two on in the ninth which gave a fitting end to a Series which did not seem to have an end.

WORLD SERIES – NEW YORK (AL) 4 SAN FRANCISCO (NL) 3

LINE SCORES

TEAM	1	2	3	4	5	6	7	8	9	10	11	12	R	H	E
Game 1 October 4 at San Francisco															
NY (AL)	2	0	0	0	0	0	1	2	1				6	11	0
SF (NL)	0	1	1	0	0	0	0	0	0				2	10	0
Ford	**O'Dell**, Larsen (8), Miller (9)														
Game 2 October 5 at San Francisco															
NY	0	0	0	0	0	0	0	0	0				0	3	1
SF	1	0	0	0	0	0	1	0	X				2	6	0
Terry, Daley (8)	**Sanford**														
Game 3 October 7 at New York															
SF	0	0	0	0	0	0	0	0	2				2	4	3
NY	0	0	0	0	0	0	3	0	X				3	5	1
Pierce, Larsen (7), Bolin (8)	**Stafford**														
Game 4 October 8 at New York															
SF	0	2	0	0	0	0	4	0	1				7	9	1
NY	0	0	0	0	0	2	0	0	1				3	9	1
Marichal, Bolin (5), **Larsen** (6), O'Dell (7)	Ford, **Coates** (7), Bridges (7)														
Game 5 October 10 at New York															
SF	0	0	1	0	1	0	0	0	1				3	8	2
NY	0	0	0	1	0	1	0	3	X				5	6	0
Sanford, Miller (8)	**Terry**														
Game 6 October 15 at San Francisco															
NY	0	0	0	0	1	0	0	1	0				2	3	2
SF	0	0	0	3	2	0	0	0	X				5	10	1
Ford, Coates (5), Bridges (8)	**Pierce**														
Game 7 October 16 at San Francisco															
NY	0	0	0	0	1	0	0	0	0				1	7	0
SF	0	0	0	0	0	0	0	0	0				0	4	1
Terry	**Sanford**, O'Dell (8)														

COMPOSITE BATTING

NAME	POS	G	AB	R	H	2B	3B	HR	RBI	BA
New York (AL)										
Totals		7	221	20	44	6	1	3	17	.199
Kubek	SS	7	**29**	2	8	1	0	0	1	.276
Tresh	OF	7	28	**5**	**9**	1	0	1	4	.321
Richardson	2B	7	27	3	4	0	0	0	0	.148
Mantle	OF	7	25	2	3	1	0	0	0	.120
Maris	OF	7	23	4	4	1	0	1	**5**	.174
Boyer	3B	7	22	2	7	1	0	1	4	.318
Howard	C	6	21	1	3	1	0	0	1	.143
Skowron	1B	6	18	1	4	0	1	0	1	.222
Terry	P	3	8	0	1	0	0	0	0	.125
Ford	P	3	7	0	0	0	0	0	0	.000
Long	1B	2	5	0	1	0	0	0	1	.200
Stafford	P	1	3	0	0	0	0	0	0	.000
Berra	C	2	2	0	0	0	0	0	0	.000
Lopez	PH	2	2	0	0	0	0	0	0	.000
Blanchard	PH	1	1	0	0	0	0	0	0	.000
Coates	P	2	0	0	0	0	0	0	0	.000
Bridges	P	2	0	0	0	0	0	0	0	.000
Daley	P	1	0	0	0	0	0	0	0	.000
San Francisco (NL)										
Totals		7	226	21	51	10	2	5	19	.226
Mays	OF	7	28	3	7	2	0	0	1	.250
Hiller	2B	7	26	4	7	**3**	0	1	**5**	.269
F. Alou	OF	7	26	2	7	1	1	0	1	.269
Davenport	3B	7	22	1	3	1	0	0	1	.136
Pagan	SS	7	19	2	7	0	0	1	2	**.368**
Cepeda	1B	5	19	1	3	1	0	0	2	.158
McCovey	1B-OF	4	15	2	3	0	1	1	1	.200
Haller	C	4	14	1	4	1	0	1	3	.286
Bailey	C	6	14	1	1	0	0	1	2	.071
M. Alou	OF	6	12	2	4	1	0	0	1	.333
Kuenn	OF	3	12	1	1	0	0	0	0	.083
Sanford	P	3	7	0	3	0	0	0	0	.429
Pierce	P	2	5	0	0	0	0	0	0	.000
O'Dell	P	3	3	0	1	0	0	0	0	.333
Marichal	P	1	2	0	0	0	0	0	0	.000
Bowman	SS	2	1	1	0	0	0	0	0	.000
Orsino	C	1	1	0	0	0	0	0	0	.000
Larsen	P	3	0	0	0	0	0	0	0	.000
Miller	P	2	0	0	0	0	0	0	0	.000
Bolin	P	2	0	0	0	0	0	0	0	.000
Nieman	PH	1	0	0	0	0	0	0	0	.000

COMPOSITE PITCHING

NAME	G	IP	H	BB	SO	W	L	SV	ERA
New York (AL)									
Totals	7	61	51	12	39	4	3	0	2.95
Terry	3	**25**	17	2	16	**2**	1	0	**1.80**
Ford	3	19.2	**24**	4	12	1	1	0	4.12
Stafford	1	9	4	2	5	1	0	0	2.00
Bridges	2	3.2	4	2	3	0	0	0	4.91
Coates	2	2.2	1	1	3	0	1	0	6.75
Daley	1	1	1	1	0	0	0	0	0.00
San Francisco (NL)									
Totals	7	61	44	21	39	3	4	1	2.66
Sanford	3	23.1	16	**8**	**19**	1	**2**	0	1.93
Pierce	2	15	8	2	5	1	1	0	2.40
O'Dell	2	12.1	12	3	9	0	1	1	4.38
Marichal	1	4	2	2	4	0	0	0	0.00
Bolin	2	2.2	4	2	2	0	0	0	6.75
Larsen	3	2.1	1	2	0	1	0	0	3.86
Miller	2	1.1	1	2	0	0	0	0	0.00

NEW YORK 1st 96-66 .593 — RALPH HOUK

NAME	G by POS	B	AGE	G	AB	R	H	2B	3B	HR	RBI	BB	SO	SB	BA	SA
TOTALS			29	162	**5644**	**817**	**1509**	240	29	199	**791**	584	842	42	**.267**	**.426**
Bill Skowron	1B135	R	31	140	478	63	129	16	6	23	80	36	99	0	.270	.473
Bobby Richardson	2B161	R	26	161	**692**	99	**209**	38	5	8	59	37	24	11	.302	.406
Tom Tresh	SS111, OF43	B	24	157	622	94	178	26	5	20	93	67	74	4	.286	.441
Clete Boyer	3B157	R	25	158	566	85	154	24	1	18	68	51	106	3	.272	.413
Roger Maris	OF154	L	27	157	590	92	151	34	1	33	100	87	78	1	.256	.485
Mickey Mantle (KJ)	OF117	B	30	123	377	96	121	15	1	30	89	**122**	78	9	.321	**.605**
Hector Lopez	OF84, 2B1, 3B1	R	29	106	335	45	92	19	1	6	48	33	53	0	.275	.391
Elston Howard	C129	R	33	136	494	63	138	23	5	21	91	31	76	1	.279	.474
Johnny Blanchard	OF47, C15, 1B2	L	29	93	246	33	57	7	0	13	39	28	32	0	.232	.419
Jack Reed	OF75	R	29	88	43	17	13	2	1	1	4	4	7	2	.302	.465
Yogi Berra	C31, OF28	L	37	86	232	25	52	8	0	10	35	24	18	0	.224	.388
Phil Linz	SS21, 3B8, 2B5, OF2	R	23	71	129	28	37	8	0	1	14	6	17	6	.287	.372
Joe Pepitone	OF32, 1B16	L	21	63	138	14	33	3	2	7	17	3	21	1	.239	.442
Tony Kubek (MS)	SS35, OF6	L	25	45	169	28	53	6	1	4	17	12	17	2	.314	.432
2 Dale Long	1B31	L	36	41	94	12	28	4	0	4	17	18	9	1	.298	.468
1 Bob Cerv	OF3	R	36	14	17	1	2	1	0	0	0	2	1	0	.118	.176

1 Billy Gardner 34 R 0-1, Jake Gibbs 23 L 0-0

NAME	T	AGE	W	L	PCT	SV	G	GS	CG	IP	H	BB	SO	ShO	ERA
TOTALS		28	**96**	66	**.593**	42	162	162	33	**1470**	1375	499	838	10	3.70
Ralph Terry	R	26	**23**	12	.657	2	43	**39**	14	**299**	257	57	176	3	3.19
Whitey Ford	L	33	17	8	.680	0	38	37	7	258	243	69	160	0	2.90
Bill Stafford	R	22	14	9	.609	0	35	33	7	213	188	77	109	2	3.68
Marshall Bridges	L	31	8	4	.667	18	52	0	0	72	49	48	66	0	3.13
Bud Daley	L	29	7	5	.583	4	43	6	0	105	105	21	55	0	3.60
Jim Coates	R	29	7	6	.538	6	50	6	0	118	119	50	67	0	4.42
Jim Bouton	R	23	7	7	.500	2	36	16	3	163	124	59	71	1	3.99
Rollie Sheldon	R	25	7	8	.467	1	34	16	2	118	136	28	54	0	5.49
Bob Turley	R	31	3	3	.500	1	24	8	0	69	68	47	42	0	4.57
Tex Clevenger	R	29	2	0	1.000	0	21	0	0	38	36	17	11	0	2.84
Luis Arroyo (SA)	L	35	1	3	.250	7	27	0	0	34	33	17	21	0	4.76
2 Hal Brown	R	37	0	1	.000	0	2	1	0	7	9	2	2	0	6.43
Jack Cullen	R	22	0	0	.000	1	2	0	0	3	2	2	2	0	0.00
Hal Reniff	R	23	0	0	.000	0	2	0	0	4	6	5	1	0	6.75
Al Downing	L	21	0	0	.000	0	1	0	0	1	0	0	1	0	0.00

MINNESOTA 2nd 91-71 .562 5 — SAM MELE

NAME	G by POS	B	AGE	G	AB	R	H	2B	3B	HR	RBI	BB	SO	SB	BA	SA
TOTALS			26	163	5561	798	1445	215	39	185	758	649	823	33	.260	.412
Vic Power	1B142, 2B2	R	30	144	611	80	177	28	2	16	63	22	35	7	.290	.421
Bernie Allen	2B158	L	23	159	573	79	154	27	7	12	64	62	82	0	.269	.403
Zoilo Versalles	SS160	R	22	160	568	69	137	18	3	17	67	37	71	5	.241	.373
Rich Rollins	3B159, SS1	R	24	159	624	96	186	23	5	16	96	75	62	3	.298	.428
Bob Allison	OF147	R	27	149	519	102	138	24	8	29	102	84	115	8	.266	.511
Lenny Green	OF156	L	28	158	619	97	168	33	3	14	63	88	36	8	.271	.402
Harmon Killebrew	OF151, 1B4	R	26	155	552	85	134	21	1	**48**	**126**	106	**142**	1	.243	.545
Earl Battey	C147	R	27	148	522	58	146	20	3	11	57	57	48	0	.280	.393
Bill Tuttle	OF104	R	32	110	124	21	26	4	1	1	13	19	14	1	.210	.282
Don Mincher	1B25	L	24	86	121	20	29	1	1	9	29	34	24	0	.240	.488
George Banks	OF17, 3B6	R	23	63	103	22	26	0	2	4	15	21	27	0	.252	.408
Johnny Goryl	2B4, SS1	R	28	37	26	6	5	0	1	2	2	2	6	0	.192	.500
Marty Martinez	SS11, 3B1	R	20	37	18	13	3	0	1	0	3	3	4	0	.167	.278
Jerry Zimmerman	C34	R	27	34	62	8	17	4	0	0	7	3	5	0	.274	.339
Hal Naragon	C9	L	33	24	35	1	8	1	0	0	3	3	1	0	.229	.257
Jim Lemon (SJ)	OF3	R	34	12	17	1	3	0	0	1	5	3	4	0	.176	.353
Jim Snyder	2B5, 1B1	R	29	12	10	1	1	0	0	0	1	0	0	0	.100	.100
Tony Oliva	OF2	L	21	9	9	3	4	1	0	0	3	3	2	0	.444	.556

NAME	T	AGE	W	L	PCT	SV	G	GS	CG	IP	H	BB	SO	ShO	ERA
TOTALS		27	91	71	.562	27	163	163	**53**	1462	1400	493	**948**	11	3.90
Camilo Pascual	R	28	20	11	.645	0	34	33	**18**	258	236	59	**206**	**5**	3.31
Jim Kaat	L	23	18	14	.563	1	39	35	16	269	243	75	173	**5**	3.14
Dick Stigman	L	26	12	5	.706	3	40	15	6	143	122	64	116	0	3.65
Jack Kralick	L	27	12	11	.522	0	39	37	7	243	239	61	139	1	3.85
Ray Moore	R	36	8	3	.727	9	49	0	0	65	55	30	58	0	4.71
Joe Bonikowski	R	21	5	7	.417	2	30	13	3	100	95	38	45	0	3.87
2 Frank Sullivan	R	32	4	1	.800	5	21	0	0	33	33	13	10	0	3.27
Lee Stange	R	25	4	3	.571	3	44	6	1	95	98	39	70	0	4.45
1 Don Lee	R	28	3	3	.500	0	9	9	1	52	51	24	28	0	4.50
Bill Pleis	L	24	2	5	.286	3	21	4	0	45	46	14	31	0	4.40
Ted Sadowski	R	26	1	1	.500	0	19	0	0	34	37	11	15	0	5.03
2 Ruben Gomez	R	34	1	1	.500	0	6	2	1	19	17	11	8	0	4.74
Georges Maranda	R	30	1	3	.250	0	32	4	0	73	69	35	36	0	4.44
2 Jim Donohue	R	23	0	1	.000	1	6	1	0	10	12	6	3	0	7.20
1 Jackie Collum	L	35	0	2	.000	0	8	3	0	15	29	11	5	0	11.40
Jim Manning	R	18	0	0	.000	0	5	1	0	7	14	1	3	0	5.14
Jerry Arrigo	L	21	0	0	.000	0	1	0	0	1	3	1	1	0	18.00
Jim Roland	L	19	0	0	.000	0	1	0	0	2	1	0	1	0	0.00

LOS ANGELES 3rd 86-76 .531 10 — BILL RIGNEY

NAME	G by POS	B	AGE	G	AB	R	H	2B	3B	HR	RBI	BB	SO	SB	BA	SA
TOTALS			27	162	5499	718	1377	232	35	137	667	602	917	46	.250	.380
Lee Thomas	1B90, OF74	L	26	160	583	88	169	21	2	26	104	55	74	6	.290	.467
Billy Moran	2B160	R	28	160	659	90	186	25	3	17	74	39	80	5	.282	.407
Joe Koppe	SS118, 2B5, 3B4	R	31	128	375	47	85	16	0	4	40	73	84	2	.227	.301
Felix Torres	3B123	R	30	127	451	44	117	19	4	11	74	28	73	0	.259	.392
George Thomas (MS)	OF51	R	24	56	181	13	43	10	2	4	12	21	37	0	.238	.381
Albie Pearson	OF160	L	27	160	614	**115**	160	29	6	5	42	95	36	15	.261	.352
Leon Wagner	OF156	L	28	160	612	96	164	21	5	37	107	50	87	7	.268	.500
Bob Rodgers	C150	B	23	155	565	65	146	34	6	6	61	45	68	1	.258	.372
Earl Averill	OF49, C6	R	30	92	187	21	41	9	0	4	22	43	47	0	.219	.332
Tom Burgess	1B35, OF2	L	34	87	143	17	28	7	1	2	13	36	20	2	.196	.301
Steve Bilko (LJ)	1B50	R	33	64	164	26	47	9	1	8	38	25	35	1	.287	.500
Jim Fregosi	SS52	R	20	58	175	15	51	3	4	3	23	18	27	2	.291	.406
Eddie Yost	3B28, 1B7	R	35	52	104	22	25	9	1	0	10	30	21	0	.240	.346
2 Gordie Windhorn	OF34	R	29	40	45	9	8	6	0	0	1	7	10	1	.178	.311
2 Billy Consolo	3B20, SS4, 2B1	R	27	28	20	4	2	0	0	0	0	3	11	2	.100	.100
Eddie Sadowski	C18	R	30	27	55	4	11	4	0	1	3	2	14	1	.200	.327
Leo Burke	OF12, 3B4, SS1	R	28	19	64	8	17	1	0	4	14	5	11	0	.266	.469
Ken Hunt (AJ-MS)	1B3	R	27	13	11	4	2	0	0	1	1	1	5	1	.182	.455
1 Marlan Coughtry	3B4, 2B2	L	27	11	22	0	4	0	0	0	2	0	6	0	.182	.182
Tom Satriano	3B5	L	21	10	19	4	8	2	0	2	6	0	1	0	.421	.842
Gene Leek (MS)	3B4	R	25	7	14	0	2	0	0	0	0	0	6	0	.143	.143
Frank Leja	1B4	L	26	7	16	0	0	0	0	0	0	1	6	0	.000	.000
Chuck Tanner	OF2	L	32	7	8	0	1	0	0	0	0	0	0	0	.125	.125

Dick Simpson 18 R 2-8, Ed Kirkpatrick 17 L 0-6

NAME	T	AGE	W	L	PCT	SV	G	GS	CG	IP	H	BB	SO	ShO	ERA
TOTALS		28	86	76	.531	**47**	162	162	23	1466	1412	616	858	**15**	3.70
Dean Chance	R	21	14	10	.583	8	50	24	6	207	195	66	127	2	2.96
Ken McBride (XJ)	R	26	11	5	.688	0	24	23	6	149	136	70	83	4	3.50
Bo Belinsky	L	25	10	11	.476	1	33	31	5	187	149	**122**	145	3	3.56
Ted Bowsfield	L	26	9	8	.529	1	34	25	1	139	154	40	52	0	4.40
2 Don Lee	R	28	8	8	.500	2	27	22	4	153	153	39	74	2	3.12
Eli Grba	R	27	8	9	.471	1	40	29	1	176	185	75	90	0	4.55
2 Dan Osinski	R	28	6	4	.600	4	33	0	0	54	45	30	44	0	2.83
Tom Morgan	R	32	5	2	.714	9	48	0	0	59	53	19	29	0	2.90
Jack Spring	L	29	4	2	.667	6	57	0	0	65	66	30	31	0	4.02
Art Fowler	R	39	4	3	.571	5	48	0	0	77	67	25	38	0	2.81
Bob Botz	R	27	2	1	.667	2	35	0	0	63	71	11	24	0	3.43
Ryne Duren	R	33	2	9	.182	8	42	3	0	71	53	57	74	0	4.44
1 Jim Donohue	R	23	1	0	1.000	0	12	1	0	24	24	11	14	0	3.75
Julio Navarro	R	26	1	1	.500	0	9	0	0	15	20	4	11	0	4.80
1 George Witt	R	28	1	1	.500	0	5	2	0	10	15	5	10	0	8.10
Fred Newman	R	20	0	1	.000	0	4	1	0	6	11	3	4	0	10.50
Bobby Darwin	R	19	0	1	.000	0	1	1	0	3	8	4	6	0	12.00
1 Joe Nuxhall	L	33	0	0	.000	0	5	0	0	5	7	5	2	0	10.80

Ron Moeller (MS) 23

DETROIT 4th 85-76 .528 10.5 — BOB SCHEFFING

NAME	G by POS	B	AGE	G	AB	R	H	2B	3B	HR	RBI	BB	SO	SB	BA	SA
TOTALS			28	161	5456	758	1352	191	36	**209**	719	**651**	894	69	.248	.411
Norm Cash	1B146, OF3	L	27	148	507	94	123	16	2	39	89	104	82	6	.243	.513
Jake Wood	2B90	R	25	111	367	68	83	10	5	8	30	33	59	24	.226	.346
Chico Fernandez	SS138, 3B2, 1B1	R	30	141	503	64	125	17	2	20	59	42	69	10	.249	.410
Steve Boros	3B105, 2B6	R	25	116	356	46	81	14	1	16	47	53	62	3	.228	.407
Al Kaline (BC)	OF100	R	27	100	398	78	121	16	6	29	94	47	39	4	.304	.593
Bill Bruton	OF145	L	36	147	561	90	156	27	5	16	74	55	67	14	.278	.430
Rocky Colavito	OF161	R	28	161	601	90	164	30	2	37	112	96	68	2	.273	.514
Dick Brown	C132	R	27	134	431	40	104	12	0	12	40	21	66	0	.241	.353
Dick McAuliffe	2B70, 3B49, SS16	L	22	139	471	50	124	20	5	12	63	64	76	4	.263	.403
Bubba Morton	OF62, 1B3	R	30	90	195	30	51	6	3	4	17	32	32	1	.262	.385
Vic Wertz	1B16	L	37	74	105	7	34	2	0	5	18	5	13	0	.324	.486
Bobo Osborne	3B13, 1B7, C1	L	26	64	74	12	17	1	0	0	7	16	25	0	.230	.243
Mike Roarke	C53	R	31	56	136	11	29	4	1	4	14	13	17	0	.213	.346
2 Bob Farley	1B6, OF6	L	24	36	50	9	8	2	0	1	4	14	10	0	.160	.260
2 Don Buddin	SS19, 2B5, 3B2	R	28	31	83	14	19	3	0	0	4	20	16	1	.229	.265
1 Charlie Maxwell	OF15, 1B1	L	35	30	67	5	13	2	0	1	9	8	10	0	.194	.269
Purnal Goldy	OF15	R	20	20	70	8	16	1	1	3	12	0	12	0	.229	.400
Frank Kostro	3B11	R	24	16	41	5	11	3	0	0	3	1	6	0	.268	.341
Reno Bertoia	2B1, SS1, 3B1	R	27	5	0	3	0	0	0	0	0	0	0	0	.000	.000
1 George Alusik		R	27	2	2	0	0	0	0	0	0	0	0	0	.000	.000

NAME	T	AGE	W	L	PCT	SV	G	GS	CG	IP	H	BB	SO	ShO	ERA
TOTALS		30	85	76	.528	35	161	161	46	1444	**1452**	503	873	8	3.81
Jim Bunning	R	30	19	10	.655	6	41	35	12	258	**262**	74	184	2	3.59
Hank Aguirre	L	30	16	8	.667	3	42	22	11	216	162	65	156	2	**2.21**
Phil Regan	R	25	11	9	.550	0	35	23	6	171	169	64	87	0	4.05
Don Mossi	L	33	11	13	.458	1	35	27	8	180	195	36	121	1	4.20
Paul Foytack	R	31	10	7	.588	0	29	21	5	144	145	86	63	1	4.38
Ron Nischwitz	L	25	4	5	.444	4	48	0	0	65	73	26	28	0	3.88
Howie Koplitz	R	24	3	0	1.000	0	10	6	1	38	54	10	10	0	5.21
Terry Fox	R	26	3	1	.750	16	44	0	0	58	48	16	23	0	1.71
Ron Kline	R	30	3	6	.333	2	36	4	0	77	88	28	47	0	4.32
Sam Jones	R	36	2	4	.333	1	30	6	1	81	77	35	73	0	3.67
Frank Lary (SA)	R	32	2	6	.250	0	17	14	2	80	98	21	41	1	5.74
Jerry Casale	R	28	1	2	.333	0	18	1	0	37	33	18	16	0	4.62
Bob Humphreys	R	26	0	1	.000	1	4	0	0	5	8	2	3	0	7.20
Doug Gallagher	L	22	0	4	.000	1	9	2	0	25	31	15	14	0	4.68
Fred Gladding	R	26	0	0	.000	0	6	0	0	5	3	2	4	0	0.00
Bill Faul	R	22	0	0	.000	0	1	0	0	2	4	3	2	0	27.00
Tom Fletcher	L	20	0	0	.000	0	1	0	0	2	2	2	1	0	0.00

CHICAGO 5th 85-77 .525 11 — AL LOPEZ

NAME	G by POS	B	AGE	G	AB	R	H	2B	3B	HR	RBI	BB	SO	SB	BA	SA
TOTALS			30	162	5514	707	1415	250	56	92	662	620	674	76	.257	.372
Joe Cunningham	1B143, OF5	L	30	149	526	91	155	32	7	8	70	101	59	3	.295	.428
Nellie Fox	2B154	L	34	157	621	79	166	27	7	2	54	38	12	1	.267	.343
Luis Aparicio	SS152	R	28	153	581	72	140	23	5	7	40	32	36	**31**	.241	.334
Al Smith	3B105, OF39	R	34	142	511	62	149	23	8	16	82	57	60	3	.292	.462
Mike Hershberger	OF135	R	22	148	427	54	112	14	2	4	46	37	36	10	.262	.333
Jim Landis	OF144	R	28	149	534	82	122	21	6	15	61	80	105	19	.228	.375
Floyd Robinson	OF155	L	26	156	600	89	187	**45**	10	11	109	72	47	4	.312	.475
Cam Carreon	C93	R	24	106	313	31	80	19	1	4	37	33	37	1	.256	.361
Sherm Lollar (JJ)	C66	R	37	84	220	17	59	12	0	2	26	32	23	1	.268	.350
Bob Sadowski	3B16, 2B12	L	25	79	130	22	30	3	3	6	24	13	22	0	.231	.438
Sammy Esposito	3B41, SS20, 2B7	R	30	75	81	14	19	1	0	0	4	17	13	0	.235	.247
2 Charlie Maxwell	OF56, 1B6	L	35	69	206	30	61	8	3	9	43	34	32	0	.296	.495
Charley Smith	3B54	R	24	65	145	11	30	4	0	2	17	9	32	0	.207	.276
Bob Roselli	C20	R	30	35	64	4	12	3	1	1	5	11	15	1	.188	.313
1 Bob Farley	1B14	L	24	35	53	7	10	1	1	1	4	13	13	0	.189	.302
Deacon Jones	1B6	L	28	18	28	3	9	2	0	0	8	4	6	0	.321	.393
J. C. Martin	C6, 1B1, 3B1	L	25	18	26	0	2	0	0	0	2	0	3	0	.077	.077
Ramon Conde	3B7	R	27	14	16	0	0	0	0	0	1	3	3	0	.000	.000
Al Weis	SS4, 2B1, 3B1	B	24	7	12	2	1	0	0	0	0	2	3	1	.083	.083
Brian McCall	OF1	L	19	4	8	2	3	0	0	2	3	0	2	0	.375	1.125
Ken Berry	OF2	R	21	3	6	2	2	0	0	0	0	0	0	0	.333	.333
Dick Kenworthy	2B2	R	21	3	4	0	0	0	0	0	0	0	0	0	.000	.000

NAME	T	AGE	W	L	PCT	SV	G	GS	CG	IP	H	BB	SO	ShO	ERA
TOTALS		29	85	77	.525	28	162	162	50	1452	1380	537	821	13	3.73
Ray Herbert	R	32	20	9	**.690**	0	35	35	12	237	228	74	115	2	3.27
Juan Pizarro	L	25	12	14	.462	1	36	32	9	203	182	97	173	1	3.81
Eddie Fisher	R	25	9	5	.643	5	57	12	2	183	169	45	88	1	3.10
John Buzhardt	R	25	8	12	.400	0	28	25	8	152	156	59	64	2	4.20
Frank Baumann	L	29	7	6	.538	4	40	10	3	120	117	36	55	1	3.38
Joe Horlen (SA)	R	24	7	6	.538	0	20	19	5	109	108	43	63	1	4.87
Early Wynn	R	42	7	15	.310	0	27	26	11	168	171	56	91	3	4.45
Dom Zanni	R	30	6	5	.545	5	44	2	0	86	67	31	66	0	3.77
Turk Lown	R	38	4	2	.667	6	42	0	0	56	58	25	40	0	3.05
Mike Joyce	R	21	2	1	.667	2	25	1	0	43	40	14	9	0	3.35
1 Russ Kemmerer	R	30	2	1	.667	0	20	0	0	28	30	11	17	0	3.86
2 Dean Stone	L	31	1	0	1.000	5	27	0	0	30	28	9	23	0	3.30
Gary Peters	L	25	0	1	.000	0	5	0	0	6	8	1	4	0	6.00
Dave DeBusschere	R	21	0	0	.000	0	12	0	0	18	5	23	8	0	2.00
Herb Score	L	29	0	0	.000	0	4	0	0	6	6	4	3	0	4.50
Verle Tiefenthaler	R	24	0	0	.000	0	3	0	0	4	6	7	1	0	9.00
Mike Degerick	R	19	0	0	.000	0	1	0	0	1	1	1	0	0	0.00
Frank Kreutzer	L	23	0	0	.000	0	1	0	0	1	0	1	1	0	0.00

CLEVELAND 6th 80-82 .494 16 — MEL McGAHA

NAME	G by POS	B	AGE	G	AB	R	H	2B	3B	HR	RBI	BB	SO	SB	BA	SA
TOTALS			27	162	5484	682	1341	202	22	180	644	502	**939**	35	.245	.388
Tito Francona	1B158	L	28	158	621	82	169	28	5	14	70	47	74	3	.272	.401
Jerry Kindall	2B154	R	27	154	530	51	123	21	1	13	55	45	107	4	.232	.349
Woodie Held	SS133, 3B5, OF1	R	30	139	466	55	116	12	2	19	58	73	107	5	.249	.406
Bubba Phillips	3B145, OF3, 2B1	R	32	148	562	53	145	26	0	10	54	20	55	4	.258	.358
Willie Kirkland	OF125	L	28	137	419	56	84	9	1	21	72	43	62	9	.200	.377
Ty Cline	OF107	L	23	118	375	53	93	15	5	2	28	28	50	5	.248	.331
Chuck Essegian	OF90	R	30	106	336	59	92	12	0	21	50	42	68	0	.274	.497
John Romano	C130	R	27	135	459	71	120	19	3	25	81	73	64	0	.261	.479
Al Luplow	OF86	L	23	97	318	54	88	15	3	14	45	36	44	1	.277	.475
Don Dillard	OF50	L	25	95	174	22	40	5	1	5	14	11	25	0	.230	.356
2 Willie Tasby	OF66, 3B1	R	29	75	199	25	48	7	0	4	17	25	41	0	.241	.337
Gene Green	OF33, 1B2	R	29	66	143	16	40	4	1	11	28	8	21	0	.280	.552
Doc Edwards	C39	R	24	53	143	13	39	6	0	3	9	9	14	0	.273	.378
Jim Mahoney	SS23, 2B8, 3B1	R	28	41	74	12	18	4	0	3	5	3	14	0	.243	.419
Dick Donovan	P34	L	34	34	89	8	16	1	0	4	9	7	32	0	.180	.326
Jack Kubiszyn	SS18, 3B1	R	25	25	59	3	10	2	0	1	2	5	7	0	.169	.254
1 Ken Aspromonte	2B6, 3B3	R	30	20	28	4	4	2	0	0	1	6	5	0	.143	.214
Max Alvis	3B12	R	24	12	51	1	11	2	0	0	3	2	13	3	.216	.255
Walt Bond	OF12	L	24	12	50	10	19	3	0	6	17	4	9	1	.380	.800
Mike de la Hoz	2B2	R	22	12	12	0	1	0	0	0	0	0	3	0	.083	.083
Hal Jones	1B4	R	26	5	16	2	5	1	0	0	1	0	4	0	.313	.375

Tommie Agee 19 R 3-14, 3 Marlan Coughtry 27 L 1-2, 1 Bob Nieman 35 R 0-1

NAME	T	AGE	W	L	PCT	SV	G	GS	CG	IP	H	BB	SO	ShO	ERA
TOTALS		27	80	82	.494	31	162	162	45	1441	1410	594	780	12	4.14
Dick Donovan	R	34	20	10	.667	0	34	34	16	251	255	47	94	**5**	3.59
Jim Perry	R	26	12	12	.500	0	35	27	7	194	213	59	74	3	4.13
Gary Bell	R	25	10	9	.526	12	57	6	1	108	104	52	80	0	4.25
Pedro Ramos	R	27	10	12	.455	1	37	27	7	201	189	85	96	2	3.72
Barry Latman	R	26	8	13	.381	5	45	21	7	179	179	72	117	1	4.17
Mudcat Grant	R	26	7	10	.412	0	26	23	6	150	128	81	90	1	4.26
Sam McDowell	L	19	3	7	.300	1	25	13	0	88	81	70	70	0	6.03
Frank Funk	R	26	2	1	.667	6	47	0	0	81	62	32	49	0	3.22
Bill Dailey	R	27	2	2	.500	1	27	0	0	43	43	17	24	0	3.56
Ron Taylor	R	24	2	2	.500	0	8	4	1	33	36	13	15	0	6.00
Wynn Hawkins (MS)	R	26	1	0	1.000	0	3	0	0	4	9	1	0	0	6.75
Floyd Weaver	R	21	1	0	1.000	0	1	1	0	5	3	0	8	0	1.80
Bob Allen	L	24	1	1	.500	4	30	0	0	31	29	25	23	0	5.81
1 Ruben Gomez	R	34	1	2	.333	1	15	4	0	45	50	25	21	0	3.40
Bob Hartman	L	24	0	1	.000	0	8	2	0	17	14	8	11	0	3.18
Dave Tyriver	R	24	0	0	.000	0	4	0	0	11	10	7	7	0	4.09
2 Jackie Collum	L	35	0	0	.000	0	1	0	0	1	4	0	1	0	18.00
1 Don Rudolph	L	30	0	0	.000	0	1	0	0	1	1	0	0	0	0.00

BALTIMORE 7th (Tie) 77-85 .475 19 — BILLY HITCHCOCK

NAME	G by POS	B	AGE	G	AB	R	H	2B	3B	HR	RBI	BB	SO	SB	BA	SA
TOTALS			28	162	5491	652	1363	225	34	156	617	516	931	45	.248	.387
Jim Gentile	1B150	L	28	152	545	80	137	21	1	33	87	77	100	1	.251	.475
Marv Breeding	2B73, SS1, 3B1	R	28	95	240	27	59	10	1	2	18	8	41	2	.246	.321
Jerry Adair	SS113, 2B34, 3B1	R	25	139	538	67	153	29	4	11	48	27	77	7	.284	.414
Brooks Robinson	3B162, SS3, 2B2	R	25	162	634	77	192	29	9	23	86	42	70	3	.303	.486
Russ Snyder	OF121	L	28	139	416	47	127	19	4	9	40	17	46	7	.305	.435
Jackie Brandt	OF138, 3B2	R	28	143	505	76	129	29	5	19	75	55	64	9	.255	.446
Boog Powell	OF112, 1B1	L	20	124	400	44	97	13	2	15	53	38	79	1	.243	.398
Gus Triandos (BG)	C63	R	31	66	207	20	33	7	0	6	23	29	43	0	.159	.280
Whitey Herzog	OF70	L	30	99	263	34	70	13	1	7	35	41	36	2	.266	.403
Dave Nicholson	OF80	R	22	97	173	25	30	4	1	9	15	27	76	3	.173	.364
Dick Williams	OF29, 1B21, 3B4	R	33	82	178	20	44	7	1	1	18	14	26	0	.247	.315
Charlie Lau	C56	L	29	81	197	21	58	11	2	6	37	7	11	1	.294	.462
1 Johnny Temple	2B71	R	33	78	270	28	71	8	1	1	17	36	22	7	.263	.311
Ron Hansen (BG)	SS64	R	24	71	196	12	34	7	0	3	17	30	36	0	.173	.255
2 Hobie Landrith	C60	L	32	60	167	18	37	4	1	4	17	19	9	0	.222	.329
Milt Pappas	P35	R	23	35	69	5	6	1	0	4	8	1	41	0	.087	.275
Earl Robinson	OF17	R	25	29	63	12	18	3	1	1	4	8	10	2	.286	.413
Barry Shetrone	OF6	L	23	21	24	3	6	1	0	1	1	0	5	0	.250	.417
1 Marv Throneberry	OF2	L	28	9	9	1	0	0	0	0	0	4	6	0	.000	.000
Bob Saverine	2B7	B	21	8	21	2	5	2	0	0	3	1	3	0	.238	.333
Pete Ward	OF6	L	22	8	21	1	3	2	0	0	2	4	5	0	.143	.238
2 Darrell Johnson	C6	R	33	6	22	0	4	0	0	0	1	0	4	0	.182	.182

Mickey McGuire 21 R 0-4, Nate Smith 27 R 2-9, Andy Etchebarren 19 R 2-6, Ozzie Virgil 29 R 0-0

NAME	T	AGE	W	L	PCT	SV	G	GS	CG	IP	H	BB	SO	ShO	ERA
TOTALS		29	77	85	.475	33	162	162	32	1462	1373	549	898	8	**3.69**
Milt Pappas	R	23	12	10	.545	0	35	32	9	205	200	75	130	1	4.04
Robin Roberts	R	35	10	9	.526	0	27	25	6	191	176	41	102	0	2.78
Steve Barber (AJ)	L	23	9	6	.600	0	28	19	5	140	145	61	89	2	3.47
Chuck Estrada	R	24	9	**17**	.346	0	34	33	6	223	199	121	165	0	3.83
Jack Fisher (SJ)	R	23	7	9	.438	1	32	25	4	152	173	56	81	0	5.09
Hoyt Wilhelm	R	38	7	10	.412	15	52	0	0	93	64	34	90	0	1.94
1 Hal Brown	R	37	6	4	.600	1	22	11	0	86	88	21	25	0	4.08
Dick Hall	R	31	6	6	.500	6	43	6	1	118	102	19	71	0	2.29
Billy Hoeft	L	30	4	8	.333	7	57	4	0	114	103	43	73	0	4.58
Wes Stock	R	28	3	2	.600	3	53	0	0	65	50	36	34	0	4.43
Art Quirk	L	24	2	2	.500	0	7	5	0	27	36	18	18	0	6.00
Dave McNally	L	19	1	0	1.000	0	1	1	1	9	2	3	4	1	0.00
John Miller	R	21	1	1	.500	0	2	1	0	10	2	5	4	0	0.90
Dick Luebke	L	27	0	1	.000	0	10	0	0	13	12	6	7	0	2.77
Jim Lehew	R	24	0	0	.000	0	6	0	0	10	10	3	2	0	1.80
Bill Short	L	24	0	0	.000	0	5	0	0	4	8	6	3	0	15.75
John Papa	R	21	0	0	.000	0	1	0	0	1	3	1	0	0	27.00

BOSTON 7th (Tie) 76-84 .475 19 — PINKY HIGGINS

NAME	G by POS	B	AGE	G	AB	R	H	2B	3B	HR	RBI	BB	SO	SB	BA	SA
TOTALS			28	160	5530	707	1429	**257**	53	146	671	525	923	39	.258	.403
Pete Runnels	1B151	L	34	152	562	80	183	33	5	10	60	79	57	3	**.326**	.456
Chuck Schilling (BH)	2B118	R	24	119	413	48	95	17	1	7	35	29	48	1	.230	.327
Ed Bressoud	SS153	R	30	153	599	79	166	40	9	14	68	46	118	2	.277	.444
Frank Malzone	3B156	R	32	156	619	74	175	20	3	21	95	35	43	0	.283	.426
Lu Clinton	OF103	R	24	114	398	63	117	24	10	18	75	34	79	2	.294	.540
Gary Geiger	OF129	L	25	131	466	67	116	18	4	16	54	67	66	18	.249	.408
Carl Yastrzemski	OF160	L	22	160	646	99	191	43	6	19	94	66	82	7	.296	.469
Jim Pagliaroni	C73	R	24	90	260	39	67	14	0	11	37	36	55	2	.258	.438
Carroll Hardy	OF105	R	29	115	362	52	78	13	5	8	36	54	68	3	.215	.345
Bob Tillman	C66	R	25	81	249	28	57	6	4	14	38	19	65	0	.229	.454
Russ Nixon (AJ)	C38	L	27	65	151	11	42	7	2	1	19	8	14	0	.278	.371
Pumpsie Green	2B18, SS5	B	28	56	91	12	21	2	1	2	11	11	18	1	.231	.341
2 Billy Gardner	2B30, 3B7, SS4	R	34	53	199	22	54	9	2	0	12	10	39	0	.271	.337
Dave Philley	OF4	B	42	38	42	3	6	2	0	0	4	5	3	0	.143	.190
Don Gile	1B14	R	27	18	41	3	2	0	0	1	3	3	15	0	.049	.122

NAME	T	AGE	W	L	PCT	SV	G	GS	CG	IP	H	BB	SO	ShO	ERA
TOTALS		28	76	84	.475	40	160	160	34	1438	1416	632	923	12	4.22
Bill Monbouquette	R	25	15	13	.536	0	35	35	11	235	227	65	153	4	3.33
Gene Conley	R	31	15	14	.517	1	34	33	9	242	238	68	134	2	3.94
Earl Wilson	R	27	12	8	.600	0	31	28	4	191	163	111	137	1	3.91
Dick Radatz	R	25	9	6	.600	**24**	**62**	0	0	125	95	40	144	0	2.23
Don Schwall	R	26	9	15	.375	0	33	32	5	182	180	121	89	1	4.95
Arnie Earley	L	29	4	5	.444	5	38	3	0	68	76	46	59	0	5.82
Ike Delock	R	32	4	5	.444	0	17	13	4	86	89	24	49	2	3.77
1 Galen Cisco	R	26	4	7	.364	0	23	9	1	83	95	50	43	0	6.72
Mike Fornieles	R	30	3	6	.333	5	42	1	0	82	96	37	36	0	5.38
Chet Nichols	L	31	1	1	.500	3	29	1	0	57	61	22	33	0	3.00
Bill MacLeod	L	20	0	1	.000	0	2	0	0	2	4	1	2	0	4.50
Pete Smith (MS)	R	22	0	1	.000	0	1	1	0	4	7	2	1	0	18.00
Hal Kolstad	R	27	0	2	.000	2	27	2	0	61	65	35	36	0	5.46
Merlin Nippert	R	23	0	0	.000	0	4	0	0	6	4	4	3	0	4.50
Wilbur Wood	L	20	0	0	.000	0	1	1	0	8	6	3	3	0	3.38

Billy Muffett 31 R 0-0, Tracy Stallard 24 R 0-0, 1 Ted Wills 28 L 0-0

KANSAS CITY 9th 72-90 .444 24 — HANK BAUER

NAME	G by POS	B	AGE	G	AB	R	H	2B	3B	HR	RBI	BB	SO	SB	BA	SA
TOTALS			27	162	5576	745	1467	220	**58**	116	691	556	803	76	.263	.386
Norm Siebern	1B162	L	28	162	600	114	185	25	6	25	117	110	88	3	.308	.495
Jerry Lumpe	2B156, SS2	L	29	156	641	89	193	34	10	10	83	44	38	0	.301	.432
Dick Howser (BH)	SS72	R	25	83	286	53	68	8	3	6	34	38	8	19	.238	.350
Ed Charles	3B140, 2B2	R	27	147	535	81	154	24	7	17	74	54	70	20	.288	.454
Gino Cimoli	OF147	R	32	152	550	67	151	20	**15**	10	71	40	89	2	.275	.420
Bobby Del Greco	OF124	R	29	132	338	61	86	21	1	9	38	49	62	4	.254	.402
Manny Jiminez	OF122	L	23	139	479	48	144	24	2	11	69	31	34	0	.301	.428
Haywood Sullivan	C94, 1B1	R	31	95	274	33	68	7	2	4	29	31	54	1	.248	.332
Wayne Causey	SS51, 3B26, 2B9	L	25	117	305	40	77	14	1	4	38	41	30	2	.252	.344
Jose Tartabull	OF85	L	23	107	310	49	86	6	5	0	22	20	19	19	.277	.329
2 George Alusik	OF50, 1B1	R	27	90	209	29	57	10	1	11	35	16	29	1	.273	.488
Joe Azcue (JJ)	C70	R	22	72	223	18	51	9	1	2	25	17	27	1	.229	.305
3 Billy Consolo	SS48	R	27	54	154	11	37	4	2	0	16	23	33	1	.240	.292
Leo Posada	OF11	R	26	29	46	6	9	1	1	0	3	7	14	0	.196	.261
Billy Bryan	C22	L	23	25	74	5	11	2	1	2	7	5	32	0	.149	.284
Deron Johnson (MS)	1B2, 3B2, OF2	R	23	17	19	1	2	1	0	0	0	3	8	0	.105	.158
John Wojcik	OF12	L	20	16	43	8	13	4	0	0	9	13	4	3	.302	.395
1 Gordie Windhorn	OF7	R	28	14	19	1	3	1	0	0	1	0	3	0	.158	.211
Bill Kern	OF3	R	27	8	16	1	4	0	0	1	1	0	3	0	.250	.438
2 Marlan Coughtry	3B3	L	27	6	11	1	2	0	0	0	1	4	3	0	.182	.182

Charlie Shoemaker 22 L 2-11, Gene Stephens (LJ) 29 L 0-4, Hector Martinez 23 R 0-1

NAME	T	AGE	W	L	PCT	SV	G	GS	CG	IP	H	BB	SO	ShO	ERA
TOTALS		27	72	90	.444	33	162	162	32	1434	1450	**655**	825	4	4.79
Ed Rakow	R	26	14	**17**	.452	1	42	35	11	235	232	98	159	2	4.25
Dave Wickersham	R	26	11	4	.733	1	30	9	3	110	105	43	61	0	4.17
John Wyatt	R	27	10	7	.588	11	59	9	0	125	121	80	106	0	4.46
Diego Segui	R	24	8	5	.615	6	37	13	2	117	89	46	71	0	3.85
Jerry Walker	R	23	8	9	.471	0	31	21	3	143	165	78	57	1	5.92
Orlando Pena	R	28	6	4	.600	0	13	12	6	90	71	27	56	1	3.00
Bill Fischer	R	31	4	12	.250	2	34	16	5	128	150	8	38	0	3.94
Dan Pfister	R	25	4	14	.222	1	41	25	2	196	175	106	123	0	4.55
Gordon Jones	R	32	3	2	.600	6	21	0	0	33	31	14	28	0	6.27
Norm Bass	R	23	2	6	.250	0	22	10	0	75	96	46	33	0	6.12
2 Moe Drabowsky	R	26	1	1	.500	0	10	3	0	28	29	10	19	0	5.14
Bob Giggie	R	28	1	1	.500	0	4	2	0	14	17	3	4	0	6.43
Bob Grim	R	32	0	1	.000	3	12	0	0	13	14	8	3	0	6.23
Jim Archer	L	30	0	1	.000	0	18	1	0	28	40	10	12	0	9.32
Granny Hamner	R	35	0	1	.000	0	3	0	0	4	10	6	0	0	9.00
Art Ditmar	R	33	0	2	.000	0	6	5	0	22	31	13	13	0	6.55
Danny McDevitt	L	29	0	3	.000	2	33	1	0	51	47	41	28	0	5.82
Bill Kunkel	R	25	0	0	.000	0	9	0	0	8	8	4	6	0	3.38
1 Dan Osinski	R	28	0	0	.000	0	4	0	0	5	8	8	4	0	16.20
Don Williams	R	30	0	0	.000	0	3	0	0	4	6	0	1	0	9.00
Rupe Toppin	R	20	0	0	.000	0	2	0	0	2	1	5	1	0	13.50
Fred Norman	L	19	0	0	.000	0	2	0	0	4	4	1	2	0	2.25

WASHINGTON 10th 60-101 .373 35.5 — MICKEY VERNON

NAME	G by POS	B	AGE	G	AB	R	H	2B	3B	HR	RBI	BB	SO	SB	BA	SA
TOTALS			29	162	5484	599	1370	206	38	132	566	466	789	**99**	.250	.373
Harry Bright	1B99, C3, 3B1	R	32	113	392	55	107	15	4	17	67	26	51	2	.273	.462
Chuck Cottier	2B134	R	26	136	443	50	107	14	6	6	40	44	57	14	.242	.341
Ken Hamlin	SS87, 2B2	R	27	98	292	29	74	12	0	3	22	22	22	7	.253	.325
Bob Johnson	3B72, SS50, 2B3, OF1	R	26	135	466	58	134	20	2	12	43	32	50	9	.288	.416
Jim King	OF101	L	29	132	333	39	81	15	0	11	35	55	37	4	.243	.387
Jimmy Piersall	OF132	R	32	135	471	38	115	20	4	4	31	39	53	12	.244	.329
Chuck Hinton	OF136, 2B12, SS1	R	28	151	542	73	168	25	6	17	75	47	66	28	.310	.472
Ken Retzer	C99	L	28	109	340	36	97	11	2	8	37	26	21	2	.285	.400
Joe Hicks	OF42	L	29	102	174	20	39	4	2	6	14	15	34	3	.224	.374
Bob Schmidt	C88	R	29	88	256	28	62	14	0	10	31	14	37	0	.242	.414
Danny O'Connell	3B41, 2B22	R	35	84	236	24	62	7	2	2	18	23	28	5	.263	.335
Johnny Schaive	3B49, 2B6	R	28	82	225	20	57	15	1	6	29	6	25	0	.253	.409
Don Lock	OF67	R	25	71	225	30	57	6	2	12	37	30	63	4	.253	.458
Bud Zipfel	1B26, OF23	L	23	68	184	21	44	4	1	6	21	17	43	1	.239	.370
1 Dale Long	1B51	L	36	67	191	17	46	8	0	4	24	18	22	5	.241	.346
Eddie Brinkman	SS38, 3B10	R	20	54	133	8	22	7	1	0	4	11	28	1	.165	.233
1 Gene Woodling	OF30	L	39	44	107	19	30	4	0	5	16	24	5	1	.280	.458
John Kennedy	SS9, 3B2	R	21	14	42	6	11	0	1	1	2	2	0	0	.262	.381
1 Willie Tasby	OF10	R	29	11	34	4	7	0	0	0	0	2	6	0	.206	.206
Ron Stillwell	2B6, SS1	R	22	6	22	5	6	0	0	0	2	2	2	0	.273	.273

NAME	T	AGE	W	L	PCT	SV	G	GS	CG	IP	H	BB	SO	ShO	ERA
TOTALS		28	60	**101**	.373	13	162	162	38	1445	1400	593	771	11	4.04
Dave Stenhouse	R	28	11	12	.478	0	34	26	9	197	169	90	123	2	3.65
2 Don Rudolph	L	30	8	10	.444	0	37	23	6	176	187	42	68	2	3.63
Claude Osteen	L	22	8	13	.381	1	28	22	7	150	140	47	59	2	3.66
Tom Cheney	R	27	7	9	.438	1	37	23	4	173	134	97	147	3	3.17
Bennie Daniels	R	30	7	16	.304	2	44	21	3	161	172	68	66	1	4.86
Marty Kutyna	R	29	5	6	.455	0	54	0	0	78	83	27	25	0	4.04
Pete Burnside	L	31	5	11	.313	2	40	20	6	150	152	51	74	0	4.44
Steve Hamilton	L	28	3	8	.273	2	41	10	1	107	103	39	83	0	3.79
Ed Hobaugh	R	28	2	1	.667	1	26	2	0	69	66	25	37	0	3.78
Jim Hannan	R	22	2	4	.333	4	42	3	0	68	56	49	39	0	3.31
Ray Rippelmeyer	R	28	1	2	.333	0	18	1	0	39	47	17	17	0	5.54
Carl Bouldin	R	22	1	2	.333	0	6	3	1	20	26	9	12	0	5.85
Freddie Green	L	28	0	1	.000	0	5	0	0	7	7	6	2	0	6.43
Bob Baird	L	20	0	1	.000	0	3	3	0	11	13	8	3	0	6.55
Jack Jenkins	R	19	0	1	.000	0	3	1	1	13	12	7	10	0	4.15
Joe McClain	R	29	0	4	.000	0	10	4	0	24	33	11	6	0	9.38

SAN FRANCISCO 1st 103-62 .624 — **AL DARK** (Defeated Los Angeles in playoff 2 games to 1)

NAME	G by POS	B	AGE	G	AB	R	H	2B	3B	HR	RBI	BB	SO	SB	BA	SA
TOTALS			27	165	5588	878	1552	235	32	204	807	523	822	73	.278	.441
Orlando Cepeda	1B160, OF2	R	24	162	625	105	191	26	1	35	114	37	97	10	.306	.518
Chuck Hiller	2B161	L	27	161	602	94	166	22	2	3	48	55	49	5	.276	.334
Jose Pagan	SS164	R	27	164	580	73	150	25	6	7	57	47	77	13	.259	.359
Jim Davenport	3B141	R	28	144	485	83	144	25	5	14	58	45	76	2	.297	.456
Felipe Alou	OF150	R	27	154	561	96	177	30	3	25	98	33	66	10	.316	.513
Willie Mays	OF161	R	31	162	621	130	189	36	5	49	141	78	85	18	.304	.615
Harvey Kuenn	OF105, 3B30	R	31	130	487	73	148	23	5	10	68	49	37	3	.304	.433
Tom Haller	C91	L	25	99	272	53	71	13	1	18	55	51	59	1	.261	.515
Ed Bailey	C75	L	31	96	254	32	59	9	1	17	45	42	42	1	.232	.476
Willie McCovey	OF57, 1B17	L	24	91	229	41	67	6	1	20	54	29	35	3	.293	.590
Matty Alou	OF57	L	23	78	195	28	57	8	1	3	14	14	17	3	.292	.390
Manny Mota	OF27, 3B7, 2B3	R	24	47	74	9	13	1	0	0	9	7	8	3	.176	.189
Ernie Bowman	2B17, 3B11, SS10	R	24	46	42	9	8	1	0	1	4	1	10	0	.190	.286
2 Bob Nieman	OF3	R	35	30	30	1	9	2	0	1	3	1	9	0	.300	.467
Carl Boles	OF7	R	27	19	24	4	9	0	0	0	1	0	6	0	.375	.375
John Orsino	C16	R	24	18	48	4	13	2	0	0	4	5	11	0	.271	.313
1 Joe Pignatano	C7	R	32	7	5	2	1	0	0	0	0	4	0	0	.200	.200
Dick Phillips	1B1	L	30	5	3	1	0	0	0	0	1	1	1	0	.000	.000
Cap Peterson	SS2	R	19	4	6	1	1	0	0	0	0	1	4	0	.167	.167

NAME	T	AGE	W	L	PCT	SV	G	GS	CG	IP	H	BB	SO	ShO	ERA
TOTALS		29	103	62	.624	39	165	165	62	1462	1399	503	886	10	3.79
Jack Sanford	R	33	24	7	.774	0	39	38	13	265	233	92	147	2	3.43
Billy O'Dell	L	29	19	14	.576	0	43	39	20	281	282	66	195	2	3.52
Juan Marichal	R	24	18	11	.621	1	37	36	18	263	233	90	153	3	3.35
Billy Pierce	L	35	16	6	.727	1	30	23	7	162	147	35	76	2	3.50
Bobby Bolin	R	23	7	3	.700	5	41	5	2	92	84	35	74	0	3.62
Don Larsen	R	32	5	4	.556	11	49	0	0	86	83	47	58	0	4.40
Mike McCormick (SA)	L	23	5	5	.500	0	28	15	1	99	112	45	42	0	5.36
Stu Miller	R	34	5	8	.385	19	59	0	0	107	107	42	78	0	4.12
Gaylord Perry	R	23	3	1	.750	0	13	7	1	43	54	14	20	0	5.23
Jim Duffalo	R	26	1	2	.333	0	24	2	0	42	42	23	29	0	3.64
Dick LeMay	L	23	0	1	.000	1	9	0	0	9	9	9	5	0	8.00
Bob Garibaldi	R	20	0	0	.000	1	9	0	0	12	13	5	9	0	5.25

LOS ANGELES 2nd 102-63 .618 1 — **WALT ALSTON** (Defeated by San Francisco in playoff 2 games to 1)

NAME	G by POS	B	AGE	G	AB	R	H	2B	3B	HR	RBI	BB	SO	SB	BA	SA
TOTALS			27	165	5628	842	1510	192	65	140	781	572	886	198	.268	.400
Ron Fairly	1B120, OF48	L	23	147	460	80	128	15	7	14	71	75	59	1	.278	.433
Jim Gilliam	2B113, 3B90, OF1	B	33	160	588	83	159	24	1	4	43	93	35	17	.270	.335
Maury Wills	SS165	B	29	165	695	130	208	13	10	6	48	51	57	104	.299	.373
Daryl Spencer	3B57, SS10	R	33	77	157	24	37	5	1	2	12	22	31	0	.236	.310
Frank Howard	OF131	R	25	141	493	80	146	25	6	31	119	39	108	1	.296	.560
Willie Davis	OF156	L	22	157	600	103	171	18	10	21	85	42	72	32	.285	.453
Tommy Davis	OF146, 3B39	R	23	163	665	120	230	27	9	27	153	33	65	18	.346	.535
Johnny Roseboro	C128	L	29	128	389	45	97	16	7	7	55	50	60	12	.249	.380
Larry Burright	2B109, SS1	R	24	115	249	35	51	6	5	4	30	21	67	4	.205	.317
Wally Moon	OF36, 1B32	L	32	95	244	36	59	9	1	4	31	30	33	5	.242	.336
Tim Harkness	1B59	L	24	92	62	9	16	2	0	2	7	10	20	1	.258	.387
Duke Snider	OF39	L	35	80	158	28	44	11	3	5	30	36	32	2	.278	.481
Lee Walls	OF17, 1B11, 3B4	R	29	60	109	9	29	3	1	0	17	10	21	1	.266	.312
Andy Carey	3B42	R	30	53	111	12	26	5	1	2	13	16	23	0	.234	.351
Doug Camilli	C39	R	25	45	88	16	25	5	2	4	22	12	21	0	.284	.523
Norm Sherry	C34	R	30	35	88	7	16	2	0	3	16	6	17	0	.182	.307
Dick Tracewski	SS4	R	27	15	2	3	0	0	0	0	0	2	0	0	.000	.000
Ken McMullen	OF2	R	20	6	11	0	3	0	0	0	0	0	3	0	.273	.273

NAME	T	AGE	W	L	PCT	SV	G	GS	CG	IP	H	BB	SO	ShO	ERA
TOTALS		26	102	63	.618	46	165	165	44	1489	1386	588	1104	8	3.61
Don Drysdale	R	25	25	9	.735	1	43	41	19	314	272	78	232	2	2.84
Johnny Podres	L	29	15	13	.536	0	40	40	8	255	270	71	178	0	3.81
Sandy Koufax (RJ)	L	26	14	7	.667	1	28	26	11	184	134	57	216	2	2.54
Stan Williams	R	25	14	12	.538	1	40	28	4	186	184	98	108	1	4.46
Ed Roebuck	R	30	10	2	.833	9	64	0	0	119	102	54	72	0	3.10
Larry Sherry	R	26	7	3	.700	11	58	0	0	90	81	44	71	0	3.20
Joe Moeller	R	29	6	5	.545	1	19	15	1	86	87	58	46	0	5.23
Ron Perranoski	L	26	6	6	.500	20	70	0	0	107	103	36	68	0	2.86
Pete Richert	L	22	5	4	.556	0	19	12	1	81	77	45	75	0	3.89
Phil Ortega	R	22	0	2	.000	1	24	3	0	54	60	39	30	0	6.83
Jack Smith	R	26	0	0	.000	1	8	0	0	10	10	4	7	0	4.50
1 Willard Hunter	L	28	0	0	.000	0	1	0	0	2	6	4	1	0	40.50

CINCINNATI 3rd 98-64 .605 3.5 — **FRED HUTCHINSON**

NAME	G by POS	B	AGE	G	AB	R	H	2B	3B	HR	RBI	BB	SO	SB	BA	SA
TOTALS			28	162	5645	802	1523	252	40	167	745	498	903	66	.270	.417
Gordy Coleman	1B128	L	27	136	476	73	132	13	1	28	86	36	68	2	.277	.485
Don Blasingame	2B137	L	30	141	494	77	139	9	7	2	35	63	44	4	.281	.340
Leo Cardenas	SS149	R	23	153	589	77	173	31	4	10	60	39	99	2	.294	.411
Eddie Kasko	3B114, SS21	R	30	134	533	74	148	26	2	4	41	35	44	3	.278	.356
Frank Robinson	OF161	R	26	162	609	134	208	51	2	39	136	76	62	18	.342	.624
Vada Pinson	OF152	L	23	155	619	107	181	31	7	23	100	45	68	26	.292	.477
Wally Post	OF90	R	32	109	285	43	75	10	3	17	62	32	67	1	.263	.498
Johnny Edwards	C130	L	24	133	452	47	115	28	5	8	50	45	70	1	.254	.392
Jerry Lynch	OF73	L	31	114	288	41	81	15	4	12	57	24	38	3	.281	.486
Marty Keough	OF71, 1B29	L	27	111	230	34	64	8	2	7	27	21	31	3	.278	.422
Joe Gaines	OF13	R	25	64	52	12	12	3	0	1	7	8	16	0	.231	.346
2 Don Zimmer	3B43, 2B17, SS1	R	31	63	192	16	48	11	2	2	16	14	30	1	.250	.359
Hank Foiles	C41	R	33	43	131	17	36	6	1	7	25	13	39	0	.275	.496
Cookie Rojas	2B30, 3B1	R	23	39	86	9	19	2	0	0	6	9	4	1	.221	.244
Don Pavletich	1B25, C2	R	23	34	63	7	14	3	0	1	7	8	18	0	.222	.317
Gene Freese (BN)	3B10	R	28	18	42	2	6	1	0	0	1	6	8	0	.143	.167
Rogelio Alvarez	1B13	R	24	14	28	1	6	0	0	0	2	1	10	0	.214	.214
Tommy Harper	3B6	R	21	6	23	1	4	0	0	0	1	2	6	1	.174	.174
1 Cliff Cook	3B4	R	25	6	5	0	0	0	0	0	0	0	2	0	.000	.000
Jesse Gonder		L	26	4	4	0	0	0	0	0	0	0	3	0	.000	.000
1 Darrell Johnson	C2	R	33	2	4	0	0	0	0	0	0	2	0	0	.000	.000

NAME	T	AGE	W	L	PCT	SV	G	GS	CG	IP	H	BB	SO	ShO	ERA
TOTALS		29	98	64	.605	35	162	162	51	1461	1397	567	964	13	3.75
Bob Purkey	R	32	23	5	.821	0	37	37	18	288	260	64	141	2	2.81
Joey Jay	R	26	21	14	.600	0	39	37	16	273	269	100	155	4	3.76
Jim O'Toole	L	25	16	13	.552	0	36	34	11	252	222	87	170	3	3.50
Jim Maloney	R	22	9	7	.563	1	22	17	3	115	90	66	105	0	3.52
Johnny Klippstein	R	34	7	6	.538	4	40	7	0	109	113	64	67	0	4.46
2 Joe Nuxhall	L	33	5	0	1.000	1	12	9	1	66	59	25	57	0	2.45
Bill Henry	L	34	4	2	.667	11	40	0	0	37	40	20	35	0	4.62
Dave Sisler	R	30	4	3	.571	1	35	0	0	44	44	26	27	0	3.89
Jim Brosnan	R	32	4	4	.500	13	48	0	0	65	76	18	51	0	3.32
Sammy Ellis	R	21	2	2	.500	0	8	4	0	28	29	29	27	0	6.75
1 Moe Drabowsky	R	26	2	6	.250	1	23	10	1	83	84	31	56	0	4.99
John Tsitouris	R	26	1	0	1.000	0	4	2	1	21	13	7	7	1	0.86
2 Ted Wills	L	28	0	2	.000	3	26	5	0	61	61	23	58	0	5.31
1 Bob Miller	L	26	0	0	.000	0	6	0	0	5	14	3	4	0	23.40
Howie Nunn	R	26	0	0	.000	0	6	0	0	10	15	3	4	0	5.40
1 Dave Hillman	R	34	0	0	.000	0	2	0	0	4	8	1	0	0	9.00

PITTSBURGH 4th 93-68 .578 8 — **DANNY MURTAUGH**

NAME	G by POS	B	AGE	G	AB	R	H	2B	3B	HR	RBI	BB	SO	SB	BA	SA
TOTALS			30	161	5483	706	1468	240	65	108	655	432	836	50	.268	.394
Dick Stuart	1B101	R	29	114	394	52	90	11	4	16	64	32	94	0	.228	.398
Bill Mazeroski	2B159	R	25	159	572	55	155	24	9	14	81	37	47	0	.271	.418
Dick Groat	SS161	R	31	161	678	76	199	34	3	2	61	31	61	2	.294	.361
Don Hoak	3B116	R	34	121	411	63	99	14	8	5	48	49	49	4	.241	.350
Roberto Clemente	OF142	R	27	144	538	95	168	28	9	10	74	35	73	6	.312	.454
Bill Virdon	OF156	L	31	156	663	82	164	27	10	6	47	36	65	5	.247	.345
Bob Skinner	OF139	L	30	144	510	87	154	29	7	20	75	76	89	10	.302	.504
Smoky Burgess	C101	L	35	103	360	38	118	19	2	13	61	31	19	0	.328	.500
Howie Goss	OF66	R	27	89	111	19	27	6	0	2	10	9	36	5	.243	.351
Donn Clendenon	1B52, OF19	R	26	80	222	39	67	8	5	7	28	26	58	16	.302	.477
2 Jim Marshall	1B26	L	30	55	100	13	22	5	1	2	12	15	19	1	.220	.350
Dick Schofield	3B20, 2B2, SS1	B	27	54	104	19	30	3	0	2	10	17	22	0	.288	.375
Don Leppert	C44	L	30	45	139	14	37	6	1	3	18	12	21	0	.266	.388
Johnny Logan	3B19	R	35	44	80	7	24	3	0	1	12	7	6	0	.300	.375
Cal Neeman	C24	R	33	24	50	5	9	1	1	1	5	3	10	0	.180	.300
Bob Bailey	3B12	R	19	14	42	6	7	2	1	0	6	6	10	1	.167	.262
Willie Stargell	OF9	L	22	10	31	1	9	3	1	0	4	3	10	0	.290	.452
Orlando McFarlane	C8	R	24	8	23	0	2	0	0	0	1	1	4	0	.087	.087
Larry Elliot	OF3	L	24	8	10	2	3	0	0	1	2	0	1	0	.300	.600
Elmo Plaskett	C4	R	24	7	14	2	4	0	0	1	3	1	3	0	.286	.500
Coot Veal		R	29	1	1	0	0	0	0	0	0	0	1	0	.000	.000

NAME	T	AGE	W	L	PCT	SV	G	GS	CG	IP	H	BB	SO	ShO	ERA
TOTALS		31	93	68	.578	41	161	161	40	1432	1433	466	897	13	3.38
Bob Friend	R	31	18	14	.563	1	39	36	13	262	280	53	144	5	3.06
Al McBean	R	24	15	10	.600	0	33	29	6	190	212	65	119	2	3.69
Vern Law	R	32	10	7	.588	0	23	20	7	139	156	27	78	2	3.95
Tom Sturdivant	R	32	9	5	.643	2	49	12	2	125	120	39	76	1	3.74
Harvey Haddix	L	36	9	6	.600	0	28	20	4	141	146	42	101	0	4.21
Earl Francis	R	25	9	8	.529	0	36	23	5	176	153	83	121	1	3.07
Roy Face	R	34	8	7	.533	28	63	0	0	91	74	18	45	0	1.88
Diomedes Olivo	L	43	5	1	.833	7	62	1	0	84	88	25	66	0	2.79
Jack Lamabe	R	25	3	1	.750	2	46	0	0	78	70	40	56	0	2.88
Joe Gibbon	L	27	3	4	.429	0	19	8	0	57	53	24	26	0	3.63
Bob Veale	L	26	2	2	.500	1	11	6	2	46	39	25	42	0	3.72
Bob Priddy	R	22	1	0	1.000	0	2	0	0	3	4	1	1	0	3.00
1 Vinegar Bend Mizell	L	31	1	1	.500	0	4	3	0	16	15	10	6	0	5.06
Tommie Sisk	R	20	0	2	.000	0	5	3	1	18	18	8	6	0	4.00
Tom Butters	R	24	0	0	.000	0	4	0	0	6	5	6	10	0	1.50

MILWAUKEE 5th 86-76 .531 15.5 — **BIRDIE TEBBETTS**

NAME	G by POS	B	AGE	G	AB	R	H	2B	3B	HR	RBI	BB	SO	SB	BA	SA
TOTALS			28	162	5458	730	1376	204	38	181	685	581	975	57	.252	.403
Joe Adcock	1B112	R	34	121	391	48	97	12	1	29	78	50	91	2	.248	.506
Frank Bolling	2B119	R	30	122	406	45	110	17	4	9	43	35	45	2	.271	.399
Roy McMillan	SS135	R	31	137	468	66	115	13	0	12	41	60	53	2	.246	.350
Eddie Mathews	3B140, 1B7	L	30	152	536	106	142	25	6	29	90	101	90	4	.265	.496
Mack Jones	OF91	L	23	91	333	51	85	17	4	10	36	44	100	5	.255	.420
Hank Aaron	OF153, 1B1	R	28	156	592	127	191	28	6	45	128	66	73	15	.323	.618
Lee Maye (IL)	OF94	L	27	99	349	40	85	10	0	10	41	25	58	9	.244	.358
Del Crandall	C90, 1B5	R	32	107	350	35	104	12	3	8	45	27	24	3	.297	.417
Tommie Aaron	1B110, OF42, 2B1, 3B1	R	22	141	334	54	77	20	2	8	38	41	58	6	.231	.374
Joe Torre	C63	R	21	80	220	23	62	8	1	5	26	24	24	1	.282	.395
2 Gus Bell	OF58	L	33	79	214	28	61	11	3	5	24	12	17	0	.285	.435
Amado Samuel	SS36, 2B28, 3B3	R	23	76	209	16	43	10	0	3	20	12	54	0	.206	.297
Lou Johnson	OF55	R	27	61	117	22	33	4	5	2	13	11	27	6	.282	.453
Howie Bedell	OF45	L	26	58	138	15	27	1	2	0	2	11	22	1	.196	.232
Denis Menke	2B20, 3B15, SS9, 1B2, OF1	R	21	50	146	12	28	3	1	2	16	16	38	0	.192	.267
2 Ken Aspromonte	2B12, 3B6	R	30	34	79	11	23	2	0	0	7	6	5	0	.291	.316
Bob Uecker	C24	R	27	33	64	5	16	2	0	1	8	7	15	0	.250	.328
Hawk Taylor (MS)	OF11	R	23	20	47	3	12	0	0	0	2	2	10	0	.255	.255
Mike Krsnich	OF3, 1B1, 3B1	R	30	11	12	0	1	1	0	0	2	0	4	0	.083	.167
Lou Klimchock		L	22	8	8	0	0	0	0	0	0	0	2	0	.000	.000
Ethan Blackaby	OF3	L	21	6	13	0	2	1	0	0	0	1	8	0	.154	.231

NAME	T	AGE	W	L	PCT	SV	G	GS	CG	IP	H	BB	SO	ShO	ERA
TOTALS		27	86	76	.531	24	162	162	59	1435	1443	407	802	10	3.68
Warren Spahn	L	41	18	14	.563	0	34	34	22	269	248	55	118	0	3.04
Bob Shaw	R	29	15	9	.625	2	38	29	12	225	223	44	124	3	2.80
Bob Hendley	L	23	11	13	.458	1	35	29	7	200	188	59	112	2	3.60
Lew Burdette	R	35	10	9	.526	2	37	19	6	144	172	23	59	1	4.88
Tony Cloninger	R	21	8	3	.727	0	24	15	4	111	113	46	69	1	4.30
Claude Raymond	R	25	5	5	.500	10	26	0	0	43	37	15	40	0	2.72
2 Jack Curtis	L	25	4	4	.500	1	30	5	0	76	82	27	40	0	4.14
Ron Piche	R	27	3	2	.600	0	14	8	2	52	54	29	28	0	4.85
Denny Lemaster	L	23	3	4	.429	0	17	12	4	87	75	32	69	1	3.00
Cecil Butler	R	24	2	0	1.000	0	9	2	1	31	26	9	22	0	2.61
Don Nottebart	R	26	2	2	.500	2	39	0	0	64	64	20	36	0	3.23
Hank Fischer	R	22	2	3	.400	4	29	0	0	37	43	20	29	0	5.35
Carl Willey	R	31	2	5	.286	1	30	6	0	73	95	20	40	0	5.42
Jim Constable	L	29	1	1	.500	1	3	2	1	18	14	4	12	1	2.00
1 Don McMahon	R	32	0	1	.000	0	2	0	0	3	3	0	3	0	6.00
1 Bob Buhl	R	33	0	1	.000	0	1	1	0	2	6	4	1	0	22.50

ST. LOUIS 6th 84-78 .519 17.5 — JOHNNY KEANE

	NAME	G by POS	B	AGE	G	AB	R	H	2B	3B	HR	RBI	BB	SO	SB	BA	SA
	TOTALS			27	163	5643	774	1528	221	31	137	707	515	846	86	.271	.394
	Bill White	1B146, OF27	L	28	159	614	93	199	31	3	20	102	58	69	9	.324	.482
	Julian Javier	2B151, SS4	R	25	155	598	97	157	25	5	7	39	47	73	26	.263	.356
	Julio Gotay	SS120, 2B8, OF2, 3B1	R	23	127	369	47	94	12	1	2	27	27	47	7	.255	.309
	Ken Boyer	3B160	R	31	160	611	92	178	27	5	24	98	75	104	12	.291	.470
	Charlie James	OF116	R	24	129	388	50	107	13	4	8	59	10	58	3	.276	.392
	Curt Flood	OF151	R	24	151	635	99	188	30	5	12	70	42	57	8	.296	.416
	Stan Musial	OF119	L	41	135	433	57	143	18	1	19	82	64	46	3	.330	.508
	Gene Oliver	C98, OF8, 1B3	R	25	122	345	42	89	19	1	14	45	50	59	5	.258	.441
	Red Schoendienst	2B21, 3B4	B	39	98	143	21	43	4	0	2	12	9	12	0	.301	.371
3	Bobby Gene Smith	OF80	R	28	91	130	13	30	9	0	0	12	7	14	1	.231	.300
	Carl Sawatski	C70	L	24	85	222	26	56	9	1	13	42	36	38	0	.252	.477
	Dal Maxvill	SS76, 3B1	R	23	79	189	20	42	3	1	1	18	17	39	1	.222	.265
	Fred Whitfield	1B38	L	24	73	158	20	42	7	1	8	34	7	30	1	.266	.475
	Jimmie Schaffer	C69	R	26	70	66	7	16	2	1	0	6	6	16	1	.242	.303
	Doug Clemens	OF34	L	23	48	93	12	22	1	1	1	12	17	19	0	.237	.301
	Minnie Minoso (BW)	OF27	R	39	39	97	14	19	5	0	1	10	7	17	4	.196	.278
1	Don Landrum	OF26	L	26	32	35	11	11	0	0	0	3	4	2	2	.314	.314
1	Alex Grammas	SS16, 2B2	R	35	21	18	0	2	0	0	0	1	1	6	0	.111	.111
1	Carl Warwick	OF10	R	25	13	23	4	8	0	0	1	4	2	2	2	.348	.478

Mike Shannon 22 R 2-15, Bob Burda 23 L 1-14, Gary Kolb 22 L 5-14, Hal Smith (IL) 31

	NAME	T	AGE	W	L	PCT	SV	G	GS	CG	IP	H	BB	SO	ShO	ERA
			28	84	78	.519	25	163	163	53	1463	1394	517	914	**17**	3.55
	Larry Jackson	R	31	16	11	.593	0	36	35	11	252	267	64	112	2	3.75
	Bob Gibson	R	26	15	13	.536	1	32	30	15	234	174	95	208	**5**	2.85
	Ernie Broglio	R	26	12	9	.571	0	34	30	11	222	193	93	132	4	3.00
	Ray Washburn	R	24	12	9	.571	0	34	25	2	176	187	58	109	1	4.09
	Curt Simmons	L	33	10	10	.500	0	31	22	9	154	167	32	74	4	3.51
	Ray Sadecki	L	21	6	8	.429	1	22	17	4	102	121	43	50	1	5.56
2	Bobby Shantz	L	36	5	3	.625	4	28	0	0	58	45	20	47	0	2.17
	Lindy McDaniel	R	26	3	10	.231	14	55	2	0	107	96	29	79	0	4.12
	Bob Duliba	R	27	2	0	1.000	2	28	0	0	39	33	17	22	0	2.08
	Ed Bauta	R	27	1	0	1.000	1	20	0	0	32	28	21	25	0	5.06
1	Paul Toth	R	27	1	0	1.000	0	6	1	1	17	18	4	5	0	5.29
2	Don Ferrarese	L	33	1	4	.200	1	38	0	0	57	55	31	45	0	2.68
	Harvey Branch	L	23	0	1	.000	0	1	1	0	5	5	5	2	0	5.40
1	John Anderson	R	29	0	0	.000	1	5	0	0	6	4	3	3	0	1.50
1	Bobby Locke	R	28	0	0	.000	0	1	0	0	2	1	2	1	0	0.00

PHILADELPHIA 7th 81-80 .503 20 — GENE MAUCH

	NAME	G by POS	B	AGE	G	AB	R	H	2B	3B	HR	RBI	BB	SO	SB	BA	SA
	TOTALS			27	161	5420	705	1410	199	39	142	658	531	923	79	.260	.390
	Roy Sievers	1B130, OF7	R	35	144	477	61	125	19	5	21	80	56	80	2	.262	.455
	Tony Taylor	2B150, SS2	R	26	152	625	87	162	21	5	7	43	68	82	20	.259	.342
	Bobby Wine	SS89, 3B20	R	23	112	311	30	76	15	0	4	25	11	49	2	.244	.331
	Don Demeter	3B105, OF63, 1B1	R	27	153	550	85	169	24	3	29	107	41	93	2	.307	.520
	Johnny Callison	OF152	L	23	157	603	107	181	26	**10**	23	83	54	96	10	.300	.491
	Tony Gonzalez (XJ)	OF114	L	25	118	437	76	132	16	4	20	63	40	82	17	.302	.494
	Ted Savage	OF109	R	26	127	335	54	89	11	2	7	39	40	66	16	.266	.373
	Clay Dalrymple	C119	L	25	123	370	40	102	13	3	11	54	70	32	1	.276	.416
	Wes Covington	OF88	L	30	116	304	36	86	12	1	9	44	19	44	0	.283	.418
	Frank Torre	1B76	L	30	108	168	13	52	8	2	0	20	24	6	1	.310	.381
	Billy Klaus	3B53, SS30, 2B11	L	33	102	248	30	51	8	2	4	20	29	43	1	.206	.302
	Ruben Amaro (MS)	SS78, 1B1	R	26	79	226	24	55	10	0	0	19	30	28	5	.243	.288
	Mel Roach	3B26, 2B9, 1B4, OF3	R	29	65	105	9	20	4	0	0	8	5	19	0	.190	.229
	Jacke Davis	OF26	R	26	48	75	9	16	0	1	1	6	4	20	1	.213	.280
	Sammy White	C40	R	33	41	97	7	21	4	0	2	12	2	16	0	.216	.320
	Bob Oldis	C30	R	34	38	80	9	21	1	0	1	10	13	10	0	.263	.313

1 Billy Consolo 27 R 2-5, John Herrnstein 24 L 1-5, Bobby Malkmus 30 R 1-5, Jimmie Coker (MS) 26 R 0-3

	NAME	T	AGE	W	L	PCT	SV	G	GS	CG	IP	H	BB	SO	ShO	ERA
			26	81	80	.503	24	161	161	43	1427	1469	574	863	7	4.28
	Art Mahaffey	R	24	19	14	.576	0	41	39	20	274	253	81	177	2	3.94
	Jack Baldschun	R	25	12	7	.632	13	67	0	0	113	95	58	95	0	2.95
	Cal McLish	R	36	11	5	.688	1	32	24	5	155	184	45	71	1	4.24
	Chris Short	L	24	11	9	.550	3	47	12	4	142	149	56	91	0	3.42
	Dennis Bennett	L	22	9	9	.500	3	31	24	7	175	144	68	149	2	3.81
	Jack Hamilton	R	23	9	12	.429	2	41	26	4	182	185	**107**	101	1	5.09
	Dallas Green	R	27	6	6	.500	1	37	10	2	129	145	43	58	0	3.84
	Jim Owens	R	28	2	4	.333	0	23	12	1	70	90	33	21	0	6.30
2	Bobby Locke	R	28	1	0	1.000	0	5	0	0	16	16	10	9	0	5.63
	Bill Smith	L	28	1	5	.167	0	24	5	0	50	59	10	26	0	4.32
1	Don Ferrarese	L	33	0	1	.000	0	5	0	0	7	9	3	6	0	7.71
1	Frank Sullivan	R	32	0	2	.000	0	19	0	0	23	38	12	12	0	6.26
	Paul Brown (IL)	R	21	0	6	.000	1	23	9	0	64	74	33	29	0	5.91
	John Boozer	R	22	0	0	.000	0	9	0	0	20	22	10	13	0	5.85
	Ed Keegan	R	22	0	0	.000	0	4	0	0	8	6	5	5	0	2.25

HOUSTON 8th 64-96 .400 36.5 — HARRY CRAFT

	NAME	G by POS	B	AGE	G	AB	R	H	2B	3B	HR	RBI	BB	SO	SB	BA	SA
	TOTALS			30	162	5558	592	1370	170	47	105	549	493	806	42	.246	.351
	Norm Larker	1B135, OF6	L	31	147	506	58	133	19	5	9	63	70	47	1	.263	.374
	Joey Amalfitano	2B110, 3B5	R	28	117	380	44	90	12	5	1	27	45	43	4	.237	.303
	Bob Lillis	SS99, 2B33, 3B9	R	32	129	457	38	114	12	4	1	30	28	23	7	.249	.300
	Bob Aspromonte	3B142, SS11, 2B1	R	24	149	534	59	142	18	4	11	59	46	54	4	.266	.376
	Roman Mejias	OF142	R	31	146	566	82	162	12	3	24	76	30	83	12	.286	.445
2	Carl Warwick	OF128	R	25	130	477	63	124	17	1	16	60	38	77	2	.260	.400
	Al Spangler	OF121	L	28	129	418	51	119	10	9	5	35	70	46	7	.285	.388
	Hal Smith	C92, 3B6, 1B2	R	31	109	345	32	81	14	0	12	35	24	55	0	.235	.380
	Jim Pendleton	OF90, 1B8, 3B3, SS2	R	38	117	321	30	79	12	2	8	36	14	57	0	.246	.371
	Billy Goodman	2B31, 3B17, 1B1	L	36	82	161	12	41	4	1	0	10	12	11	0	.255	.292
	Merritt Ranew	C58	L	24	71	218	26	51	6	8	4	24	14	43	2	.234	.390
	Pidge Browne	1B26	L	33	65	100	8	21	4	2	1	10	13	9	0	.210	.320
	J C Hartman	SS48	R	28	51	148	11	33	5	0	0	5	4	16	1	.223	.257
1	Don Buddin	SS27, 3B9	R	28	40	80	10	13	4	1	2	10	17	17	0	.163	.313
2	Johnny Temple	2B26, 3B1	R	33	31	95	14	25	4	0	0	12	7	11	1	.263	.305
	Jim Campbell	C25	R	25	27	86	6	19	4	0	3	6	6	23	0	.221	.372
	Al Heist	OF23	R	34	27	72	4	16	1	0	0	3	3	9	0	.222	.236
2	Bob Cerv	OF6	R	36	19	31	2	7	0	0	2	3	2	10	0	.226	.419
	Dave Roberts	OF12, 1B6	L	29	16	53	3	13	3	0	1	10	8	8	0	.245	.358
	Johnny Weekly	OF7	R	25	13	26	3	5	1	0	2	2	7	4	0	.192	.462

Don Taussig 30 R 5-25, Jim Busby 35 R 2-11, Ernie Fazio 20 R 1-12, Dick Gernert 33 R 5-24, Ron Davis 20 R 3-14, George Williams 22 R 3 8

	NAME	T	AGE	W	L	PCT	SV	G	GS	CG	IP	H	BB	SO	ShO	ERA
			29	64	96	.400	19	162	162	34	1454	1446	471	1047	9	3.83
	Bob Bruce	R	29	10	9	.526	0	32	27	6	175	164	82	135	0	4.06
	Dick Farrell	R	28	10	20	.333	4	43	29	11	242	210	55	203	2	3.01
	Jim Golden	R	26	7	11	.389	1	37	18	5	153	163	50	88	2	4.06
	Ken Johnson	R	29	7	16	.304	0	33	31	5	197	195	46	178	1	3.84
2	Russ Kemmerer	R	30	5	3	.625	3	36	2	0	68	72	15	23	0	4.10
2	Don McMahon	R	32	5	5	.500	8	51	0	0	77	53	33	69	0	1.52
	Hal Woodeshick	L	29	5	16	.238	0	31	26	2	139	161	54	82	1	4.40
	Jim Umbricht	R	31	4	0	1.000	2	34	0	0	67	51	17	55	0	2.01
1	Dean Stone	L	31	3	2	.600	0	15	7	2	52	61	20	31	2	4.50
	Dave Giusti	R	22	2	3	.400	0	22	5	0	74	82	30	43	0	5.59
	Bobby Tiefenauer	R	32	2	4	.333	1	43	0	0	85	91	21	60	0	4.34
	George Brunet	L	27	2	4	.333	0	17	11	2	54	62	21	36	0	4.50
	Dick Drott (SA)	R	26	1	0	1.000	0	6	1	0	13	12	9	10	0	7.62
1	Bobby Shantz	L	36	1	1	.500	0	3	3	1	21	15	5	14	0	1.29
2	George Witt	R	28	0	2	.000	0	8	2	0	15	20	9	10	0	7.20
2	John Anderson	R	29	0	0	.000	0	10	0	0	18	26	3	6	0	5.00
	Al Cicotte	R	32	0	0	.000	0	5	0	0	5	8	1	4	0	3.60

CHICAGO 9th 59-103 .364 42.5 — EL TAPPE 4-16 .200 LOU KLEIN 12-18 .400 CHARLIE METRO 43-69 .384

	NAME	G by POS	B	AGE	G	AB	R	H	2B	3B	HR	RBI	BB	SO	SB	BA	SA
	TOTALS			25	162	5534	632	1398	196	56	126	600	504	**1044**	78	.253	.377
	Ernie Banks	1B149, 3B3	R	31	154	610	87	164	20	6	37	104	30	71	5	.269	.503
	Ken Hubbs	2B159	R	20	160	661	90	172	24	9	5	49	35	**129**	3	.260	.346
	Andre Rodgers	SS133, 1B1	R	27	138	461	40	128	20	8	5	44	44	93	5	.278	.388
	Ron Santo	3B157, SS8	R	22	162	604	44	137	20	4	17	83	65	94	4	.227	.358
	George Altman	OF129, 1B16	L	29	147	534	74	170	27	5	22	74	62	89	19	.318	.511
	Lou Brock	OF106	L	23	123	434	73	114	24	7	9	35	35	96	16	.263	.412
	Billy Williams	OF159	L	24	159	618	94	184	22	8	22	91	70	72	9	.298	.466
	Dick Bertell	C76	R	26	77	215	19	65	6	2	2	18	13	30	0	.302	.377
	Bob Will	OF9	L	30	87	92	6	22	3	0	2	15	13	22	0	.239	.337
2	Don Landrum	OF55	L	26	83	238	29	67	5	2	1	15	30	31	9	.282	.332
	Moe Thacker	C65	R	28	65	107	8	20	5	0	0	9	14	40	0	.187	.234
	Jim McKnight	3B9, OF5, 2B2	R	26	60	85	6	19	0	1	0	5	2	13	0	.224	.247
	Cuno Barragan	C55	R	30	58	134	11	27	6	1	0	12	21	28	0	.201	.261
	El Tappe	C26	R	35	26	53	3	11	0	0	0	6	4	3	0	.208	.208
2	Alex Grammas	SS13, 2B3, 3B1	R	35	23	60	3	14	3	0	0	3	2	7	1	.233	.283
	Elder White	SS15, 2B1	R	27	23	53	4	8	2	0	0	1	8	11	3	.151	.189
	Nelson Mathews	OF14	R	20	15	49	5	15	2	0	2	13	5	4	3	.306	.469
	Danny Murphy	OF9	L	19	14	35	5	7	3	1	0	3	2	9	0	.200	.343
	Billy Ott	OF7	B	21	12	28	3	4	0	0	1	2	2	10	0	.143	.250

Moe Morhardt 25 L 2-16, 2 Bobby Gene Smith 28 R 5-29, Daryl Robertson 26 R 2-19, 1 Sammy Taylor 29 L 2-15, Jim McAnany 25 R 0-6

	NAME	T	AGE	W	L	PCT	SV	G	GS	CG	IP	H	BB	SO	ShO	ERA
			28	59	103	.364	26	162	162	29	1438	1509	**601**	783	4	4.54
2	Bob Buhl	R	33	12	13	.480	0	34	30	8	212	204	94	109	1	3.69
	Cal Koonce	R	21	10	10	.500	0	35	30	3	191	200	86	84	1	3.96
	Dick Ellsworth	L	22	9	20	.310	1	37	33	6	209	241	77	113	0	5.08
	Don Cardwell	R	26	7	16	.304	4	41	29	6	196	205	60	104	1	4.91
	Barney Schultz	R	35	5	5	.500	5	51	0	0	78	66	23	58	0	3.81
	Glen Hobbie	R	26	5	14	.263	0	42	23	5	162	198	62	87	0	5.22
	Don Elston	R	33	4	8	.333	8	57	0	0	66	57	32	37	0	2.45
2	Paul Toth	R	27	3	1	.750	0	6	4	1	34	29	10	11	0	4.24
	Jug Gerard	R	25	2	3	.400	3	39	0	0	59	67	28	30	0	4.88
	Bob Anderson	R	26	2	7	.222	4	57	4	0	108	111	60	82	0	5.00
	Al Lary	R	32	0	1	.000	0	15	3	0	34	42	15	18	0	7.15
	Tony Balsamo	R	24	0	1	.000	0	18	0	0	29	34	20	27	0	6.52
	Morrie Steevens	L	21	0	1	.000	0	12	1	0	15	10	11	5	0	2.40
	Jim Brewer	L	24	0	1	.000	0	6	1	0	6	10	3	1	0	9.00
1	Jack Curtis	L	25	0	2	.000	0	4	3	0	18	18	6	8	0	3.50
	Freddie Burdette	R	25	0	0	.000	1	8	0	0	10	5	8	5	0	3.60
	Jack Warner	R	21	0	0	.000	0	7	0	0	7	9	0	3	0	7.71
	George Gerberman	R	20	0	0	.000	0	1	1	0	5	3	5	1	0	1.80
	Don Prince	R	24	0	0	.000	0	1	0	0	1	0	1	0	0	0.00

NEW YORK 10th 40-120 .250 60.5 — CASEY STENGEL

	NAME	G by POS	B	AGE	G	AB	R	H	2B	3B	HR	RBI	BB	SO	SB	BA	SA
	TOTALS			30	161	5492	617	1318	166	40	139	573	**616**	991	59	.240	.361
2	Marv Throneberry	1B97	L	28	116	357	29	87	11	3	16	49	34	83	1	.244	.426
	Charlie Neal	2B85, SS39, 3B12	R	31	136	508	59	132	14	9	11	58	56	90	2	.260	.388
	Elio Chacon	SS110, 2B2, 3B1	R	25	118	368	49	87	10	3	2	27	76	64	12	.236	.296
	Felix Mantilla	3B95, SS25, 2B14	R	27	141	466	54	128	17	4	11	59	37	51	3	.275	.399
	Richie Ashburn	OF97, 2B2	L	35	135	389	60	119	7	3	7	28	81	39	12	.306	.393
	Jim Hickman	OF124	R	25	140	392	54	96	18	2	13	46	47	96	4	.245	.401
	Frank Thomas	OF126, 1B11, 3B10	R	33	156	571	69	152	23	3	34	94	48	95	2	.266	.496
	Chris Cannizzaro	C56, OF1	R	24	59	133	9	32	2	1	0	9	19	26	1	.241	.271
	Rod Kanehl	2B62, 3B30, OF20, 1B3, SS2	R	28	133	351	52	87	10	2	4	27	23	36	8	.248	.322
	Joe Christopher	OF94	R	26	119	271	36	66	10	2	6	32	35	42	11	.244	.362
2	Gene Woodling	OF48	L	39	81	190	18	52	8	1	5	24	24	22	0	.274	.405
2	Sammy Taylor (BG)	C50	L	29	68	158	12	35	4	2	3	20	23	17	0	.222	.329
	Choo Choo Coleman	C44	L	24	55	152	24	38	7	2	6	17	11	24	2	.250	.441
	Gil Hodges	1B47	R	38	54	127	15	32	1	0	9	17	15	27	0	.252	.472
	Ed Bouchee	1B19	L	29	50	87	7	14	2	0	3	10	18	17	0	.161	.287
2	Cliff Cook	3B16, OF10	R	25	40	112	12	26	6	1	2	9	4	34	1	.232	.357
	Rick Herrscher	1B10, 3B6, OF4, SS3	R	25	35	50	5	11	3	0	1	6	5	11	0	.220	.340
1	Gus Bell	OF26	L	33	30	101	8	15	2	0	1	6	10	7	0	.149	.198
2	Joe Pignatano	C25	R	32	27	56	2	13	2	0	0	2	2	11	0	.232	.268
	Sammy Drake	2B10, 3B6	B	27	25	52	2	10	0	0	0	7	6	12	0	.192	.192
1	Hobie Landrith	C21	L	32	23	45	6	13	3	0	1	7	8	3	0	.289	.422
1	Jim Marshall	1B5, OF1	L	30	17	32	6	11	1	0	3	4	3	6	0	.344	.656

Harry Chiti 29 R 8-41, John DeMerit 26 R 3-16, 1 Don Zimmer 31 R 4-52, 1 Bobby Gene Smith 28 R 3-22, Ed Kranepool 17 L 1-6, Joe Ginsberg 35 L 0-5

	NAME	T	AGE	W	L	PCT	SV	G	GS	CG	IP	H	BB	SO	ShO	ERA
			27	40	**120**	.250	10	161	161	43	1430	**1577**	571	772	4	5.04
	Roger Craig	R	31	10	**24**	.294	3	42	33	13	233	261	70	118	0	4.52
	Jay Hook	R	25	8	19	.296	0	37	34	13	214	230	71	113	0	4.84
	Al Jackson	L	26	8	20	.286	0	36	33	12	231	244	78	118	4	4.40
	Ken MacKenzie	L	28	5	4	.556	1	42	1	0	80	87	34	51	0	4.95
	Craig Anderson	R	24	3	17	.150	4	50	14	2	131	150	63	62	0	5.36
2	Bob Miller	L	26	2	2	.500	1	17	0	0	20	24	8	8	0	7.20
2	Galen Cisco	R	26	1	1	.500	0	4	2	1	19	15	11	13	0	3.32
	Ray Daviault	R	28	1	5	.167	0	36	3	0	81	92	48	51	0	6.22
2	Willard Hunter	L	28	1	6	.143	0	27	6	1	63	67	34	40	0	5.57
	Bob Miller	R	23	1	12	.077	0	33	21	1	144	146	62	91	0	4.88
	Herb Moford	R	33	0	1	.000	0	7	0	0	15	21	1	5	0	7.20
	Larry Foss	R	26	0	1	.000	0	5	1	0	12	17	7	3	0	4.50
	Bob Moorhead	R	24	0	2	.000	0	38	7	0	105	118	42	63	0	4.54
2	Vinegar Bend Mizell	L	31	0	2	.000	0	17	2	0	38	48	25	15	0	7.34
	Sherman Jones	R	27	0	4	.000	0	8	3	0	23	31	8	11	0	7.83
	Dave Hillman	R	34	0	0	.000	1	13	1	0	16	21	8	8	0	6.19
	Clem Labine	R	35	0	0	.000	0	3	0	0	4	5	1	2	0	11.25

1963 Shutting Out the Ghost of Autumns Past

The year of 1963 included the expansion of the batter's strike zone, 43-year-old Early Wynn finally winning his 300th lifetime game, and the Mets' Roger Craig losing 18 games in a row. More important, though, was the coming of baseball's finest southpaw since Lefty Grove. Putting the talent and experience of nine major league campaigns together, the Dodgers' Sandy Koufax became the premier pitcher and gate attraction of the game. By using a dazzling fastball and a curve graceful enough to rival a prima ballerina, Koufax struck his way to 25 victories, a 1.88 E.R.A., and both the MVP and Cy Young Awards.

Koufax's performance was further intensified by his recovery from the 1962 finger ailment which had placed his career in doubt. While pitching the Dodgers steadily along the pennant road with the aid of Don Drysdale, a 19-game winner, and Ron Perranoski, the brilliant relief specialist who saved 21 games while winning 16 with a 1.67 E.R.A., the only real offensive help came from Tommy Davis, Frank Howard, and Maury Wills. Davis again won the batting title, while Howard provided the sole long-ball threat. Wills, although a good distance off from his 1962 stolen base mark, managed enough thefts and a .302 batting average to hamper the opposition.

Yet, before the Dodgers could claim the National League flag, they had to contend with the likes of Bill White, Dick Groat, Ken Boyer, and Stan Musial, the kingpins of the St. Louis Cardinals. Bouncing back from an eight-game losing streak right before the All-Star break, the Cards burned up the league in early September, winning 19 of 20 games to pull within one game of the Dodgers on September 16, when both clubs squared off for a three-game series at St. Louis.

Lefty Johnny Podres cooled off the Cards with a three hitter for a 3-1 Dodger win in the first game. Then Koufax took the stage and shut out the Cards on four hits for a 4-0 second-game triumph. In the final match, St. Louis led 5-1 after seven innings, but a tiring Bob Gibson gave up three runs in the eighth and a home run to rookie Dick Nen in the ninth to send the game into extra innings. The Dodgers finally won 6-5 in 13 innings, sweeping the series and avoiding the embarrassment of a second straight late-season fold-up. The triple loss ended the Cards' dream of giving Stan Musial a World Series in his final year in uniform.

The Giants' strong bats kept them in the race until late August, but their pitching staff, weak outside of Juan Marichal, sabotaged any pennant hopes. The surprising Phillies came on strong at the end to capture fourth place, while the disappointing Reds finished fifth despite a fine rookie season by Pete Rose. At the bottom of the heap was the New York Mets, a horrendous team which drew 1,000,000 enthusiastic fans into the Polo Grounds. Managed by double-talking Casey Stengel, the Mets showcased fading stars like Duke Snider and Jimmy Piersall, and supported ace pitcher Roger Craig so sparingly that he lost 18 games in a row before he switched his uniform number to 13 and promptly won his first game in three months.

Despite serious injuries to Mickey Mantle and Roger Maris, the Yankees still managed the power to support a good pitching staff and win the American League flag by 10½ games over the Chicago White Sox. Mantle fractured his foot and then hurt his knee, and a bad back plagued Maris during the campaign, with the two sluggers appearing together in the starting lineup only 30 times all year. Manager Ralph Houk used Johnny Blanchard and Hector Lopez to take up the slack, and the duo responded with 30 combined home runs. While Joe Pepitone won the first base job in the spring and proceeded to confirm Houk's choice by belting 27 home runs, backstop Elston Howard won the MVP Award with a .287 performance spiced by 28 circuit blasts. The sound Yankee infield of Pepitone, Bobby Richardson, Tony Kubek, and Clete Boyer stayed healthy and supported the pitchers with air-tight defense. Veteran Whitey Ford paced the hurlers with 24 victories, surprising sophomore Jim Bouton won 21 games, and Ralph Terry captured 17 wins. Al Downing, recalled in June, also helped to bolster the starting staff.

The Yankees' team batting effort was underscored by the absence of any pinstriper from the league leaders, as Boston's Carl Yastrzemski and Dick Stuart, respectively, won the batting and RBI titles, and the Twins' Harmon Killebrew the home run crown. Yankee pitching ace Ford did lead the league in wins and winning percentage, and Chicago's Gary Peters, a failure in three previous big league trials, pleasantly surprised the White Sox by posting a league-low 2.33 E.R.A.

When the World Series dawned, it marked the sixth time the Yankees and Dodgers were getting together. In all but one previous attempt, the Dodgers had come up second best. Only the presence of Koufax, and the fact that the rematch was now a transcontinental affair, gave the Dodger rooters any hope that the jinx would finally be broken.

Game one in New York saw Koufax blow the Yankees apart with a record 15 strikeouts as ex-Yankee Moose Skowron made up for his poor season in the National League by driving in two runs. Johnny Podres continued the silencing of Bronx bats in the next game with a 4-1 victory finished by Perranoski and marked by a Skowron home run. Drysdale faced Bouton in a magnificent pitchers' battle in the opening of the Series in Los Angeles and came up on top of a 1-0 score. With their backs to the wall, the Yankees again faced Koufax in the fourth game and came up with two hits and a Pepitone error to lose 2-1.

It was all over, and the fans rejoiced in Brooklyn as well as Los Angeles. After the fanfare subsided, the Yankees promoted Houk to general manager and Yogi Berra to field boss, a move that would register its repercussions soon after one melodic tune would be played on a harmonica.

WORLD SERIES – LOS ANGELES (NL) 4 NEW YORK (AL) 0

LINE SCORES

TEAM	1	2	3	4	5	6	7	8	9	10	11	12	R	H	E
Game 1 October 2 at New York															
LA (NL)	0	4	1	0	0	0	0	0	0				5	9	0
NY (AL)	0	0	0	0	0	0	0	2	0				2	6	0
Koufax	**Ford**, Williams (6), Hamilton (9)														
Game 2 October 3 at New York															
LA	2	0	0	1	0	0	0	1	0				4	10	1
NY	0	0	0	0	0	0	0	0	1				1	7	0
Podres, Perranoski (9)	**Downing**, Terry (6), Reniff (9)														
Game 3 October 5 at Los Angeles															
NY	0	0	0	0	0	0	0	0	0				0	3	0
LA	1	0	0	0	0	0	0	0	X				1	4	1
Bouton, Reniff (8)	**Drysdale**														
Game 4 October 6 at Los Angeles															
NY	0	0	0	0	0	0	1	0	0				1	6	1
LA	0	0	0	0	1	0	1	0	X				2	2	1
Ford, Reniff (8)	**Koufax**														

COMPOSITE BATTING

NAME	POS	G	AB	R	H	2B	3B	HR	RBI	BA
Los Angeles (NL)										
Totals		4	117	12	25	3	2	3	12	.214
T. Davis	OF	4	15	0	**6**	0	**2**	0	2	**.400**
Wills	SS	4	15	1	2	0	0	0	0	.133
Roseboro	C	4	14	1	2	0	0	1	**3**	.143
Skowron	1B	4	13	2	5	0	0	1	**3**	.385
Gilliam	3B	4	13	**3**	2	0	0	0	0	.154
Tracewski	2B	4	13	1	2	0	0	0	0	.154
W. Davis	OF	4	12	2	2	**2**	0	0	**3**	.167
F. Howard	OF	3	10	2	3	1	0	1	1	.300
Koufax	P	2	6	0	0	0	0	0	0	.000
Podres	P	1	4	0	1	0	0	0	0	.250
Fairly	OF	4	1	0	0	0	0	0	0	.000
Drysdale	P	1	1	0	0	0	0	0	0	.000
Perranoski	P	1	0	0	0	0	0	0	0	.000
New York (AL)										
Totals		4	129	4	22	3	0	2	4	.171
Kubek	SS	4	**16**	1	3	0	0	0	0	.188
E. Howard	C	4	15	0	5	0	0	0	1	.333
Tresh	OF	4	15	1	3	0	0	1	2	.200
Mantle	OF	4	15	1	2	0	0	1	1	.133
Richardson	2B	4	14	0	3	1	0	0	0	.214
Pepitone	1B	4	13	0	2	0	0	0	0	.154
Boyer	3B	4	13	0	1	0	0	0	0	.077
Lopez	OF	3	8	1	2	**2**	0	0	0	.250
Maris	OF	2	5	0	0	0	0	0	0	.000
Linz	PH	3	3	0	1	0	0	0	0	.333
Ford	P	2	3	0	0	0	0	0	0	.000
Blanchard	OF	1	3	0	0	0	0	0	0	.000
Bright	PH	2	2	0	0	0	0	0	0	.000
Bouton	P	1	2	0	0	0	0	0	0	.000
Downing	P	1	1	0	0	0	0	0	0	.000
Berra	PH	1	1	0	0	0	0	0	0	.000
Reniff	P	3	0	0	0	0	0	0	0	.000
Williams	P	1	0	0	0	0	0	0	0	.000
Hamilton	P	1	0	0	0	0	0	0	0	.000
Terry	P	1	0	0	0	0	0	0	0	.000

COMPOSITE PITCHING

NAME	G	IP	H	BB	SO	W	L	SV	ERA
Los Angeles (NL)									
Totals	4	36	22	5	37	4	0	1	1.00
Koufax	2	**18**	**12**	3	**23**	**2**	0	0	1.50
Drysdale	1	9	3	1	9	1	0	0	**0.00**
Podres	1	8.1	6	1	4	1	0	0	1.08
Perranoski	1	.2	1	0	1	0	0	1	0.00
New York (AL)									
Totals	4	34	25	11	25	0	4	0	2.91
Ford	2	12	10	3	8	0	**2**	0	4.50
Bouton	1	7	4	**5**	4	0	1	0	1.29
Downing	1	5	7	1	6	0	1	0	5.40
Williams	1	3	1	0	5	0	0	0	0.00
Reniff	**3**	3	0	1	1	0	0	0	0.00
Terry	1	3	3	1	0	0	0	0	3.00
Hamilton	1	1	0	0	1	0	0	0	0.00

NAME	G by POS	B	AGE	G	AB	R	H	2B	3B	HR	RBI	BB	SO	SB	BA	SA
NEW YORK 1st 104-57 .646	RALPH HOUK															
TOTALS			28	161	5506	714	1387	197	35	188	666	434	808	42	.252	.403
Joe Pepitone	1B143, OF16	L	22	157	580	79	157	16	3	27	89	23	63	3	.271	.448
Bobby Richardson	2B150	R	27	151	630	72	167	20	6	3	48	25	22	15	.265	.330
Tony Kubek	SS132, OF1	L	26	135	557	72	143	21	3	7	44	28	68	4	.257	.343
Clete Boyer	3B141, SS9, 2B1	R	26	152	557	59	140	20	3	12	54	33	91	4	.251	.363
Roger Maris	OF86	L	28	90	312	53	84	14	1	23	53	35	40	1	.269	.542
Tom Tresh	OF144	B	25	145	520	91	140	28	5	25	71	83	79	3	.269	.487
Hector Lopez	OF124, 2B1	R	30	130	433	54	108	13	4	14	52	35	71	1	.249	.395
Elston Howard	C132	R	34	135	487	75	140	21	6	28	85	35	68	0	.287	.528
Jack Reed	OF89	R	30	106	73	18	15	3	1	0	1	9	14	5	.205	.274
Johnny Blanchard	OF64	L	30	76	218	22	49	4	0	16	45	26	30	0	.225	.463
Phil Linz	SS22, 3B13, OF12, 2B6	R	24	72	186	22	50	9	0	2	12	15	18	1	.269	.349
Mickey Mantle (BF)	OF52	B	31	65	172	40	54	8	0	15	35	40	32	2	.314	.622
Yogi Berra	C35	L	38	64	147	20	43	6	0	8	28	15	17	1	.293	.497
2 Harry Bright	1B35, 3B12	R	33	60	157	15	37	7	0	7	23	13	31	0	.236	.414
Pedro Gonzalez	2B7	R	24	14	26	3	5	1	0	0	1	0	5	0	.192	.231
Dale Long	1B2	L	37	14	15	1	3	0	0	0	0	1	3	0	.200	.200
Jake Gibbs	C1	L	24	4	8	1	2	0	0	0	0	0	1	0	.250	.250
CHICAGO 2nd 94-68 .580 10.5	AL LOPEZ															
TOTALS			26	162	5508	683	1379	208	40	114	648	571	896	64	.250	.365
Tommy McCraw	1B97	L	22	102	280	38	71	11	3	6	33	21	46	15	.254	.379
Nellie Fox	2B134	L	35	137	539	54	140	19	0	2	42	24	17	0	.260	.306
Ron Hansen	SS144	R	25	144	482	55	109	17	2	13	67	78	74	1	.226	.351
Pete Ward	3B154, 2B1, SS1	L	23	157	600	80	177	34	6	22	84	52	77	7	.295	.482
Floyd Robinson	OF137	L	27	146	527	71	149	21	6	13	71	62	43	4	.283	.419
Jim Landis	OF124	R	29	133	396	56	89	6	6	13	45	47	75	8	.225	.369
Dave Nicholson	OF123	R	23	126	449	53	103	11	4	22	70	63	175	2	.229	.419
J. C. Martin	C98, 1B3, 3B1	L	26	105	259	25	53	11	1	5	28	26	35	0	.205	.313
Mike Hershberger	OF119	R	23	135	476	64	133	26	2	3	45	39	39	9	.279	.361
Cam Carreon	C92	R	25	101	270	28	74	10	1	2	35	23	32	1	.274	.341
Al Weis	2B48, SS27, 3B1	B	25	99	210	41	57	9	0	0	18	18	37	15	.271	.314
Charlie Maxwell	OF24, 1B17	L	36	71	130	17	30	4	2	3	17	31	27	0	.231	.362
Joe Cunningham (BC)	1B58	L	31	67	210	32	60	12	1	1	31	33	23	1	.286	.367
3 Jim Lemon	1B25	R	35	36	80	4	16	0	1	1	8	12	32	0	.200	.263
Sherm Lollar	C23, 1B2	R	38	35	73	4	17	4	0	0	6	8	7	0	.233	.288
Deacon Jones	1B1	L	29	17	16	4	3	0	1	1	2	2	2	0	.188	.500
Don Buford	3B9, 2B2	R	26	12	42	9	12	1	2	0	5	5	7	1	.286	.405
Gene Stephens	OF5	L	30	6	18	5	7	0	0	1	2	1	3	0	.389	.556
Ken Berry	OF2, 2B1	R	22	4	5	2	1	0	0	0	0	1	1	0	.200	.200
Charley Smith	SS1	R	25	4	7	0	2	0	1	0	1	0	2	0	.286	.571
Brian McCall 20 L 0-7, 1 Sammy Esposito 31 R 0-0																
MINNESOTA 3rd 91-70 .565 13	SAM MELE															
TOTALS			27	161	5531	767	1408	223	35	225	722	547	912	32	.255	.430
Vic Power	1B124, 2B18, 3B5	R	31	138	541	65	146	28	2	10	52	22	24	3	.270	.384
Bernie Allen	2B128	L	24	139	421	52	101	20	1	9	43	38	52	0	.240	.356
Zoilo Versalles	SS159	R	23	159	621	74	162	31	13	10	54	33	66	7	.261	.401
Rich Rollins	3B132, 2B1	R	25	136	531	75	163	23	1	16	61	36	59	2	.307	.444
Bob Allison	OF147	R	28	148	527	99	143	25	4	35	91	90	109	6	.271	.533
Jimmie Hall	OF143	L	25	156	497	88	129	21	5	33	80	63	101	3	.260	.521
Harmon Killebrew	OF137	R	27	142	515	88	133	18	0	45	96	72	105	0	.258	.555
Earl Battey	C146	R	28	147	508	64	145	17	1	26	84	61	75	0	.285	.476
Lenny Green	OF119	L	29	145	280	41	67	10	1	4	27	31	21	11	.239	.325
Don Mincher	1B60	L	25	82	225	41	58	8	0	17	42	30	51	0	.258	.520
Johnny Goryl	2B34, 3B11, SS7	R	29	64	150	29	43	5	3	9	24	15	29	0	.287	.540
Jerry Zimmerman	C39	R	28	39	56	3	13	1	0	0	3	2	8	0	.232	.250
2 Vic Wertz	1B6	L	38	35	44	3	6	0	0	3	7	6	5	0	.136	.341
George Banks	3B21	R	24	25	71	5	11	4	0	3	8	9	21	0	.155	.338
2 Wally Post	OF12	R	33	21	47	6	9	0	1	2	6	2	17	0	.191	.362
Bill Tuttle	OF14	R	33	16	3	0	0	0	0	0	0	1	0	0	.000	.000
Paul Ratliff	C7	L	19	10	21	2	4	1	0	1	3	2	7	0	.190	.381
Jay Ward	3B4, OF1	R	24	9	15	0	1	1	0	0	2	1	5	0	.067	.133
1 Jim Lemon	OF4	R	35	7	17	0	2	0	0	0	1	1	5	0	.118	.118
Tony Oliva		L	22	7	7	0	3	0	0	0	1	0	2	0	.429	.429
Julio Becquer		L	31	1	1	0	0	0	0	0	0	0	0	0	.000	.000
BALTIMORE 4th 86-76 .531 18.5	BILLY HITCHCOCK															
TOTALS			27	162	5448	644	1359	207	32	146	609	469	940	97	.249	.380
Jim Gentile	1B143	L	29	145	496	65	123	16	1	24	72	76	101	1	.248	.429
Jerry Adair	2B103	R	26	109	382	34	87	21	3	6	30	9	51	3	.228	.346
Luis Aparicio	SS145	R	29	146	601	73	150	18	8	5	45	36	35	40	.250	.331
Brooks Robinson	3B160, SS1	R	26	161	589	67	148	26	4	11	67	46	84	2	.251	.365
Russ Snyder	OF130	L	29	148	429	51	110	21	2	7	36	40	48	18	.256	.364
Jackie Brandt	OF134, 3B1	R	29	142	451	49	112	15	5	15	61	34	85	4	.248	.404
Boog Powell	OF121, 1B23	L	21	140	491	67	130	22	2	25	82	49	87	1	.265	.470
John Orsino	C109, 1B3	R	25	116	379	53	103	18	1	19	56	38	53	2	.272	.475
Al Smith	OF97	R	35	120	368	45	100	17	1	10	39	32	74	9	.272	.405
Bob Saverine	OF59, 2B19, SS13	B	22	115	167	21	39	1	2	1	12	25	44	8	.234	.281
Bob Johnson	2B50, 1B8, SS7, 3B5	R	27	82	254	34	75	10	0	8	32	18	35	5	.295	.429
Joe Gaines	OF39	R	26	66	126	24	36	4	1	6	20	20	39	2	.286	.476
Dick Brown	C58	R	28	59	171	13	42	7	0	2	13	15	35	1	.246	.322
1 Charlie Lau	C8	L	30	29	48	4	9	2	0	0	6	1	5	0	.188	.229
Fred Valentine	OF10	B	28	26	41	5	11	1	0	0	1	8	5	0	.268	.293
Sam Bowens	OF13	R	24	15	48	8	16	3	1	1	9	4	5	1	.333	.500
1 Hobie Landrith	C1	L	33	2	1	0	0	0	0	0	0	0	0	0	.000	.000
CLEVELAND 5th 79-83 .488 25.5	BIRDIE TEBBETTS															
TOTALS			27	162	5496	635	1314	214	29	169	592	469	1102	59	.239	.381
Fred Whitfield	1B92	L	25	109	346	44	87	17	3	21	54	24	61	0	.251	.500
Woodie Held	2B96, OF35, SS5, 3B3	R	31	133	416	61	103	19	4	17	61	61	96	2	.248	.435
Jerry Kindall	SS46, 2B37, 1B4	R	28	86	234	27	48	4	1	5	20	18	71	3	.205	.295
Max Alvis	3B158	R	25	158	602	81	165	32	7	22	67	36	109	9	.274	.460
Willie Kirkland	OF112	L	29	127	427	51	98	13	2	15	47	45	99	8	.230	.375
Vic Davalillo (BW)	OF89	L	26	90	370	44	108	18	5	7	36	16	41	3	.292	.424
Tito Francona	OF122, 1B11	L	29	142	500	57	114	29	0	10	41	47	77	9	.228	.346
2 Joe Azcue	C91	R	23	94	320	26	91	16	0	14	46	15	46	1	.284	.466
Al Luplow	OF85	L	24	100	295	34	69	6	2	7	27	33	62	4	.234	.339
Joe Adcock	1B78	R	35	97	283	28	71	7	1	13	49	30	53	1	.251	.420
Johnny Romano (BG)	C71, OF4	R	28	89	255	28	55	5	2	10	34	38	49	4	.216	.369
Larry Brown	SS46, 2B27	R	23	74	247	28	63	6	0	5	18	22	27	4	.255	.340
Mike de la Hoz	2B34, 3B6, SS2, OF2	R	23	67	150	15	40	10	0	5	25	9	29	0	.267	.433
Willie Tasby	OF37, 2B1	R	30	52	116	11	26	3	1	4	5	15	25	0	.224	.371
2 Dick Howser	SS44	R	26	49	162	25	40	5	0	1	10	22	18	9	.247	.296
Tony Martinez	SS41	R	22	43	141	10	22	4	0	0	8	5	18	1	.156	.184
1 Gene Green	OF18	R	30	43	78	4	16	3	0	2	7	4	22	0	.205	.321
1 Ellis Burton	OF16	B	26	26	31	6	6	3	0	1	1	4	4	0	.194	.387
Bob Chance	OF14	L	22	16	52	5	15	4	0	2	7	1	10	0	.288	.481
Tommie Agee	OF13	R	20	13	27	3	4	1	0	1	3	2	9	0	.148	.296
1 Doc Edwards	C10	R	25	10	31	6	8	2	0	0	0	2	6	0	.258	.323
1 Cal Neeman	C9	R	34	9	9	0	0	0	0	0	0	1	5	0	.000	.000
3 Sammy Taylor	C2	L	30	4	10	1	3	0	0	0	1	0	2	0	.300	.300
Jim Lawrence	C2	L	24	2	0	0	0	0	0	0	0	0	0	0	.000	.000
Bob Lipski	C2	L	24	2	1	0	0	0	0	0	0	0	1	0	.000	.000

NAME	T	AGE	W	L	PCT	SV	G	GS	CG	IP	H	BB	SO	ShO	ERA
NEW YORK		27	104	57	.646	31	161	161	59	1449	1239	476	965	19	3.07
Whitey Ford	L	34	24	7	.774	1	38	37	13	269	240	56	189	3	2.74
Jim Bouton	R	24	21	7	.750	1	40	30	12	249	191	87	148	6	2.53
Ralph Terry	R	27	17	15	.531	1	40	37	18	268	246	39	114	3	3.22
Al Downing	L	22	13	5	.722	0	24	22	10	176	114	80	171	4	2.56
Stan Williams	R	26	9	8	.529	0	29	21	6	146	137	57	98	1	3.21
2 Steve Hamilton	L	29	5	1	.833	5	34	0	0	62	49	24	63	0	2.60
Hal Reniff	R	24	4	3	.571	18	48	0	0	89	63	42	56	0	2.63
Bill Stafford	R	23	4	8	.333	3	28	14	0	90	104	42	52	0	6.00
Bill Kunkel	R	26	3	2	.600	0	22	0	0	46	42	13	31	0	2.74
Marshall Bridges	L	32	2	0	1.000	1	23	0	0	33	27	30	35	0	3.82
Tom Metcalf	R	22	1	0	1.000	0	8	0	0	13	12	3	3	0	2.77
Luis Arroyo	L	36	1	1	.500	0	6	0	0	6	12	3	5	0	13.50
Bud Daley (SA)	L	30	0	0	.000	1	1	0	0	1	2	0	0	0	0.00
CHICAGO		29	94	68	.580	39	162	162	49	1469	1311	440	932	21	2.97
Gary Peters	L	26	19	8	.704	1	41	30	13	243	192	68	189	4	2.33
Juan Pizarro	L	26	16	8	.667	1	32	28	10	215	177	63	163	3	2.39
Ray Herbert	R	33	13	10	.565	0	33	33	14	225	230	35	105	7	3.24
Joe Horlen	R	25	11	7	.611	0	33	21	3	124	122	55	61	0	3.27
John Buzhardt (SA)	R	26	9	4	.692	0	19	18	6	126	100	31	59	3	2.43
Eddie Fisher	R	26	9	8	.529	0	33	15	2	121	114	28	67	1	3.94
Hoyt Wilhelm	R	39	5	8	.385	21	55	3	0	136	106	30	111	0	2.65
Dave DeBusschere	R	22	3	4	.429	0	24	10	1	84	80	34	53	1	3.11
2 Jim Brosnan	R	33	3	8	.273	14	45	0	0	73	71	22	46	0	2.84
Frank Baumann (AJ)	L	30	2	1	.667	1	24	1	0	50	52	17	31	0	3.06
Bruce Howard	R	20	2	1	.667	1	7	0	0	17	12	14	9	0	2.65
Fritz Ackley	R	26	1	0	1.000	0	2	2	0	13	7	7	11	0	2.08
Frank Kreutzer	L	24	1	0	1.000	0	1	1	0	5	3	1	0	0	1.80
Joe Shipley	R	28	0	1	.000	0	3	0	0	5	9	6	3	0	5.40
Taylor Phillips	L	30	0	0	.000	0	9	0	0	14	16	13	13	0	10.29
Mike Joyce	R	22	0	0	.000	0	6	0	0	11	13	8	7	0	8.18
1 Dom Zanni	R	31	0	0	.000	0	5	0	0	4	5	4	2	0	9.00
Fred Talbot	R	22	0	0	.000	0	1	0	0	3	2	4	2	0	3.00
MINNESOTA		27	91	70	.565	30	161	161	58	1446	1322	459	941	13	3.28
Camilo Pasqual	R	29	21	9	.700	0	31	31	18	248	205	81	202	3	2.47
Dick Stigman	L	27	15	15	.500	0	33	33	15	241	210	81	193	3	3.25
Lee Stange	R	26	12	5	.706	0	32	20	7	165	145	43	100	2	2.62
Jim Kaat	L	24	10	10	.500	1	31	27	7	178	195	38	105	1	4.20
2 Jim Perry	R	27	9	9	.500	1	35	25	5	168	167	57	65	1	3.74
Bill Pleis	L	25	6	2	.750	0	36	4	1	68	67	16	37	0	4.37
Bill Dailey	R	28	6	3	.667	21	66	0	0	109	80	19	72	0	1.98
Jim Roland	L	20	4	1	.800	0	10	7	2	49	32	27	34	1	2.57
Dwight Siebler	R	25	2	1	.667	0	7	5	2	39	25	12	22	0	2.77
Garry Roggenburk	L	23	2	4	.333	4	36	2	0	50	47	22	24	0	2.16
2 Mike Fornieles	R	31	1	1	.500	0	11	0	0	23	24	13	7	0	4.76
Jerry Arrigo	L	22	1	2	.333	0	5	1	0	16	12	4	13	0	2.81
Ray Moore	R	37	1	3	.250	2	31	1	0	39	50	17	38	0	6.92
1 Jack Kralick	R	28	1	4	.200	0	5	5	1	26	28	8	13	1	3.86
Frank Sullivan	R	33	0	1	.000	1	10	0	0	11	15	4	2	0	5.73
Fred Lasher	R	21	0	0	.000	0	11	0	0	11	12	11	10	0	4.91
Don Williams	R	27	0	0	.000	0	3	0	0	4	8	6	2	0	11.25
Gary Dotter	L	20	0	0	.000	0	2	0	0	2	0	0	2	0	0.00
BALTIMORE		28	86	76	.531	43	162	162	35	1452	1353	507	913	8	3.45
Steve Barber	L	24	20	13	.606	0	39	36	11	259	253	92	180	2	2.75
Milt Pappas	R	24	16	9	.640	0	34	32	11	217	186	69	120	4	3.03
Robin Roberts	R	36	14	13	.519	0	35	35	9	251	230	40	124	2	3.33
Wes Stock	R	29	7	0	1.000	1	47	0	0	75	69	31	55	0	3.96
Dave McNally	L	20	7	8	.467	1	29	20	2	126	133	55	78	0	4.57
Mike McCormick	L	24	6	8	.429	0	25	21	2	136	132	66	75	0	4.30
Dick Hall	R	32	5	5	.500	12	47	3	0	112	91	16	74	0	2.97
Stu Miller	R	35	5	8	.385	27	71	0	0	112	93	53	114	0	2.25
Chuck Estrada (EJ)	R	25	3	2	.600	0	8	7	0	31	26	19	16	0	4.65
John Miller	R	22	1	1	.500	0	3	2	0	17	12	14	16	0	3.18
Dean Stone	L	32	1	2	.333	1	17	0	0	19	23	10	12	0	5.21
2 Ike Delock	R	33	1	3	.250	0	7	5	0	30	25	16	11	0	5.04
Herm Starrette	R	24	0	1	.000	0	18	0	0	26	26	7	13	0	3.46
2 George Brunet	L	28	0	1	.000	1	16	0	0	20	25	9	13	0	5.40
2 Pete Burnside	L	32	0	1	.000	0	6	0	0	7	11	2	6	0	4.91
Wally Bunker	R	18	0	1	.000	0	1	1	0	4	10	3	1	0	13.50
Buster Narum	R	22	0	0	.000	0	7	0	0	9	8	5	5	0	3.00
CLEVELAND		29	79	83	.488	25	162	162	40	1469	1390	478	1018	14	3.79
2 Jack Kralick	L	28	13	9	.591	0	28	27	10	197	187	41	116	3	2.92
Mudcat Grant	R	27	13	14	.481	1	38	32	10	229	213	87	157	2	3.69
Dick Donovan	R	35	11	13	.458	0	30	30	7	206	211	28	84	3	4.24
Pedro Ramos	R	28	9	8	.529	0	36	22	5	185	156	41	169	0	3.11
Gary Bell	R	26	8	5	.615	5	58	7	0	119	91	52	98	0	2.95
Ted Abernathy	R	30	7	2	.778	12	43	0	0	59	54	29	47	0	2.90
Barry Latman	R	27	7	12	.368	2	38	21	4	149	146	52	133	2	4.95
Jerry Walker	R	24	6	6	.500	1	39	2	0	88	92	36	41	0	4.91
Sam McDowell	L	20	3	5	.375	0	14	12	3	65	63	44	63	1	4.85
Bob Allen	L	25	1	2	.333	2	43	0	0	56	58	29	51	0	4.66
Early Wynn	R	43	1	2	.333	1	20	5	1	55	50	15	29	0	2.29
Gordon Seyfried	R	25	0	1	.000	0	3	1	0	7	9	3	1	0	1.29
Ron Nischwitz	L	26	0	2	.000	1	14	0	0	17	17	8	10	0	6.35
Tommy John	L	20	0	2	.000	0	6	3	0	20	23	6	9	0	2.25
1 Jim Perry	R	27	0	0	.000	0	5	0	0	10	12	2	7	0	5.23
Jack Curtis	L	26	0	0	.000	0	4	0	0	5	8	5	3	0	18.00

DETROIT 5th 79-83 .488 25.5 — BOB SCHEFFING 24-36 .400 CHUCK DRESSEN 55-47 .539

NAME	G by POS	B	AGE	G	AB	R	H	2B	3B	HR	RBI	BB	SO	SB	BA	SA
TOTALS			28	162	5500	700	1388	195	36	148	649	**592**	908	73	.252	.382
Norm Cash	1B142	L	28	147	493	67	133	19	1	26	79	89	76	2	.270	.471
Jake Wood (RJ)	2B81, 3B1	R	26	85	351	50	95	11	2	11	27	24	61	18	.271	.407
Dick McAuliffe	SS133, 2B15	L	23	150	568	77	149	18	6	13	61	64	75	11	.262	.384
Bubba Phillips	3B117, OF5	R	33	128	464	42	114	11	2	5	45	19	42	6	.246	.310
Al Kaline	OF140	R	28	145	551	89	172	24	3	27	101	54	48	6	.312	.514
Bill Bruton	OF138	L	37	145	524	84	134	21	8	8	48	59	70	14	.256	.372
Rocky Colavito	OF159	R	29	160	597	91	162	29	2	22	91	84	78	0	.271	.437
Gus Triandos	C90	R	32	106	327	28	78	13	0	14	41	32	67	0	.239	.407
Bill Freehan	C73, 1B19	R	21	100	300	37	73	12	2	9	36	39	56	2	.243	.387
Don Wert	3B47, 2B21, SS8	R	24	78	251	31	65	6	2	7	25	24	51	3	.259	.382
Gates Brown	OF16	L	24	55	82	16	22	3	1	2	14	8	13	2	.268	.402
George Smith	2B52	R	24	52	171	16	37	8	2	0	17	18	34	4	.216	.287
Whitey Herzog	1B7, OF4	L	31	52	53	5	8	2	1	0	7	11	17	0	.151	.226
2 George Thomas	OF40, 2B1	R	25	49	109	13	26	4	1	1	11	11	22	2	.239	.321
1 Frank Kostro	3B6, 1B3, OF3	R	25	31	52	4	12	1	0	0	0	9	13	0	.231	.250
Mike Roarke	C16	R	32	23	44	5	14	0	0	0	1	2	3	0	.318	.318
1 Chico Fernandez	SS14	R	31	15	49	3	7	1	0	0	2	6	11	0	.143	.163
Willie Horton	OF9	R	20	15	43	6	14	2	1	1	4	0	8	2	.326	.488
Coot Veal	SS12	R	30	15	32	5	7	0	0	0	4	4	4	0	.219	.219
Purnal Goldy		R	25	9	8	1	2	0	0	0	0	0	4	0	.250	.250

1 Bubba Morton 31 R 1-11, 1 Vic Wertz 38 L 0-5, John Sullivan 22 L 0-5

NAME	T	AGE	W	L	PCT	SV	G	GS	CG	IP	H	BB	SO	ShO	ERA
TOTALS		28	79	83	.488	28	162	162	42	1456	1407	477	930	7	3.90
Phil Regan	R	26	15	9	.625	1	38	27	5	189	179	59	115	1	3.86
Hank Aguirre	L	31	14	15	.483	0	38	33	14	226	222	68	134	3	3.66
Jim Bunning	R	31	12	13	.480	1	39	35	6	248	245	69	196	2	3.88
Terry Fox	R	27	8	6	.571	11	46	0	0	80	81	20	35	0	3.60
Don Mossi	L	34	7	7	.500	2	24	16	3	123	110	17	68	0	3.73
Bill Faul	R	23	5	6	.455	1	28	10	2	97	93	48	64	0	4.64
Mickey Lolich	L	22	5	9	.357	0	33	18	4	144	145	56	103	0	3.56
Frank Lary	R	33	4	9	.308	0	16	14	6	107	90	26	46	0	3.28
Bob Anderson	R	27	3	1	.750	0	32	3	0	60	58	21	38	0	3.30
Denny McLain	R	19	2	1	.667	0	3	3	2	21	20	16	22	0	4.29
Willie Smith	L	24	1	0	1.000	2	11	2	0	22	24	13	16	0	4.50
Fred Gladding	R	27	1	1	.500	7	22	0	0	27	19	14	24	0	2.00
Alan Koch	R	25	1	1	.500	0	7	1	0	10	21	9	5	0	10.80
2 Tom Sturdivant	R	33	1	2	.333	2	28	0	0	55	43	24	36	0	3.76
Dick Egan	L	26	0	1	.000	0	20	0	0	21	25	3	16	0	5.14
1 Paul Foytack	R	32	0	1	.000	1	9	0	0	18	18	8	7	0	8.66
Bob Dustal	R	27	0	1	.000	0	7	0	0	6	10	5	4	0	9.00
Larry Foster	R	25	0	0	.000	0	1	0	0	2	4	1	1	0	13.50

BOSTON 7th 76-85 .472 28 — JOHNNY PESKY

NAME	G by POS	B	AGE	G	AB	R	H	2B	3B	HR	RBI	BB	SO	SB	BA	SA
TOTALS			30	161	**5575**	666	1493	**247**	34	171	623	475	954	27	.252	.400
Dick Stuart	1B155	R	30	157	612	81	160	25	4	42	118	44	144	0	.261	.521
Chuck Schilling	2B143	R	25	146	576	63	135	25	0	8	33	41	72	3	.234	.319
Ed Bressoud	SS137	R	31	140	497	61	129	23	6	20	60	52	93	1	.260	.451
Frank Malzone	3B148	R	33	151	580	66	169	25	2	15	71	31	45	0	.291	.419
Lu Clinton	OF146	R	25	148	560	71	130	23	7	22	77	49	118	0	.232	.416
Gary Geiger	OF95, 1B6	L	26	121	399	67	105	13	5	16	44	36	63	9	.263	.441
Carl Yastrzemski	OF151	L	23	151	570	91	**183**	**40**	3	14	68	**95**	72	8	**.321**	.475
Bob Tillman	C95	R	26	96	307	24	69	10	2	8	32	34	64	0	.225	.349
Roman Mejias	OF86	R	32	111	357	43	81	18	0	11	39	14	36	4	.227	.370
Russ Nixon	C76	L	28	98	287	27	77	18	1	5	30	22	32	0	.268	.390
Dick Williams	3B17, 1B11, OF7	R	34	79	136	15	35	8	0	2	12	15	25	0	.257	.360
Felix Mantilla	SS27, OF11, 2B5	R	28	66	178	27	56	8	0	6	15	20	14	2	.315	.461
Billy Gardner	2B21, 3B2	R	35	36	84	4	16	2	1	0	1	4	19	0	.190	.238
Jim Gosger	OF4	L	20	19	16	3	1	0	0	0	0	3	5	0	.063	.063
Rico Petrocelli	SS1	R	20	1	4	0	1	1	0	0	1	0	1	0	.250	.500

NAME	T	AGE	W	L	PCT	SV	G	GS	CG	IP	H	BB	SO	ShO	ERA
TOTALS		26	76	85	.472	32	161	161	29	1450	1367	539	1009	7	3.97
Bill Monbouquette	R	26	20	10	.667	0	37	36	13	267	258	42	174	1	3.81
Dick Radatz	R	26	15	6	.714	25	66	0	0	132	94	51	162	0	1.98
Earl Wilson	R	28	11	16	.407	0	37	34	6	211	184	**105**	123	3	3.75
Dave Morehead	R	20	10	13	.435	0	29	29	6	175	137	99	136	1	3.81
Jack Lamabe	R	26	7	4	.636	6	65	2	0	151	139	46	93	0	3.16
Bob Heffner	R	24	4	9	.308	0	20	19	3	125	131	36	77	1	4.25
Gene Conley (SJ)	R	32	3	4	.429	0	9	9	0	41	51	21	14	0	6.59
Arnie Earley	L	30	3	7	.300	1	53	4	0	116	124	43	97	0	4.73
1 Ike Delock	R	33	1	2	.333	0	6	6	1	32	31	12	23	0	4.50
Chet Nichols	L	32	1	3	.250	0	21	7	0	53	61	24	27	0	4.75
2 Bob Turley (SA)	R	32	1	4	.200	0	11	7	0	41	42	28	35	0	6.10
Hal Kolstad	R	28	0	2	.000	0	7	0	0	11	16	6	6	0	13.09
Wilbur Wood	L	21	0	5	.000	0	25	6	0	65	67	13	28	0	3.74
1 Mike Fornieles	R	31	0	0	.000	0	9	0	0	14	16	5	5	0	6.43
Pete Smith (MS)	R	23	0	0	.000	0	6	1	0	15	11	6	6	0	3.60
Jerry Stephenson	R	19	0	0	.000	0	1	1	0	2	5	2	3	0	9.00

KANSAS CITY 8th 73-89 .451 31.5 — ED LOPAT

NAME	G by POS	B	AGE	G	AB	R	H	2B	3B	HR	RBI	BB	SO	SB	BA	SA
TOTALS			28	162	5495	615	1356	225	38	95	582	529	829	47	.247	.353
Norm Siebern	1B131, OF16	L	29	152	556	80	151	25	2	16	83	79	82	1	.272	.410
Jerry Lumpe	2B115	L	30	157	595	75	161	26	7	5	59	58	44	3	.271	.363
Wayne Causey	SS135, 3B2	L	26	139	554	72	155	32	4	8	44	56	54	4	.280	.395
Ed Charles	3B158	R	28	158	603	82	161	28	2	15	79	58	79	15	.267	.395
Gino Cimoli	OF136	R	33	145	529	56	139	19	11	4	48	39	72	3	.263	.363
Bobby Del Greco	OF110, 3B2	R	30	121	306	40	65	7	1	8	29	40	52	1	.212	.320
Jose Tartabull	OF71	L	24	79	242	27	58	8	5	1	19	17	17	16	.240	.326
2 Doc Edwards	C63	R	25	71	240	16	60	12	0	6	35	11	23	0	.250	.375
Chuck Essegian	OF53	R	31	101	231	23	52	9	0	5	27	19	48	0	.225	.329
George Alusik (BW)	OF63	R	28	87	221	28	59	11	0	9	37	26	33	0	.267	.439
Ken Harrelson	1B34, OF28	R	21	79	226	16	52	10	1	6	23	23	58	1	.230	.363
2 Charlie Lau	C50	L	30	62	187	15	55	11	0	3	26	14	17	1	.294	.401
Manny Jimenez	OF40	L	24	60	157	12	44	9	0	0	15	16	14	0	.280	.338
Haywood Sullivan	C37	R	32	40	113	9	24	6	1	0	8	15	15	0	.212	.283
Tony La Russa	SS14, 2B3	R	18	34	44	4	11	1	1	0	1	7	12	0	.250	.318
Billy Bryan	C24	L	24	24	65	11	11	1	1	3	7	9	22	0	.169	.354
John Wojcik	OF17	L	21	19	59	7	11	0	0	0	2	8	8	2	.186	.186
2 Sammy Esposito	2B7, SS4, 3B3	R	31	18	25	3	5	1	0	0	2	3	3	0	.200	.240
1 Dick Howser	SS10	R	26	15	41	4	8	0	0	0	1	7	3	0	.195	.195
Dick Green	SS6, 2B4	R	22	13	37	5	10	2	0	1	4	2	10	0	.270	.405
Jay Hankins	OF9	L	27	10	34	2	6	0	1	1	4	0	3	0	.176	.324
Tommie Reynolds	OF5	R	21	8	19	1	1	1	0	0	0	1	7	0	.053	.105
Hector Martinez	OF3	R	24	6	14	2	4	0	0	1	3	1	3	0	.286	.500
1 Joe Azcue	C1	R	23	2	4	0	0	0	0	0	0	0	1	0	.000	.000

NAME	T	AGE	W	L	PCT	SV	G	GS	CG	IP	H	BB	SO	ShO	ERA
TOTALS		27	73	89	.451	29	162	162	35	1458	1417	540	887	11	3.92
Dave Wickersham	R	27	12	15	.444	1	38	34	4	238	244	79	118	1	4.08
Orlando Pena	R	29	12	**20**	.375	0	35	33	9	217	218	53	128	3	3.69
Bill Fischer	R	32	9	6	.600	3	45	2	0	96	86	29	34	0	3.56
Diego Segui	R	25	9	6	.600	0	38	23	4	167	173	73	116	1	3.77
Ed Rakow	R	27	9	10	.474	0	34	26	7	174	173	61	104	1	3.93
Moe Drabowsky	R	27	7	13	.350	0	26	22	9	174	135	64	109	2	3.05
John Wyatt	R	28	6	4	.600	21	63	0	0	92	83	43	81	0	3.13
Ted Bowsfield	L	27	5	7	.417	3	41	11	2	111	115	47	67	1	4.46
Jose Santiago	R	22	1	0	1.000	0	4	0	0	7	8	2	6	0	9.00
Dan Pfister (EJ)	R	26	1	0	1.000	0	3	1	0	9	8	3	9	0	2.00
Pete Lovrich	R	20	1	1	.500	0	20	1	0	21	25	10	16	0	7.71
3 Tom Sturdivant	R	33	1	2	.333	0	17	3	0	53	47	17	26	0	3.74
Dave Thies	R	26	0	1	.000	0	9	2	0	25	26	12	9	0	4.68
Fred Norman	L	20	0	1	.000	0	2	2	0	6	9	7	6	0	12.00
John O'Donoghue	L	23	0	1	.000	0	1	1	0	6	6	2	1	0	1.50
Dale Willis	R	25	0	2	.000	1	25	0	0	45	46	25	47	0	5.00
Aurelio Monteagudo	R	19	0	0	.000	0	4	0	0	7	4	3	3	0	2.57
Norm Bass	R	24	0	0	.000	0	3	1	0	8	11	9	4	0	11.25
Bill Landis	L	20	0	0	.000	0	1	0	0	2	0	1	3	0	0.00

LOS ANGELES 9th 70-91 .435 34 — BILL RIGNEY

NAME	G by POS	B	AGE	G	AB	R	H	2B	3B	HR	RBI	BB	SO	SB	BA	SA
TOTALS			27	161	5506	597	1378	208	38	95	551	448	916	43	.250	.354
Lee Thomas	1B104, OF43	L	27	149	528	52	116	12	6	9	55	53	82	6	.220	.316
Billy Moran	2B151	R	29	153	597	67	164	29	5	7	65	31	57	1	.275	.375
Jim Fregosi	SS151	R	21	154	592	83	170	29	12	9	50	36	104	2	.287	.422
Felix Torres	3B122, 1B2	R	31	138	463	40	121	32	1	4	51	30	73	1	.261	.361
Bob Perry	OF55	R	28	61	166	16	42	9	0	3	14	9	31	1	.253	.361
Albie Pearson	OF148	L	28	154	578	92	176	26	5	6	47	92	37	17	.304	.398
Leon Wagner	OF141	L	29	149	550	73	160	11	1	26	90	49	73	5	.291	.456
Bob Rodgers	C85	B	24	100	300	24	70	6	0	4	23	29	35	2	.233	.293
Bob Sadowski	OF25, 3B6, 2B4	L	26	88	144	12	36	6	0	1	22	15	34	2	.250	.313
Eddie Sadowski	C68	R	31	80	174	24	30	1	1	4	15	17	33	2	.172	.259
Joe Koppe	SS19, 3B18, 2B14, OF3	R	32	76	143	11	30	4	1	1	12	9	30	0	.210	.273
Charlie Dees	1B56	L	28	60	202	23	62	11	1	3	27	11	31	3	.307	.416
1 Ken Hunt	OF50	R	28	59	142	17	26	6	1	5	16	15	49	0	.183	.345
1 George Thomas	OF39, 3B10, 1B4	R	25	53	167	14	35	7	1	4	15	9	32	0	.210	.335
2 Frank Kostro	3B19, 1B5, OF3	R	25	43	99	6	22	2	1	2	10	6	17	0	.222	.323
2 Hank Foiles	C30	R	34	41	84	8	18	1	1	4	10	8	13	0	.214	.393
Ed Kirkpatrick	C14, OF10	L	18	34	77	4	15	5	0	2	7	6	19	1	.195	.338
Tom Satriano	3B13, C2, 1B1	L	22	23	50	1	9	1	0	0	2	9	10	0	.180	.200
3 Jimmy Piersall	OF18	R	33	20	52	4	16	1	0	0	4	5	5	0	.308	.327

NAME	T	AGE	W	L	PCT	SV	G	GS	CG	IP	H	BB	SO	ShO	ERA
TOTALS		30	70	91	.435	31	161	161	30	1455	1317	**578**	889	13	3.52
Ken McBride	R	27	13	12	.520	0	36	36	11	251	198	82	147	2	3.26
Dean Chance	R	22	13	18	.419	3	45	35	6	248	229	90	168	2	3.19
Dan Osinski	R	29	8	8	.500	0	47	16	4	159	145	80	100	1	3.28
Don Lee	R	29	8	11	.421	1	40	22	3	154	148	51	89	2	3.68
Art Fowler	R	40	5	3	.625	10	57	0	0	89	70	19	53	0	2.43
2 Paul Foytack	R	32	5	5	.500	0	25	8	0	70	68	29	37	0	3.71
Julio Navarro	R	27	4	5	.444	12	57	0	0	90	75	32	53	0	2.90
Jack Spring	L	30	3	0	1.000	2	45	0	0	38	40	9	13	0	3.08
Mel Nelson	L	27	2	3	.400	1	36	3	0	53	55	32	41	0	5.26
1 Bob Turley	R	32	2	7	.222	0	19	12	3	87	71	51	70	2	3.30
Bo Belinsky	L	26	2	9	.182	0	13	13	2	77	78	35	60	0	5.73
Bob Duliba	R	28	1	1	.500	1	6	0	0	8	3	6	4	0	1.13
Mike Lee	L	22	1	1	.500	0	6	4	0	26	30	14	11	0	3.81
Aubrey Gatewood	R	24	1	1	.500	0	4	3	1	24	12	16	13	0	1.50
Eli Grba	R	28	1	2	.333	0	12	1	0	17	14	10	5	0	4.76
Fred Newman	R	21	1	5	.167	0	12	8	0	44	56	15	16	0	5.32
Tom Morgan	R	33	0	0	.000	1	13	0	0	16	20	6	7	0	5.63
1 Ron Moeller	L	24	0	0	.000	0	3	0	0	3	5	1	2	0	6.75

WASHINGTON 10th 56-106 .346 48.5 — MICKEY VERNON 14-26 .350 2 GIL HODGES 42-80 .344

NAME	G by POS	B	AGE	G	AB	R	H	2B	3B	HR	RBI	BB	SO	SB	BA	SA
TOTALS			29	162	5446	578	1237	190	35	138	538	497	963	68	.227	.351
Bobo Osborne	1B81, 3B16	L	27	125	358	42	76	14	1	12	44	49	83	0	.212	.358
Chuck Cottier	2B85, SS24, 3B1	R	27	113	337	30	69	16	4	5	21	24	63	2	.205	.320
Eddie Brinkman	SS143	R	21	145	514	44	117	20	3	7	45	31	86	5	.228	.319
2 Don Zimmer	3B78, 2B2	R	32	83	298	37	74	12	1	13	44	18	57	3	.248	.426
Jim King	OF123	L	30	136	459	61	106	16	5	24	62	45	43	3	.231	.444
Don Lock	OF146	R	26	149	531	71	134	20	1	27	82	70	151	7	.252	.446
Chuck Hinton	OF125, 3B19, 1B6, SS2	R	29	150	566	80	152	20	12	15	55	64	79	25	.269	.426
Ken Retzer	C81	L	29	95	265	21	64	10	0	5	31	17	20	2	.242	.336
Dick Phillips	1B68, 2B5, 3B4	L	31	124	321	33	76	8	0	10	32	29	35	1	.237	.355
Minnie Minoso	OF74, 3B8	R	40	109	315	38	72	12	2	4	30	33	38	8	.229	.317
Don Leppert	C60	L	31	73	211	20	50	11	0	6	24	20	29	0	.237	.374
2 Don Blasingame	2B64	L	31	69	254	29	65	10	2	2	12	24	18	3	.256	.335
Tom Brown	1B14, OF16	B	22	61	116	8	17	4	0	1	4	11	45	2	.147	.207
1 Marv Breeding	3B29, 2B22, SS2	R	29	58	197	20	54	7	2	1	14	7	21	1	.274	.345
2 Hobie Landrith	C37	L	33	42	103	6	18	3	0	1	7	15	12	0	.175	.233
John Kennedy	3B26, SS2	R	22	36	62	3	11	1	1	0	4	6	22	2	.177	.226
1 Jimmy Piersall	OF21	R	33	29	94	9	23	1	0	1	5	6	11	4	.245	.287
2 Cal Neeman	C12	R	34	14	18	1	1	0	0	0	0	1	0	0	.056	.056
Bob Schmidt	C6	R	30	9	15	3	3	1	0	0	0	3	5	0	.200	.267
1 Lou Klimchock	2B3	L	23	9	14	1	2	0	0	0	2	0	1	0	.143	.143
2 Ken Hunt	OF5	R	28	7	20	1	4	0	0	1	4	2	6	0	.200	.350

Johnny Schaive 29 R 0-3, Barry Shetrone 24 L 0-2

NAME	T	AGE	W	L	PCT	SV	G	GS	CG	IP	H	BB	SO	ShO	ERA
TOTALS		29	56	**106**	.346	25	162	162	29	1447	**1486**	537	744	8	4.42
Claude Osteen	L	23	9	14	.391	0	40	29	8	212	222	60	109	2	3.35
Tom Cheney	R	28	8	9	.471	0	23	21	7	136	99	40	97	4	2.71
Don Rudolph	L	31	7	19	.269	1	37	26	4	174	189	36	70	0	4.55
Steve Ridzik	R	34	5	6	.455	1	20	10	0	90	82	35	47	0	4.80
Bennie Daniels	R	31	5	10	.333	1	35	24	6	169	163	58	88	1	4.37
Jim Duckworth	R	24	4	12	.250	0	37	15	2	121	131	67	66	0	6.02
Ron Kline	R	31	3	8	.273	17	62	1	0	94	85	30	49	0	2.78
Dave Stenhouse (EJ)	R	29	3	9	.250	0	16	16	2	87	90	45	47	1	4.55
2 Ron Moeller	L	24	2	0	1.000	0	8	3	0	24	31	10	10	0	6.29
2 Ed Roebuck	R	31	2	1	.667	4	26	0	0	57	63	29	25	0	3.32
Jim Hannan	R	23	2	2	.500	0	13	2	0	28	23	17	14	0	4.82
Carl Bouldin	R	23	2	2	.500	0	10	3	0	23	31	8	10	0	5.87
1 Jim Coates	R	30	2	4	.333	0	20	2	0	44	51	21	31	0	5.32
Art Quirk	L	25	1	0	1.000	0	7	3	0	21	23	8	12	0	4.29
Jim Bronstad	R	27	1	3	.250	1	25	0	0	57	66	22	22	0	5.68
1 Pete Burnside	L	32	0	1	.000	0	38	1	0	67	84	24	23	0	6.15
1 Steve Hamilton	L	29	0	1	.000	0	3	0	0	2	5	2	1	0	13.50
Jack Jenkins	R	20	0	2	.000	0	4	2	0	12	16	12	5	0	6.00
Bob Baird	L	21	0	3	.000	0	5	3	0	12	12	7	7	0	7.50
Ed Hobaugh	R	29	0	0	.000	0	9	1	0	16	20	6	11	0	6.19

LOS ANGELES 1st 99-63 .611 — WALT ALSTON

NAME	G by POS	B	AGE	G	AB	R	H	2B	3B	HR	RBI	BB	SO	SB	BA	SA
TOTALS			27	163	5428	640	1361	178	34	110	584	453	867	**124**	.251	.357
Ron Fairly	1B119, OF45	L	24	152	490	62	133	21	0	12	77	58	69	5	.271	.388
Jim Gilliam	2B119, 3B55	B	34	148	525	77	148	27	4	6	49	60	28	19	.282	.383
Maury Wills	SS109, 3B33	B	30	134	527	83	159	19	3	0	34	44	48	**40**	.302	.349
Ken McMullen	3B71, 2B1, OF1	R	21	79	233	16	55	9	0	5	28	20	46	1	.236	.339
Frank Howard	OF111	R	26	123	417	58	114	16	1	28	64	33	116	1	.273	.518
Willie Davis	OF153	L	23	156	515	60	126	19	8	9	60	25	61	25	.245	.365
Tommy Davis	OF129, 3B40	R	24	146	556	69	181	19	3	16	88	29	59	15	**.326**	.457
Johnny Roseboro	C134	L	30	135	470	50	111	13	7	9	49	36	50	7	.236	.351
Wally Moon	OF96	L	33	122	343	41	90	13	2	8	48	45	43	5	.262	.382
Dick Tracewski	SS81, 2B23	R	28	104	217	23	49	2	1	1	10	19	39	2	.226	.258
Bill Skowron	1B66, 3B1	R	32	89	237	19	48	8	0	4	19	13	49	0	.203	.287
Nate Oliver	2B57, SS2	R	22	65	163	23	39	2	3	1	9	13	25	3	.239	.307
Lee Walls	OF18, 1B5, 3B2	R	30	64	86	12	20	1	0	3	11	7	25	0	.233	.349
Doug Camilli	C47	R	26	49	117	9	19	1	1	3	10	11	22	0	.162	.265
1 Don Zimmer	3B10, 2B1, SS1	R	32	22	23	4	5	1	0	1	2	3	10	0	.217	.391
Al Ferrara	OF11	R	23	21	44	2	7	0	0	1	1	6	9	0	.159	.227
2 Marv Breeding	2B17, SS1, 3B1	R	29	20	36	6	6	0	0	0	1	2	5	1	.167	.167
Dick Nen	1B5	L	23	7	8	2	1	0	0	1	1	3	3	0	.125	.500
1 Daryl Spencer	3B3	R	33	7	9	0	1	0	0	0	0	3	2	0	.111	.111

Roy Gleason 20 B 1-1, Derrell Griffith 19 L 0-2

NAME	T	AGE	W	L	PCT	SV	G	GS	CG	IP	H	BB	SO	ShO	ERA
		26	**99**	63	**.611**	29	163	163	51	1470	1329	402	**1095**	**24**	**2.85**
Sandy Koufax	L	27	**25**	5	.833	0	40	40	20	311	214	58	**306**	**11**	**1.88**
Don Drysdale	R	26	19	17	.528	0	42	**42**	17	315	**287**	57	251	3	2.63
Ron Perranoski	L	27	16	3	**.842**	21	**69**	0	0	129	112	43	75	0	1.67
Johnny Podres	L	30	14	12	.538	1	37	34	10	198	196	64	134	5	3.55
Bob Miller	R	24	10	8	.556	1	42	23	2	187	171	65	125	0	2.89
Pete Richert	L	23	5	3	.625	0	20	12	1	78	80	28	54	0	4.50
Dick Calmus	R	19	3	1	.750	0	21	1	0	44	32	16	25	0	2.66
Nick Willhite	L	22	2	3	.400	0	8	8	1	38	44	10	28	1	3.79
1 Ed Roebuck	R	31	2	4	.333	0	29	0	0	40	54	21	26	0	4.28
Larry Sherry	R	27	2	6	.250	3	36	3	0	80	82	24	47	0	3.71
Ken Rowe	R	29	1	1	.500	1	14	0	0	28	28	11	12	0	2.89
Dick Scott	L	30	0	0	.000	2	9	0	0	12	17	3	6	0	6.75
Jack Smith	R	27	0	0	.000	0	4	0	0	8	10	2	5	0	7.88
Phil Ortega	R	23	0	0	.000	0	1	0	0	1	2	0	1	0	18.00

ST. LOUIS 2nd 93-69 .574 6 — JOHNNY KEANE

NAME	G by POS	B	AGE	G	AB	R	H	2B	3B	HR	RBI	BB	SO	SB	BA	SA
TOTALS			29	162	**5678**	**747**	**1540**	**231**	**66**	128	**697**	458	915	77	**.271**	.403
Bill White	1B162	L	29	162	658	106	200	26	8	27	109	59	100	10	.304	.491
Julian Javier	2B161	R	26	161	609	82	160	27	9	9	46	24	86	18	.263	.381
Dick Groat	SS158	R	32	158	631	85	201	**43**	11	6	73	56	58	3	.319	.450
Ken Boyer	3B159	R	32	159	617	86	176	28	2	24	111	70	90	1	.285	.454
George Altman	OF124	L	30	135	464	62	127	18	7	9	47	47	93	13	.274	.401
Curt Flood	OF158	R	25	158	**662**	112	200	34	9	5	63	42	57	17	.302	.403
Charlie James	OF101	R	25	116	347	34	93	14	2	10	45	10	64	2	.268	.406
Tim McCarver	C126	L	21	127	405	39	117	12	7	4	51	27	43	5	.289	.383
Stan Musial	OF96	L	42	124	337	34	86	10	2	12	58	35	43	2	.255	.404
Gary Kolb	OF58, 3B1, C1	L	23	75	96	23	26	1	5	3	10	22	26	2	.271	.479
1 Duke Carmel	OF38, 1B1	L	26	57	44	9	10	1	0	1	2	9	11	0	.227	.318
Carl Sawatski	C27	L	35	56	105	12	25	0	0	6	14	15	28	2	.238	.410
Dal Maxvill	SS24, 2B9, 3B3	R	24	53	51	12	12	2	0	0	3	6	11	0	.235	.275
Bob Gibson	P36	R	27	41	87	12	18	3	1	3	20	8	35	0	.207	.368
1 Gene Oliver	C35	R	27	39	102	10	23	4	0	6	18	13	19	0	.225	.441
Mike Shannon	OF26	R	23	32	26	3	8	0	0	1	2	0	6	0	.308	.423
1 Leo Burke	OF11, 3B5	R	29	30	49	6	10	2	1	1	5	4	12	0	.204	.347
Phil Gagliano	2B3, 3B1	R	21	10	5	1	2	0	0	0	1	1	1	0	.400	.400
Doug Clemens	OF3	L	24	5	6	1	1	0	0	1	2	1	2	0	.167	.667
Jack Damaska	2B1, OF1	R	25	5	5	1	1	0	0	0	1	0	4	0	.200	.200
Jerry Buchek	SS1	R	21	3	4	0	1	0	0	0	0	0	2	0	.250	.250
Dave Ricketts	C3	B	27	3	8	0	2	0	0	0	0	0	2	0	.250	.250

Corky Withrow 25 R 0-9, Red Schoendienst 40 B 0-5, Jeoff Long 21 R 1-5, Jim Beauchamp 23 R 0-3, Moe Thacker 29 R 0-4, Clyde Bloomfield 27 R 0-0, Hal Smith (IL) 32

NAME	T	AGE	W	L	PCT	SV	G	GS	CG	IP	H	BB	SO	ShO	ERA
		32	93	69	.574	32	162	162	49	1463	1329	463	978	17	3.32
Ernie Broglio	R	27	18	8	.692	0	39	35	11	250	202	90	145	5	2.99
Bob Gibson	R	27	18	9	.667	0	36	33	14	255	224	96	204	2	3.39
Curt Simmons	L	34	15	9	.625	0	32	32	11	233	209	48	127	6	2.47
Ray Sadecki	L	22	10	10	.500	1	36	28	4	193	198	78	136	1	4.10
Ron Taylor	R	25	9	7	.563	11	54	9	2	133	119	30	91	0	2.84
Bobby Shantz	L	37	6	4	.600	11	55	0	0	79	55	17	70	0	2.62
Ray Washburn	R	25	5	3	.625	0	11	11	4	64	50	14	47	2	3.09
1 Ed Bauta	R	28	3	4	.429	3	38	0	0	53	55	21	30	0	3.91
2 Lew Burdette	R	36	3	8	.273	2	21	14	3	98	106	16	45	0	3.77
2 Barney Schultz	R	36	2	0	1.000	1	24	0	0	35	36	8	26	0	3.60
Sam Jones	R	37	2	0	1.000	2	11	0	0	11	15	5	8	0	9.00
Harry Fanok	R	23	2	1	.667	1	12	0	0	26	24	21	25	0	5.19
Bob Humphreys	R	27	0	1	.000	0	9	0	0	11	11	7	8	0	4.91
Diomedes Olivo	L	44	0	5	.000	0	19	0	0	13	16	9	9	0	5.54
2 Ken MacKenzie	L	29	0	1	.000	0	8	0	0	9	9	3	7	0	4.00

SAN FRANCISCO 3rd 88-74 .543 11 — AL DARK

NAME	G by POS	B	AGE	G	AB	R	H	2B	3B	HR	RBI	BB	SO	SB	BA	SA
TOTALS			29	162	5579	725	1442	206	35	**197**	680	441	889	55	.258	**.414**
Orlando Cepeda	1B150, OF3	R	25	156	579	100	183	33	4	34	97	37	70	8	.316	.563
Chuck Hiller	2B109	L	28	111	417	44	93	10	2	6	33	20	23	3	.223	.300
Jose Pagan	SS143, 2B1, OF1	R	28	148	483	46	113	12	1	6	39	26	67	10	.234	.300
Jim Davenport	3B127, 2B22, SS1	R	29	147	460	40	116	19	3	4	36	32	87	5	.252	.333
Felipe Alou	OF153	R	28	157	565	75	159	31	9	20	82	27	87	11	.281	.474
Willie Mays	OF157, SS1	R	32	157	596	115	187	32	7	38	103	66	83	8	.314	.582
Willie McCovey	OF135, 1B23	L	25	152	564	103	158	19	5	**44**	102	50	119	1	.280	.566
Ed Bailey	C88	L	32	105	308	41	81	8	0	21	68	50	64	0	.263	.494
Harvey Kuenn	OF64, 3B53	R	32	120	417	61	121	13	2	6	31	44	38	2	.290	.374
Tom Haller	C85, OF7	L	26	98	298	32	76	8	1	14	44	34	45	4	.255	.430
Ernie Bowman	SS40, 2B26, 3B12	R	25	81	125	10	23	3	0	0	4	0	15	1	.184	.208
Matty Alou	OF20	L	24	63	76	4	11	1	0	0	2	2	13	0	.145	.158
Joey Amalfitano	2B37, 3B7	R	29	54	137	11	24	3	0	1	7	12	18	2	.175	.219
Cap Peterson	2B8, 3B5, OF3, SS1	R	20	22	54	7	14	2	0	1	2	2	13	0	.259	.352
2 Norm Larker	1B11	L	32	19	14	0	1	0	0	0	0	2	2	0	.071	.071
Jesus Alou	OF12	R	21	16	24	3	6	1	0	0	5	0	3	0	.250	.292

Jose Cardenal 19 R 1-5, Jim Ray Hart (BS-PB) 21 R 4-20, Jimmie Coker 27 R 1-5

NAME	T	AGE	W	L	PCT	SV	G	GS	CG	IP	H	BB	SO	ShO	ERA
		29	88	74	.543	30	162	162	46	1469	1380	464	954	9	3.35
Juan Marichal	R	25	**25**	8	.758	0	41	40	18	**321**	259	61	248	5	2.41
Jack Sanford	R	34	16	13	.552	0	42	**42**	11	284	273	76	158	0	3.52
Billy O'Dell	L	30	14	10	.583	1	36	33	10	222	218	70	116	3	3.16
Bobby Bolin	R	24	10	6	.625	7	47	12	2	137	128	57	134	0	3.28
Don Larsen	R	33	7	7	.500	3	46	0	0	62	46	30	44	0	3.05
Jack Fisher	R	24	6	10	.375	1	36	12	2	116	132	38	57	0	4.58
Jim Duffalo (HJ)	R	27	4	2	.667	2	34	5	0	75	56	37	55	0	2.88
Billy Pierce	L	36	3	11	.214	8	38	13	3	99	106	20	52	1	4.27
Billy Hoeft (SJ)	L	31	2	0	1.000	4	23	0	0	24	26	10	8	0	4.50
Gaylord Perry	R	24	1	6	.143	2	31	4	0	76	84	29	52	0	4.03
Bob Garibaldi	R	21	0	1	.000	1	4	0	0	8	8	4	4	0	1.13
Al Stanek	L	19	0	0	.000	0	11	0	0	13	10	12	5	0	4.85
Frank Linzy	R	22	0	0	.000	0	8	1	0	17	22	10	14	0	4.76
John Pregenzer	R	27	0	0	.000	1	6	0	0	9	8	8	5	0	5.00
Jim Constable	L	30	0	0	.000	0	4	0	0	2	3	1	1	0	4.50
Ron Herbel	R	25	0	0	.000	0	2	0	0	1	1	1	1	0	9.00

PHILADELPHIA 4th 87-75 .537 12 — GENE MAUCH

NAME	G by POS	B	AGE	G	AB	R	H	2B	3B	HR	RBI	BB	SO	SB	BA	SA
TOTALS			28	162	5524	642	1390	228	54	126	599	403	955	56	.252	.381
Roy Sievers	1B126	R	36	138	450	46	108	19	2	19	82	43	72	0	.240	.418
Tony Taylor	2B149, 3B13	R	27	157	640	102	180	20	10	5	49	42	99	23	.281	.367
Bobby Wine	SS132, 3B8	R	24	142	418	29	90	14	3	6	44	14	83	1	.215	.306
Don Hoak	3B106	R	35	115	377	35	87	11	3	6	24	27	52	5	.231	.324
Johnny Callison	OF157	L	24	157	626	96	178	36	11	26	78	50	111	8	.284	.502
Tony Gonzalez	OF151	L	26	155	555	78	170	36	12	4	66	53	68	13	.306	.436
Wes Covington	OF101	L	31	119	353	46	107	24	1	17	64	26	56	1	.303	.521
Clay Dalrymple	C142	L	26	142	452	40	114	15	3	10	40	45	55	0	.252	.365
Don Demeter	OF119, 3B43, 1B26	R	28	154	515	63	133	20	2	22	83	31	93	1	.258	.433
Ruben Amaro	SS63, 3B45, 1B5	R	27	115	217	25	47	9	2	2	19	19	31	0	.217	.304
Frank Torre	1B56	L	31	92	112	8	28	7	2	1	10	11	7	0	.250	.375
Cookie Rojas	2B25, OF1	R	24	64	77	18	17	0	1	1	2	3	8	4	.221	.286
Bob Oldis	C43	R	35	47	85	8	19	3	0	0	8	3	5	0	.224	.259
Earl Averill	C20, OF8, 1B1, 3B1	R	31	47	71	8	19	2	0	3	8	9	14	0	.268	.423
2 Jim Lemon	OF18	R	35	31	59	6	16	2	0	2	6	8	18	0	.271	.407
Cal Emery	1B2	L	26	16	19	0	3	1	0	0	0	0	2	0	.158	.211
John Herrnstein	OF2, 1B1	L	25	15	12	1	2	0	0	1	1	1	5	0	.167	.417
Dick Allen	OF7, 3B1	R	21	10	24	6	7	2	1	0	2	0	5	0	.292	.458
Wayne Graham	OF6	R	26	10	22	1	4	0	0	0	0	3	1	0	.182	.182

Billy Klaus 34 L 1-18, Mike Harrington 28 R 0-0

NAME	T	AGE	W	L	PCT	SV	G	GS	CG	IP	H	BB	SO	ShO	ERA
		27	87	75	.537	31	162	162	45	1457	1262	**553**	1052	12	3.09
Ray Culp	R	21	14	11	.560	0	34	30	10	203	148	**102**	176	5	2.97
Cal McLish	R	37	13	11	.542	0	32	32	10	210	184	56	98	2	3.26
Jack Baldschun	R	26	11	7	.611	16	65	0	0	114	99	42	89	0	2.29
Dennis Bennett (BN)	L	23	9	5	.643	1	23	16	6	119	102	33	82	1	2.65
Chris Short	L	25	9	12	.429	0	38	27	6	198	185	69	160	3	2.95
Dallas Green	R	28	7	5	.583	2	40	14	4	120	134	38	68	0	3.23
Art Mahaffey	R	25	7	10	.412	0	26	22	6	149	143	48	97	1	3.99
Ryne Duren	R	34	6	2	.750	2	33	7	1	87	65	52	84	0	3.31
Johnny Klippstein	R	35	5	6	.455	8	49	1	0	112	80	46	84	0	1.93
John Boozer	R	23	3	4	.429	1	26	8	2	83	67	33	69	0	2.93
Jack Hamilton	R	24	2	1	.667	1	19	1	0	30	22	17	23	0	5.40
Marcelino Lopez	L	19	1	0	1.000	0	4	2	0	6	8	7	2	0	6.00
Paul Brown	R	22	0	1	.000	0	6	2	0	15	15	5	11	0	4.20
Bobby Locke	R	29	0	0	.000	0	9	0	0	11	10	5	7	0	5.73

CINCINNATI 5th 86-76 .531 13 — FRED HUTCHINSON

NAME	G by POS	B	AGE	G	AB	R	H	2B	3B	HR	RBI	BB	SO	SB	BA	SA
TOTALS			26	162	5416	648	1333	225	44	122	608	474	960	92	.246	.371
Gordy Coleman	1B107	L	28	123	365	38	90	20	2	14	59	29	51	1	.247	.427
Pete Rose	2B157, OF1	B	22	157	623	101	170	25	9	6	41	55	72	13	.273	.371
Leo Cardenas	SS157	R	24	158	565	42	133	22	4	7	48	23	101	3	.235	.326
Gene Freese	3B62, OF1	R	29	66	217	20	53	9	1	6	26	17	42	4	.244	.378
Tommy Harper	OF118, 3B1	R	22	129	408	67	106	12	3	10	37	44	72	12	.260	.377
Vada Pinson	OF162	L	24	162	652	96	**204**	37	**14**	22	106	36	80	27	.313	.514
Frank Robinson	OF139, 1B1	R	27	140	482	79	125	19	3	21	91	81	69	26	.259	.442
Johnny Edwards	C148	L	25	148	495	46	128	19	4	11	67	45	93	1	.259	.380
Marty Keough	1B46, OF28	L	28	95	172	21	39	8	2	6	21	25	37	1	.227	.401
Eddie Kasko	3B48, SS15, 2B1	R	31	76	199	25	48	9	0	3	10	21	29	0	.241	.332
2 Bob Skinner	OF51	L	31	72	194	25	49	10	2	3	17	21	42	1	.253	.371
Don Pavletich	1B57, C13	R	24	71	183	18	38	11	0	5	18	17	12	0	.208	.350
2 Daryl Spencer	3B48	R	33	50	155	21	37	7	0	1	23	31	37	1	.239	.303
Ken Walters	OF21, 1B1	R	29	49	75	6	14	2	0	1	7	4	14	0	.187	.253
2 Charlie Neal	3B19, 2B1, SS1	R	32	34	64	2	10	1	0	0	3	5	15	0	.156	.172
1 Jesse Gonder	C7	L	27	31	32	5	10	2	0	3	5	1	12	0	.313	.656
1 Jerry Lynch	OF7	L	32	22	32	5	8	3	0	2	9	1	5	0	.250	.531
1 Don Blasingame	2B11, 3B2	L	31	18	31	4	5	2	0	0	0	7	5	0	.161	.226
Gene Green	C8	R	30	15	31	3	7	1	0	1	3	0	8	0	.226	.355
1 Wally Post	OF1	R	33	5	7	1	0	0	0	0	0	0	1	0	.000	.000

2 Sammy Taylor 30 L 0-6, 1 Hank Foiles 34 R 0-3, 1 Harry Bright 33 R 0-1

NAME	T	AGE	W	L	PCT	SV	G	GS	CG	IP	H	BB	SO	ShO	ERA
		30	86	76	.531	**36**	162	162	55	1440	1307	425	1048	22	3.29
Jim Maloney	R	23	23	7	.767	0	33	33	13	250	183	88	265	6	2.77
Jim O'Toole	L	26	17	14	.548	0	33	32	12	234	208	57	146	5	2.88
Joe Nuxhall	L	34	15	8	.652	2	35	29	14	217	194	39	169	2	2.61
John Tsitouris	R	27	12	8	.600	0	30	21	8	191	167	38	113	3	3.16
Joey Jay	R	27	7	18	.280	1	30	22	4	170	172	73	116	1	4.29
Bob Purkey	R	33	6	10	.375	0	21	21	4	137	143	33	55	1	3.55
Al Worthington	R	34	4	4	.500	10	50	0	0	81	75	31	55	0	3.00
2 Dom Zanni	R	31	1	1	.500	5	31	1	0	43	39	21	40	0	4.19
Bill Henry	L	35	1	3	.250	14	47	0	0	52	55	11	45	0	4.15
1 Jim Brosnan	R	33	0	1	.000	0	6	0	0	5	8	3	4	0	7.20
Jim Owens	R	29	0	2	.000	4	19	3	0	42	42	24	29	0	5.36
2 Jim Coates	R	30	0	0	.000	0	9	0	0	16	21	7	11	0	6.63

MILWAUKEE 6th 84-78 .519 15 — BOBBY BRAGAN

NAME	G by POS	B	AGE	G	AB	R	H	2B	3B	HR	RBI	BB	SO	SB	BA	SA
TOTALS			28	163	5518	677	1345	204	39	139	624	**525**	954	75	.244	.370
2 Gene Oliver	1B55, OF35, C2	R	27	95	296	34	74	12	2	11	47	27	59	4	.250	.416
Frank Bolling	2B141	R	31	142	542	73	132	18	2	5	43	41	47	2	.244	.312
Roy McMillan	SS94	R	32	100	320	35	80	10	1	4	29	17	25	1	.250	.325
Eddie Mathews	3B121, OF42	L	31	158	547	82	144	27	4	23	84	**124**	119	3	.263	.453
Hank Aaron	OF161	R	29	161	631	**121**	201	29	4	**44**	**130**	78	94	31	.319	**.586**
Mack Jones	OF80	L	24	93	228	36	50	11	4	3	22	26	59	8	.219	.342
Lee Maye	OF111	L	28	124	442	67	120	22	7	11	34	36	52	14	.271	.428
Joe Torre	C105, 1B37, OF2	R	22	142	501	57	147	19	4	14	71	42	79	1	.293	.431
Denis Menke	SS82, 3B51, 2B22, 1B1, OF1	R	22	146	518	58	121	16	4	11	50	37	106	6	.234	.344
Del Crandall	C75, 1B7	R	33	86	259	18	52	4	0	3	28	18	22	1	.201	.251
Ty Cline	OF62	L	24	72	174	17	41	2	1	0	10	10	31	2	.236	.259
Tommie Aaron	1B45, OF14, 2B6, 3B1	R	23	72	135	6	27	6	1	1	15	11	27	0	.200	.281
Don Dillard	OF30	L	26	67	119	9	28	6	4	1	12	5	21	0	.235	.378
1 Norm Larker	1B42	L	32	64	147	15	26	6	0	1	14	24	24	0	.177	.238
Len Gabrielson	OF22, 1B16, 3B3	L	23	46	120	14	26	5	0	3	15	8	23	1	.217	.333
2 Lou Klimchock	1B12	L	23	24	46	6	9	1	0	0	1	0	12	0	.196	.217
Hawk Taylor (JJ)	OF8	R	24	16	29	1	2	0	0	0	0	1	12	0	.069	.069
2 Bubba Morton	OF9	R	31	15	28	1	5	0	0	0	4	2	3	0	.179	.179
Amado Samuel	SS7, 2B4	R	24	15	17	0	3	1	0	0	0	0	4	0	.176	.235

Bob Uecker 28 R 4-16, Woody Woodward 20 R 0-2, Gus Bell 34 L 1-3, Rico Carty 24 R 0-2

NAME	T	AGE	W	L	PCT	SV	G	GS	CG	IP	H	BB	SO	ShO	ERA
		27	84	78	.519	25	163	163	**56**	**1472**	1327	489	924	18	3.26
Warren Spahn	L	42	23	7	.767	0	33	33	**22**	260	241	49	102	7	2.60
Denny Lemaster	L	24	11	14	.440	1	46	31	10	237	199	85	190	1	3.04
Bob Hendley	L	24	9	9	.500	3	41	24	7	169	153	64	105	3	3.94
Tony Cloninger	R	22	9	11	.450	1	41	18	4	145	131	63	100	2	3.79
Bob Shaw	R	30	7	11	.389	13	48	16	3	159	144	55	105	3	2.66
1 Lew Burdette	R	36	6	5	.545	0	15	13	4	84	71	24	28	1	3.64
Bob Sadowski	R	25	5	7	.417	0	19	18	5	117	99	30	72	1	2.62
Hank Fischer	R	23	4	3	.571	0	31	6	1	74	74	28	72	0	4.99
Claude Raymond	R	26	4	6	.400	5	45	0	0	53	57	27	44	0	5.43
Frank Funk	R	27	3	3	.500	0	25	0	0	44	42	13	19	0	2.66
Don Schneider	R	20	1	0	1.000	0	30	3	0	44	36	20	19	0	3.07
Ron Piche	R	28	1	1	.500	0	37	1	0	53	53	25	40	0	3.40
Bobby Tiefenauer	R	33	1	1	.500	2	12	0	0	30	20	4	22	0	1.20
Wade Blasingame	L	19	0	0	.000	0	2	0	0	3	7	2	6	0	12.00

CHICAGO 7th 82-80 .506 17 — BOB KENNEDY

NAME	G by POS	B	AGE	G	AB	R	H	2B	3B	HR	RBI	BB	SO	SB	BA	SA
TOTALS			26	162	5404	570	1286	205	44	127	530	439	1049	68	.238	.363
Ernie Banks	1B125	R	32	130	432	41	98	20	1	18	64	39	73	0	.227	.403
Ken Hubbs	2B152	R	21	154	566	54	133	19	3	8	47	39	93	8	.235	.322
Andre Rodgers	SS150	R	28	150	516	51	118	17	4	5	33	65	90	5	.229	.306
Ron Santo	3B162	R	23	162	630	79	187	29	6	25	99	42	92	6	.297	.481
Lou Brock	OF140	L	24	148	547	79	141	19	11	9	37	31	122	24	.258	.382
2 Ellis Burton	OF90	B	26	93	322	45	74	16	1	12	41	36	59	6	.230	.398
Billy Williams	OF160	L	25	161	612	87	175	36	9	25	95	68	78	7	.286	.497
Dick Bertell	C99	R	27	100	322	15	75	7	2	2	14	24	41	0	.233	.286
Don Landrum	OF57	L	27	84	227	27	55	4	1	1	10	13	42	6	.242	.282
Merritt Ranew	C37, 1B7	L	25	78	154	18	52	8	1	3	15	9	32	1	.338	.461
Nelson Mathews	OF46	R	21	61	155	12	24	3	2	4	10	16	48	3	.155	.277
Jimmie Schaffer	C54	R	27	57	142	17	34	7	0	7	19	11	35	0	.239	.437
Steve Boros	1B14, OF11	R	26	41	90	9	19	5	1	3	7	12	19	0	.211	.389
2 Leo Burke	2B10, 1B4	R	29	27	49	4	9	0	0	2	7	4	13	0	.184	.306
John Boccabella	1B24	R	22	24	74	7	14	4	1	1	5	6	21	0	.189	.311
Ken Aspromonte	2B7, 1B2	R	31	20	34	2	5	3	0	0	4	4	4	0	.147	.235
Alex Grammas	SS13	R	36	16	27	1	5	0	0	0	0	0	3	0	.185	.185
Billy Cowan	OF10	R	24	14	36	1	9	1	1	1	2	0	11	0	.250	.417

Bob Will 31 L 4-23, Jimmy Stewart 24 B 11-37, Cuno Barragan 31 R 0-1

NAME	T	AGE	W	L	PCT	SV	G	GS	CG	IP	H	BB	SO	ShO	ERA
		29	82	80	.506	28	162	162	45	1457	1357	400	851	15	3.08
Dick Ellsworth	L	23	22	10	.688	0	37	37	19	291	223	75	185	4	2.10
Larry Jackson	R	32	14	18	.438	0	37	37	13	275	256	54	153	4	2.55
Lindy McDaniel	R	27	13	7	.650	**22**	57	0	0	88	82	27	75	0	2.86
Bob Buhl	R	34	11	14	.440	0	37	34	6	226	219	62	108	0	3.38
Glen Hobbie	R	27	7	10	.412	0	36	24	4	165	172	49	94	1	3.93
Paul Toth	R	28	5	9	.357	0	27	14	3	131	115	35	66	2	3.09
Don Elston	R	34	4	1	.800	4	51	0	0	70	57	21	41	0	2.83
Jim Brewer	L	25	3	2	.600	0	29	1	0	50	59	15	35	0	4.86
Cal Koonce	R	22	2	6	.250	0	21	13	0	73	75	32	44	0	4.56
1 Barney Schultz	R	36	1	0	1.000	2	15	0	0	27	25	9	18	0	3.67
Tom Baker	R	29	0	1	.000	0	10	1	0	18	20	7	14	0	3.00
Dick LeMay	L	24	0	1	.000	0	9	1	0	15	26	4	10	0	5.40
Jack Warner	R	22	0	1	.000	0	8	0	0	23	21	8	7	0	2.74
Freddie Burdette	R	26	0	0	.000	0	4	0	0	5	5	2	1	0	3.60
Phil Murdock	R	26	0	0	.000	0	1	0	0	1	2	0	0	0	9.00

PITTSBURGH 8th 74-88 .457 25 — DANNY MURTAUGH

NAME	G by POS	B	AGE	G	AB	R	H	2B	3B	HR	RBI	BB	SO	SB	BA	SA
TOTALS			27	162	5536	567	1385	181	49	108	523	454	940	57	.250	.359
Donn Clendenon	1B151	R	27	154	563	65	155	28	7	15	57	39	**136**	22	.275	.430
Bill Mazeroski	2B138	R	26	142	534	43	131	22	3	8	52	32	46	2	.245	.343
Dick Schofield	SS117, 2B20, 3B1	B	28	138	541	54	133	18	2	3	32	69	83	2	.246	.303
Bob Bailey	3B153, SS3	R	20	154	570	60	130	15	3	12	45	58	98	10	.228	.328
Roberto Clemente	OF151	R	28	152	600	77	192	23	8	17	76	31	64	12	.320	.470
Bill Virdon	OF142	L	32	142	554	58	149	22	6	8	53	43	55	1	.269	.374
Willie Stargell	OF65, 1B16	L	23	108	304	34	74	11	6	11	47	19	85	0	.243	.428
Jim Pagliaroni	C85	R	25	92	252	27	58	5	0	11	26	36	57	0	.230	.381
Smoky Burgess	C72	L	36	91	264	20	74	10	1	6	37	24	14	0	.280	.394
2 Jerry Lynch	OF64	L	32	88	237	26	63	6	3	10	36	22	28	0	.266	.443
Ted Savage (GJ)	OF47	R	27	85	149	22	29	2	1	5	14	14	31	4	.195	.322
Johnny Logan	SS44, 3B4	R	36	81	181	15	42	2	1	0	9	23	27	0	.232	.254
Manny Mota	OF37, 2B1	R	25	59	126	20	34	2	3	0	7	7	18	0	.270	.333
Ron Brand	C33, 2B2, 3B2	R	23	46	66	8	19	2	0	1	7	10	11	0	.288	.364
1 Bob Skinner	OF32	L	31	34	122	18	33	5	5	0	8	13	22	4	.270	.393
Gene Alley	3B7, 2B4, SS4	R	22	17	51	3	11	1	0	0	0	2	12	0	.216	.235

Elmo Plaskett 25 R 3-21, Julio Gotay 24 R 1-2, Larry Elliott 25 L 0-4

NAME	T	AGE	W	L	PCT	SV	G	GS	CG	IP	H	BB	SO	ShO	ERA
		29	74	88	.457	33	162	162	34	1448	1350	457	900	16	3.10
Bob Friend	R	32	17	16	.515	0	39	38	12	269	236	44	144	4	2.34
Al McBean	R	25	13	3	.813	11	55	7	2	122	100	39	74	1	2.58
Don Cardwell	R	27	13	15	.464	0	33	32	7	214	195	52	115	2	3.07
Don Schwall	R	27	6	12	.333	0	33	24	3	168	158	74	86	2	3.32
Bob Veale	L	27	5	2	.714	3	34	7	3	78	59	40	68	2	1.04
Joe Gibbon	L	28	5	12	.294	1	37	22	5	147	147	54	110	0	3.31
Vern Law (VR)	R	33	4	5	.444	0	18	12	1	77	91	13	31	1	4.91
Earl Francis	R	26	4	6	.400	0	33	13	0	97	107	43	72	0	4.55
Harvey Haddix	L	37	3	4	.429	1	49	1	0	70	67	20	70	0	3.34
Roy Face	R	35	3	9	.250	16	56	0	0	70	75	19	41	0	3.21
Tommie Sisk	R	21	1	3	.250	1	57	4	1	108	85	45	73	0	2.92
Tom Parsons	R	23	0	1	.000	0	1	1	0	4	7	2	2	0	9.00
Tom Butters	R	25	0	0	.000	0	6	1	0	16	15	8	11	0	4.50
1 Tom Sturdivant	R	33	0	0	.000	0	3	0	0	8	8	4	6	0	6.75

HOUSTON 9th 66-96 .407 33 — HARRY CRAFT

NAME	G by POS	B	AGE	G	AB	R	H	2B	3B	HR	RBI	BB	SO	SB	BA	SA
TOTALS			26	162	5384	464	1184	170	39	62	420	456	938	39	.220	.301
Rusty Staub	1B109, OF49	L	19	150	513	43	115	17	4	6	45	59	58	0	.224	.308
Ernie Fazio	2B84, SS1, 3B1	R	21	102	228	31	42	10	3	2	5	27	70	4	.184	.281
Bob Lillis	SS124, 2B19, 3B6	R	33	147	469	31	93	13	1	1	19	15	35	3	.198	.237
Bob Aspromonte	3B131, 1B1	R	25	136	468	42	100	9	5	8	49	40	57	3	.214	.306
Carl Warwick	OF141, 1B2	R	26	150	528	49	134	19	5	7	47	49	70	3	.254	.348
Howie Goss	OF123	R	28	133	411	37	86	18	2	9	44	31	128	4	.209	.328
Al Spangler	OF113	L	29	120	430	52	121	25	4	4	27	50	38	5	.281	.386
John Bateman	C115	R	20	128	404	23	85	8	6	10	59	13	103	0	.210	.334
Pete Runnels	1B70, 2B36, 3B3	L	35	124	388	35	98	9	1	2	23	45	42	2	.253	.296
Johnny Temple	2B61, 3B19	R	34	100	322	22	85	12	1	1	17	41	24	7	.264	.317
Jim Wynn	OF53, SS21, 3B2	R	21	70	250	31	61	10	5	4	27	30	53	4	.244	.372
Jim Campbell	C42	R	26	55	158	9	35	3	0	4	19	10	40	0	.222	.316
J C Hartman	SS32	R	29	39	90	2	11	1	0	0	3	2	13	1	.122	.133
Johnny Weekly (JJ)	OF23	R	26	34	80	4	18	3	0	3	14	7	14	0	.225	.375
Brock Davis	OF14	L	19	34	55	7	11	2	0	1	2	4	10	0	.200	.291
Hal Smith	C11	R	32	31	58	1	14	2	0	0	4	2	15	0	.241	.276
Carroll Hardy	OF10	R	30	15	44	5	10	3	0	0	3	3	7	1	.227	.295
Glenn Vaughan	SS9, 3B1	B	19	9	30	1	5	0	0	0	0	2	5	1	.167	.167
Joe Morgan	2B7	L	19	8	25	5	6	0	1	0	3	5	5	1	.240	.320

Dave Adlesh 19 R 0-8, Mike White 24 R 2-7, Jerry Grote 20 R 1-5, Ivan Murrell 18 R 1-5, Aaron Pointer 21 R 1-5, John Paciorek 18 R 3-3, Sonny Jackson 18 L 0-3

NAME	T	AGE	W	L	PCT	SV	G	GS	CG	IP	H	BB	SO	ShO	ERA
		30	66	96	.407	20	162	162	36	1450	1341	378	937	16	3.44
Dick Farrell	R	29	14	13	.519	1	34	26	12	202	161	35	141	0	3.03
Don Nottebart	R	27	11	8	.579	0	31	27	9	193	170	39	118	2	3.17
Hal Woodeshick	L	30	11	9	.550	10	55	0	0	114	75	42	94	0	1.97
Ken Johnson	R	30	11	17	.393	1	37	32	6	224	204	50	148	1	2.65
Bob Bruce	R	30	5	9	.357	0	30	25	1	170	162	60	123	1	3.60
Hal Brown	R	38	5	11	.313	0	26	20	6	141	137	8	68	3	3.32
Jim Umbricht	R	32	4	3	.571	0	35	3	0	76	52	21	48	0	2.61
Chris Zachary	R	19	2	2	.500	0	22	7	0	57	62	22	42	0	4.89
Dick Drott	R	27	2	12	.143	0	27	14	2	98	95	49	58	1	4.96
Don McMahon	R	33	1	5	.167	5	49	2	0	80	83	26	51	0	4.05
Jim Dickson	R	25	0	1	.000	2	13	0	0	15	22	2	6	0	6.00
Randy Cardinal	R	21	0	1	.000	0	6	1	0	13	15	7	7	0	6.23
Jim Golden	R	27	0	1	.000	0	3	1	0	6	12	2	5	0	6.00
Jay Dahl	L	17	0	1	.000	0	1	1	0	3	7	0	0	0	15.00
1 George Brunet	L	28	0	3	.000	0	5	2	0	13	24	6	11	0	6.92
Russ Kemmerer	R	31	0	0	.000	1	17	0	0	37	48	8	12	0	5.59
Larry Yellen	R	20	0	0	.000	0	1	1	0	5	7	1	3	0	3.60
Joe Hoerner	L	26	0	0	.000	0	1	0	0	3	2	0	2	0	0.00
Danny Coombs	L	21	0	0	.000	0	1	0	0	1	3	0	0	0	27.00

NEW YORK 10th 51-111 .315 48 — CASEY STENGEL

NAME	G by POS	B	AGE	G	AB	R	H	2B	3B	HR	RBI	BB	SO	SB	BA	SA
TOTALS			27	162	5336	501	1168	156	35	96	459	457	**1078**	41	.219	.315
Tim Harkness	1B106	L	25	123	375	35	79	12	3	10	41	36	79	4	.211	.339
Ron Hunt	2B142, 3B1	R	22	143	533	64	145	28	4	10	42	40	50	5	.272	.396
Al Moran	SS116, 3B1	R	24	119	331	26	64	5	2	1	23	36	60	3	.193	.230
1 Charlie Neal	3B66, SS8	R	32	72	253	26	57	12	1	3	18	27	49	1	.225	.316
Duke Snider	OF106	L	36	129	354	44	86	8	3	14	45	56	74	0	.243	.401
Jim Hickman	OF82, 3B59	R	26	146	494	53	113	21	6	17	51	44	120	0	.229	.399
Frank Thomas	OF96, 1B15, 3B1	R	34	126	420	34	109	9	1	15	60	33	48	0	.260	.393
Choo Choo Coleman	C91, OF1	L	25	106	247	22	44	0	0	3	9	24	49	5	.178	.215
Rod Kanehl	OF58, 3B13, 2B12, 1B3	R	29	109	191	26	46	6	0	1	9	5	26	6	.241	.288
Ed Kranepool	OF55, 1B20	L	18	86	273	22	57	12	2	2	14	18	50	4	.209	.289
Joe Christopher	OF45	R	27	64	149	19	33	5	1	1	8	13	21	1	.221	.289
Norm Sherry	C61	R	31	63	147	6	20	1	0	2	11	10	26	1	.136	.184
2 Chico Fernandez	SS45, 3B5, 2B3	R	31	58	145	12	29	6	0	1	9	9	30	3	.200	.262
Joe Hicks	OF41	L	30	56	159	16	36	6	1	5	22	7	31	0	.226	.371
Cliff Cook	OF21, 3B9, 1B5	R	26	50	106	9	15	2	1	2	8	12	37	0	.142	.236
2 Duke Carmel	OF21, 1B18	L	26	47	149	11	35	5	3	3	18	16	37	2	.235	.369
2 Jesse Gonder	C31	L	27	42	126	12	38	4	0	3	15	6	25	1	.302	.405
Larry Burright	SS19, 2B15, 3B1	R	25	41	100	9	22	2	1	0	3	8	25	1	.220	.260
2 Jimmy Piersall	OF38	R	33	40	124	13	24	4	1	1	10	10	14	1	.194	.266
Ted Schreiber	3B17, SS9, 2B3	R	24	39	50	1	8	0	0	0	2	4	14	0	.160	.160
1 Sammy Taylor	C13	L	30	22	35	3	9	0	1	0	6	5	7	0	.257	.314
Dick Smith	OF10, 1B2	R	24	20	42	4	10	0	1	0	3	5	10	3	.238	.286
Pumpsie Green	3B16	B	29	17	54	8	15	1	2	1	5	12	13	0	.278	.426
Chris Cannizzaro	C15	R	25	16	33	4	8	1	0	0	4	1	8	0	.242	.273

Marv Throneberry 29 L 2-14, 1 Gil Hodges 39 R 5-22, Cleon Jones 20 R 2-15

NAME	T	AGE	W	L	PCT	SV	G	GS	CG	IP	H	BB	SO	ShO	ERA
		27	51	**111**	.315	12	162	162	42	1427	**1452**	529	806	5	4.12
Al Jackson	L	27	13	17	.433	1	37	34	11	227	237	84	142	0	3.96
Carl Willey	R	32	9	14	.391	0	30	28	7	183	149	69	101	4	3.10
Galen Cisco	R	27	7	15	.318	0	51	17	1	156	165	64	81	0	4.33
Tracy Stallard	R	25	6	17	.261	1	39	23	5	155	156	77	110	0	4.70
Roger Craig	R	32	5	**22**	.185	2	46	31	14	236	249	58	108	0	3.78
Jay Hook	R	26	4	14	.222	1	41	20	3	153	168	53	89	0	5.47
1 Ken MacKenzie	L	29	3	1	.750	3	34	0	0	58	63	12	41	0	4.97
Larry Bearnarth	R	21	3	8	.273	4	58	2	0	126	127	47	48	0	3.43
Grover Powell	L	22	1	1	.500	0	20	4	1	50	37	32	39	1	2.70
Craig Anderson	R	25	0	2	.000	0	3	2	0	9	17	3	6	0	9.00
Don Rowe	L	27	0	0	.000	0	26	1	0	55	59	21	27	0	4.25
2 Ed Bauta	R	28	0	0	.000	0	9	0	0	19	22	9	13	0	5.21
Steve Dillon	L	20	0	0	.000	0	1	0	0	2	3	0	1	0	9.00

⊖ ⊖ 1964 Play It Again, Phil ⊖ ⊖

Ralph Houk was rewarded for three straight pennants by being named general manager of the Yankees. In turn, Yogi Berra was rewarded for his 14 years of service and popularity by being named field boss. It was a move the Yankees soon regretted, as Berra proved more popular with the players than respected by them. The result was that in August, the Yankees found themselves in third place behind Baltimore and Chicago, playing sluggish ball and showing signs of never getting out of second gear. But oddly enough, the final challenge to Berra's authority provoked a new spirit via a shouting match between Berra and infielder Phil Linz. The incident took place on the team bus in mid-August over the issue whether or not Linz should play his harmonica. Berra thought not and quickly put an end to Linz's hopes for a second career. But suddenly, the apathy waned and the Yankee sun hung big and bright in the American League skies once again. Mickey Mantle returned from a leg injury in September to bolster the offense and Pedro Ramos was purchased from Cleveland to bolster a shaky bullpen. Mel Stottlemeyer, recalled in August, came on to win nine games and, along with batters, Joe Pepitone and Elston Howard, and pitchers, Whitey Ford and Jim Bouton, the Bronx Bombers were spurred on to a 22-6 September and a clinching of the pennant on the next-to-last day of the season—a pennant that was won despite the reported dissension, and injuries to Mantle, Ford, and Tony Kubek.

The White Sox made their challenge with a host of good pitching. Gary Peters, Juan Pizarro, and Joe Horlen formed the Big Three which carried an offense boasting of only one power threat, Pete Ward. The Orioles' attack packed a wallop in the form of the league's MVP, Brooks Robinson, and Boog Powell, the Bird's home run leader. Their hill staff featured 19-year-old Wally Bunker. Both clubs played well down the stretch but could not match the New York pace. Minnesota finished seventh, despite having the league's batting champ in rookie Tony Oliva and home run leader Harmon Killebrew.

The Los Angeles Angels just made the first division on the arm of Dean Chance, who won the Cy Young Award with 20 wins and a 1.65 E.R.A., and the fists of Bo Belinsky, who finished with nine victories before being suspended on August 14, for slugging a sportswriter.

In the National League, owner Gussie Busch showed his dissatisfaction with his St. Louis Cardinals' fifth-place occupancy by canning general manager Bing Devine on August 17, and rumors were rampant that manager Johnny Keane was next. But what was to come could not be seen yet, as two mid-season Devine acquisitions, outfielder Lou Brock and reliever Barney Schultz, led the Cards back into the pennant race.

The Phillies were leading the pack by 6½ games with two weeks remaining. It was enough of a lead to give Philadelphia printers the sign to ink up their presses for the first time in 14 years. But the imprint of Philadelphia on the World Series wasn't to be, as the Phillies dropped ten in a row to allow the Cards, Reds, and Giants to climb back into contention in the final week. When the dust finally settled, the Phillies and Reds found themselves staring at the pennant flag over Busch Stadium by a scant one-game margin.

The Cardinal cast was studded with starring performers. Brock joined the Cards from Chicago in June and hit a robust .348 the rest of the way. Ken Boyer led the league in RBI's and also won the MVP Award, while first baseman Bill White hit .303 and batted in 102 runs. Bob Gibson, Curt Simmons, and Ray Sadecki were outstanding starters for the Cards, and Barney Schultz was called up in August and provided top-notch relieving in the pennant drive.

The Reds finished second, despite losing their manager, Fred Hutchinson, who left the team in September with a cancer that would claim his life before another season would begin. Hutchinson's chief horses were outfielders, Frank Robinson and Vada Pinson. The disappointed Phillies were spearheaded by Johnny Callison, rookie third baseman Richie Allen, and pitching ace Jim Bunning. The Dodgers fell back into sixth place with an anemic attack, while the Braves were fifth, despite five men chalking up 20 home run performances.

Roberto Clemente of the Pirates won the batting title with a .339 mark, while Willie Mays of the Giants led in home runs with 47. Larry Jackson of the lowly Cubs won 24 games to pace the loop in victories, and Sandy Koufax of Los Angeles had the lowest E.R.A. to complete the honor roll.

In the World Series, Tim McCarver and Bobby Richardson both hit .400 in leading their teams to three victories each in the first six games. In the decisive seventh game, Keane stayed with Gibson through three Yankee home runs and was rewarded with a 7-5 victory to bring the championship back to St. Louis for the first time since 1946.

It was not until the next day, however, that the fireworks began. While Keane was announcing his resignation, citing the Devine firing and rumors of his own demise as reasons, the Yankees were revealing that Berra had been fired as manager because of his lack of control and communication with his players. The musical chairs continued into the winter, as Berra rejoined his long-time mentor Casey Stengel with the New York Mets in the capacity of player-coach, while the Yankees turned right around and hired Keane to replace Berra at the helm of the Bronx Dynasty which, unknown to Keane and the world-at-large, was on its way to crumbling.

WORLD SERIES – ST. LOUIS (NL) 4 NEW YORK (AL) 3

LINE SCORES

TEAM	1	2	3	4	5	6	7	8	9	10	11	12	R	H	E
Game 1 October 7 at St. Louis															
NY (AL)	0	3	0	0	1	0	0	1	0				5	12	2
STL (NL)	1	1	0	0	0	4	0	3	X				9	12	0
Ford, Downing (6), Sheldon (8), Mikkelsen (8) — **Sadecki**, Schultz (7)															
Game 2 October 8 at St. Louis															
NY	0	0	0	1	0	1	2	0	4				8	12	0
STL	0	0	1	0	0	0	0	1	1				3	7	0
Stottlemyre — **Gibson**, Schultz (9), G. Richardson (9), Craig (9)															
Game 3 October 10 at New York															
STL	0	0	0	0	1	0	0	0	0				1	6	0
NY	0	1	0	0	0	0	0	0	1				2	5	2
Simmons, **Schultz** (9) — **Bouton**															
Game 4 October 11 at New York															
STL	0	0	0	0	0	4	0	0	0				4	6	1
NY	3	0	0	0	0	0	0	0	0				3	6	1
Sadecki, **Craig** (1), Taylor (6) — **Downing**, Mikkelsen (7), Terry (8)															
Game 5 October 12 at New York															
STL	0	0	0	0	2	0	0	0	0	3			5	10	1
NY	0	0	0	0	0	0	0	0	2	0			2	6	2
Gibson — Stottlemyre, Reniff (8), **Mikkelsen** (8)															
Game 6 October 14 at St. Louis															
NY	0	0	0	0	1	2	0	5	0				8	10	0
STL	1	0	0	0	0	0	0	1	1				3	10	1
Bouton, Hamilton (9) — **Simmons**, Taylor (7), Schultz (8), G. Richardson (8), Humphreys (9)															
Game 7 October 15 at St. Louis															
NY	0	0	0	0	0	3	0	0	2				5	9	2
STL	0	0	0	3	3	0	1	0	X				7	10	1
Stottlemyre, Downing (5), Sheldon (5), Hamilton (7), Mikkelsen (8) — **Gibson**															

COMPOSITE BATTING

NAME	POS	G	AB	R	H	2B	3B	HR	RBI	BA
St. Louis (NL)										
Totals		7	240	32	61	8	3	5	29	.254
Brock	OF	7	30	2	9	2	0	1	5	.300
Flood	OF	7	30	5	6	0	1	0	3	.200
Shannon	OF	7	28	6	6	0	0	1	2	.214
K. Boyer	3B	7	27	5	6	1	0	2	6	.222
White	1B	7	27	2	3	1	0	0	2	.111
Groat	SS	7	26	3	5	1	1	0	1	.192
McCarver	C	7	23	4	11	1	1	1	5	.478
Maxvill	2B	7	20	0	4	1	0	0	1	.200
Gibson	P	3	9	1	2	0	0	0	0	.222
Warwick	PH	5	4	2	3	0	0	0	1	.750
Simmons	P	2	4	0	2	0	0	0	1	.500
Skinner	PH	4	3	0	2	1	0	0	1	.667
James	PH	3	3	0	0	0	0	0	0	.000
Sadecki	P	2	2	0	1	0	0	0	1	.500
Buchek	2B	4	1	1	1	0	0	0	0	1.000
Schultz	P	4	1	0	0	0	0	0	0	.000
Craig	P	2	1	0	0	0	0	0	0	.000
Taylor	P	2	1	0	0	0	0	0	0	.000
Javier	2B	1	0	1	0	0	0	0	0	.000
G. Richardson P 0-0, Humphreys P 0-0										
New York (AL)										
Totals		7	239	33	60	11	0	10	33	.251
B. Richardson	2B	7	32	3	13	2	0	0	3	.406
Linz	SS	7	31	5	7	1	0	2	2	.226
Maris	OF	7	30	4	6	0	0	1	1	.200
Pepitone	1B	7	26	1	4	1	0	1	5	.154
Mantle	OF	7	24	8	8	2	0	3	8	.333
Howard	C	7	24	5	7	1	0	0	2	.292
C. Boyer	3B	7	24	2	5	1	0	1	3	.208
Tresh	OF	7	22	4	6	2	0	2	7	.273
Stottlemyre	P	3	8	0	1	0	0	0	0	.125
Bouton	P	2	7	0	1	0	0	0	1	.143
Blanchard	PH	4	4	0	1	1	0	0	0	.250
Lopez	OF	3	2	0	0	0	0	0	0	.000
Downing	P	3	2	0	0	0	0	0	0	.000
Ford	P	1	1	0	1	0	0	0	1	1.000
Gonzalez	3B	1	1	0	0	0	0	0	0	.000
Hegan	PH	3	1	1	0	0	0	0	0	.000
Mikkelsen	P	4	0	0	0	0	0	0	0	.000
Sheldon	P	2	0	0	0	0	0	0	0	.000
Hamilton	P	2	0	0	0	0	0	0	0	.000
Terry P 0-0, Reniff P 0-0										

COMPOSITE PITCHING

NAME	G	IP	H	BB	SO	W	L	SV	ERA
St. Louis (NL)									
Totals	7	63	60	25	54	4	3	2	4.29
Gibson	3	27	23	8	31	2	1	0	3.00
Simmons	2	14.1	11	3	8	0	1	0	2.51
Sadecki	2	6.1	12	5	2	1	0	0	8.53
Craig	2	5	2	3	9	1	0	0	0.00
Taylor	2	4.2	0	1	2	0	0	1	0.00
Schultz	4	4	9	3	1	0	1	1	18.00
Humphreys	1	1	0	0	1	0	0	0	0.00
G. Richardson	2	.2	3	2	0	0	0	0	40.50
New York (AL)									
Totals	7	62	61	18	39	3	4	1	3.77
Stottlemyre	3	20	18	6	12	1	1	0	3.15
Bouton	2	17.1	15	5	7	2	0	0	1.56
Downing	3	7.2	9	2	5	0	1	0	8.22
Ford	1	5.1	8	1	4	0	1	0	8.44
Mikkelsen	4	4.2	4	2	4	0	1	0	5.79
Sheldon	2	2.2	0	2	2	0	0	0	0.00
Hamilton	2	2	3	0	2	0	0	1	4.50
Terry	1	2	2	0	3	0	0	0	0.00
Reniff	1	.1	2	0	0	0	0	0	0.00

NEW YORK 1st 99-63 .611 — YOGI BERRA

NAME	G by POS	B	AGE	G	AB	R	H	2B	3B	HR	RBI	BB	SO	SB	BA	SA
TOTALS			28	164	**5705**	730	**1442**	208	35	162	688	520	976	54	.253	.387
Joe Pepitone	1B155, OF30	L	23	160	613	71	154	12	3	28	100	24	63	2	.251	.418
Bobby Richardson	2B157, SS1	R	28	159	**679**	90	181	25	4	4	50	28	36	11	.267	.333
Tony Kubek (XJ)	SS99	L	27	106	415	46	95	16	3	8	31	26	55	4	.229	.340
Clete Boyer	3B123, SS21	R	27	147	510	43	111	10	5	8	52	36	93	6	.218	.304
Roger Maris	OF137	L	29	141	513	86	144	12	2	26	71	62	78	3	.281	.464
Mickey Mantle	OF132	B	32	143	465	92	141	25	2	35	111	99	102	6	.303	.591
Tom Tresh	OF146	B	26	153	533	75	131	25	5	16	73	73	110	13	.246	.402
Elston Howard	C146	R	35	150	550	63	172	27	3	15	84	48	73	1	.313	.455
Hector Lopez	OF103, 3B1	R	31	127	285	34	74	9	3	10	34	24	54	1	.260	.418
Phil Linz	SS55, 3B41, 2B5, OF3	R	25	112	368	63	92	21	3	5	25	43	61	3	.250	.364
Pedro Gonzalez	1B31, OF20, 3B9, 2B6	R	25	80	112	18	31	8	1	0	5	7	22	3	.277	.366
Johnny Blanchard	C25, OF14, 1B3	L	31	77	161	18	41	8	0	7	28	24	24	1	.255	.435
Archie Moore	OF8, 1B7	L	22	31	23	4	4	2	0	0	1	2	9	0	.174	.261
Harry Bright	1B2	R	34	4	5	0	1	0	0	0	0	1	1	0	.200	.200
Elvio Jiminez	OF1	R	24	1	6	0	2	0	0	0	0	0	0	0	.333	.333

Jake Gibbs 25 L 1-6, Mike Hegan L 0-5, Roger Repoz 23 L 0-1

NAME	T	AGE	W	L	PCT	SV	G	GS	CG	IP	H	BB	SO	ShO	ERA
		27	**99**	63	**.611**	**45**	164	164	46	**1507**	1312	504	989	18	3.15
Jim Bouton	R	25	18	13	.581	0	38	37	11	271	227	60	125	4	3.02
Whitey Ford	L	35	17	6	.739	1	39	36	12	245	212	57	172	8	2.13
Al Downing	L	23	13	8	.619	2	37	35	11	244	201	**120**	**217**	1	3.47
Mel Stottlemyre	R	22	9	3	.750	0	13	12	5	96	77	35	49	2	2.06
Steve Hamilton	L	30	7	2	.778	3	30	3	1	60	55	15	49	0	3.30
Pete Mikkelsen	R	24	7	4	.636	12	50	0	0	86	79	41	63	0	3.56
Ralph Terry	R	28	7	11	.389	4	27	14	2	115	130	31	77	1	4.54
Hal Reniff	R	25	6	4	.600	9	41	0	0	69	47	30	38	0	3.13
Bill Stafford	R	24	5	0	1.000	4	31	1	0	61	50	22	39	0	2.66
Rollie Sheldon	R	27	5	2	.714	1	19	12	3	102	92	18	57	0	3.62
Bud Daley (SA)	L	31	3	2	.600	1	13	3	0	35	37	25	16	0	4.63
2 Pedro Ramos	R	29	1	0	1.000	8	13	0	0	22	13	0	21	0	1.25
Stan Williams	R	27	1	5	.167	0	21	10	1	82	76	38	54	0	3.84
1 Bob Meyer	R	24	0	3	.000	0	7	1	0	18	16	12	12	0	4.91

CHICAGO 2nd 98-64 .605 1 — AL LOPEZ

NAME	G by POS	B	AGE	G	AB	R	H	2B	3B	HR	RBI	BB	SO	SB	BA	SA
TOTALS			27	162	5491	642	1356	184	40	106	586	**562**	902	75	.247	.353
Tommy McCraw	1B84, OF36	L	23	125	368	47	96	11	5	6	36	32	65	15	.261	.367
Al Weis	2B116, SS9, OF2	B	26	133	328	36	81	4	4	2	23	22	41	22	.247	.302
Ron Hansen	SS158	R	26	158	575	85	150	25	3	20	68	73	73	1	.261	.419
Pete Ward	3B138	L	24	144	539	61	152	28	3	23	94	56	76	1	.282	.473
Mike Hershberger	OF134	R	24	141	452	55	104	15	3	2	31	48	47	8	.230	.290
Jim Landis	OF101	R	30	106	298	30	62	8	4	1	18	36	64	5	.208	.272
Floyd Robinson	OF138	L	28	141	525	83	158	17	3	11	59	70	41	9	.301	.408
J. C. Martin	C120	L	27	122	294	23	58	10	1	4	22	16	30	0	.197	.279
Don Buford	2B92, 3B37	B	27	135	442	62	116	14	6	4	30	46	62	12	.262	.348
Dave Nicholson	OF92	R	24	97	294	40	60	6	1	13	39	52	126	0	.204	.364
Gene Stephens	OF59	L	31	82	141	21	33	4	2	3	17	21	28	1	.234	.355
2 Bill Skowron	1B70	R	33	73	273	19	80	11	3	4	38	19	36	0	.293	.399
Jerry McNertney	C69	R	27	73	186	16	40	5	0	3	23	19	24	0	.215	.290
Gary Peters	P37	L	27	54	120	9	25	7	0	4	19	2	29	0	.208	.367
1 Joe Cunningham	1B33	L	32	40	108	13	27	7	0	0	10	14	14	0	.250	.315
Cam Carreon (SJ)	C34	R	26	37	95	12	26	5	0	0	4	7	13	0	.274	.326
Minnie Minoso	OF5	R	41	30	31	4	7	0	0	1	5	5	3	0	.226	.323
2 Jeoff Long	1B5, OF5	R	22	23	35	0	5	0	0	0	5	4	15	0	.143	.143
Ken Berry	OF12	R	23	12	32	4	12	1	0	1	4	5	3	0	.375	.500
2 Smoky Burgess		L	37	7	5	1	1	0	0	1	1	2	0	0	.200	.800
Marv Staehle		L	22	6	5	0	2	0	0	0	2	0	0	1	.400	.400
1 Charley Smith	3B2	R	26	2	7	1	1	0	1	0	0	1	1	0	.143	.429

Charlie Maxwell 37 L 0-2, Dick Kenworthy 23 R 0-2, Jim Hicks 24 R 0-0

NAME	T	AGE	W	L	PCT	SV	G	GS	CG	IP	H	BB	SO	ShO	ERA
		29	98	64	.605	**45**	162	162	44	1468	1216	401	955	20	**2.72**
Gary Peters	L	27	**20**	8	.714	0	37	36	11	274	217	104	205	3	2.50
Juan Pizarro	L	27	19	9	.679	0	33	33	11	239	193	55	162	4	2.56
Joe Horlen	R	26	13	9	.591	0	32	28	9	211	142	55	138	2	1.88
Hoyt Wilhelm	R	40	12	9	.571	27	73	0	0	131	94	30	95	0	1.99
John Buzhardt	R	27	10	8	.556	0	31	25	8	160	150	35	97	3	2.98
Eddie Fisher	R	27	6	3	.667	9	59	2	0	125	86	32	74	0	3.02
Ray Herbert (EJ)	R	34	6	7	.462	0	20	19	1	112	117	17	40	1	3.46
Fred Talbot	R	23	4	5	.444	0	17	12	3	75	83	20	34	2	3.72
Don Mossi	L	35	3	1	.750	7	34	0	0	40	37	7	36	0	2.93
1 Frank Kreutzer	L	25	3	1	.750	1	17	2	0	40	37	18	32	0	3.35
Bruce Howard	R	21	2	1	.667	0	3	3	1	22	10	8	17	1	0.82
Frank Baumann	L	31	0	3	.000	1	22	0	0	32	40	16	19	0	6.19
Fritz Ackley	R	27	0	0	.000	0	3	2	0	6	10	4	6	0	9.00

Dave DeBusschere (MS) 23

BALTIMORE 3rd 97-65 .599 2 — HANK BAUER

NAME	G by POS	B	AGE	G	AB	R	H	2B	3B	HR	RBI	BB	SO	SB	BA	SA
TOTALS			27	163	5463	679	1357	229	20	162	632	537	1019	78	.248	.387
Norm Siebern	1B149	L	30	150	478	92	117	24	2	12	56	**106**	87	2	.245	.379
Jerry Adair	2B153	R	27	155	569	56	141	20	3	9	47	28	72	3	.248	.341
Luis Aparicio	SS145	R	30	146	578	93	154	20	3	10	37	49	51	**57**	.266	.363
Brooks Robinson	3B163	R	27	163	612	82	194	35	3	28	**118**	51	64	1	.317	.521
Sam Bowens	OF135	R	25	139	501	58	132	25	2	22	71	42	99	4	.263	.453
Jackie Brandt	OF134	R	30	137	523	66	127	25	1	13	47	45	104	1	.243	.369
Boog Powell	OF124, 1B5	L	22	134	424	74	123	17	0	39	99	76	91	0	.290	**.606**
Dick Brown	C84	R	29	88	230	24	59	6	0	8	32	12	45	2	.257	.387
Bob Johnson	SS18, 1B15, 2B15, 3B1, OF1	R	28	93	210	18	52	8	2	3	29	9	37	0	.248	.348
John Orsino	C66, 1B5	R	26	81	248	21	55	10	0	8	23	23	55	0	.222	.359
1 Willie Kirkland	OF58	L	30	66	150	14	30	5	0	3	22	17	26	3	.200	.293
2 Charlie Lau	C47	L	31	62	158	16	41	15	1	1	14	17	27	0	.259	.386
Russ Snyder (BN)	OF40	L	30	56	93	11	27	3	0	1	7	11	22	0	.290	.355
Bob Saverine	SS15, OF2	B	23	46	34	14	5	1	0	0	0	3	6	3	.147	.176
2 Gino Cimoli	OF35	R	34	38	58	6	8	3	2	0	3	2	13	0	.138	.259
Earl Robinson	OF34	R	27	37	121	11	33	5	1	3	10	7	24	1	.273	.405
1 Joe Gaines	OF5	R	27	16	26	2	4	0	0	1	2	3	7	0	.154	.269
3 Lenny Green	OF8	L	30	14	21	0	4	0	0	0	1	7	3	1	.190	.190
Lou Jackson	OF1	L	28	4	8	0	3	0	0	0	0	0	2	0	.375	.375

Paul Blair 20 R 0-1, Lou Piniella 20 R 0-1

NAME	T	AGE	W	L	PCT	SV	G	GS	CG	IP	H	BB	SO	ShO	ERA
		28	97	65	.599	41	163	163	44	1459	1292	456	939	17	3.16
Wally Bunker	R	19	19	5	**.792**	0	29	29	12	214	161	62	96	1	2.69
Milt Pappas	R	25	16	7	.696	0	37	36	13	252	225	48	157	7	2.96
Robin Roberts	R	37	13	7	.650	0	31	31	8	204	203	52	109	4	2.91
Dick Hall	R	33	9	1	.900	7	45	0	0	88	58	16	52	0	1.84
Dave McNally	L	21	9	11	.450	0	30	23	5	159	157	51	88	3	3.68
Steve Barber	L	25	9	13	.409	1	36	26	4	157	144	81	118	0	3.84
Stu Miller	R	36	7	7	.500	23	66	0	0	97	77	34	87	0	3.06
Harvey Haddix	L	38	5	5	.500	10	49	0	0	90	68	23	90	0	2.30
Chuck Estrada (EJ)	R	26	3	2	.600	0	17	6	0	55	62	21	32	0	5.24
1 Wes Stock	R	30	2	0	1.000	0	14	0	0	21	17	8	14	0	3.92
Dave Vineyard	R	23	2	5	.286	0	19	6	1	54	57	27	50	0	4.17
Frank Bertaina	L	20	1	0	1.000	0	6	4	1	26	18	13	18	1	2.77
Ken Rowe	R	30	1	0	1.000	0	6	0	0	4	10	1	4	0	9.00
Herm Starrette	R	25	1	0	1.000	0	5	0	0	11	9	6	5	0	1.64
Mike McCormick	L	25	0	2	.000	0	4	2	0	17	21	8	13	0	5.29
Sam Jones	R	38	0	0	.000	0	7	0	0	10	5	5	6	0	2.70

DETROIT 4th 85-77 .525 14 — CHUCK DRESSEN

NAME	G by POS	B	AGE	G	AB	R	H	2B	3B	HR	RBI	BB	SO	SB	BA	SA
TOTALS			28	163	5513	699	1394	199	**57**	157	658	517	912	60	.253	.395
Norm Cash	1B137	L	29	144	479	63	123	15	5	23	83	70	66	2	.257	.453
Jerry Lumpe	2B158	L	31	158	624	75	160	21	6	6	46	50	61	2	.256	.338
Dick McAuliffe	SS160	L	24	162	557	85	134	18	7	24	66	77	96	8	.241	.427
Don Wert	3B142, SS4	R	25	148	525	63	135	18	5	9	55	50	74	3	.257	.362
Al Kaline	OF136	R	29	146	525	77	154	31	5	17	68	75	51	4	.293	.469
George Thomas	OF90, 3B1	R	26	105	308	39	88	15	2	12	44	18	53	4	.286	.464
Gates Brown	OF106	L	25	123	426	65	116	22	6	15	54	31	53	11	.272	.458
Bill Freehan	C141, 1B1	R	22	144	520	69	156	14	8	18	80	36	68	5	.300	.462
Don Demeter	OF88, 1B23	R	29	134	441	57	113	22	1	22	80	17	85	4	.256	.460
Bill Bruton	OF81	L	38	106	296	42	82	11	5	5	33	32	54	14	.277	.399
Jake Wood	1B11, 2B10, 3B6, OF1	R	27	64	125	11	29	2	2	1	7	4	24	0	.232	.304
Bubba Phillips	3B22, OF1	R	34	46	87	14	22	1	0	3	6	10	13	1	.253	.368
Mike Roarke	C27	R	33	29	82	4	19	1	0	0	7	10	10	0	.232	.244
Willie Horton	OF23	R	21	25	80	6	13	1	3	1	10	11	20	0	.163	.288
George Smith	2B3	R	25	5	7	1	2	0	0	0	2	1	4	1	.286	.286
Jim Northrup	OF2	L	24	5	12	1	1	1	0	0	0	0	3	1	.083	.167
Mickey Stanley	OF4	R	21	4	11	3	3	0	0	0	1	0	1	0	.273	.273
Bill Roman	1B2	L	25	3	8	2	3	0	0	1	1	0	2	0	.375	.750
John Sullivan	C2	L	23	2	3	0	0	0	0	0	0	0	1	0	.000	.000

NAME	T	AGE	W	L	PCT	SV	G	GS	CG	IP	H	BB	SO	ShO	ERA
		27	85	77	.525	35	163	163	35	1453	1343	536	993	11	3.84
Dave Wickersham	R	28	19	12	.613	1	40	36	11	254	224	81	164	1	3.44
Mickey Lolich	L	23	18	9	.667	2	44	33	12	232	196	64	192	6	3.26
Ed Rakow	R	28	8	9	.471	3	42	13	1	152	155	59	96	0	3.73
Fred Gladding	R	28	7	4	.636	7	42	0	0	67	57	27	59	0	3.09
Larry Sherry (FJ)	R	28	7	5	.583	11	38	0	0	66	52	37	58	0	3.68
Joe Sparma	R	22	5	6	.455	0	21	11	3	84	62	45	71	2	3.00
Phil Regan	R	27	5	10	.333	1	32	21	2	147	162	49	91	0	5.02
Hank Aguirre	L	32	5	10	.333	1	32	27	3	162	134	59	88	0	3.78
Terry Fox	R	28	4	3	.571	5	32	0	0	61	77	16	28	0	3.39
Denny McLain	R	20	4	5	.444	0	19	16	3	100	84	37	70	0	4.05
2 Julio Navarro	R	28	2	1	.667	2	26	0	0	41	40	16	36	0	3.95
Johnny Seale	L	25	1	0	1.000	0	4	0	0	10	6	4	5	0	3.60
Jack Hamilton	R	25	0	1	.000	0	5	1	0	15	24	8	5	0	8.40
1 Frank Lary	R	34	0	2	.000	0	6	4	0	18	24	10	6	0	7.00
Dick Egan	L	27	0	0	.000	2	23	0	0	34	33	17	21	0	4.50
1 Alan Koch	R	26	0	0	.000	0	3	0	0	4	6	3	1	0	6.75
Bill Faul	R	24	0	0	.000	0	1	1	0	5	5	2	1	0	10.80
Fritz Fisher	L	22	0	0	.000	0	1	0	0	.1	2	2	1	0	108.00

LOS ANGELES 5th 82-80 .506 17 — BILL RIGNEY

NAME	G by POS	B	AGE	G	AB	R	H	2B	3B	HR	RBI	BB	SO	SB	BA	SA
TOTALS			27	162	5362	544	1297	186	27	102	508	472	920	49	.242	.344
Joe Adcock	1B105	R	36	118	366	39	98	13	0	21	64	48	61	0	.268	.475
Bobby Knoop	2B161	R	25	162	486	42	105	8	1	7	38	46	109	3	.216	.280
Jim Fregosi	SS137	R	22	147	505	86	140	22	9	18	72	72	87	8	.277	.463
Felix Torres	3B72, 1B3	R	32	100	277	25	64	10	0	12	28	13	56	1	.231	.397
2 Lu Clinton	OF86	R	26	91	306	30	76	18	0	9	38	31	40	3	.248	.395
Albie Pearson	OF66	L	29	107	265	34	59	5	1	2	16	35	22	6	.223	.272
Willie Smith	OF87, P15	L	25	118	359	46	108	14	6	11	51	8	39	7	.301	.465
Bob Rodgers	C146	B	25	148	514	38	125	18	3	4	54	40	71	4	.243	.313
Tom Satriano	3B38, 1B32, C25, SS2, 2B1	L	23	108	255	18	51	9	0	1	17	30	37	0	.200	.247
Jimmy Piersall	OF72	R	34	87	255	28	80	11	0	2	13	16	32	5	.314	.380
Ed Kirkpatrick	OF63	L	19	75	219	20	53	13	3	2	22	23	30	2	.242	.356
Bob Perry	OF62	R	21	70	221	19	61	8	1	3	16	14	52	1	.276	.362
2 Vic Power	1B48, 3B28, 2B5	R	32	68	221	17	55	6	0	3	13	8	14	1	.249	.317
Joe Koppe	SS31, 2B13, 3B3	R	33	54	113	10	29	4	1	0	6	14	16	0	.257	.310
1 Billy Moran	3B47, 2B3, SS1	R	30	50	198	26	53	10	1	0	11	13	20	1	.268	.328
1 Lee Thomas	OF47, 1B1	L	28	47	172	14	47	8	1	2	24	18	22	1	.273	.366
2 Lenny Green	OF23	L	30	39	92	13	23	2	0	2	4	10	8	2	.250	.337
Charlie Dees	1B12	L	29	26	26	3	2	1	0	0	1	1	4	1	.077	.115
Dick Simpson	OF16	R	20	21	50	11	7	1	0	2	4	8	15	2	.140	.280
Paul Schaal	2B9, 3B9	R	21	17	32	3	4	0	0	0	0	2	5	0	.125	.125
Rick Reichardt	OF11	R	21	11	37	0	6	0	0	0	0	1	12	1	.162	.162
Jack Hiatt	C3, 1B2	R	21	9	16	2	6	0	0	0	2	2	3	0	.375	.375
Hank Foiles		R	35	4	4	0	1	0	0	0	0	0	2	0	.250	.250

NAME	T	AGE	W	L	PCT	SV	G	GS	CG	IP	H	BB	SO	ShO	ERA
		27	82	80	.506	41	162	162	30	1451	1273	530	965	**28**	2.91
Dean Chance	R	23	**20**	9	.690	4	46	35	**15**	**278**	194	86	207	**11**	**1.65**
Fred Newman	R	22	13	10	.565	0	32	28	7	190	177	39	83	2	2.75
Bo Belinsky (ST)	L	27	9	8	.529	0	23	22	4	135	120	49	91	1	2.87
Bob Duliba	R	29	6	4	.600	9	58	0	0	73	80	22	33	0	3.58
Bob Lee	R	26	6	5	.545	19	64	5	0	137	87	58	111	0	1.51
Barry Latman	R	28	6	10	.375	2	40	18	2	138	128	52	81	1	3.85
Don Lee	R	30	5	4	.556	2	33	8	0	89	99	25	73	0	2.73
Ken McBride	R	28	4	13	.235	1	29	21	0	116	104	75	66	0	5.28
Dan Osinski	R	30	3	3	.500	2	47	4	1	93	87	39	88	1	3.48
Aubrey Gatewood	R	25	3	3	.500	0	15	7	0	60	59	12	25	0	2.25
Bill Kelso	R	24	2	0	1.000	0	10	1	1	24	19	9	21	1	2.25
George Brunet	L	29	2	2	.500	0	10	7	0	42	38	25	36	0	3.64
1 Jack Spring	L	31	1	0	1.000	0	6	0	0	3	3	3	0	0	3.00
2 Bob Meyer	R	24	1	1	.500	0	6	5	0	18	25	13	13	0	5.00
Willie Smith	L	25	1	4	.200	0	15	1	0	32	34	10	20	0	2.81
Paul Foytack	R	33	0	1	.000	0	2	0	0	2	4	2	1	0	18.00
Ed Sukla	R	21	0	1	.000	0	2	0	0	3	2	1	3	0	6.00
Art Fowler	R	41	0	2	.000	1	4	0	0	7	8	5	5	0	10.29
1 Julio Navarro	R	28	0	0	.000	1	5	0	0	9	5	5	8	0	1.93

CLEVELAND 6th (Tie) 79-83 .488 20 — BIRDIE TEBBETTS

NAME	G by POS	B	AGE	G	AB	R	H	2B	3B	HR	RBI	BB	SO	SB	BA	SA
TOTALS			27	164	5603	689	1386	208	22	164	640	500	1063	79	.247	.380
Bob Chance	1B81, OF31	L	23	120	390	45	109	16	1	14	75	40	101	3	.279	.433
Larry Brown	2B103, SS4	R	24	115	335	33	77	12	1	12	40	24	55	1	.230	.379
Dick Howser	SS162	R	27	162	637	101	163	23	4	3	52	76	39	20	.256	.319
Max Alvis (IL)	3B105	R	26	107	381	51	96	14	3	18	53	29	77	5	.252	.446
Tito Francona	OF69, 1B17	L	30	111	270	35	67	13	2	8	24	44	46	1	.248	.400
Vic Davalillo	OF143	L	27	150	577	64	156	26	2	6	51	34	77	21	.270	.354
Leon Wagner	OF163	L	30	163	641	94	162	19	2	31	100	56	121	14	.253	.434
Johnny Romano	C96, 1B1	R	29	106	352	46	85	18	1	19	47	51	83	2	.241	.460
Woodie Held	2B52, OF41, 3B30	R	32	118	364	50	86	13	0	18	49	43	88	1	.236	.420
Fred Whitfield	1B79	L	26	101	293	29	79	13	1	10	29	12	58	0	.270	.423
Chico Salmon	OF53, 2B32, 1B13	R	23	86	283	43	87	17	2	4	25	13	37	10	.307	.424
Joe Azcue	C76	R	24	83	271	20	74	9	1	4	34	16	38	0	.273	.358
2 Billy Moran	3B42, 2B15, 1B2	R	30	69	151	14	31	6	0	1	10	18	16	0	.205	.265
1 Al Smith	OF48, 3B1	R	36	61	136	15	22	1	1	4	9	8	32	0	.162	.272
1 Jerry Kindall	1B23	R	29	23	25	5	9	1	0	2	2	2	7	0	.360	.480
Al Luplow	OF5	L	25	19	18	1	2	0	0	0	1	1	8	0	.111	.111
Tommie Agee	OF12	R	21	13	12	0	2	0	0	0	0	0	3	0	.167	.167
Tony Martinez	2B4, SS1	R	23	9	14	1	3	1	0	0	2	0	2	0	.214	.286
2 George Banks	OF3, 2B1, 3B1	R	25	9	17	6	5	1	0	2	3	6	6	0	.294	.706

Paul Dicken 20 R 0-11, Wally Post 34 R 0-8, Duke Sims 23 L 0-6, Vern Fuller (BS) 20 R 0-1

NAME	T	AGE	W	L	PCT	SV	G	GS	CG	IP	H	BB	SO	ShO	ERA
TOTALS		28	79	83	.488	37	164	164	37	1488	1443	565	1162	16	3.75
Jack Kralick	L	29	12	7	.632	0	30	29	8	191	196	51	119	3	3.20
Sam McDowell	L	21	11	6	.647	1	31	24	6	173	148	100	177	2	2.71
Luis Tiant	R	23	10	4	.714	1	19	16	9	127	94	47	105	3	2.83
Gary Bell	R	27	8	6	.571	4	56	2	0	106	106	53	89	0	4.33
Sonny Siebert	R	27	7	9	.438	3	41	14	3	156	142	57	144	1	3.23
Dick Donovan	R	36	7	9	.438	1	30	23	5	158	181	29	83	0	4.56
1 Pedro Ramos	R	29	7	10	.412	0	36	19	3	133	144	26	98	1	5.14
Dom McMahon	R	34	6	4	.600	16	70	0	0	101	67	52	92	0	2.41
2 Lee Stange	R	27	4	8	.333	0	23	14	0	92	98	31	78	0	4.12
1 Mudcat Grant	R	28	3	4	.429	0	13	9	1	62	82	25	43	0	5.95
Ted Abernathy	R	31	2	6	.250	11	53	0	0	73	66	46	57	0	4.32
Tommy John	L	21	2	9	.182	0	25	14	2	94	97	35	65	1	3.93
Jerry Walker	R	25	0	1	.000	0	6	0	0	10	9	4	5	0	4.50
Tom Kelley	R	20	0	0	.000	0	6	0	0	10	9	9	7	0	5.40
Gordon Seyfried	R	26	0	0	.000	0	2	0	0	2	4	0	0	0	0.00

MINNESOTA 6th (Tie) 79-83 .488 20 — SAM MELE

NAME	G by POS	B	AGE	G	AB	R	H	2B	3B	HR	RBI	BB	SO	SB	BA	SA
TOTALS			26	163	5610	**737**	1413	227	46	**221**	**707**	553	1019	46	.252	**.427**
Bob Allison	1B93, OF61	R	29	149	492	90	141	27	4	32	86	92	99	10	.287	.553
Bernie Allen (NJ)	2B71	L	25	74	243	28	52	8	1	6	20	33	30	1	.214	.329
Zoilo Versalles	SS160	R	24	160	659	94	171	33	**10**	20	64	42	88	14	.259	.431
Rich Rollins	3B146	R	26	148	596	87	161	25	**10**	12	68	53	80	2	.270	.406
Tony Oliva	OF159	L	23	161	672	**109**	**217**	**43**	9	32	94	34	68	12	**.323**	.557
Jimmie Hall	OF137	L	26	149	510	61	144	20	3	25	75	44	112	5	.282	.480
Harmon Killebrew	OF157	R	28	158	577	95	156	11	1	**49**	111	93	135	0	.270	.548
Earl Battey	C125	R	29	131	405	33	110	17	1	12	52	51	49	1	.272	.407
Don Mincher	1B76	L	26	120	287	45	68	12	4	23	56	27	51	0	.237	.547
Jerry Zimmerman	C63	R	29	63	120	6	24	3	0	0	12	10	15	0	.200	.225
2 Jerry Kindall	2B51, SS7, 1B1	R	29	62	128	8	19	2	0	1	6	7	44	0	.148	.188
Frank Kostro	3B12, 2B7, OF2, 1B1	R	26	59	103	10	28	5	0	3	12	4	21	0	.272	.408
Johnny Goryl	2B28, 3B13	R	30	58	114	9	16	0	2	0	1	10	25	1	.140	.175
Jim Snyder	2B25	R	31	26	71	3	11	2	0	1	9	4	11	0	.155	.225
1 Lenny Green	OF7	L	30	26	15	3	0	0	0	0	0	4	6	0	.000	.000
Ron Henry	C13	R	27	22	41	4	5	1	1	2	5	2	17	0	.122	.341
1 Vic Power	1B12, 2B1	R	32	19	45	6	10	2	0	0	1	1	3	0	.222	.267
Joe McCabe	C12	R	25	14	19	1	3	0	0	0	2	0	8	0	.158	.158
Jay Ward	2B9, OF3	R	25	12	31	4	7	2	0	0	2	6	13	0	.226	.290
Bill Bethea	2B7, SS3	R	22	10	30	4	5	1	0	0	2	4	4	0	.167	.200
Rich Reese	1B1	L	22	10	7	0	0	0	0	0	0	0	1	0	.000	.000

Clyde Bloomfield 28 R 1-7, Joe Nossek 23 R 0-1, 1 George Banks 25 R 0-1

NAME	T	AGE	W	L	PCT	SV	G	GS	CG	IP	H	BB	SO	ShO	ERA
TOTALS		28	79	83	.488	29	163	163	**47**	1478	1361	545	1099	4	3.57
Jim Kaat	L	25	17	11	.607	1	36	34	13	243	231	60	171	1	3.22
Camilo Pascual	R	30	15	12	.556	0	36	36	14	267	245	98	213	1	3.30
2 Mudcat Grant	R	28	11	9	.550	1	26	23	10	166	162	36	75	1	2.82
Jerry Arrigo	L	23	7	4	.636	1	41	12	2	105	97	45	96	1	3.86
Jim Perry	R	28	6	3	.667	2	42	1	0	65	61	23	55	0	3.46
Dick Stigman	L	28	6	15	.286	0	32	29	5	190	160	70	159	1	4.03
2 Al Worthington	R	35	5	6	.455	14	41	0	0	72	47	28	59	0	1.38
Bill Pleis	L	26	4	1	.800	4	47	0	0	51	43	31	42	0	3.88
1 Lee Stange	R	27	3	6	.333	0	14	11	2	80	78	19	54	0	4.75
Dave Boswell	R	19	2	0	1.000	0	4	4	0	23	21	12	25	0	4.30
Jim Roland	L	21	2	6	.250	3	30	13	1	94	76	55	63	0	4.12
Bill Dailey (SA)	R	29	1	2	.333	0	14	0	0	15	23	17	6	0	8.40
Bill Fischer	R	33	0	1	.000	0	9	0	0	7	16	5	2	0	7.71
Jerry Fosnow	L	23	0	1	.000	0	7	0	0	11	13	8	9	0	10.64
Garland Shifflet	R	29	0	2	.000	1	10	0	0	18	22	7	8	0	4.50
2 Johnny Klippstein	R	36	0	4	.000	2	33	0	0	46	44	20	39	0	1.96
Dwight Siebler	R	26	0	0	.000	0	9	0	0	11	10	6	10	0	4.91
Bill Whitby	R	20	0	0	.000	0	4	0	0	6	8	1	2	0	9.00
Gary Dotter	L	21	0	0	.000	0	3	0	0	4	3	3	6	0	2.25
Chuck Nieson	R	21	0	0	.000	0	2	0	0	2	1	1	5	0	4.50

BOSTON 8th 72-90 .444 27 — JOHNNY PESKY 70-90 .438 BILLY HERMAN 2-0 1.000

NAME	G by POS	B	AGE	G	AB	R	H	2B	3B	HR	RBI	BB	SO	SB	BA	SA
TOTALS			27	162	5513	688	1425	**253**	29	186	648	504	917	18	**.258**	.416
Dick Stuart	1B155	R	31	156	603	73	168	27	1	33	114	37	130	0	.279	.491
Dalton Jones	2B85, SS1, 3B1	L	20	118	374	37	86	16	4	6	39	22	38	6	.230	.342
Ed Bressoud	SS158	R	32	158	566	86	166	41	3	15	55	72	99	1	.293	.456
Frank Malzone	3B143	R	34	148	537	62	142	19	0	13	56	37	43	0	.264	.372
2 Lee Thomas	OF107, 1B1	L	28	107	401	44	103	19	2	13	42	34	29	2	.257	.411
Carl Yastrzemski	OF148, 3B2	L	24	151	567	77	164	29	9	15	67	75	90	6	.289	.451
Tony Conigliaro (BA)	OF106	R	19	111	404	69	117	21	2	24	52	35	78	2	.290	.530
Bob Tillman	C131	R	27	131	425	43	118	18	1	17	61	49	74	0	.278	.445
Felix Mantilla	OF48, 2B45, 3B7, SS6	R	29	133	425	69	123	20	1	30	64	41	46	0	.289	.553
Russ Nixon	C45	L	29	81	163	10	38	7	0	1	20	14	29	0	.233	.294
Roman Mejias	OF37	R	33	62	101	14	24	3	1	2	4	7	16	0	.238	.347
Dick Williams	1B21, 3B13, OF5	R	35	61	69	10	11	2	0	5	11	7	10	0	.159	.406
Earl Wilson	P33	R	29	54	73	15	15	4	0	5	13	9	22	0	.205	.466
Chuck Schilling	2B42	R	26	47	163	18	32	6	0	0	7	15	22	0	.196	.233
1 Lu Clinton	OF35	R	26	37	120	15	31	4	3	3	6	9	33	1	.258	.417
Tony Horton	OF24, 1B8	R	19	36	126	9	28	5	0	1	8	3	20	0	.222	.286
2 Al Smith	3B11, OF8	R	36	29	51	10	11	4	0	2	7	13	10	0	.216	.412
Gary Geiger (IL)	OF4	L	27	5	13	3	5	0	1	0	1	2	2	0	.385	.538

Bob Guindon 20 L 1-8, Mike Ryan 22 R 1-3

NAME	T	AGE	W	L	PCT	SV	G	GS	CG	IP	H	BB	SO	ShO	ERA
TOTALS		26	72	90	.444	38	162	162	21	1422	1464	571	1094	9	4.50
Dick Radatz	R	27	16	9	.640	**29**	79	0	0	157	103	58	181	0	2.29
Bill Monbouquette	R	27	13	14	.481	1	36	35	7	234	258	40	120	5	4.04
Earl Wilson	R	29	11	12	.478	0	33	31	5	202	213	73	166	0	4.50
Jack Lamabe	R	27	9	13	.409	1	39	25	3	177	235	57	109	0	5.90
Dave Morehead	R	21	8	15	.348	0	32	30	3	167	156	112	139	1	4.96
Bob Heffner	R	25	7	9	.438	6	55	10	1	159	152	44	112	1	4.08
Ed Connolly	L	24	4	11	.267	0	27	15	1	81	80	64	73	1	4.89
Bill Spanswick	L	25	2	3	.400	0	29	7	0	65	75	44	55	0	6.92
Arnie Earley (EJ)	L	31	1	1	.500	1	25	3	1	50	51	18	45	0	2.70
Jay Ritchie	R	27	1	1	.500	0	21	0	0	46	43	14	35	6	2.74
Pete Charton	R	21	0	2	.000	0	25	5	0	65	67	24	37	0	5.26
Dave Gray	R	21	0	0	.000	0	9	1	0	13	18	20	17	0	9.00
1 Wilbur Wood	L	22	0	0	.000	0	4	0	0	6	13	3	5	0	16.50

WASHINGTON 9th 62-100 .383 37 — GIL HODGES

NAME	G by POS	B	AGE	G	AB	R	H	2B	3B	HR	RBI	BB	SO	SB	BA	SA
TOTALS			29	162	5396	578	1246	199	28	125	528	514	**1124**	47	.231	.348
1 Bill Skowron	1B66	R	33	73	262	28	71	10	0	13	41	11	56	0	.271	.458
Don Blasingame	2B135	L	32	143	506	56	135	17	2	1	34	40	44	8	.267	.314
Eddie Brinkman	SS125	R	22	132	447	54	100	20	3	8	34	26	99	2	.224	.336
John Kennedy	3B106, SS49, 2B2	R	23	148	482	55	111	16	4	7	35	29	119	3	.230	.324
Jim King	OF121	L	31	134	415	46	100	15	1	18	56	55	65	3	.241	.412
Don Lock	OF149	R	27	152	512	73	127	17	4	28	80	79	137	4	.248	.461
Chuck Hinton	OF131, 3B2	R	30	138	514	71	141	25	7	11	53	57	77	17	.274	.414
Mike Brumley	C132	L	25	136	426	36	104	19	2	2	35	40	54	1	.244	.312
Don Zimmer	3B87, OF4, C2, 2B1	R	33	121	341	38	84	16	2	12	38	27	94	1	.246	.411
Dick Phillips	1B61, 3B4	L	32	109	234	17	54	6	1	2	23	27	22	1	.231	.291
Fred Valentine	OF57	B	29	102	212	20	48	5	0	4	20	21	44	4	.226	.307
Chuck Cottier	2B53, 3B3, SS2	R	28	73	137	16	23	6	2	3	10	19	33	2	.168	.307
Ken Hunt	OF37	R	29	51	96	9	13	4	0	1	4	14	35	0	.135	.208
Don Leppert	C43	L	32	50	122	6	19	3	0	3	12	11	32	0	.156	.254
2 Joe Cunningham	1B41	L	32	49	126	15	27	4	0	0	7	23	13	0	.214	.246
2 Roy Sievers	1B15	R	37	33	58	5	10	1	0	4	11	9	14	0	.172	.397
2 Willie Kirkland	OF27	L	30	32	102	8	22	6	0	5	13	6	30	0	.216	.422
Ken Retzer	C13	L	30	17	32	1	3	0	0	0	1	5	4	0	.094	.094

NAME	T	AGE	W	L	PCT	SV	G	GS	CG	IP	H	BB	SO	ShO	ERA
TOTALS		29	62	100	.383	26	162	162	27	1435	1417	505	794	5	3.98
Claude Osteen	L	24	15	13	.536	0	37	36	13	257	256	64	133	0	3.33
Ron Kline	R	32	10	7	.588	14	61	0	0	81	81	21	40	0	2.33
Buster Narum	R	23	9	15	.375	0	38	32	7	199	195	73	121	2	4.30
Bernie Daniels	R	32	8	10	.444	0	33	24	3	163	147	64	73	2	3.70
Steve Ridzik	R	35	5	5	.500	2	49	3	0	112	96	31	60	0	2.89
Jim Hannan	R	24	4	7	.364	3	49	7	0	106	108	45	67	0	4.16
2 Alan Koch	R	26	3	10	.231	0	32	14	1	114	110	43	67	0	4.89
2 Frank Kreutzer	L	25	2	6	.250	0	13	9	0	45	48	23	27	0	4.77
Dave Stenhouse (AJ)	R	30	2	7	.222	1	26	14	1	88	80	39	44	0	4.81
Don Loun	L	23	1	1	.500	0	2	2	1	13	13	3	3	1	2.08
Don Rudolph	L	32	1	3	.250	0	28	8	0	70	81	12	32	0	4.11
Tom Cheney (SA)	R	29	1	3	.250	1	15	6	1	49	45	13	25	0	3.67
Jim Duckworth (SA)	R	25	1	6	.143	3	30	2	0	56	52	25	56	0	4.34
Jim Bronstad	R	28	0	1	.000	0	4	0	0	7	10	2	9	0	5.14
Marshall Bridges	L	33	0	3	.000	2	17	0	0	30	37	17	16	0	5.70
Carl Bouldin	R	24	0	3	.000	0	9	3	0	25	30	11	12	0	5.40
Howie Koplitz	R	26	0	0	.000	0	6	1	0	17	20	13	9	0	4.76
Pete Craig	R	23	0	0	.000	0	2	1	0	2	8	4	0	0	40.50
1 Ed Roebuck	R	32	0	0	.000	0	2	0	0	1	0	2	0	0	9.00

KANSAS CITY 10th 57-105 .352 42 — ED LOPAT 17-35 .327 MEL McGAHA 40-70 .364

NAME	G by POS	B	AGE	G	AB	R	H	2B	3B	HR	RBI	BB	SO	SB	BA	SA
TOTALS			27	163	5524	621	1321	216	29	166	594	548	1104	34	.239	.379
Jim Gentile	1B128	L	30	136	439	71	110	10	0	28	71	84	122	0	.251	.465
Dick Green	2B120	R	23	130	435	48	115	14	5	11	37	27	87	3	.264	.395
Wayne Causey	SS131, 2B17, 3B9	R	27	157	604	82	170	31	4	8	49	88	65	0	.281	.386
Ed Charles	3B147	R	29	150	557	69	134	25	2	16	63	64	92	12	.241	.379
Rocky Colavito	OF159	R	30	160	588	89	161	31	2	34	102	83	56	3	.274	.507
Nelson Mathews	OF154	R	22	157	573	58	137	27	5	14	60	43	**143**	2	.239	.377
Manny Jiminez	OF49	L	25	95	204	19	46	7	0	12	38	15	24	0	.225	.436
Doc Edwards	C79, 1B7	R	26	97	294	25	66	10	0	5	28	13	40	0	.224	.310
Jose Tartabull	OF59	L	25	104	100	9	20	2	0	0	3	5	12	0	.200	.220
George Alusik	OF44, 1B12	R	29	102	204	18	49	10	1	3	19	30	36	0	.240	.343
Billy Bryan	C65	L	25	93	220	19	53	9	2	13	36	16	69	0	.241	.477
Bert Campaneris	SS38, OF27, 3B6	R	22	67	269	27	69	14	3	4	22	15	41	10	.257	.375
Ken Harrelson	OF24, 1B15	R	22	49	139	15	27	5	0	7	12	13	34	0	.194	.381
1 Charlie Lau	C35	L	31	43	118	11	32	7	1	2	9	10	18	0	.271	.398
George Williams	2B20, SS2, 3B2, OF2	R	24	37	91	10	19	6	0	0	2	6	12	0	.209	.275
Tommie Reynolds	OF25, 3B3	R	22	31	94	11	19	1	0	2	9	10	22	0	.202	.277
Dave Duncan	C22	R	18	25	53	2	9	0	1	1	5	2	20	0	.170	.264
Rick Joseph	1B12, 3B3	R	24	17	54	3	12	2	0	0	1	3	11	0	.222	.259
Charlie Shoemaker	2B14	L	24	16	52	6	11	2	2	0	3	0	9	0	.212	.327
Larry Stahl	OF10	L	23	15	46	7	12	1	0	3	6	1	10	0	.261	.478
John Wojcik	OF6	L	22	6	22	1	3	0	0	0	0	2	8	0	.136	.136
1 Gino Camoli	OF4	R	34	4	9	1	0	0	0	0	0	0	1	0	.000	.000

NAME	T	AGE	W	L	PCT	SV	G	GS	CG	IP	H	BB	SO	ShO	ERA
TOTALS		27	57	**105**	.352	27	163	163	18	1456	**1516**	**614**	966	6	4.71
Orlando Pena	R	30	12	14	.462	0	40	32	5	219	231	73	184	0	4.44
John O'Donoghue	L	24	10	14	.417	0	39	32	2	174	202	65	79	1	4.91
John Wyatt	R	29	9	8	.529	20	**81**	0	0	128	111	52	74	0	3.59
Diego Segui	R	26	8	**17**	.320	0	40	35	5	217	219	94	155	2	4.56
2 Wes Stock	R	30	6	3	.667	5	50	0	0	93	69	34	101	0	1.94
Moe Drabowsky	R	28	5	13	.278	1	53	21	1	168	176	72	119	0	5.30
Ted Bowsfield	L	28	4	7	.364	0	50	9	2	119	135	31	45	1	4.08
Blue Moon Odom	R	19	1	2	.333	0	5	5	1	17	29	11	10	1	10.06
3 Bob Meyer	R	24	1	4	.200	0	9	7	2	42	37	33	30	0	3.86
Dan Pfister	R	27	1	5	.167	0	19	3	0	41	50	29	21	0	6.59
Vern Handrahan	R	25	0	1	.000	0	18	1	0	36	33	25	18	0	6.00
Jack Aker	R	23	0	1	.000	0	9	0	0	16	17	10	7	0	9.00
Ken Sanders	R	22	0	2	.000	1	21	0	0	27	23	17	18	0	3.67
Joe Grzenda	L	27	0	2	.000	0	20	0	0	25	34	13	17	0	5.40
Lew Krausse	R	21	0	2	.000	0	5	4	0	15	22	9	9	0	7.20
Aurelio Monteagudo	R	20	0	4	.000	0	11	6	0	31	40	10	14	0	9.00
Jose Santiago	R	23	0	6	.000	0	34	8	0	84	84	35	64	0	4.71
1 Tom Sturdivant	R	34	0	0	.000	0	3	0	0	4	4	1	1	0	9.00

ST. LOUIS 1st 93-69 .574 — JOHNNY KEANE

NAME	G by POS	B	AGE	G	AB	R	H	2B	3B	HR	RBI	BB	SO	SB	BA	SA
TOTALS			27	162	**5625**	715	**1531**	240	53	109	654	427	925	73	**.272**	.392
Bill White	1B160	L	30	160	631	92	191	37	4	21	102	52	103	7	.303	.474
Julian Javier	2B154	R	27	155	535	66	129	19	5	12	65	30	82	9	.241	.363
Dick Groat	SS160	R	33	161	636	70	186	35	6	1	70	44	42	2	.292	.371
Ken Boyer	3B162	R	33	162	628	100	185	30	10	24	**119**	70	85	3	.295	.489
Mike Shannon	OF88	R	24	88	253	30	66	8	2	9	43	19	54	4	.261	.415
Curt Flood	OF162	R	26	162	**679**	97	**211**	25	3	5	46	43	53	8	.311	.378
2 Lou Brock	OF102	L	25	103	419	81	146	21	9	12	44	27	87	33	.348	.527
Tim McCarver	C137	L	22	143	465	53	134	19	3	9	52	40	44	2	.288	.400
Charlie James	OF60	R	26	88	233	24	52	9	1	5	17	11	58	0	.233	.335
Carl Warwick	OF49	R	27	88	158	14	41	7	1	3	15	11	30	2	.259	.323
2 Bob Skinner	OF31	L	32	55	118	10	32	5	0	1	16	11	20	0	.271	.339
Bob Uecker	C40	R	29	40	106	8	21	1	0	1	6	17	24	0	.198	.236
Johnny Lewis	OF36	L	24	40	94	10	22	2	2	2	7	13	23	2	.234	.362
Phil Gagliano	2B12, OF2, 1B1, 3B1	R	22	40	58	5	15	4	0	1	9	3	10	0	.259	.379
Dal Maxvill	2B15, SS13, 3B1, OF1	R	25	37	26	4	6	0	0	0	4	0	7	1	.231	.231
Jerry Buchek	SS20, 2B9, 3B1	R	22	35	30	7	6	0	2	0	1	3	11	0	.200	.333
1 Doug Clemens	OF22	L	25	33	78	8	16	4	3	1	9	6	16	0	.205	.372
1 Jeoff Long	OF4, 1B3	R	22	28	43	5	10	1	0	1	4	6	18	0	.233	.326
Ed Spiezio		R	22	12	12	0	4	0	0	0	0	0	1	0	.333	.333

Joe Morgan 33 L 0-3, Hal Smith (IL) 33

NAME	T	AGE	W	L	PCT	SV	G	GS	CG	IP	H	BB	SO	ShO	ERA
		30	**93**	69	**.574**	38	162	162	47	1445	1405	410	877	10	3.43
Ray Sadecki	L	23	20	11	.645	1	37	32	9	220	232	60	119	2	3.68
Bob Gibson	R	28	19	12	.613	1	40	36	17	287	250	86	245	2	3.01
Curt Simmons	L	35	18	9	.667	0	34	34	12	244	233	49	104	3	3.43
Ron Taylor	R	26	8	4	.667	7	63	2	0	101	109	33	69	0	4.63
Roger Craig	R	33	7	9	.438	5	39	19	3	166	180	35	84	0	3.25
Mike Cuellar	L	27	5	5	.500	4	32	7	1	72	80	33	56	0	4.50
Gordie Richardson	L	24	4	2	.667	1	19	6	1	47	40	15	28	0	2.30
Ray Washburn (SA)	R	26	3	4	.429	2	15	10	0	60	60	17	28	0	4.05
1 Ernie Broglio	R	28	3	5	.375	0	11	11	3	69	65	26	36	1	3.52
Bob Humphreys	R	28	2	0	1.000	2	28	0	0	43	32	15	36	0	2.51
1 Lew Burdette	R	37	1	0	1.000	0	8	0	0	10	10	3	3	0	1.80
2 Glen Hobbie	R	28	1	2	.333	1	13	5	1	44	41	15	18	0	4.30
Barney Schultz	R	37	1	3	.250	14	30	0	0	49	35	11	29	0	1.65
1 Bobby Shantz	L	38	1	3	.250	0	16	0	0	17	14	7	12	0	3.18
Harry Fanok (SA)	R	24	0	0	.000	0	4	0	0	8	5	3	10	0	5.63
Dave Bakenhaster	R	19	0	0	.000	0	2	0	0	3	9	1	0	0	6.00
3 Jack Spring	L	31	0	0	.000	0	2	0	0	3	8	1	0	0	3.00
Dave Dowling	L	21	0	0	.000	0	1	0	0	1	2	0	0	0	0.00

CINCINNATI 2nd (Tie) 92-70 .568 1 — FRED HUTCHINSON (IL) 60-49 .550 DICK SISLER 32-21 .604

NAME	G by POS	B	AGE	G	AB	R	H	2B	3B	HR	RBI	BB	SO	SB	BA	SA
TOTALS			26	163	5561	660	1383	220	38	130	605	457	974	90	.249	.372
Deron Johnson	1B131, OF10, 3B1	R	25	140	477	63	130	24	4	21	79	37	98	4	.273	.472
Pete Rose	2B128	B	23	136	516	64	139	13	2	4	34	36	51	4	.269	.326
Leo Cardenas	SS163	R	26	163	597	61	150	22	3	0	60	41	110	4	.251	.367
Steve Boros	3B114	R	27	117	370	31	95	12	3	2	31	47	43	4	.257	.322
Frank Robinson	OF156	R	28	156	568	103	174	38	6	29	96	79	67	23	.306	.548
Vada Pinson	OF156	L	25	156	625	99	166	23	11	23	84	42	99	8	.266	.448
Tommy Harper	OF92, 3B2	R	23	102	317	42	77	5	2	4	22	39	56	24	.243	.309
Johnny Edwards	C120	L	26	126	423	47	119	23	1	7	55	34	65	1	.281	.390
Marty Keough	OF81, 1B4	L	29	109	276	29	71	9	1	9	28	22	58	1	.257	.395
Gordy Coleman	1B49	L	29	89	198	18	48	6	2	5	27	13	30	2	.242	.369
Chico Ruiz	3B49, 2B30	B	25	77	311	33	76	13	2	2	16	7	41	11	.244	.318
Mel Queen	OF20	L	22	48	95	7	19	2	0	2	12	4	19	0	.200	.284
1 Bobby Klaus	2B18, 3B11, SS3	R	26	40	93	10	17	5	1	2	6	4	13	1	.183	.323
Don Pavletich	C27, 1B1	R	25	34	91	12	22	4	0	5	11	10	17	0	.242	.451
Hal Smith	C20	R	33	32	66	6	8	1	0	0	3	12	20	1	.121	.136
1 Bob Skinner	OF12	L	32	25	59	6	13	3	0	3	5	4	12	0	.220	.424
Tony Perez	1B6	R	22	12	25	1	2	1	0	0	1	3	9	0	.080	.120
Jimmie Coker	C11	R	28	11	32	3	10	2	0	1	4	3	5	0	.313	.469

Johnny Temple 35 R 0-3, Tommy Helms 23 R 0-1

NAME	T	AGE	W	L	PCT	SV	G	GS	CG	IP	H	BB	SO	ShO	ERA
		29	92	70	.568	35	163	163	54	1467	1306	436	**1122**	14	3.07
Jim O'Toole	L	27	17	7	.708	0	30	30	9	220	194	51	145	3	2.66
Jim Maloney	R	24	15	10	.600	0	31	31	11	216	175	83	214	2	2.71
Bob Purkey	R	34	11	9	.550	1	34	25	9	190	101	49	70	2	3.03
Joey Jay	R	28	11	11	.500	2	34	23	10	183	167	36	134	0	3.39
Sammy Ellis	R	23	10	3	.769	14	52	5	2	122	101	28	125	0	2.58
Joe Nuxhall	L	35	9	8	.529	2	32	22	7	155	146	51	111	4	4.06
John Tsitouris	R	28	9	13	.409	2	37	24	6	175	178	75	146	1	3.81
Billy McCool	L	19	6	5	.545	7	40	3	0	89	66	29	87	0	2.43
Bill Henry	L	36	2	2	.500	6	37	0	0	52	31	12	28	0	0.87
1 Al Worthington	R	35	1	0	1.000	0	6	0	0	7	14	2	6	0	10.29
Jim Dickson	R	26	1	0	1.000	0	4	0	0	5	8	5	6	0	7.20
2 Ryne Duren	R	35	0	2	.000	1	26	0	0	44	41	15	39	0	2.86
Chet Nichols	L	33	0	0	.000	0	3	0	0	3	4	0	3	0	6.00

PHILADELPHIA 2nd (Tie) 92-70 .568 1 — GENE MAUCH

NAME	G by POS	B	AGE	G	AB	R	H	2B	3B	HR	RBI	BB	SO	SB	BA	SA
TOTALS			27	162	5493	693	1415	241	51	130	649	440	924	30	.258	.391
John Herrnstein	OF69, 1B68	L	26	125	303	38	71	12	4	6	25	22	67	1	.234	.360
Tony Taylor	2B150	R	28	154	570	62	143	13	6	4	46	46	74	13	.251	.316
Bobby Wine	SS108, 3B16	R	25	126	283	28	60	8	3	4	34	25	37	1	.212	.304
Dick Allen	3B162	R	22	162	632	**125**	201	38	**13**	29	91	67	**138**	3	.318	.557
Johnny Callison	OF162	L	25	162	654	101	179	30	10	31	104	36	95	6	.274	.492
Tony Gonzalez	OF119	L	27	131	421	55	117	25	3	4	40	44	74	0	.278	.380
Wes Covington	OF108	L	32	129	339	37	95	18	0	13	58	38	50	0	.280	.448
Clay Dalrymple	C124	L	27	127	382	36	91	16	3	6	46	39	40	0	.238	.343
Ruben Amaro	SS79, 1B58, 2B3, 3B3, OF1	R	28	129	299	31	79	11	0	4	34	16	37	1	.264	.341
Cookie Rojas	OF70, 2B20, SS18, 3B1, C1	R	25	109	340	58	99	19	5	2	31	22	17	1	.291	.394
Gus Triandos	C64, 1B1	R	33	73	188	17	47	9	0	8	33	26	41	0	.250	.426
Johnny Briggs	OF19, 1B1	L	20	61	66	16	17	2	0	1	6	9	12	1	.258	.333
Danny Cater (BA)	OF39, 1B7, 3B1	R	24	60	152	13	45	9	1	1	13	7	15	1	.296	.388
1 Roy Sievers	1B33	R	37	49	120	7	22	3	1	4	16	13	20	0	.183	.325
Alex Johnson	OF35	R	21	43	109	18	33	7	1	4	18	6	26	1	.303	.495
2 Frank Thomas (BG)	1B39	R	35	39	143	20	42	11	0	7	26	5	12	0	.294	.517
3 Vic Power	1B17	R	32	18	48	1	10	4	0	0	3	2	3	0	.208	.292
Adolfo Phillips	OF4	R	22	13	13	4	3	0	0	0	0	3	3	0	.231	.231
Costen Shockley	1B9	L	22	11	35	4	8	0	0	1	2	2	8	0	.229	.314

Don Hoak 36 R 0-4, Pat Corrales 23 R 0-1

NAME	T	AGE	W	L	PCT	SV	G	GS	CG	IP	H	BB	SO	ShO	ERA
		26	92	70	.568	**41**	162	162	37	1460	1402	440	1009	17	3.37
Jim Bunning	R	32	19	8	.704	2	41	39	13	284	248	46	219	5	2.63
Chris Short	L	26	17	9	.654	2	42	31	12	221	174	51	181	4	2.20
Art Mahaffey	R	26	12	9	.571	0	34	29	2	157	161	82	80	2	4.53
Dennis Bennett	L	24	12	14	.462	1	41	32	7	208	222	58	125	2	3.68
Ray Culp (SA)	R	22	8	7	.533	0	30	19	3	135	139	56	96	1	4.13
Jack Baldschun	R	27	6	9	.400	21	71	0	0	118	111	40	96	0	3.13
2 Ed Roebuck	R	32	5	3	.625	12	60	0	0	77	55	25	42	0	2.22
Rick Wise	R	18	5	3	.625	0	25	8	0	69	78	25	39	0	4.04
John Boozer	R	24	3	4	.429	2	22	3	0	60	64	18	51	0	5.10
Dallas Green	R	29	2	1	.667	0	25	0	0	42	63	14	21	0	5.79
1 Johnny Klippstein	R	36	2	1	.667	1	11	0	0	22	22	8	13	0	4.09
3 Bobby Shantz	L	38	1	1	.500	0	14	0	0	32	23	6	18	0	2.25
Cal McLish (SA)	R	38	0	1	.000	0	2	1	0	5	6	1	6	0	3.60
Bobby Locke	R	30	0	0	.000	0	8	0	0	19	21	6	11	0	2.84
Morrie Steevens	L	23	0	0	.000	0	4	0	0	3	5	1	3	0	3.00
1 Ryne Duren	R	35	0	0	.000	0	2	0	0	3	5	1	5	0	6.00
1 Gary Kroll	R	22	0	0	.000	0	2	0	0	3	3	2	2	0	3.00
Dave Bennett	R	18	0	0	.000	0	1	0	0	1	2	0	1	0	9.00

SAN FRANCISCO 4th 90-72 .556 3 — AL DARK

NAME	G by POS	B	AGE	G	AB	R	H	2B	3B	HR	RBI	BB	SO	SB	BA	SA
TOTALS			28	162	5535	656	1360	185	38	**165**	608	**505**	900	64	.246	.382
Orlando Cepeda	1B139, OF1	R	26	142	529	75	161	27	2	31	97	43	83	9	.304	.539
Hal Lanier	2B98, SS3	R	21	98	383	40	105	16	3	2	28	5	44	2	.274	.347
Jose Pagan	SS132, OF8	R	29	134	367	33	82	10	1	1	28	35	66	5	.223	.264
Jim Ray Hart	3B149, OF6	R	22	153	566	71	162	15	6	31	81	47	94	5	.286	.498
Jesus Alou (LJ)	OF108	R	22	115	376	42	103	11	0	3	28	13	35	6	.274	.327
Willie Mays	OF155, 1B1, SS1, 3B1	R	33	157	578	121	171	21	9	**47**	111	82	72	19	.296	**.607**
Willie McCovey	OF83, 1B26	L	26	130	364	55	80	14	1	18	54	61	73	2	.220	.412
Tom Haller	C113, OF3	L	27	117	388	43	98	14	3	16	48	55	51	4	.253	.428
Jim Davenport	SS64, 3B41, 2B30	R	30	116	297	24	70	10	6	2	26	29	46	2	.236	.330
Harvey Kuenn	OF88, 1B11, 3B2	R	33	111	351	42	92	16	2	4	22	35	32	0	.262	.353
Matty Alou (BW)	OF80	L	25	110	250	28	66	4	2	1	14	11	25	5	.264	.308
Duke Snider	OF43	L	37	91	167	16	35	7	0	4	17	22	40	0	.210	.323
Chuck Hiller	2B60, 3B1	L	29	80	205	21	37	8	1	1	17	17	23	1	.180	.244
Del Crandall	C65	R	34	69	195	12	45	8	1	3	11	22	21	0	.231	.328
Cap Peterson	OF10, 1B2, 2B1, 3B1	R	21	66	74	8	15	1	1	1	8	3	20	0	.203	.284
Jose Cardenal	OF16	R	20	20	15	3	0	0	0	0	0	2	3	2	.000	.000
Gil Garrido	SS14	R	23	14	25	1	2	0	0	0	1	2	7	1	.080	.080
Randy Hundley	C2	R	22	2	1	1	0	0	0	0	0	0	1	0	.000	.000

NAME	T	AGE	W	L	PCT	SV	G	GS	CG	IP	H	BB	SO	ShO	ERA
		29	90	72	.556	30	162	162	48	1476	1348	**480**	1023	17	3.19
Juan Marichal	R	26	21	8	.724	0	33	33	**22**	269	241	52	206	4	2.48
Gaylord Perry	R	25	12	11	.522	5	44	19	5	206	179	43	155	2	2.75
Bob Hendley	L	25	10	11	.476	0	30	29	4	163	161	59	104	1	3.64
Ron Herbel	R	26	9	9	.500	1	40	22	7	161	162	61	98	2	3.07
Billy O'Dell	L	31	8	7	.533	2	36	8	1	85	82	35	54	0	5.40
Bob Shaw	R	31	7	6	.538	11	61	1	0	93	105	31	57	0	3.77
Bobby Bolin	R	25	6	9	.400	1	38	23	5	175	143	77	146	3	3.24
Jim Duffalo (BR)	R	28	5	1	.833	3	35	3	1	74	57	31	55	0	2.92
Jack Sanford (SJ)	R	35	5	7	.417	1	18	17	3	106	91	37	64	1	3.31
Billy Pierce	L	37	3	0	1.000	4	34	1	0	49	40	10	29	0	2.20
John Pregenzer	R	28	2	0	1.000	0	13	0	0	18	21	11	8	0	5.00
Massanori Murakami	L	20	1	0	1.000	1	9	0	0	15	8	1	15	0	1.80
Dick Estelle	L	22	1	2	.333	0	6	6	0	42	39	23	23	0	3.00
1 Don Larsen	R	34	0	1	.000	0	6	0	0	10	10	6	6	0	4.50
Ken MacKenzie	L	30	0	0	.000	1	10	0	0	9	9	3	3	0	5.00

MILWAUKEE 5th 88-74 .543 5 — BOBBY BRAGAN

NAME	G by POS	B	AGE	G	AB	R	H	2B	3B	HR	RBI	BB	SO	SB	BA	SA
TOTALS			28	162	5591	**803**	1522	**274**	32	159	**755**	486	825	53	**.272**	**.418**
Gene Oliver	1B76, C1	R	28	93	279	45	77	15	1	13	49	17	41	3	.276	.477
Frank Bolling	2B117	R	32	120	352	35	70	11	1	5	34	21	44	0	.199	.278
Denis Menke	SS141, 2B15, 3B6	R	23	151	505	79	143	29	5	20	65	68	77	4	.283	.479
Eddie Mathews	3B128, 1B7	L	32	141	502	83	117	19	1	23	74	85	100	2	.233	.412
Hank Aaron	OF139, 2B11	R	30	145	570	103	187	30	2	24	95	62	46	22	.328	.514
Lee Maye	OF135, 3B5	L	29	153	588	96	179	**44**	5	10	74	34	54	5	.304	.447
Rico Carty	OF121	R	25	133	455	72	150	28	4	22	88	43	78	1	.330	.554
Joe Torre	C96, 1B70	R	23	154	601	87	193	36	5	20	109	36	67	2	.321	.498
Felipe Alou (KJ)	OF92, 1B18	R	29	121	415	60	105	26	3	9	51	30	41	5	.253	.395
Ty Cline	OF54, 1B6	L	25	101	116	22	35	4	2	1	13	8	22	0	.302	.397
Ed Bailey	C80	L	33	95	271	30	71	10	1	5	34	34	39	2	.262	.362
Mike de la Hoz	2B25, 3B25, SS8	R	24	78	189	25	55	7	1	4	12	14	22	1	.291	.402
Woody Woodward	2B40, SS18, 3B7, 1B1	R	21	77	115	18	24	2	1	0	11	6	28	0	.209	.243
Gary Kolb	OF14, 3B7, 2B6, C2	L	24	36	64	7	12	1	0	0	2	6	10	3	.188	.203
1 Len Gabrielson	1B12, OF2	L	24	24	38	0	7	2	0	0	1	1	8	1	.184	.237
Sandy Alomar	SS19	R	20	19	53	3	13	1	0	0	6	0	11	1	.245	.264
Lou Klimchock	3B4, 2B2	L	24	10	21	3	7	2	0	0	2	1	2	0	.333	.429
Ethan Blackaby	OF5	L	23	9	12	0	1	0	0	0	1	1	2	0	.083	.083
2 Merritt Ranew	C3	L	26	9	17	1	2	0	0	0	0	0	3	0	.118	.118
1 Roy McMillan	SS8	R	33	8	13	1	4	0	0	0	2	0	2	1	.308	.308
Bill Southworth	3B2	R	18	3	7	2	2	0	0	1	2	0	3	0	.286	.714
Gus Bell		L	35	3	3	0	0	0	0	0	0	0	1	0	.000	.000
Phil Roof	C1	R	23	1	2	0	0	0	0	0	0	0	1	0	.000	.000

NAME	T	AGE	W	L	PCT	SV	G	GS	CG	IP	H	BB	SO	ShO	ERA
		28	88	74	.543	39	162	162	45	1435	1411	452	906	14	4.11
Tony Cloninger	R	23	19	14	.576	2	38	34	15	243	206	82	163	3	3.56
Denny Lemaster	L	25	17	11	.607	1	39	35	9	221	216	75	185	3	4.15
Hank Fischer	R	24	11	10	.524	2	37	28	9	168	177	39	99	5	4.02
Wade Blasingame	L	20	9	5	.643	2	28	13	3	117	113	51	70	1	4.23
Bob Sadowski	R	26	9	10	.474	5	51	18	5	167	159	56	96	0	4.10
Warren Spahn	L	43	6	13	.316	4	38	25	4	174	204	52	78	1	5.28
Billy Hoeft	L	32	4	0	1.000	4	42	0	0	73	76	18	47	0	3.82
Bobby Tiefenauer	R	34	4	6	.400	13	46	0	0	73	61	15	48	0	3.21
Clay Carroll	R	23	2	0	1.000	1	11	1	0	20	15	3	17	0	1.80
Chi Chi Olivo	R	26	2	1	.667	5	38	0	0	60	55	21	45	0	3.75
Jack Smith	R	28	2	2	.500	0	22	0	0	31	28	11	19	0	3.77
3 Frank Lary	R	34	1	0	1.000	0	5	2	0	12	15	0	4	0	4.50
Arnie Umbach	R	21	1	0	1.000	0	1	1	0	8	11	4	7	0	3.38
Dan Schneider (XJ)	R	21	1	2	.333	0	13	5	0	36	38	13	14	0	5.50
Phil Niekro	R	25	0	0	.000	0	10	0	0	15	15	7	8	0	4.80
Dave Eilers	R	27	0	0	.000	0	6	0	0	8	11	1	1	0	4.50
Cecil Butler	R	26	0	0	.000	0	2	0	0	4	7	0	2	0	9.00
Dick Kelley (AJ)	L	24	0	0	.000	0	2	0	0	2	2	3	2	0	18.00
John Braun	R	24	0	0	.000	0	1	0	0	2	2	1	1	0	0.00

LOS ANGELES 6th (Tie) 80-82 .494 13 — **WALT ALSTON**

NAME	G by POS	B	AGE	G	AB	R	H	2B	3B	HR	RBI	BB	SO	SB	BA	SA
TOTALS			27	164	5499	614	1375	180	39	79	555	438	893	141	.250	.340
Ron Fairly	1B141	L	25	150	454	62	116	19	5	10	74	65	59	4	.256	.385
Nate Oliver	2B98, SS1	R	23	99	321	28	78	9	0	0	21	31	57	7	.243	.271
Maury Wills	SS149, 3B6	B	31	158	630	81	173	15	5	2	34	41	73	53	.275	.324
Jim Gilliam	3B86, 2B25, OF2	B	35	116	334	44	76	8	3	2	27	42	21	4	.228	.287
Frank Howard	OF122	R	27	134	433	60	98	13	2	24	69	51	113	1	.226	.432
Willie Davis	OF155	L	24	157	613	91	180	23	7	12	77	22	59	42	.294	.413
Tommy Davis	OF148	R	25	152	592	70	163	20	5	14	86	29	68	11	.275	.397
Johnny Roseboro	C128	L	31	134	414	42	119	24	1	3	45	44	61	3	.287	.372
Wes Parker	OF69, 1B31	B	24	124	214	29	55	7	1	3	10	14	45	5	.257	.341
Dick Tracewski	2B56, 3B30, SS19	R	29	106	304	31	75	13	4	1	26	31	61	3	.247	.326
Derrell Griffith	3B35, OF29	L	20	78	238	27	69	16	2	4	23	5	21	5	.290	.424
Wally Moon	OF23	L	34	68	118	8	26	2	1	2	9	12	22	1	.220	.305
Doug Camilli	C46	R	27	50	123	1	22	3	0	0	10	8	19	0	.179	.203
Lee Walls	OF6, C1	R	31	37	28	1	5	1	0	0	3	2	12	0	.179	.214
Johnny Werhas	3B28	R	26	29	83	6	16	2	1	0	8	13	12	0	.193	.241
Jeff Torborg	C27	R	22	28	43	4	10	1	1	0	4	3	8	0	.233	.302
Ken McMullen	1B13, 3B4, OF3	R	22	24	67	3	14	0	0	1	2	3	7	0	.209	.254
Bart Shirley	3B10, SS8	R	24	18	62	6	17	1	1	0	7	4	8	0	.274	.323
Willie Crawford	OF4	L	17	10	16	3	5	1	0	0	0	1	7	1	.313	.375

NAME	T	AGE	W	L	PCT	SV	G	GS	CG	IP	H	BB	SO	ShO	ERA
		26	80	82	.494	27	164	164	47	1484	1289	548	1062	19	2.95
Sandy Koufax	L	28	19	5	.792	1	29	28	15	223	154	53	223	7	1.74
Don Drysdale	R	27	18	16	.529	0	40	40	21	321	242	68	237	5	2.19
Bob Miller	R	25	7	7	.500	9	74	2	0	138	115	63	94	0	2.61
Phil Ortega	R	24	7	9	.438	1	34	25	4	157	149	56	107	3	4.01
Joe Moeller	R	21	7	13	.350	0	27	24	1	145	153	31	97	0	4.22
Ron Perranoski	L	28	5	7	.417	14	72	0	0	125	128	46	79	0	3.10
Jim Brewer	L	26	4	3	.571	1	34	5	1	93	79	25	63	1	3.00
Larry Miller	L	27	4	8	.333	0	16	14	1	80	87	28	50	0	4.16
Howie Reed	R	27	3	4	.429	1	26	7	0	90	79	36	52	0	3.20
John Purdin	R	21	2	0	1.000	0	3	2	1	16	6	6	8	1	0.56
Pete Richert	L	24	2	3	.400	0	8	6	1	35	38	18	25	1	4.11
Nick Willhite	L	23	2	4	.333	0	10	7	2	44	43	13	24	0	3.68
Bill Singer	R	20	0	1	.000	0	2	2	0	14	11	12	3	0	3.21
Johnny Podres (EJ)	L	31	0	2	.000	0	2	2	0	3	5	3	0	0	15.00

PITTSBURGH 6th (Tie) 80-82 .494 13 — **DANNY MURTAUGH**

NAME	G by POS	B	AGE	G	AB	R	H	2B	3B	HR	RBI	BB	SO	SB	BA	SA
TOTALS			28	162	5566	663	1469	225	54	121	630	408	970	39	.264	.389
Donn Clendenon	1B119	R	28	133	457	53	129	23	8	12	64	26	96	12	.282	.446
Bill Mazeroski	2B162	R	27	162	601	66	161	22	8	10	64	29	52	1	.268	.381
Dick Schofield	SS111	B	29	121	398	50	98	22	5	3	36	54	60	1	.246	.349
Bob Bailey	3B105, OF35, SS2	R	21	143	530	73	149	26	3	11	51	44	78	10	.281	.404
Roberto Clemente	OF154	R	29	155	622	95	211	40	7	12	87	51	87	5	.339	.484
Bill Virdon	OF134	L	33	145	473	59	115	11	3	3	27	30	48	1	.243	.298
Manny Mota	OF93, 2B1, C1	R	26	115	271	43	75	8	3	5	32	10	31	4	.277	.384
Jim Pagliaroni	C96	R	26	97	302	33	89	12	3	10	36	41	56	1	.295	.454
Willie Stargell	OF59, 1B50	L	24	117	421	53	115	19	7	21	78	17	92	1	.273	.501
Jerry Lynch	OF78	L	33	114	297	35	81	14	2	16	66	26	57	0	.273	.495
Gene Freese	3B72	R	30	99	289	33	65	13	2	9	40	19	45	1	.225	.377
Gene Alley	SS61, 3B3, 2B1	R	23	81	209	30	44	3	1	6	13	21	56	0	.211	.321
1 Smoky Burgess	C44	L	37	68	171	9	42	3	1	2	17	13	14	2	.246	.310
Orlando McFarlane	C35, OF1	R	26	37	78	5	19	5	0	0	1	4	27	0	.244	.308
Dave Wissman	OF10	L	23	16	27	2	4	0	0	0	0	1	9	0	.148	.148
Jerry May	C11	R	20	11	31	1	8	0	0	0	3	3	9	0	.258	.258

Rex Johnston 26 B 0-7, Julio Gotay 25 R 1-2

NAME	T	AGE	W	L	PCT	SV	G	GS	CG	IP	H	BB	SO	ShO	ERA
		28	80	82	.494	29	162	162	42	1444	1429	476	951	14	3.52
Bob Veale	L	28	18	12	.600	0	40	38	14	280	222	124	250	1	2.73
Bob Friend	R	33	13	18	.419	0	35	35	13	240	253	50	128	3	3.34
Vern Law	R	34	12	13	.480	0	35	29	7	192	203	32	93	5	3.61
Joe Gibbon	L	29	10	7	.588	0	28	24	3	147	145	54	97	0	3.67
Al McBean	R	26	8	3	.727	22	58	0	0	90	76	17	41	0	1.90
Steve Blass	R	22	5	8	.385	0	24	13	3	105	107	45	67	1	4.03
Don Schwall	R	28	4	3	.571	0	15	9	0	50	53	15	36	0	4.32
Roy Face	R	36	3	3	.500	4	55	0	0	80	82	27	63	0	5.18
Frank Bork	L	23	2	2	.500	2	33	2	0	42	51	11	31	0	4.07
Tom Butters	R	26	2	2	.500	0	28	4	0	64	52	37	58	0	2.39
Bob Priddy	R	24	1	2	.333	1	19	0	0	34	35	15	23	0	3.97
Don Cardwell (SJ)	R	28	1	2	.333	0	4	4	1	19	15	7	10	1	2.84
Tommie Sisk	R	22	1	4	.200	0	42	1	0	61	91	29	35	0	6.20
Earl Francis	R	27	0	1	.000	0	2	1	0	6	7	1	6	0	9.00
2 Wilbur Wood	L	22	0	2	.000	0	3	2	1	17	16	11	7	0	3.71
Freddie Green	L	30	0	0	.000	0	8	0	0	7	10	0	2	0	1.29
John Gelnar	R	21	0	0	.000	0	7	0	0	9	11	1	4	0	5.00

CHICAGO 8th 76-86 .469 17 — **BOB KENNEDY**

NAME	G by POS	B	AGE	G	AB	R	H	2B	3B	HR	RBI	BB	SO	SB	BA	SA
TOTALS			27	162	5545	649	1391	239	50	145	609	499	1041	70	.251	.390
Ernie Banks	1B157	R	33	157	591	67	156	29	6	23	95	36	84	1	.264	.450
Joey Amalfitano	2B86, 1B1, SS1	R	30	100	324	51	78	19	6	4	27	40	42	2	.241	.373
Andre Rodgers	SS126	R	29	129	448	50	107	17	3	12	46	53	88	5	.239	.371
Ron Santo	3B161	R	24	161	592	94	185	33	13	30	114	86	96	3	.313	.564
2 Len Gabrielson	OF68, 1B8	L	24	89	272	22	67	11	2	5	23	19	37	9	.246	.357
Billy Cowan	OF134	R	25	139	497	52	120	16	4	19	50	18	128	12	.241	.404
Billy Williams	OF162	L	26	162	645	100	201	39	2	33	98	59	84	10	.312	.532
Dick Bertell	C110	R	28	112	353	29	84	11	3	4	35	33	67	2	.238	.320
Jimmy Stewart	2B61, SS45, OF4, 3B1	B	25	132	415	59	105	17	0	3	33	49	61	10	.253	.316
Leo Burke	OF18, 2B5, 3B4, 1B2, C1	R	30	59	103	11	27	3	1	1	14	7	31	0	.262	.340
Jimmie Schaffer(BH)	C43	R	28	54	122	9	25	6	1	2	9	17	17	2	.205	.320
2 Doug Clemens	OF40	L	25	54	140	23	39	10	2	2	12	18	22	0	.279	.421
1 Lou Brock	OF52	L	25	52	215	30	54	9	2	2	14	13	40	10	.251	.340
Ellis Burton	OF29	B	27	42	105	12	20	3	2	2	7	17	22	4	.190	.314
Vic Roznovsky	C26	L	25	35	76	2	15	1	0	0	2	5	18	0	.197	.211
Ron Campbell	2B26	R	24	26	92	7	25	6	1	1	10	1	21	0	.272	.391
Billy Ott	OF10	B	23	20	39	4	7	3	0	0	1	3	10	0	.179	.256
1 Merritt Ranew	C9	L	26	16	33	0	3	0	0	0	1	2	6	0	.091	.091
Don Landrum	OF1	L	28	11	11	2	0	0	0	0	0	1	2	0	.000	.000
John Boccabella	1B5, OF2	R	23	9	23	4	9	2	1	0	6	0	3	0	.391	.565
Don Kessinger	SS4	R	21	4	12	1	2	0	0	0	0	0	1	0	.167	.167

Paul Popovich 23 R 1-1, Ken Hubbs (DD) 22

NAME	T	AGE	W	L	PCT	SV	G	GS	CG	IP	H	BB	SO	ShO	ERA
		30	76	86	.469	19	162	162	58	1445	1510	423	737	11	4.08
Larry Jackson	R	33	24	11	.686	0	40	38	19	298	265	58	148	3	3.14
Bob Buhl	R	35	15	14	.517	0	36	35	11	228	208	68	107	3	3.83
Dick Ellsworth	L	24	14	18	.438	0	37	36	16	257	267	71	148	1	3.75
2 Lew Burdette	R	37	9	9	.500	0	28	17	8	131	152	19	40	2	4.88
2 Ernie Broglio	R	28	4	7	.364	1	18	16	3	100	111	30	46	0	4.05
Cal Koonce	R	23	3	0	1.000	0	6	2	0	31	30	7	17	0	2.03
Sterling Slaughter	R	22	2	4	.333	0	20	6	1	52	64	32	32	0	5.71
Don Elston	R	35	2	5	.286	1	48	0	0	54	68	34	26	0	5.33
Freddie Burdette	R	27	1	0	1.000	0	18	0	0	20	17	10	4	0	3.15
Paul Jaeckel	R	22	1	0	1.000	1	4	0	0	8	4	3	2	0	0.00
Lindy McDaniel	R	28	1	7	.125	15	63	0	0	95	104	23	71	0	3.88
2 Bobby Shantz	L	38	0	1	.000	1	20	0	0	11	15	6	12	0	5.73
John Flavin	L	24	0	1	.000	0	5	1	0	5	11	3	5	0	12.60
Paul Toth	R	29	0	2	.000	0	4	2	0	11	15	5	0	0	8.18
1 Glen Hobbie	R	28	0	3	.000	0	8	4	0	27	39	10	14	0	8.00
Fred Norman	L	21	0	4	.000	0	8	5	0	32	34	21	20	0	6.47
Wayne Schurr	R	26	0	0	.000	0	26	0	0	48	57	11	29	0	3.75
Lee Gregory	L	26	0	0	.000	0	11	0	0	18	23	5	8	0	3.50
2 Jack Spring	L	31	0	0	.000	0	7	0	0	6	4	2	1	0	6.00
Jack Warner	R	23	0	0	.000	0	7	0	0	9	12	4	6	0	3.00
Dick Scott	L	31	0	0	.000	0	3	0	0	4	10	1	1	0	13.50

HOUSTON 9th 66-96 .407 27 — **HARRY CRAFT 61-88 .409** **LUM HARRIS 5-8 .385**

NAME	G by POS	B	AGE	G	AB	R	H	2B	3B	HR	RBI	BB	SO	SB	BA	SA
TOTALS			27	162	5303	495	1214	162	41	70	452	381	872	40	.229	.315
Walt Bond	1B76, OF71	L	26	148	543	63	138	16	7	20	85	38	90	2	.254	.420
Nellie Fox	2B115	L	36	133	442	45	117	12	6	0	28	27	13	0	.265	.319
Eddie Kasko	SS128, 3B2	R	32	133	448	45	109	16	1	0	22	37	52	4	.243	.283
Bob Aspromonte	3B155	R	26	157	553	51	155	20	3	12	69	35	54	6	.280	.392
Joe Gaines	OF81	R	27	89	307	37	78	9	7	7	34	27	69	8	.254	.397
Mike White	OF72, 2B10, 3B3	R	25	89	280	30	76	11	3	0	27	20	47	1	.271	.332
Al Spangler	OF127	L	30	135	449	51	110	18	5	4	38	41	43	7	.245	.334
Jerry Grote	C98	R	21	100	298	26	54	9	3	3	24	20	75	0	.181	.262
Bob Lillis	2B52, SS43, 3B12	R	34	109	332	31	89	11	2	0	17	11	10	4	.268	.313
Rusty Staub	1B49, OF38	L	20	89	292	26	63	10	2	8	35	21	31	1	.216	.346
John Bateman	C72	R	21	74	221	18	42	8	0	5	19	17	48	0	.190	.294
Jim Wynn	OF64	R	22	65	219	19	49	7	0	5	18	24	58	5	.224	.324
Dave Roberts	1B34, OF4	L	31	61	125	9	23	4	1	1	7	14	28	0	.184	.256
Carroll Hardy	OF41	R	31	46	157	13	29	1	1	2	12	8	30	0	.185	.242
Jim Beauchamp	OF15, 1B2	R	24	23	55	6	9	2	0	2	4	5	16	0	.164	.309
Pete Runnels	1B14	L	36	22	51	3	10	1	0	0	3	8	7	0	.196	.216
Joe Morgan	2B10	L	20	10	37	4	7	0	0	0	0	6	7	0	.189	.189
Ivan Murrell	OF5	R	19	10	14	1	2	1	0	0	1	0	6	0	.143	.214
Sonny Jackson	SS7	L	19	9	23	3	8	1	0	0	1	2	3	1	.348	.391
John Hoffman	C5	L	20	6	15	1	1	0	0	0	0	1	7	0	.067	.067
Dave Adlesh	C3	R	20	3	10	0	2	0	0	0	0	0	5	0	.200	.200

Walt Williams 20 R 0-9, Johnny Weekly 27 R 2-15, Steve Hertz 19 R 0-4, Brock Davis 20 L 0-3

NAME	T	AGE	W	L	PCT	SV	G	GS	CG	IP	H	BB	SO	ShO	ERA
		32	66	96	.407	31	162	162	30	1428	1421	353	852	9	3.41
Bob Bruce	R	31	15	9	.625	0	35	29	9	202	191	33	135	4	2.76
Dick Farrell	R	30	11	10	.524	0	32	27	7	198	196	52	117	0	3.27
Ken Johnson	R	31	11	16	.407	0	35	35	7	218	209	44	117	1	3.63
Jim Owens	R	30	8	7	.533	6	48	11	0	118	115	32	88	0	3.28
Don Nottebart	R	28	6	11	.353	0	28	24	2	157	165	37	90	0	3.90
Claude Raymond	R	27	5	5	.500	0	38	0	0	80	64	22	56	0	2.81
2 Don Larsen	R	34	4	8	.333	1	30	10	2	103	92	20	58	1	2.27
Hal Brown	R	39	3	15	.167	1	27	21	3	132	154	26	53	0	3.95
Hal Woodeshick	L	31	2	9	.182	23	61	0	0	78	73	32	58	0	2.77
Danny Coombs (MS)	L	22	1	1	.500	0	7	1	0	18	21	10	14	0	5.00
Gordon Jones	R	34	0	1	.000	0	34	0	0	50	58	14	28	0	4.14
Larry Dierker	R	17	0	1	.000	0	3	1	0	9	7	3	5	0	2.00
Chris Zachary	R	20	0	1	.000	0	1	1	0	4	6	1	2	0	9.00
Don Bradey	R	29	0	2	.000	0	3	1	0	2	6	3	2	0	22.50
Larry Yellen	R	21	0	0	.000	0	13	1	0	21	27	10	9	0	6.86
Dave Giusti	R	24	0	0	.000	0	8	0	0	26	24	8	16	0	3.12
Joe Hoerner	L	27	0	0	.000	0	7	0	0	11	13	6	4	0	4.91

Jim Umbricht (DD) 33

NEW YORK 10th 53-109 .327 40 — **CASEY STENGEL**

NAME	G by POS	B	AGE	G	AB	R	H	2B	3B	HR	RBI	BB	SO	SB	BA	SA
TOTALS			27	163	5566	569	1372	195	31	103	527	353	932	36	.246	.348
Ed Kranepool	1B104, OF6	L	19	119	420	47	108	19	4	10	45	32	50	0	.257	.393
Ron Hunt	2B109, 3B12	R	23	127	475	59	144	19	6	6	42	29	30	6	.303	.406
2 Roy McMillan	SS111	R	33	113	379	30	80	8	2	1	25	14	16	3	.211	.251
2 Charley Smith	3B85, SS36, OF13	R	26	127	443	44	106	12	0	20	58	19	101	2	.239	.402
Joe Christopher	OF145	R	28	154	543	78	163	26	8	16	76	48	92	6	.300	.466
Jim Hickman	OF113, 3B1	R	27	139	409	48	105	14	1	11	57	36	90	0	.257	.377
George Altman	OF109	L	31	124	422	48	97	14	1	9	47	18	70	4	.230	.332
Jesse Gonder	C97	L	28	131	341	28	92	11	1	7	35	29	65	0	.270	.370
Rod Kanehl	2B34, OF25, 3B19, 1B2	R	30	98	254	25	59	7	1	1	11	7	18	3	.232	.280
Hawk Taylor	C45, OF16	R	25	92	225	20	54	8	0	4	23	8	33	0	.240	.329
Larry Elliott	OF63	L	26	80	224	27	51	8	0	9	22	28	55	1	.228	.384
1 Frank Thomas	OF31, 1B19, 3B2	R	35	60	197	19	50	6	1	3	19	10	29	1	.254	.340
Chris Cannizzaro	C53	R	26	60	164	11	51	10	0	0	10	14	28	0	.311	.372
2 Bobby Klaus	3B28, 2B25, SS5	R	26	56	209	25	51	8	3	2	11	25	30	3	.244	.340
Amado Samuel	SS34, 3B17, 2B3	R	25	53	142	7	33	7	0	0	5	4	24	0	.232	.282
Dick Smith	1B18, OF13	R	25	46	94	14	21	6	1	0	3	1	29	6	.223	.309
Tim Harkness (SJ)	1B32	L	26	39	117	11	33	2	1	2	13	9	18	1	.282	.368
Johnny Stephenson	3B14, OF8	L	23	37	57	2	9	0	0	1	2	4	18	0	.158	.211
Wayne Graham	3B11	R	27	20	33	1	3	1	0	0	0	0	5	0	.091	.121
Al Moran	SS15, 3B1	R	25	16	22	2	5	0	0	0	4	2	2	0	.227	.227
Larry Burright	2B3	R	26	3	7	0	0	0	0	0	0	0	0	0	.000	.000

NAME	T	AGE	W	L	PCT	SV	G	GS	CG	IP	H	BB	SO	ShO	ERA
		26	53	109	.327	15	163	163	40	1439	1511	466	717	10	4.25
Al Jackson	L	28	11	16	.407	1	40	31	11	213	229	60	112	3	4.27
Jack Fisher	R	25	10	17	.370	0	40	34	8	228	256	56	115	1	4.22
Tracy Stallard	R	26	10	20	.333	0	36	34	11	226	213	73	118	2	3.78
Galen Cisco	R	28	6	19	.240	0	36	25	5	192	182	54	78	2	3.61
Larry Bearnarth	R	22	5	5	.500	3	44	1	0	78	79	38	31	0	4.15
Willard Hunter	L	30	3	3	.500	5	41	0	0	49	54	9	22	0	4.41
Bill Wakefield	R	23	3	5	.375	2	62	4	0	120	103	61	61	0	3.60
2 Frank Lary	R	34	2	3	.400	1	13	8	3	57	62	14	27	1	4.58
Ron Locke	L	22	1	2	.333	0	25	3	0	41	46	22	17	0	3.51
Tom Parsons	R	24	1	2	.333	0	4	2	1	19	20	6	10	0	4.26
Dennis Ribant	R	22	1	5	.167	1	14	7	1	58	65	9	35	1	5.12
2 Gary Kroll	R	22	0	1	.000	0	8	2	0	22	19	15	24	0	4.09
Craig Anderson	R	26	0	1	.000	0	4	1	0	13	21	3	5	0	5.54
Jay Hook	R	27	0	1	.000	0	3	2	0	10	17	7	5	0	9.00
Carl Willey (BJ)	R	33	0	2	.000	0	14	3	0	30	37	8	14	0	3.60
Jerry Hinsley	R	20	0	2	.000	0	9	2	0	15	21	7	11	0	8.40
Ed Bauta	R	29	0	2	.000	1	8	0	0	10	17	3	3	0	5.40
Darrell Sutherland	R	22	0	3	.000	0	10	4	0	27	32	12	9	0	7.67
2 Tom Sturdivant	R	34	0	0	.000	1	16	0	0	29	34	7	18	0	5.90
Steve Dillon	L	21	0	0	.000	0	2	0	0	3	4	2	2	0	9.00

1965 An Appointment with Disaster

Johnny Keane came to New York with all the confidence of a man hand-picked by Destiny for greatness. His journey to the city near the sea from the midlands of America had proven to be the coup of the previous year. What Keane had accomplished was simply to tell his Cardinal boss, Gussie Busch, where to get off. Keane spent the 1964 season with St. Louis and unexpectedly brought home the pennant despite seeing clouds every time he looked up into the sky which, oddly enough, resembled Busch's axe. Keane's patience with the Cardinals and himself proved the fulfillment of an age old fantasy: getting the last laugh on the boss. His decision to abandon Busch warmed the hearts of every working man in the country. Keane had further savored his personal triumph by beating Yogi Berra and the Yankees for the world's championship in 1964. Now, in 1965, he was on his way to pilot the Yankees—American League pennant winners since what seemed like time immemorial and the favorites to win an unprecedented sixth straight pennant. Such was not the case. Keane didn't know until it was too late that he had arrived just in time to preside over the collapse of an empire. The Bronx Bombers could never get untracked for Keane and skidded into sixth place, their lowest finish since 1925. Elston Howard's elbow, Tony Kubek's shoulder, and Roger Maris' hand all kept them out of action for extended periods, while little hurts cut down on Mickey Mantle's efficiency and Jim Bouton was unable to win more than four games. Keane found himself replacing the star-studded cast of 1964 with the likes of Doc Edwards, Ray Barker, and Roger Repoz. Try as he may, he could not prevent a resounding fall into the second division.

The Minnesota Twins captured 102 victories in picking up the fallen mantle of American League champion. Leading most of the way and ending with a seven-game margin over second-place Chicago, the Twins were powered by a heavy-hitting offense sparked by MVP Zoilo Versalles, batting champ Tony Oliva, and sluggers, Harmon Killebrew, Jimmie Hall, Bob Allison, and Don Mincher. Killebrew started the year on first base, but was moved to third in June so that Mincher's bat could be fit into the lineup. Ace right-hander Camilo Pascual lost six weeks due to a torn muscle in his back, but Mudcat Grant came through with a league-pacing 21 wins to take up the slack. Jim Kaat and Jim Perry contributed 30 wins between them, while reliever Al Worthington picked up ten victories and 21 saves.

The biggest story in the National League took place off the field. The directors of the Milwaukee Braves requested permission from the league to move to Atlanta, Georgia, for the 1965 season. The league ruled that due to the year remaining on the Milwaukee stadium lease and due to threatened litigation on the part of the city of Milwaukee, the Braves had to remain in Milwaukee for 1965 but could move to Dixie in 1966. The lame-duck season turned into a much-publicized fiasco, with several crowds under 1,000 and an anemic season's attendance of 555,584. The decision to leave stirred some congressmen and generated much bitterness between the baseball establishment and the public over the wooing, using, and abandoning of the Wisconsin territory in the course of 13 years.

On the field, the bat of Juan Marichal made headlines—not for hitting baseballs, but for hitting the head of Johnny Roseboro. In an August 22, Dodger-Giant contest, words between Marichal and Roseboro led to Marichal's conking the catcher on the head with his bat. When tempers subsided, Marichal and the Giants found themselves on the short end of the stick. The ace right-hander received a fine of $1,750, a suspension of nine days, and was barred from accompanying the Giants on their final trip to Los Angeles—a move that would prove costly as the two clubs were in a torrid fight for the pennant. Marichal's suspension denied him at least one start down the all-important stretch drive.

The pennant race found the Dodgers, Giants, Pirates, and Reds all in contention as September began, with the two California teams pulling away during the month with winning streaks of 13 for the Dodgers and 14 for the Giants. The final outcome saw the Dodgers take the flag by two games over their northern Californian rivals, as the temper outburst by Marichal came home to roost.

The Dodger attack was strictly popgun, along with a fantastic array of pitching. Maury Wills led the offense with a .286 mark and 94 stolen bases—which gave him the theft title for the sixth year in a row. Last in the league in home runs, the Dodger attack received a boost when the 31-year-old Lou Johnson was recalled to play left field after Tommy Davis broke an ankle. Johnson hit 12 home runs to tie Jim LeFebvre for the club lead. But what the Dodgers lacked in power, they made up for in pitching as Sandy Koufax and Don Drysdale provided an unparalleled one-two mound punch, winning 49 games between them with machine-like regularity.

The presence of Drysdale and Koufax made the Dodgers heavy Series favorites, but the Twins stunned the baseball world by defeating Drysdale and Koufax in the first two games. Claude Osteen then came on in the third game and shut out the Twins, and Drysdale and Koufax returned to give the Dodgers a 3-2 Series lead before Mudcat Grant evened it up for Minny. In game seven, Dodger manager Walter Alston deliberated on which ace to start. He choose Koufax, ignoring the two days of rest between starts for his ace-lefty, and Sandy replied with his second shutout in succession, to wrap up the crown for Los Angeles.

The 1965 season, as all the others before it, was not without its footnotes to baseball history. Casey Stengel broke his hip on the eve of his 75th birthday, an injury which finally forced the Old Professor to retire, thus ending a long managerial career which included ten pennants with the Yankees and three-and-one-half years of fun with the Mets.

A free-agent draft was instituted to help equalize the distribution of talent and to cut down on large bonus outlays to untried green talent. A new commissioner was named in General William Eckert, a man who soon became known for his lack of public presence, and the Houston Astrodome had opened in the spring—baseball's first enclosed, air-conditioned stadium. The park was billed as the Eighth Wonder of the world, and whether it was, mattered little, for it was at least enough of a conversation piece to triple Houston's attendance to 2,151,470.

WORLD SERIES – LOS ANGELES (NL) 4 MINNESOTA (AL) 3

LINE SCORES

TEAM	1	2	3	4	5	6	7	8	9	10	11	12	R	H	E
Game 1 October 6 at Minnesota															
LA (NL)	0	1	0	0	0	0	0	0	1				2	10	1
MIN (AL)	0	1	6	0	0	1	0	0	X				8	10	0
Drysdale, Reed (3), Brewer (5), Perranoski (7) — **Grant**															
Game 2 October 7 at Minnesota															
LA	0	0	0	0	0	0	1	0	0				1	7	3
MIN	0	0	0	0	0	2	1	2	X				5	9	0
Koufax, Perranoski (7), Miller (8) — **Kaat**															
Game 3 October 9 at Los Angeles															
MIN	0	0	0	0	0	0	0	0	0				0	5	0
LA	0	0	0	2	1	1	0	0	X				4	10	1
Pascual, Merritt (6), Klippstein (8) — **Osteen**															
Game 4 October 10 at Los Angeles															
MIN	0	0	0	1	0	1	0	0	0				2	5	2
LA	1	1	0	1	0	3	0	1	X				7	10	0
Grant, Worthington (6), Pleis (8) — **Drysdale**															
Game 5 October 11 at Los Angeles															
MIN	0	0	0	0	0	0	0	0	0				0	4	1
LA	2	0	2	1	0	0	2	0	X				7	14	0
Kaat, Boswell (3), Perry (6) — **Koufax**															
Game 6 October 13 at Minnesota															
LA	0	0	0	0	0	0	1	0	0				1	6	1
MIN	0	0	0	2	0	3	0	0	X				5	6	1
Osteen, Reed (6), Miller (8) — **Grant**															
Game 7 October 14 at Minnesota															
LA	0	0	0	2	0	0	0	0	0				2	7	0
MIN	0	0	0	0	0	0	0	0	0				0	3	1
Koufax — **Kaat**, Worthington (4), Klippstein (6), Merritt (7), Perry (9)															

COMPOSITE BATTING

NAME	POS	G	AB	R	H	2B	3B	HR	RBI	BA
Los Angeles (NL)										
Totals		7	234	24	64	10	1	5	21	.274
Wills	SS	7	**30**	3	**11**	**3**	0	0	3	.367
Fairly	OF	7	29	**7**	**11**	**3**	0	**2**	**6**	.379
Gilliam	3B	7	28	2	6	1	0	0	2	.214
Johnson	OF	7	27	3	8	2	0	**2**	4	.296
W. Davis	OF	7	26	3	6	0	0	0	0	.231
Parker	1B	7	23	3	7	0	1	1	2	.304
Roseboro	C	7	21	1	6	1	0	0	3	.286
Tracewski	2B	6	17	0	2	0	0	0	0	.118
Lefebvre	2B	3	10	2	4	0	0	0	0	**.400**
Koufax	P	3	9	0	1	0	0	0	1	.111
Drysdale	P	3	5	0	0	0	0	0	0	.000
Osteen	P	2	3	0	1	0	0	0	0	.333
Crawford	PH	2	2	0	1	0	0	0	0	.500
Moon	PH	2	2	0	0	0	0	0	0	.000
Kennedy	3B	4	1	0	0	0	0	0	0	.000
LeJohn	PH	1	1	0	0	0	0	0	0	.000
Reed	P	2	0	0	0	0	0	0	0	.000
Perranoski	P	2	0	0	0	0	0	0	0	.000
Miller	P	2	0	0	0	0	0	0	0	.000
Brewer	P	1	0	0	0	0	0	0	0	.000
Minnesota (AL)										
Totals		7	215	20	42	7	2	6	19	.195
Versalles	SS	7	28	3	8	1	1	1	4	.286
Oliva	OF	7	26	2	5	1	0	1	2	.192
Battey	C	7	25	1	3	0	1	0	2	.120
Mincher	1B	7	23	3	3	0	0	1	1	.130
Killebrew	3B	7	21	2	6	0	0	1	2	.286
Quilici	2B	7	20	2	4	2	0	0	1	.200
Nossek	OF	6	20	0	4	0	0	0	0	.200
Allison	OF	5	16	3	2	1	0	1	2	.125
Valdespino	OF	5	11	1	3	1	0	0	0	.273
Grant	P	3	8	3	2	1	0	1	3	.250
Hall	OF	2	7	0	1	0	0	0	0	.143
Kaat	P	3	6	0	1	0	0	0	2	.167
Rollins	PH	3	2	0	0	0	0	0	0	.000
Zimmerman	C	2	1	0	0	0	0	0	0	.000
Pascual	P	1	1	0	0	0	0	0	0	.000
Merritt	P	2	0	0	0	0	0	0	0	.000
Klippstein	P	2	0	0	0	0	0	0	0	.000
Worthington	P	2	0	0	0	0	0	0	0	.000
Perry	P	2	0	0	0	0	0	0	0	.000

Pleis P 0-0, Boswell P 0-0

COMPOSITE PITCHING

NAME	G	IP	H	BB	SO	W	L	SV	ERA
Los Angeles (NL)									
Totals	7	60	42	19	54	4	3	0	2.10
Koufax	**3**	**24**	13	**5**	**29**	**2**	1	0	**0.38**
Osteen	2	14	9	**5**	4	1	1	0	0.64
Drysdale	2	11.2	12	3	15	1	1	0	3.86
Perranoski	2	3.2	3	4	1	0	0	0	7.36
Reed	2	3.1	2	2	4	0	0	0	8.10
Brewer	1	2	3	0	1	0	0	0	4.50
Miller	2	1.1	0	0	0	0	0	0	0.00
Minnesota (AL)									
Totals	7	60	64	13	31	3	4	0	3.15
Grant	**3**	23	**22**	2	12	**2**	1	0	2.74
Kaat	**3**	14.1	18	2	6	1	**2**	0	3.77
Pascual	1	5	8	1	0	0	1	0	5.40
Worthington	2	4	2	2	2	0	0	0	0.00
Perry	2	4	5	2	4	0	0	0	4.50
Merritt	2	3.1	2	0	1	0	0	0	2.70
Klippstein	2	2.2	2	2	3	0	0	0	0.00
Boswell	1	2.2	3	2	3	0	0	0	3.38
Pleis	1	1	2	0	0	0	0	0	9.00

MINNESOTA 1st 102-60 .630 — SAM MELE

NAME	G by POS	B	AGE	G	AB	R	H	2B	3B	HR	RBI	BB	SO	SB	BA	SA
TOTALS			27	162	5488	**774**	**1396**	**257**	42	150	**711**	554	969	92	**.254**	.399
Don Mincher	1B99, OF1	L	27	128	346	43	87	17	3	22	65	49	73	1	.251	.509
Jerry Kindall	2B106, 3B10, SS7	R	30	125	342	41	67	12	1	6	36	36	97	2	.196	.289
Zoilo Versalles	SS160	R	25	160	**666**	**126**	182	**45**	**12**	19	77	41	**122**	27	.273	.462
Rich Rollins	3B112, 2B16	R	27	140	469	59	117	22	1	5	32	37	54	4	.249	.333
Tony Oliva	OF147	L	24	149	576	107	**185**	40	5	16	98	55	64	19	**.321**	.491
Jimmie Hall	OF141	L	27	148	522	81	149	25	4	20	86	51	79	14	.285	.464
Bob Allison	OF122, 1B3	R	30	135	438	71	102	14	5	23	78	73	114	10	.233	.445
Earl Battey	C128	R	30	131	394	36	117	22	2	6	60	50	23	0	.297	.409
Harmon Killebrew (EJ)	1B72, 3B44, OF1	R	29	113	401	78	108	16	1	25	75	72	69	0	.269	.501
Sandy Valdespino	OF57	L	26	108	245	38	64	8	2	1	22	20	28	7	.261	.322
Joe Nossek	OF48, 3B9	R	24	87	170	19	37	9	0	2	16	7	22	2	.218	.306
Jerry Zimmerman	C82	R	30	83	154	8	33	1	1	1	11	12	23	0	.214	.253
Frank Quilici	2B52, SS4	R	26	56	149	16	31	5	1	0	7	15	33	1	.208	.255
Andy Kosco	OF14, 1B2	R	23	23	55	3	13	4	0	1	6	1	15	0	.236	.364
Frank Kostro	2B7, 3B6, OF2	R	27	20	31	2	5	2	0	0	1	4	5	0	.161	.226
Bernie Allen (KJ)	2B10, 3B1	L	26	19	39	2	9	2	0	0	6	6	8	0	.231	.282
Cesar Tovar	2B4, 3B2, OF2, SS1	R	24	18	25	3	5	1	0	0	2	2	3	2	.200	.240
Rich Reese	1B6, OF1	L	23	14	7	0	2	1	0	0	0	2	2	0	.286	.429
Ted Uhlaender	OF4	L	25	13	22	1	4	0	0	0	1	0	2	1	.182	.182
John Sevcik	C11	R	22	12	16	1	1	1	0	0	0	1	5	0	.063	.125

NAME	T	AGE	W	L	PCT	SV	G	GS	CG	IP	H	BB	SO	ShO	ERA
		28	**102**	60	**.630**	45	162	162	32	1457	1278	503	934	12	3.14
Mudcat Grant	R	29	**21**	7	**.750**	0	41	39	14	270	252	61	142	**6**	3.30
Jim Kaat	L	26	18	11	.621	2	45	**42**	7	264	**267**	63	154	2	2.83
Jim Perry	R	29	12	7	.632	0	36	19	4	168	142	47	88	2	2.63
Al Worthington	R	36	10	7	.588	21	62	0	0	80	57	41	59	0	2.14
Johnny Klippstein	R	37	9	3	.750	5	56	0	0	76	59	31	59	0	2.25
Camilo Pascual (SA)	R	31	9	3	.750	0	27	27	5	156	126	63	96	1	3.35
Dave Boswell (IL)	R	20	6	5	.545	0	27	12	1	106	77	46	85	0	3.40
Jim Merritt	L	21	5	4	.556	2	16	9	1	77	68	20	61	0	3.16
Dick Stigman	L	29	4	2	.667	4	33	8	0	70	59	33	70	0	4.37
Bill Pleis	L	27	4	4	.500	4	41	2	0	51	49	27	33	0	3.00
Jerry Fosnow	L	24	3	3	.500	2	29	0	0	47	33	25	35	0	4.40
Garry Roggenburk	L	25	1	0	1.000	2	12	0	0	21	21	12	6	0	3.43
Mel Nelson	L	29	0	4	.000	3	28	3	0	55	57	23	31	0	4.09
Dwight Siebler	R	27	0	0	.000	0	7	1	0	15	11	11	15	0	4.20
Pete Cimino	R	22	0	0	.000	0	1	0	0	1	0	0	0	0	0.00

CHICAGO 2nd 95-67 .586 7 — AL LOPEZ

NAME	G by POS	B	AGE	G	AB	R	H	2B	3B	HR	RBI	BB	SO	SB	BA	SA
TOTALS			27	162	**5509**	647	1354	200	38	125	587	533	916	50	.246	.364
Bill Skowron	1B145	R	34	146	559	63	153	24	3	18	78	32	77	1	.274	.424
Don Buford	2B139, 3B41	B	28	155	586	93	166	22	5	10	47	67	76	17	.283	.389
Ron Hansen	SS161, 2B1	R	27	162	587	61	138	23	4	11	66	60	73	1	.235	.344
Pete Ward	3B134, 2B1	L	25	138	507	62	125	25	3	10	57	56	83	2	.247	.367
Floyd Robinson	OF153	L	29	156	577	70	153	15	6	14	66	76	51	4	.265	.385
Ken Berry	OF156	R	24	157	472	51	103	17	4	12	42	28	96	4	.218	.347
Danny Cater	OF127, 3B11, 1B3	R	25	142	514	74	139	18	4	14	55	33	65	3	.270	.403
Johnny Romano	C111, OF4, 1B2	R	30	122	356	39	86	11	0	18	48	59	74	0	.242	.424
Tommy McCraw	1B72, OF64	L	24	133	273	38	65	12	1	5	21	25	48	12	.238	.344
J. C. Martin	C112, 1B4, 3B2	L	28	119	230	21	60	12	0	2	21	24	29	2	.261	.339
Al Weis	2B74, SS7, 3B2, OF2	B	27	103	135	29	40	4	3	1	12	12	22	4	.296	.393
Smoky Burgess	C5	L	38	80	77	2	22	4	0	2	24	11	7	0	.286	.416
Dave Nicholson	OF36	R	25	54	85	11	13	2	1	2	12	9	40	0	.153	.271
1 Jimmie Schaffer	C14	R	29	17	31	2	6	3	1	0	1	3	4	0	.194	.355
2 Gene Freese	3B8	R	31	17	32	2	9	0	1	1	4	5	9	0	.281	.438
Jim Hicks	OF5	R	25	13	19	2	5	1	0	1	2	0	9	0	.263	.474
Bill Voss	OF10	L	21	11	33	4	6	0	1	1	3	3	5	0	.182	.333
Tommie Agee (BH)	OF9	R	22	10	19	2	3	1	0	0	3	2	6	0	.158	.211
Marv Staehle		L	23	7	7	0	3	0	0	0	2	0	0	0	.429	.429
Duane Josephson	C4	R	23	4	9	2	1	0	0	0	0	2	4	0	.111	.111

Dick Kenworthy 24 R 0-1, Bill Heath 26 L 0-1

NAME	T	AGE	W	L	PCT	SV	G	GS	CG	IP	H	BB	SO	ShO	ERA
		28	95	67	.586	**53**	162	162	21	**1482**	1261	460	946	14	2.99
Eddie Fisher	R	28	15	7	.682	24	**82**	0	0	165	118	43	90	0	2.40
Tommy John	L	22	14	7	.667	3	39	27	6	184	162	58	126	1	3.08
John Buzhardt	R	28	13	8	.619	1	32	30	4	189	167	56	108	1	3.00
Joe Horlen	R	27	13	13	.500	0	34	34	7	219	203	39	125	4	2.88
Gary Peters	L	28	10	12	.455	0	33	30	1	176	181	63	95	0	3.63
Bruce Howard	R	22	9	8	.529	0	30	22	1	148	123	72	120	1	3.47
Hoyt Wilhelm	R	41	7	7	.500	20	66	0	0	144	88	32	106	0	1.81
Juan Pizarro (SA)	L	28	6	3	.667	0	18	18	2	97	96	37	65	1	3.43
Bob Locker	R	27	5	2	.714	2	51	0	0	91	71	30	69	0	3.16
Ted Wills	L	31	2	0	1.000	1	15	0	0	19	17	14	12	0	2.84
2 Frank Lary	R	35	1	0	1.000	2	14	1	0	27	23	7	14	0	4.00
Greg Bollo	R	21	0	0	.000	0	15	0	0	23	12	9	16	0	3.52

BALTIMORE 3rd 94-68 .580 8 — HANK BAUER

NAME	G by POS	B	AGE	G	AB	R	H	2B	3B	HR	RBI	BB	SO	SB	BA	SA
TOTALS			27	162	5450	641	1299	227	38	125	596	529	907	67	.238	.363
Boog Powell	1B78, OF71	L	23	144	472	54	117	20	2	17	72	71	93	1	.248	.407
Jerry Adair	2B157	R	28	157	582	51	151	26	3	7	66	35	65	6	.259	.351
Luis Aparicio	SS141	R	31	144	564	67	127	20	10	8	40	46	56	26	.225	.339
Brooks Robinson	3B143	R	28	144	559	81	166	25	2	18	80	47	47	3	.297	.445
Russ Snyder	OF106	L	31	132	345	49	93	11	2	1	29	27	38	3	.270	.322
Paul Blair	OF116	R	21	119	364	49	85	19	2	5	25	32	52	8	.234	.338
Curt Blefary	OF136	L	21	144	462	72	120	23	4	22	70	88	73	4	.260	.470
Dick Brown (IL)	C92	R	30	96	255	17	59	9	1	5	30	17	53	2	.231	.333
Norm Siebern	1B76	L	31	106	297	44	76	13	4	8	32	50	49	1	.256	.407
Jackie Brandt	OF84	R	31	96	243	35	59	17	0	8	24	21	40	1	.243	.412
Bob Johnson	1B34, SS23, 3B13, 2B5	R	29	87	273	36	66	13	2	5	27	15	34	1	.242	.359
Sam Bowens	OF68	R	26	84	203	16	33	4	1	7	20	10	41	7	.163	.296
John Orsino	C62, 1B5	R	27	77	232	30	54	10	2	9	28	23	51	1	.233	.409
Charlie Lau	C35	L	32	68	132	15	39	5	2	2	18	17	18	0	.295	.409
Dave Johnson	3B9, 2B3, SS2	R	22	20	47	5	8	3	0	0	1	5	6	3	.170	.234
Mark Belanger	SS4	R	21	11	3	1	1	0	0	0	0	0	0	0	.333	.333
2 Carl Warwick	OF3	R	28	9	14	3	0	0	0	0	0	3	2	0	.000	.000
Andy Etchebarren	C5	R	22	5	6	1	1	0	0	1	4	0	2	0	.167	.667

NAME	T	AGE	W	L	PCT	SV	G	GS	CG	IP	H	BB	SO	ShO	ERA
		29	94	68	.580	41	162	162	32	1478	1268	510	939	**15**	**2.98**
Steve Barber	L	26	15	10	.600	0	37	32	7	221	177	81	130	2	2.69
Stu Miller	R	37	14	7	.667	24	67	0	0	119	87	32	104	0	1.89
Milt Pappas	R	26	13	9	.591	0	34	34	9	221	192	52	127	3	2.61
Dave McNally	L	22	11	6	.647	0	35	29	6	199	163	73	116	2	2.85
Dick Hall	R	34	11	8	.579	12	48	0	0	94	84	11	79	0	3.06
Wally Bunker	R	20	10	8	.556	2	34	27	4	189	170	58	84	1	3.38
John Miller	R	24	6	4	.600	0	16	16	1	93	75	58	71	0	3.19
Jim Palmer	R	19	5	4	.556	1	27	6	0	92	75	56	75	0	3.72
1 Robin Roberts	R	38	5	7	.417	0	20	15	5	115	110	20	63	1	3.37
Harvey Haddix	L	39	3	2	.600	1	24	0	0	34	31	23	21	0	3.44
2 Don Larsen	R	35	1	2	.333	1	27	1	0	54	53	20	40	0	2.67
Darold Knowles	L	23	0	1	.000	0	5	1	0	15	14	10	12	0	9.00
Ken Rowe	R	31	0	0	.000	0	6	0	0	13	17	2	3	0	3.46
Ed Barnowski	R	19	0	0	.000	0	4	0	0	4	3	7	6	0	2.25
Herm Starrette	R	26	0	0	.000	0	4	0	0	9	8	3	3	0	1.00
Frank Bertaina	L	21	0	0	.000	0	2	1	0	6	9	4	5	0	6.00

DETROIT 4th 89-73 .549 13 — CHUCK DRESSEN

NAME	G by POS	B	AGE	G	AB	R	H	2B	3B	HR	RBI	BB	SO	SB	BA	SA
TOTALS			27	162	5368	680	1278	190	27	162	635	554	952	57	.238	.374
Norm Cash	1B139	L	30	142	467	79	124	23	1	30	82	77	62	6	.266	.512
Jerry Lumpe	2B139	L	32	145	502	72	129	15	3	4	39	56	34	7	.257	.323
Dick McAuliffe(BW)	SS112	L	25	113	404	61	105	13	6	15	54	49	62	6	.260	.433
Don Wert	3B161, SS3, 2B1	R	26	162	609	81	159	22	2	12	54	73	71	5	.261	.363
Al Kaline (BH)	OF112, 3B1	R	30	125	399	72	112	18	2	18	72	72	49	6	.281	.471
Don Demeter	OF81, 1B34	R	30	122	389	50	108	16	4	16	58	23	65	4	.278	.463
Willie Horton	OF141, 3B1	R	22	143	512	69	140	20	2	29	104	48	101	5	.223	.490
Bill Freehan	C129	R	23	130	431	45	101	15	0	10	43	39	63	4	.234	.339
Gates Brown	OF56	L	26	96	227	33	58	14	2	10	43	17	33	6	.256	.467
Ray Oyler	SS57, 2B11, 1B1, 3B1	R	26	82	194	22	36	6	0	5	13	21	61	1	.186	.294
Jim Northrup	OF54	L	25	80	,219	20	45	12	3	2	16	12	50	1	.205	.315
George Thomas	OF59, 2B1	R	27	79	169	19	36	5	1	3	10	12	39	0	.213	.308
Jake Wood	2B20, 1B1, SS1, 3B1	R	28	58	104	12	30	3	0	2	7	10	19	3	.288	.375
John Sullivan	C29	L	24	34	86	5	23	0	0	2	11	9	13	0	.267	.337
George Smith	2B22, SS3, 3B3	R	26	32	53	6	5	0	0	1	1	3	18	0	.094	.151
Mickey Stanley	OF29	R	22	30	117	14	28	6	0	3	13	3	12	1	.239	.368
Jackie Moore	C20	R	26	21	53	2	5	0	0	0	2	6	12	0	.094	.094
Bill Roman	1B6	L	26	21	27	0	2	0	0	0	0	2	7	0	.074	.074
Wayne Redmond	OF2	R	19	4	4	1	0	0	0	0	0	1	1	0	.000	.000

NAME	T	AGE	W	L	PCT	SV	G	GS	CG	IP	H	BB	SO	ShO	ERA
		28	89	73	.549	31	162	162	**45**	1455	1283	509	1069	14	3.35
Denny McLain	R	21	16	6	.727	1	33	29	13	220	174	62	192	4	2.62
Mickey Lolich	L	24	15	9	.625	3	43	37	7	244	216	72	226	3	3.43
Hank Aguirre	L	33	14	10	.583	0	32	32	10	208	185	60	141	2	3.59
Joe Sparma	R	23	13	8	.619	0	30	28	6	167	142	75	127	0	3.18
Dave Wickersham	R	29	9	14	.391	0	34	27	8	195	179	61	109	3	3.78
Fred Gladding	R	29	6	2	.750	5	46	0	0	70	63	29	43	0	2.83
Terry Fox	R	29	6	4	.600	10	42	0	0	78	59	31	34	0	2.77
2 Orlando Pena	R	31	4	6	.400	4	30	0	0	57	54	20	55	0	2.51
Larry Sherry	R	29	3	6	.333	5	39	0	0	78	71	40	46	0	3.12
Ron Nischwitz	L	28	1	0	1.000	1	20	0	0	23	21	6	12	0	2.74
Jack Hamilton (JJ)	R	26	1	1	.500	0	4	1	0	4	6	4	3	0	15.75
Phil Regan	R	28	1	5	.167	0	16	7	1	52	57	20	37	0	5.02
Julio Navarro	R	29	0	2	.000	1	15	1	0	30	25	12	22	0	4.20
Ed Rakow	R	29	0	0	.000	0	6	0	0	13	14	11	10	0	6.23
John Hiller	L	22	0	0	.000	1	5	0	0	6	5	1	4	0	0.00
Johnny Seale	L	26	0	0	.000	0	4	0	0	3	7	2	3	0	12.00
Leo Marentette	R	24	0	0	.000	0	2	0	0	3	1	1	3	0	0.00
Vern Holtgrave	R	22	0	0	.000	0	1	0	0	3	4	2	2	0	6.00

CLEVELAND 5th 87-75 .537 15 — BIRDIE TEBBETTS

NAME	G by POS	B	AGE	G	AB	R	H	2B	3B	HR	RBI	BB	SO	SB	BA	SA
TOTALS			28	162	5469	663	1367	198	21	156	615	605	857	109	.250	.379
Fred Whitfield	1B122	L	27	132	468	49	137	23	1	26	90	16	42	2	.293	.513
2 Pedro Gonzalez	2B112, OF3, 3B2	R	26	116	400	38	101	14	3	5	39	18	57	7	.253	.340
Larry Brown	SS95, 2B26	R	25	124	438	52	111	22	2	8	40	38	62	5	.253	.368
Max Alvis	3B156	R	27	159	604	88	149	24	2	21	61	47	121	12	.247	.397
Rocky Colavito	OF162	R	31	162	592	92	170	25	2	26	**108**	**93**	63	1	.287	.468
Vic Davalillo	OF134	L	28	142	505	67	152	19	1	5	40	35	50	26	.301	.372
Leon Wagner	OF134	L	31	144	517	91	152	18	1	28	79	60	52	12	.294	.495
Joe Azcue	C108	R	25	111	335	16	77	7	0	2	35	27	54	2	.230	.269
Chuck Hinton	OF72, 1B40, 2B23, 3B1	R	31	133	431	59	110	17	6	18	54	53	65	17	.255	.448
Dick Howser	SS73, 2B17	R	28	107	307	47	72	8	2	1	6	57	25	17	.235	.283
Chico Salmon	1B28, OF17, 2B5, 3B5	R	24	79	120	20	29	8	0	3	12	5	19	7	.242	.383
Al Luplow	OF6	L	26	53	45	3	6	2	0	1	4	3	14	0	.133	.244
Duke Sims	C40	L	24	48	118	9	21	0	0	6	15	15	33	0	.178	.331
2 Phil Roof	C41	R	24	43	52	3	9	1	0	0	3	5	13	0	.173	.192
Billy Moran	2B7, SS1	R	31	22	24	1	3	0	0	0	0	2	5	0	.125	.125
Cam Carreon	C19	R	27	19	52	6	12	2	1	1	7	9	6	1	.231	.365
3 Lu Clinton	OF9	R	27	12	34	2	6	1	0	1	2	3	7	0	.176	.294
1 Ray Barker	1B3	R	29	11	6	0	0	0	0	0	0	2	2	0	.000	.000
Bill Davis		L	23	10	10	0	3	1	0	0	0	0	1	0	.300	.400
George Banks	3B1	R	26	4	5	0	1	1	0	0	0	1	3	0	.200	.400
Richie Scheinblum		B	22	4	1	1	0	0	0	0	0	0	0	0	.000	.000
Tony Martinez		R	24	4	3	0	0	0	0	0	0	0	0	0	.000	.000
Ralph Gagliano		L	18	1	0	0	0	0	0	0	0	0	0	0	.000	.000

NAME	T	AGE	W	L	PCT	SV	G	GS	CG	IP	H	BB	SO	ShO	ERA
		28	87	75	.537	41	162	162	41	1458	1254	500	**1156**	13	3.30
Sam McDowell	L	22	17	11	.607	4	42	35	14	273	178	**132**	**325**	3	**2.18**
Sonny Siebert	R	28	16	8	.667	1	39	27	4	189	139	46	191	1	2.43
Ralph Terry	R	29	11	6	.647	0	30	26	6	166	154	23	84	2	3.69
Luis Tiant	R	24	11	11	.500	1	41	30	10	196	166	66	152	2	3.54
Lee Stange	R	28	8	4	.667	0	41	12	4	132	122	26	80	2	3.34
Gary Bell	R	28	6	5	.545	17	60	0	0	104	86	50	86	0	3.03
Jack Kralick	L	30	5	11	.313	0	30	16	1	86	106	21	34	0	4.92
Steve Hargan	R	22	4	3	.571	2	17	8	1	60	55	28	37	0	3.45
Don McMahon	R	35	3	3	.500	11	58	0	0	85	79	37	60	0	3.28
Tom Kelley	R	21	2	1	.667	0	4	4	1	30	19	13	31	0	2.40
Floyd Weaver	R	24	2	2	.500	1	32	1	0	61	61	24	37	0	5.46
Jack Spring	L	32	1	2	.333	0	14	0	0	22	21	10	9	0	3.68
Dick Donovan	R	37	1	3	.250	0	12	3	0	23	32	6	12	0	5.87
3 Bobby Tiefenauer	R	35	0	5	.000	4	15	0	0	22	24	10	13	0	4.84
Mike Hedlund (JJ)	R	18	0	0	.000	0	6	0	0	5	6	5	4	0	5.40
Stan Williams	R	28	0	0	.000	0	3	0	0	4	6	3	1	0	6.75

NEW YORK 6th 77-85 .475 25 — JOHNNY KEANE

NAME	G by POS	B	AGE	G	AB	R	H	2B	3B	HR	RBI	BB	SO	SB	BA	SA
TOTALS			29	162	5470	611	1286	196	31	149	576	489	951	35	.235	.364
Joe Pepitone	1B115, OF41	L	24	143	531	51	131	18	3	18	62	43	59	4	.247	.394
Bobby Richardson	2B158	R	29	160	664	76	164	28	2	6	47	37	39	7	.247	.322
Tony Kubek	SS93, OF3, 1B1	L	28	109	339	26	74	5	3	5	35	20	48	1	.218	.295
Clete Boyer	3B147, SS2	R	28	148	514	69	129	23	6	18	58	39	79	4	.251	.424
Hector Lopez	OF75, 1B2	R	32	111	283	25	74	12	2	7	39	26	61	0	.261	.392
Tom Tresh	OF154	B	27	156	602	94	168	29	6	26	74	59	92	5	.279	.477
Mickey Mantle (SJ)	OF108	B	33	122	361	44	92	12	1	19	46	73	76	4	.255	.452
Elston Howard (AJ)	C95, 1B5, OF1	R	36	110	391	38	91	15	1	9	45	24	65	0	.233	.345
Phil Linz	SS71, 3B4, OF4, 2B1	R	26	99	285	37	59	12	1	2	16	30	33	2	.207	.277
2 Ray Barker	1B61, 3B3	L	29	98	205	21	52	11	0	7	31	20	46	1	.254	.410
Ross Moschitto	OF89	R	20	96	27	12	5	0	0	1	3	0	12	0	.185	.296
Roger Repoz	OF69	L	24	79	218	34	48	7	4	12	28	25	57	1	.220	.454
Horace Clarke	3B17, 2B7, SS1	B	25	51	108	13	28	1	0	1	9	6	6	2	.259	.296
Roger Maris (LJ-HJ)	OF43	L	30	46	155	22	37	7	0	8	27	29	29	0	.239	.439
2 Doc Edwards	C43	R	27	45	100	3	19	3	0	1	9	13	14	1	.190	.250
Art Lopez	OF16	L	28	38	49	5	7	0	0	0	0	1	6	0	.143	.143
Jake Gibbs	C21	L	26	37	68	6	15	1	0	2	7	4	20	0	.221	.324
Bob Schmidt	C20	R	32	20	40	4	10	1	0	1	3	3	8	0	.250	.350
Roy White	OF10, 2B1	B	21	14	42	7	14	2	0	0	3	4	7	2	.333	.381
1 Johnny Blanchard	C12	L	32	12	34	1	5	1	0	1	3	7	3	0	.147	.265
Bobby Murcer	SS11	L	19	11	37	2	9	0	1	1	4	5	12	0	.243	.378

Archie Moore 23 L 7-17, 1 Pedro Gonzalez 26 R 2-5, Duke Carmel 28 L 0-8

NAME	T	AGE	W	L	PCT	SV	G	GS	CG	IP	H	BB	SO	ShO	ERA
		27	77	85	.475	31	162	162	41	1460	1337	511	1001	11	3.28
Mel Stottlemyre	R	23	20	9	.690	0	37	37	18	291	250	88	155	4	2.63
Whitey Ford	L	36	16	13	.552	1	37	36	9	244	241	50	162	2	3.25
Al Downing	L	24	12	14	.462	0	35	32	8	212	185	105	179	2	3.40
Pedro Ramos	R	30	5	5	.500	19	65	0	0	92	80	27	68	0	2.93
Pete Mikkelsen	R	25	4	9	.308	1	41	3	0	82	78	36	69	0	3.29
Jim Bouton	R	26	4	15	.211	0	30	25	2	151	158	60	97	0	4.83
Steve Hamilton	L	31	3	1	.750	5	46	1	0	58	47	16	51	0	1.40
Hal Reniff	R	26	3	4	.429	3	51	0	0	85	74	48	74	0	3.81
Jack Cullen	R	25	3	4	.429	0	12	9	2	59	59	21	25	1	3.05
Bill Stafford (SA)	R	25	3	8	.273	0	22	15	1	111	93	31	71	0	3.57
Rick Beck	R	24	2	1	.667	0	3	3	1	21	22	7	10	1	2.14
Gil Blanco	L	19	1	1	.500	0	17	1	0	20	16	12	14	0	4.05
2 Bobby Tiefenauer	R	35	1	1	.500	2	10	0	0	20	19	5	15	0	3.54
1 Rollie Sheldon	R	28	0	0	.000	0	3	0	0	6	5	1	7	0	1.42
Jim Brenneman	R	24	0	0	.000	0	3	0	0	2	5	3	2	0	18.00
Mike Jurewicz	L	19	0	0	.000	0	2	0	0	2	5	1	2	0	9.00

CALIFORNIA 7th 75-87 .463 27 — BILL RIGNEY

NAME	G by POS	B	AGE	G	AB	R	H	2B	3B	HR	RBI	BB	SO	SB	BA	SA
TOTALS			27	162	5354	527	1279	200	36	92	486	443	973	107	.239	.341
Joe Adcock	1B97	R	37	122	349	30	84	14	0	14	47	37	74	2	.241	.400
Bobby Knoop	2B142	R	26	142	465	47	125	24	4	7	43	31	101	3	.269	.383
Jim Fregosi	SS160	R	23	161	602	66	167	19	7	15	64	54	107	13	.277	.407
Paul Schaal	3B153, 2B1	R	22	155	483	48	108	12	2	9	45	61	88	6	.224	.313
Albie Pearson	OF101	L	30	122	360	41	100	17	2	4	21	51	17	12	.278	.369
Jose Cardenal	OF129, 3B2, 2B1	R	21	134	512	58	128	23	2	11	57	27	72	37	.250	.367
Willie Smith	OF123, 1B2	L	26	136	459	52	120	14	9	14	57	32	60	9	.261	.423
Bob Rodgers	C128	B	26	132	411	33	86	14	3	1	32	35	61	4	.209	.266
Vic Power	1B107, 2B6, 3B2	R	33	124	197	11	51	7	1	1	20	5	13	2	.259	.320
1 Lu Clinton	OF73	R	27	89	222	29	54	12	3	1	8	23	37	2	.243	.338
Jimmy Piersall	OF41	R	35	53	112	10	30	5	2	2	12	5	15	2	.268	.402
2 Al Spangler	OF24	L	31	51	96	17	25	1	0	0	1	8	9	4	.260	.271
Tom Satriano	3B15, 2B12, C12, 1B3	L	24	47	79	8	13	2	0	1	4	10	10	1	.165	.228
Merritt Ranew	C24	L	27	41	91	12	19	4	0	1	10	7	22	0	.209	.286
Costen Shockley	1B31, OF1	L	23	40	107	5	20	2	0	2	17	9	16	0	.187	.262
Julio Gotay	2B23, 3B9, SS1	R	26	40	77	6	19	4	0	1	3	4	9	0	.247	.338
Bobby Gene Smith	OF15	R	31	23	57	1	13	3	0	0	5	2	10	0	.228	.281
Joe Koppe	2B10, SS4, 3B4	R	34	23	33	3	7	1	0	1	2	3	10	1	.212	.333
Rick Reichardt	OF20	R	22	20	75	8	20	4	0	1	6	5	12	4	.267	.360
Ed Kirkpatrick	OF19	L	20	19	73	8	19	5	0	3	8	3	9	1	.260	.452
Tom Egan	C16	R	19	18	38	3	10	0	1	0	1	3	12	0	.263	.316

Charlie Dees 30 L 5-32, 1 Phil Roof 24 R 3-22, Dick Simpson 21 R 6-27, Jackie Hernandez 24 R 2-6, Gino Cimoli 35 R 0-5

NAME	T	AGE	W	L	PCT	SV	G	GS	CG	IP	H	BB	SO	ShO	ERA
		25	75	87	.463	33	162	162	39	1442	1259	563	847	14	3.17
Dean Chance	R	24	15	10	.600	0	36	33	10	226	197	101	164	4	3.15
Marcelino Lopez	L	21	14	13	.519	1	35	32	8	215	185	82	122	1	2.93
Fred Newman	R	23	14	16	.467	0	36	36	10	261	225	64	109	2	2.93
Bob Lee	R	27	9	7	.563	23	69	0	0	131	95	42	89	0	1.92
George Brunet	L	30	9	11	.450	2	41	26	8	197	149	69	141	3	2.56
Aubrey Gatewood	R	26	4	5	.444	0	46	3	0	92	91	37	37	0	3.42
Rudy May	L	20	4	9	.308	0	30	19	2	124	111	78	76	1	3.92
Jim Coates	R	32	2	0	1.000	3	17	0	0	28	23	16	15	0	3.54
Ed Sukla	R	22	2	3	.400	3	25	0	0	32	32	10	15	0	4.50
Barry Latman	R	29	1	1	.500	0	18	0	0	32	30	16	18	0	2.81
2 Jack Sanford	R	36	1	2	.333	1	9	5	0	29	35	10	13	0	4.66
1 Don Lee	R	31	0	1	.000	0	10	0	0	14	21	5	12	0	6.43
Ron Piche	R	30	0	3	.000	0	14	1	0	20	20	12	14	0	6.75
Ken McBride (SA)	R	29	0	3	.000	0	8	4	0	22	24	14	11	0	6.14
Jim McGlothin	R	21	0	3	.000	0	3	3	1	18	18	7	9	0	3.50
Dick Wantz (DD)	R	25	0	0	.000	0	1	0	0	1	3	0	2	0	18.00

WASHINGTON 8th 70-92 .432 32 — GIL HODGES

NAME	G by POS	B	AGE	G	AB	R	H	2B	3B	HR	RBI	BB	SO	SB	BA	SA
TOTALS			29	162	5374	591	1227	179	33	136	563	570	1125	30	.228	.350
Dick Nen	1B65	L	25	69	246	18	64	7	1	6	31	19	47	1	.260	.370
Don Blasingame	2B110	L	33	129	403	47	90	8	8	1	18	35	45	5	.223	.290
Eddie Brinkman	SS150	R	23	154	444	35	82	13	2	5	35	38	82	1	.185	.257
Ken McMullen	3B142, OF8, 1B1	R	23	150	555	75	146	18	6	18	54	47	90	2	.263	.414
Woodie Held	OF106, 3B5, 2B4, SS2	R	33	122	332	46	82	16	2	16	54	49	74	0	.247	.452
Don Lock	OF136	R	28	143	418	52	90	15	1	16	39	57	115	1	.215	.371
Frank Howard	OF138	R	28	149	516	53	149	22	6	21	84	55	112	0	.289	.477
Mike Brumley	C66	L	26	79	216	15	45	4	0	3	15	20	33	1	.208	.269
Willie Kirkland	OF92	L	31	123	312	38	72	9	1	14	54	19	65	3	.231	.401
Jim King	OF88	L	32	120	258	46	55	10	2	14	49	44	50	1	.213	.430
Ken Hamlin	2B77, SS47, 3B1	R	30	117	362	45	99	21	1	4	22	33	45	8	.273	.370
Don Zimmer	3B36, C33, 2B12	R	34	95	226	20	45	6	0	2	17	26	59	2	.199	.252
Joe Cunningham	1B59	L	33	95	201	29	46	9	1	3	20	46	27	0	.229	.328
Doug Camilli	C59	R	28	75	193	13	37	6	1	3	18	16	34	0	.192	.280
Bob Chance	1B48, OF3	L	24	72	199	20	51	9	0	4	14	18	44	0	.256	.362
Joe McCabe	C11	R	26	14	27	1	5	0	0	1	5	4	13	1	.185	.296
Jim French	C13	L	23	13	37	4	11	0	0	1	7	9	5	1	.297	.378
Roy Sievers	1B7	R	38	12	21	3	4	1	0	0	0	4	3	0	.190	.238
Fred Valentine	OF11	B	30	12	29	6	7	0	0	0	1	4	5	3	.241	.241
Brant Alyea	1B3, OF1	R	24	8	13	3	3	0	0	2	6	1	4	0	.231	.692

Paul Casanova 23 R 4-13, Chuck Cottier 29 R 0-1

NAME	T	AGE	W	L	PCT	SV	G	GS	CG	IP	H	BB	SO	ShO	ERA
		29	70	92	.432	40	162	162	21	1436	1376	633	867	8	3.93
Pete Richert	L	25	15	12	.556	0	34	29	6	194	146	84	161	0	2.60
Phil Ortega	R	25	12	15	.444	0	35	29	4	180	176	97	88	2	5.10
Mike McCormick	L	26	8	8	.500	1	44	21	3	158	158	36	88	1	3.36
Ron Kline	R	33	7	6	.538	29	74	0	0	99	106	32	52	0	2.64
Steve Ridzik	R	36	6	4	.600	8	63	0	0	110	108	43	72	0	4.01
Bennie Daniels	R	33	5	13	.278	1	33	18	1	116	135	39	42	0	4.73
Howie Koplitz	R	27	4	7	.364	1	33	11	0	107	97	48	59	0	4.04
Buster Narum	R	24	4	12	.250	0	46	24	2	174	176	91	86	0	4.45
Joe Coleman	R	18	2	0	1.000	0	2	2	2	18	9	8	7	0	1.50
Jim Duckworth	R	26	2	2	.500	0	17	8	0	64	45	36	74	0	3.94
Frank Kreutzer	L	26	2	6	.250	0	33	14	2	85	73	54	65	1	4.34
2 Ryne Duren	R	36	1	1	.500	0	16	0	0	23	24	18	18	0	6.65
Jim Hannan	R	25	1	1	.500	0	4	1	1	15	18	6	5	1	4.80
Marshall Bridges	L	34	1	2	.333	0	40	0	0	57	62	25	39	0	2.68
Pete Craig	R	24	0	3	.000	0	3	3	0	14	18	8	2	0	8.36
Dallas Green	R	30	0	0	.000	0	6	2	0	14	14	3	6	0	3.21
1 Nick Willhite	L	24	0	0	.000	0	5	0	0	6	10	4	3	0	7.50
Barry Moore	L	22	0	0	.000	0	1	0	0	1	1	1	0	0	0.00
Tom Cheney (VR) 30															

BOSTON 9th 62-100 .383 40 — BILLY HERMAN

NAME	G by POS	B	AGE	G	AB	R	H	2B	3B	HR	RBI	BB	SO	SB	BA	SA
TOTALS			26	162	5487	669	1378	244	40	**165**	629	**607**	964	47	.251	**.400**
Lee Thomas	1B127, OF20	L	29	151	521	74	141	27	4	22	75	72	42	6	.271	.464
Felix Mantilla	2B123, OF27, 1B2	R	30	150	534	60	147	17	2	18	92	79	84	7	.275	.416
Rico Petrocelli	SS93	R	22	103	323	38	75	15	2	13	33	36	71	0	.232	.412
Frank Malzone	3B96	R	35	106	364	40	87	20	0	3	34	28	38	1	.239	.319
Tony Conigliaro	OF137	R	20	138	521	82	140	21	5	**32**	82	51	116	4	.269	.512
Lenny Green	OF95	L	31	119	373	69	103	24	6	7	24	48	43	8	.276	.429
Carl Yastrzemski	OF130	L	25	133	494	78	154	**45**	3	20	72	70	58	7	.312	**.536**
Bob Tillman	C106	R	28	111	368	20	79	10	3	6	35	40	69	0	.215	.307
Dalton Jones	3B81, 2B8	L	21	112	367	41	99	13	5	5	37	28	45	8	.270	.373
Ed Bressoud	SS86, 3B2, OF1	R	33	107	296	29	67	11	1	8	25	29	77	0	.226	.351
Jim Gosger	OF81	L	22	81	324	45	83	15	4	9	35	29	61	3	.256	.410
Chuck Schilling	2B41	R	27	71	171	14	41	3	2	3	9	13	17	0	.240	.333
Tony Horton	1B44	R	20	60	163	23	48	8	1	7	23	18	36	0	.294	.485
Russ Nixon	C38	L	30	59	137	11	37	5	1	0	11	6	23	0	.270	.321
Earl Wilson	P36	R	30	47	79	13	14	0	0	6	12	13	29	0	.177	.405
Mike Ryan	C33	R	23	33	107	7	17	0	1	3	9	5	19	0	.159	.262
Gary Geiger (IL-FS)	OF16	L	28	24	45	5	9	3	0	1	2	13	10	3	.200	.333

Jerry Moses 18 R 1-4, Rudy Schlesinger 22 R 0-1

NAME	T	AGE	W	L	PCT	SV	G	GS	CG	IP	H	BB	SO	ShO	ERA
		27	62	100	.383	25	162	162	33	1439	**1443**	543	993	9	4.24
Earl Wilson	R	30	13	14	.481	0	36	36	8	231	221	77	164	1	3.97
Bill Monbouquette	R	28	10	**18**	.357	0	35	35	10	229	239	40	110	2	3.69
Dave Morehead	R	22	10	**18**	.357	0	34	33	5	193	157	113	163	2	4.06
Dick Radatz	R	28	9	11	.450	22	63	0	0	124	104	53	121	0	3.92
Jim Lonborg	R	23	9	17	.346	0	32	31	7	185	193	65	113	1	4.48
Dennis Bennett	L	25	5	7	.417	0	34	18	3	142	152	53	85	0	4.37
Bob Duliba	R	30	4	2	.667	1	39	0	0	64	60	22	27	0	3.80
Jay Ritchie	R	28	1	2	.333	2	44	0	0	71	83	26	55	0	3.17
Jerry Stephenson	R	21	1	5	.167	0	15	8	0	52	62	33	49	0	6.23
Arnie Earley	L	32	0	1	.000	0	57	0	0	74	79	29	47	0	3.65
Bob Heffner	R	26	0	2	.000	0	27	1	0	49	59	18	42	0	7.16
1 Jack Lamabe	R	28	0	3	.000	0	14	0	0	25	34	14	17	0	8.28

KANSAS CITY 10th 59-103 .364 43 — MEL McGAHA 5-21 .192 HAYWOOD SULLIVAN 54-82 .397

NAME	G by POS	B	AGE	G	AB	R	H	2B	3B	HR	RBI	BB	SO	SB	BA	SA
TOTALS			25	162	5393	585	1294	186	**59**	110	546	521	1020	**110**	.240	.358
Ken Harrelson	1B125, OF4	R	23	150	483	61	115	17	3	23	66	66	112	9	.238	.429
Dick Green	2B126	R	24	133	474	64	110	15	1	15	55	50	110	0	.232	.363
Cmp'nris	SS109, OF39, 1B, 2B, 3B, C, P=1	R	23	144	678	67	156	23	**12**	6	42	41	71	**51**	.270	.382
Ed Charles	3B128, 2B1, SS1	R	30	134	480	55	129	19	7	8	56	44	72	13	.269	.388
Mike Hershberger	OF144	R	25	150	494	43	114	15	5	5	48	37	42	7	.231	.312
Jim Landis	OF108	R	31	118	364	46	87	15	1	3	36	57	84	8	.239	.310
Tommie Reynolds	OF83, 3B1	R	23	90	270	34	64	11	3	1	22	36	41	9	.237	.311
Billy Bryan	C95	L	26	108	325	36	82	11	5	14	51	29	87	0	.252	.446
Wayne Causey	SS62, 2B45, 3B35	L	28	144	513	48	134	17	8	3	34	61	48	1	.261	.343
Rene Lachemann	C75	R	20	92	216	20	49	7	1	9	29	12	57	0	.227	.394
Santiago Rosario	1B31, OF3	L	25	81	85	8	20	3	0	2	8	6	16	0	.235	.341
Jose Tartabull	OF54	L	26	68	218	28	68	11	4	1	19	18	20	11	.312	.413
Nelson Mathews	OF57	R	23	67	184	17	39	7	7	2	15	24	49	0	.212	.359
2 Johnny Blanchard	OF20, C14	L	32	52	120	10	24	2	0	2	11	8	16	0	.200	.267
Skip Lockwood	3B7	R	18	42	33	4	4	0	0	0	0	7	11	0	.121	.121
1 Jim Gentile	1B35	L	31	38	118	14	29	5	0	10	22	9	26	0	.246	.542
Larry Stahl	OF21	L	24	28	81	9	16	2	1	4	14	5	16	1	.198	.395

1 Doc Edwards 27 R 3-20, Randy Schwartz 21 L 2-7, 2 Lu Clinton 27 R 0-1, John Sanders 19 R 0-0

NAME	T	AGE	W	L	PCT	SV	G	GS	CG	IP	H	BB	SO	ShO	ERA
		27	59	**103**	.364	32	162	162	18	1433	1399	574	882	7	4.24
2 Rollie Sheldon	R	28	10	8	.556	0	32	29	4	187	180	56	105	1	3.95
Fred Talbot	R	24	10	12	.455	0	39	33	2	198	188	86	117	1	4.14
John O'Donoghue	L	25	9	**18**	.333	0	34	30	4	178	183	66	82	1	3.94
Catfish Hunter	R	19	8	8	.500	0	32	20	3	133	124	46	82	2	4.26
Don Mossi	L	36	5	8	.385	7	51	0	0	55	59	20	41	0	3.76
Diego Segui	R	27	5	15	.250	0	40	25	5	163	166	67	119	1	4.64
Jack Aker	R	24	4	3	.571	3	34	0	0	51	45	18	26	0	3.18
Jim Dickson	R	27	3	2	.600	0	68	0	0	86	68	47	54	0	3.45
Lew Krausse	R	22	2	4	.333	0	7	5	0	25	29	8	22	0	5.04
John Wyatt	R	30	2	6	.250	18	65	0	0	89	78	53	70	0	3.24
Moe Drabowsky	R	29	1	5	.167	0	14	5	0	39	44	18	25	0	4.38
Jess Hickman	R	25	0	1	.000	0	12	0	0	15	9	8	16	0	6.00
Don Buschhorn (LJ)	R	19	0	1	.000	0	12	3	0	31	36	8	9	0	4.35
Dick Joyce	L	21	0	1	.000	0	5	3	0	13	12	4	7	0	2.77
Paul Lindblad	L	23	0	1	.000	0	4	0	0	7	12	0	12	0	11.57
Wes Stock	R	31	0	4	.000	4	62	2	0	100	96	40	52	0	5.22
1 Orlando Pena	R	31	0	6	.000	0	12	5	0	35	42	13	24	0	6.88

Aurelio Monteagudo 21 R 0-0, Ron Tompkins 20 R 0-0, Jose Santiago 24 R 0-0, Satchel Paige 58 R 0-0, Tom Harrison 20 R 0-0, Blue Moon Odom 20 R 0-0, Bert Campaneris 23 R 0-0

LOS ANGELES 1st 97-65 .599 — WALT ALSTON

NAME	G by POS	B	AGE	G	AB	R	H	2B	3B	HR	RBI	BB	SO	SB	BA	SA
TOTALS			29	162	5425	608	1329	193	32	78	548	492	891	**172**	.245	.335
Wes Parker	1B154, OF1	B	25	154	542	80	129	24	7	8	51	75	95	13	.238	.352
Jim Lefebvre	2B156	B	22	157	544	57	136	21	4	12	69	71	92	3	.250	.369
Maury Wills	SS155	B	32	158	650	92	186	14	7	0	33	40	64	**94**	.286	.329
Jim Gilliam (RC)	3B80, OF22, 2B5	B	36	111	372	54	104	19	4	4	39	53	31	9	.280	.384
Ron Fairly	OF148, 1B13	L	26	158	555	73	152	28	1	9	70	76	72	2	.274	.377
Willie Davis	OF141	L	25	142	558	52	133	24	3	10	57	14	81	25	.238	.346
Lou Johnson	OF128	R	30	131	468	57	121	24	1	12	58	24	81	15	.259	.391
Johnny Roseboro	C131, 3B1	L	32	136	437	42	102	10	0	8	57	34	51	1	.233	.311
John Kennedy	3B95, SS5	R	24	104	105	12	18	3	0	1	5	8	33	1	.171	.229
Dick Tracewski	3B53, 2B14, SS7	R	30	78	186	17	40	6	0	1	20	25	30	2	.215	.263
Don Drysdale	P44	R	28	58	130	18	39	4	1	7	19	5	34	0	.300	.508
Jeff Torborg	C53	R	23	56	150	8	36	5	1	3	13	10	26	0	.240	.347
Wally Moon	OF23	L	35	53	89	6	18	3	0	1	11	13	22	2	.202	.270
Willie Crawford	OF8	L	18	52	27	10	4	0	0	0	0	2	8	2	.148	.148
Al Ferrara	OF27	R	25	41	81	5	17	2	1	1	10	9	20	0	.210	.296
Don Le John	3B26	R	31	34	78	2	20	2	0	0	7	5	13	0	.256	.282
Derrell Griffith	OF11	L	21	22	41	3	7	0	0	1	2	0	9	0	.171	.244
Tommy Davis (BN)	OF16	R	26	17	60	3	15	1	1	0	9	2	4	2	.250	.300
Hec Valle	C6	R	24	9	13	1	4	0	0	0	2	2	3	0	.308	.308

Dick Smith 26 R 0-6, Nate Oliver 24 R 1-1, Johnny Werhas 27 R 0-3

NAME	T	AGE	W	L	PCT	SV	G	GS	CG	IP	H	BB	SO	ShO	ERA
		28	**97**	65	**.599**	34	162	162	**58**	1476	1223	425	1079	**23**	**2.81**
Sandy Koufax	L	29	**26**	8	**.765**	2	43	41	**27**	**336**	216	71	**382**	8	**2.04**
Don Drysdale	R	28	23	12	.657	1	44	**42**	20	308	**270**	66	210	7	2.78
Claude Osteen	L	25	15	15	.500	0	40	40	9	287	253	78	162	1	2.79
Howie Reed	R	28	7	5	.583	1	38	5	0	78	73	27	47	0	3.12
Johnny Podres	L	32	7	6	.538	1	27	22	2	134	126	39	63	1	3.43
Ron Perranoski	L	29	6	6	.500	17	59	0	0	105	85	40	53	0	2.23
Bob Miller	R	26	6	7	.462	9	61	1	0	103	82	26	77	0	2.97
Jim Brewer (EJ)	L	27	3	2	.600	2	19	2	0	49	33	28	31	0	1.84
John Purdin	R	22	2	1	.667	0	11	2	0	23	26	13	16	0	6.65
2 Nick Willhite	L	24	2	2	.500	1	15	6	0	42	47	22	28	0	5.36
Mike Kekich	L	20	0	1	.000	0	5	1	0	10	10	13	9	0	9.90
Bill Singer	R	21	0	0	.000	0	2	0	0	1	2	2	1	0	0.00

SAN FRANCISCO 2nd 95-67 .586 2 — HERMAN FRANKS

NAME	G by POS	B	AGE	G	AB	R	H	2B	3B	HR	RBI	BB	SO	SB	BA	SA
TOTALS			27	163	5495	682	1384	169	43	159	623	476	844	47	.252	.385
Willie McCovey	1B156	L	27	160	540	93	149	17	4	39	92	88	118	0	.276	.539
Hal Lanier	2B158, SS1	R	22	159	522	41	118	15	9	0	39	21	67	2	.226	.289
2 Dick Schofield	SS93	B	30	101	379	39	77	10	1	2	19	33	50	2	.203	.251
Jim Ray Hart	3B144, OF15	R	23	160	591	91	177	30	6	23	96	47	75	6	.299	.487
Jesus Alou	OF136	R	23	143	543	76	162	19	4	9	52	13	40	8	.298	.398
Willie Mays	OF151	R	34	157	558	118	177	21	3	**52**	112	76	71	9	.317	**.645**
Matty Alou	OF103, P1	L	26	117	324	37	75	12	2	2	18	17	28	10	.231	.299
Tom Haller	C133	L	28	134	422	40	106	4	3	16	49	47	67	0	.251	.389
Jim Davenport	3B39, SS37, 2B26	R	31	106	271	29	68	14	3	4	31	21	47	0	.251	.369
2 Len Gabrielson	OF77, 1B5	L	25	88	269	36	81	6	5	4	26	26	48	4	.301	.405
Cap Peterson	OF27	R	22	63	105	14	26	7	0	3	15	10	16	0	.248	.400
Ken Henderson	OF48	B	19	63	73	10	14	1	1	0	7	9	19	1	.192	.233
Jack Hiatt	C21, 1B7	R	22	40	67	5	19	4	0	1	7	12	14	0	.284	.388
Orlando Cepeda (KJ)	1B4, OF2	R	27	33	34	1	6	1	0	1	5	3	9	0	.176	.294
Bob Burda	1B11, OF1	L	26	31	27	0	3	0	0	0	5	5	6	0	.111	.111
Bob Schroder	2B4, 3B1	L	20	31	9	4	2	0	0	0	1	1	1	0	.222	.222
1 Jose Pagan	SS26	R	30	26	83	10	17	4	0	0	5	8	9	1	.205	.253
Tito Fuentes	SS18, 2B7, 3B1	R	21	26	72	12	15	1	0	0	1	5	14	0	.208	.222
1 Ed Bailey	C12, 1B2	L	34	24	28	1	3	0	0	0	3	6	7	0	.107	.107
1 Harvey Kuenn	OF14, 1B7	R	34	23	59	4	14	0	0	0	6	10	3	3	.237	.237
2 Dick Bertell	C22	R	29	22	48	1	9	1	0	0	3	7	5	0	.188	.208
1 Chuck Hiller	2B2	L	30	7	7	1	1	0	0	1	1	0	1	0	.143	.571

Randy Hundley 23 R 1-15, Ollie Brown 21 R 2-10, Bob Barton 23 R 4-7

NAME	T	AGE	W	L	PCT	SV	G	GS	CG	IP	H	BB	SO	ShO	ERA
		30	95	67	.586	**42**	163	163	42	1465	1325	408	1060	17	3.20
Juan Marichal	R	27	22	13	.629	1	39	37	24	295	224	46	240	**10**	2.14
Bob Shaw	R	32	16	9	.640	2	42	33	6	235	213	53	148	1	2.64
Bobby Bolin	R	26	14	6	.700	2	45	13	2	163	125	56	135	0	2.76
Ron Herbel	R	27	12	9	.571	1	47	21	1	171	172	47	106	0	3.84
Frank Linzy	R	24	9	3	.750	21	57	0	0	82	76	23	35	0	1.43
Gaylord Perry	R	26	8	12	.400	1	47	26	6	196	194	70	170	0	4.18
Masanori Murakami	L	21	4	1	.800	8	45	1	0	74	57	22	85	0	3.77
1 Jack Sanford	R	36	4	5	.444	2	23	16	0	91	92	30	43	0	3.96
2 Warren Spahn	L	44	3	4	.429	0	16	11	3	72	70	21	34	0	3.38
2 Bill Henry	L	37	2	2	.500	4	35	0	0	42	40	8	35	0	3.64
Bob Priddy	R	25	1	0	1.000	0	8	0	0	10	6	2	7	0	1.80
1 Jim Duffalo	R	29	0	1	.000	0	2	0	0	.1	1	2	0	0	27.00
Bill Hands	R	25	0	2	.000	0	4	2	0	6	13	6	5	0	16.50
1 Bob Hendley	L	26	0	0	.000	0	8	2	0	15	27	13	8	0	12.60
Dick Estelle	L	23	0	0	.000	0	6	1	0	11	12	8	6	0	4.09
Matty Alou	L	26	0	0	.000	0	1	0	0	2	3	1	3	0	0.00

PITTSBURGH 3rd 90-72 .556 7 — HARRY WALKER

NAME	G by POS	B	AGE	G	AB	R	H	2B	3B	HR	RBI	BB	SO	SB	BA	SA
TOTALS			28	163	**5686**	675	1506	217	57	111	631	419	1008	51	.265	.382
Donn Clendenon	1B158, 3B1	R	29	162	612	89	184	32	14	14	96	48	128	9	.301	.467
Bill Mazeroski	2B127	R	28	130	494	52	134	17	1	6	54	18	34	2	.271	.346
Gene Alley	SS110, 2B40, 3B1	R	24	153	500	47	126	21	6	5	47	32	82	7	.252	.348
Bob Bailey	3B142, OF28	R	22	159	626	87	160	28	3	11	49	70	93	10	.256	.363
Roberto Clemente	OF145	R	30	152	589	91	194	21	14	10	65	43	78	8	**.329**	.463
Bill Virdon	OF128	L	34	135	481	58	134	22	5	4	24	30	49	4	.279	.370
Willie Stargell	OF137, 1B7	L	25	144	533	68	145	25	8	27	107	39	127	1	.272	.501
Jim Pagliaroni	C131	R	27	134	403	42	108	15	0	17	65	41	84	0	.268	.432
Manny Mota	OF95	R	27	121	294	47	82	7	6	4	29	22	32	2	.279	.384
Andre Rodgers	SS33, 3B15, 1B6, 2B1	R	30	75	178	17	51	12	0	2	25	18	28	2	.287	.388
Jerry Lynch	OF26	L	34	73	121	7	34	1	0	5	16	8	26	0	.281	.413
Del Crandall	C60	R	35	60	140	11	30	2	0	2	10	14	10	1	.214	.271
1 Gene Freese	3B19	R	31	43	80	6	21	4	0	0	8	6	18	0	.263	.313
2 Jose Pagan	3B16, SS7	R	30	42	38	6	9	1	0	0	1	1	7	1	.237	.263
Ozzie Virgil	C16, 3B7, 2B6	R	32	39	49	3	13	2	0	1	5	2	10	0	.265	.367
1 Dick Schofield	SS28	B	30	31	109	13	25	5	0	0	6	15	19	1	.229	.275
George Spriggs	OF1	L	24	9	2	5	1	0	0	0	0	0	0	2	.500	.500

Jerry May 21 R 1-2, Hal Smith 34 R 0-3, Bob Oliver 22 R 0-2

NAME	T	AGE	W	L	PCT	SV	G	GS	CG	IP	H	BB	SO	ShO	ERA
		29	90	72	.556	27	163	163	49	**1479**	1324	469	882	17	3.01
Vern Law	R	35	17	9	.654	0	29	28	13	217	182	35	101	4	2.16
Bob Veale	L	29	17	12	.586	0	39	37	14	266	221	**119**	276	7	2.84
Don Cardwell	R	29	13	10	.565	0	37	34	12	240	214	59	107	2	3.19
Don Schwall	R	29	9	6	.600	4	43	1	0	77	77	30	55	0	2.92
Bob Friend	R	34	8	12	.400	0	34	34	8	222	221	47	74	2	3.24
Tommie Sisk	R	23	7	3	.700	0	38	12	1	111	103	50	66	1	3.41
Al McBean	R	27	6	6	.500	18	62	1	0	114	111	42	54	0	2.29
Roy Face (KJ)	R	37	5	2	.714	0	16	0	0	20	20	7	19	0	2.70
Joe Gibbon	L	30	4	9	.308	1	31	15	1	106	85	34	63	0	4.50
Frank Carpin	L	26	3	1	.750	4	39	0	0	40	35	24	27	0	3.15
Wilbur Wood	L	23	1	1	.500	0	34	1	0	51	44	16	29	0	3.18
Tom Butters	R	27	0	1	.000	0	5	0	0	9	9	5	6	0	7.00
Luke Walker	L	21	0	0	.000	0	2	0	0	5	2	1	5	0	0.00

CINCINNATI 4th 89-73 .549 8 — DICK SISLER

NAME	G by POS	B	AGE	G	AB	R	H	2B	3B	HR	RBI	BB	SO	SB	BA	SA
TOTALS			26	162	5658	**825**	**1544**	**268**	**61**	183	**776**	**538**	1003	82	**.273**	**.439**
Gordy Coleman	1B89	L	30	108	325	39	98	19	0	14	57	24	38	0	.302	.489
Pete Rose	2B162	B	24	162	**670**	117	**209**	35	11	11	81	69	76	8	.312	.446
Leo Cardenas	SS155	R	26	156	557	65	160	25	11	11	57	60	100	1	.287	.431
Deron Johnson	3B159	R	26	159	616	92	177	30	7	32	**130**	52	97	0	.287	.515
Frank Robinson	OF155	R	29	156	582	109	172	33	5	33	113	70	100	13	.296	.540
Vada Pinson	OF159	L	26	159	669	97	204	34	10	22	94	43	81	21	.305	.484
Tommy Harper	OF159, 3B2, 2B1	R	24	159	646	**126**	166	28	3	18	64	78	127	35	.257	.393
Johnny Edwards	C110	L	27	114	371	47	99	22	2	17	51	50	45	0	.267	.474
Tony Perez	1B93	R	23	104	281	40	73	14	4	12	47	21	67	0	.260	.466
Don Pavletich	C54, 1B9	R	26	68	191	25	61	11	1	8	32	23	27	1	.319	.513
Art Shamsky	OF18, 1B1	L	23	64	96	13	25	4	3	2	10	10	29	1	.260	.427
Marty Keough	1B32, OF4	L	30	62	43	14	5	0	0	0	3	3	14	0	.116	.116
Chico Ruiz (BL)	3B4, SS3	B	26	29	18	7	2	1	0	0	1	0	5	1	.111	.167
Charlie James	OF7	R	27	26	39	2	8	0	0	0	2	1	9	0	.205	.205
Jimmie Coker	C19	R	29	24	61	3	15	2	0	2	9	8	16	0	.246	.377
Tommy Helms	SS8, 3B2, 2B1	R	24	21	42	4	16	2	2	0	6	3	7	1	.381	.524

Mel Queen 23 L 0-3, Lee May 22 R 0-4, Steve Boros 28 R 0-0, Fred Hutchinson (DD) 45

NAME	T	AGE	W	L	PCT	SV	G	GS	CG	IP	H	BB	SO	ShO	ERA
		28	89	73	.549	34	162	162	43	1457	1355	**587**	**1113**	9	3.89
Sammy Ellis	R	24	22	10	.688	2	44	39	15	264	222	104	183	2	3.78
Jim Maloney	R	25	20	9	.690	0	33	33	14	255	189	110	244	5	2.54
Joe Nuxhall	L	36	11	4	.733	2	32	16	5	149	142	31	117	1	3.44
Joey Jay	R	29	9	8	.529	1	37	24	4	156	150	63	102	1	4.21
Billy McCool	L	20	9	10	.474	21	62	2	0	105	93	47	120	0	4.29
John Tsitouris	R	29	6	9	.400	1	31	20	3	131	134	65	91	0	4.95
Ted Davidson	L	25	4	3	.571	1	24	1	0	69	57	17	54	0	2.22
Jim O'Toole	L	28	3	10	.231	1	29	22	2	128	154	47	71	0	5.91
1 Bill Henry	L	37	2	0	1.000	0	3	0	0	5	3	1	5	0	0.00
Jerry Arrigo	L	24	2	4	.333	2	27	5	0	54	75	30	43	0	6.17
Roger Craig	R	34	1	4	.200	3	40	0	0	64	74	25	30	0	3.66
2 Jim Duffalo	R	29	0	1	.000	0	22	0	0	44	33	30	34	0	3.48
Bobby Locke	R	31	0	1	.000	0	11	0	0	17	20	8	8	0	5.82
Dom Zanni	R	33	0	0	.000	0	8	0	0	13	7	5	10	0	1.38
Darrell Osteen	R	22	0	0	.000	0	3	0	0	3	2	4	1	0	0.00

MILWAUKEE 5th 86-76 .531 11 — BOBBY BRAGAN

NAME	G by POS	B	AGE	G	AB	R	H	2B	3B	HR	RBI	BB	SO	SB	BA	SA
TOTALS			27	162	5542	708	1419	243	28	**196**	664	408	976	64	.256	.416
Gene Oliver	1B52, C64, OF1	R	29	122	392	56	106	20	0	21	58	36	61	5	.270	.482
Frank Bolling	2B147	R	33	148	535	55	141	26	3	7	50	24	41	0	.264	.363
Woody Woodward	SS107, 2B8	R	22	112	265	17	55	7	4	0	11	10	50	2	.208	.264
Eddie Mathews	3B153	L	33	156	546	77	137	23	0	32	95	73	110	1	.251	.469
Hank Aaron	OF148	R	31	150	570	109	181	**40**	1	32	89	60	81	24	.318	.560
Mack Jones	OF133	L	26	143	504	78	132	18	7	31	75	29	122	8	.262	.510
Felipe Alou	OF91, 1B69, 3B2, SS1	R	30	143	555	80	165	29	2	23	78	31	63	8	.297	.481
Joe Torre	C100, 1B49	R	24	148	523	68	152	21	1	27	80	61	79	0	.291	.489
Ty Cline	OF86, 1B5	L	26	123	220	27	42	5	3	0	10	16	50	2	.191	.241
Rico Carty	OF73	R	26	83	271	37	84	18	1	10	35	17	44	1	.310	.494
Mike de la Hoz	SS41, 3B22, 2B10, 1B1	R	25	81	176	15	45	3	2	2	11	8	21	0	.256	.330
Denis Menke (KJ)	SS54, 1B8, 3B4	R	24	71	181	16	44	13	1	4	18	18	28	1	.243	.392
Sandy Alomar	SS39, 2B19	R	21	67	108	16	26	1	1	0	8	4	12	12	.241	.269
Lou Klimchock	1B4	L	25	34	39	3	3	0	0	0	3	2	8	0	.077	.077
2 Jesse Gonder	C13	L	29	31	53	2	8	2	0	1	5	4	9	0	.151	.245
1 Gary Kolb	OF13	L	25	24	27	3	7	0	0	0	1	1	6	0	.259	.259
Don Dillard	OF1	L	28	20	19	1	3	0	0	1	3	0	6	0	.158	.316
2 Billy Cowan	OF10	R	26	19	27	4	5	1	0	0	0	0	9	0	.185	.222
1 Lee Maye	OF13	L	30	15	53	8	16	2	0	2	7	2	6	0	.302	.453
3 Frank Thomas	1B6, OF3	R	36	15	33	3	7	3	0	0	1	2	11	0	.212	.303
3 Johnny Blanchard	OF1	L	32	10	10	1	1	0	0	1	2	2	1	0	.100	.400
Tommie Aaron	1B6	R	25	8	16	1	3	0	0	0	1	1	2	0	.188	.188
2 Jim Beauchamp	1B2	R	25	4	3	0	0	0	0	0	0	1	1	0	.000	.000

NAME	T	AGE	W	L	PCT	SV	G	GS	CG	IP	H	BB	SO	ShO	ERA
		27	86	76	.531	38	162	162	43	1448	1336	541	966	4	3.52
Tony Cloninger	R	24	24	11	.686	1	40	38	16	279	247	**119**	211	1	3.29
Wade Blasingame	L	21	16	10	.615	1	38	36	10	225	200	116	117	1	3.76
2 Ken Johnson	R	32	13	8	.619	2	29	76	8	180	165	37	123	1	3.20
Billy O'Dell	L	32	10	6	.625	18	62	1	0	111	87	30	78	0	2.19
Hank Fischer	R	25	8	9	.471	0	31	19	2	123	126	39	79	0	3.88
Denny Lemaster (SA)	L	26	7	13	.350	0	32	23	4	146	140	58	111	1	4.44
Bob Sadowski	R	27	5	9	.357	3	34	13	3	123	117	35	78	0	4.32
Phil Niekro	R	26	2	3	.400	6	41	1	0	75	73	26	49	0	2.88
Dick Kelley	L	25	1	1	.500	0	21	4	0	45	37	20	31	0	3.00
Clay Carroll	R	24	0	1	.000	1	19	1	0	35	35	13	16	0	4.37
Chi Chi Olivo	R	27	0	1	.000	0	8	0	0	13	12	5	11	0	1.38
1 Bobby Tiefenauer	R	35	0	1	.000	0	6	0	0	7	8	3	7	0	7.71
Dan Osinski	R	31	0	3	.000	6	61	0	0	83	81	40	54	0	2.82
1 Dave Eilers	R	28	0	0	.000	0	6	0	0	4	8	0	1	0	11.25

PHILADELPHIA 6th 85-76 .528 11.5 — GENE MAUCH

NAME	G by POS	B	AGE	G	AB	R	H	2B	3B	HR	RBI	BB	SO	SB	BA	SA
TOTALS			27	162	5528	654	1380	205	53	144	608	494	1091	46	.250	.384
Dick Stuart	1B143, 3B1	R	32	149	538	53	126	19	1	28	95	39	136	1	.234	.429
Tony Taylor	2B86, 3B5	R	29	106	323	41	74	14	3	3	27	22	58	5	.229	.319
Bobby Wine	SS135, 1B4	R	26	139	394	31	90	8	1	5	33	31	69	0	.228	.292
Dick Allen	3B160, SS2	R	23	161	619	93	187	31	14	20	85	74	150	15	.302	.494
Johnny Callison	OF159	L	26	160	619	93	162	25	16	32	101	57	117	6	.262	.509
Tony Gonzalez	OF104	L	28	108	370	48	109	19	1	13	41	31	52	3	.295	.457
Alex Johnson	OF82	R	22	97	262	27	77	9	3	8	28	15	60	4	.294	.443
Clay Dalrymple	C102	L	28	103	301	14	64	5	5	4	23	34	37	0	.213	.302
Cookie Rojas	2B84, OF55, SS11, C2, 1B1	R	26	142	521	78	158	25	3	3	42	42	33	5	.303	.380
Ruben Amaro	1B60, SS60, 2B6	R	29	118	184	26	39	7	0	0	15	27	22	1	.212	.250
Wes Covington	OF64	L	33	101	235	27	58	10	1	15	45	26	47	0	.247	.489
Johnny Briggs	OF66	L	21	93	229	47	54	9	4	4	23	42	44	3	.236	.362
Pat Corrales	C62	R	24	63	174	16	39	8	1	2	15	25	42	0	.224	.316
John Herrnstein	1B18, OF14	L	27	63	85	8	17	2	0	1	5	2	18	0	.200	.259
Adolfo Phillips	OF32	R	23	41	87	14	20	4	0	3	5	5	34	3	.230	.379
1 Frank Thomas	OF12, 1B11, 3B11	R	36	35	77	7	20	4	0	1	7	4	10	0	.260	.351
1 Gus Triandos	C28	R	34	30	82	3	14	2	0	0	4	9	17	0	.171	.195

Bill Sorrell 24 L 5-13, Bobby Del Greco 32 R 0-4

NAME	T	AGE	W	L	PCT	SV	G	GS	CG	IP	H	BB	SO	ShO	ERA
		30	85	76	.528	21	162	162	50	1469	1426	466	1071	18	3.53
Jim Bunning	R	33	19	9	.679	0	39	39	15	291	253	62	268	7	2.60
Chris Short	L	27	18	11	.621	2	47	40	15	297	260	89	237	5	2.82
Ray Culp	R	23	14	10	.583	0	33	30	11	204	188	78	134	2	3.22
Gary Wagner	R	25	7	7	.500	7	59	0	0	105	87	49	91	0	3.00
Ed Roebuck	R	33	5	3	.625	3	44	0	0	50	55	15	29	0	3.42
Jack Baldschun	R	28	5	8	.385	6	65	0	0	99	102	42	81	0	3.82
Ray Herbert	R	35	5	8	.385	1	25	19	4	131	162	19	51	1	3.85
Bo Belinsky	L	28	4	9	.308	1	30	14	3	110	103	48	71	0	4.83
2 Lew Burdette	R	38	3	3	.500	0	19	9	1	71	95	17	23	1	5.45
Ferguson Jenkins	R	21	2	1	.667	1	7	0	0	12	7	2	10	0	2.25
Art Mahaffey	R	27	2	5	.286	0	22	9	1	71	82	32	52	0	6.21
Grant Jackson	L	22	1	1	.500	0	6	2	0	14	17	5	15	0	7.07
Morrie Steevens	L	24	0	1	.000	0	6	0	0	3	5	4	3	0	15.00
1 Ryne Duren	R	36	0	0	.000	0	6	0	0	11	10	4	6	0	3.27

ST. LOUIS 7th 80-81 .497 16.5 — RED SCHOENDIENST

NAME	G by POS	B	AGE	G	AB	R	H	2B	3B	HR	RBI	BB	SO	SB	BA	SA
TOTALS			28	162	5579	707	1415	234	46	109	645	477	882	100	.254	.371
Bill White	1B144	L	31	148	543	82	157	26	3	24	73	63	86	3	.289	.481
Julian Javier (BG)	2B69	R	28	77	229	34	52	6	4	2	23	8	44	5	.227	.314
Dick Groat	SS148, 3B2	R	34	153	587	55	149	26	5	0	52	56	50	1	.254	.315
Ken Boyer	3B143	R	34	144	535	71	139	18	2	13	75	57	73	2	.260	.374
Mike Shannon	OF101, C4	R	25	124	244	32	54	17	3	3	25	28	46	2	.221	.352
Curt Flood	OF151	R	27	156	617	90	191	30	3	11	83	51	50	9	.310	.421
Lou Brock	OF153	L	26	155	631	107	182	35	8	16	69	45	116	63	.288	.445
Tim McCarver	C111	L	23	113	409	48	113	17	2	11	48	31	26	5	.276	.408
Phil Gagliano	2B57, OF25, 3B19	R	23	122	363	46	87	14	2	8	53	40	45	2	.240	.355
Tito Francona	OF34, 1B13	L	31	81	174	15	45	6	2	5	19	17	30	0	.259	.402
Bob Skinner	OF33	L	33	80	152	25	47	5	4	5	26	12	30	1	.309	.493
Dal Maxvill	2B49, SS12	R	26	68	89	10	12	2	0	0	10	7	15	0	.135	.202
Jerry Buchek	2B33, SS18, 3B1	R	23	55	166	17	41	8	3	3	21	13	46	1	.247	.386
Bob Uecker	C49	R	30	53	145	17	33	7	0	2	10	24	27	0	.228	.317
1 Carl Warwick	OF21, 1B4	R	28	50	77	3	12	2	1	0	6	4	18	1	.156	.208
Bob Gibson	P38	R	29	42	104	14	25	2	0	5	19	3	26	2	.240	.404
Ted Savage	OF20	R	29	30	63	7	10	3	0	1	4	6	9	1	.159	.254
Bobby Tolan	OF17	L	19	17	69	8	13	2	0	0	6	0	4	2	.188	.217

Dave Ricketts 29 B 7-29, George Kernek 25 L 9-31, Ed Spiezio 23 R 3-18

NAME	T	AGE	W	L	PCT	SV	G	GS	CG	IP	H	BB	SO	ShO	ERA
		28	80	81	.497	35	162	162	40	1461	1414	467	916	11	3.77
Bob Gibson	R	29	20	12	.625	1	38	36	20	299	243	103	270	6	3.07
Tracy Stallard	R	27	11	8	.579	0	40	26	4	194	172	70	99	1	3.39
Bob Purkey	R	35	10	9	.526	2	32	17	3	124	148	33	39	1	5.81
Ray Washburn	R	27	9	11	.450	2	28	16	1	119	114	28	67	1	3.62
Curt Simmons	L	36	9	15	.375	0	34	32	5	203	229	54	96	0	4.08
Ray Sadecki	L	24	6	15	.286	1	36	28	4	173	192	64	122	0	5.20
Larry Jaster	L	21	3	0	1.000	0	4	3	3	28	21	7	10	0	1.61
2 Hal Woodeshick	L	32	3	2	.600	15	51	0	0	60	47	27	37	0	1.80
Nelson Briles	R	21	3	3	.500	4	37	2	0	82	79	26	52	0	3.51
1 Ron Taylor	R	27	2	1	.667	1	25	0	0	44	43	15	26	0	4.50
Barney Schultz	R	38	2	2	.500	2	34	0	0	42	39	11	38	0	3.86
Don Dennis	R	23	2	3	.400	6	41	0	0	55	47	16	29	0	2.29
Steve Carlton	L	20	0	0	.000	0	15	2	0	25	27	8	21	0	2.52
Dennis Aust	R	24	0	0	.000	1	6	0	0	7	6	2	7	0	5.14
Earl Francis	R	28	0	0	.000	0	2	0	0	5	7	3	3	0	5.40

CHICAGO 8th 72-90 .444 25 — BOB KENNEDY 24-32 .429 LOU KLEIN 48-58 .453

NAME	G by POS	B	AGE	G	AB	R	H	2B	3B	HR	RBI	BB	SO	SB	BA	SA
TOTALS			27	164	5540	635	1316	202	33	134	590	532	948	65	.238	.358
Ernie Banks	1B162	R	34	163	612	79	162	25	3	28	106	55	64	3	.265	.453
Glenn Beckert	2B153	R	24	154	614	73	147	21	3	3	30	28	52	6	.239	.298
Don Kessinger	SS105	R	22	106	309	19	62	4	3	0	14	20	44	1	.201	.233
Ron Santo	3B164	R	25	164	608	88	173	30	4	33	101	88	109	3	.285	.510
Billy Williams	OF164	L	27	164	645	115	203	39	6	34	108	65	76	10	.315	.552
Don Landrum	OF115	L	29	131	425	60	96	20	4	6	34	36	84	14	.226	.334
Doug Clemens	OF105	L	26	128	340	36	75	11	0	4	26	38	53	5	.221	.288
Vic Roznovsky	C63	L	26	71	172	9	38	4	1	3	15	16	30	1	.221	.308
Jimmy Stewart	OF55, SS48	B	26	116	282	26	63	9	4	0	19	30	53	13	.223	.284
George Altman	OF45, 1B2	L	32	90	196	24	46	7	1	4	23	19	36	3	.235	.342
Joey Amalfitano	2B24, SS4	R	31	67	96	13	26	4	0	0	8	12	14	2	.271	.313
2 Ed Bailey	C54, 1B3	L	34	66	150	13	38	6	0	5	23	34	28	0	.253	.393
Chris Krug	C55	R	25	60	169	16	34	5	0	5	24	13	52	0	.201	.320
2 Harvey Kuenn	OF35, 1B1	R	34	54	120	11	26	5	0	0	6	22	13	1	.217	.258
Roberto Pena	SS50	R	25	51	170	17	37	5	1	2	12	16	19	1	.218	.294
1 Dick Bertell	C34	R	29	34	84	6	18	2	0	0	7	11	10	0	.214	.238
1 Len Gabrielson	OF14, 1B1	L	25	28	48	4	12	0	0	3	5	7	16	0	.250	.438
Harry Bright		R	35	27	25	1	7	1	0	0	4	0	8	0	.280	.320
Ellis Burton	OF12	B	28	17	40	6	7	1	0	0	4	1	10	1	.175	.200
Don Young	OF11	R	19	11	35	1	2	0	0	1	2	0	11	0	.057	.143

Leo Burke 31 R 2-10, John Boccabella 24 R 4-12, Byron Browne 22 R 0-6, Ron Campbell 25 R 0-2, Chuck Hartenstein 23 R 0-0

NAME	T	AGE	W	L	PCT	SV	G	GS	CG	IP	H	BB	SO	ShO	ERA
		29	72	90	.444	35	164	164	33	1472	1470	481	855	9	3.78
Dick Ellsworth	L	25	14	15	.483	1	36	34	8	222	227	57	130	0	3.81
Larry Jackson	R	34	14	21	.400	0	39	39	12	257	268	57	131	4	3.85
Bob Buhl	R	36	13	11	.542	0	32	31	2	184	207	57	92	0	4.40
Cal Koonce	R	24	7	9	.438	0	38	23	3	173	181	52	88	1	3.69
Bill Faul	R	25	6	6	.500	0	17	16	5	97	83	18	59	3	3.53
Lindy McDaniel	R	29	5	6	.455	2	71	0	0	129	115	47	92	0	2.58
2 Bob Hendley	L	26	4	4	.500	0	18	10	2	62	59	25	38	0	4.35
Ted Abernathy	R	32	4	6	.400	31	84	0	0	136	113	56	104	0	2.58
Bob Humphreys	R	29	2	0	1.000	0	41	0	0	66	59	27	38	0	3.14
Billy Hoeft	L	33	2	2	.500	1	29	2	1	51	41	20	44	0	2.82
Ernie Broglio	R	29	1	6	.143	0	26	6	0	51	63	46	22	0	6.88
Jack Warner	R	24	0	1	.000	0	11	0	0	16	22	9	7	0	8.44
Frank Baumann	L	32	0	1	.000	0	4	0	0	4	4	3	2	0	6.75
1 Lew Burdette	R	38	0	2	.000	0	7	3	0	20	26	4	5	0	5.40
Ken Holtzman	L	19	0	0	.000	0	3	0	0	4	2	3	3	0	2.25

HOUSTON 9th 65-97 .401 32 — LUM HARRIS

NAME	G by POS	B	AGE	G	AB	R	H	2B	3B	HR	RBI	BB	SO	SB	BA	SA
TOTALS			27	162	5483	569	1299	188	42	97	523	502	877	90	.237	.340
Walt Bond	1B74, OF38	L	27	117	407	46	107	17	2	7	47	42	51	2	.263	.366
Joe Morgan	2B157	L	21	157	601	100	163	22	12	14	40	97	77	20	.271	.418
Bob Lillis	SS104, 3B9, 2B6	R	35	124	408	34	90	12	1	0	20	20	10	2	.221	.255
Bob Aspromonte	3B146, 1B6, SS4	R	27	152	578	53	152	15	2	5	52	38	54	2	.263	.322
Rusty Staub	OF112, 1B1	L	21	131	410	43	105	20	1	14	63	52	57	3	.256	.412
Jim Wynn	OF155	R	23	157	564	90	155	30	7	22	73	84	126	43	.275	.470
2 Lee Maye	OF103	L	30	108	415	38	104	17	7	3	36	20	37	1	.251	.347
Ron Brand	C102, 3B6, OF5	R	25	117	391	27	92	6	3	2	37	19	34	10	.235	.281
Joe Gaines	OF65	R	28	100	229	21	52	8	1	6	31	18	59	4	.227	.349
2 Jim Gentile	1B68	L	31	81	227	22	55	11	1	7	31	34	72	0	.242	.392
Eddie Kasko (KJ)	SS59, 3B2	R	33	68	215	18	53	7	1	1	10	11	20	1	.247	.302
John Bateman	C39	R	22	45	142	15	28	3	1	7	14	12	37	0	.197	.380
1 Al Spangler	OF33	L	31	38	112	18	24	1	1	1	7	14	8	1	.214	.268
2 Gus Triandos	C20	R	34	24	72	5	13	2	0	2	7	5	14	0	.181	.292
1 Jim Beauchamp	OF9, 1B3	R	25	24	53	5	10	1	0	0	4	5	11	0	.189	.208
2 Frank Thomas	1B16, 3B2, OF1	R	36	23	58	7	10	2	0	3	9	3	15	0	.172	.362
Nellie Fox	3B6, 1B2, 2B1	L	37	21	41	3	11	2	0	0	1	0	2	0	.268	.317
Chuck Harrison	1B12	R	24	15	45	2	9	4	0	1	9	8	9	0	.200	.356
Dave Adlesh	C13	R	21	15	34	2	5	1	0	0	3	2	12	0	.147	.176

Norm Miller 19 L 3-15, Sonny Jackson 20 L 3-23, Mike White 26 R 0-9, Jim Mahoney 31 R 1-5, Gene Ratliff 19 R 0-4, John Hoffman 21 L 2-6

NAME	T	AGE	W	L	PCT	SV	G	GS	CG	IP	H	BB	SO	ShO	ERA
		28	65	97	.401	26	162	162	29	1461	1459	388	931	7	3.84
Dick Farrell	R	31	11	11	.500	1	33	29	8	208	202	35	122	3	3.50
Bob Bruce	R	32	9	18	.333	0	35	34	7	230	241	38	145	1	3.72
Dave Giusti	R	25	8	7	.533	3	38	13	4	131	132	46	92	1	4.33
Claude Raymond	R	28	7	4	.636	5	33	7	2	96	87	16	79	0	2.91
Larry Dierker	R	18	7	8	.467	0	26	19	1	147	135	37	109	0	3.49
Jim Owens	R	31	6	5	.545	8	50	0	0	71	64	29	53	0	3.30
2 Robin Roberts	R	38	5	2	.714	0	10	10	3	76	61	10	34	2	1.89
Don Nottebart	R	29	4	15	.211	0	29	25	3	158	166	55	77	0	4.67
1 Ken Johnson	R	32	3	2	.600	0	8	8	1	52	52	11	28	0	4.15
1 Hal Woodeshick	L	32	3	4	.429	3	27	0	0	32	27	18	22	0	3.09
Mike Cuellar	L	28	1	4	.200	2	25	4	0	56	55	21	46	0	3.54
2 Ron Taylor	R	27	1	5	.167	4	32	1	0	58	68	16	37	0	6.36
Carroll Sembera	R	23	0	1	.000	0	2	1	0	7	5	3	4	0	3.86
Danny Coombs	L	23	0	2	.000	0	26	3	0	47	54	23	35	0	4.79
Chris Zachary	R	21	0	2	.000	0	4	2	0	11	12	6	4	0	4.09
2 Jack Lamabe	R	28	0	2	.000	0	3	2	0	13	17	3	6	0	4.15
Jim Ray	R	20	0	2	.000	0	3	2	0	8	11	6	7	0	10.13
Ken MacKenzie	L	31	0	3	.000	0	21	0	0	37	46	6	26	0	3.89
2 Don Lee	R	31	0	0	.000	0	7	0	0	8	8	3	3	0	3.38

Bruce VonHoff 21 R 0-0, Don Arlich 22 L 0-0, Gordon Jones 35 R 0-0, 1 Don Larsen 35 R 0-0

NEW YORK 10th 50-112 .309 47 — CASEY STENGEL 31-64 .326 WES WESTRUM 19-48 .284

NAME	G by POS	B	AGE	G	AB	R	H	2B	3B	HR	RBI	BB	SO	SB	BA	SA
TOTALS			26	164	5441	495	1202	203	27	107	460	392	1129	28	.221	.327
Ed Kranepool	1B147	L	20	153	525	44	133	24	4	10	53	39	71	1	.253	.371
2 Chuck Hiller	2B80, OF4, 3B2	L	30	100	286	24	68	11	1	5	21	14	24	1	.238	.336
Roy McMillan	SS153	R	34	157	528	44	128	19	2	1	42	24	60	1	.242	.292
Charley Smith	3B131, SS6, 2B1	R	27	135	499	49	122	20	3	16	62	17	123	2	.244	.393
Johnny Lewis	OF142	L	25	148	477	64	117	15	3	15	45	59	117	4	.245	.384
Jim Hickman	OF91, 1B30, 3B14	R	28	141	369	32	87	18	0	15	40	27	76	3	.236	.407
Ron Swoboda	OF112	R	21	135	399	52	91	15	3	19	50	33	102	2	.228	.424
Chris Cannizzaro	C112	R	27	114	251	17	46	8	2	0	7	28	60	0	.183	.231
Joe Christopher	OF112	R	29	148	437	38	109	18	3	5	40	35	82	4	.249	.339
Bobby Klaus	2B72, SS28, 3B25	R	27	119	288	30	55	12	0	2	12	45	49	1	.191	.253
1 Billy Cowan	OF61, 2B2, SS1	R	26	82	156	16	28	8	2	3	9	4	45	3	.179	.314
Danny Napoleon	OF15, 3B7	R	23	68	97	5	14	1	1	0	7	8	23	0	.144	.175
Johnny Stephenson	C47, OF2	L	24	62	121	9	26	5	0	4	15	8	19	0	.215	.355
Ron Hunt (SJ)	2B46, 3B6	R	24	57	196	21	47	12	1	1	10	14	19	2	.240	.327
1 Jesse Gonder	C31	L	29	53	105	6	25	4	0	4	9	11	20	0	.238	.390
2 Gary Kolb	OF29, 1B1, 3B1	L	25	40	90	8	15	2	0	1	7	3	28	3	.167	.222
Cleon Jones	OF23	R	22	30	74	2	11	1	0	1	9	2	23	1	.149	.203
Hawk Taylor	C15, 1B1	R	26	25	46	5	7	0	0	4	10	1	8	0	.152	.413
2 Jimmie Schaffer	C21	R	29	24	37	0	5	2	0	0	0	1	15	0	.135	.189
Bud Harrelson	SS18	B	21	19	37	3	4	1	1	0	0	2	11	0	.108	.189
Greg Goossen	C8	R	19	11	31	2	9	0	0	1	2	1	5	0	.290	.387
Kevin Collins(SJ)	3B7, SS3	L	18	11	23	3	4	1	0	0	0	1	9	0	.174	.217
Yogi Berra	C2	L	40	4	9	1	2	0	0	0	0	0	3	0	.222	.222

NAME	T	AGE	W	L	PCT	SV	G	GS	CG	IP	H	BB	SO	ShO	ERA
		26	50	112	.309	14	164	164	29	1455	1462	498	776	11	4.06
Al Jackson	L	29	8	20	.286	1	37	31	7	205	217	61	120	3	4.35
Jack Fisher	R	26	8	24	.250	1	43	36	10	254	252	68	116	0	3.93
Gary Kroll	R	23	6	6	.500	1	32	11	1	87	83	41	62	0	4.45
Galen Cisco	R	29	4	8	.333	0	35	17	1	112	119	51	58	1	4.50
1 Warren Spahn	L	44	4	12	.250	0	20	19	5	126	140	35	56	0	4.36
Darrell Sutherland	R	23	3	1	.750	0	18	2	0	48	33	17	16	0	2.81
Larry Bearnarth	R	23	3	5	.375	1	40	3	0	61	75	28	16	0	4.57
Jim Bethke	R	18	2	0	1.000	0	25	0	0	40	41	22	19	0	4.28
Dick Selma	R	21	2	1	.667	0	4	4	1	27	22	9	26	1	3.67
Gordie Richardson	L	25	2	2	.500	2	35	0	0	52	41	16	43	0	3.81
Tug McGraw	L	20	2	7	.222	1	37	9	2	98	88	48	57	0	3.31
2 Dave Eilers	R	28	1	1	.500	2	11	0	0	18	20	4	9	0	4.00
Carl Willey	R	34	1	2	.333	0	13	3	1	28	30	15	13	0	4.18
Dennis Ribant	R	23	1	3	.250	3	19	1	0	35	29	6	13	0	3.86
1 Frank Lary	R	35	1	3	.250	1	14	7	0	57	48	16	23	0	3.00
Larry Miller	L	28	1	4	.200	0	28	5	0	57	66	25	36	0	5.05
Tom Parsons	R	25	1	10	.091	1	35	11	1	91	108	17	58	1	4.65
Bob Moorhead	R	27	0	1	.000	0	9	0	0	14	16	5	5	0	4.50
Rob Gardner	L	20	0	2	.000	0	5	4	0	28	23	7	19	0	3.21
Dennis Musgraves (EJ)	R	21	0	0	.000	0	5	1	0	16	11	7	11	0	0.56

1966 Heads You Win, Tails I Lose

Frank Robinson was a proven star. He had provided the muscle in the Cincinnati attack since first coming up to the majors in 1956. Milt Pappas was not a star, simply a good pitcher who had toiled with the Baltimore Orioles since 1957, never winning more than 16 games in one season. But Cincinnati was not happy with Robinson because of some off-field incidents and decided it was time for a trade. The Orioles were willing and made a clean swap, man for man, with Pappas for Robinson. The newspaper headlines generated much conversation. Cincinnati rooters screamed and Baltimore fans cheered. The Dodgers' Sandy Koufax was happy to see Robinson go, if only because of what his bat had done to the ace left-hander's E.R.A. When all the words were written and the throats hoarse, the consensus was that Baltimore got the best of it. Pappas defended himself and Cincinnati by saying that the trade could not be truly evaluated before several years had elapsed. Baltimore did not care what the years would prove because, by the time the 1966 season ended, it was clear they had it all.

Playing with a vengeance to prove the Cincinnati Reds wrong in trading him, the lean, confident Robinson used his first season in the American League to sweep the Triple Crown and the MVP Award, while leading the Orioles to an easy pennant victory—their first since coming to Baltimore in 1954.

After Cleveland held first place going into June, Hank Bauer's Birds flew into the lead and ran off a 13-game lead by the end of July, enough of a margin to allow the Orioles to coast home the rest of the way. Although Brooks Robinson and Boog Powell combined with the Cincinnati cast-off to give the Orioles three 100 RBI men and the league's best attack, the pitching staff was not without its problems. Dave McNally and Jim Palmer were healthy all year, but Steve Barber and Wally Bunker had to sit out parts of the season nursing bad arms. A very low total of complete games was compensated for by a standout veteran bullpen led by slow baller Stu Miller and knuckle baller Eddie Fisher.

The ascendance of the Orioles coincided with the complete collapse of the New York Yankees into last place. Maris and Mantle were no longer the feared threats they once were, Elston Howard was a mere shadow of his former self, Whitey Ford had circulatory problems in his arm and won only two games, and Tony Kubek was forced to retire before the season began because of a recurring back injury. In the course of two years, the club slipped from five straight pennants into an ignoble tenth-place finish. Manager Johnny Keane's dream of glory ended in May, as Ralph Houk left his general manager's chair to resume field director duties. At the season's end, Maris and Clete Boyer would be traded off, marking the start of a long rebuilding program for the once-masters of baseball, and Keane, troubled by his failure, would become the victim of a heart attack just as the new year got underway.

With Robinson sweeping the offensive awards, pitching leaderships went to Minnesota's Jim Kaat for the most victories and to Gary Peters of Chicago for the lowest earned run average.

The National League race was a close copy of the previous year with the Los Angeles Dodgers again nailing down the crown on the final day of the season to thwart season-long standout performances by the Giants and Pirates. In the spring, Dodger manager Walter Alston was not sure whether he would have his ace pitching duo of Sandy Koufax and Don Drysdale back in the fold. The two mound stars pulled a dramatic joint holdout, refusing to sign until both received the pacts they thought they deserved. As spring training was winding to an end, both finally signed—Koufax for $125,000 and Drysdale for $110,000.

The lack of spring training hardly hurt Koufax as he won 27 games and had a 1.73 E.R.A., both tops in the loop. But what the statistics didn't show, the arm did. As the year wound on, it was discovered that Koufax had arthritis in his pitching arm. The pain was such that only a combination of willpower and an increase in medication kept him on the mound. Further stress was placed on Koufax due to Drysdale's performance, which fell off to a mediocre 13-16 record and resulted in Koufax's having to pitch with little rest in the final game of the season to wrap up the pennant.

The Dodgers used the same formula as in 1965 to win the flag—many singles, much running, and good pitching. Maury Wills remained the inspirational leader at bat and in the field, and Jim Lefebvre and Lou Johnson came through with solid years with the bat. Tommy Davis made a partial comeback from his broken ankle by hitting .313 as a platoon left fielder. In addition to Koufax, Claude Osteen and rookie Don Sutton were solid starters, and Tiger-reject Phil Regan became the bullpen sensation of the year, earning the nickname "The Vulture" for his scavenger work in saving close games.

The Giants, sparked by Willie Mays, Willie McCovey, Juan Marichal, and Gaylord Perry, fought the Dodgers to the end but finally lost out again. Harry Walker's Pirates used a blistering attack, led by MVP Roberto Clemente and batting champ Matty Alou, to make a strong run to the top which ended three games back.

While the National League belonged to the Dodgers, the world's championship became the undisputed possession of Baltimore. The claim was made if for no other reason than the lack of Dodger run-power and the overabundance of Oriole shutout power.

The Dodgers tallied two early runs in the first game before Moe Drabowsky came out of the Birds' bullpen to pitch 6 2/3 innings of shutout relief in a 5-2 victory. The Dodgers never again would touch home, as Jim Palmer, Wally Bunker, and Dave McNally tossed shutouts in the next three games to blow the Dodgers into oblivion. Koufax appeared in the second game but could not keep up with center fielder Willie Davis' three successive errors in the fifth inning.

After the Series, the Dodgers travelled to Japan to play an exhibition slate. In the middle of the tour, Wills left the club without permission, prompting owner Walter O'Malley to trade him to the Pirates. In addition, Tommy Davis was traded to the Mets, and Koufax announced his retirement due to the arthritic elbow—marking the end to a phenomenal career in which, for his last five years, he compiled a 111-34 record, 1,444 strikeouts, and five straight E.R.A. titles.

WORLD SERIES – BALTIMORE (AL) 4 LOS ANGELES (NL) 0

LINE SCORES

TEAM	1	2	3	4	5	6	7	8	9	10	11	12	R	H	E
Game 1 October 5 at Los Angeles															
BAL (AL)	3	1	0	1	0	0	0	0	0				5	9	0
LA(NL)	0	1	1	0	0	0	0	0	0				2	3	0
McNally, **Drabowsky** (3) — **Drysdale**, Moeller (3), R. Miller (5), Perranoski (8)															
Game 2 October 6 at Los Angeles															
BAL	0	0	0	0	3	1	0	2	0				6	8	0
LA	0	0	0	0	0	0	0	0	0				0	4	6
Palmer — **Koufax**, Perranoski (7), Regan (8), Brewer (9)															
Game 3 October 8 at Baltimore															
LA	0	0	0	0	0	0	0	0	0				0	6	0
BAL	0	0	0	0	1	0	0	0	X				1	3	0
Osteen, Regan (8) — **Bunker**															
Game 4 October 9 at Baltimore															
LA	0	0	0	0	0	0	0	0	0				0	4	0
BAL	0	0	0	1	0	0	0	0	X				1	4	0
Drysdale — **McNally**															

COMPOSITE BATTING

NAME	POS	G	AB	R	H	2B	3B	HR	RBI	BA
Baltimore (AL)										
Totals		4	120	13	24	3	1	4	10	.200
Aparicio	SS	4	**16**	0	4	1	0	0	2	.250
Powell	1B	4	14	1	**5**	1	0	0	1	**.357**
F. Robinson	OF	4	14	**4**	4	0	1	**2**	**3**	.286
D. Johnson	2B	4	14	1	4	1	0	0	1	.286
B. Robinson	3B	4	14	2	3	0	0	1	1	.214
Blefary	OF	4	13	0	1	0	0	0	0	.077
Etchebarren	C	4	12	2	1	0	0	0	0	.083
Snyder	OF	3	6	1	1	0	0	0	1	.167
Blair	OF	4	6	2	1	0	0	1	1	.167
Palmer	P	1	4	0	0	0	0	0	0	.000
McNally	P	2	3	0	0	0	0	0	0	.000
Drabowsky	P	1	2	0	0	0	0	0	0	.000
Bunker	P	1	2	0	0	0	0	0	0	.000
Los Angeles (NL)										
Totals		4	120	2	17	3	0	1	2	.142
W. Davis	OF	4	**16**	0	1	0	0	0	0	.063
L. Johnson	OF	4	15	1	4	1	0	0	0	.267
Roseboro	C	4	14	0	1	0	0	0	0	.071
Parker	1B	4	13	0	3	2	0	0	0	.231
Wills	SS	4	13	0	1	0	0	0	0	.077
Lefebvre	2B	4	12	1	2	0	0	1	1	.167
T. Davis	OF	4	8	0	2	0	0	0	0	.250
Fairly	OF-1B	3	7	0	1	0	0	0	0	.143
Gilliam	3B	2	6	0	0	0	0	0	1	.000
Kennedy	3B	2	5	0	1	0	0	0	0	.200
Stuart	PH	2	2	0	0	0	0	0	0	.000
Drysdale	P	2	2	0	0	0	0	0	0	.000
Koufax	P	1	2	0	0	0	0	0	0	.000
Osteen	P	1	2	0	0	0	0	0	0	.000
Ferrara	PH	1	1	0	1	0	0	0	0	1.000
Covington	PH	1	1	0	0	0	0	0	0	.000
Barbieri	PH	1	1	0	0	0	0	0	0	.000
Perranoski	P	2	0	0	0	0	0	0	0	.000
Regan	P	2	0	0	0	0	0	0	0	.000
Moeller	P	1	0	0	0	0	0	0	0	.000
R. Miller	P	1	0	0	0	0	0	0	0	.000
Brewer	P	1	0	0	0	0	0	0	0	.000
Oliver	PR	1	0	0	0	0	0	0	0	.000

COMPOSITE PITCHING

NAME	G	IP	H	BB	SO	W	L	SV	ERA
Baltimore (AL)									
Totals	4	36	17	13	28	4	0	0	0.50
McNally	2	**11.1**	6	**7**	5	1	0	0	1.59
Palmer	1	9	4	3	6	1	0	0	**0.00**
Bunker	1	9	6	1	6	1	0	0	**0.00**
Drabowsky	1	6.2	1	2	**11**	1	0	0	0.00
Los Angeles (NL)									
Totals	4	34	24	11	17	0	4	0	2.65
Drysdale	2	10	**8**	3	6	0	**2**	0	4.50
Osteen	1	7	3	1	3	0	1	0	1.29
Koufax	1	6	6	2	2	0	1	0	1.50
Perranoski	2	3.1	4	1	2	0	0	0	5.40
R. Miller	1	3	2	2	1	0	0	0	0.00
Moeller	1	2	1	1	0	0	0	0	4.50
Regan	2	1.2	0	1	2	0	0	0	0.00
Brewer	1	1	0	0	1	0	0	0	0.00

BALTIMORE 1st 97-63 .606 — HANK BAUER

NAME	G by POS	B	AGE	G	AB	R	H	2B	3B	HR	RBI	BB	SO	SB	BA	SA
TOTALS			26	160	**5529**	**755**	**1426**	**243**	35	175	**703**	514	926	55	**.258**	**.409**
Boog Powell	1B136	L	24	140	491	78	141	18	0	34	109	67	125	0	.287	.532
Dave Johnson	2B126, SS3	R	23	131	501	47	129	20	3	7	56	31	64	3	.257	.351
Luis Aparicio	SS151	R	32	151	**659**	97	182	25	8	6	41	33	42	25	.276	.366
Brooks Robinson	3B157	R	29	157	620	91	167	35	2	23	100	56	36	2	.269	.444
Frank Robinson	OF151, 1B3	R	30	155	576	**122**	182	34	2	**49**	**122**	87	90	8	**.316**	**.637**
Paul Blair	OF127	R	22	133	303	35	84	20	2	6	33	15	36	5	.277	.416
Russ Snyder	OF104	L	32	117	373	66	114	21	5	3	41	38	37	2	.306	.413
Andy Etchebarren	C121	R	23	121	412	49	91	14	6	11	50	38	106	0	.221	.364
Curt Blefary	OF109, 1B20	L	22	131	419	73	107	14	3	23	64	73	56	1	.255	.468
Sam Bowens	OF68	R	27	89	243	26	51	9	1	6	20	17	52	9	.210	.329
Bob Johnson	2B20, 1B17, 3B3	R	30	71	157	13	34	5	0	1	10	12	24	0	.217	.268
Woodie Held	OF10, 2B5, SS3, 3B3	R	34	56	82	6	17	3	1	1	7	12	30	0	.207	.305
Vic Roznovsky	C34	L	27	41	97	4	23	5	0	1	10	9	11	0	.237	.320
Larry Haney	C20	R	23	20	56	3	9	1	0	1	3	1	15	0	.161	.232
Charlie Lau (EJ)		L	33	18	12	1	6	2	1	0	5	4	1	0	.500	.833
1 Jerry Adair	2B13	R	29	17	52	3	15	1	0	0	3	4	8	0	.288	.308
Mark Belanger	SS6	R	22	8	19	2	3	1	0	0	0	0	3	0	.158	.211
Mike Epstein	1B4	L	23	6	11	1	2	0	1	0	3	1	3	0	.182	.364
Cam Carreon	C3	R	28	4	9	2	2	2	0	0	2	3	2	0	.222	.444

NAME	T	AGE	W	L	PCT	SV	G	GS	CG	IP	H	BB	SO	ShO	ERA
		26	**97**	63	**.606**	**51**	160	160	23	1466	1267	514	1070	13	3.32
Jim Palmer	R	20	15	10	.600	0	30	30	6	208	176	91	147	0	3.46
Dave McNally	L	23	13	6	.684	0	34	33	5	213	212	64	158	1	3.17
Steve Barber (AJ)	L	27	10	5	.667	0	25	22	5	133	104	49	91	3	2.30
Wally Bunker	R	21	10	6	.625	0	29	24	3	143	151	48	89	0	4.28
Stu Miller	R	38	9	4	.692	18	51	0	0	92	65	22	67	0	2.25
Eddie Watt	R	24	9	7	.563	4	43	13	1	146	123	44	102	0	3.82
Moe Drabowsky	R	30	6	0	1.000	7	44	3	0	96	62	29	98	0	2.81
Dick Hall	R	35	6	2	.750	7	32	0	0	66	59	8	44	0	3.95
2 Eddie Fisher	R	29	5	3	.625	13	**44***	0	0	72	60	19	39	0	2.62
Gene Brabender	R	24	4	3	.571	2	31	1	0	71	57	29	62	0	3.55
John Miller	R	25	4	8	.333	0	23	16	0	101	92	58	81	0	4.72
Tom Phoebus	R	21	2	1	.667	0	3	3	2	22	16	6	17	2	1.23
1 Bill Short	L	28	2	3	.400	0	6	6	1	38	34	10	27	1	2.84
Frank Bertaina	L	22	2	5	.286	0	16	9	0	63	52	36	46	0	3.14
Ed Barnowski	R	20	0	0	.000	0	2	0	0	3	4	1	2	0	3.00

*Fisher, also with Chicago, league leader in G with 67

MINNESOTA 2nd 89-73 .549 9 — SAM MELE

NAME	G by POS	B	AGE	G	AB	R	H	2B	3B	HR	RBI	BB	SO	SB	BA	SA
TOTALS			28	162	5390	663	1341	219	33	144	611	513	844	67	.249	.382
Don Mincher	1B130	L	28	139	431	53	108	30	0	14	62	58	68	3	.251	.418
Bernie Allen	2B89, 3B2	L	27	101	319	34	76	18	1	5	30	26	40	2	.238	.348
Zoilo Versalles	SS135	R	26	137	543	73	135	20	6	7	36	40	85	10	.249	.346
Harmon Killebrew	3B108, 1B42, OF18	R	30	162	569	89	160	27	1	39	110	**103**	98	1	.281	.538
Tony Oliva	OF159	L	26	159	622	99	**191**	32	7	25	87	42	72	13	.307	.502
Ted Uhlaender	OF100	L	26	105	367	39	83	12	2	2	22	27	33	10	.226	.286
Jimmie Hall	OF103	L	28	120	356	52	85	7	4	20	47	33	66	1	.239	.449
Earl Battey	C113	R	31	115	364	30	93	12	1	4	34	43	30	4	.255	.327
Cesar Tovar	2B76, SS31, OF24	R	25	134	465	57	121	19	5	2	41	44	50	16	.260	.335
Rich Rollins	3B65, OF1, 2B2	R	28	90	269	30	66	7	1	10	40	13	34	0	.245	.390
Bob Allison	OF56	R	31	70	168	34	37	6	1	8	19	30	34	6	.220	.411
Jerry Zimmerman	C59	R	31	60	119	11	30	4	1	1	15	15	23	0	.252	.328
Andy Kosco	OF40, 1B5	R	24	57	158	11	35	5	0	2	13	7	31	0	.222	.291
Sandy Valdespino	OF23	L	27	52	108	11	19	1	1	2	9	4	24	2	.176	.259
Russ Nixon	C32	L	31	51	96	5	25	2	1	0	7	7	13	0	.260	.302
Ron Clark	3B1	R	23	5	1	1	1	0	0	0	1	0	0	0	1.000	1.000
George Mitterwald	C3	R	21	3	5	1	1	0	0	0	0	0	0	0	.200	.200

1 Joe Nossek 25 R 0-0, Rich Reese 24 L 0-2

NAME	T	AGE	W	L	PCT	SV	G	GS	CG	IP	H	BB	SO	ShO	ERA
		29	89	73	.549	28	162	162	**52**	1439	1246	**392**	1015	11	3.13
Jim Kaat	L	27	**25**	13	.658	0	41	**41**	**19**	**305**	**271**	55	205	3	2.74
Mudcat Grant	R	30	13	13	.500	0	35	35	10	249	248	49	110	3	3.25
Dave Boswell	R	21	12	5	.706	0	28	21	8	169	120	65	173	1	3.14
Jim Perry	R	30	11	7	.611	0	33	25	8	184	149	53	122	1	2.54
Camilo Pascual (SA)	R	32	8	6	.571	0	21	19	2	103	113	30	56	0	4.89
Jim Merritt	L	22	7	14	.333	3	31	18	5	114	112	33	124	1	3.38
Al Worthington	R	37	6	3	.667	16	65	0	0	91	66	27	93	0	2.47
Dwight Siebler	R	28	2	2	.500	1	23	2	0	50	47	14	24	0	3.42
Pete Cimino	R	23	2	5	.286	4	35	0	0	65	53	30	57	0	2.91
Johnny Klippstein	R	38	1	1	.500	3	26	0	0	40	35	20	26	0	3.38
1 Garry Roggenburk	L	26	1	2	.333	1	12	0	0	12	14	10	3	0	6.00
Bill Pleis	L	28	1	2	.333	0	8	0	0	9	5	4	9	0	2.00
Ron Keller	R	23	0	0	.000	0	2	0	0	5	7	1	1	0	5.40
Jim Roland	L	23	0	0	.000	0	1	0	0	2	0	0	1	0	0.00
Jim Ollom	R	20	0	0	.000	0	3	1	0	10	6	1	11	0	3.60

DETROIT 3rd 88-74 .543 10 — CHUCK DRESSEN (DD) 16-10 .615 BOB SWIFT (IL-DD) 32-25 .561 FRANK SKAFF 40-39 .506

NAME	G by POS	B	AGE	G	AB	R	H	2B	3B	HR	RBI	BB	SO	SB	BA	SA
TOTALS			27	162	5507	719	1383	224	45	**179**	682	**551**	987	41	.251	.406
Norm Cash	1B158	L	31	160	603	98	168	18	3	32	93	66	91	2	.279	.478
Jerry Lumpe	2B95	L	33	113	385	30	89	14	3	1	26	24	44	0	.231	.291
Dick McAuliffe	SS105, 3B15	L	26	124	430	83	118	16	8	23	56	66	80	5	.274	.509
Don Wert	3B150	R	27	150	559	56	150	20	2	11	70	64	69	6	.268	.370
Jim Northrup	OF113	L	26	123	419	53	111	24	6	16	58	33	52	4	.265	.465
Al Kaline	OF136	R	31	142	479	85	138	29	1	29	88	81	66	5	.288	.534
Willie Horton	OF137	R	23	146	526	72	138	22	6	27	100	44	103	1	.262	.481
Bill Freehan	C132, 1B5	R	24	136	492	47	115	22	0	12	46	40	72	5	.234	.352
Jake Wood	2B52, 3B4, 1B2	R	29	98	230	39	58	9	3	2	27	28	48	4	.252	.343
Mickey Stanley (BH)	OF82	R	23	92	235	28	68	15	4	3	19	17	20	2	.289	.426
Gates Brown	OF43	L	27	88	169	27	45	5	1	7	27	18	19	3	.266	.432
Dick Tracewski	2B70, SS3	R	31	81	124	15	24	1	1	0	7	10	32	1	.194	.218
Ray Oyler	SS69	R	27	71	210	16	36	8	3	1	9	23	62	0	.171	.252
Orlando McFarlane	C33	R	28	49	138	16	35	7	0	5	13	9	46	0	.254	.413
1 Don Demeter	OF27, 1B4	R	31	32	99	12	21	5	0	5	12	3	19	1	.212	.414
2 Earl Wilson	P23	R	31	27	64	13	15	0	2	5	17	4	25	0	.234	.531

Don Pepper 22 L 0-3, Arlo Brunsberg 25 L 1-3

NAME	T	AGE	W	L	PCT	SV	G	GS	CG	IP	H	BB	SO	ShO	ERA
		29	88	74	.543	38	162	162	36	1454	1356	520	1026	11	3.85
Denny McLain	R	22	20	14	.588	0	38	38	14	264	205	104	192	4	3.92
Mickey Lolich	L	25	14	14	.500	3	40	33	5	204	204	83	173	1	4.76
2 Earl Wilson	R	31	13	6	.684	0	23	23	8	163	126	38	133	2	2.60
Dave Wickersham	R	30	8	3	.727	1	38	14	3	141	139	54	93	0	3.19
Larry Sherry	R	30	8	5	.615	20	55	0	0	78	66	36	63	0	3.81
Bill Monbouquette	R	29	7	8	.467	0	30	14	2	103	120	22	61	1	4.72
Fred Gladding	R	30	5	0	1.000	2	51	0	0	74	62	29	57	0	3.28
Orlando Pena	R	32	4	2	.667	7	54	0	0	108	105	35	79	0	3.08
2 Johnny Podres	L	33	4	5	.444	4	36	13	2	108	106	34	53	1	3.42
Hank Aguirre	L	34	3	9	.250	0	30	14	2	104	104	26	50	0	3.81
Joe Sparma	R	24	2	7	.222	0	29	13	0	92	103	52	61	0	5.28
1 Terry Fox	R	30	0	1	.000	1	4	0	0	10	9	2	6	0	6.30
George Korince	R	20	0	0	.000	0	2	0	0	3	1	3	2	0	0.00
Bill Graham	R	29	0	0	.000	0	1	0	0	2	2	0	2	0	0.00
John Hiller	L	23	0	0	.000	0	1	0	0	2	2	2	1	0	9.00
Julio Navarro	R	30	0	0	.000	0	1	0	0	0	2	0	0	0	∞

CHICAGO 4th 83-79 .512 15 — EDDIE STANKY

NAME	G by POS	B	AGE	G	AB	R	H	2B	3B	HR	RBI	BB	SO	SB	BA	SA
TOTALS			28	163	5348	574	1235	193	40	87	524	476	872	**153**	.231	.331
Tommy McCraw	1B121, OF41	L	25	151	389	49	89	16	4	5	48	29	40	20	.229	.329
Al Weis	2B96, SS18	B	28	129	187	20	29	4	1	0	9	17	50	3	.155	.187
2 Jerry Adair	SS75, 2B50	R	29	105	370	27	90	18	2	4	36	17	44	3	.243	.335
Don Buford	3B133, 2B37, OF11	B	29	163	607	85	148	26	7	8	52	69	71	51	.244	.349
Floyd Robinson	OF113	L	30	127	342	44	81	11	2	5	35	44	32	8	.237	.325
Tommie Agee	OF159	R	23	160	629	98	172	27	8	22	86	41	127	44	.273	.447
Ken Berry	OF141	R	25	147	443	50	120	20	2	8	34	28	63	7	.271	.379
Johnny Romano	C102	R	31	122	329	33	76	12	0	15	47	58	72	0	.231	.404
Bill Skowron	1B98	R	35	120	337	27	84	15	2	6	29	26	45	1	.249	.359
Pete Ward (XJ)	OF59, 3B16, 1B5	L	26	84	251	22	55	7	1	3	28	24	49	3	.219	.291
Lee Elia	SS75	R	28	80	195	16	40	5	2	3	22	15	39	0	.205	.297
Smoky Burgess	C2	L	39	79	67	0	21	5	0	0	15	11	8	0	.313	.388
2 Wayne Causey	2B60, SS1, 3B1	L	29	78	164	23	40	8	2	0	13	24	13	2	.244	.317
J. C. Martin (BG)	C63	L	29	67	157	13	40	5	3	2	20	14	24	0	.255	.363
1 Gene Freese	3B34	R	32	48	106	8	22	2	0	3	10	8	20	2	.208	.311
Jerry McNertney	C37	R	29	44	59	3	13	0	0	0	1	7	6	1	.220	.220
Ron Hansen (XJ)	SS23	R	28	23	74	3	13	1	0	0	4	15	10	0	.176	.189
1 Danny Cater	OF18	R	26	21	60	3	11	1	1	0	4	0	10	3	.183	.233
Jim Hicks	OF10, 1B2	R	26	18	26	3	5	0	1	0	1	1	5	0	.192	.269
Buddy Bradford	OF9	R	21	14	28	3	4	0	0	0	0	2	6	0	.143	.143
Ed Stroud	OF11	L	26	12	36	3	6	2	0	0	1	2	8	3	.167	.222
Duane Josephson	C11	R	24	11	38	3	9	1	0	0	3	3	3	0	.237	.263
Dick Kenworthy	3B6	R	25	9	25	1	5	0	0	0	0	0	0	0	.200	.200
Marv Staehle	2B6	L	24	8	15	2	2	0	0	0	0	4	2	1	.133	.133

Deacon Jones 32 L 2-5, Bill Voss 22 L 0-2

NAME	T	AGE	W	L	PCT	SV	G	GS	CG	IP	H	BB	SO	ShO	ERA
		29	83	79	.512	34	163	163	38	**1475**	1229	403	896	**22**	**2.68**
Tommy John	L	23	14	11	.560	0	34	33	10	223	195	57	138	5	2.62
Gary Peters	L	29	12	10	.545	0	30	27	11	205	156	45	129	4	**1.98**
Joe Horlen	R	28	10	13	.435	1	37	29	4	211	185	53	124	2	2.43
Bruce Howard	R	23	9	5	.643	0	27	21	4	149	110	44	85	2	2.30
Bob Locker	R	28	9	8	.529	12	56	0	0	95	73	23	70	0	2.46
Juan Pizarro	L	29	8	6	.571	3	34	9	1	89	91	39	42	0	3.74
Jack Lamabe	R	29	7	9	.438	0	34	17	3	121	116	35	67	2	3.94
John Buzhardt	R	29	6	11	.353	1	33	22	5	150	144	30	66	4	3.84
Hoyt Wilhelm (BG)	R	42	5	2	.714	6	46	0	0	81	50	17	61	0	1.67
Denny Higgins	R	26	1	0	1.000	5	42	1	0	93	66	33	86	0	2.52
Fred Klages	R	22	1	0	1.000	0	3	3	0	16	9	7	6	0	1.69
1 Eddie Fisher	R	29	1	3	.250	6	**23***	0	0	35	27	17	18	0	2.31
Greg Bollo	R	22	0	1	.000	0	3	1	0	7	7	3	4	0	2.57

*Fisher, also with Baltimore, league leader in G with 67

CLEVELAND 5th 81-81 .500 17 — BIRDIE TEBBETTS 66-57 .537 GEORGE STRICKLAND 15-24 .385

NAME	G by POS	B	AGE	G	AB	R	H	2B	3B	HR	RBI	BB	SO	SB	BA	SA
TOTALS			29	162	5474	574	1300	156	25	155	536	450	914	53	.237	.360
Fred Whitfield	1B132	L	28	137	502	59	121	15	2	27	78	27	76	1	.241	.440
Pedro Gonzalez	2B104, 3B1, OF1	R	27	110	352	21	82	9	2	2	17	15	54	8	.233	.287
Larry Brown (FS)	SS90, 2B10	R	26	105	340	29	78	12	0	3	17	36	58	0	.229	.291
Max Alvis	3B157	R	28	157	596	67	146	22	3	17	55	50	98	4	.245	.378
Rocky Colavito	OF146	R	32	151	533	68	127	13	0	30	72	76	81	2	.238	.432
Vic Davalillo	OF108	L	29	121	344	42	86	6	4	3	19	24	37	8	.250	.317
Leon Wagner	OF139	L	32	150	549	70	153	20	0	23	66	46	69	5	.279	.441
Joe Azcue	C97	R	26	98	302	22	83	10	1	9	37	20	22	0	.275	.404
C. Salmon	SS61, 2B28, 1B24, OF10, 3B6	R	25	126	422	46	108	13	2	7	40	21	41	10	.256	.346
Chuck Hinton	OF104, 1B6, 2B2	R	32	123	348	46	89	9	3	12	50	35	66	10	.256	.402
Jim Landis	OF61	R	32	85	158	23	35	5	1	3	14	20	25	2	.222	.323
Dick Howser	2B26, SS26	R	29	67	140	18	32	9	1	2	4	15	23	2	.229	.350
Duke Sims (XJ)	C48	L	25	52	133	12	35	2	2	6	19	11	31	0	.263	.444
Del Crandall	C49	R	36	50	108	10	25	2	0	4	8	14	9	0	.231	.361
2 Jim Gentile	1B9	L	32	33	47	2	6	1	0	2	4	5	18	0	.128	.277
Bill Davis	1B9	L	24	23	38	2	6	1	0	1	4	6	9	0	.158	.263
Tony Curry		L	27	19	16	4	2	0	0	0	3	3	8	0	.125	.125
Buddy Booker	C12	L	24	18	28	6	6	1	0	2	5	2	6	0	.214	.464
Jose Vidal	OF11	R	26	17	32	4	6	1	1	0	3	5	11	0	.188	.281
Tony Martinez	SS5, 2B4	R	25	17	17	2	5	0	0	0	0	1	6	1	.294	.294
Vern Fuller	2B16	R	22	16	47	7	11	2	1	2	2	7	6	0	.234	.447

George Banks 27 R 1-4, Paul Dicken 22 R 0-2

NAME	T	AGE	W	L	PCT	SV	G	GS	CG	IP	H	BB	SO	ShO	ERA
		27	81	81	.500	28	162	162	49	1467	1260	489	**1111**	15	3.23
Sonny Siebert	R	29	16	8	**.667**	1	34	32	11	241	193	62	163	1	2.80
Gary Bell	R	29	14	15	.483	0	40	37	12	254	211	79	194	0	3.22
Steve Hargan	R	23	13	10	.565	0	38	21	7	192	173	45	132	3	2.48
Luis Tiant	R	25	12	11	.522	8	46	16	7	155	121	50	145	**5**	2.79
Sam McDowell (SA)	L	23	9	8	.529	3	35	28	8	194	130	102	**225**	**5**	2.88
John O'Donoghue	L	26	6	8	.429	0	32	13	2	108	109	23	49	0	3.83
Tom Kelley	R	22	4	8	.333	0	31	7	1	95	97	42	64	0	4.36
Jack Kralick	L	31	3	4	.429	0	27	4	0	68	69	20	31	0	3.84
Bob Allen	L	28	2	2	.500	5	36	0	0	51	56	13	33	0	4.24
1 Lee Stange	R	29	1	0	1.000	0	8	2	1	16	17	3	8	0	2.81
1 Don McMahon	R	36	1	1	.500	1	12	0	0	12	8	6	5	0	3.00
Bob Heffner	R	27	0	1	.000	0	5	1	0	13	12	3	7	0	3.46
George Culver	R	22	0	2	.000	0	5	1	0	10	15	7	6	0	8.10
2 Dick Radatz	R	29	0	3	.000	10	39	0	0	57	49	34	49	0	4.58

CALIFORNIA 6th 80-82 .494 18 — BILL RIGNEY

NAME	G by POS	B	AGE	G	AB	R	H	2B	3B	HR	RBI	BB	SO	SB	BA	SA
TOTALS			26	162	5360	604	1244	179	54	122	562	525	1062	80	.232	.354
Norm Siebern	1B99	L	32	125	336	29	83	14	1	5	41	63	61	0	.247	.339
Bobby Knoop	2B161	R	27	161	590	54	137	18	**11**	17	72	43	144	1	.232	.386
Jim Fregosi	SS162, 1B1	R	24	162	611	78	154	32	7	13	67	67	89	17	.252	.391
Paul Schaal	3B131	R	23	138	386	59	94	15	7	6	24	68	56	6	.244	.365
Ed Kirkpatrick	OF102, 1B3	L	21	117	312	31	60	7	4	9	44	51	67	7	.192	.327
Jose Cardenal	OF146	R	22	154	561	67	155	15	3	16	48	34	69	24	.276	.399
Rick Reichardt (IL)	OF87	R	23	89	319	48	92	5	4	16	44	27	61	8	.288	.480
Bob Rodgers	C133	B	27	133	454	45	107	20	3	7	48	29	57	3	.236	.339
Tom Satriano	C43, 1B36, 3B25, 2B4	L	25	103	226	16	54	5	3	0	24	27	32	3	.239	.288
Willie Smith	OF52	L	27	90	195	18	36	3	2	1	20	12	37	1	.185	.236
Joe Adcock	1B71	R	38	83	231	33	63	10	3	18	48	31	48	2	.273	.576
Frank Malzone	3B35	R	36	82	155	6	32	5	0	2	12	10	11	0	.206	.277
Jimmy Piersall	OF63	R	36	75	123	14	26	5	0	0	14	13	19	1	.211	.252
Jay Johnstone	OF61	L	20	61	254	35	67	12	4	3	17	11	36	3	.264	.378
Jackie Hernandez	3B11, 2B8, SS8, OF3	R	25	58	23	19	1	0	0	0	2	1	4	1	.043	.043
Jackie Warner	OF37	R	22	45	123	22	26	4	1	7	16	9	55	0	.211	.431
Bubba Morton	OF14	R	34	15	50	4	11	1	0	0	4	2	6	1	.220	.240
Chuck Vinson	1B11	L	22	13	22	3	4	2	0	1	6	5	9	0	.182	.409
Al Spangler	OF3	L	32	6	9	2	6	0	0	0	0	2	2	0	.667	.667

Willie Montanez 18 L 0-2, Tom Egan 20 R 0-11, Ed Bailey 35 L 0-5, Albie Pearson (XJ) 31 L 0-3

NAME	T	AGE	W	L	PCT	SV	G	GS	CG	IP	H	BB	SO	ShO	ERA
		28	80	82	.494	40	162	162	31	1457	1364	511	836	12	3.56
Jack Sanford	R	37	13	7	.650	5	50	6	0	108	108	27	54	0	3.83
George Brunet	L	31	13	13	.500	0	41	32	8	212	183	106	148	2	3.31
Dean Chance	R	25	12	17	.414	1	41	37	11	260	206	**114**	180	2	3.08
Lew Burdette	R	39	7	2	.778	5	54	0	0	80	80	12	27	0	3.38
Minnie Rojas	R	27	7	4	.636	10	47	2	0	84	83	15	37	0	2.89
Marcelino Lopez	L	22	7	14	.333	1	37	32	6	199	188	68	132	2	3.93
Bob Lee	R	28	5	4	.556	16	61	0	0	102	90	31	46	0	2.74
Fred Newman	R	24	4	7	.364	0	21	19	1	103	112	31	42	0	4.72
Clyde Wright	L	25	4	7	.364	0	20	13	3	91	92	25	37	1	3.76
Jim McGlothin	R	22	3	1	.750	0	19	11	0	68	79	19	41	0	4.50
Jorge Rubio	R	21	2	1	.667	0	7	4	1	27	22	16	27	1	3.00
Ed Sukla	R	23	1	1	.500	1	12	0	0	17	18	6	8	0	6.35
Jim Coates	R	33	1	1	.500	0	9	4	1	32	32	10	16	1	3.94
Bill Kelso	R	26	1	1	.500	0	5	0	0	11	11	6	11	0	2.45
2 Howie Reed	R	29	0	1	.000	1	19	1	0	43	39	15	17	0	2.93
Ramon Lopez	R	29	0	1	.000	0	4	1	0	7	4	4	2	0	5.14
Dick Egan	L	29	0	0	.000	0	11	0	0	14	17	6	11	0	4.50

Rudy May (SA) 21

KANSAS CITY 7th 74-86 .463 23 — AL DARK

NAME	G by POS	B	AGE	G	AB	R	H	2B	3B	HR	RBI	BB	SO	SB	BA	SA
TOTALS			26	160	5328	564	1259	212	**56**	70	509	421	982	132	.236	.337
1 Ken Harrelson	1B58, OF3	R	24	63	210	24	47	5	0	5	22	27	59	9	.224	.319
Dick Green	2B137, 3B2	R	25	140	507	58	127	24	3	9	62	27	101	6	.250	.363
Bert Campaneris	SS138	R	24	142	573	82	153	29	10	5	42	25	72	**52**	.267	.379
Ed Charles	3B104, 1B1, OF1	R	31	118	385	52	110	18	8	9	42	30	53	12	.286	.444
Mike Hershberger	OF143	R	26	146	538	55	136	27	7	2	57	47	37	13	.253	.340
2 Jim Gosger	OF77	L	23	88	272	34	61	14	1	5	27	37	53	5	.224	.338
Larry Stahl	OF94	L	25	119	312	37	78	11	5	5	34	17	63	5	.250	.365
Phil Roof	C123, 1B2	R	25	127	369	33	77	14	3	7	44	37	95	2	.209	.320
2 Danny Cater	1B53, 3B42, OF22	R	26	116	425	47	124	16	3	7	52	28	37	1	.292	.393
2 Roger Repoz	OF52, 1B45	L	25	101	319	40	69	10	3	11	34	44	80	3	.216	.370
2 Joe Nossek	OF78, 3B1	R	25	87	230	13	60	10	3	1	27	8	21	4	.261	.343
O. Chavarria	OF26, SS23, 2B14, 1B8, 3B5	R	25	86	191	26	46	10	0	2	10	18	43	3	.241	.325
1 Jose Tartabull	OF33	L	27	37	127	13	30	2	3	0	4	11	13	8	.236	.299
Tim Talton	C14, 1B9	L	27	37	53	8	18	3	1	2	6	1	5	0	.340	.547
Ken Suarez	C34	R	23	35	69	5	10	0	1	0	2	15	26	2	.145	.174
1 Billy Bryan	C21, 1B3	L	27	32	76	0	10	4	0	0	7	6	17	0	.132	.184
1 Wayne Causey	3B15, SS10	L	29	28	79	1	18	0	0	0	5	7	6	1	.228	.228
Ernie Fazio	2B10, SS4	R	24	27	34	3	7	0	1	0	2	4	10	1	.206	.265
Ron Stone	OF4, 1B3	L	23	26	22	2	6	1	0	0	0	0	2	1	.273	.318
Rick Monday	OF15	L	20	17	41	4	4	1	1	0	2	6	16	1	.098	.171
John Donaldson	2B9	L	23	15	30	4	4	0	0	0	1	3	4	1	.133	.133
Manny Jiminez	OF12	L	27	13	35	1	4	0	1	0	1	6	4	0	.114	.171
Sal Bando	3B7	R	22	11	24	1	7	1	1	0	1	1	3	0	.292	.417

2 Don Blasingame 34 L 3-19, Randy Schwartz 22 L 1-11, Rene Lachemann 21 R 1-5

NAME	T	AGE	W	L	PCT	SV	G	GS	CG	IP	H	BB	SO	ShO	ERA
		26	74	86	.463	47	160	160	19	1436	1281	**630**	854	11	3.55
Lew Krausse	R	23	14	9	.609	3	36	22	4	178	144	63	87	1	2.99
Jim Nash	R	21	12	1	.923	1	18	17	5	127	95	47	98	0	2.06
Catfish Hunter (IL)	R	20	9	11	.450	0	30	25	4	177	158	64	103	0	4.02
Jack Aker	R	25	8	4	.667	**32**	66	0	0	113	81	28	68	0	1.99
Blue Moon Odom	R	21	5	5	.500	0	14	14	4	90	70	53	47	2	2.50
Paul Lindblad	L	24	5	10	.333	1	38	14	0	121	138	37	69	0	4.17
1 Fred Talbot	R	25	4	4	.500	0	11	11	0	68	65	28	37	0	4.76
Chuck Dobson (SA)	R	22	4	6	.400	0	14	14	1	84	71	50	61	0	4.07
1 Rollie Sheldon	R	29	4	7	.364	0	14	13	1	69	73	26	26	1	3.13
2 Ken Sanders	R	24	3	4	.429	1	38	1	0	65	59	48	41	0	3.74
Wes Stock	R	32	2	2	.500	3	35	0	0	44	30	21	31	0	2.66
Gil Blanco	L	20	2	4	.333	0	11	8	0	38	31	36	21	0	4.74
Jim Dickson	R	28	1	0	1.000	1	24	1	0	37	37	23	20	0	5.35
1 Ralph Terry	R	30	1	5	.167	0	15	10	0	64	65	15	33	0	3.80
2 Guido Grilli	L	27	0	1	.000	1	16	0	0	16	19	11	8	0	6.75
Vern Handrahan	R	27	0	1	.000	1	16	1	0	25	20	15	18	0	4.32
Bill Edgerton	L	24	0	1	.000	0	6	1	0	8	10	7	3	0	3.38
Joe Grzenda	L	29	0	2	.000	0	21	0	0	22	28	12	14	0	3.27
2 Jim Duckworth (SA)	R	27	0	2	.000	1	8	0	0	12	14	10	10	0	9.00
1 John Wyatt	R	31	0	3	.000	2	19	0	0	24	19	16	25	0	5.25
Bill Stafford	R	26	0	4	.000	0	9	8	0	40	42	12	31	0	4.95
Aurelio Monteagudo	R	22	0	0	.000	0	6	0	0	13	12	7	3	0	2.77
Jess Hickman	R	26	0	0	.000	0	1	0	0	1	0	1	0	0	0.00

WASHINGTON 8th 71-88 .447 25.5 — GIL HODGES

NAME	G by POS	B	AGE	G	AB	R	H	2B	3B	HR	RBI	BB	SO	SB	BA	SA
TOTALS			28	159	5318	557	1245	185	40	126	525	450	**1069**	53	.234	.355
Dick Nen	1B76	L	26	94	235	20	50	8	0	6	30	28	46	0	.213	.323
Bob Saverine	2B70, 3B26, SS11, OF9	B	25	120	406	54	102	10	4	5	24	27	62	4	.251	.333
Eddie Brinkman	SS158	R	24	158	582	42	133	18	9	7	48	29	105	7	.229	.326
Ken McMullen	3B141, 1B8, OF1	R	24	147	524	48	122	19	4	13	54	44	89	3	.233	.359
Fred Valentine	OF138, 1B2	B	31	146	508	77	140	29	7	16	59	51	63	22	.276	.455
Don Lock	OF129	R	29	138	386	52	90	13	1	16	48	57	126	2	.233	.396
Frank Howard	OF135	R	29	146	493	52	137	19	4	18	71	53	104	1	.278	.442
Paul Casanova	C119	R	24	122	429	45	109	16	5	13	44	14	78	1	.254	.406
Willie Kirkland	OF68	L	32	124	163	21	31	2	1	6	17	16	50	2	.190	.325
Jim King	OF85	L	33	117	310	41	77	14	2	10	30	38	41	4	.248	.403
2 Ken Harrelson	1B70	R	24	71	250	25	62	8	1	7	28	26	53	4	.248	.372
1 Don Blasingame	2B58, SS1	L	34	68	200	18	43	9	0	1	11	18	21	2	.215	.275
Ken Hamlin	2B50, 3B1	R	31	66	158	13	34	7	1	1	16	13	21	1	.215	.291
Doug Camilli (AJ)	C39	R	29	44	107	5	22	4	0	2	8	3	19	0	.206	.299
Bob Chance	1B13	L	25	37	57	1	10	3	0	1	8	2	23	0	.175	.281
Dick Phillips	1B5	L	34	25	37	3	6	0	0	0	4	2	5	0	.162	.162
Tim Cullen	3B8, 2B5	R	24	18	34	0	8	1	0	0	0	2	8	0	.235	.265
John Orsino (EJ)	1B5, C2	R	28	14	23	1	4	1	0	0	0	0	7	0	.174	.217
Hank Allen	OF9	R	25	9	31	2	12	0	0	1	6	3	6	0	.387	.484

Jim French (LJ) 24 L 5-24, Mike Brumley 27 L 2-18, Joe Cunningham 34 L 1-8

NAME	T	AGE	W	L	PCT	SV	G	GS	CG	IP	H	BB	SO	ShO	ERA
		28	71	88	.447	35	159	159	25	1419	1282	448	866	6	3.70
Pete Richert	L	26	14	14	.500	0	36	34	7	246	196	69	195	0	3.37
Phil Ortega	R	26	12	12	.500	0	33	31	5	197	158	53	121	1	3.93
Mike McCormick	L	27	11	14	.440	0	41	32	8	216	193	51	101	3	3.46
Bob Humphreys	R	30	7	3	.700	3	58	1	0	112	91	28	88	0	2.81
Ron Kline	R	34	6	4	.600	23	63	0	0	90	79	17	46	0	2.40
Dick Lines	L	27	5	2	.714	2	53	0	0	83	63	24	49	0	2.28
Casey Cox	R	24	4	5	.444	7	66	0	0	113	104	35	46	0	3.50
Barry Moore	L	23	3	3	.500	0	12	11	1	62	55	39	28	0	3.77
Diego Segui	R	28	3	7	.300	0	21	13	1	72	82	24	54	1	5.00
Jim Hannan	R	26	3	9	.250	0	30	18	2	114	125	59	68	0	4.26
Dick Bosman	R	22	2	6	.250	0	13	7	0	39	60	12	20	0	7.62
Joe Coleman	R	19	1	0	1.000	0	1	1	1	9	6	2	4	0	2.00
Tom Cheney	R	31	0	1	.000	0	3	1	0	5	4	6	3	0	5.40
1 Jim Duckworth	R	27	0	3	.000	0	5	4	0	14	14	10	14	0	5.14
Frank Kreutzer	L	27	0	5	.000	0	9	6	0	31	30	10	24	0	6.10
Dave Baldwin	R	28	0	0	.000	0	4	0	0	7	8	1	4	0	3.86
Buster Narum	R	26	0	0	.000	0	3	0	0	3	11	4	0	0	24.00
Alan Closter	L	23	0	0	.000	0	1	0	0	.1	1	2	0	0	0.00
Pete Craig	R	25	0	0	.000	0	1	0	0	2	2	1	1	0	4.50
Howie Koplitz (SJ)	R	28	0	0	.000	0	1	0	0	2	0	1	0	0	0.00

BOSTON 9th 72-90 .444 26 — BILLY HERMAN 64-82 .438 PETE RUNNELS 8-8 .500

NAME	G by POS	B	AGE	G	AB	R	H	2B	3B	HR	RBI	BB	SO	SB	BA	SA
TOTALS			25	162	5498	655	1318	228	44	145	617	542	1020	35	.240	.376
George Scott	1B158, 3B5	R	22	162	601	73	147	18	7	27	90	65	**152**	4	.245	.433
George Smith	2B109, SS19	R	27	128	403	41	86	19	4	8	37	37	86	4	.213	.340
Rico Petrocelli	SS127, 3B5	R	23	139	522	58	124	20	1	18	59	41	99	1	.238	.383
Joe Foy	3B139, SS13	R	23	151	554	97	145	23	8	15	63	91	80	2	.262	.413
Tony Conigliaro	OF146	R	21	150	558	77	148	26	7	28	93	52	112	0	.265	.487
2 Don Demeter	OF57, 1B2	R	31	73	226	31	66	13	1	9	29	5	42	1	.292	.478
Carl Yastrzemski	OF158	L	26	160	594	81	165	**39**	2	16	80	84	60	8	.278	.431
Mike Ryan	C114	R	24	116	369	27	79	15	3	2	32	29	68	1	.214	.287
Dalton Jones	2B70, 3B3	L	22	115	252	26	59	11	5	4	23	22	27	1	.234	.365
Lenny Green	OF27	L	32	85	133	18	32	6	0	1	12	15	19	0	.241	.308
Bob Tillman	C72	R	29	78	204	12	47	8	0	3	24	22	35	0	.230	.314
George Thomas	OF48, 3B6, 1B2, C2	R	28	69	173	25	41	4	0	5	20	23	33	1	.237	.347
2 Jose Tartabull	OF46	L	27	68	195	28	54	7	4	0	11	6	11	11	.277	.354
Eddie Kasko (XJ)	SS20, 3B10, 2B8	R	34	58	136	11	29	7	0	1	12	15	19	1	.213	.287
1 Jim Gosger	OF32	L	23	40	126	16	32	4	0	5	17	15	20	0	.254	.405
Joe Christopher	OF2	R	30	12	13	1	1	0	0	0	0	2	4	0	.077	.077
Reggie Smith	OF6	B	21	6	26	1	4	1	0	0	0	0	5	0	.154	.192

Tony Horton 21 R 3-22, Mike Andrews 22 R 3-18

NAME	T	AGE	W	L	PCT	SV	G	GS	CG	IP	H	BB	SO	ShO	ERA
		28	72	**90**	.444	31	162	162	32	1464	**1402**	577	977	10	3.92
Jose Santiago	R	25	12	13	.480	2	35	28	7	172	155	58	119	1	3.66
Jim Lonborg	R	24	10	10	.500	2	45	23	3	182	173	55	131	1	3.86
2 Don McMahon	R	36	8	7	.533	9	49	0	0	78	65	38	57	0	2.65
Darrell Brandon	R	25	8	8	.500	2	40	17	5	158	129	70	101	2	3.30
2 Lee Stange	R	29	7	9	.438	0	28	19	8	153	140	43	77	2	3.35
1 Earl Wilson	R	31	5	5	.500	0	15	14	5	101	88	36	67	1	3.83
Dan Osinski	R	32	4	3	.571	2	44	1	0	67	68	28	44	0	3.63
Dennis Bennett (AJ)	L	26	3	3	.500	0	16	13	0	75	75	23	47	0	3.24
2 John Wyatt	R	31	3	4	.429	8	42	0	0	72	59	27	63	0	3.12
1 Ken Sanders	R	24	3	6	.333	2	24	0	0	47	36	28	33	0	3.83
Dick Stigman	L	30	2	1	.667	0	34	10	1	81	85	46	65	1	5.44
3 Hank Fischer	R	26	2	3	.400	0	6	5	1	31	35	11	26	0	2.90
Jerry Stephenson (SA)	R	22	2	5	.286	0	15	11	1	66	68	44	50	0	5.86
Bob Sadowski	R	28	1	1	.500	1	11	5	0	33	41	9	11	0	5.45
Dave Morehead	R	23	1	2	.333	0	12	5	0	28	31	7	20	0	5.46
2 Rollie Sheldon	R	29	1	6	.143	0	23	10	1	80	106	23	38	0	4.95
1 Dick Radatz	R	29	0	2	.000	4	16	0	0	19	24	11	19	0	4.74
1 Guido Grilli	L	27	0	1	.000	0	6	0	0	5	5	9	4	0	7.20

Pete Magrini 24 R 0-1, 2 Garry Roggenburk 26 L 0-0, 2 Bill Short 28 L 0-0

NEW YORK 10th 70-89 .440 26.5 — JOHNNY KEANE 4-16 .200 RALPH HOUK 66-73 .415

NAME	G by POS	B	AGE	G	AB	R	H	2B	3B	HR	RBI	BB	SO	SB	BA	SA
TOTALS			29	160	5330	611	1254	182	36	162	569	485	817	49	.235	.374
Joe Pepitone	1B119, OF55	L	25	152	585	85	149	21	4	31	83	29	58	4	.255	.463
Bobby Richardson	2B147, 3B2	R	30	149	610	71	153	21	3	7	42	25	28	6	.251	.330
Horace Clarke	SS63, 2B16, 3B4	B	26	96	312	37	83	10	4	6	28	27	24	5	.266	.381
Clete Boyer	3B85, SS59	R	29	144	500	59	120	22	4	14	57	46	48	6	.240	.384
Roger Maris	OF95	L	31	119	348	37	81	9	2	13	43	36	60	0	.233	.382
Mickey Mantle	OF97	B	34	108	333	40	96	12	1	23	56	57	76	1	.288	.538
Tom Tresh	OF84, 3B64	B	28	151	537	76	125	12	4	27	68	86	89	5	.233	.421
Elston Howard	C100, 1B13	R	37	126	410	38	105	19	2	6	35	37	65	0	.256	.356
Roy White	OF82, 2B2	B	22	115	316	39	71	13	2	7	20	37	43	14	.225	.345
Lu Clinton	OF63	R	28	80	159	18	35	10	2	5	21	16	27	0	.220	.403
Jake Gibbs (BG)	C54	L	27	62	182	19	47	6	0	3	20	19	16	5	.258	.341
Ray Barker	1B47	L	30	61	75	11	14	5	0	3	13	4	20	0	.187	.373
Hector Lopez	OF29	R	33	54	117	14	25	4	1	4	16	8	20	0	.214	.368
1 Roger Repoz	OF30	L	25	37	43	4	15	4	1	0	9	4	8	0	.349	.488
Steve Whitaker	OF31	L	23	31	114	15	28	3	2	7	15	9	24	0	.246	.491
2 Bill Bryan	C14, 1B3	L	27	27	69	5	15	2	0	4	5	5	19	0	.217	.420
2 Dick Schofield	SS19	B	31	25	58	5	9	2	0	0	2	9	8	0	.155	.190
Bobby Murcer	SS18	L	20	21	69	3	12	1	1	0	5	4	5	2	.174	.217

Mike Hegan 23 L 8-39, Ruben Amaro (KJ) 30 R 5-23, Mike Ferraro 21 R 5-28, John Miller 22 R 2-23, Ross Moschitto (MS) 21

NAME	T	AGE	W	L	PCT	SV	G	GS	CG	IP	H	BB	SO	ShO	ERA
		28	70	89	.440	32	160	160	29	1415	1318	443	842	7	3.42
Fritz Peterson	L	24	12	11	.522	0	34	32	11	215	196	40	96	2	3.31
Mel Stottlemyre	R	24	12	**20**	.375	1	37	35	9	251	239	82	146	3	3.80
Al Downing	L	25	10	11	.476	0	30	30	1	200	178	79	152	0	3.56
Steve Hamilton	L	32	8	3	.727	3	44	3	1	90	69	22	57	1	3.00
Dooley Womack	R	26	7	3	.700	4	42	1	0	75	52	23	50	0	2.64
2 Fred Talbot	R	25	7	7	.500	0	23	19	3	124	123	45	48	0	4.14
Hal Reniff	R	27	3	7	.300	9	56	0	0	95	80	49	79	0	3.22
Jim Bouton (SA)	R	27	3	8	.273	1	24	19	3	120	117	38	65	0	2.70
Pedro Ramos	R	31	3	9	.250	13	52	1	0	90	98	18	58	0	3.60
Whitey Ford (AJ)	L	37	2	5	.286	0	22	9	0	73	79	24	43	0	2.47
Jack Cullen	R	26	1	0	1.000	0	5	0	0	11	11	5	7	0	4.09
Stan Bahnsen	R	21	1	1	.500	1	4	3	1	23	15	7	16	0	3.52
1 Bob Friend	R	35	1	4	.200	0	12	8	0	45	61	9	22	0	4.80
Bill Henry	L	24	0	0	.000	0	2	0	0	3	0	2	3	0	0.00

Rich Beck (MS) 25

LOS ANGELES 1st 95-67 .586 — WALT ALSTON

NAME	G by POS	B	AGE	G	AB	R	H	2B	3B	HR	RBI	BB	SO	SB	BA	SA
TOTALS			29	162	5471	606	1399	201	27	108	565	430	830	94	.256	.362
Wes Parker	1B140, OF14	B	26	156	475	67	120	17	5	12	51	69	83	7	.253	.385
Jim Lefebvre	2B119, 3B40	B	23	152	544	69	149	23	3	24	74	48	72	1	.274	.460
Maury Wills	SS139, 3B4	B	33	143	594	60	162	14	2	1	39	34	60	38	.273	.308
John Kennedy	3B87, SS28, 2B15	R	25	125	274	15	55	9	2	3	24	10	64	1	.201	.281
Ron Fairly	OF98, 1B25	L	27	117	351	53	101	20	0	14	61	52	38	3	.288	.464
Willie Davis	OF152	L	26	153	624	74	177	31	6	11	61	15	68	21	.284	.405
Lou Johnson	OF148	R	31	152	526	71	143	20	2	17	73	21	75	8	.272	.414
Johnny Roseboro	C138	L	33	142	445	47	123	23	2	9	53	44	51	3	.276	.398
Tommy Davis	OF79, 3B2	R	27	100	313	27	98	11	1	3	27	16	36	3	.313	.383
Jim Gilliam	3B70, 1B2, 2B2	B	37	88	235	30	51	9	0	1	16	34	17	2	.217	.268
Nate Oliver	2B68, SS2, 3B1	R	25	80	119	17	23	2	0	0	3	13	17	3	.193	.210
Al Ferrara	OF32	R	26	63	115	15	31	4	0	5	23	9	35	0	.270	.435
Jeff Torborg	C45	R	24	46	120	4	27	3	0	1	13	10	23	0	.225	.275
Jim Barbieri	OF20	L	24	39	82	9	23	5	0	0	3	9	7	2	.280	.341
2 Dick Stuart	1B25	R	33	38	91	4	24	1	0	3	9	11	17	0	.264	.374
2 Wes Covington	OF2	L	34	37	33	1	4	0	1	1	6	6	5	0	.121	.273
Derrell Griffith	OF7	L	22	23	15	3	1	0	0	0	2	2	3	0	.067	.067
3 Dick Schofield	3B19, SS3	B	31	20	70	10	18	0	0	0	4	8	8	1	.257	.257
Bart Shirley	SS5	R	26	12	5	2	1	0	0	0	0	0	2	0	.200	.200

Willie Crawford 19 L 0-0, Tommy Hutton 20 L 0-2, Jim Campanis 22 R 0-1

NAME	T	AGE	W	L	PCT	SV	G	GS	CG	IP	H	BB	SO	ShO	ERA
		27	95	67	.586	35	162	162	52	1458	1287	356	1084	20	2.62
Sandy Koufax	L	30	27	9	.750	0	41	41	27	323	241	77	317	5	1.73
Claude Osteen	L	26	17	14	.548	0	39	38	8	240	238	65	137	3	2.85
Phil Regan	R	29	14	1	.933	21	65	0	0	117	85	24	88	0	1.62
Don Drysdale	R	29	13	16	.448	0	40	40	11	274	279	45	177	0	3.42
Don Sutton	R	21	12	12	.500	0	37	35	6	226	192	52	209	2	2.99
Ron Perranoski	L	30	6	7	.462	7	55	0	0	82	82	31	50	0	3.18
Bob Miller	R	27	4	2	.667	5	46	0	0	84	70	29	58	0	2.79
Joe Moeller	R	23	2	4	.333	0	29	8	0	79	73	14	31	0	2.51
Jim Brewer (EJ)	L	28	0	2	.000	2	13	0	0	22	17	11	8	0	3.68
Nick Willhite	L	25	0	0	.000	0	6	0	0	4	3	5	4	0	2.25
Bill Singer	R	22	0	0	.000	0	3	0	0	4	4	2	4	0	0.00
1 Johnny Podres	L	33	0	0	.000	0	1	0	0	2	2	1	1	0	0.00
1 Howie Reed	R	29	0	0	.000	0	1	0	0	2	1	0	0	0	0.00

SAN FRANCISCO 2nd 93-68 .578 1.5 — HERMAN FRANKS

NAME	G by POS	B	AGE	G	AB	R	H	2B	3B	HR	RBI	BB	SO	SB	BA	SA
TOTALS			26	161	5539	675	1373	195	31	181	627	414	860	29	.248	.392
Willie McCovey	1B145	L	28	150	502	85	148	26	6	36	96	76	100	2	.295	.586
Hal Lanier	2B112, SS41	B	23	149	459	37	106	14	2	3	37	16	49	1	.231	.290
Tito Fuentes	SS76, 2B60	R	22	100	541	63	141	21	3	9	40	9	57	6	.261	.360
Jim Ray Hart	3B139, OF17	R	24	156	578	88	165	23	4	33	93	48	75	2	.285	.510
Ollie Brown	OF114	R	22	115	348	32	81	7	1	7	33	33	66	2	.233	.319
Willie Mays	OF150	R	35	152	552	99	159	29	4	37	103	70	81	5	.288	.556
Jesus Alou	OF100	R	24	110	370	41	96	13	1	1	20	9	22	5	.259	.308
Tom Haller	C136, 1B4	L	29	142	471	74	113	19	2	27	67	53	74	1	.240	.461
Jim Davenport	SS58, 3B36, 2B21, 1B2	R	32	111	305	42	76	6	2	9	30	22	40	1	.249	.370
Len Gabrielson	OF67, 1B6	L	26	94	240	27	52	7	0	4	16	21	51	0	.217	.296
Cap Peterson	OF51, 1B2	R	23	89	190	13	45	6	1	2	19	11	32	2	.237	.311
Don Landrum	OF54	L	30	72	102	9	19	4	0	1	7	9	18	1	.186	.255
Bob Barton	C39	R	24	43	91	1	16	2	1	0	3	5	5	0	.176	.220
Ozzie Virgil	3B13, C13, 1B5, 2B2, OF2	R	33	42	89	7	19	2	0	2	9	4	12	1	.213	.303
Don Mason	2B9	L	21	42	25	8	3	0	0	1	1	0	2	0	.120	.240
Bob Burda	1B7, OF4	L	27	37	43	3	7	3	0	0	2	2	5	0	.163	.233
1 Orlando Cepeda	OF8, 1B6	R	28	19	49	5	14	2	0	3	15	4	11	0	.286	.510
Jack Hiatt	1B7	R	23	18	23	2	7	2	0	0	1	4	5	0	.304	.391
Frank Johnson	OF13	R	23	15	32	2	7	0	0	0	0	2	7	0	.219	.219
Dick Dietz	OF6	R	24	13	23	1	1	0	0	0	0	0	9	0	.043	.043
Ken Henderson	OF10	B	20	11	29	4	9	1	1	1	1	2	3	0	.310	.517

1 Dick Schofield 31 B 1-16, Bob Schroder 21 L 8-33, Dick Bertell (LJ) 32

NAME	T	AGE	W	L	PCT	SV	G	GS	CG	IP	H	BB	SO	ShO	ERA
		29	93	68	.578	27	161	161	52	1476	1370	359	973	14	3.24
Juan Marichal	R	28	25	6	.806	0	37	36	25	307	228	36	222	4	2.23
Gaylord Perry	R	27	21	8	.724	0	36	35	13	256	242	40	201	3	2.99
Bobby Bolin	R	27	11	10	.524	1	36	34	10	224	174	70	143	4	2.89
Lindy McDaniel	R	30	10	5	.667	0	64	0	0	122	103	35	93	0	2.66
Frank Linzy	R	25	7	11	.389	16	51	0	0	100	107	34	57	0	2.97
Bob Priddy	R	26	6	3	.667	1	38	3	0	91	88	28	51	0	3.96
Ron Herbel	R	28	4	5	.444	1	32	18	0	130	149	39	55	0	4.15
Joe Gibbon	L	31	4	6	.400	1	37	10	1	81	86	16	48	0	3.67
2 Ray Sadecki	L	25	3	7	.300	0	26	19	3	105	125	39	62	1	5.40
Bill Henry	L	38	1	1	.500	1	35	0	0	22	15	10	15	0	2.45
1 Bob Shaw	R	33	1	4	.200	0	13	6	0	32	45	7	21	0	6.19
2 Billy Hoeft	L	34	0	2	.000	0	4	0	0	4	4	3	3	0	6.75
Bob Garibaldi	R	24	0	0	.000	0	1	0	0	1	1	0	0	0	0.00
Rich Robertson	R	21	0	0	.000	0	1	0	0	2	3	2	2	0	9.00

Masanori Murakami (JL) 22

PITTSBURGH 3rd 92-70 .568 3 — HARRY WALKER

NAME	G by POS	B	AGE	G	AB	R	H	2B	3B	HR	RBI	BB	SO	SB	BA	SA
TOTALS			28	162	5676	759	1586	238	66	158	715	405	1011	64	.279	.428
Donn Clendenon	1B152	R	30	155	571	80	171	22	10	28	98	52	142	8	.299	.520
Bill Mazeroski	2B162	R	29	162	621	56	163	22	7	16	82	31	62	4	.262	.398
Gene Alley	SS143	R	25	147	579	88	173	28	10	7	43	27	83	8	.299	.418
Bob Bailey	3B96, OF20	R	23	126	380	51	106	19	3	13	46	47	65	5	.279	.447
Roberto Clemente	OF154	R	31	154	638	105	202	31	11	29	119	46	109	7	.317	.536
Matty Alou	OF136	L	27	141	535	86	183	18	9	2	27	24	44	23	.342	.421
Willie Stargell	OF127, 1B15	L	26	140	485	84	153	30	0	33	102	48	109	2	.315	.581
Jim Pagliaroni	C118	R	28	123	374	37	88	20	0	11	49	50	71	0	.235	.377
Manny Mota	OF96, 3B4	R	28	116	322	54	107	16	7	5	46	25	28	7	.332	.472
Jose Pagan	3B83, SS18, 2B3, OF3	R	31	109	368	44	97	15	6	4	54	13	38	0	.264	.370
Jerry Lynch	OF4	L	35	64	56	5	12	1	0	1	6	4	10	0	.214	.286
Jesse Gonder	C52	L	30	59	160	13	36	3	1	7	16	12	39	0	.225	.388
Jerry May	C41	R	22	42	52	6	13	4	0	1	2	2	15	0	.250	.385
Andre Rodgers (LJ)	SS5, 3B3, OF3, 1B2	R	31	36	49	6	9	1	0	0	4	8	7	0	.184	.204
Gene Michael	SS8, 2B2, 3B1	B	28	30	33	9	5	2	1	0	2	0	7	0	.152	.273
Dave Roberts	1B2	L	33	14	16	3	2	1	0	0	0	0	7	0	.125	.188
George Spriggs		L	25	9	7	0	1	0	0	0	0	0	3	0	.143	.143
Don Bosch	OF1	B	23	3	2	0	0	0	0	0	0	0	0	0	.000	.000

NAME	T	AGE	W	L	PCT	SV	G	GS	CG	IP	H	BB	SO	ShO	ERA
		30	92	70	.568	43	162	162	35	1463	1445	463	898	12	3.52
Bob Veale	L	30	16	12	.571	0	38	37	12	268	228	102	229	3	3.02
Vern Law (PJ)	R	36	12	8	.600	0	31	28	8	178	203	24	88	4	4.04
Woodie Fryman	L	26	12	9	.571	1	36	28	9	182	182	47	105	3	3.81
Steve Blass	R	24	11	7	.611	0	34	25	1	156	173	46	76	0	3.87
Tommie Sisk	R	24	10	5	.667	1	34	23	4	150	146	52	60	1	4.14
Pete Mikkelsen	R	26	9	8	.529	14	71	0	0	126	106	51	76	0	3.07
Roy Face	R	38	6	6	.500	18	54	0	0	70	68	24	67	0	2.70
Don Cardwell	R	30	6	6	.500	1	32	14	1	102	112	27	60	0	4.59
Al McBean	R	28	4	3	.571	3	47	0	0	87	95	24	54	0	3.21
2 Billy O'Dell	L	33	3	2	.600	4	37	2	0	71	74	23	47	0	2.79
1 Don Schwall	R	30	3	2	.600	0	11	4	0	42	31	21	24	0	2.14
Bob Purkey	R	36	0	1	.000	1	10	0	0	20	16	4	5	0	1.35
Luke Walker	L	22	0	1	.000	0	10	1	0	10	8	15	7	0	4.50
Jim Shellenback	L	22	0	0	.000	0	2	0	0	3	3	3	0	0	9.00

PHILADELPHIA 4th 87-75 .537 8 — GENE MAUCH

NAME	G by POS	B	AGE	G	AB	R	H	2B	3B	HR	RBI	BB	SO	SB	BA	SA
TOTALS			29	162	5607	696	1448	224	49	117	628	510	969	56	.258	.378
Bill White	1B158	L	32	159	577	85	159	23	6	22	103	68	109	16	.276	.451
Cookie Rojas	2B106, OF56, SS2	R	27	156	626	77	168	18	1	6	55	35	46	4	.268	.329
Dick Groat	SS139, 3B20, 1B1	R	35	155	584	58	152	21	4	2	53	40	38	2	.260	.320
Dick Allen	3B91, OF47	R	24	141	524	112	166	25	10	40	110	68	136	10	.317	.632
Johnny Callison	OF154	L	27	155	612	93	169	40	7	11	55	56	83	8	.276	.418
Johnny Briggs (XJ)	OF69	L	22	81	255	43	72	13	5	10	23	41	55	3	.282	.490
Tony Gonzalez	OF121	L	29	132	384	53	110	20	4	6	40	26	60	2	.286	.406
Clay Dalrymple	C110	L	29	114	331	30	81	13	3	4	39	60	57	0	.245	.338
Tony Taylor	2B68, 3B52	R	30	125	434	47	105	14	8	5	40	31	56	8	.242	.346
2 Harvey Kuenn	OF31, 1B13, 3B1	R	35	86	159	15	47	9	0	0	15	10	16	0	.296	.352
Jackie Brandt	OF71	R	32	82	164	16	41	6	1	1	15	17	36	0	.250	.317
Doug Clemens	OF28, 1B1	L	27	79	121	10	31	1	0	1	15	16	25	1	.256	.289
Bob Uecker	C76	R	31	78	207	15	43	6	0	7	30	22	36	0	.208	.338
Bobby Wine (XJ)	SS40, OF2	R	27	46	89	8	21	5	0	0	5	6	13	0	.236	.292
Phil Linz	3B14, SS6, 2B3	R	27	40	70	4	14	3	0	0	6	2	14	0	.200	.243
Jimmie Schaffer	C6	R	30	8	15	2	2	1	0	1	4	1	7	0	.133	.400
1 John Herrnstein	OF2	L	28	4	10	0	1	0	0	0	1	0	7	0	.100	.100

Gary Sutherland 21 R 0-3, 1 Adolfo Phillips 24 R 0-3

NAME	T	AGE	W	L	PCT	SV	G	GS	CG	IP	H	BB	SO	ShO	ERA
		29	87	75	.537	23	162	162	52	1460	1439	412	928	15	3.57
Chris Short	L	28	20	10	.667	0	42	39	19	272	257	68	177	4	3.54
Jim Bunning	R	34	19	14	.576	1	43	41	16	314	260	55	252	5	2.41
2 Larry Jackson	R	35	15	13	.536	0	35	33	12	247	243	58	107	5	2.99
Ray Culp	R	24	7	4	.636	1	34	12	1	111	106	53	100	0	5.03
Darold Knowles	L	24	6	5	.545	13	69	0	0	100	98	46	88	0	3.06
2 Bob Buhl	R	37	6	8	.429	1	32	18	1	132	156	39	59	0	4.77
Rick Wise	R	20	5	6	.455	0	22	13	3	99	100	24	58	0	3.73
2 Terry Fox	R	30	3	2	.600	4	36	0	0	44	57	17	22	0	4.50
Roger Craig	R	35	2	1	.667	1	14	0	0	23	31	5	13	0	5.48
Ray Herbert	R	36	2	5	.286	2	23	2	0	50	55	14	15	0	4.32
Joe Verbanic	R	23	1	1	.500	1	17	0	0	14	12	10	7	0	5.14
John Morris	L	24	1	1	.500	0	13	0	0	14	15	3	8	0	5.14
Gary Wagner	R	26	0	1	.000	0	5	1	0	6	8	5	2	0	9.00
Bo Belinsky	L	29	0	2	.000	0	9	1	0	15	14	5	8	0	3.00
Ed Roebuck	R	34	0	2	.000	0	6	0	0	6	9	2	5	0	6.00
John Boozer	R	26	0	0	.000	0	2	2	0	5	8	3	5	0	7.20
Grant Jackson	L	23	0	0	.000	0	2	0	0	2	2	3	0	0	4.50
Steve Ridzik	R	37	0	0	.000	0	2	0	0	2	5	1	0	0	9.00
1 Ferguson Jenkins	R	22	0	0	.000	0	1	0	0	2	3	1	2	0	4.50

ATLANTA 5th 85-77 .525 10 — BOBBY BRAGAN 52-59 .468 BILLY HITCHCOCK 33-18 .647

NAME	G by POS	B	AGE	G	AB	R	H	2B	3B	HR	RBI	BB	SO	SB	BA	SA
TOTALS			29	163	5616	782	1476	220	32	207	734	512	913	59	.263	.424
Felipe Alou	1B90, OF79, 3B3, SS1	R	31	154	666	122	218	32	6	31	74	24	51	5	.327	.533
Woody Woodward	2B79, SS73	R	23	144	455	46	120	23	3	0	43	37	54	2	.264	.327
Denis Menke	SS106, 3B39, 1B7	R	25	138	454	55	114	20	4	15	60	71	87	0	.251	.412
Eddie Mathews	3B127	L	34	134	452	72	113	21	4	16	53	63	82	1	.250	.420
Hank Aaron	OF158, 2B2	R	32	158	603	117	168	23	1	44	127	76	96	21	.279	.539
Mack Jones (SJ)	OF112, 1B1	L	27	118	417	60	110	14	1	23	66	39	85	16	.264	.468
Rico Carty	OF126, C17, 1B2, 3B1	R	27	151	521	73	170	25	2	15	76	60	74	4	.326	.468
Joe Torre	C114, 1B36	R	25	148	546	83	172	20	3	36	101	60	61	0	.315	.560
Gary Geiger	OF49	L	29	78	126	23	33	5	3	4	10	21	29	0	.262	.444
Gene Oliver (JJ)	C48, 1B5, OF2	R	30	76	191	19	37	9	1	8	24	16	43	2	.194	.377
Frank Bolling	2B67	R	34	75	227	16	48	7	0	1	18	10	14	1	.211	.256
Mike de la Hoz	3B30, 2B8, SS1	R	26	71	110	11	24	3	0	2	7	5	18	0	.218	.300
Tony Cloninger	P39	R	25	47	111	12	26	5	0	5	23	2	22	1	.234	.414
2 Ty Cline	OF19, 1B6	L	27	42	71	12	18	0	0	0	6	3	11	2	.254	.254
1 Lee Thomas	1B36	L	30	39	126	11	25	1	1	6	15	10	15	1	.198	.365
Felix Millan	2B25, SS1, 3B1	R	22	37	91	20	25	6	0	0	5	2	6	3	.275	.341
Sandy Alomar	2B21, SS5	B	22	31	44	4	4	1	0	0	2	1	10	0	.091	.114
3 John Herrnstein	OF5	L	28	17	18	2	4	0	0	0	1	0	7	0	.222	.222
1 Marty Keough	1B4, OF3	L	31	17	17	1	1	0	0	0	1	1	6	0	.059	.059
Lee Bales	2B7, 3B3	B	21	12	16	4	1	0	0	0	0	0	5	0	.063	.063
Bill Robinson	OF5	R	23	6	11	1	3	0	1	0	3	0	1	0	.273	.455
Eddie Sadowski	C3	R	34	3	9	1	1	0	0	0	1	1	1	0	.111	.111

George Kopacz 25 L 0-9, Adrian Garrett 23 L 0-3

NAME	T	AGE	W	L	PCT	SV	G	GS	CG	IP	H	BB	SO	ShO	ERA
		28	85	77	.525	36	163	163	37	1469	1430	485	884	10	3.68
Ken Johnson	R	33	14	8	.636	0	32	31	11	216	213	46	105	2	3.29
Tony Cloninger	R	25	14	11	.560	1	39	38	11	258	253	116	178	1	4.12
Denny Lemaster	L	27	11	8	.579	0	27	27	10	171	170	41	139	3	3.74
Clay Carroll	R	25	8	7	.533	11	73	3	0	144	127	29	67	0	2.38
Dick Kelley	L	26	7	5	.583	0	20	13	2	81	75	21	50	2	3.22
Pat Jarvis	R	25	6	2	.750	0	10	9	3	62	46	12	41	1	2.32
Chi Chi Olivo	R	28	5	4	.556	7	47	0	0	66	59	19	41	0	4.23
Phil Niekro	R	27	4	3	.571	2	28	0	0	50	48	23	17	0	4.14
2 Ted Abernathy	R	33	4	4	.500	4	38	0	0	66	58	36	42	0	3.88
2 Don Schwall	R	30	3	3	.500	0	11	8	0	45	44	19	27	0	4.40
Wade Blasingame (AJ)	L	22	3	7	.300	0	16	12	0	68	71	25	34	0	5.29
1 Billy O'Dell	L	33	2	3	.400	6	24	0	0	41	44	18	20	0	2.41
1 Hank Fischer	R	26	2	3	.400	0	14	8	0	48	55	14	22	0	3.94
Charlie Vaughan	L	18	1	0	1.000	0	1	1	0	7	8	3	6	0	2.57
Ron Reed	R	23	1	1	.500	0	2	2	0	8	7	4	6	0	2.25
Jay Ritchie	R	29	0	1	.000	4	22	0	0	35	32	12	33	0	4.11
Herb Hippauf	L	26	0	1	.000	0	3	0	0	3	6	1	1	0	12.00
Arnie Umbach	R	23	0	2	.000	0	22	3	0	41	40	18	23	0	3.07
2 Joey Jay	R	30	0	4	.000	1	9	8	0	30	39	20	19	0	7.80
Dan Schneider	R	23	0	0	.000	0	14	0	0	26	35	5	11	0	3.46
Cecil Upshaw	R	23	0	0	.000	0	1	0	0	3	0	3	2	0	0.00

ST. LOUIS 6th 83-79 .512 12 — RED SCHOENDIENST

NAME	G by POS	B	AGE	G	AB	R	H	2B	3B	HR	RBI	BB	SO	SB	BA	SA
TOTALS			27	162	5480	571	1377	196	61	108	533	345	977	144	.251	.368
2 Orlando Cepeda	1B120	R	28	123	452	65	137	24	0	17	58	34	68	9	.303	.469
Julian Javier	2B145	R	29	147	460	52	105	13	5	7	31	26	63	11	.228	.324
Dal Maxvill	SS128, 2B5, OF1	R	27	134	394	25	96	14	3	0	24	37	61	3	.244	.294
Charley Smith	3B107, SS1	R	28	116	391	34	104	13	4	10	43	22	81	0	.266	.396
Mike Shannon	OF129, C1	R	26	137	459	61	132	20	6	16	64	37	106	8	.288	.462
Curt Flood	OF159	R	28	160	626	64	167	21	5	10	78	26	50	14	.267	.364
Lou Brock	OF154	L	27	156	643	94	183	24	12	15	46	31	134	74	.285	.429
Tim McCarver	C148	L	24	150	543	50	149	19	13	12	68	36	38	9	.274	.424
Jerry Buchek	2B49, SS48, 3B4	R	24	100	284	23	67	10	4	4	25	23	71	0	.236	.342
Phil Gagliano	3B41, 1B8, OF5, 2B1	R	24	90	213	23	54	8	2	2	15	24	29	2	.254	.338
Tito Francona	1B30, OF9	L	32	83	156	14	33	4	1	4	17	7	27	0	.212	.327
Bob Skinner		L	34	49	45	2	7	1	0	1	5	2	17	0	.156	.244
Bobby Tolan	OF26, 1B1	L	20	43	93	10	16	5	1	1	6	6	15	1	.172	.280
Pat Corrales	C27	R	25	28	72	5	13	2	0	0	3	2	17	1	.181	.208
Ed Spiezio	3B19	R	24	26	73	4	16	5	1	2	10	5	11	1	.219	.397
Alex Johnson	OF22	R	23	25	86	7	16	0	1	2	6	5	18	1	.186	.279
George Kernek	1B16	L	26	20	50	5	12	0	1	0	3	4	9	1	.240	.280
Ted Savage	OF7	R	30	16	29	4	5	2	1	0	3	4	7	4	.172	.310
Jim Williams (MS)	SS7, 2B3	R	22	13	11	1	3	0	0	0	1	1	5	0	.273	.273

NAME	T	AGE	W	L	PCT	SV	G	GS	CG	IP	H	BB	SO	ShO	ERA
TOTALS		28	83	79	.512	32	162	162	47	1460	1345	448	892	19	3.11
Bob Gibson	R	30	21	12	.636	0	35	35	20	280	210	78	225	5	2.44
Al Jackson	L	30	13	15	.464	0	36	30	11	233	222	45	90	3	2.51
Larry Jaster	L	22	11	5	.688	0	26	21	6	152	124	45	92	5	3.26
Ray Washburn	R	28	11	9	.550	0	27	26	4	170	183	44	98	1	3.76
Joe Hoerner	L	29	5	1	.833	13	57	0	0	76	57	21	63	0	1.54
Don Dennis	R	24	4	2	.667	2	38	1	0	60	73	17	25	0	4.95
Nelson Briles	R	22	4	15	.211	6	49	17	0	154	162	54	100	0	3.21
Steve Carlton	L	21	3	3	.500	0	9	9	2	52	56	18	25	1	3.12
Hal Woodeshick	L	33	2	1	.667	4	59	0	0	70	57	23	30	0	1.93
Dick Hughes	R	28	2	1	.667	1	6	2	1	21	12	7	20	1	1.71
1 Ray Sadecki	L	25	2	1	.667	0	5	3	1	24	16	9	21	0	2.25
Jim Cosman	R	23	1	0	1.000	0	1	1	1	9	2	2	5	1	0.00
1 Curt Simmons	L	37	1	1	.500	0	10	5	1	33	35	14	14	0	4.64
Ron Piche	R	31	1	3	.250	2	20	0	0	25	21	18	21	0	4.32
Art Mahaffey	R	28	1	4	.200	1	12	5	0	35	37	21	19	0	6.43
Tracy Stallard	R	28	1	5	.167	1	20	7	0	52	65	25	35	0	5.71
Dennis Aust	R	25	0	1	.000	1	9	0	0	10	12	6	7	0	6.30
Ron Willis	R	22	0	0	.000	1	4	0	0	3	1	1	2	0	0.00

CINCINNATI 7th 76-84 .475 18 — DON HEFFNER 37-46 .446 — DAVE BRISTOL 39-38 .506

NAME	G by POS	B	AGE	G	AB	R	H	2B	3B	HR	RBI	BB	SO	SB	BA	SA
TOTALS			26	160	5521	692	1434	232	33	149	651	394	877	70	.260	.395
Tony Perez	1B75	R	24	99	257	25	68	10	4	4	39	14	44	1	.265	.381
Pete Rose	2B140, 3B16	B	25	156	654	97	205	38	5	16	70	37	61	4	.313	.460
Leo Cardenas	SS160	R	27	160	568	59	145	25	4	20	81	45	87	9	.255	.419
Tommy Helms	3B113, 2B20	R	25	138	542	72	154	23	1	9	49	24	31	3	.284	.380
Tommy Harper	OF147	R	25	149	553	85	154	22	5	5	31	57	85	29	.278	.363
Vada Pinson	OF154	L	27	156	618	70	178	35	6	16	76	33	83	18	.288	.442
Deron Johnson	OF106, 1B71, 3B18	R	27	142	505	75	130	25	3	24	81	39	87	1	.257	.461
Johnny Edwards	C98	L	28	98	282	24	54	8	0	6	39	31	42	1	.191	.284
Art Shamsky	OF74	L	24	96	234	41	54	5	0	21	47	32	45	0	.231	.521
Dick Simpson	OF64	R	22	92	84	26	20	2	0	4	14	10	32	0	.238	.405
Gordy Coleman	1B65	L	31	91	227	20	57	7	0	5	37	16	45	2	.251	.348
Don Pavletich	C55, 1B10	R	27	83	235	29	69	13	2	12	38	18	37	1	.294	.519
Chico Ruiz	3B27, OF8, SS6	B	27	82	110	13	28	2	1	0	5	5	14	1	.255	.291
Mel Queen	OF32, P7	L	24	56	55	4	7	1	0	0	5	10	12	0	.127	.145
Jimmie Coker	C39, OF2	R	30	50	111	9	28	3	0	4	14	8	5	0	.252	.387
Lee May	1B16	R	23	25	75	14	25	5	1	2	10	0	14	0	.333	.507

NAME	T	AGE	W	L	PCT	SV	G	GS	CG	IP	H	BB	SO	ShO	ERA
TOTALS		28	76	84	.475	35	160	160	28	1436	1408	490	1043	10	4.08
Jim Maloney	R	26	16	8	.667	0	32	32	10	225	174	90	216	5	2.80
Milt Pappas	R	27	12	11	.522	0	33	32	6	210	224	39	133	2	4.29
Sammy Ellis	R	25	12	19	.387	0	41	36	7	221	226	78	154	0	5.29
Billy McCool	L	21	8	8	.500	18	57	0	0	105	76	41	104	0	2.49
1 Joey Jay	R	30	6	2	.750	0	12	10	1	74	78	23	44	1	3.89
Joe Nuxhall (AJ)	L	37	6	8	.429	0	35	16	2	130	136	42	71	1	4.50
Don Nottebart	R	30	5	4	.556	11	59	1	0	111	97	43	69	0	3.08
Ted Davidson	L	26	5	4	.556	4	54	0	0	85	82	23	54	0	3.92
Jim O'Toole	L	29	5	7	.417	0	25	24	2	142	139	49	96	0	3.55
Jack Baldschun	R	29	1	5	.167	0	42	0	0	57	71	25	44	0	5.53
Darrell Osteen	R	23	0	2	.000	1	13	0	0	15	26	9	17	0	12.00
2 Hank Fischer	R	26	0	6	.000	0	11	9	0	38	53	15	24	0	6.63
Mel Queen	R	24	0	0	.000	1	7	0	0	7	11	6	9	0	6.43
Dom Zanni	R	34	0	0	.000	0	5	0	0	7	5	3	5	0	0.00
1 Jerry Arrigo	L	25	0	0	.000	0	3	0	0	7	7	3	3	0	5.14
John Tsitouris	R	30	0	0	.000	0	1	0	0	1	3	1	0	0	18.00

HOUSTON 8th 72-90 .444 23 — GRADY HATTON

NAME	G by POS	B	AGE	G	AB	R	H	2B	3B	HR	RBI	BB	SO	SB	BA	SA
TOTALS			26	163	5511	612	1405	203	35	112	570	491	885	90	.255	.365
Chuck Harrison	1B114	R	25	119	434	52	111	23	2	9	52	37	69	2	.256	.380
Joe Morgan (BK)	2B117	R	22	122	425	60	121	14	8	5	42	89	43	11	.285	.391
Sonny Jackson	SS150	L	21	150	596	80	174	6	5	3	25	42	53	49	.292	.334
Bob Aspromonte	3B149, 1B2, SS2	R	28	152	560	55	141	16	3	8	52	35	63	0	.252	.334
Rusty Staub	OF148, 1B1	L	22	153	554	60	155	28	3	13	81	58	61	2	.280	.412
Jim Wynn (EJ)	OF104	R	24	105	418	62	107	21	1	18	62	41	81	13	.256	.440
Lee Maye	OF97	L	31	115	358	38	103	12	4	9	36	20	26	4	.288	.419
John Bateman	C121	R	23	131	433	39	121	24	3	17	70	20	74	0	.279	.467
Dave Nicholson	OF90	R	26	100	280	36	69	8	4	10	31	46	92	1	.246	.411
Felix Mantilla	1B14, 3B14, 2B9, OF1	R	31	77	151	16	33	5	0	6	22	11	32	1	.219	.371
Bob Lillis	2B35, SS18, 3B6	R	36	68	164	14	38	6	0	0	11	7	4	1	.232	.268
Ron Brand	C25, 2B9, OF3, 3B1	R	26	56	123	12	30	2	0	0	10	9	13	0	.244	.260
Bill Heath	C37	L	27	55	123	12	37	6	0	0	8	9	11	1	.301	.350
1 Jim Gentile	1B43	L	32	49	144	16	35	6	1	7	18	21	39	0	.243	.444
Ron Davis	OF48	R	24	48	194	21	48	10	1	2	19	13	26	2	.247	.340
2 Gene Freese	3B4, 2B3, OF1	R	32	21	33	1	3	0	0	0	0	5	11	1	.091	.091
Nate Colbert		R	20	19	7	3	0	0	0	0	0	0	4	0	.000	.000
Aaron Pointer	OF11	R	24	11	26	5	9	1	0	1	5	5	6	1	.346	.500
Norm Miller	OF8, 3B2	L	20	11	34	1	5	0	0	1	3	2	8	0	.147	.235
Joe Gaines	OF3	R	29	11	13	4	1	1	0	0	0	3	5	0	.077	.154
Brock Davis	OF7	L	22	10	27	2	4	1	0	0	1	5	4	1	.148	.185

Greg Sims 20 B 1-6, Julio Gotay 27 R 0-5, Dave Adlesh 22 R 0-6, Bob Watson 20 R 0-1

NAME	T	AGE	W	L	PCT	SV	G	GS	CG	IP	H	BB	SO	ShO	ERA
TOTALS		28	72	90	.444	26	163	163	34	1444	1468	391	929	13	3.76
Dave Giusti	R	26	15	14	.517	0	34	33	9	210	215	54	131	4	4.20
Mike Cuellar	L	29	12	10	.545	2	38	28	11	227	193	52	175	1	2.22
Larry Dierker	R	19	10	8	.556	0	29	28	8	187	173	45	108	2	3.18
Claude Raymond	R	29	7	5	.583	16	62	0	0	92	85	25	73	0	3.13
Dick Farrell	R	32	6	10	.375	2	32	21	3	153	167	28	101	0	4.59
Jim Owens	R	32	4	7	.364	2	40	0	0	50	53	17	32	0	4.68
1 Robin Roberts	R	39	3	5	.375	1	13	12	1	64	79	10	26	1	3.80
Chris Zachary	R	22	3	5	.375	0	10	8	0	55	44	32	37	0	3.44
Bob Bruce	R	33	3	13	.188	0	25	23	1	130	160	29	71	0	5.33
1 Don Lee	R	32	2	0	1.000	1	9	0	0	18	17	4	9	0	2.50
Ron Taylor (XJ)	R	28	2	3	.400	0	36	1	0	65	89	10	29	0	5.68
Barry Latman	R	30	2	7	.222	1	31	9	1	103	88	35	74	1	2.71
Frank Carpin	L	27	1	0	1.000	0	10	0	0	6	9	6	2	0	7.50
Don Wilson	R	21	1	0	1.000	0	1	0	0	6	5	1	7	0	3.00
Carroll Sembera	R	24	1	2	.333	1	24	0	0	33	36	16	21	0	3.00
Don Arlich	L	23	0	1	.000	0	7	0	0	4	11	4	1	0	15.75
Gary Kroll	R	24	0	0	.000	0	10	0	0	24	26	11	22	0	3.75
2 Aurelio Monteagudo	R	22	0	0	.000	1	10	0	0	15	14	11	7	0	4.80
Danny Coombs	L	24	0	0	.000	0	2	0	0	3	4	0	3	0	3.00
Jim Ray	R	21	0	0	.000	0	1	0	0	0	0	1	0	0	∞

NEW YORK 9th 66-95 .410 28.5 — WES WESTRUM

NAME	G by POS	B	AGE	G	AB	R	H	2B	3B	HR	RBI	BB	SO	SB	BA	SA
TOTALS			28	161	5371	587	1286	187	35	98	534	446	992	55	.239	.342
Ed Kranepool	1B132, OF11	L	21	146	464	51	118	15	2	16	57	41	66	1	.254	.399
Ron Hunt	2B123, SS1, 3B1	R	25	132	479	63	138	19	2	3	33	41	34	8	.288	.355
Ed Bressoud	SS94, 3B32, 1B9, 2B7	R	34	133	405	48	91	15	5	10	49	47	107	2	.225	.360
Ken Boyer	3B130, 1B2	R	35	136	496	62	132	28	2	14	61	30	64	4	.266	.415
Al Luplow	OF101	L	27	111	334	31	84	9	1	7	31	38	46	2	.251	.347
Cleon Jones	OF129	R	23	139	495	74	136	16	4	8	57	30	62	16	.275	.372
Ron Swoboda	OF97	R	22	112	342	34	76	9	4	8	50	31	76	4	.222	.342
Jerry Grote	C115, 3B2	R	23	120	317	26	75	12	2	3	31	40	81	4	.237	.315
Chuck Hiller	2B45, 3B14, OF9	L	31	108	254	25	71	8	2	2	14	15	22	0	.280	.350
Billy Murphy	OF57	R	22	84	135	15	31	4	1	3	13	7	34	1	.230	.341
Roy McMillan	SS71	R	35	76	220	24	47	9	1	1	12	20	25	1	.214	.277
Larry Elliot	OF54	L	28	65	199	24	49	14	2	5	32	17	46	0	.246	.412
Johnny Lewis	OF49	L	26	65	166	21	32	6	1	5	20	21	43	2	.193	.331
Johnny Stephenson	C52, OF1	L	25	63	143	17	28	1	1	1	11	8	28	0	.196	.238
Jim Hickman (BW)	OF45, 1B17	R	29	58	160	15	38	7	0	4	16	13	34	2	.238	.356
Hawk Taylor	C29, 1B13	R	27	53	109	5	19	2	0	3	12	3	19	0	.174	.275
Bud Harrelson	SS29	B	22	33	99	20	22	2	4	0	4	13	23	7	.222	.323
1 Dick Stuart	1B23	R	33	31	87	7	19	0	0	4	13	9	26	0	.218	.356
Greg Goossen	C11	R	20	13	32	1	6	2	0	1	5	1	11	0	.188	.344
Danny Napoleon	OF10	R	24	12	33	2	7	2	0	0	0	1	10	0	.212	.273
Shaun Fitzmaurice	OF5	R	23	9	13	2	2	0	0	0	0	2	6	1	.154	.154

Choo Choo Coleman 28 L 3-16, Lou Klimchock 26 L 0-5

NAME	T	AGE	W	L	PCT	SV	G	GS	CG	IP	H	BB	SO	ShO	ERA
TOTALS		26	66	95	.410	22	161	161	37	1427	1497	521	773	9	4.17
Dennis Ribant	R	24	11	9	.550	3	39	26	10	188	184	40	84	1	3.21
2 Bob Shaw	R	33	11	10	.524	0	26	25	7	168	171	42	104	2	3.91
Jack Fisher	R	27	11	14	.440	0	38	33	10	230	229	54	127	2	3.68
Jack Hamilton	R	27	6	13	.316	13	57	13	3	149	138	88	93	1	3.93
2 Bob Friend	R	35	5	8	.385	1	22	12	2	86	101	16	30	1	4.40
Dick Selma	R	22	4	6	.400	1	30	7	0	81	84	39	58	0	4.22
Rob Gardner	L	21	4	8	.333	1	41	17	3	134	147	64	74	0	5.10
Bill Hepler	L	20	3	3	.500	0	37	3	0	69	71	51	25	0	3.52
2 Jerry Arrigo (RJ)	L	25	3	3	.500	0	17	5	0	43	47	16	28	0	3.77
Darrell Sutherland	R	24	2	0	1.000	1	31	0	0	44	60	25	23	0	4.91
Larry Bearnarth	R	24	2	3	.400	0	29	1	0	55	59	20	27	0	4.42
Tug McGraw (SA)	L	21	2	9	.182	0	15	12	1	62	72	25	34	0	5.37
Dave Eilers	R	29	1	1	.500	0	23	0	0	35	39	7	14	0	4.63
Dick Rusteck (SA)	L	24	1	2	.333	0	8	3	1	24	24	8	9	1	3.00
2 Ralph Terry	R	30	0	1	.000	1	11	1	0	25	27	11	14	0	4.68
Nolan Ryan	R	19	0	1	.000	0	2	1	0	3	5	3	6	0	15.00
Gordie Richardson	L	26	0	2	.000	1	15	1	0	19	24	6	15	0	9.00
Larry Miller	L	29	0	2	.000	0	4	1	0	8	9	4	7	0	7.88
Dallas Green	R	31	0	0	.000	0	4	0	0	5	6	2	1	0	5.40

CHICAGO 10th 59-103 .364 36 — LEO DUROCHER

NAME	G by POS	B	AGE	G	AB	R	H	2B	3B	HR	RBI	BB	SO	SB	BA	SA
TOTALS			27	162	5592	644	1418	203	43	140	603	457	998	76	.254	.380
Ernie Banks	1B130, 3B8	R	35	141	511	52	139	23	7	15	75	29	59	0	.272	.432
Glenn Beckert	2B152, SS1	R	25	153	656	73	188	23	7	1	59	26	36	10	.287	.348
Don Kessinger	SS148	B	23	150	533	50	146	8	2	1	43	26	46	13	.274	.302
Ron Santo	3B152, SS8	R	26	155	561	93	175	21	8	30	94	95	78	4	.312	.538
Billy Williams	OF162	L	28	162	648	100	179	23	5	29	91	69	61	6	.276	.461
2 Adolfo Phillips	OF111	R	24	116	416	60	109	29	1	16	36	43	135	32	.262	.452
Byron Browne	OF114	R	23	120	419	46	102	15	7	16	51	40	143	3	.243	.427
Randy Hundley	C149	R	24	149	526	50	124	22	3	19	63	35	113	1	.236	.397
George Altman	OF42, 1B4	L	33	88	185	19	41	6	0	5	17	14	37	2	.222	.335
John Boccabella (EJ)	OF33, 1B30, C5	R	25	75	206	22	47	9	0	6	25	14	39	0	.228	.359
2 Lee Thomas	1B20, OF17	L	30	75	149	15	36	4	0	1	9	14	15	0	.242	.289
Jimmy Stewart	OF15, 2B4, SS2, 3B2	B	27	57	90	4	16	4	1	0	4	7	12	1	.178	.244
Joey Amalfitano	2B12, 3B3, SS2	R	32	41	38	8	6	2	0	0	3	4	10	0	.158	.211
2 Marty Keough	OF5	L	31	33	26	3	6	1	0	0	5	5	9	1	.231	.269
Ron Campbell	SS11, 3B7	R	26	24	60	4	13	1	0	0	4	6	5	1	.217	.233
Carl Warwick	OF10	R	29	16	22	3	5	0	0	0	0	0	6	0	.227	.227
Don Bryant	C10	R	24	13	26	2	8	2	0	0	4	1	4	1	.308	.385
Chris Krug	C10	R	26	11	28	1	6	1	0	0	1	1	8	0	.214	.250
2 John Herrnstein	1B4, OF1	L	28	9	17	3	3	0	0	0	0	3	8	0	.176	.176
Bob Raudman	OF8	L	24	8	29	1	7	2	0	0	2	1	4	0	.241	.310
Roberto Pena	SS5	R	26	6	17	0	3	2	0	0	1	0	4	0	.176	.294

1 Wes Covington 34 L 1-11, 1 Ty Cline 27 L 6-17, Frank Thomas 37 R 0-5, 1 Harvy Kuenn 35 R 1-3, Paul Popovich 25 R 0-6

NAME	T	AGE	W	L	PCT	SV	G	GS	CG	IP	H	BB	SO	ShO	ERA
TOTALS		28	59	103	.364	24	162	162	28	1458	1513	479	908	6	4.33
Ken Holtzman	L	20	11	16	.407	0	34	33	9	221	194	68	171	0	3.79
Bill Hands	R	26	8	13	.381	2	41	26	0	159	168	59	93	0	4.58
Dick Ellsworth	L	26	8	22	.267	0	38	37	9	269	321	51	144	0	3.98
2 Ferguson Jenkins	R	22	6	8	.429	5	60	12	2	182	147	51	148	1	3.31
Cal Koonce	R	25	5	5	.500	2	45	5	0	109	113	35	65	0	3.80
Bob Hendley	L	27	4	5	.444	7	43	6	0	90	98	39	65	0	3.90
2 Curt Simmons	L	37	4	7	.364	0	19	10	3	77	79	21	24	1	4.09
2 Don Lee (KJ)	R	32	2	1	.667	0	16	0	0	19	28	12	7	0	7.11
Arnie Earley	L	33	2	1	.667	0	13	0	0	18	14	9	12	0	3.50
2 Robin Roberts	R	39	2	3	.400	0	11	9	1	48	62	11	28	0	6.19
Ernie Broglio	R	30	2	6	.250	1	15	11	2	62	70	38	34	0	6.39
Dave Dowling	L	23	1	0	1.000	0	1	1	1	9	10	0	3	0	2.00
Chuck Estrada	R	28	1	1	.500	0	9	1	0	12	16	5	3	0	7.50
1 Billy Hoeft	L	34	1	2	.333	3	36	0	0	41	43	14	30	0	4.61
1 Ted Abernathy	R	33	1	3	.250	4	20	0	0	28	26	17	18	0	6.11
Bill Faul	R	26	1	4	.200	0	17	6	1	51	47	18	32	0	5.12
Billy Connors	R	24	0	1	.000	0	11	0	0	16	20	7	3	0	7.31
Len Church	R	24	0	1	.000	0	4	0	0	6	10	7	3	0	7.50
1 Larry Jackson	R	35	0	2	.000	0	3	2	0	8	14	4	5	0	13.50
Rich Nye	L	21	0	2	.000	0	3	2	0	17	16	7	9	0	2.12
Chuck Hartenstein	R	24	0	0	.000	0	5	0	0	9	8	3	4	0	2.00
Fred Norman	L	23	0	0	.000	0	2	0	0	4	5	2	6	0	4.50
1 Bob Buhl	R	37	0	0	.000	0	1	1	0	2	4	1	1	0	18.00

1967 The Fury at Fenway

They called it *The Great Race,* and through the final week the battle raged with the American League pennant at stake. Four teams fought, unable to shake off any of the others. The Boston Red Sox were the darlings of fans everywhere; rising up from ninth place in 1966, they were 100-to-one shots seeking The Impossible Dream. The Chicago White Sox had no batters as high as .250, but hung in the race on pitching, defense, and spirit. The Detroit Tigers were a strong team favored by the press to win it, and the Minnesota Twins came to life after manager Sam Mele was replaced in June by Cal Ermer. All four teams remained in the running into the final week, and the torrid chase set typewriters ablaze across the country.

Eddie Stanky's Hitless Wonders from Chicago were the first to drop out, losing a doubleheader to Kansas City on September 27, to end their hopes. Minnesota entered the final weekend one game up on Boston and Detroit. Rain caused the scheduling of back-to-back doubleheaders in Detroit with the California Angels, while the Twins came into Fenway Park to play two against the Red Sox. On Saturday, the Tigers split with the Angels, while an early Minnesota lead was lost after Jim Kaat had to leave the game with an injury, and Boston pounded Twin relievers for a 6-4 victory and a tie for the top. On Sunday, the capacity Boston crowd watched Jim Lonborg defeat Dean Chance to eliminate the Twins, while the Tigers won their first game to climb to a half-game behind the Red Sox. A Detroit victory would have ended the season in a tie, but all Boston—including the Red Sox—listened to their radios, and prayed, as Detroit dropped the second game to the Angels 8-5. The Impossible Dream became a reality as Red Sox rooters floated in the celebration of their first pennant since 1946 behind freshman manager Dick Williams.

The story behind the Fenway Miracle rested on the bat, arm, and legs of Carl Yastrzemski, a good hitter with a touch of power, who spent the winter months lifting weights and the summer months converting hits into home runs and winning the coveted Triple Crown of batting and the league's MVP honors. Along with the advent of Boston's new superstar, was the pitching of Jim Lonborg, who chalked up 22 wins after never having won more than 10, and the acquisition of Ken Harrelson, who finally made his way to the Red Sox after being made a free agent by the Kansas City A's owner Charley O. Finley. Harrelson called Finley "a menace to baseball" in the year's most famous off-the-field incident, which also included the suspension of pitcher Lew Krausse and the firing of manager Al Dark.

What appeared to be a mediocre Red Sox squad responded to Yastrzemski's leadership with outstanding years by the cluster. George Scott and Rico Petrocelli shone in the infield, and Mike Andrews and Reggie Smith were stellar rookies. Catching was a problem until Elston Howard was obtained from New York in August. Tony Conigliaro was continuing his fine four year career until smashed in the face with a Jack Hamilton fastball that sidelined him for the season and left his eyesight in doubt. Infielder Jerry Adair was purchased from Chicago in June and proceeded to hit .291 and steady the infield. The parade of key acquisitions continued with Gary Bell, a key starter who won 12 games for Boston after joining them in June. Jose Santiago posted a 12-4 mark with a hot September, and John Wyatt provided a solid relief hand. The collection of odds and ends and stars blended together to win perhaps the most thrilling pennant chase in history.

The National League race proved to be a slaughter for the St. Louis Cardinals, as early challenges by the Giants and Cubs were beaten back. Orlando Cepeda, acquired a year before from the Giants, turned in an MVP performance with a .325 average, 25 homers, a league-leading 111 RBI's, and proved to be the inspirational leader of the Cardinals. Curt Flood and Lou Brock also sparked the offense, while Bob Gibson led the mound staff, until suffering a broken leg on July 15, as the result of a line drive off the bat of Roberto Clemente. The injury brought gloom over St. Louis, but the pitching staff took up the challenge, as young Steve Carlton won 14 games, 29-year-old rookie Dick Hughes won 16, and Nelson Briles came out of the bullpen to win 14 games. During the time Gibson was out, the Cardinals racked up a 36-20 mark.

San Francisco finished second to St. Louis but was hampered by poor years from Willie Mays and Juan Marichal. Jim Ray Hart took on the Giants' run-producing leadership, and Mike McCormick won 22 games in a strong comeback from a sore arm to win the National League Cy Young Award. Leo Durocher, in his second year as the Cubs manager, had his team in contention with an attack led by Ernie Banks, Ron Santo, and Billy Williams, and a hill staff aced by surprise 20-game winner Ferguson Jenkins. By the time the World Series got underway, there was still great excitement in Boston. But the outcome, which was not to be Boston's, was an anticlimactic matter after the torrid American League race.

The Cardinals and Red Sox split the first six games of the World Series with Jim Lonborg and Bob Gibson both winning two games. Game seven saw the two aces pitted against each other, with Lonborg pitching on two days' rest, and Gibson on three—a difference which was enough to have Lonborg pounded for seven runs in six innings, to give Gibson his third victory and the Cardinals their eighth Series title in their history. Yastrzemski continued his inspirational batting in the Series with a .400 mark, but Lou Brock outshined him with a .414 average, 12 hits, 8 runs, and a Series record seven stolen bases.

Although Boston's dream fell short by a single game, they at least had the satisfaction of a pennant—something made possible in part by the temperament of Charley O. Finley. All Finley could muster out of a painful season was another move for his team—this time to Oakland for the 1968 season—the city on the other side of the Golden Gate Bridge.

WORLD SERIES – ST. LOUIS (NL) 4 BOSTON (AL) 3

LINE SCORES

TEAM	1	2	3	4	5	6	7	8	9	10	11	12	R	H	E
Game 1 October 4 at Boston															
STL (NL)	0	0	1	0	0	0	1	0	0				2	10	0
BOS (AL)	0	0	1	0	0	0	0	0	0				1	6	0
B. Gibson — **Santiago**, Wyatt (8)															
Game 2 October 5 at Boston															
STL	0	0	0	0	0	0	0	0	0				0	1	1
BOS	0	0	0	1	0	1	3	0	X				5	9	0
Hughes, Willis (6), Hoerner (7), Lamabe (7) — **Lonborg**															
Game 3 October 7 at St. Louis															
BOS	0	0	0	0	0	1	1	0	0				2	7	1
STL	1	2	0	0	0	1	0	1	X				5	10	0
Bell, Waslewski (3), Stange (6), Osinski (8) — **Briles**															
Game 4 October 8 at St. Louis															
BOS	0	0	0	0	0	0	0	0	0				0	5	0
STL	4	0	2	0	0	0	0	0	X				6	9	0
Santiago, Bell (1), Stephenson (3), Morehead (5), Brett (8) — **B. Gibson**															
Game 5 October 9 at St. Louis															
BOS	0	0	1	0	0	0	0	0	2				3	6	1
STL	0	0	0	0	0	0	0	0	1				1	3	2
Lonborg — **Carlton**, Washburn (7), Willis (9), Lamabe (9)															
Game 6 October 11 at Boston															
STL	0	0	2	0	0	0	2	0	0				4	8	0
BOS	0	1	0	3	0	0	4	0	X				8	12	1
Hughes, Willis (4), Briles (5), **Lamabe** (7), Hoerner (7), Jaster (7), Washburn (7), Woodeshick (8) — Waslewski, **Wyatt** (6), Bell (8)															
Game 7 October 12 at Boston															
STL	0	0	2	0	2	3	0	0	0				7	10	1
BOS	0	0	0	0	1	0	0	1	0				2	3	1
B. Gibson — **Lonborg**, Santiago (7), Morehead (9), Osinski (9), Brett (9)															

COMPOSITE BATTING

NAME	POS	G	AB	R	H	2B	3B	HR	RBI	BA
St. Louis (NL)										
Totals		7	229	25	51	11	2	5	24	.223
Brock	OF	7	**29**	**8**	**12**	2	1	1	3	**.414**
Cepeda	1B	7	**29**	1	3	2	0	0	1	.103
Flood	OF	7	28	2	5	1	0	0	3	.179
Maris	OF	7	26	3	10	1	0	1	**7**	.385
Javier	2B	7	25	2	9	**3**	0	1	4	.360
Shannon	3B	7	24	3	5	1	0	1	2	.208
McCarver	C	7	24	3	3	1	0	0	2	.125
Maxvill	SS	7	19	1	3	0	1	0	1	.158
B. Gibson	P	3	11	1	1	0	0	1	1	.091
Ricketts	PH	3	3	0	0	0	0	0	0	.000
Briles	P	2	3	0	0	0	0	0	0	.000
Hughes	P	2	3	0	0	0	0	0	0	.000
Tolan	PH	3	2	1	0	0	0	0	0	.000
Gagliano	PH	1	1	0	0	0	0	0	0	.000
Spiezio	PH	1	1	0	0	0	0	0	0	.000
Carlton	P	1	1	0	0	0	0	0	0	.000
Bressoud	SS	2	0	0	0	0	0	0	0	.000

Lamabe P 0-0, Willis P 0-0, Washburn P 0-0, Hoerner P 0-0, Woodeschick P 0-0, Jaster P 0-0

NAME	POS	G	AB	R	H	2B	3B	HR	RBI	BA
Boston (AL)										
Totals		7	222	21	48	6	1	8	19	.216
Scott	1B	7	26	3	6	1	1	0	0	.231
Yastrzemski	OF	7	25	4	10	2	0	**3**	5	.400
Smith	OF	7	24	3	6	1	0	2	3	.250
Petrocelli	SS	7	20	3	4	1	0	2	3	.200
Jones	3B	6	18	2	7	0	0	0	1	.389
Howard	C	7	18	0	2	0	0	0	1	.111
Adair	2B	5	16	0	2	0	0	0	1	.125
Foy	3B	6	15	2	2	1	0	0	1	.133
Andrews	2B	5	13	2	4	0	0	0	1	.308
Tartabull	OF	7	13	1	2	0	0	0	0	.154
Harrelson	OF	4	13	0	1	0	0	0	1	.077
Lonborg	P	3	9	0	0	0	0	0	0	.000
Siebern	OF	3	3	0	1	0	0	0	1	.333
Santiago	P	3	2	1	1	0	0	1	1	.500
Thomas	OF	2	2	0	0	0	0	0	0	.000
R. Gibson	C	2	2	0	0	0	0	0	0	.000
Ryan	C	1	2	0	0	0	0	0	0	.000
Waslewski	P	2	1	0	0	0	0	0	0	.000
Bell	P	3	0	0	0	0	0	0	0	.000

Wyatt P 0-0, Morehead P 0-0, Osinski P 0-0, Brett P 0-0, Stephenson P 0-0, Stange P 0-0

COMPOSITE PITCHING

NAME	G	IP	H	BB	SO	W	L	SV	ERA
St. Louis (NL)									
Totals	7	61	48	17	49	4	3	0	2.66
B. Gibson	3	**27**	14	**5**	**26**	**3**	0	0	**1.00**
Briles	2	11	7	1	4	1	0	0	1.64
Hughes	2	9	9	3	7	0	1	0	5.00
Carlton	1	6	3	2	5	0	1	0	0.00
Lamabe	3	2.2	5	0	4	0	1	0	6.75
Washburn	2	2.1	1	1	2	0	0	0	0.00
Woodeshick	1	1	1	0	0	0	0	0	0.00
Willis	3	1	2	4	1	0	0	0	27.00
Hoerner	2	.2	4	1	0	0	0	0	40.50
Jaster	1	.1	2	0	0	0	0	0	0.00
Boston (AL)									
Totals	7	61	51	17	30	3	4	1	3.39
Lonborg	3	24	14	2	11	2	1	0	2.63
Santiago	3	9.2	**16**	3	6	0	**2**	0	5.59
Waslewski	2	8.1	4	2	7	0	0	0	2.16
Bell	3	5.1	8	1	1	0	1	1	5.06
Wyatt	2	3.2	1	3	1	1	0	0	4.91
Morehead	2	3.1	0	4	3	0	0	0	0.00
Stange	1	2	3	0	0	0	0	0	0.00
Stephenson	1	2	3	1	0	0	0	0	9.00
Brett	2	1.1	0	1	1	0	0	0	0.00
Osinski	2	1.1	2	0	0	0	0	0	6.75

BOSTON 1st 92-70 .568 — DICK WILLIAMS

NAME	G by POS	B	AGE	G	AB	R	H	2B	3B	HR	RBI	BB	SO	SB	BA	SA
TOTALS			25	162	5471	722	1394	216	39	158	666	522	1020	68	.255	.395
George Scott	1B152, 3B2	R	23	159	565	74	171	21	7	19	82	63	119	10	.303	.465
Mike Andrews	2B139, SS6	R	23	142	494	79	130	20	0	8	40	62	72	7	.263	.352
Rico Petrocelli	SS141	R	24	142	491	53	127	24	2	17	66	49	93	2	.259	.420
Joe Foy	3B118, OF1	R	24	130	446	70	112	22	4	16	49	46	87	8	.251	.426
Tony Conigliaro (IJ)	OF95	R	22	95	349	59	100	11	5	20	67	27	58	4	.287	.519
Reggie Smith	OF144, 2B6	B	22	158	565	78	139	24	6	15	61	57	95	16	.246	.389
Carl Yastrzemski	OF161	L	27	161	579	**112**	**189**	31	4	**44**	**121**	91	69	10	**.326**	**.622**
Mike Ryan	C79	R	25	79	226	21	45	4	2	2	27	26	42	2	.199	.261
Jose Tartabull	OF83	L	28	115	247	36	55	1	2	0	10	23	26	6	.223	.243
2 Jerry Adair	3B35, SS30, 2B23	R	30	89	316	41	92	13	1	3	26	13	35	1	.291	.367
Dalton Jones	3B30, 2B19, 1B1	L	23	89	159	18	46	6	2	3	25	11	23	0	.289	.409
George Thomas	OF43, 1B3, C1	R	29	65	89	10	19	2	0	1	6	3	23	0	.213	.270
Russ Gibson	C48	R	28	49	138	8	28	7	0	1	15	12	31	0	.203	.275
2 Elston Howard	C41	R	38	42	116	9	17	3	0	1	11	9	24	0	.147	.198
2 Norm Siebern	1B13, OF1	L	33	33	44	2	9	0	2	0	7	6	8	0	.205	.295
1 Bob Tillman	C26	R	30	30	64	4	12	1	0	1	4	3	18	0	.188	.250
3 Ken Harrelson	OF23, 1B1	R	25	23	80	9	16	4	1	3	14	5	12	1	.200	.388
1 Tony Horton	1B6	R	22	21	39	2	12	3	0	0	9	0	5	0	.308	.385
1 Don Demeter (IL)	OF12, 3B1	R	32	20	43	7	12	5	0	1	4	3	11	0	.279	.465

2 Jim Landis 33 R 1-7, Ken Poulsen 19 L 1-5

NAME	T	AGE	W	L	PCT	SV	G	GS	CG	IP	H	BB	SO	ShO	ERA
		28	**92**	70	**.568**	44	162	162	41	1459	1307	477	1010	9	3.36
Jim Lonborg	R	25	**22**	9	.710	0	39	**39**	15	273	228	83	**246**	2	3.16
Jose Santiago	R	26	12	4	.750	5	50	11	2	145	138	47	109	0	3.60
2 Gary Bell	R	30	12	8	.600	3	29	24	8	165	143	47	115	0	2.81
John Wyatt	R	32	10	7	.588	20	60	0	0	93	71	39	68	0	2.61
Lee Stange	R	30	8	10	.444	1	35	24	6	182	171	32	101	2	2.77
Dave Morehead	R	24	5	4	.556	0	10	9	1	48	48	22	40	1	4.31
Darrell Brandon	R	26	5	11	.313	3	39	19	2	158	147	59	96	0	4.16
1 Dennis Bennett	L	27	4	3	.571	0	13	11	4	70	72	22	34	1	3.86
Dan Osinski	R	33	3	1	.750	2	34	0	0	64	61	14	38	0	2.53
Jerry Stephenson	R	23	3	1	.750	1	8	6	0	40	32	16	24	0	3.83
Gary Waslewski	R	25	2	2	.500	0	12	8	0	42	34	20	20	0	3.21
Billy Rohr	L	22	2	3	.400	0	10	8	2	42	43	22	16	1	5.14
Bill Landis	L	24	1	0	1.000	0	18	1	0	26	24	11	23	0	5.19
Hank Fischer	R	27	1	2	.333	1	9	2	1	27	24	8	18	0	2.33
1 Don McMahon	R	37	1	2	.333	2	11	0	0	18	14	13	10	0	3.50
Sparky Lyle	L	22	1	2	.333	5	27	0	0	43	33	14	42	0	2.30
Galen Cisco	R	31	0	1	.000	1	11	0	0	22	21	8	8	0	3.68
Ken Brett	L	18	0	0	.000	0	1	0	0	2	3	0	2	0	4.50

DETROIT 2nd (Tie) 91-71 .562 1 — MAYO SMITH

NAME	G by POS	B	AGE	G	AB	R	H	2B	3B	HR	RBI	BB	SO	SB	BA	SA
TOTALS			28	163	5410	683	1315	192	36	152	619	**626**	994	37	.243	.376
Norm Cash	1B146	L	32	152	488	64	118	16	5	22	72	81	100	3	.242	.430
Dick McAuliffe	2B145, SS43	L	27	153	557	92	133	16	7	22	65	105	118	6	.239	.411
Ray Oyler	SS146	R	28	148	367	33	76	14	2	1	29	37	91	0	.207	.264
Don Wert	3B140, SS1	R	28	142	534	60	137	23	2	6	40	44	59	1	.257	.341
Al Kaline (BA)	OF130	R	32	131	458	94	141	28	2	25	78	83	47	8	.308	.541
Jim Northrup	OF143	L	27	144	495	63	134	18	6	10	61	43	83	7	.271	.392
Willie Horton	OF110	R	24	122	401	47	110	20	3	19	67	36	80	0	.274	.481
Bill Freehan	C147, 1B11	R	25	155	517	66	146	23	1	20	74	73	71	1	.282	.447
Mickey Stanley	OF128, 1B8	R	24	145	333	38	70	7	3	7	24	29	46	9	.210	.313
Jerry Lumpe	2B54, 3B6	L	34	81	177	19	41	4	0	4	17	16	18	0	.232	.322
Dick Tracewski	SS44, 2B12, 3B10	R	32	74	107	19	30	4	2	1	9	8	20	1	.280	.383
Lenny Green	OF44	L	33	58	151	22	42	8	1	1	13	9	17	1	.278	.364
Earl Wilson	P39	R	32	52	108	8	20	2	0	4	15	8	39	0	.185	.315
Gates Brown (WJ)	OF20	L	28	51	91	17	17	1	1	2	9	13	15	0	.187	.286
Jim Price	C24	R	25	44	92	9	24	4	0	0	8	4	10	0	.261	.304
2 Eddie Mathews	3B21, 1B13	L	35	36	108	14	25	3	0	6	19	15	23	0	.231	.426
1 Jim Landis	OF12	R	33	25	48	4	10	0	0	2	4	7	12	0	.208	.333

2 Bill Heath 28 L 4-32, 1 Jake Wood 30 R 1-20, Dave Campbell 25 R 0-2, Tom Matchick 23 L 1-6, Wayne Comer 23 R 1-3

NAME	T	AGE	W	L	PCT	SV	G	GS	CG	IP	H	BB	SO	ShO	ERA
		28	91	71	.562	40	163	163	46	1444	1230	472	1038	17	3.32
Earl Wilson	R	32	**22**	11	.667	0	39	38	12	264	216	92	184	0	3.27
Denny McLain	R	23	17	16	.515	0	37	37	10	235	209	73	161	3	3.79
Joe Sparma	R	25	16	9	.640	0	37	37	11	218	186	85	153	5	3.76
Mickey Lolich	L	26	14	13	.519	0	31	30	11	204	165	56	174	**6**	3.04
Fred Gladding	R	31	6	4	.600	12	42	1	0	77	62	19	64	0	1.99
John Hiller	L	24	4	3	.571	3	23	6	2	65	57	9	49	2	2.63
Dave Wickersham	R	31	4	5	.444	4	36	4	0	85	72	33	44	0	2.75
Johnny Podres	L	34	3	1	.750	1	21	8	0	63	58	11	34	0	3.86
Fred Lasher	R	25	2	1	.667	9	17	0	0	30	25	11	28	0	3.90
George Korince	R	21	1	0	1.000	0	9	0	0	14	10	11	11	0	5.14
Pat Dobson	R	25	1	2	.333	0	28	1	0	49	38	27	34	0	2.94
Mike Marshall	R	24	1	3	.250	10	37	0	0	59	51	20	41	0	1.98
Hank Aguirre	L	35	0	1	.000	0	31	1	0	41	34	17	33	0	2.41
1 Larry Sherry	R	31	0	1	.000	1	20	0	0	28	35	7	20	0	6.43
1 Orlando Pena	R	33	0	1	.000	0	2	0	0	2	5	0	2	0	13.50
Johnny Klippstein	R	39	0	0	.000	0	5	0	0	7	6	1	4	0	5.14
1 Bill Monbouquette	R	30	0	0	.000	0	2	0	0	2	1	0	2	0	0.00

MINNESOTA 2nd (Tie) 91-71 .562 1 — SAM MELE 25-25 .500 CAL ERMER 66-46 .589

NAME	G by POS	B	AGE	G	AB	R	H	2B	3B	HR	RBI	BB	SO	SB	BA	SA
TOTALS			28	164	5458	671	1309	**216**	48	131	619	512	976	55	.240	.369
Harmon Killebrew	1B160, 3B3	R	31	163	547	105	147	24	1	**44**	113	**131**	111	1	.269	.558
Rod Carew	2B134	L	21	137	514	66	150	22	7	8	51	37	91	5	.292	.409
Zoilo Versalles	SS159	R	27	160	581	63	116	16	7	6	50	33	113	5	.200	.282
Rich Rollins	3B97	R	29	109	339	31	83	11	2	6	39	27	58	1	.245	.342
Tony Oliva	OF146	L	27	146	557	76	161	**34**	6	17	83	44	61	11	.289	.463
Ted Uhlaender	OF118	L	27	133	415	41	107	19	7	6	49	13	45	4	.258	.381
Bob Allison	OF145	R	32	153	496	73	128	21	6	24	75	74	114	6	.258	.470
Jerry Zimmerman	C104	R	32	104	234	13	39	3	0	1	12	22	49	0	.167	.192
Cesar Tovar	OF74, 3B70, 2B36, SS9	R	26	164	**649**	98	173	32	7	6	47	46	51	19	.267	.365
Sandy Valdespino	OF65	L	28	99	97	9	16	2	0	1	3	5	22	3	.165	.216
Rich Reese	1B36, OF10	L	25	95	101	13	25	5	0	4	20	8	17	0	.248	.416
Russ Nixon	C69	L	32	74	170	16	40	6	1	1	22	18	29	0	.235	.300
Earl Battey	C41	R	32	48	109	6	18	3	1	0	8	13	24	0	.165	.211
Frank Kostro	OF3, 3B1	R	29	32	31	4	10	0	0	0	2	3	2	0	.323	.323
Jackie Hernandez	SS15, 3B13	R	26	29	28	1	4	0	0	0	3	0	6	0	.143	.143
Ron Clark (EJ)	3B16	R	24	20	60	7	10	3	1	2	11	4	9	0	.167	.350
Hank Izquierdo	C16	R	36	16	26	4	7	2	0	0	2	1	2	0	.269	.346
Walt Bond (DD)	OF3	L	29	10	16	4	5	1	0	1	5	3	1	0	.313	.563
Andy Kosco	OF7	R	25	9	28	4	4	1	0	0	4	2	4	0	.143	.179

Frank Quilici 28 R 2-19, Carroll Hardy 34 R 3-8, Graig Nettles 22 L 1-3, Pat Kelly (MS) 22 L 0-1

NAME	T	AGE	W	L	PCT	SV	G	GS	CG	IP	H	BB	SO	ShO	ERA
		28	91	71	.562	24	164	164	**58**	1461	1336	396	1089	18	3.14
Dean Chance	R	26	20	14	.588	1	41	**39**	**18**	**284**	244	68	220	5	2.73
Jim Kaat	L	28	16	13	.552	0	42	38	13	262	**269**	42	211	2	3.05
Dave Boswell	R	22	14	12	.538	0	37	32	11	223	162	107	204	3	3.27
Jim Merritt	L	23	13	7	.650	0	37	28	11	228	196	30	161	4	2.53
Jim Perry	R	31	8	7	.533	0	37	11	3	131	123	50	94	2	3.02
Al Worthington	R	38	8	9	.471	16	59	0	0	92	77	38	80	0	2.84
Ron Kline	R	35	7	1	.875	5	54	0	0	72	71	15	36	0	3.75
Mudcat Grant	R	31	5	6	.455	0	27	14	2	95	121	17	50	0	4.74
Jim Roland	L	24	0	1	.000	2	25	0	0	36	33	17	16	0	3.00
Jim Ollom	L	21	0	1	.000	0	21	2	0	35	33	11	17	0	5.40
Dwight Siebler	R	29	0	0	.000	0	2	0	0	3	4	1	0	0	3.00
Mel Nelson	L	31	0	0	.000	0	1	0	0	.1	3	0	0	0	54.00

CHICAGO 4th 89-73 .549 3 — EDDIE STANKY

NAME	G by POS	B	AGE	G	AB	R	H	2B	3B	HR	RBI	BB	SO	SB	BA	SA
TOTALS			28	162	5383	531	1209	181	34	89	491	480	849	124	.225	.320
Tommy McCraw	1B123, OF6	L	26	125	453	55	107	18	3	11	45	33	55	24	.236	.362
Wayne Causey	2B96, SS2	L	30	124	292	21	66	10	3	1	28	32	35	2	.226	.291
Ron Hansen	SS157	R	29	157	498	35	116	20	0	8	51	64	51	0	.233	.321
Don Buford	3B121, 2B51, OF1	B	30	156	535	61	129	10	9	4	32	65	51	34	.241	.316
Ken Berry	OF143	R	26	147	485	49	117	14	4	7	41	46	68	9	.241	.330
Tommie Agee	OF152	R	24	158	529	73	124	26	2	14	52	44	129	28	.234	.371
Pete Ward	OF89, 1B39, 3B22	L	27	146	467	49	109	16	2	18	62	61	109	3	.233	.392
J. C. Martin	C96, 1B1	L	30	101	252	22	59	12	1	4	22	30	41	4	.234	.337
Walt Williams	OF73	R	23	104	275	35	66	16	3	3	15	17	20	3	.240	.353
Smoky Burgess		L	40	77	60	2	8	1	0	2	11	14	8	0	.133	.250
Duane Josephson	C59	R	25	62	189	11	45	5	1	1	9	6	24	0	.238	.291
2 Rocky Colavito	OF58	R	33	60	190	20	42	4	1	3	29	25	10	1	.221	.300
2 Ken Boyer	3B33, 1B18	R	36	57	180	17	47	5	1	4	21	7	25	0	.261	.367
Jerry McNertney	C52	R	30	56	123	8	28	6	0	3	13	6	14	0	.228	.350
Dick Kenworthy	3B35	R	26	50	97	9	22	4	1	4	11	4	17	0	.227	.412
Al Weis (KJ)	2B32, SS13	B	29	50	53	9	13	2	0	0	4	1	7	3	.245	.283
Marv Staehle	2B17, SS5	L	25	32	54	1	6	1	0	0	1	4	8	1	.111	.130
1 Jerry Adair	2B27	R	30	28	98	6	20	4	0	0	9	4	17	0	.204	.245
Buddy Bradford	OF14	R	22	24	20	6	2	1	0	0	1	1	7	1	.100	.150
2 Jimmy Stewart	OF6, 2B5, SS2	B	28	24	18	5	3	0	0	0	1	1	6	1	.167	.167
2 Jim King	OF12	L	34	23	50	2	6	1	0	0	2	4	16	0	.120	.140
1 Ed Stroud	OF12	L	27	20	27	6	8	0	1	0	3	1	5	7	.296	.370

Bill Voss 23 L 2-22, 2 Sandy Alomar 23 B 3-15, 1 Bill Skowron 36 R 0-8, Rich Morales 23 R 0-10, Ed Herrmann 20 L 2-3, Cotton Nash 24 R 0-3

NAME	T	AGE	W	L	PCT	SV	G	GS	CG	IP	H	BB	SO	ShO	ERA
		30	89	73	.549	39	162	162	36	**1490**	1197	465	927	**24**	**2.45**
Joe Horlen	R	29	19	7	**.731**	0	35	35	13	258	188	58	103	**6**	**2.06**
Gary Peters	L	30	16	11	.593	0	38	36	11	260	187	91	215	3	2.28
Tommy John	L	24	10	13	.435	0	31	29	9	178	143	47	110	**6**	2.48
Hoyt Wilhelm	R	43	8	3	.727	12	49	0	0	89	58	34	76	0	1.31
Bob Locker	R	29	7	5	.583	20	**77**	0	0	125	102	23	80	0	2.09
2 Don McMahon	R	37	5	0	1.000	3	52	0	0	92	54	27	74	0	1.66
Wilbur Wood	L	25	4	2	.667	4	51	8	0	95	95	28	47	0	2.46
Jim O'Toole (SJ)	L	30	4	3	.571	0	15	10	1	54	53	18	37	1	2.83
Fred Klages	R	23	4	4	.500	0	11	9	0	45	43	16	17	0	3.80
1 John Buzhardt	R	30	3	9	.250	0	28	7	0	89	100	37	33	0	3.94
Bruce Howard	R	24	3	10	.231	0	30	17	1	113	102	52	76	0	3.42
Cisco Carlos	R	26	2	0	1.000	0	8	7	1	42	23	9	27	1	0.86
Steve Jones	L	26	2	2	.500	0	11	3	0	26	21	12	17	0	4.15
1 Jack Lamabe	R	30	1	0	1.000	0	3	0	0	5	7	1	3	0	1.80
Dennis Higgins (IJ)	R	27	1	2	.333	0	9	0	0	12	13	10	8	0	6.00
Roger Nelson	R	23	0	1	.000	0	5	0	0	7	4	0	4	0	1.29
Aurelio Monteagudo	R	23	0	1	.000	0	1	1	0	1	4	2	0	0	27.00

CALIFORNIA 5th 84-77 .522 7.5 — BILL RIGNEY

NAME	G by POS	B	AGE	G	AB	R	H	2B	3B	HR	RBI	BB	SO	SB	BA	SA
TOTALS			27	161	5307	567	1265	170	37	114	524	453	1021	40	.238	.349
Don Mincher	1B142, OF1	L	29	147	487	81	133	23	3	25	76	69	69	0	.273	.487
Bobby Knoop	2B159	R	28	159	511	51	125	18	5	9	38	44	136	2	.245	.352
Jim Fregosi	SS151	R	25	151	590	75	171	23	6	9	56	49	77	9	.290	.395
Paul Schaal	3B88, SS2, 2B1	R	24	99	272	31	51	9	1	6	20	38	39	2	.188	.294
Jimmie Hall	OF120	L	29	129	401	54	100	8	3	16	55	42	65	4	.249	.404
Jose Cardenal	OF101	R	23	108	381	40	90	13	5	6	27	15	63	10	.236	.344
Rick Reichardt	OF138	R	24	146	498	56	132	14	2	17	69	35	90	5	.265	.404
Bob Rodgers	C134, OF1	B	28	139	429	29	94	13	3	6	41	34	55	1	.219	.305
Tom Satriano	3B38, C23, 2B15, 1B5	L	26	90	201	13	45	7	0	4	21	28	25	1	.224	.318
Bubba Morton	OF61	R	35	80	201	23	63	9	3	0	32	22	29	0	.313	.388
Jay Johnstone	OF63	L	21	79	230	18	48	7	1	2	10	5	37	3	.209	.274
2 Roger Repoz	OF63	L	26	74	176	25	44	9	1	5	20	19	37	2	.250	.398
2 Bill Skowron	1B32	R	36	62	123	8	27	2	1	1	10	4	18	0	.220	.276
2 Woodie Held	3B19, OF17, SS13, 2B3	R	35	58	141	15	31	3	0	4	17	18	41	0	.220	.326
2 Johnny Werhas	3B30, 1B4, OF1	R	29	49	75	8	12	1	1	2	6	10	22	0	.160	.280
Aurelio Rodriguez	3B29	R	19	29	130	14	31	3	1	1	8	2	21	1	.238	.300
2 Hawk Taylor	C19	R	28	23	52	5	16	3	0	1	3	4	8	0	.308	.423
Orlando McFarlane	C6	R	29	12	22	0	5	0	0	0	3	1	7	0	.227	.227
1 Len Gabrielson	OF1	L	27	11	12	2	1	0	0	0	2	2	4	0	.083	.083

Ed Kirkpatrick 22 L 0-8, Don Wallace 26 L 0-6, Larry Stubing 29 L 0-5, Jimmy Piersall 37 R 0-3, Jim Hibbs 22 R 0-3, Tom Egan 21 R 0-1

NAME	T	AGE	W	L	PCT	SV	G	GS	CG	IP	H	BB	SO	ShO	ERA
		28	84	77	.552	**46**	161	161	19	1430	1246	525	892	14	3.19
Jim McGlothlin	R	23	12	8	.600	0	32	29	9	197	163	56	137	**6**	2.97
Minnie Rojas	R	28	12	9	.571	**27**	72	0	0	122	106	38	83	0	2.51
Rickey Clark	R	21	12	11	.522	0	32	30	1	174	144	69	81	1	2.59
George Brunet	L	32	11	**19**	.367	1	40	37	7	250	203	90	165	2	3.31
2 Jack Hamilton	R	28	9	6	.600	0	26	20	0	119	104	63	74	0	3.25
Bill Kelso	R	27	5	3	.625	11	69	1	0	112	85	63	91	0	2.97
Clyde Wright	L	26	5	5	.500	0	20	11	1	77	76	24	35	0	3.27
Jim Weaver	L	28	3	0	1.000	1	13	2	0	30	26	9	20	0	2.70
Bobby Locke	R	33	3	0	1.000	2	9	1	0	19	14	3	7	0	2.37
1 Jack Sanford	R	38	3	2	.600	1	12	9	0	48	53	7	21	0	4.50
Pete Cimino	R	24	3	3	.500	1	46	1	0	88	73	31	80	0	3.27
2 Curt Simmons	L	38	2	1	.667	1	14	4	1	35	44	9	13	1	2.57
Lew Burdette	R	40	1	0	1.000	1	19	0	0	18	16	0	8	0	5.00
Fred Newman (SA)	R	25	1	0	1.000	0	3	1	0	6	8	2	0	0	1.50
Jim Coates	R	34	1	2	.333	0	25	1	0	52	47	23	39	0	4.33
Ken Turner	L	23	1	2	.333	0	13	1	0	17	16	4	6	0	4.24
1 Nick Willhite	L	26	0	2	.000	0	10	7	0	39	39	16	22	0	4.38
1 Marcelino Lopez	L	23	0	2	.000	0	4	3	0	9	11	9	6	0	9.00
Jorge Rubio	R	22	0	2	.000	0	3	3	0	15	18	9	4	0	3.60
Rudy May (SA) 22															

BALTIMORE 6th (Tie) 76-85 .472 15.5 — HANK BAUER

NAME	G by POS	B	AGE	G	AB	R	H	2B	3B	HR	RBI	BB	SO	SB	BA	SA
TOTALS			27	161	5456	654	1312	215	44	138	624	531	1002	54	.240	.372
Boog Powell	1B114	L	25	125	415	53	97	14	1	13	55	55	94	1	.234	.366
Dave Johnson	2B144, 3B3	R	24	148	510	62	126	30	3	10	64	59	82	4	.247	.376
Luis Aparicio	SS131	R	33	134	546	55	127	22	5	4	31	29	44	18	.233	.313
Brooks Robinson	3B158	R	30	158	610	88	164	25	5	22	77	54	54	1	.269	.434
Frank Robinson (IJ)	OF126, 1B2	R	31	129	479	83	149	23	7	30	94	71	84	2	.311	.576
Paul Blair	OF146	R	23	151	552	72	162	27	12	11	64	50	68	8	.293	.446
Curt Blefary	OF103, 1B52	L	23	155	554	69	134	19	5	22	81	73	94	4	.242	.413
Andy Etchebarren	C110	R	24	112	330	29	71	13	0	7	35	38	80	1	.215	.318
Russ Snyder	OF69	L	33	108	275	40	65	8	2	4	23	32	48	5	.236	.324
Mark Belanger	SS38, 2B26, 3B2	R	23	69	184	19	32	5	0	1	10	12	46	6	.174	.217
Sam Bowens	OF32	R	28	62	120	13	22	2	1	5	12	11	43	3	.183	.342
Larry Haney	C57	R	24	58	164	13	44	11	0	3	20	6	28	1	.268	.390
Vic Roznovsky	C23	L	28	45	97	7	20	5	0	0	10	1	20	0	.206	.258
Dave May	OF19	L	23	36	85	12	20	1	1	1	7	6	13	0	.235	.306
Curt Motton	OF18	R	26	27	65	5	13	2	0	2	9	5	14	0	.200	.323
1 Woodie Held	2B9, 3B5, OF2	R	35	26	41	4	6	3	0	1	6	6	12	0	.146	.293
Mickey McGuire	2B4	R	26	10	17	2	4	0	0	0	2	0	2	0	.235	.235

1 Mike Epstein 24 L 2-13, 1 Charlie Lau 34 L 1-8, 1 Bob Johnson 31 R 1-3

NAME	T	AGE	W	L	PCT	SV	G	GS	CG	IP	H	BB	SO	ShO	ERA
		27	76	85	.472	36	161	161	29	1457	1218	566	1034	17	3.32
Tom Phoebus	R	22	14	9	.609	0	33	33	7	208	177	114	179	4	3.33
Jim Hardin	R	23	8	3	.727	0	19	14	5	111	85	27	64	2	2.27
Moe Drabowsky	R	31	7	5	.583	12	43	0	0	95	66	25	96	0	1.61
Dave McNally	L	24	7	7	.500	0	24	22	3	119	134	39	70	1	4.54
2 Pete Richert	L	27	7	10	.412	2	26	19	5	132	107	41	90	1	3.00
Gene Brabender	R	25	6	4	.600	0	14	14	3	94	77	23	71	1	3.35
Bill Dillman	R	22	5	9	.357	3	32	15	2	124	115	33	69	1	4.35
Eddie Fisher	R	30	4	3	.571	1	46	0	0	90	82	26	53	0	3.60
1 Steve Barber	L	28	4	9	.308	0	15	15	1	75	47	61	48	1	4.08
Jim Palmer (SA)	R	21	3	1	.750	0	9	9	2	49	34	20	23	1	2.94
Eddie Watt	R	25	3	5	.375	8	49	0	0	104	67	37	93	0	2.25
Wally Bunker	R	22	3	7	.300	1	29	9	1	88	83	31	51	0	4.09
Stu Miller	R	39	3	10	.231	8	42	0	0	81	63	36	60	0	2.56
2 Marcelino Lopez (SA)	L	23	1	0	1.000	0	4	4	0	18	15	10	15	0	2.50
1 Frank Bertaina	L	23	1	1	.500	0	5	2	0	22	17	14	19	0	3.27
2 John Buzhardt	R	30	0	1	.000	0	7	1	0	12	14	5	7	0	4.50
Mike Adamson	R	19	0	1	.000	0	3	2	0	10	9	12	8	0	8.10
Dave Leonhard	R	25	0	0	.000	1	3	2	0	14	11	6	9	0	3.21

Tom Fisher 24 R 0-0, John Miller 26 R 0-0, Paul Gilliford 22 L 0-0

WASHINGTON 6th (Tie) 76-85 .472 15.5 — GIL HODGES

NAME	G by POS	B	AGE	G	AB	R	H	2B	3B	HR	RBI	BB	SO	SB	BA	SA
TOTALS			26	161	5441	550	1211	168	25	115	521	472	1037	53	.223	.326
2 Mike Epstein	1B80	L	24	96	284	32	65	7	4	9	29	38	74	1	.229	.377
Bernie Allen	2B75	L	28	87	254	13	49	5	1	3	18	18	43	1	.193	.256
Eddie Brinkman	SS109	R	25	109	320	21	60	9	2	1	18	24	58	1	.188	.238
Ken McMullen	3B145	R	25	146	563	73	138	22	2	16	67	46	84	5	.245	.377
Cap Peterson	OF101	R	24	122	405	35	97	17	2	8	46	32	61	0	.240	.351
Fred Valentine	OF136	B	32	151	457	52	107	16	1	11	44	56	76	17	.234	.346
Frank Howard	OF141, 1B4	R	30	149	519	71	133	20	2	36	89	60	**155**	0	.256	.511
Paul Casanova	C137	R	25	141	528	47	131	19	1	9	53	17	65	1	.248	.339
Tim Cullen	SS69, 2B46, 3B15, OF1	R	25	124	402	35	95	7	0	2	31	40	47	4	.236	.269
Hank Allen	OF99	R	26	116	292	34	68	8	4	3	17	13	53	3	.233	.318
Dick Nen	1B65, OF1	L	27	110	238	21	52	7	1	6	29	21	39	0	.218	.332
Bob Saverine	2B48, SS10, 3B8, OF2	B	26	89	233	22	55	13	0	0	8	17	34	8	.236	.292
2 Ed Stroud	OF79	L	27	87	204	36	41	5	3	1	10	25	29	8	.201	.270
1 Jim King	OF31, C1	L	34	47	100	10	21	2	2	1	12	15	13	1	.210	.300
Doug Camilli	C24	R	30	30	82	5	15	1	0	2	5	4	16	0	.183	.268
Bob Chance	1B10	L	26	27	42	5	9	2	0	3	7	7	13	0	.214	.476
1 Ken Harrelson	1B23	R	25	26	79	10	16	0	0	3	10	7	15	0	.203	.316
Frank Coggins	2B19	B	23	19	75	9	23	3	0	1	8	2	17	1	.307	.387

Jim French 25 L 1-16, John Orsino 29 R 0-1

NAME	T	AGE	W	L	PCT	SV	G	GS	CG	IP	H	BB	SO	ShO	ERA
		27	76	85	.472	39	161	161	24	1473	1334	495	878	14	3.38
Camilo Pascual	R	33	12	10	.545	0	28	27	5	165	147	43	106	1	3.27
Phil Ortega	R	27	10	10	.500	0	34	34	5	220	189	57	122	2	3.03
Joe Coleman	R	20	8	9	.471	0	28	22	3	134	154	47	77	0	4.63
Casey Cox	R	25	7	4	.636	1	54	0	0	73	67	21	32	0	2.96
Barry Moore	L	24	7	11	.389	0	27	26	3	144	127	71	74	1	3.75
Bob Humphreys	R	31	6	2	.750	4	48	2	0	100	93	41	54	0	4.16
2 Frank Bertaina	L	23	6	5	.545	0	18	17	4	96	90	37	67	4	2.58
Darold Knowles	L	25	6	8	.429	14	61	1	0	113	91	52	85	0	2.71
Dick Bosman	R	23	3	1	.750	0	7	7	2	51	38	10	25	1	1.76
Bob Priddy	R	27	3	7	.300	4	46	8	1	110	98	33	57	0	3.44
Dave Baldwin	R	29	2	4	.333	12	58	0	0	69	53	20	52	0	1.70
Dick Lines	L	28	2	5	.286	4	54	0	0	86	83	24	54	0	3.35
1 Pete Richert	L	27	2	6	.250	0	11	10	1	54	49	15	41	1	4.15
Buster Narum	R	26	1	0	1.000	0	2	2	0	12	8	4	8	0	3.00
Jim Hannan	R	27	1	1	.500	0	8	2	0	22	28	7	14	0	5.32
Dick Nold	R	24	0	2	.000	0	7	3	0	20	19	13	10	0	4.95

CLEVELAND 8th 75-87 .463 17 — JOE ADCOCK

NAME	G by POS	B	AGE	G	AB	R	H	2B	3B	HR	RBI	BB	SO	SB	BA	SA
TOTALS			28	162	5461	559	1282	213	35	131	514	413	984	53	.235	.359
2 Tony Horton	1B94	R	22	106	363	35	102	13	4	10	44	18	52	3	.281	.421
Vern Fuller	2B64, SS2	R	23	73	206	18	46	10	0	7	21	19	55	2	.223	.374
Larry Brown	SS150	R	27	152	485	38	110	16	2	7	37	53	62	4	.227	.311
Max Alvis	3B161	R	29	161	637	66	163	23	4	21	70	38	107	3	.256	.403
Chuck Hinton	OF136, 2B5	R	33	147	498	55	122	19	3	10	37	43	100	6	.245	.355
Vic Davalillo	OF125	L	30	139	359	47	103	17	5	2	22	10	30	6	.287	.379
Leon Wagner	OF117	L	33	135	433	56	105	15	1	15	54	37	76	3	.242	.386
Joe Azcue	C86	R	27	86	295	33	74	12	5	11	34	22	35	0	.251	.437
Lee Maye	OF77, 2B1	L	32	115	297	43	77	20	4	9	27	26	47	3	.259	.444
Fred Whitfield	1B66	L	29	100	257	24	56	10	0	9	31	25	45	3	.218	.362
C. Salmon	2B31, 1B24, 2B24, SS14, 3B4	R	26	90	203	19	46	13	1	2	19	17	29	10	.227	.330
Duke Sims	C85	L	26	88	272	25	55	8	2	12	37	30	64	3	.202	.379
Pedro Gonzalez	2B64, 1B4, 3B4, SS3	R	28	80	189	19	43	6	0	1	8	12	36	4	.228	.275
1 Rocky Colavito	OF50	R	33	63	191	10	46	9	0	5	21	24	31	2	.241	.366
2 Don Demeter	OF35, 3B1	R	32	51	121	15	25	4	0	5	12	6	16	0	.207	.364
Gus Gil	2B49, 1B1	R	27	51	96	11	11	4	0	0	5	9	18	0	.115	.156
Willie Smith	OF4, 1B3	L	28	21	32	0	7	2	0	0	2	1	10	0	.219	.281
Richie Scheinblum	OF18	B	24	18	66	8	21	4	2	0	6	5	10	0	.318	.439
Jose Vidal	OF10	R	27	16	34	4	4	0	0	0	0	7	12	0	.118	.118

3 Jim King 34 L 3-21, Ray Fosse 20 R 1-16, Gordon Lund 26 R 2-8

NAME	T	AGE	W	L	PCT	SV	G	GS	CG	IP	H	BB	SO	ShO	ERA
		27	75	87	.463	27	162	162	49	1478	1258	559	**1189**	14	3.25
Steve Hargan	R	24	14	13	.519	0	30	29	15	223	180	72	141	**6**	2.62
Sam McDowell	L	24	13	15	.464	0	37	37	10	236	201	**123**	236	1	3.85
Luis Tiant	R	26	12	9	.571	2	33	29	9	214	177	67	219	1	2.73
Sonny Siebert	R	30	10	12	.455	4	34	26	7	185	136	54	136	1	2.38
John O'Donoghue	L	27	8	9	.471	2	33	17	5	131	120	33	81	2	3.23
George Culver	R	23	7	3	.700	3	53	1	0	75	71	31	41	0	3.96
Stan Williams	R	30	6	4	.600	1	16	8	2	79	64	24	75	1	2.62
Ed Connolly	L	27	2	1	.667	0	15	4	0	49	63	34	45	0	7.53
Steve Bailey	R	25	2	5	.286	2	32	1	0	65	62	42	46	0	3.88
1 Gary Bell	R	30	1	5	.167	0	9	9	1	61	50	24	39	0	3.69
Bobby Tiefenauer	R	37	0	1	.000	0	5	0	0	11	9	3	6	0	0.82
Jack Kralick	L	32	0	2	.000	0	2	0	0	2	4	1	1	0	9.00
2 Orlando Pena	R	33	0	3	.000	8	48	1	0	88	67	22	72	0	3.38
Bob Allen	L	29	0	5	.000	5	47	0	0	54	49	25	50	0	3.00
1 Dick Radatz	R	30	0	0	.000	0	3	0	0	3	5	2	1	0	6.00
Tom Kelley (SA)	R	23	0	0	.000	0	1	0	0	1	0	2	0	0	0.00

NEW YORK 9th 72-90 .444 20 — RALPH HOUK

NAME	G by POS	B	AGE	G	AB	R	H	2B	3B	HR	RBI	BB	SO	SB	BA	SA
TOTALS			31	163	5443	522	1225	166	17	100	473	532	**1043**	63	.225	.317
Mickey Mantle	1B131	B	35	144	440	63	108	17	0	22	55	107	113	1	.245	.434
Horace Clarke	2B140	B	27	143	588	74	160	17	0	3	29	42	64	21	.272	.316
Ruben Amaro	SS123, 3B3, 1B2	R	31	130	417	31	93	12	0	1	17	43	49	3	.223	.259
Charley Smith	3B115	R	29	135	425	38	95	15	3	9	38	32	110	0	.224	.336
Steve Whitaker	OF114	L	24	122	441	37	107	12	3	11	50	23	89	2	.243	.358
Joe Pepitone	OF123, 1B6	L	26	133	501	45	126	18	3	13	64	34	62	1	.251	.377
Tom Tresh	OF118	B	29	130	448	45	98	23	3	14	53	50	86	1	.219	.377
Jake Gibbs	C99	L	28	116	374	33	87	7	1	4	25	28	57	7	.233	.289
Bill Robinson	OF102	R	24	116	342	31	67	6	1	7	29	28	56	2	.196	.281
John Kennedy	SS36, 3B34, 2B2	R	26	78	179	22	35	4	0	1	17	17	35	2	.196	.235
Roy White	OF36, 3B17	B	23	70	214	22	48	8	0	2	18	19	25	10	.224	.290
Mike Hegan (MS)	1B54, OF10	L	24	68	118	12	16	4	1	1	3	20	40	7	.136	.212
1 Elston Howard	C48, 1B1	R	38	66	199	13	39	6	0	3	17	12	36	0	.196	.271
Dick Howser (BW)	2B22, 3B12, SS3	R	30	63	149	18	40	6	0	0	10	25	15	1	.268	.309
2 Bob Tillman	C15	R	30	22	63	5	16	1	0	2	9	7	17	0	.254	.365
Jerry Kenney	SS18	L	22	20	58	4	18	2	0	1	5	10	8	2	.310	.397
Ray Barker	1B13	L	31	17	26	2	2	0	0	0	0	3	5	0	.077	.077
Billy Bryan	C1	L	28	16	12	1	2	0	0	1	2	5	3	0	.167	.417
Ross Moschitto	OF6	R	22	14	9	1	1	0	0	0	0	1	2	0	.111	.111
Frank Fernandez (MS)	C7, OF2	R	24	9	28	1	6	2	0	1	4	2	7	1	.214	.393
Tom Shopay	OF7	L	22	8	27	2	8	1	0	2	6	1	5	2	.296	.556

Frank Tepedino 19 L 2-5, Lu Clinton 29 R 2-4, Charlie Sands 19 L 0-1, Bobby Murcer (MS) 21

NAME	T	AGE	W	L	PCT	SV	G	GS	CG	IP	H	BB	SO	ShO	ERA
		27	72	90	.444	27	163	163	37	1481	**1375**	480	898	16	3.24
Mel Stottlemyre	R	25	15	15	.500	0	36	36	10	255	235	88	151	4	2.96
Al Downing	L	26	14	10	.583	0	31	28	10	202	158	61	171	4	2.63
Fritz Peterson	L	25	8	14	.364	0	36	30	6	181	179	43	102	1	3.48
2 Bill Monbouquette	R	30	6	5	.545	1	33	10	2	133	122	17	53	1	2.37
Fred Talbot	R	26	6	8	.429	0	29	22	2	139	132	54	61	0	4.21
2 Steve Barber	L	28	6	9	.400	0	17	17	3	98	103	54	70	1	3.59
Dooley Womack	R	27	5	6	.455	18	65	0	0	97	80	35	57	0	2.41
Joe Verbanic	R	24	4	3	.571	2	28	6	1	80	74	21	39	1	2.81
Thad Tillotson	R	26	3	9	.250	2	43	5	1	98	99	39	62	0	4.04
Steve Hamilton	L	33	2	4	.333	4	44	0	0	62	57	23	55	0	3.48
Whitey Ford	L	38	2	4	.333	0	7	7	2	44	40	9	21	1	1.64
Jim Bouton	R	28	1	0	1.000	0	17	1	0	44	47	18	31	0	4.70
Cecil Perkins	R	26	0	1	.000	0	2	1	0	5	6	2	1	0	9.00
1 Hal Reniff	R	28	0	2	.000	0	24	0	0	40	40	14	24	0	4.28
Dale Roberts	L	25	0	0	.000	0	2	0	0	2	3	2	0	0	9.00

Rich Beck (MS) 26

KANSAS CITY 10th 62-99 .385 29.5 — AL DARK 52-69 .430 LUKE APPLING 10-30 .250

NAME	G by POS	B	AGE	G	AB	R	H	2B	3B	HR	RBI	BB	SO	SB	BA	SA
TOTALS			25	161	5349	533	1244	212	**50**	69	481	452	1019	**132**	.233	.330
Ramon Webster	1B83, OF15	L	24	122	360	41	92	15	4	11	51	32	44	5	.256	.411
John Donaldson	2B101, SS1	L	24	105	377	27	104	16	5	0	28	37	39	6	.276	.345
Bert Campaneris	SS145	R	25	147	601	85	149	29	6	3	32	36	82	**55**	.248	.331
Dick Green	3B59, 2B50, 1B1, SS1	R	26	122	349	26	69	12	4	5	37	30	68	6	.198	.298
Mike Hershberger	OF130	R	27	142	480	55	122	25	1	1	49	38	40	10	.254	.317
Rick Monday	OF113	L	21	124	406	52	102	14	6	14	58	42	107	3	.251	.419
Jim Gosger	OF113	L	24	134	356	31	86	14	5	5	36	53	69	5	.242	.351
Phil Roof	C113	R	26	114	327	23	67	14	5	6	24	23	85	4	.205	.333
Danny Cater	3B56, OF55, 1B44	R	27	142	529	55	143	17	4	4	46	34	56	4	.270	.340
Joe Nossek	OF63	R	26	87	166	12	34	6	1	0	10	4	26	2	.205	.253
2 Ken Harrelson	1B45	R	25	61	174	23	53	11	0	6	30	17	17	8	.305	.471
Ted Kubiak	SS20, 2B10, 3B5	B	25	53	102	6	16	2	1	0	5	12	20	0	.157	.196
Sal Bando	3B44	R	23	47	130	11	25	3	2	0	6	16	24	1	.192	.246
Tim Talton	C22, 1B1	L	28	46	59	7	15	3	1	0	5	7	13	0	.254	.339
1 Roger Repoz	OF31	L	26	40	87	9	21	6	1	2	8	12	20	4	.241	.402
Ken Suarez	C36	R	24	39	63	7	15	5	0	2	9	16	21	1	.238	.413
Ossie Chavarria	2B17, 3B7, OF3, SS2	R	26	38	59	2	6	2	0	0	4	7	16	1	.102	.136
Reggie Jackson	OF34	L	21	35	118	13	21	4	4	1	6	10	46	1	.178	.305
Dave Duncan	C32	R	21	34	101	9	19	4	0	5	11	4	50	0	.188	.376
1 Ed Charles	3B18	R	32	19	61	5	15	1	0	0	5	12	13	1	.246	.262
Joe Rudi	1B9, OF6	R	20	19	43	4	8	2	0	0	1	3	7	0	.186	.233

Allan Lewis 25 B 1-6, Hoss Bowlin 26 R 1-5

NAME	T	AGE	W	L	PCT	SV	G	GS	CG	IP	H	BB	SO	ShO	ERA
		24	62	**99**	.385	34	161	161	26	1428	1265	558	990	10	3.68
Catfish Hunter	R	21	13	17	.433	0	35	35	13	260	209	84	196	5	2.80
Jim Nash	R	22	12	17	.414	0	37	34	8	222	200	87	186	2	3.77
Chuck Dobson	R	23	10	10	.500	0	32	29	4	198	172	75	110	1	3.68
Lew Krausse	R	24	7	17	.292	6	48	19	0	160	140	67	96	0	4.28
Paul Lindblad	L	25	5	8	.385	6	46	10	1	116	106	35	83	1	3.57
Tony Pierce	L	21	3	4	.429	7	49	6	0	98	79	30	61	0	3.03
Diego Segui	R	29	3	4	.429	1	36	3	0	70	62	31	52	0	3.09
Jack Aker	R	26	3	8	.273	12	57	0	0	88	87	32	65	0	4.30
Blue Moon Odom	R	22	3	8	.273	0	29	17	0	104	94	68	67	0	5.02
Bill Edgerton	L	25	1	0	1.000	0	7	0	0	8	11	3	6	0	2.25
Bobby Rodriguez	R	25	1	1	.500	2	15	5	0	40	42	14	29	0	3.60
2 Jack Sanford	R	38	1	2	.333	0	10	1	0	22	24	14	13	0	6.55
Bill Stafford	R	27	0	1	.000	0	14	0	0	16	12	9	10	0	1.69
George Lauzerique	R	19	0	2	.000	0	3	2	0	16	11	6	10	0	2.25
Bob Duliba	R	32	0	0	.000	0	7	0	0	10	13	1	6	0	6.30
Wes Stock	R	33	0	0	.000	0	1	0	0	1	3	2	0	0	18.00

ST. LOUIS 1st 101-60 .627 — RED SCHOENDIENST

NAME	G by POS	B	AGE	G	AB	R	H	2B	3B	HR	RBI	BB	SO	SB	BA	SA
TOTALS			27	161	5566	695	1462	225	40	115	656	443	919	102	.263	.379
Orlando Cepeda	1B151	R	29	151	563	91	183	37	0	25	111	62	75	11	.325	.524
Julian Javier	2B138	R	30	140	520	68	146	16	3	14	64	25	92	6	.281	.404
Dal Maxvill	SS148, 2B7	R	28	152	476	37	108	14	4	1	41	48	66	0	.227	.279
Mike Shannon	3B122, OF6	R	27	130	482	53	118	18	3	12	77	37	89	2	.245	.369
Roger Maris	OF118	L	32	125	410	64	107	18	7	9	55	52	61	0	.261	.405
Curt Flood	OF126	R	29	134	514	68	172	24	1	5	50	37	46	2	.335	.414
Lou Brock	OF157	L	28	159	689	113	206	32	12	21	76	24	109	52	.299	.472
Tim McCarver	C130	L	25	138	471	68	139	26	3	14	69	54	32	8	.295	.452
Bobby Tolan	OF80, 1B13	L	21	110	265	35	67	7	3	6	32	19	43	12	.253	.370
Alex Johnson	OF57	R	24	81	175	20	39	9	2	1	12	9	26	6	.223	.314
Phil Gagliano	2B27, 3B25, 1B4, SS2	R	25	73	217	20	48	7	0	2	21	19	26	0	.221	.281
Ed Spiezio	3B19, OF7	R	25	55	105	9	22	2	0	3	10	7	18	2	.210	.314
Dave Ricketts	C21	B	31	52	99	11	27	8	0	1	14	4	7	0	.273	.384
Ed Bressoud	SS48, 3B1	R	35	52	67	8	9	1	1	1	1	9	18	0	.132	.224
Johnny Romano	C20	R	32	24	58	1	7	1	0	0	2	13	15	1	.121	.138
1 Ted Savage		R	31	9	8	1	1	0	0	0	0	1	3	0	.125	.125

Steve Huntz 21 B 1-6, Jim Williams 23 R 0-2

NAME	T	AGE	W	L	PCT	SV	G	GS	CG	IP	H	BB	SO	ShO	ERA
		28	101	60	.627	45	161	161	44	1465	1313	431	956	17	3.05
Dick Hughes	R	29	16	6	.727	3	37	27	12	222	164	48	161	3	2.68
Nelson Briles	R	23	14	5	.737	6	49	14	4	155	139	40	94	2	2.44
Steve Carlton	L	22	14	9	.609	1	30	28	11	193	173	62	168	2	2.98
Bob Gibson (BL)	R	31	13	7	.650	0	24	24	10	175	151	40	147	2	2.98
Ray Washburn	R	29	10	7	.588	0	27	27	3	186	190	42	98	1	3.53
Al Jackson	L	31	9	4	.692	1	38	11	1	107	117	29	43	1	3.95
Larry Jaster	L	23	9	7	.563	3	34	23	2	152	141	44	87	1	3.02
Ron Willis	R	23	6	5	.545	10	65	0	0	81	76	43	42	0	2.67
Joe Hoerner	L	30	4	4	.500	15	57	0	0	66	52	20	50	0	2.59
3 Jack Lamabe	R	30	3	4	.429	4	23	1	1	48	43	10	30	1	2.81
Hal Woodeshick	L	34	2	1	.667	2	36	0	0	42	41	28	20	0	5.14
Jim Cosman	R	24	1	0	1.000	0	10	5	0	31	21	24	11	0	3.19
Mike Torrez	R	20	0	1	.000	0	3	1	0	6	5	1	5	0	3.00

SAN FRANCISCO 2nd 91-71 .562 10.5 — HERMAN FRANKS

NAME	G by POS	B	AGE	G	AB	R	H	2B	3B	HR	RBI	BB	SO	SB	BA	SA
TOTALS			27	162	5524	652	1354	201	39	140	604	520	978	22	.245	.372
Willie McCovey	1B127	L	29	135	456	73	126	17	4	31	91	71	110	3	.276	.535
Tito Fuentes	2B130, SS5	R	23	133	344	27	72	12	1	5	29	27	61	4	.209	.294
Hal Lanier	SS137, 2B34	R	24	151	525	37	112	16	3	0	42	16	61	2	.213	.255
Jim Ray Hart	3B89, OF72	R	25	158	578	98	167	26	7	29	99	77	100	1	.289	.509
Ollie Brown	OF115	R	23	120	412	44	110	12	1	13	53	25	65	0	.267	.396
Willie Mays	OF134	R	36	141	486	83	128	22	2	22	70	51	92	6	.263	.453
Jay Alou	OF123	R	25	129	510	55	149	15	4	5	30	14	39	1	.292	.367
Tom Haller	C136, OF1	L	30	141	455	54	114	23	5	14	49	62	61	0	.241	.415
Jim Davenport	3B64, SS28, 2B12	R	33	124	295	42	81	10	3	5	30	39	50	1	.275	.380
Jack Hiatt	1B36, C3, OF2	R	24	73	153	24	42	6	0	6	26	27	37	0	.275	.431
Ken Henderson	OF52	B	21	65	179	15	34	3	0	4	14	19	52	0	.190	.274
2 Ty Cline	OF37	L	28	64	122	18	33	5	5	0	4	9	13	2	.270	.393
Bob Schroder	2B45, 3B4	L	22	62	135	20	31	4	0	0	7	15	15	1	.230	.259
Dick Dietz	C43	R	25	56	120	10	27	3	0	4	19	25	44	0	.225	.350
1 Norm Siebern	1B15, OF2	L	33	46	58	6	9	1	1	0	4	14	13	0	.155	.207
Bobby Etheridge	3B37	R	23	40	115	13	26	7	2	1	15	7	12	0	.226	.348
2 Dick Groat	SS24, 2B1	R	36	34	70	4	12	1	1	0	4	6	7	0	.171	.214
Cesar Gutierrez	SS15, 2B1	R	24	18	21	4	3	0	0	0	0	1	4	1	.143	.143
Bill Sorrell	OF5	R	26	18	17	1	3	1	0	0	1	3	2	0	.176	.235
Frank Johnson	OF3	R	24	8	10	3	3	0	0	0	0	1	2	0	.300	.300
Bob Barton	C7	R	25	7	19	0	4	0	0	0	1	0	2	0	.211	.211

Don Mason 22 L 0-3, Dave Marshall 24 L 0-0

NAME	T	AGE	W	L	PCT	SV	G	GS	CG	IP	H	BB	SO	ShO	ERA
		30	91	71	.562	25	162	162	64	1475	1283	453	990	17	2.92
Mike McCormock	L	28	22	10	.688	0	40	35	14	262	220	81	150	5	2.85
Gaylord Perry	R	28	15	17	.469	1	39	37	18	293	231	84	230	3	2.61
Juan Marichal (LJ)	R	29	14	10	.583	0	26	26	18	202	195	42	166	2	2.76
Ray Sadecki	L	26	12	6	.667	0	35	24	10	188	165	58	145	2	2.78
Frank Linzy	R	26	7	7	.500	17	57	0	0	96	67	34	38	0	1.50
Joe Gibbon	L	32	6	2	.750	1	28	10	3	82	65	33	63	1	3.07
Bobby Bolin	R	28	6	8	.429	0	37	15	0	120	120	50	69	0	4.88
Ron Herbel	R	29	4	5	.444	1	42	11	1	126	125	35	52	1	3.07
Bill Henry	L	39	2	0	1.000	2	28	1	0	22	16	9	23	0	2.05
Lindy McDaniel	R	31	2	6	.250	3	41	3	0	73	69	24	48	0	3.70
Nestor Chavez	R	19	1	0	1.000	0	2	0	0	5	4	3	3	0	0.00
Rich Robertson	R	22	0	0	.000	0	1	0	0	2	3	0	1	0	4.50
Ron Bryant	L	19	0	0	.000	0	1	0	0	4	3	0	2	0	4.50

CHICAGO 3rd 87-74 .540 14 — LEO DUROCHER

NAME	G by POS	B	AGE	G	AB	R	H	2B	3B	HR	RBI	BB	SO	SB	BA	SA
TOTALS			28	162	5463	702	1373	211	49	128	642	509	912	63	.251	.378
Ernie Banks	1B47	R	36	151	573	68	158	26	4	23	95	27	93	2	.276	.455
Glenn Beckert	2B144	R	26	146	597	91	167	32	3	5	40	30	25	10	.280	.369
Don Kessinger	SS143	B	24	145	580	61	134	10	7	0	42	33	80	6	.231	.272
Ron Santo	3B161	R	27	161	586	107	176	23	4	31	98	96	103	1	.300	.512
2 Ted Savage	OF86, 3B1	R	31	96	225	40	49	10	1	5	33	40	54	7	.218	.338
Adolfo Phillips	OF141	R	25	144	448	66	120	20	7	17	70	80	93	24	.268	.458
Billy Williams	OF162	L	29	162	634	92	176	21	12	28	84	68	67	6	.278	.481
Randy Hundley	C152	R	25	152	539	68	144	25	3	14	60	44	75	2	.267	.403
Lee Thomas	OF43, 1B10	L	31	77	191	16	42	4	1	2	23	15	22	1	.220	.283
Al Spangler	OF41	L	33	62	130	18	33	7	0	0	13	23	17	2	.254	.308
Clarence Jones	OF31, 1B13	L	23	53	135	13	34	7	0	2	16	14	33	0	.252	.348
Paul Popovich	SS31, 2B17, 3B2	R	26	49	159	18	34	4	0	0	2	9	12	0	.214	.239
Norm Gigon	2B12, OF4, 3B1	R	29	34	70	8	12	3	1	1	6	4	14	0	.171	.286
John Boccabella	OF9, 1B3, C1	R	26	25	35	0	6	1	1	0	8	3	7	0	.171	.257
Johnny Stephenson	C13	L	26	18	49	3	11	3	1	0	5	1	6	0	.224	.327
George Altman	OF4, 1B1	L	34	15	18	1	2	2	0	0	1	2	8	0	.111	.222
Byron Browne	OF8	R	24	10	19	3	3	2	0	0	2	4	5	1	.158	.263
Bob Raudman	OF8	L	25	8	26	0	4	0	0	0	1	1	4	0	.154	.154
1 Jimmy Stewart		B	28	6	6	1	1	0	0	0	1	0	0	0	.167	.167
Dick Bertell	C2	R	31	2	6	1	1	0	1	0	0	0	1	0	.167	.500

Joe Campbell 23 R 0-3, Joey Amalfitano 33 R 0-1

NAME	T	AGE	W	L	PCT	SV	G	GS	CG	IP	H	BB	SO	ShO	ERA
		26	87	74	.540	28	162	162	47	1457	1352	463	888	7	3.48
Ferguson Jenkins	R	23	20	13	.606	0	38	38	20	289	230	83	236	3	2.80
Rich Nye	L	22	13	10	.565	0	35	30	7	205	179	52	119	0	3.20
Joe Niekro	R	22	10	7	.588	0	36	22	7	170	171	32	77	2	3.34
Ken Holtzman (MS)	L	21	9	0	1.000	0	12	12	3	93	76	44	62	0	2.52
Chuck Hartenstein	R	25	9	5	.643	10	45	0	0	73	74	17	20	0	3.08
Ray Culp	R	25	8	11	.421	0	30	22	4	153	138	59	111	1	3.88
Bill Hands	R	27	7	8	.467	6	49	11	3	150	134	48	84	1	2.46
1 Curt Simmons	L	38	3	7	.300	0	17	14	3	82	100	23	31	0	4.94
1 Bob Hendley	L	28	2	0	1.000	1	7	0	0	12	17	3	10	0	6.75
1 Cal Koonce	R	26	2	2	.500	2	34	0	0	51	52	21	28	0	4.59
Bill Stoneman	R	23	2	4	.333	4	28	2	0	63	51	22	52	0	3.29
2 Dick Radatz	R	30	1	0	1.000	5	20	0	0	23	12	24	18	0	6.65
Jim Ellis	L	22	1	1	.500	0	8	1	0	17	20	9	8	0	3.18
John Upham	L	25	0	1	.000	0	5	0	0	1	4	2	2	0	45.00
Rick James	R	19	0	1	.000	0	3	1	0	5	9	2	2	0	12.60
Rob Gardner	L	22	0	2	.000	0	18	5	0	32	33	6	16	0	3.94
2 Bob Shaw	R	34	0	2	.000	0	9	3	0	22	33	9	7	0	6.14
2 Pete Mikkelsen	R	27	0	0	.000	0	7	0	0	7	9	5	0	0	6.43
Don Larsen	R	37	0	0	.000	0	3	0	0	4	5	2	1	0	9.00
Dick Calmus	R	23	0	0	.000	0	1	1	0	4	5	0	1	0	9.00
Fred Norman	L	24	0	0	.000	0	1	0	0	1	0	0	3	0	0.00

CINCINNATI 4th 87-75 .537 14.5 — DAVE BRISTOL

NAME	G by POS	B	AGE	G	AB	R	H	2B	3B	HR	RBI	BB	SO	SB	BA	SA
TOTALS			27	162	5519	604	1366	251	54	109	560	372	969	92	.248	.372
Lee May	1B81, OF48	R	24	127	438	54	116	29	2	12	57	19	80	4	.265	.422
Tommy Helms	2B88, SS46	R	26	137	497	40	136	27	4	2	35	24	41	5	.274	.356
Leo Cardenas (BH)	SS108	R	28	108	379	30	97	14	3	2	21	34	77	4	.256	.325
Tony Perez	3B139, 1B18, 2B1	R	25	156	600	78	174	28	7	26	102	33	102	0	.290	.490
Tommy Harper (BW)	OF100	R	26	103	365	55	82	17	3	7	22	43	51	23	.225	.345
Vada Pinson	OF157	L	28	158	650	90	187	28	13	18	66	26	86	26	.288	.454
Pete Rose	OF123, 2B35	B	26	148	585	86	176	32	8	12	76	56	66	11	.301	.444
Johnny Edwards	C73	L	29	80	209	10	43	6	0	2	20	16	28	1	.206	.263
Deron Johnson	1B81, 3B24	R	28	108	361	39	81	18	1	13	53	22	104	0	.224	.388
Chico Ruiz	2B56, 3B13, SS11, OF5	B	28	105	250	32	55	12	4	0	13	11	35	9	.220	.300
Art Shamsky	OF40	L	25	76	147	6	29	3	1	3	13	15	34	0	.197	.293
Don Pavletich	C66, 1B6, 3B1	R	28	74	231	25	55	14	3	6	34	21	38	2	.238	.403
Floyd Robinson	OF39	L	31	55	130	19	31	6	2	1	10	14	14	3	.238	.338
Jimmie Coker	C34	R	31	45	97	8	18	2	1	2	4	4	20	0	.186	.289
Dick Simpson	OF26	R	23	44	54	8	14	3	0	1	6	7	11	0	.259	.370
Johnny Bench	C26	R	19	26	86	7	14	3	1	1	6	5	19	0	.163	.256
2 Jake Wood	OF2	R	30	16	17	1	2	0	0	0	1	1	3	0	.118	.118
Gordy Coleman	1B2	L	32	4	7	0	0	0	0	0	0	1	0	0	.000	.000
Len Boehmer	2B1	R	26	2	3	0	0	0	0	0	0	0	0	0	.000	.000

NAME	T	AGE	W	L	PCT	SV	G	GS	CG	IP	H	BB	SO	ShO	ERA
		27	87	75	.537	39	162	162	34	1468	1328	498	1065	18	3.05
Milt Pappas	R	28	16	13	.552	0	34	32	5	218	218	38	129	3	3.34
Jim Maloney	R	27	15	11	.577	0	30	29	6	196	181	72	153	3	3.26
Gary Nolan	R	19	14	8	.636	0	33	32	8	227	193	62	206	5	2.58
Mel Queen	R	25	14	8	.636	0	31	24	6	196	155	52	154	2	2.76
Sammy Ellis	R	26	8	11	.421	0	32	27	8	176	197	67	80	1	3.84
Ted Abernathy	R	34	6	3	.667	28	70	0	0	106	63	41	88	0	1.27
Jerry Arrigo	L	26	6	6	.500	1	32	5	1	74	61	35	56	1	3.16
2 Bob Lee	R	29	3	3	.500	2	27	1	0	51	51	25	33	0	4.41
Billy McCool	L	22	3	7	.300	2	31	11	0	97	92	56	83	0	3.43
Ted Davidson (PB)	L	27	1	0	1.000	0	9	0	0	13	13	3	6	0	4.15
John Tsitouris	R	31	1	0	1.000	0	2	1	0	8	4	6	4	0	3.38
Darrell Osteen	R	24	0	2	.000	2	10	0	0	14	10	13	13	0	6.43
Don Nottebart	R	31	0	3	.000	4	47	0	0	79	75	19	48	0	1.94
Jack Baldschun	R	30	0	0	.000	0	9	0	0	13	15	9	12	0	4.15

PHILADELPHIA 5th 82-80 .506 19.5 — GENE MAUCH

NAME	G by POS	B	AGE	G	AB	R	H	2B	3B	HR	RBI	BB	SO	SB	BA	SA
TOTALS			28	162	5401	612	1306	221	47	103	553	545	1033	79	.242	.357
Bill White (FJ)	1B95	L	33	110	308	29	77	6	2	8	33	52	61	6	.250	.360
C. Rojas	2B137, OF9, C3, SS2, 3B1, P1	R	28	147	528	60	137	21	2	4	45	30	58	8	.259	.330
Bobby Wine	SS134, 1B2	R	28	135	363	27	69	12	5	2	28	29	77	3	.190	.267
Dick Allen (NJ)	3B121, 2B1, SS1	R	25	122	463	89	142	31	10	23	77	75	117	20	.307	.566
Johnny Callison	OF147	L	28	149	556	62	145	30	5	14	64	56	63	6	.261	.400
Johnny Briggs	OF94	L	23	106	332	47	77	12	4	9	30	41	72	3	.232	.373
Tony Gonzalez	OF143	L	30	149	508	74	172	23	9	9	59	47	58	10	.339	.472
Clay Dalrymple	C97	L	30	101	268	12	46	7	1	3	21	36	49	1	.172	.239
Tony Taylor	1B58, 3B44, 2B42, SS3	R	31	132	462	55	110	16	6	2	34	42	74	10	.238	.312
Don Lock	OF97	R	30	112	313	46	79	13	1	14	51	43	98	9	.252	.435
Gary Sutherland	SS66, OF25	R	22	103	231	23	57	12	1	1	19	17	22	0	.247	.320
2 Gene Oliver	C79, 1B2	R	31	85	263	29	59	16	0	7	34	29	56	2	.224	.365
Doug Clemens	OF10	R	28	69	73	2	13	5	0	0	4	8	15	0	.178	.247
Billy Cowan	OF20, 2B1, 3B1	R	28	34	59	11	9	0	0	3	6	4	14	1	.153	.305
2 Chuck Hiller	2B6	L	32	31	43	4	13	1	0	0	2	2	4	0	.302	.326
1 Tito Francona	1B24, OF1	L	33	27	73	7	15	1	0	0	3	7	10	0	.205	.219
1 Phil Linz	SS7, 3B1	R	28	23	18	4	4	2	0	1	5	2	1	0	.222	.500
1 Bob Uecker	C17	R	32	18	35	3	6	2	0	0	7	5	9	0	.171	.229
Rick Joseph	1B13	R	27	17	41	4	9	2	0	1	5	4	10	0	.220	.341
1 Jackie Brandt	OF3	R	33	16	19	1	2	1	0	0	1	0	6	0	.105	.158
1 Dick Groat	SS6	R	36	10	26	3	3	0	0	0	1	4	4	0	.115	.115

Jimmie Schaffer 31 R 0-2, Terry Harmon 23 R 0-0

NAME	T	AGE	W	L	PCT	SV	G	GS	CG	IP	H	BB	SO	ShO	ERA
		30	82	80	.506	23	162	162	46	1453	1372	403	967	17	3.10
Jim Bunning	R	35	17	15	.531	0	40	40	16	302	241	73	253	6	2.29
Larry Jackson	R	36	13	15	.464	0	40	37	11	262	242	54	139	4	3.09
Rick Wise	R	21	11	11	.500	0	36	25	6	181	177	45	111	3	3.28
Dick Hall	R	36	10	8	.556	8	48	1	1	86	83	12	49	0	2.20
2 Dick Farrell	R	33	9	6	.600	12	50	1	0	92	76	15	68	0	2.05
Chris Short (KJ)	L	29	9	11	.450	1	29	26	8	199	163	74	142	2	2.40
Dick Ellsworth	L	27	6	7	.462	0	32	21	3	125	152	36	45	1	4.39
John Boozer	R	27	5	4	.556	1	28	7	1	75	86	24	48	0	4.08
Grant Jackson	L	24	2	3	.400	1	43	4	0	84	86	43	83	0	3.86
Dallas Green	R	32	0	0	.000	0	8	0	0	15	25	6	12	0	9.00
Ruben Gomez	R	39	0	0	.000	0	7	0	0	11	8	7	9	0	4.09
Pedro Ramos	R	32	0	0	.000	0	6	0	0	8	14	8	1	0	9.00
Larry Loughlin	L	25	0	0	.000	0	3	0	0	5	9	4	6	0	16.20
Bob Buhl	R	38	0	0	.000	0	3	0	0	3	6	2	1	0	12.00
Gary Wagner	R	27	0	0	.000	0	1	0	0	2	1	0	1	0	0.00
Dick Thoenen	R	23	0	0	.000	0	1	0	0	1	2	0	0	0	9.00
Cookie Rojas	R	28	0	0	.000	0	1	0	0	1	1	0	0	0	0.00

PITTSBURGH 6th 81-81 .500 20.5 — **HARRY WALKER 42-42 .500 DANNY MURTAUGH 39-39 .500**

NAME	G by POS	B	AGE	G	AB	R	H	2B	3B	HR	RBI	BB	SO	SB	BA	SA
TOTALS			29	163	5724	679	1585	193	62	91	615	387	914	79	.277	.380
Donn Clendenon	1B123	R	31	131	478	46	119	15	2	13	56	34	107	4	.249	.370
Bill Mazeroski	2B163	R	30	163	639	62	167	25	3	9	77	30	55	1	.261	.352
Gene Alley	SS146	R	26	152	550	59	158	25	7	6	55	36	70	10	.287	.391
Maury Wills	3B144, SS2	B	34	149	616	92	186	12	9	3	45	31	44	29	.302	.365
Roberto Clemente	OF145	R	32	147	585	103	209	26	10	23	110	41	103	9	.357	.554
Matty Alou	OF134, 1B1	L	28	139	550	87	186	21	7	2	28	24	42	16	.338	.413
Willie Stargell	OF98, 1B37	L	27	134	462	54	125	18	6	20	73	67	103	1	.271	.465
Jerry May	C110	R	23	110	325	23	88	13	2	3	22	36	55	0	.271	.351
Manny Mota	OF99, 3B2	R	29	120	349	53	112	14	8	4	56	14	46	3	.321	.441
Jose Pagan	3B25, OF23, SS16, 2B2, C1	R	32	81	211	17	61	6	2	1	19	10	28	1	.289	.351
2 Al Luplow	OF25	L	28	55	103	13	19	1	0	1	8	6	14	1	.184	.223
Manny Jimenez	OF6	L	28	50	56	3	14	2	0	2	10	1	4	0	.250	.393
Andre Rodgers	1B9, 3B5, SS3, 2B2	R	32	47	61	8	14	3	0	2	4	8	18	1	.230	.377
Jim Pagliaroni (XJ)	C38	R	29	44	100	4	20	1	1	0	9	16	26	0	.200	.230
George Spriggs	OF13	L	26	38	57	14	10	1	1	0	5	6	20	3	.175	.228
Manny Sanguillen	C28	R	23	30	96	6	26	4	0	0	8	4	12	0	.271	.313
Jesse Gonder	C18	L	31	22	36	4	5	1	0	0	3	5	9	0	.139	.167
Bob Robertson	1B9	R	20	9	35	4	6	0	0	2	4	3	12	0	.171	.343

NAME	T	AGE	W	L	PCT	SV	G	GS	CG	IP	H	BB	SO	ShO	ERA
		30	81	81	.500	35	163	163	35	1458	1439	561	820	5	3.74
Bob Veale	L	31	16	8	.667	0	33	31	6	203	184	119	179	1	3.64
Tommie Sisk	R	25	13	13	.500	1	37	31	11	208	196	78	85	2	3.33
Dennis Ribant	R	25	9	8	.529	0	38	22	2	172	186	40	75	0	4.08
Juan Pizarro	L	30	8	10	.444	9	50	9	1	107	99	52	96	1	3.95
Al McBean	R	29	7	4	.636	4	51	8	5	131	118	43	54	0	2.54
Roy Face	R	39	7	5	.583	17	61	0	0	74	62	22	41	0	2.43
Steve Blass	R	25	6	8	.429	0	32	16	2	127	126	47	72	0	3.54
Billy O'Dell	L	34	5	6	.455	0	27	11	1	87	88	41	34	0	5.79
Woodie Fryman	L	27	3	8	.273	1	28	18	3	113	121	44	74	1	4.06
Bruce Dal Canton	R	25	2	1	.667	0	8	2	1	24	19	10	13	0	1.88
Vern Law	R	37	2	6	.250	0	25	10	1	97	122	18	43	0	4.18
Bob Moose	R	19	1	0	1.000	0	2	2	1	15	14	4	7	0	3.60
Jim Shellenback	L	23	1	1	.500	0	6	2	1	23	23	12	11	0	2.74
1 Pete Mikkelsen	R	27	1	2	.333	2	32	0	0	56	50	19	30	0	4.34
John Gelnar	R	24	0	1	.000	0	10	1	0	19	30	11	5	0	8.05
Bill Short	L	29	0	0	.000	1	6	0	0	2	1	1	1	0	4.50

ATLANTA 7th 77-85 .475 24.5 — **BILLY HITCHCOCK 77-82 .484 KEN SILVESTRI 0-3 .000**

NAME	G by POS	B	AGE	G	AB	R	H	2B	3B	HR	RBI	BB	SO	SB	BA	SA
TOTALS			29	162	5450	631	1307	191	29	158	596	512	947	55	.240	.372
Felipe Alou	1B85, OF5	R	32	140	574	76	157	26	3	15	43	32	50	6	.274	.408
Woody Woodward	2B120, SS16	R	24	136	429	30	97	15	2	0	25	37	51	0	.226	.270
Denis Menke	SS124, 3B3	R	26	129	418	37	95	14	3	7	39	65	62	5	.227	.325
Clete Boyer	3B150, SS6	R	30	154	572	63	140	18	3	26	96	39	81	6	.245	.423
Hank Aaron	OF152, 2B1	R	33	155	600	113	184	37	3	39	109	63	97	17	.307	.573
Mack Jones	OF126	L	28	140	454	72	115	23	4	17	50	64	108	10	.253	.434
Rico Carty	OF112, 1B9	R	28	134	444	41	113	16	2	15	64	49	70	4	.255	.401
Joe Torre	C114, 1B23	R	26	135	477	67	132	18	1	20	68	49	75	2	.277	.444
2 Tito Francona	1B56, OF6	L	33	82	254	28	63	5	1	6	25	20	34	1	.248	.346
Mike de la Hoz	2B23, 3B22, SS1	R	27	74	143	10	29	3	0	3	14	4	14	1	.203	.287
Gary Geiger	OF38	L	30	69	117	17	19	1	1	1	5	20	35	1	.162	.214
2 Bob Uecker	C59	R	32	62	158	14	23	2	0	3	13	19	51	0	.146	.215
2 Charlie Lau		L	34	52	45	3	9	1	0	1	5	4	9	0	.200	.289
Marty Martinez	SS25, 2B9, C3, 3B2, 1B1	B	25	44	73	14	21	2	1	0	5	11	11	0	.288	.342
Felix Millan	2B41	R	23	41	136	13	32	3	3	2	6	4	10	0	.235	.346
1 Gene Oliver	C14	R	31	17	51	8	10	2	0	3	6	6	8	0	.196	.412
Angel Hermoso	SS9, 2B2	R	20	11	26	3	8	0	0	0	0	2	4	1	.308	.308
Dave Nicholson	OF7	R	27	10	25	2	5	0	0	0	1	2	9	0	.200	.200
Mike Lum	OF6	L	21	9	26	1	6	0	0	0	1	1	4	0	.231	.231

Clarence Gaston 23 R 3-25, 1 Ty Cline (LJ) 28 L 0-8, Glen Clark 26 B 0-4, Jim Beauchamp 27 R 0-3

NAME	T	AGE	W	L	PCT	SV	G	GS	CG	IP	H	BB	SO	ShO	ERA
		28	77	85	.475	32	162	162	35	1454	1377	449	862	5	3.47
Pat Jarvis	R	26	15	10	.600	0	32	30	7	194	195	62	118	1	3.66
Ken Johnson	R	34	13	9	.591	0	29	29	6	210	191	38	85	0	2.74
Phil Niekro	R	28	11	9	.550	9	46	20	10	207	164	55	129	1	1.87
Denny Lemaster	L	28	9	9	.500	0	31	31	8	215	184	72	148	2	3.35
Clay Carroll	R	26	6	12	.333	0	42	7	1	93	111	29	35	0	5.52
2 Claude Raymond	R	30	4	1	.800	5	28	0	0	34	33	11	14	0	2.06
Jay Ritchie	R	30	4	6	.400	2	52	0	0	82	75	29	57	0	3.18
Tony Cloninger (IL)	R	26	4	7	.364	0	16	16	1	77	85	31	55	0	5.14
Ed Rakow	R	31	3	2	.600	0	17	3	0	39	36	15	25	0	5.31
Cecil Upshaw	R	24	2	3	.400	8	30	0	0	45	42	8	31	0	2.60
Bob Bruce	R	34	2	3	.400	1	12	7	1	39	42	15	22	0	4.85
Dick Kelley	L	27	2	9	.182	2	39	9	1	98	88	42	75	1	3.77
1 Wade Blasingame	L	23	1	0	1.000	0	10	4	0	25	27	21	20	0	4.68
Ron Reed	R	24	1	1	.500	0	3	3	0	21	21	3	11	0	3.00
Ramon Hernandez	L	26	0	2	.000	5	46	0	0	52	60	14	28	0	4.15
Jim Britton	R	23	0	2	.000	0	2	2	0	13	15	2	4	0	6.23
George Stone	L	21	0	0	.000	0	2	1	0	7	8	1	5	0	5.14
Don Schwall	R	31	0	0	.000	0	1	0	0	1	0	1	0	0	0.00

LOS ANGELES 8th 73-89 .451 28.5 — **WALT ALSTON**

NAME	G by POS	B	AGE	G	AB	R	H	2B	3B	HR	RBI	BB	SO	SB	BA	SA
TOTALS			28	162	5456	519	1285	203	38	82	465	485	881	56	.236	.332
Wes Parker	1B112, OF18	B	27	139	413	56	102	16	5	5	31	65	83	10	.247	.346
Ron Hunt	2B90, 3B8	R	26	110	388	44	102	17	3	3	33	39	24	2	.263	.345
Gene Michael	SS83	B	29	98	223	20	45	3	1	0	7	11	30	1	.202	.224
Jim Lefebvre	3B92, 2B34, 1B5	B	24	136	494	51	129	18	5	8	50	44	64	1	.261	.366
Ron Fairly	OF97, 1B68	L	28	153	486	45	107	19	0	10	55	54	51	1	.220	.321
Willie Davis	OF138	L	27	143	569	65	146	27	9	6	41	29	65	20	.257	.367
Lou Johnson (BL)	OF91	R	32	104	330	39	89	14	1	11	41	24	52	4	.270	.418
Johnny Roseboro	C107	L	34	116	334	37	91	18	2	4	24	38	33	2	.272	.374
Al Ferrara	OF94	R	27	122	347	41	96	16	1	16	50	33	73	0	.277	.467
Bob Bailey	3B65, OF27, 1B4, SS1	R	24	116	322	21	73	8	2	4	28	40	50	5	.227	.301
2 Len Gabrielson	OF68	L	27	90	238	20	62	10	3	7	29	15	41	3	.261	.416
Dick Schofield	SS69, 2B4, 3B2	B	32	84	232	23	50	10	1	2	15	31	40	1	.216	.293
Nate Oliver	2B39, SS32, OF1	R	26	77	232	18	55	6	2	0	7	13	50	3	.237	.280
Jeff Torborg	C75	R	25	76	196	11	42	4	1	2	12	13	31	1	.214	.276
Jim Hickman	OF37, 1B2, 3B2, P1	R	30	65	98	7	16	6	1	0	10	14	28	1	.163	.245
Jim Campanis	C23	R	23	41	62	3	10	1	0	2	2	9	14	0	.161	.274
Luis Alcaraz	2B17	R	26	17	60	1	14	1	0	0	3	1	13	1	.233	.250

Tommy Dean 21 R 4-28, 1 Johnny Werhas 29 R 1-7, Willie Crawford 20 L 1-4

NAME	T	AGE	W	L	PCT	SV	G	GS	CG	IP	H	BB	SO	ShO	ERA
		28	73	89	.451	24	162	162	41	1473	1421	393	967	17	3.21
Claude Osteen	L	27	17	17	.500	0	39	39	14	288	298	52	152	5	3.22
Don Drysdale	R	30	13	16	.448	0	38	38	9	282	269	60	196	3	2.74
Bill Singer	R	23	12	8	.600	0	32	29	7	204	185	61	169	3	2.65
Don Sutton	R	22	11	15	.423	1	37	34	11	233	223	57	169	3	3.94
Ron Perranoski	L	31	6	7	.462	16	70	0	0	110	97	45	75	0	2.45
Phil Regan	R	30	6	9	.400	6	55	3	0	96	108	32	53	0	3.00
Jim Brewer	L	29	5	4	.556	1	30	11	0	101	78	31	74	0	2.67
Bob Miller	R	28	2	9	.182	0	52	4	0	86	88	27	32	0	4.29
Dick Egan	L	30	1	1	.500	0	20	0	0	32	34	15	20	0	6.19
Alan Foster	R	20	0	1	.000	0	4	2	0	17	10	3	15	0	2.12
John Duffie	R	21	0	2	.000	0	2	2	0	10	11	4	6	0	2.70
Joe Moeller	R	24	0	0	.000	0	6	0	0	5	9	3	2	0	9.00
1 Bob Lee	R	29	0	0	.000	0	4	0	0	7	6	3	2	0	5.14
Bruce Brubaker	R	25	0	0	.000	0	1	0	0	1	3	0	2	0	27.00
Jim Hickman	R	30	0	0	.000	0	1	0	0	2	2	0	0	0	4.50
Sandy Koufax (RJ)		31													

HOUSTON 9th 69-93 .426 32.5 — **GRADY HATTON**

NAME	G by POS	B	AGE	G	AB	R	H	2B	3B	HR	RBI	BB	SO	SB	BA	SA
TOTALS			25	162	5506	626	1372	259	46	93	581	537	934	88	.249	.364
1 Eddie Mathews	1B79, 3B24	L	35	101	328	39	78	13	2	10	38	48	65	2	.238	.381
Joe Morgan	2B130, OF1	L	23	133	494	73	136	27	11	6	42	81	51	29	.275	.411
Sonny Jackson	SS128	L	22	129	520	67	123	18	3	0	25	36	45	22	.237	.283
Bob Aspromonte	3B133	R	29	137	486	51	143	24	5	6	58	45	44	2	.294	.401
Rusty Staub	OF144	L	23	149	546	71	182	44	1	10	74	60	47	0	.333	.473
Jim Wynn	OF157	R	25	158	594	102	148	29	3	37	107	74	137	16	.249	.495
Ron Davis	OF80	R	25	94	285	31	73	19	1	7	38	17	48	5	.256	.404
John Bateman	C71	R	24	76	252	16	48	9	0	2	17	17	53	0	.190	.250
Ron Brand	C67, 2B1, OF1	R	27	84	215	22	52	8	1	0	18	23	17	4	.242	.288
Julio Gotay	2B30, SS20, 3B3	R	28	77	234	30	66	10	2	2	15	15	30	1	.282	.368
Chuck Harrison	1B59	R	26	70	177	13	43	7	3	2	26	13	30	0	.243	.350
Norm Miller (MS)	OF53	L	21	64	190	15	39	9	3	1	14	19	42	2	.205	.300
3 Jim Landis	OF44	R	33	50	143	19	36	11	1	1	14	20	35	2	.252	.364
Doug Rader	1B36, 3B7	R	22	47	162	24	54	10	4	2	26	7	31	0	.333	.481
2 Jackie Brandt	1B14, OF6, 3B1	R	33	41	89	7	21	4	1	1	15	8	9	0	.236	.337
Dave Adlesh	C31	R	23	39	94	4	17	1	0	1	4	11	28	0	.181	.223
Bob Lillis	SS23, 2B3, 3B2	R	37	37	82	3	20	1	0	0	5	1	8	0	.244	.256
Aaron Pointer	OF22	R	25	27	70	6	11	4	0	1	10	13	26	1	.157	.257
Lee Bales	2B6, SS1	B	22	19	27	4	3	0	0	0	2	8	7	1	.111	.111
Hal King	C11	L	23	15	44	2	11	1	2	0	6	2	9	0	.250	.364

Ivan Murrell 22 R 9-29, Bob Watson 21 R 3-14, 1 Bill Heath 28 L 1-11, Joe Herrara 25 R 1-4, Alonzo Hatris 19 B 0-1

NAME	T	AGE	W	L	PCT	SV	G	GS	CG	IP	H	BB	SO	ShO	ERA
		27	69	93	.426	21	162	162	35	1446	1444	485	1060	8	4.03
Mike Cuellar	L	30	16	11	.593	1	36	32	16	246	233	63	203	3	3.04
Dave Giusti	R	27	11	15	.423	1	37	33	8	222	231	58	157	1	4.18
Don Wilson	R	22	10	9	.526	0	31	28	7	184	141	69	159	3	2.79
Dave Eilers	R	30	6	4	.600	1	35	0	0	59	68	17	27	0	3.97
Larry Dierker (MS)	R	20	6	5	.545	0	15	15	4	99	95	25	68	0	3.36
2 Wade Blasingame	L	23	4	7	.364	0	15	14	0	77	91	27	46	0	5.96
Danny Coombs	L	25	3	0	1.000	0	6	2	0	24	21	9	23	0	3.38
Barry Latman	R	31	3	6	.333	0	39	1	0	78	73	34	70	0	4.50
Bo Belinsky	L	30	3	9	.250	0	27	18	0	115	112	54	80	0	4.70
Carroll Sembera	R	25	2	6	.250	3	45	0	0	60	66	19	48	0	4.80
1 Dick Farrell	R	33	1	0	1.000	0	7	0	0	12	11	7	10	0	4.50
Pat House	L	26	1	0	1.000	1	6	0	0	4	3	0	2	0	4.50
Howie Reed	R	30	1	1	.500	0	4	2	0	18	19	2	9	0	3.50
2 Larry Sherry	R	31	1	2	.333	6	29	0	0	41	53	13	32	0	4.83
Chris Zachary	R	23	1	6	.143	0	9	7	0	36	42	12	18	0	5.75
Jim Owens	R	33	0	1	.000	0	10	0	0	11	12	2	6	0	4.09
Dan Schneider	R	24	0	2	.000	2	54	0	0	53	60	27	39	0	4.92
Tom Dukes	R	24	0	2	.000	1	17	0	0	24	25	11	23	0	5.25
Bruce Von Hoff	R	23	0	3	.000	0	10	10	0	50	52	28	22	0	4.86
1 Claude Raymond	R	30	0	4	.000	5	21	0	0	31	31	7	17	0	3.19

John Buzhardt R 30 0-0, Arnie Earley L 34 0-0

NEW YORK 10th 61-101 .377 40.5 — **WES WESTRUM 57-94 .377 SALTY PARKER 4-7 .364**

NAME	G by POS	B	AGE	G	AB	R	H	2B	3B	HR	RBI	BB	SO	SB	BA	SA
TOTALS			27	162	5417	498	1288	178	23	83	461	362	981	58	.238	.325
Ed Kranepool	1B139	L	22	141	469	37	126	17	1	10	54	37	51	0	.269	.373
Jerry Buchek	2B95, 3B17, SS9	R	25	124	411	35	97	11	2	14	41	26	101	3	.236	.375
Bud Harrelson	SS149	B	23	151	540	59	137	16	4	1	28	48	64	12	.254	.304
2 Ed Charles	3B89	R	32	101	323	32	77	13	2	3	31	24	58	4	.238	.319
Ron Swoboda	OF108, 1B20	R	23	134	449	47	126	17	3	13	53	41	96	3	.281	.419
Cleon Jones	OF115	R	24	129	411	46	101	10	5	5	30	19	57	12	.246	.331
Tommy Davis	OF149, 1B1	R	28	154	577	72	174	32	0	16	73	31	71	9	.302	.440
Jerry Grote	C119	R	24	120	344	25	67	8	0	4	23	14	65	2	.195	.253
Tommie Reynolds	OF72, 3B5, C1	B	25	101	136	16	28	1	0	2	9	11	26	1	.206	.257
2 Bob Johnson	2B39, 1B23, SS14, 3B1	R	31	90	230	26	80	8	3	5	27	12	29	1	.348	.474
Larry Stahl	OF43	L	26	71	155	9	37	5	0	1	18	8	25	2	.239	.290
John Sullivan	C57	R	26	65	147	4	32	5	0	0	6	6	13	0	.218	.252
1 Ken Boyer	3B44, 1B8	R	36	56	166	17	39	7	2	3	13	26	22	2	.235	.355
Don Bosch	OF39	B	24	44	93	7	13	0	1	0	2	5	24	3	.140	.161
1 Al Luplow	OF33	L	28	41	112	11	23	1	0	3	9	8	19	0	.205	.295
Greg Goossen	C23	R	21	37	69	2	11	1	0	0	3	4	26	0	.159	.174
1 Chuck Hiller (RJ)	2B14	L	32	25	54	0	5	3	0	0	3	2	11	0	.093	.148
2 Phil Linz	2B11, SS8, 3B1, OF1	R	28	24	58	8	12	2	0	0	1	4	10	0	.207	.241
Amos Otis	OF16, 3B1	R	20	19	59	6	13	2	0	0	1	5	13	0	.220	.254
Bob Heise	2B12, SS3, 3B2	R	20	16	62	7	20	4	0	0	3	3	1	0	.323	.387
Joe Moock	3B12	L	23	13	40	2	9	2	0	0	5	0	7	0	.225	.275
1 Hawk Taylor	C12	R	28	13	37	3	9	3	0	0	4	2	8	0	.243	.324
Ken Boswell	2B6, 3B4	L	21	11	40	2	9	3	0	1	4	1	5	0	.225	.375

Johnny Lewis 27 L 4-34, 1 Sandy Alomar 23 B 0-22, Bart Shirley 27 R 0-12, Kevin Collins 20 L 1-10,

NAME	T	AGE	W	L	PCT	SV	G	GS	CG	IP	H	BB	SO	ShO	ERA
		27	61	101	.377	19	162	162	36	1434	1369	536	893	10	3.73
Tom Seaver	R	22	16	13	.552	0	35	34	18	251	224	78	170	2	2.76
Jack Fisher	R	28	9	18	.333	0	39	30	7	220	251	64	117	1	4.70
Don Cardwell (EJ)	R	31	5	9	.357	0	26	16	3	118	112	39	71	3	3.58
Don Shaw (MS)	L	23	4	5	.444	3	40	0	0	51	40	23	44	0	3.00
Ron Taylor	R	29	4	6	.400	8	50	0	0	73	60	23	46	0	2.34
2 Hal Reniff	R	28	3	3	.500	4	29	0	0	43	42	23	21	0	3.35
2 Bob Hendley	L	28	3	3	.500	0	15	13	2	71	65	28	36	0	3.42
2 Cal Koonce	R	26	3	3	.500	0	11	6	2	45	45	7	24	1	2.80
1 Bob Shaw	R	34	3	9	.250	0	23	13	3	99	105	28	49	1	4.27
1 Jack Hamilton	R	28	2	0	1.000	1	17	1	0	31	24	16	22	0	3.77
Les Rohr	L	21	2	1	.667	0	3	3	0	17	13	9	15	0	2.12
Dick Selma	R	23	2	4	.333	2	38	4	0	81	71	36	52	0	2.78
2 Dennis Bennett	L	27	1	1	.500	0	8	6	0	26	37	7	14	0	5.19
Chuck Estrada	R	29	1	2	.333	0	9	2	0	22	28	17	15	0	9.41
Bill Graham	R	30	1	2	.333	0	5	3	1	27	20	11	14	0	2.67
Danny Frisella	R	21	1	6	.143	0	14	11	0	74	68	33	51	0	3.41
Bill Denehy	R	21	1	7	.125	0	15	8	0	54	51	29	35	0	4.67
2 Nick Willhite	L	26	0	1	.000	0	4	1	1	8	9	5	9	0	9.00
Jerry Koosman	L	24	0	2	.000	0	9	3	0	22	22	19	11	0	6.14
2 Jack Lamabe	R	30	0	3	.000	1	16	2	0	32	24	8	23	0	3.94
Tug McGraw	L	22	0	3	.000	0	4	4	0	17	13	13	18	0	7.94
Joe Grzenda	L	30	0	0	.000	0	11	0	0	17	14	8	9	0	2.12
Bill Connors	R	25	0	0	.000	0	6	1	0	13	8	5	13	0	6.23
Billy Wynne	R	23	0	0	.000	0	6	1	0	9	12	2	4	0	3.00

Ralph Terry 31 R 0-0, Jerry Hinsley 23 R 0-0, Al Schmelz 23 R 0-0

1968 The Revenge of '30

As batting had caught up with the pitcher in 1930, 1968 was to witness a reversal in what was best described as the Year of the Pitcher. The event was evidenced by plummeting batting averages, a rise in low-scoring games, 335 shutouts, and individual outstanding pitching performances. Danny McLain was perhaps the biggest story among the many pitchers who were headline news during the year. With national television present, the brash, cocky McLain fastballed his way to his 30th victory on September 14, becoming the first hurler to achieve that mark since Dizzy Dean in 1934. Winning games with a steady monotony during the season, Detroit's McLain wound up with 31 victories against 6 losses and both the MVP and Cy Young Awards.

The Tigers coasted into the American League championship with a margin of 12 games by playing consistent baseball all year. McLain acted as stopper par excellence, winning practically every fourth day to prevent any Detroit losing streak as Mickey Lolich, the lefty counterpart to McLain, finished at 17-9. At bat, veteran Al Kaline, Willie Horton, and Bill Freehan provided enough offense for the Tigers to lead the league in runs and home runs.

The rest of the teams spent the year chasing after Detroit. The Orioles, by virtue of staying a distant second all year, cost manager Hank Bauer his job during the All-Star break. He was replaced by coach Earl Weaver. As with almost every other team, Baltimore's pitching far outshone lackluster hitting. Third-place Cleveland also held a mediocre hand in terms of attack, but flashed a pair of aces on the mound. Sam McDowell cashed in on his great potential with an E.R.A. of 1.81 and the most strikeouts in the league, and Luis Tiant reversed the trend of his early mediocre career with a spectacular season, leading the league in E.R.A. with 1.60 and winning 21 games against 9 losses.

Carl Yastrzemski of Boston paced the league's batters in average, finishing fast to end at .301 and spare the league the embarrassment of no .300 hitters. Frank Howard of last-place Washington developed into a mature power threat by knocking 44 home runs to pace the loop. Hawk Harrelson, the late-season addition to Boston's 1967 champions, spent the year in Fenway Park driving in 109 runs, tops in the league, to go with 35 home runs in a ballpark perfectly proportioned for his swing.

Bob Gibson piled up the honors in the National League as he led the Cardinals to a repeat pennant by nine games over San Francisco. Gibson's blistering 1.12 was the best E.R.A. since the introduction of the lively ball in 1920 and his 13 shutouts and 268 strikeouts paced the circuit. In winning 15 straight games and pitching 28 complete games, Gibson compiled a season which won for him both the MVP and Cy Young Awards. Pitching strength made up for a slumping Cardinal offense which witnessed bad years by Orlando Cepeda, Tim McCarver, and Julian Javier. Curt Flood, Lou Brock, and Mike Shannon provided enough runs for the best pitching in the majors to win. Besides Gibson, Nelson Briles and Steve Carlton lodged good years on the mound.

With Sandy Koufax retired, Don Drysdale claimed the Dodger pitching spotlight, and all baseball watched as Big D broke long-standing records in hurling six consecutive shutouts and 58 2/3 straight scoreless innings—2 2/3 more than notched by Walter Johnson in 1913. But good Dodger pitching could boost the club no higher than seventh place, due to a .230 team batting average.

The Year of the Pitcher is well exemplified by the Giant-Cardinal games of September 17-18. Gaylord Perry no-hit the Cards on the 17th, and the next night, Ray Washburn of St. Louis came back to throw a no-hitter at San Francisco. Earlier in the season, on July 9, in the first All-Star Game played at night, yawning fans watched as the National League squeaked by their foes, 1-0. The New York Mets and Houston Astros literally sent their audience to bed with a night contest on April 15, that took six hours and six minutes before being won by Houston in the bottom of the 24th, 1-0.

The Series was billed as a battle between Gibson and McLain, but McLain simply could not keep up with the Cardinals' ace. Gibson set a record by whiffing 17 Tigers in defeating McLain 4-0 in game one, and Denny was bombed out in a 10-1, fourth-game Gibson victory. The Cards took three of the first four games, but Mickey Lolich won his second in game five, and McLain finally made the victory column by defeating Washburn in game six.

Gibson seemed unbeatable in game seven as he and Lolich locked horns in a pitcher's duel through six innings. With two Tigers on base in the seventh, Jim Northrup lined a shot to center which Curt Flood misjudged into a triple, breaking Gibson's momentum and allowing the Tigers to go on to a decisive 4-1 victory. Although Norm Cash, Al Kaline, Willie Horton, and Jim Northrup had good games at bat for the Tigers, the spotlight fell on the triumphs of Lolich and Gibson and the failure of McLain.

In December, a minor bombshell was dropped when Commissioner William Eckert was fired by the club owners. Eckert's lack of decisive leadership and poor public image led the owners to seek a younger man to lead the game through the coming years of change. The man finally selected was 42-year-old Bowie Kuhn, a Wall Street attorney who would preside over baseball's first attempt at divisional play—a move prompted by both leagues expanding to twelve teams. Although the regular 162-game schedule would be kept intact, the new set up facilitated an uneven amount of games to be played. Each league was divided into two, six-team divisions, and while teams in the same division played each other 18 times, only 12 games were scheduled with each team in the other division. The new divisional play also added another exciting, but controversial feature. Whereas finishing first was once good enough to break open the champagne and prepare for the World Series, divisional winners now had to meet in a best, three-of-five championship series to decide the pennant winner.

WORLD SERIES – DETROIT (AL) 4 ST. LOUIS (NL) 3

LINE SCORES

TEAM	1	2	3	4	5	6	7	8	9	10	11	12	R	H	E
Game 1 October 2 at St. Louis															
DET (AL)	0	0	0	0	0	0	0	0	0				0	5	3
STL (NL)	0	0	0	3	0	0	1	0	X				4	6	0
McLain, Dobson (6), McMahon (8) — **Gibson**															
Game 2 October 3 at St. Louis															
DET	0	1	1	0	0	3	1	0	2				8	13	1
STL	0	0	0	0	0	1	0	0	0				1	6	1
Lolich — **Briles**, Carlton (6), Willis (7), Hoerner (9)															
Game 3 October 5 at Detroit															
STL	0	0	0	0	4	0	3	0	0				7	13	0
DET	0	0	2	0	1	0	0	0	0				3	4	0
Washburn, Hoerner (6) — **Wilson**, Dobson (5), McMahon (6), Patterson (7), Hiller (8)															
Game 4 October 6 at Detroit															
STL	2	0	2	2	0	0	0	4	0				10	13	0
DET	0	0	0	1	0	0	0	0	0				1	5	4
Gibson — **McLain**, Sparma (3), Patterson (4), Lasher (6), Hiller (8), Dobson (8)															
Game 5 October 7 at Detroit															
STL	3	0	0	0	0	0	0	0	0				3	9	0
DET	0	0	0	2	0	0	3	0	X				5	9	1
Briles, **Hoerner** (7), Willis (7) — **Lolich**															
Game 6 October 9 at St. Louis															
DET	0	2	10	0	1	0	0	0	0				13	12	1
STL	0	0	0	0	0	0	0	0	1				1	9	1
McLain — **Washburn**, Jaster (3), Willis (3), Hughes (3), Carlton (4), Granger (7), Nelson (9)															
Game 7 October 10 at St. Louis															
DET	0	0	0	0	0	0	3	0	1				4	8	1
STL	0	0	0	0	0	0	0	0	1				1	5	0
Lolich — **Gibson**															

COMPOSITE BATTING

NAME	POS	G	AB	R	H	2B	3B	HR	RBI	BA
Detroit (AL)										
Totals		7	231	34	56	4	3	8	33	.242
Kaline	OF	7	**29**	**6**	11	2	0	**2**	**8**	.379
Northrup	OF	7	28	4	7	0	1	**2**	**8**	.250
Stanley	SS-OF	7	28	4	6	0	1	0	0	.214
McAuliffe	2B	7	27	5	6	0	0	1	3	.222
Cash	1B	7	26	5	10	0	0	1	5	.385
Freehan	C	7	24	0	2	1	0	0	2	.083
Horton	OF	7	23	**6**	7	1	1	1	3	.304
Wert	3B	6	17	1	2	0	0	0	2	.118
Lolich	P	3	12	2	3	0	0	1	2	.250
McLain	P	3	6	0	0	0	0	0	0	.000
Mathews	3B	2	3	0	1	0	0	0	0	.333
Matchick	PH	3	3	0	0	0	0	0	0	.000
Price	PH	2	2	0	0	0	0	0	0	.000
Comer	PH	1	1	0	1	0	0	0	0	1.000
Brown	PH	1	1	0	0	0	0	0	0	.000
Wilson	P	1	1	0	0	0	0	0	0	.000
Oyler	SS	4	0	0	0	0	0	0	0	.000
Tracewski	3B	2	0	1	0	0	0	0	0	.000
Dobson P 0-0, Hiller P 0-0, McMahon P 0-0, Lasher P 0-0, Patterson P 0-0, Sparma P 0-0										
St. Louis (NL)										
Totals		7	239	27	61	7	3	7	27	.255
Shannon	3B	7	**29**	3	8	1	0	1	4	.276
Brock	OF	7	28	**6**	**13**	**3**	1	**2**	6	**.464**
Flood	OF	7	28	4	8	1	0	0	2	.286
Cepeda	1B	7	28	2	7	0	0	**2**	6	.250
McCarver	C	7	27	3	9	0	**2**	1	4	.333
Javier	2B	7	27	1	9	1	0	0	3	.333
Maxvill	SS	7	22	1	0	0	0	0	0	.000
Maris	OF	6	19	5	3	1	0	0	1	.158
Gibson	P	3	8	2	1	0	0	1	2	.125
Davis	OF	2	7	0	0	0	0	0	0	.000
Briles	P	2	4	0	0	0	0	0	0	.000
Gagliano	PH	3	3	0	0	0	0	0	0	.000
Washburn	P	2	3	0	0	0	0	0	0	.000
Hoerner	P	3	2	0	1	0	0	0	0	.500
Ricketts	PH	1	1	0	1	0	0	0	0	1.000
Spiezio	PH	1	1	0	1	0	0	0	0	1.000
Edwards	PH	1	1	0	0	0	0	0	0	.000
Tolan	PH	1	1	0	0	0	0	0	0	.000
Schofield SS 0-0, Willis P 0-0, Carlton P 0-0, Granger P 0-0, Hughes P 0-0, Nelson P 0-0, Jaster P 0-0										

COMPOSITE PITCHING

NAME	G	IP	H	BB	SO	W	L	SV	ERA
Detroit (AL)									
Totals	7	62	61	21	40	4	3	0	3.48
Lolich	3	**27**	**20**	6	21	**3**	0	0	**1.67**
McLain	3	16.2	18	4	13	1	**2**	0	3.24
Dobson	3	4.2	5	1	0	0	0	0	3.86
Wilson	1	4.1	4	6	3	0	1	0	6.23
Patterson	2	3	1	1	0	0	0	0	0.00
Lasher	1	2	1	0	1	0	0	0	0.00
Hiller	2	2	6	3	1	0	0	0	13.50
McMahon	2	2	4	0	1	0	0	0	13.50
Sparma	1	.1	2	0	0	0	0	0	54.00
St. Louis (NL)									
Totals	7	62	56	27	59	3	4	1	4.65
Gibson	3	**27**	18	4	**35**	2	1	0	**1.67**
Briles	2	11.1	13	4	7	0	1	0	5.56
Washburn	2	7.1	7	**7**	6	1	1	0	9.82
Hoerner	3	4.2	5	5	3	0	1	1	3.86
Willis	3	4.1	2	4	3	0	0	0	8.31
Carlton	2	4	7	1	3	0	0	0	6.75
Granger	1	2	0	1	1	0	0	0	0.00
Nelson	1	1	0	0	1	0	0	0	0.00
Hughes	1	.1	2	0	0	0	0	0	0.00
Jaster	1	0	2	1	0	0	0	0	∞

DETROIT 1st 103-59 .636 — MAYO SMITH

NAME	G by POS	B	AGE	G	AB	R	H	2B	3B	HR	RBI	BB	SO	SB	BA	SA
TOTALS			28	164	**5490**	**671**	1292	190	39	**185**	**640**	521	964	26	.235	**.385**
Norm Cash	1B117	L	33	127	411	50	108	15	1	25	63	39	70	1	.263	.487
Dick McAuliffe	2B148, SS5	L	28	151	570	**95**	142	24	10	16	56	82	99	8	.249	.411
Ray Oyler	SS111	R	29	111	215	13	29	6	1	1	12	20	59	0	.135	.186
Don Wert	3B150	R	29	150	536	44	107	15	1	12	37	37	79	0	.200	.299
Jim Northrup	OF151	L	28	154	580	76	153	29	7	21	90	50	87	4	.264	.447
Mickey Stanley	OF130, 1B15, SS9, 2B1	R	25	153	583	88	151	16	6	11	60	42	57	4	.259	.364
Willie Horton	OF139	R	25	143	512	68	146	20	2	36	85	49	110	0	.285	.543
Bill Freehan	C138, 1B21, OF1	R	26	155	540	73	142	24	2	25	84	65	64	0	.263	.454
Al Kaline	OF74, 1B22	R	33	102	327	49	94	14	1	10	53	55	39	6	.287	.428
Dick Tracewski	SS51, 3B16, 2B14	R	33	90	212	30	33	3	1	4	15	24	51	3	.156	.236
Tom Matchick	SS59, 2B13, 1B6	L	24	80	227	18	46	6	2	3	14	10	46	0	.203	.286
Gates Brown	OF17, 1B1	L	29	67	92	15	34	7	2	6	15	12	4	0	.370	.685
Jim Price	C42	R	26	64	132	12	23	4	0	3	13	13	14	0	.174	.273
Wayne Comer	OF27, C1	R	24	48	48	8	6	0	1	1	3	2	7	0	.125	.229
Earl Wilson	P34	R	33	40	88	9	20	0	1	7	17	2	35	0	.227	.489
Eddie Mathews (XJ)	3B6, 1B6	L	36	31	52	4	11	0	0	3	8	5	12	0	.212	.385
Dave Campbell	2B5	R	26	9	8	1	1	0	0	1	2	1	3	0	.125	.500
Lenny Green	OF2	L	34	6	4	0	1	0	0	0	0	1	0	0	.250	.250
Bob Christian	1B1, OF1	R	22	3	3	0	1	1	0	0	0	0	0	0	.333	.667

NAME	T	AGE	W	L	PCT	SV	G	GS	CG	IP	H	BB	SO	ShO	ERA
TOTALS		28	**103**	59	**.636**	29	164	164	**59**	**1490**	1180	486	1115	19	2.71
Denny McLain	R	24	**31**	6	**.838**	0	41	**41**	**28**	**336**	241	63	280	6	1.96
Mickey Lolich	L	27	17	9	.654	1	39	32	8	220	178	65	197	4	3.19
Earl Wilson	R	33	13	12	.520	0	34	33	10	224	192	65	168	3	2.85
Joe Sparma	R	26	10	10	.500	0	34	31	7	182	169	77	110	1	3.71
John Hiller	L	25	9	6	.600	2	39	12	4	128	92	51	78	1	2.39
Fred Lasher	R	26	5	1	.833	5	34	0	0	49	37	22	32	0	3.31
Pat Dobson	R	26	5	8	.385	7	47	10	2	125	89	48	93	1	2.66
Jon Warden	L	22	4	1	.800	3	28	0	0	37	30	15	25	0	3.65
2 Don McMahon	R	38	3	1	.750	1	20	0	0	36	22	10	33	0	2.00
1 Dennis Ribant	R	26	2	2	.500	1	14	0	0	24	20	10	7	0	2.25
Daryl Patterson	R	24	2	3	.400	7	38	1	0	68	53	27	49	0	2.12
Les Cain	L	20	1	0	1.000	0	8	4	0	24	25	20	13	0	3.00
3 John Wyatt	R	33	1	0	1.000	2	22	0	0	30	26	11	25	0	2.40
2 Roy Face	R	40	0	0	.000	0	2	0	0	1	2	1	1	0	0.00
Jim Rooker	L	26	0	0	.000	0	2	0	0	5	4	1	4	0	3.60

BALTIMORE 2nd 91-71 .562 12 — HANK BAUER 43-37 .538 EARL WEAVER 48-34 .585

NAME	G by POS	B	AGE	G	AB	R	H	2B	3B	HR	RBI	BB	SO	SB	BA	SA
TOTALS			27	162	5275	579	1187	**215**	28	133	534	570	1019	78	.225	.352
Boog Powell	1B149	L	26	154	550	60	137	21	1	22	85	73	97	7	.249	.411
Dave Johnson	2B127, SS34	R	25	145	504	50	122	24	4	9	56	44	80	7	.242	.359
Mark Belanger	SS145	R	24	145	472	40	98	13	0	2	21	40	114	10	.208	.248
Brooks Robinson	3B162	R	31	162	608	65	154	36	6	17	75	44	55	1	.253	.416
Frank Robinson	OF117, 1B3	R	32	130	421	69	113	27	1	15	52	73	84	11	.268	.444
Paul Blair	OF132, 3B1	R	24	141	421	48	89	22	1	7	38	37	60	4	.211	.318
Curt Blefary	OF92, C40, 1B12	L	24	137	451	50	90	8	1	15	39	65	66	6	.200	.322
Andy Etchebarren (BG)	C70	R	25	74	189	20	44	11	2	5	20	19	46	0	.233	.392
Don Buford	OF65, 2B58, 3B2	B	31	130	426	65	120	13	4	15	46	57	46	27	.282	.437
Dave May	OF61	L	24	84	152	15	29	6	3	0	7	19	27	3	.191	.270
Curt Motton	OF54	R	27	83	217	27	43	7	0	8	25	31	43	1	.198	.341
Ellie Hendricks	C53	L	27	79	183	19	37	8	1	7	23	19	51	0	.202	.372
2 Fred Valentine	OF26	B	33	47	91	9	17	3	2	2	5	7	20	0	.187	.330
Larry Haney	C32	R	25	38	89	5	21	3	1	1	5	0	19	0	.236	.326
Merv Rettenmund	OF23	R	25	31	64	10	19	5	0	2	7	18	20	1	.297	.469
Chico Fernandez	SS7, 2B4	R	29	24	18	0	2	0	0	0	0	1	2	0	.111	.111
Mike Fiore	1B5, OF1	L	23	6	17	2	1	0	0	0	0	4	4	0	.059	.059
Bobby Floyd	SS4	R	24	5	9	0	1	1	0	0	1	0	3	0	.111	.222

NAME	T	AGE	W	L	PCT	SV	G	GS	CG	IP	H	BB	SO	ShO	ERA
TOTALS		26	91	71	.562	31	162	162	53	1451	1111	502	1044	16	**2.66**
Dave McNally	L	25	22	10	.688	0	35	35	18	273	175	55	202	5	1.95
Jim Hardin	R	24	18	13	.581	0	35	35	16	244	188	70	160	2	2.51
Tom Phoebus	R	23	15	15	.500	0	36	36	9	241	186	105	193	3	2.61
Dave Leonhard	R	26	7	7	.500	1	28	18	5	126	95	57	61	2	3.14
Pete Richert (MS)	L	28	6	3	.667	6	36	0	0	62	51	12	47	0	3.48
Gene Brabender	R	26	6	7	.462	3	37	15	3	125	116	48	92	2	3.31
Eddie Watt	R	26	5	5	.500	11	59	0	0	83	63	35	72	0	2.28
Roger Nelson	R	24	4	3	.571	1	19	6	0	71	49	26	70	0	2.41
Moe Drabowsky	R	32	4	4	.500	7	45	0	0	61	35	25	46	0	1.92
Wally Bunker	R	23	2	0	1.000	0	18	10	2	71	59	14	44	1	2.41
John Morris	L	26	2	0	1.000	0	19	0	0	32	19	17	22	0	2.53
Mike Adamson	R	20	0	2	.000	0	2	2	0	8	9	4	4	0	9.00
2 Bruce Howard	R	25	0	2	.000	0	10	5	0	31	30	26	19	0	3.77
John O'Donoghue	L	28	0	0	.000	2	16	0	0	22	34	7	11	0	6.14
Fred Beene	R	25	0	0	.000	0	1	0	0	1	2	1	1	0	9.00

Jim Palmer (SA) 22

CLEVELAND 3rd 86-75 .534 16.5 — AL DARK

NAME	G by POS	B	AGE	G	AB	R	H	2B	3B	HR	RBI	BB	SO	SB	BA	SA
TOTALS			28	162	5416	516	1266	210	36	75	476	427	858	115	.234	.327
Tony Horton	1B128	R	23	133	477	57	119	29	3	14	59	34	56	3	.249	.411
Vern Fuller	2B73, 3B23, SS4	R	24	97	244	14	59	8	2	0	18	24	49	2	.242	.291
Larry Brown	SS154	R	28	154	495	43	116	18	3	6	35	43	46	1	.234	.319
Max Alvis	3B128	R	30	131	452	38	101	17	3	8	37	41	91	5	.223	.327
Tommy Harper	OF115, 2B2	R	27	130	235	26	51	15	2	6	26	26	56	11	.217	.374
Jose Cardenal	OF153	R	24	157	583	78	150	21	7	7	44	39	74	40	.257	.353
Lee Maye	OF80, 1B1	L	33	109	299	20	84	13	2	4	26	15	24	0	.281	.378
Joe Azcue	C97	R	28	115	357	23	100	10	0	4	42	28	33	1	.280	.342
Duke Sims	C84, 1B31, OF4	L	27	122	361	48	90	21	0	11	44	62	68	1	.249	.399
C. Salmon	2B45, 3B18, SS15, OF13, 1B11	R	27	103	276	24	59	8	1	3	12	12	30	7	.214	.283
Dave Nelson	2B59, SS14	B	24	88	189	26	44	4	5	0	19	17	35	23	.233	.307
2 Russ Snyder	OF54, 1B1	L	34	68	217	30	61	8	2	2	23	25	21	1	.281	.364
2 Lou Johnson	OF57	R	33	65	202	25	52	11	1	5	23	9	24	6	.257	.396
2 Jimmie Hall	OF29	L	30	53	111	4	22	4	0	1	8	10	19	1	.198	.261
1 Vic Davalillo	OF49	L	31	51	180	15	43	2	3	2	13	3	19	8	.239	.317
Billy Harris	2B27, 3B10, SS1	L	24	38	94	10	20	5	1	0	3	8	22	2	.213	.287
1 Leon Wagner	OF10	L	34	38	49	5	9	4	0	0	6	6	6	0	.184	.265
Jose Vidal	OF26, 1B1	R	28	37	54	5	9	0	0	2	5	2	15	3	.167	.278
1 Willie Smith	1B7, P2, OF1	L	29	33	42	1	6	2	0	0	3	3	14	0	.143	.190
Richie Scheinblum	OF16	B	25	19	55	3	12	5	0	0	5	5	8	0	.218	.309
Ken Suarez	C12, 2B1, 3B1, OF1	R	25	17	10	1	1	0	0	0	0	1	3	0	.100	.100
Lou Klimchock	3B4, 1B1, 2B1	L	28	11	15	0	2	0	0	0	3	1	0	0	.133	.133
Lou Piniella	OF2	R	24	6	5	1	0	0	0	0	1	0	0	0	.000	.000
Russ Nagelson		L	23	5	3	0	1	0	0	0	0	2	2	0	.333	.333

Eddie Leon 21 R 0-1, Ray Fosse 21 R 0-0

NAME	T	AGE	W	L	PCT	SV	G	GS	CG	IP	H	BB	SO	ShO	ERA
TOTALS		27	86	75	.534	32	162	162	48	1464	1087	**540**	**1157**	**23**	**2.66**
Luis Tiant	R	27	21	9	.700	0	34	32	19	258	152	73	264	**9**	**1.60**
Sam McDowell	L	25	15	14	.517	0	38	37	11	269	181	**110**	**283**	3	1.81
Stan Williams	R	31	13	11	.542	9	44	24	6	194	163	51	147	2	2.51
Sonny Siebert	R	31	12	10	.545	0	31	30	8	206	145	88	146	4	2.97
Steve Hargan	R	25	8	15	.348	0	32	27	4	158	139	81	78	2	4.16
2 Vincente Romo	R	25	5	3	.625	12	40	1	0	83	43	33	54	0	1.63
Mike Paul	L	23	5	8	.385	3	36	7	0	92	72	35	87	0	3.91
Eddie Fisher	R	31	4	2	.667	4	54	0	0	95	87	17	42	0	3.84
Hal Kurtz	R	24	1	0	1.000	1	28	0	0	38	37	15	16	0	5.21
Billy Rohr	L	23	1	0	1.000	1	17	0	0	18	18	10	5	0	7.00
Horacio Pina	R	23	1	1	.500	2	12	3	0	31	24	15	24	0	1.74
Steve Bailey	R	26	0	1	.000	0	2	1	0	5	4	2	1	0	3.60
Tommy Gramly	R	23	0	1	.000	0	3	0	0	3	3	2	1	0	3.00
Rob Gardner	L	23	0	0	.000	0	5	0	0	3	5	2	6	0	6.00
Mike Hedlund	R	21	0	0	.000	0	3	0	0	2	6	2	0	0	9.00
Darrell Sutherland	R	26	0	0	.000	0	3	0	0	3	6	4	2	0	9.00
1 Willie Smith	L	29	0	0	.000	0	2	0	0	5	2	1	1	0	0.00

Tom Kelley (EJ) 24

BOSTON 4th 86-76 .531 17 — DICK WILLIAMS

NAME	G by POS	B	AGE	G	AB	R	H	2B	3B	HR	RBI	BB	SO	SB	BA	SA
TOTALS			27	162	5303	614	1253	207	17	125	558	**582**	974	76	.236	.352
George Scott	1B112, 3B6	R	24	124	350	23	60	14	0	3	25	26	88	3	.171	.237
Mike Andrews	2B139, SS4, 3B1	R	24	147	536	77	145	22	1	7	45	81	57	3	.271	.354
Rico Petrocelli	SS117, 1B1	R	25	123	406	41	95	17	2	12	46	31	73	0	.234	.374
Joe Foy	3B147, OF3	R	25	150	515	65	116	18	2	10	60	84	91	26	.225	.326
Ken Harrelson	OF132, 1B19	R	26	150	535	79	147	17	4	35	**109**	69	90	2	.275	.518
Reggie Smith	OF155	B	23	155	558	78	148	**37**	5	15	69	64	77	22	.265	.430
Carl Yastrzemski	OF155, 1B3	L	28	157	539	90	162	32	2	23	74	**119**	90	13	**.301**	.495
Russ Gibson	C74, 1B1	R	29	76	231	15	52	11	1	3	20	8	38	1	.225	.320
Dalton Jones	1B56, 2B26, 3B8	L	24	111	354	38	83	13	0	5	29	17	53	1	.234	.314
Jerry Adair	SS46, 2B12, 3B7, 1B1	R	31	74	208	18	45	1	0	2	12	9	28	0	.216	.250
Jose Tartabull (GJ)	OF43	L	29	72	139	24	39	6	0	0	6	6	5	2	.281	.324
Elston Howard	C68	R	39	71	203	22	49	4	0	5	18	22	45	1	.241	.335
Joe Lahoud	OF25	L	21	29	78	5	15	1	0	1	6	16	16	0	.192	.244
Russ Nixon	C27	L	33	29	85	1	13	2	0	0	6	7	13	0	.153	.176
Norm Siebern	1B2, OF2	L	34	27	30	0	2	0	0	0	0	0	5	0	.067	.067
2 Floyd Robinson	OF11	L	32	24	24	1	3	0	0	0	2	3	4	1	.125	.125
1 Gene Oliver	C10, OF1	R	32	16	35	2	5	0	0	0	1	4	12	0	.143	.143
George Thomas	OF9	R	30	12	10	3	2	0	0	1	1	1	3	1	.200	.500
Luis Alvarado	SS11	R	19	11	46	3	6	2	0	0	1	1	11	0	.130	.174
Jerry Moses	C6	R	21	6	18	2	6	0	0	2	4	1	4	0	.333	.667

Tony Conigliaro (IJ) 23

NAME	T	AGE	W	L	PCT	SV	G	GS	CG	IP	H	BB	SO	ShO	ERA
TOTALS		27	86	76	.531	31	162	162	55	1447	1303	523	972	17	3.33
Ray Culp	R	26	16	6	.727	0	35	30	11	216	166	82	190	6	2.92
Dick Ellsworth	L	28	16	7	.696	0	31	28	10	196	196	37	106	1	3.03
Gary Bell	R	31	11	11	.500	1	35	27	9	199	177	68	103	3	3.12
Jose Santiago (EJ)	R	27	9	4	.692	0	18	18	7	124	96	42	86	2	2.25
Sparky Lyle	L	23	6	1	.857	11	49	0	0	66	67	14	52	0	2.73
2 Juan Pizarro	L	31	6	8	.429	2	19	12	6	108	97	44	84	0	3.58
Jim Lonborg (KJ)	R	26	6	10	.375	0	23	17	4	113	89	59	73	1	4.30
Lee Stange	R	31	5	5	.500	12	50	2	1	103	89	25	53	0	3.93
Gary Waslewski	R	26	4	7	.364	2	34	11	2	105	108	40	59	0	3.69
Bill Landis (MS)	L	25	3	3	.500	3	38	1	0	60	48	30	59	0	3.15
Jerry Stephenson	R	24	2	8	.200	0	23	7	2	69	81	42	51	0	5.61
1 John Wyatt	R	33	1	2	.333	0	8	0	0	11	9	6	11	0	4.09
Dave Morehead	R	25	1	4	.200	0	11	9	3	55	52	20	28	1	2.45
Darrell Brandon	R	27	0	0	.000	0	8	0	0	13	19	9	10	0	6.23
Garry Roggenburk (SA)	L	28	0	0	.000	0	4	0	0	8	9	3	4	0	2.25
Fred Wenz	R	26	0	0	.000	0	1	0	0	1	0	2	3	0	0.00

NEW YORK 5th 83-79 .512 20 — RALPH HOUK

NAME	G by POS	B	AGE	G	AB	R	H	2B	3B	HR	RBI	BB	SO	SB	BA	SA
TOTALS			28	164	5310	536	1137	154	34	109	501	566	958	90	.214	.318
Mickey Mantle	1B131	B	36	144	435	57	103	14	1	18	54	106	97	6	.237	.398
Horace Clarke	2B139	B	28	148	579	52	133	6	1	2	26	23	46	20	.230	.254
Tom Tresh	SS119, OF27	B	30	152	507	60	99	18	3	11	52	76	97	10	.195	.308
Bobby Cox	3B132	R	27	135	437	33	100	15	1	7	41	41	85	3	.229	.316
Bill Robinson	OF98	R	25	107	342	34	82	16	7	6	40	26	54	7	.240	.380
Joe Pepitone	OF92, 1B12	L	27	108	380	41	93	9	3	15	56	37	45	8	.245	.403
Roy White	OF154	B	24	159	577	89	154	20	7	17	62	73	50	20	.267	.414
Jake Gibbs	C121	L	29	124	423	31	90	12	3	3	29	27	68	9	.213	.277
Andy Kosco	OF95, 1B28	R	26	131	466	47	112	19	1	15	59	16	71	2	.240	.382
Dick Howser	2B29, 3B2, SS1	R	31	85	150	24	23	2	1	0	3	35	17	0	.153	.180
Gene Michael	SS43, P1	B	30	61	116	8	23	3	0	1	8	2	23	3	.198	.250
Frank Fernandez	C45, OF4	R	25	51	135	15	23	6	1	7	30	35	50	1	.170	.385
Charley Smith (KJ)	3B13	R	30	46	70	2	16	4	1	1	7	5	18	0	.229	.357
2 Rocky Colavito	OF28, P1	R	34	39	91	13	20	2	2	5	13	14	17	0	.220	.451
Steve Whitaker	OF14	L	25	28	60	3	7	2	0	0	3	8	18	0	.117	.150
Mike Ferraro	3B22	R	23	23	87	5	14	0	1	0	1	2	17	0	.161	.184
Ruben Amaro	SS23, 1B22	R	32	47	41	3	5	1	0	0	0	9	6	0	.122	.146

Ellie Rodriguez 22 R 5-24, Tony Solaita 21 L 0-1, Bobby Murcer (MS) 22, Jerry Kenney (MS) 23

NAME	T	AGE	W	L	PCT	SV	G	GS	CG	IP	H	BB	SO	ShO	ERA
TOTALS		28	83	79	.512	27	164	164	45	1467	1308	424	831	14	2.79
Mel Stottlemyre	R	26	21	12	.636	0	36	36	19	279	**243**	65	140	6	2.45
Stan Bahnsen	R	23	17	12	.586	0	37	34	10	267	216	68	162	1	2.06
Fritz Peterson	L	26	12	11	.522	0	36	27	6	212	187	29	115	2	2.63
Steve Barber	L	29	6	5	.545	0	20	19	3	128	127	64	87	1	3.23
Joe Verbanic	R	25	6	7	.462	4	40	11	2	97	104	41	40	1	3.15
1 Bill Monbouquette	R	31	5	7	.417	0	17	11	2	89	92	13	32	0	4.45
2 Lindy McDaniel	R	32	4	1	.800	10	24	0	0	51	30	12	43	0	1.76
Al Downing (SJ)	L	27	3	3	.500	0	15	12	1	61	54	20	40	0	3.54
Dooley Womack	R	28	3	7	.300	2	45	0	0	62	53	29	27	0	3.19
Steve Hamilton	L	34	2	2	.500	11	40	0	0	51	37	13	42	0	2.12
2 Rocky Colavito	R	34	1	0	1.000	0	1	0	0	3	1	2	1	0	0.00
Thad Tillotson	R	27	1	0	1.000	0	7	0	0	10	11	7	1	0	4.50
Jim Bouton	R	29	1	1	.500	0	12	3	1	44	49	9	24	0	3.68
Fred Talbot	R	27	1	9	.100	0	29	11	1	99	89	42	67	0	3.36
2 John Wyatt	R	33	0	2	.000	0	7	0	0	8	7	9	6	0	2.25
John Cumberland	L	21	0	0	.000	0	1	0	0	2	3	1	1	0	9.00
Gene Michael	R	30	0	0	.000	0	1	0	0	3	5	0	3	0	0.00

OAKLAND 6th 82-80 .506 21 — BOB KENNEDY

NAME	G by POS	B	AGE	G	AB	R	H	2B	3B	HR	RBI	BB	SO	SB	BA	SA
TOTALS			25	163	5406	569	**1300**	192	40	94	522	472	1022	**147**	**.240**	.343
Danny Cater	1B121, OF20, 2B1	R	28	147	504	53	146	28	3	6	62	35	43	8	.290	.393
John Donaldson	2B98, 3B5, SS1	L	25	127	363	37	80	9	2	2	27	45	44	5	.220	.273
Bert Campaneris	SS155, OF3	R	26	159	**642**	87	**177**	25	9	4	38	50	69	**62**	.276	.361
Sal Bando	3B162, OF1	R	24	162	605	67	152	25	5	9	67	51	78	13	.251	.354
Reggie Jackson	OF151	L	22	154	553	82	138	13	6	29	74	50	**171**	14	.250	.452
Rick Monday	OF144	L	22	148	482	56	132	24	7	8	49	72	143	14	.274	.402
Mike Hershberger	OF90	R	28	99	246	23	67	9	2	5	32	21	22	8	.272	.386
Dave Duncan	C79	R	22	82	246	15	47	4	0	7	28	25	68	1	.191	.293
Jim Gosger	OF64	L	25	88	150	7	27	1	1	0	5	17	21	4	.180	.200
Dick Green	2B61, 3B1, C1	R	27	76	202	19	47	6	0	6	18	21	41	3	.233	.351
Joe Rudi	OF56	R	21	68	181	10	32	5	1	1	12	12	32	1	.177	.232
Jim Pagliaroni (BW)	C63	R	30	66	199	19	49	4	0	6	20	24	42	0	.246	.357
Ramon Webster	1B55	L	25	66	196	17	42	11	1	3	23	12	24	3	.214	.327
1 Floyd Robinson	OF18	L	32	53	81	5	20	5	0	1	14	4	10	0	.247	.346
Ted Kubiak (MS)	2B24, SS12	B	26	48	120	10	30	5	2	0	8	8	18	1	.250	.325
Catfish Hunter	P36	R	22	39	82	9	19	3	0	1	8	0	19	0	.232	.305
Joe Keough	OF29, 1B1	L	22	34	98	7	21	2	1	2	18	8	11	1	.214	.316
Phil Roof (AJ)	C32	R	27	34	64	5	12	0	0	1	2	2	15	1	.188	.234
Rene Lachemann	C16	R	23	19	60	3	9	1	0	0	4	1	11	0	.150	.167

Allan Lewis 26 B 1-4, Tony LaRussa 23 R 1-3

NAME	T	AGE	W	L	PCT	SV	G	GS	CG	IP	H	BB	SO	ShO	ERA
		24	82	80	.506	29	163	163	45	1456	1220	505	997	18	2.94
Blue Moon Odom	R	23	16	10	.615	0	32	31	9	231	179	98	143	4	2.45
Catfish Hunter	R	22	13	13	.500	1	36	34	11	234	210	69	172	2	3.35
Jim Nash	R	23	13	13	.500	0	34	33	12	229	185	55	169	6	2.28
Chuck Dobson	R	24	12	14	.462	0	35	34	11	225	197	80	168	3	3.00
Lew Krausse	R	25	10	11	.476	4	36	25	2	185	147	62	105	0	3.11
Diego Segui	R	30	6	5	.545	6	52	0	0	83	51	32	72	0	2.39
Paul Lindblad	L	26	4	3	.571	2	47	1	0	56	51	14	42	0	2.41
Jack Aker	R	27	4	4	.500	11	54	0	0	75	72	33	44	0	4.08
Ed Sprague	R	22	3	4	.429	4	47	1	0	69	51	34	34	0	3.26
Tony Pierce	L	22	1	2	.333	1	17	3	0	33	39	10	16	0	3.82
Ken Sanders	R	26	0	1	.000	0	7	0	0	11	8	8	6	0	3.27
Warren Bogle	L	21	0	0	.000	0	16	1	0	23	26	8	26	0	4.30
Rollie Fingers	R	21	0	0	.000	0	1	0	0	1	4	1	0	0	36.00
George Lauzerique	R	20	0	0	.000	0	1	0	0	1	0	1	0	0	0.00

MINNESOTA 7th 73-83 .488 24 — CAL ERMER

NAME	G by POS	B	AGE	G	AB	R	H	2B	3B	HR	RBI	BB	SO	SB	BA	SA
TOTALS			29	162	5373	562	1274	207	**41**	105	522	445	966	98	.237	.350
Rich Reese	1B87, OF15	L	26	126	332	40	86	15	2	4	28	18	36	3	.259	.352
Rod Carew	2B117, SS4	L	22	127	461	46	126	27	2	1	42	26	71	12	.273	.347
Jackie Hernandez	SS79, 1B1	R	27	83	199	13	35	3	0	2	17	9	52	5	.176	.221
Tovar	3B75, OF78, SS35, 2B18, 1B, C, P=1	R	27	157	613	89	167	31	6	6	47	34	41	35	.272	.372
Tony Oliva	OF126	L	28	128	470	54	136	24	5	18	68	45	61	10	.289	.477
Ted Uhlaender	OF129	L	28	140	488	52	138	21	5	7	52	28	46	16	.283	.389
Bob Allison	OF117, 1B17	R	33	145	469	63	116	16	8	22	52	52	98	9	.247	.456
Johnny Roseboro	C117	L	35	135	380	31	82	12	0	8	39	46	57	2	.216	.311
Ron Clark	3B52, SS43, 2B10	R	25	104	227	14	42	5	1	1	13	16	44	3	.185	.229
Harmon Killebrew (GJ)	1B77, 3B11	R	32	100	295	40	62	7	2	17	40	70	70	0	.210	.420
Frank Quilici	2B48, 3B40, SS6, 1B1	R	29	97	229	22	56	11	4	1	22	21	45	0	.245	.341
Rich Rollins	3B56	R	30	93	203	14	49	5	0	6	30	10	34	3	.241	.355
Jim Holt	OF38, 1B1	L	24	70	106	9	22	2	1	0	8	4	20	0	.208	.245
Frank Kostro	OF24, 1B5	R	30	63	108	9	26	4	1	0	9	6	20	0	.241	.296
Bruce Look	C41	L	25	59	118	7	29	4	0	0	9	20	24	0	.246	.280
Rick Renick	SS40	R	24	42	97	16	21	5	2	3	13	9	42	0	.216	.402
Graig Nettles	OF16, 3B5, 1B3	L	23	22	76	13	17	2	1	5	8	7	20	0	.224	.474

Jerry Zimmerman 33 R 5-45, Pat Kelly 23 L 4-35, George Mitterwald 23 R 7-34

NAME	T	AGE	W	L	PCT	SV	G	GS	CG	IP	H	BB	SO	ShO	ERA
		29	79	83	.488	29	162	162	46	1433	1224	414	996	14	2.89
Dean Chance	R	27	16	16	.500	1	43	39	15	292	224	63	234	6	2.53
Jim Kaat (SA)	L	29	14	12	.538	0	30	29	9	208	192	40	130	2	2.94
Jim Merritt	L	24	12	16	.429	1	38	34	11	238	207	52	181	1	3.25
Dave Boswell	R	23	10	13	.435	0	34	28	7	190	148	87	143	2	3.32
Jim Perry	R	32	8	6	.571	1	32	18	3	139	113	26	69	2	2.27
Ron Perranoski	L	32	8	7	.533	6	66	0	0	87	86	38	65	0	3.10
Jim Roland	L	25	4	1	.800	0	28	4	1	62	55	24	36	0	3.48
Al Worthington	R	39	4	5	.444	**18**	54	0	0	76	67	32	57	0	2.72
Tom Hall	L	20	2	1	.667	0	8	4	0	30	27	12	18	0	2.40
Buzz Stephen	R	23	1	1	.500	0	2	2	0	11	11	7	4	0	4.91
Ron Keller (MS)	R	25	0	1	.000	0	7	1	0	16	18	4	11	0	2.81
Danny Morris	R	22	0	1	.000	0	3	2	0	11	11	4	6	0	1.64
Bob Miller	R	29	0	3	.000	2	45	0	0	72	65	24	41	0	2.75
Cesar Tovar	R	27	0	0	.000	0	1	1	0	1	0	1	1	0	0.00

CALIFORNIA 8th (Tie) 67-95 .414 36 — BILL RIGNEY

NAME	G by POS	B	AGE	G	AB	R	H	2B	3B	HR	RBI	BB	SO	SB	BA	SA
TOTALS			28	162	5331	498	1209	170	33	83	453	447	**1080**	62	.227	.318
Don Mincher	1B113	L	30	120	399	35	94	12	1	13	48	43	65	0	.236	.368
Bobby Knoop	2B151	R	29	152	494	48	123	20	4	3	39	35	128	3	.249	.324
Jim Fregosi	SS159	R	26	159	614	77	150	21	**13**	9	49	60	101	9	.244	.365
Aurelio Rodriguez (IL)	3B70, 2B2	R	20	76	223	14	54	10	1	1	16	17	36	0	.242	.309
Roger Repoz	OF114	L	27	133	375	30	90	8	1	13	54	38	83	8	.240	.371
2 Vic Davalillo	OF86	L	31	93	339	34	101	15	4	1	18	15	34	17	.298	.375
Rick Reichardt	OF148	R	25	151	534	62	136	20	3	21	73	42	118	8	.255	.421
Bob Rodgers	C87	B	29	91	258	13	49	6	0	1	14	16	48	2	.190	.225
Chuck Hinton	1B48, OF37, 3B13, 2B9	R	34	116	267	28	52	10	3	7	23	24	61	3	.195	.333
Tom Satriano	C85, 2B14, 3B11, 1B1	L	27	111	297	20	75	9	0	8	35	37	44	0	.253	.364
Ed Kirkpatrick	OF45, C4, 1B2	L	23	89	161	23	37	4	0	1	15	25	32	1	.230	.273
Bubba Morton	OF50, 3B1	R	36	81	163	13	44	6	0	1	18	14	18	2	.270	.325
Paul Schaal (FS)	3B58	R	25	60	219	22	46	7	1	2	16	29	25	5	.210	.279
1 Jimmie Hall	OF39	L	30	46	126	15	27	3	0	1	8	16	19	1	.214	.262
Jay Johnstone	OF29	L	22	41	115	11	30	4	1	0	3	7	15	2	.261	.313
1 Woodie Held	2B5, 3B5, SS5, OF3	R	36	33	45	4	5	1	0	0	0	5	15	0	.111	.133
Chuck Cottier	3B27, 2B4	R	32	33	67	2	13	4	1	0	1	2	15	0	.194	.284
Jim Spencer	1B19	L	20	19	68	2	13	1	0	0	5	3	10	0	.191	.206
Jarvis Tatum	OF11	R	21	17	51	7	9	1	0	0	2	0	9	0	.176	.196
Tom Egan	C14	R	22	16	43	2	5	1	0	1	4	2	15	0	.116	.209

Bobby Trevino 24 R 9-40, Winston Llenas 24 R 5-39, Orlando McFarlane (LJ) 30 R 9-31, 2 Wayne Causey 31 L 0-11

NAME	T	AGE	W	L	PCT	SV	G	GS	CG	IP	H	BB	SO	ShO	ERA
		27	67	95	.414	31	162	162	29	1437	1234	519	869	11	3.43
George Brunet	L	33	13	**17**	.433	0	39	36	8	245	191	68	132	5	2.87
Clyde Wright	L	27	10	6	.625	3	41	13	2	126	123	44	71	1	3.93
Jim McGlothlin	R	24	10	15	.400	3	40	32	8	208	187	60	135	0	3.55
Sammy Ellis	R	27	9	10	.474	2	42	24	3	164	150	56	93	0	3.95
Tom Murphy	R	22	5	6	.455	0	15	15	3	99	67	28	56	0	2.18
Andy Messersmith	R	22	4	2	.667	4	28	5	2	81	44	35	74	1	2.22
Minnie Rojas (SA)	R	29	4	3	.571	6	38	0	0	55	55	15	33	0	4.25
Marty Pattin	R	25	4	4	.500	3	52	4	0	84	67	37	66	0	2.79
Jack Hamilton	R	29	3	1	.750	2	21	2	1	38	34	15	18	0	3.32
Bobby Locke	R	34	2	3	.400	2	29	0	0	36	51	13	21	0	6.50
Tom Burgmeier	L	29	1	4	.200	5	56	2	0	73	65	24	33	0	4.32
Bill Harrelson	R	22	1	6	.143	0	10	5	1	34	28	26	22	0	5.03
Rickey Clark (LJ)	R	22	1	11	.083	0	21	17	0	94	74	54	60	0	3.54
Steve Kealey	R	21	0	1	.000	0	6	0	0	10	10	5	4	0	2.70
Jim Weaver	L	29	0	1	.000	0	14	0	0	23	22	10	8	0	2.35
Dennis Bennett	L	28	0	5	.000	1	16	7	1	48	46	17	36	0	3.56
Bob Heffner	R	29	0	0	.000	0	7	0	0	8	6	6	3	0	2.25
Pete Cimino	R	25	0	0	.000	0	4	0	0	7	7	4	2	0	2.57
Larry Sherry	R	32	0	0	.000	0	3	0	0	3	7	2	2	0	6.00

CHICAGO, 8th (Tie) 67-95 .414 36 — EDDIE STANKY 34-45 .430 LES MOSS 0-2 .000 AL LOPEZ 33-48 .420

NAME	G by POS	B	AGE	G	AB	R	H	2B	3B	HR	RBI	BB	SO	SB	BA	SA
TOTALS			28	162	5405	463	1233	169	33	71	431	397	840	90	.228	.311
Tommy McCraw	1B135	L	27	136	477	51	112	16	12	9	44	36	58	20	.235	.375
Sandy Alomar	2B99, 3B27, SS9, OF1	B	24	133	363	41	92	8	2	0	12	20	42	21	.253	.287
Luis Aparicio	SS154	R	34	155	622	55	164	24	4	4	36	33	43	17	.264	.334
Pete Ward	3B77, 1B31, OF22	L	28	125	399	43	86	15	0	15	50	76	85	4	.216	.366
Buddy Bradford	OF99	R	23	103	281	32	61	11	0	5	24	23	67	8	.217	.310
Ken Berry	OF151	R	27	153	504	49	127	21	2	7	32	25	64	6	.252	.343
Tommy Davis	OF116, 1B6	R	29	132	456	30	122	5	3	8	50	16	48	4	.268	.344
Duane Josephson	C122	R	26	128	434	35	107	16	6	6	45	18	52	2	.247	.353
Jerry McNertney	C64, 1B1	R	31	74	169	18	37	4	1	3	18	18	29	0	.219	.308
1 Tim Cullen	2B71	R	26	72	155	16	31	7	0	2	13	15	23	0	.200	.284
2 Leon Wagner	OF46	L	34	69	162	14	46	8	0	1	18	21	31	2	.284	.352
Walt Williams	OF34	R	24	63	133	6	32	6	0	1	8	4	17	0	.241	.308
Bill Voss (BY)	OF55	L	24	61	167	14	26	2	1	2	15	16	34	5	.156	.216
1 Wayne Causey	2B41	L	31	59	100	8	18	2	0	0	7	14	7	0	.180	.200
Dick Kenworthy	3B38	R	27	58	122	2	27	2	0	0	2	5	21	0	.221	.238
2 Ron Hansen	3B29, SS7, 2B2	R	30	40	87	7	20	3	0	1	4	11	12	0	.230	.299
2 Woodie Held	OF33, 3B5, 2B1	R	36	40	54	5	9	1	0	0	2	5	14	0	.167	.185
1 Russ Snyder	OF22	L	34	38	82	2	11	2	0	1	5	4	16	0	.134	.195
Bill Melton	3B33	R	22	34	109	5	29	8	0	2	16	10	32	1	.266	.294
Carlos May	OF17	L	20	17	67	4	12	1	0	0	1	3	15	0	.179	.194

Gail Hopkins 25 L 8-37, Rich Morales 24 R 5-29, 1 Ken Boyer 37 R 3-24, Buddy Booker 26 L 0-5

NAME	T	AGE	W	L	PCT	SV	G	GS	CG	IP	H	BB	SO	ShO	ERA
		30	67	95	.414	**40**	162	162	20	1468	1290	451	834	11	2.75
Wilbur Wood	L	26	13	12	.520	16	**88**	2	0	159	127	33	74	0	1.87
Joe Horlen	R	30	12	14	.462	0	35	35	4	224	197	70	102	1	2.37
Tommy John (SJ)	L	25	10	5	.667	0	25	25	5	177	135	49	117	1	1.98
Jack Fisher	R	29	8	13	.381	0	35	28	2	181	176	48	80	0	2.98
Bob Locker	R	30	5	4	.556	10	70	0	0	90	78	27	62	0	2.30
Hoyt Wilhelm	R	44	4	4	.500	12	72	0	0	94	69	24	72	0	1.72
Gary Peters	L	31	4	13	.235	1	31	25	6	163	146	60	110	1	3.75
Cisco Carlos	R	27	4	14	.222	0	29	21	0	122	121	37	57	0	3.91
Bob Priddy	R	28	3	11	.214	0	35	18	2	114	106	41	66	0	3.63
1 Don McMahon	R	38	2	1	.667	0	25	0	0	46	31	20	32	0	1.96
Jerry Nyman	L	25	2	1	.667	0	8	7	1	40	38	16	27	1	2.03
Danny Lazar	L	24	0	1	.000	0	8	1	0	13	14	4	11	0	4.15
2 Dennis Ribant	R	26	0	2	.000	1	17	0	0	31	42	17	20	0	6.03
Fred Rath	R	24	0	0	.000	0	5	0	0	11	8	3	3	0	1.64
Billy Wynne	R	24	0	0	.000	0	1	0	0	2	2	2	1	0	4.50

WASHINGTON 10th 65-96 .404 37.5 — JIM LEMON

NAME	G by POS	B	AGE	G	AB	R	H	2B	3B	HR	RBI	BB	SO	SB	BA	SA
TOTALS			27	161	5400	524	1208	160	37	124	489	454	960	29	.224	.336
Mike Epstein	1B110	L	25	123	385	40	90	8	2	13	33	48	91	1	.234	.366
Bernie Allen	2B110, 3B2	L	29	120	373	31	90	12	4	6	40	28	35	2	.241	.343
1 Ron Hansen	SS81, 3B5	R	30	86	275	28	51	12	0	8	28	35	49	0	.185	.316
Ken McMullen	3B145, SS11	R	26	151	557	66	138	11	2	20	62	63	66	1	.248	.382
Ed Stroud	OF84	L	28	105	306	41	73	10	10	4	23	20	50	9	.239	.376
Del Unser	OF156, 1B1	L	23	156	635	66	146	13	7	1	30	46	66	11	.230	.277
Frank Howard	OF107, 1B55	R	31	158	598	79	164	28	3	**44**	106	54	141	0	.274	**.552**
Paul Casanova	C92	R	26	96	322	19	63	6	0	4	25	7	52	0	.196	.252
Cap Peterson	OF52	R	25	94	226	20	46	8	1	3	18	18	31	2	.204	.288
Ed Brinkman	SS74, 2B2, OF1	R	26	77	193	12	36	3	0	0	6	19	31	0	.187	.202
Gary Holman	1B33, OF10	L	24	75	85	10	25	5	1	0	7	13	15	0	.294	.376
Hank Allen	OF25, 3B16, 2B1	R	27	68	128	16	28	2	2	1	9	7	16	0	.219	.209
Frank Coggins	2B52	B	24	62	171	15	30	6	1	0	7	9	33	1	.175	.222
Jim French	C53	L	26	59	165	9	32	5	0	1	10	19	19	1	.194	.242
Sam Bowens	OF27	R	29	57	115	14	22	4	0	4	7	11	39	0	.191	.330
Brant Alyea	OF39	R	27	53	150	18	40	11	1	6	23	10	39	0	.267	.473
2 Tim Cullen	SS33, 2B16, 3B3	R	26	47	114	8	31	4	2	1	16	7	12	0	.272	.368
Billy Bryan	C28	L	29	40	108	7	22	3	0	3	8	14	27	0	.204	.315
1 Fred Valentine	OF27	B	33	37	101	11	24	2	0	3	7	6	11	1	.238	.247
Dick Billings	OF8, 3B4	R	25	12	33	3	6	1	0	1	3	5	13	0	.182	.303

Gene Martin 21 L 4-11, Doug Camilli (RC) 31

NAME	T	AGE	W	L	PCT	SV	G	GS	CG	IP	H	BB	SO	ShO	ERA
		27	65	**96**	.404	28	161	161	26	1440	**1402**	517	826	11	3.64
Camilo Pascual	R	34	13	12	.520	0	31	31	8	201	181	59	111	4	2.69
Joe Coleman	R	21	12	16	.429	0	33	33	12	223	212	51	139	2	3.27
Jim Hannan	R	28	10	6	.625	0	25	22	4	140	147	50	75	1	3.02
Frank Bertaina	L	24	7	13	.350	0	27	23	1	127	133	69	81	0	4.68
Bob Humphreys	R	32	5	7	.417	2	56	0	0	93	78	30	56	0	3.68
Phil Ortega	R	28	5	12	.294	0	31	16	1	116	115	62	57	1	4.97
Denny Higgins	R	28	4	4	.500	13	59	0	0	100	81	46	66	0	3.24
Barry Moore	L	25	4	6	.400	3	32	18	0	118	116	42	56	0	3.36
Dick Bosman	R	24	2	9	.182	1	46	10	0	139	139	35	63	0	3.69
Darold Knowles (MS)	L	26	1	1	.500	4	32	0	0	41	38	12	37	0	2.20
Steve Jones	L	27	1	2	.333	0	7	0	0	11	8	7	11	0	5.73
1 Bruce Howard	R	25	1	4	.200	0	13	7	0	49	62	23	23	0	5.36
Casey Cox	R	26	0	1	.000	0	4	0	0	8	7	0	4	0	2.25
Jerry Schoen	R	21	0	1	.000	0	1	1	0	4	6	1	1	0	6.75
Dave Baldwin	R	30	0	2	.000	5	40	0	0	42	40	12	30	0	4.07
Bill Haywood	R	31	0	0	.000	0	14	0	0	23	27	12	10	0	4.70
Bill Denehy	R	22	0	0	.000	0	3	0	0	2	4	4	1	0	9.00
Jim Miles	R	24	0	0	.000	0	3	0	0	4	8	2	5	0	13.50

ST. LOUIS 1st 97-65 .599 — RED SCHOENDIENST

NAME	G by POS	B	AGE	G	AB	R	H	2B	3B	HR	RBI	BB	SO	SB	BA	SA
TOTALS			29	162	5561	583	1383	227	**48**	73	539	378	897	110	.249	.346
Orlando Cepeda	1B154	R	30	157	600	71	149	26	2	16	73	43	96	8	.248	.378
Julian Javier	2B139	R	31	139	519	54	135	25	4	4	52	24	61	10	.260	.347
Dal Maxvill	SS151	R	29	151	459	51	116	8	5	1	24	52	71	0	.253	.298
Mike Shannon	3B156	R	28	156	576	62	153	29	2	15	79	37	114	1	.266	.401
Roger Maris	OF84	L	33	100	310	25	79	18	2	5	45	24	38	0	.255	.374
Curt Flood	OF149	R	30	150	618	71	186	17	4	5	60	33	58	11	.301	.366
Lou Brock	OF156	L	29	159	660	92	184	**46**	**14**	6	51	46	124	**62**	.279	.418
Tim McCarver	C109	L	26	128	434	35	110	15	6	5	48	26	31	4	.253	.350
Bobby Tolan	OF67, 1B9	L	22	92	278	28	64	12	1	5	17	13	42	9	.230	.335
Johnny Edwards	C54	L	30	85	230	14	55	9	1	3	29	16	20	1	.239	.326
Dick Schofield	SS43, 2B23	B	33	69	127	14	28	7	1	1	8	13	31	1	.220	.315
Phil Gagliano	2B17, 3B10, OF5	R	26	53	105	13	24	4	2	0	13	7	12	0	.229	.307
2 Ron Davis	OF25	R	26	33	79	11	14	4	2	0	5	5	17	1	.177	.278
Ed Spiezio	OF11, 3B2	R	26	29	51	1	8	0	0	0	2	5	6	1	.157	.157
1 Dick Simpson	OF22	R	24	26	56	11	13	0	0	3	8	8	21	0	.232	.393
Dave Ricketts	C1	B	32	20	22	1	3	0	0	0	1	0	3	0	.136	.136
Joe Hague	OF3, 1B2	L	24	7	17	2	4	0	0	1	1	2	2	0	.235	.412

Floyd Wicker 24 L 2-4, Ted Simmons 18 B 1-3

NAME	T	AGE	W	L	PCT	SV	G	GS	CG	IP	H	BB	SO	ShO	ERA
TOTALS		27	**97**	65	.599	32	162	162	63	1479	1282	375	971	**30**	**2.49**
Bob Gibson	R	32	22	9	.710	0	34	34	28	305	198	62	**268**	**13**	**1.12**
Nelson Briles	R	24	19	11	.633	0	33	33	13	244	251	55	141	4	2.80
Ray Washburn	R	30	14	8	.636	0	31	30	8	215	191	47	124	4	2.26
Steve Carlton	L	23	13	11	.542	0	34	33	10	232	214	61	162	5	2.99
Larry Jaster	L	24	9	13	.409	0	31	21	3	154	153	38	70	1	3.51
Joe Hoerner	L	31	8	2	.800	17	47	0	0	49	34	12	42	0	1.47
Wayne Granger	R	24	4	2	.667	4	34	0	0	44	40	12	27	0	2.25
Mel Nelson	L	32	2	1	.667	1	18	4	1	53	49	9	16	0	2.89
Mike Torrez	R	21	2	1	.667	0	5	2	0	19	20	12	6	0	2.84
Dick Hughes (SA)	R	30	2	2	.500	4	25	5	0	64	45	21	49	0	3.52
Ron Willis	R	24	2	3	.400	4	48	0	0	64	50	28	39	0	3.38
1 Hal Gilson	L	26	0	2	.000	2	13	0	0	22	27	11	19	0	4.50
2 Pete Mikkelsen	R	28	0	0	.000	0	5	0	0	16	10	7	8	0	1.13

SAN FRANCISCO 2nd 88-74 .543 9 — HERMAN FRANKS

NAME	G by POS	B	AGE	G	AB	R	H	2B	3B	HR	RBI	BB	SO	SB	BA	SA
TOTALS			27	163	5441	599	1301	162	33	108	566	**508**	904	50	.239	.341
Willie McCovey	1B146	L	30	148	523	81	153	16	4	**36**	**105**	72	71	4	.293	**.545**
Ron Hunt	2B147	R	27	148	529	79	132	19	0	2	28	78	41	6	.250	.297
Hal Lanier	SS150	B	25	151	486	37	100	14	1	0	27	12	57	2	.206	.239
Jim Davenport	3B82, SS17, 2B1	R	34	113	272	27	61	1	1	1	17	26	32	0	.224	.246
Bobby Bonds	OF80	R	22	81	307	55	78	10	5	9	35	38	84	16	.254	.407
Willie Mays	OF142, 1B1	R	37	148	498	84	144	20	5	23	79	67	81	12	.289	.488
Jesus Alou	OF105	R	26	120	419	26	110	15	4	0	39	9	23	1	.263	.317
Dick Dietz	C90	L	26	98	301	21	82	14	2	6	38	34	68	1	.272	.392
Jim Ray Hart	3B72, OF65	R	26	136	480	67	124	14	3	23	78	46	74	3	.258	.444
Ty Cline	OF70, 1B24	L	29	116	291	37	65	6	3	1	28	11	26	0	.223	.275
Jack Hiatt	C58, 1B10	R	25	90	224	14	52	10	2	4	34	41	61	0	.232	.348
Dave Marshall	OF50	L	25	76	174	17	46	5	1	1	16	20	37	2	.264	.322
Frank Johnson	3B36, OF8, SS5, 2B3	R	25	67	174	11	33	2	0	1	7	12	23	1	.190	.218
Bob Barton	C45	R	26	46	92	4	24	2	0	0	5	7	18	0	.261	.283
Ollie Brown	OF35	R	24	40	95	7	22	4	0	0	11	3	23	1	.232	.274
Nate Oliver (IL)	2B14, SS13, 3B1	R	27	36	73	3	13	2	0	0	1	1	13	0	.178	.205
Bob Schroder	2B12, SS4, 3B2	L	23	35	44	5	7	1	1	0	2	7	3	0	.159	.227
Don Mason	2B5, SS4, 3B2	L	23	10	19	3	3	0	0	0	1	1	4	1	.158	.158
Ken Henderson	OF2	B	22	3	3	1	1	0	0	0	0	2	1	0	.333	.333

NAME	T	AGE	W	L	PCT	SV	G	GS	CG	IP	H	BB	SO	ShO	ERA
TOTALS		29	88	74	.543	16	163	163	**77**	1469	1302	344	942	20	2.71
Juan Marichal	R	30	**26**	9	.743	0	38	38	**30**	**326**	**295**	46	218	5	2.43
Gaylord Perry	R	29	16	15	.516	1	39	38	19	291	240	59	173	3	2.44
Mike McCormick	L	29	12	14	.462	1	38	28	9	198	196	49	121	2	3.59
Ray Sadecki	L	27	12	**18**	.400	0	38	36	13	254	225	70	206	6	2.91
Bob Bolin	R	29	10	5	.667	0	34	19	6	177	128	46	126	3	1.98
Frank Linzy	R	27	9	8	.529	12	57	0	0	95	76	27	36	0	2.08
Rich Robertson	R	23	2	0	1.000	0	3	1	0	9	9	3	8	0	6.00
Joe Gibbon	L	33	1	2	.333	1	29	0	0	40	33	19	22	0	1.58
2 Bill Monbouquette	R	31	0	1	.000	1	7	0	0	12	11	2	5	0	3.75
1 Bill Henry	L	40	0	2	.000	0	7	1	0	5	4	3	0	0	5.40
Ron Herbel	R	30	0	0	.000	0	28	2	0	43	55	15	18	0	3.35
1 Lindy McDaniel	R	32	0	0	.000	0	12	0	0	19	30	5	9	0	7.58

CHICAGO 3rd 84-78 .519 13 — LEO DUROCHER

NAME	G by POS	B	AGE	G	AB	R	H	2B	3B	HR	RBI	BB	SO	SB	BA	SA
TOTALS			30	163	5458	612	1319	203	43	**130**	576	415	854	41	.242	.366
Ernie Banks	1B147	R	36	150	552	71	136	27	0	32	83	27	67	2	.246	.469
Glenn Beckert	2B155	R	27	155	643	**98**	189	28	4	4	37	31	20	8	.294	.369
Don Kessinger	SS159	B	25	160	655	63	157	14	7	1	32	38	86	9	.240	.287
Ron Santo	3B162	R	28	162	577	86	142	17	3	26	98	**96**	106	3	.246	.421
Jim Hickman	OF66	R	31	75	188	22	42	6	3	5	23	18	38	1	.223	.367
Adolfo Phillips	OF141	R	26	143	439	49	106	20	5	13	33	47	90	9	.241	.399
Billy Williams	OF163	L	30	163	642	91	185	30	8	30	98	48	53	4	.288	.500
Randy Hundley	C160	R	26	160	553	41	125	18	4	7	65	39	69	1	.226	.311
Al Spangler	OF48	L	34	88	177	21	48	9	3	2	18	20	24	0	.271	.390
Dick Nen	1B52	L	28	81	94	8	17	1	1	2	16	6	17	0	.181	.277
1 Lou Johnson	OF57	R	33	62	205	14	50	14	3	1	14	6	23	3	.244	.356
Jose Arcia	OF17, 2B10, SS7, 3B1	R	24	59	84	15	16	4	0	1	8	3	24	0	.190	.274
2 Willie Smith	OF38, 1B4, P1	L	29	55	142	13	39	8	2	5	25	12	33	0	.275	.465
Lee Elia	SS2, 3B1, 2B1	R	30	15	17	1	3	0	0	0	3	0	6	0	.176	.176
2 Gene Oliver	1B2, OF1, C1	R	32	8	11	1	4	0	0	0	1	3	2	0	.364	.364
John Boccabella	C4, OF1	R	27	7	14	0	1	0	0	0	1	2	2	0	.071	.071
Randy Bobb	C7	R	20	7	8	0	1	0	0	0	0	1	2	0	.125	.125
Jimmy McMath	OF3	L	18	6	14	0	2	0	0	0	2	0	6	0	.143	.143
Clarence Jones	1B1	L	24	5	2	0	0	0	0	0	0	2	1	0	.000	.000
John Felske	C3	R	26	4	2	0	0	0	0	0	0	0	1	0	.000	.000
1 Ted Savage	OF2	R	32	3	8	0	2	0	0	0	0	0	1	1	.250	.250
Vic LaRose	2B2, SS2	R	23	4	2	0	0	0	0	0	0	0	1	0	.000	.000

Johnny Stephenson 27 L 0-2, Bill Plummer 21 R 0-2

NAME	T	AGE	W	L	PCT	SV	G	GS	CG	IP	H	BB	SO	ShO	ERA
TOTALS		26	84	78	.519	32	163	163	46	1453	1399	392	894	12	3.41
Ferguson Jenkins	R	24	20	15	.571	0	40	**40**	20	308	255	65	260	3	2.63
Bill Hands	R	28	16	10	.615	0	38	34	11	259	221	36	148	4	2.88
Joe Niekro	R	23	14	10	.583	2	34	29	2	177	204	59	65	1	4.32
Ken Holtzman	L	22	11	14	.440	1	34	32	6	215	201	76	151	3	3.35
2 Phil Regan	R	31	10	5	.667	**25***	68	0	0	127	109	24	60	0	2.20
Rich Nye	L	23	7	12	.368	1	27	20	6	133	145	34	74	1	3.79
Jack Lamabe	R	31	3	2	.600	1	42	0	0	61	68	24	30	0	4.28
Chuck Hartenstein	R	26	2	4	.333	1	28	0	0	36	41	11	17	0	4.50
Gary Ross	R	20	1	1	.500	0	13	5	1	41	44	25	31	0	4.17
Darcy Fast	L	21	0	1	.000	0	8	1	0	10	8	8	10	0	5.40
Frank Reberger	R	24	0	1	.000	0	3	1	0	6	9	2	3	0	4.50
Archie Reynolds	R	22	0	1	.000	0	7	1	0	13	14	7	6	0	6.92
Bill Stoneman	R	24	0	1	.000	0	18	0	0	29	35	14	18	0	5.59
Bobby Tiefenauer	R	38	0	1	.000	1	9	0	0	13	20	2	9	0	6.23
Ramon Hernandez	L	27	0	0	.000	0	8	0	0	9	14	0	3	0	9.00
1 Pete Mikkelsen	R	28	0	0	.000	0	3	0	0	5	7	1	5	0	7.20
John Upham	L	26	0	0	.000	0	2	0	0	7	2	3	2	0	0.00
Jophery Brown	R	23	0	0	.000	0	1	0	0	2	2	1	0	0	4.50
2 Willie Smith	L	29	0	0	.000	0	1	0	0	3	0	0	2	0	0.00

***Regan, also with Los Angeles, league leader in SV with 25**

CINCINNATI 4th 83-79 .512 14 — DAVE BRISTOL

NAME	G by POS	B	AGE	G	AB	R	H	2B	3B	HR	RBI	BB	SO	SB	BA	SA
TOTALS			27	163	**5767**	**690**	**1573**	**281**	36	106	**638**	379	938	59	**.273**	**.389**
Lee May	1B122, OF33	R	25	146	559	78	162	32	1	22	80	34	100	4	.290	.469
Tommy Helms	2B127, SS2, 3B1	R	27	127	507	35	146	28	2	2	47	12	27	5	.288	.363
Leo Cardenas	SS136	R	29	137	452	45	106	13	2	7	41	36	83	2	.235	.319
Tony Perez	3B160	R	26	160	625	93	176	25	7	18	92	51	92	3	.282	.430
Pete Rose	OF148, 2B3, 1B1	B	27	149	626	94	**210**	42	6	10	49	56	76	3	**.335**	.470
Vada Pinson	OF123	L	29	130	499	60	135	29	6	5	48	32	59	17	.271	.383
Alex Johnson	OF140	R	25	149	603	79	188	32	6	2	58	26	71	16	.312	.395
Johnny Bench	C154	R	20	154	564	67	155	40	2	15	82	31	96	1	.275	.433
Mack Jones	OF60	L	29	103	234	40	59	9	1	10	34	28	46	2	.252	.427
Fred Whitfield	1B41	L	30	87	171	15	44	8	0	6	32	9	29	0	.257	.409
Chico Ruiz	2B34, 1B16, 3B5, SS3	B	29	85	139	15	36	2	1	0	9	12	18	4	.259	.288
2 Woody Woodward	SS41, 2B9, 1B1	R	25	56	119	13	29	2	0	0	10	7	23	1	.244	.261
Don Pavletich (EJ)	1B22, C5	R	29	46	98	11	28	3	1	2	11	8	23	0	.286	.398
Jim Beauchamp	OF13, 1B1	R	28	31	57	10	15	2	0	2	14	4	19	0	.263	.404
Pat Corrales	C20	R	27	20	56	3	15	4	0	0	6	6	16	0	.268	.339
Hal McRae	2B16	R	21	17	51	1	10	1	0	0	2	4	14	1	.196	.216
1 Bob Johnson	SS2, 1B1	R	32	16	15	2	4	0	0	0	1	1	2	0	.267	.267
Jimmie Schaffer	C2	R	32	4	6	0	1	0	0	0	1	0	3	0	.167	.167

NAME	T	AGE	W	L	PCT	SV	G	GS	CG	IP	H	BB	SO	ShO	ERA
TOTALS		27	83	79	.512	**38**	163	163	24	**1490**	1399	**573**	963	16	3.56
Jim Maloney	R	28	16	10	.615	0	33	32	8	207	183	80	181	5	3.61
Jerry Arrigo	L	27	12	10	.545	0	36	31	5	205	181	77	140	1	3.34
George Culver	R	24	11	16	.407	2	42	35	5	226	229	84	114	2	3.23
Ted Abernathy	R	35	10	7	.588	13	**78**	0	0	135	111	55	64	0	2.47
Gary Nolan	R	20	9	4	.692	0	23	22	4	150	105	49	111	2	2.40
2 Clay Carroll	R	27	7	7	.500	17	58	1	0	122	102	32	61	0	2.29
Bill Kelso	R	28	4	1	.800	1	35	0	0	54	56	15	39	0	4.00
2 Tony Cloninger	R	27	4	3	.571	0	17	17	2	91	81	48	65	2	4.05
Billy McCool (WJ)	L	23	3	4	.429	2	30	4	0	51	59	41	30	0	4.94
Jay Ritchie	R	31	2	3	.400	0	28	2	0	57	68	13	32	0	4.58
Bob Lee	R	30	2	4	.333	3	44	1	0	65	73	37	34	0	5.12
1 Milt Pappas	R	29	2	5	.286	0	15	11	0	63	70	10	43	0	5.57
1 Ted Davidson	L	28	1	0	1.000	0	23	0	0	22	27	7	7	0	6.14
Dan McGinn	L	24	0	1	.000	0	14	0	0	12	13	11	16	0	5.25
Mel Queen (SJ)	R	26	0	1	.000	0	5	4	0	18	25	6	20	0	6.00
John Tsitouris	R	32	0	3	.000	0	3	3	0	13	16	8	6	0	6.92

ATLANTA 5th 81-81 .500 16 — LUM HARRIS

NAME	G by POS	B	AGE	G	AB	R	H	2B	3B	HR	RBI	BB	SO	SB	BA	SA
TOTALS			29	163	5552	514	1399	179	31	80	480	414	782	83	.252	.339
Deron Johnson (BH)	1B97, 3B21	R	29	127	342	29	71	11	1	8	33	35	79	0	.208	.316
Felix Millan	2B145	R	24	149	570	49	165	22	2	1	33	22	26	6	.289	.340
Sonny Jackson (GJ)	SS99	L	23	105	358	37	81	8	2	1	19	25	35	16	.226	.268
Clete Boyer (HJ)	3B69	R	31	71	273	19	62	7	2	4	17	16	32	2	.227	.311
Hank Aaron	OF151, 1B14	R	34	160	606	84	174	33	4	29	86	64	62	28	.287	.498
Felipe Alou	OF158	R	33	160	**662**	72	**210**	37	5	11	57	48	56	12	.317	.438
Mike Lum	OF95	L	22	122	232	22	52	7	3	3	21	14	35	3	.224	.319
Joe Torre (BY)	C92, 1B29	R	27	115	424	45	115	11	2	10	55	34	72	1	.271	.377
Tito Francona	OF65, 1B33	L	34	122	346	32	99	13	1	2	47	51	45	3	.286	.347
Marty Martinez	SS54, 3B37, 2B16, C14	B	26	113	356	34	82	5	3	0	12	29	28	6	.230	.261
Tommie Aaron	OF62, 1B28, 3B1	R	28	98	283	21	69	10	3	1	25	21	37	3	.244	.311
Bob Tillman	C75	R	31	86	236	16	52	4	0	5	20	16	55	1	.220	.301
2 Bob Johnson	3B48, 2B4	R	32	59	187	15	49	5	1	0	11	10	20	0	.262	.299
Sandy Valdespino	OF20	L	29	36	86	8	20	1	0	1	4	10	20	0	.233	.279
Mike Page	OF6	L	27	20	28	1	5	0	0	0	1	1	9	0	.179	.179
Gil Garrido	SS17	R	27	18	53	5	11	0	0	0	2	2	2	0	.208	.208
3 Wayne Causey	2B6, 3B2, SS2	L	31	16	37	2	4	0	1	1	4	0	4	0	.108	.243
1 Woody Woodward	SS6, 3B2, 2B1	R	25	12	24	2	4	1	0	0	1	1	6	1	.167	.208
Ralph Garr		L	22	11	7	3	2	0	0	0	0	1	0	1	.286	.286
Walt Hriniak	C9	L	25	9	26	0	9	0	0	0	3	0	3	0	.346	.346
Dusty Baker	OF3	R	19	6	5	0	2	0	0	0	0	0	1	0	.400	.400

Rico Carty (IL) 29

NAME	T	AGE	W	L	PCT	SV	G	GS	CG	IP	H	BB	SO	ShO	ERA
TOTALS		28	81	81	.500	29	163	163	44	1474	1326	362	871	16	2.92
Pat Jarvis	R	27	16	12	.571	0	34	34	14	256	202	50	157	1	2.60
Phil Niekro	R	29	14	12	.538	2	37	34	15	257	228	45	140	5	2.59
Ron Reed	R	25	11	10	.524	0	35	28	6	202	189	49	111	1	3.34
2 Milt Pappas	R	29	10	8	.556	0	22	19	3	121	111	22	75	1	2.38
Cecil Upshaw	R	25	8	7	.533	13	52	0	0	117	98	24	74	0	2.46
George Stone	L	22	7	4	.636	0	17	10	2	75	63	19	52	0	2.76
Ken Johnson	R	35	5	8	.385	0	31	16	1	135	145	25	57	0	3.47
Jim Britton	R	24	4	6	.400	3	34	9	2	90	81	34	61	2	3.10
Claude Raymond	R	31	3	5	.375	10	36	0	0	60	56	18	37	0	2.85
Dick Kelley	L	28	2	4	.333	1	31	11	1	98	86	45	73	1	2.76
1 Tony Cloninger	R	27	1	3	.250	0	8	1	0	19	15	11	7	0	4.26
1 Clay Carroll	R	27	0	1	.000	0	10	0	0	22	26	6	10	0	4.91
Al Santorini	R	20	0	1	.000	0	1	1	0	3	4	0	0	0	0.00
Rick Kester	R	21	0	0	.000	0	5	0	0	6	8	3	9	0	6.00
2 Ted Davidson	L	28	0	0	.000	0	4	0	0	7	10	4	3	0	6.43
Skip Guinn	L	23	0	0	.000	0	3	0	0	5	3	3	4	0	3.60
Stu Miller	R	40	0	0	.000	0	2	0	0	1	1	4	1	0	36.00

PITTSBURGH 6th 80-82 .494 17 — LARRY SHEPARD

NAME	G by POS	B	AGE	G	AB	R	H	2B	3B	HR	RBI	BB	SO	SB	BA	SA
TOTALS			30	163	5569	583	1404	180	44	80	538	422	953	130	.252	.343
Donn Clendenon	1B155	R	32	158	584	63	150	20	6	17	87	47	163	10	.257	.399
Bill Mazeroski	2B142	R	31	143	506	36	127	18	2	3	42	38	38	3	.251	.312
Gene Alley	SS109, 2B24	R	27	133	474	48	116	20	2	4	39	39	78	13	.245	.321
Maury Wills	3B141, SS10	B	35	153	627	76	174	12	6	0	31	45	57	52	.278	.316
Roberto Clemente	OF131	R	33	132	502	74	146	18	12	18	57	51	77	2	.291	.482
Matty Alou	OF144	L	29	146	558	59	185	28	4	0	52	27	26	18	.332	.396
Willie Stargell	OF113, 1B13	L	28	128	435	57	103	15	1	24	67	47	105	5	.237	.441
Jerry May	C135	R	24	137	416	26	91	15	2	1	33	41	80	0	.219	.272
Manny Mota	OF92, 2B1, 3B1	R	30	111	331	35	93	10	2	1	33	20	19	4	.281	.332
Jose Pagan	3B30, OF19, SS8, 2B2, 1B1	R	33	80	163	24	36	7	1	4	21	11	32	2	.221	.350
Gary Kolb	OF25, C10, 3B4, 2B1	L	28	74	119	16	26	4	1	2	6	11	17	2	.218	.319
Manny Jiminez	OF5	L	29	66	66	7	20	1	1	1	11	6	15	0	.303	.394
Freddie Patek (BW)	SS52, OF5, 3B1	R	23	61	208	31	53	4	2	2	18	12	37	18	.255	.322
Carl Taylor	C29, OF2	R	24	44	71	5	15	1	0	0	7	10	10	1	.211	.225
Chris Cannizzaro	C25	R	30	25	58	5	14	2	2	1	7	9	13	0	.241	.397
Chuck Hiller	2B2	L	33	11	13	2	5	1	0	0	1	0	0	0	.385	.462
Bill Virdon	OF4	L	37	6	3	1	1	0	0	1	2	0	2	0	.333	1.333

Al Oliver 21 L 1-8, Richie Hebner 20 L 0-1, Bob Robertson (IL) 21

NAME	T	AGE	W	L	PCT	SV	G	GS	CG	IP	H	BB	SO	ShO	ERA
		29	80	82	.494	30	163	163	42	1487	1322	485	897	19	2.74
Steve Blass	R	26	18	6	.750	0	33	31	12	220	191	57	132	7	2.13
Bob Veale	L	32	13	14	.481	0	36	33	13	245	187	94	171	4	2.06
Ron Kline	R	36	12	5	.706	7	56	0	0	113	94	31	48	0	1.67
Al McBean	R	30	9	12	.429	0	36	28	9	198	204	63	100	2	3.59
Bob Moose	R	20	8	12	.400	3	38	22	3	171	136	41	126	3	2.74
Dock Ellis	R	23	6	5	.545	0	26	10	2	104	82	38	52	0	2.51
Tommie Sisk	R	26	5	5	.500	1	33	11	0	96	101	35	41	0	3.28
Jim Bunning	R	36	4	14	.222	0	27	26	3	160	168	48	95	1	3.88
1 Roy Face	R	40	2	4	.333	13	43	0	0	52	46	7	34	0	2.60
Dave Wickersham	R	32	1	0	1.000	1	11	0	0	21	21	13	8	0	3.43
Bruce Dal Canton	R	26	1	1	.500	2	7	0	0	17	7	6	8	0	2.12
1 Juan Pizarro	L	31	1	1	.500	0	12	0	0	11	14	10	6	0	3.27
Luke Walker (IL)	L	24	0	3	.000	3	39	2	0	62	42	39	66	0	2.03
2 Bill Henry	L	40	0	0	.000	0	10	0	0	17	29	3	9	0	7.94

LOS ANGELES 7th (Tie) 76-86 .469 21 — WALT ALSTON

NAME	G by POS	B	AGE	G	AB	R	H	2B	3B	HR	RBI	BB	SO	SB	BA	SA
TOTALS			28	162	5354	470	1234	202	36	67	434	439	980	57	.230	.319
Wes Parker	1B114, OF28	B	28	135	468	42	112	22	2	3	27	49	87	4	.239	.314
Paul Popovich	2B89, SS45, 3B7	B	27	134	418	35	97	8	1	2	25	29	37	1	.232	.270
Zoilo Versalles	SS119	R	28	122	403	29	79	16	3	2	24	26	84	6	.196	.266
Bob Bailey	3B90, SS1, OF1	R	25	105	322	24	73	9	3	8	39	38	69	1	.227	.348
Ron Fairly	OF105, 1B36	L	29	141	441	32	103	15	1	4	43	41	61	0	.234	.299
Willie Davis	OF158	L	28	160	643	86	161	24	10	7	31	31	88	36	.250	.351
Len Gabrielson	OF86	L	28	108	304	38	82	16	1	10	35	32	47	1	.270	.428
Tom Haller	C139	L	31	144	474	37	135	27	5	4	53	46	76	1	.285	.388
Jim Fairey	OF63	L	23	99	156	17	31	3	3	1	10	9	32	1	.199	.276
Jim Lefebvre (WJ)	2B62, 3B16, OF5, 1B3	B	25	84	286	23	69	12	1	5	31	26	55	0	.241	.343
2 Ken Boyer	3B34, 1B32	R	37	83	221	20	60	7	2	6	41	16	34	2	.271	.403
Willie Crawford	OF48	L	21	61	175	25	44	12	1	4	14	20	64	1	.251	.400
2 Ted Savage	OF39	R	32	61	126	7	26	6	1	2	7	10	20	1	.206	.317
Luis Alcaraz	2B20, 3B13, SS1	R	27	41	106	4	16	1	0	2	5	9	23	1	.151	.217
1 Rocky Colavito	OF33	R	34	40	113	8	23	3	0	3	11	15	18	0	.204	.310
Bart Shirley	SS21, 2B18	R	28	39	83	6	15	3	0	0	4	10	13	0	.181	.217
Jeff Torborg	C37	R	26	37	93	2	15	2	0	0	4	6	10	0	.161	.183
Bill Sudakis	3B24	B	22	24	87	11	24	4	2	3	12	15	14	1	.276	.471
Cleo James	OF2	R	27	10	10	2	2	1	0	0	0	0	6	0	.200	.300

Jim Campanis 24 R 1-11, Al Ferrara (BN) 28 R 1-7

NAME	T	AGE	W	L	PCT	SV	G	GS	CG	IP	H	BB	SO	ShO	ERA
		28	76	86	.469	31	162	162	38	1449	1293	414	994	23	2.69
Don Drysdale	R	31	14	12	.538	0	31	31	12	239	201	56	155	8	2.15
Bill Singer	R	24	13	17	.433	0	37	36	12	256	227	78	227	6	2.88
Claude Osteen	L	28	12	18	.400	0	39	36	5	254	267	54	119	3	3.08
Don Sutton	R	23	11	15	.423	1	35	27	7	208	179	59	162	2	2.60
Jim Brewer	L	30	8	3	.727	14	54	0	0	76	59	33	75	0	2.49
Mudcat Grant	R	32	6	4	.600	3	37	4	1	95	77	19	35	0	2.08
Jack Billingham	R	25	3	0	1.000	8	50	1	0	71	54	30	46	0	2.15
1 Phil Regan	R	31	2	0	1.000	0*	5	0	0	8	10	1	7	0	3.38
John Purdin	R	25	2	3	.400	2	35	1	0	56	42	21	38	0	3.05
Mike Kekich	L	23	2	10	.167	0	25	20	1	115	116	46	84	1	3.91
Alan Foster (SJ)	R	21	1	1	.500	0	3	3	0	16	11	2	10	0	1.69
Joe Moeller	R	25	1	1	.500	0	3	3	0	16	17	2	11	0	5.06
Hank Aguirre	L	36	1	2	.333	3	25	0	0	39	32	13	25	0	0.69
1 Vicente Romo	R	25	0	0	.000	0	1	0	0	1	1	0	0	0	0.00

*Regan, also with Chicago, league leader in SV with 25

PHILADELPHIA 7th (Tie) 76-86 .469 21 — GENE MAUCH 26-27 .491 GEORGE MYATT 2-0 1.000 BOB SKINNER 48-59 .449

NAME	G by POS	B	AGE	G	AB	R	H	2B	3B	HR	RBI	BB	SO	SB	BA	SA
TOTALS			29	162	5372	543	1253	178	30	100	505	462	1003	58	.233	.333
Bill White	1B111	L	34	127	385	34	92	16	2	9	40	39	79	0	.239	.361
Cookie Rojas	2B150, C1	R	29	152	621	53	144	19	0	9	48	16	55	4	.232	.306
Roberto Pena	SS133	R	28	138	500	56	130	13	2	1	38	34	63	3	.260	.300
Tony Taylor	3B138, 2B5, 1B1	R	32	145	547	59	137	20	2	3	38	39	60	22	.250	.311
Johnny Callison	OF109	L	29	121	398	46	97	18	4	14	40	42	70	4	.244	.415
Tony Gonzalez	OF117	L	31	121	416	45	110	13	4	3	38	40	42	6	.264	.337
Dick Allen	OF139, 3B10	R	26	152	521	87	137	17	9	33	90	74	161	7	.263	.520
Mike Ryan	C96	R	26	96	296	12	53	6	1	1	15	15	59	0	.179	.216
Johnny Briggs	OF65, 1B36	L	24	110	338	36	86	13	1	7	31	58	72	8	.254	.361
Don Lock	OF78	R	31	99	248	27	52	7	2	8	34	26	64	3	.210	.351
Clay Dalrymple	C80	L	31	85	241	19	50	9	1	3	26	22	57	1	.207	.290
Gary Sutherland	2B17, 3B10, SS10, OF7	R	23	67	138	16	38	7	0	0	15	8	15	0	.275	.326
Rick Joseph	1B30, 3B14, OF1	R	28	66	155	20	34	5	0	3	12	16	35	0	.219	.310
Doug Clemens	OF17	L	29	29	57	6	12	1	1	2	8	7	13	0	.211	.368
Bobby Wine (XJ)	SS25, 3B1	R	29	27	71	5	12	3	0	2	7	6	17	0	.169	.296
John Sullivan	C8	L	27	12	18	0	4	0	0	0	1	2	4	0	.222	.222
Howie Bedell		L	32	9	7	0	1	0	0	0	1	1	0	0	.143	.143
Larry Hisle	OF6	R	21	7	11	1	4	1	0	0	1	1	4	0	.364	.455
Don Money	SS4	R	21	4	13	1	3	2	0	0	2	2	4	0	.231	.385

NAME	T	AGE	W	L	PCT	SV	G	GS	CG	IP	H	BB	SO	ShO	ERA
		29	76	86	.469	27	162	162	42	1448	1416	421	935	12	3.36
Chris Short	L	30	19	13	.594	1	42	36	9	270	236	81	202	2	2.93
Larry Jackson	R	37	13	17	.433	0	34	34	12	244	229	60	127	2	2.77
Woody Fryman	L	28	12	14	.462	0	34	32	10	214	198	64	151	5	2.78
Rick Wise	R	22	9	15	.375	0	30	30	7	182	210	37	97	1	4.55
Dick Hall	R	37	4	1	.800	0	32	0	0	46	53	5	31	0	4.89
Jeff James	R	26	4	4	.500	0	29	13	1	116	112	46	83	1	4.27
Jerry Johnson	R	24	4	4	.500	0	16	11	2	81	82	29	40	0	3.22
Gary Wagner	R	28	4	4	.500	8	44	0	0	78	69	31	43	0	3.00
Dick Farrell	R	34	4	6	.400	12	54	0	0	83	83	32	57	0	3.47
John Boozer	R	28	2	2	.500	5	38	0	0	69	76	15	49	0	3.65
Grant Jackson	L	25	1	6	.143	1	33	6	1	61	59	20	49	0	2.95
Paul Brown	R	27	0	0	.000	0	2	0	0	4	6	1	4	0	9.00
Larry Colton	R	26	0	0	.000	0	1	0	0	2	3	0	2	0	4.50

NEW YORK 9th 73-89 .451 24 — GIL HODGES

NAME	G by POS	B	AGE	G	AB	R	H	2B	3B	HR	RBI	BB	SO	SB	BA	SA
TOTALS			26	163	5503	473	1252	178	30	81	434	379	1203	72	.228	.315
Ed Kranepool	1B113, OF2	L	23	127	373	29	86	13	1	3	20	19	39	0	.231	.295
Ken Boswell (BG)	2B69	L	22	75	284	37	74	7	2	4	11	16	27	7	.261	.342
Bud Harrelson	SS106	B	24	111	402	38	88	7	3	0	14	29	68	4	.219	.251
Ed Charles	3B106, 1B2	R	33	117	369	41	102	11	1	15	53	28	57	5	.276	.434
Ron Swoboda	OF125	R	24	132	450	46	109	14	6	11	59	52	113	8	.242	.373
Tommie Agee	OF127	R	25	132	368	30	80	12	3	5	17	15	103	13	.217	.307
Cleon Jones	OF139	R	25	147	509	63	151	29	4	14	55	31	98	23	.297	.452
Jerry Grote	C115	R	25	124	404	29	114	18	0	3	31	44	81	1	.282	.349
Art Shamsky	OF82, 1B17	L	26	116	345	30	82	14	4	12	48	21	58	1	.238	.406
Al Weis	SS59, 2B29, 3B2	B	30	90	274	15	47	6	0	1	14	21	63	3	.172	.204
Phil Linz	2B71	R	29	78	258	19	54	7	0	0	17	10	41	1	.209	.236
J. C. Martin	C53, 1B14	L	31	78	244	20	55	9	2	3	31	21	31	0	.225	.316
Jerry Buchek	3B37, 2B12, OF9	R	26	73	192	8	35	4	0	1	11	10	53	1	.182	.219
Kevin Collins	3B40, 2B6, SS1	L	21	58	154	12	31	5	2	1	13	7	37	0	.201	.279
Larry Stahl	OF47, 1B9	L	27	53	183	15	43	7	2	3	10	21	38	3	.235	.344
Don Bosch	OF33	B	25	50	111	14	19	1	0	3	7	9	33	0	.171	.261
Greg Goossen	1B30, C2	R	22	38	106	4	22	7	0	0	6	10	21	0	.208	.274
Mike Jorgensen	1B4	L	19	8	14	0	2	1	0	0	0	0	4	0	.143	.214
Bob Heise	SS6, 2B1	R	21	6	23	3	5	0	0	0	1	1	1	0	.217	.217
Duffy Dyer	C1	R	22	1	3	0	1	0	0	0	0	1	1	0	.333	.333

NAME	T	AGE	W	L	PCT	SV	G	GS	CG	IP	H	BB	SO	ShO	ERA
		27	73	89	.451	32	163	163	45	1483	1250	430	1014	25	2.72
Jerry Koosman	L	25	19	12	.613	0	35	34	17	264	221	69	178	7	2.08
Tom Seaver	R	23	16	12	.571	1	36	35	14	278	224	48	205	5	2.20
Dick Selma	R	24	9	10	.474	0	33	23	4	170	148	54	117	3	2.75
Don Cardwell	R	32	7	13	.350	1	29	25	5	180	156	50	82	1	2.95
Cal Koonce	R	27	6	4	.600	11	55	2	0	97	80	32	50	0	2.41
Nolan Ryan (HJ)	R	21	6	9	.400	0	21	18	3	134	93	75	133	0	3.09
Jim McAndrew	R	24	4	7	.364	0	12	12	2	79	66	17	46	1	2.28
Al Jackson	L	32	3	7	.300	3	25	9	0	93	88	17	59	0	3.68
Danny Frisella	R	22	2	4	.333	2	19	4	0	51	53	17	47	0	3.88
Ron Taylor	R	30	1	5	.167	13	58	0	0	77	64	18	49	0	2.69
Billy Connors	R	26	0	1	.000	0	9	0	0	14	21	7	8	0	9.00
Les Rohr	L	22	0	2	.000	0	2	1	0	6	9	7	5	0	4.50
Bill Short	L	30	0	3	.000	1	34	0	0	30	24	14	24	0	4.80
Don Shaw	L	24	0	0	.000	0	7	0	0	12	3	5	11	0	0.75

HOUSTON 10th 72-90 .444 25 — GRADY HATTON 23-38 .377 HARRY WALKER 49-52 .485

NAME	G by POS	B	AGE	G	AB	R	H	2B	3B	HR	RBI	BB	SO	SB	BA	SA
TOTALS			26	162	5336	510	1233	205	28	66	473	479	988	44	.231	.317
Rusty Staub	1B147, OF15	L	24	161	591	54	172	37	1	6	72	73	57	2	.291	.387
Denis Menke	2B119, SS35, 1B5, 3B4	R	27	150	542	56	135	23	6	6	56	64	81	5	.249	.347
Hector Torres	SS127, 2B1	R	22	128	466	44	104	11	1	1	24	18	64	2	.223	.258
Doug Rader	3B86, 1B5	R	23	98	333	42	89	16	4	6	43	31	51	2	.267	.393
Norm Miller	OF74	L	22	79	257	35	61	18	2	6	28	22	48	6	.237	.393
1 Ron Davis	OF52	R	26	52	217	22	46	10	1	1	12	13	48	0	.212	.281
Jim Wynn	OF153	R	26	156	542	85	146	23	5	26	67	90	131	11	.269	.474
John Bateman	C108	R	25	111	350	28	87	19	0	4	33	23	46	1	.249	.337
Bob Aspromonte	3B75, OF36, SS1, 1B1	R	30	124	409	25	92	9	2	1	46	35	57	1	.225	.264
Lee Thomas	OF48, 1B2	L	32	90	201	14	39	4	0	1	11	14	22	2	.194	.229
Julio Gotay	2B48, 3B1	R	29	75	165	9	41	3	0	1	11	4	21	1	.248	.285
2 Dick Simpson	OF49	R	24	59	177	25	33	7	2	3	11	20	61	4	.186	.299
Bob Watson (NJ)	OF40	R	22	45	140	13	32	7	0	2	8	13	32	1	.229	.321
Ron Brand	C29, 3B1, OF1	R	28	43	81	7	13	2	0	0	4	9	11	1	.160	.185
Dave Adlesh	C38	R	24	40	104	3	19	1	1	0	4	5	27	0	.183	.212
Ivan Murrell	OF15	R	23	32	59	3	6	1	1	0	3	1	17	0	.102	.153
Joe Herrera	OF17, 2B7	R	26	27	100	9	24	5	0	0	7	4	12	0	.240	.290
Hal King	C19	L	24	27	55	4	8	2	1	0	2	7	16	0	.145	.218
Nate Colbert	OF11, 1B5	R	22	20	53	5	8	1	0	0	4	1	23	1	.151	.170
Leon McFadden	SS16	R	24	16	47	2	13	1	0	0	1	6	10	1	.277	.298
Joe Morgan (KJ)	2B5, OF1	L	24	10	20	6	5	0	1	0	0	7	4	3	.250	.350
Byron Browne	OF2	R	25	10	13	0	3	0	0	0	1	4	6	0	.231	.231
John Mayberry	1B2	L	18	4	9	0	0	0	0	0	0	0	2	0	.000	.000
Danny Walton		R	20	2	2	0	0	0	0	0	0	0	1	0	.000	.000

NAME	T	AGE	W	L	PCT	SV	G	GS	CG	IP	H	BB	SO	ShO	ERA
		26	72	90	.444	23	162	162	50	1447	1362	479	1021	12	3.26
Don Wilson	R	23	13	16	.448	0	33	30	9	209	187	70	175	3	3.27
Larry Dierker	R	21	12	15	.444	0	32	32	10	234	206	89	161	1	3.31
Dave Giusti	R	28	11	14	.440	1	37	34	12	251	226	67	186	2	3.19
Denny Lemaster	L	29	10	15	.400	0	33	32	7	224	231	72	146	2	2.81
Mike Cuellar	L	31	8	11	.421	1	28	24	11	171	152	45	133	2	2.74
Danny Coombs	L	26	4	3	.571	2	40	2	0	47	52	17	29	0	3.26
John Buzhardt	R	31	4	4	.500	5	39	4	0	84	73	35	37	0	3.11
Steve Shea	R	25	4	4	.500	6	30	0	0	35	27	11	15	0	3.34
Tom Dukes	R	25	2	2	.500	4	43	0	0	53	62	28	37	0	4.25
Jim Ray	R	23	2	3	.400	1	41	2	1	81	65	25	71	0	2.67
Pat House	L	27	1	1	.500	0	18	0	0	16	21	6	6	0	7.88
Wade Blasingame (BG)	L	24	1	2	.333	1	22	2	0	36	45	10	22	0	4.75
Fred Gladding (EJ)	R	32	0	0	.000	2	7	0	0	4	8	3	2	0	15.75
2 Hal Gilson	L	26	0	0	.000	0	2	0	0	4	7	1	1	0	6.75

Carroll Sembera (JJ) 26

1969 The Miracle at Flushing Meadows

Professional baseball's centennial year began with the expansion of both leagues to 12 teams and the introduction of division play in both leagues, as Montreal and San Diego joined the National League and Seattle and Kansas City the American League. Because pitchers had become overly dominant in the game, the pitcher's mound was lowered and the strike zone shrunk to spruce up the batting. Other news' items included Hawk Harrelson, who created an uproar by refusing to report after Boston traded him to Cleveland, and only did so after a significant pay raise; Donn Clendenon, who refused to be traded to Houston by Montreal and wound up in New York; Mickey Mantle, who could no longer fight injury and age and called it quits before the season opened; Richie Allen, who spent a month on the sidelines after being suspended by Phillie manager Bob Skinner, who himself resigned in mid-season; and Ted Williams, who returned to uniform as the manager of the Washington Senators. None of these events, including the firing at season's end of Billy Martin of the Western Division champion Minnesota Twins, or the bankruptcy of the Seattle Pilots could equal the biggest surprise in baseball's long history—the miracle of the amazing Mets!

The Mets, born and nurtured in mediocrity, had never risen above ninth place since entering the National League in 1962, and a loss on opening day to the newly-minted Montreal Expos only seemed to confirm another season of futility. But manager Gil Hodges had a vision and a plan which he patiently put in motion, the result of which found the Mets trailing only the Cubs in the National League's Eastern Division as summer dawned. The first real sign of what was to come arrived in early July when the Mets took two of three games from Chicago at Shea Stadium—one of the contests being a near-perfect performance by right-hander Tom Seaver who lost his bid for immortality with one out in the ninth inning to pinch-hitter Jimmy Qualls. Then, in Chicago the next week, light-hitting Al Weis swatted two homers in two games as the Mets again took two parts of a three-game set.

A slump in early August seemed to end all hopes of a miracle as the Mets dropped to 9½ games back. But they then again caught fire, as every man on the starless club played the best ball of his career. And with Tommie Agee, Cleon Jones, and Bud Harrelson starring day after day, and Hodges skillfully platooning at every other position, the one-time doormat rushed to within 2½ games of the slumping Cubs on September 8, when the Bruins came into New York for two games. With momentum on their side, the Mets swept both games, moved into first place on September 10, and kept winning until they had amassed 100 victories and the division title.

The Mets' pitching staff boasted of young aces, Seaver and Jerry Koosman, relief bulwark Tug McGraw, and strong arms up and down a deep staff. In contrast, the Atlanta Braves copped the Western Division crown in a close race with the San Francisco Giants and MVP Willie McCovey by wielding a powerful attack featuring Hank Aaron, Orlando Cepeda, and Rico Carty, but the favored Braves fell before the Mets' steamroller, three games to none in the championship playoff.

The Baltimore Orioles began a string of American League championships by taking the Eastern crown and then icing the Minnesota Twins for the American League title. Harmon Killebrew of the Twins took the MVP Award, but a good case could have been made for Frank Robinson, Boog Powell, or Brooks Robinson, all stars for the Orioles. Mike Cuellar won 23 games after joining the Birds in an off-season trade, Jim Palmer chalked up 16 victories after two injury-plagued seasons, and Dave McNally won his first 15 decisions on the way to a 20-win season.

After dropping the first game to Cuellar, the Mets' machine rolled on with four straight wins via unbelievable catches by Agee in the second game and Ron Swoboda in the fourth game to become the unlikeliest champions in baseball history. In addition to Swoboda and the gremlins who haunted the Orioles, the winning play of the game came in the tenth inning when J. C. Martin bunted and was hit in the wrist by Pete Richert's throw to score Rod Gaspar from second after the ball ricocheted into short right field. What was not definitely known until that evening was the newspaper photograph which showed Martin running in fair territory for which he should have been declared out by umpire Shag Crawford. Yet it was the final game which best showed the winks that fate was constantly tossing in the Mets' direction. Trailing 3-0 in the sixth inning, Cleon Jones was awarded first base when shoe polish on the ball revealed he had been struck on the foot. Donn Clendenon then promptly drilled a homer over the left-field wall. Al Weis tied it up in the seventh with his first and only Shea Stadium home run, and in the eighth inning the two winning runs scored on doubles by Jones and Swoboda and two Baltimore errors. As the screaming continued long into the night, it was certain that the 5-3 victory climaxed a meteoric rise which had absolutely no worlds left to conquer.

1969 AMERICAN LEAGUE

EAST DIVISION

NAME	G by POS	B	AGE	G	AB	R	H	2B	3B	HR	RBI	BB	SO	SB	BA	SA
BALTIMORE 1st 109-53 .673	EARL WEAVER															
	TOTALS		28	162	5518	779	1465	234	29	175	722	634	806	82	.265	.414
Boog Powell	1B144	L	27	152	533	83	162	25	0	37	121	72	76	1	.304	.559
Dave Johnson	2B142, SS2	R	26	142	511	52	143	34	1	7	57	57	52	3	.280	.391
Mark Belanger	SS148	R	25	150	530	76	152	17	4	2	50	53	54	14	.287	.345
Brooks Robinson	3B156	R	32	156	598	73	140	21	3	23	84	56	55	2	.234	.395
Frank Robinson	OF134, 1B19	R	33	148	539	111	166	19	5	32	100	88	62	9	.308	.540
Paul Blair	OF150	R	25	150	625	102	178	32	5	26	76	40	72	20	.285	.477
Don Buford	OF128, 2B10, 3B6	B	32	144	554	99	161	31	3	11	64	96	62	19	.291	.417
Ellie Hendricks	C87, 1B4	L	28	105	295	36	72	5	0	12	38	39	44	0	.244	.383
Merv Rettenmund	OF78	R	26	95	190	27	47	10	3	4	25	28	28	6	.247	.395
Dave May	OF40	L	25	78	120	8	29	6	0	3	10	9	23	2	.242	.367
Andy Etchebarren	C72	R	26	73	217	29	54	9	2	3	26	28	42	1	.249	.350
Curt Motton	OF20	R	28	56	89	15	27	6	0	6	21	13	10	3	.303	.573
Chico Salmon	1B17, 2B9, SS9, 3B3, OF1	R	28	52	91	18	27	5	0	3	12	10	22	0	.297	.451
Bobby Floyd	2B15, SS15, 3B9	R	25	39	84	7	17	4	0	0	1	6	17	0	.202	.250
Clay Dalrymple	C30	L	32	37	80	8	19	1	1	3	6	13	8	0	.238	.388
Terry Crowley	1B3, OF2	L	22	7	18	2	6	0	0	0	3	1	4	0	.333	.333
DETROIT 2nd 90-72 .556 19	MAYO SMITH															
	TOTALS		29	162	5441	701	1316	188	29	182	649	578	922	35	.242	.387
Norm Cash	1B134	L	34	142	483	81	135	15	4	22	74	63	80	2	.280	.464
Dick McAuliffe (KJ)	2B72	L	29	74	271	49	71	10	5	11	33	47	41	2	.262	.458
2 Tom Tresh	SS77, OF11, 3B1	B	31	94	331	46	74	13	1	13	37	39	47	2	.224	.387
Don Wert	3B129	R	30	132	423	46	95	11	1	14	50	49	60	3	.225	.355
Al Kaline	OF118, 1B9	R	34	131	456	74	124	17	0	21	69	54	61	1	.272	.447
Jim Northrup	OF143	L	29	148	543	79	160	31	5	25	66	52	83	4	.295	.508
Willie Horton	OF136	R	26	141	508	66	133	17	1	28	91	52	93	3	.262	.465
Bill Freehan	C120, 1B20	R	27	143	489	61	128	16	3	16	49	53	55	1	.262	.405
Mickey Stanley	OF101, SS59, 1B4	R	26	149	592	73	139	28	1	16	70	52	56	8	.235	.367
Tom Matchick	2B47, 3B27, SS6, 1B2	L	25	94	298	25	72	11	2	0	32	15	51	3	.242	.292
Jim Price	C51	R	27	72	192	21	45	8	0	9	28	18	20	0	.234	.417
Ike Brown	2B45, 3B12, OF3, SS1	R	27	70	170	24	39	4	3	5	12	26	43	2	.229	.376
Dick Tracewski	SS41, 2B13, 3B6	R	34	66	79	10	11	2	0	0	4	15	20	3	.139	.165
Gates Brown	OF14	L	30	60	93	13	19	1	2	1	6	5	17	0	.204	.290
Dave Campbell	1B13, 2B5, 3B1	R	27	32	39	4	4	1	0	0	2	4	15	0	.103	.128
2 Cesar Gutierrez 26 R 12-49, 1 Ron Woods 26 R 4-15, Wayne Redmond 23 R 0-3																
BOSTON 3rd 87-75 .537 22	DICK WILLIAMS 82-71 .536 EDDIE POPOWSKI 5-4 .556															
	TOTALS		26	162	5494	743	1381	234	37	**197**	701	**658**	923	41	.251	**.415**
Dalton Jones	1B81, 3B9, 2B1	L	25	111	336	50	74	18	3	3	33	39	36	1	.220	.318
Mike Andrews	2B120	R	25	121	464	79	136	26	2	15	59	71	53	1	.293	.455
Rico Petrocelli	SS153, 3B1	R	26	154	535	92	159	32	2	40	97	98	68	3	.297	.589
George Scott	3B109, 1B53	R	25	152	549	63	139	14	5	16	52	61	74	4	.253	.384
Tony Conigliaro	OF137	R	25	141	506	57	129	21	3	20	82	48	111	2	.255	.427
Reggie Smith	OF139	B	24	143	543	87	168	29	7	25	93	54	67	7	.309	.527
Carl Yastrzemski	OF143, 1B22	L	29	162	603	96	154	28	2	40	111	101	91	15	.255	.507
Russ Gibson	C83	R	30	85	287	21	72	9	1	3	27	15	25	1	.251	.321
Joe Lahoud	OF66, 1B1	L	22	101	218	32	41	5	0	0	21	40	43	2	.188	.335
Syd O'Brien	3B53, SS15, 2B12	R	24	100	263	47	64	10	5	9	29	15	37	2	.243	.422
Dick Schofield	2B37, SS11, 3B9, OF5	B	34	94	226	30	58	9	3	2	20	29	44	0	.257	.350
Jerry Moses	C36	R	22	53	135	13	41	9	1	4	17	5	23	0	.304	.474
2 Don Lock	OF28, 1B4	R	32	53	58	8	13	1	0	1	2	11	21	0	.224	.293
2 Tom Satriano	C44	L	28	47	127	9	24	2	0	0	11	22	12	0	.189	.205
Billy Conigliaro	OF24	R	21	32	80	14	23	6	2	4	7	9	23	1	.288	.563
George Thomas (KJ)	OF12, 1B10, 3B1, C1	R	31	29	51	9	18	3	1	0	8	3	11	0	.353	.451
2 Joe Azcue	C19	R	29	19	51	7	11	2	0	0	3	4	5	0	.216	.255
1 Ken Harrelson	1B10	R	27	10	46	6	10	1	0	3	8	4	6	0	.217	.435
Luis Alvarado 20 R 0-5, Carlton Fisk 21 R 0-5, Tony Muser 21 L 1-9																

NAME	T	AGE	W	L	PCT	SV	G	GS	CG	IP	H	BB	SO	ShO	ERA
		28	**109**	53	.673	36	162	162	50	1474	1194	498	897	**20**	**2.83**
Mike Cuellar	L	32	23	11	.676	0	39	39	18	291	213	79	182	5	2.38
Dave McNally	L	26	20	7	.741	0	41	40	11	269	232	84	166	4	3.21
Jim Palmer (XJ)	R	23	16	4	**.800**	0	26	23	11	181	131	64	123	6	2.34
Tom Phoebus	R	24	14	7	.667	0	35	33	6	202	180	87	117	2	3.52
Dave Leonhard	R	27	7	4	.636	1	37	3	1	94	78	38	37	1	2.49
Pete Richert	L	29	7	4	.636	12	44	0	0	57	42	14	54	0	2.21
Jim Hardin	R	25	6	7	.462	1	30	20	3	138	128	43	64	1	3.59
Dick Hall	R	38	5	2	.714	6	39	0	0	66	49	9	31	0	1.91
Eddie Watt	R	27	5	2	.714	16	56	0	0	71	49	26	46	0	1.65
Marcelino Lopez	L	25	5	3	.625	0	27	4	0	69	65	34	57	0	4.43
Al Severinsen	R	24	1	1	.500	0	12	0	0	20	14	10	13	0	2.25
Mike Adamson	R	21	0	1	.000	0	6	0	0	8	10	6	2	0	4.50
Fred Beene	R	26	0	0	.000	0	2	0	0	3	2	1	0	0	0.00
2 Frank Bertaina	L	25	0	0	.000	0	3	0	0	6	1	3	5	0	0.00
		28	90	72	.556	28	162	162	**55**	1455	1250	586	**1032**	**20**	3.31
Denny McLain	R	25	**24**	9	.727	0	42	**41**	23	**325**	**288**	67	181	**9**	2.80
Mickey Lolich	L	28	19	11	.633	1	37	36	15	281	214	122	271	1	3.14
Earl Wilson	R	34	12	10	.545	0	35	35	5	215	209	69	150	1	3.31
Mike Kilkenny	L	24	8	6	.571	2	39	15	6	128	99	63	97	4	3.38
Joe Sparma	R	27	6	8	.429	0	23	16	3	93	78	77	41	2	4.74
Pat Dobson	R	27	5	10	.333	9	49	9	1	105	100	39	64	0	3.60
Tom Timmerman	R	29	4	3	.571	1	31	1	1	56	50	26	42	0	2.73
John Hiller	L	26	4	4	.500	4	40	8	1	99	97	44	74	1	4.00
1 Don McMahon	R	39	3	5	.375	11	34	0	0	37	25	18	38	0	3.89
Fred Lasher	R	27	2	1	.667	0	32	0	0	44	34	22	26	0	3.07
1 Dick Radatz	R	32	2	2	.500	0	11	0	0	19	14	5	18	0	3.32
Fred Scherman	L	24	1	0	1.000	0	4	0	0	4	6	0	3	0	6.75
Gary Taylor	R	23	0	1	.000	0	7	0	0	10	10	6	3	0	5.40
Daryl Patterson (MS)	R	25	0	2	.000	0	18	0	0	22	15	19	12	0	2.86
Norm McRae	R	21	0	0	.000	0	3	0	0	3	2	1	3	0	6.00
Bob Reed	R	24	0	0	.000	0	8	1	0	15	9	8	9	0	1.80
Jon Warden (SJ) 22															
		27	87	75	.537	41	162	162	30	1467	1423	**685**	935	7	3.92
Ray Culp (SA)	R	27	17	8	.680	0	32	32	9	227	195	79	172	2	3.81
2 Sonny Siebert	R	32	14	10	.583	5	43	22	2	163	151	68	127	0	3.81
Mike Nagy	R	21	12	2	.857	0	33	28	7	197	183	106	84	1	3.11
Sparky Lyle	L	24	8	3	.727	17	71	0	0	103	91	48	93	0	2.63
2 Vicente Romo	R	26	7	9	.438	11	52	11	4	127	116	50	89	1	3.19
Jim Lonborg	R	27	7	11	.389	0	29	23	4	144	148	65	100	0	4.50
Lee Stange	R	32	6	9	.400	3	41	15	2	137	137	56	59	0	3.68
Bill Landis	L	26	5	5	.500	1	45	5	0	82	82	49	50	0	5.27
Ray Jarvis	R	23	5	6	.455	1	29	12	2	100	105	43	36	0	4.77
Ken Brett	L	20	2	3	.400	0	8	8	0	39	41	22	23	0	5.31
Mike Garman	R	19	1	0	1.000	0	2	2	0	12	13	10	10	0	4.50
Fred Wenz	R	27	1	0	1.000	0	8	0	0	11	9	10	11	0	5.73
Bill Lee	L	22	1	3	.250	0	20	1	0	52	56	28	45	0	4.50
2 Gary Wagner	R	29	1	3	.250	0	6	1	0	16	18	15	9	0	6.19
3 Ron Kline	R	37	0	1	.000	1	16	0	0	17	24	17	7	0	4.76
1 Juan Pizarro	L	32	0	1	.000	2	6	0	0	9	14	6	4	0	6.00
1 Garry Roggenburk (VR)	L	29	0	1	.000	0	7	0	0	10	13	5	8	0	8.10
1 Dick Ellsworth	L	29	0	0	.000	0	2	2	0	12	16	4	4	0	3.75
Jose Santiago (EJ)	R	28	0	0	.000	0	10	0	0	8	11	4	4	0	3.38

EAST DIVISION

WASHINGTON 4th 86-76 .531 23 — TED WILLIAMS

NAME	G by POS	B	AGE	G	AB	R	H	2B	3B	HR	RBI	BB	SO	SB	BA	SA
TOTALS			28	162	5447	694	1365	171	40	148	640	630	900	52	.251	.378
Mike Epstein	1B118	L	26	131	403	73	112	18	1	30	85	85	99	2	.278	.551
Bernie Allen	2B110, 3B6	L	30	122	365	33	90	17	4	9	45	50	35	5	.247	.389
Ed Brinkman	SS150	R	27	151	576	71	153	18	5	2	43	50	42	2	.266	.325
Ken McMullen	3B154	R	27	158	562	83	153	25	2	19	87	70	103	4	.272	.425
Hank Allen	OF91, 3B6, 2B3	R	28	109	271	42	75	9	3	1	17	13	28	12	.277	.343
Del Unser	OF149	L	24	153	581	69	166	19	8	7	57	58	54	8	.286	.382
Frank Howard	OF114, 1B70	R	32	161	592	111	175	17	2	48	111	102	96	1	.296	.574
Paul Casanova	C122	R	27	124	379	26	82	9	2	4	37	18	52	0	.216	.282
Ed Stroud	OF85	L	29	123	206	35	52	5	6	4	29	30	33	12	.252	.393
Tim Cullen	2B105, SS9, 3B1	R	27	119	249	22	52	7	0	1	15	14	27	1	.209	.249
Brant Alyea	OF69, 1B3	R	28	104	237	29	59	4	0	11	40	34	67	1	.249	.405
2 Lee Maye	OF65	L	34	71	238	41	69	9	3	9	26	20	25	1	.290	.466
Jim French	C63	L	27	63	158	14	29	6	3	2	13	41	15	1	.184	.297
Gary Holman	1B11, OF3	L	25	41	31	1	5	1	0	0	2	4	7	0	.161	.194
Sam Bowens	OF30	R	30	33	57	6	11	1	0	0	4	5	14	1	.193	.211
2 Zoilo Versalles	SS13, 2B6, 3B5	R	29	31	75	9	20	2	1	0	6	3	13	1	.267	.320
Dick Billings	OF6, 3B1	R	26	27	37	3	5	0	0	0	0	6	8	0	.135	.135
Dick Smith	OF9	R	24	21	28	2	3	0	0	0	0	4	7	0	.107	.107

Doug Camilli (RC) 32 R 1-3, Toby Harrah 20 R 0-1

NAME	T	AGE	W	L	PCT	SV	G	GS	CG	IP	H	BB	SO	ShO	ERA
TOTALS		27	86	76	.531	41	162	162	28	1447	1310	656	835	10	3.49
Dick Bosman	R	25	14	5	.737	1	31	26	5	193	156	39	99	2	2.19
Casey Cox	R	27	12	7	.632	0	52	13	4	172	161	64	73	0	2.77
Joe Coleman	R	22	12	13	.480	1	40	36	12	248	222	100	182	4	3.27
Denny Higgins	R	29	10	9	.526	16	55	0	0	85	79	56	71	0	3.49
Darold Knowles (MS)	L	27	9	2	.818	13	53	0	0	84	73	31	59	0	2.25
Barry Moore	L	26	9	8	.529	0	31	25	4	134	123	67	51	0	4.30
Jim Hannan	R	29	7	6	.538	0	35	28	1	158	138	91	72	1	3.65
2 Jim Shellenbach	L	25	4	7	.364	1	30	11	2	85	87	48	50	0	4.00
Bob Humphreys	R	33	3	3	.500	5	47	0	0	80	69	38	43	0	3.04
Dave Baldwin	R	31	2	4	.333	4	43	0	0	67	57	34	51	0	4.03
1 Camilo Pascual	R	35	2	5	.286	0	14	13	0	55	49	38	34	0	6.87
2 Cisco Carlos	R	28	1	1	.500	0	6	4	0	18	23	6	5	0	4.50
1 Frank Bertaina	L	25	1	3	.250	0	14	5	0	36	43	23	25	0	6.50
Jim Miles	R	25	0	1	.000	0	10	1	0	20	19	15	15	0	6.30
Jan Dukes	L	23	0	2	.000	0	8	0	0	11	8	4	3	0	2.45
Frank Kreutzer	L	30	0	0	.000	0	4	0	0	2	3	2	2	0	4.50

NEW YORK 5th 80-81 .497 28.5 — RALPH HOUK

NAME	G by POS	B	AGE	G	AB	R	H	2B	3B	HR	RBI	BB	SO	SB	BA	SA
TOTALS			27	162	5308	562	1247	210	44	94	521	565	840	119	.235	.344
Joe Pepitone	1B132	L	28	135	513	49	124	16	3	27	70	30	42	8	.242	.442
Horace Clarke	2B156	B	29	156	641	82	183	26	7	4	48	53	41	33	.285	.367
Gene Michael	SS118	B	31	119	412	41	112	24	4	2	31	43	56	7	.272	.364
Jerry Kenney	3B83, OF31, SS10	L	24	130	447	49	115	14	2	2	34	48	36	25	.257	.311
Bobby Murcer	OF118, 3B31	L	23	152	564	82	146	24	4	26	82	50	103	7	.259	.454
Bill Robinson	OF62, 1B1	R	26	87	222	23	38	11	2	3	21	16	39	3	.171	.279
Roy White	OF126	B	25	130	448	55	130	30	5	7	74	81	51	18	.290	.426
Jake Gibbs	C66	L	30	71	219	18	49	9	2	0	18	23	30	3	.224	.283
Frank Fernandez	C65, OF14	R	26	89	229	34	51	6	1	12	29	65	68	1	.223	.415
Bobby Cox	3B56, 2B6	R	28	85	191	17	41	7	1	2	17	34	41	0	.215	.293
2 Jimmie Hall	OF50, 1B7	L	31	80	212	21	50	8	5	3	26	19	34	8	.236	.363
2 Ron Woods	OF67	R	26	72	171	18	30	5	2	1	7	22	29	2	.175	.246
1 Tom Tresh	SS41	B	31	45	143	13	26	5	2	1	9	17	23	2	.182	.266
Len Boehmer	1B21, 3B8, 2B1, SS1	R	28	45	108	5	19	4	0	0	7	8	10	0	.176	.213
1 Billy Cowan	OF14	R	30	32	48	5	8	0	0	1	3	3	9	0	.167	.229
Jim Lyttle	OF28	L	23	28	83	7	15	4	0	0	4	4	19	1	.181	.229
Tom Shopay	OF11	L	24	28	48	2	4	0	1	0	0	2	10	0	.083	.125
Thurman Munson	C25	R	22	26	86	6	22	1	2	1	9	10	10	0	.256	.349
Johnny Ellis	C15	R	20	22	62	2	18	4	0	1	8	1	11	0	.290	.403

Frank Tepedino 21 L 9-39, Dave McDonald 26 L 5-23, 1 Dick Simpson 25 R 3-11, Ron Blomberg 20 L 3-6, 1 Nate Oliver 28 R 0-1

NAME	T	AGE	W	L	PCT	SV	G	GS	CG	IP	H	BB	SO	ShO	ERA
TOTALS		27	80	81	.497	20	162	162	53	1441	1258	522	801	13	3.23
Mel Stottlemyre	R	27	20	14	.588	0	39	39	24	303	267	97	113	3	2.82
Fritz Peterson	L	27	17	16	.515	0	37	37	16	272	228	43	150	4	2.55
Stan Bahnsen	R	24	9	16	.360	1	40	33	5	221	222	90	130	2	3.83
2 Jack Aker	R	28	8	4	.667	11	38	0	0	66	51	22	40	0	2.05
Al Downing	L	28	7	5	.583	0	30	15	5	131	117	49	85	1	3.37
Bill Burbach	R	21	6	8	.429	0	31	24	2	141	112	102	82	1	3.64
Lindy McDaniel	R	33	5	6	.455	5	51	0	0	84	84	23	60	0	3.54
Mike Kekich	L	24	4	6	.400	1	28	13	1	105	91	49	66	0	4.54
Steve Hamilton	L	35	3	4	.429	2	38	0	0	57	39	21	39	0	3.32
2 Ken Johnson	R	36	1	2	.333	0	12	0	0	26	19	11	21	0	3.46
John Cumberland	L	22	0	0	.000	0	2	0	0	4	3	4	0	0	4.50
Ron Klimkowski	R	24	0	0	.000	0	3	1	0	14	6	5	3	0	0.64
1 Don Nottebart	R	33	0	0	.000	0	4	0	0	6	6	0	5	0	4.50
1 Fred Talbot	R	28	0	0	.000	0	8	0	0	12	13	6	7	0	5.25

Joe Verbanic (SA) 26

CLEVELAND 6th 62-99 .385 46.5 — AL DARK

NAME	G by POS	B	AGE	G	AB	R	H	2B	3B	HR	RBI	BB	SO	SB	BA	SA
TOTALS			27	161	5365	573	1272	173	24	119	534	535	906	85	.237	.345
Tony Horton	1B157	R	24	159	625	77	174	25	4	27	93	37	91	3	.278	.461
Vern Fuller	2B102, 3B7	R	25	108	254	25	60	11	1	4	22	20	53	2	.236	.335
Larry Brown	SS101, 3B29, 2B5	R	29	132	469	48	112	10	2	4	24	44	43	5	.239	.294
Max Alvis (KJ)	3B58, SS1	R	31	66	191	13	43	6	0	1	15	14	26	1	.225	.272
2 Ken Harrelson	OF144, 1B16	R	27	149	519	83	115	13	4	27	84	95	96	17	.222	.418
Jose Cardenal	OF142, 3B5	R	25	146	557	75	143	26	3	11	45	49	58	36	.257	.373
Russ Snyder	OF84	L	35	122	266	26	66	10	0	2	24	25	33	3	.248	.308
Duke Sims	C102, OF3, 1B1	L	28	114	326	40	77	8	0	18	45	66	80	1	.236	.426
Richie Scheinblum	OF50	B	26	102	199	13	37	5	1	1	13	19	30	0	.186	.236
Chuck Hinton	OF40, 3B14	R	35	94	121	18	31	3	2	3	19	8	22	2	.256	.388
Lou Klimchock	3B56, 2B21, C1	L	29	90	258	26	74	13	2	6	26	18	14	0	.287	.422
Cap Peterson	OF30, 3B4	R	26	76	110	8	25	3	0	1	14	24	18	0	.227	.282
1 Zoilo Versalles	2B46, 3B30, SS3	R	29	72	217	21	49	11	1	1	13	21	47	3	.226	.300
Eddie Leon	SS64	R	22	64	213	20	51	6	0	3	19	19	37	2	.239	.310
Frank Baker	OF46	L	24	52	172	21	44	5	3	3	15	14	34	2	.256	.372
Dave Nelson (LJ)	2B33, OF2	R	25	52	123	11	25	0	0	0	6	9	26	4	.203	.203
1 Lee Maye	OF28	L	34	43	108	9	27	5	0	1	15	8	15	1	.250	.333
Ray Fosse	C37	R	22	37	116	11	20	3	0	2	9	8	29	1	.172	.250
Ken Suarez	C36	R	26	36	85	7	25	5	0	1	9	15	12	1	.294	.388

1 Joe Azcue 29 R 7-24, Russ Nagelson 24 L 6-17, Lou Camilli 22 B 0-14, 1 Jimmie Hall 31 L 0-10, Jack Heidemann 19 R 0-3

NAME	T	AGE	W	L	PCT	SV	G	GS	CG	IP	H	BB	SO	ShO	ERA
TOTALS		27	62	99	.385	22	161	161	35	1437	1330	681	1000	7	3.94
Sam McDowell	L	26	18	14	.563	1	39	38	18	285	222	102	279	4	2.94
Luis Tiant	R	28	9	20	.310	0	38	37	9	250	229	129	156	1	3.71
2 Dick Ellsworth	L	29	6	9	.400	0	34	22	3	135	162	40	48	1	4.13
Stan Williams	R	32	6	14	.300	12	61	15	3	178	155	67	139	0	3.94
Mike Paul	L	24	5	10	.333	2	47	12	0	117	104	54	98	0	3.62
Steve Hargan	R	26	5	14	.263	0	32	23	1	144	145	81	76	1	5.69
Horacio Pina	R	24	4	2	.667	1	31	4	0	47	44	27	32	0	5.17
2 Juan Pizarro	L	32	3	3	.500	4	48	4	1	83	67	49	44	0	3.14
Ron Law	R	23	3	4	.429	1	35	1	0	52	68	34	29	0	5.02
Phil Hennigan	R	23	2	1	.667	0	9	0	0	16	14	4	10	0	3.38
1 Vicente Romo	R	26	1	1	.500	0	3	0	0	8	7	3	7	0	2.25
1 Sonny Siebert	R	32	0	1	.000	0	2	2	0	14	10	8	6	0	3.21
Gary Boyd	R	22	0	2	.000	0	8	3	0	11	8	14	9	0	9.00
Larry Burchart (JJ)	R	23	0	2	.000	0	29	0	0	42	42	24	26	0	4.29
1 Jack Hamilton	R	30	0	2	.000	1	20	0	0	31	37	23	13	0	4.35
Gary Kroll	R	27	0	0	.000	0	19	0	0	24	16	22	28	0	4.13

WEST DIVISION

MINNESOTA 1st 97-65 .599 — BILLY MARTIN

NAME	G by POS	B	AGE	G	AB	R	H	2B	3B	HR	RBI	BB	SO	SB	BA	SA
TOTALS			29	162	5677	790	1520	246	32	163	733	599	906	115	.268	.408
Rich Reese	1B117, OF5	L	27	132	419	52	135	24	4	16	69	23	57	1	.322	.513
Rod Carew	2B118	L	23	123	458	79	152	30	4	8	56	37	72	19	.332	.467
Leo Cardenas	SS160	R	30	160	578	67	162	24	4	10	70	66	96	5	.280	.388
Harmon Killebrew	3B105, 1B80	R	33	162	555	106	153	20	2	49	140	145	84	8	.276	.584
Tony Oliva	OF152	L	29	153	637	97	197	39	4	24	101	45	66	10	.309	.496
Cesar Tovar	OF113, 2B41, 3B20	R	28	158	535	99	154	25	5	11	52	37	37	45	.288	.415
Ted Uhlaender	OF150	L	29	152	554	93	151	18	2	8	62	44	52	15	.273	.356
Johnny Roseboro	C111	L	36	115	361	33	95	12	0	3	32	39	44	5	.263	.321
Frank Quilici	3B84, 2B36, SS1	R	30	118	144	19	25	3	1	2	12	12	22	2	.174	.250
Graig Nettles	OF54, 3B21	L	24	96	225	27	50	9	2	7	26	32	47	1	.222	.373
Chuck Manuel	OF46	L	25	83	164	14	34	6	0	2	24	28	33	1	.207	.280
Bob Allison	OF58, 1B3	R	34	81	189	18	43	8	2	8	27	29	39	2	.228	.418
Rick Renick	3B30, OF10, SS6	R	25	71	139	21	34	3	0	5	17	12	32	0	.245	.374
George Mitterwald	C63, OF1	R	24	69	187	18	48	8	0	5	13	17	47	0	.257	.380
Tom Tischinski	C32	R	24	37	47	2	9	0	0	0	2	8	8	0	.191	.191
Jim Holt	OF5, 1B1	L	25	12	14	3	5	0	0	1	2	0	4	0	.357	.571

Herm Hill 23 L 0-2, Cotton Nash 26 R 2-9, Rick Dempsey 19 R 3-6, Frank Kostro 31 R 0-2, 1 Ron Clark 26 R 1-8

NAME	T	AGE	W	L	PCT	SV	G	GS	CG	IP	H	BB	SO	ShO	ERA
TOTALS		29	97	65	.599	43	162	162	41	1498	1388	524	906	8	3.24
Jim Perry	R	33	20	6	.769	0	46	36	12	262	244	66	153	3	2.82
Dave Boswell	R	24	20	12	.625	0	39	38	10	256	215	99	190	0	3.23
Jim Kaat	L	30	14	13	.519	1	40	32	10	242	252	75	139	0	3.50
Ron Perranoski	L	33	9	10	.474	31	75	0	0	120	85	52	62	0	2.10
Tom Hall	L	21	8	7	.533	0	31	18	5	141	129	50	92	2	3.32
Dick Woodson	R	24	7	5	.583	1	44	10	2	110	99	49	66	0	3.68
Dean Chance (SA)	R	28	5	4	.556	0	20	15	1	88	76	35	50	0	2.97
Bob Miller	R	30	5	5	.500	3	48	11	1	119	118	32	57	0	3.03
Joe Grzenda	L	32	4	1	.800	3	38	0	0	49	52	17	24	0	3.86
Al Worthington (VR)	R	40	4	1	.800	3	46	0	0	61	65	20	51	0	4.57
Jerry Crider	R	27	1	0	1.000	1	21	1	0	29	31	15	16	0	4.66
Danny Morris	R	23	0	1	.000	0	3	1	0	5	5	4	1	0	5.40
Charley Wolters	R	22	0	0	.000	0	6	0	0	7	6	3	2	0	5.14
Bill Zepp	R	22	0	0	.000	0	4	0	0	5	6	4	2	0	7.20
2 Darrell Brandon	R	28	0	0	.000	0	3	0	0	3	5	3	1	0	3.00

OAKLAND 2nd 88-74 .543 9 — HANK BAUER 80-69 .537 JOHN McNAMARA 8-5 .615

NAME	G by POS	B	AGE	G	AB	R	H	2B	3B	HR	RBI	BB	SO	SB	BA	SA
TOTALS			27	162	5614	740	1400	210	28	148	680	617	953	100	.249	.376
Danny Cater	1B132, OF20, 2B4	R	29	152	584	64	153	24	2	10	76	28	40	1	.262	.361
Dick Green	2B131	R	28	136	483	61	133	25	6	12	64	53	94	2	.275	.427
Bert Campaneris	SS125	R	27	135	547	71	142	15	2	2	25	30	62	62	.260	.305
Sal Bando	3B162	R	25	162	609	106	171	25	3	31	113	111	82	1	.281	.484
Reggie Jackson	OF150	L	23	152	549	123	151	36	3	47	118	114	142	13	.275	.608
Rick Monday (BW)	OF119	L	23	122	399	57	108	17	4	12	54	72	100	12	.271	.424
Tommie Reynolds(SJ)	OF89	R	27	107	315	51	81	10	0	2	20	34	29	1	.257	.308
Phil Roof	C106	R	28	106	247	19	58	6	1	2	19	33	55	1	.235	.283
Ted Kubiak	SS42, 2B33	B	27	92	305	38	76	9	1	2	27	25	35	2	.249	.305
Jose Tartabull	OF63	L	30	75	266	28	71	11	1	0	11	9	11	3	.267	.316
Ramon Webster	1B13	L	26	64	77	5	20	0	1	1	13	12	8	0	.260	.325
Dave Duncan	C56	R	23	58	127	11	16	3	0	3	22	19	41	0	.126	.220
2 Larry Haney	C53	R	26	53	86	8	13	4	0	2	12	7	19	0	.151	.267
Mike Hershberger (SJ)	OF35	R	29	51	129	11	26	2	0	1	10	10	15	1	.202	.240
2 Bob Johnson	1B7, 2B2	R	33	51	67	5	23	1	0	1	9	3	4	0	.343	.403
Blue Moon Odom (EJ)	P32	R	24	43	79	15	21	2	1	5	16	2	24	0	.266	.506
Lew Krausse	P43	R	26	43	48	7	8	1	0	4	9	2	22	0	.167	.438
Joe Rudi	OF18, 1B11	R	22	35	122	10	23	3	1	2	6	5	16	1	.189	.277
2 Tito Francona	1B19, OF1	L	35	32	85	12	29	6	1	3	20	12	11	0	.341	.541
Bobby Brooks	OF21	R	23	29	79	13	19	5	0	3	10	20	24	0	.241	.418
Gene Tenace	C13	R	22	16	38	1	6	0	0	1	2	1	15	0	.158	.237
1 Jim Pagliaroni (BG)	C7	R	31	14	27	1	4	1	0	1	2	5	2	0	.148	.296

Bill McNulty 22 R 0-17, 1 John Donaldson (BT) 26 L 1-13, Tony LaRussa 24 R 0-8, 1 Joe Nossek 28 R 0-6, Allan Lewis 27 B 0-1

NAME	T	AGE	W	L	PCT	SV	G	GS	CG	IP	H	BB	SO	ShO	ERA
TOTALS		24	88	74	.543	36	162	162	42	1481	1356	586	887	14	3.71
Blue Moon Odom (EJ)	R	24	15	6	.714	0	32	32	10	231	179	112	150	3	2.92
Chuck Dobson	R	25	15	13	.536	0	35	35	11	235	244	80	137	1	3.87
Catfish Hunter	R	23	12	15	.444	0	38	35	10	247	210	85	150	3	3.35
Paul Lindblad	L	27	9	6	.600	9	60	0	0	78	72	33	64	0	4.15
Jim Nash (SJ)	R	24	8	8	.500	0	26	19	3	115	112	30	75	1	3.68
Lew Krausse	R	26	7	7	.500	7	43	16	4	140	134	48	85	2	4.44
Rollie Fingers	R	22	6	7	.462	12	60	8	1	119	116	41	61	1	3.71
Jim Roland	L	26	5	1	.833	1	39	3	2	86	59	46	48	0	2.20
Marcel Lachemann	R	28	4	1	.800	2	28	0	0	43	43	19	16	0	3.98
George Lauzerique	R	21	3	4	.429	0	19	8	1	61	58	27	39	0	4.72
Vida Blue	L	19	1	1	.500	1	12	4	0	42	49	18	24	0	6.21
3 Juan Pizarro	L	32	1	1	.500	1	3	0	0	8	3	3	4	0	2.25
Ed Sprague	R	23	1	1	.500	2	27	0	0	46	47	31	20	0	4.50
3 Fred Talbot	R	28	1	2	.333	1	12	2	0	19	22	7	9	0	5.21
John Wyatt	R	34	0	1	.000	0	4	0	0	8	8	6	5	0	5.63

CALIFORNIA 3rd 71-91 .438 26 — BILL RIGNEY 11-28 .282 LEFTY PHILLIPS 60-63 .488

NAME	G by POS	B	AGE	G	AB	R	H	2B	3B	HR	RBI	BB	SO	SB	BA	SA
TOTALS			26	163	5316	528	1221	151	29	88	480	516	929	54	.230	.319
Jim Spencer	1B107	L	21	113	386	39	98	14	3	10	31	26	53	1	.254	.383
2 Sandy Alomar	2B134	B	25	134	559	60	140	10	2	1	30	36	48	18	.250	.281
Jim Fregosi	SS160	R	27	161	580	78	151	22	6	12	47	93	86	9	.260	.381
Aurelio Rodriguez	3B159	R	21	159	561	47	130	17	2	7	49	32	88	5	.232	.307
Bill Voss	OF111, 1B2	L	25	133	349	33	91	11	4	2	40	35	40	5	.261	.332
Jay Johnstone	OF144	L	23	148	540	64	146	20	5	10	59	38	75	3	.270	.381
Rick Reichardt	OF136, 1B3	R	26	137	493	60	125	11	4	13	68	43	100	3	.254	.371
3 Joe Azcue	C80	R	29	80	248	15	54	6	0	1	19	27	28	0	.218	.254
Roger Repoz	OF48, 1B31	L	28	103	219	25	36	1	1	8	19	32	52	1	.164	.288
Bubba Morton	OF49, 1B1	R	37	87	172	18	42	10	1	7	32	28	29	0	.244	.436
Lou Johnson	OF45	R	34	67	133	10	27	8	0	0	9	10	19	5	.203	.263
Tom Egan (BY)	C46	R	23	46	120	7	17	1	0	5	16	17	41	0	.142	.275
1 Tom Satriano	C36, 1B5, 2B2	L	28	41	108	5	28	2	0	1	16	18	15	0	.259	.306
2 Jim Hicks	OF10, 1B8	R	29	37	48	6	4	0	0	3	8	13	18	0	.083	.271
Winston Llenas	3B9	R	25	34	47	4	8	2	0	0	0	2	10	0	.170	.213
1 Vic Davalillo	OF22, 1B3	L	32	33	71	10	11	1	1	0	1	6	5	3	.155	.197
2 Billy Cowan	OF13, 1B6	R	30	28	56	10	17	1	0	4	10	3	9	0	.304	.536
1 Bobby Knoop	2B27	R	30	27	71	5	14	1	0	1	6	13	16	1	.197	.254
Dick Stuart	1B13	R	36	22	51	3	8	2	0	1	4	3	21	0	.157	.255

Bob Rodgers 30 B 9-46, Ruben Amaro 33 R 6-27, Randy Brown 24 L 4-25, Jarvis Tatum 22 R 7-22, Marty Perez 22 R 3-13, Bob Chance 28 L 1-7, Chuck Cottier 33 R 0-2

NAME	T	AGE	W	L	PCT	SV	G	GS	CG	IP	H	BB	SO	ShO	ERA
TOTALS		28	71	91	.438	39	163	163	25	1438	1294	517	885	9	3.54
Andy Messersmith	R	23	16	11	.593	2	40	33	10	250	169	100	211	2	2.52
Rudy May	L	24	10	13	.435	2	43	25	4	180	142	66	133	0	3.45
Tom Murphy	R	23	10	16	.385	0	36	35	4	216	213	69	100	0	4.21
Jim McGlothlin	R	25	8	16	.333	0	37	35	4	201	188	58	96	1	3.18
Ken Tatum	R	25	7	2	.778	22	45	0	0	86	51	39	65	0	1.36
1 George Brunet	L	34	6	7	.462	0	23	19	2	101	98	39	56	2	3.83
1 Hoyt Wilhelm	R	45	5	7	.417	10	44	0	0	66	45	18	53	0	2.45
Eddie Fisher	R	32	3	2	.600	2	52	1	0	97	100	28	47	0	3.62
Steve Kealey	R	22	2	0	1.000	0	15	3	1	37	48	13	17	1	3.89
Pedro Borbon	R	22	2	3	.400	0	22	0	0	41	55	11	20	0	6.15
Vern Geishert	R	23	1	1	.500	1	11	3	0	31	32	7	18	0	4.65
Clyde Wright	L	28	1	8	.111	0	37	5	0	64	66	30	31	0	4.08
Lloyd Allen	R	19	0	1	.000	0	4	1	0	10	5	10	5	0	5.40
Tom Bradley	R	22	0	1	.000	0	3	0	0	2	9	0	2	0	27.00
2 Bob Priddy	R	29	0	1	.000	0	15	0	0	26	24	7	15	0	4.85
Greg Washburn	R	22	0	2	.000	0	8	2	0	11	21	5	4	0	8.18
Rickey Clark	R	23	0	0	.000	0	6	1	0	10	12	7	6	0	5.40
Phil Ortega (BJ)	R	29	0	0	.000	0	5	0	0	8	13	7	4	0	10.13
Wally Wolf	R	27	0	0	.000	0	2	0	0	2	3	3	2	0	13.50

KANSAS CITY 4th 69-93 .426 28 — JOE GORDON

NAME	G by POS	B	AGE	G	AB	R	H	2B	3B	HR	RBI	BB	SO	SB	BA	SA
TOTALS			25	163	5462	586	1311	179	32	98	538	522	901	129	.240	.338
Mike Fiore	1B91, OF13	L	24	107	339	53	93	14	1	12	35	84	63	4	.274	.428
Jerry Adair	2B109, SS8, 3B1	R	32	126	432	29	108	9	1	5	48	20	36	1	.250	.310
Jackie Hernandez	SS144	R	28	145	504	54	112	14	2	4	40	38	111	17	.222	.282
Joe Foy	3B113, 1B16, OF16, SS5, 2B3	R	26	145	519	72	136	19	2	11	71	74	75	37	.262	.370
Bob Oliver	OF98, 1B12, 3B8	R	26	118	394	43	100	8	4	13	43	21	74	5	.254	.393
Pat Kelly	OF107	L	24	112	417	61	110	20	4	8	32	49	70	40	.264	.388
Lou Piniella	OF129	R	25	135	493	43	139	21	6	11	68	33	56	2	.282	.416
Ellie Rodriguez	C90	R	23	95	267	27	63	10	0	2	20	31	26	3	.236	.296
Ed Kirkpatrick	OF82, C8, 1B2, 3B2, 2B1	L	24	120	315	40	81	11	4	14	49	43	42	3	.257	.451
Juan Rios	2B46, SS32, 3B4	R	23	87	196	20	44	5	1	1	5	7	19	1	.224	.276
Chuck Harrison	1B55	R	28	75	213	18	47	5	1	3	18	16	20	1	.221	.296
Buck Martinez (RL)	C55, OF1	R	20	72	205	14	47	6	1	4	23	8	25	0	.229	.327
Joe Keough	OF49, 1B1	L	23	70	166	17	31	2	0	0	7	13	13	5	.187	.199
Hawk Taylor	OF18, C6	R	30	64	89	7	24	5	0	3	21	6	18	0	.270	.427
Paul Schaal	3B49, 2B6, SS6	R	26	61	205	22	54	6	0	1	13	25	27	2	.263	.307
Jim Rooker	P28	R	27	34	57	7	16	3	0	4	8	1	19	0	.281	.544
Jim Campanis	C26	R	25	30	83	4	13	5	0	0	5	5	19	0	.157	.217
Luis Alcaraz	2B19, 3B2, SS1	R	28	22	79	15	20	2	1	1	7	7	9	0	.253	.342

George Spriggs 28 L 4-29, Scott Northey 22 R 16-61, Dennis Paepke 24 R 3-27, Fred Rico 24 R 6-26, Fran Healy 22 R 4-10, Billy Harris 25 L 2-7

NAME	T	AGE	W	L	PCT	SV	G	GS	CG	IP	H	BB	SO	ShO	ERA
TOTALS		27	69	93	.426	25	163	163	42	1465	1357	560	894	10	3.72
Wally Bunker	R	24	12	11	.522	2	35	31	10	223	198	62	130	1	3.23
Moe Drabowsky	R	33	11	9	.550	11	52	0	0	98	68	30	76	0	2.94
Dick Drago	R	24	11	13	.458	1	41	26	10	201	190	65	108	2	3.76
Bill Butler	L	22	9	10	.474	0	34	29	5	194	174	91	156	4	3.90
Roger Nelson	R	25	7	13	.350	0	29	29	8	193	170	65	82	1	3.31
Jim Rooker	L	27	4	16	.200	0	28	22	8	158	136	73	108	1	3.76
Tom Burgmeier	L	25	3	1	.750	0	31	0	0	54	67	21	23	0	4.17
Mike Hedlund	R	22	3	6	.333	2	34	16	1	125	123	40	74	0	3.24
Steve Jones	L	28	2	3	.400	0	20	4	0	45	45	24	31	0	4.20
Dave Morehead	R	26	2	3	.400	0	21	2	0	33	28	28	32	0	5.73
Dave Wickersham	R	33	2	3	.400	5	34	0	0	50	58	14	27	0	3.96
Galen Cisco	R	32	1	1	.500	1	15	0	0	22	17	15	18	0	3.68
Al Fitzmorris	R	23	1	1	.500	2	7	0	0	11	9	4	3	0	4.09
Don O'Riley	R	24	1	1	.500	1	18	0	0	23	32	15	10	0	7.04
Jerry Cram	R	21	0	1	.000	0	5	2	0	17	15	6	10	0	3.18
Chris Zachary	R	25	0	1	.000	0	8	2	0	18	27	7	6	0	8.00

CHICAGO 5th 68-94 .420 29 — AL LOPEZ 8-9 .471 DON GUTTERIDGE 60-85 .414

NAME	G by POS	B	AGE	G	AB	R	H	2B	3B	HR	RBI	BB	SO	SB	BA	SA
TOTALS			27	162	5450	625	1346	210	27	112	585	552	844	54	.247	.357
Gail Hopkins	1B101	L	26	124	373	52	99	13	3	8	46	50	28	2	.265	.381
2 Bobby Knoop	2B104	R	30	104	345	34	79	14	1	6	41	35	68	2	.229	.328
Luis Aparicio	SS154	R	35	156	599	77	168	24	5	5	51	66	29	24	.280	.362
Bill Melton	3B148, OF11	R	23	157	556	67	142	26	2	23	87	56	106	1	.255	.433
Walt Williams	OF111	R	25	135	471	59	143	22	1	3	32	26	33	6	.304	.374
Ken Berry	OF120	R	28	130	297	25	69	12	2	4	18	24	50	1	.232	.327
Carlos May(HJ)	OF100	L	21	100	367	62	103	18	2	18	62	58	66	1	.281	.488
Ed Herrmann	C92	L	22	102	290	31	67	8	0	8	31	30	35	0	.231	.341
Pete Ward	1B25, 3B21, OF9	L	29	105	199	22	49	7	0	6	32	33	38	0	.246	.372
Buddy Bradford (GJ)	OF88	R	24	93	273	36	70	8	2	11	27	34	75	5	.256	.421
Tommy McCraw(KJ)	1B44, OF41	L	28	93	240	21	62	12	2	2	25	21	24	1	.258	.350
Ron Hansen	2B26, 1B21, SS8, 3B7	R	31	85	185	15	48	6	1	2	22	18	25	2	.259	.335
Don Pavletich (HJ)	C51, 1B13	R	30	78	188	26	46	12	0	6	33	28	45	0	.245	.404
Woody Held	SS3, 3B3 2B1	R	37	56	63	9	9	2	0	3	6	13	19	0	.143	.317
Rich Morales	2B38, SS13, 3B1	R	25	55	121	12	26	0	1	0	6	7	18	1	.215	.231
Duane Josephson (AJ)	C47	R	27	52	162	19	39	6	2	1	20	13	17	0	.241	.321
Bob Christian	OF38	R	23	39	129	11	28	4	0	3	16	10	19	3	.217	.318
Angel Bravo	OF25	L	26	27	90	10	26	4	2	1	1	3	5	2	.289	.411

1 Sandy Alomar 25 B 13-58, Bob Spence 23 L 4-26, Chuck Brinkman 24 R 1-15, Doug Adams 25 L 3-14, Jose Ortiz 22 R 3-11

NAME	T	AGE	W	L	PCT	SV	G	GS	CG	IP	H	BB	SO	ShO	ERA
TOTALS		28	68	94	.420	25	162	162	29	1438	1470	564	810	10	4.21
Joe Horlen	R	31	13	16	.448	0	36	35	7	236	237	77	121	2	3.78
Wilbur Wood	L	27	10	11	.476	15	76	0	0	120	113	40	73	0	3.00
Gary Peters	L	32	10	15	.400	0	36	32	7	219	238	78	140	3	4.52
Tommy John	L	26	9	11	.450	0	33	33	6	232	230	90	128	2	3.26
Billy Wynne	R	25	7	7	.500	0	20	20	6	129	143	50	67	1	4.05
Dan Osinski	R	35	5	5	.500	2	51	0	0	61	56	23	27	0	3.54
1 Cisco Carlos	R	28	4	3	.571	0	25	4	0	49	52	23	28	0	5.69
Jerry Nyman	L	26	4	4	.500	0	20	10	2	65	58	39	40	1	5.26
Danny Murphy	R	26	2	1	.667	4	17	0	0	31	28	10	16	0	2.03
1 Bob Locker	R	31	2	3	.400	4	17	0	0	22	26	6	15	0	6.55
Bart Johnson	R	19	1	3	.250	0	4	3	0	22	22	6	18	0	3.27
Paul Edmondson	R	26	1	6	.143	0	14	13	1	88	72	39	46	0	3.68
Don Secrist (BH)	L	25	0	1	.000	0	19	0	0	40	35	14	23	0	6.08
Fred Rath	R	25	0	2	.000	0	3	2	0	12	11	8	4	0	7.50
Sammy Ellis	R	28	0	3	.000	0	10	5	0	29	42	16	15	0	5.90
2 Jack Hamilton	R	30	0	3	.000	0	8	0	0	12	23	7	5	0	12.00
2 Gary Bell	R	32	0	0	.000	0	23	2	0	39	48	23	26	0	6.29

Danny Lazar 25 I 0-0, 1 Bob Priddy 29 0-0, Denny O'Toole 20 R 0-0

SEATTLE 6th 64-98 .395 33 — JOE SCHULTZ

NAME	G by POS	B	AGE	G	AB	R	H	2B	3B	HR	RBI	BB	SO	SB	BA	SA
TOTALS			28	163	5444	639	1276	179	27	125	583	626	**1015**	**167**	.234	.346
Don Mincher	1B122	L	31	140	427	53	105	14	0	25	78	78	69	10	.246	.454
2 John Donaldson	2B90, 3B2, SS1	L	26	95	338	22	79	8	3	1	19	36	36	6	.234	.284
Ray Oyler	SS106	R	30	106	255	24	42	5	0	7	22	31	80	1	.165	.267
Tommy Harper	3B59, 2B59, OF26	R	28	148	537	78	126	10	2	9	41	95	90	73	.235	.311
Steve Hovley	OF84	L	24	91	329	41	91	14	3	3	20	30	34	10	.277	.365
Wayne Comer	OF139, 3B1, C1	R	25	147	481	88	118	18	1	15	54	82	79	18	.245	.380
1 Tommy Davis	OF112, 1B1	R	30	123	454	52	123	29	1	6	80	30	46	19	.271	.379
Jerry McNertney	C122	R	32	128	410	39	99	18	1	8	55	29	63	1	.241	.349
Mike Hegan	OF64, 1B19	L	26	95	267	54	78	9	6	8	37	62	61	6	.292	.461
Gus Gil	3B38, 2B18, SS12	R	29	92	221	20	49	7	0	0	17	16	28	2	.222	.253
Steve Whitaker	OF39	L	26	69	116	15	29	2	1	6	13	12	29	2	.250	.440
John Kennedy (RJ)	SS33, 3B23	R	28	61	128	18	30	3	1	4	14	14	25	4	.234	.367
Rich Rollins (KJ)	3B47, SS1	R	31	58	187	15	42	7	0	4	21	7	19	2	.225	.326
2 Ron Clark	SS38, 3B15, 2B5, 1B1	R	26	57	163	9	32	5	0	0	12	13	29	1	.196	.227
Merritt Ranew	C13, OF3, 3B1	L	31	54	81	11	20	2	0	0	4	10	14	0	.247	.272
Greg Goossen	1B31, OF2	R	23	52	139	19	43	8	1	10	24	14	29	1	.309	.597
1 Jim Gosger	OF26	L	26	39	55	4	6	2	1	1	1	6	11	2	.109	.236
Danny Walton	OF23	R	21	23	92	12	20	1	2	3	10	5	26	2	.217	.370

2 Dick Simpson 25 R 9-51, 1 Larry Haney 26 R 15-59, Fred Stanley 21 B 12-43, Gordon Lund 28 R 10-38, Jose Vidal 29 R 5-26,
2 Sandy Valdespino 30 L 8-38, 2 Jim Pagliaroni (BG) 31 R 4-27, F. Velazquez 31 R 2-16, M. Ferraro 24 R 0-4, Billy Williams 36 R 0-10

NAME	T	AGE	W	L	PCT	SV	G	GS	CG	IP	H	BB	SO	ShO	ERA
TOTALS		28	64	98	.395	33	163	163	21	1464	**1490**	653	963	6	4.35
Gene Brabender	R	27	13	14	.481	0	40	29	7	202	193	103	139	1	4.37
Diego Segui	R	31	12	6	.667	12	66	8	2	142	127	61	113	0	3.36
Marty Pattin	R	26	7	12	.368	0	34	27	2	159	166	71	126	1	5.60
2 Fred Talbot	R	28	5	8	.385	0	25	16	1	115	125	41	67	1	4.15
Steve Barber (SA)	L	30	4	7	.364	0	25	16	0	86	99	48	69	0	4.81
2 Bob Locker	R	31	3	3	.500	6	51	0	0	78	69	26	46	0	2.19
John Gelnar	R	26	3	10	.231	3	39	10	0	109	103	26	69	0	3.30
Mike Marshall	R	26	3	10	.231	0	20	14	3	88	99	35	47	1	5.11
1 Jim Bouton	R	30	2	1	.667	1	57	1	0	92	77	38	68	0	3.91
2 Dooley Womack	R	29	2	1	.667	0	9	0	0	14	15	3	8	0	2.57
John O'Donoghue	L	29	2	2	.500	6	55	0	0	70	58	37	48	0	2.96
2 Garry Roggenburk	L	29	2	2	.500	0	7	4	1	24	27	11	11	0	4.50
2 George Brunet	L	34	2	5	.286	0	12	11	2	64	70	28	37	0	5.34
1 Gary Bell	R	32	2	6	.250	2	13	11	1	61	76	34	30	1	4.72
Dick Baney	R	22	1	0	1.000	0	9	1	0	19	21	7	9	0	3.79
Mickey Fuentes	R	20	1	3	.250	0	8	4	1	26	29	16	14	0	5.19
1 Darrell Brandon	R	28	0	1	.000	0	8	1	0	15	15	16	10	0	8.40
Skip Lockwood	R	22	0	1	.000	0	6	3	0	23	24	6	10	0	3.52

Bill Edgerton 27 L 0-1, 1 Jack Aker 28 R 0-2, Bob Meyer 29 L 0-3, John Morris 27 L 0-0,
Jerry Stephenson 25 R 0-0, Gary Timberlake (MS) 20 L 0-0, Dick Bates 23 R 0-0

AMERICAN LEAGUE CHAMPIONSHIP – BALTIMORE (EAST) 3 MINNESOTA (WEST) 0

LINE SCORES

TEAM	1	2	3	4	5	6	7	8	9	10	11	12	R	H	E
Game 1 October 4 at Baltimore															
MIN	0	0	0	0	1	0	2	0	0	0	0	0	3	4	2
BAL	0	0	0	1	1	0	0	0	1	0	0	1	4	10	1
Game 2 October 5 at Baltimore															
MIN	0	0	0	0	0	0	0	0	0	0	0		0	3	1
BAL	0	0	0	0	0	0	0	0	0	0	1		1	8	0
Game 3 October 6 at Minnesota															
BAL	0	3	0	2	0	1	0	2	3				11	18	0
MIN	1	0	0	0	1	0	0	0	0				2	10	2

Game 1: Perry, **Perranoski** (9) — Cuellar, Richert (9), Watt (10), Lopez (12), **Hall** (12)

Game 2: **Boswell**, Perranoski (11) — **McNally**

Game 3: **Palmer** — **Miller**, Woodson (2), Hall (4), Worthington (5), Grzenda (6), Chance (7), Perranoski (9)

COMPOSITE BATTING

NAME	POS	G	AB	R	H	2B	3B	HR	RBI	BA
Baltimore Totals		3	123	16	36	8	1	4	15	.293
Blair	OF	3	**15**	1	6	**2**	0	1	**6**	.400
Belanger	SS	3	**15**	**4**	4	0	**1**	1	1	.267
B. Robinson	3B	3	14	1	**7**	1	0	0	0	**.500**
Buford	OF	3	14	3	4	1	0	0	1	.286
Powell	1B	3	13	2	5	0	0	1	1	.385
Johnson	2B	3	13	2	3	0	0	0	0	.231
F. Robinson	OF	3	12	1	4	2	0	0	1	.333
Hendricks	C	3	8	2	2	2	0	0	3	.250

Etchebarren C 0-4, Motton PH 1-2, May PH 0-1, Salmon PH 0-1, Rettenmund PH 0-0

NAME	POS	G	AB	R	H	2B	3B	HR	RBI	BA
Minnesota Totals		3	110	5	17	3	1	1	5	.155
Carew	2B	3	14	0	1	0	0	0	0	.071
Oliva	OF	3	13	3	5	**2**	0	**1**	2	.385
Cardenas	SS	3	13	0	2	0	**1**	0	0	.154
Tovar	OF	3	13	0	1	0	0	0	0	.077
Reese	1B	3	12	0	2	0	0	0	2	.167
Killebrew	3B	3	8	2	1	1	0	0	0	.125
Allison	OF	2	8	0	0	0	0	0	0	.000

Mitterwald C 1-7, Uhlaender OF 1-6, Roseboro C 1-5, Nettles PH 1-1, Renick PH 0-1, Manuel PH 0-0

COMPOSITE PITCHING

NAME	G	IP	H	BB	SO	W	L	SV	ERA
Baltimore Totals	3	32	17	12	27	3	0	0	1.13
McNally	1	**11**	3	5	**11**	1	0	0	**0.00**
Palmer	1	9	**10**	2	4	1	0	0	2.00
Cuellar	1	8	3	1	7	0	0	0	2.25
Watt	1	2	3	0	2	0	0	0	0.00
Richert	1	1	0	2	2	0	0	0	0.00
D. Hall	1	.2	0	0	1	1	0	0	0.00
Lopez	1	.1	1	2	0	0	0	0	0.00
Minnesota Totals	3	31.1	36	13	14	0	3	0	4.02
Boswell	1	10.2	7	**7**	4	0	1	0	0.84
Perry	1	8	6	3	3	0	0	0	3.38
Perranoski	**3**	4.2	8	0	2	0	1	0	5.79
Chance	1	2	4	0	2	0	0	0	13.50
Miller	1	1.2	5	0	0	0	1	0	5.40

Worthington 1G, Woodson 1G, Grzenda 1G, T. Hall 1G

NATIONAL LEAGUE CHAMPIONSHIP – NEW YORK (EAST) 3 ATLANTA (WEST) 0

LINE SCORES

TEAM	1	2	3	4	5	6	7	8	9	10	11	12	R	H	E
Game 1 October 4 at Atlanta															
NY	0	2	0	2	0	0	0	5	0				9	10	1
ATL	0	1	2	0	1	0	1	0	0				5	10	2
Seaver, Taylor (8)				Niekro, Upshaw (9)											
Game 2 October 5 at Atlanta															
NY	1	3	2	2	1	0	2	0	0				11	13	1
ATL	0	0	0	1	5	0	0	0	0				6	9	3
Koosman, Taylor (5), McGraw (7)				Reed, Doyle (2), Pappas (3), Britton (6), Upshaw (6), Neibauer (9)											
Game 3 October 6 at New York															
ATL	2	0	0	0	2	0	0	0	0				4	8	1
NY	0	0	1	2	3	1	0	0	X				7	14	0
Jarvis, Stone (5), Upshaw (6)				Gentry, Ryan (3)											

COMPOSITE BATTING

NAME	POS	G	AB	R	H	2B	3B	HR	RBI	BA
New York Totals		3	113	27	37	8	1	6	24	.327
Jones	OF	3	14	4	6	2	0	1	4	.429
Agee	OF	3	14	4	5	1	0	2	4	.357
Shamsky	OF	3	13	3	7	0	0	0	1	.538
Garrett	3B	3	13	3	5	2	0	1	3	.385
Boswell	2B	3	12	4	4	0	0	2	5	.333
Kranepool	1B	3	12	2	3	1	0	0	1	.250
Grote	C	3	12	3	2	1	0	0	1	.167
Harrelson	SS	3	11	2	2	1	1	0	3	.182
Martin	PH	2	2	0	1	0	0	0	2	.500
Weis	2B	3	1	0	0	0	0	0	0	.000
Gaspar	OF	3	0	0	0	0	0	0	0	.000
Atlanta Totals		3	106	15	27	9	0	5	15	.255
H. Aaron	OF	3	14	3	5	2	0	3	7	.357
Gonzalez	OF	3	14	4	5	1	0	1	2	.357
Millan	2B	3	12	2	4	1	0	0	0	.333
Cepeda	1B	3	11	2	5	2	0	1	3	.455
Didier	C	3	11	0	0	0	0	0	0	.000
Carty	OF	3	10	4	3	2	0	0	0	.300
Garrido	SS	3	10	0	2	0	0	0	0	.200
Boyer	3B	3	9	0	1	0	0	0	3	.111
Aspromonte	PH	3	3	0	0	0	0	0	0	.000
Lum	OF	2	2	0	2	1	0	0	0	1.000
T. Aaron	PH	1	1	0	0	0	0	0	0	.000

Alou PH 0-1, Jackson SS 0-0, Tillman C 0-0

COMPOSITE PITCHING

NAME	G	IP	H	BB	SO	W	L	SV	ERA
New York Totals	3	27	27	11	20	3	0	2	5.00
Ryan	1	7	3	2	7	1	0	0	2.57
Seaver	1	7	8	3	2	1	0	0	6.43
Koosman	1	4.2	7	4	5	0	0	0	11.57
Taylor	2	3.1	3	0	4	1	0	1	0.00
McGraw	1	3	1	1	1	0	0	1	0.00
Gentry	1	2	5	1	1	0	0	0	9.00
Atlanta Totals	3	26	37	10	25	0	3	0	6.92
Niekro	1	8	9	4	4	0	1	0	4.50
Upshaw	3	6.1	5	1	4	0	0	0	2.84
Jarvis	1	4.1	10	0	6	0	1	0	12.46
Pappas	1	2.1	4	0	4	0	0	0	11.57
Reed	1	1.2	5	3	3	0	1	0	21.60
Doyle	1	1	2	1	3	0	0	0	0.00
Neibauer	1	1	0	0	1	0	0	0	0.00
Stone	1	1	2	0	0	0	0	0	0.00
Britton	1	.1	0	1	0	0	0	0	0.00

EAST DIVISION

NEW YORK 1st 100-62 .617 — GIL HODGES

NAME	G by POS	B	AGE	G	AB	R	H	2B	3B	HR	RBI	BB	SO	SB	BA	SA
TOTALS			27	162	5427	632	1311	184	41	109	598	527	1089	66	.242	.351
Ed Kranepool	1B106, OF2	L	24	112	353	36	84	9	2	11	49	37	32	3	.238	.368
Ken Boswell	2B96	L	23	102	362	48	101	14	7	3	32	36	47	7	.279	.381
Bud Harrelson	SS119	B	25	123	395	42	98	11	6	0	24	54	54	1	.248	.306
Wayne Garrett	3B72, 2B47, SS9	L	21	124	400	38	87	11	3	1	39	40	75	4	.218	.268
Ron Swoboda	OF97	R	25	109	327	38	77	10	2	9	52	43	90	1	.235	.361
Tommie Agee	OF146	R	26	149	565	97	153	23	4	26	76	59	137	12	.271	.464
Cleon Jones	OF122, 1B15	R	26	137	483	92	164	25	4	12	75	64	60	16	.340	.482
Jerry Grote	C112	R	26	113	365	38	92	12	3	6	40	32	59	2	.252	.351
Rod Gaspar	OF91	B	23	118	215	26	49	6	1	1	14	25	19	7	.228	.279
Al Weis	SS52, 2B43, 3B1	R	31	103	247	20	53	9	2	2	23	15	51	3	.215	.291
Art Shamsky (XJ)	OF78, 1B9	L	27	100	303	42	91	9	3	14	47	36	32	1	.300	.488
2 Donn Clendenon	1B58, OF1	R	33	72	202	31	51	5	0	12	37	19	62	3	.252	.455
J. C. Martin	C48, 1B2	L	32	66	177	12	37	5	1	4	21	12	32	0	.209	.316
Bobby Pfeil	3B49, 2B11, OF2	R	25	62	211	20	49	9	0	0	10	7	27	0	.232	.275
Ed Charles	3B52	R	34	61	169	21	35	8	1	3	18	18	31	4	.207	.320
Amos Otis	OF35, 3B3	R	22	48	93	6	14	3	1	0	4	6	27	1	.151	.204
Duffy Dyer	C19	R	23	29	74	5	19	3	1	3	12	4	22	0	.257	.446

1 Kevin Collins 22 L 6-40, 2 Jim Gosger 26 L 2-15, Bob Heise 22 R 3-10

NAME	T	AGE	W	L	PCT	SV	G	GS	CG	IP	H	BB	SO	ShO	ERA
		26	100	62	.617	35	162	162	51	1468	1217	517	1012	28	2.99
Tom Seaver	R	24	25	7	.781	0	36	35	18	273	202	82	208	5	2.21
Jerry Koosman	L	26	17	9	.654	0	32	32	16	241	187	68	180	6	2.28
Gary Gentry	R	22	13	12	.520	0	35	35	6	234	192	81	154	3	3.42
Tug McGraw	L	24	9	3	.750	12	42	4	1	100	89	47	92	0	2.25
Ron Taylor	R	31	9	4	.692	13	59	0	0	76	61	24	42	0	2.72
Don Cardwell	R	33	8	10	.444	0	30	21	4	152	145	47	60	0	3.02
Cal Koonce	R	28	6	3	.667	7	40	0	0	83	85	42	48	0	4.99
Nolan Ryan (GJ)	R	22	6	3	.667	1	25	10	2	89	60	53	92	0	3.54
Jim McAndrew	R	25	6	7	.462	0	27	21	4	135	112	44	90	2	3.47
Jack DiLauro	L	26	1	4	.200	1	23	4	0	64	50	18	27	0	2.39
Danny Frisella	R	23	0	0	.000	0	3	0	0	5	8	3	5	0	7.20
Jesse Hudson	L	20	0	0	.000	0	1	0	0	2	2	2	3	0	4.50
1 Al Jackson	L	33	0	0	.000	0	9	0	0	11	18	4	10	0	10.64
Bob Johnson	R	26	0	0	.000	1	2	0	0	2	1	1	1	0	0.00
Les Rohr	L	23	0	0	.000	0	1	0	0	1	5	1	0	0	27.00

CHICAGO 2nd 92-70 .568 8 — LEO DUROCHER

NAME	G by POS	B	AGE	G	AB	R	H	2B	3B	HR	RBI	BB	SO	SB	BA	SA
TOTALS			30	163	5530	720	1400	215	40	142	671	559	928	30	.253	.384
Ernie Banks	1B153	R	38	155	565	60	143	19	2	23	106	42	101	0	.253	.416
Glenn Beckert (BG)	2B129	R	28	131	543	69	158	22	1	1	37	24	24	6	.291	.341
Don Kessinger	SS157	B	26	158	664	109	181	38	6	4	53	61	70	11	.273	.366
Ron Santo	3B160	R	29	160	575	97	166	18	4	29	123	96	97	1	.289	.485
Jim Hickman	OF125	R	32	134	338	38	80	11	2	21	54	47	74	2	.237	.467
Don Young	OF100	R	23	101	272	36	65	12	3	6	27	38	74	1	.239	.371
Billy Williams	OF159	L	31	163	642	103	188	33	10	21	95	59	70	3	.293	.474
Randy Hundley	C151	R	27	151	522	67	133	15	1	18	64	61	90	2	.255	.391
Willie Smith	OF33, 1B24	L	30	103	195	21	48	9	1	9	25	25	49	1	.246	.441
Al Spangler	OF58	L	35	82	213	23	45	8	1	4	23	21	16	0	.211	.315
2 Paul Popovich	2B25, SS7, 3B6, OF1	B	28	60	154	26	48	6	0	1	14	18	14	0	.312	.370
2 Nate Oliver	2B13	R	28	44	44	15	7	3	0	1	4	1	10	0	.159	.295
Jim Qualls (SJ)	OF35, 2B4	B	22	43	120	12	30	5	3	0	9	2	14	2	.250	.342
1 Adolpho Phillips	OF25	R	27	28	49	5	11	3	1	0	1	16	15	1	.224	.327
Bill Heath	C9	L	30	27	32	1	5	0	1	0	1	12	4	0	.156	.219
Ken Rudolph	C11, OF3	R	22	27	34	7	7	1	0	1	6	6	11	0	.206	.324
Oscar Gamble	OF24	L	19	24	71	6	16	1	1	1	5	10	12	0	.225	.310
Gene Oliver	C6	R	33	23	27	0	6	3	0	0	0	1	9	0	.222	.333

3 Jimmie Hall 31 L 5-24, Rick Bladt 22 R 2-13, Manny Jiminez 30 L 1-6, John Hairston 23 R 1-4, Charley Smith 31 R 0-2, Randy Bobb 21 R 0-2

NAME	T	AGE	W	L	PCT	SV	G	GS	CG	IP	H	BB	SO	ShO	ERA
		29	92	70	.568	27	163	163	58	1454	1366	475	1017	22	3.34
Ferguson Jenkins	R	25	21	15	.583	1	43	42	23	311	284	71	273	7	3.21
Bill Hands	R	29	20	14	.588	0	41	41	18	300	268	73	181	3	2.49
Ken Holtzman	L	23	17	13	.567	0	39	39	12	261	248	93	176	6	3.59
Phil Regan	R	32	12	6	.667	17	71	0	0	112	120	35	56	0	3.70
2 Dick Selma	R	25	10	8	.556	1	36	25	4	169	137	72	161	2	3.62
Ted Abernathy	R	36	4	3	.571	3	56	0	0	85	75	42	55	0	3.18
Rich Nye	L	24	3	5	.375	3	34	5	1	69	72	21	39	0	5.09
Hank Aguirre	L	37	1	0	1.000	1	41	0	0	45	45	12	19	0	2.60
Jim Colborn	R	23	1	0	1.000	0	6	2	0	15	15	9	4	0	3.00
Joe Decker	R	22	1	0	1.000	0	4	1	0	12	10	6	13	0	3.00
2 Don Nottebart	R	33	1	1	.500	0	16	0	0	18	28	7	8	0	7.00
3 Ken Johnson	R	36	1	2	.333	1	9	1	0	19	17	13	18	0	2.84
Dave Lemonds	L	20	0	1	.000	0	2	1	0	5	5	5	0	0	3.60
1 Joe Niekro	R	24	0	1	.000	0	4	3	0	19	24	6	7	0	3.79
Archie Reynolds	R	23	0	1	.000	0	2	2	0	7	11	7	4	0	2.57
Alec Distaso	R	20	0	0	.000	0	2	0	0	5	6	1	1	0	3.60
1 Gary Ross	R	21	0	0	.000	0	2	1	0	2	1	2	2	0	13.50
Darcy Fast (MS) 22															

PITTSBURGH 3rd 88-74 .543 12 — LARRY SHEPHARD 84-73 .535 ALEX GRAMMAS 4-1 .800

NAME	G by POS	B	AGE	G	AB	R	H	2B	3B	HR	RBI	BB	SO	SB	BA	SA
TOTALS			27	162	5626	725	1557	220	52	119	651	454	944	74	.277	.398
Al Oliver	1B106, OF21	L	22	129	463	55	132	19	2	17	70	21	38	8	.285	.445
Bill Mazeroski (LJ)	2B65	R	32	67	227	13	52	7	1	3	25	22	16	1	.229	.308
Freddie Patek	SS146	R	24	147	460	48	110	9	1	5	32	53	86	15	.239	.296
Richie Hebner	3B124, 1B1	L	21	129	459	72	138	23	4	8	47	53	53	4	.301	.420
Roberto Clemente	OF132	R	34	138	507	87	175	20	12	19	91	56	73	4	.345	.544
Matty Alou	OF162	L	30	162	698	105	231	41	6	1	48	42	35	22	.331	.411
Willie Stangell	OF116, 1B23	L	29	145	522	89	160	31	6	29	92	61	120	1	.307	.556
Manny Sanguillen	C113	R	25	129	459	62	139	21	6	5	57	12	48	8	.303	.407
Jose Pagan	3B44, OF23, 2B1	R	34	108	274	29	78	11	4	9	42	17	46	1	.285	.453
Carl Taylor	OF36, 1B24	R	25	104	221	30	77	10	1	4	33	31	36	0	.348	.457
Gene Alley (SJ)	2B53, SS25, 3B5	R	28	82	285	28	70	3	2	8	32	19	48	4	.246	.354
Jose Martinez	2B42, SS20, 3B5, OF2	R	26	77	168	20	45	6	0	1	16	9	32	1	.268	.321
Jerry May (SJ)	C52	R	25	62	190	21	44	8	0	7	23	9	53	1	.232	.384
Ron Davis	OF51	R	27	62	64	10	15	1	1	0	4	7	14	0	.234	.281
Bob Robertson	1B26	R	22	32	96	7	20	4	1	1	9	8	30	1	.208	.302
Dave Cash	2B17	R	21	18	61	8	17	3	1	0	4	9	9	2	.279	.361

Johnnie Jeter 24 R 9-29, Angel Mangual 22 R 1-4, Gary Kolb 29 L 3-37

NAME	T	AGE	W	L	PCT	SV	G	GS	CG	IP	H	BB	SO	ShO	ERA
		29	88	74	.543	33	162	162	39	1446	1348	553	1124	9	3.61
Steve Blass	R	27	16	10	.615	2	38	32	9	210	207	86	147	0	4.46
Bob Moose	R	21	14	3	.824	4	44	19	6	170	149	62	165	1	2.91
Bob Veale	L	33	13	14	.481	0	34	34	9	226	232	91	213	1	3.23
Dock Ellis	R	24	11	17	.393	0	35	33	8	219	206	76	173	2	3.58
1 Jim Bunning	R	37	10	9	.526	0	25	25	4	156	147	49	124	0	3.81
Bruce Dal Canton	R	27	8	2	.800	5	57	0	0	86	79	49	56	0	3.35
2 Joe Gibbon	L	34	5	1	.833	9	35	0	0	51	38	17	35	0	1.94
Chuch Hartenstein	R	27	5	4	.556	10	56	0	0	96	84	27	44	0	3.94
Luke Walker	L	25	4	6	.400	0	31	15	3	119	98	57	96	1	3.63
Lou Marone	L	23	1	1	.500	0	29	0	0	35	24	13	25	0	2.57
1 Ron Kline	R	37	1	3	.250	3	20	0	0	31	37	5	15	0	5.81
1 Pedro Ramos	R	34	0	1	.000	0	5	0	0	6	8	0	4	0	6.00
Bo Belinsky	L	32	0	3	.000	0	8	3	0	18	17	14	15	0	4.50
Frank Brosseau	R	24	0	0	.000	0	2	0	0	2	2	2	2	0	9.00
Gene Garber	R	21	0	0	.000	0	2	1	0	5	6	1	3	0	5.40
1 Jim Shellenback	L	25	0	0	.000	0	8	0	0	17	14	4	7	0	3.18

ST. LOUIS 4th 87-75 .537 13 — RED SCHOENDIENST

NAME	G by POS	B	AGE	G	AB	R	H	2B	3B	HR	RBI	BB	SO	SB	BA	SA
TOTALS			30	162	5536	595	1403	228	44	90	561	503	876	87	.253	.359
Joe Torre	1B144, C17	R	28	159	602	72	174	29	6	18	101	66	85	0	.289	.447
Julian Javier	2B141	R	32	143	493	59	139	28	2	10	42	40	74	8	.282	.408
Dal Maxvill	SS131	R	30	132	372	27	65	10	2	2	32	44	52	1	.175	.228
Mike Shannon	3B149	R	29	150	551	51	140	15	5	12	55	49	87	1	.254	.365
Vada Pinson (BW)	OF124	L	30	132	495	58	126	22	6	10	70	35	63	4	.255	.384
Curt Flood	OF152	R	31	153	606	80	173	31	3	4	57	48	57	9	.285	.366
Lou Brock	OF157	L	30	157	655	97	195	33	10	12	47	50	115	53	.298	.434
Tim McCarver	C136	L	27	138	515	46	134	27	3	7	51	49	26	4	.260	.365
Steve Huntz	SS52, 2B12, 3B6	B	23	71	139	13	27	4	0	3	13	27	34	0	.194	.288
2 Vic Davalillo	OF23, P2	L	32	63	98	15	26	3	0	2	10	7	8	1	.265	.357
Phil Gagliano	2B20, 1B9, 3B9, OF2	R	27	62	128	7	29	2	0	1	10	14	12	0	.227	.266
Bill White	1B15	L	35	49	57	7	12	1	0	0	4	11	15	1	.211	.228
Joe Hague	OF17, 1B9	L	25	40	100	8	17	2	1	2	8	12	23	0	.170	.270
Dave Ricketts	C8	B	33	30	44	2	12	1	0	0	5	4	5	0	.273	.295
Byron Browne	OF16	R	26	22	53	9	12	0	1	1	7	11	14	0	.226	.321
1 Jim Hicks	OF15	R	29	19	44	5	8	0	2	1	3	4	14	0	.182	.341
1 Bob Johnson	3B4, 1B1	R	33	19	29	1	6	0	0	1	2	2	4	0	.207	.310
2 Jerry DaVanon	SS16	R	23	16	40	7	12	3	0	1	7	6	8	0	.300	.450

Levon Lee 21 L 5-23, Tom Coulter 24 L 6-19, Ted Simmons 19 B 3-14, 2 Joe Nossek 28 R 1-5, Boots Day 21 L 0-6, Dick Hughes (SA) 31

NAME	T	AGE	W	L	PCT	SV	G	GS	CG	IP	H	BB	SO	ShO	ERA
		28	87	75	.537	26	162	162	63	1460	1289	511	1004	12	2.94
Bob Gibson	R	33	20	13	.606	0	35	35	28	314	251	95	269	4	2.18
Steve Carlton	L	24	17	11	.607	0	31	31	12	236	185	93	210	2	2.17
Nelson Briles	R	25	15	13	.536	0	36	33	10	228	218	63	126	3	3.51
Mike Torrez	R	22	10	4	.714	0	24	15	3	108	96	62	61	0	3.58
2 Mudcat Grant	R	33	7	5	.583	7	30	3	1	63	62	22	35	0	4.14
Chuck Taylor	R	27	7	5	.583	0	27	13	5	127	108	30	62	1	2.55
Dave Giusti	R	29	3	7	.300	0	22	12	2	100	96	37	62	1	3.60
Ray Washburn	R	31	3	8	.273	1	28	16	2	132	133	49	80	0	3.07
Joe Hoerner	L	32	2	3	.400	15	45	0	0	53	44	9	35	0	2.89
Sal Campisi	R	26	1	0	1.000	0	7	0	0	10	4	6	7	0	0.90
Jerry Reuss	L	20	1	0	1.000	0	1	1	0	7	2	3	3	0	0.00
1 Ron Willis	R	25	1	2	.333	0	26	0	0	32	26	19	23	0	4.22
Santiago Guzman	R	19	0	1	.000	0	1	1	0	7	9	3	7	0	5.14
Mel Nelson	L	33	0	1	.000	0	8	0	0	5	13	3	3	0	12.60
1 Gary Waslewski	R	27	0	2	.000	1	12	0	0	21	19	8	16	0	3.86
Tom Hilgendorf	L	27	0	0	.000	2	6	0	0	6	3	2	2	0	1.50
Jim Ellis	L	24	0	0	.000	0	2	1	0	5	7	3	0	0	1.80
2 Vic Davallio	L	32	0	0	.000	0	2	0	0	0	2	2	0	0	∞
Reggie Cleveland	R	21	0	0	.000	0	1	1	0	4	7	1	3	0	9.00
1 Dennis Ribrant	R	27	0	0	.000	0	1	0	0	1	4	1	0	0	18.00

PHILADELPHIA 5th 63-99 .389 37 — BOB SKINNER 44-64 .297 GEORGE MYATT 19-35 .352

NAME	G by POS	B	AGE	G	AB	R	H	2B	3B	HR	RBI	BB	SO	SB	BA	SA
TOTALS			27	162	5408	645	1304	227	35	137	593	549	1130	73	.241	.372
Dick Allen (ST)	1B117	R	27	118	438	79	126	23	3	32	89	64	144	9	.288	.573
Cookie Rojas	2B95, OF2	R	30	110	391	35	89	11	1	4	30	23	28	1	.228	.292
Don Money	SS126	R	22	127	450	41	103	22	2	6	42	43	83	1	.229	.327
Tony Taylor	3B71, 2B57, 1B10	R	33	138	557	68	146	24	5	3	30	42	62	19	.262	.339
Johnny Callison	OF129	L	30	134	495	66	131	29	5	16	64	49	73	2	.265	.440
Larry Hisle (BG)	OF140	R	22	145	482	75	128	23	5	20	56	48	152	18	.266	.459
Johnny Briggs	OF108, 1B2	L	25	124	361	51	86	20	3	12	46	64	78	9	.238	.410
Mike Ryan	C132	R	27	133	446	41	91	17	2	12	44	30	66	1	.204	.332
Deron Johnson	OF72, 3B50, 1B18	R	30	138	475	51	121	19	4	17	80	60	111	4	.255	.419
Ron Stone	OF69	L	26	103	222	22	53	7	1	1	24	29	28	3	.239	.293
Rick Joseph	3B58, 1B17, 2B1	R	29	99	264	35	72	15	0	6	37	22	57	2	.273	.398
Terry Harmon	SS38, 2B19, 3B2	R	25	87	201	25	48	8	1	0	16	22	31	1	.239	.289
Dave Watkins	C54, OF5, 3B1	R	25	69	148	17	26	2	1	4	12	22	53	2	.176	.284
Rich Barry	OF9	R	28	20	32	4	6	1	0	0	0	5	6	0	.188	.219
Gene Stone	1B5	L	25	18	28	4	6	0	1	0	0	4	9	0	.214	.286
Scott Reid	OF5	L	22	13	19	5	4	0	0	0	0	7	5	0	.211	.211
Vic Roznovsky	C2	L	30	13	13	0	3	0	0	0	1	1	4	0	.231	.231

1 Don Lock 32 R 0-4, Leroy Reams 25 L 0-1

NAME	T	AGE	W	L	PCT	SV	G	GS	CG	IP	H	BB	SO	ShO	ERA
TOTALS		26	63	99	.389	21	162	162	47	1434	1494	570	921	14	4.14
Rick Wise	R	23	15	13	.536	0	33	31	14	220	215	61	144	4	3.23
Grant Jackson	L	26	14	18	.438	1	38	35	13	253	237	92	180	4	3.34
Woodie Fryman	L	29	12	15	.444	0	36	35	10	228	243	89	150	1	4.42
Jerry Johnson	R	25	6	13	.316	1	33	21	4	147	151	57	82	2	4.29
Billy Champion	R	21	5	10	.333	1	23	20	4	117	130	63	70	2	5.00
Dick Farrell	R	35	3	4	.429	3	46	0	0	74	92	27	40	0	4.01
Jeff James	R	27	2	2	.500	0	6	5	1	32	36	14	21	0	5.34
Billy Wilson (AJ)	R	26	2	5	.286	6	37	0	0	62	53	36	48	0	3.34
Lowell Palmer	R	21	2	8	.200	0	26	9	1	90	91	47	68	1	5.20
John Boozer	R	29	1	2	.333	6	46	2	0	82	91	36	47	0	4.28
Al Raffo	R	27	1	3	.250	1	45	0	0	72	81	25	38	0	4.13
Barry Lersch	R	24	0	3	.000	2	10	0	0	18	20	10	13	0	7.00
1 Gary Wagner	R	29	0	3	.000	0	9	2	0	19	31	7	8	0	8.05
Lou Peraza	R	26	0	0	.000	0	8	0	0	9	12	2	7	0	6.00
Chris Short (XJ)	L	31	0	0	.000	0	2	2	0	10	11	4	5	0	7.20

MONTREAL 6th 52-110 .321 48 — GENE MAUCH

NAME	G by POS	B	AGE	G	AB	R	H	2B	3B	HR	RBI	BB	SO	SB	BA	SA
TOTALS			29	162	5419	582	1300	202	33	125	542	529	962	52	.240	.359
Bob Bailey (BN)	1B85, OF12, 3B1	R	26	111	358	46	95	16	6	9	53	40	76	3	.265	.419
Gary Sutherland	2B139, SS15, OF1	R	24	141	544	63	130	26	1	3	35	37	31	5	.239	.307
Bobby Wine	SS118, 1B1, 3B1	R	30	121	370	23	74	8	1	3	25	28	49	0	.200	.251
Coco Laboy	3B156	R	29	157	562	53	145	29	1	18	83	40	96	0	.258	.409
Rusty Staub	OF150	L	25	158	549	89	166	26	5	29	79	110	61	3	.302	.526
2 Adolfo Phillips (IL)	OF53	R	27	58	199	25	43	4	4	4	7	19	62	6	.216	.337
Mack Jones	OF129	L	30	135	455	73	123	23	5	22	79	67	110	6	.270	.488
Ron Brand	C84, OF2	R	29	103	287	19	74	12	0	0	20	30	19	2	.258	.300
Ty Cline	OF41, 1B17	L	30	101	209	26	50	5	3	2	12	32	22	4	.239	.321
John Bateman (RJ)	C66	R	26	74	235	16	49	4	0	8	19	12	44	0	.209	.328
2 Ron Fairly (HJ)	1B52, OF21	L	30	70	253	35	73	13	4	12	39	28	22	1	.289	.514
2 Kevin Collins	2B20, 3B16	L	22	52	96	5	23	5	1	2	12	8	16	0	.240	.375
Don Bosch (KJ)	OF32	B	26	49	112	13	20	5	0	1	4	8	20	1	.179	.250
1 Maury Wills	SS46, 2B1	B	36	47	189	23	42	3	0	0	8	20	21	15	.222	.238
Joe Herrara	OF31, 2B2, 3B1	R	27	47	126	7	36	5	0	2	12	3	14	1	.286	.373
Floyd Wicker	OF11	L	25	41	39	2	4	0	0	0	2	2	20	0	.103	.103
John Boccabella	C32	R	28	40	86	4	9	2	0	1	6	6	30	1	.105	.163
1 Donn Clendenon	1B24, OF11	R	33	38	129	14	31	6	1	4	14	6	32	0	.240	.395
1 Manny Mota	OF22	R	31	31	89	6	28	1	1	0	0	6	11	1	.315	.348
Angel Hermoso	2B18, SS6	R	22	28	74	6	12	0	0	0	3	5	10	3	.162	.162
Jim Fairey	OF13	L	24	20	49	6	14	1	0	1	6	1	7	0	.286	.367
Marv Staehle	2B4	L	27	6	17	4	7	2	0	1	1	2	0	0	.412	.706

Don Hahn 20 R 1-9, Gerry Jestadt 22 R 0-6

NAME	T	AGE	W	L	PCT	SV	G	GS	CG	IP	H	BB	SO	ShO	ERA
TOTALS		28	52	110	.321	21	162	162	26	1426	1429	702	973	8	4.33
Bill Stoneman	R	25	11	19	.367	0	42	36	8	236	233	123	185	5	4.39
Dan McGinn	L	25	7	10	.412	6	74	1	0	132	123	65	112	0	3.95
Howie Reed	R	32	6	7	.462	1	31	15	2	106	119	50	59	1	4.84
Steve Renko	R	24	6	7	.462	0	18	15	4	103	94	50	68	0	4.02
Mike Wegener	R	22	5	14	.263	0	32	26	4	166	150	96	124	1	4.39
Jerry Robertson	R	25	5	16	.238	1	38	27	3	180	186	81	133	0	3.95
Roy Face	R	41	4	2	.667	5	44	0	0	59	62	15	34	0	3.97
2 Gary Waslewski	R	27	3	7	.300	1	30	14	3	109	102	63	63	1	3.30
Don Shaw	L	25	2	5	.286	1	35	1	0	66	61	37	45	0	5.18
2 Claude Raymond	R	32	1	2	.333	1	15	0	0	22	21	8	11	0	4.09
1 Mudcat Grant	R	33	1	6	.143	0	11	10	1	51	64	14	20	0	4.76
Larry Jaster	L	25	1	6	.143	0	24	11	1	77	95	28	39	0	5.49
Carroll Sembera	R	27	0	2	.000	2	23	0	0	33	28	24	15	0	3.55
Carl Morton	R	25	0	3	.000	0	8	5	0	29	29	18	16	0	4.66
2 Dick Radatz	R	32	0	4	.000	3	22	0	0	35	32	18	32	0	5.66
Leo Marentette	R	28	0	0	.000	0	3	0	0	5	9	1	4	0	7.20
Bob Reynolds	R	22	0	0	.000	0	1	1	0	1	3	3	2	0	27.00
Steve Shea	R	26	0	0	.000	0	10	0	0	16	18	8	11	0	2.81

WEST DIVISION

ATLANTA 1st 93-69 .574 — LUM HARRIS

NAME	G by POS	B	AGE	G	AB	R	H	2B	3B	HR	RBI	BB	SO	SB	BA	SA
TOTALS			29	162	5460	691	1411	195	22	141	640	485	665	59	.258	.380
Orlando Cepeda	1B153	R	31	154	573	74	147	28	2	22	88	55	76	12	.257	.428
Felix Millan	2B162	R	25	162	652	98	174	23	5	6	57	34	35	14	.267	.345
Sonny Jackson (LJ)	SS97	L	24	98	318	41	76	3	5	1	27	35	33	12	.239	.289
Clete Boyer	3B141	R	32	144	496	57	124	16	1	14	57	55	87	3	.250	.371
Hank Aaron	OF144, 1B4	R	35	147	547	100	164	30	3	44	97	87	47	9	.300	.607
Felipe Alou	OF116	R	34	123	476	54	134	13	1	5	32	23	23	4	.282	.345
2 Tony Gonzalez	OF82	L	32	89	320	51	94	15	2	10	50	27	22	3	.294	.447
Bob Didier	C114	R	20	114	352	30	90	16	1	0	32	34	39	1	.256	.307
Mike Lum	OF89	L	23	121	168	20	45	8	0	1	22	16	18	0	.268	.333
Rico Carty	OF79	R	30	104	304	47	104	15	0	16	58	32	28	0	.342	.549
Gil Garrido	SS81	R	28	82	227	18	50	5	1	0	10	16	11	0	.220	.251
Bob Aspromonte	OF24, 3B23, SS18, 2B2	R	31	82	198	16	50	8	1	3	24	13	19	0	.253	.348
Bob Tillman	C69	R	32	69	190	18	37	5	0	12	29	18	47	0	.195	.411
1 Tito Francona	OF15, 1B7	L	35	51	88	5	26	1	0	2	22	13	10	0	.295	.375
Tommie Aaron	1B16, OF8	R	29	49	60	13	15	2	0	1	5	6	6	0	.250	.333
Ralph Garr	OF7	L	23	22	27	6	6	1	0	0	2	2	4	1	.222	.259
Darrell Evans	3B6	L	22	12	26	3	6	0	0	0	1	1	8	0	.231	.231

1 Walt Hriniak (BG) 26 L 1-7, Oscar Brown 23 R 1-4, Dusty Baker 20 R 0-7, Jim Breazeale 19 L 0-1

NAME	T	AGE	W	L	PCT	SV	G	GS	CG	IP	H	BB	SO	ShO	ERA
TOTALS		27	93	69	.574	42	162	162	38	1445	1334	438	893	7	3.53
Phil Niekro	R	30	23	13	.639	1	40	35	21	284	235	57	193	4	2.57
Ron Reed	R	26	18	10	.643	0	36	33	7	241	227	56	160	1	3.47
George Stone	L	23	13	10	.565	3	36	20	3	165	166	48	102	0	3.65
Pat Jarvis	R	28	13	11	.542	0	37	33	4	217	204	73	123	1	4.49
Jim Britton	R	25	7	5	.583	1	24	13	2	88	69	49	60	1	3.78
Cecil Upshaw	R	26	6	4	.600	27	62	0	0	105	102	29	57	0	2.91
Milt Pappas	R	30	6	10	.375	0	26	24	1	144	149	44	72	0	3.63
Paul Doyle	L	29	2	0	1.000	4	36	0	0	39	31	16	25	0	2.08
2 Hoyt Wilhelm	R	45	2	0	1.000	4	8	0	0	12	5	4	14	0	0.75
1 Claude Raymond	R	32	2	2	.500	1	33	0	0	48	56	13	15	0	5.25
Gary Neibauer	R	24	1	2	.333	0	29	0	0	58	42	31	42	0	3.88
Garry Hill	R	22	0	1	.000	0	1	1	0	2	6	1	2	0	18.00
1 Ken Johnson	R	36	0	1	.000	1	9	2	0	29	32	9	20	0	4.97
Rick Kester	R	22	0	0	.000	0	1	0	0	2	5	0	2	0	13.50
Larry Maxie	R	28	0	0	.000	0	2	0	0	3	1	1	1	0	3.00
Mike McQueen	L	18	0	0	.000	0	1	1	0	3	3	3	3	0	3.00
3 Bob Priddy	R	29	0	0	.000	0	1	0	0	2	1	1	1	0	0.00
Charlie Vaughan	L	21	0	0	.000	0	1	0	0	1	1	3	1	0	18.00

SAN FRANCISCO 2nd 90-72 .556 3 — CLYDE KING

NAME	G by POS	B	AGE	G	AB	R	H	2B	3B	HR	RBI	BB	SO	SB	BA	SA
TOTALS			28	162	5474	713	1325	187	28	136	657	711	1054	71	.242	.361
Willie McCovey	1B148	L	31	149	491	101	157	26	2	45	126	121	66	0	.320	.656
Ron Hunt	2B125, 3B1	R	28	128	478	72	125	23	3	3	41	51	47	9	.262	.341
Hal Lanier	SS150	B	26	150	495	37	113	9	1	0	35	25	68	0	.228	.251
Jim Davenport	3B104, 1B1, SS1, OF1	R	35	112	303	20	73	10	1	2	42	29	37	0	.241	.300
Bobby Bonds	OF155	R	23	158	622	120	161	25	6	32	90	81	187	45	.259	.473
Willie Mays	OF109, 1B1	R	38	117	403	64	114	17	3	13	58	49	71	6	.283	.437
Ken Henderson (LJ)	OF111, 3B3	B	23	113	374	42	84	14	4	6	44	42	64	6	.225	.332
Dick Dietz	C73	R	27	79	244	28	56	8	1	11	35	53	53	0	.230	.406
Dave Marshall	OF87	L	26	110	267	32	62	7	1	2	33	40	68	1	.232	.288
Don Mason	2B51, 3B21, SS7	L	24	104	250	43	57	4	2	0	13	36	29	1	.228	.260
Bob Burda	1B45, OF19	L	30	97	161	20	37	8	0	6	27	21	12	0	.230	.391
Jim Ray Hart	OF68, 3B3	R	27	95	236	27	60	9	0	3	26	28	49	0	.254	.331
Jack Hiatt (FJ)	C60, 1B3	R	26	69	194	18	38	4	0	7	34	48	58	0	.196	.325
Tito Fuentes (NJ)	3B36, SS30	B	25	67	183	28	54	4	3	1	14	15	25	2	.295	.366
Bobby Etheridge	3B39, SS1	R	25	56	131	13	34	9	0	1	10	19	26	0	.260	.351
Bob Barton	C49	R	27	49	106	5	18	2	0	0	1	9	19	0	.170	.189
Johnny Stephenson	C9, 3B1	L	28	22	27	2	6	2	0	0	3	0	4	0	.222	.296
1 Cesar Gutierrez	3B7, SS4	R	26	15	23	4	5	1	0	0	0	6	2	1	.217	.261
Leon Wagner	OF1	L	35	11	12	0	4	0	0	0	2	2	1	0	.333	.333

George Foster 20 R 2-5, John Harrell 21 R 3-6, Frank Johnson 26 R 1-10, Ozzie Virgil 36 R 0-1

NAME	T	AGE	W	L	PCT	SV	G	GS	CG	IP	H	BB	SO	ShO	ERA
TOTALS		29	90	72	.556	17	162	162	71	1474	1381	461	906	15	3.25
Juan Marichal	R	31	21	11	.656	0	37	36	27	300	244	54	205	8	2.10
Gaylord Perry	R	30	19	14	.576	0	40	39	26	325	290	91	233	3	2.49
Frank Linzy	R	28	14	9	.609	11	58	0	0	116	129	38	62	0	3.65
Mike McCormick	L	30	11	9	.550	0	32	28	9	197	175	77	76	0	3.34
Bob Bolin	R	30	7	7	.500	0	30	22	2	146	149	49	102	0	4.44
Ray Sadecki	L	28	5	8	.385	0	29	17	4	138	137	53	104	3	4.24
Ron Herbel	R	31	4	1	.800	1	39	4	2	87	92	23	34	0	4.03
Ron Bryant	L	21	4	3	.571	1	16	8	0	58	60	25	30	0	4.34
2 Don McMahon	R	39	3	1	.750	2	13	0	0	24	13	9	21	0	3.00
1 Joe Gibbon	L	34	1	3	.250	2	16	0	0	20	15	13	9	0	3.60
Rich Robertson	R	24	1	3	.250	0	17	7	1	44	53	21	20	1	5.52
Bob Garibaldi	R	27	0	1	.000	0	1	1	0	5	6	2	1	0	1.80
2 Ron Kline	R	37	0	2	.000	0	7	0	0	11	16	6	7	0	4.09
Mike Davison	L	23	0	0	.000	0	1	0	0	2	2	0	2	0	4.50

CINCINNATI 3rd 89-73 .549 4 — DAVE BRISTOL

NAME	G by POS	B	AGE	G	AB	R	H	2B	3B	HR	RBI	BB	SO	SB	BA	SA
TOTALS			26	163	5634	798	1558	224	42	171	750	474	1042	79	.277	.422
Lee May	1B156, OF7	R	26	158	607	85	169	32	3	38	110	45	142	5	.278	.529
Tommy Helms	2B125, SS4	R	28	126	480	38	129	18	1	1	40	18	33	4	.269	.317
Woody Woodward	SS93, 2B2	R	26	97	241	36	63	12	0	0	15	24	40	3	.261	.311
Tony Perez	3B160	R	27	160	629	103	185	31	2	37	122	63	131	4	.294	.526
Pete Rose	OF156, 2B4	B	28	156	627	120	218	33	11	16	82	88	65	7	.348	.512
Bobby Tolan	OF150	L	23	152	637	104	194	25	10	21	93	27	92	26	.305	.474
Alex Johnson	OF132	R	26	139	523	86	165	18	4	17	88	25	69	11	.315	.463
Johnny Bench	C147	R	21	148	532	83	156	23	1	26	90	49	86	6	.293	.487
Jimmy Stewart	OF66, 2B18, 3B6, SS1	B	30	119	221	26	56	3	4	4	24	19	33	4	.253	.357
Darrel Chaney	SS91	B	21	93	209	21	40	5	2	0	15	24	75	1	.191	.234
Chico Ruiz	2B39, SS29, 3B7, 1B2, OF1	B	30	88	196	19	48	4	1	0	13	14	28	4	.245	.276
Fred Whitfield	1B14	L	31	74	74	2	11	0	0	1	8	18	27	0	.149	.189
Ted Savage	OF17, 2B1	R	33	68	110	20	25	7	0	2	11	20	27	3	.227	.345
Jim Beauchamp	OF9, 1B3	R	29	43	60	8	15	1	0	1	8	5	13	0	.250	.317
Pat Corrales	C29	R	28	29	72	10	19	5	0	1	5	8	17	0	.264	.375
Danny Breeden	C3	R	27	3	8	0	1	0	0	0	1	0	3	0	.125	.125

Mike de la Hoz 29 R 0-1, Bernie Carbo 21 L 0-3, Clyde Mashore 24 R 0-1, Hal McRae (BL) 22

NAME	T	AGE	W	L	PCT	SV	G	GS	CG	IP	H	BB	SO	ShO	ERA
TOTALS		28	89	73	.549	44	163	163	23	1465	1478	611	818	11	4.11
Jim Merritt	L	25	17	9	.654	0	42	36	8	251	269	61	144	1	4.37
Jim Maloney (FJ)	R	30	12	5	.706	0	30	27	6	179	135	86	102	3	2.77
Clay Carroll	R	28	12	6	.667	7	71	4	0	151	149	78	90	0	3.52
Tony Cloninger	R	28	11	17	.393	0	35	34	6	190	184	103	103	2	5.02
Wayne Granger	R	25	9	6	.600	27	90	0	0	145	143	40	68	0	2.79
Gary Nolan (SA)	R	21	8	8	.500	0	16	15	2	109	102	40	83	1	3.55
George Culver (IL)	R	25	5	7	.417	4	32	13	0	101	117	52	58	0	4.28
2 Pedro Ramos	R	34	4	3	.571	2	38	0	0	66	73	24	40	0	5.18
Jack Fisher	R	30	4	4	.500	1	34	15	0	113	137	30	55	0	5.50
Jerry Arrigo	L	28	4	7	.364	0	20	16	1	91	89	61	35	0	4.15
2 Al Jackson	L	33	1	0	1.000	3	33	0	0	27	27	17	16	0	5.33
Mel Queen	R	27	1	0	1.000	0	2	2	0	12	7	3	7	0	2.25
Jose Pena	R	26	1	1	.500	0	6	0	0	5	10	5	3	0	18.00
John Noreiga	R	25	0	0	.000	0	5	0	0	8	12	3	4	0	5.63
2 Camilo Pascual	R	35	0	0	.000	0	5	1	0	7	14	4	3	0	9.00
2 Dennis Ribant	R	27	0	0	.000	0	7	0	0	8	6	3	7	0	1.13
Bill Short	L	31	0	0	.000	0	4	0	0	2	4	1	0	0	18.00

LOS ANGELES 4th 85-77 .525 8 — WALT ALSTON

NAME	G by POS	B	AGE	G	AB	R	H	2B	3B	HR	RBI	BB	SO	SB	BA	SA
TOTALS			27	162	5532	645	1405	185	**52**	97	584	484	823	80	.254	.359
Wes Parker (IL)	1B128, OF2	B	29	132	471	76	131	23	4	13	68	56	46	4	.278	.427
Ted Sizemore	2B118, SS46, OF1	R	24	159	590	69	160	20	5	4	46	45	40	5	.271	.342
2 Maury Wills	SS104	B	36	104	434	57	129	7	8	4	39	39	40	25	.297	.378
Bill Sudakis	3B121	B	23	132	462	50	108	17	5	14	53	40	94	3	.234	.383
Andy Kosco	OF109, 1B3	R	27	120	424	51	105	13	2	19	74	21	66	0	.248	.422
Willie Davis	OF125	L	29	129	498	66	155	23	8	11	59	33	39	24	.311	.456
Willie Crawford	OF113	L	22	129	389	64	96	17	5	11	41	49	85	4	.247	.401
Tom Haller	C132	L	32	134	445	46	117	18	3	6	39	48	58	0	.263	.357
Bill Russell	OF86	R	20	98	212	35	48	6	2	5	15	22	45	4	.226	.344
Jim Lefebvre	3B44, 2B37, 1B6	B	26	95	275	29	65	15	2	4	44	48	37	2	.236	.349
2 Manny Mota	OF80	R	31	85	294	35	95	6	4	3	30	26	25	5	.323	.401
Len Gabrielson	OF47, 1B2	L	29	83	178	13	48	5	1	1	18	12	25	1	.270	.326
Jeff Torborg	C50	R	27	51	124	7	23	4	0	0	7	9	17	1	.185	.218
Billy Grabarkewitz	SS18, 3B6, 2B3	R	23	34	65	4	6	1	1	0	5	4	19	1	.092	.138
1 Ron Fairly (HJ)	1B12, OF10	L	30	30	64	3	14	3	2	0	8	9	6	0	.219	.328
1 Paul Popovich	2B23, SS3	B	28	28	50	5	10	0	0	0	4	1	4	0	.200	.200
John Miller	OF6, 1B5, 3B2, 2B1	R	25	26	38	3	8	1	0	1	1	2	9	0	.211	.316
Tommy Hutton	1B16	L	23	16	48	2	13	0	0	0	4	5	7	0	.271	.271

Bob Stinson 23 B 3-8, Von Joshua 21 L 2-8, Bill Buckner 19 L 0-1, Bobby Valentine 19 R 0-0, Ken Boyer 38 R 7-34, Steve Garvey 20 R 1-3

NAME	T	AGE	W	L	PCT	SV	G	GS	CG	IP	H	BB	SO	ShO	ERA
		27	85	77	.525	31	162	162	47	1457	1324	420	975	20	3.08
Bill Singer	R	25	20	12	.625	1	41	40	16	316	244	74	247	2	2.34
Claude Osteen	L	29	20	15	.571	0	41	41	16	321	**293**	74	183	7	2.66
Don Sutton	R	24	17	18	.486	0	41	41	11	293	269	91	217	4	3.47
Pete Mikkelsen	R	29	7	5	.583	4	48	0	0	81	57	30	51	0	2.78
Jim Brewer	L	32	7	6	.538	20	59	0	0	88	71	41	92	0	2.56
Don Drysdale (SJ)	R	32	5	4	.556	0	12	12	1	63	71	13	24	1	4.43
2 Jim Bunning	R	37	3	1	.750	0	9	9	1	56	65	10	33	0	3.38
Alan Foster	R	22	3	9	.250	0	24	15	2	103	119	29	59	2	4.37
2 Al McBean	R	31	2	6	.250	4	31	0	0	48	46	21	26	0	3.94
Joe Moeller	R	26	1	0	1.000	1	23	4	0	51	54	13	25	0	3.35
Ray Lamb	R	24	0	1	.000	1	10	0	0	15	12	7	11	0	1.80
Bobby Darwin	R	26	0	0	.000	0	3	0	0	4	4	5	0	0	9.00
Jack Jenkins	R	26	0	0	.000	0	1	0	0	1	0	0	1	0	0.00
John Purdin	R	26	0	0	.000	0	9	0	0	16	19	12	6	0	6.19

HOUSTON 5th 81-81 .500 12 — HARRY WALKER

NAME	G by POS	B	AGE	G	AB	R	H	2B	3B	HR	RBI	BB	SO	SB	BA	SA
TOTALS			26	162	5348	676	1284	208	40	104	618	699	972	**101**	.240	.352
Curt Blefary	1B152, OF1	L	25	155	542	66	137	26	7	12	67	77	79	8	.253	.393
Joe Morgan	2B132, OF14	L	25	147	535	94	126	18	5	15	43	110	74	49	.236	.372
Denis Menke	SS131, 2B23, 1B9, 3B1	R	28	154	553	72	149	25	5	10	90	87	87	2	.269	.387
Doug Rader	3B154, 1B4	R	24	155	569	62	140	25	3	11	83	62	103	1	.246	.359
Norm Miller	OF114	L	23	119	409	58	108	21	4	4	50	47	77	4	.264	.364
Jim Wynn	OF149	R	27	149	495	113	133	17	1	33	87	**148**	142	23	.269	.507
Jesus Alou (CN)	OF112	R	27	115	452	49	112	19	4	5	34	15	30	4	.248	.341
Johnny Edwards	C151	L	31	151	496	52	115	20	6	6	50	53	69	2	.232	.333
Gary Geiger	OF65	L	32	93	125	19	28	4	1	0	16	24	34	2	.224	.272
M. Martinez	OF21, SS17, 3B15, C7, 2B1, P1	B	27	78	198	14	61	5	4	0	15	10	21	0	.308	.374
Julio Gotay	2B16, 3B1	R	30	46	81	7	21	5	0	0	9	7	13	2	.259	.321
Leon McFadden	OF17, SS8	R	25	44	74	3	13	2	0	0	3	4	9	1	.176	.203
1 Sandy Valdespino	OF29	L	30	41	119	17	29	4	0	0	12	15	19	2	.244	.277
Hector Torres (CN)	SS22	R	23	34	69	5	11	1	0	1	8	2	12	0	.159	.217
Don Bryant	C28	R	27	31	59	2	11	1	0	1	6	4	13	0	.186	.254
2 Tommy Davis	OF21	R	30	24	79	2	19	3	0	1	9	8	9	1	.241	.316

Cesar Geronimo 21 L 2-8, Bob Watson 23 R 11-40, Keith Lampard 23 L 3-12, John Mayberry 19 L 0-4

NAME	T	AGE	W	L	PCT	SV	G	GS	CG	IP	H	BB	SO	ShO	ERA
		26	81	81	.500	34	162	162	52	1436	1347	547	**1221**	11	3.60
Larry Dierker	R	22	20	13	.606	0	39	37	20	305	240	72	232	4	2.33
Don Wilson	R	24	16	12	.571	0	34	34	13	225	210	97	235	1	4.00
Denny Lemaster	L	30	13	17	.433	1	38	37	11	245	232	72	173	1	3.16
Tom Griffin	R	21	11	10	.524	0	31	31	6	188	156	93	200	3	3.54
Jim Ray	R	24	8	2	.800	0	40	13	0	115	105	48	115	0	3.91
Jack Billingham	R	26	6	7	.462	2	52	4	1	83	92	29	71	0	4.23
Fred Gladding	R	33	4	8	.333	**29**	57	0	0	73	83	27	40	0	4.19
1 Dooley Womack	R	29	2	1	.667	0	30	0	0	51	49	20	32	0	3.53
Skip Guinn	L	24	1	2	.333	0	28	0	0	27	34	21	33	0	6.67
Danny Coombs	L	27	0	1	.000	0	8	0	0	8	12	2	3	0	6.75
Dan Schneider	L	26	0	1	.000	0	6	0	0	7	16	5	3	0	14.14
2 Jim Bouton	R	30	0	2	.000	1	16	1	1	31	32	12	32	0	4.06
Wade Blasingame	L	25	0	5	.000	1	26	5	0	52	66	33	33	0	5.37
Bill Henry	L	41	0	0	.000	0	3	0	0	5	2	2	2	0	0.00
Scipio Spinks	R	21	0	0	.000	0	1	0	0	2	1	1	4	0	0.00
Bob Watkins	R	21	0	0	.000	0	5	0	0	16	13	13	11	0	5.06
2 Ron Willis	R	25	0	0	.000	0	3	0	0	2	3	0	2	0	0.00
Marty Martinez	R	27	0	0	.000	0	1	0	0	1	1	0	0	0	9.00

SAN DIEGO 6th 52-110 .321 41 — PRESTON GOMEZ

NAME	G by POS	B	AGE	G	AB	R	H	2B	3B	HR	RBI	BB	SO	SB	BA	SA
TOTALS			26	162	5357	468	1203	180	42	99	431	423	**1143**	45	.225	.329
Nate Colbert	1B134	R	23	139	483	64	123	20	9	24	66	45	123	6	.255	.482
Jose Arcia	2B68, SS37, 3B8, OF4, 1B1	R	25	120	302	35	65	11	3	0	10	14	47	14	.215	.272
Tommy Dean	SS97, 2B2	R	23	101	273	14	48	9	2	2	9	27	54	0	.176	.245
Ed Spiezio	3B98, OF1	R	27	121	355	29	83	9	0	13	43	38	64	1	.234	.369
Ollie Brown	OF148	R	25	151	568	76	150	18	3	20	61	44	97	10	.264	.412
Clarence Gaston	OF113	R	25	129	391	20	90	11	7	2	28	24	117	4	.230	.309
Al Ferrara	OF96	R	29	138	366	39	95	22	1	14	56	45	69	0	.260	.440
Chris Cannizzaro	C132	R	31	134	418	23	92	14	3	4	33	42	81	0	.220	.297
Roberto Pena	SS65, 2B33, 3B27, 1B12	R	29	139	472	44	118	16	3	4	30	21	63	0	.250	.322
Ivan Murrell	OF72, 1B2	R	24	111	247	19	63	10	6	3	25	11	65	3	.255	.381
Larry Stahl	OF37, 1B13	L	28	95	162	10	32	6	2	3	10	17	31	3	.198	.315
Van Kelly	3B49, 2B10	L	23	73	209	16	51	7	1	3	15	12	24	0	.244	.330
John Sipin (XJ)	2B60	R	22	68	229	22	51	12	2	2	9	8	44	2	.223	.319
1 Tony Gonzalez	OF49	L	32	53	182	17	41	4	0	2	8	19	24	1	.225	.280
2 Walt Hriniak	C19	R	26	31	66	4	15	0	0	0	1	8	11	0	.227	.227
Bill Davis	1B14	L	27	31	57	1	10	1	0	0	1	8	18	0	.175	.193
1 Jerry DaVanon	2B15	R	23	24	59	4	8	1	0	0	3	3	12	0	.136	.153
Jerry Morales	OF19	R	20	19	41	5	8	2	0	1	6	5	7	0	.195	.317
Sonny Ruberto	C15	R	23	19	21	3	3	0	0	0	0	1	7	0	.143	.143
Ron Slocum	2B4, 3B4, SS1	R	23	13	24	6	7	1	0	1	5	0	5	0	.292	.458
Jim Williams	OF6	R	22	13	25	4	7	1	0	0	2	3	11	0	.280	.320
Fred Kendall	C9	R	20	10	26	2	4	0	0	0	0	2	5	0	.154	.154
Rafael Robles	SS6	R	21	6	20	1	2	0	0	0	0	1	3	1	.100	.100

Chris Krug 29 R 1-17, Frankie Libran 21 R 1-10

NAME	T	AGE	W	L	PCT	SV	G	GS	CG	IP	H	BB	SO	ShO	ERA
		26	52	**110**	.321	25	162	162	16	1422	1454	592	764	9	4.24
Al Santorini	R	21	8	14	.364	0	32	30	2	185	194	73	111	1	3.94
2 Joe Niekro	R	24	8	17	.320	0	37	31	8	202	213	45	55	3	3.70
Jack Baldschun	R	32	7	2	.778	1	61	0	0	77	80	29	67	0	4.79
Clay Kirby	R	21	7	**20**	.259	0	35	35	2	216	204	100	113	0	3.79
Johnny Podres	L	36	5	6	.455	0	17	9	1	65	66	28	17	0	4.29
Dick Kelley	L	29	4	8	.333	0	27	23	1	136	113	61	96	1	3.57
Billy McCool	L	24	3	5	.375	7	54	0	0	59	59	42	35	0	4.27
2 Gary Ross	R	21	3	12	.200	3	46	7	0	110	104	56	58	0	4.17
1 Dick Selma	R	25	2	2	.500	0	4	3	1	22	19	9	20	0	4.09
Tommie Sisk	R	27	2	13	.133	6	53	13	1	143	160	48	59	0	4.78
Tom Dukes	R	26	1	0	1.000	1	13	0	0	22	26	10	15	0	7.36
Frank Reberger	R	25	1	2	.333	6	67	0	0	88	83	41	65	0	3.58
Mike Corkins	R	23	1	3	.250	0	6	4	0	17	27	8	13	0	8.47
Leon Everitt	R	22	0	1	.000	0	5	0	0	16	18	12	11	0	7.88
Steve Arlin	R	23	0	1	.000	0	4	1	0	11	13	9	9	0	9.00
1 Al McBean	R	31	0	1	.000	0	1	1	0	7	10	2	1	0	5.14
Dave Roberts	L	24	0	3	.000	1	22	5	0	49	65	19	19	0	4.78

WORLD SERIES – NEW YORK (NL) 4 BALTIMORE (AL) 1

LINE SCORES

TEAM	1	2	3	4	5	6	7	8	9	10	11	12	R	H	E
Game 1 October 11 at Baltimore															
NY (NL)	0	0	0	0	0	0	1	0	0				1	6	1
BAL (AL)	1	0	0	3	0	0	0	0	X				4	6	0
Seaver, Cardwell (6), Taylor (7)	**Cuellar**														
Game 2 October 12 at Baltimore															
NY	0	0	0	1	0	0	0	0	1				2	6	0
BAL	0	0	0	0	0	0	1	0	0				1	2	0
Koosman, Taylor (9)	**McNally**														
Game 3 October 14 at New York															
BAL	0	0	0	0	0	0	0	0	0				0	4	1
NY	1	2	0	0	0	1	0	1	X				5	6	0
Palmer, Leonhard (7)	**Gentry**, Ryan (7)														
Game 4 October 15 at New York															
BAL	0	0	0	0	0	0	0	0	1	0			1	6	1
NY	0	1	0	0	0	0	0	0	0	1			2	10	1
Cuellar, Watt (8), **Hall** (10), Richert (10)	**Seaver**														
Game 5 October 16 at New York															
BAL	0	0	3	0	0	0	0	0	0				3	5	2
NY	0	0	0	0	0	2	1	2	X				5	7	0
McNally, **Watt** (8)	**Koosman**														

COMPOSITE BATTING

NAME	POS	G	AB	R	H	2B	3B	HR	RBI	BA
New York (NL)										
Totals		5	159	15	35	8	0	6	13	.220
Grote	C	5	19	1	4	**2**	0	0	1	.211
Jones	OF	5	19	2	3	1	0	0	0	.158
Agee	OF	5	18	1	3	0	0	1	1	.167
Harrelson	SS	5	17	1	3	0	0	0	0	.176
Swoboda	OF	4	15	1	**6**	1	0	0	1	.400
Charles	3B	4	15	1	2	1	0	0	0	.133
Clendenon	1B	4	14	**4**	5	1	0	**3**	**4**	.357
Weis	2B	5	11	1	5	0	0	1	3	**.455**
Koosman	P	2	7	0	1	1	0	0	0	.143
Shamsky	OF	3	6	0	0	0	0	0	0	.000
Kranepool	1B	1	4	1	1	0	0	1	1	.250
Seaver	P	2	4	0	0	0	0	0	0	.000
Boswell	2B	1	3	1	1	0	0	0	0	.333
Gentry	P	1	3	0	1	1	0	0	2	.333
Gaspar	OF	3	2	1	0	0	0	0	0	.000
Garrett	3B	2	1	0	0	0	0	0	0	.000
Dyer	PH	1	1	0	0	0	0	0	0	.000
Martin	PH	1	0	0	0	0	0	0	0	.000
Taylor	P	2	0	0	0	0	0	0	0	.000
Cardwell	P	1	0	0	0	0	0	0	0	.000
Ryan	P	1	0	0	0	0	0	0	0	.000
Baltimore (AL)										
Totals		5	157	9	23	1	0	3	9	.146
Blair	OF	5	**20**	1	2	0	0	0	0	.100
Buford	OF	5	**20**	1	2	1	0	1	2	.100
Powell	1B	5	19	0	5	0	0	0	0	.263
B. Robinson	3B	5	19	0	1	0	0	0	2	.053
F. Robinson	OF	5	16	2	3	0	0	1	1	.188
Johnson	2B	5	16	1	1	0	0	0	0	.063
Belanger	SS	5	15	2	3	0	0	0	1	.200
Hendricks	C	3	10	1	1	0	0	0	0	.100
Etchebarren	C	2	6	0	0	0	0	0	0	.000
Cuellar	P	2	5	0	2	0	0	0	1	.400
McNally	P	2	5	1	1	0	0	1	2	.200
Dalrymple	PH	2	2	0	2	0	0	0	0	1.000
Palmer	P	1	2	0	0	0	0	0	0	.000
May	PH	2	1	0	0	0	0	0	0	.000
Motton	PH	1	1	0	0	0	0	0	0	.000
Salmon	PR	2	0	0	0	0	0	0	0	.000
Rettenmund	PR	1	0	0	0	0	0	0	0	.000
Watt	P	2	0	0	0	0	0	0	0	.000

Hall P 0-0, Leonhard P 0-0, Richert P 0-0

COMPOSITE PITCHING

NAME	G	IP	H	BB	SO	W	L	SV	ERA
New York (NL)									
Totals	5	45	23	15	28	4	1	2	1.80
Koosman	2	**17.2**	7	4	9	**2**	0	0	2.04
Seaver	2	15	12	3	9	1	1	0	3.00
Gentry	1	6.2	3	**5**	4	1	0	0	0.00
Taylor	2	2.1	0	1	3	0	0	1	0.00
Ryan	1	2.1	1	2	3	0	0	1	0.00
Cardwell	1	1	0	0	0	0	0	0	0.00
Baltimore (AL)									
Totals	5	43	35	15	35	1	4	0	2.72
Cuellar	2	16	**13**	4	**13**	1	0	0	**1.13**
McNally	2	16	11	**5**	**13**	0	1	0	2.81
Palmer	1	6	5	4	5	0	1	0	6.00
Watt	2	3	4	0	3	0	1	0	3.00
Leonhard	1	2	1	1	1	0	0	0	4.50
Hall	1	0	1	1	0	0	1	0	0.00
Richert	1	0	0	0	0	0	0	0	0.00

1970 Damned If You Do

After winning the Cy Young Award in the American League two years in a row, Denny McLain lost it all: his money, his good name, and his fastball. Commissioner Bowie Kuhn suspended the fun-loving right-hander in February for a number of incidents which besmirched baseball's reputation for uprightness. Specifically, McLain had become involved with underworld gamblers during the 1967 season, going as far as to provide monetary backing for a bookmaking operation. Previously known for his 31-win season, his egotistical conduct, and his off-season organ playing, McLain had become the center of numerous tales concerning his sorry financial state when Kuhn sentenced him to a rather light suspension ending on July 1.

The Tigers hoped to start a pennant drive upon McLain's return, and a SRO crowd packed Tiger Stadium on July 1, to see the arrogant hurler take the mound against the Yankees. McLain, though, was knocked out in the sixth inning, and a 3-5 record through August gave stark evidence to the fact that his fastball had lost its old zip during the months of turmoil. When he doused two local reporters with buckets of ice water in the Detroit clubhouse, McLain was slapped with a week's suspension by the Tigers. To cap an infamous season, Kuhn again suspended McLain on September 9, for the duration of the season for carrying a pistol in violation of the probationary conditions set by the commissioner. At the season's end, the Tigers hastily unloaded Denny in a large trade with the Washington Senators.

While McLain was being called in Kuhn's chambers, Curt Flood was presenting his antitrust suit against baseball before New York City's Federal Court. When Flood was traded by St. Louis to Philadelphia during the winter, he refused to report and, instead, filed suit against baseball's reserve clause which bound a player forever to whatever team held his contract. Flood wanted the right to sign with the team of his choice. The New York court gave Flood a negative and, while his attorneys prepared to make an appeal, he sat out the season. In a final irony, Flood joined McLain as a member of the Senators after they acquired his "reserve" from the Phillies and after he was assured that the move would not hurt his case.

Kuhn was forced to cope with other problems during the year. Baseball had to navigate through treacherous legal waters when the bankrupt Seattle franchise was shifted to Milwaukee four days before the season's opening. Houston pitcher Jim Bouton published *Ball Four,* a diary which revealed some of the hidden personal aspects of major league baseball. Kuhn duly censured Bouton, who by autumn had become a television sportscaster. Finally, a one-day strike by major league umpires during the play-offs was settled by the commissioner.

By comparison, action on the field could not equal the off-field headlines as the Cincinnati Reds used a torrid first half, and the Pittsburgh Pirates a final spurt, to each win their division titles. Freshman manager Sparky Anderson guided a Cincinnati lineup including MVP Johnny Bench, Pete Rose, Lee May, Tony Perez, and Bobby Tolan to a pennant, despite injuries to several key pitchers. The Pirates also boasted of a powerful attack but dropped the championship series to Cincinnati in three straight games.

The Baltimore Orioles and Minnesota Twins repeated as division leaders in the American League, and the Birds duplicated their three-game sweep of the Twins in the play-off. The Orioles overwhelmed their opposition, using MVP Boog Powell, Brooks Robinson, and Frank Robinson to amass runs, and 20-game winners, Mike Cuellar, Dave McNally, and Jim Palmer, to shut the opposition out. Despite injuries to Rod Carew, Dave Boswell, and Luis Tiant, the Twins repeated under new manager Bill Rigney with fine performances from Harmon Killebrew, Tony Oliva, and Cy Young winner Jim Perry.

By the time the World Series got around, baseball's foundation was a bit shaken. But, with Brooks Robinson starring both afield and at bat, and the Orioles avenging their 1969 Series loss by knocking off the Reds handily in five games, there was little doubt about professional baseball's endurance at the start of its second century.

1970 AMERICAN LEAGUE

EAST DIVISION

BALTIMORE 1st 108-54 .667 — EARL WEAVER

NAME	G by POS	B	AGE	G	AB	R	H	2B	3B	HR	RBI	BB	SO	SB	BA	SA
TOTALS			29	162	**5545**	**792**	1424	213	25	179	**748**	**717**	952	84	.257	.401
Boog Powell	1B145	L	28	154	526	82	156	28	0	35	114	104	80	1	.297	.549
Dave Johnson	2B149, SS2	R	27	149	530	68	149	27	1	10	53	66	68	2	.281	.392
Mark Belanger	SS143	R	26	145	459	53	100	6	5	1	36	52	65	13	.218	.259
Brooks Robinson	3B156	R	33	158	608	84	168	31	4	18	94	53	53	1	.276	.429
Frank Robinson	OF120, 1B7	R	34	132	471	88	144	24	1	25	78	69	70	2	.306	.520
Paul Blair	OF128, 3B1	R	26	133	480	79	128	24	2	18	65	56	93	24	.267	.438
Don Buford	OF130, 2B3, 3B3	B	33	144	504	99	137	15	2	17	66	109	55	16	.272	.411
Ellie Hendricks	C95	L	29	106	322	32	78	9	0	12	41	33	44	1	.242	.382
Merv Rettenmund	OF93	R	27	106	338	60	109	17	2	18	58	38	59	13	.322	.544
Terry Crowley	OF27, 1B23	L	23	83	152	25	39	5	0	5	20	35	26	2	.257	.388
Andy Etchebarren	C76	R	27	78	230	19	56	10	1	4	28	21	41	4	.243	.348
Chico Salmon	SS33, 2B12, 3B11, 1B2	R	29	63	172	19	43	4	0	7	22	8	30	2	.250	.395
Curt Motton	OF21	R	29	52	84	16	19	3	1	3	19	18	20	1	.226	.393
1 Dave May	OF9	L	26	25	31	6	6	0	1	1	6	4	4	0	.194	.355
Clay Dalrymple (BN)	C11	L	33	13	32	4	7	1	0	1	3	7	4	0	.219	.344
Bobby Grich	SS20, 2B9, 3B1	R	21	30	95	11	20	1	3	0	8	9	21	1	.211	.284
Don Baylor	OF6	R	21	8	17	4	4	0	0	0	4	2	3	1	.235	.235
Johnny Oates	C4	L	24	5	18	2	5	0	1	0	2	2	0	0	.278	.389
1 Bobby Floyd	SS2, 2B1	R	26	3	2	0	0	0	0	0	0	0	2	0	.000	.000
Roger Freed	1B3, OF1	R	24	4	13	0	2	0	0	0	1	3	4	0	.154	.154

NAME	T	AGE	W	L	PCT	SV	G	GS	CG	IP	H	BB	SO	ShO	ERA
		29	**108**	54	**.667**	31	162	162	**60**	**1479**	1317	469	941	12	**3.15**
Mike Cuellar	L	33	**24**	8	**.750**	0	40	**40**	**21**	298	273	69	190	4	3.47
Dave McNally	L	27	**24**	9	.727	0	40	**40**	16	296	**277**	78	185	1	3.22
Jim Palmer	R	24	20	10	.667	0	39	39	17	**305**	263	100	199	**5**	2.71
Dick Hall	R	39	10	5	.667	3	32	0	0	61	51	6	30	0	3.10
Pete Richert	L	30	7	2	.778	13	50	0	0	55	36	24	66	0	1.96
Eddie Watt	R	28	7	7	.500	12	53	0	0	55	44	29	33	0	3.27
Jim Hardin	R	26	6	5	.545	1	36	19	3	145	150	26	78	2	3.54
Tom Phoebus	R	25	5	5	.500	0	27	21	3	135	106	62	72	0	3.07
2 Moe Drabowsky	R	34	4	2	.667	1	21	0	0	33	30	15	21	0	3.82
Marcelino Lopez	L	26	1	1	.500	0	25	3	0	61	47	37	49	0	2.07
Fred Beene	R	27	0	0	.000	0	4	0	0	6	8	5	4	0	6.00
Dave Leonhard	R	28	0	0	.000	1	23	0	0	28	32	18	14	0	5.14

NEW YORK 2nd 93-69 .574 15 — RALPH HOUK

NAME	G by POS	B	AGE	G	AB	R	H	2B	3B	HR	RBI	BB	SO	SB	BA	SA
TOTALS			26	163	5492	680	1381	208	**41**	111	627	588	808	105	.251	.365
Danny Cater	1B131, 3B42, OF7	R	30	155	582	64	175	26	5	6	76	34	44	4	.301	.393
Horace Clarke	2B157	B	30	158	**686**	81	172	24	2	4	46	35	35	23	.251	.309
Gene Michael	SS123, 3B4, 2B3	B	32	134	435	42	93	10	1	2	38	50	93	3	.214	.255
Jerry Kenney	3B135, 2B2	L	25	140	404	46	78	10	7	4	35	52	44	20	.193	.282
Curt Blefary	OF79, 1B6	L	26	99	269	34	57	6	0	9	37	43	37	1	.212	.335
Bobby Murcer	OF155	L	24	159	581	95	146	23	3	23	78	87	100	15	.251	.420
Roy White	OF161	B	26	162	609	109	180	30	6	22	94	95	66	24	.296	.473
Thurman Munson	C125	R	23	132	453	59	137	25	4	6	53	57	56	5	.302	.415
Ron Woods	OF78	R	27	95	225	30	51	5	3	8	27	33	35	4	.227	.382
Jim Lyttle	OF70	L	24	87	126	20	39	7	1	3	14	10	26	3	.310	.452
Johnny Ellis	1B53, 3B5, C2	R	21	78	226	24	56	12	1	7	29	18	47	0	.248	.403
Pete Ward	1B13	R	30	66	77	5	20	2	2	1	18	9	17	0	.260	.377
Ron Hansen	SS15, 3B11, 2B1	R	32	59	91	13	27	4	0	4	14	19	9	0	.297	.473
Jake Gibbs	C44	L	31	49	153	23	46	9	2	8	26	7	14	2	.301	.542
Frank Baker	SS35	L	23	35	117	6	27	4	1	0	11	14	26	1	.231	.282
Frank Tepedino	1B1, OF1	L	22	16	19	2	6	2	0	0	2	1	2	0	.316	.421
Bobby Mitchell	OF7	R	26	10	22	1	5	2	0	0	4	2	3	0	.227	.318

NAME	T	AGE	W	L	PCT	SV	G	GS	CG	IP	H	BB	SO	ShO	ERA
		28	93	69	.574	49	163	163	36	1472	1386	451	777	6	3.24
Fritz Peterson	L	28	20	11	.645	0	39	37	8	260	247	40	127	2	2.91
Mel Stottlemyre	R	28	15	13	.536	0	37	37	14	271	262	84	126	0	3.09
Stan Bahnsen	R	25	14	11	.560	0	36	35	6	233	227	75	116	2	3.32
Lindy McDaniel	R	34	9	5	.643	29	62	0	0	112	88	23	81	0	2.01
Mike Kekich (LJ)	L	25	6	3	.667	0	26	14	1	99	103	55	63	0	4.82
Steve Kline	R	22	6	6	.500	0	16	15	5	100	99	24	49	0	3.42
Ron Klimkowski	R	25	6	7	.462	1	45	3	1	98	80	33	40	1	2.66
Jack Aker	R	29	4	2	.667	16	41	0	0	70	57	20	36	0	2.06
1 Steve Hamilton	L	36	4	3	.571	3	35	0	0	45	36	16	33	0	2.80
1 John Cumberland	L	23	3	4	.429	0	15	8	1	64	62	15	38	0	3.94
2 Mike McCormick	L	31	2	0	1.000	0	9	4	0	21	26	13	12	0	6.00
2 Gary Waslewski	R	28	2	2	.500	0	26	5	0	55	42	27	27	0	3.11
Rob Gardner	L	25	1	0	1.000	0	1	1	0	7	8	4	6	0	5.14
Joe Verbanic	R	27	1	0	1.000	0	7	0	0	16	20	12	8	0	4.50
Bill Burbach	R	22	0	2	.000	0	4	4	0	17	23	9	10	0	10.06
Loyd Colson	R	22	0	0	.000	0	1	0	0	2	3	0	3	0	4.50
Gary Jones	L	25	0	0	.000	0	2	0	0	2	3	1	2	0	0.00

BOSTON 3rd 87-75 .537 21 — EDDIE KASKO

NAME	G by POS	B	AGE	G	AB	R	H	2B	3B	HR	RBI	BB	SO	SB	BA	SA
TOTALS			25	162	5535	786	**1450**	**252**	28	**203**	743	594	855	50	**.262**	**.428**
Carl Yastrzemski	1B94, OF69	L	30	161	566	**125**	186	29	0	40	102	128	66	23	.329	**.592**
Mike Andrews	2B148	R	26	151	589	91	149	28	1	17	65	81	63	2	.253	.390
Rico Petrocelli	SS141, 3B18	R	27	157	583	82	152	31	3	29	103	67	82	1	.261	.473
George Scott (BH)	3B68, 1B59	R	26	127	480	50	142	24	5	16	63	44	95	4	.296	.467
Tony Conigliaro	OF146	R	25	146	560	89	149	20	1	36	116	43	93	4	.266	.498
Reggie Smith	OF145	B	25	147	580	109	176	32	7	22	74	51	60	10	.303	.497
Billy Conigliaro	OF108	R	22	114	398	59	108	16	3	18	58	35	73	3	.271	.462
Jerry Moses	C88, OF1	R	23	92	315	26	83	18	1	6	35	21	45	1	.263	.384
Dick Schofield	2B15, 3B15, SS3	B	35	76	139	16	26	1	2	1	14	21	26	0	.187	.245
Luis Alvarado	3B29, SS27	R	21	59	183	19	41	11	0	1	10	9	30	1	.224	.301
Tom Satriano	C51	L	29	59	165	21	39	9	1	3	13	21	23	0	.236	.358
2 John Kennedy	3B33, 2B2	R	29	43	129	15	33	7	1	4	17	6	14	0	.256	.419
2 Mike Fiore	1B17, OF2	L	25	41	50	5	7	0	0	0	4	8	4	0	.140	.140
George Thomas (RC)	OF26, 3B6	R	32	38	99	13	34	8	0	2	13	11	12	0	.343	.485
Don Pavletich	1B16, C10	R	31	32	65	4	9	1	1	0	6	10	15	1	.138	.185
Mike Derrick	OF2, 1B1	L	26	24	33	3	7	1	0	0	5	0	11	0	.212	.242
Bob Montgomery	C22	R	26	22	78	8	14	2	0	1	4	6	20	0	.179	.244
Joe Lahoud	OF13	L	23	17	49	6	12	1	0	2	5	7	6	0	.245	.388
Carmen Fanzone	3B5	R	27	10	15	0	3	1	0	0	3	2	2	0	.200	.267
1 Tom Matchick	3B2, 2B1, SS1	L	26	10	14	2	1	0	0	0	0	2	2	0	.071	.071

NAME	T	AGE	W	L	PCT	SV	G	GS	CG	IP	H	BB	SO	ShO	ERA
		28	87	75	.537	44	162	162	38	1446	1391	594	1003	8	3.87
Ray Culp	R	28	17	14	.548	0	33	33	15	251	211	91	197	1	3.05
Gary Peters	L	33	16	11	.593	0	34	34	10	222	221	83	155	4	4.05
Sonny Siebert	R	33	15	8	.652	0	33	33	7	223	207	60	142	2	3.43
Ken Brett	L	21	8	9	.471	2	41	14	1	139	118	79	155	0	4.08
Vicente Romo	R	27	7	3	.700	6	48	10	0	108	115	43	71	0	4.08
Mike Nagy	R	22	6	5	.545	0	23	20	4	129	138	64	56	0	4.47
Jim Lonborg (SJ)	R	28	4	1	.800	0	9	4	0	34	33	9	21	0	3.18
Gary Wagner	R	30	3	1	.750	7	38	0	0	40	36	19	20	0	3.38
2 Cal Koonce	R	29	3	4	.429	2	23	8	1	76	64	29	37	0	3.55
2 Bob Bolin	R	31	2	0	1.000	2	6	0	0	8	2	5	8	0	0.00
Bill Lee (MS)	L	23	2	2	.500	1	11	5	0	37	48	14	19	0	4.62
1 Lee Stange	R	33	2	2	.500	2	20	0	0	27	34	12	14	0	5.67
Roger Moret	L	20	1	0	1.000	0	3	1	0	8	7	4	2	0	3.38
Sparky Lyle	L	25	1	7	.125	20	63	0	0	67	62	34	51	0	3.90
Ray Jarvis	R	24	0	1	.000	0	15	0	0	16	17	14	8	0	3.94
Ed Phillips	R	25	0	2	.000	0	18	0	0	24	29	10	23	0	5.25
Jose Santiago (EJ)	R	29	0	2	.000	1	8	0	0	11	18	8	8	0	10.64
3 Chuck Hartenstein	R	28	0	3	.000	1	17	0	0	19	21	12	12	0	8.05
John Curtis	L	22	0	0	.000	0	1	0	0	2	4	1	1	0	13.50
Dick Mills	R	24	0	0	.000	0	2	0	0	4	6	3	3	0	2.25

DETROIT 4th 79-83 .488 29 — MAYO SMITH

NAME	G by POS	B	AGE	G	AB	R	H	2B	3B	HR	RBI	BB	SO	SB	BA	SA
TOTALS			29	162	5377	666	1282	207	38	148	619	656	825	29	.238	.374
Norm Cash	1B114	L	35	130	370	58	96	18	2	15	53	72	58	0	.259	.441
Dick McAuliffe	2B127, SS15, 3B12	L	30	146	530	73	124	21	1	12	50	101	62	5	.234	.345
Cesar Gutierrez	SS135	R	27	135	415	40	101	11	6	0	22	18	39	4	.243	.299
Don Wert	3B117, 2B2	R	31	128	363	34	79	13	0	6	33	44	56	1	.218	.303
Al Kaline	OF91, 1B52	R	35	131	467	64	130	24	4	16	71	77	49	2	.278	.450
Mickey Stanley	OF132, 1B9	R	27	142	568	83	143	21	11	13	47	45	56	10	.252	.396
Jim Northrup	OF136	L	30	139	504	71	132	21	3	24	80	58	68	3	.262	.458
Bill Freehan (XJ)	C114	R	28	117	395	44	95	17	3	16	52	52	48	0	.241	.420
Elliott Maddox	3B40, OF37, SS19, 2B1	R	22	109	258	30	64	13	4	3	24	30	42	2	.248	.364
Willie Horton (NJ)	OF96	R	27	96	371	53	113	18	2	17	69	28	43	0	.305	.601
Dalton Jones	2B35, 3B18, 1B10	L	26	89	191	29	42	7	0	6	21	33	33	1	.220	.351
Gates Brown	OF26	L	31	81	124	18	28	3	0	3	24	20	14	0	.226	.323
Ike Brown	2B23, OF4, 3B1	R	28	56	94	17	27	5	0	4	15	13	26	0	.287	.468
Jim Price	C38	R	28	52	132	12	24	4	0	5	15	21	23	0	.182	.326
Ken Szotkiewicz (KJ)	SS44	L	23	47	84	9	9	1	0	3	9	12	29	0	.107	.226
Kevin Collins	1B1	L	23	25	24	2	5	1	0	1	3	1	10	0	.208	.375
Gene Lamont	C15	L	23	15	44	3	13	3	1	1	4	2	9	0	.295	.477

2 Rus Nagelson 25 L 3-24, Tim Hosley 23 R 2-12

NAME	T	AGE	W	L	PCT	SV	G	GS	CG	IP	H	BB	SO	ShO	ERA
TOTALS		26	79	83	.488	39	162	162	33	1447	1443	623	1045	9	4.09
Mickey Lolich	L	29	14	19	.424	0	40	39	13	273	272	109	230	3	3.79
Les Cain	L	22	12	7	.632	0	29	29	5	181	167	98	156	0	3.83
Joe Niekro	R	25	12	13	.480	0	38	34	6	213	221	72	101	2	4.06
Daryl Patterson	R	26	7	1	.875	2	43	0	0	78	81	39	55	0	4.85
Mike Kilkenny	L	25	7	6	.538	0	36	21	3	129	141	70	105	0	5.16
John Hiller	L	27	6	6	.500	3	47	5	1	104	82	46	89	1	3.03
Tom Timmerman	R	30	6	7	.462	27	61	0	0	85	90	34	49	0	4.13
Fred Scherman	L	25	4	4	.500	1	48	0	0	70	61	28	58	0	3.21
1 Earl Wilson	R	35	4	6	.400	0	18	16	4	96	87	32	74	1	4.41
Denny McLain (SL)	R	26	3	5	.375	0	14	14	1	91	100	28	52	0	4.65
Bob Reed	R	25	2	4	.333	2	16	4	0	46	54	14	26	0	4.89
Dennis Saunders	R	21	1	1	.500	1	8	0	0	14	16	5	8	0	3.21
1 Fred Lasher	R	28	1	3	.250	3	12	0	0	9	10	12	8	0	5.00
Lerrin LaGrow	R	21	0	1	.000	0	10	0	0	12	16	6	7	0	7.50
Norm McRae	R	22	0	0	.000	0	19	0	0	31	26	25	16	0	2.90
Jerry Robertson	R	26	0	0	.000	0	11	0	0	15	19	5	11	0	3.60

CLEVELAND 5th 76-86 .469 32 — AL DARK

NAME	G by POS	B	AGE	G	AB	R	H	2B	3B	HR	RBI	BB	SO	SB	BA	SA
TOTALS			26	162	5463	649	1358	197	23	183	617	503	909	25	.249	.394
Tony Horton (IL)	1B112	R	25	115	413	48	111	19	3	17	59	30	54	3	.269	.453
Eddie Leon	2B141, SS23, 3B1	R	23	152	549	58	136	20	4	10	56	47	89	1	.248	.353
Jack Heidemann	SS132	R	20	133	445	44	94	14	2	6	37	34	88	2	.211	.292
Graig Nettles	3B154, OF3	L	25	157	549	81	129	13	1	26	62	81	77	3	.235	.404
Vada Pinson	OF141, 1B7	L	31	148	574	74	164	28	6	24	82	28	69	7	.286	.481
Ted Uhlaender	OF134	L	30	141	473	56	127	21	2	11	46	39	44	3	.268	.391
Roy Foster	OF131	R	24	139	477	66	128	26	0	23	60	54	75	3	.268	.468
Ray Fosse	C120	R	23	120	450	62	138	17	1	18	61	39	55	1	.307	.469
Duke Sims	C39, OF36, 1B29	L	29	110	345	46	91	12	0	23	56	46	59	0	.264	.499
Chuck Hinton	1B40, OF35, C4, 2B3, 3B2	R	36	107	195	24	62	4	0	9	29	25	34	0	.318	.477
2 Buddy Bradford	OF64, 3B1	R	25	75	163	25	32	6	1	7	23	21	43	0	.196	.374
Larry Brown	SS27, 3B17, 2B16	R	30	72	155	17	40	5	2	0	15	20	14	1	.258	.316
2 Rich Rollins	3B5	R	32	42	43	6	10	0	0	2	4	3	5	0	.233	.372
Lou Klimchock	1B5, 2B5	L	30	41	56	5	9	0	0	1	2	3	9	0	.161	.214
Vern Fuller	2B16, 3B4, 1B1	R	26	29	33	3	6	2	0	1	2	3	9	0	.182	.333
Ted Ford	OF12	R	23	26	46	5	8	1	0	1	1	3	13	0	.174	.261
John Lowenstein	2B10, 3B2, OF2, SS1	L	23	17	43	5	11	3	1	1	6	1	9	1	.256	.442
1 Russ Nagelson	OF4	L	25	17	24	3	3	1	0	1	2	3	9	0	.125	.292

Ken Harrelson (BL) 28 R 11-39, Lou Camilli 23 B 0-15

NAME	T	AGE	W	L	PCT	SV	G	GS	CG	IP	H	BB	SO	ShO	ERA
TOTALS		26	76	86	.469	35	162	162	34	1451	1333	**689**	**1076**	8	3.91
Sam McDowell	L	27	20	12	.625	0	39	39	19	**305**	236	**131**	**304**	1	2.92
Steve Hargan (SA)	R	27	11	3	.786	0	23	19	8	143	101	53	72	1	2.90
1 Dean Chance	R	29	9	8	.529	4	45	19	1	155	172	59	109	1	4.24
Phil Hennigan	R	24	6	3	.667	3	42	1	0	72	69	44	43	0	4.00
Rich Hand	R	21	6	13	.316	3	35	25	3	160	132	69	110	1	3.83
Denny Higgins	R	30	4	6	.400	11	58	0	0	90	82	54	82	0	4.00
Steve Dunning	R	21	4	9	.308	0	19	17	0	94	93	54	77	0	4.98
1 Dick Ellsworth	L	30	3	3	.500	2	29	1	0	44	49	14	13	0	4.50
1 Barry Moore	L	27	3	5	.375	0	13	12	0	70	70	46	35	0	4.24
1 Bob Miller	R	31	2	2	.500	1	15	2	0	28	35	15	15	0	4.18
Rick Austin	L	23	2	5	.286	3	31	8	1	68	74	26	53	1	4.76
Mike Paul	L	25	2	8	.200	0	30	15	1	88	91	45	70	0	4.81
Steve Mingori	L	26	1	0	1.000	1	21	0	0	20	17	12	16	0	2.70
Vince Colbert	R	24	1	1	.500	2	23	0	0	31	37	16	17	0	7.26
Jim Rittwage	R	25	1	1	.500	0	8	3	1	26	18	21	16	0	4.15
2 Fred Lasher	R	28	1	7	.125	5	43	1	0	58	57	30	44	0	4.03

WASHINGTON 6th 70-92 .432 38 — TED WILLIAMS

NAME	G by POS	B	AGE	G	AB	R	H	2B	3B	HR	RBI	BB	SO	SB	BA	SA
TOTALS			29	162	5460	626	1302	184	28	138	583	635	**989**	72	.238	.358
Mike Epstein	1B122	L	27	140	430	55	110	15	3	20	56	73	117	2	.256	.444
Tim Cullen	2B112, SS6	R	28	123	262	22	56	10	2	1	18	31	38	3	.214	.279
Ed Brinkman	SS157	R	28	158	625	63	164	17	2	1	40	60	41	8	.262	.301
2 Aurelio Rodriguez	3B136, SS7	R	22	142	547	64	135	31	5	19	76	37	81	15	.247	.426
Ed Stroud	OF118	L	30	129	433	69	115	11	5	5	32	40	79	29	.266	.349
Del Unser	OF103	L	25	119	322	37	83	5	1	5	30	30	29	1	.258	.326
Frank Howard	OF120, 1B48	R	33	161	566	90	160	15	1	**44**	**126**	**132**	125	1	.283	.546
Paul Casanova	C100	R	28	104	328	25	75	17	3	6	30	10	47	0	.229	.354
2 Rick Reichardt	OF79, 3B1	R	27	107	277	42	70	14	2	15	46	23	69	2	.253	.480
Bernie Allen	2B80, 3B12	L	31	104	261	31	61	7	1	8	29	43	21	0	.234	.360
1 Lee Maye	OF68, 3B1	L	35	96	255	28	67	12	1	7	30	21	32	4	.263	.400
2 Wayne Comer	OF58, 3B1	R	26	77	129	21	30	4	0	0	8	22	16	4	.233	.264
Jim French	C62, OF1	L	28	69	166	20	35	3	1	1	13	38	23	0	.211	.259
Tommy Grieve	OF39	R	22	47	116	12	23	5	1	3	10	14	38	0	.198	.336
Dave Nelson	2B33	R	26	47	107	5	17	1	0	0	4	7	24	2	.159	.168
Johnny Roseboro	C30	L	37	46	86	7	20	4	0	1	6	18	10	1	.233	.314
1 Hank Allen	OF17	R	29	22	38	3	8	2	0	0	4	5	9	0	.211	.263
2 Greg Goossen	1B2, OF5	R	24	21	36	2	8	3	0	0	1	2	8	0	.222	.306
1 Ken McMullen	3B15	R	28	15	59	5	12	2	0	0	3	5	10	0	.203	.237

Dick Billings 27 R 6-24, Jeff Burroughs 19 R 2-12, Dick Nen 30 L 1-5, Larry Biittner 24 L 0-2

NAME	T	AGE	W	L	PCT	SV	G	GS	CG	IP	H	BB	SO	ShO	ERA
TOTALS		28	70	**92**	.432	40	162	162	20	1458	1375	611	823	11	3.80
Dick Bosman	R	26	16	12	.571	0	36	34	7	231	212	71	134	3	3.00
Jim Hannan	R	30	9	11	.450	0	42	17	1	128	119	54	61	1	4.01
1 George Brunet	L	35	8	6	.571	0	24	20	2	118	124	48	67	1	4.42
Joe Coleman	R	23	8	12	.400	0	39	29	6	219	190	89	152	1	3.58
Casey Cox	R	28	8	12	.400	1	37	30	1	192	211	44	68	0	4.45
Jim Shellenback	L	26	6	7	.462	0	39	14	2	117	107	51	57	1	3.69
Horacio Pina	R	25	5	3	.625	6	61	0	0	71	66	35	41	0	2.79
Joe Grzenda	L	33	3	6	.333	6	49	3	0	85	86	34	38	0	4.98
Jackie Brown	R	27	2	2	.500	0	24	5	1	57	49	37	47	0	3.95
Bill Gogolewski	R	22	2	2	.500	0	8	5	0	34	33	25	19	0	4.76
Darold Knowles	L	28	2	14	.125	27	71	0	0	119	100	58	71	0	2.04
Dick Such	R	25	1	5	.167	0	21	5	0	50	48	45	41	0	7.56
Cisco Carlos	R	29	0	0	.000	0	5	0	0	6	3	4	2	0	1.50
Jan Dukes	L	24	0	0	.000	0	5	0	0	7	6	1	4	0	2.57
1 Bob Humphreys	R	34	0	0	.000	0	5	0	0	7	4	9	6	0	1.29
Pedro Ramos	R	35	0	0	.000	0	4	0	0	8	10	4	10	0	7.88
Denny Riddleberger	L	24	0	0	.000	0	8	0	0	9	7	2	5	0	1.00

WEST DIVISION

MINNESOTA 1st 98-64 .605 — BILL RIGNEY

NAME	G by POS	B	AGE	G	AB	R	H	2B	3B	HR	RBI	BB	SO	SB	BA	SA
TOTALS			28	162	5483	744	1438	230	**41**	153	694	501	905	57	**.262**	.403
Rich Reese	1B146	L	28	153	501	63	131	15	5	10	56	48	70	5	.261	.371
Danny Thompson	2B81, 3B37, SS6	R	23	96	302	25	66	9	0	0	22	7	39	0	.219	.248
Leo Cardenas	SS160	R	31	160	588	67	145	34	4	11	65	42	101	2	.247	.374
Harmon Killebrew	3B138, 1B28	R	34	157	527	96	143	20	1	41	113	128	84	0	.271	.546
Tony Oliva	OF157	L	30	157	628	96	**204**	**36**	7	23	107	38	67	5	.325	.514
Cesar Tovar	OF151, 2B8, 3B4	R	29	161	650	120	195	**36**	**13**	10	54	52	47	30	.300	.442
Jim Holt	OF130, 1B2	L	26	142	319	37	85	9	3	3	40	17	32	3	.266	.342
George Mitterwald	C117	R	25	117	369	36	82	12	2	15	46	34	84	3	.222	.388
Frank Quilici	2B73, 3B27, SS1	R	31	111	141	19	32	3	0	2	12	15	16	0	.227	.291
Brant Alyea	OF75	R	29	94	258	34	75	12	1	16	61	28	51	3	.291	.531
Rick Renick	3B30, OF25, SS1	R	26	81	179	20	41	8	0	7	25	22	29	0	.229	.391
Paul Ratliff	C53	L	26	69	149	19	40	7	2	5	22	15	51	0	.268	.443
Chuck Manuel	OF11	L	26	59	64	4	12	0	0	1	7	6	17	0	.188	.234
Rod Carew (KJ)	2B45, 1B1	L	24	51	191	27	70	12	3	4	28	11	28	4	.366	.524
Bob Allison	OF17, 1B7	R	35	47	72	15	15	5	0	1	7	14	20	1	.208	.319
Herm Hill	OF14	L	24	27	22	8	2	0	0	0	0	0	6	0	.091	.091
Tom Tischinski	C22	R	25	24	46	6	9	0	0	1	2	9	6	0	.196	.261
Minnie Mendoza	3B5, 2B4	R	36	16	16	2	3	0	0	0	2	0	1	0	.188	.188
Jim Nettles	OF11	L	23	13	20	3	5	0	0	0	0	1	5	0	.250	.250

Steve Brye 21 R 2-11, Rick Dempsey 20 R 0-7, Cotton Nash 27 R 1-4

NAME	T	AGE	W	L	PCT	SV	G	GS	CG	IP	H	BB	SO	ShO	ERA
TOTALS		27	98	64	.605	**58**	162	162	26	1448	1329	486	940	12	3.23
Jim Perry	R	34	**24**	12	.667	0	40	**40**	13	279	258	57	168	4	3.03
Jim Kaat	L	31	14	10	.583	0	45	34	4	230	244	58	120	1	3.56
Tom Hall	L	22	11	6	.647	4	52	11	1	155	94	66	184	0	2.55
Stan Williams	R	33	10	1	.909	15	68	0	0	113	85	32	76	0	1.99
Bert Blyleven	R	19	10	9	.526	0	27	25	5	164	143	47	135	1	3.18
Bill Zepp	R	23	9	4	.692	2	43	20	1	151	154	51	64	1	3.22
Luis Tiant (BS)	R	29	7	3	.700	0	18	17	2	93	84	41	50	1	3.39
Ron Perranoski	L	34	7	8	.467	**34**	67	0	0	111	108	42	55	0	2.43
Dave Boswell (XJ)	R	25	3	7	.300	0	18	15	0	69	80	44	45	0	6.39
Hal Haydel	R	25	2	0	1.000	0	4	0	0	9	7	4	4	0	3.00
Dick Woodson	R	25	1	2	.333	1	21	0	0	31	29	19	22	0	3.77
Pete Hamm	R	22	0	2	.000	0	10	0	0	16	17	7	3	0	5.63
Steve Barber	R	22	0	0	.000	2	18	0	0	27	26	18	14	0	4.67

OAKLAND 2nd 89-73 .549 9 — JOHN McNAMARA

NAME	G by POS	B	AGE	G	AB	R	H	2B	3B	HR	RBI	BB	SO	SB	BA	SA
TOTALS			28	162	5376	678	1338	208	24	171	630	584	977	**131**	.249	.392
Don Mincher	1B137	L	32	140	463	62	114	18	0	27	74	56	71	5	.246	.460
Dick Green	2B127, 3B5, C1	R	29	135	384	34	73	7	0	4	29	38	73	3	.190	.240
Bert Campaneris	SS143	R	28	147	603	97	168	28	4	22	64	36	73	**42**	.279	.448
Sal Bando	3B152	R	26	155	502	93	132	20	2	20	75	118	88	6	.263	.430
Reggie Jackson	OF142	L	24	149	426	57	101	21	2	23	66	75	**135**	26	.237	.458
Rick Monday	OF109	L	24	112	376	63	109	19	7	10	37	58	99	17	.290	.457
Felipe Alou	OF145, 1B1	R	35	154	575	70	156	25	3	8	55	32	31	10	.271	.367
Frank Fernandez	C76, OF1	R	27	94	252	30	54	5	0	15	44	40	76	1	.214	.413
Joe Rudi	OF63, 1B28	R	23	106	350	40	108	23	2	11	42	16	61	3	.309	.480
Dave Duncan	C73	R	24	86	232	21	60	7	0	10	29	22	38	0	.259	.418
2 Steve Hovley	OF42	L	25	72	100	8	19	1	0	0	1	5	11	3	.190	.200
2 Tommy Davis	OF45, 1B8	R	31	66	200	17	58	9	1	1	27	8	18	2	.290	.360
Tony LaRussa	2B44	R	25	52	106	6	21	4	1	0	6	15	19	0	.198	.255
John Donaldson	2B21, SS6, 3B1	L	27	41	89	4	22	2	1	1	11	9	6	1	.247	.326
Gene Tenace	C30	R	23	38	105	19	32	6	0	7	20	23	30	0	.305	.562
1 Tito Francona	1B6, OF1	L	36	32	33	2	8	0	0	1	6	6	6	0	.242	.333
Bob Johnson	3B6, 1B1	R	34	30	46	6	8	1	0	1	2	3	2	2	.174	.261
Jose Tartabull	OF6	L	31	24	13	5	3	2	0	0	2	0	2	1	.231	.385
Jim Driscoll	2B7, SS7	L	26	21	52	2	10	0	0	1	2	2	15	0	.192	.250
1 Roberto Pena	SS12, 3B5	R	30	19	58	4	15	1	0	0	3	3	4	1	.259	.276

Bobby Brooks 24 R 6-18, Allan Lewis 28 B 2-8, Larry Haney 27 R 0-2

NAME	T	AGE	W	L	PCT	SV	G	GS	CG	IP	H	BB	SO	ShO	ERA
TOTALS		28	89	73	.549	40	162	162	33	1443	1253	542	858	**15**	3.30
Catfish Hunter	R	24	18	14	.563	0	40	**40**	9	262	253	74	178	1	3.81
Chuck Dobson	R	26	16	15	.516	0	41	**40**	13	267	230	92	149	**5**	3.74
Diego Segui	R	32	10	10	.500	2	47	19	3	162	130	68	95	2	**2.56**
Blue Moon Odom (EJ)	R	25	9	8	.529	0	29	29	4	156	128	100	88	1	3.81
Paul Lindblad	L	28	8	2	.800	3	62	0	0	63	52	28	42	0	2.71
Rollie Fingers	R	23	7	9	.438	2	45	19	1	148	137	48	79	0	3.65
1 Mudcat Grant	R	34	6	2	.750	24	72	0	0	123	104	30	54	0	1.83
1 Al Downing	L	29	3	3	.500	0	10	6	1	41	39	22	26	0	3.95
Marcel Lachemann	R	29	3	3	.500	3	41	0	0	58	58	18	39	0	2.79
2 Bob Locker	R	32	3	3	.500	4	38	0	0	56	49	19	33	0	2.89
Jim Roland (KJ)	L	27	3	3	.500	2	28	2	0	43	28	23	26	0	2.72
Vida Blue	L	20	2	0	1.000	0	6	6	2	39	20	12	35	2	2.08
Darrell Osteen (MS)	R	27	1	0	1.000	0	3	1	0	6	9	3	3	0	6.00
Fred Talbot	R	29	0	1	.000	0	1	1	0	2	2	1	0	0	9.00
1 Roberto Rodriquez	R	29	0	0	.000	0	6	0	0	12	10	3	8	0	3.00
Dooley Womack	R	30	0	0	.000	0	2	0	0	3	4	1	3	0	15.00

CALIFORNIA 3rd 86-76 .531 12 — LEFTY PHILLIPS

NAME	G by POS	B	AGE	G	AB	R	H	2B	3B	HR	RBI	BB	SO	SB	BA	SA
TOTALS			26	162	5532	631	1391	197	40	114	598	447	922	69	.251	.363
Jim Spencer	1B142	L	22	146	511	61	140	20	4	12	68	28	61	0	.274	.399
Sandy Alomar	2B153, SS10, 3B1	B	26	162	672	82	169	18	2	2	36	49	65	35	.251	.293
Jim Fregosi	SS150, 1B6	R	28	158	601	95	167	33	5	22	82	69	92	0	.278	.459
2 Ken McMullen	3B122	R	28	124	422	50	98	9	3	14	61	59	81	1	.232	.367
Roger Repoz	OF110, 1B18	L	29	137	407	50	97	17	6	18	47	45	90	4	.238	.442
Jay Johnstone	OF100	L	24	119	320	34	76	10	5	11	39	24	53	1	.238	.403
Alex Johnson	OF156	R	27	156	614	85	202	26	6	14	86	35	68	17	.329	.459
Joe Azcue	C112	R	30	114	351	19	85	13	1	2	25	24	40	0	.242	.302
Bill Voss (BW)	OF55	L	26	80	181	21	44	4	3	3	30	23	18	2	.243	.348
Tom Egan	C79	R	24	79	210	14	50	6	0	4	20	14	67	0	.238	.324
Jarvis Tatum	OF58	R	23	75	181	28	43	7	0	0	6	17	35	1	.238	.276
Billy Cowan	OF27, 1B14, 3B2	R	31	68	134	20	37	9	1	5	25	11	29	0	.276	.470
Chico Ruiz	3B27, 2B3, SS3, 1B2, C1	B	31	68	107	10	26	3	1	0	12	7	16	3	.243	.290
Tommie Reynolds	OF32, 3B1	R	28	59	120	11	30	3	1	1	6	6	10	1	.250	.317
2 Tony Gonzalez	OF24	L	33	26	92	9	28	2	0	1	12	2	11	3	.304	.359
Doug Griffin	2B11, 3B8	R	23	18	55	2	7	1	0	0	4	6	5	0	.127	.145
1 Aurelio Rodriguez	3B17	R	22	17	63	6	17	2	2	0	7	3	6	0	.270	.365

Mickey Rivers 21 L 8-25, Ray Oyler 31 R 2-24, Tommy Silverio 24 L 0-15, 1 Rich Reichardt 27 R 1-6, Jim Hicks 30 R 1-4, Randy Brown 25 L 0-4, Marty Perez 23 R 0-3

NAME	T	AGE	W	L	PCT	SV	G	GS	CG	IP	H	BB	SO	ShO	ERA
TOTALS		26	86	76	.531	49	162	162	21	1462	1280	559	922	10	3.48
Clyde Wright	L	29	22	12	.647	0	39	39	7	261	226	88	110	2	2.83
Tom Murphy	R	24	16	13	.552	0	39	38	5	227	223	81	99	2	4.24
Andy Messersmith (VJ)	R	24	11	10	.524	5	37	26	6	195	144	78	162	1	3.00
Ken Tatum	R	26	7	4	.636	17	62	0	0	89	68	26	50	0	2.93
Rudy May	L	25	7	13	.350	0	38	34	2	209	190	81	164	2	4.00
Greg Garrett	L	23	5	6	.455	0	32	7	0	75	48	44	53	0	2.64
Dave LaRoche	L	22	4	1	.800	4	38	0	0	50	41	21	44	0	3.42
Eddie Fisher	R	33	4	4	.500	8	67	2	0	130	117	35	74	0	3.05
1 Paul Doyle	L	30	3	1	.750	5	40	0	0	42	43	21	34	0	5.14
Mel Queen	R	28	3	6	.333	9	34	3	0	60	58	28	44	0	4.20
Tom Bradley	R	23	2	5	.286	0	17	11	1	70	71	33	53	1	4.11
Steve Kealey	R	23	1	0	1.000	1	17	0	0	22	19	6	14	0	4.09
Lloyd Allen	R	20	1	1	.500	0	8	2	0	24	23	11	12	0	2.63
Wally Wolf	R	28	0	0	.000	0	4	0	0	5	3	4	5	0	5.40
Terry Cox	R	21	0	0	.000	0	3	0	0	2	4	0	3	0	4.50
Harvey Shank	R	23	0	0	.000	0	1	0	0	3	2	2	1	0	0.00

KANSAS CITY 4th (Tie) 65-97 .401 33 — CHARLIE METRO 19-33 .365 — BOB LEMON 46-64 .418

NAME	G by POS	B	AGE	G	AB	R	H	2B	3B	HR	RBI	BB	SO	SB	BA	SA
TOTALS			26	162	5503	611	1341	202	41	97	572	514	958	97	.244	.348
Bob Oliver	1B115, 3B46	R	27	160	612	83	159	24	6	27	99	42	126	3	.260	.451
2 Cookie Rojas	2B97	R	31	98	384	36	100	13	3	2	28	20	29	3	.260	.326
Jackie Hernandez	SS77	R	29	83	238	14	55	4	1	2	10	15	50	1	.231	.282
Paul Schaal	3B97, SS10, 2B6	R	27	124	380	50	102	12	3	5	35	43	39	7	.268	.355
Pat Kelly	OF110	L	26	136	452	56	106	16	1	6	38	76	105	34	.235	.314
Amos Otis	OF159	R	23	159	620	91	176	36	9	11	58	68	67	33	.284	.424
Lou Piniella	OF139, 1B1	R	26	144	542	54	163	24	5	11	88	35	42	3	.301	.424
Ed Kirkpatrick	C89, OF19, 1B16	L	25	134	424	59	97	17	2	18	62	55	65	4	.229	.406
Ellie Rodriguez	C75	R	24	80	231	25	52	8	2	1	15	27	35	2	.225	.290
Rich Severson	SS50, 2B25	B	25	77	240	22	60	11	1	1	22	16	33	0	.250	.317
Joe Keough (BL)	OF34, 1B18	L	24	57	183	28	59	6	2	4	21	23	18	1	.322	.443
Bill Sorrell	3B29, OF4, 1B3	L	29	57	135	12	36	2	0	4	14	10	13	1	.267	.370
2 Tom Matchick	SS43, 2B10, 3B1	L	26	55	158	11	31	3	2	0	11	5	23	0	.196	.241
George Spriggs	OF36	L	29	51	130	12	27	2	3	1	7	14	32	4	.208	.292
Luis Alcaraz	2B31	R	29	35	120	10	20	5	1	1	14	4	13	0	.167	.250
Jim Campanis	C13, OF1	R	26	31	54	6	7	0	0	2	2	4	14	0	.130	.241
1 Mike Fiore	1B20	L	25	25	72	6	13	2	0	0	4	13	24	1	.181	.208
2 Bobby Floyd	SS8, 3B6	R	26	14	43	5	14	4	0	0	9	4	9	0	.326	.419

Jerry Adair 33 R 4-27, Buck Martinez (MS) 21 R 1-9, Hawk Taylor 31 R 9-55

NAME	T	AGE	W	L	PCT	SV	G	GS	CG	IP	H	BB	SO	ShO	ERA
TOTALS		27	65	97	.401	25	162	162	30	1464	1346	641	915	11	3.78
Jim Rooker	L	28	10	15	.400	1	38	29	6	204	190	102	117	3	3.53
3 Ted Abernathy	R	37	9	3	.750	12	36	0	0	56	41	38	49	0	2.57
Dick Drago	R	25	9	15	.375	0	35	34	7	240	239	72	127	1	3.75
Al Fitzmorris	R	24	8	5	.615	1	43	11	2	118	112	52	47	0	4.42
Bob Johnson	R	27	8	13	.381	4	40	26	10	214	178	82	206	1	3.07
Tom Burgmeier	L	26	6	6	.500	1	41	0	0	68	59	23	43	0	3.18
Bill Butler	L	23	4	12	.250	0	25	25	2	141	117	87	75	1	3.77
Dave Morehead	R	27	3	5	.375	1	28	17	1	122	121	62	69	0	3.61
Mike Hedlund (IL)	R	23	2	3	.400	0	9	0	0	15	18	7	5	0	7.20
Wally Bunker (SJ)	R	25	2	11	.154	0	24	15	2	122	109	50	59	1	4.20
Aurelio Monteagudo	R	26	1	1	.500	0	21	0	0	27	20	9	18	0	3.00
Jim York	R	22	1	1	.500	0	4	0	0	8	5	2	6	0	3.38
1 Moe Drabowsky	R	34	1	2	.333	2	24	0	0	36	28	12	38	0	3.25
Ken Wright	R	23	1	2	.333	3	47	0	0	53	49	29	30	0	5.26
Paul Splittorff	L	23	0	1	.000	0	2	1	0	9	16	5	10	0	7.00
Roger Nelson (SA)	R	26	0	2	.000	0	4	2	0	9	18	0	3	0	10.00
Don O'Riley	R	25	0	0	.000	0	9	2	0	23	26	9	13	0	5.48

MILWAUKEE 4th (Tie) 65-97 .401 33 — DAVE BRISTOL

NAME	G by POS	B	AGE	G	AB	R	H	2B	3B	HR	RBI	BB	SO	SB	BA	SA
TOTALS			30	163	5395	613	1305	202	24	126	571	592	985	91	.242	.358
Mike Hegan	1B139, OF8	L	27	148	476	70	116	21	2	11	52	67	116	9	.244	.366
Ted Kubiak	2B91, SS73	B	28	158	540	63	136	9	6	4	41	72	51	4	.252	.313
2 Roberto Pena	SS99, 2B15, 1B7	R	30	121	416	36	99	19	1	3	42	25	45	3	.238	.310
Tommy Harper	3B128, 2B22, OF13	R	29	154	604	104	179	35	4	31	82	77	107	38	.296	.522
Russ Snyder	OF106	L	36	124	276	34	64	11	0	4	31	16	40	1	.232	.315
2 Dave May	OF99	L	26	101	342	36	82	8	1	7	31	44	56	8	.240	.330
Danny Walton	OF114	R	22	117	397	32	102	20	1	17	66	51	126	2	.257	.441
Phil Roof	C107, 1B1	R	29	110	321	39	73	7	1	13	37	32	72	3	.227	.377
Ted Savage	OF82, 1B1	R	34	114	276	43	77	10	5	12	50	57	44	10	.279	.482
Jerry McNertney	C94, 1B13	R	33	111	296	27	72	11	1	6	22	22	33	1	.243	.348
2 Bob Burda	OF64, 1B7	L	31	78	222	19	55	9	0	4	20	16	17	1	.248	.342
Gus Gil	2B38, 3B14	R	30	64	119	12	22	4	0	1	12	21	12	2	.185	.244
Max Alvis	3B36	R	32	62	115	16	21	2	0	3	12	5	20	1	.183	.278
2 Tito Francona	1B13	L	36	52	65	4	15	3	0	0	4	6	15	1	.231	.277
Mike Hershberger (SJ)	OF35	R	30	49	98	7	23	5	0	1	6	10	8	1	.235	.316
Bernie Smith	OF39	R	28	44	76	8	21	3	1	1	6	11	12	1	.276	.382
1 Steve Hovley	OF38	L	25	40	135	17	38	9	0	0	16	17	11	5	.281	.348
2 Hank Allen	OF14, 2B5, 1B4	R	29	28	61	4	14	4	0	0	4	7	5	0	.230	.295
1 John Kennedy	2B16, 3B5, SS4, 1B1	R	29	25	55	8	14	2	0	2	6	5	9	0	.255	.400
1 Greg Goossen	1B15	R	24	21	47	3	12	3	0	1	3	10	12	0	.255	.383
Floyd Wicker	OF12	L	26	15	41	3	8	1	0	1	3	1	8	0	.195	.293

1 Rich Rollins 32 R 5-25, Pete Koegel 22 R 2-8, 1 Wayne Comer 26 R 1-17, Sandy Valdespino 31 L 0-9, Fred Stanley 22 B 0-0

NAME	T	AGE	W	L	PCT	SV	G	GS	CG	IP	H	BB	SO	ShO	ERA
TOTALS		29	65	97	.401	27	163	163	31	1447	1397	587	895	2	4.21
Marty Pattin	R	27	14	12	.538	0	37	29	11	233	204	71	161	0	3.40
Lew Krausse	R	27	13	18	.419	0	37	35	8	216	235	67	130	1	4.75
Gene Brabender	R	28	6	15	.286	1	29	21	2	129	127	79	76	0	6.00
Ken Sanders	R	28	5	2	.714	13	50	0	0	92	64	25	64	0	1.76
1 Bob Bolin	R	31	5	11	.313	1	32	20	3	132	131	67	81	0	4.91
Skip Lockwood	R	23	5	12	.294	0	27	26	3	174	173	79	93	1	4.29
John Gelnar	R	27	4	3	.571	4	53	0	0	92	98	23	48	0	4.21
John Morris (IL)	L	28	4	3	.571	0	20	9	2	73	70	22	40	0	3.95
1 John O'Donoghue	L	30	2	0	1.000	0	25	0	0	23	29	9	13	0	5.09
Dave Baldwin	R	32	2	1	.667	1	28	0	0	35	25	18	26	0	2.57
2 Bob Humphreys	R	34	2	4	.333	3	23	1	0	46	37	22	32	0	3.13
2 Al Downing	L	29	2	10	.167	0	17	16	1	94	79	59	53	0	3.35
George Lauzerique	R	22	1	2	.333	0	11	4	1	35	41	14	24	0	6.94
1 Bob Locker	R	32	0	1	.000	3	28	0	0	32	37	10	19	0	3.38
Bob Meyer	L	30	0	1	.000	0	10	0	0	18	24	12	20	0	6.50
Ray Peters	R	23	0	2	.000	0	2	2	0	2	7	5	1	0	31.50
Bruce Brubaker	R	28	0	0	.000	0	1	0	0	2	2	1	0	0	9.00
2 Dick Ellsworth	L	30	0	0	.000	1	14	0	0	16	11	3	9	0	1.69
Wayne Twitchell	R	22	0	0	.000	0	2	0	0	2	3	1	5	0	9.00

Mickey Fuentes (DD) 20

CHICAGO 6th 56-106 .346 42 — DON GUTTERIDGE 49-89 .355 — JIMMY ADAIR 4-4 .500 — CHUCK TANNER 3-13 .188

NAME	G by POS	B	AGE	G	AB	R	H	2B	3B	HR	RBI	BB	SO	SB	BA	SA
TOTALS			27	162	5514	633	1394	192	20	123	587	477	872	53	.253	.362
Gail Hopkins	1B77, C8	L	27	116	287	32	82	8	1	6	29	28	19	0	.286	.383
Bobby Knoop	2B126	R	31	130	402	34	92	13	2	5	36	34	79	0	.229	.308
Luis Aparicio	SS146	R	36	146	552	86	173	29	3	5	43	53	34	8	.313	.404
Bill Melton	3B70, OF71	R	24	141	514	74	135	15	1	33	96	56	107	2	.263	.488
Walt Williams	OF79	R	26	110	315	43	79	18	1	3	15	19	30	3	.251	.343
Ken Berry	OF138	R	29	141	463	45	128	12	2	7	50	43	61	6	.276	.356
Carlos May	OF141, 1B7	L	22	150	555	83	158	28	4	12	68	79	96	12	.285	.414
Ed Herrmann	C88	L	23	96	297	42	84	9	0	19	52	31	41	0	.283	.505
Tommy McCraw	1B59, OF49	L	29	129	332	39	73	11	2	6	31	21	50	12	.220	.319
Syd O'Brien	3B68, 2B43, SS5	R	25	121	441	48	109	13	2	8	44	22	62	3	.247	.340
Duane Josephson (BG)	C84	R	28	96	285	28	90	12	1	4	41	24	28	0	.316	.407
Rich Morales	SS24, 3B20, 2B12	R	26	62	112	6	18	2	0	1	2	9	16	1	.161	.205
John Matias	OF22, 1B18	L	25	58	117	7	22	2	0	2	6	3	22	1	.188	.256
Bob Spence	1B37	L	24	46	130	11	29	4	1	4	15	11	32	0	.223	.362
Rich McKinney	3B23, SS11	R	23	43	119	12	20	5	0	4	17	11	25	3	.168	.311
1 Buddy Bradford	OF27	R	25	32	91	8	17	3	0	2	8	10	30	1	.187	.286

Ossie Blanco 24 R 13-66, Jose Ortiz 23 R 8-24, Chuck Brinkman 25 R 5-20, Bob Christian 24 R 4-15, Art Kusnyer 24 R 1-10, 2 Lee Maye 35 L 1-6

NAME	T	AGE	W	L	PCT	SV	G	GS	CG	IP	H	BB	SO	ShO	ERA
TOTALS		28	56	106	.346	30	162	162	20	1430	1554	556	762	6	4.54
Tommy John	L	27	12	17	.414	0	37	37	10	269	253	101	138	3	3.28
Jerry Janeski	R	24	10	17	.370	0	35	35	4	206	247	63	79	1	4.76
Wilbur Wood	L	28	9	13	.409	21	77	0	0	122	118	36	85	0	2.80
Joe Horlen (KJ)	R	32	6	16	.273	0	28	26	4	172	198	41	77	0	4.87
2 Bob Miller	R	31	4	6	.400	3	15	12	0	70	88	33	36	0	5.01
Jerry Crider	R	28	4	7	.364	4	32	8	0	91	101	34	40	0	4.45
Bart Johnson	R	20	4	7	.364	0	18	15	2	90	92	46	71	1	4.80
Danny Murphy	R	27	2	3	.400	5	51	0	0	81	82	49	42	0	5.67
2 Lee Stange	R	33	1	0	1.000	0	16	0	0	22	28	5	14	0	5.32
Tommie Sisk	R	28	1	1	.500	0	17	1	0	33	37	13	16	0	5.45
Floyd Weaver	R	29	1	2	.333	0	31	3	0	62	52	31	51	0	4.35
Billy Wynne	R	26	1	4	.200	0	12	9	0	44	54	22	19	0	5.32
Jim Magnuson	L	23	1	5	.167	0	13	6	0	45	45	16	20	0	4.80
Gene Rounsaville	R	25	0	1	.000	0	8	0	0	6	10	2	3	0	10.50
Jerry Arrigo (SJ)	L	29	0	3	.000	0	5	3	0	13	24	9	12	0	13.15
2 Barry Moore	L	27	0	4	.000	0	24	7	0	71	85	34	34	0	6.34

Don Secrist 26 L 0-0, 2 Steve Hamilton 36 L 0-0, Denny O'Toole 21 R 0-0, Don Eddy 23 L 0-0, Richie Maloney 20 R 0-0, Paul Edmondson (DD) 27

AMERICAN LEAGUE CHAMPIONSHIP – BALTIMORE (EAST) 3 MINNESOTA (WEST) 0

LINE SCORES

TEAM	1	2	3	4	5	6	7	8	9	10	11	12	R	H	E
Game 1 October 3 at Minnesota															
BAL	0	2	0	7	0	1	0	0	0				10	13	0
MIN	1	1	0	1	3	0	0	0	0				6	11	2
Cuellar, **D. Hall**	Perry, Zepp (4), Woodson (5), Williams (6), Perranoski (9)														
Game 2 October 4 at Minnesota															
BAL	1	0	2	1	0	0	0	0	7				11	13	0
MIN	0	0	0	3	0	0	0	0	0				3	6	2
McNally	**T. Hall**, Zepp (4), Williams (5), Perranoski (8), Tiant (9)														
Game 3 October 5 at Baltimore															
MIN	0	0	0	0	1	0	0	0	0				1	7	2
BAL	1	1	3	0	0	0	1	0	X				6	10	0
Kaat, Blyleven (3), T. Hall (5), Perry (7)	Palmer														

COMPOSITE BATTING

NAME	POS	G	AB	R	H	2B	3B	HR	RBI	BA
Baltimore										
Totals		3	109	27	36	7	0	6	24	.330
Powell	1B	3	14	2	6	2	0	1	6	.429
Blair	OF	3	13	0	1	0	0	0	0	.077
B. Robinson	3B	3	12	3	7	2	0	0	1	.583
Belanger	SS	3	12	5	4	0	0	0	1	.333
Johnson	2B	3	11	4	4	0	0	2	4	.364
F. Robinson	OF	3	10	3	2	0	0	1	2	.200
Etchebarren	C	2	9	1	1	0	0	0	0	.111
Buford	OF	2	7	2	3	1	0	1	3	.429
Hendricks	C	1	5	2	2	0	0	0	0	.400
Rettenmund	OF	1	3	1	1	0	0	0	1	.333
Minnesota										
Totals		3	101	10	24	4	1	3	10	.238
Tovar	2B-OF	3	13	2	5	0	1	0	1	.385
Oliva	OF	3	12	2	6	2	0	1	1	.500
Killebrew	1B-3B	3	11	2	3	0	0	2	4	.273
Cardenas	SS	3	11	1	2	0	0	0	1	.182
Mitterwald	C	2	8	2	4	1	0	0	2	.500
Thompson	2B	3	8	0	1	1	0	0	0	.125
Reese	1B	2	7	0	1	0	0	0	0	.143
Alyea	OF	3	7	1	0	0	0	0	0	.000

Renick 3B 1-5, Holt OF 0-5, Ratliff C 1-4, Allison PH 0-2, Quilici 2B 0-2, Carew PH 0-2, Manuel PH 0-1

COMPOSITE PITCHING

NAME	G	IP	H	BB	SO	W	L	SV	ERA
Baltimore									
Totals	3	27	24	9	22	3	0	0	3.33
McNally	1	9	6	5	5	1	0	0	3.00
Palmer	1	9	7	3	12	1	0	0	1.00
Cuellar	1	4.1	10	1	2	0	0	0	12.46
D. Hall	1	4.2	1	0	3	1	0	0	0.00
Minnesota									
Totals	3	26	36	12	19	0	3	0	7.62
Williams	2	6	2	1	2	0	0	0	0.00
T. Hall	2	5.1	6	4	6	0	1	0	6.75
Perry	2	5.1	10	1	3	0	1	0	13.50
Perranoski	2	2.1	5	1	3	0	0	0	19.29
Blyleven	1	2	2	0	2	0	0	0	0.00
Katt	1	2	6	2	1	0	1	0	9.00

Zepp 2G, Woodson 1G, Tiant 1G

NATIONAL LEAGUE CHAMPIONSHIP – CINCINNATI (WEST) 3 PITTSBURG (EAST) 0

LINE SCORES

TEAM	1	2	3	4	5	6	7	8	9	10	11	12	R	H	E
Game 1 October 3 at Pittsburgh															
CIN	0	0	0	0	0	0	0	0	0	3			3	9	0
PIT	0	0	0	0	0	0	0	0	0	0			0	8	0
Nolan, Carroll (10)	Ellis, Gibbon (10)														
Game 2 October 4 at Pittsburgh															
CIN	0	0	1	0	1	0	0	1	0				3	8	1
PIT	0	0	0	0	0	1	0	0	0				1	5	2
Merritt, Carroll (6), Gullett (6)	Walker, Giusti (8)														
Game 3 October 5 at Cincinnati															
PIT	1	0	0	0	1	0	0	0	0				2	10	0
CIN	2	0	0	0	0	0	0	1	X				3	5	0
Moose, Gibbon (8), Giusti (8)	Cloninger, Wilcox (6), Granger (9), Gullett (9)														

COMPOSITE BATTING

NAME	POS	G	AB	R	H	2B	3B	HR	RBI	BA
Cincinnati										
Totals		3	100	9	22	3	1	3	8	.220
Rose	OF	3	13	1	3	0	0	0	1	.231
Tolan	OF	3	12	3	5	0	0	1	2	.417
Perez	3B-1B	3	12	1	4	2	0	1	2	.333
May	1B	3	12	0	2	1	0	0	2	.167
Helms	2B	3	11	0	3	0	0	0	0	.273
Woodward	SS-3B	3	10	0	1	0	0	0	0	.100
Bench	C	3	9	2	2	0	0	1	1	.222
Carbo	OF	2	6	0	0	0	0	0	0	.000
McRae	OF	2	4	0	0	0	0	0	0	.000
Stewart	OF	1	2	0	0	0	0	0	0	.000
Cline	OF	2	1	2	1	0	1	0	1	1.000
Bravo	PH	1	1	0	0	0	0	0	0	.000
Concepcion	SS	3	0	0	0	0	0	0	0	.000
Pittsburgh										
Totals		3	102	3	23	6	0	0	3	.225
Clemente	OF	3	14	1	3	0	0	0	1	.214
Stargell	OF	3	12	0	6	1	0	0	1	.500
Alou	OF	3	12	1	3	1	0	0	0	.250
Sanguillen	C	3	12	0	2	0	0	0	0	.167
Oliver	1B	2	8	0	2	0	0	0	1	.250
Cash	2B	2	8	1	1	1	0	0	0	.125
Alley	SS	2	7	0	0	0	0	0	0	.000
Hebner	3B	2	6	0	4	2	0	0	0	.667
Robertson	1B	2	5	0	1	1	0	0	0	.200
Pagan	3B	1	3	0	1	0	0	0	0	.333

Patek SS 0-3, Jeter OF 0-2, Mazeroski 2B 0-2

COMPOSITE PITCHING

NAME	G	IP	H	BB	SO	W	L	SV	ERA
Cincinnati									
Totals	3	28	23	12	19	3	0	3	0.96
Nolan	1	9	8	4	6	1	0	0	0.00
Merritt	1	5.1	3	0	2	1	0	0	1.69
Cloninger	1	5	7	4	1	0	0	0	3.60
Gullett	2	3.2	1	2	3	0	0	2	0.00
Wilcox	1	3	1	2	5	1	0	0	0.00
Carroll	2	1.1	2	0	2	0	0	1	0.00
Granger	1	.2	1	0	0	0	0	0	0.00
Pittsburgh									
Totals	3	27	22	8	12	0	3	0	2.67
Ellis	1	9.2	9	4	1	0	1	0	2.79
Moose	1	7.2	4	2	4	0	1	0	3.52
Walker	1	7	5	1	5	0	1	0	1.29
Giusti	2	2.1	3	1	1	0	0	0	3.86
Gibbon	2	.1	1	0	1	0	0	0	0.00

EAST DIVISION

PITTSBURGH 1st 89-73 .549 — DANNY MURTAUGH

NAME	G by POS	B	AGE	G	AB	R	H	2B	3B	HR	RBI	BB	SO	SB	BA	SA
TOTALS			28	162	5637	729	1522	235	70	130	676	444	871	66	.270	.406
Bob Robertson	1B99, 3B5, OF3	R	23	117	390	69	112	19	4	27	82	51	98	4	.287	.564
Bill Mazeroski	2B102	R	33	112	367	29	84	14	0	7	39	27	40	2	.229	.324
Gene Alley	SS108, 2B8, 3B2	R	29	121	426	46	104	16	5	8	41	31	70	7	.244	.362
Richie Hebner	3B117	L	22	120	420	60	122	24	8	11	46	42	48	2	.290	.464
Roberto Clemente	OF104	R	35	108	412	65	145	22	10	14	60	38	66	3	.352	.556
Matty Alou	OF153	L	31	155	677	97	201	21	8	1	47	30	18	19	.297	.356
Willie Stargell	OF125, 1B1	L	30	136	474	70	125	18	3	31	85	44	119	0	.264	.511
Manny Sanguillen	C125	R	26	128	486	63	158	19	9	7	61	17	45	2	.325	.444
Al Oliver	OF80, 1B77	L	23	151	551	63	149	33	5	12	83	35	35	1	.270	.414
Jose Pagan	3B53, OF4, 1B1, 2B1	R	35	95	230	21	61	14	1	7	29	20	24	1	.265	.426
Johnnie Jeter	OF56	R	25	85	126	27	30	3	2	2	12	13	34	9	.238	.341
Freddie Patek	SS65	R	25	84	237	42	58	10	5	1	19	29	46	8	.245	.342
Dave Cash	2B55	R	22	64	210	30	66	7	6	1	28	17	25	5	.314	.419
Jerry May	C45	R	26	51	139	13	29	4	2	1	16	21	25	0	.209	.288
Gene Clines	OF7	R	23	31	37	4	15	2	0	0	3	2	5	2	.405	.459

Jose Martinez 27 R 1-20, George Kopacz 29 L 3-16, Dave Ricketts 34 B 2-11, Milt May 19 L 2-4

NAME	T	AGE	W	L	PCT	SV	G	GS	CG	IP	H	BB	SO	ShO	ERA
TOTALS		28	89	73	.549	43	162	162	36	1454	1386	625	990	13	3.70
Luke Walker	L	26	15	6	.714	3	42	19	5	163	129	89	124	3	3.04
Doc Ellis	R	25	13	10	.565	0	30	30	9	202	194	87	128	4	3.21
Bob Moose (SA)	R	22	11	10	.524	0	28	27	9	190	186	64	119	2	3.98
Steve Blass (EJ)	R	28	10	12	.455	0	31	31	6	197	187	73	120	1	3.52
Bob Veale	L	34	10	15	.400	0	34	32	5	202	189	94	178	1	3.92
Dave Giusti	R	30	9	3	.750	26	66	1	0	103	98	39	85	0	3.06
Bruce Dal Canton	R	28	9	4	.692	1	41	6	1	85	94	39	53	0	4.55
Jim Nelson	R	22	4	2	.667	0	15	10	1	68	64	38	42	1	3.44
2 Mudcat Grant	R	34	2	1	.667	0	8	0	0	12	8	2	4	0	2.25
Orlando Pena	R	36	2	1	.667	2	23	0	0	38	38	7	25	0	4.74
Dick Colpaert	R	26	1	0	1.000	0	8	0	0	11	9	8	6	0	5.73
2 George Brunet	L	35	1	1	.500	0	12	1	0	17	19	9	17	0	2.65
1 Chuck Hartenstein	R	28	1	1	.500	1	17	0	0	24	25	8	14	0	4.50
Fred Cambria	R	22	1	2	.333	0	6	5	0	33	37	12	14	0	3.55
Joe Gibbon	L	35	0	1	.000	5	41	0	0	41	44	24	26	0	4.83
John Lamb	R	23	0	1	.000	3	23	0	0	32	23	13	24	0	2.81

Gene Garber 22 R 0-3, 2 Al McBean 32 R 0-0, Lou Marone 24 L 0-0, Ed Acosta 26 R 0-0

CHICAGO 2nd 84-78 .519 5 — LEO DUROCHER

NAME	G by POS	B	AGE	G	AB	R	H	2B	3B	HR	RBI	BB	SO	SB	BA	SA
TOTALS			30	162	5491	806	1424	228	44	179	761	607	844	39	.259	.415
Ernie Banks (KJ)	1B62	R	39	72	222	25	56	6	2	12	44	20	33	0	.252	.459
Glenn Beckert	2B138, OF1	R	29	143	591	99	170	15	6	3	36	32	22	4	.288	.349
Don Kessinger	SS154	B	27	154	631	100	168	21	14	1	39	66	59	12	.266	.349
Ron Santo	3B152, OF1	R	30	154	555	83	148	30	4	26	114	92	108	2	.267	.476
Johnny Callison	OF144	L	31	147	477	65	126	23	2	19	68	60	63	7	.264	.440
Jim Hickman	OF79, 1B74	R	33	149	514	102	162	33	4	32	115	93	99	0	.315	.582
Billy Williams	OF160	L	32	161	636	137	205	34	4	42	129	72	65	7	.322	.586
Randy Hundley (KJ)	C73	R	28	73	250	13	61	5	0	7	36	16	52	0	.244	.348
Cleo James	OF90	R	29	100	176	33	37	7	2	3	14	17	24	5	.210	.324
Willie Smith	1B43, OF1	L	31	87	167	15	36	9	1	5	24	11	32	2	.216	.371
Paul Popovich	2B22, SS17, 3B16	B	29	78	186	22	47	5	1	4	20	18	18	0	.253	.355
2 Jack Hiatt	C63, 1B2	R	27	66	178	19	43	12	1	2	22	31	48	0	.242	.354
2 Joe Pepitone	OF56, 1B13	L	29	56	213	38	57	9	2	12	44	15	15	0	.268	.498
J. C. Martin	C36, 1B3	L	33	44	77	11	12	1	0	1	4	20	11	0	.156	.208
1 Jimmie Hall	OF8	L	32	28	32	2	3	1	0	0	1	4	12	0	.094	.125
2 Phil Gagliano	2B16, 1B1, 3B1	R	28	26	40	5	6	0	0	0	5	5	5	0	.150	.150
Al Spangler	OF6	L	36	21	14	2	2	1	0	1	1	3	3	0	.143	.429
3 Tommy Davis	OF10	R	31	11	42	4	11	2	0	2	8	1	1	0	.262	.452

Ken Rudolph 23 R 4-40, 1 Boots Day 22 L 2-8, Terry Hughes 21 R 1-3, Brock Davis 26 L 0-3, Adrian Garrett 27 L 0-3, Roger Metzger 22 L 0-2, Roe Skidmore 24 R 1-1

NAME	T	AGE	W	L	PCT	SV	G	GS	CG	IP	H	BB	SO	ShO	ERA
TOTALS		28	84	78	.519	25	162	162	59	1435	1402	475	1000	9	3.76
Ferguson Jenkins	R	26	22	16	.579	0	40	39	24	313	265	60	274	3	3.39
Bill Hands	R	30	18	15	.545	1	39	38	12	265	278	76	170	2	3.70
Ken Holtzman	L	24	17	11	.607	0	39	38	15	288	271	94	202	1	3.38
2 Milt Pappas	R	31	10	8	.556	0	21	20	6	145	135	36	80	2	2.67
Phil Regan	R	33	5	9	.357	12	54	0	0	76	81	32	31	0	4.74
Hank Aguirre	L	38	3	0	1.000	1	17	0	0	14	13	9	11	0	4.50
Jim Colborn	R	24	3	1	.750	4	34	5	0	73	88	23	50	0	3.58
3 Roberto Rodriquez	R	29	3	2	.600	2	26	0	0	43	50	15	46	0	5.86
Joe Decker	R	23	2	7	.222	0	24	17	1	109	108	56	79	0	4.62
Larry Gura	L	22	1	3	.250	1	20	3	1	38	35	23	21	0	3.79
1 Steve Barber	L	31	0	1	.000	0	5	0	0	6	10	6	3	0	9.00
2 Hoyt Wilhelm	R	46	0	1	.000	0	3	0	0	4	4	3	1	0	9.00
Jimmy Dunegan	R	22	0	2	.000	0	7	0	0	13	13	12	3	0	4.85
Archie Reynolds	R	24	0	2	.000	0	7	1	0	15	17	9	9	0	6.60
1 Ted Abernathy	R	37	0	0	.000	1	11	0	0	9	9	5	2	0	2.00
Jim Cosman	R	27	0	0	.000	0	1	0	0	1	3	1	0	0	27.00
3 Bob Miller	R	31	0	0	.000	2	7	1	0	9	6	6	4	0	5.00
Juan Pizarro	L	33	0	0	.000	1	12	0	0	16	16	9	14	0	4.50

NEW YORK 3rd 83-79 .512 6 — GIL HODGES

NAME	G by POS	B	AGE	G	AB	R	H	2B	3B	HR	RBI	BB	SO	SB	BA	SA
TOTALS			27	162	5443	695	1358	211	42	120	640	684	1062	118	.249	.370
Donn Clendenon	1B100	R	34	121	396	65	114	18	3	22	97	39	91	4	.288	.515
Ken Boswell	2B101	L	24	105	351	32	89	13	2	5	44	41	32	5	.254	.345
Bud Harrelson	SS156	B	26	157	564	72	137	18	8	1	42	95	74	23	.243	.309
Joe Foy	3B97	R	27	99	322	39	76	12	0	6	37	68	58	22	.236	.329
Ron Swoboda	OF100	R	26	115	245	29	57	8	2	9	40	40	72	2	.233	.392
Tommie Agee	OF150	R	27	153	636	107	182	30	7	24	75	55	156	31	.286	.469
Cleon Jones	OF130	R	27	134	506	71	140	25	8	10	63	57	87	12	.277	.417
Jerry Grote	C125	R	27	126	415	38	106	14	1	2	34	36	39	2	.255	.308
Art Shamsky	OF58, 1B56	L	28	122	403	48	118	19	2	11	49	49	33	1	.293	.432
Wayne Garrett	3B70, 2B45, SS1	L	22	114	366	74	93	17	4	12	45	81	60	5	.254	.421
Dave Marshall	OF43	L	27	92	189	21	46	10	1	6	29	17	43	4	.243	.402
Mike Jorgenson	1B50, OF10	L	21	76	87	15	17	3	1	3	4	10	23	2	.195	.356
Al Weis	2B44, SS15	R	32	75	121	20	25	7	1	1	11	7	21	1	.207	.306
Ken Singleton	OF51	B	23	69	198	22	52	8	0	5	26	30	48	1	.263	.379
Duffy Dyer	C57	R	24	59	148	8	31	1	0	2	12	21	32	1	.209	.257
Ed Kranepool	1B8	L	25	43	47	2	8	0	0	0	3	5	2	0	.170	.170

Tim Foli 19 R 4-11, Rod Gaspar 24 B 0-14, Ted Martinez 22 R 1-16, Leroy Stanton 24 R 1-4

NAME	T	AGE	W	L	PCT	SV	G	GS	CG	IP	H	BB	SO	ShO	ERA
TOTALS		26	83	79	.512	32	162	162	47	1460	1260	575	1064	10	3.45
Tom Seaver	R	25	18	12	.600	0	37	36	19	291	230	83	283	2	2.81
Jerry Koosman (EJ)	L	27	12	7	.632	0	30	29	5	212	189	71	118	1	3.14
Jim McAndrew	R	26	10	14	.417	2	32	27	9	184	166	38	111	3	3.57
Gary Gentry	R	23	9	9	.500	1	32	29	5	188	155	86	134	2	3.69
Danny Frisella	R	24	8	3	.727	1	30	1	0	66	49	34	54	0	3.00
Ray Sadecki	L	29	8	4	.667	0	28	19	4	139	134	52	89	0	3.88
Nolan Ryan	R	23	7	11	.389	1	27	19	5	132	86	97	125	2	3.41
Ron Taylor	R	32	5	4	.556	13	57	0	0	66	65	16	28	0	3.95
Tug McGraw	L	25	4	6	.400	10	57	0	0	91	77	49	81	0	3.26
2 Ron Herbel	R	32	2	2	.500	1	12*	0	0	13	14	2	8	0	1.38
2 Dean Chance	R	29	0	1	.000	1	3	0	0	2	3	2	0	0	13.50
1 Don Cardwell	R	34	0	2	.000	0	16	1	0	25	31	6	8	0	6.48
Rich Folkers	L	23	0	2	.000	2	16	1	0	29	36	25	15	0	6.52
1 Cal Koonce	R	29	0	2	.000	0	13	0	0	22	25	14	10	0	3.27

*Herbel, also with San Diego, league leader in G with 76

ST. LOUIS 4th 76-86 .469 13 — RED SCHOENDIENST

NAME	G by POS	B	AGE	G	AB	R	H	2B	3B	HR	RBI	BB	SO	SB	BA	SA
TOTALS			28	162	5689	744	1497	218	51	113	688	569	961	117	.263	.379
Dick Allen (LJ)	1B79, 3B38, OF3	R	28	122	459	88	128	17	5	34	101	71	118	5	.279	.560
Julian Javier	2B137	R	33	139	513	62	129	16	3	2	42	24	70	6	.251	.306
Dal Maxvill	SS136, 2B22	R	30	152	399	35	80	5	2	0	28	51	56	0	.201	.223
Joe Torre	3B73, C90, 1B1	R	29	161	624	89	203	27	9	21	100	70	91	2	.325	.498
Leron Lee	OF77	L	22	121	264	28	60	13	1	6	23	24	66	5	.227	.352
Jose Cardenal	OF134	R	26	148	552	73	162	32	6	10	74	45	70	26	.293	.428
Lou Brock	OF152	L	31	155	664	114	202	29	5	13	57	60	99	51	.304	.422
Ted Simmons (MS)	C79	B	20	82	284	29	69	8	2	3	24	37	37	2	.243	.317
Joe Hague	1B82, OF52	L	26	139	451	58	122	16	4	14	68	63	87	2	.271	.417
Vic Davalillo	OF54	L	33	111	183	29	57	14	3	1	33	13	19	4	.311	.437
Carl Taylor	OF46, 1B15, 3B1	R	26	104	245	39	61	12	2	6	45	41	30	5	.249	.388
Milt Ramirez	SS59, 3B1	R	20	62	79	8	15	2	1	0	3	8	9	0	.190	.241
Mike Shannon (IL)	3B31	R	30	55	174	18	37	9	2	0	22	16	20	1	.213	.287
2 Jim Beauchamp	OF10, 1B5	R	30	44	58	8	15	2	0	1	6	8	11	2	.259	.345
Bob Gibson	P34	R	34	40	109	14	33	3	1	2	19	8	25	0	.303	.404
Ed Crosby	SS35, 3B3, 2B2	L	21	38	95	9	24	4	1	0	6	7	5	0	.253	.316
1 Cookie Rojas	2B10, OF3, SS2	R	31	23	47	2	5	0	0	0	2	3	4	0	.106	.106
Luis Melendez	OF18	R	20	21	70	11	21	1	0	0	8	2	12	3	.300	.314
1 Phil Gagliano	3B6, 1B3, 2B2	R	28	18	32	0	6	0	0	0	2	1	3	0	.188	.188

Jim Campbell 27 L 3-13, Jim Kennedy 23 L 3-24, Jerry DaVanon 24 R 2-18, Jose Cruz 22 L 6-17, Joe Nossek 29 R 0-1, Jorge Rogue 20 R 0-1, Bart Zeller 28 R 0-0

NAME	T	AGE	W	L	PCT	SV	G	GS	CG	IP	H	BB	SO	ShO	ERA
TOTALS		26	76	86	.469	20	162	162	51	1476	1483	632	960	11	4.05
Bob Gibson	R	34	23	7	.767	0	34	34	23	294	262	88	274	3	3.12
Steve Carlton	L	25	10	19	.345	0	34	33	13	254	239	109	193	2	3.72
Mike Torrez	R	23	8	10	.444	0	30	28	5	179	168	103	100	1	4.22
Jerry Reuss	L	21	7	8	.467	0	20	20	5	127	132	49	74	2	4.11
Chuck Taylor	R	28	6	7	.462	8	56	7	1	124	116	31	64	1	3.12
Nelson Briles	R	26	6	7	.462	0	30	19	1	107	129	36	59	1	6.22
1 George Culver	R	26	3	3	.500	0	11	7	2	57	64	24	23	0	4.58
2 Frank Linzy	R	29	3	5	.375	2	47	0	0	61	66	23	19	0	3.69
1 Jerry Johnson	R	26	2	0	1.000	1	7	0	0	11	6	3	5	0	3.27
Al Hrabosky	L	20	2	1	.667	0	16	1	0	19	22	7	12	0	4.74
Sal Campisi	R	27	2	2	.500	4	37	0	0	49	53	37	26	0	2.94
2 Ted Abernathy	R	37	1	0	1.000	1	11	0	0	18	15	12	8	0	3.00
Santiago Guzman	R	20	1	1	.500	0	8	3	1	14	14	13	9	0	7.07
Harry Parker	R	22	1	1	.500	0	7	4	0	22	24	15	9	0	3.27
Frank Bertaina	L	26	1	2	.333	0	8	5	0	31	36	15	14	0	3.19
Bob Chlupsa	R	25	0	2	.000	0	14	0	0	16	26	9	10	0	9.00
Billy McCool	L	25	0	3	.000	1	18	0	0	22	20	16	12	0	6.14
Tom Hilgendorf	L	28	0	4	.000	3	23	0	0	21	22	13	13	0	3.86
Reggie Cleveland	R	22	0	4	.000	0	16	1	0	26	31	18	22	0	7.62

2 C. Hartenstein 28 R 0-0, Fred Norman 27 L 0-0, 1 Rich Nye 25 L 0-0

EAST DIVISION

PHILADELPHIA 5th 73-88 .453 15.5 — **FRANK LUCCHESI**

NAME	G by POS	B	AGE	G	AB	R	H	2B	3B	HR	RBI	BB	SO	SB	BA	SA
TOTALS			27	161	5456	594	1299	224	58	101	553	519	1066	72	.238	.356
Deron Johnson	1B154, 3B3	R	31	159	574	66	147	28	3	27	93	72	132	0	.256	.456
Denny Doyle	2B103	L	26	112	413	43	86	10	7	2	16	33	64	6	.208	.281
Larry Bowa	SS143, 2B1	B	24	145	547	50	137	17	6	0	34	21	48	24	.250	.303
Don Money (IJ)	3B119, SS2	L	26	120	447	66	132	25	4	14	66	43	68	4	.295	.463
Ron Stone	OF99, 1B6	L	27	123	321	30	84	12	5	3	39	38	45	5	.262	.358
Larry Hisle	OF121	R	23	126	405	52	83	22	4	10	44	53	139	5	.205	.353
Johnny Briggs (LJ)	OF95	L	26	110	341	43	92	15	7	9	47	39	65	5	.270	.434
Tim McCarver (BH)	C44	L	28	44	164	16	47	11	1	4	14	14	10	2	.287	.439
Tony Taylor	2B59, 3B38, OF18, SS1	R	34	124	439	74	132	26	9	9	55	50	67	9	.301	.462
Byron Browne	OF88	R	27	104	270	29	67	17	2	10	36	33	72	1	.248	.437
Oscar Gamble	OF74	L	20	88	275	31	72	12	4	1	19	27	37	5	.262	.345
Terry Harmon	SS35, 2B14, 3B2	R	26	71	129	16	32	2	4	0	7	12	22	6	.248	.326
Rick Joseph	OF12, 1B10, 3B9	R	30	71	119	7	27	2	1	3	10	6	28	0	.227	.336
Jim Hutto	OF22, 1B12, C5, 3B1	R	22	57	92	7	17	2	0	3	12	5	20	0	.185	.304
Mike Compton	C40	R	25	47	110	8	18	0	1	1	7	9	22	0	.164	.209
Mike Ryan (BH)	C46	R	28	46	134	14	24	8	0	2	11	16	24	0	.179	.284
Doc Edwards	C34	R	32	35	78	5	21	0	0	0	6	4	10	0	.269	.269
Scott Reid	OF18	L	23	25	49	5	6	1	0	0	1	11	22	0	.122	.143
Del Bates	C20	L	30	22	60	1	8	2	0	0	1	6	15	0	.133	.167
Willie Montanez	OF10, 1B5	L	22	18	25	3	6	0	0	0	3	1	4	0	.240	.240
Joe Lis	OF9	R	23	13	37	1	7	2	0	1	4	5	11	0	.189	.324

Sam Parrilla 27 R 2-16, Greg Luzinski 19 R 2-12, John Vukovich 22 R 1-8, Curt Flood (HO) 32

NAME	T	AGE	W	L	PCT	SV	G	GS	CG	IP	H	BB	SO	ShO	ERA
		28	73	88	.453	36	161	161	24	1461	1483	538	1047	8	4.17
Rick Wise	R	24	13	14	.481	0	35	34	5	220	253	65	113	1	4.17
Jim Bunning	R	38	10	15	.400	0	34	33	4	219	233	56	147	0	4.11
Joe Hoerner	L	33	9	5	.643	9	44	0	0	58	53	20	39	0	2.64
Chris Short	L	32	9	16	.360	1	36	34	7	199	211	66	133	2	4.30
Woodie Fryman (SA)	L	30	8	6	.571	0	27	20	4	128	122	43	97	3	4.08
Dick Selma	R	26	8	9	.471	22	73	0	0	134	108	59	153	0	2.75
Barry Lersch	R	25	6	3	.667	3	42	11	3	138	119	47	92	0	3.26
Grant Jackson	L	27	5	15	.250	0	32	23	1	150	170	61	104	0	5.28
Fred Wenz	R	28	2	0	1.000	1	22	0	0	30	27	13	24	0	4.50
Billy Wilson	R	27	1	0	1.000	0	37	0	0	58	57	33	41	0	4.81
Mike Jackson	L	24	1	1	.500	0	5	0	0	6	6	4	4	0	1.50
Lowell Palmer	R	22	1	2	.333	0	38	5	0	102	98	55	85	0	5.47
Billy Champion	R	22	0	2	.000	0	7	1	0	14	21	10	12	0	9.00
Ken Reynolds	L	23	0	0	.000	0	4	0	0	2	3	4	1	0	0.00
Bill Laxton	L	22	0	0	.000	0	2	0	0	2	2	2	2	0	13.50

MONTREAL 6th 73-89 .451 16 — **GENE MAUCH**

NAME	G by POS	B	AGE	G	AB	R	H	2B	3B	HR	RBI	BB	SO	SB	BA	SA
TOTALS			28	162	5411	687	1284	211	35	136	646	659	972	65	.237	.365
Ron Fairly (BF)	1B110, OF4	L	31	119	385	54	111	19	0	15	61	72	64	10	.288	.455
Gary Sutherland	2B97, SS15, 3B1	R	25	116	359	37	74	10	0	3	26	31	22	2	.206	.259
Bobby Wine	SS159	R	31	159	501	40	116	21	3	3	51	39	94	0	.232	.303
Coco Laboy	3B132, 2B3	R	30	137	432	37	86	26	1	5	53	31	81	0	.199	.299
Rusty Staub	OF160	L	26	160	569	98	156	23	7	30	94	112	93	12	.274	.497
Adolfo Phillips	OF75	R	28	92	214	36	51	6	3	6	21	36	51	7	.238	.379
Mack Jones	OF87	L	31	108	271	51	65	11	3	14	32	59	74	5	.240	.458
John Bateman	C137	R	27	139	520	51	123	21	5	15	68	28	75	8	.237	.383
Bob Bailey	3B48, OF44, 1B18	R	27	131	352	77	101	19	3	28	84	72	70	5	.287	.597
Marv Staehle	2B91, SS1	L	28	104	321	41	70	9	1	0	26	39	21	1	.218	.252
Jim Fairey	OF59	L	25	92	211	35	51	9	3	3	25	14	38	1	.242	.355
Jim Gosger	OF71, 1B19	L	27	91	274	38	72	11	2	5	37	35	35	5	.263	.372
Don Hahn	OF61	R	21	82	149	22	38	8	0	0	8	27	27	4	.255	.309
Ron Brand	SS19, 3B12, C9, OF5, 2B3	R	30	72	126	10	30	2	3	0	9	9	16	2	.238	.302
John Boccabella	1B33, C24, 3B1	R	29	61	145	18	39	3	1	5	17	11	24	0	.269	.407
2 Boots Day	OF35	L	22	41	108	14	29	4	0	0	5	6	18	3	.269	.306
1 Jack Hiatt	C12, 1B2	R	27	17	43	4	14	2	0	0	7	14	14	0	.326	.372
Clyde Mashore	OF10	R	25	13	25	2	4	0	0	1	3	4	11	0	.160	.280

Fred Whitfield 32 L 1-15, Jim Qualls 23 B 1-9, 1 Ty Cline (IL) 31 L 1-2, Angel Hermoso 23 R 0-1, Joe Herrara 28 R 0-1

NAME	T	AGE	W	L	PCT	SV	G	GS	CG	IP	H	BB	SO	ShO	ERA
		27	73	89	.451	32	162	162	29	1439	1434	716	914	10	4.50
Carl Morton	R	26	18	11	.621	0	43	37	10	285	281	125	154	4	3.60
Steve Renko	R	25	13	11	.542	1	41	33	7	220	203	101	142	1	4.32
Dan McGinn	L	26	7	10	.412	0	52	19	3	131	154	78	83	2	5.43
Bill Stoneman	R	26	7	15	.318	0	40	30	5	208	209	109	176	3	4.59
Howie Reed	R	33	6	5	.545	5	57	1	0	89	81	40	42	0	3.13
Claude Raymond	R	33	6	7	.462	23	59	0	0	83	76	27	68	0	4.45
John Strohmayer	R	23	3	1	.750	0	42	0	0	76	85	39	74	0	4.86
2 Rich Nye	L	25	3	2	.600	0	8	6	2	46	47	20	21	0	4.11
Mike Wegener (EJ)	R	23	3	6	.333	0	25	16	1	104	100	56	35	0	5.28
2 Mike Marshall	R	27	3	7	.300	3	24	5	0	65	56	29	38	0	3.46
Bill Dillman	R	25	2	3	.400	0	18	0	0	31	28	18	17	0	5.23
2 John O'Donoghue	L	30	2	3	.400	0	9	3	0	22	20	11	6	0	5.32
Baylor Moore	L	19	0	2	.000	0	6	2	0	10	14	8	6	0	7.20
1 Gary Waslewski	R	28	0	2	.000	0	6	4	0	25	23	15	19	0	5.04
Joe Sparma	R	28	0	4	.000	0	9	6	1	29	34	25	23	0	7.14
Ken Johnson	R	37	0	0	.000	0	3	0	0	6	9	1	4	0	7.50
Carroll Sembera	R	28	0	0	.000	0	5	0	0	7	14	11	6	0	18.00

WEST DIVISION

CINCINNATI 1st 102-60 .630 — **SPARKY ANDERSON**

NAME	G by POS	B	AGE	G	AB	R	H	2B	3B	HR	RBI	BB	SO	SB	BA	SA
TOTALS			25	162	5540	775	1498	253	45	191	726	547	984	115	.270	.436
Lee May	1B153	R	27	153	605	78	153	34	2	34	94	38	125	1	.253	.484
Tommy Helms	2B148, SS12	R	29	150	575	42	136	21	1	1	45	21	33	2	.237	.282
Dave Concepcion	SS93, 2B3	R	22	101	265	38	69	6	3	1	19	23	45	10	.260	.317
Tony Perez	3B153, 1B8	R	28	158	587	107	186	28	6	40	129	83	134	8	.317	.589
Pete Rose	OF159	B	29	159	649	120	205	37	9	15	52	73	64	12	.316	.470
Bobby Tolan	OF150	L	24	152	589	112	186	36	6	16	80	62	94	57	.316	.475
Bernie Carbo	OF119	L	22	125	365	54	113	19	3	21	63	94	77	10	.310	.551
Johnny Bench	C140, OF23, 1B12, 3B1	R	22	158	605	97	177	35	4	45	148	54	102	5	.293	.587
Jimmy Stewart	OF48, 2B18, 3B9, 1B1, C1	B	31	101	105	15	28	3	1	1	8	8	13	5	.267	.343
Woody Woodward	SS77, 3B20, 2B10, 1B2	R	27	100	264	23	59	8	3	1	14	20	21	1	.223	.288
Hal McRae	OF46, 3B6, 2B1	R	23	70	165	18	41	6	1	8	23	15	23	0	.248	.442
Angel Bravo	OF22	L	27	65	65	10	18	1	1	0	3	9	13	0	.277	.323
Darrel Chaney	SS30, 2B18, 3B3	B	22	57	95	7	22	3	0	1	4	3	26	1	.232	.295
2 Ty Cline (IL)	OF20, 1B2	L	31	48	63	13	17	7	1	0	8	12	11	1	.270	.413
Pat Corrales	C42	R	29	43	106	9	25	5	1	1	10	8	22	0	.236	.330
Frank Duffy	SS5	R	23	6	11	1	2	2	0	0	0	1	2	1	.182	.364

Bill Plummer 23 R 1-8, Jay Ward 31 R 0-3

NAME	T	AGE	W	L	PCT	SV	G	GS	CG	IP	H	BB	SO	ShO	ERA
		26	102	60	.630	60	162	162	32	1445	1370	592	843	15	3.69
Jim Merritt (EJ)	L	26	20	12	.625	0	35	35	12	234	248	53	136	1	4.08
Gary Nolan	R	22	18	7	.720	0	37	37	4	251	226	96	181	2	3.26
Wayne Simpson (SJ)	R	21	14	3	.824	0	26	26	10	176	125	81	119	2	3.02
Jim McGlothlin	R	26	14	10	.583	0	35	34	5	211	192	86	97	3	3.58
Clay Carroll	R	29	9	4	.692	16	65	0	0	104	104	27	63	0	2.60
Tony Cloninger	R	29	9	7	.563	1	30	18	0	148	136	78	56	0	3.83
Wayne Granger	R	26	6	5	.545	35	67	0	0	85	79	27	38	0	2.65
Don Gullett	L	19	5	2	.714	6	44	2	0	78	54	44	76	0	2.42
Ray Washburn	R	32	4	4	.500	0	35	3	0	66	90	48	37	0	6.95
Milt Wilcox	R	20	3	1	.750	1	5	2	1	22	19	7	13	1	2.45
Jim Maloney (FJ)	R	30	0	1	.000	1	7	3	0	17	26	15	7	0	11.12
Mel Behney (MS)	L	23	0	2	.000	0	5	1	0	10	15	8	2	0	4.50
Pedro Borbon	R	23	0	2	.000	0	12	1	0	17	21	6	6	0	6.88
Bo Belinsky	L	33	0	0	.000	0	3	0	0	8	10	6	6	0	4.50
John Noriega	R	26	0	0	.000	0	8	0	0	18	25	10	6	0	8.00

LOS ANGELES 2nd 87-74 .540 14.5 — **WALT ALSTON**

NAME	G by POS	B	AGE	G	AB	R	H	2B	3B	HR	RBI	BB	SO	SB	BA	SA
TOTALS			28	161	5606	749	1515	233	67	87	695	541	841	138	.270	.382
Wes Parker	1B161	B	30	161	614	84	196	47	4	10	111	79	70	8	.319	.458
Ted Sizemore (LJ)	2B86, OF9, SS2	R	25	96	340	40	104	10	1	1	34	34	19	5	.306	.350
Maury Wills	SS126, 3B4	B	37	132	522	77	141	19	3	0	34	50	34	28	.270	.318
Billy Grabarkewitz	3B97, SS50, 2B20	R	24	156	529	92	153	20	8	17	84	95	149	19	.289	.454
Willie Crawford	OF94	L	23	109	299	48	70	8	6	8	40	33	88	4	.234	.381
Willie Davis	OF143	L	30	146	593	92	181	23	16	8	93	29	54	38	.305	.438
Manny Mota	OF111, 3B1	R	32	124	417	63	127	12	6	3	37	47	37	11	.305	.384
Tom Haller	C106	L	33	112	325	47	93	16	6	10	47	32	35	3	.286	.465
Jim Lefebvre	2B70, 3B21, 1B1	B	27	109	314	33	79	15	1	4	44	29	42	1	.252	.344
Bill Sudakis	3B37, OF3, 1B1	B	24	94	269	37	71	11	0	14	44	35	46	4	.264	.461
Bill Russell	OF79, SS1	R	21	81	278	30	72	11	9	0	28	16	28	9	.259	.363
Andy Kosco	OF58, 1B1	R	28	74	224	21	51	12	0	8	27	1	40	1	.228	.388
Von Joshua	OF41	L	22	72	109	23	29	1	3	1	8	6	24	2	.266	.358
Jeff Torborg	C63	R	28	64	134	11	31	8	0	1	17	14	15	1	.231	.313
Len Gabrielson	OF2, 1B1	L	30	43	42	1	8	2	0	0	6	1	15	0	.190	.238
Steve Garvey	3B27, 2B1	R	21	34	93	8	25	5	0	1	6	6	17	1	.269	.355
Bill Buckner	OF20, 1B1	L	20	28	68	6	13	3	1	0	4	3	7	0	.191	.265
Gary Moore	OF5, 1B1	R	25	7	16	2	3	0	2	0	0	0	1	1	.188	.438

Tom Paciorek 23 R 2-9, Joe Ferguson 23 R 1-4, Bob Stinson 24 B 0-3

NAME	T	AGE	W	L	PCT	SV	G	GS	CG	IP	H	BB	SO	ShO	ERA
		27	87	74	.540	42	161	161	37	1459	1394	496	880	17	3.82
Claude Osteen	L	30	16	14	.533	0	37	37	11	259	280	52	114	4	3.82
Don Sutton	R	25	15	13	.536	0	38	38	10	260	251	78	201	4	4.08
Alan Foster	R	23	10	13	.435	0	33	33	7	199	200	81	83	1	4.25
Bill Singer (IL)	R	26	8	5	.615	0	16	16	5	106	79	32	93	3	3.14
Jim Brewer	L	32	7	6	.538	24	58	0	0	89	66	33	91	0	3.13
Sandy Vance	R	23	7	7	.500	0	20	18	2	115	109	37	45	0	3.13
Joe Moeller	R	27	7	9	.438	4	31	19	2	135	131	43	63	1	3.93
Ray Lamb	R	25	6	1	.857	0	35	0	0	57	59	27	32	0	3.79
Pete Mikkelsen (IL)	R	30	4	2	.667	6	33	0	0	62	48	20	47	0	2.76
Jose Pena	R	27	4	3	.571	4	29	0	0	57	51	29	31	0	4.42
1 Fred Norman	L	27	2	0	1.000	1	30	0	0	62	65	33	47	0	5.23
Mike Strahler	R	23	1	1	.500	1	6	0	0	19	13	10	11	0	1.42
Charlie Hough	R	22	0	0	.000	2	8	0	0	17	18	11	8	0	5.29
1 Al McBean	R	32	0	0	.000	0	1	0	0	1	1	0	0	0	0.00
Camilo Pascual	R	36	0	0	.000	0	10	0	0	14	12	5	8	0	2.57
Jerry Stephenson	R	26	0	0	.000	0	3	0	0	7	11	5	6	0	9.00

SAN FRANCISCO 3rd 86-76 .531 16 — **CLYDE KING** 19-23 .452 **CHARLIE FOX** 67-53 .558

NAME	G by POS	B	AGE	G	AB	R	H	2B	3B	HR	RBI	BB	SO	SB	BA	SA
TOTALS			28	162	5578	831	1460	257	35	165	773	729	1005	83	.262	.409
Willie McCovey	1B146	L	32	152	495	98	143	39	2	39	126	137	75	0	.289	.612
Ron Hunt	2B85, 3B16	R	29	117	367	70	103	17	1	6	41	44	29	1	.281	.381
Hal Lanier	SS130, 2B4, 1B2	R	27	134	438	33	101	13	1	2	41	21	41	1	.231	.279
Alan Gallagher	3B91	R	24	109	282	31	75	15	2	4	28	30	37	2	.266	.376
Bobby Bonds	OF157	R	24	157	663	134	200	36	10	26	78	77	189	48	.302	.504
Willie Mays	OF129, 1B5	R	39	139	478	94	139	15	2	28	83	79	90	5	.291	.506
Ken Henderson	OF146	B	24	148	554	104	163	35	3	17	88	87	78	20	.294	.460
Dick Dietz	C139	R	28	148	493	82	148	36	2	22	107	109	106	0	.300	.515
Tito Fuentes	2B78, SS36, 3B24	B	26	123	435	49	116	13	7	2	32	36	52	4	.267	.343
Jim Ray Hart	3B56, OF18	R	28	76	255	30	72	12	1	8	37	30	29	0	.282	.431
Frank Johnson	OF33, 1B27	R	27	67	161	25	44	1	2	3	31	19	18	1	.273	.360
Bob Heise	SS33, 2B28, 3B2	R	23	67	154	15	36	5	1	1	22	5	13	0	.234	.299
Bob Taylor	OF26, C1	L	26	63	84	12	16	0	0	2	10	12	13	0	.190	.262
Don Mason	2B14	L	25	46	36	4	5	0	0	0	1	5	7	0	.139	.139
1 Bob Burda	1B8, OF1	L	31	28	23	1	6	0	0	0	3	5	2	0	.261	.261
Russ Gibson	C23	R	31	24	69	3	16	6	0	0	6	7	12	0	.232	.319
Johnny Stephenson	C9, OF1	L	29	23	43	3	3	1	0	0	6	2	7	0	.070	.093
Jim Davenport	3B10	R	36	22	37	3	9	1	0	0	4	7	6	0	.243	.270
George Foster	OF7	R	21	9	19	2	6	1	1	1	4	2	5	0	.316	.632
Bernie Williams	OF6	R	21	7	16	2	5	2	0	0	1	2	1	1	.313	.438

Steve Whitaker 27 L 3-27, Ed Goodson 22 L 3-11

NAME	T	AGE	W	L	PCT	SV	G	GS	CG	IP	H	BB	SO	ShO	ERA
		28	86	76	.531	30	162	162	50	1458	1514	604	931	7	4.50
Gaylord Perry	R	31	23	13	.639	0	41	41	23	329	292	84	214	5	3.20
Juan Marichal (IL)	R	32	12	10	.545	0	34	33	14	243	269	48	123	1	4.11
Don McMahon	R	40	9	5	.643	19	61	0	0	94	70	45	74	0	2.97
Rich Robertson	R	25	8	9	.471	1	41	26	6	184	199	96	121	0	4.84
Frank Reberger	R	26	7	8	.467	2	45	18	3	152	178	98	117	0	5.57
Skip Pitlock	L	22	5	5	.500	0	18	15	1	87	92	48	56	0	4.66
Ron Bryant	L	22	5	8	.385	0	34	11	1	96	103	38	66	0	4.78
2 Jerry Johnson	R	26	3	4	.429	3	33	1	0	65	67	38	44	0	4.29
1 Mike McCormick	L	31	3	4	.429	2	23	11	1	78	80	36	37	0	6.23
Mike Davison	L	24	3	5	.375	1	31	0	0	36	46	22	21	0	6.50
2 John Cumberland	L	23	2	0	1.000	0	7	0	0	11	6	4	6	0	0.82
1 Frank Linzy	R	29	2	1	.667	1	20	0	0	26	33	11	16	0	6.92
Don Carrithers	R	20	2	1	.667	0	11	2	0	22	31	14	14	0	7.36
Jim Johnson	L	24	1	0	1.000	0	3	0	0	7	8	5	2	0	7.71
Miguel Puente	R	22	1	3	.250	0	6	4	1	19	25	11	14	0	8.05
Bill Faul	R	30	0	0	.000	1	7	0	0	10	15	6	6	0	7.20

HOUSTON 4th 79-83 .488 23 — HARRY WALKER

NAME	G by POS	B	AGE	G	AB	R	H	2B	3B	HR	RBI	BB	SO	SB	BA	SA
TOTALS			27	162	5574	744	1446	250	47	129	694	598	911	114	.259	.391
Bob Watson	1B83, C6, OF1	R	24	97	327	48	89	19	2	11	61	24	59	1	.272	.443
Joe Morgan	2B142	L	26	144	548	102	147	28	9	8	52	102	55	42	.268	.396
Denis Menke	SS133, 2B21, 1B5, 3B5, OF3	R	29	154	562	82	171	26	6	13	92	82	80	6	.304	.441
Doug Rader	3B154, 1B1	R	25	156	576	90	145	25	3	25	87	57	102	3	.252	.436
Jesus Alou	OF108	R	28	117	458	59	140	27	3	1	44	21	15	3	.306	.384
Cesar Cedeno	OF90	R	19	90	355	46	110	21	4	7	42	15	57	17	.310	.451
Jim Wynn	OF151	R	28	157	554	82	156	32	2	27	88	106	96	24	.282	.493
Johnny Edwards	C139	L	32	140	458	46	101	16	4	7	49	51	63	1	.221	.319
Norm Miller	OF72, C1	L	24	90	226	29	54	9	0	4	29	41	33	3	.239	.332
1 Joe Pepitone	1B50, OF28	L	29	75	279	44	70	9	5	14	35	18	28	5	.251	.470
Marty Martinez	SS29, 3B10, C6, 2B4	R	28	75	150	12	33	3	0	0	12	9	22	0	.220	.240
1 Tommy Davis	OF53	R	31	57	213	24	60	12	2	3	30	7	25	8	.282	.399
Keith Lampard	OF16, 1B2	L	24	53	72	8	17	8	1	0	5	5	24	0	.236	.375
John Mayberry	1B45	L	20	50	148	23	32	3	2	5	14	21	33	1	.216	.365
Cesar Geronimo	OF26	L	22	47	37	5	9	0	0	0	2	2	5	0	.243	.243
1 Jim Beauchamp	OF16	R	30	31	26	3	5	0	0	1	4	3	7	0	.192	.308
Hector Torres	SS22, 2B6	R	24	31	65	6	16	1	2	0	5	6	8	0	.246	.323
Larry Howard	C26, 1B2, OF1	R	25	31	88	11	27	6	0	2	16	10	23	0	.307	.443

Don Bryant 28 R 5-24, Gary Geiger 33 L 1-4, Leon McFadden 26 R 0-0

NAME	T	AGE	W	L	PCT	SV	G	GS	CG	IP	H	BB	SO	ShO	ERA
		27	79	83	.488	35	162	162	36	1456	1491	577	942	6	4.23
Larry Dierker	R	23	16	12	.571	1	37	36	17	270	263	82	191	2	3.87
Jack Billingham	R	27	13	9	.591	0	46	24	8	188	190	63	134	2	3.97
Don Wilson	R	25	11	6	.647	0	29	27	3	184	188	66	94	0	3.91
Fred Gladding	R	34	7	4	.636	18	63	0	0	71	84	24	46	0	4.06
Denny Lemaster	L	31	7	12	.368	3	39	21	3	162	169	65	103	0	4.56
Jim Ray	R	25	6	3	.667	5	52	2	0	105	97	49	67	0	3.26
Ron Cook	L	22	4	4	.500	2	41	7	0	82	80	42	50	0	3.73
Jim Bouton	R	31	4	6	.400	0	29	6	1	73	84	33	49	0	5.42
Wade Blasingame	L	26	3	3	.500	0	13	13	1	78	76	23	55	0	3.46
2 George Culver	R	26	3	3	.500	3	32	0	0	45	44	21	31	0	3.20
Tom Griffin	R	22	3	13	.188	0	23	20	2	111	118	72	72	1	5.76
Ken Forsch	R	23	1	2	.333	0	4	4	1	24	28	5	13	0	5.63
Jack DiLauro	L	27	1	3	.250	3	42	0	0	34	34	17	23	0	4.24
1 Mike Marshall	R	27	0	1	.000	0	4	0	0	5	8	4	5	0	9.00
Dan Osinski	R	36	0	1	.000	0	3	0	0	4	5	2	1	0	9.00
Scipio Spinks	R	22	0	1	.000	0	5	2	0	14	17	9	6	0	9.64
Buddy Harris	R	21	0	0	.000	0	2	0	0	6	6	0	2	0	6.00

ATLANTA 5th 76-86 .469 26 — LUM HARRIS

NAME	G by POS	B	AGE	G	AB	R	H	2B	3B	HR	RBI	BB	SO	SB	BA	SA
TOTALS			29	162	5546	736	1495	215	24	160	692	522	736	58	**.270**	.404
Orlando Cepeda	1B148	R	32	148	567	87	173	33	0	34	111	47	75	6	.305	.543
Felix Millan	2B142	R	26	142	590	100	183	25	5	2	37	35	23	16	.310	.380
Sonny Jackson	SS87	L	25	103	328	60	85	14	3	0	20	45	27	11	.259	.320
Clete Boyer	3B126, SS5	R	33	134	475	44	117	14	1	16	62	41	71	2	.246	.381
Hank Aaron	OF125, 1B11	R	36	150	516	103	154	26	1	38	118	74	63	9	.298	.574
1 Tony Gonzalez	OF119	L	33	123	430	57	114	18	2	7	55	46	45	3	.265	.365
Rico Cartly	OF133	R	31	136	478	84	175	23	3	25	101	77	46	1	**.366**	.584
Bob Tillman	C70	R	33	71	223	19	53	5	0	11	30	20	66	0	.238	.408
Mike Lum	OF98	L	24	123	291	25	74	17	5	7	28	17	43	3	.254	.399
Gil Garrido	SS80, 2B26	R	29	101	367	38	97	5	4	1	19	15	16	0	.264	.308
Hal King	C62	L	26	89	204	29	53	8	0	11	30	32	41	1	.260	.461
Bob Aspromonte	3B30, SS4, 1B1, OF1	R	32	62	127	5	27	3	0	0	7	13	13	0	.213	.236
Bob Didier	C57	B	21	57	168	9	25	2	1	0	7	12	11	1	.149	.173
Tommie Aaron	1B16, OF12	R	30	44	63	3	13	2	0	2	7	3	10	0	.206	.333
2 Jimmie Hall	OF28	L	32	39	47	7	10	2	0	2	4	2	14	0	.213	.381
Ralph Garr	OF21	L	24	37	96	18	27	3	0	0	8	5	12	5	.281	.313
Oscar Brown	OF25	R	24	28	47	6	18	2	1	1	7	7	7	0	.383	.532
Darrell Evans	3B12	L	23	12	44	4	14	1	1	0	9	7	5	0	.318	.386

Dusty Baker 21 R 7-24, Earl Williams 21 R 7-19

NAME	T	AGE	W	L	PCT	SV	G	GS	CG	IP	H	BB	SO	ShO	ERA
		29	76	86	.469	24	162	162	45	1431	1451	478	960	9	4.33
Pat Jarvis	R	29	16	16	.500	0	36	34	11	254	240	72	173	1	3.61
Jim Nash	R	25	13	9	.591	0	34	33	6	212	211	90	163	2	4.08
Phil Niekro	R	31	12	18	.400	0	34	32	10	230	222	68	168	3	4.27
George Stone	L	24	11	11	.500	0	35	30	9	207	218	50	131	2	3.87
Ron Reed (BC)	R	27	7	10	.412	0	21	18	6	135	140	39	68	0	4.40
1 Hoyt Wilhelm	R	46	6	4	.600	13	50	0	0	78	69	39	67	0	3.12
Bob Priddy	R	30	5	5	.500	8	41	0	0	73	75	24	32	0	5.42
2 Don Cardwell	R	34	2	1	.667	0	16	2	1	23	31	13	16	1	9.00
1 Milt Pappas	R	31	2	2	.500	0	11	3	1	36	44	7	25	0	6.00
Larry Jaster	L	26	1	1	.500	0	14	0	0	22	33	8	9	0	6.95
Mike McQueen	L	19	1	5	.167	1	22	8	1	66	67	31	54	0	5.59
2 Steve Barber	L	31	0	1	.000	0	5	2	0	15	17	5	11	0	4.80
Gary Neibauer	R	25	0	3	.000	0	7	0	0	13	11	8	9	0	4.85
Aubrey Gatewood	R	31	0	0	.000	0	3	0	0	2	4	2	0	0	4.50
Rick Kester	R	23	0	0	.000	0	15	0	0	32	36	19	20	0	5.63
Ron Kline	R	38	0	0	.000	1	5	0	0	6	9	2	3	0	7.50
Julio Navarro	R	34	0	0	.000	1	17	0	0	26	24	1	21	0	4.15

Cecil Upshaw (RJ) 27
Jim Britton (EJ) 26

SAN DIEGO 6th 63-99 .389 39 — PRESTON GOMEZ

NAME	G by POS	B	AGE	G	AB	R	H	2B	3B	HR	RBI	BB	SO	SB	BA	SA
TOTALS			27	162	5494	681	1353	208	36	172	629	500	**1164**	60	.246	.391
Nate Colbert	1B153, 3B1	R	24	156	572	84	148	17	6	38	86	56	150	3	.259	.509
Dave Campbell	2B153	R	28	154	581	71	127	28	2	12	40	40	115	18	.219	.336
Tommy Dean (BG)	SS55	R	24	61	158	18	35	5	1	2	13	11	29	2	.222	.304
Ed Spiezio	3B93	R	28	110	316	45	90	18	1	12	42	43	42	4	.285	.462
Ollie Brown	OF137	R	26	139	534	79	156	34	1	23	89	34	78	5	.292	.489
Clarence Gaston	OF142	R	26	146	584	92	186	26	9	29	93	41	142	4	.318	.543
Al Ferrara	OF96	R	30	138	372	44	103	15	4	13	51	46	63	0	.277	.444
Chris Cannizzaro	C110	R	32	111	341	27	95	13	3	5	42	48	49	2	.279	.378
Ivan Murrell	OF101, 1B1	R	25	125	347	43	85	9	3	12	35	17	93	9	.245	.392
Jose Arcia	SS67, 2B20, 3B9, OF7	R	26	114	229	28	51	9	3	0	17	12	36	3	.223	.288
Steve Huntz	SS57, 3B51	B	24	106	352	54	77	8	0	11	37	66	69	0	.219	.335
Ramon Webster	1B15, OF1	L	27	95	116	12	30	3	0	2	11	11	12	1	.259	.336
Bob Barton	C59	R	28	61	188	15	41	6	0	4	16	15	37	1	.218	.314
Ron Slocum	C19, SS17, 3B11, 2B9	R	24	60	71	8	10	2	2	1	11	8	24	0	.141	.268
Larry Stahl	OF20	L	29	52	66	5	12	2	0	0	3	2	14	2	.182	.212
Van Kelly	3B27, 2B1	L	24	38	89	9	15	3	0	1	9	15	21	0	.169	.236
Jerry Morales	OF26	R	21	28	58	6	9	0	1	1	4	3	11	0	.155	.241
Rafael Robles	SS23	R	22	23	89	5	19	1	0	0	3	5	11	3	.213	.225
Dave Robinson	OF13	B	24	15	38	5	12	2	0	2	6	5	4	2	.316	.526

Jim Williams 23 R 4-14, Fred Kendall 21 R 0-9

NAME	T	AGE	W	L	PCT	SV	G	GS	CG	IP	H	BB	SO	ShO	ERA
		26	63	**99**	.389	32	162	162	24	1440	1483	611	886	9	4.36
Pat Dobson	R	28	14	15	.483	1	40	34	8	251	257	78	185	1	3.76
Danny Coombs	L	28	10	14	.417	0	35	27	5	188	185	76	105	1	3.30
Clay Kirby	R	22	10	16	.385	0	36	34	6	215	198	120	154	1	4.52
Dave Roberts	L	25	8	14	.364	1	43	21	3	182	182	43	102	2	3.81
1 Ron Herbel	R	32	7	5	.583	9	**64***	1	0	111	114	39	53	0	4.95
Mike Corkins	R	24	5	6	.455	0	24	18	1	111	109	79	75	0	4.62
Ron Willis	R	26	2	2	.500	4	42	0	0	56	53	28	20	0	4.02
Gary Ross	R	22	2	3	.400	1	33	2	0	62	72	36	39	0	5.23
Steve Arlin	R	24	1	0	1.000	0	2	2	1	13	11	8	3	1	2.77
Jack Baldschun	R	33	1	0	1.000	0	12	0	0	13	24	4	12	0	10.38
2 Earl Wilson	R	35	1	6	.143	0	15	9	0	65	82	19	29	0	4.85
Tom Dukes (BR)	R	27	1	6	.143	10	53	0	0	69	62	25	56	0	4.04
Al Santorini	R	22	1	8	.111	1	21	12	0	76	91	43	41	0	6.04
2 Paul Doyle	L	30	0	2	.000	2	9	0	0	7	9	6	2	0	6.43
Jerry Nyman	L	27	0	2	.000	0	2	2	0	5	8	2	2	0	16.20
2 Roberto Rodriquez	R	29	0	0	.000	3	10	0	0	16	26	5	8	0	6.75

Dick Kelley (SJ) 30

***Herbel, also with New York, league leader in G with 76**

WORLD SERIES – BALTIMORE (AL) 4 CINCINNATI (NL) 1

LINE SCORES

TEAM	1	2	3	4	5	6	7	8	9	10	11	12	R	H	E
Game 1 October 10 at Cincinnati															
BAL (AL)	0	0	0	2	1	0	1	0	0				4	7	2
CIN (NL)	1	0	2	0	0	0	0	0	0				3	5	0
Palmer, Richert (9) — **Nolan**, Carroll (7)															
Game 2 October 11 at Cincinnati															
BAL	0	0	0	1	5	0	0	0	0				6	10	2
CIN	3	0	1	0	0	1	0	0	0				5	7	0
Cuellar, **Phoebus** (3), Drabowsky (5), Lopez (7), Hall (7) — McGlothin, **Wilcox** (5), Carroll (5), Gullett (8)															
Game 3 October 13 at Baltimore															
CIN	0	1	0	0	0	0	2	0	0				3	9	0
BAL	2	0	1	0	1	4	1	0	X				9	10	1
Cloninger, Granger (6), Gullett (7) — **McNally**															
Game 4 October 14 at Baltimore															
CIN	0	1	1	0	1	0	0	3	0				6	8	3
BAL	0	1	3	0	0	1	0	0	0				5	8	0
Nolan, Gullett (3), **Carroll** (6) — Palmer, **Watt** (8), Drabowsky (9)															
Game 5 October 15 at Baltimore															
CIN	3	0	0	0	0	0	0	0	0				3	6	0
BAL	2	2	2	0	1	0	0	2	X				9	15	0
Merritt, Granger (2), Wilcox (3), Cloninger (5), Washburn (7), Carroll (9) — **Cuellar**															

COMPOSITE BATTING

NAME	POS	G	AB	R	H	2B	3B	HR	RBI	BA
Baltimore (AL)										
Totals		5	171	33	50	7	0	10	32	.292
F. Robinson	OF	5	**22**	5	6	0	0	**2**	4	.273
B. Robinson	3B	5	21	5	**9**	**2**	0	**2**	6	.429
Blair	OF	5	19	5	**9**	1	0	0	3	**.474**
Belanger	SS	5	19	0	2	0	0	0	1	.105
Powell	1B	5	17	**6**	5	1	0	**2**	5	.294
Johnson	2B	5	16	2	5	**2**	0	0	2	.313
Buford	OF	4	15	3	4	0	0	1	1	.267
Hendricks	C	3	11	1	4	1	0	1	4	.364
Etchebarren	C	2	7	1	1	0	0	0	0	.143
Palmer	P	2	7	1	1	0	0	0	0	.143
Rettenmund	OF	2	5	2	2	0	0	1	2	.400
McNally	P	1	4	1	1	0	0	1	4	.250
Cuellar	P	2	4	0	0	0	0	0	0	.000
Salmon	PH	1	1	1	1	0	0	0	0	1.000
Crowley	PH	1	1	0	0	0	0	0	0	.000
Drabowsky	P	2	1	0	0	0	0	0	0	.000
Hall	P	1	1	0	0	0	0	0	0	.000
Lopez	P	1	0	0	0	0	0	0	0	.000

Phoebus P 0-0, Richert P 0-0, Watt P 0-0

NAME	POS	G	AB	R	H	2B	3B	HR	RBI	BA
Cincinnati (NL)										
Totals		5	164	20	35	6	1	5	20	.213
Rose	OF	5	20	2	5	1	0	1	2	.250
Bench	C	5	19	3	4	0	0	1	3	.211
Tolan	OF	5	19	5	4	1	0	1	1	.211
May	1B	5	18	**6**	7	**2**	0	**2**	**8**	.389
Helms	2B	5	18	1	4	0	0	0	0	.222
Perez	3B	5	18	2	1	0	0	0	0	.056
McRae	OF	3	11	1	5	**2**	0	0	3	.455
Concepcion	SS	3	9	0	3	0	1	0	3	.333
Carbo	OF	4	8	0	0	0	0	0	0	.000
Woodward	SS	4	5	0	1	0	0	0	0	.200
Cline	PH	3	3	0	1	0	0	0	0	.333
Nolan	P	2	3	0	0	0	0	0	0	.000
Bravo	PH	4	2	0	0	0	0	0	0	.000
Stewart	PH	2	2	0	0	0	0	0	0	.000
Cloninger	P	2	2	0	0	0	0	0	0	.000
McGlothin	P	1	2	0	0	0	0	0	0	.000
Chaney	SS	3	1	0	0	0	0	0	0	.000
Corrales	PH	1	1	0	0	0	0	0	0	.000
Carroll	P	4	1	0	0	0	0	0	0	.000
Gullett	P	3	1	0	0	0	0	0	0	.000

Merritt P 0-1, Granger P 0-0, Wilcox P 0-0, Washburn P 0-0

COMPOSITE PITCHING

NAME	G	IP	H	BB	SO	W	L	SV	ERA
Baltimore (AL)									
Totals	5	45	35	15	23	4	1	2	3.40
Palmer	2	**15.2**	**11**	**9**	9	1	0	0	4.60
Cuellar	2	11.1	10	2	5	1	0	0	3.18
McNally	1	9	9	2	5	1	0	0	3.00
Drabowsky	2	3.1	2	1	1	0	0	0	2.70
Hall	1	2.1	0	0	0	0	0	1	0.00
Phoebus	1	1.2	1	0	0	1	0	0	0.00
Watt	1	1	2	1	3	0	1	0	9.00
Lopez	1	.1	0	0	0	0	0	0	0.00
Richert	1	.1	0	0	0	0	0	1	0.00
Cincinnati (NL)									
Totals	5	43	50	20	33	1	4	0	6.70
Nolan	2	9.1	9	3	9	0	1	0	7.71
Carroll	**4**	9	5	2	**11**	1	0	0	**0.00**
Cloninger	2	7.1	10	5	4	0	1	0	7.36
Gullett	3	6.2	5	4	4	0	0	0	1.35
McGlothin	1	4.1	6	2	2	0	0	0	8.31
Wilcox	2	2	3	0	2	0	1	0	9.00
Granger	2	1.1	7	1	1	0	0	0	33.75
Merritt	1	1.2	3	1	0	0	1	0	21.60
Washburn	1	1.1	2	2	0	0	0	0	13.50

1971 Fast and Blue and Wait 'Til Next Year

In the dying days of the 1970 season, a 21-year-old southpaw with a blazing fastball gave advance notice of his stardom by pitching a no-hitter. The pitcher was Oakland's Vida Blue. By winning nine of his first ten decisions, he began the 1971 season in spectacular fashion to become a major drawing card in the American League. Despite a second-half slump due to pressure, Blue finished with a 24-8 record and pocketed the MVP and the Cy Young Awards, despite the 25-win season of Detroit's Mickey Lolich. Blue's arrival in Oakland further strengthened owner Charley Finley's squad with home-grown talent as hitting stars, Reggie Jackson and Sal Bando, and ace right-hander Catfish Hunter teamed up with the talented Blue to lead the Athletics to an easy win in the Western Division.

The California Angels, expected to contend strongly, finished fourth in a whirlpool of dissension and controversy. Alex Johnson, the eye of the Angel's storm, was fined and benched several times by manager Lefty Phillips for not hustling, and the surly outfielder, on poor terms with all his teammates, was finally suspended for the season on June 26. California's other woe was Tony Conigliaro, obtained from Boston, who retired on July 11, due to deteriorating eyesight suffered in a 1967 beaning.

The Orioles repeated as Eastern Division leaders by waltzing to a 12-game lead over runner-up Detroit. By winning their final 11 games, the Birds finished with over 100 wins for the third straight year. The pitching staff flashed four 20-win aces in Mike Cuellar, Dave McNally, Jim Palmer, and newcomer Pat Dobson, while sluggers, Frank Robinson, Brooks Robinson, and Boog Powell, were joined by Merv Rettenmund as batting stars in the Baltimore lineup. The other big story in the East was the Washington Senators; Denny McLain flopped to a 10-22 mark, Curt Flood jumped the team after only 13 games while his antitrust suit was pending before the Supreme Court, and owner Bob Short added the coup de grace by moving the financially-troubled club to Arlington, Texas, (a Dallas suburb) after the conclusion of the season. The post-season championship play-off resulted in a third-consecutive sweep by the Orioles.

Unlike the junior circuit, the National League witnessed close races. In the West, there was a tooth-and-nail fight between the rival Giants and Dodgers. San Francisco jumped out to a 10½ game lead by the end of May and, as late as September 5, held an 8½ game bulge over Los Angeles. But when Willie McCovey injured his knee, the Giants fell into a hitting slump and went into a tailspin, dropping 16 of their last 24 tilts. By September 14, the Dodgers had melted the lead to only one game—a slim lead that the Giants' pitching aces, Juan Marichal and Gaylord Perry, protected over the last two weeks of the season. With a bad knee troubling McCovey, and 40-year-old Willie Mays tiring after a good start, most of the offense generated by the Giants down the stretch came from the bat of young Bobby Bonds.

The Pittsburgh Pirates again won in the East by staving off a late-season threat from the St. Louis Cardinals and MVP Joe Torre. The Pirates' potent offense boasted of sluggers, Roberto Clemente, Willie Stargell, Manny Sanguillen, Al Oliver, and Bob Robertson, and a deep pitching staff headed by Dock Ellis and Steve Blass.

The Bucs defeated the Giants in four games to win the National League pennant, and then came back from two opening losses to defeat the favored Orioles in seven games in the World Series. The talent-laden Pirates had a myriad of heroes, but the standout performers were veterans, Roberto Clemente, a .414 swinger, and pitcher Steve Blass, whose two wins included a clutch seventh-game four-hitter.

1971 AMERICAN LEAGUE

EAST DIVISION

NAME	G by POS	B	AGE	G	AB	R	H	2B	3B	HR	RBI	BB	SO	SB	BA	SA
BALTIMORE 1st 101-57 .639		EARL WEAVER														
TOTALS			30	158	5303	**742**	1382	207	25	158	**702**	**672**	844	66	**.261**	.398
Boog Powell	1B124	L	29	128	418	59	107	19	0	22	92	82	64	1	.256	.459
Dave Johnson	2B140	R	28	142	510	67	144	26	1	18	72	51	55	3	.282	.443
Mark Belanger	SS149	R	27	150	500	67	133	19	4	0	35	73	48	10	.266	.320
Brooks Robinson	3B156	R	34	156	589	67	160	21	1	20	92	63	50	0	.272	.413
Merv Rettenmund	OF134	R	28	141	491	81	156	23	4	11	75	87	60	15	.318	.448
Paul Blair	OF138	R	27	141	516	75	135	24	8	10	44	32	94	14	.262	.397
Don Buford	OF115	B	34	122	449	**99**	130	19	4	19	54	89	62	15	.290	.477
Ellie Hendricks	C90, 1B3	L	30	101	316	33	79	14	1	9	42	39	38	0	.250	.386
Frank Robinson	OF92, 1B37	R	35	133	455	82	128	16	2	28	99	72	62	3	.287	.516
Andy Etchebarren	C70	R	28	70	222	21	60	8	0	9	29	16	40	1	.270	.428
Tom Shopay (NJ)	OF13	L	26	47	74	10	19	2	0	0	5	3	7	2	.257	.284
Chico Salmon	1B9, 2B9, 3B6, SS5	R	30	42	84	11	15	1	0	2	7	3	21	0	.179	.262
Jerry DaVanon	2B20, SS11, 3B3, 1B1	R	25	38	81	14	19	5	0	0	4	12	20	0	.235	.296
Curt Motton	OF16	R	30	38	53	13	10	1	0	4	8	10	12	0	.189	.434
Clay Dalrymple	C18	L	34	23	49	6	10	1	0	1	6	16	13	0	.204	.286
Terry Crowley	OF6, 1B2	L	24	18	23	2	4	0	0	0	1	3	4	0	.174	.174
Bobby Grich	SS5, 2B2	R	22	7	30	7	9	0	0	1	6	5	8	1	.300	.400
Don Baylor	OF1	R	22	1	2	0	0	0	0	0	1	2	1	0	.000	.000
DETROIT 2nd 91-71 .562 12		BILLY MARTIN														
TOTALS			31	162	**5502**	701	1399	214	38	**179**	562	540	854	35	.254	**.405**
Norm Cash	1B131	L	36	135	452	72	128	10	3	32	91	59	86	1	.283	.531
Dick McAuliffe	2B123, SS7	L	31	128	477	67	99	16	6	18	57	53	67	4	.208	.379
Ed Brinkman	SS159	R	29	159	527	40	120	18	2	1	37	44	54	1	.228	.275
Aurelio Rodriguez	3B153, SS1	R	23	154	604	68	153	30	7	15	39	27	93	4	.253	.401
Al Kaline	OF129, 1B5	R	36	133	405	69	119	19	2	15	54	82	57	4	.294	.462
Mickey Stanley	OF139	R	28	139	401	43	117	14	5	7	41	24	44	1	.292	.404
Willie Horton (IJ)	OF118	R	28	119	450	64	130	25	1	22	72	37	75	1	.289	.496
Bill Freehan	C144, OF1	R	29	148	516	57	143	26	4	21	71	54	48	2	.277	.465
Jim Northrup	OF108, 1B32	L	31	136	459	72	124	26	2	16	71	60	43	7	.270	.442
Dalton Jones	OF16, 3B13, 1B3, 2B1	L	27	83	138	15	35	5	0	5	11	9	21	1	.254	.399
Gates Brown	OF56	L	32	82	195	37	66	2	3	11	29	21	17	4	.338	.549
Ike Brown	1B17, OF9, 2B8, 3B4, SS1	R	29	59	110	20	28	1	0	8	19	19	25	0	.225	.482
2 Tony Taylor	2B51, 3B3	R	35	55	181	27	52	10	2	3	19	12	11	5	.287	.414
Cesar Gutierrez	SS14, 3B5, 2B2	R	28	38	37	8	7	0	0	0	4	0	3	0	.189	.189
Kevin Collins	3B4, OF2, 2B1	L	24	35	41	6	11	2	1	1	4	0	12	0	.268	.439
Jim Price (LJ)	C25	R	29	29	54	4	13	2	0	1	7	6	3	0	.241	.333
Marvin Lane	OF6	R	21	8	14	0	2	0	0	0	1	1	3	0	.143	.143
Tim Hosley	C4, 1B1	R	24	7	16	2	3	0	0	2	6	0	1	0	.188	.563
Gene Lamont	C7	L	24	7	15	2	1	0	0	0	1	0	5	0	.067	.067
John Young	1B1	L	22	2	4	1	2	1	0	0	1	0	0	0	.500	.750
BOSTON 3rd 85-77 .525 18		EDDIE KASKO														
TOTALS			28	162	5401	691	1360	**246**	28	161	650	552	871	51	.252	.397
George Scott	1B143	R	27	146	537	72	141	16	4	24	78	41	102	0	.263	.441
Doug Griffin (XJ)	2B124	R	24	125	483	51	118	23	2	3	27	31	45	11	.244	.319
Luis Aparicio	SS121	R	37	125	491	56	114	23	0	4	45	35	43	6	.232	.303
Rico Petrocelli	3B156	R	28	158	553	82	139	24	4	28	89	91	108	2	.251	.461
Billy Conigliaro	OF100	R	23	101	351	42	92	26	1	11	33	25	68	3	.262	.436
Reggie Smith	OF159	B	26	159	618	85	175	**33**	2	30	96	63	82	11	.283	.489
Carl Yastrzemski	OF146	L	31	148	508	75	129	21	2	15	70	106	60	8	.254	.392
Duane Josephson	C87	R	29	91	306	38	75	14	1	10	39	22	35	2	.245	.395
Joe Lahoud	OF69	L	24	107	256	39	55	9	3	14	32	40	45	2	.215	.438
John Kennedy	2B37, SS33, 3B5	R	30	74	272	41	75	12	5	5	22	14	42	1	.276	.412
Bob Montgomery	C66	R	27	67	205	19	49	11	2	2	24	16	43	1	.239	.341
Mike Fiore	1B12	L	26	51	62	9	11	2	0	1	6	12	14	0	.177	.258
Phil Gagliano	OF11, SS7, 3B4	R	29	47	68	11	22	5	0	0	13	11	5	0	.324	.397
Sonny Siebert	P32	R	34	32	79	10	21	3	0	6	15	1	20	0	.266	.532
Juan Beniquez	SS15	R	21	16	57	8	17	2	0	0	4	3	4	3	.298	.333
Rick Miller	OF14	L	23	15	33	9	11	5	0	1	7	8	8	0	.333	.576
Carlton Fisk	C14	R	23	14	48	7	15	2	1	2	6	1	10	0	.313	.521
Cecil Cooper	1B11	L	21	14	42	9	13	4	1	0	3	5	4	1	.310	.452
Don Pavletich	C8	R	32	14	27	5	7	1	0	1	3	5	5	0	.259	.407
Ben Oglivie	OF11	L	22	14	38	2	10	3	0	0	4	0	5	0	.263	.342
1 George Thomas	OF5	R	33	9	13	0	1	0	0	0	1	1	4	0	.077	.077
Buddy Hunter	2B6	R	23	8	9	2	2	1	0	0	0	2	1	0	.222	.333

NAME	T	AGE	W	L	PCT	SV	G	GS	CG	IP	H	BB	SO	ShO	ERA
		30	**101**	57	**.639**	22	158	158	**71**	1415	1257	416	793	15	**2.99**
Dave McNally (SA)	L	28	21	5	**.808**	0	30	30	11	224	188	58	91	1	2.89
Pat Dobson	R	29	20	8	.714	1	38	37	18	282	248	63	187	4	2.90
Mike Cuellar	L	34	20	9	.690	0	38	38	21	292	250	78	124	4	3.08
Jim Palmer	R	25	20	9	.690	0	37	37	20	282	231	106	184	3	2.68
Dick Hall	R	40	6	6	.500	1	27	0	0	43	52	11	26	0	5.02
Grant Jackson	L	28	4	3	.571	0	29	9	0	78	72	20	51	0	3.12
Eddie Watt (BH)	R	29	3	1	.750	11	35	0	0	40	39	8	26	0	1.80
Pete Richert	L	31	3	5	.375	4	35	0	0	36	26	22	35	0	3.50
Dave Leonhard	R	29	2	3	.400	1	12	6	1	54	51	19	18	1	2.83
2 Dave Boswell	R	26	1	2	.333	0	15	.1	0	25	32	15	14	0	4.32
Tom Dukes	R	28	1	5	.167	4	28	0	0	38	40	8	30	0	3.55
Orlando Pena	R	37	0	1	.000	0	5	0	0	15	16	5	4	0	3.00
1 Jim Hardin	R	27	0	0	.000	0	6	0	0	6	12	3	3	0	4.50
		27	91	71	.562	32	162	162	53	1468	1355	609	**1000**	11	3.63
Mickey Lolich	L	30	**25**	14	.641	0	45	**45**	**29**	**376**	**336**	92	**308**	4	2.92
Joe Coleman	R	24	20	9	.690	0	39	38	16	286	241	96	236	3	3.15
Fred Scherman	L	26	11	6	.647	20	69	1	1	113	91	49	46	0	2.71
Les Cain (SJ)	L	23	10	9	.526	0	26	26	3	145	121	91	118	1	4.34
Tom Timmerman	R	31	7	6	.538	4	52	2	0	84	82	37	51	0	3.86
Joe Niekro	R	26	6	7	.462	1	31	15	0	122	136	49	43	0	4.50
Mike Kilkenny (IL)	L	26	4	5	.444	1	30	11	2	86	83	44	47	0	5.02
Dean Chance	R	30	4	6	.400	0	31	14	0	90	91	50	64	0	3.50
Bill Gilbreth	L	23	2	1	.667	0	9	5	2	30	28	21	14	0	4.80
1 Jim Hannan	R	31	1	0	1.000	0	7	0	0	11	7	7	6	0	3.27
Bill Zepp	R	24	1	1	.500	2	16	4	0	32	41	17	15	0	5.06
1 Daryl Patterson	R	27	0	1	.000	0	12	0	0	9	14	6	5	0	5.00
2 Ron Perranoski	L	35	0	1	.000	2	11	0	0	18	16	3	8	0	2.50
Jack Whillock	R	28	0	2	.000	1	7	0	0	8	10	2	6	0	5.63
Bill Denehy	R	25	0	3	.000	1	31	1	0	49	47	28	27	0	4.22
1 Dave Boswell	R	26	0	0	.000	0	3	0	0	4	3	6	3	0	6.75
Jim Foor	L	22	0	0	.000	0	3	0	0	1	2	4	2	0	18.00
Chuck Seelbach	R	23	0	0	.000	0	5	0	0	4	6	7	1	0	13.50
John Hiller (IL) 28															
		29	85	77	.525	35	162	162	44	1443	**1424**	535	871	11	3.80
Sonny Siebert	R	34	16	10	.615	0	32	32	12	235	220	60	131	4	2.91
Gary Peters	L	34	14	11	.560	1	34	32	9	214	241	70	100	1	4.37
Ray Culp	R	29	14	16	.467	0	35	35	12	242	236	67	151	3	3.61
Jim Lonborg (SJ)	R	29	10	7	.588	0	27	26	5	168	167	67	100	1	4.13
Bill Lee	L	24	9	2	.818	2	47	3	0	102	102	46	74	0	2.74
Sparky Lyle	L	26	6	4	.600	16	50	0	0	52	41	23	37	0	2.77
Bob Bolin	R	32	5	3	.625	6	52	0	0	70	74	24	51	0	4.24
Roger Moret	L	21	4	3	.571	0	13	7	4	71	50	40	47	1	2.92
John Curtis	L	23	2	2	.500	0	5	3	1	26	30	6	19	0	3.12
Ken Tatum	R	27	2	4	.333	9	36	1	0	54	50	25	21	0	4.17
Mike Garman	R	21	1	1	.500	0	3	3	0	19	15	9	6	0	3.79
Mike Nagy	R	23	1	3	.250	0	12	7	0	38	46	20	9	0	6.63
Luis Tiant	R	30	1	7	.125	0	21	10	1	72	73	32	59	0	4.88
Cal Koonce	R	30	0	1	.000	0	13	1	0	21	22	11	9	0	5.57
Ken Brett	L	22	0	3	.000	1	29	2	0	59	57	35	57	0	5.34
Ray Jarvis (AJ) 25															

NEW YORK 4th 82-80 .506 21 — RALPH HOUK

NAME	G by POS	B	AGE	G	AB	R	H	2B	3B	HR	RBI	BB	SO	SB	BA	SA
TOTALS			28	162	5413	648	1377	195	43	97	607	581	717	75	.254	.360
Danny Cater	1B78, 3B52	R	31	121	428	39	118	16	5	4	50	19	25	0	.276	.364
Horace Clarke	2B156	B	31	159	625	76	156	23	7	2	41	64	43	17	.250	.318
Gene Michael	SS136	B	33	139	456	36	102	15	0	3	35	48	64	3	.224	.276
Jerry Kenney	3B109, SS5, 1B1	L	26	120	325	50	85	10	3	0	20	56	38	9	.262	.311
2 Felipe Alou	OF80, 1B42	R	36	131	461	52	133	20	6	8	69	32	24	5	.289	.410
Bobby Murcer	OF143	L	25	146	529	94	175	25	6	25	94	91	60	14	.331	.543
Roy White	OF145	B	27	147	524	86	153	22	7	19	84	86	66	14	.292	.469
Thurman Munson	C117, OF1	R	24	125	451	71	113	15	4	10	42	52	65	6	.251	.368
Johnny Ellis	1B65, C2	R	22	83	238	16	58	12	1	3	34	23	42	0	.244	.340
Jake Gibbs	C51	L	32	70	206	23	45	9	0	5	21	12	23	2	.218	.335
Ron Blomberg	OF57	L	22	64	199	30	64	6	2	7	31	14	23	2	.322	.477
Ron Hansen	3B30, 2B9, SS3	R	33	61	145	6	30	3	0	2	20	9	27	0	.207	.269
2 Ron Swoboda	OF47	R	27	54	138	17	36	2	1	2	20	27	35	0	.261	.333
Jim Lyttle	OF29	L	25	49	86	7	17	5	0	1	7	8	18	0	.198	.291
Frank Baker	SS38	L	24	43	79	9	11	2	0	0	2	16	22	3	.139	.165
1 Ron Woods	OF9	R	28	25	32	4	8	1	0	1	2	4	2	0	.250	.375
1 Curt Blefary	OF6, 1B4	L	27	21	36	4	7	1	0	1	2	3	5	0	.194	.306
Rusty Torres	OF5	B	22	9	26	5	10	3	0	2	3	0	8	0	.385	.731

2 Danny Walton 23 R 2-14, 1 Frank Tepedino 23 L 0-6, Len Boehmer 30 R 0-5

NAME	T	AGE	W	L	PCT	SV	G	GS	CG	IP	H	BB	SO	ShO	ERA
		28	82*	80	.506	12	162	162	67	1452	1382	423	707	15	3.43
Mel Stottlemyre	R	29	16	12	.571	0	35	35	19	270	234	69	132	7	2.87
Fritz Peterson	L	29	15	13	.536	1	37	35	16	274	269	42	139	4	3.05
Stan Bahnsen	R	26	14	12	.538	0	36	34	14	242	221	72	110	3	3.35
Steve Kline	R	23	12	13	.480	0	31	30	15	222	206	37	81	1	2.96
Mike Kekich	L	26	10	9	.526	0	37	24	3	170	167	82	93	0	4.08
Lindy McDaniel	R	35	5	10	.333	4	44	0	0	70	82	24	39	0	5.01
Jack Aker	R	30	4	4	.500	4	41	0	0	56	48	26	24	0	2.57
Roger Hambright	R	22	3	1	.750	2	18	0	0	27	22	10	14	0	4.33
Alan Closter	L	28	2	2	.500	0	14	1	0	28	33	13	22	0	5.14
Bill Burbach	R	23	0	1	.000	0	2	0	0	3	6	5	3	0	12.00
Gary Waslewski	R	29	0	1	.000	1	24	0	0	36	28	16	17	0	3.25
2 Jim Hardin (SJ)	R	27	0	2	.000	0	12	3	0	28	35	9	14	0	5.08
2 Rob Gardner	L	26	0	0	.000	0	2	0	0	3	3	2	2	0	3.00
Gary Jones	L	26	0	0	.000	0	12	0	0	14	19	7	10	0	9.00
Terry Ley	L	24	0	0	.000	0	6	0	0	9	9	9	7	0	5.00

*1 win by forfeit

WASHINGTON 5th 63-96 .396 38.5 — TED WILLIAMS

NAME	G by POS	B	AGE	G	AB	R	H	2B	3B	HR	RBI	BB	SO	SB	BA	SA
TOTALS			27	159	5290	537	1219	189	30	86	500	575	956	68	.230	.326
2 Don Mincher	1B88	L	33	100	323	35	94	15	1	10	45	53	52	2	.291	.437
Tim Cullen	2B78, SS62	R	29	125	403	34	77	13	4	2	26	33	47	2	.191	.258
Toby Harrah	SS116, 3B7	R	22	127	383	45	88	11	3	2	22	40	48	10	.230	.290
Dave Nelson	3B84, 2B1	R	27	85	329	47	92	11	3	5	33	23	29	17	.280	.377
Elliott Maddox	OF103, 3B12	R	23	128	258	38	56	8	2	1	18	51	42	10	.217	.275
Del Unser	OF151	L	26	153	581	63	148	19	6	9	41	59	68	11	.255	.355
Frank Howard	OF100, 1B68	R	34	153	549	60	153	25	2	26	83	77	121	1	.279	.474
Paul Casanova	C83	R	29	94	311	19	63	9	1	5	26	14	52	0	.203	.286
Tommy McCraw	OF60, 1B30	L	30	122	207	33	44	6	4	7	25	19	38	3	.213	.382
Dick Billings	C62, OF32, 3B2	R	28	116	349	32	86	14	0	6	48	21	54	2	.246	.338
Bernie Allen	2B41, 3B34	L	32	97	229	18	61	11	1	4	22	33	27	2	.266	.376
Lenny Randle	2B66	R	22	75	215	27	47	11	0	2	13	24	56	1	.219	.298
Larry Biittner	OF41, 1B3	L	25	66	171	12	44	4	1	0	16	16	20	1	.257	.292
Jeff Burroughs	OF50	R	20	59	181	20	42	9	0	5	25	22	55	1	.232	.365
Joe Foy	3B37, 2B3, SS1	R	28	41	128	12	30	8	0	0	11	27	14	4	.234	.297
Richie Scheinblum	OF13	B	28	27	49	5	7	3	0	0	4	8	5	0	.143	.204
1 Mike Epstein	1B24	L	28	24	85	6	21	1	1	1	9	12	31	1	.247	.318
Don Wert	SS7, 3B7, 2B1	R	32	20	40	2	2	1	0	0	2	4	10	0	.050	.075

Curt Flood 33 R 7-35, 2 Frank Fernandez 28 R 3-30, Jim French 29 L 6-41, Tom Ragland 25 R 4-23, Jim Mason 20 L 3-9, Dick Stelmaszek 22 L 0-9, Bill Fahey 21 L 0-8

NAME	T	AGE	W	L	PCT	SV	G	GS	CG	IP	H	BB	SO	ShO	ERA
		26	63	96*	.396	26	159	159	30	1419	1376	554	762	10	3.70
Dick Bosman	R	27	12	16	.429	0	35	35	7	237	245	71	113	1	3.72
Denny McLain	R	27	10	22	.313	0	33	32	9	217	233	72	103	3	4.27
2 Paul Lindblad	L	29	6	4	.600	8	43	0	0	84	58	29	50	0	2.57
Bill Gogolewski	R	23	6	5	.545	0	27	17	4	124	112	39	70	1	2.76
Joe Grzenda	L	34	5	2	.714	5	46	0	0	70	54	17	56	0	1.93
Casey Cox	R	29	5	7	.417	7	54	11	0	124	131	40	43	0	3.99
Pete Broberg	R	21	5	9	.357	0	18	18	7	125	104	53	89	1	3.46
Denny Riddleberger	L	25	3	1	.750	1	57	0	0	70	67	32	56	0	3.21
Jackie Brown	R	28	3	4	.429	0	14	9	0	47	60	27	21	0	5.94
Jim Shellenback	L	27	3	11	.214	0	40	15	3	120	123	49	47	1	3.53
1 Darold Knowles	L	29	2	2	.500	2	12	0	0	15	17	6	16	0	3.60
Horacio Pina	R	26	1	1	.500	2	56	0	0	58	47	31	38	0	3.57
Jerry Janeski	R	25	1	5	.167	1	23	10	0	62	72	34	19	0	4.94
Mike Thompson	R	21	1	6	.143	0	16	12	0	67	53	54	41	0	4.84

*1 loss by forfeit

CLEVELAND 6th 60-102 .370 43 — AL DARK 42-61 .408 JOHNNY LIPON 18-41 .305

NAME	G by POS	B	AGE	G	AB	R	H	2B	3B	HR	RBI	BB	SO	SB	BA	SA
TOTALS			26	162	5467	543	1303	200	20	109	507	467	868	57	.238	.342
Chris Chambliss	1B108	L	22	111	415	49	114	20	4	9	48	40	83	2	.275	.407
Eddie Leon	2B107, SS24	R	24	131	429	35	112	12	2	4	35	34	69	3	.261	.326
Jack Heidemann (KJ)	SS81	R	21	81	240	16	50	7	0	0	9	12	46	1	.208	.238
Graig Nettles	3B158	L	26	158	598	78	156	18	1	28	86	82	56	7	.261	.435
Vada Pinson	OF141, 1B3	L	32	146	566	60	149	23	4	11	35	21	58	25	.263	.376
Ted Uhlaender	OF131	L	31	141	500	52	144	20	3	2	47	38	44	3	.288	.352
Roy Foster	OF107	R	25	125	396	51	97	21	1	18	45	35	48	6	.245	.439
Ray Fosse	C126, 1B4	R	24	133	486	53	134	21	1	12	62	36	62	4	.276	.397
Chuck Hinton	1B20, OF20, C5	R	37	88	147	13	33	7	0	5	14	20	34	0	.224	.374
Gomer Hodge	1B3, 3B3, 2B2	B	27	80	83	3	17	3	0	1	9	4	19	0	.205	.277
Ted Ford	OF55	R	24	74	196	15	38	6	0	2	14	9	34	2	.194	.255
Frank Baker	OF51	L	26	73	181	18	38	12	1	1	23	12	34	1	.210	.304
Fred Stanley	SS55, 2B3	B	23	60	129	14	29	4	0	2	12	27	25	1	.225	.302
John Lowenstein (LJ)	2B29, OF18, SS3	L	24	58	140	15	26	5	0	4	9	16	28	1	.186	.307
Kurt Bevacqua	2B36, OF5, 3B3, SS2	R	24	55	137	9	28	3	1	3	13	4	28	0	.204	.307
Ken Harrelson	1B40, OF7	R	29	52	161	20	32	2	0	5	14	24	21	1	.199	.304
Ken Suarez	C48	R	28	50	123	10	25	7	0	1	9	18	15	0	.203	.285
Lou Camilli	SS23, 2B16	B	24	39	81	5	16	2	0	0	0	8	10	0	.198	.222
1 Buddy Bradford	OF18	R	26	20	38	4	6	2	1	0	3	6	10	0	.158	.263

1 Larry Brown 31 R 11-50, Jim Clark 24 R 3-18, Tony Horton (IL) 26

NAME	T	AGE	W	L	PCT	SV	G	GS	CG	IP	H	BB	SO	ShO	ERA
		25	60	102	.370	32	162	162	21	1440	1352	770	937	7	4.28
Sam McDowell	L	28	13	17	.433	1	35	31	8	215	160	153	192	2	3.39
Alan Foster	R	24	8	12	.400	0	36	26	3	182	158	82	97	0	4.15
Steve Dunning	R	22	8	14	.364	1	31	29	3	184	173	109	132	1	4.50
Vince Colbert	R	25	7	6	.538	2	50	10	2	143	140	71	74	0	3.97
Ray Lamb	R	26	6	12	.333	1	43	21	3	158	147	69	91	1	3.36
Ed Farmer	R	21	5	4	.556	4	43	4	0	79	77	41	48	0	4.33
Phil Hennigan	R	25	4	3	.571	14	57	0	0	82	80	51	69	0	4.94
Camilo Pascual	R	37	2	2	.500	0	9	1	0	23	17	11	20	0	3.13
Rich Hand (AJ)	R	22	2	6	.250	0	15	12	0	61	74	38	26	0	5.75
Mike Paul	L	26	2	7	.222	0	17	12	1	62	78	14	33	0	5.95
Mark Ballinger	R	22	1	2	.333	0	18	0	0	35	30	13	25	0	4.63
Steve Mingori	L	27	1	2	.333	4	54	0	0	57	31	24	45	0	1.42
Steve Hargan (BN)	R	28	1	13	.071	1	37	16	1	113	138	56	52	0	6.21
Chuck Machemehl	R	24	0	2	.000	3	14	0	0	18	16	15	9	0	6.50
Rick Austin	L	24	0	0	.000	1	23	0	0	23	25	20	20	0	5.09
Bob Kaiser	L	21	0	0	.000	0	5	0	0	6	8	3	4	0	4.50

WEST DIVISION

OAKLAND 1st 101-60 .627 — DICK WILLIAMS

NAME	G by POS	B	AGE	G	AB	R	H	2B	3B	HR	RBI	BB	SO	SB	BA	SA
TOTALS			27	161	5494	691	1383	195	25	160	642	542	1018	80	.252	.384
2 Mike Epstein	1B96	L	28	104	329	43	77	13	0	18	51	62	71	0	.234	.438
Dick Green	2B143, SS1	R	30	144	475	58	116	14	1	12	49	51	83	1	.244	.354
Bert Campaneris	SS133	R	29	134	569	80	143	18	4	5	47	29	64	34	.251	.323
Sal Bando	3B153	R	27	153	538	75	146	23	1	24	94	86	55	3	.271	.452
Reggie Jackson	OF145	L	25	150	567	87	157	29	3	32	80	63	161	16	.277	.508
Rick Monday	OF111	L	25	116	355	53	87	9	3	18	56	49	93	6	.245	.439
Joe Rudi	OF121, 1B5	R	24	127	513	62	137	23	4	10	52	28	62	3	.267	.386
Dave Duncan	C102	R	25	103	363	39	92	13	1	15	40	28	77	1	.253	.419
Angel Mangual	OF81	R	24	94	287	32	82	8	1	4	30	17	27	1	.286	.362
Tommy Davis	1B35, OF16, 2B3, 3B2	R	32	79	219	26	71	8	1	3	42	15	19	7	.324	.411
2 Larry Brown	SS31, 2B23, 3B10	R	31	70	189	14	37	2	1	1	9	7	19	1	.196	.233
Gene Tenace	C52, OF1	R	24	65	179	26	49	7	0	7	25	29	34	2	.274	.430
2 Mike Hegan	1B47, OF2	L	28	65	55	5	13	3	0	0	3	5	13	1	.236	.291
2 Curt Blefary	OF14, C14, 3B5, 2B2	L	27	50	101	15	22	2	0	5	12	15	15	0	.218	.386
George Hendrick	OF36	R	21	42	114	8	27	4	1	0	8	3	20	0	.237	.289
Catfish Hunter	P37	R	25	38	103	14	36	1	1	1	12	2	11	1	.350	.408
1 Don Mincher	1B27	L	33	28	92	9	22	6	1	2	8	20	14	1	.239	.391
Steve Hovley	OF11	L	26	24	27	3	3	2	0	0	3	7	9	2	.111	.185
1 Tony LaRussa		R	26	23	8	3	0	0	0	0	0	0	4	0	.000	.000
Dwain Anderson	SS10, 2B5, 3B1	R	23	16	37	3	10	2	1	0	3	5	9	0	.270	.378
Adrian Garrett	OF5	L	28	14	21	1	3	0	0	1	2	5	7	0	.143	.286

1 Felipe Alou 36 R 2-8, 13 Frank Fernandez 28 R 1-9, 2 Ramon Webster 28 L 0-5, Ron Clark 28 R 0-1

NAME	T	AGE	W	L	PCT	SV	G	GS	CG	IP	H	BB	SO	ShO	ERA
		28	101	60	.627	36	161	161	57	1469	1229	501	999	18	3.05
Vida Blue	L	21	24	8	.750	0	39	39	24	312	209	88	301	8	1.82
Catfish Hunter	R	25	21	11	.656	0	37	37	16	274	225	80	181	4	2.96
Chuck Dobson (EJ)	R	27	15	5	.750	0	30	30	7	189	185	71	100	1	3.81
Diego Segui	R	33	10	8	.556	0	26	21	5	146	122	63	81	0	3.14
Blue Moon Odom (EJ)	R	26	10	12	.455	0	25	25	3	141	147	71	69	1	4.28
Bob Locker	R	33	7	2	.778	6	47	0	0	72	68	19	46	0	2.88
2 Darold Knowles	L	29	5	2	.714	7	43	0	0	53	40	16	40	0	3.57
Rollie Fingers	R	24	4	6	.400	17	48	8	2	129	94	30	98	1	3.00
Ron Klimkowski	R	26	2	2	.500	2	26	0	0	45	37	23	25	0	3.40
2 Mudcat Grant	R	35	1	0	1.000	3	15	0	0	27	25	6	13	0	2.00
1 Paul Lindblad	L	29	1	0	1.000	0	8	0	0	16	18	2	4	0	3.94
Jim Roland	L	28	1	3	.250	1	31	0	0	45	34	19	30	0	3.20
Jim Panther	R	26	0	1	.000	0	4	0	0	6	10	5	4	0	10.50
1 Rob Gardner	L	26	0	0	.000	0	4	1	0	8	8	3	5	0	2.25
2 Daryl Patterson	R	27	0	0	.000	0	4	0	0	6	5	4	2	0	7.50
Marcel Lachemann	R	30	0	0	.000	0	1	0	0	.1	2	1	0	0	54.00

KANSAS CITY 2nd 85-76 .528 16 — BOB LEMON

NAME	G by POS	B	AGE	G	AB	R	H	2B	3B	HR	RBI	BB	SO	SB	BA	SA
TOTALS			27	161	5295	603	1323	225	40	80	573	490	819	130	.250	.353
Gail Hopkins	1B83	L	28	103	295	35	82	16	1	9	47	37	13	3	.278	.431
Cookie Rojas (BN)	2B111, SS2, OF1	R	32	115	414	56	124	22	2	6	59	39	35	8	.300	.406
Freddie Patek	SS147	R	26	147	591	86	158	21	11	6	36	44	80	49	.267	.371
Paul Schaal	3B161	R	28	161	548	80	150	31	6	11	63	103	51	7	.274	.412
Joe Keough	OF100	L	25	110	351	34	87	14	2	3	30	35	26	0	.248	.325
Amos Otis	OF144	R	24	147	555	80	167	26	4	15	79	40	74	52	.301	.443
Lou Piniella (BG)	OF115	R	27	126	448	43	125	21	5	3	51	21	43	5	.279	.368
Jerry May (BG)	C71	R	27	71	218	16	55	13	2	1	24	27	37	0	.252	.344
Bob Oliver	1B68, OF48, 3B2	R	28	128	373	35	91	12	2	8	52	14	88	0	.244	.351
Ed Kirkpatrick	OF61, C59	L	26	120	365	46	80	12	1	9	46	48	60	3	.219	.332
Bobby Knoop	2B52, 3B1	R	32	72	161	14	33	8	1	1	11	15	36	1	.205	.286
Dennis Paepke	C32, OF17	R	26	60	152	11	31	6	0	2	14	8	29	0	.204	.283
Chuck Harrison	1B39	R	30	49	143	9	31	4	0	2	21	11	19	0	.217	.287
Bobby Floyd	SS15, 2B8, 3B1	R	27	31	66	8	10	3	0	0	2	7	21	0	.152	.197
Buck Martinez	C21	R	22	22	46	3	7	2	0	0	1	5	9	0	.152	.196
1 Carl Taylor	OF12	R	27	20	39	3	7	0	0	0	3	5	13	0	.179	.179
2 Ted Savage	OF9	R	35	19	29	2	5	0	0	0	1	3	6	2	.172	.172
Sandy Valdespino	OF15	L	32	18	63	10	20	6	0	2	15	2	5	0	.317	.508
Rich Severson	2B6, SS6, 3B1	B	26	16	30	4	9	0	2	0	1	3	5	0	.300	.433

NAME	T	AGE	W	L	PCT	SV	G	GS	CG	IP	H	BB	SO	ShO	ERA
		27	85	76	.528	44	161	161	34	1420	1301	496	775	15	3.25
Dick Drago	R	26	17	11	.607	0	35	34	15	241	251	46	109	4	2.99
Mike Hedlund	R	24	15	8	.652	0	32	30	7	206	168	72	76	1	2.71
Tom Burgmeier	L	27	9	7	.563	17	67	0	0	88	71	30	44	0	1.74
Bruce Dal Canton	R	29	8	6	.571	0	25	22	2	141	144	44	58	0	3.45
Paul Splittorff	L	24	8	9	.471	0	22	22	6	144	129	35	80	3	2.69
Al Fitzmorris	R	25	7	5	.583	0	36	15	2	127	112	55	53	1	4.18
Jim York	R	23	5	5	.500	3	53	0	0	93	70	44	103	0	2.90
Ted Abernathy	R	38	4	6	.400	23	63	0	0	81	60	50	55	0	2.56
Monty Montgomery	R	24	3	0	1.000	0	3	2	0	21	16	3	12	0	2.14
Ken Wright (SJ)	R	24	3	6	.333	1	21	12	1	78	66	47	56	1	3.69
Wally Bunker	R	26	2	3	.400	0	7	6	0	32	35	6	15	0	5.06
Jim Rooker	L	29	2	7	.222	0	20	7	1	54	59	24	31	1	5.33
Lance Clemons	L	23	1	0	1.000	0	10	3	0	24	26	12	20	0	4.13
Bill Butler (EJ)	L	24	1	2	.333	0	14	6	0	44	45	18	32	0	3.48
Roger Nelson	R	27	0	1	.000	0	13	1	0	34	35	5	29	0	5.29
Mike McCormick	L	32	0	0	.000	0	4	1	0	10	14	5	2	0	9.00

CHICAGO 3rd 79-83 .488 22.5 CHUCK TANNER

NAME	G by POS	B	AGE	G	AB	R	H	2B	3B	HR	RBI	BB	SO	SB	BA	SA
TOTALS			25	162	5382	617	1346	185	30	138	568	562	870	83	.250	.373
Carlos May	1B130, OF9	L	23	141	500	64	147	21	7	7	70	62	61	16	.294	.406
Mike Andrews (BW)	2B76, 1B25	R	27	109	330	45	93	16	0	12	47	67	36	3	.282	.439
Luis Alvarado	SS71, 2B16	R	22	99	264	22	57	14	1	0	8	11	34	1	.216	.277
Bill Melton	3B148	R	25	150	543	72	146	18	2	**33**	86	61	87	3	.269	.492
Walt Williams	OF90, 3B1	R	27	114	361	43	106	17	3	8	35	24	27	5	.294	.424
Jay Johnstone	OF119	L	25	124	388	53	101	14	1	16	40	38	50	10	.260	.425
Rick Reichardt	OF128, 1B9	R	28	138	496	53	138	14	2	19	62	37	90	5	.278	.429
Ed Herrmann	C97	L	24	101	294	32	63	6	0	11	35	44	48	2	.214	.347
Rich McKinney	2B67, OF25, 3B5	R	24	114	369	35	100	11	2	8	46	35	37	0	.271	.377
Lee Richard	SS68, OF16	R	22	87	260	38	60	7	3	2	17	20	46	8	.231	.304
Tom Egan	C77, 1B1	R	25	85	251	29	60	11	1	10	34	26	94	1	.239	.410
Rich Morales	SS57, 3B18, 2B3, OF1	R	27	84	185	19	45	8	0	2	14	22	26	2	.243	.319
Mike Hershberger	OF59	R	31	74	177	22	46	9	0	2	15	30	23	6	.260	.345
Pat Kelly	OF61	L	26	67	213	32	62	6	3	3	22	36	29	14	.291	.390
Ed Stroud	OF44	L	31	53	141	19	25	4	3	0	2	11	20	4	.177	.248
Steve Huntz	2B14, SS7, 3B6	B	25	35	86	10	18	3	1	2	6	7	9	1	.209	.337

Lee Maye (SJ) 36 L 9-44, Bob Spence 25 L 4-27, Chuck Brinkman 26 R 4-20, Tony Muser 23 L 5-16, Ken Hottman 23 R 2-16, Ron Lolich 24 R 1-8

NAME	T	AGE	W	L	PCT	SV	G	GS	CG	IP	H	BB	SO	ShO	ERA
		25	79	83	.488	32	162	162	46	1450	1348	468	976	19	3.12
Wilbur Wood	L	29	22	13	.629	1	44	42	22	334	272	62	210	7	1.91
Tom Bradley	R	24	15	15	.500	2	45	39	7	286	273	74	206	6	2.96
Tommy John	L	28	13	16	.448	0	38	35	10	229	244	58	131	3	3.62
Bart Johnson	R	21	12	10	.545	14	53	16	4	178	148	111	153	0	2.93
Joe Horlen (KJ)	R	33	8	9	.471	2	34	18	3	137	150	30	82	0	4.27
Rich Hinton	L	24	3	4	.429	0	18	2	0	24	27	6	15	0	4.50
Steve Kealey	R	24	2	2	.500	6	54	1	0	77	69	26	50	0	3.86
Terry Forster	L	19	2	3	.400	1	45	3	0	50	46	23	48	0	3.96
Jim Magnuson	L	24	1	1	.500	0	15	4	0	30	30	16	11	0	4.50
Vicente Romo	R	28	1	7	.125	5	45	2	0	72	52	37	48	0	3.38
Stan Perzanowski	R	20	0	1	.000	1	5	0	0	6	14	3	5	0	12.00
Don Eddy	L	24	0	2	.000	0	22	0	0	23	19	19	14	0	2.35
Pat Jacquez	R	24	0	0	.000	0	2	0	0	2	4	2	1	0	4.50
Denny O'Toole	R	22	0	0	.000	0	1	0	0	2	0	1	2	0	0.00

CALIFORNIA 4th 76-86 .469 25.5 LEFTY PHILIPS

NAME	G by POS	B	AGE	G	AB	R	H	2B	3B	HR	RBI	BB	SO	SB	BA	SA
TOTALS			28	162	5495	511	1271	213	18	96	477	441	827	72	.231	.329
Jim Spencer	1B145	L	23	148	510	50	121	21	2	18	59	48	63	0	.237	.392
Sandy Alomar	2B137, SS28	B	27	162	**689**	77	179	24	3	4	42	41	60	39	.260	.321
Jim Fregosi (FJ)	SS74, 1B18, OF7	R	29	107	347	31	81	15	1	5	33	39	61	2	.233	.326
Ken McMullen	3B158	R	29	160	593	63	148	19	2	21	68	53	74	1	.250	.395
Roger Repoz	OF97, 1B13	L	30	113	297	39	59	11	1	13	41	60	69	3	.199	.374
Ken Berry	OF101	R	30	111	298	29	66	17	0	3	22	18	33	3	.221	.309
Tony Gonzalez	OF88	L	34	111	314	32	77	9	2	3	38	28	28	0	.245	.318
Johnny Stephenson	C88	L	30	98	279	24	61	17	0	3	25	22	21	0	.219	.312
Syd O'Brien	SS52, 2B7, 3B6, 1B1, OF1	R	26	90	251	25	50	8	1	5	21	15	33	0	.199	.299
Mickey Rivers (MS)	OF75	L	22	78	268	31	71	12	2	1	12	19	38	13	.265	.336
Tony Conigliaro (IJ)	OF72	R	26	74	266	23	59	18	0	4	15	23	52	3	.222	.335
Billy Cowan	OF40, 1B5	R	32	74	174	12	48	8	0	4	20	7	41	1	.276	.391
Jerry Moses	C63, OF1	R	24	69	181	12	41	8	2	4	15	10	34	0	.227	.359
Alex Johnson (ST)	OF61	R	28	65	242	19	63	8	0	2	21	15	34	5	.260	.318
Jeff Torborg (BG)	C49	R	29	55	123	6	25	5	0	0	5	3	6	0	.203	.244
Tommie Reynolds	OF26, 3B1	R	29	45	86	4	16	3	0	2	8	9	6	0	.186	.291
Chico Ruiz	3B3, 2B2	B	32	31	19	4	5	0	0	0	0	2	7	1	.263	.263
Bruce Christensen	SS24	L	23	29	63	4	17	1	0	0	3	6	5	0	.270	.286

Billy Parker 24 R 16-70, Art Kusnyer 25 R 2-13, Tommy Silverio 25 L 1-3, Rudy Meoli 20 L 0-3, Joe Azcue (HO) 31

NAME	T	AGE	W	L	PCT	SV	G	GS	CG	IP	H	BB	SO	ShO	ERA
		26	76	86	.469	32	162	162	39	**1481**	1246	607	904	11	3.10
Andy Messersmith	R	25	20	13	.606	0	38	38	14	277	224	121	179	4	2.99
Clyde Wright	L	30	16	17	.485	0	37	37	10	277	225	82	135	2	2.99
Rudy May (BW)	L	26	11	12	.478	0	32	31	7	208	160	87	156	2	3.03
Eddie Fisher	R	34	10	8	.556	3	57	3	0	119	92	50	82	0	2.72
Tom Murphy	R	25	6	17	.261	0	37	36	7	243	228	82	89	0	3.78
Dave LaRoche	L	23	5	1	.833	9	56	0	0	72	55	27	63	0	2.50
Lloyd Allen	R	21	4	0	.400	15	54	1	0	91	76	40	73	0	3.10
Rickey Clark	R	25	2	1	.667	1	11	7	1	44	36	28	28	1	2.86
Mel Queen	R	29	2	2	.500	4	44	0	0	66	49	29	53	0	1.77
Andy Hassler	L	19	0	3	.000	0	6	4	0	19	25	15	13	0	3.79
Jim Maloney (GJ)	R	31	0	3	.000	0	13	4	0	30	35	24	13	0	5.10
Archie Reynolds	R	25	0	3	.000	0	15	1	0	27	32	18	15	0	4.67
Fred Lasher	R	29	0	0	.000	0	2	0	0	1	4	2	0	0	36.00
Billy Wynne	R	27	0	0	.000	0	3	0	0	4	6	2	6	0	4.50

MINNESOTA 5th 74-86 .463 26.5 BILL RIGNEY

NAME	G by POS	B	AGE	G	AB	R	H	2B	3B	HR	RBI	BB	SO	SB	BA	SA
TOTALS			28	160	5414	654	**1406**	197	31	116	618	512	846	66	.260	.372
Harmon Killebrew	1B90, 3B64	R	35	147	500	61	127	19	1	28	**119**	**114**	96	3	.254	.464
Rod Carew	2B142, 3B2	L	25	147	577	88	177	16	10	2	48	45	81	6	.307	.380
Leo Cardenas	SS153	R	32	153	554	59	146	25	4	18	75	51	69	3	.264	.421
Steve Braun	3B73, 2B28, SS10, OF2	L	22	128	343	51	87	12	2	5	35	48	50	8	.254	.344
Tony Oliva (KJ)	OF121	L	31	126	487	73	164	30	3	22	81	25	44	4	**.337**	**.546**
Cesar Tovar	OF154, 3B7, 2B2	R	30	157	657	94	**204**	29	3	1	45	45	39	18	.311	.368
Jim Holt	OF106, 1B3	L	27	126	340	35	88	11	3	1	29	16	28	5	.259	.318
George Mitterwald	C120	R	26	125	388	38	97	13	1	13	44	39	104	3	.250	.389
Rich Reese	1B95, OF9	L	29	120	329	40	72	8	3	10	39	20	35	7	.219	.353
Brant Alyea	OF48	R	30	79	158	13	28	4	0	2	15	24	38	1	.177	.241
Jim Nettles	OF62	L	24	70	168	17	42	5	1	6	24	19	24	3	.250	.399
Danny Thompson (AJ)	3B17, 2B3, SS1	R	24	48	57	10	15	2	0	0	7	7	12	0	.263	.298
2 Phil Roof	C29	R	30	31	87	6	21	4	0	0	6	8	18	0	.241	.287
Steve Brye	OF28	R	22	28	107	10	24	1	0	3	11	7	15	3	.224	.318
Rick Renick (KJ)	3B7, OF7	R	27	27	45	4	10	2	0	1	8	5	14	0	.222	.333
2 George Thomas	OF11	R	33	23	30	4	8	1	0	0	2	4	3	0	.267	.300

Eric Soderholm 22 R 10-64, 1 Paul Ratliff 27 L 7-44, Paul Powell 23 R 5-31, Tom Tischinski 26 R 3-23, Chuck Manuel 27 L 2-16, Rick Dempsey 21 R 4-13

NAME	T	AGE	W	L	PCT	SV	G	GS	CG	IP	H	BB	SO	ShO	ERA
		27	74	86	.463	25	160	160	43	1417	1384	529	895	9	3.81
Jim Perry	R	35	17	17	.500	1	40	39	8	270	263	102	126	0	4.23
Bert Blyleven	R	20	16	15	.516	0	38	38	17	278	267	59	224	5	2.82
Jim Kaat	L	32	13	14	.481	0	39	38	15	260	275	47	137	4	3.32
Ray Corbin	R	22	8	11	.421	3	52	11	2	140	141	70	83	0	4.11
Hal Haydel	R	26	4	2	.667	1	31	0	0	40	33	20	29	0	4.28
1 Stan Williams	R	34	4	5	.444	4	46	1	0	78	63	44	47	0	4.15
Tom Hall	L	23	4	7	.364	9	48	11	0	130	104	58	137	0	3.32
Pete Hamm	R	23	2	4	.333	0	13	8	1	44	55	18	16	0	6.75
Steve Luebber	R	21	2	5	.286	1	18	12	0	68	73	37	35	0	5.03
Steve Barber	R	23	1	0	1.000	0	4	2	0	12	8	13	4	0	6.00
Jim Strickland	L	25	1	0	1.000	1	24	0	0	31	20	18	21	0	1.45
Bob Gebhard	R	28	1	2	.333	0	17	0	0	18	17	11	13	0	3.00
1 Ron Perranoski	L	35	1	4	.200	5	36	0	0	43	60	28	21	0	6.70
Sal Campisi	R	28	0	0	.000	0	6	0	0	4	5	4	2	0	4.50

MILWAUKEE 6th 69-92 .429 32 DAVE BRISTOL

NAME	G by POS	B	AGE	G	AB	R	H	2B	3B	HR	RBI	BB	SO	SB	BA	SA
TOTALS			27	161	5185	534	1188	160	23	104	496	543	924	82	.229	.329
2 Johnny Briggs	1B60, OF65	L	27	125	375	51	99	11	1	21	59	71	79	1	.264	.467
Ron Theobald	2B111, SS1, 3B1	R	26	126	388	50	107	12	2	1	23	38	39	11	.276	.325
Rick Auerbach	SS78	R	21	79	236	22	48	10	0	1	9	20	40	3	.203	.258
Tommy Harper	3B70, OF90, 2B1	R	30	152	585	79	151	26	3	14	52	65	92	25	.258	.385
Bill Voss	OF79	L	27	97	275	31	69	4	0	10	30	24	45	2	.251	.375
Dave May	OF142	L	27	144	501	74	139	20	3	16	65	50	59	15	.277	.425
2 Jose Cardenal	OF52	R	27	53	198	20	51	10	0	3	32	13	20	9	.258	.354
Ellie Rodriguez	C114	R	25	115	319	28	67	10	1	1	30	41	51	1	.210	.257
Roberto Pena	1B50, 3B37, SS23, 2B1	R	31	113	274	17	65	9	3	3	28	15	37	2	.237	.325
Andy Kosco	OF45, 1B29, 3B12	R	29	98	264	27	60	6	2	10	39	24	57	1	.227	.379
1 Ted Kubiak	2B48, SS39	B	29	89	260	26	59	6	5	3	17	41	31	0	.227	.323
2 Bob Heise	SS51, 3B11, 2B3, OF1	R	24	68	189	10	48	7	0	0	7	7	15	1	.254	.291
2 Frank Tepedino	1B28	L	23	53	106	11	21	1	0	2	7	4	17	2	.198	.264
1 Mike Hegan	1B45	L	28	46	122	19	27	4	1	4	11	26	19	1	.221	.369
Tom Matchick	3B41, 2B1	L	27	42	114	6	25	1	0	1	7	7	23	3	.219	.254
1 Phil Roof	C39	R	30	41	114	6	22	2	1	1	10	8	28	0	.193	.254
Rob Ellis	3B19, OF15	R	20	36	111	9	22	2	0	0	6	12	24	0	.198	.216
Bobby Mitchell	OF19	R	27	35	55	7	10	1	1	2	6	6	18	0	.182	.345
1 Danny Walton	OF19, 3B1	R	23	30	69	5	14	3	0	2	9	7	22	0	.203	.333
Al Yates	OF12	R	26	24	47	5	13	2	0	1	4	3	7	1	.277	.383
2 Paul Ratliff	C13	L	27	23	41	3	7	1	0	3	7	5	21	0	.171	.415
2 Dick Schofield	3B12, SS4, 2B2	B	36	23	28	2	3	0	0	0	1	2	8	0	.107	.179

Darrell Porter 19 L 15-70, Bernie Smith 29 R 5-36, Gus Gil 31 R 5-32, 1 Ted Savage 35 R 3-17, 1 Floyd Wicker 27 L 1-8, 1 Pete Koegel 23 R 0-3

NAME	T	AGE	W	L	PCT	SV	G	GS	CG	IP	H	BB	SO	ShO	ERA
		27	69	92	.429	32	161	161	32	1416	1303	569	795	**23**	3.38
Marty Pattin	R	28	14	14	.500	0	36	36	9	265	225	73	169	5	3.12
Bill Parsons	R	22	13	17	.433	0	36	35	12	245	219	93	139	4	3.20
Jim Slaton	R	21	10	8	.556	0	26	23	5	148	140	71	63	4	3.77
Skip Lockwood	R	24	10	15	.400	0	33	32	5	208	191	91	115	1	3.33
Lew Krausse	R	28	8	12	.400	0	43	22	1	180	164	62	92	0	2.95
Ken Sanders	R	29	7	12	.368	**31**	**83**	0	0	136	111	34	80	0	1.92
Jerry Bell	R	23	2	1	.667	0	8	0	0	15	10	6	8	0	3.00
John Morris (AJ)	L	29	2	2	.500	1	43	1	0	68	69	27	42	0	3.71
Marcelino Lopez	L	27	2	7	.222	0	31	11	0	68	64	60	42	0	4.63
2 Jim Hannan	R	31	1	1	.500	0	21	1	0	32	38	21	17	0	5.06
Dick Ellsworth	L	31	0	1	.000	0	11	0	0	15	22	7	10	0	4.80
2 Bob Reynolds	R	24	0	1	.000	0	3	0	0	6	4	3	4	0	3.00
Floyd Weaver	R	30	0	1	.000	0	21	0	0	27	33	18	12	0	7.33
Larry Bearnarth	R	29	0	0	.000	0	2	0	0	3	10	2	2	0	18.00
John Gelnar	R	28	0	0	.000	0	2	0	0	1	3	1	0	0	18.00

AMERICAN LEAGUE CHAMPIONSHIP – BALTIMORE (EAST) 3 OAKLAND (WEST) 0

LINE SCORES

TEAM	1	2	3	4	5	6	7	8	9	10	11	12	R	H	E
Game 1 October 3 at Baltimore															
OAK	0	2	0	1	0	0	0	0	0				3	9	0
BAL	0	0	0	1	0	0	4	0	X				5	7	1
Blue, Fingers (8)				**McNally**, Watt (8)											
Game 2 October 4 at Baltimore															
OAK	0	0	0	1	0	0	0	0	0				1	6	0
BAL	0	1	1	0	0	0	1	2	X				5	7	0
Hunter		**Cuellar**													
Game 3 October 5 at Oakland															
BAL	1	0	0	0	2	0	2	0	0				5	12	0
OAK	0	0	1	0	0	1	0	1	0				3	7	0
Palmer		**Segui**, Fingers (5), Knowles (7), Locker (7), Grant (8)													

COMPOSITE BATTING

NAME	POS	G	AB	R	H	2B	3B	HR	RBI	BA
Baltimore										
Totals		3	95	15	26	7	1	4	14	.274
F. Robinson	OF	3	**12**	2	1	1	0	0	1	.083
B. Robinson	3B	3	11	2	**4**	1	0	1	**3**	**.364**
Johnson	2B	3	10	2	3	**2**	0	0	0	.300
Powell	1B	3	10	**4**	3	0	0	**2**	**3**	.300
Blair	OF	3	9	1	3	1	0	0	2	.333
Belanger	SS	3	8	1	2	0	0	0	1	.250
Rettenmund	OF	3	8	0	2	1	0	0	1	.250
Buford	OF	2	7	1	3	0	1	0	0	.429
Hendricks	C	2	4	1	2	0	0	1	2	.500

Etchebarren C 0-5, Motton PH 1-1

NAME	POS	G	AB	R	H	2B	3B	HR	RBI	BA
Oakland										
Totals		3	96	7	22	8	1	3	7	.229
Jackson	OF	3	**12**	2	**4**	1	0	**2**	2	.333
Campaneris	SS	3	**12**	0	2	1	0	0	0	.167
Mangual	OF	3	**12**	1	2	1	1	0	2	.167
Bando	3B	3	11	3	**4**	**2**	0	1	1	**.364**
Davis	1B	3	8	1	3	1	0	0	0	.375
Green	2B	3	7	0	2	0	0	0	0	.286
Rudi	OF	2	7	0	1	1	0	0	0	.143
Duncan	C	2	6	0	3	1	0	0	2	.500

Epstein 1B 1-5, Monday OF 0-3, Tenace C 0-3, Blefary PH 0-1, Hegan PH 0-1

COMPOSITE PITCHING

NAME	G	IP	H	BB	SO	W	L	SV	ERA
Baltimore									
Totals	3	27	22	5	16	3	0	0	2.33
Cuellar	1	**9**	6	1	2	1	0	0	**1.00**
Palmer	1	**9**	**7**	3	**8**	1	0	0	3.00
McNally	1	7	**7**	1	5	1	0	0	3.86
Watt	1	2	2	0	1	0	0	1	0.00
Oakland									
Totals	3	25	26	13	22	0	3	0	5.40
Hunter	1	8	**7**	2	6	0	1	0	5.63
Blue	1	7	**7**	2	**8**	0	1	0	6.43
Segui	1	4.2	6	**6**	4	0	1	0	5.79
Fingers	**2**	2.1	2	1	2	0	0	0	7.71
Grant	1	2	3	0	2	0	0	0	0.00
Locker	1	.2	0	2	0	0	0	0	0.00
Knowles	1	.1	1	0	0	0	0	0	0.00

LINE SCORES

TEAM	1	2	3	4	5	6	7	8	9	10	11	12	R	H	E
Game 1 October 2 at San Francisco															
PIT	0	0	2	0	0	0	2	0	0				4	9	0
SF	0	0	1	0	4	0	0	0	X				5	7	2
Blass, Moose (6), Giusti (8) Perry															
Game 2 October 3 at San Francisco															
PIT	0	1	0	2	1	0	4	0	1				9	15	0
SF	1	1	0	0	0	0	0	0	2				4	9	0
Ellis, Miller (6), Giusti (9) Cumberland, Barr (4), McMahon (5), Carrithers (7), Bryant (7), Hamilton (9)															
Game 3 October 5 at Pittsburgh															
SF	0	0	0	0	0	1	0	0	0				1	5	2
PIT	0	1	0	0	0	0	0	1	X				2	4	1
Marichal Johnson, Giusti (9)															
Game 4 October 6 at Pittsburgh															
SF	1	4	0	0	0	0	0	0	0				5	10	0
PIT	2	3	0	0	0	4	0	0	X				9	11	2
Perry, Johnson (6), McMahon (8) Blass, Kison (3), Giusti (7)															

COMPOSITE BATTING

NAME	POS	G	AB	R	H	2B	3B	HR	RBI	BA
Pittsburgh										
Totals		4	144	24	39	4	0	8	23	.271
Cash	2B	4	**19**	**5**	**8**	**2**	0	0	1	.421
Clemente	OF	4	18	2	6	0	0	0	4	.333
Hebner	3B	4	17	3	5	1	0	2	4	.294
Robertson	1B	4	16	**5**	7	1	0	**4**	**6**	**.438**
Sanguillen	C	4	15	1	4	0	0	0	1	.267
Stargell	OF	4	14	1	0	0	0	0	0	.000
Hernandez	SS	4	13	2	3	0	0	0	1	.231
Oliver	OF	4	12	2	3	0	0	1	5	.250
Clines	OF	1	3	1	1	0	0	1	1	.333
Alley	SS	1	2	1	1	0	0	0	0	.500
Davalillo	PH	2	2	0	0	0	0	0	0	.000
Mazeroski PH 1-1, May PH 0-1, Pagan 3B 0-1										
San Francisco										
Totals		4	132	15	31	5	0	5	14	.235
Fuentes	2B	4	16	4	5	1	0	1	2	.313
Henderson	OF	4	16	3	5	1	0	0	2	.313
Mays	OF	4	15	2	4	**2**	0	1	3	.267
Dietz	C	4	15	0	1	0	0	0	0	.067
McCovey	1B	4	14	2	6	0	0	2	**6**	.429
Speier	SS	4	14	4	5	1	0	1	1	.357
Gallagher	3B	4	10	0	1	0	0	0	0	.100
Klingman	OF	4	9	0	1	0	0	0	0	.111
Bonds	OF	3	8	0	2	0	0	0	0	.250
Hart 3B 0-5, Duffy PH 0-1, Lanier 3B 0-1, Rosario PR 0-0										

COMPOSITE PITCHING

NAME	G	IP	H	BB	SO	W	L	SV	ERA
Pittsburgh									
Totals	4	35	31	16	28	3	1	3	3.34
B. Johnson	1	8	5	3	7	1	0	0	**0.00**
Blass	2	7	14	2	**11**	0	1	0	11.57
Giusti	**4**	5.1	1	2	3	0	0	3	**0.00**
Ellis	1	5	6	**4**	1	1	0	0	3.60
Kison	1	4.2	2	2	3	1	0	0	0.00
Miller	1	3	3	3	3	0	0	0	6.00
Moose	1	2	0	0	0	0	0	0	0.00
San Francisco									
Totals	4	34	39	5	33	1	3	0	2.50
Perry	2	**14.2**	**19**	3	**11**	1	1	0	6.14
Marichal	1	8	4	0	6	0	1	0	2.25
McMahon	2	3	0	0	3	0	0	0	0.00
Cumberland	1	3	7	0	4	0	1	0	9.00
Bryant	1	2	1	1	2	0	0	0	4.50
J. Johnson	1	1.1	1	1	2	0	0	0	13.50
Barr	1	1	3	0	2	0	0	0	9.00
Hamilton	1	1	1	0	3	0	0	0	9.00
Carrithers	1	0	3	0	0	0	0	0	∞

PITTSBURGH 1st 97-65 .599 DANNY MURTAUGH

NAME	G by POS	B	AGE	G	AB	R	H	2B	3B	HR	RBI	BB	SO	SB	BA	SA
TOTALS			28	162	**5674**	**788**	**1555**	223	**61**	**154**	**744**	469	919	65	.274	**.416**
Bob Robertson	1B126	R	24	131	469	65	127	18	2	26	72	60	101	1	.271	.484
Dave Cash	2B105, 3B24, SS3	R	23	123	478	79	138	17	4	2	34	46	33	13	.289	.354
Gene Alley	SS108,3B1	R	30	114	348	38	79	8	7	6	28	35	43	9	.227	.342
Richie Hebner	3B108	L	23	112	388	50	105	17	8	17	67	32	68	2	.271	.487
Roberto Clemente	OF124	R	36	132	522	82	178	29	8	13	86	26	65	1	.341	.502
Al Oliver	OF116, 1B25	L	24	143	529	69	149	31	7	14	64	27	72	4	.282	.446
Willie Stargell	OF135	L	31	141	511	104	151	26	0	**48**	125	83	**154**	0	.295	.628
Manny Sanguillen	C135	R	27	138	533	60	170	26	5	7	81	19	32	6	.319	.426
Vic Davalillo	OF61, 1B16	L	34	99	295	48	84	14	6	1	33	11	31	10	.285	.383
Gene Clines	OF74	R	24	97	273	52	84	12	4	1	24	22	36	15	.308	.392
Jackie Hernandez	SS75, 3B9	R	30	88	233	30	48	7	3	3	26	17	45	0	.206	.300
Bill Mazeroski	2B46, 3B7	R	34	70	193	17	49	3	1	1	16	15	8	0	.254	.295
Jose Pagan (BA)	3B41, OF3, 1B2	R	36	57	158	16	38	1	0	5	15	16	25	0	.241	.342
Rennie Stennett	2B36	R	20	50	153	24	54	5	4	1	15	7	9	1	.353	.458
Milt May	C31	L	20	49	126	15	35	1	0	6	25	9	16	0	.278	.429
Charlie Sands	C3	L	23	28	25	4	5	2	0	1	5	7	6	0	.200	.400

Richie Zisk 22 R 3-15, 2 Carl Taylor 27 R 2-15, Rimp Lanier 22 L 0-4, Frank Taveras 21 R 0-0

NAME	T	AGE	W	L	PCT	SV	G	GS	CG	IP	H	BB	SO	ShO	ERA
		28	**97**	65	**.599**	**48**	162	162	43	1461	1426	470	813	15	3.31
Dock Ellis	R	26	19	9	.679	0	31	31	11	227	207	63	137	2	3.05
Steve Blass	R	29	15	8	.652	0	33	33	12	240	226	68	136	**5**	2.85
Bob Moose	R	23	11	7	.611	1	30	18	3	140	169	35	68	1	4.11
Luke Walker	L	27	10	8	.556	0	28	24	4	160	157	53	86	2	3.54
Bob Johnson	R	28	9	10	.474	0	31	27	7	175	170	55	101	1	3.45
Nelson Briles	R	27	8	4	.667	1	37	14	4	136	131	35	76	2	3.04
Bob Veale	L	35	6	0	1.000	2	37	0	0	46	59	24	40	0	7.04
Bruce Kison	R	21	6	5	.545	0	18	13	2	95	93	36	60	1	3.41
1 Mudcat Grant	R	35	5	3	.625	7	42	0	0	75	79	28	22	0	3.60
Dave Giusti	R	31	5	6	.455	**30**	58	0	0	86	79	31	55	0	2.93
Jim Nelson	R	23	2	2	.500	0	17	2	0	35	27	26	11	0	2.31
3 Bob Miller	R	32	1	2	.333	3	16	0	0	28	20	13	13	0	1.29
Ramon Hernandez	L	30	0	1	.000	4	10	0	0	12	5	2	7	0	0.75
Frank Brosseau	R	26	0	0	.000	0	1	0	0	2	1	0	0	0	0.00
John Lamb (FS)	R	24	0	0	.000	0	2	0	0	4	3	1	1	0	0.00

ST. LOUIS 2nd 90-72 .556 7 RED SCHOENDIENST

NAME	G by POS	B	AGE	G	AB	R	H	2B	3B	HR	RBI	BB	SO	SB	BA	SA
TOTALS			28	163	5610	739	1542	225	54	95	686	543	757	**124**	**.275**	.385
Joe Hague	1B91, OF36	L	27	129	380	46	86	9	3	16	54	58	69	0	.226	.392
Ted Sizemore	2B93, SS39, OF15, 3B1	R	26	135	478	53	126	14	5	3	42	42	26	4	.264	.333
Dal Maxvill	SS140	R	32	142	356	31	80	10	1	0	24	43	45	1	.225	.258
Joe Torre	3B161	R	30	161	634	97	**230**	34	8	24	**137**	63	70	4	**.363**	.555
Matty Alou	OF94, 1B57	L	32	149	609	85	192	28	6	7	74	34	27	19	.315	.415
Jose Cruz	OF83	L	23	83	292	46	80	13	2	9	27	49	35	6	.274	.425
Lou Brock	OF157	L	32	157	640	**126**	200	37	7	7	61	76	107	**64**	.313	.425
Ted Simmons	C130	B	21	133	510	64	155	32	4	7	77	36	50	1	.304	.424
Julian Javier	2B80, 3B1	R	34	90	259	32	67	6	4	3	28	9	33	5	.259	.347
1 Jose Cardenal	OF83	R	27	89	301	37	73	12	4	7	48	29	35	12	.243	.379
Luis Melendez	OF66	R	21	88	173	25	39	3	1	0	11	24	29	2	.225	.254
Jim Beauchamp	1B44, OF1	R	31	77	162	24	38	8	3	2	16	9	26	3	.235	.358
Bob Burda	1B13, OF1	L	32	65	71	6	21	0	0	1	12	10	11	0	.296	.338
Jerry McNertney	C36	R	34	56	128	15	37	4	2	4	22	12	14	0	.289	.445
1 Dick Schofield	SS17, 2B13, 3B3	B	36	34	60	7	13	2	0	1	6	10	9	0	.217	.300
2 Ted Kubiak	SS17, 2B14	B	29	32	72	8	18	3	2	1	10	11	12	1	.250	.389
1 Leron Lee	OF8	L	23	25	28	3	5	1	0	1	2	4	12	0	.179	.321

Bob Stinson 25 B 4-19, Milt Ramirez 21 R 3-11, Jorge Roque 21 R 3-10, Herm Hill (DD) 25

NAME	T	AGE	W	L	PCT	SV	G	GS	CG	IP	H	BB	SO	ShO	ERA
		28	90	72	.556	22	163	163	56	1467	1482	576	911	14	3.85
Steve Carlton	L	26	20	9	.690	0	37	36	18	273	275	98	172	4	3.56
Bob Gibson	R	35	16	13	.552	0	31	31	20	246	215	76	185	**5**	3.04
Jerry Reuss	L	22	14	14	.500	0	36	35	7	211	228	109	131	2	4.78
Reggie Cleveland	R	23	12	12	.500	0	34	34	10	222	238	53	148	2	4.07
Don Shaw	L	27	7	2	.778	2	45	0	0	51	45	31	19	0	2.65
Moe Drabowsky	R	35	6	1	.857	8	51	0	0	60	45	33	49	0	3.45
Frank Linzy	R	30	4	3	.571	6	50	0	0	59	49	27	24	0	2.14
2 Stan Williams	R	34	3	0	1.000	0	10	0	0	13	13	2	8	0	1.38
Chuck Taylor	R	29	3	1	.750	3	43	1	0	71	72	25	46	0	3.55
Chris Zachary	R	27	3	10	.231	0	23	12	1	90	114	26	48	1	5.30
Denny Higgins	R	31	1	0	1.000	0	3	0	0	7	6	2	6	0	3.86
1 Mike Torrez	R	24	1	2	.333	0	9	6	0	36	41	30	8	0	6.00
Rudy Arroyo	L	21	0	1	.000	0	9	0	0	12	18	5	5	0	5.25
3 Daryl Patterson	R	27	0	1	.000	1	13	2	0	27	20	15	11	0	4.33
George Brunet	L	36	0	1	.000	0	7	0	0	9	12	7	4	0	6.00
1 Fred Norman	L	28	0	0	.000	0	4	0	0	4	7	7	4	0	11.25
2 Al Santorini	R	23	0	2	.000	2	19	5	0	50	51	19	21	0	3.78

1 Bob Reynolds 24 R 0-0, Harry Parker 23 R 0-0, Santiago Gozman 21 R 0-0, Bob Chlupsa 26 R 0-0, Al Hrabosky (MS) 21 L 0-0, Mike Jackson 25 L 0-0

CHICAGO 3rd (Tie) 83-79 .512 14 LEO DUROCHER

NAME	G by POS	B	AGE	G	AB	R	H	2B	3B	HR	RBI	BB	SO	SB	BA	SA
TOTALS			31	162	5438	637	1401	202	34	128	603	527	772	44	.258	.378
Joe Pepitone (EJ)	1B95, OF23	L	30	115	427	50	131	19	4	16	61	24	41	1	.307	.482
Glenn Beckert (RJ)	2B129	R	30	131	530	80	181	18	5	2	42	24	24	3	.342	.406
Don Kessinger	SS154	B	28	155	617	77	159	18	6	2	38	52	54	15	.258	.316
Ron Santo	3B149, OF6	R	31	154	555	77	148	22	1	21	88	79	95	4	.267	.423
Johnny Callison	OF89	L	32	103	290	27	61	12	1	8	38	36	55	2	.210	.341
Brock Davis	OF93	L	27	106	301	22	77	7	5	0	28	35	34	0	.256	.312
Billy Williams	OF154	L	33	157	594	86	179	27	5	28	93	77	44	7	.301	.505
2 Chris Cannizzaro	C70	R	33	71	197	18	42	8	1	5	23	28	24	0	.213	.340
Jim Hickman	OF69, 1B44	R	34	117	383	50	98	13	2	19	60	50	61	0	.256	.449
Paul Popovich	2B40, 3B16, SS1	B	30	89	226	24	49	7	1	4	28	14	17	0	.217	.310
Cleo James	OF48, 3B2	R	30	54	150	25	43	7	0	2	13	10	16	6	.287	.373
J. C. Martin	C43, OF1	L	34	47	125	13	33	5	0	2	17	12	16	1	.264	.352
Ferguson Jenkins	P39	R	27	39	115	13	28	7	1	6	20	7	40	0	.243	.478
Ernie Banks	1B20	R	40	39	83	4	16	2	0	3	6	6	14	0	.193	.325
Jose Ortiz	OF30	R	24	36	88	10	26	7	1	0	3	4	10	2	.295	.398
Hector Torres	SS18, 2B4	R	25	31	58	4	13	3	0	0	2	4	10	0	.224	.276
Danny Breeden	C25	R	29	25	65	3	10	1	0	0	4	9	18	0	.154	.169
Ken Rudolph	C25	R	24	25	76	5	15	3	0	0	7	6	20	0	.197	.237
Hal Breeden	1B8	R	27	23	36	1	5	1	0	1	2	2	7	0	.139	.250
4 Frank Fernandez (BG)	C16	R	28	17	41	11	7	1	0	4	4	17	15	0	.171	.488
Carmen Fanzone	OF6, 3B3, 1B2	R	28	12	43	5	8	2	0	2	5	2	7	0	.186	.372

Gene Hiser 22 L 6-29, Randy Hundley (KJ) 29 R 7-21, Bill North 23 R 6-16, Al Spangler 37 L 2-5, 1 Garry Jestadt 24 R 0-3, 3 Ramon Webster 28 L 5-16, Pat Bourque 24 L 7-37

NAME	T	AGE	W	L	PCT	SV	G	GS	CG	IP	H	BB	SO	ShO	ERA
		28	83	79	.512	13	162	162	**75**	1444	1458	411	900	17	3.61
Ferguson Jenkins	R	27	**24**	13	.649	0	39	**39**	**30**	**325**	**304**	37	263	3	2.77
Milt Pappas	R	32	17	14	.548	0	35	35	14	261	279	62	99	**5**	3.52
Bill Hands	R	31	12	18	.400	0	36	35	14	242	248	50	128	1	3.42
Ken Holtzman	L	25	9	15	.375	0	30	29	9	195	213	64	143	3	4.48
Juan Pizarro	L	34	7	6	.538	0	16	14	6	101	78	40	67	3	3.48
Phil Regan	R	34	5	5	.500	6	48	1	0	73	84	33	28	0	3.95
Joe Decker	R	24	3	2	.600	0	21	4	0	46	62	25	37	0	4.70
Burt Hooton	R	21	2	0	1.000	0	3	3	2	21	8	10	22	1	2.14
Bill Bonham	R	22	2	1	.667	0	33	2	0	60	63	36	41	0	4.65
Earl Stephenson	L	23	1	0	1.000	1	16	0	0	20	24	11	11	0	4.50
Ray Newman	L	26	1	2	.333	2	30	0	0	38	30	17	35	0	3.55
Jim Colborn	R	25	0	1	.000	0	14	0	0	10	18	3	2	0	7.20
Ron Tompkins	R	26	0	2	.000	3	35	0	0	40	31	21	20	0	4.05
Larry Gura	L	23	0	0	.000	1	6	0	0	3	6	1	2	0	6.00
1 Bob Miller	R	32	0	0	.000	0	2	0	0	7	10	1	2	0	5.14

NEW YORK 3rd (Tie) 83-79 .512 14 GIL HODGES

NAME	G by POS	B	AGE	G	AB	R	H	2B	3B	HR	RBI	BB	SO	SB	BA	SA
TOTALS			27	162	5477	588	1365	203	29	98	546	547	958	89	.249	.351
Ed Kranepool	1B108, OF11	L	26	122	421	61	118	20	4	14	58	38	33	0	.280	.447
Ken Boswell	2B109	L	25	116	392	46	107	20	1	5	40	36	31	5	.273	.367
Bud Harrelson	SS140	B	27	142	547	55	138	16	6	0	32	53	59	28	.252	.303
Bob Aspromonte	3B97	R	33	104	342	21	77	9	1	5	33	29	25	0	.225	.301
Ken Singleton	OF96	B	24	115	298	34	73	5	0	13	46	61	64	0	.245	.393
Tommie Agee	OF107	R	28	113	425	58	121	19	0	14	50	50	84	28	.285	.428
Cleon Jones	OF132	R	28	136	505	63	161	24	6	14	69	53	87	6	.319	.473
Jerry Grote	C122	R	28	125	403	35	109	25	0	2	35	40	47	1	.270	.347
Dave Marshall	OF64	L	28	100	214	28	51	9	1	3	21	26	54	3	.238	.332
Don Hahn	OF80	R	22	98	178	16	42	5	1	1	11	21	32	2	.236	.292
Tim Foli	2B58, 3B36, SS12, OF1	R	20	97	288	32	65	12	2	0	24	18	50	5	.226	.281
Donn Clendenon	1B72	R	35	88	263	29	65	10	0	11	37	21	78	1	.247	.411
Art Shamsky (XJ)	OF38, 1B1	L	29	68	135	13	25	6	2	5	18	21	18	1	.185	.370
Duffy Dyer	C53	R	25	59	169	13	39	7	1	2	18	14	45	1	.231	.320
Wayne Garrett (MS)	3B53, 2B9	L	23	56	202	20	43	2	0	1	11	28	31	1	.213	.238
Mike Jorgensen	OF31, 1B1	L	22	45	118	16	26	1	1	5	11	11	24	1	.220	.373
Ted Martinez	SS23, 2B13, 3B3, OF1	R	23	38	125	16	36	5	2	1	10	4	22	6	.288	.384

Leroy Stanton 25 R 4-21, John Milner 21 L 3-18, Al Weis 33 R 0-11, Frank Estrada 23 R 1-2

NAME	T	AGE	W	L	PCT	SV	G	GS	CG	IP	H	BB	SO	ShO	ERA
		27	83	79	.512	22	162	162	42	1466	1227	529	**1157**	13	**2.99**
Tom Seaver	R	26	20	10	.667	0	36	35	21	286	210	61	**289**	4	**1.76**
Gary Gentry	R	24	12	11	.522	0	32	31	8	203	167	82	155	3	3.24
Tug McGraw	L	26	11	4	.733	8	51	1	0	111	73	41	109	0	1.70
Nolan Ryan	R	24	10	14	.417	0	30	26	3	152	125	116	137	0	3.97
Danny Frisella	R	25	8	5	.615	12	53	0	0	91	76	30	93	0	1.98
Ray Sadecki	L	30	7	7	.500	0	34	20	5	163	139	44	120	2	2.93
Jerry Koosman (VJ)	L	28	6	11	.353	0	26	24	4	166	160	51	96	0	3.04
Charlie Williams	R	23	5	6	.455	0	31	9	1	90	92	41	53	0	4.80
Ron Taylor	R	33	2	2	.500	2	45	0	0	69	71	11	32	0	3.65
Jim McAndrew	R	27	2	5	.286	0	24	10	0	90	78	32	42	0	4.40
Buzz Capra	R	23	0	1	.000	0	3	0	0	5	3	5	6	0	9.00
Jon Matlack	L	21	0	3	.000	0	7	6	0	37	31	15	24	0	4.14
Don Rose	R	24	0	0	.000	0	1	0	0	2	2	0	1	0	0.00

MONTREAL 5th 71-90 .441 25.5 — **GENE MAUCH**

NAME	G by POS	B	AGE	G	AB	R	H	2B	3B	HR	RBI	BB	SO	SB	BA	SA
TOTALS			28	162	5335	622	1312	197	29	88	567	543	800	51	.246	.343
Ron Fairly	1B135, OF10	L	32	146	447	58	115	23	0	13	71	81	65	1	.257	.396
Ron Hunt	2B133, 3B19	R	30	152	520	89	145	20	3	5	38	58	41	5	.279	.358
Bobby Wine(BW)	SS119	R	32	119	340	25	68	9	0	1	16	25	46	0	.200	.235
Bob Bailey	3B120, OF51, 1B9	R	28	157	545	65	137	21	4	14	83	97	105	13	.251	.382
Rusty Staub	OF162	L	27	162	599	94	186	34	6	19	97	74	42	9	.311	.482
Boots Day	OF120	L	23	127	371	53	105	10	2	4	33	33	39	9	.283	.353
Jim Fairey	OF58	L	26	92	200	19	49	8	1	1	19	12	23	3	.245	.310
John Bateman	C137	R	28	139	492	34	119	17	3	10	56	19	87	1	.242	.350
Gary Sutherland	2B56, SS46, OF4, 3B2	R	26	111	304	25	78	7	2	4	26	18	12	3	.257	.332
Coco Laboy	3B35, 2B2	R	31	76	151	10	38	4	0	1	14	11	19	0	.252	.298
John Boccabella	1B37, C37, 3B2	R	30	74	177	15	39	11	0	3	15	14	26	0	.220	.333
Clyde Mashore	OF47, 3B1	R	26	66	114	20	22	5	0	1	7	10	22	1	.193	.263
2 Ron Woods	OF45	R	28	51	138	26	41	7	3	1	17	19	18	0	.297	.413
Jim Gosger	OF43, 1B6	L	28	51	102	7	16	2	2	0	8	9	17	1	.157	.216
Stan Swanson	OF38	R	27	49	106	14	26	3	0	2	11	10	13	1	.245	.330
Ron Brand	SS22, 3B4, OF4, 2B1, C1	R	31	47	56	3	12	0	0	0	1	3	5	1	.214	.214
Mack Jones	OF27	L	32	43	91	11	15	3	0	3	9	15	24	1	.165	.297
1 Ron Swoboda	OF26	R	27	39	75	7	19	4	3	0	6	11	16	0	.253	.387
Dave McDonald	1B8, OF1	L	28	24	39	3	4	2	0	1	4	4	14	0	.103	.231

Rich Hacker 23 B 4-33, Terry Humphrey 21 R 5-26

NAME	T	AGE	W	L	PCT	SV	G	GS	CG	IP	H	BB	SO	ShO	ERA
		28	71	90	.441	25	162	162	49	1434	1418	658	829	8	4.12
Bill Stoneman	R	27	17	16	.515	0	39	39	20	295	243	146	251	3	3.14
Steve Renko	R	26	15	14	.517	0	40	37	9	276	256	135	129	3	3.75
Ernie McAnally	R	24	11	12	.478	0	31	25	8	178	150	87	98	2	3.89
Carl Morton	R	27	10	18	.357	1	36	35	9	214	252	83	84	0	4.79
John Strohmayer	R	24	7	5	.583	1	27	14	2	114	124	31	56	0	4.34
Mike Marshall	R	28	5	8	.385	23	66	0	0	111	100	50	85	0	4.30
Jim Britton (EJ)	R	27	2	3	.400	0	16	6	0	46	49	27	23	0	5.67
Howie Reed	R	34	2	3	.400	0	43	0	0	57	66	24	25	0	4.26
Dan McGinn	L	27	1	4	.200	0	28	6	1	71	74	42	40	0	5.96
Claude Raymond	R	34	1	7	.125	0	37	0	0	54	81	25	29	0	4.67
John O'Donoghue	L	31	0	0	.000	0	13	0	0	17	19	7	7	0	4.76
2 Mike Torrez	R	24	0	0	.000	0	1	0	0	3	4	1	2	0	0.00

PHILADELPHIA 6th 67-95 .414 30 — **FRANK LUCCHESI**

NAME	G by POS	B	AGE	G	AB	R	H	2B	3B	HR	RBI	BB	SO	SB	BA	SA
TOTALS			26	162	5538	558	1289	209	35	123	522	499	1031	63	.233	.350
Deron Johnson	1B136, 3B22	R	32	158	582	74	154	29	0	34	95	72	146	0	.265	.490
Denny Doyle (NJ)	2B91	L	27	95	342	34	79	12	1	3	24	19	31	4	.231	.298
Larry Bowa	SS157	R	25	159	650	74	162	18	5	0	25	36	61	28	.249	.292
John Vukovich	3B74	R	23	74	217	11	36	5	0	0	14	12	34	2	.166	.189
Roger Freed	OF106, C1	R	25	118	348	23	77	12	1	6	37	44	86	0	.221	.313
Willie Montanez	OF158, 1B9	L	23	158	599	78	153	27	6	30	99	67	105	4	.255	.471
Oscar Gamble	OF80	L	21	92	280	24	62	11	1	6	23	21	35	5	.221	.332
Tim McCarver	C125	L	29	134	474	51	132	20	5	8	46	43	26	5	.278	.392
Don Money	3B68, OF40, 2B20	R	24	121	439	40	98	22	8	7	38	31	80	4	.223	.358
Ron Stone	OF51, 1B3	L	28	95	185	16	42	8	1	2	23	25	36	2	.227	.314
Terry Harmon	2B58, SS9, 3B3, 1B2	R	27	79	221	27	45	4	2	0	12	20	45	3	.204	.240
Joe Lis	OF35	R	24	59	123	16	26	6	0	6	10	16	43	0	.211	.407
Byron Browne (LJ)	OF30	R	28	58	68	5	14	3	0	3	5	8	23	0	.206	.382
B. Pfeil	3B15, C4, OF3, 1B1, 2B1, SS1	R	27	44	70	5	19	3	0	2	9	6	9	1	.271	.400
Mike Ryan	C43	R	29	43	134	9	22	5	1	3	6	10	32	0	.164	.284
Rick Wise	P38	R	25	39	97	14	23	2	1	6	15	3	34	0	.237	.464
1 Tony Taylor	2B14, 3B11, 1B2	R	35	36	107	9	25	2	1	1	5	9	10	2	.234	.299
Larry Hisle	OF27	R	24	36	76	7	15	3	0	0	3	6	22	1	.197	.237
Greg Luzinski	1B28	R	20	28	100	13	30	8	0	3	15	12	32	2	.300	.470
Mike Anderson	OF26	R	20	26	89	11	22	5	1	2	5	13	28	0	.247	.393

2 Pete Koegel 23 R 6-26, 1 Johnny Briggs 27 L 4-22

NAME	T	AGE	W	L	PCT	SV	G	GS	CG	IP	H	BB	SO	ShO	ERA
		29	67	95	.414	25	162	162	31	1471	1396	525	838	10	3.71
Rick Wise	R	25	17	14	.548	0	38	37	17	272	261	70	155	4	2.88
Woodie Fryman	L	31	10	7	.588	2	37	17	3	149	133	46	104	2	3.38
Chris Short	L	33	7	14	.333	1	31	26	5	173	182	63	95	2	3.85
Darrell Brandon	R	30	0	0	.000	1	52	0	0	83	81	47	44	0	3.90
Ken Reynolds	L	24	5	9	.357	0	35	25	2	162	163	82	81	1	4.50
Jim Bunning	R	39	5	12	.294	1	29	16	1	110	126	37	58	0	5.48
Barry Lersch	R	26	5	14	.263	0	38	30	3	214	203	50	113	0	3.79
Joe Hoerner	L	34	4	5	.444	9	49	0	0	73	57	21	57	0	1.97
Billy Wilson	R	28	4	6	.400	7	38	0	0	59	39	22	40	0	3.05
Billy Champion	R	23	3	5	.375	0	37	9	0	109	100	48	49	0	4.38
Wayne Twitchell	R	23	1	0	1.000	0	6	1	0	16	8	10	15	0	0.00
Manny Muniz	R	23	0	1	.000	0	5	0	0	10	9	8	6	0	7.20
Dick Selma (AJ)	R	27	0	2	.000	1	17	0	0	25	21	8	15	0	3.24
Lowell Palmer	R	23	0	0	.000	0	3	1	0	15	13	13	6	0	6.00

WEST DIVISION

SAN FRANCISCO 1st 90-72 .556 — **CHARLIE FOX**

NAME	G by POS	B	AGE	G	AB	R	H	2B	3B	HR	RBI	BB	SO	SB	BA	SA
TOTALS			28	162	5461	706	1348	224	36	140	653	654	1042	101	.247	.378
Willie McCovey (KJ)	1B95	L	33	105	329	45	91	13	0	18	70	64	57	0	.277	.480
Tito Fuentes	2B152	B	27	152	630	63	172	28	6	4	52	18	46	12	.273	.356
Chris Speier	SS156	R	21	157	601	74	141	17	6	8	46	56	90	4	.235	.323
Alan Gallagher	3B128	R	25	136	429	47	119	18	5	5	57	40	57	2	.277	.378
Bobby Bonds	OF154	R	25	155	619	110	178	32	4	33	102	62	137	26	.288	.512
Willie Mays	OF84, 1B48	R	40	136	417	82	113	24	5	18	61	112	123	23	.271	.482
Ken Henderson	OF138, 1B1	B	25	141	504	80	133	26	6	15	65	84	76	18	.264	.429
Dick Dietz	C135	R	29	142	453	58	114	19	0	19	72	97	86	1	.252	.419
Hal Lanier	3B83, 2B13, SS8, 1B3	R	28	109	206	21	48	8	0	1	13	15	26	0	.233	.286
Jimmy Rosario	OF67	B	27	92	192	26	43	6	1	0	13	33	35	7	.224	.266
Fran Healy	C22	R	24	47	93	10	26	3	0	2	11	15	24	1	.280	.376
Dave Kingman	1B20, OF14	R	22	41	115	17	32	10	2	6	24	9	35	5	.278	.557
1 George Foster	OF30	R	22	36	105	11	28	5	0	3	8	6	27	0	.267	.400
Bernie Williams	OF27	R	22	35	73	8	13	1	0	1	5	12	24	1	.178	.233
Frank Johnson	1B9, OF4	R	28	32	49	4	4	1	0	0	5	3	9	0	.082	.102
Jim Ray Hart	3B3, OF3	R	29	31	39	5	10	0	0	2	5	6	8	0	.256	.410
Russ Gibson	C22	R	32	25	57	2	11	1	1	1	7	2	13	0	.193	.298
2 Frank Duffy	SS6, 2B1, 3B1	R	24	21	28	4	5	0	0	0	2	0	10	0	.179	.179
Ed Goodson	1B14	L	23	20	42	4	8	1	0	0	1	2	4	0	.190	.214
1 Bob Heise	3B2	L	24	13	11	2	0	0	0	0	0	0	1	0	.000	.000

2 Floyd Wicker 27 L 3-21, Chris Arnold 23 R 3-13, Jim Howarth 24 L 3-13, Dave Rader 22 L 0-4

NAME	T	AGE	W	L	PCT	SV	G	GS	CG	IP	H	BB	SO	ShO	ERA
		28	90	72	.556	30	162	162	45	1455	1324	471	831	14	3.32
Juan Marichal	R	33	18	11	.621	0	37	37	18	279	244	56	159	4	2.94
Gaylord Perry	R	32	16	12	.571	0	37	37	14	280	255	67	158	2	2.76
Jerry Johnson	R	27	12	9	.571	18	67	0	0	109	93	48	85	0	2.97
Don McMahon	R	41	10	6	.625	4	61	0	0	82	73	37	71	0	4.06
John Cumberland	L	24	9	6	.600	2	45	21	5	185	153	55	65	2	2.92
Ron Bryant (SA)	L	23	7	10	.412	0	27	22	3	140	146	49	79	2	3.79
Don Carrithers	R	21	5	3	.625	1	22	12	2	80	77	37	41	1	4.05
Steve Stone	R	23	5	9	.357	0	24	19	2	111	110	55	63	2	4.14
Frank Reberger (RJ)	R	27	3	0	1.000	0	13	7	0	44	37	19	21	0	3.89
Steve Hamilton	L	37	2	2	.500	4	39	0	0	45	29	11	38	0	3.00
Rich Robertson	R	26	2	2	.500	1	23	6	1	61	66	31	32	0	4.57
Jim Barr	R	23	1	1	.500	0	17	0	0	35	33	5	16	0	3.60
Jim Willoughby	R	22	0	1	.000	0	2	1	0	4	8	1	3	0	9.00

LOS ANGELES 2nd 89-73 .549 1 — **WALT ALSTON**

NAME	G by POS	B	AGE	G	AB	R	H	2B	3B	HR	RBI	BB	SO	SB	BA	SA
TOTALS			28	162	5523	663	1469	213	38	95	631	489	755	76	.266	.370
Wes Parker	1B148, OF18	B	31	157	533	69	146	24	1	6	62	63	63	6	.274	.356
Jim Lefebvre	2B102, 3B7	B	28	119	388	40	95	14	2	12	68	39	55	0	.245	.384
Maury Wills	SS144, 3B4	B	38	149	601	73	169	14	3	3	44	40	44	15	.281	.329
Steve Garvey (BH)	3B79	R	22	81	225	27	51	12	1	7	26	21	33	1	.227	.382
Willie Crawford	OF97	L	24	114	342	64	96	16	6	9	40	28	49	5	.281	.442
Willie Davis	OF157	L	31	158	641	84	198	33	10	10	74	23	47	20	.309	.438
Dick Allen	OF60, 3B67, 1B28	R	29	155	549	82	162	24	1	23	90	93	113	8	.295	.468
Duke Sims	C74	L	30	90	230	23	63	7	2	6	25	30	39	0	.274	.400
Bill Buckner	OF86, 1B11	L	21	108	358	37	99	15	1	5	41	11	18	4	.277	.366
Bob Valentine	SS37, 3B23, 2B21, OF11	R	21	101	281	32	70	10	2	1	25	15	20	5	.249	.310
Manny Mota	OF80	R	33	91	269	24	84	13	5	0	34	20	20	4	.312	.398
Bill Russell	2B41, OF40, SS6	R	22	91	211	29	48	7	4	2	15	11	39	6	.227	.327
Tom Haller	C67	L	34	84	202	23	54	5	0	5	32	25	30	0	.267	.366
Billy Grabarkewitz (AJ)	2B13, 3B10, SS1	R	25	44	71	9	16	5	0	0	6	19	16	1	.225	.296
Bill Sudakis (KJ)	C19, 3B3, 1B1, OF1	B	25	41	83	10	16	3	0	3	7	12	22	0	.193	.337
Joe Ferguson	C35	R	24	36	102	13	22	3	0	2	7	12	15	1	.216	.304

Bobby Darwin 28 R 5-20, Von Joshua 23 L 0-7, Tom Paciorek 24 R 1-2, Ron Cey 23 R 0-2

NAME	T	AGE	W	L	PCT	SV	G	GS	CG	IP	H	BB	SO	ShO	ERA
		28	89	73	.549	33	162	162	48	1450	1363	399	853	18	3.23
Al Downing	L	30	20	9	.690	0	37	36	12	262	245	84	136	5	2.68
Don Sutton	R	26	17	12	.586	1	38	37	12	265	231	55	194	4	2.55
Claude Osteen	L	31	14	11	.560	0	38	38	11	259	262	63	109	4	3.51
Bill Singer	R	27	10	17	.370	0	31	31	8	203	195	71	144	1	4.17
Pete Mikkelsen	R	31	8	5	.615	5	41	0	0	74	67	17	46	0	3.65
Jim Brewer	L	33	6	5	.545	22	55	0	0	81	55	24	66	0	1.89
Doyle Alexander	R	20	6	6	.500	0	17	12	4	92	105	18	30	0	3.82
Jose Pena	R	28	2	0	1.000	1	21	0	0	43	32	18	44	0	3.56
Sandy Vance	R	24	2	1	.667	0	10	3	0	26	38	9	11	0	6.92
Bob O'Brien	L	22	2	2	.500	0	14	4	1	42	42	13	15	1	3.00
Joe Moeller	R	28	2	4	.333	1	28	1	0	66	72	12	32	0	3.82
2 Hoyt Wilhelm	R	47	0	1	.000	3	9	0	0	18	6	4	15	0	1.00
Charlie Hough	R	23	0	0	.000	0	4	0	0	4	3	3	4	0	4.50
Mike Strahler	R	24	0	0	.000	0	6	0	0	13	10	8	7	0	2.77

ATLANTA 3rd 82-80 .506 8 — **LUM HARRIS**

NAME	G by POS	B	AGE	G	AB	R	H	2B	3B	HR	RBI	BB	SO	SB	BA	SA
TOTALS			27	162	5575	643	1434	192	30	153	597	434	747	57	.257	.385
Hank Aaron	1B71, OF60	R	37	139	495	95	162	22	3	47	118	71	58	1	.327	.669
Felix Millan	2B141	R	27	143	577	65	167	20	8	2	45	37	22	11	.289	.362
Marty Perez	SS126, 2B1	R	24	130	410	28	93	15	3	4	32	25	44	1	.227	.307
Darrell Evans	3B72, OF3	L	24	89	260	42	63	11	1	12	38	39	54	2	.242	.431
Mike Lum	OF125, 1B1	L	25	145	454	56	122	14	1	13	55	47	43	0	.269	.390
Sonny Jackson	OF145	L	26	149	547	58	141	20	5	2	25	35	45	7	.258	.324
Ralph Garr	OF153	L	25	154	639	101	219	24	6	9	44	30	68	30	.343	.441
Earl Williams	C72, 3B42, 1B31	R	22	145	497	64	129	14	1	33	87	42	80	0	.260	.491
Hal King	C60	L	27	86	198	14	41	9	0	5	19	29	43	0	.207	.328
Gil Garrido	SS32, 3B28, 2B18	R	30	79	125	8	27	3	0	0	12	15	12	0	.216	.240
Orlando Cepeda (KJ)	1B63	R	33	71	250	31	69	10	1	14	44	22	29	3	.276	.492
Zoilo Versalles	3B30, SS24, 2B1	R	31	66	194	21	37	11	0	5	22	11	40	2	.191	.325
Bob Didier	C50	B	22	51	155	9	34	4	1	0	5	6	17	0	.219	.258
Clete Boyer	3B25, SS1	R	34	30	98	10	24	1	0	6	19	8	11	0	.245	.439
Dusty Baker	OF18	R	22	29	62	2	14	2	0	0	4	1	14	0	.226	.258
Oscar Brown	OF15	R	25	27	43	4	9	4	0	0	5	3	8	0	.209	.302
Tommie Aaron	1B11, 3B7	R	31	25	53	4	12	2	0	0	3	3	5	0	.226	.264
Marv Staehle	2B7, 3B1	L	29	22	36	5	4	0	0	0	1	5	4	0	.111	.111
Jim Breazeale	1B4	L	21	10	21	1	4	0	0	1	3	0	3	0	.190	.333

Leo Foster 20 R 0-10, 2 Tony LaRussa 26 R 2-7, Rico Carty (KJ) 31

NAME	T	AGE	W	L	PCT	SV	G	GS	CG	IP	H	BB	SO	ShO	ERA
		28	82	80	.506	31	162	162	40	1475	1529	485	823	11	3.75
Phil Niekro	R	32	15	14	.517	2	42	36	18	269	248	70	173	4	2.98
Ron Reed	R	28	13	14	.481	0	32	32	8	222	221	54	129	1	3.73
Cecil Upshaw	R	28	11	6	.647	17	49	0	0	82	95	28	56	0	3.51
Tom Kelley	R	27	9	5	.643	0	28	20	5	143	140	69	68	0	2.96
Jim Nash	R	26	9	7	.563	2	32	19	2	133	166	50	65	0	4.94
George Stone	L	25	6	8	.429	0	27	24	4	173	186	35	110	2	3.59
Pat Jarvis	R	30	6	14	.300	1	35	23	3	162	162	51	68	3	4.11
Mike McQueen (SA)	L	20	4	1	.800	1	17	3	0	56	47	23	38	0	3.54
Bob Priddy	R	31	4	9	.308	4	40	0	0	64	71	44	36	0	4.22
Steve Barber	L	32	3	1	.750	2	39	3	0	75	92	25	40	0	4.80
Tom House	L	24	1	0	1.000	0	11	1	0	21	20	3	11	0	3.00
Gary Neibauer	R	26	1	0	1.000	1	6	1	0	21	14	9	6	0	2.14
Ron Herbel	R	33	0	1	.000	1	25	0	0	52	61	23	22	0	5.19
1 Hoyt Wilhelm	R	47	0	0	.000	0	3	0	0	2	6	1	1	0	18.00

CINCINNATI 4th (Tie) 79-83 .488 11 SPARKY ANDERSON

NAME	G by POS	B	AGE	G	AB	R	H	2B	3B	HR	RBI	BB	SO	SB	BA	SA
TOTALS			26	162	5414	586	1306	203	28	138	542	438	907	59	.241	.366
Lee May	1B143	R	28	147	553	85	154	17	3	39	98	42	135	3	.278	.532
Tommy Helms	2B149	R	30	150	547	40	141	26	1	3	52	26	33	3	.258	.325
Dave Concepcion	SS112, 2B10, 3B7, OF5	R	23	130	327	24	67	4	4	1	20	18	51	9	.205	.251
Tony Perez	3B148, 1B44	R	29	158	609	72	164	22	3	25	91	51	120	4	.269	.438
Pete Rose	OF158	B	30	160	632	86	192	27	4	13	44	68	50	13	.304	.421
2 George Foster	OF102	R	22	104	368	39	86	18	4	10	50	23	93	7	.234	.386
Bernie Carbo	OF90	L	23	106	310	33	68	20	1	5	20	54	56	2	.219	.339
Johnny Bench	C141, 1B12, OF12, 3B3	R	23	149	562	80	134	19	2	27	61	49	83	2	.238	.423
Woody Woodward	SS85, 3B63, 2B9	R	28	136	273	22	66	9	1	0	18	27	28	4	.242	.282
Hal McRae	OF91	R	24	99	337	39	89	24	2	9	34	11	35	3	.264	.427
Jimmy Stewart	OF19, 3B9, 2B6	B	32	80	82	7	19	2	2	0	9	9	12	3	.232	.305
2 Buddy Bradford	OF66	R	26	79	100	17	20	3	0	2	12	14	23	4	.200	.290
Ty Cline	OF28, 1B2	L	32	69	97	12	19	1	0	0	1	18	16	2	.196	.206
Pat Corrales	C39	R	30	40	94	6	17	2	0	0	6	6	17	0	.181	.202
2 Al Ferrara	OF5	R	31	32	33	2	6	0	0	1	5	3	10	0	.182	.273
Willie Smith	1B10	L	32	31	55	3	9	2	0	1	4	3	9	0	.164	.255
1 Frank Duffy	SS10	R	24	13	16	0	3	1	0	0	1	1	2	0	.188	.250
Darrel Chaney	SS7, 2B1, 3B1	B	23	10	24	2	3	0	0	0	1	1	3	0	.125	.125

Bill Plummer 24 R 0-19, 1 Angel Bravo 28 L 1-5, Bobby Tolan (FJ) 25

NAME	T	AGE	W	L	PCT	SV	G	GS	CG	IP	H	BB	SO	ShO	ERA
		26	79	83	.488	38	162	162	27	1444	1298	501	750	11	3.35
Don Gullett	L	20	16	6	.727	0	35	31	4	218	196	64	107	3	2.64
Gary Nolan	R	23	12	15	.444	0	35	35	9	245	208	59	146	0	3.16
Clay Carroll	R	30	10	4	.714	15	61	0	0	94	78	42	64	0	2.49
Ross Grimsley	L	21	10	7	.588	0	26	26	6	161	151	43	67	3	3.58
Jim McGlothlin	R	27	8	12	.400	0	30	26	6	171	151	47	93	0	3.21
Wayne Granger	R	27	7	6	.538	11	70	0	0	100	94	28	51	0	3.33
Joe Gibbon	L	36	5	6	.455	11	50	0	0	64	54	32	34	0	2.95
Wayne Simpson	R	22	4	7	.364	0	22	21	1	117	106	77	61	0	4.77
Tony Cloninger	R	30	3	6	.333	0	28	8	1	97	79	49	51	1	3.90
Milt Wilcox	R	21	2	2	.500	1	18	3	0	43	43	17	21	0	3.35
Ed Sprague	R	25	1	0	1.000	0	7	0	0	11	8	1	7	0	0.00
Jim Merritt	L	27	1	11	.083	0	28	11	0	107	115	31	38	0	4.37
Greg Garrett	L	24	0	1	.000	0	2	1	0	9	7	10	2	0	1.00
Steve Blateric	R	27	0	0	.000	0	2	0	0	3	5	0	4	0	12.00
Pedro Borbon	R	24	0	0	.000	0	3	0	0	4	3	1	4	0	4.50

HOUSTON 4th (Tie) 79-83 .488 11 HARRY WALKER

NAME	G by POS	B	AGE	G	AB	R	H	2B	3B	HR	RBI	BB	SO	SB	BA	SA
TOTALS			27	162	5492	585	1319	230	52	71	547	478	888	101	.240	.340
Denis Menke	1B101, 3B32, SS17, 2B6	R	30	146	475	57	117	26	3	1	43	59	68	4	.246	.320
Joe Morgan	2B157	L	27	160	583	87	149	27	11	13	56	88	52	40	.256	.407
Roger Metzger	SS148	B	23	150	562	64	132	14	11	0	26	44	50	15	.235	.299
Doug Rader	3B135	R	26	135	484	51	118	21	4	12	56	40	112	5	.244	.378
Jim Wynn	OF116	R	29	123	404	38	82	16	0	7	45	56	63	10	.203	.295
Cesar Cedeno	OF157, 1B2	R	20	161	611	85	161	40	6	10	81	25	102	20	.264	.398
Jesus Alou	OF109	R	29	122	433	41	121	21	4	2	40	13	17	3	.279	.360
Johnny Edwards (HJ)	C104	L	33	106	317	18	74	13	4	1	23	26	38	1	.233	.309
Bob Watson	OF87, 1B45	R	25	129	468	49	135	17	3	9	67	41	56	0	.288	.395
Cesar Geronimo	OF64	L	23	94	82	13	18	2	2	1	6	5	31	2	.220	.329
Jack Hiatt (BZ)	C65, 1B1	R	28	69	174	16	48	8	1	1	16	35	39	0	.276	.351
Rich Chiles	OF27	L	21	67	119	12	27	5	1	2	15	6	20	0	.227	.336
John Mayberry	1B37	L	21	46	137	16	25	0	1	7	14	13	32	0	.182	.350
Norm Miller (BW)	OF20, C1	L	25	45	74	5	19	5	0	2	10	5	13	0	.257	.405
Marty Martinez	2B9, SS7, 1B4, 3B3	B	29	32	62	4	16	3	1	0	4	3	6	1	.258	.339
Larry Howard	C22	R	26	24	64	6	15	3	0	2	14	3	17	0	.234	.375
Ray Busse	SS5, 3B3	R	22	10	34	2	5	3	0	0	4	2	9	0	.147	.235

Derrell Thomas 20 B 0-5, Jay Schlueter 21 R 1-3

NAME	T	AGE	W	L	PCT	SV	G	GS	CG	IP	H	BB	SO	ShO	ERA
		27	79	83	.488	25	162	162	43	1471	1318	475	914	10	3.13
Don Wilson	R	26	16	10	.615	0	35	34	18	268	195	79	180	3	2.45
Larry Dierker (EJ)	R	24	12	6	.667	0	24	23	6	150	150	33	91	2	2.72
Jim Ray	R	26	10	4	.714	3	47	1	0	98	72	31	46	0	2.11
Jack Billingham	R	28	10	16	.385	0	33	33	8	228	205	68	139	3	3.39
Wade Blasingame	L	27	9	11	.450	0	30	28	2	158	177	45	93	0	4.61
Ken Forsch	R	24	8	8	.500	0	33	23	7	188	162	53	131	2	2.54
George Culver	R	27	5	8	.385	7	59	0	0	95	89	38	57	0	2.65
Fred Gladding	R	35	4	5	.444	12	48	0	0	51	51	22	17	0	2.12
J. R. Richard	R	21	2	1	.667	0	4	4	1	21	17	16	29	0	3.43
Scipio Spinks	R	23	1	0	1.000	0	5	3	1	29	22	13	26	0	3.72
Bill Greif	R	21	1	1	.500	0	7	3	0	16	18	8	14	0	5.06
Buddy Harris	R	22	1	1	.500	0	20	0	0	31	33	16	21	0	6.39
Denny Lemaster	L	32	0	2	.000	2	42	0	0	60	59	22	28	0	3.45
Ron Cook (SA)	L	23	0	4	.000	0	5	4	0	26	23	8	10	0	4.85
Tom Griffin	R	23	0	6	.000	0	10	6	0	38	44	20	29	0	4.74
Skip Guinn	L	26	0	0	.000	1	4	0	0	5	1	3	3	0	0.00
Larry Yount	R	21	0	0	.000	0	1	0	0	0	0	0	0	0	0.00

SAN DIEGO 6th 61-100 .379 28.5 PRESTON GOMEZ

NAME	G by POS	B	AGE	G	AB	R	H	2B	3B	HR	RBI	BB	SO	SB	BA	SA
TOTALS			26	161	5366	486	1250	184	31	96	447	438	966	70	.233	.332
Nate Colbert	1B153	R	25	156	565	81	149	25	3	27	84	63	119	5	.264	.462
Don Mason	2B90, 3B3	L	26	113	344	43	73	12	1	2	11	27	35	6	.212	.270
Enzo Hernandez	SS143	R	22	143	549	58	122	9	3	0	12	54	34	21	.222	.250
Ed Spiezio (KJ)	3B91, OF1	R	29	97	308	16	71	10	1	7	36	22	50	6	.231	.338
Ollie Brown	OF134	R	27	145	484	36	132	16	0	9	55	52	74	3	.273	.362
Clarence Gaston	OF133	R	27	141	518	57	118	13	9	17	61	24	121	1	.228	.386
Larry Stahl	OF75, 1B7	L	30	114	308	27	78	13	4	8	36	26	59	4	.253	.399
Bob Barton	C119	R	29	121	376	23	94	17	2	5	23	35	49	0	.250	.346
D. Campbell (LJ)	2B69, 3B40, SS4, 1B2, OF2	R	29	108	365	38	83	14	2	7	29	37	75	9	.227	.334
Ivan Murrell	OF72	R	26	103	255	23	60	6	3	7	24	7	60	5	.235	.365
2 Leron Lee	OF68	L	23	79	256	29	70	20	2	4	21	18	45	4	.273	.414
2 Garry Jestadt	3B49, 2B23, SS1	R	24	75	189	17	55	13	0	0	13	11	24	1	.291	.360
2 Angel Bravo	OF9	L	28	52	58	6	9	2	0	0	6	8	12	0	.155	.190
Fred Kendall	1B1, 3B1	R	22	49	111	2	19	1	0	1	7	7	16	1	.171	.207
Tommy Dean	SS28, 3B11, 2B1	R	25	41	70	2	8	0	0	0	1	4	13	1	.114	.114
1 Chris Cannizzaro	C19	R	33	21	63	2	12	1	0	1	8	11	10	0	.190	.254
Johnnie Jeter	OF17	R	26	18	75	8	24	4	0	1	3	2	16	2	.320	.413
Rod Gaspar	OF2	B	25	16	17	1	2	0	0	0	2	3	3	0	.118	.118
Jerry Morales	OF7	R	22	12	17	1	2	0	0	0	1	2	2	1	.118	.118
Mike Ivie	C6	R	18	6	17	0	8	0	0	0	3	1	1	0	.471	.471

1 Al Ferrara 31 R 2-17, Ron Slocum 25 R 0-18, 1 Ramon Webster 28 L 1-8, Dave Robinson 25 B 0-6

NAME	T	AGE	W	L	PCT	SV	G	GS	CG	IP	H	BB	SO	ShO	ERA
		27	61	100	.379	17	161	161	47	1438	1351	559	923	10	3.22
Clay Kirby	R	23	15	13	.536	0	38	36	13	267	213	103	231	2	2.83
Dave Roberts	L	26	14	17	.452	0	37	34	14	270	238	61	135	2	2.10
Steve Arlin	R	25	9	19	.321	0	36	34	10	228	211	103	156	4	3.47
2 Bob Miller	R	32	7	3	.700	7	38	0	0	64	53	26	36	0	1.41
Ed Acosta	R	27	3	3	.500	0	8	6	3	46	43	7	16	1	2.74
Tom Phoebus	R	26	3	11	.214	0	29	21	2	133	144	64	80	0	4.47
2 Fred Norman	L	28	3	12	.200	0	20	18	5	127	114	56	77	0	3.33
Dick Kelley	L	31	2	3	.400	2	48	1	0	60	52	23	42	0	3.45
Al Severinsen	R	26	2	5	.286	8	59	0	0	70	77	30	31	0	3.47
Mike Caldwell	L	22	1	0	1.000	0	6	0	0	7	4	3	5	0	0.00
Gary Ross	R	23	1	3	.250	0	13	0	0	24	27	11	13	0	3.00
Danny Coombs	L	29	1	6	.143	0	19	7	0	58	81	25	37	0	6.21
Jay Franklin	R	18	0	1	.000	0	3	1	0	6	5	4	4	0	6.00
Bill Laxton	L	23	0	2	.000	0	18	0	0	28	32	26	23	0	6.75
1 Al Santorini	R	23	0	2	.000	0	18	3	0	38	43	11	21	0	3.79
Mike Corkins	R	25	0	0	.000	0	8	0	0	13	14	6	16	0	3.46

WORLD SERIES – PITTSBURG (NL) 4 BALTIMORE (AL) 3

LINE SCORES

TEAM	1	2	3	4	5	6	7	8	9	10	11	12	R	H	E
Game 1 October 9 at Baltimore															
PIT (NL)	0	3	0	0	0	0	0	0	0				3	3	0
BAL (AL)	0	1	3	0	1	0	0	0	X				5	10	3
Ellis, Moose (3), Miller (7) — McNally															
Game 2 October 11 at Baltimore															
PIT	0	0	0	0	0	0	0	3	0				3	8	1
BAL	0	1	0	3	6	1	0	0	X				11	14	1
B. Johnson, Kison (4), Moose (4), Veale (5), Miller (6), Giusti (8) — Palmer, Hall (9)															
Game 3 October 12 at Pittsburgh															
BAL	0	0	0	0	0	0	1	0	0				1	3	3
PIT	1	0	0	0	0	1	3	0	X				5	7	0
Cuellar, Dukes (7), Watt (8) — Blass															
Game 4 October 13 at Pittsburgh															
BAL	3	0	0	0	0	0	0	0	0				3	4	1
PIT	2	0	1	0	0	0	1	0	X				4	14	0
Dobson, Jackson (6), Watt (7), Richert (8) — Walker, Kison (1), Giusti (8)															
Game 5 October 14 at Pittsburgh															
BAL	0	0	0	0	0	0	0	0	0				0	2	1
PIT	0	2	1	0	1	0	0	0	X				4	9	0
McNally, Leonhard (5), Dukes (6) — Briles															
Game 6 October 16 at Baltimore															
PIT	0	1	1	0	0	0	0	0	0	0			2	9	1
BAL	0	0	0	0	0	1	1	0	0	1			3	8	0
Moose, B. Johnson (6), Giusti (7), Miller (10) — Palmer, Dobson (10), McNally (10)															
Game 7 October 17 at Baltimore															
PIT	0	0	0	1	0	0	0	1	0				2	6	1
BAL	0	0	0	0	0	0	0	1	0				1	4	0
Blass — Cuellar, Dobson (9), McNally (9)															

COMPOSITE BATTING

NAME	POS	G	AB	R	H	2B	3B	HR	RBI	BA
Pittsburgh (NL)										
Totals		7	238	23	56	9	2	5	21	.235
Cash	2B	7	30	2	4	1	0	0	1	.133
Clemente	OF	7	29	3	12	2	1	2	4	.414
Sanguillen	C	7	29	3	11	1	0	0	0	.379
Robertson	1B	7	25	4	6	0	0	2	5	.240
Stargell	OF	7	24	3	5	1	0	0	1	.208
Oliver	OF	5	19	1	4	2	0	0	2	.211
Hernandez	SS	7	18	2	4	0	0	0	1	.222
Pagan	3B	4	15	0	4	2	0	0	2	.267
Hebner	3B	3	12	2	2	0	0	1	3	.167
Clines	OF	3	11	2	1	0	1	0	0	.091
Blass	P	2	7	0	0	0	0	0	0	.000
Davalillo	OF	3	3	1	1	0	0	0	0	.333
B. Johnson	P	2	3	0	0	0	0	0	0	.000
May	PH	2	2	0	1	0	0	0	1	.500
Briles	P	1	2	0	1	0	0	0	1	.500
Alley	SS	2	2	0	0	0	0	0	0	.000
Kison	P	2	2	0	0	0	0	0	0	.000
Moose	P	3	2	0	0	0	0	0	0	.000
Mazeroski	PH	1	1	0	0	0	0	0	0	.000
Sands	PH	1	1	0	0	0	0	0	0	.000
Ellis	P	1	1	0	0	0	0	0	0	.000
Giusti P 0-0, Miller P 0-0, Veale P 0-0, Walker P 0-0										
Baltimore (AL)										
Totals		7	219	24	45	3	1	5	22	.205
Rettenmund	OF	7	27	3	5	0	0	1	4	.185
D. Johnson	2B	7	27	1	4	0	0	0	3	.148
Powell	1B	7	27	1	3	0	0	0	1	.111
F. Robinson	OF	7	25	5	7	0	0	2	2	.280
Buford	OF	6	23	3	6	1	0	2	4	.261
B. Robinson	3B	7	22	2	7	0	0	0	5	.318
Belanger	SS	7	21	4	5	0	1	0	0	.238
Hendricks	C	6	19	3	5	1	0	0	1	.263
Blair	OF	4	9	2	3	1	0	0	0	.333
Shopay	PH	5	4	0	0	0	0	0	0	.000
McNally	P	4	4	0	0	0	0	0	0	.000
Palmer	P	2	4	0	0	0	0	0	2	.000
Cuellar	P	2	3	0	0	0	0	0	0	.000
Etchebarren	C	1	2	0	0	0	0	0	0	.000
Dobson	P	3	2	0	0	0	0	0	0	.000
Dukes	P	2	0	0	0	0	0	0	0	.000
Watt	P	2	0	0	0	0	0	0	0	.000
Hall P 0-0, Jackson P 0-0, Leonhard P 0-0, Richert P 0-0										

COMPOSITE PITCHING

NAME	G	IP	H	BB	SO	W	L	SV	ERA
Pittsburgh (NL)									
Totals	7	61.2	45	20	35	4	3	1	3.50
Blass	2	18	7	4	13	2	0	0	1.00
Moose	3	9.2	12	2	7	0	0	0	6.52
Briles	1	9	2	2	2	1	0	0	0.00
Kison	2	6.1	1	2	3	1	0	0	0.00
Giusti	3	5.1	3	2	4	0	0	1	0.00
B. Johnson	2	5	5	3	3	0	1	0	9.00
Miller	3	4.2	7	1	2	0	1	0	3.86
Ellis	1	2.1	4	1	1	0	1	0	15.43
Veale	1	.2	1	2	0	0	0	0	13.50
Walker	1	.2	3	1	0	0	0	0	40.50
Baltimore (AL)									
Totals	7	61	56	26	47	3	4	1	2.66
Palmer	2	17	15	9	15	1	0	0	2.65
Cuellar	2	14	11	6	10	0	2	0	3.86
McNally	4	13.2	10	5	12	2	1	0	1.98
Dobson	3	6.2	13	4	6	0	0	0	4.05
Dukes	2	4	2	0	1	0	0	0	0.00
Watt	2	2.1	4	0	2	0	1	0	3.86
Hall	1	1	0	1	0	0	0	1	0.00
Leonhard	1	1	0	1	0	0	0	0	0.00
Jackson	1	.2	0	1	0	0	0	0	0.00
Richert	1	.2	0	0	1	0	0	0	0.00

1972 Tragedy, Protest, and Finley's Moustache Brigade

Near the final day of the regular season, Pittsburgh's Roberto Clemente got his 3,000th hit. On the final day of the year, he was flying with supplies en route from his native Puerto Rico to lead a mercy mission for the earthquake victims of Managua, Nicaragua. The plane, considered unsafe, never arrived. The superstar's death ended a year which had begun with another tragedy—the death of New York Mets' manager Gil Hodges, who died of a heart attack in spring training. The news of the tragedy came at a time when the ballplayers from spring training camps all around the country walked off the diamond in protest of several issues—the main one being the conditions of their pension plan. As major league players' representative Marvin Miller negotiated with the owners and their representatives, all baseball activity remained frozen. When a settlement was finally reached, 13 days and 86 games were scratched from the regular season. The players, although winning out on the owners, lost in the Supreme Court when it finally ruled against Curt Flood's 1970 reserve clause lawsuit.

During the season, which was to include big winter trades, the trading of aging superstar Willie Mays to the Mets, and the continuing saga of Denny McLain going from the majors to the minors and the majors again, the moustache became the symbol of success. And no one wore it more stylishly than the Oakland Athletics. With half of A's owner Charley O. Finley's team sporting moustaches, as well as manager Dick Williams, the squad made it to their first pennant since 1931. Even with Vida Blue holding out well into the season and never reaching top form, Oakland outlasted a threat from the surprising Chicago White Sox, while flashing the best pitching staff in the West with Catfish Hunter and Ken Holtzman leading the starters and Rollie Fingers acing the bullpen. Reggie Jackson, Sal Bando, Joe Rudi, and Mike Epstein provided the sock in the lineup, and Bert Campaneris spark-plugged the attack by heisting 52 bases.

In the American League East, the Tigers, Orioles, Red Sox, and Yankees all stayed within a postage stamp of the top into September. But Detroit and Boston—locked in a virtual tie—were the only contenders remaining in the final days of the season. The Tigers finally clinched the crown by knocking off the Red Sox in two of three games before a cheering Detroit crowd. Personalities dominated each of the four squads in the late going: Al Kaline and his hot late season bat, former heart attack victim John Hiller's fine comeback in Detroit, Luis Tiant by his totally unexpected spectacular hurling in Boston, Bobby Murcer's home run bat in New York, and Frank Robinson, who was traded to the National League during the winter and was conspicuous by his absence in Baltimore. In the play-offs, the Tigers bowed to the A's in a thrilling five-game series.

Rod Carew of the Twins became the first American League batting champion not to hit any home runs and Chicago's Dick Allen won the home run and RBI crown and the MVP Award in his first season in the junior circuit. Another newcomer, Cleveland's Gaylord Perry, edged Detroit's Mickey Lolich and Chicago's Wilbur Wood for the Cy Young Award.

The National League produced no pennant suspense, as Pittsburgh and Cincinnati clearly outclassed their competition. While the Pirates were returning to the Eastern title for the third straight year, Cincinnati was back for Western honors after a one-year interruption on the return to form of MVP Johnny Bench, the hustling of Pete Rose, and the speed of former Houston star Joe Morgan. The individual highlight of the year, though, came from Steve Carlton, the winner of 27 games and the Cy Young Award while playing on a Philadelphia team that wound up with the worst record in the National League. An exciting play-off between the two champions ended with Cincinnati scoring the deciding run in the bottom of the ninth on a wild pitch by Pittsburgh's Bob Moose.

The World Series produced six one-run games. After the A's jumped out to a three-to-one edge in games, the Reds battled back and knotted the count before Oakland walked away victorious in a 3-2 seventh-game triumph. The unlikely Series hero was Oakland's Gene Tenace, a second-string catcher during the season, who drive in nine runs and tied a Series record with four home runs.

1972 AMERICAN LEAGUE — EAST DIVISION

DETROIT 1st 86-70 .551 — BILLY MARTIN

NAME	G by POS	B	AGE	G	AB	R	H	2B	3B	HR	RBI	BB	SO	SB	BA	SA
TOTALS			32	156	5099	558	1206	179	32	122	531	483	793	17	.237	.356
Norm Cash	1B134	L	37	137	440	51	114	16	0	22	61	50	64	0	.259	.445
Dick McAuliffe	2B116, SS3, 3B1	L	32	122	408	47	98	16	3	8	30	59	59	0	.240	.353
Ed Brinkman	SS156	R	30	156	516	42	105	19	1	6	49	38	51	0	.203	.279
Aurelio Rodriguez	3B153, SS2	R	24	153	601	65	142	23	5	13	56	28	104	2	.236	.356
Jim Northrup	OF127, 1B2	L	32	134	426	40	111	15	2	8	42	38	47	4	.261	.362
Mickey Stanley	OF139	R	29	142	435	45	102	16	6	14	55	29	49	1	.234	.395
Willie Horton	OF98	R	29	108	333	44	77	9	5	11	36	27	47	0	.231	.387
Bill Freehan	C105	R	30	111	374	51	98	18	2	10	56	48	51	0	.262	.401
Al Kaline (LJ)	OF84, 1B11	R	37	106	278	46	87	11	2	10	32	28	33	1	.313	.475
Gates Brown	OF72	L	33	103	252	33	58	5	0	10	31	26	28	3	.230	.369
Tony Taylor	2B67, 3B8, 1B1	R	36	78	228	33	69	12	4	1	20	14	34	5	.303	.404
Tom Haller	C36	L	35	59	121	7	25	5	2	2	13	15	14	0	.207	.331
Ike Brown	OF22, 1B13, 2B3, SS1, 3B1	R	30	51	84	12	21	3	0	2	10	17	23	1	.250	.357
2 Duke Sims	C25, OF4	L	31	38	98	11	31	4	0	4	19	19	18	0	.316	.480
Paul Jata	1B12, OF10, C1	R	22	32	74	8	17	2	0	0	3	7	14	0	.230	.257
Wayne Comer	OF17	R	28	27	9	1	1	0	0	0	1	0	1	0	.111	.111
2 Frank Howard	1B10, OF1	R	35	14	33	1	8	1	0	1	7	4	8	0	.242	.364
John Knox	2B4	L	23	14	13	1	1	1	0	0	0	1	2	0	.077	.154

1 Dalton Jones 28 L 0-7, Marvin Lane 22 R 0-6, Ike Blessitt 22 R 0-5, John Gamble 24 R 0-3, Joe Staton 24 L 0-2, Gene Lamont 25 L 0-0

NAME	T	AGE	W	L	PCT	SV	G	GS	CG	IP	H	BB	SO	ShO	ERA
		28	8	70	.551	33	156	156	46	1388	1212	465	952	11	2.96
Mickey Lolich	L	31	22	14	.611	0	41	41	23	327	282	74	250	4	2.50
Joe Coleman	R	25	19	14	.576	0	40	39	9	280	216	110	222	3	2.80
2 Woodie Fryman	L	32	10	3	.769	0	16	14	6	114	93	31	72	1	2.05
Chuck Seelbach	R	24	9	8	.529	14	61	3	0	112	96	39	76	0	2.89
Tom Timmerman	R	32	8	10	.444	0	34	25	3	150	121	41	88	2	2.88
Fred Scherman	L	27	7	3	.700	12	57	3	0	94	91	53	53	0	3.64
Bill Slayback	R	24	5	6	.455	0	23	13	3	82	74	25	65	1	3.18
Joe Niekro (PJ)	R	27	3	2	.600	1	18	7	1	47	62	8	24	0	3.83
Jim Foor	L	23	1	0	1.000	0	7	0	0	4	6	6	2	0	13.50
Chris Zachary	R	28	1	1	.500	1	25	1	0	38	27	15	21	0	1.42
John Hiller (IL)	L	29	1	2	.333	3	24	3	1	44	39	13	26	0	2.05
Fred Holdsworth	R	20	0	1	.000	0	2	2	0	7	13	2	5	0	12.86
Lerrin LaGrow	R	23	0	1	.000	2	16	0	0	27	22	6	9	0	1.33
Phil Meeler	R	24	0	1	.000	0	7	0	0	8	10	7	5	0	4.50
1 Ron Perranoski	L	36	0	1	.000	0	17	0	0	19	23	8	10	0	7.58
Les Cain	L	24	0	3	.000	0	5	5	0	24	18	16	16	0	3.75
Bill Gilbreth	L	24	0	0	.000	0	2	0	0	5	10	4	2	0	16.20
1 Mike Kilkenny	L	27	0	0	.000	0	1	0	0	1	1	0	0	0	9.00
Don Leshnock	L	25	0	0	.000	0	1	0	0	1	2	0	2	0	0.00
Bob Strampe	R	22	0	0	.000	0	7	0	0	5	6	7	4	0	10.80

BOSTON 2nd 85-70 .548 .5 — EDDIE KASKO

NAME	G by POS	B	AGE	G	AB	R	H	2B	3B	HR	RBI	BB	SO	SB	BA	SA
TOTALS			29	155	5208	**640**	1289	**229**	**34**	124	**594**	522	858	66	.248	**.376**
Danny Cater	1B90	R	32	92	317	32	75	17	1	8	39	15	33	0	.237	.372
Doug Griffin	2B129	R	25	129	470	43	122	12	1	2	35	45	48	9	.260	.302
Luis Aparicio (BG)	SS109	R	38	110	436	47	112	26	3	3	39	26	28	3	.257	.351
Rico Petrocelli	3B146	R	29	147	521	62	125	15	2	15	75	78	91	0	.240	.363
Reggie Smith	OF129	B	27	131	467	75	126	25	4	21	74	68	63	15	.270	.475
Tommy Harper	OF144	R	31	144	556	92	141	29	2	14	49	67	104	25	.254	.388
Carl Yastrzemski (KJ)	OF83, 1B42	L	32	125	455	70	120	18	2	12	68	67	44	5	.264	.391
Carlton Fisk	C131	R	24	131	457	74	134	28	**9**	22	61	52	83	5	.293	.538
Ben Oglivie	OF65	L	23	94	253	27	61	10	2	8	30	18	61	1	.241	.391
Rick Miller	OF75	L	24	89	98	13	21	4	1	3	15	11	27	0	.214	.367
John Kennedy	2B32, SS27, 3B11	R	31	71	212	22	52	11	1	2	22	18	40	0	.245	.335
Phil Gagliano	OF12, 3B5, 2B4, 1B2	R	30	52	82	9	21	4	1	0	10	10	13	1	.256	.329
Bob Burda	1B15, OF1	L	33	45	73	4	12	1	0	2	9	8	11	0	.164	.260
Juan Beniquez	SS27	R	22	33	99	10	24	4	1	1	8	7	11	2	.242	.333
Duane Josephson (IL)	1B16, C6	R	30	26	82	11	22	4	1	1	7	4	11	0	.268	.378
Bob Montgomery	C22	R	28	24	77	7	22	1	0	2	7	3	17	0	.286	.377
Dwight Evans	OF17	R	20	18	57	2	15	3	1	1	6	7	13	0	.263	.404
2 Andy Kosco	OF12	R	30	17	47	5	10	2	1	3	6	2	9	0	.213	.489

Cecil Cooper 22 L 4-17, Bob Gallagher 23 L 0-5, Vic Correll 26 R 2-4

NAME	T	AGE	W	L	PCT	SV	G	GS	CG	IP	H	BB	SO	ShO	ERA
		29	85	70	.548	25	155	155	48	1383	**1309**	512	918	20	3.47
Marty Pattin	R	29	17	13	.567	0	38	35	13	253	232	65	168	4	3.24
Luis Tiant	R	31	15	6	.714	3	43	19	12	179	128	65	123	6	**1.91**
Sonny Siebert	R	35	12	12	.500	0	32	30	7	196	204	59	123	3	3.81
John Curtis	L	24	11	8	.579	0	26	21	8	154	161	50	106	3	3.74
Lynn McGlothen	R	28	8	7	.533	0	22	22	4	145	135	59	112	1	3.41
Bill Lee	L	25	7	4	.636	5	47	0	0	84	75	32	43	0	3.21
Ray Culp (SJ)	R	30	5	8	.385	0	16	16	4	105	104	53	52	1	4.46
Don Newhauser	R	24	4	2	.667	4	31	0	0	37	30	25	27	0	2.43
Gary Peters	L	35	3	3	.500	1	33	4	0	85	91	38	67	0	4.34
2 Bob Veale	L	36	2	0	1.000	2	6	0	0	8	2	3	10	0	0.00
Lew Krausse	R	29	1	3	.250	1	24	7	0	61	74	28	35	0	6.34
Bob Bolin	R	33	0	1	.000	5	21	0	0	31	24	11	27	0	2.90
Mike Garman	R	22	0	1	.000	0	3	1	0	3	4	2	1	0	12.00
Ken Tatum (LJ)	R	28	0	2	.000	4	22	0	0	29	32	15	15	0	3.10
Roger Moret	L	22	0	0	.000	0	3	0	0	5	5	6	4	0	3.60
Mike Nagy	R	24	0	0	.000	0	1	0	0	2	3	0	2	0	9.00
Stan Williams	R	35	0	0	.000	0	3	0	0	4	5	1	3	0	6.75

BALTIMORE 3rd 80-74 .519 5 — EARL WEAVER

NAME	G by POS	B	AGE	G	AB	R	H	2B	3B	HR	RBI	BB	SO	SB	BA	SA
TOTALS			28	154	5028	519	1153	193	29	100	483	507	935	78	.229	.339
Boog Powell	1B133	L	30	140	465	53	117	20	1	21	81	65	92	4	.252	.434
Dave Johnson	2B116	R	29	118	376	31	83	22	3	5	32	52	68	1	.221	.335
Mark Belanger	SS105	R	28	113	285	36	53	9	1	2	16	18	53	6	.186	.246
Brooks Robinson	3B152	R	35	153	556	48	139	23	2	8	64	43	45	1	.250	.342
Merv Rettenmund	OF98	R	29	102	301	40	70	10	2	6	21	41	37	6	.233	.339
Paul Blair	OF139	R	28	142	477	47	111	20	8	8	49	25	78	7	.233	.358
Don Buford	OF105	B	35	125	408	46	84	6	2	5	22	69	83	8	.206	.267
Johnny Oates	C82	L	26	85	253	20	66	12	1	4	21	28	31	5	.261	.364
Bobby Grich	SS81, 2B45, 1B16, 3B8	R	23	133	460	66	128	21	3	12	50	53	96	13	.278	.415
Don Baylor	OF84, 1B9	R	23	102	320	33	81	13	3	11	38	29	50	24	.253	.416
Terry Crowley	OF68, 1B15	L	25	97	247	30	57	10	0	11	29	32	26	0	.231	.405
Andy Etchebarren	C70	R	29	71	188	11	38	6	1	2	21	17	43	0	.202	.277
Tom Shopay	OF3	L	27	49	40	3	9	0	0	0	2	5	12	0	.225	.225
1 Ellie Hendricks	C28	L	31	33	84	6	13	4	0	0	4	12	19	0	.155	.202
2 Tommy Davis	OF18, 1B3	R	33	26	82	9	21	3	0	0	6	6	18	2	.256	.293
Chico Salmon	1B2, 3B1	R	31	17	16	2	1	1	0	0	0	0	4	0	.063	.125
Rich Coggins	OF13	L	21	16	[illegible]	5	13	4	0	0	1	1	6	0	.333	.436

Al Bumory 25 L 4-11, Tom Matchick 28 L 2-9, Sergio Robles 26 [illegible], Enos Cabell 22 R 0-5

NAME	T	AGE	W	L	PCT	SV	G	GS	CG	IP	H	BB	SO	ShO	ERA
		28	80	74	.519	21	154	154	**62**	1372	1116	395	788	20	**2.53**
Jim Palmer	R	26	21	10	.677	0	36	36	18	274	219	70	184	3	2.07
Mike Cuellar	L	35	18	12	.600	0	35	35	17	248	197	71	132	4	2.58
Pat Dobson	R	30	16	**18**	.471	0	38	36	13	268	220	69	161	3	2.65
Dave McNally	L	29	13	17	.433	0	36	36	12	241	220	68	120	6	2.95
Doyle Alexander	R	21	6	8	.429	2	35	9	2	106	78	30	49	2	2.46
Rorie Harrison	R	25	3	4	.429	4	39	2	0	94	68	34	62	0	2.30
Eddie Watt	R	30	2	3	.400	7	38	0	0	46	30	20	23	0	2.15
Grant Jackson	L	29	1	1	.500	8	32	0	0	41	33	9	34	0	2.63
Mickey Scott	L	24	0	1	.000	0	15	0	0	23	23	5	11	0	2.74
Dave Leonhard	R	30	0	0	.000	0	14	0	0	20	20	12	7	0	4.50
Bob Reynolds	R	25	0	0	.000	0	3	0	0	10	8	7	5	0	1.80

NEW YORK 4th 79-76 .510 6.5 — RALPH HOUK

NAME	G by POS	B	AGE	G	AB	R	H	2B	3B	HR	RBI	BB	SO	SB	BA	SA
TOTALS			29	155	5168	557	1288	201	24	103	526	491	689	71	.249	.357
Ron Blomberg	1B95	L	23	107	299	36	80	22	1	14	49	38	26	0	.268	.488
Horace Clarke	2B143	B	32	147	547	65	132	20	2	3	37	56	44	18	.241	.302
Gene Michael	SS121	B	34	126	391	29	91	7	4	1	32	32	45	4	.233	.279
Celerino Sanchez	3B68	R	28	71	250	18	62	8	3	0	22	12	30	0	.248	.304
Johnny Callison	OF74	L	33	92	275	28	71	10	0	9	34	18	34	3	.258	.393
Bobby Murcer	OF151	L	26	153	585	102	171	30	7	33	96	63	67	11	.292	.537
Roy White	OF155	B	28	155	556	76	150	29	0	10	54	99	59	23	.270	.376
Thurman Munson	C132	R	25	140	511	54	143	16	3	7	46	47	58	6	.280	.364
Felipe Alou	1B95, OF15	R	37	120	324	33	90	18	1	6	37	22	27	1	.278	.395
Bernie Allen	3B44, 2B20	L	33	84	220	26	50	9	0	9	21	23	42	0	.227	.391
Rusty Torres	OF62	B	23	80	199	15	42	7	0	3	13	18	44	0	.211	.291
Ron Swoboda	OF35, 1B2	R	28	63	113	9	28	8	0	1	12	17	29	0	.248	.345
Hal Lanier	3B47, SS9, 2B3	R	29	60	103	5	22	3	0	0	6	2	13	1	.214	.243
Johnny Ellis	C25, 1B8	R	23	52	136	13	40	5	1	5	25	8	22	0	.294	.456
Jerry Kenney	SS45, 3B1	L	27	50	119	16	25	2	0	0	7	16	13	3	.210	.227
Rich McKinney	3B33	R	25	37	121	10	26	2	0	1	7	7	13	1	.215	.256

Charlie Spikes 21 R 5-34, Frank Tepedino 24 L 0-8

NAME	T	AGE	W	L	PCT	SV	G	GS	CG	IP	H	BB	SO	ShO	ERA
		29	79	76	.510	39	155	155	35	1373	1306	419	625	19	3.05
Fritz Peterson	L	30	17	15	.531	0	35	35	12	250	270	44	100	3	3.24
Steve Kline	R	24	16	9	.640	0	32	32	11	236	210	44	58	4	2.40
Mel Stottlemyre	R	30	14	18	.438	0	36	36	9	260	250	85	110	7	3.22
Mike Kekich	L	27	10	13	.435	0	29	28	2	175	172	76	78	0	3.70
Sparky Lyle	L	27	9	5	.643	35	59	0	0	108	84	29	75	0	1.92
Rob Gardner	L	27	8	5	.615	0	20	14	1	97	91	28	58	0	3.06
Lindy McDaniel	R	36	3	1	.750	0	37	0	0	68	54	25	47	0	2.25
1 Rich Hinton	L	25	1	0	1.000	0	7	3	0	17	20	8	13	0	4.76
Fred Beene	R	29	1	3	.250	3	29	1	0	58	55	24	37	0	2.33
2 Wade Blasingame	L	28	0	1	.000	0	12	1	0	17	14	11	7	0	4.24
2 Casey Cox	R	30	0	1	.000	0	5	1	0	12	13	3	4	0	4.50
Larry Gowell	R	25	0	1	.000	0	2	1	0	7	3	2	7	0	1.29
2 Jim Roland	L	29	0	1	.000	0	16	0	0	25	27	16	13	0	5.04
Ron Klimkowski	R	27	0	3	.000	1	16	2	0	31	32	15	11	0	4.06
1 Jack Aker	R	31	0	0	.000	0	4	0	0	6	5	3	1	0	3.00
Steve Blateric	R	28	0	0	.000	0	1	0	0	4	2	0	4	0	0.00
Alan Closter	L	29	0	0	.000	0	2	0	0	2	2	4	2	0	13.50
Doc Medich	R	23	0	0	.000	0	1	1	0	0	2	2	0	0	∞

CLEVELAND 5th 72-84 .462 14 — KEN ASPROMONTE

NAME	G by POS	B	AGE	G	AB	R	H	2B	3B	HR	RBI	BB	SO	SB	BA	SA
TOTALS			26	156	5207	472	1220	187	18	91	440	420	762	49	.234	.330
Chris Chambliss (LJ)	1B119	L	23	121	466	51	136	27	2	6	44	26	63	3	.292	.397
Jack Brohamer	2B132, 3B1	L	22	136	527	49	123	13	2	5	35	27	46	3	.233	.294
Frank Duffy	SS126	R	25	130	385	23	92	16	4	3	27	31	54	6	.239	.325
Graig Nettles	3B150	L	27	150	557	65	141	28	0	17	70	57	50	2	.253	.395
Buddy Bell	OF123, 3B6	R	20	132	466	49	119	21	1	9	36	34	29	5	.255	.363
Del Unser	OF119	L	27	132	383	29	91	12	0	1	17	28	46	5	.238	.277
Alex Johnson	OF95	R	29	108	356	31	85	10	1	8	37	22	40	6	.239	.340
Ray Fosse	C124, 1B3	R	25	134	457	42	110	20	1	10	41	45	46	5	.241	.354
Tommy McCraw	OF84, 1B38	L	31	129	391	43	101	13	5	7	33	41	47	12	.258	.371
Eddie Leon	2B36, SS35	R	25	89	225	14	45	2	1	4	16	20	47	0	.200	.271
Roy Foster	OF45	R	26	73	143	19	32	4	0	4	13	21	23	0	.224	.336
John Lowenstein	OF58, 1B2	L	25	68	151	16	32	8	1	6	21	20	43	2	.212	.397
Gerry Moses	C39, 1B3	R	25	52	141	9	31	3	0	4	14	11	29	0	.220	.326
Lou Camilli	SS8, 2B2	B	25	39	41	2	6	2	0	0	3	3	8	0	.146	.195
Ron Lolich	OF22	R	25	24	80	4	15	1	0	2	8	4	20	0	.188	.275
Kurt Bevacqua	OF11, 3B1	R	25	19	35	2	4	0	0	1	1	3	10	0	.114	.200

Jack Heidemann 22 R 3-20, 1 Fred Stanley 24 R 2-12, Adolfo Phillips 30 R 0-7, Larry Johnson 21 R 1-2

NAME	T	AGE	W	L	PCT	SV	G	GS	CG	IP	H	BB	SO	ShO	ERA
		26	72	84	.462	24	156	156	47	1410	1232	534	846	13	2.92
Gaylord Perry	R	33	24	16	.600	1	41	40	29	343	253	82	234	5	1.92
Dick Tidrow	R	25	14	15	.483	0	39	34	10	237	200	70	123	3	2.77
Milt Wilcox	R	22	7	14	.333	0	32	27	4	156	145	72	90	2	3.40
Steve Dunning	R	23	6	4	.600	0	16	16	1	105	98	43	52	0	3.26
Phil Hennigan (SJ)	R	26	5	3	.625	5	38	1	0	67	54	18	44	0	2.69
Ray Lamb	R	27	5	6	.455	0	34	9	0	108	101	29	64	0	3.08
4 Mike Kilkenny	L	27	4	1	.800	1	22	7	1	58	51	39	44	0	3.41
Tom Hilgendorf	L	30	3	1	.750	0	19	5	1	47	51	21	25	0	2.68
Ed Farmer	R	22	2	5	.286	7	46	1	0	61	51	27	33	0	4.43
Denny Riddleberger	L	26	1	3	.250	0	38	0	0	54	45	22	34	0	2.50
Vince Colbert	R	26	1	7	.125	0	22	11	1	75	74	38	36	1	4.56
Steve Hargan	R	29	0	3	.000	0	12	1	0	20	23	15	10	0	5.85
Steve Mingori	L	28	0	6	.000	10	41	0	0	57	67	36	47	0	3.95
Bill Butler	L	25	0	0	.000	0	6	2	0	12	9	10	6	0	1.50
Marcelino Lopez	L	28	0	0	.000	0	4	2	0	8	8	10	1	0	5.63
2 Lowell Palmer	R	24	0	0	.000	0	1	0	0	2	2	2	3	0	4.50

MILWAUKEE 6th 65-91 .417 21 — DAVE BRISTOL 10-20 .333 ROY McMILLAN 1-1 .500 DEL CRANDALL 54-70 .435

NAME	G by POS	B	AGE	G	AB	R	H	2B	3B	HR	RBI	BB	SO	SB	BA	SA
TOTALS			26	156	5124	493	1204	167	22	88	461	472	868	64	.235	.328
George Scott	1B139, 3B23	R	28	152	578	71	154	24	4	20	88	43	130	16	.266	.426
Ron Theobald	2B113	R	28	125	391	45	86	11	0	1	19	68	38	0	.220	.256
Rick Auerbach	SS153	R	22	153	554	50	121	16	3	2	30	43	62	24	.218	.269
Mike Ferraro	3B115, SS1	R	27	124	381	19	97	18	1	2	29	17	41	0	.255	.323
Joe Lahoud	OF97	L	25	111	316	35	75	9	3	12	34	45	54	3	.237	.399
Dave May	OF138	L	28	143	500	49	119	20	2	9	45	47	56	11	.238	.340
Johnny Briggs	OF106, 1B28	L	28	135	418	58	111	14	1	21	65	54	67	1	.266	.455
Ellie Rodriguez	C114	R	26	116	355	31	101	14	2	2	35	52	43	1	.285	.352
Bob Heise	2B49, 3B24, SS9	R	25	95	271	23	72	10	1	0	12	12	14	1	.266	.310
Brock Davis	OF43	L	28	85	154	17	49	2	0	0	12	12	23	6	.318	.331
Tommie Reynolds	OF41, 1B1, 3B1	R	30	72	130	13	26	5	1	2	13	10	25	0	.200	.300
3 Ollie Brown	OF56, 3B1	R	28	66	179	21	50	8	0	3	25	17	24	0	.279	.374
Billy Conigliaro (VR)	OF50	R	24	52	191	22	44	6	2	7	16	8	54	1	.230	.393
John Felske	C23, 1B8	R	30	37	80	6	11	3	0	1	5	8	23	0	.138	.213
2 Syd O'Brien	3B9, 2B7	R	27	31	58	5	12	2	0	1	5	2	13	0	.207	.293
1 Bill Voss	OF11	L	28	27	36	1	3	1	0	0	1	5	4	0	.083	.111
2 Ron Clark	2B11, 3B10	R	29	22	54	8	10	1	1	2	5	5	11	0	.185	.296
Paul Ratliff	C13	L	28	22	42	1	3	0	0	1	4	2	23	0	.071	.143
Darrell Porter	C18	L	20	18	56	2	7	1	0	1	2	5	21	0	.125	.196

2 Joe Azcue 32 R 2-14, 1 Curt Motton 31 R 1-6

NAME	T	AGE	W	L	PCT	SV	G	GS	CG	IP	H	BB	SO	ShO	ERA
		26	65	91	.417	32	156	156	37	1392	1289	486	740	14	3.45
Jim Lonborg	R	30	14	12	.538	1	33	30	11	223	197	76	143	2	2.83
Bill Parsons	R	23	13	13	.500	0	33	30	10	214	194	68	111	2	3.91
Skip Lockwood	R	25	8	15	.348	0	29	27	5	170	148	71	106	3	3.60
Jim Colborn	R	26	7	7	.500	0	39	12	4	148	135	43	97	1	3.10
Ken Brett (XJ)	L	23	7	12	.368	0	26	22	2	133	121	49	74	1	4.53
Jerry Bell (XJ)	R	24	5	1	.833	0	25	3	0	71	50	33	20	0	1.65
Earl Stephenson	L	24	3	5	.375	0	35	8	1	80	79	33	33	0	3.26
Gary Ryerson	L	24	3	8	.273	0	20	14	4	102	119	21	45	1	3.62
Frank Linzy	R	31	2	2	.500	12	47	0	0	77	70	27	24	0	3.04
Ken Sanders	R	30	2	9	.182	17	62	0	0	92	88	31	51	0	3.13
Jim Slaton	R	22	1	6	.143	0	9	8	0	44	50	21	17	0	5.52
Archie Reynolds	R	26	0	1	.000	0	5	2	0	19	26	8	13	0	7.11
Ray Newman	L	27	0	0	.000	1	4	0	0	7	4	2	1	0	1.00
2 Chuck Taylor	R	30	0	0	.000	1	5	0	0	12	8	3	5	0	1.50

WEST DIVISION

OAKLAND 1st 93-62 .600 — DICK WILLIAMS

NAME	G by POS	B	AGE	G	AB	R	H	2B	3B	HR	RBI	BB	SO	SB	BA	SA
TOTALS			27	155	5200	604	1248	195	29	134	565	463	886	87	.240	.366
Mike Epstein	1B137	L	29	138	455	63	123	18	2	26	70	68	68	0	.270	.490
Tim Cullen	2B65, 3B4, SS1	R	30	72	142	10	37	8	1	0	15	5	17	0	.261	.331
Bert Campaneris	SS148	R	30	149	625	85	150	25	2	8	32	32	88	52	.240	.325
Sal Bando	3B151, 2B1	R	28	152	535	64	126	20	3	15	77	78	55	3	.236	.368
Angel Mangual	OF74	R	25	91	272	19	67	13	2	5	32	14	48	0	.246	.364
Reggie Jackson	OF135	L	26	135	499	72	132	25	2	25	75	59	125	9	.265	.473
Joe Rudi	OF147, 3B1	R	25	147	593	94	181	32	9	19	75	37	62	3	.305	.486
Dave Duncan	C113	R	26	121	403	39	88	13	0	19	59	34	68	0	.218	.392
Mike Hegan	1B64, OF3	L	29	98	79	13	26	3	1	1	5	7	20	1	.329	.430
Gene Tenace	C49, OF9, 1B7, 2B2, 3B2	R	25	82	227	22	51	5	3	5	32	24	42	0	.225	.339
George Hendrick	OF41	R	22	58	121	10	22	1	1	4	15	3	22	3	.182	.306
2 Ted Kubiak	2B49, 3B1	B	30	51	94	14	17	4	1	0	8	9	11	0	.181	.245
Larry Brown (XJ)	2B46, 3B1	R	32	47	142	11	26	2	0	0	4	13	8	0	.183	.197
2 Don Mincher	1B11	L	34	47	54	2	8	1	0	0	5	10	16	0	.148	.167
2 Bill Voss	OF34	L	28	40	97	10	22	5	1	1	5	9	16	0	.227	.330
2 Matty Alou	OF32	L	33	32	121	11	34	5	0	1	16	11	12	2	.281	.347
2 Dal Maxvill	2B24, SS4	R	33	27	36	2	9	1	0	0	1	1	11	0	.250	.278
Dick Green (XJ)	2B26	R	31	26	42	1	12	1	1	0	3	3	5	0	.286	.357
2 Marty Martinez	2B17, SS6, 3B1	B	30	22	40	3	5	0	0	0	1	3	6	0	.125	.125
Gonzalo Marquez	1B2	L	26	23	21	2	8	0	0	0	4	3	4	1	.381	.381
Allen Lewis	OF6	B	30	24	10	5	2	1	0	0	2	0	1	8	.200	.300
1 Brant Alyea	OF8	R	31	20	31	3	6	1	0	1	2	3	5	0	.194	.323
2 Ollie Brown	OF16	R	28	20	54	5	13	1	0	1	4	6	14	1	.241	.315
Bobby Brooks	OF11	R	26	15	39	4	7	0	0	0	5	8	8	0	.179	.179

1 Ron Clark 29 R 4-15, 1 Curt Blefary 28 L 5-11, Bill McNulty 25 L 1-10, Adrian Garrett 29 L 0-11
2 Art Shamsky 30 L 0-7, 1 Dwain Anderson 24 R 0-7, Larry Haney 29 R 0-4, 2 Orlando Cepeda (KJ) 34 R 0-3

NAME	T	AGE	W	L	PCT	SV	G	GS	CG	IP	H	BB	SO	ShO	ERA
		20	93	62	.600	43	155	155	42	1418	1170	418	862	23	2.58
Catfish Hunter	R	26	21	7	.750	0	38	37	16	295	200	70	191	5	2.04
Ken Holtzman	L	26	19	11	.633	0	39	37	16	265	232	52	134	4	2.51
Blue Moon Odom	R	27	15	6	.714	0	31	30	4	194	164	87	86	2	2.51
Rollie Fingers	R	25	11	9	.550	21	65	0	0	111	85	32	113	0	2.51
Bob Locker	R	34	6	1	.857	10	56	0	0	78	69	16	47	0	2.65
Dave Hamilton	L	24	6	6	.500	0	25	14	1	101	94	31	55	0	2.94
Vida Blue (HO)	L	22	6	10	.375	0	25	23	5	151	117	48	111	4	2.80
Darold Knowles	L	30	5	1	.833	11	54	0	0	66	49	37	36	0	1.36
Joe Horlen	R	34	3	4	.429	1	32	6	0	84	74	20	58	0	3.00
1 Denny McLain	R	28	1	2	.333	0	5	5	0	22	32	8	8	0	6.14
1 Diego Segui	R	34	0	1	.000	0	7	3	0	23	25	7	11	0	3.52
2 Don Shaw	L	28	0	1	.000	0	3	0	0	5	12	2	4	0	18.00
Gary Waslewski	R	30	0	3	.000	0	8	0	0	18	12	8	8	0	2.00
2 Mike Kilkenny	L	27	0	0	.000	0	1	0	0	1	0	0	0	0	0.00
1 Jim Roland	L	29	0	0	.000	0	2	0	0	2	5	0	0	0	4.50

Chuck Dobson (EJ) 28

CHICAGO 2nd 87-67 .565 5.5 — CHUCK TANNER

NAME	G by POS	B	AGE	G	AB	R	H	2B	3B	HR	RBI	BB	SO	SB	BA	SA
TOTALS			27	154	5083	566	1208	170	28	108	528	511	991	100	.238	.346
Dick Allen	1B143, 3B2	R	30	148	506	90	156	28	5	37	113	99	126	19	.308	.603
Mike Andrews	2B145, 1B5	R	28	148	505	58	111	18	0	7	50	70	78	2	.220	.297
Rich Morales	SS86, 2B16, 3B14	R	28	110	287	24	59	7	1	2	20	19	49	2	.206	.258
2 Ed Spiezio	3B74	R	30	74	277	20	66	10	1	2	22	13	43	0	.238	.303
Pat Kelly	OF109	L	27	119	402	57	105	14	7	5	24	55	69	32	.261	.368
Rick Reichardt	OF90	R	29	101	291	31	73	14	4	8	43	28	63	2	.251	.409
Carlos May	OF145, 1B5	L	24	148	523	83	161	26	3	12	68	79	70	23	.308	.438
Ed Herrmann	C112	L	25	116	354	23	88	9	0	10	40	43	37	0	.249	.359
Jay Johnstone	OF97	L	26	113	261	27	49	9	0	4	17	25	42	2	.188	.268
Luis Alvarado	SS81, 2B16, 3B2	R	23	103	254	30	54	4	1	4	29	13	36	2	.213	.283
Walt Williams	OF57, 3B1	R	28	77	221	22	55	7	1	2	11	13	20	6	.249	.317
Bill Melton (XJ)	3B56	R	26	57	208	22	51	5	0	7	30	23	31	1	.245	.370
Jorge Orta	SS18, 2B14, 3B9	L	21	51	124	20	25	3	1	3	11	6	37	3	.202	.315
Tom Egan	C46	R	26	50	141	8	27	3	0	2	9	4	48	0	.191	.255
Jim Lyttle	OF21	L	26	44	82	8	19	5	2	0	5	1	28	0	.232	.341
Tony Muser	1B29, OF1	L	24	44	61	6	17	2	2	1	9	2	6	1	.279	.426
Buddy Bradford	OF28	R	27	35	48	13	13	2	0	2	8	4	13	3	.271	.438
Chuck Brinkman	C33	R	27	35	52	1	7	0	0	0	0	4	7	0	.135	.135

Lee Richard 23 R 7-29, Rudy Hernandez 20 R 4-21, Hank Allen 31 R 3-21, Jim Qualls 25 B 0-10, Hugh Yancy 22 R 1-9

NAME	T	AGE	W	L	PCT	SV	G	GS	CG	IP	H	BB	SO	ShO	ERA
		25	87	67	.565	42	154	154	36	1385	1269	431	936	14	3.12
Wilbur Wood	L	30	24	17	.585	0	49	49	20	377	325	74	193	8	2.51
Stan Bahnsen	R	27	21	16	.568	0	43	41	5	252	263	73	157	1	3.61
Tom Bradley	R	25	15	14	.517	0	40	40	11	260	225	65	209	2	2.98
Rich Gossage	R	20	7	1	.875	2	36	1	0	80	72	44	57	0	4.28
Terry Forster	L	20	6	5	.545	29	62	0	0	100	75	44	104	0	2.25
Dave Lemonds	L	23	4	7	.364	0	31	18	0	95	87	38	69	0	2.94
Cy Acosta	R	25	3	0	1.000	5	26	0	0	35	25	17	28	0	1.54
Vicente Romo (SA)	R	29	3	0	1.000	1	28	0	0	52	47	18	46	0	3.29
Steve Kealey	R	25	3	2	.600	4	40	0	0	57	50	12	37	0	3.32
Ken Frailing	L	24	1	0	1.000	0	4	0	0	3	3	1	1	0	3.00
2 Eddie Fisher	R	35	0	1	.000	0	6	4	0	22	31	9	10	0	4.50
2 Phil Regan	R	35	0	1	.000	0	10	0	0	13	18	6	4	0	4.15
Bart Johnson (KJ)	R	22	0	3	.000	1	9	0	0	14	18	13	9	0	9.00
2 Moe Drabowsky	R	36	0	0	.000	0	7	0	0	7	6	2	4	0	2.57
Jim Geddes	R	23	0	0	.000	0	5	1	0	10	12	10	3	0	7.20
Dan Neumeier	R	24	0	0	.000	0	3	0	0	3	2	3	0	0	9.00
Denny O'Toole	R	23	0	0	.000	0	3	0	0	5	10	2	5	0	5.40

MINNESOTA 3rd 77-77 .500 15.5 — BILL RIGNEY 36-34 .514 — FRANK QUILICI 41-43 .488

NAME	G by POS	B	AGE	G	AB	R	H	2B	3B	HR	RBI	BB	SO	SB	BA	SA
TOTALS			27	154	5234	537	1277	182	31	93	506	478	905	53	.244	.344
Harmon Killebrew	1B130	R	36	139	433	53	100	13	2	26	74	94	91	0	.231	.450
Rod Carew	2B139	L	26	142	535	61	170	21	6	0	51	43	60	12	**.318**	.379
Danny Thompson	SS144	R	25	144	573	54	158	22	6	4	48	34	57	3	.276	.356
Eric Soderholm	3B79	R	23	93	287	28	54	10	0	13	39	19	48	3	.188	.359
Cesar Tovar	OF139	R	31	141	548	86	145	20	6	2	31	39	39	21	.265	.334
Bobby Darwin	OF142	R	29	145	513	48	137	20	2	22	80	38	**145**	2	.267	.442
Steve Brye	OF93	R	23	100	253	18	61	9	3	0	12	17	38	3	.241	.300
Glenn Borgmann	C56	R	22	56	175	11	41	4	0	3	14	25	25	0	.234	.309
Rich Reese	1B98, OF13	L	30	132	197	23	43	3	2	5	26	25	27	0	.218	.330
Steve Braun	3B74, 2B20, SS11, OF9	L	23	121	402	40	116	21	0	2	50	45	38	4	.289	.356
Jim Nettles	OF78, 1B1	L	25	102	235	28	48	5	2	4	15	32	52	4	.204	.294
George Mitterwald	C61	R	27	64	163	12	30	4	1	1	8	9	37	0	.184	.239
Chuck Manuel	OF28	L	28	63	122	6	25	5	0	1	8	4	16	0	.205	.270
Phil Roof	C61	R	31	61	146	16	30	11	1	3	12	6	27	0	.205	.356
Rick Renick	OF21, 1B6, 3B4, SS1	R	28	55	93	10	16	2	0	4	8	15	25	0	.172	.323
Dan Monzon	2B13, 3B5, SS3, OF1	R	26	55	55	13	15	1	0	0	5	8	12	1	.273	.291

Rick Dempsey 22 R 8-40, Tony Oliva (KJ) 32 L 9-28, Jim Holt 28 L 12-27, Mike Adams 23 R 2-6, Bucky Guth 24 R 0-3

NAME	T	AGE	W	L	PCT	SV	G	GS	CG	IP	H	BB	SO	ShO	ERA
		26	77	77	.500	34	154	154	37	1399	1188	444	838	17	2.84
Bert Blyleven	R	21	17	17	.500	0	39	38	11	287	247	69	228	3	2.73
Dick Woodson	R	27	14	14	.500	0	36	36	9	252	193	101	150	3	2.71
Jim Perry	R	36	13	16	.448	0	35	35	5	218	191	60	85	2	3.34
Jim Kaat (BW)	L	33	10	2	.833	0	15	15	5	113	94	20	64	0	2.07
Ray Corbin	R	23	8	9	.471	0	31	19	5	162	135	53	83	3	2.61
Dave LaRoche	L	24	5	7	.417	10	62	0	0	95	72	39	79	0	2.84
Wayne Granger	R	28	4	6	.400	19	63	0	0	90	83	28	45	0	3.00
Jim Strickland	L	26	3	1	.750	3	25	0	0	36	28	19	30	0	2.50
Dave Goltz	R	23	3	3	.500	1	15	11	2	91	75	26	38	0	2.67
Bob Gebhard	R	29	0	1	.000	1	13	0	0	21	36	13	13	0	8.57
Tom Norton (EJ)	R	22	0	1	.000	0	21	0	0	32	31	14	22	0	2.81
Steve Luebber	R	22	0	0	.000	0	2	0	0	2	3	2	1	0	0.00

KANSAS CITY 4th 76-78 .494 16.5 — BOB LEMON

NAME	G by POS	B	AGE	G	AB	R	H	2B	3B	HR	RBI	BB	SO	SB	BA	SA
TOTALS			27	154	5167	580	**1317**	220	26	78	547	**534**	711	85	**.255**	.353
John Mayberry	1B146	L	22	149	503	65	150	24	3	25	100	78	74	0	.298	.507
Cookie Rojas	2B131, 3B6, SS2	R	33	137	487	49	127	25	0	3	53	41	35	2	.261	.331
Freddie Patek	SS136	R	27	136	518	59	110	25	4	0	32	47	64	33	.212	.276
Paul Schaal	3B123, SS1	R	29	127	435	47	99	19	3	6	41	61	59	1	.228	.326
Richie Scheinblum	OF119	B	29	134	450	60	135	21	4	8	66	58	40	0	.300	.418
Amos Otis	OF1[illegible]	[illegible]	[illegible]	[illegible]	[illegible]	[illegible]	[illegible]	[illegible]	[illegible]	11	[illegible]	[illegible]	[illegible]	28	.293	.413
Lou Piniella	OF150	R	28	151	574	65	179	**33**	4	11	72	34	59	7	.312	.441
Ed Kirkpatrick	C108, 1B1	L	27	113	364	43	100	15	1	9	43	51	50	3	.275	.396
Steve Hovley	OF68	L	27	105	196	24	53	5	1	3	24	24	29	3	.270	.352
Carl Taylor	C21, OF7, 1B6, 3B5	R	28	63	113	17	30	2	1	0	11	17	61	4	.265	.301
Bobby Floyd	3B30, SS29, 2B2	R	28	61	134	9	24	3	0	0	5	5	29	1	.179	.201
Jerry May	C41	R	28	53	116	10	22	5	1	1	4	14	13	0	.190	.276
Joe Keough	OF16	L	26	56	64	8	14	2	0	0	5	8	7	2	.219	.250
Gail Hopkins	1B13, 3B1	L	29	53	71	1	15	2	0	0	5	7	4	0	.211	.239
Bobby Knoop	2B33, 3B4	R	33	44	97	8	23	5	0	0	7	9	16	0	.237	.289

1 Bob Oliver 29 R 17-63, Ron Hansen 34 R 4-30, Jim Wohlford 21 R 6-25, Dennis Paepke 27 R 0-6

NAME	T	AGE	W	L	PCT	SV	G	GS	CG	IP	H	BB	SO	ShO	ERA
		28	76	78	.494	28	154	154	44	1381	1293	405	801	16	3.24
Paul Splittorff	L	25	12	12	.500	0	35	33	12	216	189	67	140	2	3.13
Dick Drago	R	27	12	17	.414	0	34	33	11	239	230	51	135	2	3.01
Roger Nelson (SJ)	R	28	11	6	.647	2	34	19	10	173	120	31	120	6	2.08
Tom Burgmeier	L	28	6	2	.750	9	51	0	0	55	67	33	18	0	4.25
Bruce Dal Canton	R	30	6	6	.500	2	36	16	1	132	135	29	75	0	3.41
Jim Rooker	L	30	5	6	.455	0	18	10	4	72	78	24	44	2	4.38
Mike Hedlund	R	25	5	7	.417	0	29	16	1	113	119	41	52	0	4.78
2 Tom Murphy	R	26	4	4	.500	1	18	9	1	70	77	16	34	1	3.09
Steve Busby	R	22	3	1	.750	0	5	5	3	40	28	8	31	0	1.58
Monte Montgomery	R	25	3	3	.500	0	9	8	1	56	55	17	24	1	3.05
Ted Abernathy	R	39	3	4	.429	5	45	0	0	58	44	19	28	0	1.71
Norm Angelini	L	24	2	1	.667	2	21	0	0	16	13	12	16	0	2.25
Al Fitzmorris	R	26	2	5	.286	3	38	2	0	101	99	28	51	0	3.74
Mike Jackson	L	26	1	2	.333	0	7	3	0	20	24	14	15	0	6.30
Ken Wright	R	25	1	2	.333	4	17	0	0	18	15	15	18	0	5.00

CALIFORNIA 5th 75-80 .484 18 — DEL RICE

NAME	G by POS	B	AGE	G	AB	R	H	2B	3B	HR	RBI	BB	SO	SB	BA	SA
TOTALS			28	155	5165	454	1249	171	26	78	420	358	850	57	.242	.330
2 Bob Oliver	1B127, OF8	R	29	134	509	47	137	20	4	19	70	27	97	4	.269	.436
Sandy Alomar	2B154, SS4	B	28	155	610	65	146	20	3	1	25	47	55	20	.239	.287
Leo Cardenas	SS150	R	33	150	551	25	123	11	2	6	42	35	73	1	.223	.283
Ken McMullen	3B137	R	30	137	472	36	127	18	1	9	34	48	59	1	.269	.369
Leroy Stanton	OF124	R	26	127	402	44	101	15	3	12	39	22	100	2	.251	.393
Ken Berry	OF116	R	31	119	409	41	118	15	3	5	39	35	47	5	.289	.377
Vada Pinson	OF134, 1B1	L	33	136	484	56	133	24	2	7	49	30	54	17	.275	.376
Art Kusnyer	C63	R	26	64	179	13	37	2	1	2	13	16	33	0	.207	.263
Jim Spencer	1B35, OF24	L	24	82	212	13	47	5	0	1	14	12	25	0	.222	.259
Johnny Stephenson	C56	L	31	66	146	14	40	3	1	2	17	11	8	0	.274	.349
Jeff Torborg (IL)	C58	R	30	59	153	5	32	3	0	0	8	14	21	0	.209	.229
Mickey Rivers	OF48	L	23	58	159	18	34	6	2	0	7	8	26	4	.214	.277
1 Andy Kosco	OF36	R	30	49	142	15	34	4	2	6	13	5	23	1	.239	.423
Winston Llenas	3B10, 2B2, OF2	R	28	44	64	3	17	3	0	0	7	3	8	0	.266	.313
2 Curt Motton	OF9	R	31	42	39	6	6	1	0	0	1	5	12	0	.154	.179
Billy Parker	3B21, 2B9, OF5, SS1	R	25	36	80	11	17	2	0	2	8	9	17	0	.213	.313
1 Syd O'Brien	3B8, SS4, 2B3, 1B1	R	27	36	39	10	7	2	0	1	1	6	10	0	.179	.308

Jack Hiatt '29 R 13-45, Doug Howard 24 R 10-38, Chris Coletta 27 L 9-30, Tommy Silverio 26 L 2-12, Roger Repoz 31 L 1-3, Billy Cowan 33 R 0-3, 1 Joe Azcue 32 R 0-2

NAME	T	AGE	W	L	PCT	SV	G	GS	CG	IP	H	BB	SO	ShO	ERA
		28	75	80	.484	16	155	155	57	1378	1109	**620**	**1000**	18	3.06
Nolan Ryan	R	25	19	16	.543	0	39	39	20	284	166	**157**	**329**	**9**	2.28
Clyde Wright	L	31	18	11	.621	0	35	35	15	251	229	80	87	2	2.98
Rudy May	L	27	12	11	.522	1	35	30	10	205	162	82	169	3	2.94
Andy Messersmith (RJ)	R	26	8	11	.421	2	25	21	10	170	125	68	142	3	2.81
2 Steve Barber	L	33	4	4	.500	2	34	3	0	58	37	30	34	0	2.02
1 Eddie Fisher	R	35	4	5	.444	4	43	1	0	81	73	31	32	0	3.78
Rickey Clark	R	26	4	9	.308	1	26	15	2	110	105	55	61	0	4.50
Lloyd Allen	R	22	3	7	.300	5	42	6	0	85	76	55	53	0	3.49
Dave Sells	R	25	2	0	1.000	0	10	0	0	16	11	5	2	0	2.81
Don Rose	R	25	1	4	.200	0	16	4	0	43	49	19	39	0	4.19
Tom Dukes (EJ)	R	29	0	1	.000	1	7	0	0	11	11	0	8	0	1.64
Alan Foster	R	25	0	1	.000	0	8	0	0	13	12	6	11	0	4.85
Paul Doyle	L	32	0	0	.000	0	2	0	0	2	2	3	4	0	0.00
Dick Lange	R	23	0	0	.000	0	2	1	0	8	7	2	8	0	4.50
1 Tom Murphy	R	26	0	0	.000	0	6	0	0	10	13	8	2	0	5.40
Mel Queen	R	30	0	0	.000	0	17	0	0	31	31	19	19	0	4.35

TEXAS 6th 54-100 .351 38.5 — TED WILLIAMS

NAME	G by POS	B	AGE	G	AB	R	H	2B	3B	HR	RBI	BB	SO	SB	BA	SA
TOTALS			26	154	5029	461	1092	166	17	56	424	503	926	**126**	.217	.290
1 Frank Howard	1B66, OF21	R	35	95	287	28	70	9	0	9	31	42	55	1	.244	.369
Lenny Randle	2B65, SS4, OF2	B	23	74	249	23	48	13	0	2	21	13	51	4	.193	.269
Toby Harrah (IL)	SS106	R	23	116	374	47	97	14	3	1	31	34	31	16	.259	.321
Dave Nelson	3B119, OF15	B	28	145	499	68	113	16	3	2	28	67	81	51	.226	.283
Ted Ford	OF119	R	25	129	429	43	101	19	1	14	50	37	80	4	.235	.382
Joe Lovitto	OF103	B	21	117	330	23	74	9	1	1	19	37	54	13	.224	.267
Elliott Maddox (BH)	OF94	R	24	98	294	40	74	7	2	0	10	49	53	20	.252	.289
Dick Billings	C92, OF41, 3B5, 1B1	R	29	133	469	41	119	15	1	5	58	29	77	1	.254	.322
Larry Biittner	1B65, OF65	L	26	137	382	34	99	18	1	3	31	29	37	1	.259	.335
2 Dalton Jones	3B23, 2B17, 1B7, OF2	L	28	72	151	14	24	2	0	4	19	10	31	1	.159	.252
Tommy Grieve	OF49	R	24	64	142	12	29	2	1	3	11	11	39	1	.204	.296
1 Don Mincher	1B59	L	34	61	191	23	45	10	0	6	39	46	23	2	.236	.382
Vic Harris	2B58, SS1	B	22	61	186	8	26	5	1	0	10	12	39	7	.140	.177
Hal King	C38	L	28	50	122	12	22	5	0	4	12	25	35	0	.180	.320
Jim Mason	SS32, 3B10	L	21	46	147	10	29	3	0	0	10	9	39	0	.197	.218
1 Ted Kubiak	2B25, SS15, 3B1	B	30	46	116	5	26	3	0	0	7	12	12	0	.224	.250
Bill Fahey	C39	L	22	39	119	8	20	2	0	1	10	12	23	4	.168	.210
3 Marty Martinez	SS5, 3B4, 2B1	B	30	26	41	3	6	1	1	0	3	2	8	0	.146	.220

Tom Ragland 26 R 10-58, Ken Suarez 29 R 5-33, Jeff Burroughs (XJ) 21 R 12-65, Jim Driscoll 28 L 0-18

NAME	T	AGE	W	L	PCT	SV	G	GS	CG	IP	H	BB	SO	ShO	ERA
		26	54	**100**	.351	34	154	154	11	1375	1258	613	868	8	3.53
Rich Hand	R	23	10	14	.417	0	30	28	2	171	139	103	109	1	3.32
Mike Paul	L	27	8	9	.471	1	49	20	1	162	149	52	108	1	3.64
Dick Bosman	R	28	8	10	.444	0	29	29	1	173	183	48	105	1	3.64
Paul Lindblad	L	30	5	8	.385	9	**66**	0	0	100	95	29	51	0	2.61
Jim Panther	R	27	5	9	.357	0	58	4	0	94	101	46	44	0	4.12
Pete Broberg	R	22	5	12	.294	1	39	25	3	176	153	85	133	2	4.30
Bill Gogolewski	R	24	4	11	.267	2	36	21	2	151	136	58	95	1	4.23
1 Casey Cox	R	30	3	5	.375	4	35	4	0	65	73	26	27	0	4.43
Jim Shellenback	L	28	2	4	.333	1	22	6	0	57	46	16	30	0	3.47
Horacio Pina	R	27	2	7	.222	15	60	0	0	76	61	43	60	0	3.20
Don Stanhouse (EJ)	R	21	2	9	.182	0	24	16	1	105	83	73	78	0	3.77
2 Rich Hinton	L	25	0	1	.000	0	5	0	0	11	7	10	4	0	2.45
Jerry Janeski	R	26	0	1	.000	0	4	1	0	13	11	7	7	0	2.77
Jan Dukes	L	26	0	0	.000	0	3	0	0	2	1	5	0	0	4.50
Steve Lawson	L	21	0	0	.000	1	13	0	0	16	13	10	13	0	2.81
3 Jim Roland	L	29	0	0	.000	0	5	0	0	3	7	2	4	0	9.00

AMERICAN LEAGUE CHAMPIONSHIP – OAKLAND (WEST) 3 DETROIT (EAST) 2

LINE SCORES

TEAM	1	2	3	4	5	6	7	8	9	10	11	12	R	H	E
Game 1 October 7 at Oakland															
DET	0	1	0	0	0	0	0	0	0	0	1		2	6	2
OAK	0	0	1	0	0	0	0	0	0	0	2		3	10	1
Lolich, Seelbach (11) — Hunter, Blue (9), **Fingers** (9)															
Game 2 October 8 at Oakland															
DET	0	0	0	0	0	0	0	0	0				0	3	1
OAK	1	0	0	0	4	0	0	0	X				5	8	0
Fryman, Zachary (5), Scherman (5), LaGrow (6), Hiller (7) — **Odom**															
Game 3 October 10 at Detroit															
OAK	0	0	0	0	0	0	0	0	0				0	7	0
DET	0	0	0	2	0	0	0	1	X				3	8	1
Holtzman, Fingers (5), Blue (6), Locker (7) — **Coleman**															
Game 4 October 11 at Detroit															
OAK	0	0	0	0	0	0	1	0	0	2			3	9	2
DET	0	0	1	0	0	0	0	0	0	3			4	10	1
Hunter, Fingers (8), Blue (9), Locker (10), **Horlen** (10), Hamilton (10) — Lolich, Seelbach (10), **Hiller** (10)															
Game 5 October 12 at Detroit															
OAK	0	1	0	1	0	0	0	0	0				2	4	0
DET	1	0	0	0	0	0	0	0	0				1	5	2
Odom, Blue (6) — **Fryman**, Hiller (9)															

COMPOSITE BATTING

NAME	POS	G	AB	R	H	2B	3B	HR	RBI	BA
Oakland										
Totals		5	170	13	38	8	0	1	10	.224
Alou	OF	5	**21**	2	**8**	**4**	0	0	2	**.381**
Rudi	OF	5	20	1	5	1	0	0	2	.250
Bando	3B	5	20	0	4	0	0	0	0	.200
Jackson	OF	5	18	1	5	1	0	0	2	.278
Tenace	C-2B	5	17	1	1	0	0	0	1	.059
Epstein	1B	5	16	1	3	0	0	1	1	.188
Green	2B	5	8	0	1	1	0	0	0	.125
Maxvill	2B-SS	5	8	0	1	0	0	0	0	.125
Campaneris	SS	2	7	**3**	3	0	0	0	0	.429
Hendrick	OF	5	7	2	1	0	0	0	0	.143
Kubiak	2B-SS	4	4	0	2	0	0	0	1	.500
Marquez	PH	3	3	1	2	0	0	0	1	.667
Mangual	PH	3	3	0	0	0	0	0	0	.000
Duncan	C	2	2	0	0	0	0	0	0	.000

Odom P-PR 1-4, Cullen SS 0-1, Mincher PH 0-1, Hegan 1B 0-1

NAME	POS	G	AB	R	H	2B	3B	HR	RBI	BA
Detroit										
Totals		5	162	10	32	6	1	4	10	.198
McAuliffe	2B-SS	5	20	**3**	4	0	0	1	1	.200
Kaline	OF	5	19	**3**	5	0	0	1	1	.263
Rodriguez	3B	5	16	0	0	0	0	0	0	.000
Cash	1B	5	15	1	4	0	0	1	2	.267
Taylor	2B	4	15	0	2	2	0	0	0	.133
Northrop	OF	5	14	0	5	0	0	0	1	.357
Sims	C-OF	4	14	0	3	2	1	0	0	.214
Freehan	C	3	12	2	3	1	0	1	**3**	.250
Horton	OF	5	10	0	1	0	0	0	0	.100
Stanley	OF	4	6	0	2	0	0	0	0	.333

Brinkman SS 1-4, I. Brown 1B 1-2, G. Brown PH 0-2, Haller PH 0-1, Knox PR 0-0, Niekro PR 0-0

COMPOSITE PITCHING

NAME	G	IP	H	BB	SO	W	L	SV	ERA
Oakland									
Totals	5	46	32	13	25	3	2	1	1.76
Hunter	2	15.1	10	**5**	9	0	0	0	1.17
Odom	2	14	5	2	5	**2**	0	0	**0.00**
Blue	**4**	5.1	4	1	5	0	0	1	**0.00**
Fingers	3	5.1	4	1	3	1	0	0	1.69
Holtzman	1	4	4	2	2	0	1	0	4.50
Locker	2	2	4	0	1	0	0	0	13.50
Hamilton	1	0	1	1	0	0	0	0	0.00
Horlen	1	0	0	1	0	0	1	0	∞
Detroit									
Totals	5	46.1	38	12	35	2	3	0	2.14
Lolich	2	**19**	**14**	**5**	10	0	1	0	1.42
Fryman	2	12.1	11	2	8	0	**2**	0	3.65
Coleman	1	9	7	3	**14**	1	0	0	**0.00**
Hiller	3	3.1	1	1	1	1	0	0	0.00
LaGrow	1	1	0	0	1	0	0	0	0.00
Seelbach	2	1	4	0	0	0	0	0	18.00
Scherman	1	.2	1	0	1	0	0	0	0.00
Zachary	1	0	0	1	0	0	0	0	∞

LINE SCORES

TEAM	1	2	3	4	5	6	7	8	9	10	11	12	R	H	E
Game 1 October 7 at Pittsburgh															
CIN	1	0	0	0	0	0	0	0	0				1	8	0
PIT	3	0	0	0	2	0	0	0	X				5	6	0
Gullett, Borbon (7) — **Blass**, R. Hernandez (9)															
Game 2 October 8 at Pittsburgh															
CIN	4	0	0	0	0	0	0	1	0				5	8	1
PIT	0	0	0	1	1	1	0	0	0				3	7	1
Billingham, **Hall** (5) — **Moose**, Johnson (1), Kison (6), R. Hernandez (7), Giusti (9)															
Game 3 October 9 at Cincinnati															
PIT	0	0	0	0	1	0	1	1	0				3	7	0
CIN	0	0	2	0	0	0	0	0	0				2	8	1
Briles, **Kison** (7), Giusti (8) — Nolan, Borbon (7), **Carroll** (7), McGlothin (9)															
Game 4 October 10 at Cincinnati															
PIT	0	0	0	0	0	0	1	0	0				1	2	3
CIN	1	0	0	2	0	2	2	0	X				7	11	1
Ellis, Johnson (6), Walker (7), Miller (8) — **Grimsley**															
Game 5 October 11 at Cincinnati															
PIT	0	2	0	1	0	0	0	0	0				3	8	0
CIN	0	0	1	0	1	0	0	0	2				4	7	1
Blass, R. Hernandez (8), **Giusti** (9), Moose (9) — Gullett, Borbon (4), Hall (6), **Carroll** (9)															

COMPOSITE BATTING

NAME	POS	G	AB	R	H	2B	3B	HR	RBI	BA
Cincinnati Totals		5	166	19	42	9	2	4	16	.253
Tolan	OF	5	**21**	3	5	1	1	0	**4**	.238
Rose	OF	5	20	1	**9**	**4**	0	0	2	**.450**
Perez	1B	5	20	0	4	1	0	0	2	.200
Geronimo	OF	5	20	2	2	0	0	1	1	.100
Morgan	2B	5	19	**5**	5	0	0	**2**	3	.263
Bench	C	5	18	3	6	1	1	1	2	.333
Menke	3B	5	16	1	4	1	0	0	0	.250
Chaney	SS	5	16	3	3	0	0	0	1	.188
Uhlaender	PH	2	2	0	1	0	0	0	0	.500
Concepcion	SS	3	2	0	0	0	0	0	0	.000
Hague PH 0-1, McRae PH 0-0, Foster PR 0-0										
Pittsburgh Totals		5	158	15	30	6	1	3	14	.190
Stennett	OF-2B	5	**21**	2	6	0	0	0	1	.286
Oliver	OF	5	20	3	5	2	1	1	3	.250
Cash	2B	5	19	0	4	0	0	0	3	.211
Clemente	OF	5	17	1	4	1	0	1	2	.235
Sanguillen	C	5	16	4	5	1	0	1	2	.313
Hebner	3B	5	16	2	3	1	0	0	1	.188
Stargell	1B-OF	5	16	1	1	1	0	0	1	.063
Alley	SS	5	16	1	0	0	0	0	0	.000
May	C	1	2	0	1	0	0	0	1	.500
Mazeroski	PH	2	2	0	1	0	0	0	0	.500
Clines PH PR 0 2, Davalillo PH 0-0, Robertson 1B 0-0, Ellis P-PR 0-1										

COMPOSITE PITCHING

NAME	G	IP	H	BB	SO	W	L	SV	ERA
Cincinnati Totals	5	44	30	9	27	3	2	0	3.07
Grimsley	1	9	2	0	5	1	0	0	**1.00**
Gullett	2	9	**12**	0	5	0	1	0	8.00
Hall	2	7.1	3	3	**8**	1	0	0	1.23
Nolan	1	6	4	1	4	0	0	0	1.50
Billingham	1	4.2	5	2	4	0	0	0	3.86
Borbon	**3**	4.1	2	0	1	0	0	0	2.08
Carroll	2	2.2	2	3	0	1	1	0	3.38
McGlothin	1	1	0	0	0	0	0	0	0.00
Pittsburgh Totals	5	43.2	42	10	28	2	3	2	3.30
Blass	2	**15.2**	**12**	**6**	5	1	0	0	1.72
Briles	1	6	6	1	3	0	0	0	3.00
Johnson	2	6	4	2	7	0	0	0	3.00
Ellis	1	5	5	1	3	0	1	0	0.00
R. Hernandez	**3**	3.1	1	0	3	0	0	1	2.70
Giusti	**3**	2.2	5	0	3	0	1	1	6.75
Kison	2	2.1	1	0	3	1	0	0	0.00
Miller	1	1	0	0	1	0	0	0	0.00
Walker	1	1	3	0	0	0	0	0	18.00
Moose	2	.2	5	0	0	0	1	0	54.00

EAST DIVISION

PITTSBURGH 1st 96-59 .619 — BILL VIRDON

NAME	G by POS	B	AGE	G	AB	R	H	2B	3B	HR	RBI	BB	SO	SB	BA	SA
TOTALS			28	155	**5490**	691	**1505**	**251**	**47**	110	654	404	871	49	**.274**	**.397**
Willie Stargell	1B101, OF32	L	32	138	495	75	145	28	2	33	112	65	129	1	.293	.558
Dave Cash	2B97	R	24	99	425	58	120	22	4	3	30	22	31	9	.282	.374
Gene Alley	SS114, 3B4	R	31	119	347	30	86	12	2	3	36	38	52	4	.248	.320
Richie Hebner	3B121	L	24	124	427	63	128	24	4	19	72	52	54	0	.300	.508
Roberto Clemente (NJ)	OF94	R	37	102	378	68	118	19	7	10	60	29	49	0	.312	.479
Al Oliver	OF138, 1B3	L	25	140	565	88	176	27	4	12	89	34	44	2	.312	.437
Vic Davalillo	OF97, 1B8	L	35	117	368	59	117	19	2	4	28	26	44	14	.318	.413
Manny Sanguillen	C127, OF2	R	28	136	520	55	155	18	8	7	71	21	38	1	.298	.404
Bob Robertson	1B89, OF23, 3B11	R	25	115	306	25	59	11	0	12	41	41	84	1	.193	.346
Rennie Stennett	2B49, OF41, SS6	R	21	109	370	43	106	14	5	3	30	9	43	4	.286	.376
Gene Clines	OF83	R	25	107	311	52	104	15	6	0	17	16	47	12	.334	.421
Jackie Hernandez	SS68, 3B4	R	31	72	176	12	33	7	1	1	14	9	43	0	.188	.256
Milt May	C33	L	21	57	139	12	39	10	0	0	14	10	13	0	.281	.353
Jose Pagan	3B32, OF2	R	37	53	127	11	32	9	0	3	8	5	17	0	.252	.394
Bill Mazeroski (XJ)	2B15, 3B3	R	35	34	64	3	12	4	0	0	3	3	5	0	.188	.250

Richie Zisk 23 R 7-37, Chuck Goggin 26 R 2-7, Frank Taveras 21 R 0-3, Fernando Gonzalez 22 R 0-2, Charlie Sands 24 L 0-1

NAME	T	AGE	W	L	PCT	SV	G	GS	CG	IP	H	BB	SO	ShO	ERA
TOTALS		28	**96**	59	**.619**	48	155	155	39	1414	1282	433	838	15	2.81
Steve Blass	R	30	19	8	.704	0	33	32	11	250	227	84	117	2	2.48
Dock Ellis	R	27	15	7	.682	0	25	25	4	163	156	33	96	1	2.71
Nelson Briles	R	28	14	11	.560	0	28	27	9	196	185	43	120	2	3.08
Bob Moose	R	24	13	10	.565	1	31	30	6	226	213	47	144	3	2.91
Bruce Kison	R	22	9	7	.563	3	32	18	6	152	123	69	102	1	3.26
Dave Giusti	R	32	7	4	.636	22	54	0	0	75	59	20	54	0	1.92
Ramon Hernandez	L	31	5	0	1.000	14	53	0	0	70	50	22	47	0	1.67
Bob Miller	R	33	5	2	.714	3	36	0	0	54	54	24	18	0	2.67
Bob Johnson	R	29	4	4	.500	3	31	11	1	116	98	46	79	0	2.95
Luke Walker (XJ)	L	28	4	6	.400	2	26	12	2	93	98	34	48	0	3.39
Jim McKee	R	25	1	0	1.000	0	2	0	0	5	2	1	4	0	0.00
Gene Garber	R	24	0	0	.000	0	4	0	0	6	7	3	3	0	7.50
1 Bob Veale	L	36	0	0	.000	0	5	0	0	9	10	7	6	0	6.00

CHICAGO 2nd 85-70 .548 11 — 1 LEO DUROCHER 46-44 .511 WHITEY LOCKMAN 39-26 .600

NAME	G by POS	B	AGE	G	AB	R	H	2B	3B	HR	RBI	BB	SO	SB	BA	SA
TOTALS			31	156	5247	685	1346	206	40	133	634	565	815	69	.257	.387
Jim Hickman	1B77, OF27	R	35	115	368	65	100	15	2	17	64	52	64	3	.272	.462
Glenn Beckert	2B118	R	31	120	474	51	128	22	2	3	43	23	17	2	.270	.344
Don Kessinger	SS146	B	29	149	577	77	158	20	6	1	39	67	44	8	.274	.334
Ron Santo (BW)	3B129, 2B3, SS1, OF1	R	32	133	464	68	140	25	5	17	74	69	75	1	.302	.487
Jose Cardenal	OF137	R	28	143	533	96	155	24	6	17	70	55	58	25	.291	.454
Rick Monday	OF134	L	26	138	434	68	108	22	5	11	42	78	102	12	.249	.399
Billy Williams	OF144, 1B5	L	34	150	574	95	191	34	6	37	122	62	59	3	.333	.606
Randy Hundley	C113	R	30	114	357	23	78	12	0	5	30	22	62	1	.218	.294
C. Fanzone	3B36, 1B21, 2B13, SS1, OF1	R	29	86	222	26	50	11	0	8	42	35	45	2	.225	.383
Joe Pepitone (VR)	1B66	L	31	66	214	23	56	5	0	8	21	13	22	1	.262	.397
Billy North	OF48	B	24	66	127	22	23	2	3	0	4	13	33	6	.181	.244
Paul Popovich (IL)	2B36, SS8, 3B1	B	31	58	129	8	25	3	2	1	11	12	8	0	.194	.271
Ken Rudolph	C41	R	25	42	106	10	25	1	1	2	9	6	14	1	.236	.321
Gene Hiser	OF15	L	23	32	46	2	9	0	0	0	4	6	8	1	.196	.196
J. C. Martin (EJ)	C17	L	35	25	50	3	12	3	0	0	7	5	9	1	.240	.300
2 Ellie Hendricks	C16	L	31	17	43	7	5	1	0	2	6	13	8	0	.116	.279

Pat Bourque 25 L 7-27, 1 Tommy Davis 33 R 7-26, 1 Art Shamsky 30 L 2-16, Dave Rosello 22 R 3-12, Al Montreuil 28 R 1-11, Jim Tyrone 23 R 0-8, Pete LaCock 20 L 3-6, Frank Fernandez 29 R 0-3, Frank Coggins 28 B 0-1, Chris Ward 23 L 0-1

NAME	T	AGE	W	L	PCT	SV	G	GS	CG	IP	H	BB	SO	ShO	ERA
TOTALS		29	85	70	.548	32	156	156	54	1399	1329	421	824	19	3.22
Ferguson Jenkins	R	28	20	12	.625	0	36	36	23	289	253	62	184	5	3.21
Milt Pappas	R	33	17	7	.708	0	29	28	10	195	187	29	80	3	2.77
Bill Hands	R	32	11	8	.579	0	32	28	6	189	168	47	96	3	3.00
Burt Hooton	R	22	11	14	.440	0	33	31	9	218	201	81	132	3	2.81
Rick Reuschel	R	23	10	8	.556	0	21	18	5	129	127	29	87	4	2.93
2 Jack Aker	R	31	6	6	.500	17	48	0	0	67	65	23	36	0	2.96
Juan Pizarro	L	35	4	5	.444	1	16	7	1	59	66	32	24	0	3.97
2 Tom Phoebus	R	27	3	3	.500	6	37	1	0	83	76	45	59	0	3.80
Joe Decker	R	25	1	0	1.000	0	5	1	0	13	9	4	7	0	2.08
Steve Hamilton	L	38	1	0	1.000	0	22	0	0	17	24	8	13	0	4.76
Bill Bonham	R	23	1	1	.500	4	19	4	0	58	56	25	49	0	3.10
1 Phil Regan	R	35	0	1	.000	0	5	0	0	4	6	2	2	0	2.25
Dan McGinn	L	28	0	5	.000	4	42	2	0	63	78	29	42	0	5.86
Clint Compton	L	21	0	0	.000	0	1	0	0	2	2	2	0	0	9.00
Larry Gura	L	24	0	0	.000	0	7	0	0	12	11	3	13	0	3.75

NEW YORK 3rd 83-73 .532 13.5 — GIL HODGES (DD) 47 YOGI BERRA 83-73 .532

NAME	G by POS	B	AGE	G	AB	R	H	2B	3B	HR	RBI	BB	SO	SB	BA	SA
TOTALS			28	156	5135	528	1154	175	31	105	490	589	**990**	41	.225	.332
Ed Kranepool	1B108, OF1	L	27	122	327	28	88	15	1	8	34	34	35	1	.269	.394
Ken Boswell	2B94	L	26	100	355	35	75	9	1	9	33	32	35	2	.211	.318
Bud Harrelson (XJ)	SS115	B	28	115	418	54	90	10	4	1	24	58	57	12	.215	.266
Jim Fregosi	3B85, SS6, 1B3	R	30	101	340	31	79	15	4	5	32	38	71	0	.232	.344
John Milner	OF91, 1B10	L	22	117	362	52	86	12	2	17	38	51	74	2	.238	.423
Tommie Agee	OF109	R	29	114	422	52	96	23	0	13	47	53	92	8	.227	.374
Cleon Jones	OF84, 1B20	R	29	106	375	39	92	15	1	5	52	30	83	1	.245	.331
Duffy Dyer	C91, OF1	R	26	94	325	33	75	17	3	8	36	28	71	0	.231	.375
Wayne Garrett	3B82, 2B22	L	24	111	298	41	69	13	3	2	29	70	58	3	.232	.315
Ted Martinez	2B47, SS42, OF15, 3B2	R	24	103	330	22	74	5	5	1	19	12	49	7	.224	.279
Dave Marshall	OF42	L	29	72	156	21	39	5	0	4	11	22	28	3	.250	.359
2 Willie Mays	OF49, 1B11	R	41	69	195	27	52	9	1	8	19	43	43	1	.267	.446
Rusty Staub (BH)	OF65	L	28	66	239	32	70	11	0	9	38	31	13	0	.293	.452
Jerry Grote (AJ)	C59, 3B3, OF1	R	29	64	205	15	43	5	1	3	21	26	27	1	.210	.288
Jim Beauchamp	1B35, OF5	R	32	58	120	10	29	1	0	5	19	7	33	0	.242	.375
Dave Schneck	OF33	L	23	37	123	7	23	3	2	3	10	10	26	0	.187	.317
Lute Barnes	2B14, SS6	R	25	24	72	5	17	2	2	0	6	6	4	0	.236	.319

Bill Sudakis (KJ) 26 B 7-49, Don Hahn 23 R 6-37, Joe Nolan 21 L 0-10

NAME	T	AGE	W	L	PCT	SV	G	GS	CG	IP	H	BB	SO	ShO	ERA
TOTALS		27	83	73	.532	41	156	156	32	**1415**	1263	486	**1059**	12	3.26
Tom Seaver	R	27	21	12	.636	0	35	35	13	262	215	77	249	3	2.92
Jon Matlack	L	22	15	10	.600	0	34	32	8	244	215	71	169	4	2.32
Jim McAndrew	R	28	11	8	.579	1	28	23	4	161	133	38	81	0	2.80
Jerry Koosman	L	29	11	12	.478	1	34	24	4	163	155	52	147	1	4.14
Tug McGraw	L	27	8	6	.571	27	54	0	0	106	71	40	92	0	1.70
Gary Gentry	R	25	7	10	.412	0	32	26	3	164	153	75	120	0	4.01
Danny Frisella	R	26	5	8	.385	9	39	0	0	67	63	20	46	0	3.36
Buzz Capra	R	24	3	2	.600	0	14	6	0	53	50	27	45	0	4.58
Ray Sadecki	L	31	2	1	.667	0	34	2	0	76	73	31	38	0	3.08
Bob Rauch	R	23	0	1	.000	1	19	0	0	27	27	21	23	0	5.00
Brent Strom	L	23	0	3	.000	0	11	5	0	30	34	15	20	0	6.90
1 Chuck Taylor	R	30	0	0	.000	2	20	0	0	31	44	9	9	0	5.52
Tommy Moore	R	23	0	0	.000	0	3	1	0	12	12	1	5	0	3.00
Hank Webb	R	22	0	0	.000	0	6	2	0	18	18	9	15	0	4.50

ST. LOUIS 4th 75-81 .481 21.5 — RED SCHOENDIENST

NAME	G by POS	B	AGE	G	AB	R	H	2B	3B	HR	RBI	BB	SO	SB	BA	SA
TOTALS			27	156	5326	568	1383	214	42	70	518	437	793	104	.260	.355
1 Matty Alou	1B66, OF39	L	33	108	404	46	127	17	2	3	31	24	23	11	.314	.389
Ted Sizemore	2B111	R	27	120	439	53	116	17	4	2	38	37	36	8	.264	.335
1 Dal Maxvill	SS95, 2B11	R	33	105	276	22	61	6	1	1	23	31	47	0	.221	.261
Joe Torre	3B117, 1B27	R	31	149	544	71	157	26	6	11	81	54	64	3	.289	.419
2 Bernie Carbo	OF92, 3B1	L	24	99	302	42	78	13	1	7	34	67	56	0	.258	.377
Jose Cruz	OF102	L	24	117	332	33	78	14	4	2	23	36	54	9	.235	.319
Lou Brock	OF149	L	33	153	621	81	193	26	8	3	42	47	93	**63**	.311	.393
Ted Simmons	C135, 1B15	B	22	152	594	70	180	36	6	16	96	29	57	1	.303	.465
Luis Melendez	OF105	R	22	118	332	32	79	11	3	5	28	25	34	5	.238	.334
Ed Crosby	SS43, 2B38, 3B14	L	23	101	276	27	60	9	1	0	19	18	27	1	.217	.257
Donn Clendenon	1B36	R	36	61	136	13	26	4	0	4	9	17	37	1	.191	.309
2 Dwain Anderson	SS43, 3B13, 2B1	R	24	57	135	12	36	41	1	1	8	8	23	0	.267	.333
Jerry McNertney	C10	R	35	39	48	3	10	3	1	0	9	6	16	0	.208	.313
Bob Gibson	P34	R	36	34	103	12	20	6	0	5	12	1	25	0	.194	.398
Jorge Roque	OF24, 1B2	R	22	32	67	3	7	2	1	1	5	6	19	1	.104	.209
1 Joe Hague	OF3	L	28	27	76	8	18	5	1	3	11	17	18	0	.237	.447
Mick Kelleher	SS23	R	24	23	63	5	10	2	1	0	1	6	15	0	.159	.222
Skip Jutze	C17	R	26	21	71	1	17	2	0	0	5	1	16	0	.239	.268
Ken Reitz	3B20	R	21	21	78	5	28	4	0	0	10	2	4	0	.359	.410
1 Mike Fiore	1B6, OF1	L	27	17	10	0	1	0	0	0	1	2	3	0	.100	.100
Bill Stein	3B4, OF4	R	25	14	35	2	11	0	1	2	3	0	7	1	.314	.543
Mike Tyson	2B11, SS2	B	22	13	37	1	7	1	0	0	0	1	9	0	.189	.216

3 Bill Voss 28 L 4-15, Ron Allen 28 B 1-11, 1 Marty Martinez 30 B 3-7, 2 Brant Alyea 31 R 3-19

NAME	T	AGE	W	L	PCT	SV	G	GS	CG	IP	H	BB	SO	ShO	ERA
TOTALS		30	75	81	.481	13	156	156	**64**	1400	1290	531	912	13	3.42
Bob Gibson	R	36	19	11	.633	0	34	34	23	278	226	88	208	4	2.46
Rick Wise	R	26	16	16	.500	0	35	35	20	269	250	71	142	2	3.11
Reggie Cleveland	R	24	14	15	.483	0	33	33	11	231	229	60	153	3	3.94
Al Santorini	R	24	8	11	.421	0	30	19	3	134	136	46	72	3	4.10
Scipio Spinks (KJ)	R	24	5	5	.500	0	16	16	6	118	96	59	93	0	2.67
2 Diego Segui	R	34	3	1	.750	9	33	0	0	56	47	32	54	0	3.05
Don Durham	R	23	2	7	.222	0	10	8	1	48	42	22	35	0	4.31
Joe Grzenda	L	35	1	0	1.000	0	30	0	0	35	46	17	15	0	5.66
Al Hrabosky	L	22	1	0	1.000	0	5	0	0	7	2	3	9	0	0.00
Charlie Hudson	L	22	1	0	1.000	0	12	0	0	12	10	7	4	0	5.25
Rich Folkers	L	25	1	0	1.000	0	9	0	0	13	12	5	7	0	3.46
2 John Cumberland	L	25	1	1	.500	0	14	1	0	22	23	7	7	0	6.55
1 Moe Drabowsky	R	36	1	1	.500	2	30	0	0	28	29	14	22	0	2.57
Denny Higgins	R	32	1	2	.333	1	15	1	0	23	19	22	20	0	3.91
Jim Bibby	R	27	1	3	.250	0	6	6	0	40	29	19	28	0	3.38
1 Don Shaw	L	28	0	1	.000	0	8	0	0	3	5	3	0	0	9.00
Ray Bare	R	23	0	1	.000	1	14	0	0	17	18	6	5	0	0.53
Lance Clemons	L	24	0	1	.000	0	3	1	0	5	8	5	2	0	10.80
Tony Cloninger	R	31	0	2	.000	0	17	0	0	26	29	19	11	0	5.19
1 Lowell Palmer	R	24	0	3	.000	0	16	2	0	35	30	26	25	0	3.86
Santiago Guzman	R	22	0	0	.000	0	1	0	0	1	1	0	0	0	9.00
Tim Plodinec	R	25	0	0	.000	0	1	0	0	.1	3	0	0	0	27.00

MONTREAL 5th 70-86 .449 26.5 — GENE MAUCH

NAME	G by POS	B	AGE	G	AB	R	H	2B	3B	HR	RBI	BB	SO	SB	BA	SA
TOTALS			27	156	5156	513	1205	156	22	91	462	474	828	68	.234	.325
Mike Jorgensen	1B76, OF28	L	28	113	372	48	86	12	3	13	47	53	75	12	.231	.384
Ron Hunt	2B122, 3B5	R	31	129	443	56	112	20	0	0	18	51	29	9	.253	.298
Tim Foli	SS148, 2B1	R	21	149	540	45	130	12	2	2	35	25	43	11	.241	.281
Bob Bailey	3B134, OF5, 1B3	R	29	143	489	55	114	10	4	16	57	59	112	6	.233	.368
Ron Fairly	OF70, 1B68	L	33	140	446	51	124	15	1	17	68	46	45	3	.278	.430
Boots Day	OF117	L	24	128	386	32	90	7	4	0	30	29	44	3	.233	.272
Ken Singleton	OF137	B	25	142	507	77	139	23	2	14	50	70	99	5	.274	.410
Terry Humphrey (LJ)	C65	R	22	69	215	13	40	8	0	1	9	16	38	4	.186	.237
Ron Woods	OF73	R	29	97	221	21	57	5	1	10	31	22	33	3	.258	.425
Clyde Mashore	OF74	R	27	93	176	23	40	7	1	3	23	14	41	6	.227	.330
Jim Fairey	OF37	L	27	86	141	9	33	7	0	1	15	10	21	1	.234	.305
John Boccabella	C73, 1B7, 3B1	R	31	83	207	14	47	8	1	1	10	9	29	1	.227	.290
Hector Torres	2B60, SS16, OF2, 3B1	R	26	83	181	14	28	4	1	2	7	13	26	0	.155	.221
2 Tim McCarver	C45, OF14, 3B6	L	30	77	239	19	60	5	1	5	20	19	14	4	.251	.343
Hal Breeden	1B26, OF1	R	28	42	87	6	20	2	0	3	10	7	15	0	.230	.356
Bobby Wine	3B21, SS4, 2B1	R	33	34	18	2	4	1	0	0	0	0	2	0	.222	.278
Coco Laboy (KJ)	3B24, 2B3, SS2	R	32	28	69	6	18	2	0	3	14	10	16	0	.261	.420
1 John Bateman	C7	R	29	18	29	0	7	1	0	0	3	3	4	0	.241	.276
Pepe Mangual	OF3	R	20	8	11	2	3	0	0	0	0	1	5	0	.273	.273

NAME	T	AGE	W	L	PCT	SV	G	GS	CG	IP	H	BB	SO	ShO	ERA
		25	70	86	.449	23	156	156	39	1401	1281	579	888	11	3.59
Mike Torrez	R	25	16	12	.571	0	34	33	13	243	215	103	112	0	3.33
Mike Marshall	R	29	14	8	.636	18	65	0	0	116	82	47	95	0	1.78
Bill Stoneman	R	28	12	14	.462	0	36	35	13	251	213	102	171	4	2.98
Balor Moore	L	21	9	9	.500	0	22	22	6	148	122	59	161	3	3.47
Carl Morton	R	28	7	13	.350	0	27	27	3	172	170	53	51	1	3.92
Ernie McAnally	R	25	6	15	.286	0	29	27	4	170	165	71	102	2	3.81
Denny Lemaster	L	33	2	0	1.000	0	13	0	0	20	28	6	13	0	7.65
Tom Walker	R	23	2	2	.500	2	46	0	0	75	71	22	42	0	2.88
John Strohmayer	R	25	1	2	.333	3	48	0	0	77	73	31	50	0	3.51
Steve Renko	R	27	1	10	.091	0	30	12	0	97	96	67	66	0	5.20
Joe Gilbert	L	20	0	1	.000	0	22	0	0	33	41	18	25	0	8.45
Hector Torres	R	26	0	0	.000	0	1	0	0	1	5	0	0	0	18.00

PHILADELPHIA 6th 59-97 .378 37.5 — FRANK LUCCHESI 26-50 .342 — PAUL OWENS 33-47 .413

NAME	G by POS	B	AGE	G	AB	R	H	2B	3B	HR	RBI	BB	SO	SB	BA	SA
TOTALS			27	156	5248	503	1240	200	36	98	469	487	930	42	.236	.344
Tommy Hutton	1B87	L	26	134	381	40	99	16	2	4	38	56	24	5	.260	.344
Denny Doyle	2B119	L	28	123	442	33	110	14	2	1	26	31	33	6	.249	.296
Larry Bowa	SS150	B	26	152	579	67	145	11	13	1	31	32	51	17	.250	.320
Don Money	3B151, SS2	R	25	152	536	54	119	16	2	15	52	41	92	5	.222	.343
Bill Robinson	OF72	R	29	82	188	19	45	9	1	8	21	5	30	2	.239	.426
Willie Montanez	OF130, 1B14	L	24	147	531	60	131	39	3	13	64	58	108	1	.247	.405
Greg Luzinski	OF145, 1B2	R	21	150	563	66	158	33	5	18	68	42	114	0	.281	.453
2 John Bateman	C80	R	29	82	252	10	56	9	0	3	17	8	39	0	.222	.294
Deron Johnson (LJ)	1B62	R	33	96	230	19	49	4	1	9	31	26	69	0	.213	.357
Oscar Gamble	OF35, 1B1	L	22	74	135	17	32	5	2	1	13	19	16	0	.237	.326
Terry Harmon	2B50, SS15, 3B5	R	28	73	218	35	62	8	2	2	13	29	28	3	.284	.367
Roger Freed	OF46	R	26	73	129	10	29	4	0	6	18	23	39	0	.225	.395
Joe Lis	1B30, OF14	R	25	62	140	13	34	6	0	6	18	30	34	0	.243	.414
Mike Ryan	C46	R	30	46	106	6	19	4	0	2	10	10	25	0	.179	.274
1 Tim McCarver	C40	L	30	45	152	14	36	8	0	2	14	17	15	1	.237	.329
Ron Stone	OF15	L	29	41	54	3	9	0	1	0	3	9	11	0	.167	.204
Pete Koegel	1B8, C5, 3B4, OF2	R	24	41	49	3	7	2	0	0	1	6	16	0	.143	.184
Mike Anderson	OF35	R	21	36	103	8	20	5	1	2	5	19	36	1	.194	.320
Byron Browne	OF9	R	29	21	21	2	4	0	0	0	0	1	8	0	.190	.190
Bob Boone	C14	R	24	16	51	4	14	1	0	1	4	5	7	1	.275	.353
Mike Schmidt	3B11, 2B1	R	22	13	34	2	7	0	0	1	3	5	15	0	.206	.294
Craig Robinson	SS4	R	23	5	15	0	3	1	0	0	0	1	2	0	.200	.267

NAME	T	AGE	W	L	PCT	SV	G	GS	CG	IP	H	BB	SO	ShO	ERA
		28	59	97	.378	15	156	156	43	1400	1318	536	927	13	3.66
Steve Carlton	L	27	27	10	.730	0	41	41	30	346	257	87	310	8	1.98
Darrell Brandon	R	31	7	7	.500	2	42	6	0	104	106	46	67	0	3.46
Wayne Twitchell	R	24	5	9	.357	1	49	15	1	140	138	56	112	1	4.05
Barry Lersch (IL)	R	27	4	6	.400	0	36	8	3	101	86	33	48	1	3.03
1 Woodie Fryman	L	32	4	10	.280	1	23	17	3	120	131	[illegible]	[illegible]	2	[illegible]
Billy Champion	R	24	4	14	.222	0	30	22	2	133	155	54	54	0	5.08
Dick Selma	R	28	2	9	.182	3	46	10	1	99	91	73	58	0	5.55
Ken Reynolds	L	25	2	15	.118	0	33	23	2	154	149	60	87	0	4.27
Chris Short (XJ)	L	34	1	1	.500	1	19	0	0	23	24	8	20	0	3.91
Billy Wilson (XJ)	R	29	1	1	.500	0	23	0	0	30	26	11	18	0	3.30
Dave Downs	R	20	1	1	.500	0	4	4	1	23	25	3	5	1	2.74
Mac Scarce	L	23	1	2	.333	4	31	0	0	37	30	20	40	0	3.41
1 Joe Hoerner	L	35	0	2	.000	3	15	0	0	22	21	5	12	0	2.05
2 Gary Neibauer	R	27	0	2	.000	0	9	2	0	19	17	14	7	0	5.21
2 Jim Nash (SJ)	R	27	0	8	.000	0	9	8	0	37	46	17	15	0	6.32
Bob Terlecki	R	27	0	0	.000	0	9	0	0	13	16	10	5	0	4.85

WEST DIVISION

CINCINNATI 1st 95-59 .617 — SPARKY ANDERSON

NAME	G by POS	B	AGE	G	AB	R	H	2B	3B	HR	RBI	BB	SO	SB	BA	SA
TOTALS			27	154	5241	707	1317	214	44	124	650	606	914	140	.251	.380
Tony Perez	1B136	R	30	136	515	64	146	33	7	21	90	55	121	4	.283	.497
Joe Morgan	2B149	L	28	149	552	122	161	23	4	16	73	115	44	58	.292	.435
Dave Concepcion	SS114, 3B9, 2B1	R	24	119	378	40	79	13	2	2	29	32	65	13	.209	.270
Denis Menke	3B130, 1B11	R	31	140	447	41	104	19	2	9	50	58	76	0	.233	.345
Cesar Geronimo	OF106	L	24	120	255	32	70	9	7	4	29	24	64	2	.275	.412
Bobby Tolan	OF149	L	26	149	604	88	171	28	5	8	82	44	88	42	.283	.386
Pete Rose	OF154	B	31	154	645	107	198	31	11	6	57	73	46	10	.307	.417
Johnny Bench	C130, OF17, 1B6, 3B4	R	24	147	538	87	145	22	2	40	125	100	84	6	.270	.541
Darrel Chaney	SS64, 2B12, 3B10	B	24	83	196	29	49	7	2	2	19	29	28	1	.250	.337
Ted Uhlaender	OF27	L	32	73	113	9	18	3	0	0	6	13	11	0	.159	.186
2 Joe Hague	1B22, OF19	L	28	69	138	17	34	7	1	4	20	20	18	1	.246	.399
Hal McRae	OF12, 3B11	R	25	61	97	9	27	4	0	5	26	2	10	0	.278	.474
George Foster	OF47	R	23	59	145	15	29	4	1	2	12	5	44	2	.200	.283
Julian Javier	3B19, 2B5, 1B1	R	35	44	91	3	19	2	0	2	12	6	11	1	.209	.297
Bill Plummer (FJ)	C35, 1B1, 3B1	R	25	38	102	8	19	4	0	2	9	4	20	0	.186	.284
1 Bernie Carbo	OF4	L	24	19	21	2	3	0	0	0	0	6	3	0	.143	.143
Sonny Ruberto	C2	R	26	2	3	0	0	0	0	0	0	0	1	0	.000	.000
1 Pat Corrales	C2	R	31	2	1	0	0	0	0	0	0	2	0	0	.000	.000

NAME	T	AGE	W	L	PCT	SV	G	GS	CG	IP	H	BB	SO	ShO	ERA
		25	95	59	.617	60	154	154	25	1413	1313	435	806	15	3.21
Gary Nolan	R	24	15	5	.750	0	25	25	6	176	147	30	90	2	1.99
Ross Grimsley	L	22	14	8	.636	1	30	28	4	198	194	50	79	1	3.05
Jack Billingham	R	29	12	12	.500	1	36	31	8	218	197	64	137	4	3.18
Tom Hall	L	24	10	1	.909	8	47	7	1	124	77	56	134	1	2.61
Jim McGlothlin	R	28	9	8	.529	0	31	21	3	145	165	49	69	1	3.91
Don Gullett	L	21	9	10	.474	2	31	16	2	135	127	43	96	0	3.93
Pedro Borbon	R	25	8	3	.727	11	62	2	0	122	115	32	48	0	3.17
Wayne Simpson	R	23	8	5	.615	0	24	22	1	130	124	49	70	0	4.15
Clay Carroll	R	31	6	4	.600	37	65	0	0	96	89	32	51	0	2.25
Ed Sprague	R	26	3	3	.500	0	33	1	0	57	55	26	25	0	4.11
Jim Merritt	L	28	1	0	1.000	0	4	1	0	8	13	2	4	0	4.50
1 Joe Gibbon	L	37	0	0	.000	0	2	0	0	.1	3	1	1	0	54.00
Dave Tomlin	L	23	0	0	.000	0	3	0	0	4	7	1	2	0	9.00

HOUSTON 2nd 84-69 .549 10.5 — HARRY WALKER 68-54 .557 — 2 LEO DUROCHER 16-15 .516

NAME	G by POS	B	AGE	G	AB	R	H	2B	3B	HR	RBI	BB	SO	SB	BA	SA
TOTALS			28	153	5267	708	1359	233	38	134	660	524	907	111	.258	.393
Lee May	1B146	R	29	148	592	87	168	31	2	29	98	52	145	3	.284	.490
Tommy Helms	2B139	R	31	139	518	45	134	20	5	5	60	24	27	4	.259	.346
Roger Metzger	SS153	B	24	153	641	84	142	12	3	2	38	60	71	23	.222	.259
Doug Rader	3B152	R	27	152	553	70	131	24	7	22	90	57	120	5	.237	.425
Jim Wynn	OF144	R	30	145	542	117	148	29	3	24	90	103	99	17	.273	.470
Cesar Cedeno	OF137	R	21	139	559	103	179	39	8	22	82	56	62	55	.320	.537
Bob Watson	OF143, 1B2	R	26	147	548	74	171	27	4	16	86	53	83	1	.312	.464
Johnny Edwards	C105	L	34	108	332	33	89	16	2	5	40	50	39	2	.268	.373
Jimmy Stewart	OF11, 1B9, SS8, 3B2	B	33	68	96	14	21	5	2	0	9	6	9	0	.219	.313
Norm Miller	OF29	L	26	67	107	18	26	4	0	4	13	13	23	1	.243	.393
Larry Howard	C53, OF1	R	27	54	157	16	35	7	0	2	13	17	30	0	.223	.306
Jesus Alou	OF23	R	30	52	93	8	29	4	1	0	11	7	5	0	.312	.376
Bob Fenwick	2B17, SS4, 3B2	R	25	36	50	7	9	3	0	0	4	3	13	0	.180	.240
Bob Stinson	C12, OF3	B	26	27	35	3	6	1	0	0	2	1	6	0	.171	.200
1 Jack Hiatt	C10	R	29	10	25	2	5	3	0	0	0	5	5	0	.200	.320
Rich Chiles	OF2	L	22	9	11	0	3	1	0	0	2	1	1	0	.273	.364
Gary Sutherland	2B1, 3B1	R	27	5	8	0	1	0	0	0	1	0	0	0	.125	.125
Cliff Johnson	C1	R	24	5	4	0	1	0	0	0	0	2	0	0	.250	.250

NAME	T	AGE	W	L	PCT	SV	G	GS	CG	IP	H	BB	SO	ShO	ERA
		27	84	69	.549	31	153	153	38	1385	1340	498	971	14	3.77
Larry Dierker	R	25	15	8	.652	0	31	31	12	215	209	51	115	5	3.39
Don Wilson	R	27	15	10	.600	0	33	33	13	228	196	66	172	3	2.68
Dave Roberts	L	27	12	7	.632	2	35	28	7	192	227	57	111	3	4.50
Jim Ray	R	27	10	9	.526	8	54	0	0	90	77	44	50	0	4.30
Jerry Reuss	L	23	9	13	.409	1	33	30	4	192	177	83	174	1	4.17
George Culver	R	28	6	2	.750	2	45	0	0	97	73	43	82	0	3.06
Ken Forsch	R	25	6	8	.429	0	30	24	1	156	163	62	113	0	3.92
Tom Griffin	R	24	5	4	.556	3	39	5	1	94	92	38	83	1	3.26
Fred Gladding	R	36	5	6	.455	14	42	0	0	49	38	12	18	0	2.76
J. R. Richard	R	22	1	0	1.000	0	4	1	0	6	10	8	8	0	13.50
Jim York	R	23	0	1	.000	0	26	0	0	36	45	18	25	0	5.25
Mike Cosgrove	L	21	0	1	.000	1	7	1	0	14	16	3	7	0	4.50
1 Wade Blasingame	L	28	0	0	.000	0	10	0	0	8	4	8	9	0	9.00
2 Joe Gibbon	L	37	0	0	.000	0	9	0	0	7	13	5	4	0	10.29

LOS ANGELES 3rd 85-70 .548 10.5 — WALT ALSTON

NAME	G by POS	B	AGE	G	AB	R	H	2B	3B	HR	RBI	BB	SO	SB	BA	SA
TOTALS			28	155	5270	584	1349	178	39	98	543	480	786	82	.256	.360
Wes Parker	1B120, OF5	B	32	130	427	45	119	14	3	4	59	62	43	3	.279	.354
Lee Lacy (KJ)	2B58	R	24	60	243	34	63	7	3	0	12	19	37	5	.259	.313
Bill Russell	SS121, OF6	R	23	129	434	47	118	19	5	4	34	34	64	14	.272	.366
Steve Garvey	3B85, 1B3	R	23	96	294	36	79	14	2	9	30	19	36	4	.269	.422
Frank Robinson	OF95	R	36	103	342	41	86	6	1	19	59	55	76	2	.251	.442
Willie Davis	OF146	L	32	149	615	81	178	22	7	19	79	27	61	20	.289	.441
Manny Mota	OF99	R	34	118	371	57	120	16	5	5	48	27	15	4	.323	.434
Chris Cannizzaro	C72	R	34	73	200	14	48	6	0	2	18	31	38	0	.240	.300
Bobby Valentine	2B49, 3B39, OF16, SS10	R	22	119	391	42	107	11	2	3	32	27	33	5	.274	.335
Bill Buckner	OF61, 1B35	L	22	105	383	47	122	14	3	5	37	17	13	10	.319	.410
Willie Crawford	OF74	L	25	96	243	28	61	7	3	8	27	35	55	4	.251	.403
Maury Wills	SS31, 3B26	B	39	71	132	16	17	3	1	0	4	10	18	1	.129	.167
Jim Lefebvre	2B33, 3B11	B	29	70	169	11	34	8	0	5	24	17	30	0	.201	.337
Billy Grabarkewitz (SJ)	3B24, 2B19, SS2	R	26	53	144	17	24	4	0	4	16	18	53	3	.167	.278
1 Duke Sims	C48	L	31	51	151	7	29	7	0	2	11	17	23	0	.192	.278
Steve Yeager	C35	R	23	35	106	18	29	0	1	4	15	16	26	0	.274	.406
Dick Dietz (BH)	C22	R	30	27	56	4	9	1	0	1	6	14	11	2	.161	.232
Tom Paciorek	1B6, OF6	R	25	11	47	4	12	4	0	1	6	1	7	1	.255	.404
Ron Cey	3B11	R	24	11	37	3	10	1	0	1	3	7	10	0	.270	.378
Dave Lopes	2B11	R	26	11	42	6	9	4	0	0	1	7	6	4	.214	.310
Terry McDermott	1B7	R	21	9	23	2	3	0	0	0	0	2	8	0	.130	.130
Joe Ferguson	C7, OF2	R	25	8	24	2	7	3	0	1	5	2	4	0	.292	.542

NAME	T	AGE	W	L	PCT	SV	G	GS	CG	IP	H	BB	SO	ShO	ERA
		32	85	70	.548	29	155	155	50	1403	1196	429	856	23	2.78
Claude Osteen	L	32	20	11	.264	0	33	33	14	252	232	69	100	4	2.64
Don Sutton	R	27	19	9	.679	0	33	33	18	273	186	63	207	9	2.08
Tommy John	L	29	11	5	.688	0	29	29	4	187	172	40	117	1	2.89
Al Downing	L	31	9	9	.500	0	31	30	7	203	196	67	117	4	2.97
Jim Brewer	L	34	8	7	.533	17	51	0	0	78	41	25	69	0	1.27
Bill Singer	R	28	6	16	.273	0	26	25	4	169	148	60	101	3	3.67
Pete Mikkelsen	R	32	5	5	.500	5	33	0	0	58	65	23	41	0	4.03
2 Ron Perranoski	L	36	2	0	1.000	0	9	0	0	17	19	8	5	0	2.65
Doug Rau	L	23	2	2	.500	0	7	3	2	33	18	11	19	0	2.18
Pete Richert	L	32	2	3	.400	6	37	0	0	52	42	18	38	0	2.25
Mike Strahler	R	25	1	2	.333	0	19	2	1	47	42	22	25	0	3.26
Hoyt Wilhelm	R	48	0	1	.000	1	16	0	0	25	20	15	9	0	4.68
Charlie Hough	R	24	0	0	.000	0	2	0	0	3	2	2	4	0	3.00
Jose Pena	R	29	0	0	.000	0	5	0	0	7	13	6	4	0	9.00

ATLANTA 4th 70-84 .455 25 — LUM HARRIS 47-57 .452 — EDDIE MATHEWS 23-27 .460

NAME	G by POS	B	AGE	G	AB	R	H	2B	3B	HR	RBI	BB	SO	SB	BA	SA
TOTALS			27	155	5278	628	1363	186	17	144	593	532	770	47	.258	.382
Hank Aaron	1B109, OF15	R	38	129	449	75	119	10	0	34	77	92	55	4	.265	.514
Felix Millan	2B120	R	28	125	498	46	128	19	3	1	38	23	28	6	.257	.313
Marty Perez	SS141	R	25	141	479	33	109	13	1	1	28	30	55	0	.228	.265
Darrell Evans	3B123	L	25	125	418	67	106	12	0	19	71	90	58	4	.254	.419
Ralph Garr	OF131	L	26	134	554	87	180	22	0	12	53	25	41	25	.325	.430
Dusty Baker	OF123	R	23	127	446	62	143	27	2	17	76	45	68	4	.321	.504
Rico Carty (LJ)	OF78	R	33	86	271	31	75	12	2	6	29	44	33	0	.277	.402
Earl Williams	C116, 3B21, 1B20	R	23	151	565	72	146	24	2	28	87	62	118	0	.258	.457
Mike Lum	OF109, 1B2	L	26	123	369	40	84	14	2	9	38	50	52	1	.228	.350
Oscar Brown	OF59	R	26	76	164	19	37	5	1	3	16	4	29	0	.226	.323
Sonny Jackson (NJ)	SS17, OF10, 3B6	L	27	60	126	20	30	6	3	0	8	7	9	1	.238	.333
Jim Breazeale	1B16, 3B1	L	22	52	85	10	21	2	0	5	17	6	12	0	.247	.447
Paul Casanova	C43	R	30	49	136	8	28	3	0	2	10	4	28	0	.206	.272
Gil Garrido	2B21, SS10, 3B3	R	31	40	75	11	20	1	0	0	7	11	6	1	.267	.280
Larvell Blanks	2B18, SS4, 3B2	R	22	33	85	10	28	5	0	1	7	7	12	0	.329	.424
1 Orlando Cepeda (KJ)	1B22	R	34	28	84	6	25	3	0	4	9	7	17	0	.298	.476
Rod Gilbreath	2B7, 3B4	R	19	18	38	2	9	1	0	0	1	2	10	1	.237	.263

Bob Didier 23 B 12-40, Rowland Office 19 L 2-5

NAME	T	AGE	W	L	PCT	SV	G	GS	CG	IP	H	BB	SO	ShO	ERA
		28	70	84	.455	27	155	155	40	1377	1412	512	732	4	4.27
Phil Niekro	R	33	16	12	.571	0	38	36	17	282	254	53	164	1	3.06
Pat Jarvis	R	31	11	7	.611	2	37	6	0	99	94	44	56	0	4.09
Ron Reed	R	29	11	15	.423	0	31	30	11	213	222	60	111	1	3.93
George Stone	L	26	6	11	.353	1	31	16	2	111	143	44	63	1	5.51
Jim Hardin	R	28	5	2	.714	2	26	9	1	80	93	24	25	0	4.39
Tom Kelley	R	28	5	7	.417	0	27	14	2	116	122	65	59	1	4.58
Ron Schueler	R	24	5	8	.385	2	37	18	3	145	122	60	96	0	3.66
Cecil Upshaw	R	29	3	5	.375	13	42	0	0	54	50	19	23	0	3.67
2 Denny McLain	R	28	3	5	.375	1	15	8	2	54	60	18	21	0	6.50
Jimmy Freeman	L	21	2	2	.500	0	6	6	1	36	40	22	18	0	6.00
1 Jim Nash	R	27	1	1	.500	1	11	4	0	31	35	25	10	0	5.52
Larry Jaster	L	28	1	1	.500	0	5	1	0	12	12	8	6	0	5.25
2 Joe Hoerner	L	35	1	3	.250	2	25	0	0	23	34	8	19	0	6.65
Mike McQueen (AJ)	L	21	0	5	.000	1	23	7	1	78	79	44	40	0	4.62
1 Steve Barber	L	33	0	0	.000	0	5	0	0	16	18	6	6	0	5.63
Tom House	L	25	0	0	.000	2	8	0	0	9	7	6	7	0	3.00
1 Gary Neibauer	R	27	0	0	.000	0	8	0	0	17	27	6	8	0	7.41

SAN FRANCISCO 5th 69-86 .445 26.5 — CHARLIE FOX

NAME	G by POS	B	AGE	G	AB	R	H	2B	3B	HR	RBI	BB	SO	SB	BA	SA
TOTALS			26	155	5245	662	1281	211	36	150	600	480	964	123	.244	.384
Willie McCovey (BA)	1B74	L	34	81	263	30	56	8	0	14	35	38	45	0	.213	.403
Tito Fuentes	2B152	B	28	152	572	64	151	33	6	7	53	39	56	16	.264	.379
Chris Speier	SS150	R	22	150	562	74	151	25	2	15	71	82	92	9	.269	.400
Alan Gallagher	3B69	R	26	82	233	19	52	3	1	2	18	33	39	2	.223	.270
Bobby Bonds	OF153	R	26	153	626	118	162	29	5	26	80	60	137	44	.259	.446
Garry Maddox	OF121	R	22	125	458	62	122	26	7	12	58	14	97	13	.266	.432
Ken Henderson	OF123	B	26	130	439	60	113	21	2	18	51	38	66	14	.257	.437
Dave Rader	C127	L	23	133	459	44	119	14	1	6	41	29	31	1	.259	.333
Dave Kingman	3B59, 1B56, OF22	R	23	135	472	65	106	17	4	29	83	51	140	16	.225	.462
Jim Howarth	OF25, 1B4	L	25	74	119	16	28	4	0	1	7	16	18	3	.235	.294
Ed Goodson (KJ)	1B42	L	24	58	150	15	42	1	1	6	30	8	12	0	.280	.420
Chris Arnold	3B17, 2B7, SS4	R	24	51	84	8	19	3	1	1	4	8	12	0	.226	.321
Bernie Williams	OF15	R	23	46	68	12	13	3	1	3	9	7	22	0	.191	.397
Fran Healy	C43	R	25	45	99	12	15	4	0	1	8	13	24	0	.152	.222
Damie Blanco	3B19, SS8, 2B3	R	30	39	20	5	7	1	0	0	2	4	3	2	.350	.400
Jim Ray Hart	3B20	R	30	24	79	10	24	5	0	5	8	6	10	0	.304	.557
Gary Matthews	OF19	R	21	20	62	11	18	1	1	4	14	7	13	0	.290	.532
1 Willie Mays	OF14	R	41	19	49	8	9	2	0	0	3	17	5	3	.184	.224

Gary Thomasson 20 L 9-27, Russ Gibson 33 R 2-12, Jimmy Rosario 28 B 0-2

NAME	T	AGE	W	L	PCT	SV	G	GS	CG	IP	H	BB	SO	ShO	ERA
		28	69	86	.445	23	155	155	44	1386	1309	507	771	8	3.69
Ron Bryant	L	24	14	7	.667	0	35	28	11	214	176	77	107	4	2.90
Sam McDowell (SJ)	L	29	10	8	.556	0	28	25	4	164	155	86	122	0	4.34
Jerry Johnson	R	28	8	6	.571	8	48	0	0	73	73	40	57	0	4.44
Jim Barr	R	24	8	10	.444	2	44	18	8	179	166	41	86	2	2.87
Jim Willoughby	R	23	6	4	.600	0	11	11	7	88	72	14	40	0	2.35
Steve Stone	R	24	6	8	.429	0	27	16	4	124	97	49	85	1	2.98
Juan Marichal	R	34	6	16	.273	0	25	24	6	165	176	46	72	0	3.71
Don Carrithers	R	22	4	8	.333	1	25	14	2	90	108	42	42	0	5.80
Don McMahon	R	42	3	3	.500	5	44	0	0	63	46	21	45	0	3.71
Frank Reberger	R	28	3	4	.429	0	20	11	2	99	97	37	52	0	4.00
Randy Moffitt	R	23	1	5	.167	4	40	0	0	71	72	30	37	0	3.68
Elias Sosa	R	22	0	1	.000	3	8	0	0	16	10	12	10	0	2.25
Charlie Williams	R	24	0	2	.000	0	3	2	0	9	14	3	3	0	9.00
1 John Cumberland	L	25	0	4	.000	0	9	6	0	25	38	7	8	0	8.64
John Morris	L	30	0	0	.000	0	7	0	0	6	9	2	5	0	4.50

SAN DIEGO 6th 58-95 .379 36.5 — PRESTON GOMEZ 4-11 .267 — DON ZIMMER 54-84 .391

NAME	G by POS	B	AGE	G	AB	R	H	2B	3B	HR	RBI	BB	SO	SB	BA	SA
TOTALS			25	153	5213	488	1181	168	38	102	452	407	976	78	.227	.332
Nate Colbert	1B150	R	26	151	563	87	141	27	2	38	111	70	127	15	.250	.508
Derrel Thomas	2B83, SS49, OF3	B	21	130	500	48	115	15	5	5	36	41	73	9	.230	.310
Enzo Hernandez	SS107, OF3	R	23	114	329	33	64	11	2	1	15	22	25	24	.195	.249
Dave Roberts	3B84, 2B20, SS3, C1	R	21	100	418	38	102	17	0	5	33	18	64	7	.244	.321
Clarence Gaston(NJ)	OF94	R	28	111	379	30	102	14	0	7	44	22	76	0	.269	.361
Johnnie Jeter	OF91	R	27	110	326	25	72	4	3	7	21	18	92	11	.221	.316
Leron Lee (BG)	OF96	L	24	101	370	50	111	23	7	12	47	29	58	2	.300	.497
Fred Kendall	C82, 1B1	R	23	91	273	18	59	3	4	6	18	11	42	0	.216	.322
Jerry Morales	OF96, 3B4	R	23	115	347	38	83	15	7	4	18	35	54	4	.239	.357
Larry Stahl	OF76, 1B1	L	31	107	297	31	67	9	3	7	20	31	67	1	.226	.347
Garry Jestadt	2B48, 3B25, SS3	R	25	92	256	15	63	5	1	6	22	13	21	0	.246	.344
2 Curt Blefary	C12, 1B6, 3B3, OF3	L	28	74	102	10	20	3	0	3	9	19	18	0	.196	.314
2 Pat Corrales	C43	R	31	44	119	6	23	0	0	0	6	11	26	0	.193	.193
2 Fred Stanley	2B21, SS17, 3B4	R	24	39	85	15	17	2	0	0	2	12	19	1	.200	.224
Dave Campbell	3B31, 2B1	R	30	33	100	6	24	5	0	0	3	11	12	0	.240	.290
Bob Barton	C29	R	30	29	88	1	17	1	0	0	9	2	19	2	.193	.205
1 Ollie Brown	OF17	R	28	23	70	3	12	2	0	0	3	5	9	0	.171	.200
1 Ed Spiezio	3B5	R	30	20	29	2	4	2	0	0	4	1	6	1	.138	.207
Rafael Robles	SS15, 3B1	R	24	18	24	1	4	0	0	0	0	0	3	0	.167	.167
Randy Elliott	OF13	R	21	14	49	5	10	3	1	0	6	2	11	0	.204	.306
Dave Hilton	3B13	R	21	13	47	2	10	2	1	0	5	3	6	1	.213	.298

Joe Goddard 21 R 7-35, John Grubb 23 L 7-21, Don Mason 27 L 2-11, Ivan Murrell 27 R 1-7, 2 Mike Fiore 27 L 0-6

NAME	T	AGE	W	L	PCT	SV	G	GS	CG	IP	H	BB	SO	ShO	ERA
		25	58	95	.379	19	153	153	39	1404	1350	618	960	17	3.78
Clay Kirby	R	24	12	14	.462	0	34	34	9	239	197	116	175	2	3.13
Steve Arlin	R	26	10	21	.323	0	38	37	12	250	217	122	159	3	3.60
Fred Norman	L	29	9	11	.450	2	42	28	10	212	195	88	167	6	3.44
Mike Caldwell	L	23	7	11	.389	2	42	20	4	164	183	49	102	2	4.01
Mike Corkins	R	26	6	9	.400	6	47	9	2	140	125	62	108	1	3.54
Bill Greif	R	22	5	16	.238	2	34	22	2	125	143	47	91	1	5.62
Gary Ross	R	24	4	3	.571	3	60	0	0	92	87	49	46	0	2.45
Ed Acosta	R	28	3	6	.333	0	46	2	0	89	105	30	53	0	4.45
Mark Schaeffer	L	24	2	0	1.000	1	41	0	0	41	52	28	25	0	4.61
1 Tom Phoebus	R	27	0	1	.000	0	1	0	0	6	3	6	8	0	7.50
Al Severinsen	R	27	0	1	.000	1	17	0	0	21	13	7	9	0	2.57
Steve Simpson	R	23	0	2	.000	2	9	0	0	11	10	8	9	0	4.91
3 Mike Kilkenny	L	27	0	0	.000	0	5	0	0	4	7	3	5	0	9.00
Ron Taylor	R	34	0	0	.000	0	4	0	0	5	9	0	0	0	12.60
Ralph Garcia	R	23	0	0	.000	0	3	0	0	5	4	3	3	0	1.80

Jay Franklin (JJ) 19

WORLD SERIES – OAKLAND (AL) 4 CINCINNATI (NL) 3

LINE SCORES

TEAM	1	2	3	4	5	6	7	8	9	10	11	12	R	H	E
Game 1 October 14 at Cincinnati															
OAK (AL)	0	2	0	0	1	0	0	0	0				3	4	0
CIN (NL)	0	1	0	1	0	0	0	0	0				2	7	0
Game 2 October 15 at Cincinnati															
OAK	0	1	1	0	0	0	0	0	0				2	9	2
CIN	0	0	0	0	0	0	0	0	1				1	6	0
Game 3 October 18 at Oakland															
CIN	0	0	0	0	0	0	1	0	0				1	4	2
OAK	0	0	0	0	0	0	0	0	0				0	3	2
Game 4 October 19 at Oakland															
CIN	0	0	0	0	0	0	0	2	0				2	7	1
OAK	0	0	0	0	1	0	0	0	2				3	10	1
Game 5 October 20 at Oakland															
CIN	1	0	0	1	1	0	0	1	1				5	8	0
OAK	0	3	0	1	0	0	0	0	0				4	7	2
Game 6 October 21 at Cincinnati															
OAK	0	0	0	0	1	0	0	0	0				1	7	1
CIN	0	0	0	1	1	1	5	0	X				8	10	0
Game 7 October 22 at Cincinnati															
OAK	1	0	0	0	0	2	0	0	0				3	6	1
CIN	0	0	0	0	1	0	0	1	0				2	4	2

Game 1: **Holtzman**, Fingers (6), Blue (7) — **Nolan**, Borbon (7), Carroll (8)

Game 2: **Hunter**, Fingers (9) — **Grimsley**, Borbon (6), Hall (8)

Game 3: **Billingham**, Carroll (9) — **Odom**, Blue (8), Fingers (8)

Game 4: Gullet, Borbon (8), **Carroll** (9) — Holtzman, Blue (8), **Fingers** (9)

Game 5: McGlothlin, Borbon (4), Hall (5), Carroll (7), **Grimsley** (8), Billingham (9) — Hunter, **Fingers** (5), Hamilton (9)

Game 6: **Blue**, Locker (6), Hamilton (7), Horlen (7) — Nolan, **Grimsley** (5), Borbon (6), Hall (7)

Game 7: Odom, **Hunter** (5), Holtzman (8), Fingers (8) — Billingham, **Borbon** (6), Carroll (6), Grimsley (7), Hall (8)

COMPOSITE BATTING

NAME	POS	G	AB	R	H	2B	3B	HR	RBI	BA
Oakland (AL)										
Totals		7	220	16	46	4	0	5	16	.209
Campaneris	SS	7	28	1	5	0	0	0	0	.179
Bando	3B	7	26	2	7	1	0	0	1	.269
Rudi	OF	7	25	1	6	0	0	1	1	.240
Alou	OF	7	24	0	1	0	0	0	0	.042
Tenace	C-1B	7	23	5	8	1	0	4	9	.348
Green	2B	7	18	0	6	2	0	0	1	.333
Epstein	1B	6	16	1	0	0	0	0	0	.000
Hendrick	OF	5	15	3	2	0	0	0	0	.133
Mangual	OF	4	10	1	3	0	0	0	1	.300
Marquez	PH	5	5	0	3	0	0	0	1	.600
Hegan	1B	6	5	0	1	0	0	0	0	.200
Duncan	C	3	5	0	1	0	0	0	0	.200
Hunter	P	3	5	0	1	0	0	0	1	.200
Holtzman	P	3	5	0	0	0	0	0	0	.000
Odom	P-PR	4	4	0	0	0	0	0	0	.000
Kubiak	2B	4	3	0	1	0	0	0	0	.333
Mincher	PH	3	1	0	1	0	0	0	1	1.000
Fingers	P	6	1	0	0	0	0	0	0	.000
Lewis	PR	6	0	2	0	0	0	0	0	.000

Blue P 0-1, Hamilton P 0-0, Horlen P 0-0, Locker P 0-0

NAME	POS	G	AB	R	H	2B	3B	HR	RBI	BA
Cincinnati (NL)										
Totals		7	220	21	46	8	1	3	21	.209
Rose	OF	7	28	3	6	0	0	1	2	.214
Tolan	OF	7	26	2	7	1	0	0	6	.269
Morgan	2B	7	24	4	3	2	0	0	1	.125
Menke	3B	7	24	1	2	0	0	1	2	.083
Perez	1B	7	23	3	10	2	0	0	2	.435
Bench	C	7	23	4	6	1	0	1	1	.261
Geronimo	OF	7	19	1	3	0	0	0	3	.158
Concepcion	SS	6	13	2	4	0	1	0	2	.308
McRae	OF	5	9	1	4	1	0	0	2	.444
Chaney	SS	4	7	0	0	0	0	0	0	.000
Billingham	P	3	5	0	0	0	0	0	0	.000
Uhlaender	PH	4	4	0	1	1	0	0	0	.250
Hague	OF	3	3	0	0	0	0	0	0	.000
Nolan	P	2	3	0	0	0	0	0	0	.000
Javier	PH	4	2	0	0	0	0	0	0	.000
Grimsley	P	4	2	0	0	0	0	0	0	.000
Hall	P	4	2	0	0	0	0	0	0	.000
Gullet	P	1	2	0	0	0	0	0	0	.000
McGlothlin	P	1	1	0	0	0	0	0	0	.000

Foster OF 0-0, Carroll P 0-0, Borbon P 0-0

COMPOSITE PITCHING

NAME	G	IP	H	BB	SO	W	L	SV	ERA
Oakland (AL)									
Totals	7	62	46	27	46	4	3	3	3.05
Hunter	3	16	12	6	11	2	0	0	2.81
Holtzman	3	12.2	11	3	4	1	0	0	2.13
Odom	2	11.1	5	6	13	0	1	0	1.59
Fingers	6	10.1	4	4	11	1	1	2	1.74
Blue	4	8.2	8	5	5	0	1	1	4.15
Hamilton	2	1.1	3	1	1	0	0	0	27.00
Horlen	1	1.1	2	2	1	0	0	0	6.75
Locker	1	.1	1	0	0	0	0	0	0.00
Cincinnati (NL)									
Totals	7	62.1	46	21	37	3	4	3	2.17
Billingham	3	13.2	6	4	11	1	0	1	0.00
Nolan	2	10.2	7	2	3	0	1	0	3.38
Hall	4	8.1	6	2	7	0	0	1	0.00
Borbon	6	7	7	2	4	0	1	0	3.86
Grimsley	4	7	7	3	2	2	1	0	2.57
Gullett	1	7	5	2	4	0	0	0	1.29
Carroll	5	5.2	6	4	3	0	1	1	1.59
McGlothlin	1	3	2	2	3	0	0	0	12.00

1973 O, Charley O.

In a season which saw Hank Aaron come within one of Babe Ruth's lifetime home run record, Nolan Ryan go beyond Sandy Koufax's single-season strikeout record, and the American League offer a rule which dramatically changed the style of play in the junior circuit, the unpredictable New York Mets stole the whole show with their late-season theatrics. If the Mets had any rival for showmanship and fanfare, it wasn't a team but an individual in Charley O. Finley, owner of the Oakland Athletics. While the Mets earned their half of the twin billing in baseball's 1973 extravaganza by proving the best of the worst in the National League's Eastern Division, Finley arrived on the balanced strength of the A's, who proved the class of the American League West.

In reaching the second World Series in their short history, the Mets waited until September before awakening to the fact that winning was an important part of baseball. Yet, in all fairness to the Amazing Nine from Flushing Meadows, several key injuries threw their balance out of wack. Shortstop Bud Harrelson, the secret to the infield, catcher Jerry Grote, and left fielder Cleon Jones all sat out at least one month with injuries and Willie Mays, who finally said good-bye to baseball after 21 years, played only 66 games as a result of injuries and age. While the Mets were suffering their woes, the senior circuit race went on as usual. But in all respects neither the race nor the finish had anything commonplace about it.

The St. Louis Cardinals started out in dismal fashion and soon found themselves in the cellar. The Pittsburgh Pirates entered the season without superstar Roberto Clemente, the victim of a tragic plane accident on December 31, 1972, and tried to fill the vacant spot in right field with the bat of catcher Manny Sanguillen—a move which kept the Pirates away from the top until they finally sent Sanguillen back behind the plate. And while the Phillies were experiencing shock with the drastic reversal of form in Steve Carlton, the 1972 Cy Young winner, Montreal had found some consistency due to the development of Ken Singleton and the super endurance of relief specialist Mike Marshall. The Cubs, once again trying for Eastern honors, and using the experience of an aging ball club, soon found themselves in the top spot as the All-Star game approached.

However, by the time the morning of August 17, arrived, St. Louis was magically transplanted in first place by three games over the Pirates and the Cubs were in fourth, 5½ back. Montreal was seemingly in the midst of a miracle with third-place occupancy and the Mets in last, 7½ off the leader. Yet neither the scramble, nor the race, was over yet, and by early September every team, including the Mets, still had a shot at the top. Then, as the Mets regulars began to return and the victories became consistent, a critical blow came to the Cardinals when their ace righty, Bob Gibson, injured his leg and was shelved until the last weekend of the season. By September 20, Pittsburgh had taken over the lead with the Cubs in fifth, four games off the pace. Only the Phillies, then 9½ back, could be counted out. Finally, on the 27th, the Mets found themselves in first and Montreal in fifth by a scant 4½ games.

During the last weekend of the regular season, Pittsburgh finally eliminated Montreal, and St. Louis beat back Philadelphia to still have a chance depending upon the outcome of the Mets-Cubs series in Chicago. Rainouts had caused the Mets to play four games in two days with the Cubs as well as force the regular season a day past its regular schedule when the Mets could only split the first two to give St. Louis, Pittsburgh and even Chicago a chance. The sky was still heavy with clouds when the Mets and Cubs took to the field on October 1st, but Jon Matlack, pitching a strong two-hit shutout gave the Mets the first game and the Eastern Division title.

For the Mets, in coming out of the mediocre rubble to post the lowest winning percentage of any pennant winner in baseball history, the credit belonged to Cy Young winner Tom Seaver, who won 19 games in posting a league-low 2.08 E.R.A., Tug McGraw, who recovered from early season lethargy to save 25 games and start the phrase, "You Gotta Believe", Jon Matlack, who won 14 games and lost a lot of tough decisions and Felix Millan, who came over from the Braves to hit .290 to keep the Mets in contention. For manager Yogi Berra, the victory couldn't have been sweeter as it quickly transformed him from inept to hero as he became the only manager besides Joe McCarthy to win pennants in both leagues.

In the National League West the furor ended early. After the Dodgers, led by several promising youngsters, gained the lead in the first half of the season, the Cincinnati Reds came on behind the MVP performance of Pete Rose, who collected 230 hits, the slugging of Tony Perez, who hit .314 with 27 home runs and 101 RBI's, Johnny Bench, who hit 25 home runs after successfully going through a winter lung operation, and Joe Morgan. Third-place San Francisco had to settle for the growing maturity of Bobby Bonds, who hit 39 home runs, and the arrival of pitcher Ron Bryant, who won a league high 24 games without the help of a single shutout. For the Braves, there was a lot of home run hitting and little pitching—all facts which were mostly obscured by Hank Aaron's drive toward Babe Ruth's lifetime home run record of 714. Aaron, who finished fourth in the league with 40 home runs, went into the last game of the season with a chance to tie the record. But with commissioner Bowie Kuhn in attendance, as well as a lot of the press, Aaron could only manage three singles and finish the year with 713 home runs. Teammate Dave Johnson, who came over from the Orioles and who never hit more than 18 home runs in the American League, surprised many by belting 43 home runs to eclipse the second baseman's home run mark set by the legendary Rogers Hornsby. Third baseman Darrell Evans finished between the two with 41 round-trippers to give Atlanta the top three spots behind league-leader Willie Stargell of Pittsburgh.

In the American League the season began with the innovation of a new rule which allowed the manager to name a "designated hitter" to bat throughout the game for the pitcher, and the move, which was designed to bolster the action, instead produced a record twelve 20-game winners. Armed with the best of this new breed, the Orioles began a resurgance which gave them the Eastern title by eight games over the Red Sox. For Baltimore, Tommy Davis found enough success in the designated hitter spot to hit .293 and Orlando Cepeda, signed by the Red Sox after Oakland released him, took top power honors for designated hitters with 20 home runs. Baltimore's return to the top was also sparked by the superb play of rookies, Al Bumbry and Rich Coggins, and the steller pitching of Jim Palmer, who posted a 22-9 season with a league-low 2.40 E.R.A. to win the Cy Young Award. For third-place Detroit, who managed to stay in the race until the Orioles started their late-season winning skein, there was some consolation in John Hiller's 38 saves— a major league record.

Over in the Western Division, the White Sox began the season by throwing knuckler-baller Wilbur Wood so often that it seemed he would have no trouble posting 40 victories. But as things turned out Wood finished at 24-20 and Chicago in fifth, 17 games back. Whatever chance Chicago might have had was lost when Dick Allen, the highest paid player in baseball, broke his leg in mid-season and was sidelined for the year. Oakland, on the other hand, had no costly injuries until late in the year, and managed to again take the Western title, this time by six games over oncoming Kansas City. Led by MVP Reggie Jackson, the A's managed their return on the arms of the division's best mound staff which consisted of starters, Jim Hunter, Ken Holtzman, and Vida Blue, and ace reliever Rollie Fingers. Also included in manager Dick Williams' star-studded cast was shortstop Bert Campaneris, third baseman Sal Bando, first baseman Gene Tenace, and young center-fielder Bill North. For the California Angels, who finished fourth, the only satisfaction came in Nolan Ryan, who hurled two no-hitters and burned his way past 383 batters to set a new major league strikeout record.

In the American League championship play-off series, Oakland and Baltimore played out the five game string before the A's emerged victorious with a 3-0 performance from Hunter. In the National League series, the number was the same, but the frenzy of the Mets' fans nearly put a premature end to play. The fans' hysteria was ignited by a fight between Rose and Harrelson in the third game. But after order had been restored, the fans' anger continued and when Rose returned to his left field position, he was bombarded by whatever objects the fans could find to throw. Finally, Rose, in a effort to save himself from injury, marched off the field. He was followed by the other Reds and only after Willie Mays, Tom Seaver, and a few other Mets went out to left field to plead with the fans did they begin to settle down. Although the hostilities continued throughout the series, the Mets, behind Tom Seaver and Tug McGraw posted a win in the fifth game to give New York the National League pennant.

By the time the World Series started Met fans were already exhausted from all the fanfare which led up to the fall classic. But their fatigue quickly diminished and their fears began when Oakland got off to an opening game extra inning victory. In the second game, the Series again went beyond the ninth frame, but this time the Mets emerged the winner. As the see-saw Series continued the Mets pitching completely cut off the A's home run power. However, the A's battled the Mets despite their failure to hit a single home run, and when Reggie Jackson's three clutch hits beat Seaver in the sixth game, the Series went into a crucial seventh game showdown. With singles hitter Bert Campaneris and Reggie Jackson both hitting two run home runs in the third inning, Oakland routed Matlack and came away with a 5-2 victory and their second straight world's championship.

Although the Series had its usual excitement and great moments of play, they were matters which became overshadowed by Finley's off-the-field maneuvers when, in the second game reserve second baseman Mike Andrews came in and committed two errors to give the Mets a victory. After the game Finley put Andrews on the disabled list and the Oakland players and the press screamed bloody murder. Andrews was restored to the active roster for the next game on orders of Commissioner Kuhn and he received a standing ovation, even from Finley, when he came out of the dugout to pinch hit. But for all the final victory, Finley lost his manager, Dick Williams, who publicly announced his displeasure with Finley's interference, and left the team after the Series was over.

BALTIMORE 1st 97-65 .599 — EARL WEAVER

NAME	G by POS	B	AGE	G	AB	R	H	2B	3B	HR	RBI	BB	SO	SB	BA	SA
TOTALS			28	162	5537	754	1474	229	**48**	119	692	**648**	752	**146**	.266	.389
Boog Powell	1B111	L	31	114	370	52	98	13	1	11	54	85	64	0	.265	.395
Bobby Grich	2B162	R	24	162	581	82	146	29	7	12	50	107	91	17	.251	.387
Mark Belanger	SS154	R	29	154	470	60	106	15	1	0	27	49	54	13	.226	.262
Brooks Robinson	3B154	R	36	155	549	53	141	17	2	9	72	55	50	2	.257	.344
Don Baylor	OF110, 1B6, DH1	R	24	118	405	64	116	20	4	11	51	35	48	32	.286	.437
Paul Blair	OF144, DH1	R	29	146	500	73	140	25	3	10	64	43	72	18	.280	.402
Rich Coggins	OF101, DH1	L	22	110	389	54	124	19	9	7	41	28	24	17	.319	.468
Earl Williams	C95, 1B42, DH2	R	24	132	459	58	109	18	1	22	83	66	107	0	.237	.425
Tommy Davis	DH127, 1B4	R	34	137	552	53	169	20	3	7	89	30	56	11	.306	.391
Al Bumbry	OF86, DH7	L	26	110	356	73	120	15	**11**	7	34	34	49	23	.337	.500
Merv Rettenmund	OF90	R	30	95	321	59	84	17	2	9	44	57	38	11	.262	.411
Andy Etchebarren	C51	R	30	54	152	16	39	9	1	2	23	12	21	1	.257	.368
Terry Crowley	DH23, OF10, 1B7	L	26	54	131	16	27	4	0	3	15	16	14	0	.206	.305
Frank Baker	SS32, 2B7, 1B1, 3B1	L	26	44	63	10	12	1	2	1	11	7	7	0	.190	.317
Ellie Hendricks (BN)	C38, DH1	L	32	41	101	9	18	5	1	3	15	10	22	0	.178	.337
Enos Cabell	1B23, 3B1	R	23	32	47	12	10	2	0	1	3	3	7	1	.213	.319
Larry Brown	3B15, 2B1	R	33	17	28	4	7	0	0	1	5	5	4	0	.250	.357
Doug DeCinces	3B8, 2B2, SS1	R	22	10	18	2	2	0	0	0	3	1	5	0	.111	.111
Jim Fuller	OF5, 1B2, DH1	R	22	9	26	2	3	0	0	2	4	1	17	0	.115	.346
Sergio Robles	C8	R	27	8	13	0	1	0	0	0	0	3	1	0	.077	.077
Curt Motton	OF1, DH1	R	35	5	6	2	2	0	0	1	4	1	1	0	.333	.833

NAME	T	AGE	W	L	PCT	SV	G	GS	CG	IP	H	BB	SO	ShO	ERA
		28	**97**	65	**.599**	26	162	162	67	1462	1297	475	715	14	**3.07**
Jim Palmer	R	27	22	9	.710	1	38	37	19	297	225	113	158	6	**2.40**
Mike Cuellar	L	36	18	13	.581	0	38	38	17	267	265	84	140	2	3.27
Dave McNally	L	30	17	17	.500	0	38	38	17	266	247	81	87	4	3.21
Doyle Alexander (EJ)	R	22	12	8	.600	0	29	26	10	175	169	52	63	0	3.86
Grant Jackson	L	30	8	0	1.000	9	45	0	0	80	54	24	47	0	1.91
Bob Reynolds	R	26	7	5	.583	9	42	1	0	111	88	31	77	0	1.95
Jesse Jefferson	R	24	6	5	.545	0	18	15	3	101	104	46	52	0	4.10
Don Hood	L	23	3	2	.600	1	8	4	1	32	31	6	18	1	3.94
Eddie Watt	R	31	3	4	.429	5	30	0	0	71	62	21	38	0	3.30
1 Orlando Pena	R	39	1	1	.500	1	11	2	0	45	36	8	23	0	4.00
Wayne Garland	R	22	0	1	.000	0	4	1	0	16	14	7	10	0	3.94
1 Mickey Scott	L	25	0	0	.000	0	1	0	0	2	2	2	2	0	4.50

BOSTON 2nd 89-73 .549 8 — EDDIE KASKO

NAME	G by POS	B	AGE	G	AB	R	H	2B	3B	HR	RBI	BB	SO	SB	BA	SA
TOTALS			29	162	5513	738	1472	235	30	147	692	581	799	114	.267	**.401**
Carl Yastrzemski	1B107, 3B31, OF14	L	33	152	540	82	160	25	4	19	95	105	58	9	.296	.463
Doug Griffin (BH)	2B113	R	26	113	396	43	101	14	5	1	33	21	42	7	.255	.323
Luis Aparicio	SS132	R	39	132	499	56	135	17	1	0	49	43	33	13	.271	.309
Rico Petrocelli (EJ)	3B99	R	30	100	356	44	87	13	1	13	45	47	64	0	.244	.396
Reggie Smith	OF104, DH8, 1B1	B	28	115	423	79	128	23	2	21	69	68	49	3	.303	.515
Tommy Harper	OF143, DH1	R	32	147	566	92	159	23	3	17	71	61	93	**54**	.281	.422
Rick Miller	OF137	L	25	143	441	65	115	17	7	6	43	51	59	12	.261	.372
Carlton Fisk	C131, DH3	R	25	135	508	65	125	21	0	26	71	37	99	7	.246	.441
Orlando Cepeda	DH142	R	35	142	550	51	159	25	0	20	86	50	81	0	.289	.444
Dwight Evans	OF113, DH2	R	21	119	282	46	63	13	1	**10**	32	40	52	5	.223	.383
John Kennedy	2B31, 3B24, DH9	R	32	67	155	17	28	9	1	1	16	12	45	0	.181	.271
Mike Guerrero	SS46, 2B24	R	23	66	219	19	51	5	2	0	11	10	21	2	.233	.274
Danny Cater	1B37, 3B21, DH3	R	33	63	195	30	61	12	0	1	24	10	22	0	.313	.390
Ben Oglivie	OF32, DH13	L	24	58	147	16	32	9	1	2	9	9	32	1	.218	.333
Bob Montgomery	C33	R	29	34	128	18	41	6	2	7	25	7	36	0	.320	.563
Cecil Cooper	1B29	L	23	30	101	12	24	2	0	3	11	7	12	1	.238	.347
Buddy Hunter	3B3, 2B2, DH1	R	25	13	7	3	3	1	0	0	2	3	1	0	.429	.571

Duane Josephson (IL) 31

NAME	T	AGE	W	L	PCT	SV	G	GS	CG	IP	H	BB	SO	ShO	ERA
		30	89	73	.549	33	162	162	67	1440	1417	499	808	10	3.65
Luis Tiant	R	32	20	13	.606	0	35	35	23	272	217	78	206	0	3.34
Bill Lee	L	26	17	11	.667	1	38	33	18	285	275	76	120	1	2.75
Marty Pattin	R	30	15	15	.500	1	34	30	11	219	238	69	119	2	4.32
Roger Moret (KJ)	L	23	13	2	.867	3	30	15	5	156	138	67	90	2	3.17
John Curtis	L	25	13	13	.500	0	35	30	10	221	225	83	101	4	3.58
Dick Pole	R	22	3	2	.600	0	12	7	0	55	70	18	24	0	5.56
Bob Bolin	R	34	3	4	.429	15	39	0	0	53	45	13	31	0	2.72
Bob Veale	L	37	2	3	.400	11	32	0	0	36	37	12	25	0	3.50
Ray Culp (SJ)	R	31	2	6	.250	0	10	9	0	50	46	32	32	0	4.50
Lynn McGlothen (KJ)	R	23	1	2	.333	0	6	3	0	23	39	8	16	0	8.22
Craig Skok	L	25	0	1	.000	1	11	0	0	29	35	11	22	0	6.21
1 Sonny Siebert	R	36	0	1	.000	0	2	0	0	2	5	1	5	0	9.00
Mike Garman	R	23	0	0	.000	0	12	0	0	22	32	15	9	0	5.32
Don Newhauser (XJ)	R	25	0	0	.000	1	9	0	0	12	9	13	8	0	0.00
Ken Tatum	R	29	0	0	.000	0	1	0	0	4	6	3	0	0	9.00

DETROIT 3rd 85-77 .525 12 — BILLY MARTIN 71-65 .522 JOE SCHULTZ 14-12 .538

NAME	G by POS	B	AGE	G	AB	R	H	2B	3B	HR	RBI	BB	SO	SB	BA	SA
TOTALS			32	162	5508	642	1400	213	32	157	592	509	722	28	.254	.390
Norm Cash	1B114, DH3	L	38	121	363	51	95	19	0	19	40	47	73	1	.262	.471
Dick McAuliffe	2B102, SS2, DH1	L	33	106	343	39	94	18	1	12	47	49	52	0	.274	.437
Eddie Brinkman	SS162	R	31	162	515	55	122	16	4	7	40	34	79	0	.237	.324
Aurelio Rodriguez	3B160, SS1	R	25	160	555	46	123	27	3	9	58	31	85	3	.222	.330
Jim Northrup	OF116	L	33	119	404	55	124	14	7	12	44	38	41	4	.307	.465
Mickey Stanley	OF157	R	30	157	602	81	147	23	5	17	57	48	65	0	.244	.384
Willie Horton	OF107, DH1	R	30	111	411	42	130	19	3	17	53	23	57	1	.316	.501
Bill Freehan	C98, 1B7, DH3	R	31	110	380	33	89	10	1	6	29	40	30	0	.234	.313
Gates Brown	DH119, OF2	L	34	125	377	48	89	11	1	12	50	52	41	1	.236	.366
Al Kaline	OF63, 1B36	R	38	91	310	40	79	13	0	10	45	29	28	4	.255	.394
Dick Sharon	OF91	R	23	91	178	20	43	9	0	7	16	10	31	2	.242	.410
Frank Howard	DH76, 1B2	R	36	85	227	26	58	9	1	12	29	24	28	0	.256	.463
Tony Taylor	2B72, 1B6, 3B4, DH2, OF1	R	37	84	275	35	63	9	3	5	24	17	29	9	.229	.338
1 Duke Sims	C68, OF6	L	32	80	252	31	61	10	0	8	30	30	36	1	.242	.377
1 Rich Reese	1B37, OF21	L	31	59	102	10	14	1	0	2	4	7	17	0	.137	.206
Ike Brown	1B21, OF12, 3B2, DH2	R	31	42	76	12	22	2	1	1	9	**15**	**13**	0	.289	.382
Tom Veryzer	SS18	R	20	18	20	1	6	0	1	0	2	2	4	0	.300	.400
Ron Cash	OF7, 3B6	R	23	14	39	8	16	1	1	0	6	5	5	0	.410	.487
John Knox	2B9	L	24	12	32	1	9	1	0	0	3	3	3	1	.281	.313

Joe Staton 25 L 4-17, Bob Didier 24 B 10-22, John Gamble 25 R 0-0, Marvin Lane 23 R 2-8

NAME	T	AGE	W	L	PCT	SV	G	GS	CG	IP	H	BB	SO	ShO	ERA
		30	85	77	.525	**46**	162	162	39	1448	1468	493	911	11	3.90
Joe Coleman	R	26	23	15	.605	0	40	40	13	288	283	93	202	2	3.53
Mickey Lolich	L	32	16	15	.516	0	42	42	17	309	315	79	214	3	3.82
Jim Perry	R	37	14	13	.519	0	35	34	7	203	225	55	66	1	4.03
John Hiller	L	30	10	5	.667	**38**	**65**	0	0	125	89	39	124	0	1.44
Woody Fryman	L	33	6	13	.316	0	34	29	1	170	200	64	119	0	5.35
2 Bob Miller	R	34	4	2	.667	1	22	0	0	42	34	22	23	0	3.43
Mike Strahler	R	26	4	5	.444	0	22	11	1	80	84	39	37	0	4.39
2 Ed Farmer	R	23	3	0	1.000	2	24	0	0	45	52	27	28	0	5.00
Fred Scherman	L	27	2	2	.500	1	34	0	0	62	59	30	28	0	4.21
Chuck Seelbach (SJ)	R	25	1	0	1.000	0	5	0	0	7	7	2	2	0	3.86
1 Tom Timmerman	R	33	1	1	.500	1	17	1	0	39	39	11	21	0	3.69
Lerrin LaGrow (SA)	R	24	1	5	.167	3	21	3	0	54	54	23	33	0	4.33
Fred Holdsworth	R	21	0	1	.000	0	5	2	0	15	13	6	9	0	6.60
Gary Ignasiak	L	22	0	0	.000	0	3	0	0	5	5	3	4	0	3.60
Bill Slayback	R	25	0	0	.000	0	3	0	0	2	5	0	1	0	4.50
Dave Lemanczyk	R	22	0	0	.000	0	1	0	0	2	4	0	0	0	13.50

NEW YORK 4th 80-82 .494 17 — RALPH HOUK

NAME	G by POS	B	AGE	G	AB	R	H	2B	3B	HR	RBI	BB	SO	SB	BA	SA
TOTALS			30	162	5492	641	1435	212	17	131	616	489	**680**	**47**	.261	**.378**
1 Felipe Alou	1B67, OF22	R	38	93	280	25	66	12	0	4	27	9	25	0	.236	.321
Horace Clarke	2B147	B	33	148	590	60	155	21	0	2	35	47	48	11	.263	.308
Gene Michael	SS129	B	34	129	418	30	94	11	1	3	47	26	51	1	.225	.278
Graig Nettles	3B157, DH2	L	28	160	552	65	129	18	0	22	81	78	**76**	0	.234	.386
1 Matty Alou	OF85, 1B40, DH1	L	34	123	497	59	147	22	1	2	28	30	43	**5**	.296	.356
Bobby Murcer	OF160	L	27	160	616	83	187	29	2	22	95	50	67	**6**	.304	.464
Roy White	OF162	B	29	162	**639**	88	157	22	3	18	60	78	81	**16**	.246	.374
Thurman Munson	C142, DH1	R	26	147	519	80	156	29	4	20	74	48	64	**4**	.301	.487
2 Jim Ray Hart	DH106	R	31	114	339	29	86	13	2	13	52	36	45	0	.254	.419
Ron Blomberg	DH55, 1B41	L	24	100	301	45	99	13	1	12	57	34	**25**	2	.329	.498
Johnny Callison	OF32, DH10	R	30	45	136	10	24	4	0	1	10	4	24	1	.176	.228
2 Mike Hegan	1B37	L	30	37	131	12	36	3	2	6	14	7	34	0	.275	**.466**
Hal Lanier	SS26, 2B8, 3B1	R	30	35	86	9	18	3	0	0	5	3	10	0	.209	.244
Celerino Sanchez	3B11, DH11, SS2, OF2	R	29	34	64	12	14	3	0	1	9	2	12	1	.219	.313
Ron Swoboda	OF20, DH4	R	29	34	43	6	5	0	0	1	2	4	18	0	.116	.186
Fred Stanley	SS21, 2B3	B	25	26	66	6	14	0	1	1	5	7	16	0	.212	.288
Otto Velez	OF23	R	22	23	77	9	15	4	0	2	7	15	24	0	.195	.325
Gerry Moses	C17, DH1	R	26	20	59	5	15	2	0	0	3	2	6	0	.254	.288
1 Bernie Allen	2B13, DH2	L	34	17	57	5	13	3	0	0	4	5	5	0	.228	.281
Rick Dempsey	C5	R	23	6	11	0	2	0	0	0	0	1	3	0	.182	.182
2 Duke Sims	DH2, C1	L	32	4	9	3	3	0	0	1	1	3	1	0	.333	.667

NAME	T	AGE	W	L	PCT	SV	G	GS	CG	IP	H	BB	SO	ShO	ERA
		30	80	82	.494	39	162	162	47	1428	1379	457	708	16	3.34
Mel Stottlemyre	R	31	16	16	.500	0	38	38	19	273	259	79	95	4	3.07
Doc Medich	R	24	14	9	.609	0	34	32	11	235	217	74	145	3	2.95
Lindy McDaniel	R	37	12	6	.667	10	47	3	1	160	148	49	93	0	2.87
2 Pat Dobson	R	31	9	8	.529	0	22	21	6	142	150	34	70	1	4.18
Fritz Peterson	L	31	8	15	.348	0	31	31	6	184	207	49	59	0	3.96
Fred Beene	R	30	6	0	1.000	1	19	4	0	91	67	27	49	0	1.68
2 Sam McDowell	L	30	5	8	.385	0	16	15	2	96	73	64	75	1	3.94
Sparky Lyle	L	28	5	9	.357	27	51	0	0	82	66	18	63	0	2.52
Steve Kline (EJ)	R	25	4	7	.364	0	14	13	2	74	76	31	19	1	4.01
1 Mike Kekich	L	28	1	1	.500	0	5	4	0	15	20	14	4	0	9.00
Tom Buskey	R	26	0	1	.000	1	8	0	0	17	18	4	8	0	5.29
Jim Magnuson	L	26	0	1	.000	0	8	0	0	27	38	9	9	0	4.33
2 Wayne Granger	R	29	0	1	.000	0	7	0	0	15	19	3	10	0	1.80
Dave Pagan	R	23	0	0	.000	0	4	1	0	13	16	1	9	0	2.77
Casey Cox	R	31	0	0	.000	0	1	0	0	3	5	1	0	0	6.00

MILWAUKEE 5th 74-88 .457 23 — DEL CRANDALL

NAME	G by POS	B	AGE	G	AB	R	H	2B	3B	HR	RBI	BB	SO	SB	BA	SA
TOTALS			26	162	5526	708	1399	229	40	145	669	563	**977**	110	.253	.388
George Scott	1B157, DH1	R	29	158	604	98	185	30	4	24	107	61	94	9	.306	.488
Pete Garcia	2B160	R	23	160	580	67	142	32	5	15	54	40	119	11	.245	.395
Tim Johnson	SS135	L	23	136	465	39	99	10	2	0	32	29	93	6	.213	.243
Don Money	3B124, SS21	R	26	145	556	75	158	28	2	11	61	53	53	22	.284	.401
Bob Coluccio	OF108, DH11	R	21	124	438	65	98	21	8	15	58	54	92	13	.224	.411
Dave May	OF152, DH2	L	29	156	624	96	189	23	4	25	93	44	78	6	.303	.473
Johnny Briggs	OF137, DH1	L	29	142	488	79	120	20	7	18	57	87	83	15	.246	.426
Darrell Porter	C90, DH19	L	21	117	350	50	89	19	2	16	67	57	85	5	.254	.457
Ollie Brown	DH82, OF4	R	29	97	296	28	83	10	1	7	32	33	53	4	.280	.392
Joe Lahoud	DH41, OF40	L	26	96	225	29	46	9	0	5	26	27	36	5	.204	.311
Ellie Rodriguez	C75, DH14	R	27	94	290	30	78	8	1	0	30	41	28	4	.269	.303
Gorman Thomas	OF50, DH3, 3B1	R	22	59	155	16	29	7	1	2	11	14	61	5	.187	.284
John Vukovich	3B40, 1B13, SS1	R	25	55	128	10	16	3	0	2	9	9	40	0	.125	.195
Bob Heise	SS29, 3B9, 1B4, 2B4, DH2	R	26	49	98	8	20	2	0	0	4	4	4	1	.204	.224
Bobby Mitchell	OF20, DH19	R	29	47	130	12	29	6	0	5	20	5	32	4	.223	.385
Wilbur Howard	OF12, DH1	B	24	16	39	3	8	0	0	0	1	2	10	0	.205	.205
John Felske	C7, 1B6	R	31	13	22	1	3	0	1	0	4	1	11	0	.136	.227
Charlie Moore	C8	R	20	8	27	0	5	0	1	0	3	2	4	0	.185	.259
Rick Auerbach	SS2	R	23	6	10	2	1	1	0	0	0	0	1	0	.100	.200

NAME	T	AGE	W	L	PCT	SV	G	GS	CG	IP	H	BB	SO	ShO	ERA
		26	74	88	.457	28	162	162	50	1454	1476	623	671	11	3.98
Jim Colborn	R	27	20	12	.625	1	43	36	22	314	297	87	135	4	3.18
Jim Slaton	R	23	13	15	.464	0	38	38	13	276	266	99	134	3	3.72
Eduardo Rodriguez	R	21	9	7	.563	5	30	6	2	76	71	47	49	0	3.32
Jerry Bell	R	25	9	9	.500	1	31	25	8	184	185	70	57	0	3.96
Skip Lockwood	R	26	5	12	.294	0	37	15	3	155	164	59	87	0	3.89
Chris Short	L	35	3	5	.375	2	42	7	0	72	86	44	44	0	5.13
Billy Champion	R	25	5	8	.385	1	37	11	2	136	139	62	67	0	3.71
Bill Parsons	R	24	3	6	.333	0	20	17	0	60	59	67	30	0	6.75
Ray Newman	L	28	2	1	.667	1	11	0	0	18	19	5	10	0	3.00
Carlos Velazquez	R	25	2	2	.500	2	18	0	0	38	46	10	12	0	2.60
Frank Linzy	R	32	2	6	.250	13	42	1	0	63	68	21	21	0	3.57
2 Rob Gardner	L	28	1	1	.500	1	10	0	0	13	17	13	5	0	9.69
Gary Ryerson	L	25	0	1	.000	0	9	4	0	23	32	7	10	0	7.83
3 Ed Sprague	R	27	0	1	.000	1	7	0	0	10	13	14	3	0	9.00
Kevin Kobel	L	19	0	1	.000	0	2	1	0	8	9	8	4	0	9.00
Ken Reynolds	R	27	0	1	.000	0	2	1	0	7	5	10	3	0	7.71

EAST DIVISION

CLEVELAND 6th 71-91 .438 26 — KEN ASPROMONTE

NAME	G by POS	B	AGE	G	AB	R	H	2B	3B	HR	RBI	BB	SO	SB	BA	SA
TOTALS			25	162	5592	680	1429	205	29	**158**	636	471	793	60	.256	.387
Chris Chambliss	1B154	L	24	155	572	70	156	30	2	11	53	58	76	4	.273	.390
Jack Brohamer	2B97	L	23	102	300	29	66	12	1	4	29	32	23	0	.220	.307
Frank Duffy (SJ)	SS115	R	26	116	361	34	95	16	4	8	50	25	41	6	.263	.396
Buddy Bell	3B154, OF2	R	21	156	631	86	169	23	7	14	59	49	47	7	.268	.393
Rusty Torres	OF114	B	24	122	312	31	64	8	1	7	28	50	62	6	.205	.304
George Hendrick (BW)	OF110	R	23	113	440	64	118	18	0	21	61	25	71	7	.268	.452
Charlie Spikes	OF111, DH26	R	22	140	506	68	120	12	3	23	73	45	103	5	.237	.409
Dave Duncan (BW)	C86, DH9	R	27	95	344	43	80	11	1	17	43	35	86	3	.233	.419
Oscar Gamble	DH70, OF37	L	22	113	390	56	104	11	3	20	44	34	37	3	.267	.464
Johnny Ellis	C72,DH38,1B12	R	24	127	437	59	118	12	2	14	68	46	57	0	.270	.403
Walt Williams	OF61, DH26	R	29	104	350	43	101	15	1	8	38	14	29	9	.289	.406
J. Lowenstein	OF51, 2B25, 3B8, DH4, 1B1	L	26	98	305	42	89	16	1	6	40	23	41	5	.292	.410
Leo Cardenas	SS67, 3B5	R	34	72	195	9	42	4	0	0	12	13	42	1	.215	.236
Tom Ragland	2B65, SS2	R	27	67	183	16	47	7	1	0	12	8	31	2	.257	.306
Ron Lolich	OF32, DH12	R	26	61	140	16	32	7	0	2	15	7	27	0	.229	.321
Tommy Smith	OF13	L	24	14	41	6	10	2	0	2	3	1	2	1	.244	.439
Ted Ford	OF10	R	26	11	40	3	9	0	1	0	3	2	7	1	.225	.275
Alan Ashby	C11	B	21	11	29	4	5	1	0	1	3	2	11	0	.172	.310
Jerry Kenney	2B5	L	28	5	16	0	4	0	1	0	2	2	0	0	.250	.375

NAME	T	AGE	W	L	PCT	SV	G	GS	CG	IP	H	BB	SO	ShO	ERA
		28	71	91	.438	21	162	162	55	**1465**	**1532**	602	883	9	4.58
Gaylord Perry	R	34	19	19	.500	0	41	41	**29**	344	315	115	238	7	3.38
Dick Tidrow	R	26	14	16	.467	0	42	40	13	275	289	95	138	2	4.42
2 Tom Timmerman	R	33	8	7	.533	2	29	15	4	124	117	54	62	0	4.93
Milt Wilcox (FJ)	R	23	8	10	.444	0	26	19	4	134	143	68	82	0	5.84
2 Ken Sanders	R	31	5	1	.833	5	15	0	0	27	18	9	14	0	1.67
Tom Hilgendorf	L	31	5	3	.625	6	48	1	1	95	87	36	58	0	3.13
Jerry Johnson	R	29	5	6	.455	5	39	1	0	60	70	39	45	0	6.15
Ray Lamb	R	28	3	3	.500	2	32	1	0	86	98	42	60	0	4.60
Brent Strom (EJ)	L	24	2	10	.167	0	27	18	2	123	134	47	91	0	4.61
2 Mike Kekich	L	28	1	4	.200	0	16	6	0	50	73	35	26	0	7.02
2 Dick Bosman	R	29	1	8	.111	0	22	17	2	97	130	29	41	0	6.22
1 Ed Farmer	R	23	0	2	.000	1	16	0	0	17	25	5	10	0	4.76
1 Steve Dunning	R	24	0	2	.000	0	4	3	0	18	17	13	10	0	6.50
Mike Kilkenny	L	28	0	0	.000	0	5	0	0	2	5	5	3	0	22.50
1 Steve Mingori	L	29	0	0	.000	0	5	0	0	12	10	10	4	0	6.00
2 Mike Jackson	L	27	0	0	.000	0	1	0	0	1	1	0	1	0	0.00

WEST DIVISION

OAKLAND 1st 94-68 .580 — DICK WILLIAMS

NAME	G by POS	B	AGE	G	AB	R	H	2B	3B	HR	RBI	BB	SO	SB	BA	SA
TOTALS			28	162	5507	**758**	1431	216	28	147	**714**	595	919	128	.260	.389
Gene Tenace	1B134, C33, DH3, 2B1	R	26	160	510	83	132	18	2	24	84	101	94	2	.259	.443
Dick Green	2B100, OF1, DH1	R	32	133	332	33	87	17	0	3	42	21	63	0	.262	.340
Bert Campaneris	SS149	R	31	151	601	89	150	17	6	4	46	50	79	34	.250	.318
Sal Bando	3B159, DH3	R	29	162	592	97	170	**32**	3	29	98	82	84	4	.287	.498
Reggie Jackson	OF145, DH3	L	27	151	539	**99**	158	28	2	**32**	**117**	76	111	22	.293	**.531**
Billy North	OF138, DH6	B	25	146	554	98	158	10	5	5	34	78	89	53	.285	.348
Joe Rudi	OF117, 1B1, DH1	R	26	120	437	53	118	25	1	12	66	30	72	0	.270	.414
Ray Fosse	C141, DH2	R	26	143	492	37	126	23	2	7	52	25	62	2	.256	.354
2 Deron Johnson	DH107, 1B23	R	34	131	464	61	114	14	2	19	81	59	116	0	.246	.407
Ted Kubiak	2B83, SS26, 3B2	B	31	106	182	15	40	6	1	3	17	12	19	1	.220	.313
1 Mike Hegan	1B56, OF3, DH3	L	31	75	71	8	13	2	0	1	5	5	17	0	.183	.254
Angel Mangual	OF50, DH14, 1B2, 2B1	R	26	74	192	20	43	4	1	3	13	8	34	1	.224	.302
Billy Conigliaro (KJ)	OF40, 2B1	R	25	48	110	5	22	2	2	0	14	9	26	1	.200	.255
Rich McKinney	3B17, 2B7, DH6, OF3	R	26	48	65	9	16	3	0	1	7	7	4	0	.246	.338
2 Vic Davalillo	1B8, DH2	L	37	38	64	5	12	1	0	0	4	3	4	0	.188	.203
2 Jesus Alou	OF21, DH6	R	32	36	108	10	33	3	0	1	11	2	6	0	.306	.361
Allen Lewis	DH6, OF1	B	31	35	0	16	0	0	0	0	0	0	0	7	–	–
1 Dal Maxvill	SS18, 2B11, 3B1	R	34	29	19	0	4	0	0	0	1	1	3	0	.211	.211
2 Pat Bourque	DH15, 1B5	L	26	23	42	8	8	4	1	2	9	15	10	0	.190	.476
Jay Johnstone	OF7, DH4, 2B2	L	27	23	28	1	3	1	0	0	3	2	4	0	.107	.143
1 Gonzalo Marquez	2B2, 1B1, OF1, DH1	L	27	23	25	1	6	1	0	0	2	0	4	0	.240	.280
2 Mike Andrews	2B9, DH2	R	29	18	21	1	4	1	0	0	0	3	1	0	.190	.238
Manny Trillo	2B16	R	22	17	12	0	3	2	0	0	3	0	4	0	.250	.417
Tim Hosley	C13	R	26	13	14	3	3	0	0	0	2	2	3	0	.214	.214
Phil Garner	3B9	R	24	9	5	0	0	0	0	0	0	0	3	0	.000	.000
3 Rico Carty	DH1	R	34	7	8	1	2	1	0	1	1	2	1	0	.250	.750
1 Jose Morales	DH3	R	28	6	14	0	4	1	0	0	1	1	5	0	.286	.357
1 Larry Haney	C2	R	30	2	2	0	1	0	0	0	0	0	0	0	.500	.500

NAME	T	AGE	W	L	PCT	SV	G	GS	CG	IP	H	BB	SO	ShO	ERA
		27	94	68	.580	41	162	162	46	1457	1311	494	797	16	3.29
Catfish Hunter (BG)	R	27	21	5	.808	0	36	36	11	256	222	69	124	3	3.34
Ken Holtzman	L	28	21	13	.618	0	40	40	16	297	275	66	157	4	2.97
Vida Blue	L	23	20	9	.690	0	37	37	13	264	214	105	158	4	3.27
Rollie Fingers	R	26	7	8	.467	22	62	2	0	127	107	39	110	0	1.91
Horacio Pina	R	28	6	3	.667	8	47	0	0	88	58	34	41	0	2.76
Dave Hamilton	L	25	6	4	.600	0	16	11	1	70	74	24	34	0	4.37
Darold Knowles	L	31	6	8	.429	9	52	5	1	99	87	49	46	1	3.09
Blue Moon Odom	R	28	5	12	.294	0	30	24	3	150	153	67	83	0	4.50
Glenn Abbott	R	22	1	0	1.000	0	5	3	1	19	16	7	6	0	3.79
Paul Lindblad	L	31	1	5	.167	2	36	3	0	78	89	28	33	0	3.69
Chuck Dobson	R	29	0	1	.000	0	1	1	0	2	6	2	3	0	9.00
1 Rob Gardner	L	28	0	0	.000	0	3	0	0	7	10	4	2	0	5.14

KANSAS CITY 2nd 88-74 .543 6 — JACK McKEON

NAME	G by POS	B	AGE	G	AB	R	H	2B	3B	HR	RBI	BB	SO	SB	BA	SA
TOTALS			28	162	5508	755	1440	239	40	114	703	644	696	105	.261	.381
John Mayberry	1B149, DH1	L	23	152	510	87	142	20	2	26	100	**122**	79	3	.278	.478
Cookie Rojas	2B137	R	34	139	551	78	152	29	3	6	69	37	38	18	.276	.372
Freddie Patek	SS135	R	28	135	501	82	117	19	5	5	45	54	63	36	.234	.321
Paul Schaal	3B121	R	30	121	396	61	114	14	3	8	42	63	45	5	.288	.399
Ed Kirkpatrick	OF108, C14, DH8	L	28	126	429	61	113	24	3	6	45	46	48	3	.263	.375
Amos Otis	OF135, DH14	R	26	148	583	89	175	21	4	26	93	63	47	13	.300	.484
Lou Piniella	OF128, DH9	R	29	144	513	53	128	28	1	9	69	30	65	5	.250	.361
Fran Healy	C92, DH1	R	26	95	279	25	77	15	2	6	34	31	56	3	.276	.409
Hal McRae	DH37, OF64, 3B2	R	26	106	338	36	79	18	3	9	50	34	38	2	.234	.385
Steve Hovley	OF79, DH15	L	28	104	232	29	59	8	1	2	24	33	34	6	.254	.323
K. Bevacqua	3B40, 2B16, DH16, OF10, 1B9	R	26	99	276	39	71	8	3	2	40	25	42	2	.257	.330
Gail Hopkins	DH36, 1B10	L	30	74	138	17	34	6	1	2	16	29	15	1	.246	.348
Carl Taylor	C63, 1B2, DH1	R	29	69	145	18	33	6	1	0	16	32	20	2	.228	.283
Frank White	SS37, 2B11	R	22	51	139	20	31	6	1	0	5	8	23	3	.223	.281
Bobby Floyd	2B25, SS24	R	29	51	78	10	26	3	1	0	8	4	14	1	.333	.397
Jim Wohlford	DH19, OF13	R	22	45	109	21	29	1	3	2	10	11	12	1	.266	.385
2 Rick Reichardt	DH31, OF7	R	30	41	127	15	28	5	2	3	17	11	28	0	.220	.362
Tom Poquette	OF20	L	21	21	28	4	6	1	0	0	3	1	4	1	.214	.250
Buck Martinez	C14	R	24	14	32	2	8	1	0	1	6	4	5	0	.250	.375
George Brett	3B13	L	20	13	40	2	5	2	0	0	0	0	5	0	.125	.175
1 Jerry May	C11	R	29	11	30	4	4	1	1	0	2	3	5	0	.133	.233
Frank Ortenzio	1B7, DH1	R	22	9	25	1	7	2	0	1	6	2	6	0	.280	.480
Keith Marshall	OF8	R	21	8	9	0	2	1	0	0	3	1	4	0	.222	.333

NAME	T	AGE	W	L	PCT	SV	G	GS	CG	IP	H	BB	SO	ShO	ERA
		27	88	74	.543	41	162	162	40	1449	1521	617	790	7	4.19
Paul Splittorff	L	26	20	11	.645	0	38	38	12	262	279	78	110	3	3.98
Steve Busby	R	23	16	15	.516	0	37	37	7	238	246	105	174	1	4.24
Dick Drago	R	28	12	14	.462	0	37	33	10	213	252	76	98	1	4.23
Gene Garber	R	25	9	9	.500	11	48	8	4	153	164	49	60	0	4.24
Al Fitzmorris	R	26	8	3	.727	0	15	13	3	89	88	25	26	1	2.83
Ken Wright	R	26	6	5	.545	0	25	12	1	81	60	82	75	0	4.89
Bruce Dal Canton	R	31	4	3	.571	3	32	3	1	97	108	46	38	0	4.82
Doug Bird	R	23	4	4	.500	20	54	0	0	102	81	30	83	0	3.00
2 Steve Mingori	L	29	3	3	.500	1	19	1	0	56	59	23	46	0	3.05
Wayne Simpson	R	24	3	4	.429	0	16	10	1	60	66	35	29	0	5.70
2 Joe Hoerner	L	36	2	0	1.000	4	22	0	0	19	28	13	15	0	5.21
Mark Littell	R	20	1	3	.250	0	8	7	1	38	44	23	16	0	5.68
1 Mike Jackson	L	27	0	0	.000	0	9	0	0	22	25	20	13	0	6.95
Norm Angelini	L	25	0	0	.000	1	7	0	0	4	2	7	3	0	4.50
Tom Burgmeier	L	29	0	0	.000	1	6	0	0	10	13	4	4	0	5.40
Barry Raziano	R	26	0	0	.000	0	2	0	0	5	6	1	0	0	5.40

MINNESOTA 3rd 81-81 .500 13 — FRANK QUILICI

NAME	G by POS	B	AGE	G	AB	R	H	2B	3B	HR	RBI	BB	SO	SB	BA	SA
TOTALS			28	162	**5625**	738	**1521**	**240**	44	120	688	598	954	87	**.270**	.393
Joe Lis	1B96, DH1	R	26	103	253	37	62	11	1	9	25	28	66	0	.245	.403
Rod Carew	2B147	L	27	149	580	98	**203**	30	**11**	6	62	62	55	41	**.350**	.471
Danny Thompson	SS95, 3B1	R	26	99	347	29	78	13	2	1	36	16	41	1	.225	.282
Steve Braun (KJ)	3B102, OF6	L	24	115	361	46	102	28	5	6	42	74	48	4	.283	.438
Larry Hisle	OF143	R	26	143	545	88	148	25	6	15	64	64	128	11	.272	.422
Bobby Darwin	OF140, DH1	R	30	145	560	69	141	20	2	18	90	46	**137**	5	.252	.391
Jim Holt	OF102, 1B33	L	29	132	441	52	131	25	3	11	58	29	43	0	.297	.442
George Mitterwald	C122, DH3	R	28	125	432	50	112	15	0	16	64	39	111	3	.259	.405
Tony Oliva	DH142	L	33	146	571	63	166	20	0	16	92	45	44	2	.291	.410
Jerry Terrell	SS81, 3B30, 2B14, OF1, DH1	R	26	124	438	43	116	15	2	1	32	21	56	13	.265	.315
Steve Brye	OF87	R	24	92	278	39	73	9	5	6	33	35	43	3	.263	.396
Harmon Killebrew (KJ)	1B57, DH9	R	37	69	248	29	60	9	1	5	32	41	59	0	.242	.347
Mike Adams	OF24, DH2	R	24	55	66	21	14	2	0	3	6	17	18	2	.212	.379
Phil Roof	C47	R	32	47	117	10	23	4	1	1	15	13	27	0	.197	.274
Dan Monzon	2B17, 3B14, OF1	R	27	39	76	10	17	1	1	0	4	11	9	1	.224	.263
Danny Walton	OF18, DH11, 3B1	R	25	37	96	13	17	1	1	4	8	17	28	0	.177	.333
Eric Soderholm	3B33, SS1	R	24	35	111	22	33	7	2	1	9	21	16	1	.297	.423
2 Rich Reese	1B17	L	31	22	23	7	4	1	1	1	3	6	6	0	.174	.435
Craig Kusick	1B11, OF2, DH2	R	24	15	48	4	12	2	0	0	4	7	9	0	.250	.292
Glenn Borgmann	C12	R	23	12	34	7	9	2	0	0	9	6	10	0	.265	.324

NAME	T	AGE	W	L	PCT	SV	G	GS	CG	IP	H	BB	SO	ShO	ERA
		27	81	81	.500	34	162	162	48	1452	1443	519	879	**18**	3.77
Bert Blyleven	R	22	20	17	.541	0	40	40	25	325	296	67	258	9	2.52
1 Jim Kaat	L	33	11	12	.478	0	29	28	7	182	206	39	93	2	4.40
Dick Woodson (SA)	R	28	10	8	.556	0	23	23	4	141	137	68	53	2	3.96
Joe Decker	R	26	10	10	.500	0	29	24	6	170	167	88	109	3	4.18
Ray Corbin	R	24	8	5	.615	14	51	7	1	148	124	60	83	0	3.04
Bill Hands	R	33	7	10	.412	2	39	15	3	142	138	41	78	1	3.49
Dave Goltz	R	24	6	4	.600	1	32	10	1	106	138	32	65	0	5.26
Dan Fife	R	23	3	2	.600	0	10	7	1	52	54	29	18	0	4.33
Bill Campbell	R	24	3	3	.500	7	28	2	0	52	44	20	42	0	3.12
1 Ken Sanders	R	31	2	4	.333	8	27	0	0	44	53	21	19	0	6.14
Vic Albury	L	26	1	0	1.000	0	14	0	0	23	13	19	13	0	2.74
Jim Strickland	L	27	0	1	.000	0	7	0	0	5	11	5	6	0	12.60
Eddie Bane	L	21	0	5	.000	2	23	6	0	60	62	30	42	0	4.95

CALIFORNIA 4th 79-83 .488 — BOBBY WINKLES

	NAME	G by POS	B	AGE	G	AB	R	H	2B	3B	HR	RBI	BB	SO	SB	BA	SA
	TOTALS			30	162	5505	629	1395	183	29	93	595	509	816	59	.253	.348
2	Mike Epstein	1B86	L	30	91	312	30	67	8	2	8	32	34	54	0	.215	.330
	Sandy Alomar	2B110, SS31	B	29	136	470	45	112	7	1	0	28	34	44	25	.238	.257
	Rudy Meoli	SS95, 3B13, 2B8	L	22	120	305	36	68	12	1	2	23	31	38	2	.223	.289
2	Alan Gallagher	3B98, 2B1, SS1	R	27	110	311	16	85	6	1	0	26	35	31	1	.273	.299
	Lee Stanton	OF107	R	27	119	306	41	72	9	2	8	34	27	88	3	.235	.356
	Ken Berry	OF129	R	32	136	415	48	118	11	2	3	36	26	50	1	.284	.342
	Vada Pinson	OF120	L	34	124	466	56	121	14	6	8	57	20	55	5	.260	.367
	Jeff Torborg (BG)	C102	R	31	102	255	20	56	7	0	1	18	21	32	0	.220	.259
	Frank Robinson	DH127, OF17	R	37	147	534	85	142	29	0	30	97	82	93	1	.266	.489
	Bob Oliver	3B49, OF47, 1B32, DH12	R	30	151	544	51	144	24	1	18	89	33	100	1	.265	.412
	Tommy McCraw	OF34, 1B25, DH8	L	32	99	264	25	70	7	0	3	24	30	42	3	.265	.326
	Winston Llenas	2B20, 3B11, OF4, DH4	R	29	78	130	16	35	1	0	1	25	10	16	0	.269	.300
2	Richie Scheinblum	OF54, DH7	B	30	77	229	28	75	10	2	3	21	35	27	0	.328	.428
1	B. Grabarkewitz	2B18, 3B12, DH5, SS1, OF1	R	27	61	129	27	21	6	1	3	9	28	27	2	.163	.295
	Johnny Stephenson	C56	L	32	60	122	9	30	5	0	1	9	7	7	0	.246	.311
	Art Kusnyer	C41	R	27	41	64	5	8	2	0	0	3	2	12	0	.125	.156
	Jerry DaVanon	SS14, 2B12, 3B7	R	27	41	49	6	12	3	0	0	2	3	9	1	.245	.306
	Billy Parker	2B32, SS3	R	26	38	102	14	23	2	1	0	7	8	23	0	.225	.265
	Bobby Valentine (BL)	SS25, OF8	R	23	32	126	12	38	5	2	1	13	5	9	6	.302	.397
	Mickey Rivers	OF29	L	23	30	129	26	45	6	4	0	16	8	11	8	.349	.457
1	Jim Spencer	1B26, DH2	L	25	29	87	10	21	4	2	2	11	9	9	0	.241	.402
	Dave Chalk	SS22	R	22	24	69	14	16	2	0	0	6	9	13	0	.232	.261
2	Dick Stelmaszek	C22	L	24	22	26	2	4	1	0	0	3	6	7	0	.154	.192
	Charlie Sands	C10	L	25	17	33	5	9	2	1	1	5	5	10	0	.273	.485
	Doug Howard	OF6, 1B1, 3B1	R	25	8	21	2	2	0	0	0	0	1	6	0	.095	.095
	Bobby Brooks	OF1	R	28	4	7	0	1	0	0	0	0	0	3	0	.143	.143

	NAME	T	AGE	W	L	PCT	SV	G	GS	CG	IP	H	BB	SO	ShO	ERA
			28	79	83	.488	19	162	162	72	1456	1351	614	1010	13	3.53
	Nolan Ryan	R	26	21	16	.568	1	41	39	26	326	238	162	383	4	2.87
	Bill Singer	R	29	20	14	.588	0	40	40	19	316	280	130	241	2	3.22
	Clyde Wright	L	32	11	19	.367	0	37	36	13	257	273	76	65	1	3.68
	Dave Sells	R	26	7	2	.778	10	51	0	0	68	72	35	25	0	3.71
	Rudy May	L	28	7	17	.292	0	34	28	10	185	177	80	134	4	4.38
2	Rich Hand	R	24	4	3	.571	0	16	6	0	55	58	21	19	0	3.60
	Steve Barber	L	34	3	2	.600	4	50	1	0	89	90	32	58	0	3.54
	Dick Lange	R	24	2	1	.667	0	17	4	1	53	61	21	27	0	4.42
	Aurelio Monteagudo	R	29	2	1	.667	3	15	0	0	30	23	16	8	0	4.20
	Frank Tanana	L	19	2	2	.500	0	4	4	2	26	20	8	22	1	3.12
	Ron Perranoski (SJ)	L	37	0	2	.000	0	8	0	0	11	11	7	5	0	4.09
	Andy Hassler	L	21	0	4	.000	0	7	4	1	32	33	19	19	0	3.66
1	Lloyd Allen	R	23	0	0	.000	1	5	0	0	9	15	5	4	0	10.00
	Terry Wilshusen	R	24	0	0	.000	0	1	0	0	.1	0	2	0	0	81.00

CHICAGO 5th 77-85 .475 17 — CHUCK TANNER

	NAME	G by POS	B	AGE	G	AB	R	H	2B	3B	HR	RBI	BB	SO	SB	BA	SA
	TOTALS			26	162	5475	652	1400	228	38	111	598	537	952	83	.256	.372
	Tony Muser	1B89, DH13, OF2	L	25	109	309	38	88	14	3	4	30	33	36	8	.285	.388
	Jorge Orta	2B122, SS1	L	22	128	425	46	113	9	10	6	40	37	87	8	.266	.376
	Eddie Leon	SS122, 2B3	R	26	127	399	37	91	10	3	3	30	34	103	1	.228	.291
	Bill Melton	3B151, DH1	R	27	152	560	83	155	29	1	20	87	75	66	4	.277	.439
	Pat Kelly	OF141, DH1	L	28	144	550	77	154	24	5	1	44	65	91	22	.280	.347
	Johnnie Jeter	OF72, DH3	R	28	89	300	38	72	14	4	7	26	9	74	4	.240	.383
	Bill Sharp	OF70, DH1	L	23	76	196	23	54	8	3	4	22	19	28	2	.276	.408
	Ed Herrmann	C114, DH2	L	26	119	379	42	85	17	1	10	39	31	55	2	.224	.354
	Carlos May	DH75, OF70, 1B2	L	25	149	553	62	148	20	0	20	96	53	73	8	.268	.412
	Luis Alvarado	2B45, SS18, 3B10, DH1	R	24	80	203	21	47	7	2	0	20	4	20	6	.232	.286
	Ken Henderson (KJ)	OF44, DH26	B	27	73	262	32	68	13	0	6	32	27	49	3	.260	.378
	Dick Allen (BL)	1B67, 2B2, DH1	R	31	72	250	39	79	20	3	16	41	33	51	7	.316	.612
	Chuck Brinkman	C63	R	28	63	139	13	26	6	0	1	10	11	37	0	.187	.252
	Jerry Hairston	OF33, 1B19, DH8	B	21	60	210	25	57	11	1	0	23	33	30	0	.271	.333
	Buddy Bradford (SJ)	OF51	R	28	53	168	24	40	3	1	8	15	17	43	4	.238	.411
1	Mike Andrews	DH30, 1B9, 2B6, 3B5	R	29	52	159	10	32	9	0	0	10	23	28	0	.201	.258
1	Rick Reichardt	OF37, DH6	R	30	46	153	15	42	8	1	3	16	8	29	2	.275	.399
	Bucky Dent	SS36, 2B3, 3B1	R	21	40	117	17	29	2	0	0	10	10	18	2	.248	.265
	Brian Downing (KJ)	OF13, C11, 3B8, DH1	R	22	34	73	5	13	1	0	2	4	10	17	0	.178	.274
	Hank Allen	3B9, 1B8, OF5, 2B1, C1	R	32	28	39	2	4	2	0	0	0	1	9	0	.103	.154
	Sam Ewing	1B4	L	24	11	20	1	3	1	0	0	2	2	6	0	.150	.200
1	Rich Morales	3B5, 2B2	R	29	7	4	1	0	0	0	0	1	1	1	0	.000	.000
	Pete Varney	C5	R	24	5	4	0	0	0	0	0	1	1	0	0	.000	.000
	Joe Keough		L	27	5	1	1	0	0	0	0	0	0	0	0	.000	.000

	NAME	T	AGE	W	L	PCT	SV	G	GS	CG	IP	H	BB	SO	ShO	ERA
			26	77	85	.475	35	162	162	48	1456	1484	574	848	15	3.86
	Wilbur Wood	L	31	24	20	.545	0	49	48	21	359	381	91	199	4	3.46
	Stan Bahnsen	R	28	18	21	.462	0	42	42	14	282	290	117	120	4	3.57
	Cy Acosta	R	26	10	6	.625	18	48	0	0	97	66	39	60	0	2.23
1	Eddie Fisher	R	36	6	7	.462	0	26	16	2	111	135	38	57	0	4.86
	Terry Forster	L	21	6	11	.353	16	51	12	4	173	174	78	120	0	3.23
	Steve Stone	R	25	6	11	.353	1	36	22	3	176	163	82	138	0	4.24
2	Jim Kaat	L	34	4	1	.800	0	7	7	3	43	44	4	16	1	4.20
	Bart Johnson	R	23	3	3	.500	0	22	9	0	81	76	40	56	0	4.11
2	Jim McGlothlin	R	29	0	1	.000	0	5	1	0	18	13	13	14	0	4.00
	Rich Gossage	R	21	0	4	.000	0	20	4	1	50	57	37	33	0	7.38
	Ken Frailing	L	25	0	0	.000	0	10	0	0	18	18	7	15	0	2.00
	Steve Kealey (SA)	R	26	0	0	.000	0	7	0	0	11	23	7	4	0	15.55
	Jim Geddes	R	24	0	0	.000	0	6	1	0	16	14	14	7	0	2.81
	Denny O'Toole	R	24	0	0	.000	0	6	0	0	16	23	3	8	0	5.63
	Dave Baldwin	R	35	0	0	.000	0	3	0	0	5	7	4	1	0	3.60
	Dave Lemonds (AJ)		24													

TEXAS 6th 57-105 .352 37 — WHITEY HERZOG 47-91 .341 DEL WILBER 1-0 1.000 BILLY MARTIN 9-14 .391

	NAME	G by POS	B	AGE	G	AB	R	H	2B	3B	HR	RBI	BB	SO	SB	BA	SA
	TOTALS			27	162	5488	619	1397	195	29	110	574	503	791	91	.255	.361
2	Jim Spencer	1B99	L	25	102	352	35	94	12	3	4	43	34	41	0	.267	.352
	Dave Nelson	2B140	R	29	142	576	71	165	24	4	7	48	34	78	43	.286	.378
	Jim Mason	SS74, 2B19, 3B1	L	22	92	238	23	49	7	2	3	19	23	48	0	.206	.290
	Tony Harrah (BG)	SS76, 3B52	R	24	118	461	64	120	16	1	10	50	46	49	10	.260	.364
	Elliott Maddox (SJ)	OF89, 3B7, DH1	R	25	100	172	24	41	1	0	1	17	29	28	5	.238	.262
	Vic Harris	OF113, 3B25, 2B18	B	23	152	555	71	138	14	7	8	44	55	81	13	.249	.342
	Jeff Burroughs	OF148, 1B3, PH1	R	22	151	526	71	147	17	1	30	85	67	88	0	.279	.487
	Ken Suarez	C90	R	30	93	278	25	69	11	0	1	27	33	16	1	.248	.299
	Alex Johnson	DH116, OF41	R	30	158	624	62	179	26	3	8	68	32	82	10	.287	.377
1	Rico Carty	OF53, DH37	R	34	86	306	24	71	12	0	3	33	36	39	2	.232	.301
	Larry Biittner	OF57, 1B20, DH3	L	27	83	258	19	65	8	2	1	12	20	21	1	.252	.310
	Bill Sudakis	3B29, 1B24, C9, DH8, OF2	B	27	82	235	32	60	11	0	15	43	23	53	0	.255	.494
	Dick Billings (BG)	C72, OF4, 1B3, DH2	R	30	81	280	17	50	11	0	3	32	20	43	1	.179	.250
	Tommy Grieve	OF59, DH1	R	25	66	123	22	38	6	0	7	21	7	25	1	.309	.528
2	Jim Fregosi	3B34, 1B10, SS6	R	31	45	157	25	42	6	2	6	16	12	31	0	.268	.446
	Pete Mackanin	SS33, 3B10	R	21	44	90	3	9	2	0	0	2	4	26	0	.100	.122
1	Mike Epstein	1B25	L	30	27	85	9	16	3	0	1	6	14	19	0	.188	.259
	Joe Lovitto	3B20, OF3	B	22	26	44	3	6	1	0	0	0	5	7	1	.136	.159
	Bill Madlock	3B21	R	22	21	77	16	27	5	3	1	5	7	9	3	.351	.532
	Lenny Randle	2B5, OF2	B	24	10	29	3	6	1	1	1	1	0	2	0	.207	.414
1	Dick Stelmaszek	C7	L	24	7	9	0	1	0	0	0	0	1	2	0	.111	.111
	Don Castle	DH3	L	23	4	13	0	4	1	0	0	2	1	3	0	.308	.385

	NAME	T	AGE	W	L	PCT	SV	G	GS	CG	IP	H	BB	SO	ShO	ERA
			25	57	105	.352	27	162	162	35	1430	1514	680	831	10	4.64
2	Jim Bibby	R	28	9	10	.474	1	26	23	11	180	121	106	155	2	3.25
2	Sonny Siebert (SJ)	R	36	7	11	.389	2	25	20	1	120	120	37	76	1	3.97
1	Mike Paul	L	28	5	4	.556	2	36	10	1	87	104	36	49	0	4.97
	Jackie Brown	R	30	5	5	.500	2	25	3	2	67	82	25	45	1	3.90
	Pete Broberg	R	23	5	9	.357	0	22	20	6	119	130	66	57	1	5.60
	Jim Merritt	L	29	5	13	.278	1	35	19	8	160	191	34	65	1	4.05
	Charlie Hudson (RJ)	L	23	4	2	.667	1	25	4	1	62	59	31	34	1	4.65
	Dave Clyde	L	18	4	8	.333	0	18	18	0	93	106	54	74	0	5.03
	Bill Gogolewski	R	25	3	6	.333	6	49	1	0	124	139	48	77	0	4.21
1	Rich Hand	R	24	2	3	.400	0	8	7	1	42	49	19	14	0	5.36
	Steve Foucault (BJ)	R	23	2	4	.333	8	32	0	0	56	54	31	28	0	3.86
1	Dick Bosman	R	29	2	5	.286	0	7	7	1	40	42	17	14	1	4.28
2	Steve Dunning	R	24	2	6	.250	0	23	12	2	94	101	52	38	0	5.36
	Rick Henninger	R	25	1	0	1.000	0	6	2	0	23	23	11	6	0	2.74
	Don Stanhouse	R	22	1	7	.125	1	21	5	1	70	70	44	42	0	4.76
	Jim Kremmel	L	25	0	2	.000	0	4	2	0	9	15	6	6	0	9.00
	Don Durham	R	24	0	4	.000	1	15	4	0	40	49	23	23	0	7.65
2	Lloyd Allen	R	23	0	6	.000	1	23	5	0	41	58	39	25	0	9.22
	Jim Shellenback	L	29	0	0	.000	0	2	0	0	2	0	0	3	0	0.00
	Rick Waits	L	21	0	0	.000	1	1	0	0	1	1	1	0	0	9.00

AMERICAN LEAGUE CHAMPIONSHIP – OAKLAND (WEST) 3 BALTIMORE (EAST) 2

LINE SCORES

TEAM	1	2	3	4	5	6	7	8	9	10	11	12	R	H	E
Game 1 October 6 at Baltimore															
OAK	0	0	0	0	0	0	0	0	0				0	5	1
BAL	4	0	0	0	0	0	1	1	X				6	12	0
Blue, Pina (1), Odom (3), Fingers (8)						Palmer									
Game 2 October 7 at Baltimore															
OAK	1	0	0	0	0	2	0	2	1				6	9	0
BAL	1	0	0	0	0	1	0	1	0				3	8	0
Hunter, Fingers (8)						McNally, Reynolds (8), Jackson (9)									
Game 3 October 9 at Oakland															
BAL	0	1	0	0	0	0	0	0	0	0	0		1	3	0
OAK	0	0	0	0	0	0	0	1	0	0	1		2	4	3
Cuellar						Holtzman									
Game 4 October 10 at Oakland															
BAL	0	0	0	0	0	0	4	1	0				5	8	0
OAK	0	3	0	0	0	1	0	0	0				4	7	0
Palmer, Reynolds (2), Watt (7), Jackson (7)						Blue, Fingers (7)									
Game 5 October 11 at Oakland															
BAL	0	0	0	0	0	0	0	0	0				0	5	2
OAK	0	0	1	2	0	0	0	0	X				3	7	0
Alexander, Palmer (4)						Hunter									

COMPOSITE BATTING

NAME	POS	G	AB	R	H	2B	3B	HR	RBI	BA
Oakland Totals		5	160	15	32	5	1	5	14	.200
Campaneris	SS	5	21	3	7	1	0	2	3	.333
Jackson	OF	5	21	0	3	0	0	0	0	.143
Rudi	OF	5	18	1	4	0	0	1	3	.222
Bando	3B	5	18	2	3	0	0	2	3	.167
Tenace	1B-C	5	17	3	4	1	0	0	0	.235
Green	2B	5	13	0	1	1	0	0	0	.077
Fosse	C	5	11	2	1	1	0	0	3	.091
Johnson	DH	4	10	0	1	0	0	0	0	.100
Mangual	OF	3	9	1	1	0	0	0	0	.111
Davalillo	1B-OF	4	8	2	5	1	1	0	1	.625
Alou	DH-PH	4	6	0	2	0	0	0	1	.333

Conigliaro OF 0-4, Kubiak 2B 0-2, Andrews DH, PH, 2B 0-1, Bourque DH 0-1, Fingers P 0-0, Blue P 0-0, Hunter P 0-0, Lewis PR 0-0, Holtzman P 0-0, Odom P 0-0, Pina P 0-0

NAME	POS	G	AB	R	H	2B	3B	HR	RBI	BA
BALTIMORE Totals		5	171	15	36	7	0	3	15	.211
Davis	DH	5	21	1	6	1	0	0	2	.286
Grich	2B	5	20	1	2	0	0	1	1	.100
Robinson	3B	5	20	1	5	2	0	0	2	.250
Williams	C-1B	5	18	2	5	2	0	1	4	.278
Blair	OF	5	18	2	3	0	0	0	0	.167
Belanger	SS	5	16	0	2	0	0	0	1	.125
Etchebarren	C	4	14	1	5	1	0	1	4	.357
Baylor	OF	4	11	3	3	0	0	0	1	.273
Rettenmund	OF	3	11	1	1	0	0	0	0	.091
Coggins	OF	2	9	1	4	1	0	0	0	.444
Brumby	OF	2	7	1	0	0	0	0	0	.000

Powell 1B 0-4, Crowley OF 0-2, Palmer P 0-0, Baker SS 0-0, Jackson P 0-0, Reynolds P 0-0, Alexander P 0-0, Brown 3B 0-0, Cuellar P 0-0, Hood PR 0-0, McNally P 0-0, Watt P 0-0

COMPOSITE PITCHING

NAME	G	IP	H	BB	SO	W	L	SV	ERA
Oakland Totals	5	46	36	16	25	3	2	1	2.74
Hunter	2	16.1	12	5	6	2	0	0	1.65
Holtzman	1	11	3	1	7	1	0	0	0.82
Blue	2	7	8	5	3	0	1	0	10.29
Odom	1	5	6	2	4	0	0	0	1.80
Fingers	3	4.2	4	2	4	0	1	1	1.93
Pina	1	2	3	1	1	0	0	0	0.00
BALTIMORE Totals	5	45	32	17	39	2	3	0	2.74
Palmer	3	14.2	11	8	15	1	0	0	1.84
Cuellar	1	10	4	3	11	0	1	0	1.80
McNally	1	7.2	7	2	7	0	1	0	5.87
Reynolds	2	5.2	5	3	5	0	0	0	3.18
Alexander	1	3.2	5	0	1	0	1	0	4.91
Jackson	2	3	0	1	0	1	0	0	0.00
Watt	1	.1	0	0	0	0	0	0	0.00

NATIONAL LEAGUE CHAMPIONSHIP– NEW YORK (EAST) 3 CINCINNATI (WEST) 2

LINE SCORES

TEAM	1	2	3	4	5	6	7	8	9	10	11	12	R	H	E
Game 1 October 6 at Cincinnati															
NY	0	1	0	0	0	0	0	0	0				1	3	0
CIN	0	0	0	0	0	0	0	1	1				2	6	0
Seaver — Billingham, Hall (9), **Borbon** (9)															
Game 2 October 7 at Cincinnati															
NY	0	0	0	1	0	0	0	0	4				5	7	0
CIN	0	0	0	0	0	0	0	0	0				0	2	0
Matlack — **Gullett**, Carroll (6), Hall (9), Bourbon (9)															
Game 3 October 8 at New York															
CIN	0	0	2	0	0	0	0	0	0				2	8	1
NY	1	5	1	2	0	0	0	0	X				9	11	1
Grimsley, Hall (2), Tomlin (3), Nelson (4), Borbon (7) — **Koosman**															
Game 4 October 9 at New York															
CIN	0	0	0	0	0	0	1	0	0	0	0	1	2	8	0
NY	0	0	1	0	0	0	0	0	0	0	0	0	1	3	2
Stone, McGraw (7), **Parker** (12) — Norman, Bullett (6), **Carroll** (10), Borbon (12)															
Game 5 October 10 at New York															
CIN	0	0	1	0	1	0	0	0	0				2	7	1
NY	2	0	0	0	4	1	0	0	X				7	13	1
Billingham, Gullett (5), Carroll (5), Grimsley (7) — **Seaver**, McGraw (9)															

COMPOSITE BATTING

NAME	POS	G	AB	R	H	2B	3B	HR	RBI	BA
New York										
Totals		5	168	23	37	5	0	3	22	.220
Garrett	3B	5	**23**	1	2	1	0	0	1	.087
Jones	OF	5	20	3	6	**2**	0	0	3	.300
Millan	2B	5	19	**5**	6	0	0	0	2	.316
Grote	C	5	19	2	4	0	0	0	2	.211
Harrelson	SS	5	18	1	3	0	0	0	2	.167
Hahn	OF	5	17	2	4	0	0	0	1	.235
Milner	1B	5	17	2	3	0	0	0	1	.176
Staub	OF	4	15	4	3	0	0	**3**	**5**	.200
Seaver	P	2	6	1	2	**2**	0	0	1	.333

Koosman P 2-4, Mays OF 1-3, Kranepool OF 1-2, Matlack P 0-2, Boswell PH 0-1, McGraw P 0-1, Stone P 0-1, Parker P 0-0

NAME	POS	G	AB	R	H	2B	3B	HR	RBI	BA
Cincinnati										
Totals		5	167	8	31	6	0	5	8	.186
Perez	1B	5	22	1	2	0	0	1	2	.091
Rose	OF	5	21	3	**8**	1	0	2	2	**.381**
Morgan	2B	5	20	1	2	1	0	0	1	.100
Bench	C	5	19	1	5	**2**	0	1	1	.263
Geronimo	OF	4	15	0	1	0	0	0	0	.067
Driessen	3B	4	12	0	2	1	0	0	1	.167
Kosco	OF	3	10	0	3	0	0	0	0	.300
Menke	SS-3B	3	9	1	2	0	0	1	1	.222
Chaney	SS	5	9	0	0	0	0	0	0	.000

Griffey OF 1-7, Armbrister OF 1-6, Stahl PH 2-4, Gagliano PH 0-3, Billingham P 0-2, Crosby SS 1-2, King PH 1-2, Gullett P 0-1, Nelson P 0-1, Norman P 0-1, Borbon P 0-0, Carroll P 0-0, Hall P 0-0, Grimsley P 0-0, Tomlin P 0-0

COMPOSITE PITCHING

NAME	G	IP	H	BB	SO	W	L	SV	ERA
New York									
Totals	5	47.1	31	13	42	3	2	1	1.34
Seaver	2	**16.2**	**13**	**5**	**17**	1	1	0	1.59
Matlack	1	9	2	3	9	1	0	0	**0.00**
Koosman	1	9	8	0	9	1	0	0	2.00
Stone	1	6.2	3	2	4	0	0	0	1.29
McGraw	2	5	4	3	3	0	0	**1**	0.00
Parker	1	1	1	0	0	0	1	0	9.00
Cincinnati									
Totals	5	46	37	19	28	2	3	1	4.50
Billingham	2	12	9	4	9	0	1	0	4.50
Gullett	3	9	4	3	6	0	1	0	2.00
Carroll	3	7	5	1	2	1	0	0	1.29
Norman	1	5	1	3	3	0	0	0	1.80
Borbon	**4**	4.2	3	0	3	1	0	**1**	0.00
Grimsley	2	3.2	7	2	3	0	1	0	11.25
Nelson	1	2.1	0	1	0	0	0	0	0.00
Tomlin	1	1.2	5	1	1	0	0	0	13.50
Hall	3	.2	3	4	1	0	0	0	45.00

EAST DIVISION

NEW YORK 1st 82-79 .509 — YOGI BERRA

NAME	G by POS	B	AGE	G	AB	R	H	2B	3B	HR	RBI	BB	SO	SB	BA	SA
TOTALS			28	161	5457	608	1345	198	24	85	553	540	805	27	.246	.338
John Milner (LJ)	1B95, OF29	L	23	129	451	69	108	12	3	23	72	62	84	1	.239	.432
Felix Millan	2B153	R	29	153	638	82	185	23	4	3	37	35	22	2	.290	.353
Bud Harrelson (BH)	SS103	B	29	106	356	35	92	12	3	0	20	48	48	5	.258	.309
Wayne Garrett	3B130, SS9, 2B6	L	25	140	504	76	129	20	3	16	58	72	74	6	.256	.403
Rusty Staub	OF152	L	29	152	585	77	163	36	1	15	76	74	52	1	.279	.421
Don Hahn	OF87	R	24	93	262	22	60	10	0	2	21	22	43	2	.229	.290
Cleon Jones (WJ)	OF92	R	30	92	339	48	88	13	0	11	48	28	51	1	.260	.395
Jerry Grote (BA)	C81, 3B2	R	30	84	285	17	73	10	2	1	32	13	23	0	.256	.316
Ed Kranepool	1B51, OF32	L	28	100	284	28	68	12	2	1	35	30	28	1	.239	.306
Ted Martinez	SS44, OF21, 2B5	R	25	92	263	34	67	11	0	1	14	13	38	3	.255	.308
Ken Boswell	3B17, 2B3	L	27	76	110	12	25	2	1	2	14	12	11	0	.227	.318
Duffy Dyer	C60	R	27	70	189	9	35	6	1	1	9	13	40	0	.185	.243
Willie Mays	OF45, 1B17	R	42	66	209	24	44	10	0	6	25	27	47	1	.211	.344
Jim Beauchamp	1B11	R	33	50	61	5	17	1	1	0	14	7	11	1	.279	.328
Ron Hodges	C40	L	24	45	127	5	33	2	0	1	18	11	19	0	.260	.299
1 Jim Fregosi	SS17, 3B17, 1B3, OF1	R	31	45	124	7	29	4	1	0	11	20	25	1	.234	.282
George Theodore (PJ)	OF33, 1B4	R	25	45	116	14	30	4	0	1	15	10	13	1	.259	.319
Jim Gosger	OF35	L	30	38	92	9	22	2	0	0	10	9	16	0	.239	.261

Dave Schneck 24 L 7-36, Rich Chiles 23 L 3-25, 2 Jerry May 29 R 2-8, Brian Ostrosser 24 L 0-5, Lute Barnes 26 R 1-2, Greg Harts 23 L 1-2

NAME	T	AGE	W	L	PCT	SV	G	GS	CG	IP	H	BB	SO	ShO	ERA
		27	82	79	.509	40	161	161	47	1465	1345	490	1027	15	3.26
Tom Seaver	R	28	19	10	.655	0	36	36	**18**	290	219	64	**251**	3	**2.08**
Jerry Koosman	L	30	14	15	.483	0	35	35	12	263	234	76	156	3	2.84
Jon Matlack	L	23	14	16	.467	0	34	34	14	242	210	99	205	3	3.20
George Stone	L	26	12	3	.800	1	27	20	2	148	157	31	77	0	2.80
Harry Parker	R	25	8	4	.667	5	38	9	0	97	79	36	63	0	3.34
Ray Sadecki	L	32	5	4	.556	1	31	11	1	117	109	41	87	0	3.38
Tug McGraw	L	28	5	6	.455	25	60	2	0	119	106	55	81	0	3.86
Jim McAndrew	R	29	3	8	.273	1	23	12	0	80	109	31	38	0	5.40
Buzz Capra	R	25	2	7	.222	4	24	0	0	42	35	28	35	0	3.86
Tommy Moore	R	24	0	1	.000	0	3	1	0	3	6	3	1	0	12.00
Craig Swan	R	22	0	1	.000	0	3	1	0	8	16	2	4	0	9.00
Phil Hennigan	R	27	0	4	.000	3	30	0	0	43	50	16	22	0	6.28
2 John Strohmayer	R	26	0	0	.000	0	7	0	0	10	13	4	5	0	8.10
Hank Webb	R	23	0	0	.000	0	2	0	0	2	2	2	1	0	9.00
Bob Apodaca	R	23	0	0	.000	0	1	0	0	0	0	2	0	0	∞
3 Bob Miller	R	34	0	0	.000	0	1	0	0	1	0	0	1	0	0.00

ST. LOUIS 2nd 81-81 .500 1.5 — RED SCHOENDIENST

NAME	G by POS	B	AGE	G	AB	R	H	2B	3B	HR	RBI	BB	SO	SB	BA	SA
TOTALS			27	162	5478	643	1418	240	35	75	592	531	796	100	.259	.357
Joe Torre	1B114, 3B58	R	32	141	519	67	149	17	2	13	69	65	78	2	.287	.403
Ted Sizemore	2B139, 3B3	R	28	142	521	69	147	22	1	1	54	68	34	6	.282	.334
Mike Tyson	SS128, 2B16	R	23	144	469	48	114	15	4	1	33	23	66	2	.243	.299
Ken Reitz	3B135,SS1	R	22	147	426	40	100	20	2	6	42	9	25	0	.235	.333
Luis Melandez	OF95	R	23	121	341	35	91	18	1	2	35	27	50	2	.267	.343
Jose Cruz	OF118	L	25	132	406	51	92	22	5	10	57	51	66	10	.227	.379
Lou Brock	OF159	L	34	160	650	110	193	29	8	7	63	15	112	**70**	.297	.398
Ted Simmons	C153, 1B6, OF2	B	23	161	619	62	192	36	2	13	91	61	47	2	.310	.438
Tim McCarver	1B77, C11	L	31	130	331	30	88	16	4	3	49	38	31	2	.266	.366
Bernie Carbo	OF94	L	25	111	308	42	88	18	0	8	40	58	52	2	.286	.422
Mick Kelleher	SS42	R	25	43	38	4	7	2	0	0	2	4	11	0	.184	.237
Bake McBride	OF17	L	24	40	63	8	19	3	0	0	5	4	10	0	.302	.349
Bill Stein	OF10, 1B2, 3B1	R	26	32	55	4	12	2	0	0	2	7	18	0	.218	.255
Jim Dwyer	OF20	L	23	28	57	7	11	1	1	0	0	1	5	0	.193	.246
2 Tommy Agee	OF19	R	30	26	62	8	11	3	1	3	7	5	13	1	.177	.403
1 Ray Busse	SS23	R	24	24	70	6	10	4	2	2	5	5	21	0	.143	.343

Tom Heintzelman 26 R 9-29, 1 Ed Crosby 24 L 5-39, 1 Dwain Anderson 25 R 2-17, 2 Dave Campbell 31 R 0-21, 2 Matty Alou 34 L 3-11, Terry Hughes 24 R 3-14, Hector Cruz 20 R 0-11, Bob Fenwick 26 R 1-6, Tommy Cruz 22 L 0-0, 2 Larry Haney 30 R 0-1, Marc Hill 21 R 0-3

NAME	T	AGE	W	L	PCT	SV	G	GS	CG	IP	H	BB	SO	ShO	ERA
		29	81	81	.500	36	162	162	42	1461	1366	486	867	14	3.25
Rick Wise	R	27	16	12	.571	0	35	34	14	259	259	59	144	5	3.37
Reggie Cleveland	R	25	14	10	.583	0	32	32	6	224	211	61	122	3	3.01
Alan Foster	R	26	13	9	.591	0	35	29	6	204	195	63	106	2	3.13
Bob Gibson (KJ)	R	37	12	10	.545	0	25	25	13	195	159	57	142	1	2.77
Diego Segui	R	35	7	6	.538	17	65	0	0	100	78	53	93	0	2.79
2 Orlando Pena	R	39	4	4	.500	6	42	0	0	62	60	14	38	0	2.18.
Rich Folkers	L	26	4	4	.500	3	39	9	1	82	74	34	44	0	3.62
Tom Murphy	R	27	3	7	.300	0	19	13	2	89	89	22	42	0	3.74
2 Eddie Fisher	R	36	2	1	.667	0	6	0	0	7	3	1	1	0	1.29
Al Hrabosky	L	23	2	4	.333	5	44	0	0	56	45	21	57	0	2.09
1 Wayne Granger	R	29	2	4	.333	5	33	0	0	47	50	21	14	0	4.21
John Andrews	L	24	1	1	.500	0	16	0	0	18	16	11	5	0	4.50
Scipio Spinks (SJ)	R	25	1	5	.167	0	8	8	0	39	39	25	25	0	4.85
Mike Nagy	R	25	0	2	.000	0	9	7	0	41	44	15	14	0	4.17
1 Jim Bibby	R	28	0	2	.000	0	6	3	0	16	19	17	12	0	9.56
2 Ed Sprague	R	27	0	0	.000	0	8	0	0	8	8	4	2	0	2.25
Al Santorini	R	25	0	0	.000	0	6	0	0	8	14	2	2	0	5.63
Mike Thompson	R	23	0	0	.000	0	2	2	0	4	1	5	3	0	0.00
Lew Krausse	R	30	0	0	.000	0	1	0	0	2	2	1	1	0	0.00

PITTSBURGH 3rd 80-82 .494 2.5 — BILL VIRDON 67-69 .493 DANNY MURTAUGH 13-13 .500

NAME	G by POS	B	AGE	G	AB	R	H	2B	3B	HR	RBI	BB	SO	SB	BA	SA
TOTALS			27	162	5608	704	1465	**257**	44	154	664	432	842	23	.261	.405
Bob Robertson	1B107	R	26	119	397	43	95	16	0	14	40	55	77	0	.239	.385
Dave Cash	2B92, 3B17	R	25	116	436	59	118	21	2	2	31	38	36	2	.271	.342
2 Dal Maxvill	SS74	R	34	74	217	19	41	4	3	0	17	22	40	0	.189	.235
Richie Hebner	3B139	L	25	144	509	73	138	28	1	25	74	56	60	0	.271	.477
Richie Zisk	OF84	R	24	103	333	44	108	23	7	10	54	21	63	0	.324	.526
Al Oliver	OF109, 1B50	L	26	158	654	90	191	38	7	20	99	22	52	6	.292	.463
Willie Stargell	OF142	L	33	148	522	106	156	**43**	3	**44**	**119**	80	129	0	.299	**.646**
Manny Sanguillen	C89, OF59	R	29	149	589	64	166	26	7	12	65	17	29	2	.282	.411
Reggie Stennett	2B84, SS43, OF5	R	22	128	466	45	113	18	3	10	55	16	63	2	.242	.358
Gene Clines (NJ)	OF77	R	26	110	304	42	80	11	3	1	23	26	36	8	.263	.329
Milt May	C79	L	22	101	283	29	76	8	1	7	31	34	26	0	.269	.378
Gene Alley	SS49, 3B8	R	32	76	158	25	32	3	2	2	8	20	28	1	.203	.285
1 Vic Davalillo	1B10, OF10	L	36	59	83	9	15	1	0	1	3	2	7	0	.181	.229
Dave Parker	OF39	L	22	54	139	17	40	9	1	4	14	2	27	1	.288	.453
Jackie Hernandez	SS49	R	32	54	73	8	18	1	2	0	8	4	12	0	.247	.315
Fernando Gonzalez	3B5	R	23	37	49	5	11	0	1	1	5	1	11	0	.224	.327

Dave Augustine 23 R 2-7, Jerry McNertney 36 R 1-4, Jim Campanis 29 R 1-6, 1 Chuck Goggin 27 B 1-1

NAME	T	AGE	W	L	PCT	SV	G	GS	CG	IP	H	BB	SO	ShO	ERA
		29	80	82	.494	**44**	162	162	26	1451	1426	564	839	11	3.71
Nelson Briles	R	29	14	13	.519	0	33	33	7	219	201	51	94	1	2.84
Bob Moose	R	25	12	13	.480	0	33	29	6	201	219	70	111	3	3.54
Dock Ellis (EJ)	R	28	12	14	.462	0	28	28	3	192	176	55	122	1	3.05
Jim Rooker	L	31	10	6	.625	5	41	18	6	170	143	52	122	3	2.86
Dave Giusti	R	32	9	2	.818	20	67	0	0	99	89	37	64	0	2.36
Luke Walker	L	29	7	12	.368	1	37	18	2	122	129	66	74	1	4.65
Bob Johnson	R	30	4	2	.667	4	50	2	0	92	98	34	68	0	3.62
Ramon Hernandez	L	32	4	5	.444	11	59	0	0	90	71	25	64	0	2.40
Bruce Kison (SA)	R	22	3	0	1.000	0	7	7	0	44	36	24	26	0	3.07
Steve Blass	R	31	3	9	.250	0	23	18	1	89	109	84	27	0	9.81
John Morlan	R	25	2	2	1.000	0	10	7	1	41	42	23	23	0	3.95
John Lamb	R	26	0	1	.000	2	22	0	0	30	37	10	11	0	6.00
Jim McKee	R	26	0	1	.000	0	15	1	0	27	31	17	13	0	5.67
Tom Dettore	R	25	0	1	.000	0	12	1	0	23	33	14	13	0	5.87
Chris Zachary	R	29	0	1	.000	1	6	0	0	12	10	1	6	0	3.00
Jim Foor	L	24	0	0	.000	0	3	0	0	1	2	1	1	0	0.00

MONTREAL 4th 79-83 .488 3.5 — GENE MAUCH

NAME	G by POS	B	AGE	G	AB	R	H	2B	3B	HR	RBI	BB	SO	SB	BA	SA
TOTALS			28	162	5369	668	1345	190	23	125	613	**695**	777	77	.251	.364
Mike Jorgensen	1B123, OF11	L	24	138	413	49	95	16	2	9	47	64	49	16	.230	.344
Ron Hunt (KJ)	2B102, 3B14	R	32	113	401	61	124	14	0	0	18	52	19	10	.309	.344
Tim Foli (BJ)	SS123, 2B2, OF1	R	22	126	458	37	110	11	0	2	36	28	40	6	.240	.277
Bob Bailey	3B146, OF2	R	30	151	513	77	140	25	4	26	86	88	99	5	.273	.489
Ken Singleton	OF161	B	26	162	560	100	169	26	2	23	103	123	91	2	.302	.479
Ron Woods	OF114	R	30	135	318	45	73	11	3	3	31	56	34	12	.230	.311
Ron Fairly	OF121, 1B5	L	34	142	413	70	123	13	1	17	49	86	33	2	.298	.458
John Boccabella	C117, 1B1	R	32	118	403	25	94	13	0	7	46	26	57	1	.233	.318
Hal Breeden	1B66	R	29	105	258	36	71	10	6	15	43	29	45	0	.275	.535
Boots Day	OF51	L	25	101	207	36	57	7	0	4	28	21	28	0	.274	.367
Pepe Frias	SS46, 2B44, 3B6, OF1	R	24	100	225	19	52	10	1	0	22	10	24	1	.231	.284
Clyde Mashore (IL)	OF44, 2B1	R	28	67	103	12	21	3	0	3	14	15	28	4	.204	.320
Larry Lintz	2B34, SS15	B	23	52	116	20	29	1	0	0	3	17	18	12	.250	.259
Jim Lyttle	OF36	L	27	49	116	12	30	5	1	4	19	9	14	0	.259	.422
Bob Stinson	C35, 3B1	B	27	48	111	12	29	6	1	3	12	17	15	0	.261	.414
Terry Humphrey	C35	R	23	43	90	5	15	2	0	1	9	5	16	0	.167	.222
Pepe Mangual	OF22	R	21	33	62	9	11	2	1	3	7	6	18	2	.177	.387

Jorge Roque 23 R 9-61, Coco Laboy 33 R 4-33, 2 Felipe Alou 38 R 10-48, 2 Bernie Allen 34 L 9-50, Tony Scott 21 B 0-1, Jim Cox 23 R 2-15, Barry Foote 21 R 4-6, 2 Jose Morales 28 R 2-5, Curt Brown 27 R 0-4

NAME	T	AGE	W	L	PCT	SV	G	GS	CG	IP	H	BB	SO	ShO	ERA
		26	79	83	.488	38	162	162	26	1452	1356	**681**	866	6	3.73
Steve Renko	R	28	15	11	.577	1	36	34	9	250	201	108	164	0	2.81
Mike Marshall	R	30	14	11	.560	**31**	**92**	0	0	179	163	75	124	0	2.66
Steve Rogers	R	23	10	5	.667	0	17	17	7	134	93	49	64	3	1.54
Mike Torrez	R	26	9	12	.429	0	35	34	3	208	207	115	90	1	4.46
Tom Walker	R	24	7	5	.583	4	54	0	0	92	95	42	68	0	3.62
Ernie McAnally	R	26	7	9	.438	0	27	24	4	147	158	54	72	0	4.04
Balor Moore	L	22	7	16	.304	0	35	32	3	176	151	109	151	1	4.50
Bill Stoneman (SJ)	R	29	4	8	.333	1	29	17	0	97	120	55	48	0	6.77
Chuck Taylor	R	31	2	0	1.000	0	8	0	0	20	17	2	10	0	1.80
Pat Jarvis (VJ)	R	32	2	1	.667	0	28	0	0	39	37	16	19	0	3.23
2 Mickey Scott	L	25	1	2	.333	0	22	0	0	24	27	9	11	0	5.25
Joe Gilbert	L	21	1	2	.333	1	21	0	0	29	30	19	17	0	4.97
1 John Strohmayer	R	26	0	1	.000	0	17	3	0	35	34	22	15	0	5.14
Craig Caskey	L	23	0	0	.000	0	9	1	0	14	15	4	6	0	5.79
John Montague	R	25	0	0	.000	0	4	0	0	8	8	2	7	0	3.38

CHICAGO 5th 77-84 .478 5 — WHITEY LOCKMAN

NAME	G by POS	B	AGE	G	AB	R	H	2B	3B	HR	RBI	BB	SO	SB	BA	SA
TOTALS			31	161	5363	614	1322	201	21	117	570	575	855	65	.247	.357
Jim Hickman	1B51, OF13	R	36	92	201	27	49	1	2	3	20	42	42	1	.244	.313
Glenn Beckert (FJ)	2B88	R	32	114	372	38	95	13	0	0	29	30	15	0	.255	.290
Don Kessinger	SS158	B	30	160	577	52	151	22	3	0	43	57	44	6	.262	.310
Ron Santo	3B146	R	33	149	536	65	143	29	2	20	77	63	97	1	.267	.440
Jose Cardenal	OF142	R	29	145	522	80	158	33	2	11	68	58	62	19	.303	.437
Rick Monday	OF148	L	27	149	554	93	148	24	5	26	56	92	124	5	.267	.469
Billy Williams	OF138, 1B19	L	35	156	576	72	166	22	2	20	86	76	72	4	.288	.438
Randy Hundley	C122	R	31	124	368	35	83	11	1	10	43	30	51	5	.226	.342
Gene Hiser	OF64	L	24	100	109	15	19	3	0	1	6	11	17	4	.174	.229
Paul Popovich	2B84, SS9, 3B1	B	32	99	280	24	66	6	3	2	24	18	27	3	.236	.300
Carmen Fanzone	3B25, 2B24, OF6	R	30	64	150	22	41	7	0	6	22	20	38	1	.273	.440
Ken Rudolph	C64	R	26	64	170	12	35	8	1	2	17	7	25	1	.206	.300
1 Pat Bourque	1B38	L	26	57	139	11	29	6	0	7	20	16	21	1	.209	.403
Cleo James	OF22	R	32	44	45	9	5	0	0	0	0	1	6	5	.111	.111
Adrian Garrett	OF7, C6	L	30	36	54	7	12	0	0	3	8	4	18	1	.222	.389
1 Joe Pepitone	1B28	L	32	31	112	16	30	3	0	3	18	8	6	3	.268	.375
2 Rico Carty	OF19	R	34	22	70	4	15	0	0	1	8	6	10	0	.214	.257
2 Gonzalo Marquez	1B18	L	27	19	58	5	13	2	0	1	4	3	4	0	.224	.310
Andy Thornton	1B9	R	23	17	35	3	7	3	0	0	2	7	9	0	.200	.286
Dave Rosello	2B13, SS1	R	23	16	38	4	10	2	0	0	2	2	4	2	.263	.316

Matt Alexander 26 B 1-5, Pete LaCock 21 L 4-16, Tom Lundstedt 24 B 0-5, Tony LaRussa 28 R 0-0

NAME	T	AGE	W	L	PCT	SV	G	GS	CG	IP	H	BB	SO	ShO	ERA
		27	77	84	.478	40	161	161	27	1438	1471	438	885	13	3.66
Rick Reuschel	R	24	14	15	.483	0	36	36	7	237	244	62	168	3	3.00
Ferguson Jenkins	R	29	14	16	.467	0	38	38	7	271	267	57	170	2	3.89
Burt Hooton	R	23	14	17	.452	0	42	34	9	240	248	73	134	2	3.68
Bob Locker	R	35	10	6	.625	18	63	0	0	106	96	42	76	0	2.55
Bill Bonham	R	24	7	5	.583	6	44	15	3	152	126	64	121	0	3.02
Milt Pappas	R	34	7	12	.368	0	30	29	1	162	192	40	48	1	4.28
Dave LaRoche	L	25	4	1	.800	4	45	0	0	54	55	29	34	0	5.83
Jack Aker	R	32	4	5	.444	12	47	0	0	64	76	23	25	0	4.08
Larry Gura	L	25	2	4	.333	0	21	7	0	65	79	11	43	0	4.85
Ray Burris	R	22	1	1	.500	0	31	1	0	65	65	27	57	0	2.91
2 Mike Paul	L	28	0	1	.000	0	11	1	0	18	17	9	6	0	3.50
1 Juan Pizarro	L	36	0	1	.000	0	2	0	0	4	6	1	3	0	11.25

PHILADELPHIA 6th 71-91 .438 11.5 — DANNY OZARK

NAME	G by POS	B	AGE	G	AB	R	H	2B	3B	HR	RBI	BB	SO	SB	BA	SA
TOTALS			26	162	5546	642	1381	218	29	134	592	476	979	51	.249	.371
Willie Montanez	1B99, OF51	L	25	146	552	69	145	16	5	11	65	46	80	2	.263	.370
Denny Doyle	2B114	L	29	116	370	45	101	9	3	3	26	31	32	1	.273	.338
Larry Bowa (BL)	SS122	B	27	122	446	42	94	11	3	0	23	24	31	10	.211	.249
Mike Schmidt	3B125, 2B4, 1B2, SS2	R	23	132	367	43	72	11	0	18	52	62	136	8	.196	.373
Bill Robinson	OF113, 3B14	R	30	124	452	62	130	32	1	25	65	27	91	5	.288	.529
Del Unser	OF136	L	28	136	440	64	127	20	4	11	52	47	55	5	.289	.427
Greg Luzinski	OF159	R	22	161	610	76	174	26	4	29	97	51	135	3	.285	.484
Bob Boone	C145	R	25	145	521	42	136	20	2	10	61	41	36	3	.261	.365
Tommy Hutton	1B71	L	27	106	247	31	65	11	0	5	29	32	31	3	.263	.368
Cesar Tovar (KJ)	3B36, OF24, 2B22	R	32	97	328	49	88	18	4	1	21	29	35	6	.268	.357
Mike Anderson (JJ)	OF67	R	22	87	193	32	49	9	1	9	28	19	53	0	.254	.451
Terry Harmon	2B43, SS19, 3B1	R	29	72	148	17	31	3	0	0	8	13	14	1	.209	.230
Mike Rogodzinski	OF16	L	25	66	80	13	19	3	0	2	7	12	19	0	.238	.350
Craig Robinson	SS42, 2B4	R	24	46	146	11	33	7	0	0	7	0	25	1	.226	.274
Jose Pagan	3B16, 1B5, OF2, 2B1	R	38	46	78	4	16	5	0	0	5	1	15	0	.205	.269
Ken Brett	P31	L	24	37	80	6	20	5	0	4	16	4	17	0	.250	.463
Mike Ryan	C27	R	31	28	69	7	16	1	2	1	5	6	19	0	.232	.348
2 Billy Grabarkewitz	2B20, 3B3, OF1	R	27	25	66	12	19	2	0	2	7	12	18	3	.288	.409
1 Deron Johnson	1B10	R	34	12	36	3	6	2	0	1	5	5	10	0	.167	.306

Jim Essian 22 R 0-3, Larry Cox 25 R 0-0

NAME	T	AGE	W	L	PCT	SV	G	GS	CG	IP	H	BB	SO	ShO	ERA
		26	71	91	.438	22	162	162	49	1447	1435	632	919	11	3.99
Wayne Twitchell	R	25	13	9	.591	0	34	28	10	223	172	99	169	5	2.50
Ken Brett	L	24	13	9	.591	0	31	25	10	212	206	74	111	1	3.44
Jim Lonborg	R	31	13	16	.448	0	38	30	6	199	218	80	106	0	4.88
Steve Carlton	L	28	13	20	.394	0	40	40	18	293	293	113	223	3	3.90
Dick Ruthven (IL)	R	22	6	9	.400	1	25	23	3	128	125	75	98	1	4.22
2 George Culver	R	29	3	1	.750	0	14	0	0	19	26	15	7	0	4.74
Barry Lersch	R	28	3	6	.333	1	42	4	0	98	105	27	51	0	4.41
Darrell Brandon	R	22	2	4	.333	2	36	0	0	56	54	25	25	0	5.46
Mike Wallace	L	22	1	1	.500	1	20	3	1	33	38	15	20	0	3.82
Dick Selma	R	29	1	1	.500	0	6	0	0	8	6	5	4	0	5.63
Billy Wilson	R	30	1	3	.250	4	44	0	0	49	54	29	24	0	6.61
Larry Christenson	R	19	1	4	.200	0	10	9	1	34	53	20	11	0	6.62
Mac Scarce	L	24	1	8	.111	12	52	0	0	71	54	47	57	0	2.41
Ron Diorio	R	26	0	0	.000	1	23	0	0	19	18	6	11	0	2.37
Dave Wallace	R	25	0	0	.000	0	4	0	0	4	13	2	2	0	20.25

Dave Downs (SA) 21

CINCINNATI 1st 99-63 .611 — SPARKY ANDERSON

NAME	G by POS	B	AGE	G	AB	R	H	2B	3B	HR	RBI	BB	SO	SB	BA	SA
TOTALS			27	162	5505	741	1398	232	34	137	686	639	947	148	.254	.383
Tony Perez	1B151	R	31	151	552	73	177	33	3	27	101	74	117	3	.314	.527
Joe Morgan	2B154	L	29	157	576	116	167	35	2	26	82	111	61	67	.290	.493
Dave Concepcion (BN)	SS88, OF2	R	25	89	328	39	94	18	3	8	46	21	55	22	.287	.433
Denis Menke	3B123, SS7, 2B5, 1B1	R	32	139	241	38	46	10	0	3	26	69	53	1	.191	.270
Bobby Tolan	OF120	L	27	129	457	42	94	14	2	9	51	27	68	15	.206	.304
Cesar Geronimo	OF130	L	25	139	324	35	68	14	3	4	33	23	74	5	.210	.309
Pete Rose	OF159	B	32	160	**680**	115	**230**	36	8	5	64	65	42	10	**.338**	.437
Johnny Bench	C134, OF23, 1B4, 3B1	R	25	152	557	83	141	17	3	25	104	83	83	4	.253	.429
Darrel Chaney	SS75, 2B14, 3B12	B	25	105	227	27	41	7	1	0	14	26	50	4	.181	.220
Dan Driessen	3B87, 1B35, OF1	L	20	102	366	49	110	15	2	4	47	24	37	8	.301	.385
Larry Stahl	OF29, 1B2	L	32	76	111	17	25	2	2	2	12	14	34	1	.225	.333
Phil Gagliano	3B7, 2B4, 1B1, OF1	R	31	63	69	8	20	2	0	0	7	13	16	0	.290	.319
Bill Plummer	C42, 3B5	R	26	50	119	8	18	3	0	2	11	18	26	1	.151	.227
Andy Kosco	OF36, 1B1	R	31	47	118	17	33	7	0	9	21	13	26	0	.280	.568
2 Ed Crosby	SS20, 2B6	L	24	36	51	4	11	1	1	0	5	7	12	0	.216	.275
Hal King	C9	L	29	35	43	5	8	0	0	4	10	6	10	0	.186	.465
1 Gene Locklear	OF5	L	23	29	26	6	5	0	0	0	0	2	5	0	.192	.192
1 Richie Scheinblum	OF19	B	30	29	54	5	12	2	0	1	8	10	4	0	.222	.315
Ken Griffey	OF21	L	23	25	86	19	33	5	1	3	14	6	10	4	.384	.570
Joe Hague	OF5, 1B4	L	29	19	33	2	5	2	0	0	1	5	5	1	.152	.212
Ed Armbrister	OF14	R	24	18	37	5	8	3	1	1	5	2	8	0	.216	.432
George Foster	OF13	R	24	17	39	6	11	3	0	4	9	4	7	0	.282	.667
Bob Barton	C2	R	31	3	1	0	0	0	0	0	0	1	0	0	.000	.000

NAME	T	AGE	W	L	PCT	SV	G	GS	CG	IP	H	BB	SO	ShO	ERA
		27	**99**	63	**.611**	43	162	162	39	1473	1389	518	801	**17**	3.40
Jack Billingham	R	30	19	10	.655	0	40	**40**	16	**293**	257	95	155	**7**	3.04
Don Gullett	L	22	18	8	.692	2	45	30	7	228	198	69	153	4	3.51
Ross Grimsley	L	23	13	10	.565	1	38	36	8	242	245	68	90	1	3.24
2 Fred Norman	L	30	12	6	.667	0	24	24	7	166	136	72	112	3	3.31
Pedro Borbon	R	25	11	4	.733	14	80	0	0	121	137	35	60	0	2.16
Tom Hall	L	25	8	5	.615	8	54	7	0	104	74	48	96	0	3.46
Clay Carroll	R	32	8	8	.500	14	53	5	0	93	111	34	41	0	3.68
Roger Nelson (EJ)	R	29	3	2	.600	0	14	8	1	55	49	24	17	0	3.44
1 Jim McGlothlin	R	29	3	3	.500	0	24	9	0	63	91	23	18	0	6.71
Dick Baney	R	26	2	1	.667	2	11	1	0	31	26	6	17	0	2.90
Dave Tomlin	L	24	1	2	.333	1	16	0	0	28	24	15	20	0	4.82
1 Ed Sprague	R	27	1	3	.250	1	28	0	0	39	35	22	19	0	5.08
Gary Nolan (SA)	R	25	0	1	.000	0	2	2	0	10	6	7	3	0	3.60

LOS ANGELES 2nd 95-66 .590 3.5 — WALT ALSTON

NAME	G by POS	B	AGE	G	AB	R	H	2B	3B	HR	RBI	BB	SO	SB	BA	SA
TOTALS			27	162	5604	675	1473	219	29	110	623	497	795	109	.263	.371
Bill Buckner	1B93, OF48	L	23	140	575	68	158	20	0	8	46	17	34	12	.275	.351
Dave Lopes	2B135, OF5, SS2, 3B1	R	27	142	535	77	147	13	5	6	37	62	77	36	.275	.351
Bill Russell	SS162	R	24	162	615	55	163	26	3	4	56	34	63	15	.265	.337
Ron Cey	3B146	R	25	152	507	60	124	18	4	15	80	74	77	1	.245	.385
Willie Crawford	OF138	L	26	145	457	75	135	26	2	14	66	78	91	12	.295	.453
Willie Davis	OF146	L	33	152	599	82	171	29	9	16	77	29	62	17	.285	.444
Manny Mota	OF74	R	35	89	293	33	92	11	2	0	23	25	12	1	.314	.365
Joe Ferguson	C122, OF20	R	26	136	487	84	128	26	0	25	88	87	81	1	.263	.470
Steve Garvey	1B76, OF10	R	24	114	349	37	106	17	3	8	50	11	42	0	.304	.438
Tom Paciorek	OF77, 1B4	R	26	96	195	26	51	8	0	5	18	11	35	3	.262	.379
Von Joshua (BW)	OF46	L	25	75	159	19	40	4	1	2	17	8	29	7	.252	.327
Lee Lacy	2B41	R	25	57	135	14	28	2	0	0	8	15	34	2	.207	.222
Steve Yeager	C50	R	24	54	134	18	34	5	0	2	10	15	33	1	.254	.336
Ken McMullen (XJ)	3B24	R	31	42	85	6	21	5	0	5	18	6	13	0	.247	.482
Chris Cannizzaro	C13	R	35	17	21	0	4	0	0	0	3	3	3	0	.190	.190

Jim Fairey 28 L 2-9, Jerry Royster 20 R 4-19, Orlando Alvarez 21 R 1-4, Paul Powell 25 R 0-1

NAME	T	AGE	W	L	PCT	SV	G	GS	CG	IP	H	BB	SO	ShO	ERA
		30	95	66	.590	38	162	162	45	**1491**	1270	461	961	15	**3.00**
Don Sutton	R	28	18	10	.643	0	33	33	14	256	196	56	200	3	2.43
Tommy John	L	30	16	7	**.696**	0	36	31	4	218	202	50	116	2	3.10
Claude Osteen	L	33	16	11	.593	0	33	33	12	237	227	61	86	3	3.30
Andy Messersmith	R	27	14	10	.583	0	33	33	10	250	196	77	177	3	2.70
Al Downing	L	32	9	9	.500	0	30	28	5	193	155	68	124	2	3.31
Jim Brewer	L	35	6	8	.429	20	56	0	0	72	58	25	56	0	3.00
Charlie Hough	R	25	4	2	.667	5	37	0	0	72	52	45	70	0	2.75
Doug Rau	L	24	4	2	.667	3	31	3	0	64	64	28	51	0	3.94
1 George Culver	R	29	4	4	.500	2	28	0	0	42	45	21	23	0	3.00
Pete Richert	L	33	3	3	.500	7	39	0	0	51	44	19	31	0	3.18
Geoff Zahn	L	27	1	0	1.000	0	6	1	0	13	5	2	9	0	1.38
Greg Shanahan	R	25	0	0	.000	1	7	0	0	16	14	4	11	0	3.38
Eddie Solomon	R	22	0	0	.000	0	4	0	0	6	10	4	6	0	7.50
Greg Heydeman	R	21	0	0	.000	0	1	0	0	2	2	1	1	0	4.50

SAN FRANCISCO 3rd 88-74 .543 11 — CHARLIE FOX

NAME	G by POS	B	AGE	G	AB	R	H	2B	3B	HR	RBI	BB	SO	SB	BA	SA
TOTALS			25	162	5537	739	1452	212	**52**	161	684	590	913	112	.262	.407
Willie McCovey	1B117	L	35	130	383	52	102	14	3	29	75	106	78	1	.266	.546
Tito Fuentes	2B160, 3B1	B	29	160	656	78	182	25	5	6	63	45	62	12	.277	.358
Chris Speier	SS150, 2B1	R	23	153	542	58	135	17	4	11	71	66	69	4	.249	.356
Ed Goodson	3B93	L	25	102	384	37	116	20	1	12	53	15	44	0	.302	.453
Bobby Bonds	OF158	R	27	160	643	**131**	182	34	4	39	96	87	**148**	43	.283	.530
Garry Maddox	OF140	R	23	144	587	81	187	30	10	11	76	24	73	24	.319	.460
Gary Matthews	OF145	R	22	148	540	74	162	22	10	12	58	58	83	17	.300	.444
Dave Rader	C148	L	24	148	462	59	106	15	4	9	41	63	22	0	.229	.338
Dave Kingman	3B60, 1B46, P2	R	24	112	305	54	62	10	1	24	55	41	122	8	.203	.479
Gary Thomasson	1B47, OF43, P2	L	21	112	235	35	67	10	4	4	30	22	43	2	.285	.413
Jim Howarth	OF33, 1B1	L	26	65	90	8	18	1	1	0	7	7	8	0	.200	.233
Mike Phillips	3B38, SS20, 2B7	L	22	63	104	18	25	3	4	1	9	6	17	0	.240	.375
Chris Arnold	C9, 2B1, 3B1	R	25	49	54	7	16	2	0	1	13	8	11	0	.296	.389
Mike Sadek	C35	R	27	39	66	6	11	1	1	0	4	11	8	1	.167	.212
Damie Blanco	3B7, SS5, 2B3	R	31	28	12	4	0	0	0	0	0	1	2	0	.000	.000
Steve Ontiveros	1B5, OF1	B	21	24	33	3	8	0	0	1	5	4	7	0	.242	.333
Bruce Miller	3B4, 2B3, SS1	R	26	12	21	1	3	0	0	0	2	2	3	0	.143	.143
1 Alan Gallagher	3B5	R	27	5	9	1	2	0	0	0	1	0	0	0	.222	.222
1 Jim Ray Hart	3B1	R	31	5	3	0	0	0	0	0	1	3	1	0	.000	.000

NAME	T	AGE	W	L	PCT	SV	G	GS	CG	IP	H	BB	SO	ShO	ERA
		28	88	74	.543	**44**	162	162	33	1452	1442	485	787	8	3.79
Ron Bryant	L	25	**24**	12	.667	0	41	39	8	270	240	115	143	0	3.53
Tom Bradley	R	26	13	12	.520	0	35	34	6	224	212	69	136	1	3.90
Juan Marichal	R	35	11	15	.423	0	34	32	9	207	231	37	87	2	3.83
Jim Barr	R	25	11	17	.393	2	41	33	8	231	240	49	88	3	3.82
Elias Sosa	R	23	10	4	.714	18	71	1	0	107	95	41	70	0	3.28
Don McMahon	R	43	4	0	1.000	6	22	0	0	30	21	7	20	0	1.50
Randy Moffitt	R	24	4	4	.500	14	60	0	0	100	86	31	65	0	2.43
Jim Willoughby	R	24	4	5	.444	1	39	12	1	123	138	37	60	1	4.68
Charlie Williams	R	25	3	0	1.000	0	12	2	0	23	32	7	11	0	6.65
John Morris (BG)	L	31	1	0	1.000	0	7	0	0	6	12	3	3	0	9.00
John D'Acquisto	R	20	1	1	.500	0	7	3	1	28	23	19	29	0	3.54
Don Carrithers	R	23	1	2	.333	0	25	3	0	58	64	35	36	0	4.81
1 Sam McDowell	L	30	1	2	.333	3	18	3	0	40	45	29	35	0	4.50
Dave Kingman	R	24	0	0	.000	0	2	0	0	4	3	6	4	0	9.00

HOUSTON 4th 82-80 .506 17 — LEO DUROCHER

NAME	G by POS	B	AGE	G	AB	R	H	2B	3B	HR	RBI	BB	SO	SB	BA	SA
TOTALS			29	162	5532	681	1391	216	35	134	634	469	962	92	.251	.376
Lee May	1B144	R	30	148	545	65	147	24	3	28	105	34	122	1	.270	.479
Tommy Helms	2B145	R	32	146	543	44	156	28	2	4	61	32	21	1	.287	.368
Roger Metzger	SS149	B	25	154	580	67	145	11	14	1	35	39	70	10	.250	.322
Doug Rader	3B152	R	28	154	574	79	146	26	0	21	89	46	97	4	.254	.409
Bob Watson	OF142, 1B26, C3	R	27	158	573	97	179	24	3	16	94	85	73	1	.312	.449
Cesar Cedeno	OF136	R	22	139	525	86	168	35	2	25	70	41	79	56	.320	.537
Jim Wynn	OF133	R	31	139	481	90	106	14	5	20	55	91	102	14	.220	.395
Skip Jutze	C86	R	27	90	278	18	62	6	0	0	18	19	37	0	.223	.245
1 Tommy Agee	OF67	R	30	83	204	30	48	5	2	8	15	16	55	2	.235	.397
Johnny Edwards (IL)	C76	L	35	79	250	24	61	10	2	5	27	19	23	1	.244	.360
Bob Gallagher	OF41, 1B1	L	24	71	148	16	39	3	1	2	10	3	27	0	.264	.338
Jimmy Stewart	3B8, OF3, 2B1	B	34	61	68	6	13	0	0	0	3	9	12	0	.191	.191
Hector Torres	SS22, 2B13	R	27	38	66	3	6	1	0	0	2	7	13	0	.091	.106
1 Jesus Alou	OF14	R	31	28	55	7	13	2	0	1	8	1	6	0	.236	.327
1 Larry Howard	C20	R	28	20	48	3	8	3	0	0	4	5	12	0	.167	.229
Gary Sutherland	2B14, SS1	R	28	16	54	8	14	5	0	0	3	3	5	0	.259	.352
2 Ray Busse	SS5, 3B3	R	24	15	17	1	1	0	0	0	0	1	12	0	.059	.059
Greg Gross	OF9	L	20	14	39	5	9	2	1	0	1	0	4	2	.231	.333
Rafael Batista	1B8	L	27	12	15	2	4	0	0	0	2	1	6	0	.267	.267
3 Dave Campbell	3B5, OF1	R	31	9	15	1	4	2	0	0	2	0	4	0	.267	.400

Cliff Johnson 25 R 6-20, Mike Easler 22 L 0-7, 1 Norm Miller (XJ) 27 L 0-3, Otis Thornton 28 R 0-3

NAME	T	AGE	W	L	PCT	SV	G	GS	CG	IP	H	BB	SO	ShO	ERA
		28	82	80	.506	26	162	162	45	1461	1389	575	907	14	3.75
Dave Roberts	L	28	17	11	.607	0	39	36	12	249	264	62	119	6	2.86
Jerry Reuss	L	24	16	13	.552	0	41	40	12	279	271	117	177	3	3.74
Don Wilson	R	28	11	16	.407	2	37	32	10	239	187	92	149	3	3.20
Ken Forsch	R	26	9	12	.429	4	46	26	5	201	197	74	149	0	4.21
J.R. Richard	R	23	6	2	.750	0	16	10	2	72	54	38	75	1	4.00
Jim Ray	R	28	6	4	.600	6	42	0	0	69	65	38	25	0	4.43
Tom Griffin (VJ)	R	25	4	6	.400	0	25	12	4	100	83	46	69	0	4.14
Jim York	R	24	3	4	.429	6	41	0	0	53	65	20	22	0	4.42
Fred Gladding	R	37	2	0	1.000	1	16	0	0	16	18	4	9	0	4.50
2 Juan Pizarro	L	36	2	2	.500	0	15	1	0	23	28	11	10	0	6.65
2 Cecil Upshaw	R	30	2	3	.400	1	35	0	0	38	38	15	21	0	4.50
Jim Crawford	L	22	2	4	.333	6	48	0	0	70	69	33	56	0	4.50
Larry Dierker (RJ + SJ)	R	26	1	1	.500	0	14	3	0	27	27	13	18	0	4.33
Mike Cosgrove	L	22	1	1	.500	0	13	0	0	10	11	8	2	0	1.80
Doug Konieczny	R	21	0	1	.000	0	2	2	0	13	12	4	6	0	5.54

ATLANTA 5th 76-85 .472 22.5 — EDDIE MATHEWS

NAME	G by POS	B	AGE	G	AB	R	H	2B	3B	HR	RBI	BB	SO	SB	BA	SA
TOTALS			29	162	**5631**	**799**	**1497**	219	34	**206**	**758**	608	870	84	**.266**	**.427**
Mike Lum	1B84, OF64	L	27	138	513	74	151	26	0	16	82	41	89	2	.294	.462
Dave Johnson	2B157	R	30	157	559	84	151	25	0	43	99	81	93	5	.270	.546
Marty Perez	SS139	R	26	141	501	66	125	15	5	8	57	49	66	2	.250	.347
Darrell Evans	3B146, 1B20	L	26	161	595	114	167	25	8	41	104	**124**	104	6	.281	.556
Hank Aaron	OF105	R	39	120	392	84	118	12	1	40	96	68	51	1	.301	.643
Dusty Baker	OF156	R	24	159	604	101	174	29	4	21	99	67	72	24	.288	.454
Ralph Garr	OF148	L	27	148	668	94	200	32	6	11	55	22	64	35	.299	.415
Johnny Oates (KJ)	C86	L	27	93	322	27	80	6	0	4	27	22	31	1	.248	.304
Sonny Jackson	OF56, SS36	L	28	117	206	29	43	5	2	0	12	22	13	6	.209	.252
Dick Dietz	1B36, C20	R	31	83	139	22	41	8	1	3	24	49	25	0	.295	.432
Paul Casanova	C78	R	31	82	236	18	51	7	0	7	18	11	36	0	.216	.335
Frank Tepedino	1B58	L	25	74	148	20	45	5	0	4	29	13	21	0	.304	.419
2 Chuck Goggin	2B19, OF6, SS5, C1	R	27	64	90	18	26	5	0	0	7	9	19	0	.289	.344
Rod Gilbreath	3B22	R	20	29	74	10	21	2	1	0	2	6	10	2	.284	.338
Oscar Brown (JJ)	OF13	R	27	22	58	3	12	3	0	0	0	3	10	0	.207	.259
Larvell Blanks	3B3, 2B2, SS2	R	23	17	18	1	4	0	0	0	0	1	3	0	.222	.222
Freddy Velasquez	C11	R	35	15	23	2	8	1	0	0	3	1	3	0	.348	.391

Jack Pierce 24 L 1-20, 2 Norm Miller (XJ) 27 L 3-8, 2 Larry Howard 28 R 1-8, Leo Foster 22 R 1-6, 2 Joe Pepitone 32 L 4-11

NAME	T	AGE	W	L	PCT	SV	G	GS	CG	IP	H	BB	SO	ShO	ERA
		28	76	85	.472	35	162	162	34	1462	1467	575	803	9	4.25
Carl Morton	R	29	15	10	.600	0	38	37	10	256	254	70	112	4	3.41
Phil Niekro	R	34	13	10	.565	4	42	30	9	245	214	89	131	1	3.31
Roric Harrison	R	26	11	8	.579	5	38	22	3	177	161	98	130	0	4.17
Ron Schueler	R	25	8	7	.533	2	39	20	4	186	179	66	124	2	3.87
Tom House	L	26	4	2	.667	4	52	0	0	67	58	31	42	0	4.70
Gary Gentry (EJ)	R	26	4	6	.400	1	16	14	3	87	74	35	42	0	3.41
Ron Reed (AJ)	R	30	4	11	.267	1	20	19	2	116	133	31	64	0	4.42
1 Pat Dobson	R	31	3	7	.300	0	12	10	1	58	73	19	23	1	4.97
Gary Niebauer	R	28	2	1	.667	0	16	1	0	21	24	19	9	0	7.29
1 Joe Hoerner (KJ)	L	36	2	2	.500	2	20	0	0	13	17	4	10	0	6.23
Max Leon	R	23	2	2	.500	0	12	1	1	27	30	9	18	0	5.33
Adrian Devine	R	21	2	3	.400	4	24	1	0	32	45	12	15	0	6.47
Jim Panther	R	28	2	3	.400	0	23	0	0	31	45	9	8	0	7.55
Joe Niekro	R	28	2	4	.333	3	20	0	0	24	23	11	12	0	4.13
Danny Frisella (SJ)	R	27	1	2	.333	8	42	0	0	45	40	23	27	0	4.20
Wenty Ford	R	26	1	2	.333	0	4	2	1	16	17	8	4	0	5.63

Tom Kelley 29 R 0-1, 1 Cecil Upshaw 30 R 0-1, Dave Cheadle 21 L 0-1, Jimmy Freeman 22 L 0-2, Alan Closter 29 L 0-0

Mike McQueen (PB) 22

SAN DIEGO 6th 60-102 .370 39 — DON ZIMMER

NAME	G by POS	B	AGE	G	AB	R	H	2B	3B	HR	RBI	BB	SO	SB	BA	SA
TOTALS			25	162	5457	548	1330	198	26	112	516	401	966	88	.244	.351
Nate Colbert	1B144	R	27	145	529	73	143	25	2	22	80	54	146	9	.270	.450
2 Rich Morales	2B79, SS10	R	29	90	244	9	40	6	1	0	16	27	36	0	.164	.197
Derrel Thomas	SS74, 2B47	B	22	113	404	41	96	7	1	0	22	34	52	15	.238	.260
Dave Roberts	3B111, 2B12	R	22	127	479	56	137	20	3	21	64	17	83	11	.286	.472
Jerry Morales	OF100	R	24	122	388	47	109	23	2	9	34	27	55	6	.281	.420
John Grubb	OF102, 3B2	L	24	113	389	52	121	22	3	8	37	37	50	9	.311	.445
Clarence Gaston	OF119	R	29	133	476	51	119	18	4	16	57	20	88	0	.250	.405
Fred Kendall	C138	R	24	145	507	39	143	22	3	10	59	30	35	3	.282	.396
Leron Lee	OF84	L	25	118	333	36	79	7	2	3	30	33	61	4	.237	.297
Ivan Murrell	OF37, 1B24	R	28	93	210	23	48	13	1	9	21	2	52	2	.229	.429
Enzo Hernandez (NJ)	SS67	R	24	70	247	26	55	2	1	0	9	17	14	15	.223	.239
Dave Hilton	3B47, 2B23	R	22	70	234	21	46	9	0	5	16	19	35	2	.197	.299
2 Gene Locklear	OF37	L	23	67	154	20	37	6	1	3	25	21	22	9	.240	.351
Dave Winfield	OF36, 1B1	R	21	56	141	9	39	4	1	3	12	12	19	0	.277	.383
2 Dwain Anderson	SS39, 3B6	R	25	53	107	11	13	0	0	0	3	14	29	2	.121	.121
Dave Marshall	OF8	L	30	39	49	4	14	5	0	0	4	8	9	0	.286	.388
1 Dave Campbell	2B27, 1B3, 2B2	R	31	33	98	2	22	3	0	0	8	7	15	1	.224	.255
Pat Corrales	C28	R	32	29	72	7	15	2	1	0	3	6	10	0	.208	.264
Don Mason	2B1	L	28	8	8	0	0	0	0	0	0	0	2	0	.000	.000
Bob Davis	C5	R	21	5	11	1	1	0	0	0	0	0	5	0	.091	.091

NAME	T	AGE	W	L	PCT	SV	G	GS	CG	IP	H	BB	SO	ShO	ERA
		26	60	**102**	.370	23	162	162	34	1430	1461	548	845	10	4.16
Steve Arlin	R	27	11	14	.440	0	34	27	7	180	196	72	98	3	5.10
Bill Greif	R	23	10	17	.370	1	36	31	9	199	181	62	120	3	3.21
Clay Kirby (SA)	R	25	8	18	.308	0	34	31	4	192	214	66	129	2	4.78
Randy Jones	L	23	7	6	.538	0	20	19	6	140	129	37	77	1	3.15
Rich Troedson	L	23	7	9	.438	1	50	18	2	152	167	59	81	0	4.26
Mike Corkins	R	27	5	8	.385	3	47	11	2	122	130	61	82	0	4.50
Mike Caldwell	L	24	5	14	.263	10	55	13	3	149	146	53	86	1	3.74
Gary Ross	R	25	4	4	.500	0	58	0	0	76	93	33	44	0	5.45
Vicente Romo	R	30	2	3	.400	7	49	1	0	88	85	46	51	0	3.68
1 Fred Norman	L	30	1	7	.125	0	12	11	1	74	72	29	49	0	4.26
Frank Snook	R	24	0	2	.000	1	18	0	0	27	19	18	13	0	3.67
1 Bob Miller	R	34	0	0	.000	0	18	0	0	31	29	12	15	0	4.06

WORLD SERIES – OAKLAND (AL) 4 NEW YORK (NL) 3

LINE SCORES

TEAM	1	2	3	4	5	6	7	8	9	10	11	12	R	H	E
Game 1 October 13 at Oakland															
NY (NL)	0	0	0	1	0	0	0	0	0				1	7	2
OAK (AL)	0	0	2	0	0	0	0	0	X				2	4	0

Matlack, McGraw (7) — **Holtzman**, Fingers (6), Knowles (9)

TEAM	1	2	3	4	5	6	7	8	9	10	11	12	R	H	E
Game 2 October 14 at Oakland															
NY	0	1	1	0	0	4	0	0	0	0	0	4	10	15	1
OAK	2	1	0	0	0	0	1	0	2	0	0	1	7	13	5

Koosman, Sadecki (3), Parker (5), **McGraw** (6), Stone (12) — Blue, Pina (6), Knowles (6), Odom (8), **Fingers** (10), Lindblad (12)

TEAM	1	2	3	4	5	6	7	8	9	10	11	12	R	H	E
Game 3 October 16 at New York (night)															
OAK	0	0	0	0	0	1	0	1	0	0	1		3	10	1
NY	2	0	0	0	0	0	0	0	0	0	0		2	10	2

Hunter, Knowles (7), **Lindblad** (9), Fingers (11) — Seaver, Sadecki (9), McGraw (9), **Parker** (11)

TEAM	1	2	3	4	5	6	7	8	9	10	11	12	R	H	E
Game 4 October 17 at New York (night)															
OAK	0	0	0	0	0	1	0	0	0				1	5	1
NY	3	0	0	3	0	0	0	0	X				6	13	1

Holtzman, Odom (1), Knowles (4), Pina (6), Lindblad (8) — **Matlack**, Sadecki (9)

TEAM	1	2	3	4	5	6	7	8	9	10	11	12	R	H	E
Game 5 October 18 at New York (night)															
OAK	0	0	0	0	0	0	0	0	0				0	3	1
NY	0	1	0	0	0	1	0	0	X				2	7	1

Blue, Knowles (6), Fingers (7) — **Koosman**, McGraw (7)

TEAM	1	2	3	4	5	6	7	8	9	10	11	12	R	H	E
Game 6 October 20 at Oakland															
NY	0	0	0	0	0	0	0	1	0				1	6	2
OAK	1	0	1	0	0	0	0	1	X				3	7	0

Seaver, McGraw (8) — **Hunter**, Knowles (8), Fingers (8)

TEAM	1	2	3	4	5	6	7	8	9	10	11	12	R	H	E
Game 7 October 21 at Oakland															
NY	0	0	0	0	0	1	0	0	1				2	8	1
OAK	0	0	4	0	1	0	0	0	X				5	9	0

Matlack, Parker (3), Sadecki (5), Stone (7) — **Holtzman**, Fingers (6), Knowles (9)

COMPOSITE BATTING

NAME	POS	G	AB	R	H	2B	3B	HR	RBI	BA
Oakland (AL)										
Totals		7	241	21	51	12	3	2	20	.212
Campaneris	SS	7	31	**6**	9	0	1	1	3	.290
Jackson	OF	7	29	3	9	**3**	1	1	**6**	.310
Rudi	OF	7	27	3	9	2	0	0	4	.333
Bando	3B	7	26	5	6	1	1	0	1	.231
Alou	OF	7	19	0	3	1	0	0	3	.158
Fosse	C	7	19	0	3	1	0	0	0	.158
Tenace	1B	7	19	0	3	1	0	0	3	.158
Green	2B	7	16	0	1	0	0	0	0	.063
Davalillo	OF-1B	6	11	0	1	0	0	0	0	.091
Johnson	1B	6	10	0	3	1	0	0	0	.300
Mangual	OF	5	6	0	0	0	0	0	0	.000
Hunter	P	2	5	0	0	0	0	0	0	.000
Blue	P	2	4	0	0	0	0	0	0	.000
Holtzman	P	3	3	2	2	2	0	0	0	.667
Fingers	P	6	3	0	1	0	0	0	0	.333
Kubiak	2B	4	3	1	0	0	0	0	0	.000
Conigliaro	PH	3	3	0	0	0	0	0	0	.000
Andrews	2B	2	3	0	0	0	0	0	0	.000
Bourque	1B	2	2	0	1	0	0	0	0	.500
Odom	P	3	1	0	0	0	0	0	0	.000
Lindblad	P	3	1	0	0	0	0	0	0	.000

Knowles P 0-0, Lewis PR 0-0, Pina P 0-0

NAME	POS	G	AB	R	H	2B	3B	HR	RBI	BA
New York (NL)										
Totals		7	261	24	66	7	2	4	16	.253
Millan	2B	7	**32**	3	6	1	1	0	1	.187
Grote	C	7	30	2	8	0	0	0	0	.267
Garrett	3B	7	30	4	5	0	0	**2**	2	.167
Hahn	OF	7	29	2	7	1	1	0	2	.241
Jones	OF	7	28	5	8	2	0	1	1	.286
Milner	1B	7	27	2	8	0	0	0	2	.296
Staub	OF	7	26	1	**11**	2	0	1	**6**	**.423**
Harrelson	SS	7	24	2	6	1	0	0	1	.250
Mays	OF	3	7	1	2	0	0	0	1	.286
Seaver	P	2	5	0	0	0	0	0	0	.000
Beauchamp	PH	4	4	0	0	0	0	0	0	.000
Matlack	P	3	4	0	1	0	0	0	0	.250
Koosman	P	2	4	0	0	0	0	0	0	.000
Boswell	PH	3	3	1	3	0	0	0	0	1.000
McGraw	P	5	3	1	1	0	0	0	0	.333
Kranepool	PH	4	3	0	0	0	0	0	0	.000
Theodore	OF	2	2	0	0	0	0	0	0	.000

Sadecki P 0-0, Parker P 0-0, Martinez PR 0-0, Stone P 0-0, Hodges PH 0-0

COMPOSITE PITCHING

NAME	G	IP	H	BB	SO	W	L	SV	ERA
Oakland (AL)									
Totals	7	66	66	26	36	4	3	4	2.32
Fingers	6	13.2	**13**	4	8	0	1	2	**0.66**
Hunter	2	13.1	11	4	6	1	0	0	2.03
Blue	2	11	10	5	6	0	1	0	4.91
Holtzman	3	10.2	**13**	3	8	**2**	1	0	4.22
Knowles	**7**	6.1	4	5	5	0	0	2	0.00
Odom	2	4.2	5	2	2	0	0	0	3.86
Lindblad	3	3.1	4	1	1	1	0	0	0.00
Pina	2	3	6	2	0	0	0	0	0.00
New York (NL)									
Totals	7	65	51	28	62	3	4	3	2.22
Matlack	3	**16.2**	10	5	11	1	**2**	0	2.16
Seaver	2	15	**13**	3	**18**	0	1	0	2.40
McGraw	5	13.2	8	**9**	14	1	0	1	2.63
Koosman	2	8.2	9	7	8	1	0	0	3.12
Sadecki	4	4.2	5	1	6	0	0	1	1.93
Parker	3	3.1	2	2	2	0	1	0	0.00
Stone	2	3	4	1	3	0	0	1	0.00

1974 Aaron in April, Oakland in October

History was made as the season began—Hank Aaron broke Babe Ruth's home run record. Aaron's feat came on the night of April 8th, when he hit home run no. 715 off of the Los Angeles Dodgers' Al Downing. The "shot" from Atlanta's stadium finally put to rest the controversy which began when Braves' owner, Bill Bartholomay, opted to save the history-making feat for Atlanta by benching Aaron in the three-game opener at Cincinnati. Commissioner Bowie Kuhn stepped in and ordered Aaron to play. He did. In his first at bat he slammed home run no. 714 off of Jack Billingham to tie Ruth's lifetime total. Of course, no other home runs were hit at Cincinnati, and the durable Aaron returned home to end the most publicized chase in baseball history at 9:07 Eastern Standard Time before a standing-room-only crowd of 53,775.

With the home run question settled, baseball returned to its divisional races. In the American League West, Oakland, despite losing manager Dick Williams after their 1973 World Series triumph, took their fourth straight divisional title, this one under the reins of Al Dark. In Dark's second turn at the helm under owner Charles O. Finley, the race was taken by five games over the improving Texas Rangers, who were helped by the acquisition of Ferguson Jenkins and the development of young Jeff Burroughs, who won the league's MVP honors. For the A's, Catfish Hunter won 25 games and Rollie Fingers chalked up 18 saves in 76 appearances. Reggie Jackson led the offense with 29 home runs, but lost the power title to Dick Allen, who finished with 32 homers despite "retiring" from the White Sox on September 14th. Two other footnotes to the A's season included the debuts of Claudell and Herb Washington, who were related by name only. Claudell, 19 years old, finished the season at .285 with only a year-and-a-half baseball experience. Herb became the game's first full-time pinch runner owing to his ability as a world class sprinter. Without any professional baseball experience, he went on to steal 29 bases in 45 attempts.

In the A.L. East, Baltimore won 28 of their last 34 games to beat the greatly improved New York Yankees by two games. After beating the Yankees in a three-game series in early September to take a half-game lead, the Orioles went on their stretch drive, which included 15 one-run victories. Other A.L. highlights included Al Kaline's 3000th hit, and Nolan Ryan's third no-hitter.

In the N.L. West, the Dodgers ruled the roost on newly acquired Mike Marshall's arm, which was strong enough to chalk up a record 106 relief appearances and win the Cy Young Award, and the bat of Steve Garvey, which produced a .312 average and 111 runs batted in, good enough to earn him MVP honors. In the East, the St. Louis Cardinals seemed to have everything with Lou Brock stealing a record 118 bases, and newly-acquired Reggie Smith driving in 100 runs, to go with Ted Simmons' 103. But the Cards could not overcome a disappointing starting staff, which featured Bob Gibson's fall to an 11-13 record in a season which saw him achieve the unique goal of recording his 3000th strikeout to join the immortal Walter Johnson in that category. As a result of the Redbirds' poor front line pitching, the Pittsburgh Pirates, led by the bats of Willie Stargell, Al Oliver, and Richie Zisk, and the arms of Jim Rooker, and Jerry Reuss won the division by a game-and-a-half.

In the playoffs, Oakland took Baltimore in three straight, and the Dodgers eliminated the Pirates in four games. For the World Series, it was a question of Los Angeles' youth against Oakland's experience. Experience prevailed as the A's won their third straight crown, 4 games to 1.

1974 AMERICAN LEAGUE

EAST DIVISION

NAME	G by POS	B	AGE	G	AB	R	H	2B	3B	HR	RBI	BB	SO	SB	BA	SA
BALTIMORE 1st 91-71 .562	EARL WEAVER															
TOTALS			28	162	5535	659	1418	226	27	116	608	509	770	145	.256	.370
Boog Powell	1B102, DH1	L	32	110	344	37	91	13	1	12	45	52	58	0	.265	.413
Bobby Grich	2B160	R	25	160	582	92	153	29	6	19	82	90	117	17	.263	.431
Mark Belanger	SS155	R	30	155	493	54	111	14	4	5	36	51	69	17	.225	.300
Brooks Robinson	3B153	R	37	153	553	46	159	27	0	7	59	56	47	2	.288	.374
Rich Coggins	OF105	L	23	113	411	53	100	13	3	4	32	29	31	26	.243	.319
Paul Blair	OF151	R	30	151	552	77	144	27	4	17	62	43	59	27	.261	.417
Don Baylor	OF129, 1B8, DH1	R	25	137	489	66	133	22	1	10	59	43	56	29	.272	.382
Earl Williams	C75, 1B47, DH1	R	25	118	413	47	105	16	0	14	52	40	79	0	.254	.395
Tommy Davis	DH155	R	35	158	626	67	181	20	1	11	84	34	49	6	.289	.377
Al Bumbry	OF67, DH7	L	27	94	270	35	63	10	3	1	19	21	46	12	.233	.304
Enos Cabell	1B28, OF22, 3B19, 2B1, DH1	R	24	80	174	24	42	4	2	3	17	7	20	5	.241	.339
Ellie Hendricks	C54, 1B1, DH1	L	33	66	159	18	33	8	2	3	8	17	25	0	.208	.340
Jim Fuller	1B4, DH2	R	23	64	189	17	42	11	0	7	28	8	68	1	.222	.392
Andy Etchebarren	C60	R	31	62	180	13	40	8	0	2	15	6	26	1	.222	.300
Frank Baker	SS17, 2B3, 3B1	L	27	24	29	3	5	1	0	0	0	3	5	0	.172	.207
Mike Reinbach	OF3, DH3	L	24	12	20	2	5	1	0	0	2	2	5	0	.250	.300
2 Bob Oliver	1B4, DH2	R	31	9	20	1	3	2	0	0	4	0	5	1	.150	.250
3 Jim Northrup	OF6, DH1	L	34	8	7	2	4	0	0	1	3	2	1	0	.571	1.000
Tim Nordbrook 24 R 4-15, Curt Motton 30 R 0-0, Doug DeCinces 23 R 0-1																
NEW YORK 2nd 89-73 .549 2	BILL VIRDON															
TOTALS			28	162	5524	671	1451	220	30	101	637	515	690	53	.263	.368
2 Chris Chambliss	1B106	L	25	100	400	38	97	16	3	6	43	23	43	0	.243	.343
2 Sandy Alomar	2B76, DH1	B	30	76	279	35	75	8	0	1	27	14	25	6	.269	.308
Jim Mason	SS152	L	23	152	440	41	110	18	6	5	37	35	87	1	.250	.352
Graig Nettles	3B154, SS1	L	29	155	566	74	139	21	1	22	75	59	75	1	.246	.403
Bobby Murcer	OF156	L	28	156	606	69	166	25	4	10	88	57	59	14	.274	.378
Elliott Maddox	OF135, 2B2, 3B1	R	26	137	466	75	141	26	2	3	45	69	48	6	.303	.386
Lou Piniella	OF130, DH6, 1B1	R	30	140	518	71	158	26	0	9	70	32	58	1	.305	.407
Thurman Munson	C137, DH4	R	27	144	517	64	135	19	2	13	60	44	66	2	.261	.381
Ron Blomberg	DH58, OF19	L	25	90	265	39	82	11	2	10	48	29	33	2	.311	.481
Roy White	OF67, DH53	B	29	136	473	68	130	19	8	7	43	67	44	15	.275	.393
Bill Sudakis	DH39, 1B33, 3B3, C1	B	28	89	259	26	60	8	0	7	39	25	48	0	.232	.344
Gene Michael	2B45, SS39, 3B2	B	35	81	177	19	46	9	0	0	13	14	24	0	.260	.311
2 Fernando Gonzalez	2B42, 3B7, SS3, DH1	R	24	51	121	11	26	5	1	1	7	7	7	0	.215	.298
Rick Dempsey	C31, OF2, DH1	R	24	43	109	12	26	3	0	2	12	8	7	1	.239	.321
Walt Williams	DH3, OF1	R	30	43	53	5	6	0	0	0	3	1	10	1	.113	.113
Fred Stanley	SS19, 2B15	R	26	33	38	2	7	0	0	0	3	3	2	1	.184	.184
Otto Velez	1B21, OF3, 3B2	R	23	27	67	9	14	1	1	2	10	15	24	0	.209	.343
1 Horace Clarke	2B20, DH1	B	34	24	47	3	11	1	0	0	1	4	5	1	.234	.255
1 Mike Hegan	1B17	L	31	18	53	3	12	2	0	2	9	5	9	1	.226	.377
2 Alex Johnson	DH6, OF1	R	31	10	28	3	6	1	0	1	2	0	3	20	.214	.357
Jim Ray Hart 32 R 1-19, 1 Duke Sims 33 L 2-15, Larry Murray 21 B 1-6, Terry Whitfield 21 L 1-5, Jim Deidel 25 R 0-2																
BOSTON 3rd 84-78 .519 7	DARRELL JOHNSON															
TOTALS			27	162	5499	**696**	1449	**236**	31	109	**658**	**569**	811	104	.264	.377
Carl Yastrzemski	1B84, OF63, DH4	L	34	148	515	**93**	155	25	2	15	79	104	48	12	.301	.445
Doug Griffin (PB)	2B91, SS1	R	27	93	312	35	83	12	4	0	33	28	21	2	.266	.330
Mike Guerrero	SS93	R	24	93	204	18	70	6	2	0	23	13	22	3	.246	.282
Rico Petrocelli	3B116, DH9	R	31	129	454	53	121	23	1	15	76	48	74	1	.267	.421
Dwight Evans	OF122, DH7	R	22	133	463	60	130	19	8	10	70	38	77	4	.281	.421
Juan Beniquez	OF97, DH4	R	24	106	389	60	104	14	3	5	32	25	61	19	.267	.357
Bernie Carbo	OF87, DH15	L	26	117	338	40	84	20	0	12	61	58	90	4	.249	.414
Carlton Fisk (KJ)	C50, DH2	R	26	52	187	36	56	12	1	11	26	24	23	5	.299	.551
Tommy Harper	OF61, DH51	R	33	118	443	66	105	15	3	5	24	46	65	28	.237	.318
Cecil Cooper	1B74, DH41	L	24	121	414	55	114	24	1	8	43	32	74	2	.275	.396
Rick Burleson	SS88, 2B31, 3B2	R	23	114	384	36	109	22	0	4	44	21	34	3	.284	.372
Rick Miller	OF105	L	26	114	280	41	73	8	1	5	23	37	47	13	.261	.350
Dick McAuliffe	2B53, 3B40, SS3, DH3	L	34	100	272	32	57	13	1	5	24	39	40	2	.210	.320
Bob Montgomery	C79, DH5	R	30	88	254	26	64	10	0	4	38	13	50	3	.252	.339
Danny Cater	1B23, DH14	R	34	56	126	14	31	5	0	5	20	10	13	1	.246	.405
Tim Blackwell	C44	B	21	44	122	9	30	1	1	0	8	10	21	1	.246	.270
Terry Hughes	3B36, DH1	R	26	41	69	5	14	2	0	1	6	6	18	0	.203	.275
Jim Rice	DH16, OF3	R	21	24	67	6	18	2	1	1	13	4	12	0	.269	.373
Fred Lynn	OF12, DH1	L	22	15	43	5	18	2	2	2	10	6	6	0	.419	.698
3 Deron Johnson	DH8	R	35	11	25	0	3	0	0	0	2	0	6	0	.120	.120
2 Tim McCarver 32 L 7-28, John Kennedy 33 R 2-15, Bob Didier 25 B 1-14, Chuck Goggin 28 B 0-1																

NAME	T	AGE	W	L	PCT	SV	G	GS	CG	IP	H	BB	SO	ShO	ERA
		27	**91**	71	**.562**	25	162	162	57	**1474**	1393	480	701	**16**	3.27
Mike Cuellar	L	37	22	10	**.688**	0	38	38	20	269	253	86	106	5	3.11
Ross Grimsley	L	24	18	13	.581	1	40	39	17	296	267	76	158	4	3.07
Dave McNally	L	31	16	10	.615	1	39	37	13	259	260	81	111	4	3.58
Bob Reynolds	R	27	7	5	.583	7	54	0	0	69	75	14	43	0	2.74
Jim Palmer (SA)	R	28	7	12	.368	0	26	26	5	179	176	69	84	2	3.27
Grant Jackson	L	31	6	4	.600	12	49	0	0	67	48	22	56	0	2.55
Doyle Alexander	R	23	6	9	.400	0	30	12	2	114	127	43	40	0	4.03
Wayne Garland	R	23	5	5	.500	1	20	6	0	91	68	26	40	0	2.97
Dave Johnson	R	25	2	2	.500	2	11	0	0	15	17	5	6	0	3.00
Jesse Jefferson	R	25	1	0	1.000	0	20	2	0	57	55	38	31	0	4.42
Don Hood	L	24	1	1	.500	1	20	2	0	57	47	20	26	0	3.47

NAME	T	AGE	W	L	PCT	SV	G	GS	CG	IP	H	BB	SO	ShO	ERA
		28	89	73	.549	24	162	162	53	1455	1402	528	829	13	3.31
Pat Dobson	R	32	19	15	.559	0	39	39	12	281	282	75	157	2	3.07
Doc Medich	R	25	19	15	.559	0	38	38	17	280	275	91	154	4	3.60
2 Dick Tidrow	R	27	11	9	.550	1	33	25	5	191	205	53	100	0	3.86
Sparky Lyle	L	28	9	3	.750	15	66	0	0	114	93	43	89	0	1.66
2 Rudy May (SJ)	L	29	8	4	.667	0	17	15	8	114	75	48	90	2	2.29
2 Mike Wallace	L	23	6	0	1.000	0	23	1	0	52	42	35	34	0	2.42
Mel Stottlemyre (SJ)	R	32	6	7	.462	0	16	15	6	113	119	37	40	0	3.58
Larry Gura	L	26	5	1	.833	0	8	8	4	56	54	12	17	2	2.41
1 Steve Kline	R	26	2	2	.500	0	4	4	0	26	26	5	6	0	3.46
Dick Woodson	R	29	1	2	.333	0	8	3	0	28	34	12	12	0	5.79
Dave Pagan	R	24	1	3	.250	0	16	6	1	49	49	28	39	0	5.14
2 Cecil Upshaw	R	31	1	5	.167	6	36	0	0	60	53	24	27	0	3.00
Sam McDowell (XJ-JT)	L	31	1	6	.143	0	13	7	0	48	42	41	33	0	4.69
Tippy Martinez	L	24	0	0	–	0	10	0	0	13	14	9	10	0	4.15
1 Fred Beene	R	31	0	0	–	1	6	0	0	10	9	2	10	0	2.70
1 Fritz Peterson	L	32	0	0	–	0	3	1	0	8	13	2	5	0	4.50
Ken Wright	R	27	0	0	–	0	3	0	0	6	5	7	2	0	3.00
Rick Sawyer	R	26	0	0	–	0	1	0	0	2	2	1	1	0	13.50
1 Tom Buskey	R	27	0	1	.000	1	4	0	0	6	10	3	3	0	6.00

NAME	T	AGE	W	L	PCT	SV	G	GS	CG	IP	H	BB	SO	ShO	ERA
		29	84	78	.519	18	162	162	**71**	1455	1462	463	751	12	3.72
Luis Tiant	R	33	22	13	.629	0	38	38	25	311	281	82	176	**7**	2.92
Bill Lee	L	27	17	15	.531	0	38	37	16	282	**320**	67	95	1	3.51
Reggie Cleveland	R	26	12	14	.462	0	41	27	10	221	234	69	103	0	4.32
Roger Moret	L	24	9	10	.474	2	31	21	10	173	158	79	111	1	3.75
Dick Drago	R	29	7	10	.412	3	33	18	8	176	165	56	90	0	3.48
Diego Segui	R	36	6	8	.429	10	58	0	0	108	106	49	76	0	4.00
Juan Marichal (XJ)	R	36	5	1	.833	0	11	9	0	57	61	14	21	0	4.89
Rick Wise (SJ)	R	28	3	4	.429	0	9	9	1	49	47	16	25	0	3.86
Steve Barr	L	22	1	0	1.000	0	1	1	1	9	7	6	3	0	4.00
Lance Clemons	L	27	1	0	1.000	0	6	0	0	6	8	4	1	0	10.50
Dick Pole	R	23	1	1	.500	1	15	2	0	45	55	13	32	0	4.20
Bob Veale	L	38	0	1	.000	2	18	0	0	13	16	4	16	0	5.54
Don Newhauser	R	26	0	1	.000	0	2	0	0	4	5	4	2	0	9.00

CLEVELAND 4th 77-85 .475 14 — KEN ASPROMONTE

	NAME	G by POS	B	AGE	G	AB	R	H	2B	3B	HR	RBI	BB	SO	SB	BA	SA
	TOTALS			25	162	5474	662	1395	201	19	131	616	432	756	79	.255	.370
	Johnny Ellis (BF)	1B69, C42, DH21	R	25	128	477	58	136	23	6	10	64	32	53	1	.285	.421
	Jack Brohamer	2B99	L	24	101	315	33	85	11	1	2	30	26	22	2	.270	.330
	Frank Duffy	SS158	R	27	158	549	62	128	18	0	8	48	30	64	7	.233	.310
	Buddy Bell (KJ)	3B115, DH1	R	22	116	423	51	111	15	1	7	46	35	29	1	.262	.352
	Charlie Spikes	OF154	R	23	155	568	63	154	23	1	22	80	34	100	10	.271	.431
	George Hendrick	OF133, DH1	R	24	139	495	65	138	23	1	19	67	33	73	6	.279	.444
	John Lowenstein	OF100, 3B28, 1B12, 2B4	L	27	140	508	65	123	14	2	8	48	53	85	36	.242	.325
	Dave Duncan	C134, 1B3, DH1	R	28	136	425	45	85	10	1	16	46	42	91	0	.200	.341
	Oscar Gamble	DH115, OF13	L	23	135	454	74	132	16	4	19	59	48	51	5	.291	.469
	Rusty Torres	OF94, DH1	B	25	108	150	19	28	2	0	3	12	13	24	2	.187	.260
	Leron Lee	OF62, DH2	L	26	79	232	18	54	13	0	5	25	15	42	3	.233	.353
3	Luis Alvarado	2B46, SS7, DH3	R	25	61	114	12	25	2	0	0	12	6	14	1	.219	.237
2	Joe Lis	1B31, 3B9, DH9, OF1	R	27	57	109	15	22	3	0	6	16	14	30	1	.202	.394
	Angel Hermoso (KJ)	2B45	R	27	48	122	15	27	3	1	0	5	7	7	2	.221	.262
2	Tommy McCraw	1B38, DH2, OF1	L	33	45	112	17	34	8	0	3	17	5	11	0	.304	.455
	Ed Crosby	3B18, SS13, 2B3	L	25	37	86	11	18	3	0	0	6	6	12	0	.209	.244
	Rico Carty	DH14, 1B8	R	34	33	91	6	33	5	0	1	16	5	9	0	.363	.451
	Tommy Smith (BA)	OF17, DH1	L	25	23	31	4	3	1	0	0	0	2	7	0	.097	.129
1	Chris Chambliss	1B17	L	25	17	67	8	22	4	0	0	7	5	5	0	.328	.388
2	Frank Robinson	DH10, 1B4	R	38	15	50	6	10	1	1	2	5	10	10	0	.200	.380

Ossie Blanco 28 R 7-36, Duane Kuiper 24 L 11-22, Johnnie Jeter 29 R 6-17, 1 Jack Heidemann 24 R 1-11, Alan Ashby 22 B 1-7, Dwain Anderson 26 R 1-3, Larry Johnson 23 R 0-0

	NAME	T	AGE	W	L	PCT	SV	G	GS	CG	IP	H	BB	SO	ShO	ERA
	TOTALS		30	77	85*	.475	27	162	162	45	1446	1419	479	650	9	3.80
	Gaylord Perry	R	35	21	13	.618	0	37	37	28	322	230	99	216	4	2.52
	Jim Perry	R	38	17	12	.586	0	36	36	8	252	242	64	71	3	2.96
2	Fritz Peterson	L	32	9	14	.391	0	29	29	3	153	187	37	52	0	4.35
	Dick Bosman	R	30	7	5	.583	0	25	18	2	127	126	29	56	1	4.11
	Tom Hilgendorf	L	32	4	3	.571	3	35	0	0	48	58	17	23	0	4.88
2	Fred Beene	R	31	4	4	.500	2	32	0	0	73	68	26	35	0	4.93
	Bob Johnson	R	31	3	4	.429	0	14	10	0	72	75	37	36	0	4.38
2	Steve Kline (EJ)	R	26	3	8	.273	0	16	11	1	71	70	31	17	0	5.07
	Milt Wilcox	R	24	2	2	.500	4	41	2	1	71	74	24	33	0	4.69
2	Steve Arlin	R	28	2	5	.286	0	11	10	1	44	59	22	20	0	6.55
2	Tom Buskey	R	27	2	6	.250	17	51	0	0	93	93	33	40	0	3.19
	Bruce Ellingsen	L	25	1	1	.500	0	16	2	0	42	45	17	16	0	3.21
	Tom Timmerman	R	34	1	1	.500	0	4	0	0	10	9	5	2	0	5.40
1	Dick Tidrow	R	27	1	3	.250	0	4	4	0	19	21	13	8	0	7.11
	Bill Gogolewski	R	26	0	0	–	0	5	0	0	14	15	2	3	0	4.50
	Jim Kern	R	25	0	1	.000	0	4	3	1	15	16	14	11	0	4.80
1	Ken Sanders	R	32	0	1	.000	1	9	0	0	11	21	5	4	0	9.82
1	Cecil Upshaw	R	31	0	1	.000	0	7	0	0	8	10	4	7	0	3.38

*1 loss by forfeit

MILWAUKEE 5th 76-86 .469 15 — DEL CRANDALL

	NAME	G by POS	B	AGE	G	AB	R	H	2B	3B	HR	RBI	BB	SO	SB	BA	SA
	TOTALS			27	162	5472	647	1335	228	49	120	612	500	909	106	.244	.369
	George Scott	1B148, DH10	R	30	158	604	74	170	36	2	17	82	59	90	9	.281	.432
	Pete Garcia	2B140	R	24	141	452	46	90	15	4	12	54	26	67	8	.199	.330
	Robin Yount	SS107	R	18	107	344	48	86	14	5	3	26	12	46	7	.250	.346
	Don Money	3B157, 2B1, DH1	R	27	159	629	85	178	32	3	15	65	62	80	19	.283	.415
	Dave May	OF121, DH8	L	30	135	477	56	108	15	1	10	42	28	73	4	.226	.325
	Bob Coluccio	OF131, DH2	R	22	138	394	42	88	13	4	6	31	43	61	15	.223	.322
	Johnny Briggs	OF149, DH2	L	30	154	554	72	140	30	8	17	73	71	102	9	.253	.428
	Darrell Porter	C117, DH9	L	22	131	432	59	104	15	4	12	56	50	88	8	.241	.377
	Bobby Mitchell	DH53, OF26	R	30	88	173	27	42	6	2	5	20	18	46	7	.243	.387
	Ken Berry	OF82, DH13	R	33	98	267	21	64	9	2	1	24	18	26	3	.240	.300
	Tim Johnson	SS64, 2B26, 3B1, OF1, DH1	L	24	93	245	25	60	7	7	0	25	11	48	4	.245	.331
2	Mike Hegan	DH37, 1B17, OF17	L	31	89	190	21	45	7	1	7	32	33	34	0	.237	.395
	Charlie Moore	C61, DH6	R	21	72	204	17	50	10	4	0	19	21	34	3	.245	.333
	Bob Hansen	DH18, 1B3	L	26	58	88	5	26	4	1	2	9	3	16	2	.295	.432
1	Deron Johnson	1B30, DH19	R	35	49	152	14	23	3	0	6	18	21	41	1	.151	.289
	John Vukovich	3B12, SS12, 2B11, 1B4	R	25	38	80	5	15	1	0	3	11	1	16	2	.188	.313
	Rob Ellis	OF11, DH9, 3B1	R	23	22	48	4	14	2	0	0	4	4	11	0	.292	.333

Sixto Lezcano 20 R 13-54, Gorman Thomas 23 R 12-46, Bobby Sheldon 23 L 2-17, Jack Lind 28 B 4-17, Felipe Alou 39 R 0-3

	NAME	T	AGE	W	L	PCT	SV	G	GS	CG	IP	H	BB	SO	ShO	ERA
	TOTALS		26	76	86	.469	24	162	162	43	1458	1476	493	621	11	3.76
	Jim Slaton	R	24	13	16	.448	0	40	35	10	250	255	102	126	3	3.92
	Billy Champion	R	26	11	4	.733	0	31	23	2	162	168	49	60	0	3.61
	Tom Murphy	R	28	10	10	.500	20	70	0	0	123	97	51	47	0	1.90
	Jim Colborn (GJ)	R	28	10	13	.435	0	33	31	10	224	230	60	83	1	4.06
	Clyde Wright	L	33	9	20	.310	0	38	32	15	232	264	54	64	0	4.42
	Ed Sprague (KJ)	R	28	7	2	.778	0	20	10	3	94	94	31	57	0	2.39
	Eduardo Rodriguez	R	22	7	4	.636	4	43	6	0	112	97	51	58	0	3.62
	Kevin Kobel	L	20	6	14	.300	0	34	24	3	169	166	54	74	2	3.99
	Billy Travers	L	21	2	3	.400	0	23	1	0	53	59	30	31	0	4.92
	Jerry Bell	R	26	1	0	1.000	0	5	0	0	14	17	5	4	0	2.57
	Bill Castro	R	20	0	0	–	0	8	0	0	18	19	5	10	0	4.50
	Larry Anderson	R	21	0	0	–	0	2	0	0	2	2	1	3	0	0.00
	Roger Miller	R	19	0	0	–	0	2	0	0	2	3	0	2	0	13.50
2	Dick Selma	R	30	0	0	–	0	2	0	0	2	5	0	2	0	22.50

DETROIT 6th 72-90 .444 19 — RALPH HOUK

	NAME	G by POS	B	AGE	G	AB	R	H	2B	3B	HR	RBI	BB	SO	SB	BA	SA
	TOTALS			30	162	5568	620	1375	200	35	131	579	436	784	67	.247	.366
	Bill Freehan	1B65, C63, DH1	R	32	130	445	58	132	17	5	18	60	42	44	2	.297	.479
	Gary Sutherland	2B147, SS10, 3B4	R	29	149	619	60	157	20	1	5	49	26	37	1	.254	.313
	Ed Brinkman	SS151, 3B2	R	32	153	502	55	111	15	3	14	54	29	71	2	.221	.347
	Aurelio Rodriguez	3B159	R	26	159	571	54	127	23	5	5	49	26	70	2	.222	.306
1	Jim Northrup	OF97	L	34	97	376	41	89	12	1	11	42	36	46	0	.237	.366
	Mickey Stanley (BH)	OF91, 1B12, 2B1	R	31	99	394	40	87	13	2	8	34	26	63	5	.221	.325
	Willie Horton (KJ)	OF64, DH1	R	31	72	238	32	71	8	1	15	47	21	36	0	.298	.529
	Jerry Moses	C74	R	27	74	198	19	47	6	3	4	19	11	38	0	.237	.359
	Al Kaline	DH146	R	39	147	558	71	146	28	2	13	64	65	75	2	.262	.389
	Ben Ogilvie	OF63, 1B10, DH4	L	25	92	252	28	68	11	3	4	29	34	38	12	.270	.385
	Gates Brown	DH13	L	35	73	99	7	24	2	0	4	17	10	15	0	.242	.384
	Dick Sharon	OF56	R	24	60	129	12	28	4	0	2	10	14	29	4	.217	.295
	Gene Lamont	C60	L	27	60	92	9	20	4	0	3	8	7	19	0	.217	.359
	Ron LeFlore	OF59	R	22	59	254	37	66	8	1	2	13	13	58	23	.260	.323
	John Knox	2B33, DH2, 3B1	L	25	55	88	11	27	1	1	0	6	6	13	5	.307	.341
	Norm Cash	1B44	L	39	53	149	17	34	3	2	7	12	19	30	1	.228	.416
	Marvin Lane	OF46, DH1	R	24	50	103	16	24	4	1	2	9	19	24	2	.233	.350
	Jim Nettles	OF41	L	27	43	141	20	32	5	1	6	17	15	26	3	.227	.404
	Reggie Sanders	1B25, DH1	R	24	26	99	12	27	7	0	3	10	5	20	1	.273	.434
	Tom Veryzer	SS20	R	21	22	55	4	13	2	0	2	9	5	8	1	.236	.382
	Ron Cash (IL)	1B17, 3B4	R	24	20	62	6	14	2	0	0	5	0	11	0	.226	.258
	Leon Roberts	OF17	R	23	17	63	5	17	3	2	0	7	3	10	0	.270	.381

Dan Meyer 21 L 10-50, John Wockenfuss 25 R 4-29, Ike Brown 32 R 0-2

	NAME	T	AGE	W	L	PCT	SV	G	GS	CG	IP	H	BB	SO	ShO	ERA
	TOTALS		29	72	90	.444	15	162	162	54	1456	1443	621	869	7	4.16
	John Hiller	L	31	17	14	.548	13	59	0	0	150	127	62	134	0	2.64
	Mickey Lolich	L	33	16	**21**	.432	0	41	41	27	308	310	78	202	3	4.15
	Joe Coleman	R	27	14	12	.538	0	41	41	11	286	272	158	177	2	4.31
	Lerrin LaGrow	R	25	8	19	.296	0	37	34	11	216	245	80	85	0	4.67
	Woody Fryman	L	34	6	9	.400	0	27	22	4	142	120	67	92	1	4.31
	Luke Walker (YJ)	L	30	5	5	.500	0	28	9	0	92	100	54	52	0	4.99
	Vern Ruhle	R	23	2	0	1.000	0	5	3	1	33	35	6	10	0	2.73
	Dave Lemanczyk	R	23	2	1	.667	0	22	3	0	79	79	44	52	0	3.99
	Bill Slayback	R	26	1	3	.250	0	16	4	0	55	57	26	23	0	4.75
	Jim Ray	R	29	1	3	.250	2	28	0	0	52	49	29	26	0	4.50
	Chuck Seelbach	R	26	0	0	–	0	4	0	0	8	9	3	0	0	4.50
	Fred Holdsworth	R	22	0	3	.000	0	8	5	0	36	40	14	16	0	4.25

WEST DIVISION

OAKLAND 1st 90-72 .556 — AL DARK

	NAME	G by POS	B	AGE	G	AB	R	H	2B	3B	HR	RBI	BB	SO	SB	BA	SA
	TOTALS			29	162	5331	689	1315	205	37	132	637	568	**876**	**164**	.247	.373
	Gene Tenace	1B106, C79, 2B3	R	27	158	484	71	102	17	1	26	73	**110**	105	2	.211	.411
	Dick Green	2B100	R	33	100	287	20	61	8	2	2	22	22	50	2	.213	.275
	Bert Campaneris	SS133, DH1	R	32	134	527	77	153	18	8	2	41	47	81	34	.290	.366
	Sal Bando	3B141, DH3	R	30	146	498	84	121	21	2	22	103	86	79	2	.243	.426
	Reggie Jackson	OF127, DH19	L	28	148	506	90	146	25	1	29	93	86	105	25	.289	.514
	Billy North	OF138, DH8	B	26	149	543	79	141	20	5	4	33	69	86	**54**	.260	.337
	Joe Rudi	OF140, 1B27, DH2	R	27	158	593	73	174	**39**	4	22	99	34	92	2	.293	.484
	Ray Fosse (XJ)	C68, DH1	R	27	69	204	20	40	8	3	4	23	11	31	1	.196	.324
2	Deron Johnson	DH50	R	35	50	174	16	34	1	2	7	23	11	37	1	.195	.345
	Angel Mangual	OF74, DH37, 3B1	R	27	115	365	37	85	14	4	9	43	17	59	3	.233	.367
	Ted Kubiak	2B71, SS19, 3B14, DH2	B	32	99	220	22	46	3	0	0	18	18	15	1	.209	.223
	Jesus Alou	DH41, OF25	R	33	96	220	13	59	8	0	2	15	5	9	0	.268	.332
	Herb Washington	DH27	R	23	92	0	29	0	0	0	0	0	0	0	29	–	–
	Larry Haney	C73, 3B3, 1B2	R	31	76	121	12	20	4	0	2	3	3	18	1	.165	.248
	Claudell Washington	DH38, OF32	L	19	73	221	16	63	10	5	0	19	13	44	6	.285	.376
1	Pat Bourque	1B39	L	27	73	96	6	22	4	0	1	16	15	20	0	.229	.302
2	Dal Maxvill	2B30, SS29, 3B1	R	35	60	52	3	10	0	0	0	2	8	10	0	.192	.192
2	Jim Holt	1B17, DH3	L	30	30	42	1	6	0	0	0	0	1	9	0	.143	.143
	Phil Garner	3B19, SS8, 2B3, DH2	R	25	30	28	4	5	1	0	0	1	1	5	1	.179	.214
	Manny Trillo (LJ)	2B21	R	23	21	33	3	5	0	0	0	2	2	8	0	.152	.152

Gaylen Pitts 28 R 10-41, Champ Summers 26 L 3-24, Vic Davalillo 38 L 4-23, John Donaldson 31 L 2-15, Tim Hosley 27 R 2-7, Rich McKinney 27 R 1-7

	NAME	T	AGE	W	L	PCT	SV	G	GS	CG	IP	H	BB	SO	ShO	ERA
	TOTALS		28	90	72	.556	28	162	162	49	1440	1322	430	755	12	**2.95**
	Catfish Hunter	R	28	**25**	12	.676	0	41	41	23	318	268	46	143	6	**2.49**
	Ken Holtzman	L	29	19	17	.528	0	39	38	9	255	273	51	117	3	3.07
	Vida Blue	L	24	17	15	.531	0	40	40	12	282	246	98	174	1	3.26
	Rollie Fingers	R	27	9	5	.643	18	**76**	0	0	119	104	29	95	0	2.65
	Dave Hamilton	L	26	7	4	.636	0	29	18	1	117	104	48	69	1	3.15
	Glenn Abbott	R	23	5	7	.417	0	19	17	3	96	89	34	38	0	3.00
	Paul Lindblad	L	32	4	4	.500	6	45	2	0	101	85	30	46	0	2.05
	Darold Knowles	L	32	3	3	.500	3	45	1	0	53	61	35	18	0	4.25
	Blue Moon Odom	R	29	1	5	.167	1	34	5	1	87	85	52	52	0	3.83
	Leon Hooten	R	26	0	0	–	0	6	0	0	8	6	4	1	0	3.38
	Bill Parsons	R	25	0	0	–	0	4	0	0	2	1	3	2	0	0.00

Bob Locker (EJ) 36

TEXAS 2nd 84-76 .525 5 — BILLY MARTIN

	NAME	G by POS	B	AGE	G	AB	R	H	2B	3B	HR	RBI	BB	SO	SB	BA	SA
	TOTALS			27	161	5449	690	1482	198	39	99	643	508	710	113	**.272**	.377
	Mike Hargrove	1B91, DH32, OF6	L	24	131	415	57	134	18	6	4	66	49	42	0	.323	.424
	Dave Nelson (BZ)	2B120, DH1	R	30	121	474	71	112	13	1	3	42	34	72	25	.236	.287
	Toby Harrah	SS158, 3B3	R	25	161	573	79	149	23	2	21	74	50	65	15	.260	.417
	Lenny Randle	3B89, 2B40, OF21, DH2, SS1	B	25	151	520	65	157	17	4	1	49	29	43	26	.302	.356
	Cesar Tovar	OF135, DH3	R	33	138	562	78	164	24	6	4	58	47	33	13	.292	.377
	Joe Lovitto	OF107, 1B5	B	23	113	283	27	63	9	3	2	26	25	36	6	.223	.297
	Jeff Burroughs	OF150, 1B2, DH1	R	23	152	554	84	167	33	2	25	**118**	91	104	2	.301	.504
	Jim Sundberg	C132	R	23	132	368	45	91	13	3	3	36	62	61	2	.247	.323
	Jim Spencer	1B60, DH54	L	26	118	352	36	98	11	4	7	44	22	27	1	.278	.392
1	Alex Johnson	OF81, DH30	R	31	114	453	57	132	14	3	4	41	28	59	20	.291	.362
	Tommy Grieve	DH40, OF38, 1B1	R	26	84	259	30	66	10	4	9	32	20	48	0	.255	.429
	Jim Fregosi	1B47, 3B32	R	32	78	230	31	60	5	0	12	34	22	41	0	.261	.439
	Larry Brown	3B47, 2B8, SS1	R	34	54	76	10	15	2	0	0	5	9	13	0	.197	.224
2	Duke Sims	C30, DH5, OF1	L	33	39	106	7	22	0	0	3	6	8	24	0	.208	.292
	Leo Cardenas	3B21, SS10, DH4	R	35	34	92	5	25	3	0	0	7	2	14	1	.272	.304

Roy Howell 20 L 11-44, 1 Dick Billings 31 R 7-31, Bill Fahey 24 L 4-16, Mike Cubbage 23 L 0-15, Tom Robson 28 R 3-13, Pete Mackanin 22 R 1-6, Bob Jones 24 L 0-5, Dave Moates 26 L 0-0

	NAME	T	AGE	W	L	PCT	SV	G	GS	CG	IP	H	BB	SO	ShO	ERA
	TOTALS		27	84*	76	.525	12	161	161	62	1434	1423	449	871	**16**	3.82
	Ferguson Jenkins	R	30	**25**	12	.676	0	41	41	**29**	328	286	45	225	6	2.83
	Jim Bibby	R	29	19	19	.500	0	41	41	11	264	255	113	149	5	4.74
	Jackie Brown	R	31	13	12	.520	0	35	26	9	217	219	74	134	2	3.57
	Steve Hargan	R	31	12	9	.571	0	37	27	8	187	202	48	98	2	3.95
	Steve Foucault	R	24	8	9	.471	12	69	0	0	144	123	40	106	0	2.25
	Dave Clyde	L	19	3	9	.250	0	28	21	4	117	129	47	52	0	4.38
2	Bill Hands	R	34	2	0	1.000	0	2	2	1	14	11	3	4	1	1.93
	Don Stanhouse	R	23	1	1	.500	0	18	0	0	31	38	17	26	0	4.94
	Jim Merritt (SA)	L	30	0	0	–	0	26	1	0	33	46	6	18	0	4.09
	Jim Shellenback	L	30	0	0	–	0	11	0	0	25	30	12	14	0	5.76
	Stan Thomas	R	24	0	0	–	0	12	0	0	14	22	6	8	0	6.43
	Jeff Terpko	R	23	0	0	–	0	3	0	0	7	6	4	3	0	1.29
	Steve Dunning	R	25	0	0	–	0	1	0	0	2	3	3	1	0	22.50
1	Lloyd Allen	R	24	0	1	.000	0	14	0	0	22	24	18	18	0	6.55
	Pete Broberg	R	24	0	4	.000	0	12	2	0	29	29	13	15	0	8.07

*1 win by forfeit

MINNESOTA 3rd 82-80 .506 8 — FRANK QUILICI

NAME	G by POS	B	AGE	G	AB	R	H	2B	3B	HR	RBI	BB	SO	SB	BA	SA
TOTALS			28	163	5632	669	1530	190	37	111	632	520	791	74	.272	.378
Craig Kusick	1B75	R	25	76	201	36	48	7	1	8	26	35	36	0	.239	.403
Rod Carew	2B148	L	28	153	599	86	218	30	5	3	55	74	49	38	.364	.446
Danny Thompson (LJ)	SS88,3B5,DH1	R	27	97	264	25	66	6	1	4	25	22	29	1	.250	.326
Eric Soderholm	3B130,SS1	R	25	141	464	63	128	18	3	10	51	48	68	7	.276	.392
Larry Hisle	OF137	R	27	143	510	68	146	20	7	19	79	48	112	12	.286	.465
Steve Brye	OF129	R	25	135	488	52	138	32	1	2	41	22	59	1	.283	.365
Bobby Darwin	OF142	R	31	152	575	67	152	13	7	25	94	37	127	1	.264	.442
Glenn Borgmann	C128	R	24	128	345	33	87	8	1	3	45	39	44	2	.252	.307
Tony Oliva	DH112	L	34	127	459	43	131	16	2	13	57	27	31	0	.285	.414
Steve Braun	OF108,3B17	L	25	129	453	53	127	12	1	8	40	56	51	4	.280	.364
Harmon Killebrew	DH57,1B33	R	38	122	333	28	74	7	0	13	54	45	61	0	.222	.360
J. Terrell	SS34,2B26,3B21,DH12,OF3,1B2	B	27	116	229	43	56	4	6	0	19	11	27	3	.245	.314
Luis Gomez	SS74,2B2,DH1	R	22	82	168	18	35	1	0	0	3	12	16	2	.208	.214
1 Jim Holt	1B67,OF5	L	30	79	197	24	50	11	0	0	16	14	16	0	.254	.310
Phil Roof	C44	R	33	44	97	10	19	1	0	2	13	6	24	0	.196	.268
Randy Hundley (KJ)	C28	R	32	32	88	2	17	2	0	0	3	4	12	0	.193	.216

2 Pat Bourque 27 L 14-64, Sergio Ferrer 23 B 16-57, 1 Joe Lis 27 R 8-41

NAME	T	AGE	W	L	PCT	SV	G	GS	CG	IP	H	BB	SO	ShO	ERA
TOTALS		27	82	80	.506	29	163	163	43	1455	1436	513	934	11	3.64
Bert Blyleven	R	23	17	17	.500	0	37	37	19	281	244	77	249	3	2.66
Joe Decker	R	26	16	14	.533	0	37	37	11	249	234	97	158	1	3.29
Dave Goltz	R	25	10	10	.500	1	28	24	5	174	192	45	89	1	3.26
Bill Campbell	R	25	8	7	.533	19	63	0	0	120	109	55	89	0	2.63
Vic Albury	L	27	8	9	.471	0	32	22	4	164	159	80	85	1	4.12
Ray Corbin	R	25	7	6	.538	0	29	15	1	112	133	40	50	0	5.30
Tom Burgmeier	L	30	5	3	.625	4	50	0	0	92	92	26	34	0	4.50
1 Bill Hands	R	34	4	5	.444	3	35	10	0	115	130	25	74	0	4.46
Bill Butler	L	24	4	6	.400	1	26	12	2	99	91	56	79	0	4.09
Tom Johnson	R	23	2	0	1.000	1	4	0	0	7	4	0	4	0	0.00
1 Dick Woodson	R	29	1	1	.500	0	5	4	0	27	30	4	12	0	4.33
Dan Fife	R	24	0	0	–	0	4	0	0	5	10	4	3	0	16.20
Jim Hughes	R	22	0	0	.000	0	2	2	1	10	8	4	8	0	5.40

CHICAGO 4th 80-80 .500 9 — CHUCK TANNER

NAME	G by POS	B	AGE	G	AB	R	H	2B	3B	HR	RBI	BB	SO	SB	BA	SA
TOTALS			27	163	5577	684	1492	225	23	135	633	519	858	64	.268	.389
Dick Allen (VR)	1B125,DH1,2B1	R	32	128	462	84	139	23	1	32	88	57	89	7	.301	.563
Jorge Orta	2B123,DH10,SS3	L	23	139	525	73	166	31	2	10	67	40	88	9	.316	.440
Bucky Dent	SS154	R	22	154	496	55	136	15	3	5	45	28	48	3	.274	.347
Bill Melton	3B123,DH11	R	28	136	495	63	120	17	0	21	63	59	60	3	.242	.404
Bill Sharp	OF99	L	24	100	320	45	81	13	2	4	24	25	37	0	.253	.344
Ken Henderson	OF162	B	28	162	602	76	176	35	5	20	95	66	112	12	.292	.467
Carlos May	OF129,DH13	L	26	149	551	66	137	19	2	8	58	46	76	8	.249	.334
Ed Herrmann	C107	L	27	107	367	32	95	13	1	10	39	16	49	1	.259	.381
Pat Kelly	DH67,OF53	L	29	122	424	60	119	16	3	4	21	46	58	18	.281	.361
Ron Santo	DH47,2B39,3B28,1B,SS1	R	34	117	375	29	83	12	1	5	41	37	72	0	.221	.299
Brian Downing	C63,OF39,DH9	R	23	108	293	41	66	12	1	10	39	51	72	0	.225	.375
Tony Muser	1B80,DH13	L	26	103	206	16	60	5	1	1	18	6	22	1	.291	.340
Jerry Hairston (LJ)	OF22,DH10	B	22	45	109	8	25	7	0	0	8	13	18	0	.229	.294
Buddy Bradford (BC)	OF32,DH1	R	29	39	96	16	32	2	0	5	10	13	11	1	.333	.510
Lee Richard	3B12,SS6,DH5,2B3,OF1	R	25	32	67	5	11	1	0	0	1	5	8	0	.164	.179
Eddie Leon	SS21,2B7,3B2,DH1	R	27	31	46	1	5	1	0	0	3	2	12	0	.109	.130
Bill Stein	3B11,DH2	R	27	13	43	5	12	1	0	0	5	7	8	0	.279	.302

Lamar Johnson 23 R 10-29, Pete Varney 25 R 7-28, Nyls Nyman 20 L 9-14, Chuck Brinkman 29 R 2-14, 1 Luis Alvarado 25 R 1-10, Hugh Yancy 24 R 0-0

NAME	T	AGE	W	L	PCT	SV	G	GS	CG	IP	H	BB	SO	ShO	ERA
TOTALS		27	80	80	.500	29	163	163	55	1466	1470	548	826	11	3.94
Jim Kaat	L	35	21	13	.618	0	42	39	15	277	263	63	142	3	2.92
Wilbur Wood	L	32	20	19	.513	0	42	42	22	320	305	80	169	1	3.60
Stan Bahnsen	R	29	12	15	.444	0	38	35	10	216	230	110	102	1	4.71
Bart Johnson	R	24	10	4	.714	0	18	18	8	122	105	32	76	2	2.73
Terry Forster	L	22	7	8	.467	24	59	1	0	134	120	48	105	0	3.63
Rich Gossage (UJ)	R	22	4	6	.400	1	39	3	0	89	92	47	64	0	4.15
Skip Pitlock	L	26	3	3	.500	1	40	5	0	106	103	55	68	0	4.42
Joe Henderson	R	27	1	0	1.000	0	5	3	0	15	21	11	12	0	8.40
Bill Moran	R	23	1	3	.250	0	15	5	0	46	57	23	17	0	4.70
Jack Kucek	R	21	1	4	.200	0	9	7	0	38	48	21	25	0	5.21
Ken Tatum	R	30	0	0	–	0	10	1	0	21	23	9	5	0	4.71
Wayne Granger	R	30	0	0	–	0	5	0	0	8	16	3	4	0	7.88
Stan Perzanowski	R	23	0	0	–	0	2	1	0	2	8	2	2	0	22.50
Francisco Barrios	R	21	0	0	–	0	2	0	0	2	7	2	2	0	27.00
Jim Otten	R	23	0	1	.000	0	5	1	0	16	22	12	11	0	5.63
2 Lloyd Allen	R	24	0	1	.000	0	6	2	0	7	7	12	3	0	10.29
Cy Acosta (IJ)	R	27	0	3	.000	3	27	0	0	46	43	18	19	0	3.72

KANSAS CITY 5th 77-85 .475 13 — JACK McKEON

NAME	G by POS	B	AGE	G	AB	R	H	2B	3B	HR	RBI	BB	SO	SB	BA	SA
TOTALS			27	162	5582	667	1448	232	42	89	623	550	768	146	.259	.364
John Mayberry	1B106,DH16	L	24	126	427	63	100	13	1	22	69	77	72	4	.234	.424
Cookie Rojas	2B141	R	35	144	542	52	147	17	1	6	60	30	43	8	.271	.339
Freddie Patek	SS149	R	29	149	537	72	121	18	6	3	38	77	69	33	.225	.298
George Brett	3B132,SS1	L	21	133	457	49	129	21	5	2	47	21	38	8	.282	.363
Jim Wohlford	OF138,DH1	R	23	143	501	55	136	16	7	2	44	39	74	16	.271	.343
Amos Otis	OF143,DH2	R	27	146	552	87	157	31	9	12	73	58	67	18	.284	.438
Vada Pinson	OF110,DH2,1B1	L	35	115	406	46	112	18	2	6	41	21	45	21	.276	.374
Fran Healy	C138	R	27	139	445	59	112	24	2	9	53	62	73	16	.252	.375
Hal McRae	DH90,OF56,3B1	R	27	148	539	71	167	36	4	15	88	54	68	11	.310	.475
Al Cowens	OF102,DH4,3B2	R	22	110	269	28	65	7	1	1	25	3	38	5	.242	.286
Frank White	2B50,SS29,3B16,DH3	R	23	99	204	19	45	6	3	1	18	5	33	3	.221	.294
Tony Solaita	1B65,DH14,OF1	L	27	96	239	31	64	12	0	7	30	35	70	0	.268	.406
Buck Martinez	C38	R	25	43	107	10	23	3	1	1	8	14	19	0	.215	.290
1 Kurt Bevacqua	1B14,3B13,2B7,DH3,SS2	R	27	39	90	10	19	0	0	0	3	9	20	1	.211	.211
2 Richie Scheinblum	DH18,OF2	B	31	36	83	7	15	2	0	0	2	8	8	0	.181	.205
Orlando Cepeda	DH26	R	36	33	107	3	23	5	0	1	18	9	16	1	.215	.290

1 Paul Schaal 31 R 6-34, Fernando Gonzalez 24 R 3-21, Dennis Paepke 29 R 2-12, Bobby Floyd 30 R 1-9, Rick Reichardt 31 R 1-1

NAME	T	AGE	W	L	PCT	SV	G	GS	CG	IP	H	BB	SO	ShO	ERA
TOTALS		30	77	85	.475	17	162	162	54	1472	1477	482	731	13	3.51
Steve Busby	R	24	22	14	.611	0	38	38	20	292	284	92	198	3	3.39
Al Fitzmorris	R	27	13	6	.684	1	34	27	9	190	189	63	53	4	2.79
Paul Splittorff	L	27	13	19	.406	0	36	36	8	226	252	75	90	1	4.10
Bruce Dal Canton	R	32	8	10	.444	0	31	22	9	175	135	82	96	2	3.14
Doug Bird	R	24	7	6	.538	10	55	1	1	92	100	27	62	0	2.74
Nelson Briles (KJ)	R	30	5	7	.417	0	18	17	3	103	118	21	41	0	4.02
Marty Pattin	R	31	3	7	.300	0	25	11	2	117	121	28	50	0	4.00
Steve Mingori	L	30	2	3	.400	2	36	0	0	67	53	23	43	0	2.82
Joe Hoerner	L	37	2	3	.400	2	30	0	0	35	32	12	24	0	3.86
1 Gene Garber	R	26	1	2	.333	1	17	0	0	28	35	13	14	0	4.82
Lindy McDaniel	R	38	1	4	.200	1	38	5	2	107	109	24	47	0	3.45
Aurelio Lopez	R	25	0	0	–	0	8	1	0	16	21	10	5	0	5.63
Dennis Leonard	R	23	0	4	.000	0	5	4	0	22	28	12	8	0	5.32

CALIFORNIA 6th 68-94 .420 22 — BOBBY WINKLES 30-44 .405 WHITEY HERZOG 2-2 .500 DICK WILLIAMS 36-48 .429

NAME	G by POS	B	AGE	G	AB	R	H	2B	3B	HR	RBI	BB	SO	SB	BA	SA
TOTALS			27	163	5401	618	1372	203	31	95	550	509	801	119	.254	.356
John Doherty	1B70,DH2	L	22	74	223	20	57	14	1	3	15	8	13	2	.256	.368
Denny Doyle	2B146,SS2	L	30	147	511	47	133	19	2	1	34	25	49	6	.260	.311
Dave Chalk	SS99,3B38	R	23	133	465	44	117	9	3	5	31	30	57	10	.252	.316
2 Paul Schaal	3B51	R	31	53	165	10	41	5	0	2	20	18	27	2	.248	.315
Lee Stanton (BH)	OF114	R	28	118	415	48	111	21	2	11	62	33	107	11	.267	.407
Mickey Rivers (BH)	OF116	L	24	118	466	69	133	19	11	3	31	39	47	30	.285	.393
Joe Lahoud	OF106,DH10	L	27	127	325	46	88	16	3	13	44	47	57	4	.271	.458
Ellie Rodriquez	C137,DH1	R	28	140	395	48	100	20	0	7	36	69	56	4	.253	.357
1 Frank Robinson	DH124,OF1	R	38	129	427	75	107	26	2	20	63	75	85	5	.251	.461
Bobby Valentine	OF62,SS36,3B15,DH4,2B1	R	24	117	371	39	97	10	3	3	39	25	25	8	.261	.329
1 Bob Oliver	1B57,3B36,OF4	R	31	110	359	22	89	9	1	8	55	16	51	2	.248	.345
Winston Llenas (KJ)	OF32,2B15,DH10,3B2	R	30	72	138	16	36	6	0	2	17	11	19	0	.261	.348
Bruce Bochte	OF39,1B24	L	23	57	196	24	53	4	1	5	26	18	23	6	.270	.378
Morris Nettles	OF54	L	22	56	175	27	48	4	0	0	8	16	38	20	.274	.297
1 Tommy McCraw	1B29,OF12	L	33	56	119	21	34	8	0	3	17	12	13	2	.286	.429
1 Sandy Alomar	SS19,2B15,3B5,OF1	B	30	46	54	12	12	0	1	0	1	2	8	2	.222	.259
Tom Egan	C41	R	28	43	94	4	11	0	0	0	4	8	40	1	.117	.117
Charlie Sands (KH)	DH21,C5	L	26	43	83	6	16	2	0	4	13	23	17	0	.193	.361
Rudy Meoli	3B20,SS8,2B1,1B1	L	23	36	90	9	22	2	0	0	3	8	10	2	.244	.267
Orlando Ramirez	SS31	R	22	31	86	4	14	0	0	0	7	6	23	2	.163	.163
2 Bob Heise	2B17,3B6,SS3	R	27	29	75	7	20	1	0	0	6	5	10	0	.267	.360

Mike Epstein 31 L 10-62, John Balaz 23 R 10-42, Doug Howard 26 R 9-39, 1 Richie Scheinblum 31 B 4-26

NAME	T	AGE	W	L	PCT	SV	G	GS	CG	IP	H	BB	SO	ShO	ERA
TOTALS		25	68	94	.420	12	163	163	64	1439	1339	649	986	13	3.52
Nolan Ryan	R	27	22	16	.579	0	42	41	26	333	221	202	367	3	2.89
Frank Tanana	L	20	14	19	.424	0	39	35	12	269	262	77	180	4	3.11
Bill Singer (XJ)	R	30	7	4	.636	0	14	14	8	109	102	43	77	0	2.97
Andy Hassler	L	22	7	11	.389	1	23	22	10	162	132	79	76	2	2.61
Dick Lange	R	25	3	8	.273	0	21	18	1	114	111	47	57	0	3.79
Luis Quintana	L	22	2	1	.667	0	18	0	0	13	17	14	11	0	4.15
2 Dick Selma	R	30	2	2	.500	1	18	0	0	23	22	17	15	0	5.09
Dave Sells	R	27	2	3	.400	2	20	0	0	39	48	16	14	0	3.69
Chuck Dobson	R	30	2	3	.400	0	5	5	2	30	39	13	16	0	5.70
Skip Lockwood	R	27	2	5	.286	1	37	2	0	81	81	32	39	0	4.33
Ed Figueroa	R	25	2	8	.200	0	25	12	5	105	119	36	49	1	3.69
Barry Raziano	R	27	1	2	.333	1	13	0	0	17	15	8	9	0	6.35
Horacio Pina	R	29	1	2	.333	0	11	0	0	12	9	3	6	0	2.25
Bill Stoneman	R	30	1	8	.111	0	13	11	0	59	78	31	33	0	6.10
2 Ken Sanders	R	32	0	0	–	1	9	0	0	10	10	3	4	0	2.70
2 Orlando Pena	R	40	0	0	–	3	4	0	0	8	6	1	5	0	0.00
Don Kirkwood	R	24	0	0	–	0	3	0	0	7	12	6	4	0	9.00
Bill Gilbreth	L	26	0	0	–	0	3	0	0	1	2	1	0	0	18.00
1 Rudy May	L	29	0	1	.000	2	18	3	0	27	29	10	12	0	7.00
John Cumberland	L	27	0	1	.000	0	17	0	0	22	24	10	12	0	3.68

AMERICAN LEAGUE CHAMPIONSHIP – OAKLAND (WEST) 3 BALTIMORE (EAST) 1

LINE SCORES

TEAM	1	2	3	4	5	6	7	8	9	10	11	12	R	H	E
Game 1 October 5 at Oakland															
BAL	1	0	0	1	4	0	0	0	0				6	10	0
OAK	0	0	1	0	1	0	0	0	1				3	9	0
Cuellar, Grimsley (9) — **Hunter**, Odom (5), Fingers (9)															
Game 2 October 6 at Oakland															
BAL	0	0	0	0	0	0	0	0	0				0	5	2
OAK	0	0	0	1	0	1	0	3	X				5	8	0
McNally, Garland (6) Reynolds (7), Jackson (8) — **Holtzman**															
Game 3 October 8 at Baltimore															
OAK	0	0	0	1	0	0	0	0	0				1	4	2
BAL	0	0	0	0	0	0	0	0	0				0	2	1
Blue — **Palmer**															
Game 4 October 9 at Baltimore															
OAK	0	0	0	0	1	0	0	0	0				2	1	0
BAL	0	0	0	0	0	0	0	0	1				1	5	1
Hunter, Fingers (8) — **Cuellar**, Grimsley (5)															

COMPOSITE BATTING

NAME	POS	G	AB	R	H	2B	3B	HR	RBI	BA
Oakland										
Totals		4	120	11	22	4	1	3	11	.183
Campaneris	SS	4	17	0	3	0	0	0	3	.176
North	CF	4	16	3	1	1	0	0	0	.063
Bando	3B	4	13	4	3	0	0	2	2	.231
Rudi	LF	4	13	0	2	0	1	0	1	.154
Fosse	C	4	12	1	4	1	0	1	3	.333
Jackson	DH-RF	4	12	0	2	1	0	0	1	.167
C. Washington	RF	4	11	1	3	1	0	0	0	.273
Tenace	1B	4	11	1	0	0	0	0	0	.000
Green	2B	4	9	0	2	0	0	0	0	.222

Mangual DH 1-4, Alou PH 1-1, Maxvill 2B 0-1, Holt 1B 0-0, H. Washington PR 0-0, Odom P-PR 0-0, Trillo PR 0-0

NAME	POS	G	AB	R	H	2B	3B	HR	RBI	BA
Baltimore										
Totals		4	124	7	22	1	0	3	7	.177
Grich	2B	4	16	2	4	1	0	1	2	.250
Davis	DH	4	15	0	4	0	0	0	1	.267
Baylor	LF	4	15	0	4	0	0	0	0	.267
Blair	CF	4	14	3	4	0	0	1	2	.286
Robinson	3B	4	12	1	1	0	0	1	1	.083
Coggins	RF	3	11	0	0	0	0	0	0	.000
Belanger	SS	4	9	0	0	0	0	0	0	.000
Powell	1B	2	8	0	1	0	0	0	1	.125
Hendricks	C	3	6	1	1	0	0	0	0	.167

Etchebarren C 2-6, Williams 1B 0-6, Cabell RF 1-4, Bumbry PH-PR 0-1, Motton PH 0-1, Baker SS 0-0, Palmer P-PR 0-0

COMPOSITE PITCHING

NAME	G	IP	H	BB	SO	W	L	SV	ERA
Oakland									
Totals	4	36	22	5	20	3	1	1	1.75
Hunter	2	11.2	11	2	6	1	1	0	4.63
Blue	1	9	2	0	7	1	0	0	0.00
Holtzman	1	9	5	2	3	1	0	0	0.00
Odom	1	3.1	1	0	1	0	0	0	0.00
Fingers	2	3	3	1	3	0	0	1	3.00
Baltimore									
Totals	4	35	22	22	16	1	3	0	1.80
Cuellar	2	12.2	9	13	6	1	1	0	2.84
Palmer	1	9	4	1	4	0	1	0	1.00
McNally	1	5.2	6	2	2	0	1	0	1.59
Grimsley	2	5.1	1	2	2	0	0	0	1.69
Reynolds	1	1.1	0	3	1	0	0	0	0.00
Garland	1	.2	1	1	0	0	0	0	0.00
Jackson	1	.1	1	0	1	0	0	0	0.00

NATIONAL LEAGUE CHAMPIONSHIP — LOS ANGELES (WEST) 3 PITTSBURGH (EAST) 1

LINE SCORES

TEAM	1	2	3	4	5	6	7	8	9	10	11	12	R	H	E
Game 1 October 5 at Pittsburgh															
LA	0	1	0	0	0	0	0	0	2				3	9	2
PIT	0	0	0	0	0	0	0	0	0				0	4	0
Sutton — Reuss, Giusti (8)															
Game 2 October 6 at Pittsburgh															
LA	1	0	0	1	0	0	0	3	0				5	12	0
PIT	0	0	0	0	0	0	2	0	0				2	8	3
Messersmith, Marshall (8) — Rooker, Giusti (8), Demery (8), Hernandez (8)															
Game 3 October 8 at Los Angeles															
PIT	5	0	2	0	0	0	0	0	0				7	10	0
LA	0	0	0	0	0	0	0	0	0				0	4	5
Kison, Hernandez (7) — Rau, Hough (1), Downing (4), Solomon (8)															
Game 4 October 9 at Los Angeles															
PIT	0	0	0	0	0	0	1	0	0				1	3	1
LA	1	0	2	0	2	2	2	3	X				12	12	0
Reuss, Brett (3), Demery (6), Giusti (7), Pizarro (8) — Sutton, Marshall (9)															

COMPOSITE BATTING

NAME	POS	G	AB	R	H	2B	3B	HR	RBI	BA
Los Angeles										
Totals		4	138	20	37	8	1	3	19	.268
Garvey	1B	4	18	4	7	1	0	2	5	.389
Russell	SS	4	18	1	7	0	0	0	3	.389
Buckner	LF	4	18	0	3	1	0	0	0	.167
Cey	3B	4	16	2	5	3	0	1	1	.313
Lopes	2B	4	15	4	4	0	1	0	3	.267
Ferguson	RF-C	4	13	3	3	0	0	0	2	.231
Wynn	CF	4	10	4	2	2	0	0	2	.200
Yeager	C	3	9	1	0	0	0	0	0	.000

Crawford RF 1-4, Mota LF 1-3, Paciorek RF 1-1, Auerbach PH 1-1, McMullen PH 0-1, Joshua PH 0-0, Lacy PR 0-0

NAME	POS	G	AB	R	H	2B	3B	HR	RBI	BA
Pittsburgh										
Totals		4	129	10	25	1	0	3	10	.194
Sanguillen	C	4	16	0	4	1	0	0	0	.250
Stennett	2B	4	16	1	1	0	0	0	0	.063
Stargell	LF	4	15	3	6	0	0	2	4	.400
Oliver	CF	4	14	1	2	0	0	0	1	.143
Hebner	3B	4	13	1	3	0	0	1	4	.231
Zisk	RF	3	10	1	3	0	0	0	0	.300
Kirkpatrick	1B	3	9	0	0	0	0	0	0	.000
Parker	RF	3	8	0	1	0	0	0	0	.125
Popovich	SS	3	5	1	3	0	0	0	0	.600
Mendoza	SS	3	5	0	1	0	0	0	1	.200
Robertson	1B	1	5	1	0	0	0	0	0	.000

Clines LF-RF 0-1, Howe PH 0-1

COMPOSITE PITCHING

NAME	G	P	H	BB	SO	W	L	SV	ERA
Los Angeles									
Totals	4	36	25	8	17	3	1	0	2.00
Sutton	2	17	7	2	13	2	0	0	0.53
Messersmith	1	7	8	3	0	1	0	0	2.57
Downing	1	4	1	1	0	0	0	0	0.00
Marshall	2	3	0	0	1	0	0	0	0.00
Hough	1	2.1	4	0	2	0	0	0	9.00
Solomon	1	2	2	1	1	0	0	0	0.00
Rau	1	0.2	3	1	0	0	1	0	27.00
Pittsburgh									
Totals	4	35	37	30	16	1	3	0	4.89
Reuss	2	9.2	7	8	3	0	2	0	3.60
Rooker	1	7	6	5	4	0	0	0	2.57
Kison	1	6.2	2	6	5	1	0	0	0.00
Hernandez	2	4.1	3	1	2	0	1	0	0.00
Giusti	3	3.1	13	5	1	0	0	0	24.00
Brett	1	2.1	3	2	1	0	0	0	9.00
Demery	2	1	3	2	0	0	0	0	27.00
Pizarro	1	0.2	0	1	0	0	0	0	0.00

EAST DIVISION

PITTSBURGH 1st 88-74 .543 — DANNY MURTAUGH

NAME	G by POS	B	AGE	G	AB	R	H	2B	3B	HR	RBI	BB	SO	SB	BA	SA
TOTALS			27	162	5702	751	1560	238	46	114	692	514	828	55	.274	.391
Bob Robertson	1B63	R	27	91	236	25	54	11	0	16	48	33	48	0	.229	.479
Rennie Stennett	2B154, OF2	R	23	157	673	84	196	29	3	7	56	32	51	8	.291	.374
Frank Taveras	SS124	R	24	126	333	33	82	4	2	0	26	25	41	13	.246	.270
Richie Hebner	3B141	L	26	146	550	97	160	21	6	18	68	60	53	0	.291	.449
Richie Zisk	OF141	R	25	149	536	75	168	30	3	17	100	65	91	1	.313	.476
Al Oliver	OF98, 1B49	L	27	147	617	96	198	38	12	11	85	33	58	10	.321	.475
Willie Stargell	OF135, 1B1	L	34	140	508	90	153	37	4	25	96	87	106	0	.301	.537
Manny Sanguillen	C151	R	30	151	596	77	171	21	4	7	68	21	27	2	.287	.371
Ed Kirkpatrick	1B59, OF14, C6	L	29	116	271	32	67	9	0	6	38	51	30	1	.247	.347
Gene Clines	OF78	R	27	107	276	29	62	5	1	0	14	30	40	14	.225	.250
Mario Mendoza	SS87	R	23	91	163	10	36	1	2	0	15	8	35	1	.221	.252
Dave Parker (LJ)	OF49, 1B6	L	23	73	220	27	62	10	3	4	29	10	53	3	.282	.409
Paul Popovich	2B12, SS10	B	33	59	83	9	18	2	1	0	5	5	10	0	.217	.265
Art Howe	3B20, SS2	R	27	29	74	10	18	4	1	1	5	9	13	0	.243	.365
2 Kurt Bevacqua	3B8, OF1	R	27	18	35	1	4	1	0	0	0	2	10	0	.114	.143
Dave Augustine	OF11	R	24	18	22	3	4	0	0	0	0	0	5	0	.182	.182

Mike Ryan 32 R 3-30, 1 Dal Maxvill 35 R 4-22, 2 Chuck Brinkman 29 R 1-7, Ken Macha 23 R 3-5, Ed Ott 22 L 0-5, Miguel Dilone 19 B 0-2

NAME	T	AGE	W	L	PCT	SV	G	GS	CG	IP	H	BB	SO	ShO	ERA
Totals		27	88	74	.543	17	162	162	51	1466	1428	543	721	9	3.49
Jerry Reuss	L	25	16	11	.593	0	35	35	14	260	259	101	105	1	3.50
Jim Rooker	L	32	15	11	.577	0	33	33	15	263	228	83	139	1	2.77
Ken Brett (EJ)	L	25	13	9	.591	0	27	27	10	191	192	52	96	3	3.30
Dock Ellis (BH)	R	29	12	9	.571	0	26	26	9	177	163	41	91	0	3.15
Bruce Kison	R	23	9	8	.529	2	40	16	1	129	123	57	71	0	3.49
Dave Giusti	R	33	7	5	.583	12	64	2	0	106	101	40	53	0	3.31
Larry Demery	R	21	6	6	.500	0	19	15	2	95	95	51	51	0	4.26
Ramon Hernandez	L	33	5	2	.714	2	58	0	0	69	68	18	33	0	2.74
Daryl Patterson	R	30	2	1	.667	1	14	0	0	21	35	9	8	0	7.29
Juan Pizarro	L	37	1	1	.500	0	7	2	0	24	20	11	7	0	1.88
Kent Tekulve	R	27	1	1	.500	0	8	0	0	9	12	5	6	0	6.00
Bob Moose (IL)	R	26	1	5	.167	0	7	6	0	36	59	7	15	0	7.50
Steve Blass	R	32	0	0	–	0	1	0	0	5	5	7	2	0	9.00
Juan Jiminez	R	25	0	0	–	0	4	0	0	4	6	2	2	0	6.75
Jim Minshall	R	26	0	1	.000	0	5	0	0	4	1	2	3	0	0.00
Jim Sadowski	R	22	0	1	.000	0	4	0	0	9	7	9	1	0	6.00
John Morlan	R	26	0	3	.000	0	39	0	0	65	54	48	38	0	4.29

ST. LOUIS 2nd 86-75 .534 1.5 — RED SCHOENDIENST

NAME	G by POS	B	AGE	G	AB	R	H	2B	3B	HR	RBI	BB	SO	SB	BA	SA
TOTALS			28	161	5620	677	1492	216	46	83	610	531	752	172	.265	.365
Joe Torre	1B139, 3B18	R	33	147	529	59	149	28	1	11	70	69	88	1	.282	.401
Ted Sizemore	2B128, SS1, OF1	R	29	129	504	68	126	17	0	2	47	70	37	8	.250	.296
Mike Tyson	SS143, 2B12	R	24	151	422	35	94	14	5	1	37	22	70	4	.223	.287
Ken Reitz	3B151, SS2	R	23	154	579	48	157	28	2	7	54	23	63	0	.271	.363
Reggie Smith	OF132, 1B1	B	29	143	517	79	160	26	9	23	100	71	70	4	.309	.528
Bake McBride	OF144	L	25	150	559	81	173	19	5	6	56	43	47	30	.309	.394
Lou Brock	OF152	L	35	153	635	105	194	25	7	3	48	61	88	118	.306	.381
Ted Simmons	C141, 1B12	B	24	152	599	66	163	33	6	20	103	47	35	0	.272	.447
Jose Cruz	OF53, 1B1	L	26	107	161	24	42	4	3	5	20	20	27	4	.261	.416
Luis Melendez	OF46, SS1	R	24	83	124	15	27	4	3	0	8	11	9	2	.218	.298
1 Tim McCarver	C21, 1B6	L	32	74	106	13	23	0	1	0	11	22	6	0	.217	.236
Jim Dwyer	OF25, 1B3	L	24	74	86	13	24	1	0	2	11	11	16	0	.279	.360
Jim Hickman	1B14, 3B1	R	37	50	60	5	16	0	0	2	4	8	10	0	.267	.367
2 Jack Heidemann	SS45, 3B1	R	24	47	70	8	19	1	0	0	3	5	10	0	.271	.286
Tom Heintzelman	2B28, 3B2, SS1	R	27	38	74	10	17	4	0	1	6	9	14	0	.230	.324

Jerry DaVanon 28 R 6-40, 2 Luis Alvarado 25 R 5-36, Keith Hernandez 20 L 10-34, 2 Ron Hunt 34 R 4-23, Marc Hill 22 R 5-21, Danny Godby 22 R 2-13, Larry Herndon 20 R 3-12, 1 Bob Heise 27 R 1-7, 3 Richie Scheinblum 31 B 2-6, 2 Dick Billings 31 R 1-5, Stan Papi 23 R 1-4, Jerry Mumphrey 21 B 0-2

NAME	T	AGE	W	L	PCT	SV	G	GS	CG	IP	H	BB	SO	ShO	ERA
Totals		29	86	75	.534	20	161	161	37	1473	1399	616	794	13	3.48
Lynn McGlothen	R	24	16	12	.571	0	31	31	8	237	212	89	142	3	2.70
Bob Gibson	R	38	11	13	.458	0	33	33	9	240	236	104	129	1	3.83
John Curtis	L	26	10	14	.417	1	33	29	5	195	199	83	89	2	3.78
Al Hrabosky	L	24	8	1	.889	9	65	0	0	88	71	38	82	0	2.97
Sonny Siebert (EJ)	R	37	8	8	.500	0	28	20	5	134	150	51	68	3	3.83
Mike Garman	R	24	7	2	.778	6	64	0	0	82	66	27	45	0	2.63
Bob Forsch	R	24	7	4	.636	0	19	14	5	100	84	34	39	2	2.97
Alan Foster	R	27	7	10	.412	0	31	25	5	162	167	61	78	1	3.89
Rich Folkers	L	27	6	2	.750	2	55	0	0	90	65	38	57	0	3.00
1 Orlando Pena	R	40	5	2	.714	1	42	0	0	45	45	20	23	0	2.60
Ray Bare	R	25	1	2	.333	0	10	3	0	24	25	9	6	0	6.00
1 Pete Richert	L	34	0	0	–	1	13	0	0	11	10	11	4	0	2.45
John Denny	R	21	0	0	–	0	2	0	0	2	3	0	1	0	0.00
Barry Lersch	R	29	0	0	–	0	1	0	0	1	3	5	0	0	54.00
2 Claude Osteen	L	34	0	2	.000	0	8	2	0	23	26	11	6	0	4.30
1 Mike Thompson	R	24	0	3	.000	0	19	4	0	38	37	35	25	0	5.68

PHILADELPHIA 3rd 80-82 .494 8 — DANNY OZARK

NAME	G by POS	B	AGE	G	AB	R	H	2B	3B	HR	RBI	BB	SO	SB	BA	SA
TOTALS			27	162	5494	676	1434	233	50	95	636	469	822	115	.261	.373
Willie Montanez	1B137, OF1	L	26	143	527	55	160	33	1	7	79	32	57	3	.304	.410
Dave Cash	2B162	R	26	162	687	89	206	26	11	2	58	46	33	20	.300	.378
Larry Bowa	SS162	B	28	162	669	97	184	19	10	1	36	23	52	39	.275	.338
Mike Schmidt	3B162	R	24	162	568	108	160	28	7	36	116	106	138	23	.282	.546
Mike Anderson	OF133, 1B1	R	23	145	395	35	99	22	2	5	34	37	75	2	.251	.354
Del Unser	OF135	L	29	142	454	72	120	18	5	11	61	50	62	6	.264	.399
Greg Luzinski (KJ)	OF82	R	23	85	302	29	82	14	1	7	48	29	76	3	.272	.394
Bob Boone	C146	R	26	146	488	41	118	24	3	3	52	35	29	3	.242	.322
Bill Robinson	OF87	R	31	100	280	32	66	14	1	5	29	17	61	5	.236	.346
Tommy Hutton	1B39, OF33	L	28	96	208	32	50	6	3	4	33	30	13	2	.240	.356
Jay Johnstone	OF59	L	28	64	200	30	59	10	4	6	30	24	28	5	.295	.475
Tony Taylor	1B7, 3B5, 2B4	R	38	62	64	5	21	4	0	2	13	6	6	0	.328	.484
Ollie Brown	OF33	R	30	43	99	11	24	5	2	4	13	6	20	0	.242	.454
1 Billy Grabarkewitz	OF5, 3B1	R	28	34	30	7	4	0	0	1	2	5	10	3	.133	.233
Larry Cox (KJ)	C29	R	26	30	53	5	9	2	0	0	4	4	9	0	.170	.208
Terry Harmon	SS7, 2B5	R	30	27	15	5	2	0	0	0	0	3	3	0	.133	.133
Alan Bannister	OF8, SS2	R	22	26	25	4	3	0	0	0	1	3	7	0	.120	.120
Jim Essian	C15, 1B1, 3B1	R	23	17	20	1	2	0	0	0	0	2	1	0	.100	.100

Mike Rogodzinski 26 L 1-15, Jerry Martin 25 R 3-14, John Stearns 22 R 1-2

NAME	T	AGE	W	L	PCT	SV	G	GS	CG	IP	H	BB	SO	ShO	ERA
Totals		28	80	82	.494	19	162	162	46	1447	1394	682	892	4	3.91
Jim Lonborg	R	32	17	13	.567	0	39	39	16	283	280	70	121	3	3.21
Steve Carlton	L	29	16	13	.552	0	39	39	17	291	249	136	240	1	3.22
Ron Schueler	R	26	11	16	.407	1	44	27	5	203	202	98	109	0	3.72
Dick Ruthven	R	23	9	13	.409	0	35	35	6	213	182	116	153	0	4.01
Wayne Twitchell (KJ)	R	26	6	9	.400	0	25	18	2	112	122	65	72	0	5.22
2 Gene Garber	R	26	4	0	1.000	4	34	0	0	48	39	31	27	0	2.06
Frank Linzy	R	33	3	2	.600	0	22	0	0	25	27	7	12	0	3.24
Mac Scarce	L	25	3	8	.273	5	58	0	0	70	72	35	50	0	5.01
2 Pete Richert (AJ)	L	34	2	1	.667	0	21	0	0	20	15	4	9	0	2.25
Ed Farmer	R	24	2	1	.667	0	14	3	0	31	41	27	20	0	8.42
Jesus Hernaiz	R	26	2	3	.400	1	27	0	0	41	53	25	16	0	5.93
George Culver	R	30	1	0	1.000	0	14	0	0	22	20	16	9	0	6.55
Tom Underwood	L	20	1	0	1.000	0	7	0	0	13	15	5	8	0	4.85
1 Mike Wallace	L	23	1	0	1.000	0	8	0	0	8	12	2	1	0	5.63
Eddie Watt	R	32	1	1	.500	6	42	0	0	38	39	26	23	0	4.03
Larry Christenson	R	20	1	1	.500	2	10	1	0	23	20	15	18	0	4.30
Ron Diorio	R	27	0	0	–	0	2	0	0	1	2	1	0	0	18.00
Erskine Thomason	R	25	0	0	–	0	1	0	0	1	0	0	1	0	0.00
Dave Wallace	R	26	0	1	.000	0	3	0	0	3	4	3	3	0	9.00

MONTREAL 4th 79-82 .491 8.5 — GENE MAUCH

NAME	G by POS	B	AGE	G	AB	R	H	2B	3B	HR	RBI	BB	SO	SB	BA	SA
TOTALS			28	151	5343	662	1355	201	29	86	610	652	812	124	.254	.350
Mike Jorgensen	1B91, OF29	L	25	131	287	45	89	16	1	11	59	70	39	3	.310	.488
Jim Cox (BH)	2B72	R	24	77	236	29	52	9	1	2	26	23	36	2	.220	.292
Tim Foli	SS120, 3B1	R	23	121	441	41	112	10	3	0	39	28	27	8	.254	.290
1 Ron Hunt	3B75, 2B31, SS1	R	33	115	403	66	108	15	0	0	26	55	17	2	.268	.305
Ken Singleton	OF143	B	27	148	511	68	141	20	2	9	74	93	84	5	.276	.376
Willie Davis	OF151	L	34	153	611	86	180	27	9	12	89	27	69	25	.295	.427
Bob Bailey	OF78, 3B68	R	31	152	507	69	142	20	2	20	73	100	107	4	.280	.446
Barry Foote	C122	R	22	125	420	44	110	23	4	11	60	35	74	2	.262	.414
Larry Lintz	2B67, SS31, 3B1	B	24	113	319	60	76	10	1	0	20	44	50	50	.238	.276
Ron Fairly	1B67, OF20	L	35	101	282	35	69	9	1	12	43	57	28	2	.245	.411
Ron Woods	OF61	R	31	90	127	15	26	0	0	1	12	17	17	6	.205	.228
Hal Breeden	1B56	R	30	79	190	14	47	13	0	2	20	24	35	0	.247	.347
Pepe Frias	SS30, 3B27, 2B15, OF3	R	25	75	112	12	24	4	1	0	7	7	10	1	.214	.268
Boots Day	OF16	L	26	52	65	8	12	0	0	0	2	5	8	0	.185	.185
Bob Stinson (BT)	C29	B	28	38	87	4	15	2	0	1	6	15	16	1	.172	.230
Larry Parrish	3B24	R	20	25	69	9	14	5	0	0	4	6	19	0	.203	.275
Pepe Mangual	OF22	R	22	23	61	10	19	3	0	0	4	5	15	5	.311	.361
2 Jim Northrup	OF13	L	34	21	54	3	13	1	0	2	8	5	9	0	.241	.370
Terry Humphrey	C17	R	24	20	52	3	10	3	0	0	3	4	9	0	.192	.250

Gary Carter 20 R 11-27, Jose Morales 29 R 7-26, Larry Biittner 28 L 7-26, Warren Cromartie 20 L 3-17, Jerry White 21 B 4-10, Jim Lyttle 28 L 3-9, Tony Scott 22 B 2-7, Pat Scanlon 21 L 1-4

NAME	T	AGE	W	L	PCT	SV	G	GS	CG	IP	H	BB	SO	ShO	ERA
Totals		25	79	82	.491	27	161	161	35	1429	1340	544	822	8	3.60
Mike Torrez	R	27	15	8	.652	0	32	30	6	186	184	84	92	1	3.58
Steve Rogers	R	24	15	22	.405	0	38	38	11	254	255	80	154	1	4.46
Steve Renko	R	29	12	16	.429	0	37	35	8	228	222	81	138	1	4.03
Dennis Blair	R	20	11	7	.611	0	22	22	4	146	113	72	76	1	3.27
Chuck Taylor	R	32	6	2	.750	11	61	0	0	108	101	25	43	0	2.17
Ernie McAnally	R	27	6	13	.316	0	25	21	5	129	126	56	79	2	4.47
Don Carrithers	R	24	5	2	.714	1	22	3	0	60	56	17	31	0	3.00
Tom Walker	R	25	4	5	.444	2	33	8	1	92	96	28	70	0	3.82
John Montague	R	26	3	4	.429	3	46	1	0	83	73	38	43	0	3.14
Don DeMola	R	21	1	0	1.000	0	25	1	0	58	46	21	47	0	3.10
Dale Murray	R	24	1	1	.500	10	32	0	0	70	46	23	31	0	1.03
Bob Gebhard	R	31	0	0	–	0	1	0	0	2	5	1	0	0	4.50
Terry Enyart	L	23	0	0	–	0	2	0	0	2	4	4	2	0	13.50
Balor Moore	L	23	0	2	.000	0	8	2	0	14	13	15	16	0	3.86

NEW YORK 5th 71-91 .438 17 — YOGI BERRA

NAME	G by POS	B	AGE	G	AB	R	H	2B	3B	HR	RBI	BB	SO	SB	BA	SA
TOTALS			28	162	5468	572	1286	183	22	96	538	597	735	43	.235	.329
John Milner	1B133	L	24	137	507	70	128	19	0	20	63	66	77	10	.252	.408
Felix Millan	2B134	R	30	136	518	50	139	15	2	1	33	31	14	5	.268	.311
Bud Harrelson (BH)	SS97	B	30	106	331	48	75	10	0	1	13	71	39	9	.227	.266
Wayne Garrett	3B144, SS9	L	26	151	522	55	117	14	3	13	53	89	96	4	.224	.337
Rusty Staub	OF147	L	30	151	561	65	145	22	2	19	78	77	39	2	.258	.406
Don Hahn	OF106	R	25	110	323	34	81	14	1	4	28	37	34	2	.251	.337
Cleon Jones (KJ)	OF120	R	31	124	461	62	130	23	1	13	60	38	79	3	.282	.421
Jerry Grote (HJ)	C94	R	31	97	319	25	82	8	1	5	36	33	33	0	.257	.335
Ted Martinez	SS75, 3B12, 2B11, OF10	R	26	116	334	32	73	15	7	2	43	14	40	3	.219	.323
Ken Boswell	2B28, 3B20, OF7	L	28	96	222	19	48	6	1	2	15	18	19	0	.216	.279
Ed Kranepool	OF33, 1B24	L	29	94	217	20	65	11	1	4	24	18	14	1	.300	.415
Dave Schneck	OF84	L	25	93	254	23	52	11	1	5	25	16	43	4	.205	.315
Duffy Dyer	C45	R	28	63	142	14	30	1	1	0	10	18	15	0	.211	.232
George Theodore	1B14, OF12	R	26	60	76	7	12	1	0	1	1	8	14	0	.158	.211
Ron Hodges	C44	L	25	59	136	16	30	4	0	4	14	19	11	0	.221	.338
Jim Gosger	OF24	L	31	26	33	3	3	0	0	0	0	3	2	0	.091	.091
Benny Ayala	OF20	R	23	23	68	9	16	1	0	2	8	7	17	0	.235	.338
Brock Pemberton	1B4	B	20	11	22	0	4	0	0	0	1	0	3	0	.182	.182
Bruce Boisclair	OF5	L	21	7	12	0	3	1	0	0	1	1	4	0	.250	.333
Rich Puig	2B3, 3B1	L	21	4	10	0	0	0	0	0	0	1	2	0	.000	.000
Ike Hampton	C1	B	22	4	4	0	0	0	0	0	1	0	1	0	.000	.000

NAME	T	AGE	W	L	PCT	SV	G	GS	CG	IP	H	BB	SO	ShO	ERA
		29	71	91	.438	14	162	162	46	1470	1433	504	908	15	3.42
Jerry Koosman	L	31	15	11	.577	0	35	35	13	265	258	85	188	0	3.36
Jon Matlack	L	24	13	15	.464	0	34	34	14	265	221	76	195	7	2.41
Tom Seaver	R	29	11	11	.500	0	32	32	12	236	199	75	201	5	3.20
Ray Sadecki	L	33	8	8	.500	0	34	10	3	103	107	35	46	1	3.41
Bob Apodaca	R	24	6	6	.500	3	35	8	1	103	92	42	54	0	3.50
Tug McGraw (SJ)	L	29	6	11	.353	3	41	4	1	89	96	32	54	1	4.15
Harry Parker	R	26	4	12	.250	4	40	16	1	131	145	46	58	0	3.92
2 Jack Aker (XJ)	R	33	2	1	.667	2	24	0	0	41	33	14	18	0	3.51
Bob Miller	R	35	2	2	.500	2	58	0	0	78	89	39	35	0	3.58
George Stone (SJ)	L	27	2	7	.222	0	15	13	1	77	103	21	29	0	5.03
Randy Sterling	R	23	1	1	.500	0	3	2	0	9	13	3	2	0	5.00
Craig Swan (EJ)	R	23	1	3	.250	0	7	5	0	30	28	21	10	0	4.50
Nino Espinosa	R	20	0	0	–	0	2	1	0	9	12	0	2	0	5.00
John Strohmayer	R	27	0	0	–	0	1	0	0	1	0	1	0	0	0.00
Jerry Cram	R	26	0	1	.000	0	10	0	0	22	22	4	8	0	1.64
Hank Webb	R	24	0	2	.000	0	3	2	0	10	15	10	8	0	7.20

CHICAGO 6th 66-96 .407 22 — WHITEY LOCKMAN 41-52 .441 JIM MARSHALL 25-44 .362

NAME	G by POS	B	AGE	G	AB	R	H	2B	3B	HR	RBI	BB	SO	SB	BA	SA
TOTALS			27	162	5574	669	1397	221	42	110	610	621	857	78	.251	.365
Billy Williams (FJ)	1B65, OF43	L	36	117	404	55	113	22	0	16	68	67	44	4	.280	.453
Vic Harris (KJ)	2B56	B	24	62	200	18	39	6	3	0	11	29	26	9	.195	.255
Don Kessinger	SS150	B	31	153	599	83	155	20	7	1	42	62	54	7	.259	.321
Bill Madlock (NJ)	3B121	R	23	128	453	65	142	21	5	9	54	42	63	11	.313	.442
Jose Cardenal	OF136	R	30	143	542	75	159	35	3	13	72	56	67	23	.293	.441
Rick Monday	OF139	L	28	142	538	84	158	19	7	20	58	70	94	7	.294	.467
Jerry Morales	OF143	R	25	151	534	70	146	21	7	15	82	46	63	2	.273	.423
Steve Swisher	C90	R	22	90	280	21	60	5	0	5	27	37	63	0	.214	.286
Andy Thornton	1B90, 3B1	R	24	107	303	41	79	16	4	10	46	48	50	2	.261	.439
Chris Ward	OF22, 1B6	L	25	92	137	8	28	4	0	1	15	18	13	0	.204	.255
George Mitterwald	C68	R	29	78	215	17	54	7	0	7	28	18	42	1	.251	.381
Carmen Fanzone	3B35, 2B10, 1B7, OF1	R	31	65	158	13	30	6	0	4	22	15	27	0	.190	.304
Dave Rosello	2B49, SS12	R	24	62	148	9	30	7	0	0	10	10	28	1	.203	.250
Jim Tyrone	OF32, 3B1	R	25	57	81	19	15	0	1	3	3	6	8	1	.185	.321
2 Billy Grabarkewitz	2B45, SS7, 3B6	R	28	53	125	21	31	3	2	1	12	21	28	1	.248	.328
Matt Alexander	3B19, OF4, 2B2	B	27	45	54	15	11	2	1	0	0	12	12	8	.204	.278
Rob Sperring	2B35, SS8	R	24	42	107	9	22	3	0	1	5	9	28	1	.206	.262
Pete LaCock	OF22, 1B11	L	22	35	110	9	20	4	1	1	8	12	16	0	.182	.264
Dick Stelmaszek	C16	L	25	25	87	4	15	2	0	1	7	10	6	0	.227	.341
Ron Dunn	2B21, 3B6	R	24	23	68	6	20	7	0	2	15	12	8	0	.294	.485
Tom Lundstedt	C22	B	25	22	32	1	3	0	0	0	0	5	7	0	.094	.094

Gene Hiser 25 L 4-17, Gonzalo Marquez 28 L 0-11, Adrian Garrett 31 L 0-8

NAME	T	AGE	W	L	PCT	SV	G	GS	CG	IP	H	BB	SO	ShO	ERA
		26	66	96	.407	26	162	162	23	1466	**1593**	576	895	6	4.28
Rick Reuschel	R	25	13	12	.520	0	41	38	8	241	262	83	160	2	4.29
Bill Bonham	R	25	11	**22**	.333	1	44	36	10	243	246	109	191	2	3.85
Steve Stone	R	26	8	6	.571	0	38	23	1	170	185	64	90	0	4.13
Burt Hooton	R	24	7	11	.389	1	48	21	3	176	214	51	94	1	4.81
Ken Frailing	L	26	6	9	.400	1	55	16	1	125	150	43	71	0	3.89
Dave LaRoche	L	26	5	6	.455	5	49	4	0	92	103	47	49	0	4.79
Jim Todd	R	26	4	2	.667	3	43	6	0	88	82	41	42	0	3.89
1 Horacio Pina	R	29	3	4	.429	4	34	0	0	47	49	28	32	0	4.02
Ray Burris	R	23	3	5	.375	1	40	5	0	75	91	26	40	0	6.60
Tom Dettore	R	26	3	5	.375	0	16	9	0	65	64	31	43	0	4.15
Oscar Zamora	R	29	3	9	.250	10	56	0	0	84	82	19	38	0	3.11
Mike Paul	L	29	0	1	.000	0	2	0	0	1	4	1	1	0	36.00
Jim Kremmel	L	26	0	2	.000	0	23	2	0	31	37	18	22	0	5.23
Herb Hutson (JJ)	R	24	0	2	.000	0	20	2	0	29	24	15	22	0	3.41

WEST DIVISION

LOS ANGELES 1st 102-60 .630 — WALT ALSTON

NAME	G by POS	B	AGE	G	AB	R	H	2B	3B	HR	RBI	BB	SO	SB	BA	SA
TOTALS			27	162	5557	**798**	1511	231	34	**139**	**744**	597	820	149	.272	**.401**
Steve Garvey	1B156	R	25	156	642	95	200	32	3	21	111	31	66	5	.312	.469
Dave Lopes	2B143	R	28	145	530	95	141	26	3	10	35	66	71	59	.266	.383
Bill Russell	SS160, OF1	R	25	160	553	61	149	18	6	5	65	53	53	14	.269	.351
Ron Cey	3B158	R	26	159	577	88	151	20	2	18	97	76	68	1	.262	.397
Willie Crawford	OF133	L	27	139	468	73	138	23	4	11	61	64	88	7	.295	.432
Jim Wynn	OF148	R	32	150	535	104	145	17	4	32	108	108	104	18	.271	.497
Bill Buckner	OF137, 1B6	L	24	145	580	83	182	30	3	7	58	30	24	31	.314	.412
Steve Yeager	C93	R	25	94	316	41	84	16	1	12	41	32	77	2	.266	.437
Joe Ferguson	C82, OF32	R	27	111	349	54	88	14	1	16	57	75	73	2	.252	.436
Tom Paciorek	OF77, 1B1	R	27	85	175	23	42	8	6	1	24	10	32	1	.240	.371
Von Joshua	OF35	L	26	81	124	11	29	5	1	1	16	7	17	3	.234	.315
Manny Mota	OF3	R	36	66	57	5	16	2	0	0	16	5	4	0	.281	.316
Lee Lacy	2B34, 3B1	R	26	48	78	13	22	6	0	0	8	2	14	2	.282	.359
Rick Auerbach	SS19, 2B10, 3B3	R	24	45	73	12	25	0	0	1	4	8	9	4	.342	.384
Ken McMullen (VR)	3B7, 2B3	R	32	44	60	5	15	1	0	3	12	2	12	0	.250	.417
Gail Hopkins	C2, 1B2	L	31	15	18	1	4	0	0	0	0	3	1	0	.222	.222
Jerry Royster	3B1, 2B1, OF1	R	21	6	0	2	0	0	0	0	0	0	0	0	–	–
John Hale	OF3	L	20	4	4	2	4	1	0	0	2	0	0	0	1.000	1.250

Chuck Manuel 30 L 1-3, Ivan DeJesus 21 R 1-3, Orlando Alvarez 22 R 0-1, Kevin Pasley 20 R 0-0

NAME	T	AGE	W	L	PCT	SV	G	GS	CG	IP	H	BB	SO	ShO	ERA
		30	**102**	60	**.630**	23	162	162	33	1465	1272	464	**943**	19	**2.97**
Andy Messersmith	R	28	**20**	6	.769	0	39	39	13	292	227	94	221	3	2.59
Don Sutton	R	29	19	9	.679	0	40	**40**	10	276	241	80	179	5	3.23
Mike Marshall	R	31	15	12	.556	**21**	**106**	0	0	208	191	56	143	0	2.42
Tommy John (EJ)	L	31	13	3	**.813**	0	22	22	5	153	133	42	78	3	2.59
Doug Rau	L	25	13	11	.542	0	36	35	3	198	191	70	126	1	3.73
Charlie Hough	R	26	9	4	.692	1	49	0	0	96	65	40	63	0	3.75
Al Downing	L	33	5	6	.455	0	21	16	1	98	94	45	63	1	3.67
Jim Brewer (XJ)	L	36	4	4	.500	0	24	0	0	39	29	10	26	0	2.54
Geoff Zahn	L	28	3	5	.375	0	21	10	1	80	78	16	33	0	2.03
Rick Rhoden	R	21	1	1	1.000	0	4	0	0	9	5	4	7	0	2.00
Greg Shanahan	R	26	0	0	–	0	4	0	0	7	7	5	2	0	3.86
Eddie Solomon	R	23	0	0	–	1	4	0	0	6	5	2	2	0	1.50
Rex Hudson	R	20	0	0	–	0	1	0	0	2	6	0	0	0	22.50

CINCINNATI 2nd 98-64 .605 4 — SPARKY ANDERSON

NAME	G by POS	B	AGE	G	AB	R	H	2B	3B	HR	RBI	BB	SO	SB	BA	SA
TOTALS			27	163	5535	776	1437	**271**	35	135	714	**693**	**940**	146	.260	.394
Tony Perez	1B157	R	32	158	596	81	158	28	2	28	101	61	112	1	.265	.460
Joe Morgan	2B142	L	30	149	512	107	150	31	3	22	67	120	69	58	.293	.494
Dave Concepcion	SS160	R	26	160	594	70	167	25	1	14	82	44	79	41	.281	.397
Dan Driessen	3B126, 1B47, OF3	L	21	150	470	63	132	23	6	7	56	48	62	10	.281	.400
George Foster	OF98	R	25	106	276	31	73	18	0	7	41	30	52	3	.264	.406
Cesar Geronimo	OF145	L	26	150	474	73	133	17	8	7	54	46	96	9	.281	.395
Pete Rose	OF163	B	33	163	652	**110**	185	**45**	7	3	51	106	54	2	.284	.388
Johnny Bench	C137, 3B36, 1B5	R	26	160	621	108	174	38	2	33	**129**	80	90	5	.280	.507
Darrell Chaney	3B81, 2B38, SS12	L	26	117	135	27	27	6	1	2	16	26	33	1	.200	.304
Ken Griffey	OF70	L	24	88	227	24	57	9	5	2	19	27	43	9	.251	.361
Terry Crowley	OF22, 1B7	L	27	84	125	11	30	12	0	1	20	10	16	1	.240	.360
Merv Rettenmund	OF69	R	31	80	208	30	45	6	0	6	28	37	39	5	.216	.332
Bill Plummer	C49, 3B1	R	27	50	120	7	27	7	0	2	10	6	21	1	.225	.333
Phil Gagliano	2B2, 3B1, 1B1	R	32	46	31	2	2	0	0	0	0	15	7	0	.065	.065
Andy Kosco (XJ)	3B8, OF1	R	32	33	37	3	7	2	0	0	5	7	8	0	.189	.243
Junior Kennedy	2B17, 3B5	R	23	22	19	2	3	0	0	0	0	6	4	0	.158	.158
Hal King	C5	L	30	20	17	1	3	1	0	0	3	3	4	0	.176	.235
Ray Knight	3B14	R	21	14	11	1	2	1	0	0	2	1	2	0	.182	.273
Ed Armbrister	OF4	R	25	9	7	0	2	0	0	0	0	1	1	0	.286	.286
Roger Freed	1B1	R	28	6	6	1	2	0	0	1	3	1	1	0	.333	.833

NAME	T	AGE	W	L	PCT	SV	G	GS	CG	IP	H	BB	SO	ShO	ERA
		27	98	64	.605	**27**	163	163	34	1466	1364	536	875	11	3.41
Jack Billingham	R	31	19	11	.633	0	36	35	8	212	233	64	103	3	3.95
Don Gullett	L	23	17	11	.607	0	36	35	10	243	201	88	183	3	3.04
Fred Norman	L	31	13	12	.520	0	35	26	8	186	170	68	141	2	3.15
Clay Carroll	R	33	12	5	.706	6	57	3	0	101	96	30	46	0	2.14
Clay Kirby	R	26	12	9	.571	0	36	35	7	231	210	91	160	1	3.27
Pedro Borbon	R	26	10	7	.588	14	73	0	0	139	133	32	53	0	3.24
Tom Carroll	R	21	4	3	.571	0	16	13	0	78	68	44	37	0	3.69
Roger Nelson (SJ)	R	30	4	4	.500	1	14	12	1	85	67	35	42	0	3.39
Tom Hall	L	26	3	1	.750	1	40	1	0	64	54	30	48	0	4.08
Will McEnaney	L	22	2	1	.667	2	24	0	0	27	24	9	13	0	4.33
Dick Baney	R	27	1	0	1.000	1	22	1	0	41	51	17	12	0	5.49
Pat Darcy	R	24	1	0	1.000	0	6	2	0	17	17	8	14	0	3.71
Rawly Eastwick	R	23	0	0	–	2	8	0	0	18	12	5	14	0	2.00
Mike McQueen	L	23	0	0	–	0	10	0	0	15	17	11	5	0	5.40
Pat Osburn	L	25	0	0	–	0	6	0	0	9	11	4	4	0	8.00

Gary Nolan (SJ) 26

ATLANTA 3rd 88-74 .543 14 — EDDIE MATHEWS 50-49 .505 CLYDE KING 38-25 .603

NAME	G by POS	B	AGE	G	AB	R	H	2B	3B	HR	RBI	BB	SO	SB	BA	SA
TOTALS			28	163	5533	661	1375	202	37	120	599	571	772	72	.249	.363
Dave Johnson	1B73, 2B71	R	31	136	454	56	114	18	0	15	62	75	59	1	.251	.390
Marty Perez	2B102, SS14, 3B6	R	27	127	447	51	116	20	5	2	34	35	51	2	.260	.340
Craig Robinson	SS142	R	25	145	452	52	104	4	6	0	29	30	57	11	.230	.265
Darrell Evans	3B160	L	27	160	571	99	137	21	3	25	79	**126**	88	4	.240	.419
Ralph Garr	OF139	L	28	143	606	87	**214**	24	**17**	11	54	28	52	26	**.353**	.503
Dusty Baker	OF148	R	25	149	574	80	147	35	0	20	69	71	87	18	.256	.422
Hank Aaron	OF89	R	40	112	340	47	91	16	0	20	69	39	29	1	.268	.491
Johnny Oates	C91	L	28	100	291	22	65	10	0	1	21	23	24	2	.223	.268
Rowland Office	OF119	L	21	131	248	20	61	16	1	3	31	16	30	5	.246	.355
Mike Lum (BY)	1B60, OF50	L	28	106	361	50	84	11	2	11	50	45	49	0	.233	.366
Frank Tepedino	1B46	L	26	78	169	11	39	5	1	0	16	9	13	1	.231	.272
Vic Correll	C59	R	28	73	202	20	48	15	1	4	29	21	38	0	.238	.381
Ivan Murrell	OF32, 1B13	R	29	73	133	11	33	1	1	2	12	5	35	0	.248	.316
Leo Foster	SS43, 2B10, 3B3, OF1	R	23	72	112	16	22	2	0	1	5	9	22	1	.196	.241
Paul Casanova	C33	R	32	42	104	5	21	0	0	0	8	5	17	0	.202	.202
Norm Miller	OF4	L	28	42	41	1	7	1	0	1	5	7	9	0	.171	.268

Jack Pierce 25 L 1-9, Larvell Blanks 24 R 2-8, Sonny Jackson 29 L 3-7, Rod Gilbreath 21 R 2-6, John Fuller 24 L 1-3

NAME	T	AGE	W	L	PCT	SV	G	GS	CG	IP	H	BB	SO	ShO	ERA
		29	88	74	.543	22	163	163	46	**1474**	1343	488	772	**21**	3.05
Phil Niekro	R	35	**20**	13	.606	1	41	39	**18**	**302**	249	88	195	6	2.38
Buzz Capra	R	26	16	8	.667	1	39	27	11	217	163	84	137	5	**2.28**
Carl Morton	R	30	16	12	.571	0	38	38	7	275	**293**	89	113	1	3.14
Ron Reed (BH)	R	31	10	11	.476	0	28	28	6	186	171	41	78	2	3.39
Tom House	L	27	6	2	.750	11	56	0	0	103	74	27	64	0	1.92
Roric Harrison (KJ)	R	27	6	11	.353	0	20	20	3	126	148	49	46	0	4.71
Lew Krausse	R	31	4	3	.571	0	29	4	0	67	65	32	27	0	4.16
Max Leon	R	24	4	7	.364	3	34	2	1	75	68	14	38	1	2.64
Joe Niekro	R	29	3	2	.600	0	27	2	0	43	36	18	31	0	3.56
Danny Frisella	R	28	3	4	.429	6	36	1	0	42	37	28	27	0	5.14
Mike Beard	L	24	0	0	–	0	6	0	0	9	5	1	7	0	3.00
Gary Gentry (EJ)	R	27	0	0	–	0	3	1	0	7	4	2	0	0	1.29
2 Mike Thompson	R	24	0	0	–	0	1	1	0	4	7	2	2	0	4.50
Jamie Easterly	L	21	0	0	–	0	3	0	0	3	6	4	0	0	15.00
1 Jack Aker	R	33	0	1	.000	0	17	0	0	17	17	9	7	0	3.71

HOUSTON 4th 81-81 .500 21 — PRESTON GOMEZ

NAME	G by POS	B	AGE	G	AB	R	H	2B	3B	HR	RBI	BB	SO	SB	BA	SA
TOTALS			27	162	5489	653	1441	222	41	110	603	471	864	108	.263	.378
Lee May	1B145	R	31	152	556	59	149	26	0	24	85	17	97	1	.268	.444
Tommy Helms	2B133	R	33	137	452	32	126	21	1	5	50	23	27	5	.279	.363
Roger Metzger	SS143	B	26	143	572	66	145	18	10	0	30	37	73	9	.253	.320
Doug Rader	3B152	R	29	152	533	61	137	27	3	17	78	60	131	7	.257	.415
Greg Gross	OF151	L	21	156	589	78	185	21	8	0	36	76	39	12	.314	.377
Cesar Cedeno	OF157	R	23	160	610	95	164	29	5	26	102	64	103	57	.269	.461
Bob Watson	OF140, 1B35	R	28	150	524	69	156	19	4	11	67	60	61	3	.298	.412
Milt May	C116	L	23	127	405	47	117	17	4	7	54	39	33	0	.289	.402
Larry Milbourne	2B87, SS8, OF4	B	23	112	136	31	38	2	1	0	9	10	14	6	.279	.309
Bob Gallagher	OF62, 1B4	L	25	102	87	13	15	2	0	0	3	12	23	1	.172	.195
Cliff Johnson	C28, 1B21	R	26	83	171	26	39	4	1	10	29	33	45	0	.228	.439
Wilbur Howard	OF50	B	25	64	111	19	24	4	0	2	5	5	18	4	.216	.306
Johnny Edwards	C32	L	36	50	117	8	26	7	1	1	10	11	12	1	.222	.325
Dave Campbell (HJ)	2B9, 1B6, 3B2, OF1	R	32	35	23	4	2	1	0	0	2	1	8	1	.087	.130
Denis Menke	1B12, 3B7, 2B3, SS2	R	33	30	29	2	3	1	0	0	1	4	10	0	.103	.138
1 Ollie Brown	OF20	R	30	27	69	8	15	1	0	3	6	4	15	0	.217	.362
Mick Kelleher	SS18	R	26	19	57	4	9	0	0	0	2	5	10	1	.158	.158
Ray Busse	3B8	R	25	19	34	3	7	1	0	0	0	3	12	0	.206	.235
Mike Easler		L	23	15	15	0	1	0	0	0	0	0	5	0	.067	.067
Skip Jutze	C7	R	28	8	13	0	3	0	0	0	1	1	1	0	.231	.231

NAME	T	AGE	W	L	PCT	SV	G	GS	CG	IP	H	BB	SO	ShO	ERA
		27	81	81	.500	18	162	162	36	1451	1396	601	738	18	3.46
Tom Griffin	R	26	14	10	.583	0	34	34	8	211	202	89	110	3	3.54
Larry Dierker	R	27	11	10	.524	0	33	33	7	224	189	82	150	3	2.89
Don Wilson	R	29	11	13	.458	0	33	27	5	205	170	100	112	4	3.07
Dave Roberts	L	29	10	12	.455	1	34	30	8	204	216	65	72	2	3.40
1 Claude Osteen	L	34	9	9	.500	0	23	21	7	138	158	47	45	2	3.72
Ken Forsch	R	27	8	7	.533	10	70	0	0	103	98	37	48	0	2.80
Mike Cosgrove	L	23	7	3	.700	2	45	0	0	90	76	39	47	0	3.50
Jerry Johnson	R	30	2	1	.667	0	34	0	0	45	47	24	32	0	4.80
Jim York	R	25	2	2	.500	1	28	0	0	38	48	19	15	0	3.32
J.R. Richard	R	24	2	3	.400	0	15	9	0	65	58	36	42	0	4.15
Fred Scherman	L	28	2	5	.286	4	53	0	0	61	67	26	35	0	4.13
Paul Siebert	L	21	1	1	.500	0	5	5	1	25	21	11	10	1	3.60
Mike Nagy	R	26	1	1	.500	0	9	0	0	13	17	5	5	0	8.31
Ramon de los Santos	L	25	1	1	.500	0	12	0	0	12	11	9	7	0	2.25
Doug Konieczny	R	22	0	3	.000	0	6	3	0	16	18	12	8	0	7.88

SAN FRANCISCO 5th 72-90 .444 — CHARLIE FOX 34-42 .447 WES WESTRUM 38-48 .442

NAME	G by POS	B	AGE	G	AB	R	H	2B	3B	HR	RBI	BB	SO	SB	BA	SA
TOTALS			25	162	5482	634	1380	228	38	93	568	548	869	107	.252	.358
Dave Kingman	1B91, 3B21, OF2	R	25	121	350	41	78	18	2	18	55	37	125	8	.223	.440
Tito Fuentes	2B103	B	30	108	390	33	97	15	2	0	22	22	32	7	.249	.297
Chris Speier	SS135, 2B4	R	24	141	501	55	125	19	5	9	53	62	64	3	.250	.361
Steve Ontiveros	3B75, 1B19, OF2	B	22	120	343	45	91	15	1	4	33	57	41	0	.265	.350
Bobby Bonds	OF148	R	28	150	567	97	145	22	8	21	71	95	134	41	.256	.434
Garry Maddox	OF131	R	24	135	538	74	153	31	3	8	50	29	64	21	.284	.398
Gary Matthews	OF151	R	23	154	561	87	161	27	6	16	82	70	69	11	.287	.442
Dave Rader	C109	L	25	113	323	26	94	16	2	1	26	31	21	1	.291	.362
Gary Thomasson	OF76, 1B15	L	22	120	315	41	77	14	3	2	29	38	56	7	.244	.327
Mike Phillips	3B34, 2B30, SS23	L	23	100	283	19	62	6	1	2	20	14	37	4	.219	.269
Ed Goodson	1B73, 3B8	L	26	98	298	25	81	15	0	6	48	18	22	1	.272	.383
Chris Arnold	2B31, 3B7, SS1	R	26	78	174	22	42	7	3	1	26	15	27	1	.241	.333
Bruce Miller	3B41, SS13, 2B9	R	27	73	198	19	55	7	1	0	16	11	15	1	.278	.323
Ken Rudolph	C56	R	27	57	158	11	41	3	0	0	10	21	15	0	.259	.278
John Boccabella	C26	R	33	29	80	6	11	3	0	0	5	4	6	0	.138	.175
Glenn Redmon	2B4	R	26	7	17	0	4	3	0	0	4	1	3	0	.235	.412
Jim Howarth	OF1	L	27	6	4	0	0	0	0	0	0	0	0	0	.000	.000
Damie Blanco		R	32	5	1	0	0	0	0	0	0	0	1	1	.000	.000

NAME	T	AGE	W	L	PCT	SV	G	GS	CG	IP	H	BB	SO	ShO	ERA
		25	72	90	.444	25	162	162	27	1439	1409	559	756	11	3.78
Mike Caldwell	L	25	14	5	.737	0	31	27	6	189	176	63	83	2	2.95
Jim Barr	R	26	13	9	.591	2	44	27	11	240	223	47	84	5	2.74
John D'Acquisto	R	21	12	14	.462	0	38	36	5	215	182	124	167	1	3.77
Elias Sosa	R	24	9	7	.563	6	68	0	0	101	94	45	48	0	3.48
Tom Bradley	R	27	8	11	.421	0	30	21	2	134	152	52	72	0	5.17
Randy Moffitt	R	25	5	7	.417	15	61	1	0	102	99	29	49	0	4.50
John Montefusco	R	24	3	2	.600	0	7	5	1	39	41	19	34	1	4.85
Ron Bryant (UJ)	L	26	3	15	.167	0	41	23	0	127	142	68	75	0	5.60
Butch Metzger	R	22	1	0	1.000	0	10	0	0	13	11	12	5	0	3.46
John Morris	L	32	1	1	.500	1	17	0	0	21	17	4	9	0	3.00
Charlie Williams	R	26	1	3	.250	0	39	7	0	100	93	31	48	0	2.79
Jim Willoughby	R	25	1	4	.200	0	18	4	0	41	51	9	12	0	4.61
Ed Halicki	R	23	1	8	.111	0	16	11	2	74	84	31	40	0	4.26
Don McMahon	R	44	0	0	–	0	9	0	0	12	13	2	5	0	3.00
Don Rose	R	27	0	0	–	0	2	0	0	1	4	1	0	0	9.00
Steve Barber	L	35	0	1	.000	1	13	0	0	14	13	12	13	0	5.14
Gary Lavelle	L	25	0	3	.000	0	10	0	0	17	14	10	12	0	2.12

SAN DIEGO 6th 60-102 .370 42 — JOHN McNAMARA

NAME	G by POS	B	AGE	G	AB	R	H	2B	3B	HR	RBI	BB	SO	SB	BA	SA
TOTALS			27	162	5415	541	1239	196	27	99	506	564	900	85	.229	.330
Willie McCovey	1B104	L	36	128	344	53	87	19	1	22	63	96	76	1	.253	.506
Derrel Thomas	2B104, 3B22, OF20, SS5	B	23	141	523	48	129	24	6	3	41	51	58	7	.247	.333
Enzo Hernandez	SS145	R	25	147	512	55	119	19	2	0	34	38	36	37	.232	.277
Dave Roberts	3B103, SS3, OF1	R	23	113	318	26	53	10	1	5	18	32	69	2	.167	.252
Dave Winfield	OF131	R	22	145	498	57	132	18	4	20	75	40	96	9	.265	.438
John Grubb	OF122, 3B2	L	25	140	444	53	127	20	4	8	42	46	47	4	.286	.403
Bobby Tolan (KJ)	OF88	L	28	95	357	45	95	16	1	8	40	20	41	7	.266	.384
Fred Kendall	C133	R	25	141	424	32	98	15	2	8	45	49	33	0	.231	.333
Nate Colbert	1B79, OF48	R	28	119	368	53	76	16	0	14	54	62	108	10	.207	.364
Clarence Gaston	OF63	R	30	106	267	19	57	11	0	6	33	16	51	0	.213	.322
Dave Hilton	3B55, 2B15	R	23	74	217	17	52	8	2	1	12	13	28	3	.240	.309
Glenn Beckert (NJ)	2B36, 3B1	R	33	64	172	11	44	1	0	0	7	11	8	0	.256	.262
Rich Morales	SS29, 2B18, 3B6, 1B1	R	30	54	61	8	12	3	0	1	5	8	6	1	.197	.295
Matty Alou	OF13, 1B2	L	35	48	81	8	16	3	0	0	3	5	6	0	.198	.235
2 Horace Clarke	2B21	B	34	42	90	5	17	1	0	0	4	8	6	0	.189	.200
Gene Locklear	OF12	L	24	39	74	7	20	3	2	1	3	4	12	0	.270	.405
Bob Barton (BG)	C29	R	32	30	81	4	19	1	0	0	7	13	19	0	.235	.247
Chris Cannizzaro	C26	R	36	26	60	2	11	1	0	0	4	6	11	0	.183	.200
Jerry Turner	OF13	L	20	17	48	4	14	1	0	0	2	3	5	2	.292	.313
Bill Almon	SS14	R	21	16	38	4	12	1	0	0	3	2	9	1	.316	.342

Mike Ivie 21 R 3-34, Randy Elliott 23 R 7-33, Bernie Williams 25 R 2-15, John Scott 22 R 1-15, Rod Gaspar 28 B 3-14

NAME	T	AGE	W	L	PCT	SV	G	GS	CG	IP	H	BB	SO	ShO	ERA
		25	60	**102**	.370	19	162	162	25	1446	1536	**715**	855	7	4.58
Larry Hardy	R	26	9	4	.692	2	76	1	0	102	129	44	57	0	4.68
Dan Spillner	R	22	9	11	.450	0	30	25	5	148	153	70	95	2	4.01
Dave Freisleben	R	22	9	14	.391	0	33	31	6	212	194	112	130	2	3.65
Bill Greif	R	24	9	19	.321	1	43	35	7	226	244	95	137	1	4.66
Randy Jones	L	24	8	**22**	.267	2	40	34	4	208	217	78	124	1	4.46
Vicente Romo	R	31	5	5	.500	9	54	1	0	71	78	37	26	0	4.56
Dave Tomlin	L	25	2	0	1.000	2	47	0	0	58	59	30	29	0	4.34
Rusty Gerhardt	L	23	2	1	.667	1	23	1	0	36	44	17	22	0	7.00
Mike Corkins (SA)	R	28	2	2	.500	0	25	2	0	56	53	32	41	0	4.82
Lowell Palmer	R	26	2	5	.286	0	22	8	1	73	68	59	52	0	5.67
Rich Troedson	L	24	1	1	.500	1	15	1	0	19	24	8	11	0	8.53
Jim McAndrew	R	30	1	4	.200	0	15	5	1	42	48	13	16	0	5.57
1 Steve Arlin	R	28	1	7	.125	1	16	12	1	64	85	37	18	0	5.91
Gary Ross	R	26	0	0	–	0	9	0	0	18	23	6	11	0	4.50
Ralph Garcia	R	25	0	0	–	0	8	0	0	10	15	7	9	0	6.30
Bill Laxton	L	26	0	1	.000	0	30	1	0	45	37	38	40	0	4.00
Mike Johnson	R	23	0	2	.000	0	18	0	0	21	29	15	15	0	4.71
Joe McIntosh	R	22	0	4	.000	0	10	5	0	37	36	17	22	0	3.65

WORLD SERIES – OAKLAND (AL) 4 LOS ANGELES (NL) 1

LINE SCORES

TEAM	1	2	3	4	5	6	7	8	9	10	11	12	R	H	E
Game 1 October 12 at Los Angeles															
OAK	0	1	0	0	1	0	0	1	0				3	6	2
LA	0	0	0	0	1	0	0	0	1				2	11	1
Holtzman, **Fingers** (5), Hunter — **Messersmith**, Marshall (9)															
Game 2 October 13 at Los Angeles															
OAK	0	0	0	0	0	0	0	0	2				2	6	0
LA	0	1	0	0	0	2	0	0	X				3	6	1
Blue, Odom (8) — **Sutton**, Marshall (9)															
Game 3 October 15 at Oakland															
LA	0	0	0	0	0	0	0	1	1				2	7	2
OAK	0	0	2	1	0	0	0	0	X				3	5	2
Downing, Brewer (4), Hough (5), Marshall (7) — **Hunter**, Fingers (8)															
Game 4 October 16 at Oakland															
LA	0	0	0	2	0	0	0	0	0				2	7	1
OAK	0	0	1	0	0	4	0	0	X				5	7	0
Messersmith, Marshall (7) — **Holtzman**, Fingers (8)															
Game 5 October 17 at Oakland															
LA	0	0	0	0	0	2	0	0	0				2	5	1
OAK	1	1	0	0	0	0	1	0	X				3	6	1
Sutton, **Marshall** (6) — Blue, **Odom** (7), Fingers (8)															

COMPOSITE BATTING

NAME	POS	G	AB	R	H	2B	3B	HR	RBI	BA
Oakland (AL)										
Totals		5	142	16	30	4	0	4	14	.211
Rudi	LF-1B	5	18	1	6	0	0	**1**	**4**	.333
Campaneris	SS	5	17	1	6	**2**	0	0	2	.353
North	CF	5	17	**3**	1	0	0	0	0	.059
Bando	3B	5	16	**3**	1	0	0	0	2	.063
Jackson	RF	5	14	**3**	4	1	0	**1**	1	.286
Fosse	C	5	14	1	2	0	0	**1**	1	.143
Green	2B	5	13	1	0	0	0	0	1	.000
Tenace	1B	5	9	0	2	0	0	0	0	.222
C. Washington	RF-CF-LF	5	7	1	4	0	0	0	0	.571
Holtzman	P	2	4	2	2	1	0	**1**	1	.500
Blue	P	2	4	0	0	0	0	0	0	.000
Holt	1B	4	3	0	2	0	0	0	2	.667
Fingers	P	4	2	0	0	0	0	0	0	.000
Hunter	P	2	2	0	0	0	0	0	0	.000
Alou	PH	1	1	0	0	0	0	0	0	.000
Mangual	PH	1	1	0	0	0	0	0	0	.000
H. Washington	PR	3	0	0	0	0	0	0	0	–
Haney	C	2	0	0	0	0	0	0	0	–
Maxvill	2B	2	0	0	0	0	0	0	0	–
Odom	P	2	0	0	0	0	0	0	0	–
Los Angeles (NL)										
Totals		5	158	11	36	4	1	4	10	.228
Garvey	1B	5	**21**	2	8	0	0	0	1	**.381**
Buckner	LF	5	20	1	5	1	0	**1**	1	.250
Russell	SS	5	18	0	4	0	**1**	0	2	.222
Lopes	2B	5	18	2	2	0	0	0	0	.111
Cey	3B	5	17	1	3	0	0	0	0	.176
Wynn	CF	5	16	1	3	1	0	**1**	2	.188
Ferguson	RF-C	5	16	2	2	0	0	**1**	2	.125
Yeager	C	4	11	0	4	1	0	0	1	.364
Crawford	RF	3	6	1	2	0	0	**1**	1	.333
Messersmith	P	2	4	0	2	0	0	0	0	.500
Joshua	PH	4	4	0	0	0	0	0	0	.000
Sutton	P	2	3	0	0	0	0	0	0	.000
Paciorek	PH-PR	3	2	1	1	1	0	0	0	.500
Lacy	PH	1	1	0	0	0	0	0	0	.000
Downing	P	1	1	0	0	0	0	0	0	.000
Marshall	P	5	0	0	0	0	0	0	0	–
Auerbach	PR	1	0	0	0	0	0	0	0	–
Brewer	P	1	0	0	0	0	0	0	0	–
Hough	P	1	0	0	0	0	0	0	0	–

COMPOSITE PITCHING

NAME	G	IP	H	BB	SO	W	L	SV	ERA
Oakland (AL)									
Totals	5	44	36	16	32	4	1	3	2.05
Blue	2	13.2	10	**7**	9	0	1	0	3.29
Holtzman	2	12	**13**	4	10	**1**	0	0	1.50
Fingers	4	9.1	8	2	6	**1**	0	**2**	1.93
Hunter	2	7.2	5	2	5	**1**	0	1	1.17
Odom	2	1.1	0	1	2	**1**	0	0	0.00
Los Angeles (NL)									
Totals	5	42	30	16	42	1	4	1	2.79
Messersmith	2	**14**	11	**7**	**12**	0	**2**	0	4.50
Sutton	2	13	9	3	**12**	**1**	0	0	2.77
Marshall	**5**	9	6	1	10	0	1	1	**1.00**
Downing	1	3.2	4	4	3	0	1	0	2.45
Hough	1	2	0	1	4	0	0	0	0.00
Brewer	1	0.1	0	0	1	0	0	0	0.00

1975 Coming Up Red

As a result of a contract dispute with Oakland owner Charles O. Finley, Catfish Hunter was made a free agent—a move which precipitated "the most celebrated auction in baseball history". The New York Yankees got Hunter for a package which cost them over $3 million. That deal, and the trade of Bobby Murcer to the Giants for Bobby Bonds, was enought to make New York a pre-season pick along with Baltimore to win the American League East. But the team taken slightly, the Boston Red Sox, came up with two sensational rookie finds and beat out the Orioles, who didn't get into high gear until the end of the season, and the Yankees, who suffered a rash of injuries. Of the two rookies—Fred Lynn and Jim Rice—Lynn took most of the headlines by playing a flawless centerfield, hitting .331 with 21 homers and 105 runs batted in, and becoming the first man to win both the MVP and rookie-of-the-year awards. Rice, althought suffering a broken wrist in late September, finished with a .309 average, 22 homers, and 102 runs batted in.

In the A.L. West, the A's seemed ripe to be overthrown without Hunter, but despite the gap in the pitching rotation and Sal Bando's poor season, the A's once again captured the Western title handily by beating back a late challenge from the Kansas City Royals. To supplement the familiar faces on the Oakland roster, Claudell Washington blossomed into a dangerous hitter and Billy Williams came over from the National League to provide power as the designated hitter.

In the N.L. East, the winner was also familiar as the Pittsburgh Pirates held off the Phillies to capture the title for the fifth time in six years. The Bucs had a balanced squad, highlighted by a seven-for-seven day at the plate by second baseman Rennie Stennett. In the West, Cincinnati put together a 41-9 record in late May to pull away from the injury-ridden defending champs, the Los Angeles Dodgers. The Reds' devastating attack—which won the division by 20 games—featured the hitting of Joe Morgan, Pete Rose, Tony Perez, and Johnny Bench, while Don Gullett spearheaded a mound staff that was the deepest in recent Cincinnati history.

The Reds continued their domination in the playoffs by taking Pittsburgh in three straight for their third pennant in six years. Oakland, also favored to win their fourth straight pennant, was surprised and embarrassed by Boston, which easily won the playoffs in three straight.

In the World Series, favorite Cincinnati was looking for their first title since 1940. Boston had also suffered a drought by not winning a Series since 1918. The Red Sox were not expected to provide much of a challenge, but they kept their season-long performance intact in a Series which proved the most exciting in years and produced a folk hero for Boston in pitcher Luis Tiant. The clubs battled back and forth, with the Reds winning three of the first five games—one on a disputed extra innings interference call. The sixth game crammed a heaping portion of drama into twelve innings, with superb fielding plays by George Foster and Dwight Evans and a three-run pinch homer by Bernie Carbo paving the way for Carlton Fisk's game-winning homer in the bottom of the twelfth for a 7-6 Boston victory. The seventh game, watched by an estimated 71 million TV viewers, saw the Reds triumph in the ninth inning on a bloop single by Joe Morgan for 4-3 win.

Beyond the Series, there were many other events which made up the year: Rod Carew won his fourth straight A.L. batting title, Frank Robinson led the Cleveland Indians as the first black manager in major league history, Nolan Ryan notched his fourth no-hitter, Juan Marichal, Mel Stottlemyre, and Bob Gibson called it quits, and Hank Aaron moved to Milwaukee as a DH, where he hit 12 homers to run his career total to 745. Death also took its toll and counted Houston pitcher Don Wilson and the game's most colorful character, Casey Stengel.

1975 AMERICAN LEAGUE

EAST DIVISION

NAME	G by POS	B	AGE	G	AB	R	H	2B	3B	HR	RBI	BB	SO	SB	BA	SA
BOSTON 1st 95-65 .594			**DARRELL JOHNSON**													
TOTALS			27	160	5448	**796**	**1500**	**284**	44	134	**756**	565	741	66	**.275**	**.417**
Carl Yastrzemski	1B140, OF8, DH2	L	35	149	543	91	146	30	1	14	60	87	67	8	.269	.405
2 Denny Doyle	2B84, 3B6, SS2	L	31	89	310	50	96	21	2	4	36	14	11	5	.310	.429
Rick Burleson	SS157, 3B1	R	24	158	580	66	146	25	1	6	62	45	44	8	.252	.329
Rico Petrocelli	3B112, DH1, SS1	R	32	115	402	31	96	15	1	7	59	41	66	0	.239	.333
Dwight Evans	OF115, DH7	R	23	128	412	61	113	24	6	13	56	47	60	3	.274	.456
Fred Lynn	OF144	L	23	145	528	**103**	175	**47**	7	21	105	62	90	10	.331	**.566**
Jim Rice	OF90, DH54	R	22	144	564	92	174	29	4	22	102	36	122	10	.309	.491
Carlton Fisk (BA)	C71, DH6	R	27	79	263	47	87	14	4	10	52	27	32	4	.331	.529
Cecil Cooper	DH54, 1B35	L	25	106	305	49	95	17	6	14	44	19	33	1	.311	.544
Bernie Carbo	OF85, DH13	L	27	107	319	64	82	21	3	15	50	83	69	2	.257	.483
Doug Griffin	2B99, SS1	R	28	100	287	21	69	6	0	1	29	18	29	2	.240	.272
Juan Beniquez	OF44, DH20, 3B14	R	25	78	254	43	73	14	4	2	17	25	26	7	.291	.402
Rick Miller	OF65	L	27	77	108	21	21	2	1	0	15	21	20	3	.194	.231
Bob Heise	3B45, 2B14, SS4, 1B1	R	28	63	126	12	27	3	0	0	21	4	6	0	.214	.238
Bob Montgomery	C53, 1B6, DH3	R	31	62	195	16	44	10	1	2	26	4	37	1	.226	.318
Tim Blackwell	C57, DH2	B	22	59	132	15	26	3	2	0	6	19	13	0	.197	.250
Tony Conigliaro (GJ)	DH15	R	30	21	57	8	7	1	0	2	9	8	9	1	.123	.246
1 Tim McCarver	C7, 1B1	L	33	12	21	1	8	2	1	0	3	1	3	0	.381	.571
Dick McAuliffe (VR)	3B7	L	35	7	15	0	2	0	0	0	1	1	2	0	.133	.133
2 Deron Johnson	1B2, DH1	R	36	3	10	2	6	0	0	1	3	2	0	0	.600	.900

Steve Dillard 23 R 2-5, Andy Merchant 24 L 2-4, Butch Hobson 23 R 1-4, Kim Andrew 21 R 1-2, Buddy Hunter 27 R 0-1

NAME	T	AGE	W	L	PCT	SV	G	GS	CG	IP	H	BB	SO	ShO	ERA
		29	95	65	.594	31	160	160	62	1437	1463	490	720	11	3.98
Rick Wise	R	29	19	12	.613	0	35	35	17	255	262	72	141	1	3.95
Luis Tiant	R	34	18	14	.563	0	35	35	18	260	262	72	142	2	4.02
Bill Lee	L	28	17	9	.654	0	41	34	17	260	274	69	78	4	3.95
Roger Moret	L	25	14	3	**.824**	1	36	16	4	145	132	76	80	1	3.60
Reggie Cleveland	R	27	13	9	.591	0	31	20	3	171	173	52	78	1	4.42
Jim Willoughby	R	26	5	2	.714	8	24	0	0	48	46	16	29	0	3.56
Dick Pole (BY)	R	24	4	6	.400	0	18	11	2	90	102	32	42	1	4.40
Dick Drago	R	30	2	2	.500	15	40	2	0	73	69	31	43	0	3.82
Diego Segui	R	37	2	5	.286	6	33	1	1	71	71	43	45	0	4.82
Jim Burton	L	25	1	2	.333	1	29	4	0	53	58	19	39	0	2.89
Rick Kreuger	L	26	0	0	–	0	2	0	0	4	3	1	1	0	4.50
Steve Barr	L	23	0	1	.000	0	3	2	0	7	11	7	2	0	2.57

NAME	G by POS	B	AGE	G	AB	R	H	2B	3B	HR	RBI	BB	SO	SB	BA	SA
BALTIMORE 2nd 90-69 .566 4.5			**EARL WEAVER**													
TOTALS			31	159	5474	682	1382	224	33	124	635	580	834	104	.252	.373
Lee May	1B144, DH2	R	32	146	580	67	152	28	3	20	99	36	91	1	.262	.424
Bobby Grich	2B150	R	26	150	524	81	136	26	4	13	57	107	88	14	.260	.399
Mark Belanger	SS152	R	31	152	442	44	100	11	1	3	27	36	53	16	.226	.276
Brooks Robinson	3B143	R	38	144	482	50	97	15	1	6	53	44	33	0	.201	.274
Ken Singleton	OF155	B	28	155	586	88	176	37	4	15	55	118	82	3	.300	.454
Paul Blair	OF138, DH1, 1B1	R	31	140	440	51	96	13	4	5	31	25	82	17	.218	.300
Don Baylor	OF135, DH7, 1B2	R	26	145	524	79	148	21	6	25	76	53	64	32	.282	.489
Dave Duncan	C95	R	29	96	307	30	63	7	0	12	41	16	82	0	.205	.345
Tommy Davis	DH111	R	36	116	460	43	130	14	1	6	57	23	52	2	.283	.357
Al Bumbry	DH48, OF39, 3B1	L	28	114	349	47	94	19	4	2	32	32	81	16	.269	.364
Ellie Hendricks	C83	L	34	85	223	32	48	8	2	8	38	34	40	0	.215	.377
Jim Northrup	OF58, DH3	L	35	84	194	27	53	13	0	5	29	22	22	0	.273	.418
2 Tony Muser	1B62	L	27	80	82	11	26	3	0	0	11	8	9	0	.317	.354
Doug DeCinces	3B34, SS13, 2B11, 1B2	R	24	61	167	20	42	6	3	4	23	13	32	0	.251	.395
Tim Nordbrook	SS36, 2B3	R	25	40	34	6	4	1	0	0	0	7	7	0	.118	.147
Tom Shopay	OF13, DH3, C1	L	30	40	31	4	5	1	0	0	2	4	7	3	.161	.194
1 Andy Etchebarren (BE)	C7	R	32	8	20	0	4	1	0	0	3	0	3	0	.200	.250

Royle Stillman 24 L 6-14, Bob Bailor 23 R 1-7, Jim Hutto 27 R 0-5, Larry Harlow 23 L 1-3

NAME	T	AGE	W	L	PCT	SV	G	GS	CG	IP	H	BB	SO	ShO	ERA
		29	90	69	.566	21	159	159	**70**	1451	1285	500	717	**19**	**3.17**
Jim Palmer	R	29	**23**	11	.676	1	39	38	25	323	253	80	193	**10**	**2.09**
Mike Torrez	R	28	20	9	.690	0	36	36	16	271	238	**133**	119	2	3.06
Mike Cuellar	L	38	14	12	.538	0	36	36	17	256	229	84	105	5	3.66
Ross Grimsley	L	25	10	13	.435	0	35	32	8	197	210	47	89	1	4.07
Doyle Alexander	R	24	8	8	.500	1	32	11	3	133	127	47	46	1	3.05
Dyar Miller	R	29	6	3	.667	8	30	0	0	46	32	16	33	0	2.74
Grant Jackson	L	32	4	3	.571	7	41	0	0	48	42	21	39	0	3.38
Paul Mitchell	R	24	3	0	1.000	0	11	4	1	57	41	19	31	0	3.63
Wayne Garland	R	24	2	5	.286	4	29	1	0	87	80	31	46	0	3.72
Mike Flanagan	L	23	0	1	.000	0	2	1	0	10	9	6	7	0	2.70
Dave Johnson	R	26	0	1	.000	0	6	0	0	9	8	7	4	0	4.00
1 Bob Reynolds	R	28	0	1	.000	0	7	0	0	6	11	1	1	0	9.00
1 Jesse Jefferson	R	26	0	2	.000	0	4	0	0	8	5	8	4	0	2.25

NAME	G by POS	B	AGE	G	AB	R	H	2B	3B	HR	RBI	BB	SO	SB	BA	SA
NEW YORK 3rd 83-77 .519 12			**BILL VIRDON 53-51 .510**				**BILLY MARTIN 30-26 .536**									
TOTALS			29	160	5415	681	1430	230	39	110	642	486	710	102	.264	.382
Chris Chambliss	1B147	L	26	150	562	66	171	38	4	9	72	29	50	0	.304	.434
Sandy Alomar	2B150	B	31	151	489	61	117	18	4	2	39	26	58	28	.239	.305
Fred Stanley	SS83, 2B33, 3B1	R	27	117	252	34	56	5	1	0	15	15	27	3	.222	.250
Graig Nettles	3B157	L	30	157	581	71	155	24	4	21	91	51	88	1	.267	.430
Bobby Bonds	OF129, DH12	R	29	145	529	93	143	26	3	32	85	89	137	30	.270	.512
Elliott Maddox (KJ)	OF55, 2B1	R	27	55	218	36	67	10	3	1	23	21	24	9	.307	.394
Roy White	OF135, 1B7, DH2	B	31	148	556	81	161	32	5	12	59	72	50	16	.290	.430
Thurman Munson	C130, DH22, 1B2, OF2, 3B1	R	28	157	597	83	190	24	3	12	102	45	52	3	.318	.429
Ron Blomberg	DH27, OF1	L	26	34	106	18	27	8	2	4	17	13	10	0	.255	.481
Jim Mason	SS93, 2B1	L	24	94	223	17	34	3	2	2	16	22	49	0	.152	.211
Walt Williams	OF31, DH17, 2B6	R	31	82	185	27	52	5	1	5	16	8	23	0	.281	.400
Ed Herrmann	DH35, C24	L	28	80	200	16	51	9	2	6	30	16	23	0	.255	.410
Lou Piniella	OF46, DH12	R	31	74	199	7	39	4	1	0	22	16	22	0	.196	.226
Rick Dempsey	C19, DH18, OF8, 3B1	R	25	71	145	18	38	8	0	1	11	21	15	0	.262	.338
Alex Johnson	DH28, OF7	R	32	52	119	15	31	5	1	1	15	7	21	2	.261	.345
Rick Bladt	OF51	R	28	52	117	13	26	3	1	1	11	11	8	6	.222	.291
2 Rich Coggins	OF36, DH9	L	24	51	107	7	24	1	0	1	6	7	16	3	.224	.262
3 Eddie Brinkman	SS29, 3B4, 2B3	R	33	44	63	2	11	4	1	0	2	3	6	0	.174	.270
Terry Whitfield	OF25, DH1	L	22	28	81	9	22	1	1	0	7	1	17	1	.272	.309
Bob Oliver	1B8, DH3, 3B1	R	32	18	38	3	5	1	0	0	1	1	9	0	.132	.158

Kerry Dineen 23 L 8-22, Dave Bergman 22 L 0-17, Otto Velez 24 R 2-8, Larry Murray 22 B 0-1, Eddie Leon 28 R 0-0

NAME	T	AGE	W	L	PCT	SV	G	GS	CG	IP	H	BB	SO	ShO	ERA
		29	83	77	.519	20	160	160	**70**	1424	1325	502	809	11	3.29
Catfish Hunter	R	29	**23**	14	.622	0	39	39	**30**	**328**	248	83	177	7	2.58
Doc Medich	R	26	16	16	.500	0	38	37	15	272	271	72	132	2	3.51
Rudy May	L	30	14	12	.538	0	32	31	13	212	179	99	146	1	3.06
Pat Dobson	R	33	11	14	.440	0	33	30	7	208	205	83	129	1	4.07
Larry Gura	L	27	7	8	.467	0	26	20	5	151	173	41	65	0	3.52
Dick Tidrow	R	28	6	3	.667	5	37	0	0	69	65	31	38	0	3.13
Sparky Lyle	L	30	5	7	.417	6	49	0	0	89	94	36	65	0	3.13
Tippy Martinez	L	25	1	2	.333	8	23	2	0	37	27	32	20	0	2.68
Dave Pagan	R	25	0	0	–	1	13	0	0	31	30	13	18	0	4.06
Rick Saywer	R	27	0	0	–	0	4	0	0	6	7	2	3	0	3.00
1 Mike Wallace	L	24	0	0	–	0	3	0	0	4	11	1	2	0	15.75
Ron Guidry	L	24	0	1	.000	0	10	1	0	16	15	9	15	0	3.38

CLEVELAND 4th 79-80 .497 15.5 — FRANK ROBINSON

NAME	G by POS	B	AGE	G	AB	R	H	2B	3B	HR	RBI	BB	SO	SB	BA	SA
TOTALS			26	159	5404	688	1409	201	25	153	643	525	667	106	.261	.392
Boog Powell	1B121,DH5	L	33	134	435	64	129	18	0	27	86	59	72	1	.297	.524
Duane Kuiper	2B87,DH1	L	25	90	346	42	101	11	1	0	25	30	26	19	.292	.329
Frank Duffy	SS145	R	28	146	482	44	117	22	2	1	47	27	60	10	.243	.303
Buddy Bell	3B153	R	23	153	553	66	150	20	4	10	59	51	72	6	.271	.376
George Hendrick	OF143	R	25	145	561	82	145	21	2	24	86	40	78	6	.258	.431
Rick Manning	OF118,DH1	L	20	120	480	69	137	16	5	3	35	44	62	19	.285	.358
Charlie Spikes	OF103,DH2	R	24	111	345	41	79	13	3	11	33	30	51	7	.229	.380
Alan Ashby	C87,1B2,DH1,3B1	B	23	90	254	32	57	10	1	5	32	30	42	3	.224	.331
Rico Carty	DH72,1B26,OF12	R	36	118	383	57	118	19	1	18	64	45	31	2	.308	.504
Oscar Gamble	OF82,DH29	L	24	121	348	60	91	16	3	15	45	53	39	11	.261	.454
Johnny Ellis	C84,DH3,1B2	R	26	92	296	22	68	11	1	7	32	14	33	0	.230	.345
Johnny Lowenstein	OF36,DH31,3B8,2B2	L	28	91	265	37	64	5	1	12	33	28	28	15	.242	.404
Jack Brohamer (PJ)	2B66	L	25	69	217	15	53	5	0	6	16	14	14	2	.244	.350
Ed Crosby	SS30,2B19,3B13	L	26	61	128	12	30	3	0	0	7	13	14	0	.234	.258
Frank Robinson (SJ)	DH42	R	39	49	118	19	28	5	0	9	24	29	15	0	.237	.508
Ken Berry	OF18,DH5	R	34	25	40	6	8	1	0	0	1	1	7	0	.200	.225
Tommy McCraw	1B16,OF3	L	34	23	51	7	14	1	1	2	5	7	7	4	.275	.451
2 Bill Sudakis	1B12,C6,DH1	B	29	20	46	4	9	0	0	1	3	4	7	0	.196	.261

1 Leron Lee 27 L 3-23, Joe Lis 28 R 4-13, Rick Cerone 21 R 3-12, Tommy Smith 26 L 1-8
Angel Hermoso (KJ) 29

NAME	T	AGE	W	L	PCT	SV	G	GS	CG	IP	H	BB	SO	ShO	ERA
		28	79	80	.497	32	159	159	37	1435	1395	599	800	6	3.84
Fritz Peterson (HJ)	L	33	14	8	.636	0	25	25	6	146	154	40	47	2	3.95
Dennis Eckersley	R	20	13	7	.650	2	34	24	6	187	147	90	152	2	2.60
2 Roric Harrison	R	28	7	7	.500	0	19	19	4	126	137	46	52	0	4.79
Eric Raich	R	23	7	8	.467	0	18	17	2	93	118	31	34	0	5.52
Rick Waits	L	23	6	2	.750	1	16	7	3	70	57	25	34	0	2.96
1 Gaylord Perry	R	36	6	9	.400	0	15	15	10	122	120	34	85	1	3.54
Don Hood	L	25	6	10	.375	0	29	19	2	135	136	57	51	0	4.40
Dave LaRoche	L	27	5	3	.625	17	61	0	0	82	61	57	94	0	2.20
Tom Buskey (XJ)	R	28	5	3	.625	7	50	0	0	77	69	29	29	0	2.57
2 Jim Bibby	R	30	5	9	.357	1	24	12	2	113	99	50	62	0	3.20
Fred Beene (SJ)	R	32	1	0	1.000	1	19	1	0	47	63	25	20	0	6.89
2 Blue Moon Odom	R	30	1	0	1.000	0	3	1	1	10	4	8	10	1	2.70
2 Jackie Brown	R	32	1	2	.333	1	25	3	1	69	72	29	41	0	4.28
Jim Kern	R	26	1	2	.333	0	13	7	0	72	60	45	55	0	3.75
1 Jim Perry	R	39	1	6	.143	0	8	6	0	38	46	18	11	0	6.63
Jim Strickland	L	29	0	0	–	0	4	0	0	5	4	2	3	0	1.80
Larry Andersen	R	22	0	0	–	0	3	0	0	6	4	2	4	0	4.50
1 Dick Bosman	R	31	0	2	.000	0	6	3	0	29	33	8	11	0	4.03
3 Bob Reynolds	R	28	0	2	.000	2	5	0	0	10	11	3	5	0	4.50

Steve Kline (EJ) 27

MILWAUKEE 5th 68-94 .420 28 — DEL CRANDALL

NAME	G by POS	B	AGE	G	AB	R	H	2B	3B	HR	RBI	BB	SO	SB	BA	SA
TOTALS			27	162	5378	675	1343	242	34	146	632	553	**922**	65	.250	.389
George Scott	1B144,3B12,3B5	R	31	158	617	86	176	26	4	**36**	**109**	51	97	6	.285	.515
Pete Garcia (XJ)	2B94,DH1	R	25	98	302	40	68	15	2	6	38	18	59	12	.225	.348
Robin Yount	SS145	R	19	147	558	67	149	28	2	8	52	33	69	12	.267	.367
Don Money (GJ)	3B99,SS7	R	28	109	405	58	112	16	1	15	43	31	51	7	.277	.432
Sixto Lezcano	OF129,DH2	R	21	134	429	55	106	19	3	11	43	46	93	5	.247	.382
2 Bill Sharp	OF124	L	25	125	373	37	95	27	3	1	34	19	26	0	.255	.351
Gorman Thomas	OF113,DH6	R	24	121	240	34	43	12	2	10	28	31	84	4	.179	.371
Darrell Porter	C124,DH2	L	23	130	409	66	95	12	5	18	60	87	77	2	.232	.418
Hank Aaron	DH128,OF3	R	41	137	465	45	109	16	2	12	60	70	51	0	.234	.355
Kurt Bevacqua	3B60,2B32,SS5,1B3,DH1	R	28	104	258	30	59	14	0	2	24	26	45	3	.229	.306
Bobby Mitchell	OF72,DH11	R	31	93	229	39	57	14	3	9	41	25	69	3	.249	.454
Mike Hegan	OF42,1B27,DH2	L	32	93	203	19	51	11	0	5	22	31	42	1	.251	.379
Charlie Moore	C47,OF22,DH1	R	22	73	241	26	70	20	1	1	29	17	31	1	.290	.394
2 Bobby Darwin (BH)	OF43,DH9	R	32	55	186	19	46	6	2	8	23	11	54	4	.247	.430
Bobby Sheldon	2B44,DH6	L	24	53	181	17	52	3	3	0	14	13	14	0	.287	.337
T. Johnson (EJ)	2B11,3B11,SS10,DH3,1B2	L	25	38	85	6	12	1	0	0	2	6	17	3	.141	.153
1 Johnny Briggs (NJ)	OF21	L	31	28	74	12	22	1	0	3	5	20	13	0	.297	.432
1 Bob Coluccio	OF22	R	23	22	62	8	12	0	1	1	5	11	11	1	.194	.274
Tommy Bianco	3B7,1B5,DH2	B	22	18	34	6	6	1	0	0	0	3	7	0	.176	.206

Jack Lind 29 B 1-20, Rob Ellis 24 R 2-7

NAME	T	AGE	W	L	PCT	SV	G	GS	CG	IP	H	BB	SO	ShO	ERA
		25	68	94	.420	34	162	162	36	1432	**1496**	624	643	10	4.34
Pete Broberg	R	25	14	16	.467	0	38	32	7	220	219	106	100	2	4.13
Jim Colborn	R	29	11	13	.458	2	36	29	8	206	215	65	79	1	4.28
Jim Slaton	R	25	11	18	.379	0	37	33	10	217	238	90	119	3	4.52
Eduardo Rodriguez	R	23	7	0	1.000	7	43	1	0	88	77	44	65	0	3.48
Billy Champion (AJ)	R	27	6	6	.500	0	27	13	3	110	125	55	40	1	5.89
Billy Travers	L	22	6	11	.353	1	28	23	5	136	130	60	57	0	4.30
Bill Castro (EJ)	R	21	3	2	.600	1	18	5	0	75	78	17	25	0	2.52
Tom Hausman	R	22	3	6	.333	0	29	9	1	112	110	47	46	0	4.10
Jerry Augustine	L	22	2	0	1.000	0	5	3	1	27	26	12	8	0	3.00
Rick Austin	L	28	2	3	.400	2	32	0	0	40	32	32	30	0	4.05
Larry Anderson	R	22	1	0	1.000	0	8	1	1	30	36	6	13	1	5.10
Ed Sprague (KJ)	R	29	1	7	.125	1	18	11	0	67	81	40	21	0	4.70
Tom Murphy (SJ)	R	29	1	9	.100	20	52	0	0	72	85	27	32	0	4.63
Pat Osburn	L	26	0	1	.000	0	6	1	0	12	19	9	1	0	5.25
Lafayette Currence	L	23	0	2	.000	0	8	1	0	19	25	14	7	0	7.58

DETROIT 6th 57-102 .358 37.5 — RALPH HOUK

NAME	G by POS	B	AGE	G	AB	R	H	2B	3B	HR	RBI	BB	SO	SB	BA	SA
TOTALS			27	159	5366	570	1338	171	39	125	546	383	872	63	.249	.366
Jack Pierce	1B49	L	26	53	170	19	40	6	1	8	22	20	40	0	.235	.424
Gary Sutherland	2B128	R	30	129	503	51	130	12	3	6	39	45	41	0	.258	.330
Tom Veryzer	SS128	R	22	128	404	37	102	13	1	5	48	23	76	2	.252	.327
Aurelio Rodriguez	3B151	R	27	151	507	47	124	20	6	13	60	30	63	1	.245	.385
Leon Roberts	OF127,DH1	R	24	129	447	51	115	17	5	10	38	36	94	3	.257	.385
Ron LeFlore	OF134	R	23	136	550	66	142	13	6	8	37	33	139	28	.258	.347
Ben Oglivie	OF86,1B5,DH2	L	26	100	332	45	95	14	1	9	36	16	62	11	.286	.416
Bill Freehan	C113,1B5	R	33	120	427	42	105	17	3	14	47	32	56	2	.246	.398
Willie Horton	DH159	R	32	159	615	62	169	13	1	25	92	44	109	1	.275	.421
Dan Meyer	OF74,1B46	L	22	122	470	56	111	17	3	8	47	26	25	8	.236	.336
Gene Michael	SS44,2B7,3B4	B	36	56	145	15	31	2	0	3	13	8	28	0	.214	.290
Mickey Stanley (RJ)	OF28,1B14,3B7,DH1	R	32	52	164	26	42	7	3	3	19	21	27	1	.256	.390
Gates Brown		L	36	47	35	1	6	2	0	1	3	9	6	0	.171	.314
1 Nate Colbert	1B44,DH1	R	29	45	156	16	23	4	2	4	18	17	52	0	.147	.276
John Knox	2B28,3B3,DH3	L	26	43	86	8	23	1	0	0	2	10	9	1	.267	.279
John Wockenfuss	C34	R	26	35	118	15	27	6	3	4	13	10	15	0	.229	.432
Billy Baldwin	OF25,DH1	L	25	30	95	8	21	3	0	4	8	5	14	2	.221	.379
Terry Humphrey (SJ)	C18	R	25	18	41	0	10	0	0	0	1	2	6	0	.244	.244
Art James	OF11	L	22	11	40	2	9	2	0	0	1	1	3	1	.225	.275

Bob Molinaro 25 L 5-19, Jerry Manuel 21 B 1-18, Chuck Scrivener 27 R 4-16, Gene Lamont 28 L 3-8

NAME	T	AGE	W	L	PCT	SV	G	GS	CG	IP	H	BB	SO	ShO	ERA
		28	57	**102**	.358	17	159	159	52	1396	**1496**	533	787	10	4.27
Mickey Lolich	L	34	12	18	.400	0	32	32	19	241	260	64	139	1	3.77
Vern Ruhle	R	24	11	12	.478	0	32	31	8	190	199	65	67	3	4.03
Joe Coleman	R	28	10	18	.357	0	31	31	6	201	234	85	125	1	5.55
Ray Bare	R	26	8	13	.381	0	29	21	6	151	174	47	71	1	4.47
Lerrin LaGrow	R	26	7	14	.333	0	32	26	7	164	183	66	75	2	4.39
Tom Walker	R	26	3	8	.273	0	36	9	1	115	116	40	60	0	4.46
Fred Arroyo	R	23	2	1	.667	0	14	2	1	53	56	22	25	0	4.58
John Hiller (AJ)	L	32	2	3	.400	14	36	0	0	71	52	36	87	0	2.15
Dave Lemanczyk (SJ)	R	24	2	7	.222	0	26	6	4	109	120	46	67	0	4.46
Ike Brookens	R	25	0	0	–	0	3	0	0	10	11	5	8	0	5.40
Tom Makowski	L	24	0	0	–	0	3	0	0	9	10	9	3	0	5.00
Steve Grilli	R	26	0	0	–	0	3	0	0	7	3	6	5	0	1.29
2 Bob Reynolds	R	28	0	2	.000	3	21	0	0	35	40	14	26	0	4.63
Ed Glynn	L	22	0	2	.000	0	3	1	0	15	11	8	8	0	4.20
Gene Pentz	R	22	0	4	.000	0	13	0	0	25	27	20	21	0	3.24

WEST DIVISION

OAKLAND 1st 98-64 .605 — AL DARK

NAME	G by POS	B	AGE	G	AB	R	H	2B	3B	HR	RBI	BB	SO	SB	BA	SA
TOTALS			29	162	5415	758	1376	220	33	151	703	609	846	183	.254	.391
Joe Rudi (RJ)	1B91,OF44,DH2	R	26	126	468	66	130	26	6	21	75	40	56	2	.278	.494
Phil Garner	2B160,SS1	R	26	160	488	46	120	21	5	6	54	30	65	4	.246	.346
Bert Campaneris	SS137	R	33	137	509	69	135	15	3	4	46	50	71	24	.265	.330
Sal Bando	3B160	R	31	160	562	64	129	24	1	15	78	87	80	7	.230	.356
Reggie Jackson	OF147,DH9	L	29	157	593	91	150	39	3	**36**	104	67	133	17	.253	.511
Billy North	OF138,DH1	B	27	140	524	74	143	17	5	1	43	81	80	30	.273	.330
Claudell Washington	OF148	L	20	148	590	86	182	24	7	10	77	32	80	40	.308	.424
Gene Tenace	C125,1B68,DH1	R	28	158	498	83	127	17	0	29	87	106	127	7	.255	.464
Billy Williams	DH145,1B7	L	37	155	520	68	127	20	1	23	81	76	68	0	.244	.419
Jim Holt	1B52,DH4,OF2	L	31	102	123	7	27	3	0	2	16	11	11	0	.220	.293
2 Ted Martinez	SS45,2B31,3B14	R	27	86	87	1	15	0	0	0	3	2	2	1	.172	.172
Ray Fosse	C82,1B1,2B1	R	28	82	136	14	19	3	2	0	12	8	19	0	.140	.191
Don Hopkins	DH20,OF5	L	23	82	6	25	1	0	0	0	0	2	0	21	.167	.167
Matt Alexander (IJ)	DH17,OF11,2B3,3B2	B	28	63	10	16	1	0	0	0	0	1	1	17	.100	.100
Angel Mangual	OF39,DH15	R	28	62	109	13	24	3	0	1	6	3	18	0	.220	.275
Larry Haney	C43,3B4	R	32	47	26	3	5	0	0	1	2	1	4	0	.192	.308
2 Tommy Harper	1B16,OF9,DH5,3B2	R	34	34	69	11	22	4	0	2	7	5	9	7	.319	.464
1 Ted Kubiak	3B7,SS7,2B6	B	33	20	28	2	7	1	0	0	4	2	2	0	.250	.286
2 Cesar Tovar	2B4,DH4,3B3,SS1	R	35	19	26	5	6	1	0	0	3	3	3	4	.231	.269

Dal Maxvill 36 R 2-10, Dennis Walling 21 L 1-8, Rich McKinney 28 R 1-7, Charlie Chant 23 R 0-5, Gaylen Pitts 29 R 1-3, Charlie Sands 27 L 1-2, Billy Grabarkewitz 28 R 0-2, Herb Washington 23 R 0-0, Tommy Sandt 24 R 0-0

NAME	T	AGE	W	L	PCT	SV	G	GS	CG	IP	H	BB	SO	ShO	ERA
		31	**98**	64	**.605**	**44**	162	162	36	1448	1267	523	784	10	3.27
Vida Blue	L	25	22	11	.667	1	39	38	13	278	243	99	189	2	3.01
Ken Holtzman	L	30	18	14	.563	0	39	38	13	266	217	108	122	2	3.15
2 Dick Bosman	R	31	11	4	.733	0	22	21	2	123	112	24	42	0	3.51
Rollie Fingers	R	28	10	6	.625	24	**75**	0	0	127	95	33	115	0	2.98
Paul Lindblad	L	33	9	1	.900	7	68	0	0	122	105	43	58	0	2.73
Jim Todd	R	27	8	3	.727	12	58	0	0	122	104	33	50	0	2.29
2 Stan Bahnsen	R	30	6	7	.462	0	21	16	2	100	88	37	49	0	3.24
Glenn Abbott	R	24	5	5	.500	0	30	15	3	114	109	50	51	1	4.26
2 Sonny Siebert (GJ)	R	38	4	4	.500	0	17	13	0	61	60	31	44	0	3.69
2 Jim Perry	R	39	3	4	.429	0	15	11	2	68	61	26	33	1	4.63
Mike Norris (EJ)	R	20	1	0	1.000	0	4	3	1	17	6	8	5	1	0.00
Dave Hamilton	L	27	1	2	.333	0	11	4	0	36	42	18	20	0	4.00
Craig Mitchell	R	21	0	1	.000	0	1	1	0	4	6	2	2	0	11.25
1 Blue Moon Odom	R	30	0	2	.000	0	7	2	0	11	19	11	4	0	12.27

KANSAS CITY 2nd 91-71 .562 7 — JACK McKEON 50-46 .521 — WHITEY HERZOG 41-25 .621

NAME	G by POS	B	AGE	G	AB	R	H	2B	3B	HR	RBI	BB	SO	SB	BA	SA
TOTALS			28	162	5491	710	1431	263	**58**	118	667	591	675	155	.261	.394
John Mayberry	1B131,DH27	L	25	156	554	95	161	38	1	34	106	**119**	73	5	.291	.547
Cookie Rojas	2B117,DH1	R	36	120	406	34	103	18	2	2	37	30	24	4	.254	.323
Freddie Patek	SS136,DH1	R	30	136	483	58	110	14	5	5	45	42	65	32	.228	.308
George Brett	3B159,SS1	L	22	159	**634**	84	**195**	35	**13**	11	89	46	49	13	.308	.456
Al Cowens	OF113,DH2	R	23	120	328	44	91	13	8	4	42	28	36	12	.277	.402
Amos Otis	OF130	R	28	132	470	87	116	26	6	9	46	66	48	39	.247	.385
Hal McRae	OF114,DH12,3B1	R	28	126	480	58	147	38	6	5	71	47	47	11	.306	.442
Buck Martinez	C79	R	26	80	226	15	51	9	2	3	23	21	28	1	.226	.323
Harmon Killebrew	DH92,1B6	R	39	106	312	25	62	13	0	14	44	54	70	1	.199	.375
Jim Wohlford	OF102,DH4	R	24	116	353	45	90	10	5	0	30	34	37	12	.255	.312
Frank White	2B67,SS42,3B4,DH2,C1	R	24	111	304	43	76	10	2	7	36	20	39	11	.250	.365
Vada Pinson	OF82,DH5,1B4	L	36	103	319	38	71	14	5	4	22	10	21	5	.223	.335
Tony Solaita	DH37,1B35	L	28	93	231	35	60	11	0	16	44	39	79	0	.260	.515
Bob Stinson	C59,OF1,1B1,2B1,DH1	B	29	63	147	18	39	9	1	1	9	18	29	1	.265	.361
Fran Healy (SJ)	C51,DH4	R	28	56	188	16	48	5	2	2	18	14	19	4	.255	.335
Rodney Scott	DH22,2B9,SS8	B	21	48	15	13	1	0	0	0	0	1	3	4	.067	.067
Jamie Quirk	OF10,3B2,DH1	L	20	14	39	2	10	0	0	1	5	2	7	0	.256	.333
Gary Martz	OF1	R	24	1	1	0	0	0	0	0	0	0	0	0	.000	.000

NAME	T	AGE	W	L	PCT	SV	G	GS	CG	IP	H	BB	SO	ShO	ERA
		29	91	71	.562	25	162	162	52	1457	1422	498	815	11	3.47
Steve Busby	R	25	18	12	.600	0	34	34	18	260	233	81	160	3	3.08
Al Fitzmorris	R	28	16	12	.571	0	35	35	11	242	239	76	78	3	3.57
Dennis Leonard	R	24	15	7	.682	0	32	30	8	212	212	90	146	0	3.78
Marty Pattin	R	32	10	10	.500	5	44	15	5	177	173	45	89	1	3.25
Doug Bird	R	25	9	6	.600	11	51	4	0	105	100	40	81	0	3.26
Paul Splittorff	L	28	9	10	.474	1	35	23	6	159	156	56	76	3	3.17
Nelson Briles (EJ)	R	31	6	6	.500	2	24	16	3	112	127	25	73	0	4.26
Lindy McDaniel (IL)	R	39	5	1	.667	1	40	0	0	78	81	24	40	0	4.15
Bob McClure	L	22	1	0	1.000	1	12	0	0	15	4	14	15	0	0.00
3 Ray Sadecki	L	34	1	0	1.000	0	5	0	0	3	5	3	0	0	3.00
Mark Littell	R	22	1	2	.333	0	7	3	1	24	19	15	19	0	3.75
George Throop	R	24	0	0	–	2	7	0	0	9	8	2	8	0	4.00
1 Bruce Dal Canton	R	33	0	2	.000	0	4	2	0	9	23	7	5	0	15.00
Steve Mingori (IL)	L	31	0	3	.000	2	36	0	0	50	42	20	25	0	2.52

TEXAS 3rd 79-83 .488 19 — BILLY MARTIN 44-51 .463 — FRANK LUCCHESI 35-32 .522

	NAME	G by POS	B	AGE	G	AB	R	H	2B	3B	HR	RBI	BB	SO	SB	BA	SA
	TOTALS			27	162	5599	714	1431	208	17	134	675	613	863	102	.256	.371
	Jim Spencer	1B99,DH25	L	27	132	403	50	107	18	1	11	47	35	43	0	.266	.397
	L. Randle	2B79,OF66,3B17,DH3,SS1,C1	B	26	156	601	85	166	24	7	4	57	57	80	16	.276	.359
	Toby Harrah	SS118,3B28,2B21	R	26	151	522	81	153	24	1	20	93	98	71	23	.293	.458
	Roy Howell	3B115,DH5	L	21	125	383	43	96	15	2	10	51	39	79	2	.251	.379
	Jeff Burroughs	OF148,DH3	R	24	152	585	81	132	20	0	29	94	79	155	4	.226	.409
	Dave Moates	OF51,DH1	L	27	54	175	21	48	9	0	3	14	13	15	9	.274	.377
	Mike Hargrove	OF96,1B48,DH12	L	25	145	519	82	157	22	2	11	62	79	66	4	.303	.416
	Jim Sundberg	C155	R	24	155	472	45	94	9	0	6	36	51	77	3	.199	.256
1	Cesar Tovar	DH69,OF31,2B1	R	34	102	427	53	110	16	0	3	28	27	25	16	.258	.316
	Tommy Grieve	OF63,DH45	R	27	118	369	46	102	17	1	14	61	22	74	0	.276	.442
	Roy Smalley	SS59,2B19,C1	B	22	78	250	22	57	8	0	3	33	30	42	4	.228	.296
	Jim Fregosi	1B54,DH13,3B4	R	33	77	191	25	50	5	0	7	33	20	39	0	.262	.398
	Mike Cubbage	2B37,3B3,DH2	L	24	58	143	12	32	6	0	4	31	18	14	0	.224	.350
	Leo Cardenas	3B43,SS5,2B3	R	36	55	102	15	24	0	0	1	5	14	12	0	.235	.284
	Joe Lovitto (VJ)	OF38,1B2,DH2,C1	B	24	50	106	17	22	3	0	1	8	13	16	2	.208	.264
1	Willie Davis	OF42	L	35	42	169	16	42	8	2	5	17	4	25	13	.249	.408

Dave Nelson (NJ) 31 R 17-80, Bill Fahey (BH) 25 L 11-37, Tom Robson 29 R 7-35, Ron Pruitt 23 R 3-17, Bob Jones 25 L 1-11, 2 Eddie Brinkman 33 R 0-2

	NAME	T	AGE	W	L	PCT	SV	G	GS	CG	IP	H	BB	SO	ShO	ERA
			30	79	83	.488	17	162	162	60	1466	1456	518	792	16	3.86
	Ferguson Jenkins	R	31	17	18	.486	0	37	37	22	270	261	56	157	4	3.93
	Gaylord Perry	R	36	12	8	.600	0	22	15	15	184	157	36	148	4	3.03
	Steve Hargan	R	32	9	10	.474	0	33	26	8	189	203	62	93	1	3.81
	Steve Foucault	R	25	8	4	.667	10	59	0	0	107	96	56	56	0	4.12
	Jim Umbarger	L	22	8	7	.533	2	56	12	3	131	134	59	50	2	4.12
	Bill Hands (XJ)	R	35	6	7	.462	0	18	18	4	110	118	28	67	1	4.01
1	Jackie Brown	R	32	5	5	.500	0	17	7	2	70	70	35	35	1	4.24
	Stan Thomas	R	25	4	4	.500	3	46	1	0	81	72	34	34	0	3.11
	Clyde Wright	L	34	4	6	.400	0	25	14	1	93	105	47	32	0	4.45
	Stan Perzanowski	R	24	3	3	.500	0	12	8	1	66	59	25	26	0	3.00
1	Jim Bibby	R	30	2	6	.250	0	12	12	4	68	73	28	31	1	5.03
	Mike Bacsik	R	23	1	2	.333	0	7	3	0	27	28	9	13	0	3.67
	Mike Kekich	L	30	0	0	–	2	23	0	0	31	33	21	19	0	3.77
	Jim Merritt (LJ)	L	31	0	0	–	0	5	0	0	4	3	0	0	0	0.00
	Jim Gideon	R	21	0	0	–	0	1	1	0	6	7	5	2	0	7.50
	Dave Clyde	L	20	0	1	.000	0	1	1	0	7	6	6	2	0	2.57
2	Tommy Moore	R	26	0	2	.000	0	12	0	0	21	31	12	15	0	8.14

MINNESOTA 4th 76-83 .478 20.5 — FRANK QUILICI

	NAME	G by POS	B	AGE	G	AB	R	H	2B	3B	HR	RBI	BB	SO	SB	BA	SA
	TOTALS			28	159	5514	724	1497	215	28	121	669	563	746	81	.271	.386
2	Johnny Briggs	1B49,OF35,DH3	L	31	87	264	44	61	9	2	7	39	60	41	6	.231	.360
	Rod Carew	2B123,1B14,DH2	L	29	143	535	89	192	24	4	14	80	64	40	35	.359	.497
	Danny Thompson	SS100,3B7,DH3,2B1	R	28	112	355	25	96	11	2	5	37	18	30	0	.270	.355
	Eric Soderholm (KJ)	3B113,DH3	R	26	117	419	62	120	17	2	11	58	53	66	3	.286	.415
	Larry Hisle (EJ)	OF58,DH14	R	28	80	255	37	80	9	2	11	51	27	39	27	.314	.494
	Dan Ford	OF120,DH3	R	23	130	440	72	123	21	1	15	59	30	79	6	.280	.434
	Lyman Bostock (BN)	OF92,DH1	L	24	98	369	52	104	21	5	0	29	28	42	2	.282	.366
	Glenn Borgmann	C125	R	25	125	352	34	73	15	2	2	33	47	59	0	.207	.278
	Tony Oliva	DH120	L	35	131	455	46	123	10	0	13	58	41	45	0	.270	.378
	Steve Braun	OF106,1B9,DH9,2B1	L	26	136	453	70	137	18	3	11	45	66	55	0	.302	.428
	J. Terrell	SS41,2B39,1B15,3B12,OF6,DH2	R	28	108	385	48	110	16	2	1	36	19	27	4	.286	.345
	Luis Gomez	SS70,2B6,DH1	R	23	89	72	7	10	0	0	0	5	4	12	0	.139	.139
	Steve Brye (BH)	OF72,DH1	R	26	86	246	41	62	13	1	9	34	21	37	2	.252	.423
	Phil Roof (LJ)	C63	R	34	63	126	18	38	2	0	7	21	9	28	0	.302	.484
	Craig Kusick	1B51	R	26	57	156	14	37	8	0	6	27	21	23	0	.237	.404
	Tom Kelly	1B43,OF2	L	24	49	127	11	23	5	0	1	11	15	22	0	.181	.244
1	Bobby Darwin	OF27,DH19	R	32	48	169	26	37	6	0	5	18	18	44	2	.219	.343
	Dave McKay	3B33	B	25	33	125	8	32	4	1	2	16	6	14	1	.256	.352

Sergio Ferrer 24 B 20-81, Danny Walton 27 B 11-63, Mike Poepping 24 R 5-37, Tom Lundstedt 26 B 3-28

	NAME	T	AGE	W	L	PCT	SV	G	GS	CG	IP	H	BB	SO	ShO	ERA
			26	76	83	.478	22	159	159	57	1423	1381	617	846	7	4.05
	Jim Hughes	R	23	16	14	.533	0	37	34	12	250	241	127	130	2	3.82
	Bert Blyleven	R	24	15	10	.600	0	35	35	20	276	219	84	233	3	3.00
	Dave Goltz	R	26	14	14	.500	0	32	32	15	243	235	72	128	1	3.67
	Vic Albury	L	28	6	7	.462	1	32	15	2	135	115	97	72	0	4.53
	Bill Butler	L	28	5	4	.556	0	23	8	1	82	100	35	55	0	5.93
	Ray Corbin (EJ)	R	26	5	7	.417	0	18	11	3	90	105	38	49	0	5.10
	Tom Burgmeier	L	31	5	8	.385	11	46	0	0	76	76	23	41	0	3.08
	Bill Campbell	R	26	4	6	.400	5	47	7	2	121	119	46	76	1	3.79
	Eddie Bane	L	23	3	1	.750	0	4	4	0	28	28	15	14	0	2.89
	Tom Johnson	R	24	1	2	.333	3	18	0	0	39	40	21	17	0	4.15
	Mark Wiley	R	27	1	3	.250	2	15	3	1	39	50	13	15	0	6.00
	Joe Decker (IL)	R	28	1	3	.250	0	10	7	1	26	25	36	8	0	8.65
	Mike Pazik	L	25	0	4	.000	0	5	3	0	20	28	10	8	0	8.10

CHICAGO 5th 75-86 .466 22.5 — CHUCK TANNER

	NAME	G by POS	B	AGE	G	AB	R	H	2B	3B	HR	RBI	BB	SO	SB	BA	SA
	TOTALS			26	161	5490	655	1400	209	38	94	604	611	800	101	.255	.358
	Carlos May	1B63,OF46,DH19	L	27	128	454	55	123	19	2	8	53	67	46	12	.271	.370
	Jorge Orta	2B135,DH2	L	24	140	542	64	165	26	10	11	83	48	67	16	.304	.450
	Bucky Dent	SS157	R	23	157	502	52	159	29	4	3	58	36	48	2	.264	.341
	Bill Melton	3B138,DH11	R	29	149	512	62	123	16	0	15	70	78	106	5	.240	.359
	Pat Kelly	OF115,DH14	L	30	133	471	73	129	21	7	9	45	58	69	18	.274	.406
	Ken Henderson	OF137,DH1	B	29	140	513	65	129	20	3	9	53	74	65	5	.251	.355
	Nyls Nyman	OF94,DH4	L	21	106	327	36	74	6	3	2	28	11	34	10	.226	.281
	Brian Downing	C137,DH1	R	24	138	420	58	101	12	1	7	41	76	75	13	.240	.324
1	Deron Johnson	DH93,1B55	R	36	148	554	66	129	25	1	18	72	48	117	0	.233	.379
	Bill Stein	2B28,3B24,DH18,OF1	R	28	76	226	23	61	7	1	3	21	18	32	2	.270	.350
	Jerry Hairston	OF59,DH8	B	23	69	219	26	62	8	0	0	23	46	23	1	.283	.320
2	Bob Coluccio (NJ)	OF59,DH1	R	23	61	161	22	33	4	2	4	13	13	34	4	.205	.329
1	Tony Muser	1B41	L	27	43	111	11	27	3	0	0	6	7	8	2	.243	.270
	Lee Richard	3B12,SS9,2B5,DH5	B	26	43	45	11	9	0	1	0	5	4	7	2	.200	.244
	Pete Varney	C34,DH2	R	26	36	107	12	29	5	1	2	8	6	28	2	.271	.393
1	Buddy Bradford	OF18,DH4	R	30	25	58	8	9	3	1	2	15	8	22	3	.155	.345
	Mike Squires	1B20	L	23	20	65	5	15	0	0	0	4	8	5	3	.231	.231
1	Bill Sharp	OF14	L	25	18	35	1	7	0	0	0	4	2	3	0	.200	.200

Chet Lemon 20 R 9-35, Lamar Johnson 24 R 6-30, 2 Jerry Moses 28 R 1-2

	NAME	T	AGE	W	L	PCT	SV	G	GS	CG	IP	H	BB	SO	ShO	ERA
			29	75	86	.466	39	161	161	34	1452	1489	655	799	7	3.93
	Jim Kaat	L	36	20	14	.588	0	43	41	12	304	321	77	142	1	3.11
	Wilbur Wood	L	33	16	20	.444	0	43	43	14	291	309	92	140	2	4.11
	Rich Gossage	R	23	9	8	.529	26	62	0	0	142	99	70	130	0	1.84
	Claud Osteen	L	35	7	16	.304	0	37	37	5	204	237	92	63	0	4.37
3	Dave Hamilton	L	27	6	5	.545	6	30	1	0	70	63	29	51	0	2.83
2	Jesse Jefferson	R	26	5	9	.357	0	22	21	1	108	100	94	67	0	5.08
1	Stan Bahnsen	R	30	4	6	.400	0	12	12	2	67	78	40	31	0	6.04
	Danny Osborn	R	29	3	0	1.000	0	24	0	0	58	57	37	38	0	4.50
	Terry Forster (EJ)	L	23	3	3	.500	4	17	1	0	37	30	24	32	0	2.19
	Rich Hinton	L	28	1	0	1.000	0	15	0	0	37	41	15	30	0	4.86
	Cecil Upshaw	R	32	1	1	.500	1	29	0	0	47	49	21	22	0	3.26
	Bill Gogolewski (XJ)	R	27	0	0	–	2	19	0	0	55	61	28	37	0	5.24
	Jim Otten	R	24	0	0	–	0	2	0	0	5	4	7	3	0	7.20
	Jack Kucek	R	22	0	0	–	0	2	0	0	4	9	4	2	0	4.50
	Chris Knapp	R	21	0	0	–	0	2	0	0	2	2	4	3	0	4.50
	Tim Stoddard	R	22	0	0	–	0	1	0	0	1	2	0	0	0	9.00
	Skip Pitlock	L	27	0	0	–	0	1	0	0	0	1	0	0	0	–
	Pete Vuckovich	R	22	0	1	.000	0	4	2	0	10	17	7	5	0	13.50
	Ken Kravec	L	23	0	1	.000	0	2	1	0	4	1	8	1	0	6.75
	Lloyd Allen	R	25	0	2	.000	0	3	2	0	5	8	6	2	0	12.60

Bart Johnson (XJ) 25

CALIFORNIA 6th 72-89 .447 25.5 — DICK WILLIAMS

	NAME	G by POS	B	AGE	G	AB	R	H	2B	3B	HR	RBI	BB	SO	SB	BA	SA
	TOTALS			26	161	5377	628	1324	195	41	55	572	593	811	220	.246	.328
	Bruce Bochte (BG)	1B105,DH1	L	24	107	375	41	107	19	3	3	48	45	43	3	.285	.376
	Jerry Remy	2B147	L	22	147	569	82	147	17	5	1	46	45	55	34	.258	.311
	Mike Miley	SS70	B	22	70	224	17	39	3	2	4	26	16	54	0	.174	.259
	Dave Chalk	3B149	R	24	149	513	59	140	24	2	3	56	66	49	6	.273	.345
	Lee Stanton	OF131,DH1	R	29	137	440	67	115	20	3	14	82	52	85	18	.261	.416
	Mickey Rivers	OF152,DH1	L	25	155	616	70	175	17	13	1	53	43	42	70	.284	.359
	Dave Collins	OF75,DH12	B	22	93	319	41	85	13	4	3	29	36	55	24	.266	.361
	Ellie Rodriguez (NJ)	C90	R	29	90	226	20	53	6	0	3	27	49	37	2	.235	.301
1	Tommy Harper	DH55,1B19,OF9	R	34	89	285	40	68	10	1	3	31	38	51	19	.239	.312
	Morris Nettles	OF90,DH9	L	23	112	294	50	68	11	0	0	23	26	57	22	.231	.296
	Joe Lahoud (XJ)	DH35,OF29	L	28	76	192	21	41	6	2	6	33	48	33	2	.214	.359
	Rudy Meoli	SS28,3B15,2B11,DH3	L	24	70	126	21	27	2	1	0	6	15	20	3	.314	.246
	Billy Smith	SS50,1B6,DH4,3B2	B	21	59	143	10	29	5	1	0	14	12	27	1	.203	.252
	Winston Llenas	2B12,OF10,1B6,DH6,3B3	R	31	56	113	6	21	4	0	0	11	10	11	0	.186	.221
	John Balaz	OF27,DH11	R	24	45	120	10	29	8	1	1	10	5	25	0	.242	.350
	Orlando Ramirez	SS40	R	23	44	100	10	24	4	1	0	4	11	22	9	.240	.300
2	Adrian Garrett	DH23,1B10,OF2,C1	L	32	37	107	17	28	5	0	0	18	14	28	3	.262	.477
2	Andy Etchebarren (BG)	C31	R	32	31	100	10	28	0	1	3	17	14	19	1	.280	.390

John Doherty 23 L 19-94, Tom Egan 29 B 16-70, Ike Hampton 23 B 10-66, 1 Bill Sudakis 29 B 7-58,
1 Bobby Vanentine 25 R 16-57, Bob Allietta (BG) 23 R 8-45, Ron Jackson 22 R 9-39, Dan Briggs 22 L 7-31, Paul Dade 23 R 6-30, 1 Denny Doyle 31 L 1-15, Danny Goodwin 21 L 1-10

	NAME	T	AGE	W	L	PCT	SV	G	GS	CG	IP	H	BB	SO	ShO	ERA
			27	72	89	.447	16	161	161	59	1453	1386	613	975	19	3.89
	Frank Tanana	L	21	16	9	.640	0	34	33	16	257	211	73	269	5	2.63
	Ed Figueroa	R	26	16	13	.552	0	33	32	10	245	213	84	139	2	2.90
	Nolan Ryan (EJ)	R	28	14	12	.538	0	28	28	10	198	152	132	186	5	3.45
	Bill Singer	R	31	7	15	.318	1	29	27	8	179	171	81	78	0	4.98
	Don Kirkwood	R	25	6	5	.545	7	44	2	0	84	85	28	49	0	3.11
	Mickey Scott	L	27	4	2	.667	1	50	0	0	68	59	18	31	0	3.31
	Dick Lange	R	26	4	6	.400	1	30	8	1	102	119	53	45	0	5.21
	Andy Hassler	L	23	3	12	.200	0	30	18	6	133	158	53	82	1	5.95
2	Jim Brewer	L	37	1	1	1.000	5	21	0	0	35	38	11	22	0	1.80
	Joe Pactwa	L	27	1	0	1.000	0	4	3	0	16	23	10	3	0	3.94
1	Dave Sells	R	28	0	0	–	0	4	0	0	8	9	8	7	0	9.00
	Steve Blateric	R	31	0	0	–	0	2	0	0	4	9	1	5	0	6.75
	Charlie Hudson	L	25	0	1	.000	0	3	1	0	6	7	4	0	0	9.00
	Gary Ross	R	27	0	1	.000	0	1	1	0	5	6	1	4	0	5.40
	Chuck Dobson	R	31	0	2	.000	0	9	2	0	28	30	13	14	0	6.75
	Sid Monge	L	24	0	2	.000	0	4	2	2	24	22	10	17	0	4.13
	Horacio Pina	R	30	0	2	.000	0	7	0	0	13	13	8	4	0	2.08
	Luis Quintana	L	23	0	2	.000	0	4	0	0	7	13	6	5	0	6.43
	Chuck Hockenberry	R	24	0	5	.000	1	16	4	0	41	48	19	15	0	5.27

AMERICAN LEAGUE CHAMPIONSHIP – BOSTON (EAST) 3 OAKLAND (WEST) 0

LINE SCORES

TEAM	1	2	3	4	5	6	7	8	9	10	11	12	R	H	E
Game 1 October 4 at Boston															
OAK	0	0	0	0	0	0	0	1	0				1	3	4
BOS	2	0	0	0	0	0	5	0	X				7	8	3
Game 2 October 5 at Boston															
OAK	2	0	0	1	0	0	0	0	0				2	10	0
BOS	0	0	0	3	0	1	1	1	X				6	12	0
Game 3 October 7 at Oakland															
BOS	0	0	0	1	3	0	0	1	0				5	11	1
OAK	0	0	0	0	0	1	0	2	0				3	6	2

Game 1: **Holtzman**, Todd (7), Lindblad (7), Bosman (7), Abbott (8) — **Tiant**

Game 2: Blue, Todd (4), **Fingers (5)** — Cleveland, **Moret (6)**, Drago (7)

Game 3: **Wise**, Drago (8) — **Holtzman**, Todd (5), Lindblad (5)

COMPOSITE BATTING

NAME		G	AB	R	H	2B	3B	HR	RBI	BA
Boston										
Totals		3	98	18	31	8	0	2	14	.316
Fisk	C	3	12	4	5	1	0	0	2	.417
Beniquez	DH	3	12	2	3	0	0	0	1	.250
Petrocelli	3B	3	12	1	2	0	0	1	2	.167
Yastrzemski	LF	3	11	4	5	1	0	1	2	.455
Lynn	CF	3	11	1	4	1	0	0	3	.364
Doyle	2B	3	11	3	3	0	0	0	2	.273
Cooper	1B	3	10	0	4	2	0	0	1	.400
Evans	RF	3	10	1	1	1	0	0	0	.100
Burleson	SS	3	9	2	4	2	0	0	1	.444
Oakland										
Totals		3	98	7	19	6	0	1	7	.194
Bando	3B	3	12	1	6	2	0	0	2	.500
Jackson	RF	3	12	1	5	0	0	1	3	.417
Rudi	1B-LF	3	12	1	3	2	0	0	0	.250
C. Washington	LF-DH	3	12	1	3	1	0	0	1	.250
Campaneris	SS	3	11	1	0	0	0	0	0	.000
North	CF	3	10	0	0	0	0	0	1	.000
Tenace	C-1B	3	9	0	0	0	0	0	0	.000
Williams	DH	3	8	0	0	0	0	0	0	.000
Garner	2B	3	5	0	0	0	0	0	0	.000

Holt 1B 1-3, Tovar 2B 1-2, Fosse C 0-2, Martinez 2B 0-0, Hopkins DH 0-0, Harper PH 0-0

COMPOSITE PITCHING

NAME	G	IP	H	BB	SO	W	L	SV	ERA
Boston									
Totals	3	27	19	9	14	3	0	2	1.67
Tiant	1	9	3	3	8	1	0	0	0.00
Wise	1	7.1	6	3	2	1	0	0	2.45
Cleveland	1	5	7	1	2	0	0	0	5.40
Drago	2	4.2	2	1	2	0	0	2	0.00
Moret	1	1	1	1	0	1	0	0	0.00
Oakland									
Totals	3	25	31	3	12	0	3	0	4.32
Holtzman	2	11	12	1	7	0	2	0	4.09
Lindblad	2	4.2	5	1	0	0	0	0	0.00
Fingers	1	4	5	1	3	0	1	0	6.75
Blue	1	3	6	0	2	0	0	0	9.00
Abbott	1	1	0	0	0	0	0	0	0.00
Todd	3	1	3	0	0	0	0	0	9.00
Bosman	1	0.1	0	0	0	0	0	0	0.00

NATIONAL LEAGUE CHAMPIONSHIP – CINCINNATI (WEST) 3 PITTSBURGH (EAST) 0

LINE SCORES

TEAM	1	2	3	4	5	6	7	8	9	10	11	12	R	H	E
Game 1 October 4 at Cincinnati															
PIT	0	2	0	0	0	0	0	0	1				3	8	0
CIN	0	1	3	0	4	0	0	0	X				8	11	0
Reuss, Brett (3), Demery (5), Ellis (7)	**Gullett**														
Game 2 October 5 at Cincinnati															
PIT	0	0	0	1	0	0	0	0	0				1	5	0
CIN	2	0	0	2	0	1	1	0	X				6	12	1
Rooker, Tekulve (5), Brett (6), Kison (7)	**Norman**, Eastwick (7)														
Game 3 October 7 at Pittsburgh															
CIN	0	1	0	0	0	0	0	2	0	2			5	6	0
PIT	0	0	0	0	0	2	0	0	1	0			3	7	2
Nolan, C. Carroll (7), McEnaney (8), **Eastwick (9)**, Borbon (10)	Candelaria, Giusti (8), **Hernandez (10)**, Tekulve (10)														

COMPOSITE BATTING

NAME	POS	G	AB	R	H	2B	3B	HR	RBI	BA
Cincinnati										
Totals		3	102	19	29	4	0	4	18	.284
Rose	3B	3	**14**	3	5	0	0	1	2	.357
Bench	C	3	13	1	1	0	0	0	0	.077
Perez	1B	3	12	**3**	**5**	0	0	**1**	**4**	.417
Griffey	RF	3	12	**3**	4	1	0	0	**4**	.333
Concepcion	SS	3	11	2	**5**	0	0	**1**	1	.455
Foster	LF	3	11	**3**	4	0	0	0	0	.364
Morgan	2B	3	11	2	3	**3**	0	0	1	.273
Geronimo	CF	3	10	0	0	0	0	0	1	.000
Rettenmund PH 0-1, Crowley PH 0-0, Armbrister PH 0-0										
Pittsburgh										
Totals		3	101	7	20	3	0	1	7	.198
Stennett	2B	3	**14**	0	3	0	0	0	0	.214
Hebner	3B	3	12	2	4	1	0	0	2	.333
Sanguillen	C	3	12	0	2	0	0	0	0	.167
Oliver	CF	3	11	1	2	0	0	**1**	2	.182
Stargell	1B	3	11	1	2	1	0	0	0	.182
Zisk	LF	3	10	0	**5**	1	0	0	0	**.500**
Parker	RF	3	10	2	0	0	0	0	0	.000
Taveras	SS	3	7	0	1	0	0	0	1	.143
Robertson	1B	3	2	0	1	0	0	0	1	.500
Randolph	2B	2	2	1	0	0	0	0	0	.000
Kirkpatrick PH 0-2, Robinson PH 0-2, Reynolds SS 0-1, Dyer PH 0-0										

COMPOSITE PITCHING

NAME	G	IP	H	BB	SO	W	L	SV	ERA
Cincinnati									
Totals	3	28	20	10	18	3	0	2	2.25
Gullett	1	**9**	**8**	2	5	**1**	0	0	3.00
Norman	1	6	4	**5**	4	**1**	0	0	1.50
Nolan	1	6	5	0	5	0	0	0	3.00
Eastwick	**2**	3.2	2	2	1	**1**	0	**1**	**0.00**
McEnaney	1	1.1	1	0	1	0	0	0	9.00
Borbon	1	1	0	0	1	0	0	**1**	0.00
C. Carroll	1	1	0	1	1	0	0	0	0.00
Pittsburgh									
Totals	3	26	29	9	28	0	3	0	6.58
Candelaria	1	7.2	3	2	**14**	0	0	0	3.38
Rooker	1	4	7	0	5	0	**1**	0	9.00
Reuss	1	2.2	4	4	1	0	**1**	0	12.00
Brett	**2**	2.1	1	0	1	0	0	0	0.00
Ellis	1	2	2	0	2	0	0	0	0.00
Kison	1	2	2	1	1	0	0	0	4.50
Demery	1	2	4	1	1	0	0	0	18.00
Tekulve	**2**	1.1	3	1	2	0	0	0	9.00
Giusti	1	1.1	0	0	1	0	0	0	0.00
Hernandez	1	0.2	3	0	0	0	**1**	0	18.00

EAST DIVISION

PITTSBURGH 1st 92-69 .571 DANNY MURTAUGH

NAME	G by POS	B	AGE	G	AB	R	H	2B	3B	HR	RBI	BB	SO	SB	BA	SA
TOTALS			28	161	5489	712	1444	255	47	**138**	669	468	832	49	.263	**.402**
Willie Stargell	1B122	L	35	124	461	71	136	32	2	22	90	58	109	0	.295	.516
Rennie Stennett	2B144	R	24	148	616	89	176	25	7	7	62	33	42	5	.286	.383
Frank Taveras	SS132	R	24	134	378	44	80	9	4	0	23	37	42	17	.212	.257
Richie Hebner	3B126	L	27	128	472	65	116	16	4	15	57	43	48	0	.246	.392
Dave Parker	OF141	L	24	148	558	75	172	35	10	25	101	38	89	8	.308	**.541**
Al Oliver	OF153,1B4	L	28	155	628	90	176	39	8	18	84	25	73	4	.280	.454
Richie Zisk	OF140	R	26	147	504	69	146	27	3	20	75	68	109	0	.290	.474
Manny Sanguillen	C132	R	31	133	481	60	158	24	3	9	58	48	31	5	.328	.451
Bill Robinson	OF57	R	32	92	200	26	56	12	2	6	33	11	36	3	.280	.450
Ed Kirkpatrick	1B28,OF14	L	30	89	144	15	34	5	0	5	16	18	22	1	.236	.375
Bob Robertson	1B27	R	28	75	124	17	34	4	0	6	18	23	25	0	.274	.452
Art Howe	3B42,SS3	R	28	63	146	13	25	9	0	1	10	15	15	1	.171	.253
Mario Mendoza	SS53,3B1	R	24	56	50	8	9	1	0	0	2	3	17	0	.180	.200
Duffy Dyer	C36	R	29	48	132	8	30	5	2	3	16	6	12	0	.227	.364
Craig Reynolds	SS30	L	22	31	76	8	17	3	0	0	4	3	5	0	.224	.263
Willie Randolph	2B14,3B1	R	20	30	61	9	10	1	0	0	3	7	6	1	.164	.180
Paul Popovich	2B8,SS8	B	34	25	40	5	8	1	0	0	1	3	2	0	.200	.225

Omar Moreno 21 R 1-6, Miguel Dilone 20 B 0-6, Ed Ott 23 L 1-5

NAME	T	AGE	W	L	PCT	SV	G	GS	CG	IP	H	BB	SO	ShO	ERA
		28	92	69	.571	31	161	161	43	1437	1302	551	768	14	3.01
Jerry Reus	L	26	18	11	.621	0	32	32	15	237	224	78	131	6	2.54
Jim Rooker	L	33	13	11	.542	0	28	28	7	197	177	76	102	1	2.97
Bruce Kison	R	24	12	11	.522	0	33	29	6	192	160	92	89	0	3.23
Ken Brett (EJ)	L	26	9	5	.643	0	23	16	4	118	110	43	47	1	3.36
John Candelaria	L	21	8	6	.571	0	18	18	4	121	95	36	95	1	2.75
Dock Ellis	R	30	8	9	.471	0	27	24	5	140	163	43	69	2	3.79
Ramon Hernandez	L	34	7	2	.778	5	46	0	0	64	62	28	43	0	2.95
Larry Demery	R	22	7	5	.583	4	45	8	1	115	95	43	59	0	2.90
Dave Giusti	R	34	5	4	.556	17	61	0	0	92	79	42	38	0	2.93
Sam McDowell	L	32	2	1	.667	0	14	1	0	35	30	20	29	0	2.83
Bob Moose (RJ)	R	27	2	2	.500	0	23	5	1	68	63	25	34	0	3.71
Kent Tekulve	R	28	1	2	.333	5	34	0	0	56	43	23	28	0	2.25
Odell Jones	R	22	0	0	–	0	2	0	0	3	1	0	2	0	0.00
Jim Minshall	R	27	0	0	–	0	1	0	0	1	0	2	2	0	0.00

PHILADELPHIA 2nd 86-76 .531 6.5 DANNY OZARK

NAME	G by POS	B	AGE	G	AB	R	H	2B	3B	HR	RBI	BB	SO	SB	BA	SA
TOTALS			27	162	5592	735	1506	**283**	42	125	687	610	**960**	126	.269	.402
2 Dick Allen	1B113	R	33	119	416	54	97	21	3	12	62	58	109	11	.233	.385
Dave Cash	2B162	R	27	162	**699**	111	**213**	40	3	4	57	56	34	13	.305	.388
Larry Bowa (BG)	SS135	B	29	136	583	79	178	18	9	2	38	24	32	24	.305	.377
Mike Schmidt	3B151,SS10	R	25	158	562	93	140	34	3	**38**	95	101	**180**	29	.249	.523
Jay Johnstone	OF101	L	29	122	350	50	115	19	2	7	54	42	39	7	.329	.454
2 Garry Maddox (BK)	OF97	R	25	99	374	50	109	25	8	4	46	36	54	24	.291	.433
Greg Luzinski	OF159	R	24	161	596	85	179	35	3	34	**120**	89	151	3	.300	.540
Bob Boone	C92,3B3	R	27	97	289	28	71	14	2	2	20	32	14	1	.246	.329
Mike Anderson	OF105,1B3	R	24	115	247	24	64	10	3	4	28	17	66	1	.259	.372
Tommy Hutton	1B71,OF12	L	29	113	165	24	41	6	0	3	24	27	10	2	.248	.339
2 Johnny Oates	C82	L	29	90	269	28	77	14	0	1	25	33	29	1	.286	.349
Ollie Brown	OF63	R	31	84	145	19	44	12	0	6	26	15	29	1	.303	.510
Tony Taylor	3B16,1B4,2B3	R	39	79	103	13	25	5	1	1	17	17	18	3	.243	.340
Jerry Martin	OF49	R	26	57	113	15	24	7	1	2	11	11	16	2	.212	.345
Terry Harmon	SS25,2B7,3B1	R	31	48	72	14	13	1	2	0	5	9	13	0	.181	.250
2 Tim McCarver	C10,1B1	L	33	47	59	6	15	2	0	1	7	14	7	0	.254	.339
Alan Bannister	OF18,SS1,2B1	R	23	24	61	10	16	3	1	0	0	1	9	2	.262	.344
1 Willie Montanez	1B21	L	27	21	84	9	24	8	0	2	16	4	12	1	.286	.452

Mike Rogodzinski 27 L 5-19, Larry Cox 27 R 1-5, 1 Don Hahn 26 R 0-5, Jim Essian 24 R 1-2, Larry Fritz 26 L 0-1, Ron Clark R 0-1

NAME	T	AGE	W	L	PCT	SV	G	GS	CG	IP	H	BB	SO	ShO	ERA
		29	86	76	.531	30	162	162	33	1455	1353	546	897	11	3.82
Steve Carlton	L	30	15	14	.517	0	37	37	14	255	217	104	192	3	3.56
Tom Underwood	L	21	14	13	.519	0	35	35	7	219	221	84	123	2	4.15
Larry Christenson	R	21	11	6	.647	1	29	26	5	172	149	45	88	2	3.66
Gene Garber	R	27	10	12	.455	14	**71**	0	0	110	104	27	69	0	3.60
Tug McGraw	L	30	9	6	.600	14	56	0	0	103	84	36	55	0	2.97
Jim Lonborg	R	33	8	6	.571	0	27	26	6	159	161	45	72	2	4.13
Tom Hilgendorf	L	33	7	3	.700	0	53	0	0	97	81	38	52	0	2.13
Wayne Twitchell	R	27	5	10	.333	0	36	20	0	134	132	78	101	0	4.43
Ron Schueler	R	27	4	4	.500	0	46	6	1	93	88	40	69	0	5.23
Dick Ruthven	R	24	2	2	.500	0	11	7	0	41	37	22	26	0	4.17
Wayne Simpson	R	26	1	0	.000	0	7	5	0	31	31	11	19	0	3.19
Joe Hoerner (FJ)	L	38	0	0	–	0	25	0	0	21	25	8	20	0	2.57
Cy Acosta	R	28	0	0	–	1	6	0	0	9	9	3	2	0	6.00
Randy Lerch	L	20	0	0	–	0	3	0	0	7	6	1	8	0	6.43
2 John Montague	R	27	0	0	–	0	3	0	0	5	8	4	1	0	9.00

NEW YORK 3rd(tie) 82-80 .506 10.5 YOGI BERRA 56-53 .514 ROY McMILLAN 26-27 .491

NAME	G by POS	B	AGE	G	AB	R	H	2B	3B	HR	RBI	BB	SO	SB	BA	SA
TOTALS			28	162	5587	646	1430	217	34	101	604	**501**	805	32	.256	.361
Ed Kranepool	1B82,OF4	L	30	106	325	42	105	16	0	4	43	27	21	1	.323	.409
Felix Millan	2B162	R	31	162	676	81	191	37	2	1	56	36	28	1	.283	.348
2 Mike Phillips	SS115,2B1	L	24	116	383	31	98	10	7	1	28	25	47	3	.256	.326
Wayne Garrett	3B94,SS3	L	27	107	274	49	73	8	3	6	34	50	45	3	.266	.383
Rusty Staub	OF153	L	31	155	574	93	162	30	4	19	105	77	55	2	.282	.448
Del Unser	OF144	L	30	147	531	65	156	18	2	10	53	37	76	4	.294	.392
Dave Kingman	OF71,1B58,3B12	R	26	134	502	65	116	22	1	36	88	34	153	7	.231	.494
Jerry Grote	C111	R	32	119	386	28	114	14	5	2	39	38	23	0	.295	.373
Joe Torre	3B83,1B24	R	34	114	361	33	89	16	3	6	35	35	55	0	.247	.357
John Milner	OF31,1B29	L	25	91	220	24	42	11	0	7	29	33	22	1	.191	.336
Gene Clines	OF60	R	28	82	203	25	46	6	3	0	10	11	21	4	.227	.286
Jesus Alou	OF20	R	33	62	102	8	27	3	0	0	11	4	5	0	.265	.294
Jack Heidemann	SS44,3B4,2B1	R	25	61	145	12	31	4	2	1	16	17	28	1	.214	.290
John Stearns	C54	R	23	59	169	25	32	5	1	3	10	17	15	4	.189	.284
Mike Vail	OF36	R	23	38	162	17	49	8	1	3	17	9	37	0	.302	.420
Bud Harrelson	SS34	B	31	34	73	5	16	2	0	0	3	12	13	0	.219	.247
Cleon Jones (KJ)	OF12	R	32	21	50	2	12	1	0	0	2	3	6	0	.240	.260

Ron Hodges 26 L 7-34, Roy Staiger 25 R 3-19, Bob Gallagher 26 L 2-15, Brock Pemberton 21 B 0-2

NAME	T	AGE	W	L	PCT	SV	G	GS	CG	IP	H	BB	SO	ShO	ERA
		27	82	80	.506	31	162	162	40	1466	1344	580	**989**	14	3.39
Tom Seaver	R	30	**22**	9	.710	0	36	36	15	280	217	88	**243**	5	2.38
Jon Matlack	R	25	16	12	.571	0	33	32	8	229	224	58	154	3	3.38
Jerry Koosman	L	32	14	13	.519	2	36	34	11	240	234	98	173	4	3.41
Hank Webb	R	25	7	6	.538	0	29	15	3	115	102	62	38	1	4.07
Randy Tate	R	22	5	13	.278	0	26	23	2	138	121	86	99	0	4.43
Tom Hall	L	27	4	3	.571	1	34	4	0	61	58	31	48	0	4.72
George Stone (SJ)	L	28	3	3	.500	0	13	11	1	57	75	21	21	0	5.05
Bob Apodaca (BZ)	R	25	3	4	.429	13	46	0	0	85	66	28	45	0	1.48
Rich Baldwin	R	22	3	5	.375	6	54	0	0	97	97	34	54	0	3.34
1 Harry Parker (SJ)	R	27	2	3	.400	2	18	1	0	35	37	19	22	0	4.37
Ken Sanders	R	33	1	1	.500	5	29	0	0	43	31	14	8	0	2.30
Skip Lockwood	R	28	1	3	.250	2	24	0	0	48	28	25	61	0	1.50
Craig Swan	R	24	1	3	.250	0	6	6	0	31	38	12	19	0	6.39
Mac Scarce	L	26	0	0	–	0	1	0	0	0	1	0	0	0	–
Jerry Cram	R	27	0	0	.000	0	4	0	0	5	7	2	2	0	5.40
Nino Espinosa	R	21	0	1	.000	0	2	0	0	3	8	1	2	0	18.00

ST. LOUIS 3rd (tie) 82-80 .506 10.5 RED SCHOENDIENST

NAME	G by POS	B	AGE	G	AB	R	H	2B	3B	HR	RBI	BB	SO	SB	BA	SA
TOTALS			28	163	**5597**	662	**1527**	239	46	81	619	444	649	116	**.273**	.375
Reggie Smith	OF69,1B66,3B1	B	30	135	477	67	144	26	3	19	76	63	59	9	.302	.488
Ted Sizemore	2B153	R	30	153	562	56	135	23	1	3	49	45	37	1	.240	.301
Mike Tyson	SS95,2B24,3B5	R	25	122	368	45	98	16	3	2	37	24	39	5	.266	.342
Ken Reitz	3B160	R	24	161	592	43	159	25	1	5	63	22	54	1	.269	.340
2 Willie Davis	OF89	L	35	98	350	41	102	19	6	6	50	14	27	10	.291	.431
Bake McBride (SJ)	OF107	L	26	116	413	70	124	10	9	5	36	34	52	26	.300	.404
Lou Brock	OF128	L	36	136	528	78	163	27	6	3	47	38	64	56	.309	.400
Ted Simmons	C154,1B2,OF2	B	25	157	581	80	193	32	3	18	100	63	35	1	.332	.491
Luis Melendez	OF89	R	25	110	291	33	77	8	5	2	27	16	25	3	.265	.347
Ron Fairly	1B56,OF20	L	36	107	229	32	69	13	2	7	37	45	22	0	.301	.467
Keith Hernandez	1B56	L	21	64	188	20	47	8	2	3	20	17	26	0	.250	.362
Mike Guerrero	SS64	R	25	64	184	17	44	9	0	0	11	10	7	0	.239	.288
2 Buddy Bradford	OF25	R	30	50	81	12	22	1	0	4	15	12	24	0	.272	.432
Ken Rudolph	C31	R	28	44	80	5	16	2	0	1	6	3	10	0	.200	.263
1 Eddie Brinkman	SS24	R	33	28	75	6	18	4	0	1	6	7	10	0	.240	.333
Hector Cruz	3B12,OF6	R	22	23	48	7	7	2	2	0	6	2	4	0	.146	.271
Danny Cater	1B12	R	35	22	35	3	8	2	0	0	2	1	3	0	.229	.286
1 Jim Dwyer	OF9	L	25	21	31	4	6	1	0	0	1	4	6	0	.194	.226

Doug Howard 27 R 6-29, 1 Ted Martinez 27 R 4-21, 2 Larry Lintz 25 B 5-18, Jerry Mumphrey 22 B 6-16, 2 Don Hahn 26 R 1-8, Mick Kelleher 27 R 0-4, Dick Billings 32 R 0-3

NAME	T	AGE	W	L	PCT	SV	G	GS	CG	IP	H	BB	SO	ShO	ERA
		27	82	80	.506	36	163	163	33	1455	1452	571	824	13	3.57
Bob Forsch	R	25	15	10	.600	0	34	34	7	230	213	70	108	4	2.86
Lynn McGlothen	R	25	15	13	.536	0	35	34	9	239	231	97	146	2	3.92
Al Hrabosky	L	25	13	3	**.813**	**22**	65	0	0	97	72	33	82	0	1.67
John Denny	R	22	10	7	.588	0	25	24	3	136	149	51	72	2	3.97
2 Ron Reed	R	32	9	8	.529	0	24	24	7	176	181	37	99	2	3.22
John Curtis	L	27	8	9	.471	1	39	18	4	147	151	65	67	0	3.43
Harry Rasmussen	R	23	5	5	.500	0	14	13	2	81	86	20	59	1	3.78
Mike Garman	R	25	3	8	.273	10	66	0	0	79	73	48	48	0	2.39
Bob Gibson	R	39	3	10	.231	2	22	14	1	109	120	62	60	0	5.04
1 Ray Sadecki	L	34	1	0	1.000	0	8	0	0	11	13	7	8	0	3.27
2 Mike Wallace	L	24	0	0	–	0	9	0	0	9	9	5	6	0	2.00
1 Tommy Moore	R	26	0	0	–	0	10	0	0	19	15	12	6	0	3.79
Mike Barlow	R	27	0	0	–	0	9	0	0	8	11	3	2	0	4.50
Ryan Kurosaki	R	22	0	0	–	0	7	0	0	13	15	7	6	0	7.62
Ken Reynolds	L	28	0	1	.000	0	10	0	0	17	12	11	7	0	1.59
Greg Terlecky	R	23	0	1	.000	0	20	0	0	30	38	12	13	0	4.50
2 Harry Parker	R	27	0	1	.000	1	14	0	0	19	21	10	13	0	6.16
2 Ron Bryant	L	27	0	1	.000	0	10	1	0	9	20	7	7	0	16.00
1 Elias Sosa	R	25	0	3	.000	0	14	1	0	27	22	14	15	0	4.00

EAST DIVISION

CHICAGO 5th (tie) 75-87 .463 17.5 — JIM MARSHALL

NAME	G by POS	B	AGE	G	AB	R	H	2B	3B	HR	RBI	BB	SO	SB	BA	SA
TOTALS			27	162	5470	712	1419	229	41	95	645	650	802	67	.259	.368
Andy Thornton (BW)	1B113, 3B2	R	25	120	372	70	109	21	4	18	60	88	63	3	.293	.516
Manny Trillo	2B153,SS1	R	24	154	545	55	135	12	2	7	70	45	78	1	.248	.316
Don Kessinger	SS140, 3B13	B	32	154	601	77	146	26	10	0	46	68	47	4	.243	.319
Bill Madlock	3B128	R	24	130	514	77	182	29	7	7	64	42	34	9	**.354**	.479
Jose Cardenal	OF151	R	31	154	574	85	182	30	2	9	68	77	50	34	.317	.423
Rick Monday	OF131	L	29	136	491	89	131	29	4	17	60	83	95	8	.267	.446
Jerry Morales	OF151	R	26	153	578	62	156	21	0	12	91	50	65	3	.270	.369
Steve Swisher	C93	R	23	93	254	20	54	16	2	1	22	30	57	1	.213	.303
Pete LaCock	1B53, OF26	L	23	106	249	30	57	8	1	6	30	37	27	0	.229	.341
George Mitterwald	C59,1B10	R	30	84	200	19	44	4	3	5	26	19	42	0	.220	.345
Champ Summers	OF18	L	27	76	91	14	21	5	1	1	16	10	13	0	.231	.341
Rob Sperring	3B22,2B17,SS16,OF8	R	25	65	144	25	30	4	1	1	9	16	31	0	.208	.271
Tim Hosley	C53	R	28	62	141	22	36	7	0	6	20	27	25	1	.255	.433
Vic Harris	OF11,3B7,2B5	B	25	51	56	6	10	0	0	0	5	6	7	0	.179	.179
Gene Hiser	OF18,1B1	L	26	45	62	11	15	3	0	0	6	11	7	0	.242	.290
Ron Dunn	3B11,OF2,2B1	R	25	32	44	2	7	3	0	1	6	6	17	0	.159	.295
Dave Rosello	SS19	R	25	19	58	7	15	2	0	1	8	9	8	0	.259	.345
Joe Wallis	OF15	L	23	16	56	9	16	2	2	1	4	5	14	2	.286	.446
1 Adrian Garrett	1B4	L	32	16	21	1	2	0	0	1	6	1	8	0	.095	.238
Jim Tyrone	OF8	R	26	11	22	0	5	0	1	0	3	1	4	1	.227	.318

NAME	T	AGE	W	L	PCT	SV	G	GS	CG	IP	H	BB	SO	ShO	ERA
TOTALS		28	75	87	.463	33	162	162	27	1444	1587	551	850	8	4.49
Ray Burris	R	24	15	10	.600	0	36	35	8	238	259	73	108	2	4.12
Bill Bonham	R	26	13	15	.464	0	38	36	7	229	254	109	165	2	4.72
Steve Stone	R	27	12	8	.600	0	33	32	6	214	198	80	139	1	3.95
Rick Reuschel	R	26	11	**17**	.393	1	38	37	6	234	244	67	155	0	3.73
Darold Knowles	L	33	6	9	.400	15	58	0	0	88	107	36	63	0	5.83
Oscar Zamora (XJ)	R	30	5	2	.714	10	52	0	0	71	84	15	28	0	5.07
Tom Dettore	R	27	5	4	.556	0	36	5	0	85	88	31	46	0	5.40
Buddy Schultz	L	24	2	0	1.000	0	6	0	0	6	11	5	4	0	6.00
Ken Frailing	L	27	2	5	.286	1	41	0	0	53	61	26	39	0	5.43
2 Geoff Zahn (SJ)	L	29	2	7	.222	1	16	10	0	63	67	26	21	0	4.43
Ken Crosby	R	27	1	0	1.000	0	9	0	0	8	10	7	6	0	3.38
Paul Reuschel	R	28	1	3	.250	5	28	0	0	36	44	13	12	0	3.50
Donnie Moore	R	21	0	0	–	0	4	1	0	9	12	4	8	0	4.00
Eddie Solomon	R	24	0	0	–	0	6	0	0	7	7	6	3	0	1.29
Milt Wilcox	R	25	0	1	.000	0	25	0	0	38	50	17	21	0	5.68
Bob Locker	R	37	0	1	.000	0	22	0	0	33	38	16	14	0	4.91
Eddie Watt	R	33	0	1	.000	0	6	0	0	6	14	8	6	0	13.50
1 Burt Hooton	R	25	0	2	.000	0	3	3	0	11	18	4	5	0	8.18
Willie Prall	L	25	0	2	.000	0	3	3	0	15	21	8	7	0	8.40

MONTREAL 5th (tie) 75-87 .463 17.5 — GENE MAUCH

NAME	G by POS	B	AGE	G	AB	R	H	2B	3B	HR	RBI	BB	SO	SB	BA	SA
TOTALS			25	162	5518	601	1346	216	31	98	542	579	954	108	.244	.348
Mike Jorgensen	1B133,OF6	L	26	144	445	58	116	18	0	18	67	79	75	3	.261	.422
Pete Mackanin	2B127,SS1,3B1	R	23	130	448	59	101	19	6	12	44	31	99	11	.225	.375
Tim Foli	SS151,2B1	R	24	152	572	64	136	25	2	1	29	36	49	13	.238	.294
Larry Parrish	3B143,2B1,SS1	R	21	145	532	50	146	32	5	10	65	28	74	4	.274	.410
Gary Carter	OF92,C66,3B1	R	21	144	503	58	136	20	1	17	68	72	83	5	.270	.416
Pepe Mangual	OF138	R	23	140	514	84	126	16	2	9	45	74	115	33	.245	.337
Larry Biittner	OF93	L	29	121	346	34	109	13	5	3	28	34	33	2	.315	.408
Barry Foote	C115	R	23	118	387	25	75	16	1	7	30	17	48	0	.194	.295
Bob Bailey (BH)	OF61,3B3	R	32	106	227	23	62	5	0	5	30	46	38	4	.273	.361
Jose Morales	1B27,OF6,C5	R	30	93	163	18	49	6	1	2	24	14	21	0	.301	.387
Tony Scott	OF71	B	23	92	143	19	26	4	2	0	11	12	38	5	.182	.238
2 Jim Dwyer	OF52	L	25	60	175	22	50	7	1	3	20	23	30	4	.286	.389
Pat Scanlon	3B28,1B1	L	22	60	109	5	20	3	1	2	15	17	25	0	.183	.284
Pepe Frias (BZ)	SS29,3B11,2B7	R	26	51	64	4	8	2	0	0	4	3	13	0	.125	.156
1 Larry Lintz	2B39,SS2	B	25	46	132	18	26	0	0	0	3	23	18	17	.197	.197
Jim Lyttle	OF16	L	29	44	55	7	15	4	0	0	6	13	6	0	.273	.345
Jerry White	OF30	B	22	39	97	14	29	4	1	2	7	10	7	5	.299	.423
2 Nate Colbert	1B22	R	29	38	81	10	14	4	1	4	11	5	31	0	.173	.395
Hal Breeden	1B12	R	31	24	37	4	5	2	0	0	1	7	5	0	.135	.189
1 Rich Coggins (IL)	OF10	L	24	13	37	1	10	3	1	0	4	1	7	0	.270	.405
Ellis Valentine	OF11	R	20	12	33	2	12	4	0	1	3	2	1	0	.364	.576

Jim Cox 25 R 7-27, Bombo Rivera 22 R 1-9, Larry Johnson 24 R 1-3

NAME	T	AGE	W	L	PCT	SV	G	GS	CG	IP	H	BB	SO	ShO	ERA
TOTALS		27	75	87	.463	25	162	162	30	**1480**	1448	665	831	12	3.72
Dale Murray (IL)	R	25	15	8	.652	9	63	0	0	111	134	39	43	0	3.97
Steve Rogers	R	25	11	12	.478	0	35	35	12	252	248	88	137	3	3.29
Woody Fryman	L	35	9	12	.429	3	38	20	7	157	141	68	118	3	3.32
Dan Warthen	L	22	8	6	.571	3	40	18	2	168	130	87	128	0	3.11
Dennis Blair	R	21	8	15	.348	0	30	27	1	163	150	106	82	0	3.81
Steve Renko	R	30	6	12	.333	1	31	25	3	170	175	76	99	1	4.08
Don Carrithers (SJ)	R	25	5	3	.625	0	19	14	5	101	90	38	37	2	3.30
2 Fred Scherman	L	29	4	3	.571	0	34	7	0	76	84	41	43	0	3.55
Don DeMola	R	22	4	7	.364	1	60	0	0	98	92	42	63	0	4.13
Dave McNally (VR)	L	32	3	6	.333	0	12	12	0	77	88	36	36	0	5.26
Chuck Taylor	R	33	2	2	.500	6	54	0	0	74	72	24	29	0	3.53
Don Stanhouse	R	24	0	0	–	0	4	3	0	13	19	11	5	0	8.31
Chip Lang	R	22	0	0	–	0	1	1	0	2	2	3	2	0	9.00
1 John Montague	R	27	0	1	.000	2	12	0	0	18	23	6	9	0	5.50

WEST DIVISION

CINCINNATI 1st 108-54 .667 — SPARKY ANDERSON

NAME	G by POS	B	AGE	G	AB	R	H	2B	3B	HR	RBI	BB	SO	SB	BA	SA
TOTALS			28	162	5581	**840**	1515	278	37	124	**779**	**691**	916	**168**	.271	.401
Tony Perez	1B132	R	33	137	511	74	144	28	3	20	109	54	101	1	.282	.466
Joe Morgan	2B142	L	31	146	498	107	163	27	6	17	94	**132**	52	67	.327	.508
Dave Concepcion	SS130,3B6	R	27	140	507	62	139	23	1	5	49	39	51	33	.274	.353
Pete Rose	3B137,OF35	B	34	162	662	**112**	210	**47**	4	7	74	89	50	0	.317	.432
Ken Griffey	OF119	L	25	132	463	95	141	15	9	4	46	67	67	16	.305	.402
Cesar Geronimo	OF148	L	27	148	501	69	129	25	5	6	53	48	97	13	.257	.363
George Foster	OF125,1B1	R	26	134	463	71	139	24	4	23	78	40	73	2	.300	.518
Johnny Bench	C121,OF19,1B9	R	27	142	530	83	150	39	1	28	110	65	108	11	.283	.519
Merv Rettenmund	OF61,3B1	R	32	93	188	24	45	6	1	2	19	35	22	5	.239	.314
Doug Flynn	3B40,2B30,SS17	R	24	89	127	17	34	7	0	1	20	11	13	3	.268	.346
Dan Driessen	1B41,OF29	L	22	88	210	38	59	8	1	7	38	35	30	10	.281	.429
Darrel Chaney	SS34,2B23,3B13	L	27	71	160	18	35	6	0	2	26	14	38	3	.219	.294
Terry Crowley	OF4,1B4	L	28	66	71	8	19	6	0	1	11	7	6	0	.268	.394
Bill Plummer	C63	R	28	65	159	17	29	7	0	1	19	24	28	1	.182	.245
Ed Armbrister	OF19	R	26	59	65	9	12	1	0	0	2	5	19	3	.185	.200
John Vukovich	3B31	R	27	31	38	4	8	3	0	0	2	4	5	0	.211	.289
Don Werner	C7	R	22	7	8	0	1	0	0	0	0	0	0	0	.125	.125

NAME	T	AGE	W	L	PCT	SV	G	GS	CG	IP	H	BB	SO	ShO	ERA
TOTALS		28	**108**	54	**.667**	**50**	162	162	22	1459	1422	487	663	8	3.37
Don Gullett (BG)	L	24	15	4	.789	0	22	22	8	160	127	56	98	3	2.42
Gary Nolan	R	27	15	9	.625	0	32	32	5	211	202	29	74	1	3.16
Jack Billingham	R	32	15	10	.600	0	33	32	5	208	222	76	79	0	4.11
Fred Norman	L	32	12	4	.750	0	34	26	2	188	163	84	119	0	3.73
Pat Darcy	R	25	11	5	.688	1	27	22	1	131	134	59	46	0	3.57
Clay Kirby	R	27	10	6	.625	0	26	19	1	111	113	54	48	0	4.70
Pedro Borbon	R	27	9	5	.643	5	67	0	0	125	145	21	29	0	2.95
Clay Carroll	R	34	7	5	.583	7	56	2	0	96	93	32	44	0	2.63
Will McEnaney	L	23	5	2	.714	15	70	0	0	91	92	23	48	0	2.47
Rawly Eastwick	R	24	5	3	.625	**22**	58	0	0	90	77	25	61	0	2.60
Tom Carroll	R	22	4	1	.800	0	12	7	0	47	52	26	14	0	4.98
1 Tom Hall	L	27	0	0	–	0	2	0	0	2	2	2	3	0	0.00

LOS ANGELES 2nd 88-74 .543 20 — WALT ALSTON

NAME	G by POS	B	AGE	G	AB	R	H	2B	3B	HR	RBI	BB	SO	SB	BA	SA
TOTALS			27	162	5453	648	1355	217	31	118	606	611	825	138	.248	.365
Steve Garvey	1B160	R	26	160	659	85	210	38	6	18	95	33	66	11	.319	.476
Dave Lopes	2B137,OF24,SS14	R	29	155	618	108	162	24	6	8	41	91	93	**77**	.262	.359
Bill Russell (BH-KJ)	SS83	R	26	84	252	24	52	9	2	0	14	23	28	5	.206	.258
Ron Cey	3B158	R	27	158	566	72	160	29	2	25	101	78	74	5	.283	.473
Willie Crawford	OF113	L	28	124	373	46	98	15	2	9	46	49	43	5	.263	.386
Jim Wynn	OF120	R	33	130	412	80	102	16	0	18	58	110	77	7	.248	.417
Bill Buckner (NJ)	OF72	L	25	92	288	30	70	11	2	6	31	17	15	8	.243	.358
Steve Yeager	C135	R	26	135	452	34	103	16	1	12	54	40	75	2	.228	.347
Lee Lacy	2B43,OF43,SS1	R	27	101	306	44	96	11	5	7	40	22	29	5	.314	.451
Rick Auerbach (NJ)	SS81,2B1,3B1	R	25	85	170	18	38	9	0	0	12	18	22	3	.224	.276
John Hale	OF68	L	21	71	204	20	43	7	0	6	22	26	51	1	.211	.333
Joe Ferguson (BW)	C35,OF34	R	28	66	202	15	42	2	1	5	23	35	47	2	.208	.302
Ivan DeJesus	SS63	R	22	63	87	10	16	2	1	0	2	11	15	1	.184	.230
Tom Paciorek	OF54	R	28	62	145	14	28	8	0	1	5	11	29	4	.193	.269
Henry Cruz	OF41	L	23	53	94	8	25	3	1	0	5	7	6	1	.266	.319
Manny Mota	OF5	R	37	52	49	3	13	1	0	0	10	5	1	0	.265	.286
2 Leron Lee	OF4	L	27	48	43	2	11	4	0	0	2	3	9	0	.256	.349
Ken McMullen	3B11,1B3	R	33	39	46	4	11	1	1	2	14	7	12	0	.239	.435

Jerry Royster 22 R 9-36, Chuck Manuel 31 L 2-15, Paul Powell 27 R 2-10, Joe Simpson 23 L 2-6, Orlando Alvarez 23 R 0-4

NAME	T	AGE	W	L	PCT	SV	G	GS	CG	IP	H	BB	SO	ShO	ERA
TOTALS		29	88	74	.543	21	162	162	**51**	1470	1215	448	894	**18**	**2.92**
Andy Messersmith	R	29	19	14	.576	1	42	**40**	**19**	**322**	244	96	213	**7**	2.29
2 Burt Hooton	R	25	18	7	.720	0	31	30	12	224	172	64	148	4	2.81
Don Sutton	R	30	16	13	.552	0	35	35	11	254	202	62	175	4	2.87
Doug Rau	L	26	15	9	.625	0	38	38	8	258	227	61	151	2	3.10
Mike Marshall (VJ)	R	32	9	14	.391	13	57	0	0	109	98	39	64	0	3.30
1 Jim Brewer	L	37	3	1	.750	2	21	0	0	33	44	12	21	0	5.18
Rick Rhoden	R	22	3	3	.500	0	26	11	1	99	94	32	40	0	3.09
Charlie Hough	R	27	3	7	.300	4	38	0	0	61	43	34	34	0	2.95
Al Downing	L	34	2	1	.667	1	22	6	0	75	59	28	39	0	2.88
Dennis Lewallyn	R	21	0	0	–	0	2	0	0	3	1	0	0	0	0.00
Stan Wall	L	24	0	1	.000	0	10	0	0	16	12	7	6	0	1.69
1 Geoff Zahn	L	29	0	1	.000	0	2	0	0	3	2	5	1	0	9.00
Juan Marichal	R	37	0	1	.000	0	2	2	0	6	11	5	1	0	13.50
2 Dave Sells	R	28	0	2	.000	0	5	0	0	7	6	3	1	0	3.86

Tommy John (EJ) 32

SAN FRANCISCO 3rd 80-81 .497 27.5 — WES WESTRUM

NAME	G by POS	B	AGE	G	AB	R	H	2B	3B	HR	RBI	BB	SO	SB	BA	SA
TOTALS			25	161	5447	659	1412	235	45	84	606	604	775	99	.259	.365
2 Willie Montanez	1B134	L	27	135	518	52	158	26	2	8	85	45	50	5	.305	.409
Derrell Thomas	2B141,OF1	B	24	144	540	99	149	21	9	6	48	57	56	28	.276	.381
Chris Speier	SS136,3B1	R	25	141	487	60	132	30	5	10	69	70	50	4	.271	.415
Steve Ontiveros	3B89,OF8,1B4	B	23	108	325	21	94	16	0	3	31	55	44	2	.289	.366
Bobby Murcer	OF144	L	29	147	526	80	157	29	4	11	91	91	45	9	.298	.432
Von Joshua	OF117	L	27	129	507	75	161	25	10	7	43	32	75	20	.318	.448
Gary Matthews (BG)	OF113	R	24	116	425	67	119	22	3	12	58	65	53	13	.280	.431
Dave Rader	C94	L	26	98	292	39	85	15	0	5	31	32	30	1	.291	.394
Gary Thomasson	OF74,1B17	L	23	114	326	44	74	12	3	7	32	37	48	9	.227	.347
Bruce Miller	3B68,2B21,SS6	R	28	99	309	22	74	6	3	1	31	15	26	0	.239	.288
Marc Hill	C60,3B1	R	23	72	182	14	39	4	0	5	23	25	27	0	.214	.319
Glenn Adams	OF25	L	27	61	90	10	27	2	1	4	15	11	25	1	.300	.478
Mike Sadek	C38	R	29	42	106	14	25	5	2	0	9	14	14	1	.236	.321
Jake Brown	OF14	R	27	41	43	6	9	3	0	0	4	5	13	0	.209	.279
1 Ed Goodson	1B16,3B13	L	27	39	121	10	25	7	0	1	8	7	14	0	.207	.289
Chris Arnold	2B4,OF4	R	27	29	41	4	8	0	0	0	0	4	8	0	.195	.195
2 Craig Robinson	SS12,2B9	R	26	29	29	4	2	1	0	0	0	2	6	0	.069	.103
John LeMaster	SS22	R	21	22	74	4	14	4	0	2	9	4	15	2	.189	.324
1 Garry Maddox	OF13	R	25	17	52	4	7	1	0	1	4	6	3	1	.135	.212
1 Mike Phillips	2B6,3B6	L	24	10	31	3	6	0	0	0	1	6	4	1	.194	.194

Jack Clarke 19 R 4-17, Horace Speed 23 R 2-15, Gary Alexander 22 R 0-3

NAME	T	AGE	W	L	PCT	SV	G	GS	CG	IP	H	BB	SO	ShO	ERA
TOTALS		25	80	81	.497	24	161	161	37	1433	1406	612	856	9	3.74
John Montefusco	R	25	15	9	.625	0	35	34	10	244	210	86	215	4	2.88
Jim Barr	R	27	13	14	.481	0	35	33	12	244	244	58	77	2	3.06
Pete Falcone	L	21	12	11	.522	0	34	32	3	190	171	111	131	1	4.17
Ed Halicki	R	24	9	13	.409	0	24	23	7	160	143	59	153	2	3.49
Mike Caldwell	L	26	7	13	.350	1	38	21	4	163	194	48	57	0	4.80
Gary Lavelle	L	26	6	3	.667	8	65	0	0	82	80	48	51	0	2.96
Charlie Williams	R	27	5	3	.625	3	55	2	0	98	94	66	45	0	3.49
Randy Moffitt	R	26	4	5	.444	11	55	0	0	74	73	32	39	0	3.89
Dave Heaverlo	R	24	3	1	.750	1	42	0	0	64	62	31	35	0	2.39
Tom Bradley	R	28	2	3	.400	0	13	6	0	42	57	18	13	0	6.21
John D'Acquisto (EJ)	R	22	2	4	.333	0	10	6	0	28	29	34	22	0	10.29
Rob Dressler	R	21	1	0	1.000	0	3	2	1	16	17	4	6	0	1.13
Greg Minton	R	23	1	1	.500	0	4	2	0	17	19	11	6	0	6.88
Tommy Toms	R	23	0	1	.000	0	7	0	0	10	13	6	6	0	6.30

1 Ron Bryant (VR) 27

SAN DIEGO 4th 71-91 .438 37 — JOHN McNAMARA

NAME	G by POS	B	AGE	G	AB	R	H	2B	3B	HR	RBI	BB	SO	SB	BA	SA
TOTALS			28	162	5429	552	1324	215	22	78	505	506	754	85	.244	.335
Willie McCovey	1B115	L	37	122	413	43	104	17	0	23	68	57	80	1	.252	.460
Tito Fuentes	2B142	B	31	146	565	57	158	21	3	4	43	25	51	8	.280	.349
Enzo Hernandez	SS111	R	26	116	344	37	75	12	2	0	19	26	25	20	.218	.265
2 Ted Kubiak	3B64,2B11,1B1	B	33	87	196	13	44	5	0	0	14	24	18	3	.224	.250
Dave Winfield	OF138	R	23	143	509	74	136	20	2	15	76	69	82	23	.267	.403
John Grubb	OF139	L	26	144	553	72	149	36	2	4	38	59	59	2	.269	.363
Bobby Tolan	OF120,1B27	L	29	147	506	58	129	19	4	5	43	28	45	11	.255	.338
Fred Kendall	C85	R	26	103	286	26	57	12	1	0	24	26	28	0	.199	.248
Hector Torres	SS75,3B42,2B16	R	29	112	352	31	91	12	0	5	26	22	32	2	.259	.335
Mike Ivie	1B78,3B61,C1	R	22	111	377	36	94	16	2	8	46	20	63	4	.249	.366
Gene Locklear	OF51	L	25	100	237	31	76	11	1	5	27	22	26	4	.321	.439
Dick Sharon	OF57	R	25	91	160	14	31	7	0	4	20	26	35	0	.194	.313
Randy Hundley	C51	R	33	74	180	7	37	5	1	2	14	19	29	0	.206	.278
Bob Davis	C43	R	23	43	128	6	30	3	2	0	7	11	31	0	.234	.289
3 Don Hahn	OF26	R	26	34	26	7	6	1	2	0	3	10	2	1	.231	.423
Dave Roberts	3B30,2B5	R	24	33	113	7	32	2	0	2	12	13	19	3	.283	.354
John Scott	OF1	R	23	25	9	6	0	0	0	0	0	0	2	2	.000	.000
Steve Huntz	3B16,2B2	B	29	22	53	3	8	4	0	0	4	7	8	0	.151	.226
1 Jerry Moses	C5	R	28	13	19	1	3	2	0	0	1	2	3	0	.158	.263
Jerry Turner	OF4	L	21	11	22	1	6	0	0	0	0	2	1	0	.273	.273
Glenn Beckert (NJ)	3B4	R	34	9	16	2	6	1	0	0	0	1	0	0	.375	.438

2 Bobby Valentine 25 R 2-15, Bill Almon 22 R 4-10, Dave Hilton (IL) 24 R 0-8

NAME	T	AGE	W	L	PCT	SV	G	GS	CG	IP	H	BB	SO	ShO	ERA
		26	71	91	.438	20	162	162	40	1463	1494	521	713	12	3.48
Randy Jones	L	25	20	12	.625	0	37	36	18	285	242	56	103	6	2.24
Brent Strom (EJ)	L	26	8	8	.500	0	18	16	6	120	103	33	56	2	2.55
Joe McIntosh	R	23	8	15	.348	0	37	28	4	183	195	60	71	1	3.69
Rich Folkers	L	28	6	11	.353	0	45	15	4	142	155	39	87	0	4.18
Dan Spillner	R	23	5	13	.278	1	37	25	3	167	194	63	104	0	4.26
Dave Freisleben	R	23	5	14	.263	0	36	27	4	181	206	82	77	1	4.28
Dave Tomlin	L	26	4	2	.667	1	67	0	0	83	87	31	48	0	3.25
Bill Greif	R	25	4	6	.400	9	59	1	0	72	74	38	43	0	3.88
Alan Foster (SJ)	R	28	3	1	.750	0	17	4	1	45	41	21	20	0	2.40
Jerry Johnson	R	31	3	1	.750	0	21	4	0	54	60	31	18	0	5.17
1 Sonny Siebert	R	38	3	2	.600	0	6	6	0	27	37	10	10	0	4.33
Butch Metzger	R	23	1	0	1.000	0	4	0	0	5	6	4	6	0	7.20
Danny Frisella	R	29	1	6	.143	9	65	0	0	98	86	51	67	0	3.12
Larry Hardy	R	27	0	0	–	0	3	0	0	3	8	2	3	0	12.00

ATLANTA 5th 67-94 .416 40.5 — CLYDE KING 58-76 .433 — CONNIE RYAN 9-18 .333

NAME	G by POS	B	AGE	G	AB	R	H	2B	3B	HR	RBI	BB	SO	SB	BA	SA
TOTALS			26	161	5424	583	1323	179	28	107	541	543	759	55	.244	.346
Earl Williams	1B90,C11	R	26	111	383	42	92	13	0	11	50	34	63	0	.240	.360
Marty Perez (BG)	2B116,SS7	R	28	120	461	50	127	14	2	2	34	37	44	2	.275	.328
Larvell Blanks	SS129,2B12	R	25	141	471	49	110	13	3	3	38	38	43	4	.234	.293
Darrell Evans	3B156,1B3	L	28	156	567	82	138	22	2	22	73	105	106	12	.243	.406
Rowland Office	OF107	L	22	126	355	30	103	14	1	3	30	23	41	2	.290	.361
Dusty Baker	OF136	R	26	142	494	63	129	18	2	19	72	67	57	12	.261	.421
Ralph Garr	OF148	L	29	151	625	74	174	26	11	6	31	44	50	14	.278	.384
Vic Correll	C97	R	29	103	325	37	70	12	2	11	39	42	66	0	.215	.360
Mike Lum	1B60,OF38	L	29	124	364	32	83	8	2	8	36	39	38	2	.228	.327
Rod Gilbreath	2B52,3B10,SS1	R	22	90	202	24	49	3	1	2	16	24	26	5	.243	.297
Dave May	OF53	L	31	82	203	28	56	8	0	12	40	25	27	1	.276	.493
Biff Pocoroba	C62	R	21	67	188	15	48	7	1	1	22	20	11	0	.255	.319
Clarence Gaston	OF35,1B1	R	31	64	141	17	34	4	0	6	15	17	33	1	.241	.397
2 Ed Goodson	1B13,3B1	L	27	47	76	5	16	2	0	1	8	2	8	0	.211	.276
Rob Belloir	SS38,2B1	R	26	43	105	11	23	2	1	0	9	7	8	0	.219	.257
Bob Beall	1B8	B	27	20	31	2	7	2	0	0	1	6	9	0	.226	.290
1 Craig Robinson	SS7	R	26	10	17	1	1	0	0	0	0	0	5	0	.059	.059
1 Johnny Oates	C6	L	29	8	18	0	4	1	0	0	0	1	4	0	.222	.278

Frank Tepedino 27 L 0-7, Joe Nolan 24 L 1-4, Dave Johnson 32 R 1-1, 1 Dick Allen (RR) 33

NAME	T	AGE	W	L	PCT	SV	G	GS	CG	IP	H	BB	SO	ShO	ERA
		29	67	94	.416	24	161	161	32	1430	**1543**	519	669	4	3.91
Carl Morton	R	31	17	16	.515	0	39	39	11	278	**302**	82	78	2	3.50
Phil Niekro	R	36	15	15	.500	0	39	37	13	276	285	72	144	1	3.20
Tom House	L	28	7	7	.500	11	58	0	0	79	79	36	36	0	3.19
Mike Beard	L	25	4	0	1.000	0	34	2	0	70	71	28	27	0	3.21
1 Ron Reed	R	32	4	5	.444	0	10	10	1	75	93	16	40	0	4.20
Buzz Capra (SJ)	R	27	4	7	.364	0	12	12	5	78	77	28	35	0	4.27
1 Roric Harrison	R	28	3	4	.429	1	15	7	2	55	58	19	22	0	4.75
Max Leon	R	25	2	1	.667	6	50	1	0	85	90	33	53	0	4.13
Elias Sosa	R	25	2	2	.500	2	43	0	0	62	70	29	31	0	4.50
2 Ray Sadecki	L	34	2	3	.400	1	25	5	0	66	73	21	24	0	4.23
2 Bruce Dal Canton	R	33	2	7	.222	3	26	9	0	67	63	24	38	0	3.36
Jamie Easterly	L	22	2	9	.182	0	21	13	0	69	73	42	34	0	4.96
Adrian Devine	R	23	1	0	1.000	0	5	2	0	16	19	7	8	0	4.50
Gary Gentry	R	28	1	1	.500	0	7	2	0	20	25	8	10	0	4.95
3 Blue Moon Odom	R	30	1	7	.125	0	15	10	0	56	78	28	30	0	7.07
Preston Hanna	R	20	0	0	–	0	4	0	0	6	7	5	2	0	1.50
Pablo Torrealba	L	27	0	1	.000	0	6	0	0	7	7	3	5	0	1.29
Frank LaCorte	R	23	0	3	.000	0	3	2	0	14	13	6	10	0	5.14
Mike Thompson	R	25	0	6	.000	0	16	10	0	52	60	32	42	0	4.67

HOUSTON 6th 64-97 .398 43.5 — PRESTON GOMEZ 47-80 .370 — BILL VIRDON 17-17 .500

NAME	G by POS	B	AGE	G	AB	R	H	2B	3B	HR	RBI	BB	SO	SB	BA	SA
TOTALS			26	162	5515	664	1401	218	**54**	84	606	523	762	133	.254	.359
Bob Watson	1B118,OF9	R	29	132	485	67	157	27	1	18	85	40	50	3	.324	.495
Rob Andrews	2B94,SS6	R	22	103	277	29	66	5	4	0	19	31	34	12	.238	.285
Roger Metzger	SS126	B	27	127	450	54	102	7	9	2	26	41	39	4	.227	.296
Doug Rader	3B124,SS2	R	30	129	448	41	100	23	2	12	48	42	101	5	.223	.364
Wilbur Howard	OF95	B	26	121	392	62	111	16	8	0	21	21	67	32	.283	.365
Cesar Cedeno (RJ)	OF131	R	24	131	500	93	144	31	3	13	63	62	52	50	.288	.440
Greg Gross	OF121	L	22	132	483	67	142	14	10	0	41	63	37	2	.294	.364
Milt May	C102	L	24	111	386	29	93	15	1	4	52	26	41	1	.241	.316
Cliff Johnson	1B47,C41,OF1	R	27	122	340	52	94	16	1	20	65	46	64	1	.276	.506
Jose Cruz	OF94	L	27	120	315	44	81	15	2	9	49	52	44	6	.257	.403
Enos Cabell	OF67,1B25,3B22	R	25	117	348	43	92	17	6	2	43	18	53	12	.264	.365
Ken Boswell	2B31,3B23	L	29	86	178	16	43	8	2	0	21	30	12	0	.242	.309
Larry Milbourne	2B43,SS22	B	24	73	151	17	32	1	2	1	9	6	14	1	.212	.265
Tommy Helms	2B42,3B3,SS1	R	34	64	135	7	28	2	0	0	14	10	8	0	.207	.222
Skip Jutze	C47	R	29	51	93	9	21	2	0	0	6	2	4	1	.226	.247
Jerry DaVanon	SS21,2B9,3B3	R	29	32	97	15	27	4	2	1	10	16	7	2	.278	.392
Art Gardner	OF8	L	22	13	31	3	6	0	0	0	2	1	8	1	.194	.194

Rafael Batista 29 L 3-10, Mike Easler 24 L 0-5, Jesus de la Rosa 21 R 1-3

NAME	T	AGE	W	L	PCT	SV	G	GS	CG	IP	H	BB	SO	ShO	ERA
		27	64	**97**	.398	25	162	162	39	1458	1436	**679**	839	6	4.04
Larry Dierker	R	28	14	16	.467	0	34	34	14	232	225	91	127	2	4.00
J.R. Richard	R	25	12	10	.545	0	33	31	7	203	178	**138**	176	1	4.39
Dave Roberts	L	29	8	14	.364	1	32	27	7	198	182	73	101	0	4.27
Joe Niekro	R	30	6	4	.600	4	40	4	1	88	79	39	54	1	3.07
Doug Konieczny	R	23	6	13	.316	0	32	29	4	171	184	87	89	1	4.47
Jim York	R	26	4	4	.500	0	19	4	0	47	43	25	17	0	3.83
Ken Forsch (NJ)	R	28	4	8	.333	2	34	9	2	109	114	30	54	0	3.22
Jim Crawford	L	24	3	5	.375	4	44	2	0	87	92	37	37	0	3.62
Tom Griffin (HJ)	R	27	3	8	.273	0	17	13	3	79	89	46	56	1	5.35
Wayne Granger	R	31	2	5	.286	5	55	0	0	74	76	23	30	0	3.65
Mike Cosgrove	L	24	1	2	.333	5	32	3	1	71	62	37	32	0	3.04
Jose Sosa	R	22	1	3	.250	1	25	2	0	47	51	23	31	0	4.02
1 Fred Scherman	L	29	0	1	.000	0	16	0	0	16	21	4	13	0	5.06
Paul Siebert	L	22	0	2	.000	2	7	2	0	18	20	6	6	0	3.00
Mike Stanton	R	22	0	2	.000	1	7	2	0	17	20	20	16	0	7.41

WORLD SERIES — CINCINNATI (NL) 4 BOSTON (AL) 3

LINE SCORES

TEAM	1	2	3	4	5	6	7	8	9	10	11	12	R	H	E
Game 1 October 11 at Boston															
CIN (NL)	0	0	0	0	0	0	0	0	0				0	5	0
BOS (AL)	0	0	0	0	0	0	6	0	X				6	12	0
Gullett, Carroll (7), McEnaney (7) — **Tiant**															
Game 2 October 12 at Boston															
CIN	0	0	0	1	0	0	0	0	2				3	7	1
BOS	1	0	0	0	0	1	0	0	0				2	7	0
Billingham, Borbon (6), McEnaney (7), **Eastwick (8)** — Lee, **Drago (9)**															
Game 3 October 14 at Cincinnati															
BOS	0	1	0	0	0	1	1	0	2	0			5	10	2
CIN	0	0	0	2	3	0	0	0	0	1			6	7	0
Wise, Burton (5), Cleveland (5), **Willoughby (7)**, Moret (10) — Nolan, Darcy (5), Carroll (7), McEnaney (7), **Eastwick (9)**															
Game 4 October 15 at Cincinnati															
BOS	0	0	0	5	0	0	0	0	0				5	11	1
CIN	2	0	0	2	0	0	0	0	0				4	9	1
Tiant — **Norman**, Borbon (4), Carroll (5), Eastwick (7)															
Game 5 October 16 at Cincinnati															
BOS	1	0	0	0	0	0	0	0	1				2	5	0
CIN	0	0	0	1	1	3	0	1	X				6	8	0
Cleveland, Willoughby (6), Pole (8), Segui (8) — **Gullett**, Eastwick (9)															
Game 6 October 21 at Boston															
CIN	0	0	0	0	3	0	2	1	0	0	0	0	6	14	0
BOS	3	0	0	0	0	0	0	3	0	0	0	1	7	10	1
Nolan, Norman (3), Billingham (3), Carroll (5), Borbon (6), Eastwick (8), McEnaney (9), **Darcy (10)** — Tiant, Moret (8), Drago (9), **Wise (12)**															
Game 7 October 22 at Boston															
CIN	0	0	0	0	0	2	1	0	1				4	9	0
BOS	0	0	3	0	0	0	0	0	0				3	5	2
Gullett, Billingham (6), **Carroll (8)**, McEnaney (9) — Lee, Moret (7), Willoughby (7), **Burton (9)**, Cleveland (9)															

COMPOSITE BATTING

NAME	POS	G	AB	R	H	2B	3B	HR	RBI	BA
Cincinnati (NL)										
Totals		7	244	29	59	9	3	7	29	.242
Foster	LF	7	29	1	8	1	0	0	2	.276
Bench	C	7	29	5	6	2	0	1	4	.207
Perez	1B	7	28	4	5	0	0	**3**	**7**	.179
Concepcion	SS	7	28	3	5	1	0	1	4	.179
Rose	3B	7	27	3	**10**	1	**1**	0	2	**.370**
Morgan	2B	7	27	4	7	1	0	0	3	.259
Griffey	RF	7	26	4	7	**3**	**1**	0	4	.269
Geronimo	CF	7	25	3	7	0	**1**	2	3	.280
Gullett	P	3	7	1	2	0	0	0	0	.286
Rettenmund	PH	3	3	0	0	0	0	0	0	.000
Crowley	PH	2	2	0	1	0	0	0	0	.500
Billingham	P	3	2	0	0	0	0	0	0	.000
Chaney	PH	2	2	0	0	0	0	0	0	.000
Driessen	PH	2	2	0	0	0	0	0	0	.000
McEnaney	P	5	1	0	1	0	0	0	0	1.000
Armbrister	PH	4	1	1	0	0	0	0	0	.000
Eastwick	P	5	1	0	0	0	0	0	0	.000
Borbon	P	3	1	0	0	0	0	0	0	.000
Nolan	P	2	1	0	0	0	0	0	0	.000
Norman	P	2	1	0	0	0	0	0	0	.000

Darcy P 0-1, Carroll P 0-0

NAME	POS	G	AB	R	H	2B	3B	HR	RBI	BA
Boston (AL)										
Totals		7	239	30	60	7	2	6	30	.251
Doyle	2B	7	**30**	3	8	1	**1**	0	0	.267
Yastrzemski	LF-1B	7	29	**7**	9	0	0	0	4	.310
Petrocelli	3B	7	26	3	8	1	0	0	4	.308
Lynn	CF	7	25	3	7	1	0	1	5	.280
Fisk	C	7	25	5	6	0	0	2	4	.240
Evans	RF	7	24	3	7	1	**1**	1	5	.292
Burleson	SS	7	24	1	7	1	0	0	2	.292
Cooper	1B	5	19	0	1	1	0	0	1	.053
Beniquez	LF	3	8	0	1	0	0	0	1	.125
Tiant	P	3	8	2	2	0	0	0	0	.250
Carbo	LF	4	7	3	3	1	0	2	4	.429
Lee	P	2	6	0	1	0	0	0	0	.167
Miller	LF	3	2	0	0	0	0	0	0	.000
Cleveland	P	3	2	0	0	0	0	0	0	.000
Wise	P	2	2	0	0	0	0	0	0	.000
Griffin	PH	1	1	0	0	0	0	0	0	.000
Montgomery	PH	1	1	0	0	0	0	0	0	.000

Moret P 0-0, Willoughby P 0-0, Drago P 0-0, Segui P 0-0, Pole P 0-0

COMPOSITE PITCHING

NAME	G	IP	H	BB	SO	W	L	SV	ERA
Oakland (AL)									
Totals	7	65	60	30	40	4	3	2	3.88
Gullett	3	18.2	19	**10**	**15**	1	**1**	0	4.34
Billingham	3	9	8	5	7	0	0	0	**1.00**
Eastwick	**5**	8	6	3	4	**2**	0	**1**	2.25
McEnaney	**5**	6.2	3	2	5	0	0	**1**	2.70
Nolan	2	6	6	1	2	0	0	0	6.00
Carroll	**5**	5.2	4	2	3	1	0	0	3.18
Norman	2	4	8	3	2	0	1	0	9.00
Darcy	2	4	3	2	1	0	1	0	4.50
Borbon	3	3	3	2	1	0	0	0	6.00
Boston (AL)									
Totals	7	65.1	59	25	30	3	4	0	3.86
Tiant	3	**25**	**25**	8	12	**2**	0	0	3.60
Lee	2	14.1	12	3	7	0	0	0	3.14
Cleveland	3	6.2	7	3	5	0	1	0	6.75
Willoughby	3	6.1	3	0	2	0	1	0	0.00
Wise	2	5.1	6	2	2	1	0	0	8.44
Drago	2	4	3	1	1	0	**1**	0	2.25
Moret	3	1.2	2	3	1	0	0	0	0.00
Segui	1	1	0	0	0	0	0	0	0.00
Burton	2	1	1	3	0	0	**1**	0	9.00
Pole	1	0	0	2	0	0	0	0	∞

USE NAME – GIVEN NAMES (NICKNAMES)	TEAM BY YEAR	BIRTH DATE	BIRTH PLACE	DEATH DATE	B	T	HGT	WGT	G	AB	R	H	2B	3B	HR	RBI	BB	SO	SB	BA	SA
					LIFETIME BATTING TOTALS																
Aaron, Hank-Henry Louis (Hammering Hank)	54-65MilN 67-74AtlN 75MilA	2- 5-34	Mobile, Ala.		R	R	6'	180	3213	12093	2152	3709	616	98	745	2262	1367	1345	240	.307	.559
Aaron, Tommie-Tommie Lee	62-63, 65MilN 68-71AtlN	8- 5-39	Mobile, Ala.		R	R	6'	200	437	944	102	216	42	6	13	94	86	145	9	.229	.327
Adair, Jerry-Kenneth Jerry	58-66BalA 66-67ChiA 67-68BosA 69-70KCA	12-17-36	Sand Springs, Okla.		R	R	6'	180	1165	4019	378	1022	163	19	57	366	208	499	29	.254	.347
Adams, Doug-Harold Douglas	69ChiA	1-27-43	Blue River, Wis.		L	R	6'3	195	8	14	1	3	0	0	0	1	1	3	0	.214	.214
Adams, Glenn-Glenn Charles	75SFN	10- 4-47	Northbridge, Mass.		L	R	6'	185	61	90	10	27	2	1	4	15	11	25	1	.300	.478
Adams, Mike-Robert Michael	72-73MinA	7-24-48	Cincinnati, Ohio		R	R	5'9	180	58	72	21	16	2	0	3	6	17	19	2	.222	.375
Adlesh, Dave-David George	63-68HouN	7-15-43	Long Beach, Cal.		R	R	6'	167	106	256	9	43	3	1	1	11	18	80	0	.168	.199
Agee, Tommie-Tommie Lee	62-64CleA 65-67ChiA 68-72NYN 73HouN 73StLN	8- 9-42	Magnolia, Ala.		R	R	5'11	190	1129	3912	558	999	170	27	130	433	342	918	167	.255	.412
Alcaraz, Luis-Angel Luis [Acosta]	67-68LAN 69-70KCA	6-20-41	Humacao, P.R.		R	R	5'9	165	15	365	30	70	9	2	4	29	21	58	2	.192	.260
Alexander, Gary-Gary Wayne (Sleepy)	75SFN	3-27-53	Los Angeles, Cal.		R	R	6'2	195	3	3	1	0	0	0	0	0	1	2	0	.000	.000
Alexander, Matt-Matthew (Sonny)	73-74ChiN 75OakA	1-30-47	Shreveport, La.		B	R	5'11	170	120	69	35	13	2	1	0	1	14	14	27	.188	.246
Allen, Bernie-Bernard Keith	62-66MinA 67-71WasA 72-73NYA 73MonN	4-16-39	East Liverpool, Ohio		L	R	6'	180	1139	3404	357	815	140	21	73	351	360	424	13	.239	.357
Allen, Dick-Richard Anthony	63-69PhiN 70StLN 71LAN 72-74ChiA 75PhiN	3- 8-42	Wampum, Pa.		R	R	5'11	187	1610	5863	1028	1727	300	78	331	1039	833	1457	121	.295	.542
Allen, Hank-Harold Andrew	66-70WasA 70MilA 72-73ChiA	7-23-40	Wampum, Pa.		R	R	6'	190	389	881	104	212	27	9	6	57	49	128	15	.241	.312
Allen, Ron-Ronald Frederick	72StLN	12-23-43	Wampum, Pa.		B	R	6'3	210	7	11	2	1	0	0	1	1	3	5	0	.091	.364
Alley, Gene-Leonard Eugene	63-73PitN	7-10-40	Richmond, Va.		R	R	5'10	160	1195	3927	442	999	140	44	55	342	300	632	63	.254	.354
Allietta, Bob-Robert George	75CalA	5- 1-52	New Bedford, Mass.		R	R	6'	188	21	45	4	8	1	0	1	2	1	6	0	.178	.267
Allison, Bob-William Robert	58-60WasA 61-70MinA	7-11-34	Raytown, Mo.		R	R	6'3	220	1541	5032	811	1281	216	53	256	796	795	1033	84	.255	.471
Almon, Bill-William Francis	74-75SDN	11-21-52	Providence, R.I.		R	R	6'3	180	21	48	4	16	1	0	0	3	2	10	1	.333	.354
Alomar, Sandy-Santos [Conde]	64-65MilN 66AtlN 67NYN 67-69ChiA 69-74CalA	10-19-43	Salinas, P.R.		B	R	5'9	155	1321	4485	514	1101	118	19	11	260	280	450	211	.245	.288
	74-75NYA				Bats right 65-66, part of 64																
Alou (Rojas), Felipe-Felipe Rojas [Alou]	58-63SFN 64-65MilN 66-69AtlN	5-12-35	Haina, Dom. Rep.		R	R	6'1	195	2082	7339	985	2101	359	49	206	852	423	706	107	.286	.433
	70-71OakA 72-73NYA 73MonN 74MilA																				
Alou (Rojas), Jesus-Jesus Maria Rojas [Alou] (Jay)	63-68SFN 69-73HouN	3-24-42	Haina, Dom. Rep.		R	R	6'2	190	1261	4163	438	1160	161	25	30	348	126	255	31	.279	.351
	73-74OakA 75NYN																				
Alou (Rojas), Matty-Mateo Rojas (Alou)	60-65SFN 66-70PitN 71-72StLN 72OakA	12-22-38	Haina, Dom. Rep.		L	L	5'9	160	1667	5789	780	1777	236	50	31	427	311	377	156	.307	.381
	73NYA 73StLN 74SDN																				
Altman, George-George Lee	59-62ChiN 63StLN 64NYN 65-67ChiN	3-20-33	Goldsboro, N.C.		L	R	6'4	200	991	3091	409	832	132	34	101	403	268	572	52	.269	.432
Alusik, George-George Joseph (Turk, Glider)	58, 61-62DetA 62-64KCA	2-11-35	Ashley, Pa.		R	R	6'3	180	298	652	75	167	31	2	23	93	73	103	1	.256	.416
Alvarado, Luis-Luis Cesar [Martinez] (Pimba)	68-70BosA 71-74ChiA 74StLN	1-15-49	Lajas, P.R.		R	R	5'9	162	444	1115	111	236	42	4	5	81	46	154	11	.212	.270
	74CleA																				
Alvarez, Orlando-Jesus Manuel Orlando [Monge] (Nenin)	73-75LAN	2-28-52	Rio Grande, P.R.		R	R	6'	175	10	9	0	1	1	0	0	0	0	2	0	.111	.222
Alvarez, Rogelio-Rogelio [Hernandez] (Gorrego)	60, 62CinN	4-18-38	Pinar del Rio, Cuba		R	R	5'11	183	17	37	2	7	0	0	0	2	1	13	0	.189	.189
Alvis, Max-Roy Maxwell	62-69CleA 70MilA	2- 2-38	Jasper, Tex.		R	R	5'11	185	1013	3629	421	895	142	22	111	373	262	662	43	.247	.390
Alyea, Brant-Garrabrant Ryerson	63,68-69WasA 70-71MinA 72OakA 72StLN 72OakA	12- 8-40	Passaic, N.J.		R	R	6'3	215	371	866	100	214	33	2	38	148	100	210	5	.247	.421
Amalfitano, Joey-John Joseph	54-55NYN 60-61SFN 62HouN 63SFN 64-67ChiN	1-23-34	San Pedro, Cal.		R	R	5'11	175	643	1715	248	418	67	19	9	123	185	224	19	.244	.321
Amaro, Ruben-Ruben [Mora]	58StLN 60-65PhiN 66-68NYA 69CalA	1- 6-36	Veracruz, Mexico		R	R	5'11	170	940	2155	211	505	75	13	8	156	227	280	11	.234	.292
Anderson, Dwain-Dwain Cleaven (D)	71-72OakA 72-73StLN 73SDN 74CleA	11-23-47	Oakland, Cal.		R	R	6'	180	149	306	33	62	6	2	1	14	32	70	2	.201	.244
Anderson, Mike-Michael Allen	71-75PhiN	6-22-51	Florence, S.C.		R	R	6'2	200	409	1027	110	254	51	8	22	100	105	258	4	.247	.377
Andrew, Kim-Kim Darrell	75BosA	11-14-53	Burbank, Cal.		R	R	5'11	165	2	2	0	1	0	0	0	0	0	0	0	.500	.500
Andrews, Mike-Michael Jay	66-70BosA 71-73ChiA 73OakA	7- 9-43	Los Angeles, Cal.		R	R	6'3	195	893	3116	441	803	140	4	66	316	458	390	19	.258	.369
Andrews, Rob-Robert Patrick	75HouN	12-11-52	Santa Monica, Cal.		R	R	5'11	180	103	277	29	66	5	4	0	19	31	34	12	.238	.285
Aparicio, Luis-Luis Ernesto [Monteil] (Little Louie)	56-62ChiA 63-67BalA	4-29-34	Maracaibo, Venezuela		R	R	5'9	160	2599	10230	1335	2677	394	92	83	791	735	742	506	.262	.343
	68-70ChiA 71-73BosA																				
Arcia, Jose-Jose Raimundo [Orta] (Flaco)	68ChiN 69-70SDN	8-22-43	Havana, Cuba		R	R	6'3	170	293	615	78	132	24	6	1	35	29	107	17	.215	.278
Ardell, Danny-Daniel Miers	61LAA	5-27-41	Seattle, Wash.		L	L	6'2	190	7	4	1	1	0	0	0	0	1	2	0	.250	.250
Armbrister, Ed-Edison Rosanda	73-75CinN	7- 4-48	Nassau, Bahamas		R	R	6'3	175	86	109	14	22	4	1	1	7	8	28	3	.202	.284
Arnold, Chris-Christopher Paul	71-75SFN	11- 6-47	Long Beach, Cal.		R	R	5'11	185	213	366	43	88	12	4	4	46	36	60	1	.240	.328
Ashby, Alan-Alan Dean	73-75CleA	7- 8-51	Long Beach, Cal.		B	R	6'1	190	111	290	37	63	11	1	6	35	33	55	3	.217	.324
Aspromonte, Bob-Robert Thomas	56BknN 60-61LAN 62-68HouN 69-70AtlN 71NYN	6-19-38	Brooklyn, N.Y.		R	R	6'2	190	1324	4369	386	1103	135	26	60	457	333	459	19	.252	.336
Auerbach, Rick-Frederick, Steven (Reindeer)	71-73MilA 74-75LAN	2-15-50	Glendale, Cal.		R	R	6'	175	368	1043	104	233	36	3	4	55	89	134	34	.223	.275
Augustine, Dave-David Ralph (Augie)	73-74PitN	11-28-49	Follansbee, W. Va.		R	R	6'2	178	29	29	4	6	1	0	0	0	0	6	0	.207	.241
Averill, Earl-Earl Douglas	56, 58CleA 59-60ChiN 60ChiA 61-62LAA 63PhiN	9- 9-31	Cleveland, Ohio		R	R	5'10	200	449	1031	137	249	41	0	44	159	162	220	3	.242	.409
Ayala, Benny-Benigno [Felix]	74NYN	2- 7-51	Yauco, P.R.		R	R	6'1	195	23	68	9	16	1	0	2	8	7	17	0	.235	.338
Azcue, Joe-Jose Joaquin [Lopez]	60CinN 62-63KCA 63-69CleA 69BosA 69-70CalA	8-18-39	Cienfuegos, Cuba		R	R	6'	195	909	2828	201	712	94	9	50	304	207	344	5	.252	.344
	71HO 72CalA 72MilA																				
Bailey, Bob-Robert Sherwood	62-66PitN 67-68LAN 69-75MonN	10-13-42	Long Beach, Cal.		R	R	6'1	185	1768	5783	734	1489	223	41	177	730	805	1070	82	.257	.402
Bailor, Bob-Robert Michael (Buzz)	75BalA	7-10-51	Connellsville, Pa.		R	R	5'10	165	5	7	0	1	0	0	0	0	1	0	0	.143	.143
Baker, Dusty-Johnnie B	68-75AtlN	6-15-49	Riverside, Cal.		R	R	6'2	190	628	2216	311	616	111	8	77	324	253	306	58	.278	.440
Baker, Frank-Frank	69-71CleA	1-11-44	Bartow, Fla.		L	R	5'10	188	125	353	39	82	17	4	4	38	26	68	2	.232	.337
Baker, Frank-Frank Watts	70-71NYA 73-74BalA	10-29-46	Meridian, Miss.		L	R	6'2	185	146	288	28	55	8	3	1	24	40	60	4	.191	.250
Balaz, John-John Larry (Blazer)	74-75CalA	11-24-50	Toronto, Canada		R	R	6'3	185	59	162	14	39	8	1	2	15	7	35	0	.241	.340
Baldwin, Billy-Robert Harvey	75DetA	6- 9-50	Tazewell, Va.		L	L	6'	180	30	95	8	21	3	0	4	8	5	14	2	.221	.379
Bales, Lee-Wesley Owen	66AtlN 67HouN	12- 4-44	Los Angeles, Cal.		R	R	5'10	165	31	43	8	4	0	0	0	2	0	12	1	.093	.093
Bando, Sal-Salvatore Leonard	66-67KCA 68-75OakA	2-13-44	Cleveland, Ohio		R	R	6'	210	1310	4595	662	1179	194	23	165	712	716	628	40	.257	.417
Banks, Ernie-Ernest	53-71ChiN	1-31-31	Dallas, Tex.		R	R	6'1	180	2528	9421	1305	2583	407	90	512	1636	763	1236	50	.274	.500
Banks, George-George Edward	62-64MinA 64-66CleA	9-24-38	Pacolet Mills, S.C.		R	R	5'11	185	106	201	33	44	6	2	9	27	37	59	0	.219	.403
Bannister, Alan-Alan	74-75PhiN	9- 3-51	Montebello, Cal.		R	R	5'11	170	50	86	14	19	3	1	0	1	4	16	2	.221	.279
Barbieri, Jim-James Patrick	66LAN	9-15-41	Schenectady, N.Y.		L	R	5'7	155	39	82	9	23	5	0	0	3	9	7	2	.280	.341
Barker, Ray-Raymond Herrell (Buddy)	60BalA 65CleA 65-67NYA	3-12-36	Martinsburg, W. Va.		L	R	6'	192	192	318	34	68	16	0	10	44	29	76	1	.214	.358
Barnes, Lute-Luther Owen	72-73NYN	4-28-47	Forest City, Iowa		R	R	5'10	162	27	74	7	18	2	2	0	7	6	5	0	.243	.324
Barragan, Cuno-Facundo Anthony	61-63ChiN	6-20-32	Sacramento, Cal.		R	R	5'11	180	69	163	14	33	6	1	1	14	23	36	0	.202	.270
Barry, Rich-Richard Donovan	69PhiN	9-12-40	Berkeley, Cal.		R	R	6'4	205	20	32	4	6	1	0	0	0	5	6	0	.188	.219
Barton, Bob-Robert Wilbur	65-69SFN 70-72SDN 73CinN 74SDN	7-30-41	Norwood, Ohio		R	R	6'	185	393	1049	54	237	31	3	9	66	87	168	3	.226	.287
Bateman, John-John Alvin	63-68HouN 69-72MonN 72PhiN	7-21-42	Killeen, Tex.		R	R	6'3	215	1017	3330	250	765	123	18	81	375	172	610	10	.230	.350
Bates, Del-Delbert Oakley (Butch)	70PhiN	6-12-40	Seattle, Wash.		L	R	6'3	210	22	60	1	8	2	0	0	1	6	15	0	.133	.167
Batista (Roble), Rafael-Rafael [Bastista]	73,75HouN	11-21-45	Ingenio Consuelo, D.R.		L	L	6'1	190	22	25	2	7	1	0	0	2	1	10	0	.280	.320
Battey, Earl-Earl Jesse	55-59ChiA 60WasA 61-67MinA	1- 5-35	Los Angeles, Cal.		R	R	6'1	215	1141	3586	393	969	150	17	104	449	421	470	13	.270	.409
Baumer, Jim-James Sloan	49ChiA 61CinN	1-29-31	Tulsa, Okla.		R	R	6'2	185	18	34	2	7	1	1	0	2	2	10	0	.206	.294
Baylor, Don-Donald Edward	70-75BalA	6-28-49	Austin, Tex.		R	R	6'1	195	511	1757	246	482	76	14	57	229	164	222	118	.274	.431
Beall, Bob-Robert Brooks	75AtlN	4-24-48	Portland, Ore.		B	L	5'11	180	20	31	2	7	2	0	0	1	6	9	0	.226	.290
Beauchamp, Jim-James Edward	63StLN 64-65HouN 65MilN 67AtlN 68-69CinN 70HouN	8-21-39	Vinita, Okla.		R	R	6'2	205	393	661	79	153	18	4	14	90	54	150	6	.231	.334
	70-71StLN 72-73NYN																				
Beckert, Glenn-Glenn Alfred	65-73ChiN 74-75SDN	12-10-40	Pittsburgh, Pa.		R	R	6'1	190	1320	5208	685	1473	196	31	22	360	260	243	49	.283	.341
Bedell, Howie-Howard William	62MilN 68PhiN	9-29-35	Clearfield, Pa.		L	R	6'1	185	67	145	15	28	1	2	0	3	12	22	1	.193	.228
Belanger, Mark-Mark Henry	65-75BalA	6- 8-44	Pittsfield, Mass.		R	R	6'2	180	1252	3857	452	889	110	20	16	258	384	559	105	.230	.282
Bell, Buddy-David Gus	72-75CleA	8-27-51	Pittsburgh, Pa.		R	R	6'2	190	457	2073	252	549	79	13	40	200	169	177	19	.265	.373
Belloir, Rob-Robert Edward	75AtlN	7-13-48	Heidelberg, Germany		R	R	5'10	165	43	105	11	23	2	1	0	9	7	8	0	.219	.257
Bench, Johnny-Johnny Lee	67-75CinN	12- 7-47	Oklahoma City, Okla.		R	R	6'1	197	1236	4595	695	1246	236	18	240	855	516	751	40	.271	.487
Beniquez, Juan-Juan Jose [Torres]	71-72, 74-75BosA	5-13-50	San Sebastian, P.R.		R	R	5'11	160	233	801	121	219	34	8	8	62	60	102	31	.273	.366
Bergman, Dave-David Bruce	75NYA	6- 6-53	Evanston, Ill.		L	L	6'3	185	7	17	0	0	0	0	0	0	2	4	0	.000	.000
Berry, Ken-Allen Kent	62-70ChiA 71-73CalA 74MilA 75CleA	5-10-41	Kansas City, Mo.		R	R	6'	185	1383	4156	422	1053	150	23	58	343	298	569	45	.253	.342
Bertell, Dick-Richard George	60-65ChiN 65SFN 66KJ 67ChiN	11-21-35	Oak Park, Ill.		R	R	6'	200	444	1310	91	327	34	9	10	112	106	188	2	.250	.312
Bethea, Bill-William Lamar (Spot)	64MinA	1- 1-42	Houston, Tex.		R	R	6'	175	10	30	4	5	1	0	0	2	4	4	0	.167	.200
Bevacqua, Kurt-Kurt Anthony (Dirty)	71-72CleA 73-74KCA 74PitN 75MilA	1-23-47	Miami Beach, Fla.		R	R	6'1	185	334	831	91	185	26	4	8	81	69	146	7	.223	.292
Bianco, Tommy-Thomas Anthony (Toby)	75MilA	12-16-52	Rockville Centre, N.Y.		B	R	5'11	190	18	34	6	6	1	0	0	0	3	7	0	.176	.206
Biittner, Larry-Lawrence David (Butch)	70-71WasA 72-73TexA 74-75MonN	7-27-45	Fort Dodge, Iowa		L	L	6'2	205	427	1185	101	324	44	9	7	90	99	113	5	.273	.343
Billings, Dick-Richard Arlin (Rich)	68-71WasA 72-74TexA 74-75StLN	12- 4-42	Detroit, Mich.		R	R	6'1	195	400	1231	101	280	44	1	16	142	87	207	6	.227	.304
Blackaby, Ethan- Ethan Allen	62, 64MilN	7-24-40	Cincinnati, Ohio		L	L	5'11	190	15	25	0	3	1	0	0	1	2	10	0	.120	.160
Blackwell, Tim-Timothy P	74-75BosA	8-19-52	San Diego, Cal.		B	R	5'11	180	103	254	24	56	4	3	0	14	29	34	1	.220	.260
Bladt, Rick-Richard Alan	69ChiN 75NYA	12- 9-46	Santa Cruz, Cal.		R	R	6'1	160	62	130	14	28	3	1	1	12	11	13	6	.215	.277

USE NAME – GIVEN NAMES (NICKNAMES)	TEAM BY YEAR	BIRTH DATE	BIRTH PLACE	DEATH DATE	B	T	HGT	WGT	G	AB	R	H	2B	3B	HR	RBI	BB	SO	SB	BA	SA
Blair, Paul-Paul L.D. (Motormouth)	64-75BalA	2- 1-44	Cushing, Okla.		R	R	6'	170	1555	5231	708	1354	253	51	123	551	398	767	152	.259	.397
					Bats Both part of 71																
Blanchard, Johnny-John Edwin	55,59-65NYA 65KCA 65MilN	2-26-33	Minneapolis, Minn.		L	R	6'1	198	516	1193	137	285	36	2	67	200	136	163	2	.239	.441
Blanco, Damie-Damaso [Caripe]	72-74SFN	12-11-41	Curiepe, Venezuela		R	R	5'9	160	72	33	9	7	1	0	0	2	5	6	3	.212	.242
Blanco, Ossie-Oswaldo (Carlos Osvaldo) [Dias]	70ChiA 74CleA	9- 8-45	Caracas, Venezuela		R	R	6'	185	52	102	5	20	1	0	0	9	10	18	0	.196	.206
Blanks, Larvell-Larvell (Sugar Bear, Scooter)	72-75AtlN	1-28-50	Del Rio, Tex.		R	R	5'8	164	194	582	60	144	18	3	4	46	46	58	4	.247	.309
Blefary, Curt,Curtis LeRoy	65-68BalA 69HouN 70-71NYA 71-72OakA 72SDN	7- 5-43	Brooklyn, N.Y.		L	R	6'2	200	863	2489	340	583	78	15	101	324	456	444	16	.234	.399
Blessitt, Ike-Isaiah	72DetA	9-30-49	Detroit, Mich.		R	R	5'10	185	4	5	0	0	0	0	0	0	0	2	0	.000	.000
Blomberg, Ron-Ronald Mark (Boomer)	69,71-75NYA	8-23-48	Atlanta, Ga.		L	R	6'1	205	399	1175	168	355	60	8	47	204	129	117	6	.302	.487
Bloomfield, Clyde-Clyde Stalcup (Bud)	63StLN 64MinA	1- 5-36	Oklahoma City, Okla.		R	R	5'11	175	8	7	1	1	0	0	0	0	0	0	0	.143	.143
Bobb, Randy-Mark Randall	68-69ChiN	1- 1-48	Los Angeles, Cal.		R	R	6'1	195	10	10	0	1	0	0	0	0	1	3	0	.100	.100
Boccabella, John-John Dominic	63-68ChiN 69-73MonN 74SFN	6-29-41	San Francisco, Cal.		R	R	6'1	195	551	1462	117	320	56	5	26	148	96	246	3	.219	.317
Bochte, Bruce Anton	74-75CalA	11-12-50	Pasadena, Cal.		L	L	6'3	190	164	571	65	160	23	4	8	74	63	66	9	.280	.377
Boehmer, Len-Leonard Joseph Stephen	67CinN 69,71NYA	6-28-41	Flint Hill, Mo.		R	R	6'1	192	50	116	5	19	4	0	0	7	8	10	0	.163	.198
Boisclair, Bruce-Bruce Armand (Bo)	74NYN	12- 9-52	Putnam, Conn.		L	L	6'3	195	7	12	0	3	1	0	0	1	1	4	0	.250	.333
Boles, Carl-Carl Theodore	62SFN	10-31-34	Center Point, Ark.		R	R	5'11	185	19	24	4	9	0	0	0	1	0	6	0	.375	.375
Bond, Walt-Walter Franklin	60-62CleA 64-65HouN 67MinA	10-19-37	Denmark, Tenn.	9-14-67	L	R	6'7	228	365	1199	149	307	40	11	41	179	106	175	10	.256	.410
Bonds, Bobby-Bobby Lee	68-74SFN 75NYA	3-15-46	Riverside, Cal.		R	R	6'1	195	1159	4576	858	1249	214	45	218	637	589	1153	295	.273	.482
Booker, Buddy-Richard Lee	66CleA 68ChiA	5-28-42	Lynchburg, Va.		L	R	5'10	170	23	33	6	6	1	0	2	5	3	8	0	.182	.394
Boone, Bob-Robert Raymond	72-75PhiN	11-19-47	San Diego, Cal.		R	R	6'2	200	404	1349	115	339	59	7	16	137	113	86	8	.251	.341
Borgmann, Glenn-Glenn Dennis	72-75MinA	5-25-50	Paterson, N.J.		R	R	6'2	208	321	906	85	210	29	3	8	101	117	138	2	.232	.297
Boros, Steve-Stephen	57-58,61-62DetA 63ChiN 64-65CinN	9- 3-36	Flint, Mich.		R	R	6'	185	422	1255	141	308	50	7	26	149	181	174	11	.245	.359
Bosch, Don-Donald John	66PitN 67-68NYN 69MonN	7-15-42	San Francisco, Cal.		B	R	5'10	165	146	318	34	52	6	1	4	13	22	77	4	.164	.226
Bostock, Lyman-Lyman Wesley	75MinA	11-22-50	Birmingham, Ala.		L	R	6'1	175	98	369	52	104	21	5	0	29	28	42	2	.282	.366
Boswell, Ken-Kenneth George	67-74NYN 75HouN	2-23-46	Austin, Tex.		L	R	6'	170	747	2294	249	571	82	17	31	214	242	219	26	.249	.340
Bourque, Pat-Patrick Daniel	71-73ChiN 73-74OakA 74MinA	3-23-47	Worcester, Mass.		L	L	6'	220	201	405	36	87	17	2	12	61	58	73	1	.215	.356
Bowa, Larry-Lawrence Robert	70-75PhiN	12- 6-45	Sacramento, Cal.		B	R	5'10	155	876	3474	409	900	94	46	4	187	160	275	142	.259	.316
Bowens, Sam-Samuel Edward	63-67BalA 68-69WasA	3-23-39	Wilmington, N.C.		R	R	6'1	188	479	1287	141	287	48	6	45	143	100	293	25	.223	.375
Bowlin, Hoss-Lois Weldon	67KCA	12-10-40	Paragould, Ark.		R	R	5'9	155	2	5	0	1	0	0	0	0	0	0	0	.200	.200
Bowman, Ernie-Ernest Ferrell	61-63SFN	7-28-37	Johnson City, Tenn.		R	R	5'10	160	165	205	29	39	4	2	1	10	2	33	3	.190	.244
Boyer, Clete-Cletus LeRoy	55-57KCA 59-66NYA 67-71AtlN	2- 8-37	Cassville, Mo.		R	R	6'	180	1725	5780	645	1396	200	33	162	654	470	931	41	.242	.372
Boyer, Ken-Kenton Lloyd	56-65StLN 66-67NYN 67-68ChiA 68-69LAN	5-20-31	Liberty, Mo.		R	R	6'2	200	2034	7455	1104	2143	318	68	282	1141	713	1017	105	.287	.462
Bradford, Buddy-Charles William	66-70ChiA 70-71CleA 71CinN 72-75ChiA 75StLN	7-25-44	Mobile, Ala.		R	R	5'11	190	642	1443	204	328	45	6	48	161	165	374	30	.227	.367
Brand, Ron-Ronald George	63PitN 65-68HouN 69-71MonN	1-30-40	Los Angeles, Cal.		R	R	5'7	170	568	1345	108	322	34	7	3	106	112	126	20	.239	.282
Brandt, Jackie-John George	56StLN 56NYN 57MS 58-59SFN 60-65BalA 66-67PhiN 67HouN	4-28-34	Omaha, Neb.		R	R	5'11	175	1221	3895	540	1020	175	37	112	485	351	574	45	.262	.412
Braun, Steve-Stephen Russell	71-75MinA	5- 8-48	Trenton, N.J.		L	R	5'10	180	629	2012	260	569	91	11	32	212	289	242	20	.283	.387
Bravo, Angel-Angel Alfonso [Urdaneta]	69ChiA 70-71CinN 71SDN	8- 4-42	Maracaibo, Venezuela		L	L	5'8	155	149	218	26	54	7	3	1	12	20	31	2	.248	.321
Breazeale, Jim-James Leo	69,71-72AtlN 73BN	10- 3-49	Houston, Tex.		L	R	6'2	210	64	107	12	25	2	0	6	20	8	15	0	.234	.421
Breeden, Danny-Danny Richard	69CinN 71ChiN	6-27-42	Albany, Ga.		R	R	6'	185	28	73	3	11	1	0	0	5	9	21	0	.151	.164
Breeden, Hal-Harold Noel	71ChiN 72-75MonN	6-28-44	Albany, Ga.		R	L	6'2	205	273	608	61	148	28	6	21	76	69	107	0	.243	.413
Breeding, Marv-Marvin Eugene	60-62BalA 63WasA 63LAN	3- 8-34	Decatur, Ala.		R	R	6'	175	415	1268	154	317	50	5	7	92	66	180	19	.250	.314
Bressoud, Ed-Edward Francis	56-57NYN 58-61SFN 62-65BosA 66NYN 67StLN	5- 2-32	Los Angeles, Cal.		R	R	6'1	180	1186	3672	443	925	184	40	94	365	359	723	9	.252	.401
Brett, George-George Howard	73-75KCA	5-15-53	Wheeling, W. Va.		L	R	6'1	190	305	1131	135	329	58	18	13	136	67	92	21	.291	.408
Brickell, Fritzie-Fritz Darrell	58-59NYA 61LAA	3-19-35	Wichita, Kans.	10-15-65	R	R	5'5	157	41	88	7	16	1	0	1	7	7	19	0	.182	.227
Briggs, Dan-Daniel Lee	75CalA	11-18-52	Scotia, Cal.		L	L	6'	180	13	31	3	7	1	0	1	3	2	6	0	.226	.355
Briggs, Johnny-John Edward	64-71PhiN 71-75MilA 75MinA	3-10-44	Paterson, N.J.		L	L	6'1	200	1366	4117	602	1041	170	43	139	507	663	786	64	.253	.416
Bright, Harry-Harry James	58-60PitN 61-62WasA 63CinN 63-64NYA 65ChiN	9-22-29	Kansas City, Mo.		R	R	6'	190	336	839	99	214	31	4	32	126	65	133	2	.255	.416
Brinkman, Chuck-Charles Ernest	69-74ChiA 74PitN	9-16-44	Cincinnati, Ohio		R	R	6'1	185	148	267	22	46	7	0	1	12	23	60	0	.172	.210
Brinkman, Eddie-Edwin Albert	61-70WasA 71-74DetA 75StLN 75TexA 75NYA	12- 8-41	Cincinnati, Ohio		R	R	6'	170	1845	6045	552	1355	201	38	59	461	444	845	30	.224	.299
Brock, Lou-Louis Clark	61-64ChiN 64-75StLN	6-18-39	El Dorado, Ark.		L	L	5'11	170	2130	8652	1381	2551	416	126	138	737	656	1509	809	.295	.420
Brohamer, Jack-John Anthony (The Hammer)	72-75CleA	2-26-50	Maywood, Cal.		L	R	5'9	163	408	1359	126	327	41	4	17	110	99	105	7	.241	.314
					Bats Both part of 72																
Brooks, Bobby-Robert (Hammer)	69-70,72OakA 73CalA	11- 1-45	Los Angeles, Cal.		R	R	5'9	175	55	143	19	33	6	0	5	20	29	42	0	.231	.378
Brown, Curt-Curtis (Bubba)	73MonN	9-14-45	Scaramento, Cal.		R	R	6'	183	1	4	0	0	0	0	0	0	0	0	0	.000	.000
Brown, Dick-Richard Ernest	57-59CleA 60ChiA 61-62DetA 63-65BalA	1-17-35	Shinnston, W. Va.	4-17-70	R	R	6'2	190	636	1866	175	455	62	3	62	223	117	356	7	.244	.380
Brown, Gates-William James	63-75DetA	5- 2-39	Crestline, Ohio		L	R	5'11	230	1051	2262	330	582	78	19	84	322	242	275	33	.257	.420
Brown, Ike-Isaac	69-74DetA	4-13-42	Memphis, Tenn.		R	R	6'1	195	280	536	85	137	15	4	20	65	90	130	3	.256	.410
Brown, Jake-Jerald Ray	75SFN	3-22-48	Sumrall, Miss.		R	R	6'2	200	41	43	6	9	3	0	0	4	5	13	0	.209	.279
Brown, Larry-Larry Leslie	63-71CleA 71-72OakA 73BalA 74TexA	3- 1-40	Shinnston, W. Va.		R	R	5'10	170	1129	3449	331	803	108	13	47	254	317	414	22	.233	.313
Brown, Ollie-Ollie Lee	65-68SFN 69-72SDN 72OakA 72-73MilA 74HouN 74-75PhiN	2-11-44	Tuscaloosa, Ala.		R	R	6'2	200	1076	3363	369	894	131	9	96	411	277	569	27	.226	.396
Brown, Oscar-Oscar Lee	69-73AtlN	2- 8-46	Long Beach, Cal.		R	R	6'	175	160	310	34	77	14	2	4	28	17	55	0	.248	.345
Brown, Randy-Edwin Randolph	69-70CalA	8-29-44	Leesburg, Fla.		L	R	5'7	170	18	29	3	4	1	0	0	0	6	1	0	.138	.172
Brown, Tom-Thomas William 64-69 played in N.F.L.	63WasA	12-12-40	Laureldale, Pa.		B	L	6'1	190	61	116	8	17	4	0	1	4	11	45	2	.147	.207
Browne, Byron-Byron Ellis (By)	65-67ChiN 68HouN 69StLN 70-72PhiN	12-27-42	St. Joseph, Mo.		R	R	6'2	200	349	869	94	205	37	10	30	102	101	273	5	.236	.405
Browne, Pidge-Prentice Almont	62HouN	3-21-29	Peekskill, N.Y.		L	L	6'	190	65	100	8	21	4	2	1	10	13	9	0	.210	.320
Brumley, Mike-Tony Mike	64-66WasA	7-10-38	Granite, Okla.		L	R	5'10	195	224	660	52	151	24	2	5	50	60	89	2	.229	.294
Brunsberg, Arlo-Arlo Adolph	66DetA	8-15-40	Fertile, Minn.		L	R	6'	195	2	3	1	1	1	0	0	0	0	0	0	.333	.667
Bryan, Billy-William Ronald	61-66KCA, 66-67NYA 68WasA	12- 4-38	Morgan, Ga.		L	R	6'4	210	374	968	86	209	32	9	41	125	91	283	0	.216	.395
Bryant, Don-Donald Ray	66ChiN 69-70HouN	7-13-41	Jasper, Fla.		R	R	6'5	210	59	109	6	24	3	0	1	13	6	25	1	.220	.275
Brye, Steve-Stephen Robert	70-75MinA	2- 4-49	Alameda, Cal.		R	R	6'	190	450	1383	161	360	65	10	20	133	104	196	12	.260	.365
Buchek, Jerry-Gerald Peter	61,63-66StLN 67-68NYN	5- 9-42	St. Louis, Mo.		R	R	5'11	185	421	1177	96	259	35	11	22	108	75	312	5	.220	.325
Buckner, Bill-William Joseph	69-75LAN	12-14-49	Vallejo, Cal.		L	L	6'	185	619	2253	271	644	93	10	31	217	95	111	65	.286	.377
Buford, Don-Donald Alvin	63-67ChiA 68-72BalA	2- 2-37	Linden, Tex.		B	R	5'7	160	1256	4553	718	1203	157	44	93	418	672	575	200	.264	.379
Bumbry, Al-Alonza Benjamin (Bumblebee)	72-75BalA	4-21-47	Fredericksburg, Va.		L	R	5'8	170	327	986	160	281	44	19	10	85	87	176	52	.285	.399
Burda, Bob-Edward Robert	62StLN 65-66,69-70SFN 70MilA 71StLN 72BosA	7-16-38	St. Louis, Mo.		L	L	5'11	180	388	634	53	142	21	0	13	78	70	65	2	.224	.319
Burgess, Tom-Thomas Roland (Tim)	54StLN 62LAA	9- 1-27	London, Canada		L	L	6'	180	104	164	19	29	8	1	2	14	39	29	2	.177	.274
Burke, Leo-Leo Patrick	58-59BalA 61-62LAA 63StLN 63-65ChiN	5- 6-34	Hagerstown, Md.		R	R	5'11	185	165	301	33	72	7	2	9	45	21	79	0	.239	.365
Burleson, Rick-Richard Paul (The Rooster)	74-75BosA	4-19-51	Lynwood, Cal.		R	R	5'10	160	272	964	102	255	47	1	10	106	66	78	11	.265	.346
Burright, Larry-Larry Allen (Possum)	62LAN 63-64NYN	7-10-37	Roseville, Ill.		R	R	5'11	170	159	356	44	73	8	6	4	33	29	92	5	.205	.295
Burroughs, Jeff-Jeffrey Alan	70-71WasA 72-75TexA	3- 7-51	Long Beach, Cal.		R	R	6'2	200	542	1923	261	502	80	3	90	326	266	429	7	.261	.446
Burton, Ellis-Ellis Narrington	58,60StLN 63CleA 63-65ChiN	8-12-36	Los Angeles, Cal.		B	R	5'11	160	215	556	79	120	24	4	17	59	65	117	11	.216	.365
Busse, Ray-Raymond Edward	71HouN 73StLN 73-74HouN	9-25-48	Daytona Beach, Fla.		R	R	6'4	185	68	155	12	23	8	2	2	9	11	54	0	.148	.265
Cabell, Enos-Enos, Milton (Big E)	72-74BalA 75HouN	10- 8-49	Fort Riley, Kans.		R	R	6'5	190	232	574	79	144	23	8	6	64	28	80	18	.251	.350
Callison, Johnny-John Wesley	58-59ChiA 60-69PhiN 70-71ChiN 72-73NYA	3-12-39	Qualls, Okla.		L	R	5'10	180	1886	6652	926	1757	321	89	226	840	650	1064	74	.264	.441
Camilli, Doug-Douglas Joseph	60-64LAN 65-67WasA 68RC 69WasA	9-22-36	Philadelphia, Pa.		R	R	5'11	195	313	767	56	153	22	4	18	80	56	146	0	.199	.309
Camilli, Lou-Louis Steven	69-72CleA	9-24-46	El Paso, Tex.		B	R	5'10	175	107	151	7	22	4	0	0	3	13	23	0	.146	.172
Campaneris, Bert-Dagoberto [Blanco] (Campy)	64-67KCA 68-75OakA	3- 9-42	Pueblo Nuevo, Cuba		R	R	5'10	160	1646	6644	916	1745	256	69	69	477	441	853	512	.263	.353
Campanis, Jim-James Alexander	66-68LAN 69-70KCA 73PitN	2- 9-44	New York, N.Y.		R	R	6'	195	113	217	13	32	6	0	4	9	19	49	0	.147	.230
Campbell, Dave-David Wilson	67-69DetA 70-73SDN 73StLN 73-74HouN	1-14-42	Manistee, Mich.		R	R	6'1	180	428	1252	128	267	54	4	20	89	102	254	29	.213	.311
Campbell, Jim-James Robert	70StLN	1-10-43	Hartsville, S.C.		L	R	6'2	205	13	13	0	3	0	0	0	1	0	3	0	.231	.231
Campbell, Jim-James Robert	62-63HouN	6-24-37	Palo Alto, Cal.		R	R	6'	190	82	244	15	54	7	0	7	25	16	63	0	.221	.336
Campbell, Joe-Joseph Earl	67ChiN	3-10-44	Louisville, Ky.		R	R	6'1	175	1	3	0	0	0	0	0	0	0	3	0	.000	.000
Campbell, Ron-Ronald Thomas	64-66ChiN	4- 5-40	Chattanooga, Tenn.		R	R	6'1	180	52	154	11	38	7	1	1	14	7	26	1	.247	.325
Cannizzaro, Chris-Christopher John	60-61StLN, 62-65NYN 68PitN 69-71SDN 71ChiN 72-73LAN 74SDN	5- 3-38	Oakland, Cal.		R	R	6'	190	739	1950	132	458	66	12	18	169	241	354	3	.235	.309
Carbo, Bernie-Bernardo	69-72CinN 72-73StLN 74-75BosA	8- 5-47	Detroit, Mich.		L	R	6'	185	688	1966	277	516	111	8	68	304	410	405	45	.262	.431
Cardenal (Domec), Jose-Jose Rosario Domec [Cardenal]	63-64SFN 65-67CalA 68-69CleA 70-71StLN 71MilA 72-75ChiN	10- 7-43	Matanzas, Cuba		R	R	5'10	150	1603	5836	788	1607	274	43	121	655	500	702	297	.275	.392

USE NAME – GIVEN NAMES (NICKNAMES)	TEAM BY YEAR	BIRTH DATE	BIRTH PLACE	DEATH DATE	B	T	HGT	WGT	G	AB	R	H	2B	3B	HR	RBI	BB	SO	SB	BA	SA
Cardenas, Leo-Leonardo Lazaro [Alfonso] (Chico)	60-68CinN 69-71MinA 72CalA 73CleA 74-75TexA	12-17-38	Matanzas, Cuba		R	R	5'11	160	1941	6705	662	1725	285	49	118	689	522	1135	39	.257	.367
Carew, Rod-Rodney Cline	67-75MinA	10- 1-45	Gatun, Panama		L	R	6'	175	1172	4450	640	1458	212	52	46	473	399	547	172	.328	.430
Carmel, Duke-Leon James	59-60,63StLN 63NYN 65NYA	4-23-37	New York, N.Y.		L	L	6'3	202	124	227	22	48	7	3	4	23	27	60	3	.211	.322
Carreon, Cam-Camilo [Garcia]	59-64ChiA 65CleA 66BalA	8- 6-37	Colton, Cal.		R	R	6'1	198	354	986	113	260	43	4	11	114	97	117	3	.264	.349
Carter, Gary-Gary Edmund (Kid)	74-75MonN	4- 8-54	Culver City, Cal.		R	R	6'2	200	153	530	63	147	20	2	18	74	73	85	7	.277	.425
Carty, Rico-Ricardo Adolfo Jacobo	63-65MilN 66-67AtlN 68IL 69-70AtlN 71KJ 72AtlN 73TexA 73ChiN 73OakA 74-75CleA	9- 1-39	San Pedro de Macoris, Dom. Rep.		R	R	6'2	190	1095	3604	477	1110	174	11	133	573	416	465	15	.308	.473
Casanova, Paul-Paulino [Ortiz]	65-71WasA 72-74AtlN	12-31-41	Colon, Cuba		R	R	6'4	200	859	2786	214	627	87	12	50	252	101	430	2	.225	.319
Cash, Dave-David	69-73PitN 74-75PhiN	6-11-48	Utica, N.Y.		R	R	6'	175	744	2996	434	878	136	31	14	242	234	201	64	.293	.373
Cash, Norm-Norman Dalton	58-59ChiA 60-74DetA	11-10-34	Justiceburg, Tex.		L	L	6'	190	2089	6705	1046	1820	241	41	377	1103	1043	1091	43	.271	.488
Cash, Ron-Ronald Forrest	73-74DetA	11-20-49	Atlanta, Ga.		R	R	6'	185	34	101	14	30	3	1	0	11	5	16	0	.297	.347
Castle, Don-Donald Hardy	73TexA	2- 1-50	Kokomo, Ind.		L	L	6'2	195	4	13	0	4	1	0	0	2	1	3	0	.308	.385
Cater, Danny-Danny Anderson	64PhiN 65-66ChiA 66-67KCA 68-69OakA 70-71NYA 72-74BosA 75StLN	2-25-40	Austin, Tex.		R	R	6'	185	1289	4451	491	1229	191	29	64	517	254	406	26	.276	.375
Causey, Wayne-James Wayne	55-57BalA 61-66KCA 66-68ChiA 68CalA 68AtlN	12-26-36	Ruston, La.		L	R	5'10	175	1105	3244	357	819	130	26	35	285	390	341	12	.252	.341
Cedeno, Cesar-Cesar Eugenito [Encarnacion]	70-75HouN	2-25-51	Santo Domingo, Dom. Rep.		R	R	6'2	190	820	3160	508	926	195	28	103	440	263	455	255	.293	.470
Cepeda, Orlando-Orlando Manuel [Penne] (The Baby Bull, Cha-Cha)	58-66SFN 66-68StLN 69-72AtlN 72OakA 73BosA 74KCA	9-17-37	Ponce, P.R.		R	R	6'2	210	2124	7927	1131	2351	417	27	379	1365	588	1169	142	.297	.499
Cerone, Rick-Richard Aldo	75CleA	5-11-54	Newark, N.J.		R	R	5'11	190	7	12	1	3	1	0	0	0	1	0	0	.250	.333
Cey, Ron-Ronald Charles (The Penguin)	71-75LAN	2-15-48	Tacoma, Wash.		R	R	5'10	185	482	1689	223	445	68	8	59	281	235	231	7	.263	.418
Chacon, Elio-Elio [Rodriguez]	60-61CinN 62NYN	10-26-36	Caracas, Venezuela		R	R	5'10	170	228	616	89	143	15	5	4	39	111	109	20	.232	.292
Chalk, Dave-David Lee (Shaver, Chalker)	73-75CalA	8-30-50	Del Rio, Tex.		R	R	5'10	175	306	1027	117	273	35	5	8	93	105	119	16	.266	.333
Chambliss, Chris-Carroll Christopher	71-74CleA 74-75NYA	12-26-48	Dayton, Ohio		L	R	6'2	200	664	2482	282	696	135	15	41	267	181	320	9	.280	.396
Chance, Bob-Robert	63-64CleA 65-67WasA 69CalA	9-10-40	Statesboro, Ga.		L	R	6'2	217	277	747	76	195	34	1	24	112	68	195	3	.261	.406
Chaney, Darrel-Darrel Lee	69-75CinN	3- 9-48	Hammond, Ind.		B	R	6'2	188	536	1046	131	217	34	6	7	95	123	253	11	.207	.272
					Bats Left 74-75, part of 73																
Chant, Charlie-Charles Joseph	75OakA	8- 7-51	Bell Gardens, Cal.		R	R	6'	190	5	5	1	0	0	0	0	0	0	0	0	.000	.000
Charles, Ed-Edwin Douglas (The Glider)	62-67KCA 67-69NYN	4-29-35	Daytona Beach, Fla.		R	R	5'10	170	1005	3428	438	917	147	30	86	421	332	525	86	.263	.397
Chavarria, Ossie-Osvaldo [Quijano]	66-67KCA	8- 5-40	Colon, Panama		R	R	5'11	160	124	250	28	52	12	0	2	14	25	59	4	.208	.280
Chiles, Rich-Richard Francis	71-72HouN 73NYN	11-22-49	Sacramento, Cal.		L	L	5'11	170	84	155	14	33	8	1	2	18	7	23	0	.213	.316
Christensen, Bruce-Bruce Ray	71CalA	2-22-48	Madison, Wis.		L	R	5'11	160	29	63	4	17	1	0	0	3	6	5	0	.270	.286
Christian, Bob-Robert Charles	68DetA 69-70ChiA	10-17-45	Chicago, Ill.	2-20-74	R	R	5'10	180	54	147	13	33	5	0	4	19	11	23	3	.224	.340
Christopher, Joe-Joseph O'Neal	59-61PitN 62-65NYN 66BosA	12-13-35	Frederiksted, V.I.		R	R	5'10	175	638	1667	224	434	68	17	29	173	157	277	29	.260	.374
Cipriani, Frank-Frank Dominick	61KCA	4-14-41	Buffalo, N.Y.		R	R	6'	180	13	36	2	9	0	0	0	2	2	4	0	.250	.250
Clark, Glen-Glen Ester	67AtlN	3-17-41	Austin, Tex.		B	R	6'1	190	4	4	0	0	0	0	0	0	0	1	0	.000	.000
Clark, Jack-Jack Anthony	75SFN	11-10-55	New Brighton, Pa.		R	R	6'2	176	8	17	3	4	0	0	0	2	1	2	1	.235	.235
Clark, Jim-James Edward	71CleA	4-30-47	Kansas City, Kans.		R	R	6'1	190	13	18	2	3	0	1	0	0	2	7	0	.167	.278
Clark, Ron-Ronald Bruce	66-68MinA 69SeaA 71-72OakA 72MilA 75PhiN	1-14-43	Fort Worth, Tex.		R	R	5'11	175	230	530	40	100	16	3	5	43	41	98	4	.189	.258
Clarke, Horace-Horace Meredith (Hoss)	65-74NYA 74SDN	6- 2-40	Frederiksted, V.I.		B	R	5'9	175	1272	4813	548	1230	150	23	27	304	365	362	151	.256	.313
Clemens, Doug-Douglas Horace	60-64StLN 64-65ChiN 66-68PhiN	6- 9-39	Leesport, Pa.		L	R	6'	180	452	920	99	211	34	7	12	88	114	166	6	.229	.321
Clemente, Roberto-Roberto Walker	55-72PitN	8-18-34	Carolina, P.R.	12-31-72	R	R	5'11	180	2433	9454	1416	3000	440	166	240	1305	621	1230	83	.317	.475
Clendenon, Donn-Donn Alvin (Clink)	61-68PitN 69MonN 69-71NYN 72StLN	7-11-35	Neosho, Mo.		R	R	6'4	210	1362	4648	594	1273	192	57	159	682	379	1140	90	.274	.442
Cline, Ty-Tyrone Alexander	60-62CleA 63-65MilN 66ChiN 66-67AtlN 67-68SFN 69-70MonN 70-71CinN	6-15-39	Hampton, S.C.		L	L	6'	170	892	1834	251	437	53	25	6	125	153	262	22	.238	.304
Clines, Gene-Eugene Anthony (Road Runner)	70-74PitN 75NYN	10- 6-46	San Pablo, Cal.		R	R	5'9	175	534	1404	204	391	51	17	2	91	107	185	55	.278	.343
Clinton, Lu-Lucien Louis	60-64BosA 64LAA 65CalA 65KCA 65CleA 66-67NYA	10-13-37	Ponca City, Okla.		R	R	6'1	185	691	2153	270	532	112	31	65	269	188	418	12	.247	.418
Coggins, Frank-Franklin (Swish)	67-68WasA 72ChiN	5-22-44	Griffin, Ga.		B	R	6'2	187	87	247	25	53	9	1	1	15	12	50	2	.215	.271
Coggins, Rich-Richard Allen	72-74BalA 75MonN 75NYA	12- 7-50	Indianapolis, Ind.		L	L	5'9	170	303	983	120	271	40	13	12	84	66	83	46	.276	.379
Coker, Jimmie-Jimmie Goodwin	58-62PhiN 63SFN 64-67CinN	3-28-36	Holly Mill, S.C.		R	R	5'11	200	233	592	44	137	15	4	16	70	55	99	1	.231	.351
Colavito, Rocky-Rocco Domenico	55-59CleA 60-63DetA 64KCA 65-67CleA 67ChiA 68LAN 68NYA	8-10-33	Bronx, N.Y.		R	R	6'3	195	1841	6503	971	1730	283	21	374	1159	951	880	19	.266	.489
Colbert, Nate-Nathan	66,68HouN 69-74SDN 75DetA 75MonN	4- 9-46	St. Louis, Mo.		R	R	6'2	210	988	3369	476	815	139	25	171	514	373	883	49	.242	.450
Coleman, Choo Choo-Clarence	61PhiN 62-63,66NYN	8-25-37	Orlando, Fla.		L	R	5'9	165	201	462	51	91	8	2	9	30	37	85	7	.197	.281
Coleman, Gordy-Gordon Calvin	59CleA 60-67CinN	7- 5-34	Rockville, Md.		L	R	6'3	208	773	2384	282	650	102	11	98	387	177	333	9	.273	.448
Coletta, Chris-Christopher Michael	72CalA	8- 2-44	Brooklyn, N.Y.		L	L	5'11	185	14	30	5	9	1	0	1	7	1	4	0	.300	.433
Collins, Dave-David S.	75CalA	10-20-52	Rapid City, S.D.		B	L	5'11	175	93	319	41	85	13	4	3	29	36	55	24	.266	.361
Collins, Kevin-Kevin Michael (Casey)	65,67-69NYN 69MonN 70-71DetA	8- 4-46	Springfield, Mass.		L	R	6'2	190	201	388	30	81	17	4	6	34	20	97	1	.209	.320
Coluccio, Bob-Robert Pasquali (The Macaroni Pony)	73-75MilA 75ChiA	10- 2-51	Centralia, Wash.		R	R	5'11	185	345	1055	137	231	38	15	26	107	121	198	33	.219	.357
Comer, Wayne-Harry Wayne	67-68DetA 69SeaA 70MilA 70WasA 72DetA	2- 3-44	Shenandoah, Va.		R	R	5'10	175	316	687	119	157	22	2	16	67	106	106	22	.229	.336
Compton, Mike-Michael Lynn	70PhiN	8-15-44	Stamford, Tex.		R	R	5'10	180	47	110	8	18	0	1	1	7	9	22	0	.164	.209
Concepcion, Dave-David Ismael [Benitez]	70-75CinN	6-17-48	Ocumare de la C., Venez.		R	R	6'2	173	739	2399	273	615	89	14	31	245	177	346	128	.256	.344
Conde, Ramon-Ramon Luis (Witto)	62ChiA	12-29-34	Juana Diaz, P.R.		R	R	5'8	172	14	16	0	0	0	0	0	1	3	3	0	.000	.000
Conigliaro, Billy-William Michael	69-71BosA 72MilA 73OakA	8-15-47	Revere, Mass.		R	R	6'	178	347	1130	142	289	56	10	40	128	86	244	9	.256	.429
Conigliaro, Tony-Anthony Richard	64-67BosA 68IJ 69-70BosA 71CalA 72-74IJ 75BosA	1- 7-45	Revere, Mass.		R	R	6'3	190	876	3221	464	849	139	23	166	516	287	629	20	.264	.476
Cook, Cliff-Raymond Clifford	59-62CinN 62-63NYN	8-20-36	Dallas, Tex.		R	R	6'	185	163	398	33	80	17	3	7	35	26	136	2	.201	.312
Cooper, Cecil-Cecil Celester (Flash)	71-75BosA	12-20-49	Washington Co., Tex.		L	L	6'2	188	283	879	125	250	48	8	25	103	55	128	5	.284	.443
Corrales, Pat-Patrick	64-65PhiN 66StLN 68-72CinN 72-73SDN	3-20-41	Los Angeles, Cal.		R	R	6'	195	300	767	63	166	28	3	4	54	75	167	1	.216	.276
Correll, Vic-Victor Crosby	72BosA 74-75AtlN	2- 5-46	Washington, D.C.		R	R	5'10	185	177	531	58	120	27	2	15	69	63	105	0	.226	.369
Cottier, Chuck-Charles Keith	59-60MilA 61DetA 61-65WasA 68-69CalA	1- 8-36	Delta, Colo.		R	R	5'10	175	580	1584	168	348	63	17	19	127	137	248	28	.220	.317
Coughtry, Marlan-James Marlan	60BosA 62LAA 62KCA 62CleA	9-11-34	Hollywood, Cal.		L	R	6'1	170	35	54	5	10	0	0	0	4	10	18	0	.185	.185
Coulter, Tom-Thomas Lee (Chip)	69StLN	6- 5-45	Steubenville, Ohio		B	R	5'10	172	6	19	3	6	1	1	0	4	2	6	0	.316	.474
Covington, Wes-John Wesley	56-61MilN 61ChiA 61KCA 61-65PhiN 66ChiN 66LAN	3-27-32	Laurinburg, N.C.		L	R	6'1	205	1075	2978	355	832	128	17	131	499	247	414	7	.279	.466
Cowan, Billy-Billy Rolland	63-64ChiN 65NYN 65MilN 67PhiN 69NYA 69-72CalA	8-28-38	Calhoun City, Miss.		R	R	6'	170	493	1190	131	281	44	8	40	125	50	297	17	.236	.387
Cowens, Al-Alfred Edward	74-75KCA	10-25-51	Los Angeles, Cal.		R	R	6'2	205	230	597	72	156	20	9	5	67	31	74	17	.261	.350
Cox, Bobby-Robert Joe	68-69NYA	5-21-41	Tulsa, Okla.		R	R	5'11	180	220	628	50	141	22	2	9	58	75	126	3	.225	.309
Cox, Jim-James Charles	73-75MonN	5-28-50	Bloomington, Ill.		R	R	5'11	175	97	278	31	61	11	1	3	31	25	42	3	.219	.299
Cox, Larry-Larry Eugene	73-75PhiN	9-11-47	Bluffton, Ohio		R	R	5'11	190	42	58	5	10	2	0	0	5	5	9	1	.172	.207
Crawford, Willie-Willie Murphy	64-75LAN	9- 7-46	Los Angeles, Cal.		L	L	6'1	197	989	2793	437	748	125	29	74	335	360	581	45	.268	.413
Cromartie, Warren-Warren Livingston (Cro)	74MonN	9-29-53	Miami Beach, Fla.		L	L	6'	185	8	17	2	3	0	0	0	0	3	3	1	.176	.176
Crosby, Ed-Edward Carlton (Spider)	70,72-73StLN 73CinN 74-75CleA	5-26-49	Long Beach, Cal.		L	R	6'2	175	295	675	67	148	22	4	0	44	55	74	1	.219	.264
Crowley, Terry-Terrence Michael	69-73BalA 74-75CinN	2-16-47	Staten Island, N.Y.		L	L	6'	180	409	767	94	182	37	0	21	99	104	96	3	.237	.368
Cruz, Hector-Hector Louis [Dilan] (Haiti)	73,75StLN	4- 2-53	Arroyo, P.R.		R	R	5'11	180	34	59	8	7	2	2	0	6	3	7	0	.119	.220
Cruz, Henry-Henry [Acosta] (Papo)	75LAN	2-27-52	Christiansted, V.I.		L	L	6'	173	53	94	8	25	3	1	0	5	7	6	1	.266	.319
Cruz, Jose-Jose [Dilan] (Cheo)	70-74StLN 75HouN	8- 8-47	Arroyo, P.R.		L	L	6'	175	565	1523	200	379	69	16	35	177	212	226	35	.249	.384
Cruz, Tommy-Cirilo T. [Dilan] (Cuki)	73StLN	2-15-51	Arroyo, P.R.		L	L	5'9	170	3	0	1	0	0	0	0	0	0	0	0	–	–
Cubbage, Mike-Michael Lee	74-75TexA	7-21-50	Charlottesville, Va.		L	R	6'	182	67	158	12	32	6	0	4	21	18	18	0	.203	.316
Cullen, Tim-Timothy Leo	66-67WasA 68ChiA 68-71WasA 72OakA	2-16-42	San Francisco, Cal.		R	R	6'1	185	700	1761	155	387	57	9	9	134	147	219	10	.220	.278
Dade, Paul-Lonnie Paul (Executioner)	75CalA	12- 7-51	Seattle, Wash.		R	R	6'	190	11	30	5	6	4	0	0	1	6	7	0	.200	.333
Dalrymple, CLay-Clayton Errol	60-68PhiN 69-71BalA	12- 3-36	Chico, Cal.		L	R	6'	190	1079	3042	243	710	98	23	55	327	387	403	3	.233	.335
Damaska, Jack-Jack Lloyd	63StLN	8-21-37	Beaver Falls, Pa.		R	R	5'11	168	5	5	1	1	0	0	0	1	0	4	0	.200	.200
Darwin, Bobby-Arthur Bobby Lloyd (See P 61-73)	62LAA 69,71LAN 72-75MinA 75MilA	2-16-43	Los Angeles, Cal.		R	R	6'2	200	563	2024	232	518	66	11	79	309	152	517	14	.256	.417
Davalillo, Vic-Victor Jose [Rodriguez]	63-68CleA 68-69CalA 69-70StLN 71-73PitN 73-74OakA	7-31-36	Cabimas, Venezuela		L	L	5'7	150	1323	3859	488	1075	156	36	35	312	207	408	121	.279	.365
DaVanon, Jerry-Frank Gerald	69SDN 69-70StLN 71BalA 73CalA 74StLN 75HouN	8-21-45	Oceanside, Cal.		R	R	5'11	175	192	384	52	86	18	2	2	30	46	66	3	.224	.297
Davenport, Jim-James Houston	58-70SFN	8-17-33	Siluria, Ala.		R	R	5'11	175	1501	4427	552	1142	177	37	77	456	382	673	16	.258	.367
Davis, Bill-Arthur Willard	65-66CleA 69SDN	6- 6-42	Graceville, Minn.		L	L	6'7	222	64	105	3	19	3	0	1	5	14	28	0	.181	.238
Davis, Bob-Robert John Eugene (Stinger)	73,75SDN	3- 1-52	Pryor, Okla.		R	R	6'	190	48	139	7	31	3	2	0	7	11	36	0	.223	.273
Davis, Brock-Bryshear Barnett	63-64,66HouN 70-71ChiN 72MilA	10-19-43	Oakland, Cal.		L	L	5'10	160	243	543	46	141	12	5	1	43	57	73	7	.260	.308
Davis, Jacke-Jacke Sylvester	62PhiN	3- 5-36	Carthage, Tex.		R	R	5'11	190	48	75	9	16	0	1	1	6	4	20	1	.213	.280
Davis, Ron-Ronald Everette	62,66-68HouN 68StLN 69PitN	10-21-41	Roanoke Rapids, N.C.		R	R	6'	175	295	853	96	199	44	6	10	79	56	160	9	.233	.334

USE NAME – GIVEN NAMES (NICKNAMES)	TEAM BY YEAR	BIRTH DATE	BIRTH PLACE	DEATH DATE	B	T	HGT	WGT	G	AB	R	H	2B	3B	HR	RBI	BB	SO	SB	BA	SA
Davis, Tommy-Herman Thomas	59-66LAN 67NYN 68ChiN 69SeaA 69-70HouN 70OakA 70ChiN 71OakA 72ChiN 72-75BalA	3-21-39	Brooklyn, N.Y.		R	R	6'2	195	1919	6985	794	2058	267	36	150	1026	365	736	136	.295	.408
Davis, Willie-William Henry	60-73LAN 74MonN 75TexA 75StLN	4-15-40	Mineral Springs, Ark.		L	L	6'2	185	2245	8625	1147	2415	375	127	177	1005	395	936	383	.280	.414
Day, Boots-Charles Frederick	69StLN 70ChiN 70-74MonN	8-31-47	Ilion, N.Y.		L	L	5'9	165	471	1151	146	295	28	6	8	98	95	141	15	.256	.312
Dean, Tommy-Tommy Douglas	67LAN 69-71SDN	8-30-45	Iuka, Miss.		R	R	6'	165	215	529	35	95	15	3	4	25	42	105	3	.180	.242
DeCinces, Doug-Douglas Vernon	73-75BalA	8-29-50	Burbank, Cal.		R	R	6'2	193	72	186	22	44	6	3	4	26	15	37	0	.237	.366
Dees, Charlie-Charles Henry	63-64LAA 65CalA	6-24-35	Birmingham, Ala.		L	L	6'1	173	98	260	27	69	12	1	3	29	13	43	5	.265	.354
Deidel, Jim-James Lawrence	74NYA	6- 6-49	Denver, Colo.		R	R	6'2	215	2	2	0	0	0	0	0	0	0	0	0	.000	.000
DeJesus, Ivan-Ivan [Alvarez]	74-75LAN	1- 9-53	Stanturce, P.R.		R	R	5'11	169	66	90	11	17	2	1	0	2	11	17	1	.189	.233
de la Hoz, Mike-Miguel Angel	60-63CleA 64-65MilN 66-67AtlN 69CinN	10- 2-39	Havana, Cuba		R	R	5'11	173	494	1114	116	280	42	5	25	115	56	130	2	.251	.365
de la Rosa, Jesus-Jesus	75HouN	7-28-53	Santo Domingo, Dom. Rep.		R	R	6'1	153	3	3	1	1	1	0	0	0	0	0	0	.333	.667
Del Greco, Bobby-Robert George	52,56PitN 56StLN 57ChiN 57-58NYA 60-61PhiN 61-63KCA 65PhiN	4- 7-33	Pittsburgh, Pa.		R	R	5'10	185	731	1982	271	454	95	11	42	169	271	372	16	.229	.352
DeMerit, John-John Stephen (Thumper)	57-59,61MilN 62NYN	1- 8-36	West Bend, Wis.		R	R	6'1	195	93	132	21	23	3	0	3	7	8	33	1	.174	.265
Demeter, Don-Donald Lee	56BknN 58-61LAN 61-63PhiN 64-66DetA 66-67BosA 67CleA	6-25-35	Oklahoma City, Okla.		R	R	6'4	190	1109	3443	467	912	147	17	163	563	180	658	22	.265	.459
Dempsey, Rick-John Rikard	69-72MinA 73-75NYA	9-13-49	Fayetteville, Tenn.		R	R	6'	180	161	331	34	81	14	0	3	23	39	35	1	.245	.314
Dent, Bucky-Russell Earl	73-75ChiA	11-25-51	Savannah, Ga.		R	R	5'11	175	351	1215	124	324	46	7	8	113	74	114	7	.267	.336
Derrick Mike-James Michael	70BosA	9-19-43	Columbia, S.C.		L	R	6'	190	24	33	3	7	1	0	0	5	0	11	0	.212	.242
Dicken, Paul-Paul Franklin	64,66CleA	10- 2-43	Deland, Fla.		R	R	6'5	195	13	13	0	0	0	0	0	0	0	6	0	.000	.000
Didier, Bob-Robert Daniel	69-72AtlN 73DetA 74BosA	2-16-49	Hattiesburg, Miss.		B	R	6'	190	247	751	56	172	25	4	0	51	59	72	2	.229	.273
Dietz, Dick-Richard Allen (Mule)	66-71SFN 72LAN 73AtlN	9-18-41	Crawfordsville, Ind.		R	R	6'1	195	646	1829	226	478	89	6	66	301	381	402	4	.261	.425
Dillard, Don-David Donald	59-62CleA 63,65MilN	1- 8-37	Greenville, S.C.		L	R	6'1	200	272	476	59	116	16	5	14	47	32	85	0	.244	.387
Dillard, Steve-Stephen Bradley	75BosA	12- 8-51	Memphis, Tenn.		R	R	6'1	180	1	5	2	2	0	0	0	0	0	0	1	.400	.400
Dilone, Miguel-Miguel Angel [Reyes] (Euelo)	74-75PitN	11- 1-54	Santiago, Dom. Rep.		B	R	5'11	155	30	8	11	0	0	0	0	0	1	1	4	.000	.000
Dineen, Kerry-Kerry Michael	75NYA	7- 1-52	Englewood, N.J.		L	L	5'11	165	7	22	3	8	1	0	0	1	2	1	0	.364	.409
Doherty, John-John Michael (Pup)	74-75CalA	8-22-51	Auburn, Mass.		L	L	5'10	185	104	317	27	76	17	1	4	27	18	25	3	.240	.338
Donaldson, John-John David	66-67KCA 68-69OakA 69SeaA 70,74OakA	5- 5-43	Charlotte, N.C.		L	R	5'11	160	405	1225	96	292	35	11	4	86	132	133	19	.238	.295
Downing, Brian-Brian Jay	73-75ChiA	10- 9-50	Los Angeles, Cal.		R	R	5'10	185	280	787	104	180	25	2	19	84	137	164	13	.248	.338
Doyle, Denny-Robert Dennis	70-73PhiN 74-75CalA 75BosA	1-17-44	Glasgow, Ky.		L	R	5'10	170	690	2403	252	606	85	17	14	162	154	221	28	.252	.319
Drake, Sammy-Samuel Harrison	60-61ChiN 62NYN	10- 7-34	Little Rock, Ark.		B	R	5'11	175	53	72	8	11	0	0	0	7	8	17	0	.153	.153
Driessen, Dan-Daniel (The Cobra)	73-75CinN	7-29-51	Hilton Head, S.C.		L	R	5'11	187	340	1046	150	301	46	9	18	141	107	129	29	.288	.401
Driscoll, Jim-James Bernard (J.D.)	70OakA 72TexA	5-14-44	Medford, Mass.		L	R	5'11	175	36	70	2	10	0	0	1	2	4	18	0	.143	.186
Duffy, Frank-Frank Thomas	70-71CinN 71SFN 72-75CleA	10-14-46	Oakland, Cal.		R	R	6'1	180	590	1832	168	442	75	10	20	175	115	233	30	.241	.326
Duncan, Dave-David Edwin	64,67KCA 68-72OakA 73-74CleA 75BalA	9-26-45	Dallas, Tex.		R	R	6'2	195	836	2601	254	559	72	4	106	324	227	621	5	.215	.367
Dunn, Ron-Ronald Ray	74-75ChiN	1-24-50	Oklahoma City, Okla.		R	R	5'11	180	55	112	8	27	10	0	3	21	18	25	0	.241	.411
Dwyer, Jim-James Edward	73-75StLN 75MonN	1- 3-50	Evergreen Park, Ill.		L	L	5'10	175	183	349	46	91	10	2	5	32	39	57	4	.261	.344
Dyer, Duffy, Don Robert	68-74NYN 75PitN	8-15-45	Dayton, Ohio		R	R	6'	200	423	1182	90	260	40	9	19	113	105	248	2	.220	.317
Easler, Mike-Michael Anthony	73-75HouN	11-29-50	Cleveland, Ohio		L	R	6'	195	26	27	1	1	0	0	0	0	2	10	0	.037	.037
Edwards, Doc-Howard Rodney	62-63CleA 63-65KCA 65NYA 70PhiN	12-10-37	Red Jacket, W. Va.		R	R	6'2	215	317	906	69	216	33	0	15	87	53	109	1	.238	.325
Edwards, Johnny-John Alban	61-67CinN 68StLN 69-74HouN	6-10-38	Columbus, Ohio		L	R	6'4	220	1470	4577	430	1106	202	32	81	524	465	635	15	.242	.353
Egan, Tom-Thomas Patrick	65-70CalA 71-72ChiA 74-75CalA	6- 9-46	Los Angeles, Cal.		R	R	6'4	218	373	979	74	196	25	3	22	91	80	336	1	.200	.299
					Bats Both 75, part of 74																
Elia, Lee-Lee Constantine	66ChiA 68ChiN	7-16-37	Philadelphia, Pa.		R	R	5'11	184	95	212	17	43	5	2	3	25	15	45	0	.203	.288
Elliot, Larry-Lawrence Lee	62-63PitN 64,66NYN	3- 5-38	San Diego, Cal.		L	L	6'2	200	157	437	53	103	22	2	15	56	45	105	1	.236	.398
Elliott, Randy-Randy Lee	72,74SDN	6- 5-51	Oxnard, Cal.		R	R	6'2	200	27	82	10	17	4	1	1	8	9	20	0	.207	.317
Ellis, Johnny-John Charles	69-72NYA 73-75CleA	8-21-48	New London, Conn.		R	R	6'2	220	582	1872	194	494	79	12	47	260	142	265	1	.264	.394
Ellis, Rob-Robert Walker	71,74-75MilA	7- 3-50	Grand Rapids, Mich.		R	R	6'	182	64	166	16	38	4	0	0	10	16	35	0	.229	.253
Emery, Cal-Calvin Wayne	63PhiN	6-28-37	Centre Hall, Pa.		L	L	6'2	205	16	19	0	3	1	0	0	0	0	2	0	.158	.211
Epstein, Mike-Michael Peter	66-67BalA 67-71WasA 71-72OakA 73TexA 73-74CalA	4- 4-43	Bronx, N.Y.		L	L	6'3	230	907	2854	362	695	93	16	130	380	448	645	7	.244	.424
Essegian, Chuck-Charles Abraham	58PhiN 59StLN 59-60LAN, 61BalA 61KCA 61-62CleA 63KCA	8- 9-31	Boston, Mass.		R	R	5'11	200	404	1018	139	260	45	4	47	150	97	233	0	.255	.446
Essian, Jim-James Sarkis	73-75PhiN 75ChiA	1- 2-51	Detroit, Mich.		R	R	6'1	187	21	24	2	3	0	0	0	1	3	2	0	.125	.125
Estrada, Frank-Francisco [Soto]	71NYN	2-12-48	Navojoa, Mexico		R	R	5'8	185	1	2	0	1	0	0	0	0	0	0	0	.500	.500
Etchebarren, Andy-Andrew Auguste	62,65-75BalA 75CalA	6-20-43	Whittier, Cal.		R	R	6'1	195	761	2252	218	528	89	14	49	272	209	471	10	.234	.352
Etheridge, Bobby-Bobby Lamar (Luke)	67,69SFN	11-25-43	Greenville, Miss.		R	R	5'9	170	96	246	26	60	16	2	2	25	26	38	0	.244	.350
Evans, Darrell-Darrell Wayne (Dee)	69-75AtlN	5-26-47	Pasadena, Cal.		L	R	6'2	200	715	2481	411	631	92	15	119	385	492	423	28	.254	.447
Evans, Dwight-Dwight Michael (Dewey)	72-75BosA	11- 3-51	Santa Monica, Cal.		R	R	6'3	210	398	1214	169	321	59	16	34	164	132	202	12	.264	.423
Ewing, Sam-Samuel James	73ChiA	4- 9-49	Lewisburg, Tenn.		L	R	6'3	205	11	20	1	3	1	0	0	2	2	6	0	.150	.200
Fahey, Bill-William Roger	71WasA 72,74-75TexA	6-14-50	Detroit, Mich.		L	R	6'	200	68	180	12	35	3	1	1	13	13	34	4	.194	.239
Fairey, Jim-James Burke	68LAN 69-72MonN 73LAN	9-22-44	Orangeburg, S.C.		L	L	5'10	190	399	766	86	180	25	7	7	75	47	122	6	.235	.313
Fairly, Ron-Ronald Ray	58-69LAN 69-74MonN 75StLN	7-12-38	Macon, Ga.		L	L	5'10	175	2131	6335	826	1694	273	31	183	909	937	764	35	.267	.407
Fanzone, Carmen-Carmen Ronald	70BosA 71-74ChiN	8-30-42	Detroit, Mich.		R	R	6'	200	237	588	66	132	27	0	20	94	74	119	3	.224	.372
Farley, Bob-Robert Jacob	61SFN 62ChiA 62DetA	11-15-37	Watsontown, Pa.		L	L	6'2	200	84	123	19	20	3	1	2	9	30	28	0	.163	.252
Fazio, Ernie-Ernest Joseph	62-63HouN 66KCA	1-25-42	Oakland, Cal.		R	R	5'7	165	141	274	37	50	10	4	2	8	33	85	5	.182	.270
Felske, John-John Frederick (Big John)	68ChiN 72-73MilA	5-30-42	Chicago, Ill.		R	R	6'3	195	54	104	7	14	3	1	1	9	9	35	0	.135	.212
Fenwick, Bob-Robert Richard (Bloop)	72HouN 73StLN	12-10-46	Okinawa, Ryukyu Is.		R	R	5'8	165	41	56	7	10	3	0	0	5	3	15	0	.179	.232
Ferguson, Joe-Joseph Vance	70-75LAN	9-19-46	San Francisco, Cal.		R	R	6'2	200	362	1168	168	288	48	2	49	181	213	222	6	.247	.417
Fernandez, Chico-Lorenzo Marto [Mosquera]	68BalA	4-23-39	Havana, Cuba		R	R	5'10	160	24	18	0	2	0	0	0	0	1	2	0	.111	.111
Fernandez, Frank-Frank	67-69NYA 70-71OakA 71WasA 71-72ChiN	4-16-43	Staten Island, N.Y.		R	R	6'	185	285	737	92	145	21	2	39	116	164	231	4	.199	.395
Ferrara, Al-Alfred John (The Bull)	63,65-68LAN 69-71SDN 71CinN	12-22-39	Brooklyn, N.Y.		R	R	6'1	210	574	1382	148	358	60	7	51	198	156	286	0	.259	.423
Ferraro, Mike-Michael Dennis	66,68NYA 69SeaA 72MilA	8-14-44	Kingston, N.Y.		R	R	5'11	175	162	500	28	116	18	2	2	30	23	61	0	.232	.288
Ferrer, Sergio (Cucho)	74-75MinA	1-29-51	Santurce, P.R.		B	R	5'7	145	56	138	26	36	3	3	0	2	11	17	6	.261	.326
Fiore, Mike-Michael Garry Joseph	68BalA 69-70KCA 70-71BosA 72StLN 72SDN	10-11-44	Brooklyn, N.Y.		L	L	6'	175	254	556	75	126	18	10	13	50	124	115	5	.227	.333
Fisk, Carlton-Carlton Ernest (Pudge)	69,71-75BosA	12-26-47	Bellows Falls, Vt.		R	R	6'2	200	413	1468	229	417	76	15	71	216	141	249	20	.284	.501
Fitzmaurice, Shaun-Shaun Earle	66NYN	8-25-42	Worcester, Mass.		R	R	6'	180	9	13	2	2	0	0	0	0	2	6	1	.154	.154
Flood, Curt-Curtis Charles	56-57CinN 58-69StLN 70HO 71WasA	1-18-38	Houston, Tex.		R	R	5'9	165	1759	6357	851	1861	271	44	85	636	444	609	88	.293	.389
Floyd, Bobby-Robert Nathan	68-70BalA 71-74KCA	10-20-43	Hawthorne, Cal.		R	R	6'1	180	214	425	40	93	17	1	0	26	28	99	2	.219	.264
Flynn, Doug-Robert Douglas	75CinN	4-18-51	Lexington, Ky.		R	R	5'11	165	89	127	17	34	7	0	1	20	11	13	3	.268	.346
Foli, Tim-Timothy John (Crazy Horse)	70-71NYN 72-75MonN	12- 8-50	Culver City, Cal.		R	R	6'	180	650	2310	219	557	70	9	5	164	135	211	43	.241	.286
Foote, Barry-Barry Clifton	73-75MonN	2-16-52	Smithfield, N.C.		R	R	6'3	210	249	813	69	189	39	6	18	91	52	122	2	.232	.362
Ford, Dan-Darrell Glenn	75MinA	5-19-52	Los Angeles, Cal.		R	R	6'1	185	130	440	72	123	21	1	15	59	30	79	7	.280	.434
Ford, Ted-Theodore Henry	70-71CleA 72TexA 73CleA	2- 7-47	Vineland, N.J.		R	R	5'10	180	240	711	66	156	26	2	17	68	51	134	7	.219	.333
Fosse, Ray-Raymond Earl	67-72CleA 73-75OakA	4- 4-47	Marion, Ill.		R	R	6'2	215	726	2357	239	588	95	10	53	261	172	308	14	.249	.366
Foster, George-George Arthur	69-71SFN 71-75CinN	12- 1-48	Tuscaloosa, Ala.		R	R	6'2	195	474	1420	176	374	73	10	50	203	110	302	14	.263	.435
Foster, Leo-Leonard Norris	71,73-74AtlN	2- 2-51	Covington, Ky.		R	R	5'11	162	84	128	18	23	3	0	1	5	9	25	1	.180	.227
Foster, Roy-Roy	70-72CleA	7-29-45	Bixby, Okla.		R	R	6'	185	337	1016	136	257	51	1	45	118	110	146	9	.253	.438
Foy, Joe-Joseph Anthony	66-68BosA 69KCA 70NYN 71WasA	2-21-43	New York, N.Y.		R	R	6'	215	716	2484	355	615	102	16	58	291	390	405	99	.248	.372
Francona, Tito-John Patsy	56-57BalA 58ChiA 58DetA 59-64CleA 65-66StLN 67PhiN 67-69AtlN 69-70OakA 70MilA	11- 4-33	Aliquippa, Pa.		L	L	5'11	190	1719	5121	650	1395	224	34	125	656	544	694	46	.272	.403
Freed, Roger-Roger Vernon	70BalA 71-72PhiN 74CinN	6- 2-46	Los Angeles, Cal.		R	R	6'	210	201	496	34	110	16	1	13	59	71	130	0	.222	.337
Freehan, Bill-William Ashley	61,63-75DetA	11-29-41	Detroit, Mich.		R	R	6'3	208	1703	5836	684	1527	231	34	195	731	614	726	24	.262	.413
Fregosi, Jim-James Louis	61-64LAA 65-71CalA 72-73NYN 73-75TexA	4- 4-42	San Francisco, Cal.		R	R	6'2	195	1775	6286	810	1668	254	77	145	672	672	1042	72	.265	.399
French, Jim-Richard James	65-71WasA	8-13-41	Warren, Ohio		L	R	5'8	180	234	607	53	119	17	4	5	51	121	78	3	.196	.262
Frias, Pepe-Jesus Maria [Andujar]	73-75MonN	7-14-48	San Pedro de Macoris, Dom. Rep.		R	R	5'9	160	226	401	35	84	16	2	0	33	20	47	2	.209	.259
Fritz, Larry-Lawrence Joseph (Zeb)	75PhiN	2-14-49	East Chicago, Ind.		L	L	6'2	220	1	1	0	0	0	0	0	0	0	0	0	.000	.000
Fuentes, Tito-Rigoberto [Peat]	65-67,69-74SFN 75SDN	1- 4-44	Havana, Cuba		B	R	5'11	180	1200	4388	474	1158	173	36	38	349	241	456	71	.264	.346
					Bats Right 65-67, part of 70																
Fuller, Jim-James Hardy	73-74BalA	11-28-50	Bethesda, Md.		R	R	6'4	220	73	215	19	45	11	0	9	32	9	85	1	.209	.386
Fuller, John-John Edward (Turkey)	74AtlN	1-29-50	Lynwood, Cal.		L	L	6'3	185	3	3	1	1	0	0	0	0	0	0	0	.333	.333
Fuller, Vern-Vernon Gordon	64,66-70CleA	3- 1-44	Menomonie, Wis.		R	R	6'1	170	325	785	67	182	33	4	14	65	73	172	6	.232	.338
Gabrielson, Len-Leonard Gary	60,63-64MilN 64-65ChiN 65-66SFN 67CalA 67-70LAN	2-14-40	Oakland, Cal.		L	R	6'4	215	708	1764	178	446	64	12	37	176	145	315	20	.253	.366

USE NAME – GIVEN NAMES (NICKNAMES)	TEAM BY YEAR	BIRTH DATE	BIRTH PLACE	DEATH DATE	LIFETIME BATTING TOTALS																
					B	T	HGT	WGT	G	AB	R	H	2B	3B	HR	RBI	BB	SO	SB	BA	SA
Gagliano, Phil-Philip Joseph	63-70StLN 70ChiN 71-72BosA 73-74CinN	12-27-41	Memphis, Tenn.		R	R	6'1	185	702	1411	150	336	50	7	14	159	163	184	5	.238	.313
Gagliano, Ralph-Ralph Michael	65CleA	10-18-46	Memphis, Tenn		L	R	5'11	170	1	0	0	0	0	0	0	0	0	0	0	–	–
Gaines, Joe-Arnesta Joe	60-62CinN 63-64BalA 64-66HouN	11-22-36	Bryant, Tex.		R	R	6'1	190	362	771	104	186	25	9	21	95	81	197	14	.241	.379
Gallagher, Alan-Alan Mitchell Edward George Patrick Henry (Dirty Al)	70-73SFN 73CalA	10-19-45	San Francisco, Cal.		R	R	6'	185	442	1264	114	333	42	9	11	130	138	164	7	.263	.337
Gallagher, Bob-Robert Collins	72BosA 73-74HouN 75NYN	7- 7-48	Newton, Mass.		L	L	6'4	190	213	255	34	56	6	1	2	13	16	56	1	.220	.275
Gamble, John-John Robert	72-73DetA	2-10-48	Reno, Nev.		R	R	5'10	165	13	3	1	0	0	0	0	0	0	0	0	.000	.000
Gamble, Oscar-Oscar Charles	69ChiN 70-72PhiN 73-75CleA	12-20-49	Ramer, Ala.		L	R	5'11	160	647	1953	268	509	72	18	63	208	212	227	29	.261	.413
Garcia, Pete-Pedro Modesto [Delfi] (Chicken)	73-75MilA	4-17-50	Guayama, P.R.		R	R	5'10	175	399	1334	153	300	62	11	33	146	84	245	31	.225	.362
Gardner, Art-Arthur Junior	75HouN	9-21-52	Madden, Miss.		L	L	5'11	175	13	31	3	6	0	0	0	2	1	8	1	.194	.194
Garner, Phil-Philip Mason (Gar)	73-75OakA	4-30-49	Jefferson City, Tenn.		R	R	5'10	180	199	621	60	126	22	5	6	55	31	73	5	.240	.336
Garr, Ralph-Ralph Allen (Flip, Road Runner)	68-75AtlN	12-12-45	Monroe, La.		L	R	5'11	185	800	3222	420	1022	132	40	49	247	157	291	137	.317	.429
Garrett, Adrian-Henry Adrian	66AtlN 70ChiN 71-72OakA 73-75ChiN 75CalN	1- 3-43	Brooksville, Fla.		L	R	6'3	185	134	228	26	45	5	0	11	34	26	71	4	.197	.364
Garrett, Wayne-Ronald Wayne	69-75NYN	12- 3-47	Brooksville, Fla.		L	R	6'	175	803	2566	353	611	85	19	51	269	430	439	26	.238	.346
Garrido, Gil-Gil Gonzalo	64SFN 68-72AtlN	6-26-41	Panama, Panama		R	R	5'9	160	334	872	81	207	14	5	1	51	61	54	2	.237	.268
Garvey, Steve-Steven Patrick	69-75LAN	12-22-48	Tampa, Fla.		R	R	5'10	192	644	2265	288	672	118	15	64	318	121	261	22	.297	.447
Gaspar, Rod-Rodney Earl	69-70NYN 71,74SDN	4- 3-46	Long Beach, Cal.		B	L	5'11	165	148	260	35	54	6	1	1	17	33	29	0	.208	.250
Gaston, Clarence-Clarence Edwin (Cito)	67AtlN 69-74SDN 75AtlN	3-17-44	San Antonio, Tex.		R	R	6'3	210	839	2781	287	709	97	30	83	332	164	633	11	.255	.401
Geiger, Gary-Gary Merle	58CleA 59-65BosA 66-67AtlN 69-70HouN	4- 4-37	San Ridge, Ill.		L	R	6'	168	954	2569	388	633	91	29	77	283	341	466	62	.246	.394
Gentile, Jim-James Edward (Diamond Jim)	57BknN 58LAN 60-63BalA 64-65KCA	6- 3-34	San Francisco, Cal.		L	L	6'4	210	936	2922	434	759	113	6	179	549	475	663	3	.260	.486
	65-66HouN 66CleA																				
Geronimo, Cesar-Cesar Francisco [Zorrilla]	69-71HouN 72-75CinN	3-11-48	El Seibo, Dom. Rep.		L	L	6'1	165	726	1681	235	429	68	25	22	177	148	370	31	.255	.365
Gibbs, Jake-Jerry Dean	62-71NYA	11- 7-38	Grenada, Miss.		L	R	6'	185	538	1639	157	382	53	8	25	146	120	231	28	.233	.321
Gibson, Russ-John Russell	67-69BosA 70-72SFN	5- 6-39	Fall River, Mass.		R	R	6'1	195	264	794	49	181	34	4	8	78	44	123	2	.228	.311
Gigon, Norm-Norman Phillip	67ChiN	5-12-38	Teaneck, N.J.		R	R	6'	195	34	70	8	12	3	1	1	6	5	14	0	.171	.286
Gil, Gus-Tomas Gustavo [Guillen]	67CleA 69SeaA 70-71MilA	4-19-40	Caracas, Venezuela		R	R	5'10	180	221	468	46	87	16	0	1	37	56	63	5	.186	.226
Gilbreath, Rod-Rodney Joe	72-75AtlN	9-24-52	Laurel, Miss.		R	R	6'1	180	140	320	38	81	6	2	2	19	34	46	8	.253	.303
Gleason, Roy-Roy William	63LAN	4- 9-43	Melrose Park, Ill.		B	R	6'5	220	8	1	3	1	1	0	0	0	0	0	0	1.000	2.000
Godby, Danny-Danny Ray (Deacon)	74StLN	11- 4-46	Logan, W. Va.		R	R	6'	185	13	13	2	2	0	0	0	1	3	4	0	.154	.154
Goddard, Joe-Joseph Harold	72SDN	7-23-50	Beckley, W. Va.		R	R	6'	182	12	35	0	7	2	0	0	2	5	9	0	.200	.257
Goggin, Chuck-Charlis Francis	72-73PitN 73Atl 74BosA	7- 7-45	Pompano Beach, Fla.		B	R	5'11	165	72	99	19	29	5	0	0	7	10	21	0	.293	.343
Goldy, Purnal-Purnal William	62-63DetA	11-28-37	Camden, N.J.		R	R	6'5	200	29	78	9	18	1	1	3	12	0	16	0	.231	.385
Gomez, Luis-Luis	74-75MinA	8-19-51	Guadalajara, Mexico		R	R	5'9	150	171	240	25	45	1	0	0	8	16	28	2	.188	.192
Gonder, Jesse-Jesse Lemar	60-61NYA 62-63CinN 63-65NYN 65MilN 66-67PitN	1-20-36	Monticello, Ark.		L	R	5'10	190	395	876	73	220	28	2	26	94	72	184	1	.251	.377
Gonzalez, Fernando-Jose Fernando [Quinones]	72-73PitN 74KCA 74NYA	6-19-50	Arecibo, P.R.		R	R	5'10	170	100	193	17	40	6	2	2	14	8	24	1	.207	.290
Gonzalez, Pedro-Pedro	63-65NYA 65-67CleA	12-12-38	San Pedro de Macoris, D.R.		R	R	6'	175	407	1084	99	264	39	6	8	70	52	176	22	.244	.313
Gonzalez, Tony-Andres Antonio [Gonzalez]	60CinN 60-68PhiN 69-70AtlN 70-71CalA	8-28-36	Central Canagua, Cuba		L	R	5'11	178	1559	5195	690	1485	238	57	103	615	467	706	79	.286	.413
Goodson, Ed-James Edward	70-75SFN 75AtlN	1-25-48	Pulaski, Va.		L	R	6'3	185	371	1082	97	291	46	2	26	148	52	106	1	.269	.387
Goodwin, Danny-Danny Kay	75CalA	9- 2-53	Peoria, Ill.		L	R	6'1	195	4	10	0	1	0	0	0	0	0	5	0	.100	.100
Goossen, Greg-Gregory Bryant	65-68NYN 69SeaA 70MilA 70WasA	12-14-45	Los Angeles, Cal.		R	R	6'1	210	193	460	33	111	24	1	13	44	42	112	1	.241	.383
Goryl, Johnny-John Albert	57-59ChiN 62-64MinA	10-21-33	Cumberland, R.I.		R	R	5'10	175	276	595	79	134	19	10	16	48	64	106	2	.225	.371
Gosger, Jim-James Charles	63,65-66BosA 66-67KCA 68OakA 69SeaA 69NYN	11- 6-42	Port Huron, Mich.		L	L	5'11	185	705	1815	197	411	67	16	30	177	217	316	25	.226	.331
	70-71MonN 73-74NYN																				
Goss, Howie-Howard Wayne	62PitN 63HouN	11- 1-34	Wewoka, Okla.		R	R	6'4	204	222	522	56	113	24	2	11	54	40	164	9	.216	.333
Gotay, Julio-Julio Enrique [Sanchez]	60-62StlLN 63-64PitN 65CalA 66-69HouN	6- 9-39	Fajardo, P.R.		R	R	6'	180	389	988	106	257	38	3	6	70	61	127	12	.260	.323
Grabarkewitz, Billy-Billy Cordell	69-72LAN 73CalA 73-74PhiN 74ChiN 75OakA	1-18-47	Lockhart, Tex.		R	R	5'10	175	466	1161	189	274	41	12	28	141	202	321	33	.236	.364
Graham, Wayne-Wayne Leon	63PhiN 64NYN	4- 6-37	Yoakum, Tex.		R	R	6'	200	30	55	2	7	1	0	0	0	3	6	0	.127	.145
Green, Dick-Richard Larry	63-67KCA 68-75OakA	4-21-41	Sioux City, Iowa		R	R	5'10	180	1288	4007	427	960	139	23	80	422	343	785	26	.240	.346
Green, Gene-Gene Leroy	57-59StLN 60BalA 61WasA 62-63CleA 63CinN	6-26-33	Los Angeles, Cal.		R	R	6'2	200	408	1151	130	307	49	7	46	160	89	185	2	.267	.441
Green, Lenny-Leonard Charles	57-59BalA 59-60WasA 61-64MinA 64LAA 64BalA	1- 6-34	Detroit, Mich.		L	L	5'11	175	1136	2956	461	788	138	27	47	253	368	260	78	.267	.379
	65-66BosA 67-68DetA																				
Grich, Bobby-Robert Anthony	70-75BalA	1-15-49	Muskegon, Mich.		R	R	6'2	185	642	2272	339	592	106	23	57	253	371	421	63	.261	.403
Grieve, Tommy-Thomas Alan	70WasA 72-75TexA	3- 4-48	Pittsfield, Mass.		R	R	6'2	195	379	1009	122	258	40	7	36	135	74	224	2	.256	.416
Griffey, Ken-George Kenneth	73-75CinN	4-10-50	Donora, Pa.		L	L	6'	190	245	776	138	231	29	15	9	79	100	120	29	.298	.409
Griffin, Doug-Douglas Lee	70CalA 71-75BosA	6- 4-47	South Gate, Cal.		R	R	6'1	160	578	2003	195	500	68	12	7	161	149	190	31	.250	.306
Griffith, Derrell-Robert Derrell	63-66LAN	12-12-43	Anadarko, Okla.		L	R	6'	168	124	296	33	77	16	2	5	27	7	33	5	.260	.378
Groat, Dick-Richard Morrow	52PitN 53-54MS 55-62PitN 63-65StLN 66-67PhiN	11- 4-30	Wilkinsburg, Pa.		R	R	5'11	170	1929	7484	829	2138	352	67	39	707	490	512	14	.286	.366
52-53 played in N.B.A.	67SFN																				
Gross, Greg-Gregory Eugene	73-75HouN	8- 1-52	York, Pa.		L	L	5'11	170	302	1111	150	336	37	19	0	78	143	80	16	.302	.370
Grote, Jerry-Gerald Wayne	63-64HouN 66-75NYN	10- 6-42	San Antonio, Tex.		R	R	5'10	185	1195	3746	302	930	135	18	34	347	337	556	13	.248	.321
Grubb, John-John Maywood	72-75SDN	8- 4-48	Richmond, Va.		L	R	6'3	185	404	1407	181	404	79	10	20	118	143	159	15	.287	.400
Guerrero, Mike-Mario Miguel [Abud] (Mickey)	73-74BosA 75StLN	9-28-49	Santo Domingo, Dom. Rep.		R	R	5'9	160	223	687	54	165	20	4	0	45	33	50	5	.240	.281
Guindon, Bob-Robert Joseph	64BosA	9- 4-43	Brookline, Mass.		L	L	6'2	185	5	8	0	1	1	0	0	0	1	4	0	.125	.250
Guth, Bucky-Charles Henry	72MinA	8-18-47	Baltimore, Md.		R	R	6'1	180	3	3	1	0	0	0	0	0	0	0	0	.000	.000
Gutierrez, Cesar-Cesar Dario (Cocoa)	67,69SFN 69-71DetA	1-26-43	Coro, Venezuela		R	R	5'9	155	223	545	61	128	13	6	0	26	30	51	7	.235	.281
Hacker, Rich-Richard Warren	71MonN	10- 6-47	Belleville, Ill.		B	R	6'1	170	16	33	2	4	1	0	0	2	3	12	0	.121	.151
Hague, Joe-Joe Clarence	68-72StLN 72-73CinN	4-25-44	Huntington, W. Va.		L	L	6'	195	430	1195	141	286	41	10	40	163	177	222	4	.239	.391
Hahn, Don-Donald Antone	69-70MonN 71-74NYN 75PhiN 75StLN 75SDN	11-16-48	San Francisco, Cal.		R	R	6'1	185	454	997	104	235	38	4	7	74	122	158	11	.236	.303
Hairston, Jerry-Jerry Wayne	73-75ChiA	2-16-52	Birmingham, Ala.		B	R	5'10	185	174	538	59	144	26	1	0	54	92	71	1	.268	.320
Hairston, Johnny-John Louis	69ChiN	8-29-45	Birmingham, Ala.		R	R	6'2	200	3	4	0	1	0	0	0	0	0	2	0	.250	.250
Hale, John-John Steven	74-75LAN	8- 5-53	Fresno, Cal.		L	R	6'2	200	75	208	22	47	8	0	6	26	26	51	1	.226	.351
Hall, Jimmie-Jimmie Randolph	63-66MinA 67-68CalA 68-69CleA 69NYA 69-70ChiN	3-17-38	Mount Holly, N.C.		L	R	6'	175	968	2848	387	724	100	24	121	391	287	529	38	.254	.434
	70AtlN																				
Haller, Tom-Thomas Frank	61-67SFN 68-71LAN 72DetA	6-23-37	Lockport, Ill.		L	R	6'4	205	1294	3935	411	1011	153	31	134	504	477	593	14	.257	.414
Hamlin, Ken-Kenneth Lee	57,59PitN 60KCA 61LAA 62,65-66WasA	5-18-35	Detroit, Mich.		R	R	5'10	170	468	1340	143	323	53	4	11	89	125	146	17	.241	.311
Hampton, Ike-Isaac Bernard	74NYN 75CalA	8-22-51	Camden, S.C.		B	R	6'1	185	35	70	8	10	3	0	0	5	7	20	0	.143	.186
Haney, Larry-Wallace Larry	66-68BalA 69SeaA 69-70,72-73OakA 73StLN 74-75OakA	11-19-42	Charlottesville, Va.		R	R	6'2	195	325	610	49	128	26	1	12	52	26	118	3	.210	.315
Hankins, Jay-Jay Nelson	61,63KCA	11- 7-35	St. Louis Co., Mo.		L	R	5'7	170	86	207	25	38	0	4	4	10	8	20	2	.184	.280
Hansen, Bob-Robert Joseph	74MilA	5-26-48	Boston, Mass.		L	L	6'	195	58	88	8	26	4	1	2	9	3	16	2	.295	.432
Hansen, Ron-Ronald Lavern	58-62BalA 63-67ChiA 68WasA 68-69ChiA 70-71NYA 72KCA	4- 5-38	Oxford, Neb.		R	R	6'3	200	1384	4311	446	1007	166	17	106	501	551	643	9	.234	.351
Hardy, Carroll-Carroll William	58-60CleA 60-62BosA 63-64HouN 67MinA	5-18-33	Sturgis, S.D.		R	R	6'	190	433	1117	172	251	47	10	17	113	122	222	13	.225	.330
56 played in N.F.L.																					
Hargrove, Mike-Dudley Michael	74-75TexA	10-26-49	Perryton, Texas		L	L	6'	195	276	934	139	291	40	8	15	128	128	108	4	.312	.420
Harkness, Tim-Thomas William	61-62LAN 63-64NYN	12-23-37	Lachine, Canada		L	L	6'2	182	259	562	59	132	18	4	14	61	58	118	7	.235	.356
Harlow, Larry-Larry Duane	75BalA	11-31-51	Colorado Springs, Colo.		L	L	6'2	185	4	3	1	1	0	0	0	0	0	1	0	.333	.333
Harmon, Terry-Terry Walter	67,69-75PhiN	4-12-44	Toledo, Ohio		R	R	6'2	180	465	1004	139	233	26	11	2	61	108	156	14	.232	.286
Harper, Tommy-Tommy	62-67CinN 68CleA 69SeaA 70-71MilA 72-74BosA 75CalA 75OakA	10-14-40	Oak Grove, La.		R	R	5'9	165	1764	6192	964	1591	251	36	145	560	743	1064	404	.257	.379
Harrah, Toby-Colbert Dale	69,71WasA 72-75TexA	10-26-48	Sissonville, W.Va.		R	R	6'	180	681	2314	320	607	88	10	54	270	268	264	74	.262	.379
Harrell, John-John Robert	69SFN	11-27-47	Long Beach, Cal.		R	R	6'2	190	2	6	0	3	0	0	0	2	2	1	0	.500	.500
Harrelson, Bud-Derrel McKinley	65-75NYN	6- 6-44	Niles, Cal.		B	R	5'11	155	1097	3762	431	897	105	39	4	204	483	511	101	.238	.290
					Bats Right - 65, part of 75																
Harrelson, Ken-Kenneth Smith (Hawk)	63-66KCA 66-67WasA 67KCA 67-69BosA	9- 4-41	Woodruff, S.C.		R	R	6'2	190	900	2941	374	703	94	14	131	421	382	677	53	.239	.414
	69-71CleA																				
Harrington, Mickey-Charles Michael	63PhiN	10- 8-34	Hattiesburg, Miss.		R	R	6'4	205	1	0	0	0	0	0	0	0	0	0	0	–	–
Harris, Alonzo-Alonzo (Candy)	67HouN	9-17-47	Selma, Ala.		L	R	6'	160	6	1	0	0	0	0	0	0	0	1	0	.000	.000
Harris, Billy-James William	68CleA 69KCA	11-24-43	Hamlet, N.C.		B	R	6'	175	43	101	11	22	6	1	0	3	8	23	2	.218	.297
Harris, Vic-Victor Lanier	72-73TexA 74-75ChiN	3-27-50	Los Angeles, Cal.		L	R	6'	170	326	995	103	213	25	11	8	70	102	153	29	.214	.285
Harrison, Chuck-Charles William	65-67HouN 69,71KCA	4-25-41	Abilene, Tex.		R	R	5'10	210	328	1012	94	241	43	6	17	126	85	147	3	.238	.343
Hart, Jim Ray-James Ray	63-73SFN 73-74NYA	10-30-41	Hookerton, N.C.		R	R	5'11	190	1125	3783	518	1052	148	29	170	578	380	573	17	.278	.467
Hartman, J.C.-J.C.	62-63HouN	4-15-34	Cottonton, Ala.		R	R	6'	175	90	238	13	44	8	0	0	8	6	29	2	.185	.210
Harts, Greg-Gregory Rudolph	73NYN	4-21-50	Atlanta, Ga.		L	L	6'	168	3	2	0	1	0	0	0	0	0	0	0	.500	.500
Healy, Fran-Francis Xavier	69KCA 71-72SFN 73-75KCA	9- 6-46	Holyoke Mass.		R	R	6'5	220	388	1114	122	282	52	6	20	124	135	201	24	.253	.364
Heath, Bill-William Chris	65ChiA 66-67HouN 67DetA 69ChiN	3-10-39	Yuba City, Cal.		L	R	5'8	175	112	199	13	47	6	1	0	13	26	22	1	.236	.276
Hebner, Richie-Richard Joseph	68-75PitN	1-26-47	Brighton, Mass.		L	R	6'1	195	905	3226	480	907	153	35	113	431	338	384	15	.281	.455

USE NAME – GIVEN NAMES (NICKNAMES)	TEAM BY YEAR	BIRTH DATE	BIRTH PLACE	DEATH DATE	B	T	HGT	WGT	G	AB	R	H	2B	3B	HR	RBI	BB	SO	SB	BA	SA
Hegan, Mike-James Michael	64,66-67NYA 69SeaA 70-71MilA 71-73OakA 73-74NYA 74-75MilA	7-21-42	Cleveland, Ohio		L	L	6'1	188	850	1806	243	441	69	15	46	195	276	418	31	.244	.375
Heidemann, Jack-Jack Seale	69-72,74CleA 74StLN 75NYN	7-11-49	Brenham, Tex.		R	R	6'	175	347	934	82	198	26	4	7	65	70	179	4	.212	.271
Heintzelman, Tom-Thomas Kenneth	73-74StLN	11- 3-46	St. Charles, Mo.		R	R	6'	185	61	103	15	26	4	0	1	6	12	17	0	.252	.320
Heise, Bob-Robert Lowell	67-69NYN 70-71SFN 71-73MilA 74StLN 74CalA 75BosA	5-12-47	San Antonio, Tex.		R	R	6'	175	413	1026	88	252	39	2	1	76	44	67	3	.246	.290
Heist, Al-Alfred Michael	60-61ChiN 62HouN	10- 5-27	Brooklyn, N.Y.		R	R	6'2	185	177	495	63	126	20	6	8	46	52	72	6	.255	.368
Held, Woody-Woodson George	54,57NYA 57-58KCA 58-64CleA 65WasA 66-67BalA 67-68CalA 68-69ChiA	3-25-32	Sacramento, Cal.		R	R	5'10	180	1390	4019	524	963	150	22	179	559	509	944	14	.240	.421
Helms, Tommy-Tommy Van	64-71CinN 72-75HouN	5- 5-41	Charlotte, N.C.		R	R	5'10	170	1337	4839	399	1302	216	20	32	459	217	287	33	.269	.342
Henderson, Ken-Kenneth Joseph	65-72SFN 73-75ChiA	6-15-46	Carroll, Iowa		B	R	6'2	185	1049	3532	488	924	169	25	96	450	450	595	79	.262	.405
Hendrick, George-George Andrew	71-72OakA 73-75CleA	10-18-49	Los Angeles, Cal.		R	R	6'3	195	497	1731	229	450	67	5	68	237	104	264	22	.260	.422
Hendricks, Ellie-Elrod Jerome	68-72BalA 72ChiN 73-75BalA	12-22-40	Charlotte Amalie, V.I.		L	R	6'1	175	633	1726	192	383	62	7	56	215	216	291	1	.222	.363
Henry, Ron-Ronald Baxter	61,64MinA	8- 7-36	Chester, Pa.		R	R	6'1	180	42	69	5	9	1	1	2	8	4	24	0	.130	.261
Hermoso, Angel-Angel Remigio (Remy)	67AtlN 69-70MonN 74CleA 75KJ	10- 1-46	Caracas, Venezuela		R	R	5'9	155	91	223	25	47	3	1	0	8	14	21	6	.211	.233
Hernandez, Enzo-Enzo Octavio [Martinez]	71-75SDN	2-12-49	Valle de Guanape, Venez.		R	R	5'8	155	590	1981	209	435	53	11	1	89	157	134	117	.220	.259
Hernandez, Jackie-Jacinto [Zulueta]	65-66CalA 67-68MinA 69-70KCA 71-73PitN	9-11-40	Central Tinguaro, Cuba		R	R	6'	170	618	1480	153	308	37	9	12	121	93	324	25	.208	.270
Hernandez, Keith-Keith (Chicano)	74-75StLN	10-20-53	San Francisco, Cal.		L	L	6'	183	78	222	23	57	9	4	3	22	24	34	2	.257	.374
Hernandez, Rudy-Rodolfo [Acosta]	72ChiA	10-18-51	Empalme, Mexico		R	R	5'8	150	8	21	0	4	0	0	0	1	0	3	0	.190	.190
Herndon, Larry-Larry Darnell (Hondo)	74StLN	11- 3-53	Sunflower, Miss.		R	R	6'3	188	12	1	3	1	0	0	0	0	0	0	0	1.000	1.000
Herrera, Joe-Jose Concepcion [Ontiveros] (Loco)	67-68HouN 69-70MonN	4- 8-42	San Lorenzo, Venezuela		R	R	5'9	175	80	231	16	61	10	0	2	20	7	28	1	.264	.333
Herrmann, Ed-Edward Martin	67,69-74ChiA 75NYA	8-27-46	San Diego, Cal.		L	R	6'1	205	725	2184	222	535	72	4	74	264	211	295	5	.245	.383
Herrnstein, John-John Ellett	62-66PhiN 66ChiN 66AtlN	3-31-38	Hampton, Va.		L	L	6'3	215	239	450	52	99	14	4	8	34	29	115	1	.220	.322
Herrscher, Rick-Richard Franklin	62NYN	11- 3-36	St. Louis, Mo.		R	R	6'2	187	35	50	5	11	3	0	1	6	5	11	0	.220	.340
Hershberger, Mike-Norman Michael	61-64ChiA 65-67KCA 68-69OakA 70MilA 71ChiA	10- 9-39	Massillon, Ohio		R	R	5'10	180	1150	3572	398	900	150	22	26	344	319	311	74	.252	.328
Hertz, Steve-Stephen Allan	64HouN	2-26-45	Dayton, Ohio		R	R	6'	195	5	4	2	0	0	0	0	0	0	3	0	.000	.000
Hiatt, Jack-Jack E.	64LAA 65-69SFN 70MonN 70ChiN 71-72HouN 72CalA	7-27-42	Bakersfield, Cal.		R	R	6'2	190	483	1142	110	287	51	5	22	154	224	395	0	.251	.363
Hibbs, Jim-James Kerr	67CalA	9-10-44	Klamath Falls, Ore.		R	R	6'	190	3	3	0	0	0	0	0	0	0	2	0	.000	.000
Hickman, Jim-James Lucius	62-66NYN 67LAN 68-73ChiN 74StLN	5-10-37	Henning, Tenn.		R	R	6'3	195	1421	3974	518	1002	163	25	159	560	491	832	17	.252	.426
Hicks, Jim-James Edward	64-66ChiA 69StLN 69-70CalA	5-18-40	East Chicago, Ind.		R	R	6'3	205	93	141	16	23	1	3	5	14	18	48	0	.163	.319
Hicks, Joe-William Joseph	59-60ChiA 61-62WasA 63NYN	4- 7-33	Ivy, Va.		L	R	6'	180	212	416	41	92	11	3	12	39	29	73	3	.221	.349
Hill, Herm-Herman Alexander	69-70MinA	10-12-45	Tuskegee, Ala.	12-14-70	L	R	6'2	190	43	24	12	2	0	0	0	0	0	7	1	.083	.083
Hill, Marc-Marc Kevin	73-74StLN 75SFN	2-18-52	Elsberry, Mo.		R	R	6'3	205	83	206	16	44	5	0	5	25	29	33	0	.214	.311
Hiller, Chuck-Charles Joseph (Iron Hands)	61-65SFN 65-67NYN 67PhiN 68PitN	10- 1-34	Johnsburg, Ill.		L	R	5'11	170	704	2121	253	516	76	9	20	152	157	187	14	.243	.316
Hilton, Dave-John David	72-75SDN	9-15-50	Uvalde, Tex.		R	R	6'	180	161	506	40	108	19	3	6	33	35	69	6	.213	.298
Hinton, Chuck-Charles Edward	61-64WasA 65-67CleA 68CalA 69-71CleA	5- 3-34	Rocky Mount, N.C.		R	R	6'1	180	1353	3968	518	1048	152	47	113	443	416	685	130	.264	.412
Hiser, Gene-Gene Taylor	71-75ChiN	12-11-48	Baltimore, Md.		L	L	5'11	170	206	263	34	53	7	0	1	18	32	43	6	.202	.240
Hisle, Larry-Larry Eugene	68-71PhiN 73-75MinA	5- 5-47	Portsmouth, Ohio		R	R	6'2	193	680	2284	327	604	103	24	75	297	246	592	64	.264	.429
Hobson, Butch-Clell Lavern	75BosA	8- 7-51	Bessemer, Ala.		R	R	6'1	193	2	4	0	1	0	0	0	0	0	2	0	.250	.250
Hodge, Gomer-Harold Morris	71CleA	4- 3-44	Rutherfordton, N.C.		B	R	6'2	190	80	83	3	17	3	0	1	9	4	19	0	.205	.277
Hodges, Ron-Ronald Wray	73-75NYN	6-22-49	Rocky Mount, Va.		L	R	6'1	185	113	297	24	70	7	0	7	36	31	36	0	.236	.330
Hoffman, John-John Edward (Pork Chop)	64-65HouN	10-31-43	Aberdeen, S.D.		L	R	6'	190	8	21	2	3	0	0	0	1	1	10	0	.143	.143
Holman, Gary-Gary Richard	68-69WasA	1-25-44	Long Beach, Cal.		L	L	6'1	200	116	116	11	30	6	1	0	9	17	22	0	.259	.328
Holt, Jim-James William	68-74MinA 74-75OakA	5-27-44	Graham, N.C.		L	R	6'	195	703	1609	174	426	62	10	19	175	92	164	8	.265	.351
Hopkins, Don-Donald (Hoppy)	75OakA	1- 9-52	West Point, Miss.		L	R	6'1	175	82	6	25	1	0	0	0	0	2	0	21	.167	.167
Hopkins, Gail-Gail Eason	68-70ChiA 71-73KCA 74LAN	2-19-43	Tulsa, Okla.		L	R	5'10	198	514	1219	142	324	47	6	25	145	160	83	6	.266	.376
Horton, Tony-Anthony Darrin	64-67BosA 67-70CleA 71IL	12- 6-44	Santa Monica, Cal.		R	R	6'3	210	636	2228	251	597	102	15	76	297	140	319	12	.268	.430
Horton, Willie-Willie Wattison	63-75DetA	10-18-42	Arno, Va.		R	R	5'11	210	1400	5000	631	1384	194	31	248	830	420	872	14	.277	.477
Hosley, Tim-Timothy Kenneth	70-71DetA 73-74OakA 75ChiN	5-10-47	Spartanburg, S.C.		R	R	5'11	190	100	190	31	46	7	0	9	31	30	37	1	.242	.421
Hottman, Ken-Kenneth Roger	71ChiA	5- 7-48	Stockton, Cal.		R	R	5'11	200	6	16	1	2	0	0	0	0	1	2	0	.125	.125
Hovley, Steve-Stephen Eugene (Orbie)	69SeaA 70MilA 70-71OakA 72-73KCA	12-18-44	Ventura, Cal.		L	L	5'9	180	436	1019	122	263	39	5	8	88	116	128	29	.258	.330
Howard, Doug-Douglas Lynn	72-74CalA 75StLN	2- 6-48	Salt Lake City, Utah		R	R	6'3	185	58	127	12	27	1	1	1	9	4	17	1	.213	.260
Howard, Elston-Elston Gene (Ellie)	55-67NYA 67-68BosA	2-23-29	St. Louis, Mo.		R	R	6'2	200	1605	5363	619	1471	218	50	167	762	373	786	9	.274	.427
Howard, Frank-Frank Oliver (Hondo, The Capital Punisher)	58-64LAN 65-71WasA 72TexA 72-73DetA	8- 8-36	Columbus, Ohio		R	R	6'7	275	1902	6488	864	1774	245	35	382	1119	782	1460	8	.273	.499
Howard, Larry-Lawrence Rayford	70-73HouN 73AtlN	6- 6-45	Columbus, Ohio		R	R	6'2	205	133	365	36	86	19	0	6	47	37	85	0	.236	.337
Howard, Wilbur-Wilbur Leon (Whistle)	73MilA 74-75HouN	1- 8-49	Lowell, N. C.		B	R	6'2	180	201	542	84	143	20	8	2	27	28	95	36	.264	.341
Howarth, Jim-James Eugene	71-74SFN	5- 7-47	Biloxi, Miss.		L	L	5'11	180	152	226	27	49	6	1	1	16	26	29	3	.217	.265
Howe, Art-Arthur Henry (Hank)	74-75PitN	12-15-46	Pittsburgh, Pa.		R	R	6'2	185	92	220	23	43	13	1	2	15	24	28	1	.195	.291
Howell, Roy-Roy Lee	74-75TexA	12-18-53	Lompoc, Cal.		L	R	6'	190	138	427	45	107	16	2	11	54	41	89	2	.251	.375
Howser, Dick-Richard Dalton	61-63KCA 63-66CleA 67-68NYA	5-14-37	Miami, Fla.		R	R	5'8	155	789	2483	398	617	90	17	16	165	387	186	105	.248	.318
Hriniak, Walt-Walter John	68-69AtlN 69SDN	5-22-43	Natick, Mass.		L	R	5'11	180	47	99	4	25	0	0	0	4	10	15	0	.253	.253
Hubbs, Ken-Kenneth Douglas	61-63ChiN	12-23-41	Riverside, Cal.	2-13-64	R	R	6'2	175	324	1255	148	310	44	13	14	98	74	230	11	.247	.336
Hughes Terry-Terry Wayne	70ChiN 73StLN 74BosA	5-13-49	Spartanburg, S.C.		R	R	6'1	185	54	86	6	18	3	0	1	7	7	22	0	.209	.279
Humphrey, Terry-Terryal Gene	71-74MonN 75DetA	8- 4-49	Chickasha, Okla.		R	R	6'3	190	159	424	22	80	14	0	2	23	27	73	4	.189	.236
Hundley, Randy-Cecil Randolph	64-65SFN 66-73ChiN 74MinA 75SDN	6- 1-42	Martinsville, Va.		R	R	5'11	170	1046	3420	308	810	116	13	82	380	270	560	12	.237	.350
Hunt, Ken-Kenneth Lawrence	59-60NYA 61-63LAA 63-64WasA	7-13-34	Grand Forks, N.D.		R	R	6'1	205	310	782	107	177	42	4	33	111	85	222	9	.226	.417
Hunt, Ron-Ronald Kenneth	63-66NYN 67LAN 68-70SFN 71-74MonN 74StLN	2-23-41	St. Louis, Mo.		R	R	6'	186	1483	5235	745	1429	223	23	39	370	555	382	65	.273	.347
Hunter, Buddy-Harold James	71,73,75BosA	8- 9-47	Omaha, Neb.		R	R	5'10	178	22	17	5	5	2	0	0	2	5	2	0	.294	.412
Huntz, Steve-Steven Michael	67,69StLN 70SDN 71ChiA 75SDN	12- 3-45	Cleveland, Ohio		R	R	6'1	204	237	636	81	131	19	1	16	60	108	122	1	.206	.314
Hutto, Jim-James Neamon	70PhiN 75BalA	10-17-47	Norfolk, Va.		R	R	6'	200	61	97	7	17	2	0	3	12	5	22	0	.175	.289
Hutton, Tommy-Thomas George	66,69LAN 72-75PhiN	4-20-46	Los Angeles, Cal.		L	L	5'11	180	468	1051	129	268	39	5	16	128	150	85	12	.255	.347
Ivie, Mike-Michael Wilson (Moose)	71,74-75SDN	8- 8-52	Atlanta, Ga.		R	R	6'3	210	129	428	37	105	16	2	9	52	23	72	4	.245	.355
Izquierdo, Hank-Enrique Roberto [Valdes]	67MinA	3-20-31	Matanzas, Cuba		R	R	5'11	175	16	26	4	7	0	0	0	2	1	2	0	.269	.346
Jackson, Reggie-Reginald Martinez	67KCA 68-75OakA	5-18-46	Wyncote, Pa.		L	L	6'	200	1231	4350	714	1154	220	26	254	733	600	1129	143	.265	.503
Jackson, Ron-Ronnie (Pop)	75CalA	5- 9-53	Birmingham, Ala.		R	R	6'	200	13	39	2	9	2	0	0	2	2	10	1	.231	.282
Jackson, Sonny-Roland Thomas	63-67HouN 68-74AtlN	7- 9-44	Washington, D.C.		L	R	5'9	155	936	3055	396	767	81	28	7	162	250	265	126	.251	.303
Jacobs, Lamar-Lamar Gary (Jake)	60WasA 61MinA	6- 9-37	Youngstown, Ohio		R	R	6'	175	10	10	0	2	0	0	0	0	0	2	0	.200	.200
James, Art-Arthur (Spider)	75DetA	8- 2-52	Detroit, Mich.		L	L	6'	170	11	40	2	9	2	0	0	1	1	3	1	.225	.275
James, Charlie-Charles Wesley	60-64StLN 65CinN	12-22-37	St. Louis, Mo.		R	R	6'1	195	510	1406	158	358	56	9	29	172	48	260	7	.255	.369
James, Cleo-Cleo Joel	68LAN 70-71,73ChiN	8-31-40	Clarksdale, Miss.		R	R	5'10	176	208	381	69	87	15	2	5	27	28	52	16	.228	.318
Jata, Paul-Paul	72DetA	9- 4-49	Queens, N.Y.		R	R	6'1	195	32	74	8	17	2	0	0	3	7	14	0	.230	.257
Javier, Julian-Manuel Julian [Liranzo] (Hoolie, The Phantom)	60-71StLN 72CinN	8- 9-36	San Francisco de Mac., D.R.		R	R	6'1	175	1622	5722	722	1469	216	55	78	506	314	812	135	.257	.355
Jestadt, Garry-Garry Arthur	69MonN 71ChiN 71-72SDN	3-19-47	Chicago, Ill.		R	R	6'2	188	176	454	33	118	18	1	6	36	24	45	1	.260	.344
Jeter, Johnnie-Johnnie	69-70PitN 71-72SDN 73ChiA 74CleA	10-24-44	East Point, La.		R	R	6'1	186	336	873	108	213	27	10	18	69	46	237	28	.244	.360
Jiminez, Elvio-Felix Elvio	64NYA	1- 6-40	San Pedro de Macoris, D.R.		R	R	5'9	170	1	6	0	2	0	0	0	0	0	0	0	.333	.333
Jiminez, Manny-Manuel Emilio	62-64,66KCA, 67-68PitN 69ChiN	11-19-38	San Pedro de Macoris, D.R.		L	R	6'1	190	429	1003	90	273	43	4	26	144	75	97	0	.272	.401
Johnson, Alex-Alexander	64-65PhiN 66-67StLN 68-69CinN 70-71CalA 72CleA 73-74TexA 74-75NYA	12- 7-42	Helena, Ark.		R	R	6'	205	1197	4194	509	1216	165	31	72	480	225	577	89	.290	.396
Johnson, Bob-Robert Wallace	60KCA 61-62WasA 63-67BalA 67NYN 68CinN 68AtlN 69StLN 69-70OakA	3- 4-36	Omaha, Neb.		R	R	5'10	180	874	2307	254	628	88	11	44	230	156	291	24	.272	.377
Johnson, Cliff-Clifford (Top Cat, Boomer)	72-75HouN	7-22-47	San Antonio, Tex.		R	R	6'4	227	217	535	84	140	22	2	32	100	81	116	1	.262	.490
Johnson, Dave-David Allen	65-72BalA 73-75AtlN	1-30-43	Orlando, Fla.		R	R	6'1	180	1289	4503	522	1170	230	16	124	553	521	627	32	.260	.401
Johnson, Deron-Deron Roger	60-61NYA 61-62KCA 64-67CinN 68AtlN 69-73PhiN 73OakA 74MilA 74OakA 74BosA 75ChiA 75BosA	7-17-38	San Diego, Cal.		R	R	6'2	205	1750	5902	703	1442	246	32	245	923	580	1307	11	.244	.421
Johnson, Frank-Frank Herbert	66-71SFN	7-22-42	El Paso, Tex.		R	R	6'1	165	196	436	47	92	4	2	4	43	37	60	2	.211	.256
Johnson, Lamar-Lamar	74-75ChiA	9- 2-50	Bessemer, Ala.		R	R	6'2	215	18	59	3	16	3	0	1	3	1	8	0	.271	.373
Johnson, Larry-Larry Doby	72,74CleA 75MonN	8-17-50	Cleveland, Ohio		R	R	6'	184	3	5	1	2	1	0	0	1	1	2	0	.400	.600
Johnson, Lou-Louis Brown (Slick, Sweet Lou)	60ChiN 61LAA 62MilN 65-67LAN 68ChiN 68CleA 69CalA	9-22-34	Lexington, Ky.		R	R	5'11	170	677	2049	244	529	97	14	48	232	110	320	50	.258	.389
Johnson, Tim-Timothy Evald	73-75MilA	7-22-49	Grand Forks, N.D.		L	R	6'3	180	267	795	70	171	18	9	0	59	46	158	13	.215	.260
Johnston, Rex-Rex David	60 played in N.F.L. 64PitN	11- 8-37	Colton, Cal.		B	R	6'1	202	14	7	1	0	0	0	0	0	3	0	0	.000	.000
Johnstone, Jay-John William	66-70CalA 71-72ChiA 73OakA 74-75PhiN	11-20-45	Manchester, Conn.		L	R	6'1	185	894	2686	323	694	106	23	59	272	216	379	36	.258	.381
Jones, Bob-Robert Oliver	74-75TexA	10-11-49	Elkton, Md.		L	L	6'2	190	11	16	2	1	0	0	0	0	3	4	0	.063	.063

USE NAME – GIVEN NAMES (NICKNAMES)	TEAM BY YEAR	BIRTH DATE	BIRTH PLACE	DEATH DATE	B	T	HGT	WGT	G	AB	R	H	2B	3B	HR	RBI	BB	SO	SB	BA	SA
									LIFETIME BATTING TOTALS												
Jones, Clarence-Clarence Woodrow	67-68ChiN	11- 7-42	Zanesville, Ohio		L	L	6'2	205	58	137	13	34	7	0	2	16	16	34	0	.248	.343
Jones, Cleon-Cleon Joseph	63,65-75NYN	8- 4-42	Plateau, Ala.		R	L	6'	190	1201	4223	563	1182	182	33	93	521	355	697	91	.280	.405
Jones, Dalton-James Dalton	64-69BosA 70-72DetA 72TexA	12-10-43	McComb, Miss.		L	R	6'1	180	907	2329	268	548	91	19	41	237	191	309	20	.235	.343
Jones, Deacon-Grover William	62-63,66ChiA	4-18-34	White Plains, N.Y.		L	R	5'10	190	40	49	7	14	2	1	1	10	6	8	0	.286	.429
Jones, Hal-Harold Marion	61-62CleA	4- 9-36	Louisiana, Mo.		R	R	6'2	194	17	51	4	11	1	0	2	5	2	16	0	.216	.353
Jones, Mack-Mack (Mack the Knife)	61-63,65MilN 66-67AtlN 68CinN 69-71MonN	11- 6-38	Atlanta, Ga.		L	R	6'1	190	1002	3091	495	778	132	31	133	415	383	756	65	.252	.444
Jorgensen, Mike-Michael	68,70-71NYN 72-75MonN	8-16-48	Passaic, N.J.		L	L	6'	195	655	1736	231	431	67	8	59	235	287	289	37	.248	.398
Joseph, Rick-Ricardo Emelindo	64KCA 67-70PhiN	8-24-39	San Pedro de Macoris, D.R.		R	R	6'1	192	270	633	69	154	26	1	13	65	51	141	2	.243	.349
Josephson, Duane-Duane Charles	65-70ChiA 71-72BosA 73IL	6- 3-42	New Hampton, Iowa		R	R	6'	190	470	1505	147	388	58	12	23	164	92	174	2	.258	.358
Joshua, Von-Von Everett	69-71,73-74LAN 75SFN	5- 1-48	Oakland, Cal.		L	L	5'10	170	382	914	132	261	35	15	11	84	53	148	33	.286	.393
Jutze, Skip-Alfred Henry	72StLN 73-75HouN	5-28-46	Queens, N.Y.		R	R	6'	195	170	455	28	103	10	0	0	30	23	58	0	.226	.248
Kaline, Al-Albert William	53-74DetA	12-19-34	Baltimore, Md.		R	R	6'1	180	2834	10116	1622	3007	498	75	399	1583	1277	1020	137	.297	.480
Kanehl, Roderick Edwin (Hot Rod)	62-64NYN	4- 1-34	Wichita, Kans.		R	R	6'1	180	340	796	103	192	22	3	6	47	35	80	17	.241	.300
Kasko, Eddie-Edward Michael	57-58StLN 59-63CinN 64-65HouN 66,M70-73BosA	6-27-32	Linden, N.J.		R	R	6'	180	1077	3546	411	935	146	13	22	261	265	353	31	.264	.331
Kelleher, Mick-Michael Dennis	72-73StLN 74HouN 75StLN	7-25-47	Seattle, Wash.		R	R	5'9	176	92	162	13	26	4	1	0	5	15	37	1	.160	.198
Kelly, Pat-Harold Patrick	67-68MinA 69-70KCA 71-75ChiA	7-30-44	Philadelphia, Pa.		L	L	6'1	185	853	3065	419	789	119	30	37	228	388	502	178	.257	.352
Kelly, Tom-Jay Thomas (Red)	75MinA	8-15-50	Graceville, Minn.		L	L	5'11	185	49	127	11	23	5	0	1	11	15	22	0	.181	.244
Kelly, Van-Van Howard	69-70SDN	3-18-46	Charlotte, N.C.		L	R	5'11	180	111	298	25	66	10	1	4	24	27	45	0	.221	.302
Kendall, Fred-Fred Lyn	69-75SDN	1-31-49	Torrance, Cal.		R	R	6'1	185	543	1636	109	380	53	10	25	154	125	159	4	.232	.323
Kenders, Al-Albert Daniel George	61PhiN	4- 4-37	Barrington, N.J.		R	R	6'	185	10	23	0	4	1	0	0	1	1	0	0	.174	.217
Kennedy, Jim-James Earl	70StLN	11- 1-46	Tulsa, Okla.		L	R	5'9	160	12	24	1	3	0	0	0	0	0	0	0	.125	.125
Kennedy, John-John Edward	62-64WasA 65-66LAN 67NYA 69SeaA 70MilA 70-74BosA	5-29-41	Chicago, Ill.		R	R	6'	185	856	2110	237	475	77	17	32	185	142	461	0	.225	.323
Kennedy, Junior-Junior Raymond	74CinN	8- 9-50	Fort Gibson, Okla.		R	R	6'	180	22	19	2	3	0	0	0	0	6	4	0	.158	.158
Kenney, Jerry-Gerald T.	67NYA 68MS 69-72NYA 73CleA	6-30-45	St. Louis, Mo.		L	R	6'1	170	465	1369	165	325	38	13	7	103	184	139	59	.237	.299
Kenworthy, Dick-Richard Lee	62,64-68ChiA	4- 1-41	Red Oak, Iowa		R	R	5'9	170	125	251	12	54	6	1	4	13	10	42	0	.215	.295
Keough, Joe-Joseph William	68OakA 69-72KCA 73ChiA	1- 7-46	Pomona, Cal.		L	L	6'	185	332	863	95	212	26	5	9	81	87	75	9	.246	.319
Keough, Marty-Richard Martin	56-60BosA 60CleA 61WasA 62-65CinN 66AtlN 66ChiN	4-14-35	Oakland, Cal.		L	L	6'	180	841	1796	256	434	71	23	43	176	164	318	26	.242	.379
Kern, Bill-William George	62KCA	2-28-35	Coplay, Pa.		R	R	6'2	184	8	16	1	4	0	0	1	1	0	3	0	.250	.438
Kernek, George-George Boyd	65-66StLN	1-12-40	Holdenville, Okla.		L	L	6'3	190	30	81	11	21	3	2	0	6	6	13	1	.259	.346
Kessinger, Don-Donald Eulon	64-75ChiN	7-17-42	Forrest City, Ark.		B	R	6'1	170	1648	6355	769	1619	201	71	11	431	550	629	92	.255	.314
					Bats Right 64-65																
Killebrew, Harmon-Harmon Clayton (Killer)	54-60WasA 61-74MinA 75KCA	6-29-36	Payette, Idaho		R	R	6'	210	2435	8147	1283	2086	290	24	573	1584	1559	1699	19	.256	.509
Kindall, Jerry-Gerald Donald (Slim)	56-58,60-61ChiN 62-64CleA 64-65MinA	5-27-35	St. Paul, Minn.		R	R	6'2	175	742	2057	211	439	83	9	44	198	145	535	17	.213	.327
					Bats Both part of 60																
King, Hal-Harold	67-68HouN 70-71AtlN 72TexA 73-74CinN	2- 1-44	Oviedo, Fla.		L	R	6'1	200	322	683	67	146	26	3	24	82	104	158	0	.214	.366
King, Jim-James Hubert	55-56ChiN 57StLN 58SFN 61-67WasA 67ChiA 67CleA	8-27-32	Elkins, Ark.		L	R	6'	190	1125	2918	374	699	112	19	117	401	363	401	23	.240	.411
Kingman, Dave-David Arthur	71-74SFN 75NYN	12-21-48	Pendleton, Ore.		R	R	6'6	210	543	1744	242	394	77	10	113	305	172	575	44	.226	.476
Kirkland, Willie-Willie Charles	58-60SFN 61-63CleA 64BalA 64-66WasA	2-17-34	Siluria, Ala.		L	R	6'1	206	1149	3494	443	837	134	29	148	509	323	648	52	.240	.422
Kirkpatrick, Ed-Edgar Leon	62-64LAA 65-68CalA 69-73KCA 74-75PitN	10- 8-44	Spokane, Wash.		L	R	5'11	195	1158	3168	382	756	127	18	84	395	420	478	30	.239	.370
Klaus, Bobby-Robert Francis	64CinN 64-65NYN	12-27-37	Spring Grove, Ill.		R	R	5'10	170	215	590	65	123	25	4	6	29	74	92	5	.208	.295
Klimchock, Lou-Louis Stephen	58-61KCA 62MilN 63WasA 63-65MilN 66NYN 68-70CleA	10-15-39	Hostetter, Pa.		L	R	5'11	180	318	669	64	155	21	3	13	69	31	71	0	.232	.330
Knight, Ray-Charles Ray (Knight Train)	74CinN	12-28-52	Albany, Ga.		R	R	6'2	185	14	11	1	2	1	0	0	2	1	2	0	.182	.273
Knoop, Bobby-Robert Frank	64LAA 65-69CalA 69-70ChiA 71-72KCA	10-18-38	Sioux City, Iowa		R	R	6'1	180	1153	3622	337	856	129	29	56	331	305	833	16	.236	.334
Knox, John-John Clinton	72-75DetA	7-26-48	Newark, N.J.		L	R	6'	170	124	219	21	60	4	1	0	11	20	27	7	.274	.301
Koegel, Pete-Peter John (Jolly)	70-71MilA 71-72PhiN	7-31-47	Mineola, N.Y.		R	R	6'6	230	62	86	6	15	3	0	1	5	11	28	0	.174	.244
Kolb, Gary-Gary Alan	60,62-63StLN 64-65MilN 65NYN 68-69PitN	3-13-40	Rock Falls, Ill.		L	R	6'	194	293	450	63	94	9	6	6	29	46	104	10	.209	.296
Kopacz, George-George Felix	66AtlN 70PitN	2-26-41	Chicago, Ill.		L	L	6'1	195	16	25	2	3	0	0	0	0	1	10	0	.120	.120
Koppe (Kopchia), Joe-Joseph	58MilN 59-61PhiN 61-64LAA 65CalA	10-19-30	Detroit, Mich.		R	R	5'10	165	578	1606	202	379	61	12	19	141	209	345	16	.236	.324
Kosco, Andy-Andrew John	65-67MinA 68NYA 69-70LAN 71MilA 72CalA 72BosA	10- 5-41	Youngstown, Ohio		R	R	6'3	205	668	1963	204	464	75	8	73	267	99	350	5	.236	.394
	73-74CinN																				
Kostro, Frank-Frank Jerry	62-63DetA 63LAA 64-65,67-69MinA	8- 4-37	Windber, Pa.		R	R	6'2	190	266	467	40	114	17	2	5	37	33	85	0	.244	.321
Kranepool, Ed-Edward Emil	62-75NYN	11- 8-44	Bronx, N.Y.		L	L	6'3	205	1474	4504	447	1165	184	24	93	489	375	493	13	.259	.370
Krsnich, Mike-Michael	60,62MilN	9-24-31	West Allis, Wis.		R	R	6'1	190	15	21	0	4	2	0	0	4	0	4	0	.190	.286
Krug, Chris-Everett Ben	65-66ChiN 69SDN	12-25-39	Los Angeles, Cal.		R	R	6'4	200	79	214	17	41	6	0	5	25	15	66	0	.192	.290
Kubek, Tony-Anthony Christopher	57-65NYA	10-12-36	Milwaukee, Wis.		L	R	6'3	190	1092	4167	522	1109	178	30	57	373	217	441	29	.266	.364
Kubiak, Ted-Theodore Rodger	67KCA 68-69OakA 70-71MilA 71StLN 72TexA	5-12-42	New Brunswick, N.J.		B	R	6'	175	881	2235	222	535	56	19	13	176	246	244	13	.239	.299
	72-75OakA 75SDN																				
Kubiszyn, Jack-Jack Joseph	61-62CleA	12-19-36	Buffalo, N.Y.		R	R	5'11	170	50	101	7	19	2	0	1	2	7	12	0	.188	.238
Kuiper, Duane-Duane E.	74-75CleA	6-19-50	Racine, Wis.		L	R	6'	173	100	368	49	112	13	1	0	29	32	28	20	.304	.345
Kusick, Craig-Craig Robert (Kooz)	73-75MinA	9-30-48	Milwaukee, Wis.		R	R	6'3	225	148	405	54	97	17	1	14	57	63	68	0	.240	.390
Kusnyer, Art-Arthur William	70ChiA 71-73CalA	12-19-45	Akron, Ohio		R	R	6'2	200	115	266	18	48	4	1	2	16	18	52	0	.180	.226
Laboy, Coco-Jose Alberto [Guilbe]	69-73MonN	7- 3-39	Ponce, P.R.		R	R	5'10	170	420	1247	108	291	62	2	28	166	97	220	0	.233	.354
Lachemann, Rene-Rene George	65-66KCA 68OakA	5- 4-45	Los Angeles, Cal.		R	R	6'	198	118	281	23	59	9	1	9	33	13	69	0	.210	.345
LaCock, Pete-Ralph Pierre	72-75ChiN	1-17-52	Burbank, Cal.		L	L	6'2	205	157	381	43	84	13	2	7	45	50	46	1	.220	.320
Lacy, Lee-Leondaus	72-75LAN	4-10-48	Longview, Tex.		R	R	6'1	180	266	762	105	209	26	8	7	68	58	114	14	.274	.357
Lahoud, Joe-Joseph Michael	69-71BosA 72-74MilA 75CalA	4-14-47	Danbury, Conn.		L	L	6'1	198	664	1659	215	373	56	11	62	201	270	290	18	.225	.384
Lamont, Gene-Gene William	70-72,74-75DetA	12-25-46	Rockford, Ill.		L	R	6'1	195	87	159	15	37	8	1	4	14	9	35	1	.233	.371
Lampard, Keith-Christopher Keith	69-70HouN	12-20-45	Warrington, England		L	R	6'2	195	62	84	10	20	8	1	1	7	5	27	0	.238	.393
Landis, Jim-James Henry	57-64ChiA 65KCA 66CleA 67DetA 67BosA 67HouN	3- 9-34	Fresno, Cal.		R	R	6'1	180	1346	4288	625	1061	169	50	93	467	588	767	139	.247	.375
Landrum, Don-Donald LeRoy	57PhiN 60-62StLN 62-65ChiN 66SFN	2-16-36	Santa Rosa, Cal.		L	R	6'	180	456	1160	151	272	36	8	12	75	104	200	36	.234	.310
Lane, Marvin-Marvin	71-74DetA	1-18-50	Sandersville, Ga.		R	R	5'11	180	72	131	20	28	4	1	3	12	22	31	2	.214	.328
Lanier, Hal-Harold Clifton	64-71SFN 72-73NYA	7- 4-42	Denton, N.C.		R	R	6'2	186	1196	3703	297	843	111	20	8	273	136	436	11	.228	.275
					Bats Both 66, 68-70, part of 67																
Lanier, Rimp-Lorenzo	71PitN	10-19-48	Tuskegee, Ala.		L	R	5'8	150	6	4	0	0	0	0	0	0	0	1	0	.000	.000
LaRose, Vic-Victor Raymond	68ChiN	12-23-44	Los Angeles, Cal.		R	R	5'11	180	4	2	0	0	0	0	0	0	0	1	0	.000	.000
LaRussa, Tony-Anthony	63KCA 68-71OakA 71AtlN 73ChiN	10- 4-44	Tampa, Fla.		R	R	6'	180	132	176	15	35	5	2	0	7	23	37	0	.199	.250
Lau, Charlie-Charles Richard	56,58-59DetA 60-61MilN 61-63BalA 63-64KCA	4-12-33	Romulus, Mich.		L	R	6'	190	527	1170	105	298	63	9	16	140	109	150	3	.255	.365
	64-67BalA 67AtlN																				
Lawrence, Jim-James Ross	63CleA	2-12-39	Hamilton, Canada		L	R	6'1	185	2	0	0	0	0	0	0	0	0	0	0	–	–
Lee, Leron-Leron	69-71StLN 71-73SDN 74-75CleA 75LAN	3- 4-48	Bakersfield, Cal.		L	R	6'1	196	591	1672	172	398	83	12	31	150	131	306	19	.238	.358
Leek, Gene-Eugene Harold	59CleA 61-62LAA	7-15-36	San Diego, Cal.		R	R	6'	185	77	249	23	55	12	1	6	25	9	0	0	.221	.349
Lefebvre, Jim-James Kenneth (Frenchy)	65-72LAN	1- 7-43	Hawthorne, Cal.		B	R	6'	180	922	3014	313	756	126	18	74	404	322	447	8	.251	.378
LeFlore, Ron-Ronald	74-75DetA	6-16-52	Detroit, Mich.		R	R	6'	198	195	804	103	208	21	7	10	50	46	197	51	.259	.340
LeJohn, Don-Donald Everett	65LAN	5-13-34	Daisytown, Pa.		R	R	5'10	175	34	78	2	20	2	0	0	7	5	13	0	.256	.282
LeMaster, John-Johnnie Lee (Peanut)	75SFN	6-19-54	Portsmouth, Ohio		R	R	6'2	160	22	74	4	14	4	0	2	9	4	15	2	.189	.324
Lemon, Chet-Chester Earl	75ChiA	2-12-55	Jackson, Miss.		R	R	6'	190	9	35	2	9	2	0	0	1	2	6	1	.257	.314
Leon, Eddie-Eduardo Antonio	68-72CleA 73-74ChiA 75NYA	8-11-46	Tucson, Ariz.		R	R	6'	175	601	1862	165	440	51	10	24	159	156	358	7	.236	.313
Leppert, Don-Donald George	61-62PitN 63-64WasA	10-19-31	Indianapolis, Ind.		L	R	6'2	220	190	532	46	122	22	2	15	59	44	93	0	.229	.363
Lewis, Allan-Allan Sydney	67KCA 68-70,72-73OakA	12-12-41	Colon, Panama		B	R	6'	170	156	29	47	6	1	0	1	3	1	4	44	.207	.345
Lewis, Johnny-Johnny Joe	64StLN 65-67NYN	8-10-39	Greenville, Ala.		L	R	6'1	189	266	771	97	175	24	6	22	74	95	194	8	.227	.359
Lezcano, Sixto-Sixto Joaquin (Tato)	74-75MilA	11-28-53	Arecibo, P.R.		R	R	5'11	170	149	483	60	119	21	3	13	52	50	102	6	.246	.383
Libran, Frankie-Francisco [Rosas]	69SDN	5- 6-48	Mayaquez, P.R.		R	R	6'	168	10	10	1	1	1	0	0	1	1	2	0	.100	.200
Lillis, Bob-Robert Perry	58-61LAN 61StLN 62-67HouN	6- 2-30	Altadena, Cal.		R	R	5'11	160	817	2328	198	549	68	9	3	137	99	116	23	.236	.277
Lind, Jack-Jackson Hugh	74-75MilA	6- 8-46	Denver, Colo.		B	R	6'	175	26	37	5	5	2	0	0	1	4	14	1	.135	.135
Lintz, Larry-Larry (Candy Man)	73-75MonN 75StLN	10-10-49	Martinez, Cal.		B	R	5'10	150	238	585	104	136	12	1	0	27	87	88	83	.232	.256
Linz, Phil-Philip Francis (Supersub)	62-65NYA 66-67PhiN 67-68NYN	6- 4-39	Baltimore, Md.		R	R	6'1	180	519	1372	185	322	64	4	11	96	112	195	13	.235	.311
Lipski, Bob-Robert Peter	63CleA	7- 7-38	Scranton, Pa.		L	R	6'1	180	2	1	0	0	0	0	0	0	0	1	0	.000	.000
Lis, Joe-Joseph Anthony	70-72PhiN 73-74MinA 74-75CleA	8-15-46	Somerville, N.J.		R	R	6'	195	327	716	91	163	30	1	30	84	101	199	1	.228	.398
Llenas, Winston-Winston Enriquillo [Davila] (Chilote)	68,69,72-75CalA	9-23-43	Santiago, Dom. Rep.		R	R	5'10	170	300	531	50	122	17	0	3	61	38	69	0	.230	.279
Lock, Don-Don Wilson	62-66WasA 67-69PhiN 69BosA	7-27-36	Wichita, Kans.		R	R	6'2	205	921	2695	359	642	92	12	122	373	373	776	30	.238	.417
Locklear, Gene-Gene (Chief)	73CinN 73-75SDN	7-19-49	Lumberton, N.C.		L	R	5'10	170	235	491	64	138	20	4	9	55	49	65	13	.281	.393
Lockwood, Skip-Claude Edward (See P 61-75)	65KCA 69SeaA 70-73MilA 74CalA	8-17-46	Roslindale, Mass.		R	R	6'1	195	166	214	11	29	2	0	2	7	16	56	0	.136	.173
	75NYN																				

USE NAME – GIVEN NAMES (NICKNAMES)	TEAM BY YEAR	BIRTH DATE	BIRTH PLACE	DEATH DATE	B	T	HGT	WGT	G	AB	R	H	2B	3B	HR	RBI	BB	SO	SB	BA	SA
					LIFETIME BATTING TOTALS																
Lolich, Ron-Ronald John	71ChiA 72-73CleA	9-19-46	Portland, Ore.		R	R	6'1	195	87	228	20	48	9	0	4	23	11	49	0	.211	.303
Long, Jeoff-Jeoffrey Keith	63-64StLN 64ChiA	10- 9-41	Covington, Ky.		R	R	6'1	200	56	83	5	16	1	0	1	9	10	34	0	.193	.241
Look, Bruce-Bruce Michael	68MinA	6- 9-43	Lansing, Mich.		L	R	5'11	183	59	118	7	29	4	0	0	9	20	24	0	.246	.280
Look, Dean-Dean Zachary	62 played in A.F.L. 61ChiA	7-23-37	Lansing, Mich.		R	R	5'11	185	3	6	0	0	0	0	0	0	0	1	0	.000	.000
Lopes, Dave-David Earl (Davey)	72-75LAN	5- 3-46	East Providence, R.I.		R	R	5'9	175	453	1725	286	459	67	14	24	114	226	247	176	.266	.363
Lopez, Art-Arturo	65NYA	5- 8-37	Mayaguez, P.R.		L	L	5'9	170	38	49	5	7	0	0	0	0	1	6	0	.143	.143
Lovitto, Joe-Joseph	72-75TexA	1- 6-51	San Pedro, Cal.		B	L	6'	190	306	763	70	165	22	4	4	53	80	113	22	.216	.271
Lowenstein, John-John Lee (Steiner)	70-75CleA	1-27-47	Wolf Point, Mont.		L	R	6'1	175	472	1412	180	345	51	6	37	157	141	234	60	.244	.368
Lum, Mike-Michael Ken-Wai	67-75AtlN	10-27-45	Honolulu, Hawaii		L	L	6'	180	1001	2778	320	701	105	18	68	333	270	371	11	.252	.377
Lumpe, Jerry-Jerry Dean	56-59NYA 59-63KCA 64-67DetA	6- 2-33	Lincoln, Mo.		L	R	6'2	185	1371	4912	620	1314	190	52	47	454	428	411	20	.268	.356
Lund, Gordon-Gordon Thomas	67CleA 69SeaA	2-23-41	Iron Mountain, Mich.		R	R	5'11	170	23	46	5	12	1	0	0	1	7	7	1	.261	.283
Lundstedt, Tom-Thomas Robert	73-74ChiN 75MinA	4-10-49	Davenport, Iowa		B	R	6'4	205	44	65	3	6	0	0	0	1	9	13	0	.092	.092
Luplow, Al-Alvin David	61-65CleA 66-67NYN 67PitN	3-13-39	Saginaw, Mich.		L	R	5'10	185	481	1243	147	292	34	6	33	125	127	213	8	.235	.352
Luzinski, Greg-Gregory Michael (Bull)	70-75PhiN	11-22-50	Chicago, Ill.		R	R	6'1	220	593	2183	269	625	116	13	91	348	226	513	11	.286	.476
Lynn, Fred-Fredric Michael	74-75BosA	2-23-52	Chicago, Ill.		L	L	6'1	185	160	571	108	193	49	9	23	115	68	96	10	.338	.576
Lyttle, Jim-James Lawrence	69-71NYA 72ChiA 73-75MonN	5-20-46	Hamilton, Ohio		L	R	6'	185	326	557	62	138	30	4	8	57	46	114	4	.248	.359
Macha, Ken-Kenneth Edward	74PitN	9-29-50	Monroeville, Pa.		R	R	6'3	210	5	5	1	3	1	0	0	1	0	0	0	.600	.800
MacKenzie, Gordon-Henry Gordon	61KCA	7- 9-37	St. Petersburg, Fla.		R	R	5'11	175	11	24	1	3	0	0	0	1	1	6	0	.125	.125
Mackanin, Pete-Peter	73-74TexA 75MonN	8- 1-51	Chicago, Ill.		R	R	6'2	190	176	544	63	111	21	7	12	46	35	127	11	.204	.335
Maddox, Elliott-Elliott	70DetA 71WasA 72-73TexA 74-75NYA	12-21-47	East Orange, N.J.		R	R	5'10	180	627	1666	243	443	65	13	9	137	249	237	52	.266	.337
Maddox, Garry-Garry Lee	72-75SFN 75PhiN	9- 1-49	Cincinnati, Ohio		R	R	6'3	190	520	2009	271	558	113	28	36	234	109	291	83	.278	.416
Madlock, Bill-William	73TexA 74-75ChiN	1-12-51	Memphis, Tenn.		R	R	5'11	185	279	1044	158	351	55	15	17	123	91	106	23	.336	.466
Mahoney, Jim-James Thomas (Moe)	59BosA 61WasA 62CleA 65HouN	5-26-34	Englewood, N.J.		R	R	6'	175	120	210	32	48	4	1	4	15	11	47	1	.229	.314
Malkmus, Bobby-Robert Edward	57MilN 58-59WasA 60-62PhiN	7- 4-31	Newark, N.J.		R	R	5'9	175	268	572	69	123	15	5	8	46	38	90	3	.215	.301
Malzone, Frank-Frank James	55-65BosA 66CalA	2-28-30	Bronx, N.Y.		R	R	5'10	180	1441	5428	647	1486	239	21	133	728	337	434	14	.274	.399
Mangual, Angel-Angel Luis [Guilbe]	69PitN 71-75OakA	3-19-47	Juana Diaz, P.R.		R	R	5'10	178	442	1229	122	302	43	8	22	124	59	186	5	.246	.347
Mangual, Pepe-Jose Manuel [Guilbe]	72-75MonN	5-23-52	Ponce, P.R.		R	R	5'9	170	204	648	105	159	21	3	12	56	86	153	40	.245	.343
Manning, Rick-Richard Eugene	75CleA	9- 2-54	Niagara Falls, N.Y.		L	R	6'1	180	120	480	69	137	16	5	3	35	44	62	19	.285	.358
Mantilla, Felix-Felix Lamela	56-61MilN 62NYN 63-65BosA 66HouN	7-29-34	Isabela, P.R.		R	R	6'	170	969	2707	360	707	97	10	89	330	256	352	27	.261	.403
Manuel, Chuck-Charles Fuqua	69-72MinA 74-75LAN	1- 4-44	North Fork, W. Va.		L	R	6'4	200	242	384	25	76	12	0	4	43	40	77	1	.198	.260
Manuel, Jerry-Jerry	75DetA	12-24-53	Hahira, Ga.		B	R	6'	165	6	18	0	1	0	0	0	0	0	4	0	.056	.056
Maris, Roger-Roger Eugene	57-58CleA 58-59KCA 60-66NYA 67-68StLN	9-10-34	Fargo, N.D.		L	R	6'	200	1463	5101	826	1325	195	42	275	851	652	733	21	.260	.476
Marquez, Gonzalo-Gonzalo Enrique [Moya]	72-73OakA 73-74ChiN	3-31-46	Carupano, Venezuela		L	L	5'11	190	76	115	9	27	3	0	1	10	7	14	1	.235	.287
Marshall, Dave-David Lewis	67-69SFN 70-72NYN 73SDN	1-14-43	Artesia, Cal.		L	R	6'1	192	490	1049	123	258	41	4	16	114	133	239	22	.246	.338
Marshall, Keith-Keith Alan	73KCA	7- 2-51	San Francisco, Cal.		R	R	6'2	185	8	9	0	2	1	0	0	3	1	4	0	.222	.333
Martin, Gene-Thomas Eugene	68WasA	1-12-47	Americus, Ga.		L	R	6'	190	9	11	1	4	1	0	1	1	0	1	0	.364	.727
Martin, J.C.-Joseph Clifton	59-67ChiN 68-69NYN 70-72ChiN	12-13-36	Axton, Va.		L	R	6'2	188	908	2189	189	487	82	12	32	230	201	299	9	.222	.315
Martin, Jerry-Jerry Lindsey	74-75PhiN	5-11-49	Columbia, S.C.		R	R	6'1	195	70	127	17	27	8	1	2	12	12	21	2	.213	.339
Martinez, Buck-John Albert	69-71,73-75KCA	11- 7-48	Redding, Cal.		R	R	5'10	190	237	625	45	137	21	4	9	61	54	87	1	.219	.309
Martinez, Hector-Rodolfo Hector	62-63KCA	5-11-39	Las Villas, Cuba		R	R	5'10	160	7	15	2	4	0	0	1	3	1	4	0	.267	.467
Martinez, Jose-Jose [Azcuiz]	69-70PitN	7-26-42	Cardenas, Cuba		R	R	6'	178	96	188	21	46	6	0	1	16	10	37	1	.245	.293
Martinez, Marty-Orlando [Oliva]	62MinA 67-68AtlN 69-71HouN 72StLN 72OakA	8-23-41	Batabano, Cuba		R	R	6'	175	436	945	97	230	19	11	0	57	70	107	7	.243	.287
	72TexA				Bats Right - 62																
Martinez, Ted-Teodoro Noel [Encarnacion]	70-74NYN 75StLN 75OakA	12-10-47	Central Barahona, Dom. Rep.		R	R	6'	160	455	1176	112	270	38	14	5	91	45	163	20	.230	.298
					Bats Both part of 73-74																
Martinez, Tony-Gabriel Antonio	63-66CleA	3-18-41	Perico, Cuba		R	R	5'10	165	73	175	13	30	5	0	0	10	6	26	2	.171	.200
Martz, Gary-Gary Arthur (Sugar Bear)	75KCA	1-10-51	Spokane, Wash.		R	R	6'4	210	1	1	0	0	0	0	0	0	0	0	0	.000	.000
Mashore, Clyde-Clyde Wayne	69CinN 70-73MonN	5-29-45	Concord, Cal.		R	R	6'	190	241	419	67	87	15	1	8	47	43	102	11	.208	.305
Mason, Don-Donald Stetson	66-70SFN 71-73SDN	12-20-44	Boston, Mass.		L	R	5'11	160	336	696	102	143	16	3	3	27	70	80	8	.205	.250
Mason, Jim-James Percy	71WasA 72-73TexA 74-75NYA	8-14-50	Mobile, Ala.		L	R	6'2	190	387	1057	91	225	31	10	10	82	90	226	1	.213	.289
Matchick, Tom-John Thomas	67-69DetA 70BosA 70KCA 71MilA 72BalA	9- 7-43	Hazelton, Pa.		L	R	6'1	173	292	826	63	178	21	6	4	64	39	148	6	.215	.270
Mathews, Nelson-Nelson Elmer	60-63ChiN 64-65KCA	7-21-41	Columbia, Ill.		R	R	6'4	195	306	978	93	218	39	14	22	98	88	248	8	.223	.359
Matias, John-John Roy (Gido)	70ChiA	8-15-44	Honolulu, Hawaii		L	L	5'11	180	58	117	7	22	2	0	2	6	3	22	1	.188	.256
Matthews, Gary-Gary Nathaniel	72-75SFN	7- 5-50	San Fernando, Cal.		R	R	6'2	200	438	1588	239	460	72	12	44	212	200	218	41	.290	.433
Maxvill, Dal-Charles Dallan	62-72StLN 72-73OakA 73-74PitN 74-75OakA	2-18-39	Granite City, Ill.		R	R	5'11	157	1423	3443	302	748	79	24	6	252	370	538	7	.217	.259
May, Carlos-Carlos	68-75ChiA	5-17-48	Birmingham, Ala.		L	R	5'11	210	982	3570	479	989	152	20	85	476	447	503	80	.277	.402
May, Dave-David LaFrance	67-70BalA 70-74MilA 75AtlN	12-23-43	New Castle, Del.		L	R	5'10	195	984	3035	380	777	107	16	84	356	276	416	50	.256	.385
May, Jerry-Jerry Lee	64-70PitN 71-73KCA 73NYN	12-14-43	Staunton, Va.		R	R	6'2	200	556	1527	120	357	63	10	15	130	157	293	1	.234	.318
May, Lee-Lee Andrew (Mo)	65-71CinN 72-74HouN 75BalA	5-23-43	Birmingham, Ala.		R	R	6'3	205	1355	5114	673	1395	258	20	248	836	317	1052	23	.273	.477
May, Milt-Milton Scott	70-73PitN 74-75HouN	8- 1-50	Gary, Ind.		L	R	6'	190	450	1343	133	362	52	6	24	178	118	129	1	.270	.371
Mayberry, John-John Claiborn	68-71HouN 72-75KCA	2-18-50	Detroit, Mich.		L	L	6'3	220	688	2292	349	610	98	10	119	403	431	364	13	.266	.473
Maye, Lee-Arthur Lee	59-65MilN 65-66HouN 67-69CleA 69-70WasA 70-71ChiA	12-11-34	Tuscaloosa, Ala.		L	R	6'2	190	1298	4048	533	1109	190	39	94	419	282	481	59	.274	.410
Mays, Willie-Willie (Say Hay)	51-52NYN 53MS 54-57NYN 58-72SFN 72-73NYN	5- 6-31	Westfield, Ala.		R	R	5'11	180	2992	10881	2062	3283	523	140	660	1903	1463	1526	338	.302	.557
Mazeroski, Bill-William Stanley (Maz)	56-72PitN	9- 5-36	Wheeling, W. Va.		R	R	5'11	187	2163	7755	769	2016	294	62	138	853	447	703	27	.260	.367
McAuliffe, Dick-Richard John	60-73DetA 74-75BosA	11-29-39	Hartford, Conn.		L	R	5'11	176	1763	6185	888	1530	231	71	197	697	882	974	63	.247	.403
McBride, Bake-Arnold Ray	73-75StLN	2- 3-49	Fulton, Mo.		L	R	6'2	190	306	1035	159	316	32	14	11	97	81	109	56	.305	.395
McCabe, Joe-Joseph Robert	64MinA 65WasA	8-27-38	Indianapolis, Ind.		R	R	6'	190	28	46	2	8	0	0	1	7	4	21	1	.174	.239
McCall, Brian-Brian Allen (Bam)	62-63ChiA	1-25-43	Kentfield, Cal.		L	L	5'10	170	7	15	3	3	0	0	2	3	1	4	0	.200	.600
McCarver, Tim-James Timothy	59-69StLN 70-72PhiN 72MonN 73-74StLN 74-75BosA	10-16-41	Memphis, Tenn.		L	R	6'1	193	1551	4917	503	1334	203	51	86	558	437	361	52	.271	.386
	75PhiN																				
McCovey, Willie-Willie Lee (Stretch)	59-73SFN 74-75SDN	1-10-38	Mobile, Ala.		L	L	6'4	215	2092	6676	1081	1840	287	44	458	1296	1169	1251	22	.276	.538
McCraw, Tommy-Tommy Lee	63-70ChiA 71WasA 72CleA 73-74CalA 74-75CleA	11-21-40	Malverne, Ark.		L	L	6'	183	1468	3956	484	972	150	42	75	404	332	544	143	.246	.362
McDermott, Terry-Terrence Michael	72LAN	3-20-51	Rockville Centre, N.Y.		R	R	6'4	205	9	23	2	3	0	0	0	0	2	8	0	.130	.130
McDonald, Dave-David Bruce	69NYA 71MonN	5-20-43	New Albany, Ind.		L	R	6'3	215	33	62	3	9	3	0	1	6	6	19	0	.145	.242
McFadden, Leon-Leon	68-70HouN	4-26-44	Little Rock, Ark.		R	R	6'2	195	62	121	5	26	3	0	0	4	12	20	2	.215	.240
McFarlane, Orlando-Orlando deJesus [Quesada]	62,64PitN 66DetA 67-68CalA	6-28-38	Oriente, Cuba		R	R	6'	180	124	292	22	70	12	0	5	20	20	93	0	.240	.332
McGuire, Mickey-Mickey C.	62,67BalA	1-18-41	Dayton, Ohio		R	R	5'10	170	16	21	2	4	0	0	0	2	0	2	0	.190	.190
McKay, Dave-David Lawrence	75MinA	3-14-50	Vancouver, Canada		R	R	6'2	195	33	125	8	32	4	1	2	16	6	14	1	.256	.352
McKinney, Rich-Charles Richard	70-71ChiA 72NYA 73-75OakA	11-22-46	Piqua, Ohio		R	R	5'11	187	255	688	66	164	21	2	14	79	61	81	4	.238	.336
McKnight, Jim-James Arthur	60,62ChiN	7- 1-36	Bee Branch, Ark.		R	R	6'1	185	63	91	6	21	0	1	0	6	2	14	0	.231	.253
McMath, Jimmy-Jimmy Lee (Mac)	68ChiN	8-10-49	Tuscaloosa, Ala.		L	L	6'1	195	3	14	0	2	0	0	0	2	0	6	0	.143	.143
McMullen, Ken-Kenneth Lee	62-64LAN 65-70WasA 70-72CalA 73-75LAN	6- 1-42	Oxnard, Cal.		R	R	6'3	190	1422	4809	533	1201	159	23	146	564	473	749	19	.250	.383
McNertney, Jerry-Gerald Edward	64,66-68ChiA 69SeaA 70MilA 71-72StLN 73PitN	8- 7-36	Boone, Iowa		R	R	6'1	190	590	1423	129	337	51	6	27	163	119	199	3	.237	.338
McNulty, Bill-William Francis	69,72OakA	8-29-46	Sacramento, Cal.		R	R	6'4	205	9	27	0	1	0	0	0	0	2	11	0	.037	.037
McRae, Hal-Harold Abraham	68CinN 69BL 70-72CinN 73-75KCA	7-10-46	Avon Park, Fla.		R	R	5'11	180	627	2007	262	560	127	16	51	294	167	235	28	.279	.434
Mejias, Roman-Roman Gomez	55,57-61PitN 62HouN 63-64BosA	8- 9-30	Rio Damuji, Cuba		R	R	6'	185	627	1768	212	449	57	12	54	202	89	238	20	.254	.391
Melendez Luis-Luis Antonio [Santana]	70-75StLN	8-11-49	Aibonito, P.R.		R	R	6'1	165	541	1331	151	334	45	13	9	117	105	159	17	.251	.325
Melton, Bill-William Edwin	68-75ChiA	7- 7-45	Gulfport, Miss.		R	R	6'2	200	976	3497	448	901	134	6	154	535	419	595	20	.258	.432
Mendoza, Mario-Mario [Aizpuru] (Coruco)	74-75PitN	12-26-50	Chihuahua, Mexico		R	R	5'11	177	147	213	18	45	2	2	0	17	11	52	1	.211	.239
Mendoza, Minnie-Cristobal Rigoberto [Carreras]	70MinA	11-16-33	Ceiba del Agua, Cuba		R	R	6'	180	16	16	2	3	0	0	0	2	0	1	0	.188	.188
Menke, Denis-Denis John	62-65MilN 66-67AtlN 68-71HouN 72-73CinN 74HouN	7-21-40	Algona, Iowa		R	R	6'	185	1598	5071	605	1270	225	40	101	606	698	853	35	.250	.370
Meoli, Rudy-Rudolph Bartholomew	71,73-75CalA	5- 1-51	Troy, N.Y.		L	R	5'9	165	233	524	57	117	16	2	2	32	54	69	7	.223	.273
Merchant, Andy-James Anderson	75BosA	8-30-50	Mobile, Ala.		L	R	5'11	190	1	4	1	2	0	0	0	0	1	0	0	.500	.500
Metzger, Roger-Roger Henry	70ChiN 71-75HouN	10-10-47	Fredericksburg, Tex.		B	R	6'	165	728	2807	335	666	62	47	5	155	221	303	61	.237	.298
					Bats Left - 70																
Meyer, Dan-Daniel Thomas	74-75DetA	8- 3-52	Hamilton, Ohio		L	R	5'11	180	135	520	61	121	18	4	11	54	27	26	9	.233	.346
Michael, Gene-Eugene Richard (The Stick)	66PitN 67LAN 68-74NYA 75DetA	6- 2-38	Kent, Ohio		B	R	6'2	183	973	2806	249	642	86	12	15	226	234	421	22	.229	.284
Milbourne, Larry-Lawrence William	74-75HouN	2-14-51	Port Norris, N.J.		B	R	6'	160	185	287	48	70	3	3	1	18	16	28	7	.244	.286
Miley, Mike-Michael Wilfred	75CalA	3-30-53	Yazoo City, Miss.		B	R	6'1	180	70	224	17	39	3	2	4	26	16	54	0	.174	.259
Millan, Felix-Felix Bernardo [Martinez] (The Cat)	66-72AtlN 73-75NYN	8-21-43	Yabucoa, P.R.		R	R	5'11	172	1250	4946	604	1389	193	34	19	347	259	214	64	.281	.345

USE NAME – GIVEN NAMES (NICKNAMES)	TEAM BY YEAR	BIRTH DATE	BIRTH PLACE	DEATH DATE	B	T	HGT	WGT	G	AB	R	H	2B	3B	HR	RBI	BB	SO	SB	BA	SA
					LIFETIME BATTING TOTALS																
Miller, Bruce-Charles Bruce	73-75SFN	3- 4-47	Fort Wayne, Ind.		R	R	6'1	185	184	528	40	132	13	4	1	49	28	44	1	.250	.295
Miller, John-John Allen	66NYA 69LAN	3-14-44	Alhambra, Cal.		R	R	5'11	195	32	61	4	10	1	0	2	3	2	18	0	.164	.279
Miller, Norm-Norman Calvin	65-73HouN 73-74AtlN	2- 5-46	Los Angeles, Cal.		L	R	5'10	185	540	1364	166	325	68	10	24	159	160	265	16	.238	.356
Miller, Rick-Richard Alan	71-75BosA	4-19-48	Grand Rapids, Mich.		L	L	6'1	185	438	960	149	241	36	10	15	102	128	161	28	.251	.356
Milner, John-John David (The Hammer)	71-75NYN	12-28-49	Atlanta, Ga.		L	L	6'	185	483	1558	216	367	55	5	67	203	212	260	14	.236	.406
Mincher, Don-Donald Ray	60WasA 61-66MinA 67-68CalA 69SeaA 70-71OakA 71WasA 72TexA 72OakA	6-24-38	Huntsville, Ala.		L	R	6'3	205	1400	4026	530	1003	176	16	200	643	606	668	24	.249	.450
Mitchell, Bobby-Robert Vance	70NYA 71,73-75MilA	10-22-43	Norristown, Pa.		R	R	6'3	195	273	609	86	143	29	6	21	91	56	168	14	.235	.406
Mitterwald, George-George Eugene	66,68-73MinA 74-75ChiN	6- 7-45	Berkeley, Cal.		R	R	6'2	205	676	1993	192	475	64	7	62	230	178	471	10	.238	.371
Moates, Dave-David Allan (Motor)	74-75TexA	1-30-48	Great Lakes, Ill.		L	L	5'9	170	55	175	21	48	9	0	3	14	13	15	9	.274	.377
Molinaro, Bob-Robert Joseph	75DetA	5-21-50	Newark, N.J.		L	R	6'	185	6	19	2	5	0	1	0	1	1	0	0	.263	.368
Monday, Rick-Robert James	66-67KCA 68-71OakA 72-75ChiN	11-20-45	Batesville, Ark.		L	L	6'3	195	1204	4076	619	1087	178	49	136	472	622	973	85	.267	.434
Money, Don-Donald Wayne	68-72PhiN 73-75MilA	6- 7-47	Washington, D.C.		R	R	6'1	190	937	3475	420	903	163	22	83	369	306	511	62	.260	.391
Montanez, Willie-Guillermo [Naranjo]	66CalA 70-75PhiN 75SFN	4- 1-48	Catano, P.R.		L	L	6'	185	776	2838	328	777	149	17	71	411	253	418	17	.274	.413
Montgomery, Bob-Robert Edward	70-75BosA	4-16-44	Nashville, Tenn.		R	R	6'2	200	297	937	94	234	40	5	18	124	49	203	5	.250	.361
Montreuil, Al-Allan Arthur	72ChiN	8-23-43	New Orleans, La.		R	R	5'4	158	5	11	0	1	0	0	0	0	1	4	0	.091	.091
Monzon, Dan-Daniel Francisco	72-73MinA	5-17-46	Bronx, N.Y.		R	R	5'10	182	94	131	23	32	2	1	0	9	19	21	2	.244	.275
Moock, Joe-Joseph Geoffrey	67NYN	3-12-44	Plaquemine, La.		L	R	6'1	180	13	40	2	9	2	0	0	5	0	7	0	.225	.275
Moore, Archie-Archie Francis	64-65NYA	8-30-41	Upper Darby, Pa.		L	L	6'2	190	40	40	5	11	4	0	1	5	6	13	0	.275	.450
Moore, Charlie-Charles William (Butch)	73-75MilA	6-21-53	Birmingham, Ala.		R	R	5'11	185	153	472	43	125	30	6	1	51	40	69	4	.265	.360
Moore, Gary-Gary Douglas	70LAN	2- 4-45	Tulsa, Okla.		R	L	5'10	190	7	16	2	3	0	2	0	0	0	1	1	.188	.438
Moore, Jackie-Jackie Spencer	65DetA	2-19-39	Jay, Fla.		R	R	6'	180	21	53	2	5	0	0	0	2	6	12	0	.094	.094
Morales, Jerry-Julio Ruben [Torres]	69-73SDN 74-75ChiN	2-18-49	Yabucoa, P.R.		R	R	5'10	165	600	1963	229	513	82	17	42	236	168	257	16	.261	.385
Morales, Jose-Jose Manuel [Hernandez] (Shady)	73OakA 73-75MonN	12-30-44	Frederiksted, V.I.		R	R	5'11	205	129	208	21	62	11	1	3	30	16	33	0	.298	.404
Morales, Rich-Richard Angelo	67-73ChiA 73-74SDN	9-20-43	San Francisco, Cal.		R	R	5'11	170	480	1053	81	205	26	3	6	5	95	159	7	.195	.242
Moran, Al-Richard Alan	63-64NYN	12- 5-38	Detroit, Mich.		R	R	6'1	190	135	353	28	69	5	2	1	27	38	62	3	.195	.229
Moran, Billy-William Nelson	58-59CleA 61-64LAA 64-65CleA	11-27-33	Montgomery, Ala.		R	R	5'11	185	634	2076	242	545	88	10	28	202	133	218	10	.263	.355
Moreno, Omar-Omar Renan [Quintero]	75PitN	10-24-53	Chiriqui, Panama		R	L	6'2	180	6	6	1	1	0	0	0	0	1	1	1	.167	.167
Morgan, Joe-Joe Leonard	63-71HouN 72-75CinN	9-19-43	Bonham, Tex.		L	R	5'7	155	1492	5406	983	1501	252	73	142	594	1063	594	445	.278	.430
Morhardt, Moe-Meredith Goodwin	61-62ChiN	1-16-37	Manchester, Conn.		L	L	6'1	185	25	34	4	7	0	0	0	3	5	13	0	.206	.206
Morton, Bubba-Wycliffe Nathaniel	61-63DetA 63MilN 66-69CalA	12-13-31	Washington, D.C.		R	R	5'10	175	451	928	117	248	37	8	14	128	111	143	7	.267	.370
Moschitto, Ross-Rosario Allen	65NYA 66MS 67NYA	2-15-45	Fresno, Cal.		R	R	6'2	175	110	36	3	6	0	0	1	3	1	14	0	.167	.250
Moses, Jerry-Gerald Braheen	65,68-70BosA 71CalA 72CleA 73NYA 74DetA 75SDN 75ChiA	8- 9-46	Yazoo City, Miss.		R	R	6'3	210	385	1072	89	269	48	8	25	109	63	184	1	.251	.381
Mota, Manny-Manuel Rafael [Geronimo]	62SFN 63-68PitN 69MonN 69-75LAN	2-18-38	Santo Domingo, Dom. Rep.		R	R	5'10	170	1345	3606	487	1091	120	52	30	410	266	307	49	.303	.390
Motton, Curt-Curtell Howard	67-71BalA 72MilA 72CalA 73-74BalA	9-24-40	Darnell, La.		R	R	5'8	170	316	567	85	121	20	1	25	89	86	116	5	.213	.384
Mumphrey, Jerry-Jerry Wayne	74-75StLN	9- 9-52	Tyler, Tex.		B	R	6'2	180	16	18	4	6	2	0	0	1	4	3	0	.333	.444
Munson, Thurman-Thurman Lee	69-75NYA	6- 7-47	Akron, Ohio		R	R	5'11	190	871	3134	417	896	129	22	69	386	303	369	26	.286	.407
Murcer, Bobby-Bobby Ray	65-66NYA 67-68MS 69-74NYA 75SFN	5-20-46	Oklahoma City, Okla.		L	R	5'11	175	1105	4113	610	1169	186	32	151	633	498	518	78	.284	.455
Murphy, Billy-William Eugene	66NYN	5- 7-44	Pineville, La.		R	R	6'1	190	84	135	15	31	4	1	3	13	7	34	1	.230	.341
Murphy, Danny-Daniel Francis (See P 61-75)	60-62ChiN 69-70ChiA	8-23-42	Beverly, Mass.		L	R	5'11	185	117	130	18	23	5	1	4	13	11	29	0	.177	.323
Murray, Larry-Larry (Slick)	74-75NYA	4- 1-53	Chicago, Ill.		B	R	6'	178	12	2	2	0	0	0	0	0	0	0	0	.000	.000
Murrell, Ivan-Ivan Augustus	63-64,67-68HouN 69-73SDN 74AtlN	4-24-45	Almirante, Panama		R	R	6'2	195	564	1306	126	308	41	15	33	123	44	342	20	.236	.366
Muser, Tony-Anthony Joseph	69BosA 71-75ChiA 75BalA	8- 1-47	Van Nuys, Cal.		L	L	6'2	185	392	794	84	224	27	7	6	75	58	83	12	.282	.356
Nagelson, Russ-Russell Charles (Rusty)	68-70CleA 70DetA	9-19-44	Cincinnati, Ohio		L	R	6'	205	62	76	9	16	1	0	1	4	13	20	0	.211	.263
Napoleon, Danny-Daniel	65-66NYN	1-11-42	Claysburg, Pa.		R	R	5'11	190	80	130	7	21	3	1	0	7	9	33	0	.162	.200
Nash, Cotton-Charles Francis 64-65 played in N.B.A. 67-68 played in A.B.A.	67ChiA 69-70MinA	7-24-42	Jersey City, N.J.		R	R	6'6	220	13	16	2	3	0	0	0	2	3	3	0	.188	.188
Nelson, Dave-David Earl	68-69CleA 70-71WasA 72-75TexA	6-20-44	Fort Sill, Okla.		R	R	5'10	160	708	2377	308	585	70	16	19	190	199	355	171	.246	.313
					Bats Both part of 68																
Nen, Dick-Richard LeRoy	63LAN 65-67WasA 68ChiN 70WasA	9-24-39	South Gate, Cal.		L	L	6'2	205	367	826	70	185	23	3	21	107	77	152	1	.224	.335
Nettles, Graig-Graig	70-72CleA 73-75NYA	8-20-44	San Diego, Cal.		L	R	6'	180	1061	3707	474	917	134	10	148	499	447	489	15	.247	.409
Nettles, Jim-James William	70-72MinA 74DetA	3- 2-47	San Diego, Cal.		L	L	6'	190	228	564	68	127	15	4	16	56	67	107	10	.225	.351
Nettles, Morris-Morris	74-75CalA	1-26-52	Los Angeles, Cal.		L	L	6'1	175	168	469	77	116	15	0	0	31	42	95	42	.247	.279
Nicholson, Dave-David Lawrence	60,62BalA 63-65ChiA 66HouN 67AtlN	8-29-39	St. Louis, Mo.		R	R	6'2	215	538	1419	184	301	32	12	61	179	219	573	6	.212	.381
Nixon, Russ-Russell Eugene	57-60CleA 60-65BosA 66-67MinA 68BosA	2-19-35	Cleveland, Ohio		L	R	6'1	195	906	2504	215	670	115	19	27	266	154	279	0	.268	.361
Nolan, Joe-Joseph William	72NYN 75AtlN	5-12-51	St. Louis, Mo.		L	R	6'	180	8	14	0	1	0	0	0	0	2	3	0	.071	.071
Nordbrook, Tim-Timothy Charles	74-75BalA	7- 7-49	Baltimore, Md.		R	R	6'1	178	46	49	10	8	1	0	0	1	9	9	1	.163	.184
North, Billy-William Alex	71-72ChiN 73-75OakA	5-15-48	Seattle, Wash.		B	R	5'11	185	509	1764	276	471	49	18	10	114	245	294	144	.267	.332
					Bats Right - 71																
Northey, Scott-Scott Richard	69KCA	10-15-46	Philadelphia, Pa.		R	R	6'	175	20	61	11	16	2	2	1	7	7	19	6	.262	.410
Northrup, Jim-James Thomas	64-74DetA 74MonN 74-75BalA	11-24-39	Breckenridge, Mich.		L	R	6'3	190	1392	4692	603	1254	218	42	153	610	449	635	39	.267	.429
Nossek, Joe-Joseph Rudolph	64-66MinA 66-67KCA 69OakA 69-70StLN	11- 8-40	Cleveland, Ohio		R	R	6'	178	295	579	47	132	25	4	3	53	19	72	8	.228	.301
Nyman, Nyls-Nyls Wallace Rex	74-75ChiA	3- 7-54	Detroit, Mich.		L	L	6'	172	111	341	41	83	8	4	2	32	11	35	11	.243	.308
Oates, Johnny-Johnny Lane	70,72BalA 73-75AtlN 75PhiN	1-21-46	Sylva, N.C.		L	R	5'11	185	381	1171	99	297	43	2	10	96	109	119	9	.254	.319
O'Brien, Syd, Sydney Lloyd	69BosA 70ChiA 71-72CalA 72MilA	12-18-44	Compton, Cal.		R	R	6'1	185	378	1052	135	242	35	8	24	100	60	155	5	.230	.347
Office, Rowland-Rowland Johnie	72,74-75AtlN	10-25-52	Sacramento, Cal.		L	L	6'	170	259	608	51	166	30	2	6	61	40	73	7	.273	.359
Oglivie, Ben-Benjamin Ambrosio (Junie)	71-73BosA 74-75DetA	2-11-49	Colon, Panama		L	L	6'2	175	358	1022	118	266	47	7	23	108	77	198	25	.260	.387
Oldis, Bob-Robert Carl	53-55WasA 60-61PitN 62-63PhiN	1- 5-28	Preston, Iowa		R	R	6'1	185	135	236	20	56	6	0	1	22	20	22	0	.237	.275
Oliva, Tony-Pedro [Lopez]	62-75MinA	7-20-40	Pinar del Rio, Cuba		L	R	6'2	190	1609	6178	867	1891	326	48	219	931	446	632	86	.306	.481
Olivares, Ed-Edward Balzac	60-61StLN	11- 5-38	Mayaguez, P.R.		R	R	5'11	180	24	35	2	5	0	0	0	1	0	7	1	.143	.143
Oliver, Al-Albert (Scoop)	68-75PitN	10-14-46	Portsmouth, Ohio		L	L	6'	195	1027	4015	552	1168	225	45	104	574	197	376	35	.291	.447
Oliver, Bob-Robert Lee	65PitN 69-72KCA 72-74CalA 74BalA 75NYA	2- 8-43	Shreveport, La.		R	R	6'3	205	817	2914	293	745	102	19	94	419	156	562	17	.256	.400
Oliver, Gene-Eugene George	59,61-63StLN 63-65MilN 66-67AtlN 67PhiN 68BosA 68-69ChiN	3-22-36	Moline, Ill.		R	R	6'2	225	786	2216	268	546	111	5	93	320	215	420	24	.246	.427
Oliver, Nate-Nathaniel (Pee Wee)	63-67LAN 68SFN 69NYA 69ChiN	12-13-40	St. Petersburg, Fla.		R	R	5'10	160	410	954	107	216	24	5	2	45	72	172	17	.226	.268
Ontiveros, Steve-Steven Robert (Onti)	73-75SFN	10-26-51	Bakersfield, Cal.		B	R	6'	190	252	701	69	193	31	1	8	69	116	92	2	.275	.357
Orsino, John-John Joseph (Horse)	61-62SFN 63-65BalA 66-67WasA	4-22-38	Teaneck, N.J.		R	R	6'3	215	332	1014	114	252	44	5	40	123	92	191	3	.249	.420
Orta, Jorge-Jorge [Nunez]	72-75ChiA	11-26-50	Mazatlan, Mexico		L	R	5'10	170	458	1616	203	469	69	23	30	201	131	279	36	.290	.417
Ortenzio, Frank-Frank Joseph (Moose)	73KCA	2-24-51	Fresno, Cal.		R	R	6'1	220	9	25	1	7	2	0	1	6	2	6	0	.280	.480
Ortiz, Jose-Jose Luis [Irizarry] (Polilla)	69-70ChiA 71ChiN	6-25-47	Ponce, P.R.		R	R	5'9	155	67	123	14	37	9	1	0	6	7	12	3	.301	.390
Osborne, Bobo-Lawrence Sidney	57-59,61-62DetA 63WasA	10-12-35	Chattahoochie, Ga.		L	R	6'1	205	359	763	93	157	30	2	17	86	104	171	2	.206	.317
Ostrosser, Brian-Brian Leonard	73NYN	6-17-49	Hamilton, Canada		L	R	6'	175	4	5	0	0	0	0	0	0	0	2	0	.000	.000
Otis, Amos-Amos Joseph	67,69NYN 70-75KCA	4-26-47	Mobile, Ala.		R	R	5'11	170	942	3472	521	976	173	35	84	408	356	402	184	.281	.424
Ott, Billy-William Joseph	62,64ChiN	11-23-40	New York, N.Y.		B	R	6'1	180	32	67	7	11	3	0	1	3	5	20	0	.164	.254
Ott, Ed-Nathan Edward	74-75PitN	7-11-51	Muncy, Pa.		L	R	5'11	180	12	10	1	1	0	0	0	0	0	1	0	.100	.100
Oyler, Ray-Raymond Francis	65-68DetA 69SeaA 70CalA	8- 4-38	Indianapolis, Ind.		R	R	5'11	170	542	1265	110	221	39	6	15	86	135	359	2	.175	.251
Paciorek, John-John Francis	63HouN	2-11-45	Detroit, Mich.		R	R	6'2	200	1	3	4	3	0	0	0	3	2	0	0	1.000	1.000
Paciorek, Tom-Thomas Marian (Wimpy)	70-75LAN	11- 2-46	Detroit, Mich.		R	R	6'4	215	264	573	69	136	29	6	8	54	33	106	9	.237	.351
Paepke, Dennis-Dennis Ray	69,71-72,74KCA	4-17-45	Long Beach, Cal.		R	R	6'	202	80	197	13	36	7	0	2	14	12	36	0	.183	.249
Pagan, Jose-Jose Antonio [Rodriguez]	59-65SFN 65-72PitN 73PhiN	5- 5-35	Barceloneta, P.R.		R	R	5'9	170	1326	3689	387	922	138	26	52	372	244	510	46	.250	.344
Page, Mike-Michael Randy	68AtlN	7-12-40	Woodruff, S.C.		L	R	6'2	210	20	28	1	5	0	0	0	1	1	9	0	.179	.179
Pagliaroni, Jim-James Vincent (Pag)	55BosA 56-57MS 60-62BosA 63-67PitN 68-69OakA 69SeaA	12- 8-37	Dearborn, Mich.		R	R	6'4	210	849	2465	269	622	98	7	90	326	330	494	4	.252	.407
Papi, Stan-Stanley Gerard	74StLN	2- 4-51	Fresno, Cal.		R	R	6'	165	8	4	0	1	0	0	0	1	0	0	0	.250	.250
Parker, Billy-William David (Wee Willie)	71-73CalA	1-14-47	Hayneville, Ala.		R	R	5'8	168	94	252	29	56	4	2	3	21	19	60	1	.222	.290
Parker, Dave-David Gene	73-75PitN	6- 9-51	Calhoun, Miss.		L	R	6'5	225	275	917	119	274	54	14	33	144	50	169	12	.299	.496
Parker, Wes-Maurice Wesley	64-72LAN	11-13-39	Evanston, Ill.		B	L	6'1	180	1288	4157	548	1110	194	32	64	470	532	615	60	.267	.375
Perrilla, Sammy-Samuel	70PhiN	6-12-43	Santurce, P.R.		R	R	5'11	200	11	16	0	2	1	0	0	0	1	4	0	.125	.188
Parrish, Larry-Larry Alton (Gov)	74-75MonN	11-10-53	Winter Haven, Fla.		R	R	6'3	190	170	601	59	160	37	5	10	69	34	93	4	.266	.394
Pasley, Kevin-Kevin Patrick (Ragna)	74LAN	7-22-53	Bronx, N.Y.		R	R	6'	190	1	0	0	0	0	0	0	0	0	0	0	–	–
Patek, Freddie-Frederick Joseph (The Flea, Moochie)	68-70PitN 71-75KCA	10- 9-44	Seguin, Tex.		R	R	5'4	160	995	3535	478	837	120	39	27	265	358	510	224	.237	.316

USE NAME – GIVEN NAMES (NICKNAMES)	TEAM BY YEAR	BIRTH DATE	BIRTH PLACE	DEATH DATE	B	T	HGT	WGT	G	AB	R	H	2B	3B	HR	RBI	BB	SO	SB	BA	SA
Pavletich, Don-Donald Stephen	57CinN 58MS 59,62-68CinN 69ChiA 70-71BosA	7-13-38	Milwaukee, Wis.		R	R	5'11	213	536	1373	163	349	73	8	46	193	148	237	5	.254	.420
Pearson, Albie-Albert Gregory	58-59WasA 59-60BalA 61-64LAA 65-66CalA	9-12-34	Alhambra, Cal.		L	L	5'5	140	988	3077	485	831	130	24	28	214	477	195	77	.270	.355
Pemberton, Brock-Brock	74-75NYN	11- 5-53	Tulsa, Okla.		B	L	6'2	195	13	24	0	4	0	0	0	1	0	4	0	.167	.167
Pena, Roberto-Roberto Cesar [Ramirez]	65-66ChiN 68PhiN 69SDN 70OakA 70-71MilA	4-17-40	Santo Domingo, Dom. Rep.		R	R	5'8	175	587	1907	174	467	65	10	13	154	114	235	10	.245	.310
Pepitone, Joe-Joseph Anthony (Pepi)	62-69NYA 70HouN 70-73ChiN 73AtlN	10- 9-40	Brooklyn, N.Y.		L	L	6'2	195	1397	5097	606	1315	158	35	219	721	302	526	41	.258	.432
Pepper, Don-Donald Hoyte	66DetA	10- 8-43	Saratoga Springs, N.Y.		L	L	6'4	215	4	3	0	0	0	0	0	0	0	1	0	.000	.000
Perez, Marty-Martin Roman	69-70CalA 71-75AtlN	2-28-47	Visalia, Cal.		R	R	5'11	160	675	2314	231	573	77	16	17	188	178	261	7	.248	.317
Perez, Tony-Atanacio [Rigal]	64-75CinN	5-14-42	Ciego de Avila, Cuba		R	R	6'2	195	1589	5799	811	1653	281	48	258	1024	563	1150	29	.285	.484
Perry, Bob-Melvin Gray	63-64LAA	9-14-34	New Bern, N.C.		R	R	6'2	180	131	387	35	103	17	1	6	30	23	83	2	.266	.362
Peterson, Cap-Charles Andrew	62-66SFN 67-68WasA 69CleA	8-15-42	Tacoma, Wash.		R	R	6'2	195	536	1170	106	269	44	5	19	122	101	195	4	.230	.325
Petrocelli, Rico-Americo Peter	63,65-75BosA	6-27-43	Brooklyn, N.Y.		R	R	6'	185	1468	5150	636	1301	230	21	207	749	627	888	10	.253	.426
Pfiel, Bobby-Robert Raymond	69NYN 71PhiN	11-13-43	Passaic, N.J.		R	R	6'1	180	106	281	25	68	12	0	2	19	13	36	1	.242	.306
Phillips, Adolfo-Adolfo Emilio [Lopez]	64-66PhiN 66-69ChiN 69-70MonN 72CleA	12-16-41	Bethania, Panama		R	R	6'1	175	649	1875	270	463	86	21	59	173	251	485	82	.247	.410
Phillips, Dick-Richard Eugene	62SFN 63-64,66WasA	11-24-31	Racine, Wis.		L	R	6'	185	263	595	54	136	14	1	12	60	59	63	2	.229	.316
Phillips, Mike-Michael Dwaine	73-75SFN 75NYN	8-19-50	Beaumont, Tex.		L	R	6'1	184	289	801	71	191	19	12	4	58	51	105	8	.238	.307
Pierce, Jack-Lavern Jack	73-74AtlN 75DetA	6- 2-49	Laurel, Miss.		L	R	6'3	215	70	199	20	42	6	1	8	22	22	48	0	.211	.372
Piniella, Lou-Louis Victor	64BalA 68CleA 69-73KCA 74-75NYA	8-28-43	Tampa, Fla.		R	R	6'1	190	924	3293	337	931	157	22	54	441	201	345	23	.283	.393
Pinson, Vada-Vada Edward	58-68CinN 69StLN 70-71CleA 72-73CalA 74-75KCA	8-11-38	Memphis, Tenn.		L	L	5'11	180	2469	9645	1366	2757	485	127	256	1170	574	1196	305	.286	.442
Pitts, Gaylen-Gaylen Richard	74-75OakA	6- 6-46	Wichita, Kans.		R	R	6'	190	28	44	5	11	4	0	0	4	5	4	0	.250	.341
Plaskett, Elmo-Elmo Alexander	62-63PitN	6-27-38	Frederiksted, V.I.		R	R	5'10	195	17	35	3	7	0	0	1	5	1	8	0	.200	.286
Plummer, Bill-William Francis	68ChiN 70-75CinN	3-21-47	Oakland, Cal.		R	R	6'2	200	219	529	40	94	21	0	7	49	52	102	3	.178	.257
Pocoroba, Biff-Biff	75AtlN	7-25-53	Burbank, Cal.		R	R	5'10	175	67	188	15	48	7	1	1	22	20	11	0	.255	.319
					Bats Both part of 75																
Poepping, Mike-Michael Harold	75MinA	8- 7-50	Little Falls, Minn.		R	R	6'6	230	14	37	0	5	1	0	0	1	5	7	0	.135	.162
Pointer, Aaron-Aaron Elton (Hawk)	[illegible]HouN	4-19-42	Little Rock, Ark.		R	R	6'2	185	40	101	11	21	5	0	2	15	18	33	2	.208	.317
Popovich, Paul-Paul Edward	64,66-67ChiN 68-69LAN 69-73ChiN 74-75PitN	8-18-40	Flemington, W.Va.		B	R	6'	175	681	1732	176	403	42	9	14	134	127	151	0	.200	[illegible]
					Bats Right - 64, 66-67																
Poquette, Tom-Thomas Arthur (Pierre)	73KCA	10-30-51	Eau Claire, Wis.		L	R	5'11	178	21	28	4	6	1	0	0	3	1	4	1	.214	.250
Porter, Darrell-Darrell Ray (Dee)	71-73MilA	1-17-52	Joplin, Mo.		L	R	6'	193	418	1317	181	310	49	11	49	194	210	291	17	.235	.401
Posada, Leo-Leopoldo Jesus [Hernandez] (Popy)	60-62KCA	4-15-36	Havana, Cuba		R	R	5'11	175	155	426	51	109	11	7	8	58	46	105	1	.256	.371
Poulsen, Ken-Ken Sterling	67BosA	8- 4-47	Van Nuys, Cal.		L	R	6'1	190	5	5	0	1	1	0	0	0	0	2	0	.200	.400
Powell, Boog-John Wesley	61-74BalA 75CleA	8-17-41	Lakeland, Fla.		L	R	6'4	250	1997	6347	860	1703	261	11	330	1149	948	1174	19	.268	.469
Powell, Paul-Paul Ray	71MinA 73,75LAN	3-19-48	San Angelo, Tex.		R	R	5'11	185	30	42	9	7	1	0	1	2	4	15	0	.167	.262
Prescott, Bobby-George Bertrand	61KCA	3-27-31	Colon, Panama		R	R	5'11	180	10	12	0	1	0	0	0	0	2	5	0	.083	.083
Price, Jim-Jimmie William	67-71DetA	10-13-41	Harrisburg, Pa.		R	R	6'	192	261	602	58	129	22	0	18	71	62	70	0	.214	.341
Pruitt, Ron-Ronald Ralph	75TexA	10-21-51	Flint, Mich.		R	R	6'	185	14	17	2	3	0	0	0	0	1	3	0	.176	.176
Puig, Rich-Richard Gerald	74NYN	3-16-53	Tampa, Fla.		L	R	5'10	165	4	10	0	0	0	0	0	0	1	2	0	.000	.000
Qualls, Jim-James Robert	69ChiN 70MonN 72ChiA	10- 9-46	Exeter, Cal.		B	R	5'10	158	63	139	13	31	5	3	0	10	2	16	2	.223	.309
Queen, Mel-Melvin Douglas (See P 61-75)	64-69CinN 70-72CalA	3-26-42	Johnson City, N.Y.		L	R	6'1	190	269	274	20	49	7	0	2	25	21	50	2	.179	.226
Quilici, Frank-Frank Ralph (Guido)	65,67-70,M72-75MinA	5-11-39	Chicago, Ill.		R	R	6'1	175	405	682	78	146	23	6	5	53	66	120	3	.214	.287
Quirk, Jamie-James Patrick	75KCA	10-22-54	Whittier, Cal.		L	R	6'4	190	14	39	2	10	0	0	1	5	2	7	0	.256	.333
Rader, Dave-David Martin	71-75SFN	12-26-48	Claremore, Okla.		L	R	5'11	165	495	1540	168	404	60	7	21	139	155	104	3	.262	.351
Rader, Doug-Douglas Lee (The Red Rooster)	67-75HouN	7-30-44	Chicago, Ill.		R	R	6'2	208	1178	4234	520	1060	197	30	108	600	402	848	32	.250	.388
Ragland, Tom-Thomas	71WasA 72TexA 73CalA	6-16-46	Talladega, Ala.		R	R	5'10	160	101	264	20	61	9	1	0	14	13	47	2	.231	.273
Ramirez, Milt-Milton [Barbosa] (Ramrod)	70-71StLN	4- 2-50	Mayaguez, P.R.		R	R	5'10	150	66	90	10	18	2	1	0	3	10	10	0	.200	.244
Ramirez, Orlando-Orlando Neal	74-75CalA	9-28-51	Cartagena, Colombia		R	R	5'9	174	75	186	14	38	4	1	0	11	17	45	11	.204	.237
Randle, Lenny-Leonard Shenoff	71WasA 72-75TexA	2-12-49	Long Beach, Cal.		B	R	5'10	175	466	1614	203	424	66	12	10	141	123	232	47	.263	.337
					Bats Right - 71, part of 72																
Randolph, Willie-William Larry	75PitN	7- 6-54	Holly Hill, S.C.		R	R	5'11	165	30	61	9	10	1	0	0	3	7	6	1	.164	.180
Ranew, Merritt-Merritt Thomas	62HouN 63-64ChiN 64MilN 65CalA 69SeaA	5-10-38	Albany, Ga.		L	R	5'11	175	269	594	68	147	20	9	8	54	42	120	3	.247	.352
Ratliff, Gene-Kelly Eugene	65HouN	9-28-45	Macon, Ga.		R	R	6'5	185	4	4	0	0	0	0	0	0	0	4	0	.000	.000
Ratliff, Paul-Paul Hawthorne	63,70-71MinA 71-72MilA	1-23-44	San Diego, Cal.		L	R	6'2	190	145	297	28	61	10	2	12	42	28	119	0	.205	.374
Raudman, Bob-Robert Joyce (Shorty)	66-67ChiN	3-14-42	Erie, Pa.		L	L	5'9	190	16	55	1	11	2	0	0	3	2	8	0	.000	.236
Reams, Leroy-Leroy (Cat)	69PhiN	8-11-43	Wabbaseka, Ark.		L	R	6'2	190	1	1	0	0	0	0	0	0	0	1	0	.000	.000
Redmon, Glenn-Glenn Vincent (Red)	74SFN	1-11-48	Detroit, Mich.		R	R	5'11	178	7	17	0	4	3	0	0	4	1	3	0	.235	.412
Redmond, Wayne-Howard Wayne	65,69DetA	1-25-45	Athens, Ala.		R	R	5'10	165	9	7	1	0	0	0	0	0	1	3	0	.000	.000
Reed, Jack-John Burwell	61-63NYA	2- 2-33	Silver City, Miss.		R	R	6'1	185	222	129	39	30	5	2	1	6	14	22	7	.233	.326
Reese, Rich-Richard Benjamin	64-72MinA 73DetA 73MinA	9-29-41	Leipsic, Ohio		L	L	6'3	185	866	2019	248	512	73	17	52	245	158	270	16	.254	.384
Reichardt, Rick-Frederick Carl	64LAA 67-70CalA 70WasA 71-73ChiA 73-74KCA	3-16-43	Madison, Wis.		R	R	6'3	215	997	3307	391	864	109	24	116	445	263	672	40	.261	.414
Reid, Scott-Scott Donald	69-70PhiN	1- 7-47	Chicago, Ill.		L	R	6'1	195	38	68	10	10	1	0	0	1	18	27	0	.147	.162
Reinback, Mike-Michael Wayne (Rhino)	74BalA	8- 6-49	San Diego, Cal.		L	R	6'2	195	12	20	2	5	1	0	0	2	2	5	0	.250	.300
Reitz, Ken-Kenneth John (The Zamboni Machine)	72-75StLN	6-24-51	San Francisco, Cal.		R	R	6'	186	483	1675	136	444	77	5	18	169	56	146	1	.265	.349
Remy, Jerry-Gerald Peter	75CalA	1- 8-52	Fall River, Mass.		L	R	5'9	165	147	569	82	147	17	5	1	46	45	55	34	.258	.311
Renick, Rick-Warren Richard	68-72MinA	3-16-44	London, Ohio		R	R	6'	188	276	553	71	122	20	2	20	71	63	142	0	.221	.373
Repoz, Roger-Roger Allen	64-66NYA 66-67KCA 67-72CalA	8- 3-40	Bellingham, Wash.		L	L	6'3	190	831	2145	257	480	73	19	82	260	280	499	26	.224	.390
Rettenmund, Merv-Mervin Weldon	68-73BalA 74-75CinN	6- 6-43	Flint, Mich.		R	R	5'11	195	743	2101	331	575	94	14	58	277	341	303	62	.274	.415
Retzer, Ken-Kenneth Leo	61-64WasA	4-30-34	Wood River, Ill.		L	R	6'	185	237	690	65	182	25	2	14	72	52	50	5	.264	.367
Reynolds, Craig-Gordon Craig	75PitN	12-27-52	Houston, Tex.		L	R	6'1	175	31	76	8	17	3	0	0	4	3	5	0	.224	.263
Reynolds, Tommie-Tommie D.	63-65KCA 67NYN 69OakA 70-71CalA 72MilA	8-15-41	Arizona, La.		R	R	6'2	190	513	1170	141	265	35	5	12	87	117	166	12	.226	.296
					Bats Both part of 67																
Rice, Jim-James Edward	74-75BosA	3- 8-53	Anderson, S.C.		R	R	6'1	200	168	631	98	192	31	5	23	115	40	134	10	.304	.479
Richard, Lee-Lee Edward (Bee-Bee)	71-72,74-75ChiA	9-18-48	Lafayette, La.		R	R	5'11	165	173	401	59	87	8	4	2	24	29	68	11	.217	.272
Richardson, Bobby-Robert Clinton	55-66NYA	8-19-35	Sumter, S.C.		R	R	5'9	170	1412	5386	643	1432	196	37	34	390	262	243	73	.266	.335
Ricketts, Dave-David William	63,65-69StLN 70PitN	7-12-35	Pottstown, Pa.		B	R	6'2	190	130	213	15	53	9	0	1	20	10	13	0	.249	.305
Rico, Fred-Alfredo [Cruz] (Rock)	69KCA	7- 4-44	Jerome, Ariz.		R	R	5'10	190	12	26	2	6	2	0	0	2	9	10	0	.231	.308
Rios, Juan-Juan O. [Velez]	69KCA	7-14-45	Mayaguez, P.R.		R	R	6'3	188	87	196	20	44	5	1	1	5	7	19	1	.224	.276
Rivera, Bombo-Jesus Manuel [Torres]	75MonN	8- 2-52	Ponce, P.R.		R	R	5'9	187	5	9	1	1	0	0	0	0	2	3	0	.111	.111
Rivers, Mickey-John Milton (Swift)	70-75CalA	10-31-48	Miami, Fla.		L	L	5'10	165	456	1663	220	466	62	32	5	122	120	169	126	.280	.365
Roarke, Mike-Michael Thomas	61-64DetA	11- 8-30	West Warwick, R.I.		R	R	6'2	195	194	491	41	113	11	2	6	44	45	61	0	.230	.297
Roberts, Dave-David Leonard	62,64HouN 66PitN	6-30-33	Panama, Panama		L	L	6'	172	91	194	15	38	8	1	1	17	22	43	0	.196	.278
Roberts, Dave-David Wayne	72-75SDN	2-17-51	Lebanon, Ore.		R	R	6'3	205	373	1328	127	324	49	4	33	127	80	235	23	.244	.361
Roberts, Leon-Leon Kauffman	74-75DetA	1-22-51	Kalamazoo, Mich.		R	R	6'3	198	146	510	56	132	20	7	10	45	39	104	3	.259	.384
Robertson, Bob-Robert Eugene	67,69-75PitN	10- 2-46	Frostburg, Md.		R	R	6'1	210	689	1953	255	507	83	7	104	314	274	475	7	.260	.469
Robertson, Daryl-Daryl Berdine	62ChiN	1- 5-36	Cripple Creek, Colo.		R	R	6'	184	9	19	0	2	0	0	0	2	2	10	0	.105	.105
Robinson, Bill-William Henry	66AtlN 67-69NYA 72-74PhiN 75PitN	6-26-43	McKeesport, Pa.		R	R	6'2	200	714	2037	228	487	100	16	60	241	130	368	27	.239	.392
Robinson, Brooks-Brooks Calbert (The Vacuum Cleaner)	55-75BalA	5-18-37	Little Rock, Ark.		R	R	6'1	190	2801	10391	1213	2795	472	66	264	1342	848	962	28	.269	.403
Robinson, Craig-Craig George	72-73PhiN 74-75AtlN 75SFN	8-21-48	Abington, Pa.		R	R	5'9	165	235	659	68	143	13	6	0	36	33	95	12	.217	.255
Robinson, Dave-David Tanner	70-71SDN	5-22-46	Minneapolis, Minn.		B	L	6'1	186	22	44	5	12	2	0	2	6	6	7	2	.273	.455
Robinson, Earl-Earl John	58LAN 61-62,64BalA	11- 3-36	New Orleans, La.		R	R	6'1	190	170	421	63	113	20	5	12	44	47	92	7	.268	.425
Robinson, Floyd-Floyd Andrew	60-66ChiA 67CinN 68OakA 68BosA	5- 9-36	Prescott, Ark.		L	R	5'9	175	1012	3284	458	929	140	36	67	426	408	282	42	.283	.409
Robinson, Frank-Frank (The Judge)	56-65CinN 66-71BalA 72LAN 73-74CalA 74-75,M75CleA	8-31-35	Beaumont, Tex.		R	R	6'1	190	2772	9939	1824	2928	528	72	583	1802	1409	1520	204	.295	.538
Robles, Rafael-Rafael Radames [Natera] (Orlando)	69-70,72SDN	10-20-47	Ingenio Quisquaya, Dom. R.		R	R	6'1	165	47	133	7	25	1	0	0	3	6	17	4	.188	.195
Robles, Sergio-Sergio [Valenzuela]	72-73BalA	4-16-46	Magdalena, Mexico		R	R	6'1	190	10	18	0	2	0	0	0	0	3	1	0	.111	.111
Robson, Tom-Thomas James	74-75TexA	1-15-46	Rochester, N.Y.		R	R	6'4	220	23	48	5	10	1	0	0	4	5	6	0	.208	.229
Rodgers, Andre-Kenneth Andre Ian (Andy)	57NYN 58-60SFN, 61-64ChiN 65-67PitN	12- 2-34	Nassau, Bahamas		R	R	6'3	195	854	2521	268	628	112	23	45	245	290	507	22	.249	.365
Rodgers, Bob-Robert Leroy	61-64LAA 65-69CalA	8-16-38	Delaware, Ohio		B	R	6'2	190	932	3033	259	704	114	18	31	288	234	409	17	.232	.312
Rodriguez, Aurelio-Aurelio [Ituarte]	69-70CalA 70WasA 71-75DetA	12-28-47	Cananea, Mexico		R	R	5'10	180	1200	4362	425	1036	186	37	83	418	233	647	33	.238	.354
Rodriguez, Ellie-Eliseo [Delgado]	68NYA 69-70KCA 71-73MilA 74-75CalA	5-24-46	Fajardo, P.R.		R	R	5'11	185	739	2107	210	519	76	6	16	194	313	279	17	.246	.311
Rogodzinski, Mike-Michael George	73-75PhiN	2-22-48	Evanston, Ill.		L	R	6'	185	93	114	17	25	4	0	2	12	17	23	0	.219	.307
Rojas, Cookie-Octavio Victor [Rivas]	62CinN 63-69PhiN 70StLN 70-75KCA	3- 6-39	Havana, Cuba		R	R	5'10	165	1695	6021	695	1589	239	24	54	567	380	457	71	.264	.338

USE NAME – GIVEN NAMES (NICKNAMES)	TEAM BY YEAR	BIRTH DATE	BIRTH PLACE	DEATH DATE	B	T	HGT	WGT	G	AB	R	H	2B	3B	HR	RBI	BB	SO	SB	BA	SA
									LIFETIME BATTING TOTALS												
Rollins, Rich-Richard John (Red)	61-68MinA 69SeaA 70MilA 70CleA	4-16-38	Mt. Pleasant, Pa.		R	R	5'10	185	1002	3303	419	887	125	20	77	399	266	411	17	.269	.388
Roman, Bill-William Anthony	64-65DetA	10-11-38	Detroit, Mich.		L	L	6'4	190	24	35	2	5	0	0	1	1	2	9	0	.143	.229
Romano, Johnny-John Anthony (Honey)	58-59ChiA 60-64CleA 65-66ChiA 67StLN	8-23-34	Hoboken, N.J.		R	R	5'11	205	905	2767	355	706	112	10	129	417	414	485	7	.255	.443
Roof, Phil-Phillip Anthony	61,64MilN 65CalA 65CleA 66-67KCA 68-69OakA	3- 5-41	Paducah, Ky.		R	R	6'3	200	832	2091	189	452	66	13	43	206	182	494	11	.216	.322
	70-71MilA 71-75MinA																				
Roque, Jorge-Jorge [Vargas]	70-72StLN 73MonN	4-28-50	Ponce, P.R.		R	R	6'	185	65	139	14	19	4	1	2	12	10	40	4	.137	.223
Rosario, Jimmy-Angel Ramon	71-72SFN	5- 5-44	Bayamon, P.R.		B	R	5'11	170	99	194	27	43	6	1	0	13	33	35	7	.222	.263
Rosario, Santiago-Santiago	65KCA	7-25-39	Guayanilla, P.R.		L	L	5'11	165	81	85	8	20	3	0	2	8	6	16	0	.235	.341
Rose, Pete-Peter Edward (Charlie Hustle)	63-75CinN	4-14-41	Cincinnati, Ohio		B	R	5'11	192	1992	8221	1339	2547	441	95	124	775	871	773	97	.310	.432
Roseboro, Johnny-John	57BknN 58-67LAN 68-69MinA 70WasA	5-13-33	Ashland, Ohio		L	R	5'11	195	1585	4847	512	1206	190	44	104	548	547	677	67	.249	.371
Roselli, Bob-Robert Edward	55-56,58MilN 61-62ChiA	12-10-31	San Francisco, Cal.		R	R	5'11	185	68	114	8	25	7	1	2	10	12	31	1	.219	.351
Rosello, Dave-David [Rodriguez]	72-75ChiN	6-26-50	Mayaguez, P.R.		R	R	5'11	160	102	256	22	58	11	0	2	23	24	42	3	.227	.293
Royster, Jerry-Jeron Kennis (The Bird)	73-75LAN	10-18-52	Sacramento, Cal.		R	R	6'	165	29	55	5	13	2	1	0	3	1	8	2	.236	.309
Roznovsky, Vic-Victor Joseph	64-65ChiN 66-67BalA 69PhiN	10-19-38	Shiner, Tex.		L	R	6'	180	205	455	22	99	15	1	4	38	32	83	1	.218	.281
Ruberto, Sonny-John Edward	69SDN 72CinN	10- 2-46	Staten Island, N.Y.		R	R	5'11	175	21	24	3	3	0	0	0	0	1	8	0	.125	.125
Rudi, Joe-Joseph Oden	67KCA 68-75OakA	9- 7-46	Modesto, Cal.		R	R	6'2	200	906	3300	412	911	178	28	98	428	205	460	15	.276	.436
Rudolph, Ken-Kenneth Victor	69-73ChiN 74SFN 75StLN	12-29-46	Rockford, Ill.		R	R	6'1	185	279	664	51	143	19	2	6	57	50	107	2	.215	.277
Ruiz, Chico-Hiraldo Sablon	64-69CinN 70-71CalA	12- 5-38	Santo Domingo, Cuba	2- 9-72	B	R	6'	170	565	1150	133	276	37	10	2	69	58	164	34	.240	.295
Russell, Bill-William Ellis	69-75LAN	10-21-48	Pittsburg, Kans.		R	R	6'	180	805	2555	281	650	96	31	20	227	193	320	67	.254	.340
					Bats Both - 71																
Ryan, Mike-Michael James	64-67BosA 68-73PhiN 74PitN	11-25-41	Haverhill, Mass.		R	R	6'2	210	636	1920	146	370	60	12	28	161	152	370	4	.193	.280
Sadek, Mike-Michael George	73,75SFN	5-30-46	Minneapolis, Minn.		R	R	5'10	165	81	172	20	36	6	3	0	13	25	22	2	.209	.279
Sadowski, Bob-Robert Frank (Sid)	60StLN 61PhiN 62ChiA 63LAA	1-15-37	St. Louis, Mo.		L	R	6'	175	184	329	38	73	9	3	7	46	33	63	3	.222	.331
Sadowski, Eddie-Edward Roman	60BosA 61-63LAA 66AtlN	1-19-32	Pittsburgh, Pa.		R	R	5'11	175	217	495	55	100	20	1	12	39	39	94	5	.202	.319
Salmon, Chico-Ruthford Eduardo	64-68CleA 69-72BalA	12- 3-40	Colon, Panama		R	R	5'10	160	658	1667	202	415	70	6	31	149	89	233	46	.249	.354
Samuel, Amado-Amado Ruperto	62-63MilN 64NYN	12- 6-38	San Pedro de Macoris, D.R.		R	R	6'1	170	144	368	23	79	18	0	3	25	16	82	0	.215	.288
Sanchez, Celerino-Celerino [Perez]	72-73NYA	2- 3-44	Villa Cardel, Mexico		R	R	5'11	190	105	314	30	76	11	3	1	31	14	42	1	.242	.306
Sanders, John-John Frank	65KCA	11-20-45	Grand Island, Neb.		R	R	6'2	200	1	0	0	0	0	0	0	0	0	0	0	–	–
Sanders, Reggie-Reginald Jerome (Doctor)	74DetA	9- 9-49	Birmingham, Ala.		R	R	6'2	210	26	99	12	27	7	0	3	10	5	20	1	.273	.434
Sands, Charlie-Charles Duane	67NYA 71-72PitN 73-74CalA 75OakA	12-17-47	Newport News, Va.		L	R	6'2	220	93	145	15	31	6	1	6	23	36	35	0	.214	.393
Sandt, Tommy-Thomas James (Mr. Boot)	75OakA	12-22-50	Brooklyn, N.Y.		R	R	5'11	180	1	0	0	0	0	0	0	0	0	0	0	–	–
Sanguillen, Manny-Manuel DeJesus [Magan]	67,69-75PitN	3-21-44	Colon, Panama		R	R	6'	193	994	3760	447	1149	159	43	54	469	159	262	26	.306	.414
Santo, Ron-Ronald Edward	60-73ChiN 74ChiA	2-25-40	Seattle, Wash.		R	R	6'	194	2243	8143	1138	2254	365	67	342	1331	1108	1343	35	.277	.464
Satriano, Tom-Thomas Victor Nicholas (Satch)	61-64LAA 65-69CalA 69-70BosA	8-28-40	Pittsburgh, Pa.		L	R	6'1	185	674	1623	130	365	53	5	21	157	214	225	7	.225	.303
Savage, Ted-Theodore Ephesian	62PhiN 63PitN 65-67StLN 67-68ChiN 68LAN	2-21-36	Venice, Ill.		R	R	6'1	185	642	1375	202	321	51	11	34	163	200	242	49	.233	.361
	69CinN 70-71MilA 71KCA																				
Saverine, Bob-Robert Paul (Rabbit)	59,62-64BalA 66-67WasA	6- 2-41	Norwalk, Conn.		B	R	5'10	160	379	861	114	206	27	6	6	47	73	149	23	.239	.305
Scanlon, Pat-James Patrick	74-75MonN	9-23-52	Minneapolis, Minn.		L	R	6'1	180	62	113	6	21	3	1	2	15	17	26	0	.186	.283
Schaal, Paul-Paul	64LAA 65-68CalA 69-74KCA 74CalA	3- 3-43	Pittsburgh, Pa.		R	R	5'11	185	1128	3555	436	869	132	26	57	323	516	466	43	.244	.344
Schaffer, Jimmie-Jimmie Ronald	61-62StLN 63-64ChiN 65ChiA 65NYN 66-67PhiN	4- 5-36	Limeport, Pa.		R	R	5'9	185	304	574	53	128	28	3	11	56	49	127	3	.223	.340
	68CinN																				
Schaive, Johnny-John Edward	58-60,62-63WasA	2-25-34	Springfield, Ill.		R	R	5'8	175	114	323	25	75	18	1	6	32	7	40	0	.232	.350
Scheinblum, Richie-Richard Alan	65,67-69CleA 71WasA 72KCA 73CinN 73-74CalA	11- 5-42	New York, N.Y.		B	R	6'1	180	462	1218	131	320	52	9	13	127	149	135	0	.263	.352
	74KCA 74StLN																				
Schilling, Chuck-Charles Thomas	61-65BosA	10-25-37	Brooklyn, N.Y.		R	R	5'10	170	541	1969	230	470	76	5	23	146	176	236	11	.239	.317
Schlesinger, Rudy-William Cordes	65BosA	11- 5-42	Cincinnati, Ohio		R	R	6'2	175	1	1	0	0	0	0	0	0	0	0	0	.000	.000
Schlueter, Jay-Jay D. (Slushy)	71HouN	7-31-49	Phoenix, Ariz.		R	R	6'	185	7	3	1	1	0	0	0	0	0	1	0	.333	.333
Schmidt, Mike-Michael Jack	72-75PhiN	9-27-49	Dayton, Ohio		R	R	6'2	195	465	1531	246	379	73	10	93	266	274	469	60	.248	.491
Schneck, Dave-David Lee	72-74NYN	6-18-49	Allentown, Pa.		L	L	5'10	195	143	413	32	82	14	4	8	35	27	73	4	.199	.310
Schofield, Dick-John Richard (Ducky)	53-58StLN 58-65PitN 65-66SFN 66NYA	1- 7-35	Springfield, Ill.		B	R	5'9	163	1321	3083	394	699	113	20	21	211	390	525	12	.227	.297
	66-67LAN 68StLN 69-70BosA 71StLN 71MilA																				
Schreiber, Ted-Theodore Henry	63NYN	7-11-38	Brooklyn, N.Y.		R	R	5'11	175	39	50	1	8	0	0	0	2	4	14	0	.160	.160
Schroder, Bob-Robert James	65-68SFN	12-30-44	Ridgefield, N.J.		L	R	6'	175	138	221	29	48	5	1	0	12	23	21	1	.217	.249
Schwartz, Randy-Douglas Randall	65-66KCA	2- 9-44	Los Angeles, Cal.		L	L	6'3	230	16	18	0	3	0	0	0	2	1	7	0	.167	.167
Scott, George-George Charles	66-71BosA 72-75MilA	2-23-44	Greenville, Miss.		R	R	6'2	215	1516	5485	684	1485	223	42	202	776	514	1041	65	.271	.437
Scott, John-John Henry	74-75SDN	1-24-52	Tunica, Miss.		R	R	6'3	175	39	24	9	1	0	0	0	0	0	6	3	.042	.042
Scott, Rodney-Rodney Darrell (Cool Breeze)	75KCA	10-16-53	Indianapolis, Ind.		B	R	6'	160	48	15	13	1	0	0	0	0	1	3	4	.067	.067
Scott, Tony-Anthony	73-75MonN	9-18-51	Cincinnati, Ohio		B	R	6'	167	122	151	23	28	4	2	0	12	13	42	6	.185	.238
Scrivener, Chuck-Wayne Allison	75DetA	10- 3-47	Alexandria, Va.		R	R	5'9	155	4	16	0	4	1	0	0	0	0	1	1	.250	.313
Sevcik, John-Joseph	65MinA	7-11-42	Oak Park, Ill.		R	R	6'2	205	12	16	1	1	1	0	0	0	1	5	0	.063	.125
Severson, Rich-Richard Allen	70-71KCA	1-18-45	Artesia, Cal.		R	R	6'	174	93	270	26	69	11	3	1	23	19	38	0	.256	.330
Shamsky, Art-Arthur Louis	65-67CinN 68-71NYN 72ChiN 72OakA	10-14-41	St. Louis, Mo.		L	L	6'1	180	665	1686	194	426	60	15	68	233	188	254	5	.253	.427
Shannon, Mike-Thomas Michael (Moonman)	62-70StLN	7-15-39	St. Louis, Mo.		R	R	6'3	195	882	2780	313	710	116	23	68	367	224	525	19	.255	.387
Sharon, Dick-Richard Louis	73-74DetA 75SDN	4-15-50	San Mateo, Cal.		R	R	6'2	200	242	467	46	102	20	0	13	46	50	95	6	.218	.345
Sharp, Bill-William Howard	73-75ChiA 75MilA	1-18-50	Lima, Ohio		L	L	5'10	178	319	924	106	237	48	8	9	84	65	94	2	.256	.355
Sheldon, Bobby-Bob Mitchell	74-75MilA	11-27-50	Montebello, Cal.		L	R	6'	170	83	158	21	54	4	4	0	14	17	16	0	.273	.333
Sherry, Norm-Norman Burt	59-62LAN 63NYN	7-16-31	New York, N.Y.		R	R	5'11	180	194	497	45	107	9	1	18	69	37	102	1	.215	.346
Shirley, Bart-Barton Arvin	64,66LAN 67NYN 68LAN	1- 4-40	Corpus Christi, Tex.		R	R	5'10	183	75	162	15	33	4	1	0	11	14	28	0	.204	.241
Shockley, Costen-John Costen	64PhiN 65CalA	2- 8-42	Georgetown, Del.		L	L	6'2	200	51	142	9	28	2	0	3	19	11	24	0	.197	.275
Shoemaker, Charlie-Charles Landis	61-62,64KCA	8-10-39	Los Angeles, Cal.		L	R	5'10	155	28	89	12	23	4	2	0	4	2	13	0	.258	.348
Shopay, Tom-Thomas Michael	67,69NYA 71-72,75BalA	2-21-45	Bristol, Conn.		L	R	5'9	160	172	220	21	45	4	1	2	15	15	41	7	.205	.259
Siebern, Norm-Norman Leroy	56,58-59NYA 60-63KCA 64-65BalA 66CalA 67SFN	7-26-33	St. Louis, Mo.		L	R	6'2	205	1406	4481	662	1217	206	38	132	636	708	749	18	.272	.423
	67-68BosA																				
Silverio, Tommy-Tomas Roberto	70-72CalA	10-14-45	Santiago, Dom. Rep.		L	L	5'10	170	31	30	2	3	0	0	0	0	2	9	0	.100	.100
Simmons, Ted-Ted Lyle (Simba)	68-75StLN	8- 9-49	Highland Park, Mich.		B	R	5'11	193	844	3204	371	956	177	24	77	494	275	263	7	.298	.441
Simpson, Dick-Richard Charles	62,64LAA 65CalA 66-67CinN 68StLN 68HouN	7-28-43	Washington, D.C.		R	R	6'4	176	288	518	94	107	19	2	15	56	64	174	10	.207	.338
	69NYA 69SeaA																				
Simpson, Joe-Joe Allen	75LAN	12-31-51	Purcell, Okla.		L	L	6'3	175	9	6	3	2	0	0	0	0	0	2	0	.333	.333
Sims, Duke-Duane B.	64-70CleA 71-72LAN 72-73DetA 73-74NYA 74TexA	6- 5-41	Salt Lake City, Utah		L	R	6'2	210	843	2422	263	580	80	6	100	310	338	483	6	.239	.401
Sims, Greg-Gregory Emmett	66HouN	6-28-46	San Francisco, Cal.		B	R	6'	190	7	6	1	1	0	0	0	0	1	3	0	.167	.167
Singleton, Ken-Kenneth Wayne	70-71NYN 72-74MonN 75BalA	6-10-47	New York, N.Y.		B	R	6'4	215	791	2660	389	750	119	10	79	344	495	468	16	.282	.423
Sipin, John-John White	69SDN	8-29-46	Watsonville, Cal.		R	R	6'1	175	68	229	22	51	12	2	2	9	8	44	2	.223	.319
Sizemore, Ted-Theodore Crawford	69-70LAN 71-75StLN	4-15-45	Gadsden, Ala.		R	R	5'10	170	934	3434	408	914	123	17	16	310	341	229	37	.266	.326
Skidmore, Roe-Robert Roe (Cotton)	70ChiN	10-30-45	Decatur, Ill.		R	L	6'3	210	1	1	0	1	0	0	0	0	0	0	0	1.000	1.000
Skowron, Bill-William Joseph (Moose)	54-62NYA 63LAN 64WasA 64-67ChiA 67CalA	12-18-30	Chicago, Ill.		R	R	5'11	195	1658	5547	681	1566	243	53	112	888	383	870	16	.282	.459
Slocum, Ron-Ronald Reece	69-71SDN	7- 2-45	Modesto, Cal.		R	R	6'2	185	80	113	15	17	3	2	2	16	8	37	0	.150	.265
Smalley, Roy-Roy Frederick III	75TexA	10-25-52	Los Angeles, Cal.		B	R	6'1	180	78	250	22	57	8	0	3	33	30	42	4	.228	.296
Smith, Bernie-Calvin Bernard	70-72MilA	9- 4-41	Ponchatoula, La.		R	R	5'8	164	59	112	9	26	4	1	2	9	11	17	1	.232	.339
Smith, Billy-Billy Edward (The Kid)	75CalA	7-14-53	Jonesboro, La.		B	R	6'2	183	59	143	10	29	5	1	0	14	12	27	1	.203	.252
Smith, Charley-Charles William	60-61LAN 61PhiN 62-64ChiA 64-65NYN 66StLN	9-15-37	Charleston, S.C.		R	R	6'1	176	771	2484	228	594	83	18	69	281	130	565	7	.239	.370
	67-68NYA 69ChiN																				
Smith, Dick-Richard Arthur	63-64NYN 65LAN	5-17-39	Lebanon, Ore.		R	R	6'2	205	76	142	18	31	6	2	0	7	6	42	9	.218	.289
Smith, Dick-Richard Kelly	69WasA	8-25-44	Lincolnton, N.C.		R	R	6'5	200	21	28	2	3	0	0	0	0	4	7	0	.107	.107
Smith, George-George Cornelius	63-65DetA 66BosA	7- 7-38	St. Petersburg, Fla.		R	R	5'10	170	217	634	64	130	27	6	9	57	59	142	9	.205	.309
Smith, Nate-Nathaniel Beverly	62BalA	4-26-35	Chicago, Ill.		R	R	5'11	170	5	9	3	2	1	0	0	0	1	4	0	.222	.333
Smith, Reggie-Carl Reginald	66-73BosA 74-75StLN	4- 2-45	Shreveport, La.		B	R	6'	190	1292	4774	738	1368	256	45	191	712	559	627	97	.287	.479
Smith, Tommy-Tommy Alexander	73-75CleA	8- 1-48	Albemarle, N.C.		L	R	6'4	225	45	80	10	14	3	0	2	5	3	10	1	.175	.288
Smith, Willie-Willie (Wonderful Willie) (See P 61-75)	63DetA 64LAA 65-66CalA	2-11-39	Anniston, Ala.		L	L	6'	182	691	1654	171	410	63	21	46	211	107	284	20	.248	.395
	67-68CleA 68-70ChiN 71CinN																				
Snyder, Jim-James Robert	61-62,64MinA	8-15-32	Dearborn, Mich.		R	R	6'1	185	41	86	4	12	2	0	1	10	4	12	0	.140	.198
Snyder, Russ-Russell Henry	59-60KCA 61-67BalA 68ChiA 68-69CleA 70MilA	6-22-34	Oak, Neb.		L	R	6'1	190	1365	3631	488	984	150	29	42	319	294	438	58	.271	.363
Soderholm, Eric-Eric Thane	71-75MinA	9-24-48	Cortland, N.Y.		R	R	6'	187	407	1345	184	345	56	7	36	161	151	215	14	.257	.389
Solaita, Tony-Tolia	68NYA 74-75KCA	1-15-47	Nuuyli, Amer. Samoa		L	L	6'	210	190	471	66	124	23	0	23	74	74	150	0	.263	.459
Sorrell, Bill-William	65PhiN 67SFN 70KCA	10-14-40	Morehead, Ky.		L	R	6'	190	85	185	15	44	3	0	5	17	15	16	1	.238	.335

USE NAME – GIVEN NAMES (NICKNAMES)	YEAR BY TEAM	BIRTH DATE	BIRTH PLACE	DEATH DATE	B	T	HGT	WGT	G	AB	R	H	2B	3B	HR	RBI	BB	SO	SB	BA	SA
									LIFETIME BATTING TOTALS												
Southworth, Bill-William Frederick	64MilN	11-10-45	Madison, Wis.		R	R	6'2	205	3	7	2	2	0	0	1	2	0	3	0	.286	.714
Spangler, Al-Albert Donald	59-61MilN 62-65HouN 65-66CalA 67-71ChiN	7- 8-33	Philadelphia, Pa.		L	L	6'	175	912	2267	307	594	87	26	21	175	295	234	37	.262	.351
Speed, Horace-Horace Arthur	75SFN	10- 4-51	Los Angeles, Cal.		R	R	6'1	180	17	15	2	2	1	0	0	1	1	8	0	.133	.200
Speier, Chris-Chris Edward	71-75SFN	6-28-50	Alameda, Cal.		R	R	6'1	180	742	2693	321	684	108	22	53	310	336	365	24	.254	.369
Spence, Bob-John Robert	69-71ChiA	2-10-46	San Diego, Cal.		L	R	6'4	215	72	183	13	37	5	1	4	19	16	47	0	.202	.306
Spencer, Jim-James Lloyd	68-73CalA 73-75TexA	7-30-47	Hanover, Pa.		L	L	6'2	195	889	2881	296	739	106	19	65	322	217	332	2	.257	.374
Sperring, Rob-Robert Walter	74-75ChiN	10-10-49	San Francisco, Cal.		R	R	6'1	185	107	251	34	52	7	1	2	14	25	59	1	.207	.267
Spiezio, Ed-Edward Wayne	64-68StLN 69-72SDN 72ChiA	10-31-41	Joliet, Ill.		R	R	5'11	180	554	1544	126	367	56	4	39	174	135	245	16	.238	.355
Spikes, Charlie-Leslie Charles	72NYA 73-75CleA	1-23-51	Bogalusa, La.		R	R	6'3	215	420	1453	174	358	49	7	56	189	110	267	22	.246	.405
Spriggs, George-George Herman	65-67PitN 69-70KCA	5-22-41	Newell, Md.		L	R	5'11	175	130	225	35	43	5	5	1	12	23	63	9	.191	.271
Squires, Mike-Michael Lynn	75ChiA	3- 5-52	Kalamazoo, Mich.		L	L	5'11	185	20	65	5	15	0	0	0	4	8	5	3	.231	.231
Staehle, Marv-Marvin Gustave	64-67ChiA 69-70MonN 71AtlN	3-13-42	Oak Park, Ill.		L	R	5'10	165	185	455	53	94	12	1	1	33	54	35	4	.207	.244
Stahl, Larry-Larry Floyd	64-66KCA 67-68NYN 69-72SDN 73CinN	6-29-41	Belleville, Ill.		L	L	6'	180	730	1721	167	400	58	19	36	163	142	357	22	.232	.351
Staiger, Roy-Roy Joseph	75NYN	1- 6-50	Tulsa, Okla.		R	R	6'	195	13	19	2	3	1	0	0	0	0	4	0	.158	.211
Stanley, Fred-Frederick Blair	69SeaA 70MilA 71-72CleA 72SDN 73-75NYA	8-13-47	Farnhamville, Iowa		R	R	5'10	170	304	625	75	137	14	3	3	41	75	100	7	.219	.266
					Bats Both 69-71																
Stanley, Mickey-Mitchell Jack	64-75DetA	7-20-42	Grand Rapids, Mich.		R	R	6'1	190	3104	4437	562	1097	166	46	102	440	330	496	42	.247	.374
Stanton Lee-Leroy Bobby (Baby Bull)	70-71NYN 72-75CalA	4-10-46	Latta, S.C.		R	R	6'1	200	510	1588	202	404	66	11	45	219	136	384	33	.254	.395
Stargell, Willie-Wilver Dornel	62-75PitN	3- 6-40	Earlsboro, Okla.		L	L	6'3	225	1753	6164	956	1750	344	49	368	1197	718	1497	12	.284	.535
Staton, Joe-Joseph	72-73DetA	3- 8-48	Seattle, Wash.		L	L	6'4	178	15	19	3	4	0	0	0	3	0	4	1	.211	.211
Staub, Rusty-Daniel Joseph (Le Grand Orange)	63-68HouN 69-71MonN 72-75NYN	4- 1-44	New Orleans, La.		L	R	6'2	205	1837	6582	845	1840	338	37	197	937	878	666	37	.280	.432
Stearns, John-John Hardin	74PhiN 75NYN	8-21-51	Denver, Colo.		R	R	5'11	185	60	171	25	33	5	1	3	10	17	15	4	.193	.287
Stein, Bill-William Allen	72-73StLN 74-75ChiA	1-21-47	Battle Creek, Mich.		R	R	5'10	175	135	359	34	96	10	2	5	31	32	65	3	.267	.348
Stelmaszek, Dick-Richard Francis	71WasA 73TexA 73CalA 74ChiN	10- 8-48	Chicago, Ill.		L	R	6'1	200	60	88	4	15	3	0	1	10	17	18	0	.170	.239
Stennett, Rennie-Renaldo Antonio [Porte]	71-75PitN	4- 5-51	Colon, Panama		R	R	5'11	178	597	2278	285	645	91	22	28	218	97	208	20	.283	.379
Stephenson, Johnny-John Herman	64-66NYN 67-68ChiN 69-70SFN 71-73CalA	4-13-41	South Portsmouth, Ky.		L	R	5'11	180	451	989	83	214	37	3	12	93	63	118	0	.216	.296
Stewart, Jimmy-James Franklin	63-67ChiN 67ChiA 69-71CinN 72-73HouN	6-11-39	Opelika, Ala.		B	R	6'	165	777	1420	164	336	45	14	8	112	139	218	38	.237	.305
Stillman, Royle-Royle Eldon	75BalA	1- 2-51	Santa Monica, Cal.		L	L	5'10	175	13	14	1	6	0	0	0	1	1	3	0	.429	.429
Stillwell, Ron-Ronald Roy	61-62WasA	12- 3-39	Los Angeles, Cal.		R	R	5'11	165	14	38	8	8	1	0	0	3	3	6	0	.211	.237
Stinson, Bob-Gorrell Robert	69-70LAN 71StLN 72HouN 73-74MonN 75KCA	10-11-45	Elkin, N.C.		B	R	5'11	180	201	410	42	96	19	2	5	32	52	76	2	.234	.327
					Bats Right - 69																
Stone, Gene-Eugene Daniel	69PhiN	1-16-44	Pacoima, Cal.		L	L	5'11	190	18	28	4	6	0	1	0	0	4	9	0	.214	.286
Stone, Ron-Harry Ronald	69-72PhiN	9- 9-42	Corning, Cal.		L	L	6'2	195	388	804	73	194	28	8	6	89	101	122	11	.241	.318
Stroud, Ed-Edwin Marvin (The Creeper)	66-67ChiA 67-70WasA 71ChiA	10-31-39	La Pine, Ala.		L	R	5'11	175	629	1353	209	320	37	28	14	100	129	224	72	.237	.336
Stuart, Dick-Richard Lee (Dr. Strangeglove)	58-62PitN 63-64BosA 65PhiN 66NYN 66LAN 69CalA	11- 7-32	San Francisco, Ca.		R	R	6'4	212	1112	3997	506	1055	157	30	228	743	301	957	2	.264	.489
Stubing, Larry-Lawrence George	67CalA	3-11-38	Bronx, N.Y.		L	L	6'3	220	5	5	0	0	0	0	0	0	0	4	0	.000	.000
Suarez, Ken-Kenneth Raymond	66-67KCA 68-69,71CleA 72-73TexA	4-12-43	Tampa, Fla.		R	R	5'9	175	295	661	57	150	29	1	5	58	99	97	4	.227	.297
Sudakis, Bill-William Paul (Suds)	68-71LAN 72NYN 73TexA 74NYA 75CalA 75CleA	3-27-46	Joliet, Ill.		B	R	6'1	190	530	1548	177	362	56	7	59	214	172	313	9	.234	.393
Sullivan, Haywood-Haywood Cooper	55,57BosA 58JJ 59-60BosA 61-63,M65KCA	12-15-30	Donalsonville, Ga.		R	R	6'4	215	312	851	94	192	30	5	13	87	109	140	2	.226	.318
Sullivan, John-John Peter	63-65DetA 67NYN 68PhiN	1- 3-41	Somerville, N.J.		L	L	6'	195	116	259	9	59	5	0	2	18	19	45	0	.228	.270
Summers, Champ-John J	74OakA 75ChiN	6-15-48	Bremerton, Wash.		L	R	6'2	205	96	115	16	24	6	1	1	19	11	18	0	.209	.304
Sundberg, Jim-James Howard (Sunny)	74-75TexA	5-18-51	Galesburg, Ill.		R	R	6'	190	287	840	90	185	22	3	9	72	113	138	5	.220	.286
Sutherland, Gary-Gary Lynn (Suds)	66-68PhiN 69-71MonN 72-73HouN 74-75DetA	9-27-44	Glendale, Cal.		R	R	6'	185	840	2763	283	679	99	8	22	213	185	185	11	.246	.311
Swanson, Stan-Stanley Lawrence	71MonN	5-19-44	Yuba City, Cal.		R	R	5'10	175	49	106	14	26	3	0	2	11	10	13	1	.245	.330
Swisher, Steve-Steven Eugene	74-75ChiN	8- 9-51	Parkersburg, W. Va.		R	R	6'2	205	183	534	41	114	21	2	6	49	67	120	1	.213	.294
Swoboda, Ron-Ronald Alan (Rocky)	65-70NYN 71MonN 71-73NYA	6-30-44	Baltimore, Md.		R	R	6'2	205	927	2581	285	624	87	24	73	344	299	647	20	.242	.379
Szotkiewicz, Ken-Kenneth John (Sock)	70DetA	2-25-47	Wilmington, Del.		L	R	6'	170	47	84	9	9	1	0	3	9	12	29	0	.107	.226
Talton, Tim-Marion Lee	66-67KCA	1-14-39	Pikeville, N.C.		L	R	6'3	200	83	112	15	33	6	2	2	11	8	18	0	.295	.438
Tartabull, Jose-Jose Guzman [Milages]	62-66KCA 66-68BosA 69-70OakA	11-27-38	Cienfuegos, Cuba		L	L	5'11	165	749	1857	247	484	56	24	2	107	115	136	81	.261	.320
Tatum, Jarvis-Jarvis	68-70CalA	10-11-46	Fresno, Cal.		R	R	6'	185	102	254	37	59	8	0	0	8	17	50	1	.232	.264
Taussig, Don-Donald Franklin	58SFN 61StLN 62HouN	2-19-32	New York, N.Y.		R	R	6'	190	153	263	38	69	14	5	4	30	21	53	2	.262	.399
Taveras, Frank-Frank Crisotomo [Fabian]	71-72,74-75PitN	12-24-49	Las Matas, Dom. Rep.		R	R	6'	160	265	714	77	162	13	6	0	49	63	84	30	.227	.262
Taylor, Bob-Robert Lee (T-Bone)	70SFN	3-20-44	Leland, Miss.		L	R	5'9	182	63	84	12	16	0	0	2	10	12	13	0	.190	.262
Taylor, Carl-Carl Means	68-69PitN 70StLN 71KCA 71PitN 72-73KCA	1-20-44	Sarasota, Fla.		R	R	6'2	200	411	846	113	225	31	6	10	115	136	130	12	.266	.352
Taylor, Hawk-Robert Dale	57-58,61-63MilN 64-67NYN 67CalA 69-70KCA	4- 3-39	Metropolis, Ill.		R	R	6'1	195	394	724	56	158	25	0	16	82	36	146	0	.218	.319
Taylor, Tony-Antonio Nemesio [Sanchez]	58-60CinN 60-71PhiN 71-73DetA 74-75PhiN	12-19-35	Central Alava, Cuba		R	R	5'9	180	2169	7557	1003	2001	297	86	75	595	612	1076	234	.265	.357
Tenace (Tennaci), Gene (Fiore Gino)-Fury Gene	69-75OakA	10-10-46	Russellton, Pa.		R	R	6'	195	677	2047	305	499	70	6	99	323	394	447	13	.244	.429
Tepedino, Frank-Frank Ronald	67,69-71NYA 71MilA 72NYA 73-75AtlN	11-23-47	Brooklyn, N.Y.		L	L	5'11	190	265	507	50	122	13	1	6	58	33	61	4	.241	.306
Terrell, Jerry-Jerry Wayne	73-75MinA	7-13-46	Waseca, Minn.		R	R	6'	165	348	1052	134	282	35	10	2	87	51	110	20	.268	.326
					Bats Both part of 74																
Thacker, Moe-Morris Benton	58,60-62ChiN 63StLN	5-21-34	Louisville, Ky.		R	R	6'3	205	158	260	20	46	7	0	2	20	40	81	1	.177	.227
Theobald, Ron-Ronald Merle	71-72MilA	7-28-43	Oakland, Cal.		R	R	5'8	165	251	779	95	193	23	2	2	42	106	77	11	.248	.290
Theodore, George-George Basil (The Stork)	73-74NYN	11-13-47	Salt Lake City, Utah		R	R	6'5	195	105	192	21	42	5	0	2	16	18	27	3	.219	.276
Thomas, Derrel-Derrel Osbon	71HouN 72-74SDN 75SFN	1-14-51	Los Angeles, Cal.		B	R	6'	160	533	1972	236	489	67	21	14	147	183	241	59	.248	.325
Thomas, George-George Edward	57-58,61DetA 61-63LAA 63-65DetA 66-71BosA 71MinA	11-29-37	Minneapolis, Minn.		R	R	6'3	190	685	1688	203	430	71	9	46	202	138	343	13	.255	.389
Thomas, Gorman-James Gorman	73-75MilA	12-12-50	Charleston, S.C.		R	R	6'2	205	197	441	60	84	23	3	14	50	53	160	13	.190	.351
Thomas, Lee-James Leroy	61NYA 61-64LAA 64-65BosA 66AtlN 66-67ChiN 68HouN	2- 5-36	Peoria, Ill.		L	L	6'2	195	1027	3324	405	847	111	22	106	428	332	397	25	.255	.397
Thomasson, Gary-Gary Leah	72-75SFN	7-29-51	San Diego, Cal.		L	L	6'2	190	356	903	125	227	37	11	13	92	98	154	18	.251	.360
Thompson, Danny-Danny Leon	70-75MinA	2- 1-47	Wichita, Kans.		R	R	6'	180	596	1898	168	479	63	11	14	175	104	208	5	.252	.319
Thornton, Andy-Andre (Thor)	73-75ChiN	8-13-49	Tuskegee, Ala.		R	R	6'2	205	244	710	114	195	40	8	28	108	143	122	5	.275	.472
Thornton, Otis-Otis Benjamin	73HouN	6-30-45	Docena, Ala.		R	R	6'1	200	2	3	0	0	0	0	0	1	0	2	0	.000	.000
Tillman, Bob-John Robert	62-67BosA 67NYA 68-70AtlN	3-24-37	Nashville, Tenn.		R	R	6'4	205	775	2329	189	540	68	10	79	282	228	510	1	.232	.371
Tischinski, Tom-Thomas Arthur	69-71MinA	7-12-44	Kansas City, Mo.		R	R	5'10	190	82	116	8	21	2	0	1	6	18	18	0	.181	.224
Tolan, Bobby-Robert	65-68StLN 69-70CinN 71FJ 72-73CinN 74-75SDN	11-19-45	Los Angeles, Cal.		L	L	5'11	180	1086	3855	530	1029	162	33	79	450	246	532	182	.267	.388
Torborg, Jeff-Jeffrey Allen	64-70LAN 71-73CalA	11-26-41	Plainfield, N.J.		R	R	6'	195	574	1391	78	297	42	3	8	101	103	189	3	.214	.265
Torre, Joe-Joseph Paul	60-65MilN 66-68AtlN 69-74StLN 75NYN	7-18-40	Brooklyn, N.Y.		R	R	6'2	205	2069	7513	958	2238	331	56	246	1145	756	1049	22	.298	.455
Torres, Felix-Felix [Sanchez]	62-64LAA	5- 1-32	Ponce, P.R.		R	R	5'11	182	365	1191	109	302	61	5	27	153	71	202	2	.254	.281
Torres, Hector-Hector Epitacio [Marroquin]	68-70HouN 71ChiN 72MonN 73HouN 75SDN	9-16-45	Monterrey, Mexico		R	R	6'	175	457	1257	107	269	33	4	9	74	72	165	4	.214	.268
Torres, Rusty-Rosendo [Hernandez]	71-72NYA 73-74CleA	9-30-48	Aguadilla, P.R.		B	R	5'11	180	318	687	70	144	20	1	15	56	81	138	8	.210	.307
Tovar (Perez), Cesar-Cesar Leonardo [Tovar] (Pepi)	65-72MinA 73PhiN 74-75TexA 75OakA	7- 3-40	Caracas, Venezuela		R	R	5'9	155	1446	5485	831	1532	252	55	46	429	405	403	225	.279	.370
Tracewski, Dick-Richard Joseph	62-65LAN 66-69DetA	2- 3-35	Eynon, Pa.		R	R	5'11	170	614	1231	148	262	31	9	8	91	134	253	15	.213	.272
Tresh, Tom-Thomas Michael	61-69NYA 69DetA	9-20-37	Detroit, Mich.		B	R	6'1	185	1192	4251	595	1041	179	34	153	530	550	698	45	.245	.411
Trevino, Bobby-Carlos [Castro]	68CalA	8-15-43	Monterrey, Mexico		R	R	6'2	185	17	40	1	9	1	0	0	1	2	9	0	.225	.250
Trillo (Marcano), Manny-Jesus Manuel Marcano [Trillo]	73-74OakA 75ChiN	12-25-50	Caripito, Venezuela		R	R	6'1	160	192	590	58	143	14	2	7	75	47	90	1	.242	.308
Turner, Jerry-John Webber	73-74SDN	1-17-54	Texarkana, Ark.		L	L	5'9	175	28	70	5	20	1	0	0	2	5	6	2	.286	.300
Tyrone, Jim-James Vernon	72,74-75ChiN	1-29-49	Alice, Tex.		R	R	6'1	185	81	111	20	20	0	2	3	6	7	15	3	.180	.297
Tyson, Mike-Michael Ray (Rocky)	72-75StLN	1-13-50	Rocky Mount, N.C.		R	R	5'9	175	430	1296	129	313	46	12	4	107	70	184	11	.242	.305
					Bats Both part of 72																
Uecker, Bob-Robert George	62-63MilN 64-65StLN 66-67PhiN 67AtlN	1-26-35	Milwaukee, Wis.		R	R	6'1	190	297	731	65	146	22	0	14	74	96	167	0	.200	.287
Uhlaender, Ted-Theodore Otto	65-69MinA 70-71CleA 72CinN	10-21-39	Chicago Heights, Ill.		L	R	6'2	190	908	2932	343	772	114	21	36	285	202	277	52	.263	.353
Unser, Del-Delbert Bernard	73-74PhiN 75NYN	12- 9-44	Decatur, Ill.		L	L	6'1	180	1138	3927	465	1037	124	33	55	341	355	456	51	.264	.354
Vail, Mike-Michael Lewis	75NYN	11-10-51	San Francisco, Cal.		R	R	6'1	180	38	162	17	49	8	1	3	17	9	37	0	.302	.420
Valdespino, Sandy-Hilario [Borroto]	65-67MinA 68AtlN 69HouN 69SeaA 70MilA 71KCA	1-14-39	San Jose de las Lajas, Cuba		L	L	5'8	170	382	765	96	176	23	3	7	67	57	129	14	.230	.295
Valentine, Bobby-Robert John	69,71-72LAN 73-75CalA 75SDN	5-13-50	Stamford, Conn.		R	R	5'10	185	407	1241	134	330	38	9	9	115	80	90	17	.266	.333
Valentine, Ellis-Ellis Clarence	75MonN	7-30-54	Helena, Ark.		R	R	6'4	205	12	33	2	12	4	0	1	3	2	4	0	.364	.576
Valentine, Fred-Fred Lee (Squeaky)	59,63BalA 64-68WasA 68BalA	1- 9-35	Clarksdale, Miss.		B	R	6'1	190	533	1458	180	360	56	10	36	138	156	228	47	.247	.373
Valle, Hector-Hector Jose	65LAN	10-27-40	Vega Baja, P.R.		R	R	5'9	180	9	13	1	4	0	0	0	2	2	3	0	.308	.308
Varney, Pete-Richard Fred	73-75ChiA	4-10-49	Roxbury, Mass.		R	R	6'3	220	50	141	13	36	5	1	2	10	8	36	2	.255	.348
Vaughan, Glenn-Glenn Edward (Sparky)	63HouN	2-16-44	Compton, Cal.		B	R	5'11	170	9	30	1	5	0	0	0	0	2	5	1	.167	.167
Velazquez, Freddy-Frederico Antonio	69SeaA 73AtlN	12- 6-37	Santo Domingo, Dom. Rep.		R	R	6'1	190	21	39	3	10	3	0	0	5	2	6	0	.256	.333
Velez, Otto-Otoniel [Fronceschi]	73-75NYA	11-29-50	Ponce, P.R.		R	R	6'	185	56	154	18	31	5	1	4	17	32	48	0	.201	.325

USE NAME – GIVEN NAMES (NICKNAMES)	TEAM BY YEAR	BIRTH DATE	BIRTH PLACE	DEATH DATE	B	T	HGT	WGT	G	AB	R	H	2B	3B	HR	RBI	BB	SO	SB	BA	SA
					LIFETIME BATTING TOTALS																
Versalles, Zoilo-Zoilo Casanova [Rodriguez] (Zorro)	59-60WasA 61-67MinA 68LAN 69CleA 69WasA 71AtlN	12-18-39	Vedado, Cuba		R	R	5'10	165	1400	5141	650	1246	230	63	95	471	318	810	97	.242	.367
Veryzer, Tom-Thomas Martin	73-75DetA	2-11-53	Port Jefferson, N.Y.		R	R	5'11	175	168	479	42	121	15	2	7	59	30	88	3	.253	.336
Vidal, Jose-Jose [Nicolas] (Papito)	66-68CleA 69SeaA	4- 3-40	Batey Lechugas, Dom. Rep.		R	R	6'	190	88	146	20	24	1	2	3	10	18	46	4	.164	.260
Vinson, Chuck-Charles Anthony	66CalA	1- 5-44	Washington, D.C.		L	L	6'3	207	13	22	3	4	2	0	1	6	5	9	0	.182	.409
Vose, Bill-William Edward	65-68ChiA 69-70CalA 71-72MilA 72OakA 72StLN	10-31-43	Glendale, Cal.		L	L	6'2	160	475	1177	119	267	29	10	19	127	117	167	13	.227	.317
Vukovich, John-John Christopher	70-71PhiN 73-74MilA 75CinN	7-31-47	Sacramento, Cal.		R	R	6'1	190	201	471	31	76	12	0	5	36	27	95	4	.161	.219
Wagner, Leon-Leon Lamar (Daddy Wags)	58-59SFN 60StLN 61-63LAA 64-68CleA 68ChiA 69SFN	5-13-34	Chattanooga, Tenn.		L	R	6'1	195	1352	4426	636	1202	150	15	211	669	435	656	54	.272	.455
Wallace, Don-Donald Allen	67CalA	8-25-40	Sapulpa, Okla.		L	R	5'8	165	23	6	2	0	0	0	0	0	3	2	0	.000	.000
Walling, Dennis-Dennis Martin	75OakA	4-17-54	Neptune, N.J.		L	R	6'1	185	6	8	0	1	1	0	0	2	0	4	0	.125	.160
Wallis, Joe-Harold Joseph (Tarzan)	75ChiN	1- 9-52	East St. Louis, Ill.		L	R	5'10	195	16	56	9	16	2	2	1	4	5	14	2	.286	.446
Walton, Danny-Daniel James	68HouN 69SeaA 70-71MilA 71NYA 73,75MinA	7-14-47	Los Angeles, Cal.		R	R	6'	195	256	733	67	166	27	4	28	103	84	228	4	.226	.389
					Bats Both - 75, part of 71																
Ward, Chris-Chris Gilbert	72,74ChiN	5-18-49	Oakland, Cal.		L	L	6'	175	93	138	8	28	4	0	1	15	18	13	0	.203	.254
Ward, Jay-John Francis	63-64MinA 70CinN	9- 9-38	Brookfield, Mo.		R	R	6'1	185	27	49	4	8	3	0	0	4	9	19	0	.163	.224
Ward, Pete-Peter Thomas	62BalA 63-69ChiA 70NYA	7-26-39	Montreal, Canada		L	R	6'1	190	973	3060	345	776	136	17	98	427	371	539	20	.254	.405
Warner, Jackie-John Joseph	66CalA	8- 1-43	Monrovia, Cal.		R	R	6'	180	45	123	22	26	4	1	7	16	9	55	0	.211	.431
Warwick, Carl-Carl Wayne	61LAN 61-62StLN 62-63HouN 64-65StLN 65BalA 66ChiN	2-27-37	Dallas, Tex.		R	L	5'10	170	530	1462	168	363	51	10	31	149	127	241	13	.248	.360
Washington, Claudell-Claudell	74-75OakA	8-31-54	Los Angeles, Cal.		L	L	6'1	190	221	811	102	245	34	12	10	96	45	124	46	.302	.411
Washington, Herb-Herbert	74-75OakA	11-16-50	Flint, Mich.		R	R	6'1	170	105	0	33	0	0	0	0	0	0	0	31	–	–
Watkins, Dave-David Roger	69PhiN	3-15-44	Owensboro, Ky.		R	R	5'10	185	69	148	17	26	2	1	4	12	22	53	2	.176	.284
Watsons, Bob-Robert Jose (Bull)	66-75HouN	4-10-46	Los Angeles, Cal.		R	R	6'1	200	885	3120	421	933	143	17	84	473	322	422	10	.299	.437
Webster, Ramon-Ramon Alberto	67KCA 68-69OakA 70-71SDN 71OakA 71ChiN	8-31-42	Colon, Panama		L	L	6'	185	380	778	76	190	31	6	17	98	70	94	9	.244	.365
Weekly, Johnny-Johnny	62-64HouN	6-14-37	Waterproof, La.	11-24-74	R	R	6'	200	53	121	7	25	4	0	5	19	15	21	0	.207	.364
Weis, Al-Albert John	62-67ChiA 68-71NYN	4- 2-38	Franklin Square, N.Y.		B	R	6'	160	800	1578	195	346	45	11	7	115	117	299	55	.219	.275
					Bats Right 69-71																
Werhas, Johnny-John Charles (Peaches)	64-65,67LAN 67CalA	2- 7-38	Highland Park, Mich.		R	R	6'2	200	89	168	15	29	3	2	2	14	24	39	0	.173	.260
Werner, Don-Donald Paul	75CinN	3- 8-53	Appleton, Wis.		R	R	6'1	185	7	8	0	1	0	0	0	0	0	0	0	.125	.125
Wert, Don-Donald Ralph	63-70DetA 71WasA	7-29-38	Strasburg, Pa.		R	R	5'10	168	1110	3840	417	929	129	15	77	366	389	529	22	.242	.343
Whitaker, Steve-Stephen Edward	66-68NYA 69SeaA 70SFN	5- 7-43	Tacoma, Was.		L	R	6'	180	266	758	73	174	20	6	24	85	54	174	4	.230	.367
White, Bill-William DeKova	56SFN 57MS 58SFN 59-65StLN 66-68PhiN 69StLN	1-28-34	Lakewood, Fla.		L	L	6'	195	1673	5972	843	1706	278	65	202	870	596	927	103	.286	.455
White, Elder-Elder Lafayette	62ChiN	12-23-34	Colerain, N.C.		R	R	5'11	165	23	53	4	8	2	0	0	1	8	11	3	.151	.189
White, Frank-Frank (Academy Frank)	73-75KCA	9- 4-50	Greenville, Miss.		R	R	5'11	165	261	647	82	152	22	6	8	59	33	95	17	.235	.325
White, Jerry-Jerome Cardell	74-75MonN	8-23-52	Shirley, Mass.		B	R	5'10	164	48	107	14	33	5	2	2	9	10	7	8	.308	.449
White, Mike-Hoyner Michael	63-65HouN	12-18-38	Detroit, Mich.		R	R	5'8	160	100	296	30	78	11	3	0	27	21	49	1	.264	.321
White, Roy-Roy Hilton	65-75NYA	12-27-43	Los Angeles, Cal.		B	R	5'11	170	1398	4954	720	1398	227	43	121	571	711	543	172	.272	.409
Whitfield, Fred-Fred Dwight	62StLN 63-67CleA 68-69CinN 70MonN	1- 7-38	Vandiver, Ala.		L	L	6'1	190	817	2284	242	578	93	8	108	356	139	371	7	.253	.443
Whitfield, Terry-Terry Bertland	74-75NYA	1-12-53	Blythe, Cal.		L	R	6'1	195	30	86	9	23	1	1	0	7	1	18	1	.267	.302
Wicker, Floyd-Floyd Euliss	68StLN 69MonN 70-71MilA 71SFN	9-12-43	Burlington, N.C.		L	R	6'2	175	81	113	10	18	1	0	1	6	7	33	0	.159	.195
Williams, Bernie-Bernard	70-72SFN 74SDN	10- 8-48	Akaneda, Cal.		R	R	6'1	180	102	172	23	33	6	1	4	15	21	53	2	.192	.308
Williams, Billy-Billy Leo	59-74ChiN 75OakA	6-15-38	Whistler, Ala.		L	R	6'1	175	2368	8999	1374	2637	422	88	415	1434	987	1002	86	.293	.498
Williams, Billy-William	69SeaA	6-13-33	Newberry, S.C.		R	R	6'3	195	4	10	1	0	0	0	0	0	1	3	0	.000	.000
Williams, Earl-Earl Craig	70-72AtlN 73-74BalA 75AtlN	7-14-48	Newark, N.J.		R	R	6'4	220	667	2336	287	588	89	4	108	364	247	451	0	.252	.432
Williams, George-George	61PhiN 62HouN 64KCA	10-23-39	Detroit, Mich.		R	R	5'11	165	59	135	15	31	7	0	0	5	10	17	0	.230	.281
Williams, Jim-James Alfred	69-70SDN	4-29-47	Zachary, La.		R	R	6'3	190	24	39	8	11	1	0	0	2	4	14	1	.282	.308
Williams, Jim-James Francis	66-67StLN	10- 4-43	Santa Maria, Cal.		L	R	5'10	170	14	13	1	3	0	0	0	1	1	6	0	.231	.231
Williams, Walt-Walter Allen (No Neck)	64HouN 67-72ChiA 73CleA 74-75NYA	12-19-43	Brownwood, Tex.		R	R	5'6	180	842	2373	284	640	106	11	33	173	126	211	34	.270	.365
Willis, Maury-Maurice Morning	59-66LAN 67-68PitN 69MonN 69-72LAN	10- 2-32	Washington, D.C.		B	R	5'11	165	1942	7588	1067	2134	177	71	20	458	552	684	586	.281	.331
Windhorn, Gordie-Gordon Ray	59NYA 61LAN 62KCA 62LAA	12-19-33	Watseka, Ill.		R	R	6'1	185	95	108	20	19	9	1	2	8	11	19	1	.176	.333
Wine, Bobby-Robert Paul	60,62-68PhiN 69-72MonN	9-17-38	New York, N.Y.		R	R	6'1	187	1164	3172	249	682	104	16	30	268	214	538	7	.215	.286
Winfield, Dave-David Mark (The Rave)	73-75SDN	10- 3-51	St. Paul, Minn.		R	R	6'6	220	344	1148	140	307	42	7	38	163	121	197	32	.267	.416
Wissman, Dave-David Alvin	64PitN	2-17-41	Greenfield, Mass.		L	R	6'2	178	16	27	2	4	0	0	0	0	1	9	0	.148	.148
Withrow, Corky-Raymond Wallace	63StLN	11-28-37	High Coal, W. Va.		R	R	6'3	197	6	9	0	0	0	0	0	1	0	2	0	.000	.000
Wockenfuss, John-John Bilton (Fuss)	74-75DetA	2-27-49	Welch, W. Va.		R	R	6'	190	48	147	16	31	7	3	4	15	13	17	0	.211	.381
Wohlford, Jim-James Eugene	72DetA 73-75KCA	2-28-51	Visalia, Cal.		R	R	5'10	172	319	988	124	261	28	15	4	84	86	129	33	.264	.335
Wojcik, John-John Joseph	62-64KCA	4- 6-42	Olean, N.Y.		L	R	6'	175	41	124	16	27	4	0	0	11	23	20	5	.218	.250
Wood, Jake-Jacob	61-67DetA 67CinN	6-22-37	Elizabeth, N.J.		R	R	6'1	170	608	1877	279	469	53	26	35	168	159	362	79	.250	.362
Woods, Jim-James Jerome (Woody)	57ChiN 60-61PhiN	9-17-39	Chicago, Ill.		R	R	6'	175	36	82	11	17	3	0	3	12	7	28	0	.207	.354
Woods, Ron-Ronald Lawrence	69DetA 69-71NYA 71-74MonN	2- 1-43	Hamilton, Ohio		R	R	5'10	168	582	1247	162	290	34	12	26	130	175	171	27	.233	.342
Woodward, Woody-William Frederick	63-65MilN 66-68AtlN 68-71CinN	9-23-42	Miami, Fla.		R	R	6'2	185	880	2187	208	517	79	14	1	148	169	301	14	.236	.287
Wynn, Jim-James Sherman (The Toy Cannon)	63-73HouN 74-75LAN	3-12-42	Hamilton, Ohio		R	R	5'9	170	1706	6010	1013	1536	261	36	273	885	1065	1269	205	.256	.447
Yancy, Hugh-Hugh	72,74ChiA	10-10-49	Sarasota, Fla.		R	R	5'11	180	4	9	0	1	0	0	0	0	0	0	0	.111	.111
Yastrzemski, Carl-Carl Michael (Yaz)	61-75BosA	8-22-39	Southampton, N.Y.		L	R	6'	180	2266	8302	1331	2413	466	48	317	1261	1348	1051	145	.291	.473
Yates, Al-Albert Arthur (Bunny)	71MilA	4-26-45	Jersey City, N.J.		R	R	6'3	210	24	47	5	13	2	0	1	4	3	7	1	.277	.383
Yeager, Steve-Stephen Wayne	72-75LAN	11-24-48	Huntington, W. Va.		R	R	6'	195	318	1008	111	250	37	3	30	120	103	211	5	.248	.380
Young, Don-Donald Wayne	65,69ChiN	10-18-45	Houston, Tex.		R	R	6'2	185	112	307	37	67	12	3	7	29	38	85	1	.218	.345
Young, John-John Thomas	71DetA	2- 9-49	Los Angeles, Cal.		L	L	6'3	215	2	4	1	2	1	0	0	1	0	0	0	.500	.750
Yount, Robin-Robin R.	74-75MilA	9-16-55	Danville, Ill.		R	R	6'2	170	254	902	115	235	42	7	11	78	45	115	19	.261	.359
Zeller, Bart-Barton Wallace	70StLN	7-22-41	Chicago Heights, Ill.		R	R	6'1	190	1	0	0	0	0	0	0	0	0	0	0	–	–
Zimmerman, Jerry-Gerald Robert	61CinN 62-68MinA	9-21-34	Omaha, Neb.		R	R	6'2	185	483	994	60	203	22	2	3	72	78	154	1	.204	.239
Zipfel, Bud-Marion Sylvester	61-62WasA	11-18-38	Belleville, Ill.		L	R	6'3	200	118	354	38	78	11	6	10	39	32	92	2	.220	.370
Zisk, Richie-Richard Walter	71-75PitN	2- 6-49	Brooklyn, N.Y.		R	R	6'1	205	423	1425	194	432	84	13	48	235	165	280	1	.303	.481

		BIRTH		DEATH	LIFETIME PITCHING TOTALS																	BATTING TOTALS			
USE NAME – GIVEN NAMES (NICKNAMES)	TEAM BY YEAR	DATE	BIRTH PLACE	DATE	B	T	HGT	WGT	W	L	PCT	SV	G	GS	CG	IP	H	BB	SO	ShO	ERA	AB	H	HR	BA
Abbott, Glenn-William Glenn	73-75OakA	2-16-51	Little Rock, Ark.		R	R	6'6	210	11	12	.478	0	54	35	7	229	214	91	95	1	3.69				
Abernathy, Ted-Theodore Wade	55-57,60WasA 64-65CleA 65-66ChiN 67AtlN	3- 6-33	Stanley, N.C.		R	R	6'4	205	63	69	.477	148	681	34	7	1148	1010	592	765	2	3.46	181	25	0	.138
	67-68CinN 69-70ChiN 70StLN 70-72KCA																								
Ackley, Fritz-Florian Frederick	63-64ChiA	4-10-37	Hayward, Wis.		L	R	6'1	202	1	0	1.000	0	5	4	0	19	17	11	17	0	4.26	6	2	0	.333
Acosta, Cy-Cecilio [Miranda]	72-74ChiA 75PhiN	11-22-46	El Sabino, Mexico		R	R	5'10	176	13	9	.591	27	107	0	0	187	143	77	109	0	2.65	7	0	0	.000
Acosta, Ed-Eduardo Elixbet [Montenegro] (Coca-Cola)	70PitN 71-72SDN	3- 9-44	Boquete, Panama		B	R	6'5	223	6	9	.400	1	57	8	3	138	153	39	70	1	4.04	29	1	0	.034
					Bats Right - 70																				
Adamson, Mike-John Michael	67-69BalA	9-13-47	San Diego, Cal.		R	R	6'2	190	0	4	.000	0	11	4	0	26	28	22	14	0	7.27	6	2	0	.333
Aguirre, Hank-Henry John	55-57CleA 58-67DetA 68LAN 69-70ChiN	1-31-32	Azusa, Cal.		R	L	6'4	205	75	72	.510	33	447	149	44	1376	1216	479	856	9	3.24	388	33	0	.085
					Bats Both 65-70																				
Aker, Jack-Jackie Delane (Chief)	64-67KCA 68OakA 69SeaA 69-72NYA	7-13-40	Tulare, Cal.		R	R	6'2	190	47	45	.511	123	495	0	0	746	679	274	404	0	3.28	92	7	0	.076
	72-73ChiN 74AtlN 74NYN																								
Albury, Vic-Victor	73-75MinA	5-12-47	Key West, Fla.		L	L	6'	192	15	16	.484	1	78	37	6	322	287	196	170	1	4.19	1	0	0	.000
Alexander, Doyle-Doyle Lafayette	71LAN 72-75BalA	9- 5-50	Cordova, Ala.		R	R	6'3	200	38	39	.494	3	143	70	21	620	606	190	228	3	3.47	58	11	0	.190
Allen, Bob-Robert Gray	61-63,66-67CleA	10-23-37	Tatum, Tex.		L	L	6'2	185	7	12	.368	19	204	0	0	274	288	132	199	0	4.11	31	4	0	.129
Allen, Lloyd-Lloyd Cecil	69-73CalA 73-74TexA 74-75ChiA	5- 8-50	Merced, Cal.		R	R	6'1	185	8	25	.242	22	159	19	0	297	291	196	194	0	4.70	40	8	1	.200
Andersen, Larry-Larry Eugene	75CleA	5- 6-53	Portland, Ore.		R	R	6'3	200	0	0	–	0	3	0	0	6	4	2	4	0	4.50				
Anderson, Craig-Norman Craig	61StLN 62-64NYN	7- 1-38	Washington, D.C.		R	R	6'2	205	7	23	.233	5	82	17	2	192	226	81	94	0	5.11	47	7	0	.149
Anderson, John-John Charles	58PhiN 60BalA 62StLN 62HouN	11-23-32	St. Paul, Minn.		R	R	6'1	190	0	0	–	1	24	1	0	45	64	14	19	0	6.40	5	0	0	.000
Anderson, Larry-Lawrence Dennis	74-75MilA	12- 3-52	Maywood, Cal.		R	R	6'4	200	1	0	1.000	0	10	1	1	32	38	7	16	1	4.78				
Andrews, John-John Richard	73StLN	2- 9-49	Monterey Park, Cal.		L	L	5'10	180	1	1	.500	0	16	0	0	18	16	11	5	0	4.50	2	1	0	.500
Angelini, Norm-Norman Stanley	72-73KCA	9-24-47	San Francisco, Cal.		L	L	5'11	180	2	1	.667	3	28	0	0	20	15	19	19	0	2.70	2	0	0	.000
Apodaca, Bob-Robert John	73-75NYN	1-31-50	Los Angeles, Cal.		R	R	5'10	175	9	10	.474	16	82	8	1	188	158	72	99	0	2.63	36	7	0	.194
Archer, Jim-James William	61-62KCA	5-25-32	Max Meadows, Va.		R	L	6'	190	9	16	.360	5	57	28	9	233	244	70	122	2	3.94	64	5	0	.078
Arlich, Don-Donald Louis	65-66HouN	2-15-43	Wayne, Mich.		L	L	6'2	185	0	1	.000	0	8	1	0	10	16	5	1	0	8.10	3	0	0	.000
Arlin, Steve-Stephen Ralph	69-74SDN 74CleA	9-25-45	Seattle, Wash.		R	R	6'3	195	34	67	.337	1	141	123	32	790	792	353	463	11	4.32	230	32	0	.139
Arrigo, Jerry-Gerald William	61-64MinA 65-66CinN 66NYN 67-69CinN	6-12-41	Chicago, Ill.		L	L	6'1	195	35	40	.467	4	194	80	9	620	605	291	433	3	4.14	179	27	1	.151
	70ChiA																								
Arroyo, Fred-Fernando	75DetA	3-21-52	Sacramento, Cal.		R	R	6'2	185	2	1	.667	0	14	2	1	53	56	22	25	0	4.50				
Arroyo, Rudy-Rudolph (Yo-Yo)	71StLN	6-19-50	New York, N.Y.		R	L	6'2	190	0	1	.000	0	9	0	0	12	18	5	5	0	5.25	1	0	0	.000
Augustine, Jerry-Gerald Lee	75MilA	7-24-52	Green Bay, Wis.		L	L	6'	190	2	0	1.000	0	5	3	1	27	26	12	8	0	3.00				
Aust, Dennis-Dennis Kay	65-66StLN	11-25-40	Tecumseh, Neb.		R	R	5'11	180	0	1	.000	2	15	0	0	17	18	8	14	0	5.82	2	0	0	.000
Austin, Rick-Rick Gerald	70-71CleA	10-27-46	Seattle, Wash.		R	L	6'4	200	4	9	.308	5	86	8	1	131	131	78	103	1	4.60	19	2	0	.105
Bacsik, Mike-Michael James	75TexA	4- 1-52	Dallas, Tex.		R	R	6'2	190	1	2	.333	0	7	3	0	27	28	9	13	0	3.67				
Bahnsen, Stan-Stanley Raymond	66,68-71NYA 72-75ChiA 75OakA	12-15-44	Council Bluffs, Iowa		R	R	6'2	195	116	117	.498	2	309	285	69	1903	1850	689	793	14	3.53	394	47	0	.119
Bailey, Steve-Steven John	67-68CleA	2-12-42	Bronx, N.Y.		R	R	6'1	194	2	6	.250	2	34	2	0	70	66	44	47	0	3.86	10	0	0	.000
Baird, Bob-Robert Allen	62-63WasA	1-16-42	Knoxville, Tenn.	4-11-74	L	L	6'4	195	0	4	.000	0	8	6	0	23	25	15	10	0	7.04	6	1	0	.167
Bakenhaster, Dave-David Lee	64StLN	3- 5-45	Columbus, Ohio		R	R	5'10	168	0	0	–	0	2	0	0	3	9	1	0	0	6.00				
Baker, Tom-Thomas Henry	63ChiN	5- 6-34	Port Townsend, Wash.		L	L	6'	195	0	1	.000	0	10	1	0	18	20	7	14	0	3.00	3	0	0	.000
Baldschun, Jack-Jack Edward	61-65PhiN 66-67CinN 69-70SDN	10-16-36	Greenville, Ohio		R	R	6'1	182	48	41	.539	60	457	0	0	704	687	298	555	0	3.69	78	7	0	.090
Baldwin, Dave-David George	66-69WasA 70MilA 73ChiA	3-30-38	Tucson, Ariz.		R	R	6'2	205	6	11	.353	22	176	0	0	225	190	89	164	0	3.08	15	1	0	.067
Baldwin, Rick-Rickey Alan	75NYN	6- 1-53	Fresno, Cal.		L	R	6'3	175	3	5	.375	6	54	0	0	97	97	34	54	0	3.34	15	3	0	.200
Ballinger, Mark-Mark Alan	71CleA	1-31-49	Glendale, Cal.		R	R	6'6	205	1	2	.333	0	18	0	0	35	30	13	25	0	4.63	5	1	0	.200
Balsamo, Tony-Anthony Fred	62ChiN	11-21-37	Brooklyn, N.Y.		R	R	6'2	185	0	1	.000	0	18	0	0	29	34	20	27	0	6.52	5	1	0	.200
Bane, Eddie-Edward Norman	73,75MinA	3-22-52	Chicago, Ill.		R	L	5'10	165	3	6	.333	2	27	10	0	88	90	45	56	0	4.30				
Baney, Dick-Richard Lee	69SeaA 73-74CinN	11- 1-46	Fullerton, Cal.		R	R	6'	200	4	1	.800	3	42	3	0	91	98	30	38	0	4.25	16	2	0	.125
Barber, Steve-Stephen David	60-66BalA 67-68NYA 69SeaA 70ChiN	2-22-39	Takoma Park, Md.		L	L	6'	200	121	106	.533	13	466	272	59	1998	1818	950	1309	21	3.36	563	65	5	.115
	70-72AtlN 72-73CalA 74SFN																								
Barber, Steve-Steven Lee	70-71MinA	3-13-48	Grand Rapids, Mich.		R	R	6'1	190	1	0	1.000	2	22	2	0	39	34	31	18	0	5.08	7	0	0	.000
Bare, Ray-Raymond Douglas	72,74StLN 75DetA	4-15-49	Miami, Fla.		R	R	6'2	193	9	16	.360	1	53	24	6	192	217	62	82	1	4.31	5	1	0	.200
Barlow, Mike-Michael Roswell	75StLN	4-30-48	Stamford, N.Y.		L	R	6'6	210	0	0	.360	0	9	0	0	8	11	3	2	0	4.50				
Barnowski, Ed-Edward Anthony	65-66BalA	8-23-45	Scranton, Pa.		R	R	6'2	200	0	0	–	0	6	0	0	7	7	8	8	0	2.57				
Barr, Jim-James Leland	71-75SFN	2-10-48	Los Angeles, Cal.		R	R	6'2	215	46	51	.474	6	181	111	39	929	906	200	351	12	3.15	266	46	1	.173
Barr, Steve-Steven Charles	74-75BosA	9- 8-51	St. Louis, Mo.		L	L	6'4	200	1	1	.500	0	4	3	1	16	18	13	5	0	3.38				
Barrios, Francisco-Francisco Xavier	74ChiA	6-10-53	Hermosillo, Mexico		R	R	6'3	200	0	0	–	0	2	0	0	2	7	2	2	0	27.00				
Bass, Norm-Norman Delaney	64 played in A.F.L. 61-63KCA	1-21-39	Laurel, Miss.		R	R	6'3	205	13	17	.433	0	65	34	6	254	271	137	111	2	5.31	82	8	1	.098
Bates, Dick-Charles Richard	69SeaA	10- 7-45	McArthur, Ohio		L	R	6'1	190	0	0	–	0	1	0	0	2	3	3	3	0	22.50				
Bauta, Ed-Eduardo [Galvez]	60-63StLN 63-64NYN	1- 6-35	Florida, Cuba		R	R	6'3	200	6	6	.500	11	97	0	0	149	148	70	89	0	4.35	17	3	0	.176
Beard, Mike-Michael Richard	74-75AtlN	6-21-50	Little Rock, Ark.		L	L	6'1	185	4	0	1.000	0	40	2	0	79	76	29	34	0	3.19	9	1	0	.111
Bearnarth, Larry-Lawrence Donald	63-66NYN 71MilA	9-11-41	New York, N.Y.		R	R	6'2	203	13	21	.382	8	173	7	0	323	350	135	124	0	4.12	62	10	0	.161
Beck, Rich-Richard Henry	65NYA 66-67MS	1-21-41	Pasco, Wash.		B	R	6'3	190	2	1	.667	0	3	3	1	21	22	7	10	1	2.14	7	0	0	.000
Beene, Fred-Freddy Ray	68-70BalA 72-74NYA 74-75CleA	11-24-42	Angleton, Tex.		B	R	5'9	150	12	7	.632	8	112	6	0	289	274	111	156	0	3.61	9	0	0	.000
					Bats Right - 68																				
Behney, Mel-Melvin Brian	70CinN	9- 2-47	Newark, N.J.		L	L	6'2	180	0	2	.000	0	5	1	0	10	15	8	2	0	4.50	1	0	0	.000
Belinsky, Bo-Robert	62-64LAA 65-66PhiN 67HouN 69PitN 70CinN	12- 7-36	New York, N.Y.		L	L	6'2	190	28	51	.354	2	146	102	14	665	603	323	476	4	4.10	206	27	0	.131
Bell, Gary-Gary	58-67CleA 67-68BosA 69SeaA 69ChiA	11-17-36	San Antonio, Tex.		R	R	6'1	196	121	117	.508	51	519	233	71	2015	1794	842	1378	9	3.68	569	105	1	.185
Bell, Jerry-Jerry Houston	71-74MilA	10- 6-47	Madison, Tenn.		B	R	6'4	195	17	11	.607	1	69	28	8	284	262	114	89	0	3.26	14	1	0	.071
Bennett, Dave-David Hans	64PhiN	11- 7-45	Berkeley, Cal.		R	R	6'5	195	0	0	–	0	1	0	0	1	2	0	1	0	9.00				
Bennett, Dennis-Dennis John	62-65PhiN 65-67BosA 67NYN 68CalA	10- 5-39	Oakland, Cal.		L	L	6'3	205	43	47	.478	6	182	127	28	863	850	281	572	6	3.69	277	46	4	.166
Bertaina, Frank-Frank Louis	64-67BalA 67-69WasA 69BalA 70StLN	4-14-44	San Francisco, Cal.		L	L	6'	185	19	29	.396	0	99	76	6	412	399	214	280	5	3.84	126	16	1	.127
Bethke, Jim-James Charles	65NYN	11- 5-46	Falls City, Neb.		R	R	6'3	185	2	0	1.000	0	25	0	0	40	41	22	19	0	4.28	4	0	0	.000
Bibby, Jim-James Blair	72-73StLN 73-75TexA 75CleA	10-29-44	Franklinton, N.C.		R	R	6'5	225	36	49	.424	2	115	97	28	681	596	333	437	8	4.02	10	1	0	.100
Billingham, Jack-John Eugene (The Blade)	68LAN 69-71HouN 72-75CinN	2-21-43	Orlando, Fla.		R	R	6'4	210	97	75	.564	11	326	200	54	1501	1450	489	864	19	3.53	444	39	0	.088
Bird, Doug-James Douglas	73-75KCA	3- 5-50	Corona, Cal.		R	R	6'3	180	20	16	.556	41	160	5	1	299	281	97	226	0	3.01				
Blair, Dennis-Dennis Herman	74-75MonN	6- 5-54	Middletown, Ohio		R	R	6'5	190	19	22	.463	0	52	49	5	309	263	178	158	1	3.55	100	13	0	.130
Blanco, Gil-Gilbert Henry	65NYA 66KCA	12-15-45	Phoenix, Ariz.		L	L	6'5	205	3	5	.375	0	28	9	0	58	47	48	35	0	4.50	12	2	0	.167
Blasingame, Wade-Wade Allen	63-65MilN 66-67AtlN 67-72HouN 72NYA	11-22-43	Deming, N.M.		L	L	6'1	190	46	51	.474	5	222	128	16	864	891	372	512	2	4.52	265	44	3	.166
Blass, Steve-Stephen Robert	64,66-74PitN	4-18-42	Canaan, Conn.		R	R	6'	175	103	76	.575	2	282	231	57	1599	1558	597	896	16	3.62	546	94	1	.172
Blateric, Steve-Stephen Lawrence	71CinN 72NYA 75CalA	3-20-44	Denver, Colo.		R	R	6'3	200	0	0	–	0	5	0	0	11	16	1	13	0	5.73	1	0	0	.000
Blue, Vida-Vida Rochelle	69-75OakA	7-28-49	Mansfield, La.		B	L	6'	195	92	54	.630	2	198	187	69	1368	1098	470	992	21	2.89	172	17	1	.099
					Bats Left - 69																				
Blyleven (Blijleven), Bert-Rik Aalbert	70-75MinA	4- 6-51	Zeist, Netherlands		R	R	6'3	200	95	85	.528	0	216	213	97	1611	1416	403	1327	24	2.78	235	34	0	.145
Bogle, Warren-Warren Frederick	68OakA	10-19-46	Passaic, N.J.		L	L	6'4	220	0	0	–	0	16	1	0	23	26	8	26	0	4.30	5	0	0	.000
Bolin, Bobby-Bobby Donald	61-69SFN 70MilA 70-73BosA	1-29-39	Hickory Grove, S.C.		R	R	6'4	210	88	75	.540	50	495	164	32	1576	1364	597	1175	10	3.40	423	69	6	.163
Bollo, Greg-Gregory Gene	65-66ChiA	11-16-43	Detroit, Mich.		R	R	6'4	183	0	1	.000	0	18	1	0	30	19	12	20	0	3.30	1	0	0	.000
Bonham, Bill-William Gordon	71-75ChiN	10- 1-48	Glendale, Cal.		R	R	6'3	195	34	44	.436	11	177	93	20	742	745	343	567	4	3.95	235	37	0	.157
Bonikowski, Joe-Joseph Peter	62MinA	1-16-41	Philadelphia, Pa.		R	R	6'	175	5	7	.417	2	30	13	3	100	95	38	45	0	3.87	27	4	0	.148
Boozer, John-John Morgan	62-64,66-69PhiN	7- 6-39	Columbia, S.C.		R	R	6'3	205	14	16	.467	15	171	22	3	394	414	139	282	0	4.09	74	12	0	.162
Borbon, Pedro-Pedro [Rodriguez]	69CalA 70-75CinN	12- 2-46	Valverde de Mao, D.R.		R	R	6'2	185	40	24	.625	44	319	3	0	569	509	138	220	0	3.26	92	18	0	.196
Bork, Frank-Frank Bernard	64PitN	7-13-40	Buffalo, N.Y.		R	L	6'2	175	2	2	.500	2	33	2	0	42	51	11	31	0	4.07	5	1	0	.200
Bosman, Dick-Richard Allen	66-71WasA 72-73TexA 73-75CleA 75OakA	2-17-44	Kenosha, Wis.		R	R	6'2	200	78	83	.484	2	279	214	29	1478	1476	393	724	10	3.64	329	41	0	.125
Boswell, Dave-David Wilson	64-70MinA 71DetA 71BalA	1-20-45	Baltimore, Md.		R	R	6'3	185	68	56	.548	0	205	151	37	1065	858	481	882	6	3.52	367	74	4	.202
Botz, Bob-Robert Allen (Butterball)	62LAA	4-28-35	Milwaukee, Wis.		R	R	5'11	170	2	1	.667	2	35	0	0	63	71	11	24	0	3.43	9	0	0	.000
Bouldin, Carl-Carl Edward	61-64WasA	9-17-39	Germantown, Ky.		B	R	6'2	180	3	8	.273	0	27	10	1	71	96	30	36	0	6.21	21	0	0	.000
					Bats Left - 61																				
Bouton, Jim-James Alan	62-68NYA 69SeaA 69-70HouN	3- 8-39	Newark, N.J.		R	R	6'	185	61	60	.505	6	299	139	34	1208	1106	414	710	11	3.55	340	35	0	.103
Bowsfield, Ted-Edward Oliver	58-60BosA 60CleA 61-62LAA 63-64KCA	1-10-36	Vernon, Canada		R	L	6'1	190	37	39	.487	6	215	86	12	663	699	259	326	4	4.34	173	22	0	.127
Boyd, Gary-Gary Lee	69CleA	8-22-46	Pasadena, Cal.		R	R	6'4	200	0	2	.000	0	8	3	0	11	8	14	9	0	9.00	1	0	0	.000
Brabender, Gene-Eugene Mathew (Bender)	66-68BalA 69SeaA 70MilA	8-16-41	Madison, Wis.		R	R	6'5	225	35	43	.449	6	151	80	15	621	570	282	440	4	4.25	187	19	2	.102
Bradey, Don-Donald Eugene	64HouN	10- 4-34	Charlotte, N.C.		R	R	5'9	180	0	2	.000	0	3	1	0	2	6	3	2	0	22.50				
Bradley, Tom-Thomas William (Fly)	69-70CalA 71-72ChiA 73-75SFN	3-16-47	Asheville, N.C.		R	R	6'3	185	55	61	.474	2	183	151	27	1018	999	311	691	10	3.72	332	48	1	.145
Branch, Harvey-Harvey Alfred	62StLN	2- 8-39	Memphis, Tenn.		R	L	6'	175	0	1	.000	0	1	1	0	5	5	5	2	0	5.40	1	0	0	.000
Brandon, Darrell-Darrell G. (Bucky)	66-68BosA 69SeaA 69MinA 71-73PhiN	7- 8-40	Nacogdoches, Tex.		R	R	6'2	200	28	37	.431	13	228	43	7	590	556	275	354	2	4.04	122	20	0	.164
Braun, John-John Paul	64MilN	12-26-39	Madison, Wis.		R	R	6'5	218	0	0	–	0	1	0	0	2	2	1	1	0	0.00				

USE NAME – GIVEN NAMES (NICKNAMES)	TEAM BY YEAR	BIRTH DATE	BIRTH PLACE	DEATH DATE	B	T	HGT	WGT	W	L	PCT	SV	G	GS	CG	IP	H	BB	SO	ShO	ERA	AB	H	HR	BA
					LIFETIME PITCHING TOTALS																	BATTING TOTALS			
Brenneman, Jim-James LeRoy	65NYA	2-13-41	San Diego, Cal.		R	R	6'2	180	0	0	–	0	3	0	0	2	5	3	2	0	18.00				
Brett, Ken-Kenneth Alven	67-69-71BosA 72MilA 73PitN 74-75PitN	9-18-48	Brooklyn, N.Y.		L	L	6'	195	52	50	.510	3	186	114	27	893	848	354	565	6	4.07	324	87	10	.269
Brewer, Jim-James Thomas	60-63ChiN 64-75LAN 75CalA	11-17-37	Merced, Cal.		L	L	6'1	186	66	64	.508	130	571	35	1	1024	878	354	794	1	3.07	140	21	0	.150
Brice, Alan-Alan Healey	61ChiA	10- 1-37	New York, N.Y.		R	R	6'5	215	0	1	.000	0	3	0	0	3	4	3	3	0	0.00				
Bridges, Marshall-Marshall (Sheriff)	59-60StLN 60-61CinN 62-63NYA	6- 2-31	Jackson, Miss.		R	L	6'1	188	23	15	.605	25	206	5	1	346	315	191	302	0	3.75	59	7	1	.119
	64-65WasA				Bats Both 59-61																				
Briles, Nelson-Nelson Kelley (Nellie)	65-70StLN 71-73PitN 74-75KCA	8- 5-43	Dorris, Cal.		R	R	5'11	195	108	95	.532	19	374	225	54	1736	1740	449	976	15	3.36	469	72	3	.154
Britton, Jim-James Allan	67-69AtlN 70EJ 71MonN	3-25-44	N. Tonawanda, N.Y.		R	R	6'5	225	13	16	.448	4	76	30	4	237	214	112	148	3	3.99	55	7	0	.127
Broberg, Pete-Peter Sven	71WasA 72-74TexA 75MilA	3- 2-50	West Palm Beach, Fla.		R	R	6'3	205	29	50	.367	1	129	97	23	669	635	323	394	6	4.48	95	9	1	.095
Broglio, Ernie-Ernest Gilbert	59-64StLN 64-66ChiN	8-27-35	Berkeley, Cal.		R	R	6'2	200	77	74	.510	2	259	184	52	1337	1216	587	849	18	3.74	431	68	0	.158
Bronstad, Jim-James Warren	59NYA 63-64WasA	6-22-36	Fort Worth, Tex.		R	R	6'3	196	1	7	.125	3	45	3	0	93	110	37	45	0	5.52	17	0	0	.000
Brookens, Ike-Edward Dwain	75DetA	11- 3-49	Chambersburg, Pa.		R	R	6'3	170	0	0	–	0	3	0	0	10	11	5	8	0	5.40				
Brosseau, Frank-Franklin Lee	69,71PitN	7-31-44	Drayton, N.D.		R	R	6'2	200	0	0	–	0	3	0	0	4	3	2	2	0	4.50				
Brown, Jackie-Jackie Gene	70-71WasA 73-75TexA 75CleA	5-31-43	Holdenville, Okla.		R	R	6'2	195	29	30	.492	3	140	53	15	528	552	227	323	4	4.04	28	4	0	.143
Brown, Jophery-Jophery Clifford	68ChiN	1-22-45	Grambling, La.		L	R	6'2	190	0	0	–	0	1	0	0	2	2	1	0	0	4.50				
Brown, Paul-Paul Dwayne	61-63,68PhiN	6-18-41	Fort Smith, Ark.		R	R	6'1	190	0	8	.000	1	36	12	0	93	108	47	45	0	6.00	17	4	0	.235
Brubaker, Bruce-Bruce Ellsworth	67LAN 70MilA	12-29-41	Harrisburg, Pa.		R	R	6'1	198	0	0	–	0	2	0	0	3	5	1	2	0	15.00				
Bruce, Bob-Robert James	59-61DetA 62-66HouN 67AtlN	5-16-33	Detroit, Mich.		R	R	6'3	210	49	71	.408	1	219	167	26	1123	1146	340	733	6	3.85	346	52	0	.150
Bruckbauer, Fred-Frederick John	61MinA	5-27-38	New Ulm, Minn.		R	R	6'1	185	0	0	–	0	1	0	0	0	3	1	0	0	∞				
Brunet, George-George Stuart (Lefty)	56-57,59-60KCA 60-61MilN 62-63HouN	6- 8-35	Houghton, Mich.		R	L	6'1	200	69	93	.426	4	324	213	39	1431	1303	581	921	15	3.62	418	37	3	.089
	63BalA 64LAA 65-69CalA 69SeaA 70WasA 70PitN 71StLN																								
Bryant, Ron-Ronald Raymond	67,69-74SFN 75StLN	11-12-47	Redlands, Cal.		B	L	6'1	195	57	56	.504	1	205	132	23	918	874	379	509	6	4.02	291	48	0	.165
Bunker, Wally-Wallace Edward	63-68BalA 69-71KCA	1-25-45	Seattle, Wash.		R	R	6'2	197	60	52	.536	5	206	152	34	1086	976	334	569	5	3.51	331	31	0	.094
Bunning, Jim-James Paul David	55-63DetA 64-67PhiN 68-69PitN 69LAN	10-23-31	Southgate, Ky.		R	R	6'3	200	224	184	.549	16	591	519	151	3759	3433	1000	2855	40	3.27	1275	213	7	.167
	70-71PhiN																								
Burbach, Bill-William David	69-71NYA	8-22-47	Dickeyville, Wis.		R	R	6'4	215	6	11	.353	0	37	28	2	161	141	116	95	1	4.47	47	4	0	.085
Burchart, Larry-Larry Wayne (Turk)	69CleA	2- 8-46	Tulsa, Okla.		R	R	6'3	205	0	2	.000	1	29	0	0	42	42	24	26	0	4.29				
Burdette, Freddie-Freddie Thomason	62-64ChiN	9-15-36	Moultrie, Ga.		R	R	6'1	170	1	0	1.000	1	30	0	0	35	27	20	10	0	3.34	2	1	0	.500
Burgmeier, Tom-Thomas Henry (Bugs)	68CalA 69-73KCA 74-75MinA	8- 2-43	St. Paul, Minn.		L	L	5'11	185	35	31	.530	48	348	2	0	516	510	184	240	0	3.58	66	14	0	.212
Burnside, Pete-Peter Willits	55,57NYN 58SFN 59-60DetA 61-63WasA 63BalA	7- 2-30	Evanston, Ill.		R	L	6'2	180	19	36	.345	7	196	64	14	569	607	230	303	3	4.79	132	10	0	.076
Burris, Ray-Bertram Ray	73-75ChiN	8-22-50	Idabel, Okla.		R	R	6'5	200	19	16	.543	1	107	41	8	378	415	126	205	2	4.40	102	17	0	.167
Burton, Jim-Jim Scott (Eric)	75BosA	10-27-49	Royal Oak, Mich.		R	L	6'3	195	1	2	.333	1	29	4	0	53	58	19	39	0	2.89				
Busby, Steve-Steven Lee	72-75KCA	9-29-49	Burbank, Cal.		R	R	6'2	205	59	42	.584	0	114	114	48	830	791	286	563	7	3.45	15	3	0	.200
Buschhorn, Don-Donald Lee	65KCA	4-29-46	Independence, Mo.		L	R	6'	170	0	1	.000	0	12	3	0	31	36	8	9	0	4.35	4	2	0	.500
Buskey, Tom-Thomas William (Husky)	73-74NYA 74-75CleA	2-20-47	Harrisburg, Pa.		R	R	6'3	218	7	11	.389	26	113	0	0	193	190	69	80	0	3.22				
Butler, Bill-William Franklin	69-71KCA 72CleA 74-75MinA	3-12-47	Hyattsville, Md.		L	L	6'2	210	23	34	.404	1	128	82	10	572	536	297	403	5	4.11	117	6	0	.051
Butler, Cecil-Cecil Dean	62,64MilN	10-23-37	Dallas, Ga.		R	R	6'4	195	2	0	1.000	0	11	2	1	35	33	9	24	0	3.34	8	0	0	.000
Butters, Tom-Thomas Arden	62-65PitN	4- 8-38	Delaware, Ohio		R	R	6'2	195	2	3	.400	0	43	5	0	95	81	56	85	0	3.13	15	3	0	.200
Buzhardt, John-John William	58-59ChiN 60-61PhiN 62-67ChiA 67BalA	8-15-36	Prosperity, S.C.		R	R	6'2	195	71	96	.425	7	326	200	44	1489	1425	457	678	15	3.67	445	60	0	.135
	67-68HouN																								
Cain, Les-Leslie	68,70-72DetA	1-13-48	San Luis Obispo, Cal.		L	L	6'1	200	23	19	.548	0	68	64	8	374	331	225	303	1	3.97	137	21	2	.153
Caldwell, Mike-Ralph Michael	71-73SDN 74-75SFN	1-22-49	Tarboro, N.C.		R	L	6'	185	34	43	.442	13	172	81	17	672	703	216	333	5	3.80	193	29	0	.150
Calmus, Dick-Richard Lee	67ChiN	1- 7-44	Los Angeles, Cal.		R	R	6'4	187	3	1	.750	0	22	2	0	48	37	16	26	0	3.19	8	1	0	.125
Campbell, Bill-William Richard	73-75MinA	8- 9-44	Highland Park, Mich.		R	R	6'3	185	15	16	.484	31	138	9	2	293	272	121	153	1	3.19	1	0	0	.000
Cambria, Fred-Frederick Dennis	70PitN	1-22-48	Queens, N.Y.		R	R	6'2	195	1	2	.333	0	6	5	0	33	37	12	14	0	3.55	10	2	0	.200
Campisi, Sal-Salvatore John	69-70StLN 71MinA	8-11-42	Brooklyn, N.Y.		R	R	6'2	210	3	2	.600	4	50	0	0	63	62	47	35	0	2.71	1	0	0	.000
Candelaria, John-John Robert (Candy)	75PitN	11- 6-53	Brooklyn, N.Y.		L	L	6'7	215	8	6	.571	0	18	18	4	121	95	36	95	1	2.75	43	6	0	.140
Capra, Buzz-Lee William	71-73NYN 74-75AtlN	10- 1-47	Chicago, Ill.		R	R	5'11	170	25	25	.500	5	92	45	16	395	328	172	258	5	3.24	105	15	0	.143
Cardinal, Randy-Conrad Seth	63HouN	3-30-42	Brooklyn, N.Y.		R	R	6'1	190	0	1	.000	0	6	1	0	13	15	7	7	0	6.23	2	0	0	.000
Cardwell, Don-Donald Eugene	57-60PhiN 60-62ChiN 63-66PitN 67-70NYN	12- 7-35	Winston-Salem, N.C.		R	R	6'4	210	102	138	.425	7	410	301	72	2122	2009	671	1211	17	3.92	698	94	15	.135
	70AtlN																								
Carlos, Cisco-Francisco Manuel	67-69ChiA 69-70WasA	9-17-40	Monrovia, Cal.		R	R	6'3	205	11	18	.379	0	73	36	1	235	222	79	119	1	3.75	62	4	0	.065
Carlton, Steve-Stephen Noman	65-71StLN 72-75PhiN	12-22-44	Miami, Fla.		L	L	6'4	210	148	119	.554	1	347	329	145	2450	2185	889	1916	31	3.10	827	155	6	.187
Carpin, Frank-Frank Dominic	65PitN 66HouN	9-14-38	Brooklyn, N.Y.		L	L	5'10	172	4	1	.800	4	49	0	0	46	44	30	29	0	3.72	1	0	0	.000
Carrithers, Don-Donald Eugene	70-73SFN 74-75MonN	9-15-49	Lynwood, Cal.		R	R	6'3	205	22	19	.537	3	124	48	9	411	426	183	201	3	4.38	116	23	0	.198
Carroll, Clay-Clay Palmer (Hawk)	64-65MilN 66-68AtlN 68-75CinN	5- 2-41	Clanton, Ala.		R	R	6'1	205	87	64	.576	132	641	27	1	1171	1136	387	605	0	2.98	197	26	1	.132
Carroll, Tom-Thomas Michael	74-75CinN	11- 5-52	Utica, N.Y.		L	R	6'4	185	8	4	.667	0	28	20	0	125	120	70	51	0	4.18	40	4	0	.100
Caskey, Craig-Craig Douglas	73MonN	12-11-49	Visalia, Cal.		B	L	5'11	180	0	0	–	0	9	1	0	14	15	4	6	0	5.79	1	0	0	.000
Castro, Bill-William Radhames	74-75MilA	12-13-53	Santiago, Dom. Rep.		R	R	6'	170	3	2	.600	1	26	5	0	93	97	22	35	0	2.90				
Champion, Billy-Buford Billy	69-72PhiN 73-75MilA	9-18-47	Shelby, N.C.		R	R	6'4	190	34	49	.410	2	192	99	13	781	838	341	352	3	4.61	99	14	1	.141
Chance, Dean-Wilmer Dean	61-64LAA 65-66CalA 67-69MinA 70CleA 70NYN	6- 1-41	Wayne, Ohio		R	R	6'3	204	128	115	.529	23	406	294	83	2148	1864	739	1534	33	2.92	662	44	0	.066
	71DetA																								
Charton, Pete-Frank Lane	64BosA	12-21-42	Jackson, Tenn.		L	R	6'2	190	0	2	.000	0	25	5	0	65	67	24	37	0	5.26	10	1	0	.100
Chavez, Nestor-Isaias [Silva]	67SFN	7- 6-47	Chacao, Venezuela	3-16-69	R	R	6'	170	1	0	1.000	0	2	0	0	5	4	3	3	0	0.00	1	0	0	.000
Cheadle, Dave-David Baird	73AtlN	2-19-52	Greensboro, N.C.		L	L	6'3	205	0	1	.000	0	2	0	0	2	2	3	2	0	18.00				
Cheney, Tom-Thomas Edgar	57StLN 58MS 59StLN 60-61PitN 61-64WasA	10-14-34	Morgan, Ga.		R	R	5'11	170	19	29	.396	2	115	71	13	466	382	245	345	8	3.77	133	18	0	.135
	65VR 66WasA																								
Chlupsa, Bob Robert Joseph	70-71StLN	2-16-45	New York, N.Y.		R	R	6'7	220	0	2	.000	0	15	0	0	18	29	9	11	0	9.00				
Christenson, Larry-Larry Richard (Chris)	73-75PhiN	11-10-53	Everett, Wash.		R	R	6'4	220	13	11	.542	3	49	36	6	229	222	80	117	2	4.17	71	14	2	.197
Church, Len-Leonard	66ChiN	3-21-42	Chicago, Ill.		B	R	6'	190	0	1	.000	0	4	0	0	6	10	7	3	0	7.50	1	0	0	.000
Cimino, Pete-Peter William	65-66MinA 67-68CalA	10-17-42	Philadelphia, Pa.		R	R	6'2	195	5	8	.385	5	86	1	0	161	133	65	139	0	3.07	18	5	0	.278
Cisco, Galen-Galen Bernard	61-62BosA 62-65NYN 67BosA 69KCA	3- 7-36	St. Mary's, Ohio		R	R	6'	200	25	56	.302	2	192	78	9	658	681	281	325	3	4.57	164	21	0	.128
Clark, Rickey-Rickey Charles	67-69,71-72CalA	3-21-46	Mt. Clemens, Mich.		R	R	6'2	170	19	22	.463	2	96	70	4	432	371	213	236	2	3.38	126	13	0	.103
Clemons, Lance-Lance Levis	71KCA 72StLN 74BosA	7- 6-47	Philadelphia, Pa.		L	L	6'2	210	2	1	.667	0	19	4	0	35	42	21	23	0	6.17	8	2	1	.250
Cleveland, Reggie-Reginald Leslie	69-73StLN 74-75BosA	5-23-48	Swift Current, Canada		R	R	6'1	200	65	64	.504	0	188	148	40	1099	1123	314	629	9	4.02	232	49	0	.211
Cloninger, Tony-Tony Lee	61-65MilN 66-68AtlN 68-71CinN 72StLN	8-13-40	Lincoln, N.C.		R	R	6'	210	113	97	.538	6	352	247	63	1768	1643	798	1120	13	4.07	621	119	11	.192
Closter, Alan-Alan Edward	66WasA 71-72NYA 73AtlN	6-15-43	Creighton, Neb.		L	L	6'2	190	2	2	.500	0	21	1	0	34	43	43	27	0	6.88	7	0	0	.000
Clyde, Dave-David Eugene	73-75TexA	4-22-55	Kansas City, Kans.		L	L	6'1	190	7	18	.280	0	47	40	4	217	241	107	128	0	4.60				
Coates, Jim-James Alton	56,59-62NYA 63WasA 63CinN 65-67CalA	8- 4-32	Farnham, Va.		R	R	6'4	192	43	22	.662	18	247	46	13	683	650	286	396	4	4.01	160	21	0	.131
Colbert, Vince-Vincent Norman	70-72CleA	2-20-45	Washington, D.C.		R	R	6'4	200	9	14	.391	4	95	21	3	249	251	125	127	1	4.55	51	8	0	.157
Colborn, Jim-James William	69-71ChiN 72-75MilA	5-22-46	Santa Paula, Cal.		R	R	6'	195	52	47	.525	7	205	115	44	990	998	290	450	7	3.66	55	4	0	.073
Coleman, Joe-Joseph Howard	65-70WasA 71-75DetA	2- 3-47	Boston, Mass.		R	R	6'3	195	129	118	.522	1	334	312	91	2192	2039	839	1523	18	3.67	444	46	0	.104
Colpaert, Dick-Richard Charles	70PitN	1- 3-44	Fraser, Mich.		R	R	5'10	175	1	0	1.000	0	8	0	0	11	9	8	6	0	5.73				
Colson, Loyd-Loyd Albert	70NYA	11- 4-47	Wellington, Tex.		R	R	6'1	190	0	0	–	0	1	0	0	2	3	0	3	0	4.50				
Colton, Larry-Lawrence Robert	68PhiN	6- 8-42	Los Angeles, Cal.		L	R	6'3	200	0	0	–	0	1	0	0	2	3	0	2	0	4.50				
Compton, Clint-Robert Clinton	72ChiN	11- 1-50	Montgomery, Ala.		L	L	5'11	178	0	0	–	0	1	0	0	2	2	2	0	0	9.00				
Connolly, Ed-Edward Joseph Jr.	64BosA 67CleA	12- 3-39	Brooklyn, N.Y.		L	L	6'1	190	6	12	.333	0	42	19	1	130	143	98	118	1	5.88	29	5	0	.172
Connors, Billy-William Joseph	66ChiN 67-68NYN	11- 2-41	Schenectady, N.Y.		R	R	6'1	185	0	2	.000	0	26	1	0	43	49	19	24	0	7.53	2	1	0	.500
Cook, Ron-Ronald Wayne	70-71HouN	7-11-47	Jefferson, Tex.		L	L	6'1	190	4	8	.333	2	46	11	0	108	103	50	60	0	4.00	25	6	0	.240
Coombs, Danny-Daniel Bernard	63-69HouN 70-71SDN	3-23-42	Lincoln, Me.		R	L	6'4	200	19	27	.413	2	144	5	2	393	433	162	249	1	4.08	100	14	0	.140
Corbin, Ray-Alton Ray	71-75MinA	2-12-49	Live Oak, Fla.		R	R	6'3	202	36	38	.486	17	181	63	12	652	638	261	348	3	3.84	83	11	0	.133
Corkins, Mike-Michael Patrick	69-74SDN	5-25-46	Riverside, Cal.		L	L	6'1	195	19	28	.404	9	157	44	5	459	458	248	335	1	4.39	119	24	5	.202
Cosgrove, Mike-Michael John	72 75HouN	2-17-51	Phoenix, Ariz.		L	L	6'1	180	9	7	.563	8	97	4	1	185	165	87	88	0	3.31	33	3	0	.091
Cosman, Jim-James Henry	66-65StLN 70ChiN	2-19-43	Brockport, N.Y.		R	R	6'4	210	2	0	1.000	0	12	6	1	41	26	27	16	1	3.07	11	1	0	.091
Cox, Casey-Joseph Casey	66-71WasA 72TexA 72-73NYA	7- 3-41	Long Beach, Cal.		R	R	6'5	200	39	42	.481	20	308	59	5	762	772	234	297	0	3.70	151	15	0	.099
Cox, Terry-Terry Lee	70CalA	3-30-49	Odessa, Tex.		R	R	6'5	235	0	0	–	0	3	0	0	2	4	0	3	0	4.50				
Craig, Pete-Peter Joel	64-66WasA	7-10-40	La Salle, Canada		L	R	6'5	220	0	3	.000	0	6	4	0	18	28	13	3	0	11.82	3	2	0	.667
Craig, Roger-Roger Lee	55-57BknN 58-61LAN 62-63NYN 64StLN 65CinN	2- 7-31	Durham, N.C.		R	R	6'4	200	74	98	.430	19	368	186	58	1537	1528	522	803	7	3.82	448	38	0	.085
	66PhiN																								
Cram, Jerry-Gerald Allen	69KCA 74-75NYN	12- 9-47	Los Angeles, Cal.		R	R	6'	180	0	3	.000	0	19	2	0	44	44	12	20	0	2.66	6	1	0	.167
Crawford, Jim-James Frederick (Catfish)	73,75HouN	9-29-50	Chicago, Ill.		L	L	6'3	200	5	9	.357	10	92	2	0	157	161	70	93	0	4.01	30	8	0	.267
Crosby-Ken-Kenneth Stewart	75ChiN	12-16-47	New Denver, Canada		R	R	6'3	188	1	0	1.000	0	9	0	0	8	10	7	6	0	3.38				
Cuellar, Mike-Miguel Angel [Santana]	59CinN 64StLN 65-68HouN 69-75BalA	5- 8-37	Las Villas, Cuba		L	L	5'11	175	181	116	.609	10	425	359	170	2697	2400	769	1597	35	3.05	661	76	7	.115
Cueto, Bert-Dagoberto [Concepcion]	61MinA	8-14-37	San Luis, Cuba		R	R	6'4	170	1	3	.250	0	7	5	0	21	27	10	5	0	7.29	5	0	0	.000

USE NAME – GIVEN NAMES (NICKNAMES)	TEAM BY YEAR	BIRTH DATE	BIRTH PLACE	DEATH DATE	LIFETIME PITCHING TOTALS																	BATTING TOTALS			
					B	T	HGT	WGT	W	L	PCT	SV	G	GS	CG	IP	H	BB	SO	ShO	ERA	AB	H	HR	BA
Cullen, Jack-John Patrick	62,65-66NYA	10- 6-39	Newark, N.J.		R	R	5'11	170	4	4	.500	1	19	9	2	73	72	28	34	1	3.08	23	3	0	.130
Culp, Ray-Raymond Leonard	63-66PhiN 67ChiN 68-73BosA	8- 6-41	Elgin, Tex.		R	R	6'	200	122	101	.547	1	322	268	80	1897	1677	752	1411	22	3.58	602	74	1	.123
Culver, George-George Raymond	66-67CleA 68-69CinN 70StLN 70-72HouN 73LAN 73-74PhiN	7- 8-43	Salinas, Cal.		R	R	6'2	195	48	49	.495	23	335	57	7	789	793	352	451	2	3.62	161	20	0	.124
Cumberland, John-John Sheldon	68-70NYA 70-72SFN 72StLN 74CalA	5-10-47	Westbrook, Me.		R	L	6'	185	15	16	.484	2	110	36	6	335	312	103	137	2	3.81	91	9	0	.099
Currence, Lafayette-Delancy Lafayette	75MilA	12- 3-51	Rock Hill, S.C.		B	L	5'11	175	0	2	.000	0	8	1	0	19	25	14	7	0	7.58				
Curtis, Jack-Jack Patrick	61-62ChiN 62MilN 63CleA	1-11-37	Rhodhiss, N.C.		L	L	5'10	175	14	19	.424	1	69	35	6	279	328	89	108	0	4.84	82	15	2	.183
Curtis, Jack-John Duffield	70-73BosA 74-75StLN	3- 9-48	Newton, Mass.		L	L	6'2	185	44	46	.489	2	139	101	28	745	770	288	383	9	3.64	163	24	0	.147
D'Acquisto, John-John Francis (D)	73-75SFN	12-24-51	San Diego, Cal.		R	R	6'2	205	15	19	.441	0	55	45	6	271	234	177	218	1	4.42	87	8	1	.092
Dahl, Jay-Jay Steven	63HouN	12- 6-45	San Bernardino, Cal.	6-20-65	B	L	5'10	183	0	1	.000	0	1	1	0	3	7	0	0	0	15.00				
Dailey, Bill William Garland	61-62CleA 63-64MinA	5-13-35	Arlington, Va.		R	R	6'3	185	10	7	.588	22	119	0	0	186	162	59	109	0	2.76	26	5	1	.192
Dal Canton, Bruce-John Bruce	67-70PitN 71-75KCA 75AtlN	6-15-42	California, Pa.		R	R	6'2	205	48	42	.533	16	266	82	15	833	807	336	440	2	3.68	141	15	0	.106
Daniels, Bennie-Bennie	57-60PitN 61-65WasA	6-17-32	Tuscaloosa, Ala.		L	R	6'1	205	45	76	.372	5	230	139	26	997	1004	383	471	5	4.44	300	51	5	.170
Darcy, Pat-Patrick Leonard	74-75CinN	5-12-50	Troy, Ohio		L	R	6'4	195	12	5	.706	1	33	24	1	148	151	67	60	0	3.59	50	5	0	.100
Darwin, Bobby-Arthur Bobby Lee	62LAA 69LAN	2-16-43	Los Angeles, Cal.		R	R	6'2	200	0	1	.000	0	4	1	0	7	12	9	6	0	10.29	(See B 61-75)			
Daviault, Ray-Raymond Joseph Robert	62NYN	5-27-34	Montreal, Canada		R	R	6'1	170	1	5	.167	0	36	3	0	81	92	48	51	0	6.22	15	1	0	.067
Davidson, Ted-Thomas Eugene	65-68CinN 68AtlN	10- 4-39	Las Vegas, Nev.		R	L	6'	192	11	7	.611	5	114	1	0	195	189	54	124	0	3.69	31	0	0	.000
Davison, Mike-Michael Lynn	69-70SFN	8- 4-45	Galesburg, Ill.		L	L	6'1	170	3	5	.375	1	32	0	0	38	48	22	21	0	6.39	1	0	0	.000
DeBusschere, Dave-David Albert 62-74 played in N.B.A.	62-63ChiA 64MS	10-16-40	Detroit, Mich.		R	R	6'6	225	3	4	.429	0	36	10	1	102	85	57	61	1	2.91	22	1	0	.045
Decker, Joe-George Henry	69-72ChiN 73-75MinA	6-16-47	Storm Lake, Iowa		R	R	6'1	180	34	36	.486	0	134	92	19	625	615	312	401	4	4.06	46	8	1	.174
Degerick, Mike-Michael Arthur	61-62ChiA	4- 1-43	New York, N.Y.		R	R	6'2	178	0	0	–	0	2	0	0	3	3	2	0	0	3.00				
de los Santos, Ramon-Ramon [Genera] (Pinta Cora)	74HouN	5-19-49	Santo Domingo, D.R.		L	L	6'2	183	1	1	.500	0	12	0	0	12	11	9	7	0	2.25				
Demery, Larry-Lawrence Calvin	74-75PitN	6- 4-53	Bakersfield, Cal.		R	R	6'	172	13	9	.591	4	64	23	3	210	190	94	110	0	3.51	57	8	0	.140
De Mola, Don-Donald John (Mole)	74-75MonN	7- 5-52	Glen Cove, N.Y.		R	R	6'2	185	5	7	.417	1	85	1	0	150	138	63	110	0	3.90	12	0	0	.000
Denehy, Bill-William Francis	67NYN 68WasA 71DetA	3-31-46	Middletown, Conn.		B	R	6'3	200	1	10	.091	1	49	0	0	105	102	61	63	0	4.54	11	0	0	.000
					Bats Left - 71																				
Dennis, Don-Donald Ray	65-66StLN	3- 3-42	Uniontown, Kans.		R	R	6'2	190	6	5	.545	8	79	1	0	115	120	33	54	0	3.68	17	3	0	.176
Denny, John-John Allen	74-75StLN	11- 8-52	Prescott, Ariz.		R	R	6'3	185	10	7	.588	0	27	24	3	138	152	51	73	2	3.91	44	10	0	.227
Dettore, Tom-Thomas Anthony	73PitN 74-75ChiN	11-17-47	Canonsburg, Pa.		L	R	6'4	210	8	10	.444	0	64	15	0	173	185	76	102	0	4.99	48	11	0	.229
Devine, Adrian-Paul Adrian	73,75AtlN	12- 2-51	Galveston, Tex.		R	R	6'4	197	3	3	.500	4	29	3	0	48	64	19	23	0	5.81	9	1	0	.111
Dickson, Jim-James Edward	63HouN 64CinN 65-66KCA	4-20-38	Portland, Ore.		L	R	6'1	185	5	3	.625	3	109	1	0	143	135	77	86	0	4.34	7	1	0	.143
Dierker, Larry-Lawrence Edward	64-75HouN	9-22-46	Hollywood, Cal.		R	R	6'4	205	124	103	.546	1	317	292	99	2108	1919	623	1375	21	3.24	717	98	3	.137
DiLauro, Jack-Jack Edward	69NYN 70HouN	5- 3-43	Akron, Ohio		B	L	6'2	185	2	7	.222	4	65	4	0	98	84	35	50	0	3.03	14	0	0	.000
Dillman, Bill-William Howard	67BalA 70MonN	5-25-45	Trenton, N.J.		R	R	6'2	180	7	12	.368	3	50	15	2	155	143	51	86	1	4.53	33	5	0	.152
Dillon, Steve-Stephen Edward	63-64NYN	3-20-43	Bronx, N.Y.		L	L	5'10	160	0	0	–	0	3	0	0	5	7	2	3	0	9.00				
Diorio, Ron-Ronald Michael (D.O.)	73PhiN 74ChiN	7-15-46	Waterbury, Conn.		R	R	6'6	212	0	0	–	1	25	0	0	20	20	7	11	0	3.15				
Distaso, Alec-Alec John	69ChiN	12-23-48	Los Angeles, Cal.		R	R	6'2	200	0	0	–	0	2	0	0	5	6	1	1	0	3.60				
Dobson, Chuck-Charles Thomas	66-67KCA 68-71OakA 72EJ 73OakA 74-75CalA	1-10-44	Kansas City, Mo.		R	R	6'4	200	74	69	.517	0	202	190	49	1258	1174	486	758	11	3.78	511	63	0	.123
Dobson, Pat-Patrick Edward	67-69DetA 70SDN 71-72BalA 73AtlN 73-75NYA	2-12-42	Depew, N.Y.		R	R	6'3	200	103	105	.495	18	346	227	68	1769	1662	535	1103	14	3.35	317	39	0	.123
Donohue, Jim-James Thomas	61DetA 61-62LAA 62MinA	10-31-38	St. Louis, Mo.		R	R	6'4	190	3	4	.429	7	70	9	0	156	152	82	116	0	4.27	34	5	0	.147
Dotter, Gary-Gary Richard	61,63-64MinA	8- 7-42	St. Louis, Mo.		L	L	6'1	180	0	0	–	0	7	0	0	12	9	7	10	0	5.25	1	0	0	.000
Dowling, Dave-David Barclay	64StlN 66ChiN	8-23-42	Baton Rouge, La.		R	L	6'2	180	1	0	1.000	0	2	1	1	10	12	0	3	0	1.80	2	0	0	.000
Downing, Al-Alphonso Erwin	61-69NYA 70OakA 70MilA 71-75LAN	6-28-41	Trenton, N.J.		R	L	5'11	180	122	104	.540	3	376	313	73	2202	1881	899	1586	24	3.17	710	91	2	.128
Downs, Dave-David Ralph	72PhiN 73SA	6-21-52	Logan, Utah		R	R	6'6	220	1	1	.500	0	4	4	1	23	25	3	5	1	2.74	8	2	0	.250
Doyle, Paul-Paul Sinnott	69AtlN 70CalA 70SDN 72CalA	10- 2-39	Philadelphia, Pa.		L	L	5'11	172	5	3	.625	11	87	0	0	90	85	46	65	0	3.80	7	0	0	.000
Drabowsky, Moe-Myron Walter	56-60ChiN 61MilN 62CinN 62-65KCA 66-68BalA 69-70KCA 70BalA 71-72StLN 72ChiA	7-21-35	Ozanna, Poland		R	R	6'3	190	88	105	.456	55	589	154	33	1640	1441	702	1162	6	3.71	420	68	3	.162
Drago, Dick-Richard Anthony	69-73KCA 74-75BosA	6-25-45	Toledo, Ohio		R	R	6'1	190	70	82	.461	19	255	180	61	1383	1296	397	710	6	3.53	273	21	0	.077
Dressler, Rob-Robert Alan	75SFN	2- 2-54	Portland, Ore.		R	R	6'3	190	1	0	1.000	0	3	2	1	16	17	4	6	0	1.13	4	0	0	.000
Drysdale, Don-Donald Scott (Big D)	56-57BknN 58-69LAN	7-23-36	Van Nuys, Cal.		R	R	6'5	215	209	166	.557	6	518	465	167	3432	3084	855	2486	49	2.95	1169	218	29	.186
Duckworth, Jim-James Raymond	63-66WasA 66KCA	5-24-39	National City, Cal.		R	R	6'4	194	7	25	.219	4	97	29	2	267	256	148	220	0	5.26	59	2	0	.034
Duffalo, Jim-James Francis	61-65SFN 65CinN	11-25-35	Helvetia, Pa.		R	R	6'1	180	15	8	.652	6	141	14	2	298	248	155	210	0	3.38	63	8	1	.127
Duffie, John-John Brown	67LAN	10- 4-45	Greenwood, S.C.		R	R	6'7	210	0	2	.000	0	2	2	0	10	11	4	6	0	2.70	2	0	0	.000
Dukes, Jan-Noble Jan	69-70WasA 72TexA	8-16-45	Cheyenne, Wyo.		L	L	5'11	180	0	2	.000	0	16	0	0	20	15	10	7	0	2.70	1	0	0	.000
Dukes, Tom-Thomas Earl	67-68HouN 69-70SDN 71BalA 72CalA	8-31-42	Knoxville, Tenn.		R	R	6'2	200	5	16	.238	21	161	0	0	217	226	82	169	0	4.35	21	2	0	.095
Duliba, Bob-Robert John	59-60,62StLN 63-64LAA 65BosA 67KCA	1- 9-35	Glen Lyon, Pa.		R	R	5'10	180	17	12	.586	14	176	0	0	258	257	96	129	0	3.45	26	1	0	.038
Dunnegan, Jimmy-James William	70ChiN	8- 6-47	Burlington, Iowa		R	R	6'1	205	0	2	.000	0	7	0	0	13	13	12	3	0	4.85	4	1	0	.250
Dunning, Steve-Steven John	70-73CleA 73-74TexA	5-15-49	Denver, Colo.		R	R	6'2	205	20	35	.364	1	94	77	6	497	485	274	310	1	4.64	119	24	4	.202
Duren, Ryne-Rinold George	54BalA 57KCA 58-61NYA 61-62LAA 63-64PhiN 64CinN 65PhiN 65WasA	2-22-29	Cazenovia, Wis.		R	R	6'2	194	27	44	.380	57	311	32	2	590	443	392	630	1	3.83	114	7	0	.061
Durham, Don-Donald Gary	72StLN 73TexA	3-21-49	Yosemite, Ky.		R	R	6'	170	2	11	.154	1	25	12	1	88	91	45	58	0	5.83	14	7	2	.500
Dustal, Bob-Robert Andrew	63DetA	9-28-35	Sayreville, N.J.		R	R	6'	172	0	1	.000	0	7	0	0	6	10	5	4	0	9.00				
Earley, Arnie-Arnold Carl	60-65BosA 66ChiN 67HouN	6- 4-33	Lincoln Park, Mich.		L	L	6'1	195	12	20	.375	14	223	10	1	381	400	184	310	0	4.49	51	8	0	.157
Easterly, Jamie-James Morris	74-75AtlN	2-17-53	Houston, Tex.		B	L	5'9	170	2	9	.182	0	24	13	0	72	79	46	34	0	5.38	18	1	0	.056
Eastwick, Rawly-Rawlins Jackson	75CinN	10-24-50	Camden, N.J.		R	R	6'2	175	5	3	.625	24	66	0	0	108	89	29	75	0	2.50	16	1	0	.063
Eckersley, Dennis-Dennis Lee	75CleA	10- 3-54	Oakland, Cal.		R	R	6'2	190	13	7	.650	2	34	24	6	187	147	90	152	2	2.60				
Eddy, Don-Donald Eugene	70-71ChiA	10-25-46	Mason City, Iowa		R	L	5'11	180	0	2	.000	0	29	0	0	35	29	25	23	0	2.31	1	1	0	1.000
Edgerton, Bill-William Albert	66-67KCA 69SeaA	8-16-41	South Bend, Ind.		L	L	6'2	185	1	2	.333	0	17	1	0	20	31	10	11	0	4.95				
Edmondson, Paul-Paul Michael	69ChiA	2-12-43	Kansas City, Kans.	2-13-70	R	R	6'5	195	1	6	.143	0	14	13	1	88	72	39	46	0	3.68	29	5	0	.172
Egan, Dick-Richard Wallis	63-64DetA 66CalA 67LAN	3-24-37	Berkeley, Cal.		L	L	6'4	193	1	2	.333	2	74	0	0	101	109	41	68	0	5.17	5	0	0	.000
Eilers, Dave-David Louis	64-65MilN 65-66NYN 67HouN	12- 3-36	Oldenberg, Tex.		R	R	5'11	188	8	6	.571	3	81	0	0	124	146	29	52	0	4.43	9	1	0	.111
Ellingsen, Bruce-H. Bruce	74CleA	4-26-49	Pocatello, Idaho		L	L	6'	180	1	1	.500	0	16	2	0	42	45	17	16	0	3.21				
Ellis, Dock-Dock Phillip	68-75PitN	3-11-45	Los Angeles, Cal.		B	R	6'3	205	96	80	.545	0	228	207	51	1424	1347	436	868	12	3.16	462	63	0	.136
Ellis, Jim-James Russell	67ChiN 69StLN	3-25-45	Tulare, Cal.		R	L	6'2	185	1	1	.500	0	10	2	0	22	27	12	8	0	2.86	5	1	0	.200
Ellis, Sammy-Samuel Joseph	62,64-67CinN 68CalA 69ChiA	2-11-41	Youngstown, Ohio		L	R	6'1	182	63	58	.521	18	229	140	35	1004	967	378	677	3	4.15	299	31	0	.104
Ellsworth, Dick-Richard Clark	58,60-66ChiN 67PhiN 68-69BosA 69-70CleA 70-71MilA	3-22-40	Lusk, Wyo.		L	L	6'3	195	115	137	.456	5	407	310	87	2156	2274	595	1140	9	3.72	673	59	0	.088
Enyart, Terry-Terry Gene (Earthquake)	74MonN	10-10-50	Ironton, Ohio		R	L	6'2	200	0	0	–	0	2	0	0	2	4	4	2	0	13.50				
Espinosa, Nino-Arnulfo Acevedo	74-75NYN	8-15-53	Villa Altagracia, D.R.		R	R	6'1	180	0	1	.000	0	4	1	0	12	20	1	4	0	8.25	2	1	0	.500
Estelle, Dick-Richard Henry	64-65SFN	1-18-42	Lakewood, N.J.		B	L	6'2	170	1	2	.333	0	12	7	0	53	51	31	29	0	3.23	16	1	0	.063
Estrada, Chuck-Charles Leonard	60-64BalA 66ChiN 67NYN	2-15-38	San Luis Obispo, Cal.		L	R	6'1	185	50	44	.532	2	146	105	24	764	652	416	535	2	4.08	232	30	1	.129
Everitt, Leon-Edward Leon	69SDN	1-12-47	Marshall, Tex.		B	R	6'2	190	0	1	.000	0	5	0	0	16	18	12	11	0	7.88	3	0	0	.000
Face, Roy-Elroy Leon	53,55-68PitN 68DetA 69MonN	2-20-28	Stephentown, N.Y.		B	R	5'8	155	104	95	.523	193	848	27	6	1375	1347	362	877	0	3.48	194	31	0	.160
					Bats Right 53-59																				
Falcone, Pete-Peter	75SFN	10- 1-53	Brooklyn, N.Y.		L	L	6'2	185	12	11	.522	0	34	32	3	190	171	111	131	1	4.17	65	4	0	.062
Fanok, Harry-Harry Michael (The Flame Thrower)	63-64StLN	5-11-40	Whippany, N.J.		B	R	6'	185	2	1	.667	1	16	0	0	35	29	24	35	0	5.14	6	2	0	.333
Farmer, Ed-Edward Joseph (The Raven)	71-73CleA 73DetA 74PhiN	10-18-49	Evergreen Park, Ill.		R	R	6'4	205	12	12	.500	14	143	8	0	233	246	127	139	0	5.06	30	3	0	.100
Farrell, Dick-Richard Joseph (Turk)	56-61PhiN 61LAN 62-67HouN 67-69PhiN	4- 8-34	Boston, Mass.		R	R	6'4	215	106	111	.488	83	590	134	41	1704	1628	468	1177	5	3.45	436	59	4	.135
Fast, Darcy-Darcy Rae	68ChiN 69MS	3-10-47	Dallas, Ore.		L	L	6'3	195	0	1	.000	0	8	1	0	10	8	8	10	0	5.40	3	0	0	.000
Faul, Bill-William Alvan	62-64DetA 65-66ChiN 70SFN	4-21-40	Cincinnati, Ohio		R	R	5'10	184	12	16	.429	2	71	33	8	262	247	95	164	3	4.71	72	7	0	.097
Fife, Dan-Danny Wayne	73-74MinA	10- 5-49	Harrisburg, Ill.		R	R	6'2	190	3	2	.600	0	14	7	1	57	64	33	21	0	5.37				
Figueroa, Ed-Eduardo [Padilla]	74-75CalA	10-14-48	Ciales, P.R.		R	R	6'	195	18	21	.462	0	58	44	21	350	332	120	188	3	3.14				
Fingers, Rollie-Roland Glen	68-75OakA	8-25-46	Steubenville, Ohio		R	R	6'4	190	54	50	.519	116	432	37	4	881	741	253	671	2	2.97	118	23	2	.195
Fischer, Hank-Henry William (Bulldog)	62-65MilN 66AtlN 66CinN 66-67BosA	1-11-40	Yonkers, N.Y.		R	R	6'	190	30	39	.435	7	168	77	14	546	587	174	369	5	4.24	152	18	0	.118
Fisher, Eddie-Eddie Gene	59-61SFN 62-66ChiA 66-67BalA 68CleA 69-72CalA 72-73ChiA 73StLN	7-16-36	Shreveport, La.		R	R	6'2	200	85	70	.548	81	690	63	7	1541	1398	438	812	2	3.40	246	30	0	.122
Fisher, Fritz-Frederick Brown	64DetA	11-28-41	Adrian, Mich.		L	L	6'1	180	0	0	–	0	1	0	0	1	2	2	1	0	108.00				
Fisher, Jack-John Howard (Fat Jack)	59-62BalA 63SFN 64-67NYN 68ChiA 69CinN	3- 4-39	Frostburg, Md.		R	R	6'2	225	86	139	.382	9	400	265	62	1977	2061	605	1017	9	4.06	594	74	1	.125
Fisher, Tom-Thomas Gene	67BalA	4- 4-43	Cleveland, Ohio		R	R	6'	180	0	0	–	0	2	0	0	3	2	2	1	0	0.00				
Fitzmorris, Al-Alan James	69-75KCA	3-21-46	Buffalo, N.Y.		B	R	6'2	190	55	37	.598	7	208	103	27	878	848	303	311	9	3.56	99	24	0	.242
Flanagan, Mike-Michael Kendall	75BalA	12-16-51	Manchester, N.H.		L	L	6'1	185	0	1	.000	0	2	1	0	10	9	6	7	0	2.70				
Flavin, John-John Thomas	64ChiN	5- 7-42	Albany, Cal.		L	L	6'2	208	0	1	.000	0	5	1	0	5	11	3	5	0	12.60				
Fletcher, Tom-Thomas Wayne	62DetA	6-28-42	Elmira, N.Y.		B	L	6'	170	0	0	–	0	1	0	0	2	2	2	1	0	0.00	1	0	0	.000

USE NAME – GIVEN NAMES (NICKNAMES)	TEAM BY YEAR	BIRTH DATE	BIRTH PLACE	DEATH DATE	B	T	HGT	WGT	W	L	PCT	SV	G	GS	CG	IP	H	BB	SO	ShO	ERA	AB	H	HR	BA
Folkers, Rich-Richard Nevin	70NYN 72-74StLN 75SDN	10-17-46	Waterloo, Iowa		L	L	6'2	180	17	19	.472	7	159	24	5	356	342	141	210	0	3.92	73	11	0	.151
Foor, Jim-James Emerson	71-72DetA 73PitN	1-13-49	St. Louis, Mo.		L	L	6'2	185	1	0	1.000	0	13	0	0	6	10	11	5	0	12.00				
Ford, Wenty-Percival Edmund Wentworth	73AtlN	11-25-46	Nassau, Bahamas		R	R	6'	180	1	2	.333	0	4	2	1	16	17	8	4	0	5.63	5	2	0	.400
Forsch, Bob-Robert Herbert	74-75StLN	1-13-50	Sacramento, Cal.		R	R	6'4	200	22	14	.611	0	53	48	12	330	297	104	147	6	2.89	107	31	1	.290
Forsch, Ken-Kenneth Roth	70-75HouN	9-8-46	Sacramento, Cal.		R	R	6'4	205	36	45	.444	16	217	86	16	781	762	261	508	2	3.47	197	19	0	.096
Forster, Terry-Terry Jay	71-75ChiA	1-14-52	Sioux Falls, S.D.		L	L	6'3	210	24	30	.444	74	234	17	4	494	445	217	409	0	3.13	25	12	0	.480
Fosnow, Jerry-Gerald Eugene	64-65MinA	9-21-40	Deshler, Ohio		R	L	6'4	195	3	4	.429	2	36	0	0	58	46	33	44	0	5.59	5	0	0	.000
Foss, Larry-Larry Curtis	61PitN 62NYN	4-18-36	Castleton, Kans.		R	R	6'2	187	1	2	.333	0	8	4	0	27	32	18	12	0	5.33	7	1	0	.143
Foster, Alan-Alan Benton	67-70LAN 71-72CleA 73-74StLN 75SDN	12-8-46	Pasadena, Cal.		R	R	6'	180	45	57	.441	0	191	137	24	941	913	346	470	5	3.78	277	34	0	.123
Foster, Larry-Larry Lynn	63DetA	12-24-37	Lansing, Mich.		L	R	6'	185	0	0	–	0	1	0	0	2	4	1	1	0	13.50				
Foucault, Steve-Steven Raymond (Foucy)	73-75TexA	10-3-49	Duluth, Minn.		L	R	6'	210	18	17	.514	30	160	0	0	307	273	126	190	0	3.20				
Fox, Terry-Terrence Edward	60MilN 61-66DetA 66PhiN	7-31-35	Chicago, Ill.		R	R	6'	175	29	19	.604	59	248	0	0	396	379	124	185	0	3.00	65	8	0	.123
Frailing, Ken-Kenneth Douglas	72-73ChiA 74-75ChiN	1-19-48	Marion, Wis.		L	L	6'	187	9	14	.391	2	110	16	1	199	232	77	126	0	4.12	38	9	0	.237
Francis, Earl-Earl Coleman	60-64PitN 65StLN	7-14-36	Slab Fork, W. Va.		R	R	6'2	210	16	23	.410	0	103	52	5	405	398	181	263	1	3.78	122	21	1	.172
Franklin, Jay-John William	71SDN 72JJ	3-16-53	Arlington, Va.		R	R	6'3	200	0	1	.000	0	3	1	0	6	5	4	4	0	6.00	1	0	0	.000
Freeman, Jimmy-Jimmy Lee	72-73AtlN	6-29-51	Carlsbad, N.M.		L	L	6'4	180	2	4	.333	1	19	11	1	73	90	47	38	0	6.90	26	3	0	.115
Freisleben, Dave-David James	74-75SDN	10-30-51	Coraopolis, Pa.		R	R	6'	200	14	28	.333	0	69	58	10	393	400	194	207	3	3.94	112	15	0	.134
Frisella, Danny-Daniel Vincent	67-72NYN 73-74AtlN 75SDN	3-4-46	San Francisco, Cal.		L	R	6'	190	29	38	.433	47	301	17	0	529	480	239	417	0	3.40	77	14	0	.182
Fryman, Woody-Woodrow Thompson	66-67PitN 68-72PhiN 72-74DetA 75MonN	4-15-40	Ewing, Ky.		R	L	6'3	200	92	106	.465	8	336	252	60	1717	1684	602	1151	22	3.83	442	61	2	.138
Fuentes, Mickey-Miguel [Pinet]	69SeaA	5-10-49	Loiza Aldea, P.R.	12-9-70	R	R	6'	160	1	3	.250	0	8	4	1	26	29	16	14	0	5.19	6	2	0	.333
Funk, Frank-Franklin Ray	60-62CleA 63MilN	8-30-35	Washington, D.C.		R	R	6'	180	20	17	.541	18	137	0	0	249	210	85	150	0	3.00	45	3	0	.067
Gabler, John-John Richard (Gabe)	59-60NYA 61WasA	10-2-30	Kansas City, Mo.		B	R	6'2	170	7	12	.368	5	53	14	0	164	171	79	63	0	4.39	42	6	0	.143
Gallagher, Doug-Douglas Eugene	62DetA	2-21-40	Fremont, Ohio		R	L	6'3	205	0	4	.000	1	9	2	0	25	31	15	14	0	4.68	6	2	0	.333
Garber, Gene-Henry Eugene	69-70,72PitN 73-74KCA 74-75PhiN	11-13-47	Elizabethtown, Pa.		R	R	5'10	175	24	26	.480	30	191	8	4	372	377	134	183	0	3.90	20	4	0	.200
Garcia, Ralph-Ralph	72,74SDN	12-14-48	Los Angeles, Cal.		R	R	6'1	195	0	0	–	0	11	0	0	15	19	10	12	0	4.80				
Gardner, Rob-Richard Frank	65-66NYN 67ChiN 68CleA 70NYA 71OakA	12-19-44	Binghamton, N.Y.		R	L	6'1	180	14	18	.438	2	109	42	4	332	345	133	193	0	4.34	87	12	0	.138
	71-72NYA 73OakA 73MilA																								
Garibaldi, Bob-Robert Ray	62-63,66,69SFN	3-3-42	Stockton, Cal.		L	R	6'4	210	0	2	.000	2	15	1	0	26	28	11	14	0	3.12	4	0	0	.000
Garland, Wayne-Marcus Wayne	73-75BalA	10-26-50	Nashville, Tenn.		R	R	6'1	212	7	11	.389	5	53	8	0	194	162	64	96	0	3.39				
Garman, Mike-Michael Douglas	69,71-73BosA 74-75StLN	9-16-49	Caldwell, Idaho		R	R	6'3	210	12	12	.500	16	150	6	0	217	203	101	119	0	3.15	23	5	0	.217
Garrett, Greg-Gregory	70CalA 71CinN	3-12-47	Atascadero, Cal.		B	L	6'	210	5	7	.417	0	34	8	0	84	55	54	55	0	2.46	18	2	0	.111
Gatewood, Aubrey-Aubrey Lee	63-64LAA 65CalA 70AtlN	11-17-38	Little Rock, Ark.		R	R	6'1	170	8	9	.471	0	68	13	1	178	166	67	75	0	2.78	42	5	0	.119
Gebhard, Bob-Robert Henry	71-72MinA 74MonN	1-3-43	Lamberton, Minn.		R	R	6'2	210	1	3	.250	1	31	0	0	41	58	24	26	0	5.93				
Geddes, Jim-James Lee	72-73ChiA	3-23-49	Columbus, Ohio		R	R	6'2	200	0	0	–	0	11	2	0	26	26	24	10	0	4.50	1	0	0	.000
Geishert, Vern-Vernon William	69CalA	1-10-46	Madison, Wis.		R	R	6'2	215	1	1	.500	1	11	3	0	31	32	7	18	0	4.65	9	0	0	.000
Gelnar, John-John Richard	64,67PitN 69SeaA 70-71MilA	6-25-43	Granite, Okla.		R	R	6'2	185	7	14	.333	7	111	11	0	230	245	62	126	0	4.19	37	3	0	.081
Gentry, Gary-Gary Edward	69-72NYN 73-75AtlN	10-6-46	Phoenix, Ariz.		R	R	6'1	180	46	49	.484	2	157	138	25	903	770	369	615	8	3.56	285	27	0	.095
Gerard, Jug-David Frederick	62ChiN	8-6-36	New York, N.Y.		R	R	6'2	205	2	3	.400	3	39	0	0	59	67	28	30	0	4.88	8	3	0	.375
Gerberman, George-George Alois	62ChiN	3-8-42	El Campo, Tex.		R	R	6'	180	0	0	–	0	1	1	0	5	3	5	1	0	1.80	1	0	0	.000
Gerhardt, Rusty-Allen Russell	74SDN	8-13-50	Baltimore, Md.		B	L	5'9	174	2	1	.667	1	23	1	0	36	44	17	22	0	7.00	6	1	0	.167
Gibbon, Joe-Joseph Charles	60-65PitN 66-69SFN 69-70PitN 71-72CinN	4-10-35	Hickory, Miss.		R	L	6'4	210	61	65	.484	32	419	127	20	1119	1053	414	743	4	3.52	263	38	0	.144
	72HouN				Bats Both 67-68																				
Gibson, Bob-Robert (Hoot, Gibby)	59-75StLN	11-19-35	Omaha, Neb.		R	R	6'1	190	251	174	.591	6	528	482	255	3885	3379	1336	3117	56	2.91	1328	274	24	.206
Gideon, Jim-James Leslie	75TexA	9-26-53	Taylor, Tex.		R	R	6'4	190	0	0	–	0	1	1	0	6	7	2	5	0	7.50				
Gilbert, Joe-Joe Dennis	72-73MonN	4-20-52	Jasper, Tex.		R	L	6'1	165	1	3	.250	1	43	0	0	62	71	37	42	0	6.82	5	0	0	.000
Gilbreth, Bill-William Freeman	71-72DetA 74CalA	9-3-47	Abilene, Tex.		L	L	6'	190	2	1	.667	0	14	5	2	36	40	26	16	0	6.75	12	2	0	.167
Gilliford, Paul-Paul Gant (Gorilla)	67BalA	1-12-45	Bryn Mawr, Pa.		R	L	5'11	210	0	0	–	0	2	0	0	3	6	1	2	0	12.00				
Gilson, Hal-Harold (Lefty)	68StLN 68HouN	2-9-42	Los Angeles, Cal.		R	L	6'5	195	0	2	.000	2	15	0	0	25	34	12	20	0	5.04	4	0	0	.000
Giusti, Dave-David John	62,64-68HouN 69StLN 70-75PitN	11-27-39	Seneca Falls, N.Y.		R	R	5'11	195	92	84	.523	132	568	133	35	1575	1511	509	1036	9	3.55	406	77	4	.190
Gladding, Fred-Fred Earl	61-67DetA 68-73HouN	6-28-36	Flat Rock, Mich.		L	R	6'1	225	48	34	.585	109	450	1	0	600	566	223	394	0	3.36	63	1	0	.016
Glynn, Ed-Edward Paul	75DetA	6-3-53	Queens, N.Y.		R	R	6'3	180	0	2	.000	0	3	1	0	15	11	8	8	0	4.20				
Gogolewski, Bill-William Joseph (Go-Go)	70-71WasA 72-73TexA 74CleA 75ChiA	10-26-47	Oshkosh, Wis.		L	R	6'4	205	15	24	.385	9	144	44	6	502	496	200	301	1	4.02	79	10	0	.127
Golden, Jim-James Edward	60-61LAN 62-63HouN	3-20-36	Eldon, Mo.		L	R	6'	175	9	13	.409	1	69	20	5	208	233	76	115	2	4.54	60	13	0	.217
Goltz, Dave-David Allan	72-75MinA	6-23-49	Pelican Rapids, Minn.		R	R	6'1	200	33	31	.516	3	107	77	23	612	640	175	320	2	3.69	29	3	0	.103
Gossage, Rick-Richard Michael	72-75ChiA	7-5-51	Colorado Springs, Colo.		R	R	6'3	215	20	19	.513	29	158	8	1	361	320	198	284	0	3.71	16	0	0	.000
Gowell, Larry-Lawrence Clyde	72NYA	5-2-47	Lewiston, Me.		R	R	6'2	190	0	1	.000	0	2	1	0	7	3	2	7	0	1.29	1	1	0	1.000
Graham, Bill-William Albert	66DetA 67NYN	1-21-37	Flemingsburg, Ky.		R	R	6'3	217	1	2	.333	0	6	3	1	29	22	11	16	0	2.48	8	1	0	.125
Gramly, Tommy-Bert Thomas	68CleA	4-19-45	Dallas, Tex.		R	R	6'3	175	0	1	.000	0	3	0	0	3	3	2	1	0	3.00				
Granger, Wayne-Wayne Allan	68StLN 69-71CinN 72MinA 73StLN 73NYA	3-15-44	Springfield, Mass.		R	R	6'2	165	34	35	.493	106	424	0	0	608	600	185	297	0	3.11	65	7	1	.108
	74ChiA 75HouN																								
Grant, Mudcat-James Timothy	58-64CleA 64-67MinA 68LAN 69MonN	8-13-35	Lacoochee, Fla.		R	R	6'1	186	145	119	.549	53	571	293	89	2441	2292	849	1267	18	3.63	759	135	0	.178
	69StLN 70OakA 70-71PitN 71OakA																								
Gray, Dave-David Alexander	64BosA	1-7-43	Ogden, Utah		R	R	6'1	190	0	0	–	0	9	1	0	13	18	20	17	0	9.00	1	1	0	1.000
Grba, Eli-Eli	59-60NYA 61-63LAA	8-9-34	Chicago, Ill.		R	R	6'2	210	28	33	.459	4	135	75	10	536	513	284	255	0	4.48	160	35	4	.219
Green, Dallas-George Dallas	60-64PhiN 65WasA 66NYN 67PhiN	8-4-34	Newport, Del.		L	R	6'5	210	20	22	.476	4	185	46	12	562	647	197	268	2	4.26	142	17	0	.120
Gregory, Lee-Grover LeRoy	64ChiN	6-2-38	Bakersfield, Cal.		L	L	6'1	180	0	0	–	0	11	0	0	18	23	5	8	0	3.50	131	1	0	.077
Greif, Bill-William Briley	71HouN 72-75SDN	4-25-50	Fort Stockton, Tex.		R	R	6'5	205	29	59	.330	13	179	92	18	638	660	250	405	5	4.32	154	12	0	.078
Griffin, Tom-Thomas James	69-75HouN	2-22-48	Los Angeles, Cal.		R	R	6'3	210	40	57	.412	3	179	121	24	821	784	404	619	9	4.11	247	45	6	.182
Grilli, Guido-Guido John	66BosA 66KCA	1-9-39	Memphis, Tenn.		L	L	6'	188	0	2	.000	1	22	0	0	20	24	20	12	0	7.20	2	1	0	.500
Grilli, Steve-Stephen Joseph	75DetA	5-2-49	Brooklyn, N.Y.		R	R	6'2	170	0	0	–	0	3	0	0	7	3	6	4	0	1.29				
Grimsley, Ross-Ross Albert Jr.	71-73CinN 74-75BalA	1-7-50	Topeka, Kans.		L	L	6'3	200	65	51	.560	3	169	161	43	1094	1067	284	483	10	3.36	199	19	0	.095
Grzenda, Joe-Joseph Charles	61DetA 64,66KCA 67NYN 69MinA 70-71WasA	6-8-37	Scranton, Pa.		R	L	6'2	180	14	13	.519	14	219	3	0	309	323	120	173	0	3.99	30	2	0	.067
	72StLN																								
Guidry, Ron-Ronald Ames (Gator)	75NYA	8-28-50	Lafayette, La.		L	L	5'11	160	0	1	.000	0	10	1	0	16	15	9	15	0	3.38				
Guinn, Skip-Drannon Eugene	68AtlN 70-71HouN	10-25-44	St. Charles, Mo.		R	L	5'10	180	1	2	.333	1	35	0	0	37	38	27	40	0	5.35	3	0	0	.000
Gullett, Don-Donald Edward	70-75CinN	1-5-51	Lynn, Ky.		R	L	6'	190	80	41	.661	10	213	136	31	1062	903	364	713	13	3.03	338	66	0	.195
Gura, Larry-Lawrence Cyril	70-73ChiN 74-75NYA	11-26-47	Joliet, Ill.		B	L	6'	185	15	16	.484	1	88	38	10	325	358	91	161	2	3.66	27	3	0	.111
					Bats Right -70																				
Guzman, Santiago-Santiago Donovan	69-72StLN	7-25-49	San Pedro de Mac., D.R.		R	R	6'1	180	1	2	.333	0	12	5	1	32	30	18	29	0	4.50	9	2	0	.222
Halicki, Ed-Edward Louis (Big Ed)	74-75SFN	10-4-50	Newark, N.J.		R	R	6'7	228	10	21	.323	0	40	34	9	234	227	90	193	2	3.73	78	12	1	.154
Hall, Dick-Richard Wallace (Turkey Neck)	55-57PitN 58VR 59PitN 60KCA	9-27-30	St. Louis, Mo.		R	R	6'6	205	93	75	.554	68	495	74	20	1259	1152	236	741	3	3.32	(See B 46-60)			
	61-66BalA 67-68PhiN 69-71BalA																								
Hall, Tom-Tom Edward (The Blade)	68-71MinA 72-75CinN 75NYN	11-23-47	Thomasville, N.C.		L	L	6'	158	50	31	.617	31	316	63	7	811	619	353	760	3	3.21	192	31	0	.161
Hambright, Roger-Roger Dee	71NYA	3-26-49	Sunnyside, Wash.		R	R	5'10	180	3	1	.750	3	18	0	0	27	22	10	14	0	4.33	2	1	0	.500
Hamilton, Dave-David Edward	72-75OakA 75ChiA	12-13-47	Seattle, Wash.		L	L	6'1	170	26	21	.553	6	111	48	3	393	377	150	229	1	3.34	26	4	0	.154
Hamilton, Jack-Jack Edwin	62-63PhiN 64-65DetA 66-67NYN 67-68CalA	12-25-38	Burlington, Iowa		R	R	6'	205	32	40	.444	20	218	65	8	612	597	348	357	2	4.53	150	16	1	.107
	69CleA 69ChiA																								
Hamilton, Steve-Steven Absher	61CleA 62-63WasA 63-70NYA 70ChiA 71SFN	11-30-33	Columbia, Ky.		L	L	6'7	200	40	31	.563	42	421	17	3	662	556	214	531	1	3.06	112	14	0	.125
58-60 played in N.B.A.	72ChiN																								
Hamm, Pete-Peter Whitfield	70-71MinA	9-20-47	Buffalo, N.Y.		R	R	6'5	215	2	6	.250	0	23	8	1	60	72	25	19	0	6.43	12	3	0	.250
Hand, Rich-Richard Allen	70-71CleA 72-73TexA 73CalA	7-10-48	Bellevue, Wash.		R	R	6'1	195	24	39	.381	3	104	78	6	488	452	250	278	1	4.00	109	16	0	.147
Handrahan, Vern-James Vernon	64-66KCA	11-27-38	Charlottetown, Canada		R	R	6'2	185	0	2	.000	1	34	2	0	61	53	40	36	0	5.31	12	2	0	.167
Hands, Bill-William Alfred	65SFN 66-72ChiN 73-74MinA 74-75TexA	5-6-40	Hackensack, N.J.		R	R	6'2	195	111	110	.502	14	374	260	72	1951	1896	492	1088	17	3.35	472	37	0	.078
Hanna, Preston-Preston Lee	75AtlN	9-10-54	Pensacola, Fla.		R	R	6'1	195	0	0	–	0	4	0	0	6	7	5	2	0	1.50				
Hannan, Jim-James John	62-70WasA 71DetA 71MilA	1-7-40	Jersey City, N.J.		R	R	6'3	205	41	48	.461	7	276	101	9	822	807	406	438	4	3.88	209	19	0	.091
Hardin, Jim-James Warren	67-71BalA 71NYA 72AtlN	8-6-43	Morris Chapel, Tenn.		R	R	6'	190	43	32	.573	4	164	100	28	752	691	202	408	7	3.18	234	24	3	.103
Hardy, Larry-Howard Lawrence	74-75SDN	1-10-48	Goose Creek, Tex.		R	R	5'11	170	9	4	.692	2	79	1	0	105	137	46	60	0	4.89	10	0	0	.000
Hargan, Steve-Steven Lowell	65-72CleA 74-75TexA	9-8-42	Fort Wayne, Ind.		R	R	6'3	175	77	93	.453	3	291	197	53	1429	1359	621	789	16	3.80	319	42	1	.132
Harrelson, Bill-William Charles	68CalA	11-17-45	Tahlequah, Okla.		B	R	6'5	215	1	6	.143	0	10	5	1	34	28	26	22	0	5.03	10	1	0	.100
Harris, Buddy-Walter Francis	70-71HouN	12-5-48	Philadelphia, Pa.		R	R	6'7	250	1	1	.500	0	22	0	0	37	39	16	23	0	6.32	3	0	0	.000
Harrison, Roric-Roric Edward (Duke)	72BalA 73-75AtlN 75CleA	9-20-46	Los Angeles, Cal.		R	R	6'3	200	30	34	.469	10	131	70	12	578	572	246	312	0	4.17	124	15	6	.121
Harrison, Tom-Thomas James	65KCA	1-18-45	Trail, Canada		R	R	6'3	200	0	0	–	0	1	0	0	1	2	1	0	0	9.00				
Hartenstein, Chuck-Charles Oscar (Twiggy)	65-68ChiN 69-70PitN 70StLN	5-26-42	Seguin, Tex.		R	R	5'11	165	17	17	.500	23	174	0	0	270	277	83	120	0	4.17	37	2	0	.054
	70BosA																								
Hartman, Bob-Robert Louis	59MilN 62CleA	8-28-37	Kenosha, Wis.		R	L	5'11	185	0	1	.000	0	11	2	0	19	20	10	12	0	5.21	7	0	0	.000

					LIFETIME PITCHING TOTALS																	BATTING TOTALS			
USE NAME – GIVEN NAMES (NICKNAMES)	TEAM BY YEAR	BIRTH DATE	BIRTH PLACE	DEATH DATE	B	T	HGT	WGT	W	L	PCT	SV	G	GS	CG	IP	H	BB	SO	ShO	ERA	AB	H	HR	BA
Hassler, Andy-Andrew Earl	71,73-75CalA	10-18-51	Texas City, Tex.		L	L	6'5	200	10	30	.250	1	66	48	17	346	348	166	190	3	4.06	5	0	0	.000
Hausman, Tom-Thomas Matthew	75MilA	3-31-53	Mobridge, S.D.		R	R	6'5	200	3	6	.333	0	29	9	1	112	110	47	46	0	4.10				
Hawkins, Wynn-Wynn Firth (Hawk)	60-62CleA	2-20-36	East Palestine, Ohio		R	R	6'3	195	12	13	.480	1	48	30	4	203	216	99	90	1	4.17	57	6	0	.105
Haydel, Hal-John Harold	70-71MinA	7- 9-44	Houma, La.		R	R	6'	190	6	2	.750	1	35	0	0	49	40	24	33	0	4.04	6	3	1	.500
Haywood, Bill-William Kiernan	68WasA	4-21-37	Colon, Panama		R	R	6'3	205	0	0	–	0	14	0	0	23	27	12	10	0	4.70				
Heaverlo, Dave-David Wallace (Kojak)	75SFN	8-25-50	Ellensburg, Wash.		R	R	6'1	190	3	1	.750	1	42	0	0	64	62	31	35	0	2.39	4	2	0	.500
Hedlund, Mike-Michael David (Red)	65,68CleA 69-62KCA	8-11-46	Dallas, Tex.		R	R	6'1	190	25	24	.510	2	113	62	9	466	440	167	211	1	3.55	138	17	0	.123
					Bats Both 68-69																				
Heffner, Bob-Robert Frederic (Butch)	63-65BosA 66CleA 68CalA	9-13-38	Allentown, Pa.		R	R	6'4	200	1	21	.344	6	114	31	4	354	360	107	241	2	4.50	94	12	1	.128
Heiser, Roy-Leroy Barton	61WasA	6-22-42	Baltimore, Md.		R	R	6'4	190	0	0	–	0	3	0	0	6	6	9	1	0	6.00	2	0	0	.000
Heman, Russ-Russell Frederick	61CleA 61LAA	2-10-33	Olive, Cal.		R	R	6'4	205	0	0	–	1	12	0	0	20	12	10	6	0	2.70	2	0	0	.000
Henderson, Joe-Joseph Lee (Fresno Joe)	74ChiA	7- 4-46	Lake Cormorant, Miss.		L	R	6'2	185	1	0	1.000	0	5	3	0	15	21	11	12	0	8.40	1	0	0	.000
Hendley, Bob-Charles Robert	61-63MilN 64-65SFN 65-67ChiN 67NYN	4-30-39	Macon, Ga.		R	L	6'2	195	48	52	.480	12	216	126	25	879	864	329	522	6	3.97	243	23	1	.095
Hennigan, Phil-Phillip Winston	69-72CleA 73NYN	4-10-46	Jasper, Tex.		R	R	6'	185	17	14	.548	26	176	2	0	280	267	133	188	0	4.27	30	3	0	.100
Henninger, Rick-Richard Lee	73TexA	1-11-48	Hastings, Neb.		R	R	6'7	225	1	0	1.000	0	6	2	0	23	23	11	6	0	2.74				
Henry, Bill-William Francis	66NYA	2-15-42	Long Beach, Cal.		L	L	6'3	195	0	0	–	0	2	0	0	3	0	2	3	0	0.00				
Henry, Bill-William Rodman	52-55BosA 58-59ChiN 60-65CinN 65-68SFN	10-15-27	Alice, Tex.		L	L	6'2	187	46	50	.479	90	527	44	12	914	842	296	619	2	3.26	203	36	0	.177
	68PitN 69HouN																								
Hepler, Bill-William Lewis	66NYN	9-25-45	Covington, Va.		L	L	6'	160	3	3	.500	0	37	3	0	69	71	51	25	0	3.52	14	3	0	.214
Herbel, Ron-Ronald Samuel	63-69SFN 70SDN 70NYN 71AtlN	1-16-38	Denver, Colo.		R	R	6'1	195	42	37	.532	16	331	79	11	895	945	285	447	3	3.82	206	6	0	.029
Hernaiz, Jesus-Jesus Rafael (Chuito)	74PhiN	1- 8-48	Santurce, P.R.		R	R	6'2	175	2	3	.400	1	27	0	0	41	53	25	16	0	5.93	2	0	0	.000
Hernandez, Ramon-Ramon Gonzalez	67AtlN 68ChiN 71-75PitN	8-31-40	Carolina, P.R.		B	L	5'11	180	21	12	.636	41	280	0	0	366	330	109	225	0	2.78	36	5	0	.139
Heydeman, Greg-Gregory George	73LAN	1- 2-52	Carmel, Cal.		R	R	6'2	205	0	0	–	0	1	0	0	2	2	1	1	0	4.50				
Hickman, Jess-Jesse Owens	65-66KCA	2-18-40	Lecompte, La.		R	R	6'2	186	0	1	.000	0	13	0	0	16	9	9	16	0	5.63				
Higgins, Denny-Dennis Dean	66-67ChiA 68-69WasA 70CleA 71-72StLN	8- 4-39	Jefferson City, Mo.		R	R	6'3	190	22	23	.489	46	241	2	0	205	186	134	179	0	3.78	58	9	0	.155
Hilgendorf, Tom-Thomas Eugene	69-70StLN 72-74CleA 75PhiN	3-10-42	Clinton, Iowa		R	L	6'1	187	19	14	.576	12	184	6	2	314	302	127	173	0	3.04	27	5	0	.185
Hill, Garry-Garry Alton	69AtlN	11- 3-46	Rutherfordton, N.C.		R	R	6'2	195	0	1	.000	0	1	1	0	2	6	1	2	0	18.00				
Hiller, John-John Frederick	65-70DetA 71IL 72-75DetA	4- 8-43	Toronto, Canada		R	L	6'1	190	53	43	.552	81	339	34	9	794	642	303	666	5	2.55	100	11	0	.110
Hinsley, Jerry-Jerry Dean	64,67NYN	4- 9-44	Hugo, Okla.		R	R	5'11	165	0	2	.000	0	11	2	0	20	27	11	14	0	7.20	1	0	0	.000
Hinton, Rich-Richard Michael	71ChiA 72NYA 72TexA 75ChiA	5-22-47	Tucson, Ariz.		L	L	6'2	185	5	5	.500	0	45	5	0	89	95	39	62	0	4.45	6	1	0	.167
Hippauf, Herb-Herbert August	66AtlN	5- 9-40	New York, N.Y.		R	L	6'	180	0	1	.000	0	3	0	0	3	6	1	1	0	12.00				
Hobaugh, Ed-Edward Russell	61-63WasA	6-27-34	Kittanning, Pa.		R	R	6'	175	9	10	.474	1	61	21	3	211	228	95	115	0	4.35	55	7	1	.127
Hockenberry, Chuck-Charles Marion	75CalA	12-15-50	LaCrosse, Wis.		B	R	6'1	192	0	5	.000	1	16	4	0	41	48	19	15	0	5.27				
Hoerner, Joe-Joseph Walter	63-64HouN 66-69StLN 70-72PhiN 72-73AtlN	11-12-36	Dubuque, Iowa		R	L	6'1	200	39	30	.565	91	444	0	0	522	469	159	392	0	2.74	59	6	1	.102
	73-74KCA 75PhiN																								
Holdsworth, Fred-Fredrick William	72-74DetA	5-29-52	Detroit, Mich.		R	R	6'1	190	0	5	.000	0	15	9	0	58	66	22	30	0	5.90	3	1	0	.333
Holtgrave, Vern-Lavern George (Woody)	65DetA	10-18-42	Aviston, Ill.		R	R	6'1	183	0	0	–	0	1	0	0	3	4	2	2	0	6.00				
Holtzman, Ken-Kenneth Dale	65-71ChiN 72-75OakA	11- 3-45	St. Louis, Mo.		R	L	6'2	190	151	124	.549	1	348	336	108	2360	2202	719	1438	26	3.28	554	87	2	.157
Hood, Don-Donald Harris	73-74BalA 75CleA	10-16-49	Florence, S.C.		L	L	6'3	192	10	13	.435	2	57	25	3	224	214	83	95	1	4.10				
Hook, Jay-James Wesley	57-61CinN 62-64NYN	11-18-36	Waukegan, Ill.		L	R	6'2	185	29	62	.319	1	160	112	30	754	808	275	394	2	5.22	225	34	0	.151
Hooten, Leon-Michael Leon	74OakA	4- 4-48	Downey, Cal.		R	R	5'11	175	0	0	–	0	6	0	0	8	6	4	1	0	3.38				
Hooton, Burt-Burt Carlton (Night Owl)	71-75ChiN 75LAN	2- 7-50	Greenville, Tex.		R	R	6'1	210	52	51	.505	1	160	122	35	890	861	283	535	11	3.49	272	30	2	.110
Horlen, Joe-Joel Edward	61-71ChiA 72OakA	8-14-37	San Antonio, Tex.		R	R	6'	170	116	117	.498	4	361	290	59	2003	1829	554	1065	18	3.55	618	83	0	.134
Hough, Charlie-Charles Oliver	70-75LAN	1- 5-48	Honolulu, Hawaii		R	R	6'2	195	16	13	.552	12	138	0	0	253	183	135	183	0	3.38	37	6	0	.162
House, Pat-Patrick Lory	67-68HouN	9- 1-40	Boise, Idaho		L	L	6'3	185	2	1	.667	1	24	0	0	20	24	6	8	0	7.20				
House, Tom-Thomas Ross	71-75AtlN	4-29-47	Seattle, Wash.		L	L	5'11	185	18	11	.621	26	185	1	0	279	238	103	160	0	3.06	35	9	0	.257
Howard, Bruce-Bruce Ernest	63-67ChiA 68WasA 68BalA	1- 2-53	Salisbury, Md.		B	R	6'2	180	26	31	.456	1	120	75	7	529	449	239	349	4	3.18	147	17	1	.116
Hrabosky, Al-Alan Thomas (The Mad Hungarian)	70-75StLN	7-21-49	Oakland, Cal.		L	L	5'11	185	26	9	.743	36	196	1	0	269	214	102	242	0	2.34	36	7	0	.194
Hudson, Charlie-Charles	72StLN 73TexA 75CalA	8-18-49	Ada, Okla.		L	L	6'3	190	5	3	.625	1	40	5	1	80	76	42	38	1	5.06				
Hudson, Jesse-Jesse James	69NYN	7-22-48	Mansfield, La.		R	L	6'2	170	0	0	–	0	1	0	0	2	2	2	3	0	4.50				
Hudson, Rex-Rex Haughton	74LAN	8-11-53	Tulsa, Okla.		B	R	5'10	170	0	0	–	0	1	0	0	2	6	0	0	0	22.50				
Hughes, Dick-Richard Henry	66-68StLN 69SA	2-13-38	Stephens, Ark.		R	R	6'3	195	20	9	.690	8	68	34	13	307	221	76	230	4	2.79	98	12	0	.122
Hughes, Jim-James Michael	74-75MinA	7- 2-51	Los Angeles, Cal.		R	R	6'3	190	16	16	.500	0	39	36	13	260	249	131	138	2	3.88				
Humphreys, Bob-Robert William	62DetA 63-64StLN 65ChiN 66-70WasA 70MilA	8-18-35	Covington, Va.		R	R	5'10	170	27	21	.563	20	319	4	0	568	482	219	364	0	3.34	61	8	0	.131
Hunt, Ken-Kenneth Raymond	61CinN	12-14-38	Ogden, Utah		R	R	6'4	200	9	10	.474	0	29	22	4	136	130	66	75	0	3.97	39	7	0	.179
Hunter, Catfish-James Augustus	65-67KCA 68-74OakA 75NYA	4- 8-46	Hertford, N.C.		R	R	6'	195	184	127	.592	1	402	379	146	2784	2327	770	1697	38	3.06	657	149	6	.227
Hunter, Willard-Willard Mitchell	62LAN 62,64NYN	3-18-34	Newark, N.J.		R	L	6'2	180	4	9	.308	5	69	6	1	114	127	47	63	0	5.68	14	4	0	.286
Hutson, Herb-George Herbert	74ChiN	7-17-49	Savannah, Ga.		R	R	6'1	205	0	2	.000	0	20	2	0	29	24	15	22	0	3.41	2	0	0	.000
Ignasiak, Gary-Gary Raymond (Iggy)	73DetA	9- 1-50	Mt. Clemens, Mich.		R	L	5'11	185	0	0	–	0	3	0	0	5	5	3	4	0	3.60				
Jackson, Al-Alvin Neil	59,61PitN 62-65NYN 66-67StLN 68-69NYN 69CinN	12-25-35	Waco, Tex.		L	L	5'10	170	67	99	.404	10	302	184	54	1389	1449	407	738	14	3.98	435	69	1	.159
Jackson, Grant-Grant Dwight (Buck)	65-70PhiN 71-75BalA	9-28-42	Fostoria, Ohio		B	L	6'	190	46	54	.460	39	350	79	15	878	820	320	658	4	3.52	185	23	2	.124
					Bats Left 71-75																				
Jackson, Larry-Lawrence Curtis	55-62StLN 63-66ChiN 66-68PhiN	6- 2-31	Nampa, Idaho		R	R	6'1	190	194	183	.515	20	558	429	149	3262	3206	824	1709	37	3.40	1089	170	2	.156
Jackson, Mike-Michael Warren	70PhiN 71StLN 72-73KCA 73CleA	3-27-46	Paterson, N.J.		L	L	6'3	197	2	3	.400	0	23	3	0	50	57	38	33	0	5.76	7	0	0	.000
Jacquez, Pat-Patrick Thomas (Wahoo)	71ChiA	4-23-47	Stockton, Cal.		R	R	6'	200	0	0	–	0	2	0	0	2	4	2	1	0	4.50	1	0	0	.000
Jaeckel, Paul-Paul Henry (Jake)	64ChiN	4- 1-42	East Los Angeles, Cal.		R	R	5'10	170	1	0	1.000	1	4	0	0	8	4	3	2	0	0.00	1	0	0	.000
James, Jeff-Jeffrey Lynn (Jesse)	68-69PhiN	9-29-41	Indianapolis, Ind.		R	R	6'3	195	6	6	.500	0	35	18	2	148	148	60	104	1	4.50	44	6	0	.136
James, Johnny-John Philip	58,60-61NYA, 61LAA	7-23-33	Bonner's Ferry, Ala.		L	R	5'10	160	5	3	.625	2	66	3	0	119	107	84	73	0	4.76	17	0	0	.000
James, Rick-Richard Lee	67ChiN	10-11-47	Sheffield, Ala.		R	R	6'2	205	0	1	.000	0	3	1	0	5	9	2	2	0	12.60	1	0	0	.000
Janeski, Jerry-Gerard Joseph	70ChiA 71WasA 72TexA	4-18-46	Pasadena, Cal.		R	R	6'4	205	11	23	.324	1	62	46	4	281	330	104	105	1	4.71	82	8	0	.098
Jarvis, Pat-Robert Patrick	66-73AtlN 73MonN	3-18-41	Carlyle, Ill.		R	R	5'10	180	85	73	.538	3	249	169	42	1283	1180	380	755	8	3.58	405	49	0	.121
Jarvis, Ray-Raymond Arnold	69-70BosA	5-10-46	Providence, R.I.		R	R	6'2	198	5	7	.417	1	44	12	2	116	122	57	44	0	4.66	29	2	0	.069
Jaster, Larry-Larry Edward	65-68StLN 69MonN 70,72AtlN	1-13-44	Midland, Mich.		L	L	6'3	190	35	33	.414	3	138	80	15	597	579	178	313	7	3.65	171	29	0	.170
Jay, Joey-Joseph Richard	53-55,57-60MilN 61-66CinN 66AtlN	8-15-35	Middletown, Conn.		B	R	6'4	228	99	91	.521	7	310	203	63	1546	1460	607	999	16	3.77	483	55	2	.114
					Bats Right - 53																				
Jefferson, Jesse-Jesse Harrison	73-75BalA 75ChiA	3- 3-49	Midlothian, Va.		R	R	6'3	195	12	16	.429	0	64	38	4	273	264	186	154	0	4.52				
Jenkins, Ferguson-Ferguson Arthur	65-66PhiN 66-73ChiN 74-75TexA	12-13-43	Chatham, Canada		R	R	6'5	210	191	139	.579	7	426	366	190	2900	2562	590	2202	37	3.17	776	125	13	.161
Jenkins, Jack-Warren Washington	62-63WasA 69LAN	12-22-42	Covington, Va.		R	R	6'2	205	0	3	.000	0	8	3	1	26	28	19	16	0	4.85	7	1	0	.143
Jiminez, Juan-Juan Antonio	74PitN	3- 8-49	La Torre, Dom. Rep.		R	R	6'1	184	0	0	–	0	4	0	0	4	6	2	2	0	6.75				
John, Tommy-Thomas Edward	63-64CleA 65-71ChiA 72-74LAN 75EJ	5-22-43	Terre Haute, Ind.		R	L	6'3	185	114	106	.518	3	355	318	71	2164	1989	633	1273	28	2.97	691	112	4	.162
Johnson, Bart-Clair Barth	69-74ChiA 75XJ	1- 3-50	Torrance, Cal.		R	R	6'5	215	30	30	.500	15	124	61	14	507	461	248	383	3	3.59	93	20	0	.215
Johnson, Bob-Robert Dale	69NYN 70KCA 71-73PitN 74CleA	4-25-43	Aurora, Ill.		L	R	6'4	220	28	32	.467	12	168	76	18	671	620	255	491	2	3.35	154	14	0	.091
Johnson, Dave-David Charles	74-75BalA	10- 4-48	Abilene, Tex.		R	R	6'2	185	2	3	.400	2	17	0	0	24	25	12	10	0	3.38				
Johnson, Jerry-Jerry Michael	68-69PhiN 70StLN 70-72SFN 73CleA 74HouN 75SDN	12- 3-43	Miami, Fla.		R	R	6'3	200	45	44	.506	36	298	38	7	646	649	309	408	2	4.21	119	15	0	.126
Johnson, Jim-James Brian	70SFN	11- 3-45	Muskegon, Mich.		L	L	6'	180	1	0	1.000	0	3	0	0	7	8	5	2	0	7.71	2	0	0	.000
Johnson, Ken-Kenneth Travis	58-61KCA 61CinN 62-65HouN 65MilN	6-16-33	West Palm Beach, Fla.		R	R	6'4	210	91	106	.462	9	334	231	50	1736	1670	413	1042	7	3.46	534	61	2	.114
	66-69AtlN 69NYA 69ChiN 70MonN																								
Johnson, Mike-Michael Norton	74SDN	3- 2-51	Slayton, Minn.		R	R	6'1	190	0	2	.000	0	18	0	0	21	29	15	15	0	4.71				
Johnson, Tom-Thomas Raymond	74-75MinA	4- 2-51	St. Paul, Minn.		R	R	6'1	185	3	2	.600	4	22	0	0	46	44	21	21	0	3.52				
Jones, Gary-Gareth Howell	70-71NYA	6-12-45	Huntington Park, Cal.		L	L	6'	190	0	0	–	0	14	0	0	16	22	8	12	0	7.87	1	0	0	.000
Jones, Odell-Odell	75PitN	1-13-53	Tulare, Cal.		R	R	6'3	175	0	0	–	0	2	0	0	3	1	0	2	0	0.00				
Jones, Randy-Randall Leo	73-75SDN	1-12-50	Fullerton, Cal.		R	L	6'	177	35	40	.467	2	97	89	28	633	588	171	304	8	3.17	194	29	0	.149
Jones, Sherman-Sherman Jarvis (Roadblock)	60SFN 61CinN 62NYN	2-10-35	Winton, N.C.		L	R	6'4	205	2	6	.250	3	48	5	0	110	119	46	53	0	4.75	25	7	0	.280
Jones, Steve-Steven Howell	67ChiA 68WasA 69KCA	4-22-41	Huntington Park, Cal.		L	L	5'10	175	5	7	.417	0	42	3	0	80	74	43	59	0	4.50	13	2	0	.154
Joyce, Dick-Richard Edward	65KCA	11-18-43	Portland, Me.		L	L	6'5	225	0	1	.000	0	5	3	0	13	12	4	7	0	2.77	4	0	0	.000
Joyce, Mike-Michael Lewis	62-63ChiA	2-12-41	Detroit, Mich.		R	R	6'2	193	2	1	.667	2	31	1	0	54	53	22	16	0	4.33	7	3	0	.429
Jurewicz, Mike-Michael Allen	65NYA	9-20-45	Buffalo, N.Y.		B	L	6'3	205	0	0	–	0	2	0	0	2	5	1	2	0	9.00				
Kaat, Jim-James Lee	59-60WasA 61-73MinA 73-75ChiA	11- 7-38	Zeeland, Mich.		L	L	6'4	215	235	187	.557	6	576	520	163	3636	3610	873	2151	28	3.30	1011	193	14	.191
Kaiser, Bob-Robert Thomas (Chisel)	71CleA	4-29-50	Cincinnati, Ohio		B	L	5'10	175	0	0	–	0	5	0	0	6	8	3	4	0	4.50				
Kealey, Steve-Steven William	68-70CalA 71-73ChiA	5-13-47	Torrance, Cal		R	R	6'	195	8	5	.615	11	139	4	1	214	219	69	126	1	4.29	26	3	1	.115
Keegan, Ed-Edward Charles	59PhiN 61KCA 62PhiN	7- 8-39	Camden, N.J.		R	R	6'3	165	0	3	.000	1	13	3	0	23	31	23	11	0	9.00	3	0	0	.000
Kekich, Mike-Michael Dennis	65,68LAN 69-73NYA 73CleA 75TexA	4- 2-45	San Diego, Cal.		R	L	6'2	200	34	47	.420	3	194	110	8	770	785	391	436	1	4.48	209	25	0	.120
Keller, Ron-Ronald Lee	66,68MinA	6- 3-43	Indianapolis, Ind.		R	R	6'2	200	0	1	.000	0	9	1	0	21	25	5	12	0	3.43	2	0	0	.000

USE NAME – GIVEN NAMES (NICKNAMES)	TEAM BY YEAR	BIRTH DATE	BIRTH PLACE	DEATH DATE	LIFETIME PITCHING TOTALS																	BATTING TOTALS			
					B	L	HGT	WGT	W	L	PCT	SV	G	GS	CG	IP	H	BB	SO	ShO	ERA	AB	H	HR	BA
Kelley, Dick-Richard Anthony	64-65MilN 66-68AtlN 69,71SDN	1- 8-40	Brighton, Mass.		R	L	6'	185	18	30	.375	5	188	61	5	520	453	315	369	5	3.39	125	12	0	.096
Kelley, Tom-Thomas Henry	64-67CleA 68EJ 71-73AtlN	1- 5-44	Manchester, Conn		R	R	6'1	190	20	22	.476	0	104	45	9	408	400	207	234	1	3.75	116	11	0	.095
Kelso, Bill-William Eugene	64LAA 66-67CalA 68CinN	2-19-40	Kansas City, Mo.		R	R	6'4	215	12	5	.706	12	119	2	1	201	171	93	162	1	3.13	34	2	0	.059
Kern, Jim-James Lester	74-75CleA	3-15-49	Gladwin, Mich.		R	R	6'6	190	1	3	.250	0	17	10	1	87	76	59	66	0	3.93				
Kester, Rick-Richard Lee	68-70AtlN	7- 7-46	Iola, Kans.		R	R	6'	190	0	0	–	0	21	0	0	40	49	22	31	0	6.08	9	0	0	.000
Kilkenny, Mike-Michael David	69-72DetA 72OakA 72SDN 72-73CleA	4-11-45	Bradford, Canada		R	L	6'3	175	23	18	.561	4	139	54	12	409	387	224	301	4	4.44	114	8	0	.070
Kirby, Clay-Clayton Laws	69-73SDN 74-75CinN	6-25-48	Washington, D.C.		R	R	6'3	175	74	96	.435	0	239	224	42	1471	1349	650	1010	8	3.73	460	46	0	.100
Kirk, Bill-William Partlemore	61KCA	7-19-35	Coatesville, Pa.		L	L	6'	165	0	0	–	0	1	1	0	3	6	1	3	0	12.00				
Kirkwood, Don-Donald Paul (Red)	74-75CalA	9-24-49	Pontiac, Mich.		R	R	6'3	178	6	5	.545	7	47	2	0	91	97	34	53	0	3.56				
Kison, Bruce-Bruce Eugene	71-75PitN	2-18-50	Pasco, Wash.		R	R	6'5	180	39	31	.557	5	130	83	15	612	535	270	348	2	3.31	192	24	0	.125
Klages, Fred-Frederick Albert Anthony	66-67ChiA	10-31-43	Ambridge, Pa.		R	R	6'2	185	5	4	.556	0	14	12	0	61	52	23	23	0	3.25	18	3	0	.167
Klimkowski, Ron-Ronald Bernard	69-70NYA 71OakA 72NYA	3- 1-45	Jersey City, N.J.		R	R	6'2	190	8	12	.400	4	90	6	1	188	155	76	79	1	2.92	33	3	0	.091
Kline, Ron-Ronald Lee	52PitN 53-54MS 55-59PitN 60StLN 61LAA	3- 9-32	Callery, Pa.		R	R	6'3	205	114	144	.442	108	736	203	44	2078	2113	731	989	8	3.86	491	45	0	.092
	61-62DetA 63-66WasA 67MinA 68-69PitN 69SFN 69BosA 70AtlN																								
Kline, Steve-Steven Jack	70-74NYA 71CleA 75EJ	10- 6-47	Wenatchee, Wash.		R	R	6'3	205	43	45	.489	0	113	105	34	729	687	159	243	6	3.17	170	21	0	.124
Knapp, Chris-Robert Christian	75ChiA	9-16-53	Cherry Point, N.C.		R	R	6'4	200	0	0	–	0	2	0	0	2	2	4	3	0	4.50				
Knowles, Darold-Darold Duane	65BalA 66PhiN 67-71WasA 71-74OakA 75ChiN	12- 9-41	Brunswick, Mo.		L	L	6'	185	51	56	.477	118	555	8	1	846	775	371	588	1	3.13	110	13	0	.118
Kobel, Kevin-Kevin Richard	73-74MilA	10- 2-53	Buffalo, N.Y.		R	L	6'1	190	6	15	.286	0	36	25	3	177	175	62	78	2	4.22				
Koch, Alan-Alan Goodman	63-64DetA 64WasA	3-25-38	Decatur, Ala.		R	R	6'4	195	4	11	.267	0	42	15	1	128	137	55	73	0	5.41	35	10	0	.286
Kolstad, Hal-Harold Everette	62-63BosA	6- 1-35	Rice Lake, Wis.		R	R	5'9	190	0	4	.000	2	34	2	0	72	81	41	42	0	6.63	19	1	0	.053
Konieczny, Doug-Douglas James (Dr. Kono)	73-75HouN	9-27-51	Detroit, Mich.		R	R	6'3	216	6	17	.261	0	40	32	4	200	214	103	103	1	4.82	58	8	0	.138
Koonce, Cal-Calvin Lee	62-67ChiN 67-70NYN 70-71BosA	11-18-40	Fayetteville, N.C.		R	R	6'1	190	47	49	.490	24	334	90	9	972	972	368	504	3	3.78	239	24	0	.100
Koosman, Jerry-Jerome Martin	67-75NYN	12-23-42	Appleton, Minn.		R	L	6'2	205	108	92	.540	3	270	250	82	1839	1660	589	1247	22	3.01	566	67	0	.118
Koplitz, Howie-Howard Dean	64-66WasA	5- 4-38	Oshkosh, Wis.		R	R	5'10	190	9	7	.563	1	54	19	2	176	187	80	87	0	4.19	51	6	0	.118
Korince, George-George Eugene (Moose)	66-67DetA	1-10-46	Ottawa, Canada		R	R	6'3	210	1	0	1.000	0	11	0	0	17	11	14	13	0	4.24	1	0	0	.000
Koufax, Sandy-Sanford	56-57BknN 58-66LAN 67RJ	12-30-35	Brooklyn, N.Y.		R	L	6'2	205	167	85	.655	9	397	314	137	2325	1754	817	2396	40	2.76	776	75	2	.097
Kralick, Jack-Jack Francis	61-63MinA 63-67CleA	6- 1-35	Youngstown, Ohio		L	L	6'2	180	67	65	.508	1	235	169	45	1218	1238	318	668	12	3.56	382	62	4	.162
Krausse, Lew-Lewis Bernard Jr.	61,64-67KCA 68-69OakA 70-71MilA	4-25-43	Media, Pa.		R	R	6'1	185	68	91	.428	21	321	167	21	1285	1205	493	721	5	4.00	354	49	6	.138
	72BosA 73StLN 74AtlN																								
Kravec, Ken-Kenneth Peter	75ChiA	7-29-51	Cleveland, Ohio		L	L	6'1	185	0	1	.000	0	2	1	0	4	1	8	1	0	6.75				
Kremmel, Jim-James Louis	73TexA 74ChiN	2- 8-48	Belleville, Ill.		L	L	6'1	185	0	4	.000	0	27	4	0	40	52	24	28	0	6.08	3	0	0	.000
Kreuger, Rick-Richard Allen	75BosA	11- 3-48	Grand Rapids, Mich.		R	L	6'2	185	0	0	–	0	2	0	0	4	3	1	1	0	4.50				
Kreutzer, Frank-Franklin James	62-64ChiA 64-66,69WasA	2- 7-39	Buffalo, N.Y.		R	L	6'1	175	8	18	.308	1	78	32	2	210	194	109	151	1	4.41	51	4	1	.078
Kroll, Gary-Gary Melvin	64PhiN 64-65NYN 66HouN 69CleA	7- 8-41	Culver City, Cal.		R	R	6'6	220	6	7	.462	1	71	13	1	160	147	91	138	0	4.22	32	4	0	.125
Kucek, Jack-John Andrew Charles	74-75ChiA	6- 8-53	Warren, Ohio		R	R	6'2	200	1	4	.200	0	11	7	0	42	57	25	27	0	5.41				
Kunkel, Bill-William Gustave James	61-62KCA 63NYA	7- 7-36	Hoboken, N.J.		R	R	6'1	187	6	6	.500	4	89	2	0	143	153	49	83	0	4.28	14	3	0	.214
Kurosaki, Ryan-Ryan Yoshitomo	75StLN	7- 3-52	Honolulu, Hawaii		R	R	5'10	170	0	0	–	0	7	0	0	13	15	7	6	0	7.62	1	0	0	.000
Kurtz, Hal-Harold James (Bud)	68CleA	8-20-43	Washington, D.C.		R	R	6'3	205	1	0	1.000	1	28	0	0	38	37	15	16	0	5.21	4	0	0	.000
Kutyna, Marty-Marion James	59-60KCA 61-62WasA	11-14-32	Philadelphia, Pa.		R	R	6'	190	14	16	.467	8	159	6	0	290	301	108	110	0	3.88	47	9	0	.191
Lachemann, Marcel-Marcel Ernest	69-71OakA	6-13-41	Los Angeles, Cal.		R	R	6'1	185	7	4	.636	5	70	0	0	101	103	38	55	0	3.48	10	0	0	.000
LaCorte, Frank-Frank Joseph	75AtlN	10-13-51	San Jose, Cal.		R	R	6'1	185	0	3	.000	0	3	2	0	14	13	6	10	0	5.14	5	0	0	.000
LaGrow, Lerrin-Lerrin Harris	70,72-75DetA	7- 8-48	Phoenix, Ariz.		R	R	6'5	230	16	40	.286	5	116	63	18	473	520	181	209	2	4.41	1	0	0	.000
Lamabe, Jack-John Alexander	62PitN 63-65BosA 65HouN 66-67ChiA	10- 3-36	Farmingdale, N.Y.		R	R	6'1	198	33	41	.446	15	285	49	7	710	753	238	434	3	4.25	156	15	1	.096
	67NYN 67StLN 68ChiN																								
Lamb, John-John Andrew	70-71,73PitN	7-20-46	Sharon, Conn.		R	R	6'3	180	0	2	.000	5	47	0	0	66	63	24	36	0	4.09	7	0	0	.000
Lamb, Ray-Raymond Richard	69-70LAN 71-73CleA	12-28-44	Glendale, Cal.		R	R	6'1	170	20	23	.465	4	154	31	3	424	417	174	258	1	3.54	69	4	0	.058
Landis, Bill-William Henry	63KCA 67-69BosA	10- 8-42	Hanford, Cal.		L	L	6'2	178	9	8	.529	4	102	7	0	170	154	91	135	0	4.45	19	0	0	.000
Lang, Chip-Robert David	75MonN	8-21-52	Pittsburgh, Pa.		R	R	6'4	205	0	0	–	0	1	1	0	2	2	3	2	0	9.00				
Lange, Dick-Richard Otto	72-75CalA	9- 1-48	Harbor Beach, Mich.		R	R	5'10	195	9	15	.375	1	70	31	3	277	298	123	137	0	4.45	3	0	0	.000
LaRoche, Dave-David Eugene	70-71CalA 72MinA 73-74ChiN 75CleA	5-14-48	Colorado Springs, Colo.		L	L	6'2	200	28	19	.596	49	311	4	0	445	388	220	363	0	3.50	61	9	0	.148
Lary, Al-Alfred Allen	54-55,62ChiN	9-26-29	Northport, Ala.		R	R	6'3	185	0	1	.000	0	16	4	0	40	45	22	22	0	6.53	8	2	0	.250
Lasher, Fred-Frederick Walter	63MinA 67-70DetA 70CleA 71CalA	8-19-41	Poughkeepsie, N.Y.		R	R	6'3	190	11	13	.458	22	151	1	0	202	179	110	148	0	3.88	32	2	0	.063
Latman, Barry-Arnold Barry	57-59ChiA 60-63CleA 64LAA 65CalA 66-67HouN	5-21-36	Los Angeles, Cal.		R	R	6'3	210	59	68	.465	16	344	134	28	1219	1130	489	829	10	3.91	332	48	2	.145
Lauzerique, George-George Albert	67KCA 68-69OakA 70MilA	7-22-47	Havana, Cuba		R	R	6'1	180	4	8	.333	0	34	14	2	113	110	48	73	0	5.02	33	4	1	.121
Lavelle, Gary-Gary Robert (Pudge)	74-75SFN	1- 3-49	Scranton, Pa.		B	L	6'1	198	6	6	.500	8	75	0	0	99	94	58	63	0	2.82	11	1	0	.091
Law, Ron-Ronald David	69CleA	3-14-46	Hamilton, Canada		R	R	6'1	178	3	4	.429	1	35	1	0	52	68	34	29	0	5.02	7	1	0	.143
Lawson, Steve-Steven George	72TexA	12-28-50	Oakland, Cal.		R	L	6'2	190	0	0	–	1	13	0	0	16	13	10	13	0	2.81	1	1	0	.100
Laxton, Bill-William Harry	70PhiN 71,74SDN	1- 5-48	Camden, N.J.		L	L	6'2	190	0	3	.000	0	51	1	0	75	71	66	65	0	4.32	5	1	0	.200
Lazar, Danny-John Don	68-69ChiA	11-14-43	East Chicago, Ind.		L	L	6'1	190	0	1	.000	0	17	4	0	34	35	15	20	0	5.56	6	0	0	.000
Lee, Bill-William Francis (The Spaceman)	69-75BosA	12-28-46	Burbank, Cal.		L	L	6'3	220	70	46	.603	9	242	113	51	1102	1150	332	474	6	3.41	60	8	1	.133
Lee, Bob-Robert Dean (Horse)	64LAA 65-66CalA 67LAN 67-68CinN	11-26-37	Ottumwa, Iowa		R	R	6'3	235	25	23	.521	63	269	7	0	402	402	190	315	0	2.71	67	7	1	.104
Lee, Don-Donald Edward	57-58DetA 60WasA 61-62MinA 62-64LAA 65CalA	2-26-34	Globe, Ariz.		R	R	6'4	205	40	44	.476	11	244	97	13	828	827	281	467	4	3.61	226	37	1	.164
	65-66HouN 66ChiN																								
Lee, Mike-Michael Randall	60CleA 63LAA	5-19-41	Bell, Cal.		L	L	6'5	220	1	1	.500	0	13	4	0	35	36	25	17	0	3.34	7	0	0	.000
Lehew, Jim-James Anthony	61-62BalA	8-19-37	Baltimore, Md.		R	R	6'	185	0	0	–	0	8	0	0	12	11	3	2	0	1.50	1	0	0	.000
Lemanczyk, Dave-David Lawrence (Mule)	73-75DetA	8-17-50	Syracuse, N.Y.		R	R	6'5	230	4	8	.333	0	49	9	4	190	203	90	119	0	4.36				
Lemaster, Denny-Denver Clayton	62-65MilN 66-67AtlN 68-71HouN 72MonN	2-25-39	Corona, Cal.		R	L	6'1	182	90	105	.462	8	357	249	66	1788	1703	600	1305	14	3.58	552	72	4	.130
LeMay, Dick-Richard Paul	61-62SFN 63ChiN	8-28-38	Cincinnati, Ohio		L	L	6'3	190	3	8	.273	4	45	6	1	107	100	49	69	0	4.21	28	2	0	.071
Lemonds, Dave-David Lee	69ChiN 72ChiA 73AJ	7- 5-48	Charlotte, N.C.		L	L	6'1	180	4	8	.333	0	33	19	0	100	92	43	69	0	2.97	26	3	0	.115
Leon, Max-Maximino [Molino]	73-75AtlN	2- 4-50	Ponta Coza Acula, Mex.		R	R	5'9	158	8	10	.444	9	96	4	2	187	188	56	109	1	3.71	31	7	0	.226
Leonard, Dennis-Dennis Patrick	74-75KCA	5- 8-51	Brooklyn, N.Y.		R	R	6'1	195	15	11	.577	0	37	34	8	234	240	102	153	0	3.92				
Leonhard, Dave-David Paul	67-72BalA	1-22-42	Arlington, Va.		R	R	5'11	170	16	14	.533	5	117	29	7	336	287	150	146	4	3.16	77	12	0	.156
Lerch, Randy-Randy Louis	75PhiN	10- 9-54	Sacramento, Cal.		L	L	6'3	170	0	0	–	0	3	0	0	7	6	1	8	0	6.43				
Lersch, Barry-Barry Lee	69-73PhiN 74StLN	9- 7-44	Denver, Colo.		B	R	6'	175	18	32	.360	6	169	53	9	570	536	172	317	1	3.82	133	15	0	.113
					Bats Left 73-74																				
Leshnock, Don-Donald Lee	72DetA	11-25-46	Youngstown, Ohio		R	L	6'3	195	0	0	–	0	1	0	0	1	2	0	2	0	0.00				
Lewallyn, Dennis-Dennis Dale	75LAN	8-11-53	Pensacola, Fla.		R	R	6'4	200	0	0	–	0	2	0	0	3	1	0	0	0	0.00				
Ley, Terry-Terrence Richard	71NYA	2-21-47	Portland, Ore.		L	L	6'	190	0	0	–	0	6	0	0	9	9	9	7	0	5.00				
Lindblad, Paul-Paul Aaron	65-67KCA 68-71OakA 71WasA 72TexA 73-75OakA	8- 9-41	Chanute, Kans.		L	L	6'1	185	57	52	.523	53	523	30	1	942	881	368	554	1	3.18	133	26	0	.195
Lines, Dick-Richard George	66-67WasA	8-17-38	Montreal, Canada		R	L	6'1	175	7	7	.500	6	107	0	0	169	146	48	103	0	2.82	19	1	0	.053
Linzy, Frank-Frank Alfred	63,65-70SFN 70-71StLN 72-73MilA 74PhiN	9-15-40	Fort Gibson, Okla,		R	R	6'1	195	62	55	.530	111	516	2	0	817	790	282	358	0	2.85	121	18	1	.149
Littell, Mark-Mark Alan (Country)	73,75KCA	1-17-53	Cape Girardeau, Mo.		L	R	6'3	210	2	5	.286	0	15	10	2	62	63	38	35	0	4.94				
Locke, Bobby-Lawrence Donald	59-61CleA 62StLN 62-64PhiN 65CinN	3- 3-34	Rowe's Run, Pa.		R	R	5'11	185	16	15	.516	10	165	23	2	416	432	165	194	2	4.02	98	25	1	.255
	67-68CalA																								
Locke, Ron-Ronald Thomas	64NYN	4- 4-42	Wakefield, R.I.		R	L	5'11	168	1	2	.333	0	25	3	0	41	46	22	17	0	3.51	5	0	0	.000
Locker, Bob-Robert Awtry	65-69ChiA 69SeaA 70MilA 70-72OakA 73ChiN	3-15-38	George, Iowa		B	R	6'3	200	57	39	.594	95	576	0	0	878	776	257	577	0	2.76	95	7	0	.074
	74EJ 75ChiN				Bats Right 65-67																				
Lockwood, Skip-Claude Edward	69SeaA 70-73MilA 74CalA 75NYN	8-17-46	Roslindale, Mass.		R	R	6'1	195	31	63	.330	3	193	105	16	859	809	363	511	5	3.68	(See B 61-75)			
Lolich, Mickey-Michael Stephen (Michigan Fats)	63-75DetA	9-12-40	Portland, Ore.		B	L	6'1	210	207	175	.542	10	508	459	190	3363	3093	1014	2679	39	3.45	758	83	0	.109
Lonborg, Jim-James Reynold	65-71BosA 72MilA 73-75PhiN	4-16-42	Santa Maria, Cal.		R	R	6'5	210	120	112	.517	3	341	288	77	1963	1887	674	1226	13	3.82	620	83	0	.134
Lopez, Aurelio-Aurelio Rios (Yeyo)	74KCA	9-21-48	Tecamachalco, Mexico		R	R	6'	200	0	0	–	0	8	1	0	16	21	10	5	0	5.63				
Lopez, Marcelino-Marcelino Pons (Lito)	63PhiN 65-67CalA 67,69-70BalA	9-23-43	Havana, Cuba		R	L	6'3	205	31	40	.437	2	171	93	14	653	591	317	426	3	3.62	181	31	1	.171
	71MilA 72CleA																								
Lopez, Ramon-Jose Ramon [Hevia]	66CalA	5-26-37	Las Villas, Cuba		R	R	6'	175	0	1	.000	0	4	1	0	7	4	4	2	0	5.14				
Loughlin, Larry-Larry John	67PhiN	8-16-41	Tacoma, Wash.		L	L	6'1	190	0	0	–	0	3	0	0	5	9	4	5	0	16.20	1	1	0	1.000
Loun, Don-Donald Nelson	64WasA	11- 9-40	Frederick, Md.		R	L	6'2	185	1	1	.500	0	2	2	1	13	13	3	3	1	2.08	4	0	0	.000
Lovrich, Pete-Peter	63KCA 64-65MS	10-16-42	Blue Island, Ill.		R	R	6'4	200	1	1	.500	0	20	1	0	21	25	10	16	0	7.71				
Luebber, Steven-Stephen Lee	71-72MinA	7- 9-49	Clinton, Mo.		R	R	6'3	195	2	5	.286	1	20	12	0	70	76	39	36	0	4.89	19	1	0	.053
Luebke, Dick-Richard Raymond	62BalA	4- 8-35	Chicago, Ill.	12- 4-74	R	L	6'4	200	0	1	.000	0	10	0	0	13	12	6	7	0	2.77				
Lyle, Sparky-Albert Walter	67-71BosA 72-75NYA	7-22-44	DuBois, Pa.		L	L	6'1	182	50	41	.549	152	485	0	0	724	628	259	567	0	2.52	71	12	0	.169
Machemehl, Chuck-Charles Walter	71CleA	4-20-47	Brenham, Tex.		R	R	6'4	216	0	2	.000	3	14	0	0	18	16	15	9	0	6.50	2	1	0	.500
MacKenzie, Ken-Kenneth Purvis	60-61MilN 62-63NYN 63StLN 64SFN 65HouN	3-10-34	Gore Bay, Canada		R	L	6'	185	8	10	.444	5	129	1	0	207	231	63	142	0	4.83	36	4	0	.111
MacLeod, Bill-William Daniel	62BosA	5-13-42	Gloucester, Mass.		L	L	6'2	190	0	1	.000	0	2	0	0	2	4	1	2	0	4.50				
Maestri, Hector-Hector Anibal	60WasA 61WasA	4-19-35	Havana, Cuba		R	R	5'10	158	0	1	.000	0	2	1	0	8	7	3	3	0	1.13	1	0	0	.000

USE NAME – GIVEN NAMES (NICKNAMES)	TEAM BY YEAR	BIRTH DATE	BIRTH PLACE	DEATH DATE	B	T	HGT	WGT	W	L	PCT	SV	G	GS	CG	IP	H	BB	SO	ShO	ERA	AB	H	HR	BA
									LIFETIME PITCHING TOTALS													BATTING TOTALS			
Magnuson, Jim-James Robert	70-71ChiA 73NYA	8-18-46	Marinette, Wis.		R	L	6'2	195	2	7	.222	0	36	10	0	102	113	41	40	0	4.59	15	0	0	.000
Magrini, Pete-Peter Alexander	66BosA	6- 8-42	San Francisco, Cal.		R	R	6'	195	0	1	.000	0	3	1	0	7	8	8	3	0	10.29	3	0	0	.000
Mahaffey, Art-Arthur	60-65PhiN 66StLN	6- 4-38	Cincinnati, Ohio		R	R	6'2	200	59	64	.480	1	185	148	46	998	959	368	639	9	4.18	313	42	3	.134
Makowski, Tom-Thomas Anthony	75DetA	12-22-50	Buffalo, N.Y.		R	L	5'11	185	0	0	–	0	3	0	0	9	10	3	9	0	5.00				
Maloney, Jim-James William	60-70CinN 71CalA	6- 2-40	Fresno, Cal.		L	R	6'2	200	134	84	.615	4	302	262	74	1849	1518	810	1605	30	3.19	628	126	7	.201
Manning, Jim-James Benjamin	62MinA	7-21-43	L'Anse, Mich.		R	R	6'1	185	0	0	–	0	5	1	0	7	14	1	3	0	5.14	1	0	0	.000
Maranda, Georges-Georges Henri	60SFN 62MinA	1-15-32	Levis, Canada		R	R	6'2	195	2	7	.222	0	49	8	0	124	119	65	64	0	4.50	28	6	0	.214
Marentette, Leo-Leo John	65DetA 69MonN	2-18-41	Detroit, Mich.		R	R	6'2	200	0	0	–	0	5	0	0	8	10	2	7	0	4.50	1	0	0	.000
Marichal, Juan-Juan Antonio [Sanchez]	60-73SFN 74BosA 75LAN	10-20-37	Laguna Verde, D.R.		R	R	6'	190	243	142	.631	2	471	457	244	3506	3153	709	2303	52	2.89	1231	202	4	.164
Marone, Lou-Louis Stephen	69-70PitN	12- 3-45	San Diego, Cal.		R	L	5'10	185	1	1	.500	0	30	0	0	37	26	13	25	0	2.68				
Marshall, Mike-Michael Grant	67DetA 69SeaA 70HouN 70-73MonN 74-75LAN	1-15-43	Adrian, Mich.		R	R	5'10	180	64	74	.464	119	471	19	3	940	848	355	642	1	3.04	171	33	1	.193
Martinez, Tippy-Felix Anthony	74-75NYA	5-31-50	La Junta, Colo.		L	L	5'10	175	1	2	.333	8	33	2	0	50	41	41	30	0	3.06				
Matlack, Jon-Jonathan Trumpour	70-75NYN	1-19-50	West Chester, Pa.		L	L	6'3	200	58	56	.509	0	142	138	44	1017	921	319	747	17	2.87	303	37	0	.122
Maxie, Larry-Larry Hans	69AtlN	10-10-40	Upland, Cal.		R	R	6'4	220	0	0	–	0	2	0	0	3	1	1	1	0	3.00				
May, Rudy-Rudolph	65CalA 66-67SA 69-74CalA 74-75NYA	7-18-44	Coffeyville, Kans.		L	L	6'2	205	73	92	.442	5	279	216	56	1464	1225	631	1079	15	3.47	278	33	0	.119
McAnally, Ernie-Ernest Lee	71-74MonN	8-15-46	Mt. Pleasant, Tex.		R	R	6'1	195	30	49	.380	0	112	97	21	624	599	268	351	6	4.02	204	27	1	.132
McAndrew, Jim-James Clement	68-73NYN 74SDN	1-11-44	Lost Nation, Iowa		R	R	6'2	185	37	53	.411	4	161	110	20	771	712	213	424	6	3.65	201	20	0	.100
McBean, Al-Alvin O'Neal	61-68PitN 69SDN 69-70LAN 70PitN	5-15-38	Charlotte Amalie, V.I.		R	R	5'11	175	67	50	.573	63	409	76	22	1072	1058	365	575	5	3.13	264	52	3	.197
McBride, Ken-Kenneth Faye	59-60ChiA 61-64LAA 65CalA	8-12-35	Huntsville, Ala.		R	R	6'1	195	40	50	.444	3	151	122	28	808	717	363	503	7	3.79	264	38	1	.144
McClain, Joe-Joe Fred	61-62WasA	5- 5-33	Johnson City, Tenn.		R	R	6'	183	8	22	.267	1	43	33	7	236	254	59	82	2	4.42	75	15	0	.200
McCLure, Bob-Robert Craig (Mac)	75KCA	4-29-53	Oakland, Cal.		B	L	5'11	170	1	0	1.000	1	12	0	0	15	4	14	15	0	0.00				
McCool, Billy-William John	64-68CinN 69SDN 70StLN	7-14-44	Batesville, Ind.		R	L	6'2	200	32	42	.432	58	292	20	0	528	447	272	471	0	3.60	101	7	0	.069
McCormick, Mike-Michael Francis	56-57NYN 58-62SFN 63-64BalA 65-66WasA 67-70SFN 70NYA 71KCA	9-29-38	Pasadena, Cal.		L	L	6'2	195	134	128	.511	12	484	333	91	2381	2281	795	1321	33	3.73	738	115	7	.156
McDaniel, Lindy-Lyndall Dale	55-62StLN 63-65ChiN 66-68SFN 68-73NYA 74-75KCA	12-13-35	Hollis, Okla.		R	R	6'3	195	141	119	.542	172	987	74	18	2140	2099	623	1361	2	3.45	376	56	3	.149
McDowell, Sam-Samuel Edward Thomas (Sudden Sam)	61-71CleA 72-73SFN 73-74NYA 75PitN	9-21-42	Pittsburgh, Pa.		L	L	6'5	215	141	134	.513	14	425	346	103	2492	1948	1312	2453	23	[illegible]	774	119	[illegible]	.154
McEnaney, Will-William Henry	74-75CinN	2-14-52	Springfield, Ohio		L	L	6'	180	7	3	.700	17	94	0	0	118	116	32	61	0	2.90	14	0	0	.000
McGinn, Dan-Daniel Michael	68CinN 69-71MonN 72ChiN	11-29-43	Omaha, Neb.		L	L	6'	200	15	30	.333	10	210	28	4	409	442	225	293	2	5.11	91	15	1	.165
McGlothen, Lynn-Lynn Everratt	72-73BosA 74-75StLN	3-27-50	Monroe, La.		L	R	6'2	185	40	34	.541	0	94	90	21	642	617	253	416	6	3.52	216	32	0	.148
McGlothlin, Jim-James Milton	65-69CalA 70-73CinN 73ChiA	10- 6-43	Los Angeles, Cal.		R	R	6'1	185	67	77	.465	2	256	201	36	1300	1247	418	544	8	3.61	380	48	3	.126
McGraw, Tug-Frank Edwin	65-67,69-73NYN 75PhiN	8-30-44	Martinez, Cal.		R	L	6'	180	56	61	.477	100	417	36	5	896	769	386	673	1	3.14	170	29	1	.171
					Bats Both part of 73																				
McIntosh, Joe-Joseph Anthony	74-75SDN	8- 4-51	Billings, Mont.		B	R	6'2	190	8	19	.296	0	47	33	4	220	231	77	93	1	3.68	58	9	0	.155
McKee, Jim-James Marion	72-73PitN	2- 1-47	Columbus, Ohio		R	R	6'7	230	1	1	.500	0	17	1	0	32	33	18	17	0	4.78	4	0	0	.000
McLain, Denny-Dennis Dale	63-70DetA 71WasA 72OakA 72AtlN	3-29-44	Chicago, Ill.		R	R	6'1	185	131	91	.590	2	280	264	105	1809	1646	548	1282	29	3.54	617	82	1	.133
McMahon, Don-Donald John	57-62MilN 62-63HouN 64-66CleA 66-67BosA 67-68ChiA 68-69DetA 69-74SFN	1- 4-30	Brooklyn, N.Y.		R	R	6'2	215	90	68	.570	153	874	2	0	1312	1054	579	1003	0	2.97	168	23	0	.137
McNally, Dave-David Arthur	62-74BalA 75MonN	10-31-42	Billings, Mont.		R	L	5'11	195	184	119	.607	2	424	396	120	2730	2488	826	1512	33	3.24	731	97	9	.133
McQueen, Mike-Michael Robert	69-72AtlN 73BP 74CinN	8-30-50	Oklahoma City, Okla.		L	L	6'	188	5	11	.313	3	73	19	2	218	212	112	140	0	4.67	63	13	0	.206
McRae-Norm-Norman	69-70DetA	9-26-47	Elizabeth, N.J.		R	R	6'2	200	0	0	–	0	22	0	0	34	28	26	19	0	3.18	1	0	0	.000
Medich, Doc-George Francis	72-75NYA	12- 9-48	Aliquippa, Pa.		R	R	6'5	225	49	40	.551	0	111	108	43	787	765	239	431	9	3.40				
Meeler, Phil-Charles Phillip	72DetA	7- 3-48	South Boston, Va.		R	R	6'5	225	0	1	.000	0	7	0	0	8	10	7	5	0	4.50	2	0	0	.000
Merritt, Jim-James Joseph	65-68MinA 69-72CinN 73-75TexA	12- 3-43	Altadena, Cal.		L	L	6'2	180	81	96	.458	7	297	192	56	1484	1468	322	932	9	3.65	397	56	4	.141
Messersmith, Andy-John Alexander	68-72CalA 73-75LAN	8- 6-45	Toms River, N.J.		R	R	6'1	200	112	77	.593	14	282	235	84	1837	1373	609	1379	24	2.65	606	106	4	.175
Metcalf, Tom-Thomas John	63NYA	7-16-40	Amherst, Wis.		R	R	6'2	174	1	0	1.000	0	8	0	0	13	12	3	3	0	2.77				
Metzger, Butch-Clarence Edward	74SFN 75SDN	5-23-52	Lafayette, Ind.		R	R	6'1	185	2	0	1.000	0	14	0	0	18	17	16	11	0	4.50				
Meyer, Bob-Robert Bernard	64NYA 64LAA 64KCA 69SeaA 70MilA	8- 4-39	Toledo, Ohio		R	L	6'2	185	2	12	.143	0	38	18	3	129	142	80	92	0	4.40	35	2	0	.057
Mikkelsen, Pete-Peter James	64-65NYA 66-67PitN 67-68ChiN 68StLN 69-72LAN	10-25-39	Staten Island, N.Y.		R	R	6'2	210	45	40	.529	49	364	3	0	653	576	250	436	0	3.38	83	11	0	.133
Miles, Jim-James Charlie	68-69WasA	8- 8-43	Grenada, Miss.		R	R	6'2	210	0	1	.000	0	13	1	0	24	27	17	20	0	7.50	3	1	0	.333
Miller(Gmeinweisser), Bob-Robert Lane	57,59-61StLN 62NYN 63-67LAN 68-69MinA 70CleA 70ChiA 70-71ChiN 71SDN 71-72PitN 73SDN 73DetA 73-74NYN	2-18-39	St. Louis, Mo.		R	R	6'1	190	69	81	.460	52	694	99	7	1552	1487	608	895	0	3.37	299	33	0	.110
Miller, Dyar-Dyar K. (D)	75BalA	5-29-46	Batesville, Ind.		R	R	6'1	195	6	3	.667	8	30	0	0	46	32	33	16	0	2.74				
Miller, John-John Ernest	62-63,65-67BalA	5-30-41	Baltimore, Md.		R	R	6'2	210	12	14	.462	0	46	35	1	227	188	138	178	0	3.89	73	7	0	.096
Miller, Larry-Larry Don	64LAN 65-66NYN	6-19-37	Topeka, Kans.		L	L	6'1	195	5	14	.263	0	48	20	1	145	162	57	93	0	4.72	39	10	0	.256
Miller, Roger-Roger Wesley (Killer)	74MilA	8- 1-54	Connellsville, Pa.		R	R	6'2	215	0	0	–	0	2	0	0	2	3	0	2	0	13.50				
Miller, Stu-Stuart Leonard	53-54,56StLN 56PhiN 57NYN 58-62SFN 63-67BalA 68AtlN	12-26-27	Northampton, Mass.		R	R	5'11	165	105	103	.505	154	704	93	24	1694	1522	600	1164	5	3.24	369	49	0	.133
Mills, Dick-Richard Alan	70BosA	1-29-45	Boston, Mass.		R	R	6'3	200	0	0	–	0	2	0	0	4	6	3	3	0	2.25				
Mingori, Steve-Stephen Bernard	70-73CleA 73-75KCA	2-29-44	Kansas City, Mo.		L	L	5'10	170	7	17	.292	20	212	1	0	319	279	148	226	0	2.88	12	2	0	.167
Minshall, Jim-James Edward (Minnie)	74-75PitN	7- 4-47	Covington, Ky.		R	R	6'6	215	0	1	.000	0	6	0	0	5	1	4	5	0	0.00				
Minton, Greg-Gregory Brian	75SFN	7-29-51	Lubbock, Tex.		B	R	6'2	190	1	1	.500	0	4	2	0	17	19	11	6	0	6.88	6	0	0	.000
Mitchell, Craig-Craig Seton	75OakA	4-14-54	Santa Rosa, Cal.		R	R	6'3	190	0	1	.000	0	1	1	0	4	6	2	2	0	11.25				
Mitchell, Paul-Paul Michael	75BalA	8-19-50	Worcester, Mass.		R	R	6'1	195	3	0	1.000	0	11	4	1	57	41	19	31	0	3.63				
Moeller, Joe-Joseph Douglas	62,64-71LAN	2-15-43	Blue Island, Ill.		R	R	6'5	192	26	36	.419	7	166	74	4	583	596	176	307	1	4.01	155	20	0	.129
Moeller, Ron-Ronald Ralph (The Kid)	56,58BalA 61LAA 62MS 63LAA 63WasA	10-13-38	Cincinnati, Ohio		L	L	6'	180	6	9	.400	0	52	22	1	153	174	100	104	1	5.76	39	8	0	.205
Moffitt, Randy-Randall James	72-75SFN	10-13-48	Long Beach, Cal.		R	R	6'2	190	14	21	.400	44	216	1	0	347	330	122	190	0	3.61	55	9	0	.164
Moloney, Rich-Richard Henry	70ChiA	6- 7-50	Brookline, Mass.		R	R	6'3	195	0	0	–	0	1	0	0	1	2	0	1	0	0.00				
Monbouquette, Bill-William Charles (Monbo)	58-65BosA 66-67DetA 67-68NYA 68SFN	8-11-36	Medford, Mass.		R	R	5'11	195	114	112	.504	3	343	263	78	1962	1995	462	1122	18	3.68	582	60	0	.103
Monge, Sid-Isidro Pedroza	75CalA	4-11-51	Agua Prieta, Mexico		B	L	6'2	185	0	2	.000	0	4	2	2	24	22	17	10	0	4.13				
Montague, John-John Evans	73-75MonN 75PhiN	9-12-47	Newport News, Va.		R	R	6'2	205	3	5	.375	5	65	1	0	114	112	49	60	0	3.79	12	1	0	.083
Monteagudo, Aurelio-Aurelio Faustino [Cintra]	63-66KCA 66HouN 67ChiA 70KCA 73CalA	11-19-43	Caibarien, Cuba		R	R	5'11	185	3	7	.300	4	72	7	0	131	122	62	58	0	5.08	10	2	0	.200
Montefusco, John-John Joseph (Count)	74-75SFN	5-25-50	Long Branch, N.J.		R	R	6'	180	18	11	.621	0	42	39	11	283	251	99	249	5	3.15	94	11	1	.117
Montejo, Manny-Manuel (Pete)	61DetA	10-16-36	Havana, Cuba		R	R	5'11	166	0	0	–	0	12	0	0	16	13	6	15	0	3.94				
Montgomery, Monty-Monty Bryson	71-72KCA	9- 1-46	Albermarle, N.C.		R	R	6'3	205	6	3	.667	0	12	10	1	77	71	20	36	1	2.81	24	3	0	.125
Moore, Balor-Balor Lilbon (Butch)	70,72-74MonN	1-25-51	Smithville, Tex.		L	L	6'2	185	16	29	.356	0	71	58	9	348	300	191	334	4	4.11	113	12	0	.106
Moore, Barry-Robert Barry	65-69WasA 70CleA 70ChiA	4- 3-43	Statesville, N.C.		L	L	6'1	190	26	37	.413	3	140	99	8	600	577	300	278	1	4.15	179	27	0	.151
Moore, Donnie-Donnie Ray	75ChiN	2-13-54	Lubbock, Tex.		L	R	6'	170	0	0	–	0	4	1	0	9	12	4	8	0	4.00	3	0	0	.000
Moore, Tommy-Tommy Joe	72-73NYN 75StLN 75TexA	7- 7-48	Lynwood, Cal.		R	R	5'11	180	0	3	.000	0	27	2	0	55	64	28	27	0	5.73	5	2	0	.400
Moorhead, Bob-Charles Robert	62,65NYN	1-23-38	Chambersburg, Pa.		R	R	6'1	208	0	3	.000	0	47	7	0	119	134	47	68	0	4.54	22	1	0	.045
Moose, Bob-Robert Ralph	67-75PitN	10- 9-47	Export, Pa.		R	R	6'	200	73	62	.541	9	236	158	35	1217	1208	355	789	13	3.48	385	53	0	.138
Moran, Bill-Carl William (Bugs)	74ChiA	9-26-50	Portsmouth, Va.		R	R	6'4	210	1	3	.250	0	15	5	0	46	57	23	17	0	4.70				
Morehead, Dave-David Michael (Moe)	67-68BosA 69-70KCA	9- 5-42	San Diego, Cal.		R	R	6'1	195	40	64	.385	1	177	134	19	821	730	463	627	6	4.14	244	31	0	.127
Moret, Roger-Rogelio [Torres]	70-75BosA	9-16-49	Guayama, P.R.		B	L	6'4	170	41	18	.695	6	116	60	23	558	490	272	334	5	3.44	27	2	0	.074
Morlan, John-John Glen	73-74PitN	11-12-47	Columbus, Ohio		R	R	5'11	185	2	5	.286	0	49	7	1	106	96	71	61	0	4.16	18	2	0	.111
Morris, Danny-Danny Walker	68-69MinA	6-11-46	Greenville, Ky.		R	R	6'1	200	0	2	.000	0	6	3	0	16	16	8	7	0	2.81	3	0	0	.000
Morris, John-John Wallace	66PhiN 68BalA 69SeaA 70-71MilA 72-74SFN	8-23-41	Lewes, Del.		R	L	6'2	200	11	7	.611	2	132	10	2	233	227	86	137	0	3.94	31	6	0	.194
Morton, Carl-Carl Wendle	69-72MonN 73-75AtlN	1-18-44	Kansas City, Mo.		R	R	6'	200	83	83	.500	1	229	218	50	1509	1581	520	608	12	3.69	506	78	7	.154
Mudrock, Phil-Philip Ray	63ChiN	6-12-37	Louisville, Colo.		R	R	6'2	198	0	0	–	0	1	0	0	1	2	0	0	0	9.00				
Muniz, Manny-Manuel [Rodriquez]	71PhiN	12-31-47	Caguas, P.R.		R	R	5'11	175	0	1	.000	0	5	0	0	10	9	8	6	0	7.20	1	0	0	.000
Murakami, Masanori-Masanori	64-65SFN 66JL	5- 6-44	Otsuki, Japan		L	L	6'	180	5	1	.833	9	54	1	0	89	65	23	100	0	3.44	16	2	0	.125
Murphy, Danny-Daniel Francis	69-70ChiA	8-23-42	Beverly, Mass.		L	R	5'11	185	4	4	.500	9	68	0	0	112	110	59	58	0	4.66	(See B 61-75)			
Murphy, Tom-Thomas Andrew	68-72CalA 72KCA 73StLN 74-75MilA	12-30-45	Cleveland, Ohio		R	R	6'3	205	55	82	.401	41	292	146	22	1149	1092	384	501	3	3.63	289	42	0	.145
Murray, Dale-Dale Albert (Spud, Tex)	74-75MonN	2- 2-50	Cuero, Tex.		R	R	6'4	205	16	9	.640	19	95	0	0	181	180	62	74	0	2.83	24	3	0	.125
Musgraves, Dennis-Dennis Eugene	65NYN	12-25-43	Indianapolis, Ind.		R	R	6'4	188	0	0	–	0	5	1	0	16	11	7	11	0	0.56	2	0	0	.000
Nagy, Mike-Michael Timothy	69-72BosA 73StLN 74HouN	3-25-48	Bronx, N.Y.		R	R	6'3	195	20	13	.606	0	87	62	11	420	431	210	170	1	4.14	133	18	0	.135
Narum, Buster-Leslie Ferdinand	64-67WasA	11-16-40	Philadelphia, Pa.		R	R	6'1	194	14	27	.341	0	96	58	9	397	298	177	220	2	4.44	118	7	3	.059
Nash, Jim-James Edwin (Jumbo)	66-67KCA 68-69OakA 70-72AtlN 72PhiN	2- 9-45	Hawthorne, Nev.		R	R	6'5	225	68	64	.515	4	201	177	36	1107	1050	401	771	11	3.59	375	38	4	.101
Navarro, Julio-Julio [Ventura] (Whiplash)	62-64LAA 64-66DetA 70AtlN	1- 9-36	Vieques, P.R.		R	R	6'	190	7	9	.438	17	130	1	0	211	191	70	151	0	3.67	34	5	0	.147
Neibauer, Gary-Gary Wayne	69-72AtlN 72PhiN 73AtlN	10-29-44	Billings, Mont.		R	R	6'3	200	4	8	.333	1	75	4	0	149	135	87	81	0	4.77	29	2	1	.069
Nelson, Jim-James Lorin	70-71PitN	7- 4-47	Birmingham, Ala.		R	R	6'	182	6	4	.600	0	32	12	1	103	91	64	53	1	3.06	26	7	0	.269
Nelson, Mel-Melvin Frederick	60StLN 63LAA 65,67MinA 68-69StLN	5-30-36	San Diego, Cal.		R	L	6'	185	4	10	.286	5	93	11	1	174	184	69	98	0	4.40	34	5	0	.147

USE NAME – GIVEN NAMES (NICKNAMES)	TEAM BY YEAR	BIRTH DATE	BIRTH PLACE	DEATH DATE	B	T	HGT	WGT	W	L	PCT	SV	G	GS	CG	IP	H	BB	SO	ShO	ERA	AB	H	HR	BA
									LIFETIME PITCHING TOTALS													BATTING TOTALS			
Nelson, Roger-Roger Eugene (Spider)	67ChiA 68BalA 70-72KCA 73-74CinN	6- 7-44	Altadena, Cal.		R	R	6'3	200	29	32	.475	4	132	77	20	627	512	186	367	7	3.07	180	23	0	.128
Neumeier, Dan-Daniel George	72ChiA	3- 9-48	Shawano, Wis.		R	R	6'5	230	0	0	–	0	3	0	0	3	2	3	0	0	9.00	1	0	0	.000
Newhauser, Don-Donald Louis	72-74BosA	11- 7-47	Miami, Fla.		R	R	6'4	215	4	3	.571	5	42	0	0	53	44	42	37	0	2.38	2	0	0	.000
Newman, Fred-Frederick William	62-64LAA 65-67CalA	2-21-42	Boston, Mass.		R	R	6'3	210	33	39	.458	0	108	93	18	610	589	154	254	4	3.41	183	28	2	.153
Newman, Ray-Raymond Francis	71ChiN 72-73MilA	6-20-45	Evansville, Ind.		L	L	6'5	215	3	3	.500	4	45	0	0	63	53	24	46	0	3.00	7	1	0	.143
Niekro, Joe-Joseph Frankling	67-68ChiN 69SDN 70-72DetA 73-74AtlN 75HouN	11- 7-44	Martins Ferry, Ohio		R	R	6'1	190	64	67	.489	11	285	147	25	1105	1169	339	469	9	3.86	292	46	0	.158
Niekro, Phil-Philip Henry	64-65MilN 66-75AtlN	4- 1-39	Blaine, Ohio		R	R	6'1	180	145	122	.543	27	438	300	131	2492	2135	653	1511	26	2.87	796	127	5	.160
Nieson, Chuck-Charles Bassett	64MinA	9-24-42	Hanford, Cal.		R	R	6'2	185	0	0	–	0	2	0	0	2	1	1	5	0	4.50				
Nippert, Merlin-Merlin Lee	62BosA	9- 1-38	Mangum, Okla.		R	R	6'1	175	0	0	–	0	4	0	0	6	4	4	3	0	4.50				
Nischwitz, Rob-Ronald Lee	61-62DetA 63CleA 65DetA	7- 1-37	Dayton, Ohio		B	L	6'3	205	5	8	.385	6	88	1	0	116	124	48	58	0	4.19	18	5	0	.278
Nolan, Gary-Gary Lynn	67-73CinN 74SJ 75CinN	5-27-48	Herlong, Cal.		R	R	6'3	197	91	57	.615	0	203	200	38	1379	1189	372	894	13	2.88	435	64	1	.147
Nold, Dick-Richard Louis	67WasA	5- 4-43	San Francisco, Cal.		R	R	6'2	190	0	2	.000	0	7	3	0	20	19	13	10	0	4.95	3	0	0	.000
Noriega, John-John Alan	69-70CinN	12-20-43	Ogden, Utah		R	R	6'4	185	0	0	–	0	13	0	0	26	37	13	10	0	7.27	4	1	0	.250
Norman, Fred-Fredie Hubert	62-63KCA 64,66-67ChiN 70LAN 70-71StLN 71-73SDN 73-75CinN	8-20-42	San Antonio, Tex.		L	L	5'8	170	52	57	.477	3	217	140	33	1067	975	468	753	11	3.75	322	40	0	.124
					Bats Both 71-73																				
Norris, Mike-Michael Kevin	75OakA	3-19-55	San Francisco, Cal.		R	R	6'2	175	1	0	1.000	0	4	3	1	17	6	5	8	1	0.00				
Norton, Tom-Thomas John	72MinA	4-26-50	Elyria, Ohio		R	R	6'2	200	0	1	.000	0	21	0	0	32	31	14	22	0	2.81				
Nottebart, Don-Donald Edward	60-62MilN 63-65HouN 66-67CinN 69NYA 69ChiN	1-23-36	West Newton, Mass.		R	R	6'1	195	36	51	.414	21	296	89	16	927	902	283	525	2	3.66	238	32	0	.134
Nunn, Howie-Howard Ralph	59StLN 61-62CinN	10-18-35	Westfield, N.C.		R	R	6'	185	4	3	.571	0	46	0	0	69	73	42	50	0	5.09	10	2	0	.000
Nye, Rich-Richard Raymond	66-69ChiN 70StLN 70MonN	8- 4-44	Oakland, Cal.		L	L	6'4	185	26	31	.456	4	113	63	16	478	472	140	267	1	3.71	158	30	0	.190
Nyman, Jerry-Gerald Smith	68-69ChiA 70SDN	11-23-42	Logan, Utah		L	L	5'10	165	6	7	.462	0	30	19	3	110	104	57	69	1	4.58	33	3	0	.091
O'Brien, Bob-Robert Allen	71LAN	4-23-49	Pittsburgh, Pa.		L	L	5'10	172	2	2	.500	0	14	4	1	42	42	13	15	1	3.00	9	1	0	.111
O'Dell, Billy-William Oliver (Digger)	54BalA 55MS 56-59BalA 60-64SFN 65MilN 66AtlN 66-67PitN	2-10-33	Whitmere, S.C.		B	L	5'11	170	105	100	.512	48	479	199	63	1816	1697	556	1133	13	3.30	528	66	2	.125
Odom, Blue Moon-Johnny Lee	64-67KCA 68-75OakA 75CleA 75AtlN	5-29-45	Macon, Ga.		R	R	6'	178	82	83	.497	1	287	225	40	1479	1331	768	839	15	3.66	405	79	12	.195
O'Donoghue, John-John Eugene	63-65KCA 66-67CleA 68BalA 69SeaA 70MilA 70-71MonN	10- 7-39	Kansas City, Mo.		R	L	6'4	210	39	55	.415	10	257	96	13	751	780	260	377	4	4.07	206	35	3	.170
Olivio, Chi Chi-Federico Emilio [Maldonato]	61,64-65MilN 66AtlN	3-18-28	Guayabin, Dom. Rep.		R	R	6'2	215	7	6	.538	12	96	0	0	141	129	50	98	0	3.96	13	2	0	.154
Olivo, Diomedes-Diomedes Antonio [Maldonato]	60,62PitN 63StLN	1-22-19	Guayabin, Dom. Rep.		L	L	6'1	195	5	6	.455	7	85	1	0	107	112	39	85	0	3.11	17	3	0	.176
Ollom, Jim-James Donald	66-67MinA	7- 8-45	Snohomish, Wash.		L	R	6'4	210	0	1	.000	0	24	3	0	45	39	12	28	0	5.00	7	1	0	.143
O'Riley, Don-Donald Lee	69-70KCA	3-12-45	Topeka, Kans.		R	R	6'3	205	1	1	.500	1	27	2	0	46	58	24	23	0	6.26	6	0	0	.000
Ortega, Phil-Filomeno Coronado	60-64LAN 65-68WasA 69CalA	10- 7-39	Gilbert, Ariz.		R	R	6'2	185	46	62	.426	2	204	141	20	952	884	378	549	9	4.42	253	29	0	.115
Osborn, Danny-Danny Leon (Ozzie)	75ChiA	6-19-46	Springfield, Mo.		R	R	6'2	195	3	0	1.000	0	24	0	0	58	57	38	37	0	4.50				
Osburn, Pat-Larry Pat (Oz)	74CinN 75MilA	5- 4-49	Murray, Ky.		L	L	6'2	190	0	1	.000	0	12	1	0	21	30	13	5	0	6.43	2	0	0	.000
Osinski, Dan-Daniel	62KCA 62-64LAA 65MilN 66-67BosA 69ChiA 70HouN	11-17-33	Chicago, Ill.		R	R	6'1	190	29	28	.509	18	324	21	5	590	556	264	400	2	2.34	98	12	0	.122
Osteen, Claude-Claude Wilson	57,59-61CinN 61-64WasA 65-73LAN 74HouN 74StLN 75ChiA	8- 9-39	Caney Springs, Tenn.		L	L	5'11	170	196	195	.501	1	541	488	140	3460	3471	940	1612	40	3.30	1093	207	8	.189
Osteen, Darrell-Milton Darrell	65-67CinN 70OakA	2-14-43	Oklahoma City, Okla.		R	R	6'1	175	1	4	.200	3	29	1	0	38	47	29	34	0	8.05	5	1	0	.200
O'Toole, Denny-Dennis Joseph	69-73ChiA	3-13-49	Chicago, Ill.		R	R	6'3	195	0	0	–	0	15	0	0	30	43	10	22	0	5.10				
O'Toole, Jim-James Jerome	58-66CinN 67ChiA	1-10-37	Chicago, Ill.		B	L	6'	200	98	84	.538	4	270	238	58	1615	1545	546	1039	8	3.57	538	67	0	.125
Otten, Jim-James Edward	74-75ChiA	7- 1-51	Lewiston, Mont.		R	R	6'2	185	0	1	.000	0	7	1	0	21	26	19	14	0	6.00				
Owens, Jim-James Philip (Bear)	55-56PhiN 57MS 58-62PhiN 63CinN 64-67HouN	1-16-34	Gifford, Pa.		R	R	5'11	195	42	68	.382	21	286	103	21	886	932	340	516	1	4.31	218	22	0	.101
Pactwa, Joe-Joseph Martin (Packy)	75CalA	6- 2-48	Hammond, Ind.		L	L	5'10	185	1	0	1.000	0	4	3	0	16	23	10	3	0	3.94				
Pagan, Dave-David Percy	73-75NYA	9-15-49	Nipawin, Canada		R	R	6'2	180	1	3	.250	1	33	7	1	93	95	42	66	0	4.45				
Palmer, Jim-James Alvin	65-67BalA 68SA 69-75BalA	10-15-45	New York, N.Y.		R	R	6'3	195	152	80	.655	3	307	281	123	2189	1783	769	1372	36	2.63	489	85	3	.174
Palmer, Lowell-Lowell Raymond	69-71PhiN 72StLN 72CleA 74SDN	8-18-47	Sacramento, Cal.		R	R	6'1	195	5	18	.217	0	106	25	2	317	302	202	239	1	5.28	82	10	1	.122
Panther, Jim-James Edward	71OakA 72TexA 73AtlN	3- 1-45	Burlington, Iowa		R	R	6'1	195	7	13	.350	0	85	4	0	131	156	60	66	0	5.22	9	1	0	.111
Papa, John-John Paul	61-62BalA	12- 5-40	Bridgeport, Conn.		R	R	5'11	190	0	0	–	0	3	0	0	2	5	4	3	0	22.50				
Pappas, Milt-Milton Edward	57-65BalA 66-68CinN 68-70AtlN 70-73ChiN	5-11-39	Detroit, Mich.		R	R	6'3	205	209	164	.560	4	520	465	129	3186	3046	858	1728	43	3.40	1073	132	20	.123
Parker, Harry-Harry William	70-71StLN 73-75NYN 75StLN	9-14-47	Highland, Ill.		R	R	6'3	190	15	21	.417	12	121	30	1	308	312	128	167	0	3.94	70	6	0	.086
Parsons, Bill-William Raymond	71-73MilA 74OakA	8-17-48	Riverside, Cal.		R	R	6'6	200	29	36	.446	0	93	82	22	521	473	231	282	2	3.89	139	23	1	.165
Parsons, Tom-Thomas Anthony (Long Tom)	63PitN 64-65NYN	9-13-39	Lakeville, Conn.		R	R	6'7	210	2	13	.133	1	40	14	2	114	135	25	70	1	4.74	27	1	0	.037
Pascual, Camilo-Camilo Alberto [Lus]	54-60WasA 61-66MinA 67-69WasA 69CinN 70LAN 71CleA	1-20-34	Havana, Cuba		R	R	5'11	185	174	170	.506	10	529	404	132	2930	2703	1069	2167	36	3.63	967	198	0	.205
Patterson, Daryl-Daryl Alan	68-71DetA 71OakA 71StLN 74PitN	11-21-43	Coalinga, Cal.		L	R	6'4	192	11	9	.550	11	142	3	0	231	223	119	142	0	4.09	35	0	0	.000
Pattin, Marty-Martin William	68CalA 69SeaA 70-71MilA 72-73BosA 74-75KCA	4- 6-43	Charleston, Ill.		R	R	5'11	180	84	87	.491	9	300	187	53	1507	1426	459	948	13	3.68	309	38	2	.123
Paul, Mike-Michael George	68-71CleA 72-73TexA 73-74ChiN	4-18-45	Detroit, Mich.		L	L	6'	175	27	48	.360	8	228	77	5	627	619	246	452	1	3.92	148	17	0	.115
Pazik, Mike-Michael Joseph	75MinA	1-26-50	Lynn, Mass.		L	L	6'2	190	0	4	.000	0	5	3	0	20	28	10	8	0	8.10				
Pena, Jose-Jose [Gutierrez] (Peluche)	69CinN 70-72LAN	12- 3-42	Ciudad Juarez, Mex.		R	R	6'2	190	7	4	.636	5	61	0	0	112	106	58	82	0	4.98	11	3	0	.273
Pena, Orlando-Orlando Gregorio [Guevara]	58-60CinN 62-65KCA 65-67DetA 67CleA 70PitN 71,73BalA 73-74StLN 74-75CalA	11-17-33	Victoria de las Tunas, Cuba		R	R	5'11	170	56	77	.421	40	427	93	21	1203	1175	352	818	4	3.70	264	36	2	.136
Pentz, Gene-Eugene David (Gino)	75DetA	6-21-53	Johnstown, Pa.		R	R	6'	205	0	4	.000	0	13	0	0	25	27	20	21	0	3.24				
Peraza, Luis-Luis [Rios]	69PhiN	6-17-43	Rio Piedras, P.R.		R	R	5'11	185	0	0	–	0	8	0	0	9	12	2	7	0	6.00	1	0	0	.000
Perkins, Cecil-Cecil Boyce	67NYA	12- 1-40	Baltimore, Md.		R	R	6'	175	0	1	.000	0	2	1	0	5	6	2	1	0	9.00	1	0	0	.000
Perranoski, Ron-Ronald Peter	61-67LAN 68-71MinA 71-72DetA 72LAN 73CalA	4- 1-36	Paterson, N.J.		L	L	6'	185	79	74	.516	179	737	1	0	1176	1097	468	687	0	2.79	167	16	0	.096
Perry, Gaylord-Gaylord Jackson	62-71SFN 72-75CleA 75TexA	9-15-38	Williamston, N.C.		R	R	6'4	210	216	174	.554	11	523	438	236	3610	3136	947	2527	42	2.88	870	115	4	.132
Perry, Jim-James Evan	59-63CleA 63-72MinA 73DetA 74-75CleA 75OakA	10-30-35	Williamston, N.C.		B	R	6'4	200	215	174	.553	10	630	447	109	3287	3127	998	1580	32	3.44	889	117	5	.199
Perzanowski, Stan-Stanley	71,74ChiA 75TexA	8-25-50	East Chicago, Ind.		B	R	6'3	190	3	4	.429	1	19	9	1	74	81	30	33	0	4.26	2	0	0	.000
Peters, Gary-Gary Charles	59-69ChiA 70-72BosA	4-21-37	Grove City, Pa.		L	L	6'2	200	124	103	.546	5	359	286	79	2081	1894	706	1420	23	3.25	807	179	19	.222
Peters, Ray-Raymond James	70MilA	8-27-46	Buffalo, N.Y.		R	R	6'6	220	0	2	.000	0	2	2	0	2	7	5	1	0	31.50				
Peterson, Fritz (Fred Ingels)-Fritz Fred	66-74NYA 74-75CleA	2- 8-42	Chicago, Ill.		B	L	6'	190	132	128	.508	1	342	319	90	2154	2137	409	992	20	3.25	515	82	2	.159
Pfister, Dan-Daniel Albin	61-64KCA	12-20-36	Planifield, N.J.		R	R	6'	187	6	19	.240	1	65	29	2	248	238	142	156	0	4.50	74	12	0	.162
Phillips, Ed-Norman Edwin	70BosA	9-20-44	Ardmore, Okla.		R	R	6'2	198	0	2	.000	0	18	0	0	24	29	10	23	0	5.25	3	0	0	.000
Phoebus, Tom-Thomas Harold	66-70BalA71-72SDN 72ChiN	4- 7-42	Baltimore, Md.		R	R	5'8	185	56	52	.519	6	201	149	29	1030	888	489	725	11	3.33	335	57	2	.171
Piche, Ron-Ronald Jacques	60-63MilN 65CalA 66StLN	5-22-35	Verdun, Canada		R	R	5'11	165	10	16	.385	12	134	11	3	221	216	123	157	0	4.19	42	1	0	.024
Pierce, Tony-Tony Michael	67KCA 68OakA	1-29-46	Brunswick, Ga.		R	L	6'1	190	4	6	.400	8	66	9	0	131	118	40	77	0	3.23	26	0	0	.000
Pina, Horacio-Horacio [Garcia]	68-69CleA 70-71WasA 72TexA 73OakA 74ChiN 74CalA	3-12-45	Matamoros de la Laguna, Mexico		R	R	6'2	177	23	23	.500	38	312	7	0	430	358	216	274	0	3.27	26	5	0	.192
Pitlock, Skip-Lee Patrick	70SFN 74-75ChiA	11- 6-47	Chicago, Ill.		L	L	6'3	190	8	8	.500	1	59	20	1	193	196	103	124	0	4.52	25	2	1	.080
Pizarro, Juan-Juan Ramon [Cordova]	57-60MilN 61-66ChiA 67-68PitN 68-69BosA CleA 69OakA 70-73ChiN 73HouN 74PitN	2- 7-37	Santurce, P.R.		L	L	5'11	185	131	105	.555	28	488	245	79	2035	1807	888	1520	17	3.43	658	133	8	.202
Pleis, Bill-William	61-66MinA	8- 5-37	St. Louis, Mo.		L	L	5'10	175	21	16	.568	13	190	10	1	280	269	126	184	0	4.08	50	8	0	.160
Plodinex, Tim-Timothy Alfred	72StLN	1-27-47	Aliquippa, Pa.		R	R	6'4	200	0	0	–	0	1	0	0	1	3	0	0	0	27.00				
Pole, Dick-Richard Henry	73-75BosA	10-30-50	Trout Creek, Mich.		R	R	6'3	215	8	9	.471	1	45	20	2	190	227	63	98	1	4.69				
Powell, Grover-Grover David	63NYN	10-10-40	Sayre, Pa.		L	L	5'10	175	1	1	.500	0	20	4	1	50	37	32	39	1	2.70	10	2	0	.200
Prall, Willie-Wilfred Anthony	75ChiN	4-20-50	Hackensack, N.J.		L	L	6'3	195	0	2	.000	0	3	3	0	15	21	8	7	0	8.40	4	0	0	.000
Pregenzer, John-John Arthur	63-64SFN	8- 2-35	Burlington, Wis.		R	R	6'5	220	2	0	1.000	1	19	0	0	27	29	19	13	0	5.00				
Priddy, Bob-Robert Simpson	62,64PitN 65-66SFN 67WasA 68-69ChiA 69CalA 69-71AtlN	12-10-39	Pittsburgh, Pa.		R	R	6'1	200	24	38	.387	18	249	29	3	535	518	198	294	0	4.00	95	13	1	.137
Prince, Don-Donald Mark	62ChiN	4- 5-38	Clarkton, N.C.		R	R	6'4	200	0	0	–	0	1	0	0	1	0	1	0	0	0.00				
Puente, Miguel-Miguel Antonio [Aguilar]	70SFN	5- 8-48	San Luis Potosi, Mex.		R	R	6'	165	1	3	.250	0	6	4	1	19	25	11	14	0	8.05	7	0	0	.000
Purdin, John-John Nolan	64-65,68-69LAN	7-16-42	Lynx, Ohio		R	R	6'2	185	6	4	.600	2	58	5	1	111	93	52	68	1	3.89	16	4	0	.250
Queen, Mel-Melvin Douglas	66-69CinN 70-72CalA	3-26-42	Johnson City, N.Y.		L	R	6'1	190	20	17	.541	14	140	33	6	390	336	143	306	2	3.14	(See B 61-75)			
Quintana, Luis-Luis Joaquin	74-75CalA	11-25-51	Vega Baja, P.R.		L	L	6'2	184	0	0	–	0	22	0	0	20	30	20	16	0	4.95				
Quirk, Art-Arthur Lincoln	62BalA 63WasA	4-11-38	Providence, R.I.		R	L	5'11	170	3	2	.600	0	14	8	0	48	59	26	30	0	5.25	11	2	0	.182
Radatz, Dick-Richard Raymond (The Monster)	62-66BosA 66-67CleA 67ChiN 69DetA 69MonN	4- 2-37	Detroit, Mich.		R	R	6'6	235	52	43	.547	122	381	0	0	694	532	296	745	0	3.13	145	19	1	.131
Raffo, Al-Albert Martin	69PhiN	11-27-41	San Francisco, Cal.		R	R	6'5	210	1	3	.250	1	45	0	0	72	81	25	38	0	4.13	6	1	0	.167
Raich, Eric-Eric James (Big E)	75CleA	11- 1-51	Detroit, Mich.		R	R	6'4	220	7	8	.467	0	18	17	2	93	118	31	34	0	5.52				
Rakow, Ed-Edward Charles (Rock)	60LAN 61-63KCA 64-65DetA 67AtlN	5-30-36	Pittsburgh, Pa.		B	R	5'11	178	36	47	.434	5	195	90	20	760	771	304	484	3	4.33	226	19	0	.084
					Bats Right 60-61																				
Ramos, Pedro-Pedro [Guerra]	55-60WasA 61MinA 62-64CleA 64-66NYA 67PhiN 69PitN 69CinN 70WasA	4-28-35	Pinar del Rio, Cuba		B	R	6'	175	117	160	.422	55	582	268	73	2355	2364	724	1305	13	4.08	703	109	15	.155
					Bats Right 55-59																				
Rasmussen, Harry-Harold Ralph	75StLN	3-22-52	Racine, Wis.		R	R	6'3	205	5	5	.500	0	14	13	2	81	86	20	59	1	3.78	26	4	0	.154
Rath, Fred-Frederick Helsher	68-69ChiA	9- 1-43	Little Rock, Ark.		R	R	6'3	200	0	2	.000	0	8	2	0	23	19	11	7	0	4.70	3	0	0	.000
Rau, Doug-Douglas James	72-75LAN	12-15-48	Columbus, Tex.		L	L	6'2	180	34	24	.586	3	112	79	13	553	500	170	347	3	3,37	169	28	0	.166

USE NAME – GIVEN NAMES (NICKNAMES)	TEAM BY YEAR	BIRTH DATE	BIRTH PLACE	DEATH DATE	B	T	HGT	WGT	W	L	PCT	SV	G	GS	CG	IP	H	BB	SO	ShO	ERA	AB	H	HR	BA
							LIFETIME PITCHING TOTALS															BATTING TOTALS			
Rauch, Bob-Robert John	72NYN	6-16-49	Brookings, S.D.		R	R	6'4	205	0	1	.000	1	19	0	0	27	27	21	23	0	5.00	3	0	0	.000
Ray, Jim-James Francis (Sting)	65-66,68-73HouN 74DetA	12- 1-44	Rock Hill, S.C.		R	R	6'1	194	45	30	.600	25	308	20	1	618	541	271	407	0	3.61	117	16	0	.137
Raymond, Claude-Joseph Claude Marc (Frenchy)	59ChiA 61-63MilN 64-67HouN 67-69AtlN 69-71MonN	5- 7-37	St. Jean, Canada		R	R	5'10	180	46	53	.465	83	449	7	2	720	711	225	497	0	3.66	101	11	0	.109
Raziano, Barry-Barry John	73KCA 74CalA	2- 5-47	New Orleans, La.		B	R	5'11	185	1	2	.333	1	15	0	0	22	21	9	9	0	6.14				
Reberger, Frank-Frank Beall (Crane)	68ChiN 69SDN 70-72SFN	6- 7-44	Caldwell, Idaho		L	R	6'5	210	14	15	.483	8	148	37	5	389	404	197	258	0	4.51	100	23	0	.230
Reed, Bob-Robert Edward	69-70DetA	1-12-45	Boston, Mass.		R	R	5'10	175	2	4	.333	2	24	5	0	61	63	22	35	0	4.13	14	2	0	.143
Reed, Howie-Howard Dean	58-60KCA 64-66LAN 66CalA 67HouN 69-71MonN	12-21-36	Dallas, Tex.		R	R	6'1	200	26	29	.473	9	229	35	3	516	510	208	268	1	3.72	91	6	1	.066
Reed, Ron-Ronald Lee 65-67 played in N.B.A.	66-75AtlN 75StLN	11- 2-42	LaPorte, Ind.		R	R	6'6	215	89	96	.481	1	242	227	54	1594	1605	390	877	8	3.69	527	78	0	.148
Regan, Phil-Phillip Raymond (The Vulture)	60-65DetA 66-68LAN 68-72ChiN 72ChiA	4- 6-37	Otsego, Mich.		R	R	6'3	200	96	81	.542	92	551	105	20	1373	1392	447	743	1	3.83	321	49	1	.153
Reniff, Hal-Harold Eugene (Porky)	61-67NYA 67NYN	7- 2-38	Warren, Ohio		R	R	6'	215	21	23	.477	45	276	0	0	470	383	242	314	0	3.27	52	5	0	.096
Renko, Steve-Steven	69-75MonN	2-10-44	Kansas City, Kans.		R	R	6'5	230	68	81	.456	3	233	191	40	1347	1247	621	806	6	3.92	469	106	6	.226
Reuschel, Paul-Paul Richard	75ChiN	1-12-47	Quincy, Ill.		R	R	6'4	230	1	3	.250	5	28	0	0	36	44	13	12	0	3.50	4	0	0	.000
Reuschel, Ricky-Ricky Eugene	72-75ChiN	5-16-49	Quincy, Ill.		R	R	6'3	230	48	52	.480	1	136	129	26	841	879	241	570	9	3.56	280	50	1	.179
Reuss, Jerry-Jerry	69-71StLN 72-73HouN 74-75PitN	6-19-49	St. Louis, Mo.		L	L	6'5	200	81	70	.536	1	198	193	57	1313	1293	540	795	15	3.72	426	58	0	.136
Reynolds, Archie-Archie Edward	68-70ChiN 71CalA 72MilA	1- 3-46	Glendale, Cal.		R	R	6'2	205	0	8	.000	0	36	7	0	81	100	49	47	0	5.78	11	3	0	.273
Reynolds, Bob-Robert Allen	69MonN 71StLN 71MilA 72-75BalA 75DetA 75CleA	1-21-47	Seattle, Wash.		R	R	6'2	205	14	16	.467	21	140	2	0	254	255	82	167	0	3.15	4	0	0	.000
Reynolds, Ken-Kenneth Lee	70-72MinA 73MilA 75StLN	1- 4-47	Trevose, Pa.		L	L	6'	186	7	26	.212	0	84	49	4	342	332	167	179	1	4.29	92	18	0	.196
Rhoden, Rick-Richard Alan	74-75LAN	5-16-53	Boynton Beach, Fla.		R	R	6'3	195	4	3	.571	0	30	11	1	108	99	36	47	0	3.00	30	3	0	.100
Ribant, Dennis-Dennis Joseph	64-66NYN 67PitN 68DetA 68ChiA 69StLN 69CinN	9-20-41	Detroit, Mich.		R	R	5'11	175	24	29	.453	9	149	56	13	519	536	126	241	2	3.87	159	31	0	.195
Richard, J.R.-James Rodney (High Rise)	71-75HouN	3- 7-50	Vienna, La.		R	R	6'8	230	23	16	.590	0	72	55	10	367	317	236	330	2	4.37	130	23	2	.177
Richardson, Gordie-Gordon Clark	64StLN 65-66NYN	7-19-39	Colquitt, Ga.		R	L	6'	185	6	6	.500	4	69	7	1	118	105	37	86	0	4.04	21	1	0	.048
Richert, Pete-Peter Gerard	62-64LAN 65-67WasA 67-71BalA 72-73LAN 74StLN 74PhiN	10-29-39	Floral Park, N.Y.		L	L	6'	180	80	73	.523	51	429	122	22	1166	959	424	925	3	3.19	297	43	1	.145
Riddleberger, Denny-Dennis Michael	70-71WasA 72CleA	11-22-45	Clifton Forge, Va.		R	L	6'3	197	4	4	.500	1	103	0	0	133	119	56	95	0	2.77	8	0	0	.000
Rippelmeyer, Ray-Raymond Roy	62WasA	7- 9-33	Valmeyer, Ill.		[illegible]	[illegible]	[illegible]	[illegible]	1	[illegible]	.333	0	18	1	0	39	47	17	17	0	5.54	6	3	1	.500
Ritchie, Jay-Jay Seay	64-65BosA 66-67AtlN 68CinN	11-20-36	Salisbury, N.C.		R	R	6'4	190	8	13	.381	8	167	2	0	291	301	94	212	0	3.43	[illegible]	7	0	[illegible]
Rittwage, Jim-James Michael William	70CleA	10-23-44	Cleveland, Ohio		R	R	6'3	190	1	1	.500	0	8	3	1	26	18	21	16	0	4.15	8	3	0	.375
Roberts, Dale-Dale (Mountain Man)	67NYA	4-12-42	Owenton, Ky.		R	L	6'4	180	0	0	–	0	2	0	0	2	3	2	0	0	9.00				
Roberts, Dave-David Arthur	69-71SDN 72-75HouN	9-11-44	Gallipolis, Ohio		L	L	6'3	190	69	78	.469	6	242	181	51	1344	1374	370	659	15	3.43	448	84	5	.188
Robertson, Jerry-Jerry Lee	70DetA	10-13-43	Winchester, Kans.		B	R	6'2	205	5	16	.238	1	49	27	3	195	205	86	144	0	3.92	56	5	0	.089
Robertson, Rich-Richard Paul	66-71SFN	10-14-44	Albany, Cal.		R	R	6'2	210	13	14	.481	2	86	40	8	302	333	153	184	1	4.95	86	8	2	.093
Rodriguez, Eduardo [Reyes] (Volanta)	73-75MilA	3- 6-52	Barceloneta, P.R.		R	R	6'	185	23	11	.676	16	116	13	2	276	245	142	172	0	3.49	1	1	0	1.000
Rodriguez, Roberto-Roberto Munoz	67KCA 70OakA 70SDN 70ChiN	11-29-41	Caracas, Venezuela		R	R	6'3	185	3	2	.600	5	57	5	0	112	128	37	91	0	4.82	12	1	1	.083
Rogers, Steve-Stephen Douglas	73-75MonN	10-26-49	Jefferson City, Mo.		R	R	6'1	175	36	39	.480	0	90	90	30	640	596	217	355	7	2.74	197	28	0	.142
Roggenburk, Garry-Garry Earl	63,65-66MinA 66,68-69BosA 69SeaA	4-16-40	Cleveland, Ohio		R	L	6'6	205	6	9	.400	7	79	6	1	126	132	64	56	0	3.64	20	2	0	.100
Rohr, Billy-William Joseph	67BosA 68CleA	7- 1-45	San Diego, Cal.		L	L	6'3	170	3	3	.500	1	27	8	2	60	61	32	21	1	5.70	11	0	0	.000
Rohr, Les-Leslie Norvin	67-69NYN	3- 5-46	Lowestoft, England		L	L	6'5	205	2	3	.400	0	6	4	0	24	27	17	20	0	3.75	6	0	0	.000
Rojas, Minnie-Minervo Alejandro [Landin]	66-68CalA	11-26-38	Remedios, Cuba		R	R	6'1	188	23	16	.590	43	157	2	0	261	244	68	153	0	3.00	41	3	0	.073
Roland, Jim-James Ivan	62-64,66-68MinA 69-72OakA 72NYA 72TexA	12-14-42	Franklin, N.C.		R	L	6'3	185	19	17	.528	9	216	29	6	450	358	229	272	1	3.22	84	6	0	.071
Romo, Vicente-Vicente [Navarro] (Huevo)	68LAN 68-69CleA 69-70BosA 71-72ChiA 73-74SDN	5-21-43	Santa Rosalia, Mexico		R	R	6'1	185	31	31	.500	51	320	26	4	610	544	267	392	1	3.39	116	17	1	.147
Rooker, Jim-James Phillip	68DetA 69-72KCA 73-75PitN	9-23-41	Lakeview, Ore.		R	L	6'	195	59	72	.450	6	208	147	47	1103	1015	435	667	12	3.39	366	79	5	.216
Rose, Don-Donald Gary	71NYN 72CalA 74SFN	3-19-47	Covina, Cal.		R	R	6'3	185	1	4	.200	0	19	4	0	46	55	20	40	0	4.11	10	2	1	.200
Ross, Gary-Gary Douglas	68-69ChiN 69-74SDN 75CalA	9-16-47	McKeesport, Pa.		R	R	6'1	185	15	27	.357	7	235	16	1	430	457	222	245	0	4.19	61	7	0	.115
Rounsaville, Gene-Virl Gene	70ChiN	9-27-44	Konawa, Okla.		R	R	6'3	205	0	1	.000	0	8	0	0	6	10	2	3	0	10.50				
Rowe, Don-Donald Howard	63NYN	4- 3-36	Brawley, Cal.		L	L	6'	180	0	0	–	0	26	1	0	55	59	21	27	0	4.25	13	3	0	.231
Rowe, Ken-Kenneth Darrell	63LAN 64-65BalA	12-31-33	Ferndale, Mich.		R	R	6'2	205	2	1	.667	1	26	0	0	45	55	14	19	0	3.60	6	1	0	.167
Rubio, Jorge-Jorge Jesus [Chavez]	66-67CalA	4-23-45	Mexicali, Mexico		R	R	6'3	200	2	3	.400	0	10	7	1	42	40	25	31	1	3.21	11	1	0	.091
Rudolph, Don-Frederick Donald	57-59ChiA 59CinN 62CleA 62-64WasA	8-16-31	Baltimore, Md.	9-12-68	L	L	5'11	195	18	32	.360	3	124	57	10	450	485	102	182	2	4.00	120	20	1	.167
Ruhle, Vern-Vernon Gerald	74-75DetA	1-25-51	Midland, Mich.		R	R	6'1	185	13	12	.520	0	37	36	11	223	234	73	75	3	3.83				
Rusteck, Dick-Richard Frank	66NYN	7-12-41	Chicago, Ill.		R	L	6'1	175	1	2	.333	0	8	3	1	24	24	8	9	1	3.00	5	0	0	.000
Ruthven, Dick-Richard David	73-75PhiN	3-27-51	Sacramento, Cal.		R	R	6'2	185	17	24	.415	1	71	65	9	382	344	213	277	1	4.10	119	20	0	.168
Ryan, Nolan-Lynn Nolan	66,68-71NYN 72-75CalA	1-31-47	Refugio, Tex.		R	R	6'2	200	105	98	.517	3	255	220	95	1651	1146	997	1748	23	3.06	261	35	0	.134
Ryerson, Gary-Gary Lawrence	72-73MilA	6-17-48	Los Angeles, Cal.		R	L	6'1	180	3	9	.250	0	29	18	4	125	151	28	55	1	4.39	23	1	0	.043
Sadecki, Ray-Raymond Michael	60-66StLN 66-69SFN 70-74NYN 75StLN 75AtlN 75KCA	12-26-40	Kansas City, Kans.		L	L	5'11	185	133	130	.506	6	520	327	85	2456	2408	896	1566	20	3.78	789	151	5	.191
Sadowski, Bob-Robert F.	63-65MilN 66BosA	2-19-38	Pittsburgh, Pa.		R	R	6'2	195	20	27	.426	8	115	54	13	440	416	130	257	1	3.87	129	13	0	.101
Sadowski, Jim-James Michael	74PitN	8- 7-51	Pittsburgh, Pa.		R	R	6'3	200	0	1	.000	0	4	0	0	9	7	9	1	0	6.00	1	0	0	.000
Sadowski, Ted-Theodore	60WasA 61-62MinA	4- 1-36	Pittsburgh, Pa.		R	R	6'1	190	2	3	.400	1	43	2	0	84	103	31	39	0	5.79	13	2	0	.154
Sanders, Ken-Kenneth George	64KCA 66BosA 66KCA 68OakA 70-72MilA 73MinA 73-74CleA 74CalA 75NYN	7- 8-41	St. Louis, Mo.		R	R	5'11	180	28	43	.394	85	374	1	0	607	522	243	342	0	3.00	51	6	0	.118
Sanford, Jack-John Stanley	56-58PhiN 59-65SFN 65-67CalA 67KCA	5-18-29	Wellesley Hills, Mass.		R	R	6'	190	137	101	.576	11	388	293	76	2047	1907	737	1182	14	3.69	665	105	3	.158
Santiago, Jose-Jose Rafael [Alfonso]	63-65KCA 66-70BosA	8-15-40	Juana Diaz, P.R.		R	R	6'2	185	0	2	.000	1	163	0	0	19	29	12	12	0	7.58	162	28	1	.173
Santorini, Al-Alan Joel	68AtlN 69-71SDN 71-73StLN	5-19-48	Irvington, N.J.		R	R	6'	190	17	38	.309	3	127	70	5	494	533	194	268	4	4.28	137	15	1	.109
Saunders, Dennis-Dennis James (Buttons)	70DetA	1- 4-49	Alhambra, Cal.		B	R	6'3	200	1	1	.500	1	8	0	0	14	16	5	8	0	3.21	5	0	0	.000
Sawyer, Rich-Richard Clyde (Buzz)	74-75NYA	4- 7-48	Bakersfield, Cal.		R	R	6'2	205	0	0	–	0	5	0	0	8	9	3	4	0	5.63				
Scarce, Mac-Guerrant McCurdy	72-74PhiN 75NYN	4- 8-49	Danville, Va.		L	L	6'3	190	5	18	.217	21	142	0	0	178	157	102	147	0	3.64	17	0	0	.000
Schaeffer, Mark-Mark Philip	72SDN	6- 5-48	Santa Monica, Cal.		L	L	6'6	220	2	0	1.000	1	41	0	0	41	52	28	25	0	4.61	3	0	0	.000
Scherman, Fred-Frederick John	69-73DetA 74-75HouN 75MonN	7-25-44	Dayton, Ohio		L	L	6'1	195	31	24	.564	38	315	8	1	497	480	231	279	0	3.57	78	10	0	.128
Schmelz, Al-Alan George	67NYN	11-12-43	Whittier, Cal.		R	R	6'4	210	0	0	–	0	2	0	0	3	4	1	2	0	3.00				
Schneider, Dan-Daniel Louis	63-64MilN 66AtlN 67,69HouN	8-29-42	Evansville, Ind.		L	L	6'3	170	2	5	.286	2	117	8	0	166	185	70	86	0	4.72	29	5	0	.172
Schueler, Ron-Ronald Richard	72-73AtlN 74-75PhiN	4-18-48	Catherine, Kans.		R	R	6'4	210	28	35	.444	5	166	71	13	627	591	264	398	2	3.98	158	27	0	.171
Schoen, Jerry-Gerald Thomas	68WasA	1-15-47	New Orleans, La.		R	R	6'3	215	0	1	.000	0	1	1	0	4	6	1	1	0	6.75	1	0	0	.000
Schultz, Barney-George Warren	55StLN 59DetA 61-63ChiN 63-65StLN	8-15-26	Beverly, N.J.		R	R	6'2	200	20	20	.500	35	227	0	0	347	303	116	264	0	3.63	33	4	0	.121
Schultz, Buddy-Charles Budd	75ChiN	9-19-50	Cleveland, Ohio		R	L	5'11	170	2	0	1.000	0	6	0	0	6	11	5	4	0	6.00				
Schurr, Wayne-Wayne Allen	64ChiN	8- 6-37	Garrett, Ind.		R	R	6'4	185	0	0	–	0	26	0	0	48	57	11	29	0	3.75	5	0	0	.000
Schwall, Don-Donald Bernard	61-62BosA 63-66PitN 66-67AtlN	3- 2-36	Wilkes-Barre, Pa.		R	R	6'6	200	49	48	.505	4	172	103	18	744	710	391	408	5	3.71	234	34	0	.145
Scott, Dick-Richard Lewis	63LAN 64ChiN	3-15-33	Portsmouth, N.H.		R	L	6'2	200	0	0	–	2	12	0	0	16	27	4	7	0	8.44				
Scott, Mickey-Ralph Robert	72-73BalA 73MonN 75CalA	7-25-47	Weimar, Germany		L	L	6'1	175	5	5	.500	1	88	0	0	117	111	34	55	0	3.62	4	0	0	.000
Seale, Johnny-Johnny Ray (The Durango Kid)	64-65DetA	11-14-38	Edgewater, Colo.		L	L	5'10	155	1	0	1.000	0	8	0	0	13	13	6	8	0	5.54	1	0	0	.000
Seaver, Tom-George Thomas	67-75NYN	11-17-44	Fresno, Cal.		R	R	6'1	195	168	96	.636	1	319	314	148	2447	1940	657	2099	34	2.46	798	124	6	.155
Secrist, Don-Donald Lavern	69-70ChiA	2-26-44	Seattle, Wash.		L	L	6'2	195	0	1	.000	0	28	0	0	55	54	26	32	0	5.89	7	1	0	.143
Seelbach, Chuck-Charles Frederick	71-74DetA	3-20-48	Lakewood, Ohio		R	R	6'	185	10	8	.556	14	85	3	0	131	118	51	79	0	3.37	21	3	0	.143
Sequi, Diego-Diego Pablo [Gonzalez]	62-65KCA 66WasA 67KCA 68OakA 69SeaA 70-72OakA 72-73StLN 74-75BosA	8-17-37	Holguin, Cuba		R	R	6'	190	92	104	.469	69	597	164	28	1697	1548	743	1207	7	3.69	384	58	4	.151
Sells, Dave-David Wayne	72-75CalA 75LAN	9-18-46	Vacaville, Cal.		R	R	5'11	185	11	7	.611	12	90	0	0	138	146	67	49	0	3.91	1	1	0	1.000
Selma, Dick-Richard Jay	65-68NYN 69SDN 69ChiN 70-73PhiN 74CalA 74MilA	11- 4-43	Santa Ana, Cal.		R	R	5'11	160	42	54	.438	31	307	76	11	841	734	381	681	6	3.62	203	35	0	.172
					Bats Both part of 66																				
Sembera, Carroll-Carroll William	65-67HouN 69-70MonN	7-26-41	Shiner, Tex.		R	R	6'	160	3	11	.214	6	99	1	0	140	149	73	94	0	4.69	15	2	0	.133
Severinsen, Al-Albert Henry	69BalA 71-72SDN	11- 9-44	Brooklyn, N.Y.		R	R	6'3	220	3	7	.300	9	88	0	0	111	104	47	53	0	3.08	5	1	0	.200
Seyfried, Gordon-Gordon Clay	63-64CleA	7- 4-37	Long Beach, Cal.		R	R	6'	185	0	1	.000	0	5	1	0	10	13	3	1	0	0.90	2	0	0	.000
Shanahan, Greg-Paul Gregory (Shany)	73-74LAN	12-11-47	Eureka, Cal.		R	R	6'2	190	0	0	–	1	11	0	0	23	21	9	13	0	3.52	1	0	0	.000
Shank, Harvey-Harvey Tillman	70CalA	7-29-46	Toronto, Canada		R	R	6'4	220	0	0	–	0	1	0	0	3	2	2	1	0	0.00				
Shaw, Bob-Robert John	57-58DetA 58-61ChiA 61KCA 62-63MilN 64-66SFN 66-67NYN 67ChiN	6-29-33	Bronx, N.Y.		R	R	6'2	195	108	98	.524	32	430	223	55	1779	1837	511	880	14	3.52	519	69	0	.133
Shaw, Don-Donald Wellington	67-68NYN 69MonN 71-72StLN 72OakA	2-23-44	Pittsburgh, Pa.		L	L	6'	180	13	14	.489	6	138	1	0	188	166	101	123	0	4.02	15	0	0	.000
Shea, Steve-Steven Francis	68HouN 69MonN	12- 5-42	Worcester, Mass.		R	R	6'3	215	4	4	.500	6	40	0	0	51	45	19	26	0	3.18	6	0	0	.000
Sheldon, Rollie-Roland Frank	61-62,64-65NYA 65-66KCA 66BosA	12-17-36	Putnam, Conn.		R	R	6'4	190	38	36	.514	2	160	101	17	725	741	207	371	4	4.08	209	20	0	.096
Shellenback, Jim-James Philip	66-67,69PitN 69-71WasA 72-74TexA	11-18-43	Riverside, Cal.		L	L	6'2	200	16	30	.348	2	160	48	8	449	433	195	219	2	3.75	104	13	0	.125
Sherry, Larry-Lawrence	58-63LAN 64-67DetA 67HouN 68CalA	7-25-35	Los Angeles, Cal.		R	R	6'2	200	53	44	.546	82	416	16	2	799	747	374	606	1	3.67	148	25	3	.169
Shifflett, Garland-Garland Jessie (Duck)	57WasA 65MinA	3-28-35	Elkton, Va.		R	R	5'10	165	0	2	.000	1	16	1	0	26	28	17	10	0	6.23	4	0	0	.000
Short, Bill-William Ross	60NYA 62,66BalA 66BosA 67PitN 68NYN 69CinN	11-27-37	Kingston, N.Y.		L	L	5'9	170	5	11	.313	2	73	16	3	131	130	64	71	1	4.74	32	4	0	.125

USE NAME – GIVEN NAMES (NICKNAMES)	TEAM BY YEAR	BIRTH DATE	BIRTH PLACE	DEATH DATE	B	T	HGT	WGT	W	L	PCT	SV	G	GS	CG	IP	H	BB	SO	ShO	ERA	AB	H	HR	BA
									LIFETIME PITCHING TOTALS													BATTING TOTALS			
Short, Chris-Christopher Joseph	59-72PhiN 73MilA	9-19-37	Milford, Del.		R	L	6'4	213	135	132	.506	18	501	308	88	2324	2215	806	1629	24	3.43	697	88	0	.126
					Bats Both 70-71																				
Siebert, Paul–Paul Edward	74-75HouN	6- 5-53	Minneapolis, Minn.		L	L	6'2	205	1	3	.250	2	12	7	1	43	41	17	16	1	3.35	9	0	0	.000
Siebert, Sonny-Wilfred Charles	64-69CleA 69-73BosA 73TexA 74StLN	1-14-37	St. Mary's, Mo.		R	R	6'3	205	140	114	.551	16	399	307	67	2152	1919	692	1511	21	3.21	660	114	12	.173
	75SDN 75OakA																								
Siebler, Dwight-Dwight Leroy	63-67MinA	8- 5-37	Columbus, Neb.		R	R	6'2	184	4	3	.571	1	48	8	2	118	97	44	71	0	3.43	27	2	0	.074
Simpson, Steve-Steven Edward	72SDN	8-30-48	St. Joseph, Mo.		R	R	6'2	205	0	2	.000	2	9	0	0	11	10	8	9	0	4.91				
Simpson, Wayne-Wayne Kirby	70-72CinN 73KCA 75PhiN	12- 2-48	Los Angeles, Cal.		R	R	6'3	215	30	19	.612	0	95	84	13	514	452	53	298	2	4.03	153	12	0	.078
Singer, Bill-William Robert (The Singer Throwing Machine)	64-72LAN	4-24-44	Los Angeles, Cal.		R	R	6'4	200	103	109	.486	2	273	260	89	1877	1648	646	1385	20	3.25	413	45	0	.109
	73-75CalA																								
Sisk, Tommie-Tommie Wayne	62-68PitN 69SDN 70ChiA	4-12-42	Ardmore, Okla.		R	R	6'3	195	40	49	.449	10	316	99	19	928	937	358	441	4	3.92	235	22	0	.094
Skok, Craig-Craig Richard	73BosA	9- 1-47	Dobbs Ferry, N.Y.		R	L	6'	190	0	1	.000	1	11	0	0	29	35	11	22	0	6.21				
Slaton, Jim-James Michael	71-75MilA	6-19-50	Long Beach, Cal.		R	R	6'1	185	48	63	.432	0	150	137	30	935	949	383	459	13	4.05	57	6	0	.105
Slaughter, Sterling-Sterling F. (Stu)	64ChiN	11-18-41	Danville, Ill.		R	R	5'11	165	2	4	.333	0	20	6	1	52	64	32	32	0	5.71	12	1	0	.083
Slayback, Bill-William Grover	72-74DetA	2-21-48	Hollywood, Cal.		R	R	6'4	190	6	9	.400	0	42	17	3	139	136	51	89	1	3.82	23	4	0	.174
Smith, Bill-William Garland	58-59StLN 62PhiN	6- 8-34	Washington, D.C.		L	L	6'	190	1	6	.143	1	32	6	0	68	82	17	34	0	4.24	14	2	0	.143
Smith, Jack-Jack Hatfield	62-63LAN 64MilN	11-15-35	Pikeville, Ky.		R	R	6'	185	2	2	.500	1	34	0	0	49	48	17	31	0	4.59	6	1	0	.167
Smith, Pete-Pete Luke	62-63BosA	3-19-40	Natick, Mass.		R	R	6'2	190	0	1	.000	0	7	2	0	19	19	8	7	0	6.63	3	0	0	.000
Smith, Willie-Willie (Wonderful Willie)	63DetA 64LAA 68CleA 68ChiN	2-11-39	Anniston, Ala.		L	L	6'	182	2	4	.333	2	29	3	0	62	60	24	39	0	3.05	(See B 61-75)			
Snook, Frank-Frank Walter (Snooker)	73SDN	3-28-49	Somerville, N.J.		R	R	6'2	180	0	2	.000	1	18	0	0	27	19	18	13	0	3.67	2	0	0	.000
Solomon, Eddie-Eddie (King)	73-74LAN 75ChiN	2- 9-51	Perry, Ga.		R	R	6'3	205	0	0	–	1	14	0	0	19	22	12	11	0	3.32	1	0	0	.000
Sosa, Elias-Elias [Martinez]	72-74SFN 75StLN 75AtlN	6-10-50	La Vega, Dom. Rep.		R	R	6'2	198	21	17	.553	29	204	2	0	314	291	101	174	0	3.58	48	4	0	.083
Sosa, Jose-Jose Ynocencio	75HouN	12-28-52	Santo Domingo, D.R.		R	R	6'	190	1	3	.250	1	25	2	0	47	51	23	31	0	4.02	9	3	1	.333
Spanswick, Bill-William Henry	64BosA	7- 8-38	Springfield, Mass.		L	L	6'3	195	2	3	.400	0	29	7	0	65	75	44	55	0	6.92	14	4	0	.286
Sparma, Joe-Joseph Blase	64-69DetA 70MonN	2- 4-42	Massillon, Ohio		R	R	6'1	194	52	52	.500	0	183	142	31	865	774	436	586	10	3.94	269	32	0	.119
Spillner, Dan-Daniel Ray	74-75SDN	11-27-51	Casper, Wyo.		R	R	6'1	195	14	24	.368	1	67	50	8	315	347	133	199	2	4.14	88	7	0	.080
Spinks, Scipio-Scipio Ronald	69-71HouN 72-73StLN	7-12-47	Chicago, Ill.		R	R	6'2	190	7	12	.362	0	35	29	7	202	175	107	154	0	3.70	65	11	1	.169
Splittorff, Paul-Paul William	70-75KCA	10- 8-46	Evansville, Ind.		L	L	6'3	205	62	61	.504	1	168	153	44	1016	1021	316	506	12	3.54	121	22	0	.182
Sprague, Ed-Edward Nelson	68-69OakA 71-73CinN 73StLN 73-75MilA	9-16-45	Boston, Mass.		R	R	6'4	200	17	21	.447	9	195	23	3	401	392	203	188	0	3.77	22	1	0	.045
Spring, Jack-Jack Russell	55PhiN 57BosA 58WasA 61-64LAA 64ChiN	3-11-33	Spokane, Wash.		R	L	6'1	185	12	5	.706	8	155	5	0	186	195	78	86	0	4.26	28	3	0	.107
	64StLN 65CleA																								
Sprout, Bob-Robert Samuel	61LAA	12- 5-41	Florin, Pa.		L	L	6'	165	0	0	–	0	1	1	0	4	4	3	2	0	4.50				
Stafford, Bill-William Charles	60-65NYA 66-67KCA	8-13-39	Catskill, N.Y.		R	R	6'1	188	43	40	.518	9	186	104	18	786	707	270	449	6	3.52	245	38	0	.155
Stallard, Tracy-Evan Tracy	60-62BosA 63-64NYN 65-66StLN	8-31-37	Coeburn, Va.		R	R	6'5	204	30	57	.345	4	183	104	21	765	716	343	477	3	4.16	245	27	0	.110
Stanek, Al-Albert Wilfred (Lefty)	63SFN	12-24-43	Springfield, Mass.		L	L	5'11	190	0	0	–	0	11	0	0	13	10	12	5	0	4.85	1	0	0	.000
Stange, Lee-Albert Lee	61-64MinA 64-66CleA 66-70BosA 70ChiA	10-27-36	Chicago, Ill.		R	R	5'10	170	62	61	.504	21	359	115	32	1216	1172	344	718	8	3.56	305	24	0	.079
Stanhouse, Don-Donald Joseph	72-74TexA 75MonN	2-12-51	DuQuoin, Ill.		R	R	6'3	190	4	17	.190	1	67	24	2	219	210	145	151	0	4.52	31	4	0	.129
Stanton, Mike-Michael Thomas	75HouN	9-25-52	St. Louis, Mo.		R	R	6'3	195	0	2	.000	1	7	2	0	17	20	20	16	0	7.41	4	1	0	.250
Starrette, Herm-Herman Paul	63-65BalA	11-20-38	Statesville, N.C.		R	R	6'	175	1	1	.500	0	27	0	0	46	43	16	21	0	2.54	5	0	0	.000
Steevens, Morrie-Morris Dale	62ChiN 64-65PhiN	10- 7-40	Salem, Ill.		L	L	6'2	175	0	2	.000	0	22	1	0	21	20	16	11	0	4.29	1	0	0	.000
Stenhouse, Dave-David Rotchford	62-64WasA	9-12-33	Westerly, R.I.		R	R	6'	195	16	28	.364	1	76	56	12	372	339	174	214	3	4.14	103	11	0	.107
Stephen, Buzz-Louis Roberts	68MinA	7-13-44	Porterville, Cal.		R	R	6'4	205	1	1	.500	0	2	2	0	11	11	7	4	0	4.91	3	0	0	.000
Stephenson, Earl-Chester Earl	71ChiN 72MilA	7-31-47	Benson, N.C.		L	L	6'3	190	4	5	.444	1	51	8	1	100	103	44	44	0	3.51	20	0	0	.000
Stephenson, Jerry-Jerry Joseph	63,65-68BosA 69SeaA 70LAN	10- 6-43	Detroit, Mich.		L	R	6'2	195	8	19	.296	1	67	33	3	239	265	145	184	0	5.72	65	15	0	.231
Sterling, Randy-Randall Wayne	74NYN	4-21-51	Key West, Fla.		B	R	6'3	195	1	1	.500	0	3	2	0	9	13	3	2	0	5.00	2	0	0	.000
Stigman, Dick-Richard Lewis	60-61CleA 62-65MinA 66BosA	1-24-36	Nimrod, Minn.		R	L	6'3	200	46	54	.460	16	235	119	30	923	819	406	755	5	4.03	282	32	0	.113
Stock, Wes-Wesley Gay	59-64BalA 64-67KCA	4-10-34	Longview, Wash.		R	R	6'2	188	27	13	.675	22	321	3	0	518	434	215	365	0	3.60	59	3	0	.051
Stoddard, Tim-Timothy Paul	75ChiA	1-24-53	East Chicago, Ind.		R	R	6'7	240	0	0	–	0	1	0	0	1	2	0	0	0	9.00				
Stone, George-George Heard	67-72AtlN 73-75NYN	7- 9-46	Ruston, La.		L	L	6'3	210	60	57	.513	5	203	145	24	1020	1119	270	590	5	3.89	339	72	1	.212
Stone, Steve-Steven Michael	71-72SFN 73ChiA 74-75ChiN	7-14-47	Euclid, Ohio		R	R	5'10	175	37	42	.468	1	158	112	16	795	753	330	415	4	3.93	198	19	0	.096
Stoneman, Bill-William Hambly	67-68ChiN 69-73MonN 74CalA	4- 7-44	Oak Park, Ill.		R	R	5'10	170	54	85	.388	5	245	170	46	1238	1182	602	934	15	4.08	338	29	0	.086
Stottlemyre, Mel-Melvin Leon	64-74NYA	11-13-41	Hazelton, Mo.		R	R	6'1	185	164	139	.541	1	360	356	152	2662	2435	809	1257	40	2.97	749	120	7	.160
Strahler, Mike-Michael Wayne	70-72LAN 73DetA	3-14-47	Chicago, Ill.		R	R	6'4	185	6	8	.429	1	53	13	2	159	149	79	80	0	3.57	20	4	0	.200
Strampe, Bob-Robert Edwin	72DetA	6-13-50	Janesville, Wis.		B	R	6'1	185	0	0	–	0	7	0	0	5	6	7	4	0	10.80				
Strickland, Jim-James Michael	71-73MinA 75CleA	6-12-46	Los Angeles, Cal.		L	L	6'	175	4	2	.667	4	60	0	0	77	63	44	60	0	2.69	4	1	0	.250
Strohmayer, John-John Emery	70-73MonN 73-74NYN	10-13-46	Belle Fourche, S.D.		R	R	6'	180	11	9	.550	4	142	17	2	313	329	128	200	0	4.46	50	10	0	.200
Strom, Brent-Brent Terry	72NYN 73CleA 75SDN	10-14-48	San Diego, Cal.		R	L	6'3	190	10	21	.323	0	56	39	8	273	271	95	167	2	3.96	36	3	0	.083
Such, Dick-Richard Stanley	70WasA	10-15-44	Sanford, N.C.		L	R	6'4	200	1	5	.167	0	21	5	0	50	48	45	41	0	7.56	13	3	0	.231
Sukla, Ed-Edward Anthony	64LAA 65-66CalA	3- 3-43	Long Beach, Cal.		R	R	5'11	170	3	5	.375	4	39	0	0	52	52	17	26	0	5.19	1	0	0	.000
Sutherland, Darrell-Darrell Wayne	64-66NYN 68CleA	11-14-41	Glendale, Cal.		R	R	6'4	170	5	4	.556	1	62	6	0	122	131	58	50	0	4.80	21	5	0	.238
Sutton, Don-Donald Howard	66-75LAN	4- 2-45	Clio, Ala.		R	R	6'1	190	155	126	.552	3	367	353	110	2544	2170	653	1913	40	3.02	842	135	0	.160
Swan, Craig-Craig Steven	73-75NYN	11-30-50	Van Nuys, Cal.		R	R	6'3	225	2	7	.222	0	16	12	0	69	82	36	33	0	5.87	20	4	0	.200
Talbot, Fred-Frederick Lealand	63-64ChiA 65-66KCA 66-69NYA 69SeaA	6-28-41	Washington, D.C.		R	R	6'2	200	38	56	.404	1	195	126	12	854	844	334	449	4	4.12	241	42	4	.174
	69-70OakA																								
Tanana, Frank-Frank Daryl	73-75CalA	7- 3-53	Detroit, Mich.		L	L	6'3	190	32	30	.516	0	77	72	30	552	493	158	471	10	2.89				
Tate, Randy-Randall Lee	75NYN	10- 3-52	Florence, Ala.		R	R	6'3	195	5	13	.278	0	26	23	2	138	121	86	99	0	4.43	41	0	0	.000
Tatum, Ken-Kenneth Ray	69-70CalA 71-73BosA 74ChiA	4-25-44	Alexandria, La.		R	R	6'2	205	16	12	.571	52	176	2	0	283	274	117	156	0	2.93	45	11	4	.244
Taylor, Chuck-Charles Gilbert	69-71StLN 72NYN 72MilA 73-75MonN	4-18-42	Murfreesboro, Tenn.		R	R	6'2	195	26	17	.605	31	274	21	6	567	538	149	268	2	2.97	98	16	0	.163
Taylor, Gary-Gary William	69DetA	10-19-45	Detroit, Mich.		R	R	6'2	190	0	1	.000	0	7	0	0	10	10	6	3	0	5.40	1	0	0	.000
Taylor, Ron-Ronald Wesley	62CleA 63-65StLN 65-66HouN 67-71NYN 72SDN	12-13-37	Toronto, Canada		R	R	6'1	195	45	43	.511	72	491	17	3	799	794	209	464	0	3.93	116	12	0	.103
Tekulve, Kent-Kenton Charles	74-75PitN	3- 5-47	Cincinnati, Ohio		R	R	6'4	175	2	3	.400	5	42	0	0	65	55	28	34	0	2.77	11	1	0	.091
Terlecki, Bob-Robert Joseph	72PhiN	2-14-45	Trenton, N.J.		R	R	5'9	183	0	0	–	0	9	0	0	13	16	10	5	0	4.85				
Terlecky, Greg-Gregory John	75StLN	3-20-52	Culver City, Cal.		R	R	6'3	195	0	1	.000	0	20	0	0	30	38	12	13	0	4.50	3	1	0	.333
Terpko, Jeff-Jeffrey Michael	74TexA	10-16-50	Sayre, Pa.		R	R	6'	180	0	0	–	0	3	0	0	7	6	4	3	0	1.29				
Terry, Ralph-Ralph Willard	56-57NYA 57-59KCA 59-64NYA 65KCA 66-67NYN	1- 9-36	Big Cabin, Okla.		R	R	6'3	195	107	99	.519	11	338	257	75	1850	1748	446	1000	20	3.62	593	95	1	.160
Thies, Dave-David Robert	63KCA	3-21-37	Minneapolis, Minn.		R	R	6'4	205	0	1	.000	0	9	2	0	25	26	12	9	0	4.68	6	2	0	.333
Thoenen, Dick-Richard Crispin	67PhiN	1- 9-44	Mexico, Mo.		R	R	6'6	215	0	0	–	0	1	0	0	1	2	0	0	0	9.00				
Thomas, Stan-Stanley Brown	74-75TexA	7-11-49	Rumford, Me.		R	R	6'2	185	4	4	.500	3	58	1	0	95	94	40	54	0	3.60				
Thomason, Erskine-Melvin Erskine	74PhiN	8-13-48	Laurens, S.C.		R	R	6'1	190	0	0	–	0	1	0	0	1	0	0	1	0	0.00				
Thompson, Mike-Michael Wayne	71WasA 73-74StLN 74-75AtlN	9- 6-49	Denver, Colo.		R	R	6'3	205	1	15	.063	0	54	29	0	165	158	128	113	0	4.85	41	4	0	.098
Throop, George-George Lynford (Bird)	75KCA	11-24-50	Pasadena, Cal.		R	R	6'7	205	0	0	–	2	7	0	0	9	8	2	8	0	4.00				
Tiant, Luis-Luis Clemente [Vega]	64-69CleA 70MinA 71-75BosA	11-23-40	Marianao, Cuba		R	R	6'	187	158	120	.568	15	401	314	144	2387	1984	802	1597	37	3.05	496	81	5	.163
Tidrow, Dick-Richard William	72-74CleA 74-75NYA	5-14-47	San Francisco, Cal.		R	R	6'4	220	46	46	.500	6	155	103	28	791	780	262	407	5	3.74	70	7	0	.100
Tiefenauer, Bobby-Bobby Gene	52,55StLN 60CleA 61StLN 62HouN	10-10-29	Desloge, Mo.		R	R	6'2	185	9	25	.265	23	179	0	0	316	312	87	204	0	3.84	39	1	0	.026
	63-65MilN 65NYA 65,67CleA 68ChiN																								
Tiefenthaler, Verle-Verle Matthew	62ChiA	7-11-37	Breda, Iowa		L	R	6'1	190	0	0	–	0	3	0	0	4	6	7	1	0	9.00				
Tillotson, Thad-Thaddeus Asa	67-68NYA	12-20-40	Merced, Cal.		R	R	6'2	195	4	9	.308	2	50	5	1	108	110	46	63	0	4.08	17	1	0	.059
Timberlake, Gary-Gary Dale	69SeaA	8- 9-48	Laconia, Ind.		R	L	6'2	205	0	0	–	0	2	2	0	6	7	9	4	0	7.50	1	0	0	.000
Timmerman (Timmermann), Tom-Thomas Henry	69-72DetA 73-74CleA	5-12-40	Breese, Ill.		R	R	6'4	215	35	35	.500	35	228	44	8	548	508	208	315	2	3.78	88	8	0	.091
Todd, Jim-James Richard	74ChiN 75OakA	9-21-47	Lancaster, Pa.		L	R	6'2	195	12	5	.706	15	101	6	0	210	186	74	92	0	2.96	16	0	0	.063
Tomlin, Dave-David Allen	72-73CinN 74-75SDN	6-22-49	Maysville, Ky.		L	L	6'2	185	7	4	.636	4	133	0	0	199	205	77	99	0	3.48	12	1	0	.083
Tompkins, Ron-Ronald Everett (Stretch)	65KCA 71ChiN	11-27-44	San Diego, Cal.		R	R	6'4	198	0	2	.000	3	40	1	0	50	40	24	24	0	3.96	1	0	0	.000
Toms, Tommy-Thomas Howard	75SFN	10-15-51	Charlottesville, Va.		R	R	6'4	190	0	1	.000	0	7	0	0	10	13	6	6	0	6.30				
Toppin, Rube-Ruperto	62KCA	12- 7-41	Panama, Panama		R	R	6'1	185	0	0	–	0	2	0	0	2	1	5	1	0	13.50	1	1	0	1.000
Torrealba, Pablo, Pablo Arnoldo	75AtlN	4-28-48	Barquismeto, Venez.		L	L	5'9	165	0	1	.000	0	6	0	0	7	7	3	5	1	1.29	1	1	0	1.000
Torrez, Mike-Michael Augustine	67-71StLN 71-74MonN 75BalA	8-28-46	Topeka, Kans.		R	R	6'5	220	81	59	.579	0	209	185	46	1259	1178	644	595	5	3.70	337	58	0	.172
Toth, Paul-Paul Louis	62StLN 62-64ChiN	6-30-35	McRoberts, Ky.		R	R	6'1	192	9	12	.429	0	43	21	5	193	177	54	82	2	3.78	58	6	0	.103
Travers, Billy-William Edward	74-75MilA	10-27-52	Norwood, Miss.		L	L	6'6	185	8	14	.364	1	51	24	5	189	189	90	88	0	4.48				
Troedson, Rich-Richard LaMonte	73-74SDN	5- 1-50	Palo Alto, Cal.		L	L	6'2	190	8	10	.444	2	65	19	2	171	191	67	92	0	4.47	41	7	0	.171
Tsitouris, John-John Philip	57DetA 58-60KCA 62-68CinN	5- 4-36	Monroe, N.C.		R	R	6'	175	34	38	.472	3	149	84	18	662	653	260	432	5	4.13	198	22	0	.111
Turner, Ken-Kenneth Charles	67CalA	8-17-43	Framingham, Mass.		R	L	6'2	190	1	2	.333	0	13	1	0	17	16	4	6	0	4.24	4	0	0	.000
Twitchell, Wayne-Wayne Lee	70MilA 71-75PhiN	3-10-48	Portland, Ore.		R	R	6'6	220	30	37	.448	1	152	82	13	627	675	309	474	6	3.70	172	18	0	.105

USE NAME – GIVEN NAMES (NICKNAMES)	TEAM BY YEAR	BIRTH DATE	BIRTH PLACE	DEATH DATE	LIFETIME PITCHING TOTALS																	BATTING TOTALS			
					B	T	HGT	WGT	W	L	PCT	SV	G	GS	CG	IP	H	BB	SO	ShO	ERA	AB	H	HR	BA
Tyriver, Dave-David Burton	62CleA	10-31-37	Oshkosh, Wis.		R	R	6'	175	0	0	–	0	4	0	0	11	10	7	7	0	4.09	3	0	0	.000
Umbach, Arnie-Arnold William	64MilN 66AtlN	12- 6-42	Williamsburg, Va.		R	R	6'1	180	1	2	.333	0	23	4	0	49	51	22	30	0	3.12	8	1	0	.125
Umbarger, Jim-James Harold	75TexA	2-17-53	Burbank, Cal.		L	L	6'6	200	8	7	.533	2	56	12	3	131	134	59	50	2	4.12				
Umbricht, Jim-James	59-61PitN 62-63HouN	9-17-30	Chicago, Ill.	4- 8-64	R	R	6'4	215	9	5	.643	3	88	7	0	194	155	71	133	0	3.06	28	5	0	.179
Underwood, Tom-Thomas Gerald	74-75PhiN	12-22-53	Kokomo, Ind.		L	L	5'11	170	15	13	.536	0	42	35	7	232	236	89	131	2	4.19	75	9	0	.120
Upham, John-John Leslie	67-68ChiN	12-29-41	Windsor, Canada		L	L	6'	180	0	1	.000	0	7	0	0	8	6	5	4	0	5.63	13	4	0	.308
Upshaw, Cecil-Cecil Lee	66-69AtlN 70RJ 71-73AtlN 73HouN 74CleA 74NYA 75ChiA	10-22-42	Spearsville, La.		R	R	6'6	205	34	36	.486	86	348	0	0	563	545	177	323	0	3.13	75	12	1	.160
Vance, Sandy-Gene Covington	70-71LAN	1- 5-47	Lamar, Colo.		R	R	6'2	180	9	8	.529	0	30	21	2	141	147	46	56	0	3.83	42	7	0	.167
Vaughan, Charlie-Charles Wayne	66,69AtlN	10- 6-47	Mercedes, Tex.		R	L	6'1	185	1	0	1.000	0	2	1	0	8	9	6	7	0	4.50	4	1	0	.250
Veale, Bob-Robert Andrew	62-72PitN 72-74BosA	10-28-35	Birmingham, Ala.		B	L	6'6	218	120	95	.558	21	397	255	78	1926	1684	858	1703	20	3.07	630	72	0	.114
Velasquez, Carlos-Carlos [Quinones]	73MilA	3-22-48	Loiza, P.R.		R	R	5'11	180	2	2	.500	2	18	0	0	38	46	10	12	0	2.61				
Verbanic, Joe-Joseph Michael	66PhiN 67-68NYA 69SA 70NYA	4-24-43	Washington, Pa.		R	R	6'	165	12	11	.522	6	92	17	3	207	210	84	94	2	3.26	46	5	0	.109
Vineyard, Dave-David Kent	64BalA	2-25-41	Clay, W. Va.		R	R	6'	165	2	5	.286	0	19	6	1	54	57	27	50	0	4.17	12	2	0	.167
Von Hoff, Bruce-Bruce Frederick	65,67HouN	11-17-43	Oakland, Cal.		R	R	6'3	195	0	3	.000	0	13	10	0	53	55	30	23	0	5.09	15	1	0	.067
Vuckovich, Pete-Peter Dennis	75ChiA	10-27-52	Johnstown, Pa.		R	R	6'4	215	0	1	.000	0	4	2	0	10	17	7	5	0	13.50				
Wagner, Garry-Gary Edward	65-69PhiN 69-70BosA	6-28-40	Bridgeport, Ill.		R	R	6'4	190	15	19	.441	22	162	4	0	266	250	126	174	0	3.72	37	3	0	.081
Waits, Rick-Michael Richard	73TexA 75CleA	5-15-52	Atlanta, Ga.		B	L	6'3	195	6	2	.750	2	17	7	3	71	58	26	34	0	3.04				
Wakefield, Bill-William Sumner	64NYN	5-24-41	Kansas City, Mo.		R	R	6'	175	3	5	.375	2	62	4	0	120	103	61	61	0	3.60	24	4	0	.167
Walker, Jerry-Jerry Allen	57-60BalA 61-62KCA 63-64CleA	2-12-39	Ada, Okla.		B	R	6'1	195	37	44	.457	13	190	90	16	747	734	341	326	4	4.36	252	58	4	.230
					Bats Right 63-64																				
Walker, Luke-James Luke	65-66,68-73PitN 74-75DetA	9- 2-43	DeKalb, Tex.		L	L	6'2	200	48	55	.466	9	279	109	17	941	879	448	618	7	3.74	218	11	0	.050
Walker, Tom-Robert Thomas	72-74MonN	11- 7-48	Tampa, Fla.		R	R	6'1	190	13	12	.520	8	133	8	1	259	262	92	180	0	3.47	26	3	0	.115
Wall, Stan-Stanley Arthur	75LAN	6-16-51	Butler, Mo.		L	L	6'	175	0	1	.000	0	10	0	0	16	12	7	6	0	1.69				
Wallace, Dave-David William	73-74PhiN	9- 7-47	Waterbury, Conn.		R	R	5'10	185	0	1	.000	0	7	0	0	7	17	5	5	0	15.43				
Wallace, Mike-Michael Sherman	73-74PhiN 74-75NYA 75StLN	2- 3-51	Gastonia, N.C.		L	L	6'2	200	8	1	.889	1	63	4	1	106	112	58	63	0	3.57	4	0	0	.000
Walters, Charlie-Charles Leonard	69MinA	2-21-47	Minneapolis, Minn.		R	R	6'4	190	0	0	–	0	6	0	0	7	6	3	2	0	5.14				
Wantz, Dick-Richard Carter	65CalA	4-11-40	South Gate, Cal.	5-14-65	R	R	6'5	175	0	0	–	0	1	0	0	1	3	0	2	0	18.00				
Warden, Jon-Jonathan Edgar (Warbler)	68DetA 69SJ	10- 1-46	Columbus, Ohio		B	L	6'	205	4	1	.800	3	28	0	0	37	30	15	25	0	3.65	2	0	0	.000
Warner, Jack-Jack Dyer	62-65ChiN	7-12-40	Brandywine, W. Va.		R	R	5'11	190	0	2	.000	0	33	0	0	55	64	21	23	0	5.07	5	1	0	.200
Warthen, Dan-Daniel Dean	75MonN	12- 1-52	Omaha, Neb.		R	L	6'	190	8	6	.571	3	40	18	2	168	130	87	128	0	3.11	51	6	0	.118
Washburn, Greg-Gregory James	69CalA	12- 3-46	Coal City, Ill.		R	R	6'	190	0	2	.000	0	8	2	0	11	21	1	4	0	8.18				
Washburn, Ray-Ray Clark	61-69StLN 70CinN	5-11-38	Pasco, Wash.		R	R	6'2	200	72	64	.529	5	239	166	25	1208	1208	354	700	10	3.54	361	38	1	.105
Waslewski, Gary-Gary Lee	67-68BosA 69StLN 69-70MonN 70-71NYA 72OakA	7-21-41	Meriden, Conn.		R	R	6'4	195	11	26	.297	5	152	42	5	411	368	197	229	1	3.44	88	4	0	.045
Watkins, Bob-Robert Cecil	69HouN	3-12-48	San Francisco, Cal.		R	R	6'2	190	0	0	–	0	5	0	0	16	13	13	11	0	5.06	2	0	0	.000
Watt, Eddie-Edward Dean	66-73BalA 74PhiN 75ChiN	4- 4-42	Lamoni, Iowa		R	R	5'10	190	38	36	.514	80	411	13	1	660	530	254	462	0	2.90	100	19	3	.190
Weaver, Floyd-David Floyd	62,65CleA 70ChiA 71MilA	5-12-41	Ben Franklin, Tex.		R	R	6'4	195	4	5	.444	1	85	5	0	155	149	73	108	0	5.23	20	2	0	.100
Weaver, Jim-James Brian (Fluff)	67-68CalA	2-19-39	Lancaster, Pa.		L	L	6'	178	3	1	.750	1	27	2	0	53	48	19	28	0	2.55	7	0	0	.000
Webb, Hank-Henry Gaylon Matthew	72-75NYN	5-21-50	Copiague, N.Y.		R	R	6'2	175	7	8	.467	0	40	19	3	145	137	83	62	1	4.41	39	8	0	.205
Wegener, Mike-Michael Denis	69-70MonN	10- 8-46	Denver, Colo.		R	R	6'4	215	8	20	.286	0	57	42	5	270	250	152	267	1	4.73	88	17	0	.193
Wenz, Fred-Frederick Charles (Fireball)	68-69BosA 70PhiN	8-26-41	Bound Brook, N.J.		R	R	6'3	214	3	0	1.000	1	31	0	0	42	36	25	38	0	4.71	5	0	0	.000
Whillock, Jack-Jack Franklin	71DetA	11- 4-42	Searcy, Okla.		R	R	6'3	195	0	2	.000	0	7	0	0	8	10	2	6	0	5.63	1	0	0	.000
Whitby, Bill-William Edward	64MinA	7-29-43	Crewe, Va.		R	R	6'1	190	0	0	–	0	4	0	0	6	8	1	2	0	9.00	1	0	0	.000
Wickersham, Dave-David Clifford	60-63KCA 64-67DetA 68PitN 69KCA	9-27-35	Erie, Pa.		R	R	6'3	195	68	57	.544	18	283	124	29	1123	1071	384	638	5	3.66	324	28	0	.086
Wilcox, Milt-Milton Edward	70-71CinN 72-74CleA 75ChiN	4-20-50	Honolulu, Hawaii		R	R	6'2	190	22	30	.423	6	147	53	10	464	474	205	260	3	4.44	62	11	0	.177
Wiley, Mark-Mark Eugene (Coyote)	75MinA	2-28-48	National City, Cal.		R	R	6'2	203	1	3	.250	2	15	3	1	39	50	13	15	0	6.00				
Wilhelm, Hoyt-James Hoyt	52-56NYN 57StLN 57-58CleA 58-62BalA 63-68ChiA 69CalA 69-70AtlN 70ChiN 71AtlN 71-72LAN	7-26-23	Huntersville, N.C.		R	R	6'	190	143	122	.540	227	1070	52	20	2253	1757	778	1610	5	2.52	432	38	1	.088
Willey, Carl-Carlton Francis	58-62MilN 63-65NYN	6- 6-31	Cherryfield, Me.		R	R	6'	175	38	58	.396	1	199	117	28	876	830	326	493	11	3.76	263	26	2	.099
Willhite, Nick-Jon Nicholas	63-64LAN 65WasA 65-66LAN 67CalA 67NYN	1-27-41	Tulsa, Okla.		L	L	6'2	195	6	12	.333	1	58	29	3	182	195	75	118	1	4.55	43	7	0	.163
Williams, Charlie-Charles Prosek	71NYN 72-75SFN	10-11-47	Queens, N.Y.		R	R	6'3	200	14	14	.500	3	140	22	1	320	325	148	160	0	4.02	66	8	0	.121
Williams, Don-Donald Reid (Dino)	63MinA	9- 2-35	Los Angeles, Cal.		R	R	6'5	218	0	0	–	0	3	0	0	4	8	6	2	0	11.25				
Williams, Stan-Stanley Wilson	58-62LAN 63-64NYA 65,67-69CleA 70-71MinA 71StLN 72BosA	9-14-36	Enfield, N.H.		R	R	6'5	230	109	94	.537	43	482	208	42	1763	1527	748	1305	11	3.48	502	59	5	.114
Willis, Dale-Dale Jerome	63KCA	5-29-38	Calhoun, Ga.		R	R	5'11	165	0	2	.000	1	25	0	0	45	46	25	47	0	5.00	6	1	0	.167
Willis, Ron-Ronald Earl	66-69StLN 69HouN 70SDN	7-12-43	Willisville, Tenn.		R	R	6'2	185	11	12	.478	19	188	0	0	239	209	119	128	0	3.31	25	4	0	.160
Willoughby, Jim-James Arthur	71-74SFN 75BosA	1-31-49	Salinas, Cal.		R	R	6'2	200	16	16	.500	9	94	28	8	304	315	77	144	1	3.88	66	10	1	.152
Wills, Ted-Theodore Carl	62CinN 65ChiA	2- 9-34	Fresno, Cal.		L	L	6'2	200	8	11	.421	5	83	13	2	186	210	97	133	0	5.52	44	11	0	.250
Wilshusen, Terry-Terry Wayne (Dizzy)	73CalA	3-22-49	Atascadero, Cal.		R	R	6'2	205	0	0	–	0	1	0	0	.1	0	2	0	0	81.00				
Wilson, Billy-William Harlan	69-73PhiN	9-21-42	Pomeroy, Ohio		R	R	6'2	200	9	15	.375	17	179	0	0	258	229	131	171	0	4.22	24	2	0	.083
Wilson, Don-Donald Edward	66-74HouN	2-12-45	Monroe, La.	1- 5-75	R	R	6'3	205	104	92	.531	2	270	245	78	1748	1479	640	1283	20	3.15	597	87	1	.146
Wilson, Earl (Earl Lawrence)-Robert Earl	59-60,62-66BosA 66-70DetA 70SDN	10- 2-34	Ponchatoula, La.		R	R	6'3	216	121	109	.526	0	338	310	69	2052	1863	796	1452	13	3.69	740	144	35	.195
Wise, Rick-Richard Charles	64,66-71PhiN 72-73StLN 74-75BosA	9-13-45	Jackson, Mich.		R	R	6'2	195	129	120	.518	0	333	291	104	2075	2112	545	1169	21	3.56	585	121	15	.207
Wolf, Wally-Walter Beck	69-70CalA	1- 5-42	Los Angeles, Cal.		R	R	6'	190	0	0	–	0	6	0	0	7	6	7	7	0	7.71				
Womack, Dooley-Horace Guy	66-68NYA 69HouN 69SeaA 70OakA	8-25-39	Columbia, S.C.		L	R	6'	170	19	18	.514	24	193	1	0	302	253	111	177	0	2.95	31	7	0	.226
Wood, Wilbur-Wilbur Forrester	61-64BosA 64-65PitN 67-75ChiA	10-22-41	Cambridge, Mass.		R	L	6'	190	143	135	.514	57	592	245	100	2337	2205	589	1269	22	3.03	422	27	0	.064
Woodeshick, Hal-Harold Joseph	58DetA 58CleA 59-61WasA 61DetA 62-65HouN 65-67StLN	8-24-32	Wilkes-Barre, Pa.		R	L	6'3	200	44	62	.415	61	427	62	7	847	816	389	484	1	3.56	174	16	0	.092
Woodson, Dick-Richard Lee	69-70,72-74MinA 74NYA	3-30-45	Oelwein, Iowa		R	R	6'5	205	34	32	.515	2	137	76	15	589	522	253	315	5	3.47	117	9	0	.077
Worthington, Al-Allan Fulton (Red)	53-54,56-57NYN 58-59SFN 60BosA 60ChiA 63-64ChiN 64-69MinA	2- 5-29	Birmingham, Ala.		R	R	6'2	205	75	82	.478	110	602	69	11	1245	1130	527	834	3	3.39	255	35	1	.137
Wright, Clyde-Clyde	66-73CalA 74MilA 75TexA	2-20-41	Jefferson City, Tenn.		R	L	6'1	195	100	111	.474	3	329	235	67	1729	1679	550	667	9	3.50	378	69	4	.183
Wright, Ken-Kenneth Warren	70-73KCA 74NYA	9- 4-46	Pensacola, Fla.		R	R	6'2	230	11	15	.423	8	113	24	2	236	195	180	181	1	4.54	28	2	0	.071
Wyatt, John-John Thomas	61-66KCA 66-68BosA 68NYA 68DetA 69OakA	4-19-35	Chicago, Ill.		R	R	5'11	205	42	44	.488	103	435	9	0	686	600	346	540	0	3.48	83	4	0	.048
Wynne, Bill-Billy Vernon	67NYN 68-70ChiA 71 CalA	7-31-43	Williams, N.C.		L	R	6'3	205	8	11	.421	0	42	30	6	188	217	78	97	1	4.31	55	6	0	.109
Yellen, Larry-Lawrence Alan	63-64HouN	1- 4-43	Brooklyn, N.Y.		R	R	5'11	190	0	0	–	0	14	2	0	26	34	11	12	0	6.23	5	0	0	.000
York, Jim-James Harlan	70-71KCA 72-75HouN	8-27-47	Maywood, Cal.		R	R	6'3	200	15	17	.469	10	171	4	0	275	276	128	188	0	3.73	40	2	1	.050
Yount, Larry-Lawrence King	71HouN	2-15-50	Houston, Tex.		R	R	6'3	195	0	0	–	0	1	0	0	0	0	0	0	0	–				
Zachary, Chris-William Christopher	63-67HouN 69KCA 71StLN 72DetA 73PitN	2-19-44	Knoxville, Tenn.		L	R	6'2	200	10	29	.256	2	108	40	1	321	344	122	184	1	4.51	83	15	0	.181
Zahn, Geoff-Geoffrey Clayton	73-75LAN 75ChiN	12-19-45	Baltimore, Md.		L	L	6'1	185	6	13	.316	1	45	21	1	159	152	49	64	2	3.06	40	6	0	.150
Zamora, Oscar-Oscar Joseph	74-75ChiN	9-23-44	Camaguey, Cuba		R	R	5'10	178	8	12	.400	20	108	0	0	155	166	34	66	0	4.01	17	3	0	.176
Zanni, Dom-Dominick Thomas	58-59,61SFN 62-63ChiA 63,65-66CinN	3- 1-32	Bronx, N.Y.		R	R	5'11	180	9	6	.600	10	111	3	0	182	155	85	148	0	3.81	25	7	0	.280
Zepp, Bill-William Clinton	69-70MinA 71DetA	7-22-46	Detroit, Mich.		R	R	6'2	185	10	5	.667	4	63	24	1	188	201	72	81	1	3.64	49	6	0	.122

Leaders and Features

Baseball's great magnetism has always been in the sheer numbers the sport produces. It is an attraction which no other sport can come close to matching. Although there has been repeated criticism of the lack of action of the game, no fan has ever delighted more than when a batting average is remembered and thrown up in conversation—baseball's advantage in that respect is also its disadvantage. It is a game of innings, not time, and the interest of the fan is more determined on his ability to appreciate the subtlety of play than the speed or violence present in other sports. For these reasons, it is important to realize that baseball is a season, not a single game, and that as the performance of the individuals on a team are followed, so grows the great interest in the sport.

The statistics which are part of the game of baseball are designed in a unique way as to give each man on a team a measure of his performance. It is also in this area where baseball has its great advantage over other sports. A .333 batting average, for example, tells that the player was successful one-third of the time, just as an earned run average is an excellent indication of a pitcher's effectiveness. In this respect, there are statistics for every act performed on the field—a yardstick of independence not to be found in any other sport.

Baseball is by no means perfect in its representation of the individuals who perform their tasks, it is simply endowed with a greater and more accurate means for comparison than other sports. Because of the varied statistical categories available, it is possible to measure men who are separated by decades. For this reason, statistics such as Ty Cobb's lifetime batting average of .367 and Babe Ruth's hitting a home run every 11.8 times at bat are not dated numbers. The fan could, for instance, from these two percentages envision how these two immortals might fare on the playing field today. Even with playing conditions drastically altered from fifty years ago, the continuity of the sport remains uninterrupted due to its unique set of statistical information. Along these lines the assumption could be made that even if in a hundred years from now someone was to scan through the records, he could come very close to recreating a player's performance. In the case of Tom Seaver, a few of the things which could be immediately learned is that he had an excellent fastball (number of strikeouts), good control (balls on base vs. innings pitched), and endurance (complete games vs. games started).

On the following pages are many categories of single-season and lifetime leaders, as well as special features dealing with the World Series and other aspects of baseball. Although they do not tell the entire story of baseball, they are more than endless columns of numbers. For if they only inspire the human aspect of the people they represent, they have achieved a sound purpose.

Note: On certain of the lifetime categories, active players who are approaching the minimum needed to qualify for that category may be included. This does not mean that the ranking listed for the active player is truly his lifetime ranking in that category.

YEARLY PENNANT LEADERS

AMERICAN LEAGUE

TEAM (WORLD SERIES WINS)	Manager	Won	Lost	Pct.	Games Ahead	Bat Age	Pitch Age	Year
Chicago	Clark Griffith	83	53	.610	4	30	26	1901
Philadelphia	Connie Mack	83	53	.610	5	29	26	1902
Boston(5)	Jimmy Collins	91	47	.659	14.5	30	28	1903
Boston	Jimmy Collins	95	59	.617	1.5	31	29	1904
Philadelphia(1)	Connie Mack	92	56	.622	2	29	25	1905
Chicago(4)	Fielder Jones	93	58	.616	3	29	27	1906
Detroit(0)	Hughie Jennings	92	58	.613	1.5	26	30	1907
Detroit(1)	Hughie Hennings	90	63	.588	.5	27	27	1908
Detroit(3)	Hughie Jennings	98	54	.645	3.5	27	27	1909
Philadelphia(4)	Connie Mack	102	48	.680	14.5	28	27	1910
Philadelphia(4)	Connie Mack	101	50	.669	13.5	27	29	1911
Boston(4)	Jake Stahl	105	47	.691	14	27	25	1912
Philadelphia(4)	Connie Mack	96	57	.627	6.5	25	25	1913
Philadelphia(0)	Connie Mack	99	53	.651	8.5	26	25	1914
Boston(4)	Bill Carrigan	101	50	.669	2.5	27	25	1915
Boston(4)	Bill Carrigan	91	63	.591	2	27	26	1916
Chicago(4)	Pants Rowland	100	54	.649	9	26	28	1917
Boston(4)	Ed Barrow	75	51	.595	2.5	29	25	1918
Chicago(3)	Kid Gleason	88	52	.629	3.5	28	30	1919
Cleveland(5)	Tris Speaker	98	56	.636	2	29	28	1920
New York(3)	Miller Huggins	98	55	.641	4.5	28	28	1921
New York(0)	Miller Huggins	94	60	.610	1	29	27	1922
New York(4)	Miller Huggins	98	54	.645	16	29	29	1923
Washington(4)	Bucky Harris	92	62	.597	2	28	29	1924
Washington(3)	Bucky Harris	96	55	.636	8.5	30	32	1925
New York(3)	Miller Huggins	91	63	.591	3	27	30	1926
New York(4)	Miller Huggins	110	44	.714	19	28	31	1927
New York(4)	Miller Huggins	101	53	.656	2.5	28	29	1928
Philadelphia(4)	Connie Mack	104	46	.693	18	29	31	1929
Philadelphia(4)	Connie Mack	102	52	.662	8	28	32	1930
Philadelphia(3)	Connie Mack	107	45	.704	13.5	28	29	1931
New York(4)	Joe McCarthy	107	47	.695	13	28	29	1932
Washington(1)	Joe Cronin	99	53	.651	7	30	30	1933
Detroit(3)	Mickey Cochrane	101	53	.656	7	28	28	1934
Detroit(4)	Mickey Cochrane	93	58	.616	3	29	28	1935
New York(4)	Joe McCarthy	102	51	.667	19.5	28	30	1936
New York(4)	Joe McCarthy	102	52	.662	13	28	30	1937
New York(4)	Joe McCarthy	99	53	.651	9.5	28	30	1938
New York(4)	Joe McCarthy	106	45	.702	17	27	30	1939
Detroit(3)	Del Baker	90	64	.584	1	30	27	1940
New York(4)	Joe McCarthy	101	53	.656	17	27	29	1941
New York(1)	Joe McCarthy	103	51	.669	9	28	30	1942
New York(4)	Joe McCarthy	98	56	.636	13.5	29	31	1943
St. Louis(2)	Luke Sewell	89	65	.578	1	30	31	1944
Detroit(4)	Steve O'Neill	88	65	.575	1.5	33	29	1945
Boston(3)	Joe Cronin	104	50	.675	12	30	31	1946
New York(4)	Bucky Harris	97	57	.630	12	30	30	1947
Cleveland(4)	Lou Boudreau	97	58	.626	1	28	30	1948
Defeated Boston in 1 game playoff								
New York(4)	Casey Stengel	97	57	.630	1	28	30	1949
New York(4)	Casey Stengel	98	56	.636	3	29	31	1950
New York(4)	Casey Stengel	98	56	.636	5	28	31	1951
New York(4)	Casey Stengel	95	59	.617	2	27	31	1952
New York(4)	Casey Stengel	99	52	.656	8.5	29	32	1953
Cleveland(0)	Al Lopez	111	43	.721	8	30	30	1954
New York(3)	Casey Stengel	96	58	.623	3	28	28	1955
New York(4)	Casey Stengel	97	57	.630	9	28	27	1956
New York(3)	Casey Stengel	98	56	.636	8	29	28	1957
New York(4)	Casey Stengel	92	62	.597	10	27	29	1958
Chicago(2)	Al Lopez	94	60	.610	5	30	32	1959
New York(3)	Casey Stengel	97	57	.630	8	28	29	1960
New York(4)	Ralph Houk	109	53	.673	8	28	27	1961
New York(4)	Ralph Houk	96	66	.593	5	29	28	1962
New York(0)	Ralph Houk	104	57	.646	10.5	28	27	1963
New York(3)	Yogi Berra	99	63	.611	1	28	27	1964
Minnesota(3)	Sam Mele	102	60	.630	7	27	28	1965
Baltimore(4)	Hank Bauer	97	63	.606	9	26	26	1966
Boston(3)	Dick Williams	92	70	.568	1	25	28	1967
Detroit(4)	Mayo Smith	103	59	.636	12	28	28	1968
Baltimore(1)	Earl Weaver	109	53	.673	19	28	28	1969
Won Championship Series over Minnesota (3 games to none)								
Baltimore(4)	Earl Weaver	108	54	.667	15	29	29	1970
Won Championship Series over Minnesota (3 games to none)								
Baltimore(3)	Earl Weaver	101	57	.639	12	30	30	1971
Won Championship Series over Oakland (3 games to none)								
Oakland(4)	Dick Williams	93	62	.600	5.5	27	28	1972
Won Championship Series over Detroit (3 games to 2)								
Oakland(4)	Dick Williams	94	68	.580	6	28	27	1973
Won Championship Series over Baltimore (3 games to 2)								
Oakland(4)	Al Dark	90	72	.556	5	29	28	1974
Won Championship Series over Baltimore (3 games to 1)								
Boston(3)	Darrell Johnson	95	65	.594	4.5	27	28	1975
Won Championship Series over Oakland (3 games to 0)								

NOTE: BOLD FACE DENOTES TEAM WINNING WORLD SERIES

NATIONAL LEAGUE

Year	TEAM (WORLD SERIES WINS)	Manager	Won	Lost	Pct.	Games Ahead	Bat Age	Pitch Age
1901	Pittsburgh	Fred Clarke	90	49	.647	1.5	29	28
1902	Pittsburgh	Fred Clarke	103	36	.741	27.5	28	28
1903	Pittsburgh(3)	Fred Clarke	91	49	.650	6.5	27	31
1904	New York	John McGraw	106	47	.693	13	29	26
1905	**New York(4)**	John McGraw	105	48	.686	9	30	27
1906	Chicago(2)	Frank Chance	116	36	.763	20	27	27
1907	**Chicago(4)**	Frank Chance	107	45	.704	17	28	29
1908	**Chicago(4)**	Frank Chance	99	55	.643	1	29	30
1909	**Pittsburgh(4)**	Fred Clarke	110	42	.724	6.5	28	30
1910	Chicago(1)	Frank Chance	104	50	.675	13	30	29
1911	New York(2)	John McGraw	99	54	.647	7.5	26	26
1912	New York(3)	John McGraw	103	48	.682	10	26	27
1913	New York(1)	John McGraw	101	51	.664	12.5	26	28
1914	**Boston(4)**	George Stallings	94	59	.614	10.5	24	24
1914 FEDERAL LEAGUE	Indianapolis	Bill Phillips	88	65	.575	1.5	27	29
1915	Philadelphia(1)	Pat Moran	90	62	.592	7	28	27
1915 FEDERAL LEAGUE	Chicago	Joe Tinker	86	66	.566	0	26	31
1916	Brooklyn(1)	Wilbert Robinson	94	60	.610	2.5	29	29
1917	New York(2)	John McGraw	98	56	.636	10	28	29
1918	Chicago(2)	Fred Mitchell	84	45	.651	10.5	[illegible]	[illegible]
1919	**Cincinnati(5)**	Pat Moran	96	44	.686	9	29	28
1920	Brooklyn(2)	Wilbert Robinson	93	61	.604	7	31	29
1921	**New York(5)**	John McGraw	94	59	.614	4	27	30
1922	**New York(4)**	John McGraw	93	61	.604	7	28	27
1923	New York(2)	John McGraw	95	58	.621	4.5	27	27
1924	New York(3)	John McGraw	93	60	.608	1.5	28	26
1925	**Pittsburgh(4)**	Bill McKechnie	95	58	.621	8.5	28	32
1926	**St. Louis(4)**	Rogers Hornsby	89	65	.578	2	27	29
1927	Pittsburgh(0)	Donie Bush	94	60	.610	1.5	28	31
1928	St. Louis(0)	Bill McKechnie	95	59	.617	2	28	31
1929	Chicago(1)	Joe McCarthy	98	54	.645	10.5	30	30
1930	St. Louis(2)	Gabby Street	92	62	.597	2	29	31
1931	**St. Louis(4)**	Gabby Street	101	53	.656	13	29	31
1932	Chicago(0)	R. Hornsby(53-44) C. Grimm(37-20)	90	64	.584	4	28	31
1933	**New York(4)**	Bill Terry	91	61	.599	5	29	31
1934	**St. Louis(4)**	Frankie Frisch	95	58	.621	2	28	30
1935	Chicago(2)	Charlie Grimm	100	54	.649	4	27	27
1936	New York(2)	Bill Terry	92	62	.597	5	29	28
1937	New York(1)	Bill Terry	85	57	.625	3	28	28
1938	Chicago(0)	C. Grimm(45-36) G. Hartnett(44-27)	89	63	.586	2	29	31
1939	Cincinnati(0)	Bill McKechnie	97	57	.630	4.5	29	29
1940	**Cincinnati(4)**	Bill McKechnie	100	53	.654	12	28	29
1941	Brooklyn(1)	Leo Durocher	100	54	.649	2.5	28	31
1942	**St. Louis(4)**	Billy Southworth	106	48	.688	2	26	26
1943	St. Louis(1)	Billy Southworth	105	49	.682	18	27	27
1944	**St. Louis(4)**	Billy Southworth	105	49	.682	14.5	27	28
1945	Chicago(3)	Charlie Grimm	98	56	.636	3	29	32
1946	**St. Louis(4)**	Eddie Dyer	98	58	.628	2	27	29
	Defeated Brooklyn in Playoff (2 games to none)							
1947	Brooklyn(3)	Sukeforth(1-0) Shotton(93-60)	94	60	.610	5	28	26
1948	Boston(2)	Billy Southworth	91	62	.595	6.5	30	31
1949	Brooklyn(1)	Burt Shotton	97	57	.630	1	27	25
1950	Philadelphia(0)	Eddie Sawyer	91	63	.591	2	27	27
1951	New York(2)	Leo Durocher	98	59	.624	1	27	28
	Defeated Brooklyn in Playoff (2 games to 1)							
1952	Brooklyn(3)	Chuck Dressen	96	57	.627	4.5	30	27
1953	Brooklyn(2)	Chuck Dressen	105	49	.682	13	29	28
1954	**New York(4)**	Leo Durocher	97	57	.630	5	28	30
1955	**Brooklyn(4)**	Walt Alston	98	55	.641	13.5	30	26
1956	Brooklyn(3)	Walt Alston	93	61	.604	1	32	27
1957	**Milwaukee(4)**	Fred Haney	95	59	.617	8	28	28
1958	Milwaukee(3)	Fred Haney	92	62	.597	8	29	29
1959	**Los Angeles(4)**	Walt Alston	88	68	.564	2	28	27
	Defeated Milwaukee in Playoff (2 games to none)							
1960	**Pittsburgh(4)**	Danny Murtaugh	95	59	.617	7	29	29
1961	Cincinnati(1)	Fred Hutchinson	93	61	.604	4	27	26
1962	San Francisco(3)	Al Dark	103	62	.624	1	27	29
	Defeated Los Angeles in Playoff (2 games to 1)							
1963	**Los Angeles(4)**	Walt Alston	99	63	.611	6	27	26
1964	**St. Louis(4)**	Johnny Keane	93	69	.574	1	27	30
1965	**Los Angeles(4)**	Walt Alston	97	65	.599	2	29	28
1966	Los Angeles(0)	Walt Alston	95	67	.586	1.5	29	27
1967	**St. Louis(4)**	Red Schoendienst	101	60	.627	10.5	27	28
1968	St. Louis(3)	Red Schoendienst	97	65	.599	9	29	27
1969	**New York(4)**	Gil Hodges	100	62	.617	8	27	26
	Won Championship Series over Atlanta (3 games to none)							
1970	Cincinnati(1)	Sparky Anderson	102	60	.630	14.5	25	26
	Won Championship Series over Pittsburgh (3 games to none)							
1971	**Pittsburgh(4)**	Danny Murtaugh	97	65	.599	7	28	28
	Won Championship Series over San Francisco (3 games to 1)							
1972	Cincinnati(3)	Sparky Anderson	95	59	.617	10.5	27	25
	Won Championship Series over Pittsburgh (3 games to 2)							
1973	New York(3)	Yogi Berra	82	79	.509	1.5	28	27
	Won Championship Series over Cincinnati (3 games to 2)							
1974	Los Angeles(1)	Walt Alston	102	60	.630	4	27	30
	Won Championship Series over Pittsburgh (3 games to 1)							
1975	**Cincinnati(4)**	Sparky Anderson	108	54	.667	20	28	27
	Won Championship Series over Pittsburgh (3 games to 0)							

YEARLY BATTING LEADERS

AT-BATS

American League			National League	
Waldron-Was. + Mil.	598	1901	Burkett-St.L.	601
Parent-Bos.	567	1902	Dolan-Bkn.	592
Dougherty-Bos.	590	1903	Beaumont-Pit.	613
Dougherty-Bos. + N.Y.	647	1904	Beaumont-Pit.	615
Stone-St.L.	632	1905	Abbaticchio-Bos.	610
Flick-Cle.	624	1906	Bennett-St.L.	595
Donahue-Chi.	609	1907	Shannon-N.Y.	585
Crawford-Det.	591	1908	Grant-Phi.	598
Hartzell-St.L.	595	1909	Grant-Phi.	631
Lajoie-Cle.	591	1910	Hoblitzell-Cin.	611
Milan-Was.	616	1911	Hoblitzell-Cin.	622
Foster-Was.	618	1912	Campbell-Bos.	624
Crawford-Det.	610	1913	Carey-Pit.	620
Foster-Was.	616	1914	Carey-Pit.	593
Foster-Was.	618	1915	Burns-N.Y.	622
Shotton-St.L.	618	1916	Burns-N.Y.	623
Cobb-Det.	588	1917	Chase-Cin.	602
Foster-Was.	519	1918	Hollocher-Chi.	509
Weaver-Chi.	571	1919	Olson-Bkn.	590
Sisler-St.L.	631	1920	Stock-St.L.	639
Tobin-St.L.	671	1921	Olson-Bkn.	652
Rice-Was.	633	1922	Maranville-Pit.	672
Dugan-N.Y.	644	1923	Statz-Chi.	655
Jamieson-Cle.	644			
Rice-Was.	646	1924	Wright-Pit.	616
Simmons-Phi.	658	1925	Adams-Chi.	627
Rice-Was.	641	1926	Adams-Chi.	624
Combs-N.Y.	648	1927	Adams-Chi.	647
Lind-Cle.	650	1928	L.Waner-Pit.	659
Johnson-Det.	640	1929	L.Waner-Pit.	662
Oliver-Bos.	646	1930	Douthit-St.L.	664
Averill-Cle.	627	1931	L.Waner-Pit.	681
Simmons-Phi.	670	1932	Critz-N.Y.	659
Cramer-Phi.	661	1933	Fullis-Phi.	647
Cramer-Phi.	649	1934	Rothrock-St.L.	647
Cramer-Phi.	644	1935	Moore-N.Y.	681
Finney-Phi.	653	1936	Jensen-Pit.	696
Lewis-Was.	668	1937	Medwick-St.L.	633
Cramer-Bos.	658	1938	McCormick-Cin.	640
Crosetti-N.Y.	656	1939	Brown-St.L.	645
Cramer-Bos.	661	1940	F.McCormick-Cin.	618
Cramer-Was.	660	1941	Rucker-N.Y.	622
Cramer-Det.	630	1942	Brown-St.L.	606
Wakefield-Det.	633	1943	Holmes-Bos.	629
Rocco-Cle.	653	1944	Williams-Cin.	653
Stirnweis-N.Y.	632	1945	Clay-Cin.	656
Pesky-Bos.	621	1946	Musial-St.L.	624
Pesky-Bos.	638	1947	Schoendienst-St.L.	659
DiMaggio-Bos.	648	1948	Rojek-Pit.	641
Mitchell-Cle.	640	1949	Ashburn-Phi.	662
			Hamner-Phi.	662
Kell-Det.	641	1950	Schoendienst-St.L.	642
DiMaggio-Bos.	639	1951	Furillo-Bkn.	667
Fox-Chi.	648	1952	Adams-Cin.	637
Kuenn-Det.	679	1953	Dark-N.Y.	647
Kuenn-Det.	656	1954	Dark-N.Y.	644
Fox-Chi.	636	1955	Bruton-Mil.	636
Fox-Chi.	649	1956	Temple-Cin.	632
Gardner-Bal.	644	1957	Blasingame-St.L.	650
Malzone-Bos.	627	1958	Banks-Chi.	617
Fox-Chi.	624	1959	Pinson-Cin.	648
Fox-Chi.	605	1960	Pinson-Cin.	652
Robinson-Bal.	668	1961	Wills-L.A.	613
Richardson-N.Y.	692	1962	Wills-L.A.	695
Richardson-N.Y.	630	1963	Altman-St.L.	662
Richardson-N.Y.	679	1964	Flood-St.L.	679
Versalles-Min.	666	1965	Rose-Cin.	670
Aparicio-Bal.	659	1966	Alou-Atl.	666
Tovar-Min.	649	1967	Brock-St.L.	689
Campaneris-Oak.	642	1968	Alou-Atl.	662
Clarke-N.Y.	641	1969	Alou-Pit.	698
Clarke-N.Y.	686	1970	Alou-Pit.	677
Alomar-Cal.	689	1971	Bowa-Phi.	650
Campaneris-Oak.	625	1972	Rose-Cin.	645
White-N.Y.	639	1973	Rose-Cin.	680
Money-Mil.	629	1974	Cash-Phi.	687
Brett-K.C.	634	1975	Cash-Phi.	699

1914 FEDERAL LEAGUE	Swacina-Bal.	617
1915 FEDERAL LEAGUE	Tobin-St.L.	623

HITS

American League			National League	
Lajoie-Phi.	229	1901	Burkett-St.L.	228
Hickman-Bos + Cle.	194	1902	Beaumont-Pit.	194
Dougherty-Bos.	195	1903	Beaumont-Pit.	209
Lajoie-Cle.	211	1904	Beaumont-Pit.	185
Stone-St.L.	187	1905	Seymour-Cin.	219
Lajoie-Cle.	214	1906	Steinfeldt-Chi.	176
Cobb-Det.	212	1907	Beaumont-Bos.	187
Cobb-Det.	188	1908	Wagner-Pit.	201
Cobb-Det.	216	1909	Doyle-N.Y.	172
Lajoie-Cle.	227	1910	Byrne-Pit.	178
			Wagner-Pit.	178
Cobb-Det.	248	1911	Miller-Bos.	192
Cobb-Det.	227	1912	Zimmerman-Chi.	207
Jackson-Cle.	197	1913	Cravath-Phi.	179
Speaker-Bos.	193	1914	Magee-Phi.	171
Cobb-Det.	208	1915	Doyle-N.Y.	189
Speaker-Cle.	211	1916	Chase-Cin.	184
Cobb-Det.	225	1917	Groh-Cin.	182
Burns-Phi.	178	1918	Hollocher-Chi.	161
Cobb-Det.	191	1919	Olson-Bkn.	164
Veach-Det.	191			
Sisler-St.L.	257	1920	Hornsby-St.L.	218
Heilmann-Det.	237	1921	Hornsby-St.L.	235
Sisler-St.L.	246	1922	Hornsby-St.L.	250
Jamieson-Cle.	222	1923	Frisch-N.Y.	223
Rice-Was.	216	1924	Hornsby-St.L.	227
Simmons-Phi.	253	1925	Bottomley-St.L.	227
Burns-Cle.	216	1926	Brown-Bos.	201
Rice-Was.	216			
Combs-N.Y.	231	1927	P.Waner-Pit.	237
Manush-St.L.	241	1928	Lindstrom-N.Y.	231
Alexander-Det.	215	1929	O'Doul-Phi.	254
Gehringer-Det.	215			
Hodapp-Cle.	225	1930	Terry-N.Y.	254
Gehrig-N.Y.	211	1931	L.Waner-Pit.	214
Simmons-Phi.	216	1932	Klein-Phi.	226
Manush-Was.	221	1933	Klein-Phi.	223
Gehringer-Det.	214	1934	P.Waner-Pit.	217
Vosmik-Cle.	216	1935	Herman-Chi.	227
Averill-Cle.	232	1936	Medwick-St.L.	223
Bell-St.L.	218	1937	Medwick-St.L.	237
Vosmik-Bos.	201	1938	McCormick-Cin.	209
Rolfe-N.Y.	213	1939	McCormick-Cin.	209
Cramer-Bos.	200	1940	Hack-Chi.	191
McCosky-Det.	200		F.McCormick-Cin.	191
Radcliffe-St.L.	200			
Travis-Was.	218	1941	Hack-Chi.	186
Peksy-Bos.	205	1942	Slaughter-St.L.	188
Wakefield-Det.	200	1943	Musial-St.L.	220
Stirnweiss-N.Y.	205	1944	Cavarretta-Chi.	197
			Musial-St.L.	197
Stirnweiss-N.Y.	195	1945	Holmes-Bos.	224
Pesky-Bos.	208	1946	Musial-St.L.	228
Pesky-Bos.	207	1947	Holmes-Bos.	191
Dillinger-St.L.	207	1948	Musial-St.L.	230
Mitchell-Cle.	203	1949	Musial-St.L.	207
Kell-Det.	218	1950	Snider-Bkn.	199
Kell-Det.	191	1951	Ashburn-Phi.	221
Fox-Chi.	192	1952	Musial-St.L.	194
Kuenn-Det.	209	1953	Ashburn-Phi.	205
Fox-Chi.	201	1954	Mueller-N.Y.	212
Kuenn-Det.	201			
Kaline-Det.	200	1955	Kluszewski-Cin.	192
Kuenn-Det.	196	1956	Aaron-Mil.	200
Fox-Chi.	196	1957	Schoendienst-N.Y. + Mil.	200
Fox-Chi.	187	1958	Ashburn-Phi.	215
Kuenn-Det.	198	1959	Aaron-Mil.	223
Minoso-Chi.	184	1960	Mays-S.F.	190
Cash-Det.	193	1961	Pinson-Cin.	208
Richardson-N.Y.	209	1962	Davis-L.A.	230
Yastrzemski-Bos.	183	1963	Pinson-Cin.	204
Oliva-Min.	217	1964	Clemente-Pit.	211
			Flood-St.L.	211
Oliva-Min.	185	1965	Rose-Cin.	209
Oliva-Min.	191	1966	Alou-Atl.	218
Yastrzemski-Bos.	189	1967	Clemente-Pit.	209
Campaneris-Oak.	177	1968	Alou-Atl.	210
			Rose-Cin.	210
Oliva-Min.	197	1969	Alou-Pit.	231
Oliva-Min.	204	1970	Rose-Cin.	205
			Williams-Chi.	205
Tovar-Min.	204	1971	Torre-St.L.	230
Rudi-Oak.	181	1972	Rose-Cin.	198
Carew-Min.	203	1973	Rose-Cin.	230
Carew-Min.	218	1974	Garr-Atl.	214
Brett-K.C.	195	1975	Cash-Phi.	213

1914 FEDERAL LEAGUE	Kauff-Ind.	211
1915 FEDERAL LEAGUE	Tobin-St.L.	186

RUNS

American League			National League	
Lajoie-Phi.	145	1901	Burkett-St.L.	139
Fultz-Phi.	109	1902	Wagner-Pit.	105
Hartsel-Phi.	109			
Dougherty-Bos.	106	1903	Beaumont-Pit.	137
Dougherty-Bos. + N.Y.	113	1904	Browne-N.Y.	99
Davis-Phi.	92	1905	Donlin-N.Y.	124
Flick-Cle.	98	1906	Chance-Chi.	103
			Wagner-Pit.	103
Crawford-Det.	102	1907	Shannon-N.Y.	104
McIntyre-Det.	105	1908	Tenney-N.Y.	101
Cobb-Det.	116	1909	Leach-Pit.	126
Cobb-Det.	106	1910	Magee-Phi.	110
Cobb-Det.	147	1911	Sheckard-Chi.	121
Collins-Phi.	137	1912	Bescher-Cin.	120
Collins-Phi.	125	1913	Carey-Pit.	99
			Leach-Chi.	99
Collins-Phi.	122	1914	Burns-N.Y.	100
Cobb-Det.	144	1915	Cravath-Phi.	89
Cobb-Det.	113	1916	Burns-N.Y.	105
Bush-Det.	112	1917	Burns-N.Y.	103
Chapman-Cle.	84	1918	Groh-Cin.	88
Ruth-Bos.	102	1919	Burns-N.Y.	86
Ruth-N.Y.	158	1920	Burns-N.Y.	115
Ruth-N.Y.	177	1921	Hornsby-St.L.	131
Sisler-St.L.	134	1922	Hornsby-St.L.	141
Ruth-N.Y.	151	1923	Youngs-N.Y.	121
Ruth-N.Y.	143	1924	Frisch-N.Y.	121
			Hornsby-St.L.	121
Mostil-Chi.	135	1925	Cuyler-Pit.	144
Ruth-N.Y.	139	1926	Cuyler-Pit.	113
Ruth-N.Y.	158	1927	Hornsby-N.Y.	133
			L.Waner-Pit.	133
Ruth-N.Y.	163	1928	P.Waner-Pit.	142
Gehringer-Det.	131	1929	Hornsby-Chi.	156
Simmons-Phi.	152	1930	Klein-Phi.	158
Gehrig-N.Y.	163	1931	Klein-Phi.	121
			Terry-N.Y.	121
Foxx-Phi.	151	1932	Klein-Phi.	152
Gehrig-N.Y.	138	1933	Martin-St.L.	122
Gehringer-Det.	134	1934	P.Waner-Pit.	122
Gehrig-N.Y.	125	1935	Galan-Chi.	133
Gehrig-N.Y.	167	1936	Vaughan-Pit.	122
DiMaggio-N.Y.	151	1937	Medwick-St.L.	111
Greenberg-Det.	149	1938	Ott-N.Y.	116
Rolfe-N.Y.	139	1939	Werber-Cin.	115
Williams-Bos.	134	1940	Vaughan-Pit.	113
Williams-Bos.	135	1941	Reiser-Bkn.	117
Williams-Bos.	141	1942	Ott-N.Y.	118
Case-Was.	102	1943	Vaughan-Bkn.	112
Stirnweiss-N.Y.	125	1944	Nicholson-Chi.	116
Stirnweiss-N.Y.	107	1945	Stanky-Bkn.	128
Williams-Bos.	142	1946	Musial-St.L.	124
Williams-Bos.	125	1947	Mize-N.Y.	137
Henrich-N.Y.	138	1948	Musial-St.L.	135
Williams-Bos.	150	1949	Reese-Bkn.	132
DiMaggio-Bos.	131	1950	Torgeson-Bos.	120
DiMaggio-Bos.	113	1951	Kiner-Pit.	124
			Musial-St.L.	124
Doby-Cle.	104	1952	Hemus-St.L.	105
			Musial-St.L.	105
Rosen-Cle.	115	1953	Snider-Bkn.	132
Mantle-N.Y.	129	1954	Musial-St.L.	120
			Snider-Bkn.	120
Smith-Cle.	123	1955	Snider-Bkn.	126
Mantle-N.Y.	132	1956	Robinson-Cin.	122
Mantle-N.Y.	121	1957	Aaron-Mil.	118
Mantle-N.Y.	127	1958	Mays-S.F.	121
Yost-Det.	115	1959	Pinson-Cin.	131
Mantle-N.Y.	119	1960	Bruton-Mil.	112
Mantle-N.Y.	132	1961	Mays-S.F.	129
Maris-N.Y.	132			
Pearson-L.A.	115	1962	Robinson-Cin.	134
Allison-Min.	99	1963	Aaron-Mil.	121
Oliva-Min.	109	1964	Allen-Phi.	125
Versalles-Min.	126	1965	Harper-Cin.	126
F. Robinson-Bal.	122	1966	Alou-Atl.	122
Yastrzemski-Bos.	112	1967	Aaron-Atl.	113
			Brock-St.L.	113
McAuliffe-Det.	95	1968	Beckert-Chi	98
Jackson-Oak.	123	1969	Bonds-S.F.	120
			Rose-Cin	120
Yastrzemski-Bos.	125	1970	Williams-Chi.	137
Buford-Bal.	99	1971	Brock-St.L.	126
Murcer-N.Y.	102	1972	Morgan-Cin.	122
Jackson-Oak.	90	1973	Bonds-S.F.	131
Yastrzemski-Bos.	93	1974	Rose-Cin.	110
Lynn-Bos.	103	1975	Rose-Cin.	112

1914 FEDERAL LEAGUE	Kauff-Ind.	120
1915 FEDERAL LEAGUE	Borton-St.L.	97

YEARLY BATTING LEADERS

DOUBLES

AMERICAN LEAGUE			NATIONAL LEAGUE	
Lajoie-Phi.	48	1901	Beckley-Cin.	39
			Wagner-Pit.	39
Davis-Phi.	43	1902	Wagner-Pit.	33
Seybold-Phi.	43	1903	Clarke-Pit.	32
			Mertes-N.Y.	32
			Steinfeldt-Cin.	32
Lajoie-Cle.	50	1904	Wagner-Pit.	44
Davis-Phi.	47	1905	Seymour-Cin.	40
Lajoie-Cle.	49	1906	Wagner-Pit.	38
Davis-Phi.	37	1907	Wagner-Pit.	38
Cobb-Det.	36	1908	Wagner-Pit.	39
Crawford-Det.	35	1909	Wagner-Pit.	39
Lajoie-Cle.	51	1910	Byrne-Pit.	43
Cobb-Det.	47	1911	Konetchy-St.L.	38
Speaker-Bos.	53	1912	Zimmerman-Chi.	41
Jackson-Cle.	39	1913	Smith-Bkn.	40
Speaker-Bos.	46	1914	Magee-Phi.	39
Veach-Det.	40	1915	Doyle-N.Y.	40
Graney-Cle.	41	1916	Niehoff-Phi.	42
Speaker-Cle.	41			
Cobb-Det.	44	1917	Groh-Cin.	39
Speaker-Cle.	33	1918	Groh-Cin.	28
Veach-Det.	45	1919	Youngs-N.Y.	31
Speaker-Cle.	50	1920	Hornsby-St.L.	44
Speaker-Cle.	52	1921	Hornsby-St.L.	44
Speaker-Cle.	48	1922	Hornsby-St.L.	46
Speaker-Cle.	59	1923	Roush-Cin.	41
Heilmann-Det.	45	1924	Hornsby-St.L.	43
J. Sewell-Cle.	45			
McManus-St.L.	44	1925	Bottomley-St.L.	44
Burns-Cle.	64	1926	Bottomley-St.L.	40
Gehrig-N.Y.	52	1927	Stephenson-Chi.	46
Gehrig-N.Y.	47	1928	P.Waner-Pit.	50
Manush-St.L.	47			
Gehringer-Det.	45	1929	Frederick-Bkn.	52
Johnson-Det.	45			
Manush-St.L.	45			
Hodapp-Cle.	51	1930	Klein-Phi.	59
Webb-Bos.	67	1931	Adams-St.L.	46
McNair-Phi.	47	1932	P.Waner-Pit.	62
Cronin-Was.	45	1933	Klein-Phi.	44
Greenberg-Det.	63	1934	Allen-Phi.	42
			Cuyler-Chi.	42
Vosmik-Cle.	47	1935	Herman-Chi.	57
Gehringer-Det.	60	1936	Medwick-St.L.	64
Bell-St.L.	51	1937	Medwick-St.L.	56
Cronin-Bos.	51	1938	Medwick-St.L.	47
Rolfe-N.Y.	46	1939	Slaughter-St.L.	52
Greenberg-Det.	50	1940	F.McCormick-Cin.	44
Boudreau-Cle.	45	1941	Mize-St.L.	39
			Reiser-Bkn.	39
Kolloway-Chi.	40	1942	Marion-St.L.	38
Wakefield-Det.	38	1943	Musial-St.L.	48
Boudreau-Cle.	45	1944	Musial-St.L.	51
Moses-Chi.	35	1945	Holmes-Bos.	47
Vernon-Was.	51	1946	Musial-St.L.	50
Boudreau-Cle.	45	1947	Miller-Cin.	38
Williams-Bos.	44	1948	Musial-St.L.	46
Williams-Bos.	39	1949	Musial-St.L.	41
Kell-Det.	56	1950	Schoendienst-St.L.	43
Kell-Det.	36	1951	Dark-N.Y.	41
Mele-Was.	36			
Yost-Was.	36			
Fain-Phi.	43	1952	Musial-St.L.	42
Vernon-Was.	43	1953	Musial-St.L.	53
Vernon-Was.	33	1954	Musial-St.L.	41
Kuenn-Det.	38	1955	Aaron-Mil.	37
			Logan-Mil.	37
Piersall-Bos.	40	1956	Aaron-Mil.	34
Gardner-Bal.	36	1957	Hoak-Cin.	39
Minoso-Chi.	36			
Kuenn-Det.	39	1958	Cepeda-S.F.	38
Kuenn-Det.	42	1959	Pinson-Cin.	47
Francona-Cle.	36	1960	Pinson-Cin.	37
Kaline-Det.	41	1961	Aaron-Mil.	39
Robinson-Chi.	45	1962	Robinson-Cin.	51
Yastrzemski-Bos.	40	1963	Groat-St.L.	43
Oliva-Min.	43	1964	Maye-Mil.	44
Versalles-Min.	45	1965	Aaron-Mil.	40
Yastrzemski-Bos.	45			
Yastrzemski-Bos.	39	1966	Callison-Phi.	40
Oliva-Min.	34	1967	Staub-Hou.	44
Smith-Bos.	37	1968	Brock-St.L.	46
Oliva-Min.	39	1969	Alou-Pit.	41
Oliva-Min.	36	1970	Parker-L.A.	47
Otis-K.C.	36			
Tovar-Min.	36			
Smith-Bos.	33	1971	Cedeno-Hou.	40
Piniella-K.C.	33	1972	Cedeno-Hou.	39
			Montanez-Phi.	39
Bando-Oak.	32	1973	Stargell-Pit.	43
Garcia-Mil.	32			
Rudi-Oak.	39	1974	Rose-Cin.	45
Lynn-Bos.	47	1975	Rose-Cin.	47

1914 FEDERAL LEAGUE — Kauff-Ind. 44

1915 FEDERAL LEAGUE — Evans-Bkn. + Bal. 34

TRIPLES

AMERICAN LEAGUE			NATIONAL LEAGUE	
Keister-Bal.	21	1901	Sheckard-Bkn.	19
Williams-Bal.	21			
Williams-Bal.	21	1902	Crawford-Cin.	23
Crawford-Det.	25	1903	Wagner-Pit.	19
Stahl-Bos.	22	1904	Lumley-Bkn.	18
Flick-Cle.	19	1905	Seymour-Cin.	21
Flick-Cle.	22	1906	Clarke-Pit.	13
			Schulte-Chi.	13
Flick-Cle.	18	1907	Alperman-Bkn.	16
			Ganzel-Cin.	16
Cobb-Det.	20	1908	Wagner-Pit.	19
Baker-Phi.	19	1909	Mitchell-Cin.	17
Crawford-Det.	19	1910	Mitchell-Cin.	18
Cobb-Det.	24	1911	Doyle-N.Y.	25
Jackson-Cle.	26	1912	Wilson-Pit.	36
Crawford-Det.	23	1913	Saier-Chi.	21
Crawford-Det.	26	1914	Carey-Pit.	17
Crawford-Det.	19	1915	Long-St.L.	25
Jackson-Chi.	21	1916	Hinchman-Pit.	16
Cobb-Det.	23	1917	Hornsby-St.L.	17
Cobb-Det.	14	1918	Daubert-Bkn.	15
Veach-Det.	17	1919	Myers-Bkn.	14
			Southworth-Pit.	14
Jackson-Chi.	20	1920	Myers-Bkn.	22
Shanks-Was.	19	1921	Hornsby-St.L.	18
			Powell-Bos.	18
Sisler-St.L.	18	1922	Daubert-Cin.	22
Goslin-Was.	18	1923	Carey-Pit.	19
Rice-Was.	18		Traynor-Pit.	19
Pipp-N.Y.	19	1924	Roush-Cin.	21
Goslin-Was.	20	1925	Cuyler-Pit.	26
Gehrig-N.Y.	20	1926	P.Waner-Pit.	22
Combs-N.Y.	23	1927	P.Waner-Pit.	17
Combs-N.Y.	21	1928	Bottomley-St.L.	20
Gehringer-Det.	19	1929	L.Waner-Pit.	20
Combs-N.Y.	22	1930	Comorosky-Pit.	23
Johnson-Det.	19	1931	Terry-N.Y.	20
Cronin-Was.	18	1932	Herman-Cin.	19
Manush-Was.	17	1933	Vaughan-Pit.	19
Chapman-N.Y.	13	1934	Medwick-St.L.	18
Vosmik-Cle.	20	1935	Goodman-Cin.	18
Averill-Cle.	15	1936	Goodman-Cin.	14
DiMaggio-N.Y.	15			
Rolfe-N.Y.	15			
Kreevich-Chi.	16	1937	Vaughan-Pit.	17
Walker-Chi.	16			
Heath-Cle.	18	1938	Mize-St.L.	16
Lewis-Was.	16	1939	Herman-Chi.	18
McCosky-Det.	19	1940	Vaughan-Pit.	15
Heath-Cle.	20	1941	Reiser-Bkn.	17
Spence-Was.	15	1942	Slaughter-St.L.	17
Lindell-N.Y.	12	1943	Musial-St.L.	20
Moses-Chi.	12			
Lindell-N.Y.	16	1944	Barrett-Pit.	19
Stirnweiss-N.Y.	16			
Stirnweiss-N.Y.	22	1945	Olmo-Bkn.	13
Edwards-Cle.	16	1946	Musial-St.L.	20
Henrich-N.Y.	13	1947	Walker-St.L. + Phi.	16
Henrich-N.Y.	14	1948	Musial-St.L.	18
Mitchell-Cle.	23	1949	Musial-St.L.	13
			Slaughter-St.L.	13
DiMaggio-Bos.	11	1950	Ashburn-Phi.	14
Doerr-Bos.	11			
Evers-Det.	11			
Minoso-Cle. + Chi.	14	1951	Bell-Pit.	12
			Musial-St.L.	12
Avila-Cle.	11	1952	Thomson-N.Y.	14
Rivera-Chi.	16	1953	Gilliam-Bkn.	17
Minoso-Chi.	18	1954	Mays-N.Y.	13
Carey-N.Y.	11	1955	Long-Pit.	13
Mantle-N.Y.	11		Mays-N.Y.	13
Jensen-Bos.	11	1956	Bruton-Mil.	15
Lemon-Was.	11			
Minoso-Chi.	11			
Simpson-K.C.	11			
Bauer-N.Y.	9	1957	Mays-N.Y.	20
McDougald-N.Y.	9			
Simpson-K.C. + N.Y.	9			
Power-K.C. + Cle.	10	1958	Ashburn-Phi.	13
Allison-Was.	9	1959	Moon-L.A.	11
			Neal-L.A.	11
Fox-Chi.	10	1960	Bruton-Mil.	13
Wood-Det.	14	1961	Altman-Chi.	12
Cimoli-K.C.	15	1962	Callison-Phi.	10
			Davis-L.A.	10
			Virdon-Pit.	10
			Wills-L.A.	10
Versalles-Min.	13	1963	Pinson-Cin.	14
Rollins-Min.	10	1964	Allen-Phi.	13
Versalles-Min.	10		Santo-Chi.	13
Campaneris-Oak.	12	1965	Callison-Phi.	16
Versalles-Min.	12			
Knoop-Cal.	11	1966	McCarver-St.L.	13
Blair-Bal.	12	1967	Pinson-Cin.	13
Fregosi-Bal.	13	1968	Brock-St.L.	14
Unser-Was.	8	1969	Clemente-Pit.	12
Tovar-Cin.	13	1970	Davis-L.A.	16
Patek-K.C.	11	1971	Metzger-Hou.	11
			Morgan-Hou.	11
Fisk-Bos.	9	1972	Bowa-Phi.	13
Rudi-Oak.	9			
Bumbry-Bal.	11	1973	Metzger-Hou.	14
Carew-Min.	11			
Rivers-Cal.	11	1974	Garr-Atl.	17
Brett-K.C.	13	1975	Garr-Atl.	11
Rivers-Cal.	13			

1914 FEDERAL LEAGUE — Esmond-Ind. 15; Evans-Bkn. 15

1915 FEDERAL LEAGUE — Mann-Chi. 19

HOME RUNS

AMERICAN LEAGUE			NATIONAL LEAGUE	
Lajoie-Phi.	14	1901	Crawford-Cin.	16
Seybold-Phi.	16	1902	Leach-Pit.	6
Freeman-Bos.	13	1903	Sheckard-Bkn.	9
Davis-Phi.	12	1904	Lumley-Bkn.	9
Davis-Phi.	8	1905	Odwell-Cin.	9
Davis-Phi.	12	1906	Jordan-Bkn.	12
Davis-Phi.	8	1907	Brain-Bos.	10
Crawford-Det.	7	1908	Jordan-Bkn.	12
Cobb-Det.	9	1909	Murray-N.Y.	7
Stahl-Bos.	10	1910	Beck-Bos.	10
			Schulte-Chi.	10
Baker-Phi.	11	1911	Schulte-Chi.	21
Baker-Phi.	10	1912	Zimmerman-Chi.	14
Baker-Phi.	12	1913	Cravath-Phi.	19
Baker-Phi.	9	1914	Cravath-Phi.	19
Roth-Chi. + Cle.	7	1915	Cravath-Phi.	24
Pipp-N.Y.	12	1916	Robertson-N.Y.	12
			Williams-Chi.	12
Pipp-N.Y.	9	1917	Cravath-Phi.	12
			Robertson-N.Y.	12
Ruth-Bos.	11	1918	Cravath-Phi.	8
Walker-Phi.	11			
Ruth-Bos.	29	1919	Cravath-Phi.	12
Ruth-N.Y.	54	1920	Williams-Phi	15
Ruth-N.Y.	59	1921	Kelly-N.Y.	23
Williams-St.L.	39	1922	Hornsby-St.L.	42
Ruth-N.Y.	41	1923	Williams-Phi.	41
Ruth-N.Y.	46	1924	Fournier-Bkn.	27
Meusel-N.Y.	33	1925	Hornsby-St.L.	39
Ruth-N.Y.	47	1926	Wilson-Chi.	21
Ruth-N.Y.	60	1927	Williams-Phi.	30
			Wilson-Chi.	30
Ruth-N.Y.	54	1928	Bottomley-St.L.	31
			Wilson-Chi.	31
Ruth-N.Y.	46	1929	Klein-Phi.	43
Ruth-N.Y.	49	1930	Wilson-Chi.	56
Gehrig-N.Y.	46	1931	Klein-Phi.	31
Ruth-N.Y.	46			
Foxx-Phi.	58	1932	Klein-Phi.	38
			Ott-N.Y.	38
Foxx-Phi.	48	1933	Klein-Phi.	28
Gehrig-N.Y.	49	1934	Collins-St.L.	35
			Ott-N.Y.	35
Foxx-Phi.	36	1935	Berger-Bos.	34
Greenberg-Det.	36			
Gehrig-N.Y.	49	1936	Ott-N.Y.	33
DiMaggio-N.Y.	46	1937	Medwick-St.L.	31
			Ott-N.Y.	31
Greenberg-Det.	58	1938	Ott-N.Y.	36
Foxx-Bos.	35	1939	Mize-St.L.	28
Greenberg-Det.	41	1940	Mize-St.L.	43
Williams-Bos.	37	1941	Camilli-Bkn.	34
Williams-Bos.	36	1942	Ott-N.Y.	30
York-Det.	34	1943	Nicholson-Chi.	29
Etten-N.Y.	22	1944	Nicholson-Chi.	33
Stephens-St.L.	24	1945	Holmes-Bos.	28
Greenberg-Det.	44	1946	Kiner-Pit.	23
Williams-Bos.	32	1947	Kiner-Pit.	51
			Mize-N.Y.	51
DiMaggio-N.Y.	39	1948	Kiner-Pit.	40
			Mize-N.Y.	40
Williams-Bos.	43	1949	Kiner-Pit.	54
Rosen-Cle.	37	1950	Kiner-Pit.	47
Zernial-Chi. + Phi.	33	1951	Kiner-Pit.	42
Doby-Cle.	32	1952	Kiner-Pit.	37
			Sauer-Chi.	37
Rosen-Cle.	43	1953	Mathews-Bos.	47
Doby-Cle.	32	1954	Kluszewski-Cin.	49
Mantle-N.Y.	37	1955	Mays-N.Y.	51
Mantle-N.Y.	52	1956	Snider-Bkn.	43
Sievers-Was.	42	1957	Aaron-Mil.	44
Mantle-N.Y.	42	1958	Banks-Chi.	47
Colavito-Cle.	42	1959	Mathews-Mil.	46
Killebrew-Was.	42			
Mantle-N.Y.	40	1960	Banks-Chi.	41
Maris-N.Y.	61	1961	Cepeda-S.F.	46
Killebrew-Min.	48	1962	Mays-S.F.	49
Killebrew-Min.	45	1963	Aaron-Mil.	44
			McCovey-S.F.	44
Killebrew-Min.	49	1964	Mays-S.F.	47
Conigliaro-Bos.	32	1965	Mays-S.F.	52
F.Robinson-Bal.	49	1966	Aaron-Atl.	44
Killebrew-Min.	44	1967	Aaron-Atl.	39
Yastrzemski-Bos.	44			
Howard-Was.	44	1968	McCovey-S.F.	36
Killebrew-Min.	49	1969	McCovey-S.F.	45
Howard-Was.	44	1970	Bench-Cin.	45
Melton-Chi.	33	1971	Stargell-Pit.	48
Allen-Chi.	37	1972	Bench-Cin.	40
Jackson-Oak.	32	1973	Stargell-Pit.	44
Allen-Chi.	32	1974	Schmidt-Phi.	36
Jackson-Oak.	36	1975	Schmidt-Phi.	38
Scott-Mil.	36			

1914 FEDERAL LEAGUE — Kenworthy-K.C. 15; Zwilling-Chi. 15

1915 FEDERAL LEAGUE — Chase-Buf. 17

YEARLY BATTING LEADERS

BASES ON BALLS

AMERICAN LEAGUE			NATIONAL LEAGUE	
Hoy-Chi.	86	1901	Thomas-Phi.	100
Hartsel-Phi.	87	1902	Thomas-Phi.	107
Barrett-Det.	74	1903	Thomas-Phi.	107
Barrett-Det.	79	1904	Thomas-Phi.	102
Hartsel-Phi.	121	1905	Huggins-Cin.	103
Hartsel-Phi.	88	1906	Thomas-Phi.	107
Hartsel-Phi.	106	1907	Huggins-Cin.	83
			Thomas-Phi.	83
Hartsel-Phi.	93	1908	Bresnahan-N.Y.	83
Bush-Det.	88	1909	Clarke-Pit.	80
Bush-Det.	78	1910	Huggins-St.L.	116
Bush-Det.	98	1911	Sheckard-Chi.	147
Bush-Det.	117	1912	Sheckard-Chi.	122
Shotton-St.L.	99	1913	Bescher-Cin.	94
Bush-Det.	112	1914	Huggins-St.L.	105
Collins-Chi.	119	1915	Cravath-Phi.	86
Shotton-St.L.	111	1916	Groh-Cin.	84
Graney-Cle.	94	1917	Burns-N.Y.	75
Chapman-Cle.	84	1918	Carey-Pit.	62
Graney-Cle.	105	1919	Burns-N.Y.	82
Ruth-N.Y.	148	1920	Burns-N.Y.	76
Ruth-N.Y.	144	1921	Burns-N.Y.	80
Witt-N.Y.	89	1922	Carey-Pit.	80
Ruth-N.Y.	170	1923	Burns-Cin.	101
Ruth-N.Y.	142	1924	Hornsby-St.L.	89
Kamm-Chi.	90	1925	Fournier-Bkn.	86
Mostil-Chi.	90			
Ruth-N.Y.	144	1926	Wilson-Chi.	69
Ruth-N.Y.	138	1927	Hornsby-N.Y.	86
Ruth-N.Y.	135	1928	Hornsby-Chi.	107
Bishop Phi.	120	1929	Ott-N.Y.	113
Ruth-N.Y.	136	1930	Wilson-Chi.	105
Ruth-N.Y.	128	1931	Ott-N.Y.	80
Ruth-N.Y.	130	1932	Ott-N.Y.	100
Ruth-N.Y.	114	1933	Ott-N.Y.	75
Foxx-Phi.	111	1934	Vaughan-Pit.	94
Gehrig-N.Y.	132	1935	Vaughan-Pit.	97
Gehrig-N.Y.	130	1936	Vaughan-Pit.	118
Gehrig-N.Y.	127	1937	Ott-N.Y.	102
Foxx-Bos.	119	1938	Camilli-Bkn.	119
Greenberg-Det.	111	1939	Camilli-Bkn.	110
Clift-St.L.	111			
Keller-N.Y.	106	1940	Fletcher-Pit.	119
Williams-Bos.	145	1941	Fletcher-Pit.	118
Williams-Bos.	145	1942	Ott-N.Y.	109
Keller-N.Y.	106	1943	Galan-Bkn.	103
Etten-N.Y.	97	1944	Galan-Bkn.	101
Cullenbine-Cle. + Det.	112	1945	Stanky-Bkn.	148
Williams-Bos.	156	1946	Stanky-Bkn.	137
Williams-Bos.	162	1947	Greenberg-Pit.	104
			Reese-Bkn.	104
Williams-Bos.	126	1948	Elliott-Bos.	131
Williams-Bos.	162	1949	Kiner-Pit.	117
Yost-Was.	141	1950	Stankey-N.Y.	144
Williams-Bos.	143	1951	Kiner-Pit.	137
Yost-Was.	129	1952	Kiner-Pit.	110
Yost-Was.	123	1953	Musial-St.L.	105
Williams-Bos.	136	1954	Ashburn-Phi.	125
Mantle-N.Y.	113	1955	Mathews-Mil.	109
Yost-Was.	151	1956	Snider-Bkn.	99
Mantle-N.Y.	146	1957	Ashburn-Phi.	94
			Temple-Cin.	94
Mantle-N.Y.	129	1958	Ashburn-Phi.	97
Yost-Det.	135	1959	Gilliam-L.A.	96
Yost-Det.	125	1960	Ashburn-Phi.	116
Mantle-N.Y.	126	1961	Mathews-Mil.	93
Mantle-N.Y.	122	1962	Mathews-Mil.	101
Yastrzemski-Bos.	95	1963	Mathews-Mil.	124
Siebern-Bal.	106	1964	Santo-Chi.	86
Colavito-Cle.	93	1965	Morgan-Hou.	97
Killebrew-Min.	103	1966	Santo-Chi.	95
Killebrew-Min.	131	1967	Santo-Chi.	96
Yastrzemski-Bos.	119	1968	Santo-Chi.	96
Killebrew-Min.	145	1969	Wynn-Hou.	148
Howard-Was.	132	1970	McCovey-S.F.	137
Killebrew-Min.	114	1971	Mays-S.F.	112
Allen-Chi.	99	1972	Morgan-Cin.	115
White-N.Y.	99			
Mayberry-K.C.	122	1973	Evans-Atl.	124
Tenace-Oak.	110	1974	Evans-Atl.	126
Mayberry-K.C.	119	1975	Morgan-Cin.	132

1914 FEDERAL LEAGUE Wickland-Chi. 81
1915 FEDERAL LEAGUE Borton-St.L. 92

STRIKEOUTS

AMERICAN LEAGUE			NATIONAL LEAGUE	
		1910	Hummel-Bkn.	70
		1911	Bescher-Cin.	78
			Coulson-Bkn.	78
		1912	McDonald-Bos.	91
Moeller-Was.	103	1913	Burns-N.Y.	74
Williams-St.L.	120	1914	Merkle-N.Y.	80
Lavan-St.L.	83	1915	Baird-Pit.	88
Pipp-N.Y.	82	1916	Cravath-Phi.	89
Roth-Cle.	73	1917	Williams-Chi.	78
Ruth-Bos.	58	1918	Paskert-Chi.	49
			Youngs-N.Y.	49
Shannon-Phi. + Bos.	70	1919	Powell-Bos.	79
Ward-N.Y.	84	1920	Kelly-N.Y.	92
Meusel-N.Y.	88	1921	Powell-Bos.	85
Dykes-Phi.	98	1922	Parkinson-Phi.	93
Ruth-N.Y.	93	1923	Grantham-Chi.	92
Ruth-N.Y.	81	1924	Grantham-Chi.	63
McManus-St.L.	69	1925	Hartnett-Chi.	77
Lazzeri-N.Y.	96	1926	Friberg-Phi.	77
Ruth-N.Y.	89	1927	Wilson-Chi.	70
Ruth-N.Y.	87	1928	Wilson-Chi.	94
Foxx-Phi.	70	1929	Wilson-Chi.	83
Foxx-Phi.	66	1930	Wilson-Chi.	86
Morgan-Cle.	66			
Foxx-Phi.	84	1931	Cullop-Cin.	86
Campbell-St.L. + Chi.	104	1932	Wilson-Bkn.	85
Foxx-Phi.	93	1933	Berger-Bos.	77
Clift-St.L.	100	1934	Camilli-Chi. + Phi.	94
Foxx-Phi.	99	1935	Camilli-Phi.	113
Foxx-Phi.	119	1936	Brubaker-Pit.	96
Crosetti-N.Y.	105	1937	DiMaggio-Bos.	111
Crosetti-N.Y.	97	1938	DiMaggio-Bos.	134
Greenberg-Det.	95	1939	Camilli-Bkn.	107
Chapman-Phi.	96	1940	Ross-Bos.	127
Foxx-Bos.	103	1941	Camilli-Bkn.	115
Gordon-N.Y.	95	1942	DiMaggio-Pit.	87
Laabs-St.L.	105	1943	DiMaggio-Pit.	126
Seerey-Cle.	99	1944	DiMaggio-Pit.	83
Seerey-Cle.	97	1945	DiMaggio-Pit.	91
Keller-N.Y.	101	1946	Kiner-Pit.	109
Seerey-Cle.	101			
Joost-Phi.	110	1947	Nicholson-Chi.	83
Seerey-Cle. + Chi.	102	1948	Sauer-Cin.	85
Kokos-St.L.	91	1949	Snider-Bkn.	92
Zernial-Chi.	110	1950	Smalley-Chi.	114
Zernial-Chi. + Phi.	101	1951	Hodges-Bkn.	99
Doby-Cle.	111	1952	Mathews-Bos.	115
Mantle-N.Y.	111			
Doby-Cle.	121	1953	Bilko-St.L.	125
Mantle-N.Y.	107	1954	Snider-Bkn.	96
Zauchin-Bos.	105	1955	Post-Cin.	102
Lemon-Was.	138	1956	Post-Cin.	124
Lemon-Was.	94	1957	Snider-Bkn.	104
Lemon-Was.	120	1958	Anderson-Phi.	95
Mantle-N.Y.	120			
Mantle-N.Y.	126	1959	Post-Phi.	101
Mantle-N.Y.	125	1960	Herrara-Phi.	136
Wood-Det.	141	1961	Stuart-Pit.	121
Killebrew-Min.	142	1962	Hubbs-Chi.	129
Nicholson-Chi.	175	1963	Clendenon-Pit.	136
Mathews-K.C.	143	1964	Allen-Phi.	138
Versalles-Min.	122	1965	Allen-Phi.	150
Scott-Bos.	152	1966	Browne-Chi.	143
Howard-Was.	155	1967	Wynn-Hou.	137
Jackson-Oak.	171	1968	Clendenon-Pit.	163
Jackson-Oak.	142	1969	Bonds-S.F.	187
Jackson-Oak.	135	1970	Bonds-S.F.	189
Jackson-Oak.	161	1971	Stargell-Pit.	154
Darwin-Min.	145	1972	May-Hou.	145
Darwin-Min.	137	1973	Bonds-S.F.	148
Darwin-Min.	127	1974	Schmidt-Phi.	138
Burroughs-Tex.	155	1975	Schmidt-Phi.	180

STOLEN BASES

AMERICAN LEAGUE			NATIONAL LEAGUE	
Isbell-Chi.	52	1901	Wagner-Pit.	48
Hartsell-Phi.	47	1902	Wagner-Pit.	43
Bay-Cle.	45	1903	Chance-Chi.	67
			Sheckard-Bkn.	67
Flick-Cle.	42	1904	Wagner-Pit.	53
Hoffman-Phi.	46	1905	Devlin-N.Y.	59
			Maloney-Chi.	59
Anderson-Was.	39	1906	Chance-Chi.	57
Flick-Cle.	39			
Cobb-Det.	49	1907	Wagner-Pit.	61
Dougherty-Chi.	47	1908	Wagner-Pit.	53
Cobb-Det.	76	1909	Bescher-Cin.	54
Collins-Phi.	81	1910	Bescher-Cin.	70
Cobb-Det.	83	1911	Bescher-Cin.	80
Milan-Was.	88	1912	Bescher-Cin.	67
Milan-Was.	74	1913	Carey-Pit.	61
Maisel-N.Y.	74	1914	Burns-N.Y.	62
Cobb-Det.	96	1915	Carey-Pit.	36
Cobb-Det.	68	1916	Carey-Pit.	63
Cobb-Det.	55	1917	Carey-Pit.	46
Sisler-St.L.	45	1918	Carey-Pit.	58
Collins-Chi.	33	1919	Burns-N.Y.	40
Rice-Was.	63	1920	Carey-Pit.	52
Sisler-St.L.	35	1921	Frisch-N.Y.	49
Sisler-St.L.	51	1922	Carey-Pit.	51
Collins-Chi.	49	1923	Carey-Pit.	51
Collins-Chi.	42	1924	Carey-Pit.	49
Mostil-Chi.	43	1925	Carey-Pit.	46
Mostil-Chi.	35	1926	Cuyler-Pit.	35
Sisler-St.L.	27	1927	Frisch-St.L.	48
Myer-Bos.	30	1928	Cuyler-Chi.	37
Gehringer-Det.	27	1929	Cuyler-Chi.	43
McManus-Det.	23	1930	Cuyler-Chi.	37
Chapman-N.Y.	61	1931	Frisch-St.L.	28
Chapman-N.Y.	38	1932	Klein-Phi.	20
Chapman-N.Y.	27	1933	Martin-St.L.	26
Werber-Bos.	40	1934	Martin-St.L.	23
Werber-Bos.	29	1935	Galan-Chi.	22
Lary-St.L.	37	1936	P.Martin-St.L.	23
Chapman-Was. + Bos.	35	1937	Galan-Chi.	23
Werber-Phi.	35			
Crosetti-N.Y.	27	1938	Hack-Chi.	16
Case-Was.	51	1939	Hack-Chi.	17
			Handley-Pit.	17
Case-Was.	35	1940	Frey-Cin.	22
Case-Was.	33	1941	Murtaugh-Phi.	18
Case-Was.	44	1942	Reiser-Bkn.	20
Case-Was.	61	1943	Vaughan-Bkn.	20
Stirnweiss-N.Y.	55	1944	Barnett-Pit.	28
Stirnweiss-N.Y.	33	1945	Schoendienst-St.L.	26
Case-Cle.	28	1946	Reiser-Bkn.	34
Dillinger-St.L.	34	1947	Robinson-Bkn.	29
Dillinger-St.L.	28	1948	Ashburn-Phi.	32
Dillinger-St.L.	20	1949	Robinson-Bkn.	37
DiMaggio-Bos.	15	1950	Jethroe-Bos.	35
Minoso-Cle. + Chi.	31	1951	Jethroe-Bos.	35
Minoso-Chi.	22	1952	Reese-Bkn.	30
Minoso-Chi.	25	1953	Bruton-Mil.	26
Jensen-Bos.	22	1954	Bruton-Mil.	34
Rivera-Chi.	25	1955	Bruton-Mil.	25
Aparicio-Chi.	21	1956	Mays-N.Y.	40
Aparicio-Chi.	28	1957	Mays-N.Y.	38
Aparicio-Chi.	29	1958	Mays-S.F.	31
Aparicio-Chi.	56	1959	Mays-S.F.	27
Aparicio-Chi.	51	1960	Wills-L.A.	50
Aparicio-Chi.	53	1961	Wills-L.A.	35
Aparicio-Chi.	31	1962	Wills-L.A.	104
Aparicio-Bal.	40	1963	Wills-L.A.	40
Aparicio-Bal.	57	1964	Wills-L.A.	53
Campaneris-Oak.	51	1965	Wills-L.A.	94
Campaneris-Oak.	52	1966	Brock-St.L.	74
Campaneris-Oak.	55	1967	Brock-St.L.	52
Campaneris-Oak.	62	1968	Brock-St.L.	62
Harper-Sea.	73	1969	Brock-St.L.	53
Campaneris-Oak.	42	1970	Tolan-Cin.	57
Otis-K.C.	52	1971	Brock-St.L.	64
Campaneris-Oak.	52	1972	Brock-St.L.	63
Harper-Bos.	54	1973	Brock-St.L.	70
North-Oak.	54	1974	Brock-St.L.	118
Rivers-Cal.	70	1975	Lopes-L.A.	77

1914 FEDERAL LEAGUE Kauff-Ind. 75
1915 FEDERAL LEAGUE Kauff-Bkn. 55

YEARLY BATTING LEADERS

BATTING AVERAGE

AMERICAN LEAGUE			NATIONAL LEAGUE	
Lajoie-Phi.	.422	1901	Burkett-St.L.	.382
Delahanty-Was.	.376	1902	Beaumont-Pit.	.357
Lajoie-Cle.	.355	1903	Wagner-Pit.	.355
Lajoie-Cle.	.381	1904	Wagner-Pit.	.349
Flick-Cle.	.306	1905	Seymour-Cin.	.377
Stone-St.L.	.358	1906	Wagner-Pit.	.339
Cobb-Det.	.350	1907	Wagner-Pit.	.350
Cobb-Det.	.324	1908	Wagner-Pit.	.354
Cobb-Det.	.377	1909	Wagner-Pit.	.339
Cobb-Det.	.385	1910	Magee-Phi.	.331
Cobb-Det.	.420	1911	Wagner-Pit.	.334
Cobb-Det.	.410	1912	Zimmerman-Chi.	.372
Cobb-Det.	.390	1913	Daubert-Bkn.	.350
Cobb-Det.	.368	1914	Daubert-Bkn.	.329
Cobb-Det.	.369	1915	Doyle-N.Y.	.320
Speaker-Cle.	.386	1916	Chase-Cin.	.339
Cobb-Det.	.383	1917	Roush-Cin.	.341
Cobb-Det.	.382	1918	Wheat-Bkn.	.335
Cobb-Det.	.384	1919	Roush-Cin.	.321
Sisler-St.L.	.407	1920	Hornsby-St.L.	.370
Heilmann-Det.	.394	1921	Hornsby-St.L.	.397
Sisler-St.L.	.420	1922	Hornsby-St.L.	.401
Heilmann-Det.	.403	1923	Hornsby-St.L.	.384
Ruth-N.Y.	.378	1924	Hornsby-St.L.	.424
Heilmann-Det.	.393	1925	Hornsby-St.L.	.403
Manush-Det.	.378	1926	Hargrave-Cin.	.353
Heilmann-Det.	.398	1927	P.Waner-Pit.	.380
Goslin-Was.	.379	1928	Hornsby-Bos.	.387
Fonseca-Cle.	.369	1929	O'Doul-Phi.	.398
Simmons-Phi.	.381	1930	Terry-N.Y.	.401
Simmons-Phi.	.390	1931	Hafey-St.L.	.350
Alexander-Det. + Bos.	.367	1932	O'Doul-Bkn.	.368
Foxx-Phi.	.356	1933	Klein-Phi.	.368
Gehrig-N.Y.	.363	1934	P.Waner-Pit.	.362
Myer-Was.	.349	1935	Vaughan-Pit.	.385
Appling-Chi.	.388	1936	P.Waner-Pit.	.373
Gehringer-Det.	.371	1937	Medwick-St.L.	.374
Foxx-Bos.	.349	1938	Lombardi-Cin.	.342
DiMaggio-N.Y.	.381	1939	Mize-St.L.	.349
DiMaggio-N.Y.	.352	1940	Garms-Pit.	.355
Williams-Bos.	.406	1941	Reiser-Bkn.	.343
Williams-Bos.	.356	1942	Lombardi-Bos.	.330
Appling-Chi.	.328	1943	Musial-St.L.	.357
Boudreau-Cle.	.327	1944	Walker-Bkn.	.357
Stirnweiss-N.Y.	.309	1945	Cavarretta-Chi.	.355
Vernon-Was.	.353	1946	Musial-St.L.	.365
Williams-Bos.	.343	1947	Walker-St.L. + Phi.	.363
Williams-Bos.	.369	1948	Musial-St.L.	.376
Kell-Det.	.343	1949	Robinson-Bkn.	.342
Goodman-Bos.	.354	1950	Musial-St.L.	.346
Fain-Phi.	.344	1951	Musial-St.L.	.355
Fain-Phi.	.327	1952	Musial-St.L.	.336
Vernon-Was.	.337	1953	Furillo-Bkn.	.344
Avila-Cle.	.341	1954	Mays-N.Y.	.345
Kaline-Det.	.340	1955	Ashburn-Phi.	.338
Mantle-N.Y.	.353	1956	Aaron-Mil.	.328
Williams-Bos.	.388	1957	Musial-St.L.	.351
Williams-Bos.	.328	1958	Ashburn-Phi.	.350
Kuenn-Det.	.353	1959	Aaron-Mil.	.355
Runnels-Bos.	.320	1960	Groat-Pit.	.325
Cash-Det.	.361	1961	Clemente-Pit.	.351
Runnels-Bos.	.326	1962	Davis-L.A.	.346
Yastrzemski-Bos.	.321	1963	Davis-L.A.	.326
Oliva-Min.	.323	1964	Clemente-Pit.	.339
Oliva-Min.	.321	1965	Clemente-Pit.	.329
F.Robinson-Bal.	.316	1966	Alou-Pit.	.342
Yastrzemski-Bos.	.326	1967	Clemente-Pit.	.357
Yastrzemski-Bos.	.301	1968	Rose-Cin.	.335
Carew-Min.	.332	1969	Rose-Cin.	.348
Johnson-Cal.	.329	1970	Carty-Atl.	.366
Oliva-Min.	.337	1971	Torre-St.L.	.363
Carew-Min.	.318	1972	Williams-Chi.	.333
Carew-Min.	.350	1973	Rose-Cin.	.338
Carew-Min.	.364	1974	Garr-Atl.	.353
Carew-Min.	.359	1975	Madlock-Chi.	.354

1914 FEDERAL LEAGUE Kauff-Ind. .370
1915 FEDERAL LEAGUE Kauff-Bkn. .342

SLUGGING AVERAGE

AMERICAN LEAGUE			NATIONAL LEAGUE	
Lajoie-Phi.	.635	1901	Sheckard-Bkn.	.536
Delahanty-Was.	.590	1902	Wagner-Pit.	.467
Lajoie-Cle.	.533	1903	Clarke-Pit.	.532
Lajoie-Cle.	.554	1904	Wagner-Pit.	.520
Flick-Cle.	.466	1905	Seymour-Cin.	.559
Stone-St.L.	.496	1906	Lumley-Bkn.	.477
Cobb-Det.	.473	1907	Wagner-Pit.	.513
Cobb-Det.	.475	1908	Wagner-Pit.	.542
Cobb-Det.	.517	1909	Wagner-Pit.	.489
Cobb-Det.	.554	1910	Magee-Phi.	.507
Cobb-Det.	.621	1911	Schulte-Chi.	.534
Cobb-Det.	.586	1912	Zimmerman-Chi.	.571
Jackson-Cle.	.551	1913	Cravath-Phi.	.568
Cobb-Det.	.513	1914	Magee-Phi.	.509
Fournier-Chi.	.491	1915	Cravath-Phi.	.510
Speaker-Cle.	.502	1916	Wheat-Bkn.	.461
Cobb-Det.	.571	1917	Hornsby-St.L.	.484
Ruth-Bos.	.555	1918	Roush-Cin.	.455
Ruth-Bos.	.657	1919	Myers-Bkn.	.436
Ruth-N.Y.	.847	1920	Hornsby-St.L.	.559
Ruth-N.Y.	.846	1921	Hornsby-St.L.	.639
Ruth-N.Y.	.672	1922	Hornsby-St.L.	.722
Ruth-N.Y.	.764	1923	Hornsby-St.L.	.627
Ruth-N.Y.	.739	1924	Hornsby-St.L.	.696
Williams-St.L.	.613	1925	Hornsby-St.L.	.756
Ruth-N.Y.	.737	1926	Williams-Phi.	.568
Ruth-N.Y.	.772	1927	Hafey-St. L.	.590
Ruth-N.Y.	.709	1928	Hornsby-Bos.	.632
Ruth-N.Y.	.697	1929	Hornsby-Chi.	.679
Ruth-N.Y.	.732	1930	Wilson-Chi.	.723
Ruth-N.Y.	.700	1931	Klein-Phi.	.584
Foxx-Phi.	.749	1932	Klein-Phi.	.646
Foxx-Phi.	.703	1933	Klein-Phi.	.602
Gehrig-N.Y.	.706	1934	Collins-St.L.	.615
Foxx-Phi.	.636	1935	Vaughan-Pit.	.607
Gehrig-N.Y.	.696	1936	Ott-N.Y.	.588
DiMaggio-N.Y.	.673	1937	Medwick-St.L.	.641
Foxx-Bos.	.704	1938	Mize-St.L.	.614
Foxx-Bos.	.694	1939	Mize-St.L.	.626
Greenberg-Det.	.670	1940	Mize-St.L.	.636
Williams-Bos.	.735	1941	Reiser-Bkn.	.558
Williams-Bos.	.648	1942	Mize-N.Y.	.521
York-Det.	.527	1943	Musial-St.L.	.562
Doerr-Bos.	.528	1944	Musial-St.L.	.549
Stirnweiss-N.Y.	.476	1945	Holmes-Bos.	.577
Williams-Bos.	.667	1946	Musial-St.L.	.587
Williams-Bos.	.634	1947	Kiner-Pit.	.639
Williams-Bos.	.615	1948	Musial-St.L.	.702
Williams-Bos.	.650	1949	Kiner-Pit.	.658
DiMaggio-N.Y.	.585	1950	Musial-St.L.	.596
Williams-Bos.	.556	1951	Kiner-Pit.	.627
Doby-Cle.	.541	1952	Musial-St.L.	.538
Rosen-Cle.	.613	1953	Snider-Bkn.	.627
Williams-Bos.	.635	1954	Mays-N.Y.	.667
Mantle-N.Y.	.611	1955	Mays-N.Y.	.659
Mantle-N.Y.	.705	1956	Snider-Bkn.	.598
Williams-Bos.	.731	1957	Mays-N.Y.	.626
Colavito-Cle.	.620	1958	Banks-Chi.	.614
Kaline-Det.	.530	1959	Aaron-Mil.	.636
Maris-N.Y.	.581	1960	Robinson-Cin.	.595
Mantle-N.Y.	.687	1961	Robinson-Cin.	.611
Mantle-N.Y.	.605	1962	Robinson-Cin.	.624
Killebrew-Min.	.555	1963	Aaron-Mil.	.586
Powell-Bal.	.606	1964	Mays-S.F.	.607
Yastrzemski-Bos.	.536	1965	Mays-S.F.	.645
F. Robinson-Bal.	.637	1966	Allen-Phi.	.632
Yastrzemski-Bos.	.622	1967	Aaron-Atl.	.573
Howard-Was.	.552	1968	McCovey-S.F.	.545
Jackson-Oak.	.608	1969	McCovey-S.F.	.656
Yastrzemski-Bos.	.592	1970	McCovey-S.F.	.612
Oliva-Min.	.546	1971	Aaron-Atl.	.669
Allen-Chi.	.603	1972	Williams-Chi.	.606
Jackson-Oak.	.531	1973	Stargell-Pit.	.646
Allen-Chi.	.563	1974	Schmidt-Phi.	.546
Lynn-Bos.	.566	1975	Parker-Pit.	.541

1914 FEDERAL LEAGUE Evans-Bkn. .556
1915 FEDERAL LEAGUE Kauff-Bkn. .509

RUNS BATTED IN

AMERICAN LEAGUE			NATIONAL LEAGUE	
Lajoie-Phi.	125	1901	Wagner-Pit.	126
Freeman-Bos.	121	1902	Wagner-Pit.	91
Freeman-Bos.	104	1903	Mertes-N.Y.	104
Lajoie-Cle.	102	1904	Dahlen-N.Y.	80
Davis-Phi.	83	1905	Seymour-Cin.	121
Davis-Phi.	96	1906	Nealon-Pit.	83
			Steinfeldt-Chi.	83
Cobb-Det.	119	1907	Magee-Phi.	85
Cobb-Det.	108	1908	Wagner-Pit.	109
Cobb-Det.	107	1909	Wagner-Pit.	100
Crawford-Det.	120	1910	Magee-Phi.	123
Cobb-Det.	127	1911	Schulte-Chi.	107
			Wilson-Pit.	107
Baker-Phi.	130	1912	Wagner-Pit.	102
Baker-Phi.	117	1913	Cravath-Phi.	128
Crawford-Det.	104	1914	Magee-Phi.	103
Crawford-Det.	112	1915	Cravath-Phi.	115
Veach-Det.	112			
Pratt-St.L.	103	1916	Zimmerman-Chi. + N.Y.	83
Veach-Det.	103	1917	Zimmerman-N.Y.	102
Veach-Det.	78	1918	Magee-Cin.	76
Ruth-Bos.	114	1919	Myers-Bkn.	73
Ruth-N.Y.	137	1920	Hornsby-St.L.	94
			Kelly-N.Y.	94
Ruth-N.Y.	171	1921	Hornsby-St.L.	126
Williams-St.L.	155	1922	Hornsby-St.L.	152
Ruth-N.Y.	131	1923	Meusel-N.Y.	125
Goslin-Was.	129	1924	Kelly-N.Y.	136
Meusel-N.Y.	138	1925	Hornsby-St.L.	143
Ruth-N.Y.	145	1926	Bottomley-St.L.	120
Gehrig-N.Y.	175	1927	P.Waner-Pit.	131
Gehrig-N.Y.	142	1928	Bottomley-St.L.	136
Ruth-N.Y.	142			
Simmons-Phi.	157	1929	Wilson-Chi.	159
Gehrig-N.Y.	174	1930	Wilson-Chi.	190
Gehrig-N.Y.	184	1931	Klein-Phi.	121
Foxx-Phi.	169	1932	Hurst-Phi.	143
Foxx-Phi.	163	1933	Klein-Phi.	120
Gehrig-N.Y.	165	1934	Ott-N.Y.	135
Greenberg-Det.	170	1935	Berger-Bos.	130
Trosky-Cle.	162	1936	Medwick-St.L.	138
Greenberg-Det.	183	1937	Medwick-St.L.	154
Foxx-Bos.	175	1938	Medwick-St.L.	122
Williams-Bos.	145	1939	McCormick-Cin.	128
Greenberg-Det.	150	1940	Mize-St.L.	137
DiMaggio-N.Y.	125	1941	Camilli-Bkn.	120
Williams-Bos.	137	1942	Mize-N.Y.	110
York-Det.	118	1943	Nicholson-Chi.	128
Stephens-St.L.	109	1944	Nicholson-Chi.	122
Etten-N.Y.	111	1945	Walker-Bkn.	124
Greenberg-Det.	127	1946	Slaughter-St.L.	130
Williams-Bos.	114	1947	Mize-N.Y.	138
DiMaggio-N.Y.	155	1948	Musial-St.L.	131
Stephens-Bos.	159	1949	Kiner-Pit.	127
Williams-Bos.	159			
Dropo-Bos.	144	1950	Ennis-Phi.	126
Stephens-Bos.	144			
Zernial-Chi. + Phi.	129	1951	Irvin-N.Y.	121
Rosen-Cle.	105	1952	Sauer-Chi.	121
Rosen-Cle.	145	1953	Campanella-Bkn.	142
Doby-Cle.	126	1954	Kluszewski-Cin.	141
Boone-Det.	116	1955	Snider-Bkn.	136
Jensen-Bos.	116			
Mantle-N.Y.	130	1956	Musial-St.L.	109
Sievers-Was.	114	1957	Aaron-Mil.	132
Jensen-Bos.	122	1958	Banks-Chi.	129
Jensen-Bos.	112	1959	Banks-Chi.	143
Maris-N.Y.	112	1960	Aaron-Mil.	126
Maris-N.Y.	142	1961	Cepeda-S.F.	142
Killebrew-Min.	126	1962	Davis-L.A.	153
Stuart-Bos.	118	1963	Aaron-Mil.	130
Robinson-Bal.	118	1964	Boyer-St.L.	119
Colavito-Cle.	108	1965	Johnson-Cin.	130
F. Robinson-Bal.	122	1966	Aaron-Atl.	127
Yastrzemski-Bos.	121	1967	Cepeda-St.L.	111
Harrelson-Bos.	109	1968	McCovey-S.F.	105
Killebrew-Min.	140	1969	McCovey-S.F.	126
Howard-Was.	126	1970	Bench-Cin.	148
Killebrew-Min.	119	1971	Torre-St.L.	137
Allen-Chi.	113	1972	Bench-Cin.	125
Jackson-Oak.	117	1973	Stargell-Pit.	119
Burroughs-Tex.	118	1974	Bench-Cin.	129
Scott-Mil.	109	1975	Luzinski-Phi.	120

1914 FEDERAL LEAGUE Esmond-Ind. 107
1915 FEDERAL LEAGUE Zwilling-Chi. 94

YEARLY PITCHING LEADERS

WINS

AMERICAN LEAGUE			NATIONAL LEAGUE	
Young-Bos.	33	1901	Donovan-Bkn.	25
Young-Bos.	32	1902	Chesbro-Pit.	28
Young-Bos.	28	1903	McGinnity-N.Y.	31
Chesbro-N.Y.	41	1904	McGinnity-N.Y.	35
Waddell-Phi.	26	1905	Mathewson-N.Y.	32
Orth-N.Y.	27	1906	McGinnity-N.Y.	27
Joss-Cle.	27	1907	Mathewson-N.Y.	24
White-Chi.	27			
Walsh-Chi.	40	1908	Mathewson-N.Y.	37
Mullin-Det.	29	1909	Brown-Chi.	27
Coombs-Phi.	31	1910	Mathewson-N.Y.	27
Coombs-Phi.	28	1911	Alexander-Phi.	28
Wood-Bos.	34	1912	Cheney-Chi.	26
			Marquard-N.Y.	26
Johnson-Was.	36	1913	Seaton-Phi.	27
Johnson-Was.	28	1914	Alexander-Phi.	27
			Rudolph-Bos.	27
Johnson-Was.	27	1915	Alexander-Phi.	31
Johnson-Was.	25	1916	Alexander-Phi.	33
Cicotte-Chi.	28	1917	Alexander-Phi.	30
Johnson-Was.	23	1918	Vaughn-Chi.	22
Cicotte-Chi.	29	1919	J.Barnes-N.Y.	25
Bagby-Cle.	31	1920	Alexander-Chi.	27
Mays-N.Y.	27	1921	Cooper-Pit.	22
Shocker-St.L.	27		Grimes-Bkn.	22
Rommel-Phi.	27	1922	Rixey-Cin.	25
Uhle-Cle.	26	1923	Luque-Cin.	27
Johnson-Was.	23	1924	Vance-Bkn.	28
Lyons-Chi.	21	1925	Vance-Bkn.	22
Rommel-Phi.	21			
Uhle-Cle.	27	1926	Donahue-Cin.	20
			Kremer-Pit.	20
			Meadows-Pit.	20
			Rhem-St.L.	20
Hoyt-N.Y.	22	1927	Root-Chi.	26
Lyons-Chi	22			
Grove-Phi.	24	1928	Benton-N.Y.	25
Pipgras-N.Y.	24		Grimes-Pit.	25
Earnshaw-Phi.	24	1929	Malone-Chi.	22
Grove-Phi.	28	1930	Kremer-Pit.	20
			Malone-Chi.	20
Grove-Phi.	31	1931	Elliott-Phi.	19
			Hallihan-St.L.	19
			Meine-Pit.	19
Crowder-Was.	26	1932	Warneke-Chi.	22
Crowder-Was.	24	1933	Hubbell-N.Y.	23
Grove-Phi.	24			
Gomez-N.Y.	26	1934	D.Dean-St.L.	30
Ferrell-Bos.	25	1935	D.Dean-St.L.	28
Bridges-Det.	23	1936	Hubbell-N.Y.	26
Gomez-N.Y.	21	1937	Hubbell-N.Y.	22
Ruffing-N.Y.	21	1938	Lee-Chi.	22
Feller-Cle.	24	1939	Walters-Cin.	27
Feller-Cle.	27	1940	Walters-Cin.	22
Feller-Cle.	25	1941	Higbe-Bkn.	22
			Wyatt-Bkn.	22
Hughson-Bos.	22	1942	M.Cooper-St.L.	22
Chandler-N.Y.	20	1943	Cooper-St.L.	21
Trout-Det.	20		Riddle-Cin.	21
			Sewell-Pit.	21
Newhouser-Det.	29	1944	Walters-Cin.	23
Newhouser-Det.	25	1945	Barrett-Bos. + St.L.	23
Feller-Cle.	26	1946	Pollet-St.L.	21
Newhouser-Det.	26			
Feller-Cle.	20	1947	Blackwell-Cin.	22
Newhouser-Det.	21	1948	Sain-Bos.	24
Parnell-Bos.	25	1949	Spahn-Bos.	21
Lemon-Cle.	23	1950	Spahn-Bos.	21
Feller-Cle.	22	1951	Jansen-N.Y.	23
			Maglie-N.Y.	23
Shantz-Phi.	24	1952	Roberts-Phi.	28
Porterfield-Was.	22	1953	Roberts-Phi.	23
			Spahn-Mil.	23
Lemon-Cle.	23	1954	Roberts-Phi.	23
Wynn-Cle.	23			
Ford-N.Y.	18	1955	Roberts-Phi.	23
Lemon-Cle.	18			
Sullivan-Bos.	18			
Lary-Det.	21	1956	Newcombe-Bkn.	27
Bunning-Det.	20	1957	Spahn-Mil.	21
Pierce-Chi.	20			
Turley-N.Y.	21	1958	Friend-Pit.	22
			Spahn-Mil.	22
Wynn-Chi.	22	1959	Burdette-Mil.	21
			Jones-S.F.	21
			Spahn-Mil.	21
Estrada-Bal.	18	1960	Broglio-St.L.	21
Perry-Cle.	18		Spahn-Mil.	21
Ford-N.Y.	25	1961	Jay-Cin.	21
			Spahn-Mil.	21
Terry-N.Y.	23	1962	Drysdale-L.A.	25
Ford-N.Y.	24	1963	Koufax-L.A.	25
			Marichal-S.F.	25
Chance-L.A.	20	1964	Jackson-Chi.	24
Peters-Chi.	20			
Grant-Min.	21	1965	Koufax-L.A.	26
Kaat-Min.	25	1966	Koufax-L.A.	27
Lonborg-Bos.	22	1967	McCormick-S.F.	22
Wilson-Det.	22			
McLain-Det.	31	1968	Marichal-S.F.	26
McLain-Det.	24	1969	Seaver-N.Y.	25
Cuellar-Bal.	24	1970	Gibson-St.L.	23
McNally-Bal.	24		Perry-S.F.	23
Perry-Min.	24			
Lolich-Det.	25	1971	Jenkins-Chi.	24
Perry-Cle.	24	1972	Carlton-Phi.	27
Wood-Chi.	24			
Wood-Chi.	24	1973	Bryant-S.F.	24
Hunter-Oak.	25	1974	Messersmith-L.A.	20
Jenkins-Tex.	25		Niekro-Atl.	20
Hunter-N.Y.	23	1975	Seaver-N.Y.	23
Palmer-Bal.	23			

1914 FEDERAL LEAGUE	Hendrix-Chi.	29
1915 FEDERAL LEAGUE	McConnell-Chi.	25

LOSSES

AMERICAN LEAGUE			NATIONAL LEAGUE	
Dowling-Mil. + Cle.	27	1901	Taylor-N.Y.	27
Dinneen-Bos.	21	1902	Yerkes-St.L.	21
Flaherty-Chi.	25	1903	Pittinger-Bos.	22
Townsend-Was.	27	1904	Jones-Bkn.	25
			Willis-Bos.	25
Glade-St.L.	24	1905	Willis-Bos.	29
Harris-Bos.	21	1906	Dorner-Cin. + Bos.	26
Young-Bos.	21			
Orth-N.Y.	21	1907	McGlynn-St.L.	25
Pelty-St.L.	21			
Lake-N.Y.	22	1908	Raymond-St.L.	25
Groom-Was.	26	1909	Ferguson-Bos.	23
Walsh-Chi.	20	1910	Bell-Bkn.	27
Powell-St.L.	19	1911	Moore-Phi.	19
			Steele-St.L.	19
Ford-N.Y.	21	1912	Tyler-Bos.	22
Scott-Chi.	20	1913	Griner-St.L.	22
Weilman-St.L.	20			
Benz-Chi.	19	1914	Ames-Cin.	23
Wyckoff-Phi.	22	1915	Schneider-Cin.	19
Bush-Phi.	24	1916	Meadows-St.L.	23
Groom-St.L.	19	1917	Barnes-Bos.	21
Sothoron-St.L.	19			
Cicotte-Chi.	19	1918	Marquard-Bkn.	18
Perry-Phi.	19		Oeschger-Phi.	18
Harper-Was.	21	1919	Rudolph-Bos.	18
Perry-Phi.	25	1920	Rixey-Phi.	22
Rommel-Phi.	23	1921	Smith-Phi.	20
Harriss-Phi.	20	1922	Luque-Cin.	23
Pillette-Det.	19	1923	Cooper-Pit.	19
Rommel-Phi.	19			
Ehmke-Bos.	17	1924	Barnes-Bos.	20
Ferguson-Bos.	17			
Shaute-Cle.	17			
Jones-N.Y.	21	1925	Grimes-Bkn.	19
Gaston-St.L.	18	1926	Petty-Bkn.	17
Zahniser-Bos.	18		Root-Chi.	17
Harriss-Bos.	21	1927	Scott-Phi.	21
Ruffing-Bos.	25	1928	Brandt-Bos.	21
Ruffing-Bos.	22	1929	Clark-Bkn.	19
Gaston-Bos.	20	1930	French-Pit.	18
Russell-Bos.	20		Frey-Cin.	18
Caraway-Chi.	24	1931	Johnson-Cin.	19
Gray-St.L.	24			
Hadley-Chi. + St.L.	21	1932	Carroll-Cin.	19
Lyons-Chi.	21	1933	Derringer-St.L. + Cin.	27
Newsom-St.L.	20	1934	Johnson-Cin.	22
Newsom-St.L. + Was.	18	1935	Cantwell-Bos.	25
Rhodes-Phi.	20	1936	Walters-Phi.	21
Kelly-Phi.	21	1937	LaMaster-Phi.	19
Caster-Phi.	20	1938	Mulcahy-Phi.	20
Kennedy-Det. + St.L.	20	1939	Butcher-Pit.	17
			Klinger-Phi. + Pit.	17
Caster-Phi.	19	1940	Mulcahy-Phi.	22
Leonard-Was.	19			
Newsom-Det.	20	1941	Sewell-Pit.	17
Smith-Chi.	20	1942	Tobin-Bos.	21
Harris-Phi.	21	1943	Andrews-Bos.	20
Dietrich-Chi.	17	1944	Raffensberger-Phi.	20
Wynn-Was.	17			
Newsom-Phi.	20	1945	Barrett-Phi.	20
Fowler-Phi.	16	1946	Koslo-N.Y.	19
Knerr-Phi.	16			
Marchildon-Phi.	16			
Newhouser-Det.	17	1947	Schmitz-Chi.	18
Sanford-St.L.	21	1948	Leonard-Phi.	17
Calvert-Was.	17	1949	Fox-Cin.	19
Garver-St.L.	17			
Hudson-Was.	17			
Kellner-Phi.	20	1950	Rush-Chi.	20
Gray-Det.	14	1951	Minner-Chi.	17
Kellner-Phi.	14		Raffensberger-Cin.	17
Lemon-Cle.	14		Ramsdell-Cin.	17
Pierce-Chi.	14			
Pillette-St.L.	14			
Trout-Det.	14			
Houtteman-Det.	20	1952	Dickson-Pit.	21
Byrd-Phi.	20	1953	Dickson-Pit.	19
			Hacker-Chi.	19
Larsen-Bal.	21	1954	Dickson-Phi.	20
Wilson-Bal.	18	1955	Jones-Chi.	20
Ditmar-K.C.	22	1956	Kline-Pit.	18
			Roberts-Phi.	18
Stobbs-Was.	20	1957	Roberts-Phi.	22
Ramos-Was.	18	1958	Kline-Pit.	16
Ramos-Was.	19	1959	Friend-Pit.	19
Ramos-Was.	18	1960	Hobbie-Chi.	20
Ramos-Min.	20	1961	Friend-Pit.	19
			Mahaffey-Phi.	19
Estrada-Bal.	17	1962	Craig-N.Y.	24
Rakow-K.C.	17			
Pena-K.C.	20	1963	Craig-N.Y.	22
Segui-K.C.	17	1964	Stallard-N.Y.	20
Monbouquette-Bos.	18	1965	Fisher-N.Y.	24
Morehead-Bos.	18			
O'Donoghue-K.C.	18			
Stottlemyre-N.Y.	20	1966	Ellsworth-Chi.	22
Brunet-Cal.	19	1967	Fisher-N.Y.	18
Brunet-Cal.	17	1968	Osteen-L.A.	18
			Sadecki-S.F.	18
Tiant-Cle.	20	1969	Kirby-S.D.	20
Lolich-Det.	19	1970	Carlton-St.L.	19
McLain-Was.	22	1971	Arlin-S.D.	19
Dobson-Bal.	18	1972	Arlin-S.D.	21
Stottlemyre-N.Y.	18			
Bahnsen-Chi.	21	1973	Carlton-Phi.	20
Lolich-Det.	21	1974	Bonham-Chi.	22
			Jones-S.D.	22
Wood-Chi.	20	1975	R. Reuschel-Chi.	17

1914 FEDERAL LEAGUE	Groom-St.L.	20
1915 FEDERAL LEAGUE	Quinn-Bal.	22

WINNING PERCENTAGE

AMERICAN LEAGUE			NATIONAL LEAGUE	
Griffith-Chi.	.774	1901	Chesbro-Pit.	.667
Waddell-Phi.	.774	1902	Chesbro-Pit.	.824
Young-Bos.	.757	1903	Leever-Pit.	.781
Chesbro-N.Y.	.774	1904	McGinnity-N.Y.	.814
Coakley-Phi.	.741	1905	Mathewson-N.Y.	.800
Plank-Phi.	.792	1906	Reulbach-Chi.	.826
Donovan-Det.	.862	1907	Reulbach-Chi.	.810
Walsh-Chi.	.727	1908	Reulbach-Chi.	.774
Mullin-Det.	.763	1909	Cammitz-Pit.	.806
			Mathewson-N.Y.	.806
Bender-Phi.	.821	1910	Cole-Chi.	.833
Gregg-Cle.	.767	1911	Marquard-N.Y.	.774
Wood-Bos.	.872	1912	Hendrix-Pit.	.727
Johnson-Was.	.837	1913	Humphries-Chi.	.800
Bender-Phi.	.850	1914	James-Bos.	.788
Ruth-Bos.	.750	1915	Alexander-Phi.	.756
Cicotte-Chi.	.696	1916	Hughes-Bos.	.842
Russell-Chi.	.750	1917	Schupp,N.Y.	.750
Jones-Bos.	.762	1918	Hendrix-Chi.	.741
Cicotte-Chi.	.806	1919	Ruether-Cin.	.760
Bagby-Cle.	.721	1920	Grimes-Bkn.	.676
Mays-N.Y.	.750	1921	Doak-St.L.	.714
Bush-N.Y.	.788	1922	Donohue-Cin.	.667
Pennock-N.Y.	.760	1923	Luque-Cin.	.771
Johnson-Was.	.767	1924	Yde-Pit.	.842
Coveleski-Was.	.800	1925	Sherdel-St.L.	.714
Uhle-Cle.	.711	1926	Kremer-Pit.	.769
Hoyt-N.Y.	.759	1927	Benton-Bos. + N.Y.	.708
Crowder-St.L.	.808	1928	Benton-N.Y.	.735
Grove-Phi.	.769	1929	Root-Chi.	.760
Grove-Phi.	.848	1930	Fitzsimmons-N.Y.	.731
Grove-Phi.	.886	1931	Derringer-St.L.	.692
Allen-N.Y.	.810	1932	Warneke-Chi.	.786
Grove-Phi.	.750	1933	Cantwell-Bos.	.667
Gomez-N.Y.	.839	1934	D.Dean-St.L.	.811
Auker-Det.	.720	1935	Lee-Chi.	.769
Pearson-N.Y.	.731	1936	Hubbell-N.Y.	.813
Allen-Cle.	.938	1937	Hubbell-N.Y.	.733
Ruffing-N.Y.	.750	1938	Lee-Chi.	.710
Grove-Bos.	.789	1939	Derringer-Cin.	.781
Rowe-Det.	.842	1940	Fitzsimmons-Bkn.	.889
Gomez-N.Y.	.750	1941	Riddle-Cin.	.826
Bonham-N.Y.	.808	1942	French-Bkn.	.789
Chandler-N.Y.	.833	1943	Cooper-St.L.	.724
Hughson-Bos.	.783	1944	Wilks-St.L.	.810
Newhouser-Det.	.735	1945	Brecheen-St.L.	.789
Ferriss-Bos.	.806	1946	Dickson-St.L.	.714
Reynolds-N.Y.	.704	1947	Jansen-N.Y.	.808
Kramer-Bos.	.783	1948	Brecheen-St.L.	.741
Kinder-Bos.	.793	1949	Roe-Bkn.	.714
Raschi-N.Y.	.724	1950	Maglie-N.Y.	.818
Feller-Cle.	.733	1951	Roe-Bkn.	.880
Shantz-Phi.	.774	1952	Wilhelm-N.Y.	.833
Lopat-N.Y.	.800	1953	Erskine-Bkn.	.769
Consuegra-Chi.	.842	1954	Antonelli-N.Y.	.750
Byrne-N.Y.	.762	1955	Newcombe-Bkn.	.800
Ford-N.Y.	.760	1956	Newcombe-Bkn.	.794
Donovan-Chi.	.727	1957	Buhl-Mil.	.720
Turley-N.Y.	.750	1958	Burdette-Mil.	.667
			Spahn-Mil.	.667
Shaw-Chi.	.750	1959	Face-Pit.	.947
Perry-Cle.	.643	1960	Broglio-St.L.	.700
Ford-N.Y.	.862	1961	Podres-L.A.	.783
Herbert-Chi.	.690	1962	Purkey-Cin.	.821
Ford-N.Y.	.774	1963	Perranoski-L.A.	.842
Bunker-Bal.	.792	1964	Koufax-L.A.	.792
Grant-Min.	.750	1965	Koufax-L.A.	.765
Siebert-Cle.	.667	1966	Marichal-S.F.	.806
Horlen-Chi.	.731	1967	Hughes-St.L.	.727
McLain-Det.	.838	1968	Blass-Pit.	.750
Palmer-Bal.	.800	1969	Seaver-N.Y.	.781
Cuellar-Bal.	.750	1970	Gibson-St.L.	.767
McNally-Bal.	.808	1971	Gullett-Cin.	.727
Hunter-Oak.	.750	1972	Nolan-Cin.	.750
Hunter-Oak.	.808	1973	John-L.A.	.696
Cuellar-Bal.	.688	1974	John-L.A.	.813
Moret-Bos.	.824	1975	Hrabosky-St.L.	.813

1914 FEDERAL LEAGUE	Ford-Buf.	.778
1915 FEDERAL LEAGUE	McConnell-Chi.	.714

YEARLY PITCHING LEADERS

GAMES PITCHED

AMERICAN LEAGUE			NATIONAL LEAGUE	
McGinnity-Bal.	48	1901	Donovan-Bkn.	45
			Powell-St.L.	45
			Taylor-N.Y.	45
Young-Bos.	45	1902	Willis-Bos.	51
Plank-Phi.	43	1903	McGinnity-N.Y.	55
Chesbro-N.Y.	55	1904	McGinnity-N.Y.	51
Waddell-Phi.	46	1905	McGinnity-N.Y.	46
			Pittenger-Phi.	46
Chesbro-N.Y.	49	1906	McGinnity-N.Y.	45
Walsh-Chi.	56	1907	McGinnity-N.Y.	47
Walsh-Chi.	66	1908	Mathewson-N.Y.	56
Smith-Chi.	51	1909	Brown-Chi.	50
Coombs-Phi.	45	1910	Mattern-Bos.	51
Johnson-Was.	45			
Walsh-Chi.	45			
Walsh-Chi.	56	1911	Brown-Chi.	53
Walsh-Chi.	62	1912	Benton-Cin.	50
Russell-Chi.	51	1913	Cheney-Chi.	54
Johnson-Was.	51	1914	Cheney-Chi.	50
Coveleski-Det.	50	1915	Hughes-Bos.	50
Faber-Chi.	50			
Davenport-St.L.	59	1916	Meadows-Pit.	51
Danforth-Chi.	50	1917	Douglas-Chi.	51
Bagby-Cle.	45	1918	Grimes-Bkn.	40
Mogridge-N.Y.	45			
Shaw-Was.	45	1919	Tuero-St.L.	45
Bagby-Cle.	48	1920	Haines-St.L.	47
Mays-N.Y.	49'	1921	Scott-Bos.	47
Rommel-Phi.	51	1922	North-St.L.	53
Rommel-Phi.	56	1923	Jonnard-N.Y.	45
			Ryan-N.Y.	45
Marberry-Was.	50	1924	Kremer-Pit.	41
			Morrison-Pit.	41
Marberry-Was.	55	1925	Morrison-Pit.	44
Marberry-Was.	64	1926	Scott-N.Y.	50
Braxton-Was.	59	1927	Root-Chi.	48
			Scott-Phi.	48
Marberry-Was.	48	1928	Grimes-Pit.	48
Marberry-Was.	49	1929	Bush-Chi.	50
Grove-Phi.	50	1930	Elliott-Phi.	48
Hadley-Was.	55	1931	Elliott-Phi.	52
Marberry-Was.	54	1932	French-Pit.	47
Crowder-Was.	52	1933	Dean-St.L.	48
Russell-Was.	54	1934	Davis-Phi.	51
Van Atta-N.Y. + St.L.	58	1935	Jorgens-Phi.	53
Van Atta-St.L.	52	1936	D.Dean-St.L.	51
			Derringer-Cin.	51
Brown-Chi.	53	1937	Mulcahy-Phi.	56
Humphries-Cle.	45	1938	Brown-Pit.	51
			Coffman-N.Y.	51
Brown-Chi.	61	1939	Shoun-St.L.	53
Feller-Cle.	43	1940	Shoun-St.L.	40
Feller-Cle.	44	1941	Higbe-St.L.	48
Haynes-Chi.	40	1942	Adams-N.Y.	61
Brown-Bos.	49	1943	Adams-N.Y.	70
Heving-Cle.	63	1944	Adams-N.Y.	65
Berry-Phi.	52	1945	Karl-Phi.	67
Feller-Cle.	48	1946	Trinkle-N.Y.	48
Klieman-Cle.	58	1947	Trinkle-N.Y.	62
Page-N.Y.	55	1948	Gumbert-Cin.	61
Page-N.Y.	60	1949	Wilks-St.L.	59
Harris-Was.	53	1950	Konstanty-Phi.	74
Kinder-Bos.	63	1951	Wilks-St.L. + Pit.	48
Kennedy-Chi.	47	1952	Wilhelm-N.Y.	71
Kinder-Bos.	69	1953	Wilhelm-N.Y.	68
Dixon-Was. + Phi.	54	1954	Hughes-Bkn.	60
Narleski-Cle.	60	1955	Labine-Bkn.	60
Zuverink-Bal.	62	1956	Face-Pit.	68
Zuverink-Bal.	56	1957	Lown-Chi.	67
Clevenger-Was.	55	1958	Elston-Chi.	69
Staley-Chi.	67	1959	Elston-Chi.	65
			Henry-Chi.	65
Fornieles-Bos.	70	1960	Face-Pit.	68
Arroyo-N.Y.	65	1961	Baldshun-Phi.	65
Radatz-Bos.	62	1962	Perranoski-L.A.	70
Miller-Bal.	71	1963	Perranoski-L.A.	69
Wyatt-K.C.	81	1964	Miller-L.A.	74
Fisher-Chi.	82	1965	Abernathy-Chi.	84
Fisher-Chi. + Bal.	67	1966	Carroll-Atl.	73
Locker-Chi.	77	1967	Abernathy-Cin.	70
			Perranoski-L.A.	70
Wood-Chi.	88	1968	Abernathy-Cin.	78
Wood-Chi.	76	1969	Granger-Cin.	90
Wood-Chi.	77	1970	Herbel-S.D. + N.Y.	76
Sanders-Mil.	83	1971	Granger-Cin.	70
Lindblad-Tex.	66	1972	Carroll-Cin.	65
			Marshall-Mon.	65
Hiller-Det.	65	1973	Marshall-Mon.	92
Fingers-Oak.	76	1974	Marshall-L.A.	106
Fingers-Oak.	75	1975	Garber-Phi.	71

1914	FEDERAL LEAGUE	C. Hendrix-Chi.	49
		Falkenberg-Ind.	49
1915	FEDERAL LEAGUE	Davenport-St.L.	55

EARNED RUN AVERAGE

AMERICAN LEAGUE			NATIONAL LEAGUE	
Young-Bos.	1.63	1901	Tannehill-Pit.	2.18
Siever-Det.	1.91	1902	Taylor-Chi.	1.33
Moore-Cle.	1.77	1903	Leever-Pit.	2.06
Joss-Cle.	1.59	1904	McGinnity-N.Y.	1.61
Waddell-Phi.	1.48	1905	Mathewson-N.Y.	1.27
White-Chi.	1.52	1906	Brown-Chi.	1.04
Walsh-Chi.	1.60	1907	Pfiester-Chi.	1.15
Joss-Cle.	1.16	1908	Mathewson-N.Y.	1.43
Krause-Phi.	1.39	1909	Mathewson-N.Y.	1.14
Walsh-Chi.	1.27	1910	McQuillan-Phi.	1.60
Gregg-Cle.	1.81	1911	Mathewson-N.Y.	1.99
Johnson-Was.	1.39	1912	Tesreau-N.Y.	1.96
Johnson-Was.	1.09	1913	Mathewson-N.Y.	2.06
Leonard-Bos.	1.01	1914	Doak-St.L.	1.72
Wood-Bos.	1.49	1915	Alexander-Phi.	1.22
Ruth-Bos.	1.75	1916	Alexander-Phi.	1.55
Cicotte-Chi.	1.53	1917	Alexander-Phi.	1.86
Johnson-Was.	1.27	1918	Vaughn-Chi.	1.71
Johnson-Was.	1.49	1919	Alexander-Chi.	1.72
Shawkey-N.Y.	2.45	1920	Alexander-Chi.	1.91
Faber-Chi.	2.48	1921	Doak-St.L.	2.58
Faber-Chi.	2.80	1922	Ryan-N.Y.	3.00
S.Coveleski-Cle.	2.76	1923	Luque-Cin.	1.93
Johnson-Was.	2.72	1924	Vance-Bkn.	2.16
S.Coveleski-Was.	2.84	1925	Luque-Cin.	2.63
Grove-Phi.	2.51	1926	Kremer-Pit.	2.61
Moore-N.Y.	2.28	1927	Kremer-Pit.	2.47
Braxton-Was.	2.52	1928	Vance-Bkn.	2.09
Grove-Phi.	2.82	1929	Walker-N.Y.	3.08
Grove-Phi.	2.54	1930	Vance-Bkn.	2.61
Grove-Phi.	2.05	1931	Walker-N.Y.	2.26
Grove-Phi.	2.84	1932	Warneke-Chi.	2.37
Pearson-Cle.	2.33	1933	Hubbell-N.Y.	1.66
Gomez-N.Y.	2.33	1934	Hubbell-N.Y.	2.30
Grove-Bos.	2.70	1935	Blanton-Pit.	2.59
Grove-Bos.	2.81	1936	Hubbell-N.Y.	2.31
Gomez-N.Y.	2.33	1937	Turner-Bos.	2.38
Grove-Bos.	3.07	1938	Lee-Chi.	2.66
Grove-Bos.	2.54	1939	Walters-Cin.	2.29
Feller-Cle.	2.62	1940	Walters-Cin.	2.48
Lee-Chi.	2.37	1941	Riddle-Cin.	2.24
Lyons-Chi.	2.10	1942	W.Cooper-St.L.	1.77
Chandler-N.Y.	1.64	1943	Pollet-St.L.	1.75
Trout-Det.	2.12	1944	Heusser-Cin.	2.38
Newhouser-Det.	1.81	1945	Borowy-Chi.	2.14
Newhouser-Det.	1.94	1946	Pollett-St.L.	2.10
Chandler-N.Y.	2.46	1947	Spahn-Bos.	2.33
Bearden-Cle.	2.43	1948	Brecheen-St.L.	2.24
Parnell-Bos.	2.78	1949	Koslo-N.Y.	2.50
Wynn-Cle.	3.20	1950	Hearn-St.L. + N.Y.	2.49
Rogovin-Det. + Chi.	2.78	1951	Nichols-Bos.	2.88
Reynolds-N.Y.	2.07	1952	Wilhelm-N.Y.	2.43
Lopat-N.Y.	2.43	1953	Spahn-Mil.	2.10
Garcia-Cle.	2.64	1954	Antonelli-N.Y.	2.29
Pierce-Chi.	1.97	1955	Friend-Pit.	2.84
Ford-N.Y.	2.47	1956	Burdette-Mil.	2.71
Shantz-N.Y.	2.45	1957	Podres-Bkn.	2.66
Ford-N.Y.	2.01	1958	Miller-S.F.	2.47
Wilhelm-Bal.	2.19	1959	S.Jones-S.F.	2.82
Baumann-Chi.	2.68	1960	McCormick-S.F.	2.70
Donovan-Was.	2.40	1961	Spahn-Mil.	3.01
Aguirre-Det.	2.21	1962	Koufax-L.A.	2.54
Peters-Chi.	2.33	1963	Koufax-L.A.	1.88
Chance-L.A.	1.65	1964	Koufax-L.A.	1.74
McDowell-Cle.	2.18	1965	Koufax-L.A.	2.04
Peters-Chi.	1.98	1966	Koufax-L.A.	1.73
Horlen-Chi.	2.06	1967	Niekro-Atl.	1.87
Tiant-Cle.	1.60	1968	Gibson-St.L.	1.12
Bosman-Was.	2.19	1969	Marichal-S.F.	2.10
Segui-Oak.	2.56	1970	Seaver-N.Y.	2.81
Blue-Oak.	1.82	1971	Seaver-N.Y.	1.76
Tiant-Bos.	1.91	1972	Carlton-Phi.	1.98
Palmer-Bal.	2.40	1973	Seaver-N.Y.	2.08
Hunter-Oak.	**2.49**	**1974**	**Capra-Atl.**	**2.28**
Palmer-Bal.	**2.09**	**1975**	**Jones-S.D.**	**2.24**

1914	FEDERAL LEAGUE	C. Hendrix-Chi.	1.69
1015	FEDERAL LEAGUE	Moseley-Nwk.	1.91

SAVES

AMERICAN LEAGUE			NATIONAL LEAGUE	
Hoffer-Cle.	3	1901	Donovan-Bkn.	3
McGinnity-Bal.	3		Powell-St.L.	3
Powell-St.L.	3	1902	Willis-Bos.	3
Mullin-Det.	3	1903	Lundren-Chi.	3
			Miller-N.Y.	3
Patten-Was.	2	1904	McGinnity-N.Y.	6
Waddell-Phi.	4	1905	Elliott-N.Y.	6
Bender-Phi.	3	1906	Ferguson-N.Y.	7
Hess-Cle.	3			
Walsh-Chi.	3			
Dinneen-St.L.	4	1907	McGinnity-N.Y.	4
Walsh-Chi.	7	1908	Brown-Chi.	5
			Mathewson-N.Y.	5
Arellanes-Bos.	8	1909	Brown-Chi.	7
Walsh-Chi.	6	1910	Brown-Chi.	7
			Gaspar-Cin.	7
Walsh-Chi.	7	1911	Brown-Chi.	13
Walsh-Chi.	10	1912	Sallee-St.L.	6
Bender-Phi.	12	1913	Cheney-Chi.	11
Bentley-Was.	4	1914	Ames-St.L.	6
Dauss-Det.	4		Sallee-Cin.	6
Faber-Chi.	4			
Leonard-Bos.	1			
Mitchell-St.L.	4			
Shaw-Was.	4			
Mays-Bos.	6	1915	Hughes-Bos.	9
Shawkey-N.Y.	9	1916	Ames-St.L.	8
Danforth-Chi.	11	1917	Sallee-N.Y.	4
Bagby-Cle.	6	1918	Anderson-N.Y.	3
			Cooper-Pit.	3
			Oeschger-Phi.	3
			Toney-Cin. + N.Y.	3
Russell-N.Y. + Bos.	6	1919	Tuero-St.L.	4
Kerr-Chi.	5	1920	Sherdel-St.L.	6
Shocker-St.L.	5			
Mays-N.Y.	7	1921	North-St.L.	7
Middleton-Det.	7			
Uhle-Cle.	5	1922	Jonnard-N.Y.	5
Russell-Was.	9	1923	Jonnard-N.Y.	5
Marberry-Was.	15	1924	May-Cin.	6
Marberry-Was.	15	1925	Bush-Pit.	4
			Morrison-Pit.	4
Marberry-Was.	22	1926	Davies-N.Y.	6
Braxton-Was.	13	1927	Sherdel-St.L.	6
Moore-N.Y.	13			
Hoyt-N.Y.	8	1928	Haid-St.L.	5
			Sherdel-St.L.	5
Marberry-Was.	11	1929	Bush-Chi.	8
			Morrison-Bkn.	8
Grove-Phi.	9	1930	Bell-St.L.	8
Moore-Bos.	10	1931	Quinn-Bkn.	15
Marberry-Was.	13	1932	Quinn-Bkn.	8
Russell-Was.	13	1933	Collins-Phi.	6
Russell-Was.	7	1934	Hubbell-N.Y.	8
Knott-St.L.	7	1935	Leonard-Bkn.	8
Malone-N.Y.	9	1936	D.Dean-St.L.	11
Brown-Chi.	18	1937	Brown-Pit.	7
			Melton-N.Y.	7
Murphy-N.Y.	11	1938	Coffman-N.Y.	12
Murphy-N.Y.	19	1939	Bowman-St.L.	9
			Shoun-St.L.	9
Benton-Det.	17	1940	Beggs-Cin.	7
			Brown-N.Y.	7
			Brown-Pit.	7
Murphy-N.Y.	15	1941	Brown-N.Y.	8
Murphy-N.Y.	11	1942	Casey-Bkn.	13
Maltzberger-Chi.	14	1943	Webber-Bkn.	10
Berry-Phi.	12	1944	Adams-N.Y.	13
Caster-St.L.	12			
Maltzberger-Chi.	12			
Turner-N.Y.	10	1945	Adams-N.Y.	15
			Karl-Phi.	15
Klinger-Bos.	9	1946	Raffensberger-Phi.	6
Klieman-Cle.	17	1947	Casey-Bkn.	18
Page-N.Y.	17			
Christopher-Cle.	17	1948	Gumbert-Cin.	17
Page-N.Y.	27	1949	Wilks-St.L.	9
Harris-Was.	15	1950	Konstanty-Phi.	22
Kinder-Bos.	14	1951	Wilks-St.L. + Pit.	13
Dorish-Chi.	11	1952	Brazle-St.L.	16
Kinder-Bos.	27	1953	Brazle-St.L.	18
Sain-N.Y.	22	1954	Hughes-Bkn.	24
Narleski-Cle.	19	1955	Meyer-Phi.	16
Zuverink-Bal.	16	1956	Labine-Bkn.	19
Grim-N.Y.	19	1957	Labine-Bkn.	17
Duren-N.Y.	20	1958	Face-Pit.	20
Lown Chi.	15	1959	McDaniel-St.L.	15
			McMahon-Mil.	15
Fornieles-Bos.	14	1960	McDaniel-St.L.	26
Klippstein-Cle.	14			
Arroyo-N.Y.	29	1961	Miller-S.F.	17
Radatz-Bos.	24	1962	Face-Pit.	28
Miller-Bal.	27	1963	McDaniel-Chi.	22
Radatz-Bos.	29	1964	Woodeshick-Hou.	23
Kline-Was.	29	1965	Abernathy-Chi.	31
Aker-K.C.	32	1966	Regan-L.A.	21
Rojas-Cal.	27	1967	Abernathy-Cin.	28
Worthington-Min.	18	1968	Regan-L.A. + Chi.	25
Perranoski-Min.	31	1969	Gladding-Hou.	29
Perranoski-Min.	34	1970	Granger-Cin.	35
Sanders-Mil.	31	1971	Giusti-Pit.	30
Lyle-N.Y.	35	1972	Carroll-Cin.	37
Hiller-Det.	38	1973	Marshall-Mon.	31
Forster-Chi.	24	1974	Marshall-L.A.	21
Gossage-Chi.	26	1975	Eastwick-Cin.	22
			Hrabosky-St.L.	22

1914	FEDERAL LEAGUE	Ford-Buf.	6
1915	FEDERAL LEAGUE	Bedient-Buf.	10

YEARLY PITCHING LEADERS

SHUTOUTS

AMERICAN LEAGUE			NATIONAL LEAGUE	
Young-Bos. Griffith-Chi.	5	1901	Chesbro-Pit. Orth-Phi. Willis-Bos.	6
Joss-Cle.	5	1902	Chesbro-Pit. Mathewson-N.Y.	8
Young-Bos.	7	1903	Leever-Pit.	7
Young-Bos.	10	1904	McGinnity-N.Y.	9
Killian-Det.	8	1905	Mathewson-N.Y.	8
Walsh-Chi.	10	1906	Brown-Chi.	9
Plank-Phi.	8	1907	Overall-Chi.	8
Walsh-Chi.	12	1908	Mathewson-N.Y.	11
Walsh-Chi.	8	1909	Overall-Chi.	9
Coombs-Phi.	13	1910	Brown-Chi.	7
Johnson-Was.	6	1911	Alexander-Phi.	7
Plank-Phi.	6			
Wood-Bos.	12	1912	Rucker-Bkn.	6
Johnson-Was.	12	1913	Alexander-Phi.	7
Johnson-Was.	10	1914	Tesreau-N.Y.	8
Johnson-Was.	7	1915	Alexander-Phi.	12
Scott-Chi.	7			
Ruth-Bos.	9	1916	Alexander-Phi.	16
Coveleski-Cle.	9	1917	Alexander-Phi.	8
Johnson-Was.	8	1918	Tyler-Chi.	8
Mays-Bos.	8		Vaughn-Chi.	8
Johnson-Was.	7	1919	Alexander-Chi.	9
Mays-N.Y.	6	1920	Adams-Pit.	8
Jones-Bos.	5	1921	Alexander-Chi. Douglas-N.Y.	3
			Fillingim-Bos. Luque-Cin.	3
			Mitchell-Bkn. Morrison-Pit.	3
			Oeschger-Bos.	3
Uhle-Cle.	5	1922	Morrison-Pit. Vance-Bkn.	5
Coveleski-Cle.	5	1923	Luque-Cin.	6
Johnson-Was.	6	1924	Barnes-Bos. Cooper-Pit. Kremer-Pit.	4
			Rixey-Cin. Sothoren-St.L. Yde-Pit.	4
Lyons-Chi.	5	1925	Carlson-Phi. Luque-Cin. Vance-Bkn.	4
Wells Det.	4	1926	Donohue-Cin.	5
Lisenbee-Was.	4	1927	Haines-St.L.	6
Pennock-N.Y.	5	1928	Blake-Chi. Grimes-Pit. Lucas-Cin.	4
			McWeeney-Bkn. Vance-Bkn.	4
Blaeholder-St.L. Gray-St.L.	4	1929	Malone-Chi.	5
Crowder-St.L. MacFayden-Bos.	4			
Earnshaw-Phi. Pipgras-N.Y.	3	1930	Root-Chi. Vance-Bkn.	4
Brown-Cle.				
Earnshaw-Phi. Grove-Phi.	3	1931	Walker-N.Y.	6
Bridges-Det. Grove-Phi.	4	1932	Dean-St.L. Swetonic-Pit.	4
			Warneke-Chi.	4
Hildebrand-Cle.	6	1933	Hubbell-N.Y.	10
Gomez-N.Y. Harder-Cle.	6	1934	D. Dean-St.L.	7
Rowe-Det.	6	1935	Blanton-Pit. Fitzsimmons-N.Y.	4
			French-Chi. Mungo-Bkn. Weaver-Pit.	4
Grove-Bos.	6	1936	Blanton-Pit. Carleton-Chi.	4
			French-Chi. Lee-Chi. Smith-N.Y.	4
			Walters-Phi. Warneke-Chi.	4
Gomez-N.Y.	6	1937	Fette-Bos. Grissom-Cin. Turner-Bos.	5
Gomez-N.Y. Leonard-Was.	3	1938	Lee-Chi.	9
Ruffing-N.Y. Wilson-Bos.	3			
Ruffing-N.Y.	5	1939	Fette-Bos.	6
Feller-Cle. Lyons-Chi.	4	1940	Lohrman-N.Y. Salvo-Bos. Wyatt-Bkn.	5
Milnar-Cle.	4			
Feller-Cle.	6	1941	Wyatt-Bkn.	7
Bonham-N.Y.	6	1942	Cooper-St.L.	10
Chandler-N.Y. Trout-Det.	5	1943	Bithorn-Chi.	7
Trout-Det.	7	1944	Cooper-St.L.	7
Newhouser-Det.	8	1945	Passeau-Chi.	5
Feller-Cle.	10	1946	Blackwell-Cin.	6
Feller-Cle.	5	1947	Spahn-Bos.	7
Lemon-Cle.	10	1948	Brecheen-St.L.	7
Kinder-Bos. Trucks-Det.	6	1949	Heintzelman-Phi. Newcombe-Bkn.	5
			Pollet-St.L. Raffensberger-Cin.	5
Houtteman-Det.	4	1950	Hearn-N.Y. Jansen-St.L. + N.Y.	5
			Maglie-N.Y. Roberts-Phi.	5
Reynolds-N.Y.	7	1951	Spahn-Bos.	7
Garcia-Cle. Reynolds-N.Y.	6	1952	Raffensberger-Cin. Simmons-Phi.	6
Porterfield-Was.	9	1953	Haddix-St.L.	6
Garcia-Cle. Trucks-Chi.	5	1954	Antonelli-N.Y.	6
Hoeft-Det.	7	1955	Nuxhall-Cin.	5
Score-Cle.	5	1956	Burdette-Mil.	6
Wilson-Chi.	5	1957	Podres-Bkn.	6
Ford-N.Y.	7	1958	Willey-Mil.	4
Pascual-Was.	6	1959	Antonelli-S.F. Buhl-Mil.	4
			Burdette-Mil. Craig-L.A.	4
			Drysdale-L.A. Jones-S.F. Spahn-Mil.	4
Ford-N.Y. Perry-Cle. Wynn-Chi.	4	1960	Sanford-S.F.	6
Barber-Bal. Pascual-Min.	8	1961	Jay-Cin. Spahn-Mil.	4
Donovan-Cle. Kaat-Min.	5	1962	Friend-Pit. Gibson-St.L.	5
Pascual-Min.	5			
Herbert-Chi.	7	1963	Koufax-L.A.	11
Chance-L.A.	11	1964	Koufax-L.A.	7
Grant-Min.	6	1965	Marichal-S.F.	10
John-Chi. McDowell-Cle.	5	1966	Bunning-Phi. Gibson-St.L.	5
Tiant-Cle.	5		Jackson-Phi. Jaster-St.L.	5
			Koufax-L.A. Maloney-Cin.	5
Hargan-Cle. Horlen-Chi.	6	1967	Bunning-Phi.	6
John-Chi. Lolich-Det.	6			
McGlothlin-Cal.	6			
Tiant-Cle.	9	1968	Gibson-St.L.	13
McLain-Det.	9	1969	Marichal-S.F.	8
Dobson-Oak. Palmer-Bal.	5	1970	Perry-S.F.	5
Blue-Oak.	8	1971	Pappas-Chi. Downing-L.A. Blass-Pit.	5
			Gibson-St.L.	
Ryan-Cal.	9	1972	Sutton-L.A.	9
Blyleven-Min.	9	1973	Billingham-Cin.	7
Tiant-Bos.	7	1974	Matlack-N.Y.	7
Palmer-Bal.	7	1975	Messersmith-L.A.	7

1914 FEDERAL LEAGUE Falkenberg-Ind. 9
1915 FEDERAL LEAGUE Davenport-St.L. 10

BASES ON BALLS

AMERICAN LEAGUE			NATIONAL LEAGUE	
Fraser-Phi.	132	1901	Donovan-Bkn.	152
Moore-Chi.	101	1902	Pittinger-Bos.	128
Mullin-Det.	106	1903	Pittinger-Bos.	143
Mullin-Det.	131	1904	Pittinger-Bos.	144
Mullin-Det.	138	1905	Fraser-Bos.	149
Mullin-Det.	108	1906	Scanlan-Bkn.	127
Falkenberg-Was.	108			
Smith-Chi.	111	1907	McGlynn-St.L.	112
Dygert-Phi.	97	1908	Rucker-Bkn.	125
Groom-Was.	105	1909	Mattern-Bos.	108
			Moore-Phi.	108
Morgan-Phi.	117	1910	Harmon-St.L.	133
Knapp-Cle.	136	1911	Harmon-St.L.	181
Kahler-Cle.	121	1912	O'Toole-Pit.	159
Gregg-Cle.	124	1913	Seaton-Phi.	136
Shaw-Was.	137	1914	Cheney-Chi.	140
Wyckoff-Phi.	165	1915	Dale-Cin.	107
Myers-Phi.	168	1916	Mamaux-Pit.	136
Shaw-Was.	123	1917	Schneider-Cin.	119
Mogridge-N.Y.	116	1918	Schneider-Cin.	117
Ehmke-Det.	107	1919	Ruether-Cin.	83
Davis-St.L.	149	1920	Schupp-St.L.	127
Davis-St.L.	123	1921	Oeschger-Bos.	97
Collins-Bos.	103	1922	Ring-Phi.	103
Vangilder-St.L.	120	1923	Ring-Phi.	115
Bush-N.Y.	109	1924	Ring-Phi.	108
Grove-Phi.	131	1925	Ring-Phi.	119
Uhle-Cle.	118	1926	Blake-Chi.	92
Whitehill-Det.	105	1927	Root-Chi.	117
Johnson-N.Y.	104	1928	McWeeney-Bkn.	114
Earnshaw-Phi.	125	1929	Blake-Chi.	130
Earnshaw-Phi.	139	1930	Hallahan-St.L.	126
Ferrell-Cle.	130	1931	Hallahan-St.L.	112
Hadley-Chi. + St.L.	171	1932	Mungo-Bkn.	115
Hadley-St.L.	141	1933	Hallahan-St.L.	98
Newsom-St.L.	149	1934	Mungo-Bkn.	104
Cain-Phi. + St.L.	123	1935	Parmelee-N.Y.	97
Kennedy-Chi.	147	1936	Mungo-Bkn.	118
Newsom-Was. + Bos.	167	1937	Mulcahy-Phi.	97
Feller-Cle.	208	1938	Bryant-Chi.	125
Feller-Cle.	142	1939	Higbe-Chi. + Phi.	123
Chase-Was.	143	1940	Higbe-Phi.	121
Feller-Cle.	194	1941	Higbe-Bkn.	132
Marchildon-Phi.	140	1942	Melton-Phi.	114
Newhouser-Det.	111	1943	Vander Meer-Cin.	162
Gentry-Det.	108	1944	Javery-Bos.	118
			Voiselle-N.Y.	118
Reynolds-Cle.	130	1945	Gregg-Bkn.	120
Feller-Cle.	153	1946	Kennedy-N.Y.	116
Marchildon-Phi.	141	1947	Higbe-Bkn. + Pit.	122
Wight-Chi.	135	1948	Vander Meer-Cin.	124
Byrne-N.Y.	179	1949	Wehmeier-Cin.	117
Byrne-N.Y.	160	1950	Wehmeier-Cin.	135
Byrne-N.Y. + St.L.	150	1951	Spahn-Bos.	107
Wynn-Cle.	132	1952	Mizell-St.L.	103
			Wehmeier-Cin.	103
Parnell-Bos.	116	1953	Lindell-Pit. + Phi.	139
Turley-Bal.	181	1954	Gomez-N.Y.	109
Turley-N.Y.	177	1955	Jones-Chi.	185
Foytack-Det.	142	1956	Jones-Chi.	115
Moore-Bal.	112	1957	Drott-Chi.	129
Turley-N.Y.	128	1958	Jones-St.L.	107
Wynn-Chi.	119	1959	Jones-S.F.	109
Barber-Bal.	113	1960	Buhl-Mil.	103
Estrada-Bal.	132	1961	Gibson-St.L.	119
Belinsky-L.A.	122	1962	Hamilton-Phi.	107
Wilson-Bos.	105	1963	Culp-Phi.	102
Downing-N.Y.	120	1964	Veale-Pit.	124
McDowell-Cle.	132	1965	Cloninger-Mil.	119
			Veale-Pit.	119
Chance-Cal.	114	1966	Cloninger-Atl.	116
McDowell-Cle.	123	1967	Veale-Pit.	119
McDowell-Cle.	110	1968	Veale-Pit.	94
Tiant-Cle.	129	1969	Stoneman-Mon.	123
McDowell-Cle.	131	1970	Morton-Mon.	125
McDowell-Cle.	153	1971	Stoneman-Mon.	146
Ryan-Cal.	157	1972	Arlin-S.D.	122
Ryan-Cal.	162	1973	Reuss-Hou.	117
Ryan-Cal.	202	1974	Carlton-Phi.	136
Torrez-Bal.	133	1975	Richard-Hou.	138

1914 FEDERAL LEAGUE Lafitte-Bkn. 127
1915 FEDERAL LEAGUE Schulz-Buf. 149

STRIKEOUTS

AMERICAN LEAGUE			NATIONAL LEAGUE	
Young-Bos.	158	1901	Hahn-Cin.	239
Waddell-Phi.	210	1902	Willis-Bos.	225
Waddell-Phi.	302	1903	Mathewson-N.Y.	267
Waddell-Phi.	349	1904	Mathewson-N.Y.	212
Waddell-Phi.	287	1905	Mathewson-N.Y.	206
Waddell-Phi.	196	1906	Beebe-Chi. + St.L.	171
Waddell-Phi.	232	1907	Mathewson-N.Y.	178
Walsh-Chi.	269	1908	Mathewson-N.Y.	259
Smith-Chi.	177	1909	Overall-Chi.	205
Johnson-Was.	313	1910	Moore-Phi.	185
Walsh-Chi.	255	1911	Marquard-N.Y.	237
Johnson-Was.	303	1912	Alexander-Phi.	195
Johnson-Was.	243	1913	Seaton-Phi.	168
Johnson-Was.	225	1914	Alexander-Phi.	214
Johnson-Was.	203	1915	Alexander-Phi.	241
Johnson-Was.	228	1916	Alexander-Phi.	167
Johnson-Was.	188	1917	Alexander-Phi.	201
Johnson-Was.	162	1918	Vaughn-Chi.	148
Johnson-Was.	147	1919	Vaughn-Chi.	141
Coveleski-Cle.	133	1920	Alexander-Chi.	173
Johnson-Was.	143	1921	Grimes-Bkn.	136
Shocker-St.L.	149	1922	Vance-Bkn.	134
Johnson-Was.	130	1923	Vance-Bkn.	197
Johnson-Was.	158	1924	Vance-Bkn.	262
Grove-Phi.	116	1925	Vance-Bkn.	221
Grove-Phi.	194	1926	Vance-Bkn.	140
Grove-Phi.	174	1927	Vance-Bkn.	184
Grove-Phi.	183	1928	Vance-Bkn.	200
Grove-Phi.	170	1929	Malone-Chi.	166
Grove-Phi.	209	1930	Hallahan-St.L.	177
Grove-Phi.	175	1931	Hallahan-St.L.	159
Ruffing-N.Y.	190	1932	Dean-St.L.	191
Gomez-N.Y.	163	1933	Dean-St.L.	199
Gomez-N.Y.	158	1934	D. Dean-St.L.	195
Bridges-Det.	163	1935	D. Dean-St.L.	182
Bridges-Det.	175	1936	Mungo-Bkn.	238
Gomez-N.Y.	194	1937	Hubbell-N.Y.	159
Feller-Cle.	240	1938	Bryant-Chi.	135
Feller-Cle.	246	1939	Passeau-Phi. + Chi.	137
			Walters-Cin.	137
Feller-Cle.	261	1940	Higbe-Phi.	137
Feller-Cle.	260	1941	Vander Meer-Cin.	202
Hughson-Bos.	113	1942	Vander Meer-Cin.	186
Newsom-Was.	113			
Reynolds-Cle.	151	1943	Vander Meer-Cin.	174
Newhouser-Det.	187	1944	Voiselle-N.Y.	161
Newhouser-Det.	212	1945	Roe-Pit.	148
Feller-Cle.	348	1946	Schmitz-Chi.	135
Feller-Cle.	196	1947	Blackwell-Cin.	193
Feller-Cle.	164	1948	Brecheen-St.L.	149
Trucks-Det.	153	1949	Spahn-Bos.	151
Lemon-Cle.	170	1950	Spahn-Bos.	191
Raschi-N.Y.	164	1951	Newcombe-Bkn.	164
			Spahn-Bos.	164
Reynolds-N.Y.	160	1952	Spahn-Bos.	183
Pierce-Chi.	186	1953	Roberts-Phi.	198
Turley-Bal.	185	1954	Roberts-Phi.	185
Score-Cle.	245	1955	Jones-Chi.	198
Score-Cle.	263	1956	Jones-Chi.	176
Wynn-Cle.	184	1957	Sanford-Phi.	188
Wynn-Chi.	179	1958	Jones-St.L.	205
Bunning-Det.	201	1959	Drysdale-L.A.	242
Bunning-Det.	201	1960	Drysdale-L.A.	246
Pascual-Min.	221	1961	Koufax-L.A.	269
Pascual-Min.	206	1962	Drysdale-L.A.	232
Pascual-Min.	202	1963	Koufax-L.A.	306
Downing-N.Y.	217	1964	Veale-Pit.	250
McDowell-Cle.	325	1965	Koufax-L.A.	382
McDowell-Cle.	225	1966	Koufax-L.A.	317
Lonborg-Bos.	246	1967	Bunning-Phi.	253
McDowell-Cle.	283	1968	Gibson-St.L.	268
McDowell-Cle.	279	1969	Jenkins-Chi.	273
McDowell-Cle.	304	1970	Seaver-N.Y.	283
Lolich-Det.	308	1971	Seaver-N.Y.	289
Ryan-Cal.	329	1972	Carlton-Phi.	310
Ryan-Cal.	383	1973	Seaver-N.Y.	251
Ryan-Cal.	367	1974	Carlton-Phi.	240
Tanana-Cal.	269	1975	Seaver-N.Y.	243

1914 FEDERAL LEAGUE Falkenberg-Ind. 236
1915 FEDERAL LEAGUE Davenport-St.L. 229

SINGLE SEASON LEADERS

(numbers after individual name indicates number of times that individual appears within a specific category; the bold indicates the individual appearing most within a category)

BATTING AVERAGE

1	Rogers Hornsby-1	St.L.	NL	1924	.424
2	Nap Lajoie-1	Phi.	AL	1901	.422
3	George Sisler-1	St.L.	AL	1922	.420
4	Ty Cobb-1	Det.	AL	1911	.420
5	Ty Cobb-2	Det.	AL	1912	.410
6	Joe Jackson-1	Cle	AL	1911	.408
7	George Sisler-2	St.L.	AL	1920	.407
8	Ted Williams-1	Bos	AL	1941	.406
9	Rogers Hornsby-2	St.L.	NL	1925	.403
10	Harry Heilmann-1	Det.	AL	1923	.403
11	Rogers Hornsby-3	St.L.	NL	1922	.401
12	Bill Terry	N.Y.	NL	1930	.401
13	Ty Cobb-3	Det.	AL	1922	.401
14	Lefty O'Doul-1	Phi.	NL	1929	.398
15	Harry Heilmann-2	Det.	AL	1927	.398
16	Rogers Hornsby-4	St.L.	NL	1921	.397
17	Joe Jackson-2	Cle.	AL	1912	.395
18	Harry Heilman-3	Det.	AL	1921	.394
19	Babe Ruth-1	N.Y.	AL	1923	.393
20	Harry Heilmann-4	Det.	AL	1925	.393
21	Babe Herman-1	Bkn.	NL	1930	.393
22	Al Simmons-1	Phi.	AL	1927	.392
23	Ty Cobb-4	Det.	AL	1913	.390
24	Al Simmons-2	Phi.	AL	1931	.390
25	Tris Speaker-1	Cle.	AL	1925	.389
26	Ty Cobb-5	Det.	AL	1921	.389
27	Ted Williams-2	Bos.	AL	1957	.388
28	Luke Appling	Chi.	AL	1936	.388
29	Tris Speaker-2	Cle.	AL	1920	.383
30	Rogers Hornsby-5	Bos.	NL	1928	.387
31	Tris Speaker-3	Cle.	AL	1916	.386
32	Chuck Klein	Phi.	NL	1930	.386
33	Ty Cobb-6	Det.	AL	1910	.385
34	Arky Vaughan	Pit.	NL	1935	.385
35	Rogers Hornsby-6	St.L.	NL	1923	.384
36	Al Simmons-3	Phi.	AL	1925	.384
37	Ty Cobb-7	Det.	AL	1919	.384
38	Nap Lajoie-2	Cle.	AL	1910	.384
39	Tris Speaker-4	Bos.	AL	1912	.383
40	Ty Cobb-8	Det.	AL	1917	.383
41	Lefty O'Doul-2	Phi.	NL	1930	.383
42	Ty Cobb-9	Det.	AL	1918	.382
43	Joe Jackson-3	Chi.	AL	1920	.382
44	Jesse Burkett	St.L.	NL	1901	.382
45	Babe Herman-2	Bkn.	NL	1929	.381
46	Joe DiMaggio	N.Y.	AL	1939	.381
47	Nap Lajoie-3	Cle.	AL	1904	.381
48	Al Simmons-4	Phi.	AL	1930	.381
49	Paul Waner	Pit.	NL	1927	.380
50	Rogers Hornsby-7	Chi.	NL	1929	.380
51	Tris Speaker-5	Cle.	AL	1923	.380
52	Goose Goslin	Was.	AL	1928	.379
	Fred Lindstrom	N.Y.	NL	1930	.379
54	Lou Gehrig	N.Y.	AL	1930	.379
55	Ty Cobb-10	Det.	AL	1925	.378
56	Sam Crawford	Det.	AL	1911	.378
	Babe Ruth-2	N.Y.	AL	1924	.378
58	Tris Speaker-6	Cle.	AL	1922	.378
59	Earl Averill	Cle.	AL	1936	.378
60	Babe Ruth-3	N.Y.	AL	1921	.378
	Heinie Manush-1	St.L.	AL	1928	.378
62	Heinie Manush-2	Det.	AL	1926	.378
63	Cy Seymour	Cin.	NL	1905	.377
	Ty Cobb-11	Det.	AL	1909	.377
65	Stan Musial	St.L.	NL	1948	.376
66	Ed Delahanty	Was.	AL	1902	.376
67	Babe Ruth-4	N.Y.	AL	1920	.375
68	Zack Wheat	Bkn.	NL	1924	.375

SLUGGING AVERAGE

1	Babe Ruth-1	N.Y.	AL	1920	.847
2	Babe Ruth-2	N.Y.	AL	1921	.846
3	Babe Ruth-3	N.Y.	AL	1927	.777
4	Lou Gehrig-1	N.Y.	AL	1927	.765
5	Babe Ruth-4	N.Y.	AL	1923	.764
6	Rogers Hornsby-1	St.L.	NL	1925	.756
7	Jimmie Foxx-1	Phi.	AL	1932	.749
8	Babe Ruth-5	N.Y.	AL	1924	.739
9	Babe Ruth-6	N.Y.	AL	1926	.737
10	Ted Williams-1	Bos.	AL	1941	.735
11	Babe Ruth-7	N.Y.	AL	1930	.732
12	Ted Williams-2	Bos.	AL	1957	.731
13	Hack Wilson	Chi.	NL	1930	.723
14	Rogers Hornsby-2	St.L.	NL	1922	.722
15	Lou Gehrig-2	N.Y.	AL	1930	.721
16	Babe Ruth-8	N.Y.	AL	1928	.709
17	Al Simmons	Phi.	AL	1930	.708
18	Lou Gehrig-3	N.Y.	AL	1934	.706
19	Mickey Mantle-1	N.Y.	AL	1956	.705
20	Jimmie Foxx-2	Bos.	AL	1938	.704
21	Jimmie Foxx-3	Phi.	AL	1933	.703
22	Stan Musial	St.L.	NL	1948	.702
23	Babe Ruth-9	N.Y.	AL	1931	.700
24	Babe Ruth-10	N.Y.	AL	1929	.697
25	Lou Gehrig-4	N.Y.	AL	1936	.696
26	Rogers Hornsby-3	St.L.	NL	1924	.696
27	Jimmie Foxx-4	Bos.	AL	1939	.694
28	Chuck Klein-1	Phi.	NL	1930	.687
	Mickey Mantle-2	N.Y.	AL	1961	.687
30	Hank Greenberg-1	Det.	AL	1938	.683
31	Rogers Hornsby-4	Chi.	NL	1929	.679
32	Babe Herman	Bkn.	NL	1930	.678
33	Joe DiMaggio	N.Y.	AL	1937	.673
34	Babe Ruth-11	N.Y.	AL	1922	.672
35	Joe DiMaggio	N.Y.	AL	1939	.671
36	Hank Greenberg-2	Det.	AL	1940	.670
37	Hank Aaron	Atl.	NL	1971	.669
38	Hank Greenberg-3	Det.	AL	1937	.668
39	Ted Williams-3	Bos.	AL	1946	.667
40	Willie Mays-1	N.Y.	NL	1954	.667
41	Mickey Mantle-3	N.Y.	AL	1957	.665
42	Lou Gehrig-5	N.Y.	AL	1931	.662
43	Norm Cash	Det.	AL	1961	.662
44	Babe Ruth-12	N.Y.	AL	1932	.661
45	Willie Mays-2	N.Y.	NL	1955	.659
46	Ralph Kiner	Pit.	NL	1949	.658
47	Chuck Klein-2	Phi.	NL	1929	.657
48	Babe Ruth-13	Bos.	AL	1919	.657
49	Willie McCovey	S.F.	NL	1969	.656
50	Jimmie Foxx-5	Phi.	AL	1934	.653
51	Chick Hafey	St.L.	NL	1930	.652
52	Rudy York	Det.	AL	1937	.651
53	Ted Williams-4	Bos.	AL	1949	.650

HITS

1	George Sisler-1	St.L.	AL	1920	257
2	Lefty O'Doul	Phi.	NL	1929	254
	Bill Terry-1	N.Y.	NL	1930	254
4	Al Simmons	Phi.	AL	1925	253
5	Rogers Hornsby-1	St.L.	NL	1922	250
	Chuck Klein-1	Phi.	NL	1930	250
7	Ty Cobb-1	Det.	AL	1911	248
8	George Sisler-2	St.L.	AL	1922	246
9	Heinie Manush	St.L.	AL	1928	241
	Babe Herman	Bkn.	NL	1930	241
11	Harry Heilmann-1	Det.	AL	1921	237
	Paul Waner	Pit.	NL	1927	237
	Joe Medwick	St.L.	NL	1937	237
14	Jack Tobin	St.L.	AL	1921	236
15	Rogers Hornsby-2	St.L.	NL	1921	235
16	Lloyd Waner	Pit.	NL	1929	234
17	Joe Jackson-1	Cle.	AL	1911	233
18	Earl Averill	Cle.	AL	1936	232
19	Earle Combs	N.Y.	AL	1927	231
	Fred Lindstrom	N.Y.	NL	1928	231
	Matty Alou	Pit.	NL	1969	231
22	Stan Musial-1	St.L.	NL	1948	230
	Tommy Davis	L.A.	NL	1962	230
	Joe Torre	St.L.	NL	1971	230
	Pete Rose	Cin.	NL	1973	230
26	Nap Lajoie-1	Phi.	AL	1901	229
	Rogers Hornsby-3	Chi.	NL	1929	229
28	Jesse Burkett	St.L.	NL	1901	228
	Kiki Cuyler	Chi.	NL	1930	228
	Stan Musial-2	St.L.	NL	1946	228
31	Nap Lajoie-2	Cle.	AL	1910	227
	Ty Cobb-2	Det.	AL	1912	227
	Rogers Hornsby-4	St.L.	NL	1924	227
	Sam Rice	Was.	AL	1925	227
	Jim Bottomley	St.L.	NL	1925	227
	Billy Herman	Chi.	NL	1935	227
	Charlie Gehringer	Det.	AL	1936	227
38	Joe Jackson-2	Cle.	AL	1912	226
	Bill Terry-2	N.Y.	NL	1929	226
	Chuck Klein-2	Phi.	NL	1932	226
41	Ty Cobb-3	Det.	AL	1917	225
	Harry Heilmann-2	Det.	AL	1925	225
	Johnny Hodapp	Cle.	AL	1930	225
	Bill Terry-3	N.Y.	NL	1932	225

DOUBLES

1	Earl Webb	Bos.	AL	1931	67
2	George Burns-1	Cle.	AL	1926	64
	Joe Medwick-1	St.L.	NL	1936	64
4	Hank Greenberg-1	Det.	AL	1934	63
5	Paul Waner-1	Pit.	NL	1932	62
6	Charie Gehringer-1	Det.	AL	1936	60
7	Tris Speaker-1	Cle.	AL	1923	59
	Chuck Klein-1	Phi.	NL	1930	59
9	Billy Herman-1	Chi.	NL	1935	57
	Billy Herman-2	Chi.	NL.	1936	57
11	Joe Medwick-2	St.L.	NL	1937	56
	George Kell	Det.	AL	1950	56
13	Gee Walker	Det.	AL	1936	55
14	Tris Speaker-2	Bos.	AL	1912	53
	Al Simmons	Phi.	AL	1926	53
	Paul Waner-2	Pit.	NL	1936	53
	Stan Musial-1	St.L.	NL	1953	53
18	Tris Speaker-3	Cle.	AL	1921	52
	Tris Speaker-4	Cle.	AL	1926	52
	Lou Gehrig	N.Y.	AL	1927	52
	Johnny Frederick	Bkn.	NL	1929	52
	Enos Slaughter	St.L.	NL	1939	52
23	Nap Lajoie-1	Cle.	AL	1910	51
	George Burns-1	Cle.	AL	1927	51
	Johnny Hodapp	Cle.	AL	1930	51
	Beau Bell	St.L.	AL	1937	51
	Joe Cronin	Bos.	AL	1938	51
	Stan Musial-2	St.L.	NL	1944	51
	Mickey Vernon	Was.	AL	1946	51
	Frank Robinson	Cin.	NL	1962	51
31	Nap Lajoie-2	Cle.	AL	1904	50
	Tris Speaker-5	Cle.	AL	1920	50
	Harry Heilmann	Det.	AL	1927	50
	Paul Waner-3	Pit.	NL	1928	50
	Kiki Cuyler	Chi.	NL	1930	50
	Chuck Klein-2	Phi.	NL	1932	50
	Charlie Gehringer-2	Det.	AL	1934	50
	Ben Chapman	NY-Was.	AL	1936	50
	Odell Hale	Cle.	AL	1936	50
	Hank Greenberg-2	Det.	AL	1940	50
	Stan Musial-3	St.L.	NL	1946	50
	Stan Spence	Was.	AL	1946	50

TRIPLES

1	Owen Wilson	Pit.	NL	1911	36
2	Joe Jackson-1	Cle.	AL	1912	26
	Sam Crawford-1	Det.	AL	1914	26
	Kiki Cuyler	Pit.	NL	1925	26
5	Sam Crawford-2	Det.	AL	1903	25
	Larry Doyle	N.Y.	NL	1911	25
	Tom Long	St.L.	NL	1915	25
8	Ty Cobb-1	Det.	AL	1911	24
9	Sam Crawford-3	Cin.	NL	1902	23
	Ty Cobb-2	Det.	AL	1912	23
	Sam Crawford-4	Det.	AL	1913	23
	Ty Cobb-3	Det.	AL	1917	23
	Earle Combs-1	N.Y.	AL	1927	23
	Adam Comorosky	Pit.	NL	1930	23
	Dale Mitchell	Cle.	AL	1949	23
16	Bill Bradley	Cle.	AL	1903	22
	Chick Stahl	Bos.	AL	1904	22
	Elmer Flick	Cle.	AL	1906	22
	Birdie Cree	N.Y.	AL	1911	22
	Mike Mitchell	Cin.	NL	1911	22
	Tris Speaker	Bos.	AL	1913	22
	Hy Myers	Bkn.	NL	1920	22
	Jake Daubert	Cin.	NL	1922	22
	Paul Waner	Pit.	NL	1926	22
	Earle Combs-2	N.Y.	AL	1930	22
	Stuffy Stirnweiss	N.Y.	AL	1945	22
27	Bill Keister	Bal.	AL	1901	21
	Jimmy Williams-1	Bal.	AL	1901	21
	Jimmy Williams-2	Bal.	AL	1902	21
	Buck Freeman-1	Bos.	AL	1903	21
	Cy Seymour	Cin.	NL	1905	21
	Wildfire Schulte	Chi.	NL	1911	21
	Frank Baker	Phi.	AL	1912	21
	Sam Crawford-5	Det.	AL	1912	21
	Vic Saier	Chi.	NL	1913	21
	Joe Jackson-2	Chi.	AL	1916	21
	Edd Roush	Cin.	NL	1924	21
	Earle Combs-3	N.Y.	AL	1928	21
39	Buck Freeman-2	Bos.	AL	1902	20
	Tommy Leach	Pit.	NL	1902	20
	Ty Cobb-4	Det.	AL	1908	20
	Red Murray	N.Y.	NL	1912	20
	Honus Wagner	Pit.	NL	1912	20
	Dots Miller	Pit.	NL	1913	20
	Rogers Hornsby	St.L.	NL	1920	20
	Joe Jackson-3	Chi.	AL	1920	20
	Rabbit Maranville	Pit.	NL	1924	20
	Goose Goslin	Was.	AL	1925	20
	Lou Gehrig	N.Y.	AL	1926	20
	Curt Walker	Cin.	NL	1926	20
	Jim Bottomley	St.L.	NL	1928	20
	Heinie Manush	St.L.	AL	1928	20
	Lloyd Waner	Pit.	NL	1929	20
	Bill Terry	N.Y.	NL	1931	20
	Joe Vosmik	Cle.	AL	1935	20
	Jeff Heath	Cle.	AL	1941	20
	Stan Musial-1	St.L.	NL	1943	20
	Stan Musial-2	St.L.	NL	1946	20
	Willie Mays	N.Y.	NL	1957	20

HOME RUNS

1	Roger Maris	N.Y.	AL	1961	61
2	Babe Ruth-1	N.Y.	AL	1927	60
3	Babe Ruth-2	N.Y.	AL	1921	59
4	Jimmie Foxx-1	Phi.	AL	1932	58
	Hank Greenberg-1	Det.	AL	1938	58
6	Hack Wilson	Chi.	NL	1930	56
7	Babe Ruth-3	N.Y.	AL	1920	54
	Babe Ruth-4	N.Y.	AL	1928	54
	Ralph Kiner-1	Pit.	NL	1949	54
	Mickey Mantle-1	N.Y.	AL	1961	54
11	Mickey Mantle-2	N.Y.	AL	1956	52
	Willie Mays-1	S.F.	NL	1965	52
13	Ralph Kiner-2	Pit.	NL	1947	51
	Johnny Mize-1	N.Y.	NL	1947	51
	Willie Mays-2	N.Y.	NL	1955	51
16	Jimmie Foxx-2	Bos.	AL	1938	50
17	Babe Ruth-5	N.Y.	AL	1930	49
	Lou Gehrig-1	N.Y.	AL	1934	49
	Lou Gehrig-2	N.Y.	AL	1936	49
	Ted Kluszewski-1	Cin.	NL	1954	49
	Willie Mays-3	S.F.	NL	1962	49
	Harmon Killebrew-1	Min.	AL	1964	49
	Frank Robinson	Bal.	AL	1966	49
	Harmon Killebrew-2	Min.	AL	1969	49
25	Jimmie Foxx-3	Phi.	AL	1933	48
	Harmon Killebrew-3	Min.	AL	1962	48
	Frank Howard-1	Was.	AL	1969	48
	Willie Stargell-1	Pit.	NL	1971	48
29	Babe Ruth-6	N.Y.	AL	1926	47
	Lou Gehrig-3	N.Y.	AL	1927	47
	Ralph Kiner-3	Pit.	NL	1950	47
	Eddie Mathews-1	Mil.	NL	1953	47
	Ted Kluszewski-2	Cin.	NL	1955	47
	Ernie Banks-1	Chi.	NL	1958	47
	Willie Mays-4	S.F.	NL	1964	47
	Reggie Jackson	Oak.	AL	1969	47
	Hank Aaron-1	Atl.	NL	1971	47
38	Babe Ruth-7	N.Y.	AL	1924	46
	Babe Ruth-8	N.Y.	AL	1929	46
	Lou Gehrig-4	N.Y.	AL	1931	46
	Babe Ruth-9	N.Y.	AL	1931	46
	Joe DiMaggio	N.Y.	AL	1937	46
	Eddie Mathews-2	Mil.	NL	1959	46
	Orlando Cepeda	S.F.	NL	1961	46
	Jim Gentile	Bal.	AL	1961	46
	Harmon Killebrew-4	Min.	AL	1961	46
47	Ernie Banks-2	Chi.	NL	1959	45
	Rocky Colavito-1	Det.	AL	1961	45
	Hank Aaron-2	Mil.	NL	1962	45
	Harmon Killebrew-5	Min.	AL	1963	45
	Willie McCovey-1	S.F.	NL	1969	45
	Johnny Bench-1	Cin.	NL	1970	45
53	Jimmie Foxx-4	Phi.	AL	1934	44
	Hank Greenberg-2	Det.	AL	1946	44
	Ernie Banks-3	Chi.	NL	1955	44
	Hank Aaron-3	Mil.	NL	1957	44
	Hank Aaron-4	Mil.	NL	1963	44
	Willie McCovey-2	S.F.	NL	1963	44
	Hank Aaron-5	Atl.	NL	1966	44
	Harmon Killebrew-6	Min.	AL	1967	44
	Carl Yastrzemski-1	Bos.	AL	1967	44
	Frank Howard-2	Was.	AL	1968	44
	Hank Aaron-6	AtL.	NL	1969	44
	Frank Howard-3	Was.	AL	1970	44
	Willie Stargell-2	Pit.	NL	1973	44
66	Chuck Klein-1	Phi.	NL	1929	43
	Johnny Mize-2	St.L.	NL	1940	43
	Ted Williams	Bos.	AL	1949	43
	Al Rosen	Cle.	AL	1953	43
	Duke Snider-1	Bkn.	NL	1956	43
	Ernie Banks-4	Chi.	NL	1957	43
	Dave Johnson	Atl.	NL	1973	43
73	Rogers Hornsby	St.L.	NL	1922	42
	Mel Ott	N.Y.	NL	1929	42
	Hal Troskey	Cle.	AL	1936	42
	Ralph Kiner-4	Pit.	NL	1951	42
	Duke Snider-2	Bkn.	NL	1953	42
	Gus Zernial	Phi.	AL	1953	42
	Gil Hodges-1	Bkn.	NL	1954	42
	Duke Snider-3	Bkn.	NL	1955	42
	Roy Sievers	Was.	AL	1957	42
	Mickey Mantle-3	N.Y.	AL	1958	42
	Rocky Colavito-2	Cle.	AL	1959	42
	Harmon Killebrew-7	Was.	AL	1959	42
	Dick Stuart	Bos.	AL	1963	42
	Billy Williams	Chi.	NL	1970	42
87	Babe Ruth-10	N.Y.	AL	1923	41
	Cy Williams	Phi.	NL	1923	41
	Lou Gehrig-5	N.Y.	AL	1930	41
	Babe Ruth-11	N.Y.	AL	1932	41
	Jimmie Foxx-5	Bos.	AL	1936	41
	Hank Greenberg-3	Det.	AL	1940	41
	Roy Campanella	Bkn.	NL	1953	41
	Willie Mays-5	N.Y.	NL	1954	41
	Hank Sauer	Chi.	NL	1954	41
	Eddie Mathews-3	Mil.	NL	1955	41
	Rocky Colavito-3	Cle.	AL	1958	41
	Ernie Banks-5	Chi.	NL	1960	41
	Norm Cash	Det.	AL	1961	41
	Harmon Killebrew-8	Min.	AL	1970	41
	Darrell Evans	AtL.	NL	1973	41
102	Chuck Klein-2	Phi.	NL	1930	40
	Hank Greenberg-4	Det.	AL	1937	40
	Johnny Mize-3	N.Y.	NL	1948	40
	Gil Hodges-2	Bkn.	NL	1951	40
	Ted Kluszewski-3	Cin.	NL	1953	40
	Eddie Mathews-4	Mil.	NL	1954	40
	Duke Snider-4	Bkn.	NL	1954	40
	Wally Post	Cin.	NL	1955	40
	Duke Snider-5	Bkn.	NL	1957	40
	Hank Aaron-7	Mil.	NL	1960	40
	Mickey Mantle-4	N.Y.	AL	1960	40
	Willie Mays-6	S.F.	NL	1961	40
	Dick Allen	Phi.	NL	1966	40
	Rico Petrocelli	Bos.	AL	1969	40
	Carl Yastrzemski-2	Bos.	AL	1969	40
	Tony Perez	Cin.	NL	1970	40
	Carl Yastrzemski-3	Bos.	AL	1970	40
	Johnny Bench-2	Cin.	NL	1972	40
	Hank Aaron-8	Atl.	NL	1973	40

SINGLE SEASON LEADERS

RUNS BATTED IN

1	Hack Wilson–1	Chi.	NL	1930	190
2	Lou Gehrig–1	N.Y.	AL	1931	184
3	Hank Greenberg–1	Det.	AL	1937	183
4	Lou Gehrig–2	N.Y.	AL	1927	175
	Jimmie Foxx–1	Bos.	AL	1938	175
6	Lou Gehrig–3	N.Y.	AL	1930	174
7	Babe Ruth–1	N.Y.	AL	1921	171
8	Chuck Klein–1	Phi.	NL	1930	170
	Hank Greenberg–2	Det.	AL	1935	170
10	Jimmie Foxx–2	Phi.	AL	1932	169
11	Joe DiMaggio–1	N.Y.	AL	1937	167
12	Al Simmons–1	Phi.	AL	1930	165
	Lou Gehrig–4	N.Y.	AL	1934	165
14	Babe Ruth–2	N.Y.	AL	1927	164
15	Babe Ruth–3	N.Y.	AL	1931	163
	Jimmie Foxx–3	Phi.	AL	1933	163
17	Hal Trosky–1	Cle.	AL	1936	162
18	Hack Wilson–2	Chi.	NL	1929	159
	Lou Gehrig–5	N.Y.	AL	1937	159
	Vern Stephens–1	Bos.	AL	1949	159
	Ted Williams–1	Bos.	AL	1949	159
22	Al Simmons–2	Phi.	AL	1929	157
23	Jimmie Foxx–4	Phi.	AL	1930	156
24	Ken Williams	St.L.	AL	1922	155
	Joe DiMaggio–2	N.Y.	AL	1948	155
26	Babe Ruth–4	N.Y.	AL	1929	154
	Joe Medwick	St.L.	NL	1937	154
28	Babe Ruth–5	N.Y.	AL	1930	153
	Tommy Davis	L.A.	NL	1962	153
30	Rogers Hornsby–1	St.L.	NL	1922	152
	Lou Gehrig–6	N.Y.	AL	1936	152
32	Mel Ott	N.Y.	NL	1929	151
	Lou Gehrig–7	N.Y.	AL	1932	151
	Al Simmons–3	Phi.	AL	1932	151
35	Hank Greenberg–3	Det.	AL	1940	150
36	Rogers Hornsby–2	Chi.	NL	1929	149
37	Johnny Bench	Cin.	NL	1970	148
38	Hank Greenberg–4	Det.	AL	1938	146
39	Babe Ruth–6	N.Y.	AL	1926	145
	Chuck Klein–2	Phi.	NL	1929	145
	Ted Williams–2	Bos.	AL	1939	145
	Al Rosen	Cle.	AL	1953	145
43	Walt Dropo	Bos.	AL	1950	144
	Vern Stephens–2	Bos.	AL	1950	144
45	Rogers Hornsby–3	St.L.	NL	1925	143
	Don Hurst	Phi.	NL	1932	143
	Earl Averill	Cle.	AL	1931	143
	Jimmie Foxx–5	Bos.	AL	1936	143
	Ernie Banks	Chi.	NL	1959	143
50	Lou Gehrig–8	N.Y.	AL	1928	142
	Babe Ruth–7	N.Y.	AL	1928	142
	Hal Trosky–2	Cle.	AL	1934	142
	Roy Campanella	Bkn.	NL	1953	142
	Orlando Cepeda	S.F.	NL	1961	142
	Roger Maris	N.Y.	AL	1961	142
56	Ted Kluszewski	Cin.	NL	1954	141
	Jim Gentile	Bal.	AL	1961	141
	Willie Mays	S.F.	NL	1961	141
59	Joe DiMaggio–3	N.Y.	AL	1938	140
	Rocky Colavito	Det.	AL	1961	140
	Harmon Killebrew	Min.	AL	1969	140

RUNS

1	Babe Ruth–1	N.Y.	AL	1921	177
2	Lou Gehrig–1	N.Y.	AL	1936	167
3	Babe Ruth–2	N.Y.	AL	1928	163
	Lou Gehrig–2	N.Y.	AL	1931	163
5	Babe Ruth–3	N.Y.	AL	1920	158
	Babe Ruth–4	N.Y.	AL	1927	158
	Chuck Klein–1	Phi.	NL	1930	158
8	Rogers Hornsby–1	Chi.	NL	1929	156
9	Kiki Cuyler–1	Chi.	NL	1930	155
10	Lefty O'Doul	Phi.	NL	1929	152
	Woody English	Chi.	NL	1930	152
	Chuck Klein–2	Phi.	NL	1932	152
	Al Simmons–1	Phi.	AL	1930	152
14	Babe Ruth–5	N.Y.	AL	1923	151
	Jimmie Foxx	Phi.	AL	1932	151
	Joe DiMaggio	N.Y.	AL	1937	151
17	Babe Ruth–6	N.Y.	AL	1930	150
	Ted Williams–1	Bos.	AL	1949	150
19	Lou Gehrig–3	N.Y.	AL	1927	149
	Babe Ruth–7	N.Y.	AL	1931	149
	Hank Greenberg–1	Det.	AL	1938	149
22	Ty Cobb	Det.	AL	1911	147
23	Hack Wilson	Chi.	NL	1930	146
24	Nap Lajoie	Phi.	AL	1901	145
	Harlond Clift	St.L.	AL	1936	145
26	Ty Cobb–2	Det.	AL	1915	144
	Kiki Cuyler–2	Pit.	NL	1925	144
	Charlie Gehringer–1	Det.	AL	1930	144
	Al Simmons–2	Phi.	AL	1932	144
	Charlie Gehringer–2	Det.	AL	1936	144
	Hank Greenberg–2	Det.	AL	1938	144
32	Babe Ruth–8	N.Y.	AL	1924	143
	Lou Gehrig–4	N.Y.	AL	1930	143
	Babe Herman	Bkn.	NL	1930	143
	Earle Combs	N.Y.	AL	1932	143
	Red Rolfe	N.Y.	AL	1937	143
37	Paul Waner	Pit.	NL	1928	142
	Ted Williams–2	Bos.	AL	1946	142
39	Rogers Hornsby–2	St.L.	NL	1922	141
	Ted Williams–3	Bos.	AL	1942	141
41	Max Carey	Pit.	NL	1922	140
	Earl Averill	Cle.	AL	1931	140

TOTAL BASES

1	Babe Ruth–1	N.Y.	AL	1921	457
2	Rogers Hornsby–1	St.L.	NL	1922	450
3	Lou Gehrig–1	N.Y.	AL	1927	447
4	Chuck Klein–1	Phi.	NL	1930	445
5	Jimmie Foxx–1	Phi.	AL	1932	438
6	Stan Musial–1	St.L.	NL	1948	429
7	Hack Wilson	Chi.	NL	1930	423
8	Chuck Klein–2	Phi.	NL	1932	420
9	Lou Gehrig–2	N.Y.	AL	1930	419
10	Joe DiMaggio	N.Y.	AL	1937	418
11	Babe Ruth–2	N.Y.	AL	1927	417
12	Babe Herman	Bkn.	NL	1930	416
13	Rogers Hornsby–2	Chi.	NL	1929	410
	Lou Gehrig–3	N.Y.	AL	1931	410
15	Lou Gehrig–4	N.Y.	AL	1934	409
16	Joe Medwick	St.L.	NL	1937	406
17	Chuck Klein–3	Phi.	NL	1929	405
	Hal Trosky	Cle.	AL	1936	405
19	Jimmie Foxx–2	Phi.	AL	1933	403
	Lou Gehrig–5	N.Y.	AL	1936	403
21	Hank Aaron	Mil.	NL	1959	400
22	George Sisler	St.L.	AL	1920	399
	Babe Ruth–3	N.Y.	AL	1923	399
24	Jimmie Foxx–3	Bkn.	AL	1938	398
25	Lefty O'Doul	Phi.	NL	1929	397
	Hank Greenberg–1	Det.	AL	1937	397
27	Al Simmons	Phi.	AL	1925	392
	Al Simmons	Phi.	AL	1930	392
	Bill Terry	N.Y.	NL	1930	392
30	Babe Ruth–4	N.Y.	AL	1924	391
31	Hank Greenberg–2	Det.	AL	1935	389
32	Babe Ruth–5	N.Y.	AL	1920	388
33	Earl Averill	Cle.	AL	1936	385
34	Hank Greenberg–3	Det.	AL	1938	384
	Hank Greenberg–4	Det.	AL	1940	384
36	Stan Musial–2	St.L.	NL	1949	382
	Willie Mays–1	N.Y.	NL	1955	382
	Willie Mays–2	S.F.	NL	1962	382
39	Rogers Hornsby–3	St.L.	NL	1925	381
40	Babe Ruth–6	N.Y.	AL	1928	380
	Frank Robinson	Cin.	NL	1962	380
42	Babe Ruth–7	N.Y.	AL	1930	379
	Ernie Banks	Chi.	NL	1958	379
44	Rogers Hornsby–4	St.L.	NL	1921	378
	Duke Snider	Bkn.	NL	1954	378
46	Willie Mays–3	N.Y.	NL	1954	377
47	Mickey Mantle	N.Y.	AL	1956	376

BATTER'S BASES ON BALLS

1	Babe Ruth–1	N.Y.	AL	1923	170
2	Ted Williams–1	Bos.	AL	1947	162
	Ted Williams–2	Bos.	AL	1949	162
4	Ted Williams–3	Bos.	AL	1946	156
5	Eddie Yost–1	Was.	AL	1956	151
6	Eddie Joost	Phi.	AL	1949	149
7	Babe Ruth–2	N.Y.	AL	1920	148
	Eddie Stanky–1	Bkn.	NL	1945	148
	Jim Wynn	Hou.	NL	1969	148
10	Jimmy Sheckard	Chi.	NL	1911	147
11	Mickey Mantle–1	N.Y.	AL	1955	146
12	Ted Williams–4	Bos.	AL	1941	145
	Ted Williams–5	Bos.	AL	1942	145
	Harmon Killebrew–1	Min.	AL	1969	145
15	Babe Ruth–3	N.Y.	AL	1921	144
	Babe Ruth–4	N.Y.	AL	1926	144
	Eddie Stanky–2	N.Y.	NL	1950	144
	Ted Williams–6	Bos.	AL	1951	144
19	Babe Ruth–5	N.Y.	AL	1924	142
20	Eddie Yost–2	Was.	AL	1950	141
21	Babe Ruth–6	N.Y.	AL	1927	138
22	Eddie Stanky–3	Bkn.	NL	1946	137
	Roy Cullenbine	Det.	AL	1947	137
	Ralph Kiner	Pit.	NL	1951	137
	Willie McCovey	S.F.	NL	1970	137
26	Babe Ruth–7	N.Y.	AL	1930	136
	Ferris Fain–1	Phi.	AL	1949	136
	Ted Williams–7	Bos.	AL	1954	136
29	Babe Ruth–8	N.Y.	AL	1928	135
	Eddie Yost–3	Det.	AL	1959	135
31	Lou Gehrig–1	N.Y.	AL	1935	132
	Ferris Fain–2	Phi.	AL	1950	132
	Frank Howard	Was.	AL	1970	132
	Joe Morgan	Cin.	NL	1975	132
35	Bob Elliott	Bos.	NL	1948	131
	Eddie Yost–4	Was.	AL	1954	131
	Harmon Killebrew–2	Min.	AL	1967	131
	Babe Ruth–9	N.Y.	AL	1932	130
	Lou Gehrig–2	N.Y.	AL	1936	130
40	Eddie Yost–5	Was.	AL	1952	129
	Mickey Mantle–2	N.Y.	AL	1958	129
42	Max Bishop	Phi.	AL	1929	128
	Max Bishop–2	Phi.	AL	1930	128
	Babe Ruth–10	N.Y.	AL	1931	128
	Harmon Killebrew–3	Min.	AL	1970	128
	Carl Yastrzemski	Bos.	AL	1970	128
47	Lou Gehrig–3	N.Y.	AL	1937	127
	Eddie Stanky–4	N.Y.	NL	1951	127
49	Lu Blue	St.L.	AL	1929	126
	Ted Williams–8	Bos.	AL	1948	126
	Eddie Yost–6	Was.	AL	1951	126
	Mickey Mantle–3	N.Y.	AL	1961	126
	Darrell Evans	Atl.	NL	1974	126
54	Richie Ashburn	Phi.	NL	1954	125
	Eddie Yost–7	Det.	AL	1960	125

BATTER'S STRIKEOUTS

1	Bobby Bonds–1	S.F.	NL	1970	189
2	Bobby Bonds–2	S.F.	NL	1969	187
3	Mike Schmidt–1	Phi.	NL	1975	180
4	Dave Nicholson	Chi.	AL	1963	175
5	Reggie Jackson–1	Oak.	AL	1968	171
6	Donn Clendenon–1	Pit.	NL	1968	163
7	Dick Allen–1	Phi.	NL	1968	161
	Reggie Jackson–2	Oak.	AL	1971	161
9	Tommie Agee–1	N.Y.	NL	1970	156
10	Frank Howard	Was.	AL	1967	155
	Jeff Burroughs	Tex.	AL	1975	155
12	Willie Stargell	Pit.	NL	1971	154
13	Dave Kingman–1	N.Y.	NL	1975	153
	George Scott	Bos.	AL	1966	152
	Larry Hisle–1	Phi.	NL	1969	152
16	Don Lock–1	Was.	AL	1963	151
	Greg Luzinski–1	Phi.	NL	1975	151
18	Dick Allen–2	Phi.	NL	1965	150
	Nate Colbert–1	S.D.	NL	1970	150
20	Billy Grabarkewitz	L.A.	NL	1970	149
21	Bobby Bonds–3	S.F.	NL	1973	148
22	Deron Johnson	Phi.	NL	1971	146
	Nate Colbert–2	S.D.	NL	1973	146
24	Bobby Darwin–1	Min.	AL	1972	145
25	Dick Stuart–1	Bos.	AL	1963	144
	Bobby Knoop–1	Cal.	AL	1966	144
	Dick Allen–3	Phi.	NL	1969	144
	Lee May–1	Hou.	NL	1972	144
29	Nelson Mathews	K.C.	AL	1963	143
	Byron Browne	Chi.	NL	1966	143
	Rick Monday	Oak.	AL	1968	143
32	Harmon Killebrew–1	Min.	AL	1962	142
	Donn Clendenon–2	Pit.	NL	1966	142
	Reggie Jackson–3	Oak.	AL	1969	142
	Lee May–2	Cin.	NL	1969	142
	Jim Wynn–1	Hou.	NL	1969	142
	Clarence Gaston	S.D.	NL	1970	142
38	Jake Wood	Det.	AL	1961	141
	Frank Howard–2	Was.	AL	1968	141
40	Dave Kingman–2	S.F.	NL	1972	140
41	Larry Hisle–2	Phi.	NL	1970	139
	Ron LeFlore	Det.	AL	1975	139
43	Jim Lemon	Was.	AL	1956	138
	Dick Allen–4	Phi.	NL	1964	138
	Mike Schmidt–2	Phi.	NL	1974	138
46	Don Lock–2	Was.	AL	1964	137
	Tommie Agee–2	N.Y.	NL	1967	137
	Jim Wynn–2	Hou.	NL	1967	137
	Bobby Bonds–4	S.F.	NL	1971	137
	Bobby Bonds–5	S.F.	NL	1972	137
	Bobby Darwin–2	Min.	AL	1973	137
	Bobby Bonds–6	N.Y.	AL	1975	137
53	Pancho Herrera	Phi.	NL	1960	136
	Donn Clendenon–3	Pit.	NL	1963	136
	Dick Stuart–2	Phi.	NL	1965	136
	Dick Allen–5	Phi.	NL	1966	136
	Bobby Knoop–2	Cal.	AL	1967	136
	Mike Schmidt–3	Phi.	NL	1973	136
59	Harmon Killebrew	Min.	AL	1964	135
	Adolfo Phillips	Phil. & Chi.	NL	1966	135
	Reggie Jackson–4	Oak.	AL	1970	135
	Lee May–3	Cin.	NL	1971	135
	Greg Luzinski–2	Phi.	NL	1973	135

STOLEN BASES

1	Lou Brock–1	St.L.	NL	1974	118
2	Maury Wills–1	L.A.	NL	1962	104
3	Ty Cobb–1	Det.	AL	1915	96
4	Maury Wills–2	L.A.	NL	1965	94
5	Clyde Milan–1	Was.	AL	1912	88
6	Ty Cobb–2	Det.	AL	1911	83
7	Eddie Collins–1	Phi.	AL	1910	81
8	Bob Bescher–1	Cin.	NL	1911	80
9	Dave Lopes–1	L.A.	NL	1975	77
10	Ty Cobb–3	Det.	AL	1909	76
11	Benny Kauff–1	Ind.	FL	1914	75
12	Clyde Milan–2	Was.	AL	1913	74
	Fritz Maisel	N.Y.	AL	1914	74
	Lou Brock–2	St.L.	NL	1966	74
15	Tommy Harper	Sea.	AL	1969	73
16	Bob Bescher–2	Cin.	NL	1910	70
	Lou Brock–3	St.L.	NL	1973	70
	Mickey Rivers	Cal.	AL	1975	70
19	Ty Cobb	Det.	AL	1916	68
20	Frank Chance–1	Chi.	NL	1903	67
	Jimmy Sheckard	Bkn.	NL	1903	67
	Eddie Collins–2	Phi.	AL	1909	67
	Bob Bescher–3	Cin.	NL	1912	67
	Joe Morgan–1	Cin.	NL	1973	67
	Joe Morgan–2	Cin.	NL	1975	67
26	Ty Cobb–5	Det.	AL	1910	65
27	Lou Brock–4	St.L.	NL	1971	64
28	Eddie Collins–3	Phi.	AL	1912	63
	Max Carey–1	Pit.	NL	1916	63
	Sam Rice	Was.	AL	1920	63
	Lou Brock–5	St.L.	NL	1965	63
	Lou Brock–6	St.L.	NL	1972	63
33	Danny Moeller	Was.	AL	1913	62
	George Burns	N.Y.	NL	1914	62
	Lou Brock–7	St.L.	NL	1968	62
	Bert Campaneris–1	Oak.	AL	1968	62
	Bert Campaneris–2	Oak.	AL	1969	62
38	Honus Wagner	Pit.	NL	1901	61
	Josh Devore	N.Y.	NL	1911	61
	Ty Cobb–6	Det.	AL	1912	61
	Max Carey–2	Pit.	NL	1913	61
	Ben Chapman	N.Y.	AL	1931	61
	George Case	Was.	AL	1943	61
	Art Devlin	N.Y.	NL	1905	59
	Billy Maloney	Chi.	NL	1905	59
	Dave Lopes–2	L.A.	NL	1974	59
47	Clyde Milan–3	Was.	AL	1911	58
	Eddie Collins–4	Phi.	AL	1914	58
	Max Carey–3	Pit.	NL	1918	58
	Joe Morgan–3	Cin.	NL	1972	58
	Joe Morgan–4	Cin.	NL	1974	58
52	Honus Wagner	Pit.	NL	1905	57
	Frank Chance–2	Chi.	NL	1906	57
	Red Murray	N.Y.	NL	1910	57
	Hap Myers	Bos.	NL	1913	57
	Luis Aparicio–1	Bal.	AL	1964	57
	Bobby Tolan	Cin.	NL	1970	57
	Cesar Cedeno–1	Hou.	NL	1974	57
59	Wally Moses	Chi.	AL	1943	56
	Luis Aparicio–2	Chi.	AL	1959	56
	Cesar Cedeno–2	Hou.	NL	1973	56
	Lou Brock–8	St.L.	NL	1975	56
63	Sherry Magee	Phi.	NL	1906	55
	Eddie Collins–5	Phi.	AL	1913	55
	Benny Kauff–2	Bkn.	FL	1915	55
	Ty Cobb–7	Det.	AL	1917	55
	Snuffy Stirnweiss	N.Y.	AL	1944	55
	Bert Campaneris–3	Oak.	AL	1967	55
	Cesar Cedeno–3	Hou.	NL	1972	55

SINGLE SEASON LEADERS

WINS

1	Jack Chesbro–1	N.Y.	AL	1904	41
2	Ed Walsh	Chi.	AL	1908	40
3	Christy Mathewson–1	N.Y.	NL	1908	37
4	Walter Johnson–1	Was.	AL	1913	36
5	Joe McGinnity–1	N.Y.	NL	1904	35
6	Smokey Joe Wood	Bos.	AL	1912	34
7	Cy Young–1	Bos.	AL	1901	33
	Christy Mathewson–2	N.Y.	NL	1904	33
	Pete Alexander–1	Phi.	NL	1916	33
10	Cy Young–2	Bos.	AL	1902	32
	Christy Mathewson–3	N.Y.	NL	1905	32
	Walter Johnson–2	Was.	AL	1912	32
13	Joe McGinnity–2	N.Y.	NL	1903	31
	Jack Coombs–1	Phi.	AL	1910	31
	Pete Alexander–2	Phi.	NL	1915	31
	Jim Bagby	Cle.	AL	1920	31
	Lefty Grove–1	Phi.	AL	1931	31
	Denny McLain	Det.	AL	1968	31
19	Christy Mathewson–4	N.Y.	NL	1903	30
	Pete Alexander–3	Phi.	NL	1917	30
	Dizzy Dean–1	St.L.	NL	1934	30
22	Three Finger Brown	Chi.	NL	1908	29
	George Mullin	Det.	AL	1909	29
	Claude Hendrix	Chi.	FL	1914	29
	Eddie Cicotte–1	Chi.	AL	1919	29
	Hal Newhouser	Det.	AL	1944	29
27	Jack Chesbro–2	Pit.	NL	1902	28
	Cy Young–3	Bos.	AL	1903	28
	Pete Alexander–4	Phi.	NL	1911	28
	Jack Coombs–2	Phi.	AL	1911	28
	Walter Johnson–3	Was.	AL	1914	28
	Eddie Cicotte–2	Chi.	AL	1917	28
	Dazzy Vance	Bkn.	NL	1924	28
	Lefty Grove–2	Phi.	AL	1930	28
	Dizzy Dean–2	St.L.	NL	1935	28
	Robin Roberts	Phi.	NL	1952	28

LOSSES

1	Vic Willis–1	Bos.	NL	1905	29
2	Pete Dowling	Mil. & Cle.	AL	1901	27
	Dummy Taylor	N.Y.	NL	1901	27
	Jack Townsend	Was.	AL	1904	27
	George Bell	Bkn.	NL	1910	27
	Paul Derringer	St.L. & Cin.	NL	1933	27
7	Gus Dorner	Bos. & Cin.	NL	1906	26
	Bob Groom	Was.	AL	1909	26
9	Patsy Flaherty	Chi.	AL	1903	25
	Oscar Jones	Bkn.	NL	1904	25
	Vic Willis–2	Bos.	NL	1904	25
	Harry McIntire	Bkn.	NL	1905	25
	Irv Young	Bkn.	NL	1906	25
	Stony McGlynn	St.L.	NL	1907	25
	Bugs Raymond	St.L.	NL	1908	25
	Walter Johnson	Was.	AL	1909	25
	Scott Perry	Phi.	AL	1920	25
	Red Ruffing	Bos.	AL	1928	25
	Ben Cantwell	Bos.	NL	1935	25
20	Chick Fraser	Phi.	NL	1904	24
	George Mullin	Det.	AL	1904	24
	Fred Glade	St.L.	AL	1905	24
	Cliff Curtis	Bos.	NL	1910	24
	Bullet Joe Bush	Phi.	AL	1916	24
	Pat Caraway	Chi.	AL	1931	24
	Sam Gray	St.L.	AL	1931	24
	Roger Craig	N.Y.	NL	1962	24
	Jack Fisher	N.Y.	NL	1965	24
29	Long Tom Hughes	Chi.	AL	1901	23
	Casey Patten	Was.	AL	1903	23
	Jack Cronin	Bkn.	NL	1904	23
	Beany Jacobson	Was.	AL	1904	23
	Orvie Overall	Cin.	NL	1905	23
	Kaiser Wilhelm	Bos.	NL	1905	23
	Vive Lindaman	Bos.	NL	1906	23
	Irv Young–2	Bos.	NL	1907	23
	Cecil Ferguson	Bos.	NL	1909	23
	Buster Brown	Bos.	NL	1910	23
	Red Ames	Cin.	NL	1914	23
	Lee Meadows	St.L.	NL	1916	23
	Elmer Myers	Phi.	AL	1916	23
	Rollie Naylor	Phi.	AL	1920	23
	Eddie Rommel	Phi.	AL	1921	23
	Dolf Luque	Cin.	NL	1922	23

WINNING PERCENTAGE
(Minimum 15 Wins)

1	Roy Face	Pit.	NL	1959	.947
2	Johnny Allen–1	Cle.	AL	1937	.938
3	Freddie Fitzsimmons	Bkn.	NL	1940	.889
4	Lefty Grove–1	Phi.	AL	1931	.886
5	Preacher Roe	Bkn.	NL	1951	.880
6	Smokey Joe Wood	Bos.	AL	1912	.872
7	Wild Bill Donovan	Det.	AL	1907	.862
	Whitey Ford	N.Y.	AL	1961	.862
9	Chief Bender–1	Phi.	AL	1914	.850
10	Lefty Grove–2	Phi.	AL	1930	.848
11	Tom Hughes	Bos.	NL	1916	.842
	Emil Yde	Pit.	NL	1924	.842
	Schoolboy Rowe	Det.	AL	1940	.842
	Sandy Consuegra	Chi.	AL	1954	.842
	Ralph Terry	N.Y.	AL	1961	.842
	Ron Perranoski	L.A.	NL	1963	.842
17	Lefty Gomez	N.Y.	AL	1934	.839
18	Denny McLain	Det.	AL	1968	.838
19	Walter Johnson	Was.	AL	1913	.837
20	King Cole	Chi.	NL	1910	.833
	Spud Chandler	N.Y.	AL	1943	.833
	Hoyt Wilhelm	N.Y.	NL	1952	.833
	Sandy Koufax	L.A.	NL	1963	.833
24	Ed Reulbach–1	Chi.	NL	1906	.826
	Elmer Riddle	Cin.	NL	1941	.826
26	Jack Chesbro	Pit.	NL	1902	.824
	Dazzy Vance	Bkn.	NL	1924	.824
28	Chief Bender–2	Phi.	AL	1910	.821
	Bob Purkey	Cin.	NL	1962	.821
30	Sal Maglie	N.Y.	NL	1950	.818
31	Joe McGinnity	N.Y.	NL	1904	.814
32	Three Finger Brown	Chi.	NL	1906	.813
	Russ Ford	N.Y.	AL	1910	.813
	Eddie Plank	Phi.	AL	1912	.813
	Carl Hubbell	N.Y.	NL	1936	.813
36	Dizzy Dean	St.L.	NL	1934	.811
37	Ed Reulbach–2	Chi.	NL	1907	.810
	Doc Crandall	N.Y.	NL	1910	.810
	Johnny Allen–2	N.Y.	AL	1932	.810
	Ted Wilks	St.L.	NL	1944	.810
41	General Crowder	St.L.	AL	1928	.808
	Bobo Newsom	Det.	AL	1940	.808
	Ernie Bonham	N.Y.	AL	1942	.808
	Larry Jansen	N.Y.	NL	1947	.808
	Dave McNally	Bal.	AL	1971	.808
	Catfish Hunter	Oak.	AL	1973	.808
47	Howie Camnitz	Pit.	NL	1909	.806
	Christy Mathewson–1	N.Y.	NL	1909	.806
	Eddie Cicotte	Chi.	AL	1919	.806
	Boo Ferriss	Bos.	AL	1946	.806
	Juan Marichal	S.F.	NL	1966	.806
52	Ed Doheny	Pit.	NL	1902	.800
	Christy Mathewson–2	N.Y.	NL	1905	.800
	Bert Humphries	Chi.	NL	1913	.800
	Stan Coveleski	Was.	AL	1925	.800
	Firpo Marberry	Was.	AL	1931	.800
	Robin Roberts	Phi.	NL	1952	.800
	Ed Lopat	N.Y.	AL	1953	.800
	Don Newcombe	Bkn.	NL	1955	.800
	Jim Palmer	Bal.	AL	1969	.800

STRIKEOUTS

1	Nolan Ryan–1	Cal.	AL	1973	383
2	Sandy Koufax–1	L.A.	NL	1965	382
3	Nolan Ryan–2	Cal.	AL	1974	367
4	Rube Waddell–1	Phi.	AL	1904	349
5	Bob Feller–1	Cle.	AL	1946	348
6	Nolan Ryan–3	Cal.	AL	1972	329
7	Sam McDowell–1	Cle.	AL	1965	325
8	Sandy Koufax–2	L.A.	NL	1966	317
9	Walter Johnson–1	Was.	AL	1910	313
10	Steve Carlton	Phi.	NL	1972	310
11	Mickey Lolich–1	Det.	AL	1971	308
12	Sandy Koufax–3	L.A.	NL	1963	306
13	Sam McDowell–2	Cle.	AL	1970	304
14	Walter Johnson–2	Was.	AL	1912	303
15	Rube Waddell–2	Phi.	AL	1903	302
16	Vida Blue	Oak.	AL	1971	301
17	Tom Seaver–1	N.Y.	NL	1971	289
18	Rube Waddell–3	Phi.	AL	1905	287
19	Sam McDowell–3	Cle.	AL	1968	283
	Tom Seaver–2	N.Y.	NL	1970	283
21	Denny McLain	Det.	AL	1968	280
22	Sam McDowell–4	Cle.	AL	1969	279
23	Bob Veale–1	Pit.	NL	1965	276
24	Hal Newhouser	Det.	AL	1946	275
25	Bob Gibson–1	St.L.	NL	1970	274
	Ferguson Jenkins–1	Chi.	NL	1970	274
27	Ferguson Jenkins–2	Chi.	NL	1969	273
28	Mickey Lolich–2	Det.	AL	1969	271
29	Bob Gibson–2	St.L.	NL	1965	270
30	Ed Walsh–1	Chi.	AL	1908	269
	Sandy Koufax–4	L.A.	NL	1961	269
	Bob Gibson–3	St.L.	NL	1969	269
	Frank Tanana	Cal.	AL	1975	269
34	Jim Bunning–1	Phi.	NL	1965	268
	Bob Gibson–4	St.L.	NL	1968	268
36	Christy Mathewson–1	N.Y.	NL	1903	267
37	Jim Maloney	Cin.	NL	1963	265
38	Luis Tiant	Cle.	AL	1968	264
39	Herb Score	Cle.	AL	1956	263
	Ferguson Jenkins–3	Chi.	NL	1971	263
41	Dazzy Vance	Bkn.	NL	1924	262
42	Bob Feller–2	Cle.	AL	1940	261
43	Bob Feller–3	Cle.	AL	1941	260
	Ferguson Jenkins–4	Chi.	NL	1968	260
45	Christy Mathewson–2	N.Y.	NL	1908	259
46	Ed Walsh–2	Chi.	AL	1910	258
	Smokey Joe Wood	Bos.	AL	1912	258
	Bert Blyleven	Min.	AL	1973	258
49	Ed Walsh–3	Chi.	AL	1911	255
50	Ed Walsh–4	Chi.	AL	1912	254
51	Jim Bunning–2	Phi.	NL	1967	253
52	Jim Bunning–3	Phi.	NL	1966	252
53	Don Drysdale	L.A.	NL	1963	251
	Bill Stoneman	Mon.	NL	1971	251
	Tom Seaver–3	N.Y.	NL	1973	251
56	Bob Veale–2	Pit.	NL	1964	250
	Mickey Lolich–3	Det.	AL	1972	250

BASES ON BALLS

1	Bob Feller–1	Cle.	AL	1938	208
2	Nolan Ryan–1	Cal.	AL	1974	202
3	Bob Feller–2	Cle.	AL	1941	194
4	Bobo Newsom–1	St.L.	AL	1938	192
5	Sam Jones	Chi.	NL	1955	185
6	Bob Harmon	St.L.	NL	1911	181
	Bob Turley–1	Bal.	AL	1954	181
8	Tommy Byrne–1	N.Y.	AL	1949	179
9	Bob Turley–2	N.Y.	AL	1955	177
10	Bump Hadley	Chi. & St.L.	AL	1932	171
11	Elmer Myers	Phi.	AL	1916	168
12	Bobo Newsom–2	Was. & Bos.	AL	1937	167
13	Weldon Wyckoff	Phi.	AL	1915	165
14	Earl Moore	Phi.	NL	1911	164
15	Johnny Vander Meer	Cin.	NL	1943	162
	Nolan Ryan–2	Cal.	AL	1973	162
17	Tommy Byrne–2	N.Y.	AL	1950	160
18	Marty O'Toole	Pit.	NL	1912	159
19	Joe Coleman	Det.	AL	1974	158
20	Grover Lowdermilk	St.L. & Det.	AL	1915	157
	Nolan Ryan–3	Cal.	AL	1972	157
22	Herb Score	Cle.	AL	1955	154
23	Bob Feller–3	Cle.	AL	1946	153
	Sam McDowell	Cle.	AL	1971	153
25	Wild Bill Donovan	Bkn.	NL	1901	152
26	Tommy Byrne–3	N.Y. &St.L.	AL	1951	150

EARNED RUN AVERAGE
(Minimum to 1950 10 Complete Games; after 1950 1 inning pitched per scheduled game)

1	Dutch Leonard	Bos.	AL	1914	1.01
2	T.F. Brown–1	Chi.	NL	1906	1.04
3	Walter Johnson–1	Was.	AL	1913	1.05
4	Bob Gibson	St.L.	NL	1968	1.12
5	Christy Mathewson–1	N.Y.	NL	1909	1.14
6	Jack Pfeister–1	Chi.	NL	1907	1.15
7	Addie Joss–1	Cle.	AL	1908	1.16
8	Carl Lundgren	Chi.	NL	1907	1.17
9	Pete Alexander–1	Phi.	NL	1915	1.22
10	Cy Young–1	Bos.	AL	1908	1.26
11	Christy Mathewson–2	N.Y.	NL	1905	1.27
	Ed Walsh–1	Chi.	AL	1910	1.27
	Walter Johnson–2	Was.	AL	1918	1.27
14	Jack Coombs	Phi.	AL	1910	1.30
15	T.F. Brown–2	Chi.	NL	1909	1.31
16	Jack Taylor	Chi.	NL	1902	1.33
17	Walter Johnson–3	Was.	AL	1910	1.35
18	T.F. Brown–3	Chi.	NL	1907	1.39
	Harry Krause	Phi.	AL	1909	1.39
	Walter Johnson–4	Was.	AL	1910	1.39
	Walter Johnson–5	Was.	AL	1912	1.39
22	Ed Walsh–2	Chi.	AL	1909	1.41
23	Ed Reulbach–1	Chi.	NL	1905	1.42
	Orvie Overall	Chi.	NL	1908	1.42
	Ed Walsh–3	Chi.	AL	1909	1.42
26	Christy Mathewson–3	N.Y.	NL	1908	1.43
27	T.F. Brown–4	Chi.	NL	1908	1.47
28	Rube Waddell–1	Phi.	AL	1905	1.48
29	Smokey Joe Wood	Bos.	AL	1915	1.49
	Walter Johnson–6	Was.	AL	1919	1.49
31	Doc White	Chi.	AL	1905	1.52
	George McQuillan–1	Phi.	NL	1908	1.52
33	Eddie Cicotte	Chi.	AL	1917	1.53
34	Pete Alexander–2	Phi.	NL	1916	1.55
	Cy Morgan	Phi.	AL	1910	1.55
	Walter Johnson–7	Was.	AL	1916	1.55
37	Jack Pfeister–2	Chi.	NL	1906	1.56
	Howie Camnitz–1	Pit.	NL	1908	1.56
39	Fred Toney	Cin.	NL	1915	1.57
40	Chief Bender	Phi.	AL	1910	1.58
	Rube Marquard	Bkn.	NL	1916	1.58
42	Addie Joss–2	Cle.	AL	1904	1.59
	Barney Pelty	St.L.	AL	1906	1.59
44	Ed Walsh–4	Chi.	AL	1907	1.60
	George McQuillan–2	Phi.	NL	1910	1.60
	Luis Tiant	Cle.	AL	1968	1.60
47	Joe McGinnity	N.Y.	NL	1904	1.61
48	Rube Waddell–2	Phi.	AL	1904	1.62
	Howie Camnitz–2	Pit.	NL	1909	1.62
	Ray Collins	Bos.	AL	1910	1.62
51	Cy Young–2	Bos.	AL	1901	1.63
52	Ed Summers	Det.	AL	1908	1.64
	Ernie Shore	Bos.	AL	1915	1.64
	Spud Chandler	N.Y.	AL	1943	1.64
55	Ed Reulbach–2	Chi.	NL	1906	1.65
	Walter Johnson–8	Was.	AL	1908	1.65
	Rube Kroh	Chi.	NL	1909	1.65
	Russ Ford	N.Y.	AL	1910	1.65
	Rube Foster	Bos.	AL	1914	1.65

SINGLE SEASON LEADERS

GAMES PITCHED

1	Mike Marshall-1	L.A.	NL	1974	106
2	Mike Marshall-2	Mon.	NL	1973	92
3	Wayne Granger-1	Cin.	NL	1969	90
4	Wilbur Wood-1	Chi	AL	1968	88
5	Ted Abernathy-1	Chi.	NL	1965	84
6	Ken Sanders	Mil.	AL	1971	83
7	Eddie Fisher	Chi.	AL	1965	82
8	Jack Wyatt	K.C.	AL	1964	81
9	Mudcat Grant	Oak. & Pit.	AL-NL	1970	80
	Pedro Borbon-1	Cin.	NL	1973	80
11	Dick Radatz	Bos.	AL	1964	79
12	Hal Woodeshick	Hou. & St.L.	NL	1965	78
	Ted Abernathy-2	Cin.	NL	1968	78
14	Bob Locker-1	Chi.	AL	1967	77
	Wilbur Wood-2	Chi.	AL	1970	77
16	Wilbur Wood-3	Chi.	AL	1969	76
	Ron Herbel	S.D. & N.Y.	NL	1970	76
	Rollie Fingers-1	Oak.	AL	1974	76
	Larry Hardy	S.D.	NL	1974	76
20	Ron Perranoski-1	Min.	AL	1969	75
	Rollie Fingers-2	Oak.	AL	1975	75
22	Jim Konstanty	Phi.	NL	1950	74
	Bob Miller	L.A.	NL	1964	74
	Ron Kline	Was.	AL	1965	74
	Dan McGinn	Mon.	NL	1969	74
26	Hoyt Wilhelm-1	Chi.	AL	1964	73
	Clay Carroll-1	Atl.	NL	1966	73
	Phil Regan-1	L.A. & Chi.	NL	1968	73
	Jim Bouton	Sea. & Hou.	AL-NL	1969	73
	Dick Selma	Phi.	NL	1970	73
	Pedro Borbon-2	Cin.	NL	1974	73
32	Ron Perranoski-2	L.A.	NL	1964	72
	Minnie Rojas	Cal.	AL	1967	72
	Hoyt Wilhelm-2	Chi.	AL	1968	72
35	Hoyt Wilhelm-3	N.Y.	NL	1952	71
	Stu Miller	Bal.	AL	1963	71
	Jack Baldschun	Phi.	NL	1964	71
	Lindy McDaniel	Chi.	NL	1965	71
	Pete Mikkelsen	Pit.	NL	1966	71
	Clay Carroll-2	Cin.	NL	1969	71
	Sparky Lyle	Bos.	AL	1969	71
	Phil Regan-2	Chi.	NL	1969	71
	Darold Knowles	Was.	AL	1970	71
	Elias Sosa	S.F.	NL	1973	71
	Gene Garber	Phi.	NL	1975	71
46	Ace Adams	N.Y.	NL	1943	70
	Mike Fornieles	Bos.	AL	1960	70
	Ron Perranoski-3	L.A.	NL	1962	70
	Don McMahon	Cle.	AL	1964	70
	Ted Abernathy-3	Cin.	NL	1967	70
	Ron Perranoski-4	L.A.	NL	1967	70
	Bob Locker-2	Chi.	AL	1968	70
	Wayne Granger-2	Cin.	NL	1971	70
	Tom Murphy	Mil.	AL	1974	70
	Ken Forsch	Hou.	NL	1974	70

GAMES STARTED

1	Jack Chesbro	N.Y.	AL	1904	51
2	Ed Walsh-1	Chi.	AL	1908	49
	Wilbur Wood-1	Chi.	AL	1972	49
4	Joe McGinnity	N.Y.	NL	1903	48
	Wilbur Wood-2	Chi.	AL	1973	48
6	Vic Willis	Bos.	NL	1902	46
	Rube Waddell	Phi.	AL	1904	46
	Christy Mathewson	N.Y.	NL	1904	46
	Ed Walsh-2	Chi.	AL	1907	46
	Dave Davenport	St.L.	FL	1915	46
11	Jack Powell	N.Y.	AL	1904	45
	Pete Alexander	Phi.	NL	1916	45
	Mickey Lolich	Det.	AL	1971	45

COMPLETE GAMES

1	Jack Chesbro	N.Y.	AL	1904	48
2	Vic Willis	Bos.	NL	1902	45
3	Joe McGinnity	N.Y.	NL	1903	44
4	George Mullin	Det.	AL	1904	42
	Ed Walsh	Chi.	AL	1908	42
6	Noodles Hahn	Cin.	NL	1901	41
	Cy Young-1	Bos.	AL	1902	41
	Irv Young	Bos.	NL	1905	41
9	Cy Young-2	Bos.	AL	1904	40

INNINGS PITCHED

1	Ed Walsh-1	Chi.	AL	1908	464
2	Jack Chesbro	N.Y.	AL	1904	455
3	Joe McGinnity-1	N.Y.	NL	1903	434
4	Ed Walsh-2	Chi.	AL	1907	422
5	Vic Willis	Bos.	NL	1902	410
6	Joe McGinnity-2	N.Y.	NL	1904	408
7	Ed Walsh-3	Chi.	AL	1912	393
	Dave Davenport	St.L.	FL	1915	393
9	Christy Mathewson-1	N.Y.	NL	1908	391
10	Jack Powell	N.Y.	AL	1904	390
11	Togie Pittinger	Bos.	NL	1902	389
	Pete Alexander-1	Phi.	NL	1916	389
13	Pete Alexander-2	Phi.	NL	1917	388
14	Cy Young-1	Bos.	AL	1902	385
15	Rube Waddell	Phi.	AL	1904	383
16	Joe McGinnity-3	Bal.	AL	1901	382
	George Mullin	Det.	AL	1904	382
18	Cy Young-2	Bos.	AL	1904	380
19	Irv Young	Bos.	NL	1905	378
20	Oscar Jones	Bkn.	NL	1904	377
	Cy Falkenberg	Ind.	FL	1914	377
	Wilbur Wood	Chi.	AL	1972	377
23	Pete Alexander-3	Phi.	NL	1915	376
	Mickey Lolich	Det.	AL	1971	376
25	Noodles Hahn	Cin.	NL	1901	375
26	Walter Johnson-1	Was.	AL	1910	374
27	Walter Johnson-2	Was.	AL	1914	372
28	Cy Young-3	Bos.	AL	1901	371
	Bill Dinneen	Bos.	AL	1902	371
	Walter Johnson-3	Was.	AL	1916	371
	Bob Feller	Cle.	AL	1946	371
32	Ed Walsh-4	Chi.	AL	1910	370
33	Ed Walsh-5	Chi.	AL	1911	369
34	Christy Mathewson-2	N.Y.	NL	1904	368
	Walter Johnson-4	Was.	AL	1912	368
36	Pete Alexander-4	Phi.	NL	1911	367
37	Christy Mathewson-3	N.Y.	NL	1903	366
38	Frank Smith	Chi.	AL	1909	365
39	Pete Alexander-5	Chi.	NL	1920	363
40	Claude Hendrix	Chi.	FL	1914	362
41	George McQuillan	Phi.	NL	1908	360

FEWEST HITS ALLOWED PER 9 INNINGS PITCHED

(Minimum - 1 inning pitched per scheduled game)

1	Nolan Ryan-1	Cal.	AL	1972	5.26
2	Luis Tiant	Cle.	AL	1968	5.30
3	Ed Reulbach	Chi.	NL	1906	5.33
4	Carl Lundgren	Chi.	NL	1907	5.65
5	Dutch Leonard	Bos.	AL	1914	5.69
6	Tommy Byrne	N.Y.	AL	1949	5.74
7	Dave McNally	Bal.	AL	1968	5.77
8	Sandy Koufax-1	L.A.	NL	[illegible]	[illegible]
9	Russ Ford	N.Y.	AL	1910	5.82
10	Al Downing	N.Y.	AL	1963	5.83
11	Bob Gibson	St.L.	NL	1968	5.84
12	Herb Score	Cle.	AL	1956	5.86
13	Sam McDowell-1	Cle.	AL	1965	5.87
14	Ed Walsh	Chi.	AL	1910	5.89
15	Nolan Ryan-2	Cal.	AL	1974	5.97
16	Walter Johnson	Was.	AL	1913	5.98
17	Vida Blue	Oak.	AL	1971	6.03
18	San McDowell-2	Cle.	AL	1966	6.03
19	Sam McDowell-3	Cle.	AL	1968	6.06
20	Pete Alexander	Phi.	NL	1915	6.06
21	Joe Horlen	Chi.	AL	1964	6.06
22	Andy Messersmith	Cal.	AL	1969	6.08
23	Stan Coveleski	Cle.	AL	1917	6.10
24	Catfish Hunter	Oak.	AL	1972	6.10
25	Bob Turley-1	N.Y.	AL	1955	6.12
26	Don Sutton	L.A.	NL	1972	6.13
27	Bob Turley-2	N.Y.	AL	1957	6.14
28	Three Finger Brown	Chi.	NL	1908	6.17
29	Sandy Koufax-2	L.A.	NL	1963	6.19
30	Sandy Koufax-3	L.A.	NL	1964	6.22

MOST STRIKEOUTS PER 9 INNINGS PITCHED

(Minimum - 1 inning pitched per scheduled game)

1	Sam McDowell-1	Cle.	AL	1965	10.71
2	Nolan Ryan-1	Cal.	AL	1973	10.57
3	Sandy Koufax-1	L.A.	NL	1962	10.57
4	Sam McDowell-2	Cle.	AL	1966	10.44
5	Nolan Ryan-2	Cal.	AL	1972	10.43
6	Sandy Koufax-2	L.A.	NL	1965	10.23
7	Sandy Koufax-3	L.A.	NL	1960	10.13
8	Nolan Ryan-3	Cal.	AL	1974	9.92
9	Herb Score-1	Cle.	AL	1955	9.71
10	Jim Maloney	Cin.	NL	1963	9.54
11	Herb Score-2	Cle.	AL	1956	9.51
12	Sam McDowell-3	Cle.	AL	1968	9.47
13	Sandy Koufax-4	L.A.	NL	1961	9.46
14	Frank Tanana	Cal.	AL	1975	9.42
15	Don Wilson	Hou.	NL	1969	9.40
16	Bob Veale	Pit.	NL	1965	9.34
17	Dave Boswell	Min.	AL	1966	9.21
18	Luis Tiant-1	Cle.	AL	1967	9.21
19	Luis Tiant-2	Cle.	AL	1958	9.21
20	Sam McDowell-4	Cle.	AL	1964	9.21
21	Sonny Siebert	Cle.	AL	1965	9.10
22	Tom Seaver	N.Y.	NL	1971	9.09
23	Sandy Koufax-5	L.A.	NL	1964	9.00

SAVES

1	John Hiller	Det.	AL	1973	38
2	Clay Carroll	Cin.	NL	1972	37
3	Wayne Granger-1	Cin.	NL	1970	35
	Sparky Lyle-1	N.Y.	AL	1972	35
5	Ron Perranoski-1	Min.	AL	1970	34
6	Jack Aker	K.C.	AL	1966	32
7	Ted Abernathy-1	Chi.	NL	1965	31
	Ron Perranoski-2	Min.	AL	1969	31
	Ken Sanders	Mil.	AL	1971	31
	Mike Marshall	Mon.	NL	1973	31
11	Dave Giusti-1	Pit.	NL	1971	30
12	Luis Arroyo	N.Y.	AL	1961	29
	Dick Radatz-1	Bos.	AL	1964	29
	Ron Kline	Was.	AL	1965	29
	Fred Gladding	Hou.	NL	1969	29
	Lindy McDaniel-1	N.Y.	AL	1970	29
	Terry Forster	Chi.	AL	1972	29
18	Roy Face	Pit.	NL	1962	28
	Ted Abernathy-2	Cin.	NL	1967	28
20	Joe Page	N.Y.	AL	1949	27
	Ellis Kinder	Bos.	AL	1953	27
	Stu Miller	Bal.	AL	1963	27
	Hoyt Wilhelm	Chi.	AL	1964	27
	Minnie Rojas	Cal.	AL	1967	27
	Wayne Granger-2	Cin.	NL	1969	27
	Cecil Upshaw	Atl.	NL	1969	27
	Darold Knowles	Was.	AL	1970	27
	Tom Timmerman	Det.	AL	1970	27
	Tug McGraw-1	N.Y.	NL	1972	27
	Sparky Lyle-2	N.Y.	AL	1973	27
31	Lindy McDaniel-2	St.L.	NL	1960	26
	Dave Giusti-2	Pit.	NL	1970	26
	Gene Gossage	Chi.	AL	1975	26
34	Dick Radatz-2	Bos.	AL	1963	25
	Phil Regan	L.A. & Chi.	NL	1968	25
	Tug McGraw-2	N.Y.	NL	1973	25

SHUTOUTS

1	Pete Alexander-1	Phi.	NL	1916	16
2	Jack Coombs	Phi.	AL	1910	13
	Bob Gibson	St.L.	NL	1968	13
4	Ed Walsh-1	Chi.	AL	1908	12
	Walter Johnson-1	Was.	AL	1913	12
	Pete Alexander-2	Phi.	NL	1915	12
7	Christy Mathewson	N.Y.	NL	1908	11
	Sandy Koufax	L.A.	NL	1963	11
	Dean Chance	L.A.	AL	1964	11
10	Cy Young	Bos.	AL	1904	10
	Ed Walsh-2	Chi.	AL	1906	10
	Smokey Joe Wood	Bos.	AL	1912	10
	Walter Johnson-2	Was.	AL	1914	10
	Dave Davenport	St.L.	FL	1915	10
	Carl Hubbell	N.Y.	NL	1933	10
	Mort Cooper	St.L.	NL	1942	10
	Bob Feller	Cle	AL	1946	10
	Bob Lemon	Cle.	AL	1948	10
	Juan Marichal	S.F.	NL	1965	10
	Jim Palmer	Bal.	AL	1975	10

LIFETIME LEADERS — BATTING

Players with Lifetime BATTING AVERAGE of .300 or higher
(Minimum of 10 major league seasons and 4000 At Bats)

		First	Last	AB	Hits	B.A.
1	Ty Cobb	1905	1928	11437	4192	.367
2	Rogers Hornsby	1915	1937	8173	2930	.358
3	Joe Jackson	1908	1920	4981	1774	.356
4	Pete Browning	1882	1894	4795	1664	.347
5	Ed Delahanty	1888	1903	7493	2593	.346
6	Willie Keeler	1892	1910	8570	2955	.345
7	Billy Hamilton	1888	1901	6262	2157	.344
8	Ted Williams	1939	1960	7706	2654	.344
9	Tris Speaker	1907	1928	10208	3515	.344
10	Dan Brouthers	1879	1904	6682	2288	.342
11	Jesse Burkett	1890	1905	8389	2872	.342
12	Babe Ruth	1914	1935	8399	2873	.342
13	Harry Heilmann	1914	1932	7787	2660	.342
14	Bill Terry	1923	1936	6428	2193	.341
15	George Sisler	1915	1930	8267	2812	.340
16	Lou Gehrig	1923	1939	8001	2721	.340
17	Nap Lajoie	1896	1916	9589	3251	.339
18	Riggs Stephenson	1921	1934	4508	1515	.336
19	Al Simmons	1924	1944	8761	2927	.334
20	Cap Anson	1876	1897	9067	3022	.333
21	Paul Waner	1926	1945	9459	3152	.333
22	Eddie Collins	1906	1930	9949	3311	.333
23	Sam Thompson	1885	1906	5972	1984	.332
24	Stan Musial	1941	1963	10972	3630	.331
25	Heinie Manush	1923	1939	7653	2524	.330
26	Hugh Duffy	1888	1906	7026	2313	.329
27	Honus Wagner	1897	1917	10427	3430	.329
28	Tip O'Neill	1883	1892	4254	1389	.327
29	Jimmie Foxx	1925	1945	8134	2646	.325
30	Earle Combs	1924	1935	5748	1866	.325
31	Joe DiMaggio	1936	1951	6821	2214	.325
32	Babe Herman	1926	1945	5603	1818	.324
33	Joe Medwick	1932	1948	7635	2471	.324
34	Denny Lyons	1897	1897	4236	1368	.323
35	Edd Roush	1913	1931	7361	2377	.323
36	Sam Rice	1915	1934	9269	2987	.322
37	Ross Youngs	1917	1926	4627	1491	.322
38	Joe Kelley	1891	1908	6989	2245	.321
39	Kiki Cuyler	1921	1938	7161	2299	.321
40	Charlie Gehringer	1924	1942	8860	2839	.320
41	Chuck Klein	1928	1944	6486	2076	.320
42	Pie Traynor	1920	1937	7559	2416	.320
43	Mickey Cochrane	1925	1937	5169	1652	.320
44	George Van Haltren	1887	1903	8007	2528	.319
45	Ken Williams	1915	1929	4860	1552	.319

		First	Last	AB	Hits	B.A.
46	Roger Connor	1880	1897	7732	2460	.318
47	Earl Averill	1929	1941	6359	2020	.318
48	Arky Vaughan	1932	1948	6622	2103	.318
49	Roberto Clemente	1955	1972	9454	3000	.317
50	Chick Hafey	1924	1937	4625	1466	.317
51	Zack Wheat	1909	1927	9106	2884	.317
52	Lloyd Waner	1927	1945	7772	2459	.316
53	Frankie Frisch	1919	1937	9112	2880	.316
54	Goose Goslin	1921	1938	8654	2735	.316
55	Elmer Flick	1898	1910	5597	1765	.315
56	Fred Clarke	1894	1915	8584	2703	.315
57	Bibb Falk	1920	1931	4656	1463	.314
58	Cecil Travis	1933	1947	4914	1544	.314
59	Mike Tiernan	1887	1899	5878	1843	.314
60	Hank Greenberg	1930	1947	5193	1628	.313
61	Hughie Jennings	1891	1918	4884	1530	.313
62	Jack Fournier	1912	1927	5207	1631	.313
63	Elmer Smith	1886	1901	4675	1462	.313
64	Bill Dickey	1928	1946	6300	1969	.313
65	Cupid Childs	1888	1901	5624	1757	.312
66	Jim O'Rourke	1876	1904	7368	2300	.312
67	Johnny Mize	1936	1953	6443	2011	.312
68	Joe Sewell	1920	1933	7132	2226	.312
69	Barney McCosky	1939	1953	4172	1301	.312
70	Bing Miller	1921	1936	6212	1937	.312
71	Fred Lindstrom	1924	1936	5611	1747	.311
72	Jackie Robinson	1947	1956	4877	1518	.311
73	Baby Doll Jacobson	1915	1927	5507	1714	.311
74	Rip Radcliff	1934	1943	4074	1267	.311
75	Ginger Beaumont	1899	1910	5647	1754	.311
76	Irish Meusel	1914	1927	4900	1521	.310
77	Luke Appling	1930	1950	8857	2749	.310
78	Bobby Veach	1912	1925	6659	2064	.310
79	**Pete Rose**	**1963**		**8221**	**2547**	**.310**
80	John Stone	1928	1938	4490	1391	.310
81	Jim Bottomley	1922	1937	7471	2313	.310
82	Sam Crawford	1889	1917	9579	2964	.309
83	Bob Meusel	1920	1930	5475	1693	.309
84	Jake Beckley	1888	1907	9476	2930	.309
85	Jimmy Ryan	1885	1903	8165	2524	.309
86	Ted Larkin	1884	1893	4691	1450	.309
87	Jack Tobin	1914	1927	6173	1908	.309
88	Spud Davis	1928	1945	4255	1312	.308
89	Richie Ashburn	1948	1962	8365	2574	.308
90	Steve Brodie	1890	1902	5686	1749	.308

		First	Last	AB	Hits	B.A.
91	Stuffy McInnis	1909	1927	7872	2406	.308
92	Joe Vosmik	1930	1944	5472	1682	.307
93	Harry Stovey	1880	1893	6072	1866	.307
94	King Kelly	1878	1893	5901	1813	.307
95	Frank Baker	1908	1922	5985	1838	.307
96	Buck Ewing	1880	1897	5318	1633	.307
97	George Burns	1914	1929	6573	2018	.307
98	Matty Alou	1960	1974	5789	1777	.307
99	Hack Wilson	1923	1934	4760	1461	.307
100	**Hank Aaron**	**1954**		**12093**	**3709**	**.307**
101	Johnny Pesky	1942	1954	4745	1455	.307
102	Chick Stahl	1897	1906	5062	1552	.307
103	George Kell	1943	1957	6702	2054	.306
104	Dixie Walker	1931	1949	6740	2064	.306
105	**Tony Oliva**	**1962**		**6178**	**1891**	**.306**
106	Ernie Lombardi	1931	1947	5855	1792	.306
107	Billy Herman	1931	1947	7707	2345	.304
108	Patsy Donovan	1890	1907	7450	2266	.304
109	Mel Ott	1926	1947	9456	2876	.304
110	Cy Seymour	1896	1913	5657	1720	.304
111	Ed McKean	1887	1899	6842	2079	.304
112	Curt Walker	1919	1930	4858	1475	.304
113	Deacon White	1876	1890	5294	1607	.304
114	Charlie Jamieson	1915	1932	6560	1990	.303
115	Jake Daubert	1910	1924	7673	2326	.303
116	Buddy Myer	1925	1941	7038	2131	.303
117	Harvey Kuenn	1952	1966	6913	2092	.303
118	George Gore	1879	1892	5324	1611	.303
119	Hal Trosky	1933	1946	5161	1561	.302
120	George Grantham	1922	1934	4989	1508	.302
121	Ben Chapman	1930	1946	6478	1958	.302
122	Carl Reynolds	1927	1939	4495	1357	.302
123	Tommy Holmes	1942	1952	4992	1507	.302
124	Willie Mays	1951	1973	10881	3283	.302
125	Jack Doyle	1889	1905	6013	1814	.302
126	Joe Cronin	1926	1945	7577	2285	.302
127	Stan Hack	1932	1947	7278	2193	.301
128	Oyster Burns	1884	1895	4615	1388	.301
129	Mike Griffin	1887	1898	5908	1775	.300
130	Paul Hines	1876	1891	6207	1864	.300
131	Wally Berger	1930	1940	5163	1550	.300
132	Ethan Allen	1926	1938	4418	1325	.300
133	Enos Slaughter	1938	1959	7946	2383	.300
134	Hardy Richardson	1879	1892	5593	1676	.300
135	Billy Goodman	1947	1962	5644	1691	.300

Players with 2000 or more HITS

		First	Last	Hits
1	Ty Cobb	1905	1928	4192
2	**Hank Aaron**	**1954**		**3709**
3	Stan Musial	1941	1963	3630
4	Tris Speaker	1907	1928	3515
5	Honus Wagner	1897	1917	3430
6	Eddie Collins	1906	1930	3311
7	Willie Mays	1951	1973	3283
8	Nap Lajoie	1896	1916	3251
9	Paul Waner	1926	1945	3152
10	Cap Anson	1876	1897	3022
11	Al Kaline	1953	1974	3007
12	Roberto Clemente	1955	1972	3000
13	Sam Rice	1915	1934	2987
14	Sam Crawford	1899	1917	2964
15	Willie Keeler	1892	1910	2955
16	Jake Beckley	1888	1907	2930
	Rogers Hornsby	1915	1937	2930
18	**Frank Robinson**	**1956**		**2928**
19	Al Simmons	1924	1944	2927
20	Zack Wheat	1909	1927	2884
21	Frankie Frisch	1919	1937	2880
22	Mel Ott	1926	1947	2876
23	Babe Ruth	1914	1935	2873
24	Jesse Burkett	1890	1905	2872
25	Charlie Gehringer	1924	1942	2839
26	George Sisler	1915	1930	2812
27	**Brooks Robinson**	**1955**		**2795**
28	**Vada Pinson**	**1958**		**2757**
29	Luke Appling	1930	1950	2749
30	Goose Goslin	1921	1938	2735
31	Lou Gehrig	1923	1939	2721
32	Doc Cramer	1929	1948	2705
33	Fred Clarke	1894	1915	2703
34	George Davis	1890	1909	2683

		First	Last	Hits
35	Luis Aparicio	1956	1973	2677
36	Max Carey	1910	1929	2665
37	Nellie Fox	1947	1965	2663
38	Harry Heilmann	1914	1932	2660
39	Ted Williams	1939	1960	2654
40	Jimmie Foxx	1925	1945	2646
41	Lave Cross	1887	1907	2645
42	**Billy Williams**	**1959**		**2637**
43	Rabbit Maranville	1912	1935	2605
44	Ed Delahanty	1888	1903	2593
45	Ernie Banks	1953	1971	2583
46	Richie Ashburn	1948	1962	2574
47	George Van Haltren	1887	1903	2558
48	**Lou Brock**	**1961**		**2551**
49	**Pete Rose**	**1963**		**2547**
50	Heinie Manush	1923	1939	2524
	Jimmy Ryan	1885	1903	2524
52	Mickey Vernon	1939	1960	2495
53	Bill Dahlen	1891	1911	2478
54	Joe Medwick	1932	1948	2471
55	Harry Hooper	1909	1925	2466
56	Roger Connor	1880	1897	2460
57	Lloyd Waner	1927	1945	2459
58	Red Schoendienst	1945	1963	2449
59	Pie Traynor	1920	1937	2416
60	**Willie Davis**	**1960**		**2415**
	Mickey Mantle	1951	1968	2415
62	**Carl Yastrzemski**	**1961**		**2413**
63	Duffy McInnis	1909	1927	2406
64	Enos Slaughter	1938	1959	2383
65	Edd Roush	1912	1931	2377
66	Orlando Cepeda	1958	1974	2351
67	Joe Judge	1915	1934	2350

		First	Last	Hits
68	Billy Herman	1931	1947	2345
69	Jake Daubert	1910	1924	2326
70	Eddie Mathews	1952	1968	2315
71	Jim Bottomley	1922	1937	2313
	Hugh Duffy	1888	1906	2313
73	Bobby Wallace	1894	1918	2308
74	Jim O'Rourke	1876	1904	2300
75	Charlie Grimm	1916	1936	2299
	Kiki Cuyler	1921	1938	2299
77	Dan Brouthers	1879	1904	2288
78	Biddy McPhee	1882	1899	2287
79	Joe Cronin	1926	1945	2285
80	Patsy Donovan	1890	1907	2266
81	Jimmy Dykes	1918	1939	2256
82	Ron Santo	1960	1974	2254
83	Tommy Corcoran	1890	1907	2248
84	Joe Kelley	1891	1908	2245
85	Fred Tenney	1894	1911	2239
86	**Joe Torre**	**1960**		**2238**
87	Joe Sewell	1920	1933	2226
88	Joe DiMaggio	1936	1951	2214
89	Joe Kuhel	1930	1947	2212
90	Stan Hack	1932	1947	2193
	Bill Terry	1923	1936	2193
92	Pee Wee Reese	1940	1958	2170
93	Sherry Magee	1904	1919	2169
94	Dick Bartell	1927	1946	2165
95	Billy Hamilton	1888	1901	2157
96	Hal Chase	1905	1919	2156
97	Yogi Berra	1946	1965	2150
98	Ed Konetchy	1907	1921	2146
99	Tommy Leach	1898	1918	2144
100	Ken Boyer	1955	1969	2143

		First	Last	Hits
101	Herman Long	1889	1904	2142
102	Dick Groat	1952	1967	2138
	Wally Moses	1935	1951	2138
104	Maury Wills	1959	1972	2134
105	Buddy Myer	1925	1941	2131
106	Monte Ward	1878	1894	2122
107	Duke Snider	1947	1964	2116
108	Arky Vaughan	1932	1948	2103
109	Felipe Alou	1958	1974	2101
110	Clyde Milan	1907	1922	2099
111	Jimmy Sheckard	1897	1913	2097
112	Harvey Kuenn	1952	1966	2092
113	Al Dark	1946	1960	2089
114	Harmon Killebrew	1954	1975	2086
115	Ed McKean	1887	1899	2079
116	George Burns	1911	1925	2077
117	Chuck Klein	1928	1944	2076
118	Dummy Hoy	1888	1902	2067
119	Dixie Walker	1931	1949	2064
	Bobby Veach	1912	1925	2064
121	Del Ennis	1946	1959	2063
122	Bob Elliott	1939	1953	2061
123	**Tommy Davis**	**1959**		**2058**
124	George Kell	1943	1957	2054
125	Bob Johnson	1933	1945	2051
126	Bobby Doerr	1937	1951	2042
127	Jack Glasscock	1879	1895	2038
128	Earl Averill	1929	1941	2020
129	George Burns	1914	1929	2018
130	Bill Mazeroski	1956	1972	2016
131	Johnny Mize	1936	1953	2011
132	Dave Bancroft	1915	1930	2004
133	**Tony Taylor**	**1958**		**2001**

Players active at the end of the 1975 season are shown in **bold face.**

LIFETIME LEADERS — BATTING

Players with 250 or more HOME RUNS

		First	Last	HR
1	**Hank Aaron**	**1954**		**745**
2	Babe Ruth	1914	1935	714
3	Willie Mays	1951	1973	660
4	**Frank Robinson**	**1956**		**583**
5	Harmon Killebrew	1954	1975	573
6	Mickey Mantle	1951	1968	536
7	Jimmie Foxx	1925	1945	534
8	Ted Williams	1939	1960	521
9	Eddie Mathews	1952	1968	512
	Ernie Banks	1953	1971	512
11	Mel Ott	1926	1947	511
12	Lou Gehrig	1923	1939	493
13	Stan Musial	1941	1963	475
14	**Billy Williams**	**1959**		**458**
15	**Billy Williams**	**1959**		**415**
16	Duke Snider	1947	1964	407
17	Al Kaline	1953	1974	399
18	Frank Howard	1958	1973	382
19	Orlando Cepeda	1958	1974	379
20	Norm Cash	1958	1974	377
21	Rocky Colavito	1955	1968	374
22	Gil Hodges	1943	1963	370
23	Ralph Kiner	1946	1955	369
24	**Willie Stargell**	**1962**		**368**
25	Joe DiMaggio	1936	1951	361
26	Johnny Mize	1936	1953	359
27	Yogi Berra	1946	1965	358
28	Ron Santo	1960	1974	342
29	Joe Adcock	1950	1966	336
30	**Dick Allen**	**1963**		**331**
	Hank Greenberg	1930	1947	331
32	**Boog Powell**	**1961**		**330**
33	Roy Sievers	1949	1965	318
34	**Carl Yastrzemski**	**1961**		**317**
35	Al Simmons	1924	1944	307
36	Rogers Hornsby	1915	1937	301
37	Chuck Klein	1928	1944	300
38	Del Ennis	1946	1959	288
	Bob Johnson	1933	1945	288
	Hank Sauer	1941	1959	288
41	Frank Thomas	1951	1966	286
42	Ken Boyer	1955	1969	282
43	Ted Kluszewski	1947	1961	279
44	Rudy York	1934	1948	277
45	Roger Maris	1957	1968	275
46	**Jim Wynn**	**1963**		**273**
47	Vic Wertz	1947	1963	266
48	**Brooks Robinson**	**1955**		**264**
	Bobby Thomson	1946	1960	264
50	**Tony Perez**	**1964**		**258**
51	**Vada Pinson**	**1958**		**256**
	Bob Allison	1958	1970	256
53	**Reggie Jackson**	**1967**		**254**
54	Joe Gordon	1938	1950	253
	Larry Doby	1947	1959	253
56	Cy Williams	1912	1930	251

Players with 18 or fewer AT BATS per HOME RUN
(Minimum of 10 major league seasons and 4000 At Bats)

		First	Last	AB/HR
1	Babe Ruth	1914	1935	11.76
2	Ralph Kiner	1946	1955	14.11
3	Harmon Killebrew	1954	1975	14.22
4	**Willie McCovey**	**1959**		**14.50**
5	Ted Williams	1939	1960	14.79
6	Mickey Mantle	1951	1968	15.12
7	Jimmie Foxx	1925	1945	15.23
8	Hank Greenberg	1930	1947	15.69
9	Lou Gehrig	1923	1939	16.23
10	**Hank Aaron**	**1954**		**16.23**
11	Willie Mays	1951	1973	16.49
12	Hank Sauer	1941	1959	16.65
13	Eddie Mathews	1952	1968	16.68
14	**Willie Stargell**	**1962**		**16.75**
15	Frank Howard	1958	1973	16.98
16	**Frank Robinson**	**1956**		**17.06**
17	Roy Campanella	1948	1957	17.38
18	Rocky Colavito	1955	1968	17.39
19	Gus Zernial	1949	1959	17.43
20	Duke Snider	1947	1964	17.59
21	**Dick Allen**	**1963**		**17.71**
22	Norm Cash	1958	1974	17.79
23	Johnny Mize	1936	1953	17.95

Players with 150 or more TRIPLES

		First	Last	3B
1	Sam Crawford	1899	1917	312
2	Ty Cobb	1905	1928	297
3	Honus Wagner	1897	1917	252
4	Jake Beckley	1888	1907	246
5	Roger Connor	1880	1897	227
6	Tris Speaker	1907	1928	223
7	Fred Clarke	1894	1915	219
8	Dan Brouthers	1879	1904	212
9	Paul Waner	1926	1945	190
10	Joe Kelley	1891	1908	189
11	Eddie Collins	1906	1930	186
12	Harry Stovey	1880	1893	185
	Jesse Burkett	1890	1905	185
14	Sam Rice	1915	1934	184
15	Ed Delahanty	1888	1903	182
	Edd Roush	1913	1931	182
17	Ed Konetchy	1907	1921	181
18	Buck Ewing	1880	1897	179
19	Rabbit Maranville	1912	1935	177
	Stan Musial	1941	1963	177
21	Goose Goslin	1921	1938	173
22	Zack Wheat	1909	1927	172
23	Biddy McPhee	1882	1899	170
	Tommy Leach	1898	1918	170
25	Elmer Flick	1898	1910	169
	Rogers Hornsby	1915	1937	169
27	Joe Jackson	1908	1920	168
28	George Davis	1890	1909	167
29	Bill Dahlen	1891	1911	166
	Sherry Magee	1904	1919	166
	Roberto Clemente	1955	1972	166
32	Jake Daubert	1910	1924	165
33	George Sisler	1915	1930	164
	Pie Traynor	1920	1937	164
35	Nap Lajoie	1896	1916	163
36	Lou Gehrig	1923	1939	162
37	Harry Hooper	1909	1925	160
	Heinie Manush	1923	1939	160
39	Mike Tiernan	1887	1899	159
	George Van Haltren	1887	1903	159
	Max Carey	1910	1929	159
	Joe Judge	1915	1934	159
43	Kiki Cuyler	1921	1938	157
44	Sam Thompson	1885	1906	156
45	Kip Selbach	1894	1906	154
	Earle Combs	1924	1935	154
47	Ed McKean	1887	1899	153
	Jimmy Ryan	1885	1903	153
	Willie Keeler	1892	1910	153
50	Tommy Corcoran	1890	1907	151
	Harry Heilmann	1914	1932	151
	Jim Bottomley	1922	1937	151

Players with 400 or more DOUBLES

		First	Last	2B
1	Tris Speaker	1907	1928	793
2	Stan Musial	1941	1963	725
3	Ty Cobb	1905	1928	724
4	Honus Wagner	1897	1917	651
5	Nap Lajoie	1896	1916	650
6	**Hank Aaron**	**1954**		**616**
7	Paul Waner	1926	1945	603
8	Charlie Gehringer	1924	1942	574
9	Harry Heilmann	1914	1932	542
10	Rogers Hornsby	1915	1937	541
11	Joe Medwick	1932	1948	540
12	Al Simmons	1924	1944	539
13	Lou Gehrig	1923	1939	535
14	Cap Anson	1876	1897	530
15	**Frank Robinson**	**1956**		**528**
16	Ted Williams	1939	1960	525
17	Willie Mays	1951	1973	523
18	Joe Cronin	1926	1945	514
19	Ed Delahanty	1888	1903	508
20	Babe Ruth	1914	1935	506
21	Goose Goslin	1921	1938	500
22	Al Kaline	1953	1974	498
23	Sam Rice	1915	1934	497
24	Heinie Manush	1923	1939	491
25	Mickey Vernon	1939	1960	490
26	Mel Ott	1926	1947	488
27	Billy Herman	1931	1947	486
28	**Vada Pinson**	**1958**		**485**
29	Zack Wheat	1909	1927	476
30	**Brooks Robinson**	**1955**		**472**
31	**Carl Yastrzemski**	**1961**		**466**
	Frankie Frisch	1919	1937	466
33	Jim Bottomley	1922	1937	465
34	Jimmie Foxx	1925	1945	458
35	Jake Beckley	1888	1907	455
	Sam Crawford	1899	1917	455
37	Jimmy Dykes	1918	1939	453
38	Dan Brouthers	1879	1904	446
39	George Burns	1914	1929	444
40	George Davis	1890	1909	442
	Dick Bartell	1927	1946	442
42	**Pete Rose**	**1963**		**441**
43	Luke Appling	1930	1950	440
	Roberto Clemente	1955	1972	440
45	Jimmy Ryan	1885	1903	439
46	Eddie Collins	1906	1930	437
47	Joe Sewell	1920	1933	436
48	Wally Moses	1935	1951	435
49	Joe Judge	1915	1934	433
50	Roger Connor	1880	1897	429
51	Red Schoendienst	1945	1963	427
52	Sherry Magee	1904	1919	425
	George Sisler	1915	1930	425
54	**Billy Williams**	**1959**		**422**
55	Max Carey	1910	1929	419
56	Orlando Cepeda	1958	1974	417
57	**Lou Brock**	**1961**		**416**
58	Enos Slaughter	1938	1959	413
59	Joe Kuhel	1930	1947	412
60	Ben Chapman	1930	1946	407
	Ernie Banks	1953	1971	407
62	Bill Dahlen	1891	1911	403
63	Lave Cross	1887	1907	402
64	Marty McManus	1920	1934	401
	Earl Averill	1929	1941	401

Players with 1000 or more EXTRA BASE HITS

		First	Last	XBH
1	**Hank Aaron**	**1954**		**1459**
2	Stan Musial	1941	1963	1377
3	Babe Ruth	1914	1935	1356
4	Willie Mays	1951	1973	1323
5	Lou Gehrig	1923	1939	1190
6	**Frank Robinson**	**1956**		**1188**
7	Ty Cobb	1905	1928	1139
8	Tris Speaker	1907	1928	1133
9	Jimmie Foxx	1925	1945	1117
	Ted Williams	1939	1960	1117
11	Mel Ott	1926	1947	1071
12	Rogers Hornsby	1915	1937	1011
13	Ernie Banks	1953	1971	1009
14	Honus Wagner	1897	1917	1004

Players with 4000 or more TOTAL BASES

		First	Last	TB
1	**Hank Aaron**	**1954**		**6756**
2	Stan Musial	1941	1963	6134
3	Willie Mays	1951	1973	6066
4	Ty Cobb	1905	1928	5864
5	Babe Ruth	1914	1935	5793
6	**Frank Robinson**	**1956**		**5349**
7	Tris Speaker	1907	1928	5105
8	Lou Gehrig	1923	1939	5059
9	Mel Ott	1926	1947	5041
10	Jimmie Foxx	1925	1945	4956
11	Honus Wagner	1897	1917	4888
12	Ted Williams	1939	1960	4884
13	Al Kaline	1953	1974	4852
14	Rogers Hornsby	1915	1937	4712
15	Ernie Banks	1953	1971	4706
16	Al Simmons	1924	1944	4685
17	Mickey Mantle	1951	1968	4511
18	Roberto Clemente	1955	1972	4492
19	**Billy Williams**	**1959**		**4880**
20	Paul Waner	1926	1945	4474
21	Nap Lajoie	1896	1916	4473
22	Eddie Mathews	1952	1968	4349
23	Sam Crawford	1899	1917	4334
24	Goose Goslin	1921	1938	4325
25	**Vada Pinson**	**1958**		**4264**
26	Eddie Collins	1906	1930	4261
27	Charlie Gehringer	1924	1942	4257
28	**Brooks Robinson**	**1955**		**4191**
29	Harmon Killebrew	1954	1975	4143
30	Jake Beckley	1888	1907	4138
31	Zack Wheat	1909	1927	4100
32	Cap Anson	1876	1897	4094
33	Harry Heilmann	1914	1932	4053

Players with Lifetime SLUGGING AVERAGE of .500 or higher
(Minimum of 10 major league seasons and 4000 At Bats)

		First	Last	AB	TB	S.A.
1	Babe Ruth	1914	1935	8399	5793	.690
2	Ted Williams	1939	1960	7706	4884	.634
3	Lou Gehrig	1923	1939	8001	5059	.632
4	Jimmie Foxx	1925	1945	8134	4956	.609
5	Hank Greenberg	1930	1947	5193	3142	.605
6	Joe DiMaggio	1936	1951	6821	3948	.579
7	Rogers Hornsby	1915	1937	8173	4712	.577
8	Johnny Mize	1936	1953	6443	3621	.562
9	Stan Musial	1941	1963	10972	6134	.559
10	**Hank Aaron**	**1954**		**12093**	**6756**	**.559**
11	Willie Mays	1951	1973	10881	6066	.557
12	Mickey Mantle	1951	1968	8102	4511	.557
13	Ralph Kiner	1946	1955	5205	2852	.548
14	Hack Wilson	1923	1934	4760	2593	.545
15	Chuck Klein	1928	1944	6486	3522	.543
16	**Dick Allen**	**1963**		**5863**	**3176**	**.542**
17	Duke Snider	1947	1964	7161	3865	.540
18	**Frank Robinson**	**1956**		**9939**	**5349**	**.538**
19	**Willie McCovey**	**1959**		**6676**	**3589**	**.538**
20	Al Simmons	1924	1944	8761	4685	.535
21	**Willie Stargell**	**1962**		**6164**	**3296**	**.535**
22	Earl Averill	1929	1941	6359	3391	.533
23	Mel Ott	1926	1947	9456	5041	.533
24	Babe Herman	1926	1945	5603	2980	.532
25	Ken Williams	1915	1929	4860	2579	.531
26	Chick Hafey	1924	1937	4625	2433	.526
27	Hal Trosky	1933	1946	5161	2692	.522
28	Wally Berger	1930	1940	5163	2693	.522
29	Harry Heilmann	1914	1932	7787	4053	.520
30	Dan Brouthers	1879	1904	6682	3476	.520
31	Joe Jackson	1908	1920	4981	2579	.518
32	Ty Cobb	1905	1928	11437	5864	.513
33	Eddie Mathews	1952	1968	8539	4349	.509
34	Jeff Heath	1936	1949	4937	2512	.509
35	Harmon Killebrew	1954	1975	8147	4143	.509
36	Bob Johnson	1933	1945	6920	3501	.506
37	Bill Terry	1923	1936	6428	3251	.506
38	Joe Medwick	1932	1948	7635	3852	.505
39	Sam Thompson	1885	1906	5972	3006	.503
40	Ed Delahanty	1888	1903	7493	3765	.502
41	Jim Bottomley	1922	1937	7471	3737	.500
42	Tris Speaker	1907	1928	10208	5105	.500
43	Goose Goslin	1921	1938	8654	4325	.500
44	Roy Campanella	1948	1957	4205	2101	.500
45	Ernie Banks	1953	1971	9421	4706	.500

Players active at the end of the 1975 season are shown in **bold face.**

LIFETIME LEADERS — BATTING

1500 or more RUNS SCORED

		First	Last	Runs
1	Ty Cobb	1905	1928	2245
2	Babe Ruth	1914	1935	2174
3	**Hank Aaron**	**1954**		**2152**
4	Willie Mays	1951	1973	2062
5	Stan Musial	1941	1963	1949
6	Lou Gehrig	1923	1939	1888
7	Tris Speaker	1907	1928	1881
8	Mel Ott	1926	1947	1859
9	**Frank Robinson**	**1956**		**1824**
10	Eddie Collins	1906	1930	1818
11	Ted Williams	1939	1960	1798
12	Charlie Gehringer	1924	1942	1774
13	Jimmie Foxx	1925	1945	1751
14	Honus Wagner	1897	1917	1740
15	Cap Anson	1876	1897	1728
16	Willie Keeler	1892	1910	1720
17	Jesse Burkett	1890	1905	1708
18	Billy Hamilton	1888	1901	1690
19	Mickey Mantle	1951	1968	1677
20	Biddy McPhee	1882	1899	1674
21	George Van Haltren	1887	1903	1650
22	Jimmy Ryan	1885	1903	1640
23	Paul Waner	1926	1945	1626
24	Al Kaline	1953	1974	1622
25	Fred Clarke	1894	1915	1620
26	Roger Connor	1880	1897	1607
27	Jake Beckley	1888	1907	1601
28	Ed Delahanty	1888	1903	1596
29	Bill Dahlen	1891	1911	1594
30	Rogers Hornsby	1915	1937	1579
31	Hugh Duffy	1888	1906	1555
32	George Davis	1890	1909	1546
33	Max Carey	1910	1929	1545
34	Frankie Frisch	1919	1937	1532
35	Tom Brown	1883	1898	1524
36	Sam Rice	1915	1934	1514
37	Dan Brouthers	1879	1904	1513
38	Eddie Mathews	1952	1968	1509
39	Al Simmons	1924	1944	1507
40	Nap Lajoie	1896	1916	1502

Players with 1300 or more RUNS BATTED IN

		First	Last	RBI
1	**Hank Aaron**	**1954**		**2262**
2	Babe Ruth	1914	1935	2212
3	Lou Gehrig	1923	1939	1991
4	Stan Musial	1941	1963	1951
5	Ty Cobb	1905	1928	1933
6	Jimmie Foxx	1925	1945	1921
7	Willie Mays	1951	1973	1903
8	Cap Anson	1876	1897	1879
9	Mel Ott	1926	1947	1860
10	Ted Williams	1939	1960	1839
11	Al Simmons	1924	1944	1827
12	**Frank Robinson**	**1956**		**1802**
13	Ernie Banks	1953	1971	1636
14	Goose Goslin	1921	1938	1609
15	Harmon Killebrew	1954	1975	1584
	Rogers Hornsby	1915	1937	1584
17	Al Kaline	1953	1974	1583
18	Jake Beckley	1888	1907	1574
19	Harry Heilmann	1914	1932	1537
	Joe DiMaggio	1936	1951	1537
21	Tris Speaker	1907	1928	1527
22	Sam Crawford	1899	1917	1524
23	Mickey Mantle	1951	1968	1509
24	Ed Delahanty	1888	1903	1464
25	Eddie Mathews	1952	1968	1453
26	**Billy Williams**	**1959**		**1434**
27	George Davis	1890	1909	1432
28	Yogi Berra	1946	1965	1430
29	Charlie Gehringer	1924	1942	1427
30	Joe Cronin	1926	1945	1423
31	Jim Bottomley	1922	1937	1422
32	Joe Medwick	1932	1948	1383
33	Orlando Cepeda	1958	1974	1365
34	**Brooks Robinson**	**1955**		**1342**
35	Johnny Mize	1936	1953	1337
36	Duke Snider	1947	1964	1333
37	Ron Santo	1960	1974	1331
38	Roger Connor	1880	1897	1323
39	Mickey Vernon	1939	1960	1311
40	Paul Waner	1926	1945	1309
41	Roberto Clemente	1955	1972	1305
42	Enos Slaughter	1938	1959	1304
43	Hugh Duffy	1888	1906	1301

Players with 5 or fewer AT BATS per RUN BATTED IN

		First	Last	AB/RBI
1	Babe Ruth	1914	1935	3.79
2	Lou Gehrig	1923	1939	4.02
3	Hank Greenberg	1930	1947	4.07
4	Ted Williams	1939	1960	4.19
5	Jimmie Foxx	1925	1945	4.23
6	Joe DiMaggio	1936	1951	4.44
7	Hack Wilson	1923	1934	4.48
8	Sam Thompson	1885	1906	4.60
9	Al Simmons	1924	1944	4.80
10	Johnny Mize	1936	1953	4.82
11	Cap Anson	1876	1897	4.83
12	Roy Campanella	1948	1957	4.91

Players with 350 or more STOLEN BASES since 1898

(*Started major league career before 1898 – before 1898 a stolen base could be awarded when a runner advanced an extra base on a hit or an out.)

		First	Last	SB
1	Ty Cobb	1905	1928	892
2	**Lou Brock**	**1961**		**809**
3	Eddie Collins	1906	1930	743
4	Max Carey	1910	1929	738
5	Honus Wagner	*1898	1917	703
6	Maury Wills	1959	1972	586
7	**Bert Campaneris**	**1964**		**512**
8	Luis Aparicio	1956	1973	506
9	Clyde Milan	1907	1922	494
10	Jimmy Sheckard	*1898	1913	474
11	**Joe Morgan**	**1963**		**445**
12	Sherry Magee	1904	1919	441
13	Tris Speaker	1907	1928	433
14	Bob Bescher	1908	1918	427
15	Frankie Frisch	1919	1937	419
16	Frank Chance	1898	1914	405
	Donie Bush	1908	1923	405
18	**Tommy Harper**	**1962**		**404**
19	**Willie Davis**	**1960**		**383**
	George Burns	1911	1925	383
21	Sam Mertes	*1898	1906	376
22	Fred Clarke	*1898	1915	375
	Harry Hooper	1909	1925	375
	George Sisler	1915	1930	375
25	Nap Lajoie	*1898	1916	367
	Sam Crawford	1899	1917	367
27	Tommy Leach	1898	1918	364
28	Hal Chase	1905	1919	363
29	Sam Rice	1915	1934	351

Players with 2300 or more GAMES PLAYED

		First	Last	Games
1	**Hank Aaron**	**1954**		**3213**
2	Ty Cobb	1905	1928	3034
3	Stan Musial	1941	1963	3026
4	Willie Mays	1951	1973	2992
5	Al Kaline	1953	1974	2834
6	Eddie Collins	1906	1930	2826
7	**Brooks Robinson**	**1955**		**2801**
8	Honus Wagner	1897	1917	2792
9	Tris Speaker	1907	1928	2789
10	**Frank Robinson**	**1956**		**2772**
11	Mel Ott	1926	1947	2730
12	Rabbit Maranville	1912	1935	2670
13	Luis Aparicio	1956	1973	2599
14	Paul Waner	1926	1945	2549
15	Ernie Banks	1953	1971	2528
16	Sam Crawford	1899	1917	2517
17	Babe Ruth	1914	1935	2503
18	Nap Lajoie	1896	1916	2480
19	Max Carey	1910	1929	2476
20	**Vada Pinson**	**1958**		**2469**
21	Bill Dahlen	1891	1911	2442
22	Harmon Killebrew	1954	1975	2435
23	Roberto Clemente	1955	1972	2433
24	Luke Appling	1930	1950	2422
25	Zack Wheat	1909	1927	2410
26	Mickey Vernon	1939	1960	2409
27	Sam Rice	1915	1934	2404
28	Mickey Mantle	1951	1968	2401
29	Eddie Mathews	1952	1968	2391
30	Bobby Wallace	1894	1918	2385
31	Jake Beckley	1888	1907	2383
32	Enos Slaughter	1938	1959	2380
33	George Davis	1890	1909	2378
34	**Billy Williams**	**1959**		**2368**
35	Nellie Fox	1947	1965	2367
36	Charlie Gehringer	1924	1942	2323
37	Jimmie Foxx	1925	1945	2317
38	Frankie Frisch	1919	1937	2310
39	Harry Hooper	1909	1925	2308

Players with 9000 or more AT BATS

		First	Last	AB
1	**Hank Aaron**	**1954**		**12093**
2	Ty Cobb	1905	1928	11437
3	Stan Musial	1941	1963	10972
4	Willie Mays	1951	1973	10881
5	Honus Wagner	1897	1917	10427
6	**Brooks Robinson**	**1955**		**10391**
7	Luis Aparicio	1956	1973	10230
8	Tris Speaker	1907	1928	10208
9	Al Kaline	1953	1974	10116
10	Rabbit Maranville	1912	1935	10078
11	Eddie Collins	1906	1930	9949
12	**Frank Robinson**	**1956**		**9939**
13	**Vada Pinson**	**1958**		**9645**
14	Nap Lajoie	1896	1916	9589
15	Sam Crawford	1899	1917	9579
16	Jake Beckley	1888	1907	9476
17	Paul Waner	1926	1945	9459
18	Mel Ott	1926	1947	9456
19	Roberto Clemente	1955	1972	9454
20	Ernie Banks	1953	1971	9421
21	Max Carey	1910	1929	9363
22	Sam Rice	1915	1934	9269
23	Nellie Fox	1947	1965	9232
24	Doc Cramer	1929	1948	9140
25	Frankie Frisch	1919	1937	9112
26	Zack Wheat	1909	1927	9106
27	Cap Anson	1876	1897	9067
28	Lave Cross	1887	1907	9065
29	George Davis	1890	1909	9027
30	Bill Dahlen	1891	1911	9019

Players with 1000 or more BASES ON BALLS

		First	Last	BB
1	Babe Ruth	1914	1935	2056
2	Ted Williams	1939	1960	2019
3	Mickey Mantle	1951	1968	1734
4	Mel Ott	1926	1947	1708
5	Eddie Yost	1944	1962	1614
6	Stan Musial	1941	1963	1599
7	Harmon Killebrew	1954	1975	1559
8	Lou Gehrig	1923	1939	1510
9	Eddie Collins	1906	1930	1503
10	Willie Mays	1951	1973	1463
11	Jimmie Foxx	1925	1945	1452
12	Eddie Mathews	1952	1968	1444
13	**Frank Robinson**	**1956**		**1409**
14	Tris Speaker	1907	1928	1381
15	**Hank Aaron**	**1954**		**1367**
16	**Carl Yastrzemski**	**1961**		**1348**
17	Luke Appling	1930	1950	1302
18	Al Kaline	1953	1974	1277
19	Ty Cobb	1905	1928	1249
20	Pee Wee Reese	1940	1958	1210
21	Richie Ashburn	1948	1962	1198
22	Billy Hamilton	1888	1901	1187
23	Charlie Gehringer	1924	1942	1185
24	**Willie McCovey**	**1959**		**1169**
25	Max Bishop	1924	1935	1153
26	Harry Hooper	1909	1925	1136
27	Jimmy Sheckard	1897	1913	1135
28	Ron Santo	1960	1974	1108
29	Lu Blue	1921	1933	1092
	Stan Hack	1932	1947	1092
31	Paul Waner	1926	1945	1090
32	Bob Johnson	1933	1945	1073
33	Harlond Clift	1934	1945	1070
34	**Jim Wynn**	**1963**		**1065**
35	Bill Dahlen	1891	1911	1064
36	**Joe Morgan**	**1963**		**1063**
37	Joe Cronin	1926	1945	1059
38	Norm Cash	1958	1974	1043
39	Eddie Joost	1936	1955	1041
40	Max Carey	1910	1929	1040
41	Rogers Hornsby	1915	1937	1038
42	Jim Gilliam	1953	1966	1036
43	Jesse Burkett	1890	1905	1029
44	Enos Slaughter	1938	1959	1018
45	Ralph Kiner	1946	1955	1011
46	Dummy Hoy	1888	1902	1004
47	Miller Huggins	1904	1916	1002
	Roger Connor	1880	1897	1002

Players with 1000 or more STRIKEOUTS

		First	Last	SO
1	Mickey Mantle	1951	1968	1710
2	Harmon Killebrew	1954	1975	1699
3	Willie Mays	1951	1973	1526
4	**Frank Robinson**	**1956**		**1520**
5	**Lou Brock**	**1961**		**1509**
6	**Willie Stargell**	**1962**		**1497**
7	Eddie Mathews	1952	1968	1487
8	Frank Howard	1958	1973	1460
9	**Dick Allen**	**1963**		**1457**
10	**Hank Aaron**	**1954**		**1345**
11	Ron Santo	1960	1974	1343
12	Babe Ruth	1914	1935	1330
13	Jimmie Foxx	1925	1945	1311
14	**Deron Johnson**	**1960**		**1307**
15	**Jim Wynn**	**1963**		**1269**
16	**Willie McCovey**	**1959**		**1251**
17	Duke Snider	1947	1964	1237
18	Ernie Banks	1953	1971	1236
19	Roberto Clemente	1955	1972	1230
20	**Vada Pinson**	**1958**		**1196**
21	**Boog Powell**	**1961**		**1174**
22	Orlando Cepeda	1958	1974	1169
23	**Bobby Bonds**	**1968**		**1153**
24	**Tony Perez**	**1964**		**1150**
25	Donn Clendenon	1961	1972	1140
26	Gil Hodges	1943	1963	1137
27	**Leo Cardenas**	**1960**		**1135**
28	**Reggie Jackson**	**1967**		**1129**
29	Norm Cash	1958	1974	1091
30	**Tony Taylor**	**1958**		**1076**
31	**Bob Bailey**	**1962**		**1070**
32	**Tommy Harper**	**1962**		**1064**
	Johnny Callison	1958	1973	1064
34	Joe Adcock	1950	1966	1059
35	**Lee May**	**1965**		**1052**
36	**Carl Yastrzemski**	**1961**		**1051**
37	**Joe Torre**	**1960**		**1049**
38	**Jim Fregosi**	**1961**		**1042**
39	Bob Allison	1958	1970	1033
40	Al Kaline	1953	1974	1020
41	Ken Boyer	1955	1969	1017
42	Larry Doby	1947	1959	1011
43	**Billy Williams**	**1959**		**1002**

Players active at the end of the 1975 season are shown in **bold face**.

LIFETIME LEADERS — PITCHING

Pitchers with 200 or more WINS

		First	Last	Wins	Losses	Pct.
1	Cy Young	1890	1911	511	313	.620
2	Walter Johnson	1907	1927	416	279	.599
3	Christy Mathewson	1900	1916	374	187	.667
4	G.C. "Pete" Alexander	1911	1930	373	208	.642
5	Warren Spahn	1942	1965	363	245	.597
6	Kid Nichols	1890	1906	362	203	.641
7	Jim Galvin	1879	1892	361	309	.539
8	Tim Keefe	1880	1893	342	224	.604
9	John Clarkson	1882	1894	327	176	.650
10	Eddie Plank	1901	1917	325	193	.627
11	Mickey Welch	1880	1892	311	207	.600
12	Old Hoss Radbourn	1881	1891	308	191	.617
13	Lefty Grove	1925	1941	300	141	.680
	Early Wynn	1939	1963	300	244	.551
15	Tony Mullane	1881	1894	286	213	.573
	Robin Roberts	1948	1966	286	245	.539
17	Red Ruffing	1924	1947	273	225	.548
18	Burleigh Grimes	1916	1934	270	212	.560
19	Bob Feller	1936	1956	266	162	.621
	Gus Weyhing	1887	1901	266	229	.537
	Eppa Rixey	1912	1933	266	251	.515
22	Jim McCormick	1878	1887	264	214	.552
23	Ted Lyons	1923	1946	260	230	.531
24	Red Faber	1914	1933	254	212	.545
25	Carl Hubbell	1928	1943	253	154	.622
26	Bob Gibson	1959	1975	251	174	.591
27	Joe McGinnity	1899	1908	248	144	.633
	Amos Rusie	1889	1901	248	170	.593
	Jack Quinn	1909	1933	248	219	.531
	Jack Powell	1897	1912	248	255	.493
31	Juan Marichal	1960	1975	243	142	.631
	Vic Willis	1898	1910	243	203	.545
33	Herb Pennock	1912	1934	240	161	.599
34	Three Finger Brown	1903	1916	239	127	.653
35	Waite Hoyt	1918	1938	237	182	.566
36	Whitey Ford	1950	1967	236	106	.690
37	Clark Griffith	1891	1914	235	143	.622
	Jim Kaat	**1959**		**235**	**187**	**.557**
39	Charlie Buffinton	1882	1892	230	151	.604
40	George Mullin	1902	1915	229	192	.544
41	Sad Sam Jones	1914	1935	228	216	.514
42	Will White	1877	1886	227	167	.576
43	Jim Bunning	1955	1971	224	184	.549
44	Mel Harder	1928	1947	223	186	.545
	Paul Derringer	1931	1945	223	212	.513
46	Hooks Dauss	1912	1926	221	182	.548
47	Earl Whitehill	1923	1939	218	185	.541
48	Bob Caruthers	1884	1892	217	101	.682
	Freddie Fitzsimmons	1925	1943	217	146	.598
50	Stan Coveleski	1912	1928	216	143	.602
	Gaylord Perry	**1962**		**216**	**174**	**.554**
	Wilbur Cooper	1912	1926	216	178	.548
53	Jim Perry	1959	1975	215	174	.553
54	Billy Pierce	1945	1964	211	169	.555
	Bobo Newsom	1929	1953	211	222	.487
56	Chief Bender	1903	1925	210	128	.621
	Jesse Haines	1918	1937	210	158	.571
58	Eddie Cicotte	1905	1920	209	149	.584
	Milt Pappas	1957	1973	209	164	.560
	Don Drysdale	1956	1969	209	166	.557
61	Carl Mays	1915	1929	207	127	.620
	Bob Lemon	1946	1958	207	128	.618
	Hal Newhouser	1939	1955	207	150	.580
	Mickey Lolich	**1963**		**207**	**175**	**.542**
65	Silver King	1886	1897	206	152	.575
66	Jack Stivetts	1889	1899	205	128	.616
	Adonis Terry	1884	1897	205	197	.510
68	Lew Burdette	1950	1967	203	144	.585
	Al Orth	1895	1909	203	183	.526
70	Charlie Root	1923	1941	201	160	.557
	Rube Marquard	1908	1925	201	177	.532
72	George Uhle	1919	1936	200	166	.546

Pitchers with Lifetime WINNING PERCENTAGE of .600 or higher
(Minimum 100 Wins)

		First	Last	Wins	Losses	Pct.
1	Spud Chandler	1937	1947	109	43	.717
2	Whitey Ford	1950	1967	236	106	.690
3	Dave Foutz	1884	1894	149	67	.690
4	Bob Caruthers	1884	1892	217	101	.682
5	Lefty Grove	1925	1941	300	141	.680
6	Smokey Joe Wood	1908	1920	115	57	.669
7	Christy Mathewson	1900	1916	374	187	.667
	Vic Raschi	1946	1955	132	66	.667
9	Larry Corcoran	1880	1887	173	90	.658
10	Sal Maglie	1945	1958	119	62	.657
11	Sam Leever	1898	1910	193	101	.656
12	**Jim Palmer**	**1965**		**152**	**80**	**.655**
13	Sandy Koufax	1955	1966	165	87	.655
14	Johnny Allen	1932	1944	142	75	.654
15	Three Finger Brown	1903	1916	239	127	.653
16	John Clarkson	1882	1894	327	176	.650
17	Lefty Gomez	1930	1943	189	102	.649
18	Dizzy Dean	1930	1947	150	83	.644
19	G.C. "Pete" Alexander	1911	1930	373	208	.642
20	Kid Nichols	1890	1906	362	203	.641
21	Fred Goldsmith	1879	1884	117	66	.639
22	**Tom Seaver**	**1967**		**168**	**96**	**.636**
23	Deacon Phillippe	1899	1911	187	108	.634
24	Joe McGinnity	1899	1908	248	144	.633
25	Ed Reulbach	1905	1917	182	106	.632
26	Juan Marichal	1960	1975	243	142	.631
27	Mort Cooper	1938	1949	128	75	.631
28	Allie Reynolds	1942	1954	182	107	.630
29	Eddie Plank	1901	1917	325	193	.627
30	Ray Kremer	1924	1933	143	85	.627
31	Addie Joss	1902	1910	159	95	.626
32	Tommy Bond	1876	1884	192	115	.625
33	Don Newcombe	1949	1960	149	90	.623
34	Firpo Marberry	1923	1936	147	89	.623
35	Doc Crandall	1908	1918	102	62	.622
36	Clark Griffith	1891	1914	235	143	.622
37	Carl Hubbell	1928	1943	253	154	.622
38	Bob Feller	1936	1956	266	162	.621
39	Chief Bender	1903	1925	210	128	.621
40	Mel Parnell	1947	1956	123	75	.621
41	Cy Young	1890	1911	511	313	.620
42	Jesse Tannehill	1894	1911	194	119	.620
43	Carl Mays	1915	1929	207	127	.620
44	Bob Lemon	1946	1958	207	128	.618
45	Monte Pearson	1932	1941	100	62	.617
46	Old Hoss Radbourn	1881	1891	308	191	.617
47	Nig Cuppy	1892	1901	161	100	.617
48	Urban Shocker	1916	1928	188	117	.616
49	Jack Stivetts	1889	1899	205	128	.616
50	Jeff Tesreau	1912	1918	115	72	.615
51	Jim Maloney	1960	1971	134	84	.615
52	Lon Warneke	1930	1945	192	121	.613
53	Schoolboy Rowe	1933	1949	158	101	.610
54	Carl Erskine	1948	1959	122	78	.610
55	**Mike Cuellar**	**1959**		**181**	**116**	**.609**
56	Monte Ward	1878	1894	158	102	.608
57	Dave McNally	1962	1975	184	119	.607
58	Art Nehf	1915	1929	184	120	.605
59	Hooks Wiltse	1904	1915	138	90	.605
60	Tim Keefe	1880	1893	342	224	.604
61	Charlie Buffinton	1882	1892	230	151	.604
62	Jack Chesbro	1899	1909	198	130	.604
63	Ed Walsh	1904	1917	194	128	.602
64	Preacher Roe	1938	1954	127	84	.602
65	Stan Coveleski	1912	1928	216	143	.602
66	Wes Ferrell	1927	1941	193	128	.601
67	Mickey Welch	1880	1892	311	207	.600

Lifetime DIFFERENCE in WINNING PERCENTAGE

Baseball executives have long used the comparison between a pitcher's winning percentage and the winning percentage of his team as a measure of the pitcher's performance. This list shows this comparison on a lifetime basis for all pitchers with 150 or more wins whose careers ended since 1900. The "Pct" column is the pitcher's lifetime winning percentage. The "Team" column is his team's winning percentage, the average of the winning percentages of the teams he pitched for each year weighted by the number of his decisions each year. "Diff" is "Pct" minus "Team", without the decimal points.

		First	Last	Pct	Team	Diff
1	**Tom Seaver**	**1967**		**.636**	**.499**	**137**
2	G.C. "Pete" Alexander	1911	1930	.642	.534	108
3	Walter Johnson	1907	1927	.599	.496	103
4	Lefty Grove	1925	1941	.680	.585	95
5	Clark Griffith	1891	1914	.622	.530	92
6	Cy Young	1890	1911	.620	.531	89
7	Jesse Tannehill	1894	1911	.620	.532	88
	Eddie Rommel	1920	1932	.590	.502	88
	Sandy Koufax	1955	1966	.655	.567	88
	Addie Joss	1902	1910	.626	.538	88
11	Wes Ferrell	1927	1941	.601	.515	86
	Schoolboy Rowe	1933	1949	.610	.524	86
13	Whitey Ford	1950	1967	.690	.605	85
	Dazzy Vance	1915	1935	.585	.500	85
15	Dizzy Dean	1930	1947	.644	.560	84
16	Urban Shocker	1916	1928	.616	.533	83
17	Juan Marichal	1960	1975	.633	.553	80
18	Christy Mathewson	1900	1916	.667	.588	79
	Red Lucas	1923	1938	.538	.459	79
20	Ted Lyons	1923	1946	.531	.459	72
21	**Catfish Hunter**	**1965**		**.592**	**.526**	**66**
22	Amos Rusie	1889	1901	.593	.529	64
	Ed Walsh	1904	1917	.602	.538	64
24	Carl Hubbell	1928	1943	.622	.559	63
	Ferguson Jenkins	**1965**		**.579**	**.516**	**63**
	Claude Passeau	1935	1947	.519	.456	63
27	Theo Breitenstein	1891	1901	.496	.434	62
28	Dutch Leonard	1933	1953	.513	.452	61
29	Bob Feller	1936	1956	.621	.562	59
	Bob Gibson	1959	1975	.591	.532	59
31	Hippo Vaughn	1908	1921	.565	.508	57
	Slim Sallee	1908	1921	.547	.490	57
	Jim Palmer	**1965**		**.655**	**.598**	**57**
34	Three Finger Brown	1903	1916	.653	.598	55
35	Warren Spahn	1942	1965	.597	.543	54
36	Joe McGinnity	1899	1908	.633	.582	51
	Jeff Pfeffer	1911	1924	.585	.534	51
38	Art Nehf	1915	1929	.605	.555	50
	Virgil Trucks	1941	1958	.567	.517	50
	Luis Tiant	**1964**		**.568**	**.518**	**50**
41	Sam Leever	1898	1910	.656	.607	49
	Camilo Pascual	1954	1971	.506	.457	49
43	Eddie Plank	1901	1917	.627	.579	48
	Red Faber	1914	1933	.545	.497	48
	Robin Roberts	1948	1966	.539	.491	48
	Rube Waddell	1897	1910	.587	.539	48
47	Bucky Walters	1934	1950	.553	.506	47
	Jack Chesbro	1899	1909	.604	.557	47
	Tommy Bridges	1930	1946	.584	.537	47
	Mike Cuellar	**1959**		**.609**	**.562**	**47**
51	Lon Warneke	1930	1945	.613	.567	46
	Allie Reynolds	1942	1954	.630	.584	46
53	Lee Meadows	1915	1929	.511	.468	43
54	Herb Pennock	1912	1934	.599	.557	42
	Wilbur Cooper	1912	1926	.548	.506	42
	George Uhle	1919	1936	.546	.504	42
	Wild Bill Donovan	1898	1918	.575	.533	42
58	Kid Nichols	1890	1906	.641	.600	41
	Babe Adams	1906	1926	.581	.540	41
60	Chief Bender	1903	1925	.621	.581	40
	Mel Stottlemyre	1964	1974	.541	.501	40
62	Freddie Fitzsimmons	1925	1943	.598	.559	39
	Stan Coveleski	1912	1928	.602	.563	39
64	Hal Newhouser	1939	1955	.580	.542	38
65	Earl Whitehill	1923	1939	.541	.504	37
	Vern Law	1950	1967	.524	.487	37
67	Jim Bunning	1955	1971	.549	.513	36
	Burleigh Grimes	1916	1934	.560	.524	36
69	Al Orth	1895	1909	.526	.491	35
	Carl Mays	1915	1929	.620	.585	35
71	Gus Weyhing	1887	1901	.537	.503	34
	Nig Cuppy	1892	1901	.617	.583	34
73	Hooks Dauss	1912	1926	.548	.516	32
	Milt Pappas	1957	1973	.560	.528	32
75	**Jim Kaat**	**1959**		**.557**	**.526**	**31**
	Gaylord Perry	**1962**		**.554**	**.523**	**31**
	Jim Perry	1959	1975	.553	.522	31
78	Lew Burdette	1950	1967	.585	.555	30
79	Eddie Cicotte	1905	1920	.584	.555	29
	Ed Lopat	1944	1955	.597	.568	29
81	Jack Taylor	1898	1907	.519	.492	27
82	Howard Ehmke	1915	1930	.500	.474	26
	Bill Doak	1912	1929	.518	.492	26
84	Curt Davis	1934	1946	.547	.522	25
85	Jesse Haines	1918	1937	.571	.547	24
86	General Crowder	1926	1936	.592	.569	23
	Bob Lemon	1946	1958	.618	.595	23
88	George Mullin	1902	1915	.544	.522	22
	Doc White	1901	1913	.551	.529	22
90	**Mickey Lolich**	**1963**		**.542**	**.521**	**21**
	Ed Reulbach	1905	1917	.632	.611	21
92	Larry Jackson	1955	1968	.515	.495	20
	Deacon Phillippe	1899	1911	.634	.614	20
	Dave McNally	1962	1975	.607	.587	20
95	Bobo Newsom	1929	1953	.487	.469	18
96	Mel Harder	1928	1947	.545	.528	17
	Murry Dickson	1939	1959	.487	.470	17
98	Jack Quinn	1909	1933	.533	.517	16
	Sad Sam Jones	1914	1935	.514	.498	16
100	Red Donahue	1893	1906	.499	.485	14
	Vic Willis	1898	1910	.545	.531	14
102	Earl Moore	1901	1914	.517	.505	12
103	Eppa Rixey	1912	1933	.515	.504	11
	Billy Pierce	1945	1964	.555	.544	11
	Bill Sherdel	1918	1932	.531	.520	11
	Hal Schumacher	1931	1946	.566	.555	11
107	Early Wynn	1939	1963	.551	.542	9
	Don Drysdale	1956	1969	.556	.547	9
	Don Sutton	**1966**		**.552**	**.543**	**9**
	Ken Holtzman	**1965**		**.549**	**.540**	**9**
111	Lefty Gomez	1930	1943	.649	.641	8
	Chick Fraser	1896	1909	.458	.450	8
	Guy Bush	1923	1945	.564	.556	8
114	Bob Buhl	1953	1967	.557	.550	7
115	Brickyard Kennedy	1892	1903	.528	.522	6
116	Paul Derringer	1931	1945	.513	.508	5
	Joe Bush	1912	1928	.516	.511	5
	Rube Marquard	1908	1925	.532	.527	5
	Bill Dinneen	1898	1909	.494	.489	5
120	**Claude Osteen**	**1957**		**.501**	**.498**	**3**
	Jesse Barnes	1915	1927	.507	.504	3
122	Jack Powell	1897	1912	.493	.491	2
	Bob Shawkey	1913	1927	.569	.567	2
	Tom Zachary	1918	1936	.492	.490	2
125	Pink Hawley	1892	1901	.482	.482	0
126	Curt Simmons	1947	1967	.513	.514	−1
127	Bob Friend	1951	1966	.461	.463	−2
128	Red Ruffing	1924	1947	.548	.551	−3
129	Rube Benton	1910	1925	.518	.522	−4
130	Waite Hoyt	1918	1938	.566	.672	−6
	Jack Coombs	1906	1920	.587	.593	−6
132	Red Ames	1903	1919	.523	.531	−8
	Bill Lee	1934	1947	.518	.526	−8
134	Willis Hudlin	1926	1944	.503	.514	−11
135	Charlie Root	1923	1941	.557	.570	−13
136	Dolf Luque	1914	1935	.519	.533	−14
137	Larry French	1929	1942	.535	.552	−17
138	Dizzy Trout	1939	1957	.514	.533	−19
139	Bump Hadley	1926	1941	.494	.517	−23
140	Rube Walberg	1923	1937	.525	.598	−73

Pitchers active at the end of the 1975 season are shown in **bold face.**

LIFETIME LEADERS — PITCHING

Pitchers with Lifetime EARNED RUN AVERAGE of 2.50 or lower since 1893
(Minimum of 1500 Innings Pitched)

		First	Last	ERA
1	Ed Walsh	1904	1917	1.82
2	Addie Joss	1902	1910	1.88
3	Joe Wood	1908	1920	2.03
4	Three Finger Brown	1903	1916	2.06
5	Christy Mathewson	1900	1916	2.13
6	Rube Waddell	1897	1910	2.16
7	Walter Johnson	1907	1927	2.17
8	Orvie Overall	1905	1913	2.23
9	Ed Reulbach	1905	1917	2.28
10	Jim Scott	1909	1917	2.32
11	Eddie Plank	1901	1917	2.34
12	Eddie Cicotte	1905	1920	2.37
13	Ed Killian	1903	1910	2.38
14	Doc White	1901	1913	2.38
15	Nap Rucker	1907	1916	2.42
16	Jeff Tesreau	1912	1918	2.43
17	Chief Bender	1903	1925	2.46
18	**Tom Seaver**	**1967**		**2.46**
19	Sam Leever	1898	1910	2.47
20	Lefty Leifield	1905	1920	2.47
21	Hooks Wiltse	1904	1915	2.48
22	Hippo Vaughn	1908	1921	2.49
23	Bob Ewing	1902	1912	2.49

Pitchers with 40 or more SHUTOUTS

		First	Last	ShO
1	Walter Johnson	1907	1927	112
2	G.C. "Pete" Alexander	1911	1930	88
3	Cy Young	1890	1911	77
	Christy Mathewson	1900	1916	77
5	Eddie Plank	1901	1917	67
6	Warren Spahn	1942	1965	63
7	Ed Walsh	1904	1917	58
8	Bob Gibson	1959	1975	56
	Pud Galvin	1879	1892	56
	Three Finger Brown	1903	1916	56
11	Juan Marichal	1960	1975	52
12	Rube Waddell	1897	1910	50
	Vic Willis	1898	1910	50
14	Early Wynn	1939	1963	49
	Don Drysdale	1956	1969	49
16	Kid Nichols	1890	1906	48
17	Jack Powell	1897	1912	47
18	Doc White	1901	1913	46
19	Addie Joss	1902	1910	45
	Red Ruffing	1924	1947	45
	Robin Roberts	1948	1966	45
	Whitey Ford	1950	1967	45
23	Babe Adams	1906	1926	44
	Bob Feller	1936	1956	44
25	Milt Pappas	1957	1973	43
26	**Gaylord Perry**	**1962**		**42**
	Bucky Walters	1934	1950	42
28	Mickey Welch	1880	1892	41
	Chief Bender	1903	1925	41
40	**Don Sutton**	**1966**		**40**
	Claude Osteen	**1957**		**40**
	Ed Reulbach	1905	1917	40
	Hippo Vaughn	1908	1921	40
	Larry French	1929	1942	40
	Sandy Koufax	1955	1966	40
	Jim Bunning	1955	1971	40
	Mel Stottlemyre	1964	1974	40

Pitchers with 2000 or more STRIKEOUTS

		First	Last	SO
1	Walter Johnson	1907	1927	3506
2	Bob Gibson	1959	1975	3117
3	Jim Bunning	1955	1971	2855
4	Cy Young	1890	1911	2803
5	**Mickey Lolich**	**1963**		**2679**
6	Warren Spahn	1942	1965	2583
7	Bob Feller	1936	1956	2581
8	**Gaylord Perry**	**1962**		**2527**
9	Tim Keefe	1880	1893	2521
10	Christy Mathewson	1900	1916	2502
11	Don Drysdale	1956	1969	2486
12	Sam McDowell	1961	1975	2453
13	Sandy Koufax	1955	1966	2396
14	Robin Roberts	1948	1966	2357
15	Early Wynn	1939	1963	2334
16	Rube Waddell	1897	1910	2316
17	Juan Marichal	1960	1975	2303
18	Lefty Grove	1925	1941	2266
19	Eddie Plank	1901	1917	2246
20	**Ferguson Jenkins**	**1965**		**2202**
21	G.C. "Pete" Alexander	1911	1930	2199
22	Camilo Pascual	1954	1971	2167
23	**Jim Kaat**	**1959**		**2151**
24	**Tom Seaver**	**1967**		**2099**
25	Bobo Newsom	1929	1953	2082
26	Dazzy Vance	1915	1935	2045

Pitchers with 1250 or more BASES ON BALLS

		First	Last	BB
1	Early Wynn	1939	1963	1775
2	Bob Feller	1936	1956	1764
3	Bobo Newsom	1929	1953	1732
4	Amos Rusie	1889	1901	1704
5	Gus Weyhing	1887	1901	1566
6	Red Ruffing	1924	1947	1541
7	Bump Hadley	1926	1941	1442
8	Warren Spahn	1942	1965	1434
9	Earl Whitehill	1923	1939	1431
10	Tony Mullane	1881	1894	1409
11	Walter Johnson	1907	1927	1404
12	Sad Sam Jones	1914	1935	1396
13	Bob Gibson	1959	1975	1336
14	Chick Fraser	1896	1909	1332
15	Sam McDowell	1961	1975	1312
16	Mark Baldwin	1887	1893	1307
17	Adonis Terry	1884	1897	1301
18	Mickey Welch	1880	1892	1297
19	Burleigh Grimes	1916	1934	1295
20	Kid Nichols	1890	1906	1268
21	Joe Bush	1912	1928	1263
22	Allie Reynolds	1942	1954	1261
23	Bob Lemon	1946	1958	1251

Pitchers with 100 or more SAVES

		First	Last	SV
1	Hoyt Wilhelm	1952	1972	227
2	Roy Face	1953	1969	193
3	Ron Perranoski	1961	1973	179
4	Lindy McDaniel	1955	1975	172
5	Stu Miller	1952	1968	154
6	Don McMahon	1957	1974	153
7	**Sparky Lyle**	**1967**		**152**
8	Ted Abernathy	1955	1972	148
9	**Dave Giusti**	**1962**		**132**
	Clay Carroll	**1964**		**132**
11	**Jim Brewer**	**1960**		**130**
12	Jack Aker	1964	1974	123
13	Dick Radatz	1962	1969	122
14	**Rollie Fingers**	**1968**		**119**
15	**Mike Marshall**	**1967**		**119**
16	**Darold Knowles**	**1965**		**118**
17	Frank Linzy	1963	1974	111
18	Al Worthington	1953	1969	110
19	Fred Gladding	1961	1973	109
20	Ron Kline	1952	1970	108
21	Johnny Murphy	1932	1947	107
22	**Wayne Granger**	**1968**		**106**
23	John Wyatt	1961	1969	103
24	Ellis Kinder	1946	1957	102
25	Firpo Marberry	1923	1936	101

Pitchers with 200 or more LOSSES

		First	Last	Losses
1	Cy Young	1890	1911	313
2	Pud Galvin	1879	1892	309
3	Walter Johnson	1907	1927	279
4	Jack Powell	1897	1912	255
5	Eppa Rixey	1912	1933	251
6	Warren Spahn	1942	1965	245
	Robin Roberts	1948	1966	245
8	Early Wynn	1939	1963	244
9	Ted Lyons	1923	1946	230
	Bob Friend	1951	1966	230
11	Gus Weyhing	1887	1901	229
12	Red Ruffing	1924	1947	225
13	Tim Keefe	1880	1893	224
14	Bobo Newsom	1929	1953	222
15	Jack Quinn	1909	1933	219
16	Sad Sam Jones	1914	1935	216
17	Jim McCormick	1878	1887	214
18	Tony Mullane	1881	1894	213
19	Burleigh Grimes	1916	1934	212
	Red Faber	1914	1933	212
	Paul Derringer	1931	1945	212
22	G.C. "Pete" Alexander	1911	1930	208
	Chick Fraser	1896	1909	208
24	Mickey Welch	1880	1892	207
25	Jim Whitney	1881	1890	204
26	Kid Nichols	1890	1906	203
	Vic Willis	1898	1910	203

Pitchers with 600 or more GAMES PITCHED

		First	Last	Games
1	Hoyt Wilhelm	1952	1972	1070
2	Lindy McDaniel	1955	1975	987
3	Cy Young	1890	1911	906
4	Don McMahon	1957	1974	874
5	Roy Face	1953	1969	848
6	Walter Johnson	1907	1927	802
7	Jack Quinn	1909	1933	757
8	Warren Spahn	1942	1965	750
9	Ron Perranoski	1961	1973	737
10	Ron Kline	1952	1970	736
11	Johnny Klippstein	1950	1967	711
12	Stu Miller	1952	1968	704
13	Pud Galvin	1879	1892	697
14	G.C. "Pete" Alexander	1911	1930	696
15	Bob Miller	1957	1974	694
16	Eppa Rixey	1912	1933	692
17	Early Wynn	1939	1963	691
18	Eddie Fisher	1959	1973	690
19	Ted Abernathy	1955	1972	681
20	Robin Roberts	1948	1966	676
21	Waite Hoyt	1918	1938	675
22	Red Faber	1914	1933	669
23	Sad Sam Jones	1914	1935	647
24	**Clay Carroll**	**1964**		**641**
25	Dutch Leonard	1933	1953	640
	Gerry Staley	1947	1961	640
27	Christy Mathewson	1900	1916	634
28	Charlie Root	1923	1941	632
29	Jim Perry	1959	1975	630
30	Lew Burdette	1950	1967	626
31	Murry Dickson	1939	1959	625
32	Red Ruffing	1924	1947	624
33	Eddie Plank	1901	1917	622
34	Kid Nichols	1890	1906	621
35	Herb Pennock	1912	1934	617
36	Lefty Grove	1925	1941	616
37	Burleigh Grimes	1916	1934	615
38	Bob Friend	1951	1966	602
	Al Worthington	1953	1969	602
40	Tim Keefe	1880	1893	600
	Bobo Newsom	1929	1953	600

Pitchers with 500 or more GAMES STARTED

		First	Last	GS
1	Cy Young	1890	1911	816
2	Pud Galvin	1879	1892	682
3	Walter Johnson	1907	1927	666
4	Warren Spahn	1942	1965	665
5	Early Wynn	1939	1963	612
6	Robin Roberts	1948	1966	609
7	G.C. "Pete" Alexander	1911	1930	598
8	Tim Keefe	1880	1893	594
9	Kid Nichols	1890	1906	562
10	Eppa Rixey	1912	1933	552
11	Christy Mathewson	1900	1916	551
12	Mickey Welch	1880	1892	548
13	Red Ruffing	1924	1947	536
14	Eddie Plank	1901	1917	527
15	Jim Bunning	1955	1971	519
16	John Clarkson	1882	1894	518
17	Jack Powell	1897	1912	517
18	Tony Mullane	1881	1894	505
19	Old Hoss Radbourn	1881	1891	503
	Gus Weyhing	1887	1901	503

Pitchers with 300 or more COMPLETE GAMES

		First	Last	CG
1	Cy Young	1890	1911	750
2	Pud Galvin	1879	1892	639
3	Tim Keefe	1880	1893	552
4	Kid Nichols	1890	1906	533
5	Walter Johnson	1907	1927	532
6	Mickey Welch	1880	1892	524
7	Old Hoss Radbourn	1881	1891	489
8	John Clarkson	1882	1894	485
9	Tony Mullane	1881	1894	469
10	Jim McCormick	1878	1887	466
11	Gus Weyhing	1887	1901	448
12	G.C. "Pete" Alexander	1911	1930	439
13	Christy Mathewson	1900	1916	434
14	Jack Powell	1897	1912	424
15	Eddie Plank	1901	1917	410
16	Will White	1877	1886	394
17	Amos Rusie	1889	1901	392
18	Vic Willis	1898	1910	388
19	Warren Spahn	1942	1965	382
20	Jim Whitney	1881	1890	377
21	Adonis Terry	1884	1897	358
22	Ted Lyons	1923	1946	356
23	George Mullin	1902	1915	353
24	Charlie Buffinton	1882	1892	351
25	Chick Fraser	1896	1909	342
25	Clark Griffith	1891	1914	337
27	Red Ruffing	1924	1947	335
28	Silver King	1886	1897	329
29	Al Orth	1895	1909	324
30	Bill Hutchison	1889	1897	319
31	Joe McGinnity	1899	1908	314
	Burleigh Grimes	1916	1934	314
33	Red Donahue	1893	1906	312
34	Guy Hecker	1882	1890	310
35	Bill Dinneen	1898	1909	306
36	Robin Roberts	1948	1966	305
37	Theo Breitenstein	1891	1901	300
	Lefty Grove	1925	1941	300

Pitchers with 4000 or more INNINGS PITCHED

		First	Last	IP
1	Cy Young	1890	1911	7357
2	Pud Galvin	1879	1892	5941
3	Walter Johnson	1907	1927	5926
4	Warren Spahn	1942	1965	5246
5	G.C. "Pete" Alexander	1911	1930	5189
6	Kid Nichols	1890	1906	5061
7	Tim Keefe	1880	1893	5052
8	Mickey Welch	1880	1892	4781
9	Christy Mathewson	1900	1916	4778
10	Robin Roberts	1948	1966	4689
11	Early Wynn	1939	1963	4566
12	Tony Mullane	1881	1894	4545
13	John Clarkson	1882	1894	4537
14	Old Hoss Radbourn	1881	1891	4535
15	Eddie Plank	1901	1917	4507
16	Eppa Rixey	1912	1933	4494
17	Jack Powell	1897	1912	4387
18	Red Ruffing	1924	1947	4342
19	Gus Weyhing	1887	1901	4324
20	Jim McCormick	1878	1887	4275
21	Burleigh Grimes	1916	1934	4177
22	Ted Lyons	1923	1946	4162
23	Red Faber	1914	1933	4087

Pitchers active at the end of the 1975 season are shown in **bold face.**

TEAM LEADERS

(Single Season)

WINNING PERCENTAGE (.700)

1	Chicago	NL 1906	.763
2	Pittsburgh	NL 1902	.741
3	Pittsburgh	NL 1909	.724
4	Cleveland	AL 1954	.721
5	New York	AL 1927	.714
6	Chicago	NL 1907	.704
	Philadelphia	AL 1931	.704
8	New York	AL 1939	.702

WINS (100)

1	Chicago	NL 1906	116
2	Cleveland	AL 1954	111
3	Pittsburgh	NL 1909	110
	New York	AL 1927	110
5	New York	AL 1961	109
	Baltimore	AL 1969	109
7	Baltimore	AL 1970	108
8	Cincinnati	NL 1975	108
9	Chicago	NL 1907	107
	Philadelphia	AL 1931	107
	New York	AL 1932	107
12	New York	NL 1904	106
	New York	AL 1939	106
	St. Louis	NL 1942	106
15	New York	NL 1905	105
	Boston	AL 1912	105
	St. Louis	NL 1943	105
	St. Louis	NL 1944	105
	Brooklyn	NL 1953	105
20	Chicago	NL 1909	104
	Chicago	NL 1910	104
	Philadelphia	AL 1929	104
	Brooklyn	NL 1942	104
	Boston	AL 1946	104
	New York	AL 1963	104
26	Pittsburgh	NL 1902	103
	New York	NL 1912	103
	New York	AL 1942	103
	New York	AL 1954	103
	San Francisco	NL 1962	103
	Detroit	AL 1968	103
32	Philadelphia	AL 1910	102
	Philadelphia	AL 1930	102
	New York	AL 1936	102
	New York	AL 1937	102
	Los Angeles	NL 1962	102
	Minnesota	AL 1965	102
	Cincinnati	NL 1970	102
	Los Angeles	NL 1974	102
40	Philadelphia	AL 1911	101
	New York	NL 1913	101
	Boston	AL 1915	101
	New York	AL 1928	101
	St. Louis	NL 1931	101
	Detroit	AL 1934	101
	New York	AL 1941	101
	Detroit	AL 1961	101
	St. Louis	NL 1967	101
	Baltimore	AL 1971	101
	Oakland	AL 1971	101
51	Detroit	AL 1915	100
	Chicago	AL 1917	100
	Chicago	NL 1935	100
	Cincinnati	NL 1940	100
	Brooklyn	NL 1941	100
	New York	NL 1969	100

LOSSES (105)

1	New York	NL 1962	120
2	Philadelphia	AL 1916	117
3	Boston	NL 1935	115
4	Washington	AL 1904	113
5	Pittsburgh	NL 1952	112
	New York	NL 1965	112
7	Boston	AL 1932	111
	St. Louis	AL 1939	111
	Philadelphia	NL 1941	111
	New York	NL 1963	111
11	Washington	AL 1909	110
	Montreal	NL 1969	110
	San Diego	NL 1969	110
14	Philadelphia	AL 1915	109
	Philadelphia	NL 1928	109
	Philadelphia	NL 1942	109
	New York	NL 1964	109
18	Boston	NL 1909	108
	St. Louis	AL 1937	108
	Philadelphia	NL 1945	108
21	St. Louis	AL 1910	107
	St. Louis	AL 1911	107
	Boston	NL 1911	107
	Baltimore	FL 1915	107
	Boston	AL 1926	107
	Philadelphia	NL 1961	107
27	Philadelphia	AL 1920	106
	Philadelphia	NL 1939	106
	Washington	AL 1963	106
	Chicago	AL 1970	106
31	Boston	AL 1906	105
	St. Louis	NL 1908	105
	Boston	AL 1925	105
	Philadelphia	NL 1938	105
	Philadelphia	AL 1943	105
	Philadelphia	AL 1946	105
	Kansas City	AL 1964	105
	Texas	AL 1973	105

SAVES (41)

1	Cincinnati	NL 1970	60
	Cincinnati	NL 1972	60
3	Minnesota	AL 1970	58
4	Chicago	AL 1965	53
5	Baltimore	AL 1966	51
6	Cincinnati	NL 1975	50
7	California	AL 1970	49
	New York	AL 1970	49
9	Pittsburgh	NL 1971	48
	Pittsburgh	NL 1972	48
11	Los Angeles	AL 1962	47
	Kansas City	AL 1966	47
13	Los Angeles	NL 1962	46
	Baltimore	AL 1967	46
	Detroit	AL 1973	46
16	Chicago	AL 1964	45
	New York	AL 1964	45
	Minnesota	AL 1965	45
	St. Louis	NL 1967	45
20	Boston	AL 1967	44
	Cincinnati	NL 1969	44
	Boston	AL 1970	44
	Kansas City	AL 1971	44
	Pittsburgh	NL 1973	44
	San Francisco	NL 1973	44
	Oakland	AL 1975	44
27	Baltimore	AL 1963	43
	Pittsburgh	NL 1966	43
	Minnesota	AL 1969	43
	Pittsburgh	NL 1970	43
	Oakland	AL 1972	43
	Cincinnati	NL 1973	43
32	New York	AL 1957	42
	New York	AL 1960	42
	New York	AL 1962	42
	San Francisco	NL 1965	42
	Atlanta	NL 1969	42
	Los Angeles	NL 1970	42
	Chicago	AL 1972	42
39	Pittsburgh	NL 1958	41
	Pittsburgh	NL 1962	41
	Baltimore	AL 1964	41
	Los Angeles	AL 1964	41
	Philadelphia	NL 1964	41
	Baltimore	AL 1965	41
	Cleveland	AL 1965	41
	Boston	AL 1969	41
	Washington	AL 1969	41
	New York	NL 1972	41
	Kansas City	AL 1973	41
	Oakland	AL 1973	41

PITCHER'S STRIKEOUTS (1050)

1	Houston	NL 1969	1221
2	Cleveland	AL 1967	1189
3	Cleveland	AL 1964	1162
4	Cleveland	AL 1968	1157
	New York	NL 1971	1157
6	Cleveland	AL 1965	1156
7	Pittsburgh	NL 1969	1124
8	Los Angeles	NL 1960	1122
	Cincinnati	NL 1964	1122
10	Detroit	AL 1968	1115
11	Cincinnati	NL 1965	1113
12	Cleveland	AL 1966	1111
13	Los Angeles	NL 1961	1105
14	Los Angeles	NL 1962	1104
15	Minnesota	AL 1964	1099
16	Los Angeles	NL 1963	1095
17	Boston	AL 1964	1094
18	Minnesota	AL 1967	1089
19	Los Angeles	NL 1966	1084
20	Los Angeles	NL 1965	1079
21	Los Angeles	NL 1959	1077
22	Cleveland	AL 1970	1076
23	Philadelphia	NL 1965	1071
24	Baltimore	AL 1966	1070
25	Detroit	AL 1965	1069
26	Cincinnati	NL 1967	1065
27	Los Angeles	NL 1964	1064
	New York	NL 1970	1064
29	San Francisco	NL 1965	1060
	Houston	NL 1967	1060
31	New York	NL 1972	1059
32	Philadelphia	NL 1963	1052

SHUTOUTS (25)

1	Chicago	AL 1906	32
2	Chicago	NL 1909	31
3	Chicago	NL 1907	30
	St. Louis	NL 1968	30
5	Chicago	NL 1906	28
	Los Angeles	AL 1964	28
	New York	NL 1969	28
8	Cleveland	AL 1906	27
	Philadelphia	AL 1907	27
	Chicago	NL 1908	27
	Philadelphia	AL 1909	27
12	Chicago	AL 1904	26
	Philadelphia	AL 1904	26
	Pittsburgh	NL 1906	26
	Chicago	AL 1909	26
	Boston	AL 1914	26
	St. Louis	NL 1944	26
	Cleveland	AL 1948	26
19	Chicago	NL 1910	25
	Boston	AL 1918	25
	New York	NL 1968	25

EARNED RUN AVERAGE (2.25)

1	Chicago	NL 1907	1.73
2	Chicago	NL 1909	1.75
3	Chicago	NL 1906	1.76
4	Philadelphia	AL 1910	1.78
5	Philadelphia	AL 1909	1.92
6	Chicago	AL 1905	1.99
7	Chicago	AL 1910	2.01
8	Cleveland	AL 1908	2.02
9	Chicago	NL 1905	2.04
	Chicago	AL 1909	2.04
11	Pittsburgh	NL 1909	2.07
12	Cleveland	AL 1906	2.09
13	Philadelphia	NL 1908	2.10
14	Boston	AL 1904	2.12
	Pittsburgh	NL 1908	2.12
	Brooklyn	NL 1916	2.12
17	Chicago	AL 1906	2.13
18	Chicago	NL 1908	2.14
	New York	NL 1908	2.14
	Washington	AL 1918	2.14
21	St. Louis	AL 1908	2.15
22	Chicago	AL 1917	2.16
23	New York	NL 1904	2.17
	Philadelphia	NL 1915	2.17
25	Chicago	NL 1918	2.18
26	Philadelphia	AL 1905	2.19
	Boston	NL 1916	2.19
28	Boston	AL 1917	2.20
29	Chicago	NL 1902	2.21
	Pittsburgh	NL 1906	2.21
	Chicago	NL 1919	2.21
32	Cleveland	AL 1904	2.22
	Chicago	AL 1907	2.22
	Chicago	AL 1908	2.22
35	St. Louis	AL 1906	2.23
	Cincinnati	NL 1919	2.23

RUNS SCORED (900)

1	New York	AL 1931	1067
2	New York	AL 1936	1065
3	New York	AL 1930	1062
4	Boston	AL 1950	1027
5	St. Louis	NL 1930	1004
6	New York	AL 1932	1002
7	Chicago	NL 1930	998
8	Chicago	NL 1929	982
9	Philadelphia	AL 1932	981
10	New York	AL 1937	979
11	New York	AL 1927	975
12	New York	AL 1939	967
13	New York	AL 1938	966
14	New York	NL 1930	959
15	Detroit	AL 1934	958
16	Brooklyn	NL 1953	955
17	Philadelphia	AL 1930	951
18	New York	AL 1921	948
19	Philadelphia	NL 1930	944
20	Detroit	AL 1937	935
21	New York	AL 1933	927
22	Detroit	AL 1929	926
23	Cleveland	AL 1921	925
24	Cleveland	AL 1936	921
	Detroit	AL 1936	921
26	Chicago	AL 1936	920
27	Detroit	AL 1935	919
28	New York	AL 1950	914
29	Pittsburgh	NL 1925	912
30	Boston	AL 1948	907
31	Pittsburgh	NL 1929	904
32	Detroit	AL 1925	903
33	Boston	AL 1938	902
34	Philadelphia	AL 1929	901

HITS (1640)

1	Philadelphia	NL 1930	1783
2	New York	NL 1930	1769
3	St. Louis	NL 1930	1732
4	Detroit	AL 1921	1724
5	Chicago	NL 1930	1722
6	Cleveland	AL 1936	1715
7	Pittsburgh	NL 1922	1698
8	St. Louis	AL 1922	1693
	Philadelphia	NL 1929	1693
10	New York	AL 1930	1683
11	New York	AL 1936	1676
12	Detroit	AL 1929	1671
13	New York	AL 1931	1667
14	Boston	AL 1950	1665
15	Pittsburgh	NL 1929	1663
16	New York	NL 1922	1661
17	Philadelphia	AL 1925	1659
	Pittsburgh	NL 1928	1659
19	Cleveland	AL 1921	1656
20	St. Louis	AL 1921	1655
	Chicago	NL 1929	1655
22	Cleveland	AL 1930	1654
	Brooklyn	NL 1930	1654
24	St. Louis	AL 1920	1651
	Pittsburgh	NL 1925	1651
26	Pittsburgh	NL 1927	1648
27	New York	AL 1927	1644
	Detroit	AL 1934	1644
29	Detroit	AL 1922	1641

DOUBLES (310)

1	St. Louis	NL 1930	373
2	Cleveland	AL 1930	358
3	Cleveland	AL 1936	357
4	Cleveland	AL 1921	355
5	St. Louis	NL 1931	353
6	Detroit	AL 1934	349
7	Philadelphia	NL 1930	345
8	Chicago	NL 1931	340
	Cleveland	AL 1934	340
10	Detroit	AL 1929	339
11	Cleveland	AL 1926	333
12	St. Louis	NL 1936	332
	St. Louis	NL 1939	332
14	Philadelphia	NL 1932	330
15	St. Louis	AL 1937	327
16	Detroit	AL 1936	326
17	Cleveland	AL 1935	324
18	Philadelphia	AL 1928	323
19	Cleveland	AL 1927	321
	Cleveland	AL 1931	321
21	Cleveland	AL 1922	320
22	Philadelphia	AL 1930	319
23	Pittsburgh	NL 1925	316
24	Detroit	AL 1924	315
	New York	AL 1936	315
26	Chicago	AL 1926	314
27	Detroit	AL 1940	312
28	Philadelphia	AL 1931	311
29	Chicago	NL 1929	310
	St. Louis	NL 1929	310
	Cleveland	AL 1932	310

TRIPLES (100)

1	Pittsburgh	NL 1912	129
2	Pittsburgh	NL 1924	122
3	Cincinnati	NL 1926	120
4	Pittsburgh	NL 1930	119
5	Pittsburgh	NL 1929	116
6	Boston	AL 1903	113
7	Baltimore	AL 1901	111
	Pittsburgh	NL 1923	111
	Cincinnati	NL 1924	111
10	Pittsburgh	NL 1903	110
	Pittsburgh	NL 1922	110
	New York	AL 1930	110
13	Philadelphia	AL 1912	108
14	Baltimore	AL 1902	107
15	Philadelphia	AL 1910	106
	Pittsburgh	NL 1911	106
	St. Louis	AL 1921	106
	Pittsburgh	NL 1926	106
19	Boston	AL 1904	105
	Cincinnati	NL 1911	105
	Pittsburgh	NL 1925	105
22	Boston	AL 1901	104
	Pittsburgh	NL 1921	104
24	New York	NL 1911	103
	New York	AL 1927	103
26	Pittsburgh	NL 1904	102
	Chicago	AL 1915	102
28	Cincinnati	NL 1905	101
	Chicago	NL 1911	101
	Boston	AL 1913	101
	Detroit	AL 1913	101
32	Chicago	AL 1916	100
	Cincinnati	NL 1917	100
	Detroit	AL 1921	100
	Boston	NL 1921	100
	Detroit	AL 1927	100
	Pittsburgh	NL 1928	100
	Washington	AL 1932	100

HOME RUNS (185)

1	New York	AL 1961	240
2	Minnesota	AL 1963	225
3	New York	NL 1947	221
	Cincinnati	NL 1956	221
	Minnesota	AL 1964	221
6	Detroit	AL 1962	209
7	Brooklyn	NL 1953	208
8	Atlanta	NL 1966	207
9	Atlanta	NL 1973	206
10	San Francisco	NL 1962	204
11	Boston	AL 1970	203
12	Brooklyn	NL 1955	201
13	Milwaukee	NL 1957	199
	New York	AL 1962	199
15	San Francisco	NL 1963	197
	Boston	AL 1969	197
17	Milwaukee	NL 1965	196
18	Brooklyn	NL 1950	194
19	New York	AL 1960	193
20	Cincinnati	NL 1970	191
21	New York	AL 1956	190
22	Los Angeles	AL 1961	189
23	Milwaukee	NL 1961	188
	New York	AL 1963	188
26	Cincinnati	NL 1957	187
26	Brooklyn	NL 1954	186
	New York	NL 1954	186
	Boston	AL 1964	186
29	Minnesota	AL 1962	185
	Detroit	AL 1968	185

BATTER'S BASES ON BALLS (700)

1	Boston	AL 1949	835
2	Boston	AL 1948	823
3	Philadelphia	AL 1949	783
4	St. Louis	AL 1941	775
5	New York	AL 1932	766
6	Detroit	AL 1947	762
7	Boston	AL 1951	756
8	Detroit	AL 1949	751
9	New York	AL 1938	749
10	New York	AL 1931	748
11	Brooklyn	NL 1947	732
12	New York	AL 1949	731
13	San Francisco	NL 1970	729
14	Boston	AL 1957	727
15	Cleveland	AL 1955	723
16	Detroit	AL 1950	722
17	Boston	AL 1950	719
18	Baltimore	AL 1970	717
19	San Francisco	NL 1969	711
20	New York	AL 1937	709
21	Boston	AL 1955	707
22	Chicago	AL 1949	702
23	New York	AL 1939	701
24	New York	AL 1933	700
	New York	AL 1934	700
	New York	AL 1936	700

BATTER'S STRIKEOUTS (1000)

1	New York	NL 1968	1203
2	San Diego	NL 1970	1164
3	San Diego	NL 1969	1143
4	Philadelphia	NL 1969	1130
5	New York	NL 1965	1129
6	Washington	AL 1965	1125
7	Washington	AL 1964	1124
8	Kansas City	AL 1964	1104
9	Cleveland	AL 1963	1102
10	Philadelphia	NL 1965	1091
11	New York	NL 1969	1089
12	California	AL 1968	1080
13	New York	NL 1963	1078
14	Washington	AL 1966	1069
15	Los Angeles	AL 1961	1068
16	Philadelphia	NL 1970	1066
17	Cleveland	AL 1964	1063
18	California	AL 1966	1062
	New York	NL 1970	1062
20	Pittsburgh	NL 1960	1054
	San Francisco	NL 1969	1054
22	Chicago	NL 1963	1049
23	Chicago	NL 1962	1044
24	New York	AL 1967	1043
25	Cincinnati	NL 1969	1042
	San Francisco	NL 1971	1042
27	Chicago	NL 1964	1041
28	Washington	AL 1967	1037
29	Philadelphia	NL 1967	1033
30	Philadelphia	NL 1971	1031
31	Chicago	NL 1961	1027
32	Oakland	AL 1968	1022
33	California	AL 1967	1021
34	Kansas City	AL 1966	1020
	Boston	AL 1966	1020
	Boston	AL 1967	1020
37	Baltimore	AL 1964	1019
	Minnesota	AL 1964	1019
	Kansas City	AL 1967	1019
	Baltimore	AL 1968	1019
41	Oakland	AL 1971	1018
42	Seattle	AL 1969	1015
43	Pittsburgh	NL 1966	1011
44	Pittsburgh	NL 1965	1008
45	San Francisco	NL 1970	1005
46	Cincinnati	NL 1965	1003
	Philadelphia	NL 1968	1003

STOLEN BASES (250)

1	New York	NL 1911	347
2	New York	NL 1912	319
3	Cincinnati	NL 1910	310
4	New York	NL 1913	296
5	New York	NL 1905	291
6	Cincinnati	NL 1911	289
7	New York	NL 1906	288
	New York	AL 1910	288
9	Washington	AL 1913	287
10	New York	NL 1904	283
	Chicago	NL 1906	283
12	New York	NL 1910	282
13	Chicago	AL 1901	280
	Detroit	AL 1909	280
	Cincinnati	NL 1909	280
16	Detroit	AL 1911	276
17	Washington	AL 1912	274
18	Brooklyn	NL 1903	273
	Indianapolis	FL 1914	273
20	New York	AL 1911	270
	Detroit	AL 1912	270
22	Chicago	NL 1905	267
23	Chicago	AL 1902	265
24	New York	NL 1903	264
	Pittsburgh	NL 1907	264
26	Chicago	NL 1903	259
27	Philadelphia	AL 1912	258
28	New York	AL 1914	251

BATTING AVERAGE (.300)

1	New York	NL 1930	.319
2	Detroit	AL 1921	.316
3	Philadelphia	NL 1930	.315
4	St. Louis	NL 1930	.314
5	St. Louis	AL 1922	.313
6	Pittsburgh	NL 1928	.309
	Philadelphia	NL 1929	.309
	Chicago	NL 1930	.309
	New York	AL 1930	.309
10	St. Louis	AL 1920	.308
	Cleveland	AL 1921	.308
	St. Louis	NL 1921	.308
	Pittsburgh	NL 1922	.308
14	Philadelphia	AL 1925	.307
	Pittsburgh	NL 1925	.307
	New York	AL 1927	.307
17	Detroit	AL 1922	.305
	Pittsburgh	NL 1927	.305
19	St. Louis	AL 1921	.304
	New York	NL 1922	.304
	Brooklyn	NL 1930	.304
	Cleveland	AL 1930	.304
	Cleveland	AL 1936	.304
24	Cleveland	AL 1920	.303
	Washington	AL 1925	.303
	Philadelphia	AL 1927	.303
	Chicago	NL 1929	.303
	Pittsburgh	NL 1929	.303
	Pittsburgh	NL 1930	.303
30	Detroit	AL 1925	.302
	Washington	AL 1930	.302
	Boston	AL 1950	.302
33	St. Louis	NL 1922	.301
	Cleveland	AL 1923	.301
35	New York	AL 1921	.300
	Detroit	AL 1923	.300
	New York	NL 1924	.300
	Detroit	AL 1934	.300
	Detroit	AL 1936	.300
	New York	AL 1936	.300

SLUGGING AVERAGE (.435)

1	New York	AL 1927	.489
2	New York	AL 1930	.488
3	New York	AL 1936	.483
4	Chicago	NL 1930	.481
5	Brooklyn	NL 1953	.474
6	New York	NL 1930	.473
7	St. Louis	NL 1930	.471
8	Philadelphia	NL 1929	.467
9	New York	AL 1921	.464
	Boston	AL 1950	.464
11	Cleveland	AL 1936	.461
12	Philadelphia	NL 1930	.458
13	New York	AL 1931	.457
	Philadelphia	AL 1932	.457
15	New York	AL 1937	.456
16	St. Louis	AL 1922	.455
17	Brooklyn	NL 1930	.454
	New York	AL 1932	.454
	New York	NL 1947	.454
20	Detroit	AL 1929	.453
21	Chicago	NL 1929	.452
	Philadelphia	AL 1930	.452
	Detroit	AL 1937	.452
24	Philadelphia	AL 1929	.451
	New York	AL 1939	.451
26	New York	AL 1928	.450
	New York	AL 1929	.450
28	Pittsburgh	NL 1930	.449
	Boston	AL 1940	.449
30	Pittsburgh	NL 1925	.448
	Brooklyn	NL 1955	.448
32	New York	AL 1938	.446
33	St. Louis	NL 1925	.445
34	St. Louis	NL 1922	.444
	Brooklyn	NL 1950	.444
	Brooklyn	NL 1954	.444
37	Philadelphia	NL 1932	.442
	Detroit	AL 1940	.442
	Milwaukee	NL 1957	.442
40	New York	AL 1950	.441
	Cincinnati	NL 1956	.441
	New York	AL 1961	.441
	San Francisco	NL 1962	.441
44	New York	AL 1933	.440
	Philadelphia	NL 1933	.440
46	St. Louis	AL 1925	.439
	Cincinnati	NL 1965	.439
48	St. Louis	NL 1929	.438
49	St. Louis	NL 1921	.437
50	New York	AL 1926	.437
51	Philadelphia	AL 1928	.436
	New York	NL 1929	.436
	Boston	AL 1939	.436
	Cincinnati	NL 1970	.436
55	Philadelphia	AL 1931	.435
	Detroit	AL 1935	.435

WORLD SERIES LEADERS

BATTING AVERAGE

(Lifetime) (Minimum 50 At Bats)

1	Pepper Martin	.418
2	Lou Brock	.391
3	Hank Aaron	.364
4	Frank Baker	.363
5	R. Clemente	.362
6	Lou Gehrig	.361
7	C. Yastrzemski	.352
8	Earle Combs	.350
9	Stan Hack	.348
10	Joe Jackson	.345

(Individual) (Minimum 2.5 At Bats Per Game)

4g	.625	Babe Ruth-NYA	1928
5g	.500	Larry McLean-NYN	1913
	.500	Joe Gordon-NYA	1941
6g	.500	Dave Robertson-NYN	1917
	.500	Billy Martin-NYA	1953
7g	.500	Pepper Martin-StLN	1931
	.500	Johnny Lindell-NYA	1947
8g	.400	Buck Herzog-NYN	1912

(Team)

4g	.313	New York-A.L.	1932
5g	.316	Philadelphia-A.L.	1910
6g	.302	New York-A.L.	1936
7g	.338	New York-A.L.	1960
8g	.270	New York-N.L.	1912

SLUGGING AVERAGE

(Lifetime) (Minimum 50 At Bats)

1	Babe Ruth	.744
2	Lou Gehrig	.731
3	Al Simmons	.658
4	Lou Brock	.655
5	Pepper Martin	.636
6	Hank Greenberg	.624
7	Charlie Keller	.611
8	Jimmie Foxx	.609
9	Hank Aaron	.600
10	Duke Snider	.594

(Individual) (Minimum 2.5 At Bats Per Game)

4g	1.727	Lou Gehrig-NYA	1928
5g	.929	Joe Gordon-NYA	1941
6g	1.000	Babe Ruth-NYA	1923
7g	.913	Gene Tenace-OakA	1972
8g	.600	Buck Herzog-NYN	1912

(Team)

4g	.530	New York-A.L.	1928
5g	.509	Baltimore-A.L.	1970
6g	.484	New York-A.L.	1953
7g	.528	New York-A.L.	1960
8g	.401	Boston-A.L.	1903

HITS

(Lifetime)

1	Yogi Berra	71
2	Mickey Mantle	59
3	Frankie Frisch	58
4	Joe DiMaggio	54
5	Hank Bauer	46
	Pee Wee Reese	46
7	Gil McDougald	45
	Phil Rizzuto	45
9	Lou Gehrig	43
10	Eddie Collins	42
	Elston Howard	42
	Babe Ruth	42

(Individual)

4g	10	Babe Ruth-NYA	1928
5g	9	Eddie Collins-PhiA	1910
	9	Frank Baker-PhiA	1910
	9	Frank Baker-PhiA	1913
	9	Heinie Groh-NYN	1922
	9	Jo-Jo Moore-NYN	1937
	9	Bobby Richardson-NYA	1961
	9	Paul Blair-BalA	1970
	9	Brooks Robinson-BalA	1970
6g	12	Billy Martin-NYA	1953
7g	13	Bobby Richardson-NYA	1964
	13	Lou Brock-StLN	1968
8g	12	Buck Herzog-NYN	1912
	12	Joe Jackson-ChiA	1919

(Team)

4g	45	New York-A.L.	1932
5g	56	Philadelphia-A.L.	1910
6g	65	New York-A.L.	1936
7g	91	New York-A.L.	1960
8g	74	New York-N.L.	1912

RUNS

(Lifetime)

1	Mickey Mantle	42
2	Yogi Berra	41
3	Babe Ruth	37
4	Lou Gehrig	30
5	Joe DiMaggio	27
6	Roger Maris	26
7	Elston Howard	25
8	Gil McDougald	23
9	Jackie Robinson	22
10	Hank Bauer	21
	Phil Rizzuto	21
	Duke Snider	21
	Gene Woodling	21

(Individual)

4g	9	Babe Ruth-NYA	1928
	9	Lou Gehrig-NYA	1932
5g	6	Frank Baker-PhiA	1910
	6	Danny Murphy-PhiA	1910
	6	Harry Hooper-BosA	1916
	6	Al Simmons-PhiA	1929
	6	Lee May-CinN	1970
	6	Boog Powell-BalA	1970
6g	8	Babe Ruth-NYA	1923
	8	Jack Powell-NYA	1936
7g	8	Tommy Leach-PitN	1909
	8	Pepper Martin-StLN	1934
	8	Billy Johnson-NYA	1947
	8	Bobby Richardson-NYA	1960
	8	Mickey Mantle-NYA	1960
	8	Mickey Mantle-NYA	1964
	8	Lou Brock-StLN	1967
8g	8	Freddy Parent-BosA	1903

(Team)

4g	37	New York-A.L.	1932
5g	35	Philadelphia-A.L.	1910
6g	43	New York-A.L.	1936
7g	55	New York-A.L.	1960
8g	39	Boston-A.L.	1903

HOME RUNS

(Lifetime)

1	Mickey Mantle	18
2	Babe Ruth	15
3	Yogi Berra	12
4	Duke Snider	11
5	Lou Gehrig	10
6	Joe DiMaggio	8
	Frank Robinson	8
	Bill Skowron	8
9	Hank Bauer	7
	Goose Goslin	7
	Gil McDougald	7

(Individual)

4g	4	Lou Gehrig-NYA	1928
5g	3	Donn Clendenon-NYN	1969
6g	3	Babe Ruth-NYA	1923
	3	Ted Kluszewski-ChiA	1959
7g	4	Babe Ruth-NYA	1926
	4	Duke Snider-BknN	1952
	4	Duke Snider-BknN	1955
	4	Hank Bauer-NYA	1958
	4	Gene Tenace-OakA	1972
8g	2	Patsy Dougherty-BosA	1903

(Team)

4g	9	New York-A.L.	1928
5g	10	Baltimore-A.L.	1970
6g	9	New York-A.L.	1953
7g	12	New York-A.L.	1956
8g	2	Boston-A.L.	1903
	2	New York-A.L.	1921
	2	New York-N.L.	1921

RUNS BATTED IN

(Lifetime)

1	Mickey Mantle	40
2	Yogi Berra	39
3	Lou Gehrig	35
4	Babe Ruth	33
5	Joe DiMaggio	30
6	Bill Skowron	29
7	Duke Snider	26
8	Hank Bauer	24
	Bill Dickey	24
	Gil McDougald	24

(Individual)

4g	9	Lou Gehrig-NYA	1928
5g	9	Danny Murphy-PhiA	1910
6g	10	Ted Kluszewski-ChiA	1959
7g	12	Bobby Richardson-NYA	1960
8g	8	Pat Duncan-CinN	1919

(Team)

4g	36	New York-A.L.	1932
5g	32	Baltimore-A.L.	1970
6g	41	New York-A.L.	1936
7g	54	New York-A.L.	1960
8g	34	Boston-A.L.	1912

DOUBLES

(Lifetime)

1	Yogi Berra	10
	Frankie Frisch	10
3	Jack Barry	9
	Pete Fox	9
	Carl Furillo	9
6	Lou Gehrig	8
	Duke Snider	8
8	11 tied with	7

(Individual)

4g	3	Hank Gowdy-BosN	1914
	3	Babe Ruth-NYA	1928
5g	4	Eddie Collins-PhiA	1910
6g	5	Chick Hafey-StLN	1930
7g	6	Pete Fox-DetA	1934
8g	4	Buck Herzog-NYN	1912
	4	Red Murray-NYN	1912
	4	Buck Weaver-ChiA	1919
	4	George Burns-NYN	1921

(Team)

4g	9	Philadelphia-A.L.	1914
5g	19	Philadelphia-A.L.	1910
6g	15	Philadelphia-A.L.	1911
7g	19	St. Louis-N.L.	1946
8g	14	Boston-A.L.	1912
	14	New York-N.L.	1912

TRIPLES

(Lifetime)

1	Billy Johnson	4
	Tommy Leach	4
	Tris Speaker	4
4	Hank Bauer	3
	Bobby Brown	3
	Buck Freeman	3
	Frankie Frisch	3
	Lou Gehrig	3
	Billy Martin	3
	Tim McCarver	3
	Bob Meusel	3
	Freddy Parent	3
	Chick Stahl	3

(Individual)

4g	2	Lou Gehrig-NYA	1927
	2	Tommy Davis-LAN	1963
5g	2	Eddie Collins-PhiA	1913
	2	Bobby Brown-NYA	1949
6g	2	George Rohe-ChiA	1906
	2	Bob Meusel-NYA	1923
	2	Billy Martin-NYA	1953
7g	3	Billy Johnson-NYA	1947
8g	4	Tommy Leach-PitN	1903

(Team)

4g	2	Boston-N.L.	1914
	2	New York-A.L.	1927
	2	Chicago-N.L.	1932
	2	Los Angeles-N.L.	1963
5g	6	Boston-A.L.	1916
6g	4	New York-N.L.	1917
	4	New York-A.L.	1923
	4	New York-A.L.	1953
7g	5	St. Louis-N.L.	1934
	5	New York-A.L.	1947
8g	16	Boston-A.L.	1903

AT BATS

(Lifetime)

1	Yogi Berra	259
2	Mickey Mantle	230
3	Joe DiMaggio	199
4	Frankie Frisch	197
5	Gil McDougald	190
6	Hank Bauer	188
7	Phil Rizzuto	183
8	Elston Howard	171
9	Pee Wee Reese	169
10	Roger Maris	152

(Individual)

4g	19	Mark Koenig-NYA	1928
5g	23	Hal Janvrin-BosA	1916
	23	Jo-Jo Moore-NYN	1937
	23	Bobby Richardson-NYA	1961
6g	28	Jo-Jo Moore-NYN	1936
7g	33	Bucky Harris-WasA	1924
	33	Sam Rice-WasA	1925
8g	36	Jimmy Collins-BosA	1903

(Team)

4g	146	Chicago-N.L.	1932
5g	178	New York-A.L.	1942
6g	215	New York-A.L.	1936
7g	269	New York-A.L.	1960
8g	282	Boston-A.L.	1903

STOLEN BASES

(Lifetime)

1	Lou Brock	14
	Eddie Collins	14
3	Frank Chance	10
	Phil Rizzuto	10
5	Frankie Frisch	9
	Honus Wagner	9
7	Johnny Evers	8
8	Pepper Martin	7
	Joe Tinker	7
10	4 tied with	6

(Individual)

4g	2	Charlie Deal-BosN	1914
	2	Rabbit Maranville-BosN	1914
	2	Tony Lazzeri-NYA	1928
	2	Bob Meusel-NYA	1928
	2	Frankie Frisch-StLN	1928
	2	Billy Jurges-ChiN	1932
5g	6	Jimmy Slagle-ChiN	1907
6g	3	Joe Tinker-ChiN	1903
	3	Eddie Collins-ChiA	1917
7g	7	Lou Brock-StLN	1967
	7	Lou Brock-StLN	1968
8g	4	Josh Devore-NYN	1912

(Team)

4g	9	Boston-N.L.	1914
5g	16	Chicago-N.L.	1907
6g	9	Chicago-N.L.	1906
7g	18	Pittsburgh-N.L.	1909
8g	12	New York-N.L.	1912

BASES ON BALLS

(Lifetime)

1	Mickey Mantle	43
2	Babe Ruth	33
3	Yogi Berra	32
4	Phil Rizzuto	30
5	Lou Gehrig	26
6	Mickey Cochrane	25
7	Jim Gilliam	23
8	Jackie Robinson	21
9	Gil McDougald	20
10	Joe DiMaggio	19
	Gene Woodling	19

(Individual)

4g	7	Hank Thompson-NYN	1954
5g	7	Jimmy Sheckard-ChiN	1910
	7	Mickey Cochrane-PhiA	1929
	7	Joe Gordon-NYA	1941
6g	8	Babe Ruth-NYA	1923
7g	11	Babe Ruth-NYA	1926
	11	Gene Tenace-OakA	1973
8g	7	Josh Devore-NYN	1912
	7	Ross Youngs-NYN	1921

(Team)

4g	23	New York-A.L.	1932
5g	24	New York-A.L.	1961
6g	26	New York-A.L.	1936
	26	New York-A.L.	1951
7g	38	New York-A.L.	1947
8g	27	New York-A.L.	1921

STRIKEOUTS

(Lifetime)

1	Mickey Mantle	54
2	Elston Howard	37
3	Duke Snider	33
4	Babe Ruth	30
5	Gil McDougald	29
6	Bill Skowron	26
7	Hank Bauer	25
8	Bob Meusel	24
9	Joe DiMaggio	23
	George Kelly	23
	Tony Kubek	23
	Frank Robinson	23

(Individual)

4g	7	Bob Meusel-NYA	1927
5g	8	Rogers Hornsby-ChiN	1929
	8	Duke Snider-BknN	1949
6g	9	Billy Sullivan-ChiA	1906
	9	Jim Bottomley-StLN	1930
7g	11	Eddie Mathews-MilN	1958
	11	Wayne Garrett-NYN	1973
8g	10	George Kelly-NYN	1921

(Team)

4g	37	New York-A.L.	1963
5g	50	Chicago-N.L.	1929
6g	49	St. Louis-A.L.	1944
7g	62	Oakland-A.L.	1973
8g	45	Pittsburgh-N.L.	1903

WORLD SERIES LEADERS

WINS

(Lifetime)

1	Whitey Ford	10
2	Bob Gibson	7
	Allie Reynolds	7
	Red Ruffing	7
5	Chief Bender	6
	Lefty Gomez	6
	Waite Hoyt	6
8	Three Finger Brown	5
	Jack Coombs	5
	Christy Mathewson	5
	Herb Pennock	5
	Vic Raschi	5

(Individual)

4g	2	Bill James–BosN	1914
	2	Dick Rudolph–BosN	1914
	2	Waite Hoyt–NYA	1928
	2	Red Ruffing–NYA	1938
	2	Sandy Koufax–LAN	1963
5g	3	Christy Mathewson–NYN	1905
	3	Jack Coombs–PhiA	1910
6g	3	Red Faber–ChiA	1917
7g	3	Babe Adams–PitN	1909
	3	Stan Coveleski–CleA	1920
	3	Harry Brecheen–StLN	1946
	3	Lew Burdette–MilN	1957
	3	Bob Gibson–StLN	1967
	3	Mickey Lolich–DetA	1968
8g	3	Bill Dinneen–BosA	1903
	3	Deacon Phillippe–PitN	1903
	3	Smokey Joe Wood–BosA	1912

STRIKEOUTS

(Lifetime)

1	Whitey Ford	94
2	Bob Gibson	92
3	Allie Reynolds	62
4	Sandy Koufax	61
	Red Ruffing	61
6	Chief Bender	59
7	George Earnshaw	56
8	Waite Hoyt	49
9	Christy Mathewson	48
10	Bob Turley	46

(Individual)

4g	23	Sandy Koufax–LAN	1963
5g	18	Christy Mathewson–NYN	1905
6g	20	Chief Bender–PhiA	1911
7g	35	Bob Gibson–StLN	1968
8g	28	Bill Dinneen–BosA	1903

(Team)

4g	37	Los Angeles–N.L.	1963
5g	50	Philadelphia–A.L.	1929
6g	49	St. Louis–N.L.	1944
7g	62	New York–N.L.	1973
8g	45	Boston–A.L.	1903

GAMES PITCHED

(Lifetime)

1	Whitey Ford	22
2	Rollie Fingers	16
3	Allie Reynolds	15
	Bob Turley	15
5	Clay Carroll	14
6	Clem Labine	13
7	Waite Hoyt	12
	Art Nehf	12
9	5 tied with	11

(Individual)

4g	3	Larry French–ChiN	1938
	3	Jim Konstanty–PhiN	1950
	3	Don Mossi–CleA	1954
	3	Hal Reniff–NYA	1963
5g	5	Mike Marshall–LAN	1974
6g	4	Red Faber–ChiA	1917
	4	Larry Sherry–LAN	1959
	4	Gerry Staley–ChiA	1959
7g	7	Darold Knowles–OakA	1973
8g	5	Deacon Phillippe–PitN	1903

MOST BASES ON BALLS ALLOWED

(Lifetime)

1	Whitey Ford	34
2	Art Nehf	32
	Allie Reynolds	32
4	Bob Turley	29
5	Paul Derringer	27
	Red Ruffing	27
7	Burleigh Grimes	26
8	Jim Palmer	25
	Vic Raschi	25
10	Carl Erskine	24

(Individual)

4g	8	Bob Lemon–CleA	1954
5g	14	Jack Coombs–PhiA	1910
6g	11	Lefty Tyler–ChiN	1918
	11	Lefty Gomez–NYA	1936
	11	Allie Reynolds–NYA	1951
7g	11	Walter Johnson–WasA	1924
	11	Bill Bevens–NYA	1947
8g	13	Art Nehf–NYN	1921

(Team)

4g	23	Chicago–N.L.	1932
5g	24	Cincinnati–N.L.	1961
6g	26	New York–N.L.	1936
	26	New York–N.L.	1951
7g	38	Brooklyn–N.L.	1947
8g	27	New York–N.L.	1921

COMPLETE GAMES

(Lifetime)

1	Christy Mathewson	10
2	Chief Bender	9
3	Bob Gibson	8
4	Whitey Ford	7
	Red Ruffing	7
6	Waite Hoyt	6
	George Mullin	6
	Art Nehf	6
	Eddie Plank	6
10	Three Finger Brown	5
	George Earnshaw	5
	Walter Johnson	5
	Carl Mays	5
	Deacon Phillippe	5
	Allie Reynolds	5

(Individual)

4g	2	Dick Rudolph–BosN	1914
	2	Waite Hoyt–NYA	1928
	2	Red Ruffing–NYA	1938
	2	Sandy Koufax–LAN	1963
5g	3	Christy Mathewson–NYN	1905
	3	Jack Coombs–PhiA	1910
6g	3	Chief Bender–PhiA	1911
	3	Hippo Vaughn–ChiN	1918
7g	3	Babe Adams–PitN	1909
	3	George Mullin–DetA	1909
	3	Stan Coveleski–CleA	1920
	3	Walter Johnson–WasA	1925
	3	Bobo Newsom–DetA	1940
	3	Lew Burdette–MilN	1957
	3	Bob Gibson–StLN	1967
	3	Bob Gibson–StLN	1968
	3	Mickey Lolich–DetA	1968
8g	5	Deacon Phillippe–PitN	1903

SAVES

(Lifetime)

1	Rollie Fingers	6
2	Johnny Murphy	4
	Allie Reynolds	4
4	Roy Face	3
	Firpo Marberry	3
	Herb Pennock	3
7	Lefty Grove	2
	Dick Hall	2
	Darold Knowles	2
	Bob Kuzava	2
	Clem Labine	2
	Joe Page	2
	Larry Sherry	2
	Ron Taylor	2

(Individual)

4g	2	Herb Pennock–NYA	1932
5g	2	Lefty Grove–PhiA	1929
	2	Rollie Fingers–OakA	1974
6g	2	Larry Sherry–LAN	1959
7g	3	Roy Face–PitN	1960
8g	0		

(Team)

4g	2	New York–N.L.	1932
	2	New York–N.L.	1954
5g	3	Oakland–A.L.	1974
6g	2	New York–A.L.	1923
	2	New York–A.L.	1936
	2	Chicago–A.L.	1959
	2	Los Angeles–N.L.	1959
7g	4	Oakland–A.L.	1973
8g	0		

INNINGS PITCHED

(Lifetime)

1	Whitey Ford	146
2	Christy Mathewson	102
3	Red Ruffing	86
4	Chief Bender	85
5	Waite Hoyt	84
6	Bob Gibson	81
7	Art Nehf	79
8	Allie Reynolds	77
9	George Earnshaw	63
10	Bullet Joe Bush	61

(Individual)

4g	18	Dick Rudolph–BosN	1914
	18	Waite Hoyt–NYA	1928
	18	Red Ruffing–NYA	1938
	18	Sandy Koufax–LAN	1963
5g	27	Christy Mathewson–NYN	1905
	27	Jack Coombs–PhiA	1910
6g	27	Christy Mathewson–NYN	1911
	27	Red Faber–ChiA	1917
	27	Hippo Vaughn–ChiN	1918
7g	32	George Mullin–DetA	1909
8g	44	Deacon Phillippe–PitN	1903

SHUTOUTS

(Lifetime)

1	Christy Mathewson	4
2	Three Finger Brown	3
	Whitey Ford	3
4	Lew Burdette	2
	Bill Dinneen	2
	Bob Gibson	2
	Wild Bill Hallahan	2
	Sandy Koufax	2
	Art Nehf	2
	Allie Reynolds	2

(Individual)

4g	1	accomplished 7 times	
5g	2	Christy Mathewson–NYN	1905
6g	1	accomplished 12 times	
7g	2	Lew Burdette–MilN	1957
	2	Whitey Ford–NYA	1960
	2	Sandy Koufax–LAN	1965
8g	2	Bill Dinneen–BosA	1903

(Team)

4g	3	Baltimore–A.L.	1966
5g	4	New York–N.L.	1905
6g	2	New York–N.L.	1917
	2	Chicago–A.L.	1959
7g	3	Los Angeles–N.L.	1965
8g	2	Boston–A.L.	1903
	2	Cincinnati–N.L.	1919
	2	New York–A.L.	1921

GAMES STARTED

(Lifetime)

1	Whitey Ford	22
2	Waite Hoyt	11
	Christy Mathewson	11
4	Chief Bender	10
	Red Ruffing	10
6	Bob Gibson	9
	Art Nehf	9
	Allie Reynolds	9

BATTER'S GAMES

(Lifetime)

1	Yogi Berra	75
2	Mickey Mantle	65
3	Elston Howard	54
4	Hank Bauer	53
	Gil McDougald	53
6	Phil Rizzuto	52
7	Joe DiMaggio	51
8	Frankie Frisch	50
9	Pee Wee Reese	44
10	Roger Maris	41
	Babe Ruth	41

LOSSES

(Lifetime)

1	Whitey Ford	8
2	Bullet Joe Bush	5
	Rube Marquard	5
	Christy Mathewson	5
	Eddie Plank	5
	Schoolboy Rowe	5
7	11 tied with	4

(Individual)

8g	3	Lefty Williams	1919

A pitcher has lost 2 games in one World Series 61 times.

FEWEST HITS ALLOWED

(Team)

4g	17	Baltimore–A.L.	1966
5g	23	New York–N.L.	1969
6g	32	Chicago–N.L.	1918
7g	42	New York–A.L.	1956
	42	Los Angeles–N.L.	1965
8g	50	New York–N.L.	1921

FEWEST BASES ON BALLS ALLOWED

(Team)

4g	4	New York–N.L.	1927
5g	5	New York–N.L.	1905
6g	4	New York–N.L.	1911
7g	9	Philadelphia–A.L.	1931
8g	13	Pittsburgh–N.L.	1903

EARNED RUN AVERAGE

(Lifetime)

(Minimum 25 Innings Pitched)

1	Harry Brecheen	0.83
2	Babe Ruth	0.87
3	Sherry Smith	0.89
4	Sandy Koufax	0.95
5	Hippo Vaughn	1.00
6	Monte Pearson	1.01
7	Christy Mathewson	1.06
8	Babe Adams	1.29
9	Eddie Plank	1.32
10	Rollie Fingers	1.35

(Team)

4g	0.50	Baltimore–A.L.	1966
5g	0.00	New York–N.L.	1905
6g	1.04	Chicago–N.L.	1918
7g	0.88	Cleveland–A.L.	1920
8g	1.62	Cincinnati–N.L.	1919

NO-HITTERS SINCE 1901

Year	Date	H/A		Pitcher	Score
1901	May 9	H		Earl Moore(Cle) vs. Chi(AL), no-hitter for 9 innings. Lost in 10th on 2 hits.	2-4
	July 15	A		Christy Mathewson(NY) vs. St.L(NL)	5-0
1902	Sept. 20	H (1st Game)		Jim Callahan(Chi) vs. Det(AL)	3-0
1903	Sept. 14	A (2nd Game)		Red Ames(NY) vs. St.L.(NL) 5 innings	5-0
	Sept. 18	A (2nd Game)		Chick Fraser(Phi) vs. Chi(NL)	10-0
1904	May 5	H		**Cy Young**(Bos) vs. Phi.(AL)	3-0
	June 11	A		Bob Wicker(Chi) vs. NY(NL), no-hitter for 9.1 innings. Won in 12th on one-hitter.	1-0
	Aug. 17	H		Jesse Tannehill(Bos) vs. Chi.(AL)	6-0
1905	June 13	A	2	Christy Mathewson(NY) vs. Chi.(NL)	1-0
	July 22	A (1st game)		Weldon Henley(Phi) vs. St.L(AL)	6-0
	Aug. 15	H		Rube Waddell(Phi) vs. St.L(AL) 5 innings	2-0
	Sept. 6	A (2nd game)		Frank Smith(Chi) vs. Det(AL)	15-0
	Sept. 27	H (1st game)		Bill Dinneen(Bos) vs. Chi(AL)	2-0
1906	May 1	A		John Lush(Phi) vs. Bkn(NL)	6-0
	July 20	A		Mal Eason(Bkn) vs. St.L.(NL)	2-0
	Aug. 1	H		Harry McIntire(Bkn) vs. Pit(NL), no-hitter for 10.2 innings. Lost in 13th on 4 hits.	0-1
	Aug. 24	H (2nd game)		John Weimer(Cin) vs. Bkn(NL) 7 innings	1-0
	Sept. 24	A (2nd game)		Stony McGlynn(St.L) vs. Bkn(NL) 7 innings	1-1
	Sept. 26	A (2nd game)		Lefty Leifield(Pit) vs. Phi(NL) 6 innings	8-0
1907	May 8	H		Big Jeff Pfeffer(Bos) vs. Cin(NL)	6-0
	May 26	H		Ed Walsh(Chi) vs. NY(AL) 5 innings	8-1
	Aug. 11	H (2nd game)		**Ed Karger**(St.L) vs. Bos(NL) 7 innings	4-0
	Aug. 23	A (2nd game)		Howie Camnitz(Pit) vs. NY(NL) 5 innings	1-0
	Sept. 20	H		Nick Maddox(Pit) vs. Bkn(NL)	2-1
	Oct. 5	A (2nd game)		**Rube Vickers** (Phil) vs. Was(AL) 5 innings	4-0
1908	June 30	A	2	Cy Young(Bos) vs. NY(AL)	8-0
	July 4	H (A.M. game)		Hooks Wiltse(NY) vs. Phi(NL)	1-0
	Aug. 6	A	2	John Lush(St.L) vs. Bkn(NL) 6 innings	2-0
	Sept. 5	H (2nd game)		Nap Rucker(Bkn) vs. Bos(NL)	6-0
	Sept. 18	H		Dusty Rhoades(Cle) vs. Bos(AL)	2-1
	Sept. 20	H	2	Frank Smith(Chi) vs. Phi(AL)	1-0
	Oct. 2	H		**Addie Joss**(Cle) vs. Chi(AL)	1-0
1909	Apr. 15	H	2	Red Ames(NY) vs. Bkn(NL) no hitter for 9.1 innings. Lost in 13th on 7 hits	0-3
1910	Apr. 20	A	2	Addie Joss(Cle) vs. Chi(AL)	1-0
	May 12	H		Chief Bender(Phi) vs. Cle(AL)	4-0
	July 31	A (2nd game)		King Cole(Chi) vs. St.L(NL) 7-innings	4-0
	Aug. 30	H (2nd game)		Tom Hughes(NY) vs. Cle(AL), no-hitter for 9.1 innings. Lost in 11th on 7 hits.	0-5
1911	July 20	H (1st game)		Smokey Joe Wood(Bos) vs. St.L(AL)	5-0
	Aug. 27	H	2	Ed Walsh(Chi) vs. Bos(AL)	5-0
1912	July 4	H (P.M. game)		George Mullin(Det) vs. St.L(AL)	7-0
	Aug. 20	H (2nd game)		Carl Cashion(Was) vs. Cle(AL) 6 innings	2-0
	Aug. 30	A		Earl Hamilton(St.L) vs. Det(AL)	5-1
	Sept. 6	A (1st game)		Jeff Tesreau(NY) vs. Phi(NL)	3-0
1914	May 14	A		Jim Scott(Chi) vs. Cle(AL), no-hitter for 9 innings. Lost in 10th on 2 hits.	0-1

Year	Date	H/A		Pitcher	Sco
1914	May 31	H		Joe Benz(Chi) vs. Cle(AL)	6-1
	Sept. 9	H (2nd game)		George Davis(Bos) vs. Phi(NL)	7-0
	Sept. 19	H		Ed Lafitte(Bkn) vs. KC(FL)	6-2
1915	Apr. 15	H		Rube Marquard(NY) vs. Bkn(NL)	2-0
	Apr. 24	A		Frank Allen(Pit) vs. StL(FL)	2-0
	May 25	A		Claude Hendrix(Chi) vs. Pit(FL)	10-0
	Aug. 16	A		Alex Main(KC) vs. Buf(FL)	5-0
	Aug. 31	A (1st game)		Jimmy Lavender(Chi) vs. NY(NL)	2-0
	Sept. 7	H		Dave Davenport(StL) vs. Chi(FL)	3-0
1916	Jun. 16	H	2	Tom Hughes(Bos) vs. Pit(NL)	2-0
	Jun. 21	H		Rube Foster(Bos) vs. NY(AL)	2-0
	Aug. 26	H		Bullet Joe Bush(Phi) vs. Cle(AL)	5-0
	Aug. 30	H		Dutch Leonard(Bos) vs. St.L(AL)	4-0
1917	Apr. 14	A		Ed Cicotte(Chi) vs. St.L(AL)	11-0
	Apr. 24	A		George Mogridge(NY) vs. Bos(AL)	2-1
	May 2	A		Fred Toney(Cin) vs. Chi(NL) 10 innings	1-0
	May 2	A		Hippo Vaughn(Chi) vs. Cin(NL) no hitter for 9.1 innings. Lost in 10th on 2 hits.	0-1
	May 5	H		Ernie Koob(St.L) vs. Chi(AL)	1-0
	May 6	H (2nd game)		Bob Groom(St.L) vs. Chi(AL)	3-0
	June 23	H (1st game)		**Ernie Shore**(Bos) vs. Was(AL), did not start game. Ruth walked the first batter and was ejected from the game. Shore relieved, the base runner was out stealing. Shore given credit for a perfect game facing only 26 batters.	4-0
1918	June 23	A	2	Dutch Leonard(Bos) vs. Det(AL)	5-0
1919	May 11	H		Hod Eller(Cin) vs. St.L(NL)	6-0
	Sept. 10	A (1st game)		Ray Caldwell(Cle) vs. NY(AL)	3-0
1920	July 1	A		Walter Johnson(Was) vs. Bos(AL)	1-0
1922	Apr. 30	A		**Charlie Robertson**(Chi) vs. Det(AL)	2-0
	May 7	H		Jesse Barnes(NY) vs. Phi(NL)	6-0
1923	Sept. 4	A		Sad Sam Jones(NY) vs. Phi(AL)	2-0
	Sept. 7	A		Howard Ehmke(Bos) vs. Phi(AL)	4-0
1924	July 17	H		Jesse Haines(St.L) vs. Bos(NL)	5-0
	Aug. 25	H	2	Walter Johnson(Was) vs. St.L(AL) 7 innings	2-0
1925	Sept. 13	H (1st game)		Dazzy Vance(Bkn) vs. Phi(NL)	10-1
1926	Aug. 21	A		Ted Lyons(Chi) vs. Bos(AL)	6-0
1929	May 8	H		Carl Hubbell(NY) vs. Pit(NL)	11-0
1931	Apr. 29	H		Wes Ferrell(Cle) vs. St.L(AL)	9-0
	Aug. 8	H		Bob Burke(Was) vs. Bos(AL)	5-0
1934	Sept. 18	H		Bobo Newsom(St.L) vs. Bos(AL), no-hitter for 9.2 innings. Lost in 10th on 1 hit.	1-2
	Sept. 21	A (2nd game)		Paul Dean (St.L) vs. Bkn(NL)	3-0
1935	Aug. 31	H		Vern Kennedy(Chi) vs. Cle(AL)	5-0
1937	June 1	H		Bill Kietrich(Chi) vs. St.L(AL)	8-0
	Aug. 27	H		Fred Frankhouse(Bkn) vs. Cin(NL) 7.2 innings	5-0
1938	June 11	H		Johnny Vander Meer(Cin) vs. Bos(NL)	3-0
	June 15	H	2	Johnny Vander Meer(Cin) vs. Bkn(NL)	6-0
	Aug. 27	H (2nd game)		Monte Pearson(NY) vs. Cle(AL)	13-0
1940	Apr. 16	A		Bob Feller(Cle) vs. Chi(AL)	1-0

NO HITTERS SINCE 1901

Year	Date	H/A		Pitcher	Score
1940	Apr. 30	A		Tex Carleton(Bkn) vs. Cin(NL)	3-0
	Aug. 5	H (2nd game)		John Whitehead(St.L) vs. Det(AL) 6 innings	4-0
1941	Aug. 30	A		Lon Warneke(St.L) vs. Cin(NL)	2-0
1944	Apr. 27	H		Jim Tobin(Bos) vs. Bkn(NL)	2-0
	May 15	H		Clyde Shoun(Cin) vs. Bos(NL)	1-0
	June 22	H (2nd game)	2	Jim Tobin(Bos) vs. Phi(NL) 5 innings	7-0
1945	Sept. 9	H (2nd game)		Dick Fowler(Phi) vs. St.L(AL)	1-0
1946	Apr. 23	H		Ed Head(Bkn) vs. Bos(NL)	5-0
	Apr. 30	A	2	Bob Feller(Cle) vs. NY(AL)	1-0
1947	June 18	H		Ewell Blackwell(Cin) vs. Bos(NL)	6-0
	July 10	H (1st game)		Don Black(Cle) vs. Phi(AL)	3-0
	Sept. 3	H		Bill McCahan(Phi) vs. Was(AL)	3-0
1948	June 30	A		Bob Lemon(Cle) vs. Det(AL)	2-0
	Sept. 9	A		Rex Barney(Bkn) vs. NY(NL)	2-0
1950	Aug. 11	H		Vern Bickford(Bos) vs. Bkn(NL)	7-0
1951	May 6	A (2nd game)		Cliff Chambers(Pit) vs. Bos(NL)	3-0
	July 1	H (1st game)	3	Bob Feller(Cle) vs. Det(AL)	2-1
	July 12	A		Allie Reynolds(NY) vs. Cle(AL)	1-0
	Sept. 28	H (1st game)	2	Allie Reynolds(NY) vs. Bos(AL)	8-0
1952	May 15	H		Virgil Trucks(Det) vs. Was(AL)	1-0
	June 19	H		Carl Erskine(Bkn) vs. Chi(NL)	5-0
	Aug. 25	A	2	Virgil Trucks(Det) vs. NY(AL)	1-0
1953	May 6	H		Bobo Holloman(St.L) vs. Phi(AL)	6-0
1954	June 12	H		Jim Wilson(Mil) vs. Phi(NL)	2-0
1955	May 12	H		Sam Jones(Chi) vs. Pit(NL)	4-0
1956	May 12	H	2	Carl Erskine(Bkn) vs. NY(NL)	3-0
	July 14	H		Mel Parnell(Bos) vs. Chi(AL)	4-0
	Sept. 25	H		Sal Maglie(Bkn) vs. Phi(NL)	5-0
	Oct. 8	H		**Don Larsen**(NY) vs. Bkn **World Series Game**	2-0
1957	Aug. 20	H (2nd game)		Bob Keegan(Chi) vs. Was(AL)	6-0
1958	July 20	A (1st game)		Jim Bunning(Det) vs. Bos(AL)	3-0
	Sept. 20	H		Hoyt Wilhelm(Bal) vs. NY(AL)	1-0
1959	May 26	A		**Harvey Haddix**(Pit) vs. Mil(NL) Perfect game for 12 innings. Lost in 13th on 1 hit.	0-1
	June 12	A		Mike McCormick(SF) vs. Phi(NL) 5 innings	3-0
	Sept. 26	A (1st game)	2	Sam Jones(SF) vs. St.L(NL) 7 innings	4-0
1960	May 15	H (2nd game)		Don Cardwell(Chi) vs. St.L(NL)	4-0
	Aug. 15	H		Lew Burdette(Mil) vs. Phi(NL)	1-0
	Sept. 16	H		Warren Spahn(Mil) vs. Phi(NL)	4-0
1961	Apr. 28	H	2	Warren Spahn(Mil) vs. SF(NL)	1-0
1962	May 5	H		Bo Belinsky(LA) vs. Bal(AL)	2-0
	June 26	H		Earl Wilson(Bos) vs. LA(AL)	2-0
	June 30	H		Sandy Koufax(LA) vs. NY(NL)	5-0
	Aug. 1	A		Bill Monboquette(Bos) vs. Chi(AL)	1-0
	Aug. 26	H		Jack Kralick(Min) vs. KC(AL)	1-0
1963	May 11	H	2	Sandy Koufax(LA) vs. SF(NL)	8-0
	May 17	H		Don Nottebart(Hou) vs. Phi(NL)	4-1
	June 15	H		Juan Marichal(SF) vs. Hou(NL)	1-0

Year	Date	H/A		Pitcher	Score
1964	Apr. 23	H		Ken Johnson(Hou) vs. Cin(NL)	0-1
	June 4	A	3	Sandy Koufax(LA) vs. Phi(NL)	3-0
	June 21	A (1st game)	2	**Jim Bunning**(Phi) vs. NY(NL)	6-0
1965	June 14	H		Jim Maloney(Cin) vs. NY(NL) no-hitter for 10 innings. Lost in 11th (2 hits)	0-1
	Aug. 19	A (1st game)	2	Jim Maloney(Cin) vs. Chi(NL)	1-0
	Sept. 9	H	**4**	**Sandy Koufax**(LA) vs. Chi(NL)	1-0
	Sept. 16	H		Dave Morehead(Bos) vs. Cle(AL)	2-0
1966	June 10	H		Sonny Siebert(Cle) vs. Was(AL)	2-0
1967	June 18	H		Don Wilson(Hou) vs. AtL(NL)	2-0
	Aug. 6	H		Dean Chance(Min) vs. Bos(AL) 5 innings	2-0
	Aug. 25	A (2nd game)	2	Dean Chance(Min) vs. Cle(AL)	2-1
	Sept. 10	H (1st game)		Joel Horlen(Chi) vs. Det(AL)	6-0
1968	Apr. 27	H		Tom Phoebus(Bal) vs. Bos(AL)	6-0
	May 8	H		**Catfish Hunter**(Oak) vs. Min(AL)	4-0
	July 29	A (2nd game)		George Culver(Cin) vs. Phi(NL)	6-1
	Sept. 17			Gaylord Perry(SF) vs. St.L(NL)	1-0
	Sept. 18	A		Ray Washburn(St.L) vs. SF(NL)	2-0
1969	Apr. 17	A		Bill Stoneman(Mon) vs. Phi(NL)	7-0
	Apr. 30	H	3	Jim Maloney(Cin) vs. Hou(NL)	10-0
	May 1	A	2	Don Wilson(Hou) vs. Cin(NL)	4-0
	Aug. 13	H		Jim Palmer(Bal) vs. Oak(AL)	8-0
	Aug. 19	H		Ken Holtzman (Chi) vs. Atl(NL)	3-0
	Sept. 20	A		Bob Moose(Pit) vs. NY(NL)	4-0
1970	June 12	A (1st game)		Dock Ellis(Pit) vs. SD(NL)	2-0
	July 3	H		Clyde Wright(Cal) vs. Oak(AL)	4-0
	July 20	H		Bill Singer(LA) vs. Phi(NL)	5-0
	Sept. 21	H		Vida Blue(Oak) vs. Min(AL)	6-0
1971	June 3	H	2	Ken Holtzman(Chi) vs. Cin(NL)	1-0
	June 23	A		Rick Wise(Phi) vs. Cin(NL)	4-0
	Aug. 14	A		Bob Gibson(St.L) vs. Pit(NL)	11-0
1972	Apr. 16	H		Burt Hooton(Chi) vs. Phi(NL)	1-0
	Sept. 2	H		Milt Pappas(Chi) vs. SD(NL)	8-0
	Oct. 2	H	2	Bill Stoneman(Mon) vs. NY(NL)	7-0
1973	Apr. 27	A		Steve Busby(KC) vs. Det(AL)	3-0
	May 15	A		Nolan Ryan(Cal) vs. KC(AL)	3-0
	July 15	A	2	Nolan Ryan(Cal) vs. Det(AL)	6-0
	July 30	A		Jim Bibby(Tex) vs. Oak(AL)	6-0
	Aug. 5	H		Phil Niekro(Atl) vs. SD(NL)	9-0
1974	June 19	A	2	Steve Busby(KC) vs. Mil(AL)	2-0
	July 19	H		Dick Bosman(Cle) vs. Oak(AL)	4-0
	Sept. 28	H	3	Nolan Ryan(Cal) vs. Min(AL)	4-0
1975	June 1	H	4	Nolan Ryan(Cal) vs. Bal(AL)	1-0
	Aug. 24	H		Ed Halicki(SF) vs. NY(NL)	6-0
				Combination No-hitters	
1906	Aug. 29	H		Jim Dygert-3 innings (Phi) vs. Chi(AL) Rube Waddell-2 innings	4-3
1956	May 26	A		Johnny Klippstein-7 innings Hersh Freeman-1 inning Joe Black-1.2 innings (Cin)vs. Mil(NL) no-hitter for 9.2 innings. Lost in 11th on 3 hits.	1-2
1967	Apr. 30	H (1st game)		Steve Barber-8.2 innings (Bal) vs. Det(AL) Stu Miller-.1 inning	1-2
1975	Sept. 28	H		Vida Blue-5 innings(Oak) vs. Cal(AL) Glenn Abbott-1 inning Paul Lindblad-1 inning Rollie Fingers-2 innings	

Bold Number-Denotes more than one no hitter for the pitcher.

Bold Name-Denotes all pitchers who have hurled a perfect game.

AWARDS

CHALMERS AWARD

AMERICAN LEAGUE		NATIONAL LEAGUE
Ty Cobb-Det.	1911	Wildfire Schulte-Chi.
Tris Speaker-Bos.	1912	Larry Doyle-N.Y.
Walter Johnson-Was.	1913	Jake Daubert-Bkn.
Eddie Collins-Phi.	1914	Johnny Evers-Bos.

TRIPLE CROWN WINNERS

Year	Name-Team (League)	HR	RBI's	B.Avg.
1887	Tip O'Neill-St.L.(AA)	14*	123	.442
1894	Hugh Duffy-Bos.(NL)	18	145	.438
1901	Nap Lajoie-Phi.(AL)	14	125	.422
1909	Ty Cobb-Det.(AL)	9	107	.377
1922	Rogers Hornsby-St.L.(NL)	42	152	.401
1925	Rogers Hornsby-St.L.(NL)	39	143	.403
1933	Jimmie Foxx-Phi.(AL)	48	163	.356
1933	Chuck Klein-Phi.(NL)	28	120	.368
1934	Lou Gehrig-N.Y.(AL)	49	165	.363
1937	Joe Medwick-St.L.(NL)	31*	154	.374
1942	Ted Williams-Bos.(AL)	36	137	.356
1947	Ted Williams-Bos.(AL)	32	114	.343
1956	Mickey Mantle-N.Y.(AL)	52	130	.353
1966	Frank Robinson-Bal.(AL)	49	122	.316
1967	Carl Yastrzemski-Bos.(AL)	44*	121	.326

*=tied for lead

LEAGUE AWARDS

AMERICAN LEAGUE		NATIONAL LEAGUE
George Sisler-St.L.	1922	No selection made
Babe Ruth-N.Y.	1923	No selection made
Walter Johnson-Was.	1924	Dazzy Vance-Bkn.
Roger Peckinpaugh-Was.	1925	Rogers Hornsby-St.L.
George Burns-Cle.	1926	Bob O'Farrell-St.L.
Lou Gehrig-N.Y.	1927	Paul Waner-Pit.
Mickey Cochrane-Phi.	1928	Jim Bottomley-St.L.
No selection made	1929	Rogers Hornsby-Chi.

M.V.P. AWARDS

Selected by the Baseball Writers Association of America
(* Unanimous selection)

AMERICAN LEAGUE		Points	Year	NATIONAL LEAGUE		Points
Lefty Grove-Phi.	p	78	1931	Frankie Frisch-St.L.	2b	65
Jimmie Foxx-Phi.	1b	75	1932	Chuck Klein-Phi.	of	78
Jimmie Foxx-Phi.	1b	74	1933	Carl Hubbell-N.Y.	p	77
Mickey Cochrane-Det.	c	67	1934	Dizzy Dean-St.L.	p	78
Hank Greenberg-Det.	1b	*80	1935	Gabby Hartnett-Chi.	c	75
Lou Gehrig-N.Y.	1b	73	1936	Carl Hubbell-N.Y.	p	60
Charlie Gehringer-Det.	2b	78	1937	Joe Medwick-St.L.	of	70
Jimmie Foxx-Bos.	1b	305	1938	Ernie Lombardi-Cin.	c	229
Joe DiMaggio-N.Y.	of	280	1939	Bucky Walters-Cin.	p	303
Hank Greenberg-Det.	1b	292	1940	Frank McCormick-Cin.	1b	274
Joe DiMaggio-N.Y.	of	291	1941	Dolph Camilli-Bkn.	1b	300
Joe Gordon-N.Y.	2b	270	1942	Mort Cooper-St.L.	p	263
Spud Chandler-N.Y.	p	246	1943	Stan Musial-St.L.	of	267
Hal Newhouser-Det.	p	236	1944	Marty Marion-St.L.	ss	190
Hal Newhouser-Det.	p	236	1945	Phil Cavarretta-Chi.	1b	279
Ted Williams-Bos.	of	224	1946	Stan Musial-St.L.	1b	319
Joe DiMaggio-N.Y.	of	202	1947	Bob Elliott-Bos.	3b	205
Lou Boudreau-Cle.	ss	324	1948	Stan Musial-St.L.	of	303
Ted Williams-Bos.	of	272	1949	Jackie Robinson-Bkn.	2b	264
Phil Rizzuto-N.Y.	ss	284	1950	Jim Konstanty-Phi.	p	286
Yogi Berra-N.Y.	c	184	1951	Roy Campanella-Bkn.	c	243
Bobby Shantz-Phi.	p	280	1952	Hank Sauer-Chi.	of	226

AMERICAN LEAGUE		Points	Year	NATIONAL LEAGUE		Points
Al Rosen-Cle.	3b	*336	1953	Roy Campanella-Bkn.	c	297
Yogi Berra-N.Y.	c	230	1954	Willie Mays-N.Y.	of	283
Yogi Berra-N.Y.	c	218	1955	Roy Campanella-Bkn.	c	226
Mickey Mantle-N.Y.	of	*336	1956	Don Newcombe-Bkn.	p	223
Mickey Mantle-N.Y.	of	233	1957	Hank Aaron-Mil.	of	239
Jackie Jensen-Bos.	of	233	1958	Ernie Banks-Chi.	ss	283
Nellie Fox-Chi.	2b	295	1959	Ernie Banks-Chi.	ss	232.5
Roger Maris-N.Y.	of	225	1960	Dick Groat-Pit.	ss	276
Roger Maris-N.Y.	of	202	1961	Frank Robinson-Cin.	of	219
Mickey Mantle-N.Y.	of	234	1962	Maury Wills-L.A.	ss	209
Ellie Howard-N.Y.	c	248	1963	Sandy Koufax-L.A.	p	237
Brooks Robinson-Bal.	3b	269	1964	Ken Boyer-St.L.	3b	243
Zoilo Versales-Min.	ss	275	1965	Willie Mays-S.F.	of	224
Frank Robinson-Bal.	of	*280	1966	Roberto Clemente-Pit.	of	218
Carl Yastrzemski-Bos.	of	275	1967	Orlando Cepeda-St.L.	1b	*280
Denny McLain-Det.	p	*280	1968	Bob Gibson-St.L.	p	242
Harmon Killebrew-Min.	1b-3b	294	1969	Willie McCovey-S.F.	1b	265
Boog Powell-Bal.	1b	234	1970	Johnny Bench-Cin.	c	326
Vida Blue-Oak.	p	268	1971	Joe Torre-St.L.	3b	318
Dick Allen-Chi.	1b	321	1972	Johnny Bench-Cin.	c	263
Reggie Jackson-Oak.	of	336	1973	Pete Rose-Cin.	of	274
Jeff Burroughs-Tex.	of	248	1974	Steve Garvey-L.A.	lb	270
Fred Lynn	of	326	1975	Joe Morgan-Cin.	2b	321.5

ROOKIE OF THE YEAR AWARDS

(* Unanimous selection)

AMERICAN LEAGUE		Votes	Year	NATIONAL LEAGUE		Votes
Combined selection			1947	Jackie Robinson-Bkn.	1b	
Combined selection			1948	Al Dark-Bos.	ss	
Roy Sievers-St.L.	of	10	1949	Don Newcombe-Bkn.	p	21
Walt Dropo-Bos.	1b	15	1950	Sam Jethroe-Bos.	of	11
Gil McDougald-N.Y.	3b	13	1951	Willie Mays-N.Y.	of	18
Harry Byrd-Phil.	p	9	1952	Joe Black-Bkn.	p	19
Harvey Kuenn-Det.	ss	23	1953	Jim Gilliam-Bkn.	2b	11
Bob Grim-N.Y.	p	15	1954	Wally Moon-St.L.	of	17
Herb Score-Cle.	p	18	1955	Bill Virdon-St.L.	of	15
Luis Aparicio-Chi.	ss	22	1956	Frank Robinson-Cin.	of	*24
Tony Kubek-N.Y.	inf-of	23	1957	Jack Sanford-Phi.	p	16
Albie Pearson-Was.	of	14	1958	Orlando Cepeda-S.F.	1b	*21
Bob Allison-Was.	of	18	1959	Willie McCovey-S.F.	1b	*24
Ron Hansen-Bal.	ss	22	1960	Frank Howard-L.A.	of	12

AMERICAN LEAGUE		Votes	Year	NATIONAL LEAGUE		Votes
Don Schwall-Bos.	p	7	1961	Billy Williams-Chi.	of	10
Tommy Tresh-N.Y.	of-ss	13	1962	Ken Hubbs-Chi.	2b	19
Gary Peters-Chi.	p	10	1963	Pete Rose-Cin.	2b	17
Tony Oliva-Min.	of	19	1964	Dick Allen-Phi.	3b	18
Curt Blefary-Bal.	of	12	1965	Jim Lefebvre-L.A.	2b	13
Tommie Agee-Chi.	of	16	1966	Tommy Helms-Cin.	3b	12
Rod Carew-Min.	2b	19	1967	Tom Seaver-N.Y.	p	11
Stan Bahnsen-N.Y.	p	17	1968	Johnny Bench-Cin.	c	10.5
Lou Piniella-K.C.	of	9	1969	Ted Sizemore-L.A.	2b	14
Thurman Munson-N.Y.	c	23	1970	Carl Morton-Mon.	p	11
Chris Chambliss-Cle.	1b	11	1971	Earl Williams-Atl.	c	18
Carlton Fisk-Bos.	c	*24	1972	Jon Matlack-N.Y.	p	19
Al Bumbry-Bal.	of	13.5	1973	Gary Matthews-S.F.	of	11
Mike Hargrove-Tex.	lb	16.5	1974	Bake McBride-St.L.	of	16
Fred Lynn-Bos.	of	23.5	1975	John Montefusco-S.F.	P	12

CY YOUNG MEMORIAL AWARDS

(For Pitchers only)
(* Unanimous selection)

Year		Votes
1956	Don Newcombe-Bkn.(N)	10
1957	Warren Spahn-Mil.(N)	15
1958	Bob Turley-N.Y.(A)	5
1959	Early Wynn-Chi.(A)	13
1960	Vern Law-Pit.(A)	8
1961	Whitey Ford-N.Y.(A)	9
1962	Don Drysdale-L.A.(N)	14
1963	Sandy Koufax-L.A.(N)	*20
1964	Dean Chance-L.A.(A)	17
1965	Sandy Koufax-L.A.(N)	*20
1966	Sandy Koufax-L.A.(N)	*20

AMERICAN LEAGUE	Votes	Year	NATIONAL LEAGUE	Votes
Jim Lonborg-Bos.	18	1967	Mike McCormick-S.F.	18
Denny McLain-Det.	*20	1968	Bob Gibson-St.L.	*20
Mike Cuellar-Bal.	10	1969	Tom Seaver-N.Y.	23
Denny McLain-Det.	10			
Jim Perry-Min.	55	1970	Bob Gibson-St.L.	118
Vida Blue-Oak.	98	1971	Ferguson Jenkins-Chi.	97
Gaylord Perry-Cle.	64	1972	Steve Carlton-Phi.	*120
Jim Palmer-Bal.	88	1973	Tom Seaver-N.Y.	71
Catfish Hunter-Oak.	90	1974	Mike Marshall-L.A.	96
Jim Palmer-Bal.	98	1975	Tom Seaver-N.Y.	98

HALL OF FAME

B.B.W.A.A.=Baseball Writers Association of America (75% of ballots cast necessary for election)
*Selected for the Hall of Fame as non-player.
Number in parenthesis denotes ballots cast.
[R] – Elected in runoff election.

1936 B.B.W.A.A.(226):
- Ty Cobb(222)
- Honus Wagner(215)
- Babe Ruth(215)
- Christy Mathewson(205)
- Walter Johnson(189)

1937 B.B.W.A.A.(201):
- Nap Lajoie(168)
- Tris Speaker(165)
- Cy Young(153)

Centennial Commission:
- *Morgan B. Bulkeley
- *Ban Johnson
- Connie Mack
- John McGraw
- George Wright

1938 B.B.W.A.A.(262):
- Pete Alexander(212)

Centennial Commission
- *Alexander Cartwright
- *Henry Chadwick

1939 B.B.W.A.A.(274):
- George Sisler(235)
- Eddie Collins(213)
- Willie Keeler(207)
- Lou Gehrig(by special election)

Comm. on Old-timers:
- Cap Anson
- Charlie Comiskey
- Candy Cummings
- Buck Ewing
- Hoss Radbourne
- Al Spaulding

1942 B.B.W.A.A.(233):
- Rogers Hornsby(182)

1944 Comm. on Old-timers:
- *Judge Kenesaw M. Landis

1945 Comm. on Old-timers:
- Roger Bresnahan
- Dan Brouthers
- Fred Clarke
- Jimmie Collins
- Ed Delahanty
- Hugh Duffy
- Hughie Jennings
- Mike Kelly
- Jim O'Rourke
- Wilbert Robinson

1946 Comm. on Old-timers:
- Jesse Burkett
- Frank Chance
- Jack Chesbro
- Johnny Evers
- Clark Griffith
- Tom McCarthy
- Joe McGinnity
- Eddie Plank
- Joe Tinker
- Rube Waddell
- Ed Walsh

1947 B.B.W.A.A.(161):
- Carl Hubbell(140)
- Frank Frisch(136)
- Mickey Cochrane(128)
- Lefty Grove(123)

1948 B.B.W.A.A.(121):
- Herb Pennock(94)
- Pie Traynor(93)

1949 B.B.W.A.A.(187):
- Charlie Gehringer(159)[R]

Comm. on Old-timers:
- Three-Finger Brown
- Kid Nichols

1951 B.B.W.A.A.(226):
- Mel Ott(197)
- Jimmie Foxx(179)

1952 B.B.W.A.A.(234):
- Harry Heilmann(203)
- Paul Waner(195)

1953 B.B.W.A.A.(264):
- Dizzy Dean(209)
- Al Simmons(199)

Comm. on Veterans:
- *Ed Barrow
- Chief Bender
- *Tom Connolly
- *Bill Klem
- Bobby Wallace
- *Harry Wright

1954 B.B.W.A.A.(252):
- Rabbit Maranville(209)
- Bill Dickey(202)
- Bill Terry(195)

1955 B.B.W.A.A.(251):
- Joe DiMaggio(223)
- Ted Lyons(217)
- Dazzy Vance(205)
- Gabby Hartnett(195)

Comm. on Veterans:
- Frank Baker
- Ray Schalk

1956 B.B.W.A.A.(193):
- Hank Greenberg(164)
- Joe Cronin(152)

1957 Comm. on Veterans:
- Sam Crawford
- *Joe McCarthy

1959 Comm. on Veterans:
- Zack Wheat

1961 Comm. on Veterans:
- Max Carey
- Billy Hamilton

1962 B.B.W.A.A.(160):
- Bob Feller(150)
- Jackie Robinson(124)

Comm. on Veterans:
- *Bill McKechnie
- Edd Roush

1963 Comm. on Veterans:
- John Clarkson
- Elmer Flick
- Sam Rice
- Eppa Rixey

1964 B.B.W.A.A.(225) Special runoff election:
- Luke Appling(189)

Comm. on Veterans:
- Red Faber
- Burleigh Grimes
- Miller Huggins
- Tim Keefe
- Heinie Manush
- John Ward

1965 Comm. on Veterans:
- Pud Galvin

1966 B.B.W.A.A.(302):
- Ted Williams(282)

Comm. on Veterans:
- Casey Stengel

1967 B.B.W.A.A.(306):
- Red Ruffing(266)[R]

Comm. on Veterans:
- Branch Rickey
- Lloyd Waner

1968 B.B.W.A.A.(283):
- Joe Medwick(240)

Comm. on Veterans:
- Kiki Cuyler
- Goose Goslin

1969 B.B.W.A.A.(340):
- Stan Musial(317)
- Roy Campanella(270)

Comm. on Veterans:
- Stan Coveleski
- Waite Hoyt

1970 B.B.W.A.A.(300):
- Lou Boudreau(232)

Comm. on Veterans:
- Earle Combs
- Ford Frick
- Jesse Haines

1971 Comm. on Veterans:
- Jake Beckley
- Dave Bancroft
- Chick Hafey
- Harry Hooper
- Joe Kelley
- Rube Marquard
- *George Weiss

Special Committee on Negroe Leagues:
- Satchel Paige

1972 B.B.W.A.A.(396):
- Sandy Koufax(344)
- Yogi Berra(339)
- Early Wynn(301)

Comm. on Veterans:
- Lefty Gomez
- *Will Harridge
- Ross Youngs

Special Committee on Negroe Leagues:
- Josh Gibson
- Buck Leonard

1973 B.B.W.A.A.(380):
- Warren Spahn(316)

Comm. on Veterans:
- *Billy Evans
- George Kelly
- Mickey Welch

Special Committee on Negro Leagues:
- Monte Irvin

Special waiver of 5-year waiting period:
- Roberto Clemente

1974 B.B.W.A.A.(365)
- Mickey Mantle(322)
- Whitey Ford(284)

1974 B.B.W.A.A.(365)
- Mickey Mantle(322)
- Whitey Ford(284)

Comm. on Veterans:
- Jim Bottomley
- *Jocko Conlan
- Sam Thompson

Special Committee on Negro Leagues:
- Cool Papa Bell

1975 B.B.W.A.A.(362)
- Ralph Kiner(273)

Comm. on Veterans:
- Earl Averill
- *Bucky Harris
- Billy Herman

Special Committee on Negro Leagues:
- Judy Johnson

The Designated Hitter

In a dramatic move to increase fan interest as well as offense in the game, the American League, in 1973, initiated the "designated hitter" ruling. Technically, the ruling states that in the batting order, instead of the pitcher, a designated hitter may be substituted who will bat but not play the field. Such a designated hitter could be placed anywhere in the batting order, and does not preclude the use of a pinch hitter, either for the designated hitter, or anyone else in the lineup.

Of course the repercussions of such a move could hardly begin to be measured, and even before spring training was underway, the controversy began. To the diehards of the game, it was a devasting decision, and their claim that Babe Ruth might have forever gone undiscovered was indeed a valid cry. But for those who thought the approach to be an imaginative and fresh one, it was a welcome change, and at the year's end it seemed that the ruling would not be a temporary one.

For the ball player, the rule had certain immediate, but opposing effects. While it obviously prolonged the careers of certain players, who through age or injury could no longer play the field, it became more difficult for fringe players to break into the lineup, as there was less of a need for pinch hitters. Statistically, scoring and hitting increased, but not significantly when compared to 1969-71.

Ironically, the rule had a greater effect on pitching than batting as the entire relationship between the starting pitcher and the relief pitcher changed. Without having to remove a starting pitcher in a tight game—a fact of life common for most of baseball—the American League in 1973 produced a record twelve 20-game winners. Along with this figure was an even more impressive statistic. The American League moundsmen finished 31.6% of their games when compared to the National League's 23.0%, a substantial difference. The new rule also made Nolan Ryan's record-breaking performance of 383 strikeouts even more notable considering he was not able to strike out opposing pitchers throughout 1973.

The following table of statistics has been designed to show the effect of the designated hitter ruling in several important categories. The statistics which include both leagues, are charted from the expansion year of 1969 in order to give a more valid evaluation of the statistical material. 1972 is shown separately because of the player strike which affected playing statistics for that year.

NATIONAL LEAGUE 69-71	NATIONAL LEAGUE 72	NATIONAL LEAGUE 73-75		AMERICAN LEAGUE 69-71	AMERICAN LEAGUE 72	AMERICAN LEAGUE 73-75
8.32	7.81	8.28	Runs per game (both teams)	8.08	6.93	8.45
.253	.248	.255	Batting Average	.247	.239	.258
1.57	1.46	1.40	Home Runs per game (both teams)	1.67	1.26	1.51
11.5	11.3	10.4	Strikeouts per game (both teams)	11.1	11.0	9.9
26.5	27.3	22.5	% Complete Games	23.5	27.0	32.5
7.6	8.8	7.1	% Shutouts	7.0	10.4	7.4

NON-PLAYING MANAGERS

Men who managed in the major leagues since 1901 and who never played major league baseball or who played in the major leagues only before 1901 (except Frank Dwyer and Biddy McPhee whose records are shown on page 16)

USE NAME—GIVEN NAMES (NICKNAMES)	TEAM BY YEAR	Birth Date	Birth Place	Death Date	B	T	Hgt	Wgt	PLAYING RECORD					
									Positions	G	HR	BA	W	L
Adair, Bill-Marion Danne	M70ChiA	2-10-16	Mobile, Ala.				5'8	190						
Armour, Bill-William R.	02-04CleA M05-06DetA	9- 3-69	Homestead, Pa.	12- 2-22										
Bancroft, Frank-Frank Carter	M80WorN M81-82DetN M83CleN M84-85ProvN M87PhiAA M89IndN M02CinN	5- 9-46	Lancaster, Mass.	3-31-21										
Barrow, Ed-Edward Grant (Cousin Ed)	M03-04DetA M18-20BosA	5-10-68	Springfield, Ill.	12-15-53										
Bezdek, Hugo-Hugo Francis 37-38 Head Coach in N.F.L.	M17-19PitN	4- 1-83	Prague, Czechoslovakia	9-19-52										
Bristol, Dave-James David	M66-69CinN M70-72MilA	6-23-33	Macon, Ga.				5'11	175						
Buckenberger, Al-Albert C.	M89-90ColAA M92-94PitN M95StLN M02-04BosN	1-31-61	Detroit, Mich.	7- 1-17										
Cantillon, Joe-Joe (Pongo Joe)	M07-09WasA	8-19-61	Janesville, Wis.	1-31-30										
Fogel, Horace-Horace S.	M87IndN M02NYN	3- 2-61	Macungie, Pa.	11-15-28										
Fuchs, Judge-Emil Edwin	M29BosN	4-17-78	New York, N.Y.	12- 5-61										
Hanlon, Ned-Edward Hugh	80CleN 81-88DetN 89,M89PitN 90,M90PitP 91,M91PitN 92,M92-98BalN M99-05BknN M06-07CinN	8-22-57	Montville, Conn.	4-14-37	L	L	5'11	170	OF	1267	30	.260		
Himsl, Vedie-Avitus Bernard	M61ChiN	4- 2-17	Plevna, Mont.				6'1	200						
Huff, George-George A.	M07BosA	6-11-72	Champaign, Ill.	10- 1-36										
Keane, Johnny-John Joseph	M61-64StLN M65-66NYA	11- 3-11	St. Louis, Mo.	1- 6-67			5'10	165						
Loftus, Tom-Thomas Joseph	77StLN 83StLAA M84MilU M88CleAA 89CleN M90-91CinN M00-01ChiN M02-03WasA	11-15-56	Jefferson City, Mo.	4-16-10	R	R		168	OF	9	0	.182		
Lucchesi, Frank-Frank Joseph	M70-72PhiN M75TexA	4-24-27	San Francisco, Cal.											
Mack (McGillicuddy), Connie-Cornelius Alexander (The Tall Tactician)	86-89WasN 90BufP 91-96,M94-96PitN M01-50PhiA	12-22-62	East Brookfield, Mass.	2- 8-56	R	R	6'2	170	C	696	5	.249		
Manning, Jimmy-James H.	84-85BosN 85-87DetN 89KCAA M01WasA	1-31-62	Fall River, Mass.	10-22-29		L			OF-2B	364	8	.215		
McCallister, Jack-John	M27CleA	1-19-79	Marietta, Ohio	10-18-46										
McCarthy, Joe-Joseph Vincent (Marse Joe)	M26-30ChiN M31-46NYA M48-50BosA	4-21-87	Philadelphia, Pa.				5'8	190						
McCloskey, John-John Joseph (Honest John)	M95-96LouN M06-08StLN	4- 4-62	Louisville, Ky.	11-17-40										
McGaha, Mel-Fred Melvin 48-49 played in B.A.A.	M62CleA M64-65KCA	9-26-26	Bastrop, La.				6'2	210						
McKeon, Jack-John Aloysius	M73-75KCA	11-23-30	South Amboy, N.J.				5'8	190						
McNamara, John-John Francis	M69-70OakA M74-75SDN	6- 4-32	Sacramento, Cal.				5'10	175						
Murray, Billy-William Jeremiah	M07-09PhiN	4-13-64	Peabody, Mass.	3-25-37										
O'Day, Hank-Henry Francis	84TolAA 85PitAA 86-89WasN 89NYN 90NYP M12CinN M14ChiN	7- 8-62	Chicago, Ill.	7- 2-35		R			P	232	1	.190	70	110
Owens, Paul-Paul Francis	M72PhiN	2- 7-24	Salamanca, N.Y.											
Ozark, Danny-Daniel Leonard	M73-75PhiN	11-26-23	Buffalo, N.Y.				6'3	205						
Phillips, Lefty-Harold Ross	M69-72CalA	6-16-19	Los Angeles, Cal.				5'11	192						
Robison, Stanley-Matthew Stanley	M05StLN	-57	Dubuque, Iowa	3-24-11										
Rowland, Pants-Clarence Henry	M15-18ChiA	2-12-79	Platteville, Wis.	5-17-69										
Sawyer, Eddie-Edwin Milby	M48-52,58-60PhiN	9-10-10	Westerly, R.I.				6'	210						
Selee, Frank-Frank Gibson	M90-01BosN M02-05ChiN	10-26-59	Amherst, N.H.	7- 5-09										
Shepard, Larry-Lawrence William	M68-69PitN	4- 3-19	Lakewood, Ohio				5'11	180						
Shettsline, Bill-William Joseph	M98-02PhiN	10-25-63	Philadelphia, Pa.	2-22-33										
Stallings, George-George Tweedy (The Miracle Man)	90BknN 97-98,M97-98PhiN M01DetA M09-10NYA M13-20BosN	11-17-67	Augusta, Ga.	5-13-29	R	R	5'10	180	C-OF-1B	7	0	.100		
Tighe, Jack-John Thomas	M57-58DetA	8- 9-13	Kearny, N.J.				5'8	170						
Weaver, Earl-Earl Sidney	M68-75BalA	8-14-30	St. Louis, Mo.				5'7	175						
Winkles, Bobby-Bobby Brooks (Winks)	M73-74CalA	3-11-30	Tuckerman, Ark.				5'9	166						

The Black, Latin, White Report

The question which is constantly asked concerns the role of the Black athlete in baseball: What would the game have been like had his presence always been felt? After conducting a statistical study to at least answer the question in a technical sense, an even greater question comes to mind: What would the game of baseball be like today if the Black athlete was still barred from the diamonds of professional baseball?

When the first professional baseball league, the National Association, made its debut in 1871 there were no Blacks to be found amongst the players. Although there was no "official" discrimination against the Black athlete, this practice continued through 1945 with the exception of only one interruption in the "color line" in 1884 when two brothers, Fleet and Welday Walker, played for Toledo in the American Association—a league which was then considered to be major. Finally, in 1946 Branch Rickey, general manager of the Brooklyn Dodgers, signed Jackie Robinson, an infielder from the Negro Leagues, and assigned him to Montreal, a Dodger farm team. This move, marked as an "experiment", was met with a flood of hostility, clamor, and publicity as could be anticipated. But Robinson's playing, persistence, and attitude was such that he was promoted to the Dodgers in 1947. Robinson, at 28, played well enough not only to be named Rookie of the Year, but also to help Brooklyn to a pennant.

Robinson's success led to four other Blacks joining the ranks of major league baseball that year. While Hank Thompson and Willard Brown joined the St. Louis Browns, Dan Bankhead joined Robinson on the Dodgers late in the year, and Larry Doby came to the Cleveland Indians. A year later other Blacks were introduced, the most notable being the legendary Satchel Paige, who joined Cleveland after two decades of pitching brilliance in the Negro Leagues. The stage was thus set and by the 1950's the gates opened even wider. Finally, by the 1960's not only had the Black athlete become an established part of the national game, but also to stand among the leaders in the achievement of his craft.

For those men who learned to ply their trade in the Negro Leagues it was a frustrating and difficult life. Salaries and recognition could never equal their White counterparts, and the structure, which included a Negro American and Negro National League, was a separate but unequal phenomenon of American life. As to the question of whether or not the Black athlete could have performed alongside the White athlete on the diamonds of professional baseball, the answer would seem to be a resounding, "yes". The Negro Leagues, in addition to playing in major league ballparks, also included many of the star players who participated in post-season barnstorming exhibition games with White major leaguers. The accounts of these games indicate that the Black players certainly had the talent to play major league baseball. One example of the Black athletes' ability during these years of discrimination can be traced to Josh Gibson, reportedly the "Babe Ruth" of the Negro Leagues. Gibson, a right-handed power hitter, was said to have hit many a home run drive down the 401-foot left field line while playing in Griffith Stadium, home of the former Washington Senators. But Gibson's feats, as that of so many other Black athletes, are unconfirmed facts because the statistical data were never compiled for the Negro Leagues. However, from 1947 to the present, there is a vast amount of data which now makes it possible to evaluate the performance and impact of the Black athlete in major league baseball. For this study, in addition to the Black and White player, the Latin ballplayer was also taken into consideration. The study itself has been broken down into three major categories due to the expansion in baseball throughout the years. In 1947-1960 there were 16 teams; in 1961-1968 there were 18 to 20 teams, and from 1969 to 1975 there were 24 teams. What was done was a tabulation for *all* players, regulars and substitutes.

BATTING (excluding Pitchers)

												Average per 550 At Bats				
		At Bats	Hits	Doubles	Triples	Home Runs	Stolen Bases	Bat. Avg.	Slug. Avg.	At Bats per Yr.	AB/Yr. Pct.	Hits	2B	3B	Home Runs	Stolen Bases
1947-60	White	966,564	252,438	40,844	8,261	23,210	7,864	.261	.393	69,040	88	144	24	5	13	4
	Black	83,702	23,417	3,682	990	3,002	1,574	.280	.455	5,979	7.6	154	22	7	20	10
	Latin	50,568	13,498	2,059	542	943	1,024	.267	.385	3,612	4.6	147	23	6	10	11
1961-68	White	511,463	128,357	19,920	3,512	13,030	3,992	.251	.380	63,933	64	138	21	4	14	4
	Black	174,176	46,771	7,192	1,644	5,370	4,317	.269	.421	21,772	22	148	23	5	17	14
	Latin	107,441	28,634	4,379	893	1,999	2,253	.267	.380	13,430	14	147	22	5	10	12
1969-75	White	488,677	122,794	18,961	2,894	11,004	4,789	.251	.369	69,811	56	138	21	3	12	5
	Black	237,343	64,486	10,167	1,847	7,019	6,714	.272	.419	33,906	27	149	24	4	16	16
	Latin	134,525	35,598	5,398	975	2,025	2,303	.265	.364	19,218	16	146	22	4	8	11

—From 1947-1960, Black and Latin hitters accounted for only 12% of all at bats, excluding pitchers. By the period 1969-1975, this figure had risen to 43%.

—Black and Latin players have consistently had a higher batting average than the White major leaguers.

—Black hitters have consistently had a higher slugging average than either the Whites or the Latins. For each of the three periods this differential has been at least 40 points.

—The Blacks and the Latins have dominated the stolen base statistics. Since 1961, the Black and Latin players have maintained an average of one stolen base for every 35-50 at bats. The White players have stolen one base for every 110-130 at bats.

On the right of the above statistics the information is shown in terms of one average major league season of 550 at bats. This makes it easier to compare the figures and they clearly show that the average Black hitter has produced more hits, more home runs, and more stolen bases than the average White hitter.

–In the 26 years since the Black man entered major league baseball, three Black stars (Hank Aaron, Willie Mays and Frank Robinson) have taken first, third and fourth places in lifetime home runs.

–Another Black star, Lou Brock, became the first man besides Ty Cobb to steal more than 800 bases. Seven men have more than 350 stolen bases since 1940. All seven are either Black or Latin.

–National League batting has been dominated recently by Black stars. In the last 15 years only 4 batting championships, 1 slugging championship and 4 home run titles have been won by White players.

PITCHING

		Wins	Losses	Pct.	Saves	Innings Pitched	Hits Allowed	Bases on Balls	Strike-outs	E.R.A.	Innings Pitched per yr.	% IP/Yr.	Hits per 9IP	BB per 9IP	SO per 9IP
1947-60	White	16,118	16,209	.499	4,443	290,047	287,714	117,873	138,255	3.98	20,718	93.8	8.93	3.66	4.29
	Black	498	416	.545	111	7,999	7,585	3,084	4,780	3.90	571	2.6	8.53	3.43	5.38
	Latin	624	615	.504	163	11,310	11,301	4,234	5,769	3.89	808	3.6	8.99	3.37	4.59
1961-68	White	11,091	11,272	.496	4,440	201,467	189,559	68,391	127,342	3.56	25,183	87.8	8.47	3.06	5.69
	Black	789	721	.522	168	13,553	12,077	5,175	9,702	3.39	1,694	5.9	8.02	3.44	6.44
	Latin	868	755	.535	353	14,345	12,996	4,667	10,104	3.34	1,793	6.3	8.15	2.93	6.34
1969-75	White	11,626	11,936	.493	4,497	211,287	202,552	78,889	125,493	3.63	30,184	87.0	8.63	3.36	5.35
	Black	1,111	943	.541	184	18,630	16,666	7,146	13,075	3.47	2,661	7.7	8.05	3.45	6.32
	Latin	760	618	.552	367	12,543	11,721	4,839	7,063	3.51	1,792	5.2	8.41	3.47	5.07

–There have been far fewer Black and Latin pitchers than hitters. For the period 1969-1975, Whites still account for 87% of the innings pitched in the major leagues.

–The few Black and Latin major league pitchers have, as a group, consistently won more games than they lost.

–Since 1961 Black and Latin pitchers have achieved a slightly lower earned run average than the White pitchers.

–The Black pitchers have maintained a better ratio of hits allowed to innings pitched and strikeouts to innings pitched than the White pitchers.

These illustrations are only the highlights of the statistical compilation. Careful study of the above tables will reveal many other facts and relationships. As to the more intriguing question of the reasons for the differences in these figures, the authors of this book leave this area of speculation to sociologists, psychologists, and fans. It is the intention of the authors that these facts, rather than causing racial divisions, only help to show the contribution of all men to the game of baseball. Further, that these facts may help us all to visualize what some of the records and statistics of major league baseball might be if the sport had been open to all men for all time.